Hoover's Handbook of

American Business
2011

Austin, Texas

Hoover's Handbook of American Business 2011 is intended to provide readers with accurate and authoritative information about the enterprises covered in it. Hoover's researched all companies and organizations profiled, and in many cases contacted them directly so that companies represented could provide information. The information contained herein is as accurate as we could reasonably make it. In many cases we have relied on third-party material that we believe to be trustworthy, but were unable to independently verify. We do not warrant that the book is absolutely accurate or without error. Readers should not rely on any information contained herein in instances where such reliance might cause financial loss. The publisher, the editors, and their data suppliers specifically disclaim all warranties, including the implied warranties of merchantability and fitness for a specific purpose. This book is sold with the understanding that neither the publisher, the editors, nor any content contributors are engaged in providing investment, financial, accounting, legal, or other professional advice.

The financial data (Historical Financials sections) in this book are from a variety of sources. Morningstar, Inc., provided selected data for the Historical Financials sections of publicly traded companies. For private companies and for historical information on public companies prior to their becoming public, we obtained information directly from the companies or from trade sources deemed to be reliable. Hoover's, Inc., is solely responsible for the presentation of all data.

Many of the names of products and services mentioned in this book are the trademarks or service marks of the companies manufacturing or selling them and are subject to protection under US law. Space has not permitted us to indicate which names are subject to such protection, and readers are advised to consult with the owners of such marks regarding their use. Hoover's is a trademark of Hoover's, Inc.

A D&B COMPANY

10 9 8 7 6 5 4 3 2 1

Publishers Cataloging-in-Publication Data

Hoover's Handbook of American Business 2011

    Includes indexes.

    ISBN: 978-1-57311-143-0

    ISSN 1055-7202

    1. Business enterprises — Directories. 2. Corporations — Directories.

HF3010 338.7

Hoover's Company Information is also available on the Internet at Hoover's Online (www.hoovers.com). A catalog of Hoover's products is available on the Internet at www.hooversbooks.com.

The Hoover's Handbook series is produced for Hoover's Business Press by:

Sycamore Productions, Inc.
5808 Balcones Drive, Suite 205
Austin, Texas 78731
info@syprod.com

Cover design is by John Baker. Electronic prepress and printing are by Sheridan Books, Inc., Ann Arbor, Michigan.

U.S. AND WORLD BOOK SALES

Hoover's, Inc.
5800 Airport Blvd.
Austin, TX 78752
Phone: 512-374-4500
Fax: 512-374-4538
e-mail: orders@hoovers.com
Web: www.hooversbooks.com

EUROPEAN BOOK SALES

William Snyder Publishing Associates
5 Five Mile Drive
Oxford OX2 8HT
England
Phone & fax: +44-186-551-3186
e-mail: snyderpub@aol.com

Hoover's, Inc.

Founder: Gary Hoover
President: Hyune Hand
VP Technology: Mamie Jones
VP Business Excellence: Jeff Cross
VP Product Management and Development: Ken Maranian
Interim VP Marketing: James Rogers
VP Product Development, D&B Digital: Gregory (Greg) Stern
VP Advertising Sales and Operations: Mark Walters
VP Sales: Tom Wickersham
Director Acquisitions: Amy Bible
Senior Director Account Services: Ron M. Chipman
Leader Strategy and Customer Insights: Katherine (Katie) Bullard

(For the latest updates on Hoover's, please visit: http://hoovers.com/global/corp)

EDITORIAL

Director, Editorial: Greg Perliski
Senior Editors: Adrianne Argumaniz, Larry Bills, Jason Cother, Barbara-Anne Mansfield, Barbara Redding, Dennis Sutton
Team Leads: Danny Cummings and Matt Saucedo
Editors: Chelsea Adams, Adam Anderson, Victoria Bernard, Alex Biesada, Joe Bramhall, James Bryant, Ryan Caione, Jason Cella, Catherine Colbert, Tami Conner, Nancy Daniels, Bobby Duncan, Lesley Epperson, Rachel Gallo, Chris Hampton, Stuart Hampton, Jim Harris, Laura Huchzermeyer, Chris Huston, Jessica Jimenez, Linnea Anderson Kirgan, Sylvia Lambert, Anne Law, Josh Lower, John MacAyeal, Kathryn Mackenzie, Rebecca Mallett, Erin McInnis, Michael McLellan, Barbara Murray, Nell Newton, Lynett Oliver, Tracey Panek, Rachel Pierce, David Ramirez, Diane Ramirez, Mark Richardson, Melanie Robertson, Patrice Sarath, Amy Schein, Nikki Sein, Seth Shafer, Lee Simmons, Anthony Staats, Tracy Uba, Vanessa Valencia, Randy Williams, David Woodruff
QA Editors: Carrie Geis, Rosie Hatch, Diane Lee, John Willis
Editorial Customer Advocates: Adi Anand and Kenny Jones

HOOVER'S BUSINESS PRESS

Distribution Manager: Rhonda Mitchell
Customer Support and Fulfillment Manager: Michael Febonio

ABOUT HOOVER'S, INC. – THE BUSINESS INFORMATION AUTHORITY℠

Hoover's, a D&B company, provides its customers the fastest path to business with insight and actionable information about companies, industries, and key decision makers, along with the powerful tools to find and connect to the right people to get business done. Hoover's provides this information for sales, marketing, business development, and other professionals who need intelligence on U.S. and global companies, industries, and the people who lead them. Hoover's unique combination of editorial expertise and one-of-a-kind data collection with user-generated and company-supplied content gives customers a 360-degree view and competitive edge. This information, along with powerful tools to search, sort, download, and integrate the content, is available through Hoover's (http://www.hoovers.com), the company's premier online service. Hoover's is headquartered in Austin, Texas.

Abbreviations

AFL-CIO – American Federation of Labor and Congress of Industrial Organizations

AMA – American Medical Association

AMEX – American Stock Exchange

ARM – adjustable-rate mortgage

ASP – application services provider

ATM – asynchronous transfer mode

ATM – automated teller machine

CAD/CAM – computer-aided design/computer-aided manufacturing

CD-ROM – compact disc – read-only memory

CD-R – CD-recordable

CEO – chief executive officer

CFO – chief financial officer

CMOS – complementary metal oxide silicon

COO – chief operating officer

DAT – digital audiotape

DOD – Department of Defense

DOE – Department of Energy

DOS – disk operating system

DOT – Department of Transportation

DRAM – dynamic random-access memory

DSL – digital subscriber line

DVD – digital versatile disc/digital video disc

DVD-R – DVD-recordable

EPA – Environmental Protection Agency

EPROM – erasable programmable read-only memory

EPS – earnings per share

ESOP – employee stock ownership plan

EU – European Union

EVP – executive vice president

FCC – Federal Communications Commission

FDA – Food and Drug Administration

FDIC – Federal Deposit Insurance Corporation

FTC – Federal Trade Commission

FTP – file transfer protocol

GATT – General Agreement on Tariffs and Trade

GDP – gross domestic product

HMO – health maintenance organization

HR – human resources

HTML – hypertext markup language

ICC – Interstate Commerce Commission

IPO – initial public offering

IRS – Internal Revenue Service

ISP – Internet service provider

kWh – kilowatt-hour

LAN – local-area network

LBO – leveraged buyout

LCD – liquid crystal display

LNG – liquefied natural gas

LP – limited partnership

Ltd. – limited

mips – millions of instructions per second

MW – megawatt

NAFTA – North American Free Trade Agreement

NASA – National Aeronautics and Space Administration

NASDAQ – National Association of Securities Dealers Automated Quotations

NATO – North Atlantic Treaty Organization

NYSE – New York Stock Exchange

OCR – optical character recognition

OECD – Organization for Economic Cooperation and Development

OEM – original equipment manufacturer

OPEC – Organization of Petroleum Exporting Countries

OS – operating system

OSHA – Occupational Safety and Health Administration

OTC – over-the-counter

PBX – private branch exchange

PCMCIA – Personal Computer Memory Card International Association

P/E – price to earnings ratio

RAID – redundant array of independent disks

RAM – random-access memory

R&D – research and development

RBOC – regional Bell operating company

RISC – reduced instruction set computer

REIT – real estate investment trust

ROA – return on assets

ROE – return on equity

ROI – return on investment

ROM – read-only memory

S&L – savings and loan

SCSI – Small Computer System Interface

SEC – Securities and Exchange Commission

SEVP – senior executive vice president

SIC – Standard Industrial Classification

SOC – system on a chip

SVP – senior vice president

USB – universal serial bus

VAR – value-added reseller

VAT – value-added tax

VC – venture capitalist

VoIP – Voice over Internet Protocol

VP – vice president

WAN – wide-area network

WWW – World Wide Web

Contents

List of Lists

Companies Profiled

Companies Profiled (continued)

Companies Profiled (continued)

Companies Profiled (continued)

About Hoover's Handbook of American Business 2011

In these tough economic times, it pays to have all the facts, whether you're making business, financial, or employment decisions. When you need information about companies, the 21st edition of *Hoover's Handbook of American Business* is the place to turn for answers. Throughout its history, it has stood as one of America's respected sources of business information, packed with the information you need.

We at Hoover's Business Press pledge we will continue our work to add more value to this already valuable resource. So search away for the business information you need to make the important decisions facing you. Leave the fact-finding and digging and the sorting and sifting to the editors at Hoover's.

Hoover's Handbook of American Business is the first of our four-title series of handbooks that covers, literally, the world of business. The series is available as an indexed set, and also includes *Hoover's Handbook of World Business, Hoover's Handbook of Private Companies,* and *Hoover's Handbook of Emerging Companies.* This series brings you information on the biggest, fastest-growing, and most influential enterprises in the world.

HOOVER'S ONLINE FOR BUSINESS NEEDS

In addition to the 2,550 companies featured in our handbooks, comprehensive coverage of more than 40,000 business enterprises is available in electronic format on our website, Hoover's Online (www.hoovers.com). Our goal is to provide one site that offers authoritative, updated intelligence on US and global companies, industries, and the people who shape them. Hoover's has partnered with other prestigious business information and service providers to bring you all the right business information, services, and links in one place.

We welcome the recognition we have received as a provider of high-quality company information — online, electronically, and in print — and continue to look for ways to make our products more available and more useful to you.

We believe that anyone who buys from, sells to, invests in, lends to, competes with, interviews with, or works for a company should know all there is to know about that enterprise. Taken together, this book and the other Hoover's products and resources represent the most complete source of basic corporate information readily available to the general public.

This latest version of *Hoover's Handbook of American Business* contains, as always, profiles of the largest and most influential companies in the United States. Each of the companies profiled here was chosen because of its important role in American business. For more details on how these companies were selected, see the section titled "Using Hoover's Handbooks."

HOW TO USE THIS BOOK

This book has four sections:

1. "Using Hoover's Handbooks" describes the contents of our profiles and explains the ways in which we gather and compile our data.

2. "A List-Lover's Compendium" contains lists of the largest, smallest, best, most, and other superlatives related to companies involved in American business.

3. The company profiles section makes up the largest and most important part of the book — 750 profiles of major US enterprises.

4. Three indexes complete the book. The first sorts companies by industry groups, the second by headquarters location. The third index is a list of all the executives found in the Executives section of each company profile.

As always, we hope you find our books useful. We invite your comments via phone (512-374-4500), fax (512-374-4538), mail (5800 Airport Boulevard, Austin, Texas 78752), or e-mail (custsupport@hoovers.com).

The Editors,
Austin, Texas,
October 2010

Using Hoover's Handbooks

SELECTION OF THE COMPANIES PROFILED

The 750 enterprises profiled in this book include the largest and most influential companies in America. Among them are:

- more than 710 publicly held companies, from 3M to Zions Bancorporation
- more than 30 large private enterprises (such as Cargill and Mars)
- several mutual and cooperative organizations (such as State Farm and Ace Hardware)
- a selection of other enterprises (such as Kaiser Foundation Health Plan, the US Postal Service, and the Tennessee Valley Authority) that we believe are sufficiently large and influential enough to warrant inclusion.

In selecting these companies, our foremost question was "What companies will our readers be most interested in?" Our goal was to answer as many questions as we could in one book — in effect, trying to anticipate your curiosity. This approach resulted in four general selection criteria for including companies in the book:

1. Size. The 500 or so largest American companies, measured by sales and by number of employees, are included in the book. In general, these companies have sales in excess of $2 billion, and they are the ones you will have heard of and the ones you will want to know about. These are the companies at the top of the *FORTUNE*, *Forbes*, and *Business Week* lists. We have made sure to include the top private companies in this number.

2. Growth. We believe that relatively few readers will be going to work for, or investing in, the railroad industry. Therefore, only a few railroads are in the book. On the other hand, we have included a number of technology firms, as well as companies that provide medical products and services — pharmaceutical and biotech companies, health care insurers, and medical device makers.

3. Visibility. Most readers will have heard of the Hilton Worldwide and Harley-Davidson companies. Their service or consumer natures make them household names, even though they are not among the corporate giants in terms of sales and employment.

4. Breadth of coverage. To show the diversity of economic activity, we've included, among others, a professional sports team, one ranch, the Big Four accounting firms, and one of the largest law firms in the US. We feel that these businesses are important enough to enjoy at least "token" representation. While we might not emphasize certain industries, the industry leaders are present.

ORGANIZATION

The profiles are presented in alphabetical order. This alphabetization is generally word by word, which means that Legg Mason precedes Leggett & Platt. You will find the commonly used name of the enterprise at the beginning of the profile; the full, legal name is found in the Locations section. If a company name is also a person's name, like Walt Disney, it will be alphabetized under the first name; if the company name starts with initials, like J. C. Penney or H.J. Heinz, look for it under the combined initials (in the above examples, JC and HJ, respectively). Basic financial data is listed under the heading Historical Financials; also included is the exchange on which the company's stock is traded if it is public, the ticker symbol used by the stock exchange, and the company's fiscal year-end.

The annual financial information contained in the profiles is current through fiscal year-ends occurring as late as May 2010. We have included certain nonfinancial developments, such as officer changes, through September 2010.

OVERVIEW

In the first section of the profile, we have tried to give a thumbnail description of the company and what it does. The description will usually include information on the company's strategy, reputation, and ownership. We recommend that you read this section first.

HISTORY

This extended section, included for almost all companies in the book, reflects our belief that every enterprise is the sum of its history and that you have to know where you came from in order to know where you are going. While some companies have limited historical awareness, we think the vast majority of the enterprises in this book have colorful backgrounds. We have tried to focus on the people who made the enterprises what they are today. We have found these histories to be full of twists and ironies; they make fascinating reading.

EXECUTIVES

Here we list the names of the people who run the company, insofar as space allows. In the case of public companies, we have shown the ages and total compensation of key officers. In some cases the published data is for the previous year although the company has announced promotions or retirements since year-end. Total compensation is the sum of salary, bonus, and the value of any other benefits, such as stock options or deferred compensation.

Although companies are free to structure their management titles any way they please, most modern corporations follow standard practices. The ultimate power in any corporation lies with the shareholders, who elect a board of directors, usually including officers or "insiders" as well as individuals from outside the company. The chief officer, the person on whose desk the buck stops, is usually called the chief executive officer (CEO). Often, he or she is also the chairman of the board.

As corporate management has become more complex, it is common for the CEO to have a "right-hand person" who oversees the day-to-day operations of the company, allowing the CEO plenty of time to focus on strategy and long-term issues. This right-hand person is usually designated the chief operating officer (COO) and is often the president of the company. In other cases one person is both chairman and president.

A multitude of other titles exists, including chief financial officer (CFO), chief administrative officer, and vice chairman. We have always tried to include the CFO, the chief legal officer, and the chief human resources or personnel officer. Our best advice is that officers' pay levels are clear indicators of who the board of directors thinks are the most important members of the management team.

The people named in the Executives section are indexed at the back of the book.

The Executives section also includes the name of the company's auditing (accounting) firm, where available.

LOCATIONS

Here we include the company's full legal name and its headquarters, street address, telephone and fax numbers, and Web site, as available. The back of the book includes an index of companies by headquarters locations.

In some cases we have also included information on the geographic distribution of the company's business, including sales and profit data. Note that these profit numbers, like those in the Products/Operations section below, are usually operating or pretax profits rather than net profits. Operating profits are generally those before financing costs (interest income and payments) and before taxes, which are considered costs attributable to the whole company rather than to one division or part of the world. For this reason the net income figures (in the Historical Financials section) are usually much lower, since they are after interest and taxes. Pretax profits are after interest but before taxes.

Headquarters for companies that are incorporated in Bermuda, but whose operational headquarters are in the US, are listed under their US address.

PRODUCTS/OPERATIONS

This section lists as many of the company's products, services, brand names, divisions, subsidiaries, and joint ventures as we could fit. We have tried to include all its major lines and all familiar brand names. The nature of this section varies by company and the amount of information available. If the company publishes sales and profit information by type of business, we have included it.

COMPETITORS

In this section we have listed companies that compete with the profiled company. This feature is included as a quick way to locate similar companies and compare them. The universe of competitors includes all public companies and all private companies with sales in excess of $500 million. In a few instances we have identified smaller private companies as key competitors.

HISTORICAL FINANCIALS

Here we have tried to present as much data about each enterprise's financial performance as we could compile in the allocated space. The information varies somewhat from industry to industry and is less complete in the case of private companies that do not release data (although we have always tried to provide annual sales and employment). There are a few industries, venture capital and investment banking, for example, for which revenue numbers are unavailable as a rule.

The following information is generally present.

A 5-year table, with relevant annualized compound growth rates, covers:
- Sales — fiscal year sales (year-end assets for most financial companies)
- Net income — fiscal year net income (before accounting changes)
- Net profit margin — fiscal year net income as a percent of sales (as a percent of assets for most financial firms)
- Employees — fiscal year-end or average number of employees
- Stock price — the fiscal year close
- P/E — high and low price/earnings ratio
- Earnings per share — fiscal year earnings per share (EPS)
- Dividends per share — fiscal year dividends per share
- Book value per share — fiscal year-end book value (common shareholders' equity per share)

The information on the number of employees is intended to aid the reader interested in knowing whether a company has a long-term trend of increasing or decreasing employment. As far as we know, we are the only company that publishes this information in print format.

The numbers on the left in each row of the Historical Financials section give the month and the year in which the company's fiscal year actually ends. Thus, a company with a March 31, 2010, year-end is shown as 3/10.

In addition, we have provided in graph form a stock price history for most public companies. The graphs, covering up to five years, show the range of trading between the high and the low price, as well as the closing price for each fiscal year. Generally, for private companies, we have graphed net income, or, if that is unavailable, sales.

Key year-end statistics in this section generally show the financial strength of the enterprise, including:

- Debt ratio (long-term debt as a percent of shareholders' equity)
- Return on equity (net income divided by the average of beginning and ending common shareholders' equity)
- Cash and cash equivalents
- Current ratio (ratio of current assets to current liabilities)
- Total long-term debt (including capital lease obligations)

- Number of shares of common stock outstanding
- Dividend yield (fiscal year dividends per share divided by the fiscal year-end closing stock price)
- Dividend payout (fiscal year dividends divided by fiscal year EPS)
- Market value at fiscal year-end (fiscal year-end closing stock price multiplied by fiscal year-end number of shares outstanding)

Per share data has been adjusted for stock splits. The data for public companies has been provided to us by Morningstar, Inc. Other public company information was compiled by Hoover's, which takes full responsibility for the content of this section.

In the case of private companies that do not publicly disclose financial information, we usually did not have access to such standardized data. We have gathered estimates of sales and other statistics from numerous sources.

Hoover's Handbook of

American Business

A List-Lover's Compendium

The 300 Largest Companies by Sales in
Hoover's Handbook of American Business 2011

Rank	Company	Sales ($ mil.)	Rank	Company	Sales ($ mil.)	Rank	Company	Sales ($ mil.)
1	Wal-Mart Stores	408,214	51	MetLife, Inc.	41,058	101	Staples, Inc.	24,276
2	Exxon Mobil	310,586	52	Safeway Inc.	40,851	102	Google Inc.	23,651
3	Chevron Corporation	171,636	53	SUPERVALU INC.	40,597	103	Macy's, Inc.	23,489
4	General Electric	156,783	54	Kraft Foods	40,386	104	International Paper	23,366
5	ConocoPhillips	152,840	55	SYSCO Corporation	36,853	105	Accenture Ltd	23,171
6	Bank of America	150,450	56	The Walt Disney Company	36,149	106	3M Company	23,123
7	AT&T Inc.	123,018	57	Cisco Systems	36,117	107	Deere & Company	23,112
8	Ford Motor	118,308	58	Comcast Corporation	35,756	108	McDonald's Corporation	22,745
9	Cargill, Incorporated	116,579	59	Intel Corporation	35,127	109	Schlumberger Limited	22,702
10	JPMorgan Chase	115,632	60	Aetna Inc.	34,764	110	New York Life Insurance Company	22,246
11	Hewlett-Packard	114,552	61	FedEx Corporation	34,734	111	Tech Data Corporation	22,100
12	Berkshire Hathaway	112,493	62	Northrop Grumman	33,755	112	Motorola, Inc.	22,044
13	McKesson Corporation	108,702	63	News Corporation	32,778	113	Fluor Corporation	21,990
14	Citigroup Inc.	108,006	64	Prudential Financial	32,688	114	Eli Lilly	21,836
15	Verizon Communications	107,808	65	Caterpillar Inc.	32,396	115	Coca-Cola Enterprises	21,645
16	General Motors	104,589	66	Sprint Nextel	32,260	116	The DIRECTV Group	21,565
17	Koch Industries	100,000	67	State Farm Mutual	32,064	117	Ernst & Young Global	21,400
18	Cardinal Health	99,512	68	The Allstate Corporation	32,013	118	IGA, Inc.	21,000
19	CVS Caremark	98,729	69	General Dynamics	31,981	119	Emerson Electric	20,915
20	Wells Fargo	98,636	70	Bechtel Group	31,400	120	TJX Companies	20,288
21	American International Group	96,004	71	Sunoco, Inc.	31,312	121	KPMG International	20,110
22	International Business Machines	95,758	72	Liberty Mutual	31,094	122	AMR Corporation	19,917
23	UnitedHealth Group	87,138	73	The Coca-Cola Company	30,990	123	U.S. Bancorp	19,490
24	Procter & Gamble	78,938	74	Humana Inc.	30,960	124	PNC Financial Services	19,231
25	The Kroger Co.	76,733	75	Honeywell International	30,908	125	Kimberly-Clark	19,115
26	US Postal Service	74,932	76	Abbott Laboratories	30,765	126	NIKE, Inc.	19,014
27	AmerisourceBergen	71,760	77	Morgan Stanley	30,070	127	Bristol-Myers Squibb	18,808
28	Costco Wholesale	71,422	78	HCA Inc.	30,052	128	Plains All American Pipeline	18,520
29	Archer-Daniels-Midland	69,207	79	Mars, Incorporated	30,000	129	Alcoa Inc.	18,439
30	The Boeing Company	68,281	80	Hess Corporation	29,569	130	CIGNA Corporation	18,414
31	Valero Energy	68,144	81	Ingram Micro	29,515	131	Aflac Incorporated	18,254
32	Home Depot	66,176	82	Johnson Controls	28,497	132	J. C. Penney	17,556
33	Target Corporation	65,357	83	Delta Air Lines	28,063	133	Exelon Corporation	17,318
34	WellPoint, Inc.	65,028	84	Merck & Co.	27,428	134	Tyco International	17,237
35	Walgreen Co.	63,335	85	Oracle Corporation	26,820	135	Kohl's Corporation	17,178
36	Microsoft Corporation	62,484	86	American Express	26,730	136	Whirlpool Corporation	17,099
37	Johnson & Johnson	61,897	87	Tyson Foods	26,704	137	Tesoro Corporation	16,872
38	Medco Health Solutions	59,804	88	PricewaterhouseCoopers	26,171	138	Altria Group	16,824
39	Marathon Oil	54,139	89	DuPont	26,109	139	UAL Corporation	16,335
40	United Technologies	52,920	90	Deloitte Touche Tohmatsu	26,100	140	Goodyear Tire & Rubber	16,301
41	Dell Inc.	52,902	91	Time Warner	25,785	141	Avnet, Inc.	16,230
42	Goldman Sachs	51,673	92	CHS Inc.	25,730	142	Kmart Corporation	16,219
43	Pfizer Inc.	50,009	93	Rite Aid	25,669	143	Computer Sciences Corporation	16,128
44	Best Buy	49,694	94	Enterprise Products Partners	25,511	144	Manpower Inc.	16,039
45	Lowe's Companies	47,220	95	Raytheon Company	24,881	145	Capital One Financial	15,951
46	United Parcel Service	45,297	96	Express Scripts	24,749	146	Medtronic, Inc.	15,817
47	Lockheed Martin	45,189	97	Hartford Financial Services	24,701	147	Southern Company	15,743
48	Dow Chemical	44,875	98	Travelers Companies	24,680	148	Health Net	15,713
49	PepsiCo, Inc.	43,232	99	Publix Super Markets	24,515	149	NextEra Energy	15,643
50	Apple Inc.	42,905	100	Amazon.com	24,509	150	L-3 Communications	15,615

SOURCE: HOOVER'S, INC., DATABASE, AUGUST 2010

The 300 Largest Companies by Sales in
Hoover's Handbook of American Business 2011 (continued)

Rank	Company	Sales ($ mil.)
151	Constellation Energy	15,599
152	Occidental Petroleum	15,531
153	Cox Enterprises	15,400
154	Colgate-Palmolive	15,327
155	Xerox Corporation	15,179
156	Dominion Resources	15,131
157	Freeport-McMoRan Copper & Gold	15,040
158	General Mills	14,797
159	Arrow Electronics	14,684
160	Halliburton Company	14,675
161	Amgen Inc.	14,642
162	Progressive Corporation	14,564
163	The Gap	14,197
164	Union Pacific	14,143
165	The AES Corporation	14,119
166	Loews Corporation	14,117
167	EMC Corporation	14,026
168	Burlington Northern Santa Fe	14,016
169	Illinois Tool Works	13,877
170	Highmark Inc.	13,694
171	American Electric Power	13,489
172	PG&E Corporation	13,399
173	Carnival Corporation	13,157
174	Consolidated Edison	13,032
175	The Chubb Corporation	13,016
176	CBS Corporation	13,015
177	FirstEnergy Corp.	12,967
178	FMR LLC	12,937
179	Sara Lee	12,881
180	TIAA-CREF	12,740
181	Duke Energy	12,731
182	Kellogg Company	12,575
183	Baxter International	12,562
184	Public Service Enterprise Group	12,406
185	Edison International	12,361
186	ARAMARK Corporation	12,298
187	Kaiser Foundation Health Plan	12,268
188	PPG Industries	12,239
189	Office Depot	12,145
190	ConAgra Foods	12,079
191	Eaton Corporation	11,873
192	Dollar General	11,796
193	Waste Management	11,791
194	Monsanto Company	11,724
195	Omnicom Group	11,721
196	Thomson Reuters	11,707
197	Jabil Circuit	11,685
198	DISH Network	11,664
199	Navistar International	11,569
200	Jacobs Engineering	11,467
201	World Fuel Services	11,295
202	Tennessee Valley Authority	11,255
203	Smithfield Foods	11,203
204	Nucor Corporation	11,190
205	Danaher Corporation	11,185
206	Dean Foods	11,158
207	ONEOK, Inc.	11,112
208	United States Steel	11,048
209	Marriott International	10,908
210	ITT Corporation	10,905
211	SAIC, Inc.	10,846
212	YUM! Brands	10,836
213	BB&T Corporation	10,818
214	Cummins, Inc.	10,800
215	AutoNation, Inc.	10,758
216	Entergy Corporation	10,746
217	Wakefern Food	10,600
218	Textron Inc.	10,500
219	H. J. Heinz Company	10,495
220	Marsh & McLennan	10,493
221	US Airways	10,458
222	Texas Instruments	10,427
223	SunTrust Banks	10,420
224	QUALCOMM	10,416
225	Land O'Lakes	10,409
226	Avon Products	10,383
227	Southwest Airlines	10,350
228	Parker Hannifin	10,309
229	BJ's Wholesale Club	10,187
230	Thermo Fisher Scientific	10,110
231	Unum Group	10,091
232	Genuine Parts	10,058
233	Progress Energy	9,885
234	R.R. Donnelley	9,857
235	Western Digital	9,850
236	Seagate Technology	9,805
237	Starbucks Corporation	9,775
238	Lear Corporation	9,740
239	Baker Hughes	9,664
240	Xcel Energy	9,644
241	Fifth Third Bancorp	9,450
242	State Street Corporation	9,362
243	URS Corporation	9,249
244	Regions Financial	9,087
245	GameStop Corp.	9,078
246	CSX Corporation	9,041
247	Tenet Healthcare	9,014
248	Anadarko Petroleum	9,000
249	Praxair, Inc.	8,956
250	S.C. Johnson	8,880
251	Automatic Data Processing	8,867
252	Principal Financial	8,849
253	Weatherford International	8,827
254	A&P	8,814
255	eBay Inc.	8,727
256	Limited Brands	8,632
257	Nordstrom, Inc.	8,627
258	Apache Corporation	8,615
259	Lincoln National	8,499
260	CNA Financial	8,472
261	Reynolds American	8,419
262	CenterPoint Energy	8,281
263	Bank of New York Mellon	8,279
264	Air Products and Chemicals	8,256
265	Williams Companies	8,255
266	Republic Services	8,199
267	Boston Scientific	8,188
268	Ashland Inc.	8,106
269	Sempra Energy	8,106
270	Owens & Minor	8,038
271	Whole Foods Market	8,032
272	Devon Energy	8,015
273	DTE Energy	8,014
274	Peter Kiewit Sons'	8,000
275	Norfolk Southern	7,969
276	Crown Holdings	7,938
277	Bed Bath & Beyond	7,829
278	Masco Corporation	7,792
279	Cablevision Systems	7,773
280	Hilton Worldwide	7,770
281	Newmont Mining	7,705
282	Chesapeake Energy	7,702
283	Advance Publications	7,630
284	Dole Food	7,620
285	Eastman Kodak	7,606
286	Aon Corporation	7,595
287	Campbell Soup	7,586
288	C.H. Robinson Worldwide	7,577
289	PPL Corporation	7,556
290	CarMax, Inc.	7,470
291	Quest Diagnostics	7,455
292	Family Dollar Stores	7,401
293	Winn-Dixie Stores	7,367
294	Ball Corporation	7,345
295	Estée Lauder	7,324
296	The Shaw Group	7,280
297	V.F. Corporation	7,220
298	OfficeMax	7,212
299	Ross Stores	7,184
300	Becton, Dickinson	7,161

The 300 Most Profitable Companies in
Hoover's Handbook of American Business 2011

Rank	Company	Net Income ($ mil.)	Rank	Company	Net Income ($ mil.)	Rank	Company	Net Income ($ mil.)
1	Exxon Mobil	19,280	51	Ford Motor	2,962	101	American Electric Power	1,370
2	Microsoft Corporation	18,760	52	Exelon Corporation	2,707	102	Automatic Data Processing	1,333
3	Wal-Mart Stores	14,848	53	Home Depot	2,661	103	Best Buy	1,317
4	International Business Machines	13,425	54	Gilead Sciences	2,636	104	The Boeing Company	1,312
5	Goldman Sachs	13,385	55	News Corporation	2,539	105	CIGNA Corporation	1,305
6	Merck & Co.	12,901	56	Time Warner	2,517	106	Dominion Resources	1,304
7	Procter & Gamble	12,736	57	Target Corporation	2,488	107	New York Life Insurance Company	1,290
8	AT&T Inc.	12,535	58	PNC Financial Services	2,403	108	Medco Health Solutions	1,280
9	Wells Fargo	12,275	59	General Dynamics	2,394	109	Aetna Inc.	1,277
10	Johnson & Johnson	12,266	60	eBay Inc.	2,389	110	McKesson Corporation	1,263
11	JPMorgan Chase	11,652	61	Visa Inc	2,353	111	Praxair, Inc.	1,254
12	Charter Communications	11,366	62	Colgate-Palmolive	2,291	112	Entergy Corporation	1,251
13	General Electric	11,241	63	U.S. Bancorp	2,205	113	PG&E Corporation	1,234
14	Bristol-Myers Squibb	10,681	64	Baxter International	2,205	114	Becton, Dickinson	1,232
15	Chevron Corporation	10,483	65	The Chubb Corporation	2,183	115	TJX Companies	1,214
16	Pfizer Inc.	8,644	66	Honeywell International	2,153	116	Kellogg Company	1,212
17	Apple Inc.	8,235	67	United Parcel Service	2,152	117	FedEx Corporation	1,184
18	Berkshire Hathaway	8,055	68	American Express	2,130	118	Publix Super Markets	1,161
19	Hewlett-Packard	7,660	69	Monsanto Company	2,109	119	Halliburton Company	1,155
20	The Coca-Cola Company	6,824	70	Newmont Mining	2,093	120	CSX Corporation	1,152
21	Google Inc.	6,520	71	Corning Incorporated	2,008	121	Danaher Corporation	1,152
22	Bank of America	6,276	72	Walgreen Co.	2,006	122	Cardinal Health	1,152
23	Oracle Corporation	6,135	73	Kimberly-Clark	1,994	123	Sempra Energy	1,122
24	Cisco Systems	6,134	74	Raytheon Company	1,976	124	The Gap	1,102
25	PepsiCo, Inc.	5,946	75	NIKE, Inc.	1,907	125	EMC Corporation	1,088
26	Abbott Laboratories	5,746	76	Union Pacific	1,898	126	Costco Wholesale	1,086
27	ConocoPhillips	4,858	77	Carnival Corporation	1,790	127	Duke Energy	1,085
28	WellPoint, Inc.	4,746	78	Lowe's Companies	1,783	128	YUM! Brands	1,071
29	Amgen Inc.	4,605	79	The AES Corporation	1,755	129	Progressive Corporation	1,058
30	McDonald's Corporation	4,551	80	DuPont	1,755	130	SYSCO Corporation	1,056
31	Constellation Energy	4,503	81	Emerson Electric	1,724	131	HCA Inc.	1,054
32	Intel Corporation	4,369	82	Burlington Northern Santa Fe	1,721	132	Humana Inc.	1,040
33	Eli Lilly	4,329	83	Southern Company	1,708	133	Norfolk Southern	1,034
34	United Technologies	3,829	84	Archer-Daniels-Midland	1,707	134	Enterprise Products Partners	1,031
35	UnitedHealth Group	3,822	85	Northrop Grumman	1,686	135	Liberty Mutual	1,023
36	CVS Caremark	3,696	86	Noble Corporation	1,679	136	The DIRECTV Group	1,007
37	Verizon Communications	3,651	87	NextEra Energy	1,615	137	FirstEnergy Corp.	1,006
38	Comcast Corporation	3,638	88	Public Service Enterprise Group	1,592	138	Waste Management	994
39	Travelers Companies	3,622	89	QUALCOMM	1,592	139	Kohl's Corporation	991
40	Freeport-McMoRan Copper & Gold	3,534	90	Accenture Ltd	1,590	140	Reynolds American	962
41	Cargill, Incorporated	3,334	91	General Mills	1,531	141	Illinois Tool Works	947
42	The Walt Disney Company	3,307	92	Aflac Incorporated	1,497	142	Edison International	945
43	Altria Group	3,208	93	Texas Instruments	1,470	143	Spectrum Brands	943
44	3M Company	3,193	94	Marathon Oil	1,463	144	Precision Castparts	925
45	Schlumberger Limited	3,142	95	MasterCard Incorporated	1,463	145	L-3 Communications	911
46	Medtronic, Inc.	3,099	96	Dell Inc.	1,433	146	Amazon.com	902
47	Prudential Financial	3,090	97	Morgan Stanley	1,406	147	Franklin Resources	897
48	Kraft Foods	3,028	98	Loews Corporation	1,383	148	Caterpillar Inc.	895
49	Lockheed Martin	3,024	99	Western Digital	1,382	149	Capital One Financial	884
50	Occidental Petroleum	2,966	100	Diamond Offshore Drilling	1,376	150	H. J. Heinz Company	882

SOURCE: HOOVER'S, INC., DATABASE, AUGUST 2010

The 300 Most Profitable Companies in
Hoover's Handbook of American Business 2011 (continued)

Rank	Company	Net Income ($ mil.)	Rank	Company	Net Income ($ mil.)	Rank	Company	Net Income ($ mil.)
151	Consolidated Edison	879	201	EOG Resources	547	251	Ball Corporation	388
152	Deere & Company	874	202	CONSOL Energy	540	252	Simon Property Group	387
153	Northern Trust	864	203	The Clorox Company	537	253	McDermott International	387
154	The Allstate Corporation	854	204	DTE Energy	535	254	Adobe Systems	387
155	BB&T Corporation	853	205	American Financial Group	531	255	Eaton Corporation	385
156	Unum Group	853	206	Mattel, Inc.	529	256	Equity Residential	382
157	Thermo Fisher Scientific	850	207	CenturyTel, Inc.	511	257	CHS Inc.	381
158	Express Scripts	828	208	Parker Hannifin	509	258	GameStop Corp.	377
159	Computer Sciences Corporation	817	209	AmerisourceBergen	503	259	Hasbro, Inc.	375
160	Kaiser Foundation Health Plan	816	210	The Lubrizol Corporation	501	260	CenterPoint Energy	372
161	Lear Corporation	814	211	SAIC, Inc.	497	261	Rowan Companies	368
162	Omnicom Group	793	212	Republic Services	495	262	Sara Lee	364
163	Aon Corporation	792	213	The J. M. Smucker Company	494	263	Williams Companies	361
164	Charles Schwab	787	214	priceline.com	490	264	C.H. Robinson Worldwide	361
165	St. Jude Medical	777	215	Xerox Corporation	485	265	Xilinx, Inc.	358
166	CA Technologies	771	216	CNA Financial	481	266	Dover Corporation	356
167	Quest Diagnostics	766	217	Polo Ralph Lauren	480	267	Gannett Co.	355
168	Progress Energy	761	218	H&R Block	479	268	SCANA Corporation	355
169	Hess Corporation	740	219	Paychex, Inc.	477	269	Whirlpool Corporation	354
170	Staples, Inc.	739	220	Fiserv, Inc.	476	270	Helmerich & Payne	354
171	Fifth Third Bancorp	737	221	C. R. Bard, Inc.	460	271	Macy's, Inc.	350
172	Campbell Soup	736	222	V.F. Corporation	459	272	Sigma-Aldrich Corporation	347
173	Coca-Cola Enterprises	731	223	Joy Global	455	273	Hormel Foods	343
174	McGraw-Hill	731	224	Brown-Forman Corporation	449	274	Cephalon, Inc.	343
175	Tennessee Valley Authority	726	225	Limited Brands	448	275	Dollar General	339
176	ConAgra Foods	723	226	Intuit Inc.	447	276	Northeast Utilities	336
177	Molson Coors Brewing	723	227	Pitney Bowes	445	277	Windstream Corporation	335
178	Symantec Corporation	714	228	Ross Stores	443	278	Crown Holdings	334
179	Fluor Corporation	685	229	Nordstrom, Inc.	441	279	Henry Schein	333
180	Forest Laboratories	682	230	Cooper Industries	439	280	SLM Corporation	325
181	International Paper	681	231	The Hershey Company	436	281	Dun & Bradstreet	322
182	Xcel Energy	681	232	Sherwin-Williams	436	282	Navistar International	320
183	Dow Chemical	676	233	T. Rowe Price Group	434	283	ONEOK, Inc.	306
184	AutoZone, Inc.	657	234	Cincinnati Financial	432	284	McCormick & Company	300
185	Principal Financial	646	235	W.W. Grainger	431	285	Advanced Micro Devices	293
186	ITT Corporation	644	236	Cummins, Inc.	428	286	Family Dollar Stores	291
187	TD Ameritrade	644	237	PPG Industries	426	287	Ralcorp Holdings	290
188	DISH Network	636	238	PPL Corporation	426	288	EarthLink, Inc.	287
189	MBIA Inc.	634	239	DaVita Inc.	423	289	Newell Rubbermaid	286
190	Air Products and Chemicals	631	240	Genzyme Corporation	422	290	Cablevision Systems	285
191	Avon Products	626	241	Baker Hughes	421	291	CarMax, Inc.	282
192	Allergan, Inc.	624	242	Ecolab Inc.	417	292	Jefferies Group	280
193	Ameren Corporation	612	243	SanDisk Corporation	415	293	Weatherford International	280
194	Goodrich Corporation	611	244	BMC Software	406	294	Alliant Techsystems	279
195	Bed Bath & Beyond	600	245	Torchmark Corporation	405	295	DENTSPLY International	274
196	Apollo Group	598	246	Darden Restaurants	405	296	Protective Life	272
197	Yahoo! Inc.	598	247	Jacobs Engineering	400	297	URS Corporation	269
198	Plains All American Pipeline	579	248	Genuine Parts	400	298	NASDAQ OMX Group	266
199	State Farm Mutual	570	249	SUPERVALU INC.	393	299	Hewitt Associates	265
200	Discovery Communications	559	250	Starbucks Corporation	391	300	Tiffany & Co.	265

The 300 Most Valuable Public Companies in
Hoover's Handbook of American Business 2011

Rank	Company	Market Value* ($ mil.)	Rank	Company	Market Value ($ mil.)	Rank	Company	Market Value ($ mil.)
1	Exxon Mobil	347,210	51	Altria Group	40,908	101	Accenture Ltd	23,295
2	Microsoft Corporation	199,119	52	Colgate-Palmolive	39,925	102	Newmont Mining	23,295
3	Wal-Mart Stores	198,207	53	The Boeing Company	39,606	103	General Mills	23,193
4	Google Inc.	197,591	54	Freeport-McMoRan Copper & Gold	37,771	104	Prudential Financial	23,188
5	Johnson & Johnson	177,414	55	Target Corporation	37,759	105	Simon Property Group	23,068
6	Procter & Gamble	170,252	56	Apache Corporation	37,583	106	Dominion Resources	22,929
7	Apple Inc.	169,329	57	News Corporation	36,303	107	Duke Energy	22,695
8	JPMorgan Chase	165,792	58	Gilead Sciences	36,288	108	Franklin Resources	22,644
9	AT&T Inc.	165,629	59	Caterpillar Inc.	35,931	109	Yahoo! Inc.	22,624
10	International Business Machines	165,101	60	EMC Corporation	35,911	110	Charles Schwab	22,462
11	Berkshire Hathaway	162,767	61	Baxter International	35,000	111	Costco Wholesale	22,387
12	General Electric	161,758	62	NIKE, Inc.	34,961	112	Marathon Oil	22,156
13	Chevron Corporation	154,796	63	Ford Motor	34,393	113	NextEra Energy	21,903
14	Bank of America	151,110	64	UnitedHealth Group	34,268	114	State Street Corporation	21,851
15	Pfizer Inc.	146,723	65	Bank of New York Mellon	33,957	115	Aflac Incorporated	21,717
16	Wells Fargo	140,622	66	Burlington Northern Santa Fe	33,604	116	Kellogg Company	20,097
17	The Coca-Cola Company	131,639	67	MasterCard Incorporated	33,497	117	Enterprise Products Partners	20,080
18	Cisco Systems	125,702	68	Walgreen Co.	32,971	118	Hess Corporation	19,869
19	Intel Corporation	113,587	69	Time Warner	32,760	119	Thermo Fisher Scientific	19,430
20	Oracle Corporation	113,442	70	Exelon Corporation	32,303	120	Deere & Company	19,351
21	Merck & Co.	112,309	71	Dow Chemical	32,047	121	Norfolk Southern	19,323
22	Hewlett-Packard	110,795	72	Devon Energy	31,973	122	Raytheon Company	19,274
23	PepsiCo, Inc.	96,729	73	Union Pacific	31,794	123	Allergan, Inc.	19,118
24	Citigroup Inc.	95,902	74	Texas Instruments	31,147	124	Adobe Systems	18,425
25	Verizon Communications	87,557	75	Lowe's Companies	30,942	125	CSX Corporation	18,409
26	Goldman Sachs	87,057	76	Anadarko Petroleum	30,882	126	Motorola, Inc.	18,111
27	Abbott Laboratories	83,362	77	eBay Inc.	30,875	127	Precision Castparts	18,018
28	Schlumberger Limited	77,668	78	DuPont	30,522	128	Automatic Data Processing	17,826
29	ConocoPhillips	75,755	79	Honeywell International	30,271	129	BB&T Corporation	17,580
30	QUALCOMM	72,202	80	Emerson Electric	30,157	130	Capital One Financial	17,513
31	McDonald's Corporation	66,457	81	Corning Incorporated	30,155	131	Baker Hughes	17,368
32	Occidental Petroleum	66,070	82	MetLife, Inc.	28,992	132	Archer-Daniels-Midland	17,214
33	United Technologies	64,487	83	The DIRECTV Group	28,907	133	Johnson Controls	17,210
34	Amazon.com	60,241	84	PNC Financial Services	27,736	134	McKesson Corporation	17,183
35	3M Company	58,955	85	Medco Health Solutions	27,715	135	Tyco International	17,160
36	Visa Inc	58,058	86	Southern Company	27,679	136	Staples, Inc.	17,124
37	United Parcel Service	56,836	87	Lockheed Martin	27,314	137	Chesapeake Energy	16,934
38	Amgen Inc.	54,191	88	Halliburton Company	27,305	138	Public Service Enterprise Group	16,823
39	The Walt Disney Company	52,520	89	Carnival Corporation	26,453	139	American Electric Power	16,680
40	American Express	48,754	90	FedEx Corporation	26,261	140	PG&E Corporation	16,625
41	Kraft Foods	47,403	91	Kimberly-Clark	26,077	141	Air Products and Chemicals	16,489
42	Comcast Corporation	47,319	92	General Dynamics	25,930	142	Alcoa Inc.	16,462
43	Medtronic, Inc.	47,315	93	Dell Inc.	25,262	143	Northrop Grumman	16,432
44	Home Depot	47,067	94	EOG Resources	24,662	144	Applied Materials	16,384
45	Monsanto Company	45,333	95	Praxair, Inc.	24,580	145	YUM! Brands	16,331
46	CVS Caremark	43,748	96	Danaher Corporation	24,539	146	Waste Management	16,331
47	Bristol-Myers Squibb	43,300	97	Illinois Tool Works	24,163	147	Becton, Dickinson	16,275
48	U.S. Bancorp	43,155	98	Express Scripts	23,438	148	The Allstate Corporation	16,159
49	Morgan Stanley	41,350	99	Travelers Companies	23,434	149	The Chubb Corporation	16,071
50	Eli Lilly	41,179	100	WellPoint, Inc.	23,301	150	Broadcom Corporation	15,845

*Market value at the latest available fiscal year-end

SOURCE: HOOVER'S, INC., DATABASE, AUGUST 2010

Rank	Company	Market Value ($ mil.)	Rank	Company	Market Value ($ mil.)	Rank	Company	Market Value ($ mil.)
151	Kohl's Corporation	15,510	201	Campbell Soup	10,536	251	Expeditors International	7,402
152	TJX Companies	15,507	202	Noble Corporation	10,414	252	DTE Energy	7,358
153	Entergy Corporation	15,490	203	Ecolab Inc.	10,401	253	Micron Technology	7,327
154	Reynolds American	15,442	204	McGraw-Hill	10,358	254	The J. M. Smucker Company	7,296
155	Starbucks Corporation	15,283	205	Hartford Financial Services	10,335	255	C. R. Bard, Inc.	7,295
156	Best Buy	15,218	206	Aon Corporation	10,330	256	Fiserv, Inc.	7,277
157	Loews Corporation	15,203	207	Paychex, Inc.	10,316	257	Plains All American Pipeline	7,210
158	H. J. Heinz Company	14,907	208	SunTrust Banks	10,143	258	Mattel, Inc.	7,187
159	Nucor Corporation	14,721	209	L-3 Communications	9,953	259	Cooper Industries	7,143
160	FirstEnergy Corp.	14,160	210	Marriott International	9,887	260	Constellation Energy	7,103
161	Sempra Energy	13,875	211	CIGNA Corporation	9,758	261	Xilinx, Inc.	6,983
162	Activision Blizzard	13,820	212	Xcel Energy	9,754	262	SAIC, Inc.	6,965
163	The Kroger Co.	13,760	213	C.H. Robinson Worldwide	9,741	263	Starwood Hotels & Resorts	6,953
164	Diamond Offshore Drilling	13,683	214	PPG Industries	9,668	264	AutoZone, Inc.	6,922
165	Boston Scientific	13,652	215	Equity Residential	9,575	265	Parker Hannifin	6,918
166	T. Rowe Price Group	13,651	216	Apollo Group	9,566	266	El Paso Corporation	6,918
167	Avon Products	13,512	217	CBS Corporation	9,564	267	Western Digital	6,916
168	Symantec Corporation	13,362	218	Valero Energy	9,472	268	W.W. Grainger	6,871
169	SYSCO Corporation	13,299	219	Intuit Inc.	9,329	269	Cerner Corporation	6,800
170	Weatherford International	13,265	220	DISH Network	9,302	270	BMC Software	6,788
171	PACCAR Inc	13,235	221	Weyerhaeuser Company	9,129	271	Vulcan Materials	6,756
172	Aetna Inc.	13,232	222	ITT Corporation	9,122	272	Macy's, Inc.	6,724
173	Genzyme Corporation	13,079	223	Cummins, Inc.	9,116	273	Sherwin-Williams	6,707
174	Consolidated Edison	12,810	224	Delta Air Lines	8,977	274	SanDisk Corporation	6,667
175	Northern Trust	12,686	225	Forest Laboratories	8,955	275	Ameren Corporation	6,660
176	The Gap	12,413	226	NVIDIA Corporation	8,806	276	NYSE Euronext	6,603
177	Williams Companies	12,325	227	Discovery Communications	8,729	277	Fortune Brands	6,582
178	PPL Corporation	12,232	228	Agilent Technologies	8,611	278	Advanced Micro Devices	6,530
179	CA Technologies	12,110	229	Stanley Black & Decker	8,534	279	Estée Lauder	6,502
180	Progressive Corporation	12,061	230	Southwest Airlines	8,509	280	Cablevision Systems	6,497
181	St. Jude Medical	12,042	231	Computer Sciences Corporation	8,405	281	Unum Group	6,497
182	Marsh & McLennan	11,978	232	Molson Coors Brewing	8,396	282	CNA Financial	6,458
183	Omnicom Group	11,798	233	Polo Ralph Lauren	8,350	283	Sara Lee	6,454
184	Progress Energy	11,777	234	The Hershey Company	8,129	284	International Game Technology	6,403
185	International Paper	11,704	235	Safeway Inc.	8,124	285	Regions Financial	6,308
186	Xerox Corporation	11,701	236	V.F. Corporation	8,064	286	Cliffs Natural Resources	6,242
187	Edison International	11,332	237	Fluor Corporation	8,051	287	AmerisourceBergen	6,240
188	TD Ameritrade	11,308	238	Goodrich Corporation	8,049	288	Limited Brands	6,185
189	CONSOL Energy	11,245	239	Cardinal Health	7,943	289	McAfee, Inc.	6,164
190	Brown-Forman Corporation	11,030	240	United States Steel	7,913	290	Electronic Arts	6,163
191	Bed Bath & Beyond	10,980	241	Lincoln National	7,880	291	Fastenal Company	6,139
192	CenturyTel, Inc.	10,915	242	The Clorox Company	7,863	292	Sigma-Aldrich Corporation	6,133
193	Republic Services	10,843	243	Citrix Systems	7,779	293	Whirlpool Corporation	6,131
194	Sprint Nextel	10,795	244	Dover Corporation	7,767	294	CenterPoint Energy	6,119
195	ConAgra Foods	10,706	245	Fifth Third Bancorp	7,764	295	Rockwell Automation	6,075
196	Quest Diagnostics	10,700	246	Frontier Communications	7,748	296	Darden Restaurants	6,033
197	Eaton Corporation	10,675	247	Principal Financial	7,686	297	DaVita Inc.	6,027
198	Coca-Cola Enterprises	10,655	248	Analog Devices	7,637	298	Genuine Parts	5,983
199	The AES Corporation	10,568	249	Nordstrom, Inc.	7,567	299	Harley-Davidson	5,935
200	priceline.com	10,568	250	Humana Inc.	7,428	300	H&R Block	5,920

The 300 Largest Employers in
Hoover's Handbook of American Business 2011

Rank	Company	Employees	Rank	Company	Employees	Rank	Company	Employees
1	Manpower Inc.	3,028,000	51	KPMG International	140,235	101	Lear Corporation	75,000
2	Wal-Mart Stores	2,100,000	52	Lockheed Martin	140,000	102	3M Company	74,835
3	US Postal Service	663,238	53	Marriott International	137,000	103	Abbott Laboratories	73,000
4	Kelly Services	487,900	54	The Gap	135,000	104	Mars, Incorporated	70,000
5	United Parcel Service	408,000	55	Kmart Corporation	133,000	105	Coca-Cola Enterprises	70,000
6	International Business Machines	399,409	56	Kohl's Corporation	133,000	106	Eaton Corporation	70,000
7	McDonald's Corporation	385,000	57	Johnson Controls	130,000	107	Goodyear Tire & Rubber	69,000
8	Target Corporation	351,000	58	Hilton Worldwide	130,000	108	State Farm Mutual	68,000
9	YUM! Brands	350,000	59	Emerson Electric	129,000	109	Wendy's/Arby's Group	67,500
10	The Kroger Co.	334,000	60	Procter & Gamble	127,000	110	Whirlpool Corporation	67,000
11	Home Depot	317,000	61	Honeywell International	122,000	111	L-3 Communications	67,000
12	General Electric	304,000	62	Northrop Grumman	120,700	112	Cracker Barrel Old Country Store	66,000
13	Hewlett-Packard	304,000	63	Tyson Foods	117,000	113	Cisco Systems	65,550
14	CVS Caremark	295,000	64	Pfizer Inc.	116,500	114	Omnicom Group	63,000
15	Bank of America	284,000	65	Johnson & Johnson	115,500	115	Western Digital	62,500
16	AT&T Inc.	282,720	66	H&R Block	110,400	116	MGM Resorts	62,000
17	Wells Fargo	281,000	67	Comcast Corporation	107,000	117	Morgan Stanley	61,388
18	Citigroup Inc.	269,000	68	Tyco International	106,000	118	Jabil Circuit	61,000
19	Berkshire Hathaway	257,000	69	Oracle Corporation	105,000	119	Royal Caribbean Cruises	60,300
20	ARAMARK Corporation	255,000	70	Liberty Mutual	100,000	120	AutoZone, Inc.	60,000
21	Lowe's Companies	239,000	71	Merck & Co.	100,000	121	The Brink's Company	59,400
22	Walgreen Co.	238,000	72	Rite Aid	97,500	122	Alcoa Inc.	59,000
23	Verizon Communications	222,900	73	Kraft Foods	97,000	123	GameStop Corp.	59,000
24	JPMorgan Chase	222,316	74	American International Group	96,000	124	Regis Corporation	59,000
25	General Motors	217,000	75	Dell Inc.	96,000	125	Illinois Tool Works	59,000
26	United Technologies	206,700	76	Chevron Corporation	95,500	126	American Express	58,300
27	PepsiCo, Inc.	203,000	77	Computer Sciences Corporation	94,000	127	U.S. Bancorp	58,229
28	Ford Motor	198,000	78	Caterpillar Inc.	93,813	128	DuPont	58,000
29	HCA Inc.	192,000	79	The Coca-Cola Company	92,800	129	Tenet Healthcare	57,613
30	Safeway Inc.	186,000	80	Limited Brands	92,100	130	R.R. Donnelley	56,800
31	Best Buy	180,000	81	IGA, Inc.	92,000	131	International Paper	56,100
32	Accenture Ltd	177,000	82	General Dynamics	91,700	132	Kimberly-Clark	56,000
33	Darden Restaurants	174,000	83	Staples, Inc.	91,095	133	PNC Financial Services	55,820
34	Deloitte Touche Tohmatsu	168,651	84	ABM Industries	91,000	134	Kindred Healthcare	54,100
35	Robert Half	166,900	85	Microsoft Corporation	89,000	135	MetLife, Inc.	54,000
36	PricewaterhouseCoopers	163,545	86	Kaiser Foundation Health Plan	84,845	136	Xerox Corporation	53,600
37	Macy's, Inc.	161,000	87	Carnival Corporation	84,800	137	Apollo Group	53,498
38	SFN Group	161,000	88	Delta Air Lines	81,106	138	Motorola, Inc.	53,000
39	SUPERVALU INC.	160,000	89	Exxon Mobil	80,700	139	Whole Foods Market	52,500
40	Cargill, Incorporated	159,000	90	Abercrombie & Fitch	80,000	140	Dow Chemical	52,195
41	The Boeing Company	157,100	91	UnitedHealth Group	80,000	141	Weatherford International	52,000
42	J. C. Penney	154,000	92	Koch Industries	80,000	142	Marsh & McLennan	52,000
43	TJX Companies	154,000	93	Dollar General	79,800	143	Parker Hannifin	51,639
44	Starwood Hotels & Resorts	145,000	94	Intel Corporation	79,800	144	Deere & Company	51,300
45	Ernst & Young Global	144,441	95	AMR Corporation	78,900	145	News Corporation	51,000
46	The Walt Disney Company	144,000	96	Brinker International	77,100	146	Halliburton Company	51,000
47	Starbucks Corporation	142,000	97	Cox Enterprises	77,000	147	Wakefern Food	50,000
48	Costco Wholesale	142,000	98	Schlumberger Limited	77,000	148	Winn-Dixie Stores	50,000
49	Publix Super Markets	142,000	99	Dole Food	75,800	149	Baxter International	49,700
50	FedEx Corporation	141,000	100	Raytheon Company	75,000	150	Nordstrom, Inc.	48,000

SOURCE: HOOVER'S, INC., DATABASE, AUGUST 2010

The 300 Largest Employers in
Hoover's Handbook of American Business 2011 (continued)

Rank	Company	Employees	Rank	Company	Employees	Rank	Company	Employees
151	Smithfield Foods	48,000	201	Aon Corporation	36,200	251	CB Richard Ellis Group	29,000
152	Blockbuster Inc.	48,000	202	Fluor Corporation	36,152	252	Marathon Oil	28,855
153	Seagate Technology	47,000	203	YRC Worldwide	36,000	253	Norfolk Southern	28,593
154	Family Dollar Stores	47,000	204	Jack in the Box	35,700	254	Freeport-McMoRan Copper & Gold	28,400
155	SYSCO Corporation	47,000	205	Avery Dennison	35,700	255	Cooper Industries	28,255
156	UAL Corporation	47,000	206	Big Lots	35,600	256	Archer-Daniels-Midland	28,200
157	Danaher Corporation	46,600	207	Molex Incorporated	35,519	257	Humana Inc.	28,100
158	SAIC, Inc.	46,200	208	Masco Corporation	35,400	258	SunTrust Banks	28,001
159	Res-Care, Inc.	45,700	209	Thermo Fisher Scientific	35,400	259	Capital One Financial	28,000
160	V.F. Corporation	45,700	210	Gannett Co.	35,000	260	Bristol-Myers Squibb	28,000
161	Ross Stores	45,600	211	Barnes & Noble	35,000	261	Hartford Financial Services	28,000
162	Automatic Data Processing	45,000	212	Aetna Inc.	35,000	262	Universal Corporation	28,000
163	URS Corporation	45,000	213	Burlington Northern Santa Fe	35,000	263	The Shaw Group	28,000
164	PetSmart, Inc.	45,000	214	Cummins, Inc.	34,900	264	Cablevision Systems	27,940
165	Hyatt Hotels Corporation	45,000	215	Southwest Airlines	34,726	265	Bon-Ton Stores	27,600
166	A&P	45,000	216	NIKE, Inc.	34,400	266	Mohawk Industries	27,400
167	Bob Evans Farms	44,086	217	Baker Hughes	34,400	267	Con-way Inc.	27,400
168	Bechtel Group	44,000	218	Health Management Associates	33,700	268	Advance Publications	27,200
169	Union Pacific	43,531	219	Pitney Bowes	33,004	269	Dean Foods	27,157
170	Waste Management	43,400	220	General Mills	33,000	270	Charming Shoppes	27,000
171	EMC Corporation	43,200	221	Thomson Reuters	32,850	271	The AES Corporation	27,000
172	Quest Diagnostics	43,000	222	McKesson Corporation	32,500	272	Mattel, Inc.	27,000
173	Medtronic, Inc.	43,000	223	Goldman Sachs	32,500	273	State Street Corporation	27,000
174	United States Steel	43,000	224	DaVita Inc.	32,500	274	Monsanto Company	27,000
175	Bank of New York Mellon	42,200	225	BB&T Corporation	32,400	275	Texas Instruments	26,584
176	Volt Information Sciences	42,000	226	Travelers Companies	32,000	276	Praxair, Inc.	26,164
177	Prudential Financial	41,943	227	Textron Inc.	32,000	277	Southern Company	26,112
178	Burger King Holdings	41,320	228	Estée Lauder	31,300	278	American Greetings	26,000
179	Dillard's, Inc.	41,300	229	US Airways	31,300	279	Boston Scientific	26,000
180	Avon Products	41,000	230	Republic Services	31,000	280	Williams-Sonoma	26,000
181	Sara Lee	41,000	231	OfficeMax	31,000	281	Ecolab Inc.	25,931
182	Bed Bath & Beyond	41,000	232	Time Warner	31,000	282	Unisys Corporation	25,600
183	Office Depot	41,000	233	First American Financial	30,922	283	CBS Corporation	25,580
184	WellPoint, Inc.	40,500	234	Kellogg Company	30,900	284	EMCOR Group	25,000
185	Eli Lilly	40,360	235	Newmont Mining	30,400	285	Progressive Corporation	24,661
186	ITT Corporation	40,200	236	CSX Corporation	30,088	286	DISH Network	24,500
187	FMR LLC	40,000	237	Sun Healthcare	30,029	287	ConAgra Foods	24,400
188	Interpublic Group	40,000	238	ConocoPhillips	30,000	288	Amazon.com	24,300
189	Sprint Nextel	40,000	239	Regions Financial	30,000	289	Fortune Brands	24,248
190	PPG Industries	39,900	240	Cheesecake Factory	30,000	290	Goodrich Corporation	24,000
191	American Eagle Outfitters	39,400	241	Cintas Corporation	30,000	291	Dana Holding	24,000
192	Federal-Mogul	39,000	242	Collective Brands	30,000	292	Corning Incorporated	23,500
193	Jacobs Engineering	38,900	243	H. J. Heinz Company	29,600	293	BJ's Wholesale Club	23,500
194	Foot Locker	38,764	244	Cardinal Health	29,600	294	The DIRECTV Group	23,300
195	Sanmina-SCI	38,602	245	Dover Corporation	29,300	295	Hertz Global Holdings	23,050
196	Colgate-Palmolive	38,100	246	CIGNA Corporation	29,300	296	Hewitt Associates	23,000
197	Apple Inc.	36,800	247	Sherwin-Williams	29,220	297	DineEquity, Inc.	22,900
198	The Allstate Corporation	36,800	248	Becton, Dickinson	29,116	298	Ryder System	22,900
199	RadioShack	36,700	249	McDermott International	29,000	299	Medco Health Solutions	22,850
200	Jones Lang LaSalle	36,600	250	Genuine Parts	29,000	300	Avis Budget Group	22,700

The 100 Fastest-Growing Companies by Sales Growth in
Hoover's Handbook of American Business 2011

Rank	Company	Annual % Change*	Rank	Company	Annual % Change	Rank	Company	Annual % Change
1	HCA Inc.	274.4%	36	Bon-Ton Stores	23.4%	71	ADC Telecommunications	16.7%
2	Hilton Worldwide	116.5%	37	BE Aerospace	23.1%	72	General Cable	16.5%
3	NYSE Euronext	75.6%	38	Western Digital	22.7%	73	QUALCOMM	16.4%
4	Windstream Corporation	56.0%	39	CommScope, Inc.	22.6%	74	JDS Uniphase	16.1%
5	Hologic, Inc.	54.4%	40	The Shaw Group	22.2%	75	Jones Lang LaSalle	16.1%
6	Discovery Communications	50.0%	41	Schnitzer Steel Industries	22.2%	76	Cephalon, Inc.	16.0%
7	Wendy's/Arby's Group	49.0%	42	CHS Inc.	21.2%	77	Bechtel Group	15.9%
8	DineEquity, Inc.	42.0%	43	Humana Inc.	21.1%	78	Guess?, Inc.	15.8%
9	Mylan Inc.	42.0%	44	The J. M. Smucker Company	20.9%	79	Oshkosh Corporation	15.7%
10	NASDAQ OMX Group	40.3%	45	Sun Healthcare	20.9%	80	Tetra Tech	15.5%
11	Google Inc.	40.1%	46	TD Ameritrade	20.6%	81	Sanderson Farms	15.5%
12	Thermo Fisher Scientific	40.0%	47	Panera Bread	20.6%	82	Citrix Systems	15.4%
13	Freeport-McMoRan Copper & Gold	37.7%	48	Baldor Electric	20.6%	83	Urban Outfitters	15.4%
14	Gilead Sciences	36.4%	49	Enterprise Products Partners	20.1%	84	Bank of America	15.3%
15	MetroPCS Communications	35.3%	50	US Airways	19.8%	85	Apollo Group	15.3%
16	McDermott International	35.1%	51	DaVita Inc.	19.7%	86	SEACOR Holdings	15.2%
17	Apple Inc.	32.5%	52	SUPERVALU INC.	19.6%	87	Moog Inc.	15.2%
18	Itron, Inc.	32.2%	53	Weatherford International	19.5%	88	Newmont Mining	15.0%
19	Diamond Offshore Drilling	31.3%	54	Jacobs Engineering	19.4%	89	MasterCard Incorporated	14.8%
20	GameStop Corp.	30.9%	55	PriceSmart, Inc.	19.3%	90	Delta Air Lines	14.7%
21	Activision Blizzard	30.7%	56	CenturyTel, Inc.	19.0%	91	Whole Foods Market	14.3%
22	Amazon.com	30.3%	57	Valassis Communications	18.7%	92	Esterline Technologies	14.3%
23	Republic Services	30.1%	58	McAfee, Inc.	18.2%	93	Watson Pharmaceuticals	14.1%
24	AT&T Inc.	29.4%	59	Allergan, Inc.	18.0%	94	CACI International	13.9%
25	CVS Caremark	27.8%	60	Cinemark Holdings	18.0%	95	Broadcom Corporation	13.9%
26	Noble Corporation	27.4%	61	ARAMARK Corporation	17.8%	96	Manitowoc Company	13.8%
27	Visa Inc	26.9%	62	Archer-Daniels-Midland	17.8%	97	United Natural Foods	13.8%
28	Koch Industries	25.7%	63	UnitedHealth Group	17.7%	98	Fluor Corporation	13.7%
29	Wells Fargo	25.0%	64	eBay Inc.	17.7%	99	Harris Corporation	13.6%
30	PNC Financial Services	24.9%	65	MasTec, Inc.	17.6%	100	Owens & Minor	13.6%
31	priceline.com	24.8%	66	McKinsey & Company	17.5%			
32	Peter Kiewit Sons'	24.3%	67	DeVry Inc.	16.9%			
33	Helmerich & Payne	24.0%	68	Joy Global	16.9%			
34	URS Corporation	24.0%	69	Oracle Corporation	16.9%			
35	Ralcorp Holdings	23.5%	70	Monsanto Company	16.8%			

*These rates are compounded annualized increases, and may have resulted from acquisitions or one-time gains. If less than 5 years of data are available, growth is for the years available.

SOURCE: HOOVER'S, INC., DATABASE, AUGUST 2010

The 100 Fastest-Growing Companies by Employment Growth in
Hoover's Handbook of American Business 2011

Rank	Company	Annual % Change*	Rank	Company	Annual % Change	Rank	Company	Annual % Change
1	DineEquity, Inc.	124.8%	36	Amazon.com	19.3%	71	Public Service Enterprise Group	13.1%
2	The Shaw Group	95.9%	37	CB Richard Ellis Group	18.9%	72	EMC Corporation	13.0%
3	Hilton Worldwide	54.9%	38	Kansas City Southern	18.8%	73	Chevron Corporation	12.8%
4	Windstream Corporation	54.7%	39	CVS Caremark	18.8%	74	UGI Corporation	12.8%
5	Mylan Inc.	50.8%	40	World Fuel Services	17.9%	75	Bank of America	12.6%
6	Hologic, Inc.	46.1%	41	AAR CORP.	17.7%	76	Brightpoint, Inc.	12.6%
7	Itron, Inc.	45.6%	42	Baldor Electric	17.2%	77	Avery Dennison	12.1%
8	priceline.com	39.4%	43	Oracle Corporation	16.9%	78	Lincoln National	11.8%
9	Google Inc.	36.7%	44	Urban Outfitters	16.9%	79	General Cable	11.5%
10	Activision Blizzard	34.3%	45	McAfee, Inc.	16.7%	80	Oshkosh Corporation	11.5%
11	Thermo Fisher Scientific	32.5%	46	Holly Corporation	16.7%	81	URS Corporation	11.4%
12	Merck & Co.	32.3%	47	Schnitzer Steel Industries	16.6%	82	Delphi Financial Group	11.4%
13	SUPERVALU INC.	32.2%	48	Enterprise Products Partners	16.6%	83	Royal Caribbean Cruises	11.2%
14	SanDisk Corporation	31.8%	49	Wells Fargo	16.3%	84	Jabil Circuit	11.1%
15	CenturyTel, Inc.	30.8%	50	Nucor Corporation	15.9%	85	Cinemark Holdings	11.1%
16	Chesapeake Energy	29.8%	51	Bank of New York Mellon	15.8%	86	Citrix Systems	11.0%
17	CommScope, Inc.	29.8%	52	Mars, Incorporated	15.7%	87	Watson Pharmaceuticals	11.0%
18	Wendy's/Arby's Group	27.9%	53	DeVry Inc.	15.7%	88	Adobe Systems	10.9%
19	Koch Industries	27.8%	54	J. Crew Group	15.3%	89	Humana Inc.	10.7%
20	Liberty Mutual	26.5%	55	QUALCOMM	14.7%	90	Moog Inc.	10.7%
21	The DIRECTV Group	26.2%	56	Broadcom Corporation	14.6%	91	Markel Corporation	10.7%
22	TD Ameritrade	26.1%	57	American Eagle Outfitters	14.4%	92	EOG Resources	10.7%
23	Western Digital	26.1%	58	Cisco Systems	14.3%	93	AT&T Inc.	10.6%
24	NASDAQ OMX Group	24.7%	59	NYSE Euronext	14.3%	94	Medco Health Solutions	10.5%
25	Republic Services	24.3%	60	Plains All American Pipeline	14.2%	95	United Natural Foods	10.5%
26	PNC Financial Services	21.8%	61	ARAMARK Corporation	14.2%	96	Polo Ralph Lauren	10.4%
27	Apple Inc.	21.6%	62	Briggs & Stratton	14.0%	97	PriceSmart, Inc.	10.3%
28	MetroPCS Communications	20.7%	63	The Coca-Cola Company	14.0%	98	Ralcorp Holdings	10.1%
29	Weatherford International	20.0%	64	Green Bay Packers	13.8%	99	Genzyme Corporation	10.0%
30	Valassis Communications	19.9%	65	Highmark Inc.	13.6%	100	Delta Air Lines	9.8%
31	Dynegy Inc.	19.5%	66	Jones Lang LaSalle	13.6%			
32	McDermott International	19.5%	67	Allergan, Inc.	13.2%			
33	Gilead Sciences	19.3%	68	Apollo Group	13.1%			
34	Hewlett-Packard	19.3%	69	Manitowoc Company	13.1%			
35	Newmont Mining	19.3%	70	Monsanto Company	13.1%			

*These rates are compounded annualized increases, and may have resulted from acquisitions or one-time gains. If less than 5 years of data are available, growth is for the years available.

SOURCE: HOOVER'S, INC., DATABASE, AUGUST 2010

50 Shrinking Companies by Sales Growth in
Hoover's Handbook of American Business 2011

Rank	Company	Annual % Change*	Rank	Company	Annual % Change	Rank	Company	Annual % Change
1	KB Home	(33.7%)	21	NVR, Inc.	(15.0%)	41	La-Z-Boy	(11.4%)
2	Beazer Homes USA	(33.0%)	22	Eastman Kodak	(14.6%)	42	Masco Corporation	(11.4%)
3	Lennar Corporation	(31.1%)	23	State Farm Mutual	(14.2%)	43	Liz Claiborne	(11.2%)
4	IAC/InterActiveCorp	(30.1%)	24	General Motors	(14.2%)	44	Denny's Corporation	(11.2%)
5	Altria Group	(29.7%)	25	Molson Coors Brewing	(13.9%)	45	IDT Corporation	(11.1%)
6	Weyerhaeuser Company	(29.7%)	26	AutoNation, Inc.	(13.5%)	46	USG Corporation	(10.9%)
7	D.R. Horton	(28.3%)	27	EarthLink, Inc.	(13.5%)	47	Terex Corporation	(10.8%)
8	The Ryland Group	(28.2%)	28	Synovus Financial	(13.4%)	48	VeriSign, Inc.	(10.5%)
9	PulteGroup	(27.4%)	29	Lear Corporation	(13.1%)	49	Calpine Corporation	(10.2%)
10	Avis Budget Group	(27.2%)	30	Leggett & Platt	(12.9%)	50	Olin Corporation	(10.2%)
11	Hovnanian Enterprises	(26.1%)	31	Morgan Stanley	(12.7%)			
12	Toll Brothers	(25.8%)	32	Solutia Inc.	(12.4%)			
13	E. W. Scripps	(24.8%)	33	Time Warner	(12.3%)			
14	Alberto-Culver	(20.2%)	34	Plains All American Pipeline	(12.2%)			
15	Tyco International	(18.8%)	35	Thor Industries	(12.2%)			
16	Sanmina-SCI	(18.5%)	36	HealthSouth Corporation	(12.1%)			
17	ArvinMeritor	(17.6%)	37	Motorola, Inc.	(12.1%)			
18	Brunswick Corporation	(17.3%)	38	YRC Worldwide	(11.8%)			
19	PACCAR Inc	(15.8%)	39	Dana Holding	(11.7%)			
20	Furniture Brands International	(15.4%)	40	The Timken Company	(11.7%)			

*These rates are compounded and annualized and may have resulted from divestitures. If less than 5 years of data are available, rates are for the years available.

SOURCE: HOOVER'S, INC., DATABASE, AUGUST 2010

50 Shrinking Companies by Employment Growth in
Hoover's Handbook of American Business 2011

Rank	Company	Annual % Change*	Rank	Company	Annual % Change	Rank	Company	Annual % Change
1	Administaff, Inc.	(61.5%)	21	PulteGroup	(19.2%)	41	VeriSign, Inc.	(13.1%)
2	Altria Group	(52.7%)	22	Tyco International	(19.1%)	42	Imation Corp.	(12.9%)
3	IAC/InterActiveCorp	(41.9%)	23	ArvinMeritor	(17.9%)	43	Borders Group	(12.7%)
4	Alberto-Culver	(39.8%)	24	Alcoa Inc.	(17.8%)	44	Spectrum Brands	(12.7%)
5	Beazer Homes USA	(33.4%)	25	Trinity Industries	(17.1%)	45	HealthSouth Corporation	(12.2%)
6	KB Home	(32.4%)	26	Halliburton Company	(16.7%)	46	United Rentals	(12.1%)
7	IDT Corporation	(30.4%)	27	NVR, Inc.	(16.0%)	47	The Timken Company	(11.4%)
8	Avis Budget Group	(28.1%)	28	Sprint Nextel	(15.9%)	48	La-Z-Boy	(11.3%)
9	Lennar Corporation	(27.2%)	29	E. W. Scripps	(15.0%)	49	Werner Enterprises	(11.1%)
10	Hovnanian Enterprises	(26.8%)	30	YRC Worldwide	(14.7%)	50	Winn-Dixie Stores	(11.1%)
11	Weyerhaeuser Company	(26.1%)	31	Warnaco Group	(14.6%)			
12	Sara Lee	(26.0%)	32	SFN Group	(14.6%)			
13	The Ryland Group	(25.0%)	33	Cardinal Health	(14.3%)			
14	D.R. Horton	(24.3%)	34	FedEx Corporation	(14.2%)			
15	Time Warner	(22.9%)	35	Dana Holding	(14.1%)			
16	EarthLink, Inc.	(22.6%)	36	Brunswick Corporation	(14.1%)			
17	Toll Brothers	(22.0%)	37	Leggett & Platt	(13.5%)			
18	Eastman Kodak	(20.7%)	38	Furniture Brands International	(13.5%)			
19	NACCO Industries	(20.4%)	39	Smurfit-Stone Container	(13.2%)			
20	Denny's Corporation	(20.1%)	40	Masco Corporation	(13.1%)			

*These rates are compounded and annualized and may have resulted from divestitures. If less than 5 years of data are available, rates are for the years available.

SOURCE: HOOVER'S, INC., DATABASE, AUGUST 2010

The *FORTUNE* 500 Largest US Corporations

Rank	Company	Sales ($ mil.)	Rank	Company	Sales ($ mil.)	Rank	Company	Sales ($ mil.)
1	Wal-Mart Stores	408,214.0	51	MetLife	41,098.0	101	Staples	24,275.5
2	Exxon Mobil	284,650.0	52	Safeway	40,850.7	102	Google	23,650.6
3	Chevron	163,527.0	53	Kraft Foods	40,386.0	103	Macy's	23,489.0
4	General Electric	156,779.0	54	Freddie Mac	37,614.0	104	International Paper	23,366.0
5	Bank of America Corp.	150,450.0	55	Sysco	36,853.3	105	Oracle	23,252.0
6	ConocoPhillips	139,515.0	56	Apple	36,537.0	106	3M	23,123.0
7	AT&T	123,018.0	57	Walt Disney	36,149.0	107	Deere	23,112.4
8	Ford Motor	118,308.0	58	Cisco Systems	36,117.0	108	McDonald's	22,744.7
9	J.P. Morgan Chase & Co.	115,632.0	59	Comcast	35,756.0	109	Tech Data	22,099.9
10	Hewlett-Packard	114,552.0	60	FedEx	35,497.0	110	Motorola	22,063.0
11	Berkshire Hathaway	112,493.0	61	Northrop Grumman	35,291.0	111	Fluor	21,990.3
12	Citigroup	108,785.0	62	Intel	35,127.0	112	Eli Lilly	21,836.0
13	Verizon Communications	107,808.0	63	Aetna	34,764.1	113	Coca-Cola Enterprises	21,645.0
14	McKesson	106,632.0	64	New York Life Insurance	34,014.3	114	Bristol-Myers Squibb	21,634.0
15	General Motors	104,589.0	65	Prudential Financial	32,688.0	115	Northwestern Mutual	21,602.6
16	American International Group	103,189.0	66	Caterpillar	32,396.0	116	DirecTV Group	21,565.0
17	Cardinal Health	99,612.9	67	Sprint Nextel	32,260.0	117	Emerson Electric	20,915.0
18	CVS Caremark	98,729.0	68	Allstate	32,013.0	118	Nationwide	20,751.0
19	Wells Fargo	98,636.0	69	General Dynamics	31,981.0	119	TJX	20,288.4
20	International Business Machines	95,758.0	70	Morgan Stanley	31,515.0	120	AMR	19,917.0
21	UnitedHealth Group	87,138.0	71	Liberty Mutual Insurance Group	31,094.0	121	U.S. Bancorp	19,490.0
22	Procter & Gamble	79,697.0	72	Coca-Cola	30,990.0	122	GMAC	19,403.0
23	Kroger	76,733.2	73	Humana	30,960.4	123	PNC Financial Services Group	19,231.0
24	AmerisourceBergen	71,789.0	74	Honeywell International	30,908.0	124	Nike	19,176.1
25	Costco Wholesale	71,422.0	75	Abbott Laboratories	30,764.7	125	Murphy Oil	19,138.0
26	Valero Energy	70,035.0	76	News Corp.	30,423.0	126	Kimberly-Clark	19,115.0
27	Archer Daniels Midland	69,207.0	77	HCA	30,052.0	127	Alcoa	18,745.0
28	Boeing	68,281.0	78	Sunoco	29,630.0	128	Plains All American Pipeline	18,520.0
29	Home Depot	66,176.0	79	Hess	29,569.0	129	Cigna	18,414.0
30	Target	65,357.0	80	Ingram Micro	29,515.4	130	AFLAC	18,254.4
31	WellPoint	65,028.1	81	Fannie Mae	29,065.0	131	Time Warner Cable	17,868.0
32	Walgreen	63,335.0	82	Time Warner	28,842.0	132	USAA	17,557.6
33	Johnson & Johnson	61,897.0	83	Johnson Controls	28,497.0	133	J.C. Penney	17,556.0
34	State Farm Insurance Cos.	61,479.6	84	Delta Air Lines	28,063.0	134	Exelon	17,318.0
35	Medco Health Solutions	59,804.2	85	Merck	27,428.3	135	Kohl's	17,178.0
36	Microsoft	58,437.0	86	DuPont	27,328.0	136	Whirlpool	17,099.0
37	United Technologies	52,920.0	87	Tyson Foods	27,165.0	137	Altria Group	16,824.0
38	Dell	52,902.0	88	American Express	26,730.0	138	Computer Sciences	16,739.9
39	Goldman Sachs Group	51,673.0	89	Rite Aid	26,289.5	139	Tesoro	16,589.0
40	Pfizer	50,009.0	90	TIAA-CREF	26,278.0	140	UAL	16,335.0
41	Marathon Oil	49,403.0	91	CHS	25,729.9	141	Goodyear Tire & Rubber	16,301.0
42	Lowe's	47,220.0	92	Enterprise GP Holdings	25,510.9	142	Avnet	16,229.9
43	United Parcel Service	45,297.0	93	Massachusetts Mutual Life Insurance	25,423.6	143	Manpower	16,038.7
44	Lockheed Martin	45,189.0	94	Philip Morris International	25,035.0	144	Capital One Financial	15,980.1
45	Best Buy	45,015.0	95	Raytheon	24,881.0	145	Southern	15,743.0
46	Dow Chemical	44,945.0	96	Express Scripts	24,748.9	146	Health Net	15,713.2
47	Supervalu	44,564.0	97	Hartford Financial Services	24,701.0	147	FPL Group	15,643.0
48	Sears Holdings	44,043.0	98	Travelers Cos.	24,680.0	148	L-3 Communications	15,615.0
49	International Assets Holding	43,604.4	99	Publix Super Markets	24,515.0	149	Constellation Energy	15,598.8
50	PepsiCo	43,232.0	100	Amazon.com	24,509.0	150	Occidental Petroleum	15,531.0

SOURCE: *FORTUNE*, MAY 3, 2010

The *FORTUNE* 500 Largest US Corporations (continued)

Rank	Company	Sales ($ mil.)	Rank	Company	Sales ($ mil.)	Rank	Company	Sales ($ mil.)
151	Colgate-Palmolive	15,327.0	201	TRW Automotive Holdings	11,614.0	251	Pepco Holdings	9,259.0
152	Xerox	15,179.0	202	Navistar International	11,569.0	252	URS	9,249.1
153	Dominion Resources	15,131.0	203	Jacobs Engineering Group	11,467.4	253	Tenet Healthcare	9,215.0
154	Freeport-McMoRan Copper & Gold	15,040.0	204	Sun Microsystems	11,449.0	254	Regions Financial	9,087.1
155	General Mills	14,691.3	205	World Fuel Services	11,295.2	255	GameStop	9,078.0
156	AES	14,690.0	206	Nucor	11,190.3	256	Lincoln National	9,071.8
157	Arrow Electronics	14,684.1	207	Danaher	11,184.9	257	Genworth Financial	9,069.0
158	Halliburton	14,675.0	208	Dean Foods	11,158.4	258	XTO Energy	9,064.0
159	Amgen	14,642.0	209	Oneok	11,111.7	259	CSX	9,041.0
160	Medtronic	14,599.0	210	Liberty Global	11,110.4	260	Anadarko Petroleum	9,000.0
161	Progressive	14,563.6	211	United States Steel	11,048.0	261	Devon Energy	8,960.0
162	Gap	14,197.0	212	AutoNation	11,015.6	262	Praxair	8,956.0
163	Smithfield Foods	14,190.5	213	Marriott International	10,908.0	263	NRG Energy	8,952.0
164	Union Pacific	14,143.0	214	ITT	10,904.5	264	Harrah's Entertainment	8,907.4
165	Loews	14,123.0	215	SAIC	10,847.0	265	Automatic Data Processing	8,867.1
166	EMC	14,025.9	216	Yum Brands	10,836.0	266	Principal Financial	8,849.1
167	Burlington Northern Santa Fe	14,016.0	217	BB&T Corp.	10,818.0	267	eBay	8,727.4
168	Coventry Health Care	13,993.3	218	Cummins	10,800.0	268	Assurant	8,700.5
169	Illinois Tool Works	13,903.6	219	Entergy	10,745.7	269	Limited Brands	8,632.5
170	Viacom	13,619.0	220	Textron	10,548.0	270	Nordstrom	8,627.0
171	Toys "R" Us	13,568.0	221	Marsh & McLennan	10,493.0	271	Apache	8,614.8
172	American Electric Power	13,489.0	222	US Airways Group	10,458.0	272	Reynolds American	8,419.0
173	PG&E Corp.	13,399.0	223	Texas Instruments	10,427.0	273	Air Products & Chemicals	8,381.4
174	Pepsi Bottling	13,219.0	224	SunTrust Banks	10,420.0	274	Bank of New York Mellon Corp.	8,345.0
175	Consolidated Edison	13,031.6	225	Qualcomm	10,416.0	275	CenterPoint Energy	8,281.0
176	Chubb	13,016.0	226	Land O'Lakes	10,408.5	276	Williams	8,255.0
177	CBS	13,014.6	227	Liberty Media	10,398.0	277	Smith International	8,218.6
178	ConAgra Foods	12,980.8	228	Avon Products	10,382.8	278	Republic Services	8,199.1
179	FirstEnergy	12,967.0	229	Southwest Airlines	10,350.0	279	Boston Scientific	8,188.0
180	Sara Lee	12,881.0	230	Parker Hannifin	10,309.0	280	Ashland	8,106.0
181	Duke Energy	12,731.0	231	Mosaic	10,298.0	280	Sempra Energy	8,106.0
182	National Oilwell Varco	12,712.0	232	BJ's Wholesale Club	10,187.0	282	Paccar	8,086.5
183	Continental Airlines	12,586.0	233	H.J. Heinz	10,148.1	283	Owens & Minor	8,037.6
184	Kellogg	12,575.0	234	Thermo Fisher Scientific	10,109.7	284	Whole Foods Market	8,031.6
185	Baxter International	12,562.0	235	Unum Group	10,091.0	285	DTE Energy	8,014.0
186	Public Service Enterprise Group	12,406.0	236	Genuine Parts	10,057.5	286	Discover Financial Services	7,985.7
187	Edison International	12,361.0	237	Guardian Life Ins. Co. of America	10,040.9	287	Norfolk Southern	7,969.0
188	Qwest Communications	12,311.0	238	Peter Kiewit Sons'	9,985.0	288	Ameriprise Financial	7,946.0
189	Aramark	12,297.9	239	Progress Energy	9,885.0	289	Crown Holdings	7,938.0
190	PPG Industries	12,239.0	240	R.R. Donnelley & Sons	9,857.4	290	Icahn Enterprises	7,865.0
191	Community Health Systems	12,149.7	241	Starbucks	9,774.6	291	Masco	7,858.0
192	Office Depot	12,144.5	242	Lear	9,739.6	292	Cablevision Systems	7,773.3
193	KBR	12,105.0	243	Baker Hughes	9,664.0	293	Huntsman	7,763.0
194	Eaton	11,873.0	244	Xcel Energy	9,644.3	294	Synnex	7,756.3
195	Dollar General	11,796.4	245	Penske Automotive Group	9,558.1	295	Newmont Mining	7,737.0
196	Waste Management	11,791.0	246	Energy Future Holdings	9,546.0	296	Chesapeake Energy	7,701.9
197	Monsanto	11,740.0	247	Great Atlantic & Pacific Tea	9,516.2	297	Eastman Kodak	7,606.0
198	Omnicom Group	11,720.7	248	Fifth Third Bancorp	9,450.0	298	Aon	7,595.0
199	Jabil Circuit	11,684.5	249	State Street Corp.	9,362.0	299	Campbell Soup	7,586.0
200	DISH Network	11,664.2	250	First Data	9,313.8	300	PPL	7,585.0

The *FORTUNE* 500 Largest US Corporations (continued)

Rank	Company	Sales ($ mil.)	Rank	Company	Sales ($ mil.)	Rank	Company	Sales ($ mil.)
301	C.H. Robinson Worldwide	7,577.2	351	Fortune Brands	6,205.4	401	Pacific Life	5,211.0
302	Integrys Energy Group	7,499.8	352	AECOM Technology	6,192.4	402	Terex	5,205.0
303	Quest Diagnostics	7,455.2	353	Symantec	6,149.9	403	Universal Health Services	5,202.4
304	Western Digital	7,453.0	354	SLM	6,144.7	404	Amerigroup	5,188.1
305	Family Dollar Stores	7,400.6	355	DaVita	6,108.8	405	Sanmina-SCI	5,177.5
306	Winn-Dixie Stores	7,367.0	356	KeyCorp	6,068.0	406	Jarden	5,152.6
307	Ball	7,345.3	357	MeadWestvaco	6,049.0	407	Tutor Perini	5,152.0
308	Estée Lauder	7,323.8	358	Interpublic Group	6,027.6	408	Mutual of Omaha Insurance	5,149.6
309	Shaw Group	7,279.7	359	Virgin Media	6,013.6	409	Avis Budget Group	5,131.0
310	VF	7,220.3	360	MGM Mirage	5,978.6	410	Autoliv	5,120.7
311	Darden Restaurants	7,217.5	361	First American Corp.	5,972.8	411	MasterCard	5,098.7
312	Becton Dickinson	7,216.7	362	Avery Dennison	5,952.7	412	Mylan	5,092.8
313	OfficeMax	7,212.1	363	McGraw-Hill	5,951.8	413	Western Union	5,083.6
314	Bed Bath & Beyond	7,208.3	364	Enbridge Energy Partners	5,905.4	414	Celanese	5,082.0
315	Kinder Morgan	7,185.2	365	Ecolab	5,900.6	415	Eastman Chemical	5,047.0
316	Ross Stores	7,184.2	366	Fidelity National Financial	5,857.7	416	Telephone & Data Systems	5,020.7
317	Pilgrim's Pride	7,113.8	367	Dover	5,831.0	417	Polo Ralph Lauren	5,018.9
318	Hertz Global Holdings	7,101.5	368	Global Partners	5,818.4	418	Auto-Owners Insurance	5,017.1
319	Sherwin-Williams	7,094.2	369	UGI	5,737.8	419	Core-Mark Holding	5,015.6
320	Ameren	7,090.0	370	Gannett	5,613.0	420	Western & Southern Financial Group	5,014.4
321	Reinsurance Group of America	7,066.8	371	Harris	5,599.6	421	Applied Materials	5,013.6
322	Owens-Illinois	7,066.5	372	Barnes & Noble	5,596.3	422	Anixter International	4,982.4
323	CarMax	7,028.3	373	Newell Rubbermaid	5,577.6	423	CenturyTel	4,974.2
324	Gilead Sciences	7,011.4	374	Smurfit-Stone Container	5,574.0	424	Atmos Energy	4,969.1
325	Precision Castparts	6,913.8	375	Pitney Bowes	5,569.2	425	Universal American	4,963.5
326	Visa	6,911.0	376	CC Media Holdings	5,551.9	426	Ryder System	4,957.6
327	Commercial Metals	6,883.4	377	Emcor Group	5,547.9	427	SPX	4,935.9
328	WellCare Health Plans	6,878.2	378	Dr Pepper Snapple Group	5,531.0	428	Foot Locker	4,854.0
329	AutoZone	6,816.8	379	Weyerhaeuser	5,528.0	429	O'Reilly Automotive	4,847.1
330	Western Refining	6,807.4	380	SunGard Data Systems	5,508.0	430	Harley-Davidson	4,838.6
331	Dole Food	6,782.7	381	CH2M Hill	5,499.3	431	Holly	4,834.3
332	Charter Communications	6,755.0	382	Pantry	5,472.0	432	Micron Technology	4,803.0
333	Stryker	6,723.1	383	Domtar	5,465.0	432	Owens Corning	4,803.0
334	Goodrich	6,685.6	384	Clorox	5,450.0	434	EOG Resources	4,787.0
335	Visteon	6,685.0	385	Northeast Utilities	5,439.4	435	Black & Decker	4,775.1
336	NiSource	6,652.9	386	Oshkosh	5,433.3	436	Big Lots	4,726.8
337	AGCO	6,630.4	387	Mattel	5,430.8	437	Spectra Energy	4,725.0
338	Calpine	6,564.0	388	Energy Transfer Equity	5,417.3	438	Starwood Hotels & Resorts	4,712.0
339	Henry Schein	6,546.3	389	Advance Auto Parts	5,412.6	439	United Stationers	4,710.3
340	Hormel Foods	6,533.7	390	Advanced Micro Devices	5,403.0	440	TravelCenters of America	4,699.8
341	Affiliated Computer Services	6,523.2	391	Corning	5,395.0	441	BlackRock	4,699.3
342	Thrivent Financial for Lutherans	6,514.8	392	Mohawk Industries	5,344.0	442	Laboratory Corp. of America	4,694.7
343	Yahoo	6,460.3	393	PetSmart	5,336.4	443	Health Management Associates	4,687.3
344	American Family Insurance Group	6,453.4	394	Reliance Steel & Aluminum	5,318.1	444	NYSE Euronext	4,687.0
345	Sonic Automotive	6,349.7	395	Hershey	5,298.7	445	St. Jude Medical	4,681.3
346	Peabody Energy	6,313.9	396	YRC Worldwide	5,282.8	446	Tenneco	4,649.0
347	Omnicare	6,242.7	397	Dollar Tree	5,231.2	447	El Paso	4,631.0
348	Dillard's	6,226.6	398	Dana Holding	5,228.0	448	Wesco International	4,624.0
349	W.W. Grainger	6,222.0	399	Cameron International	5,223.2	449	Consol Energy	4,621.9
350	CMS Energy	6,212.0	400	Nash-Finch	5,212.7	450	ArvinMeritor	4,617.0

The *FORTUNE* 500 Largest US Corporations (continued)

Rank	Company	Sales ($ mil.)	Rank	Company	Sales ($ mil.)	Rank	Company	Sales ($ mil.)
451	NCR	4,612.0	471	Biogen Idec	4,377.3	491	Fiserv	4,224.0
452	Unisys	4,597.7	472	AbitibiBowater	4,366.0	492	Host Hotels & Resorts	4,216.0
453	Lubrizol	4,586.3	473	Flowserve	4,365.3	493	H&R Block	4,213.4
454	Alliant Techsystems	4,583.2	474	Airgas	4,349.5	494	Electronic Arts	4,212.0
455	Washington Post	4,569.7	475	Conseco	4,341.4	495	Franklin Resources	4,194.1
456	Las Vegas Sands	4,563.1	476	Rockwell Automation	4,332.5	496	Wisconsin Energy	4,193.2
457	Group 1 Automotive	4,525.7	477	Kindred Healthcare	4,326.3	497	Northern Trust Corp.	4,193.1
458	Genzyme	4,515.5	478	American Financial Group	4,320.6	498	MDU Resources Group	4,176.5
459	Allergan	4,503.6	479	Kelly Services	4,314.8	499	CB Richard Ellis Group	4,165.8
460	Broadcom	4,490.3	480	Spectrum Group International	4,293.3	500	Blockbuster	4,161.8
461	Agilent Technologies	4,481.0	481	RadioShack	4,276.0			
462	Rockwell Collins	4,470.0	482	CA	4,271.0			
463	W.R. Berkley	4,431.2	483	Con-way	4,269.2			
464	PepsiAmericas	4,421.3	484	Erie Insurance Group	4,255.4			
465	Charles Schwab	4,414.0	485	Casey's General Stores	4,251.5			
466	Dick's Sporting Goods	4,412.8	486	Centene	4,248.0			
467	FMC Technologies	4,405.4	487	Sealed Air	4,242.8			
468	NII Holdings	4,397.6	488	Frontier Oil	4,237.2			
469	General Cable	4,385.2	489	Scana	4,237.0			
470	Graybar Electric	4,377.9	490	Live Nation Entertainment	4,232.0			

The *Forbes* Largest Private Companies in the US

Rank	Company	Sales ($ mil.)	Rank	Company	Sales ($ mil.)	Rank	Company	Sales ($ mil.)
1	Cargill	106,300	51	Keystone Foods	6,540	101	Roundy's Supermarkets	3,900
2	Koch Industries	100,000	52	Bloomberg	6,100	102	Edward Jones	3,860
3	Chrysler	47,600	53	Hexion Specialty Chemicals	6,090	103	Michaels Stores	3,820
4	GMAC Financial Services	35,450	54	McKinsey & Co.	6,000	104	Hyatt Hotels Corporation	3,800
5	Bechtel	31,400	55	Wawa	5,830	105	InterTech Group	3,800
6	Mars	30,000	56	DeBruce Grain	5,760	106	VWR Funding	3,760
7	HCA	28,370	57	Allegis Group	5,740	107	Stater Bros.	3,750
8	PricewaterhouseCoopers	26,200	58	MBM	5,700	108	Schneider National	3,700
9	Publix Super Markets	24,110	59	Guardian Industries	5,600	109	Neiman Marcus Group	3,640
10	Ernst & Young	21,400	60	SunGard Data Systems	5,600	110	Burlington Coat Factory	3,570
11	US Foodservice	19,810	61	CH2M Hill Cos.	5,590	111	Brightstar	3,570
12	C&S Wholesale Grocers	19,330	62	Kohler	5,500	112	HT Hackney	3,550
13	Flying J	18,000	63	Ergon	5,430	113	Walsh Group	3,530
14	Pilot Travel Centers	17,280	64	Graybar Electric	5,400	114	Schwan Food	3,530
15	Love's Travel Stops & Country Stores	16,500	65	Aleris International	5,300	115	Raley's	3,530
16	Tenaska Energy	16,000	66	McJunkin Red Man	5,260	116	Central National-Gottesman	3,500
17	TransMontaigne	15,950	67	Freescale Semiconductor	5,230	117	Eby-Brown	3,500
18	Cox Enterprises	15,400	68	Gulf States Toyota	5,100	118	Belk	3,500
19	H.E. Butt Grocery	15,100	69	Kinray	5,100	119	McCarthy Building Cos.	3,480
20	Meijer	13,880	70	Save Mart Supermarkets	5,000	120	Hensel Phelps Construction	3,440
21	Toys "R" Us	13,720	71	Unisource Worldwide	5,000	121	Parsons	3,440
22	Fidelity Investments	12,900	72	Hearst	4,810	122	Consolidated Elec Distributors	3,430
23	Aramark	12,470	73	Charmer Sunbelt Group	4,800	123	Bass Pro Shops	3,400
24	Enterprise Rent-A-Car	12,100	74	Wegmans Food Markets	4,800	124	Colonial Group	3,400
25	Reyes Holdings	11,800	75	Clark Enterprises	4,700	125	Swift Transportation	3,400
26	Energy Future Holdings	11,360	76	Tishman Construction	4,690	126	JohnsonDiversey	3,320
27	Platinum Equity	11,350	77	Perdue	4,600	127	ServiceMaster	3,310
28	Transammonia	11,210	78	Southwire	4,600	128	US Oncology	3,300
29	Dollar General	10,460	79	International Automotive Components	4,500	129	Golub	3,300
30	JM Family Enterprises	10,100	80	Oxbow	4,500	130	Sheetz	3,240
31	Kiewit Corporation	10,040	81	Levi Strauss & Co.	4,400	131	Gilbane	3,210
32	Harrah's Entertainment	9,370	82	Booz Allen Hamilton	4,400	132	Black & Veatch	3,200
33	Performance Food Group	9,300	83	Mansfield Oil	4,400	133	Vanguard Health Systems	3,200
34	Cumberland Farms	8,900	84	Pro-Build Holdings	4,400	134	Berry Plastics	3,190
35	S.C. Johnson & Son	8,880	85	Republic National Distributing Company	4,400	135	Medline Industries	3,190
36	First Data	8,810	86	J.R. Simplot	4,400	136	LPL Investment Holdings	3,120
37	Murdock Holding Company	8,490	87	NewPage	4,360	137	Dot Foods	3,100
38	Southern Wine & Spirits	8,400	88	Carlson Cos.	4,330	138	E&J Gallo Winery	3,100
39	Alticor	8,200	89	Scoular	4,300	139	JD Heiskell & Co.	3,100
40	Giant Eagle	8,150	90	Avaya	4,200	140	International Data Group	3,050
41	CDW	8,070	91	Tribune Company	4,200	141	Structure Tone	3,030
42	Menard	7,900	92	WinCo Foods	4,200	142	Sports Authority	3,030
43	Hilton Worldwide	7,770	93	Whiting-Turner Contracting	4,150	143	Alex Lee	3,000
44	Sinclair Oil	7,750	94	Manor Care	4,130	144	Ashley Furniture Industries	3,000
45	QuikTrip	7,730	95	Hallmark Cards	4,020	145	Glazer's Wholesale Drug	3,000
46	Advance Publications	7,630	96	Golden State Foods	4,000	146	OSI Group	3,000
47	Capital Group Cos.	7,630	97	Kingston Technology Company	4,000	147	Sabre Holdings	3,000
48	Hy-Vee	7,050	98	Renco Group	4,000	148	Boise Cascade	2,980
49	Gordon Food Service	6,800	99	OSI Restaurant Partners	3,960	149	Grocers Supply	2,950
50	RaceTrac Petroleum	6,680	100	Red Apple Group	3,950	150	O'Neal Steel	2,930

SOURCE: *FORBES*, OCTOBER 28, 2010

The *Forbes* Largest Private Companies in the US (continued)

Rank	Company	Sales ($ mil.)	Rank	Company	Sales ($ mil.)	Rank	Company	Sales ($ mil.)
151	Amsted Industries	2,910	186	Travelport	2,530	221	Foster Farms	2,200
152	General Parts	2,910	187	Biomet	2,500	222	HP Hood	2,200
153	JELD-WEN	2,900	188	Andersen	2,500	223	Merit Energy	2,200
154	Schreiber Foods	2,900	189	Bausch & Lomb	2,500	224	Skadden, Arps	2,200
155	ABC Supply	2,880	190	Hunt Construction Group	2,500	225	Affinia Group	2,180
156	Hunt Consolidated/Hunt Oil	2,870	191	Schnuck Markets	2,500	226	Ingram Industries	2,160
157	Drummond	2,870	192	SHI International	2,440	227	Metals USA	2,160
158	M. A. Mortenson	2,830	193	Camac International	2,430	228	Brasfield & Gorrie	2,140
159	Demoulas Super Markets	2,800	194	Discount Tire	2,410	229	Flex-N-Gate	2,140
160	Quintiles Transnational	2,800	195	Boston Consulting Group	2,400	230	W.L. Gore & Associates	2,130
161	Rich Products	2,800	196	Ebsco Industries	2,400	231	WinWholesale	2,110
162	Sammons Enterprises	2,800	197	Fry's Electronics	2,400	232	84 Lumber	2,100
163	Zachry Construction	2,800	198	Smart & Final	2,400	233	Infor	2,100
164	J.E. Dunn Construction Group	2,760	199	J M Smith	2,360	234	Newegg.com	2,100
165	G-I Holdings	2,750	200	Parsons Brinckerhoff	2,340	235	Plastipak Holdings	2,100
166	Interstate Bakeries	2,700	201	Day & Zimmermann	2,320	236	Young's Market	2,050
167	Services Group of America	2,700	202	Iasis Healthcare	2,320	237	Bartlett & Co.	2,040
168	Houchens Industries	2,700	203	Guitar Center	2,300	238	Kum & Go	2,030
169	Ben E. Keith	2,700	204	Arctic Slope Regional	2,300	239	Univision Communications	2,020
170	Quality King Distributors	2,680	205	Life Care Centers of America	2,290	240	Vizio	2,010
171	Follett	2,660	206	Brookshire Grocery	2,270	241	Roll International	2,010
172	Apex Oil	2,640	207	NTK Holdings	2,270	242	D&H Distributing	2,000
173	Leprino Foods	2,600	208	Quad/Graphics	2,270	243	Bashas'	2,000
174	Maines Paper & Food Service	2,600	209	AMC Entertainment	2,270	244	Heico Cos.	2,000
175	Mary Kay	2,600	210	Academy Sports & Outdoors	2,260	245	Holiday Companies	2,000
176	Cooper-Standard Automotive	2,600	211	SAS Institute	2,260	246	J.M. Huber	2,000
177	Graham Packaging Holdings	2,580	212	Sequa	2,250	247	Sun Products	2,000
178	Golden Living	2,580	213	West Corp.	2,250	248	UniGroup	2,000
179	Asplundh Tree Expert	2,580	214	Dresser	2,240			
180	Wilbur-Ellis	2,580	215	ShopKo Stores	2,220			
181	Reader's Digest Association	2,560	216	Soave Enterprises	2,220			
182	Rosen's Diversified	2,560	217	Genesis HealthCare	2,210			
183	World Wide Technology	2,560	218	Bi-Lo Holdings	2,200			
184	Petco Animal Supplies	2,550	219	Delaware North Cos.	2,200			
185	Milliken & Co.	2,540	220	Electro-Motive Diesel	2,200			

Top 20 in CEO Compensation

Rank	Name	Company	Total Pay* ($ mil.)
1	H. Lawrence Culp Jr.	Danaher	141.4
2	Lawrence J. Ellison	Oracle	130.2
3	Aubrey K. McClendon	Chesapeake Energy	114.3
4	Ray R. Irani	Occidental Petroleum	103.1
5	David C. Novak	YUM! Brands	76.5
6	John C. Martin	Gilead Sciences	60.4
7	Sol J. Barer	Celgene	59.3
8	Keith A. Hutton	XTO Energy	54.8
9	Richard C. Adkerson	Freeport Copper	48.8
10	Jen-Hsun Huang	Nvidia	31.4
11	Ivan G. Seidenberg	Verizon Communications	30.9
12	Louis C. Camilleri	Philip Morris International	30.1
13	Ralph Lauren	Polo Ralph Lauren	30.1
14	Howard D. Schultz	Starbucks	29.2
15	Robert W. Selander	MasterCard	29.0
16	Laurence D. Fink	BlackRock	28.2
17	J. Wayne Leonard	Entergy	27.3
18	Leslie Moonves	CBS	26.5
19	Hugh Grant	Monsanto	26.1
20	Gregg L. Engles	Dean Foods	25.5

*Includes salary, bonus, and long-term compensation

SOURCE: *FORBES*, APRIL 28, 2010

Top 20 Most Powerful Women in Business

Rank	Name	Position
1	Indra Nooyi	Chairman and CEO, PepsiCo
2	Irene Rosenfeld	Chairman and CEO, Kraft Foods
3	Patricia Woertz	Chairman and CEO, Archer Daniels Midland
4	Angela Braly	Chairman and CEO, WellPoint
5	Andrea Jung	Chairman and CEO, Avon Products
6	Oprah Winfrey	Chairman, Harpo and OWN
7	Ellen Kullman	Chairman and CEO, DuPont
8	Ginni Rometty	SVP, Sales, Marketing, and Strategy, IBM
9	Ursula Burns	Chairman and CEO, Xerox
10	Carol Bartz	President and CEO, Yahoo!
11	Safra Catz	Co-president, Oracle
12	Sherilyn McCoy	Group chairman, Johnson & Johnson
13	Melanie Healey	Group president, Procter & Gamble
14	Ann Livermore	EVP, HP Enterprise Business, Hewlett-Packard
15	Anne Sweeney	President, Disney-ABC Television Group
16	Sheryl Sandberg	COO, Facebook
17	Carol Meyrowitz	President and CEO, TJX Cos.
18	Judy McGrath	Chairman and CEO, MTV Networks, Viacom
19	Barbara Desoer	President, Home Loans, Bank of America
20	Charlene Begley	CEO, GE Home and Business Solutions

SOURCE: *FORTUNE*, OCTOBER 18, 2010

Forbes Greatest US Fortunes

Rank	Name	Age	Net Worth ($ bil.)	Source
1	Bill Gates	54	54.0	Microsoft
2	Warren Buffett	80	45.0	Berkshire Hathaway
3	Larry Ellison	66	27.0	Oracle
4	Christy Walton	55	24.0	Wal-Mart
5	Charles Koch	74	21.5	Manufacturing, energy
5	David Koch	70	21.5	Manufacturing, energy
7	Jim Walton	62	20.1	Wal-Mart
8	Alice Walton	61	20.0	Wal-Mart
9	S. Robson Walton	66	19.7	Wal-Mart
10	Michael Bloomberg	68	18.0	Bloomberg
11	Larry Page	37	15.0	Google
11	Sergey Brin	37	15.0	Google
13	Sheldon Adelson	77	14.7	Casinos, hotels
14	George Soros	80	14.2	Hedge funds
15	Michael Dell	45	14.0	Dell
16	Steve Ballmer	54	13.1	Microsoft
17	Paul Allen	57	12.7	Microsoft, investments
18	Jeff Bezos	46	12.6	Amazon
19	Anne Cox Chambers	90	12.5	Cox Enterprises
20	John Paulson	54	12.4	Hedge funds

SOURCE: *FORBES*, SEPTEMBER 16, 2010

Forbes 20 Most Powerful Celebrities

Rank	Name	Earnings ($ mil.)
1	Oprah Winfrey	315.0
2	Beyonce Knowles	87.0
3	James Cameron	210.0
4	Lady Gaga	62.0
5	Tiger Woods	105.0
6	Britney Spears	64.0
7	U2	130.0
8	Sandra Bullock	56.0
9	Johnny Depp	75.0
10	Madonna	58.0
11	Simon Cowell	80.0
12	Taylor Swift	45.0
13	Miley Cyrus	48.0
14	Kobe Bryant	48.0
15	Jay-Z	63.0
16	Black Eyed Peas	48.0
17	Bruce Springsteen	70.0
18	Angelina Jolie	20.0
19	Rush Limbaugh	58.5
20	Michael Jordan	55.0

Forbes' rankings are based on income and media recognition (Web prominence, magazine covers, radio/TV and newspaper coverage)

SOURCE: *FORBES*, JUNE 28, 2010

Advertising Age's Top 50 Media Companies by Revenue

Rank	Company	Headquarters	2009 Media Revenue ($ mil.)
1	Comcast Corp.	Philadelphia	32,090
2	DirecTV	El Segundo, CA	19,030
3	Walt Disney Co.	Burbank, CA	18,160
4	Time Warner	New York	17,180
5	News Corp.	New York	16,100
6	Time Warner Cable	New York	15,980
7	NBC Universal (General Electric)	New York	11,750
8	Dish Network Corp.	Englewood, CO	11,540
9	AT&T	Dallas	11,400
10	Cox Enterprises	Atlanta	11,330
11	CBS Corp.	New York	10,470
12	Viacom	New York	9,800
13	Google	Mountain View, CA	7,910
14	Advance Publications	New York	6,740
15	Verizon Communications	New York	6,200
16	Charter Communications	St. Louis	6,040
17	Cablevision Systems Corp.	Bethpage, NY	5,990
18	Gannett Co.	McLean, VA	4,790
19	Clear Channel Communications	San Antonio	3,860
20	Sony Corp.	New York/Tokyo	3,710
21	Yahoo!	Sunnyvale, CA	3,540
22	Hearst Corp.	New York	3,250
23	Tribune Co.	Chicago	3,180
24	A&E Television Networks	New York	2,580
25	SuperMedia	Dallas/Fort Worth Airport, TX	2,510
26	Sirius XM Radio	New York	2,390
27	AOL	New York	2,380
28	The New York Times Co.	New York	2,280
29	Activision Blizzard Corp.	Santa Monica, CA	2,220
30	Dex One Corp.	Cary, NC	2,200
31	Discovery Communications	Silver Spring, MD	2,140
32	Valassis Communications	Livonia, MI	2,090
33	Electronic Arts	Redwood City, CA	2,030
34	Univision Communications	Los Angeles	1,970
35	Scripps Networks Interactive	Knoxville, TN	1,760
36	The Washington Post Co.	Washington, DC	1,700
37	Yell Group	Uniondale, NY/Reading, UK	1,680
38	Microsoft Corp.	Redmond, WA	1,590
39	Liberty Media Corp.	Englewood, CO	1,580
40	Suddenlink Communications	St. Louis	1,570
41	McClatchy Co.	Sacramento, CA	1,470
42	Mediacom Communications Corp.	Middletown, NY	1,350
43	MediaNews Group (Affiliated Media)	Denver	1,290
44	Lions Gate Entertainment Corp.	Santa Monica, CA	1,270
45	Meredith Corp.	Des Moines, IA	1,090
46	Lamar Advertising Co.	Baton Rouge, LA	1,060
47	IAC/InterActiveCorp	New York	1,040
48	Insight Communications Co.	New York	829
49	Lee Enterprises	Davenport, IA	829
50	RDA Holding Co.	New York	724

Source: *ADVERTISING AGE*, SEPTEMBER 27, 2010

STORES' Top 20 US Retailers

Rank	Company	Headquarters	2009 Revenue ($ mil.)
1	Wal-Mart	Bentonville, AR	304,939
2	Kroger	Cincinnati	76,733
3	Target	Minneapolis	63,435
4	Walgreen	Deerfield, IL	63,335
5	The Home Depot	Atlanta	59,176
6	Costco	Issaquah, WA	56,548
7	CVS Caremark	Woonsocket, RI	55,355
8	Lowe's	Mooresville, NC	47,220
9	Sears Holdings	Hoffman Estates, IL	44,043
10	Best Buy	Richfield, MN	37,314
11	Safeway	Pleasanton, CA	34,980
12	SUPERVALU	Eden Prairie, MN	31,637
13	Rite Aid	Camp Hill, PA	25,669
14	Publix	Lakeland, FL	24,515
15	Macy's	Cincinnati	23,489
16	Ahold USA	Carlisle, PA	22,825
17	McDonald's	Oak Brook, IL	22,240
18	Delhaize America	Salisbury, NC	18,994
19	J.C. Penney	Plano, TX	17,556
20	Kohl's	Menomonee Falls, WI	17,178

SOURCE: *STORES*, JULY 2010

Supermarket News' Top 20 Supermarket Companies

Rank	Company	Headquarters	2009 Estimated Revenue ($ mil.)
1	Wal-Mart Stores	Bentonville, AR	262,000
2	Kroger Co.	Cincinnati	76,000
3	Costco Wholesale Corp.	Issaquah, WA	71,400
4	Supervalu	Minneapolis	41,300
5	Safeway	Pleasanton, CA	40,800
6	Loblaw Cos.	Toronto	29,900
7	Publix Super Markets	Lakeland, Fl	24,300
8	Ahold USA	Quincy, MA	22,300
9	C&S Wholesale Grocers	Keene, NH	19,000
10	Delhaize America	Salisbury, NC	19,000
11	7-Eleven	Dallas	17,500
12	H.E. Butt Grocery Co.	San Antonio	15,000
13	Meijer Inc.	Grand Rapids, MI	14,100
14	Sobeys	Stellarton, Nova Scotia	12,700
15	Dollar General Corp.	Goodlettsville, TN	11,800
16	Wakefern Food Corp.	Keasbey, NJ	11,700
17	Metro	Montreal	10,700
18	BJ's Wholesale Club	Natick, MA	10,200
19	A&P	Montvale, NJ	9,100
20	Giant Eagle	Pittsburgh	8,200

SOURCE: *SUPERMARKET NEWS*, JANUARY 25, 2010

Top 20 Bank Holding Companies

Rank	Company	Headquarters	2009 Total Assets ($ mil.)
1	Bank of America Corporation	Charlotte, NC	2,366,086.9
2	JPMorgan Chase & Co.	New York	2,014,019.0
3	Citigroup Inc.	New York	1,937,656.0
4	Wells Fargo & Company	San Francisco	1,225,862.0
5	Goldman Sachs Group Inc.	New York	883,529.0
6	Morgan Stanley	New York	809,456.0
7	MetLife, Inc.	New York	573,907.1
8	Barclays Group US Inc.	Wilmington, DE	356,186.0
9	Taunus Corporation	New York	348,586.0
10	HSBC North America Holdings Inc.	New York	333,998.0
11	U.S. Bancorp	Minneapolis	283,243.0
12	PNC Financial Services Group, Inc.	Pittsburgh	261,769.3
13	Bank of New York Mellon Corporation	New York	235,944.0
14	Capital One Financial Corporation	McLean, VA	197,488.7
15	Ally Financial Inc.	Detroit	176,814.0
16	Suntrust Banks, Inc.	Atlanta	170,668.5
17	State Street Corporation	Boston	160,664.2
18	TD Bank US Holding Company	Portland, ME	159,058.4
19	BB&T Corporation	Winston-Salem, NC	155,083.1
20	American Express Company	New York	142,729.4

SOURCE: FEDERAL RESERVE SYSTEM, JUNE 30, 2010

Top 20 US Law Firms

Rank	Law Firm	2009 Gross Revenue ($ mil.)	Number of Lawyers
1	Baker & McKenzie	2,112.0	3,949
2	Skadden	2,100.0	1,860
3	Latham & Watkins	1,821.0	1,880
4	Jones Day	1,520.0	2,469
5	Kirkland & Ellis	1,428.0	1,411
6	Sidley Austin	1,357.0	1,588
7	White & Case	1,307.0	1,890
8	Weil Gotshal	1,233.0	1,212
9	Greenberg Traurig	1,173.0	1,707
10	Mayer Brown	1,118.0	1,657
11	Morgan Lewis	1,068.5	1,315
12	K&L Gates	1,034.5	1,705
13	DLA Piper US	1,014.5	1,251
14	Gibson Dunn	995.0	983
14	Sullivan & Cromwell	995.0	700
16	Cleary Gottlieb	965.0	992
17	Reed Smith	942.0	1,427
18	Wilmer	941.0	933
19	Dewey & LeBoeuf	914.0	1,054
20	Paul Hastings	889.0	917

SOURCE: *AMERICAN LAWYER*, MAY 1, 2010

Top 20 Tax & Accounting Firms by US Revenue

Rank	Firm	Headquarters	2009 US Revenue ($ mil.)
1	Deloitte & Touche	New York	10,722.0
2	Ernst & Young	New York	7,620.0
3	PricewaterhouseCoopers	New York	7,369.4
4	KPMG	New York	5,076.0
5	RSM/McGladrey & Pullen	Bloomington, MN	1,460.7
6	Grant Thornton	Chicago	1,147.8
7	BDO	Chicago	620.0
8	CBIZ/Mayer Hoffman McCann	Cleveland	600.7
9	Crowe Horwath	Oak Brook Terrace, IL	508.0
10	BKD	Springfield, MO	393.0
11	Moss Adams	Seattle	323.0
12	Plante & Moran	Southfield, MI	301.2
13	Baker Tilly Virchow Krause	Chicago	260.0
14	Clifton Gunderson	Milwaukee	251.0
15	J.H. Cohn	Roseland, NJ	235.0
16	UHY Advisors	Chicago	234.4
17	Marcum	Melville, NY	233.8
18	LarsonAllen	Minneapolis	218.0
19	Dixon Hughes	High Point, NC	200.0
20	Reznick Group	Bethesda, MD	189.6

SOURCE: *ACCOUNTING TODAY*, MARCH 12, 2010

FORTUNE's 100 Best Companies to Work for in America

Rank	Company	US Employees	Rank	Company	US Employees	Rank	Company	US Employees
1	SAS	5,487	36	Container Store	3,233	71	PricewaterhouseCoopers	29,387
2	Edward Jones	37,079	37	Aflac	4,353	72	McCormick and Company	2,799
3	Wegmans Food Markets	36,770	38	Scooter Store	2,173	73	American Express	27,265
4	Google	N.A.	39	TDIndustries	1,588	74	Children's Healthcare of Atlanta	6,536
5	Nugget Market	1,342	40	Scripps Health	11,444	75	Perkins Coie	1,680
6	DreamWorks Animation SKG	1,825	41	QuikTrip	10,311	76	Balfour Beatty Construction	1,514
7	NetApp	5,033	42	Adobe Systems	4,065	77	Baker Donelson	1,127
8	Boston Consulting Group	1,737	43	Salesforce.com	2,361	78	Mattel	5,293
9	Qualcomm	12,255	44	Ernst & Young	24,815	79	Meridian Health	7,099
10	Camden Property Trust	1,743	45	USAA	21,999	80	Build-A-Bear Workshop	4,588
11	Robert W. Baird & Co.	2,286	46	OhioHealth	12,128	81	Atlantic Health	7,114
12	Bingham McCutchen	1,859	47	J. M. Smucker	4,521	82	Marriott International	110,091
13	W. L. Gore & Associates	5,764	48	FactSet Research Systems	1,322	83	S. C. Johnson & Son	3,343
14	Recreational Equipment	8,640	49	Mercedes-Benz USA	1,612	84	Accenture	30,000
15	Zappos.com	1,300	50	King's Daughters Medical Center	3,263	85	Arkansas Children's Hospital	3,733
16	Cisco	37,276	51	Microsoft	54,923	86	Publix Super Markets	139,578
17	Methodist Hospital System	11,145	52	Booz Allen Hamilton	21,303	87	National Instruments	2,568
18	Whole Foods Market	47,478	53	Nordstrom	45,853	88	KPMG	20,972
19	Genentech	11,146	54	Paychex	12,456	89	Bright Horizons	14,497
20	Devon Energy	3,912	55	Mayo Clinic	41,839	90	General Mills	16,681
21	NuStar Energy	1,375	56	CarMax	13,030	91	FedEx	218,770
22	Johnson Financial Group	1,316	57	DPR Construction	1,142	92	Gilbane	1,934
23	Umpqua Bank	1,836	58	Four Seasons Hotels	12,345	93	Starbucks Coffee	116,357
24	Goldman Sachs Group	12,243	59	Monsanto	10,772	94	Intuit	6,710
25	Novo Nordisk	3,360	60	Indiana Regional Medical Center	1,200	95	Orrick Herrington & Sutcliffe	1,481
26	CHG Healthcare Services	1,142	61	Brocade Communications Systems	2,873	96	LifeBridge Health	6,350
27	Scottrade	2,409	62	Kimley-Horn	1,808	97	Herman Miller	5,186
28	JM Family Enterprises	3,772	63	Southern Ohio Medical Center	2,286	98	Intel	43,905
29	Quicken Loans	2,893	64	Stew Leonard's	2,037	99	Winchester Hospital	2,027
30	Alston & Bird	1,842	65	Arnold & Porter	1,295	100	Colgate-Palmolive	5,366
31	PCL Construction Enterprises	3,970	66	Plante & Moran	1,547			
32	Baptist Health South Florida	11,729	67	EOG Resources	1,725			
33	Shared Technologies	1,243	68	Men's Wearhouse	14,764			
34	Chesapeake Energy	7,720	69	MITRE	6,572			
35	American Fidelity Assurance Co.	1,502	70	Deloitte	39,065			

SOURCE: *FORTUNE*, FEBRUARY 8, 2010

Top 20 Black-Owned Businesses*

Rank	Company	2009 Revenue ($ mil.)
1	World Wide Technology Inc.	2,200.0
2	CAMAC International Corp.	1,200.0
3	Bridgewater Interiors L.L.C.	1,092.6
4	ACT-1 Group	998.7
5	ZeroChaos	727.0
6	MV Transportation Inc.	705.0
7	TAG Holdings L.L.C.	533.0
8	RLJ Development L.L.C.	528.7
9	Manna Inc.	502.0
10	Barden Cos. Inc.	405.0
11	Anderson-Dubose Co.	382.1
12	Thompson Hospitality Corp.	321.0
13	H.J. Russell & Co.	316.1
14	Harpo Inc.	315.0
15	Converge	279.4
16	Global Automotive Alliance L.L.C.	275.0
17	Radio One Inc.	272.0
18	Piston Automotive	247.8
19	PRWT Services Inc.	215.0
20	1 Source Consulting Inc.	210.7

*Industrial and service companies only

SOURCE: *BLACK ENTERPRISE*, JUNE, 2010

Top 20 Hispanic-Owned Businesses

Rank	Company	2009 Revenue ($ mil.)
1	Molina Healthcare Inc.	3,700.0
2	Brightstar Corp.	2,757.0
3	MasTec Inc.	1,623.5
4	International Bancshares Corp.	728.4
5	Crossland Construction Co. Inc.	527.5
6	Ruiz Foods Inc	500.0
7	Quirch Foods Co.	500.0
8	Greenway Ford Inc.	439.0
9	Group O Inc.	438.6
10	Pan-American Life Insurance Group	427.0
11	Fred Loya Insurance	419.3
12	G&A Partners	375.5
13	Ancira Enterprises Inc.	374.0
14	Goodman Networks Inc.	365.0
15	Lopez Foods Inc.	357.0
16	The Diez Group	319.0
17	Navarro Discount Pharmacies	316.0
18	Urbieta Oil Inc.	306.0
19	Venoco Inc.	272.2
20	Blackstone Calling Card Inc.	258.0

SOURCE: *HISPANIC BUSINESS*, JUNE 2010

Top 10 Companies for Female Executives

Rank	Company	Headquarters	2009 Revenue ($ mil.)
1	Abbott	Abbott Park, IL	30,764.7
2	Aetna	Hartford, CT	34,764.1
3	American Express Company	New York	26,730.0
4	Fleishman-Hillard	St. Louis, MO	—
5	General Mills	Minneapolis	14,691.3
6	IBM Corporation	Armonk, NY	95,758.0
7	Johnson & Johnson	New Brunswick, NJ	61,897.0
8	Marriott International	Bethesda, MD	10,908.0
9	Office Depot	Boca Raton, FL	12,144.5
10	WellPoint	Indianapolis	65,028.1

SOURCE: NATIONAL ASSOCIATION OF FEMALE EXECUTIVES, MARCH 2, 2010

FORTUNE's 10 Most Admired Companies

Rank	Company	CEO	2009 Revenue ($ mil.)
1	Apple	Steven P. Jobs	42,905.0
2	Google	Eric E. Schmidt	23,650.6
3	Berkshire Hathaway	Warren E. Buffett	112,493.0
4	Johnson & Johnson	William C. Weldon	61,897.0
5	Amazon.com	Jeffrey P. Bezos	24,509.0
6	Procter & Gamble	Robert A. McDonald	79,029.0
7	Toyota Motor	Akio Toyoda	204,443.1
8	Goldman Sachs Group	Lloyd C. Blankfein	51,673.0
9	Wal-Mart Stores	Michael T. Duke	405,607.0
10	Coca-Cola	Muhtar Kent	30,990.0

SOURCE: *FORTUNE*, MARCH 22, 2010

Hoover's Handbook of

American Business

The Companies

3M Company

Loath to be stuck on one thing, 3M makes everything from masking tape to asthma inhalers. The diversified company makes products through six operating segments: consumer and office; display and graphics; electro and communications; health care (through 3M Health Care); industrial and transportation; and safety, security, and protection services. Well-known brands include Post-it Notes, Scotch tapes, Scotchgard fabric protectors, Scotch-Brite scouring pads, and Filtrete home air filters. 3M has operations in more than 60 countries.

The company has been making adjustments in costs, staffing, and capital projects to stay ahead in times of economic slowdown. 3M typically takes a conservative approach to managing its assets. For 2009 it cut about one-third of its capital spending plans and eliminated thousands of jobs across all geographic markets due to a tough recession. As a technology-driven company, however, it continues to make research and development a top priority, investing significantly in new product development efforts.

In 2010 the company expanded its consumer and office label business by acquiring a majority stake in Japanese-based A-One, the top label brand in Asia and the second largest worldwide. 3-M entered the US labels market in 2009 through its Post-it and 3M brands, and the acquisition of A-One will expand its presence to the global market.

That same year 3M acquired J.R. Phoenix Ltd., a manufacturer of hand hygiene and skin care products for health care and professional use. The majority of J.R. Phoenix products are sold under the Laura Line brand in Canada. The deal expanded 3M's line of hand hygiene skin care products to the health care market in Canada. The company also acquired UK-based Dailys Ltd., a global supplier of non-woven disposable chemical protective coveralls for industrial use.

Its 2008 acquisition of protection products maker Aearo Technologies is helping 3M's sales growth in the area of safety, security, and protection services. 3M gained a line of hearing and eye protection products for the occupational health and safety market. It added to this unit in 2010 with the purchase (through its 3M Canada subsidiary) of MTI PolyFab, which makes thermal and acoustic insulation for aerospace products. The company is also attempting to capitalize on its purchase of Beiersdorf subsidiary Futuro, which makes medical products, such as wraps, elastic bandages, and compression hosiery.

HISTORY

Five businessmen in Two Harbors, Minnesota, founded Minnesota Mining and Manufacturing (3M) in 1902 to sell corundum to grinding-wheel manufacturers. The company soon needed to raise working capital. Co-founder John Dwan offered his friend Edgar Ober 60% of 3M's stock. Ober persuaded Lucius Ordway, VP of a plumbing business, to help underwrite 3M. In 1905 the two took over the company and moved it to Duluth.

In 1907 future CEO William McKnight joined 3M as a bookkeeper. Three years later the plant moved to St. Paul. The board of directors declared a dividend to shareholders in the last quarter of 1916, and 3M hasn't missed a dividend since. The next two products 3M developed — Scotch-brand masking tape (1925) and Scotch-brand cellophane tape (1930) — assured its future.

McKnight introduced one of the first employee pension plans in 1931, and in the late 1940s he implemented a vertical management structure. 3M introduced the first commercially viable magnetic recording tape in 1947.

In 1950, after a decade of work and $1 million in development costs, 3M employee Carl Miller completed the Thermo-Fax copying machine, which was the foundation of 3M's duplicating division.

Products in the 1960s included 3M's dry-silver microfilm, photographic products, carbonless papers, overhead projection systems, and medical and dental products. The company moved into pharmaceuticals, radiology, energy control, and office markets in the 1970s and 1980s.

A 3M scientist developed Post-it Notes (1980) because he wanted to attach page markers to his church hymnal. Recalling that a colleague had developed an adhesive that wasn't very sticky, he brushed some on paper and began a product line that now generates hundreds of millions of dollars each year.

In 1990 the company bought sponge maker O-Cel-O. But not all of its inventions have brought 3M good news. In 1995, along with fellow silicone breast-implant makers Baxter International and Bristol-Myers Squibb, it agreed to settle thousands of personal-injury claims related to implants. The companies paid an average of $26,000 per claim.

3M spun off its low-profit imaging and data-storage businesses in 1996 as Imation Corp. and closed its audiotape and videotape businesses. The next year 3M sold its National Advertising billboard business to Infinity Outdoor for $1 billion and its Media Network unit (a printer of advertising inserts) to Time Warner.

The company created the 3M Nexcare brand for its line of first-aid and home health products in 1998. To regain earnings growth, 3M closed about 10% of its plants in the US and abroad; it also discontinued unprofitable product lines.

3M bought Polaroid's Technical Polarizer and Display Films business and a controlling stake in Germany-based Quante AG (telecom systems) in 2000. In addition, the company decided to halt the manufacture of many of its Scotchgard-brand repellent products due to research revealing that one of the compounds (perfluorooctane sulfonate) used in the manufacturing process is "persistent and pervasive" in the environment and in people's bloodstreams. As 2000 drew to a close, 3M named GE executive James McNerney to succeed L. D. DeSimone as its chairman and CEO.

3M in 2001 announced plans to cut 6,000 jobs and authorized a stock buy-back program of up to $2.5 billion. The company changed its legal name from Minnesota Mining and Manufacturing Company to 3M Company that year. By the end of that year, the company had cut more than 8,500 jobs — 11% of its total workforce.

CEO McNerney left 3M in 2005 to join Boeing in the same capacity and was replaced by George Buckley, formerly of the Brunswick Corporation.

That year, the company made a billion-dollar acquisition of liquid filtration producer CUNO.

3M signaled a new strategic direction in 2006 when it sold its pharmaceutical operations in pieces. The sales totaled about $2.1 billion.

The company then ran through another string of acquisitions in 2007, buying companies such as Unifam, Lingualcare, Innovative Paper Technologies, and Diamond Productions.

EXECUTIVES

Chairman, President, and CEO: George W. Buckley, age 63, $14,935,793 total compensation
EVP Consumer and Office Business: Joe E. Harlan, age 50, $2,686,414 total compensation
EVP Health Care Business: Brad T. Sauer, age 51, $3,353,798 total compensation
EVP International Operations: Inge G. Thulin, age 56, $3,531,116 total compensation
EVP Industrial and Transportation Business: Hak Cheol (H. C.) Shin, age 53
EVP Research and Development and CTO: Frederick J. Palensky, age 60
EVP Safety, Security, and Protection Services Business: Jean Lobey, age 58, $3,433,584 total compensation
EVP Display and Graphics Business: Michael A. Kelly, age 53
EVP Electro and Communications Business: Joaquin Delgado, age 50
SVP and CFO: Patrick D. (Pat) Campbell, age 57, $4,489,848 total compensation
SVP Human Resources: Angela S. Lalor, age 44
SVP Marketing and Sales: Robert D. MacDonald, age 59
SVP Strategy and Corporate Development: Roger H. D. Lacey, age 60
SVP Corporate Supply Chain Operations: John K. Woodworth, age 59
SVP Legal Affairs and General Counsel: Marschall I. Smith, age 65
VP and CIO: Ernest (Ernie) Park, age 56
VP and Treasurer: Janet L. Yeomans
VP, Corporate Controller, and Chief Accounting Officer: David W. Meline, age 52
President and CEO, Aearo Technologies: Michael A. McLain
President and General Manager, 3M Purification: Timothy B. (Tim) Carney, age 57
President, 3M New Ventures: Stefan Gabriel
Deputy General Counsel and Secretary: Gregg M. Larson
Director Investor Relations: Matt Ginter
Public Relations and Corporate Communications: Mary Clemens
Auditors: PricewaterhouseCoopers LLP

LOCATIONS

HQ: 3M Company
3M Center, St. Paul, MN 55144
Phone: 651-733-1110   **Fax:** 651-733-9973
Web: www.mmm.com

2009 Sales

	$ mil.	% of total
US	8,509	37
Asia/Pacific	6,120	26
Europe, Africa & Middle East	5,972	26
Latin America & Canada	2,516	11
Other regions	6	—
Total	**23,123**	**100**

PRODUCTS/OPERATIONS

2009 Sales

	$ mil.	% of total
Industrial & Transportation	7,116	30
Health Care	4,294	18
Consumer & Office	3,471	15
Safety, Security & Protection Services	3,180	14
Display & Graphics	3,132	13
Electro & Communications	2,276	10
Corporate	12	—
Adjustments	(358)	—
Total	**23,123**	**100**

Selected Segments and Products

Industrial and Transportation
- Automotive aftermarket products
- Automotive products
- Closures for disposable diapers
- Coated and nonwoven abrasives
- Films
- Filtration products
- Specialty adhesives
- Tapes

Health Care
- Dental products
- Drug delivery systems
- Health information systems
- Infection prevention
- Medical and surgical supplies
- Microbiology products
- Skin health products

Safety, Security, and Protection
- Commercial cleaning products
- Consumer safety products
- Corrosion protection products
- Floor matting
- Occupational health and safety products
- Safety and security products
- Track and trace products

Consumer and Office
- Carpet and fabric protectors
- Commercial cleaning products
- Fabric protectors (Scotchgard)
- High-performance cloth (Scotch-Brite)
- Home-improvement products
- Repositionable notes (Post-it)
- Scour pads (Scotch-Brite)
- Sponges (O-Cel-O)
- Tape (Scotch)

Display and Graphics
- Commercial graphics systems
- Optical films for electronic display
- Specialty film and media products
- Traffic control materials

Electro and Communications
- Insulating and splicing products for electronics, telecommunications, and electrical industries
- Packaging and interconnection devices

COMPETITORS

ACCO Brands
Avery Dennison
BASF SE
Bayer AG
Beiersdorf
Bostik
Corning
DuPont
GE
H.B. Fuller
Henkel
Honeywell International
Illinois Tool Works
International Specialty Products
Johnson & Johnson
Kimberly-Clark
Ricoh Company
RPM International
S.C. Johnson
Sealed Air Corp.

HISTORICAL FINANCIALS

Company Type: Public

Income Statement

FYE: December 31

	REVENUE ($ mil.)	NET INCOME ($ mil.)	NET PROFIT MARGIN	EMPLOYEES
12/09	23,123	3,193	13.8%	74,835
12/08	25,269	3,460	13.7%	79,183
12/07	24,462	4,096	16.7%	76,239
12/06	22,923	3,851	16.8%	75,333
12/05	21,167	3,234	15.3%	69,315
Annual Growth	2.2%	(0.3%)	—	1.9%

2009 Year-End Financials

Debt ratio: 39.9%	No. of shares (mil.): 713
Return on equity: 28.2%	Dividends
Cash ($ mil.): 3,040	Yield: 2.5%
Current ratio: 2.20	Payout: 45.1%
Long-term debt ($ mil.): 5,097	Market value ($ mil.): 58,955

Stock History

NYSE: MMM

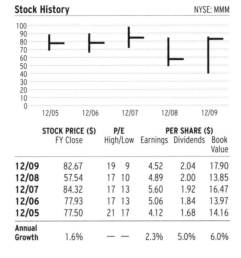

	STOCK PRICE ($) FY Close	P/E High/Low		PER SHARE ($) Earnings	Dividends	Book Value
12/09	82.67	19	9	4.52	2.04	17.90
12/08	57.54	17	10	4.89	2.00	13.85
12/07	84.32	17	13	5.60	1.92	16.47
12/06	77.93	17	13	5.06	1.84	13.97
12/05	77.50	21	17	4.12	1.68	14.16
Annual Growth	1.6%	—	—	2.3%	5.0%	6.0%

A. Schulman, Inc.

A. Schulman adds color to plastic resins but keeps them from getting red hot. Schulman adds chemicals to basic plastics such as polypropylene, polyethylene, and PVC to give them color and desired characteristics like flexibility or the ability to retard flame. Its products include color and additive concentrates, engineered compounds (such as reinforced plastics), and value-added PVC. Customers include makers of plastics and auto parts, with more than a third of its sales to packaging manufacturers. At the end of 2009 the company acquired ICO in a deal that valued the plastics maker at $190 million. The deal was designed to expand both Schulman's global presence and its masterbatch and molding businesses.

Schulman has spent much of the latter half of the decade dealing with investors who have questioned the direction of the company, sought to name directors to the board, and advocated for a merger or sale. The process began when investment firm the Barington Group demanded the right to name a director. Its success spurred another investor group, Ramius Capital, to offer up its own set of directors for A. Schulman's early-2008 elections. Ramius, like Barington, was eager to get Schulman to consider a sale or merger of the company, or, at the very least, a change in the company strategy that had led to continually disappointing results. Ultimately, Ramius won the right to nominate candidates for the board.

Encouraged by the investors and their representative board members, the company idled one manufacturing facility and sold another in 2008; it also brought in UBS to explore possibilities of selling part or all of the company. (An offer from an unidentified buyer was turned down in mid-2008.) Schulman also began to seek a partner for its Invision line of plastic sheet products, which it deemed sufficiently different from everything else the company makes as to warrant an outside collaborator. It never found a satisfactory offer, though, and simply discontinued the line and shut down the operation in 2009. (It still does manufacture a line of resins under the Invision brand name, however.)

HISTORY

Alex Schulman founded A. Schulman in 1928 as a rubber brokerage. In 1937 he hired William Zekan as an office boy after meeting the 18-year-old caddie on a golf course. With rubber in short supply during WWII, A. Schulman began using scrap plastic. Zekan was appointed head of the firm's New York sales office in 1947 and became #2 in the company in 1953.

A. Schulman abandoned the scrap market in the 1950s to focus on plastic compounds. Schulman died in 1962 and Zekan headed the company, taking it public in 1972. A. Schulman set up a joint venture in 1988 with Mitsubishi to supply plastic compounds to Honda, Nissan, and Toyota.

Zekan died in 1991 and was replaced by company veteran Terry Haines. He expanded A. Schulman through acquisitions that included Diffusion Plastique from Atochem (subsidiary of Elf Aquitaine, now called TOTAL) in 1991 and Exxon's ComAlloy International in 1994. The next year the company bought a polymer unit from J. M. Huber and polypropylene interests from Eastman Chemical.

A. Schulman opened its first plant in Asia in 1997. The next year it cut production to compensate for an industry slowdown. The company also bought an Italy-based distributor and agreed to supply all of the color concentrate for Procter & Gamble's molded white containers. In 1999 A. Schulman spent $35 million to renovate manufacturing facilities. It joined DuPont that year to make bumper fascias and other moldings for cars such as the Dodge Neon.

As pricing pressures continued in 2000, A. Schulman moved to cut its costs by closing a number of sales offices and its plant in Akron, Ohio. The company's 2001 sales were hurt by the weakening economy, especially in the US, where capacity utilization was down by 5%. Although A. Schulman's sales remained flat in 2002, the company managed to boost profits mostly through a workforce reduction and the closing of more costly facilities.

Haines and other members of management came under fire with investors' criticism that began in 2007, and Haines stepped down early in 2008. He was replaced by director Joseph Gingo, a former Goodyear executive.

EXECUTIVES

Chairman, President, and CEO; EVP and COO, North America: Joseph M. (Joe) Gingo, age 64, $2,966,022 total compensation
SVP Marketing and Chief Marketing Officer: Paul R. Boulier, age 57
VP, CFO, and Treasurer: Paul F. DeSantis, age 46, $890,008 total compensation
VP Global Supply Chain and Chief Procurement Officer: Gary A. Miller, age 63
VP, General Counsel, and Secretary: David C. Minc, age 60
VP Global Human Resources: Kim L. Whiteman, age 53
General Manager and COO, Europe: Bernard Rzepka, age 50, $1,104,482 total compensation
General Manager and COO, Asia: Derek R. Bristow, age 49
General Manager and COO, Americas: Gustavo Perez
General Manager, Engineered Plastics, North America: Oliver Stahl

General Manager, North America Resin Distribution: Ronald Wells
Director, New Business Applications; General Manager, Invision: Dennis C. Smith
North American Human Resources Director: Cathy Brown
Director, Corporate Communications and Investor Relations: Jennifer K. Beeman
Auditors: PricewaterhouseCoopers LLP

LOCATIONS

HQ: A. Schulman, Inc.
3550 W. Market St., Akron, OH 44333
Phone: 330-666-3751 **Fax:** 330-668-7204
Web: www.aschulman.com

2009 Sales

	$ mil.	% of total
Germany	408.2	32
US	192.6	15
Other countries	678.5	53
Total	**1,279.3**	**100**

PRODUCTS/OPERATIONS

2009 Sales

	$ mil.	% of total
Europe	935.9	73
North American Engineered Plastics	121.7	10
North American Masterbatch	108.5	8
North American Distribution Services	67.9	5
Asia	45.3	4
Total	**1,279.3**	**100**

COMPETITORS

Albemarle
Ampacet
Clariant
DuPont
Ferro
Georgia Gulf
PolyOne
RTP Company
Shintech International
Spartech

HISTORICAL FINANCIALS

Company Type: Public

Income Statement

FYE: August 31

	REVENUE ($ mil.)	NET INCOME ($ mil.)	NET PROFIT MARGIN	EMPLOYEES
8/09	1,279	(3)	—	2,000
8/08	1,984	18	0.9%	2,200
8/07	1,787	23	1.3%	2,471
8/06	1,616	33	2.0%	2,480
8/05	1,436	32	2.2%	2,399
Annual Growth	**(2.8%)**	**—**	**—**	**(4.4%)**

2009 Year-End Financials

Debt ratio: 27.9%
Return on equity: —
Cash ($ mil.): 229
Current ratio: 2.59
Long-term debt ($ mil.): 102
No. of shares (mil.): 31
Dividends
  Yield: 3.0%
  Payout: —
Market value ($ mil.): 632

Stock History

NASDAQ (GS): SHLM

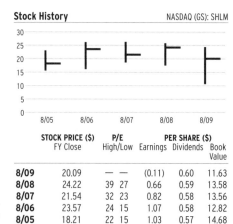

	STOCK PRICE ($) FY Close	P/E High/Low		PER SHARE ($) Earnings	Dividends	Book Value
8/09	20.09	—	—	(0.11)	0.60	11.63
8/08	24.22	39	27	0.66	0.59	13.58
8/07	21.54	32	23	0.82	0.58	13.56
8/06	23.57	24	15	1.07	0.58	12.82
8/05	18.21	22	15	1.03	0.57	14.68
Annual Growth	**2.5%**	**—**	**—**	**—**	**1.3%**	**(5.7%)**

A&P

Once one of the biggest baggers of groceries in the US, The Great Atlantic & Pacific Tea Company (A&P) has been reduced to a handful of regional grocery chains. It runs about 430 supermarkets in eight eastern states and the District of Columbia. In addition to its mainstay A&P chain, the firm now operates seven others, including Super Fresh along the East Coast from New Jersey to Virginia and The Food Emporium and Waldbaum chains in the New York and New Jersey area. A&P acquired its longtime rival in the Northeast, Pathmark Stores, for about $1.4 billion in 2007. The Pathmark purchase added about 140 stores, but has yet to reverse A&P's lagging fortunes. Germany's Tengelmann Group owns about 41% of ailing A&P.

Amid mounting losses — both before and after the Pathmark purchase — Tengelmann's CEO Karl-Erivan Haub announced in August 2010 that A&P will eventually be combined with another retailer. Haub, who said Tengelmann plans to hold a stake in the combined company, did not say what company A&P will ultimately be merged with.

Haub's statement, rapid turnover in A&P's executive suite, and the recent announcement that A&P plans to shutter 25 stores, demonstrates Tenglemann's growing frustration with A&P's ongoing poor performance. Clearly, Pathmark was not the answer to A&P's problems. Tengelmann and former Pathmark owner Yucaipa, which holds a 28% stake in the ailing company, have worked with A&P on a turnaround strategy. In addition to revenue-generation and cost-reduction initiatives, the company named Sam Martin as its incoming president and CEO. Martin joins A&P from OfficeMax, where he served as COO since 2007. Prior to his stint at OfficeMax, Martin served as COO of Wild Oats Markets (prior to its purchase by Whole Foods) and held positions at ShopKo and Fred Meyer: both have substantial grocery businesses. Martin is A&P's third CEO in the past nine months. He succeeds Ron Marshall, who joined the ailing grocery chain in February from bookseller Borders. (Marshall succeeded Eric Claus, who left the

company in October 2009.) In addition to reversing declining same-store sales at A&P-owned chains, Martin is charged with pursuing capital-raising opportunities, including sale-leaseback transactions and the sale of some of the company's noncore assets. Indeed, in September A&P was reported to be considering the sale of its upscale Food Emporium chain. With about 15 stores in Manhattan, Food Emporium is considered one of A&P's most salable assets. Analysts estimate it could fetch more than $200 million.

Under Marshall, the chain in March launched a "Lower Price Project" (LPP) and recruited morning talk show host Kelly Ripa to promote it. The LPP is rolling out 10,000 lower everyday prices at the company's A&P, Waldbaum, and SuperFresh stores.

A&P's purchase of Pathmark created a chain with stores in the New York, New Jersey, Philadelphia, and Baltimore-Washington, DC, metropolitan areas. A&P, which has mostly focused on suburban settings, hopes to benefit from Pathmark's success in urban locations and has repositioned Pathmark as its "price-impact" banner. The addition of Pathmark rounds out the grocery chain's multi-format strategy, which includes upscale gourmet (Food Emporium), fresh (A&P, Walbaum, and SuperFresh), and discount (Food Basics) stores.

A&P exited the Canadian market in 2005 to help ease its substantial debt load and raise funds to reinvest in its aging US stores. More recently, the regional grocery chain exited several US markets, including Louisiana (Sav-A-Center) and Michigan (Farmer Jack), to focus on its core business in the Northeast.

HISTORY

George Gilman and George Hartford of Augusta, Maine, set up shop in 1859 on New York City's docks to sell tea at a 50% discount by eliminating middlemen. The Great American Tea Company advertised by drawing a red wagon through the city's streets. By 1869 the company, renamed The Great Atlantic & Pacific Tea Company (A&P), had 11 stores offering discounted items.

Gilman retired in 1878, and Hartford brought in his sons George and John. In 1912, when the company had 400 stores, John opened a store on a low-price, cash-and-carry format, without customer credit or premiums, which proved popular. When the company passed to the sons four years later, A&P had more than 1,000 cash-and-carry stores.

The company expanded at a phenomenal pace during the 1920s and 1930s, growing to 15,900 stores by the mid-1930s; however, a movement by small retailers to restrict chain stores tarnished the country's view of A&P in particular. To improve the company's image, John initiated innovative marketing and customer service policies.

A&P grew in the 1940s by converting its stores to supermarkets, but an antitrust suit in 1949 and the company's reluctance to carry more nonfood items pushed it into decline. Management shut stores in California and Washington to shore up its northeastern business.

In 1975, after a long period of poor sales and failed discount format attempts, the board named former Albertson's president Jonathan Scott as CEO. (He eventually left A&P to become CEO of American Stores, which was later acquired by Albertson's.) Scott closed stores and reduced the workforce, but the company's sales increases failed to keep ahead of inflation, and A&P lost $52 million in 1978.

A year later the Hartford Foundation sold its A&P holdings to the German Tengelmann Group (owned by the Haub family), which in 1980 appointed English-born James Wood as CEO. A&P made several acquisitions, including Super Fresh (1982), Kohl's (1983), Ontario's Miracle Food Mart (1990), and Atlanta's Big Star (1992).

Rivals' superior supermarkets stripped away market share in New York City, Long Island, and Detroit in the early 1990s. In response, A&P closed hundreds of old stores, remodeled several hundred more, and planned openings of larger stores.

A 14-week strike in 1994 resulted in a complete shutdown of all 63 Miracle stores in Canada. In addition to lost sales, the company paid $17 million in labor settlement costs. In 1995 A&P began converting its Canadian Food Basics stores to franchises.

Christian Haub replaced Wood as CEO in 1998 (and became chairman in mid-2001), and A&P stepped up its modernization efforts.

A&P in 1999 exited the Richmond, Virginia and Atlanta markets. The grocer boosted its presence in New Orleans with its purchase of six Schwegmann's stores, which were later converted to the Sav-A-Center banner. A&P saw four executive officers leave in six months in 2000, including COO Michael Larkin. Early in 2001 former Nabisco exec Elizabeth Culligan became COO. Also that year A&P shuttered 31 of 39 unprofitable stores slated for closure.

Following the discovery in May 2002 of accounting irregularities related to the timing for recognition of vendor allowances and inventory accounting, in July A&P restated — and improved — its financial results for 1999 and 2000 and adjusted its 2001 results. In October the company reorganized its retail operations into two business units: A&P US and A&P Canada. Concurrently, COO Culligan left the company and Brian Piwek was named president and CEO of A&P US; Eric Claus, formerly of Co-op Atlantic, joined the grocery chain as president and CEO of A&P Canada. A&P froze hiring and deferred all pay raises for US non-union employees in late 2002.

In April 2003 A&P completed the sale of its northern New England stores, including eight A&P stores to GU Family Markets; four stores in the Springfield, Massachusetts, area to Big Y Foods; and a single store to Belmont Avenue Markets. The company also sold seven Kohl's Supermarkets in Madison, Wisconsin, to The Copps Corporation (a subsidiary of Roundy's, Inc.) and closed 23 Kohl's Food Stores in Milwaukee in August. Overall, asset sales in 2003 reaped about $285 million, which A&P used to lower debt.

In January 2004 A&P completed the sale of its Eight O'Clock Coffee division to a San Francisco-based private equity firm, Gryphon Investors, for about $108 million.

In October 2004 A&P settled a class action lawsuit with 29 franchisees of its Food Basics chain in Ontario, Canada. The retailer agreed to pay $32 million to purchase stores from the franchisees involved in the dispute. In November the company combined its corporate and US operating management structures, elevating Piwek to president and COO of The Great Atlantic & Pacific Tea Company. Piwek was formerly president and CEO of the corporation's US operating division.

In August 2005 A&P sold its 236-store Canadian division, A&P Canada, to rival METRO INC. for approximately $1.5 billion, reducing its operations to the northeastern and mid-Atlantic US states. Haub became executive chairman, handing his CEO title to Eric Claus, who previously headed A&P Canada. Also during the year the company closed about 35 stores in Michigan and Ohio.

In November 2006 A&P acquired six former Clemens Family Markets locations from C&S, which had recently purchased them from Clemens. The stores, all in the Philadelphia area, reopened as Super Fresh stores.

A&P completed the shutdown of its Michigan operations in July 2007 with the sale of 45 Farmer Jack stores to Kroger and the closure of about 20 other stores there. On the plus side, in November the grocery company acquired New York City-based wine retailer Best Cellars. Also in November, A&P sold all of its approximately 11.7 million shares of METRO Inc. for about $347 million to help fund its acquisition of Pathmark, which closed in December 2007 for some $1.4 billion. (As of December 2007, 86% of the combined company was held by A&P shareholders and 14% by former Pathmark investors.) Also in 2007, A&P sold most of its Sav-A-Center stores in the Greater New Orleans area to Louisiana-based Rouse's Supermarket and other buyers and ceased operations in the remaining Sav-A-Center stores. A&P shuttered about 10 stores in 2008.

After four years at the helm, Eric Claus stepped down as CEO. Executive chairman Haub said a "change in leadership was warranted and appropriate" as sales have continued to decline. In February 2010, former Borders Group CEO Ron Marshall took the top spot. Marshall left the company in July and was succeeded by Sam Martin, a former COO of OfficeMax and Wild Oats Markets.

EXECUTIVES

Chairman: Christian W. E. Haub, age 45, $2,289,361 total compensation
Vice Chairman and Chief Strategy Officer: Andreas Guldin, age 48, $2,305,281 total compensation
President and CEO: Samuel M. (Sam) Martin III, age 53
EVP Operations: Paul Hertz, age 41
SVP, CFO, and Treasurer: Brenda M. Galgano, age 41, $1,319,269 total compensation
SVP, General Counsel, and Secretary: Christopher (Chris) McGarry, age 43
SVP; General Manager, The Food Emporium: Hans Heer, age 50
VP and Corporate Controller: Melissa Sungela, age 44
VP Treasury Services: Krystyna Lack
Senior Director Public Relations: Laura La Bruno
Auditors: PricewaterhouseCoopers LLP

LOCATIONS

HQ: The Great Atlantic & Pacific Tea Company, Inc.
2 Paragon Dr., Montvale, NJ 07645
Phone: 201-573-9700　　**Fax:** 201-505-3054
Web: www.aptea.com

2010 Stores

	No.
New York	169
New Jersey	151
Pennsylvania	41
Maryland	27
Connecticut	25
Delaware	13
District of Columbia	1
Massachusetts	1
Virginia	1
Total	**429**

PRODUCTS/OPERATIONS

2010 Sales

	$ mil.	% of total
Fresh	4,402.0	50
Pathmark	3,855.3	44
Gourmet	273.1	3
Other (includes liquor stores)	283.2	3
Total	**8,813.6**	**100**

Selected Store Names

A&P	Super Foodmart
Best Cellars	Super Fresh
Food Basics	The Food Emporium
Pathmark	Waldbaum
Pathmark Sav-a-Center	

Selected Private-Label Brands

America's Choice	Master Choice
Hartford Reserve	Pathmark
Health Pride	Savings Plus

COMPETITORS

Acme Markets	Safeway
D'Agostino Supermarkets	Shaw's
Delhaize America	Stew Leonard's
Foodarama Supermarkets	Stop & Shop
Genuardi's	SUPERVALU
Giant Food	Trader Joe's
Gristede's Foods	Village Super Market
King Kullen Grocery	Wakefern Food
Kings Super Markets	Walgreen
Kroger	Wal-Mart
Red Apple Group	Wegmans
Rite Aid	Whole Foods

HISTORICAL FINANCIALS

Company Type: Public

Income Statement

FYE: Last Saturday in February

	REVENUE ($ mil.)	NET INCOME ($ mil.)	NET PROFIT MARGIN	EMPLOYEES
2/10	8,814	(877)	—	45,000
2/09	9,516	(140)	—	48,000
2/08	6,401	(161)	—	51,000
2/07	6,850	27	0.4%	38,000
2/06	8,740	393	4.5%	38,000
Annual Growth	**0.2%**	**—**		**4.3%**

2010 Year-End Financials

Debt ratio: —　　　　　　No. of shares (mil.): 56
Return on equity: —　　　Dividends
Cash ($ mil.): 252　　　　Yield: 0.0%
Current ratio: 1.28　　　　Payout: —
Long-term debt ($ mil.): 1,457　Market value ($ mil.): 408

Stock History

NYSE: GAP

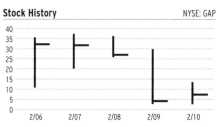

	STOCK PRICE ($) FY Close	P/E High/Low		PER SHARE ($) Earnings	Dividends	Book Value
2/10	7.27	—	—	(29.34)	0.00	(9.42)
2/09	4.07	—	—	(5.41)	0.00	4.76
2/08	27.08	—	—	(4.22)	0.00	7.44
2/07	31.80	58	32	0.64	0.00	7.67
2/06	32.26	4	1	9.64	0.00	11.96
Annual Growth	**(31.1%)**	**—**	**—**	**—**	**—**	**—**

AAR CORP.

On much more than a wing and a prayer, AAR provides a wide range of products and services for the aerospace and defense industries. The company's Aviation Supply Chain unit (40% of sales) buys and sells a variety of engine and airframe parts and components and offers inventory management services, as well as selling and leasing used commercial jet aircraft. Structures & Systems makes in-plane cargo loading and handling products, while Maintenance, Repair, & Overhaul (MRO) provides engineering services to commercial and military aircraft customers. Customers include airlines, business aircraft operators, cargo carriers, aviation OEMs, and militaries. The US Department of Defense accounts for about 45% of sales.

In the past AAR's fortunes have taken their cue primarily from the commercial aviation industry; however, government-related business is becoming more important to the company as part of its diversification strategy. Over the last decade AAR has set out to achieve a more equitable balance between its commercial and defense segments, with commercial representing 54% to defense's 46%. This strategy allows the company to weather individual economic market downturns. Even within the military market, the company's diverse offerings have shored up one another, depending on government budgeting. For example, even though DoD spending is fairly flat in 2010, the US Department of Homeland Security's spending is increasing.

AAR's Aviation Supply Chain segment is also benefiting from increased government business. In April 2010 AAR acquired Aviation Worldwide Services (AWS), a provider of expeditionary airlift services and aircraft modifications conducted primarily under government contract. The deal is valued at $200 million and includes both of the company's operating subsidiaries — Presidential Airways and STI Aviation. AWS brings a fleet of 58 aircraft, which has been deployed in Afghanistan. The acquisition expands AAR's offerings to government customers engaged in national defense, nation building efforts, and humanitarian relief projects.

Also on the military front, AAR became the exclusive provider of composite interiors for the Sikorsky S-92 and H-60 helicopter programs in 2010; the two-year contract deal is valued at $6 million. Multiply that amount by 100, and you'll know the value of AAR's largest deal in company history — in 2009 it was awarded a $600 million contract (over 9 years) to provide supply chain and logistics services, as well as maintenance operations for Northrop Grumman's KC-10 air-to-air tanker aircraft program.

Additionally, in mid-2009 AAR announced the formation of a joint venture which includes AAR, Johnson Global Services (a subsidiary of Magic Johnson Enterprises), and Zaccanelli Investment. The new joint venture, AAR Global Solutions, LLC, will expand the company's participation in the government and defense services markets.

The trend for more maintenance and repair outsourcing has also been a boon for AAR, which experienced an increase in consolidated sales for this segment. Increases were attributed to a greater number of commercial customers, increased demand for airframe maintenance and landing gear overhaul, and successful marketing efforts in international markets.

HISTORY

Ira Allen Eichner began selling aircraft radios and instruments out of his car in 1951; in 1955 he incorporated his business as Allen Aircraft Radio. He opened a maintenance facility in Oklahoma City in 1959 and moved into aircraft overhaul. The firm entered Europe in 1965, became AAR in 1966, and went public the next year. AAR began selling commercial aircraft in 1973 and expanded into manufacturing with the 1981 acquisition of Brooks & Perkins. AAR flew high and fast during the late 1980s, but lost altitude in the recession of the early 1990s as the airline industry hit a major air pocket.

The company restructured in 1993, and AAR rose again along with a resurgent airline industry. In 1997 AAR bought Cooper Aviation Industries, Avsco Aviation Service, and ATR International (composite structures and parts). It bought 14 used 747s from British Airways and inked maintenance deals with the US Air Force, Hughes, and GE. A loading systems contract with FedEx provided more lift. In 1998 AAR won a $67 million deal to maintain aircraft for the US Marshals Service and the Immigration and Naturalization Service. It also sold its floor maintenance equipment business (AAR PowerBoss) to Minuteman International.

In 1999 AAR gained investment and technology potential when it formed Aviation Inventory Management Co. with GE Capital Aviation and GE Engine Services. The following year AAR announced a deal with Societe Internationale de Telecommunication Aeronautiques (SITA), an air-transport information technology cooperative, to sell airline and aerospace products and services online, but later in 2000 it decreased its stake in the venture (Aerospan.com).

Late in 2001 AAR formed a joint venture, Spairwise, L.L.C., with Air France Industries (AFI) to provide component management support to operators of Airbus A320 family of aircraft in North and Central America. In 2002 the company inked a three-year deal to supply American Airlines with parts. As sales slumped in 2003, AAR made several refinancing moves to improve liquidity.

In early 2007 AAR bolstered its MRO operations with the purchase of Reebair Aircraft. Based in Arkansas, the business operates under the name AAR Aircraft Services — Hot Springs.

In 2008 the company acquired Avborne Heavy Maintenance, which provides maintenance services for Airbus and Boeing aircraft; it is part of AAR's MRO operations. The prior year AAR bought Brown International, a provider of engineering, design, manufacturing, and systems integration services to the aerospace industry. Brown International is being integrated into AAR's Structures and Systems division. It also purchased Summa Technology, Inc., a provider of machining, fabrication, welding, engineering, and test services. Some of Summa's projects have included the Space Shuttle, Tomahawk cruise missiles, air defense systems, and even lawn tractors. Summa operates as part of AAR's Structures and Systems division. AAR exited its non-core industrial turbine business.

EXECUTIVES

Chairman and CEO: David P. Storch, age 57, $4,030,130 total compensation
President, COO, and Director: Timothy J. Romenesko, age 53, $1,697,279 total compensation
SVP Government and Defense Business Development: Donald J. (Don) Wetekam

Group VP Structures and Systems Segment: Terry D. Stinson, age 68, $1,137,542 total compensation
Group VP Maintenance, Repair, and Overhaul (MRO): Dany Kleiman
Group VP Government and Defense Services; President, AWS: Randy J. Martinez, age 53
Group VP Aircraft Sales and Leasing: John Johnson
VP, CFO, and Treasurer: Richard J. (Rick) Poulton, age 45, $922,761 total compensation
VP Commercial Development: James J. Clark, $1,116,464 total compensation
VP Human Resources: Timothy O. Skelly
VP and CIO: Kevin M. Larson
VP Tax: Michael K. Carr
VP and Chief Commercial Officer: Peter K. Chapman
VP, General Counsel, and Secretary: Robert J. (Bob) Regan, age 52
VP, Controller, and Chief Accounting Officer: Michael J. Sharp
VP Defense Programs: David E. Prusiecki
Director, Corporate Communications: Chris Mason
President, Aviation Worldwide Services: Jeffrey (Jeff) Schloesser
Auditors: KPMG LLP

LOCATIONS

HQ: AAR CORP.
1100 N. Wood Dale Rd., Wood Dale, IL 60191
Phone: 630-227-2000 **Fax:** 630-227-2039
Web: www.aarcorp.com

2010 Sales

	% of total
US	79
Other countries	21
Total	**100**

PRODUCTS/OPERATIONS

2010 Sales

	$ mil.	% of total
Aviation supply chain	406.0	30
Structures & systems	449.9	34
Maintenance, repair & overhaul	301.3	22
Government & defense services	194.9	14
Total	**1,352.1**	**100**

2010 Sales

	$ mil.	% of total
Sales from products	1,067.5	79
Sales from services	245.2	18
Sales from leasing	39.4	3
Total	**1,352.1**	**100**

Selected Products

Cargo handling systems
Composites structures
Containers, shelters, pallets
Precision machined parts

Selected Services

Aircraft maintenance and modification
Component repair
Logistics support
Parts distribution
Supply chain management

Selected Divisions and Subsidiaries

Aircraft Sales and Leasing
AAR Aircraft & Engine Sales & Leasing, Inc.

Aviation Supply Chain
AAR Allen Services, Inc.
AAR International, Inc.
AAR Parts Trading, Inc.
AAR Services, Inc.

Maintenance, Repair, and Overhaul
AAR Aircraft Services
AAR Allen Services, Inc.
AAR Services, Inc.

Structures and Systems
AAR Manufacturing, Inc.

HISTORICAL FINANCIALS

Company Type: Public

Income Statement

FYE: May 31

	REVENUE ($ mil.)	NET INCOME ($ mil.)	NET PROFIT MARGIN	EMPLOYEES
5/10	1,352	43	3.2%	6,340
5/09	1,424	79	5.5%	5,930
5/08	1,385	75	5.4%	5,400
5/07	1,061	59	5.5%	3,900
5/06	897	35	3.9%	3,300
Annual Growth	10.8%	5.3%	—	17.7%

2010 Year-End Financials

Debt ratio: 45.0%
Return on equity: 6.2%
Cash ($ mil.): 79
Current ratio: 2.65
Long-term debt ($ mil.): 336
No. of shares (mil.): 39
Dividends
Yield: 0.0%
Payout: —
Market value ($ mil.): 778

Stock History

NYSE: AIR

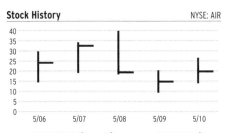

	STOCK PRICE ($) FY Close	P/E High/Low		PER SHARE ($) Earnings	Dividends	Book Value
5/10	19.70	22	12	1.16	0.00	18.92
5/09	14.70	11	5	1.87	0.00	16.64
5/08	19.28	22	11	1.76	0.00	14.82
5/07	32.50	24	14	1.40	0.00	12.52
5/06	24.08	31	16	0.94	0.00	10.71
Annual Growth	(4.9%)	—	—	5.4%	—	15.3%

Aaron's, Inc.

For all those customers who desire a desk, seek a sofa, or wish for a washer, Aaron's rents — and sells — all of the above and more. One of the leading furniture rental and rent-to-own companies in the US (behind industry leader Rent-A-Center), Aaron's purveys home and office furnishings, electronics, computers, and appliances through more than 1,675 eponymous stores in the US, Puerto Rico, and Canada. Its MacTavish Furniture Industries unit makes most of the firm's furniture and bedding at a dozen plants in the US. In addition, Aaron's leases tires, rims, and wheels through its RIMCO chain of about 20 locations. Founded in 1955, the firm changed its name from Aaron Rents to Aaron's in 2009.

The change followed the disposal of Aaron's Corporate Furnishings business, its home and office furniture rental division, to rival CORT Business Services in 2008. The rebranding effort mirrors Aaron's shift from a conventional rent-to-own business to one that specializes in the growing area of sales and lease ownership. Its stores are primarily frequented by the credit-impaired, and with less-than-ideal economic conditions lingering in the US, demand has grown for its quality-of-life-enhancing goods.

Furniture and electronics rental is Aaron's bread and butter, with two-thirds of sales derived from these two segments each year. In 2009 Aaron's revenue grew by 10% to nearly $1.8 billion while profits rose by 25% to $112 million. Since 2005 the firm's sales have grown by more than 50%, and its profits have nearly doubled.

As Aaron's balance sheet has strengthened, so too has its retail footprint. The company has added more than 700 company-operated and franchised locations since 2005, and it is poised to continue growing at a quickened pace. In 2009 Aaron's added 45 company-operated stores and more than 90 franchised locations. That year the purchase of its largest franchisee, 35-store Rosey Rentals (completed in December 2008), added to its company-owned store network, and its franchise count was boosted when Kelly's Sales & Leasing agreed to convert its roughly 20-store chain in North Carolina and Virginia to the Aaron's banner. In 2008 Aaron's rolled out nearly 25 company-operated stores while franchisees opened 20 locations. Aaron's typically targets existing markets and selected new markets to launch company-owned stores; the franchise program helps to extend its brand to new markets that the firm does not have immediate plans of entering.

The furniture company saw its management shift in mid-2008, months prior to unloading Aaron's Corporate Furnishings business. Robert Loudermilk Jr., the son of chairman and former CEO Charles Loudermilk, was promoted to chief executive of the company.

Charles Loudermilk owns about 60% of the company. T. Rowe Price Associates holds a roughly 10% stake.

HISTORY

Aaron of Aaron Rents is the Betty Crocker of the furniture rental world (i.e., there is no Aaron). The firm was named to appear first in the Yellow Pages. Charles Loudermilk and his mother Addie founded Aaron Rents in 1955 with 300 folding chairs. Loudermilk opened the second store in Atlanta in the early 1960s and then a third in 1964.

The company ventured outside Atlanta for the first time by opening a Baltimore store in 1967. After acquiring MacTavish Furniture Industries in 1971, it became the only rental company with manufacturing facilities. The firm went public in 1982. Aaron Rents launched its rent-to-own business in 1987 and began franchising the stores in 1992.

In 1998 the company joined the NYSE. Aaron Rents also opened several furniture warehouses in Florida, Georgia, Ohio, and Texas to speed delivery time to rental stores. It opened its first Aaron's Plus retail and rent-to-own store in Sandersville, Georgia. It also bought California-based Lamps Forever to add designer accessories to its offerings.

Aaron Rents continued to expand through 1999. In 2000 the company made its first move outside the US with its purchase of 10 stores in Puerto Rico. Aaron Rents purchased 52 locations from bankrupt furniture chain Heilig-Meyers in 2001. In 2002 Aaron Rents bought Sight 'n Sound Appliance Centers, a specialty retailer of furniture, appliances, and consumer electronics.

In November 2003 Aaron Rents entered into an agreement with Rosey Rentals to convert 31 of its stores to franchised Aaron Rents stores. In June 2004 Aaron Rents acquired 26 rental stores from privately held Easy Way. Several months later (September 2004) the company acquired 25 stores from Home Express. Overall, the company opened 68 company-operated stores and 79 new franchised outlets in 2004.

Aaron Rents acquired the rental contracts and merchandise of 19 stores from rival Rent-A-Center for about $4.4 million in 2005, and acquired 33 stores on the East Coast from Prime Time Rentals in 2007 (with about half of those stores changed to the Aaron format and the rest merged into existing Aaron stores).

In June 2008 Robert Loudermilk Jr., the son of chairman and ex-CEO Charles Loudermilk, was promoted to chief executive of the company. In November Aaron's sold its corporate furnishings unit (Aaron Corporate Furnishings) to Berkshire Hathaway's CORT Business Services for about $72 million. As a result, Aaron Rents exited the rent-to-rent market. In December, the firm acquired its franchisee Rosey Rentals in a cash transaction. It changed its name and ticker symbol in April 2009.

EXECUTIVES

Chairman: R. Charles Loudermilk Sr., age 82, $1,712,064 total compensation
President, CEO, and Director: Robert C. Loudermilk Jr., age 50, $1,038,683 total compensation
COO and Director: William K. Butler Jr., age 57, $958,791 total compensation
EVP, CFO, and Director: Gilbert L. Danielson, age 63, $890,068 total compensation
Senior Group VP and Secretary: James L. Cates, age 59
SVP Merchandising and Logistics, Aaron's Sales and Lease Ownership Division: Mitchell S. (Mitch) Paull
VP Franchising, Sales and Lease Ownership Division: K. Todd Evans, age 46, $452,415 total compensation
VP Internal Audit: James C. Johnson
VP Internal Security: Danny Walker Sr.
VP Finance, Aaron's Sales and Lease Ownership Division: Steven A. (Steve) Michaels
VP and General Counsel: Elizabeth L. Gibbs, age 48
VP and Corporate Controller: Robert P. Sinclair Jr
VP Manufacturing: Michael W. Jarnagin
VP and CIO: B. Lee Landers Jr., age 50
VP Employee Relations: D. Chad Strickland
Auditors: Ernst & Young LLP

LOCATIONS

HQ: Aaron's, Inc.
309 E. Paces Ferry Rd. NE, Atlanta, GA 30305
Phone: 404-231-0011 **Fax:** 678-402-3560
Web: www.aaronrents.com

PRODUCTS/OPERATIONS

2009 Sales

	$ mil.	% of total
Leasing & Fees	1,310.7	75
Nonretail sales	328.0	19
Franchising	52.9	3
Retail sales	43.4	2
Other	17.8	1
Total	**1,752.8**	**100**

2009 Stores

	No.
Company-owned	1,082
Franchised	597
Office furniture	15
RIMCO	18
Total	**1,712**

2009 Sales

	% of total
Electronics	37
Furniture	30
Appliances	15
Computers	14
Other	4
Total	**100**

Selected Rental Equipment

Automotive
  Tires
  Wheel rims
Office
  Accessories
  Business equipment
  Chairs
  Conference tables
  Credenzas
  Desks
  Sofas
Residential
  Appliances
  Dining room, living room, and bedroom furniture
  Electronics

COMPETITORS

Best Buy
Bestway
Brook Furniture Rental
Rent-A-Center
Rooms To Go
Sears
W. S. Badcock

HISTORICAL FINANCIALS

Company Type: Public

Income Statement

FYE: December 31

	REVENUE ($ mil.)	NET INCOME ($ mil.)	NET PROFIT MARGIN	EMPLOYEES
12/09	1,753	113	6.4%	10,000
12/08	1,593	90	5.7%	9,600
12/07	1,495	80	5.4%	9,600
12/06	1,327	79	5.9%	8,400
12/05	1,126	58	5.2%	7,600
Annual Growth	**11.7%**	**18.0%**	**—**	**7.1%**

2009 Year-End Financials

Debt ratio: —
Return on equity: 13.7%
Cash ($ mil.): 110
Current ratio: 0.40
Long-term debt ($ mil.): —
No. of shares (mil.): 81
Dividends
  Yield: 0.2%
  Payout: 3.6%
Market value ($ mil.): 1,497

Stock History NYSE: AAN

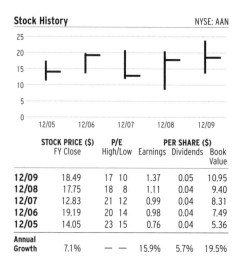

	STOCK PRICE ($) FY Close	P/E High/Low		PER SHARE ($) Earnings	Dividends	Book Value
12/09	18.49	17	10	1.37	0.05	10.95
12/08	17.75	18	8	1.11	0.04	9.40
12/07	12.83	21	12	0.99	0.04	8.31
12/06	19.19	20	14	0.98	0.04	7.49
12/05	14.05	23	15	0.76	0.04	5.36
Annual Growth	**7.1%**	**—**	**—**	**15.9%**	**5.7%**	**19.5%**

Abbott Laboratories

Filling baby bottles and soothing aching joints are a habit for Abbott. Abbott Laboratories is one of the US's top health care products makers. The company's pharmaceuticals include HIV treatment Norvir, rheumatoid arthritis therapy Humira, and Depakote to treat epilepsy and bipolar disorder. Its nutritional products division makes such well-known brands as Similac infant formula and the Ensure line of nutrition supplements. Abbott also makes diagnostic instruments and tests, including the FreeStyle diabetes care line, as well as vascular medical devices such as its Xience drug-eluting stents.

Abbott's pharmaceuticals division focuses on the therapeutic areas of immunology, oncology, neuroscience, metabolic disorders, and infectious disease. Humira is the division's big hit, and considerable R&D and marketing money is dedicated to expanding uses for the drug, as well as for new cholesterol drugs. One such drug is Trilipix, a cholesterol and lipid fibrate therapy, approved in 2008.

Like all pharmaceutical giants, the company knows the pains of patent expiration. It is facing the patent expiration of many of its top sellers between 2011 and 2016 (Aluvia, TriCor, Niaspan, Humira) and sales of top-seller Depakote have already been hit by generic competition. Abbott is hoping new candidates in its R&D pipeline, as well as expanded uses for drugs like Humira, will help make up some of those losses.

In early 2010 Abbott made a bold move for growth by paying some €4.5 billion ($6.2 billion) to acquire the pharmaceuticals business of Belgian chemical group Solvay. The purchase added therapies for cardiovascular, gastrointestinal, and neurological ailments, as well as hormone therapies.

In mid-2010 the company agreed to a deal worth roughly $4 billion to buy Piramal Healthcare's branded generic-medicine unit in India. The buy will make Abbott India's largest drugmaker, giving the company about a 7% share of the market and the rights to some 350 brands.

To keep drug development focused on its core areas (immunology, oncology, neuroscience,

metabolic disorders, and infectious disease) Abbott sold its share of TAP Pharmaceutical Products to Takeda Pharmaceutical in 2008. Takeda paid more than $1.5 billion for Abbott's share in TAP, taking home best-selling acid-reflux treatment Prevacid and the TAP development.

Abbott is still intent on pursuing growth in its non-pharmaceutical divisions. Its medical device operations got a boost with the 2009 purchase of Advanced Medical Optics for about $2.8 billion. It is a leading provider of surgical equipment and products for cataract and vision correction procedures (including LASIK equipment), as well as contact lens care products.

Until mid-2009 Abbott was embroiled in a decade-long intellectual property rights lawsuit with Medtronic over certain patents related to coronary stent and stent-delivery systems. Medtronic eventually agreed to pay $400 million to Abbott to settle the lawsuit.

HISTORY

Dr. Wallace Abbott started making his dosimetric granule (a pill that supplied uniform quantities of drugs) at his home outside Chicago in 1888. Aggressive marketing earned Abbott the American Medical Association's criticism, though much of the medical profession supported him.

During WWI, Abbott scientists synthesized anesthetics previously available only from Germany. Abbott improved its research capacity in 1922 by buying Dermatological Research Laboratories; in 1928 it bought John T. Milliken and its well-trained sales force. Abbott went public in 1929.

Salesman DeWitt Clough became president in 1933. International operations began in the mid-1930s with branches in Argentina, Brazil, Cuba, Mexico, and the UK.

Abbott was integral to the WWII effort; the US made only 28 pounds of penicillin in 1943 before the company began to ratchet up production. Consumer, infant, and nutritional products (such as Selsun Blue shampoo, Murine eye drops, and Similac formula) joined the roster in the 1960s. The FDA banned Abbott's artificial sweetener Sucaryl in 1970, saying it might be carcinogenic, and in 1971 millions of intravenous solutions were recalled following contamination deaths.

Robert Schoellhorn became CEO in 1979; profits increased but research and development was cut. In the 1980s Abbott began selling Japanese-developed pharmaceuticals in the US.

Duane Burnham became CEO in 1989; under his conservative management the company received FDA approvals to market insomnia treatment ProSom (1990), hypertension drug Hytrin for enlarged prostates (1994), and ulcer treatment Prevacid and central nervous system disorder treatment Depakote (1995).

Abbott bought MediSense, a maker of blood sugar self-tests for diabetics, in 1996; it also paid $32.5 million to settle claims by 17 states of infant formula price-fixing. In 1997 FTC action prompted Abbott to stop claiming that doctors recommended its Ensure nutritional supplement for healthy adults. That year the FDA allowed Abbott to use Norvir to treat HIV and AIDS in children, after approving its use in adults in a record 72 days in 1996.

In 1999 FDA fined the company $100 million and pulled 125 of its medical diagnostic kits off the market, citing quality assurance problems. In 2000 the FDA approved Gengraf, a drug that fights organ transplant rejection, and Kaletra, a promising protease inhibitor designed to combat AIDS. Insider Miles White was named chairman and CEO in 2001. That same year Abbott bought Knoll Pharmaceuticals, a pharmaceutical unit of German chemicals giant BASF, and also purchased Vysis, thereby acquiring that company's worldwide distribution network and adding its products for the evaluation and management of cancer, prenatal disorders, and other genetic diseases to its portfolio of diagnostics.

The FDA thwarted the company's launch of new diagnostic products in 2002 by declaring that Abbott's Chicago manufacturing plant was not up to snuff.

Abbot ceased selling attention deficit drug Cylert in early 2005, citing declining sales, concurrent with a consumer advocacy group's complaint that the drug caused more than 20 cases of liver failure. The FDA withdrew approval for the drug later that year.

Though diagnostics (including lab tests for HIV, cancer, and pregnancy) were once the core of Abbott's product line, acquisitions have shifted the company's focus toward pharmaceuticals. As part of this refocusing, Abbott sold its Abbott Spine subsidiary to Zimmer Holdings in 2008.

EXECUTIVES

Chairman and CEO: Miles D. White, age 55, $26,213,996 total compensation
EVP Finance and CFO: Thomas C. (Tom) Freyman, age 55, $9,561,227 total compensation
EVP Medical Devices: John M. Capek, age 48, $5,341,407 total compensation
EVP, General Counsel, and Secretary: Laura J. Schumacher, age 46, $5,724,060 total compensation
EVP Corporate Development: Richard W. Ashley, age 66
EVP Diagnostic Products: Edward L. Michael, age 53
EVP Nutritional Products: Holger A. Liepmann, age 58
SVP Medical Optics: James V. (Jim) Mazzo, age 52, $10,394,085 total compensation
SVP Global Strategic Marketing and Services, Pharmaceutical Products Group: Mary T. Szela, age 46
SVP Pharmaceuticals, Manufacturing, and Supply: John C. Landgraf, age 57
SVP Pharmaceuticals Research and Development: John M. Leonard, age 52
SVP Human Resources: Stephen R. (Steve) Fussell, age 52
SVP International Pharmaceuticals: Carlos Alban, age 47
SVP US Pharmaceuticals: Donald V. Patton Jr., age 57
VP Information Technology: Preston T. Simons
VP and Chief Ethics and Compliance Officer: Robert E. Funck
VP Investor Relations: John B. Thomas
VP and Treasurer: Valentine Yien, age 56
VP and Controller: Greg W. Linder, age 53
Divisional VP External Communications, Corporate Public Affairs: Melissa Brotz
President, Abbott Biotech Ventures: James L. Tyree, age 56, $6,232,208 total compensation
Auditors: Deloitte & Touche LLP

LOCATIONS

HQ: Abbott Laboratories
100 Abbott Park Rd., Abbott Park, IL 60064
Phone: 847-937-6100   **Fax:** 847-937-9555
Web: www.abbott.com

2009 Sales

	$ mil.	% of total
US	14,453	47
Netherlands	1,801	6
Japan	1,590	5
Germany	1,481	5
Italy	1,172	4
Spain	970	3
France	959	3
Canada	902	3
UK	779	2
Other countries	6,658	22
Total	**30,765**	**100**

PRODUCTS/OPERATIONS

2009 Sales

	$ mil.	% of total
Pharmaceuticals	16,486	54
Nutritionals	5,284	17
Diagnostics	3,578	12
Vascular	2,692	9
Other	2,725	8
Total	**30,765**	**100**

Selected Products

Pharmaceutical
  Azmacort (asthma)
  Biaxin (anti-infective)
  Depakote (epileptic seizures, bipolar disorder, migraines)
  Humira (rheumatoid arthritis, psoriasis, Crohn's disease)
  Kaletra (HIV)
  Lupron (pain related to endometriosis, prostate cancer)
  Marinol (appetite stimulator and antiemetic, from Solvay)
  Meridia (obesity)
  Niaspan (high cholesterol)
  Norvir (HIV)
  Omnicef (antibiotic)
  Synthroid (hyperthyroidism)
  TriCor (dyslipidemia)
  Trilipix (cholesterol)
  Zemplar (chronic kidney failure)
Diagnostic
  Abbott PRISM (high-volume blood-screening system)
  ARCHITECT c8000 (clinical chemistry system)
  Cell-Dyn (hematology systems and reagents)
  Emboshield (embolism protection in stenting procedures)
  FreeStyle (glucose monitoring meters, test strips, data management software, and accessories)
  OraQuick Advance (antibody detection/HIV)
  PathVysion (breast cancer diagnostic test)
  StarClose (vascular closure system)
  UroVysion (bladder cancer)
Nutritional
  AdvantEdge (nutritional supplements)
  Alimentum (infant formula)
  Ensure (adult nutrition)
  Glucerna (nutritional beverage for diabetics)
  Isomil (soy-based infant formula)
  Jevity (liquid food for enteral feeding)
  Myoplex (nutritional supplements)
  Pedialyte (pediatric electrolyte solution)
  PediaSure (children's nutrition)
  Similac (infant formula)
  ZonePerfect (nutritional bars)
Medical Devices (former vascular division)
  Acculink/Accunet (carotid stent)
  Asahi (coronary guidewires)
  Balance Middleweight (coronary guidewire)
  Multi-Link Vision (coronary metallic stent)
  StarClose (vessel closure)
  Xience V (drug-eluting stent)
  Voyager (balloon dilation products)

COMPETITORS

Amgen
Angiotech Pharmaceuticals
AstraZeneca
Bard
Baxter International
Bayer AG
Becton, Dickinson
Boston Scientific
Bristol-Myers Squibb
Cordis
Crucell
Eli Lilly
Eurand NV
Genentech
GlaxoSmithKline
Johnson & Johnson
Medtronic CardioVascular
Merck
Mylan
Nestlé
Novartis
Pfizer
Roche Holding
Sandoz International GmbH
Sanofi-Aventis
Shionogi & Co.
Solvay
Teva Pharmaceuticals
Watson Pharmaceuticals

HISTORICAL FINANCIALS

Company Type: Public

Income Statement
FYE: December 31

	REVENUE ($ mil.)	NET INCOME ($ mil.)	NET PROFIT MARGIN	EMPLOYEES
12/09	30,765	5,746	18.7%	73,000
12/08	29,528	4,881	16.5%	69,000
12/07	25,914	3,606	13.9%	68,000
12/06	22,476	1,717	7.6%	66,663
12/05	22,338	3,372	15.1%	59,735
Annual Growth	**8.3%**	**14.3%**	**—**	**5.1%**

2009 Year-End Financials

Debt ratio: 49.3%
Return on equity: 28.5%
Cash ($ mil.): 8,809
Current ratio: 1.79
Long-term debt ($ mil.): 11,266

No. of shares (mil.): 1,544
Dividends
  Yield: 2.9%
  Payout: 42.3%
Market value ($ mil.): 83,362

Stock History
NYSE: ABT

	STOCK PRICE ($) FY Close	P/E High/Low		PER SHARE ($) Earnings	Dividends	Book Value
12/09	53.99	16	11	3.69	1.56	14.80
12/08	53.37	20	15	3.12	1.40	11.32
12/07	56.15	26	21	2.31	1.27	11.51
12/06	48.71	45	35	1.12	1.16	9.10
12/05	39.43	23	17	2.16	1.09	9.34
Annual Growth	**8.2%**	**—**	**—**	**14.3%**	**9.4%**	**12.2%**

ABC, Inc.

Some *Desperate Housewives*, a *Modern Family*, and a group of doctors schooled in *Grey's Anatomy* call this network home. ABC operates the #3 television network in the US (behind CBS and FOX), with more than 230 affiliates (including 10 corporate-owned stations). ABC also owns an 80% stake in ESPN, a leader in cable sports broadcasting with a stable of channels, including ESPN2, ESPN Classic, and ESPN News, as well as its flagship channel. (Publisher Hearst owns the remaining 20% of ESPN.) In addition, it operates publisher Hyperion. ABC is the cornerstone of Disney-ABC Television Group, the TV division of parent Walt Disney.

Like its broadcasting brethren, ABC generates the bulk of its revenue through advertising so it is constantly focused on the performance of its television programming, particularly its prime-time schedule.

Appealing to a mass audience has always been a difficult and challenging task, but ABC's quest for larger audience share is made even more difficult by the largely entrenched positions of the major broadcast networks. CBS has a virtual lock on the top position thanks to a schedule anchored by the *CSI* franchise, while FOX wields the ratings juggernaut known as *American Idol*. The 2009-10 season produced few breakout hits for ABC aside from the comedy *Modern Family*, and the network bid a fond farewell to hit series *Lost*, which ended its run after six seasons.

In addition to weak ratings, the network has been hurt by the worsening economy with its slowed ad spending. In an effort to reduce costs, Disney-ABC Television announced hundreds of job cuts early in 2009, while the network's news division was forced to eliminate several hundred positions early the following year.

Paul Lee took over as head of ABC Entertainment Group in 2010, replacing Steve McPherson who resigned. Lee previously oversaw ABC Family, helping that cable channel expand its audience through investments in original programming. McPherson helped shepherd ABC through a revival with the help of shows such as *Lost* and *Desperate Housewives* after taking charge of ABC Entertainment in 2004. However, reported personality conflicts within Disney-ABC Television led to his departure.

Parent Walt Disney, meanwhile, has been actively trying to exploit new digital distribution channels to generate new revenue streams for its television business. The media conglomerate became a partner in video site Hulu along with NBC Universal and News Corporation in 2009. The deal saw Disney take a 30% stake in the joint venture and made ABC shows available on Hulu. The network was one of the first to distribute full-length episodes online through its own ABC.com site. ABC also sells shows through Apple's iTunes store. (Apple head honcho Steve Jobs is the largest shareholder in Disney, with a 7% stake.)

HISTORY

ABC was launched in 1927 by RCA as the Blue Network. A sister network to NBC (now owned by General Electric), Blue Network was sold to Life Savers candy magnate Edward J. Noble in 1943 after an FCC ruling that prohibited ownership of more than one network. Renamed the American Broadcasting Company (ABC) three years later, ABC struggled with just 100 radio stations in its network and no big stars. By 1953 the company had expanded into television with 14 affiliates. That year United Paramount Theatres, led by Leonard Goldenson, bought ABC for $25 million.

To compete with CBS and NBC, Goldenson turned to Hollywood. He signed a $40 million deal with Walt Disney in 1953 that gave ABC access to the Disney film library and an exclusive programming alliance. The network turned to other studios for programming such as *77 Sunset Strip* and *Maverick*. During the 1960s ABC fended off takeover attempts by ITT and Howard Hughes, and in the 1970s it pioneered the long-form mini-series with *Roots* and *Rich Man, Poor Man*. Hit shows, including *Happy Days* and *Charlie's Angels*, helped put the network on top during the 1976 season. In 1984 the company bought cable sports channel ESPN. (It sold 20% of ESPN to Hearst in 1991.) The next year ABC was sold to Capital Cities Communications for $3.5 billion.

Founded by Frank Smith as Hudson Valley Broadcasting, Capital Cities had started out as a bankrupt TV station in Albany, New York. In 1957 it acquired a second station in Raleigh, North Carolina; changed its name; and went public in 1964. Smith died in 1966, and Thomas Murphy took over as chairman and CEO. The company bought magazine publisher Fairchild Publications in 1968 and newspapers such as the *Fort Worth Star-Telegram* and *Kansas City Star* in the 1970s. By the 1980s Capital Cities had revenues of more than $1 billion.

During the early 1990s Capital Cities/ABC saw ratings soar with such hits as *Roseanne* and *Home Improvement*. Robert Iger was appointed president in 1994. Two years later Disney bought the company for $19 billion, selling off its newspapers for $1.65 billion. In 1998 ABC agreed to pay $9.2 billion for National Football League broadcast rights through 2005. In addition, Patricia Fili-Krushel was named president of ABC Television, making her the first woman to head a major broadcast network. Iger was named chairman of ABC in 1999, and ESPN chief Steven Bornstein took over as president.

In 1999 Disney sold ABC's Fairchild magazine unit to Advance Publications for about $650 million. Bornstein left late that year to head Disney's GO.com (now Disney Online). In early 2000 Iger was named president and COO of Disney, leaving broadcast president Robert Callahan in charge. Fili-Krushel later resigned.

Negotiations over rebroadcast rights between Disney and Time Warner Cable went south in 2000 and ABC broadcasts were briefly suspended for about 3.5 million viewers. (Time Warner Cable was later admonished by the FCC for dropping the stations during sweeps periods.)

Callahan resigned from ABC in 2001, and Bornstein returned from Disney Internet to become broadcast group president. Later Disney bought the Fox Family Channel, renamed ABC Family, and the international assets of the Fox Kids Network (later rebranded as JETIX) from News Corp. and Haim Saban for $5.2 billion.

Bornstein resigned as president in mid-2002.

In 2007 Disney spun off the radio broadcasting operations of ABC, including ABC Radio Network (later Citadel Media), which merged with Citadel Broadcasting. The $2.7 billion merger left Disney shareholders owning most of the combined company.

EXECUTIVES

Co-Chairman, Disney Media Networks; President, Disney-ABC Television Group: Anne M. Sweeney
Co-Chairman, Disney Media Networks; President, ESPN and ABC Sports: George W. Bodenheimer, age 51
EVP Marketing, ABC Entertainment Group: Michael (Mike) Benson
EVP and CFO, ABC Television Network and ABC Television Studios: James L. (Jim) Hedges
EVP Network Scripted Creative, ABC Entertainment Group: Suzanne Patmore-Gibbs
EVP Business Affairs and Administration, ABC Entertainment Group: Jana Winograde
EVP Comedy, ABC Entertainment Group: Samie Kim Falvey
EVP Worldwide Technology and Operations, Disney-ABC Television Group: Vince Roberts
EVP Development and Current Programs, ABC Entertainment: Francie Calfo
EVP Global Communications, Disney/ABC Television Group: Kevin Brockman
EVP Planning, Scheduling, and Distribution, ABC Entertainment Group: Jeffrey D. (Jeff) Bader
EVP Marketing, ABC Entertainment: Marla Provencio
SVP Human Resources, Disney and ABC Television Group: Steve Milovich
SVP Legal Affairs, ABC and ABC Television Studios: Milinda McNeely
President, Broadcast Operations and Engineering: Preston A. Davis
President, ABC Owned Television Stations: Rebecca Campbell
President, ABC Sales: Geri Wang
President, ABC Entertainment Group: Paul Lee
President, ABC News: David Westin
President, Hyperion: Ellen Archer, age 47
Senior Advisor to Office of Co-Chairman: Mark Pedowitz
Auditors: PricewaterhouseCoopers LLP

LOCATIONS

HQ: ABC, Inc.
77 W. 66th St., New York, NY 10023
Phone: 212-456-7777   **Fax:** 212-456-1424
Web: abc.go.com

PRODUCTS/OPERATIONS

Selected Network Shows
20/20
Better Together (Fall 2010)
Body of Proof (Fall 2010)
Brothers & Sisters
Castle
Cougar Town
Dancing With The Stars
Desperate Housewives
Detroit 1-8-7 (Fall 2010)
Extreme Makeover: Home Edition
Grey's Anatomy
The Middle
Modern Family
My Generation (Fall 2010)
No Ordinary Family (Fall 2010)
Private Practice
Secret Millionaire (Fall 2010)
Shark Tank
V
The Whole Truth (Fall 2010)

Television Stations
KABC (Los Angeles)
KFSN (Fresno, CA)
KGO (San Francisco)
KTRK (Houston)
WABC (New York City)
WJRT (Flint, MI)
WLS (Chicago)
WPVI (Philadelphia)
WTVD (Raleigh-Durham-Fayetteville, NC)
WTVG (Toledo, OH)

Abercrombie & Fitch

Trading on its century-old name, Abercrombie & Fitch (A&F) sells upscale men's, women's, and kids' casual clothes and accessories — quite a change from when the company outfitted Ernest Hemingway and Teddy Roosevelt for safaris. A&F operates some 1,100 stores in the US, Canada, and Europe, and also sells via its catalog and online. Its carefully selected college-age sales staff and use of 20-something models imbue its stores with an upscale fraternity house feel. A&F runs a fast-growing chain of some 525 teen stores called Hollister Co., and a chain targeted at boys and girls ages seven to 14 called abercrombie kids. Its just-for-women brand, Gilly Hicks, launched in 2008 and has about 15 stores.

The downturn in the economy has been hard on A&F, which saw sales plummet 16% in 2009 after falling 6% in 2008. The company's practice of not discounting in-season products probably made things worse as the newly-thrifty bypassed its stores in favor of lower-priced competitors, such as American Eagle Outfitters and The Buckle. Indeed, A&F was forced to reconsider its full-price strategy after reporting a 24% decline in revenue for the quarter ended May 2009. Only then did it announce that it would cut prices to spur sales. Another casualty of the sick retail economy was the company's high-end RUEHL chain, which closed the last of its 29 stores in January 2010. The decision to pull the plug on RUEHL, a Greenwich Village-inspired concept for the post-college set that debuted in 2005, and its e-commerce business, came after the chain suffered a steep drop-off in same-store sales.

Overall, the company saw double-digit sales declines over all of its retail brands in 2009 (with the exception of Gilly Hicks which is too new to warrant a meaningful comparison).

Bright spots in an otherwise difficult year included the opening of A&F's first stores in Italy, Germany, and Japan. The company is looking abroad for profitable growth with stores in Fukuoka, Japan and Copenhagen slated to debut in 2010. After opening its first Hollister stores in the UK in 2008, the company plans to add another 30 international mall-based Hollister shops, including in two or more new countries, in the later half of 2010. At home, A&F opened two new Gilly Hicks shops, an Aussie-inspired purveyor of bras and underwear for young women. The new chain competes with Victoria's Secret Pink line of intimate apparel for young women.

A&F is searching for a new president and COO following the resignation of Robert Singer, after only 15 months with the company. Singer's abrupt departure was due to a disagreement over the company's international expansion strategy.

Abercrombie's e-commerce business, which operates websites for all of its store brands, has grown to account for about 10% of net sales.

HISTORY

Scotsman David Abercrombie began selling camping equipment in lower Manhattan in 1892. Joined by lawyer Ezra Fitch, Abercrombie & Fitch (A&F) soon established itself as the purveyor of outdoors equipment for the very rich. A&F supplied Theodore Roosevelt and Ernest Hemingway for safaris and provided gear for Charles Lindbergh and polar explorer Richard Byrd. In 1917 the company moved into a 12-story edifice in Manhattan that included a log cabin (which Fitch lived in) and a casting pool.

A&F thrived through the 1960s. Mounted animal heads adorned its New York store, which offered 15,000 types of lures and 700 different shotguns. However, by the 1970s A&F's core customers were as extinct or endangered as the animals they had hunted, and the company struggled to find new markets. In 1977 A&F filed for bankruptcy. A year later sports retailer Oshman's (now The Sports Authority) bought the company and expanded the number of stores while providing an eclectic assortment of goods. In 1988 clothing retailer The Limited bought A&F, then with about 25 stores, and shifted the company's emphasis to apparel.

Michael Jeffries took over in 1992 and transformed the still money-losing chain into an outfitter for college students. The new *jefe* micromanaged, issuing a 29-page book on everything from how A&F salespeople (who earned around $6 an hour) must look to exactly how many sweaters can be placed in a stack. Draconian perhaps, but the strategy worked, and A&F returned to profitability in fiscal 1995. The company went public in 1996 with more than 110 stores.

In 1998 The Limited spun off its remaining 84% stake. Also that year A&F sued rival American Eagle Outfitters, claiming it illegally copied A&F's clothing and approach (the suit was dismissed in 1999), and it raised the hackles of Mothers Against Drunk Driving with a catalog article entitled "Drinking 101." The company got attention of a different sort in 1999 when the SEC launched an investigation after A&F leaked sales figures to an analyst before they were made available to the public. In 2000 A&F launched its new teen store concept called Hollister Co.

A&F continued to push the envelope with its A&F Quarterly in summer 2001. Under the theme "Let Summer Begin," the catalog featured naked and half-naked models having "wet 'n' wild summer fun" and T-shirts logos that read "I Have a Big One" and "Get on the Stick."

The company pushed a little further in Spring 2002 with a line of T-shirts portraying Asian caricatures. Vocal protests from Asian groups forced A&F to pull the T-shirts from its shelves and issue an apology. Later that spring, A&F may have pushed a little too hard. A line of children's-sized thong underwear bearing sexually suggestive messages caused a furor among family-advocacy groups.

In December 2003 Abercrombie & Fitch toned down with the discontinuation of its popular and racy A&F Quarterly magazine, which targeted consumers aged 18-24. In September 2004 it launched a young professionals' brand called RUEHL. The stores target customers aged 22 to 30, traditionally J. Crew and Banana Republic customers, offering hip styles at lower prices.

In May 2005 A&F established a Japanese subsidiary company called ANF. In November the company opened its first RUEHL Accessories store, a tiny (600 sq. ft.) shop on Manhattan's Bleecker Street. Also in November the company opened its first off-mall, flagship store on New York's Fifth Avenue at 56th Street.

In late 2007 the retailer launched an e-commerce site for its RUEHL concept. Soon after, in January 2008, the company launched its newest brand, Gilly Hicks, with a store opening in Natick, Massachusetts. The company also opened its first Hollister stores in malls in the UK in 2008.

EXECUTIVES

Chairman and CEO: Michael S. (Mike) Jeffries, age 65, $36,335,644 total compensation
EVP Planning and Allocation: Leslee K. Herro, age 49, $2,534,706 total compensation
EVP and CFO: Jonathan E. Ramsden, age 45, $743,859 total compensation
EVP Sourcing: Diane Chang, age 54, $2,534,610 total compensation
SVP Design: Katherine M. Rigby
SVP Store Operations: Lawrence E. (Larry) Honig, age 62
SVP Human Resources: Ron Grzymkowski
SVP Store Construction: Abed W. Karaze
SVP Allocation: Rebecca F. Lee
SVP Supply Chain: John A. Singleton
SVP, General Counsel, and Secretary: Ronald A. Robins Jr.
SVP Store Operations: Amy L. Zehrer
SVP Real Estate: David L. Leino, age 43
SVP Diversity and Inclusion: Todd Corley
SVP Design: Molly Hunt
SVP Technical Design: Mark D. Kabbes
VP Finance: Brian P. Logan, $502,646 total compensation
VP Brand Protection: Shane Berry
Senior Counsel: David S. Cupps, age 73, $875,954 total compensation
Manager Investor Relations: Eric M. Cerny
Auditors: PricewaterhouseCoopers LLP

LOCATIONS

HQ: Abercrombie & Fitch Co.
  6301 Fitch Path, New Albany, OH 43054
Phone: 614-283-6500   **Fax:** 614-283-6710
Web: www.abercrombie.com

2010 US Stores

	No.
California	133
Texas	98
Florida	73
New York	56
Illinois	48
Pennsylvania	48
New Jersey	41
Ohio	40
Michigan	33
Massachusetts	33
North Carolina	30
Virginia	28
Indiana	26
Georgia	25
Tennessee	24
Washington	24
Connecticut	22
Minnesota	22
Maryland	19
Missouri	18
Arizona	17
Wisconsin	16
Louisiana	15
South Carolina	15
Kentucky	14
Nevada	14
Oregon	14
Alabama	13
Colorado	12
New Hampshire	11
Oklahoma	10
Other states	78
Total	**1,070**

2010 International Stores

	No.
Canada	12
UK	11
Italy	3
Germany	1
Japan	1
Total	**28**

PRODUCTS/OPERATIONS

2010 Sales

	$ mil.	% of total
Hollister	1,287.2	44
Abercrombie & Fitch	1,272.3	43
abercrombie kids	343.2	12
Gilly Hicks	25.9	1
Total	**2,928.6**	**100**

Selected Products

Backpacks	Jackets	Skirts
Belts	Jeans	Sweaters
Caps	Outerwear	Swimwear
Footwear	Pants	Tank tops
Fragrances	Shirts	Underwear
Hats	Shorts	

COMPETITORS

Aéropostale	Lands' End
American Eagle Outfitters	Levi Strauss
Bath & Body Works	L.L. Bean
Benetton	Macy's
Body Shop	Nordstrom
The Buckle	Pacific Sunwear
Dillard's	Polo Ralph Lauren
Express LLC	Quiksilver
The Gap	Target
Guess?	Tommy Hilfiger
H&M	Urban Outfitters
J. Crew	Victoria's Secret Stores
La Senza	Wet Seal

HISTORICAL FINANCIALS

Company Type: Public

Income Statement

FYE: Saturday nearest January 31

	REVENUE ($ mil.)	NET INCOME ($ mil.)	NET PROFIT MARGIN	EMPLOYEES
1/10	2,929	0	0.0%	80,000
1/09	3,540	272	7.7%	83,000
1/08	3,750	476	12.7%	99,000
1/07	3,318	422	12.7%	86,400
1/06	2,785	334	12.0%	76,100
Annual Growth	**1.3%**	**(82.7%)**	**—**	**1.3%**

2010 Year-End Financials

Debt ratio: 3.9%
Return on equity: 0.0%
Cash ($ mil.): 680
Current ratio: 2.75
Long-term debt ($ mil.): 71
No. of shares (mil.): 88
Dividends
  Yield: 2.2%
  Payout: —
Market value ($ mil.): 2,782

Stock History

NYSE: ANF

	STOCK PRICE ($) FY Close	P/E High/Low		PER SHARE ($) Earnings	Dividends	Book Value
1/10	31.54	—	—	0.00	0.70	20.72
1/09	17.85	27	4	3.05	0.70	20.92
1/08	79.59	16	13	5.20	0.70	18.35
1/07	79.54	18	11	4.59	0.70	15.93
1/06	66.39	20	12	3.66	0.60	11.28
Annual Growth	**(17.0%)**	**—**	**—**	**—**	**3.9%**	**16.4%**

ABM Industries

Many businesses hope to clean up, but diversified facilities services contractor ABM Industries counts on it. Through its primary business unit, ABM Janitorial, the company offers cleaning services to owners and operators of office buildings, hospitals, manufacturing plants, schools, shopping centers, and transportation facilities throughout the US and in Canada and Puerto Rico. Through other units, ABM Industries provides security services and maintains mechanical, electrical, and plumbing systems. Ampco System Parking operates more than 1,800 parking lots and garages, mainly at airports across 35 states, while ABM Security Services provides security officers and security systems monitoring services.

Like other conglomerates in the business services sector, ABM has grown mainly by acquiring local and regional operating companies and their client rosters. It has also stayed focused on strengthening its core cleaning, parking, and security services operations. ABM generates cost savings by centralizing many business functions, such as marketing, sales, and accounting. This strategy also allows ABM to increase sales by more effectively leveraging its diverse portfolio of service offerings.

In 2010 ABM strengthened its janitorial segment through the acquisition of Diversco, a provider of outsourced facility services serving industrial and manufacturing clients. The deal broadened ABM Janitorial's client base and geographic reach and added security services to its list of offerings. ABM had previously enhanced this segment significantly in 2007 by acquiring rival facility services company OneSource Services. It paid about $390 million for OneSource, which posted revenue of about $825 million for the year ended March 31, 2007. The operations of OneSource, including more than 10,000 commercial accounts in the US, Canada, and Puerto Rico, were integrated into those of ABM Janitorial throughout 2008.

In 2009 ABM kept the acquisition engine running when it snatched up several cleaning and engineering businesses — Control Building Services, Control Engineering Services, and TTF Assets — located primarily in New Jersey and New York. Collectively these businesses generate annual revenues of about $50 million and cater to the commercial, institutional, and pharmaceutical industries.

ABM also periodically gauges and adjusts its mix of holdings. In order to focus on its core operations, in late 2008 the company sold the operating assets of its Amtech Lighting Services business to a unit of OSRAM SYLVANIA for about $34 million.

HISTORY

Morris Rosenberg invested $4.50 in a bucket and cleaning tools and began cleaning San Francisco storefront windows in 1909. Later that year he purchased Chicago Window Cleaning for $300 and, armed with new supplies and a Ford Model T, began offering annual cleaning contracts. He changed the company's name to American Building Maintenance in 1913 to emphasize its broadening services. By 1920 the company had established three west coast offices, and it became the first contractor to clean a major college campus when it signed an agreement with Stanford University in 1921.

The company added cleaning supplies to its offerings in 1927 with the acquisition of Easterday Janitorial Supply Company and continued to grow, even during the Great Depression, by providing cleaning services cheaper than its clients could provide for themselves. ABM expanded to the East Coast in 1932. Morris Rosenberg died in 1935, leaving the company to his oldest son Theodore, who bought electrical services company Alta Electric the following year. During WWII ABM cleaned Navy ships and wired amphibious vehicles called Water Buffaloes. By the end of the war, it operated 17 offices in the US and Canada.

Now called American Building Maintenance Industries, the company went public in 1962 with Theodore serving as chairman and younger brother Sydney as CEO. To diversify its services, ABM Industries stepped up its acquisition pace in the late 1960s, buying Ampco Auto Parks (1967, parking facilities), Commercial Air Conditioning (1968, equipment maintenance), and General Elevator Corporation (1969, elevator maintenance and repair).

ABM Industries continued to expand its business into diverse services and regions through a three-decade buying spree. In 1981 the company combined its air-conditioning, elevator, lighting, and energy services into American Technical Services Company (Amtech) to better focus on the high-growth tech and energy businesses. A management-led buyout of the company failed in 1990 on opposition from the Rosenberg brothers. Although ABM Industries' president stepped down and several lawsuits were filed following the aborted LBO, the company continued to post impressive sales and profit numbers.

The company shortened its name to ABM Industries in 1994, the same year William Steele was named CEO. Sydney Rosenberg retired as chairman in 1997, marking the end of family control. The following year the company formed a Facility Services division to provide one-stop shopping for all of its services. It moved into landscaping services in 1999 with the purchase of Commercial Landscape Systems. The following year Steele stepped down as CEO and Henrik Slipsager, a former executive of Dutch services giant ISS, was tapped as the company's new chief.

In 2001 ABM sold off its Easterday Janitorial Supply subsidiary to AmSan West. ABM acquired six companies in 2001 and 2002, including Lakeside Building Maintenance, a large Midwestern janitorial contractor. In 2003 the company sold its Amtech Elevator Services to Otis Elevator Company for $112 million. Two years later, the company sold its CommAir Mechanical Services unit to Carrier Corp.

In 2005 ABM sold the last of its mechanical operations, divesting its water treatment business to San Joaquin Chemicals. ABM made one of the biggest deals in its history in 2007 when it obtained rival facility services company OneSource Services, paying about $390 million. A year later it also divested its Amtech Lighting Services operations.

EXECUTIVES

Chairman: Maryellen C. Herringer, age 66
President, CEO, and Director: Henrik C. Slipsager, age 55, $3,126,296 total compensation
EVP; President, ABM Facility Services: Steven M. Zaccagnini, age 48, $1,029,353 total compensation
EVP and CFO: James S. Lusk, age 54, $1,098,539 total compensation
EVP; President, ABM Janitorial Services: James P. (Jim) McClure, age 52, $1,495,063 total compensation
SVP, General Counsel, and Secretary: Sarah H. McConnell, age 45, $646,574 total compensation
SVP and Chief Marketing Officer: Gary R. Wallace, age 59
SVP, Chief Accounting Officer, and Controller: Dean A. Chin, age 42
SVP Human Resources: Erin M. Andre, age 50
SVP: David L. Farwell, age 48
VP and Treasurer: D. Anthony Scaglione
VP Corporate Communications: Anthony (Tony) Mitchell
President, Ampco System Parking: Mark Muglich
President, ABM Security Services: Chris Hansen
Auditors: KPMG LLP

LOCATIONS

HQ: ABM Industries Incorporated
551 5th Ave., Ste. 300, New York, NY 10176
Phone: 212-297-0200 **Fax:** 212-297-0375
Web: www.abm.com

PRODUCTS/OPERATIONS

2009 Sales

	$ mil.	% of total
Janitorial	2,382.0	69
Parking	457.5	13
Security	334.6	9
Engineering	305.7	9
Corporate	2.0	—
Total	**3,481.8**	**100**

COMPETITORS

AlliedBarton Security
ARAMARK
Central Parking
Comfort Systems USA
Guardsmark
Healthcare Services
Impark
ISS A/S
ServiceMaster
Sodexo USA
Standard Parking
Temco Service Industries
UGL Unicco

HISTORICAL FINANCIALS

Company Type: Public

Income Statement

FYE: October 31

	REVENUE ($ mil.)	NET INCOME ($ mil.)	NET PROFIT MARGIN	EMPLOYEES
10/09	3,482	54	1.6%	91,000
10/08	3,624	45	1.3%	100,000
10/07	2,843	52	1.8%	107,000
10/06	2,793	93	3.3%	75,000
10/05	2,588	58	2.2%	73,000
Annual Growth	7.7%	(1.6%)	—	5.7%

2009 Year-End Financials

Debt ratio: 25.1%
Return on equity: 8.2%
Cash ($ mil.): 34
Current ratio: 1.81
Long-term debt ($ mil.): 173
No. of shares (mil.): 52
Dividends
  Yield: 2.8%
  Payout: 49.5%
Market value ($ mil.): 977

Stock History

NYSE: ABM

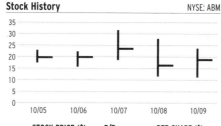

	STOCK PRICE ($) FY Close	P/E High/Low		PER SHARE ($) Earnings	Dividends	Book Value
10/09	18.78	22	11	1.05	0.52	13.20
10/08	16.33	31	14	0.88	0.50	12.38
10/07	23.52	30	18	1.04	0.48	11.64
10/06	19.86	12	9	1.88	0.44	10.40
10/05	19.73	20	16	1.15	0.42	9.15
Annual Growth	(1.2%)	—	—	(2.2%)	5.5%	9.6%

Accenture Ltd

For Accenture, the accent is on trying to help businesses improve their performance. The world's largest consulting firm, Accenture offers management consulting, information technology and systems integration, and business process outsourcing (BPO) services to customers around the globe. The company divides its practices into five main operating groups — communications and high technology, financial services, public service, products, and resources — that encompass more than 15 industries. Accenture, which is domiciled in Dublin but headquartered in New York, operates from more than 200 locations in about 50 countries.

Accenture disperses its advice widely — no single operating group accounts for substantially more than a quarter of the firm's sales. Similarly, Accenture has diversified its operations geographically. As with the rest of the outsourcing services industry, Accenture is looking to India, Brazil, China, Japan, and the Philippines as key areas for expansion. Adhering to this strategy, in mid-2008 Accenture acquired ATAN, an industrial and automation services provider based in Brazil that caters to the mining, energy, and utilities sectors. It snatched up SOPIA, a Tokyo-based consulting firm specializing in Oracle systems integration, earlier that year. Accenture also obtained RiskControl, another consulting company based in Brazil, in early 2010.

Accenture also added to its transportation and travel services operations in 2008 when it bought AddVal Technology. AddVal provides software and technology used for freight order management, and the deal enhanced Accenture's ability to integrate and simplify its clients' freight management services capabilities.

In late 2009 Accenture obtained the Symbian professional services unit of Nokia. The unit offers engineering and support services for the Symbian operating system, one of the world's most widely used operating systems for smart phones. The acquisition furthered Accenture's penetration into the cutting-edge smart phone support services market.

Like many global companies, in 2009 Accenture was affected by shrinking demand for its services due to clients cutting back in the midst of the economic downturn.

HISTORY

Accenture traces its history back to the storied accounting firm of Arthur Andersen & Co. Founded by Northwestern University professor and accounting legend Arthur Andersen in 1913, the firm's expanding scope of operations led it into forensic accounting and advising clients on financial reporting processes, forming the basis for a management consulting arm. Arthur Andersen led the firm until his death in 1947. His successor, Leonard Spacek, split off the consulting operations as a separate unit in 1954.

The consulting business grew quickly during the 1970s and 1980s, thanks in part to an orgy of US corporate re-engineering. By 1988 consulting accounted for 40% of Andersen's sales. Chafing at sharing profits with the auditors (who faced growing price pressures and a rising tide of legal action due to the accounting irregularities of their clients), the consultants sought more power within the firm. The result was a 1989 restructuring that established Andersen

Worldwide (later Andersen) as the parent of two independent units, Arthur Andersen and Andersen Consulting (AC). The growing revenue imbalance between the operations remained unresolved, however, and a year later Arthur Andersen poured gas on the flames by establishing its own business consultancy.

Meanwhile, AC continued to expand during the 1990s by forming practices focused on manufacturing, finance, and government. It addressed the shift from mainframes to PCs by forming alliances with technology heavyweights Hewlett-Packard, Sun Microsystems, and Microsoft. In 1996 AC teamed up with Internet service provider BBN (acquired by GTE in 1997) to form ServiceNet, a joint venture to develop Internet commerce and other systems.

The Andersen family feud took a turn for the worse in 1997 with the retirement of CEO Lawrence Weinbach. A deadlocked vote for a new leader led the board to appoint accounting partner Robert Grafton as CEO, angering the consulting partners. Later that year AC asked the International Chamber of Commerce to negotiate a breakup of Andersen Worldwide. George Shaheen, to whom many attributed the heightened tensions between the units, resigned as CEO of AC in 1999 and was replaced by Joe Forehand.

While the separation dispute dragged on, the consulting business grew and diversified amid increasing consolidation in the industry. In 1999 the company moved into e-commerce venture funding with the formation of Andersen Consulting Ventures, and in 2000 it inked partnership deals with Microsoft (Microsoft system implementation services), Sun Microsystems (for B2B Internet office supply sales), and BT (Internet-based human resources services).

That year an international arbitrator finally approved AC's separation from its parent, ruling that the consultancy must change its name and pay Andersen Worldwide $1 billion (far less than the $15 billion demanded by the accounting partners). Renamed Accenture, the company went public in 2001. While the new name (a made-up word) might have struck some as a marketing challenge, having an identity distinct from that of its former parent proved to be a stroke of luck for Accenture. Andersen broke apart in 2002 after becoming embroiled in the accounting scandals of energy giant Enron.

In 2004 Accenture successfully bid on a $10 billion, 10-year contract to create a system to identify visitors and immigrants coming into the country. Dubbed US-VISIT (United States Visitor and Immigrant Status Indicator Technology), the system was to be employed by the Department of Homeland Security to prevent terrorists from entering the US. However, Accenture's bid nearly ran afoul of congressional critics who tried to pass spending amendments barring firms headquartered outside the US from winning security-related business.

Forehand stepped down as CEO of Accenture in 2004 and was replaced by company veteran William Green. Forehand remained chairman until he retired in 2006, when Green was named to that post, as well.

Accenture acquired Capgemini's North American health practice in 2005 for $175 million in order to strengthen its offerings to hospitals and health care systems. In 2006 the firm expanded its outsourcing operations by buying NaviSys, a leading provider of software for the life insurance industry, along with key assets of Kansas-based accountant Savista.

EXECUTIVES

Chairman and CEO: William D. (Bill) Green, age 57, $18,277,100 total compensation
COO: Johan G. (Jo) Deblaere, age 48
CFO: Pamela J. Craig, age 52, $5,876,053 total compensation
CTO and Managing Director, Technology: Donald J. (Don) Rippert
Chief Marketing and Communications Officer: Roxanne Taylor
Chief Strategy and Corporate Development Officer: Karl-Heinz Flöther, age 57, $6,678,758 total compensation
General Counsel, Secretary and Chief Compliance Officer: Julie S. Sweet, age 43
Chief Human Resources Officer: Jill B. Smart
Group Chief Executive, Health and Public Service: Stephen J. (Steve) Rohleder, age 52, $6,697,269 total compensation
Group Chief Executive, Financial Services: Pierre Nanterme, age 50
Group Chief Executive, Resources: Alexander (Sander) van 't Noordende, age 46
Group Chief Executive, Products: Gianfranco Casati, age 50
Group Chief Executive, Technology: Kevin M. Campbell, age 49, $5,546,991 total compensation
Group Chief Executive, Communications and High Tech: Martin I. (Marty) Cole, age 53
Group Chief Executive, Global Markets and Management Consulting: Mark Foster, age 50
Group Chief Executive, Business Process Outsourcing: Michael J. (Mike) Salvino
Group Chief Executive, North America: Robert N. (Bob) Frerichs, age 58
Senior Managing Director, Strategic Initiatives; CEO, Accenture Interactive: R. Timothy S. (Tim) Breene, age 60
Senior Manager, Corporate Communications: Ben J. Geschwind
Senior Director, Investor Relations: David Straube
Executive Director, Office of the CEO: Lori L. Lovelace
Principal Accounting Officer and Controller: Anthony G. (Tony) Coughlan, age 52
Director, Public Relations: Fred J. Hawrysh
Auditors: KPMG LLP

LOCATIONS

HQ: Accenture plc
  1345 Avenue of the Americas, New York, NY 10105
Phone: 917-452-4400   **Fax:** 917-527-9915
Web: www.accenture.com

2009 Sales

	% of total
Europe, the Middle East & Africa	45
Americas	44
Asia/Pacific	11
Total	**100**

PRODUCTS/OPERATIONS

2009 Sales

	% of total
Products	26
Communications & high tech	22
Financial services	20
Resources	18
Government	14
Total	**100**

2009 Sales

	% of total
Consulting	58
Outsourcing	42
Total	**100**

Selected Practice Areas

Communications and high technology
  Communications
  Electronics and high technology
  Media and entertainment
Products
  Automotive
  Consumer goods and services
  Health and life sciences
  Industrial equipment
  Retail
  Transportation and travel services
Financial services
  Banking
  Capital markets
  Insurance
Resources
  Chemicals
  Energy
  Natural resources
  Utilities
Government

Selected Services

Business consulting
  Customer relationship management
  Finance and performance management
  Human performance
  Strategy
  Supply chain management
Outsourcing
  Application outsourcing
  Business process outsourcing (BPO)
    Customer contact
    Finance and accounting
    Human resources
    Learning
    Procurement
  Infrastructure outsourcing
Systems integration and technology
  Enterprise architecture
  Information management
  Infrastructure consulting
  Intellectual property
  Research and development

COMPETITORS

Bain & Company
Booz Allen
Boston Consulting
Capgemini
Capgemini US
Charteris
Computer Sciences Corp.
Deloitte Consulting
HP Enterprise Services
IBM
McKinsey & Company
Perot Systems
Siemens AG
Unisys

HISTORICAL FINANCIALS

Company Type: Public

Income Statement

FYE: August 31

	REVENUE ($ mil.)	NET INCOME ($ mil.)	NET PROFIT MARGIN	EMPLOYEES
8/09	23,171	1,590	6.9%	177,000
8/08	25,314	1,692	6.7%	186,000
8/07	21,453	1,243	5.8%	170,000
8/06	18,228	973	5.3%	140,000
8/05	17,094	941	5.5%	123,000
Annual Growth	**7.9%**	**14.0%**	**—**	**9.5%**

2009 Year-End Financials

Debt ratio: 0.0%
Return on equity: 58.6%
Cash ($ mil.): 4,542
Current ratio: 1.46
Long-term debt ($ mil.): 0

No. of shares (mil.): 706
Dividends
  Yield: 1.5%
  Payout: 20.5%
Market value ($ mil.): 23,295

Stock History   NYSE: ACN

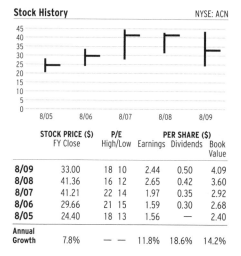

	STOCK PRICE ($) FY Close	P/E High/Low	PER SHARE ($) Earnings	Dividends	Book Value
8/09	33.00	18 10	2.44	0.50	4.09
8/08	41.36	16 12	2.65	0.42	3.60
8/07	41.21	22 14	1.97	0.35	2.92
8/06	29.66	21 15	1.59	0.30	2.68
8/05	24.40	18 13	1.56	—	2.40
Annual Growth	**7.8%**	**— —**	**11.8%**	**18.6%**	**14.2%**

Ace Hardware

Luckily, Ace has John Madden up its sleeve. Despite the growth of warehouse-style competitors, Ace Hardware has remained a household name, thanks to ads featuring Madden, a former Oakland Raiders football coach and retired TV commentator. By sales the company is the #1 hardware cooperative in the US, ahead of Do It Best. Ace dealer-owners operate about 4,600 Ace Hardware stores, home centers, and lumber and building materials locations in all 50 US states and about 60 other countries. From about 15 warehouses Ace distributes such products as electrical and plumbing supplies, garden equipment, hand tools, housewares, and power tools. Its paint division is also a major paint manufacturer in the US.

Amid the global economic downturn, Ace said its business has been fortunate because of its "relative recession resistance." Although the company's network of retail stores has been shrinking, its profits have remained relatively steady. In 2008 about 120 Ace Hardware stores opened while about 240 closed, resulting in a loss of about 120 locations. As it turns out, sales at new stores have outpaced those at closed locations.

The company is making strides to boost its bottom line, starting with helping shoppers locate hard-to-find items. In 2009 Ace launched Aisle411, a free product-location service that can be accessed via phone, similar to dialing for information. The company launched the service after learning that shoppers who were unable to find a product either left (about 20% of the time) or asked store associates for assistance (about 60%), which created a high demand for staff attention.

Challenged by big-box chains such as The Home Depot and Lowe's, Ace rolled out its "next generation" store concept, which involves signage with detailed product descriptions and different flooring to set off departments, among other features. The company is also focusing on

opening smaller neighborhood stores to entice customers who would rather not drive to edge-of-town big-box chains. In mid-2010 the hardware store chain became the first retailer — besides Sears and Kmart stores — to sell Craftsman brand tools.

HISTORY

A group of Chicago-area hardware dealers — William Stauber, Richard Hesse, Gern Lindquist, and Oscar Fisher — decided in 1924 to pool their hardware buying and promotional costs. In 1928 the group incorporated as Ace Stores, named in honor of the superior WWI fliers dubbed aces. Hesse became president the following year, retaining that position for the next 44 years. The company also opened its first warehouse in 1929, and by 1933 it had 38 dealers.

The organization had 133 dealers in seven states by 1949. In 1953 Ace began to allow dealers to buy stock in the company through the Ace Perpetuation Plan. During the 1960s Ace expanded into the South and West, and by 1969 it had opened distribution centers in Georgia and California — its first such facilities outside Chicago. In 1968 it opened its first international store in Guam.

By the early 1970s the do-it-yourself market began to surge as inflation pushed up plumber and electrician fees. As the market grew, large home center chains gobbled up market share from independent dealers such as those franchised through Ace. In response, Ace and its dealers became a part of a growing trend in the hardware industry — cooperatives.

Hesse sold the company to its dealers in 1973 for $6 million (less than half its book value), and the following year Ace began operating as a cooperative. Hesse stepped down in 1973. In 1976 the dealers took full control when the company's first Board of Dealer-Directors was elected.

After signing up a number of dealers in the eastern US, Ace had dealers in all 50 states by 1979. The co-op opened a plant to make paint in Matteson, Illinois, in 1984. By 1985 Ace had reached $1 billion in sales and had initiated its Store of the Future Program, allowing dealers to borrow up to $200,000 to upgrade their stores and conduct market analyses. Former head coach John Madden of the National Football League's Oakland Raiders signed on as Ace's mouthpiece in 1988.

A year later the co-op began to test ACENET, a computer network that allowed Ace dealers to check inventory, send and receive e-mail, make special purchase requests, and keep up with prices on commodity items such as lumber. In 1990 Ace established an International Division to handle its overseas stores. (It had been exporting products since 1975.) EVP and COO David Hodnik became president in 1995. That year the co-op added a net of 67 stores, including a three-store chain in Russia. Expanding further internationally, Ace signed a five-year joint-supply agreement in 1996 with Canadian lumber and hardware retailer Beaver Lumber. Hodnik added CEO to his title in 1996.

Ace fell further behind its old rival, True Value, in 1997 when ServiStar Coast to Coast and True Value merged to form TruServ (renamed True Value in 2005), a hardware giant that operated more than 10,000 outlets at the completion of the merger.

Late in 1997 Ace launched an expansion program in Canada. (The co-op already operated distribution centers in Ontario and Calgary.) In

1999 Ace merged its lumber and building materials division with Builder Marts of America to form a dealer-owned buying group to supply about 2,700 retailers. Ace gained 208 member outlet stores in 2000, but saw 279 member outlets terminated. The next year it gained 220, but lost 255.

Sodisco-Howden bought all the shares of Ace Hardware Canada in February 2003. To better serve international members, Ace opened its first international buying office, in Hong Kong, in April 2004.

In all, the company added 131 new stores in 2005. That year, after 33 years with the company, David F. Hodnik retired as president and CEO of Ace Hardware. He was succeeded by COO Ray A. Griffith.

In 2007 Griffith sent a letter to Ace's retailers, saying the company was considering changing from a cooperative to a traditional corporation to become more competitive and to better fuel growth. Shortly after, the company announced an accounting shortfall of about $150 million, or nearly half of its equity, which was uncovered while Ace prepared to convert formats. The error turned out to be an accident by a mid-level employee.

EXECUTIVES

Chairman: David S. Ziegler
President and CEO: Ray A. Griffith, age 56
EVP: Rita D. Kahle
SVP Supply Chain and Retail Support:
Lori L. Bossmann, age 49
SVP and CFO: Dorvin D. Lively, age 50
VP Merchandising, Marketing, Advertising, and Paint:
John J. Surane, age 41
VP International Finance: Pete Ting
VP Retail Support: Rick A. Whitson, age 55
VP and CIO: Michael G. (Mike) Elmore
VP Human Resources and Communications:
Jimmy Alexander
VP Retail Operations and New Business:
Kane C. Calamari
VP Business Development, International and Retail Training: John S. Venhuizen, age 38
Manager Public Relations: Christopher Boniface
Auditors: Ernst & Young LLP

LOCATIONS

HQ: Ace Hardware Corporation
  2200 Kensington Ct., Oak Brook, IL 60523
Phone: 630-990-6600   **Fax:** 630-990-6838
Web: www.acehardware.com

2009 Sales

	$ mil.	% of total
US	3,281.6	95
Other countries	175.6	5
Total	**3,457.2**	**100**

PRODUCTS/OPERATIONS

2009 Sales

	$ mil.	% of total
Merchandise	3,183.0	92
Retail	274.2	8
Total	**3,457.2**	**100**

HISTORICAL FINANCIALS

Company Type: Cooperative

Income Statement				FYE: Saturday nearest December 31
	REVENUE ($ mil.)	NET INCOME ($ mil.)	NET PROFIT MARGIN	EMPLOYEES
12/09	3,457	96	2.8%	4,500
12/08	3,864	86	2.2%	4,800
12/07	3,971	87	2.2%	4,800
12/06	3,770	107	2.8%	5,000
12/05	3,466	100	2.9%	4,976
Annual Growth	(0.1%)	(1.2%)	—	(2.5%)

Net Income History

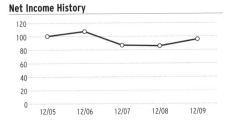

Activision Blizzard

Video game maker Activision Blizzard is a firm believer that action speaks louder than words. The video game publisher is best known for title franchises such as *World of Warcraft*, *Guitar Hero*, *Tony Hawk*, and *Call of Duty*. It also makes games based on licensed properties from LucasArts (*Star Wars*), Marvel (*Spider-Man* and *X-Men*), and DreamWorks Animation (*Shrek*). Its titles are produced for console game systems and handheld devices from Sony, Microsoft, and Nintendo, as well as games for Apple's iPhone. Vivendi acquired a majority stake in the company in a deal valued at $9.8 billion; it then combined Activision with Vivendi Games (and its Blizzard Entertainment division) to form Activision Blizzard.

Part of Vivendi's strategy behind the Activision purchase was to leverage Activision's existing relationships with movie and media companies, which can lead to profitable video game tie-ins to films and their sequels. Vivendi also was eager to add Activision's *Guitar Hero* franchise to its stable of titles.

While *Guitar Hero* (and related games it spawned such as *Band Hero* and *DJ Hero*) was a boon to sales in 2008, momentum in that genre of interactive music games began to slow in 2009. *DJ Hero* sales failed to meet expectations amid an industry-wide slump in video game sales

in 2009; some analysts have predicted that the popularity of music games may have peaked, with the high cost of peripherals such as guitars, drums, and microphones limiting growth past the core population of gamers that have already purchased them.

In addition to the *World of Warcraft* series offered through its Blizzard business, the company has tapped its *Call of Duty* and *Guitar Hero* franchises as key strategic titles; the three franchises accounted for 68% of Activision Blizzard's revenues in fiscal 2009. *Call of Duty: Modern Warfare 2* was released in 2009 and was the top-selling video game in the US that year, raking in more than $1 billion in worldwide sales. As of late 2009 the *Call of Duty* franchise had sold more than 55 million units worldwide and generated about $3 billion in total sales.

In early 2010 the company reorganized its operations into four units; Blizzard remained an independent unit with a new division created to handle *Call of Duty*, another to manage company-owned titles such as *Guitar Hero* and *Tony Hawk*, and a third new unit to oversee licensed properties.

Activision-Blizzard owns the exclusive rights to develop and publish video games based on Marvel's comic book and film franchises: *Spider-Man*, *X-Men*, *Fantastic Four*, and *Iron Man*. It has a similar deal with DreamWorks Animation that grants the company the exclusive rights to publish games based on existing properties, such as *Shrek* and *Madagascar*. Activision-Blizzard has also struck licensing deals and strategic partnerships with Mattel, Harrah's Entertainment, and Hasbro.

Like many major video game publishers, Activision Blizzard also maintains a distribution business that provides warehousing, logistical, and distribution services for its own games as well as for third-party publishers. The company's distribution operations are focused on European markets.

HISTORY

James Levy and four former Atari software designers founded Activision in 1979 to supply game cartridges to Atari. The company went public in 1983. Despite Activision's initial success, Atari's downfall in the 1980s left the company struggling to stay afloat. Levy departed in 1987, and in 1988 new management renamed the company Mediagenic and attempted to transform it into a maker of PC software. Three years later BHK, headed by Robert Kotick, bought a controlling interest in Mediagenic. The company then reorganized under Chapter 11 bankruptcy and changed its name back to Activision.

By 1996 Activision's heavy investment in game development put the company back in the black. The company enhanced its international profile the next year through acquisitions of Take Us! Marketing & Consulting (software for German markets) and UK software distributor CentreSoft. Activision's growth continued in 1998 with its acquisition of Head Games Publishing (sports-oriented CD-ROM games). That year Activision obtained the rights to distribute LucasArts' PC and PlayStation games and expanded its list of game titles through agreements with companies such as Disney, Marvel, and Viacom.

The company's acquisitive streak continued in 1999 with purchases of Expert Software (budget-priced game software) and Elsinore Multimedia (Windows-based games). That year it

introduced *Tony Hawk's Pro Skater,* which went on to sell more than 3.5 million copies. Its successes did not keep the company from posting a loss in 2000, however, and as its stock price began sinking, Activision restructured its operations and closed Expert Software. With a focus on its existing brands and other proven properties, including new Tony Hawk titles, the company experienced record growth while the rest of the industry suffered from sluggish sales. Activision also began developing titles for next-generation game systems such as Sony's PlayStation 2 and Microsoft's Xbox.

In 2001 the company bought action and action-sports game developer Treyarch Invention. The following year Activision bought the remaining 60% of Grey Matter Interactive Studios it didn't already own.

In 2002 Activision acquired 30% of Infinity Ward, the developer of *Call of Duty*; in 2003 the company bought the other 70%.

In 2007 the company acquired Bizarre Creations (the company behind the *Project Gotham Racing* and *Geometry Wars* franchises) and Red Octane (*Guitar Hero*). It also purchased network middleware developer DemonWare.

In 2008 Activision Blizzard sold its game studio Massive Entertainment (publishers of the *World in Conflict* franchise) to UbiSoft. It also sold Swordfish Studios and Wanako Studios and closed Sierra Entertainment. That same year Activision-Blizzard beefed up its music genre offerings with the purchase of Freestyle Games, and also strengthened its development capabilities for Nintendo titles with the acquisition of Budcat Creations.

Continuing to pare down its operations, in 2009-2010 the company closed its RedOctane, Luxoflux, and Shaba Games studios.

EXECUTIVES

LOCATIONS

2009 Sales

	$ mil.	% of total
North America	2,217	52
Europe	1,798	42
Asia/Pacific	263	6
Other	1	—
Total	**4,279**	**100**

PRODUCTS/OPERATIONS

2009 Sales

	$ mil.	% of total
Product sales	3,080	72
Subscription, licensing & other	1,199	28
Total	**4,279**	**100**

2009 Sales by Segment

	% of total
Activision	66
Blizzard	25
Distribution	9
Total	**100**

Selected Titles and Franchises

Bakugan
Band Hero
Call of Duty
DJ Hero
Guitar Hero
Spider-Man
Tony Hawk
True Crime
World of Warcraft

COMPETITORS

Capcom
Disney Interactive Studios
Eidos
Electronic Arts
Konami
Lucasfilm Entertainment
Microsoft
Namco Limited
Nintendo
SEGA
Sony
Square Enix
Take-Two
THQ
Ubisoft

HISTORICAL FINANCIALS

Company Type: Public

Income Statement

FYE: December 31

	REVENUE ($ mil.)	NET INCOME ($ mil.)	NET PROFIT MARGIN	EMPLOYEES
12/09	4,279	113	2.6%	7,000
12/08*	3,026	(107)	—	7,000
3/08	2,898	345	11.9%	2,640
3/07	1,513	86	5.7%	2,125
3/06	1,468	42	2.9%	2,149
Annual Growth	**30.7%**	**28.1%**	**—**	**34.3%**

*Fiscal year change

2009 Year-End Financials

Debt ratio: —
Return on equity: 1.0%
Cash ($ mil.): 2,768
Current ratio: 2.13
Long-term debt ($ mil.): —
No. of shares (mil.): 1,244
Dividends
  Yield: —
  Payout: —
Market value ($ mil.): 13,820

Stock History

NASDAQ (GS): ATVI

	STOCK PRICE ($) FY Close	P/E High/Low		PER SHARE ($) Earnings	Dividends	Book Value
12/09	11.11	146	90	0.09	—	8.65
12/08*	8.64	—	—	(0.11)	—	9.27
3/08	13.65	27	15	0.55	—	1.57
3/07	9.47	69	37	0.14	—	1.13
3/06	6.89	129	76	0.07	—	0.99
Annual Growth	**12.7%**	**—**	**—**	**6.5%**	**—**	**72.1%**

*Fiscal year change

ADC Telecommunications

The transmission overhauls ADC Telecommunications performs don't leave grease stains on the driveway. The company provides broadband data access and infrastructure equipment. Its products — central office service platforms, broadband switches and routers, and wireless gear — are used to transmit voice and data signals and connect communications providers with their subscribers. ADC also provides network management software and integration services. Customers include AT&T, Ciena, Graybar Electric, Time Warner Cable, and Verizon Communications. In July 2010 Tyco Electronics agreed to buy ADC for about $1.25 billion.

The combination of ADC and Tyco Electronics will create a leading provider of broadband connectivity products that reaches across all geographic regions. While ADC has a solid market position in the Americas and China, the deal will bolster its business in Europe and India, where Tyco does more business. In addition, ADC — which has struggled at times with uneven operating results — will be able to expand more quickly as part of a larger organization with deep pockets.

ADC's two largest customers, AT&T and Verizon, together accounted for 38% of its revenues in fiscal 2009.

Along with many of its rivals, the global recession in 2008-2009 impacted ADC adversely, with sales declining and costs as a percentage of net sales rising. As a result the company undertook a series of restructuring initiatives that have included reducing its workforce, closing facilities, discontinuing certain product lines, and selling its APS Germany services unit.

The company's product strategy has included expanding its wireless and fiber-based products lines, and growing its presence in developing markets such as China and Russia. In addition to its internal development efforts, ADC has pursued acquisitions to that end. It acquired LGC

Wireless, a provider of in-building wireless networks, for about $169 million. In a bid to grow its presence in China, ADC purchased Century Man Communication in 2008. The acquisition of Century Man, which makes communication distribution frames, also provided ADC with manufacturing facilities in China.

HISTORY

Engineer Ralph Allison founded Audio Development Company (ADC) in 1935 to make devices to test hearing. The company soon diversified into products for the broadcast industry before Allison's departure in 1949, the year ADC sold its audiometer unit.

In 1961 ADC merged with power supply maker Magnetic Controls, becoming ADC Magnetic Controls. In 1970 the Bell family, founders of General Mills and 51% owners of ADC, recruited Honeywell executive Charles Denny as president and CEO. He turned the company into a telephone equipment maker. ADC benefited from the 1983 AT&T breakup, when the Baby Bells began buying equipment from outside sources. ADC sold its struggling power supply business in 1984 and became ADC Telecommunications.

Denny stepped down as president in 1990 and as CEO in 1991 after leading two decades of annual 20% compound earnings. Ex-AT&T executive William Cadogan took over both positions. ADC's acquisitions let it fill market niches not addressed by larger companies. Profit margins rose as ADC expanded from copper-based telecom gear to fiber-optic, wireless, and digital technologies.

Deregulation positioned the company to benefit from increased industry competition. In the mid-1990s ADC began using acquisitions to fuel global and wireless expansion, including Finland's Solitra Oy (1996), signaling and control expert NewNet (1997), and Israel-based digital loop system maker Teledata Communications (1998). Other 1998 purchases expanded its systems integration business and optical component line.

The company's spree continued in 1999, when it bought Hadax (remote test and access systems), NVision (TV distribution and switching products), Pathway (ATM transmission), Austria-based Phasor Electronics (cable TV transmission products), Spectracom (optical components), and Ireland-based Saville Systems (billing and customer care software).

In 2000 ADC further diversified its product line by acquiring chief rival and digital subscriber line (DSL) specialist PairGain Technologies for $1.6 billion, wireless communications software maker Centigram, and privately held cable and DSL access equipment maker Broadband Access Systems; these purchases totalled over $4 billion.

The company eliminated about 40% of staff in 2001 due to an industrywide downturn in sales. Cadogan retired and Richard Roscitt (another ex-AT&T executive) took the reins that year. Roscitt has his work cut out for him as Cadogan had built up a head of steam for ADC after a decade at the helm. Under his leadership ADC made more than 20 acquisitions from 1996 that expanded the company's geographic reach and its broadband access product lines. The shopping spree left the company overextended as the market took a turn for the worse.

That year the company sold the units responsible for its high-speed WAN access, digital TV broadcasting, and broadband wireless transmission equipment to Platinum Equity. It also sold its radio-frequency filtration equipment business, Solitra, and its enhanced services unit (SS7 signaling gateways and wireless and unified messaging software).

As part of its restructuring around core businesses, the company continued to shed employees and close facilities (it shuttered more than 40 locations worldwide) through the end of 2002.

ADC acquired copper and fiber-optic cable maker KRONE Group from GenTek in 2004 for an estimated $350 million; the deal supported the company's effort to broaden its portfolio of cabling products and increase its presence in such emerging markets as China and India.

The company also divested operations in 2004. ADC sold its billing and customer service software (Singl.eView) to Intec Telecom. It sold its cable modem termination system product line (Cuda) and related software (FastFlow) to BigBand Networks.

In 2006 ADC agreed to acquire communications equipment manufacturer Andrew in a stock deal valued at roughly $2 billion, but Andrew withdrew from the merger when falling stock prices devalued the deal by about 40%.

EXECUTIVES

Chairman, President, and CEO: Robert E. (Bob) Switz, age 63, $3,305,683 total compensation
VP and CFO: James G. (Jim) Mathews, age 58, $754,541 total compensation
VP and President, Global Connectivity Solutions: Patrick D. (Pat) O'Brien, age 46, $825,352 total compensation
VP; President, Network Solutions Business Unit: Richard B. (Dick) Parran Jr., age 53, $639,888 total compensation
VP and Chief Administrative Officer: Laura N. Owen, age 53, $642,918 total compensation
VP and Controller: Steven G. Nemitz, age 35
VP and CIO; President, Professional Services Business Unit: Christopher Jurasek, age 43
VP Asia Pacific Sales, Marketing, and Customer Service: John Dulin
VP and General Manager, China: Nii Quaye
VP Product Management: John Spindler
VP and CTO: Michael H. Day
VP, General Counsel, and Secretary: Jeffrey D. (Jeff) Pflaum, age 50
VP Tax: Bradley V. Crary
VP Go-to-Market, Americas and Global: Kimberly S. Hartwell, age 47
Director Investor Relations: Jon Oberle
Auditors: Ernst & Young LLP

LOCATIONS

HQ: ADC Telecommunications, Inc.
13625 Technology Dr., Eden Prairie, MN 55344
Phone: 952-938-8080   **Fax:** 952-917-1717
Web: www.adc.com

2009 Sales

	$ mil.	% of total
Americas		
US	590.8	59
Canada, Central & South America	68.8	7
Europe, Middle East & Africa		
Germany	33.6	4
Other countries	136.6	17
Asia Pacific	95.1	13
Total	**996.7**	**100**

PRODUCTS/OPERATIONS

2009 Sales

	$ mil.	% of total
Connectivity	787.1	79
Professional services	136.3	14
Network solutions	73.3	7
Total	**996.7**	**100**

Selected Products

Connectivity
Broadcast and entertainment network connectors
Digital distribution frame (DDF) and digital signal cross-connect (DSX) modules, panels, and bays
FTTX fiber distribution and access terminals, splitters, multiplexers
Fiber distribution panels and frames
Power distribution and protection panels
RF signal amplifiers, combiners, couplers, and splitters
Structured cabling

Wireline
Last-mile data transport
Optical tranport for voice protocols

Wireless
Base stations, controllers, and mobile switching centers
Cell site amplifiers
In-building wireless networking equipment
Outdoor wireless applications and cellular base station hotels

COMPETITORS

3M
ADTRAN
Alcatel-Lucent
CommScope
Corning
Ericsson
Fujikura Ltd.
Furukawa Electric
KGP Logistics
MasTec
NEC
Nexans
Nokia Siemens Networks
Panduit
Powerwave Technologies
Telect
Tyco

HISTORICAL FINANCIALS

Company Type: Public

Income Statement

FYE: September 30

	REVENUE ($ mil.)	NET INCOME ($ mil.)	NET PROFIT MARGIN	EMPLOYEES
9/09*	997	(747)	—	9,050
10/08	1,456	(42)	—	10,600
10/07	1,322	106	8.0%	9,050
10/06	1,282	72	5.6%	8,600
10/05	1,169	111	9.5%	8,200
Annual Growth	**(3.9%)**	**—**	**—**	**2.5%**

*Fiscal year change

Stock History

NASDAQ (GS): ADCT

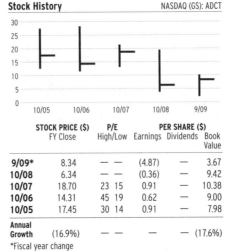

	STOCK PRICE ($) FY Close	P/E High/Low		PER SHARE ($) Earnings	Dividends	Book Value
9/09*	8.34	—	—	(4.87)	—	3.67
10/08	6.34	—	—	(0.36)	—	9.42
10/07	18.70	23	15	0.91	—	10.38
10/06	14.31	45	19	0.62	—	9.00
10/05	17.45	30	14	0.91	—	7.98
Annual Growth	**(16.9%)**	—	—	**—**	**—**	**(17.6%)**

*Fiscal year change

Administaff, Inc.

Administaff handles the payroll so you don't have to. The company is one of the leading professional employer organizations (PEOs) in the US, providing small and midsized companies such services as payroll and benefits administration, workers' compensation programs, personnel records management, and employee recruiting. As a PEO, it is a co-employer of its clients' workers. Administaff also offers Web-based services through its Employee Service Center and operates a business-to-business e-commerce site. Most of its client companies are engaged in the administration, financial, consulting, and computer services industries.

Administaff has almost 50 sales offices serving more than 20 US markets (expansion plans call for 90 offices in 40 markets). Its business in Texas accounts for about 30% of sales, while California represents its second-largest market, accounting for 16%. Administaff's long-term goal is to handle human resource services for about 10% of the small and midsized businesses in the US. The company also focuses on maintaining a consistent client retention rate, which has averaged 79% over the last five years. Like many other companies in the PEO industry, however, Administaff was stung by the nationwide reductions in employment levels in 2009.

The company has been strengthening its software offerings through acquisitions. In 2010 Administaff acquired OneMind Connect, which does business as ExpensAble. Catering to small and midsized businesses, ExpensAble provides expense management software used to automate expense reporting across a company's organization. Later that year Administaff purchased the assets and operations of Galaxy Technologies, a provider of time and attendance software solutions. Administaff made the acquisition to supplement its core human resources services.

HISTORY

Gerald McIntosh and Paul Sarvadi founded Administaff in 1986. The two entrepreneurs saw growth potential in employee leasing, despite the industry's image problems (Sarvadi had worked briefly for James Borgelt, who founded several Dallas-area employee leasing firms and was sentenced to three years in prison in 1996 for stealing from clients).

By 1991 Administaff had become one of the largest employee leasing companies in the US. That year it joined 17 other leasing companies in filing a suit against the Texas State Board of Insurance, which had tried to prohibit leasing companies from buying workers' compensation insurance. Regulators claimed leasing companies were touting their services as a way to avoid high workers' comp premiums. In 1993 a compromise law allowed employee leasing companies to buy workers' comp insurance based on the clients' on-the-job accident history.

With about 1,500 clients, Administaff went public in 1997. The following year the company formed a marketing agreement with American Express, under which the travel and financial services giant refers smaller business clients to Administaff for a fee. It began offering Web-based services during 1999 with Administaff Assistant (now Employee Service Center) and launched Internet portal site bizzport (now My MarketPlace) in 2000. It also began building its fourth service center in Los Angeles (completed in 2002). By the next year the company's client roster had grown to more than 4,000 companies.

In 2002 Administaff acquired the assets of Virtual Growth Incorporated, which provided outsourced accounting services. Also that year it launched (with IBM) HR PowerHouse, a human resources website targeting small businesses. In 2005 it bought HRTools.com.

EXECUTIVES

Chairman and CEO: Paul J. Sarvadi, age 53, $2,440,136 total compensation
President and Director: Richard G. Rawson, age 61, $1,579,994 total compensation
EVP COO and Client Services Officer: A. Steve Arizpe, age 52, $1,605,205 total compensation
EVP Sales and Marketing: Jay E. Mincks, age 56, $1,449,244 total compensation
SVP Strategic Planning: Mark W. Allen
SVP Legal, General Counsel, and Secretary: Daniel D. Herink, age 43
SVP Property and Casualty Products and Services: Ronald M. McGee
SVP Service Operations: Gregory R. (Greg) Clouse
SVP Finance, CFO, and Treasurer: Douglas S. (Doug) Sharp, age 48, $1,123,350 total compensation
SVP Enterprise and Technology Solutions: Samuel G. (Sam) Larson
SVP Client Selection and Pricing: Roger L. Gaskamp
SVP Marketing and Corporate Communications: Jason Cutbirth
SVP Corporate Human Resources: Betty L. Collins
Auditors: Ernst & Young LLP

LOCATIONS

HQ: Administaff, Inc.
19001 Crescent Springs Dr., Kingwood, TX 77339
Phone: 281-358-8986 **Fax:** 281-348-3718
Web: www.administaff.com

2009 Sales

	$ mil.	% of total
Southwest	518.8	31
Northeast	369.8	22
West	321.9	20
Central	248.6	15
Southeast	182.9	11
Other	11.1	1
Total	**1,653.1**	**100**

PRODUCTS/OPERATIONS

Selected Products and Services

Benefits and payroll administration
e-business services
Employee recruiting and selection
Employer liability management
Health insurance programs
Performance management
Personnel records management
Training and development
Workers' compensation programs

COMPETITORS

ADP
All Staff HR Group
CompuPay
Kelly Services
Paychex
TeamStaff
TriNet Group

HISTORICAL FINANCIALS

Company Type: Public

Income Statement

FYE: December 31

	REVENUE ($ mil.)	NET INCOME ($ mil.)	NET PROFIT MARGIN	EMPLOYEES
12/09	1,653	17	1.0%	1,950
12/08	1,724	46	2.7%	2,060
12/07	1,570	48	3.0%	117,301
12/06	1,390	47	3.3%	104,325
12/05	1,170	30	2.6%	88,780
Annual Growth	**9.0%**	**(13.8%)**	**—**	**(61.5%)**

2009 Year-End Financials

Debt ratio: —
Return on equity: 7.7%
Cash ($ mil.): 227
Current ratio: 1.44
Long-term debt ($ mil.): —
No. of shares (mil.): 26
Dividends
 Yield: 2.2%
 Payout: 78.8%
Market value ($ mil.): 618

Stock History

NYSE: ASF

	STOCK PRICE ($) FY Close	P/E High/Low		PER SHARE ($) Earnings	Dividends	Book Value
12/09	23.59	46	27	0.66	0.52	8.52
12/08	21.68	18	7	1.79	0.48	7.96
12/07	28.28	25	16	1.74	0.44	7.59
12/06	42.77	36	18	1.64	0.36	8.73
12/05	42.05	43	10	1.12	0.28	6.97
Annual Growth	**(13.5%)**	**—**	**—**	**(12.4%)**	**16.7%**	**5.2%**

Adobe Systems

Adobe Systems' role as a leading desktop publishing software provider is well documented. The company offers the ubiquitous Acrobat Reader (distributed free of charge), a tool that displays portable document format (PDF) files on the Internet. The company's Web and print publishing products include Photoshop, Illustrator, and PageMaker. Adobe's offerings also include print technology geared toward manufacturers, as well as Web design (Dreamweaver) and electronic book publishing software. Its InDesign publishing package provides professional layout and design applications. Adobe's Professional Services group offers implementation, training, and support.

In 2009 the company purchased Web analytics provider Omniture in a $1.8 billion deal. Adobe will use Omniture's technology to bolster its product offerings so that it can offer customers an integrated product to create, manage, and track the usage and performance of a wide variety of Web-based content, including videos, Web pages, podcasts, and more. The following year the company announced plans to purchase Day Software Holding for about $240 million; the deal will expand Adobe's enterprise content

management product line and add tools for social collaboration and digital asset management.

Graphics and Web designers, technical writers, photographers, and other publishing professionals use Adobe's products to create online and print-based documents. The company's largest product segment, Creative Solutions, accounts for more than half of Adobe's revenues; products in the segment include InDesign, a professional page layout product that competes primarily against Quark's XPress product, as well as its popular Photoshop image editor.

Though products designed for creative professionals remain Adobe's bread and butter, the company continues to expand its market focus. Adobe launched a beta version of Acrobat.com, an online collaboration service for the enterprise market, in 2008. The following year it moved the site to a subscription-based model, charging for shared access to PDF creation applications and other productivity tools.

Though Adobe generates the majority of its sales through Web and print products, the company's activities aren't limited to developing its own software. Adobe has investments in more than 30 companies (including Convio and PSS Systems) whose products and services complement its own.

HISTORY

When Charles Geschke hired John Warnock as chief scientist for Xerox's new graphics and imaging lab, he set the stage for one of the world's largest software makers. While at the Xerox lab, the pair developed the PostScript computer language, which tells printers how to reproduce digitized images on paper. When Xerox refused to market it, the duo left that company and started Adobe (named after a creek near their homes in San Jose, California) in 1982.

Their original plan was to produce an electronic document processing system based on PostScript, but the company changed direction when Apple whiz Steve Jobs hired it to co-design the software for his company's LaserWriter printer. A year later Adobe went public. Meanwhile, PostScript was pioneering the desktop publishing industry by enabling users to laser print nearly anything they created on a computer.

In 1987 the company branched into the European market with the establishment of subsidiary Adobe Systems Europe. It also entered the PC market by adapting PostScript for IBM's operating system. Two years later the company began marketing its products in Asia.

Adobe grew throughout the 1990s by acquiring other software firms, including OCR Systems and Nonlinear Technologies (1992), and AH Software and Science & Art (1993). In 1993 the company began licensing its PostScript software to printer manufacturers; it also started marketing its Acrobat software.

Adobe bought Aldus (1994), whose PageMaker software had been instrumental in establishing the desktop publishing market. (PageMaker's success depended on the font software that Adobe made, and the two companies had a history of cooperation.) Next the company bought Frame Technology (FrameMaker publishing software, 1995), but that acquisition proved disastrous. Frame sales plummeted, partly the result of Adobe's move to eliminate Frame's technical support operations. Adobe's purchase of Web toolmaker Ceneca Communications that year was more fruitful.

In 1996 Adobe spun off its pre-press applications operations as Luminous. That year its licensing sales suffered a blow when one of its largest customers, Hewlett-Packard, introduced a clone version of PostScript. Also in 1997, for the first time, Adobe's revenues from Windows-based software exceeded those of its once-dominant Macintosh-based software.

In 1998 a takeover attempt by competitor Quark proved unsuccessful. Drooping sales that year, which Adobe blamed on the Asian crisis (but which some analysts blamed on its product strategy), prompted the company to shed a layer of executives, 10% of its workforce, and its Adobe Enterprise Publishing Services and Image Club Graphics units. Its 1999 acquisition of GoLive Systems expanded its Web publishing product line. That year Adobe released professional page layout application InDesign, which immediately spurred the biggest backlog in the company's history.

The company boosted its electronic book offerings by acquiring software maker Glassbook. In 2002, in a move to expand its ePaper division, Adobe purchased electronic forms provider Accelio for $72 million. In early 2003, in order to expand its digital video offerings, the company acquired the assets of digital audio tools-maker Syntrillium Software.

In 2004 the company acquired OKYZ, a Paris-based maker of 3D collaboration software; the acquisition added 3D technology to Adobe's Intelligent Document Platform.

Adobe acquired rival Macromedia for approximately $3.4 billion in stock late in 2005. Macromedia's popular website design and animation tools included Dreamweaver and Flash. Adobe acquired Trade and Technologies France (TTF), a developer of CAD data interoperability software, in 2006.

Adobe acquired publishing software provider Scene7 in 2007. It also purchased online word processing software developer Virtual Ubiquity.

EXECUTIVES

Co-Chairman: John E. Warnock, age 69
Co-Chairman: Charles M. (Chuck) Geschke, age 70
President, CEO, and Director: Shantanu Narayen, age 48, $6,663,781 total compensation
EVP and CFO: Mark S. Garrett, age 52, $2,339,732 total compensation
SVP and CTO: Kevin M. Lynch, age 43, $2,638,227 total compensation
SVP Print and Classic Publishing Solutions Business Unit; Managing Director, India Research and Development: Naresh Gupta
SVP Worldwide Field Operations: Matthew A. (Matt) Thompson, age 51, $2,022,386 total compensation
SVP; General Manager, Digital Media Solutions: John P. (Johnny) Loiacono, age 48, $2,145,990 total compensation
SVP, General Counsel, and Secretary: Karen O. Cottle, age 60
SVP; General Manager, Digital Enterprise Solutions: Robert M. (Rob) Tarkoff, age 41
SVP and CIO: Gerri Martin-Flickinger
SVP; General Manager, Creative and Interactive Business Solutions: David Wadhwani
SVP Human Resources: Donna Morris
SVP Corporate Marketing and Communications: Ann Lewnes
SVP and Chief Software Architect, Advanced Technology Labs: Tom Malloy
SVP Engineering Technologies Group: Digby Horner
SVP Corporate Development: Paul Weiskopf
VP and Principal Accounting Officer: Richard T. Rowley, age 51
VP Investor Relations: Mike Saviage
Auditors: KPMG LLP

LOCATIONS

HQ: Adobe Systems Incorporated
345 Park Ave., San Jose, CA 95110
Phone: 408-536-6000   **Fax:** 408-537-6000
Web: www.adobe.com

2009 Sales

	$ mil.	% of total
Americas	1,383	46
Europe, Middle East & Africa	929	32
Asia	634	22
Total	**2,946**	**100**

PRODUCTS/OPERATIONS

2009 Sales

	$ mil.	% of total
Products	2,759	94
Services	187	6
Total	**2,946**	**100**

2009 Sales

	$ mil.	% of total
Creative solutions	1,702	58
Knowledge worker solutions	623	21
Enterprise	236	8
Platform	181	6
Print & publishing	178	6
Omniture	26	1
Total	**2,946**	**100**

COMPETITORS

ACD Systems	Nexaweb
Apple Inc.	Nikon
ArcSoft	Nuance Communications
Autodesk	Oracle
Avid Technology	Pegasystems
Bare Bones Software	Pinnacle Systems
Canon	Quark
Citrix Systems	RealNetworks
Corel	SAS Institute
Coremetrics	Sonic Solutions
Dell	Sony
Eastman Kodak	TIBCO Software
Google	Ultimus
Hewlett-Packard	WebEx
IBM	Webtrends
Lombardi Software	Xara
Microsoft	Yahoo!
Monotype	Zinio Systems

HISTORICAL FINANCIALS

Company Type: Public

Income Statement

FYE: Friday nearest November 30

	REVENUE ($ mil.)	NET INCOME ($ mil.)	NET PROFIT MARGIN	EMPLOYEES
11/09	2,946	387	13.1%	8,660
11/08	3,580	872	24.4%	7,335
11/07	3,158	724	22.9%	6,959
11/06	2,575	506	19.6%	6,082
11/05	1,966	603	30.7%	5,734
Annual Growth	**10.6%**	**(10.5%)**	**—**	**10.9%**

2009 Year-End Financials

Debt ratio: 20.4%	No. of shares (mil.): 525
Return on equity: 8.3%	Dividends
Cash ($ mil.): 999	Yield: 0.0%
Current ratio: 2.93	Payout: —
Long-term debt ($ mil.): 1,000	Market value ($ mil.): 18,425

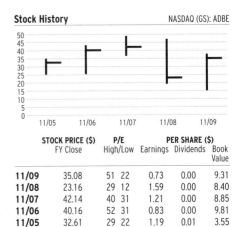

Stock History   NASDAQ (GS): ADBE

	STOCK PRICE ($) FY Close	P/E High/Low	PER SHARE ($) Earnings	Dividends	Book Value
11/09	35.08	51 22	0.73	0.00	9.31
11/08	23.16	29 12	1.59	0.00	8.40
11/07	42.14	40 31	1.21	0.00	8.85
11/06	40.16	52 31	0.83	0.00	9.81
11/05	32.61	29 22	1.19	0.01	3.55
Annual Growth	**1.8%**	**— —**	**(11.5%)**	**—**	**27.3%**

Advance Publications

The drumbeat urging this company forward is the drone of printing presses. Advance Publications is a leading newspaper and magazine publisher with several dozen titles. Its portfolio of about 20 newspapers includes *The Star-Ledger* (New Jersey), *The Cleveland Plain Dealer*, and namesake *Staten Island Advance*, as well as more than 40 weekly titles published by American City Business Journals. Through Condé Nast, Advance Publications owns a bevy of magazines including *The New Yorker*, *Vanity Fair*, and *Wired*. Other operations and interests include online content (Condé Nast Digital) and cable television. Patriarch Sam Newhouse started the family-owned business with the purchase of the *Staten Island Advance* in 1922.

Through acquisitions, creative development, and aggressive promotion, Advance Publications has built a formidable estate of media properties. Its newspapers serve generally smaller markets in about 10 states, while its magazine empire has focused on special interest topics such as fashion, food, interior decorating, and technology. Along the way, the Newhouse family, under the leadership of media mogul brothers Si and Donald, has made a place for itself among such publishing elite as the Grahams (The Washington Post Company), the Hearsts (The Hearst Corporation), and the Sulzbergers (New York Times).

Advance Publications' focus on editorial content means most of its revenue comes from advertising and subscriptions. However, the publishing business has been in decline for several years as readers turn to the Internet and other sources for their news and information. The downturn in the economy has only added to those problems. In response, the company has looked for ways to reduce operating costs at its papers and magazines, including staff cuts and mandatory furloughs. Its flagship *Star-Ledger* laid off about 40% of its workforce late in 2008.

Condé Nast, meanwhile, has had to shutter some of its under-performing titles. In 2009 the unit closed its venerable *Gourmet* magazine (launched in 1940) along with *Cookie* and *Modern Bride*. Other casualties have included *Domino* and *Condé Nast Portfolio*. (The company kept Portfolio.com alive under the auspices of American City Business Journals.) Advance Publications has been investing in online media through Condé Nast Digital. The subsidiary operates websites including Epicurious.com, STYLE.com, and the WiredDigital family of sites.

One bright spot has been the company's interests in cable television. Affiliate Advance/Newhouse controls more than 25% of Discovery Communications (DCI), a leading programmer with popular networks such as Animal Planet, the Science Channel, and its flagship Discovery Channel. DCI went public in 2008 after Advance/Newhouse combined its interests with those of Liberty Media chief John Malone. Advance/Newhouse also owns cable system operator Bright House Networks through a partnership with Time Warner Cable.

HISTORY

Solomon Neuhaus (later Samuel I. Newhouse) got started in the newspaper business after dropping out of school at age 13. He went to work at the *Bayonne Times* in New Jersey and was put in charge of the failing newspaper in 1911; he managed to turn the paper around within a year. In 1922 he bought the *Staten Island Advance* (founded in 1886) and formed the Staten Island Advance Company in 1924. After buying up more papers, he changed the name of the company to Advance Publications in 1949. By the 1950s the company had local papers in New York, New Jersey (including *The Star-Ledger*), and Alabama.

In 1959 Newhouse bought magazine publisher Condé Nast as an anniversary gift for his wife. (He joked that she had asked for a fashion magazine, so he bought her *Vogue.*) His publishing empire continued to grow with the addition of the *Times-Picayune* (New Orleans) in 1962 and *The Cleveland Plain Dealer* in 1967. In 1976 the company paid more than $300 million for Booth Newspapers, publisher of eight Michigan papers and *Parade Magazine.*

Newhouse died in 1979, leaving his sons Si and Donald to run the company, which encompassed more than 30 newspapers, a half-dozen magazines, and 15 cable systems. The next year Advance bought book publishing giant Random House from RCA. Si resurrected the Roaring Twenties standard *Vanity Fair* in 1983 and added *The New Yorker* under the Condé Nast banner in 1985. The Newhouses scored a victory over the IRS in 1990 after a long-running court battle involving inheritance taxes. Condé Nast bought Knapp Publications (*Architectural Digest*) in 1993 and Advance later acquired American City Business Journals in 1995.

In 1998 the company sold the increasingly unprofitable Random House to Bertelsmann for about $1.2 billion. It later bought hallmark Internet magazine *Wired* (though it passed on Wired Ventures' Internet operations). That year revered *New Yorker* editor Tina Brown, credited with jazzing up the publication's content and increasing its circulation, left the magazine; staff writer and Pulitzer Prize winner David Remnick was named as Brown's replacement.

In 1999 Advance joined Donrey Media Group (now called Stephens Media Group), E.W. Scripps, Hearst Corporation, and MediaNews Group to purchase the online classified advertising network AdOne. It also bought Walt Disney's trade publishing unit, Fairchild Publications, for $650 million.

In 2001 Condé Nast bought a majority stake in Miami-based Ideas Publishing Group (Spanish language versions of US magazines). Also that year Advance bought four golf magazines, including *Golf Digest,* from the New York Times Company for $430 million. Condé Nast picked up *Modern Bride* magazine from PRIMEDIA in 2002.

Richard Diamond, a Newhouse relative who'd been publisher of the *Staten Island Advance* since 1979, died in 2004. The following year, Condé Nast launched home magazine *Domino* and lifestyle title *Cookie* targeting the mommy set.

Affiliate Advance/Newhouse combined its stake in cable programmer Discovery Communications with the interests of John Malone (head of Liberty Media) in 2008 to spin off Discovery as a public company. A downturn in the economy that year led to a sharp decline in ad revenue for many of Advance Publications' newspaper and magazine titles. *The Star-Ledger* was forced to cut about 40% of its workforce to reduce costs. Condé Nast, meanwhile, shuttered several titles in 2009, including *Cookie, Domino, Gourmet,* and *Modern Bride.*

EXECUTIVES

Chairman and CEO; Chairman Condé Nast Publications: Samuel I. (S. I.) Newhouse Jr., age 82
President: Donald E. Newhouse, age 80
CFO Advance Publications and President Advance Finance Group LLC: Thomas S. (Tom) Summer, age 56
CEO Condé Nast: Charles H. (Chuck) Townsend
COO and CFO Condé Nast: John Bellando
CEO Parade Publications: John E. (Jack) Haire, age 57
Chairman Advance.net: Steven Newhouse, age 52
President and CEO American City Business Journals: Whitney Shaw
President Condé Nast: Robert (Bob) Sauerberg
President CondéNet Nast Digital: Sarah Chubb
President Advance Internet: Peter Weinberger
President Local Digital Strategy, Advance Internet: Randy Siegel

LOCATIONS

HQ: Advance Publications, Inc.
950 Fingerboard Rd., Staten Island, NY 10305
Phone: 718-981-1234 **Fax:** 718-981-1456
Web: www.advance.net

PRODUCTS/OPERATIONS

Selected Operations
Newspapers
The Cleveland Plain-Dealer
The Oregonian (Portland)
The Star-Ledger (Newark, New Jersey)
Staten Island Advance (New York)
The Times-Picayune (New Orleans)

Magazines
Allure
Architectural Digest
Bon Appétit
Condé Nast Traveler
Details
Glamour
Golf Digest
GQ
Lucky
Men's Vogue
The New Yorker
Self
Teen Vogue
Vanity Fair
Vogue
W
Wired
Other interests
Bright House Networks (cable system operator)
Discovery Communications (cable television channels, 25%)

COMPETITORS

American Express
Crain Communications
Gannett
Hearst Corporation
Lagardère Active
McClatchy Company
MediaNews
Meredith Corporation
New York Times
News Corp.
North Jersey Media
Philadelphia Media
Time Inc.
Tribune Company
Washington Post

HISTORICAL FINANCIALS
Company Type: Private

Income Statement				FYE: December 31
	ESTIMATED REVENUE ($ mil.)	NET INCOME ($ mil.)	NET PROFIT MARGIN	EMPLOYEES
12/08	7,630	—	—	27,200
12/07	7,970	—	—	29,100
12/06	7,700	—	—	28,000
12/05	7,315	—	—	30,000
Annual Growth	1.4%	—	—	(3.2%)

Revenue History

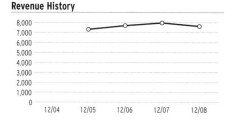

Advanced Micro Devices

Advanced Micro Devices (AMD) made some advances in its battle against Intel but hasn't capitalized on those gains. AMD ranks #2 in PC and server microprocessors, far behind its archrival. Though Intel commands about three-quarters of the world processor market, AMD at times eroded that market share thanks to the popularity of its Athlon and Opteron processor families. The company also makes embedded processors and other chips for communications and networking applications. Hewlett-Packard is AMD's biggest customer, and Chinese OEMs account for nearly half of the company's sales. In 2009 AMD split its operations, spinning off a manufacturing venture.

AMD reached a $1.25 billion legal settlement with Intel in 2009, resolving a longstanding antitrust lawsuit, which accused its archrival of using improper subsidies and coercion methods to secure sales from computer manufacturers. Also that year the European Commission fined Intel about $1.44 billion based on complaints brought by AMD, alleging that Intel paid hidden rebates to PC makers to use only Intel processors in their products, and not AMD's processors. Intel is appealing the ruling.

The settlement between the companies and the spinoff of its manufacturing operations should free AMD to focus on product development and marketing. Intel remains a fearsome and formidable competitor, although it's paid the price of greater regulatory scrutiny around the world for its business practices. Pinning its hopes on the Fusion integrated processors due out in 2011, AMD wants to become more competitive with its archrival on a number of fronts.

AMD has attacked Intel's dominant market share with a lineup of microprocessors led by the high-performance Athlon. One of the company's first releases, Opteron, competes with the likes of Intel's Itanium chip in the server market. Opterons power servers made by HP, IBM, and Sun Microsystems; Dell, long an Intel-only house, is making servers based on Opterons.

In 2008 AMD struck a deal with the Advanced Technology Investment Company (ATIC) of Abu Dhabi to form a new semiconductor manufacturing company, GLOBALFOUNDRIES, that took over AMD's wafer fabrication facilities in Germany and the US.

As part of the transaction for spinning off GLOBALFOUNDRIES, Mubadala Development paid about $125 million to buy 58 million new shares of common stock and warrants for 35 million additional shares, raising the investment firm's stake in AMD to around 20%. It received a seat on the AMD board as well. Mubadala Development is the strategic-investment arm of Abu Dhabi's government, part of the United Arab Emirates.

Seeing sales slow across all business segments in 2008, as did many chip makers, AMD cut about 13% of its global workforce, more than 2,200 employees. The company eliminated another 1,100 jobs in early 2009, 900 through layoffs and the remainder through attrition and the sale of a business unit.

HISTORY

Silicon Valley powerhouse Fairchild Camera & Instrument axed marketing whiz Jerry Sanders, reportedly for wearing a pink shirt on a sales call to IBM. In 1969 Sanders and seven friends started a semiconductor company (just as his former boss, Intel co-founder Robert Noyce, had done a year earlier) based on chip designs licensed from other companies.

Advanced Micro Devices (AMD) went public in 1972. Siemens, eager to enter the US semiconductor market, paid $30 million for nearly 20% of AMD in 1977. (Siemens had sold off its stake by 1991.) In 1982 AMD inked a deal with Intel that let AMD make exact copies of Intel's iAPX86 microprocessors, used in IBM and compatible PCs. By the mid-1980s the company was developing its own chips. In 1987 AMD sued Intel for breaking the 1982 agreement that allowed AMD to second-source Intel's new 386 chips. Intel countersued for copyright infringement when AMD introduced versions of Intel's 287 math coprocessor (1990), 386 chip (1991), and 486 chip (1993).

After a federal jury decided in AMD's favor in the 287 math coprocessor case in 1994, AMD and Intel settled their legal differences in 1995. Each agreed to pay damages, and AMD won a perpetual license to the microcode of Intel's 386 and 486 chips. AMD's K5 microprocessor (a rival of Intel's Pentium) hit the market in 1996 — more than a year late.

In 1996 AMD bought microprocessor developer NexGen Microsystems. AMD unveiled its K6 microprocessor the next year, but had trouble increasing production to meet demand. In 1999 AMD sold programmable logic chip unit Vantis to Lattice Semiconductor. The company debuted its Athlon (K7) chip in 1999 to positive reviews and soon won Compaq Computer and IBM as customers.

Early in 2000 AMD named Hector Ruiz (former head of Motorola's semiconductor operations) president and COO — and thus heir apparent — to Sanders. Improved manufacturing processes, increased sales of high-end Athlons, and a worldwide shortage of flash memory helped AMD turn a profit (and a big one) in 2000, its first since 1995. In the face of a dismal slump in the global chip business, though, AMD cut costs in 2001 by closing two chip plants in Texas and by cutting about 2,300 jobs — 15% of its total workforce — there and in Malaysia.

In 2002 Sanders handed over the CEO reins to Ruiz. In 2003 AMD joined long-time joint-venture partner Fujitsu in forming a new company, called FASL (later renamed Spansion), to pool the two chip makers' flash memory operations. AMD also bought National Semiconductor's Information Appliance unit, which made the Geode line of system-on-a-chip devices.

In 2004 Ruiz succeeded Sanders as chairman as well. AMD filed an antitrust suit against Intel in 2005, alleging that the chip giant had used improper subsidies and coercion to secure sales.

In 2006 AMD acquired ATI Technologies for about $5.4 billion in cash and stock. A year later, the company wrote off $1.3 billion in impaired goodwill on the deal.

After seven consecutive quarters of losses, Hector Ruiz stepped aside as CEO in mid-2008. He remained executive chairman. Dirk Meyer was promoted to CEO to succeed him; Meyer, a 13-year veteran of AMD, was promoted to president and COO of the company in 2006.

EXECUTIVES

Chairman: Bruce L. Claflin, age 58
President, CEO, and Director: Derrick R. (Dirk) Meyer, age 48, $4,547,527 total compensation
EVP, COO, and Chief Administrative Officer: Robert J. (Bob) Rivet Sr., age 55, $5,978,418 total compensation
EVP Legal, Corporate, and Public Affairs: Thomas M. (Tom) McCoy, age 59, $1,124,384 total compensation
SVP and CFO: Thomas J. Seifert, age 46, $1,740,885 total compensation
SVP Human Resources and Chief Talent Officer: Allen Sockwell
SVP and Chief Sales Officer: Emilio Ghilardi, age 52, $2,570,669 total compensation
SVP and CIO: Ahmed Mahmoud
SVP and General Manager: Rick Bergman, age 46
SVP and Chief Marketing Officer: Nigel Dessau, age 45
SVP and Chief Strategy Officer: Marty Seyer
VP Fusion Experience Program: Manju Hegde
Corporate VP Technology Development: Chekib Akrout, age 52
Auditors: Ernst & Young LLP

LOCATIONS

HQ: Advanced Micro Devices, Inc.
1 AMD Place, Sunnyvale, CA 94088
Phone: 408-749-4000
Web: www.amd.com

2009 Sales

	$ mil.	% of total
China	2,445	45
Europe	934	17
US	704	13
Japan	306	6
Other countries	1,014	19
Total	**5,403**	**100**

PRODUCTS/OPERATIONS

2009 Sales

	$ mil.	% of total
Computing Solutions	4,131	77
Graphics	1,206	22
Other	66	1
Total	**5,403**	**100**

Selected Products

Computing
  Microprocessors (Athlon, Opteron, Phenom, Sempron, and Turion lines)
  Motherboard reference design kits and chipsets

Graphics
  Embedded graphics processing units for digital TVs and mobile devices
  Macintosh, notebook, and desktop PC graphics processors (Radeon)
  Motherboard chipsets (for AMD and Intel processors)
  PC TV (ATI TV Wonder, ATI Theater)
  Server and workstation graphics processing units

Personal connectivity
  Embedded processors (Geode line)
  Networking chips

COMPETITORS

Analog Devices
Applied Micro Circuits
ARM Holdings
Atmel
Broadcom
Centaur Technology
Epson
Fairchild Semiconductor
Freescale Semiconductor
Hitachi
IBM Microelectronics
Imagination Technologies
Infineon Technologies
Intel
LSI Corp.
Marvell Technology
Matrox Electronic Systems
MediaTek
MIPS Technologies
NVIDIA
NXP Semiconductors
Pixelworks
QUALCOMM
Samsung Electronics
SANYO Semiconductor
Sigma Designs
Silicon Image
Silicon Integrated Systems
Silicon Motion
Sony
STMicroelectronics
Texas Instruments
Toshiba Semiconductor
VIA Technologies

HISTORICAL FINANCIALS

Company Type: Public

Income Statement

FYE: Last Sunday in December

	REVENUE ($ mil.)	NET INCOME ($ mil.)	NET PROFIT MARGIN	EMPLOYEES
12/09	5,403	293	5.4%	10,400
12/08	5,808	(3,098)	—	14,700
12/07	6,013	(3,379)	—	16,420
12/06	5,649	(166)	—	16,500
12/05	5,848	166	2.8%	9,860
Annual Growth	(2.0%)	15.3%	—	1.3%

2009 Year-End Financials

Debt ratio: 656.2%
Return on equity: 103.5%
Cash ($ mil.): 1,657
Current ratio: 1.93
Long-term debt ($ mil.): 4,252

No. of shares (mil.): 675
Dividends
  Yield: —
  Payout: —
Market value ($ mil.): 6,530

Stock History

NYSE: AMD

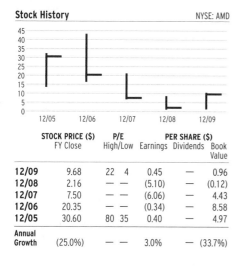

	STOCK PRICE ($) FY Close	P/E High	P/E Low	Earnings	Dividends	Book Value
12/09	9.68	22	4	0.45	—	0.96
12/08	2.16	—	—	(5.10)	—	(0.12)
12/07	7.50	—	—	(6.06)	—	4.43
12/06	20.35	—	—	(0.34)	—	8.58
12/05	30.60	80	35	0.40	—	4.97
Annual Growth	(25.0%)	—	—	—	—	(33.7%)

The AES Corporation

The right place at the right time — Is it kismet? No, it's AES, one of the world's leading independent power producers. The company has interests in more than 120 generation facilities in about 30 countries throughout the Americas, Asia, Africa, Europe, and the Middle East that give it a combined net generating capacity of 43,000 MW. AES sells electricity to utilities and other energy marketers through wholesale contracts or on the spot market. AES also sells power directly to customers worldwide through its interests in distribution utilities, mainly in Latin America. In 2009 the company had 3,000 MW of power plants under development in 10 countries.

To reduce carbon emissions the company is also developing alternative energy power plants, including wind, hydro, and biomass. In 2005 it began a business, AES Wind Generation, and by 2010 had 30 plants with more than 1,400 MW of generating capacity in operation in four countries. The company is one of the largest producers of wind power in the US. It also has some 300 MW of wind generation under construction outside the US.

In 2008 it formed AES Solar Energy, a joint venture with investment firm Riverstone Holdings. The project has begun commercial operations at nine solar plants in Spain, generating some 33 MW of power.

In a bid to further diversify its fuel sources in 2010, AES acquired Premier Power Limited, owner of the 1,246 MW natural gas-fired Ballylumford Power Station in County Antrim, Northern Ireland for £102 million ($166 million). The PPL transaction will give AES a total capacity of 1,868 MW, operating approximately 15 percent of the generation capacity in Northern Ireland and the Republic of Ireland.

However, AES is still fond of older methods of power generation. AES has earmarked $150 million to build a coal-fueled power plant in El Salvador. The 250 MW plant will be the first of its kind in the Latin American country. Owning four of the five electricity distribution companies in El Salvador, AES controls nearly 80% of the country's electric distribution utility.

In 2008 the company boosted its assets in the Philippines, acquiring the 660 MW Masinloc coal-fired power plant in Barangay Bula, Zambales Province, Luzon, for $930 million. To raise cash, that year AES sold the AES Ekibastuz power plant and Maikuben coal mine in Kazakhstan to Kazakhmys PLC for $1.1 billion.

AES has faced controversy in Brazil, where an unstable power market has caused the company to default on debts incurred from its purchases of stakes in local utilities (as well as bankrupt telecom firm Eletronet) in recent years. To restructure its debt with Banco Nacional de Desenvolvimento Economico e Social (BNDES), AES completed a deal in 2007 in which the firm's interests in AES Eletropaulo, AES Uruguaiana, AES Tiete, and AES Sul have been placed into a new holding company (Brasiliana Energia). AES owns 50.1% of the new company, while BNDES holds 49.9%.

HISTORY

Applied Energy Services (AES) was founded in 1981, three years after passage of the Public Utilities Regulation Policies Act, which enabled small power firms to enter electric generation markets formerly dominated by utility monopolies. Co-founders Roger Sant and Dennis Bakke, who had served in President Nixon's Federal Energy Administration, saw that an independent power producer (IPP) could make money by generating cheap power in large volumes to sell to large power consumers and utilities.

AES set about building massive cogeneration plants (producing both steam and electricity) in 1983. The first plant, Deepwater, went into operation near Houston in 1986. By 1989 AES had three plants on line, and it then opened plants in Connecticut and Oklahoma. In 1991 the company, formally renamed AES, went public, but one plant's falsified emissions reports caused AES's stock to plummet in 1992.

Facing environmental groups' opposition to new power plant construction and an overall glut in the US power market, AES bought interests in two Northern Ireland plants in 1992 and began expanding into Latin America in 1993. Also in 1993 AES set up a separately traded subsidiary, AES China Generating Co., to focus on Chinese development projects. AES won a plant development contract with the Puerto Rico Electric Power Authority (1994) and a bid to privatize an Argentine hydrothermal company (1995).

In 1996 AES began adding stakes in electric utility and distribution companies to its portfolio, including interests in formerly state-owned Brazilian electric utilities Light-Serviços de Eletricidade (1996) and CEMIG (1997); one Brazilian and two Argentine distribution companies (1997); and a distribution company in El Salvador (1998).

AES almost doubled its revenues after buying Destec Energy's international operations from NGC (now Dynegy) in 1997. By the next year, prospects in international markets were dimming, so AES turned to the US market again. It bought three California plants from Edison International and arranged for The Williams Companies to supply natural gas to the facilities and market the electricity generated. AES also won a bid to buy six plants from New York State Electric & Gas (now Energy East) affiliate NGE.

Also in 1998, despite black days in many world markets, AES bought 90% of Argentine electric distribution company Edelap and a 45% stake in state-owned Orissa Power Generation in India.

Boosting its presence in the UK, AES bought the Drax power station, a 3,960-MW coal-fired plant, from National Power in 1999. It also bought a majority stake in Brazilian data transmission company Eletronet from Brazil's government-owned utility ELETROBRÁS. In 2000 AES increased its interests in Brazilian power distributors. It also gained a 73% stake (later expanded to 87%) in Venezuelan electric utility Grupo EDC in a $1.5 billion hostile takeover.

The next year AES bought IPALCO, the parent of Indianapolis Power & Light, in a $3 billion deal. Also in 2001 AES acquired the outstanding shares of Chilean generation company Gener, in which it previously held a 60% stake.

In 2002 AES sold its 24% interest in Light Serviços de Eletricidade (Light) to Electricité de France (EDF) in exchange for a 20% stake in Brazilian utility Eletropaulo (increasing its stake in Eletropaulo to 70%).

In 2007 the company acquired two 230 MW petroleum coke-fired power generation facilities in Tamuin, Mexico. It also bought a 51% stake in Turkish power generator IC ICTAS Energy Group.

EXECUTIVES

Chairman: Philip A. Odeen, age 74
President, CEO, and Director: Paul T. Hanrahan, age 52, $8,812,490 total compensation
EVP, General Counsel, and Secretary: Brian A. Miller, age 44, $2,088,124 total compensation
EVP and COO: Andrés R. Gluski, age 52, $3,664,147 total compensation
EVP and CFO: Victoria D. Harker, age 45, $2,794,084 total compensation
EVP; President, Latin America and Africa: Andrew M. Vesey
EVP and Chief Risk Officer: Richard (Rich) Santoroski
EVP; Regional President, North America: Edward (Ned) Hall, $2,045,904 total compensation
SVP and CIO: Elizabeth Hackenson, age 49
VP Investor Relations: Ahmed Pasha
Director External Communications: Meghan Dotter
Director Government and Regulatory Affairs, AES Southland: Julie Gill
President, AES Southland: Eric Pendergraft
CEO, Greenhouse Gas Services: Mauricio Vargas
Auditors: Ernst & Young LLP

LOCATIONS

HQ: The AES Corporation
4300 Wilson Blvd., 11th Fl., Arlington, VA 22203
Phone: 703-522-1315   **Fax:** 703-528-4510
Web: www.aes.com

2009 Sales

	$ mil.	% of total
Latin America		
Utilities	6,092	43
Generation	3,651	26
North America		
Generation	1,940	14
Utilities	1,086	8
Europe		
Generation	720	5
Asia		
Generation	643	4
Adjustments	(13)	—
Total	**14,119**	**100**

PRODUCTS/OPERATIONS

2009 Sales

	$ mil.	% of total
Regulated	7,816	55
Non-regulated	6,303	45
Total	**14,119**	**100**

Selected Electric Utilities and Distribution Companies

AES CLESA (electric utility, El Salvador)
AES Edelap (electric utility, Argentina)
AES Eden (electric utility, Argentina)
AES Edes (electric utility, Argentina)
AES Gener (electric generation, Chile)
AES India Private Ltd.
AES SeaWest, Inc.
Brasiliana Energia
    AES Sul Distribuidora Gaucha de Energia SA (AES
        Sul, electric utility, Brazil)
    AES Tiete (power generation, Brazil)
    AES Uruguaiana (power generation, Brazil)
    Eletropaulo Metropolitana Eletricidade de São Paulo
        S.A. (AES Electropaulo, electric distribution, Brazil)
CAESS (electric utility, El Salvador)
Companhia Energética de Minas Gerais (CEMIG, Brazil)
EEO (electric utility, El Salvador)
IC ICTAS Energy Group (power generation, Turkey)
IPALCO Enterprises, Inc. (holding company)

COMPETITORS

Alliant Energy	Huadian Power
Bonneville Power	IBERDROLA
Calpine	Indeck Energy
CenterPoint Energy	International Power
CMS Energy	MidAmerican Energy
CPFL Energia	Mirant
Duke Energy	NextEra Energy
Dynegy	Nicor
Edison International	NRG Energy
El Paso Corporation	PG&E Corporation
Endesa S.A.	Public Service Enterprise
Energias de Portugal	Group
Energy Future	RRI Energy
Enersis	Sempra Energy
Entergy	Siemens AG
E.ON UK	SUEZ-TRACTEBEL
Exelon	Xcel Energy

HISTORICAL FINANCIALS

Company Type: Public

Income Statement

FYE: December 31

	REVENUE ($ mil.)	NET INCOME ($ mil.)	NET PROFIT MARGIN	EMPLOYEES
12/09	14,119	1,755	12.4%	27,000
12/08	16,070	1,234	7.7%	25,000
12/07	13,588	(95)	—	28,000
12/06	12,299	240	2.0%	32,000
12/05	11,086	632	5.7%	30,000
Annual Growth	**6.2%**	**29.1%**	**—**	**(2.6%)**

2009 Year-End Financials

Debt ratio: 383.8%
Return on equity: 42.1%
Cash ($ mil.): 1,809
Current ratio: 1.33
Long-term debt ($ mil.): 17,943
No. of shares (mil.): 794
Dividends
    Yield: 0.0%
    Payout: —
Market value ($ mil.): 10,568

Stock History

NYSE: AES

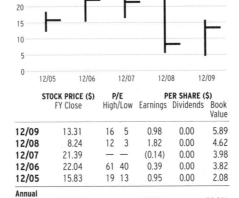

	STOCK PRICE ($) FY Close	P/E High/Low		PER SHARE ($) Earnings	Dividends	Book Value
12/09	13.31	16	5	0.98	0.00	5.89
12/08	8.24	12	3	1.82	0.00	4.62
12/07	21.39	—	—	(0.14)	0.00	3.98
12/06	22.04	61	40	0.39	0.00	3.82
12/05	15.83	19	13	0.95	0.00	2.08
Annual Growth	**(4.2%)**	**—**	**—**	**0.8%**	**—**	**29.8%**

Aetna Inc.

Life, death, health, or injury — Aetna's got an insurance policy to cover it. The company, one of the largest health insurers in the US, also offers life, disability, and long-term care insurance, as well as retirement savings products. Its Health Care division offers HMO, PPO, point of service (POS), health savings account (HSA), and traditional indemnity coverage, along with dental, vision, behavioral health, and Medicare plans, to groups and individuals. The division covers some 19 million medical members. Aetna's Group Insurance segment sells life, disability, and long-term care insurance nationwide. And its Large Case Pensions segment offers pensions, annuities, and other retirement savings products.

Outside its core medical plan offerings, Aetna provides a number of specialty health insurance products. It is one of the largest dental insurance providers in the country, serving some 14 million members. The company also operates a pharmacy benefit management (PBM) division, which includes Aetna Specialty Pharmacy (delivery of high-tech medications to patients with chronic diseases) and Aetna Rx Home Delivery (mail-order pharmacy services). Aetna Student Health (formerly Chickering Group)

specializes in health programs for college students, and Cofinity is a third-party provider of network management services. The company also offers special coverage for expatriates through its Aetna Global Benefits group, which handles international business.

Though the company primarily provides insurance through large, employer-sponsored programs, it has stepped up its marketing efforts to individuals and small businesses in response to increasing product demand in these segments. Another growth area is Medicare and Medicaid plans: The company has expanded Medicaid services to about a dozen states through subsidiary Schaller Anderson. Aetna also offers Medicare prescription drug coverage (known as Part D) nationwide and is expanding the geographic markets in which it offers privately administered Medicare Advantage health plans. However, in 2010 the Centers for Medicare and Medicaid ordered Aetna to temporarily cease marketing and enrollment efforts for new Medicare patients while it resolves compliance issues related to changes in the company's prescription drug coverage.

Aetna has also been working to expand coverage of expatriates through AGB. Aetna positioned the group to take a major leap forward when it set up a representative office in China in mid-2008, the beginning of a two-year process of becoming licensed to sell insurance in the world's largest market.

HISTORY

Hartford, Connecticut, businessman and judge Eliphalet Bulkeley started Connecticut Mutual Life Insurance in 1846. Agents gained control of the firm the following year. Undeterred, Bulkeley and a group of Hartford businessmen founded Aetna Life Insurance in 1853 as a spinoff of Aetna Fire Insurance. Among its offerings was coverage for slaves, a practice for which the company apologized in 2000.

A nationwide agency network fueled early growth at Aetna, which expanded in the 1860s by offering a participating life policy, returning dividends to policyholders based on investment earnings. (This let Aetna compete with mutual life insurers.) In 1868 Aetna became the first firm to offer renewable term life policies.

Eliphalet's son, Morgan, became president in 1879. Aetna moved into accident (1891), health (1899), workers' compensation (1902), and auto and other property insurance (1907) during his 43-year tenure. He served as Hartford mayor, Connecticut governor, and US senator, all the while leading Aetna.

By 1920 the company sold marine insurance, and by 1922 it was the US's largest multiline insurer. Aetna overexpanded its nonlife lines (particularly autos) during the 1920s, threatening its solvency. It survived the Depression by restricting underwriting and rebuilding reserves. After WWII the firm expanded into group life, health, and accident insurance. In 1967 it reorganized into holding company Aetna Life and Casualty.

The 1960s, 1970s, and 1980s were go-go years: The company added lines and bought and sold everything from an oil services firm to commercial real estate. The boom period led to a bust and a 1991 reorganization in which Aetna eliminated 8,000 jobs, withdrew from such lines as auto insurance, and sold its profitable American Reinsurance.

To take advantage of the boom in retirement savings, in 1995 it got permission to set up bank AE Trust to act as a pension trustee. Aetna sold its property/casualty, behavioral managed care (1997), and individual life insurance (1998) businesses. It then expanded overseas and bought U.S. Healthcare and New York Life's NYLCare managed health business (1998).

Controversy marred 1998. Contract terms — including a "gag" clause against discussing uncovered treatments — prompted 400 Texas doctors to leave its system; defections followed in Kentucky and West Virginia. Consumers balked over Aetna's refusal to cover some treatments, including experimental procedures and advanced fertility treatments. One group sued for false advertising.

The American Medical Association that year decried Aetna's plan to buy Prudential's health care unit as anticompetitive; in 1999 the government required Aetna to sell operations, including NYLCare, to gain approval. Also in 1999 Aetna became the second insurer (after Humana) to be sued for misleading clients about treatment decisions; it reached a settlement the next year with the State of Texas over capitation, physician incentives, and other matters.

In 2000 Aetna restated earnings for seven previous quarters at the behest of the SEC. Flagging earnings prompted CEO Richard Huber to resign; William Donaldson, one of the founders of Donaldson, Lufkin & Jenrette, took his place.

John "Jack" Rowe took over the helm as CEO in 2001. In 2002 the company returned to operating profitability after reducing its workforce, raising premiums, and restructuring critical operations. The following year it bought a mail-order pharmacy facility from Eckerd Health Services, and in 2004 formed Aetna Specialty Pharmacy, a joint venture with Priority Healthcare (now CuraScript), to provide mail-order drugs to consumers with chronic diseases.

Ronald Williams succeeded Jack Rowe as CEO in 2006.

In 2007 Aetna acquired Schaller Anderson in 2007 and transferred its existing Medicaid operations to the new subsidiary.

EXECUTIVES

Chairman and CEO: Ronald A. (Ron) Williams, age 60, $18,058,162 total compensation
President: Mark T. Bertolini, age 53, $12,627,800 total compensation
Chief of Staff, Office of the Chairman and CEO and Head Mergers and Acquisitions Integration: Kay Mooney
EVP, CFO, and Chief Enterprise Risk Officer: Joseph M. Zubretsky, age 53, $8,739,195 total compensation
SVP and General Counsel: William J. Casazza, age 54, $3,959,027 total compensation
SVP Marketing, Product, and Communications: Robert E. Mead
SVP and Chief Medical Officer: Lonny Reisman, age 54, $1,468,516 total compensation
SVP Human Resources: Elease E. Wright
SVP Innovation, Technology, and Service Operations and CIO: Margaret M. (Meg) McCarthy, age 56
Head International Business: Sandip Patel, age 43
National Medical Director Racial and Ethnic Equality: Wayne Rawlins
Chief Nursing Officer: Susan M. Kosman
Auditors: KPMG LLP

LOCATIONS

HQ: Aetna Inc.
151 Farmington Ave., Hartford, CT 06156
Phone: 860-273-0123
Web: www.aetna.com

PRODUCTS/OPERATIONS

2009 Sales

	$ mil.	% of total
Health care	32,073.3	92
Group insurance	2,143.0	6
Large group pensions	547.8	2
Total	**34,764.1**	**100**

Selected Subsidiaries

Active Health Management, Inc. (ActiveHealth)
Aetna Health Holdings, LLC
  AET Health Care Plan, Inc.
  Aetna Dental Inc.
  Aetna Health Management, LLC
  Aetna Rx Home Delivery, LLC
  Aetna Specialty Pharmacy, LLC
  Aetna Student Health Agency Inc.
  Cofinity, Inc.
  Schaller Anderson
Aetna Financial Holdings, LLC
  Aetna Behavioral Health, LLC
  Aetna Capital Management, LLC
  Aetna Integrated Informatics, Inc.
  Horizon Behavioral Services, LLC
Aetna International Inc.
  Aetna Global Benefits
  Aetna Life & Casualty (Bermuda) Limited
Aetna Life Insurance Company
  Aetna Government Health Plans, LLC
  AHP Holdings, Inc.
Aetna Health and Life Insurance Company
Aetna Health Insurance Company
Aetna Health Insurance Company of New York
Aetna Risk Indemnity Company Limited (Bermuda)

COMPETITORS

AMERIGROUP
BioScrip
Blue Cross
Caremark Pharmacy Services
Catalyst Health Solutions
Centene
CIGNA
Coventry Health Care
DeCare Dental
Delta Dental Plans
Express Scripts
Guardian Life
Health Net
HealthSpring
Highmark
Humana
Kaiser Foundation Health Plan
Magellan Health
Medco Health
MetLife
Molina Healthcare
Principal Financial
Prudential
UnitedHealth Group
USAA
Walgreen
WellPoint

HISTORICAL FINANCIALS

Company Type: Public

Income Statement

FYE: December 31

	REVENUE ($ mil.)	NET INCOME ($ mil.)	NET PROFIT MARGIN	EMPLOYEES
12/09	34,764	1,277	3.7%	35,000
12/08	30,951	1,384	4.5%	35,500
12/07	27,600	1,831	6.6%	35,200
12/06	25,146	1,702	6.8%	30,000
12/05	22,492	1,635	7.3%	28,200
Annual Growth	**11.5%**	**(6.0%)**	**—**	**5.5%**

2009 Year-End Financials

Debt ratio: 38.3%
Return on equity: 14.4%
Cash ($ mil.): 1,204
Current ratio: 0.81
Long-term debt ($ mil.): 3,640
No. of shares (mil.): 417
Dividends
  Yield: 0.1%
  Payout: 1.4%
Market value ($ mil.): 13,232

Stock History

NYSE: AET

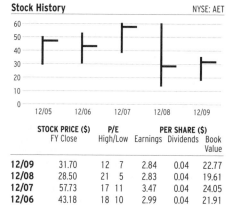

	STOCK PRICE ($) FY Close	P/E High/Low		PER SHARE ($) Earnings	Dividends	Book Value
12/09	31.70	12	7	2.84	0.04	22.77
12/08	28.50	21	5	2.83	0.04	19.61
12/07	57.73	17	11	3.47	0.04	24.05
12/06	43.18	18	10	2.99	0.04	21.91
12/05	47.15	18	11	2.70	0.02	24.21
Annual Growth	**(9.4%)**	**—**	**—**	**1.3%**	**18.9%**	**(1.5%)**

Aflac Incorporated

Would you buy insurance from a duck? Aflac counts on it! To help clients lessen the financial losses during periods of disability or illness, Aflac sells supplemental health and life insurance policies, including coverage for accidents, intensive care, dental, vision, and short-term disability, as well as for specific conditions, primarily cancer. It is a leading supplier of supplemental insurance in the US and is an industry leader in Japan's cancer-insurance market (with 14 million policies in force). Aflac, which is marketed through — and is an acronym for — American Family Life Assurance Company, sells policies that pay cash benefits for hospital confinement, emergency treatment, and medical appliances.

Despite its US roots, Aflac makes more than 70% of its insurance sales in Japan, where its policies fill in gaps not covered by the national health insurance system. Its reliance on Japan has a downside: The company is vulnerable to currency fluctuations between the dollar and yen. It also faces increased competition due to deregulation of Japan's insurance industry. However, as in the US, Japanese consumers are seeing more health care costs being shifted onto their shoulders, making Aflac's products more attractive.

In Japan, Aflac primarily sells through an agency system in which a corporation forms a subsidiary to sell Aflac insurance to its employees. In the face of Japan's deregulated life insurance industry, the company has also had a marketing alliance with Dai-ichi Life Insurance, one of the country's largest life insurers, since 2000. Changes in regulations now allow the company to sell through banks and post offices, and it has also opened retail shops where consumers can purchase directly from sales associates.

In the US, Aflac sells mainly through the workplace, with employers deducting premiums from paychecks. Building on its strong brand recognition — due, largely, to the company's popular

TV ads featuring a valiant spokes-duck — Aflac has invested in its US business by adding more sales associates and expanding its distribution to include insurance brokers.

To build up its US large-group business, in late 2009 Aflac paid $100 million to purchase Continental American Insurance. Continental's payroll-deducted insurance products are distributed through brokers and marketing groups.

Chairman and CEO Dan Amos holds 9% of the company his father and uncles founded.

HISTORY

American Family Life Assurance Company (AFLAC) was founded in Columbus, Georgia, in 1955 by brothers John, Paul, and William Amos to sell life, health, and accident insurance. Competition was fierce, and the little company did poorly. With AFLAC nearing bankruptcy, the brothers looked for a niche.

The polio scares of the 1940s and 1950s had spawned insurance coverage written especially against that disease; the Amos brothers (whose father was a cancer victim) took a cue from that concept and decided to sell cancer insurance. In 1958 they introduced the world's first cancer-expense policy. It was a hit, and by 1959 the company had written nearly a million dollars in premiums and expanded across state lines.

The enterprise grew quickly during the 1960s, especially after developing its cluster-selling approach in the workplace, where employers were usually willing to make payroll deductions for premiums. By 1971 the company was operating in 42 states.

While visiting the World's Fair in Osaka in 1970, John Amos decided to market supplemental cancer coverage to the Japanese, whose national health care plan left them exposed to considerable expense from cancer treatment. After four years the company finally won approval to sell in Japan since the policies did not threaten existing markets and because the Amoses found notable backers in the insurance and medical industries. AFLAC became one of the first US insurance companies to enter the Japanese market, and it enjoyed an eight-year monopoly on the cancer market. Back in the US, in 1973 AFLAC organized a holding company and began buying television stations in the South and Midwest.

The 1980s were marked by US and state government inquiries into dread disease insurance. Critics said such policies were a poor value because they were relatively expensive and covered only one disease. However, the inquiries led nowhere and demand for such insurance increased, bringing new competition. In the 1980s AFLAC's scales tilted: US growth slowed, while business grew in Japan, which soon accounted for most of the company's sales.

In 1990 John Amos died of cancer and was replaced as CEO by his nephew Dan. Two years later the company officially renamed itself Aflac (partly because Dan planned to increase the company's US profile and so many US companies already used the name "American").

Aflac has sought to supplement its cancer insurance by introducing new products and improving old ones to encourage policyholders to add on or trade up. Its Japanese "living benefit" product, which includes lump sum payments for heart attacks and strokes, struck a chord with the aging population.

Connecticut in 1997 repealed its ban on specified-disease insurance; New York eventually

followed suit. Also that year Aflac sold its seven TV stations to Raycom Media to focus on insurance.

The company boosted its name recognition in the US from 2% in 1990 to more than 56%, primarily through advertising, including slots during the 1998 Olympic Winter Games and NASCAR races.

Accident/disability premiums surpassed cancer premiums in the US for the first time in the company's history in 2000. The Aflac duck made its first appearance in a 2001 Japanese commercial for accident insurance. Shortly thereafter, it debuted in the US, where it quickly achieved advertising-icon status.

EXECUTIVES

Chairman and CEO: Daniel P. (Dan) Amos, age 58, $13,591,511 total compensation
President, CFO, Treasurer, and Director; EVP, Aflac: Kriss Cloninger III, age 62, $5,730,339 total compensation
President, Aflac and COO, Aflac US: Paul S. Amos II, age 34, $2,539,625 total compensation
President and COO, Aflac Japan: Tohru Tonoike, age 59, $2,810,407 total compensation
EVP, General Counsel, and Corporate Secretary, Aflac Incorporated and Aflac; Director Legal and Governmental Relations, Aflac: Joey M. Loudermilk, age 56, $2,200,840 total compensation
EVP and Chief Administrative Officer, Aflac: Teresa L. White, age 43
EVP Corporate Services: Audrey Boone Tillman, age 45
EVP and Deputy CFO: Martin A. Durant III, age 61
SVP and CIO: Gerald W. Shields
SVP Investments and Chief Investment Officer, Aflac: W. Jeremy (Jerry) Jeffery, age 59
SVP Financial Services and Chief Accounting Officer, Aflac Incorporated and Aflac; Treasurer, Aflac: Ralph A. Rogers Jr., age 61
SVP Financial Reporting: Peter T. Adams
SVP Investor Relations: Kenneth S. (Ken) Janke Jr., age 51
SVP Investment and Risk Management: William R. Wright Jr., age 57
SVP and Director Governmental Relations: Phillip J. (Jack) Friou
SVP Customer Assurance Organization: Laree Daniel
SVP and Chief Marketing Officer: M. Jeffrey (Jeff) Charney
SVP and Counsel; Director Governmental and Legal Affairs, Aflac International: Andrew J. (Andy) Conrad
Director Human Resources: Janet P. Baker
President and CEO, Communicorp: James C. Woodall
Auditors: KPMG LLP

LOCATIONS

HQ: Aflac Incorporated
 1932 Wynnton Rd., Columbus, GA 31999
Phone: 706-323-3431 **Fax:** 706-324-6330
Web: www.aflac.com

PRODUCTS/OPERATIONS

2009 Revenues

	$ mil.	% of total
Aflac Japan	14,486	74
Aflac US	4,953	25
Corporate	137	1
Other business	51	—
Realized investment losses	(1,212)	—
Adjustments	(161)	—
Total	**18,254**	**100**

COMPETITORS

American Fidelity Assurance	Colonial Life & Accident
American National Insurance	Meiji Yasuda Life
Asahi Mutual Life	MetLife
CNO Financial	Nippon Life Insurance
	Taiyo Life
	Torchmark

HISTORICAL FINANCIALS

Company Type: Public

Income Statement

FYE: December 31

	ASSETS ($ mil.)	NET INCOME ($ mil.)	INCOME AS % OF ASSETS	EMPLOYEES
12/09	84,106	1,497	1.8%	8,057
12/08	79,331	1,254	1.6%	7,949
12/07	65,805	1,634	2.5%	8,048
12/06	59,805	1,483	2.5%	7,411
12/05	56,361	1,483	2.6%	6,970
Annual Growth	**10.5%**	**0.2%**	**—**	**3.7%**

2009 Year-End Financials

Equity as % of assets: 10.0%
Return on assets: 1.8%
Return on equity: 19.9%
Long-term debt ($ mil.): 483
No. of shares (mil.): 470
Dividends
 Yield: 2.4%
 Payout: 35.1%
Market value ($ mil.): 21,717
Sales ($ mil.): 18,254

Stock History

NYSE: AFL

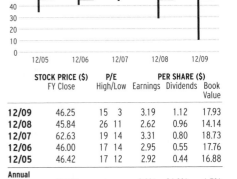

	STOCK PRICE ($) FY Close	P/E High/Low		PER SHARE ($) Earnings	Dividends	Book Value
12/09	46.25	15	3	3.19	1.12	17.93
12/08	45.84	26	11	2.62	0.96	14.14
12/07	62.63	19	14	3.31	0.80	18.73
12/06	46.00	17	14	2.95	0.55	17.76
12/05	46.42	17	12	2.92	0.44	16.88
Annual Growth	**(0.1%)**	**—**	**—**	**2.2%**	**26.3%**	**1.5%**

AGCO Corporation

AGCO's annual harvests may be smaller than those of larger rivals John Deere and CNH Global, but it still reaps profits worldwide. AGCO makes tractors, combines, hay tools, sprayers, forage equipment, and replacement parts. It sells through a global network of about 2,800 dealers and distributors. It also makes diesel engines, gears, and generators through its AGCO Sisu Power unit. Brand names include Massey Ferguson, Challenger, Valtra (Finland-based), and Fendt (Germany-based). The company offers financing services to customers and dealers through a joint venture with Netherlands-based Rabobank. AGCO sells products in some 140 countries; more than 80% of sales are generated outside the US.

AGCO is investing in production capacity and dealer training in regions with high growth potential, including China, Brazil, Russia, and Africa. In 2010 the company will open two manufacturing facilities in China, where it already has an established aftersales service and replacement parts operations. Though Russia and other Eastern European markets remain weak due to credit constraints, the company has seen conditions improve in Brazil, where government financing plans for small farms have stimulated demand for lower horsepower tractors.

The company is focused on developing technologically advanced equipment to deal with challenges facing the agricultural industry, particularly in emerging markets, such as population growth, changing diets, and scarcity of land.

During 2009 AGCO restructured in order to reduce costs and bring inventory levels in line with lower global market demand. The company made headcount reductions at manufacturing facilities and administrative offices in the US, UK, France, Germany, and Finland. It announced plans to close a facility in Denmark by July 2010, and transfer those operations to its joint venture in Italy. AGCO also instituted temporary plant shutdowns in all of its factories, cut production, and reduced both its company and dealer inventories.

The company develops products incorporating the latest technologies in machine control and precision farming. Auto-Guide (Satellite) Navigation and FIELDSTAR offer hands-free steering navigation assistance. Its e3 SCR (selective catalytic reduction) engine injects an organic compound into the exhaust stream that increases the fuel efficiency of the engine while reducing emissions. AGCO Tractors offer high-power PowerMaxx CVT (continuously variable transmission), as well as diesel engines, which improve the efficiency of harvesting and farming equipment.

HISTORY

In 1861 American Edward Allis purchased the bankrupt Reliance Works, a leading Milwaukee-based manufacturer of sawmills and flour-milling equipment. Under shrewd management, The Reliance Works of Edward P. Allis & Co. weathered financial troubles — bankruptcy in the Panic of 1873 — but managed to renegotiate its debt and recover. By the time Allis died in 1889, Reliance Works employed some 1,500 workers.

The company branched into different areas of manufacturing in the late 19th century, and by the 20th century the Edward P. Allis Co. (as it was then known) was the world leader in steam engines. In 1901 the company merged with another manufacturing giant, Fraser & Chalmers, to form the Allis-Chalmers Company. In the 1920s and 1930s, Allis-Chalmers entered the farm equipment market.

Although overshadowed by John Deere and International Harvester (IH), Allis-Chalmers made key contributions to the industry — the first rubber-tired tractor (1932) and the All-Crop harvester. Allis-Chalmers spun off its farm equipment business in the 1950s, and phased out several unrelated products. The company, with its orange-colored tractors, expanded and prospered from the 1940s through the early 1970s. Then the chafing farm economy of the late 1970s and early 1980s hurt Allis-Chalmers' sales.

After layoffs and a plant shutdown in 1984, the company was purchased in 1985 by German machinery maker Klockner-Humbolt-Deutz (KHD), who moved the company (renamed Deutz-Allis) to Georgia. In the mid-1980s low food prices hurt farmers and low demand hurt the equipment market. KHD was never able to bring profits up to a satisfactory level, and in 1990 the German firm sold the unit to the US management in a buyout led by Robert Ratliff.

Ratliff believed the company could succeed by acquiring belly-up equipment makers, turning them around, and competing on price.

Renamed AGCO, the company launched a buying spree in 1991 that included Fiat's Hesston (1991), White Tractor (1991), the North American distribution rights for Massey Ferguson (1993), and White-New Idea (1993). The bumper crop of product growth enabled AGCO to slice into the market share of competitors Deere and Case. AGCO went public in 1992. Its 1994 purchase of the remainder of Massey Ferguson (with 20% of the world market) vaulted AGCO to prominence among the world's leading farm equipment makers.

In 1997 it acquired German farm equipment makers Fendt and Dronniberg. It also picked up Deutz Argentina, a supplier of agricultural equipment, engines, and vehicles, as part of an effort to expand into Latin and South America.

AGCO entered the agricultural sprayer market in 1998 by acquiring the Spra-Coupe line from Ingersoll-Rand and the Willmar line from Cargill. A worldwide drop in farm equipment sales caused AGCO to cut about 10% of its workforce. In 1999 the company announced it was permanently closing an Ohio plant and would cease production at a Texas plant. The next year AGCO closed its Missouri plant and trimmed its workforce by about 5%.

In 2002 AGCO suffered a tragic loss when president and CEO John Shumejda and SVP Ed Swingle were killed in an airplane accident in the UK.

In early 2004 AGCO added Valtra, a global tractor and off-road engine maker, to its fold for about $750 million. In 2004 chairman Robert Ratliff handed Martin Richenhagen the president and CEO titles he had taken on after the death of Shumejda.

Late in 2006 AGCO announced a new growth initiative dubbed "Always Growing." The strategy makes some basic assumptions about the trends emerging in global agriculture. They include: the increase in mega-farms, exponential growth in certain developing countries, increased demand for biofuels in developed nations, and increasingly advanced technology.

EXECUTIVES

Chairman, President, and CEO: Martin H. Richenhagen, age 57, $5,853,703 total compensation
SVP and CFO: Andrew H. (Andy) Beck, age 46, $1,304,379 total compensation
SVP Manufacturing and Quality: Hans-Bernd Veltmaat, age 55, $947,136 total compensation
SVP Human Resources: Lucinda B. Smith, age 43
SVP Engineering: Garry L. Ball, age 62
SVP and General Manager, North America: Robert B. Crain, age 50, $1,948,302 total compensation
SVP and General Manager, South America: André M. Carioba, age 58, $2,041,359 total compensation
SVP and General Manager, EAME and Australia/New Zealand: Gary L. Collar, age 53, $1,254,488 total compensation
SVP Materials Management Worldwide: David L. Caplan, age 62
SVP Strategy and Integration and General Manager, Eastern Europe and Asia: Hubertus M. Mühlhäuser, age 40, $1,064,720 total compensation
SVP Global Sales and Marketing and Product Management: Randall G. (Randy) Hoffman, age 58
VP, Corporate Secretary, and General Counsel: Debra Kuper
VP and CIO: Robert (Bob) Greenberg, age 56
Director Investor Relations: Greg Peterson
Director: Luiz F. Furlan, age 64
Auditors: KPMG LLP

LOCATIONS

HQ: AGCO Corporation
4205 River Green Pkwy., Duluth, GA 30096
Phone: 770-813-9200   **Fax:** 770-813-6118
Web: www.agcocorp.com

2009 Sales

	$ mil.	% of total
Europe, Africa & Middle East	3,782.1	57
North America	1,442.7	22
South America	1,167.1	18
Asia/Pacific	238.5	3
Total	**6,630.4**	**100**

PRODUCTS/OPERATIONS

2009 Sales

	$ mil.	% of total
Tractors	4,393.4	66
Replacement parts	939.9	14
Combines	377.3	6
Application equipment	252.2	4
Other machinery	667.6	10
Total	**6,630.4**	**100**

Selected Products

Application equipment
Combines
Commercial grounds care
Compact tractors
Hay and forage
Implements, attachments, and material handling
Lawn and garden
Power generation
Pre-owned equipment
Row crop and arable tractors
Seeding and tillage
Specialty tractors
Track tractors and articulated 4WD
Utility tractors

Selected Brand Names

AGCO Allis
AGCO SISU POWER
AGCO Tractors
Challenger
Fendt
Gleaner
Hesston
Massey Ferguson
RoGator
SpraCoupe
Sunflower
TerraGator
Valtra
White Planters
Wilmar

COMPETITORS

Buhler Industries	Komatsu
Caterpillar	Kubota
CNH Global	Mahindra
Deere	Toro Company
Fiat	

HISTORICAL FINANCIALS

Company Type: Public

Income Statement

	REVENUE ($ mil.)	NET INCOME ($ mil.)	NET PROFIT MARGIN	EMPLOYEES
12/09	6,630	136	2.0%	14,500
12/08	8,425	400	4.7%	15,600
12/07	6,828	246	3.6%	13,700
12/06	5,435	(65)	—	12,800
12/05	5,450	32	0.6%	13,000
Annual Growth	**5.0%**	**44.0%**	**—**	**2.8%**

FYE: December 31

Stock History NYSE: AGCO

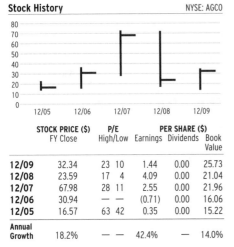

	STOCK PRICE ($) FY Close	P/E High/Low		PER SHARE ($) Earnings	Dividends	Book Value
12/09	32.34	23	10	1.44	0.00	25.73
12/08	23.59	17	4	4.09	0.00	21.04
12/07	67.98	28	11	2.55	0.00	21.96
12/06	30.94	—	—	(0.71)	0.00	16.06
12/05	16.57	63	42	0.35	0.00	15.22
Annual Growth	18.2%	—	—	42.4%	—	14.0%

Agilent Technologies

Agilent Technologies keeps scientists on their toes. A maker of scientific testing equipment, Agilent supplies a slew of bioanalytical and electronic measurement tools, including data generators, multimeters, and oscilloscopes. Operations straddle electronic test and measurement instruments (the largest in the world), bioanalytical measurement, and a semiconductor and board test business. The company offers centralized lab research, too. Agilent's 25,000 customers include global giants in communications, electronics, life sciences, and chemical analysis, such as Cisco, Dow Chemical, GlaxoSmithKline, Intel, Merck, and Samsung.

That Agilent is a leader in the test and measurement equipment industry should come as no surprise — it is the original business started by technology pioneers William Hewlett and David Packard. Hewlett-Packard spun off the business in 1999 so that it could focus on its computer products operations.

Spying lucrative, and potentially more stable, opportunities in the life science industry, Agilent in 2010 bought Varian, a maker of instruments for measuring biological and physical attributes, for about $1.5 billion in cash. The transformational deal — the largest acquisition in Agilent's history — diversifies Agilent's product portfolio into such fields as nuclear magnetic resonance, and imaging and vacuum technology, targeting life sciences, environmental, and energy industries. In order to satisfy antitrust regulators, Agilent sold Varian's micro gas chromatography business to INFICON. In 2010 Bruker bought three of Varian's instrument businesses: gas chromatography triple-quadrupole mass spectrometry, inductively coupled plasma mass spectrometry, and laboratory gas chromatography.

Being a leader has not spared the company from tough times. Agilent restructured operations in 2009, aiming to shrink costs by $310 million a year. The company cut about 3,800 positions, a reduction in force of nearly 20% since 2008.

The company sold its Network Solutions business (including network protocol test and drive test products) in 2010 to JDS Uniphase (JDSU) for $165 million in cash. Earlier in the year the company sold its Hycor Biomedical subsidiary.

In the meantime, Agilent is investing in research and development — albeit a smaller amount than in previous years. Pouring in more than $600 million in 2009 into R&D led to new products in oscilloscopes, gas chromatography, and mass spectrometry and microarrays.

HISTORY

Agilent Technologies was formed in 1999 when Hewlett-Packard (HP) split off its measurement business. But Agilent's roots run as deep as HP's — Agilent's core products served as the original business of Stanford-trained electrical engineers William Hewlett and David Packard. The friends started HP in 1939 as a test and measurement equipment maker. Their first product, developed in Packard's garage (Hewlett was living in a rented cottage behind Packard's house) was an audio oscillator for testing sound equipment; Walt Disney Studios bought eight to help make the animation classic *Fantasia*.

Demand for electronic test equipment during WWII pushed sales from $34,000 in 1940 (when HP had three employees and eight products) to nearly $1 million three years later. The company entered the microwave field in 1943, creating signal generators for the Naval Research Laboratory. Its postwar line of microwave test products made it a market leader for signal generation equipment.

Expanding beyond the US in the late 1950s, HP established a plant in West Germany. The company went public in 1957. It entered the medical field in 1961 with the purchase of Sanborn, and the analytical instrumentation business in 1965 with the purchase of F&M Scientific. In the 1970s president Hewlett and chairman Packard began shifting HP's focus toward the computer market. Late in that decade they stepped back from day-to-day management (they would retire in 1987 and 1992, respectively).

Sales hit $3 billion in 1980. In 1991 HP broadened its communications component offerings when it bought Avantek. HP moved into the DNA analysis field in 1994 with pharmaceutical research and health care products. Packard died in 1996. In 1997 HP bought Heartstream, maker of an automatic external defibrillator.

In 1999 HP formed Agilent as a separate company for its test and measurement and other non-computer operations, which by then accounted for 16% of sales. Edward Barnholt, a 30-year HP veteran, was named CEO of the new company. In a move to energize its computer business, HP spun off 15% of Agilent to the public in November 1999. The remainder was distributed to HP shareholders in mid-2000.

In 2000 Philips Electronics agreed to buy Agilent's Healthcare Solutions unit for $1.7 billion. (After lengthy scrutiny from US and European regulators, the deal was completed in mid-2001.)

In a move to bolster its networking business, Agilent completed its $665 million acquisition of network management software maker Objective Systems Integrators in early 2001. The company

also implemented cost-cutting measures such as temporary pay cuts. Later that year, in the face of harsh market conditions, Agilent announced two separate layoffs of 4,000 employees each, representing a total staff reduction of about 18%. Hewlett died the same year.

Barnholt retired early in 2005; Agilent's COO, Bill Sullivan, was tapped to replace him as president and CEO.

Later in 2005 Agilent sold its semiconductor operations to two buyout firms — Kohlberg Kravis Roberts & Co. and Silver Lake Partners — for approximately $2.7 billion. Agilent sold its stake in Lumileds Lighting (LEDs) to Philips for $950 million. It also spun off its memory and system-on-a-chip (SoC) test system operations with an IPO in 2006; the new company was called Verigy.

Late in 2007 and into 2008, the company began expanding its product portfolio, primarily to grow its newly created Life Sciences and Chemical Analysis business. Through a series of acquisitions, including Velocity11, TILL Photonics, RVM Scientific, and MTS Systems, Agilent added laboratory robotics, optical microscopy, gas chromatography, and nanoindentation solutions products.

In mid-2007 Agilent acquired Stratagene, a developer of life science research and diagnostic products, for about $252 million in cash.

It also acquired in late 2007 the operations of Velocity11, which made laboratory robotics for the life sciences market.

EXECUTIVES

Chairman: James G. Cullen, age 67
President, CEO, and Director: William P. (Bill) Sullivan, age 59, $7,570,515 total compensation
SVP; President, Chemical Analysis Group: Michael R. (Mike) McMullen, age 48, $1,599,439 total compensation
SVP and CFO: Didier Hirsch, age 58
SVP, General Counsel, and Secretary: Marie Oh Huber, age 48
SVP; President, Life Sciences Group: Nicholas H. (Nick) Roelofs, age 51, $1,489,130 total compensation
SVP Human Resources: Jean M. Halloran, age 57, $1,924,977 total compensation
SVP; President, Electronic Measurement Group: Ronald S. (Ron) Nersesian, age 50, $1,773,146 total compensation
VP and Chief Infrastructure Officer: Rick Burdsall, age 47
VP and General Manager, Sales, Service, and Support Organization, Electronic Measurements Group: Saleem N. Odeh, age 59
VP Finance and Business Development, Life Sciences and Chemical Analysis Group: Alicia Rodriguez
VP and CTO, Agilent Laboratories: Darlene J. Solomon
VP Corporate Development and Strategy: Shiela Barr Robertson
VP and Treasurer: Hilliard C. Terry III, age 41
VP and General Manager, Worldwide Sales, Marketing and Support Organization, Life Sciences and Chemical Analysis Group: Lonnie G. (Lon) Justice
VP and General Manager, Electronic Instruments Business Unit: Gooi Soon Chai, age 48
Manager Corporate Media Relations: Amy Flores
Auditors: PricewaterhouseCoopers LLP

LOCATIONS

HQ: Agilent Technologies, Inc.
5301 Stevens Creek Blvd., Santa Clara, CA 95051
Phone: 408-345-8886 **Fax:** 408-345-8474
Web: www.agilent.com

2009 Sales

	$ mil.	% of total
US	1,495	33
China	598	13
Japan	476	11
Rest of the World	1,912	43
Total	**4,481**	**100**

PRODUCTS/OPERATIONS

2009 Sales

	$ mil.	% of total
Electronic measurement	2,257	50
Bio-analytical measurement	2,063	46
Semiconductor & board test	161	4
Total	**4,481**	**100**

2009 Sales by Revenue Type

	$ mil.	% of total
Products	3,566	80
Services & other	915	20
Total	**4,481**	**100**

Selected Products

Electronic Test and Measurement
  Generators, sources, supplies
    AC power sources / power analyzers
    Data generators and analyzers
    DC electronic loads
    DC power supplies
    Function / Arbitrary waveform generators
    Pulse pattern generators
    Signal generators
  Oscilloscopes, analyzers, meters
    Bit error ratio test (BERT) solutions
    DC power analyzers
    Digital multimeters, voltmeters
    Digitizers
    Dynamic signal analyzers, mechanical and physical test
    EMI/EMC, phase noise, physical layer test
    Frequency counters and time-to-digital converts
    Impedance analyzers
    LCR and resistance meters
    Logic Analyzers
    Network analyzers
    Noise figure analyzers and noise sources
    Oscilloscopes
    Parameter and device analyzers, curve tracers
    Power meters and power sensors
    Protocol analyzers and exercisers
    Signal and spectrum analyzers
  Software
    Agilent EEsof EDA design and simulation software
    Agilent IO libraries suite
    Agilent license manager
    Agilent VEE
    Calibration and adjustment software
    Fault detective
    Instrument connectivity
    Instrument software
    Test optimization and diagnostics

Life Sciences and Chemical Analysis
  Clinical diagnostics
    Allergy testing
    Autoimmune testing
    Infectious disease
    Urinalysis
  Columns and supplies
  Informatics and software
  Instruments and systems
    Automation solutions
    DNA microarrays
    Electrophoresis
    Gas chromatography
    ICP-MS
    Lab-on-a-chip
    Liquid chromatography
    Mass spectrometry
    PCR and QPCR
    Spectroscopy
  Reagents, standards and kits
    Cloning and competent cells
    DNA microarrays
    DNA target enrichment
    Instrument standards and kits
    Mutagenesis
    Nucleic acid purification and analysis
    PCR and reverse transcription
    Protein expression and analysis
    Protein preparation
    Real-time/quantitative PCR
    Total RNA and cDNA libraries

COMPETITORS

Advantest	Ixia
Aeroflex	LeCroy
Affymetrix	Life Technologies
AMETEK	McAfee
Anritsu	MDS
Ansoft	National Instruments
Applied Materials	PerkinElmer
AWR	Rohde & Schwarz
Beckman Coulter	Shimadzu
Bio-Rad Labs	Spirent
Bruker	Tektronix
Dionex	telent
EXFO	Teradyne
Fluke Corporation	Thermo Fisher Scientific
GE Healthcare	W. R. Grace
HEIDENHAIN Corp.	Waters Corp.
IBM Software	Yokogawa Electric

HISTORICAL FINANCIALS

Company Type: Public

Income Statement

FYE: October 31

	REVENUE ($ mil.)	NET INCOME ($ mil.)	NET PROFIT MARGIN	EMPLOYEES
10/09	4,481	(31)	—	16,800
10/08	5,774	693	12.0%	19,600
10/07	5,420	638	11.8%	19,400
10/06	4,973	3,307	66.5%	18,700
10/05	5,139	327	6.4%	21,000
Annual Growth	**(3.4%)**	**—**	**—**	**(5.4%)**

2009 Year-End Financials

Debt ratio: 115.9%
Return on equity: —
Cash ($ mil.): 2,479
Current ratio: 3.53
Long-term debt ($ mil.): 2,904

No. of shares (mil.): 348
Dividends
  Yield: —
  Payout: —
Market value ($ mil.): 8,611

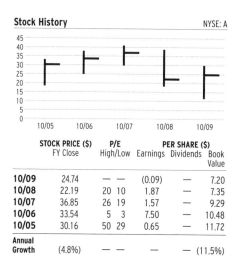

Stock History   NYSE: A

	STOCK PRICE ($) FY Close	P/E High/Low		PER SHARE ($) Earnings	Dividends	Book Value
10/09	24.74	—	—	(0.09)	—	7.20
10/08	22.19	20	10	1.87	—	7.35
10/07	36.85	26	19	1.57	—	9.29
10/06	33.54	5	3	7.50	—	10.48
10/05	30.16	50	29	0.65	—	11.72
Annual Growth	**(4.8%)**	**—**	**—**	**—**	**—**	**(11.5%)**

Air Products and Chemicals

Much like Jumpin' Jack Flash, business at Air Products and Chemicals is a gas gas gas. The company provides gases such as argon, hydrogen, nitrogen, and oxygen to manufacturers, health care facilities, and other industries. Not all is light and airy, however. It also makes gas containers and equipment that separates air, purifies hydrogen, and liquefies gas. Air Products' largest segment is Merchant Gases, which manufactures atmospheric, process, and specialty gases delivered from tanker, truck and trailer or even directly for the customer through on-site plants. The company's Tonnage Gases segment serves the global refining and chemical industries. In 2010 the company made a $7 billion offer for rival Airgas.

The company had spent months in negotiations with Airgas before coming public with its offer, which consisted of $5.1 billion in cash and the assumption of debt. Airgas had been reluctant to accept the offer, considering it too low. Air Products was hoping to add Airgas' strong network of regional industrial gas distributors and retail outlets. Ever optimistic, Air Products extended its tender offer to Airgas stockholders three times, the last into mid-October 2010.

The move for Airgas marked a big change in Air Products' acquisitions plan. In the latter half of the decade, the company had made a strategic move into Europe. It also divested its chemicals and US health care gases businesses, continuing a trend toward building up the company's international business. In 2002 Air Products achieved only a third of its total sales from outside the US; by 2008 that percentage had risen to more than half.

Air Products, through a joint venture with Technip, is building a hydrogen production facility in Sichuan, China, for PetroChina Company. The deal will be the first time a state-owned refinery in China has outsourced its hydrogen production. The plant will produce more than 90 million cubic feet per day of hydrogen and will be operational in 2012. Air Products also formed a joint venture in 2010 with First Abu Dhabi Management Services. Air Products will have a 49% stake in the venture, Air Products Gulf Gas LLC, which will expand its business presence in the Middle East.

HISTORY

In the early 1900s Leonard Pool, the son of a boilermaker, began selling oxygen to industrial users. By the time he was 30, he was district manager for Compressed Industrial Gases. In the late 1930s Pool hired engineer Frank Pavlis to help him design a cheaper, more efficient oxygen generator. In 1940 they had the design, and Pool established Air Products in Detroit (initially sharing space with the cadavers collected by his brother, who was starting a mortuary science college). The company was based on a simple, breakthrough concept: the provision of on-site gases. Instead of delivering oxygen in cylinders, Pool proposed to build oxygen-generating facilities near large-volume gas users and then lease them, reducing distribution costs.

Although industrialists encouraged Pool to pursue his ideas, few orders were forthcoming, and the company faced financial crisis. The outbreak of WWII got the company out of difficulty, as the US military became a major customer. During the war the company moved to Chattanooga, Tennessee, for the available labor.

The end of the war brought with it another downturn as demand dried up. By waiting at the Weirton Steel plant until a contract was signed, Pool won a contract for three on-site generators. Weirton was nearly the company's only customer. Pool relocated the company to Allentown, Pennsylvania, to be closer to the Northeast's industrial market, where he could secure more contracts with steel companies.

The Cold War and the launching of the Sputnik satellite in 1957 propelled the company's growth. Convinced that Soviet rockets were powered by liquid hydrogen, the US government asked Air Products to supply it with the volatile fuel. The company entered the overseas market that year through a joint venture with Butterley (UK), to which it licensed its cryogenic processes and equipment. The company went public in 1961 and formed a subsidiary in Belgium in 1964.

Air Products diversified into chemicals when it bought Houdry Process (chemicals and chemical-plant maintenance, 1962) and Airco's chemicals and plastics operations in the 1970s. The company continued to diversify in the mid-1980s as it built large-scale plants for its environmental- and energy-systems business and added Anchor Chemical and the industrial chemicals unit of Abbott Labs.

In 1995 and 1996 Air Products expanded into China and other countries by winning 20 contracts with semiconductor makers. It bought Carburos Metalicos, Spain's #1 industrial gas supplier, in 1996. To focus on its core gas and chemical lines, the company shed most of its environmental- and energy-systems business.

Expanding further in Europe, Air Products bought the methylamines and derivatives unit of UK-based Imperial Chemical Industries (ICI) in 1997. The company sold its remaining interest in American Ref-Fuel (a waste-to-energy US operation). In 1998 Air Products bought Solkatronic Chemicals and opened a methylamines plant in Florida to complement its ICI purchase.

The company boosted its European presence in 2001 with the acquisition of Messer Griesheim's (Germany) respiratory home-care

business and 50% of AGA's Netherlands industrial gases operations.

Air Products was hurt by the slowdown in manufacturing, primarily in the electronics and steel industries, which are major customers for gases. Its chemical revenues also were hurt by pressure on pricing. To improve profits, the company initiated cost cuts, including job cuts (about 10% of its employees) and divestitures such as its US packaged gas business.

The company broadened its health care operations in late 2002 by acquiring American Homecare Supply (now called Air Products Healthcare), which serves the home health care industry with medical gases and related equipment.

In 2007 Air Products made a small but strategic move into Eastern Europe. The company took advantage of Linde's sell-off of some BOC assets after the German company bought BOC in 2006. Air Products acquired the Polish Gazy SP for just under $500 million with the hopes of moving into the Central and Eastern European markets to take advantage of the migration of manufacturing to the region.

EXECUTIVES

Chairman, President, and CEO: John E. McGlade, age 56, $10,946,246 total compensation
SVP and CFO: Paul E. Huck, age 60, $2,827,752 total compensation
SVP and General Counsel: John Stanley, age 51
SVP Human Resources and Communications: Lynn C. Minella, age 52, $1,585,808 total compensation
SVP and General Manager, Merchant Gases: Robert D. Dixon, age 51, $1,727,790 total compensation
SVP Supply Chain: John W. Marsland, age 44
SVP and General Manager, Tonnage Gases, Equipment, and Energy: Stephen J. Jones, age 49
VP and Chief Risk Officer: Diane L. Sheridan
VP and CTO: Montgomery (Monty) Alger
VP Information Technology and CIO: Richard Boocock
VP and Corporate Controller: M. Scott Crocco, age 46
VP Corporate Communications: Elizabeth L. (Betsy) Klebe
President, Air Products Korea: Soo-Yon Lee
President, Air Products Japan: Eugene Crossland
President, Air Products San Fu Co.: Allen Wei Long Chien
Director, Investor Relations: Simon R. Moore
Corporate Secretary and Chief Governance Officer: Mary Afflerbach
Manager, Corporate Public Relations: Beth Mentesana
Auditors: KPMG LLP

LOCATIONS

HQ: Air Products and Chemicals, Inc.
7201 Hamilton Blvd., Allentown, PA 18195
Phone: 610-481-4911   **Fax:** 610-481-5900
Web: www.airproducts.com

2009 Sales

	$ mil.	% of total
US	3,779.8	46
Europe	2,765.1	33
Asia	1,294.2	16
Canada	238.6	3
Latin America	178.5	2
Total	**8,256.2**	**100**

PRODUCTS/OPERATIONS

2009 Sales

	$ mil.	% of total
Merchant Gases	3,610.6	44
Tonnage Gases	2,573.6	31
Electronics & Performance Materials	1,582.2	19
Equipment & Energy	489.8	6
Total	**8,256.2**	**100**

Selected Products and Services

Industrial Gases
  Argon
  Carbon dioxide
  Carbon monoxide
  Helium
  Hydrogen
  Nitrogen
  Oxygen
  Synthesis gas
Equipment and Services
  Air-pollution control systems
  Air-separation equipment
  Hydrogen-purification equipment
  Natural gas-liquefaction equipment

COMPETITORS

Aceto
Airgas
BASF SE
L'Air Liquide
The Linde Group
Messer Group
Praxair
Taiyo Nippon Sanso

HISTORICAL FINANCIALS

Company Type: Public

Income Statement

FYE: September 30

	REVENUE ($ mil.)	NET INCOME ($ mil.)	NET PROFIT MARGIN	EMPLOYEES
9/09	8,256	631	7.6%	18,900
9/08	10,415	910	8.7%	21,100
9/07	10,038	1,036	10.3%	22,100
9/06	8,850	730	8.2%	20,700
9/05	8,144	712	8.7%	19,500
Annual Growth	0.3%	(3.0%)	—	(0.8%)

2009 Year-End Financials

Debt ratio: 77.5%	No. of shares (mil.): 213
Return on equity: 12.9%	Dividends
Cash ($ mil.): 488	Yield: 2.3%
Current ratio: 1.20	Payout: 60.5%
Long-term debt ($ mil.): 3,716	Market value ($ mil.): 16,489

Stock History

NYSE: APD

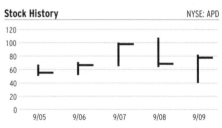

	STOCK PRICE ($) FY Close	P/E High/Low		PER SHARE ($) Earnings	Dividends	Book Value
9/09	77.58	27	14	2.96	1.79	22.55
9/08	68.49	26	16	4.15	1.70	23.67
9/07	97.76	21	14	4.64	1.48	25.86
9/06	66.37	22	17	3.18	1.34	23.17
9/05	55.14	21	17	3.08	1.25	21.53
Annual Growth	8.9%	—	—	(1.0%)	9.4%	1.2%

Airgas, Inc.

Airgas has floated to the top of the industrial gas distribution industry by buying up more than 400 companies since its founding in 1986. The company's North American network of more than 1,100 locations includes retail stores, gas fill plants, specialty gas labs, production facilities, and distribution centers. Airgas distributes argon, hydrogen, nitrogen, oxygen, and a variety of medical and specialty gases, as well as dry ice and protective equipment (hard hats, goggles). Its Merchant Gases unit operates air-separation plants that produce oxygen, nitrogen, and argon. It also sells welding machines and produces acetylene and nitrous oxide. Rival Air Products offered to buy Airgas for $7 billion in 2010.

Air Products had approached Airgas late the year before, hoping to buy its distribution rival and add Airgas' nationwide network of retail outlets. The offer consisted of $5.1 billion in cash and another $1.9 billion of assumed debt. Founder and CEO Peter McCausland, whose family owns about 10% of Airgas, and the Board of Directors repeatedly rejected the offers as undervaluing Airgas. Ever optimistic, Air Products extended its tender offer to Airgas stockholders three times in 2010.

It is the largest gas distributor in the country with a 25% market share. Almost all of the company's sales come from distributing bulk gases (nitrogen, oxygen, argon, helium), gas cylinders, and welding equipment. Airgas also distributes dry ice. The industrial manufacturing and repair and maintenance industries account for about a quarter each of the company's sales; customers primarily make fabricated metal products, industrial transportation and equipment, chemical products, and primary metal products. Other industries served include medical and health services, agriculture, mining, repair and maintenance, and wholesale trade.

The company continually strives to grow its business through acquisitions, adding 10-15 companies annually. In 2008 the company acquired 14 companies, including Refron, a US-based reseller and distributor of refrigerants and a provider of technical services and refrigerant reclamation services. Airgas acquired six businesses in 2010, including Tri-Tech, an independent distributor with 16 locations throughout Florida, Georgia and South Carolina and annual sales of $31 million.

HISTORY

In the early 1980s Peter McCausland was a corporate attorney involved in mergers and acquisitions for Messer Griesheim, a large German industrial gas producer. When the German firm declined McCausland's recommendation in 1982 to buy Connecticut Oxygen, he raised money from private sources and bought it himself. He acquired other distributors and then left Messer Griesheim in 1987 to run Airgas full-time.

Airgas began buying mostly small local and regional gas distributors in the US. By 1994 strategy shifted to purchasing larger "superregional" distributors such as Jimmie Jones Co. and Post Welding Supply of Alabama, which added about $70 million combined to the company's revenues.

Airgas then began "rolling up" additional similar businesses. In 1995 it bought more than 25 companies, and two years later it added more

than 20 gas distributors. Also in 1997 Airgas expanded its manufacturing capabilities by building five plants that could fast-fill whole pallets of gas cylinders (the old, manual system rolls cylinders two at a time). By 2000 the company had about 100 cylinder fill plants.

Struggling to integrate acquisitions while dealing with softening markets, Airgas began a companywide realignment in 1998. To that end, it sold its calcium carbide and carbon products operations to former partner Elkem ASA later that year; the company also consolidated 34 hubs into 16 regional companies and sold its operations in Poland and Thailand to Germany-based Linde in 1999.

In 2000 Airgas acquired distributor Mallinckrodt's Puritan-Bennett division (gas products for medical uses) with 36 locations in the US and Canada. The company also acquired the majority of Air Products' US packaged gas business, excluding its electronic gases and magnetic resonance imaging-related helium operations, in 2002.

In 2004 and 2005 it bought units from giants like Air Products and Chemicals, BOC, and LaRoche Industries. In 2006 Airgas continued to build with the purchase of 10 businesses, including Union Industrial Gas, which supplies Texas and much of the Southwest, and then Linde's US bulk gas business for $495 million the next year. Linde, in the process of integrating its 2006 acquisition of BOC, then sold to Airgas a portion of its US packaged gas business for $310 million.

EXECUTIVES

Chairman and CEO: Peter McCausland, age 60, $3,062,832 total compensation
EVP and COO: Michael L. (Mike) Molinini, age 59, $1,059,437 total compensation
Division President, West: Max D. Hooper, age 50
Division President, East: B. Shaun Powers, age 58, $624,436 total compensation
SVP and CFO: Robert M. McLaughlin, age 53, $683,013 total compensation
SVP, Tonnage and Merchant Gases: Thomas S. Thoman
SVP and CIO: Robert A. Dougherty, age 52
SVP Corporate Development: Leslie J. Graff, age 49, $600,876 total compensation
SVP and General Counsel: Robert H. Young Jr., age 59
SVP Distribution Operations: Michael E. Rohde
SVP Human Resources: Dwight T. Wilson, age 54
SVP Corporate Accounts: Patrick M. Visintainer, age 46
SVP Medical: Kelly P. Justice
SVP Sales and Marketing: Ronald J. (Ron) Stark
SVP, Specialty Gases and Life Sciences: James A. Muller
VP Communications and Investor Relations: R. Jay Worley
Director Investor Relations: Barry Strzelec
Auditors: KPMG LLP

LOCATIONS

HQ: Airgas, Inc.
259 N. Radnor-Chester Rd., Ste. 100
Radnor, PA 19087
Phone: 610-687-5253   **Fax:** 610-687-1052
Web: www.airgas.com

PRODUCTS/OPERATIONS

2010 Sales

	$ mil.	% of total
Distribution	3,467.3	90
Other operations	420.9	10
Adjustments	(24.2)	—
Total	**3,864.0**	**100**

2010 Sales

	$ mil.	% of total
Gas & rentals	2,496.8	65
Hardgoods	1,367.2	35
Total	**3,864.0**	**100**

Selected Products and Services

Products
  Carbon dioxide
  Dry ice
  Industrial gases
  Argon
  Helium
  Hydrogen
  Liquid oxygen
  Nitrogen
  Nitrous oxide
  Oxygen
  Safety equipment
  Specialty gases
Services
  Container rental
  Welding equipment rental

Subsidiaries

Airgas Dry Ice/Carbonic
Airgas East
Airgas Great Lakes
Airgas Gulf States
Airgas Intermountain
Airgas Kendeco Tool Crib
Airgas Mid America
Airgas Mid South
Airgas Nitrous Oxide
Airgas Nor Pac
Airgas North Central
Airgas Northern California & Nevada
Airgas Rutland Tool
Airgas Safety
Airgas South
Airgas Southwest
Airgas Specialty Gases
Airgas West
Puritan Medical Products
Red-D-Arc

COMPETITORS

Air Products
American Air Liquide
L'Air Liquide
Lincoln Electric
Matheson Tri-Gas
Praxair Distribution
Valley National Gases
W.W. Grainger

HISTORICAL FINANCIALS

Company Type: Public

Income Statement

FYE: March 31

	REVENUE ($ mil.)	NET INCOME ($ mil.)	NET PROFIT MARGIN	EMPLOYEES
3/10	3,864	196	5.1%	14,000
3/09	4,350	261	6.0%	14,000
3/08	4,017	223	5.6%	14,500
3/07	3,205	154	4.8%	11,500
3/06	2,830	126	4.5%	10,300
Annual Growth	**8.1%**	**11.7%**	**—**	**8.0%**

2010 Year-End Financials

Debt ratio: 83.5%
Return on equity: 11.7%
Cash ($ mil.): 47
Current ratio: 1.50
Long-term debt ($ mil.): 1,499
No. of shares (mil.): 84
Dividends
  Yield: 1.2%
  Payout: 32.5%
Market value ($ mil.): 5,323

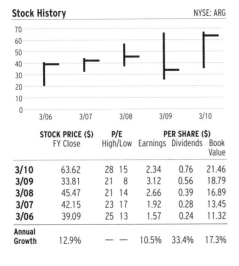
	STOCK PRICE ($) FY Close	P/E High/Low		PER SHARE ($) Earnings	Dividends	Book Value
3/10	63.62	28	15	2.34	0.76	21.46
3/09	33.81	21	8	3.12	0.56	18.79
3/08	45.47	21	14	2.66	0.39	16.89
3/07	42.15	23	17	1.92	0.28	13.45
3/06	39.09	25	13	1.57	0.24	11.32
Annual Growth	12.9%	—	—	10.5%	33.4%	17.3%

AirTran Holdings

Need to be transported by air with a low fare? AirTran Holdings may be the ticket. Through its main subsidiary, AirTran Airways, the company offers low-cost passenger transportation to more than 60 cities, mainly in the eastern US but also in Puerto Rico, Aruba, Mexico, and the Bahamas. The airline operates from its primary hub in Atlanta and secondary hubs in Baltimore, Milwaukee, and Orlando, Florida. AirTran maintains a fleet of about 140 Boeing aircraft, including the 717 and the 737. It is a leading carrier in the Atlanta market, behind Delta, which handles the largest share of the traffic at Hartsfield-Jackson Atlanta International Airport.

The carrier successfully blends a couple of industry models. It often offers lower fares than Delta, but unlike low-fare leader Southwest Airlines, AirTran Airways provides reserved seats and business-class service. In addition, it relies on its Atlanta hub more than Southwest relies on any single airport. Like Southwest, AirTran Airways has been able to maintain a lower cost structure than many of its larger rivals.

High fuel prices combined with a severe slump in travel demand and a global economic recession have hurt AirTran and the rest of the airline industry. In 2008 AirTran took a beating, mainly from bad fuel-hedging bets — turning in a $266 million loss that year. (Fuel-hedging is when airlines lock in a predetermined price for future jet fuel purchases.) In response, AirTran adjusted its heading contracts, reduced capacity, and delayed delivery of about 20 Boeing 737s. The new aircraft, originally scheduled to be delivered from 2009 through 2011, will instead be added to the carrier's fleet in 2013 and 2014.

Following the trend among discount carriers, AirTran soared to a $134 million profit in 2009, as bigger rival airlines recorded losses. AirTran was well positioned in the market as skittish consumers sought budget fares and fuel prices leveled out. A big contributor to its banner year in 2009 was a boost in "other revenues," which included fees for extras such as transporting pets and unaccompanied minors, liquor sales, priority seat selection, and (unlike Southwest) checked baggage. AirTran's other revenues

increased about 80% or $113 million in 2009 compared to the year prior.

At a time when other airlines are shrinking their networks, AirTran added some 25 non-stop routes in 2009 including flights to new cities in Pennsylvania, North Carolina, New Jersey, Missouri, West Virginia, Florida, Tennessee, Aruba, Mexico, and the Bahamas. It continued the trend in 2010 with new service to Montego Bay, Jamaica; Gulfport, Mississippi; and Lexington, Kentucky.

AirTran made a move to further extend its reach into the Midwest by forming a marketing agreement with regional carrier SkyWest Airlines in 2009. Through the partnership, AirTran and SkyWest provide non-stop service from Milwaukee to about 20 destinations.

AirTran also has a marketing partnership with Frontier Airlines. AirTran and Frontier refer passengers to each other and credit miles from one another's frequent flier programs. Potential customers on the AirTran Web site can go to Frontier to book flights to destinations not served by AirTran, and vice-versa.

HISTORY

What today is AirTran Holdings began in 1992 when airline veterans Robert Priddy, Maurice Gallagher, and Timothy Flynn founded ValuJet, basing it in Atlanta. By year's end the company operated six aircraft on 34 daily flights to Fort Lauderdale, Jacksonville, Orlando, and Tampa, Florida. By late 1994 it flew 22 jets between 16 cities, mainly in the Southeast. ValuJet continued to expand, linking Washington, DC, to Chicago and Montreal in 1995 and to New York in 1996.

In May 1996 a ValuJet DC-9 crashed in the Florida Everglades, killing all 110 people aboard. The FAA reviewed the company's safety and maintenance procedures after the crash, forcing the airline to shut down for 15 weeks. ValuJet resumed flights in September, offering $19 one-way flights to lure back passengers. Turnaround specialist Joseph Corr, formerly of TWA and Continental Airlines, came aboard in November as CEO to help ValuJet change its course.

To recover passenger bookings, the airline joined the SABRE computer reservation system in 1997, sparking a 60% increase in SABRE bookings. That year ValuJet acquired AirTran Airways through its purchase of Airways Corporation, rebranded itself as AirTran Airlines, kicked off an advertising campaign to overhaul its image, and moved to Orlando. In 1999 Joseph Leonard, a former Eastern Airlines executive, succeeded Corr as CEO. That year AirTran began to replace aging aircraft by taking delivery of new Boeing 717 regional jets, becoming the first airline to use that new aircraft model.

AirTran made an effort to acquire ailing industry giant TWA in 2000, but talks between the two airlines ended shortly after they began. Also that year AirTran transferred to the American Stock Exchange from the NASDAQ.

An effort to acquire Chicago landing slots from bankrupt ATA fell short in 2004 as rival Southwest Airlines outbid AirTran to gain additional space at Midway Airport.

In 2007 AirTran tried to expand by buying smaller rival Midwest Air Group, but its bids were rejected by Midwest's board, which wanted the company to remain independent. Midwest instead accepted an offer from an investment group led by TPG Capital. Late that year the airline stopped offering cargo service.

President Bob Fornaro was promoted to CEO in 2007, succeeding Joe Leonard. Leonard had served as CEO since 1999, the same year Fornaro was hired as president. Fornaro additionally took on the role of chairman in June 2008.

EXECUTIVES

Chairman, President, and CEO, AirTran Holdings and AirTran Airways: Robert L. (Bob) Fornaro, age 57, $2,000,353 total compensation
EVP Operations and Customer Service, AirTran Airways: Klaus Goersch, age 44
EVP Corporate Development and Finance, AirTran Airways: Steven A. (Steve) Rossum, age 46, $1,174,447 total compensation
EVP Corporate Affairs, AirTran Airways: Stephen J. Kolski, age 69, $812,807 total compensation
SVP, General Counsel, and Secretary, AirTran Holdings and AirTran Airways: Richard P. Magurno, age 66, $776,658 total compensation
SVP Human Resources and Administration, AirTran Airways: Loral Blinde
SVP Customer Service, AirTran Airways: Alfred J. (Jack) Smith III, age 58,
SVP Information Services and CIO, AirTran Airways: Rocky Wiggins, age 51
SVP Finance, Treasurer, and CFO, AirTran Holdings and AirTran Airways: Arne G. Haak, age 42, $802,617 total compensation
SVP Marketing and Planning, AirTran Airways: Kevin P. Healy
VP Inflight Service, AirTran Airways: Peggy Sauer-Clark
VP Maintenance and Engineering, AirTran Airways: Kirk Thornburg
VP Flight Operations, AirTran Airways: Jeff Miller
VP Marketing and Sales, AirTran Airways: Tad Hutcheson
VP and Chief Accounting Officer, AirTran Airways: Mark W. Osterberg, age 56
Senior Director Strategic Planning, AirTran Airways: John Kirby
Director Corporate Safety, AirTran Airways: Capt. Jean-Pierre (J. P.) Dagon $785,523 total compensation
Auditors: Ernst & Young LLP

LOCATIONS

HQ: AirTran Holdings, Inc.
9955 AirTran Blvd., Orlando, FL 32827
Phone: 407-318-5600   **Fax:** 407-318-5900
Web: www.airtran.com

PRODUCTS/OPERATIONS

2009 Sales

	$ mil.	% of total
Passenger	2,088.9	89
Other	252.5	11
Total	**2,341.4**	**100**

COMPETITORS

AMR Corp.
Continental Airlines
Delta Air Lines
JetBlue
Midwest Air
Southwest Airlines
Spirit Airlines
UAL
US Airways

HISTORICAL FINANCIALS

Company Type: Public

Income Statement

	REVENUE ($ mil.)	NET INCOME ($ mil.)	NET PROFIT MARGIN	EMPLOYEES
12/09	2,341	135	5.8%	8,070
12/08	2,553	(274)	—	8,000
12/07	2,310	53	2.3%	8,500
12/06	1,893	16	0.8%	7,700
12/05	1,451	2	0.1%	6,900
Annual Growth	12.7%	198.4%	—	4.0%

2009 Year-End Financials

Debt ratio: 185.7%
Return on equity: 36.0%
Cash ($ mil.): 543
Current ratio: 1.04
Long-term debt ($ mil.): 932

No. of shares (mil.): 135
Dividends
  Yield: —
  Payout: —
Market value ($ mil.): 707

Stock History

NYSE: AAI

	STOCK PRICE ($) FY Close	P/E High/Low	PER SHARE ($) Earnings	Dividends	Book Value
12/09	5.22	9 3	0.95	—	3.71
12/08	4.44	— —	(2.51)	—	1.82
12/07	7.16	23 13	0.56	—	3.30
12/06	11.74	111 53	0.17	—	2.83
12/05	16.03	835 370	0.02	—	2.60
Annual Growth	(24.5%)	— —	162.5%	—	9.3%

AK Steel Holding

Automobile sales help AK Steel's business keep rolling, though it has begun to branch out to the infrastructure and manufacturing industries. The company manufactures carbon, stainless, and electrical steel. It sells hot- and cold-rolled carbon steel to construction companies, steel distributors and service centers, and automotive and industrial machinery producers. AK Steel also sells cold-rolled and aluminum-coated stainless steel to automakers. The company produces electrical steels (iron-silicon alloys with unique magnetic properties) for makers of power transmission and distribution equipment. In addition, it makes carbon and stainless steel tubular products through AK Tube.

The steel industry has been consolidating for years as troubled companies have been snapped up by market leaders. AK Steel was outbid in a couple of major acquisition efforts early in the decade, and analysts have since speculated that the company itself may be an acquisition candidate. AK Steel has maintained its independence, however, in part because of its status as a leading supplier of some high-grade niche products, such as components of stainless steel exhaust systems for carmakers.

In recent years the company has increased the production capacity at many of its facilities. Total investments have been about $70 million and have improved AK Steel's electrical and tubular steel output. The company's sales to automobile makers have declined as a percentage of total sales, mostly due to its ability to raise prices for its other products, boosting revenue for those other segments. These capacity increases should only help that trend continue.

The company's 2009 sales were hit hard by the global economic downturn, specifically by declines in the construction and automobile markets. Falling steel prices also had a negative effect on AK Steel's bottom line. In 2009 AK Steel laid off some 1,500 salaried employees — 23% of its workforce — due to the downturn in the economy. The company said a steep drop in customer orders made the cuts necessary.

HISTORY

George Verity, who was in the roofing business in Cincinnati around the turn of the century, often had trouble getting sheet metal, so in 1900 he founded his own steel company, American Rolling Mill. His first plant, in Middletown, Ohio, was followed by a second production facility 11 years later in Ashland, Kentucky. Plant superintendent John Tytus, whose family was in paper milling, applied those rolling techniques to make American Rolling Mill's steel more uniform in thickness.

In 1926 Columbia Steel developed a process to overcome several production problems inherent in the Tytus method, and in 1930 American Rolling Mill bought Columbia Steel. The company changed its name to Armco Steel in 1948.

Armco began diversifying in the 1950s and continued diversifying until the early 1980s. Subsidiaries were involved in coal, oil, and gas-drilling equipment and insurance and financial services, among other things. In 1978 the company changed its name to Armco Inc.

Armco began shedding subsidiaries in the early 1980s. Sales and market share increased as the company approached the billion-dollar mark at the end of the decade. In 1989 Armco formed Armco Steel Company with Japan's Kawasaki Steel Corporation.

Armco's sales reached $1.3 billion in 1991, though the high operating expenses in the steel industry of the 1990s kept profits low. Armco began looking outside the company for help, and in 1992 it persuaded retired steel executive Tom Graham to head the company. Graham brought with him another industry veteran, Richard Wardrop, who would succeed Graham as CEO in 1995. After evaluating the company's holdings, the two divested more than 10 subsidiaries and divisions. Armco also worked on improving quality and customer service, with special emphasis placed on timely delivery.

In 1994 Armco's limited partnership with Kawasaki was altered and AK Steel Holding Corporation was formed, with AK Steel Corporation as its main subsidiary and the Middletown and Ashland plants as its production base. The holding company went public the same year, raising more than $650 million, enabling the company to pay off its debt.

AK Steel Holding moved its headquarters to Middletown, Ohio, in 1995. Despite many naysayers, Graham then pushed a plan to build a state-of-the-art $1.1 billion steel production facility. Many doubted the wisdom of going into long-term debt so soon after coming out of the hole

— especially when a similar facility had produced lackluster results for Inland Steel. Graham stuck by his plant, and in 1997 ground was broken on the facility in Spencer County near Rockport, Indiana (Rockport Works). Graham retired that year, and Wardrop took over as chairman.

In 1998 the company opened its Rockport Works cold-rolling mill and began operating a hot-dip galvanizing and galvannealing line. The next year AK Steel bought former parent Armco for $842 million. AK Steel acquired welded steel tubing maker Alpha Tube Corporation (renamed AK Tube LLC) in 2001. In late 2001 the company took a charge of $194 million for losses in its pension fund, which had been battered by a weak stock market and lowered interest rates.

AK Steel sold its Sawhill Tubular Division to John Maneely Company (Collingswood, NJ) for roughly $50 million in 2002.

AK Steel offered to purchase National Steel, which was operating under Chapter 11 bankruptcy protection. However, AK Steel's bid was trumped in 2003 by one from U.S. Steel that included a ratified labor agreement with the United Steelworkers of America. AK Steel also lost out in an effort to acquire Rouge Industries (later Severstal North America).

Chairman and CEO Wardrop and president John Hritz left their posts in September 2003. CFO James Wainscott was named president and CEO, and Robert Jenkins became chairman. (Wainscott succeeded Jenkins as chairman in January 2006.)

In an effort to reduce its debt, AK Steel in 2004 sold its Douglas Dynamics unit, a maker of snow and ice removal equipment, for $260 million, and its Greens Port Industrial Park, a 600-acre development in Houston, for $75 million.

In 2007 the company moved its corporate headquarters to West Chester, Ohio.

EXECUTIVES

Chairman, President, and CEO:
James L. (Jim) Wainscott, age 53,
$11,214,896 total compensation
EVP, General Counsel, and Secretary: David C. Horn,
age 58, $3,658,609 total compensation
EVP and Operating Officer: John F. Kaloski, age 60,
$3,210,427 total compensation
SVP Finance and CFO: Albert E. Ferrara Jr., age 61,
$2,568,998 total compensation
VP Carbon Steel Operations: Keith J. Howell
VP Specialty Steel Operations: Kirk W. Reich, age 42
VP Sales and Customer Service: Douglas W. Gant,
age 51, $2,394,831 total compensation
VP Business Planning and Development:
Roger K. Newport, age 45
VP Human Resources: Lawrence F. Zizzo Jr., age 61
VP Government and Public Relations: Alan H. McCoy,
age 58
Chief Accounting Officer and Controller:
Richard S. Williams, age 51
Auditors: Deloitte & Touche LLP

LOCATIONS

HQ: AK Steel Holding Corporation
  9227 Centre Pointe Dr., West Chester, OH 45069
Phone: 513-425-5000   **Fax:** 513-425-2676
Web: www.aksteel.com

2009 Sales

	$ mil.	% of total
US	3,309.8	81
Other countries	767.0	19
Total	**4,076.8**	**100**

PRODUCTS/OPERATIONS

2009 Sales

	$ mil.	% of total
Carbon steel	2,207.6	54
Stainless & electrical steel	1,736.2	43
Tubular steel & other	133.0	3
Total	**4,076.8**	**100**

2009 Sales

	% of total
Automotive	36
Distributors & converters	33
Industry & manufacturing	31
Total	**100**

COMPETITORS

ArcelorMittal USA
Dofasco
Kobe Steel USA
Nucor
Steel Dynamics
Union Electric Steel
United States Steel
Worthington Industries

HISTORICAL FINANCIALS

Company Type: Public

Income Statement

	REVENUE ($ mil.)	NET INCOME ($ mil.)	NET PROFIT MARGIN	EMPLOYEES
12/09	4,077	(75)	—	6,500
12/08	7,644	4	0.1%	6,800
12/07	7,003	388	5.5%	6,900
12/06	6,069	12	0.2%	7,000
12/05	5,647	(1)	—	8,000
Annual Growth	**(7.8%)**	**—**	**—**	**(5.1%)**

FYE: December 31

2009 Year-End Financials

Debt ratio: 68.8%
Return on equity: —
Cash ($ mil.): 462
Current ratio: 2.20
Long-term debt ($ mil.): 606

No. of shares (mil.): 110
Dividends
  Yield: 0.9%
  Payout: —
Market value ($ mil.): 2,347

Stock History

NYSE: AKS

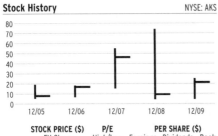

	STOCK PRICE ($) FY Close	P/E High/Low		PER SHARE ($) Earnings	Dividends	Book Value
12/09	21.35	—	—	(0.68)	0.20	8.01
12/08	9.32	1,827	130	0.04	0.20	8.81
12/07	46.24	16	5	3.46	0.00	7.96
12/06	16.90	157	69	0.11	0.00	3.79
12/05	7.95	—	—	(0.02)	0.00	2.01
Annual Growth	**28.0%**	**—**	**—**	**—**	**—**	**41.4%**

Alaska Air Group

Whether you want to capture a Kodiak moment or down a daiquiri by the Sea of Cortez, an Alaska Air Group unit can fly you there. Through primary subsidiary, Alaska Airlines, and regional carrier Horizon Air, the group flies to about 90 destinations in the US (mainly western states including Alaska and Hawaii), Canada, and Mexico. The group has hubs in Seattle and Portland, Oregon. (Alaska Airlines has additional hubs in Los Angeles and Anchorage, Alaska, while Horizon also flies from Boise, Idaho.) Alaska Airlines has a fleet of some 115 Boeing 737 jets and Horizon Air operates some 20 jets and 40 turboprops.

Like other US airlines, Alaska Air Group has had to fight to make a profit as fuel costs skyrocketed, passenger and cargo demand plunged, and the economy slid into a recession. As part of the group's cost-control programs, both airlines are moving to one model of aircraft (Alaska Airlines transitioned to an all-737 fleet in 2008 and Horizon Air is moving toward a fleet of all Bombardier Q400s). The airlines have also cut flight frequency and capacity, and revamped some routes.

With limited exposure on costly international routes and fuel prices leveling off, Alaska Air Group weathered 2009 better than some of its larger rivals. The Group turned in a profit for 2009, with a net income of about $121 million — a novelty among airlines during the economic slowdown and an improvement from the loss of $135 million the year prior. Fees for extra services that were once free, such as a new $15 charge for the first bag checked, also helped the group. The baggage fee generated some $47 million in 2009.

Alaska Airlines' dominance in the Alaska air travel market and strong presence on the West Coast have made it an attractive code-sharing partner for airlines such as Air France, American, Delta, Korean Air, and KLM. (Code-sharing enables airlines to sell tickets on one another's flights and thereby offer passengers more destinations.) Such partnerships extend Alaska Airlines' reach well beyond its service area.

Alaska Airlines hopes to grow mainly by increasing the frequency of flights within its existing route structure, but also by adding service to new markets as demand warrants. The carrier added new non-stop routes to Las Vegas; Maui and Kona, Hawaii; Austin, Texas; Houston; Atlanta; and Chicago in 2009.

HISTORY

Pilot Mac McGee started McGee Airways in 1932 to fly cargo between Anchorage and Bristol Bay, Alaska. He joined other local operators in 1937 to form Star Air Lines, which began airmail service between Fairbanks and Bethel in 1938. In 1944, a year after buying three small airlines, Star adopted the name Alaska Airlines.

The company expanded to include freight service to Africa and Australia in 1950. This expansion, coupled with the seasonal nature of the airline's business, caused losses in the early 1970s. Developer Bruce Kennedy gained control of the board, turning the firm around by the end of 1973. But the Civil Aeronautics Board forced the carrier to drop service to northwestern Alaska in 1975, and by 1978 it served only 10 Alaskan cities and Seattle.

Kennedy became CEO the next year. The 1978 Airline Deregulation Act allowed Alaska Air to move into new areas as well as regain the routes it had lost. By 1982 it was the largest airline flying between Alaska and the lower 48 states.

In 1985 the airline reorganized, forming Alaska Air Group as its holding company. The next year Alaska Air Group bought Jet America Airlines (expanding its routes eastward to Chicago, St. Louis, and Dallas) and Seattle-based Horizon Air Industries (which served 30 Northwest cities). When competition in the East and Midwest cut profits in 1987, Kennedy shut down Jet America to focus on West Coast operations.

To counterbalance summer traffic to Alaska, the airline began service to two Mexican resorts in 1988. Fuel prices and sluggish traffic hurt 1990 earnings, but Alaska Air Group stayed in the black, unlike many other carriers. Kennedy retired as chairman and CEO in 1991.

That year the airline began service to Canada and seasonal flights to two Russian cities. Neil Bergt's MarkAir airline declared war, cutting fares and horning in on Alaska Air Group's territory. Alaska Air Group's profits were slashed, and MarkAir went into bankruptcy.

Alaska Air extended Russian flights to year-round in 1994. The airline began service to Vancouver in 1996. That year it became the first major US carrier to use the GPS satellite navigation system. In 1997 it added service to more than a dozen new cities but halted service to Russia because of that country's economic woes in 1998.

Alaska Air Group and Dutch airline KLM agreed to a marketing alliance in 1998 that included reciprocal frequent-flier programs and code-sharing, and in 1999 it added code-sharing agreements with several major airlines, including American and Continental. Alaska Airlines developed an online check-in system, a first among US carriers.

In 2000 an Alaska Airlines MD-83 crashed into the Pacific Ocean near Los Angeles, killing all 88 people on board. A federal investigation of Alaska Airlines' maintenance practices found deficiencies, but the FAA eventually accepted the airline's plan to tighten safety standards.

Like most carriers in the latter part of 2001, Alaska Airlines cut back its flights as a result of reduced demand after the September 11 terrorist attacks. As demand slowly returned in 2002, Alaska Airlines began to add new destinations and increase the number of flights on some established routes.

In 2005 Alaska Airlines announced plans to buy 35 Boeing 737-800s between 2006 and 2011.

EXECUTIVES

Chairman, President, and CEO, Alaska Air Group; Chairman and CEO, Alaska Airlines: William S. (Bill) Ayer, age 55, $4,570,757 total compensation

President, Horizon Air: Glenn S. Johnson, age 51, $1,988,596 total compensation

President, Alaska Airlines: Bradley D. (Brad) Tilden, age 49, $2,259,770 total compensation

EVP Operations and COO, Alaska Airlines: Benito (Ben) Minicucci, age 43, $1,306,118 total compensation

CFO: Brandon S. Pedersen, age 43

SVP Alaska, Alaska Airlines: William L. (Bill) MacKay

VP Safety, Alaska Air Group and Alaska Airlines: Thomas W. (Tom) Nunn

VP Legal and Corporate Affairs, General Counsel, and Corporate Secretary, Alaska Air Group and Alaska Airlines: Keith Loveless, age 53

VP Planning and Revenue Management, Alaska Airlines: Andrew R. Harrison

VP Finance and Treasurer, Alaska Air Group and Alaska Airlines: John F. (Jay) Schaefer Jr.

VP Human Resources and Labor Relations, Alaska Airlines: Kelley J. Dobbs, age 43
VP Customer Service, Airports, Alaska Airlines: Jeffrey M. Butler
VP Information and Technology, Alaska Airlines: Kris M. Kutchera
VP Maintenance and Engineering, Alaska Airlines: Frederick L. Mohr
VP Customer Innovation and Alaskaair.com, Alaska Airlines: Stephen B. Jarvis
VP Flight Operations, Alaska Airlines: Gary L. Beck
VP Marketing, Alaska Airlines: Joseph A. (Joe) Sprague
Managing Director Investor Relations and Assistant Corporate Secretary, Alaska Air Group and Alaska Airlines: Shannon K. Alberts
Auditors: KPMG LLP

LOCATIONS

HQ: Alaska Air Group, Inc.
19300 International Blvd., Seattle, WA 98188
Phone: 206-392-5040   **Fax:** 206-392-2804
Web: www.alaskaair.com

PRODUCTS/OPERATIONS

2009 Sales

	$ mil.	% of total
Passenger	3,092.1	91
Freight & mail	95.9	3
Other	211.8	6
Total	**3,399.8**	**100**

2009 Sales

	$ mil.	% of total
Alaska Airlines	3,006.0	82
Horizon Airlines	654.4	18
Other	1.1	—
Adjustments	(261.7)	—
Total	**3,399.8**	**100**

COMPETITORS

ACE Aviation
Aeromexico
Allegiant Travel
AMR Corp.
Continental Airlines
Delta Air Lines
JetBlue
Mesa Air
SkyWest
Southwest Airlines
UAL
US Airways
Virgin America
WestJet

HISTORICAL FINANCIALS

Company Type: Public

Income Statement   FYE: December 31

	REVENUE ($ mil.)	NET INCOME ($ mil.)	NET PROFIT MARGIN	EMPLOYEES
12/09	3,400	122	3.6%	12,440
12/08	3,663	(136)	—	14,143
12/07	3,506	125	3.6%	14,710
12/06	3,334	(53)	—	14,485
12/05	2,975	85	2.8%	13,768
Annual Growth	**3.4%**	**9.5%**	**—**	**(2.5%)**

2009 Year-End Financials

Debt ratio: 194.8%
Return on equity: 15.9%
Cash ($ mil.): 164
Current ratio: 1.30
Long-term debt ($ mil.): 1,699
No. of shares (mil.): 36
Dividends
  Yield: 0.0%
  Payout: —
Market value ($ mil.): 1,238

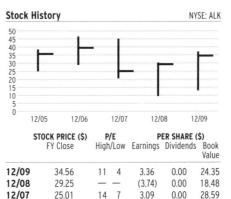

Stock History   NYSE: ALK

	STOCK PRICE ($) FY Close	P/E High/Low		PER SHARE ($) Earnings	Dividends	Book Value
12/09	34.56	11	4	3.36	0.00	24.35
12/08	29.25	—	—	(3.74)	0.00	18.48
12/07	25.01	14	7	3.09	0.00	28.59
12/06	39.50	—	—	(1.39)	0.00	24.72
12/05	35.72	—	—	(0.01)	0.00	23.11
Annual Growth	**(0.8%)**	**—**	**—**	**—**	**—**	**1.3%**

Alberto-Culver

From the bathroom to the kitchen to the laundry room, Alberto-Culver has you covered. The company makes products for hair care (Alberto VO5, Nexxus, TRESemmé), skin care (St. Ives, Noxzema), and personal care (FDS); sweeteners and seasonings (Sugar Twin, Mrs. Dash); home care (Kleen Guard); and laundry-care items (Static Guard). Alberto-Culver's products are developed, manufactured, and marketed in the US and in more than 100 other countries. The company also makes beauty products for other US companies under private label. Alberto-Culver's 2008 acquisition of the Noxzema brand from Procter & Gamble (P&G) has helped the company to ride out the recession.

The Noxzema brand contributed nearly 4% of Alberto-Culver's 2009 sales. Higher sales of TRESemmé (3.6% increase), Nexxus (1.1%), and Noxzema products allowed the hair care company to log a more than 6% rise in revenue within its US segment. Alberto-Culver's international sales were flat in 2009, however, due to foreign currency fluctuations, despite selling more TRESemmé, St. Ives, and Nexxus items.

Alberto-Culver generates most of its sales — some 94% in 2009 — from beauty care products. Peddling food and household items accounted for the rest of its revenue. To safeguard its top products category, the company has been expanding its business in the skin care market. To that end, it acquired Simple Health & Beauty, a leading skin care products company in the UK, for about £240 million (about $390 million) in December 2009. The purchase also strengthens Alberto-Culver's presence in the UK, its largest foreign market.

To maintain its momentum, Alberto-Culver is consolidating some of its US facilities in 2010 to streamline its operations. Activities at a California plant will transfer to a new plant in Arkansas and some workers will lose their jobs. The consumer products company also is shedding ancillary businesses. In 2008 Alberto-Culver sold its Cederroth unit, which served Nordic countries, to CapMan.

Dwarfed by consumer products and beauty care giants, such as P&G, Alberto-Culver had been spending millions to boost its marketing efforts as one of its key strategies to maintain "consumer awareness" of its major brands.

The Lavin and Bernick families run Alberto-Culver and control about 14% of the voting rights. Bernice Lavin, who founded the company with her husband, Leonard, died in October 2007. Neuberger Berman, LLC, owns about a 7% stake in the company.

HISTORY

Alberto VO5 Conditioning Hairdressing (featuring five vital oils in a water-free base) was developed in the early 1950s by a chemist named Alberto to rejuvenate the coiffures of Hollywood's movie stars from the damage of harsh studio lights. In 1955, 36-year-old entrepreneur Leonard Lavin and his wife, Bernice, borrowed $400,000, bought the Los Angeles-based firm that made VO5 from Blaine Culver, and relocated it to Chicago. That year Alberto-Culver implemented a key component of its corporate strategy — aggressive marketing — by running the first television commercial for VO5. Within three years Alberto VO5 led its category. In 1959 the company expanded its product line by buying TRESemmé Hair Color.

Lavin built a new plant and headquarters in Melrose Park, Illinois, in 1960, took the company public in 1961, and formed an international marketing division. A series of product innovations included Alberto VO5 Hair Spray (1961), New Dawn Hair Color (the first shampoo-in, permanent hair color; 1963), Consort Hair Spray for Men (1965), and FDS (1966). Acquisitions in 1969 included low-calorie sugar substitute SugarTwin and 10-store beauty supply chain Sally Beauty Supply.

Alberto-Culver restyled TV advertising in 1972 by putting two 30-second ads in a 60-second spot (it later pioneered the "split 30," back-to-back 15-second ads for two different products). It launched TCB (an ethnic hair care line) in 1975 and Static Guard antistatic spray in 1976.

The firm developed a series of food-substitute products in the 1980s, including Mrs. Dash (1983) and Molly McButter (1987). It also expanded the fast-growing Sally chain to the UK (1987). Lavin's son-in-law Howard Bernick succeeded him as president and COO in 1988.

By 1990 the Sally chain had about 800 stores, many added through the purchases of smaller chains. It bought the bankrupt Milo Beauty & Barber Supply chain (about 90 stores) in 1991. That year Alberto-Culver also bought Cederroth International, a Swedish maker of health and hygiene goods. Bernick became CEO in 1994, though Lavin stayed on as chairman.

In 1995 Lavin's daughter, Carol Bernick, became head of Alberto-Culver USA and led the division to more than $300 million in sales.

The 1,500-store Sally chain opened its first 10 outlets in Japan through a joint venture in 1995 and acquired a small chain in Germany the next year. Also in 1996 Alberto-Culver made its largest acquisition ever, paying $110 million for St. Ives Laboratories, maker of St. Ives Swiss Formula hair and skin care products.

In 1997 the consumer products division cut nearly 25% of its product line to focus on its best-sellers. In 1999 the company bought Argentina-based La Farmaco, a personal care products company, and professional products distributor Heil Beauty Supply. In March Alberto-Culver bought Pro-Line, a maker of personal care products targeting ethnic hair care.

In October 2004 founder and chairman Leonard Lavin stepped down after 49 years as chairman, passing his title to his daughter, Carol Lavin Bernick. Leonard Lavin became chairman emeritus and director of the firm. A director since 1955, Bernice Lavin retired from the board in late January 2005.

Alberto-Culver bought California's Nexxus Products Company in May 2005 and spun off its entire retail operations business, including Sally Beauty and Beauty Systems Group, into a separately traded company in late 2006. As part of the deal, Alberto-Culver spun off its beauty supply business into a stand-alone company renamed Sally Beauty Holdings, Inc., and paid shareholders a one-time dividend of $25 per share upon completion. Private-equity firm Clayton, Dubilier & Rice bought a 47.5% stake in Sally Beauty for at least $575 million. Alberto-Culver shareholders own the rest.

Nordic-based private-equity firm, CapMan, purchased Cederroth, a wholly owned subsidiary of Alberto-Culver, in July 2008. Selling off Cederroth has allowed Alberto-Culver to focus on catering to its TRESemmé, Nexxus, Alberto VO5, and St. Ives brands.

EXECUTIVES

Chairman: Carol Lavin Bernick, age 57, $2,938,709 total compensation
Chairman Emeritus: Leonard H. Lavin, age 90
EVP and CFO: Ralph J. Nicoletti, age 51, $1,553,840 total compensation
SVP, General Counsel, and Secretary: Gary P. Schmidt, age 58
President, United States: Kenneth C. (Casey) Keller Jr., age 48
President, International: Richard J. Hynes, age 62, $1,237,494 total compensation
President, Global Brands: Gina R. Boswell, age 47, $1,188,512 total compensation
President, CEO, and Director: V. James Marino, age 59, $4,080,395 total compensation
Auditors: KPMG LLP

LOCATIONS

HQ: Alberto-Culver Company
2525 Armitage Ave., Melrose Park, IL 60160
Phone: 708-450-3000   **Fax:** 708-450-3409
Web: www.alberto.com

2009 Sales

	$ mil.	% of total
US	917.0	64
International	516.9	36
Total	**1,433.9**	**100**

PRODUCTS/OPERATIONS

2009 Sales

	$ mil.	% of total
Beauty care	1,349.4	94
Non-beauty	84.5	6
Total	**1,433.9**	**100**

Selected Brands

Alberto VO5 (hair care products)
Bliw (liquid hand soap, Europe)
Consort (hair care products)
Farmaco (soap, Latin America)
FDS (feminine deodorant spray)
Grumme Tvattsapa (detergent, Europe)
Jordan (toothbrushes, Europe)
Just For Me (ethnic personal care products)
L300 (skin care products, Europe)
Molly McButter (butter-flavored sprinkles)
Motions (ethnic hair care products)
Mrs. Dash (salt-free seasoning)
Nexxus (hair care products)
Noxzema (skin care products)
St. Ives (hair care and skin care products)
Salve (adhesive bandages, Europe)
Samarin (antacids, Europe)
Seltin (salt substitute, Europe)
Soft & Beautiful (ethnic personal care products)
Static Guard (anti-static spray)
SugarTwin (sugar substitute)
Suketter (sugar substitute, Europe)
TCB (ethnic hair care products)
TRESemmé (hair care products)
Veritas (soap, Latin America)

COMPETITORS

Alticor
Avlon
Avon
Bristol-Myers Squibb
Colgate-Palmolive
Combe
Cumberland Packing
Del Laboratories
The Dial Corporation
Estée Lauder
Helen of Troy
Johnson & Johnson
Johnson Publishing
L'Oréal
Mary Kay
McCormick & Company
Nu Skin
Orly International
Procter & Gamble
Regis Corporation
Revlon
Schwarzkopf & Henkel
Shiseido
Unilever

HISTORICAL FINANCIALS

Company Type: Public

Income Statement

FYE: September 30

	REVENUE ($ mil.)	NET INCOME ($ mil.)	NET PROFIT MARGIN	EMPLOYEES
9/09	1,434	119	8.3%	2,500
9/08	1,444	228	15.8%	2,700
9/07	1,542	78	5.1%	3,800
9/06	3,772	205	5.4%	3,800
9/05	3,531	211	6.0%	19,000
Annual Growth	**(20.2%)**	**(13.3%)**	**—**	**(39.8%)**

2009 Year-End Financials

Debt ratio: 0.0%
Return on equity: 10.3%
Cash ($ mil.): 470
Current ratio: 3.14
Long-term debt ($ mil.): 0
No. of shares (mil.): 99
Dividends
  Yield: 1.0%
  Payout: 24.2%
Market value ($ mil.): 2,731

Stock History

NYSE: ACV

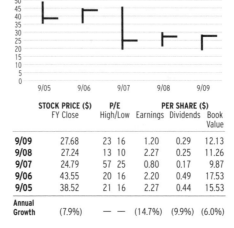

	STOCK PRICE ($) FY Close	P/E High/Low		PER SHARE ($) Earnings	Dividends	Book Value
9/09	27.68	23	16	1.20	0.29	12.13
9/08	27.24	13	10	2.27	0.25	11.26
9/07	24.79	57	25	0.80	0.17	9.87
9/06	43.55	20	16	2.20	0.49	17.53
9/05	38.52	21	16	2.27	0.44	15.53
Annual Growth	**(7.9%)**	**—**	**—**	**(14.7%)**	**(9.9%)**	**(6.0%)**

Alcoa Inc.

Alcoa is among the world's top producers of alumina (aluminum's principal ingredient, processed from bauxite) and aluminum. Its vertically integrated operations include bauxite mining, alumina refining, and aluminum smelting; primary products include alumina and its chemicals, automotive components, and sheet aluminum for beverage cans. The company's non-aluminum products include fiber-optic cables. Major markets include the aerospace, automotive, and construction industries. A truly global company, Alcoa does about half of its business in the US; it operates in more than 30 countries, with Europe and Brazil being its largest international markets.

Alcoa expanded its home building products portfolio in 2010 when it acquired window and door maker Traco. The privately held company became part of Alcoa's building and construction systems business. The Cranberry, Pennsylvania-based business employs about 650 people.

Alcoa is looking to the future and has established a presence in both China and the Middle East. Alcoa owns more than a dozen operating locations in China and expanded a rolling mill there in 2008. It also joined the Chinese aluminum giant in obstructing BHP Billiton's takeover of Rio Tinto; in early 2008, Alcoa and Chinalco acquired 9% of Rio Tinto for $14 billion. (Alcoa's portion of that deal was $1.2 billion.)

Expanding into the Middle East, in 2009 the company announced that it and Saudi Arabian mining company Ma'aden will invest $10.8 billion in a joint venture to build an aluminum industrial complex in Saudi Arabia. Alcoa will hold 25% of the joint venture.

The firm has divested its packaging business, which had accounted for more than 10% of sales, to New Zealand private investment firm the Rank Group. Those businesses, sold in 2008, included closure systems, Reynolds Wrap, and Reynolds Food Packaging. The Rank Group, which already had significant global holdings in packaging companies, paid Alcoa $2.7 billion for the operations. The company did hold onto its aluminum sheet for beverage cans operations.

Alcoa formed a soft-alloy extrusion joint venture with Sapa Group (part of Orkla) in 2008, called Sapa AB. It is the world's largest aluminum shaper and was originally owned equally by Orkla and Alcoa. The two companies also co-owned a joint venture, through Orkla subsidiary Elkem, called Elkem Aluminum. In 2009 Alcoa and Orkla exchanged ownership stakes in the two JVs, with Alcoa taking full ownership of Elkem Aluminum and Orkla doing the same with Sapa AB.

HISTORY

In 1886 two chemists, one in France and one in the US, simultaneously discovered an inexpensive process for aluminum production. The American, Charles Hall, pursued commercial applications. Two years later, with an investor group led by Captain Alfred Hunt, Hall formed the Pittsburgh Reduction Company. Its first salesman, Arthur Davis, secured an initial order for 2,000 cooking pots.

In 1889 the Mellon Bank loaned the company $4,000. In 1891 the firm recapitalized, with the Mellon family holding 12% of the stock.

Davis led the business after Hunt died in 1899 and stayed on until 1957 (he died in 1962 at age 95). It introduced aluminum foil (1910) and developed new applications for aluminum in products such as airplanes and cars. It became the Aluminum Company of America in 1907.

By the end of WWI, Alcoa had integrated backward into bauxite mining and forward into end-use production. By the 1920s the Mellons had raised their stake to 33%. The government and Alcoa had debated antitrust issues in court for years since the smelting patent expired in 1912. Finally a 1946 federal ruling forced the company to sell many operations built during WWII, as well as its Canadian subsidiary (Alcan).

In the competitive aluminum industry of the 1960s, Alcoa's lower-cost production helped it seize market share, especially in beverage cans. In the 1970s Alcoa began offering engineered products such as aerospace components, and in the 1980s it invested in research, acquisitions, and plant modernization.

Paul O'Neill (former president of International Paper) arrived as CEO in 1987 and shifted the company's focus back to aluminum. Sales and earnings set records the next two years but plunged afterward, reflecting a weak global economy and record-low aluminum prices. Then the fall of the Soviet Union in the early 1990s led to a worldwide glut as Russian exports soared.

In 1994 Alcoa cut its production as part of a two-year accord with Western and Russian producers. Alcoa formed a joint venture with Shanghai Aluminum Fabrication Plant in China. Alcoa bought #3 US aluminum producer Alumax for $3.8 billion in 1998, but only after divesting its cast-plate operations.

Known by the nickname "Alcoa" since the late 1920s, the company adopted that as its official name in 1999. O'Neill retired as CEO in 1999; COO Alain Belda succeeded him.

In 2000 Alcoa bought aluminum extrusion maker Excel Extrusions from Noranda (now called Falconbridge) and paid $4.5 billion for Reynolds Metals after agreeing to divest some assets — including all of Reynolds' alumina refineries — to satisfy regulators. Late in 2000 President-elect George W. Bush named Alcoa's chairman Paul O'Neill to be treasury secretary. (O'Neill subsequently resigned the post in December 2002.)

Alcoa sold its majority stake in the Worsley alumina refinery (Australia) to BHP Billiton in 2001 for about $1.5 billion as part of its refinery divestments. Treasury Secretary O'Neill completed the sale of his more than $90 million worth of Alcoa stock and options in June.

Late in the year Alcoa agreed to buy an 8% stake in Aluminium Corporation of China (Chalco). The deal gave Alcoa a seat on the board and 27% of Chalco's initial public offering.

In 2003 Alcoa acquired Camargo Correa Group's 41% stake in the South American businesses of Alcoa, including its largest subsidiary in the group — Alcoa Aluminio S.A. (Brazil) — and operations in Argentina, Chile, Colombia, Peru, Uruguay, and Venezuela. Faced with lower aluminum prices in its aerospace, industrial-gas-turbine, and nonresidential construction markets, Alcoa decided to divest under-performing businesses primarily in its automotive, packaging, and specialty chemicals units.

In 2006 the company sold its Home Exteriors unit to Ply Gem Industries; it also sold its aerospace service business to ThyssenKrupp.

EXECUTIVES

President, CEO, and Director: Klaus Kleinfeld, age 52, $11,897,153 total compensation
EVP and CTO: Mohammad A. Zaidi
EVP; Group President, Engineered Products and Solutions: William F. (Bill) Christopher, age 55, $4,099,159 total compensation
EVP and CFO: Charles D. (Chuck) McLane Jr., age 56, $4,507,142 total compensation
EVP; President, Global Rolled Products, Hard Alloy Extrusions, and Asia: Helmut Wieser, age 56, $3,210,810 total compensation
EVP Business Development: J. Michael (Mike) Schell, age 62, $3,461,210 total compensation
EVP; Group President, Global Primary Products: John G. Thuestad, age 49
EVP and Chief Legal and Compliance Officer: Nicholas J. DeRoma, age 63
VP, Secretary, and Corporate Governance Counsel: Donna C. Dabney, age 59
VP and General Counsel: Kurt R. Waldo, age 54
VP Human Resources: John D. (Jack) Bergen
VP; President, Alcoa Power and Propulsion: Raymond B. (Ray) Mitchell
VP; President, Global Primary Products, Australia: Alan Cransberg
VP; President, Global Primary Metals Technology and Manufacturing: Jean-Pierre Gilardeau
VP; President, Latin America and Caribbean: Franklin L (Frank) Feder
VP; President, Global Primary Products — Growth, Energy, Bauxite, and Africa: Kenneth (Ken) Wisnoski, age 55
VP; President, North American Rolled Products: Michael G. (Mick) Wallis
President, Alcoa Europe and President, Global Primary Products Europe: Marcos Ramos, age 51
President, Growth Initiatives: Kevin B. Kramer, age 50
President, Alcoa Foundation: Paula Davis
Manager Corporate Communications: Joyce Saltzman
Auditors: PricewaterhouseCoopers LLP

LOCATIONS

HQ: Alcoa Inc.
390 Park Ave., New York, NY 10022
Phone: 212-836-2600   **Fax:** 212-836-2815
Web: www.alcoa.com

2009 Sales

	$ mil.	% of total
US	9,546	52
Australia	2,287	12
Spain	1,099	6
The Netherlands	1,002	5
Brazil	897	5
Other countries	3,608	20
Total	**18,439**	**100**

PRODUCTS/OPERATIONS

2009 Sales

	$ mil.	% of total
Flat-rolled Products	6,069	32
Primary Metals	5,252	29
Engineered Products & Solutions	4,689	25
Alumina	2,161	12
Corporate	268	2
Total	**18,439**	**100**

Selected Products

Flat-rolled products (light gauge sheet products, such as rigid container sheet and foil, for the packaging market; sheet and plate mill products for the transportation, building, and construction markets)
Primary aluminum (smelted from alumina, which is derived from bauxite)
Engineered products and solutions (aluminum wheels, forgings, castings, investment castings, fasteners)
Alumina and chemicals (bauxite, alumina, alumina-based chemicals, transportation services for bauxite and alumina)

Selected Operations

Alcoa Aluminum Deutschland, Inc.
Alcoa Europe S.A.
Alcoa Latin American Holdings Corporation
Alcoa (Shanghai) Aluminum Products Ltd.
Alcoa World Alumina — Atlantic
Alcoa World Alumina and Chemicals — Australia
Cordant Technologies Holding Company
Halco (Mining) Inc. (45%)
Howmet International Inc.
Kawneer Company

COMPETITORS

BHP Billiton
Chinalco
Corus Group
Crown Holdings
Hayes Lemmerz
Hydro Aluminium
Nippon Light Metal
Ormet
Quanex Building Products
Rio Tinto Alcan
RUSAL
Superior Industries

HISTORICAL FINANCIALS

Company Type: Public

Income Statement

FYE: December 31

	REVENUE ($ mil.)	NET INCOME ($ mil.)	NET PROFIT MARGIN	EMPLOYEES
12/09	18,439	(1,090)	—	59,000
12/08	26,901	(74)	—	87,000
12/07	30,748	2,564	8.3%	107,000
12/06	30,379	2,248	7.4%	123,000
12/05	26,159	1,235	4.7%	129,000
Annual Growth	**(8.4%)**	**—**	**—**	**(17.8%)**

2009 Year-End Financials

Debt ratio: 72.6%	No. of shares (mil.): 1,021
Return on equity: —	Dividends
Cash ($ mil.): 1,481	Yield: 1.6%
Current ratio: 1.30	Payout: —
Long-term debt ($ mil.): 8,974	Market value ($ mil.): 16,462

Stock History

NYSE: AA

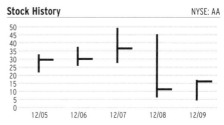

	STOCK PRICE ($) FY Close	P/E High/Low		PER SHARE ($) Earnings	Dividends	Book Value
12/09	16.12	—	—	(1.23)	0.26	12.16
12/08	11.26	—	—	(0.09)	0.68	11.49
12/07	36.55	17	10	2.95	0.68	15.68
12/06	30.01	14	10	2.57	0.60	14.33
12/05	29.57	23	16	1.40	0.60	13.10
Annual Growth	**(14.1%)**			**—**	**(18.9%)**	**(1.8%)**

Allegheny Technologies

Allegheny Technologies, Inc. (ATI) manufactures stainless and specialty steels, nickel- and cobalt-based alloys and superalloys, titanium and titanium alloys, tungsten materials, and such exotic alloys as niobium and zirconium. The company's flat-rolled products (sheet, strip, and plate) account for a great majority of its sales. Its high-performance metals unit produces metal bar, coil, foil, ingot, plate, rod, and wire. Allegheny Technologies' largest markets include aerospace, the chemical process, and oil and gas industries. Three-fourths of its sales are in the US.

After achieving record sales in 2006 and 2007 in a booming economy, ATI's sales slipped the next year and plummeted in 2009 as a global recession saddled the company with the twin burdens of low prices for its products and a slump in demand, especially of its flat-rolled products, which lost nearly half of it sales from the previous year.

To respond, ATI is working on a back-to-basics strategy — expanding its international customer base; targeting key, large customers for customized service; investing in research and development; and introducing high-value specialty products. In 2009 these products (including exotic alloys, titanium and titanium alloys, and nickel-based alloys and specialty alloys) accounted for 61% of the company's total sales (up from 42% in 2002).

Boosting its specialty products portfolio, ATI acquired the Research and Compaction Metals divisions of Crucible Materials in 2009 for about $40 million. The company won the rights to the division at auction; Crucible entered Chapter 11 bankruptcy protection earlier in 2009. ATI combined the units to form a new subsidiary called ATI Powder Metals.

ATI was formed as a result of the 1996 merger of Teledyne and stainless-steel producer Allegheny Ludlum.

HISTORY

Allegheny Ludlum Steel began in 1938 when Allegheny Steel Company (founded in Pennsylvania in 1898) and Ludlum Steel Company (founded in New Jersey in 1854) merged. Allegheny Steel veteran W. F. Detwiler became Allegheny Ludlum Steel's first chairman. During WWII the company developed heat-resisting alloys for aircraft turbine engines.

After the war the focus was on stainless steel and flat-rolled silicon electrical steel used to make electrical transformers. In 1956 the company doubled its capacity for making specialty alloys and installed the industry's first semi-automated system for working hot steel. It expanded outside the US by opening a plant in Belgium in the 1960s.

The company adopted the name Allegheny Ludlum Industries in 1970 and, after diversifying, sold its specialty steel division in a management-led buyout that formed Allegheny Ludlum Steel (1980). In 1986 it became Allegheny Ludlum Corp. It went public in 1987.

Henry Singleton and George Kozmetsky, former Litton Industries executives, invested $225,000 each in 1960 to found Teledyne to make electronic aircraft components. First year sales of $4.5 million grew to nearly $90 million by 1964. Kozmetsky left the firm in 1966.

Under Singleton, Teledyne bought more than 100 successful manufacturing and technology firms in defense-related areas such as engines, unmanned aircraft, specialty metals, and computers. Teledyne also moved into offshore oil-drilling equipment, insurance and finance, and the Water Pik line of oral-care products.

Teledyne spun off its Argonaut Insurance unit in 1986 and left the insurance business entirely with its 1990 spinoff of Unitrin. Its defense businesses were caught in a 1989 fraud probe, and the company paid $4.4 million in restitution. In 1991 Teledyne consolidated its 130 operations into 21 companies. It paid a $13 million fine in 1995 on charges of knowingly selling zirconium to a Chilean arms manufacturer for use in cluster bombs sold to Iraq.

Despite Teledyne's rebuff of holding company WHX's 1994 takeover offer, in 1996 WHX came back with a new proposal that led to the $3.2 billion merger of Teledyne and Allegheny Ludlum in 1997. Also in 1997 CEO William Rutledge was succeeded by former Allegheny Ludlum CEO Richard Simmons. Allegheny and Bethlehem Steel entered into a bidding war for steelmaker Lukens. Bethlehem won but in 1998 granted exclusive access to or sold most of Lukens' stainless-steel operations to Allegheny. The company also bought UK-based Sheffield Forgemasters Group's aerospace division and titanium producer Oregon Metallurgical.

Allegheny restructured to focus on specialty metals in 1999, changing its name to Allegheny Technologies. The company sold Ryan Aeronautical (aerial drones) to Northrop Grumman, its mining equipment business to Astec Industries, and its lift-truck-making business to Terex. It spun off its consumer oral-hygiene business as Water Pik Technologies and its remaining aerospace businesses as Teledyne Technologies. Lockheed Martin executive Thomas Corcoran became president and CEO in 1999 but abruptly resigned in late 2000. That same year the company bought Baker Hughes' tungsten carbide products unit. VC Robert Bozzone served as chairman and CEO until insider James Murdy was named CEO in 2001.

In order to cut costs, in 2001 Allegheny Technologies closed a plant in Pennsylvania, made workforce cuts, and sold its North American titanium distribution operations to management.

In 2002 the company had another round of workforce cuts (around 275 employees), mostly in its flat-rolled products unit. The following year Allegheny Technologies formed a joint venture with Russian-based VSMPO AVISMA to make a range of commercially pure titanium products.

Patrick Hassey, a retired Alcoa EVP, took over as CEO in 2003 and became chairman as well the next year.

Allegheny Technologies purchased J&L Specialty Steel, one of its competitors, for an undisclosed price in 2004. Other buys that year included two plants in Pennsylvania and Ohio from Arcelor. Still it initiated cost-cutting efforts aimed at saving $200 million a year, announcing in 2004 cuts of more than 950 jobs at Allegheny Ludlum. The plants acquired from Arcelor lost more than 300 of their workforce.

To offset rapidly rising costs in raw materials, energy, health care, and transportation, the company increased prices on several of its metal grades. Those price increases helped ATI achieve record sales in 2006 and 2007.

EXECUTIVES

LOCATIONS

HQ: Allegheny Technologies Incorporated
 1000 Six PPG Pl., Pittsburgh, PA 15222
Phone: 412-394-2800 **Fax:** 412-394-3034
Web: www.alleghenytechnologies.com

2009 Sales

	$ mil.	% of total
US	2,104.4	69
China	185.2	6
Germany	123.2	4
UK	118.5	4
Canada	114.2	4
France	91.9	3
Italy	53.8	2
India	36.2	1
Japan	33.1	1
Other countries	194.4	6
Total	**3,054.9**	**100**

PRODUCTS/OPERATIONS

2009 Sales

	$ mil.	% of total
Flat-Rolled Products	1,516.1	50
High-Performance Metals	1,300.0	42
Engineered Products	238.8	8
Total	**3,054.9**	**100**

Selected Operations and Products

Flat-Rolled Products
 Allegheny Ludlum (stainless steel, nickel-based alloys, titanium, silicon electrical steels, tool steels, high-tech alloy and titanium plate)
 Allegheny Rodney (stainless steel strip)
 Shanghai STAL Precision Stainless Steel Company Ltd. (60%, precision-rolled strip stainless steel, with Baosteel Group)
 Uniti LLC (50%, industrial titanium maker, owned jointly with the Russian metals maker VSMPO-AVISMA)

High-Performance Metals
 Allvac (nickel-based alloys and superalloys, cobalt-based alloys and superalloys, titanium and titanium-based alloys, specialty steel)
 Allvac Ltd. (UK) (nickel-based alloys and superalloys, cobalt-based alloys and superalloys, specialty steel)
 Wah Chang/Oremet (zirconium, zirconium chemicals, hafnium, niobium, tantalum, titanium and titanium-based alloys)

Engineered Products
    Casting Service (large gray iron castings, large ductile
        iron castings)
    Metalworking Products (cutting tools and tungsten
        carbide products)
    Portland Forge (carbon forgings, alloy steel forgings,
        nonferrous forgings)
    Rome Metals (processor of titanium, zirconium, nickel
        alloy, and other specialty metals)

COMPETITORS

A. M. Castle
AK Steel Holding Corporation
Carpenter Technology
Eramet
Kennametal
Nippon Steel
Nucor
Olympic Steel
Ryerson
Special Metals
ThyssenKrupp Steel
Timken
Titanium Metals
United States Steel

HISTORICAL FINANCIALS

Company Type: Public

Income Statement

FYE: December 31

	REVENUE ($ mil.)	NET INCOME ($ mil.)	NET PROFIT MARGIN	EMPLOYEES
12/09	3,055	32	1.0%	8,500
12/08	5,310	566	10.7%	9,600
12/07	5,453	747	13.7%	9,700
12/06	4,940	572	11.6%	9,500
12/05	3,540	362	10.2%	9,300
Annual Growth	(3.6%)	(45.6%)	—	(2.2%)

2009 Year-End Financials

Debt ratio: 51.6%
Return on equity: 1.6%
Cash ($ mil.): 709
Current ratio: 3.20
Long-term debt ($ mil.): 1,038

No. of shares (mil.): 99
Dividends
    Yield: 1.6%
    Payout: 225.0%
Market value ($ mil.): 4,413

Stock History

NYSE: ATI

	STOCK PRICE ($) FY Close	P/E High/Low		PER SHARE ($) Earnings	Dividends	Book Value
12/09	44.77	145	53	0.32	0.72	20.41
12/08	25.53	15	3	5.67	0.72	19.90
12/07	86.40	16	11	7.26	0.57	22.56
12/06	90.68	18	6	5.59	0.43	15.14
12/05	36.08	10	5	3.57	0.28	8.11
Annual Growth	5.5%	—	—	(45.3%)	26.6%	25.9%

Allergan, Inc.

Don't let the name fool you, Allergan can't help you with that runny nose. Instead, the company is a leading maker of eye care, skin care, and aesthetic products, including best-selling pharmaceutical Botox. Originally used to treat muscle spasms (as well as eye spasms and misalignment), Botox has found another, more popular application in diminishing facial wrinkles. Allergan's eye care products include medications for glaucoma, allergic conjunctivitis, and chronic dry eye. Skin care products include treatments for acne, wrinkles, and psoriasis. Allergan also sells implants used in breast augmentation and weight-loss surgery. Its eye care segment, featuring such products as Alphagan, Restasis, and Refresh, comprises about half of Allergan's product sales.

Allergan is focused on acquiring and developing niche pharmaceuticals, as well as discovering new uses for its existing ones to expand its market share and replace older products nearing patent expiration. As competition from other anti-wrinkle drugs ramps up, the company is eyeing new possible uses for Botox, including treatments for pain management, neuromuscular conditions, and urology conditions.

A new use for another existing drug came to Allergan's glaucoma drug Lumigan in late 2008. One of the drug's side effects turned out to be eyelash growth, so the company ran it through testing and received FDA approval for that use. Re-formulated for use on eyelashes, the drug was renamed Latisse.

Allergan also received FDA approval for Trivaris, an injectable steroid for the treatment of retinal disease, in 2008. The following year the FDA gave its nod for two more proprietary drugs: Ozurdex, another injectable retinal therapy targeting macular edema (vascular swelling of the eye), and Acuvail, an ophthalmic pain treatment for cataract surgery recovery.

To bolster its ongoing exploration of Botox (as well as some of its other products) for new conditions and to diversify its product lines ahead of patent expirations, Allergan has been actively engaged in making acquisitions and entering into licensing agreements. The company acquired private firm Esprit Pharma, which markets overactive bladder treatment Sanctura through a partnership with Indevus.

In 2010 Allergan and Serenity Pharmaceuticals made an agreement to develop and commercialize a treatment for nocturia, which causes frequent nighttime urination.

Other notable buys include acne gel treatment Aczone from struggling competitor QLT for $150 million which strengthened Allergan's dermatology portfolio, and the 2010 buy of Serica Technologies' cosmetic and reconstructive surgery unit.

Despite the slew of acquisitions, the company has also initiated some restructuring measures to combat sluggish sales. Many of Allergan's products, including Refresh, Botox Cosmetic, Juvéderm, Latisse, to a large extent the Natrelle line of breast implants, and to a lesser extent the Lap-Band System, have limited reimbursement or are not reimbursable by governmental or other health care plans and instead are partially or wholly paid for directly by the consumer, making the company particularly vulnerable to market conditions in which people are looking to cut costs.

HISTORY

In 1950 Gavin Herbert set up a small ophthalmic business above one of his drugstores in Los Angeles. Chemist Stanley Bly invented the company's first product, antihistamine eye drops called Allergan. The company adopted the name of the eye drops and expanded the business and the product range. Herbert's son Gavin Jr., then a USC student, helped with the business.

By 1960 Allergan was a $1 million company; it moved into the contact lens solution market with its Liquifilm product that year. In 1964 it developed its first foreign distributorship in Iraq, and the following year it started its first foreign subsidiary in Canada. International expansion and limited competition for hard contact lens care products sustained sales growth around 20% throughout the 1960s.

Allergan went public in 1971. During the 1970s the company became Bausch & Lomb's contractual supplier of Hydrocare lens solution and enzymatic cleaner for soft contact lenses. By 1975 Allergan had about a third of the hard contact lens care market. When Gavin Sr. died in 1978, Gavin Jr. succeeded him as president and CEO and also became chairman. By 1979 revenues topped $62 million.

SmithKline bought Allergan in 1980 just as the soft contact lens market boomed. In 1984 SmithKline acquired International Hydron, the #2 soft contact lens maker behind Bausch & Lomb; International Hydron became part of Allergan in 1987.

The next year the company acquired the rights to a botulinum toxin product called Oculinum, which would later evolve into Botox.

In 1989 SmithKline merged with Beecham and spun off Allergan.

By the early 1990s the contact lens and lens care markets had begun to mature, leading to a company restructuring and a new focus on specialty pharmaceuticals. In 1992 Allergan sold its North and South American contact lens businesses; the rest of its contact lens businesses were sold in 1993.

The company boosted its presence in the intraocular lens market with the 1994 purchase of Ioptex Research. The next year Allergan recalled about 400,000 bottles of contact lens solution because of potential eye irritation.

In 1995 Allergan acquired cataract surgery equipment maker Optical Micro Systems and the contact lens care business of Pilkington Barnes Hind. That year the government probed the company for exporting the botulism toxin in Botox — it feared the product's use in biological weapons — but did not press charges.

In 1996 it was discovered that Allergan's Botox could be used to lessen facial wrinkles.

In 1997 Allergan received approval for a handful of new products, including its multifocus eye lens for cataract patients, acne and psoriasis treatment Tazorac, and glaucoma treatment Alphagan.

The company restructured in 1998, cutting jobs and closing about half of its manufacturing plants. In 2000 Botox was approved by the FDA to treat cervical dystonia.

In 2003, Allergan bought ophthalmic drug company Oculex Pharmaceuticals, which makes the Posurdex implanted drug delivery device, and Bardeen Sciences, which had a complementary drug pipeline.

Subsidiary Advanced Medical Optics was spun off in 2004.

EXECUTIVES

Chairman Emeritus: Gavin S. Herbert, age 77
Chairman and CEO: David E. I. Pyott, age 56,
$11,994,315 total compensation
Vice Chairman: Herbert W. Boyer, age 73
President: F. Michael (Mike) Ball, age 54,
$3,912,795 total compensation
**EVP Research and Development and Chief Scientific
Officer:** Scott M. Whitcup, age 50,
$3,660,721 total compensation
EVP Finance and Business Development and CFO:
Jeffrey L. Edwards, age 49,
$3,276,384 total compensation
EVP Global Technical Operations:
Raymond H. (Ray) Diradoorian, age 52
**EVP, Chief Administrative Officer, Secretary, and Chief
Ethics Officer:** Douglas S. Ingram, age 47,
$3,121,730 total compensation
SVP and Corporate Controller: James F. Barlow, age 51
**SVP Global Development and Chief Scientific Officer,
BOTOX:** Mitchell F. Brin
SVP Treasury and Investor Relations:
James M. (Jim) Hindman
Global Corporate Communications: Caroline Van Hove
President and General Manager, Allergan Canada:
Kevin Skule
Auditors: Ernst & Young LLP

LOCATIONS

HQ: Allergan, Inc.
2525 Dupont Dr., Irvine, CA 92612
Phone: 714-246-4500   **Fax:** 714-246-6987
Web: www.allergan.com

2009 Sales

	% of total
US	65
Europe	19
Latin America	6
Asia/Pacific	6
Other regions	4
Total	**100**

PRODUCTS/OPERATIONS

2009 Sales

	$ mil.	% of total
Specialty pharmaceuticals		
Eye care pharmaceuticals	2,100.6	47
Botox/neuromodulator	1,309.6	29
Skin care	208.0	5
Urologics	65.6	1
Medical devices		
Breast aesthetics	287.5	6
Obesity intervention	258.2	6
Facial aesthetics	218.1	5
Corporate & other revenues	56.0	1
Total	**4,503.6**	**100**

Selected Products

Specialty Pharmaceuticals
Eye care
Acular (allergic conjunctivitis)
Acuvail (post-surgery pain)
Alocril (allergic conjunctivitis)
Botox (eye twitching)
Combigan (glaucoma, ocular hypertension)
Elestat (allergic conjunctivitis)
Lumigan (glaucoma)
Ozurdex (macular edema)
Pred Forte (ophthalmic anti-inflammatory)
Refresh (chronic dry eye disease)
Restasis (chronic dry eye disease)
Trivaris (corticosteroid for inflammation)
Zymar (bacterial conjunctivitis)
Neuromodular
Botox (neuromuscular disorder treatment)
Botox Cosmetic (wrinkle reduction)

Skin care
Aczone (acne treatment)
Avage (skin wrinkles or discoloration)
Azelex (acne treatment)
Clinique Medical (post-treatment creams)
Finacea (rosacea)
Fluoroplex (keratoses)
M.D. Forte (line of alpha hydroxy acid products)
Prevage (skin lines or wrinkles and protection)
Tazorac (treatment for acne and psoriasis)
Vivite (anti-aging)
Urologics
Sanctura (overactive bladder)
Medical devices
Breast Aesthetics
CUI (implants)
Inspira (implants)
Natrelle (implants)
Tissue expanders
Obesity intervention
Lap-Band (stomach implant)
Facial aesthetics
CosmoDerm and CosmoPlast (dermal filler)
Juvederm (dermal fillers)
Latisse (eyelash enhancer)
Zyderm and Zyplast (dermal fillers)

COMPETITORS

Alcon
Astellas
Bausch & Lomb
CIBA VISION
Cooper Companies
Galderma Laboratories
GlaxoSmithKline
Hoffmann-La Roche
Ipsen
Johnson & Johnson
L'Oréal
Medicis Pharmaceutical
Merck
Novartis
Nycomed US
Pfizer
Procter & Gamble
Q-Med
Sanofi-Aventis
Solta Medical
Stiefel Laboratories
Watson Pharmaceuticals

HISTORICAL FINANCIALS

Company Type: Public

Income Statement

FYE: December 31

	REVENUE ($ mil.)	NET INCOME ($ mil.)	NET PROFIT MARGIN	EMPLOYEES
12/09	4,504	624	13.9%	8,300
12/08	4,403	579	13.1%	8,740
12/07	3,939	499	12.7%	7,886
12/06	3,063	(127)	—	6,772
12/05	2,319	386	16.6%	5,055
Annual Growth	**18.0%**	**12.8%**	**—**	**13.2%**

2009 Year-End Financials

Debt ratio: 30.9%
Return on equity: 14.1%
Cash ($ mil.): 1,947
Current ratio: 3.83
Long-term debt ($ mil.): 1,491
No. of shares (mil.): 303
Dividends
Yield: 0.3%
Payout: 9.9%
Market value ($ mil.): 19,118

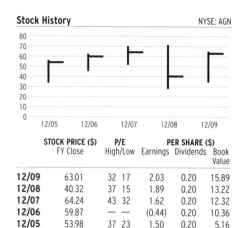

Stock History

NYSE: AGN

	STOCK PRICE ($) FY Close	P/E High/Low	PER SHARE ($) Earnings	Dividends	Book Value
12/09	63.01	32 17	2.03	0.20	15.89
12/08	40.32	37 15	1.89	0.20	13.22
12/07	64.24	43 32	1.62	0.20	12.32
12/06	59.87	— —	(0.44)	0.20	10.36
12/05	53.98	37 23	1.50	0.20	5.16
Annual Growth	3.9%	— —	7.9%	0.0%	32.5%

Alliance One International

Alliance One International keeps one eye on the world's tobacco farmers and the other eye on the cigarette makers. The company is a leading global leaf-tobacco merchant, behind its slightly larger rival Universal Corporation. Alliance One buys leaf tobacco directly from growers in about 45 countries. In 2010 Alliance One purchased more than a third of its tobacco from South American farmers. It also processes flue-cured, burley, and oriental tobaccos and sells them to large multinational cigarette and cigar manufacturers, including Philip Morris International (PMI) and Japan Tobacco, in some 90 countries. Alliance One was formed through the 2005 merger of tobacco processor DIMON and Standard Commercial.

PMI (spun off by Altria in 2008), British American Tobacco, and Japan Tobacco are currently Alliance One's three largest customers. However, Japan Tobacco in 2010 acquired a pair of leaf processors in Malawi and Brazil and formed a joint venture to obtain US tobacco leaf. The move could reduce tobacco volumes that Japan Tobacco purchases from Alliance One, as a result.

Alliance One has seen its revenue hurt by the latest trends in tobacco purchasing. While demand for tobacco in the US drops as the number of smokers decreases, more cigarette companies are choosing to buy their tobacco either directly from farmers or from merchants overseas rather than through domestic auctions. Under the direct contract buying system, the purchaser generally agrees to buy a farmer's entire crop. This is a riskier proposition for buyers because they assume the risk of matching the amount and grades of tobacco purchased with their customers' (the cigarette manufacturers) demands. If they miscalculate, they are stuck with excess inventory.

To provide its customers with a less-expensive leaf tobacco, Alliance One has expanded internationally, as prices in the US are artificially supported by the government, which has driven away foreign buyers in general. Alliance One generated some 58% of its 2010 tobacco sales in Europe while the US accounted for about 14% of its revenues. Other markets for Alliance One include Asia, Africa, Canada, Europe, Mexico, and South America.

Alliance One (then DIMON) joined other major cigarette manufacturers in settling a class-action lawsuit from tobacco farmers who alleged the company and others conspired to keep tobacco prices artificially low. The firm made no admission of guilt but agreed to pay $6 million as its share of the $200 million settlement.

HISTORY

DIMON was formed with the 1995 merger of Dibrell Brothers and Monk-Austin, two of the US's leading leaf-tobacco dealers. Founded in 1873 by Alphonso and Richard Dibrell, Dibrell Brothers bought and processed tobacco in the South and sold it in North America, expanding overseas during the 1920s. Early sales were for traditional uses such as chewing tobacco and cigars, and the company began doing business with large US cigarette makers in the early 1930s.

Publicly traded by the end of WWII, Dibrell Brothers diversified in the 1960s and 1970s, adding makers of ice-cream freezers (Richmond Cedar Works) and wooden lamps (Dunning Industries) and a chain of steakhouses (Kentucky Rib-Eye) but exited those businesses by 1990. Throughout the 1970s Dibrell Brothers established operations in Latin America, the Far East, India, and Italy. It moved into Zimbabwe in 1980 and the next year acquired B.V. Tabak Export & Import Compagnie, a Dutch tobacco firm with holdings in Brazil, the Dominican Republic, West Germany, and Zimbabwe.

In another diversification effort, Dibrell Brothers acquired 54% of Florimex Worldwide in 1987 (buying the rest during the next three years). The flower distributor helped boost sales in 1988. In the 1990s the firm's tobacco fortunes picked up with the growing demand for American-blend tobacco from countries in areas such as Eastern Europe, which previously only had access to high-tar cigarettes.

In 1995 Dibrell Brothers reached an agreement to combine with Monk-Austin, the product of a 1990 merger between tobacco firms A.C. Monk and the Austin Company. Founded by A. C. Monk in 1907, A.C. Monk & Company had interests in North Carolina tobacco plants. Subsequent members of the Monk family expanded its operations. It acquired rival Austin Company in 1990 and went public two years later. In 1993 Monk-Austin acquired tobacco trader T.S. Ragsdale; beefed up its operations in Brazil, Malawi, and Zimbabwe; and began building a tobacco processing plant in China. The company won a contract from R.J. Reynolds Tobacco in 1994 to supply all the domestic leaf tobacco that Reynolds requires.

Upon completion of the 1995 merger of Dibrell Brothers and Monk-Austin, Dibrell Brothers CEO Claude Owen became CEO of the newly formed company, DIMON Inc. Also that year the company acquired tobacco operations in Bulgaria, Greece, Italy, and Turkey and reached an agreement to buy and process leaf tobacco for Lorillard Tobacco. DIMON recorded a $30 million loss for the year, largely because of restructuring costs.

The company acquired #4 tobacco merchant Intabex Holdings Worldwide in 1997 for about $246 million. That year the firm extended its relationship with R.J. Reynolds, agreeing to

process all of its tobacco. In 1998 DIMON sold Florimex to U.S.A. Floral Products for $90 million, in part to finance debt from the purchase of Intabex. Sales were slowed that year and in 1999 by a worldwide glut of leaf tobacco.

In 1999 DIMON settled a lawsuit it had filed against Intabex's owners and management for allegedly misrepresenting its value; the purchase price was reduced by $50 million. In 2000 the company acquired Greece-based facility operator Austro-Hellenique to expand its operations in that country.

DIMON's sales decreased somewhat the next year as the company transitioned to direct contract buying (as opposed to buying tobacco at auction). In May 2005 DIMON and Standard Commercial merged and became Alliance One International. In August 2007 Brian Harker, chairman, resigned.

EXECUTIVES

Chairman, President, and CEO:
Robert E. (Pete) Harrison, age 56,
$2,688,418 total compensation
EVP and CFO: Robert A. Sheets, age 55,
$989,177 total compensation
EVP Global Operations: J. Henry Denny, age 60
EVP Business Strategy and Relationship Management:
J. Pieter Sikkel, age 46, $1,257,441 total compensation
SVP, Chief Legal Officer, and Secretary: Henry C. Babb,
age 65, $837,644 total compensation
SVP Human Resources: Michael K. McDaniel, age 60
SVP and CIO: William D. Pappas, age 57
VP Corporate Audit Services: B. Holt Ward
VP and Controller: Hampton R. Poole Jr., age 58
VP International Risk: Dennis A. Paren
VP and Treasurer: Joel L. Thomas
VP Compensation and Benefits: Laura D. Jones
Auditors: Deloitte & Touche LLP

LOCATIONS

HQ: Alliance One International, Inc.
8001 Aerial Center Pkwy., Morrisville, NC 27560
Phone: 919-379-4300   **Fax:** 919-379-4346
Web: www.aointl.com

2010 Sales

	$ mil.	% of total
Belgium	491.0	21
US	323.5	14
Russia	132.6	6
China	129.8	6
Netherlands	123.7	5
Germany	121.0	5
Indonesia	73.4	3
Other	913.2	40
Total	**2,308.3**	**100**

PRODUCTS/OPERATIONS

2010 Sales

	$ mil.	% of total
Sales & other operating revenues	2,238.1	97
Processing & other revenues	70.2	3
Total	**2,308.3**	**100**

COMPETITORS

Altadis
British American Tobacco
Japan Tobacco
Universal Corporation

HISTORICAL FINANCIALS

Company Type: Public

Income Statement				FYE: March 31
	REVENUE ($ mil.)	NET INCOME ($ mil.)	NET PROFIT MARGIN	EMPLOYEES
3/10	2,308	80	3.5%	5,000
3/09	2,258	133	5.9%	4,400
3/08	2,012	17	0.8%	4,700
3/07	1,979	(21)	—	4,700
3/06	2,113	(447)	—	5,400
Annual Growth	**2.2%**	**—**	**—**	**(1.9%)**

2010 Year-End Financials

Debt ratio: 202.1%	No. of shares (mil.): 97
Return on equity: 22.3%	Dividends
Cash ($ mil.): 130	Yield: 0.0%
Current ratio: 2.35	Payout: —
Long-term debt ($ mil.): 789	Market value ($ mil.): 495

Stock History

NYSE: AOI

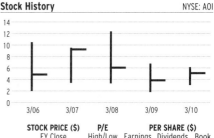

	STOCK PRICE ($) FY Close	P/E High/Low		PER SHARE ($) Earnings	Dividends	Book Value
3/10	5.09	8	4	0.78	0.00	4.02
3/09	3.84	4	1	1.49	0.00	3.36
3/08	6.04	64	18	0.19	0.00	2.18
3/07	9.23	—	—	(0.25)	0.00	2.32
3/06	4.86	—	—	(5.51)	0.10	2.20
Annual Growth	**1.2%**	**—**	**—**	**—**	**—**	**16.2%**

Alliant Techsystems

Space is not the final frontier for Alliant Techsystems (ATK), as long as its aerospace offerings are paving new paths for the company's technological endeavors. ATK is a leading manufacturer of solid-propulsion rocket motors, force protection systems, laser warning systems, and strategic and defense missiles. ATK builds motors for unmanned space launch vehicles such as the Trident II and the Delta II. ATK is also a top supplier of ammunition — from small-caliber rounds to tank ammunition — to the US and its allies. Additional lethal offerings include anti-tank mines, aircraft weapons systems, and high-tech weapons components. The US government accounts for more than 60% of sales.

Significant customers include the US Army, US Air Force, US Navy, and NASA. Expanding its customer base to state and municipal sectors, the company provides the Speer and Federal Premium branded ammunition to law enforcement agencies. It courts commercial customers with a lineup of sport shooting accessories, through the RCBS and Weaver brands, as well as reloading equipment, smokeless powder, and gun care products, among others.

Looking to expand its presence in the growing domestic and international security market, in

April 2010 ATK purchased Blackhawk Products Group, giving the company a recognized brand of tactical gear and a track record in product design and development. The deal builds upon its 2009 acquisition of Eagle Industries, which established ATK's expertise as a maker of nylon gear and equipment. Combined, the two companies form the core of ATK's Security and Sporting group.

Partnerships are also on ATK's radar. In 2010 the company announced a partnership with Lockheed Martin to upgrade and operate small satellite launchers, a new business for ATK. The deal is part of the company's strategy to woo new customers for its solid-rocket booster business, which has been used primarily to launch the soon-to-be-retired space shuttles.

ATK's investment in research and development focuses on durable, lightweight composite materials that promise to lower the cost and improve performance of aircraft. In addition, its introduction of missile and laser warning systems (AN/AAR-47) is gaining approval for use on military aircraft.

In 2009 ATK's chairman and CEO Dan Murphy resigned for personal reasons. General Ron Fogleman was named chairman. Fogleman is a company director with an impressive Pentagon resume. Mark DeYoung, a 25-year ATK veteran, took the helm as president and CEO in 2010.

HISTORY

Alliant Techsystems (ATK) was formed in 1990 when Honeywell spun off its defense-related businesses to shareholders. Honeywell's roots in the defense business go back to 1941, when it was known as Honeywell-Minnesota. A maker of consumer electronics products such as switches, buttons, and appliances, Honeywell joined the war effort and began producing tank periscopes, turbo engine regulators, automatic ammunition firing control devices, and automatic bomb-release systems.

After WWII Honeywell-Minnesota found that the Cold War provided a reliable and profitable income stream for defense contractors. By 1964 the company had focused on electronics systems. Provisions for the Vietnam War boosted sales, but the fall of Saigon led to downsizing.

When the Iron Curtain fell in the late 1980s, Honeywell's defense operations misfired and ran up huge losses. Honeywell sought to sell its defense businesses as an independent subsidiary, but was unable to obtain an acceptable bid.

Honeywell spun off Alliant Techsystems to shareholders in 1990 under Toby Warson, the CEO of Honeywell's UK subsidiary. A former naval commander, Warson began with about 8,300 employees and lots of bureaucratic layers; he quickly cut about 800 administrative jobs.

Although the Soviet Union and its Eastern Bloc allies had collapsed, a new threat raised its head: Iraq. Cutbacks in the defense budget meant that advanced high-dollar systems were put on the back burner while cheaper alternatives, such as improved ammunition, were moved to the front. During the Gulf War, ATK's ordnance contributions included 120mm uranium-tipped anti-tank shells, 25mm shells for the Bradley Fighting Vehicle, and the 30mm bullets used by Apache helicopters and A-10 Warthog anti-tank planes.

Warson cut another 800 jobs after the Gulf War and reduced the number of management layers from 14 to seven. ATK divested its only non-munitions unit, Metrum Information Storage (data recording and storage devices), in 1992. Metrum had incurred setbacks that caused the company to write off millions of dollars. ATK expanded into additional aerospace markets and achieved vertical integration in propellant production in 1995 with the purchase of the aerospace division of Hercules Incorporated, a maker of space rocket motors, strategic and tactical weapons systems, and ordnance.

ATK refocused on its core operations in 1997 and jettisoned its marine systems group (torpedoes, underwater surveillance systems). The next year the company was awarded a $1 billion contract to make components for Boeing's Delta IV rockets. In 1999 chairman and CEO Dick Schwartz retired from the company and was replaced by retired Navy admiral Paul David Miller.

Miller consolidated plants, improved manufacturing processes, and bought back more than 1.3 million shares of ATK's stock in 2000. While the conventional munitions segment posted slight sales declines that year, primarily due to reduced sales of tactical tank ammunition as the US Army transitioned into the next-generation tank round, Miller's efforts led to greater company profitability. In 2001 ATK acquired Thiokol Propulsion Corp. In September Alliant bought the defense unit of Safety Components International that makes metallic belt links for ammunition. In December the company added another acquisition to the mix with the purchase of the ammunitions unit of Blount International.

In 2003 Dan Murphy became CEO, with Miller remaining as chairman. (Miller retired in 2005 and Murphy assumed that role, as well.)

Acquisitions in 2004 included national security specialist Mission Research Corporation (now ATK Mission Research), and PSI Group, a maker of propellant systems and satellite parts.

In 2006 Alliant sold its lithium battery business to EnerSys for an undisclosed sum. The following year, the company bought Swales Aerospace, a provider of satellite components and small spacecraft, as it continued to diversify into the space business.

EXECUTIVES

Chairman: Gen. Ronald R. (Ron) Fogelman, age 68
President, CEO, and Director: Mark W. DeYoung, age 51, $2,440,772 total compensation
SVP Washington Operations: Steven J. Cortese, age 48, $1,070,639 total compensation
SVP, General Counsel, and Secretary: Keith D. Ross, age 53, $1,322,856 total compensation
SVP and CFO: John L. Shroyer, age 46, $1,683,427 total compensation
SVP; President, Armament Systems: Karen Davies, age 51
SVP; President, Aerospace Systems: Blake E. Larson, age 50, $1,445,409 total compensation
SVP; President, Security and Sporting: Ronald P. (Ron) Johnson, age 47
SVP Business Development: Jay Tibbets
SVP Human Resources and Administrative Services: Paula J. Patineau, age 56
SVP Communications and Investor Relations: Mark L. Mele, age 53

VP and General Manager, ATK Advanced Weapons: Bruce DeWitt
VP Corporate Development: Michael B. Dolby, age 49
VP Communications, ATK Aerospace Systems: George Torres
VP and General Manager, ATK Small Caliber Systems: Mark Hissong
VP and Regional Director, Middle East and Africa: Robert C. Faille Jr.
VP Investor Relations and Treasurer: Steven P. (Steve) Wold
VP Corporate Communications: Bryce Hallowell
Director Investor Relations: Jeff Huebschen
Auditors: Deloitte & Touche LLP

LOCATIONS

HQ: Alliant Techsystems Inc.
7480 Flying Cloud Dr., Minneapolis, MN 55344
Phone: 952-351-3000   **Fax:** 952-351-3009
Web: www.atk.com

PRODUCTS/OPERATIONS

2010 Sales

	$ mil.	% of total
Armament Systems	2,164.7	45
Space Systems	1,373.9	29
Mission Systems	1,269.1	26
Total	**4,807.7**	**100**

2010 Sales by Customer

	% of total
US Army	28
NASA	18
US Navy	11
US Air Force	7
Other US government	5
Commercial & foreign	31
Total	**100**

COMPETITORS

Aerojet	Lockheed Martin
Allied Defense Group	Lockheed Martin Missiles
BAE Systems Inc.	Metal Storm
Boeing	Nexter
DAC Technologies	Northrop Grumman
E'Prime Aerospace	Olin
GenCorp	Raytheon
General Dynamics	SpaceDev
ITT Corp.	Teledyne Technologies
Kaman Aerospace	

HISTORICAL FINANCIALS

Company Type: Public

Income Statement

FYE: March 31

	REVENUE ($ mil.)	NET INCOME ($ mil.)	NET PROFIT MARGIN	EMPLOYEES
3/10	4,808	279	5.8%	18,000
3/09	4,583	155	3.4%	19,000
3/08	4,172	222	5.3%	17,000
3/07	3,565	184	5.2%	16,000
3/06	3,217	154	4.8%	15,200
Annual Growth	**10.6%**	**16.0%**	**—**	**4.3%**

2010 Year-End Financials

Debt ratio: 172.8%
Return on equity: 39.4%
Cash ($ mil.): 394
Current ratio: 2.18
Long-term debt ($ mil.): 1,380

No. of shares (mil.): 33
Dividends
  Yield: —
  Payout: —
Market value ($ mil.): 2,687

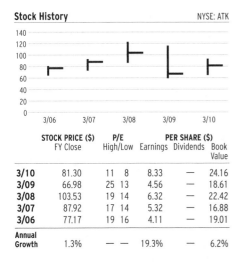

Stock History
NYSE: ATK

	STOCK PRICE ($) FY Close	P/E High/Low		PER SHARE ($) Earnings	Dividends	Book Value
3/10	81.30	11	8	8.33	—	24.16
3/09	66.98	25	13	4.56	—	18.61
3/08	103.53	19	14	6.32	—	22.42
3/07	87.92	17	14	5.32	—	16.88
3/06	77.17	19	16	4.11	—	19.01
Annual Growth	**1.3%**	**—**	**—**	**19.3%**	**—**	**6.2%**

The Allstate Corporation

Ya gotta hand it to Allstate. The "good hands" company has managed to work its way to the top of the insurance pile. The company is the second-largest personal lines insurer in the US, just behind rival State Farm. Its Allstate Protection segment sells auto, homeowners, property/casualty, and life insurance products in Canada and the US. Allstate Financial provides life insurance through subsidiaries Allstate Life, American Heritage Life, and Lincoln Benefit Life. It also provides investment products, targeting affluent and middle-income consumers. Allstate Motor Club provides emergency road service and, adding to its repertoire, the company also offers the nationwide online Allstate Bank.

Allstate has rolled together all of its property/casualty operations to form Allstate Protection, and bundled all of its life insurance, annuities, and banking services into Allstate Financial. Selling primarily private passenger auto and homeowners insurance, Allstate Protection accounts for some 90% of total premiums.

Allstate maintains a network of about 12,300 exclusive agencies which sell its Allstate-branded insurance products. Independent agencies sell the company's Deerbrook and Encompass-branded products as well as its Allstate lines. Consumers can also purchase some products by telephone and over the Internet. Its financial products are sold through its exclusive agencies, independent agents, banks, and broker dealers.

The company has disposed of the majority of its operations outside North America (including Allstate Investments in Japan and the direct auto business in Germany and Italy), focusing on its core markets in Canada and the US.

Despite trying to slim down and refocus, as the US economy weakened, Allstate Financial suffered right alongside its financial services brethren, taking a loss of $1.72 billion in 2008. However, when the US Treasury offered Allstate a piece of the Troubled Asset Relief Program in 2009, the insurer politely turned it down citing its strong capital and liquidity. Instead the company has undergone a number of initiatives to reduce its financial risk, especially in the area of natural catastrophes.

After racking up billions of dollars worth of losses in the wake of Hurricanes Katrina, Rita, Wilma, Ike, and Gustav, and to brace itself for future hurricane seasons, the company has upped its reinsurance and has stopped writing new homeowners policies for properties along the Gulf Coast, Connecticut, Delaware, and New Jersey. The company has also increased its premium rates in Florida. To address the many Allstate Floridian customers whose homeowner policies wouldn't be renewed, the company struck an agreement with Royal Palm Insurance Company. Royal Palm offers property policies, sold through Allstate agencies.

Customers in earthquake-prone areas now also must look elsewhere for new optional earthquake coverage. Allstate no longer offers it, and in California the company has made changes to its homeowners underwriting requirements in order to reduce its exposure to claims for fires following earthquakes.

HISTORY

Allstate traces its origins to a friendly game of bridge played in 1930 on a Chicago-area commuter train by Sears president Robert Wood and a friend, insurance broker Carl Odell. The insurance man suggested Sears sell auto insurance through the mail. Wood liked the idea, financed the company, and in 1931 put Odell in charge (that hand of bridge must have shown Wood that Odell was no dummy). The company was named Allstate, after one of Sears' tire brands. Allstate was born just as Sears was beginning its push into retailing, and Allstate went with it, selling insurance out of all the new Sears stores.

Growth was slow during the Depression and WWII, but the postwar boom was a gold mine for both Sears and Allstate. Suburban development made cars a necessity; 1950s prudence necessitated car insurance; and Sears made it easy to buy the insurance at their stores and, increasingly, at freestanding agencies.

In the late 1950s Allstate added home and other property/casualty insurance lines. It also went into life insurance — in-force policies zoomed from zero to $1 billion in six years, the industry's fastest growth ever.

Sears formed Allstate Enterprises in 1960 as an umbrella for all its noninsurance operations. In 1970 that firm bought its first savings and loan (S&L). The insurer continued to acquire other S&Ls and to add subsidiaries throughout the 1970s and 1980s.

This strategy dovetailed with Sears' strategy, which was to become a diversified financial services company. In 1985 Sears introduced the Discover Card through Allstate's Greenwood Trust Company. However, by the late 1980s it was obvious Sears would never be a financial services giant. Moreover, it was losing so much in retailing that by 1987 Allstate was the major contributor to corporate net income. Sears began to dismantle its financial empire in the 1990s.

Allstate also suffered from a backlash against high insurance rates. When Massachusetts instituted no-fault insurance in 1989, Allstate stopped writing new auto insurance there. Later the company had to refund $110 million to customers to settle a suit with California over rate rollbacks required by 1988's Proposition 103.

Allstate went public in 1993, when Sears sold about 20% of its stake. That year it began reducing its operations in Florida to protect itself against high losses from hurricanes. Two years later the retailer sold its remaining interest to its shareholders. Also in 1995 Allstate sold 70% of PMI, its mortgage insurance unit, to the public.

In 1996 Allstate worked to reduce its exposure to hurricane and earthquake losses. (Together, Hurricane Andrew and the Northridge quake helped account for almost $4 billion in casualty losses.) It created a Florida-only subsidiary that would buy reinsurance to protect against losses that could arise from another major hurricane.

In 1998 Allstate sold its real estate portfolio for nearly $1 billion and opened a savings bank. In 2000 Allstate restructured, cutting some 10% of its staff (some 4,000 jobs) and turning its agents into independent contractors.

In coastal counties of New York, Allstate attempted to limit homeowner policies by only renewing the policies of customers who also held other types of insurance with the company. The New York Insurance Superintendent found the company to be in violation with the state's insurance laws in mid-2007 and pressured Allstate to offer quotes to more than 55,000 former customers who had been dropped.

EXECUTIVES

Chairman, President, and CEO: Thomas J. Wilson II, age 52, $10,420,560 total compensation
SVP and Chief Marketing Officer, Allstate Insurance: Mark R. LaNeve, age 50
SVP and General Counsel; SVP, General Counsel, and Assistant Secretary, Allstate Insurance: Michele Coleman Mayes, age 60, $2,456,017 total compensation
SVP and Chief Investment Officer, Allstate Insurance: Judith P. (Judy) Greffin, age 49, $3,232,770 total compensation
SVP and CIO, Allstate Insurance: Catherine S. Brune, age 56
VP and CFO; SVP and CFO, Allstate Insurance: Don Civgin, age 48, $2,636,726 total compensation
VP Internal Audit, Allstate Insurance: Kathleen Swain, age 49
SVP Sales and Customer Service, Allstate Insurance: Joseph J. Richardson Jr., age 49
SVP Human Resources, Allstate Insurance: James D. DeVries, age 46
SVP Corporate Relations, Allstate Insurance: Joan H. Walker, age 62
SVP Claims, Allstate Insurance: Michael J. Roche, age 58
SVP Product Operations, Allstate Insurance: Steven P. Sorenson, age 45
President, Allstate Protection; SVP, Allstate Insurance: Joseph P. (Joe) Lacher Jr., age 40
President and CEO, Allstate Financial; SVP, Allstate Insurance: Matthew E. (Matt) Winter, age 53
Managing Director and Chief Risk Officer, Allstate Investments: Peruvemba Satish, age 45
Auditors: Deloitte & Touche LLP

LOCATIONS

HQ: The Allstate Corporation
2775 Sanders Rd., Northbrook, IL 60062
Phone: 847-402-5000   **Fax:** 866-532-3029
Web: www.allstate.com

PRODUCTS/OPERATIONS

2009 Sales

	$ mil.	% of total
Property/liability insurance premiums	26,194	81
Net investment income	4,444	13
Life & annuity premiums & contract charges	1,958	6
Realized capital gains & losses	(583)	—
Total	**32,013**	**100**

2009 Premiums

	% of total
Standard auto	64
Homeowners	23
Non-standard auto	4
Other personal lines	9
Total	**100**

Selected Subsidiaries

Allstate Bank
Allstate Insurance Company of Canada
Allstate Life Insurance Company
Deerbrook Insurance Company
Encompass Insurance Company
Kennett Capital, Inc.
Lincoln Benefit Life Company
Northbrook Indemnity Company
Pafco Insurance Company (Canada)
Pembridge America Inc.
Roadway Protection Auto Club, Inc.
Sterling Collision Centers, Inc.

COMPETITORS

Chubb Corp
Farmers Group
GEICO
Hanover Insurance
The Hartford
MetLife
Nationwide
Progressive Corporation
Prudential
State Farm
Torchmark
Travelers Companies
USAA

HISTORICAL FINANCIALS

Company Type: Public

Income Statement

FYE: December 31

	ASSETS ($ mil.)	NET INCOME ($ mil.)	INCOME AS % OF ASSETS	EMPLOYEES
12/09	132,652	854	0.6%	36,800
12/08	134,798	(1,679)	—	38,900
12/07	156,408	4,636	3.0%	38,000
12/06	157,554	4,900	3.1%	37,900
12/05	156,072	1,752	1.1%	38,300
Annual Growth	(4.0%)	(16.4%)	—	(1.0%)

2009 Year-End Financials

Equity as % of assets: 12.6%
Return on assets: 0.6%
Return on equity: 5.8%
Long-term debt ($ mil.): 5,910
No. of shares (mil.): 538
Dividends
Yield: 2.7%
Payout: 50.6%
Market value ($ mil.): 16,159
Sales ($ mil.): 32,013

Stock History

NYSE: ALL

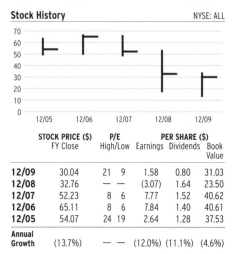

	STOCK PRICE ($) FY Close	P/E High	P/E Low	PER SHARE ($) Earnings	PER SHARE ($) Dividends	PER SHARE ($) Book Value
12/09	30.04	21	9	1.58	0.80	31.03
12/08	32.76	—	—	(3.07)	1.64	23.50
12/07	52.23	8	6	7.77	1.52	40.62
12/06	65.11	8	6	7.84	1.40	40.61
12/05	54.07	24	19	2.64	1.28	37.53
Annual Growth	(13.7%)	—	—	(12.0%)	(11.1%)	(4.6%)

Altria Group

The house the Marlboro Man built, Altria Group, owns the largest cigarette company in the US. Altria operates its cigarette business through subsidiary Philip Morris USA, which sells Marlboro — the world's best-selling cigarette brand since 1972. Altria controls about half of the US tobacco market. It manufactures cigarettes under the Parliament, Virginia Slims, and Basic cigarette brands. While still firmly hooked on cigarettes, Altria is transitioning from primarily a cigarette manufacturer to a purveyor of a variety of tobacco products, including cigars and smokeless tobacco products. It has made a number of strategic acquisitions, including smokeless tobacco maker UST in early 2009.

The all-cash purchase of UST was worth more than $11 billion. Purchasing UST brought popular brands Copenhagen and Skoal into Altria's fold and gave the company a leading position in the smokeless tobacco market. Also part of the UST deal, Altria acquired UST's machine-made cigar operation, as well as its Ste. Michelle Wine Estates. (Other liquid holdings include a 27% stake in brewer SABMiller.)

As a premium brand, Marlboro has long been a profit driver for Philip Morris. But a decline in the brand's popularity among younger smokers (ages 18 to 25) has Altria and investors worried because Marlboro accounts for about 70% of Altria's operating income. In response, Altria is introducing new versions of Marlboro (some lower priced) designed to widen its appeal among younger smokers.

A given in an industry that peddles dangerous products, Altria is in a haze over lawsuits, with about 125 cases pending as of early 2010. Altria and its Big Tobacco rivals continue to try to resolve lawsuits over smoking-related illnesses, which account for the majority of cases pending against Philip Morris and Altria. The industry has reached settlements with US states amounting to nearly $250 billion, and a number of civil suits are pending.

Historic legislation enacted in 2009 turned over the regulation of tobacco products to the U.S. Food and Drug Administration, which will now have unprecedented authority to regulate tobacco products, including marketing, labeling, and nicotine content. Altria has pledged to work constructively with the FDA and supported the passage of the legislation.

HISTORY

Philip Morris opened his London tobacco store in 1847 and by 1854 was making his own cigarettes. Morris died in 1873, and his heirs sold the firm to William Thomson just before the turn of the century. Thomson introduced his company's cigarettes to the US in 1902. American investors bought the rights to leading Philip Morris brands in 1919, and in 1925 the new company, Philip Morris & Co., introduced Marlboro, which targeted women smokers and produced modest sales.

When the firm's larger competitors raised their prices in 1930, Philip Morris Companies countered by introducing inexpensive cigarettes that caught on with Depression-weary consumers. By 1936 it was the fourth-biggest cigarette maker.

The firm acquired Benson & Hedges in 1954. It signed ad agency Leo Burnett, which promptly initiated the Marlboro Man campaign. Under Joseph Cullman (who became president in 1957), Philip Morris experienced tremendous growth overseas. After dipping to sixth place among US tobacco companies in 1960, it rebounded at home, thanks to Marlboro's growing popularity among men (Marlboro became the #1 cigarette brand in the world in 1972).

In 1970 Philip Morris bought the nation's seventh-largest brewer, Miller Brewing, and with aggressive marketing it vaulted to #2 among US beer makers by 1980. To protect itself against a shrinking US tobacco market, in 1985 Philip Morris paid $5.6 billion for General Foods (Kool-Aid, Post, Stove Top). In 1988 it bought Kraft (Miracle Whip, Velveeta). The next year Philip Morris joined Kraft with General Foods.

In 1994 Australian Geoffrey Bible became CEO. By late 1998 the company and its rivals had settled tobacco litigation with most states, agreeing to pay about $250 billion over 25 years to receive protection from further state suits.

In 1999 the US government filed a massive lawsuit against Big Tobacco, and Philip Morris admitted — no kidding — that smoking increases the risk of getting cancer and other illnesses. In 2000 Philip Morris vowed to appeal after a state court awarded $74 billion in punitive damages to Florida smokers. The court later ruled that Philip Morris, Lorillard, and the Liggett Group would pay at least $709 million in the case regardless of the outcome.

In December 2000 Philip Morris completed its purchase of Nabisco Holdings for $18.9 billion. In June 2001 Philip Morris spun off Kraft Foods in what was the second-largest IPO in US history; it retained an 84% stake in the company and 97% of the voting rights.

In April 2002 CFO Louis Camilleri succeeded Bible as CEO; in September Camilleri became chairman upon Bible's retirement. In July 2002 Philip Morris sold Miller Brewing to South African Breweries for $5.6 billion ($3.6 billion in SAB stock and the assumption of $2 billion in Miller debt) in July 2002.

In the ongoing saga of tobacco-related litigation, Philip Morris said it would appeal an October 2002 verdict by a California jury that ordered the company to pay $28 billion in punitive damages (later reduced to $28 million). In January 2003 Philip Morris changed its name to Altria Group in an effort to distance itself from its tobacco litigation. In April a Florida appeals court threw out the state's multibillion-dollar judgment (made in 2000) against Philip Morris USA and four other US tobacco companies.

In 2003 Philip Morris USA lost an Illinois lawsuit, which claimed the company's use of the word "light" was misleading and violated Illinois consumer fraud laws. The judge ordered Philip Morris USA to pay damages of $10 billion and post a $12 billion bond. The Illinois Supreme Court has lowered the bond to $7 billion and agreed to hear Philip Morris USA's appeal.

In mid-2006 Altria unseated Roger Deromedi from Kraft's top spot and appointed Irene Rosenfeld to head the company. The executive realignment was part of Altria's plan to spin off Kraft.

In 2007 Altria completed the spinoff of Kraft Foods to Altria shareholders. A year later Altria spun off its Philip Morris International arm, also to shareholders, and moved its headquarters from New York City's Park Avenue to Richmond, Virginia.

EXECUTIVES

Chairman and CEO: Michael E. (Mike) Szymanczyk, age 61, $12,444,162 total compensation
EVP Strategy and Business Development: Howard A. Willard III, age 46
EVP and CFO: David R. (Dave) Beran, age 55, $7,681,326 total compensation
EVP and CTO: John R. (Jack) Nelson, age 58, $4,137,107 total compensation
EVP: Craig A. Johnson, age 57, $3,966,717 total compensation
EVP and General Counsel: Denise F. Keane, age 58, $5,502,197 total compensation
EVP and CFO, Ste. Michelle Wine Estates: Sheila A. Newlands
EVP and Chief Compliance and Administrative Officer: Martin J. Barrington, age 56, $6,077,190 total compensation
EVP Sales and Marketing, Ste. Michelle Wine Estates: Glenn D. Yaffa
SVP Marketing, Altria Client Services: Nancy B. Lund, age 57
SVP Human Resources and Compliance, Altria Client Services: Charles (Charlie) Whitaker
SVP Human Resources, Altria Client Services: Kevin Benner
President and CEO, Philip Morris Capital Corporation: John Mulligan
President and CEO, John Middleton: Craig Schwartz
President and CEO, Philip Morris USA Inc.: William F. (Billy) Gifford Jr., age 39
President and CEO, Ste. Michelle Wine Estates: Theodor P. (Ted) Baseler, age 55
President and CEO, U.S. Smokeless Tobacco Company: Peter P. Paoli
Corporate Secretary and Senior Assistant General Counsel: W. Hildebrandt (Brandt) Surgner
Auditors: PricewaterhouseCoopers LLP

LOCATIONS

HQ: Altria Group, Inc.
6601 W. Broad St., Richmond, VA 23230
Phone: 804-274-2200   **Fax:** 804-484-8231
Web: www.altria.com

PRODUCTS/OPERATIONS

2009 Sales

	$ mil.	% of total
Cigarettes	20,919	89
Smokeless products	1,366	6
Cigars	520	2
Wine	403	2
Financial services	348	1
Excise taxes of products	(6,732)	—
Total	**16,824**	**100**

Selected Subsidiaries

John Middleton Co.
Philip Morris Capital Corp.
Philip Morris USA Inc.
Ste. Michelle Wine Estates Ltd.
U.S. Smokeless Tobacco Company LLC

COMPETITORS

Altadis	Loews
Anheuser-Busch	Lorillard
Anheuser-Busch InBev	Molson Coors
British American Tobacco	North Atlantic Trading
Constellation Brands	Ravenswood Winery
E. & J. Gallo	Reynolds American
Foster's Americas	Sebastiani Vineyards
Heineken	Swedish Match
Japan Tobacco	Vector Group

HISTORICAL FINANCIALS

Company Type: Public

Income Statement

FYE: December 31

	REVENUE ($ mil.)	NET INCOME ($ mil.)	NET PROFIT MARGIN	EMPLOYEES
12/09	16,824	3,208	19.1%	10,000
12/08	15,957	4,930	30.9%	10,400
12/07	38,051	9,786	25.7%	84,000
12/06	70,324	12,022	17.1%	175,000
12/05	68,920	10,435	15.1%	199,000
Annual Growth	(29.7%)	(25.5%)	—	(52.7%)

2009 Year-End Financials

Debt ratio: 274.9%	No. of shares (mil.): 2,084
Return on equity: 93.0%	Dividends
Cash ($ mil.): 1,871	Yield: 6.7%
Current ratio: 0.72	Payout: 85.7%
Long-term debt ($ mil.): 11,185	Market value ($ mil.): 40,908

Stock History

NYSE: MO

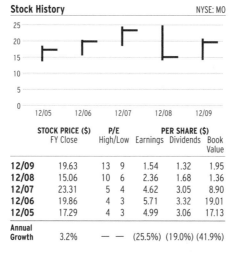

	STOCK PRICE ($) FY Close	P/E High	P/E Low	Earnings	Dividends	Book Value
12/09	19.63	13	9	1.54	1.32	1.95
12/08	15.06	10	6	2.36	1.68	1.36
12/07	23.31	5	4	4.62	3.05	8.90
12/06	19.86	4	3	5.71	3.32	19.01
12/05	17.29	4	3	4.99	3.06	17.13
Annual Growth	3.2%	—	—	(25.5%)	(19.0%)	(41.9%)

Amazon.com

What started as Earth's biggest bookstore has rapidly become Earth's biggest anything store. Expansion has propelled Amazon.com in innumerable directions. Its website offers millions of books, music, and movies (which account for most of its sales), not to mention auto parts, toys, electronics, home furnishings, apparel, health and beauty aids, prescription drugs, and groceries. Shoppers can download e-books, games, MP3s, and films to their computers or handheld devices, including Amazon's own portable reader, the Kindle. Amazon also offers products and services, such as self-publishing, online advertising, e-commerce platform, and a co-branded credit card. The firm acquired Zappos.com in 2009.

Aside from its investment in apparel and footwear retailing, Amazon has been going toe-to-toe with booksellers, stirring up interest (and boosting its revenues) with its Kindle reader and selection of more than 500,000 electronic book titles. Rivals of the Kindle include the Sony Reader, Apple iPad, and Barnes & Noble Nook. Those companies as well as Simon & Schuster and Borders Group are also competing with Amazon for e-book sales. Pricing for e-books has proven to be a thorny issue, however. In

2010 Amazon agreed to halt heavy discounting of titles from Simon & Schuster, Macmillan, and others ahead of the iPad launch. The concern, however, is that if control over pricing shifts from Amazon to the publisher, the Internet retailer could lose its cost-cutting advantage.

Amazon also has engaged Wal-Mart.com in pricing battles over books, movies, electronics, and toys in an effort to win over bargain hunters during the economic downturn.

As an online retailer, Amazon has transformed itself over the years by expanding the scope of its offerings. From its core segment of entertainment products (books, music, and movies), the company has expanded its marketplace to include just about everything else. The merchandise it features is purchased for resale from vendors, and hundreds of third-party sellers (individuals and retailers like The Gap, Nordstrom, and Lands' End) also peddle their wares on Amazon.com.

The company acquired digital audiobooks publisher Audible for about $300 million in early 2008. Later in 2008 Amazon purchased Abe-Books, an online retailer of more than 110 million primarily used, rare, and out-of-print books.

The company beefed up its digital offerings in 2008 with the launch of Amazon Video On Demand, a service that gives customers the option to stream or download ad-free digital movies and TV shows on Macs or PCs. Amazon also owns The Internet Movie Database, one of the Web's top information sites for historical movie and television research.

Bezos owns about 20% of the firm.

HISTORY

Jeff Bezos was researching the Internet in the early 1990s for hedge fund D.E. Shaw. He realized that book sales would be a perfect fit with e-commerce because book distributors already kept meticulous electronic lists. Bezos, who as a teen had dreamed of entrepreneurship in outer space, took the idea to Shaw. The company passed on the idea, but Bezos ran with it, trekking cross country to Seattle (close to a facility owned by major book distributor Ingram) and typing up a business plan along the way.

Bezos founded Amazon.com in 1994. After months of preparation, he launched a website in July 1995 (Douglas Hofstadter's *Fluid Concepts and Creative Analogies* was its first sale); it had sales of $20,000 a week by September. Bezos and his team kept working with the site, pioneering features that now seem mundane, such as one-click shopping, customer reviews, and e-mail order verification.

Amazon.com went public in 1997. Moves to cement the Amazon.com brand included becoming the sole book retailer on AOL's website and Netscape's commercial channel.

In 1998 the company launched its online music and video stores, and it began to sell toys and electronics. Amazon.com also expanded its European reach with the purchases of online booksellers in the UK and Germany, and it acquired the Internet Movie Database.

By midyear Amazon.com had attracted so much attention that its market capitalization equaled the combined values of profitable bricks-and-mortar rivals Barnes & Noble and Borders Group, even though their combined sales were far greater than the upstart's. Late that year Amazon.com formed a promotional link with Hoover's, publisher of this profile.

Amazon.com began conducting online auctions in early 1999 and partnered with venerable auction house Sotheby's. In 2000 Amazon.com inked a 10-year deal with Toysrus.com to set up a co-branded toy and video game store. (The partnership came to a bitter end in 2006 after Toys "R" Us sued Amazon.com when it began selling toys from other companies.) Also that year Amazon.com added foreign-language sites for France and Japan.

In 2001 Amazon.com cut 15% of its workforce as part of a restructuring plan that also forced a $150 million charge. In 2002 the firm introduced clothing sales, featuring hundreds of retailers including names such as The Gap, Nordstrom, and Lands' End.

The company launched its Search Inside the Book feature in 2003. The tool allows customers to search the text inside books for more relevant search returns. At launch, the search feature covered more than 120,000 books from over 190 publishers. Amazon.com expanded into China in 2004 with the purchase of Joyo.com. The company acquired shopping site Shopbop.com in 2006, boosting its apparel offerings. In November the Internet book seller introduced an electronic portable book reader called the Kindle ($399).

In May 2008 Amazon invested in The Talk Market, a user-generated TV Shopping Channel. In June the firm launched an online office supplies store and sewed up the acquisition of the online fabrics retailer Fabrics.com.

In June 2009 Amazon agreed to pay Toys "R" Us $51 million to settle a dispute dating back to 2004. The settlement was related to a partnership that gave the toy seller exclusive rights to supply some of the toys on Amazon's site. In November Amazon completed its $888 million acquisition of shoe e-tailer Zappos.com.

EXECUTIVES

Chairman, President, and CEO: Jeffrey P. (Jeff) Bezos, age 46, $1,781,840 total compensation
SVP Worldwide Operations: Marc A. Onetto, age 59, $4,598,107 total compensation
SVP and CFO: Thomas J. (Tom) Szkutak, age 49, $163,200 total compensation
SVP, General Counsel, and Secretary: L. Michelle Wilson, age 46
SVP Web Services: Andrew R. Jassy, age 42
SVP North American Retail: Jeffrey A. (Jeff) Wilke
SVP Ecommerce Platform: H. Brian Valentine, age 50, $3,877,118 total compensation
SVP Business Development: Jeffrey M. Blackburn
SVP Seller Services: Sebastian J. Gunningham, age 47, $439,887 total compensation
SVP Worldwide Digital Media: Steven Kessel, age 44
SVP International Retail: Diego Piacentini, age 49, $230,905 total compensation
VP and CTO: Werner Vogels
VP, Worldwide Controller, and Principal Accounting Officer: Shelley L. Reynolds, age 45, $613,432 total compensation
CEO, Zappos: Anthony C. (Tony) Hsieh, age 35
CEO, Audible: Donald R. Katz
CEO, IMDb.com: Col Needham
Auditors: Ernst & Young LLP

LOCATIONS

HQ: Amazon.com, Inc.
   1200 12th Ave. South, Ste. 1200, Seattle, WA 98144
Phone: 206-266-1000
Web: www.amazon.com

2009 Sales

	$ mil.	% of total
North America	12,828	52
Other countries	11,681	48
Total	**24,509**	**100**

PRODUCTS/OPERATIONS

2009 Sales

	$ mil.	% of total
Media	12,774	52
Electronics & other general merchandise	11,082	45
Other	653	3
Total	**24,509**	**100**

Selected Departments

Apparel, shoes, and jewelry
Books
   Books
   Kindle books
   Textbooks
   Magazines
Computers and office
   Computers and accessories
   Office products and supplies
   PC games
   Software
Digital downloads
   Amazon shorts
   Game downloads
   Kindle Store
   MP3 downloads
Electronics
   Audio, TV, and home theater
   Camera, photo, and video
   Car electronics and GPS
   Cell phones and service
   Home appliances
   MP3 and media players
   Musical instruments
   Video games
Grocery, health, and beauty
   Beauty
   Gourmet food
   Grocery
   Health and personal care
   Natural and organic
Home and garden
   Bedding and bath
   Furniture and decor
   Home appliances
   Home improvement
   Kitchen and dining
   Patio, lawn, and garden
   Pet supplies
   Vacuums and storage
Kindle
   Books
   Blogs
   Magazines
   Newspapers
Movies, music, and games
   Blu-ray
   Movies and TV
   Music
   Musical instruments
   Video games
   Video On Demand
Sports and outdoors
   Action sports
   Camping and hiking
   Cycling
   Exercise and fitness
   Golf
   Team sports
Tools, auto, and industrial
   Automotive
   Home improvement
   Industrial and scientific
   Lighting and electrical
   Motorcycle and ATV
   Outdoor power equipment
   Plumbing fixtures
   Power and hand tools
Toys, kids, and baby
   Apparel (kids and baby)
   Books
   Movies
   Music
   Toys and games

COMPETITORS

AutoNation	HSN
AutoZone	IAC
Barnes & Noble	Indigo Books & Music
Best Buy	J. C. Penney
Bidz.com	Lowe's
Blockbuster Inc.	Macy's
Bluefly	Netflix
Books-A-Million	Nine West
Borders Group	Office Depot
Build-A-Bear	OfficeMax
Buy.com	Overstock.com
Collective Brands	Peapod, LLC
Columbia House	PPR SA
DSW	Provide Gifts
eBay	Rack Room Shoes
Finish Line	Sears
Foot Locker	Shoe Carnival
The Gap	shoebuy.com
Google	Staples
GSI Commerce	Target
Hastings Entertainment	TJX Companies
Hollywood Media	Walmart.com
Home Depot	Yahoo!

HISTORICAL FINANCIALS

Company Type: Public

Income Statement

FYE: December 31

	REVENUE ($ mil.)	NET INCOME ($ mil.)	NET PROFIT MARGIN	EMPLOYEES
12/09	24,509	902	3.7%	24,300
12/08	19,166	645	3.4%	20,700
12/07	14,835	476	3.2%	17,000
12/06	10,711	190	1.8%	13,900
12/05	8,490	333	3.9%	12,000
Annual Growth	**30.3%**	**28.3%**	**—**	**19.3%**

2009 Year-End Financials

Debt ratio: 2.1%
Return on equity: 22.8%
Cash ($ mil.): 3,444
Current ratio: 1.33
Long-term debt ($ mil.): 109
No. of shares (mil.): 448
Dividends
   Yield: —
   Payout: —
Market value ($ mil.): 60,241

Stock History

NASDAQ (GS): AMZN

	STOCK PRICE ($) FY Close	P/E High/Low		PER SHARE ($) Earnings	Dividends	Book Value
12/09	134.52	72	23	2.04	—	11.74
12/08	51.28	62	23	1.49	—	5.97
12/07	92.64	90	32	1.12	—	2.67
12/06	39.46	108	57	0.45	—	0.96
12/05	47.15	60	36	0.84	—	0.55
Annual Growth	**30.0%**	**—**	**—**	**24.8%**	**—**	**115.0%**

AMERCO

U-Haul, u-work, u-strain, u-hurt . . . u-sure you don't want to spend the extra money for movers? If not, there's AMERCO, whose principal subsidiary, U-Haul International, rents its orange-and-white trucks, trailers, and vehicle tow devices and sells packing supplies to do-it-yourself movers through some 15,000 independent dealers and 1,400 company-owned centers in the US and Canada. AMERCO also owns self-storage facilities managed by U-Haul, and it provides property and casualty insurance to U-Haul customers through Republic Western Insurance. Aside from U-Haul, the firm's Oxford Life unit provides annuities, Medicare supplement, and life insurance coverage. AMERCO was founded in 1945 as U-Haul Trailer Rental.

The company has been working to recover its financial footing following dips in revenues and profits. Amid the economic downturn, the firm has seen demand for its U-Haul equipment rentals, self-storage, and related moving products and services slide. (U-Haul accounts for about 90% of AMERCO's sales.) Also revenues generated by property management fees, property and casualty insurance premiums, and investment and interest income have fallen.

AMERCO has been working to strengthen its core moving and storage business by making U-Haul rental equipment, self-storage facilities, and related products and services more accessible and convenient to customers. In 2008 the company introduced the U-Box service, which provides on-demand storage container delivery and warehousing. The firm plans to reinvest some $210 million in its fleet in 2011. (U-Haul's rental fleet consists of about 100,000 trucks, 75,000 trailers, and 35,000 tow devices.) To help customers get on the road, U-Haul's eMove website connects users with independent moving and self-storage companies that provide services such as packing, loading, and unloading. The company aims to improve the capabilities of its eMove.com and uhaul.com sites as the Web has become a major sales channel.

AMERCO is 55%-owned by the founding Schoen family. The company is led by chairman and president Edward "Joe" Shoen.

HISTORY

Leonard Samuel (L.S.) Shoen earned his nickname, "Slick," as a poor kid trying to make a buck during the Depression. In 1945, as a Navy veteran, he started U-Haul International in Ridgefield, Washington, to serve long-distance do-it-yourself movers who could not return a truck to its origin. Shoen bought used equipment and hit the road, convincing gas station owners to act as agents.

Shoen and his first wife, Anna Mary, who died in 1957, had six children. In 1958 Shoen remarried and with his second wife, Suzanne, had five children. Shoen bestowed stock on all his offspring but neglected to keep a controlling interest. In the 1960s Shoen brought his sons into the company.

U-Haul moved to Phoenix in 1967. Two years later it bought Oxford Life Insurance Co. Shoen formed AMERCO in 1971 as U-Haul's parent. The oil crunch of the 1970s caused U-Haul's network to shrink as gas stations closed, so the company opened its own agencies. New competitors entered the market, and the company's share of business dropped to below 50%. Shoen took AMERCO into debt to diversify into general consumer rentals. The company also established real estate and insurance subsidiaries.

Shoen's second wife divorced him after the out-of-wedlock birth of his 12th child in 1977. His brief marriage to the mother ended in divorce, and he remarried again (and, later, yet again). Meanwhile, Shoen tapped his eldest son Sam for help in pursuing the diversification strategy. In 1979 sons Edward "Joe" and Mark left the company in dispute. Sam became president.

In 1986 Joe and Mark gained the support of enough siblings to constitute a voting majority and ousted their father and brother. L. S. and Sam almost regained control two years later but were outmaneuvered by Joe, who as chairman issued enough stock to a few loyal employees to shift the balance. Then the outside faction sued the people who had been directors in 1988 over issuance of the stock.

Joe refocused on the self-moving business and began upgrading the fleet, reducing the average age of the equipment from 11 to 5 years. In 1993 AMERCO preferred stock began trading on the NYSE, and the next year its common stock was listed on Nasdaq.

In the meantime, the lawsuit moved glacially through the courts. In 1994 the 1988 directors were found to have wrongfully excluded dissenting family members from the board. An initial award of $1.47 billion was later reduced to $462 million, due from the 1988 directors individually. However, they declared bankruptcy, and AMERCO indemnified them for the award. So in 1996 the company issued new stock and sold (and leased back) tens of thousands of vehicles and trailers to fulfill the judgment. In return, the dissenting family faction (including founder L. S.) gave up their 48% stake in AMERCO.

In 1997 AMERCO held its first stockholders' meeting since 1993. The next year Joe lost an appeal to overturn a ruling that he had acted with malice in dealing with family members in the 1988 stock transaction; he was ordered to pay $7 million in punitive damages to relatives, exclusive of the $462 million previously awarded.

In 1999 founder L.S. died at age 83 in a one-car accident believed to be suicide. In 2001 the company debuted its online storage reservation system. AMERCO denied reports published in August 2002 by the Financial Times that the Securities and Exchange Commission was investigating AMERCO's accounts and probing why it dismissed PricewaterhouseCoopers, its auditor of 24 years. The company failed to make a $100 million debt principal payment in October 2002.

AMERCO announced in March 2003 that it had obtained a four-year $865.8 million credit facility. The following month the company filed suit against PricewaterhouseCoopers, alleging negligence and fraud in its audit work. AMERCO disclosed in May that federal securities regulators were investigating its financial statements. (The investigation ended in 2006 with no action being taken against the company.)

Amid its financial difficulties, the company filed for Chapter 11 bankruptcy protection in June 2003. Nine months later, in March 2004, AMERCO emerged from bankruptcy.

EXECUTIVES

Chairman and President: Edward J. (Joe) Shoen, age 61, $764,933 total compensation
Principal Accounting Officer; Chief Accounting Officer, AMERCO: Jason A. Berg, age 37, $205,349 total compensation
Treasurer, AMERCO and U-Haul: Gary B. Horton, age 66
President, U-Haul: John C. (JT) Taylor, age 52
EVP U-Haul Field Operations: Ronald C. Frank, age 69
EVP U-Haul Field Operations: Robert R. Willson, age 59
VP U-Haul Business Consultants: Mark V. Shoen, age 59, $625,506 total compensation
VP U-Haul Business Consultants and Director: James P. Shoen, age 50, $622,141 total compensation
Controller, U-Haul: Robert T. Peterson, age 59
President, Oxford Life Insurance: Mark A. Haydukovich, age 53
President, Amerco Real Estate: Carlos Vizcarra, age 63
President, Republic Western Insurance: Richard M. Amoroso, age 51, $348,010 total compensation
General Counsel: Laurence J. (Larry) De Respino, age 49
Director Investor Relations: Jennifer K. Flachman
Auditors: BDO Seidman, LLP

LOCATIONS

HQ: AMERCO
1325 Airmotive Way, Ste. 100, Reno, NV 89502
Phone: 775-688-6300   **Fax:** 775-688-6338
Web: www.amerco.com

2010 Sales

	$ mil.	% of total
US	1,887.0	94
Canada	115.0	6
Total	**2,002.0**	**100**

PRODUCTS/OPERATIONS

2010 Sales

	$ mil.	% of total
Moving & storage	1,728.9	87
Life insurance	134.3	7
Investments & interest	50.0	2
Property & casualty insurance	27.6	1
Property management fees	21.6	1
Other	39.6	2
Total	**2,002.0**	**100**

Selected Operating Units

AMERCO Real Estate Company (real estate)
Oxford Life Insurance Company
Republic Western Insurance Company (property and casualty insurance)
SAC Holding II Corporation (owns self-storage properties managed by U-Haul)
U-Haul International, Inc. (self-moving truck and trailer rental, self-storage unit rental, sales of packing supplies)

COMPETITORS

AIG
Allstate
Atlas Van Lines
Atlas World Group
Avis Budget
Extra Space
The Hartford
MetLife
Mobile Mini
National Van Lines
Penske Truck Leasing
PODS Enterprises
Prudential
Public Storage
SIRVA
Sovran
UniGroup
United Van Lines
U-Store-It
Zipcar

HISTORICAL FINANCIALS

Company Type: Public

Income Statement

FYE: March 31

	REVENUE ($ mil.)	NET INCOME ($ mil.)	NET PROFIT MARGIN	EMPLOYEES
3/10	2,002	66	3.3%	17,600
3/09	1,992	13	0.7%	17,700
3/08	2,049	68	3.3%	18,500
3/07	2,086	91	4.3%	18,000
3/06	2,107	121	5.8%	17,500
Annual Growth	(1.3%)	(14.2%)	—	0.1%

2010 Year-End Financials

Debt ratio: —
Return on equity: 8.6%
Cash ($ mil.): 244
Current ratio: 0.62
Long-term debt ($ mil.): —

No. of shares (mil.): 20
Dividends
Yield: 0.0%
Payout: —
Market value ($ mil.): 1,065

Stock History

NASDAQ (GS): UHAL

	STOCK PRICE ($) FY Close	P/E High/Low		PER SHARE ($) Earnings	Dividends	Book Value
3/10	54.29	21	11	2.74	0.00	41.46
3/09	33.53	2,997	1,095	0.02	0.00	36.60
3/08	57.09	30	17	2.78	0.00	38.68
3/07	69.99	29	16	3.72	0.00	36.62
3/06	98.97	20	8	5.19	0.00	35.48
Annual Growth	(13.9%)	—	—	(14.8%)	—	4.0%

Ameren Corporation

Ameren provides the power that makes much of the American Midwest run. The holding company distributes electricity to 2.4 million customers and natural gas to almost 1 million customers in Missouri and Illinois through utility subsidiaries. Ameren has a generating capacity of more than 16,500 MW (primarily coal-fired), most of which is controlled by utility AmerenUE and nonregulated subsidiary Ameren-Energy Resources Generating Company. Ameren also operates a nuclear power facility, three hydroelectric plants, and several turbine combustion facilities.

In addition to operating power plants, AmerenEnergy Resources procures natural gas for its affiliated companies, builds new power plants, and provides long-term energy supply contracts. Another subsidiary, Ameren Energy Inc., markets and trades electricity to wholesale and retail customers and provides risk management and other energy-related services.

In 2010 the company announced plans by the end of the year to combine AmerenIP, Ameren-CIPS, and AmerenCILCO into one entity, Ameren Illinois Co., in order to streamline operations and reduce confusion among customers. The three Illinois utilities have operated as a single business since 2004 and deliver energy to 1.2 million power and 813,000 natural gas customers in more than 1,100 communities. Ameren serves its Missouri customers through AmerenUE. The company also operates some 21,000 miles of natural gas distribution and transmission lines.

To comply with federal requirements to separate ownership of power generation and transmission businesses, Ameren has transferred control of its subsidiaries' transmission assets to Midwest Independent Transmission System Operator, a regional transmission organization that coordinates power across 15 Midwestern states and one Canadian Province.

Thomas R. Voss was named president and CEO of Ameren in 2009. He previously served as CEO of AmerenUE. He replaced Gary Rainwater, who stepped down after serving in the top post for five years and a total of 30 years with the company.

HISTORY

More than 30 St. Louis companies had built a chaotic grid of generators and power lines throughout the city by 1900. Two years later many of them merged into the Union Company, which attracted national notice when it lit the St. Louis World's Fair in the first broad demonstration of electricity's power. In 1913 the company, by then named Union Electric (UE), began buying electricity from an Iowa dam 150 miles away — the greatest distance power had ever been transmitted in such quantity.

UE pushed into rural Missouri and began buying and building fossil-fuel plants. Despite a slowdown during the Depression, UE built Bagnell Dam on Missouri's Osage River in the early 1930s to gather power for a hydroelectric plant. At the onset of WWII, construction began on new plants with larger generators and lower production costs; however, demand for electricity lagged. In the late 1940s UE compensated by joining a "power pool," a system of utilities with interconnected transmission lines that shared electricity.

Growth in the 1950s came from acquisitions, including Missouri Power & Light (1950) and Missouri Edison (1954). During the 1960s and 1970s, UE built five new plants, including the Labadie plant (2,300 MW), one of the largest coal-fired plants in the US.

UE began producing nuclear energy in 1984 at its Callaway nuke. High costs and the expenses of a scrapped second plant caused UE to battle the Missouri Public Service Commission throughout the 1980s for rate increases.

Charles Mueller became president in 1993 and CEO one year later. He oversaw continued staff reductions and cost cutting through the 1990s in an increasingly competitive market. In 1997 UE expanded into Illinois through its purchase of CIPSCO, which owned utility Central Illinois Public Service Company (CIPS).

CIPS began as a Mattoon, Illinois, streetcar company in the early 1900s. The firm bought Mattoon's electric power plant in 1904 and began growing its power business, buying small electric companies in the 1920s and 1930s. CIPS built five generating units in the 1940s and 1950s and became part-owner (along with UE) of Electric Energy Inc., which built a power plant on the Ohio River. The company bought Illinois Electric and Gas Company in the 1960s and the state's Gas Utilities in the 1980s. To prepare for competition under deregulation, CIPS created holding company CIPSCO in the 1990s to diversify.

UE's purchase of CIPSCO expanded its geographic scope, and the new company was named Ameren in 1997 to reflect its American energy focus. The next year the company committed to adding generating capacity through several natural gas-fired combustion turbines. It joined nine other utilities to form the Midwest Independent System Operator to manage their transmission needs.

In 1999 Ameren bought a 245-mile railroad line between St. Louis and Kansas City to help the area's economic development. Looking for new opportunities in deregulated energy markets, the company purchased Data & Metering Specialties.

In 2000 Ameren created subsidiary Ameren-Energy Generating to operate its nonregulated power plants and affiliate AmerenEnergy Marketing to sell the generating facilities' power. When deregulation took effect in Illinois in 2002, the company transferred AmerenCIPS' power plants to AmerenEnergy Generating. In 2003 Ameren acquired CILCORP, the holding company for electric and gas utility Central Illinois Light (now operating as AmerenCILCO), from independent power producer AES in a $1.4 billion deal. To further expand its utility operations, Ameren acquired power and gas utility Illinois Power from Dynegy in a $2.3 billion deal in 2004. As part of the agreement, Ameren gained Dynegy's 20% stake in power generator Electric Energy, in which Ameren already held a 60% stake.

In 2007 Ameren subsidiary AmerenUE moved into wind power operations by agreeing to buy 100 MW of wind power from Horizon Wind Energy's Rail Splitter Wind Farm located near Delavan, Illinois.

EXECUTIVES

Chairman: Gary L. Rainwater, age 63, $5,046,122 total compensation
President, CEO, and Director: Thomas R. Voss, age 62, $1,807,585 total compensation
SVP, CFO, and Chief Accounting Officer: Martin J. Lyons Jr., age 43, $784,398 total compensation
SVP and Chief Nuclear Officer, AmerenUE: Adam C. Heflin
SVP, General Counsel, and Secretary: Steven R. Sullivan, age 49, $1,124,603 total compensation
SVP Regulatory Affaris and Financial Services, AmerenCILCO, AmerenCIPS, and AmerenIP: Craig D. Nelson, age 55
SVP Corporate Planning and Business Risk Management: Michael L. Moehn, age 40
SVP Communications and Brand Management: Karen Foss, age 65
VP and Controller: Bruce Steinke
Chairman, President, and CEO, CILCO, CIPS, and IP: Scott A. Cisel, age 56, $1,351,822 total compensation
Chairman, President, and CEO, Ameren Energy Resources Company; Chairman and President, Ameren Energy Resources Generating Company: Charles D. Naslund, age 57, $1,181,278 total compensation
President, Ameren Energy Marketing: Andrew M. Serri, age 48
President and CEO, AmerenUE: Warner L. Baxter, age 48, $1,431,169 total compensation
President and CEO, Ameren Services: Daniel F. Cole, age 56
President, Ameren Energy Fuels and Services: Michael G. Mueller, age 46
Auditors: PricewaterhouseCoopers LLP

LOCATIONS

HQ: Ameren Corporation
 1901 Chouteau Ave., St. Louis, MO 63103
Phone: 314-621-3222   **Fax:** 314-554-3801
Web: www.ameren.com

PRODUCTS/OPERATIONS

2009 Fuel Mix

	% of total
Coal	83
Nuclear	13
Hydro	3
Natural gas	1
Total	**100**

2009 Sales

	$ mil.	% of total
Electric	5,909	83
Gas	1,181	17
Total	**7,090**	**100**

Selected Subsidiaries

AmerenEnergy, Inc. (power marketing and trading, risk management, and energy services)
AmerenEnergy Resources Company (holding company)
 AmerenEnergy Development Company (power plant development)
 AmerenEnergy Generating Company (nonregulated power generation)
 AmerenEnergy Fuels and Services Company (natural gas procurement)
 AmerenEnergy Marketing Company (retail and wholesale energy marketing, long-term power supply contracts)
Ameren Services Company (provides support services for Ameren and subsidiaries)
Central Illinois Public Service Company (AmerenCIPS, electric and gas utility)
CILCORP Incorporated (holding company)
 Central Illinois Light Company (AmerenCILCO, electric and gas utility)
 AmerenEnergy Resources Generating Company (formerly Central Illinois Generation, nonregulated power generation)
Illinois Power Company (AmerenIP, electric and gas utility)
Union Electric Company (AmerenUE, electric and gas utility)

COMPETITORS

AES
AmerenIP
Atmos Energy
CenterPoint Energy
Empire District Electric
Exelon
Great Plains Energy
MidAmerican Energy
Midwest Generation
Nicor
Southern Union

HISTORICAL FINANCIALS

Company Type: Public

Income Statement

FYE: December 31

	REVENUE ($ mil.)	NET INCOME ($ mil.)	NET PROFIT MARGIN	EMPLOYEES
12/09	7,090	612	8.6%	9,780
12/08	7,839	605	7.7%	9,524
12/07	7,546	618	8.2%	9,069
12/06	6,880	547	8.0%	8,988
12/05	6,780	628	9.3%	9,136
Annual Growth	**1.1%**	**(0.6%)**	**—**	**1.7%**

2009 Year-End Financials

Debt ratio: 101.1%
Return on equity: 8.2%
Cash ($ mil.): 622
Current ratio: 1.66
Long-term debt ($ mil.): 7,943
No. of shares (mil.): 238
Dividends
 Yield: 5.5%
 Payout: 55.4%
Market value ($ mil.): 6,660

Stock History

NYSE: AEE

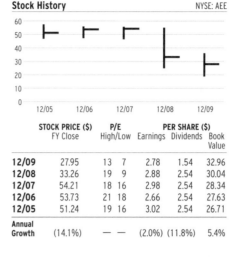

	STOCK PRICE ($) FY Close	P/E High/Low		PER SHARE ($) Earnings	Dividends	Book Value
12/09	27.95	13	7	2.78	1.54	32.96
12/08	33.26	19	9	2.88	2.54	30.04
12/07	54.21	18	16	2.98	2.54	28.34
12/06	53.73	21	18	2.66	2.54	27.63
12/05	51.24	19	16	3.02	2.54	26.71
Annual Growth	**(14.1%)**	**—**	**—**	**(2.0%)**	**(11.8%)**	**5.4%**

American Eagle Outfitters

It was once a purveyor of outdoor gear, but American Eagle Outfitters now feathers its nest with polos and khakis. The mall-based retailer sells casual apparel and accessories (shirts, jeans, shorts, sweaters, skirts, footwear, belts, bags) aimed at men and women ages 15-25. The chain operates about 1,100 stores in all 50 US states, Puerto Rico, Canada, and now in the Middle East. Virtually all of the company's products bear its private-label brand names: American Eagle Outfitters, aerie, 77kids, and (for now) MARTIN + OSA. Direct sales come from the company's website and its *AE* magazine, a lifestyle publication that doubles as a catalog.

American Eagle has weathered the recession better than many of its rivals, including Abercrombie & Fitch (A&F). Its relatively low prices, compared with A&F and other chains, apparently resonated with value-conscious shoppers.

The chain continued to add stores in 2009 — although at a much reduced rate compared to 2008, when it opened more than 120 shops. Notably, in late 2009 the retailer opened a flagship store in New York's Times Square, one of just five new locations added in 2009 (net of closings). Going forward, it plans to open more than a dozen American Eagle Outfitters stores, 20 aerie shops, and the 77kids shops in 2010. In its first foray outside of North America, the company opened stores in Dubai and Kuwait City in March 2010 via a franchise agreement with M.H. Al-shaya Co., a leading retailer in the region. More American Eagle Outfitters store openings are planned in international markets over the next several years.

The retailer has grown by opening new stores and launching retail concepts for customers outside its core 15-to-25-year-old audience. The apparel chain's latest online launch — which is slated to debut in stores in 2010 — is an upscale apparel brand for children ages two to 10 called 77kids by American Eagle. The first five 77kids stores are slated to open in 2010. A casual sportswear concept targeting 28-to-40-year-old women and men — called MARTIN + OSA — debuted in 2006 but never took root. Soon after the banner logged some $44 million in after-tax losses during fiscal 2009, American Eagle opted in early 2010 to put the concept and the MARTIN + OSA business to bed. As part of the move, it plans to shutter all 28 MARTIN + OSA stores and its online business in 2010.

Other American Eagle businesses have fared much better. An intimate apparel sub-brand called "aerie by American Eagle" also took flight in 2006. The line includes bras, boxers, camis, hoodies, panties, and personal care products targeted at the 15-to-25 female set. Aerie, which competes directly with the PINK line of intimate apparel by Victoria's Secret, is available in about 135 stand-alone aerie by American Eagle stores as well as within AE stores. The company also entered the fragrance game with a pair of scents for men and women, under the American Eagle Real banner, that debuted in AE stores in 2006.

HISTORY

Retail Ventures, an operator of specialty clothing stores owned by the Silverman family, founded the first American Eagle Outfitters (AE) store in 1977. Another retailing clan, the Schottenstein family (led by Jerome, who died in 1992), bought a 50% stake in Retail Ventures when the Silvermans encountered financial difficulties in 1980. The Schottenstein family had built a retail empire by buying and revamping dying retail chains (holdings include Value City Department and Furniture stores). The retailer returned to financial health and expanded rapidly in the late 1980s.

In 1991 the Schottensteins acquired the remainder of Retail Ventures, and with it, 153 American Eagle Outfitters stores. The company had been running up substantial losses, so the Schottensteins brought in new management and took the company public in 1994 as American Eagle Outfitters, with about 170 stores. AE opened more than 80 stores the following year.

Former president and CEO Sam Forman bought the company's 32-store outlet division in 1995 and attained a license to continue to operate the stores under the American Eagle Outlets name. Two years later AE acquired New York-based Prophecy, an apparel-sourcing firm (the Schottenstein family was Prophecy's majority owner).

In recent years AE has toned down its rugged, value-conscious image in favor of a collegiate look. One result: In 1998 across-the-mall nemesis Abercrombie & Fitch sued the company, claiming AE copied product designs as well as the look of its stores; the suit wound its way up through the courts and was dismissed three times in four years.

The company crossed the border into Canada in 2000 with the purchase of 160 Thrifty/Bluenotes and Braemar stores and distribution facilities from Canada's Dylex Limited, all for about $74 million. In 2001 the Braemer stores were converted to American Eagle Outfitters. American Eagle Outfitters opened 81 new US stores in 2001, and it introduced the American Eagle brand to Canada with 46 new stores there.

In 2003 Jim O'Donnell was named CEO and Roger S. Markfield became vice chairman and president. Previously, the duo had been co-CEOs of the company. About a year later American Eagle Outfitters sold its Bluenotes apparel chain in Canada to Stitches owner Michael Gold. In 2005 American Eagle Outfitters had nests in all 50 states with the opening of a pair of stores in Alaska.

The fall of 2006 was a busy time for the company with the launch of MARTIN + OSA (a casual sportswear concept targeting 28-to-40-year-old women and men), and the debut of an intimate apparel sub brand called "aerie by American Eagle." The aerie line includes bras, panties, and personal care products for 15-to-25-year-old females. Two years later the company's new concept for kids ages two to 10 — called 77kids by American Eagle — debuted online in fall 2008. American Eagle in March 2010 announced plans to shutter its MARTIN + OSA business when it failed to meet performance expectations.

EXECUTIVES

Chairman: Jay L. Schottenstein, age 55
Vice Chairman and Executive Creative Director:
Roger S. Markfield, age 68,
$6,252,894 total compensation
CEO and Director: James V. (Jim) O'Donnell, age 69,
$17,946,756 total compensation
Chief Merchandising Officer: Tana Ward
EVP and Chief Design Officer: LeAnn Nealz, age 53,
$2,301,145 total compensation
EVP and COO, New York Design Center:
Michael R. Rempell, age 36
EVP and CFO: Joan H. Hilson, age 50,
$1,967,421 total compensation
EVP Human Resources: Thomas A. (Tom) DiDonato,
age 51
EVP Supply Chain and Real Estate; President,
American Eagle Outfitters Foundation:
Joseph E. Kerin, age 64, $1,934,022 total compensation
EVP International: Christopher Fiore
EVP Store Operations: Dennis R. Parodi, age 58
VP Investor Relations: Judy Meehan
Auditors: Ernst & Young LLP

LOCATIONS

HQ: American Eagle Outfitters, Inc.
77 Hot Metal St., Pittsburgh, PA 15203
Phone: 412-432-3300 **Fax:** 412-432-3955
Web: www.ae.com

2010 Sales

	$ mil.	% of total
US	2,715.6	91
International	274.9	9
Total	**2,990.5**	**100**

2010 Stores

	No.
US	
California	89
Texas	72
Pennsylvania	66
New York	62
Florida	50
Ohio	40
Illinois	37
Michigan	35
Georgia	34
Massachusetts	33
Virginia	29
North Carolina	31
New Jersey	28
Tennessee	24
Indiana	22
Minnesota	22
Maryland	21
Washington	20
Missouri	19
Alabama	18
Connecticut	18
Wisconsin	18
Arizona	16
South Carolina	16
Colorado	14
Louisiana	14
Iowa	13
Kentucky	13
Oklahoma	12
Utah	12
Oregon	11
Kansas	10
West Virginia	9
Arkansas	9
New Hampshire	8
Mississippi	8
Nebraska	8
Other states	54
Canada	88
Total	**1,103**

PRODUCTS/OPERATIONS

2010 Stores

	No.
American Eagle Outfitters	938
aerie	137
MARTIN + OSA	28
Total	**1,103**

Selected Products

Accessories
Cargo pants
Footwear
Graphic T-shirts
Khakis
Outerwear
Polo shirts
Rugby shirts
Swimwear

COMPETITORS

Abercrombie & Fitch	Lands' End
Aéropostale	Levi Strauss
Bath & Body Works	Liz Claiborne
Benetton	L.L. Bean
The Buckle	Macy's
Calvin Klein	Nautica Apparel
The Children's Place	Nordstrom
Columbia Sportswear	Pacific Sunwear
Dillard's	Polo Ralph Lauren
Fossil, Inc.	Reitmans
The Gap	Target
Guess?	Tommy Hilfiger
Gymboree	Tween Brands
Hot Topic	Urban Outfitters
Hudson's Bay	VF
J. C. Penney	Victoria's Secret Direct
J. Crew	Victoria's Secret Stores

HISTORICAL FINANCIALS

Company Type: Public

Income Statement

FYE: Saturday nearest January 31

	REVENUE ($ mil.)	NET INCOME ($ mil.)	NET PROFIT MARGIN	EMPLOYEES
1/10	2,991	169	5.7%	39,400
1/09	2,989	179	6.0%	37,500
1/08	3,055	400	13.1%	38,700
1/07	2,794	387	13.9%	27,600
1/06	2,309	294	12.7%	23,000
Annual Growth	**6.7%**	**(12.9%)**	**—**	**14.4%**

2010 Year-End Financials

Debt ratio: —   No. of shares (mil.): 205
Return on equity: 11.3%   Dividends
Cash ($ mil.): 694   Yield: 2.5%
Current ratio: 2.85   Payout: 49.4%
Long-term debt ($ mil.): —   Market value ($ mil.): 3,264

Stock History

NYSE: AEO

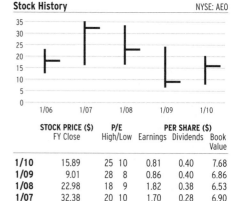

	STOCK PRICE ($) FY Close	P/E High/Low	PER SHARE ($) Earnings	Dividends	Book Value
1/10	15.89	25 10	0.81	0.40	7.68
1/09	9.01	28 8	0.86	0.40	6.86
1/08	22.98	18 9	1.82	0.38	6.53
1/07	32.38	20 10	1.70	0.28	6.90
1/06	17.99	18 10	1.26	0.18	5.63
Annual Growth	**(3.1%)**	**— —**	**(10.5%)**	**22.1%**	**8.1%**

American Electric Power

American Electric Power (AEP) takes its slice of the US power pie out of Middle America. The holding company is one of the largest power generators and distributors in the US. AEP owns the nation's largest electricity transmission system, a network of almost 39,000 miles. Its electric utilities serve 5.2 million customers in 11 states and have about 39,000 MW of largely coal-fired generating capacity. AEP is a top wholesale energy company; it markets and trades electricity, natural gas, and other commodities and has stakes in independent power plants. Other operations include natural gas transportation, storage, and processing, and barge transportation services.

AEP's transmission system serves 10% of the electricity demand in the Eastern Interconnection (which covers 38 eastern and central US states and eastern Canada), and 11% of the power demand in ERCOT (which covers most of Texas). Seeking to run cleaner, more efficient power plants, AEP has earmarked $3.7 billion through 2010 for upgrades at its coal-fired generating plants, and an additional $1.5 billion through 2020.

Although only a small percentage of its power generation comes from renewables (such as wind and hydro), the company is investing heavily in wind power to ramp up its clean energy sources in response to carbon reduction legislation in many of the states its serves. By the end of 2009 AEI was operating 310 MW of wind power facilities and had about 180 MW of long-term purchase power agreements for wind power.

As part of utility deregulation, AEP had been expanding its merchant energy activities; however, due to the collapse of the energy trading industry (spurred by Enron's collapse and the ensuing financial scrutiny of other top marketers), AEP has scaled back its nonregulated operations. The firm has shut down or sold its European trading operations, but it continues to participate in wholesale energy transactions in regions of the US where it owns assets.

HISTORY

In 1906 Richard Breed, Sidney Mitchell, and Henry Doherty set up American Gas & Electric (AG&E) in New York to buy 23 utilities from Philadelphia's Electric Company of America. With properties in seven northeastern US states, AG&E began acquiring and merging small electric properties, creating the predecessors of Ohio Power (1911), Kentucky Power (1919), and Appalachian Power (1926). AG&E also bought the predecessor of Indiana Michigan Power (1925).

By 1926 the company was operating in Indiana, Kentucky, Michigan, Ohio, Virginia, and West Virginia. In 1935 AG&E engineer Philip Sporn, later known as the Henry Ford of power, introduced his high-voltage, high-velocity circuit breaker. AG&E picked up Kingsport Power in 1938.

Becoming president in 1947, Sporn began an ambitious building program that continued through the 1960s. Plants designed by AG&E (renamed American Electric Power in 1958) were among the world's most efficient, and electric rates stayed 25%–38% below the national average.

AEP bought Michigan Power in 1967, six years after Donald Cook succeeded Sporn as president. Cook, who refused to attach scrubbers to the smokestacks of coal-fired plants, was criticized in the early 1970s by environmental protesters. AEP's first nuclear plant, named in Cook's honor, went on line in Michigan in 1975. He retired in 1976.

The firm moved from New York to Columbus, Ohio, in 1980 after buying what is now Columbus Southern Power (formed in 1883). It set up AEP Generating in 1982 to provide power to its electric utilities.

AEP began converting its second nuke, Zimmer, to coal in 1984. In 1992 AEP finally began installing scrubbers at its coal-fired Gavin plant in Ohio after being ordered to comply with the Clean Air Act. It also cleaned up its image by planting millions of trees in 1996.

AEP formed AEP Communications after Congress passed the Telecommunications Act of 1996. The next year AEP jumped into the UK's deregulated electric market; AEP and New Century Energies (now Xcel Energy) bought Yorkshire Electricity for $2.8 billion. However, a $109 million UK windfall tax on the transaction — and increased wholesale competition — hurt AEP's bottom line.

As the normally staid electric industry succumbed to merger mania, AEP agreed in 1997 to buy Central and South West (CSW) of Texas in a $6.6 billion deal. AEP's sales would nearly double, and CSW was to bring its own UK utility, SEEBOARD, and other overseas holdings.

In 1998 AEP bought a 20% stake in Pacific Hydro, an Australian power producer, and CitiPower, an Australian electric distribution company. AEP also bought Equitable Resources' Louisiana natural gas midstream operations, including an intrastate pipeline. In 1999 China's Pushan Power Plant (70%-owned by AEP) began operations. Environmental concerns resurfaced that year when the EPA sued the utility, alleging its old coal-powered plants, which had been grandfathered from the Clean Air Act, had been quietly upgraded to extend their lives.

Regulators approved the company's acquisition of CSW in 2000, but AEP had to agree to relinquish control of its 22,000 miles of transmission lines to an independent operator. The CSW deal closed later that year. (However, the SEC's approval of the deal was challenged by a federal appeals court in 2002.)

AEP sold its 50% stake in Yorkshire Power Group to Innogy (now RWE npower) in 2001. AEP became one of the largest US barge operators that year when it bought MEMCO Barge Line from Progress Energy. It also purchased two UK coal-fired power plants (4,000 MW) from Edison Mission Energy, a subsidiary of Edison International.

In 2002 AEP sold its UK utility, SEEBOARD, to Electricité de France in a $2.2 billion deal; it also sold its Australian utility, CitiPower, to a consortium led by Cheung Kong Infrastructure and Hongkong Electric. The following year AEP sold two of its competitive Texas retail electric providers (WTU Retail Energy and CPL Retail Energy) to UK utility Centrica. The company sold two UK power plants to Scottish and Southern Energy in 2004, and it sold a 50% stake in a third UK plant to Scottish Power.

AEP settled an eight-year lawsuit with the US government in 2007 and agreed to pay more than $4.6 billion to reduce hazardous air pollution from 16 coal-burning power plants.

EXECUTIVES

Chairman, President, and CEO:
Michael G. (Mike) Morris, age 63,
$7,539,278 total compensation
COO: Carl L. English, age 63,
$2,583,989 total compensation
EVP And CFO: Brian X. Tierney, age 42,
$1,453,985 total compensation
EVP Generation: Nicholas K. (Nick) Akins, age 49
EVP Environment, Safety and Health, and Facilities:
Dennis E. Welch, age 58
SVP, Chief Accounting Officer, and Controller:
Joseph M. Buonaiuto
SVP and Chief Nuclear Officer, Cook Nuclear Plant:
Lawrence J. (Larry) Weber, age 60
SVP, General Counsel, and Secretary:
D. Michael (Mike) Miller, age 62
SVP Shared Services: Barbara Radous
SVP Governmental Affairs: Anthony P. Kavanagh
SVP Fossil and Hydro Generation: Mark McCullough, age 51
SVP Regulatory Services: Richard E. (Rich) Munczinski, age 57
SVP Fuel, Emissions, and Logistics: Timothy K. Light, age 52
SVP Investor Relations and Treasurer:
Charles E. (Chuck) Zebula, age 50
VP and CIO: Pablo A. Vegas, age 37
VP Corporate Communications: Dale E. Heydlauff, age 49

President and COO, Indiana Michigan Power:
Paul Chodak III, age 46
President, AEP Utilities: Robert P. (Bob) Powers, age 52,
$2,485,998 total compensation
President, AEP Transmission: Susan Tomasky, age 56,
$2,806,260 total compensation
President and COO, AEP Texas: A. Wade Smith, age 46
President and COO, Kentucky Power:
Gregory G. Pauley, age 58
President and COO, AEP Ohio; President and COO, Columbus Southern Power and Ohio Power:
Joseph (Joe) Hamrock, age 46
President and COO, Appalachian Power:
Charles R. Patton, age 50
President and COO, Southwestern Electric Power:
Venita McCellon-Allen, age 50
President and COO, Public Service Company of Oklahoma: J. Stuart Solomon, age 48
Auditors: Deloitte & Touche LLP

LOCATIONS

HQ: American Electric Power Company, Inc.
1 Riverside Plaza, Columbus, OH 43215
Phone: 614-716-1000   **Fax:** 614-716-1823
Web: www.aep.com

PRODUCTS/OPERATIONS

2009 Sales

	$ mil.	% of total
Retail	10,391	77
Wholesale	1,849	14
Other	1,249	9
Total	**13,489**	**100**

Selected Subsidiaries

AEP Energy Services, Inc. (energy marketing and trading)
AEP Generating Co. (electricity generator, marketer)
AEP Retail Energy (retail energy marketing in deregulated territories)
AEP Texas Central Company (formerly Central Power and Light, electric utility)
AEP Texas North Company (formerly West Texas Utilities, electric utility)
AEP Towers (wireless communications towers)
Appalachian Power Company (electric utility)
Columbus Southern Power Company (electric utility)
Indiana Michigan Power Company (electric utility)
Kentucky Power Company (electric utility)
Kingsport Power Company (electric utility)
Ohio Power Company (electric utility)
Public Service Company of Oklahoma (electric utility)
Southwestern Electric Power Company (electric utility)
Wheeling Power Company (electric utility)

Utility Distribution/Customer Service Divisions

AEP Ohio (handles distribution, customer service, and external affairs functions for Columbus Southern Power Company, Ohio Power Company, and Wheeling Power Company)
AEP Texas (handles distribution, customer service, and external affairs functions for AEP Texas Central Company and AEP Texas North Company)
Appalachian Power (handles distribution, customer service, and external affairs functions for Appalachian Power Company and Kingsport Power Company)
Indiana Michigan Power (handles distribution, customer service, and external affairs functions for Indiana Michigan Power Company)
Kentucky Power (handles distribution, customer service, and external affairs functions for Kentucky Power Company)
Public Service Company of Oklahoma (handles distribution, customer service, and external affairs functions for Public Service Company of Oklahoma)
Southwestern Electric Power Company (handles distribution, customer service, and external affairs functions for Southwestern Electric Power Company)

HISTORICAL FINANCIALS

Company Type: Public

Income Statement				FYE: December 31
	REVENUE ($ mil.)	NET INCOME ($ mil.)	NET PROFIT MARGIN	EMPLOYEES
12/09	13,489	1,370	10.2%	21,673
12/08	14,440	1,380	9.6%	21,912
12/07	13,380	1,168	8.7%	20,861
12/06	12,622	1,002	7.9%	20,442
12/05	12,111	1,056	8.7%	19,630
Annual Growth	2.7%	6.7%	—	2.5%

2009 Year-End Financials

Debt ratio: 119.9%
Return on equity: 11.5%
Cash ($ mil.): 579
Current ratio: 0.89
Long-term debt ($ mil.): 15,757

No. of shares (mil.): 479
Dividends
Yield: 4.7%
Payout: 55.4%
Market value ($ mil.): 16,680

Stock History

NYSE: AEP

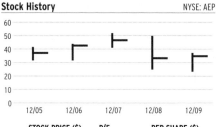

60							
50							
40							
30							
20							
10							
0							
	12/05	12/06		12/07	12/08	12/09	

	STOCK PRICE ($) FY Close	P/E High	P/E Low	PER SHARE ($) Earnings	PER SHARE ($) Dividends	PER SHARE ($) Book Value
12/09	34.79	12	8	2.96	1.64	27.41
12/08	33.28	14	7	3.42	1.64	22.43
12/07	46.56	19	15	2.72	1.58	21.02
12/06	42.58	17	13	2.53	1.50	19.63
12/05	37.09	20	16	2.08	1.42	18.96
Annual Growth	(1.6%)	—	—	9.2%	3.7%	9.7%

American Express

American Express makes money even if you do leave home without it. The company is one of the world's largest travel agencies, but it is better known for its charge cards and revolving credit cards. And yes, the company still issues traveler's checks and publishes such magazines as *Food & Wine* and *Travel + Leisure* through its American Express Publishing unit. Its travel agency operations have thousands of locations worldwide, and its Travelers Cheque Group is the world's largest issuer of traveler's checks. But the company's charge and credit cards are its bread and butter; American Express has some 88 million cards in circulation worldwide.

Discount fees paid by merchants account for about half of the company's revenues. American Express has focused on adding merchants and pushing for more widespread acceptance of its cards. Previously known primarily as a travel and entertainment card, American Express now does more business on the retail side. It has also courted businesses that typically accept cash or check payments, including construction, industrial, and pharmaceutical firms.

After suffering losses during the economic downturn in 2008, American Express implemented cost-cutting measures, including cutting nearly 10% of its work force. The company also converted to a bank holding structure, affording it access to the US government's bank bailout funds as it faced increased credit losses and write-offs of nonperforming customer accounts. (Bank subsidiaries Centurion Bank and AEBFSB issue revolving credit cards and consumer charge cards.) The company received some $3.4 billion from the Troubled Asset Relief Fund (TARP) in early 2009; it repaid the debt within months. The restructuring may also make it easier for American Express to merge with another lender.

In 2010, American Express acquired Internet-based payment platform Revolution Money for $300 million. The platform provides online payments and issues reloadable, prepaid cards.

That same year it sold its minority stake in American Express Incentive Services, which issues AmEx-branded prepaid cards, to Maritz.

Warren Buffett's Berkshire Hathaway owns about 13% of American Express.

HISTORY

In 1850 Henry Wells and his two main competitors combined their delivery services to form American Express. When directors refused to expand to California in 1852, Wells and VP William Fargo formed Wells Fargo while remaining at American Express.

American Express merged with Merchants Union Express in 1868 and developed a money order to compete with the government's postal money order. Fargo's difficulty in cashing letters of credit in Europe led to the offering of Travelers Cheques in 1891.

During WWI the US nationalized and consolidated all express delivery services, compensating the owners. After the war, American Express incorporated as an overseas freight and financial services and exchange provider (the freight operation was sold in 1970). In 1958 the company introduced the American Express charge card. It bought Fireman's Fund American Insurance

(sold gradually between 1985 and 1989) and Equitable Securities in 1968.

James Robinson, CEO from 1977 to 1993, hoped to turn American Express into a financial services supermarket. The company bought brokerage Shearson Loeb Rhoades in 1981 and investment banker Lehman Brothers in 1984, among others. In 1987 it introduced Optima, a revolving credit card, to compete with MasterCard and Visa; with no experience in underwriting credit cards, it was badly burned by losses.

Most of the financial units were combined as Shearson Lehman Brothers. But the financial services supermarket never came to fruition, and losses in this area brought a steep drop in earnings in the early 1990s. Harvey Golub was brought in as CEO in 1993 to restore stability.

The company sold its brokerage operations as Shearson (to Travelers, now Citigroup) and spun off investment banking as Lehman Brothers in 1994. In late 1996 it teamed with Advanta Corp. to allow Advanta Visa and MasterCard holders to earn points in the American Express Membership Rewards program. The move sparked a lawsuit from Visa and MasterCard, which prohibit their member banks from doing business with American Express. This move set off a spate of lawsuits culminating in the US Justice Department filing an antitrust suit against Visa and MasterCard. A federal judge sided with the Justice Department in 2001.

In 1997 Kenneth Chenault became president and COO, putting him in line to succeed Golub. In 2000 the company established a headquarters in Beijing to develop business in China.

In 2001 Chenault replaced Golub as chairman and CEO. American Express was hit hard that year by bad investments in below-investment grade bonds by its money-management unit, which shaved about $1 billion from earnings.

Amex acquired Rosenbluth International, a leading global travel management company with corporate travel operations in 15 countries, in 2003. The firm underwent a mild shakedown in 2004 when it cut 2.5% of its workforce in a restructuring that included the company's business travel operations; the move also included the sale of its banking operations in Bangladesh, Egypt, Luxembourg, and Pakistan.

In 2004 the company announced a milestone agreement with Industrial and Commercial Bank of China (ICBC), one of the biggest banks in China, to issue the first American Express-branded credit cards in that country.

To focus on its travel and credit card operations, the company in 2005 spun off Ameriprise Financial (formerly American Express Financial Advisors), which provides insurance, mutual funds, investment advice, and brokerage and asset management services.

In separate transactions toward that same end, American Express sold its Tax and Business Services division to H&R Block and its UK-based American Express Financial Services Europe to TD Waterhouse (now part of TD AMERITRADE).

In 2007, American Express reached a $2.5 billion settlement with Visa and other defendants including JPMorgan Chase, Capital One, U.S. Bancorp, and Wells Fargo, dropping them from the lawsuit alleging the companies conspired to block American Express from the bank-issued card business in the US. The following year it reached a $1.8 billion settlement with Mastercard, the final remaining defendant in the suit.

American Express sold the international operations of American Express Bank to Stanchart in 2008.

EXECUTIVES

Chairman and CEO; CEO, American Express Centurion Bank: Kenneth I. (Ken) Chenault, age 58, $17,398,568 total compensation
Vice Chairman and CEO, Business-to-Business: Edward P. (Ed) Gilligan, age 50, $12,722,885 total compensation
EVP and CFO: Daniel T. (Dan) Henry, age 60, $5,006,994 total compensation
EVP Corporate and External Affairs: Thomas Schick, age 63
EVP Human Resources: L. Kevin Cox, age 45
EVP and General Counsel: Louise M. Parent, age 59
Chief Risk Officer; President, Risk, Information Management, and Banking Group: Ashwini (Ash) Gupta, age 56
Chief Marketing Officer and Head, Global Advertising and Brand Management: John D. Hayes, age 55
Group President, Global Services and CIO: Stephen J. (Steve) Squeri, age 51, $9,503,131 total compensation
President, International Consumer and Small Business Services: Douglas E. Buckminster
President and CEO, Amex Bank of Canada; President and General Manager, Amex Canada: Howard Grosfield
President, American Express OPEN: Susan Sobbott
President, Enterprise Growth: Daniel H. (Dan) Schulman, age 51
President, American Express Foundation: Timothy J. McClimon
President and CEO, Consumer Services: Judson C. (Jud) Linville, age 52
President, Global Merchant Services: William H. (Bill) Glenn
SVP Investor Relations: Ron Stovall
VP Department of Corporate Social Responsibility: Judy Tenzer
Director Public Affairs and Communication, Corporate and Marketing Communications: Sarah B. Meron
Secretary: Carol V. Schwartz
Auditors: PricewaterhouseCoopers LLP

LOCATIONS

HQ: American Express Company
World Financial Center, 200 Vesey St.
New York, NY 10285
Phone: 212-640-2000
Web: www.americanexpress.com

PRODUCTS/OPERATIONS

2009 Sales

	$ mil.	% of total
Discount revenue	13,389	50
Interest & fees on loans	4,468	17
Net card fees	2,151	8
Travel commissions & fees	1,594	6
Other commissions & fees	1,778	7
Net securitization income	400	1
Other interest	863	3
Other	2,087	8
Total	**26,730**	**100**

COMPETITORS

Bank of America
Barclays
BCD Travel
Capital One
Citibank
Discover
Expedia
HSBC
JPMorgan Chase
JTB Corp.
MasterCard
Ovation Travel Group
PayPal
Visa Inc
Western Union

HISTORICAL FINANCIALS

Company Type: Public

Income Statement   FYE: December 31

	ASSETS ($ mil.)	NET INCOME ($ mil.)	INCOME AS % OF ASSETS	EMPLOYEES
12/09	124,088	2,130	1.7%	58,300
12/08	126,074	2,699	2.1%	66,000
12/07	149,830	4,012	2.7%	67,700
12/06	127,853	3,707	2.9%	65,400
12/05	113,960	3,734	3.3%	65,800
Annual Growth	**2.2%**	**(13.1%)**	**—**	**(3.0%)**

2009 Year-End Financials

Equity as % of assets: 11.6%
Return on assets: 1.7%
Return on equity: 16.2%
Long-term debt ($ mil.): 52,338
No. of shares (mil.): 1,203
Dividends
Yield: 1.8%
Payout: 46.8%
Market value ($ mil.): 48,754
Sales ($ mil.): 26,730

Stock History   NYSE: AXP

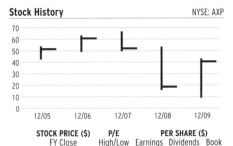

	STOCK PRICE ($) FY Close	P/E High/Low		Earnings	PER SHARE ($) Dividends	Book Value
12/09	40.52	27	6	1.54	0.72	11.97
12/08	18.55	23	7	2.33	0.72	9.84
12/07	52.02	20	15	3.36	0.63	9.17
12/06	60.67	21	17	2.99	0.57	8.74
12/05	51.46	18	15	2.97	0.48	8.77
Annual Growth	**(5.8%)**	**—**	**—**	**(15.1%)**	**10.7%**	**8.1%**

American Financial Group

American Financial Group (AFG) insures businessmen in pursuit of the great American Dream. Through the Great American Insurance Group of companies and its flagship Great American Insurance Company, AFG offers commercial property/casualty insurance focused on specialties such as workers' compensation, professional liability, ocean and inland marine, and multiperil crop insurance. The company also provides surety coverage for contractors and risk management services. For individuals and employers AFG provides supplemental medical insurance products, and a wide range of annuities sold through its Great American Financial Resources (GAFRI) subsidiary.

The company operates about 25 autonomous property/casualty businesses (making up the Great American Insurance Group) that service niche industry policies and report into a central administration organization. Policies are marketed through a network of independent agents and brokers. Property/casualty policies account for more than 80% of AFG's annual premiums, with operations divided into segments including

property and transportation (marine, crops, and commercial auto), specialty casualty (professional, excess and surplus, and general liabilities), specialty financial (fidelity and surety, risk management), workers' compensation, and other specialty offerings.

GAFRI offers fixed, variable, and indexed annuity products and supplemental life and health insurance policies through a handful of underwriting companies, including Great American Life Insurance, Annuity Investors Life Insurance, Loyal American Life Insurance, and United Teacher Associates Insurance. Products are marketed through managing general agents, financial advisors, and independent brokers.

AFG is engaged in non-insurance operations, primarily commercial real estate holdings in Cincinnati and Pittsburgh and resorts and hotels in states including Florida, Louisiana, Maryland, New Hampshire, and South Carolina.

The founding Lindner family owns more than 20% of AFG.

HISTORY

When his father became ill in the mid-1930s, Carl Lindner Jr. dropped out of high school to take over his family's dairy business. He built it into a large ice-cream store chain called United Dairy Farmers. Lindner branched out in 1955 with Henthy Realty, and in 1959 he bought three savings and loans. The next year Lindner changed the company's name to American Financial Corp. (AFC). He took it public in 1961, using the proceeds to buy United Liberty Life Insurance (1963) and Provident Bank (1966).

Lindner also formed the American Financial Leasing & Services Company in 1968 to lease airplanes, computers, and other equipment. In 1969 the company acquired Phoenix developer Rubenstein Construction and renamed it American Continental. AFC bought several life, casualty, and mortgage insurance firms in the 1970s, including National General, parent of Great American Insurance Group, later the core of AFC's insurance segment. The company also moved into publishing by buying 95% of the *Cincinnati Enquirer*, paperback publisher Bantam Books, and hardback publisher Grosset & Dunlap.

But the publishing interests soon went back on the block, as Lindner concentrated on insurance, which was then suffering from an industry wide slowdown. In addition to selling the *Enquirer*, AFC spun off American Continental in 1976. American Continental's president was Charles Keating, who had joined AFC in 1972 and whose brother published the *Enquirer*. Keating (who was later jailed, released, then eventually pleaded guilty in connection with the failure of Lincoln Savings) underwent an SEC investigation during part of his time at AFC for alleged improprieties at Provident Bank. The bank was spun off in 1980.

Lindner took AFC private in 1981. That year, following a strategy of bottom-feeding, the firm began building its interest in the non-railroad assets of Penn Central, the former railroad that had emerged from bankruptcy as an industrial manufacturer. Later that decade AFC increased its ownership in United Brands (later renamed Chiquita Brands International) from 29% to 45%. Lindner installed himself as CEO and reversed that company's losses. In 1987 AFC acquired a TV company, Taft Communications (renamed Great American Communications), entailing a heavy debt load. To reduce its debt, AFC trimmed its holdings, including Circle K, Hunter S&L, and an interest in Scripps Howard Broadcasting.

Great American Communications went bankrupt in 1992 and emerged the next year as Citicasters Inc. (sold 1996). In 1995 Lindner created American Financial Group to effect the merger of AFC and Premier Underwriters, of which he owned 42%. The result was American Financial Group (AFG).

Lindner's bipartisan political donations gained publicity when it became known that his gifts to Republicans had brought support in a dispute with the European Union over the banana trade. The next year AFG sold some noncore units, including software consultancy Millennium Dynamics and its commercial insurance operations. In 1999 AFG bought direct-response auto insurer Worldwide Insurance Company as part of its efforts to build depth in the highly commodified auto insurance market.

In 2000 American Financial Group agreed to pay $75 million over the next 30 years to get its name on the Cincinnati Reds' new stadium, known as Great American Ball Park. In 2001 AFG sold its Japanese property/casualty division to Japanese insurer Mitsui Marine & Fire (now Mitsui Sumitomo Insurance).

The company shed some commercial lines to concentrate on its property/casualty and life and annuities businesses. To refine its mix, AFG transferred Atlanta Casualty Company, Infinity Insurance Company, Leader Insurance Company, and Windsor Insurance Company into 40%-owned Infinity Property and Casualty, which went public in 2003. In 2004 the business exchanged its stake in Provident Financial Group for a holding in National City Corporation.

Founder, chairman, and legendary businessman Carl Lindner Jr., who was also part owner of the Cincinnati Reds, retired as CEO in 2005 and was succeeded by two of his sons, Carl Lindner III and Craig Lindner, who shared the CEO job.

EXECUTIVES

Chairman: Carl H. Lindner Jr., age 90
Co-President, Co-CEO, and Director: S. Craig Lindner, age 55, $5,958,276 total compensation
Co-President, Co-CEO, and Director: Carl H. Lindner III, age 56, $5,917,156 total compensation
SVP, General Counsel, and Director: James E. Evans, age 64, $2,587,122 total compensation
SVP and CFO: Keith A. Jensen, age 59, $1,777,158 total compensation
SVP Taxes: Thomas E. Mischell, age 62, $1,418,450 total compensation
VP: Sandra W. Heimann
VP: Karen Holley Horrell, age 54
VP and Treasurer: David J. Witzgall
VP and CIO: Piyush K. Singh
VP Taxation: Kathleen J. Brown
VP and Controller: Robert H. Ruffing
VP and Deputy General Counsel: James C. Kennedy
Assistant VP Investor Relations: Diane P. Weidner
VP, Assistant General Counsel, and Secretary: Karl J. Grafe
VP Internal Audit: Robert E. Dobbs
Auditors: Ernst & Young LLP

LOCATIONS

HQ: American Financial Group, Inc.
1 E. 4th St., Cincinnati, OH 45202
Phone: 513-579-2121   **Fax:** 513-412-0200
Web: www.afginc.com

PRODUCTS/OPERATIONS

2009 Premiums

	% of total
Property/casualty	
Property & transportation	32
Specialty casualty	26
Specialty financial	18
California workers' compensation	6
Other specialty	2
Life, accident & health	16
Total	**100**

COMPETITORS

ACE Limited	LSW
AIG	Markel
Allianz	MetLife
Allianz Life	Midland National Life
Arch Capital	Munich Re Group
Aviva	Mutual of Omaha
Bankers Life and Casualty	Philadelphia Insurance
Chubb Corp	RLI
Cincinnati Financial	Travelers Companies
CNA Financial	W. R. Berkley
The Hartford	Wells Fargo
HCC Insurance	XL Group plc
ING	Zenith National
Liberty Mutual	Zurich Financial Services

HISTORICAL FINANCIALS

Company Type: Public

Income Statement

FYE: December 31

	ASSETS ($ mil.)	NET INCOME ($ mil.)	INCOME AS % OF ASSETS	EMPLOYEES
12/09	27,683	531	1.9%	6,900
12/08	26,428	196	0.7%	600
12/07	25,808	383	1.5%	500
12/06	25,101	453	1.8%	5,200
12/05	22,816	207	0.9%	6,100
Annual Growth	5.0%	26.6%	—	3.1%

2009 Year-End Financials

Equity as % of assets: 13.7%	
Return on assets: 2.0%	Dividends
Return on equity: 16.9%	Yield: 2.1%
Long-term debt ($ mil.): 828	Payout: 11.7%
No. of shares (mil.): 111	Market value ($ mil.): 2,775
	Sales ($ mil.): 4,321

Stock History

NYSE: AFG

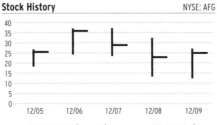

	STOCK PRICE ($) FY Close	P/E High/Low		PER SHARE ($) Earnings	Dividends	Book Value
12/09	24.95	6	3	4.45	0.52	34.00
12/08	22.88	19	8	1.67	0.50	22.39
12/07	28.88	12	8	3.10	0.40	27.39
12/06	35.91	10	7	3.75	0.37	26.34
12/05	25.54	15	11	1.75	0.33	22.10
Annual Growth	(0.6%)	—	—	26.3%	12.0%	11.4%

American Greetings

American Greetings has been building its sturdy house of cards for more than a century. The #2 US maker of greeting cards (behind Hallmark), the company makes American Greetings, Carlton Cards, and Gibson Greetings brand missives. While greeting cards make up about 70% of sales, the company also produces DesignWare party goods, Plus Mark gift wrap, and DateWorks calendars. The company's AG Interactive subsidiary distributes online greeting cards and other interactive media. The family of chairman Morry Weiss controls about 45% of the company's voting stock.

The company's core business continues to rest on traditional greeting cards and other printed products, a market segment that has largely consolidated around Hallmark and American Greetings. However, technology is rapidly changing the way people communicate and interact, putting the greeting card business into competition with online social networks such as Facebook and photo sharing services such as Flickr (owned by Yahoo!). In response, the company is focused on developing and acquiring interactive technologies and other new products to expand its offerings. AG Interactive boasts about 4 million subscribers who have unlimited access to its e-cards and ringtones. At the same time, American Greetings continues to expand its traditional cards business through organic development and acquisitions. In 2009 the company acquired Chicago-based Recycled Paper Greetings out of bankruptcy to expand its line of humor cards.

American Greetings has been keen to cut costs and divest under-performing or non-core assets. Most significantly the company sold its chain of more than 340 retail stores to California-based Schurman Fine Papers in 2009. The divestment was part of an effort by American Greetings to focus on its core greeting cards and other media products. (The retail outlets continue to operate under the banners American Greetings, Carlton Cards, and Papyrus.) As part of the deal, American Greetings acquired Schurman's wholesale supply business that distributes Papyrus branded products to other mass merchants. American Greetings also closed down its party goods operations that year and signed a supply deal with Amscan to supply the greeting card company with party products.

The company put on hold its plans to sell some of its branded characters in 2010. American Greetings had agreed to sell its Strawberry Shortcake and Care Bears properties to Toronto-based animation giant Cookie Jar Group for about $195 million, but after delays and much legal wrangling the two sides settled their dispute and terminated the sale.

In 2010 the company signaled that it might move its headquarters out from the Cleveland suburb of Brooklyn after voters there approved a hike in city payroll taxes. American Greetings has been headquartered in the Cleveland area since its beginnings in 1906 and moved to its present location in the 1950s.

HISTORY

In 1906 Polish immigrant Jacob Sapirstein founded Sapirstein Greeting Card Company and began selling postcards from a horse-drawn wagon. The outbreak of WWI and the resulting separation of families helped spur demand for the company's products. The impact of the war also helped shape the company's future: After an embargo was imposed on cards produced in Germany, Sapirstein decided to begin manufacturing his own cards.

Sapirstein's sons eventually joined the burgeoning company and, in 1940, after adopting the American Greetings Publishers name, the company's sales topped $1 million. The company incorporated as American Greetings in 1944 and went public in 1952. It introduced Hi Brows, a line of funny studio cards, in 1956 and broke ground on a 1.5-million-sq.-ft. headquarters building the same year.

In 1960 Sapirstein's son, Irving Stone (all three Sapirstein sons changed their surname to Stone, a derivative of Sapirstein) was appointed president, and Jacob Sapirstein became chairman. The ubiquitous Holly Hobbie made her first appearance on greeting cards in 1967 (within a decade, she had become the world's most popular licensed female character). In 1968 American Greetings' sales exceeded $100 million.

American Greetings introduced the Ziggy character in 1972 and launched Plus Mark, a maker of seasonal wrapping paper, boxed cards, and accessories six years later. Irving Stone succeeded his father as chairman and CEO in 1978, and Morry Weiss, Irving Stone's son-in-law, was appointed president.

With the success of Holly Hobbie licensing, American Greetings was prompted to create its own licensing division in 1980. In 1982 it introduced the Care Bears, licensed characters that appeared in animated films. Following the death of Jacob Sapirstein in 1987 (at age 102), Morry Weiss became chairman and CEO, and Irving Stone became founder-chairman.

In 1993 the company bought Magnivision (nonprescription reading glasses). It ventured onto the Internet two years later, when it began offering online greeting cards.

Its acquisitions of greeting card companies Camden Graphics and Hanson White in 1998 helped American Greetings double its presence in the UK. As part of an international restructuring plan, in 1999 the company shuttered a Canadian plant, eliminating 650 jobs.

Founder-chairman Irving Stone died in early 2000 at the age of 90. Also that year American Greetings paid $175 million for smaller rival Gibson Greetings, along with that company's stake in Egreetings Network. In 2001 the company bought the remaining shares of Egreetings Network, folding the business into its online operations; later that year it did the same with Excite-Home's BlueMountain.com e-mail cards unit.

In 2003 CEO Morry Weiss and president James Spira resigned from the management of the company. Weiss retained his chairman title and Spira remained on the board. Morry's sons, Zev and Jeffrey, became CEO and president, respectively. In late 2004 the company closed one of its plants in Tennessee and laid off 450 people.

The company sold its educational products unit Learning Horizons in 2007 to a portfolio company of Evolution Capital Partners. American Greetings expanded its digital media operations with the 2007 acquisition of photo sharing website Webshots from CNET Networks for $45 million. The following year it purchased PhotoWorks for nearly $30 million.

EXECUTIVES

Chairman: Morry Weiss, age 69, $2,886,223 total compensation
CEO and Director: Zev Weiss, age 43, $1,463,808 total compensation
President, COO, and Director: Jeffrey M. (Jeff) Weiss, age 46, $2,552,346 total compensation
SVP and CFO: Stephen J. Smith, age 46, $1,362,384 total compensation
SVP, General Counsel, and Secretary: Catherine M. (Cathy) Kilbane, age 47
SVP Creative and Merchandising: Thomas H. Johnston, age 62
SVP and General Manager, AG Interactive: Michael Waxman-Lenz
SVP and CIO: Douglas W. (Doug) Rommel, age 54
SVP Human Resources: Brian T. McGrath, age 59
SVP Wal-Mart Team; President, Carlton Cards Limited (Canada): Robert C. Swellie, age 58
SVP International and Managing Director, UK Greetings: John S.N. Charlton, age 63
SVP Executive Sales and Marketing Officer: John W. Beeder, age 50, $1,727,753 total compensation
SVP Enterprise Resource Planning: Erwin Weiss, age 61
SVP and Executive Supply Chain Officer: Michael L. Goulder, age 50, $690,595 total compensation
VP and Corporate Controller: Joseph B. Cipollone, age 51
CEO, Recycled Paper Greetings: Jude Rake, age 48
Executive Director Product Development: Kelly Ricker
Executive Director New Product Concept: Carol Miller
Auditors: Ernst & Young LLP

LOCATIONS

HQ: American Greetings Corporation
1 American Rd., Cleveland, OH 44144
Phone: 216-252-7300   **Fax:** 216-252-6778
Web: corporate.americangreetings.com

2010 Sales

	$ mil.	% of total
US	1,266.9	77
UK	209.1	13
Other countries	159.9	10
Total	**1,635.9**	**100**

PRODUCTS/OPERATIONS

2010 Sales

	$ mil.	% of total
Greeting cards		
Everyday products	764.2	47
Seasonal cards	368.8	22
Gift packaging	221.2	14
Other	281.7	17
Total	**1,635.9**	**100**

2010 Sales

	$ mil.	% of total
Social expression products		
North America	1,235.2	75
International	254.0	16
AG Interactive	80.5	5
Retail stores	11.8	1
Other	54.4	3
Total	**1,635.9**	**100**

Selected Products and Operations

Greeting cards
  American Greetings
  Carlton Cards
  Gibson
  Just For You
  Papyrus
  Recycled Paper Greetings
  Tender Thoughts

Gift packaging and other
  DateWorks (calendars)
  DesignWare (party goods)
  Plus Mark (gift wrap)
AG Interactive (online and interactive media)
  AmericanGreetings.com
  BlueMountain.com
  Egreetings.com
  Kiwee.com
  PhotoWorks
  Webshots

COMPETITORS

AOL
Carte Blanche Greetings
CSS Industries
Eastman Kodak
Facebook
Google
Hallmark
International Greetings
MySpace
NobleWorks
Pomegranate Communications
Quotable Cards
Shutterfly
Snapfish
SPS Studios
Taylor Corporation
Yahoo!

HISTORICAL FINANCIALS

Company Type: Public

Income Statement

FYE: Last day in February

	REVENUE ($ mil.)	NET INCOME ($ mil.)	NET PROFIT MARGIN	EMPLOYEES
2/10	1,636	82	5.0%	26,000
2/09	1,691	(228)	—	26,600
2/08	1,777	83	4.7%	27,300
2/07	1,745	42	2.4%	9,400
2/06	1,886	84	4.5%	29,500
Annual Growth	**(3.5%)**	**(0.8%)**	**—**	**(3.1%)**

2010 Year-End Financials

Debt ratio: 51.7%
Return on equity: 14.0%
Cash ($ mil.): 138
Current ratio: 1.82
Long-term debt ($ mil.): 329
No. of shares (mil.): 40
Dividends
  Yield: 1.9%
  Payout: 17.7%
Market value ($ mil.): 763

Stock History

NYSE: AM

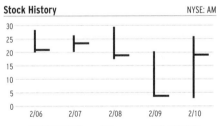

	STOCK PRICE ($) FY Close	P/E High	P/E Low	Earnings	Dividends	Book Value
2/10	19.07	13	2	2.03	0.36	15.89
2/09	3.73	—	—	(4.89)	0.60	13.22
2/08	18.82	19	12	1.52	0.40	23.57
2/07	23.38	37	29	0.71	0.32	25.30
2/06	20.98	24	18	1.16	0.32	30.49
Annual Growth	**(2.4%)**	**—**	**—**	**15.0%**	**3.0%**	**(15.0%)**

American International Group

Even to this day American International Group (AIG) is one of the world's largest insurance firms. While it remains in the spotlight for staggering losses and government bailouts, the company's subsidiaries are still providing general property/casualty insurance, life insurance and retirement services, and some financial services to commercial, institutional, and individual customers in the US and more than 130 countries around the world. Some of its non-insurance activities include financing commercial aircraft leasing and port operations in the US. After $182 billion in bailouts, the US government holds more than 80% of the company, and its future and holdings remain in a state of flux.

If all goes to its current plan, the company will be left with its profitable US and foreign commercial property/casualty businesses. To put a better face on those assets, AIG created a new independently managed company to hold them and named it Chartis. In addition to good old property/casualty, AIG will also hang on to its domestic life insurance and retirement services businesses. It will also keep some foreign life insurance businesses around as well.

The company's grand old HSB Group (industrial equipment insurance) was sold to Munich Re for $739 million, and Zurich Financial Services paid $1.9 billion for US personal auto insurer 21st Century Insurance in 2009. The company then handed over its US life insurance finance businesses to First Insurance Funding in exchange for $679 million, and has agreed to sell a chunk of its asset management businesses to Hong Kong-based Pacific Century Group for $500 million.

AIG has agreed to sell its Taiwan unit Nan Shan Life to Hong Kong-based Primus Financial for $2.2 billion. AIG has also announced that it will sell its Asia-based American Life Insurance Company (ALICO) to MetLife for $6.8 billion in cash and $8.7 billion in equity (effectively giving AIG a 20% stake in MetLife).

AIG is winding down the operations of its AIG Financial Products subsidiary, the unit whose astonishing losses brought the company to its knees. The unit has quit writing new business and has sold several key investments, including its 50% stake in London City Airport. It has also divested a $1.9 billion portfolio of energy and infrastructure assets.

In mid-2009 Robert Benmosche (a former MetLife executive) was named CEO of the company — the fifth in five years — and Harvey Golub was named non-executive chairman. In mid-2010 Golub stepped down and was replaced as chairman by Robert (Steve) Miller.

Among the many concerns for Benmosche to contemplate: with government strings attached to AIG's corporate purse, top executive salaries have been gutted and rival insurers have lured away half of the company's top level executives. Loyal executives are being expected to balance the biscuit on their noses — most of their reduced pay is coming in the form of stock that they'll have to hang onto for several years before liquidating.

HISTORY

Former ice cream parlor owner Cornelius Starr founded property/casualty insurer American Asiatic Underwriters in Shanghai in 1919. After underwriting business for other insurers, Starr began selling life insurance policies to the Chinese in 1921 (foreign companies were loath to do so despite the longevity of the Chinese). In 1926 he opened a New York office specializing in foreign risks incurred by American companies. As WWII loomed, Starr moved his base to the US; when the war cut off business in Europe, he focused on Latin America. After a brief postwar return to China, the company was kicked out by the communist government.

In the 1950s the company began providing disability, health, and life insurance and pension plans for employees who moved from country to country. Starr chose his successor, Maurice "Hank" Greenberg, in 1967 and died the next year. Greenberg, who had come aboard in 1960 to develop overseas operations, took over the newly formed American International Group, a holding company for Starr's worldwide collection of insurance concerns. Greenberg's policy of achieving underwriting profits forced the company to use tight fiscal discipline. AIG went public in 1969.

By 1975 AIG was the largest foreign life insurer in much of Asia and the only insurer with global sales and support facilities. AIG's underwriting policies saved it when price wars from 1979 to 1984 brought heavy losses to most insurers. In 1987 AIG became the second US-owned insurer (after Chubb) to enter the traditionally closed South Korean market.

The 1980s saw AIG begin investment operations in Asia, increase its presence in health care, and form a financial services group. The firm resumed its Chinese operations in 1993 after triumphing over stiff opposition from state-owned monopolies.

In 2001 AIG agreed to be the business sponsor for the troubled Chiyoda Mutual Life Insurance Company; it also bought American General to bolster AIG's share of the lucrative US retirement-planning market.

The insurer paid out about $800 million in claims related to the attacks on the World Trade Center. Legal settlements forced the company to take a $1.8 billion charge in 2003 in a move that surprised analysts and sent shock waves throughout the industry, causing other large insurance stocks to plummet.

Legal woes continued to befall AIG in 2004, when two company executives pleaded guilty to charges of involvement in an alleged price-fixing scheme that also involved insurance broker Marsh and insurer ACE. AIG also reached a $126 million settlement with federal regulators in 2004 over allegations the insurer sold products and services used to help customers improve their financial appearance.

In 2004 AIG came under investigation by the Office of the Attorney General for the State of New York, the New York Insurance Department, and the SEC into possible accounting irregularities and the company's use of offshore reinsurers. In early 2005 Greenberg was forced to step down as CEO. Former vice chairman and co-COO Martin Sullivan was named to succeed him. Soon after, Greenberg — the man most associated with the company — was forced to give up his chairman's seat as well.

As a result of the allegations, which included accounting irregularities, fraud, and bid-rigging, and along with acknowledging some wrongdoing, in 2006 the company agreed to pay a $1.6 billion settlement to the three agencies.

EXECUTIVES

Chairman: Robert S. (Steve) Miller Jr., age 68
President, CEO, and Director:
  Robert H. (Bob) Benmosche, age 65,
  $2,706,530 total compensation
EVP and CFO: David L. Herzog, age 50,
  $6,741,465 total compensation
**EVP Legal, Compliance, Regulatory Affairs, and
  Government Affairs and General Counsel:**
  Thomas A. (Tom) Russo, age 66
EVP Financial Services: William N. (Bill) Dooley, age 57
EVP Foreign General Insurance:
  Nicholas C. (Nick) Walsh, age 59,
  $9,338,687 total compensation
EVP AIG Property Casualty Group: Kristian P. Moor,
  age 50, $10,404,838 total compensation
EVP Life Insurance: Mark A. Wilson, age 43
EVP Finance, Risk, and Investments: Peter D. Hancock,
  age 51
SVP Divestiture: Alain Karaoglan
SVP Human Resources and Communications:
  Jeffrey J. Hurd, age 43
SVP and Chief Administrative Officer:
  Michael R. Cowan
SVP Strategic Planning: Brian T. Schreiber, age 44
SVP and Chief Risk Officer: Robert E. Lewis, age 58
SVP, Secretary, and Deputy General Counsel:
  Kathleen E. Shannon, age 60
SVP Communications: Christina Pretto
SVP and Chief Investment Officer: Monika Machon,
  age 49
VP and Director Investor Relations:
  Charlene M. Hamrah
**Chairman, International Life and Retirement Services;
  Chairman, American Life Insurance Company, and
  Chairman, American International Assurance
  Company Limited:** Rodney O. (Rod) Martin Jr., age 57,
  $10,193,191 total compensation
Chairman and CEO, Global Investment Group:
  Win J. Neuger, age 60, $6,354,969 total compensation
President and CEO, American General Life Companies:
  Mary Jane B. Fortin
**President and CEO, Domestic Life and Retirement
  Services:** Jay S. Wintrob, age 52
Auditors: PricewaterhouseCoopers LLP

LOCATIONS

HQ: American International Group, Inc.
  70 Pine St., New York, NY 10270
Phone: 212-770-7000   **Fax:** 212-509-9705
Web: www.aigcorporate.com

2009 Sales

	$ mil.	% of total
North America	37,228	39
Asia	35,180	37
Other regions	23,596	24
Total	**96,004**	**100**

PRODUCTS/OPERATIONS

2009 Sales

	$ mil.	% of total
Premiums & other considerations	64,702	63
Net investment income	25,239	25
Net realized capital losses	(6,854)	—
Unrealized market valuation gains	1,418	1
Other income	11,499	11
Total	**96,004**	**100**

2009 Sales

	$ mil.	% of total
General insurance	35,039	37
Domestic life insurance & retirement services	11,366	12
Foreign life insurance & retirement s ervices	32,937	34
Financial services	9,576	10
Other, consolidation & eliminations	7,086	7
Total	**96,004**	**100**

Selected Subsidiaries

Domestic Life Insurance & Retirement Services
  American General Life Insurance Company (American General)
  American General Life and Accident Insurance Company (AGLA)
  SunAmerica Annuity & Life Assurance Company (SunAmerica Annuity)
  The United States Life Insurance Company in the City of New York (USLIFE)
  The Variable Annuity Life Insurance Company (VALIC)
  Western National Life Insurance Company (Western National)
Financial Services
  AIG Credit Corp. (A.I. Credit)
  AIG Consumer Finance Group (AIGCFG)
  AIG Financial Products Corp. (AIGFP)
  American General Finance, Inc. (AGF)
  International Lease Finance Corporation (ILFC)
Foreign Life Insurance & Retirement Services
  AIG Edison Life Insurance Company
  AIG Star Life Insurance Co., Ltd.
  American International Assurance Company, Limited (AIA)
  American Life Insurance Company (ALICO)
  The Philippine American Life & General Insurance Company (Philamlife)
General Insurance
  American Home Assurance Company
  American International Reinsurance Company Limited (AIRCO)
  AIU Insurance Company (AIUI)
  Chartis Overseas, Ltd.
  Lexington Insurance Company
  National Union Fire Insurance Company of Pittsburgh, Pa (National Union)
  New Hampshire Insurance Company

COMPETITORS

ACE Limited
AEGON
Allianz
AXA
Berkshire Hathaway
Chubb Corp
CNA Financial
General Re
Hanover Insurance
The Hartford
ING
John Hancock Financial Services
Liberty Mutual
Manulife Financial
MetLife
Nationwide
New York Life
Northwestern Mutual
Prudential
Tokio Marine
Travelers Companies
Zurich Financial Services

HISTORICAL FINANCIALS

Company Type: Public

Income Statement

FYE: December 31

	ASSETS ($ mil.)	NET INCOME ($ mil.)	INCOME AS % OF ASSETS	EMPLOYEES
12/09	847,585	(12,313)	—	96,000
12/08	860,418	(99,289)	—	116,000
12/07	1,060,505	6,200	0.6%	116,000
12/06	979,414	14,014	1.4%	106,000
12/05	853,370	10,477	1.2%	97,000
Annual Growth	**(0.2%)**	**—**	**—**	**(0.3%)**

2009 Year-End Financials

Equity as % of assets: 0.0%
Return on assets: —
Return on equity: —
Long-term debt ($ mil.): 141,472
No. of shares (mil.): 135
Dividends
  Yield: 0.0%
  Payout: —
Market value ($ mil.): 4,051
Sales ($ mil.): 96,004

Stock History

NYSE: AIG

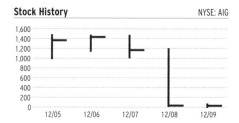

	STOCK PRICE ($) FY Close	P/E High/Low		PER SHARE ($) Earnings	Dividends	Book Value
12/09	29.98	—	—	(90.48)	0.00	516.73
12/08	31.40	—	—	(756.80)	12.40	390.08
12/07	1,166.00	31	21	47.80	14.60	708.97
12/06	1,433.20	14	11	107.20	12.60	752.46
12/05	1,364.60	18	13	79.80	11.00	638.79
Annual Growth	**(61.5%)**	**—**	**—**	**—**	**—**	**(5.2%)**

American Water Works

Water, water, everywhere — and American Water Works wants to own it. The company, once a subsidiary of German utility giant RWE, is by far the largest public water utility in the US. Through its regulated utilities and its contract services division, American Water Works serves about 16 million consumers in 32 US states, plus Manitoba and Ontario. The company also provides wastewater treatment in some of its service areas. Its regulated operations account for 90% of sales. Nonregulated subsidiary American Water Works Service provides contract management services for water and wastewater systems. In 2008 RWE spun off American Water Works, but retained a majority stake, which has been reduced to about 25%.

Boosting its presence in the industrial contract market, in 2009 the company acquired Environmental Management Corporation (EMC) from Linde. EMC has 55 water and wastewater contract operations with industrial and municipal customers in the US and Canada.

In 2007 the company's New Jersey American Water unit acquired S.J. Services Inc., expanding the parent company's service area and customer base deeper into Southern New Jersey. The next year saw its Pennsylvania American

Water subsidiary acquire the Claysville-Donegal Joint Municipal Authority water and wastewater systems. Those two states provide almost half of the company's regulated business.

Jeffry Sterba was named president and CEO of American Water Works in 2010. He was previously the chairman of PNM Resources, which operates two electric utilities and a power-generation subsidiary in New Mexico. He replaced Donald Correll, who resigned.

HISTORY

American Water Works was founded in 1886 as the American Water Works & Guarantee Company. By the time it became American Water Works & Electric (AWW&E) in 1914, it ranked among the giant US utility holding companies and owned a bevy of unrelated electric, gas, and water companies, as well as California real estate. While AWW&E was growing, John H. Ware Jr., an eighth-grade dropout, bought water companies nationwide, including Northeastern Water.

After the 1929 stock market crash ruined many utilities, the federal government passed the Public Utility Holding Company Act of 1935 to break up and regulate the powerful trusts that controlled the nation's electric and gas utilities. AWW&E tried to fight the act in the courts (but filed a reorganization plan in 1937, the first utility holding company to do so, and divested its California land holdings. The Supreme Court upheld the act in 1946, and the company put its electric utilities and its highly profitable water properties up for sale as American Water Works Co., Inc.

Ware submitted the only bid in 1947, and his Northeastern Water paid $13 million for a 51% share of a company with assets of more than $180 million. The company went public that year.

A few years after buying American Water Works, Ware spun off its electric holdings. In 1960 Ware retired as chairman and was replaced by his son, John Ware III. Three years later, Northeastern Water and American Water Works merged their operations, and in 1976 the company moved to Voorhees, New Jersey.

The federal government, which had started regulating water quality in 1974, continued to pass tougher and tougher water laws — making it harder for smaller players to survive. After decades of buying and selling small water companies, American Water Works entered a period of consolidation and integration that helped it survive the economic downturn of the late 1960s and 1970s. By 1984, the year John Ware III retired, American had 33 operating units (it had acquired more than 150 companies since the 1930s). Ware was replaced by Philadelphia banker Sam Ballam. In 1987 Marilyn Ware Lewis, daughter of John Ware III, became chairman, bringing the company back into the family's purview.

In 1998 James Barr took over as CEO. Barr, who had started at American Water Works as a 20-year-old records clerk, recognized opportunity in new federal water-quality rules that forced municipalities to upgrade their old and ailing water systems. Lacking the resources to make all the repairs themselves, many were turning to the private sector. That year American Water Works began scouting for acquisitions and completed 22.

The next year the company bought National Enterprises, a family-owned water utility operator that served 1.5 million customers in Missouri, Indiana, Illinois, and New York. The 1999

$700 million acquisition was the largest in the history of the US water utility industry. American Water Works topped it, however, later that year when it agreed to acquire the water and wastewater businesses of Citizens Utilities (now Citizens Communications); the acquisition was completed in 2002 in a $979 million deal.

In 2000 American Water Works agreed to buy California water utility SJW for about $480 million, but the companies terminated the deal in 2001 because of delays in obtaining approval from California regulators.

Unfazed by the collapse of the SJW deal, American Water Works in 2001 bought the North American operations of Enron's Azurix water unit. American Water Works also agreed to sell water utilities in Connecticut, Massachusetts, New York, and New Hampshire to UK-based Kelda Group and its US subsidiary, Aquarion; the deal was completed in 2002 for $224 million.

In September 2001 the company agreed to be acquired by RWE for $4.6 billion in cash and $4 billion in assumed debt; the deal was completed in 2003. Chairman Marilyn Ware Lewis and CEO James Barr both left the company upon completion of the acquisition; Thames Water CEO Bill Alexander inherited both positions. Later in 2003 Thames Water's Jeremy Pelczer took over the chief executive's role as president of American Water Works; Alexander remained chairman.

The company was acquired by RWE in 2003.

EXECUTIVES

Chairman: George MacKenzie Jr., age 61
President, CEO, and Board Member:
Jeffry E. (Jeff) Sterba, age 54
CTO; President, American Water Works Service Company and American Water Services:
John S. Young, age 56, $1,608,402 total compensation
President and COO, Regulated Operations:
Walter J. Lynch, age 47, $1,336,041 total compensation
SVP Corporate Communications and External Affairs:
Laura L. Monica, age 53
SVP Corporate and Business Development:
William D. (Bill) Patterson, age 55
SVP, Eastern Division; President, Kentucky American Water: Nick O. Rowe, age 52
SVP and CFO: Ellen C. Wolf, age 56, $1,433,402 total compensation
SVP Human Resources: Sean G. Burke, age 54
SVP, Western Division: David Baker
SVP, General Counsel, and Secretary: Kellye L. Walker
VP and CIO: Emily Ashworth
VP Investor Relations: Edward D. Vallejo
VP and Controller: Mark Chesla, age 50
Director Communications: Maureen Duffy
Auditors: PricewaterhouseCoopers LLP

LOCATIONS

HQ: American Water Works Company, Inc.
1025 Laurel Oak Rd., Voorhees, NJ 08043
Phone: 856-346-8200   **Fax:** 856-346-8440
Web: www.amwater.com

PRODUCTS/OPERATIONS

2009 Sales

	$ mil.	% of total
Regulated	2,207.3	90
Non-regulated	257.7	10
Adjustments	(24.3)	—
Total	**2,440.7**	**100**

Selected Subsidiaries

Arizona American Water
California American Water
Hawaii American Water
Illinois American Water
Indiana American Water
Iowa American Water
Kentucky American Water
Long Island Americam Water
Missouri American Water
New Jersey American Water
New Mexico American Water
Ohio American Water
Pennsylvania American Water
Tennessee American Water
Virginia American Water
West Virginia American Water

COMPETITORS

American States Water
Aqua America
Aquarion
California Water Service
Connecticut Water Service
Indianapolis Water
Memphis Light
Middlesex Water
Severn Trent
SJW
SouthWest Water
SRP
United Water Inc.
Utilities, Inc.
Veolia Environnement

HISTORICAL FINANCIALS

Company Type: Public

Income Statement

FYE: December 31

	REVENUE ($ mil.)	NET INCOME ($ mil.)	NET PROFIT MARGIN	EMPLOYEES
12/09	2,441	(233)	—	7,700
12/08	2,337	(562)	—	7,300
12/07	2,214	(343)	—	7,000
12/06	2,093	(162)	—	6,900
12/05	2,137	(325)	—	—
Annual Growth	**3.4%**	**—**	**—**	**3.7%**

2009 Year-End Financials

Debt ratio: 132.8%
Return on equity: —
Cash ($ mil.): 22
Current ratio: 0.82
Long-term debt ($ mil.): 5,312
No. of shares (mil.): 175
Dividends
Yield: 3.7%
Payout: —
Market value ($ mil.): 3,917

Stock History

NYSE: AWK

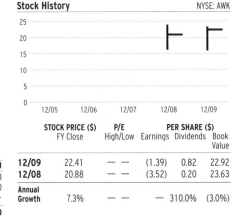

	STOCK PRICE ($) FY Close	P/E High/Low	PER SHARE ($)		
			Earnings	Dividends	Book Value
12/09	22.41	— —	(1.39)	0.82	22.92
12/08	20.88	— —	(3.52)	0.20	23.63
Annual Growth	**7.3%**	**— —**	**—**	**310.0%**	**(3.0%)**

AmeriCredit Corp.

AmeriCredit gives credit where it's not necessarily due. The company purchases loans made by about 10,000 franchised and independent auto dealers primarily to consumers with less-than-ideal credit histories. It typically finances low-mileage, late-model used cars (about 80% of all loans), and the occasional new automobile. The company periodically transfers its loans to securitization trusts, retains the servicing, and reinvests the proceeds in new loans. Post-credit market meltdown, the lender owns some $11 billion in managed auto receivables. It operates about 15 credit centers in suburban areas near car dealerships. General Motors is acquiring AmeriCredit for some $3.5 billion in an effort to boost sales.

By acquiring the lender, GM will once again own an in-house finance arm — which it hasn't had since it sold control of the former GMAC in 2006. The transaction should help the automaker increase sales to underserved nonprime buyers and leasing customers. Currently, investment firms Leucadia and Fairholme Funds each own about 25% of AmeriCredit.

Going into 2008, AmeriCredit's plans for growth included making more direct-to-consumer loans, adding leasing programs, and expanding in Canada. However, credit market conditions took a nosedive as loan defaults increased, and the company revised its strategies. It raised its minimum credit score requirements for new loans, closed more than half of its credit centers, and eliminated about 1,000 staff positions. AmeriCredit also stopped issuing loans directly to customers, stopped providing lease financing through its dealership network, and discontinued operations in Canada.

For fiscal 2009 the company originated $1.29 billion in loans compared to $6.29 billion for the same period in 2008. Originating loans became tough when AmeriCredit's main funding source, the asset-backed securities market, froze up. The company did manage a bit of an in-house thaw when it secured a line of credit through 2010 that will allow it to fund up to $1 billion in loans.

HISTORY

AmeriCredit began in 1986 as UrCarco — used car lots offering both sales and financing to customers with poor credit. It was the inspiration of Cash America pawnshop executives Jack Daugherty and Clifton Morris, who financed UrCarco with four other investors and created the nation's first chain of used car lots. The company's 1989 IPO met with great success, but the excitement was short-lived; after quadrupling in size to 20 lots, UrCarco became mired in huge losses from poor underwriting and bad loans on top of declining car sales. In 1991 the company began reinventing itself, completely restructuring after receiving $10 million from Rainwater Management.

In 1992 UrCarco changed its name to AmeriCredit, liquidated its used car business, and expanded its indirect lending services. The company improved its underwriting by adopting a credit-risk scorecard in 1994 (with assistance from credit-scoring industry leader Fair Isaac Corporation). In 1996 AmeriCredit acquired California-based Rancho Vista Mortgage (it became AmeriCredit Corporation of California) and established a home equity lending operation, making and acquiring loans through a network of mortgage brokers.

The late 1990s provided some challenges. AmeriCredit survived the subprime market meltdown of 1997 and faced continuing criticism for its accounting practices. In 1999 it formed an alliance with Chase Manhattan (now JPMorgan Chase) to provide subprime financing to auto dealers who do business with Chase. That year it discontinued its mortgage operations and liquidated its AmeriCredit Corporation of California subsidiary to focus on its auto lending.

In 2001 it teamed with JPMorgan Chase, Wells Fargo, and other finance companies to launch DealerTrack, an online system that allows dealers to submit loan applications electronically to various lenders and receive faster responses.

EXECUTIVES

Chairman: Clifton H. Morris Jr., age 74, $1,170,519 total compensation
President, CEO, and Director: Daniel E. (Dan) Berce, age 56, $1,798,534 total compensation
EVP, CFO, and Treasurer: Chris A. Choate, age 46, $836,964 total compensation
EVP and Controller: James Fehleison
EVP Structured Finance: Susan Sheffield
EVP Dealer Services: Kyle R. Birch, $574,258 total compensation
EVP, Chief Credit and Risk Officer: Steven P. Bowman, age 42, $662,632 total compensation
EVP Consumer Services: Brian S. Mock, $574,510 total compensation
VP Investor Relations: Caitlin DeYoung
Secretary: J. Michael May
Auditors: Deloitte & Touche LLP

LOCATIONS

HQ: AmeriCredit Corp.
801 Cherry St., Ste. 3900, Fort Worth, TX 76102
Phone: 817-302-7000   **Fax:** 817-302-7101
Web: www.americredit.com

PRODUCTS/OPERATIONS

2009 Sales

	$ mil.	% of total
Finance charges	1,902.7	91
Other	179.7	9
Total	**2,082.4**	**100**

COMPETITORS

Capital One Auto Finance
Consumer Portfolio
Credit Acceptance
First Investors Financial Services
HSBC Finance
Nicholas Financial
United PanAm Financial
World Acceptance

HISTORICAL FINANCIALS

Company Type: Public

Income Statement

FYE: June 30

	ASSETS ($ mil.)	NET INCOME ($ mil.)	INCOME AS % OF ASSETS	EMPLOYEES
6/09	11,984	14	0.1%	3,064
6/08	16,547	(69)	—	3,832
6/07	17,811	360	2.0%	4,831
6/06	13,068	306	2.3%	4,025
6/05	10,947	286	2.6%	3,653
Annual Growth	**2.3%**	**(53.0%)**	**—**	**(4.3%)**

2009 Year-End Financials

Equity as % of assets: 17.2%	Dividends
Return on assets: 0.1%	Yield: —
Return on equity: 0.7%	Payout: —
Long-term debt ($ mil.): 554	Market value ($ mil.): 1,823
No. of shares (mil.): 135	Sales ($ mil.): 2,082

Stock History

NYSE: ACF

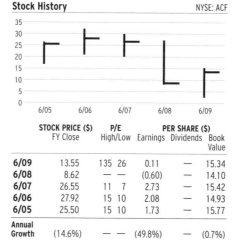

	STOCK PRICE ($) FY Close	P/E High/Low		PER SHARE ($) Earnings	Dividends	Book Value
6/09	13.55	135	26	0.11	—	15.34
6/08	8.62	—	—	(0.60)	—	14.10
6/07	26.55	11	7	2.73	—	15.42
6/06	27.92	15	10	2.08	—	14.93
6/05	25.50	15	10	1.73	—	15.77
Annual Growth	**(14.6%)**	**—**	**—**	**(49.8%)**	**—**	**(0.7%)**

AmeriGas Partners

America has a gas with AmeriGas Partners. Purveying propane has propelled the company to its position as one of the top two US retail propane marketers (rivaling Ferrellgas for the #1 slot). It serves 1.3 million residential, commercial, industrial, agricultural, motor fuel, and wholesale customers from about 1,200 locations in 50 states. AmeriGas also sells propane-related supplies and equipment and exchanges prefilled portable tanks for empty ones. The company stores propane in Arizona, California, and Virginia and distributes its products through an interstate carrier structure that runs across the US and in Canada. Utility holding company UGI owns 44% of AmeriGas.

In 2008 the enterprise bought Penn Fuel Propane and four other companies, boosting its customer base by 42,000 and its annual propane output by 20 million gallons.

AmeriGas is also growing internally through the expansion of its prefilled propane business (cylinder exchange) located at about 25,000 retail locations in the US.

HISTORY

The forerunner of AmeriGas Partners was set up in 1959, when UGI subsidiary Ugite Gas entered the liquefied petroleum gas market in Maryland and Pennsylvania. By the early 1970s the company had expanded into eight states, and in 1977 AmeriGas was formed to replace Ugite Gas.

In the 1980s UGI began to focus more on propane. AmeriGas became one of the industry's leading players when it acquired Cal Gas in 1987, and three years later UGI merged AmeriGas with AP Propane. In 1993 UGI acquired a stake in propane marketer Petrolane, and the next year it formed AmeriGas Partners to acquire AmeriGas Propane, AmeriGas Propane-2 (another UGI unit), and Petrolane.

In 1995 UGI sold 42% of AmeriGas Partners to the public. AmeriGas Partners acquired Hawaii's Oahu Gas Service, Pur-Gas Service in Florida, and Enderby Gas in Texas the next year. In 1997 it acquired 14 firms in Florida, Georgia, Illinois, Louisiana, Mississippi, and South Carolina. The next year it bought 10 more companies and expanded its prefilled propane tank operations by more than 4,000 locations.

AmeriGas gained retail propane operations in five western states from All Star Gas in 2000. The next year the company paid $202 million for NiSource's Columbia Energy Group propane businesses. In 2003 AmeriGas purchased the propane distribution assets of Active Propane, Rocky Mountain LP, and Noreika Gas, as well as three propane distribution outlets from Suburban Propane Partners. Later that year, the company purchased the retail propane distribution business of Horizon Propane.

In a consolidating industry, the fuel supplier has pursued a strategy of growth through acquisitions. In 2007 the company acquired Royal Dutch Shell's US retail propane operations. It also purchased All Star Gas.

EXECUTIVES

Chairman, AmeriGas Propane: Lon R. Greenberg, age 58, $9,948,066 total compensation
Vice Chairman, AmeriGas Propane: John L. Walsh, age 53, $3,762,308 total compensation
President, CEO, and Director, AmeriGas Propane: Eugene V. N. Bissell, age 55, $2,234,201 total compensation
VP, Secretary, and General Counsel, AmeriGas Propane: Robert H. Knauss, age 55, $2,200,217 total compensation
VP Finance and CFO, AmeriGas Propane: Jerry E. Sheridan, age 43, $791,929 total compensation
VP Sales Operations, AmeriGas Propane: William G. Robey
VP Operations Support, AmeriGas Propane: Kevin Rumbelow, age 48
VP Field Operations, AmeriGas Propane: Randy A. Hannigan, age 59
VP and CIO, AmeriGas Propane: Richard W. Fabrizio
VP Sales and Marketing, AmeriGas Propane: Andrew J. Peyton, age 41
VP Human Resources, AmeriGas Propane: William D. Katz, age 55
VP and Treasurer, AmeriGas Propane: Robert W. (Bob) Krick
VP, AmeriGas Cylinder Exchange: Joseph B. Powers
Investor and Media Relations, AmeriGas Propane: Brenda Blake
Chief Accounting Officer and Controller, AmeriGas Propane: William J. Stanczak, age 53
Auditors: PricewaterhouseCoopers LLP

LOCATIONS

HQ: AmeriGas Partners, L.P.
460 N. Gulph Rd., King of Prussia, PA 19406
Phone: 610-337-7000   **Fax:** 610-992-3259
Web: www.amerigas.com

PRODUCTS/OPERATIONS

2009 Sales

	$ mil.	% of total
Propane		
Retail	1,976.0	87
Wholesale	115.9	5
Other	168.2	8
Total	**2,260.1**	**100**

Selected Subsidiaries

AmeriGas Eagle Finance Corp.
AmeriGas Finance Corp.
AmeriGas Propane, L.P. (99%)
  AmeriGas Eagle Propane, Inc.
    AmeriGas Eagle Holdings, Inc.
      Active Propane of Wisconsin LLC
  AmeriGas Eagle Propane, L.P. (99%)
    AmeriGas Eagle Parts & Service, Inc.
  AmeriGas Propane Parts & Service, Inc.
AP Eagle Finance Corp.

COMPETITORS

Energy Transfer
Ferrellgas Partners
Piedmont Natural Gas
Southern States
Star Gas Partners
Suburban Propane

HISTORICAL FINANCIALS

Company Type: Public

Income Statement

FYE: September 30

	REVENUE ($ mil.)	NET INCOME ($ mil.)	NET PROFIT MARGIN	EMPLOYEES
9/09	2,260	225	9.9%	5,950
9/08	2,815	158	5.6%	5,900
9/07	2,277	191	8.4%	6,200
9/06	2,119	91	4.3%	5,900
9/05	1,963	61	3.1%	6,000
Annual Growth	3.6%	38.6%	—	(0.2%)

2009 Year-End Financials

Debt ratio: —
Return on equity: —
Cash ($ mil.): 59
Current ratio: 0.75
Long-term debt ($ mil.): 783

No. of shares (mil.): 57
Dividends
  Yield: 7.3%
  Payout: 73.0%
Market value ($ mil.): 2,057

Stock History

NYSE: APU

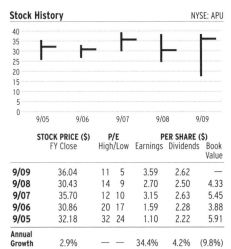

	STOCK PRICE ($) FY Close	P/E High/Low		PER SHARE ($) Earnings	Dividends	Book Value
9/09	36.04	11	5	3.59	2.62	—
9/08	30.43	14	9	2.70	2.50	4.33
9/07	35.70	12	10	3.15	2.63	5.45
9/06	30.86	20	17	1.59	2.28	3.88
9/05	32.18	32	24	1.10	2.22	5.91
Annual Growth	2.9%	—	—	34.4%	4.2%	(9.8%)

AmerisourceBergen

AmerisourceBergen is *the* source for many of North America's pharmacies and health care providers. The company serves as a go-between for drugmakers and the pharmacies, doctors' offices, hospitals, and other health care providers that dispense drugs. Operating primarily in the US and Canada, it distributes generic, branded, and over-the-counter pharmaceuticals, as well as some medical supplies and other products, using its network of more than two dozen facilities. Its specialty distribution unit focuses on sensitive and complex biopharmaceuticals, such as cancer drugs, vaccines, and plasma products. The company also has some pharmaceutical packaging operations.

AmerisourceBergen has one division through which it operates a number of business segments. The Pharmaceutical Distribution division is comprised of three operating segments which include AmerisourceBergen Drug Corporation (ABDC), AmerisourceBergen Specialty Group (ABSG), and AmerisourceBergen Packaging Group (ABPG).

ABDC is the business arm that distributes generic and brand-name pharmaceuticals, over-the-counter products, and home health care supplies and equipment to medical providers and pharmacies throughout North America.

ABSG is the company's specialty distribution operations. AmerisourceBergen intends to continue growing the unit that delivers drugs for particular diseases (especially cancer) to the doctors who administer them.

The unit also provides marketing and other services to drugmakers, helping them successfully launch new biotech drugs. Other services to pharmaceutical manufacturers include consulting and reimbursement support.

The specialty packaging group (ABPG) provides contracting packaging services to drug manufacturers in North America and the UK. The company sells its products through an in-house sales force that is organized regionally and specialized by health care provider type.

AmerisourceBergen expanded into Canada through several key acquisitions that made it that country's second-largest drug distributor.

AmerisourceBergen tapped into the growing market for electronic health records (EHR) in 2010 by offering consulting services to hospitals and other health care providers looking to go digital with EHRs.

Along with tapping into new markets, the company has also worked to streamline its existing operations by expanding some distribution facilities while closing others. Since 2001, the firm has cut its distribution facility network in half — from 51 to 26 facilities. It chose to close operations with administrative redundancies and could be easily consolidated into other, existing facilities.

HISTORY

In 1977 Cleveland millionaire and horse racing enthusiast Tinkham Veale went into the drug wholesaling business. His company, Alco Standard (now IKON Office Solutions), already owned chemical, electrical, metallurgical, and mining companies, but by the late 1970s the company was pursuing a strategy of zeroing in on various types of distribution businesses.

Alco's first drug wholesaler purchase was The Drug House (Delaware and Pennsylvania); next was Duff Brothers (Tennessee). The company then bought further wholesalers in the South, East, and Midwest. Its modus operandi was to buy small, well-run companies for cash and Alco stock and leave the incumbent management in charge.

By the early 1980s Alco was the US's third-largest wholesale drug distributor and growing quickly (28% between 1983 and 1988) at a time of mass consolidation in the industry (the number of wholesalers dropped by half between 1980 and 1992). In 1985 Alco Standard spun off its drug distribution operations as Alco Health Services, retaining 60% ownership.

Alco Health boosted its sales above $1 billion mostly via acquisitions and expanded product lines. The company offered marketing and promotional help to its independent pharmacy customers (which were beleaguered by the growth of national discounters) and also targeted hospitals, nursing homes, and clinics.

The US was in the midst of its LBO frenzy in 1988, but an Alco management group failed in its attempt. Rival McKesson then tried to acquire Alco Health, but that deal fell through for antitrust reasons. Later in 1988 management turned for backing to Citicorp Venture Capital in another buyout attempt. This time the move succeeded, and a new holding company, Alco Health Distribution, was formed.

In 1993 Alco Health was named as a defendant in suits by independent pharmacies charging discriminatory pricing policies; a ruling the next year limited its liability. To move away from a reliance on independent drugstores, Alco Health began targeting government entities and others. Alco Health went public as AmeriSource Health in 1995. Throughout the next year, AmeriSource made a series of acquisitions to move into related areas, including inventory management technology, drugstore pharmaceutical supplies, and disease-management services for pharmacies.

In 1997 AmeriSource acquired Alabama-based Walker Drug for $140 million, adding 1,500 independent and chain drugstores in the Southeast to its customer list. That same year, McKesson once again made an offer to buy AmeriSource, this time for $2.4 billion, while two other major wholesale distributors, Cardinal Health and Bergen Brunswig, reached a similar pact. The deals were scrapped in 1998 when the Federal Trade Commission voted against both pacts, and a federal judge supported that decision.

Later that year AmeriSource signed a five-year deal to become the exclusive pharmaceutical supplier to not-for-profit Sutter Health; in 1999 it renewed similar contracts with the US Department of Veterans Affairs and Pharmacy Provider Services Corporation.

In 2001 AmeriSource bought Bergen Brunswig, and the combined company renamed itself AmerisourceBergen.

In 2005, the company acquired Trent Drugs (Wholesale), a Canadian pharmaceutical wholesaler, and renamed it AmerisourceBergen Canada. The following year, it acquired Canadian pharmaceutical distributors Asenda Pharmaceutical Supplies (Western Canada), and Rep-Pharm (Central and Eastern Canada).

In 2006 the company acquired I.G.G. of America, a specialty pharmacy focusing on blood derivative IVIG. It also purchased medical education and analytical research firm Network for Medical Communications & Research.

EXECUTIVES

Chairman: Richard C. Gozon, age 71
President, CEO, and Director: R. David (Dave) Yost, age 62, $7,641,062 total compensation
EVP and CFO: Michael D. DiCandilo, age 48, $2,999,824 total compensation
EVP; President, AmerisourceBergen Drug Corporation: Steven H. Collis, age 48, $2,644,437 total compensation
EVP and General Manager, International Oncology Network: Mark Santos
SVP, General Counsel, and Secretary: John G. Chou, age 53, $906,920 total compensation
SVP Retail Sales and Marketing: Jerry Cline
SVP Strategy and Corporate Development: David M. Senior
SVP and CIO: Thomas H. Murphy
SVP Supply Chain Management: Antonio R. (Tony) Pera, age 52
SVP Operations: David W. (Dave) Neu
VP Corporate and Investor Relations: Michael N. Kilpatric
VP and Corporate Controller: Tim G. Guttman
VP and Corporate Treasurer: J. F. (Jack) Quinn
Director Corporate and Investor Relations: Barbara A. Brungess
Auditors: Ernst & Young LLP

LOCATIONS

HQ: AmerisourceBergen Corporation
1300 Morris Dr., Chesterbrook, PA 19087
Phone: 610-727-7000   **Fax:** 610-727-3600
Web: www.amerisourcebergen.com

PRODUCTS/OPERATIONS

2009 Sales

	$ mil.	% of total
Pharmaceutical distribution	70,052	98
Bulk deliveries to customer warehouses	1,707.9	2
Total	**71,759.9**	**100**

Selected Subsidiaries and Units

AmerisourceBergen Drug Corporation
  AmerisourceBergen Canada Corporation

AmerisourceBergen Packaging Group
  Anderson Packaging
  Brecon Pharmaceutical Limited
  American Health Packaging

AmerisourceBergen Specialty Group

COMPETITORS

Accredo Health
BioScrip
Cardinal Health
Covance
Covidien
CuraScript
Express Scripts
FFF Enterprises
H. D. Smith Wholesale Drug
Henry Schein
Kinray
McKesson
Medline Industries
Owens & Minor
PSS World Medical
Quality King
UPS Logistics Technologies
US Oncology
Watson Pharmaceuticals

HISTORICAL FINANCIALS

Company Type: Public

Income Statement

FYE: September 30

	REVENUE ($ mil.)	NET INCOME ($ mil.)	NET PROFIT MARGIN	EMPLOYEES
9/09	71,760	503	0.7%	10,300
9/08	70,190	251	0.4%	10,900
9/07	66,074	469	0.7%	11,300
9/06	61,203	468	0.8%	14,700
9/05	54,577	309	0.6%	13,400
Annual Growth	**7.1%**	**13.0%**	**—**	**(6.4%)**

2009 Year-End Financials

Debt ratio: 43.3%
Return on equity: 18.6%
Cash ($ mil.): 1,009
Current ratio: 1.05
Long-term debt ($ mil.): 1,177
No. of shares (mil.): 279
Dividends
  Yield: 0.9%
  Payout: 12.7%
Market value ($ mil.): 6,240

Stock History

NYSE: ABC

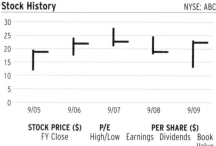

	STOCK PRICE ($) FY Close	P/E High/Low		PER SHARE ($) Earnings	Dividends	Book Value
9/09	22.38	14	8	1.66	0.21	9.74
9/08	18.83	32	24	0.77	0.15	9.72
9/07	22.67	22	17	1.25	0.10	11.12
9/06	21.93	21	16	1.13	0.04	14.85
9/05	18.75	31	20	0.62	0.03	15.35
Annual Growth	**4.5%**	**—**	**—**	**27.9%**	**62.7%**	**(10.7%)**

Amgen Inc.

Amgen is among the biggest of the biotech big'uns, and it's determined to get even bigger. The company uses cellular biology and medicinal chemistry to target cancers, kidney ailments, inflammatory disorders, and metabolic diseases. Anti-anemia drugs Epogen and Aranesp account for more than one-third of its sales. Enbrel, another leading drug, treats rheumatoid arthritis and is one of the best-selling drugs in this multi-billion-dollar market. The company has a healthy drug pipeline, as well as marketing alliances with Japanese brewer and drugmaker Kirin, Johnson & Johnson, and other pharmaceutical companies. Amgen sells its products primarily through wholesale distributors in North America and Europe.

Amgen's newer drugs also account for a majority of the company's revenues. Enbrel, Neulasta (a treatment for low white-blood-cell counts), and Aranesp each account for about 20% of annual revenues.

In addition to being a key player in the rheumatoid arthritis market, top seller Enbrel also treats psoriasis and other related conditions. Enbrel's sales have climbed as the FDA has approved the drug to be used for these larger patient populations. Enbrel is co-marketed in the US and Canada with Pfizer, which also controls international marketing rights.

However, another blockbuster, Aranesp, has experienced decreasing sales in recent years following damaging reports of adverse effects of the drug on the heart, as well as increased risks for cancer patients. As a result of the reports, the FDA required changes in Aranesp's and Epogen's warning labels in early 2007, and Medicare restricted Aranesp's use in chemotherapy patients mid-year. Revenues from Aranesp have dropped from $3.6 billion in 2007 to $2.6 billion in 2009.

Amgen has been restructuring to absorb the sales losses. The company cut its workforce by about 15% between mid-2007 and the end of 2009; it also rationalized its manufacturing facilities and reduced R&D efforts. In 2008 Amgen sold two noncore oncology products (Kepivance and Stemgen) and licensed rights to rheumatoid arthritis drug Kineret to Swedish firm Biovitrum. It also sold its Japanese unit and formed a co-development partnership with that country's top drugmaker, Takeda Pharmaceutical, in a deal worth up to $1.2 billion.

Although many of the biotech's products enjoy years of patent protection, Amgen continues to launch new products that may best its bestsellers. Nplate (romiplostim) for autoimmune bleeding disorder ITP, or immune thrombocytopenic purpura, was given FDA approval in 2008. Pipeline candidate Prolia (denosumab) is awaiting FDA approval for bone loss associated with hormone therapy in breast and prostate cancer patients. Other R&D efforts target cancer, inflammation, kidney disease, and neurological, cardiovascular, and bone and blood disorders. In 2009 the company licensed a cardiac development program from Cytokinetics.

HISTORY

Amgen was formed as Applied Molecular Genetics in 1980 by a group of scientists and venture capitalists to develop health care products based on molecular biology. George Rathmann, a VP at Abbott Laboratories and researcher at UCLA, became the company's CEO and first employee. Rathmann decided to develop a few potentially profitable products rather than conduct research. The firm initially raised $19 million.

Amgen operated close to bankruptcy until 1983, when company scientist Fu-Kuen Lin cloned the human protein erythropoietin (EPO), which stimulates the body's red blood cell production. Amgen went public that year. It formed a joint venture with Kirin Brewery in 1984 to develop and market EPO. The two firms also collaborated on recombinant human granulocyte colony stimulating factor (G-CSF, later called Neupogen), a protein that stimulates the immune system.

Amgen joined Johnson & Johnson subsidiary Ortho Pharmaceutical (now Ortho-McNeil Pharmaceutical) in a marketing alliance in 1985 and created a tie with Roche in 1988. Fortunes soared in 1989 when the FDA approved Epogen (the brand name of EPO) for anemia. (It is most commonly used to counter side effects of kidney dialysis.)

In 1991 Amgen received approval to market Neupogen to chemotherapy patients. A federal court ruling also gave it a US monopoly for EPO. The following year Amgen won another dispute, forcing a competitor to renounce its US patents for G-CSF. Amgen hired MCI veteran Kevin Sharer as president in 1992. Neupogen's usage was expanded in 1993 to include treatment of severe chronic neutropenia (low white blood cell count).

In 1993 Amgen became the first American biotech to gain a foothold in China through an agreement with Kirin Pharmaceuticals to sell Neupogen (under the name Gran) and Epogen there. The purchase of Synergen in 1994 added another research facility, accelerating the pace of and increasing the number of products in research and clinical trials. Amgen's new drug Stemgen for breast cancer patients undergoing chemotherapy was recommended for approval by an FDA advisory committee in 1998.

Amgen had to swallow a couple of tough legal pills in 1998. First, a dispute with J&J over Amgen's 1985 licensing agreement with Ortho Pharmaceutical ended when an arbiter ordered Amgen to pay about $200 million. Later that year, however, Amgen won a legal battle with J&J over the rights to a promising anemia drug.

In 2000 the firm won EU and US approval for Aranesp, an updated version of Epogen; Amgen in 2002 teamed with former J&J marketing partner Fresenius to sell Aranesp in Germany and take some market share away from J&J. Meanwhile, an arbitration committee found J&J had breached its contract with Amgen when it sold Procrit to the dialysis market, which Amgen had reserved for itself in their 1985 licensing deal.

In 2003 the company bought leukemia and rheumatoid arthritis drugs maker Immunex. As part of the FTC's blessing on the $10.3 billion union, Amgen and Immunex licensed some technologies to encourage competition. Merck Serono gained access to Enbrel data, and Regeneron Pharmaceuticals licensed some interleukin inhibitor rights.

In 2004 Amgen spent $1.3 billion to purchase the remaining 79% of cancer treatment technology maker Tularik that it did not already own.

In 2006 Amgen acquired Abgenix, a company that manufactures human therapeutic antibodies. Vectibix, Abgenix's treatment for colorectal cancer, was approved by the FDA that year. It also acquired Avidia, a developer of treatments for inflammation and autoimmune diseases.

EXECUTIVES

Chairman and CEO: Kevin W. Sharer, age 62, $15,345,717 total compensation
President and COO: Robert (Bob) Bradway, age 47, $5,142,505 total compensation
Acting CFO: Michael A. Kelly, age 53
EVP Research and Development: Roger M. Perlmutter, age 57, $5,342,569 total compensation
EVP Operations: Fabrizio Bonanni, age 63, $4,933,019 total compensation
EVP Global Commercial Operations: George J. Morrow, age 58, $5,673,895 total compensation
SVP Human Resources: Brian M. McNamee, age 53
SVP Research and Development:
Joseph P. (Joe) Miletich, age 58
SVP, General Counsel, and Secretary: David J. Scott, age 57
SVP Discovery Research: David Lacey
SVP and CIO: Thomas (Tom) Flanagan, age 60
SVP International Commercial Operations:
Rolf K. Hoffmann
SVP and Chief Compliance Officer: Anna S. Richo, age 49
SVP Global Regulatory Affairs and Safety:
Paul R. Eisenberg
SVP and International Chief Medical Officer:
Willard H. Dere
SVP Research: David L. (Dave) Lacey
SVP Global Government and Corporate Affairs:
David W. Beier, age 61

VP Global Regulatory Affairs and Corporate Chief Medical Officer: Sean E. Harper
VP Investor Relations: Arvine Sood
VP Corporate Communications and Philanthropy:
Phyllis J. Piano
VP Finance and Chief Accounting Officer:
Thomas Dittrich, age 46
Senior Director Marketing Operations:
Jeanne Fitzgerald
Auditors: Ernst & Young LLP

LOCATIONS

HQ: Amgen Inc.
1 Amgen Center Dr., Thousand Oaks, CA 91320
Phone: 805-447-1000   **Fax:** 805-447-1010
Web: www.amgen.com

2009 Sales

	$ mil.	% of total
US	11,421	78
Other countries	3,221	22
Total	**14,642**	**100**

PRODUCTS/OPERATIONS

2009 Sales

	$ mil.	% of total
Product sales		
Enbrel	3,493	23
Neulasta	3,355	23
Aranesp	2,652	18
Epogen	2,569	18
Neupogen	1,288	9
Sensipar	651	5
Other products	343	2
Other	291	2
Total	**14,642**	**100**

Products

Top sellers
Enbrel (rheumatoid arthritis, psoriasis)
Neulasta (chemotherapy-induced neutropenia — low white blood cells)
Aranesp (chemotherapy-induced anemia and chronic renal failure anemia, sustained duration Epogen)
Epogen (anemia in chronic renal failure)
Neupogen (neutropenia)
Sensipar (also known as Mimpara, chronic kidney disease)
Other drugs
Nplate (romiplostim for autoimmune bleeding disorder ITP, or immune thrombocytopenic purpura)
Vectibix (monoclonal antibody for colorectal cancer)

COMPETITORS

Abbott Labs
Affymax
Astellas
AstraZeneca
Baxter International
Bayer HealthCare Pharmaceuticals
Biogen Idec
Bristol-Myers Squibb
Cephalon
Chugai
Eli Lilly
Fresenius Medical Care
Genzyme

GlaxoSmithKline
Hospira
Incyte
Johnson & Johnson
Merck
Merck KGaA
Novartis
Pfizer
Roche Holding
Sanofi-Aventis
Shire
Takeda Pharmaceutical
Teva Pharmaceuticals
UCB

HISTORICAL FINANCIALS

Company Type: Public

Income Statement

FYE: December 31

	REVENUE ($ mil.)	NET INCOME ($ mil.)	NET PROFIT MARGIN	EMPLOYEES
12/09	14,642	4,605	31.5%	17,200
12/08	15,003	4,196	28.0%	16,900
12/07	14,771	3,166	21.4%	17,500
12/06	14,268	2,950	20.7%	20,100
12/05	12,430	3,674	29.6%	16,500
Annual Growth	4.2%	5.8%	—	1.0%

2009 Year-End Financials

Debt ratio: 46.8%
Return on equity: 21.4%
Cash ($ mil.): 2,884
Current ratio: 4.89
Long-term debt ($ mil.): 10,601

No. of shares (mil.): 958
Dividends
Yield: —
Payout: —
Market value ($ mil.): 54,191

Stock History

NASDAQ (GS): AMGN

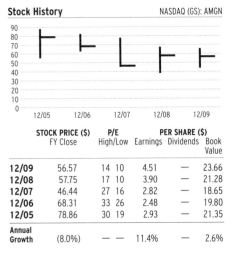

	STOCK PRICE ($) FY Close	P/E High/Low		PER SHARE ($) Earnings	Dividends	Book Value
12/09	56.57	14	10	4.51	—	23.66
12/08	57.75	17	10	3.90	—	21.28
12/07	46.44	27	16	2.82	—	18.65
12/06	68.31	33	26	2.48	—	19.80
12/05	78.86	30	19	2.93	—	21.35
Annual Growth	(8.0%)	—	—	11.4%	—	2.6%

Amkor Technology

Amkor Technology is more than amicable about lending a helping hand with microchip packaging. The company claims a top spot in contract packaging/assembly and testing services for semiconductor manufacturers. Packaging involves dicing semiconductor wafers into separate chips, die bonding, wire bonding, and encapsulating chips in protective plastic. Amkor's testing procedures verify current, function, timing, and voltage. The company has some 250 customers worldwide, including big semiconductor companies and electronics OEMs, such as Altera, Intel, IBM, LSI Corp., QUALCOMM, STMicroelectronics, Texas Instruments, and Toshiba.

Amkor operates in a naturally competitive, cyclical industry. Its business is established largely on high-volume manufacturing processes and in developing new, tailored packaging and test technologies. Patents associated with packaging computer chips are scrutinized particularly closely. Amkor was hit in 2009 with nearly $61 million in damages when an arbitration panel of the International Chamber of Commerce ruled that the company infringed Tessera's patented packaging technology.

The semiconductor industry went into a tailspin in 2009, as the global recession held down sales of consumer electronics and other electronic products. As a result, business for contractors like Amkor was slashed. Spiraling cancellations, deferrals, and a slowdown in orders, plus a downward pressure on prices, drove the company to squeeze operating costs. Lowering headcount by 11% in 2009 came after layoffs in 2008, which eliminated about 1,500 jobs, nearly 20% of its workforce.

Amkor also diversified and expanded its facilities to production centers in China, Japan, the Philippines, Singapore, South Korea, and Taiwan.

Founder and chairman James Kim and his family own about 56% of Amkor Technology. Kim became executive chairman in 2009, while Ken Joyce, previously president and COO, took over as CEO.

HISTORY

Kim Joo-Jin (James Kim), the oldest of seven children, came to the US from South Korea in 1955 to study business. A year later his father started electronics firm Anam Industrial, and in 1968 James Kim (chairman and CEO) founded Amkor (short for "American-Korean") Electronics as its US marketing agent.

To lessen its dependence on the volatile semiconductor market, Anam Industrial began diversifying in 1975, first into watch making, and eventually into banking, construction, environmental services, and electronics. (James Kim's wife, Agnes, began selling electronic watches and calculators from a kiosk near the family home in Pennsylvania; the business grew into the Electronics Boutique chain, now part of GameStop.)

James Kim joined the board of California semiconductor maker VLSI Technology (now part of NXP, formerly Philips Semiconductors) in 1982, leading the company into the application-specific integrated circuit market. Anam Industrial, meanwhile, continued to grow along with the semiconductor industry. By 1990 it had 50% of the world's semiconductor package assembly business, and was only one unit of South Korean *chaebol* (family-run, non-legal conglomerate) Anam Group. That year the group took over a plant in Manila from Advanced Micro Devices and established Amkor/Anam Pilipinas on that site. It also acquired Scotland-based ITEQ Europe Ltd., Europe's leading semiconductor assembly contractor.

During the early 1990s Anam Industrial developed the tape-automated bonding manufacturing process. When the senior Kim retired in 1992, James Kim also became head of the Anam Group.

In 1993 Amkor licensed ball-grid array (BGA) packaging technology from Motorola. At the time BGA — in which tiny balls of solder are used for connections, instead of fragile lead wires — was still an emerging standard. By 1995 Amkor had become a leader in BGA packaging. That year the company announced that it would build the US's first independent BGA facility, in Arizona (it opened in 1999).

Anam Industrial began building its fourth semiconductor assembly plant in 1996, this one in the Philippines, with a production goal of 50 million chips per month. In 1997 Amkor opened its complementary metal oxide semiconductor wafer (CMOS) plant near Seoul, using Texas Instruments' technology, as part of a 10-year cooperative agreement. It also created Amkor Industries to consolidate the various Amkor companies. Also that year Amkor/Anam formed an agreement with Acer and Taiwan Semiconductor Manufacturing to build a semiconductor assembly and test facility in Taiwan.

Amkor was originally the US marketing arm of South Korean manufacturer Anam Industrial Co., and it went public in 1998. That year Anam Industrial changed its name to Anam Semiconductor and announced plans to divest its noncore businesses to focus on chip packaging. After purchasing Anam's four packaging plants in 1999 and 2000, Amkor retained exclusive rights to the output of Anam's remaining semiconductor wafer foundry. In 2002, though, Amkor sold almost half of its formerly controlling stake in Anam to Korean foundry operator Dongbu; in 2003 it completed its divestment of Anam and exited the wafer fabrication business.

In 2002 Amkor acquired the Japan-based chip assembly business of Citizen Watch. In 2004, Amkor struck a major agreement with IBM under which Amkor acquired IBM properties in China and Singapore, and would supply the computing giant with assembly and test services.

The US Securities and Exchange Commission in 2004 opened an informal inquiry into stock trading by certain Amkor insiders and other people, covering a period from June 2003 to July 2004. In 2005 the SEC probe was upgraded to a formal inquiry. The former general counsel of the company, who resigned in 2005, was indicted in Pennsylvania for alleged violations of securities laws.

In 2006 Amkor's board created a special committee to review the company's historical practices in granting stock options from May 1998. The committee found, as was the practice at many other high-tech firms, that the grant dates of certain stock options differed from the recorded dates of the grants and the actual dates of the grants. The company restated eight years of financial results as a result. The SEC inquiry later ended without any charges, enforcement actions, or penalties for Amkor.

EXECUTIVES

Executive Chairman: James J. Kim, age 74, $584,539 total compensation
President, CEO, and Director: Kenneth T. (Ken) Joyce, age 62, $538,306 total compensation
EVP and CFO: Joanne Solomon, age 43, $366,462 total compensation
EVP Worldwide Manufacturing Operations; President, Amkor Technology Korea: JooHo Kim, age 57, $465,030 total compensation
EVP Assembly and Test: James M. (Jim) Fusaro, age 47, $425,032 total compensation
EVP Worldwide Sales: Michael J. (Mike) Lamble, age 54
EVP, Chief Administrative Officer, General Counsel, and Corporate Secretary: Gil C. Tilly, age 56, $487,615 total compensation
EVP New Business Strategy and Corporate Development: Eric R. Larson, age 54
VP Business Development: Lee Smith
VP Advanced Process Development: Miguel Jimarez
Corporate VP Business Planning and Corporate Development: Dave Lawton
Senior Director Corporate Communications: Gregory (Greg) Johnson
Auditors: PricewaterhouseCoopers LLP

LOCATIONS

HQ: Amkor Technology, Inc.
1900 S. Price Rd., Chandler, AZ 85286
Phone: 480-821-5000　　**Fax:** 480-821-8276
Web: www.amkor.com

2009 Sales

	$ mil.	% of total
US	753.8	35
Singapore	482.3	22
Japan	260.5	12
Taiwan	138.8	6
South Korea	76.8	4
China & Hong Kong	52.3	2
Other countries	414.6	19
Total	**2,179.1**	**100**

PRODUCTS/OPERATIONS

2009 Sales

	$ mil.	% of total
Packaging services	1,933.6	89
Testing & other services	245.5	11
Total	**2,179.1**	**100**

2009 Sales

	$ mil.	% of total
Packaging services		
Chip scale package	695.1	32
Leadframe	587.2	27
Ball grid array	500.2	23
Other packaging	152.5	7
Test services	244.1	11
Total	**2,179.1**	**100**

Selected Services

Semiconductor packaging
　Advanced leadframe (plastic mold with thermal, electrical characteristics)
　Laminate (plastic or tape rather than leadframe substrate)
　Traditional leadframe (plastic mold with metal leads)
Test services (analog, digital logic, and mixed-signal semiconductor devices)

COMPETITORS

Advanced Semiconductor Engineering
ChipMOS
FlipChip International
Kingston Technology
Orient Semiconductor
PSi Technologies
Shinko Electric
Siliconware Precision Industries
STATS ChipPAC
Tessera
UTAC

HISTORICAL FINANCIALS

Company Type: Public

Income Statement				FYE: December 31
	REVENUE ($ mil.)	NET INCOME ($ mil.)	NET PROFIT MARGIN	EMPLOYEES
12/09	2,179	156	7.2%	18,200
12/08	2,659	(457)	—	20,500
12/07	2,739	220	8.0%	21,600
12/06	2,729	170	6.2%	22,700
12/05	2,100	(137)	—	24,000
Annual Growth	0.9%	—	—	(6.7%)

2009 Year-End Financials

Debt ratio: 351.0%　　No. of shares (mil.): 183
Return on equity: 50.3%　　Dividends
Cash ($ mil.): 395　　　　　Yield: —
Current ratio: 1.54　　　　　Payout: —
Long-term debt ($ mil.): 1,345　Market value ($ mil.): 1,313

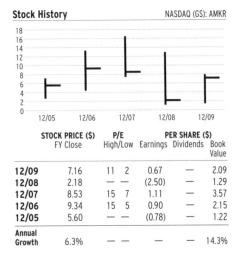

	STOCK PRICE ($) FY Close	P/E High/Low		PER SHARE ($) Earnings	Dividends	Book Value
12/09	7.16	11	2	0.67	—	2.09
12/08	2.18	—	—	(2.50)	—	1.29
12/07	8.53	15	7	1.11	—	3.57
12/06	9.34	15	5	0.90	—	2.15
12/05	5.60	—	—	(0.78)	—	1.22
Annual Growth	6.3%	—	—	—	—	14.3%

AMR Corporation

AMR knows America's spacious skies — and lots of others. Its main subsidiary is American Airlines, one of the largest airlines in the world. Together with sister company American Eagle and regional carriers that operate as American Connection, American Airlines serves some 250 destinations in about 40 countries in the Americas, Europe, and the Asia/Pacific region. The overall fleet exceeds 900 aircraft; American Airlines operates about 625 jets. The carrier extends its geographic reach through code-sharing arrangements. It is part of the Oneworld global marketing alliance, along with British Airways, Cathay Pacific, Iberia, Qantas, and other airlines.

American Airlines looks to "fly profitably" by expanding its services to such destinations as the Asia/Pacific region, particularly China (where the number of direct flights from the US is limited by law). About 40% of AMR's revenues are garnered from flights to international destinations. In 2010 American Airlines also joined with JAL in applying for approval from regulatory authorities to cooperatively provide flights between North America and Asia.

The carrier is jockeying to strengthen its transatlantic operations. American Airlines has formed alliances with British Airways and Iberia on flights between North America and Europe.

AMR was able to navigate the airline industry downturn that followed the September 11, 2001, terrorist attacks without making a stop in bankruptcy court. American Airlines reduced its capacity, its fleet, and its workforce, as well as won concessions from its unions; in the meantime, the parent company lost money for five straight years — and piled up debt — before posting profits in 2006 and 2007. The gains were followed by alarming net losses of more than $2 billion in 2008, and $1.5 billion in 2009, primarily driven by a drop in traffic and passenger yields (tied to ticket discounting).

Cost control continues to be a focus for AMR, especially as fuel prices remain volatile. The carrier reduced its mainline seating capacity by 7% in 2009, including grounding its Airbus A300 fleet and clipping the wings of some of its Embraer RJ-135 aircraft. These moves followed

American Airlines 12% cut in late 2008, which targeted the retirement of about 75 aircraft and the elimination of thousands of jobs. In addition, American Airlines has maintained its slate of passenger service charges, introduced in 2008. Besides fees for checked baggage, items in the "other" category include services charges, flight change charges, onboard food sales, as well as upgrades to first class on the day of departure, and day-passes to the carrier's Admirals Club lounge.

Even as the company works to cut costs and shore up revenue, the carrier has had to address maintenance issues. After an inspection by the Federal Aviation Administration found problems with the way wiring was bundled in aircraft wheel wells, American Airlines canceled more than 3,000 flights over several days in April 2008 in order to re-inspect its fleet of MD-80s. In a separate case, the FAA in August 2008 proposed a $7.1 million fine against American Airlines for allegedly flying airplanes that had not been properly maintained and for allegedly failing to follow drug- and alcohol-testing procedures for employees. The carrier is contesting the agency's findings.

HISTORY

In 1929 Sherman Fairchild created a New York City holding company called the Aviation Corporation (AVCO), combining some 85 small airlines in 1930 to create American Airways. In 1934 the company had its first dose of financial trouble after the government suspended private airmail for months. Corporate raider E. L. Cord took over and named the company American Airlines.

Cord put former AVCO manager C. R. Smith in charge, and American became the leading US airline in the late 1930s. The Douglas DC-3, built to Smith's specifications, was introduced by American in 1936 and became the first commercial airliner to pay its way on passenger revenues alone.

After WWII American bought Amex Airlines, which flew to northern Europe, but another financial crisis prompted Amex's sale in 1950. The airline introduced Sabre, the first automated reservations system, in 1964. Smith left American four years later to serve as secretary of commerce in the Johnson administration.

In 1979, the year after airline industry deregulation, American moved to Dallas/Fort Worth. Former CFO Bob Crandall became president in 1980 (and later, CEO). Using Sabre to track mileage, he introduced the industry's first frequent-flier program (AAdvantage). In 1982 American created AMR as its holding company. After acquiring commuter airline Nashville Eagle in 1987, AMR established American Eagle.

In 1996 AMR spun off nearly 20% of Sabre. Crandall retired in 1998 (after a major airline strike was averted only by President Clinton's intervention) and was replaced by Donald Carty. American also bought Reno Air, and concerns about integrating the smaller airline culminated in American pilots calling in sick for a week in 1999. The union was later ordered to pay almost $46 million in compensation.

To focus on its airlines, AMR sold its executive aviation services, ground services, and call center units in 1999. That year nine people died when an American jet tried to land in Arkansas during a storm and slid off the runway. Also in 2000 AMR spun off the rest of Sabre. In 2001 AMR moved to become a stronger competitor to UAL by buying the assets of troubled rival TWA for $742 million.

Also in 2001 American Airlines lost two aircraft that were used in the September 11 terrorist attacks on the World Trade Center in New York and the Pentagon in Washington, DC. In anticipation of reduced demand for air travel, AMR announced a 20% reduction in flights and layoffs of at least 20,000 employees. Later that year another American Airlines jet crashed in New York, killing all 260 passengers.

In August 2002 the carrier set about reducing its capacity by 9% and reducing its workforce by some 7,000 employees. It also simplified its fleet by retiring its Fokker-100 jets ahead of schedule.

Carty resigned in 2003 after rankling union leaders by failing to disclose executive compensation perquisites during labor negotiations aimed at keeping the airline giant out of bankruptcy. Carty was replaced as CEO by former president and COO Gerard Arpey. Director Edward Brennan, a former chairman and CEO of Sears, Roebuck & Co., was named non-executive chairman. Brennan relinquished the chairman role to Arpey in 2004, but remained a director.

To take advantage of demand for travel to the Asia/Pacific region, American Airlines began nonstop service from Chicago to Shanghai in April 2006.

EXECUTIVES

Chairman and CEO, AMR and American Airlines: Gerard J. Arpey, age 51, $3,419,239 total compensation
President, AMR and American Airlines: Thomas W. (Tom) Horton, age 49, $2,231,878 total compensation
EVP; EVP Operations, American Airlines: Robert W. (Bob) Reding, age 60, $1,928,269 total compensation
EVP; EVP Marketing, American Airlines; President and CEO, American Eagle: Daniel P. Garton, age 52, $2,068,792 total compensation
SVP and CFO, AMR and American Airlines: Isabella D. (Bella) Goren, age 50
SVP Information Technology and CIO, American Airlines: Monte E. Ford, age 50
SVP, General Counsel, and Chief Compliance Officer, AMR and American Airlines: Gary F. Kennedy Sr., age 54, $1,430,746 total compensation
SVP, Customer Service, American Eagle: Jonathan D. (Jon) Snook
SVP Airport Services, American Airlines: Thomas R. (Tom) Del Valle
SVP Maintenance and Engineering, American Airlines: James B. (Jim) Ream, age 54
SVP Human Resources, American Airlines: Jeffery J. Brundage, age 56
VP Corporate Communications and Advertising, American Airlines: Roger C. Frizzell
President, AAdvantage Marketing Programs, American Airlines: Robert J. (Rob) Friedman
Managing Director, Investor Relations: Chris Ducey
Auditors: Ernst & Young LLP

LOCATIONS

HQ: AMR Corporation
4333 Amon Carter Blvd., Fort Worth, TX 76155
Phone: 817-963-1234   **Fax:** 817-967-4162
Web: www.aa.com

2009 Sales

	$ mil.	% of total
US	11,974	60
Latin America	4,114	21
Atlantic	2,973	15
Pacific	856	4
Total	**19,917**	**100**

American Airlines Hub Locations
Chicago (O'Hare)
Dallas/Fort Worth (DFW)
Miami
St. Louis
San Juan, Puerto Rico

PRODUCTS/OPERATIONS

2009 Sales

	$ mil.	% of total
Passenger		
American Airlines	15,037	76
Regional affiliates	2,012	10
Cargo	578	3
Other	2,290	11
Total	**19,917**	**100**

COMPETITORS

Air France-KLM
AirTran Holdings
Alaska Air
China Southern Airlines
Continental Airlines
Delta Air Lines
FedEx
Frontier Airlines
Greyhound
JetBlue
Mesa Air
Pinnacle Airlines
SkyWest
Southwest Airlines
UAL
UPS
US Airways
Virgin Atlantic Airways

HISTORICAL FINANCIALS

Company Type: Public

Income Statement

FYE: December 31

	REVENUE ($ mil.)	NET INCOME ($ mil.)	NET PROFIT MARGIN	EMPLOYEES
12/09	19,917	(1,468)	—	78,900
12/08	23,766	(2,071)	—	84,100
12/07	22,935	504	2.2%	85,500
12/06	22,563	231	1.0%	86,600
12/05	20,712	(861)	—	88,400
Annual Growth	(1.0%)	—	—	(2.8%)

2009 Year-End Financials

Debt ratio: —
Return on equity: —
Cash ($ mil.): 153
Current ratio: 0.86
Long-term debt ($ mil.): 10,583

No. of shares (mil.): 333
Dividends
Yield: —
Payout: —
Market value ($ mil.): 2,574

Stock History

NYSE: AMR

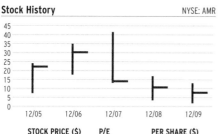

	STOCK PRICE ($) FY Close	P/E High/Low		PER SHARE ($) Earnings	Dividends	Book Value
12/09	7.73	—	—	(4.99)	—	(10.48)
12/08	10.67	—	—	(7.98)	—	(8.81)
12/07	14.03	23	8	1.78	—	7.98
12/06	30.23	35	19	0.98	—	(1.82)
12/05	22.23	—	—	(5.21)	—	(4.44)
Annual Growth	(23.2%)			—	—	—

Anadarko Petroleum

Anadarko Petroleum has ventured beyond its original area of operation — the Anadarko Basin — to explore for, develop, produce, and market oil, natural gas, natural gas liquids, and related products worldwide. The large independent company has proved reserves of 1 billion barrels of crude oil and 7.8 trillion cu. ft. of natural gas, more than 89% of which are located in the US. Other activities include coal, trona, and mineral mining. Anadarko operates a handful of gas-gathering systems in the Mid-Continent. Internationally, the company has substantial oil and gas interests in Algeria, Brazil, China, Indonesia, Mozambique, and West Africa.

Anadarko bulked up its core assets in 2009, announcing nine major deepwater discoveries (primarily in the Gulf of Mexico) and adding some 314 million barrels of oil equivalent in proved reserves. The additional reserves helped fulfill the company's plans for future revenue growth, partially mitigating a poor financial performance in 2009, which saw a decline in total revenues caused by the economic recession, low commodity prices, and the global slump in oil demand.

The company held a minority stake in the ill-fated *Deepwater Horizon* rig in the Gulf of Mexico, operated by BP. Despite attempts by BP to make Anadarko liable for part of the clean up costs related to the devastating oil spill, Anadarko has rebuffed such claims, citing BP's negligence.

In addition to growing its oil and gas reserves by exploring in high-potential, proven basins, the company is seeking to maintain a tight ship financially. To create greater financial flexibility, in 2008 Anadarko spun off midstream unit Western Gas Partners, though it still held on to about 60% of the company. The deal allows Anadarko to focus on its core exploration and production operations, while generating cash from the midstream unit through its ownership stake. In 2009 it sold $210 million of midstream assets located in the Powder River Basin to Western Gas Partners.

Taking advantage of a low price asset, the next year Anadarko and Newfield Exploration bought properties in the Maverick Basin in Texas for $310 million from bankrupt TXCO.

In the years following its acquisitions of Kerr McGee and Western Gas Resources — for which Anadarko spent almost $25 billion in 2006 — the company went on something of a selling spree. Anadarko eventually pocketed more than $15 billion from the sale of assets in Canada, the Gulf of Mexico, the Mid-Continent region of the US, and the Middle East to improve its liquidity.

HISTORY

In 1959 the Panhandle Eastern Pipe Line Company set up Anadarko (named after the Anadarko Basin) to carry out its gas exploration and production activities. The new company was also formed to take advantage of a ruling by the Federal Power Commission (now the Federal Energy Regulatory Commission) to set lower price ceilings for producing properties owned by pipeline companies.

The company grew rapidly during the early 1960s, largely because of its gas-rich namesake. It bought Ambassador Oil of Fort Worth, Texas, in 1965 — adding interests in 19 states in the US and Canada. The firm also relocated from Kansas to Fort Worth.

Anadarko began offshore exploration in the Gulf of Mexico in 1970 and focused there early in the decade. After moving to Houston in 1974, Anadarko increased its oil exploration activities when the energy crisis led to higher gas prices. A deal with Amoco (now part of BP) led to major finds on Matagorda Island, off the Texas coast, in the early 1980s.

To realize shareholder value, Panhandle spun off Anadarko in 1986 — separating transmission from production. At the time more than 90% of Anadarko's reserves were natural gas. The next year Anadarko made new discoveries in Canada.

Low domestic natural gas prices led Anadarko overseas. It signed a production-sharing agreement with Algeria's national oil and gas firm, SONATRACH, in 1989. The deal covered 5.1 million acres in the Sahara. Two years later Anadarko began operating in the South China Sea and in Alaska's North Slope.

Back home, the company spent $190 million in 1992 for properties in West Texas, and in 1993 Anadarko began divesting noncore assets. Along with some of its partners, the company also discovered oil in the Mahogany Field offshore Louisiana. Production from Mahogany began in 1996.

In 1997 Anadarko added exploration acreage in the North Atlantic and Tunisia. The next year it made two major oil and gas discoveries in the Gulf of Mexico. Anadarko decided to sell some of its noncore Algerian assets in 1999 and teamed up with Texaco (later acquired by Chevron) in a joint exploration program in the Gulf of Mexico, offshore Louisiana. The next year the company acquired Union Pacific Resources in a $5.7 billion stock swap.

Anadarko expanded its presence in western Canada in 2001 by buying Berkley Petroleum for more than $1 billion in cash and assumed debt; a smaller purchase that year, Gulfstream Resources Canada, landed Anadarko in the Persian Gulf and added 70 million barrels of oil equivalent to its reserves.

Expanding its presence and asset base in the lucrative resource plays in the Rocky Mountains and the deepwater Gulf of Mexico, in 2006 Anadarko acquired midstream operator Western Gas and fellow explorer Kerr-McGee for about $26 billion.

EXECUTIVES

Chairman Emeritus: Robert J. Allison Jr., age 71
Chairman and CEO: James T. (Jim) Hackett, age 56, $27,466,776 total compensation
President and COO: R. A. (Al) Walker, age 53, $9,877,515 total compensation
SVP Finance and CFO: Robert G. Gwin, age 47, $8,050,942 total compensation
SVP, General Counsel, and Chief Administrative Officer: Robert K. (Bobby) Reeves Sr., age 53, $4,669,974 total compensation
SVP Worldwide Operations:
Charles A. (Chuck) Meloy Sr., age 50, $11,578,417 total compensation
SVP Worldwide Exploration: Robert P. (Bob) Daniels, age 51, $8,956,126 total compensation
VP; President and CEO, Western Gas Holdings: Donald R. Sinclair
VP and Chief Accounting Officer: M. Cathy Douglas, age 54
VP Corporate Development: Katie Jackson
VP Operations: Donald H. MacLiver
VP E&P Services: Robert D. Abendschein
VP Exploration: Douglas P. Hazlett

VP Marketing and Minerals: David C. Bretches
VP Gulf of Mexico: Darrell E. Hollek
VP and Chief Information Officer: Mario M. Coll III, age 49
VP International Exploration: Frank J. Patterson
VP, Deputy General Counsel, and Corporate Secretary: David L. Siddall
VP Exploration: Stuart C. Strife
VP Human Resources: Julia A. Struble
VP Finance and Treasurer: Bruce W. Busmire, age 53
VP Investor Relations and Communications: John Colglazier
Auditors: KPMG LLP

LOCATIONS

HQ: Anadarko Petroleum Corporation
1201 Lake Robbins Dr., The Woodlands, TX 77380
Phone: 832-636-1000   **Fax:** 832-636-8220
Web: www.anadarko.com

2009 Sales

	% of total
US	82
Algeria	14
Other countries	4
Total	**100**

PRODUCTS/OPERATIONS

2009 Sales

	$ mil.	% of total
Oil & Gas Exploration & Production	7,946	86
Midstream	941	10
Marketing	379	4
Adjustments	(266)	—
Total	**9,000**	**100**

COMPETITORS

Adams Resources
Apache
BP
Cabot Oil & Gas
Chesapeake Energy
Chevron
Cimarex
ConocoPhillips
Devon Energy
EOG
Exxon Mobil
Hunt Consolidated
Jones Energy
Key Energy
National Fuel Gas
Noble Energy
Pioneer Natural Resources
Royal Dutch Shell

HISTORICAL FINANCIALS

Company Type: Public

Income Statement

FYE: December 31

	REVENUE ($ mil.)	NET INCOME ($ mil.)	NET PROFIT MARGIN	EMPLOYEES
12/09	9,000	(103)	—	4,300
12/08	15,723	3,261	20.7%	4,300
12/07	15,892	3,781	23.8%	4,000
12/06	10,187	4,854	47.6%	5,200
12/05	7,100	2,471	34.8%	3,300
Annual Growth	**6.1%**	**—**	**—**	**6.8%**

2009 Year-End Financials

Debt ratio: 64.0%
Return on equity: —
Cash ($ mil.): 3,531
Current ratio: 1.59
Long-term debt ($ mil.): 12,748

No. of shares (mil.): 495
Dividends
  Yield: 0.6%
  Payout: —
Market value ($ mil.): 30,882

Stock History

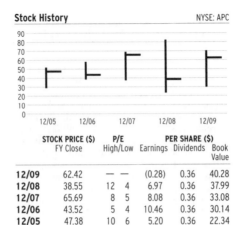

NYSE: APC

	STOCK PRICE ($) FY Close	P/E High	P/E Low	Earnings	Dividends	Book Value
12/09	62.42	—	—	(0.28)	0.36	40.28
12/08	38.55	12	4	6.97	0.36	37.99
12/07	65.69	8	5	8.08	0.36	33.08
12/06	43.52	5	4	10.46	0.36	30.14
12/05	47.38	10	6	5.20	0.36	22.34
Annual Growth	**7.1%**	**—**	**—**	**—**	**0.0%**	**15.9%**

Analog Devices

Analog Devices, Inc. (ADI) is fluent in both analog and digital. The company is a leading maker of analog (linear and mixed-signal) and digital integrated circuits (ICs), including digital signal processors (DSPs). Its linear ICs translate real-world phenomena such as pressure, temperature, and sound into digital signals. ADI's thousands of chip designs are used in industrial process controls, medical and scientific instruments, communications gear, computers, and consumer electronics devices. ADI's chips go into high-tech goods from such companies as Ericsson, Mitsubishi Electric, Philips, Siemens, and Sony. Customers outside the US account for more than three-quarters of ADI's sales. The company has manufacturing facilities in Ireland, the Philippines, and the US.

Reacting to lower sales as global demand for industrial and consumer products plummeted, ADI aggressively reduced expenses in 2008 and 2009. The company consolidated its two US wafer fabrication facilities and its two fabs in Ireland. ADI outsources some of its wafer fabrication, primarily to Taiwan Semiconductor Manufacturing Company. ADI also cut staff as it reorganized its product development and support programs to focus on expanding applications for its core analog and DSP products.

ADI has faced declining demand across all of its product lines; the most dramatic drops in demand came from the industrial (automotive, process control, and instrumentation) and consumer electronics (digital cameras, video game consoles, and other home entertainment products) markets. The company is looking to growth industries to expand uses for its products, including medical imaging and portable medical instruments, as well as energy management applications such as utility meters, wind turbines, light-emitting diodes (LED) backlights, and portable power devices.

Throughout brutal years-long market downturns that affect all parts of the semiconductor industry, ADI continues to keep R&D spending high — about 20% of sales — to promote new product development. The company is among the most consistently profitable ventures in the semiconductor industry.

ADI leveraged its early analog know-how by integrating mixed-signal technology onto DSPs in time to catch the Internet tidal wave. At the same time, the company widened its focus, pioneering tiny silicon devices called micromachines or MEMS, primarily accelerometers used in air bags.

In early 2008 ADI sold the assets of its Othello radio and SoftFone baseband chipset product lines, as well as certain cellular handset baseband support operations, to MediaTek for approximately $350 million in cash. The company continues to support the wireless handset market through its high-performance analog chips, MEMS devices, and programmable DSPs.

HISTORY

Ray Stata, an MIT graduate and Hewlett-Packard veteran, and Matthew Lorber founded Analog Devices, Inc. (ADI) in 1965 to make amplifiers for strengthening electrical signals. The company soon expanded into converters used to control machinery and take measurements, and went public in 1968. Lorber left the company that year and went on to found several startups, including Printer Technology, Torque Systems, and Copley Controls.

In 1969 ADI began manufacturing semiconductors. Stata become chairman and CEO in 1973. In 1977 he launched the influential Massachusetts High Technology Council to fight taxes that he felt were restricting the growth of high-tech firms.

During the early 1980s ADI acquired stakes in several technology firms, including Charles River Data Systems (microcomputer hardware and software), Jupiter Systems (color graphics computers), Photodyne (fiber-optics test instruments), and Tau-Tron (high-speed digital instrumentation). In the mid-1980s ADI's profits declined as Japanese competitors acquired market share.

In 1990 the company acquired Precision Monolithics, a maker of passive electronic components. The next year ADI introduced the world's first commercial micromachine, an automotive air-bag trigger.

In 1992 ADI formed a joint venture with Hewlett-Packard to develop mixed-signal chips. The company extended its global reach in 1996 by acquiring Mosaic Microsystems, a UK radio-frequency design company. It also formed Washington State-based chip producer WaferTech with Taiwan Semiconductor Manufacturing and others. Also in 1996 company veteran Jerald Fishman became ADI's president and CEO; Stata remained chairman.

In 1998 ADI acquired MediaLight, a Toronto-based developer of digital subscriber line software. ADI also sold its disk drive integrated circuit business to Adaptec for about $27 million. The next year the company bought White Mountain DSP (development software for DSPs) and Edinburgh Portable Compilers (software compilers for embedded applications).

In 2000 and early 2001, ADI completed a string of acquisitions, headlined by the purchases of Ireland-based BCO Technologies ($163 million; wafers for optical components) and Chiplogic ($68 million; broadband networking chips for voice and video). ADI sold its 4% stake in WaferTech to joint venture partner TSMC in 2000.

ADI and CEO Jerry Fishman came under the scrutiny of the US Securities and Exchange

Commission in 2006 when it targeted a number of publicly held companies for stock options violations. The company received a subpoena that year from a federal grand jury in New York investigating backdating and other options abuses from 1998 to 2001. The company and CEO Jerry Fishman reached a final settlement with the SEC in 2008. Without admitting or denying the commission's findings from a year-long investigation, the company paid a civil penalty of $3 million, while Fishman paid $1 million.

Early in 2006 ADI sold its network processor business to Ikanos Communications for $30 million in cash. The product line accounted for about 2% of ADI's sales.

Later that year ADI acquired Integrant Technologies, a Korean company specializing in high-performance analog circuits for reconfigurable radio-frequency signal processing, for about $127 million in cash. Integrant's low-power radio tuners allowed computers, consumer electronics devices, and mobile handsets to receive digital TV and digital radio broadcasts.

EXECUTIVES

Chairman: Ray Stata, age 75
President, CEO, and Director:
Jerald G. (Jerry) Fishman, age 64,
$2,938,218 total compensation
VP Finance and CFO: David A. (Dave) Zinsner, age 41,
$2,417,773 total compensation
VP Research and Development and CTO:
Samuel H. Fuller, age 63
VP Strategic Market Segments Group: Vincent Roche,
age 49, $1,243,517 total compensation
VP Worldwide Manufacturing: Robert R. (Rob) Marshall,
age 55, $1,660,054 total compensation
VP, General Counsel, and Secretary:
Margaret K. (Marnie) Seif, age 48
VP Core Products and Technologies Group:
Robert P. (Robbie) McAdam, age 58,
$1,773,369 total compensation
CIO: Peter Forte
VP Industrial and Instrumentation:
Michael (Mike) Britchfield
VP Healthcare: Pat O'Doherty
VP Analog Technology: David (Dave) Robertson
VP, Controller, and Chief Accounting Officer:
Seamus Brennan, age 58
VP Marketing: Emre Onder
VP Automotive: Thomas Wessel
VP Power Management: Peter Henry
VP MEMS and Sensors: Mark Martin
VP Consumer and Communications Infrastructure:
John Hussey
VP Planning, Logistics, and Quality:
Gerry (Ger) Dundon
Auditors: Ernst & Young LLP

LOCATIONS

HQ: Analog Devices, Inc.
1 Technology Way, Norwood, MA 02062
Phone: 781-329-4700
Web: www.analog.com

2009 Sales

	$ mil.	% of total
Asia/Pacific		
China	376.1	19
Japan	349.9	17
Other countries	291.8	14
Europe	502.6	25
Americas		
US	401.6	20
Other countries	92.9	5
Total	**2,014.9**	**100**

PRODUCTS/OPERATIONS

2009 Sales

	$ mil.	% of total
Analog signal processing products		
Converters	960.5	48
Amplifiers	501.8	25
Other analog	261.1	13
Power management & reference	118.2	6
Digital signal processor products		
General-purpose DSPs	167.1	8
Other DSPs	6.2	—
Total	**2,014.9**	**100**

2009 Sales by Market

	$ mil.	% of total
Industrial	1,049.2	52
Communications	512.9	25
Consumer	400.3	20
Computer	52.5	3
Total	**2,014.9**	**100**

Selected Products

Integrated Circuits (ICs)
  Analog
    Amplifiers
    Analog signal processing devices
    Comparators
    Data converters
    Interface circuits
    Power management ICs
    Voltage references
  Digital signal processing (DSP) devices
  Multifunction mixed-signal devices
Assembled Products
  Hybrid products (mounted and packaged chips and
    discrete components)
  Multichip modules
  Printed circuit board modules
Micromachined Products
  Accelerometers

COMPETITORS

Analogic
Broadcom
Cirrus Logic
Conexant Systems
Custom Sensors & Technologies
DENSO
DSP Group
Fairchild Semiconductor
Freescale Semiconductor
Hittite Microwave
Infineon Technologies
Integrated Device Technology
International Rectifier
Intersil
Linear Technology
Marvell Technology
Maxim Integrated Products
Micrel
Microchip Technology
Microsemi
National Semiconductor
NXP Semiconductors
ON Semiconductor
Panasonic Electronic Devices
Qualcomm CDMA
Robert Bosch
ROHM
Semtech
Silicon Image
Silicon Labs
Siliconix
Skyworks
Standard Microsystems
STMicroelectronics
Texas Instruments

HISTORICAL FINANCIALS

Company Type: Public

Income Statement

FYE: Saturday nearest October 31

	REVENUE ($ mil.)	NET INCOME ($ mil.)	NET PROFIT MARGIN	EMPLOYEES
10/09	2,015	248	12.3%	8,300
10/08	2,583	786	30.4%	9,000
10/07	2,546	497	19.5%	9,600
10/06	2,573	550	21.4%	9,800
10/05	2,389	415	17.4%	8,800
Annual Growth	**(4.2%)**	**(12.1%)**	**—**	**(1.5%)**

2009 Year-End Financials

Debt ratio: 15.0%
Return on equity: 10.0%
Cash ($ mil.): 640
Current ratio: 6.44
Long-term debt ($ mil.): 380
No. of shares (mil.): 298
Dividends
  Yield: 3.1%
  Payout: 94.1%
Market value ($ mil.): 7,637

Stock History

NYSE: ADI

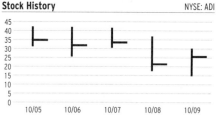

	STOCK PRICE ($) FY Close	P/E High/Low	PER SHARE ($) Earnings	Dividends	Book Value
10/09	25.63	35 18	0.85	0.80	8.49
10/08	21.36	14 7	2.67	0.76	8.12
10/07	33.46	27 21	1.50	0.70	7.85
10/06	31.82	28 18	1.48	0.56	11.53
10/05	34.78	39 29	1.08	0.32	12.39
Annual Growth	**(7.3%)**	**— —**	**(5.8%)**	**25.7%**	**(9.0%)**

Anixter International

Psssst, need to get wired? Anixter International's got connections. The company is a distributor of communication products used to connect voice, video, data, and security systems. It sells more than 450,000 products, including electrical and electronic wire, cable, fasteners, and security system components, through a global network of sales and distribution centers. The company's 230-plus warehouses stock products from more than 7,000 suppliers. Some 70 sales centers cater to such markets as education, government, health care, manufacturing, retail, and transportation. Among its 100,000 customers, Anixter also serves contractors and integrators who install and maintain communications networks and data centers.

International, national, regional, and local OEMs number among Anixter's customers, as well. They procure wire, cable, fasteners, and other small components to help finish the manufacturing of their own products, typically with short lead times. Anixter's massive distribution capacity is central to delivering goods whenever and wherever its customers demand — often within 24 hours. In addition to turn-on-a-dime delivery, the company's reach has cultivated a broad customer base; no one customer accounts for more than 3% of sales, and no one industry accounts for more than 11%. Not content, however, to rest on its distribution might, Anixter moves beyond solely aggregating and marketing products to offering a slate of inventory management services for customers, as well as testing facilities for its suppliers.

The company's operations are driven organically through both product and service expansions. At the same time, Anixter doesn't hesitate to go after niche acquisition opportunities that promise to expand its technical expertise. In 2008 Anixter acquired the assets and operations of Quality Screw & Nut (also known as QSN Industries) and its Quality Screw de Mexico subsidiary for about $80 million. The acquisition augments Anixter's geographic reach and manufacturing capacity in bolts, screws, and cold formed components, with the addition of nearly 20 facilities in the US, and Mexico. Anixter also benefits from an enhanced portfolio that courts OEMs in a variety of vertical markets.

Later that year the company purchased the assets and operations of World Class Wire & Cable for some $62 million. It bought France's Sofrasar SA, too, and Germany's Camille Gergen GmbH & Co., KG and Camille Gergen Verwaltungs GmbH. The European firms are fastener distributors and give subsidiaries Anixter Fasteners and Anixter Pentacon more muscle to supply fasteners and aerospace hardware, respectively, to OEMs throughout the world.

Billionaire financier Samuel Zell, Anixter's chairman, holds around 14% of Anixter. Zell has held this post since 1985.

HISTORY

Anixter International was founded in 1957 by two brothers, Alan and Bill Anixter, along with a small group of employees in Evanston, Illinois. The company was known as Anixter Brothers at the time and supplied distributors and wholesalers looking for an alternative to buying wire and cable in bulk quantities directly from manufacturers.

In 1967 the company went public on the American Stock Exchange. Anixter became an international company when Anixter United Kingdom was formed in 1972. That decade saw its continued growth throughout North America.

In 1987 holding company Itel bought Anixter, which had since moved into the data communications business to round out its expertise in electrical wire and cable. Itel was led by Chicago financier Samuel Zell, who had become chairman in 1985.

Zell and vice chairman Rod Dammeyer, former Household International CFO, acquired Great Lakes International (marine dredging, 1986), Anixter Bros. (wire and cable, 1986), Pullman (railcars, 1988), and a minority stake in Santa Fe Southern Pacific (railroad, 1988). Other acquisitions included Flexi-Van Leasing (1987), the assets of Evans Asset Holding (railcars, 1987), and B.C. Hydro (rail freight line, 1988). By 1988 Itel was North America's leading railcar leasing company.

In the 1990s Itel repositioned itself, selling its container-leasing business (1990) and its Itel Distribution Systems and Great Lakes Dredge & Deck Co. (1991). When the smoke cleared, Anixter was the company's core operation. Anixter spun off its cable television products subsidiary, ANTEC, in 1993. Also that year Dammeyer replaced Zell as Itel's CEO.

Itel's focus became developing new markets in the burgeoning global communications industry. The company sold its remaining rail leasing interests in 1994. The next year Itel sold its stake in Santa Fe Energy Resources and changed its name to Anixter.

When an ANTEC subsidiary merged with cable TV equipment firm TSX Corp. in 1997, Anixter's ownership in ANTEC was reduced to 19%. That year the company joined with security software maker Check Point Software Technologies to provide network security products in Europe.

Anixter sold its ANTEC holdings in 1998 to finance the repurchase of its common stock, and bought Pacer Electronics, an electrical and data cabling distributor. Also that year, company veteran Robert Grubbs became CEO.

The next year Anixter sold its European network integration business to Persetel Q Data Holdings of South Africa and its data network design and consulting unit to Ameritech for $200 million in cash. It also sold North America Integration and Asia Pacific Integration, completing the dissolution of its integration segment by the close of 1999.

In 2000 Anixter formed a consortium with Panduit, Rockwell Automation, and Siemens for the production of industrially hardened Ethernet connectors. Anixter signed an agreement to distribute network cabling products for IBM in 2001.

In 2002 Anixter was named as a *Forbes* "Platinum 400" company, chosen by the magazine's editors as one of America's "best-performing" corporations by industry. Later that year it acquired Pentacon (now Anixter Pentacon), a fastener distribution company.

More fastener acquisitions followed: Walters Hexagon in 2003, DDI in 2004, Infast Group in 2005, MFU in 2006, and Eurofast and Total Supply Solutions in 2007.

Robert Grubbs retired as president and CEO in mid-2008. The board designated EVP/COO Robert Eck, a 17-year veteran of Anixter, as his successor.

EXECUTIVES

Chairman: Samuel (Sam) Zell, age 68
President, CEO, and Director: Robert J. Eck, age 51, $2,682,494 total compensation
EVP Finance and CFO: Dennis J. Letham, age 58, $2,882,117 total compensation
SVP Global Finance: Ted A. Dosch, age 50, $825,199 total compensation
VP and Controller: Terrance A. Faber, age 58, $838,019 total compensation
VP Human Resources: Rodney A. Smith, age 52, $481,615 total compensation
VP and Treasurer, Anixter International and Anixter Inc.: Rodney A. Shoemaker, age 52
VP Taxes: Philip F. Meno, age 51
VP, General Counsel, and Secretary; General Counsel and Secretary, Anixter Inc.: John A. Dul, age 48, $759,812 total compensation
VP Marketing Communications: Dawn Marks
VP Internal Audit: Nancy C. Ross-Dronzek, age 49
Auditors: Ernst & Young LLP

LOCATIONS

HQ: Anixter International Inc.
2301 Patriot Blvd., Glenview, IL 60026
Phone: 224-521-8000   **Fax:** 224-521-8100
Web: www.anixter.com

2009 Sales

	$ mil.	% of total
North America		
US	3,030.9	61
Canada	579.1	12
Europe	907.2	18
Other regions	465.2	9
Total	**4,982.4**	**100**

PRODUCTS/OPERATIONS

Selected Products and Services

Products
  Aerospace hardware
  Electrical wire and cable (power cable)
  Electronic wire and cable (coax)
  Fasteners and connectors ("C" class)
  Industrial networking communications
  Network cabling (copper and fiber)
  Networking, wireless and voice electronics
  Security (video surveillance, access control)
Supply chain services
  Database tracking
  Deployment
  Inventory management
  Logistics
  Product enhancement and packaging
  Sourcing

COMPETITORS

Border States Electric	Lawson Products
Consolidated Electrical	Precision Industries
Crescent Electric Supply	Rexel
Gexpro	Sonepar
Graybar Electric	WESCO International
Kirby Risk	

HISTORICAL FINANCIALS

Company Type: Public

Income Statement			FYE: Friday nearest December 31
	REVENUE ($ mil.)	**NET INCOME** ($ mil.)	**NET PROFIT MARGIN**	**EMPLOYEES**
---	---	---	---	---
12/09	4,982	(29)	—	7,811
12/08	6,137	196	3.2%	8,645
12/07	5,853	254	4.3%	8,000
12/06	4,939	209	4.2%	7,500
12/05	3,847	90	2.3%	6,800
Annual Growth	6.7%	—	—	3.5%

2009 Year-End Financials

Debt ratio: 80.2%   No. of shares (mil.): 34
Return on equity: —   Dividends
Cash ($ mil.): 112   Yield: —
Current ratio: 3.06   Payout: —
Long-term debt ($ mil.): 821   Market value ($ mil.): 1,592

Stock History

NYSE: AXE

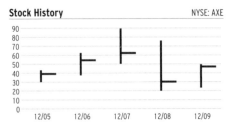

	STOCK PRICE ($)	P/E		PER SHARE ($)		
	FY Close	High	Low	Earnings	Dividends	Book Value
12/09	47.10	—	—	(0.83)	—	30.31
12/08	30.12	15	4	5.07	—	30.65
12/07	62.27	15	9	6.00	—	31.01
12/06	54.30	13	8	4.86	—	28.47
12/05	39.12	19	14	2.22	—	20.91
Annual Growth	4.8%	—	—	—	—	9.7%

AnnTaylor Stores

At AnnTaylor, basic black is as appreciated by its customers as its classic styles. The company (named for a fictional person) is a national retailer of upscale women's clothing designed exclusively for its stores. Its Ann Taylor and LOFT shops offer apparel, shoes, and accessories. Targeting fashion-conscious career women, Ann Taylor operates about 900 stores (more than 500 are LOFT outlets) in some 45 US states, the District of Columbia, and Puerto Rico. Most are located in malls or upscale retail centers. LOFT stores offer their own label of mid-priced casual apparel, while Ann Taylor Factory and LOFT Outlet stores sell clearance merchandise. AnnTaylor also has its own e-commerce website.

The deep recession in the US, combined with especially weak sales of women's apparel, has led AnnTaylor to undertake an aggressive restructuring plan that includes the shuttering of about 175 underperforming stores by the end of 2010. (As of January 2010, the retailer had shuttered about 100 of the shops marked for closure.) While the company is closing Ann Taylor locations, which target career women, it continues to open LOFT locations (launched in 1999) and to convert Ann Taylor shops to the LOFT format. It is also opening LOFT Outlet shops (20 are slated to open in 2010), which sell discounted merchandise. The restructuring plan is expected to generate about $125 million in annual cost savings by the end of 2010, with savings of about $65 million in 2009. Indeed, while sales plunged more than 16% last year, the company was able to substantially trim its losses versus the previous year through cost cutting, effective inventory management (which led to less discounting), and other measures.

In addition to cost cutting, AnnTaylor has appointed a new leadership team to breathe new life into its aging brand. A new merchandising strategy that features core items — such as "the perfect pencil skirt" and "perfect pants" — paired with more frequently restocked complementary companion pieces is helping to keep inventories lean.

Ann Taylor stores are on average 5,300 sq. ft., LOFT stores are about 5,900 sq. ft., and the factory stores are around 7,300 sq. ft. About 75% of its core Ann Taylor stores are located in shopping malls and upscale retail centers. The company's three flagship stores are located in Chicago, New York City, and San Francisco. AnnTaylor's products are made in about 15 countries, with about 40% originating in China. The fast-growing Ann Taylor LOFT format quickly overtook its more mature sister chain (in terms of the number of outlets) as American women adopted a more casual style of dress. LOFT stores eventually outperformed Ann Taylor stores.

HISTORY

AnnTaylor Stores started out in 1954 as a shop on Chapel Street in New Haven, Connecticut. Founder Robert Liebskind targeted women who would later be called "preppie," using the conservative (and fictitious) Ann Taylor name. The stores proliferated in New England. In 1977 Liebskind sold out to Garfinckel, Brooks Brothers, Miller & Rhodes, which in 1981 was bought by Allied Stores. Under Allied, AnnTaylor was the top performer, thanks in large part to the merchandising savvy of Sally Frame Kasaks, who was president from 1983 to 1985.

Campeau Corporation made a hostile takeover of Allied in 1985. Heavily in debt, and with ill-fated designs on the bigger prize of Federated Department Stores, Campeau mined AnnTaylor for cash and then sold it in 1988 for $420 million to private investors and the division's management. AnnTaylor had suffered from image drift under Campeau, and its new management continued to ignore the company's target career-woman customer; in addition, the chain was slow to see the trend toward more casual career dressing.

In 1991 AnnTaylor went public, but it continued to founder under high debt load and a fuzzy fashion image. Kasaks returned as CEO that year and transformed the store name into a brand name with original designs. She also added shoe stores and a lower-priced apparel concept (Ann Taylor LOFT). The company's fashion sense became a problem again — cropped T-shirts didn't fit in with the workplace attire its customers sought — and AnnTaylor suffered a loss in fiscal 1996. Kasaks was ousted that year.

New CEO Patrick Spainhour and new president Patricia DeRosa quickly led AnnTaylor to another turnaround. They closed the shoe stores in 1997 and refocused the company's designs. The company opened 29 Ann Taylor LOFT stores in 1999 in pursuit of younger, more cost-conscious consumers. In early 2001 DeRosa left the company.

AnnTaylor attempted a short-lived cosmetic line in 2000, which it discontinued in 2001.

In 2004 the company opened five new Ann Taylor stores and 75 Ann Taylor LOFT stores.

In June 2005 the company completed its move to its new headquarters in Times Square Tower in New York City. In August the New York retailer announced it had entered into a trademark licensing agreement with China's Guangzhou Pan Yu San Yuet Fashion Manufactory Ltd. that owns rights to use the Ann Taylor name in China. In September chairman and CEO J. Patrick Spainhour retired and was succeeded as CEO by the company's president Kay Krill. Ronald W. Hovsepian, a director of the company since 1998, became chairman.

In May 2006 COO Laura Weil resigned after less than a year with the company. (Weil had joined AnnTaylor Stores from American Eagle Outfitters in 2005.)

Ann Taylor LOFT's e-commerce site debuted in November 2007. Overall in 2007 the company added more than 50 LOFT stores and about a dozen Ann Taylor shops.

In another bid to grow, the apparel and accessories retailer has launched a beauty division that sells fragrances and skin care products. In October 2008 AnnTaylor appointed two top executives — a head designer and an executive over its stores — in its effort to breathe new life into its collections and outlets.

EXECUTIVES

Chairman: Ronald W. (Ron) Hovsepian, age 49
President, CEO, and Director: Katherine L. (Kay) Krill, age 55, $9,112,292 total compensation
EVP, CFO, and Treasurer: Michael J. (Mike) Nicholson, age 43, $2,647,923 total compensation
EVP Human Resources: Mark Morrison
EVP, General Counsel, and Secretary:
  Barbara K. Eisenberg, age 64
EVP and Chief Supply Chain Officer: Paula J. Zusi
SVP and CIO: Michael Kingston
SVP Real Estate: George R. (Buck) Sappenfield, age 59
SVP Design, AnnTaylor Stores: Lisa Axelson
SVP, Sourcing AnnTaylor Stores: Philippa Abeles

SVP, General Merchandise Manager, Ann Taylor Stores:
  Sonya Lee
VP Investor Relations: Judith A. Pirro
VP and Controller: Dominick J. Reis, age 48
VP, Corporate Facilities: Darrell DeVoe
VP Corporate Communications: Catherine Fisher
President, AnnTaylor Stores: Christine M. Beauchamp, age 40, $3,841,743 total compensation
President, Corporate Operations: Brian E. Lynch, age 52, $4,212,165 total compensation
President, LOFT: Gary P. Muto, age 50, $4,527,535 total compensation
Auditors: Deloitte & Touche LLP

LOCATIONS

HQ: AnnTaylor Stores Corporation
  7 Times Sq., 15th Fl., New York, NY 10036
Phone: 212-541-3300   **Fax:** 212-541-3379
Web: www.anntaylor.com

PRODUCTS/OPERATIONS

2010 Stores

	No.
LOFT	506
Ann Taylor	291
Ann Taylor Factory	92
LOFT Outlet	18
Total	**907**

2010 Sales

	$ mil.	% of total
LOFT	939.9	51
Ann Taylor	456.6	25
Other	432.0	24
Total	**1,828.5**	**100**

Selected Store Formats

Ann Taylor (upscale specialty stores selling women's apparel)
Ann Taylor Factory Store (clearance stores for Ann Taylor merchandise)
LOFT (mid-priced specialty stores selling women's apparel)
LOFT Outlet (clearance stores for Ann Taylor LOFT merchandise)

COMPETITORS

Banana Republic
Benetton
Bernard Chaus
Brand Matter
Brooks Brothers
Caché
Calvin Klein
Chico's FAS
Dillard's
Donna Karan
The Gap
J. Crew
J. Jill Group
Jones Apparel
Lands' End
Liz Claiborne
Macy's
New York & Company
Nordstrom
Polo Ralph Lauren
Saks
St. John Knits
Talbots
Urban Outfitters

HISTORICAL FINANCIALS

Company Type: Public

Income Statement

FYE: Saturday nearest January 31

	REVENUE ($ mil.)	NET INCOME ($ mil.)	NET PROFIT MARGIN	EMPLOYEES
1/10	1,829	(18)	—	18,800
1/09	2,195	(334)	—	18,400
1/08	2,397	97	4.1%	18,400
1/07	2,343	143	6.1%	17,700
1/06	2,073	82	4.0%	16,900
Annual Growth	(3.1%)	—	—	2.7%

2010 Year-End Financials

Debt ratio: —
Return on equity: —
Cash ($ mil.): 204
Current ratio: 1.83
Long-term debt ($ mil.): —

No. of shares (mil.): 59
Dividends
  Yield: —
  Payout: —
Market value ($ mil.): 738

Stock History

NYSE: ANN

	STOCK PRICE ($) FY Close	P/E High/Low		PER SHARE ($) Earnings	Dividends	Book Value
1/10	12.56	—	—	(0.32)	—	7.10
1/09	4.92	—	—	(5.82)	—	7.08
1/08	25.13	26	12	1.53	—	14.28
1/07	34.50	23	16	1.98	—	17.86
1/06	33.32	31	19	1.13	—	17.60
Annual Growth	(21.6%)	—	—	—	—	(20.3%)

A. O. Smith

Aerosmith has a lot of fans — A. O. Smith has a lot of fan motors. The company makes the guts of buildings, i.e., residential and commercial water heaters and electric motors. Its Water segment makes residential gas and electric water heaters and commercial water-heating systems. Electrical products include pump motors for home water systems, swimming pools, and hot tubs; fan motors for furnaces and air conditioners; and hermetic motors for compressors and commercial refrigeration units. Routes to retail shelves include private-label agreements with Lowe's and Sears. Members of the founding Smith family control the company.

A. O. Smith was impacted by the economic downturn in 2008-2009, with sales falling as poor market conditions affected demand for the company's products. Its US residential and commercial water heater sales were down due to lower housing and commercial construction, though the damage was tempered to some degree by replacement system sales to the commercial market. In China, where construction has remained strong, sales of water products were up nearly 20%. The water segment also benefitted from increases in pricing for systems, as well as strength in sales of high-efficiency

products. Sales of electrical products were down nearly 30%, due to weakness in the housing and commercial construction markets.

The company's dual exposure to commercial as well as residential builders has minimized the drag from the US housing slowdown on its bottom line. In addition, with a portion of the company's sales driven by commercial water heaters to China, A. O. Smith's international operations lend some stability.

A. O. Smith manufactures a significant portion of its products outside of the US, primarily in Mexico and China. The company sells its wares in more than 60 countries worldwide. Its commercial water heaters are sold through independent wholesale plumbing distributors. Typical end-users are restaurants, hotels, laundries, car washes, and small businesses.

The tap on China's residential and commercial water markets is being turned up. In November 2009 the company acquired an 80% stake in the water treatment activities of Hong Kong-based Tianlong Holding Co. Ltd. Tianlong offers an established product line of reverse osmosis (RO) products. A.O. Smith's entry into supplying RO water filtration products to China and neighboring export markets with Tianlong is filtered through a newly created foreign subsidiary, A.O. Smith (Shanghai) Water Treatment Products.

The company also sees opportunities in India, where the company opened a sales office to import products specifically designed for the Indian market in 2008. Later that year A. O. Smith began construction of a plant near Bangalore, the technology capital of India.

Smith Investment Company (SICO), the Smith family firm, and A. O. Smith completed a tax-free stock transaction in late 2008. Family members placed their shares in A. O. Smith into a voting trust and will refrain for three years from taking any significant action on the ownership of A. O. Smith without the approval of the company's board.

HISTORY

Charles Jeremiah Smith founded a machine shop in 1874 to make parts for baby carriages. The business expanded into making bicycles, and by 1895 it was a global leader in bicycle parts. The Smith family sold the firm in 1899. Charles' eldest son, Arthur, began tinkering with car frames, and by 1902 he had a breakthrough design. Arthur bought the company back in 1904 to make car frames and incorporated it as A. O. Smith.

A huge 1906 contract from Ford Motor spurred Arthur to retool the factory, increasing production tenfold. In 1921 A. O. Smith unveiled the first automated assembly line for car frames. Dubbed the Mechanical Marvel, it could produce a frame every eight seconds and did so for the next 40 years.

The firm began production of the first glass-lined residential water heaters in 1939. Acquisitions over the next decade allowed A. O. Smith to enter the electric motor market, and in 1959 it established a plastics unit for its fiberglass pipe.

In 1986 A. O. Smith expanded its electric motor business when it bought Westinghouse's small-motor division. The company doubled the size of its tank business by buying Peabody TecTank (dry storage tanks) the next year. Company veteran Robert O'Toole was named CEO in 1989.

A. O. Smith sold its auto business in 1997 and bought private motor producer UPPCO. The company became the #1 North American maker

of compressor motors for the air-conditioning industry with its 1998 purchase of a General Electric motor unit. In 1999 it bought the electric-motor unit of Magnetek, doubling the size of its pump motor business.

In 2000 the company sold its fluid handling (fiberglass pipe) business to Varco International (Texas). The next year A. O. Smith sold its storage products business to CST Industries (Kansas).

A. O. Smith elected to sell some 3.5 million shares of its common stock in early 2002, with the intention of repaying a portion of its debt. To expand its manufacturing capabilities, the company acquired an electric motor maker in China from the Changheng Group (air-moving motors for the Chinese air-conditioning market). A. O. Smith also pumped up its water systems by acquiring privately held State Industries (water heaters), which contributed about $313 million to its annual net sales. The same year A. O. Smith bought the assets of the Athens Products division of Electrolux.

In 2003 A. O. Smith again expanded its global motor manufacturing business, buying the assets of Taicang Special Motor Co., Ltd., a maker of hermetic electric motors based in China. Two years later the company bought another Chinese motor manufacturer, Yueyang Special Electrical Machinery.

O'Toole retired at the end of 2005 and company president Paul Jones was named CEO.

In 2006 A. O. Smith acquired GSW, a Canadian supplier of water heaters, for about $320 million in cash. The acquisition gave A. O. Smith entree as a supplier to home improvement giant Lowe's.

Later that year the company sold GSW Building Products, a manufacturer of vinyl rain ware systems, to Euramax International. GSW Building Products employed about 100 people in Barrie, Ontario, and posted 2005 sales of $30 million. A. O. Smith received net proceeds of about $11.3 million from the sale.

EXECUTIVES

Chairman and CEO: Paul W. Jones, age 61, $6,272,372 total compensation
EVP; President, Water Products: Ajita G. Rajendra, age 58, $2,175,660 total compensation
EVP and CFO: Terry M. Murphy, age 61, $1,988,057 total compensation
EVP; President, Electrical Products: Christopher L. (Chris) Mapes, age 48, $1,495,893 total compensation
EVP, General Counsel, and Secretary: James F. Stern, age 47, $841,984 total compensation
SVP Finance and Controller: John J. Kita, age 54
SVP and CIO: Randall S. (Randy) Bednar, age 57
SVP Human Resources and Public Affairs: Mark A. Petrarca, age 46, $1,244,708 total compensation
SVP Corporate Development: Steve W. Rettler, age 55
VP Investor Relations and Treasurer: Patricia K. Ackerman
VP Corporate Development: Malcolm B. Kinnaird
President and General Manager, China: Wilfridus Brouwer
Auditors: Ernst & Young LLP

LOCATIONS

HQ: A. O. Smith Corporation
11270 W. Park Place, Ste. 170
Milwaukee, WI 53224
Phone: 414-359-4000   **Fax:** 414-359-4115
Web: www.aosmith.com

2009 Sales

	$ mil.	% of total
US	1445.4	73
China	261.3	13
Canada	168.2	8
Other countries	116.6	6
Total	**1,991.5**	**100**

PRODUCTS/OPERATIONS

2009 Sales

	$ mil.	% of total
Water products	1,375.0	69
Electrical products	620.4	31
Adjustments	(3.9)	—
Total	**1,991.5**	**100**

Selected Divisions and Products

Water products
  Commercial water heaters
  Copper tube boilers
  Residential water heaters

Electric products
  Fractional horsepower electric motors
  Hermetic electric motors
  Integral horsepower A/C and D/C electric motors

COMPETITORS

AMETEK
AMTROL
Baldor Electric
Bradford White
Emerson Electric
EXX
Franklin Electric
GE
Hayward Industries
Indesit
Kinetek
Lindeteves-Jacoberg
Lochinvar
Paloma Co.
Pentair
RBS Global
Regal Beloit
Tecumseh Products
WEG Electric Motors

HISTORICAL FINANCIALS

Company Type: Public

Income Statement

FYE: December 31

	REVENUE ($ mil.)	NET INCOME ($ mil.)	NET PROFIT MARGIN	EMPLOYEES
12/09	1,992	90	4.5%	16,067
12/08	2,305	82	3.6%	15,350
12/07	2,312	88	3.8%	16,800
12/06	2,161	77	3.5%	18,000
12/05	1,689	47	2.8%	17,650
Annual Growth	**4.2%**	**17.8%**	**—**	**(2.3%)**

2009 Year-End Financials

Debt ratio: 30.1%	No. of shares (mil.): 51
Return on equity: 12.7%	Dividends
Cash ($ mil.): 76	Yield: 1.8%
Current ratio: 1.51	Payout: 22.7%
Long-term debt ($ mil.): 232	Market value ($ mil.): 2,194

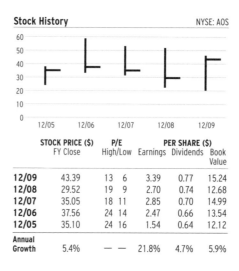

Stock History

NYSE: AOS

	STOCK PRICE ($) FY Close	P/E High/Low		PER SHARE ($) Earnings	Dividends	Book Value
12/09	43.39	13	6	3.39	0.77	15.24
12/08	29.52	19	9	2.70	0.74	12.68
12/07	35.05	18	11	2.85	0.70	14.99
12/06	37.56	24	14	2.47	0.66	13.54
12/05	35.10	24	16	1.54	0.64	12.12
Annual Growth	**5.4%**	**—**	**—**	**21.8%**	**4.7%**	**5.9%**

Aon Corporation

Aon (the name means "oneness" in Gaelic) is one of the world's leading insurance brokerages, as well as a top reinsurance broker. The company operates in two major segments: commercial brokerage and consulting services. The company's Aon Risk Services brokerage unit provides retail property/casualty, liability, workers' compensation, and other insurance products for groups and businesses, as well as risk management services. Aon Benfield handles reinsurance brokerage and analysis services to protect insurers from losses on traditional and specialty property/casualty policies. Aon's consulting unit, Aon Consulting Worldwide, specializes in employee benefits administration.

Aon provides its brokerage and consulting services from more than 500 offices in about 120 countries; the US and Europe are its largest markets. The insurance and reinsurance brokerage operations together account for more than 80% of sales. Aon Risk Services provides retail insurance brokerage services (placing policies on behalf of insurance companies for a commission) to small to large corporations and other professional organizations, as well as to individuals; it also provides risk identification and assessment, cost-control and claims management, and other administrative services.

Market conditions such as fluctuating insurance rates and strong competition are causes for the ongoing restructuring efforts, which include an approximate 10% workforce reduction between 2007 and the end of 2010.

The company has exited its older but smaller insurance underwriting segment, which offered supplementary health, accident, and life insurance and included founder W. Clement Stone's original insurance underwriting business, Combined Insurance. Aon in 2008 sold the Combined Insurance unit to ACE Limited for nearly $2.6 billion.

At the same time, Aon has been working to expand in its core business areas. In 2008 Aon acquired UK-based Benfield Group in a $1.75 billion deal to strengthen its European reinsurance brokerage operations. It then merged Benfield Group with its existing Aon Re

Global operations and renamed the new business Aon Benfield.

The company also continues to expand its retail insurance brokerage network through purchases of smaller agencies. For instance in 2009 Aon acquired 14 businesses, including Polish auto insurance brokerage firm Dom Brokerski Progres and US construction policy brokerage business Allied North America.

In one of its largest deals yet, Aon announced in 2010 that it will spend $4.9 billion to acquire human resource and benefits outsourcing firm Hewitt Associates. The deal will triple the size of the company's existing human resources operations and allow it to compete with similar operations of its rival Marsh & McLennan.

HISTORY

Aon's story begins with the birth of W. Clement Stone around the turn of the 20th century. At age six he started working as a paperboy in Chicago. The young Stone devoured the optimistic messages of the 19th-century Horatio Alger novels, which detailed the successes of plucky, enterprising heroes.

Stone's mother bought a small Detroit insurance agency and in 1918 brought her son into the business. Young Stone sold low-cost, low-benefit accident insurance, underwriting and issuing policies on-site. The next year he founded his own agency, the Combined Registry Co. While selling up to 122 policies per day, he recruited a nationwide force of agents.

As the Depression took hold, Stone reduced the company's workforce and improved training. Forced by his son's respiratory illness to winter in the South, Stone followed the sun to Arkansas and Texas. In 1939 he bought American Casualty Insurance Co. of Dallas. It was consolidated with other purchases as the Combined Insurance Co. of America in 1947.

The company grew through the 1950s and 1960s, continuing to sell health and accident policies. In the 1970s Combined expanded overseas despite being hit hard by the recession.

In 1982, after 10 years of stagnant growth under Clement Stone Jr., the elder Stone (then 79) resumed control until the completion of a merger with Ryan Insurance Co. allowed him to transfer power to Patrick Ryan.

Ryan, the son of a Wisconsin Ford dealer, had started his company as an auto credit insurer in 1964. In 1976 the company bought the insurance brokerage units of the Esmark conglomerate. Ryan's less-personal management style differed radically from Stone's rah-rah boosterism, but the men's shared interest in philanthropy helped seal the deal.

Ryan focused on insurance brokering and added more upscale insurance products. He also trimmed staff and took other cost-cutting measures, and in 1987 he changed Combined's name to Aon. In 1995 the company sold its remaining direct life insurance holdings to focus on consulting. The following year it began offering hostile takeover insurance policies to small and midsized companies.

In 1997 it bought The Minet Group, as well as troubled insurance brokerage Alexander & Alexander Services in a deal that made Aon (temporarily) the largest insurance broker worldwide. The firm made no US buys in 1998, but doubled its employee base with purchases including Spain's largest retail insurance broker, Gil y Carvajal, and the formation of Aon Korea, the first non-Korean firm of its kind to be licensed there.

In 2000 the company decided to cut 6% of its workforce as part of a restructuring effort.

Aon was hit hard by the attacks on the World Trade Center (where it was headquartered) in 2001; the company lost some 175 employees.

Aon teamed up with the Giuliani Group, former New York mayor Rudolph Giuliani's consulting firm, to provide business risk assessment and crisis management services in 2002.

In 2004-2005 Aon, along with other brokers including Marsh & McLennan and Willis Group Holdings, fell under regulatory investigation. At issue was the practice of insurance companies' payments to brokers (known as contingent commissions). The payments were thought to bring a conflict of interest, swaying broker decisions on behalf of carriers, rather than customers.

The bid-rigging investigation resulted in a $190 million settlement with regulators in three states and a shakeup of top management. Patrick Ryan stepped down as CEO and was replaced by McKinsey executive Gregory Case. Ryan remained as executive chairman until his retirement in 2008. Lester Knight was then elected to serve as non-executive chairman.

Aon sold its Aon Warranty Group division, including Virginia Surety, to Onex for $710 million in late 2006.

EXECUTIVES

Chairman: Lester B. Knight, age 52
President, CEO, and Director: Gregory C. (Greg) Case, age 47, $10,409,171 total compensation
COO; Chairman, Aon Consulting Worldwide: Andrew M. Appel, age 45, $6,678,014 total compensation
EVP and CFO: Christa Davies, age 38, $3,811,663 total compensation
EVP and General Counsel: Peter Lieb, age 53
EVP, Chief Administrative Officer, and Head, Global Strategy: Gregory J. (Greg) Besio, age 52
Global CTO: Adam Stanley
Global Chief Marketing and Communications Officer: Philip B. Clement
SVP and Head Human Resources: Jeremy G. O. Farmer, age 60
VP, Associate General Counsel, and Secretary: Jennifer L. Kraft
VP Investor Relations: Scott L. Malchow
VP Global Public Relations: David P. Prosperi
Chairman and CEO, Aon Risk Services: Stephen P. (Steve) McGill, age 51, $5,565,717 total compensation
CEO, Aon Consulting; COO, Aon Benfield: Baljit (Bal) Dail, age 43, $4,036,751 total compensation
CEO, Aon Consulting Asia Pacific: Edouard Merette Jr.
CEO, UK: Robert (Rob) Brown
CEO Marine, Global: Steve Beslity
CEO, U.S. Retail, Aon Risk Services: Eric Andersen
CEO, Aon Consulting Europe, Middle East, Africa, and UK: Robert Middleton
Chairman and CEO, Aon Asia Pacific: Bernard S. Y. Fung, age 56
Chairman, U.S. Retail, Aon Risk Services; Head, Aon Brokerage Group: Warren Mula
Auditors: Ernst & Young LLP

LOCATIONS

HQ: Aon Corporation
Aon Center, 200 E. Randolph St., Chicago, IL 60601
Phone: 312-381-1000   **Fax:** 312-381-6032
Web: www.aon.com

2009 Sales

	$ mil.	% of total
Americas		
US	2,789	37
Other countries	905	12
Europe, Middle East & Africa		
UK	1,289	17
Other countries	1,965	26
Asia/Pacific	647	8
Total	**7,595**	**100**

PRODUCTS/OPERATIONS

2009 Sales

	$ mil.	% of total
Risk & insurance brokerage services	6,305	83
Consulting	1,267	16
Other	49	1
Adjustments	(26)	—
Total	**7,595**	**100**

Selected Subsidiaries

Risk and insurance brokerage
Aon Benfield Inc. (formerly Aon Re Global, Inc.)
Aon Holdings International BV (Netherlands)
Aon Limited (UK)
Aon Risk Services Companies, Inc.
Aon Specialty (formerly Benfield Corporate Risk)
Cananwill, Inc.

Consulting
Aon Consulting Worldwide, Inc.

COMPETITORS

Accenture
Alexander Forbes
Alliant
Arthur Gallagher
BB&T
Boston Consulting
Brown & Brown
Citigroup
Clark Consulting
CRC Insurance
Equifax
Heath Lambert
Hewitt Associates
Hub International
IMA Financial Group
Jardine Lloyd
The Lockton Companies
Marsh & McLennan
Meadowbrook Insurance
National Financial Partners
RFIB Group
Towergate Partnership
Towers Watson
USI
Wells Fargo Insurance Services
Willis Group Holdings

HISTORICAL FINANCIALS

Company Type: Public

Income Statement   FYE: December 31

	REVENUE ($ mil.)	NET INCOME ($ mil.)	NET PROFIT MARGIN	EMPLOYEES
12/09	7,595	792	10.4%	36,200
12/08	7,631	1,462	19.2%	37,700
12/07	7,471	864	11.6%	42,500
12/06	8,954	719	8.0%	43,100
12/05	9,837	737	7.5%	46,600
Annual Growth	**(6.3%)**	**1.8%**	**—**	**(6.1%)**

2009 Year-End Financials

Debt ratio: 37.1%
Return on equity: 14.8%
Cash ($ mil.): 217
Current ratio: 1.11
Long-term debt ($ mil.): 1,998
No. of shares (mil.): 269
Dividends
Yield: 1.6%
Payout: 23.3%
Market value ($ mil.): 10,330

	STOCK PRICE ($) FY Close	P/E High/Low		PER SHARE ($) Earnings	Dividends	Book Value
12/09	38.34	18	14	2.57	0.60	19.97
12/08	45.68	10	7	4.86	0.60	19.71
12/07	47.69	19	13	2.69	0.60	23.09
12/06	35.34	20	15	2.13	0.60	19.37
12/05	35.95	17	10	2.17	0.60	19.68
Annual Growth	**1.6%**	**—**	**—**	**4.3%**	**0.0%**	**0.4%**

Apache Corporation

There's more than a patch of oil in Apache's portfolio. Apache is an oil and gas exploration and production company with onshore and offshore operations in North America and in Argentina, Australia, Egypt, and the UK (offshore in the North Sea). The company has estimated proved reserves of about 2.4 billion barrels of oil equivalent, mostly from five North American regions: the Gulf of Mexico, the Gulf Coast of Texas and Louisiana, the Permian Basin in West Texas, the Anadarko Basin in Oklahoma, and Canada's Western Sedimentary Basin. Of its international operations, Apache's assets in Egypt and the North Sea are the largest. Shell is Apache's largest customer, accounting for 18% of sales in 2009.

While the US represents more than 35% of the company's production and reserves, Apache is well aware that growth in the region will not be coming from drilling more wells. With that in mind, Apache says that domestic expansion will come largely through acquisitions. In 2010 is seized on one such opportunity, buying Gulf of Mexico shelf assets from Devon Energy (which is shedding assets to raise cash) for $1 billion. The acquisition adds some 41 million barrels of proved reserves and some 477,200 acres to Apache's asset base.

It also agreed to buy Mariner Energy for $2.7 billion, giving the company an entry into the deepwater Gulf of Mexico. The deal is seen as a natural extension of the company's commitment to develop the Gulf of Mexico as a primary area of production, and anticipates a rebounding economy and an increasing demand for oil.

With BP looking to raise cash to defray the cost of its rig disaster in the Gulf of Mexico, in 2010 Apache took the opportunity to buy BP assets in Canada, Egypt, and the US (Permian Basin) for about $7 billion. The deal boosts Apache's estimated proved reserves by 385 million barrels of oil equivalent.

In Canada the company moved in 2010 to expand its supply base by agreeing to buy 51% of a proposed liquefied natural gas (LNG) export terminal in British Columbia operated by Kitimat LNG Inc.

In 2009 Apache founder Raymond Plank retired as chairman of the company. He had been its chief executive from Apache's founding in 1954 until his retirement in 2002, when he remained as chairman. CEO Steven Farris took up the additional title of chairman when Plank stepped down completely.

HISTORY

Originally, Raymond Plank wanted to start a magazine. Then it was an accounting and tax-assistance service. Plank and his co-founding partner, Truman Anderson, had no experience in any of these occupations, but their accounting business succeeded. In the early 1950s Plank and Anderson branched out again, founding APA, a partnership to invest in new ventures, including oil and gas exploration. The partnership founded Apache Oil in Minnesota in 1954. Investors put up the money, and Apache managed the drilling, spreading the risk over several projects.

As problems with government regulations in the oil industry mounted during the 1960s, Apache diversified into real estate. The real estate operations were pivotal in driving a wedge between Plank and Anderson. In 1963 Anderson called a board meeting to ask the directors to fire Plank. Instead, Anderson resigned, and Plank took over.

Apache's holdings soon encompassed 24 firms, including engineering, electronics, farming, and water-supply subsidiaries. Understanding that its fortunes were tied to varying oil and gas prices, the company reassessed its diversified structure in the 1970s. When the energy crisis rocketed oil prices skyward, Apache sold its non-energy operations, which would have been hurt by the price increases.

Apache formed Apache Petroleum in 1981 as an investment vehicle to take advantage of tax laws favoring limited partnerships. Initially the strategy was a success, but it fell victim in the mid-1980s to a one-two punch: Oil prices sank like a rock, and Congress put an end to the tax advantage. After suffering its first loss in 1986, Apache reorganized into a conventional exploration and production company.

Still under Plank's leadership, the company began steadily buying oil and gas properties and companies in 1991. That year it purchased oil and gas sites with more than 100 million barrels of reserves from Amoco and put the wells back into production. By buying Hadson Energy Resources, which operated fields in western Australia, Apache gained entry into the relatively unexplored region in 1993.

In 1995 Apache merged with Calgary, Canada-based DEKALB Energy (later renamed DEK Energy) and continued picking up properties. It bought $600 million worth of US reserves from Texaco (acquired by Chevron in 2001) that year. In 1996 it expanded its Chinese operations and bought Phoenix Resource Companies, which operated solely in Egypt. A 1998 agreement with Texaco expanded its Chinese acreage thirtyfold. Apache also bought oil and gas properties and production facilities in waters off western Australia from a Mobil unit.

Apache joined with FX Energy and Polish Oil & Gas in 1998 to begin exploratory drilling in Poland. It also worked with XCL and China National Oil & Gas Exploration & Development in Bohai Bay, though the project was slowed by a dispute between Apache and XCL over costs.

Apache agreed in 2000 to buy assets in western Canada and Argentina with proved reserves of more than 700 billion cu. ft. of natural gas equivalent from New Zealand's Fletcher Challenge Energy. To help pay for the $600 million acquisition, which closed in 2001, Apache sold $100 million in stock to Shell, which acquired other Fletcher Challenge Energy assets. Apache bought the Canadian assets of Phillips Petroleum (later ConocoPhillips) for $490 million in 2000 and acquired the Egyptian assets of Repsol YPF for $410 million in 2001.

Late in 2002 in a move aimed at boosting its natural gas production by more than 10%, Apache acquired 234,000 net acres of land in southern Louisiana for $260 million.

Apache acquired UK and US oil and gas assets in 2003 from BP for $1.3 billion. The main prize was the Forties field, one of the North Sea's oldest discoveries (dating back to the early 1970s) and its largest.

In 2004 it acquired more than two dozen mature US and Canadian fields from Exxon Mobil for $347 million and Gulf of Mexico properties from Anadarko Petroleum for $525 million. In 2005 Hurricane Katrina destroyed eight of its 241 Gulf rigs.

EXECUTIVES

Chairman and CEO: G. Steven (Steve) Farris, age 61, $7,689,513 total compensation
Co-COO; President International: Rodney J. Eichler, age 60, $7,713,060 total compensation
Co-COO; President, North America; President, Apache Canada: John A. Crum, age 57, $7,226,139 total compensation
President and Principal Financial Officer: Roger B. Plank, age 53, $7,773,222 total compensation
EVP and Technology Officer: Michael S. (Mike) Bahorich, age 53, $3,590,628 total compensation
EVP and General Counsel: P. Anthony Lannie, age 55
EVP Corporate Reservoir Engineering: W. Kregg Olson, age 56
EVP; Community Outreach, US Gulf Coast: Jon A. Jeppesen, age 62
SVP Policy and Governance: Sarah B. Teslik, age 56
VP Planning and Investor Relations: Thomas P. (Tom) Chambers, age 54
VP Human Resources: Margery M. (Margie) Harris, age 49
VP and Controller: Rebecca A. (Becky) Hoyt, age 45
VP Tax: Jon W. Sauer, age 49
VP Oil and Gas Marketing: Janine J. McArdle, age 49
VP Information Technology: Aaron Merrick, age 47
VP and Treasurer: Matthew W. (Matt) Dundrea, age 56
VP Business Development: David L. French, age 40
VP Security: Alex C. De Alvarez, age 46
VP Environmental, Health, and Safety: David Carmony
Corporate Secretary: Cheri L. Peper, age 56
Director Public Affairs: William (Bill) Mintz
Director Investor Relations: Rob Rayphole
President, Apache Canada; Region VP, Australia, and Managing Director, Apache Energy: Timothy O. (Tim) Wall, age 47
Auditors: Ernst & Young LLP

LOCATIONS

HQ: Apache Corporation
2000 Post Oak Blvd., Ste. 100, Houston, TX 77056
Phone: 713-296-6000   **Fax:** 713-296-6496
Web: www.apachecorp.com

2009 Sales

	$ mil.	% of total
US	3,049.7	35
Egypt	2,553.1	30
UK (North Sea)	1,368.8	16
Canada	877.2	10
Australia	363.4	4
Argentina	361.7	4
Other	40.9	1
Total	**8,614.8**	**100**

PRODUCTS/OPERATIONS

2009 Sales

	$ mil.	% of total
Oil & gas production	8,573.9	99
Other	40.9	1
Total	**8,614.8**	**100**

Selected Subsidiaries

Apache Canada Ltd.
Apache Energy Limited
Apache International, Inc.
Apache North Sea Limited
Apache Overseas, Inc.
DEK Energy Company

COMPETITORS

Adams Resources
Anadarko Petroleum
BP
Chesapeake Energy
Chevron
Devon Energy
El Paso Corporation
EOG
Exxon Mobil
Forest Oil
Helmerich & Payne
Hess Corporation
Jones Energy
Qatargas
Royal Dutch Shell
Santos Ltd
XTO Energy

HISTORICAL FINANCIALS

Company Type: Public

Income Statement

FYE: December 31

	REVENUE ($ mil.)	NET INCOME ($ mil.)	NET PROFIT MARGIN	EMPLOYEES
12/09	8,615	(284)	—	3,452
12/08	12,328	712	5.8%	3,639
12/07	9,978	2,812	28.2%	3,521
12/06	8,289	2,553	30.8%	3,150
12/05	7,584	2,624	34.6%	2,805
Annual Growth	**3.2%**	**—**	**—**	**5.3%**

2009 Year-End Financials

Debt ratio: 31.4%
Return on equity: —
Cash ($ mil.): 2,048
Current ratio: 1.92
Long-term debt ($ mil.): 4,950
No. of shares (mil.): 364
Dividends
  Yield: 0.6%
  Payout: —
Market value ($ mil.): 37,583

Stock History

NYSE: APA

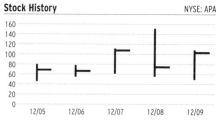

	STOCK PRICE ($) FY Close	P/E High/Low		PER SHARE ($) Earnings	Dividends	Book Value
12/09	103.17	—	—	(0.87)	0.60	43.31
12/08	74.53	71	27	2.09	0.60	45.32
12/07	107.54	13	8	8.39	0.60	42.21
12/06	66.51	10	7	7.64	0.45	36.21
12/05	68.52	10	6	7.84	0.34	28.94
Annual Growth	**10.8%**	**—**	**—**	**—**	**15.3%**	**10.6%**

Apollo Group

Apollo's creed could be that we all deserve the chance to advance. The for-profit group provides educational programs and services through a number of subsidiaries, including online stalwart University of Phoenix, which also has physical campuses in North America and Europe. The largest private university in the US, the University of Phoenix accounts for some 95% of Apollo's sales. Other schools include Western International University (graduate and undergraduate courses) and Insights Schools (online high school education for homeschooled students). Apollo has more than 440,000 degreed students, or students enrolled in degree programs ranging from the associate's to the doctoral level.

Other subsidiaries include College for Financial Planning Institutes, which offers financial planner certification and graduate programs, and Institute for Professional Development, which consults with schools seeking to expand and develop programs for working adults. Meritus University was established in 2008 to offer online degree programs in Canada.

Apollo Group joined together with private equity firm Carlyle Group in 2007 to create international arm Apollo Global. In Latin America, the unit acquired Chile's Universidad de Artes, Ciencias y Comunicación and Mexico's Universidad Latinoamericana. In 2009 it acquired UK-based BPP, a provider of legal and financial professional training. Apollo Global plans to invest in BPP's growth, enabling it to grow in the UK and throughout Europe. Also in 2009, Apollo Group upped its stake in Apollo Global from 80% to 86%.

Charles Edelstein, formerly an investment banker with Credit Suisse, was named Apollo Group's CEO in 2008. The following year, global strategy leader Gregory Capelli was named co-CEO to share leadership duties with Edelstein. Capelli was also named chairman.

Founder and executive chairman John Sperling and his son, vice chairman Peter Sperling, together own about 50% of Apollo.

HISTORY

The son of Missouri sharecroppers, John Sperling had an early interest in higher education for the working class. Following WWII he attended Reed College on the GI Bill and eventually received a PhD in economic history from Cambridge. He started the Institute for Professional Development in 1973 to offer nontraditional programs designed for working adults. Sperling's program was rejected by San Jose State University, where he was a tenured professor, so he took his idea to the University of San Francisco. There he designed a curriculum program for firefighters, police officers, and other workers. Within two years, the program had 2,500 students, but the regional accrediting board accused him of running a diploma mill and yanked his accreditation.

Sperling moved to Arizona (which falls under a different accrediting board), where he founded The University of Phoenix in 1976. The university received accreditation in 1978; its first graduating class had eight students. It expanded into new states through the 1980s, and in 1989 it added distance learning to its services using its own dial-up computer network. The company went public as Apollo Group in 1994.

To further expand its reach, Apollo bought Western International University (founded in 1978) in 1995 and the College for Financial Planning from National Endowment of Financial Education in 1997. That year it formed Apollo Learning Group to offer high-tech training programs. The University of Phoenix received approval to offer its first doctoral program in 1998, a doctor of management degree. The next year Apollo made its first entry into the northeast US when it was approved by the state of Pennsylvania. It also expanded and upgraded its online operations that year, centralizing its operations in Phoenix.

In 2001 the university introduced FlexNet, courses that combined classroom and online instruction. The weakening economy in 2001 and 2002 benefited Apollo: As jobs became more scarce, many professionals sought further education as a competitive advantage. In 2003 the school received state approval to offer courses in New Jersey.

Although it denied the claims, in 2004 Apollo agreed to pay almost $10 million in fines after a US Department of Education inquiry claimed that University of Phoenix recruiters had used unethical or illegal tactics to enroll unqualified students.

Longtime chairman and CEO Todd Nelson resigned two years later. Founder John Sperling was appointed acting chairman and Brian Mueller, president of The University of Phoenix, became the company's president and principal executive.

The company also entered the K-12 market in 2006 when it acquired Insight Schools, an online education content provider for homeschooled students.

Brian Mueller left as the company's president in 2008 to head the much-smaller Grand Canyon Education. Investment banker Charles Edelstein was named CEO (a position that had been vacant for more than two years). Apollo Group named Gregory Cappelli as co-CEO in 2009 to share leadership duties with Edelstein.

EXECUTIVES

Chairman: John G. Sperling, age 89, $6,413,371 total compensation
Vice Chairman: Peter V. Sperling, age 50
Co-CEO and Director: Charles B. (Chas) Edelstein, age 50, $11,283,002 total compensation
Co-CEO and Director; Chairman, Apollo Global: Gregory W. Cappelli, age 42, $7,316,585 total compensation
President and COO: Joseph L. (Joe) D'Amico, age 60, $6,458,570 total compensation
EVP, General Counsel, and Secretary: P. Robert (Bob) Moya, age 65, $2,131,436 total compensation
EVP and Chief Marketing and Product Development Officer; President and CEO, Aptimus: Robert W. (Rob) Wrubel, age 48, $3,235,849 total compensation
EVP External Affairs and Director: Terri C. Bishop, age 56
SVP, CFO, and Treasurer: Brian L. Swartz, age 37, $1,346,494 total compensation
SVP and Chief Human Resources Officer: Frederick J. (Fred) Newton III, age 54
VP, Chief Accounting Officer, and Controller: Gregory J. Iverson, age 34
VP Finance: Larry Fleischer
President, University of Phoenix: William J. (Bill) Pepicello, age 60
Director Public Affairs: Manny Rivera
Investor Relations: Allyson Pooley
Auditors: Deloitte & Touche LLP

LOCATIONS

HQ: Apollo Group, Inc.
4025 S. Riverpoint Pkwy., Phoenix, AZ 85040
Phone: 480-966-5394
Web: www.apollogrp.edu

2009 Sales

	$ mil.	% of total
US	3,900.2	98
Latin America	54.5	2
UK	13.1	—
Other	6.4	—
Total	**3,974.2**	**100**

PRODUCTS/OPERATIONS

2009 Sales

	$ mil.	% of total
Tuition & educational services	3,835.7	92
Educational materials	226.4	5
Services	83.2	2
Other	28.3	1
Adjustments	(199.4)	—
Total	**3,974.2**	**100**

2009 Sales by Segment

	$ mil.	% of total
University of Phoenix	3,766.6	95
Apollo Global	67.3	2
Insight Schools	20.6	—
Other schools	116.9	3
Other	2.8	—
Total	**3,974.2**	**100**

2009 Enrollment by Age

	% of total
23 to 29	34
30 to 39	31
22 & under	15
40 to 49	15
50 & over	5
Total	**100**

Selected Subsidiaries

The College for Financial Planning Institutes Corporation
Insight Schools, Inc.
Institute for Professional Development
Meritus University, Inc.
The University of Phoenix, Inc.
Western International University, Inc.

COMPETITORS

Capella Education
Career Education
Corinthian Colleges
DeVry
Education Management
ITT Educational
Laureate Education
Strayer Education
UTI

HISTORICAL FINANCIALS

Company Type: Public

Income Statement

FYE: August 31

	REVENUE ($ mil.)	NET INCOME ($ mil.)	NET PROFIT MARGIN	EMPLOYEES
8/09	3,974	598	15.1%	53,498
8/08	3,141	477	15.2%	44,647
8/07	2,724	409	15.0%	36,418
8/06	2,478	415	16.7%	36,416
8/05	2,252	445	19.8%	32,666
Annual Growth	**15.3%**	**7.7%**	**—**	**13.1%**

2009 Year-End Financials

Debt ratio: 11.0%
Return on equity: 60.1%
Cash ($ mil.): 968
Current ratio: 1.07
Long-term debt ($ mil.): 128

No. of shares (mil.): 148
Dividends
Yield: —
Payout: —
Market value ($ mil.): 9,566

Stock History

NASDAQ (GS): APOL

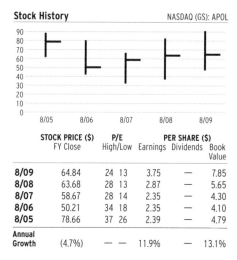

	STOCK PRICE ($)	P/E		PER SHARE ($)		
	FY Close	High/Low	Earnings	Dividends	Book Value
8/09	64.84	24 13	3.75	—	7.85
8/08	63.68	28 13	2.87	—	5.65
8/07	58.67	28 14	2.35	—	4.30
8/06	50.21	34 18	2.35	—	4.10
8/05	78.66	37 26	2.39	—	4.79
Annual Growth	(4.7%)	— —	11.9%	—	13.1%

Apple Inc.

Apple aims for nothing short of a revolution, whether in personal computing or digital media distribution. The company's desktop and laptop computers — all of which feature its OS X operating system — include its Mac mini, iMac, and MacBook for the consumer and education markets, and more powerful Mac Pro and MacBook Pro for high-end consumers and professionals involved in design and publishing. Apple scored a runaway hit with its digital music players (iPod) and online music store (iTunes). Other products include mobile phones (iPhone), servers (Xserve), wireless networking equipment (AirPort), and publishing and multimedia software.

The company came through the global recession with increased sales and profits in fiscal 2009, although harsh economic conditions reduced sales of computers and consumer electronics for many other companies. Decreased sales for Apple's desktop computers and iPods during 2009 were greatly offset by higher sales for the iPhone and related products (which more than tripled from fiscal 2008) and for portable computers. Apple is seeing increased competition in the smartphone market, however, with some consumers finding merit in alternative handsets from a variety of manufacturers.

In 2010 Apple unveiled a tablet computer, the iPad, that it hopes will prove to be another game-changer in consumer electronics, like the iPod and the iPhone. With a touchscreen display measuring about 10 inches, the iPad could fill a market niche between notebook computers and smartphones.

The graphical interface and form factor of Apple's computers reflect the aesthetic of co-founder and CEO Steve Jobs, who long championed the importance of visually attractive, user-friendly design. The features that distinguish Macs allowed the company to maintain a loyal following willing to pay premium prices.

However, despite market share gains made in recent years, Apple still trails far behind top Window-based PC vendors, such as Hewlett-Packard and Dell.

In 2003 Apple launched an online music service called the iTunes Music Store that let computer users purchase and download songs for 99 cents each. Apple later expanded the online offerings to include music videos, audio books, movies, television shows, and other content. In 2008 Apple became the top music retailer by volume in the US market, surpassing Wal-Mart.

Taking a leaf from its experience with iTunes, Apple opened another online market in 2008, the App Store, to offer applications created by third-party software developers for the iPhone and the iPod touch. By the end of 2009, there were more than 100,000 applications available through the App Store, many of them free and others costing small amounts, with thousands more being added each month.

In an effort to boost brand awareness and its appeal among consumers, the company operates more than 200 Apple retail stores across the US and 50-plus stores in other countries. Apple generates nearly 20% of its sales through its retail channel.

HISTORY

College dropouts Steve Jobs and Steve Wozniak founded Apple in 1976 in California's Santa Clara Valley. After Jobs' first sales call brought an order for 50 units, the duo built the Apple I in his garage and sold it without a monitor, keyboard, or casing. Demand convinced Jobs there was a distinct market for small computers, and the company's name (a reference to Jobs' stint on an Oregon farm) and the computer's user-friendly look and feel set it apart from others.

By 1977 Wozniak added a keyboard, color monitor, and eight peripheral device slots (which gave the machine considerable versatility and inspired numerous third-party add-on devices and software). Sales jumped from $7.8 million in 1978 to $117 million in 1980, the year Apple went public. In 1983 Wozniak left the firm and Jobs hired PepsiCo's John Sculley as president. Apple rebounded from failed product introductions that year by unveiling the Macintosh in 1984. After tumultuous struggles with Sculley, Jobs left in 1985 and founded NeXT Software, a designer of applications for developing software. That year Sculley ignored Microsoft founder Bill Gates' appeal for Apple to license its products and make the Microsoft platform an industry standard.

In 1986 Apple blazed the desktop publishing trail with its Mac Plus and LaserWriter printers. The following year it formed the software firm that later became Claris. The late 1980s brought new competition from Microsoft, whose Windows operating system (OS) featured a graphical interface akin to Apple's. Apple sued but lost its claim to copyright protection in 1992.

In 1993 Apple unveiled the Newton handheld computer, but sales were slow. Earnings fell drastically, so the company trimmed its workforce. (Sculley was among the departed.) In 1996 it hired Gilbert Amelio, formerly of National Semiconductor, as CEO, but sales kept dropping and it subsequently cut about 30% of its workforce, canceled projects, and trimmed research costs. Meanwhile Apple's board ousted Amelio and Jobs took the position back on an interim basis.

In 2000, after two-and-a-half years as the semi-permanent executive in charge, Jobs took the

"interim" out of his title. Apple introduced a digital music player called the iPod in 2001.

In 2002 Apple introduced a new look for its iMac line; featuring a half-dome base and a flat-panel display supported by a pivoting arm, the redesign was the first departure from the original (and, at the time, radical) all-in-one design since iMac's debut in 1998.

Apple announced it would begin incorporating Intel chips into its PC lines in 2005; the transition was completed the following year. Late in 2005 Apple, Motorola, and Cingular Wireless (now AT&T Mobility) announced the debut of a mobile phone with iTunes functionality. In 2006 Apple reached a settlement in a dispute with Creative Technology over technology used in digital music players; Apple agreed to pay the company $100 million in exchange for a license to use Creative's patent related to navigation and organization. Late in 2006 Apple acquired UK-based Proximity, a developer of software used to manage digital audio and video assets.

Apple unveiled a mobile phone offering called the iPhone early in 2007. To reflect the growing breadth of its product portfolio, the company announced it would change its name from Apple Computer to simply Apple.

The company kicked off 2008 with the release of an updated Apple TV device in conjunction with a new iTunes movie rental service.

EXECUTIVES

Chairman: William V. (Bill) Campbell, age 69
CEO and Director: Steven P. (Steve) Jobs, age 55, $1 total compensation
COO: Timothy D. (Tim) Cook, age 49, $14,001,040 total compensation
SVP and CFO: Peter Oppenheimer, age 47, $10,269,720 total compensation
SVP Industrial Design: Jonathan Ive
SVP iPhone Software Engineering and Platform Experience: Scott Forstall, age 41, $13,804,755 total compensation
SVP Mac Hardware Engineering: Robert (Bob) Mansfield, age 49, $13,996,589 total compensation
SVP Operations: Jeff Williams
SVP Software Engineering: Bertrand Serlet, age 49
SVP Retail: Ronald B. (Ron) Johnson, age 51
SVP, General Counsel, and Secretary: D. Bruce Sewell, age 51
SVP Worldwide Product Marketing: Philip W. Schiller, age 49
Manager Worldwide Sales and Services Strategy: Jenni Burgess
Senior Public Relations Manager: Jennifer Bowcock
Auditors: Ernst & Young LLP

LOCATIONS

HQ: Apple Inc.
1 Infinite Loop, Cupertino, CA 95014
Phone: 408-996-1010   **Fax:** 408-974-2113
Web: www.apple.com

2009 Sales

	$ mil.	% of total
Americas	18,887	44
Europe	11,810	28
Retail	6,656	16
Japan	2,279	5
Other	3,273	7
Total	**42,905**	**100**

PRODUCTS/OPERATIONS

2009 Sales

	$ mil.	% of total
Computers		
Portable	9,535	22
Desktops	4,324	10
Music-related products		
iPod	8,091	19
iTunes Music Store & other	4,036	9
iPhone & related products & services	13,033	30
Peripherals & other hardware	1,475	3
Software, services & other	2,411	7
Total	**42,905**	**100**

Selected Products

Hardware
Desktop computers (iMac, Mac mini, Power Macintosh)
Displays (Cinema, Studio)
External hard drives (Time Capsule)
Keyboards
Mice (Mighty Mouse)
Mobile phones (iPhone)
Portable computers (MacBook, MacBook Air, MacBook Pro)
Portable digital music player (iPod, iPod nano, iPod shuffle, iPod touch)
Rack-mount servers (Xserve)
Stereo systems (iPod Hi-Fi)
Storage systems (Xserve RAID)
Tablet computers (iPad)
Web cams (iSight)
Wireless networking systems (AirPort)

Software
Multimedia (DVD Studio Pro, FinalCut, GarageBand, iDVD, iLife suite, iMovie, iPhoto, iTunes, Quicktime, Soundtrack)
Networking (Apple Remote Desktop, AppleShare IP)
Operating system (OS X)
Personal productivity (AppleWorks, FileMaker, iWork, Keynote, Pages)
Server (Mac OS X Server)
Storage area network (SAN) file system (Xsan)
Web browser (Safari)

Online Services
.Mac
Applications for iPad, iPhone, iPod touch (App Store)
E-books (iBooks)
Electronic greeting cards (iCard)
E-mail (Webmail)
Online multimedia store (iTunes)
Personal Web page creation (HomePage)
Remote network storage (iDisk)
Software (antivirus, backup)
Technical support

COMPETITORS

Acer	Motorola
Adobe Systems	MTV Networks
Amazon.com	Napster
Archos	NEC
Best Buy	Netflix
Blockbuster Inc.	Nokia
Bose	Palm, Inc.
Cisco Systems	Panasonic Corp
Comcast	Philips Electronics
Creative Technology	RealNetworks
Dell	Red Hat
D-Link	Research In Motion
eMusic.com	Samsung Electronics
Ericsson	SanDisk
Fujitsu Technology	Seagate Technology
Solutions	Sharp Electronics
Google	Sony
Hewlett-Packard	Sony Ericsson Mobile
HTC Corporation	Symbian
IBM	Target
Iriver	Time Warner Cable
Kyocera	Toshiba
Lenovo	Wal-Mart
LG Electronics	Western Digital
MediaNet Digital	Yahoo!
Microsoft	

HISTORICAL FINANCIALS

Company Type: Public

Income Statement

FYE: Last Friday in September

	REVENUE ($ mil.)	NET INCOME ($ mil.)	NET PROFIT MARGIN	EMPLOYEES
9/09	42,905	8,235	19.2%	36,800
9/08	32,479	4,834	14.9%	35,100
9/07	24,006	3,496	14.6%	21,600
9/06	19,315	1,989	10.3%	17,787
9/05	13,931	1,335	9.6%	16,820
Annual Growth	**32.5%**	**57.6%**	**—**	**21.6%**

2009 Year-End Financials

Debt ratio: —
Return on equity: 31.3%
Cash ($ mil.): 5,263
Current ratio: 2.74
Long-term debt ($ mil.): —
No. of shares (mil.): 914
Dividends
Yield: 0.0%
Payout: —
Market value ($ mil.): 169,329

Stock History

NASDAQ (GS): AAPL

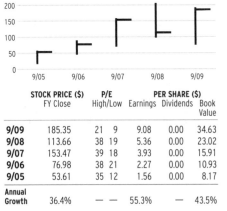

	STOCK PRICE ($) FY Close	P/E High/Low		PER SHARE ($) Earnings	Dividends	Book Value
9/09	185.35	21	9	9.08	0.00	34.63
9/08	113.66	38	19	5.36	0.00	23.02
9/07	153.47	39	18	3.93	0.00	15.91
9/06	76.98	38	21	2.27	0.00	10.93
9/05	53.61	35	12	1.56	0.00	8.17
Annual Growth	**36.4%**	**—**	**—**	**55.3%**	**—**	**43.5%**

Applied Industrial Technologies

Just imagine getting lost in *that* warehouse. Applied Industrial Technologies distributes millions of industrial parts made by thousands of manufacturers. The short list includes bearings, power transmission components, hydraulic and pneumatic components, fabricated rubber products, and linear motion systems. It sells primarily through some 460 service centers peppering the US, Canada, and Mexico. Customers are concentrated in maintenance repair operations (MRO) and OEM markets. Applied also operates regional mechanical, rubber, and fluid power shops that offer a slate of services, from engineering design to conveyor belt repair, to such industrial giants as Vulcan Materials and Goodyear Engineered Products.

Applied has expanded its service and supply center reach through a flurry of focused acquisitions. The company purchased Ontario-based SCS Supply Group, as well as UZ Engineered Products, an Ohio-based MRO distributor — both companies were brought into the company's fold in mid-2010. In 2008 the company picked up Fluid Power Resource (FPR). Along with FPR

came seven distribution businesses (Bay Advanced Technologies, Carolina Fluid Components, DTS Fluid Power, FluidTech, Hughes HiTech, Hydro Air, and Power Systems) and 19 locations. The deals give Applied additional product scope in the areas of fluid power design, as well as the integration of hydraulics with electronics. It also deepens the company's geographic presence throughout North America.

The company relies on a local presence to deliver much of its bottom line. In addition to Applied Industrial Technologies, the service centers operate under the Bearing & Transmission, B&T Rubber, Groupe GLM (Canada), Applied México, and Rafael Benitez Carrillo (Puerto Rico) trade names. The company offers fluid power services through businesses such as Air Draulics, Atelier, and Dees Fluid.

HISTORY

In 1928 founder Joseph Bruening bought the Cleveland office of Detroit Ball Bearing and incorporated his own company as Ohio Ball Bearing. His company acquired a reputation for aggressive acquisitions and maintaining a large inventory. In 1952 the firm bought bearings makers in three other states and changed its name to Bearings Specialists and then to Bearings. By 1973 the company had operations in 25 states. After a serious sales slump in the mid-1980s, former Diamond Shamrock executive John Dannemiller was hired as COO in 1988. He became CEO four years later.

Dannemiller revitalized the company by diversifying its product line, primarily through acquisitions. By 1995 non-bearings technologies accounted for 55% of the company's revenues, up from 35% in 1989. After expanding the company's product lines to include drive systems, rubber products, and fluid power components, it started competing in a broader $21 billion market, rather than the $1.7 billion market for bearings alone.

The company adopted the Applied Industrial Technologies name in 1997. That year it made its largest acquisition to date with the purchase of Invetech, a Detroit distributor with 88 branches in 19 states. It also bought Midwest Rubber and Supply of Denver. Applied broadened its product lines in 1998 by acquiring specialized distributors of bearings and mechanical- and electrical-drive systems. The company closed out the century by shutting down 28 underperforming facilities.

To streamline its businesses, in 2000 Applied reorganized its field sales and service organizations into two product platforms — industrial products and fluid power. It also acquired 21 bearing and power transmission service centers, three rubber fabrication centers, and 15 fluid power facilities from Canada's Dynavest Corp. In 2001 Applied added four facilities in Mexico with its purchase of Baleros Industriales, SA de CV (BISA), a distributor of bearings and power transmission products.

Late in 2002 Applied acquired Canadian industrial parts distributor Industrial Equipment Co., Ltd. Mexico-based Rodamientos y Bandas de la Laguna (industrial product distribution) was acquired the following year for a reported $2.8 million.

In 2006 Applied bought Minnesota Bearing Company, which distributed bearings and power transmission products.

EXECUTIVES

Chairman and CEO: David L. Pugh, age 61,
$9,896,063 total compensation
President and COO: Benjamin J. (Ben) Mondics, age 51,
$1,058,430 total compensation
VP, CFO, and Treasurer: Mark O. Eisele, age 52,
$1,036,254 total compensation
VP, General Counsel, and Secretary: Fred D. Bauer,
age 43, $654,882 total compensation
VP Supply Chain Management: Jeffrey A. Ramras,
age 54, $762,754 total compensation
VP Marketing and Strategic Accounts:
Thomas E. Armold, age 54
VP Information Technology: Lonny D. Lawrence, age 47
**VP Government Business and Chief Administrative
Officer:** Michael L. Coticchia, age 46
VP Human Resources: Barbara D. Emery, age 51
VP Operational Excellence: Mary E. Kerper, age 59
VP Communications and Learning: Richard C. Shaw,
age 60
VP Acquisitions and Global Business Development:
Todd A. Barlett, age 54
**President and COO, Applied Industrial Technologies
Ltd., Canada:** Ronald A. Sowinski, age 49
Corporate Controller: Daniel T. (Dan) Brezovec, age 48
Manager Public Relations: Julie A. Kho
Auditors: Deloitte & Touche LLP

LOCATIONS

HQ: Applied Industrial Technologies, Inc.
1 Applied Plaza, Cleveland, OH 44115
Phone: 216-426-4000   **Fax:** 216-426-4845
Web: www.appliedindustrial.com

2009 Sales

	$ mil.	% of total
US	1,674.7	87
Canada	197.8	10
Mexico	50.6	3
Total	**1,923.1**	**100**

PRODUCTS/OPERATIONS

2009 Sales

	$ mil.	% of total
Industrial products	1,422.5	74
Fluid power products	500.6	26
Total	**1,923.1**	**100**

Selected Products

Bearings
　Plane bearings
　Rolling element bearings
　　Ball bearings
　　Mounted and unmounted bearings
　　Roller bearings
Drive Components and Systems
　Electrical components
　　Electric motors (AC, DC)
　　Motor starters
　　Photoelectrics, encoders, sensors
　　Variable speed controllers (AC, DC)
　　Servo motion controllers
　Mechanical components
　　Belt drive components
　　Chain drive components
　　Clutch/brake mechanicals
　　Coupling and U joints
　　Material handling products
　　Open gears
　　Speed reducers and gear motors
Fluid Power
　Accessories (gauges, ball valves, accumulators,
　　subplates, manifold, hose and fittings, hydraulic oil)
　Cylinders
　Filters
　Motors
　Power supplies
　Pumps
　Valves

Linear Technologies
　Bellows
　Cable and hose carriers
　Controls
　Gearheads
　Linear motors
　Precision balls
　Precision mechanical components
　Steps and servo motors
Rubber Products
　Belt drive components
　Conveyor belting and accessories
　Hydraulic hose, fittings, and equipment
　Industrial hose and fittings
　Power transmission belts
　Rubber shop services
Specialty Products
　Analytical tools
　Chemicals (adhesives, lubricants, paints, sealants)
　Fluid sealing products (seals, gaskets)
　General mill supplies
　Maintenance tools
　Precision mechanical components
Shop Services
　Cylinder repair and manufacturing
　Fluid cleanliness consulting
　Hydraulic pump and motor repair
　Hydraulic servo and proportional valve services
　Mechanical repair and maintenance services
　Pneumatic circuit services
　Rubber shop services

COMPETITORS

Commercial Solutions
Dana Holding
DXP Enterprises
Fastenal
Fenner
General Parts
Genuine Parts
Hillman Companies
Horizon Solutions
Ingersoll-Rand Industrial Technologies
Kaman
Kaydon
Mark IV
McMaster-Carr
Motion Industries
MSC Industrial Direct
NN Inc.
Parker Hannifin
Premier Farnell
SKF
Tomkins
Tuthill
W.W. Grainger

HISTORICAL FINANCIALS

Company Type: Public

Income Statement

FYE: June 30

	REVENUE ($ mil.)	NET INCOME ($ mil.)	NET PROFIT MARGIN	EMPLOYEES
6/09	1,923	42	2.2%	4,673
6/08	2,090	96	4.6%	4,805
6/07	2,014	86	4.3%	4,635
6/06	1,901	72	3.8%	4,683
6/05	1,717	55	3.2%	4,415
Annual Growth	**2.9%**	**(6.5%)**	**—**	**1.4%**

2009 Year-End Financials

Debt ratio: 14.8%
Return on equity: 8.4%
Cash ($ mil.): 28
Current ratio: 3.36
Long-term debt ($ mil.): 75
No. of shares (mil.): 42
Dividends
　Yield: 3.0%
　Payout: 60.6%
Market value ($ mil.): 834

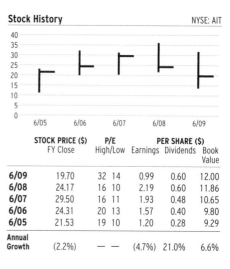

Stock History

NYSE: AIT

	STOCK PRICE ($) FY Close	P/E High/Low	PER SHARE ($) Earnings	Dividends	Book Value
6/09	19.70	32 14	0.99	0.60	12.00
6/08	24.17	16 10	2.19	0.60	11.86
6/07	29.50	16 11	1.93	0.48	10.65
6/06	24.31	20 13	1.57	0.40	9.80
6/05	21.53	19 10	1.20	0.28	9.29
Annual Growth	**(2.2%)**	**— —**	**(4.7%)**	**21.0%**	**6.6%**

Applied Materials

Today, semiconductor manufacturing; tomorrow, the world — of alternative energy sources. Applied Materials is, by far, the world's largest maker of semiconductor production equipment. With its 2006 acquisition of Applied Films, the company moved into the market for equipment used in making solar power cells. Applied's machines vie for supremacy in many segments of the chip-making process, including deposition (layering film on wafers), etching (removing portions of chip material to allow precise construction of circuits), and semiconductor metrology and inspection equipment.

A down cycle in the highly cyclical semiconductor manufacturing industry — combined with the global economic downturn and tight credit markets in the last half of 2008 and first half of 2009 — caused demand for the equipment that Applied makes to plummet.

In response, Applied cut costs through temporary plant shutdowns and workforce reductions of about 12%, or 2,000 positions, in 2009. The job cuts were on top of 2008 layoffs of about 1,000 jobs, a 7% cutback.

As semiconductors are incorporated into more and more products — from kitchen appliances to cars and TVs — demand for ever-smaller and more complex chips grows. Just as quickly, chip-making machinery becomes obsolete, which can be good news for Applied's sales. To keep up with the chip industry's constant drive toward smaller circuits, larger wafers, and new technologies such as copper interconnects, Applied relies heavily R&D efforts. The company spends around 15% on R&D each year.

The company has used a combination of acquisitions and internal development to bolster its moves into the few areas of chip manufacturing — such as atomic layer deposition equipment — where it wasn't already a major player.

Applied sees a bright future in the market for solar photovoltaic (PV) production equipment. In 2009 the company bought Advent Solar, a developer of technologies used to streamline production of crystalline silicon PV modules. Applied plans to use Advent's assembly and process innovations to develop equipment that reduces the cost of PV module manufacturing. Advent is part of Applied's Energy and Environmental Solutions Group.

Late in 2009 Applied purchased Semitool for about $364 million in cash. The acquisition of Semitool, which makes electrochemical plating and wafer surface preparation equipment, gives Applied a broader range of products and access to new customers in the semiconductor packaging market. The deal fuels Applied's industry lead in advanced semiconductor packaging equipment for mobile devices.

HISTORY

Applied Materials was founded in 1967 in Mountain View, California, as a maker of chemical vapor deposition systems for fabricating semiconductors. After years of rapid growth, the company went public in 1972. Two years later it purchased wafer maker Galamar Industries.

In 1975 Applied Materials suffered a 45% drop in sales as the semiconductor industry (and the US economy) contracted. Financial and managerial problems plagued the company following the recession, so in 1976 James Morgan, a former division manager for conglomerate Textron, was chosen to replace founder Michael McNeilly as CEO. Two years later Morgan also became chairman.

After selling Galamar (1977) and other non-core units and extending the company's line of credit, Morgan announced a plan to move into Japan. The company's first joint venture, Applied Materials Japan, was set up in 1979.

Morgan's hunch that Japan would become a semiconductor hub paid off. His early arrival, plus his attention to Japanese ways of doing business, put Applied way ahead of its American competitors. Morgan wrote *Cracking the Japanese Market* about his experiences doing business in Japan, which came to account for one-sixth of the company's sales.

When another slump hit the chip industry in 1985, Morgan revved up research and development. With two separate manufacturing technologies poised to compete, Morgan essentially bet on the fast but unproven one-at-a-time, multiple-chamber method (as opposed to the batch process system). The resulting Precision 5000 series machines revolutionized the industry and catapulted Applied Materials to the top of it. Applied's sales passed the $1 billion mark for the first time in 1993.

Shaking off an industry slump, in 1996 Applied acquired two Israeli companies, Opal (scanning electronic microscopes used in wafer inspection) and Orbot Instruments (wafer and photomask inspection systems), to grab nearly 5% of the crowded chip inspection tools market.

In early 2000 Applied began its move into photolithography — one of the few industry segments in which it didn't operate — by acquiring Etec Systems, a leading maker of semiconductor mask pattern generation equipment, for nearly $2 billion.

A sharp global downturn in the chip industry led the company in early 2001 to take a variety of cost-cutting measures (including executive pay cuts, a voluntary separation plan, and temporary plant shutdowns) that stopped short of layoffs. Later that year, though, Applied let go about 2,000 employees — about 10% of its workforce — in response to continuing poor conditions in the chip market. Late that year the

company enacted another 10% layoff, this one affecting 1,700 workers. It repeated the move late in 2002 as the chip industry's worst-ever slump stretched across two full years.

In 2003 longtime Intel executive Michael Splinter succeeded Morgan as CEO; Morgan remained chairman (until 2008, when Splinter became chairman as well).

In 2006 Applied acquired Applied Films, a supplier of thin-film deposition equipment, for around $464 million. The company delved further into the solar energy market with the 2007 acquisition of HCT Shaping Systems for about $483 million. HCT supplied equipment for making the crystalline silicon wafers that go into producing solar cells.

Applied continued to add to its solar equipment portfolio, however, adding Baccini SpA (material handling automation systems for ultrathin silicon wafers) in 2008. The following year, Applied bought Advent Solar, which develops processes and technologies used to streamline PV module production.

EXECUTIVES

Chairman, President, and CEO: Michael R. (Mike) Splinter, age 59, $6,571,219 total compensation
EVP and CFO: George S. Davis, age 52, $2,386,309 total compensation
SVP, CTO, and General Manager, Energy and Environmental Solutions and Display: Mark R. Pinto, age 50, $2,718,358 total compensation
SVP and General Manager, Silicon Systems: Randhir Thakur, age 47
SVP, General Counsel, and Corporate Secretary: Joseph J. Sweeney, age 61
SVP Worldwide Operations and Supply Chain: Joseph G. (Joe) Flanagan, age 38
SVP and Chief of Staff: Manfred Kerschbaum, age 55, $2,619,263 total compensation
VP Investor Relations: Michael Sullivan
VP Global Human Resources: Mary E. Humiston, age 45
Director Public Relations: Betty Newboe
President, Applied Solar Business: Charles Gay
Auditors: KPMG LLP

LOCATIONS

HQ: Applied Materials, Inc.
   3050 Bowers Ave., Santa Clara, CA 95052
Phone: 408-727-5555   **Fax:** 408-748-9943
Web: www.appliedmaterials.com

2009 Sales

	$ mil.	% of total
Asia/Pacific		
Taiwan	1,025.8	21
Japan	718.6	14
South Korea	663.8	13
China	635.4	13
Other countries	251.8	5
North America	965.6	19
Europe	752.6	15
Total	**5,013.6**	**100**

PRODUCTS/OPERATIONS

2009 Sales

	$ mil.	% of total
Silicon	1,960.2	39
Applied Global Services	1,396.6	28
Energy & Environmental Solutions	1,155.1	23
Display	501.7	10
Total	**5,013.6**	**100**

Selected Products

Chemical mechanical polishing/planarization systems (wafer polishing)
Deposition systems (deposit layers of conducting and insulating material on wafers)
   Dielectric deposition (chemical vapor deposition, or CVD)
   Metal (CVD, electroplating, or physical vapor deposition)
   Silicon and thermal deposition
   Sputtering (physical vapor deposition) for solar cells
   Thin-film silicon solar cells
   Web coating for flexible solar cells
Etch systems (remove portions of a wafer surface for circuit construction)
Inspection systems (defect review for reticles — patterned plates which hold precise images of chip circuit patterns — and wafers)
Ion implant systems (implant ions into wafer surface to change conductive properties)
Manufacturing process optimization software
Metrology systems
   CD-SEM (scanning electron microscope system)
   Optical monitoring systems (for glass or web coating systems)
Rapid thermal processing systems (heat wafers to change electrical characteristics)

COMPETITORS

AIXTRON
ASM International
Aviza Technology
Axcelis Technologies
Dainippon Screen
Ebara
EG Systems
FEI
FSI International
GT Solar
Hitachi
Hitachi Kokusai Electric
Intevac
KLA-Tencor
Lam Research
Mattson Technology
Micronic Laser Systems
Nanometrics
Nikon
Novellus
Rudolph Technologies
Semitool
Spire Corp.
Sumitomo Heavy Industries
Sumitomo Metal Industries
Tegal
Tokyo Electron
ULVAC
Varian Semiconductor
Veeco Instruments
Zygo

HISTORICAL FINANCIALS

Company Type: Public

Income Statement

FYE: Last Sunday in October

	REVENUE ($ mil.)	NET INCOME ($ mil.)	NET PROFIT MARGIN	EMPLOYEES
10/09	5,014	(305)	—	13,032
10/08	8,129	961	11.8%	15,410
10/07	9,735	1,710	17.6%	15,328
10/06	9,167	1,517	16.5%	14,072
10/05	6,992	1,210	17.3%	12,576
Annual Growth	**(8.0%)**	**—**	**—**	**0.9%**

2009 Year-End Financials

Debt ratio: 2.8%
Return on equity: —
Cash ($ mil.): 1,576
Current ratio: 2.93
Long-term debt ($ mil.): 201

No. of shares (mil.): 1,343
Dividends
   Yield: 2.0%
   Payout: —
Market value ($ mil.): 16,384

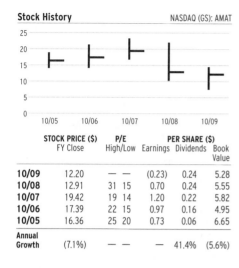

	STOCK PRICE ($)	P/E		PER SHARE ($)		
	FY Close	High/Low	Earnings	Dividends	Book Value
10/09	12.20	— —	(0.23)	0.24	5.28
10/08	12.91	31 15	0.70	0.24	5.55
10/07	19.42	19 14	1.20	0.22	5.82
10/06	17.39	22 15	0.97	0.16	4.95
10/05	16.36	25 20	0.73	0.06	6.65
Annual Growth	(7.1%)	— —	—	41.4%	(5.6%)

ARAMARK Corporation

Keeping employees fed and clothed is one mark of this company. ARAMARK is the world's #3 contract foodservice provider (behind Compass Group and Sodexo) and the #2 uniform supplier (behind Cintas) in the US. It offers corporate dining services and operates concessions at many sports arenas and other entertainment venues, while its ARAMARK Refreshment Services unit is a leading provider of vending and beverage services. The company also provides facilities management services. Through ARAMARK Uniform and Career Apparel, the company supplies uniforms for health care, public safety, and technology workers. Founded in 1959, ARAMARK is owned by an investment group led by chairman and CEO Joseph Neubauer.

Like its outsourcing rivals, ARAMARK competes primarily through bids to provide services to specific clients. It is generally engaged through long-term contracts that are renewed on a periodic basis. Most of ARAMARK's contracts allow the company to retain all revenue from its operations while paying a commission to the client; it also works under management fee arrangements under which clients bear some of the financial risk for expenses. In addition, the company's uniform and apparel division also sells products (outerwear, safety gear, work wear) directly to customers.

ARAMARK's foodservices units have wide-ranging operations throughout the US and in 20 other countries. In particular, it is a large player in the events concessions segment with hospitality contracts serving more than 80 professional and college sports facilities along with more than 30 convention centers. Other units focus on schools, universities, health care facilities, and correctional facilities.

Keen on international expansion, the company has focused on Europe and Asia, including the burgeoning market in China where it provided catering and other foodservices for the 2008 Olympic Games in Beijing. That same year ARAMARK acquired The Patman Group, expanding its reach into India. International markets now account for more than 25% of the company's revenue.

Neubauer took the company private in 2007 for $8.3 billion, including the assumption of $2 billion in debt, with the backing of such investment firms as Goldman Sachs, CCMP Capital, Thomas H. Lee Partners, and Warburg Pincus. (The executive himself already owned 40% of ARAMARK.) The deal marked the second such transaction for the company, having been taken private by Neubauer and a management group in the 1980s.

HISTORY

Davre Davidson began his career in foodservice by selling peanuts from the backseat of his car in the 1930s. He landed his first vending contract with Douglas Aircraft (later McDonnell Douglas, now part of Boeing) in 1935. Through that relationship, Davidson met William Fishman of Chicago, who had vending operations in the Midwest. Davidson and Fishman merged their companies in 1959 to form Automatic Retailers of America (ARA). Davidson became chairman and CEO of the new company; Fishman served as president.

Focusing on candy, beverage, and cigarette machines, ARA became the leading vending machine company in the US by 1961, with operations in 38 states. Despite slimmer profit margins, ARA moved into food vending in the early 1960s. It acquired 150 foodservice businesses between 1959-1963, quickly becoming a leader in the operation of cafeterias at colleges, hospitals, and work sites. The company (which changed its name to ARA Services in 1966) grew so rapidly that the FTC stepped in; ARA agreed to restrict future food vending acquisitions.

ARA provided foodservices at the 1968 Summer Olympics in Mexico City, beginning a long-term relationship with the amateur sports event. The company also diversified into publication distribution that year, and in 1970 it expanded into janitorial and maintenance services. A foray into residential care for the elderly began in 1973 (and ended in 1993 with the sale of the subsidiary). ARA also entered into emergency room staffing services (sold 1997). The company expanded into child care (National Child Care Centers) in 1980.

CFO Joseph Neubauer became CEO in 1983 and was named chairman in 1984. To avoid a hostile takeover shortly thereafter, he led a $1.2 billion leveraged buyout. After the buyout, ARA began refining its core operations. It acquired Szabo (correctional foodservices) in 1986, Children's World Learning Centers in 1987, and Coordinated Health Services (medical billing services) in 1993.

ARA changed its name to ARAMARK in 1994 as part of an effort to raise its profile with its ultimate customers, the public. The company's concession operations suffered from long work stoppages in baseball (1994) and hockey (1995). ARAMARK acquired Galls (North America's #1 supplier of public safety equipment) in 1996, and in 1997 announced plans to become 100% employee-owned.

With the new millennium the company was focused on expansion, buying the food and beverage concessions business of conglomerate Ogden Corp. for $236 million. The company penned a 10-year deal with Boeing in 2000 to supply foodservices to about 100 locations, one of the biggest foodservice contracts ever. It also bought Wackenhut's Correctional Foodservice Management division.

ARAMARK continued its expansion with the purchase of ServiceMaster's management services division in 2001 for about $800 million — opening doors in non-food management, groundskeeping, and custodial services. In late 2001 ARAMARK went public.

In 2002 it paid $100 million for Premier, Inc.'s Clinical Technology Services, which maintains and repairs clinical equipment in about 170 hospitals and health care facilities in the US.

In 2003 ARAMARK exited the child care business when it sold its Educational Resources unit (operator of Children's World Learning Centers) to Michael Milken's Knowledge Learning Corporation for $225 million. Longtime executive Bill Leonard was named president and CEO that year, with Neubauer taking on the title of executive chairman.

Expanding its Canadian presence in cleanroom services in 2004, ARAMARK acquired Toronto-based Cleanroom Garments. That same year, ARAMARK made its first foray into China by acquiring a 90% stake in Bright China Service Industries, a facilities services firm. After a brief reign, Leonard resigned that year and Neubauer returned to being CEO of the company.

EXECUTIVES

Chairman and CEO: Joseph (Joe) Neubauer, age 68, $5,176,043 total compensation
EVP and CFO; Group Executive, ARAMARK Uniform and Career Apparel: L. Frederick Sutherland, age 58, $2,611,301 total compensation
EVP; President ARAMARK Uniform and Career Apparel (AUCA): Thomas J. Vozzo, age 47, $2,026,068 total compensation
EVP Human Resources: Lynn B. McKee, age 54, $1,916,608 total compensation
EVP and Chief Globalization Officer; President, ARAMARK International: Ravi K. Saligram, age 53, $2,011,240 total compensation
EVP; Group President, Global Food, Hospitality, and Facilities Services: Andrew C. Kerin, age 46, $2,280,631 total compensation
SVP Higher Education: Michael Leone
SVP, Controller, and Chief Accounting Officer: Joseph M. (Joe) Munnelly, age 45
SVP, Treasurer, and Director: Christopher S. (Chris) Holland, age 43
President, SeamlessWeb: Jonathan Zabusky
President, ARAMARK Healthcare: Timothy (Tim) Campbell
President, ARAMARK Correctional Services: Scott Parrill
Group President, ARAMARK Healthcare: John Babiarz
Corporate Executive Chef, Sports and Entertainment: Brian Stapleton
Auditors: KPMG LLP

LOCATIONS

HQ: ARAMARK Corporation
ARAMARK Tower, 1101 Market St.
Philadelphia, PA 19107
Phone: 215-238-3000   **Fax:** 215-238-3333
Web: www.aramark.com

2009 Sales

	$ mil.	% of total
US	9,286.8	76
International	3,011.1	24
Total	**12,297.9**	**100**

PRODUCTS/OPERATIONS

2009 Sales

	$ mil.	% of total
Food & support services		
North America	8,393.5	68
International	2,326.7	19
Uniform & career apparel	1,577.7	13
Total	**12,297.9**	**100**

Selected Operations

Food and support services
ARAMARK Colleges and Universities
ARAMARK Conference Centers
ARAMARK Convention Centers
ARAMARK Correctional Services
ARAMARK Cultural Attractions
ARAMARK Facility Services
ARAMARK Food Services
ARAMARK Healthcare
ARAMARK Higher Education
ARAMARK Innovative Dining Solutions
ARAMARK Parks and Resorts
ARAMARK Refreshment Services (vending services)
ARAMARK Senior Living
ARAMARK Sports and Entertainment

Uniform and career apparel
ARAMARK Cleanroom Services
ARAMARK Uniform & Career Apparel
Galls (tactical equipment and apparel)

COMPETITORS

ABM Industries
Autogrill
Centerplate
Cintas
Compass Group
Delaware North
Elior
G&K Services
Healthcare Services
ISS A/S
Serco
Sodexo
SSP
UniFirst

HISTORICAL FINANCIALS

Company Type: Private

Income Statement

FYE: Friday nearest September 30

	REVENUE ($ mil.)	NET INCOME ($ mil.)	NET PROFIT MARGIN	EMPLOYEES
9/09	12,298	(7)	—	255,000
9/08	13,470	40	0.3%	260,000
9/07	12,384	31	0.2%	250,000
Annual Growth	**(0.3%)**	**—**	**—**	**1.0%**

Net Income History

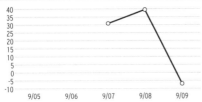

Arch Coal

What powers your power company? Perhaps Arch Coal. About half of the electricity generated in the US comes from coal, and Arch Coal is one of the country's largest coal producers, behind industry leader Peabody Energy. Arch Coal produces about 126 million tons of coal a year from about 20 mines in the western US and Central Appalachia; the company has proved and probable reserves of 2.8 billion tons. Steam coal — low-ash coal used by electric utilities to produce steam in boilers — accounts for the vast majority of the company's sales. To store and ship its Appalachian coal, the company operates the Arch Coal Terminal near the Ohio River.

In 2009 the company acquired Rio Tinto's Jacobs Ranch mine in the Powder River Basin of Wyoming for $760 million. The mine had been included in Rio Tinto spinoff Cloud Peak Energy. Arch Coal said it intends to combine the Jacobs Ranch mine with its own Black Thunder property, thereby creating the world's largest coal-mining complex.

Arch Coal acquired a 35% stake in Tenaska's Trailblazer Energy Center project in West Texas in 2010. The project will generate some 600 MW of electricity from coal, utilizing carbon capture technology that will sequester up to 90% of the plants carbon emissions. Secondarily, the plant will serve as a source of carbon dioxide for use in enhanced crude oil recovery systems. Arch Coal will provide coal for the project from its Powder River Basin operations.

HISTORY

Raised in the Oklahoma oil patch, J. Fred Miles founded the Swiss Drilling Company in 1910 and started wildcatting oil wells. Unable to compete against the low prices offered by Standard Oil, Miles moved his company in 1916 to eastern Kentucky and acquired control of 200,000 acres of oil land. With powerful backers such as the Armours of Chicago, Swiss Oil Company soon became one of the leading oil companies in Kentucky.

In the early 1920s the company's oil wells started to play out during a postwar depression. Miles fought back by expanding into refining, buying Tri-State Refining in 1930. The company changed its name in 1936 to Ashland Oil and Refining Company, a business that turned a profit even during the darkest days of the Depression. Miles didn't survive the transition, however. By 1926 Ashland was outperforming its parent, and investors eased Miles out the corporate door.

Pearl Harbor only brought more success to a business the American war machine needed to fuel its ships, planes, and tanks. Although peace brought the inevitable recession, America's postwar love affair with the automobile helped Ashland continue to thrive.

During the 1950s, Ashland's refineries ran at near capacity. In 1969 Merle Kelce and Guy Heckman, along with help from Ashland, formed Arch Mineral. Ashland had decided that it needed to diversify and lessen its dependence on oil refining. The Hunt family of Dallas, Texas, put their money into the venture in 1971, and in the following years the company bought Southwestern Illinois Coal Corporation, USX's Lynch Properties, Diamond Shamrock Coal, and Lawson-Hamilton Properties. By the end of 1996, the company owned some 1.5 billion tons of recoverable coal reserves.

Ashland struck out on its own in the coal business in 1975, forming Ashland Coal. Ashland Coal then began a series of acquisitions lasting 15 years. The company bought Addington Brothers Mining (1976), Hobet Mining and Construction (1977), Saarbergwerke (1981), Coal-Mac (1989), Mingo Logan (1990), and Dal-Tex Coal (1992). Growing through that binge of acquisitions, the company went public in 1988.

In 1997 Arch Mineral and Ashland Coal merged into Arch Coal, an entity that consolidated Ashland's coal assets. Ashland kept a 58% stake. In 1998 Arch Coal purchased Atlantic Richfield's (ARCO) US coal operations for $1.14 billion, making itself the second-largest coal producer in the US. That year Arch Coal also created Arch Western Resources, a joint venture in which Arch Coal owns 99% and ARCO owns 1%.

Regulatory pressures and low coal prices in 1999 forced the company to close three mines — the Dal-Tex in West Virginia and two surface mines in Kentucky.

Arch Coal recorded a $346 million loss in 1999. To recover from the profit plunge and benefit from increased demand as utilities complied with Clean Air Act mandates, the company boosted production at its low-sulfur coal Black Thunder mine in Wyoming. In 2000 Ashland reduced its stake in Arch Coal to 12%; it sold the remainder of its stock the next year.

In 2002 Arch Coal and WPP Group formed a partnership, Natural Resource Partners, which went public that October. The next year Arch Coal sold a portion of its stake back to Natural Resource's management for $115 million, and by 2004 Arch Coal had divested its remaining holdings in the partnership.

In 2005 Arch Coal sold four of its mining operations in southern West Virginia to Magnum Coal, a company backed by affiliates of investment firm ArcLight Capital. The sale was part of Arch Coal's strategy of focusing on its core areas, the Central Appalachian Basin and the Powder River Basin. In 2004 the company acquired Triton Coal and its mines in the Powder River Basin. Conversely, Arch Coal dipped its toe into the increasingly important Illinois Basin region with the acquisition of a one-third interest in Knight Hawk Coal.

EXECUTIVES

Chairman and CEO: Steven F. Leer, age 57, $3,548,277 total compensation
President, COO, and Director: John W. Eaves, age 52, $2,015,411 total compensation
SVP and CFO: John T. Drexler, age 40, $1,037,372 total compensation
SVP Strategic Development: C. Henry Besten Jr., age 61, $2,381,535 total compensation
SVP Law, Secretary, and General Counsel: Robert G. (Bob) Jones, age 53
SVP Operations: Paul A. Lang, age 49, $1,685,364 total compensation
VP and CIO: David E. Hartley
VP Business Development: David B. Peugh, age 55
VP Marketing and Trading: David N. Warnecke, age 54, $1,173,983 total compensation
VP Human Resources: Sheila B. Feldman, age 55
VP and Chief Accounting Officer: John W. Lorson
VP External Affairs, Western Region: Greg Schaefer
VP Market Research: Andy Blumenfeld
VP Tax: C. David Steele
VP Government, Investor, and Public Affairs: Deck S. Slone, age 46
VP Safety: Anthony S. Bumbico
President, Eastern Operations: Robert W. (Bob) Shanks
President and General Manager, Thunder Basin: Kenneth (Ken) Cochran
Auditors: Ernst & Young LLP

LOCATIONS

HQ: Arch Coal, Inc.
1 CityPlace Dr., Ste. 300, St. Louis, MO 63141
Phone: 314-994-2700 **Fax:** 314-994-2878
Web: www.archcoal.com

2009 Sales

	$ mil.	% of total
Powder River Basin	1,205.5	47
Central Appalachia	829.9	32
Western Bituminous	540.7	21
Total	**2,576.1**	**100**

PRODUCTS/OPERATIONS

Selected Operations

Central Appalachia
  Coal-Mac (West Virginia)
  Lone Mountain (Kentucky)

Western United States
  Arch of Wyoming (Wyoming)
  Black Thunder/Jacobs Ranch (Wyoming)
  Coal Creek (Wyoming)
  Dugout Canyon (Utah)
  Skyline (Utah)
  SUFCO (Utah)
  West Elk (Colorado)

COMPETITORS

Alliance Resource	James River Coal
Alpha Natural Resources	Massey Energy
CONSOL Energy	Patriot Coal
Drummond Company	Peabody Energy
International Coal	Penn Virginia

HISTORICAL FINANCIALS

Company Type: Public

Income Statement

FYE: December 31

	REVENUE ($ mil.)	NET INCOME ($ mil.)	NET PROFIT MARGIN	EMPLOYEES
12/09	2,576	42	1.6%	4,601
12/08	2,984	354	11.9%	4,300
12/07	2,414	175	7.2%	4,030
12/06	2,500	261	10.4%	4,050
12/05	2,509	38	1.5%	3,700
Annual Growth	0.7%	2.6%	—	5.6%

2009 Year-End Financials

Debt ratio: 87.2%	No. of shares (mil.): 162
Return on equity: 2.2%	Dividends
Cash ($ mil.): 61	Yield: 1.6%
Current ratio: 1.09	Payout: 128.6%
Long-term debt ($ mil.): 1,845	Market value ($ mil.): 3,615

Stock History

NYSE: ACI

	STOCK PRICE ($) FY Close	P/E High/Low		PER SHARE ($) Earnings	Dividends	Book Value
12/09	22.25	92	42	0.28	0.36	13.02
12/08	16.29	32	4	2.45	0.34	10.64
12/07	44.93	37	23	1.21	0.27	9.43
12/06	30.03	31	14	1.80	0.22	8.40
12/05	39.75	235	95	0.17	0.16	7.29
Annual Growth	(13.5%)	—	—	13.3%	22.5%	15.6%

Archer-Daniels-Midland

Archer-Daniels-Midland (ADM) knows how to grind and squeeze a fortune out of humble plants. It is one of the world's largest processors of oilseeds, corn, and wheat. Its main offerings include soybean and other oilseed products. From corn, it produces syrups, sweeteners, citric and lactic acids, and ethanol, among other products. ADM also produces wheat flour for bakeries and pasta makers; cocoa and chocolate products for confectioners; animal-feed ingredients for farmers, and malt for brewers. It operates one of the world's largest crop origination and transportation networks, through which it connects crops and their markets across the globe.

With some 240 plants located worldwide, ADM processes the three largest crops in the US — corn, soybeans, and wheat — for sale to food, beverage, and chemical companies. About one-third of the company's sales come from its oilseed products, including vegetable oils, animal feeds, and emulsifiers. ADM also makes vitamin E, textured vegetable protein (TVP), and cotton cellulose pulp (for making paper).

The company continues to introduce value-added products. A line of trans-free fats and oils, NovaLipid, allows the production of margarines, shortenings, and other products with near zero levels of trans-fatty acids. It also makes cholesterol-lowering CardioAid plant sterols, which can be added to such food as sauces, pasta, beverages, and cereals. More dried edible bean products were added to ADM's Vegefull line in 2009 in order to meet the growing demand for increased protein and fiber in food.

However, as an agricultural commodities-based business, ADM saw its raw materials costs rise significantly in 2009. Increased corn prices cut into its ethanol, sweeteners, and starches revenue, although this was partially offset by ADM increasing prices for its sweeteners and starches.

In addition, the decrease in demand for gasoline, lower gasoline prices, as well as an excess of ethanol throughout the industry cut into ADM's ethanol revenue. And finally, in 2009 the market for agricultural commodities, freight, and other ADM products was weaker due to the global economic downturn.

In addition to agriculture, ADM has other business interests, including banking and tortilla making. It owns Hickory Point Bank and Trust Company, which is located in Deactur, Illinois, and a 23% interest in Mexico's Gruma, the world's largest producer of corn flour and tortillas.

HISTORY

John Daniels began crushing flaxseed to make linseed oil in 1878, and in 1902 he formed Daniels Linseed Company in Minneapolis. George Archer, another flaxseed crusher, joined the company the following year. In 1923 the company bought Midland Linseed Products and became Archer Daniels Midland (ADM). ADM kept buying oil processing companies in the Midwest during the 1920s. It also started to research the chemical composition of linseed oil.

ADM entered the flour milling business in 1930 when it bought Commander-Larabee (then the #3 flour miller in the US). In the 1930s the company discovered a method for extracting lecithin (an emulsifier food additive used in candy and other products) from soybean oil, significantly lowering its price.

The enterprise grew rapidly following WWII. By 1949 it was the leading processor of linseed oil and soybeans in the US and was fourth in flour milling. During the early 1950s ADM began foreign expansion in earnest.

In 1966 the company's leadership passed to Dwayne Andreas, a former Cargill executive who had purchased a block of Archer family stock. Andreas focused ADM on soybeans, including the production of textured vegetable protein, a cheap soybean by-product used in foodstuffs.

Andreas' restructuring paved the way for productivity and expansion. In 1971 the company acquired Corn Sweeteners (glutens, high-fructose syrups). Other acquisitions included Tabor (grain, 1975) and Colombian Peanut (1981). ADM formed a grain-marketing joint venture with GROWMARK in 1985.

In 1995 the FBI — aided by ADM executive-turned-informer Mark Whitacre — joined a federal investigation of lysine and citric acid price-fixing by the company. The next year ADM agreed to plead guilty to two criminal charges of price-fixing and paid $100 million in penalties, a record at that time for a US criminal antitrust case. Whitacre later lost his immunity when convicted of defrauding ADM out of $9 million. He and two other ADM executives, including one-time ADM heir apparent Michael Andreas, were tried and convicted in 1998 and sentenced to prison in 1999.

Meanwhile, ADM continued to grow. In 1997 it acquired W. R. Grace's cocoa business and, after naming Allen Andreas (Dwayne's nephew) as CEO, bought 42% of Canada-based United Grain Growers. Dwayne turned over the chairman post to Allen in early 1999. In 2000 ADM was again cited for involvement in the price-fixing of lysine and was fined $45 million by the European Commission.

In 2002 ADM acquired Minnesota Corn Processors (MCP), its chief competitor in the ethanol market. In 2003 ADM reached a settlement with the US government regarding violations of the Clean Air Act and agreed to pay approximately $340 million to clean up air pollution at 52 of its midwestern food-processing plants. ADM announced a joint research agreement with Volkswagen AG in 2004 in order to develop next-generation, clean, renewable biodiesel fuels for the auto industry.

In mid-2004 ADM agreed to shell out $400 million to settle a class-action antitrust lawsuit claiming the company conspired to fix the price of high fructose corn syrup between the years of 1991 and 1995. Syrup customers involved in the suit included Coca-Cola and PepsiCo. Faced with potential damage awards of nearly $5 billion, the company chose to settle before going to trial.

In 2006 the company named Patricia Woertz CEO. Woertz joined ADM after having served as an EVP at energy giant Chevron. With her appointment, ADM became the largest publicly traded US company to be headed by a woman.

In 2006 ADM (along with two Dutch companies, Akzo Nobel and Avebe) was found guilty of price fixing in the cleaning agent sodium gluconate sector by an EU court. ADM was fined almost $13 million.

In 2007 long-time chairman G. Allen Andreas stepped down and was replaced by Woertz.

EXECUTIVES

Chairman, President, and CEO: Patricia A. (Pat) Woertz, age 57, $15,466,064 total compensation
President, ADM Alliance Nutrition: Terry Myers
EVP and CFO: Steven R. (Steve) Mills, age 54, $3,228,505 total compensation
EVP, Secretary, and General Counsel: David J. Smith, age 54, $4,280,570 total compensation
EVP Commercial and Production: John D. Rice, age 55, $5,246,499 total compensation
SVP and Senior Advisor Global Corn:
Edward A. Harjehausen, age 59, $2,758,645 total compensation
SVP Human Resources: Michael (Mike) D'Ambrose, age 52
SVP Toepfer and ADM Value Creation Team:
Lewis W. Batchelder, age 64, $4,086,258 total compensation
VP and Controller: John P. Stott, age 42
VP Human Resources: F. Kathie Whitley
VP Government Relations: Shannon S. Herzfeld, age 57
VP Global Oilseeds: Mark N. Zenuk, age 42
VP, Global Oleo Chemicals: Mike Livergood
VP Corn Processing: Dennis C. Riddle, age 62
VP Investor Services: Chris Damilatis
VP Corporate Communications: Victoria A. Podesta, age 53
VP Investor Relations: Dwight E. Grimestad
VP Compliance and Ethics: Scott A. Roney, age 45
President, Oilseeds: Matthew J. Jansen, age 43
Advisor, Office of the Chairman: Kris Lutt
Auditors: Ernst & Young LLP

LOCATIONS

HQ: Archer-Daniels-Midland Company
4666 Faries Pkwy., Decatur, IL 62525
Phone: 217-424-5200   **Fax:** 217-424-6196
Web: www.admworld.com

2009 Sales

	$ mil.	% of total
US	35,485	51
Germany	7,431	11
Other countries	26,291	38
Total	**69,207**	**100**

PRODUCTS/OPERATIONS

2009 Sales

	$ mil.	% of total
Agricultural services	34,351	47
Oilseeds processing	24,627	34
Corn processing	7,803	11
Other	5,535	8
Adjustment	(3,109)	—
Total	**69,207**	**100**

Selected Products

Animal Feed
  Corn germ meal
  Corn gluten feed
  Corn gluten meal
  Corn oil
  Condensed fermented corn extractives
  Distillers dried grain
  Wet distillers grains
  Whet corn gluten feed
Food
  Acidulants
  Beverage alcohol
  Cocoa and chocolate products
  Edible beans and bean ingredients
  Fiber
  Flour and whole grains
  Lecithin
  Natural-source vitamin E
  Oils and fats
  Plant sterols
  Polyols and gums
  Proteins
  Rice
  Soy isoflavones
  Starches
  Sweeteners

Fuel and Industrial
  Acidulants
  Chemical intermediates
  Emulsifiers and thickeners
  Ethanol
  Industrial oils
  Polymers
  Solvents
  Starches

Selected Services

Agriculture
  Grain merchandising
  Grain milling
  Grain processing
Information
  Billing and invoicing
  Inventory
  Logistics
  Payment
  Product search
Transportation
  Land
    Rail
    Truck
  Water
    Ocean
    River

COMPETITORS

Abengoa Bioenergy	Green Plains
Ag Processing Inc.	Hain Celestial
AGRI Industries	Hershey
Agrium	Liberty Vegetable Oil
Ajinomoto	Little Sioux Corn
Andersons	Processors
Barry Callebaut	Louis Dreyfus Group
Bartlett and Company	Malt Products Corporation
Bayer CropScience	MGP Ingredients
Brenntag North America	Monsanto Company
Buckeye Technologies	Nestlé
Bunge Limited	Nisshin Oillio
Cargill	Northern Growers
CHS	Omega Protein
Corn Products	Pacific Ethanol
International	Pioneer Hi-Bred
Cosun	Renewable Energy Group
CP Kelco	Riceland Foods
Danisco A/S	Südzucker
Dow AgroSciences	Scoular
DuPont Agriculture	Syngenta
& Nutrition	Tate & Lyle
General Mills	Viterra Inc.

HISTORICAL FINANCIALS

Company Type: Public

Income Statement

FYE: June 30

	REVENUE ($ mil.)	NET INCOME ($ mil.)	NET PROFIT MARGIN	EMPLOYEES
6/09	69,207	1,707	2.5%	28,200
6/08	69,816	1,802	2.6%	27,600
6/07	44,018	2,162	4.9%	27,300
6/06	36,596	1,312	3.6%	26,800
6/05	35,944	1,044	2.9%	25,641
Annual Growth	17.8%	13.1%	—	2.4%

2009 Year-End Financials

Debt ratio: 57.8%
Return on equity: 12.6%
Cash ($ mil.): 1,055
Current ratio: 2.18
Long-term debt ($ mil.): 7,800

No. of shares (mil.): 643
Dividends
  Yield: 2.0%
  Payout: 20.4%
Market value ($ mil.): 17,214

Stock History

NYSE: ADM

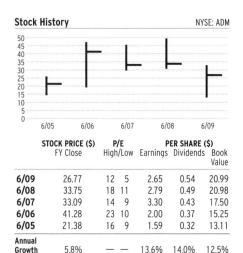

	STOCK PRICE ($) FY Close	P/E High/Low		PER SHARE ($) Earnings	Dividends	Book Value
6/09	26.77	12	5	2.65	0.54	20.99
6/08	33.75	18	11	2.79	0.49	20.98
6/07	33.09	14	9	3.30	0.43	17.50
6/06	41.28	23	10	2.00	0.37	15.25
6/05	21.38	16	9	1.59	0.32	13.11
Annual Growth	5.8%	—	—	13.6%	14.0%	12.5%

Arrow Electronics

Arrow Electronics knows its target market. The company is a leading global distributor of electronic components and computer products, alongside rival Avnet. It sells semiconductors, passive components, interconnect products, and computer peripherals from about 900 suppliers to more than 125,000 OEMs, contract manufacturers, and commercial customers. Arrow also provides value-added services, such as materials planning, design and engineering, inventory management, and contract manufacturing. The company operates from more than 300 locations in some 50 countries. It distributes products made by such manufacturers as Cree, Panasonic, Microsoft, and Intel.

Arrow's customers are primarily manufacturers in industries such aerospace and defense, computers, gaming, industrial equipment, instrumentation, medical and scientific devices, networking, optoelectronics, and telecommunications equipment, as well as resellers of computer systems. Electronic components account for about two-thirds of sales. Its Enterprise Computing Solutions (ECS) business — which sells hardware, software, storage, and security products to more than 18,000 value-added resellers — makes up the remainder. ECS has added professional consulting, cloud computing and managed services, and technical training as the business unit expands its support for resellers and systems integrators beyond hardware sales.

Faced with the challenge of a worldwide recession, the company restructured its operations in 2009 by reducing headcount by about 1,925 positions (about 15% of total workforce) and closing around 28 facilities worldwide. In 2008, it eliminated approximately 750 positions and closed nine facilities.

Arrow expands its vast product lines and global presence primarily through acquisitions. It purchased UK-based value-added reseller Sphinx Group in mid-2010 in order to boost its presence in Europe and firm up ties with suppliers in the region. Late the previous year, the company bought aerospace interconnect distributor A.E. Petsche Company.

Later in 2010 the company announced plans to purchase Shared Technologies, a provider of managed communications and enterprise services.

President and COO Michael Long, an Arrow executive since 1991, was promoted to CEO in May 2009, succeeding William Mitchell, who remained as executive chairman. Mitchell, who served as CEO for six years, retired as chairman at the end of 2009 after helping in the management transition. Long replaced Mitchell as chairman.

HISTORY

Arrow Radio began in 1935 in New York City as an outlet for used radio equipment. In the mid-1960s the company was selling various home entertainment products and wholesaling electronic parts. In 1968 three Harvard Business School graduates got Arrow in their sights. Duke Glenn, Roger Green, and John Waddell led a group of investors that acquired the company for $1 million in borrowed money. The three also bought a company that reclaimed lead from used car batteries.

With the money they made in the lead reclamation business, the trio enlarged Arrow's wholesale electronics distribution inventory. The company expanded rapidly during the 1970s, primarily through internal growth, and by 1977 it had become the US's fourth-largest electronics distributor. In 1979 Arrow bought the #2 US distributor, Cramer Electronics. Although the purchase of West Coast-based Cramer was financed with junk bonds and left Arrow deeply in debt, revenues doubled. Arrow went public in 1979.

One year later a hotel fire killed 13 members of Arrow's senior management, including Glenn and Green. Waddell, who had remained at company headquarters to answer questions about a stock split announced that day, was named acting CEO. Company stock fell 19% the first day it traded after the fire and another 14% before the end of the month. Adding to the company's woes, a slump hit the electronics industry in 1981. That year Arrow's board lured Alfred Stein to leave Motorola and to lead the company's new management team as president and CEO; Waddell remained chairman.

Stein did not mesh with Arrow, and in early 1982 the board fired him and put Waddell in charge again. By 1983 the industry slump was over, and Arrow was temporarily back in the black. However, another industry downturn led to significant losses between 1985 and 1987.

In the mid-1980s Arrow began a major global expansion, acquiring in 1985 a 40% interest in Germany's largest electronics distributor, Spoerle Electronic (Arrow owned the company by 2000). President Stephen Kaufman, a former McKinsey & Company consultant, was named CEO in 1986 (Waddell remained VC). Arrow bought Kierulff Electronics, the fourth-largest US distributor, in 1988, and Lex Electronics, the third-largest, three years later.

Arrow expanded into Asia in 1993 with the acquisition of Hong Kong-based Components Agents and New Zealand's Components+Instrumentation in 1995.

In 1999 Arrow acquired passive components distributor Richey Electronics and the Electronics Distribution Group of Bell Industries. Kaufman stepped down from the CEO post in 2000; company president Francis Scricco was named to the position. Later in 2000 Arrow purchased Wyle Components and Wyle Systems (both North American computer products distributors) from German utility giant E.ON.

Facing a broad downturn in the electronics industry, the company in 2001 laid off 1,500 employees. In 2002 Scricco resigned as CEO; Kaufman left his post as chairman to take the reins once again as CEO and director Daniel Duval stepped in as chairman. Later that year Kaufman retired and Duval was named CEO.

Early in 2003 former Solectron executive Bill Mitchell took over as president and CEO; Duval remained chairman. Mitchell added chairman to his title in 2006 when Duval stepped down from that post (but remained a director).

In 2007 Arrow bought the computer distribution business of Agilysys for $485 million in cash.

That same year Arrow also expanded into Japan for the first time, buying a Tokyo-based distributor of semiconductor and multimedia products, Universe Electron Corp., and establishing a Japanese subsidiary.

In 2008 Arrow further expanded into the Asia/Pacific region when it acquired the electronic components distribution business of Achieva Ltd., a deal that gave it operations in eight Southeast Asian countries.

EXECUTIVES

Chairman, President, and CEO: Michael J. (Mike) Long, age 51, $5,063,453 total compensation
Vice Chairman: John C. Waddell, age 72
EVP Finance and Operations and CFO: Paul J. Reilly, age 53, $3,052,022 total compensation
SVP Human Resources: John P. McMahon, age 57, $1,662,538 total compensation
SVP and Chief Strategy Officer: M. Catherine (Cathy) Morris, age 51
SVP, General Counsel, and Secretary: Peter S. Brown, age 59, $2,188,282 total compensation
VP; EVP, Arrow Europe, Middle East, Africa, and South America: Jan M. Salsgiver
VP Global Operations and Value Added Services: Ernest (Ernie) Keith
VP and CIO: Vincent P. (Vin) Melvin, age 46
VP Vertical Markets: Tom Flanagan
VP Supplier Marketing and Asset: David West
VP and Treasurer: Michael J. Taunton, age 54
President, Arrow Global Components: Peter T. Kong, age 59, $2,377,698 total compensation
President, Arrow Americas Components: Vincent (Vinnie) Vellucci
President, Arrow Enterprise Computing Solutions, North America: Richard Severa
President, Arrow Global Enterprise Computing Solutions: Andrew S. (Andy) Bryant, age 54
President, Arrow Asia-Pacific Components: Simon Yu
President, Arrow Enterprise Computing Solutions, Europe, Middle East, and Africa: Laurent Sadoun, age 44
President, Arrow Europe, Middle East, and Africa Components: Brian P. McNally
Director External Communications: John Hourigan
Auditors: Ernst & Young LLP

LOCATIONS

HQ: Arrow Electronics, Inc.
50 Marcus Dr., Melville, NY 11747
Phone: 631-847-2000 **Fax:** 631-847-2222
Web: www.arrow.com

2009 Sales

	$ mil.	% of total
North America	7,017	48
Europe, Middle East, Africa & South America	4,288	29
Asia/Pacific	3,379	23
Total	**14,684**	**100**

PRODUCTS/OPERATIONS

2009 Sales

	$ mil.	% of total
Global components	9,751	66
Global enterprise computing systems	4,933	34
Total	**14,684**	**100**

Selected Products and Services

Computer Products
  Communication control equipment
  Controllers
  Design systems
  Desktop computers
  Flat-panel displays
  Microcomputer boards and systems
  Monitors
  Printers
  Servers
  Software
  Storage products
  System chassis and enclosures
  Workstations
Electronic Components
  Capacitors
  Connectors
  Potentiometers
  Power supplies
  Relays
  Resistors
  Switches
Services
  Analysis, implementation, and support
  Component design
  Contract manufacturing
  Forecast and order management
  Inventory management

COMPETITORS

Avnet
Digi-Key
ePlus
Future Electronics
Heilind Electronics
Ingram Micro
Newark InOne
N.F. Smith
Nu Horizons Electronics
Richardson Electronics
SYNNEX
Tech Data
TTI Inc.
WPG Holdings
Yosun

HISTORICAL FINANCIALS

Company Type: Public

Income Statement

FYE: December 31

	REVENUE ($ mil.)	NET INCOME ($ mil.)	NET PROFIT MARGIN	EMPLOYEES
12/09	14,684	124	0.8%	11,300
12/08	16,761	(614)	—	12,700
12/07	15,985	408	2.6%	12,600
12/06	13,577	388	2.9%	12,000
12/05	11,164	254	2.3%	11,400
Annual Growth	**7.1%**	**(16.5%)**	**—**	**(0.2%)**

2009 Year-End Financials

Debt ratio: 43.7%
Return on equity: 4.4%
Cash ($ mil.): 1,137
Current ratio: 1.75
Long-term debt ($ mil.): 1,276

No. of shares (mil.): 118
Dividends
  Yield: 0.0%
  Payout: —
Market value ($ mil.): 3,489

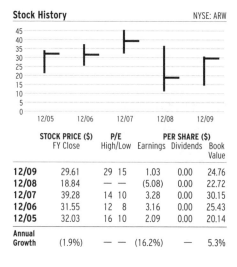

	STOCK PRICE ($)	P/E		PER SHARE ($)		
	FY Close	High/Low		Earnings	Dividends	Book Value
12/09	29.61	29	15	1.03	0.00	24.76
12/08	18.84	—	—	(5.08)	0.00	22.72
12/07	39.28	14	10	3.28	0.00	30.15
12/06	31.55	12	8	3.16	0.00	25.43
12/05	32.03	16	10	2.09	0.00	20.14
Annual Growth	(1.9%)	—	—	(16.2%)	—	5.3%

ArvinMeritor

Whether it's building axles or drum brakes for big rigs or buses, this company's products are meritorious. ArvinMeritor makes products such as axles, brakes, drivelines, suspension systems, and aftermarket transmissions for commercial truck, trailer, off-highway, construction, military, bus, and specialty vehicle manufacturers. It also makes door and roof systems for light vehicle makers. In order to focus on the more profitable commercial vehicle and industrial market segments, ArvinMeritor divested its Light Vehicle Systems (LVS) business in 2010.

In 2009 ArvinMeritor also sold its chassis business (Gabriel Ride Control Products North America) to OpenGate Capital, a private-equity firm. In addition, the company sold its Meritor Suspension Systems Company (MSSC), along with its 51% stake in Gabriel de Venezuela (shock absorbers, struts, exhaust systems, and suspension modules for the South American market) to its joint venture partner, a subsidiary of Mitsubishi Steel.

Slammed by production cutbacks due to overcapacity and falling demand in the global auto industry, ArvinMeritor started looking for ways to tighten its belt. Starting in 2009 the company laid off about 2,800 employees worldwide, more than 10% of its workforce. It closed a brake plant and a coil spring operation in Canada, and announced that its commercial truck machining and casting facility in Kentucky would be closed in early 2010.

As ArvinMeritor looks to grow its core businesses — the Commercial Truck, Industrial, and Aftermarket & Trailer segments — the company is also working to identify adjacent industries, products, and technologies that provide opportunities for diversification, such as the military market. Current efforts include a venture with Lockheed Martin and BAE SYSTEMS for work on the Joint Light Tactical Vehicle program for the US Defense Department.

ArvinMeritor continues to invest in emerging markets — specifically focused on South America, China, and India — where growth has continued in spite of the economic downturn. In Bangalore, India, the company established a new research and development center. The site will spearhead the design and testing of axles and brakes destined for Asia/Pacific. In addition, it will provide engineering support for operations in North and South America, and in Europe.

HISTORY

ArvinMeritor's earliest progenitor was the Wisconsin Parts Company, a small axle plant Willard Rockwell bought in 1919 to build a truck axle he had designed himself. In 1953 Rockwell merged Wisconsin Parts with Standard Steel and Spring and Timken-Detroit Axle to form Rockwell Spring and Axle Company. Timken-Detroit was a 1909 spinoff of the Timken Roller Bearing Axle Company, whose buggy springs predated the invention of the automobile.

Rockwell Spring and Axle changed its name in 1958 to Rockwell-Standard Corp. In 1967 Rockwell-Standard took over North American Aviation. North American Aviation needed to improve its public image by burrowing into a reputable company after the Apollo space capsule it had built ignited during a ground test, killing all three astronauts aboard. The new company, called North American Rockwell, was headed by Willard.

North American Rockwell made car and truck parts, tools, printing presses, industrial sewing machines, and electronic flight and navigation instruments. In 1973 North American Rockwell bought Willard Rockwell Jr.'s Rockwell Manufacturing and changed its name once again, to Rockwell International (now Rockwell Automation).

Under Willard Jr.'s leadership, Rockwell bought a number of high-risk businesses. During one period in the early 1970s, the company was losing a million dollars a day. Willard Jr. retired in 1979, and Robert Anderson, who had come to Rockwell in 1968 from Chrysler Corporation, became chairman. Anderson moved the company away from the high-profile consumer market that Willard Jr. had been so keen on. He also required all company divisions to submit profit goals. Under Anderson's management, Rockwell's debt fell dramatically.

In 1986 Rockwell brought out a new line of single-speed and two-speed drive axles for heavy vehicles, and in 1989 it introduced a family of nine- and 13-speed on-highway transmissions. The next year the company's Meritor WABCO unit (a joint venture with American Standard Companies) began supplying antilock brakes for trailers and tractors.

In the 1990s Rockwell's automotive division began growing through acquisitions and overseas expansion. It bought Czech auto parts maker Skoda Miada Boleslav in 1993 and Dura Automotive Systems' window-regulator business in 1995. The next year the division entered into a joint venture with China's Xuzhou Construction Machinery Axle and Case Co.

Rockwell spun off Meritor Automotive in 1997 as an independent, publicly traded company. The new company derived its name from the Latin word "meritum," meaning service, worth, and benefit. In 1999 Meritor bought UK-based LucasVarity's heavy vehicle braking system division; Volvo's heavy-duty truck axle unit; and Euclid Industries, which makes replacement parts for medium- and heavy-duty trucks.

In 2000 Meritor acquired Arvin Industries. Renamed ArvinMeritor, the combined companies formed an automotive systems titan with $7.5 billion in sales. Later that year ArvinMeritor announced that it would reduce its worldwide workforce by about 4% (1,500) because of a slump in the heavy truck industry.

In 2004 the company announced plans to exit the aftermarket business in order to focus on the needs of its OEM customers. That year ArvinMeritor sold its coil coating operations.

In 2006 ArvinMeritor sold its light vehicle aftermarket Purolator filters business to Robert Bosch and MANN+HUMMEL. Soon afterward the company sold its North American light vehicle aftermarket exhaust business to IMCO (International Muffler Company). The company also sold its light vehicle aftermarket motion control business to AVM Industries LLC.

The company formed a joint venture in China to build sunroofs for Chinese-built Volkswagens, and established two more joint ventures in France to provide AB Volvo with commercial vehicle drive axles.

In 2007 the company sold its emissions technologies business to One Equity Partners, an affiliate of JPMorgan Chase, for about $310 million. Later in 2007 ArvinMeritor sold its light vehicle aftermarket European exhaust division to Klarius Group of the UK.

EXECUTIVES

Chairman, President, and CEO: Charles G. (Chip) McClure Jr., age 57, $4,263,279 total compensation
SVP and COO: Carsten Reinhardt, age 43, $1,480,635 total compensation
SVP and CFO: Jeffrey A. (Jay) Craig, age 51, $793,138 total compensation
SVP Human Resources: Larry Ott
SVP Communications: Linda Cummins, age 63
SVP and General Counsel: Vernon G. Baker II, age 57, $998,990 total compensation
SVP Strategic Initiatives: Mary Lehmann, age 52
VP and Corporate Secretary: Barbara Novak
VP; President, Aftermarket & Trailer: Joe Mejaly
VP and General Manager, Specialty Products: Christopher Kete
VP Sales and Marketing, Light Vehicle Systems: Sherry Welsh
VP; President, Industrial: Tim Bowes
VP and Treasurer: Kevin Nowlan
Senior Director, Corporate Communications and Media Relations: Krista Sohm
Senior Director Investor Relations: Brett Penzkofer
Director Global Brand Management and Marketing Communications: Dave Giroux
Auditors: Deloitte & Touche LLP

LOCATIONS

HQ: ArvinMeritor, Inc.
2135 W. Maple Rd., Troy, MI 48084
Phone: 248-435-1000   **Fax:** 248-435-1393
Web: www.arvinmeritor.com

2009 Sales

	$ mil.	% of total
North America		
US	1,616.0	39
Mexico	246.0	6
Canada	91.0	2
Europe		
France	437.0	11
Sweden	204.0	5
Germany	111.0	3
Other countries	615.0	15
Asia/Pacific	424.0	10
South America	364.0	9
Total	**4,108.0**	**100**

PRODUCTS/OPERATIONS

2009 Sales

	$ mil.	% of total
Commercial truck	1,348.0	33
Light vehicle systems	1,033.0	25
Aftermarket & trailer	949.0	23
Industrial	778.0	19
Total	**4,108.0**	**100**

Selected Products

Commercial Vehicle Systems
  Axles
  Brakes
  Brake wheel-end components (hubs, drums, and
    rotors)
  Clutches
  Drivelines
  Exhaust products
  Ride control products
  Shock absorbers
  Suspension systems
  Trailer products (including axles and air suspension
    products)
  Universal joints
Light Vehicle Systems
  Door systems
    Actuators
    Fuel flap locking devices
    Latches
    Window regulators
  Roof systems

COMPETITORS

Accuride	Magna International
AISIN World Corp.	MAN
American Axle &	Mitsui
Manufacturing	Robert Bosch
ASC Inc.	SAF-HOLLAND
AxleTech International	SOGEFI
Benteler Group	Superior Industries
Boler	Tenneco
BorgWarner	Titan International
Borla Performance	Topy
Industries	Tower Automotive
Carlisle Companies	Trane Inc.
Dana Holding	TRW Automotive
Delphi Automotive	Valeo
Dura Automotive	Visteon
Eaton	Voith
Faurecia	Westinghouse Air Brake
Federal-Mogul	Williams Controls
Haldex	ZF Friedrichshafen
Hayes Lemmerz	

HISTORICAL FINANCIALS

Company Type: Public

Income Statement
FYE: Sunday nearest September 30

	REVENUE ($ mil.)	NET INCOME ($ mil.)	NET PROFIT MARGIN	EMPLOYEES
9/09	4,108	(1,212)	—	13,200
9/08	7,167	(101)	—	19,800
9/07	6,449	(219)	—	18,000
9/06	9,195	(175)	—	27,500
9/05	8,903	12	0.1%	29,000
Annual Growth	**(17.6%)**	**—**	**—**	**(17.9%)**

2009 Year-End Financials

Debt ratio: —
Return on equity: —
Cash ($ mil.): 95
Current ratio: 1.02
Long-term debt ($ mil.): 1,080

No. of shares (mil.): 94
Dividends
  Yield: 1.3%
  Payout: —
Market value ($ mil.): 736

Stock History
NYSE: ARM

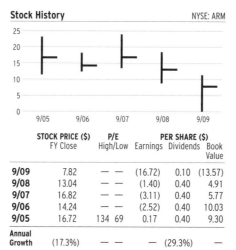

	STOCK PRICE ($) FY Close	P/E High	P/E Low	Earnings	Dividends	Book Value
9/09	7.82	—	—	(16.72)	0.10	(13.57)
9/08	13.04	—	—	(1.40)	0.40	4.91
9/07	16.82	—	—	(3.11)	0.40	5.77
9/06	14.24	—	—	(2.52)	0.40	10.03
9/05	16.72	134	69	0.17	0.40	9.30
Annual Growth	**(17.3%)**	**—**	**—**	**—**	**(29.3%)**	**—**

Ashland Inc.

Ashland's five business units are built on chemicals and cars. Ashland Distribution, which represents almost half of its business, buys chemicals and plastics and then blends and repackages them for distribution in Europe and North America. Ashland Performance Materials makes specialty resins, polymers, and adhesives. Ashland's Water Technologies unit provides chemical and nonchemical products for commercial, industrial, and municipal water treatment facilities. Consumer Markets, led by subsidiary Valvoline, runs an oil-change chain and markets Valvoline motor oil and Zerex antifreeze. Ashland Aqualon Functional Ingredients makes additives for the coatings, food, personal care, and pharmaceutical industries.

Ashland agreed in 2010 to form a 50-50 joint venture with Sud-Chemie AG to produce foundry chemicals. Sud-Chemie will manage the operation, called ASK Chemicals GmbH, which will be headquartered in Germany.

In 2008 Ashland paid $3.3 billion to buy specialty chemicals company Hercules, which added greatly to its water treatment and resins businesses. That move was just the latest in a series of transactions in the latter half of the decade that transformed Ashland from a multi-industry conglomerate into strictly a chemicals operation. Among other moves, the company sold its half of a refining joint venture with Marathon Oil and construction unit APAC.

The deal provided Ashland, already with a healthy international business, with even more of a global presence. The company now achieves more than a third of its sales from outside the US.

HISTORY

After moving to Kentucky in 1917, Fred Miles formed the Swiss Oil Company. In 1924 Swiss Oil bought a refinery in Catlettsburg, a rough town near sedate Ashland, and created a unit called Ashland Refining. Miles battled Swiss Oil directors for control, lost, and resigned in 1927.

Swiss Oil bought Tri-State Refining in 1930 and Cumberland Pipeline's eastern Kentucky pipe network in 1931. Swiss Oil changed its name to Ashland Oil and Refining in 1936. After

WWII it bought small independent oil firms, acquiring the Valvoline name in 1950 by buying Freedom-Valvoline.

The firm formed Ashland Chemical in 1967 after buying Anderson-Prichard Oil (1958), United Carbon (1963), and ADM Chemical (1967). Ashland Chemical changed its name to Ashland Oil. It added the SuperAmerica convenience store chain (1970) and started exploring for oil in Nigeria after OPEC nations raised oil prices.

Scandal hit in 1975, the year Ashland Coal was formed. CEO Orin Atkins admitted to ordering Ashland executives to make illegal contributions to the 1972 Nixon presidential campaign. Atkins was deposed in 1981 after the company made questionable payments to highly placed "consultants" with connections to oil-rich Middle Eastern governments. In 1988 Atkins was arrested for trying to fence purloined documents regarding litigation between Ashland and the National Iranian Oil Company (NIOC). Ashland, which launched the federal investigation that led to Atkins' arrest, settled with NIOC in 1989. Atkins pleaded guilty and received probation.

Ashland went on a shopping spree in the 1990s. The company bought Permian (crude oil gathering and marketing) in 1991 and merged it into Scurlock Oil. In 1992 Ashland Chemical bought most of Unocal's chemical distribution business, and two years later it bought two companies that produce chemicals for the semiconductor industry. Also in 1994 Ashland made a promising oil discovery in Nigeria.

The company, by then named Ashland Inc., spent $368 million on 14 acquisitions to expand its energy and chemical divisions in 1995. It received a $75 million settlement with Columbia Gas System (now Columbia Energy Group) for abrogated natural gas contracts resulting from Columbia's bankruptcy.

In 1996 president Paul Chellgren became CEO and, with the company under shareholder fire, began a major reorganization. The next year Arch Mineral and Ashland Coal combined to form Arch Coal, with Ashland owning 58%. Also that year Ashland made more than a dozen acquisitions to bolster its chemical and construction businesses. Its exploration unit, renamed Blazer Energy, was sold to Norway's Statoil for $566 million.

Ashland joined USX-Marathon (now Marathon Oil) in 1998 to create Marathon Ashland Petroleum (now called Marathon Petroleum). It bought 20 companies, including Eagle One Industries, a maker of car-care products, and Masters-Jackson, a group of highway construction companies. Ashland reduced its holdings in Arch Coal from 58% to 12% in 2000; it sold the remainder in early 2001.

In 2002 the company was jolted when Chellgren was forced to retire after violating a company policy prohibiting romantic office relationships. James O'Brien replaced Chellgren.

Ashland had a record year in 2001 but was hampered in 2002 by smaller profits from MAP, which was hurt by reduced demand for petroleum products and tighter margins. Ashland Distribution also hurt the bottom line, which led Ashland to reorganize that unit's management and sales teams.

After that record year Ashland came back to earth with much smaller profits in 2002 and the next year; APAC, particularly, was hit hard in 2003. The construction division swung from $120 million in profits in 2002 to a loss of more than $40 million in 2003; the company attributes the decline to unusual weather conditions, which can greatly affect the construction business more than others. (The pendulum swung back into the black in 2004 with more than $100 million in operating income.)

The company commenced a grand reorganization of its business soon after that. Beginning in 2005 it sold its former petroleum refining joint venture (with Marathon Oil), re-named Marathon Petroleum Company; acquired car cleaning products maker Car Brite for Valvoline; purchased Degussa's water treatment business (operating as Stockhausen); and bought adhesives and coatings company Northwest Coatings. Another big deal, though, provided a complementary book end to the sale of Marathon Petroleum. In 2006 Ashland sold construction unit APAC (which supplied highway materials, built bridges, and paved streets) to Oldcastle Materials for $1.3 billion. The move, coming as it did on the heels of the divestiture of MAP, transformed Ashland into solely a chemicals company.

EXECUTIVES

Chairman and CEO: James J. (Jim) O'Brien Jr., age 55, $5,147,623 total compensation
SVP and CFO: Lamar M. Chambers, age 55, $1,766,768 total compensation
SVP and General Counsel: David L. Hausrath, age 57, $1,627,900 total compensation
VP; President, Ashland Performance Materials; President, Global Supply Chain and Environmental, Health and Safety (EH&S): Theodore L. (Ted) Harris, age 44, $1,263,648 total compensation
VP; President, Consumer Markets: Samuel J. (Sam) Mitchell Jr., age 48, $1,383,821 total compensation
VP and Treasurer: J. Kevin Willis
VP Corporate Development: John W. (Jack) Joy
VP; President, Water Technologies: Paul C. Raymond III, age 47
VP Tax: Scott A. Gregg
VP; President, Ashland Distribution: Robert M. Craycraft II, age 40
VP; President, Functional Ingredients: John E. Panichella, age 51
VP and Controller: J. William Heitman, age 56
VP Human Resources and Communications: Susan B. Esler, age 48
VP Environmental, Health and Safety: Karen T. Murphy
VP and Chief Information and Administrative Services Officer: Anne T. Schumann, age 49
VP Information Systems: Kristy J. Folkwein
VP and Chief Growth Officer; SVP and General Manager, Retail Business, Valvoline: Walter H. Solomon, age 49
Assistant General Counsel and Corporate Secretary: Linda L. Foss
Manager Public Relations: James E. (Jim) Vitak
Director Investor Relations: Eric N. Boni
Auditors: Ernst & Young LLP

LOCATIONS

HQ: Ashland Inc.
50 E. RiverCenter Blvd., Covington, KY 41011
Phone: 859-815-3333   **Fax:** 859-815-5053
Web: www.ashland.com

2009 Sales

	$ mil.	% of total
US	5,083	63
Other countries	3,023	37
Total	**8,106**	**100**

PRODUCTS/OPERATIONS

2009 Sales

	$ mil.	% of total
Distribution	3,020	37
Water Technologies	1,652	20
Consumer Markets	1,650	20
Performance Materials	1,106	13
Functional Ingredients	812	10
Adjustments	(134)	—
Total	**8,106**	**100**

COMPETITORS

Aceto
Arkema
BASF SE
BP Lubricants USA
Brenntag
Chemtura
Cytec
DuPont
Harcros Chemicals
HELM U.S.
Hexion
Hydrite
Jiffy Lube
SABIC Innovative Plastics
Univar

HISTORICAL FINANCIALS

Company Type: Public

Income Statement

FYE: September 30

	REVENUE ($ mil.)	NET INCOME ($ mil.)	NET PROFIT MARGIN	EMPLOYEES
9/09	8,106	71	0.9%	14,700
9/08	8,381	167	2.0%	11,900
9/07	7,834	230	2.9%	11,700
9/06	7,277	407	5.6%	11,700
9/05	9,860	2,004	20.3%	20,900
Annual Growth	(4.8%)	(56.6%)	—	(8.4%)

2009 Year-End Financials

Debt ratio: 42.9%
Return on equity: 2.1%
Cash ($ mil.): 352
Current ratio: 1.58
Long-term debt ($ mil.): 1,537
No. of shares (mil.): 79
Dividends
Yield: 0.7%
Payout: 31.3%
Market value ($ mil.): 3,393

Stock History

NYSE: ASH

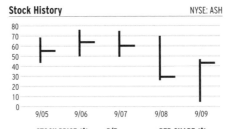

	STOCK PRICE ($) FY Close	P/E High	P/E Low	PER SHARE ($) Earnings	PER SHARE ($) Dividends	PER SHARE ($) Book Value
9/09	43.22	48	6	0.96	0.30	45.65
9/08	29.24	26	10	2.63	1.10	40.79
9/07	60.21	21	14	3.60	1.10	40.18
9/06	63.78	13	9	5.64	1.10	39.44
9/05	55.24	3	2	26.85	1.10	47.63
Annual Growth	(6.0%)	—	—	(56.5%)	(27.7%)	(1.1%)

AT&T Inc.

Through its subsidiaries, affiliates, and operating companies, holding company AT&T is the industry-leading provider of wireline voice communications services in the US. Customers in 22 states use AT&T-branded telephone, Internet, and computer telephone services; it also sells digital TV under the U-verse brand. Key markets include California, Illinois, and Texas. The company's corporate, government, and public sector clients use its range of conferencing, managed network, and wholesale communications services. Subsidiary AT&T Mobility is the nation's second-largest wireless carrier by both sales and subscriptions (after Verizon Wireless). It provides mobile voice and data services to about 85 million subscribers.

Since the purchase of Cingular Wireless and the establishment of AT&T Mobility in 2007, AT&T has pushed its mobile services through increased advertising and marketing efforts that tout the benefits of the mobile Internet. A key component of this has been an exclusive five-year partnership with Apple to carry the iPhone in the US since its debut in the summer of 2007. AT&T has reaped significant rewards from this partnership, which has driven growth and profits of its wireless business, and been instrumental in helping the company become the top US seller of smartphones. The company also gets more money from each subscriber on average than do other carriers.

The winds of change are blowing however in the wireless industry as the AT&T network struggles to handle the increased data demands of its iPhone toting subscribers. Top rival Verizon has also stepped up its smartphone game and grabbed market share by partnering with Motorola to roll out new phones based on Google's Android mobile operating system.

AT&T in mid-2010 purchased assets in 18 states from Verizon Wireless for about $2.3 billion in cash. The deal was part of a previously announced regulatory requirement for Verizon that stipulated that the company had to divest some of its holdings in order to meet approval from the US Department of Justice for its acquisition of Alltel in early 2009. AT&T gained about 1.6 million largely rural customers in the deal as it continues to make investments in the wireless side of its business.

AT&T's organic wireline improvement efforts include a $4.4 billion initiative to build a fiber-optic network, using fiber-to-the-home (FTTH) or fiber-to-the-premises (FTTP) technology, which will enable the company to offer IP-based video, broadband Internet, and VoIP services over a single line. The service (dubbed U-verse) is used by about 2 million high-definition TV subscribers and is intended to increase the appeal of AT&T's bundled communications and video packages over major cable network operators that also offer communications services.

HISTORY

In 1878 a dozen customers signed up for the first telephone exchange in St. Louis (later Bell Telephone Company of Missouri). That exchange and the Missouri and Kansas Telephone Company later merged into Southwestern Bell, which became a regional arm of the AT&T monopoly in 1917.

The old AT&T was broken up in 1984, and Southwestern Bell emerged as a regional Bell operating company (RBOC) with local phone service rights in five states, a cellular company, a directory business, and a stake in R&D arm Bellcore (now Telcordia). In 1987 the company bought paging and cellular franchises from Metromedia.

Edward Whitacre, a Texan who had worked his way from measuring phone wire to an executive spot at Southwestern Bell, became CEO in 1990. That year the RBOC joined with France Telecom and Mexican conglomerate Grupo Carso to purchase 20% of Teléfonos de México (Telmex), the former state monopoly.

The company was renamed SBC Communications in 1994. The federal Telecommunications Act passed in 1996 and in 1997 SBC acquired Pacific Telesis, the parent of Pacific Bell and Nevada Bell. SBC bought Southern New England Telecommunications (SNET) in 1998, gaining a foothold on the East Coast. The next year the company bought Comcast's cellular operations and took a minority stake in Williams Communications Group (now WilTel Communications) — the first significant investment in a long-distance carrier by a Baby Bell.

SBC completed the $62 billion purchase of Ameritech in 1999, after weathering a year-long regulatory review. The acquisition extended SBC's local access dominance into five Midwestern states, but about half of Ameritech's wireless business was sold as a condition of the deal. SBC agreed to provide competitive local phone service in 30 cities outside its home territory by 2002 to win regulatory approval. Also in 1999 the company announced plans to spend $6 billion over three years to make its networks capable of delivering high-speed digital subscriber line (DSL) Internet access to 80% of its customers.

In 2000 SBC combined its US wireless operations with those of BellSouth to form Cingular Wireless, a carrier with operations in 38 states. Also in 2000 the FCC approved SBC's application to sell long-distance service in Texas, and the company racked up more than a million long-distance customers in less than six months.

In 2001 SBC won approval to offer long-distance in Arkansas, Kansas, Missouri, and Oklahoma, but was fined $69 million by the FCC for failing to meet standards for opening its local networks to competitors. The company expanded its long-distance network to include Texas and Connecticut, and entered the lucrative California market, after receiving regulatory approval on a 3-1 vote by the FCC in late 2002.

The recession and what SBC officials called an "outmoded regulatory scheme" drove the company to cut expenses, including deep cuts in its workforce in 2002 and 2003. It sold its 16% stake in Bell Canada to BCE for $3.2 billion and in 2003 it sold its 15% stake in France's Cegetel (now SFR) to Vodafone Group. It also sold stakes in international holdings, including TDC (for about $2.1 billion).

In 2004 Cingular Wireless acquired AT&T Wireless in a cash deal valued at $41 billion, creating the #1 US wireless operator, toppling former market leader Verizon Wireless. Also that year the company sold its interest in a directory publishing partnership in Illinois and Indiana to partner R. H. Donnelley for about $1.45 billion.

SBC acquired AT&T Corp. in 2005 and took that company's more well-known name — AT&T Inc. Whitacre handed over the chief executive reins to COO Randall Stephenson in 2007.

EXECUTIVES

Chairman, President, and CEO: Randall L. Stephenson, age 49, $29,230,506 total compensation
President and CEO, AT&T Operations: John T. Stankey, age 47, $13,033,148 total compensation
President and CEO, AT&T Mobility and Consumer Markets: Ralph de la Vega, age 58, $6,150,645 total compensation
Group President, Corporate Strategy and Development: Forrest E. Miller, age 57, $5,517,097 total compensation
SEVP and General Counsel: Wayne Watts, age 56
SEVP Executive Operations: James W. (Jim) Callaway, age 63
SEVP and CFO: Richard G. (Rick) Lindner, age 55, $10,941,270 total compensation
SEVP Human Resources: William A. (Bill) Blase Jr., age 54
SEVP and Global Marketing Officer: Catherine M. (Cathy) Coughlin, age 52
SEVP External and Legislative Affairs, AT&T Services, Inc: James W. (Jim) Cicconi, age 57, $9,263,762 total compensation
EVP Enterprise Business Sales, AT&T Operations: José M. Gutiérrez, age 45
EVP, AT&T Entertainment Services: Scott C. Helbing
CTO: John M. Donovan
SVP and Chief Security Officer: Edward G. Amoroso
SVP Public Affairs and Chief Sustainability Officer: Charlene Lake
SVP Corporate Development: Rick Moore
SVP Enterprise Information Technology: Michele M. Macauda
SVP and Controller: John J. Stephens, age 50
SVP and Secretary: Ann Effinger Meuleman
SVP Talent Development and Chief Development Officer: Cynthia J. (Cindy) Brinkley, age 50
SVP Corporate Real Estate, AT&T Operations: Mark Schleyer
SVP Investor Relations: Richard C. (Rich) Dietz, age 59
SVP Corporate Communications: Larry Solomon
Auditors: Ernst & Young LLP

LOCATIONS

HQ: AT&T Inc.
208 S. Akard St., Dallas, TX 75202
Phone: 210-821-4105
Web: www.att.com

PRODUCTS/OPERATIONS

2009 Sales

	% of total
Wireless	40
Wireline	
Voice	27
Data	22
Other	11
Total	**100**

Selected Services

Voice
  Local
  Long-distance
  Wholesale

Data
  Application management
  Data equipment sales
  Data storage
  Database management
  Dedicated Internet service
  Digital television
  Directory and operator assistance
  Disaster recovery
  Enterprise networking
  Hardware and operating system management
  Internet access and network integration
  Managed Web hosting
  Network design
  Network implementation
  Network installation
  Network integration
  Network management
  Outsourcing
  Packet services
  Private lines
  Satellite video
  Switched and dedicated transport
  Voice-over-IP networks
  Wholesale networking
  WiFi

COMPETITORS

Cablevision Systems	Global Crossing
CenturyTel	Level 3 Communications
Charter Communications	Qwest Communications
Comcast	Sprint Nextel
Consolidated	TDS Metrocom
Communications	Telephone & Data Systems
Cox Communications	T-Mobile USA
DIRECTV	tw telecom
DISH Network	U.S. Cellular
EarthLink	Verizon

HISTORICAL FINANCIALS

Company Type: Public

Income Statement

FYE: December 31

	REVENUE ($ mil.)	NET INCOME ($ mil.)	NET PROFIT MARGIN	EMPLOYEES
12/09	123,018	12,535	10.2%	282,720
12/08	124,028	12,867	10.4%	301,000
12/07	118,928	11,951	10.0%	310,000
12/06	63,055	7,356	11.7%	302,000
12/05	43,862	4,786	10.9%	189,000
Annual Growth	29.4%	27.2%	—	10.6%

2009 Year-End Financials

Debt ratio: 63.5%   No. of shares (mil.): 5,909
Return on equity: 12.6%   Dividends
Cash ($ mil.): 3,802   Yield: 5.9%
Current ratio: 0.66   Payout: 77.8%
Long-term debt ($ mil.): 64,720 Market value ($ mil.): 165,629

Stock History

NYSE: T

	STOCK PRICE ($) FY Close	P/E High/Low		PER SHARE ($) Earnings	Dividends	Book Value
12/09	28.03	14	10	2.12	1.65	17.24
12/08	28.50	19	10	2.16	2.01	16.31
12/07	41.56	22	16	1.94	1.42	19.52
12/06	35.75	19	13	1.89	1.00	19.55
12/05	24.49	18	15	1.42	1.30	9.26
Annual Growth	3.4%	—	—	10.5%	6.1%	16.8%

Autodesk, Inc.

Autodesk has creative designs on moving past the desks of architects. The company is a provider of computer-aided design (CAD) software. Its flagship AutoCAD product is used primarily by architects and engineers to design, draft, and model products and buildings. Autodesk's other products include geographic information systems (GIS) packages for mapping and precision drawing software for drafting. The company also develops multimedia tools for digital content creation, including applications for animation, film editing, and creating special effects. In addition, Autodesk offers professional consulting and training services.

Autodesk has strategically pursued acquisitions that both round out its product lines and intellectual property as well as deals that expand its customer base in key industries and geographical locations. In early 2009 Autodesk purchased ALGOR, a provider of digital prototyping tools, and in January 2010 the company bought the Dynamite visualization software line from 3AM Solutions. In 2010 it also purchased Illuminate Labs, which provides lighting technology for video game makers.

The company is also focusing on moving its customers from its 2-D to 3-D modeling products (which typically carry a higher price tag) as well as working to shift clients to its subscription licensing program, which results in a more efficient sales process and greater customer loyalty.

Autodesk relies heavily on its network of about 1,700 resellers and distributors worldwide; its indirect sales channel was responsible for 86% of sales in fiscal 2009.

Autodesk spun off its Location Services business in 2009. Retaining a minority stake, it sold the unit to Hale Capital Partners, which formed a new company called LocationLogic. The company also announced in 2009 a restructuring effort that included plans to reduce its workforce by about 10%.

HISTORY

John Walker founded Autodesk in 1982 as a diversified PC software supplier, and when he bought the software rights to AutoCAD from inventor Michael Riddle, Autodesk took off. While competitors went after more complex computer systems, Autodesk focused on PC software. When PC sales boomed in the early 1980s, the firm was there to take advantage of a growing market. Autodesk went public in 1985.

The company established a multimedia unit and released its first animation tool, 3D Studio, in 1990. In 1993 Autodesk acquired 3-D graphics specialist Ithaca Software. That year Autodesk lost a trade secret lawsuit to Vermont Microsystems and was ordered to pay $25.5 million; the fine was later lowered to $7.8 million.

In 1996 the company spun off its multimedia unit as Kinetix, geared toward 3-D PC and Web applications. Continuing its acquisition drive, Autodesk bought interior decorating software developer Creative Imaging Technologies in 1996 and rival CAD software developer Softdesk in 1997.

In an effort to expand its presence in the entertainment software realm, the company bought digital video effects and editing tools maker Discreet Logic for $520 million in 1999. Later that year Autodesk bolstered its geographic information systems division by acquiring Canadian mapping software company VISION*Solutions from WorldCom for $26 million. Product delays helped prompt Autodesk that year to reorganize into four divisions, and cut 350 jobs — about 10% of its workforce.

Late in 1999 the firm spun off Buzzsaw.com, an Internet portal aimed at the design and construction industry. The next year Autodesk spun off its second portal, RedSpark, targeting the manufacturing industry.

In 2001 the company re-acquired the 60% stake in Buzzsaw.com it had previously spun off. The next year Autodesk acquired architectural software provider Revit Technology for about $130 million. As part of a larger restructuring, the company also discontinued its RedSpark portal operations.

Autodesk continues to focus on leveraging its products online, targeting the manufacturing and construction industries. In 2002 the company acquired privately held CAiCE Software. With the purchase, Autodesk formed a Transportation Group to develop applications for designing highways, airports, and railroads.

The company made two small acquisitions in early 2003, both of which were absorbed within Autodesk's Manufacturing Solutions Division. Linius Technologies developed software allowing wire harness designers to develop 3-D prototypes. VIA Development provided electrical schematics, wire diagram, and controls engineering automation software.

Autodesk completed its acquisition of 3-D graphics software developer Alias Systems for $197 million in cash early in 2006. Also that year the company purchased construction and facility project management software developer Constructware for $46 million and it took a stake in engineering software developer Hanna Strategies; in late 2007 Autodesk purchased the rest of Hanna Strategies in order to strengthen its development of digital prototyping products.

In 2008 the company acquired Moldflow, 3D Geo GmbH (3-D urban models software), Hanna Strategies Holdings (software development), Softimage (3-D technology for films and games), and Robobat (analysis engines).

EXECUTIVES

Chairman: Crawford W. Beveridge, age 64
President, CEO, and Director: Carl Bass, age 52, $6,230,916 total compensation
EVP Sales and Services: George M. Bado, $2,001,901 total compensation
EVP and CFO: Mark J. Hawkins, age 52, $2,790,318 total compensation
Chief Education Officer and EVP Location Services Division: Joseph H. (Joe) Astroth, age 54
SVP and Chief Marketing Officer: Chris Bradshaw, age 46
SVP Media and Entertainment: Marc Petit, age 44
SVP Platform Solutions and Emerging Business: Amar Hanspal, age 45
SVP Manufacturing: Robert (Buzz) Kross, age 56, $1,262,482 total compensation
SVP Human Resources: Jan Becker, age 57, $1,370,659 total compensation
SVP Architecture, Engineering and Construction: Jay Bhatt, age 40, $1,647,828 total compensation
SVP, General Counsel, and Secretary: Pascal W. Di Fronzo, age 44
SVP Strategic Planning and Operations: Moonhie K. Chin, age 52
SVP Americas Sales: Steven (Steve) Blum
VP Corporate Communications: Pamela L. (Pam) Pollace
Director Investor Relations: David V. Gennarelli
Auditors: Ernst & Young LLP

LOCATIONS

HQ: Autodesk, Inc.
111 McInnis Pkwy., San Rafael, CA 94903
Phone: 415-507-5000   **Fax:** 415-507-5100
Web: usa.autodesk.com

2010 Sales

	$ mil.	% of total
Europe, Middle East & Africa	671	39
Americas	655	38
Asia/Pacific	388	23
Total	**1,714**	**100**

PRODUCTS/OPERATIONS

2010 Sales

	$ mil.	% of total
License & other	981	57
Maintenance	733	43
Total	**1,714**	**100**

Selected Software

2-D and 3-D mechanical design (Mechanical Desktop)
3-D modeling and animation (3ds max)
Architectural design tools (AutoCAD Architectural Desktop)
Computer-aided design tool (AutoCAD)
Digital editing (fire)
Geographic data analysis (Autodesk World)
Low-cost 2-D CAD tool (AutoCAD LT)
Mapmaking and engineering-based analysis (AutoCAD Map)
Online digital image processing system (inferno)
Online, nonlinear editing and finishing (smoke)
Precision drawing tool (AutoSketch)
Production application for broadcast market (frost)
Real-time, nonlinear, digital image processing system (flame)

COMPETITORS

Adobe Systems
Advanced Visual Systems
ANSYS
Apple Inc.
Avid Technology
Axion
Bentley Systems
Dassault
ESRI
Google
Intergraph
Mentor Graphics
Moldflow
MSC.Software
Nemetschek North America
Parametric Technology
PlanGraphics
Siemens PLM Software
SofTech
Sony
Tele Atlas
Vero Software
Vizrt

HISTORICAL FINANCIALS

Company Type: Public

Income Statement

	REVENUE ($ mil.)	NET INCOME ($ mil.)	NET PROFIT MARGIN	EMPLOYEES
1/10	1,714	58	3.4%	6,800
1/09	2,315	184	7.9%	7,800
1/08	2,172	356	16.4%	7,300
1/07	1,840	290	15.7%	5,169
1/06	1,523	329	21.6%	4,813
Annual Growth	**3.0%**	**(35.2%)**	**—**	**9.0%**

FYE: January 31

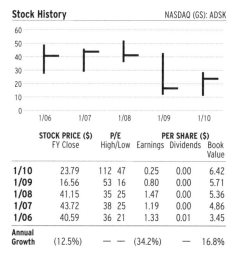
Automatic Data Processing

The original outsourcer, Automatic Data Processing (ADP) has still got it. ADP is one of the largest payroll and tax filing processors in the world, serving about 570,000 clients. Employer services account for the majority of the company's sales; ADP also provides inventory and other computing and data services to some 25,000 auto, motorcycle, truck, and recreational vehicle dealers. Other offerings include accounting, auto collision estimates for insurers, employment background checks, desktop applications support, and business development training services. ADP also provides outsourcing services to Broadridge Financial Solutions, the former brokerage services division it spun off in 2007.

The data processing giant's employer services segment has proven somewhat resilient in economic hard times as clients outsource more human resource functions. Like most players involved with the auto industry, however, ADP's dealer services felt the effects of the recession as the volume of vehicle purchases drastically declined throughout 2009. To prepare for the hit, ADP restructured the segment's cost structure. Additionally, early in the year the company bought Automaster, a Finnish company specializing in vehicle dealer and importer management systems. The acquisition allowed ADP to expand into new markets including the Nordic region, Central and Eastern Europe, and Russia.

A short time later ADP set its sights on China when it purchased a majority share in ChinaLink Professional Services, a firm providing outsourced human resources based in Shanghai. In late 2009 ADP snatched up HRinterax, an HR support services firm catering exclusively to small businesses.

In January 2010 ADP expanded into Canada with the acquisition of DO2 Technologies. Based in Calgary, DO2 Technologies provides electronic invoicing software that assists users with integrating purchase orders, processing transactions, and approving payments.

Months later, ADP announced it was buying Workscape, a provider of software that performs human resources management and benefits administration functions. The deal is projected to enhance ADP's own ability to provide benefits and administration functions, primarily for larger organizations. Workscape caters to 3.5 million users with services deployed in more than 180 countries.

Not one to rest, in the summer of 2010, ADP also acquired online car marketing agency Cobalt for about $400 million.

HISTORY

In 1949, 22-year-old Henry Taub started Automatic Payrolls, a manual payroll preparation service in Paterson, New Jersey. Taub's eight accounts created gross revenue of around $2,000 that year. In 1952 his brother Joe joined the company, and a childhood friend, Frank Lautenberg, took a pay cut to become its first salesman.

Automatic Payrolls grew steadily during the 1950s. In 1961 the company went public and changed its name to Automatic Data Processing (ADP). The next year it offered back-office services to brokerage houses and bought its first computer. The company's sales reached $1 million in 1962.

During the 1970s ADP bought more than 30 companies in Brazil, the UK, and the US — all involved in data and payroll processing or financial services. Its stock began trading on the NYSE in 1970. By 1971 revenue had reached $50 million. Lautenberg became CEO in 1975.

ADP bought more than 25 businesses during the 1980s in Canada, Germany, and the US. Its purchases of stock information provider GTE Telenet (1983) and Bunker Ramo's information system business (1986) brought the company 45,000 stock quote terminals in brokerages such as E.F. Hutton, Dean Witter, and Prudential-Bache. When Lautenberg resigned to become one of New Jersey's US senators in 1983, Josh Weston, who had joined the company as a VP in 1970, replaced him.

By 1985 ADP sales had climbed to $1 billion. That year Taub retired. The company installed 15,000 computer workstations at brokerages in 1986; it began installing more than 38,000 new integrated workstations at Merrill Lynch and Shearson Lehman three years later. ADP shed units, including its Canadian stock quote and Brazilian businesses, in 1989 and 1990.

After being deterred from major acquisitions by the inflated prices of the late 1980s, the company bought BankAmerica's 17,000-client Business Services division (1992) and Industry Software's back-office and international equities business (1993). In 1994 the company purchased Peachtree Software (accounting and payroll software for small companies), National Bio Systems (medical bill auditing), and V-Crest (auto dealership management systems). ADP acquired chief rival AutoInfo and its network of 3,000 salvage yards the next year, and further expanded into Western Europe with its purchase of Paris-based computing services firm GSI.

The buying binge continued in 1996 with acquisitions including Global Proxy Services (proxy processing services), Health Benefits

America (benefits management), and Merrin Financial (automated securities trade order management). Former Deloitte & Touche partner Arthur Weinbach, an ADP executive since 1980, was named CEO that year. ADP was ordered in an antitrust settlement in 1997 to help re-create AutoInfo as a viable competitor to its salvage yard business.

Weston retired in 1998; Weinbach was named chairman. The company also filed to spin off Peachtree to the public, but in early 1999 it sold the unit to UK-based software firm The Sage Group. The buying spree continued that year; ADP's largest purchase was The Vincam Group, an employment management contractor.

In 2000 the company acquired Cunningham Graphics, a provider of printing services to the financial services industry, and Traver Technologies, which offers consulting and training services to automobile dealers in the US. In 2003 the company bought ProBusiness Services, a payroll and human resource processing service provider, for about $500 million. The next year ADP purchased EDS's Automotive Retail Group, a provider of dealer management systems, as well as ProQuest Business Solutions' DMS business.

In 2006 Weinbach retired as chairman and CEO, and former president and COO Gary Butler was elevated to top executive at that time. The same year, ADP sold its Claims Services Group (CSG) to Solera and GTCR Golder Rauner for $975 million.

PRODUCTS/OPERATIONS

2009 Sales

	$ mil.	% of total
Employer services	6,587.7	72
Dealer services	1,348.6	15
PEO services	1,185.8	13
Other	19.5	—
Adjustments	(274.5)	—
Total	**8,867.1**	**100**

Selected Services

Dealer Services
  Business management
  Computer systems sales
  Employee productivity training
  Hardware maintenance
  Manufacturer and dealer data communications
    networks
  Software licensing and support
  Vehicle registration services

Employer Services
  401(k) record keeping and reporting
  Benefits administration and outsourcing
  Employment screening and background checks
  Human resource record keeping and reporting
  Payroll processing
  Tax filing
  Unemployment compensation management

COMPETITORS

Administaff	Hewitt Associates
Avatar Systems	HP Enterprise Services
CBIZ	Intuit
Ceridian	Paychex
Computer Sciences Corp.	Reynolds and Reynolds
Enertia Software	TriNet Group

HISTORICAL FINANCIALS

Company Type: Public

Income Statement

FYE: June 30

	REVENUE ($ mil.)	NET INCOME ($ mil.)	NET PROFIT MARGIN	EMPLOYEES
6/09	8,867	1,333	15.0%	45,000
6/08	8,777	1,236	14.1%	47,000
6/07	7,800	1,139	14.6%	46,000
6/06	8,882	1,554	17.5%	46,000
6/05	8,500	1,055	12.4%	44,000
Annual Growth	**1.1%**	**6.0%**	**—**	**0.6%**

2009 Year-End Financials

Debt ratio: 0.8%
Return on equity: 25.6%
Cash ($ mil.): 2,265
Current ratio: 1.10
Long-term debt ($ mil.): 43

No. of shares (mil.): 503
Dividends
  Yield: 3.6%
  Payout: 48.7%
Market value ($ mil.): 17,826

Stock History

NASDAQ (GS): ADP

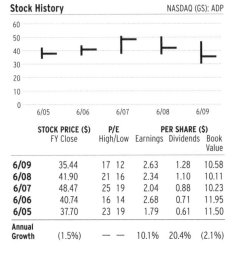

	STOCK PRICE ($) FY Close	P/E High/Low		PER SHARE ($) Earnings	Dividends	Book Value
6/09	35.44	17	12	2.63	1.28	10.58
6/08	41.90	21	16	2.34	1.10	10.11
6/07	48.47	25	19	2.04	0.88	10.23
6/06	40.74	16	14	2.68	0.71	11.95
6/05	37.70	23	19	1.79	0.61	11.50
Annual Growth	**(1.5%)**	**—**	**—**	**10.1%**	**20.4%**	**(2.1%)**

AutoNation, Inc.

AutoNation wants to instill patriotic fervor in the fickle car-buying public. The brainchild of entrepreneur and ex-chairman Wayne Huizenga (Waste Management, Blockbuster Video), Auto-Nation is the #1 car dealer in the US (ahead of Penske Automotive Group and Group 1 Automotive). The firm owns about 250 new-vehicle franchises (down from 300 in 2008) in 15 states, and it conducts online sales through AutoNation.com and individual dealer websites. AutoNation operates under different brands in local markets (including Mike Shad in Jacksonville, Florida, and Go in Colorado). In addition to auto sales, AutoNation provides maintenance and repair services, sells auto parts, and finances and insures vehicles.

With vehicle sales in a ditch as a result of the deep recession and tight credit in the US, AutoNation's revenue declined. Sales of new vehicles (more than 50% of AutoNation's total sales) were hit harder than used vehicles, which also declined steeply. Indeed, new vehicle sales would have been worse if not for the US government's "cash for clunkers" program.

Sales at the company's domestic franchises, relative to its import and luxury dealerships, have been particularly hard hit. (Not surprisingly, the auto dealer is finding it especially hard to sell new vehicles in California and Florida.) Over the past decade AutoNation has increased the percentage of import and luxury cars it sells.

While AutoNation sells more than 30 different brands of new vehicles, its core car brands are Toyota, Ford, Honda, Nissan, General Motors, Mercedes, BMW, and Chrysler. With Chrysler and GM (together with Ford) comprising the company's domestic franchise business, the Chrysler and GM bankruptcies have been a major headache for the autodealer. It saw seven of its 16 Chrysler dealerships close in 2009 as a result of the automaker's shuttering of nearly 800 dealerships nationwide.

The economic turmoil has caused AutoNation and other megadealers to put the brakes on acquisitions and divest domestic-brand dealerships. Historically, AutoNation has been a driving force in the consolidation of the US car-sales business. It clusters dealerships within markets so that they can share inventory, cross-sell to customers, and reduce marketing costs — basically cutting and combining costs in an attempt to become the auto industry's Wal-Mart.

Billionaire investor and former AutoNation director Edward Lampert has been steadily increasing his stake in AutoNation through his hedge fund ESL Investments, which in 2009 owned about 47% of the company's shares.

HISTORY

AutoNation started in 1980 as Republic Resources, which brokered petroleum leases, did exploration and production, and blended lubricants. In 1989, after oil prices crashed and a stockholder group tried to force Republic into liquidation, Browning-Ferris Industries (BFI) founder Thomas Fatjo gained control of the company and refocused it on a field he knew well — solid waste. He renamed the firm Republic Waste.

Michael DeGroote, founder of BFI rival Laidlaw, bought into Republic in 1990. (Fatjo left the next year.) DeGroote's investment funded more acquisitions. Republic moved into hazardous waste in 1992, just before the industry nosedived due to stringent new environmental rules. In 1994 Republic spun off its hazardous-waste operations as Republic Environmental Systems, and Republic's stock began rising immediately.

That attracted the attention of Wayne Huizenga, who had founded Waste Management and Blockbuster Video. To him, Republic was not merely a midsized solid-waste firm. No, Huizenga saw Republic as a publicly traded vehicle that could allow him to tap into the stock market to fund his latest project: an integrated, nationwide auto dealer — a first for the highly fragmented and localized industry.

In 1995 Republic bought Hudson Management, a trash business owned by Huizenga's brother-in-law, and Huizenga bought a large interest in Republic. As a result, Huizenga took control of Republic's board. The firm became Republic Industries, and DeGroote stepped back from active management.

Huizenga's investment helped Republic acquire more waste businesses, and his name brought a flood of new investors. The firm diversified with electronic security acquisitions, but growth in this field faltered with a failed bid to buy market leader ADT in 1996. (Republic sold its security division to Ameritech in 1997.)

By 1996 Huizenga's still-separate auto concept, AutoNation, was operational, with 55 automobile franchises and seven used-car stores. Republic bought Alamo Rent A Car and National Car Rental System, and in 1997 AutoNation was bought by Republic. The combined company continued buying dealerships and car rental firms at a sizzling rate.

Republic spun off its solid-waste operations to the public in 1998 as Republic Services. That year Republic bought or agreed to buy 181 new-car franchises, opened nine AutoNation USA dealerships, and opened 62 CarTemps USA insurance-replacement locations.

Republic became AutoNation in 1999 and announced plans to spin off its rental division. In September 1999 Mike Jackson, the former president and CEO of Mercedes-Benz USA, was named CEO of AutoNation. In December the company closed most of its poorly performing used-car superstores and laid off about 1,800 employees.

In May 2000 AutoNation acquired AutoVantage, an online car-buying service linking more than 900 dealerships. Later the company completed its spinoff of ANC Rental (Alamo, National, and CarTemps, with more than 3,400 rental car locations worldwide), making AutoNation a pure-play auto retailer.

In 2001 AutoNation closed its auto-loan unit to further focus on car sales. Huizenga retired as chairman of the company at the end of 2002. Jackson assumed the chairmanship while continuing in his role as CEO.

In March 2003 AutoNation agreed to pay the IRS about $470 million in relation to the tax treatment of some 1997-1999 transactions. It bought a dealership that accounts for some 10% of Mercedes-Benz USA sales, Glauser Mercedes-Benz in Sarasota, Florida, in May 2004. The dealership is now called Mercedes-Benz of Sarasota.

In early 2008 the company acquired Don Mackey BMW in Tucson, Arizona, and renamed the dealership BMW Tucson.

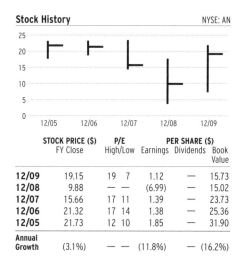
AutoZone, Inc.

Imagine that you are in your garage making some weekend car repairs. The wheel cylinders are leaking . . . the brake shoe adjuster nut is rusted solid . . . you're about to enter . . . the AutoZone. With some 4,230 stores in the US and Puerto Rico, AutoZone is the nation's #1 auto parts chain. It also operates more than 185 stores in Mexico. AutoZone stores sell hard parts (alternators, engines, batteries), maintenance items (oil, antifreeze), accessories (car stereos, floor mats), and non-automotive merchandise under brand names as well as under private labels, including Duralast and Valucraft. AutoZone's commercial sales program distributes parts and other products to garages, dealerships, and other businesses.

AutoZone also loans tools and sells merchandise and diagnostic and repair advice online. In addition to auto parts, the stores also offer diagnostic testing for starters, alternators, and batteries. (The shops do not sell tires or perform general auto repairs.) AutoZone's ALLDATA unit sells automotive diagnostic and repair software to more than 70,000 repair facilities.

The recession in the US has been good for business at AutoZone as cash-strapped consumers deferred new car purchases in 2008 and 2009 in favor of keeping old clunkers on the road. Sales and profits rose in fiscal 2009 and same-store-sales (considered the best indicator of a retailer's performance) rose 4.4% in fiscal 2009 versus just 0.4% in the previous year.

AutoZone has grown quickly through a series of acquisitions over the past several years but now is focused on internal growth and development. Among the factors AutoZone considers when opening new stores — at a rate of 150 to 200 per year — is how many cars in an area are OKVs or "our kind of vehicles," that is, cars older than seven years and no longer under their manufacturers' warranty. (With the US auto industry in the tank, more and more consumers are driving older cars.) AutoZone is also growing quickly in Mexico, where cars are even older — and in need of more repairs — than in the US.

ESL Partners, controlled by Edward Lampert, owns about 41% of the company. In December 2006 Lampert stepped down from AutoZone's board, sparking speculation that ESL might sell its stake in the company. However, Lampert has said that ESL plans to remain a significant shareholder in AutoZone for the foreseeable future.

HISTORY

Joseph "Pitt" Hyde took over the family grocery wholesale business, Malone & Hyde (established 1907) in 1968. He expanded into specialty retailing, opening drugstores, sporting goods stores, and supermarkets, but his fortunes began to race on Independence Day 1979, when he opened his first Auto Shack auto parts store in Forrest City, Arkansas.

Using retailing behemoth Wal-Mart as a model, Hyde concentrated on smaller markets in the South and Southeast, emphasizing everyday low prices and centralized distribution operations. He stressed customer service to provide his do-it-yourself customers with expert advice on choosing parts. While a number of retailers have tried to copy Wal-Mart's successful model, Hyde had an inside track: Before starting Auto Shack he served on Wal-Mart's board for seven years.

Auto Shack had expanded into seven states by 1980, and by 1983 it had 129 stores in 10 states. The next year Malone & Hyde's senior management, with investment firm Kohlberg Kravis Roberts (KKR), took the company private in an LBO. Auto Shack continued to expand, reaching 192 stores in 1984.

A year later Auto Shack introduced its Express Parts Service, the first service in the industry to offer a toll-free number and overnight delivery of parts. The following year it introduced another first: a limited lifetime warranty on its merchandise. Also in 1986 Auto Shack introduced its own Duralast line of auto products.

The company was spun off to Malone & Hyde's shareholders in 1987, and Malone & Hyde's other operations were sold. Auto Shack brought its electronic parts catalog online that year. The company changed its name to AutoZone in 1987, in part to settle a lawsuit with RadioShack. By this time it had 390 stores in 15 states.

The company went public in 1991. By the end of that year, it had nearly 600 stores and five distribution centers. The company topped $1 billion in sales in 1992. The next year it opened new distribution centers in Illinois and Tennessee and closed its Memphis operation.

AutoZone began selling to commercial customers such as service stations and repair shops in 1996. It also acquired auto diagnostic software company ALLDATA. Hyde stepped down as CEO that year and as chairman in 1997 and was replaced by COO Johnston (John) Adams.

The company made several key purchases in 1998. It acquired Chief Auto Parts for $280 million, adding 560 stores (most in California) that were converted to AutoZones in 1999. It also purchased Adap and its 112 Auto Palace stores in the Northeast, heavy-duty truck parts distributor TruckPro, and (from Pep Boys) 100 Express stores. Also in 1998 AutoZone opened its first store in Mexico (Nuevo Laredo).

Hyde sold much of his stake by early 1999. Late that year AutoZone expanded its board of directors to 10 members, making room for increasingly active longtime shareholder Edward Lampert.

In January 2001 Steve Odland, formerly COO at supermarket retailer Ahold USA, succeeded Adams as chairman and CEO. In December 2001

AutoZone sold its TruckPro subsidiary to an investor group led by Paratus Capital Management of Boston and New York.

Odland resigned in 2005 to become CEO of Office Depot. He was replaced by Bill Rhodes, AutoZone's former EVP of Store Operations and Commercial. In fiscal 2009 the company opened 40 new stores in Mexico, more than doubling its presence there since 2005.

EXECUTIVES

Chairman, President, and CEO:
William C. (Bill) Rhodes III, age 45,
$3,208,830 total compensation
CFO, EVP Finance, IT and Store Development:
William T. (Bill) Giles, age 51,
$1,653,877 total compensation
EVP Merchandising, Marketing and Supply Chain:
James A. (Jim) Shea, age 65,
$1,561,051 total compensation
EVP, Secretary and General Counsel:
Harry L. Goldsmith, age 59,
$1,408,987 total compensation
Corporate Development Officer: Robert D. (Bob) Olsen, age 57, $1,632,585 total compensation
SVP Human Resources: Timothy W. Briggs, age 49
SVP and Store Operations: Thomas B. Newbern, age 48
SVP and CIO: Jon A. Bascom, age 53
SVP Supply Chain: William W. Graves, age 50
SVP Merchandising: Mark A. Finestone, age 49
SVP Marketing: Lisa R. Kranc, age 57
SVP, Controller: Charlie Pleas III, age 45
SVP Commercial: Larry M. Roesel, age 53
VP Goverment and Community Relations:
Raymond A. Pohlman
VP Treasury, Investor Relations, and Tax:
Brian L. Campbell
Auditors: Ernst & Young LLP

LOCATIONS

HQ: AutoZone, Inc.
123 S. Front St., Memphis, TN 38103
Phone: 901-495-6500   **Fax:** 901-495-8300
Web: www.autozone.com

2009 Stores

	No.
US	
Texas	525
California	447
Ohio	219
Illinois	208
Florida	196
Georgia	175
North Carolina	164
Tennessee	150
Michigan	145
Indiana	137
Arizona	119
New York	114
Pennsylvania	109
Louisiana	108
Missouri	100
Alabama	97
Virginia	87
Mississippi	85
Kentucky	78
South Carolina	75
Oklahoma	67
Massachusetts	66
Colorado	62
New Jersey	61
Arkansas	59
New Mexico	58
Washington	53
Wisconsin	50
Nevada	49
Maryland	39
Utah	39
Kansas	38
Connecticut	35
Oregon	27
Other states	190
Mexico	188
Total	**4,417**

PRODUCTS/OPERATIONS

2009 Sales

	$ mil.	% of total
Auto parts stores	6,671.9	98
Other	144.9	2
Total	**6,816.8**	**100**

Selected Merchandise

Accessories
  Car stereos
  Floor mats
  Lights
  Mirrors
Hard Parts
  Alternators
  Batteries
  Brake shoes and pads
  Carburetors
  Clutches
  Engines
  Spark plugs
  Starters
  Struts
  Water pumps
Maintenance Items
  Antifreeze
  Brake fluid
  Engine additives
  Oil
  Power steering fluid
  Transmission fluid
  Waxes
  Windshield wipers
Other
  Air fresheners
  Dent filler
  Hand cleaner
  Paint
  Repair manuals
  Tools

Selected Brands

ALLDATA
AutoZone
Duralast
Duralast Gold
Valucraft

COMPETITORS

Advance Auto Parts
CARQUEST
Costco Wholesale
Fisher Auto Parts
Genuine Parts
Goodyear Tire & Rubber
Kmart
O'Reilly Automotive
Pep Boys
Sears
Target
Wal-Mart

HISTORICAL FINANCIALS

Company Type: Public

Income Statement

FYE: Last Saturday in August

	REVENUE ($ mil.)	NET INCOME ($ mil.)	NET PROFIT MARGIN	EMPLOYEES
8/09	6,817	657	9.6%	60,000
8/08	6,523	642	9.8%	57,000
8/07	6,170	596	9.7%	55,000
8/06	5,948	569	9.6%	53,000
8/05	5,711	571	10.0%	52,000
Annual Growth	**4.5%**	**3.6%**	**—**	**3.6%**

2009 Year-End Financials

Debt ratio: —
Return on equity: —
Cash ($ mil.): 93
Current ratio: 0.95
Long-term debt ($ mil.): 2,727
No. of shares (mil.): 47
Dividends
  Yield: —
  Payout: —
Market value ($ mil.): 6,922

Stock History

NYSE: AZO

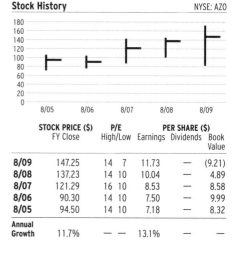

	STOCK PRICE ($) FY Close	P/E High/Low		Earnings	PER SHARE ($) Dividends	Book Value
8/09	147.25	14	7	11.73	—	(9.21)
8/08	137.23	14	10	10.04	—	4.89
8/07	121.29	16	10	8.53	—	8.58
8/06	90.30	14	10	7.50	—	9.99
8/05	94.50	14	10	7.18	—	8.32
Annual Growth	**11.7%**	**—**	**—**	**13.1%**	**—**	**—**

Avery Dennison

Avery Dennison is easy to label: It's a global leader in the making of adhesive labels used on packaging, mailers, and other items. Pressure-sensitive adhesives and materials account for more than half of the company's sales. Under the Avery Dennison and Fasson brands, the company makes papers, films, and foils coated with adhesive and sold in rolls to printers. The company also makes school and office products (Avery, Marks-A-Lot, HI-LITER) such as notebooks, three-ring binders, markers, fasteners, business forms, tickets, tags, and imprinting equipment. Perhaps its most widely used products are the self-adhesive stamps used by the US Postal Service since 1974.

The company, which operates manufacturing facilities and sales offices around the world, has been expanding its international operations through acquisitions, especially in China. The expansion benefitted the company to such an extent that the ratio of Avery Dennison's US sales to its international sales went from 60-40 in 2001 to less than 35-65 in 2008. The company has also expanded in India; its operations in China and India focus on local printers that supply local demand. Avery Dennison is also expanding in Japan, where it has invested in a new distribution center.

In 2007 the company made a major move to expand its Retail Information Services unit, which offers products and services to retailers such as the design and production of labels and tags, as well as supply-chain management services. Avery Dennison spent $1.3 billion to buy Paxar, whose strength in the European market greatly enhances Avery Dennison's own, mostly US, business. The next year it acquired the Taiwanese label maker DM Label Group, which operates in five Asian countries, as well as the US.

Responding to the decreased demand caused by a slumping global economy in 2009 Avery Dennison announced that it was cutting about 10% of its workforce (about 3,600 jobs), and taking other measures to reduce costs.

HISTORY

Avery Dennison was created in 1990 by the merger of Avery International and Dennison Manufacturing. In 1935 Stanton Avery founded Kum-Kleen Products, which would become Avery International. After a fire destroyed the plant's equipment in 1938, Avery, who had renamed the company Avery Adhesives, improved the machinery used in making the labels.

During and after WWII, Avery Adhesives shifted toward the industrial market for self-adhesives. The company incorporated in 1946. At that time Avery Adhesives sold 80% of its production, consisting of industrial labels, to manufacturers that labeled their own products.

The company lost its patent rights for self-adhesive labels in 1952, transforming the firm and the entire industry. As a result, a new division was created — the Avery Paper Company (later renamed Fasson) — to produce and market self-adhesive base materials.

Avery Adhesives went public in 1961. Three years later it had four divisions: label products, base materials, Rotex (hand-operated embossing machines), and Metal-Cal (anodized and etched aluminum foil for nameplates). Renamed Avery International in 1976, the company closed some manufacturing facilities and cut 8% of its workforce in the late 1980s.

In 1990 Avery International merged with Dennison Manufacturing. Dennison was started in 1844 by the father-and-son team of Andrew and Aaron Dennison to produce jewelry boxes. By 1849 Aaron's younger brother, Eliphalet Whorf (E.W.), was running the business and expanding it into tags, labels, and tissue paper. Dennison was incorporated in 1878 with $150,000 in capital.

By 1911 Dennison sold tags, gummed labels, paper boxes, greeting cards, sealing wax, and tissue paper, and it had stores in Boston, Chicago, New York City, Philadelphia, St. Louis, and London. Henry Dennison, E.W.'s grandson, was president from 1917 to 1952.

From the 1960s to the 1980s, Dennison spent heavily on research and development and helped to develop such products as electronic printers and pregnancy test supplies. In the mid-1980s the firm reorganized its operations, selling seven businesses, closing four others, and focusing on stationery, systems, and packaging.

In addition to office products and product identification and control systems, the 1990 merger combined Dennison's office products operations in France (Doret and Cheval Ordex) with Avery International's sizable self-adhesive base materials business.

Avery Dennison sold its 50% interest in a Japanese label converting company, Toppan, in 1996, clearing the way to develop its own businesses in Asia. In 1997 an alliance with Taiwanese rival Four Pillars turned sour when Avery Dennison accused the company of stealing trade secrets. (Two executives at Four Pillars were convicted of corporate espionage in 1999.)

President and COO Philip Neal was promoted to CEO in 1998. (He became chairman in 2000.) In 1999, adhering to its goal of global expansion, Avery Dennison formed office products joint ventures in Germany with Zweckform Buro-Produkte and in Japan with Hitachi Maxell.

Record 1998 sales and earnings were dampened by the news of slowing growth, and in 1999 Avery Dennison closed five plants and began laying off workers. Later that year the company bought Stimsonite, a maker of reflective highway safety products.

In early 2000 Avery Dennison began a $40 million expansion of its Chinese manufacturing operations, while eliminating 1,500 jobs worldwide. Later in the year the company agreed to jointly package instant imaging and labeling products with Polaroid. Several acquisitions in 2001 included CD Stomper (CD and DVD labels and software). Avery Dennison continued its acquisitive ways in 2002, acquiring Jackstadt (German maker of pressure-sensitive adhesive materials), RVL Packaging (maker of woven and printed labels and other tags for the apparel and retail industries), and L&E Packaging (key supplier and printer for RVL).

In 2003 the company sold its European package label converting business (including plants in Denmark and France) to label and packaging company CCL Industries. As part of the deal, Avery Dennison began to supply pressure-sensitive base materials to CCL Industries. The divestiture was part of the company's strategy to concentrate its efforts in adhesive materials, office products, and retail information services.

Phillip Neal retired as chairman and CEO in 2005 and was replaced by director Kent Kresa as chairman and by Dean Scarborough as president and CEO.

EXECUTIVES

Chairman, President, and CEO: Dean A. Scarborough, age 54, $8,058,747 total compensation
EVP Business Development: Daniel R. O'Bryant, age 52, $2,462,817 total compensation
SVP and Chief Human Resources Officer: Anne Hill, age 50
SVP and CFO: Mitchell R. Butier, age 38
SVP, General Counsel, and Secretary: Susan C. Miller, age 50
SVP Corporate Strategy and Technology: Robert M. Malchione, age 52, $1,682,538 total compensation
SVP and CIO: Richard W. (Rich) Hoffman
SVP Corporate Communications and Advertising: Diane B. Dixon, age 58
SVP New Growth Platforms: John M. Sallay, age 53
Group VP Office Products: Timothy G. (Tim) Bond, age 52
Group VP, Specialty Materials and Converting: Timothy S. Clyde, age 47, $1,878,893 total compensation
Group VP Roll Materials: Donald A. (Don) Nolan, age 49, $1,849,249 total compensation
VP and CTO: David N. Edwards
VP Retail Information Services: R. Shawn Neville, age 47
VP and Treasurer: Karyn E. Rodriguez, age 50
VP, Controller, and Chief Accounting Officer: Lori J. Bondar
Auditors: PricewaterhouseCoopers LLP

LOCATIONS

HQ: Avery Dennison Corporation
150 N. Orange Grove Blvd., Pasadena, CA 91103
Phone: 626-304-2000   **Fax:** 626-304-2192
Web: www.averydennison.com

2009 Sales

	$ mil.	% of total
US	2,026.4	34
Europe	1,949.4	33
Asia	1,236.8	20
Latin America	394.2	7
Other regions	345.9	6
Total	**5,952.7**	**100**

PRODUCTS/OPERATIONS

2009 Sales

	$ mil.	% of total
Pressure-Sensitive Materials	3,300.0	56
Retail Information Services	1,323.2	22
Office & Consumer Products	849.3	14
Other specialty converting businesses	480.2	8
Total	**5,952.7**	**100**

Selected Products

Pressure-Sensitive Adhesives and Materials
  Base materials
    Paper and film materials
    Pressure-sensitive coated papers, films, and foils
    Proprietary film face materials
  Graphic products
    Durable cast and reflective films
    Metallic dispersion products
    Proprietary woodgrain film laminates
    Specialty print-receptive films
  Performance polymers products
    Solvent- and emulsion-based acrylic polymer adhesives, top coats, protective coatings
  Specialty tape products
    Single- and double-coated tapes and transfer adhesives
Consumer and Converted Products
  Binder and presentation dividers
  Computer software
  Custom label products (pressure-sensitive and heat-seal labels)
  Inkjet and laser print card and index products
  Label machines (imprinting, dispensing, attaching)
  Labels (copier, data processing, inkjet, and laser printer)
  Markers and highlighters
  Presentation and organizing systems
  Self-adhesive battery labels and postage stamps
  Sheet protectors
  Tags (graphic and bar-coded)
  Three-ring binders

Selected Brands

Avery
Avery Dennison
Fasson
HI-LITER
Index Maker
Marks-A-Lot
Stabilo
Zweckform

COMPETITORS

3M
ACCO Brands
Bemis
Bostik
Brady Corporation
Checkpoint Systems
Esselte
Fortune Brands
H.B. Fuller
Newell Rubbermaid
Standard Register
UPM-Kymmene

HISTORICAL FINANCIALS

Company Type: Public

Income Statement		FYE: Saturday nearest December 31		
	REVENUE ($ mil.)	NET INCOME ($ mil.)	NET PROFIT MARGIN	EMPLOYEES
12/09	5,953	(747)	—	35,700
12/08	6,710	266	4.0%	36,000
12/07	6,308	304	4.8%	37,300
12/06	5,576	367	6.6%	22,700
12/05	5,474	226	4.1%	22,600
Annual Growth	**2.1%**	**—**	**—**	**12.1%**

2009 Year-End Financials

Debt ratio: 79.9%
Return on equity: —
Cash ($ mil.): 138
Current ratio: 0.93
Long-term debt ($ mil.): 1,089

No. of shares (mil.): 110
Dividends
  Yield: 3.3%
  Payout: —
Market value ($ mil.): 4,030

Stock History

NYSE: AVY

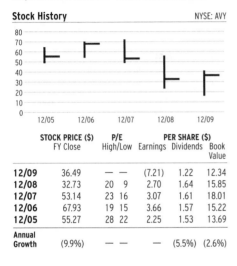

	STOCK PRICE ($) FY Close	P/E High/Low		PER SHARE ($) Earnings	Dividends	Book Value
12/09	36.49	—	—	(7.21)	1.22	12.34
12/08	32.73	20	9	2.70	1.64	15.85
12/07	53.14	23	16	3.07	1.61	18.01
12/06	67.93	19	15	3.66	1.57	15.22
12/05	55.27	28	22	2.25	1.53	13.69
Annual Growth	(9.9%)	—	—	—	(5.5%)	(2.6%)

Avis Budget Group

Whether you're a business traveler on an expense account or you're on a family vacation and you're counting every penny, Avis Budget Group has a car rental brand for you. The company's Avis Rent A Car unit, which targets corporate and leisure travelers at the high end of the market, has 2,200 locations in the Americas and the Asia/Pacific region. Budget Rent A Car, marketed to those who watch costs closely, rents cars from 2,700 locations in the same regions and trucks from 2,550 dealers in the US. Avis Budget Group, formerly known as Cendant, changed its name in 2006 after spinning off its hotel operations (Wyndham Worldwide) and its real estate division (Realogy) and selling its travel unit (Travelport).

Although Avis and Budget maintain separate brand identities, the companies share a global fleet of more than 320,000 vehicles and an administrative infrastructure. Like several of their rivals, Avis and Budget are working to open more facilities outside airports to compete in the insurance replacement and general use markets, where Enterprise has gained a leadership position. Off-airport revenue represents about a fifth of Avis Budget Group's overall domestic car rental business.

Demand for the company's airport rentals is largely dependent on airline passenger volumes, which declined in 2009, 2008, and 2007 due to the weak economy and turmoil in the airline industry as a result of volatile jet fuel prices.

Investment firm FMR LLC owns about 15% of Avis Budget Group.

HISTORY

Cendant began life through the 1997 merger of CUC International and HFS. A giant in hospitality, HFS was cobbled together as Hospitality Franchise Systems by LBO specialist Blackstone Group in 1992. With brands including Days Inn, Ramada,

and Howard Johnson, HFS went public that year. In 1995 HFS bought real estate firm Century 21. The next year it added Electronic Realty Associates (ERA) and Coldwell Banker. Also in 1996, HFS acquired the Super 8 Motels brand, as well as car-rental firm Avis (founded by Warren Avis in 1946, it went through a succession of owners until acquired by HFS). The next year HFS sold 75% of Avis' #1 franchisee to the public and later bought relocation service firm PHH.

In an attempt to leverage the power of his brands, HFS CEO Henry Silverman began looking at direct marketing giant CUC International. CUC was founded in 1973 as Comp-U-Card America by Walter Forbes and other investors envisioning a computer-based home shopping network. During the 1980s CUC developed as a discount direct marketer and catalog-based shopping club. It went public in 1983 with 100,000 members. CUC saw explosive growth as it signed up 7.6 million members between 1989 and 1993. In 1996 CUC acquired Rent Net, an online apartment rental service, and later bought entertainment software publishers Davidson & Associates and Sierra On-Line. In 1997 CUC bought software maker Knowledge Adventure and launched online shopping site NetMarket.

CUC and HFS completed their $14.1 billion merger in December 1997 with Silverman as CEO and Forbes as chairman. While the name Cendant was derived from "ascendant," the marriage quickly headed in the opposite direction. Accounting irregularities from before the merger that had inflated CUC's revenue and pretax profit by about $500 million were revealed in 1998. Cendant's stock price tumbled, taking a $14 billion hit in one day. Forbes resigned that summer. Silverman quickly took action and began to sell off operations. Cendant Software, National Leisure Group, and Match.com all were sold that year for a total of about $1.4 billion. The company also acquired Jackson Hewitt, the US's #2 tax-preparation firm, and UK-based National Parking.

In 1999 the company sold its fleet business, including PHH Vehicle Management Services, to Avis Rent A Car for $5 billion and sold its Entertainment Publications unit, the world's largest coupon book marketer and publisher, to The Carlyle Group. Cendant later paid $2.8 billion in one of the largest shareholder class action lawsuit settlements. (Accounting firm Ernst & Young also settled with Cendant shareholders for $335 million.)

In 2001 Cendant sought to expand its travel holdings with a slew of acquisitions. Its purchases included timeshare resort firm Fairfield Communities ($690 million); travel services firm Galileo International ($2.4 billion); and online travel reservation service Cheap Tickets ($425 million). In late 2001 Cendant cut some 6,000 jobs to improve its bottom line and announced that during the next year or so it would cut an additional 10,000 jobs and eliminate about 7% of its franchised hotels.

In 2002 the company purchased car-rental company Budget Rent A Car for about $110 million, then slashed costs by closing facilities and laying off more than 450 employees.

In 2004 Cendant's Jackson Hewitt subsidiary filed for its IPO. Also that year, former chairman Walter Forbes and former vice chairman E. Kirk Shelton went to trial on federal fraud and conspiracy charges stemming from pre-merger accounting irregularities that were discovered in 1998. (Shelton was found guilty of multiple counts of fraud in 2005.) CFO Ronald Nelson

was named president, taking over for Henry Silverman, who remained chairman and CEO.

Also in 2004 Cendant acquired online travel firm Orbitz in a deal valued at about $1.25 billion. As 2004 wound to a close Cendant completed the acquisition of the Ramada International Hotels & Resorts brand and franchising operations from Marriott International.

Cendant in 2005 spun off its mortgage operations, PHH Mortgage, and fleet management (PHH Arval) businesses. Also that year Cendant spun off Wright Express (payment processing and information services for fleet management) in an IPO and sold its marketing services division to Apollo Management for about $1.8 billion.

The divestitures that began in 2005 culminated in the unwinding of the Cendant conglomerate the next year. It spun off its hotel and real estate operations and sold its travel services division in 2006, reconfiguring itself around its rental car businesses and renaming itself Avis Budget Group. Silverman became chairman and CEO of the company's real estate business, Realogy, and Nelson took over as chairman and CEO of the slimmed-down Avis Budget Group, which took on its new name in September 2006.

The founder of Avis Rent A Car, Warren Avis, died in April 2007 at the age of 92.

EXECUTIVES

Chairman, President, CEO, and COO:
Ronald L. (Ron) Nelson, age 58,
$2,265,789 total compensation
Vice Chairman: F. Robert (Bob) Salerno, age 56,
$2,331,474 total compensation
EVP and Chief Administrative Officer:
Mark J. Servodidio, age 44,
$773,027 total compensation
EVP and CFO: David B. Wyshner, age 42,
$1,473,436 total compensation
EVP and General Counsel: Michael K. Tucker
EVP Operations: Larry De Shon, age 50
**EVP, General Counsel, and Corporate Compliance
Officer:** Karen C. Sclafani, age 58
EVP International Operations: Patric Siniscalchi,
age 60, $769,006 total compensation
EVP Sales and Marketing: Thomas M. (Tom) Gartland,
age 52
EVP Strategy and Pricing: W. Scott Deaver, age 58
SVP and CIO: Gerard Insall
SVP Properties: Robert Bouta
SVP and Chief Accounting Officer: Brett D. Weinblatt,
age 41
SVP and Secretary: Jean M. Sera
SVP Marketing: Becky Alseth
SVP Global Travel and Partnership Sales: Kaye E. Ceille
SVP Commercial Sales: Robert (Bob) Lambert
SVP Fleet Services: Edward Gitlitz
VP Corporate Communications and Public Affairs:
John Barrows
Auditors: Deloitte & Touche LLP

LOCATIONS

HQ: Avis Budget Group, Inc.
  6 Sylvan Way, Parsippany, NJ 07054
Phone: 973-496-4700
Web: www.avisbudgetgroup.com

2009 Sales

	$ mil.	% of total
US	4,323	84
Other countries	808	16
Total	**5,131**	**100**

PRODUCTS/OPERATIONS

2009 Sales

	$ mil.	% of total
Domestic car rental	3,967	77
International car rental	808	16
Truck rental	354	7
Corporate & other	2	—
Total	**5,131**	**100**

2009 Sales by Brand

	% of total
Avis	61
Budget	32
Budget Truck	7
Total	**100**

COMPETITORS

Dollar Thrifty Automotive
Enterprise Rent-A-Car
Hertz
Penske Truck Leasing
Ryder System
Zipcar

HISTORICAL FINANCIALS

Company Type: Public

Income Statement

FYE: December 31

	REVENUE ($ mil.)	NET INCOME ($ mil.)	NET PROFIT MARGIN	EMPLOYEES
12/09	5,131	(47)	—	22,700
12/08	5,984	(1,124)	—	26,000
12/07	5,986	(916)	—	30,000
12/06	5,689	(1,930)	—	30,000
12/05	18,236	1,349	7.4%	84,800
Annual Growth	**(27.2%)**	**—**	**—**	**(28.1%)**

2009 Year-End Financials

Debt ratio: 2,924.8%
Return on equity: —
Cash ($ mil.): 482
Current ratio: 1.35
Long-term debt ($ mil.): 6,493
No. of shares (mil.): 103
Dividends
Yield: 0.0%
Payout: —
Market value ($ mil.): 1,349

Stock History

NYSE: CAR

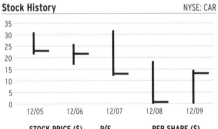

	STOCK PRICE ($) FY Close	P/E High/Low		PER SHARE ($) Earnings	Dividends	Book Value
12/09	13.12	—	—	(0.46)	0.00	2.16
12/08	0.70	—	—	(11.04)	0.00	0.90
12/07	13.00	—	—	(8.88)	0.00	14.24
12/06	21.69	—	—	(19.82)	1.10	23.75
12/05	22.96	2	2	12.60	4.00	109.77
Annual Growth	**(13.1%)**	**—**	**—**	**—**	**—**	**(62.6%)**

Avnet, Inc.

If you're after an electronic component, Avnet probably has it. The company is one of the world's largest distributors of electronic components and computer products, alongside rival Arrow Electronics. Avnet's suppliers include 300-plus component and systems makers; the company distributes these suppliers' products to some 100,000 manufacturers and resellers. Avnet Electronics Marketing offers semiconductors and other components. Avnet Technology Solutions provides computer products and services to resellers, large end-users, systems integrators, and software vendors. The company distributes products in more than 70 countries.

Facing tough global market conditions and reduced demand for products, in addition to its yearly acquisition integration costs, in 2009 Avnet restructured its business by closing about 45 facilities, more than half of them located in the Americas, and cutting staff worldwide.

Even in the market's worst troughs, Avnet continues to buy complementary businesses as a means of pushing into new markets. In 2010 the company acquired rival Bell Microproducts for about $630 million in assumed debt and cash. Avnet was attracted to Bell Micro's strong presence in fast-growing Latin America (which accounts for around 17% of Bell's sales), as well as its position in data center products and embedded systems. Also that year, Avnet bought a majority stake in Asian distributor Unidux, continuing a run of acquistions in the region the previous year, and tripling the business of Avnet Electronics Marketing in Japan.

Avnet acquired certain assets of Vietnam-based IT distributor Sunshine Joint Stock Company in 2009 and integrated it into its Technology Solutions Asia business. Additionally, the company bought a controlling interest in Vanda Group, a systems integrator and software applications developer based in China, from Hutchinson Whampoa. Vanda complemented Avnet Technology Solutions' recently launched distribution business in China, adding a vertically integrated service offering and extensive base of customers in the banking, financial services, telecommunications, and government markets. It also let Avnet expand its reach across China, Hong Kong, and Macau, where Vanda had a strong local brand.

Earlier in 2009 Avnet acquired Abacus Group, a European component distributor based in the UK. Avnet bought Tokyo-based components distributor Nippon Denso Industry Co., Ltd., in 2008. Nippon Denso adds new semiconductor suppliers and design-in engineering expertise; the acquisition doubled Avnet Electronics Marketing's business in Japan, one of the world's largest markets for electronic components.

The company acquired Horizon Technology Group in 2008 for about $150 million. Horizon is a distributor and integrator of IT products in Ireland and the UK.

HISTORY

In 1921, before the advent of commercial battery-operated radios, Charles Avnet started a small ham radio replacement parts distributorship in Manhattan, selling parts to designers, inventors, and ship-to-shore radio users on docked ships. The stock market crash in 1929 left the business strapped; it went bankrupt in 1931. A few years later Avnet founded another company,

making car radio kits and antennas. But competition got the best of him, and that company also went bankrupt.

During WWII Charles, joined by his sons Lester and Robert, founded Avnet Electronic Supply to sell parts to government and military contractors. After the war the company bought and sold surplus electrical and electronic parts. A contract from Bendix Aviation spurred company growth, and Avnet opened a West Coast warehouse. In 1955 the company incorporated as Avnet Electronics Supply, with Robert as chairman and CEO and Lester as president. Sales reached $1 million that year, although the company lost $17,000. It changed its name to Avnet Electronics in 1959.

In 1960 Avnet made its first acquisition, British Industries, and went public. Acquisitions continued throughout the 1960s with Hamilton Electro (1962), Fairmount Motor Products (1963), Carol Wire & Cable (1968), and Time Electronic Sales (1968).

To acknowledge its diversification into motors and other products, the company again changed its name, to Avnet, Inc., in 1964. Robert Avnet died the next year and Lester took over as chairman; Lester died in 1970.

In 1973 Intel, which had introduced the microprocessor, signed Avnet as a distributor, and by 1979 Avnet's sales had topped $1 billion. A soft 1982 market caused price declines that led Avnet to sell its wire and cable business. The company consolidated many of its operations to its Arizona headquarters in 1987.

During 1991 and 1992 Avnet spent more than $100 million for acquisitions strategic to the European market. In 1993 the company outbid Wyle Laboratories for Hall-Mark Electronics, the US's third-largest distributor; it also acquired Penstock, the top US distributor of microwave radio-frequency products, in 1994. Thanks to its purchases, Avnet was Europe's #2 electronics distributor by 1994, despite having had almost no European operations prior to 1990.

The company continued to expand globally in 1995, acquiring Hong Kong distributor WKK Semiconductor, among others. Also that year it began selling off its non-electronics operations.

In 1998 president and COO Roy Vallee became chairman and CEO. In 1999 Avnet acquired rival Marshall Industries for about $760 million.

In 2000 Avnet acquired IBM midrange server distributor Savoir Technology Group, making Avnet the leading distributor of IBM midrange products. Later that year the company acquired a part of Germany-based EBV Group (semiconductor distribution) and RKE (computer products and services), both from German utility giant E.ON, in a cash deal worth about $740 million.

In 2001 Avnet acquired smaller rival Kent Electronics for about $600 million. Also that year the company bought Chinese competitor Sunrise Technology.

In an effort to reduce costs during a global downturn in the electronics industry, Avnet reduced its headcount by about 1,100 people in 2003 and 2004. In 2005 the company established Avnet Managed Technologies (AMT) to offer IT services to small and mid-sized businesses.

In 2007 Avnet acquired Access Distribution, the computer products distribution business of General Electric. Access Distribution specialized in computer hardware made by Sun Microsystems.

In 2008 Avnet acquired Nippon Denso Industry Co., Ltd., a Tokyo-based value-added distributor.

EXECUTIVES

Chairman and CEO: Roy A. Vallee, age 57,
$3,825,799 total compensation
President and COO: Richard (Rick) Hamada, age 51,
$1,600,740 total compensation
SVP, CFO, and Assistant Secretary:
Raymond (Ray) Sadowski, age 55,
$1,655,932 total compensation
SVP and Chief Operational Excellence Officer:
Steven C. (Steve) Church, age 60
SVP, General Counsel, and Assistant Secretary:
David R. Birk, age 63, $1,111,637 total compensation
**SVP; SVP and Director Administrative Services for
Shared Business Services:** Patrick (Pat) Jewett
SVP and CIO: Stephen R. (Steve) Phillips, age 46
SVP; President, Avnet Electronics Marketing:
Harley M. Feldberg, age 56,
$1,465,627 total compensation
SVP; President, Avnet Technology Solutions:
Philip R. (Phil) Gallagher, age 48
Corporate VP; President, Avnet Logistics Services:
James N. (Jim) Smith, age 63
**Corporate VP; President, Electronics Marketing,
Europe, Middle East, and Africa:** Patrick Zammit
VP; President, Technology Solutions, Asia Pacific:
K. P. Tang
VP; President, Electronics Marketing, Asia:
Stephen Wong
VP; President, Avnet Technology Solutions, Americas:
Jeff Bawol
VP; Chief Human Resources Officer:
MaryAnn G. Miller, age 52
VP and Chief Communications Officer:
Allen W. (Al) Maag
VP and Chief Tax Officer: Jill M. Wysolmierski
VP Public Relations: Michelle Gorel
VP, Assistant General Counsel, and Secretary: Jun Li
VP Investor Relations: Vincent (Vince) Keenan
**President, Avnet Technology Solutions, Europe, Middle
East, and Africa:** Dick Borsboom
President, Avnet Electronics Marketing Americas:
Edward J. (Ed) Smith
Auditors: KPMG LLP

LOCATIONS

HQ: Avnet, Inc.
2211 S. 47th St., Phoenix, AZ 85034
Phone: 480-643-2000   **Fax:** 480-643-7370
Web: www.avnet.com

2009 Sales

	$ mil.	% of total
Americas	7,572.2	47
Europe, Middle East & Africa	5,268.4	32
Asia/Pacific	3,389.3	21
Total	**16,229.9**	**100**

PRODUCTS/OPERATIONS

2009 Sales

	$ mil.	% of total
Avnet Electronics Marketing	9,192.8	57
Avnet Technology Solutions	7,037.1	43
Total	**16,229.9**	**100**

2009 Sales

	$ mil.	% of total
Semiconductors	8,324.0	51
Computer products	6,393.4	39
Connectors	735.2	5
Passives, electromechanical & other	777.3	5
Total	**16,229.9**	**100**

Selected Operations

Avnet Electronics Marketing (component distribution)
  Avnet Cilicon (semiconductors)
    Analog
    Communications
    Digital Signal Processors (DSPs)
    Discrete
    Memory
    Microprocessors and microcontrollers
    Optoelectronics
    Programmable logic
    Standard logic
  Avnet IP&E (interconnect, passive, and
    electromechanical devices)
  Design Chain Services (integrated circuit and systems-
    level design services)
  Supply Chain Services
    Asset management
    Demand planning
    Information services
    Logistics
    Order management
    Warehousing
  Production Supplies & Test (electronics production
    supplies and test equipment)
Avnet Technology Solutions (computer distribution and
  information technology services)
  Avnet Hall-Mark (computers, software, storage, and
    services to resellers)
  Avnet Applied Computing
    Products
      Displays
      Memory devices
      Motherboards
      Networking equipment
      Peripherals
      Point-of-sale
      Processors
      Software
      Storage
      Wireless
    Supply chain services
      Financing
      Integration
      Logistics
      Materials management
      Technical service
  Avnet Computing Components (microprocessors for
    systems integrators)

COMPETITORS

Arrow Electronics
Digi-Key
Future Electronics
Heilind Electronics
Ingram Micro
N.F. Smith
Nu Horizons Electronics
Premier Farnell
Richardson Electronics
Sager Electrical
SYNNEX
Tech Data
TTI Inc.
WPG Holdings

HISTORICAL FINANCIALS

Company Type: Public

Income Statement

FYE: Friday nearest June 30

	REVENUE ($ mil.)	NET INCOME ($ mil.)	NET PROFIT MARGIN	EMPLOYEES
6/09	16,230	(1,123)	—	12,900
6/08	17,953	499	2.8%	12,800
6/07	15,681	393	2.5%	11,700
6/06	14,254	205	1.4%	10,900
6/05	11,067	168	1.5%	9,800
Annual Growth	**10.0%**	**—**	**—**	**7.1%**

2009 Year-End Financials

Debt ratio: 34.3%
Return on equity: —
Cash ($ mil.): 944
Current ratio: 2.09
Long-term debt ($ mil.): 947
No. of shares (mil.): 152
Dividends
  Yield: 0.0%
  Payout: —
Market value ($ mil.): 3,193

Stock History

NYSE: AVT

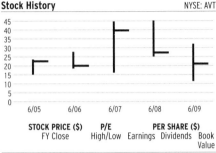

	STOCK PRICE ($) FY Close	P/E High/Low		PER SHARE ($) Earnings	Dividends	Book Value
6/09	21.03	—	—	(7.44)	0.00	18.18
6/08	27.28	14	8	3.27	0.00	27.23
6/07	39.64	17	6	2.63	0.00	22.40
6/06	20.02	20	14	1.39	0.00	18.65
6/05	22.53	17	11	1.39	0.00	13.81
Annual Growth	**(1.7%)**	**—**	**—**	**—**	**—**	**7.1%**

Avon Products

"Avon calling" — calling for a younger crowd, overseas reps, and improved global operational efficiencies. Avon Products, the world's largest direct seller of cosmetics and beauty-related items, is busy building a global brand and enticing younger customers to buy its products. Direct selling remains the firm's *modus operandi*, but sales also come from catalogs and a website. Its products include cosmetics, fragrances, toiletries, jewelry, apparel, home furnishings, and more. With sales operations and distribution in more than 100 countries and territories, Avon boasts about 6.2 million independent representatives.

Avon's ongoing restructuring that initially began in late 2005 has involved purging staff, streamlining global manufacturing, and adjusting its supply chain with regard to procurement and distribution. As part of its newer business re-organization, kicked off in 2009, Avon plans to shut down two plants (one in Ohio and another in Germany) by 2013 following the closing of a distribution center in Illinois in spring 2010.

To the company's benefit, rising unemployment in the US is creating a rising tide of willing recruits for Avon and other direct sellers. While its number of sales reps continues to grow, its office staff has shrunk in recent years. By late 2007 the firm had already trimmed its employee ranks by 10% and management by nearly 30%. In 2008 the firm shed another 4,000 jobs (about 6% of its workforce).

In mid-2010 the company agreed to acquire Silpada Designs, a Kansas-based direct seller of sterling silver jewelry with operations in the US, Canada, and the UK, for $650 million. The Silpada deal follows a pair of acquisitions Avon made earlier that year: UK-based Liz Earle Beauty, which develops skin care products made of botanical ingredients, and the Tiny Tillia brand, composed of bath and body care products for babies. Both purchases help to broaden

Avon's brand portfolio, especially as demand for natural personal care products has increased in recent years.

Despite resistance from China for years, Avon has been trying to get its foot in the country's door. In 1998 China banned direct selling because consumers there found it difficult to distinguish between companies that direct sell and those with pyramid schemes. The beauty firm sees China as an untapped gold mine and in 2005 was given approval from the government to test its direct selling in parts of China, specifically the cities of Beijing and Tianjin and the province of Guangdong. Avon now retains a direct-selling license there.

Capital Research Global Investors holds about a 10% interest in Avon Products.

HISTORY

In the 1880s book salesman David McConnell gave small bottles of perfume to New York housewives who listened to his sales pitch. The perfume was more popular than the books, so in 1886 McConnell created the California Perfume Company and hired women to sell door-to-door. (He renamed the company Avon Products in 1939 after being impressed by the beauty of Stratford-upon-Avon in England.) Through the 1950s these women, mostly housewives seeking extra income, made Avon a major force in the cosmetics industry.

From the 1960s until the mid-1980s, Avon was the world's largest cosmetics company, known for its appeal to middle-class homemakers. But the company hit hard times in 1974 — the recession made many of its products too pricey for blue-collar customers, and women were leaving home for the workforce. Discovering that Avon's traditional products had little appeal for younger women, Avon began an overhaul of its product line, introducing the Colorworks line for teenagers with the slogan, "It's not your mother's makeup."

Avon acquired prestigious jeweler Tiffany & Co. in 1979 (sold 1984) to help improve the company's image. To boost profits, it entered the retail prestige fragrance business by launching a joint venture with Liz Claiborne (1985) and buying Giorgio Armani (1987, the Giorgio Beverly Hills retail operations were sold in 1994). But Liz Claiborne dissolved the joint venture when Avon bought competitor Parfums Stern in 1987 (sold 1990). It sold 40% of Avon Japan (started 1969) to the Japanese public that year.

Avon Color cosmetics were introduced in 1988, and sleepwear, preschool toys, and videos followed in 1989. It introduced apparel in 1994 and the next year worked with designer Diane Von Furstenberg to launch a line of clothing. Mattel and Avon joined forces in 1996 to sell toys — Winter Velvet Barbie became Avon's most successful product introduction ever.

Passing over several high-ranking female executives (the company felt they weren't ready), Avon made Charles Perrin its CEO in mid-1998. Andrea Jung, the brain behind the makeover, became president. In 1999 Jung became Avon's first female CEO by replacing the retiring Perrin. Former Goodyear and Rubbermaid CEO Stanley Gault was elected chairman of the board. In March 2000 Avon announced an alliance with Swiss pharmaceutical group Roche to develop a line of women's vitamins and nutritional products (its first) launched in 2001.

In September 2001 Jung was elected chairman of the board. In 2002, as part of a move to improve operating efficiencies, Avon closed its jewelry manufacturing plant in San Sebastian, Puerto Rico. It now outsources its full jewelry line by purchasing finished goods from Asia. In another cost-cutting move, Avon laid off 3,500 employees, or 8% of its workforce, in March 2002. The next month Avon announced the closing of production operations in Northampton, UK, and a shift of these operations to its facility in Garwolin, Poland.

As part of its focus on the younger market, in 2003 Avon launched a new cosmetics line called "mark." — targeted to the 16 to 24 age group. Named for young women making their mark on the world, the line includes 300 products, such as cosmetics, skin care, fragrance, accessories, jewelry, and handbags. In 2004 Avon agreed to acquire a 20% stake in its two Chinese joint ventures with Masson Group.

EXECUTIVES

Chairman, President, and CEO: Andrea Jung, age 51, $11,055,012 total compensation
Vice Chairman, CFO, and Chief Strategy Officer: Charles W. (Chuck) Cramb, age 63, $3,602,029 total compensation
EVP Latin America and Central and Eastern Europe: Charles M. Herington, age 50, $2,780,514 total compensation
SVP Western Europe, Middle East & Africa, Asia-Pacific, and China: Bennett R. (Ben) Gallina, age 55, $2,547,985 total compensation
SVP and CIO: Donagh Herlihy
SVP Human Resources and Corporate Responsibility: Lucien Alziari, age 50
SVP Global Communications: Nancy Glaser
SVP and President, North America: Geralyn R. Breig, age 47
SVP Global Direct Selling and Business Model Innovation: John P. Higson, age 51
SVP Global Insights and Marketing Intelligence: Mike Schwartz
Group VP and Corporate Controller: Stephen Ibbotson, age 50
SVP Global Supply Chain: John F. Owen, age 52
SVP, General Counsel, and Corporate Secretary: Kim K.W. Rucker, age 43
SVP and Global Brand President: Jeri B. Finard, age 50
Manager Corporate and Media Relations: Sharon A. Samuel
Auditors: PricewaterhouseCoopers LLP

LOCATIONS

HQ: Avon Products, Inc.
1345 Avenue of the Americas, New York, NY 10105
Phone: 212-282-5000 **Fax:** 212-282-6049
Web: www.avoncompany.com

2009 Sales

	$ mil.	% of total
Latin America	4,103.2	40
North America	2,262.7	22
Central & Eastern Europe	1,500.1	14
Western Europe, Middle East & Africa	1,277.8	12
Asia/Pacific	885.6	9
China	353.4	3
Total	**10,382.8**	**100**

2009 Sales

	$ mil.	% of total
US	1,864.4	18
Brazil	1,817.1	18
All other	6,701.3	64
Total	**10,382.8**	**100**

PRODUCTS/OPERATIONS

2009 Sales

	$ mil.	% of total
Beauty	7,408.4	71
Fashion	1,768.0	17
Home	1,108.3	11
Other revenue	98.1	1
Total	**10,382.8**	**100**

Selected Collections

Advance Techniques
Anew
Avon Color
Avon Naturals
Avon Solutions
Avon Wellness
Beyond Color
Fragrance
   Christian LaCroix Absynthe
   Christian Lacroix Rouge
   Derek Jeter Driven
   Extraordinary
   mark
   Today, Tomorrow, Always
   U by Ungaro for Her
   U by Ungaro for Him
Skin So Soft

COMPETITORS

Alberto-Culver	Johnson & Johnson
Alticor	Johnson Publishing
Amway China	Kracie
Bath & Body Works	L'Oréal
BeautiControl	LVMH
Beiersdorf	Macy's
Body Shop	Mary Kay
Chanel	Murad, Inc.
Clarins	Nu Skin
Colgate-Palmolive	Perrigo
Coty Inc.	Prestige Cosmetics
Dana Classic Fragrances	Procter & Gamble
Del Laboratories	Revlon
Dillard's	Sara Lee
Elizabeth Arden Inc	Shaklee
Enesco	Shiseido
Estée Lauder	Target
Forever Living	Tupperware Brands
Hanover Direct	Unilever
J. C. Penney	Wal-Mart
Jafra	

HISTORICAL FINANCIALS

Company Type: Public

Income Statement

	REVENUE ($ mil.)	NET INCOME ($ mil.)	NET PROFIT MARGIN	EMPLOYEES
				FYE: December 31
12/09	10,383	626	6.0%	41,000
12/08	10,690	875	8.2%	42,000
12/07	9,939	531	5.3%	42,000
12/06	8,677	478	5.5%	40,300
12/05	8,150	848	10.4%	49,000
Annual Growth	6.2%	(7.3%)	—	(4.4%)

2009 Year-End Financials

Debt ratio: 195.0%
Return on equity: 64.3%
Cash ($ mil.): 1,312
Current ratio: 1.84
Long-term debt ($ mil.): 2,482
No. of shares (mil.): 429
Dividends
  Yield: 2.7%
  Payout: 57.9%
Market value ($ mil.): 13,512

Stock History

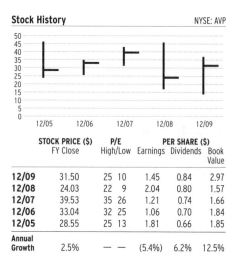

	STOCK PRICE ($) FY Close	P/E High/Low		PER SHARE ($) Earnings	Dividends	Book Value
12/09	31.50	25	10	1.45	0.84	2.97
12/08	24.03	22	9	2.04	0.80	1.57
12/07	39.53	35	26	1.21	0.74	1.66
12/06	33.04	32	25	1.06	0.70	1.84
12/05	28.55	25	13	1.81	0.66	1.85
Annual Growth	2.5%	—	—	(5.4%)	6.2%	12.5%

Baker & McKenzie

Baker & McKenzie believes big is good and bigger is better. One of the world's largest law firms, it has about 3,900 attorneys practicing from some 70 offices — from Bangkok to Berlin to Buenos Aires — in almost 40 countries. It offers expertise in a wide range of practice areas, including antitrust, intellectual property, international trade, mergers and acquisitions, project finance, and tax law. Baker & McKenzie's client list includes big companies from numerous industries, including banking and finance, construction, and technology, as well as smaller enterprises.

Baker & McKenzie is known for the geographic scope of its practice — some 80% of the firm's attorneys work outside the US. The firm touts its widespread network of offices as an advantage for clients with multinational interests. The firm's recent expansion includes opening an office in Abu Dhabi, United Arab Emirates, in February 2009.

The vast scale of Baker & McKenzie's operations increases the firm's exposure to liability, however, and that concern led Baker & McKenzie to reorganize itself as a Swiss Verein. Under the Verein structure, which is used by accounting firms such as Deloitte Touche Tohmatsu, Baker & McKenzie's member firms operate as separate entities, insulating the parent firm from liability. Baker & McKenzie was the first international law firm to organize itself as a Verein.

HISTORY

Russell Baker traveled from his native New Mexico to Chicago on a railroad freight car to attend law school. Upon graduation in 1925 he started practicing law with his classmate Dana Simpson under the name Simpson & Baker. Inspired by Chicago's role as a manufacturing and agricultural center for the world and influenced by the international focus of his alma mater, the University of Chicago, Baker dreamed of creating an international law practice. He began developing an expertise in international law, and in 1934 Abbott Laboratories retained him to handle its worldwide legal affairs. Baker was on his way to fulfilling his dream.

Baker joined forces with Chicago litigator John McKenzie in 1949, forming Baker & McKenzie. In 1955 the firm opened its first foreign office in Caracas, Venezuela, to meet the needs of its expanding US client base. Over the next 10 years it branched out into Asia, Australia, and Europe, with offices in London, Manila, Paris, and Tokyo. Baker's death in 1979 neither slowed the firm's growth nor changed its international character. The next year it expanded into the Middle East and opened its 30th office in 1982 (Melbourne). To manage the sprawling law firm, Baker & McKenzie created the position of chairman of the executive committee in 1984.

In late 1991 the firm dropped the Church of Scientology as a client, losing an estimated $2 million in business. It was speculated that pressure from client Eli Lilly (maker of the drug Prozac, which Scientologists actively oppose) influenced the decision. In 1992 Baker & McKenzie was ordered to pay $1 million for wrongfully firing an employee who later died of AIDS. (The case became the basis for the 1993 film *Philadelphia*.) The firm fought the verdict but eventually settled for an undisclosed amount in 1995.

In 1994 Baker & McKenzie closed its Los Angeles office (the former MacDonald, Halsted & Laybourne; acquired 1988) amid considerable rancor. Also that year a former secretary at the firm received a $7.1 million judgment for sexual harassment by a partner. (A San Francisco Superior Court judge later reduced the award to $3.5 million.)

John Klotsche, a senior partner from the firm's Palo Alto, California, office, was appointed chairman in 1995. The following year the firm began a major expansion into California's Silicon Valley as part of an initiative to serve technology companies around the world. It also expanded its Warsaw, Poland, office through a merger with the Warsaw office of Dickinson, Wright, Moon, Van Dusen & Freman.

In 1998 Baker & McKenzie formed a special unit in Singapore to deal with business generated by the financial troubles in Asia. The opening of offices in Taiwan and Azerbaijan in 1998 brought the firm's total number of offices to 59. Klotsche stepped down in 1999 as the firm celebrated its 50th anniversary; Christine Lagarde replaced him. In early 2001 Baker & McKenzie created a joint venture practice with Singapore-based associate firm Wong & Leow. Also that year it merged with Madrid-based Briones Alonso y Martin to create the largest independent law firm in Spain.

Lagarde stepped down as executive chairman in 2004, and John Conroy was chosen to lead the firm.

EXECUTIVES

Chairman: John J. Conroy Jr.
Global COO: Greg Walters
Global CFO: Robert S. Spencer
Global Director Practice Groups: Dave Southern
Global Director Talent Management: Vicki Kelley
Global Director Knowledge Management: Michael Campbell
Global Director Organizational Effectiveness: Jason Marty
Global Director Strategic Capabilities: David Tabolt
Global Director Communications: Mark Bain
Global Director Information Systems: Martin Telfer
Member Executive Committee, Hong Kong: Tan Poh Lee
Member Executive Committee, London: Beatriz P. de Araujo
Member Executive Committee, San Francisco: Peter J. Engstrom

Member Executive Committee, Mexico City: Raymundo E. Enriquez
Member Executive Committee, Dallas: Alan G. Harvey
Member Executive Committee, Tokyo: Jeremy D. Pitts
General Counsel: Edward J. Zulkey
Senior Public Relations Coordinator: Jessica Benzon

LOCATIONS

HQ: Baker & McKenzie, LLP
1 Prudential Plaza, 130 E. Randolph Dr., Ste. 2500
Chicago, IL 60601
Phone: 312-861-8800   **Fax:** 312-861-8823
Web: www.bakernet.com

PRODUCTS/OPERATIONS

Selected Practice Areas

Antitrust and competition
Automotive
Banking and finance
Dispute resolution
Employment
Environment and climate change
Financial restructuring and insolvency
Insurance
Intellectual property
IT/communications
Major projects: Energy, mining, and infrastructure
Mergers and acquisitions
Pharmaceuticals and health care
Private equity
Real estate
Securities
Tax
Trade and commerce

COMPETITORS

Clifford Chance
DLA Piper
Hogan Lovells
Jones Day
Kirkland & Ellis
Latham & Watkins
Mayer Brown
McDermott Will & Emery
Shearman & Sterling
Sidley Austin
Skadden, Arps
Sullivan & Cromwell
Weil, Gotshal & Manges
White & Case

HISTORICAL FINANCIALS

Company Type: Private

Income Statement

FYE: June 30

	REVENUE ($ mil.)	NET INCOME ($ mil.)	NET PROFIT MARGIN	EMPLOYEES
6/09	2,110	—	—	9,700
6/08	2,190	—	—	9,700
6/07	1,829	—	—	9,600
6/06	1,522	—	—	9,503
6/05	1,352	—	—	8,500
Annual Growth	11.8%	—	—	3.4%

Revenue History

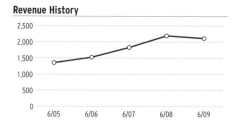

Baker Hughes

Baker Hughes cooks up a baker's dozen of products and services for the global petroleum market. Through its Drilling and Evaluation segment, Baker Hughes makes products and services used to drill oil and natural gas wells. Through its Completion and Production segment, the company provides equipment and services used from the completion phase through the productive life of oil and natural gas wells. The company tests potential well sites and drills and operates the wells; it also makes bits and drilling fluids and submersible pumps, and provides equipment and well services. In a major industry consolidation, in 2010 Baker Hughes acquired oil field services titan BJ Services for $5.5 billion.

The acquisition expands Baker Hughes portfolio, adding pressure pumping into its product offering, giving it a stronger platform for international growth, and the ability to better compete for large integrated project contracts in the unconventional gas and deepwater markets. In particular, the purchase strengthens the company's integrated services and expand its reservoir capabilities. To meet regulatory requirements, Baker Hughes agreed to sell a number of assets including two stimulation vessels and other sand control and stimulation services operating in the Gulf of Mexico.

Prior to the BJ Services deal the Drilling and Evaluation segment consisted of Baker Hughes Drilling Fluids (drilling fluids), Hughes Christensen (drill bits), INTEQ (directional drilling, measurement-while-drilling and logging-while-drilling) and Baker Atlas (downhole well logging and services).

Baker Hughes' Completion and Production segment includes Baker Oil Tools (completion, workover and fishing equipment), Baker Petrolite (oilfield specialty chemicals such as drilling fluids and stimulation additives), and Centrilift (electric submersible and progressing cavity pumps).

HISTORY

Howard Hughes Sr. developed the first oil well drill bit for rock in 1909. Hughes and partner Walter Sharp opened a plant in Houston, and their company, Sharp & Hughes, soon had a near monopoly on rock bits. When Sharp died in 1912, Hughes bought his partner's half of the company, incorporating as Hughes Tool. Hughes held 73 patents when he died in 1924; the company passed to Howard Hughes Jr.

It is estimated that between 1924 and 1972 Hughes Tool provided Hughes Jr. with $745 million in pretax profits, which he used to diversify into movies (RKO), airlines (TWA), and Las Vegas casinos. In 1972 he sold the company to the public for $150 million. After 1972 the company expanded into tools for aboveground oil production. In 1974, under the new leadership of chairman James Leach, Hughes bought the oil field equipment business of Borg-Warner.

In 1913 drilling contractor Carl Baker organized the Baker Casing Shoe Company in California to collect royalties on his three oil tool inventions. The firm began to make its own products in 1918, and during the 1920s it expanded nationally, opened global trade, and formed Baker Oil Tools (1928). The company grew in the late 1940s and the 1950s as oil drilling boomed.

During the 1960s Baker prospered, despite fewer US well completions. Foreign sales increased. From 1963 to 1975 Baker bought oil-related companies Kobe, Galigher, Ramsey Engineering, and Reed Tool.

US expenditures for oil services fell between 1982 and 1986 from $40 billion to $9 billion. In 1987 both Baker and Hughes faced falling revenues. The two companies merged to form Baker Hughes. By closing plants and combining operations, the venture became profitable by the end of 1988. The company bought Eastman Christensen (the world leader in directional and horizontal drilling equipment) and acquired the instrumentation unit of Tracor Holdings in 1990.

Baker Hughes spun off BJ Services (pumping services) to the public in 1991 and sold the Eastern Hemisphere operations of Baker Hughes Tubular Services (BHTS) to Tuboscope. It sold the Western Hemisphere operations of BHTS to ICO the following year.

Also in 1992 Baker Hughes bought Teleco Oilfield Services, a pioneer in directional drilling techniques, from Sonat. The next year the company consolidated its drilling-technology businesses into a single unit, Baker Hughes INTEQ.

In 1996 company veteran Max Lukens became CEO. He replaced James Woods as chairman the next year.

Baker Hughes allied with Schlumberger's oil field service operations in 1996. In a move to boost its oil field chemicals business the company bought Petrolite in 1997 and rival Western Atlas for $3.3 billion in 1998, strengthening its land-based seismic data business (#1 in that market) and testing business. A downturn in the Asian economy, disruptions from tropical storms, and slumping oil prices caused oil companies to reduce demand for Baker Hughes' products. The company suffered a big loss in 1998 and in response trimmed its workforce by about 15% in 1999.

In 2000 Lukens stepped down after accounting blunders caused the company to restate earnings. Company director and Newfield Exploration Company CEO Joe Foster replaced him as acting CEO until Michael Wiley was named to that office. Baker Hughes combined its seismic oil and gas exploration business with that of Schlumberger to create WesternGeco in early 2001.

In 2003 the company formed QuantX, a wellbore instrumentation joint venture company with Expro International. Cornerstone Pipeline Management was acquired in an effort to expand the pipeline inspection services provided by its Baker Petrolite division.

In 2004 Michael Wiley retired from his position as chairman and CEO of Baker Hughes. Chad Deaton, formerly president and CEO of Hanover Compressor, was named chairman and CEO to replace him.

In late 2005 the company acquired Scotland-based Zeroth Technologies, a company that manufactures expandable metal sealing elements.

In early 2006 Baker Hughes acquired Nova Technology, a Louisiana-based company that supplies monitoring and chemical injection systems for use in offshore gas and oil well operations.

To raise cash, in 2006 Baker Hughes divested its 30% stake in seismic services provider WesternGeco, selling out to joint-venture partner Schlumberger.

EXECUTIVES

Chairman and CEO: Chad C. Deaton, age 57, $8,315,147 total compensation
President and COO: Martin S. Craighead, age 50, $2,840,439 total compensation
SVP and CFO: Peter A. Ragauss, age 52, $3,092,360 total compensation
SVP and General Counsel: Alan R. Crain Jr., age 58, $2,184,530 total compensation
VP Global Marketing: Maria Claudia Borras
VP Human Resources: Didier Charreton, age 46
VP, Chief Compliance Officer, and Senior Deputy General Counsel: Jay G. Martin, age 58
VP and Controller: Alan J. Keifer, age 55
VP and CIO: Clifton N. B. (Clif) Triplett, age 51
VP Investor Relations: Gary R. Flaharty
VP and Chief Security Officer, Health, Safety, Environment, and Security: Russell J. (Russ) Cancilla, age 58
President, BJ Services: John A. (Andy) O'Donnell, age 61, $1,393,906 total compensation
President, Drilling and Evaluation: Scott Schmidt
President, US Land: Paul S. Butero, age 53
President, Industrial Portfolio: Patrick (Pat) Marfone
President, Integrated Operations: Rusty McNicoll
President, Reservoir Development Services: John Harris
President, Fluids and Chemicals: Jim Macdonald
President, Completion and Production: Neil Harrop
Secretary: Sandra E. Alford
Auditors: Deloitte & Touche LLP

LOCATIONS

HQ: Baker Hughes Incorporated
2929 Allen Pkwy., Ste. 2100, Houston, TX 77019
Phone: 713-439-8600   **Fax:** 713-439-8699
Web: www.bakerhughes.com

2009 Sales

	$ mil.	% of total
North America	3,584	37
Europe, Africa, Russia & the Caspian	2,925	30
Middle East & Asia/Pacific	2,021	21
Latin America	1,134	12
Total	**9,664**	**100**

PRODUCTS/OPERATIONS

2009 Sales

	$ mil.	% of total
Completion & production	5,059	52
Drilling & evaluation	4,605	48
Total	**9,664**	**100**

Selected Operations

Drilling and Evaluation
Baker Atlas (downhole data acquisition, processing and analysis; pipe recovery)
Baker Hughes Drilling Fluids (drilling fluids)
Hughes Christensen (oil well drill bits)
INTEQ (conventional and rotary directional drilling, measurement-while-drilling and logging-while-drilling)
Completion and Production
Baker Oil Tools (completion, workover, and fishing technologies and services)
Baker Petrolite (specialty chemicals for petroleum, transportation, and refining)
Centrilift (electric submersible pumps and downhole oil/water separation)

COMPETITORS

Aker Solutions	Petroleum Geo-Services
CE Franklin	Precision Drilling
CGGVeritas	Pride International
FMC	Schlumberger
Halliburton	Smith International
John Wood Group	Technip
Nabors Well Services	TETRA Technologies
Nalco	Weatherford International
National Oilwell Varco	Wenzel Downhole Tools

HISTORICAL FINANCIALS

Company Type: Public

Income Statement

FYE: December 31

	REVENUE ($ mil.)	NET INCOME ($ mil.)	NET PROFIT MARGIN	EMPLOYEES
12/09	9,664	421	4.4%	34,400
12/08	11,864	1,635	13.8%	39,800
12/07	10,428	1,514	14.5%	35,800
12/06	9,027	2,419	26.8%	34,600
12/05	7,186	879	12.2%	29,100
Annual Growth	7.7%	(16.8%)	—	4.3%

2009 Year-End Financials

Debt ratio: 24.5%
Return on equity: 6.0%
Cash ($ mil.): 1,595
Current ratio: 3.86
Long-term debt ($ mil.): 1,785
No. of shares (mil.): 429
Dividends
Yield: 1.5%
Payout: 44.1%
Market value ($ mil.): 17,368

Stock History

NYSE: BHI

	STOCK PRICE ($) FY Close	P/E High/Low		PER SHARE ($) Earnings	Dividends	Book Value
12/09	40.48	35	19	1.36	0.60	16.98
12/08	32.07	17	5	5.30	0.56	15.87
12/07	81.10	21	13	4.73	0.52	14.70
12/06	74.66	12	8	7.27	0.52	12.22
12/05	60.78	25	16	2.57	0.47	10.95
Annual Growth	(9.7%)	—	—	(14.7%)	6.3%	11.6%

Baldor Electric

Electricity drives Baldor Electric's sales — and its products. The company manufactures industrial AC and DC electric motors, controls, and speed drives that power products ranging from material handling conveyors to fluid handling pumps. Other products include industrial grinders, buffers, polishing lathes, and generators. Baldor Electric sells to OEMs primarily in the agricultural and semiconductor equipment industries and to independent distributors for resale as replacement parts. The company has some 75 sales offices and warehouses in North America and abroad. It maintains manufacturing plants in Canada, China, Mexico, the UK, and the US. Baldor Electric gets most of its sales in the US.

Not immune to the global economic downturn, Baldor's business was particularly affected in 2009, with sales down by 22% and profits off by nearly 40%, causing cost-cutting measures that included an elimination of about 900 jobs (a workforce reduction of about 11%). The cutbacks were expected to achieve approximately $80 million in cost savings in 2009.

Another vulnerability is the company's reliance on independent distributors, in addition to its direct sales force and manufacturer sales representatives. Its worldwide distributor network has about 10,000 locations. Approximately half of Baldor's US sales goes through distributors. Most of the company's distribution agreements are not exclusive and may be cancelled by the distributor after a short notice period.

Baldor Electric is expanding its geographic footprint, particularly in Asia, with acquisitions of Reliance Electric Company from Rockwell Automation in 2007 and Canada-based Poulies Maska in 2008. Both deals gave Baldor manufacturing operations in high-growth China and additional industrial electric motors and mechanical power transmission products. The company is also focused on organic growth through new product development, especially in the area of energy-efficient motors. On average, it releases 250 new products per year.

It is also attempting to accelerate the integration of recently acquired businesses. Reliance Electric was completely absorbed, though Baldor sells motor products under the Baldor-Reliance brand name.

HISTORY

Electrical engineer Edwin Ballman and master machinist Emil Doerr founded Baldor in 1920 in St. Louis. The company took its name from the last names of the founders. Baldor gained popularity for building fully enclosed motors that included ball bearings. It struggled through the Depression, expanding its line with custom motors, battery chargers, and grinders. After WWII, demand for Baldor's products accelerated. In 1956 the company moved to Fort Smith, Arkansas. It went public in 1976 and built market strength in part through acquisitions, including Lectron (solid-state motor starters, 1986) and Powertron (DC electric motors, 1988).

The company's energy-efficient electric motors sold well in the early 1990s. In 1994 Baldor acquired Grant Gear's line of gear-speed reducers, and in 1997 the company bought Optimised Control (motion controls, UK). Baldor was named one of FORTUNE's 100 Best Companies to Work for in America in 1998. That year Baldor acquired linear-motor maker Northern Magnetics. The next year John McFarland, a 30-year company veteran, was named CEO (a position left vacant since 1997).

In 2000 Baldor acquired Pow'R Gard Generator Corporation, a manufacturer of generators and generator sets, for $40 million. The company closed its drives plant in Plymouth, Minnesota, and consolidated it with its plant in Fort Smith, Arkansas, in 2001. In 2003 Baldor acquired the US-based Energy Dynamics, Inc., a manufacturer of industrial generators. The following year the company created Baldor Power Finance, a subsidiary to assist customers with financing and leasing Baldor's larger generators.

In 2005 Baldor acquired the 40% minority interest in Australian Baldor Pty. Ltd. that it did not previously own, making the Australian company a wholly owned subsidiary.

Roland Boreham Jr., the company's CEO from 1978 to 1981 and its chairman from 1981 through 2004, died in 2006. He was associated with Baldor Electric for 58 years, first working for his father, a Baldor grinder representative.

In 2007 Baldor acquired most of Rockwell Automation Power Systems for about $1.8 billion in cash and stock. The company purchased the Reliance Electric motors and motor repair services businesses from Rockwell Automation, along with the Dodge mechanical power transmission products business. Rockwell Automation kept the Reliance Electric and Reliance brand drives business. Baldor exchanged $1.75 billion in cash and 1.58 million shares of its common stock for the Rockwell Automation business segment.

Soon after acquiring the Reliance Electric motor business, Baldor moved to close the Reliance Electric plant in Madison, Indiana, shifting production to plants in Arkansas and Oklahoma. Baldor also sold the Reliance Electric power services business — which maintains, repairs, and supports Reliance motors — to avoid competing with existing customers. Baldor absorbed Reliance Electric, though it sells motor products under the Baldor-Reliance brand name.

EXECUTIVES

Chairman and CEO: John A. McFarland, age 59, $1,139,539 total compensation
President, COO, Secretary, and Director: Ronald E. (Ron) Tucker, age 53, $740,672 total compensation
CFO and Secretary: George E. Moschner, age 51, $429,052 total compensation
EVP Motor Sales: Randy L. Colip, age 51, $381,158 total compensation
EVP Business Integration: Edward L. (Ed) Ralston, age 40, $396,455 total compensation
EVP Materials: Gene J. Hagedorn, age 63
EVP Operations: Randal G. (Randy) Waltman, age 60
EVP Engineering: Ronald W. Thurman, age 55
VP Drives: Thomas A. (Tom) Mascari, age 58
VP Information Services: Mark L. Shackelford, age 50
VP Human Resources: Jason W. Green, age 40
VP Manufacturing, Dodge: William Ramsbey
VP Engineering: William Pizzichil
VP Marketing: Randall P. Breaux, age 47
VP Audit Services: Larry L. Johnston, age 45
VP Generators: Jeffery R. (Jeff) Hubert, age 56
VP Dodge Marketing: Robert Nemecek
VP Investor Relations: Tracy L. Long, age 44
Treasurer and Corporate Controller: Bryant G. Dooly Jr., age 48
Auditors: Ernst & Young LLP

LOCATIONS

HQ: Baldor Electric Company
5711 R. S. Boreham, Jr. St., Fort Smith, AR 72901
Phone: 479-646-4711   **Fax:** 479-648-5792
Web: www.baldor.com

2009 Sales

	$ mil.	% of total
US	1,253.4	82
Other countries	270.7	18
Total	**1,524.1**	**100**

PRODUCTS/OPERATIONS

2009 Sales

	% of total
Industrial electric motors	64
Mechanical power transmission products	29
Other (including generators, drives & metal stampings)	7
Total	**100**

Selected Products

Drives
  Linear and rotary servo motors
  Motion control products
Generators
  Emergency and standby generators
  Industrial towable generators
  Mobile light towers
  Peak-shaving generators
  Portable generators
  Prime power generators

Mechanical power transmission
  Bushings
  Conveyor pulleys
  Helical & worm gearings
  Mounted bearings
  Sheaves
Motors
  AC motors (up to 15,000 horsepower)
  DC motors (up to 3,000 horsepower)
  Integral gear motors

COMPETITORS

A. O. Smith
Altra Holdings
AMETEK
Bodine Electric
Bosch Rexroth Corp.
China Electric
Converteam
Emerson Electric
Franklin Electric
GE
Johnson Electric
Kinetek
Magnetek
Regal Beloit
Rexnord
Rockwell Automation
Siemens Industry Automation
SKF
TB Wood's
TECO-Westinghouse
TM GE Automation Systems
Toshiba
WEG Electric Motors

HISTORICAL FINANCIALS

Company Type: Public

Income Statement

FYE: Saturday nearest December 31

	REVENUE ($ mil.)	NET INCOME ($ mil.)	NET PROFIT MARGIN	EMPLOYEES
12/09	1,524	60	3.9%	7,250
12/08	1,955	99	5.1%	7,891
12/07	1,825	94	5.2%	8,083
12/06	811	48	5.9%	3,950
12/05	722	43	6.0%	3,841
Annual Growth	20.6%	8.6%	—	17.2%

2009 Year-End Financials

Debt ratio: 125.1%
Return on equity: 6.8%
Cash ($ mil.): 15
Current ratio: 3.11
Long-term debt ($ mil.): 1,156

No. of shares (mil.): 47
Dividends
  Yield: 2.4%
  Payout: 53.1%
Market value ($ mil.): 1,320

Stock History

NYSE: BEZ

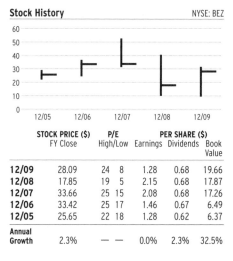

	STOCK PRICE ($) FY Close	P/E High/Low		PER SHARE ($) Earnings	Dividends	Book Value
12/09	28.09	24	8	1.28	0.68	19.66
12/08	17.85	19	5	2.15	0.68	17.87
12/07	33.66	25	15	2.08	0.68	17.26
12/06	33.42	25	17	1.46	0.67	6.49
12/05	25.65	22	18	1.28	0.62	6.37
Annual Growth	2.3%	—		0.0%	2.3%	32.5%

Ball Corporation

The well-rounded Ball Corporation pitches packaging to companies producing food, beverage, and household products. Food and beverage packaging includes aluminum and steel cans, and some polyethylene terephthalate (PET) plastic bottles. A large part of Ball's packaging revenue derives from long-term contracts with SABMiller and bottlers of Pepsi-Cola and Coca-Cola brands in North America, Europe, China, Brazil, and Argentina. Ball Aerospace & Technologies manufactures an array of systems, from remote sensing satellites to telescopes, surveillance, and antenna and video devices.

The global economic downturn in 2008 and 2009 coupled with the ripple effect of reduced consumer demand has put a dent in Ball's metal beverage packaging net sales across all regions. Shoring up revenue, the company has pinched operating costs, cut its workforce, streamlined manufacturing processes, and increased prices. Ball sold its Plastic Packaging Americas business in mid-2010 for $280 million to Amcor, Australia's packaging giant. The company shuttered metal beverage can plants, as well, in Missouri and Puerto Rico, its aluminum beverage can manufacturing plant in Washington, and aerosol can facilities in California and Georgia.

In mid-2010 Ball acquired Neuman Aluminum, a North American manufacturer of aluminum disks (commonly called slugs) used to produce an array of packaging for beverage, personal care, household, and other products. Its two plants, in Virginia and Quebec, manufacture aerosol cans, collapsible tubes, beverage bottles, and technical impact extrusions.

Ball purchased four US beverage can plants in 2009 from Anheuser-Busch InBev for $575.7 million; the plants are located in Georgia, Ohio, Wisconsin, and Florida, and produce a whopping 10 billion aluminum beverage cans and an equal number of beverage can ends per year. Two-thirds of the cans are sold to major soft drink producers, and the remainder to AB InBev.

Ball is also tapping growing demand in developing geographies. Through its 50-50 Brazilian joint venture, Latapack-Ball Embalagens, Ltda., Ball completed a new beverage can plant and added can capacity at an existing one in 2009. In addition, Ball raised its stake from 35% to 100% in Chinese joint venture Jianlibao Group Co.

Before the economy turned south, Ball made several sizeable acquisitions. It acquired US Can's US and Argentinean operations for $550 million. The deal, which included 10 US plants and two Argentinean plants, made Ball the US's largest maker of aerosol cans.

HISTORY

The Ball Corporation began in 1880 when Frank Ball and his four brothers started making wood-jacket tin cans to store and transport kerosene and other materials. In 1884 the company switched to tin-jacketed glass containers for kerosene lamps. The lamps, however, were soon displaced by Thomas Edison's electric light bulb.

The Ball brothers then learned that the patent to the original sealed-glass storage container (the Mason jar) had expired. By 1886 the brothers had entered the sealed-jar business and imprinted their jars with the Ball name. In their first year, they made 12,500 jars and sparked a patent war with the two reigning jar producers,

who asserted that they controlled the correct patents and threatened to sue. The Ball lawyers proved that the patents had expired, and the jar remained Ball's mainstay for many years.

The company began diversifying, but a 1947 antitrust ruling prohibited it from buying additional glass subsidiaries. Ball decided to take advantage of the space race by buying Control Cells (aerospace science research) in 1957; that operation became Ball Brothers Research Corporation (later Ball Aerospace Systems Division). The Soviets launched Sputnik that year, igniting a massive US scientific effort in 1958, and Ball won federal contracts to make equipment for the US space program.

Ball established its metal beverage-container business in 1969 when it bought Jeffco Manufacturing of Colorado. The operation soon won contracts to supply two-piece cans to Budweiser, Coca-Cola, Dr Pepper, Pepsi, and Stroh's Beer.

John Fisher became president and CEO in 1971. The last company president who was a member of the Ball family, Fisher wanted Ball to diversify. He took the company public in 1972 to fund his efforts. That year he acquired a Singapore-based petroleum equipment company. Next he led Ball into agricultural irrigation systems and prefabricated housing. In 1974 Ball acquired a small California computer firm, which formed the basis of its telecommunications division.

Fisher retired in 1981. Ball's metal-container business suffered in the late 1980s from overcapacity and price wars in its industry. In 1989 the company's aerospace division was hard hit by $10 million in losses on an Air Force contract and by cuts in defense spending.

Ball spun off its Alltrista canning supplies subsidiary to shareholders in 1993 and purchased Heekin Can, a manufacturer for the food, pet food, and aerosol markets. That year Ball's $50 million mirror system corrected the Hubble Space Telescope's blurred vision. The company entered the polyethylene terephthalate (PET) container business in 1995 and placed its glass-container business into a newly formed company, Ball-Foster Glass Container, and the next year sold its stake to its partner, French materials company Saint-Gobain Group.

Ball sold its aerosol-can business to BWAY Corp in 1996. It acquired M.C. Packaging of Hong Kong in 1997. Ball popped the top on another big deal in 1998 when it bought Reynolds Metals' aluminum-can business (Reynolds is now owned by Alcoa). In 1999 and 2000 the company closed four can plants in an effort to improve an imbalance in supply and demand.

In 2001 Ball and ConAgra Grocery Products formed a joint venture, Ball Western Can Company, to make metal food containers. Also that year subsidiary Ball Aerospace & Technologies landed a $260 million contract with the US Air Force, and Ball's president and COO, David Hoover, was named CEO. That November, Ball entered into a joint venture with Coors Brewing Co. called Rocky Mountain Metal Container to operate Coors' can facilities, making 4.5 billion cans per year.

In 2003 Ball completed its purchase of German can maker Schmalbach-Lubeca (renamed Ball Packaging Europe) for about $890 million. The deal made Ball the second-largest can maker in Europe.

EXECUTIVES

Chairman and CEO: R. David Hoover, age 63,
$9,615,275 total compensation
President, COO, and Director: John A. Hayes, age 44,
$3,644,055 total compensation
EVP and COO, Global Packaging Operations:
Raymond J. Seabrook, age 58,
$2,779,473 total compensation
EVP Administration and Corporate Secretary:
David A. Westerlund, age 59,
$2,627,134 total compensation
SVP and CFO: Scott C. Morrison, age 47
SVP Corporate Relations: Harold L. Sohn, age 63
VP Information Technology and Services:
Leroy J. Williams Jr., age 44
VP and Controller: Shawn M. Barker, age 42
**VP, General Counsel, and Assistant Corporate
Secretary:** Charles E. Baker, age 52
VP Administration and Compliance: Lisa A. Pauley,
age 48
VP Financial Reporting and Tax: Douglas K. Bradford,
age 52
**President, Ball Metal Beverage Packaging Division,
Americas:** Michael L. Hranicka, age 42
President, Ball Asia Pacific: Colin Gillis, age 56
President and CEO, Ball Aerospace & Technologies:
David L. (Dave) Taylor, age 58
President, Ball Packaging Europe: Gerrit Heske, age 45
President, Ball Plastic Packaging Division, Americas:
Larry J. Green, age 62
Director Investor Relations: Ann T. Scott
Auditors: PricewaterhouseCoopers LLP

LOCATIONS

HQ: Ball Corporation
10 Longs Peak Dr., Broomfield, CO 80021
Phone: 303-469-3131   **Fax:** 303-460-2127
Web: www.ball.com

2009 Sales

	$ mil.	% of total
US	5,184.4	71
Foreign	2,160.9	29
Total	**7,345.3**	**100**

PRODUCTS/OPERATIONS

2009 Sales

	$ mil.	% of total
Metal beverage packaging, Americas & Asia	2,888.8	39
Metal beverage packaging, Europe	1,739.5	24
Metal food & household products packaging, Americas	1,392.9	19
Plastic packaging, Americas	634.9	9
Aerospace & technologies	689.2	9
Total	**7,345.3**	**100**

Selected Products

Aerospace and Technologies
  Products
    Anti-blooming technology
    Conformal, low observable, reflector, silhouette, and
      tactical antennas
    Electro-optical sensors
    Fast-steering mirrors
    Hubble, James Webb, and Spitzer space telescope
    Laser communications
    Mk 20 all-light-level television, RS 170 CCD, and
      Seasparrow low light level camera
    Pointing and tracking
    Remote sensing
    Solar backscatter utraviolet radiometer
    Vac Kote lubricants
    Video products
    Wireless communications

Packaging
  Aerosol and Specialty
    Aerosol cans
    Custom-shaped aerosol cans
    Decorative custom metal tins
    General line metal cans
    Oblong metal cans
    Round metal paint cans
  Metal Beverage
    Two-piece metal beverage containers
  Metal Food
    Two- and three-piece metal food containers
  Plastic
    HDPE beverage and concentrate bottles
    PET plastic beverage and food containers
    Polypropylene food and beverage containers

COMPETITORS

Alcoa
Amcor
Anchor Glass
Boeing
BWAY
CLARCOR
Consolidated Container
Constar International
Crown Holdings
Orbital Sciences
Owens-Illinois
Rexam
Rio Tinto Alcan
Rockwell Collins
Saint-Gobain Containers
Sequa
Silgan
Teledyne Technologies
Tetra Laval

HISTORICAL FINANCIALS

Company Type: Public

Income Statement

FYE: December 31

	REVENUE ($ mil.)	NET INCOME ($ mil.)	NET PROFIT MARGIN	EMPLOYEES
12/09	7,345	388	5.3%	14,500
12/08	7,562	320	4.2%	14,500
12/07	7,390	281	3.8%	15,500
12/06	6,622	330	5.0%	15,500
12/05	5,751	262	4.5%	13,100
Annual Growth	**6.3%**	**10.4%**	**—**	**2.6%**

2009 Year-End Financials

Debt ratio: 144.4%
Return on equity: 29.1%
Cash ($ mil.): 211
Current ratio: 1.35
Long-term debt ($ mil.): 2,284
No. of shares (mil.): 92
Dividends
  Yield: 0.8%
  Payout: 9.8%
Market value ($ mil.): 4,773

Stock History

NYSE: BLL

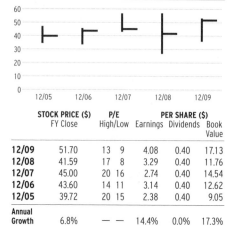

	STOCK PRICE ($) FY Close	P/E High/Low		PER SHARE ($) Earnings	Dividends	Book Value
12/09	51.70	13	9	4.08	0.40	17.13
12/08	41.59	17	8	3.29	0.40	11.76
12/07	45.00	20	16	2.74	0.40	14.54
12/06	43.60	14	11	3.14	0.40	12.62
12/05	39.72	20	15	2.38	0.40	9.05
Annual Growth	**6.8%**	**—**	**—**	**14.4%**	**0.0%**	**17.3%**

Bank of America

Welcome to the machine. One of the largest banks in the US by assets (along with Citigroup and JPMorgan Chase), Bank of America also boasts one of the country's most extensive branch networks with more than 5,900 locations covering some 40 states from coast to coast. Its core services include consumer and small business banking, credit cards, and asset management. In early 2009 Bank of America paid some $50 billion in stock for Merrill Lynch, which had been crippled by the global credit crisis. The acquisition of the once-mighty investment bank known as "The Bull," which has an extensive retail brokerage network, beefs up Bank of America's wealth management, investment banking, and international business.

However, the Merrill Lynch deal also brought Bank of America a fair share of headaches. With the approval of Bank of America leadership, the failed investment bank gave early bonuses worth billions to its executives, prompting angry Bank of America shareholders and lawmakers to cry foul. The Securities and Exchange Commission slapped Bank of America with a $33 million fine for misleading shareholders about the bonuses. That fine was rejected by a federal judge in 2009 and the matter was ordered to go to trial. Bank of America ultimately agreed to pay $150 million in a settlement.

Then-CEO Ken Lewis in particular came under fire for not disclosing how bleak Merrill Lynch's financial condition was prior to the purchase; Lewis in turn said he had been implicitly pressured by the government to keep the troubles under wraps to prevent the deal from collapsing. Director Walter Massey was named chairman and Lewis stepped down at the end of the year. Brian Moynihan, the head of consumer and small business banking, succeeded Lewis as CEO. Longtime Dupont CEO, Charles Holliday took over as chairman in 2010, replacing the retiring Massey.

Shortly after acquiring Merrill Lynch, the company began implementing a restructuring plan to cut the combined group's total workforce by some 30,000 (approximately 10% of employees) within three years.

In an effort to boost the economy and stimulate lending, the US government in 2008 bought some $250 billion worth of preferred shares in the country's top banks. Approximately $45 billion of that was slated for Bank of America ($20 billion more than the original investment total). Bank of America finished paying back the debt in late 2009.

Bank of America sold private bank First Republic, which it gained with the Merrill Lynch acquisition, to an investor group led by bank management and private investors General Atlantic and Colony Capital for around $1 billion. The bank also sold the long-term asset management business of its mutual fund manager Columbia Management to Ameriprise for some $1.2 billion.

The company acquired troubled lender Countrywide Financial in 2008. The acquisition made Bank of America the largest residential mortgage lender and servicer in the US. The company also settled a lawsuit contending that Countrywide engaged in deceptive lending practices.

HISTORY

Bank of America predecessor NationsBank was formed as the Commercial National Bank in 1874 by citizens of Charlotte, North Carolina. In 1901 George Stephens and Word Wood formed what became American Trust Co. The banks merged in 1957 to become American Commercial Bank, which in 1960 merged with Security National to form North Carolina National Bank.

In 1968 the bank formed holding company NCNB, which by 1980 was the largest bank in North Carolina. Under the leadership of Hugh McColl, who became chairman in 1983, NCNB became the first southern bank to span six states.

NCNB profited from the savings and loan crisis of the late 1980s by managing assets and buying defunct thrifts at fire-sale prices. The company nearly doubled its assets in 1988, when the FDIC chose it to manage the shuttered First Republicbank, then Texas' largest bank. The company renamed itself NationsBank in 1991.

A 1993 joint venture with Dean Witter and Discover to open securities brokerages in banks led to complaints that customers were not fully informed of the risks of some investments and that brokers were paying rebates to banking personnel for customer referrals. Dean Witter withdrew from the arrangement in 1994, and SEC investigations and a class-action lawsuit ensued. NationsBank settled the lawsuit for about $30 million the next year. (The company agreed to pay nearly $7 million to settle similar charges in 1998.)

Enter BankAmerica. Founded in 1904 as Bank of Italy, BankAmerica had once been the US's largest bank but had fallen behind as competitors consolidated. The company's board of directors was pondering ways to become more competitive, and in 1998 decided a merger was the best way; NationsBank obliged.

After the merger, the combined firm announced it would write down a billion-dollar bad loan to D.E. Shaw & Co., which followed the same Russian-investment-paved path of descent as Long-Term Capital Management. David Coulter (head of the old BankAmerica, which made the loan) took the fall for the loss, resigning as president; the balance of power shifted to the NationsBank side in 1999 when Kenneth Lewis took the post. In early 1999 the bank changed its name to Bank of America.

In 2003 Bank of America's mutual fund chief Robert Gordon was among several employees who left the firm amidst a New York attorney general's investigation into hedge fund client Canary Capital Partners, which allegedly had access to Bank of America's trading platform to make illegal after-hours trades of the company's erstwhile Nations Funds. Bank of America also paid $10 million for failing to provide documents to the SEC during its investigation of the scandal, the largest-ever fine levied by the regulatory body for such an infraction. Meanwhile, the company acquired northeastern banking behemoth FleetBoston for some $50 billion in 2004.

In 2005 the company struck a deal with regulators to implement tighter controls, cut fees charged to investors, exit the mutual fund clearing business, and pay more than $500 million in fines. Also that year, Bank of America remitted another $460 million to settle investor claims that it did not adequately conduct due diligence when underwriting bonds of doomed telecom firm WorldCom in 2001 and 2002.

Bank of America previously fattened up by purchasing northeastern banking behemoth FleetBoston for some $50 billion in 2004 and credit card giant MBNA for approximately $35 billion in cash and stock in early 2006.

EXECUTIVES

Chairman: Charles O. (Chad) Holliday Jr., age 63
President, CEO, and Director: Brian T. Moynihan, age 50, $6,511,468 total compensation
EVP and CFO: Charles H. (Chuck) Noski, age 57
CTO: Marc Gordon
General Counsel: Edward O'Keefe, age 55
Deputy General Counsel and Secretary: Alice A. Herald
Chief Risk Officer: Bruce Thompson
Global Strategy and Marketing Officer: Anne M. Finucane
Global Human Resources Executive: Andrea B. Smith, age 42
Global Director Banking and Markets: Paula Dominick
Global Head Trading Risk Analytics: Greg Ransom
Chairman, Global Mergers and Acquisitions: Steven Baronoff, age 50
Executive Vice Chairman, Global Corporate and Investment Bank: Stefan M. Selig, age 47
President, Consumer, Small Business, and Card Banking: Joe L. Price, $6,118,608 total compensation
President, Home Loans: Barbara J. Desoer, age 57, $7,415,847 total compensation
President, Global Technology and Operations: Catherine P. (Cathy) Bessant
President, Global Commercial Banking: David C. Darnell
Head Global Markets and Research Technology: Michael Dubno, age 47
Head Marketing, Global Wealth and Investment Management Division: Claire Huang
Chief Accounting Officer: Neil A. Cotty
Director Investor Relations: Kevin Stitt
Auditors: PricewaterhouseCoopers LLP

LOCATIONS

HQ: Bank of America Corporation
100 N. Tryon St., Charlotte, NC 28255
Phone: 704-386-5681   **Fax:** 704-386-6699
Web: www.bankofamerica.com

PRODUCTS/OPERATIONS

2009 Sales

	$ mil.	% of total
Interest		
Loans & leases, including fees	48,703	32
Debt securities	12,947	9
Trading account assets	7,944	5
Other	8,322	5
Noninterest		
Trading account profits	12,235	8
Investment & brokerage services	11,919	8
Service charges	11,038	7
Equity investments	10,014	7
Mortgage banking	8,791	6
Card income	8,353	6
Investment banking	5,551	4
Other	4,633	3
Total	**150,450**	**100**

2009 Assets

	$ mil.	% of total
Cash & short-term investments	145,541	6
Federal funds sold & securities borrowed or purchased under agreements to resell	189,933	8
Trading account assets	182,206	8
Derivative assets	80,689	4
Mortgage-backed securities	234,039	11
Other debt securities	77,402	3
Net loans & leases	862,928	39
Goodwill	86,314	4
Customer & other receivables	81,996	4
Other	282,251	13
Total	**2,223,299**	**100**

COMPETITORS

Bank of New York Mellon
BB&T
Capital One
Citigroup
Citizens Financial Group
Goldman Sachs
HSBC
HSBC USA
JPMorgan Chase
KeyCorp
Morgan Stanley
PNC Financial
RBC Financial Group
State Street
SunTrust
UnionBanCal
U.S. Bancorp
Wells Fargo

HISTORICAL FINANCIALS

Company Type: Public

Income Statement

	ASSETS ($ mil.)	NET INCOME ($ mil.)	INCOME AS % OF ASSETS	EMPLOYEES
				FYE: December 31
12/09	2,223,299	6,276	0.3%	284,000
12/08	1,817,943	4,008	0.2%	243,000
12/07	1,715,746	14,982	0.9%	210,000
12/06	1,459,737	21,133	1.4%	203,425
12/05	1,291,803	16,465	1.3%	176,638
Annual Growth	**14.5%**	**(21.4%)**	**—**	**12.6%**

2009 Year-End Financials

Equity as % of assets: 8.7%
Return on assets: 0.3%
Return on equity: 3.8%
Long-term debt ($ mil.): 438,521
No. of shares (mil.): 10,034
Dividends
  Yield: 0.3%
  Payout: —
Market value ($ mil.): 151,110
Sales ($ mil.): 150,450

Stock History

NYSE: BAC

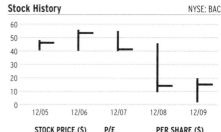

	STOCK PRICE ($) FY Close	P/E High/Low		PER SHARE ($) Earnings	Dividends	Book Value
12/09	15.06	—	—	(0.29)	0.04	23.07
12/08	14.08	82	18	0.55	2.24	17.65
12/07	41.26	16	12	3.30	2.40	14.63
12/06	53.39	12	9	4.59	2.12	13.48
12/05	46.15	12	10	4.04	1.90	10.12
Annual Growth	**(24.4%)**	**—**	**—**	**—**	**(61.9%)**	**22.9%**

Bank of New York Mellon

Big Apple, meet Iron City. The Bank of New York cemented its status as one of the world's largest securities servicing firms with the 2007 acquisition of Pittsburgh-based Mellon Financial. The merger also fit in with the company's other areas of focus, including asset management and corporate trust and treasury services. It was The Bank of New York's third attempt to acquire Mellon. Now known as The Bank of New York Mellon (BNY Mellon), the firm has about $20 trillion in assets under custody and some $1 trillion of assets under management. Its Pershing subsidiary is a leading securities clearing firm. BNY Mellon has a presence in about 35 countries.

Subsidiaries BNY Mellon Asset Management and Mellon Capital Management serve institutional investors, while the company's wealth management business courts high-net-worth individuals and families, as well as endowments and foundations. Other operations include mutual fund manager Dreyfus, foreign exchange, investment banking, and issuer services related to American Depository Receipts (ADRs). BNY Mellon also has interests in boutique money managers Standish and UK-based Newton.

BNY Mellon has been on a steady march toward global expansion. It especially has its sights set on Germany, Australia, China, South Korea, India, Brazil, and the Middle East. In 2010 it acquired PNC's Global Investment Servicing business, a provider of custody, fund accounting, transfer agency, and outsourcing solutions for asset managers and financial advisors, for some $2.3 billion in cash, stock, and debt. The acquisition, which doubled BNY Mellon's European asset base, was designed to enhance the company's position supporting fund managers and financial advisors around the world. The company also arranged to buy out Canadian Imperial Bank of Commerce's 50% stake in Toronto-based trust and custody joint venture CIBC Mellon. BNY Mellon also plans to expand its wealth management business in Canada through the acquisition of Toronto-based I(3) Advisors, which has more than $3 billion in assets.

The Bank of New York jettisoned much of its traditional banking services for more lucrative fee-based securities and financial services, swapping virtually all its retail branches in metropolitan New York for JPMorgan Chase's corporate trust business in 2006. Both units were valued at more than $2 billion each. The company followed the trade with the sale of Mellon 1st Business Bank to U.S. Bancorp in 2008.

HISTORY

In 1784 Alexander Hamilton (at 27, already a Revolutionary War hero and economic theorist) and a group of New York merchants and lawyers founded New York City's first bank, The Bank of New York (BNY). Hamilton saw a need for a credit system to finance the nation's growth and to establish credibility for the new nation's chaotic monetary system.

Hamilton became US secretary of the treasury in 1789 and soon negotiated the new US government's first loan — for $200,000 — from BNY. The bank later helped finance the War of 1812 by raising $16 million and the Civil War by loaning the government $150 million. In 1878 BNY became a US Treasury depository for the sale of government bonds.

The bank's conservative fiscal policies and emphasis on commercial banking enabled it to weather economic turbulence in the 19th century. In 1922 it merged with New York Life Insurance and Trust (formed in 1830 by many of BNY's directors) to form Bank of New York and Trust. The bank survived the crash of 1929 and remained profitable, paying dividends throughout the Depression. In 1938 it reclaimed its Bank of New York name.

During the mid-20th century, BNY expanded its operations and its reach through acquisitions, including Fifth Avenue Bank (trust services, 1948) and Empire Trust (serving developing industries, 1966). In 1968 the bank created holding company The Bank of New York Company to expand statewide with purchases such as Empire National Bank (1980).

BNY relaxed its lending policies in the 1980s and began to build its fee-for-service side, boosting its American Depositary Receipts business by directly soliciting European companies and seeking government securities business. The bank bought New York rival Irving Trust in a 1989 hostile takeover and in 1990 began buying other banks' credit card portfolios.

As the economy cooled in the early 1990s, BNY's book of highly leveraged transactions and nonperforming loans suffered, so the company sold many of those loans.

In the mid-1990s BNY bought processing and trust businesses and continued to build its retail business in the suburbs. It pared noncore operations, selling its mortgage banking unit (and in 1998 moved its remaining mortgage operations into a joint venture with Alliance Mortgage); credit card business (1998); and factoring and asset-based lending operations (1999). In late 1997 and again in 1998, the bank tried to woo Mellon Bank (now Mellon Financial) into a merger but was rejected; it had better luck in 2006.

The growth of the firm's custody services accelerated in the late 1990s. In 1997 BNY bought operations from Wells Fargo, Signet Bank (now part of First Union), and NationsBank (now Bank of America). By 1998 BNY had bought some two dozen corporate trust businesses. Two years later it acquired the trust operations of Royal Bank of Scotland and Barclays Bank.

Scandal rocked the firm in 1999 when the US began investigating the possible flow of money related to Russian organized crime; the following year a former bank executive admitted to having laundered about $7 billion through BNY. The bank reached a non-prosecution agreement in the US in 2005 and, four years later, agreed to a $14 million settlement with Russia.

In 2000 BNY bought the corporate trust business of Dai-Ichi Kangyo Bank (now part of Mizuho Financial) and Harris Trust and Savings Bank. Purchases in 2002 included equity research firm Jaywalk, institutional trader Francis P. Maglio & Co., and a pair of Boston-area asset managers for high-net-worth individuals, Gannet Welsh & Kotler and Beacon Fiduciary Advisors. BNY bought Pershing from Credit Suisse First Boston in 2003.

Fallout from the money laundering scandal lingered. In 2006 the Federal Reserve accused the bank of not tightening its own controls to prevent a recurrence of illegal activity.

EXECUTIVES

Chairman and CEO: Robert P. (Bob) Kelly, age 55, $14,046,435 total compensation
President and Director: Gerald L. Hassell, age 58, $6,394,264 total compensation
Head Global Operations and Technology: Kurt D. Woetzel
SEVP and CFO: Thomas P. (Todd) Gibbons, age 51, $4,058,141 total compensation
SEVP and General Counsel: Jane C. Sherburne
SEVP; CEO, Financial Markets and Treasury Services: Karen B. Peetz
SEVP; CEO, Pershing: Richard F. (Rich) Brueckner
SEVP and Chief Risk Officer: Brian G. Rogan
SEVP; CEO, Alternative and Broker-Dealer Services: Arthur (Art) Certosimo
CIO: John A. Fiore, age 58
Chief Auditor; EVP and Chief Auditor, The Bank of New York: James (Jim) Vallone
Chief Investment Officer, BNY Mellon Wealth Management: Leo P. Grohowski
EVP and Treasurer: Scott Freidenrich
EVP and Deputy General Counsel: Matthew Biben
EVP Broker-Dealer Services & Alternative Investment Services: Andrew M. Gordon
EVP; CEO Treasury Services: Eric D. Kamback
EVP and Head Corporate Affairs: R. Jeep Bryant
EVP Wealth Management: Donald J. (Don) Heberle
EVP and Head, Enterprise-Wide Market Risk: Robert R. Rupp, age 56
Chief Human Resources Officer: Lisa B. Peters
CEO, BNY Mellon Shareowner Services: Samir Pandiri, age 47
CEO, BNY Mellon Corporate Trust: Scott Posner
CEO, Depositary Receipts: Michael Cole-Fontayn
CEO, I(3) Advisors: June Ntazinda
CEO, Broker-Dealer Services: James Malgieri
CEO, BNY Mellon Wealth Management: Lawrence (Larry) Hughes
CEO, The Dreyfus Corporation: Jon Baum
Chairman, Asia/Pacific Region: Christopher R. (Chris) Sturdy
Chairman, Europe; Chief Global Client Management Officer and Co-CEO, BNY Mellon Asset Servicing: Timothy F. (Tim) Keaney
Co-Head Integration: Steven G. Elliott, age 63, $5,338,703 total compensation
Managing Director and Head Investor Relations: Stephen Lackey
Corporate Communications: Kevin Heine
Corporate Secretary: Arlie R. Nogay
Auditors: KPMG LLP

LOCATIONS

HQ: The Bank of New York Mellon Corporation
1 Wall St., 10th Fl., New York, NY 10286
Phone: 212-495-1784   **Fax:** 212-809-9528
Web: www.bnymellon.com

PRODUCTS/OPERATIONS

2009 Sales

	$ mil.	% of total
Interest		
Securities	1,748	13
Loans	943	7
Other	816	6
Noninterest		
Securities servicing fees		
Asset servicing	2,573	19
Issuer services	1,463	10
Clearing services	962	7
Asset & wealth management fees	2,639	19
Foreign exchange & other trading activities	1,036	7
Treasury services	519	4
Distribution & servicing	397	3
Other	735	5
Adjustments	(5,552)	—
Total	**8,279**	**100**

Selected Subsidiaries and Business Lines

Alcentra (sub-investment-grade debt asset management)
Ankura Capital (Australian equities)
Blackfriars Asset Management (emerging markets and global fixed income)
BNY Mellon Asset Management (institutional asset management)
BNY Mellon Cash Investment Strategies (money market funds)
The Boston Company (equity asset management)
Dreyfus (mutual funds)
EACM Advisors (fund of funds)
Harmon Investment Group (Asian equity management)
Ivy Investment Management (fund of hedge funds management)
Mellon Capital Management
Mellon Global Alternative Investments
Newton (active investment management)
Pershing (securities clearing)
Urdang (global real estate investment management)
Walter Scott (global equity investment management)
WestLB Mellon (European and global fixed income)

COMPETITORS

Bank of America
Barclays
BlackRock
Citigroup
Credit Suisse (USA)
Deutsche Bank
HSBC
JPMorgan Chase
Northern Trust
PNC Financial
State Street
UBS

HISTORICAL FINANCIALS

Company Type: Public

Income Statement

FYE: December 31

	ASSETS ($ mil.)	NET INCOME ($ mil.)	INCOME AS % OF ASSETS	EMPLOYEES
12/09	212,224	(1,083)	—	42,200
12/08	237,512	1,445	0.6%	42,900
12/07	197,656	2,219	1.1%	42,100
12/06	103,370	3,011	2.9%	22,961
12/05	102,074	1,571	1.5%	23,451
Annual Growth	20.1%	—	—	15.8%

2009 Year-End Financials

Equity as % of assets: 13.7%
Return on assets: —
Return on equity: —
Long-term debt ($ mil.): 17,711
No. of shares (mil.): 1,214
Dividends
Yield: 1.8%
Payout: —
Market value ($ mil.): 33,957
Sales ($ mil.): 8,279

Stock History

NYSE: BK

	STOCK PRICE ($) FY Close	P/E High/Low	PER SHARE ($) Earnings	Dividends	Book Value
12/09	27.97	— —	(1.16)	0.51	23.87
12/08	28.33	41 17	1.20	0.96	23.10
12/07	48.76	23 17	2.18	0.92	24.22
12/06	39.37	10 8	3.93	0.86	9.55
12/05	31.85	17 13	2.03	0.82	8.13
Annual Growth	(3.2%)	— —	—	(11.2%)	30.9%

Barnes & Noble

Barnes & Noble does business — big business — by the book. As the #1 bookseller in the US, it operates about 1,355 bookstores, including 720 Barnes & Noble superstores and another 635 college bookstores, in all 50 states and Washington, DC. Stores are typically 10,000 to 60,000 sq. ft. in size and stock between 60,000 and 200,000 book titles. Many locations contain Starbucks cafes as well as music departments with more than 30,000 titles. In cyberspace, the firm conducts business through Barnesandnoble.com (BN.com), which generates about 10% of revenue. In 2009 Barnes & Noble introduced the Nook e-book reader. Under pressure from shareholders, the company announced in 2010 it would consider selling itself.

The announcement comes amid increasing demand for digital books and plummeting profits (net income fell from $150 million in 2007 to $36 million in 2010, a 75% drop). Barnes & Noble is working to reposition its business from the traditional store-based model to one focused on e-commerce, however, it noted that future investment in digital technology would affect profits in 2011.

Barnes & Noble's prospective buyers include founder and chairman Leonard Riggio, who owns about 30% of the firm's stock, and billionaire investor Ron Burkle, whose investment group Yucaipa holds a nearly 20% stake.

Joining the likes of Amazon.com and Sony, Barnes & Noble developed its own digital book reader. The Nook features a 6-inch color screen made by E-Ink and allows users to share titles. (Barnes & Noble's e-bookstore features more than 1 million titles.) The company has reported strong Nook sales at its bookstores since it became available. It also acquired electronic bookseller Fictionwise for nearly $16 million in 2009.

In another strategic move, the bookseller reunited in 2009 with its sister company, Barnes & Noble College Booksellers. The two companies had operated independently since Barnes & Noble went public in 1993. Barnes & Noble paid more than $595 million for the roughly 625-location college bookseller to increase its cash flow by purchasing a business that is less vulnerable to economic cycles than its own. Barnes & Noble also gained entry to the small but growing market for electronic textbooks through the purchase.

Aiming to trim its costs as the economic downturn lingers, Barnes & Noble closed the last of its B. Dalton bookstores in early 2010.

After recording both lower sales and profits in 2009, Barnes & Noble replaced CEO Steve Riggio in early 2010 with William Lynch, who had served as president of BN.com. Lynch put e-commerce at the forefront of the company's growth track since joining in 2009 and was largely responsible in the purchase of Fictionwise, introducing the Nook, and rolling out Barnes & Noble's e-bookstore. Steve Riggio remains vice chairman of Barnes & Noble.

HISTORY

Barnes & Noble dates back to 1873 when Charles Barnes went into the used-book business in Wheaton, Illinois. By the turn of the century, he was operating a thriving bookselling operation in Chicago. His son William took over as president in 1902. William sold his share in the firm in 1917 (to C. W. Follett, who built Follett

Corp.) and moved to New York City, where he bought an interest in established textbook wholesalers Noble & Noble. The company was soon renamed Barnes & Noble. It first sold mainly to colleges and libraries, providing textbooks and opening a large Fifth Avenue shop. Over the next three decades, Barnes & Noble became one of the leading booksellers in the New York region.

Enter Leonard Riggio, who worked at a New York University bookstore to help pay for night school. He studied engineering but got the itch for bookselling. In 1965, at age 24, he borrowed $5,000 and opened Student Book Exchange NYC, a college bookstore. Beginning in the late 1960s, he expanded by buying other college bookstores.

In 1971 Riggio paid $1.2 million for the Barnes & Noble store on Fifth Avenue. He soon expanded the store, and in 1974 he began offering jaw-dropping, competitor-maddening discounts of up to 40% for best-sellers. Acquiring Marlboro Books five years later, the company entered the mail-order and publishing business.

By 1986 Barnes & Noble had grown to about 180 outlets (including 142 college bookstores). Along with Dutch retailer Vendex, that year it bought Dayton Hudson's B. Dalton mall bookstore chain (about 800 stores), forming BDB Holding Corp. (Vendex had sold its shares by 1997.) In 1989 the company acquired the Scribner's Bookstores trade name and the Bookstop/Bookstar superstore chain. BDB began its shift to superstore format and streamlined its operations to integrate Bookstop and Doubleday (acquired in 1990) into its business.

BDB changed its name to Barnes & Noble in 1991. With superstore sales booming, the retailer went public in 1993 (the college stores remained private). It bought 20% of Canadian bookseller Chapters (now Indigo Books) in 1996 (sold in 1999). The bookseller went online in 1997, and in 1998 sold a 50% stake in its Web operation subsidiary to Bertelsmann (which it re-purchased in 2003) in an attempt to strengthen both companies in the battle against online rival Amazon.com.

In 1999 barnesandnoble.com went public and Barnes & Noble bought small book publisher J.B. Fairfax International USA, which included coffee-table book publisher Michael Friedman Publishing Group. Later that year Barnes & Noble bought a 49% stake in book publishing portal iUniverse.com (later cut to 22%). It also bought Riggio's financially struggling Babbage's Etc., a chain of about 500 Babbage's, GameStop, and Software Etc. stores for $215 million.

Babbage's Etc. (renamed GameStop, Inc.) acquired video game retailer Funco for $161.5 million in 2000.

The company completed an IPO of its GameStop unit in 2003, reducing its ownership interest to about 63%. Leonard also handed over the CEO title to his brother, Steve Riggio.

In 2003 Barnes & Noble beefed up its self-publishing efforts by purchasing Sterling Publishing, a specialist in how-to and craft books. Also, Barnes & Noble's half-owned *BOOK* magazine shut down. In 2004 Barnes & Noble exited the video game retailing business when it spun off its remaining shares in GameStop.

CEO Steve Riggio was replaced by William Lynch, president of Barnes&Noble.com, in 2010. Riggio remained vice chairman of the company.

EXECUTIVES

Chairman: Leonard S. (Len) Riggio, age 69,
$715,021 total compensation
Vice Chairman: Stephen (Steve) Riggio, age 55,
$3,041,891 total compensation
CEO: William J. Lynch Jr., age 40,
$15,709,965 total compensation
CEO Retail: Mitchell S. Klipper, age 52,
$14,477,928 total compensation
CFO: Joseph J. Lombardi, age 48,
$2,048,263 total compensation
EVP Operations and Customer Service: Dan Gilbert
EVP Textbooks and Digital Education: Tracey Weber
EVP Distribution and Logistics: William F. Duffy, age 54
EVP e-Commerce Operations: Kevin M. Frain
SVP Corporate Communications and Public Affairs:
Mary Ellen Keating, age 53,
$787,600 total compensation
VP and CIO: Christopher (Chris) Grady-Troia, age 58
VP and Director Stores: Mark Bottini, age 50
VP and Corporate Controller: Allen W. Lindstrom,
age 43
VP Barnes & Noble Development: David S. Deason,
age 51, $1,010,309 total compensation
VP Human Resources: Michelle Smith, age 57
VP and Chief Merchandising Officer: Jaime Carey,
age 49
Director Investor Relations: Andy Milevoj
President, Sterling Publishing: Marcus E. Leaver,
age 40
Auditors: BDO Seidman, LLP

LOCATIONS

HQ: Barnes & Noble, Inc.
122 5th Ave., New York, NY 10011
Phone: 212-633-3300   **Fax:** 212-675-0413
Web: www.barnesandnobleinc.com

2010 US Retail Stores

	No.
California	87
Texas	57
New York	48
Florida	45
Illinois	30
Pennsylvania	27
New Jersey	25
Virginia	25
Georgia	22
Michigan	22
Arizona	21
North Carolina	21
Minnesota	20
Ohio	19
Washington	19
Massachusetts	18
Colorado	17
Indiana	14
Missouri	14
Connecticut	13
Maryland	13
South Carolina	11
Wisconsin	11
Tennessee	10
Utah	10
Alabama	8
Iowa	8
Oregon	8
Kentucky	7
Louisiana	7
Arkansas	5
Kansas	5
Nevada	5
Oklahoma	5
Other states	43
Total	**720**

PRODUCTS/OPERATIONS

2010 Stores

	No.
B&N Retail	720
B&N College	637
Total	**1,357**

2010 Sales

	$ mil.	% of total
B&N Stores	4,320.3	75
B&N College	836.5	14
B&N.com	572.8	10
Other	81.0	1
Total	**5,810.6**	**100**

COMPETITORS

Amazon.com
Best Buy
Book-of-the-Month Club
Books-A-Million
Borders Group
Buy.com
Costco Wholesale
Half Price Books
Hastings Entertainment
HMV
Hudson Group
Sony
Wal-Mart

HISTORICAL FINANCIALS

Company Type: Public

Income Statement

FYE: Saturday nearest April 30

	REVENUE ($ mil.)	NET INCOME ($ mil.)	NET PROFIT MARGIN	EMPLOYEES
4/10*	5,811	37	0.6%	35,000
1/09	5,122	76	1.5%	37,000
1/08	5,411	136	2.5%	40,000
1/07	5,261	151	2.9%	39,000
1/06	5,103	147	2.9%	39,000
Annual Growth	**3.3%**	**(29.3%)**	**—**	**(2.7%)**

*Fiscal year change

2010 Year-End Financials

Debt ratio: 28.9%
Return on equity: 4.0%
Cash ($ mil.): 61
Current ratio: 1.00
Long-term debt ($ mil.): 260
No. of shares (mil.): 59
Dividends
  Yield: 4.5%
  Payout: 158.7%
Market value ($ mil.): 1,297

Stock History

NYSE: BKS

	STOCK PRICE ($) FY Close	P/E High/Low		PER SHARE ($) Earnings	Dividends	Book Value
4/10*	22.04	46	26	0.63	1.00	15.32
1/09	16.42	26	8	1.32	0.90	15.66
1/08	33.93	22	13	2.03	0.60	18.26
1/07	38.93	22	15	2.17	0.60	19.79
1/06	42.42	22	15	2.03	0.30	18.96
Annual Growth	**(15.1%)**	**—**	**—**	**(25.4%)**	**35.1%**	**(5.2%)**

*Fiscal year change

Baxter International

Why choose between making drugs and making medical equipment? Baxter International does it all. The company makes a wide variety of medical products across its three divisions, including drugs and vaccines, dialysis equipment, and IV supplies. Its BioScience segment makes protein and plasma therapies to treat hemophilia and immune disorders, as well as vaccines and biological sealants used to close surgical wounds. Baxter is a leading maker of intravenous (IV) supplies and systems via its Medication Delivery segment; the segment also makes infusion pumps and inhaled anesthetics. Baxter's Renal division makes dialyzers and other products for the treatment of end-stage renal disease (ESRD).

The company's BioScience segment gets most of its sales from recombinant proteins and plasma products used to treat hemophilia and immune disorders. Recombinant proteins are useful because they are derived from DNA that is manufactured in the laboratory (meaning greater access to supply). Among Baxter's BioScience products are hemophilia therapy Advate and Aralast NP, a plasma-derived drug for hereditary emphysema.

The BioScience unit also makes vaccines for infectious diseases, such as tick-borne encephalitis and meningococcal meningitis. Baxter received authorization from the European Commission in 2009 to market its pandemic influenza vaccine Celvapan H1N1 in Europe.

Much of the company's R&D efforts are focused in the BioScience segment. It has an ongoing collaboration with Nektar Therapeutics, for example, to development blood-clotting proteins using Nektar's PEGylation technology. And it is working on other products in areas such as regenerative medicine and adult stem cell therapies. To jump into the bone grafting market, the company spent some $330 million to acquire UK-based ApaTech in 2010. ApaTech's bone grafting materials are already approved and sold in the US and Europe.

Medication Delivery makes intravenous drug delivery systems, infusion pumps, and anesthesia products. Products include inhaled and injectable anesthetics, as well as premixed drugs and parenteral nutrition products that are administered intravenously.

Along with dialyzers — dialysis equipment used primarily in hospitals or clinics — Baxter's Renal division makes home-use dialyzers that use a technology called peritoneal dialysis. The company is betting on the growth of peritoneal dialysis and other home-use technologies, especially in developing markets that don't have the medical infrastructure needed for clinically administered dialysis.

The Renal division is also a leading supplier of heparin, an anticoagulant used during dialysis and in critical care situations such as heart surgery. In 2008 Baxter halted production of heparin, however, after hundreds of bad reactions (including several deaths) occurred in patients using the drug. Subsequent investigations focused on raw heparin supplied to Baxter by a Chinese factory, which apparently added a cheaper ingredient into the drug which contaminated it.

HISTORY

Idaho surgeon Ralph Falk, his brother Harry, and California physician Donald Baxter formed Don Baxter Intravenous Products in 1931 to distribute the IV solutions Baxter made in Los Angeles. Two years later the company opened its first plant, located outside Chicago. Ralph Falk bought Baxter's interest in 1935 and began R&D efforts leading to the first sterilized vacuum-type blood collection device (1939), which could store blood for weeks instead of hours. Product demand during WWII spurred sales above $1.5 million by 1945.

In 1949 the company created Travenol Laboratories to make and sell drugs. Baxter went public in 1951 and began an acquisition program the next year. In 1953 failing health caused both Falks to give control to William Graham, a manager since 1945. Under Graham's leadership, Baxter absorbed Wallerstein (1957); Fenwal Labs (1959); Flint, Eaton (1959); and Dayton Flexible Products (1967).

In 1975 Baxter's headquarters moved to Deerfield, Illinois. In 1978 the company debuted the first portable dialysis machine and had $1 billion in sales. Vernon Loucks Jr. became CEO two years later. Baxter claimed the title of the world's leading hospital supplier in 1985 when it bought American Hospital Supply (a Baxter distributor from 1932 to 1962). Offering more than 120,000 products and an electronic system that connected customers with some 1,500 vendors, Baxter captured nearly 25% of the US hospital supply market in 1988. That year it became Baxter International.

In 1992 Baxter spun off Caremark (home infusion therapy and mail-order drugs) but kept a division that controlled 75% of the world's dialysis machine market.

In 1993 Baxter pleaded guilty (and was temporarily suspended from selling to the Veterans Administration) to bribing Syria to remove Baxter from a blacklist for trading in Israel.

The company entered the US cardiovascular perfusion services market in 1995 with the purchases of PSICOR and SETA. Baxter, along with two other silicone breast-implant makers, agreed to settle thousands of claims (at an average of $26,000 each) from women suffering side-effects from the implants.

Buys in 1997 boosted Baxter's presence in Europe and its share of the open-heart-surgery devices market. That year it agreed to pay about 20% of a $670 million legal settlement in a suit relating to hemophiliacs infected with HIV from blood products. In response to concerns posed by shareholders, Baxter in 1999 said it would phase out the use of PVC (polyvinyl chloride) in some products by 2010.

In 2001 Baxter withdrew dialysis equipment from Spain and Croatia after patients who used its products died. It also ended production of two types of dialyzers that were sold there. As the number of deaths mounted to more than 50 in seven countries, Baxter began facing lawsuits; it later settled with the families of many of the patients. In September 2002 the FDA issued a warning when several patients died after using Baxter's Meridian dialysis machines.

Robert L. Parkinson, Jr. took over as chairman and CEO in 2004. Parkinson succeeded Harry M. Jansen Kraemer, Jr.

In 2005 the FDA seized Baxter's existing inventories of previously recalled 6,000 Colleague Volumetric Infusion Pumps and nearly 1,000 Syndeo PCA Syringe Pumps; the federal agency resorted to these measures after the company did not fix production and design problems with the pumps in a suitable amount of time.

EXECUTIVES

Chairman and CEO: Robert L. Parkinson Jr., age 59, $14,361,305 total compensation
Corporate VP, CFO, and Treasurer: Robert J. Hombach, age 44
Corporate VP; President, Renal: Robert M. Davis, age 43, $3,342,327 total compensation
Corporate VP; President, BioScience: Joy A. Amundson, age 55, $3,433,735 total compensation
Corporate VP; President, Medication Delivery: Peter J. Arduini, age 45, $3,029,627 total compensation
Corporate VP; President, Latin America: Carlos Alonso
Corporate VP; President, Europe: Peter Nicklin
Corporate VP; President, Asia/Pacific: Gerald Lema, age 49
Corporate VP and President, International: Ludwig Hantson, age 47
Corporate VP and CIO: Karenann K. Terrell, age 48
Corporate VP and Chief Scientific Officer: Norbert G. Riedel, age 52
Corporate VP and General Counsel: David P. Scharf, age 42
Corporate VP and Controller: Michael J. Baughman, age 45
Corporate VP Manufacturing: James Michael Gatling, age 60
Corporate VP Human Resources: Jeanne K. Mason, age 54
Corporate VP, Associate General Counsel, and Corporate Secretary: Stephanie A. Shinn
Corporate VP Quality: Phillip L. Batchelor
Corporate/General Media Contact: Deborah Spak
Corporate VP Investor Relations: Mary Kay Ladone
Auditors: PricewaterhouseCoopers LLP

LOCATIONS

HQ: Baxter International Inc.
1 Baxter Pkwy., Deerfield, IL 60015
Phone: 847-948-2000   **Fax:** 847-948-2016
Web: www.baxter.com

2009 Sales

	$ mil.	% of total
International	7,245	58
United States	5,317	42
Total	**12,562**	**100**

PRODUCTS/OPERATIONS

2009 Sales

	$ mil.	% of total
BioScience	5,573	44
Medication Delivery	4,649	37
Renal	2,266	18
Transition services to Fenwal	74	1
Total	**12,562**	**100**

Selected Products

BioScience
  Advate (hemophilia A)
  Aralast (hereditary emphysema)
  Biosurgical sealants
  IGIV therapies (immune disorders)
  Vaccines
Medication Delivery
  Infusion pumps
  Inhaled anesthesia
  Injectable anesthesia
  IV fluids and medications
  IV tubing and access devices
  Parenteral nutrition products
Renal
  Hemodialysis equipment
  Peritoneal dialysis equipment

COMPETITORS

Abraxis BioScience
APP Pharmaceuticals
Bayer HealthCare
Becton, Dickinson
Biogen Idec
CareFusion
Covidien
CSL Behring
Fresenius Medical Care
Gambro AB
Grifols
Hospira
Johnson & Johnson
Novartis
Novo Nordisk
Pfizer
Roche Holding
Sanofi Pasteur
Sorin
Talecris
Terumo
ZymoGenetics

HISTORICAL FINANCIALS

Company Type: Public

Income Statement

FYE: December 31

	REVENUE ($ mil.)	NET INCOME ($ mil.)	NET PROFIT MARGIN	EMPLOYEES
12/09	12,562	2,205	17.6%	49,700
12/08	12,348	2,014	16.3%	48,500
12/07	11,263	1,707	15.2%	46,000
12/06	10,378	1,396	13.5%	48,000
12/05	9,849	956	9.7%	47,000
Annual Growth	**6.3%**	**23.2%**	**—**	**1.4%**

2009 Year-End Financials

Debt ratio: 47.8%
Return on equity: 32.9%
Cash ($ mil.): 2,786
Current ratio: 1.85
Long-term debt ($ mil.): 3,440
No. of shares (mil.): 596
Dividends
  Yield: 1.8%
  Payout: 29.8%
Market value ($ mil.): 35,000

Stock History

NYSE: BAX

	STOCK PRICE ($) FY Close	P/E High/Low		Earnings	PER SHARE ($) Dividends	Book Value
12/09	58.68	17	13	3.59	1.07	12.06
12/08	53.59	23	15	3.16	0.91	10.44
12/07	58.05	23	18	2.61	0.72	11.60
12/06	46.39	23	16	2.13	0.58	10.52
12/05	37.65	27	22	1.52	0.58	7.21
Annual Growth	**11.7%**	**—**	**—**	**24.0%**	**16.5%**	**13.7%**

BB&T Corporation

Big, Bold & Temerarious? That might be an apt description of BB&T, the banking company that covers the Southeast like kudzu. The company serves consumers, small to midsized businesses, and government entities through more than 1,800 branches. Its flagship subsidiary, Branch Banking and Trust (also known as BB&T), is one of North Carolina's oldest banks and a leading originator of residential mortgages in the Southeast. In addition to deposit accounts and loans, the company offers insurance, mutual funds, discount brokerage, wealth management, and financial planning services. Business services include leasing, factoring, and investment banking (through Scott & Stringfellow).

BB&T's bulk allows it to trump smaller competitors, yet the company maintains decentralized regional management of its banks, giving them a community bank feel. Once a serial acquirer of smaller banks throughout the Southeast, BB&T has cooled its jets in recent years amid the sputtering economy. Its only acquisition of 2008 was that of the failed Haven Trust Bank in Georgia in an FDIC-assisted transaction.

In another FDIC-assisted acquisition of a failed bank, albeit on a much larger scale, BB&T assumed ownership of more than 350 bank branches in Alabama, Florida, Georgia, Texas, and Nevada, as well as assets and customer deposits, from Colonial BancGroup, which was shut down by regulators in 2009. In early 2010 BB&T sold the Nevada assets, deposits, and branches from that transaction to U.S. Bancorp.

Virtually all of the loans acquired in the Colonial transaction are covered by loss-sharing agreements with the FDIC, but BB&T still has exposure to the depressed real estate markets in Georgia; Florida; Washington, DC; and coastal portions of the Carolinas, and has increased its provisions for loan losses.

BB&T remains an inveterate buyer of small insurance agencies (about 85 acquired since 1995) and asset managers throughout the Southeast, casting itself as a one-stop financial products shop. BB&T has also continued its strategy of purchasing niche financial services companies that offer products that can be sold at its bank branches.

Its 2007 purchase of AFCO Credit boosted the insurance premium financing operations of BB&T's specialized lending segment; it also expanded BB&T's reach into Canada for the first time, through AFCO's sister company CAFO. AFCO grew again with the acquisition of Cananwill in 2009. BB&T also acquired Collateral Real Estate Capital, which it folded into its existing commercial mortgage operations and renamed the whole thing Grandbridge Real Estate Capital.

Longtime CEO John Allison stepped down at the end of 2008; he remained chairman of the company through 2009. Former COO Kelly King was named Allison's successor as CEO and chairman of the board. The executive moves capped a five-year executive management transition plan that the company established in 2003.

HISTORY

In 1872 Alpheus Branch, son of a wealthy planter, founded Branch and Company, a mercantile business, in Wilson, North Carolina. He and Thomas Jefferson Hadley, who was organizing a public school system, created the Branch and Hadley bank later that same year. The private bank helped rebuild farms and small businesses after the Civil War.

In 1887 Branch bought out Hadley and changed the bank's name to Branch and Company, Bankers. Two years later Branch secured a state trust charter for the Wilson Banking and Trust Company. He never got the business running, however, and died in 1893. The trust charter was amended to change the name to Branch Banking and Company, and Branch and Company, Bankers, was folded into it in 1900.

In 1907 the bank finally got its trust operations running and began calling itself Branch Banking and Trust Company. In 1922 it opened its first insurance department; the next year it started its mortgage loan activities.

BB&T survived the 1929 stock market crash with the help of the Post Office. Nervous customers withdrew their funds from BB&T and other banks and deposited them in postal savings accounts, unaware that BB&T was the local Post Office's bank and the withdrawn funds went right back to the bank. BB&T opened six more branches between 1929 and 1933.

After WWII, consumerism skyrocketed, resulting in more car loans and mortgages. During the 1960s and 1970s the bank embarked on a series of mergers and acquisitions, forming the thin end of a buying wedge that would widen significantly in the coming decades.

By 1994, BB&T was the fourth-largest bank in North Carolina. In 1995 it merged with North Carolina's fifth-largest bank, Southern National Corp., founded in 1897.

With banking regulations loosening to allow different types of operations, BB&T in 1997 made several acquisitions, including banks, thrifts, and securities brokerage Craigie.

BB&T's 1998 activities included three bank acquisitions that pushed it into metro Washington, DC. The company also increased holdings in fields such as insurance sales, venture capital for Southern businesses, and investment banking (through its acquisition of Scott & Stringfellow Financial, the South's oldest NYSE member).

In 1999 Craigie was melded into Scott & Stringfellow. That year BB&T bought several insurance companies and small banks. The company continued its march through the South the following year, buying several Georgia banks and Tennessee's BankFirst. In 2001 BB&T purchased South Carolina's FirstSpartan Financial, multibank holding company Century South Banks, Maryland-based FCNB Corporation, and western Georgia's Community First Banking Company. To bolster its presence in the Washington, DC, market, it bought Virginia Capital Bancshares and F&M National.

BB&T purchased Alabama-based Cooney, Rikard & Curtin, a wholesale insurance broker active in 45 states, in 2002. Also that year it added about 100 branches in Kentucky after buying MidAmerica Bancorp and AREA Bancshares, and entered the coveted Florida market following its purchase of Regional Financial, the privately held parent of First South Bank.

Acquisitions continued the following three years, as the bank swallowed First Virginia Banks, among other targets. It took a break in 2005 to assimilate its holdings before joining the acquisition hunt in 2006 with deals for banks in Georgia (Main Street Banks) and Tennessee (First Citizens Bancorp), and in South Carolina (Coastal Financial) in 2007.

EXECUTIVES

Chairman and CEO: Kelly S. King, age 61, $5,145,917 total compensation
COO: Christopher L. (Chris) Henson, age 49, $1,794,490 total compensation
SEVP and CFO: Daryl N. Bible, age 49, $1,071,614 total compensation
SEVP and Manager, Operations Division: C. Leon Wilson III, age 55, $1,950,674 total compensation
SEVP and Chief Marketing Officer: Steven B. (Steve) Wiggs, age 52
SEVP and Manager, Deposit Services: Donna C. Goodrich, age 47
SEVP and Manager, Banking Network: Ricky K. Brown, age 53
SEVP and Manager, Administrative Services; President, Branch Banking and Trust Company: Robert E. (Rob) Greene, age 60, $2,460,615 total compensation
SEVP and Manager, Enterprise Risk Manager: Barbara F. Duck, age 43
SEVP and Chief Risk Officer: Clarke R. Starnes III, age 51
EVP and CIO: Paul W. Johnson
EVP and Chief Commercial Credit Officer: J. Tol Broome Jr.
EVP and Chief Compliance Officer: Rebecca J. (Becky) Jenkins
EVP and Chief Retail Credit Officer: Alexander (Alex) Jung
EVP and Chief Loan Operations Officer: Carla D. Fox
Chief Agency Executive Officer and President, BB&T Insurance Services: Wes Dasher
EVP and Chief Technology Officer: Gary R. Coleman
EVP, General Counsel, Corporate Secretary, and Chief Corporate Governance Officer: Frances Jones, age 47
SVP and Chief Corporate Communications Officer: Cynthia Williams
EVP and Corporate Controller: Cynthia B. (Cindy) Powell
EVP and Treasurer: Hal S. Johnson
SVP Investor Relations: Tamera Gjesdal, age 46
Auditors: PricewaterhouseCoopers LLP

LOCATIONS

HQ: BB&T Corporation
200 W. 2nd St., Winston-Salem, NC 27101
Phone: 336-733-2000   **Fax:** 336-733-2470
Web: www.bbt.com

2009 Branches

	No.
Virginia	392
North Carolina	360
Florida	307
Georgia	178
Maryland	130
South Carolina	116
Alabama	91
Kentucky	90
West Virginia	78
Tennessee	57
Texas	22
Washington, DC	12
Total	**1,833**

PRODUCTS/OPERATIONS

2009 Sales

	$ mil.	% of total
Interest		
Loans & leases, including fees	5,547	51
Securities & other	1,337	13
Noninterest		
Insurance	1,047	10
Service charges on deposits	690	6
Mortgage banking	658	6
Investment banking & brokerage fees		
& commissions	346	3
Other nondeposit fees & commissions	229	2
Checkcard fees	227	2
Net securities gains	199	2
Bankcard fees & merchant discounts	156	2
Trust & investment advisory	139	1
Other	243	2
Total	**10,818**	**100**

2009 Assets

	$ mil.	% of total
Cash & equivalents	2,919	2
Mortgage-backed securities	26,670	16
Other securities	7,875	5
Net loans & leases	103,607	62
Other	24,693	15
Total	**165,764**	**100**

Selected Subsidiaries and Affiliates

BB&T Asset Management, Inc.
BB&T Bankcard Corporation
BB&T Equipment Finance Corporation
BB&T Financial, FSB
BB&T Insurance Services, Inc.
BB&T Investment Services, Inc.
Branch Banking and Trust Company
Grandbridge Real Estate Capital LLC
Lendmark Financial Services, Inc.
McGriff, Seibels & Williams, Inc.
Prime Rate Premium Finance Corporation, Inc.
AFCO
Regional Acceptance Corporation
Scott & Stringfellow, Inc.
Stanley, Hunt, DuPree & Rhine, Inc.

COMPETITORS

Bank of America
BankAtlantic
Capital One
Fifth Third
First Citizens BancShares
First Horizon
JPMorgan Chase
PNC Financial
RBC Bank
Regions Financial
SunTrust
Synovus Financial
United Bankshares
Wells Fargo

HISTORICAL FINANCIALS
Company Type: Public

Income Statement
FYE: December 31

	ASSETS ($ mil.)	NET INCOME ($ mil.)	INCOME AS % OF ASSETS	EMPLOYEES
12/09	165,764	853	0.5%	32,400
12/08	152,015	1,519	1.0%	29,600
12/07	132,618	1,734	1.3%	29,400
12/06	121,351	1,528	1.3%	29,300
12/05	109,170	1,654	1.5%	27,700
Annual Growth	11.0%	(15.3%)	—	4.0%

2009 Year-End Financials

Equity as % of assets: 9.8%	Dividends
Return on assets: 0.5%	Yield: 3.6%
Return on equity: 5.9%	Payout: 80.0%
Long-term debt ($ mil.): 21,376	Market value ($ mil.): 17,580
No. of shares (mil.): 693	Sales ($ mil.): 10,818

Stock History
NYSE: BBT

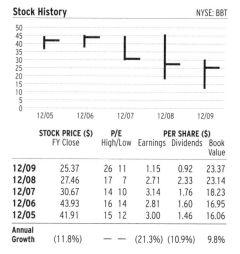

	STOCK PRICE ($) FY Close	P/E High/Low		PER SHARE ($) Earnings	Dividends	Book Value
12/09	25.37	26	11	1.15	0.92	23.37
12/08	27.46	17	7	2.71	2.33	23.14
12/07	30.67	14	10	3.14	1.76	18.23
12/06	43.93	16	14	2.81	1.60	16.95
12/05	41.91	15	12	3.00	1.46	16.06
Annual Growth	(11.8%)	—	—	(21.3%)	(10.9%)	9.8%

BE Aerospace

BE Aerospace (B/E) ensures that travelers truly enjoy air travel. A leading maker of cabin components for commercial, business jets, and military aircraft, B/E's offerings include aircraft seats, coffeemakers, refrigeration equipment, galley structures, and emergency oxygen systems. In addition to its three business segments — Consumables Management, Commercial Aircraft, and Business Jet — B/E also provides maintenance and repair services for cabin interior products, converts passenger aircraft into freighters, and distributes aerospace fasteners. B/E aftermarket operations and military demand represent approximately 50% of its revenues. B/E sells its products to most major airlines and aviation OEMs.

Consumables Management provides for the distribution of aerospace fasteners and consumables, which includes aircraft food and beverage preparation products and storage equipment. B/E offers a single point of contact for the entire program and a full range of technical capabilities. The company processes over 8,000 orders daily destined to more than 1,700 locations worldwide. It stocks 275,000 parts in 40 locations to serve customers, which include commercial, business jet, and military OEMs, aerospace manufacturers, and aftermarket customers, through its inventory programs.

The recession of 2009 created an air pocket in sales due to business jet manufacturers reducing new aircraft orders by as much as 50%; demand for commercial spare parts and consumables decreased by approximately 30%, as well. The company responded by reducing its headcount by around 24% and implementing cost savings initiatives.

The economic headwinds hit after the company put a strategic twist in its business mix in mid-2008. To boost its aftermarket business, it acquired the assets of Honeywell's consumable

solutions (HCS) distribution business for $1.15 billion in cash and stock; with the HCS acquisition, B/E's consumable products and commercial aircraft spare parts business now represents about half of revenues. The transaction included about $900 million in cash and 6 million common shares of B/E Aerospace. The HCS business distributes parts and supplies to aviation industry manufacturers, airlines, and aircraft repair and overhaul facilities. The combination of HCS and B/E's Consumables Management segment allows for distribution to every major aerospace fastener manufacturer in the world.

Commercial Aircraft offers seating products, interior systems, and engineering services for narrow and wide body aircraft. B/E makes aircraft seating for first and premium (including lie-flat seat beds) and economy classes; it also makes spares and replacement parts for aircraft seats. It offers galley equipment, including water boilers, liquid containers, and ovens. B/E also provides a wide array of interior system components including cabin lighting, and other interior components.

B/E provides complete interior packages through its Business Jets segment. Products include seating for super first class accommodations. The company also manufactures lighting systems, air valves and oxygen delivery systems along with sidewalls, bulkheads, credenzas, closets, galley inserts, lavatories, and tables.

HISTORY

Investors led by Amin Khoury founded BE Aerospace (B/E) in 1987. The name came from the group's first purchase: Bach Engineering. Khoury took B/E public in 1989.

In 1992 B/E bought PTC Aerospace (seats) and Aircraft Products (galley structures and beverage makers) from the Pullman Company; it also acquired the UK's largest maker of aircraft seats, Flight Equipment and Engineering Ltd. The company bought several US firms in 1993.

B/E posted losses in fiscal 1995 and 1996, primarily because of the costs of a writedown related to the introduction of its interactive Multimedia Digital Distribution System (MDDS), as the airline industry was slumping. To compete, B/E focused on broadening its product lines and boosting sales through upgrades, maintenance, and other services.

With the airline industry rebounding, B/E began to recover. In 1998 it acquired companies producing oxygen-delivery systems, aircraft cabin interiors and products, aircraft galley equipment, and aircraft lighting. The next year the company sold a 51% interest in its In-Flight Entertainment business to Sextant Avionique. In late 1999 B/E reported production problems in its seat manufacturing operations, prompting airlines to find other suppliers.

B/E exited the in-flight entertainment business in 2000. Throughout the year, production problems in its seating manufacturing operations impacted earnings, leading to a loss. The following year the company closed five facilities and cut its workforce by about 20% soon after the terrorist attacks of September 11, 2001, as demand for aircraft cabin interior products slumped drastically. To buffer itself somewhat from the aircraft interior market, B/E acquired aerospace fastener distributor M & M Aerospace Hardware in 2001. Faced with continued weakness, B/E continued to seek cost savings and consolidation, closing 21 facilities by the end of 2002.

In 2006 the company acquired Draeger Aerospace GmbH from Cobham plc. Draeger is a provider of oxygen delivery systems for commercial and military aircraft. Later that year the company bolstered its fasteners business with the purchase of New York Fasteners Corp., a privately held distributor of aerospace fasteners and hardware. The deal was valued at about $66 million. The acquisitions had the two-fold impact of expanding both B/E's customer base and its product line breadth.

The company expected to gain aftermarket business as airlines refurbished their aircraft interiors in response to increased passenger traffic, increased airline capacity, and stiff competition. A spike in new aircraft orders in 2007 drove demand for BE Aerospace's OEM products. Thanks to these conditions, the company enjoyed record sales in 2007.

EXECUTIVES

Chairman and CEO: Amin J. Khoury, age 71, $7,561,486 total compensation
President and COO: Michael B. Baughan, age 50, $2,158,959 total compensation
SVP, CFO, and Treasurer: Thomas P. McCaffrey, age 55, $2,137,275 total compensation
VP Sales and Marketing: Linwood Lewis
VP Law, General Counsel, and Secretary: Ryan M. Patch, $1,415,431 total compensation
VP and General Manager, Business Jet Segment: Wayne R. Exton, age 46, $961,563 total compensation
VP and General Manager, Fastener Distribution: Robert A. Marchetti, age 67, $1,326,923 total compensation
VP and General Manager, Commercial Aircraft Products: Werner Lieberherr, age 49, $1,168,341 total compensation
VP Human Resources: R. J. Landry
VP Finance and Controller: Stephen R. Swisher, age 51
VP Investor Relations: Greg Powell
Auditors: Deloitte & Touche LLP

LOCATIONS

HQ: BE Aerospace, Inc.
1400 Corporate Center Way, Wellington, FL 33414
Phone: 561-791-5000   **Fax:** 561-791-7900
Web: www.beaerospace.com

2009 Sales

	$ mil.	% of total
US	943.3	49
Asia, Pacific Rim, Middle East & Other	545.1	28
Europe	449.3	23
Total	**1,937.7**	**100**

PRODUCTS/OPERATIONS

2009 Sales

	$ mil.	% of total
Commercial Aircraft	911.3	47
Consumables Management	798.1	41
Business Jet	228.3	12
Total	**1,937.7**	**100**

Selected Products and Services

Consumables management
De-icing systems
Freighter conversions
Galley inserts and chilling systems
Lighting systems
Oxygen systems
Seating products
Structures

COMPETITORS

Alabama Aircraft	Martin-Baker Aircraft
Anixter Aerospace	Premium Aircraft Interiors
Boeing	TIMCO Aviation
DeCrane	Wesco Aircraft Hardware
EADS	Zodiac Aerospace
Israel Aerospace Industries	

HISTORICAL FINANCIALS

Company Type: Public

Income Statement

FYE: December 31

	REVENUE ($ mil.)	NET INCOME ($ mil.)	NET PROFIT MARGIN	EMPLOYEES
12/09	1,938	142	7.3%	5,500
12/08	2,110	(99)	—	6,485
12/07	1,678	147	8.8%	6,298
12/06	1,128	86	7.6%	5,058
12/05	844	85	10.0%	3,980
Annual Growth	**23.1%**	**13.8%**	**—**	**8.4%**

2009 Year-End Financials

Debt ratio: 70.4%
Return on equity: 10.5%
Cash ($ mil.): 120
Current ratio: 4.83
Long-term debt ($ mil.): 1,019
No. of shares (mil.): 102
Dividends
  Yield: —
  Payout: —
Market value ($ mil.): 2,404

Stock History

NASDAQ (GS): BEAV

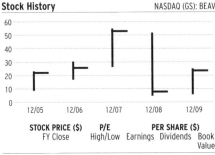

	STOCK PRICE ($) FY Close	P/E High/Low		PER SHARE ($) Earnings	Dividends	Book Value
12/09	23.50	17	4	1.43	—	14.15
12/08	7.69	—	—	(1.05)	—	12.38
12/07	52.90	33	16	1.66	—	12.30
12/06	25.68	27	16	1.10	—	6.90
12/05	22.00	16	7	1.39	—	5.57
Annual Growth	**1.7%**	**—**	**—**	**0.7%**	**—**	**26.3%**

Beazer Homes USA

Beazer Homes USA builds for the middle-class buyer who's ready to make the move into the white-picket-fence scene. Building homes with an average price of about $230,900, the company courts the entry-level, move-up, and active adult markets. Beazer Homes USA focuses on high-growth regions in the Southeast, Mid-Atlantic, and West; it closed on some 4,300 homes in 2009 (down from more than 18,000 homes closed in 2006). It also provides title insurance services in some markets.

Company design centers offer homebuyers limited customization for such features as appliances, cabinetry, flooring, fixtures, and wall coverings. Like most large homebuilders, Beazer subcontracts to build its homes.

Although new construction had been going gangbusters for much of the early part of the

21st century, the housing bubble sprang a leak in 2006 and deflated the following year. Beazer has since struggled to survive amid the housing slump and federal investigations into its dealings. In 2008 Beazer settled with the Securities and Exchange Commission, which had investigated the company for allegedly violating federal securities laws. Beazer did not admit guilt in the matter and was not fined by the agency, but agreed to comply with all SEC securities regulations in the future.

In another investigation in 2009, federal authorities agreed not to prosecute Beazer after the company agreed to pay up to $55 million in restitution and expenses related to a mortgage fraud scheme in North Carolina. The SEC also returned that year to file a fraud complaint against a former Beazer accounting officer. The company restated its financial results from 2006 and 2007 following the SEC probe.

There was more bad news: Beazer faced rising mortgage defaults and cancellation rates as the subprime mortgage market collapsed and took the housing market with it. As credit markets around the world froze and foreclosure properties gave qualified home buyers more shopping options, builders like Beazer were forced to survive on plummeting revenues. The company failed to turn a profit in 2007, 2008 or 2009.

Beazer responded by exiting the mortgage origination business, reorganizing its overhead structure, cutting about 25% of its employees, and exiting some of its land options. It also exited selected markets in California, Colorado, Indiana, Kentucky, North Carolina, Ohio, South Carolina, and Tennessee.

Beazer sees a long, slow climb up from the bottom of the housing market, with continued losses in 2010, with a possible return to profitability after that. Recovery will hinge on a drop in the supply of foreclosed homes on the market, a significant drop in the unemployment rate, and improvements in the availability of financing.

Institutional investors, including BlackRock and Highbridge International, are the largest shareholders of Beazer Homes USA.

HISTORY

Beazer Homes USA traces its roots to a construction business started in the late 1950s in Bath, England, by the Beazer family. Its operations grew to include homebuilding, quarrying, contracting, and real estate. In 1985 Beazer moved into the US and expanded throughout the Southeast through a series of acquisitions.

In 1988 the company bought US aggregates company Koppers in a deal that gave Beazer a presence in US building materials but also left it deep in debt. That debt, plus a recession, had Beazer struggling by 1991, when it was acquired by UK-based Hanson PLC. Hanson spun off the US homebuilding portion of Beazer in 1994 as Beazer Homes USA, which has continued to expand geographically through acquisitions in growth markets. In 1995 it bought Bramalea Homes Texas.

Beazer continued its march across the Sunbelt in 1996, buying homebuilders in Arizona, Florida, and Texas, and it established Beazer Mortgage. During that year Beazer ran into trouble in Nevada, where cost overruns dragged down the company's 1997 results. That year Beazer acquired Florida homebuilder Calton and formed a joint venture with Mexico's Corporacion GEO to build affordable housing; however, the venture was closed in 2000. The next year it bought Snow

Construction of Florida and entered the Mid-Atlantic market by buying Kvaerner's US homebuilding arm, Trafalgar House.

In 2001 the company moved into Colorado by buying Denver-based builder Sanford Homes. The next year Beazer acquired Crossman Communities in a $500 million cash and stock deal, which contributed to a 2% increase in new orders for fiscal 2003. Overall, new orders were up 20% that year, breaking the company's record. The company also had a record 7,426 homes (valued at $1.6 billion) in its backlog. Beazer continued to break its own record through 2004 with annual revenues nearing the $4 billion mark, along with a 36.5% increase in annual earnings. Its backlog that year exceeded 8,400 homes.

In 2005 Beazer entered new markets in California (Fresno), Florida (Sarasota), Georgia (Savannah), Indiana (Ft. Wayne), New Mexico (Albuquerque), and New York (Orange County) and closed on more than 18,100 homes. It ended the year with more than 9,200 homes (worth more than $2.7 billion) in backlog.

Like most US homebuilders, the company began to feel the pinch of a downturn in the markets in 2007, as the boom in housing prices began a prolonged downturn. By 2008, Beazer began to see a significant drop in sales, due to a weakened economy and rising mortgage foreclosures. By the end of the decade, the company was forced to abandon many of the markets it had expanded into in the late 1990s and early- to mid-2000s.

EXECUTIVES

Chairman: Brian C. Beazer, age 75
President, CEO, and Director: Ian J. McCarthy, age 57, $6,430,253 total compensation
EVP and COO: Michael H. (Mike) Furlow, age 59, $3,163,533 total compensation
EVP and CFO: Allan P. Merrill, age 44, $2,571,244 total compensation
EVP and General Counsel: Kenneth F. (Ken) Khoury, age 59, $2,571,244 total compensation
SVP National Purchasing, Planning and Design: Tony L. Callahan
SVP and Chief Accounting Officer: Robert L. Salomon
SVP and CIO: Cindy B. Tierney
SVP and Acting General Counsel: Peggy J. Caldwell
SVP and Chief Marketing Officer: Kathi James
SVP Human Resources: Fred Fratto
VP and Treasurer: Jeffrey S. (Jeff) Hoza
VP: Deborah Danzig
VP: Darr Smith
Auditors: Deloitte & Touche LLP

LOCATIONS

HQ: Beazer Homes USA, Inc.
1000 Abernathy Rd., Ste. 1200, Atlanta, GA 30328
Phone: 770-829-3700　　**Fax:** 770-481-2808
Web: www.beazer.com

2009 Homebuilding Sales by Region

	% of total
West	41
East	41
Southeast	18
Total	**100**

2009 Homes Closed

	No.
West	1,916
East	1,573
Southeast	841
Total	**4,330**

PRODUCTS/OPERATIONS

2009 Sales

	$ mil.	% of total
Homebuilding	1,000.0	100
Land & lot sales	3.4	—
Financial services	1.8	—
Total	**1,005.2**	**100**

COMPETITORS

D.R. Horton
Hovnanian Enterprises
KB Home
Lennar
M.D.C.
Meritage Homes
NVR
PulteGroup
The Ryland Group
Standard Pacific
Toll Brothers
William Lyon Homes

HISTORICAL FINANCIALS

Company Type: Public

Income Statement

FYE: September 30

	REVENUE ($ mil.)	NET INCOME ($ mil.)	NET PROFIT MARGIN	EMPLOYEES
9/09	1,005	(189)	—	901
9/08	2,074	(952)	—	1,444
9/07	3,491	(411)	—	2,619
9/06	5,462	389	7.1%	4,234
9/05	4,995	263	5.3%	4,578
Annual Growth	**(33.0%)**	**—**	**—**	**(33.4%)**

2009 Year-End Financials

Debt ratio: 752.2%
Return on equity: —
Cash ($ mil.): 507
Current ratio: 27.23
Long-term debt ($ mil.): 1,479

No. of shares (mil.): 76
Dividends
　Yield: 0.0%
　Payout: —
Market value ($ mil.): 423

Stock History

NYSE: BZH

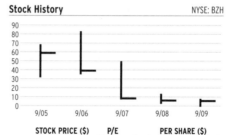

	STOCK PRICE ($) FY Close	P/E High	P/E Low	PER SHARE ($) Earnings	PER SHARE ($) Dividends	PER SHARE ($) Book Value
9/09	5.59	—	—	(4.90)	0.00	2.60
9/08	5.98	—	—	(24.69)	0.00	4.95
9/07	8.25	—	—	(10.70)	0.40	17.49
9/06	39.04	9	4	8.89	0.40	22.49
9/05	58.67	11	6	5.87	0.27	19.88
Annual Growth	**(44.4%)**	**—**	**—**	**—**	**—**	**(39.9%)**

Bechtel Group

Whether the job is raising an entire city or razing a nuclear power plant, you can bet the Bechtel Group will be there to bid on the business. The engineering, construction, and project management company serves the energy, transportation, communications, mining, oil and gas, and government services sectors. It operates worldwide and has participated in such historic projects as the construction of Hoover Dam and the cleanup of the Chernobyl nuclear plant. Bechtel's Oil, Gas & Chemical business unit and Bechtel National, its government contracts group, are its leading revenue producers. The group is in its fourth generation of leadership by the Bechtel family, with chairman and CEO Riley Bechtel at the helm.

Bechtel has made a name for itself by participating in mega-projects. In addition to providing its core project management and design services, it offers such services as environmental restoration and remediation, telecommunications infrastructure (installing cable-optic networks and constructing data centers), and project financing through Bechtel Enterprises.

Bechtel has completed projects in some 50 countries on all seven continents. Its diverse portfolio of clients and markets served helped the company weather the global economic crisis. The company's revenues did slip slightly in 2009 as some projects were scaled back or delayed and clients reduced capital spending. However, Bechtel found plenty of work building rail systems, roads, airports, oil refineries, power plants, mines, liquefied natural gas terminals, and telecom networks, in addition to managing projects for the US government.

The company sees a bright future in the sustainable energy market. In 2009 Bechtel partnered with BrightSource Energy to build a 440-megawatt solar power plant in the Mojave Desert. Bechtel also is building a clean coal power plant in Indiana. While sustainable energy is gaining ground, Bechtel still gets most its work from the oil, gas, and chemicals industry.

In Europe, the group has expanded its rail business by working on High Speed One, the high-speed rail line connecting London with the Channel Tunnel and the UK's first major new railroad project in a century. It is also managing the upgrade of the UK's West Coast main line and has joined a consortium to renovate part of London's 140-year-old subway.

HISTORY

In 1898, 25-year-old Warren Bechtel left his Kansas farm to grade railroads in the Oklahoma Indian territories, then followed the rails west. Settling in Oakland, California, he founded his own contracting firm. Foreseeing the importance of roads, oil, and power, he won big projects such as the Northern California Highway and the Bowman Dam. By 1925, when he incorporated his company as W.A. Bechtel & Co., it ranked as the West's largest construction company. In 1931 Bechtel helped found the consortium that built Hoover Dam.

Under the leadership of Steve Bechtel (president after his father's death in 1933), the company obtained contracts for large infrastructure projects such as the San Francisco-Oakland Bay Bridge. Noted for his friendships with influential people, including Dwight Eisenhower, Adlai

Stevenson, and Saudi Arabia's King Faisal, Steve developed projects that spanned nations and industries, such as pipelines in Saudi Arabia and numerous power projects. By 1960, when Steve Bechtel Jr. took over, the company was operating on six continents.

In the next two decades, Bechtel worked on transportation projects — such as San Francisco's Bay Area Rapid Transit (BART) system and the Washington, DC, subway system — and power projects, including nuclear plants. After the 1979 Three Mile Island accident, Bechtel tried its hand at nuclear cleanup. With nuclear power no longer in vogue, it focused on other markets, such as mining in New Guinea (gold and copper, 1981-84) and China (coal, 1984). Bechtel's Jubail project in Saudi Arabia, begun in 1976, raised an entire industrial port city on the Persian Gulf.

The US recession and rising developing-world debt of the early 1980s sent Bechtel reeling. It cut its workforce by 22,000 and stemmed losses by piling up small projects.

Riley Bechtel, great-grandson of Warren, became CEO in 1990. After the 1991 Gulf War, Bechtel extinguished Kuwait's flaming oil wells and worked on the oil-spill cleanup. During the decade it also worked on such projects as the Channel tunnel (Chunnel) between England and France, a new airport in Hong Kong, and pipelines in the former Soviet Union.

Bechtel was part of the consortium contracted in 1996 to build a high-speed passenger rail line between London and the Chunnel. International Generating (InterGen), Bechtel's joint venture with Pacific Gas and Electric (PG&E), was chosen to help build Mexico's first private power plant. In 1996 Bechtel bought PG&E's share of InterGen, then sold a 50% stake in InterGen to a unit of Royal Dutch Shell in early 1997.

In 1998 Bechtel joined Battelle and Electricité de France in project management of a long-term plan to stabilize the damaged reactor of the Chernobyl nuclear plant in Ukraine.

The next year Bechtel was hired to decommission the Connecticut Yankee nuclear plant.

Bechtel expanded its telecommunications operations in 2001 to provide turnkey network implementation services in Europe, the Middle East, and Asia. As part of a consortium with UK facilities management giants Jarvis and Amey, Bechtel began work in 2002 on a 30-year project to modernize part of London's aging subway system. In 2005 Bechtel and Shell Oil sold InterGen, its power production joint venture, to AIG Highstar Capital for about $1.75 billion.

Bechtel was one of the companies that received contracts to help rebuild Iraq's infrastructure beginning in 2003, but it exited that country in 2006 as its contracts expired.

Among Bechtel's more traditional (perhaps notorious) infrastructure projects was its involvement in the "Big Dig," Boston's Central Artery/Tunnel project. Bechtel, in a joint venture with Parsons Brinckerhoff, served as lead contractor on the $14.6 billion project, which was the subject of much dispute over cost overruns and safety issues. After a death occurred in which the ceiling collapsed on a motorist, the National Transportation Safety Board said that Bechtel was partially at fault. Bechtel/Parsons Brinckerhoff paid a $450 million settlement which included a provision removing any criminal liability.

EXECUTIVES

Chairman Emeritus: Stephen D. (Steve) Bechtel Jr., age 85
Chairman and CEO: Riley P. Bechtel, age 57
Vice Chairman: Adrian Zaccaria, age 64
President, COO, and Director: Bill Dudley, age 57
CFO and Director: Peter Dawson
CIO and Manager Information Systems and Technology: Geir Ramleth
General Counsel, Secretary and Director: Judith Miller
President, Nuclear Power: Carl Rau
President, Bechtel National: David Walker
President, Oil, Gas, and Chemicals Business Unit: Jim Jackson
President, Mining and Metals Global Business Unit: Andy Greig
President, Power Global Business Unit: Jack Futcher
President, Bechtel Systems & Infrastructure: Scott Ogilvie
President, Civil Global Business Unit, and Director: Mike Adams
Manager Engineering, Procurement & Construction Functions, and Human Resources: John MacDonald
Manager Engineering: Tom Patterson
Manager Corporate Affairs: Jock Covey
Auditors: PricewaterhouseCoopers LLP

LOCATIONS

HQ: Bechtel Group, Inc.
50 Beale St., San Francisco, CA 94105
Phone: 415-768-1234   **Fax:** 415-768-9038
Web: www.bechtel.com

PRODUCTS/OPERATIONS

Selected Services

Construction
Development and financing
Engineering and technology
Procurement
Project management
Safety
Sustainability and environment

Selected Markets

Civil infrastructure (airports, rail, highways, heavy civil)
Communications (wireless and other telecommunications)
Mining and metals
Oil, gas, and chemicals (Design and construction for chemical, petrochemical, LNG and natural gas plants, and pipelines)
Power electrical (gas, oil, coal, and nuclear power plants)
U.S. Government Services (defense, space, demilitarization, security, nuclear, and environmental restoration and remediation services)

COMPETITORS

Aker Solutions	Jacobs Engineering
AMEC	Kajima
Balfour Construction	Lummus Technology
Black & Veatch	Marelich Mechanical
Bouygues	Parsons Corporation
CH2M HILL	Peter Kiewit Sons'
Chiyoda Corp.	RWE
EIFFAGE	Schneider Electric
Fluor	Shaw Group
Foster Wheeler	Siemens AG
Groupe SNEF	Skanska
Halliburton	Technip
HOCHTIEF	Tutor Perini
Honeywell Technology	Uhde
Solutions	URS
Hyundai Engineering	VINCI
ITOCHU	Weston Solutions

HISTORICAL FINANCIALS

Company Type: Private

Income Statement

FYE: December 31

	REVENUE ($ mil.)	NET INCOME ($ mil.)	NET PROFIT MARGIN	EMPLOYEES
12/08	31,400	—	—	44,000
12/07	27,000	—	—	42,500
12/06	20,500	—	—	40,000
12/05	18,100	—	—	40,000
12/04	17,378	—	—	40,000
Annual Growth	**15.9%**	**—**	**—**	**2.4%**

Revenue History

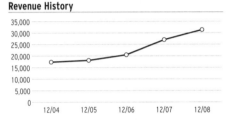

Beckman Coulter

Like the nerdiest kid in school, Beckman Coulter never saw a test it didn't love. The company makes more than 600 diagnostic testing systems and supplies, from simple blood tests to complicated genetic diagnostic tools. Its wares are used by hospital and other clinical laboratories to suss out diseases and monitor their progression. Its clinical products include immunoassay, clinical chemistry, and hematology systems, as well as products in the growing field of molecular diagnostics. In addition to its systems for diagnosing patients, Beckman Coulter makes products used by life sciences researchers, including those at academic research centers and drug companies, to understand disease and develop new therapies.

Beckman Coulter has installed more than 200,000 of its systems around the world. Along with instruments, it sells reagents and other consumable testing supplies that provide recurring revenue over the life of a system; nearly 80% of revenue comes from recurring sales, mostly to midsized to large hospitals.

Beckman Coulter markets its products in more than 160 countries. The company's international growth strategy focuses on committing resources to developing markets such as China and India. Additionally, the company is the North American distributor of Instrumentation Laboratory's hemostasis (blood disorder testing) products, sold mainly under the ACL brand.

The company tries to stay ahead of the competition by developing improved and new systems that cost-effectively perform high volumes of tests for its health care and life sciences clients. In 2008 it launched UniCel DxI 800 system, a fully automated immunochemistry (chemical tests on immune system proteins) system for high-volume clinical laboratories. Beckman Coulter has announced plans to invest $30 million per year until 2012 towards the creation of an enhanced automated molecular diagnostic (genetic testing) system that will allow for complex molecular testing in clinical labs. It is also developing new tests, with a focus on the growing fields of immunoassay and molecular diagnostic products.

Beckman Coulter has gained new technologies and products through acquisitions as well. In 2009 the company acquired the lab-based diagnostics systems business of Olympus' life sciences unit. The $800 million purchase expanded its chemistry product lines.

HISTORY

Arnold Beckman created his first chemistry lab as a child in a shed his blacksmith father had built for him. Beckman studied chemical engineering, worked at Bell Labs (now part of Lucent Technologies), and then earned his doctorate in photochemistry in 1928 from the California Institute of Technology. In 1935, while teaching at CalTech and working as a consultant, Beckman created a special ink for the National Postage Meter Company. He formed the National Inking Appliance Company (later National Technical Laboratories), which was 90%-owned by National Postage Meter and 10%-owned by Beckman.

In 1935 Beckman also created a device for a Southern California citrus processor that measured lemon juice acidity. Beckman's acidity, or pH, meter soon became a standard tool in chemical laboratories. In 1941 he debuted a wavelength spectrum analysis system, a forerunner of today's analytical precision and chemical analysis instruments. That year the company's sales topped $250,000.

The company became Beckman Instruments in 1950 and went public two years later. During that period the company created products for aerospace, military, and industrial markets. However, it increasingly focused on the medical and research niches, and during the 1960s it introduced glucose analyzers and protein peptide sequencers. By 1975 Beckman Instruments' annual sales neared $230 million.

An 82-year-old Beckman sold his company to SmithKline in 1982, creating SmithKline Beckman. In 1988 Louis Rosso, who as president had guided Beckman's move into life sciences and diagnostics, was named CEO. SmithKline Beckman in 1989 merged with UK pharmaceuticals pioneer Beecham Group, becoming SmithKline Beecham. (That company merged with Glaxo Wellcome to become GlaxoSmithKline plc in 2000.) Beckman, operating as a unit within SmithKline Beecham, suffered financially as a result of cuts in health care spending. SmithKline Beecham spun the company off that year as a medical and research market instrument maker.

New products and cost controls returned Beckman Instruments to health. The company restructured in 1993 (taking write-offs in 1993 and 1994), then launched a buying spree. It acquired Genomyx, a maker of DNA sequencing products, in 1996. In late 1997 the company acquired Coulter, which served the same hospitals and medical offices as Beckman — only with hematology products — for $1.2 billion.

Wallace Coulter in 1948 discovered a new technology for blood cell analysis, dubbed the Coulter Principle. With brother Joe, an electrical engineer, Wallace (who died in 1998) began producing the Coulter Counter cell and particle analyzer. The brothers formed Coulter Electronics in 1958. Over the years the private company made tests to detect everything from colon cancer to strep throat, but it became best known for blood cell analysis diagnostic systems.

Beckman Instruments' purchase of Coulter, which led to job cuts (13% of its workforce), caused losses for 1997. The next year the company changed its name to Beckman Coulter. John Wareham, an executive with Beckman since the early 1980s, replaced Rosso as CEO.

The addition of the Coulter product lines enabled the company to win 1999 contracts from several regional health care networks and large purchasing organizations. In 2000 the company closed plants in Argentina, Brazil, and Hong Kong. In 2005 the firm reduced its workforce and exited some development projects, including tests for mad cow disease and sepsis. The same year Beckman Coulter bought Diagnostic Systems Laboratories, a maker of specialty diagnostics in the areas of reproductive endocrinology and cardiovascular risk assessment.

In 2007 it introduced a new system (the UniCel DxI 600 Access system) intended for mid-sized hospitals who want to perform more tests in-house rather than outsourcing them. Later that year it acquired the flow cytometry business of Danish diagnostics firm Dako, adding two high-end flow cytometry systems to its portfolio of products.

EXECUTIVES

Chairman, President, and CEO: Scott Garrett, age 60, $6,133,784 total compensation
EVP Chemistry, Discovery, and Instrument Systems Development: Scott Atkin, age 46, $1,423,490 total compensation
EVP Worldwide Commercial Operations: Robert W. (Bob) Kleinert Jr., age 58, $1,448,651 total compensation
SVP and CFO: Charles P. (Charlie) Slacik, age 55, $1,551,534 total compensation
SVP Quality and Regulatory Affairs: Clair K. O'Donovan
SVP, General Counsel, and Secretary: Arnold A. Pinkston, age 51, $1,357,024 total compensation
SVP Strategy, Business Development, and Communications: Paul Glyer, age 53, $1,434,453 total compensation
SVP Human Resources; Chairman, Beckman Coulter Japan: J. Robert Hurley, age 60, $1,340,456 total compensation
SVP Supply Chain Management: Pamela A. (Pam) Miller, age 55
VP, Controller, and Chief Accounting Officer: Carolyn D. Beaver, age 52
VP Cellular Analysis: Cynthia Collins, age 51
VP Immunoassay and Molecular Diagnostics: Richard S. Creager, age 57
VP and Medical Director: Peter Heseltine
Corporate Communications: Mary F. Luthy
Investor Relations Officer: Cynthia Skoglund
Auditors: KPMG LLP

LOCATIONS

HQ: Beckman Coulter, Inc.
250 S. Kraemer Blvd., Brea, CA 92822
Phone: 714-993-5321   **Fax:** 714-773-8111
Web: www.beckmancoulter.com

2009 Sales

	$ mil.	% of total
US	1,580.4	49
Europe	731.4	22
Asia/Pacific	477.6	15
Emerging Markets (Eastern Europe, Russia, Middle East, Africa & India)	270.2	8
Other	201.0	6
Total	**3,260.6**	**100**

PRODUCTS/OPERATIONS

2009 Sales

	$ mil.	% of total
Clinical Diagnostics		
Chemistry & clinical automation	1,055.1	32
Cellular analysis	935.3	29
Immunoassay & molecular diagnostics	798.3	25
Life Science	472.0	14
Adjustments	(0.1)	—
Total	**3,260.6**	**100**

COMPETITORS

Abbott Labs
Agilent Technologies
Alere
BD Biosciences
Bio-Rad Labs
Caliper Life Sciences
GE Healthcare
Genzyme Diagnostics
Hitachi High-Technologies
Illumina
Life Technologies Corporation
Ortho-Clinical Diagnostics
PerkinElmer
Roche Diagnostics
Shimadzu
Siemens Healthcare Diagnostics
Sysmex Amer
Thermo Fisher Scientific
Waters Corp.

HISTORICAL FINANCIALS

Company Type: Public

Income Statement

FYE: December 31

	REVENUE ($ mil.)	NET INCOME ($ mil.)	NET PROFIT MARGIN	EMPLOYEES
12/09	3,261	147	4.5%	11,800
12/08	3,099	194	6.3%	11,000
12/07	2,761	211	7.7%	10,500
12/06	2,529	187	7.4%	10,340
12/05	2,444	151	6.2%	10,416
Annual Growth	**7.5%**	**(0.6%)**	**—**	**3.2%**

2009 Year-End Financials

Debt ratio: 66.6%
Return on equity: 8.7%
Cash ($ mil.): 289
Current ratio: 2.32
Long-term debt ($ mil.): 1,306
No. of shares (mil.): 69
Dividends
Yield: 1.1%
Payout: 31.7%
Market value ($ mil.): 4,531

Stock History

NYSE: BEC

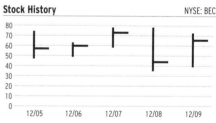

	STOCK PRICE ($) FY Close	P/E High/Low		PER SHARE ($) Earnings	Dividends	Book Value
12/09	65.44	33	18	2.18	0.69	28.32
12/08	43.94	26	12	3.01	0.68	20.74
12/07	72.80	23	18	3.30	0.64	20.82
12/06	59.80	21	17	2.92	0.60	16.67
12/05	56.90	32	21	2.32	0.56	17.25
Annual Growth	**3.6%**	**—**	**—**	**(1.5%)**	**5.4%**	**13.2%**

Becton, Dickinson

Don't worry, you'll only feel a slight prick if Becton, Dickinson (BD) is at work. The company's BD Medical segment is one of the top manufacturers of syringes and other injection and infusion devices. BD Medical also makes IV catheters and syringes, prefillable drug delivery systems, self-injection devices for diabetes patients, and surgical instruments (scalpels and anesthesia trays, for instance). The BD Diagnostics segment offers tools for collecting specimens and the equipment and reagents to detect diseases in them. Finally, Becton Dickinson caters to researchers through its BD Biosciences unit, which makes reagents, antibodies, cell imaging systems, and labware used in basic and clinical research.

BD has manufacturing, marketing, and warehousing operations all over the world. Though the company has increased sales in international markets, where its main products include various types of needles and syringes, diagnostic and blood collection systems, and disposable labware, the US remains its largest market segment.

BD has been cashing in on the increased emphasis on safety in health care delivery. BD Medical has introduced a number of safety-engineered devices that prevent accidental needlesticks, and thus exposure to infected blood; sales of the devices are growing, particularly in international markets. One new addition to its safety syringe lineup is the BD AutoShield Pen Needle, a safety needle used with insulin injection pens. Additionally, BD Diagnostics makes safety-engineered blood collection equipment, including the BD Vacutainer system.

The Diagnostics segment has also been working on tests that aim to reduce the spread of health care-associated infections (usually infections acquired as the result of a hospital stay), as well as to detect STDs and cancers. In 2009 BD acquired test and processing equipment maker Handylab for $275 million to enhance its infection-testing operations, as well as to expand in the molecular (gene-based) diagnostic testing market.

Through its BD Biosciences unit, BD makes a variety of research and clinical testing products for drug developers, life sciences researchers, and diagnostics laboratories. Its products include flow cytometry (cell sorting) systems, monoclonal antibodies (single-source proteins) and kits for cellular analysis, and cell culture media. Additionally, BD Biosciences' Discovery Labware segment makes pipettes, tubes, and other basic equipment used in laboratories.

BD made a move to streamline the medical division in 2010 when it agreed to sell its ophthalmic systems unit, as well as certain surgical blade and catheter products, to private equity firm RoundTable Healthcare Partners.

HISTORY

Maxwell Becton and Fairleigh Dickinson established a medical supply firm in New York in 1897. In 1907 the company moved to New Jersey and became one of the first US firms to make hypodermic needles.

During WWI, Becton, Dickinson (BD) made all-glass syringes and introduced the cotton elastic bandage. After the war, its researchers designed an improved stethoscope and created specialized hypodermic needles. The company supplied medical equipment to the armed forces during WWII. Becton and Dickinson helped establish Fairleigh Dickinson Junior College (now Fairleigh Dickinson University) in 1942. The company continued to develop products such as the Vacutainer blood-collection apparatus, its first medical laboratory aid.

After the deaths of Dickinson (1948) and Becton (1951), their respective sons, Fairleigh Jr. and Henry, took over. The company introduced disposable hypodermic syringes in 1961. BD went public in 1963 to raise money for new expansion. In the 1960s the company opened plants in Brazil, Canada, France, and Ireland and climbed aboard the conglomeration bandwagon by diversifying into such businesses as industrial gloves (Edmont, 1966) and computer systems (Spear, 1968). BD also went on a major acquisition spree in its core fields during the 1960s and 1970s, buying more than 25 medical supply, testing, and lab companies by 1980.

Wesley Howe, successor to Fairleigh Dickinson Jr., expanded foreign sales in the 1970s. Howe thwarted a takeover by the diversifying oil giant Sun Company (now Sunoco) in 1978 and began to sell BD's nonmedical businesses in 1983, ending with the 1989 sale of Edmont. Acquisitions, including Deseret Medical (IV catheters, surgical gloves and masks; 1986), sharpened BD's focus on medical and surgical supplies.

In the 1990s BD formed a number of alliances and ventures, including a 1991 agreement to make and market Baxter International's InterLink needleless injection system, which reduces the risk of accidental needle sticks, and a 1993 joint venture with NeXagen (now part of Gilead Sciences) to make and market in vitro diagnostics. As tuberculosis reemerged in the US as a serious health threat, the firm improved its TB-detection and drug-resistance test systems, which cut testing time from as much as seven weeks to less than two.

In 1996 BD introduced GlucoWatch (a glucose monitoring device developed by Cygnus), and acquired the diagnostic business and brand name of MicroProbe (now Epoch Pharmaceuticals).

Previously known on Wall Street as a homely company that focused on cutting costs, BD changed its image with a string of acquisitions beginning in 1997. The firm acquired PharMingen (biomedical research reagents) and Difco Laboratories (microbiology media), which broadened its product lines. BD also collaborated with Nanogen on diagnosis products for infectious disease.

In 1998 BD settled a lawsuit by a health care worker claiming that BD continued selling conventional syringes that could spread disease through accidental needle sticks instead of promoting safer technology. BD still faced several lawsuits from health workers who had sustained needle sticks. In 1999 the firm joined forces with Millennium Pharmaceuticals to develop cancer tests and treatments; it also bought genetic test maker Clontech Laboratories.

During 2006 the company acquired GeneOhm Sciences which develops molecular diagnostic testing systems specifically for the rapid detection of bacterial organisms that cause health care-associated infections in hospitalized patients, including MRSA (methicillin resistant *Staphylococcus aureus*) and Group B Strep (rapid testing for bacteria). That same year the company also acquired the 93% of TriPath Imaging that it didn't already own for $350 million.

EXECUTIVES

Chairman and CEO: Edward J. (Ed) Ludwig, age 58, $9,121,382 total compensation
Vice Chairman: John R. Considine, age 59, $2,981,269 total compensation
President and COO: Vincent A. Forlenza, age 56, $3,576,313 total compensation
EVP and CFO: David V. Elkins, age 41, $1,166,554 total compensation
EVP: William A. Kozy, age 58, $3,151,079 total compensation
EVP: Gary M. Cohen, age 51
SVP and CTO: Scott P. Bruder, age 47
SVP Human Resources: Donna M. Boles, age 56
SVP Corporate Medical Affairs: David T. Durack, age 64
SVP Corporate Regulatory and External Affairs: Patricia B. Shrader, age 59
SVP and General Counsel: Jeffrey S. Sherman, age 54
VP and Chief Intellectual Property Counsel and Assistant Secretary: David W. Highet
VP and Chief Ethics and Compliance Officer: Patti E. Russell
VP, Corporate Secretary and Public Policy: Dean J. Paranicas
VP Investor Relations: Zachary A. (Zac) Nagle
VP and Treasurer: Richard K. Berman
VP and Controller: William A. Tozzi
Director Corporate Communications: Colleen T. White
Auditors: Ernst & Young LLP

LOCATIONS

HQ: Becton, Dickinson and Company
1 Becton Dr., Franklin Lakes, NJ 07417
Phone: 201-847-6800　　**Fax:** 201-847-6475
Web: www.bd.com

2009 Sales

	$ mil.	% of total
US	3,204.7	45
Europe	2,478.3	34
Other	1,477.9	21
Total	**7,160.9**	**100**

PRODUCTS/OPERATIONS

2009 Sales

	$ mil.	% of total
BD Medical		
Medical surgical systems	1,984.9	28
Pharmaceutical systems	952.5	13
Diabetes care	715.0	10
Ophthalmic systems	78.5	1
BD Diagnostics		
Preanalytical systems	1,143.4	16
Diagnostic systems	1,082.8	15
BD Biosciences		
Cell analysis	904.5	13
Discovery labware	299.3	4
Total	**7,160.9**	**100**

Selected Products

Medical
　Anesthesia needles
　Critical care monitoring systems
　Hypodermic needles and syringes
　Intravenous catheters
　Insulin syringes and pen needles
　OEM products
　Ophthalmic surgical instruments
　Prefillable drug-delivery systems
　Safety needles and syringes
　Sharps disposal systems
　Surgical blades and scalpels

Diagnostics
  Bar-code systems for patient identification and data capture
  Blood culturing systems
  Cytology systems (for cervical cancer screening)
  Immunodiagnostic test kits
  Microorganism identification systems
  Molecular diagnostics (for infectious disease testing)
  Rapid diagnostic assays
  Safety-engineered blood collection devices
  Sample collection products
  Specimen management systems
Biosciences
  Cell growth and screening products
  Cellular imaging and analysis systems
  Clinical and research laboratory software
  Labware (tubes, pipettes, Petri dishes, etc.)
  Molecular biology reagents (for study of genes)
  Monoclonal antibodies (for biomedical research)
  Other research reagents

COMPETITORS

Abbott Labs
Affymetrix
Agilent Technologies
Alere
B. Braun Melsungen
Bard
Baxter International
Beckman Coulter
bioMérieux
Bio-Rad Labs
Boston Scientific
Covidien
Dako
Gen-Probe
Genzyme Diagnostics
Harvard Bioscience
Hologic
Hospira
Johnson & Johnson
Kimberly-Clark Health
Life Technologies Corporation
Meridian Bioscience
Novo Nordisk
Retractable Technologies
Roche Diagnostics
Safety Syringes
Siemens Healthcare Diagnostics
Terumo
Thermo Fisher Scientific
Third Wave Technologies
Trinity Biotech

HISTORICAL FINANCIALS

Company Type: Public

Income Statement

FYE: September 30

	REVENUE ($ mil.)	NET INCOME ($ mil.)	NET PROFIT MARGIN	EMPLOYEES
9/09	7,161	1,232	17.2%	29,116
9/08	7,156	1,127	15.7%	28,300
9/07	6,360	890	14.0%	28,018
9/06	5,835	752	12.9%	26,990
9/05	5,415	722	13.3%	25,571
Annual Growth	7.2%	14.3%	—	3.3%

2009 Year-End Financials

Debt ratio: 28.9%
Return on equity: 24.4%
Cash ($ mil.): 1,394
Current ratio: 2.61
Long-term debt ($ mil.): 1,488
No. of shares (mil.): 233
Dividends
  Yield: 1.9%
  Payout: 26.5%
Market value ($ mil.): 16,275

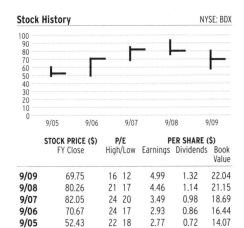

	STOCK PRICE ($) FY Close	P/E High/Low		PER SHARE ($) Earnings	Dividends	Book Value
9/09	69.75	16	12	4.99	1.32	22.04
9/08	80.26	21	17	4.46	1.14	21.15
9/07	82.05	24	20	3.49	0.98	18.69
9/06	70.67	24	17	2.93	0.86	16.44
9/05	52.43	22	18	2.77	0.72	14.07
Annual Growth	7.4%	—	—	15.9%	16.4%	11.9%

Bed Bath & Beyond

Bed Bath & Beyond (BBB) has everything you need to play "house" for real. It's the #1 superstore domestics retailer in the US with about 965 BBB stores throughout the US, Puerto Rico, and Canada. The stores' floor-to-ceiling shelves stock better-quality (brand-name and private-label) goods in two main categories: domestics (bed linens, bathroom and kitchen items) and home furnishings (cookware and cutlery, small household appliances, picture frames, and more). BBB relies exclusively on circulars, mailings, and word-of-mouth for advertising. The company also operates three smaller specialty chains: some 60 Christmas Tree Shops; 45 Harmon discount health and beauty shops; and 30 buybuy Baby locations.

After a not-so-great 2008, business improved in 2009 with net sales up more than 8% and same-store sales increasing by more than 4%. While liquidation sales at former archrival Linens 'n Things in late 2008 hurt BBB's 2008 results, it appears the company is reaping long-term benefits from its rival's demise.

New store openings — more than 60 in 2009 — and acquisitions account for much of the retail chain's growth. Its buybuy Baby format (acquired in 2007), which sells infant and toddler merchandise, doubled in size in 2009. Going forward the company plans to continue to grow its retail footprint, adding BBB stores in existing markets and growing its Christmas Tree and buybuy Baby retail formats from coast to coast. Management believes there is ultimately room for more than 1,300 BBB stores throughout North America.

BBB is also branching out into Canada and Mexico. The company opened its first international store in Richmond Hill, Ontario, in late 2007 and now has more than 15 stores in several Canadian provinces. BBB also has a joint venture with Mexican retailer Home & More that operates a pair of Home & More stores. BBB's 50% equity stake cost the company about $4 million. BBB anticipates the joint venture will be a springboard for future growth in Mexico.

The retailer's decentralized structure allows store managers to have more control than their peers at other retailers (and the company has less manager turnover). BBB cuts costs by locating its stores in strip shopping centers, freestanding buildings, and off-price malls, rather than in pricier regional malls. To cut costs further, its vendors ship merchandise directly to the stores, eliminating the expense of a central distribution center and reducing warehousing costs.

T. Rowe Price owns 13% of BBB's stock.

HISTORY

Warren Eisenberg and Leonard Feinstein, both employed by a discounter called Arlan's, brainstormed an idea in 1971 for a chain of stores offering only home goods. They were betting that customers were, in Feinstein's words, interested in a "designer approach to linens and housewares." The two men started two small linens stores (about 2,000 sq. ft) named bed n bath, one in New York and one in New Jersey.

Expansion came at a fairly slow pace as the company moved only into California and Connecticut by 1985. By then the time was right for such a specialty retailer: Department stores were cutting back on their houseware lines to focus on the more profitable apparel segment, and baby boomers were spending more leisure time at their homes (and more money on spiffing them up). Eisenberg and Feinstein opened a 20,000-sq.-ft. superstore in 1985 that offered a full line of home furnishings. The firm changed its name to Bed Bath & Beyond (BBB) two years later in order to reflect its new offerings.

With the successful superstore format, the company built all new stores in the larger design. BBB grew rapidly; square footage quadrupled between 1992 and 1996. The company went public in 1992. That year it eclipsed the size of its previous stores when it opened a 50,000-sq.-ft. store in Manhattan. (It later enlarged this store to 80,000 sq. ft.; the company's stores now average 42,000 sq. ft.)

BBB's management has attributed its success, in part, to the leeway it gives its store managers, who monitor inventory and have the freedom to try new products and layouts. One example often cited by the company is the case of a manager who decided to sell glasses by the piece instead of in sets. Sales increased 30%, and the whole chain incorporated the practice.

The retailer opened 28 new stores in 1996, 33 in 1997 (its first-ever billion-dollar sales year), and 45 in 1998.

In 1999 the company dipped a toe into the waters of e-commerce by agreeing to buy a stake in Internet Gift Registries, which operates the WeddingNetwork website. The company later began offering online sales and bridal registry services. Keeping up its rapid expansion pace, the company opened 70 stores in 1999, 85 in 2000, and 95 in 2001.

In 2002 BBB acquired Harmon Stores, a health and beauty aid retailer with 29 stores in three states. It acquired Christmas Tree Shops, a giftware and household items retailer with 23 stores in six states, for $200 million in 2003.

In March 2007 BBB acquired buybuy BABY, which operates eight stores on the East Coast, for $67 million. The retailer opened its first Canadian location in Ontario, north of Toronto, in December. In 2008 BBB added three more stores in Canada and its first locations in Mexico, via a joint venture there, under the Home & More banner.

EXECUTIVES

Co-Chairman: Leonard (Lenny) Feinstein, age 73,
$4,238,496 total compensation
Co-Chairman: Warren Eisenberg, age 79,
$4,173,538 total compensation
CEO and Director: Steven H. (Steve) Temares, age 51,
$8,697,028 total compensation
President and Chief Merchandising Officer:
Arthur (Art) Stark, age 55,
$2,662,214 total compensation
CFO and Treasurer; President, Buy Buy Baby:
Eugene A. (Gene) Castagna, age 44,
$2,194,170 total compensation
SVP Investor Relations: Ronald (Ron) Curwin, age 75
SVP Stores: Matthew Fiorilli, age 53
VP and CIO: Robert Claybrook
VP Technology and Operations: Kevin M. Wanner
VP Marketing: Rita Little
VP and Corporate Counsel: Michael J. Callahan
VP Tax: Hal R. Shapiro
VP Store and Financial Systems: Robert A. Roe
VP and Controller: Robyn M. D'Elia
VP Human Resources: Concetta Van Dyke
VP Corporate Development; President, Harmon Stores:
G. William Waltzinger Jr.
VP Legal and General Counsel: Allan N. Rauch
**VP Corporate Operations and Chief Strategy Officer;
President, BBB Canada:** Richard C. (Rich) McMahon
President, Christmas Tree Shops: Todd Johnson
Director Public Relations: Bari Fagin
Auditors: KPMG LLP

LOCATIONS

HQ: Bed Bath & Beyond Inc.
650 Liberty Ave., Union, NJ 07083
Phone: 908-688-0888   **Fax:** 908-688-6483
Web: www.bedbathandbeyond.com

2010 Stores

	No.
California	108
New York	87
New Jersey	80
Texas	77
Florida	76
Illinois	42
Massachusetts	42
Ohio	39
Pennsylvania	39
Michigan	35
Virginia	31
North Carolina	30
Arizona	27
Georgia	27
Colorado	25
Connecticut	23
Indiana	21
Washington	21
Maryland	20
Tennessee	20
Missouri	14
Alabama	13
Louisiana	13
New Hampshire	13
South Carolina	13
Utah	12
Wisconsin	10
Minnesota	9
Oregon	9
Iowa	8
Kansas	8
Kentucky	8
Nevada	8
Arkansas	7
Idaho	7
Maine	7
Mississippi	7
Oklahoma	7
Other states	41
Canada	16
Total	**1,100**

PRODUCTS/OPERATIONS

2010 Stores

	No.
Bed Bath & Beyond	965
Christmas Tree Shops	61
Harmon Face Values	45
buybuy Baby	29
Total	**1,100**

Selected Merchandise

Domestics
  Bath accessories
    Hampers
    Shower curtains
    Towels
  Bed linens
    Bedspreads
    Pillows
    Sheets
  Kitchen textiles
    Cloth napkins
    Dish towels
    Placemats
    Tablecloths
  Window treatments
Home Furnishings
  Basic housewares
    Accessories (lamps, chairs, accent rugs)
    General housewares (brooms, ironing boards)
    Small appliances (blenders, coffeemakers, vacuums)
    Storage items (hangers, organizers, shoe racks)
  General home furnishings
    Artificial plants and flowers
    Candles
    Gift wrap
    Picture frames
    Seasonal merchandise
    Wall art
  Kitchen and tabletop items
    Cookware
    Cutlery
    Flatware
    Gadgets
    Glassware
    Serveware

COMPETITORS

Anna's Linens	Kmart
Art.com	Macy's
Babies "R" Us	Pier 1 Imports
Burlington Coat Factory	Ross Stores
The Children's Place	Saks
Container Store	Sears
Cost Plus	Sensational Beginnings
Dillard's	Target
Euromarket Designs	TJX Companies
Garden Ridge	Tuesday Morning
Gymboree	Wal-Mart
IKEA	Williams-Sonoma
J. C. Penney	

HISTORICAL FINANCIALS

Company Type: Public

Income Statement

FYE: Saturday nearest February 28

	REVENUE ($ mil.)	NET INCOME ($ mil.)	NET PROFIT MARGIN	EMPLOYEES
2/10	7,829	600	7.7%	41,000
2/09	7,208	425	5.9%	37,000
2/08	7,049	563	8.0%	39,000
2/07	6,617	594	9.0%	35,000
2/06	5,810	573	9.9%	33,000
Annual Growth	**7.7%**	**1.2%**	**—**	**5.6%**

2010 Year-End Financials

Debt ratio: 2.8%
Return on equity: 18.0%
Cash ($ mil.): 1,096
Current ratio: 3.10
Long-term debt ($ mil.): 103

No. of shares (mil.): 264
Dividends
  Yield: —
  Payout: —
Market value ($ mil.): 10,980

Stock History

	STOCK PRICE ($) FY Close	P/E High/Low		Earnings	PER SHARE ($) Dividends	Book Value
2/10	41.61	19	8	2.30	—	13.84
2/09	21.30	21	10	1.64	—	11.37
2/08	28.34	20	12	2.10	—	9.71
2/07	39.89	21	15	2.09	—	10.04
2/06	36.04	24	18	1.92	—	8.57
Annual Growth	**3.7%**	**—**	**—**	**4.6%**	**—**	**12.7%**

Belden Inc.

Can you hear me, now? If you didn't, Belden can help. The company designs, makes, and markets thousands of signal transmission products to hook up entertainment, residential, industrial, and security markets. Its lineup includes flat and optical fiber cables, coaxial and multi-conductor cables, connectivity and active components. Connecting access points to area networks, Belden cable is the wire in wireless. It produces connectors, patch panels, and interconnect hardware for end-to-end structured cabling solutions, and industrial and data networking uses, largely outside of the US. Distributors are core customers — Anixter accounts for more than 15% of sales; Belden also sells to OEMs and systems integrators.

Since the company's founding more than a hundred years ago, Belden has focused on markets that required highly differentiated, high performance products. Acquisitions as well as partnerships that expand Belden's offerings have played a role in driving the company's growth. The economic downturn coupled with slumping sales to distributors, however, has forced the company to make hard choices to regain its financial footing.

Belden's restructuring included streamlining manufacturing, marketing, and support activities. The company closed a plant in Midlothian, Virginia, and moved production to the facility in Tijuana, Mexico. The cost-cutting measures slashed approximately 1,800 jobs, a 20% reduction in staff.

Partnerships have helped Belden continue to launch new products, specifically relating to industrial network security. In August 2009 the company announced a cooperative technology agreement with Byres Security Inc. (BSI), a dominant player in industrial cyber security for petrochemical and manufacturing sectors. Belden's expertise is in automation, while BSI specializes in protecting companies from cyber and network threats.

Strategic acquisitions, too, are shoring up sales. A $136 million deal in 2008 for Trapeze Networks, a maker of wireless local area networking equipment and software paid off. The acquisition opened up new competitive frontiers for Belden; Trapeze has since scored distribution agreements with two of the largest cabling infrastructure distributors in North America.

In addition, Belden is pushing for growth through earlier investments. In 2007 it acquired Hong Kong cable maker LTK Wiring for $195 million. The purchase deepens its Asia/Pacific presence for launching cable products and internal wiring (used in consumer electronics). On the European shore, it purchased the assets of German connector-maker Lumberg Automation. Belden also diversified its business with a $260 million deal for Hirschmann. The Germany-based company makes electronic control and safety products, as well as Ethernet connectors.

HISTORY

When Joseph Belden couldn't find the silk-wrapped, magnetic wire needed for telephone coils, he decided to make it himself and founded Belden Manufacturing Company in Chicago in 1902. Thomas Edison was one of the company's early customers. Rubber-covered and enamel-coated wire used by the fledgling electricity industry, and later in radio cars and electrical appliances, spurred the company's growth. During the 1950s Belden began making products for data processing and television.

The company changed its name to Belden Corporation in 1966, and in 1981 it was purchased by Cooper Industries. During that period Belden established its presence in the computer industry. Cooper spun off Belden in 1993. The following year Belden moved its headquarters to St. Louis.

Belden has expanded its product line through acquisitions. Purchases have included American Electric Cordsets and Pope Cable and Wire, BV (a unit of Netherlands-based Philips Electronics) in 1995, Intech Cable (1996), the wire division of Alpha Wire (1997), and Cowen Cable (1997). Belden bought Pacific Dunlop's (now Ansell Limited) Australia-based Olex cable business in 1998. The deal included a factory in Melbourne, Belden's first manufacturing operation in the Asia/Pacific region.

In 2000 Belden won a major contract with SBC Communications for $700 million to supply copper telecommunications cable over the next five years. And to further expand its overseas presence, Belden purchased the metallic communications cable operations division of the UK-based Corning Communications. The following year Belden sold its 70% stake in MCTec (a Netherlands-based company specializing in coatings for medical applications) to STS Biopolymers for $1.4 million. The company also reduced its workforce by nearly 17% during 2001. The trend continued the following year when Belden closed its Kingston, Ontario, plant.

Cable Design Technologies (CDT) was founded as Intercole Automation in 1980 by William Coleman. The company initially made wire and cable and materials-handling systems. In 1988 the company, by then known as CDT, was bought by current chairman Bryan Cressey's investment firm. Acquisitions fueled CDT's growth. The company bought Mohawk Wire & Cable, an early developer of wiring for computer and cable networks (1986), and Montrose Products, a maker of specialty electronics cable (1988).

Acquisitive CDT continued its buying trend during the 1990s. In 1991 it bought European cable distributor Anglo-American Cable. CDT went public in 1993, and the following year the company purchased the struggling Nya NEK Kabel AB (cable, Sweden). In 1996 CDT boosted its presence in the telecom market with its $90 million purchase of the communications cable and network wiring products business of Northern Telecom (now Nortel Networks).

CDT gained footholds in the aircraft and wireless communications markets in 1997 with its purchases of specialty cable and wire manufacturers Dearborn Wire & Cable and Barcel Wire & Cable. In 1998 CDT expanded its international reach by buying Örebro (wire and cable, Sweden) and 80% of Germany-based HEW-KABEL (cable). Citing a decline in the telecommunications industry, CDT reduced its workforce by 900 jobs in 2001.

Belden CDT Inc. was born in 2004 when the merger of Cable Design Technologies and Belden was completed. As part of the merger agreement, Belden CDT exited the North American telecommunications market by selling its communications assets to Superior Essex.

The company changed its name from Belden CDT Inc. to Belden Inc. in 2007.

EXECUTIVES

Chairman: Bryan C. Cressey, age 60
President, CEO, and Director: John S. Stroup, age 44, $4,960,649 total compensation
EVP Asia/Pacific Operations: Naresh Kumra, age 39, $1,447,464 total compensation
EVP EMEA Operations and Global Connectivity: Christoph Gusenleitner
EVP Americas Operations and Global Cable Products: Denis Suggs, age 44, $1,072,479 total compensation
SVP Finance, CFO, and Chief Accounting Officer: Gray G. Benoist, age 57, $1,829,327 total compensation
SVP Global Sales and Marketing: Steven R. (Steve) Biegacki, age 51
SVP Human Resources: Cathy O. Staples, age 59
SVP, Secretary, and General Counsel: Kevin L. Bloomfield, age 58, $1,127,385 total compensation
VP Business Development: Daniel Krawczyk
VP Financial Planning and Analysis and Treasurer: Henk Derksen
VP Internal Audit: Stephen H. Johnson, age 60
VP Global Manufacturing: Richard (Dick) Kirschner, age 59
Investor Relations: Frank Milano
President, Trapeze Networks: Dhrupad Trivedi
Auditors: Ernst & Young LLP

LOCATIONS

HQ: Belden Inc.
7733 Forsyth Blvd., Ste. 800, St. Louis, MO 63105
Phone: 314-854-8000   **Fax:** 314-854-8001
Web: www.beldencdt.com

2009 Sales

	$ mil.	% of total
Americas	766.6	54
Europe, Middle East, Africa	345.2	24
Asia/Pacific	250.3	18
Wireless	53.2	4
Total	**1,415.3**	**100**

PRODUCTS/OPERATIONS

2009 Sales

	$ mil.	% of total
Cable products	1,039.5	74
Networking products	232.0	16
Connectivity products	143.8	10
Total	**1,415.3**	**100**

Selected Products

Active connectivity products
  Fiber-optic interfaces and media converters
  Industrial Ethernet switches
  Load moment indicators
Composite cables
Connectors
Copper cables
  Coaxial cables
  Ribbon cables
  Shielded and unshielded twisted-pair cables
  Stranded cables
Fiber-optic cables
Heat-shrinkable tubing
Lead and hookup wires
Multiconductor cables
Wire management products

COMPETITORS

ADC Telecommunications	International Wire
Alcatel-Lucent	JDS Uniphase
AmerCable	Kalas Manufacturing
Bekaert Corp.	Kongsberg Power Products
Belkin	Southwire
CommScope	Sumitomo Electric
Corning	Superior Essex
Fujikura Ltd.	SWCC SHOWA
Furukawa Electric	Tyco
General Cable	W.L. Gore

HISTORICAL FINANCIALS

Company Type: Public

Income Statement

FYE: December 31

	REVENUE ($ mil.)	NET INCOME ($ mil.)	NET PROFIT MARGIN	EMPLOYEES
12/09	1,415	(25)	—	6,200
12/08	2,006	(361)	—	7,500
12/07	2,033	137	6.7%	9,500
12/06	1,496	66	4.4%	5,400
12/05	1,352	48	3.5%	6,100
Annual Growth	1.1%	—	—	0.4%

2009 Year-End Financials

Debt ratio: 98.7%
Return on equity: —
Cash ($ mil.): 309
Current ratio: 2.14
Long-term debt ($ mil.): 544
No. of shares (mil.): 47
Dividends
  Yield: 0.9%
  Payout: —
Market value ($ mil.): 1,025

Stock History

NYSE: BDC

	STOCK PRICE ($) FY Close	P/E High/Low	PER SHARE ($) Earnings	Dividends	Book Value
12/09	21.92	— —	(0.53)	0.20	11.79
12/08	20.88	— —	(8.08)	0.20	12.21
12/07	44.50	22 14	2.73	0.20	22.94
12/06	39.09	30 17	1.37	0.20	18.05
12/05	24.43	27 18	0.96	0.20	15.26
Annual Growth	(2.7%)	— —	—	0.0%	(6.3%)

Bemis Company

Thanks to companies like Bemis, delectables such as potato chips and snack cakes have a longer shelf life than most marriages. Bemis makes a broad line of flexible packaging materials, including polymer films, barrier laminates, and paper-bag packaging, nearly 60% of which are used by the food industry to bundle all manner of edibles. In addition to bags, Bemis produces pressure-sensitive products, ranging from label paper and graphic films to thin-film adhesives. Bemis' core customer, the food industry, represents 85% of sales; the company also sells to the agricultural, chemical, medical, personal care, and printing industries. With 84 facilities in 13 countries, the US accounts for some two-thirds of sales.

The company's major customers — including Kimberly-Clark, Procter & Gamble, Sara Lee, Nestlé, Kraft, General Mills, Energizer Batteries, and Hormel Foods — are themselves engaged in a fiercely competitive market where packaging counts in wooing consumer dollars. Bemis' dominant presence in the flexible packaging sector positions the package-maker to expand its lineup of premium, proprietary products. Moreover, the food industry, which has traditionally avoided the boom and bust cycles that plague other markets, offers a partial buffer to Bemis' bottom line.

The global economic recession, begun in 2008, has tripped tradition, though. Worldwide consumer demand plunged during 2009. Marshalling a mix of value-added products, along with production efficiencies and lower raw material costs, Bemis realized an uptick in cash flow from operations of more than 60%.

Bemis' resilience in the tough times is due, in part, to a series of strategic acquisitions that have broadened its manufacturing footprint, particularly in Mexico and South America. Bemis acquired Alcan Packaging Food Americas from mining group Rio Tinto for $1.2 billion. The purchase — which adds 23 flexible packaging facilities in Argentina, Brazil, Mexico, as well as New Zealand, Canada, and the US — was completed after Bemis agreed to divest certain US assets, as ordered by US Department of Justice.

In 2008 the company celebrated its 150-year anniversary. Bemis makes no secret that its longevity is tied to how it defines itself; its business is in material science, namely, using polymer resins to create base structures to fit customers' needs. Thinking outside of the bag, the company developed a platform for rigid polyester packaging. Bemis continues to expand its capabilities for the medical device packaging market; a converting plant is established in Suzhou, China, to garner new opportunities.

HISTORY

Judson Moss Bemis founded J. M. Bemis and Company, Bag Manufacturers, in St. Louis in 1858. The 25-year-old received advice and equipment from cousin Simeon Farwell, who owned an established bag-making factory. St. Louis' role as a trading center supported by major railroads and the Mississippi River helped Bemis' business. The company introduced preprinted and machine-sewn flour sacks to the city's millers, and by the end of its first year it was making about 4,000 sacks a day. In its second year Edward Brown, a relative of Farwell's, became Bemis' partner, and the firm was renamed Bemis and Brown.

During the Civil War, Brown opened an office in Boston to make the most of fluctuating exchange rates. Bemis also began trading in raw cotton (priced sky-high because of the war), and it started recycling burlap shipping bags into gunnysacks. The company soon began producing its own burlap sacks from imported jute.

Stephen Bemis, Judson's brother, became a partner in the firm in 1870 and took over its St. Louis operations. Judson joined Brown in Boston, where he could be involved in commodity purchases and financial operations. Soon after, he bought out Brown's share of the firm for an amount considered extravagant at the time — $300,000.

By the early 1880s Bemis Bros. and Co. was the US's #2 bag maker. It opened a second factory in 1881 in Minneapolis, which was home to such companies as General Mills and Pillsbury. During the late 1800s and the early 1900s, Bemis opened plants throughout the US.

Judson retired in 1909, but the company continued to be run by Bemis family members. In 1914 the company entered the emerging industry of paper milling and paper-bag making, but it continued to focus on textile packaging until WWII, when shortages of cotton and jute resulted in an expanded role for paper packaging and led to the development of polyethylene packaging. By the 1950s Bemis' core products were paper and plastic packaging. In 1959 the company opened its own R&D facility. During the late 1950s and 1960s Bemis made several important acquisitions, including Curwood (packaging for medical products) and MACtac (pressure-sensitive materials). The company was renamed Bemis Company in 1965.

Bemis sold more than $100 million of noncore businesses during the 1970s and 1980s. In its effort to become an industry leader, the company began a major capital expansion program. Bemis' sales topped $1 billion in 1988.

Bemis bought candy-packaging producer Milprint, Inc., in 1990; Princeton Packaging's bakery-packaging business in 1993; and Banner Packaging in 1995. In 1996 Bemis introduced the on-battery tester, developed with Eveready. Bemis' medical packaging segment was rejuvenated that year with the purchase of Malaysia-based Perfecseal.

In 1998 Bemis acquired Belgium's Techy International, which became Bemis' base for sales and distribution in Europe. Bemis invested more than $100 million to modernize its packaging manufacturing and printing operations in 1999.

The company opened its pocketbook again in 2002, purchasing the Clysar shrink film business of DuPont (with operations in both the US and Europe) for more than $140 million. The purchase gave Bemis a worldwide reach for its shrink bags, film, and heat-set packaging products.

In 2004 Bemis acquired flexible packaging assets in Mexico from Masterpak S.A. de C.V. The company also restructured its Pressure Sensitive Materials division, which included the closing of two facilities.

Bemis restructured its operations to reduce costs during 2006; the move primarily consisted of manufacturing facility consolidations that resulted in seven plant closings.

Intent on strengthening its market presence in South America, Bemis bought a majority stake in Brazil-based Dixie Toga, one of the country's largest packaging companies. Bemis had originally purchased a one-third interest in Dixie Toga in 1998.

EXECUTIVES

Chairman: Jeffrey H. (Jeff) Curler, age 59, $2,677,954 total compensation
President, CEO, and Director: Henry J. Theisen, age 56, $5,705,955 total compensation
EVP and Director: Gene C. Wulf, age 59, $2,081,089 total compensation
SVP: Eugene H. (Gene) Seashore Jr., age 60, $1,332,809 total compensation
VP and CFO: Scott Ullem, age 43, $1,700,560 total compensation
VP and Controller: Stanley A. Jaffy, age 61, $1,544,106 total compensation
VP Operations; President and CEO, Morgan Adhesives Company: William F. Austen, age 51, $2,023,776 total compensation
VP, General Counsel, and Secretary: Sheri H. Edison, age 52
VP Operations: Robert F. Hawthorne, age 60
VP Global Sales Development: Chris Martin
VP Human Resources: Timothy S. Fliss
VP and Treasurer: Melanie E. R. Miller, age 46
VP Operations; President, Curwood: James W. (Jim) Ransom, age 50
President, Bemis Clysar: Steve Moore
President, MACtac Americas: James Peruzzi
President, Perfecseal: Paul R. Verbeten
President, Dixie Toga: Nelson Fazenda
President, Bemis Mexico: Robert Mescal
President, Milprint/Banner: Donald E. Nimis
President, Polyethylene Packaging Division: Peter R. Mathias
President, Paper Packaging: Gregory J. Derhaag
Public Relations Specialist: Kristi Pavletich
President, Bemis Flexible Packaging Europe: Marc Dussart
Auditors: PricewaterhouseCoopers LLP

LOCATIONS

HQ: Bemis Company, Inc.
1 Neenah Center, 4th Fl., Neenah, WI 54956
Phone: 920-727-4100   **Fax:** 920-527-7600
Web: www.bemis.com

2009 Sales

	$ mil.	% of total
North America		
US	2,272.0	65
Canada	9.9	—
South America	591.7	17
Europe	545.9	15
Other regions	95.1	3
Total	**3,514.6**	**100**

PRODUCTS/OPERATIONS

2009 Sales

	$ mil.	% of total
Flexible packaging	2,986.2	85
Pressure sensitive materials	537.4	15
Adjustments	(9.0)	—
Total	**3,514.6**	**100**

Selected Products

Barrier laminate and products
Blown film and cast film
Bundling films
Bonding and mounting tapes
Carton sealing tape
Coextruded film
Cold laminates and mounting films
Controlled atmosphere packaging
Decorative products
Digital print media
EZ Open Packaging
Flexible polymer film
Flexographic printing
In-line overlamination
Label products
Labelstock
Laminate/Barrier laminate
Modified atmosphere packaging
Monolayer film
Multiwall paper bag
Pouches and bags
Pre-diecut labels
Pressure sensitive materials
Prime labels
Rigid Packaging
Rollstock
Rotogravure printing
Screen print
Sheets for offset and digital printing
Shrink film/ Barrier shrink film
Signage materials
Specialty labels
Specialty tapes
Stretch film
Thermal laminates
Thermoformed plastic packaging
UV inhibitors
Variable information printing

COMPETITORS

3M	Pactiv
Amcor	Pliant Corporation
Avery Dennison	Printpack
Bryce Corporation	Ricoh Americas
Cantex	Sealed Air Corp.
Dow Chemical	Smurfit-Stone Container
DuPont	Sonoco Products
Exopack	Southern Film Extruders
Green Bay Packaging	UPM-Kymmene
Hood Packaging	Wausau Paper
International Paper	Winpak
Intertape Polymer	

HISTORICAL FINANCIALS

Company Type: Public

Income Statement

FYE: December 31

	REVENUE ($ mil.)	NET INCOME ($ mil.)	NET PROFIT MARGIN	EMPLOYEES
12/09	3,515	147	4.2%	20,400
12/08	3,779	166	4.4%	15,400
12/07	3,649	182	5.0%	15,678
12/06	3,639	176	4.8%	15,700
12/05	3,474	163	4.7%	15,900
Annual Growth	0.3%	(2.4%)	—	6.4%

2009 Year-End Financials

Debt ratio: 68.1%
Return on equity: 9.3%
Cash ($ mil.): 1,066
Current ratio: 3.82
Long-term debt ($ mil.): 1,228

No. of shares (mil.): 109
Dividends
 Yield: 3.0%
 Payout: 65.2%
Market value ($ mil.): 3,234

Stock History

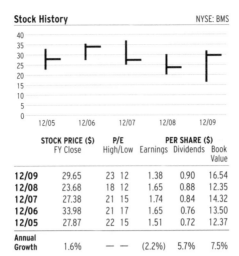

NYSE: BMS

	STOCK PRICE ($) FY Close	P/E High/Low		PER SHARE ($) Earnings	Dividends	Book Value
12/09	29.65	23	12	1.38	0.90	16.54
12/08	23.68	18	12	1.65	0.88	12.35
12/07	27.38	21	15	1.74	0.84	14.32
12/06	33.98	21	17	1.65	0.76	13.50
12/05	27.87	22	15	1.51	0.72	12.37
Annual Growth	1.6%	—	—	(2.2%)	5.7%	7.5%

Benchmark Electronics

Benchmark Electronics is setting a benchmark for electronics manufacturing services (EMS). The company, which provides contract manufacturing services to electronics makers, produces complex printed circuit boards and related electronics systems and subsystems. Its customers include manufacturers of computers, industrial control equipment, medical devices, telecommunications systems, and test and measurement instruments. Benchmark also offers design, direct order fulfillment, distribution, engineering, materials management, and testing services. The company gets about three-quarters of its revenues in the US.

The EMS market is prone to the economic pressures facing the electronics industry in general, and the global recession and credit crisis helped drive down sales of electronics, especially in 2009. Benchmark felt those effects, absorbing a 19% drop in revenues for the year. The company's business peaked in 2006-07, and Benchmark went into the red during 2008 on lower sales. With careful attention to costs, the company was able to return to profitability in 2009, despite the still lower revenues. Benchmark attributed the profits to a better product mix and increased efficiencies in operations.

Benchmark benefits from the continuing push toward outsourced manufacturing, which helps major electronics firms cut costs. In order to expand globally in the competitive and rapidly consolidating EMS market — where giants such as Flextronics, Hon Hai (Foxconn), and Jabil Circuit dominate — the company has acquired several smaller businesses and added manufacturing facilities in China and Romania and engineering design teams in Asia and Latin America, where it can operate less expensively. Benchmark now has some 25 facilities worldwide and ranks among the top 10 EMS providers.

The company is focusing on expanding its footprint in military and aerospace markets. In 2008 Benchmark worked with iRobot to provide its engineering design and services to support behavior-based robots, which help people complete complex and dangerous tasks. Later that year the company contracted with Silicon Graphics International (formerly Silicon Graphics or SGI) to create the Pleiades computer system for NASA, which will support the development of the space agency's future space fleet. Benchmark provided printed circuit board assembly, systems integration, and functional testing for the project.

Helping along the EMS consolidation trend, Benchmark in 2007 acquired PEMSTAR, an EMS provider that counted IBM and Motorola among its largest customers. The acquisition of Pemstar expanded its customer base and added value to its engineering and systems integration capabilities. The company exchanged stock and assumed debt in a transaction valued at around $300 million.

HISTORY

Benchmark Electronics was formed in 1979 as Electronics, Inc., to produce patient monitoring equipment. It was incorporated in 1981 as a wholly owned subsidiary of medical implant maker Intermedics, which pioneered surface-mount technology in pacemakers. In 1986 Intermedics sold 90% of Benchmark's stock to Electronic Investors Corp. (EIC), a company formed by Intermedics executives Donald Nigbor, Steven Barton, and Cary Fu. (Nigbor began serving as president.) In 1988 EIC became Benchmark, and Mason & Hangar (engineering and construction) bought 60% of the company. Benchmark went public in 1990.

In 1994 the company moved its headquarters from Clute, Texas, to a larger plant in nearby Angleton. Benchmark made its first acquisition — electronics contract manufacturer EMD Technologies — in 1996. In 1998 the company acquired Hudson, New Hampshire-based electronics firm Lockheed Commercial Electronics (which later became Benchmark's Hudson Division). That year, despite a prolonged slump in the electronics industry and turmoil in Asian markets, Benchmark's sales grew more than 50%.

The company acquired Stratus Computer Ireland, a Dublin, Ireland-based subsidiary of Ascend Communications, in 1999. (Lucent Technologies bought Ascend later that year.) The deal included a three-year contract to supply systems integration services to Ascend. Later that year Benchmark acquired J.M. Huber's AVEX Electronics subsidiary, then sued Huber for misrepresenting AVEX's operations.

In 2000 Benchmark sold a manufacturing plant in Sweden that it inherited from its AVEX acquisition. In 2001 John Custer stepped aside as chairman, and CEO Nigbor took his place. Fu, who had been an EVP, became president and COO of the company. Also that year Benchmark opened a systems integration facility in Singapore, expanding its geographic reach and its service capabilities. In 2002 Benchmark acquired the UK and Thailand operations of ACT Manufacturing for $46 million.

In 2004 Benchmark split the roles of chairman and CEO in an effort to improve corporate governance. Nigbor remained chairman, and Fu was promoted to CEO. The company opened its third manufacturing site in Thailand, a systems integration facility, in 2005.

Co-founders Steven Barton and Donald Nigbor retired in 2008, remaining on the company's board until the 2009 annual meeting. CEO Cary Fu succeeded Nigbor as chairman.

EXECUTIVES

Chairman and CEO: Cary T. Fu, age 61,
  $2,719,004 total compensation
President: Gayla J. Delly, age 50,
  $927,734 total compensation
CFO: Donald F. Adam, age 46,
  $927,734 total compensation
Group President: Jon J. King
Group President: Douglas H. (Doug) Hebard
General Counsel and Corporate Secretary:
  Kenneth S. Barrow
Auditors: KPMG LLP

LOCATIONS

HQ: Benchmark Electronics, Inc.
  3000 Technology Dr., Angleton, TX 77515
Phone: 979-849-6550 **Fax:** 979-848-5270
Web: www.bench.com

2009 Sales by Origin

	$ mil.	% of total
Americas	1,279.6	59
Asia	724.6	33
Europe	182.0	8
Adjustments	(96.9)	—
Total	**2,089.3**	**100**

2009 Sales by Destination

	$ mil.	% of total
US	1,549.3	74
Europe	331.8	16
Asia	171.4	8
Other regions	36.8	2
Total	**2,089.3**	**100**

PRODUCTS/OPERATIONS

2009 Sales

	% of total
Computers & related products	39
Telecommunication equipment	23
Industrial control equipment	20
Medical devices	14
Testing & instrumentation products	4
Total	**100**

Services

Circuit assembly, box build, and depot repair
Design
Distribution
Engineering
Materials procurement and management
Packaging
Prototyping
Quality analysis
Systems integration
Testing
TIME (secure Web-based information system for
  customers)

COMPETITORS

AsteelFlash
Celestica
CTS Corp.
DDi Corp.
Flextronics
Hon Hai
Jabil
Nam Tai
Plexus
Sanmina-SCI
Saturn Electronics
SigmaTron
SMTC Corp.
Sparton
Suntron
SYNNEX
TTM Technologies
Universal Scientific
Viasystems

HISTORICAL FINANCIALS
Company Type: Public

Income Statement

	REVENUE ($ mil.)	NET INCOME ($ mil.)	NET PROFIT MARGIN	EMPLOYEES
12/09	2,089	54	2.6%	9,849
12/08	2,590	(136)	—	10,522
12/07	2,916	93	3.2%	10,920
12/06	2,907	112	3.8%	9,548
12/05	2,257	81	3.6%	8,972
Annual Growth	**(1.9%)**	**(9.6%)**	**—**	**2.4%**

FYE: December 31

2009 Year-End Financials

Debt ratio: 1.0%
Return on equity: 5.0%
Cash ($ mil.): 421
Current ratio: 3.53
Long-term debt ($ mil.): 11
No. of shares (mil.): 62
Dividends
  Yield: —
  Payout: —
Market value ($ mil.): 1,177

Stock History

NYSE: BHE

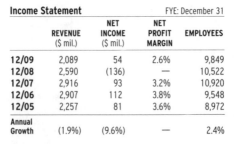

	STOCK PRICE ($) FY Close	P/E High/Low		PER SHARE ($) Earnings	Dividends	Book Value
12/09	18.91	24	10	0.83	—	17.53
12/08	12.77	—	—	(2.02)	—	16.98
12/07	17.73	21	13	1.28	—	20.70
12/06	24.36	17	12	1.71	—	15.83
12/05	22.42	18	13	1.25	—	13.60
Annual Growth	**(4.2%)**	**—**	**—**	**(9.7%)**	**—**	**6.6%**

Berkshire Hathaway

Berkshire Hathaway is where Warren Buffett, the world's second-richest man (behind his good buddy Bill Gates), spreads his risk by investing in a variety of industries, from insurance and utilities to apparel and food, and building materials to jewelry and furniture retailers. Its core insurance subsidiaries include National Indemnity, GEICO Corporation, and reinsurance giant General Re. The company also owns Dairy Queen, Fruit of the Loom, Johns Manville, Clayton Homes, Helzberg Diamonds, McLane Company, and MidAmerican Energy Holdings. Known as the Oracle of Omaha, Buffett holds more than a quarter of Berkshire Hathaway, which owns more than 70 firms and has stakes in more than a dozen others.

But even oracles are not immune to a market downturn, as Berkshire Hathaway endured its worst-ever year in 2008, partially because of declines in its residential construction and retail businesses and an ill-timed investment in ConocoPhillips as oil and gas prices spiked.

In 2008 Berkshire Hathaway acquired a nearly 20% stake in railroad operator Burlington Northern Santa Fe. It was also in on the massive Mars buyout of Wrigley, which netted Berkshire a more than 10% stake in Wrigley.

Relatively quiet for much of 2007, Berkshire Hathaway announced on Christmas Day of that year that it would buy a 60% stake in manufacturing and service conglomerate The Marmon Group from the founding Pritzker family for some $4.5 billion, the largest cash purchase in Berkshire's history. The deal closed in 2008; Berkshire will acquire the remaining 40% in stages over the next several years.

Under the guidance of the plainspoken Buffett, who pens his annual shareholder's letter in the first person and dubbed his company's annual meeting a "Woodstock for Capitalists," the firm proudly eschews get-rich-quick financial swashbuckling in favor of a measured, no-frills approach to growth. He's refused to split the company's shares or buy back any, and Berkshire Hathaway is by far the most expensive stock in the US. Buffett seeks out large companies with consistent earnings and easy-to-understand business models. Most acquisitions are made with cash, and most firms retain their management after the transaction.

Berkshire Hathaway also holds a significant portion of the ubiquitous Coca-Cola, which it plans to hold "forever." Stakes in companies such as American Express, Johnson & Johnson, Kraft Foods, The Washington Post Company, and Wells Fargo help round out the company's holdings. In 2008 Berkshire Hathaway announced it would invest $5 billion to prop up Goldman Sachs. Berkshire Hathaway also holds warrants to acquire an additional $5 billion of Goldman Sachs common stock.

A week after the Goldman Sachs investment deal, Berkshire Hathaway announced that it also would invest $3 billion in the massive conglomerate General Electric. It continued to invest in companies hit by the economic crisis in 2009 with a $2.6 billion investment in Swiss Re.

HISTORY

Warren Buffett bought his first stock — three shares of Cities Service — at age 11. In the 1950s he studied at Columbia University under famed investor Benjamin Graham. Graham's axioms: Use quantitative analysis to discover companies whose intrinsic worth exceeds their stock prices; popularity is irrelevant; the market will vindicate the patient investor.

In 1956 Buffett, then 25, founded Buffett Partnership. Its $105,000 in initial assets multiplied as the company bought Berkshire Hathaway (textiles, 1965) and National Indemnity (insurance, 1967). When Buffett nixed the partnership in 1969 because he believed stocks were overvalued, value per share had risen 30-fold.

Buffett continued investing under the Berkshire Hathaway name, looking for solid businesses, such as See's Candies (1972), advertising agencies (Interpublic, Ogilvy & Mather), newspapers (*Washington Post*, *Boston Globe*, and *Buffalo News*), and television (Capital Cities/ABC, 1985).

Buffett bought Nebraska Furniture Mart (1983) and Scott Fetzer (*World Book* encyclopedias and Kirby vacuum cleaners, 1986). The scale of investments grew as the company bought stakes in Salomon Brothers (investment banking, 1987), Gillette (1989), American Express (1991), Coca-Cola (1988-89), and Wells Fargo (1989-91). Buffett increased Berkshire Hathaway's insurance holdings, including an 82% stake in Central States Indemnity (credit insurance, 1992) and a total buyout of GEICO (1996).

In 1996, as the company's share price soared toward $35,000 — easily the highest per-share priced security in the US, outsiders threatened to start a mutual fund to invest in Berkshire Hathaway stock. In response, Buffett created a class B stock that was 1/30th the price of the class A.

In 2000 the company's purchases included furniture rental company CORT Business Services; boot maker Justin Industries; paint maker Benjamin Moore and Co.; and more than 80% of Shaw Industries, the world's largest carpet maker. The next year Buffett did a little housekeeping: He dumped 80% of his Disney stock after Mickey's earnings slipped, and sold most of the firm's holdings in Fannie Mae and Freddie Mac.

Berkshire's insurance and reinsurance businesses — especially General Re — took a hard hit from the 9/11 terrorist attacks. In a mea culpa that's rare for modern CEOs but not for him, Buffett said in his annual letter to shareholders that he had considered the risk of terrorism but hadn't adequately acted upon it.

Berkshire went on to acquire Albecca, Fruit of the Loom (pulling the garment manufacturer out of chapter 11), Garan, The Pampered Chef, and CTB during 2002.

In an interesting and contrary (and, it turns out, profitable) move, Berkshire Hathaway began investing in foreign currencies in 2002 as a result of the US's trade deficit and the weak value of the dollar. It expanded this position in 2003, encompassing some $12 billion in exchange contracts. Berkshire bought grocery distributor McLane Company from Wal-Mart for $1.5 billion the same year.

Buffett's wife, Susan, died in 2004. She had been a member of the board of directors and owned about 3% of the company.

In 2006 it bought 80% of ISCAR Metalworking, an Israel-based maker of metal-cutting tools and the first foreign company in which Berkshire has a controlling stake.

Also in 2006 Buffett announced a donation of 85% of his Berkshire Hathaway stock (worth some $44 billion) to five charitable organizations, with the Bill & Melinda Gates Foundation, led by his close friends, getting the largest portion by far.

EXECUTIVES

Chairman and CEO: Warren E. Buffett, age 79, $175,000 total compensation
Vice Chairman; Chairman and CEO, Wesco Financial: Charles T. (Charlie) Munger, age 86, $100,000 total compensation
SVP and CFO: Marc D. Hamburg, age 60, $874,750 total compensation
VP: Sharon L. Heck
VP and Controller: Daniel J. Jaksich
VP: Mark D. Millard
Secretary: Forrest N. Krutter, age 55
Director Taxes: Jo Ellen Rieck
Director Internal Auditing: Rebecca K. Amick
President and CEO, MidAmerican Energy Holdings: Gregory E. (Greg) Abel, age 47
Chairman, President, and CEO, NetJets; Chairman, MidAmerican Energy Holdings; Chairman, Johns Manville: David L. (Dave) Sokol, age 53
Chairman and CEO, General Re Corp.: Franklin (Tad) Montross IV
Chairman, President, and CEO, GEICO: Olza M. (Tony) Nicely, age 67
Auditors: Deloitte & Touche LLP

LOCATIONS

HQ: Berkshire Hathaway Inc.
3555 Farnam St., Ste. 1440, Omaha, NE 68131
Phone: 402-346-1400 **Fax:** 402-346-3375
Web: www.berkshirehathaway.com

PRODUCTS/OPERATIONS

2009 Sales

	$ mil.	% of total
Insurance & other		
Sales & service revenues	62,555	56
Insurance premiums earned	27,884	25
Other investment income	2,341	2
Utilities & energy	11,443	10
Finance & financial products	8,270	7
Total	**112,493**	**100**

2009 Sales by Segment

	$ mil.	% of total
McLane Company	31,207	28
GEICO	13,576	12
MidAmerican	11,443	10
Berkshire Hathaway Reinsurance Group	6,706	6
General Re	5,829	5
Investment income	5,223	5
Marmon	5,067	4
Finance & financial products	4,587	4
Shaw Industries	4,011	4
Berkshire Hathaway Primary Group	1,773	2
Other businesses	21,380	19
Other	1,691	1
Total	**112,493**	**100**

Major Equity Investments

American Express (12.7%)
BYD Company (9.9%)
Coca-Cola (8.6%)
ConocoPhillips (2.5%)
Kraft Foods (8.8%)
Procter & Gamble (2.9%)
Tesco plc (3%)
U.S. Bancorp (4.0%)
Washington Post Co. (18.7%)
Wells Fargo & Co. (6.5%)

Subsidiaries and Selected Holdings

Acme Building Brands (face brick and other building materials)
Albecca (custom framing products)
Applied Underwriters (workers' compensation)
Ben Bridge Jeweler (jewelry retailer)
Benjamin Moore (architectural and industrial paint)
Berkshire Hathaway Assurance Corporation
Berkshire Hathaway Credit Corporation
Berkshire Hathaway International Insurance Limited (UK)
Berkshire Hathaway Life Insurance Company of Nebraska
BH Finance (proprietary investment strategies)
Borsheim Jewelry Company (jewelry retailer)
Burlington Northern Santa Fe (railroad)
Business Wire (news service)
California Insurance Company
Central States Indemnity Co. of Omaha (credit and disability insurance)
Clayton Homes (manufactured housing and financing)
CORT (provider of rental furniture, accessories, and related services)
CTB International (manufacturer of equipment and systems for poultry, hog, and egg production)
Fechheimer Brothers (uniforms and accessories)
Fiserv Inc. (payments processing)
FlightSafety International (high technology training to operators of aircraft and ships)
Forest River (recreational vehicles)
Fruit of the Loom (apparel)
Garan (apparel)
GEICO (property/casualty insurance)
General Re Corporation (property/casualty reinsurance)
H.H. Brown Shoe Company
Helzberg's Diamond Shops (jewelry retailer)
International Dairy Queen, Inc. (licensing and servicing Dairy Queen Stores)
Iscar (cutting tools, Israel)
Johns Manville (building and equipment insulation)
Johnson & Johnson (health care products)
Jordan's Furniture (retailing home furnishings)
Justin Brands (western footwear and apparel)
Marmon Holdings (manufacturing and service)
McLane Company (wholesale distribution of groceries and non-food items)

Medical Protective Company (Med Pro; professional liability insurer)
MidAmerican Energy Holdings Company
MiTek (building components)
National Indemnity Company (specialty insurance)
Nebraska Furniture Mart (retailing home furnishings)
NetJets (fractional ownership programs for general aviation aircraft)
The Pampered Chef (kitchenware and housewares)
Precision Steel Warehouse (steel service center)
R.C. Willey Home Furnishings (home furnishings retailer)
Richline Group (jewelry manufacturer)
Russell Corporation (sportswear)
Scott Fetzer Company (manufacture and distribution of diversified products)
See's Candies (boxed chocolates and other confectionery products)
Shaw Industries (carpets and rugs)
Star Furniture (home furnishings retailer)
TTI, Inc. (electronics distribution)
Wesco Financial (investment holdings)
Wells Lamont (glove manufacturer)
World Book (encyclopedias)

COMPETITORS

AEA Investors	HM Capital Partners
Allstate	KKR
Apollo Advisors	Lincoln Financial Group
Bain Capital	Loews
Blackstone Group	Munich Re Group
The Carlyle Group	Onex
Chubb Corp	Progressive Corporation
CIGNA	State Farm
CNA Financial	TPG
The Hartford	

HISTORICAL FINANCIALS

Company Type: Public

Income Statement

FYE: December 31

	REVENUE ($ mil.)	NET INCOME ($ mil.)	NET PROFIT MARGIN	EMPLOYEES
12/09	112,493	8,055	7.2%	257,000
12/08	107,786	4,994	4.6%	246,000
12/07	118,245	13,213	11.2%	233,000
12/06	98,539	11,015	11.2%	217,000
12/05	81,663	8,528	10.4%	192,000
Annual Growth	**8.3%**	**(1.4%)**	**—**	**7.6%**

2009 Year-End Financials

Debt ratio: 28.9%
Return on equity: 6.7%
Cash ($ mil.): 30,558
Current ratio: —
Long-term debt ($ mil.): 37,909
No. of shares (mil.): 2
Dividends
Yield: —
Payout: —
Market value ($ mil.): 162,767

Stock History

NYSE: BRK.A

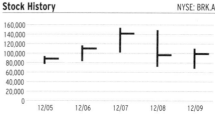

	STOCK PRICE ($) FY Close	P/E High/Low		PER SHARE ($) Earnings	Dividends	Book Value
12/09	99,200.00	21	13	5,193.00	—	79,901.61
12/08	96,600.00	46	23	3,224.00	—	66,594.02
12/07	141,600.00	18	13	8,548.00	—	73,582.10
12/06	109,990.00	16	12	7,144.00	—	66,077.20
12/05	88,620.00	17	14	5,538.00	—	55,755.97
Annual Growth	**2.9%**	**—**	**—**	**(1.6%)**	**—**	**9.4%**

Best Buy

The biggest consumer electronics outlet in the US is also the best — Best Buy, that is. The company operates more than 1,400 stores throughout the US and Canada, and another 2,600 stores in Europe, China, and now Turkey, mostly under the Best Buy, Best Buy Mobile, and The Car Phone Warehouse banners. The stores sell a wide variety of electronic gadgets, movies, music, computers, and appliances. In addition to selling products, Best Buy offers installation and maintenance services, technical support, and subscriptions for cell phone and Internet services. As the dominant consumer electronics chain in the US, following the demise of rival Circuit City, Best Buy is looking abroad for growth.

Following the formation of a joint venture with Britain's The Carphone Warehouse (TCW) in 2008, the retailer now operates more stores outside the US than within. In Europe, it runs more than 2,450 shops under The Carphone Warehouse and The Phone House banners. The stores sell mobile phones and related accessories, including subscription services, in more than half a dozen countries, including Spain, France, Germany, and the UK. Best Buy acquired 50% of TCW's European and US retail interests for about $2.2 billion in mid-2008. The purchase created a 50-50 joint venture company designed to speed Best Buy's expansion in Europe and TCW's retail business in the US.

While Best Buy has benefited from the liquidation of Circuit City, the deep recession that led to its rival's elimination also hurt Best Buy's financial results. With Circuit City out of the picture, Best Buy still faces stiff competition from Amazon.com, which has experienced rapid growth in consumer electronics sales, low-price leader Wal-Mart Stores, and Costco Wholesale, among many others.

China is an attractive growth market for the US consumer electronics retailer. In 2009 it acquired one of China's largest appliance and consumer electronics retailers, Jiangsu Five Star Appliance Co. The first Best Buy China (BBC) store opened in early 2007 and currently there are about 160 Five Star stores in China and a half a dozen BBC stores in Shanghai. However, other global retailers are also eyeing China. Indeed, Germany's largest retailer Metro AG, plans to enter the Chinese market with its Media Markt and Saturn chains of consumer electronics stores.

Other retail concepts operated by Best Buy include: eight Magnolia Audio and Video stores in California and Washington state that sell high-end audio and video products and services; and some 35 Pacific Sales Kitchen and Bath Centers, which sell high-end kitchen appliances, plumbing fixtures, and home entertainment products, mostly in the California market.

Best Buy's founder and chairman Richard Schulze owns about 17% of the company's shares.

HISTORY

Tired of working for a father who ignored his ideas on how to improve the business (electronics distribution), Dick Schulze quit. In 1966, with a partner, he founded Sound of Music, a Minnesota home/car stereo store. Schulze bought out his partner in 1971 and began to expand the chain. While chairing a school board, Schulze saw declining enrollment and realized his target customer group, 15- to 18-year-old males, was shrinking. In the early 1980s he broadened his product line and targeted older, more affluent customers by offering appliances and VCRs.

After a 1981 tornado destroyed his best store (but not its inventory), Schulze spent his entire marketing budget to advertise a huge parking-lot sale. The successful sale taught him the benefits of strong advertising and wide selection combined with low prices. In 1983 Schulze changed the company's name to Best Buy and began to open larger superstores. The firm went public two years later.

Buoyed by the format change and the fast-rising popularity of the VCR, Best Buy grew rapidly. Between 1984 and 1987 it expanded from eight stores to 24, and sales jumped from $29 million to $240 million. In 1988 another 16 stores opened and sales jumped by 84%. But Best Buy began to butt heads with many expanding consumer electronics retailers, and profits took a beating.

To set Best Buy apart from its competitors, in 1989 Schulze introduced the Concept II warehouse-like store format. Thinking that customers could buy products without much help, Schulze cut payroll by taking sales staff off commission and reducing the number of employees per store by about a third. Customers were happy, but many of Best Buy's suppliers, believing sales help was needed to sell products, pulled their products from Best Buy stores. The losses didn't seem to hurt Best Buy; it took on Sears and Montgomery Ward in the Chicago market in 1989 and continued expanding.

In 1994 the company debuted Concept III, an even larger store format. Best Buy opened 47 new stores in 1995 but found itself swimming in debt. In 1997 it realized it had overextended itself with its expansion, super-sized stores, and financing promotions. Best Buy underwent a speedy, massive makeover by scaling back expansion and doing away with its policy of "no money down, no monthly payments, no interest" (and next-to-no profits).

In early 2001 Best Buy bought The Musicland Group (at the time, operator of more than 1,300 Sam Goody, Suncoast, On Cue, and Media Play music stores) for about $425 million. The company began its international expansion in 2002 with its $377 million acquisition of Future Shop, Canada's leading consumer electronics retailer.

In June 2002 Schulze turned over his responsibilities as CEO to vice chairman Brad Anderson; Schulze remained as chairman of the board. Best Buy acquired Geek Squad, a computer support provider, for $3 million the same year.

Best Buy shut down more than 100 Musicland stores (90 Sam Goody music stores and 20 Suncoast video stores) and laid off about 700 employees in January 2003; in June it sold the entire Musicland subsidiary (then about 1,100 stores) to an affiliate of investment firm Sun Capital Partners. Three years later Best Buy purchased Pacific Sales Kitchen and Bath Centers, which sells appliances and offers assistance on residential remodeling, for $410 million.

To enhance its technology product offering for small businesses, Best Buy acquired Seattle-based Speakeasy, a provider of broadband voice, data, and IT services in 2008.

CEO Brad Anderson retired in mid-2009 and COO and longtime employee Brian Dunn took over as CEO.

EXECUTIVES

Chairman: Richard M. (Dick) Schulze, age 69
CEO and Director: Brian J. Dunn, age 49, $10,232,060 total compensation
Enterprise EVP; President, Americas: Michael A. (Mike) Vitelli, age 54, $2,419,901 total compensation
Enterprise EVP; President, Americas: Shari L. Ballard, age 43, $2,920,168 total compensation
Enterprise EVP; President, Asia: Kalendu (Kal) Patel, age 46
Enterprise EVP and Chief Administrative Officer: Timothy R. (Tim) Sheehan, age 45
EVP Finance and CFO: James L. (Jim) Muehlbauer, age 48, $2,958,211 total compensation
EVP and Chief Human Resources Officer: Carol A. Surface, age 44
EVP and Chief Marketing Officer: Barry Judge, age 47
CIO and Enterprise SVP: Neville Roberts, age 42
SVP Communications, Public Affairs, and Corporate Responsibility: Paula Prahl
SVP and CFO U.S. Strategic Business Unit and Treasurer: Ryan D. Robinson, age 44
SVP, General Counsel, and Assistant Secretary: Joseph M. Joyce, age 58
SVP Human Capital US Channels: Steve Hurst
SVP Merchandising: Michael Mohan
VP, Controller, and Chief Accounting Officer: Susan S. Grafton, age 53
VP Investor Relations: Bill Seymour
CEO, Best Buy Europe: Scott Wheway, age 43, $1,805,939 total compensation
President, Best Buy Mobile: Shawn Score
President and COO, Best Buy Canada: Michael J. (Mike) Pratt, age 42
Director Public Relations: Susan Busch
Secretary and Director: Elliot S. Kaplan, age 73
Auditors: Deloitte & Touche LLP

LOCATIONS

HQ: Best Buy Co., Inc.
7601 Penn Ave. South, Richfield, MN 55423
Phone: 612-291-1000   **Fax:** 612-292-4001
Web: www.bestbuyinc.com

2010 Sales

	$ mil.	% of total
US	37,314	75
International	12,380	25
Total	**49,694**	**100**

PRODUCTS/OPERATIONS

2010 US Stores

	No.
Best Buy	1,069
Best Buy Mobile	74
Pacific Sales	35
Magnolia Audio Video	8
Geek Squad	6
Total	**1,192**

2010 International Stores

	No.
Best Buy Europe	2,453
Canada	
Future Shop	144
Best Buy	64
Best Buy Mobile	4
China	
Five Star	158
Best Buy	6
Mexico	
Best Buy	5
Turkey	
Best Buy	1
Total	**2,835**

2010 US Sales

	% of total
Consumer electronics	39
Home office	34
Entertainment software	16
Services	6
Appliances	4
Other	1
Total	**100**

Selected Products

Consumer Electronics
  Audio
    Car stereos
    Home theater audio systems
    MP3 players
    Satellite radio systems
  Video
    Digital cameras and camcorders
    DVD players
    Televisions
Home Office
  Computers
  Networking equipment
  Office furniture
  Printers
  Scanners
  Supplies
  Telephones
Entertainment Software
  CDs
  Computer software
  DVDs
  Subscription plans
  Video game hardware and software
Appliances
  Dishwashers
  Microwave ovens
  Refrigerators
  Stoves and ranges
  Vacuum cleaners
  Washers and dryers

COMPETITORS

Amazon.com
Apple Inc.
ARTISTdirect
Audible, Inc.
Barnes & Noble
Borders Group
Brilliant Digital Entertainment
Brookstone
Buy.com
Buzz Media
Conn's
Costco Wholesale
Dell
DSG International
eMusic.com
Fry's Electronics
Gateway, Inc.
Hastings Entertainment
HMV
Home Depot
Kesa Electricals
Lowe's
MediaNet Digital
METRO AG
MSN
MySpace
Office Depot
OfficeMax
RadioShack
RealNetworks
Sears Holdings
Sony Music
Staples
Systemax
Target
Trans World Entertainment
Virgin Group
Wal-Mart
Yahoo!

HISTORICAL FINANCIALS

Company Type: Public

Income Statement

FYE: Saturday nearest end of February

	REVENUE ($ mil.)	NET INCOME ($ mil.)	NET PROFIT MARGIN	EMPLOYEES
2/10	49,694	1,317	2.7%	180,000
2/09	45,015	1,003	2.2%	155,000
2/08	40,023	1,407	3.5%	150,000
2/07	35,934	1,377	3.8%	140,000
2/06	30,848	1,140	3.7%	128,000
Annual Growth	12.7%	3.7%	—	8.9%

2010 Year-End Financials

Debt ratio: 17.5%
Return on equity: 24.0%
Cash ($ mil.): 1,826
Current ratio: 1.18
Long-term debt ($ mil.): 1,104
No. of shares (mil.): 417
Dividends
  Yield: 1.5%
  Payout: 18.1%
Market value ($ mil.): 15,218

Stock History

NYSE: BBY

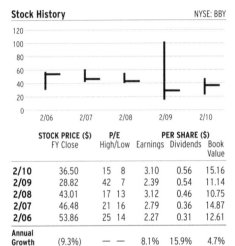

	STOCK PRICE ($) FY Close	P/E High	P/E Low	PER SHARE ($) Earnings	PER SHARE ($) Dividends	PER SHARE ($) Book Value
2/10	36.50	15	8	3.10	0.56	15.16
2/09	28.82	42	7	2.39	0.54	11.14
2/08	43.01	17	13	3.12	0.46	10.75
2/07	46.48	21	16	2.79	0.36	14.87
2/06	53.86	25	14	2.27	0.31	12.61
Annual Growth	(9.3%)	—	—	8.1%	15.9%	4.7%

Big Lots

Big Lots believes that a product's shelf life depends solely on which shelf it's on. The company is the nation's #1 broadline closeout retailer, with some 1,360 Big Lots stores (down from a high of 1,500 at the start of 2005) in 47 states. (More than one-third of its stores are located in California, Florida, Ohio, and Texas.) It sells a variety of brand-name products that have been overproduced, returned, discontinued, or result from liquidations, typically at 20%–40% below discounters' prices, as well as private-label items and furniture. Its wholesale division, Big Lots Wholesale, sells its discounted merchandise to a variety of retailers, manufacturers, distributors, and other wholesalers.

Big Lots added more than 20 locations in 2009, marking its first year of net store growth in quite some time. The company took advantage of attractive terms in the soft commercial real estate market to grow its retail presence. The chain has also experimented with a new store layout at about 60 locations across the US. The new format puts food and other consumables front and center, to capitalize on the trend of shoppers trading down from supermarkets to deep discounters to fulfill their basic needs.

Key to the retailer's turnaround is its *What's Important Now Strategy* (or WIN strategy, for short), which focuses on merchandising, real estate, and cost structure. Big Lots credits WIN with increasing its profitability. Going forward, the firm expects to enter the next phase of the plan: a growth phase. To that end, the retailer plans to add 40 stores (net of closing) in 2010 and continue to increase profits. Longer term, the closeout retailer plans to add as many as 140 stores over the next three years.

Big Lots, which buys truckloads of orphaned bric-a-brac (discontinued, overproduced, and outdated items) at steep discounts from stores and manufacturers, was able to take advantage of the many bankruptcies and liquidations resulting from the deep recession to stock its shelves at attractive prices.

New York-based investment firm BlackRock owns about 10% of Big Lots.

HISTORY

As a kid growing up in Columbus, Ohio, Russian-born Sol Shenk (pronounced "Shank") couldn't stand to pay full price for anything. His frugality blossomed into a knack for buying low and wholesaling. After a failed effort to make auto parts, Shenk began the precursor to Consolidated Stores in 1967, backed by brothers Alvin, Saul, and Jerome Schottenstein. The company started by wholesaling closeout auto parts and buying retailers' closeout items to sell to other retailers. By 1971 Shenk had branched into retailing, selling closeout auto parts through a small chain of Corvair Auto Stores.

One of Shenk's sons suggested they devote space in the Corvair stores to closeout merchandise other than car parts. Sales surged, and Shenk decided to sell the Corvair outlets and focus on closeout stores. The first Odd Lots opened in 1982. Consolidated grew more than 100% annually for the next three years. By 1986, the year after it went public, the company was opening two stores a week in midsized markets around the Midwest.

Shenk found that people would buy anything as long as the price was right. Two years after the mania for Rubik's Cubes ended, Odd Lots bought 6 million of the puzzles (once priced at $8) at 8 cents apiece, marked them up 500%, and sold them all.

By 1987 the company had nearly 300 Odd Lots/Big Lots stores. But runaway growth had created massive inventory shortages and losses as disappointed customers stopped browsing the company's sparsely stocked shelves. The woes coincided with a falling-out with the Schottensteins. Shenk retired in 1989.

Apparel and electronics retail executive William Kelley was named chairman and CEO the next year. Kelley returned Consolidated to its closeout roots and increased sales through acquisitions and creating new discount chains.

Consolidated doubled its size in 1996 with the $315 million purchase of more than 1,000 struggling Kay-Bee Toys (now KB Toys) stores from Melville Corp. The expansion continued with the 1998 purchase of top closeout competitor Mac Frugal's Bargains — Closeouts. (Mac Frugal's had nearly bought Consolidated in 1989 before Consolidated board members vetoed the deal.) The $1 billion acquisition of Mac Frugal's gave Consolidated another 326 western stores under the Pic 'N' Save and Mac Frugal's names.

In 1999 Consolidated combined its online toy sales operations with those of BrainPlay.com to form KBkids.com. In mid-2000 Kelley was ousted as CEO, handing the title over to CFO Michael Potter.

In December 2000 the company sold KB Toys (including KBkids.com) to a group led by KB management and global private equity firm Bain Capital for about $300 million. In mid-2001 the company changed its name to Big Lots and began converting all stores to that name to establish a national brand. Big Lots bought the inventory of bankrupt Internet home furnishings giant Living.com in June.

In 2002 the company completed converting 434 stores to the Big Lots banner, including 380 stores previously operating under the names of Odd Lots, Mac Frugal's, and Pic 'N' Save. The name changes were part of a larger initiative to broaden the appeal of closeout retailing and to establish a unified national brand.

In 2004 the company opened about 100 new stores and continued to add furniture departments to its existing stores.

Potter stepped down in July 2005. He was succeeded by Steven S. Fishman who became the company's chairman, CEO, and president. Fishman is a veteran of the Pamida, Frank's Nursery & Crafts, and Rhodes Furniture retail chains. Also that year, Kelley unsuccessfully sought to join the Big Lots' board by asking large shareholders to elect him. Overall, the company shuttered 174 stores in 2005. Store closures continued in 2006 with a net loss of 25 locations.

In late 2006 the company reached tentative settlements of two employee-related class action suits, including one by some 1,400 Big Lots employees in Louisiana and Texas who alleged that they were wrongly classified as managers so that they could be denied overtime pay. The settlements amounted to nearly $10 million. (In February 2004 Big Lots settled a similar suit brought by more than 1,000 California employees by agreeing to pay $10 million.)

EXECUTIVES

Chairman, President, and CEO:
Steven S. (Steve) Fishman, age 58,
$9,786,526 total compensation
EVP and CFO: Joe R. Cooper, age 52,
$1,728,493 total compensation
EVP Merchandising: John C. Martin, age 59,
$1,732,455 total compensation
EVP Supply Chain Management and CIO:
Lisa M. Bachmann, age 48,
$1,736,822 total compensation
EVP Legal and Real Estate, General Counsel, and Secretary: Charles W. Haubiel II, age 44
SVP Store Operations: Christopher T. Chapin, age 46
SVP Marketing: Robert C. Claxton, age 55
SVP Big Lots Capital and Wholesale:
Norman J. (Norm) Rankin, age 53
SVP and General Merchandise Manager, Consumables, Hardlines, and Play and Wear: Steven R. Smart
SVP Distribution and Transportation Services:
Harold A. (Hal) Wilson, age 61
SVP and General Merchandise Manager, Furniture, Seasonal, and Home Divisions: Robert S. Segal, age 55
VP Human Resources Services: Jo L. Roney
VP and Treasurer: Jared A. Poff
VP and Controller: Paul A. Schroeder, age 44
VP Information Technology Development:
Gregory W. Wilmer
Auditors: Deloitte & Touche LLP

LOCATIONS

HQ: Big Lots, Inc.
300 Phillipi Rd., Columbus, OH 43228
Phone: 614-278-6800   **Fax:** 614-278-6676
Web: www.biglots.com

2010 Stores

	No.
California	174
Texas	114
Florida	107
Ohio	101
Pennsylvania	67
North Carolina	63
Georgia	57
New York	47
Tennessee	46
Indiana	43
Kentucky	40
Michigan	40
Virginia	36
Arizona	35
Illinois	33
South Carolina	30
Alabama	26
Missouri	24
Louisiana	22
Colorado	20
Washington	20
West Virginia	18
Oklahoma	16
Massachusetts	15
Mississippi	15
Maryland	13
New Jersey	13
New Mexico	13
Oregon	12
Arkansas	11
Nevada	11
Utah	11
Wisconsin	10
Kansas	9
Connecticut	8
Maine	7
New Hampshire	6
Other states	28
Total	**1,361**

PRODUCTS/OPERATIONS

2010 Sales

	$ mil.	% of total
Consumables	1,456.4	31
Home	717.7	15
Furniture	716.8	15
Hardlines	677.8	14
Seasonal	591.3	13
Other	566.8	12
Total	**4,726.8**	**100**

COMPETITORS

99 Cents Only	Michaels Stores
Amazon.com	Quality King
BJ's Wholesale Club	Ross Stores
Costco Wholesale	Salvation Army
Dollar General	Sears
Dollar Tree	Simply Amazing
Family Dollar Stores	Target
Fred's	TJX Companies
Goodwill Industries	Tuesday Morning
J. C. Penney	Variety Wholesalers
Jo-Ann Stores	Walgreen
Kmart	Wal-Mart
Liquidation World	

HISTORICAL FINANCIALS

Company Type: Public

Income Statement				FYE: Saturday nearest January 31
	REVENUE ($ mil.)	NET INCOME ($ mil.)	NET PROFIT MARGIN	EMPLOYEES
1/10	4,727	200	4.2%	35,600
1/09	4,645	152	3.3%	37,000
1/08	4,656	159	3.4%	38,153
1/07	4,743	124	2.6%	38,738
1/06	4,430	(10)	—	43,985
Annual Growth	**1.6%**	**—**	**—**	**(5.2%)**

2010 Year-End Financials

Debt ratio: —	No. of shares (mil.): 81
Return on equity: 22.6%	Dividends
Cash ($ mil.): 284	Yield: 0.0%
Current ratio: 2.07	Payout: —
Long-term debt ($ mil.): —	Market value ($ mil.): 2,306

Stock History   NYSE: BIG

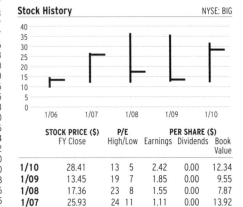

	STOCK PRICE ($) FY Close	P/E High/Low		PER SHARE ($) Earnings	Dividends	Book Value
1/10	28.41	13	5	2.42	0.00	12.34
1/09	13.45	19	7	1.85	0.00	9.55
1/08	17.36	23	8	1.55	0.00	7.87
1/07	25.93	24	11	1.11	0.00	13.92
1/06	13.37	—	—	(0.09)	0.00	13.29
Annual Growth	**20.7%**	**—**	**—**	**—**	**—**	**(1.8%)**

BJ's Wholesale Club

"Exclusive membership" has never been as common as it is at BJ's Wholesale Club. The firm is the nation's #3 membership warehouse club (behind leaders Costco and SAM'S CLUB) and #1 in New England, with more than nine million members and some 185 locations in 15 states, mostly along the Eastern Seaboard. Food, including canned, fresh, and frozen items, accounts for about two-thirds of sales at BJ's. The remainder comes from general merchandise, including apparel, housewares, office equipment, small appliances, and gas. BJ's also offers auto and home insurance, travel and other services through its website. Unlike its major rivals, BJ's targets individual retail customers rather than small businesses.

Laura Sen, who was promoted to CEO in early 2009, took the helm at BJ's amid a prolonged economic downturn, curbed discretionary spending, increased price competition, and significant price deflation on certain key food items, such as eggs, milk, and produce. BJ's is looking to strengthen its position in food sales. Indeed BJ'S, which counts supermarkets among it main competitors, aims to be customers' first stop for groceries, offering smaller package sizes and lower prices than supermarkets. BJ's is also diversifying its selection with organic produce, fresh and frozen appetizers, desserts, and restaurant-branded items. The company believes that the gains it makes through sales of these items will be sustained when the economy recovers.

Like its rivals, BJ's requires membership to its warehouses that span about 113,000 sq. ft. (although it does operate about 20 warehouses that average a mere 72,000 sq. ft. in small cities). To distinguish itself, BJ's employs a liberal membership policy and has added other consumer-minded accoutrements, such as brake, muffler, and tire service, food courts with brand-name fast-food restaurants, one-hour photo processing, and optical stores.

It is also upgrading many of its clubs. Planned improvements include upgrading decor, moving expanded health and beauty aids departments to the front of the stores, and improving presentation in its fresh food departments. BJ's operates about 105 gas stations and is planning to add more.

Mutual fund company FMR owns about 14% of BJ's common stock.

HISTORY

In 1984, with Price Club (now part of Costco) thriving and Wal-Mart Stores' SAM'S CLUB beginning to dot the horizon, Zayre Corp. opened BJ's Wholesale Club, New England's first warehouse club. Zayre, a Massachusetts-based chain of discount department stores, placed the first store in Medford, Massachusetts, and named the operation after top executive Mervin Weich's wife, Barbara Jane. In return for an annual membership fee, customers could buy a mix of goods priced at around 8%-10% above what they cost BJ's.

Zayre's bought the California-based Home-Club chain of home improvement warehouses in 1986 and combined HomeClub with BJ's to form Zayre's warehouse division. Weich was replaced by John Levy the next year.

By mid-1987 BJ's had 15 stores and more than half a billion dollars in annual sales. Over the next few years, the chain expanded into 11 states in the Northeast and Midwest, including stores in the Chicago area. Despite the chain's rapid growth — or because of it — BJ's failed to post profits.

A debt-burdened Zayre began shifting its focus to its moderate-priced chains (including T.J. Maxx and Hit or Miss) during the late 1980s. In 1989 it spun off its warehouse division to shareholders and renamed it Waban (after a nearby Massachusetts town). Zayre was renamed TJX Companies.

Waban cracked the $1 billion sales mark in 1990. During the early 1990s the company moved into the midwestern US, but its stores failed to thrive. In 1991 it closed one of its four Chicago stores and in 1992 turned the other three into HomeBase stores.

Also during those years, BJ's added fresh meats, bakery items, optical departments, and travel agents to its stores. In 1993 Herbert Zarkin, BJ's president, replaced Levy as CEO. That year BJ's had 52 stores and 2.6 million members; its sales reached $2 billion. A new inventory scanning system implemented by the company helped cut costs.

Once again, however, strong sales didn't add up to big profits. In 1993 BJ's per-store profits were far below those of its competitors, primarily due to intense competition and a regional recession. Two years later it became the first warehouse club to accept MasterCard and issued its own store-brand version of that card. BJ's added nine stores in 1995, 10 the next year, and four in 1997.

Meanwhile, Waban was struggling with HomeBase, which was still failing to show a profit due to restructuring charges. In 1997

Waban spun off BJ's Wholesale Club — its star performer — to keep it from being undervalued; Waban then changed its name to HomeBase. Also in 1997 John Nugent was named BJ's CEO.

BJ's began adding gas stations at several of its northeastern stores in 1998. Also that year it introduced its private-label products under the Executive Choice and Berkley & Jensen names. BJ's entered North Carolina in 1999.

In September 2002 CEO Nugent resigned and was replaced by Michael T. Wedge, formerly an executive vice president of the company. In November two clubs in Columbus, Ohio, and a third in Florida shut down. BJ's entered the Atlanta market in 2002 with four clubs there.

In June 2005 BJ's agreed to settle charges brought by the Federal Trade Commission alleging the company failed to protect information on thousands of its customers. Without admitting guilt the company agreed to implement new security procedures and to periodic audits of those procedures.

In 2006 Mike Wedge resigned as CEO after four years in that position. He was succeeded, on an interim basis, by chairman Herb Zarkin. (Zarkin was permanently reappointed to the job in March 2007.) In February 2007 BJ's closed its two Pro Foods Restaurant Supply stores and discontinued in-store pharmacy sales.

Zarkin stepped down as CEO in early 2009, but retained the chairman's title. President and COO Laura Sen succeeded Zarkin as chief executive of BJ'S.

EXECUTIVES

Chairman: Herbert J. (Herb) Zarkin, age 71, $4,328,400 total compensation
President, CEO, and Director: Laura J. Sen, age 53, $4,913,627 total compensation
EVP and CFO: Frank D. Forward, age 55, $1,742,949 total compensation
EVP, General Counsel, and Secretary: Lon F. Povich, age 50, $1,620,363 total compensation
EVP Club Operations: Thomas F. Gallagher, age 58, $1,733,182 total compensation
EVP Merchandising and Logistics: Christina M. (Chris) Neppl, age 49, $1,604,136 total compensation
SVP and General Merchandising Manager Consumables and Perishables: Bruce L. Graham, age 57
SVP and Director Field Operations: Cornel Catuna
SVP and Director Sales Operations: Kenneth A. Hayes
SVP Finance: Robert Eddy, age 37
SVP and Director of Marketing and E-Commerce: Michael P. Atkinson
SVP and General Manager General Merchandise: Mark S. Titlebaum, age 46
SVP and Director Logistics: Peter Amalfi
SVP and Treasurer: Carol Stone
VP Public Relations: Julie Somers
VP and Manager Investor Relations: Cathleen M. (Cathy) Maloney
Creative Director: Susan Kurnas
Auditors: PricewaterhouseCoopers LLP

LOCATIONS

HQ: BJ's Wholesale Club, Inc.
1 Mercer Rd., Natick, MA 01760
Phone: 508-651-7400   **Fax:** 508-651-6114
Web: www.bjs.com

2010 Locations

	No.
New York	37
Florida	29
Massachusetts	20
New Jersey	20
Pennsylvania	15
Connecticut	11
Virginia	10
Maryland	9
Georgia	8
North Carolina	8
New Hampshire	6
Ohio	6
Rhode Island	3
Delaware	3
Maine	2
Total	**187**

PRODUCTS/OPERATIONS

2010 Sales

	% of total
Food	65
General merchandise	35
Total	**100**

2010 Sales

	$ mil.	% of total
Retail sales	9,954.4	98
Membership fees	181.9	2
Other	50.7	—
Total	**10,187.0**	**100**

Selected Merchandise

Food
  Baked goods
  Canned goods
  Dairy products
  Dry grocery items
  Fresh produce
  Frozen foods
  Meat and fish
General Merchandise
  Apparel
  Auto accessories
  Books
  Computer software
  Consumer electronics
  Greeting cards
  Hardware
  Health and beauty aids
  Household paper products and cleaning supplies
  Housewares
  Jewelry
  Office equipment
  Office supplies
  Seasonal items
  Small appliances
  Tires
  Toys

COMPETITORS

Aurora Wholesalers	Publix
Best Buy	Sam's Club
Big Lots	Sears
Costco Wholesale	Shaw's
Family Dollar Stores	Staples
Hannaford Bros.	Stop & Shop
IGA	Target
J. C. Penney	Wal-Mart
Kmart	Weis Markets
Office Depot	Winn-Dixie
Pathmark Stores	

HISTORICAL FINANCIALS

Company Type: Public

Income Statement
FYE: Saturday nearest January 31

	REVENUE ($ mil.)	NET INCOME ($ mil.)	NET PROFIT MARGIN	EMPLOYEES
1/10	10,187	132	1.3%	23,500
1/09	10,027	135	1.3%	22,000
1/08	9,005	123	1.4%	20,800
1/07	8,480	72	0.8%	21,200
1/06	7,950	129	1.6%	20,300
Annual Growth	6.4%	0.7%	—	3.7%

2010 Year-End Financials

Debt ratio: 0.9%
Return on equity: 13.1%
Cash ($ mil.): 59
Current ratio: 1.17
Long-term debt ($ mil.): 9

No. of shares (mil.): 54
Dividends
  Yield: —
  Payout: —
Market value ($ mil.): 1,819

Stock History
NYSE: BJ

	STOCK PRICE ($) FY Close	P/E High/Low		PER SHARE ($) Earnings	Dividends	Book Value
1/10	33.79	16	11	2.42	—	19.20
1/09	28.68	19	12	2.28	—	18.29
1/08	32.39	21	14	1.90	—	18.21
1/07	30.54	31	23	1.08	—	18.95
1/06	32.14	19	14	1.87	—	18.87
Annual Growth	1.3%	—	—	6.7%	—	0.4%

Blockbuster Inc.

When it comes to renting movies, this company's goal is to remain a Blockbuster. Blockbuster is the world's largest video rental chain, with more than 6,500 company-owned or franchised stores in some 17 countries (about 62% are in the US). The chain rents more than 1 billion videos, DVDs, and video games through its Blockbuster Video outlets each year. Customers also can make rentals, purchases, and watch instant downloads through its website Blockbuster Online, which competes with the likes of Netflix and Redbox. The firm is shuttering hundreds of stores and has plans to divest its foreign operations (about a third of revenues) to focus on its North American business as it navigates toward a digital future.

Blockbuster is struggling to make the transition from a store-based distribution system to a multi-channel approach to content delivery that includes by-mail, vending, or digital download options. During 2009 the digital entertainment division partnered with Samsung Electronics America to allow owners of Samsung's next generation high-definition TVs to rent Blockbuster DVDs with the press of a button on the remote control. The rentals, which cost $2 to $4 apiece and are available for 24 hours, are piped over high-speed Internet connections. The on-demand service launched in the fall of 2009. Through a 2009 alliance with TiVo, Blockbuster also provides a video-on-demand service.

Taking a page from competitor Redbox's strategy book, the company began installing Blockbuster Express-branded DVD kiosks for video rentals via a deal with ATM manufacturer NCR. The blue vending machine-style kiosks are set up in supermarkets, convenience stores, and other retail locations. Eventually, Blockbuster plans to install about 10,000 kiosks.

In an effort to expand its online offerings, Blockbuster announced a partnership with digital media firm Sonic Solutions in 2009. The two companies are working together to offer movies-on-demand for PCs, cell phones, TVs connected to the Internet, and other electronic devices.

In response to the growing popularity of Netflix, Blockbuster launched its Blockbuster Online service where members can rent unlimited DVDs online and have them delivered via postal mail for a monthly fee. (Netflix filed suit against Blockbuster in 2006, claiming the video giant's online service violates Netflix's patent on such a video rental system. The two settled their differences in a confidential deal in 2007.)

Hedge fund manager and activist investor Carl Icahn owns 17% of Blockbuster's Class A shares and nearly 8% of its double-voting Class B shares. He resigned his seat on the company's board (held since 2005) in 2010, citing guidelines regarding limits on how many directorships one person should have.

HISTORY

After selling his computing services company, David Cook turned to operating flashy, computerized video rental stores, opening his first in 1985 and adopting the moniker Blockbuster Entertainment in 1986. Entrepreneur Wayne Huizenga took over in 1987, injecting $18 million into Blockbuster and buying the company outright by the end of the year. Huizenga's acquisitions rapidly expanded the number of Blockbuster stores to 130. Other acquisitions (including Major Video, a 175-store chain, and Erol's, the US's third-largest video chain) increased the number of stores to 1,500 by 1990.

Blockbuster became the largest video renter in the UK in 1992 through the purchase of 875-unit Cityvision. It also branched into music retailing that year when it bought the Sound Warehouse and Music Plus chains and created Blockbuster Music. The following year it acquired a majority stake in Spelling Entertainment, then was itself acquired in 1994 by Viacom for $8.4 billion. Viacom took Spelling Entertainment under its wing and formed a division for its new chain of video stores called Blockbuster Entertainment Group. Following the deal, Huizenga left the company.

Over the next few years, Blockbuster experienced a rash of poor business decisions and executive departures, starting with Steven Berrard (CEO after Viacom's 1994 takeover), who resigned in 1996 to head Huizenga's used-car operations. Wal-Mart veteran Bill Fields replaced him and started promoting the retailer as a "neighborhood entertainment center," selling videotapes (instead of renting them), books, CDs, gift items, and music. The company moved its headquarters from Florida to Dallas in 1997, a move many employees refused to make.

Fields resigned later that year and John Antioco replaced him as chairman and CEO. Antioco's reign began with Viacom taking a $300 million charge related to the turmoil at Blockbuster. He immediately started unraveling many of Fields' efforts, especially his focus on non-rental operations. Antioco also set the video rental industry on its ear in 1997 by forcing the movie studios into a revenue-sharing agreement that replaced the standard practice of buying rental copies for as much as $120 each. By 1999 Viacom spun off a minority stake in Blockbuster.

In 2004 the company launched a $700 million takeover bid for rival Hollywood Entertainment. Hollywood refused to consider the offer and eventually agreed to a purchase by its smaller rival, Movie Gallery, in 2005. In response, Blockbuster launched a hostile bid for Hollywood, raising its offer to $1.3 billion. Hollywood's directors rejected the Blockbuster offer and urged their shareholders to do the same. Blockbuster later abandoned the takeover effort. Movie Gallery completed its purchase of Hollywood later that year, creating a strong #2 in the industry.

Trying to sway customers, Blockbuster eliminated late fees on all of its traditional, in-store rentals in the US and Canada in a promotional plan in 2005. It heavily marketed the plan to the tune of about $60 million and lost more than $500 million in late fee revenues. Shortly after its implementation, however, many Blockbuster franchisors dropped the promotion and returned to charging late fees.

In July 2007 James Keyes, formerly president and CEO of convenience store operator 7-Eleven, joined Blockbuster as chairman and chief executive. He succeeded John Antioco. In September the company laid off 145 employees nationwide, including workers at its corporate headquarters.

In an ill-fated bid to diversify beyond the movie rental industry, Blockbuster in 2008 made a $1.3 billion offer to buy now-defunct Circuit City Stores. The company withdrew the bid in July, however, after reviewing Circuit City's books and announcing that the deal didn't make sense due to market conditions.

EXECUTIVES

Chairman and CEO: James W. (Jim) Keyes, age 55, $1,150,000 total compensation
EVP and CFO: Thomas M. Casey, age 51, $1,000,522 total compensation
SVP Merchandising, Distribution, and Logistics: David (Dave) Podeschi, $1,009,635 total compensation
SVP North American Store Operations: Roger Dunlap
SVP: Kevin Lewis, age 39
SVP: Thomas Kurrikoff, age 46
VP, Secretary, and General Counsel: Rod J. McDonald, age 48
Director Investor Relations: Kellie Nugent
Auditors: PricewaterhouseCoopers LLP

LOCATIONS

HQ: Blockbuster Inc.
1201 Elm St., Dallas, TX 75270
Phone: 214-854-3000   **Fax:** 214-854-3677
Web: www.blockbuster.com

2009 Sales

	$ mil.	% of total
Domestic	2,857.7	70
International	1,204.7	30
Total	**4,062.4**	**100**

PRODUCTS/OPERATIONS

2009 Sales

	$ mil.	% of total
Rental revenues	3,085.9	76
Merchandise sales	956.1	23
Other revenues	20.4	1
Total	**4,062.4**	**100**

COMPETITORS

Amazon.com
Apple Inc.
Barnes & Noble
Best Buy
Borders Group
Comcast
DIRECTV
DISH Network
GameStop
Hastings Entertainment
iN DEMAND
Kroger
Movie Gallery
Netflix
Redbox
Starz Entertainment
Target
Time Warner Cable
Trans World Entertainment
Wal-Mart

HISTORICAL FINANCIALS

Company Type: Public

Income Statement

FYE: December 31

	REVENUE ($ mil.)	NET INCOME ($ mil.)	NET PROFIT MARGIN	EMPLOYEES
12/09	4,062	(558)	—	48,000
12/08	5,288	(374)	—	58,561
12/07	5,542	(74)	—	59,643
12/06	5,524	55	1.0%	67,300
12/05	5,864	(588)	—	72,600
Annual Growth	(8.8%)	—	—	(9.8%)

2009 Year-End Financials

Debt ratio: —
Return on equity: —
Cash ($ mil.): 189
Current ratio: 1.13
Long-term debt ($ mil.): 856

No. of shares (mil.): 218
Dividends
Yield: 0.0%
Payout: —
Market value ($ mil.): 146

Stock History

Pink Sheets: BLOKA

	STOCK PRICE ($) FY Close	P/E High/Low		PER SHARE ($) Earnings	Dividends	Book Value
12/09	0.67	—	—	(2.93)	0.00	(1.44)
12/08	1.26	—	—	(2.01)	0.00	0.98
12/07	3.90	—	—	(0.45)	0.00	3.01
12/06	5.29	24	14	0.23	0.00	3.41
12/05	3.75	—	—	(3.20)	0.04	2.90
Annual Growth	(35.0%)	—	—	—	—	—

BMC Software

BMC doesn't stand for Business Mismanagement Cure, but it could. BMC Software is a leading provider of enterprise management software used for a variety of functions, including recovery and storage management, business process scheduling and integration, service management, and application and database performance management. BMC provides tools designed to manage enterprise servers, speed up and monitor databases, eliminate unplanned outages, and recover system assets. It also provides professional services such as consulting and systems integration. BMC sells directly and through channel partners worldwide.

The company is made up of two primary units: Enterprise Service Management (ESM) and Mainframe Service Management (MSM). ESM primarily provides software for service assurance and automation. ESM also encompasses BMC's professional services unit. MSM provides tools for mainframe database management and monitoring. Geographically, the company's sales are roughly split between US and international customers.

BMC continues to expand past its core expertise in mainframe management and utility software with an emphasis on ESM products. The company augmented its ESM offerings by acquiring data center automation specialist BladeLogic for about $850 million in 2008. That purchase provided BMC with application release management, configuration automation and compliance, and server provisioning tools. In 2010 BMC bolstered its Java-based offerings when it acquired Phurnace Software, a provider of automation software used to deploy and configure Java applications. It also bought middleware provider MQSoftware and IT discovery software company Tideway Systems.

The company supports both mainframe and distributed computer systems. BMC helps companies in such industries as financial services, telecommunications, and transportation — many of which rely heavily on mainframe computing — to integrate data stored on mainframes with business services.

BMC maintains technology alliances with such companies as Dell, EMC, Oracle, and Symantec. Its systems integration partners include Accenture, EDS, and Wipro.

HISTORY

BMC was launched in 1980 by Scott Boulett, John Moores, and Dan Cloer, with their initials giving the company its name. Its first product was designed to improve communications between IBM databases with connected terminals and PCs.

Through an aggressive telemarketing campaign boasted of internally as "telemuscle," the company's utility software was snapped up by a chunk of the *FORTUNE* 500, which used it to boost the performance of wall-sized IBM mainframes and database systems. The company started an international expansion in 1984, opening an office in Germany. BMC went public in 1988.

Two years later COO Max Watson replaced Richard Hosley as president and CEO. Hosley stayed on as vice chairman until 1992, when Watson assumed that title as well. Moores, the only founder who held a position with the company, resigned as chairman that year.

In the early 1990s Watson navigated BMC's transition toward networked PC systems as corporate customers began eschewing mainframes. In 1994 BMC bought PATROL Software, adding a network-based performance optimization product that would later become one of the company's flagship lines.

Using acquisitions to expand, the company in 1996 forged an alliance with Sun Microsystems to develop platform management software. The company bought software specialist DataTools in 1997 and system performance analysis software specialist BGS Systems in 1998.

In 1999 the company doubled its size when it bought rival management software maker Boole & Babbage for about $900 million and Israeli software developer New Dimension Software for about $675 million. Along with these acquisitions came a corporate reinvention that included a new logo and revamped product divisions.

In 2000 BMC increased its e-commerce offerings by acquiring Evity, a provider of Web transaction monitoring services. Early in 2001, Watson brought Robert Beauchamp on board, passing the president and CEO titles to him. Watson later stepped down as chairman as well, and was replaced by Garland Cupp.

The next year the company restructured, trimming its workforce by about 15%.

In 2003 the company purchased the Remedy unit of troubled software provider Peregrine Systems for about $350 million. After investing heavily in developing its storage management software line, BMC exited that business. BMC also expanded its business service management product line through the purchase of IT Masters for about $43 million. It acquired McAfee's (formerly Network Associates) Magic Solutions business unit in 2004.

Also in 2004 BMC acquired Marimba for about $239 million. The following year the company purchased Calendra, a provider of workflow and directory management software, and OpenNetwork Technologies, a maker of Web access management applications.

The company acquired Identify Software, a developer of application problem resolution software, for about $150 million in cash in 2006. The purchase of Identify augmented BMC's transaction management offerings. In 2007 BMC purchased business services management software providers ProactiveNet and Emprisa Networks.

EXECUTIVES

Chairman and CEO; President, Enterprise Service Management: Robert E. (Bob) Beauchamp, age 50, $12,092,843 total compensation
SVP Strategy and Corporate Development: James W. (Jim) Grant, age 61, $3,294,724 total compensation
SVP Administration: Hollie Castro, age 41, $2,800,028 total compensation
SVP and CFO: Stephen B. (Steve) Solcher, age 50, $3,211,771 total compensation
SVP Worldwide Sales and Services: John D. McMahon, age 54, $3,099,820 total compensation
SVP; President, Mainframe Service Management: William D. (Bill) Miller, age 60, $3,727,822 total compensation

SVP, General Counsel, and Secretary: Denise M. Clolery, age 54
SVP Business Operations: D. Stephen Goddard Jr., age 54
VP, Controller, and Chief Accounting Officer: T. Cory Bleuer, age 40
Director, Global Communications: Mark Stouse
VP Products, Enterprise Service Management: Paul Avenant
Auditors: Ernst & Young LLP

LOCATIONS

HQ: BMC Software, Inc.
2101 CityWest Blvd., Houston, TX 77042
Phone: 713-918-8800   **Fax:** 713-918-8000
Web: www.bmc.com

PRODUCTS/OPERATIONS

2010 Sales

	$ mil.	% of total
Maintenance	1,024	54
Licenses	758	38
Professional services	129	8
Total	**1,911**	**100**

Selected Products

Enterprise Service Management (ESM)
   Application management
   Database management
   Infrastructure management
   Service management
   Security management
   Transaction management

Mainframe Service Management (MSM)
   Data management
   Infrastructure management
   Enterprise scheduling and output management

COMPETITORS

CA Technologies
Compuware
Hewlett-Packard
IBM
McAfee
Microsoft
Oracle
SAP

HISTORICAL FINANCIALS

Company Type: Public

Income Statement

FYE: March 31

	REVENUE ($ mil.)	NET INCOME ($ mil.)	NET PROFIT MARGIN	EMPLOYEES
3/10	1,911	406	21.2%	6,100
3/09	1,872	238	12.7%	5,800
3/08	1,732	314	18.1%	5,800
3/07	1,580	216	13.7%	6,000
3/06	1,498	102	6.8%	6,200
Annual Growth	**6.3%**	**41.3%**	**—**	**(0.4%)**

2010 Year-End Financials

Debt ratio: 24.6%
Return on equity: 33.3%
Cash ($ mil.): 1,369
Current ratio: 1.40
Long-term debt ($ mil.): 341
No. of shares (mil.): 179
Dividends
   Yield: —
   Payout: —
Market value ($ mil.): 6,788

Stock History

NASDAQ (GS): BMC

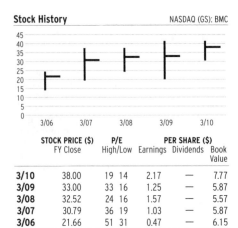

	STOCK PRICE ($) FY Close	P/E High/Low		PER SHARE ($) Earnings	Dividends	Book Value
3/10	38.00	19	14	2.17	—	7.77
3/09	33.00	33	16	1.25	—	5.87
3/08	32.52	24	16	1.57	—	5.57
3/07	30.79	36	19	1.03	—	5.87
3/06	21.66	51	31	0.47	—	6.15
Annual Growth	**15.1%**	**—**	**—**	**46.6%**	**—**	**6.0%**

Bob Evans Farms

This farm is focused on cooks in the kitchen rather than seeds in the ground. Bob Evans Farms is a leading full-service restaurant company with more than 710 locations operating under the names Bob Evans and Mimi's Café. Its namesake chain includes about 570 family-style restaurants in 20 states that are best known for breakfast items such as bacon, eggs, hotcakes, and sausage products. Its Mimi's Café casual dining chain, operated through subsidiary SWH Corporation, serves American-style dishes at more than 145 locations. In addition to its restaurants, Bob Evans Farms markets its own sausage and bacon products under the Bob Evans and Owens brands at supermarkets and other grocery retailers.

With its two distinct restaurant concepts, the company is able to target different segments of the dining market. The Bob Evans chain is a well-established brand in its core Midwestern markets that strives to offer affordable dining in a family-friendly atmosphere. It competes primarily with national family dining chains Denny's and IHOP (owned by DineEquity), as well as such regional brands as Frisch's Big Boy (Frisch's Restaurants) and Steak n' Shake (Biglari Holdings). Mimi's Café, meanwhile, targets a somewhat more upscale customer with a New Orleans-inspired menu and slightly higher prices. Operating mostly in California, it sees competition from casual dining heavyweights Darden Restaurants (Olive Garden, Red Lobster) and The Cheesecake Factory, as well as the Marie Callender chain.

The recession presented major challenges to many dining businesses during 2009, and Bob Evans Farms was no exception. The company struggled with steep declines at its Mimi's Café restaurants due to that concept's higher menu prices and concentration in the hard-hit California market. Its flagship chain, especially locations in Michigan and Ohio, also saw declines in traffic due mostly to the poor economy. In response, Bob Evans Farms focused on cutting operating costs to make up for lost sales, an effort that was aided by declines in food costs.

The company also pulled back on expansion plans as part of its cost reduction effort. (Bob Evans Farms does not franchise any of its restaurants, meaning it must bear the cost of any new construction.)

While managing its declines has been a big part of the company's focus, Bob Evans Farms is also working to spur new sales through increased efforts at marketing and menu development. The Bob Evans chain is marketing a new carry-out service to appeal to busy families who still want to dine at home, and it plans to offer an online ordering system to make carry-out meals a more convenient option. Mimi's Café, meanwhile, revamped its menu in 2010 with more than 40 new items.

The company's sausage products operation, meanwhile, continues to promote the Bob Evans brand in the supermarket aisles. The company also makes a variety of fully cooked pork products along with refrigerated and frozen food items, including mashed potatoes, macaroni and cheese, and main dish entrées. The sausage business is dominated by brands such as Johnsonville and Jimmy Dean (Sara Lee).

HISTORY

In 1946 Bob Evans opened the Bob Evans Steak House in Gallipolis, Ohio. The trucker's diner featured sausage made from hogs raised on Evans' own farm. In 1953 he and some friends and family members established the company as Bob Evans Farm Sales. By 1957, 14 trucks were delivering Bob Evans Farms sausage to southern and central Ohio customers overnight. When it went public in 1963, the company covered all of Ohio. Dan Evans, Bob's cousin, took over as CEO in 1971, when the business had just five restaurants. Dan oversaw much of the company's growth (more than 300 units by 1994), but a dispute between the cousins in 1986 led to Bob's resignation as president.

In 1987 the company acquired Texas-based Owens Country Sausage (later Owens Foods) for $16 million. Stewart Owens, whose family had started the business in 1928, continued to run the subsidiary as its president and COO. Bob Evans diversified in 1991 by acquiring salad maker Mrs. Giles Country Kitchens. A year later it bought Hickory Specialties (charcoal products; sold in 2001) and launched a new restaurant line, Cantina del Rio, to compete in the growing Mexican-food market. In 1995 Owens became president and COO of the company.

With high pork prices and consumer preferences for lower-fat foods putting pressure on restaurant sales, the company closed its Cantina del Rio chain in 1996. (It also reduced the fat content of its sausage from 40% to 25%-30%.) The next year Bob Evans Farms slowed down its expansion to focus on improving existing locations and revising menus to feature homier items. These changes, combined with declining hog prices, returned Bob Evans to steady growth in 1998.

Stewart Owens took over as CEO in 2000, becoming the first person outside the Evans family to lead the company. (He was named chairman the next year.) That same year the company rebuffed shareholders (and founder Bob Evans) who, angry that the company's stock hadn't moved since 1985, called for the firm's sale. The following year Bob Evans Farms opened 30 new restaurants. Bob Evans' daughter Deborrah Donskoy again called for the sale of the company and again shareholders voted down the proposal.

Bob Evans opened its 500th restaurant in 2002 as expansion began to accelerate during the company's 50th year in business. In 2004 the company acquired SWH Corporation, owner of the Mimi's Café casual-dining chain, for $182 million. It also opened about 40 new Bob Evans restaurants.

Owens resigned from the company in 2005; he was replaced as chairman by Robert Rabold. (After a battle with cancer, Owens died in 2008 at the age of 53.) Longtime executive Larry Corbin was called out of retirement to serve as interim president and CEO until the company brought in Steven Davis as a permanent replacement for Owens in 2006. Davis previously served as president of the Long John Silver's and A&W chains for fast-food giant YUM! Brands. Rabold died of a heart attack later that year and Davis took on the added responsibility of chairman.

Founder Bob Evans died in 2007 at age 89.

EXECUTIVES

Chairman and CEO: Steven A. (Steve) Davis, age 52, $3,262,198 total compensation
President and Chief Restaurant Operations Officer, Restaurants: Harvey Brownlee Jr., age 48
President and Chief Concept Officer, Mimi's Café: Timothy J. (Tim) Pulido, age 55, $482,937 total compensation
President and Chief Concept Officer, Bob Evans Restaurants: Randall L. (Randy) Hicks, age 50, $990,964 total compensation
CFO, Treasurer, and Assistant Secretary: Tod P. Spornhauer, age 44
SVP Marketing, Mimi's Café: Mimi Somerman
SVP Bob Evans Restaurant Marketing: Mary L. Cusick, age 54
SVP Human Resources: Joseph R. (Joe) Eulberg, age 52
SVP Supply Chain Management: Richard D. Hall, age 54
VP, General Counsel, and Secretary: Mary L. Garceau, age 37
Auditors: Ernst & Young LLP

LOCATIONS

HQ: Bob Evans Farms, Inc.
3776 S. High St., Columbus, OH 43207
Phone: 614-491-2225   **Fax:** 614-492-4949
Web: www.bobevans.com

2010 Locations

	No.
Ohio	197
Florida	60
Indiana	59
California	58
Michigan	51
Pennsylvania	39
Maryland	31
West Virginia	30
Missouri	26
Kentucky	24
Virginia	21
Illinois	19
North Carolina	16
Arizona	12
Texas	11
Colorado	8
New York	8
Delaware	7
Tennessee	6
Kansas	5
Nevada	5
South Carolina	5
Other states	17
Total	**715**

PRODUCTS/OPERATIONS

2010 Sales

	$ mil.	% of total
Restaurants	1,411.1	80
Food products	351.9	20
Adjustments	(36.2)	—
Total	**1,726.8**	**100**

2010 Locations

	No.
Bob Evans Restaurants	569
Mimi's Café	146
Total	**715**

COMPETITORS

Biglari Holdings	Frisch's
Boston Market	Golden Corral
Brinker	Hormel
Buffets Holdings	Johnsonville Sausage
Carlson Restaurants	O'Charley's
Catalina Restaurant Group	OSI Restaurant Partners
Cheesecake Factory	Perkins & Marie
Cracker Barrel	Callender's
Darden	Ruby Tuesday
Denny's	Sara Lee
DineEquity	Smithfield Foods
Eat'n Park	Tyson Fresh Meats

HISTORICAL FINANCIALS

Company Type: Public

Income Statement

FYE: Last Friday in April

	REVENUE ($ mil.)	NET INCOME ($ mil.)	NET PROFIT MARGIN	EMPLOYEES
4/10	1,727	70	4.1%	44,086
4/09	1,751	(5)	—	46,495
4/08	1,737	65	3.7%	49,149
4/07	1,655	61	3.7%	51,092
4/06	1,585	55	3.5%	50,810
Annual Growth	**2.2%**	**6.4%**	**—**	**(3.5%)**

2010 Year-End Financials

Debt ratio: 23.4%
Return on equity: 11.4%
Cash ($ mil.): 18
Current ratio: 0.40
Long-term debt ($ mil.): 149
No. of shares (mil.): 31
Dividends
  Yield: 2.2%
  Payout: 29.8%
Market value ($ mil.): 947

Stock History

NASDAQ (GS): BOBE

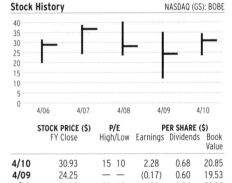

	STOCK PRICE ($) FY Close	P/E High/Low		PER SHARE ($) Earnings	Dividends	Book Value
4/10	30.93	15	10	2.28	0.68	20.85
4/09	24.25	—	—	(0.17)	0.60	19.53
4/08	28.07	20	12	1.95	0.56	20.02
4/07	36.70	23	15	1.66	0.54	23.04
4/06	28.86	20	13	1.52	0.48	23.02
Annual Growth	**1.7%**	**—**	**—**	**10.7%**	**9.1%**	**(2.4%)**

The Boeing Company

The world's largest aerospace company, Boeing is the #2 maker of large commercial jets (behind rival Airbus) and the #2 defense contractor behind Lockheed Martin. Boeing's business units include Commercial Airplanes and Boeing Defense, Space & Security (BDS; composed of Military Aircraft, Network & Space Systems, and Global Services & Support). The company also provides financing and leasing services to both commercial and military/aerospace customers through its Boeing Capital Corporation. The US DoD generates about 80% of BDS revenues; NASA and international defense agencies, as well as satellite markets, are also customers.

A short list of Boeing's Military Aircraft products include the F/A-18 Hornet, the CH-47 Chinook, the F-15 Strike Eagle, F-22 Raptor, the C-17 Globemaster III transport, the AH-64 Apache helicopter, and Airborne Early Warning and Control. Its Network & Space Systems (a business within Boeing Defense, Space & Security) helps customers integrate systems and operations using its Airborne Laser, Combat Team Modernization, and Satellite Systems. Included in this segment are communications satellites, missiles, the International Space Station, and the Space Shuttle (with Lockheed).

The recession's impact on orders for new commercial airliners forced Boeing to rachet back operations and eliminate about 10,000 jobs worldwide in 2009. However, by March 2010 the company gained an uptick in demand and announced plans to increase production on its 747 and 777 programs. It also voiced its optimism that 2010 would be a year of economic recovery.

Boeing's commercial aircraft include the new 737, 747, 767, 777, and the 787 Dreamliner, which took its inaugural flight in mid-December 2009 from Paine Field in Washington State.

Boeing Defense, Space & Security also scored a piece of the military spending pie dedicated to homeland security and the conflicts in the Middle East. Specifically, the Network & Space Systems business has enjoyed healthy gains. Contract wins include an expansion of the Army's Future Combat Systems program and a contract to develop the next-generation maritime multi-role airplane for the Navy. With an eye toward expanding its presence in cyber and intelligence markets, Boeing acquired Argon ST for approximately $775 million. The Virginia-based developer specializes in sensor and networks that capture and analyze real-time situational awareness.

HISTORY

Bill Boeing, who had already made his fortune in Washington real estate, built his first airplane in 1916 with naval officer Conrad Westervelt. His Seattle company, Pacific Aero Products, changed its name to Boeing Airplane Company the next year.

During WWI Boeing built training planes for the US Navy and began the first international airmail service (between Seattle and Victoria, British Columbia). The company added a Chicago-San Francisco route in 1927 and established an airline subsidiary, Boeing Air Transport. The airline's success was aided by Boeing's Model 40A, the first plane to use Frederick Rentschler's new air-cooled engine.

Rentschler and Boeing combined their companies as United Aircraft and Transport in 1929 and introduced the all-metal airliner in 1933. The next year new antitrust rules forced United to sell portions of its operations as United Air Lines and United Aircraft (later United Technologies). This left Boeing Airplane (as it was known until 1961) with the manufacturing concerns.

During WWII Boeing produced such planes as the B-17 "Flying Fortress" and B-29 bombers. At one point the company was producing 362 planes per month for the war effort.

Between 1935 and 1965 Boeing's commercial planes included the Model 314 Clipper, the Model 307 Stratoliner (with the first pressurized cabin), and the 707 (the first successful jetliner) and 727. In the 1960s it built the rockets used in the Apollo space program. The company delivered the first 737 in 1967. The 747 (the first jumbo jet) also went into production in the late 1960s.

Boeing expanded its information services and aerospace capabilities by establishing Boeing Computer Services in 1970. World fuel shortages and concern over aircraft noise prompted Boeing to design the efficient 757 and 767 models in the late 1970s.

Boeing bought Rockwell's aerospace and defense operations in 1996. The next year it purchased rival and leading military aircraft maker McDonnell Douglas for $16 billion.

Boeing acquired Hughes Electronics' (now The DIRECTV Group) satellite-making unit in a $3.85 billion deal in 2000. Boeing officially moved its corporate headquarters from Seattle to Chicago in September 2001. The airline industry was rocked on the 11th of that month, when terrorists crashed hijacked commercial jets in New York City, near Washington, DC, and in rural Pennsylvania. As airlines reduced their flight schedules in the aftermath, Boeing announced that it would lay off 20,000-30,000 people (about 30% of its commercial aviation workforce) by the end of 2002 (12,000 by the end of 2001 and 8,000 more by mid-2002).

Boeing was found to have obtained a 1998 launch contract with the help of confidential Lockheed Martin documents, and in 2003 was barred from bidding on launch contracts for almost two years. Even higher-profile was the scandal in which Boeing recruited Darleen Druyun — then the Air Force's #2 procurement officer — for a high-level position with Boeing, thus violating conflict of interest laws. She reportedly shared inside information with Boeing and helped the company land a contract for 100 767 refueling tankers. The deal eventually collapsed under the weight of the scandal. Michael Sears, Boeing's former CFO, was sentenced to four months in prison for his role in the incident; Druyun received nine months. Chairman and CEO Phil Condit resigned in the wake of the scandals and was replaced by Harry Stonecipher in December of 2003.

Stonecipher was forced to resign in March of 2005 when an internal investigation revealed that he had been having an extramarital relationship with another Boeing executive. CFO James A. Bell served as interim president and CEO until W. James McNerney Jr., former head of 3M, was named chairman, president, and CEO.

In 2005 Boeing bought aviation services and parts distributor Aviall Inc. for $1.7 billion.

A terminated employee blew the whistle on Boeing for scalping taxpayers; he claimed that the company padded billing records at a San Antonio maintenance plant for Air Force planes. Despite denying the charges, Boeing settled the lawsuit in 2009 by paying $2 million to the US Justice Department.

EXECUTIVES

Chairman, President, and CEO:
W. James (Jim) McNerney Jr., age 61,
$19,443,472 total compensation
EVP and General Counsel: J. Michael Luttig, age 55,
$3,743,647 total compensation
EVP; President and CEO, Boeing Defense, Space, and Security: Dennis A. Muilenburg, age 46
EVP; President and CEO, Boeing Commercial Airplanes: James F. (Jim) Albaugh, age 59,
$5,602,378 total compensation
EVP and CFO: James A. Bell, age 61,
$6,778,282 total compensation
SVP Office of Internal Governance: Wanda Denson-Low, age 53
SVP Business Development and Strategy; President, Boeing International: Shepard W. (Shep) Hill, age 57,
$2,279,738 total compensation
SVP Human Resources and Administration:
Richard D. (Rick) Stephens, age 57
SVP Communications: Thomas J. (Tom) Downey, age 45
SVP Engineering, Operations, and Technology and CTO: John J. Tracy, age 55
SVP Government Operations: Timothy J. (Tim) Keating, age 48
Chief Investment Officer: Andrew Ward, age 39
VP Information Technology and CIO: John Hinshaw
VP Investor Relations, Financial Planning and Analysis: Diana Sands, age 44
President, Phantom Works, Boeing Defense, Space & Security: Darryl W. Davis
President, Boeing Military Aircraft, Boeing Defense, Space & Security: Christopher M. (Chris) Chadwick, age 49
President, Network and Space Systems, Defense, Space & Security: Roger A. Krone, age 54
President, Australia: Ian Thomas, age 43
President, Global Services and Support, Boeing Defense, Space & Security: Anthony M. Parasida, age 54
President, Boeing Japan: Mike Denton
Auditors: Deloitte & Touche LLP

LOCATIONS

HQ: The Boeing Company
100 N. Riverside Plaza, Chicago, IL 60606
Phone: 312-544-2000   **Fax:** 312-544-2082
Web: www.boeing.com

2009 Sales

	$ mil.	% of total
Americas		
US	39,498	58
Latin America, Caribbean & other	963	1
Canada	493	1
Asia/Pacific		
China	4,888	7
Other mainland countries	7,536	11
Oceania	1,447	2
Europe	7,516	11
Middle East	5,338	8
Africa	602	1
Total	**68,281**	**100**

PRODUCTS/OPERATIONS

2009 Sales

	$ mil.	% of total
Commercial Airplanes	34,051	50
Integrated Defense Systems		
Boeing Military Aircraft	14,057	20
Network & Space Systems	10,877	16
Global Services & Support	8,727	13
Boeing Capital Corporation	660	1
Other	165	—
Adjustments	(256)	—
Total	**68,281**	**100**

2009 Sales by Type

	$ mil.	% of total
Products	57,032	84
Services	11,249	16
Total	**68,281**	**100**

Selected Products and Services

Commercial Airplanes
737 Next Generation (short-to-medium-range two-engine jet)
747 (long-range four-engine jet)
767 (medium-to-long-range two-engine jet)
777 (long-range two-engine jet)
787 (long-range, super-efficient, 200-250 passenger capacity)
Business jets

Military Aircraft and Missile Systems
AH-64D Apache helicopter
AV-8B Harrier II
C-17 Globemaster III
C-40 Clipper (military transport)
CH-47 Chinook
F/A-15 Strike Eagle
F/A-18E/F Super Hornet
Harpoon Missile
T-45 Flight Training System
V-22 Osprey tilt-rotor aircraft
Various classified projects
X-51 (for Mach 5 travel)

Space and Communications
737 AEW&C (Airborne Early Warning and Control)
Global Positioning System satellites (GPS)
International Space Station (contractor to NASA)
National Missile Defense Lead Systems Integrator (NMDD LSI)
Space Shuttle
Various classified projects

COMPETITORS

AgustaWestland	Goodrich Corp.
Airbus	Kaman
BAE SYSTEMS	Lockheed Martin
Bombardier	Northrop Grumman
Dassault Aviation	Raytheon
EADS	Rockwell Collins
Embraer	Textron
Finmeccanica	Thales
GE Aviation	United Technologies
General Dynamics	

HISTORICAL FINANCIALS

Company Type: Public

Income Statement

FYE: December 31

	REVENUE ($ mil.)	NET INCOME ($ mil.)	NET PROFIT MARGIN	EMPLOYEES
12/09	68,281	1,312	1.9%	157,100
12/08	60,909	2,672	4.4%	162,200
12/07	66,387	4,074	6.1%	159,300
12/06	61,530	2,215	3.6%	154,000
12/05	54,845	2,555	4.7%	153,000
Annual Growth	5.6%	(15.3%)	—	0.7%

2009 Year-End Financials

Debt ratio: 574.1%
Return on equity: 314.6%
Cash ($ mil.): 9,215
Current ratio: 1.07
Long-term debt ($ mil.): 12,217

No. of shares (mil.): 732
Dividends
Yield: 3.1%
Payout: 91.3%
Market value ($ mil.): 39,606

Stock History

NYSE: BA

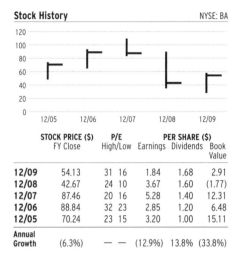

	STOCK PRICE ($) FY Close	P/E High/Low		PER SHARE ($) Earnings	Dividends	Book Value
12/09	54.13	31	16	1.84	1.68	2.91
12/08	42.67	24	10	3.67	1.60	(1.77)
12/07	87.46	20	16	5.28	1.40	12.31
12/06	88.84	32	23	2.85	1.20	6.48
12/05	70.24	23	15	3.20	1.00	15.11
Annual Growth	(6.3%)	—	—	(12.9%)	13.8%	(33.8%)

Bon-Ton Stores

Fashion hounds lost in the wilds from Maine to Montana can take refuge in The Bon-Ton Stores. The company operates more than 275 department stores under eight nameplates, including the Bon-Ton, Elder-Beerman, and Carson Pirie Scott banners, in some two dozen states. The stores sell branded (Calvin Klein, Estée Lauder, Liz Claiborne, Nautica, and Waterford) and private-label women's, children's, and men's clothing; accessories; cosmetics; and home furnishings. Bon-Ton acquired the 142-store Northern Department Store Group (NDSG) from Saks in 2006, doubling its store count. The Bon-Ton Stores was founded in 1898 by the Grumbacher family, and today is controlled by chairman Tim Grumbacher.

While the $1.05 billion acquisition of the NDSG from Saks transformed The Bon-Ton into the second-largest regional department store chain in the US (behind Dillard's), it also increased the company's debt load, not long before the US economy entered a deep recession and retail slump. Indeed, the downturn in the economy and changes in where people shop — more are choosing specialty and discount chains over full-line department stores — have led to falling sales and store closures at The Bon-Ton in recent years. Sales fell more than 5% in 2009 vs. 2008, following a 7% decline in the year earlier period. Sales of better apparel and furniture have been especially hard hit, while more moderately priced apparel and accessories performed better. While the company says it's cautiously optimistic that the economy will improve in 2010, it does not plan on opening any new stores. Instead, management is taking a conservative approach, better suited to today's difficult retail environment, and focusing on controlling costs and improving liquidity.

CEO Bud Bergren, whose employment contract was extended in 2009 to run through 2011, has said about 20 of the company's stores are unprofitable. The weakest-performing stores are in areas affected by layoffs in the auto industry, including central Pennsylvania, Ohio, and Indiana. (The company shuttered three stores in 2009, including a pair of stores in Ohio.) To lure shoppers, the retailer is shifting its marketing message to emphasize value-priced merchandise.

HISTORY

The Bon-Ton began in York, Pennsylvania, in 1898 when Sam Grumbacher and his son Max opened a one-room millinery and dry goods store, naming it for the French term for good taste. Max's son Tom joined the company — S. Grumbacher & Son — in 1931, assisted his mother and brother in guiding the business through the Depression, and took charge in the early 1940s. A second store opened in 1946, and the company expanded gradually over the next four decades, entering Maryland, New York, and West Virginia.

Tom's son Tim became CEO in 1985. S. Grumbacher & Son bought Pomeroy's, an 11-store Pennsylvania chain, from Allied Stores two years later. With 33 stores and eager to fund further expansion, the company went public in 1991 as The Bon-Ton Stores. It doubled in size in 1994 by buying 35 stores — including 20 Hess stores in Georgia, New Jersey, New York, and Pennsylvania from Crown Holding and 10-store Buffalo, New York-based Adam, Meldrum & Anderson — for about $106 million.

Growing fast but losing money in the process, the chain hired May Department Stores executive Heywood Wilansky as CEO — the first from outside the family — in 1995. To get Bon-Ton back on track, Wilansky closed 10 stores and began upgrading merchandise and using fewer vendors. In 1997 he reaffirmed the company's commitment to stick to smaller markets as it opens new stores.

To celebrate its centennial in 1998, Bon-Ton opened a store in Westfield, Massachusetts, its first location in New England. It opened seven stores in New England and New Jersey the next year. In 2000, following a management restructuring, Tim Grumbacher reassumed the position of CEO when Wilansky retired.

Bon-Ton steadily increased its sales of private-label merchandise from 9.8% in 2000 to nearly 11% in 2002. In October 2003 it bought The Elder-Beerman Stores (67 department stores and two furniture stores in nine states) for $92.8 million.

In July 2005 the company sold its private-label credit card business to HSBC Retail Services for about $316 million (minus $226 million in accounts receivable), closed its corporate credit department, and eliminated about 85 jobs. Under the terms of the deal, HSBC administers the credit card business and pays Bon-Ton a portion of the revenue generated from future credit card sales.

In March 2006 Bon-Ton completed the acquisition of Saks' Northern Department Store Group. As a result, it operated 279 department stores with some $3.4 billion in annual sales. That October the company purchased four Detroit-area Parisian department stores from Belk, which had acquired the chain from Saks.

Late to the online party, Bon-Ton launched an e-commerce sales channel in October 2007.

EXECUTIVES

Executive Chairman: M. Thomas (Tim) Grumbacher, age 70, $2,021,185 total compensation
Vice Chairman and President, Merchandising: Anthony J. (Tony) Buccina, age 59, $1,655,537 total compensation
Vice Chairman, Stores, Visual, Construction, Real Estate, Distribution & Logistics, Loss Prevention: Stephen R. (Steve) Byers, age 56, $1,099,896 total compensation
President, CEO, and Director: Byron L. (Bud) Bergren, age 63, $2,790,737 total compensation
EVP, CFO, and Principal Accounting Officer: Keith E. Plowman, age 52, $989,402 total compensation
EVP Sales Promotion and Marketing: Barbara J. Schrantz, age 51
EVP Human Resources, Corporate Procurement and Operations, and Information Services: Dennis R. Clouser, age 57
SVP Stores: John S. Farrell
SVP and CIO: James (Jim) Lance
SVP Human Resource Operations: Denise M. Domian, age 45
SVP Merchandise Planning and Internet Marketing: Jimmy D. Mansker, age 40
SVP and General Merchandise Manager, Center Core and Children's: Joyce Armeli
SVP and General Merchandise Manager, Men's and Home: Michael (Mike) Nemoir
SVP and General Merchandise Manager, Ready-to-Wear: Kiki Lockwood
SVP Distribution and Logistics: James (Jim) Rawlins
SVP, Treasurer, Risk Management and Credit: H. Todd Dissinger, age 52
VP Public and Investor Relations: Mary M. Kerr
VP and Controller: Jeff Miller
VP, General Counsel, and Secretary: Robert E. Stern
Auditors: KPMG LLP

LOCATIONS

HQ: The Bon-Ton Stores, Inc.
2801 E. Market St., York, PA 17402
Phone: 717-757-7660 **Fax:** 717-751-3108
Web: www.bonton.com

PRODUCTS/OPERATIONS

2010 Sales

	% of total
Women's apparel	26
Home	17
Cosmetics	13
Men's apparel	12
Accessories	9
Shoes	9
Children's apparel	7
Intimate apparel	4
Juniors' apparel	3
Total	**100**

2010 Stores

	No.
Bon-Ton	69
Elder-Beerman	56
Younkers	49
Herberger's	40
Carson Pirie Scott	34
Boston Store	14
Bergner's	13
Parisian	3
Total	**278**

Selected Private Labels

Breckenridge
Consensus
Cuddle Bear
Karen Neuberger Home
Kenneth Roberts
Laura Ashley
Relativity
Ruff Hewn
Studio Works
Victor by Victor Alfaro

COMPETITORS

Belk
Boscov's
Dillard's
The Gap
J. C. Penney
J. Crew
J. Jill Group
Kohl's
Lands' End
Loehmann's
Macy's
Sears
Target
Von Maur
Wal-Mart
Williams-Sonoma

HISTORICAL FINANCIALS

Company Type: Public

Income Statement

FYE: Saturday nearest January 31

	REVENUE ($ mil.)	NET INCOME ($ mil.)	NET PROFIT MARGIN	EMPLOYEES
1/10	3,035	(4)	—	27,600
1/09	3,225	(170)	—	29,100
1/08	3,468	12	0.3%	32,700
1/07	3,456	47	1.4%	33,000
1/06	1,308	26	2.0%	33,500
Annual Growth	23.4%	—	—	(4.7%)

2010 Year-End Financials

Debt ratio: 717.2%
Return on equity: —
Cash ($ mil.): 19
Current ratio: 1.91
Long-term debt ($ mil.): 1,017

No. of shares (mil.): 19
Dividends
Yield: 0.0%
Payout: —
Market value ($ mil.): 166

Stock History

NASDAQ (GS): BONT

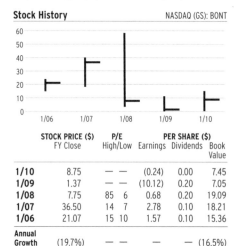

	STOCK PRICE ($) FY Close	P/E High/Low		PER SHARE ($) Earnings	Dividends	Book Value
1/10	8.75	—	—	(0.24)	0.00	7.45
1/09	1.37	—	—	(10.12)	0.20	7.05
1/08	7.75	85	6	0.68	0.20	19.09
1/07	36.50	14	7	2.78	0.10	18.21
1/06	21.07	15	10	1.57	0.10	15.36
Annual Growth	(19.7%)	—	—	—	—	(16.5%)

Borders Group

If you want John Updike or Janet Jackson to go with your java, Borders is for you. The #2 bookstore operator in the US (after Barnes & Noble), Borders Group runs more than 500 Borders superstores in about 45 states and Puerto Rico, as well as about 175 small-format shops under the Waldenbooks, Borders Express, and Borders Outlet banners. Its bookstores offer up to 170,000 book, music, and movie titles and regularly host live literary events and musician showcases to attract customers. The chain also peddles products via its website. Faced with declining sales due to the ailing book business, Borders sold its Paperchase stationery and gift business in the UK in 2010.

Borders sold Paperchase (acquired in 2004) to British private equity firm Primary Capital for £31 million (about $47 million), which the ailing bookseller will use to retire debt.

Operating within the mature bookselling industry, Borders has changed up its business strategy in recent years in response to declining revenues. The retailer posted $2.8 billion in sales in 2010, a roughly 30% drop from its high point of about $4 billion in 2007. The results reflect reduced consumer spending on discretionary entertainment products amid the economic downturn. They also indicate a shift in format preferences, from traditional (such as hardcover books, CDs) to digital (e-books, MP3s). As such, Borders has shifted its emphasis from opening new superstores to boosting the productivity of its existing locations, strengthening Web retailing operations, and developing a strategy to compete in the growing e-reader market. It has also been divesting its international holdings, closing underperforming stores, and shrinking the size of its Waldenbooks chain.

Borders, which has been looking for the funds to transform its brand, raised $25 million through a private sale to a business entity controlled by Bennett LeBow, chairman of Vector Group and an executive recognized for his restructuring expertise. When the deal was completed in May 2010, LeBow became Borders Group's executive chairman and CEO, replacing Richard McGuire, who resigned from the board.

Prior to the LeBow deal, Borders was able to slash its debt load and expenses. The company reduced the size of its workforce by almost 1,000 jobs, cut down its inventory, and curbed capital expenditures by about 80%. It also shuttered half a dozen underperforming Borders superstores and about 210 Waldenbooks stores in 2009. (The firm plans to pare the Waldenbooks chain down to 50-60 locations.)

Borders has also trimmed its overseas holdings to ease cash flow. In 2008 it sold Borders stores in Australia, New Zealand, and Singapore to book retailer A&R Whitcoulls Group. The divestiture of the bookseller's Asia/Pacific holdings follows the sale of its Borders (UK) subsidiary to Risk Capital Partners a year earlier.

Following the lead of Amazon.com and Barnes and Noble, Borders is getting in on e-book retailing. Instead of releasing a branded reading device like its rivals, however, the company partnered with e-bookseller Kobo to develop a "device neutral" reading application, meaning it can be used on smartphones, computers, and other electronic devices. Kobo is also helping to develop Borders.com's e-bookstore, which will feature more than 2 million titles.

HISTORY

Brothers Louis and Tom Borders founded their first bookstore in 1971 in Ann Arbor, Michigan. The store originally sold used books but soon added new books. As titles were added, Louis developed tracking systems for the growing inventory. It's been said that the former MIT student stumbled upon the system while trying to create a software program to predict horse race winners. In the mid-1970s the brothers formed Book Inventory Systems to market the system to other independent bookstores.

Through the late 1970s and early 1980s, the brothers focused on building the service part of their business, but by the mid-1980s they were having trouble finding enough large, independent bookstore customers. Refocusing on retail, they opened their second store (Birmingham, Michigan) in 1985.

They had five stores by 1988 and hired Robert DiRomualdo (president of cheese log chain Hickory Farms) to run Borders and mount a national expansion. Discount retailer Kmart bought Book Inventory Systems (including 19 Borders bookstores) in 1992.

Kmart already owned Waldenbooks, which had been founded in 1933 and named for the Massachusetts pond that inspired Thoreau. Started by Larry Hoyt as a book rental library, Waldenbooks had 250 outlets by 1948. In 1968 the bookseller opened its first all-retail bookstore in Pittsburgh.

By placing stores in the growing number of US shopping malls, Waldenbooks expanded rapidly during the 1970s. In 1979 the company hired former Procter & Gamble executive Harry Hoffman to run the company. Hoffman drew the ire of traditionalists in the book retailing industry because he focused on best sellers instead of literary works. Hoffman also added nonbook items such as greeting cards to the stores' merchandise mix.

In 1981 Waldenbooks became the first bookseller to operate in all 50 states. Kmart acquired the chain three years later. As part of a plan to revive its discount business, in 1995 Kmart spun off Borders Group (which by this time included Waldenbooks, Borders, and part of Planet Music, formerly CD Superstore) to the public. Borders consolidated its three divisions under one roof and bought the rest of Planet Music (closed in 1997). With mall traffic slowing nationally, Borders CEO DiRomualdo steered the company away from Waldenbooks and toward superstores.

Moving beyond its existing borders, the company acquired the UK chain Books etc., opened a store in Singapore in 1997, and entered Australia the next year. Borders finally began offering books, music, and videos through its borders.com website in 1998, three years after Amazon.com began selling online.

Philip Pfeffer, a former top executive with publisher Random House and book distributor Ingram (part of Ingram Industries) who succeeded DiRomualdo as CEO in late 1998, was forced out five months later, in part for being slow to address the company's lagging efforts online. In 1999 Greg Josefowicz, the former president of Albertson's Jewel-Osco division, was named CEO.

In 2001 Borders turned over its specialty-book operations to distributor Ingram Industries. Also that year Borders laid off its entire borders.com workforce and struck a deal to have the online unit run by rival Amazon.com; the co-branded website debuted in August 2001.

In 2002 DiRomualdo stepped down as chairman, and Josefowicz assumed the role.

International expansion continued in 2005 when Borders boosted its stake in Paperchase Products to 97%. The following year, Josefowicz announced that he planned to retire from the company by the end of 2007. When George Jones was hired in mid-2006 to lead the company, Josefowicz stepped down.

In October 2007 Borders opened its first stand-alone Paperchase shop in Boston. Also that year the company sold its Borders (UK) business, which included about 70 Borders superstores and Books etc. stores in the UK and Ireland, to book retailer A&R Whitcoulls Group.

In 2008 Borders established its own proprietary website, ending its agreement with e-tailing giant Amazon.com.

Amid declining sales, Borders replaced CEO Jones in January 2009 with Ron Marshall, a turn-around expert and founder of the private equity firm Wildridge Capital Management. Marshall left in January 2010. With an injection of $25 million in private funding from a business controlled by Bennett LeBow, Borders in May 2010 appointed LeBow as its executive chairman and CEO. In July it sold its UK stationery and gifts business, Paperchase Products, to the British private equity firm Primary Capital. Borders will continue to buy and sell Paperchase gifts and stationery products in its US stores.

EXECUTIVES

Chairman and CEO: Bennett S. LeBow, age 72
President; President and CEO, Borders, Inc.:
Michael J. (Mike) Edwards, age 50,
$761,944 total compensation
EVP, General Counsel, and Secretary:
Thomas D. (Tom) Carney, age 63,
$302,340 total compensation
EVP and CFO; COO Borders, Inc.: Mark R. Bierley,
age 43, $976,749 total compensation
SVP Merchandising, Non-Book: Gary Bale
SVP and CIO: D. Scott Laverty, age 50,
$297,866 total compensation
SVP Store Operations: James M. (Jim) Frering, age 48
SVP Marketing: William (Bill) Dandy
SVP Human Resources: Rosalind (Roz) Thompson,
age 60
**SVP Merchandising, Adult Trade, Children's, and
Bargain:** Larry Norton, age 51
SVP Merchandising Planning and Supply Chain:
Andi Lobdell
VP Real Estate: Tony Grant
VP Customer Loyalty: Dan Angus, age 38
VP Marketing: Joanna Goldstein, age 34
Media Contact: Mary Davis
Investor Contact: Brenda Rutkey
Auditors: Ernst & Young LLP

LOCATIONS

HQ: Borders Group, Inc.
100 Phoenix Dr., Ann Arbor, MI 48108
Phone: 734-477-1100   **Fax:** 734-477-1285
Web: www.bordersgroupinc.com

2010 Borders Stores

	No.
California	80
Illinois	36
New York	28
Florida	25
Pennsylvania	24
Texas	23
Ohio	19
Michigan	18
Massachusetts	16
New Jersey	15
Georgia	15
Virginia	15
Colorado	13
Indiana	13
Washington	13
Arizona	11
Connecticut	11
Maryland	11
Missouri	11
North Carolina	10
Hawaii	8
Minnesota	7
Nevada	7
Oregon	7
Tennessee	7
Kansas	6
Wisconsin	6
Kentucky	5
New Mexico	5
Iowa	4
New Hampshire	4
Oklahoma	4
District of Columbia	3
Louisiana	3
Maine	3
Montana	3
Nebraska	3
Utah	3
Other states	13
Total	**508**

PRODUCTS/OPERATIONS

2010 Sales

	% of total
Borders	81
Waldenbooks	14
International	5
Total	**100**

COMPETITORS

Amazon.com
Barnes & Noble
Best Buy
Blockbuster Inc.
Books-A-Million
Columbia House
Half Price Books
Hastings Entertainment
HMV
Movie Gallery
Wal-Mart
WHSmith

HISTORICAL FINANCIALS

Company Type: Public

Income Statement

FYE: Saturday nearest January 31

	REVENUE ($ mil.)	NET INCOME ($ mil.)	NET PROFIT MARGIN	EMPLOYEES
1/10	2,824	(109)	—	20,600
1/09	3,275	(187)	—	25,600
1/08	3,821	(157)	—	29,500
1/07	4,114	(151)	—	33,600
1/06	4,079	101	2.5%	35,500
Annual Growth	(8.8%)	—	—	(12.7%)

2010 Year-End Financials

Debt ratio: 4.2%
Return on equity: —
Cash ($ mil.): 37
Current ratio: 1.07
Long-term debt ($ mil.): 7
No. of shares (mil.): 60
Dividends
  Yield: 0.0%
  Payout: —
Market value ($ mil.): 52

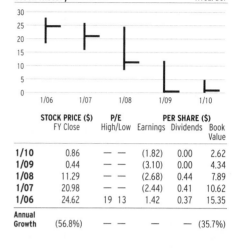

Stock History   NYSE: BGP

	STOCK PRICE ($) FY Close	P/E High/Low		Earnings	PER SHARE ($) Dividends	Book Value
1/10	0.86	—	—	(1.82)	0.00	2.62
1/09	0.44	—	—	(3.10)	0.00	4.34
1/08	11.29	—	—	(2.68)	0.44	7.89
1/07	20.98	—	—	(2.44)	0.41	10.62
1/06	24.62	19	13	1.42	0.37	15.35
Annual Growth	(56.8%)	—	—	—	—	(35.7%)

BorgWarner Inc.

If suburbanites need four-wheel-drive vehicles to turbocharge their urban drive, that's OK with BorgWarner, a leading maker of engine and drivetrain products for the world's major automotive manufacturers. Products include turbochargers, air pumps, timing chain systems, four-wheel-drive and all-wheel-drive transfer cases (primarily for light trucks and SUVs), and transmission components. Its largest customers include Volkswagen, Ford, and Daimler.

BorgWarner operates about 60 manufacturing and technical facilities worldwide. The company gets around 70% of sales from outside the US; more than half of sales come from its European operations.

BorgWarner's operations in Europe got a boost in May 2010 when, after four years of majority ownership, the company bought the remaining shares it did not own in BERU, a Germany-based maker of diesel cold-start systems and cabin heaters, spark plugs and ignition coils for gasoline engines, and sensors. BorgWarner bought about 60% of BERU in 2005, and in 2007 increased its ownership to more than 80%. The following year it took control of the company. The end of 2009 was fast approaching when BERU was formally delisted from the German stock exchange, integrated into BorgWarner, and renamed BorgWarner BERU Systems GmbH.

BorgWarner continued to expand its product line and reach further into Europe in 2010. In April the company bought Spanish emissions equipment maker Dytech ENSA. Dytech has locations in Spain, Portugal, and India, and sells to a wide range of customers across Europe and Asia. Its exhaust gas recirculation (EGR) coolers, tubes, and integrated modules are used in automotive and commercial vehicles to reduce NOx (nitrogen oxide) and particulate matter emissions, meeting stringent European standards.

The products fit well with BorgWarner's engine air management, turbochargers, and valves.

BorgWarner was in high gear early in 2008, when the company made some rosy predictions for the year's performance. The worldwide economic downturn that accelerated in the second half of 2008 obliterated those optimistic projections. The company finished the year with fourth-quarter revenues down about a third from the year before, though sales were off only slightly for the full year. It posted a small loss for 2008, its first annual loss since 2002.

The company responded to the loss with a variety of cost-cutting measures, including the elimination of about 4,400 jobs (around one-quarter of the worldwide workforce), putting European plants on four-day work weeks, and shutting down all operations for a month at the end of 2008. (In 2009 the company cut an additional 760 jobs worldwide.)

BorgWarner has been savvy about winning new business from customers outside the US, such as AUDI, Honda, Hyundai, Kia, and VW. The company's strategy is to follow market share as it shifts away from Detroit and toward Asia and Europe. BorgWarner generates more business from Volkswagen and Daimler than it does from General Motors and Chrysler, and sales in Germany outstrip those in the US.

HISTORY

BorgWarner traces its roots to the 1928 merger of major Chicago auto parts companies Borg & Beck (clutches), Warner Gear (transmissions), Mechanics Universal Joint, and Marvel Carburetor. The newly named Borg-Warner Corporation quickly began buying other companies, including Ingersoll Steel & Disc (agricultural blades and discs) and Norge (refrigerators).

The company survived the Depression largely through the contributions of its Norge and Ingersoll divisions. In the latter 1930s the company purchased Calumet Steel (1935) and US Pressed Steel (1937), along with several other companies.

During the early 1940s Borg-Warner made parts for planes, trucks, and tanks. Between 1942 and 1945 it produced more than 1.6 million automotive transmissions and gained the experience and manufacturing capacity to handle the postwar car boom. Its 1948 contract with Ford Motor to build half of its transmissions resulted in massive growth.

Roy Ingersoll, president of the Ingersoll Steel & Disc division, assumed leadership of Borg-Warner in 1950 and embarked on a major diversification plan. Borg-Warner's 1956 purchases included York, Humphreys Manufacturing, Industrial Crane & Hoist, Dittmer Gear, and the Chemical Process Company, among others. James Bert became president in 1968 and continued diversification.

Borg-Warner entered the security business in 1978 by buying Baker Industries (armored transport under the Wells Fargo name). In 1980 Borg-Warner sold its Ingersoll Products division. It acquired Burns International Security Services in 1982 and spun off York to its shareholders in 1986.

In the face of a 1987 takeover attempt, Merrill Lynch Capital Partners organized an LBO and took the company private, assuming $4.5 billion in debt. Borg-Warner then sold everything but its automotive and security units, including its

chemical group to General Electric for $2.3 billion (1988) and its credit unit, Chilton, to TRW for $330 million (1989).

The firm went public again in 1993 as Borg-Warner Security; it spun off Borg-Warner Automotive to its shareholders. (Borg-Warner Security changed its name to Burns International Services in 1999.) In 1995 Borg-Warner Automotive formed a joint venture in India (Divgi-Warner) to make transmissions and purchased the precision-forged products division of Federal-Mogul.

To expand its air- and fluid-control business, the company acquired Holley Automotive, Coltec Automotive, and Performance Friction Products from component maker Coltec Industries in 1996.

In 1999 Borg-Warner Automotive bought the Fluid Power Division (automotive cooling systems) of Eaton. The company changed its name to BorgWarner in 2000.

In 2005 BorgWarner purchased a controlling 60% stake in Germany's BERU AG.

Although it attempted to insulate itself from Detroit's woes, few could have predicted the massive 2006 production cuts at Chrysler, Ford, and GM. To adjust, late in 2006 BorgWarner said it would cut about 800 jobs at 19 facilities in the US, Canada, and Mexico — or about 13% of its total North American workforce.

In 2007 BorgWarner increased its stake in BERU to 80%, and took control of the company the following year.

EXECUTIVES

Chairman and CEO: Timothy M. (Tim) Manganello, age 60, $9,095,493 total compensation
EVP, CFO, Chief Administration Officer, and Director: Robin J. Adams, age 56, $3,675,285 total compensation
EVP; Group President and General Manager, Engine Group: Roger J. Wood, age 47, $2,351,913 total compensation
VP; President and General Manager, BorgWarner BERU Systems: Thomas Waldhier, age 47, $2,810,524 total compensation
VP; Group President and General Manager, Drivetrain Group: John G. Sanderson, age 57, $2,047,830 total compensation
VP and Chief Compliance Officer: Laurene H. Horiszny
VP Marketing, Public Relations, Communications, and Government Affairs: Scott Gallett, age 43
VP; President and General Manager of BorgWarner Morse TEC: James R. Verrier, age 47
VP, General Counsel, and Secretary: John J. Gasparovic, age 52
VP and CIO: Jamal M. Farhat
VP and Treasurer: Jan A. Bertsch, age 53
VP; President and General Manager, BogWarner TorqTransfer Systems: Daniel J. (Dan) CasaSanta, age 55
VP and Controller: Ronald T. (Ron) Hundzinski
VP Human Resources: Jan McAdams
VP Advanced Engine Engineering: Wolfgang Bullmer
VP Advanced Drivetrain Engineering: Bill Kelley
VP Business Development and M&A: Christopher H. (Chris) Vance
VP and Chief Procurement Officer: John J. McGill
Director Marketing and Public Relations: Erika Nielsen
Director Investor Relations: Ken Lamb
Auditors: PricewaterhouseCoopers LLP

LOCATIONS

HQ: BorgWarner Inc.
3850 Hamlin Rd., Auburn Hills, MI 48326
Phone: 248-754-9200   **Fax:** 248-754-9397
Web: www.bwauto.com

2009 Sales

	$ mil.	% of total
Europe		
Germany	1,419.9	36
Hungary	292.4	7
France	229.5	6
Other countries	282.9	7
US	1,090.4	28
South Korea	212.4	5
Other regions	434.3	11
Total	**3,961.8**	**100**

PRODUCTS/OPERATIONS

2009 Sales

	$ mil.	% of total
Engine	2,868.3	72
Drivetrain	1,093.5	28
Total	**3,961.8**	**100**

2009 Sales by Market

	% of total
Light vehicle	75
Commercial vehicle	17
Aftermarket replacement parts	8
Total	**100**

Selected Products

Engine Group
  Air-control valves
  Chain tensioners and snubbers
  Complete engine induction systems
  Complex solenoids and multi-function modules
  Crankshaft and camshaft sprockets
  Diesel cabin heaters
  Diesel cold starting systems (glow plugs and instant starting systems)
  Electric air pumps
  Engine hydraulic pumps
  Exhaust gas-recirculation (EGR) coolers, modules, tubes, and valves
  Fan clutches
  Fans and fan drives
  Front-wheel and four-wheel-drive chain and timing-chain systems
  High-temperature sensors (for exhaust gas aftertreatment systems)
  Ignition coils
  Intake manifolds
  On-off fan drives
  Single-function solenoids
  Spark plugs
  Throttle bodies
  Throttle position sensors
  Tire pressure sensors
  Transfer cases
  Turbochargers
Drivetrain Group
  Four-wheel-drive and all-wheel-drive transfer cases
  Friction plates
  One-way clutches
  Torque converter lock-up clutches
  Transmission bands

Selected Joint Ventures

BERU Korea Co. Ltd. (51%, South Korea, ignition coils and pumps)
Borg-Warner Shenglong (Ningbo) Co. Ltd. (70%, China, fans and fan drives)
BorgWarner TorqTransfer Systems Beijing Co. Ltd. (80%, China, transfer cases)
BorgWarner Transmission Systems Korea, Inc. (60%, South Korea, transmission components)
BorgWarner United Transmission Systems Co. Ltd. (66%, China, transmission components)
Divgi-Warner Limited (60%, India, transfer cases and automatic locking hubs)
SeohanWarner Turbo Systems Ltd. (71%, South Korea, turbochargers)

HISTORICAL FINANCIALS

Company Type: Public

Income Statement

FYE: December 31

	REVENUE ($ mil.)	NET INCOME ($ mil.)	NET PROFIT MARGIN	EMPLOYEES
12/09	3,962	27	0.7%	12,500
12/08	5,264	(36)	—	13,800
12/07	5,329	289	5.4%	17,700
12/06	4,585	212	4.6%	17,400
12/05	4,294	240	5.6%	17,400
Annual Growth	(2.0%)	(42.1%)	—	(7.9%)

2009 Year-End Financials

Debt ratio: 35.4%
Return on equity: 1.3%
Cash ($ mil.): 357
Current ratio: 1.48
Long-term debt ($ mil.): 773

No. of shares (mil.): 114
Dividends
  Yield: 0.4%
  Payout: 52.2%
Market value ($ mil.): 3,788

Stock History

NYSE: BWA

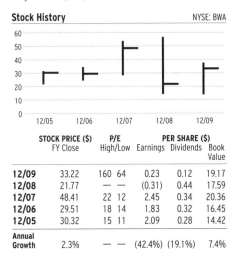

	STOCK PRICE ($) FY Close	P/E High/Low		PER SHARE ($) Earnings	Dividends	Book Value
12/09	33.22	160	64	0.23	0.12	19.17
12/08	21.77	—	—	(0.31)	0.44	17.59
12/07	48.41	22	12	2.45	0.34	20.36
12/06	29.51	18	14	1.83	0.32	16.45
12/05	30.32	15	11	2.09	0.28	14.42
Annual Growth	2.3%	—	—	(42.4%)	(19.1%)	7.4%

Boston Scientific

Boston Scientific knows that nothing is simple in matters of the heart. It makes medical supplies and devices used to diagnose and treat conditions in a variety of medical fields, with an emphasis on cardiology and cardiac rhythm management. It also makes devices used for gynecology and urology (endosurgery group) and pain management (neuromodulation). Its 13,000-plus products, made in a dozen factories worldwide, include defibrillators, catheters, coronary and urethral stents, pacemakers, biopsy forceps and needles, and urethral slings.

Cardiovascular products, which are used in procedures that affect the heart and systems carrying blood, account for more than half of Boston Scientific's sales. The cardiovascular segment includes the company's interventional cardiology and cardiac rhythm management businesses. The endosurgery product line is responsible for almost all the rest, addressing the areas of endoscopy, urology, and gynecology. The company's newest segment, neuromodulation devices (for the treatment of chronic pain), accounts for a small percentage of revenues.

Boston Scientific built its cardiac rhythm management business out of one significant acquisition: its winning bid of $28 billion to acquire Guidant in 2006. However, shortly after the acquisition, the Guidant purchase exploded like a trick cigar and Boston Scientific was hit with thousands of lawsuits over Guidant's implantable cardioverter defibrillator (ICD) devices. Over the years the resulting settlements have cost the company more than $240 million, and in 2009 Boston Scientific agreed to pay out another $296 million to the Department of Justice on behalf of Guidant after it plead guilty to misdemeanor charges related to incomplete reports filed with the FDA.

At the same time that Guidant's defibrillators were in the news, drug-coated stents began drawing negative attention — including many made by Boston Scientific. Stents, small implanted devices that prop open blood vessels and arteries, are part of the company's interventional cardiology business — a key source of revenues. Drug-coated stents that hold open blood vessels *and* slowly dispense plaque-fighting drugs have been touted as a one-two punch to fight atherosclerosis, and Boston Scientific was among the first heavyweights in the ring. However, a few years after their introduction, safety concerns were raised over the possibility that the devices may pose a risk for increased blood clots, and the company saw sales of its drug-coated stents dip.

The company took another hit in 2008 when it lost a patent infringement suit filed by competitor Johnson & Johnson and was fined $700 million by a US District Court. Boston Scientific initially appealed the ruling, which involved the company's NIR coronary stent (a product it no longer sells), but a year later it agreed to pay $716 million in exchange for a partial settlement with J&J. In early 2010 Boston Scientific settled another chunk of stent-related patent litigation (including battles over its TAXUS Express and TAXUS Liberté patents) by agreeing to pay J&J a whopping $1.7 billion.

While reorganizing and disposing of noncore businesses, the company named former Zimmer executive Ray Elliott to the post of CEO in mid-2009. He replaced Jim Tobin, who retired after holding the role for more than 10 years.

While asthma hasn't been on top of Boston Scientific's list of medical conditions to address, the company has announced it will spend some $193 million to acquire Asthmatx. The purchase will bring in that company's newly approved Alair system which uses heat to reduce the amount of smooth muscle in the airways of severe asthma patients. The acquisition will be the first in the company's strategy to realign its portfolio, while taking advantage of its sales and marketing infrastructure.

HISTORY

Many medical companies start near a hospital, but Boston Scientific's roots sprouted at a children's soccer game where two dads found common ground. John Abele and Peter Nicholas had complementary interests: Wharton MBA Nichols wanted to run his own company; philosophy and physics graduate Abele wanted a job that would help people.

In 1979 the two men founded Boston Scientific to buy medical device maker Medi-Tech. Abele and Nichols had to borrow half a million dollars from a bank and raise an additional $300,000. Medi-Tech's primary product was a steerable catheter, a soft-tipped device that could be maneuvered within the body. The catheter revolutionized gallstone operations in the early 1970s, and Boston Scientific expanded on the success of the product. The company adapted it for a slew of new procedures for the heart, lungs, intestines, and other organs.

Boston Scientific's sales were healthy in 1983, but the firm still lacked funds. It eagerly accepted $21 million from Abbott Laboratories in exchange for a 20% stake. New FDA regulations slowed product introduction and put a crimp in the company's growth. Boston Scientific found a legal loophole in the late 1980s to avoid lengthy delays: The company described its products in the vaguest possible terms so upgraded devices were considered similar enough to predecessors to escape the in-depth scrutiny of the new approval process. Still, Abele and Nicholas had to mortgage their personal properties to stay afloat before this linguistic legerdemain helped to clear government red tape. Boston Scientific returned to profitability in 1991 and went public the next year, buying back Abbott Laboratories' interest in the company as well.

Boston Scientific acquired a bevy of medical device companies in 1995, doubling its sales. Among them were SCIMED Life Systems, which specialized in cardiology products; Heart Technology, a maker of systems to treat coronary atherosclerosis; and Meadox Medicals, which made arterial grafts.

The 1998 purchase of stent maker Schneider Worldwide fattened Boston Scientific's pipeline and payroll; the company in 1999 cut 14% of workers. That year a federal judge ruled that the company's Bandit PTCA catheter infringed on a Guidant patent. In 2000 the company settled with Guidant and the two companies agreed to license products to each other.

In spite of ongoing patent infringement suits, Boston Scientific has continued to develop new products and acquire smaller companies. The firm bought Advanced Stent Technologies, which develops stents for bifurcated heart vessels (a condition caused by the branching of one vessel into two), in 2005. Boston Scientific also acquired CryoVascular Systems, which produced an angioplasty device used to treat atherosclerotic disease that was distributed by Boston Scientific.

The acquisition of Rubicon Medical later that year brought noninvasive stent delivery systems and other less-invasive endovascular devices to the company's product portfolio. Boston Scientific also acquired a portfolio of endoscopic (throat and esophageal) stents from Teleflex subsidiary Willy Rusch GmbH in 2005.

In 2008 the company sold its fluid management business (angiography and angioplasty products), and its venous access business, which makes blood stream access implants, to Avista Capital Partners for $425 million.

EXECUTIVES

Chairman: Peter M. (Pete) Nicholas, age 68
President, CEO, and Director: J. Raymond (Ray) Elliott, age 60, $33,472,734 total compensation
EVP and COO: Samuel R. (Sam) Leno, age 64, $2,269,722 total compensation
EVP and CFO: Jeffrey D. (Jeff) Capello, age 45
EVP; President, Rhythm and Vascular Group: William H. (Hank) Kucheman, age 60
EVP, Chief Administrative Officer, Secretary, and General Counsel: Timothy A. (Tim) Pratt, age 60, $1,689,921 total compensation
EVP Global Operations: Kenneth J. (Ken) Pucel, age 43
SVP International: David McFaul, age 53, $3,784,867 total compensation
SVP Global Sales Operations: Stephen F. (Steve) Moreci, age 58, $1,613,405 total compensation
SVP; President, Urology and Women's Health: John B. Pedersen, age 47
SVP; President, Endovascular Unit: Joseph M. (Joe) Fitzgerald
SVP; President, Neuromodulation: J. Michael Onuscheck, age 43
SVP; President, Endoscopy: Michael P. (Mike) Phalen, age 50
SVP and Chief Compliance Officer: Jean F. Lance, age 48
SVP and Corporate Controller: Daniel J. (Dan) Brennan
SVP Quality: Brian R. Burns, age 45
SVP Corporate Communications: Paul Donovan, age 53
SVP Restructuring and Integration: Larry Neumann
SVP Human Resources: Andrew N. (Andy) Milani II, age 50
President, Europe, Middle East, and Africa: Frederick D. (Fred) Hrkac
President, Neurovascular: Mark H. Paul
President, Boston Scientific Japan: Maulik Nanavaty
Auditors: Ernst & Young LLP

LOCATIONS

HQ: Boston Scientific Corporation
1 Boston Scientific Place, Natick, MA 01760
Phone: 508-650-8000 **Fax:** 508-650-8910
Web: www.bostonscientific.com

2009 Sales

	$ mil.	% of total
US	4,675	57
Europe, Middle East, Africa	1,837	22
Japan	988	12
Intercontinental	677	9
Divested businesses	11	—
Total	**8,188**	**100**

PRODUCTS/OPERATIONS

2009 Sales

	$ mil.	% of total
Cardiovascular group	3,520	43
Cardiac rhythm management	2,562	31
Endosurgery group	1,462	19
Neurovascular group	348	4
Neuromodulation	285	3
Divested businesses	11	—
Total	**8,188**	**100**

Selected Products

Cardiovascular
  Interventional Cardiology
    Liberté bare-metal stents
    PolarCath peripheral dilation system
    PROMUS drug-eluting stents
    TAXUS drug-eluting stents
    WALLSTENT carotid artery stents
  Cardiac Rhythm Management (CRM)
    ACUITY steerable left ventricular leads
    COGNIS pulse generator
    CONFIENT ICD (implantable cardiac defibrillator)
    LATITUDE Patient Management System
    TELIGEN ICD
  Other cardiovascular
    Cutting Balloon dilation device
    FilterWire EZ embolic protection system
    iLab ultrasound imaging catheter system
    Maverick balloon catheters
Endoscopy
  DuoTome SideLite laser treatment system (prostate intervention)
  Hydro ThermAblator system (excessive uterine bleeding)
  Prolieve Thermodilatation System (prostate intervention)
  Radial Jaw 4 single-use biopsy forceps (gastrointestinal)
  SpyGlass direct visualization system (pancreatic system)
Neuromodulation
  Precision Spinal Cord Stimulation system (chronic pain)

COMPETITORS

Abbott Labs
American Medical Systems
Bard
Cook Group
Edwards Lifesciences
ev3
Johnson & Johnson
LeMaitre Vascular
Medtronic
St. Jude Medical
ZOLL

HISTORICAL FINANCIALS

Company Type: Public

Income Statement

FYE: December 31

	REVENUE ($ mil.)	NET INCOME ($ mil.)	NET PROFIT MARGIN	EMPLOYEES
12/09	8,188	(1,025)	—	26,000
12/08	8,050	(2,036)	—	24,800
12/07	8,357	(495)	—	27,500
12/06	7,821	(3,577)	—	28,600
12/05	6,283	628	10.0%	19,800
Annual Growth	**6.8%**	**—**	**—**	**7.0%**

2009 Year-End Financials

Debt ratio: 48.1%
Return on equity: —
Cash ($ mil.): 864
Current ratio: 1.34
Long-term debt ($ mil.): 5,915
No. of shares (mil.): 1,517
Dividends
  Yield: —
  Payout: —
Market value ($ mil.): 13,652

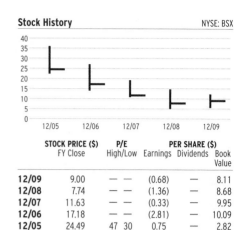

Stock History   NYSE: BSX

	STOCK PRICE ($) FY Close	P/E High/Low	PER SHARE ($) Earnings	Dividends	Book Value
12/09	9.00	— —	(0.68)	—	8.11
12/08	7.74	— —	(1.36)	—	8.68
12/07	11.63	— —	(0.33)	—	9.95
12/06	17.18	— —	(2.81)	—	10.09
12/05	24.49	47 30	0.75	—	2.82
Annual Growth	**(22.1%)**	**— —**	**—**	**—**	**30.2%**

Boyd Gaming

A key ingredient for Boyd Gaming's success is — or was — stardust. One of the country's leading casino operators, Boyd demolished the iconic Stardust Resort and Casino on the Las Vegas Strip to make way for the Echelon Place; the development is currently on hiatus. Boyd has some 15 properties, which include locations in Florida, Indiana, Illinois, Louisiana, Mississippi, and Nevada; together they have some 21,000 slot machines and 450 table games. Boyd also owns 50% of Atlantic City's Borgata Hotel Casino. The company's significant $1.3 billion purchase of Coast Casinos in 2004 created the fifth-largest gaming company in the US. Chairman William S. Boyd and his family own more than 35% of Boyd Gaming.

The company's $4.8 billion Echelon Place is planned to be a megacasino, spanning more than 60 acres. The project also includes a hotel joint venture with Morgans Hotel Group. Boyd has suspended construction on the project, citing a Las Vegas market that has been battered amid unemployment, foreclosures, and a drastic decline in tourism. It has stated that it plans to resume construction in three to five years, after credit markets fully recover and consumer spending resumes at a steady pace.

Despite a weak economy that has gripped the entire nation, Boyd has been cautiously expanding in other markets as well. It added a new hotel at its Blue Chip Casino, Hotel & Spa property in Indiana. The expansion, completed in 2009, included a spa and fitness center, additional meeting and event space, and new dining and nightlife venues. The Water Club, an 800-room boutique hotel expansion project at the Borgata property, opened in 2008. Boyd rival MGM Resorts International owns 50% of Borgata, and has put its half of the Atlantic City resort up for sale.

HISTORY

Boyd Gaming patriarch Sam Boyd may have caught the gambling bug early in life: His grandfather reportedly played poker with the outlaw Jesse James. After a stint working on gambling ships during the 1930s, Boyd arrived in Las Vegas in 1941 with less than $100 in his pockets and started running a penny roulette wheel. After years of saving half of what he made, Boyd invested $10,000 for an interest in the Sahara Hotel in 1952. He and his son William purchased the Eldorado Club in Henderson, Nevada, ten years later. Together, they founded Boyd Gaming in 1974 and opened the California Hotel in downtown Vegas the following year. In 1979 they opened Sam's Town on Las Vegas' Boulder Strip.

In 1985 the Boyds bought the Stardust (then a mob-tainted casino on the Las Vegas Strip) and acquired the Fremont Hotel and Casino near their California Hotel. Boyd Gaming was incorporated in 1988 as a holding company, and William was appointed chairman and CEO. Sam Boyd died in 1993, the same year that Boyd Gaming went public.

The company opened three casinos in Mississippi and Louisiana in 1994. That year it began managing the Treasure Chest Casino, a riverboat casino in Louisiana (it also owned a 15% stake). Two years later it acquired the Par-A-Dice Gaming riverboat casino in East Peoria, Illinois. When a federal investigation of Louisiana governor Edwin Edwards pointed toward Robert Guidry, a principal in the Treasure Chest operation, Boyd bought the remaining 85% it didn't already own. (Guidry pleaded guilty in 1998 to making payoffs to Edwards.)

In 1999 the company spent $23 million to renovate the aging Stardust, which later signed Vegas icon Wayne Newton to a 10-year engagement (a contract reportedly worth about $250 million). Boyd Gaming also gained its first foothold in Atlantic City that year when it formed a joint venture with Mirage Resorts (now owned by MGM Resorts) to build The Borgata (Italian for "village"), a 2,000-room, $1 billion casino resort. Renovation work at its Sam's Town casinos during 2000 ended Boyd's streak of earnings growth. The next year the company bought the Delta Downs racetrack near Lake Charles, Louisiana. The renamed Delta Downs Racetrack and Casino opened its casino in 2002. That year the company also purchased Isle of Capri's Tunica, Mississippi, property, adjacent to Sam's Town, for $7.5 million.

In 2004 Boyd acquired Coast Casinos for $1.3 billion. (Boyd later ditched Coast's South Coast Casino due to underperformance.) Several Boyd properties in Louisiana were temporarily closed in the wake of Hurricane Katrina, which hit the Gulf Coast in August 2005.

The company expanded in 2007 with the purchase of a jai alai facility in Dania Beach, Florida. The $152.5 million deal included about 50 acres of related land. Also that year Boyd began construction on Echelon, a multibillion-dollar Las Vegas Strip development project. In 2008 it announced a delay in the project, citing a deteriorating economy.

EXECUTIVES

Chairman: William S. (Bill) Boyd, age 78, $2,837,371 total compensation
President, CEO, and Director: Keith E. Smith, age 49, $3,362,451 total compensation
Vice Chairman, EVP, and Chief Diversity Officer: Marianne Boyd Johnson, age 51
EVP and COO: Paul J. Chakmak, age 45, $1,985,547 total compensation
EVP, Secretary, and General Counsel: Brian A. Larson, age 54

EVP, Chief Business Development Officer, and Director; President and CEO, Echelon Resorts: Robert L. (Bob) Boughner, age 57, $2,649,836 total compensation
SVP, CFO, and Treasurer: Josh Hirsberg, age 48, $748,299 total compensation
SVP Operations, Midwest and South Region: Christopher R. Gibase
SVP Operations, Nevada Region: Stephen S. Thompson
SVP Administration: William J. (Bill) Noonan
SVP Design and Construction: Tom Ballance
VP Internal Audit: Michael Bond
VP Human Resources: Robert Gerst
VP and Chief Accounting Officer: Ellie J. Bowdish, age 42
VP Technology and Systems: Paula Eylar, age 47
VP Strategic Procurement: Richard A. (Rick) Darnold
VP Information Systems: Dennis J. (Denny) Frey
VP Government and Community Affairs: Gina B. Polovina
Auditors: Deloitte & Touche LLP

LOCATIONS

HQ: Boyd Gaming Corporation
3883 Howard Hughes Pkwy., 9th Fl.
Las Vegas, NV 89169
Phone: 702-792-7200   **Fax:** 702-792-7313
Web: www.boydgaming.com

2009 Sales

	% of total
Las Vegas	
Downtown	14
Other	39
Midwest & South	47
Total	**100**

Select Operating Markets and Locations

Las Vegas
  California Hotel and Casino
  Eldorado Casino
  Fremont Hotel and Casino
  Gold Coast
  Jokers Wild Casino
  Main Street Station Casino, Brewery and Hotel
  The Orleans
  Sam's Town Las Vegas
  Suncoast
Other markets
  Blue Chip Hotel & Casino (riverboat casino; Michigan City, IN)
  Par-A-Dice Hotel and Casino (East Peoria, IL)
  Sam's Town Hotel and Gambling Hall (Tunica, MI)
  Treasure Chest Casino (riverboat casino; Kenner, LA)
Other operations
  Delta Downs (horse racing track; Lake Charles, LA)
  Vacations Hawaii (travel agency)

PRODUCTS/OPERATIONS

2009 Sales

	$ mil.	% of total
Gaming	1,372.1	75
Food & beverage	229.4	13
Room	122.3	7
Other	100.4	5
Adjustments	(183.2)	—
Total	**1,641.0**	**100**

COMPETITORS

Ameristar Casinos
Circus and Eldorado
Harrah's Entertainment
Isle of Capri Casinos
Las Vegas Sands
MGM Resorts
Pinnacle Entertainment
Rio All-Suite Hotel & Casino
Station Casinos
Tropicana Entertainment
Wynn Resorts

HISTORICAL FINANCIALS

Company Type: Public

Income Statement

FYE: December 31

	REVENUE ($ mil.)	NET INCOME ($ mil.)	NET PROFIT MARGIN	EMPLOYEES
12/09	1,641	4	0.3%	15,400
12/08	1,781	(223)	—	16,000
12/07	1,997	303	15.2%	16,900
12/06	2,193	117	5.3%	18,300
12/05	2,223	161	7.2%	23,400
Annual Growth	(7.3%)	(59.8%)	—	(9.9%)

2009 Year-End Financials

Debt ratio: 222.8%
Return on equity: 0.4%
Cash ($ mil.): 93
Current ratio: 0.65
Long-term debt ($ mil.): 2,577
No. of shares (mil.): 86
Dividends
  Yield: 0.0%
  Payout: —
Market value ($ mil.): 722

Stock History

NYSE: BYD

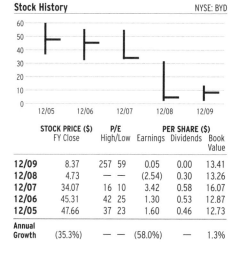

	STOCK PRICE ($) FY Close	P/E High/Low		PER SHARE ($) Earnings	Dividends	Book Value
12/09	8.37	257	59	0.05	0.00	13.41
12/08	4.73	—	—	(2.54)	0.30	13.26
12/07	34.07	16	10	3.42	0.58	16.07
12/06	45.31	42	25	1.30	0.53	12.87
12/05	47.66	37	23	1.60	0.46	12.73
Annual Growth	(35.3%)	—	—	(58.0%)	—	1.3%

Briggs & Stratton

It's no BS, Briggs & Stratton knows outdoor housework. For power equipment, the company is #1 among manufacturers of air-cooled gas engines. Lawn and garden OEMs Husqvarna Outdoor Products, MTD, and Deere are key engine customers; generator, pressure washer, and pump makers are less so. Replacement engines and parts are made for aftermarkets, too. Engines are sold worldwide direct through sales and service arms. Subsidiary Briggs & Stratton Power Products also produces generators, pressure washers, mowers, and other outdoor tools, retailed through Lowe's, Home Depot, and Sears, as well as independent dealers. Briggs & Stratton engine and power product facilities dot the US, Europe, Australia, and China.

Briggs & Stratton's manufacturing muscle is tested by weakening demand, precipitated by global economic recession and mounting competition. Its revenue relies upon engine orders from OEMs of outdoor power equipment. Exposed to consumer spending, Briggs & Stratton's power product revenue hinges on the health of big-box retailers, such as Wal-Mart and Home Depot. The company has attempted to shore up weaknesses in both engine and outdoor power product markets by branding initiatives that focus on the value and dependability of Briggs & Stratton goods.

Operating costs, which might otherwise chip away at revenues, are vertically contained. Briggs & Stratton integrates manufacture of many of its core components with its engine production. Moreover, because facilities are spread across largely non-union employment regions, wages are less aggressive. Internationally, the company expanded its capacity in 2008 by acquiring Australia's Victa Lawncare, a manufacturer of lawn and garden power equipment. Victa operates as a subsidiary of Briggs & Stratton Australia Pty. Limited, and promises to increase the company's manufacturing might, as well as market share, both in Australia and globally. Domestically, however, the company reined in activities in 2008 and 2009. It shuttered two power product facilities in Wisconsin, and one engine facility in Missouri, transferring work to other sites in the US and China.

Spreading out its manufacturing capacity horizontally, Briggs & Stratton has entered into several joint ventures. It makes components for punch presses and rewind starters for Starting Industrial of Japan, and Daihatsu Motor Company, and from its China-based facility, two-cycle engines for The Toro Company. Briggs and Stratton also teams up with Mitsubishi Heavy Industries (MHI) to distribute MHI's air cooled gas engines internationally.

President and COO Todd Teske was promoted to CEO in January 2010, replacing the retiring John Shiely, as part of a planned succession. Shiely remained chairman.

HISTORY

In 1909 inventor Stephen Foster Briggs and grain merchant Harold Stratton gathered $25,000 and founded Briggs & Stratton to produce a six-cylinder, two-cycle engine that Briggs had developed while in college. However, the engine proved too expensive for mass production. A brief foray into the auto assembly business also failed as the company skirted bankruptcy. But in 1910 Briggs received a patent for a single-spark gas engine igniter. It wasn't a runaway success, but the company had found its niche making automotive electrical components. By 1920 Briggs & Stratton was the largest US producer of specialty lights, ignitions, regulators, and starting switches. These specialties accounted for two-thirds of the firm's total business through the mid-1930s.

The company acquired the A. O. Smith Motor Wheel (a gasoline-driven wheel designed to be attached to bicycles) and the Flyer (a two-passenger vehicle similar to a buckboard) in 1919. Neither product was successful and both were soon sold, but the company gained crucial knowledge and experience. In 1923 Briggs & Stratton introduced a stationary version of the Motor Wheel designed to power washing machines, garden tractors, and lawn mowers. The company continued to diversify, moving into the auto lock business in 1924. Its die-cast cylinder lock outsold competitors' brass models, and by the end of the decade, Briggs & Stratton had the lion's share of the market. The company formed BASCO to make auto body hardware. Briggs & Stratton bought Evinrude Outboard Motor Company in 1928, but sold the business within a year.

As with many other industrial manufacturers, Briggs & Stratton benefited from the onset of WWII: The war triggered an insatiable need for the company's products. Its wartime contributions included airplane ignition switches, artillery ammunition, and engines for generators, pumps, compressors, fans, repair shops, emergency hospitals, and mobile kitchens.

After the war Briggs & Stratton focused on small engines for lawn and garden equipment, and soon it dominated the market. In 1953 the company introduced an aluminum die-cast engine that was lighter than competing models and could withstand greater operating temperatures and pressures. Baby boomers' parents fueled sales, and the small market attracted little competition; Briggs & Stratton thrived making air-cooled engines and automobile components, such as locks and switches.

By the end of the 1970s sales had risen to about $590 million and, as the low-cost producer in the industry, the company was without a rival. During the early 1980s, however, Japanese companies (including Honda, Kawasaki, Mitsubishi, and Suzuki) entered the market after motorcycle sales crested. As a result of the strong dollar, these new competitors were able to provide engines to equipment makers at less expense than could Briggs & Stratton; the company suffered a decline in the late 1980s.

The company experienced a resurgence during the early 1990s. Frederick Stratton Jr., grandson of the co-founder, took over as president in 1992, and Briggs & Stratton benefited from a dollar that was weak relative to the yen. In mid-2001 Stratton Jr. stepped down as president (he remained chairman until 2003) and COO John Shiely became president and CEO. Shiely succeeded Stratton as chairman in 2003.

Briggs & Stratton acquired the assets of Murray Inc. in 2005. In early 2007 Briggs & Stratton decided to close its engine manufacturing plant in Rolla, Missouri, and to transfer production to facilities in China and elsewhere in the US. Later that year the company elected to shutter its factory in Port Washington, Wisconsin.

EXECUTIVES

Chairman: John S. Shiely, age 57, $4,569,696 total compensation
President, CEO, and Director: Todd J. Teske, age 45, $1,293,252 total compensation
SVP and CFO: David J. Rodgers, age 39
SVP; President, Engine Power Products Group: Joseph C. Wright, age 51
SVP and President, Yard Power Products Group: Vincent R. Shiely Jr., age 50
SVP Administration: Thomas R. Savage, age 62, $1,296,626 total compensation
SVP: James E. (Jim) Brenn, age 62, $1,156,779 total compensation
SVP Sales and Customer Support: William H. Reitman, age 54, $752,571 total compensation
SVP Business Development, Briggs & Stratton Power Products Group, LLC: James H. Deneffe
SVP Operations Support: Michael D. Schoen, age 50
SVP; President, Home Power Products Group: Harold L. Redman, age 46
VP, General Counsel, and Secretary: Robert F. Heath, age 62
VP and General Manager, International, International Power Products Group: Edward J. Wajda
VP Human Resources: Jeffrey G. Mahloch
VP Marketing: Randall R. Carpenter
Director Corporate Communications: Laura Timm
Auditors: PricewaterhouseCoopers LLP

LOCATIONS

HQ: Briggs & Stratton Corporation
12301 W. Wirth St., Wauwatosa, WI 53222
Phone: 414-259-5333   **Fax:** 414-259-5773
Web: www.briggsandstratton.com

2009 Sales

	$ mil.	% of total
US	1,589.2	76
Other countries	503.0	24
Total	**2,092.2**	**100**

PRODUCTS/OPERATIONS

2009 Sales

	$ mil.	% of total
Engines	1,414.1	61
Power Products	892.9	39
Adjustments	(214.8)	—
Total	**2,092.2**	**100**

Selected Brands and Products

Brands
  Briggs & Stratton
  Brute
  Classic
  Craftsman
  Ferris
  Giant Vac
  John Deere
  Murray
  Simplicity
  Snapper
  Troy-Bilt
  Victa
Products
  Engines
    Garden tillers
    Generators
    Pressure washers
    Pumps
    Riding lawn mowers
    Snow throwers
    Walk-behind lawn mowers
  Power products
    Generators (portable and standby)
    Lawn and garden powered equipment
    Pressure washers
    Snow throwers

COMPETITORS

Aura Systems
Blount International
Campbell Hausfeld
Coleman
Deere
DeVilbiss
Dewey Electronics
Exmark Manufacturing
Generac Holdings
Graco
Honda
Kawasaki Heavy Industries
Kohler
Kubota Engine America
Metalcraft
Suzuki Motor
Tecumseh Products
Toro Company
Tradewinds Power

HISTORICAL FINANCIALS

Company Type: Public

Income Statement

FYE: Sunday nearest June 30

	REVENUE ($ mil.)	NET INCOME ($ mil.)	NET PROFIT MARGIN	EMPLOYEES
6/09	2,092	32	1.5%	6,847
6/08	2,151	23	1.1%	7,145
6/07	2,157	0	0.0%	3,693
6/06	2,542	102	4.0%	3,874
6/05	2,655	117	4.4%	4,058
Annual Growth	**(5.8%)**	**(27.7%)**	**—**	**14.0%**

2009 Year-End Financials

Debt ratio: 40.5%
Return on equity: 4.2%
Cash ($ mil.): 16
Current ratio: 2.86
Long-term debt ($ mil.): 281
No. of shares (mil.): 50
Dividends
  Yield: 5.8%
  Payout: 120.3%
Market value ($ mil.): 668

Stock History

NYSE: BGG

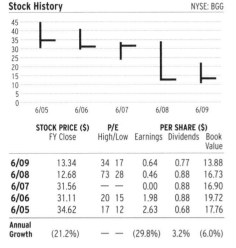

	STOCK PRICE ($) FY Close	P/E High/Low		PER SHARE ($) Earnings	Dividends	Book Value
6/09	13.34	34	17	0.64	0.77	13.88
6/08	12.68	73	28	0.46	0.88	16.73
6/07	31.56	—	—	0.00	0.88	16.90
6/06	31.11	20	15	1.98	0.88	19.72
6/05	34.62	17	12	2.63	0.68	17.76
Annual Growth	(21.2%)	—	—	(29.8%)	3.2%	(6.0%)

Brightpoint, Inc.

Brightpoint makes money moving mobiles. The company is a top global distributor of mobile phones and other wireless products, acting as a middleman between manufacturers and wireless service providers. It ships the equipment to companies that sell mobile phones and accessories, including wireless carriers, dealers, and retailers; customers include Vodafone, Best Buy, and Sprint Nextel. Brightpoint also offers a range of services that includes warehousing, product fulfillment, purchasing, contract manufacturing, call center outsourcing, customized packaging, activation, and Web marketing. The company gets more than half of its sales in the region of Europe, the Middle East, and Africa.

Brightpoint's largest suppliers include Nokia (20% of total units handled), Motorola (19%), and Samsung (16%). Other brands sold by the company include Apple, High Tech Computer (HTC), Kyocera, LG Electronics, Research In Motion, and Sony Ericsson.

Feeling the pinch of the global recession in 2009, Brightpoint reduced its workforce by nearly 11% as sales fell by almost one-third. The company was able to remain profitable, however, albeit by the customary paper-thin margin. Brightpoint has a limited number of customers and suppliers, and the loss of any significant customer or supplier could negatively affect the company's competitiveness. Mobile operators are consolidating on a global basis, leaving fewer customers for Brightpoint.

The company continues to broaden its selection of services by forming new alliances with telecom and computing equipment makers. Brightpoint has also grown through acquisitions. The company acquired the assets of CellStar's operations serving the US and Latin America for approximately $62 million in cash in

2007. It also purchased Dangaard Telecom, a Danish mobile phone distributor with subsidiaries in 14 countries, for about $385 million in stock.

HISTORY

Robert Laikin started in the portable phone business in 1985, when he established Century Car Phones (later renamed Century Cellular Network). The company grew rapidly but demand grew faster, and by 1989 Laikin's business was having trouble keeping up. That year he and Daniel Koerselman, a salesman for a car phone accessory company, started Wholesale Cellular to supply Century and others with phones. Laikin stepped down as president of Century in 1993. Wholesale Cellular went public a year later and changed its name to Brightpoint in 1995.

That year Brightpoint moved into the foreign market by forming partnerships with UK and India technology companies. It improved its distribution capabilities in North and South America by merging with Philadelphia-based Allied Communications in 1996. The next year Brightpoint further augmented its international operations by acquiring businesses in Hong Kong, Sweden, and Venezuela. It also bought the remaining 20% minority interests of its joint ventures in China, the UK, and Australia. Brightpoint continued its focus on international markets in 1998 with the acquisitions of distributors in the Netherlands and Taiwan.

Facing continuing pressures from resellers, the company in 1999 announced a restructuring plan that curtailed the global expansion, and divested its operations in Argentina, Poland, and the UK; its joint ventures in China; its accessories company in Hong Kong; and its distribution center in the Netherlands. A shareholder lawsuit was filed that summer, charging that Brightpoint withheld news of its mounting troubles in Asia and Latin America from shareholders and institutional investors (the suit was dismissed in 2001).

Despite an extension of the company's US distribution agreement with Nokia, the restructuring contributed to annual losses for Brightpoint in 1999. By 2000 the company had added new pacts and contract extensions on five continents. That year Brightpoint was awarded a patent for its wireless fulfillment system; the company promptly filed a patent infringement suit against chief rival CellStar.

Later in 2001 Brightpoint announced a joint venture with Hong Kong-based wireless communications company Chinatron; the venture, called Brightpoint China, was established to distribute wireless phones to customers in China. The deal was completed in 2002. Within months, however, Brightpoint sold its 50% stake to its joint venture partner in return for a minority stake in Chinatron. In 2004 Brightpoint sold its operations in Ireland to Celtic Telecom. Two years later it purchased fellow wireless product distributor Trio Industries.

EXECUTIVES

Chairman and CEO: Robert J. Laikin, age 46, $2,605,074 total compensation
President, Brightpoint Europe, Middle East, and Africa: Anurag Gupta, age 45
President, Americas: J. Mark Howell, age 45, $1,324,317 total compensation
President, Asia/Pacific: R. Bruce Thomlinson, age 48, $1,064,177 total compensation

EVP and CIO: John Alexander (Jac) du Plessis Currie, age 45, $978,022 total compensation
EVP, General Counsel, and Secretary: Steven E. Fivel, age 49, $933,827 total compensation
EVP, CFO, and Treasurer: Anthony W. (Tony) Boor, age 47, $1,385,659 total compensation
SVP, Chief Accounting Officer, and Controller: Vincent Donargo, age 49
SVP Human Resources: Annette Cyr
Controller, EMEA: Ryan Willman
Director Investor and Public Relations: Thomas Ward
Director Finance, Brightpoint Business Services: Stephen Babbage
Auditors: Ernst & Young LLP

LOCATIONS

HQ: Brightpoint, Inc.
7635 Interactive Way, Ste. 200
Indianapolis, IN 46278
Phone: 317-707-2355   **Fax:** 317-707-2512
Web: www.brightpoint.com

2009 Sales

	$ mil.	% of total
Europe, Middle East & Africa	1,676.4	53
Asia/Pacific	868.5	27
Americas	640.4	20
Total	**3,185.3**	**100**

PRODUCTS/OPERATIONS

2009 Sales

	$ mil.	% of total
Product distribution	2,827.5	89
Logistics services	357.8	11
Total	**3,185.3**	**100**

Selected Suppliers

Audiovox
High Tech Computer (HTC)
Kyocera
LG Electronics
Logitech
Motorola
Nokia
Novatel Wireless
Palm
Plantronics
Research In Motion
Samsung Electronics
SanDisk
SANYO
Sierra Wireless
Sony Ericsson
UTStarcom

Services

Channel development
  Outbound sales
  Product marketing
  Field training and support
  Merchandising
  Credit determination
  Co-op funds disbursement/tracking
  Commissions management
  Sales incentive programs
  VAR programs
Logistics services
  Inventory management
  Kitting and packaging
  Device programming
  Bulk and end user order processing
  Returns management and processing
  Receivables management
  Credit services
Subscriber services
  Customer contact center
  E-business solutions
  Outbound marketing
  Fulfillment services

HISTORICAL FINANCIALS

Company Type: Public

Income Statement

FYE: December 31

	REVENUE ($ mil.)	NET INCOME ($ mil.)	NET PROFIT MARGIN	EMPLOYEES
12/09	3,185	27	0.8%	2,705
12/08	4,641	(342)	—	3,032
12/07	4,300	47	1.1%	3,269
12/06	2,425	36	1.5%	2,112
12/05	2,140	10	0.5%	1,683
Annual Growth	10.5%	26.5%	—	12.6%

2009 Year-End Financials

Debt ratio: 35.0%
Return on equity: 10.1%
Cash ($ mil.): 81
Current ratio: 1.25
Long-term debt ($ mil.): 97

No. of shares (mil.): 70
Dividends
 Yield: —
 Payout: —
Market value ($ mil.): 518

Stock History

NASDAQ (GS): CELL

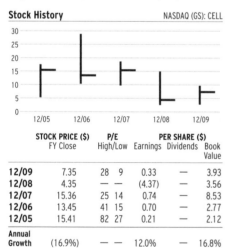

	STOCK PRICE ($) FY Close	P/E High/Low		PER SHARE ($) Earnings	Dividends	Book Value
12/09	7.35	28	9	0.33	—	3.93
12/08	4.35	—	—	(4.37)	—	3.56
12/07	15.36	25	14	0.74	—	8.53
12/06	13.45	41	15	0.70	—	2.77
12/05	15.41	82	27	0.21	—	2.12
Annual Growth	(16.9%)	—	—	12.0%	—	16.8%

Brinker International

More than a few Chili's heat up this restaurant business. One of the world's largest casual dining companies, Brinker International operates and franchises about 1,500 Chili's Grill & Bar locations in about 30 countries. Trailing only Applebee's as the largest full-service restaurant chain, Chili's specializes in southwestern-style dishes with a menu featuring fajitas, margarita grilled chicken, and its popular baby back ribs. About 670 of the eateries are operated by franchisees, including more than 200 international locations. In addition to its flagship chain, Brinker operates Maggiano's Little Italy, a casual Italian chain with more than 40 units, and it owns a stake in Romano's Macaroni Grill.

Brinker has become a leading force in the casual dining industry by successfully developing restaurant brands that appeal to middle America with ethnic-inspired menus and affordable prices. It also spends heavily on marketing to promote its restaurants over rival chains, with limited-time offers and value pricing deals playing key roles in attracting new customers. Brinker's large base of corporate-run locations allows it to have more control over customer service and food quality throughout its chains.

Responding to the recession and weak consumer spending, the company slowed the pace of its expansion in the US, opening about 40 new locations during fiscal 2009, down from about 90 new units the previous year. Most of the new eateries added were franchised Chili's outlets. More than 50 under-performing locations were closed. Brinker did add more than 40 new dining units outside the US.

Brinker is also investing in upgrades for its flagship Chili's chain, hoping to improve the profitability of the restaurants as well as service speed and customer satisfaction. Its plans call for a new kitchen design and point-of-sale information systems intended to reduce costs and make food preparation quicker. Brinker is also targeting international markets for future Chili's expansion, with plans to open more than 400 new restaurants outside the US by 2014.

To help the company focus on its flagship casual-dining concept, Brinker has been disposing of its small chains. The company sold On The Border, a Tex-Mex dining concept with about 160 locations, to an affiliate of Golden Gate Capital for about $180 million in 2010. The private equity firm previously acquired an 80% stake in Romano's Macaroni Grill from Brinker for more than $130 million in 2008.

The company is named for founder Norman Brinker. A pioneer of the casual-dining industry, he died in 2009 at the age of 78.

HISTORY

Norman Brinker pioneered the so-called "casual-dining" segment in 1966 when he opened his first Steak & Ale in Dallas. In 1971 he took the company public and watched it grow to more than 100 locations by 1976 when Pillsbury bought the chain. After serving as president of Pillsbury Restaurant Group (which included Burger King, Poppin' Fresh Restaurants, and Steak & Ale), Brinker left in 1983 to take over Chili's, a chain of southwestern-styled eateries founded by Larry Lavine in 1975. With plans to develop the company into a major chain, Brinker took Chili's public in 1984.

The company began recruiting joint venture and franchise partners. It also expanded the Chili's menu to include items such as fajitas, staking the company's growth on aging baby boomers who were looking for something more than fast food. Stymied in attempts to regain control of his former S&A Restaurant (later acquired by Metromedia) and to acquire such fast-food chains as Taco Cabana and Flyer's Island Express, Brinker decided to focus on the casual, low-priced restaurant market. In 1989 Chili's acquired Knoxville, Tennessee-based Grady's Goodtimes and Romano's Macaroni Grill, a small Italian chain founded by Texas restaurateur Phil Romano in 1988. Reflecting the expansion of its restaurant offerings, the company changed its name to Brinker International in 1990.

Brinker introduced Spageddies (a casual, lower-priced pasta restaurant) in 1992. With two Italian-cuisine chains in his network, the entrepreneur began to take on rival Olive Garden. Brinker suffered a major head injury in 1993 while playing polo, leaving him comatose for two weeks. Despite the traumatic event and poor early prognosis, he made a rapid recovery and returned to running the company. In 1994 Brinker International expanded to cash in on the popularity of Mexican food. It acquired Cozymel's Coastal Mexican Grill that year and bought the $50 million, 21-unit On The Border Mexican-food chain in 1995.

That year Brinker retired as CEO and was replaced by Ronald McDougall. McDougall sold Grady's and Spageddies to Quality Dining, since they no longer fit the company's overall strategy, and acquired two restaurant concepts (Corner Bakery and Maggiano's Little Italy) from Rich Melman's Lettuce Entertain You Enterprises.

The company began a major overhaul of Chili's menu in 1997, led by Brian Kolodziej, a 34-year-old former chef at Dallas' ritzy Mansion on Turtle Creek hotel. Two years later Brinker began expanding into Guatemala, Saudi Arabia, and Mexico. McDougall was named vice chairman in 1999 and eventually replaced Brinker as chairman the following year.

In 2001 the company gained complete control of Big Bowl and bought a 40% stake in Rockfish Seafood Grill. With an emphasis on company-owned restaurants, Brinker purchased 47 Chili's and On The Border restaurants from New England Restaurant Co. and 39 Chili's restaurants from Sydran Services in 2001.

In 2003 Brinker sold Cozymel's Coastal Mexican Grill to a group that included restaurateur Jack Baum, former HP Enterprise Services (then known as Electronic Data Systems) president Morton H. Meyerson, and their investment firm 2M Companies. McDougall stepped down from the executive ranks in early 2004, with company president Doug Brooks taking the reins as CEO.

Brinker reached an historic milestone in 2005 when it opened its 1,000th Chili's location. Company president Wilson Craft resigned that year after only 20 months on the job. The company also began shedding some of its emerging concepts to focus on its core brands, selling Big Bowl Asian Kitchen to Lettuce Entertain You in 2005 and shedding Corner Bakery the following year in a deal with upscale Italian operator Il Fornaio. Also in 2006, Brinker sold its stake in Rockfish Seafood Grill back to that chain's founders.

The company shed a majority of its Romano's business in 2008, selling an 80% stake in the Italian-themed chain to private equity firm Golden Gate Capital. The deal was worth more than $130 million.

EXECUTIVES

Chairman, President, and CEO:
Douglas H. (Doug) Brooks, age 57,
$3,412,603 total compensation
EVP and Chief PeopleWorks Officer:
Valerie L. Davisson, age 48
EVP and CFO: Charles M. (Chuck) Sonsteby, age 56,
$2,389,150 total compensation
EVP Brand Solutions: Michael B. (Happy) Webberman,
age 49, $1,377,334 total compensation
**EVP, Chief Administrative Officer, General Counsel,
and Secretary:** Roger F. Thomson, age 60,
$1,771,633 total compensation
SVP Global Business Development and COO:
Carin L. Stutz, age 53
SVP and Assistant General Counsel: Jeffrey A. Hoban
SVP Information Solutions: Michael L. Furlow
SVP and Controller: David R. Doyle
SVP Finance: Guy J. Constant
SVP; President, Global Business Development:
John Reale, age 55
VP Franchise Business Development:
Donald L. Reyburn
President, Maggiano's Little Italy: Steve Provost
**President, Chili's Grill & Bar and On The Border
Mexican Grill & Cantina:** Wyman T. Roberts, age 50
Auditors: KPMG LLP

LOCATIONS

HQ: Brinker International, Inc.
6820 LBJ Fwy., Ste. 200, Dallas, TX 75240
Phone: 972-980-9917   **Fax:** 972-770-9593
Web: www.brinker.com

2009 Locations

	No.
US	1,488
International	201
Total	**1,689**

PRODUCTS/OPERATIONS

2009 Locations

	No.
Chili's Grill & Bar	1,485
On The Border Mexican Grill & Cantina	160
Maggiano's Little Italy	44
Total	**1,689**

2009 Locations

	No.
Company-owned	1,024
Franchised	665
Total	**1,689**

COMPETITORS

Biglari Holdings	Hooters
Carlson Restaurants	OSI Restaurant Partners
Cheesecake Factory	Perkins & Marie
Cracker Barrel	Callender's
Darden	Ruby Tuesday
Denny's	Texas Roadhouse
DineEquity	

HISTORICAL FINANCIALS

Company Type: Public

Income Statement

FYE: Last Wednesday in June

	REVENUE ($ mil.)	NET INCOME ($ mil.)	NET PROFIT MARGIN	EMPLOYEES
6/09	3,621	79	2.2%	77,100
6/08	4,235	52	1.2%	100,400
6/07	4,377	230	5.3%	113,900
6/06	4,151	212	5.1%	110,800
6/05	3,913	160	4.1%	108,500
Annual Growth	**(1.9%)**	**(16.1%)**	**—**	**(8.2%)**

2009 Year-End Financials

Debt ratio: 112.4%
Return on equity: 12.8%
Cash ($ mil.): 94
Current ratio: 0.90
Long-term debt ($ mil.): 727
No. of shares (mil.): 103
Dividends
  Yield: 2.6%
  Payout: 57.1%
Market value ($ mil.): 1,747

Stock History

NYSE: EAT

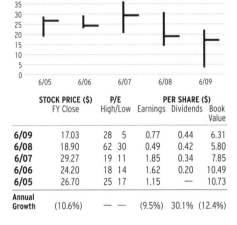

	STOCK PRICE ($) FY Close	P/E High/Low		PER SHARE ($) Earnings	Dividends	Book Value
6/09	17.03	28	5	0.77	0.44	6.31
6/08	18.90	62	30	0.49	0.42	5.80
6/07	29.27	19	11	1.85	0.34	7.85
6/06	24.20	18	14	1.62	0.20	10.49
6/05	26.70	25	17	1.15	—	10.73
Annual Growth	**(10.6%)**	**—**	**—**	**(9.5%)**	**30.1%**	**(12.4%)**

The Brink's Company

Teetering on the brink of a security disaster? The Brink's Company can help. It is the largest and oldest operator and logistics supplier of armored cars used in transporting cash for banks and retailers (85% of sales). Brink's also provides various other security-related services — such as ATM management, secure long-distance transportation of valuables, and guarding services, including airport security — which government agencies avail themselves of. The company serves customers in more than 50 countries. Its operations include more than 800 facilities and some 15,500 vehicles. Globally known, the company garners more than 70% of its revenues outside of North America.

Seven of Brink's operations (Brazil, Colombia, France, Germany, the Netherlands, the US, and Venezuela) account for nearly three-quarters of the company's business. In 2009 the company expanded its Brazilian operations with the purchase of Sebival for approximately $47 million. Sebival is a leading provider of cash-in-transit (CIT) and payment processing services in midwestern Brazil. Brink's also picked up a controlling interest in another company south of the border, a Panama armored transportation business.

Reaching around the world, Brink's also increased its ownership in an Indian cash handling and secure logistics operation, Brink's Arya, from 40% to 78%. Based in Mumbai, India, the majority stake gives Brink's a strong toehold in one of Asia's largest cash services markets. Investments in the Asia/Pacific region grew, as well, with the acquisition of majority ownership in ICD Limited, a commercial security service based in China, with branches in Hong Kong, India, Singapore, and Australia. Other acquisitions in 2009 included an 80% stake in a Russian secure logistics company.

The company's evolution includes previous control of Brink's Home Security (BHS). Its installation and monitoring alarm systems service accounted for some 15% of sales. Brink's began reviewing shareholder proposals for alternative options for the company in 2007 and hired consulting firm Monitor Company Group to help in a re-examination of strategic moves. It subsequently spun off BHS into a separate publicly traded company in order to focus on its core secure transportation, cash logistics, and other commercial security services.

HISTORY

The Brink's Company was originally the Pennsylvania Coal Company, founded in 1838 in Pittston, Pennsylvania. In 1901 it was acquired by the Erie Railroad, which itself was purchased by the Alleghany Corp. in 1916.

In the late 1920s intense competition in the coal industry and antitrust concerns prevented Alleghany's expansion. Alleghany created the Pittston Company in 1930 and offered Pittston stock to Alleghany stockholders while retaining a controlling interest. At its founding, Pittston acquired United States Distributing Corp., which owned a trucking firm, warehouses, a wholesale coal distributor, and a Wyoming mining company.

But coal consumption was falling. In 1944 the company began mining bituminous coal (which was increasingly used by industry and utilities), and in the 1950s it entered the fuel oil market. Its trucking and warehousing businesses also expanded, accounting for 43% of net income by 1954. Pittston gained its independence that year: Alleghany purchased a railroad, which raised antitrust concerns and forced the company to sell its 50% stake in Pittston.

Seeking other revenue sources, in 1956 Pittston acquired a 22% stake in (and subsequently control of) the world's largest armored car company, Chicago-based Brink's. Brink's had begun as a delivery company in 1859 and started making payroll deliveries in 1891. Pittston acquired the entire company in 1962.

By the early 1970s Pittston was the #1 exporter of metallurgical coal, used in steel manufacturing. The OPEC oil embargo and the energy crisis of the 1970s increased demand for coal; in 1976 some 90% of company profits were coal-related. However, by the late 1970s labor disputes and a steel industry slump decreased profits dramatically.

Meanwhile, Brink's suffered from rising costs and increased competition in the 1970s. In 1976 a federal grand jury investigated possible antitrust violations in the armored car business. Brink's paid nearly $6 million the following year to settle antitrust charges. The company diversified further in the 1980s, setting up Brink's Home Security (1984) after selling its warehousing operations. Pittston also entered the highly competitive airfreight express business by purchasing Burlington Air Express (1982).

Pittston began trading as two tracking stocks in 1993: Pittston Services Group (security and transportation) and Pittston Minerals Group (mining). In 1996, to further rationalize its business structure, Pittston split its security and transportation unit into two distinct businesses, each with its own tracking stock: Pittston Brink's Group and Pittston Burlington Group (later BAX Global).

Expanding globally, Brink's formed a transportation venture in 1997 with Switzerland's Zurcher Freilager, a freight-handling company. It also bought out affiliates in the Netherlands and Hong Kong in 1997 and in France and Germany in 1998. In 1999 BHS formed Brink's Mobile Security to provide wireless tracking systems for vehicles.

With its Pittston Minerals unit beset by a growing number of worker-injury lawsuits (black lung and other claims), The Pittston Company in 2000 made plans to exit the coal mining business to minimize future liability. Also that year the company abandoned its tracking stock structure.

In 2002 the company sold some of its coal assets to Braxton-Clay Land & Mineral and Massey Energy, and by the end of the year Pittston had ceased active involvement in the coal business. By 2004 Pittston had sold its remaining natural resources interests, which included natural gas and timber operations.

Also in 2003 the company changed its name to The Brink's Company to reflect its transformation from a conglomerate into a company focused solely on security.

In 2006 the company sold its BAX Global unit, which arranges for the delivery of overnight and second-day freight from business to business in more than 120 countries, to Deutsche Bahn for $1.1 billion. The Brink's Company then sold Air Transport International, formerly a part of BAX Global, to Cargo Holdings International. Its Brink's Home Security was spun off in 2008.

EXECUTIVES

Chairman, President, and CEO; CEO, Brink's, Incorporated: Michael T. Dan, age 59, $5,462,476 total compensation
VP and Chief Administrative Officer: Frank T. Lennon, age 68, $1,295,254 total compensation
VP and CFO: Joseph W. (Joe) Dziedzic, age 42, $1,954,803 total compensation
VP and General Counsel: McAlister C. Marshall II, age 40, $869,163 total compensation
VP Tax: Lisa M. Landry
VP Risk Management and Insurance: Arthur E. Wheatley, age 67
Treasurer: Jonathan A. Leon, age 43
Secretary: Michael J. McCullough
Controller: Matthew A. P. Schumacher, age 51, $520,634 total compensation
President, Brink's Europe, Middle East and Africa: Michael J. (Mike) Cazer, age 42, $1,438,151 total compensation
President, Brink's Canada: Peter Panaritis
Auditors: KPMG LLP

LOCATIONS

HQ: The Brink's Company
1801 Bayberry Ct., Richmond, VA 23226
Phone: 804-289-9600   **Fax:** 804-289-9770
Web: www.brinkscompany.com

2009 Sales

	$ mil.	% of total
Europe, Middle East & Africa	1,257	40
Latin America	905	29
North America	894	29
Asia/Pacific	79	2
Total	**3,135**	**100**

PRODUCTS/OPERATIONS

Selected Clients

Banks
Financial institutions
Government agencies
Jewelers
Mints
Retailers

Selected Services

Automated teller machine (ATM) replenishment and servicing
Cash logistics (supply chain management of cash)
Cash-in-transit (CIT) armored car transportation
Global Services (arranging secure long-distance transportation of valuables)
Guarding services (including airport security)

COMPETITORS

Dunbar Armored
G4S
Garda Cash Logistics
Loomis AB
Prosegur
Rochester Armored Car
Securitas

HISTORICAL FINANCIALS

Company Type: Public

Income Statement

FYE: December 31

	REVENUE ($ mil.)	NET INCOME ($ mil.)	NET PROFIT MARGIN	EMPLOYEES
12/09	3,135	232	7.4%	59,400
12/08	3,164	183	5.8%	56,900
12/07	3,219	137	4.3%	53,900
12/06	2,838	587	20.7%	48,700
12/05	2,549	148	5.8%	45,800
Annual Growth	**5.3%**	**11.9%**	**—**	**6.7%**

2009 Year-End Financials

Debt ratio: 32.2%
Return on equity: 61.9%
Cash ($ mil.): 143
Current ratio: 1.33
Long-term debt ($ mil.): 172
No. of shares (mil.): 47
Dividends
  Yield: 1.6%
  Payout: 9.5%
Market value ($ mil.): 1,142

Stock History

NYSE: BCO

	STOCK PRICE ($) FY Close	P/E High/Low		PER SHARE ($) Earnings	Dividends	Book Value
12/09	24.34	8	5	4.21	0.40	11.40
12/08	26.88	10	5	3.93	0.40	4.56
12/07	32.94	13	10	2.92	0.36	22.30
12/06	35.25	3	2	11.64	0.21	16.07
12/05	26.42	11	7	2.50	0.10	17.85
Annual Growth	**(2.0%)**	**—**	**—**	**13.9%**	**41.4%**	**(10.6%)**

Bristol-Myers Squibb

Pharmaceutical giant Bristol-Myers Squibb (BMS) makes big bucks on matters of the heart. The company's blockbuster cardiovascular lineup includes heart disease drug Plavix and Avapro for hypertension. BMS also makes antipsychotic medication Abilify and HIV treatments Reyataz and Sustiva. Most of the its sales come from products in the therapeutic areas of cardiovascular, immunoscience, metabolics, neuroscience, oncology, and virology.

BMS' largest international markets are Canada, France, Germany, Italy, Japan, Mexico, and Spain. Its top customers are drug distributors McKesson (25% of sales), Cardinal Health (20%), and AmerisourceBergen (15%).

BMS is engaged in a multi-year restructuring effort to focus solely on its biopharmaceutical and specialty drug operations. The plan calls for the company to divest its nonpharmaceutical operations, shutter more than half of its manufacturing and packing facilities, and trim its workforce by at least 10%.

As part of the restructuring, BMS sold its Medical Imaging unit to private equity firm Avista Capital Partners for $525 million in 2008. Also in 2008 Avista Capital Partners and Nordic Capital paid $4.1 billion to acquire BMS' ConvaTec ostomy and wound-care subsidiary. Then in 2009 the company divested its Mead Johnson subsidiary, which sold Enfamil infant formula and other nutritional products for children.

While on one hand BMS is busy restructuring and trimming, the company is also anxious to buttress its pharmaceutical pipeline by netting new drug candidates through acquisitions. In 2009 BMS acquired one of its development collaborators, Medarex, for about $2.4 billion. The purchase netted BMS a portfolio of other oncology and immunology treatments, as well as access to Medarex's antibody technology.

Collaborations are also an important part of BMS' development and marketing strategy. French drugmaker Sanofi-Aventis manufactures and distributes several of the company's products, including Plavix and Avapro. Japanese drug firm Otsuka Pharmaceutical co-promotes the schizophrenia treatment Abilify and certain oncology products. BMS also works with Allergan for the development and commercialization of AGN-209323, an early-stage, orally administered small molecule in clinical development for neuropathic pain.

Though narrowing its focus will help BMS in its quest to become a pharmaceutical juggernaut, it also increases the company's vulnerability to the loss of patent protection (and thus market exclusivity) on its best-selling drugs. Most notably Plavix and Avapro, which accounted for about 40% of the company's sales in 2009, will see their patents expire in 2011 and 2012, respectively.

Lead candidates in the BMS pipeline include Apixaban for blood clots and kidney transplant drug Belatacept. Its Onglyza treatment for type 2 diabetes (developed with AstraZeneca) received FDA approval in mid-2009. Other recently approved drugs in the company's cabinet include Orencia (rheumatoid arthritis), Ixempra (cancer), and Emsam, a treatment for major depressive disorder developed with Somerset Pharmaceuticals (a subsidiary of Mylan Laboratories).

HISTORY

Bistol-Myers Squibb is the product of a merger of rivals. Squibb was founded by Dr. Edward Squibb in New York City in 1858. He developed techniques for making pure ether and chloroform; he turned the business over to his sons in 1891.

Sales of $414,000 in 1904 grew to $13 million by 1928. The company supplied penicillin and morphine during WWII. In 1952 it was bought by Mathieson Chemical, which in turn was bought by Olin Industries in 1953, forming Olin Mathieson Chemical. Squibb maintained its separate identity.

From 1968 to 1971 Olin Mathieson went through repeated reorganizations and adopted the Squibb name. Capoten and Corgard, two major cardiovascular drugs, were introduced in the late 1970s. Capoten was the first drug engineered to attack a specific disease-causing mechanism. Squibb formed a joint venture with Denmark's Novo (now Novo Nordisk) in 1982 to sell insulin.

William Bristol and John Myers founded Clinton Pharmaceutical in Clinton, New York, in 1887 (renamed Bristol-Myers in 1900) to sell bulk pharmaceuticals. The firm made antibiotics after the 1943 purchase of Cheplin Biological Labs. It began expanding overseas in the 1950s and eventually bought Clairol (1959); Mead Johnson (drugs, infant and nutritional formula; 1967); and Zimmer (orthopedic implants, 1972). Bristol-Myers launched new drugs to treat cancer (Platinol, 1978) and anxiety (BuSpar, 1986). That year it acquired biotech companies Oncogen and Genetic Systems.

The firm bought Squibb in 1989. In 1990 the new company bought arthroscopy products and implant business lines and joined Eastman Kodak and Elf Aquitaine to develop new heart drugs in 1993. Despite these initiatives, earnings slipped. In 1994 company veteran Charles Heimbold became CEO and moved to increase profits. In 1995 the company, along with fellow silicone breast implant makers 3M and Baxter International, agreed to settle thousands of personal injury claims at an average of $26,000 per claim.

Facing an antitrust suit filed by independent drugstores, BMS and other major drugmakers agreed in 1996 to charge pharmacies the same prices as managed care groups for medications.

The firm bought a 20% stake in ImClone to collaborate on the development of cancer drug Erbitux and to stay on top of the cancer drug market. Instead, BMS found itself embroiled in the controversy over insider information and stock deals surrounding the biotech. Persistence paid off, however; Erbitux was approved by the FDA in 2004.

Analgesics Excedrin and Bufferin had made the company a household name, but in 2005 the company sold its US and Canadian consumer products operations to Novartis. The deal also meant saying goodbye to such brands as Comtrex (cold medications), Choice (blood sugar monitoring supplies), and Keri (lotions, skin care).

In mid-2006 Canadian generics maker Apotex managed to flood the market with a generic version of Plavix for several weeks. The release of the drug followed bungled attempts by BMS to negotiate a deal with Apotex that would have kept it off the market. The debacle led to federal investigations into whether that deal violated antitrust laws and also resulted in the ouster of CEO Peter Dolan (replaced by James Cornelius). BMS ultimately wound up paying more than $150 million to settle lawsuits and agreed that it would report any future deals struck with generics makers.

EXECUTIVES

Chairman: James M. (Jim) Cornelius, age 66, $18,221,434 total compensation
President, CEO, and Director: Lamberto Andreotti, age 59, $9,005,321 total compensation
CFO: Charles Bancroft, age 50
SVP and Chief Procurement Officer: Quentin L. Roach
SVP Strategic Transactions Group: Jeremy Levin
SVP Human Resources: Anthony McBride
SVP, Secretary, and General Counsel: Sandra Leung, age 49
SVP Corporate and Business Communications and Chief Communications Officer: Robert T. (Bob) Zito, age 56
SVP Global and US Oncology: Giovanni Caforio
SVP Global Regulatory Services: Richard L. Wolgemuth, age 64
SVP Global Development, Medical Affairs, and Research and Development: Brian Daniels
VP and Treasurer: Jeffrey Galik
VP Human Resources: Sandra J. Holleran
VP Investor Relations: John Elicker
President BMS Foundation: John Damonti
President Mead Johnson Nutritionals: Stephen W. (Steve) Golsby, age 55
President Emerging Markets and Asia/Pacific: John E. Celentano, age 49
President Americas: Anthony C. (Tony) Hooper, age 55, $5,027,369 total compensation
President Technical Operations and Global Support Functions: Carlo de Notaristefani, age 52
President Global Commercialization and Europe: Béatrice Cazala
Auditors: Deloitte & Touche LLP

LOCATIONS

HQ: Bristol-Myers Squibb Company
345 Park Ave., New York, NY 10154
Phone: 212-546-4000 **Fax:** 212-546-4020
Web: www.bms.com

2009 Sales

	$ mil.	% of total
US	11,909	58
Europe, Middle East & Africa	4,206	22
Pacific	1,393	12
Other Western Hemisphere	1,300	8
Total	**18,808**	**100**

PRODUCTS/OPERATIONS

2009 Sales

	$ mil.	% of total
Pharmaceuticals		
Plavix	6,146	33
Abilify	2,592	14
Reyataz	1,401	7
Avapro	1,283	7
Sustiva	1,277	7
Baraclude	734	4
Erbitux	683	4
Orencia	602	3
Sprycel	421	2
Ixempra	109	1
Onglyza	24	—
Other	3,536	18
Total	**18,808**	**100**

Selected Pharmaceuticals

Cardiovascular
  Avapro
  Plavix

Immunoscience
  Orencia

Psychiatric disorders
  Abilify

Oncology
  Erbitux
  Ixempra
  Sprycel

Virology
  Baraclude
  Reyataz
  Sustiva

COMPETITORS

Abbott Labs	Merck
Amgen	Mylan
Apotex	Novartis
AstraZeneca	Pfizer
Biogen Idec	Ranbaxy Laboratories
Boehringer Ingelheim	Roche Holding
Eli Lilly	Sandoz International
Forest Labs	Sanofi-Aventis
Genentech	Teva Pharmaceuticals
GlaxoSmithKline	Watson Pharmaceuticals
Johnson & Johnson	

HISTORICAL FINANCIALS

Company Type: Public

Income Statement

FYE: December 31

	REVENUE ($ mil.)	NET INCOME ($ mil.)	NET PROFIT MARGIN	EMPLOYEES
12/09	18,808	10,681	56.8%	28,000
12/08	20,597	5,247	25.5%	35,000
12/07	19,348	2,165	11.2%	42,000
12/06	17,914	1,585	8.8%	43,000
12/05	19,207	3,000	15.6%	43,000
Annual Growth	**(0.5%)**	**37.4%**	**—**	**(10.2%)**

2009 Year-End Financials

Debt ratio: 41.3%
Return on equity: 78.9%
Cash ($ mil.): 7,683
Current ratio: 2.21
Long-term debt ($ mil.): 6,130
No. of shares (mil.): 1,715
Dividends
  Yield: 5.0%
  Payout: 23.4%
Market value ($ mil.): 43,300

Stock History

NYSE: BMY

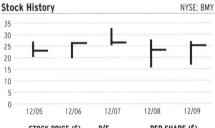

	STOCK PRICE ($) FY Close	P/E High/Low		PER SHARE ($) Earnings	Dividends	Book Value
12/09	25.25	5	3	5.34	1.25	8.66
12/08	23.25	10	6	2.63	1.24	7.14
12/07	26.52	30	24	1.09	1.15	6.16
12/06	26.32	33	25	0.81	1.12	5.83
12/05	22.98	18	14	1.52	1.12	6.54
Annual Growth	**2.4%**	**—**	**—**	**36.9%**	**2.8%**	**7.3%**

Broadcom Corporation

Broadcom harbors broad ambitions for its semiconductors' impact on broadband communications: it wants them to drive every part of the high-speed wired and wireless networks of the future. The core applications for its integrated circuits (ICs) are digital set-top boxes, cable modems, servers, and networking gear for homes and offices. Broadcom also makes semiconductors for carrier access, DSL, and wireless communications equipment, including mobile phones. Customers include 3Com, Apple, Cisco, Dell, Hewlett-Packard, IBM, LG, Motorola, Nokia, and Samsung Electronics.

In 2010 Broadcom bought Teknovus, a maker of Ethernet passive optical networking (EPON) components, for about $123 million. EPON technology is used to speed the transfer of data across fiber-optic cables. The acquisition is one among a slew of deals that support Broadcom's plans to expand its offerings for infrastructure markets, particularly for sectors engaged in transmitting data over cellular networks. Later that year it also purchased Innovision Research & Technology, a provider of custom IC design and production for RFID, EPC, and Near Field Communications applications.

Late in 2009 the company acquired Dune Networks for about $178 million. Dune Networks is a privately held fabless semiconductor company that develops switch fabric products for data center networking equipment. The acquisition will beef up Broadcom's roster of network equipment products.

Also in 2009 Broadcom reached a legal settlement with rival QUALCOMM, agreeing to dismiss their patent litigation and granting each other certain rights under their patent portfolios. Among other terms, QUALCOMM will pay Broadcom $891 million in cash over four years, with $200 million due by mid-2009.

Broadcom continues to churn out new chips for wired and wireless communications, and for networking equipment, as well. Broadcom offers a variety of "combo chips" for the wireless handset market, chips that combine Bluetooth, Global Positioning System (GPS), and FM radio capabilities on one device. The iSuppli market research firm sees GPS growing significantly as a handset feature by 2012, to more than 543 million units. Bluetooth is forecast to make it into some 1.2 billion units in that year, while FM will be featured in 901 million units.

To diversify and widen its product portfolio, Broadcom stoked its acquisition program. The company in 2008 acquired AMD's digital TV (DTV) chip line.

Co-founders Henry Samueli and Henry Nicholas each hold about 30% of the voting power in the fabless semiconductor company.

Criminal and civil charges brought against Nicholas, Samueli, and other executives related to alleged backdating of stock option grants were all dismissed in 2009, as a federal judge found there were insufficient legal grounds for the cases. A separate sensational case alleging that Nicholas helped distribute illicit drugs was dismissed in 2010, with both criminal and civil charges dropped.

HISTORY

Henry Samueli and Henry Nicholas began their partnership at UCLA as professor and student, respectively, although the two had earlier worked together as product designers for technology specialist TRW's military integrated circuit operation. In 1988 Samueli helped found copper line-based data transmission firm PairGain Technologies (now part of ADC Telecommunications). Though only in his 20s, Nicholas was PairGain's director of microelectronics.

Convinced that the fastest microchip would own the market for devices combining computers, televisions, and phones, Samueli and Nicholas left PairGain in 1991 to found Broadcom. The duo accepted no venture capital; they wanted to be able to offer heady stock options to potential employees.

Broadcom's pioneering chip efforts soon attracted the attention of larger companies. In 1993 Broadcom introduced an advanced chip for cable boxes that was chosen by Scientific-Atlanta for use in its pioneering interactive cable television trials for Time Warner. The company began shipping production quantities of its chips in 1994. Other early customers included Analog Devices, Intel, Rockwell, and the US Air Force.

Intel invested $5 million in Broadcom in 1994, and Broadcom formed chip development alliances with Hewlett-Packard in 1995 and with Northern Telecom (now Nortel Networks) in 1996.

In 1997 Broadcom unveiled chipsets that enabled different manufacturers' cable modem equipment to work together; the chips soon became the industry standard. The company went public in 1998 in an IPO that made more than 200 of its employees millionaires (and made Samueli and Nicholas billionaires).

Flush with IPO cash, in 1999 Broadcom began beefing up its technology through acquisitions. The spree continued through 2000 and into 2001, as the company spent almost $10 billion to round out its product offerings and acquire new engineering talent.

In 2002 the company acquired Mobilink Telecom, a maker of chipsets for wireless devices, in a deal initially valued at about $190 million. Late that year, the company laid off about 500 workers — a sixth of its staff — in the face of brutal industry conditions.

Early in 2003 the intensely driven and energetic Nicholas resigned as president and CEO, citing his wish to stave off divorce. (Nicholas retired from the company's board in mid-2003.) Board member and interim COO Alan Ross succeeded Nicholas as president and CEO.

When the market picked up by 2004, Broadcom picked up the pace of its acquisitions. It bought Sand Video, which designed video compression chips; Zyray Wireless, which designed baseband co-processor chips; and Alphamosaic, which designed multimedia processors. Early in 2005 it acquired wireless chip designer Zeevo. It then purchased Siliquent Technologies, a developer of processors used in network interface controllers.

Philips Semiconductors (now NXP) president and CEO Scott McGregor succeeded Ross as president and CEO at the beginning of 2005.

In 2007 the company paid about $143 million in cash to buy Global Locate, a developer of Global Positioning System (GPS) and assisted GPS semiconductors and software. Global Locate's products were used in wireless handsets and in personal navigation devices made by TomTom, a leading GPS product vendor.

EXECUTIVES

Chairman: John E. Major, age 64
President, CEO, and Director: Scott A. McGregor, age 53, $10,171,525 total compensation
EVP and CFO: Eric K. Brandt, age 47, $3,951,500 total compensation
EVP and General Manager, Wireless Connectivity Group: Robert A. (Bob) Rango, age 49, $3,917,984 total compensation
EVP, General Counsel, and Secretary: Arthur Chong, age 56, $377,489 total compensation
EVP Worldwide Sales: Thomas F. (Tom) Lagatta, age 52, $1,771,792 total compensation
EVP Human Resources: Terri L. Timberman, age 52
EVP and General Manager, Broadband Communications Group: Daniel A. (Dan) Marotta, age 49, $3,817,564 total compensation
EVP Corporate Services and CIO: Kenneth E. (Ken) Venner, age 47
EVP and General Manager, Enterprise Networking Group: Rajiv Ramaswami, age 44
EVP Operations and Central Engineering: Neil Y. Kim, age 51
CTO: Henry Samueli, age 55, $2,182,638 total compensation
SVP Infrastructure Technologies: Nariman Yousefi, $3,784,267 total compensation
SVP and General Manager, Mobile Platforms: Scott A. Bibaud, age 47
SVP, Corporate Controller, and Principal Accounting Officer: Robert L. Tirva, age 44, $875,069 total compensation
VP Corporate Communications and Investor Relations: T. Peter Andrew, age 43
Auditors: KPMG LLP

LOCATIONS

HQ: Broadcom Corporation
5300 California Ave., Irvine, CA 92617
Phone: 949-926-5000 **Fax:** 949-926-6589
Web: www.broadcom.com

2009 Sales

	% of total
Asia/Pacific	91
US	5
Europe	3
Other regions	1
Total	**100**

PRODUCTS/OPERATIONS

2009 Sales

	$ mil.	% of total
Mobile & wireless	1,720.0	38
Broadband communications	1,525.2	34
Enterprise networking	1,055.5	24
Other	189.6	4
Total	**4,490.3**	**100**

2009 Sales

	$ mil.	% of total
Product revenue	4,272.7	95
Income from QUALCOMM patent agreement	170.6	4
Licensing revenue	47.0	1
Total	**4,490.3**	**100**

Selected Markets and Products

Broadband processors (processors for broadband networking equipment)
Cable modems (high-speed data transmission and media access control devices)
Cable set-top boxes (graphics and video decoders, modulators and demodulators, and single-chip set-top box ICs)
Carrier access (VoIP broadband telephony chips)
Digital subscriber lines (DSLs; broadband transceivers and loop emulators)
Enterprise networking (Ethernet controllers, security processors, repeaters, switches, transceivers, and matching software for LANs)
Home networking (iLine controllers and chipsets)

Optical networking (wide-area and metropolitan-area network products — including amplifiers, framer/mappers, receivers, and transceivers — addressing various Ethernet and SONET/SDH protocols)

Servers (ServerWorks ICs that speed the input/output functions of servers, storage platforms, network appliances, and workstations)

Software (OpenVoIP Product Suite used in networking gateways, cable modems, ADSL modems, LAN PBXs, and computer telephony systems)

Wireless communications (Bluetooth chipsets and digital broadcast satellite, terrestrial digital broadcast, and broadband fixed wireless television receivers)

COMPETITORS

AMD
Analog Devices
Applied Micro Circuits
Atheros
Cirrus Logic
Conexant Systems
CSR plc
Cypress Semiconductor
Emulex
Entropic Communications
Freescale Semiconductor
Fujitsu Semiconductor
Gennum
Himax
IBM Microelectronics
Infineon Technologies
Intel
Intersil
LSI Corp.
Marvell Technology
MediaTek
Mindspeed
National Semiconductor
NVIDIA
NXP Semiconductors
Oki Semiconductor
PMC-Sierra
QLogic
QUALCOMM
RF Micro Devices
Samsung Electronics
ST-Ericsson
STMicroelectronics
Texas Instruments
Toshiba Semiconductor
VIA Technologies
Zarlink

HISTORICAL FINANCIALS

Company Type: Public

Income Statement

FYE: December 31

	REVENUE ($ mil.)	NET INCOME ($ mil.)	NET PROFIT MARGIN	EMPLOYEES
12/09	4,490	65	1.5%	7,407
12/08	4,658	215	4.6%	7,402
12/07	3,776	213	5.6%	6,347
12/06	3,668	379	10.3%	5,233
12/05	2,671	412	15.4%	4,287
Annual Growth	13.9%	(36.9%)	—	14.6%

2009 Year-End Financials

Debt ratio: —	No. of shares (mil.): 504
Return on equity: 1.7%	Dividends
Cash ($ mil.): 1,397	Yield: —
Current ratio: 2.54	Payout: —
Long-term debt ($ mil.): —	Market value ($ mil.): 15,845

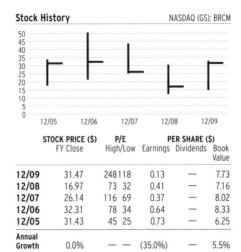

Stock History

NASDAQ (GS): BRCM

	STOCK PRICE ($) FY Close	P/E High/Low		PER SHARE ($) Earnings	Dividends	Book Value
12/09	31.47	248	118	0.13	—	7.73
12/08	16.97	73	32	0.41	—	7.16
12/07	26.14	116	69	0.37	—	8.02
12/06	32.31	78	34	0.64	—	8.33
12/05	31.43	45	25	0.73	—	6.25
Annual Growth	0.0%	—	—	(35.0%)	—	5.5%

Brown Shoe Company

There's no business like the retail and wholesale shoe business for Brown Shoe Company. Brown Shoe operates more than 1,100 Famous Footwear stores in the US and Guam, about 240 Naturalizer stores in the US and Canada, and a dozen F.X. LaSalle stores around Montreal, as well as shops in China. Besides its venerable Buster Brown line, its brands include Aerosoles, Connie, LifeStride, and Nickels; it also sells Dr. Scholl's and Disney licensed footwear. The company distributes footwear worldwide through more than 2,000 retailers, including independent, chain (DSW), and department stores (Sears). Brown Shoe is opening new stores, closing underperforming ones, and updating styles to appeal to younger bipeds.

To satisfy its strategy of attracting younger shoppers, the company has invested in its own portfolio of profitable businesses that provide youth-inspired items. In mid-2010 Brown Shoe acquired the remaining 50% stake in Edelman Shoe it didn't already own. The upscale, hip footwear, which includes sandals, sneakers, and high-heel clogs, are sold in luxury retailers Nordstrom and Bloomingdale's. As part of the agreement, Sam Edelman and Libby Edelman will retain their respective roles as president of the Sam Edelman division and head of marketing.

The retailer has been shuttering underperforming stores at both Famous Footwear and its specialty shoe store chains. Indeed, it has closed more than 110 underperforming Naturalizer stores in North America over the past five years in a bid to improve profitability. Besides culling unprofitable locations, other cost-cutting efforts include a 14% reduction in its domestic workforce and changes to its compensation structure.

The company's wholesale division (about 30% of sales) distributes footwear to department stores (Macy's, Nordstrom, and Dillard's), mass merchandisers (Wal-Mart and Target), and independent retailers, primarily in the US and Canada, but also in about 35 other countries.

International expansion, with a focus on China, is also on Brown Shoe's to-do list. The company's majority-owned subsidiary, B&H Footwear Limited, operates about 15 stores in several of China's largest cities. In 2010 B&H plans to open another three stores in China. Also, through a joint venture with China's Hongguo International Holdings, the company operates 30-plus stores there and plans to open about 15 more in 2010.

Key to Brown Shoe's future are its Famous Footwear, Naturalizer, and Dr. Scholl's businesses. The mall-based Famous Footwear stores sell Brown Shoe's own brand and name-brand footwear under the Nike, Skechers, Dr. Scholl's, Timberland, and Rockport labels, among many others. Brown Shoe has been expanding its Famous Footwear business and introducing new styles, including a line designed by musicians Fergie (Fergalicious), and Carlos Santana (Carlos), to appeal to younger customers.

HISTORY

Salesman George Brown began mass-producing women's shoes in St. Louis in 1878, unusual at a time when the shoe industry was firmly entrenched in New England. With the financial backing of partners Alvin Bryan and Jerome Desnoyers, Brown hired five shoemakers and opened Bryan, Brown and Company. The firm's fashionable first shoes were a pleasant contrast to the staid, black shoes typical of New England and were an instant success. The enterprise grew rapidly, and in 1893 Brown, by then the sole remaining partner, renamed the operation Brown Shoe Company. By 1900 sales had reached $4 million.

Company executive John Bush introduced cartoonist Richard Outcault's Buster Brown comic strip character in 1902 at the St. Louis World's Fair as a trademark for Brown's children's shoes. Bush failed to purchase the exclusive rights, and Buster Brown became the trademark for scores of products, even cigars and whiskey.

Brown Shoe became a public company in 1913 and introduced its second brand, Naturalizer, in 1927. During the Great Depression, company VP Clark Gamble developed the concept, later commonplace, of having salesmen sell only specific branded shoe lines instead of traveling with samples of all the company's shoes. Brown Shoe modernized its operations and entered the retailing business during the 1950s by purchasing Wohl Shoe, Regal Shoe, and G. R. Kinney (sold in 1963 to Woolworth because of antitrust litigation). The first Naturalizer store opened in Jamaica, New York, in 1954.

Diversifying, Brown Shoe bought Cloth World stores (1970), Eagle Rubber (toys and sporting goods, 1971), Hedstrom (bicycles and equipment, 1971), Meis Brothers (department stores, 1972), and Outdoor Sports Industries (1979), among others. It became the Brown Group in 1972.

The company acquired the 32-store Famous Footwear chain in 1981 and expanded it rapidly (especially from 1990 to 1995, when it added more than 500 stores, reaching a total of about 815). In 1985 the company sold its recreational products segment and in 1989 shed all of its specialty retailers except Cloth World.

As the US shoe manufacturing industry fell prey to cheaper foreign imports, Brown Group in 1991 and 1992 closed nine US shoe factories, cutting capacity in half. It discontinued its Wohl Leased Shoe Department business in 1994 and, still facing declining sales and profits, closed five shoe factories and discontinued its Connie and Regal footwear chains. Brown Group also sold its Cloth World chain and discontinued its Maryland Square catalog business.

Brown Group continued its restructuring in 1995, closing its last five plants in the US (it still has two in Canada). In 1999 Brown Group changed its name back to Brown Shoe Company.

In 2000 the company opened 92 new Famous Footwear stores and added another 26 stores to that chain through its purchase of the Mil-Mar chain and bought a majority interest in e-tailer Shoes.com. The company opened another 100 mostly large-format Famous Footwear stores in 2001 and closed 100 smaller stores.

In 2003 the company gained licensure of the Bass label from Phillips-Van Heusen. In April 2005 Brown Shoe acquired Boston-based Bennett Footwear Holdings for about $205 million. The company has closed more than 100 Naturalizer stores since early 2005. In late 2006 the shoe store operator closed all but one of its Via Spiga stores. (The last store was shuttered in 2007.)

In June 2007 Brown Shoe and China's Hong-guo International Holdings formed a joint venture company (51% owned by Brown Shoe) called B&H Footwear, to launch the Naturalizer and Via Spiga brands there.

EXECUTIVES

Chairman and CEO: Ronald A. (Ron) Fromm, age 59, $3,235,228 total compensation
President, COO, and Director: Diane M. Sullivan, age 54, $1,805,061 total compensation
SVP Consumer and Retail Business Development: John R. Mazurk
SVP Wholesale, Better and Image Brands: Jay Schmidt
SVP Specialty Brands: Clay Jenkins
SVP and CIO: Joseph (Joe) Caro, age 47
SVP and CFO: Mark E. Hood, age 57, $814,715 total compensation
SVP, General Counsel, and Corporate Secretary: Michael I. Oberlander, age 41
SVP and Chief Talent Officer: Douglas W. (Doug) Koch, age 58
VP License Branding: Margie Connelly
Division President, Wholesale, Product and Sourcing: Daniel R. (Dan) Friedman
Division President, Famous Footwear: Richard M. (Rick) Ausick, age 56, $1,141,164 total compensation
Division President, Wholesale: Mark D. Lardie, age 49, $873,194 total compensation
Manager Public Relations: Erin Conroy
Director Investor Relations: Ken Golden
Auditors: Ernst & Young LLP

LOCATIONS

HQ: Brown Shoe Company, Inc.
  8300 Maryland Ave., St. Louis, MO 63105
Phone: 314-854-4000   **Fax:** 314-854-4274
Web: www.brownshoe.com

2010 Sales

	$ mil.	% of total
US	1,978.7	88
Far East	190.7	9
Canada	72.5	3
Total	**2,241.9**	**100**

2010 Country of Origin

	Mil. of pairs	% of total
China	51.0	98
Brazil	0.8	2
Other countries	0.4	—
Total	**52.2**	**100**

PRODUCTS/OPERATIONS

2010 Sales

	% of total
Women's	59
Men's	26
Children's	11
Accessories	4
Total	**100**

2010 Stores

	No.
Famous Footwear	1,129
Naturalizer	238
Brown Shoe Closet	16
F.X. LaSalle	13
Other (includes China stores)	15
Total	**1,411**

2010 Sales

	% of total
Retail (includes e-commerce sales)	72
Wholesale	28
Total	**100**

Selected Products

Children's shoes
  Airborne
  Barbie (licensed)
  Bass
  Bob the Builder (licensed)
  Buster Brown
  Chill Chasers by Buster Brown
  Disney Standard Characters (licensed)
  Kim Possible (licensed)
  Mary-Kate and Ashley (licensed)
  Power Rangers (licensed)
  Red Goose
  Star Wars (licensed)
  That's So Raven (licensed)
  Winnie The Pooh (licensed)
  Zoey 101 (licensed)
Men's shoes
  Bass
  Basswood
  Big Country
  Brown Shoe
  Dr. Scholl's (licensed)
  F.X. LaSalle
  FX
  Francois Xavier Collection
  Natural Soul
  Regal
  TX Traction
  Via Spiga
Women's shoes
  AirStep
  Bass
  Basswood
  Carlos by Carlos Santana (licensed)
  Connie
  Dr. Scholl's (licensed)
  Eurosole
  Eurostep
  Fanfares
  F.X. LaSalle
  FX
  Francois Xavier Collection
  Hot Kiss (licensed)
  LifeStride
  LS Studio
  Maserati
  Naturalizer
  NaturalSport
  Nickels
  Original Dr. Scholl's (licensed)
  TX Traction
  Vision Comfort
  VS by Via Spiga
  Zodiac

COMPETITORS

Berkshire Hathaway
Collective Brands
Dillard's
DSW
Foot Locker
Genesco
Iconix Brand Group
J. C. Penney
Kenneth Cole
Kmart
Macy's
Nine West
Nordstrom
Phillips-Van Heusen
Rack Room Shoes
Reebok
Ross Stores
Saks
Sears
Shoe Carnival
Target
TJX Companies
Wal-Mart
Zappos.com

HISTORICAL FINANCIALS

Company Type: Public

Income Statement

FYE: Saturday nearest January 31

	REVENUE ($ mil.)	NET INCOME ($ mil.)	NET PROFIT MARGIN	EMPLOYEES
1/10	2,242	10	0.4%	12,100
1/09	2,276	(133)	—	12,400
1/08	2,360	60	2.6%	13,100
1/07	2,471	66	2.7%	12,700
1/06	2,292	41	1.8%	12,800
Annual Growth	**(0.6%)**	**(30.6%)**	**—**	**(1.4%)**

2010 Year-End Financials

Debt ratio: 37.3%	No. of shares (mil.): 43
Return on equity: 2.4%	Dividends
Cash ($ mil.): 126	Yield: 2.3%
Current ratio: 1.71	Payout: 127.3%
Long-term debt ($ mil.): 150	Market value ($ mil.): 532

Stock History

NYSE: BWS

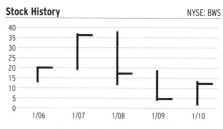

	STOCK PRICE ($) FY Close	P/E High/Low		PER SHARE ($) Earnings	Dividends	Book Value
1/10	12.25	59	9	0.22	0.28	9.27
1/09	4.69	—	—	(3.21)	0.28	9.08
1/08	17.19	28	9	1.37	0.28	12.87
1/07	36.23	24	13	1.51	0.21	12.06
1/06	20.01	21	14	0.97	0.18	10.00
Annual Growth	**(11.5%)**	**—**	**—**	**(31.0%)**	**11.7%**	**(1.9%)**

Brown-Forman Corporation

Don't blame Brown-Forman (B-F) employees if the company Christmas party gets out of control; they have lots to drink on hand. The company's portfolio of mid-priced to super-premium brands includes such well-known spirits as Jack Daniel's, Canadian Mist, Finlandia, and Southern Comfort. Its wine labels include Fetzer and Korbel. Jack Daniel's is the company's leading brand and is the largest-selling American whiskey in the world (by volume). Offering some 35 brands of wines and spirits, the company's beverages are available in more than 135 countries throughout the world. The founding Brown family, including former chairman Owsley Brown II, controls the company.

Headquartered in Louisville, Kentucky, Brown-Forman has found global success by introducing Jack Daniel's and other labels into new markets overseas. The company's principal export markets are Australia, Canada, China, France, Germany, Italy, Japan, Mexico, Poland, Russia, South Africa, Spain, and the UK. In the UK, it partners with competitor Bacardi to sell a combined portfolio of both companies' products. And although B-F is an international company, 47% of its sales are generated in the US.

As part of its ongoing review of its offerings, in 2008 Brown-Forman sold the Italian wine brands Bolla and Fontana to Gruppo Italiano Vini. The decision was in line with the company's strategy of concentrating on opportunities for growth and increasing shareholder value by building its brands and expanding into international markets. However, due to the sluggish worldwide economy, B-F has switched one of its growth strategies to pushing its markets at home rather than internationally. It designed new labeling for its super premium Tequila Herradura brand in 2010 and introduced a new Southern Comfort choice — Southern Comfort Sweet Tea ready-to-pour products.

Jack Daniel's is B-F's most important brand, however, and despite the continued global economic malaise, B-F saw net sales for the Jack Daniel's family of brands grow by 8% in 2010 when compared to 2009. (The brand family includes Jack Daniel's Tennessee Whiskey, Gentleman Jack, Jack Daniel's Single Barrel, and Jack Daniel's RTD [ready-to-drink] products such as Jack Daniel's & Cola, Jack Daniel's & Ginger, and Jack Daniel's Country Cocktails.)

HISTORY

George Brown and John Forman opened the Brown-Forman Distillery in Louisville, Kentucky, in 1870 to produce Old Forester-brand bourbon. Old Forester sold well through the end of the century, in part because of the company's innovative packaging (safety seals and quality guarantees on the bottles). When Forman died in 1901, Brown bought his interest in the company.

Old Forester continued to be successful under the Brown family. Brown-Forman obtained government approval to produce alcohol for medicinal purposes during Prohibition. In 1923 it made its first acquisition, Early Times, but stored its whiskey in a government warehouse (removed only by permit). The firm went public in 1933 and re-established the Old Forester image as an alcoholic beverage after the repeal of Prohibition.

During WWII the government greatly curtailed alcoholic beverage production (alcohol was needed for the war effort). The company compensated by providing alcohol for wartime rubber and gunpowder production. In 1941 Brown-Forman correctly predicted that the war would be over by the end of 1945 and started the four-year aging process for its bourbon. As a result, Early Times dominated the whiskey market after the war.

In 1956 Brown-Forman expanded beyond Old Forester by purchasing Lynchburg, Tennessee-based Jack Daniel's (sour mash whiskey). The company retained the simple, black Jack Daniel's label and promoted the image of a small Tennessee distillery for the brand.

Brown-Forman continued to expand its alcohol line during the 1960s and 1970s, acquiring Korbel (champagne and brandy, 1965), Quality Importers (Ambassador Scotch, Ambassador Gin, and Old Bushmills Irish Whisky; 1967), Bolla and Cella (wines, 1968), and Canadian Mist (blended whiskey, 1971). In 1979 it purchased Southern Comfort (a top-selling liqueur).

Non-beverage acquisitions included Lenox (a leading US maker of fine china, crystal, gifts, and Hartmann luggage; 1983), Kirk Stief (silver and pewter, 1990), and Dansk International Designs (china, crystal, silver, and the high-quality Gorham line; 1991). Brown-Forman launched Gentleman Jack Rare Tennessee Whiskey in 1988, the first new whiskey from its Jack Daniel's distillery in more than 100 years.

The company acquired Jekel Vineyards in 1991 and the next year bought Fetzer Vineyards. In 1993 Owsley Brown II succeeded his brother Lee as CEO. A year later Moore County, Tennessee, voters approved a referendum that allowed whiskey sales in Lynchburg (home of Jack Daniel's) for the first time since Prohibition. Also in 1995 Brown-Forman formed a joint venture with Jagatjit Industries, India's third-largest spirits producer. In 1997 Brown-Forman bought an 80% stake in Sonoma-Cutrer Vineyards in 1999 (and later bought the rest).

The company stirred up fans of Jack Daniel's in 2004 when it announced that it had reduced the alcohol content of Jack Daniel's Black Label whiskey from 90 proof to 80 proof. Due to a difficult competitive market in the US tabletop and giftware industries, Brown-Forman sold its Lenox subsidiary in 2005 to Department 56 for about $190 million in cash. Brown-Forman introduced the wine label Virgin Vines that year. And finally, 2005 saw Paul Varga succeed Owsley Brown as CEO. Brown remained chairman. (Brown retired from the company in 2007, at which time Varga assumed the role of chairman.)

In 2006 the company purchased Chambord Liqueur (a black raspberry liqueur) from Charles Jacquin et Cie and it also acquired Australian spirits and winemaker Swift + Moore. The company snapped its suitcase shut that year as well, with the sale of its Hartmann luggage subsidiary to investment firm Clarion Capital Partners.

In order to concentrate solely on the alcoholic beverage business, in 2007 B-F sold its remaining non-liquor-related business — jewelry, collectibles, and gift seller Brooks & Bentley. And boosting its presence in the tequila market that year, it acquired Mexican company Grupo Industrial Herradura for $876 million in cash. The distiller makes premium tequila brands, including Herradura and el Jimador.

EXECUTIVES

Chairman and CEO: Paul C. Varga, age 46, $7,695,600 total compensation
Vice Chairman and Executive Director Corporate Affairs, Strategy, Diversity, and Human Resources: James S. (Jim) Welch Jr., age 51, $2,553,504 total compensation
President, North American Region: Michael J. (Mike) Keyes
EVP and COO: Mark I. McCallum, age 55, $2,253,511 total compensation
EVP and CFO: Donald C. Berg, age 55, $2,411,072 total compensation
EVP and Chief Marketing Officer: John K. (Kris) Sirchio, age 44
EVP Global Business Development: James L. (Jim) Bareuther, age 64, $1,930,551 total compensation
EVP, General Counsel, and Secretary: Matthew E. Hamel, age 50, $1,487,892 total compensation
SVP and Chief Production Officer: Jill A. Jones, age 45
SVP and Chief of Staff: Philip A. (Phil) Lichtenfels
SVP, Managing Director, Western Europe and Africa, and Director: G. Garvin Brown IV, age 41
SVP Global Human Resources: Lisa P. Steiner
SVP and Director Finance, Accounting, and Technology: Jane C. Morreau, age 51
VP and Director Corporate Communications and Public Relations: Phil Lynch
Chief Diversity Officer: Ralph de Chabert
Assistant VP and Director Investor Relations: Ben Marmor
Auditors: PricewaterhouseCoopers LLP

LOCATIONS

HQ: Brown-Forman Corporation
850 Dixie Hwy., Louisville, KY 40210
Phone: 502-585-1100   **Fax:** 502-774-7876
Web: www.brown-forman.com

2010 Sales

	% of total
US	47
Europe	27
Other	26
Total	**100**

PRODUCTS/OPERATIONS

2010 Sales

	% of total
Spirits	90
Wine	10
Total	**100**

Selected Products and Brands

Spirits
  Antiguo Tequila
  Canadian Mist Blended Canadian Whisky
  Chambord Liqueur
  Don Eduardo Tequila
  Early Times Bourbon
  Early Times Kentucky Whisky
  el Jimador Tequila
  Finlandia Vodka
  Gentleman Jack
  Herradura Tequila
  Jack Daniel's Country Cocktails
  Jack Daniel's Ready-to-Drinks
  Jack Daniel's Ready-to-Pours
  Jack Daniel's Single Barrel Whiskey
  Jack Daniel's Tennessee Whiskey
  New Mix Ready-to-Drinks
  Old Forester Straight Bourbon Whisky
  Pepe Lopez Tequilas
  Southern Comfort
  Southern Comfort Ready-to-Drinks
  Tuaca Liqueur
  Woodford Reserve Kentucky Straight Bourbon Whiskey

Wine
Bel Arbor Wines
Bonterra Vineyards Wine
Fetzer Wines
Five Rivers Wines
Jekel Vineyards Wines
Korbel California Champagnes
Little Black Dress Wines
Sanctuary Wines
Sonoma-Cutrer Wines

Selected Subsidiaries

BFC Tequila Limited (Ireland)
Canadian Mist Distillers, Limited (Canada)
Chambord Liqueur Royale de France (France)
Clintock Limited (Ireland)
Distillerie Tuoni e Canepa Srl (Italy)
Early Times Distillers Company
Fetzer Vineyards
Finlandia Vodka Worldwide Ltd. (Finland)
Jack Daniel's Properties, Inc.
Longnorth Limited (Ireland)
Sonoma-Cutrer Vineyards, Inc.
Southern Comfort Properties, Inc.
Valle de Amatitan, S.A. de C.V. (Mexico)
Woodford Reserve Stables, L.L.C.

COMPETITORS

Bacardi
Beam Global Spirits & Wine
Blavod
Campari
Castle Brands
Constellation Brands
Corby Distilleries
Diageo
Diageo Chateau & Estate Wines
E. & J. Gallo
Fortune Brands
Foster's Group
Jackson Family Wines
Jose Cuervo
LVMH
Paramount Distillers
Pernod Ricard
Rémy Cointreau
Skyy
Smith Bowman Distillery
Suntory Holdings
Taittinger
United Spirits
V&S

HISTORICAL FINANCIALS

Company Type: Public

Income Statement

FYE: April 30

	REVENUE ($ mil.)	NET INCOME ($ mil.)	NET PROFIT MARGIN	EMPLOYEES
4/10	2,469	449	18.2%	3,900
4/09	2,481	435	17.5%	4,100
4/08	2,582	440	17.0%	4,466
4/07	2,218	389	17.5%	4,400
4/06	1,976	320	16.2%	3,750
Annual Growth	5.7%	8.8%	—	1.0%

2010 Year-End Financials

Debt ratio: 26.8%
Return on equity: 24.2%
Cash ($ mil.): 232
Current ratio: 2.80
Long-term debt ($ mil.): 508

No. of shares (mil.): 184
Dividends
  Yield: 2.0%
  Payout: 48.3%
Market value ($ mil.): 11,030

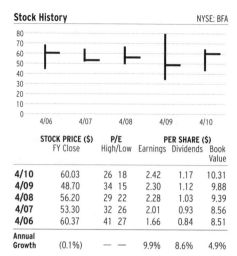

Stock History   NYSE: BFA

	STOCK PRICE ($) FY Close	P/E High/Low		PER SHARE ($) Earnings	Dividends	Book Value
4/10	60.03	26	18	2.42	1.17	10.31
4/09	48.70	34	15	2.30	1.12	9.88
4/08	56.20	29	22	2.28	1.03	9.39
4/07	53.30	32	26	2.01	0.93	8.56
4/06	60.37	41	27	1.66	0.84	8.51
Annual Growth	(0.1%)	—	—	9.9%	8.6%	4.9%

Brunswick Corporation

Brunswick's business is everyone else's free time. A global manufacturer of marine, recreation, and fitness products, the company's primary business, marine engines, includes outboard, inboard, and sterndrive engines, propellers, and engine control systems. The company also makes and markets pleasure boats, from fiberglass boats to sports fishing convertibles, offshore fishing boats, and pontoons. Its fitness business pushes treadmills, total body cross trainers, stair climbers, and stationary bicycles under brands Life Fitness, ParaBody, and Hammer Strength. Brunswick's bowling and billiards activities produce game equipment and operate more than 100 fun centers, featuring bowling, billiards, and dining.

Despite the company's global footprint and diversified lineup, the economic downturn coupled with the contraction in commercial and consumer spending on non-essentials has all but capsized Brunswick's operations. The company is shoring up its sunken bottom line with an unwavering focus on conserving cash. The effort includes cost-cutting through production dial-backs, plant consolidations, and sell-offs.

During 2010 and 2011 engine manufacturing operations are being consolidated and transferred from Stillwater, Oklahoma, to a plant in Fond du Lac, Wisconsin. The move falls on the heels of Brunswick's heavy cuts to its boat operations, including resizing the boat business' marine service, parts, and accessories activities under the marine engine segment (Mercury Marine). During 2009 Brunswick shuttered its manufacturing facilities in Knoxville, Tennessee, and Pipestone, Minnesota. Properties in Cape Canaveral, Florida, and Navassa, North Carolina, were put on the sale rack. In 2008 it sold off of its interest in Albemarle Boats and closed six facilities. Along with the plant closures, reductions to its workforce have been made — from 2008 to 2009 head-cuts totaled nearly 25%.

Brunswick's industry position is the result of several deals made to boost its marine segment. In 2006 the company acquired Cabo Yachts, which builds offshore sports fishing boats, and the Great American Marina near St. Petersburg,

Florida, in partnership with Marine-Max. The company also pocketed marine parts and accessories dealer Kellogg Marine, and 51% of Valiant rigid inflatable boats in Europe. Two of the company's earliest acquisitions, Land 'N' Sea and Attwood Corp, formed the backbone of Brunswick's marine focus. The company has formed several joint ventures, too; Cummins MerCruiser Diesel Marine LLC, a partnership between Brunswick and Cummins Marine (a division of Cummins, Inc.) supplies integrated diesel marine propulsion units to commercial and recreational marine markets.

In the area of fitness, Brunswick's Life Fitness segment jockeys for the lead in supplying equipment worldwide to health clubs as well as professional sports facilities, the military and government organizations, hotels, and schools.

The company's bowling and billiards business is its smallest, albeit oldest, segment. It manufactures a full line of bowling and billiard products, from balls to aftermarkets parts, and capital equipment such as bowling lanes and furniture. This niche, along with its relatively budget-light target market, has offered a certain amount of immunity from the recession's impact.

HISTORY

Swiss immigrant woodworker John Brunswick built his first billiard table in 1845 in Cincinnati. In 1874 he formed a partnership with Julius Balke, and a decade later they teamed with H. W. Collender to form Brunswick-Balke-Collender Company.

Following Brunswick's death, son-in-law Moses Bensinger became president. The company diversified into bowling equipment during the 1880s. Bensinger's son, B. E., followed as president (1904) and led the company into wood and rubber products, phonographs, and records. (Al Jolson recorded "Sonny Boy" on the Brunswick label.) Brunswick went public after WWI.

By 1930 Brunswick focused on bowling and billiards, sports that had seedy reputations during the 1920s and 1930s. When B. E. died in 1935, his son Bob became CEO and launched a massive promotional campaign to make his meal tickets respectable.

Bob's brother Ted succeeded him as CEO in 1954. Bowling equipment rival AMF introduced the first automatic pinsetter in 1952, and Brunswick followed four years later, capturing the lead by 1958. Brunswick diversified, adding Owens Yacht, MacGregor (sporting goods, 1958), Aloe (medical supplies, 1959), Mercury (marine products, 1961), and Zebco (fishing equipment, 1961). The company adopted its present name in 1960.

Bowling sales plummeted in the 1960s, and Brunswick cut costs by selling unprofitable units and focusing on new products such as an automatic scorer. Acquisitions in the 1970s brought Brunswick into the medical diagnostics and energy and transportation markets. In 1983 the company cut corporate staff in half and promoted the marine business.

Brunswick sparked an industrywide consolidation trend in 1986 by buying Bayliner and Ray Industries (boats), followed by Kiekhaefer Aeromarine (marine propulsion engines, 1990) and Martin Reel Company (fly reels, 1991). In 1992 Brunswick and Tracker Marine (a Missouri-based boat manufacturer) formed a partnership to build boats and marine equipment.

In 1993 Brunswick began selling its businesses in the automotive, electronics, and defense industries.

Brunswick expanded its outdoor recreation business in 1996 by purchasing Nelson/Weather Rite (camping equipment) from Roadmaster Industries along with Roadmaster's bicycle business. Also that year Brunswick acquired the Boston Whaler line of saltwater boats from Meridian Sports. In 1997 the company bought Igloo Holdings (coolers) and Bell Sports' (now Easton-Bell Sports) Mongoose bicycle unit.

The company lost antitrust lawsuits in 1999 that totaled nearly $300 million. However, all but two cases (with judgments of $65 million) were overturned on appeal.

In early 2001 Brunswick cut some jobs and rolled its bicycle business over to Pacific Cycle. Stung by the US's economic slowdown, the company announced 500 more job cuts in its powerboat division, even as it acquired Princecraft Boats from Outboard Marine.

Early in 2002 Brunswick closed the sale of its European fishing business to Zebco Sports Europe Ltd.

Brunswick acquired the Crestliner, Lowe, and Lund lines of aluminum boats from Genmar Holdings for a reported $191 million.

EXECUTIVES

Chairman and CEO: Dustan E. (Dusty) McCoy, age 60, $3,137,801 total compensation
SVP and CFO: Peter B. Hamilton, age 63, $625,846 total compensation
VP and Chief Human Resources Officer: B. Russell (Russ) Lockridge, age 60, $776,659 total compensation
VP and Controller: Alan L. Lowe, age 58, $676,337 total compensation
VP; President, Mercury Marine: Mark D. Schwabero, age 57
VP; President, Brunswick Bowling and Billiards: Warren N. Hardie, age 59
VP; President, Brunswick Marine in EMEA: John C. Pfeifer, age 44
VP Tax: Judith P. Zelisko, age 58
VP; VP Global Boat Operations: Stephen M. Wolpert, age 55
VP and President, Mercury Marine Sales, Marketing and Commercial Operations: Kevin S. Grodzki, age 54
VP; President, Brunswick Boat Group: Andrew E. (Andy) Graves, age 50, $722,131 total compensation
VP Investor and Corporate Relations: Bruce J. Byots, age 51
VP; President, Latin America Group: William J. Gress
VP and Treasurer: William L. Metzger, age 48
VP Audit: Tina A. Hotop
VP, General Counsel, and Secretary: Kristin M. Coleman, age 41
Director Public and Financial Relations: Daniel (Dan) Kubera
President, Sea Ray Group: Robert J. Parmentier, age 48
President, Life Fitness: Christopher E. (Chris) Clawson
Auditors: Ernst & Young LLP

LOCATIONS

HQ: Brunswick Corporation
1 N. Field Ct., Lake Forest, IL 60045
Phone: 847-735-4700 **Fax:** 847-735-4765
Web: www.brunswick.com

2009 Sales

	$ mil.	% of total
US	1,607.4	58
Other countries	1,168.7	42
Total	**2,776.1**	**100**

PRODUCTS/OPERATIONS

2009 Sales

	$ mil.	% of total
Marine		
Marine engine	1,425.0	50
Boat	615.7	21
Fitness	496.8	17
Bowling & billiards	337.0	12
Adjustments	(98.4)	—
Total	**2,776.1**	**100**

Selected Products

Boats
  Boat parts and accessories
  Freshwater fishing and utility boats
  General recreation boats
  Motor yachts
  Pontoon and deck boats
  Rigid inflatable and inflatable boats
  Saltwater fishing boats
  Sport fishing convertibles
Billiards
  Air hockey
  Billiards tables and accessories
Bowling
  Bowling centers
  Bowling equipment and services
  Bowling products and accessories
  Virtual bowling
Marine engines
  Engine parts and accessories
  Inboard, stern drive, and jet drive engines
  Trolling motors
  Outboard engines
Fitness
  Commercial equipment
  Home products

COMPETITORS

AMF Bowling
Bowl America
Cigarette Racing Team
Dave & Buster's
Fountain Powerboat
Giant Manufacturing
Honda
Marine Products Corp.
Yamaha

HISTORICAL FINANCIALS

Company Type: Public

Income Statement

FYE: December 31

	REVENUE ($ mil.)	NET INCOME ($ mil.)	NET PROFIT MARGIN	EMPLOYEES
12/09	2,776	(586)	—	15,003
12/08	4,709	(788)	—	19,760
12/07	5,671	112	2.0%	29,920
12/06	5,665	134	2.4%	28,000
12/05	5,924	385	6.5%	27,500
Annual Growth	**(17.3%)**	**—**	**—**	**(14.1%)**

2009 Year-End Financials

Debt ratio: 399.1%
Return on equity: —
Cash ($ mil.): —
Current ratio: 1.61
Long-term debt ($ mil.): 839
No. of shares (mil.): 89
Dividends
  Yield: 0.4%
  Payout: —
Market value ($ mil.): 1,126

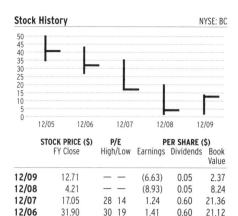

Stock History

NYSE: BC

	STOCK PRICE ($) FY Close	P/E High/Low		PER SHARE ($) Earnings	Dividends	Book Value
12/09	12.71	—	—	(6.63)	0.05	2.37
12/08	4.21	—	—	(8.93)	0.05	8.24
12/07	17.05	28	14	1.24	0.60	21.36
12/06	31.90	30	19	1.41	0.60	21.12
12/05	40.66	13	9	3.90	0.60	22.33
Annual Growth	**(25.2%)**	**—**	**—**	**—**	**(46.3%)**	**(42.9%)**

Burger King Holdings

This king rules one whopper of a fast-food empire. Burger King Holdings operates the world's #2 hamburger chain based on locations (behind McDonald's) with more than 12,000 restaurants in the US and more than 70 other countries. In addition to its popular Whopper sandwich, the chain offers a selection of burgers, chicken sandwiches, salads, and breakfast items, along with beverages, desserts, and sides. Many of the eateries are stand-alone locations offering dine-in seating and drive-through services; the chain also includes units in high-traffic locations such as airports and shopping malls. More than 1,400 of the fast food restaurants are company-owned, while the rest are owned and operated by franchisees.

Like most other giants of the fast-food industry, Burger King has expanded its nationwide and international presence primarily through franchising. The franchising model has allowed the company to build its far-flung network of restaurants without the costs of construction and acquiring real estate. Franchise operators pay Burger King a percentage of sales in royalties for the right to use the brand name and other intellectual property while agreeing to adhere to policies designed to ensure each restaurant offers the same level of service and food quality. Burger King's relatively small estate of corporate locations account for almost three-quarters of the company's sales.

The company has focused its product development and marketing efforts to appeal primarily to customers in the 18- to 34-year-old male demographic. It has added a number of premium-priced items to its menu, including the Steakhouse Burger made with Angus beef. Meanwhile, the company has used a number of online marketing techniques, including viral videos, to reach its target audience.

With the recession taking a bite out of the dining industry, Burger King has slowed its expansion efforts. The company added 115 new restaurants to its chain during fiscal 2009, down from more than 280 new locations added the previous year. Late that year, the chain reach a milestone with the opening of its 12,000th

Burger King unit. It has also been focused on attracting additional sales during breakfast, though Burger King has not taken on rival McDonald's in the morning coffee business. In addition, the company has introduced a new restaurant concept called the Whopper Bar, a smaller-sized outlet targeting urban areas with a limited burger menu.

Burger King was founded by James McLamore and David Edgerton in 1954. Investment firms TPG Capital, Bain Capital, and Goldman Sachs together own more than 30% of the company.

HISTORY

In 1954 restaurant veterans James McLamore and David Edgerton opened the first Burger King in Miami. Three years later, the company added the Whopper sandwich (which then sold for 37 cents) to its menu of hamburgers, shakes, and sodas. Burger King used television to help advertise the Whopper (its first TV commercial appeared in 1958). During its infancy, Burger King was the first chain to offer dining rooms.

In order to expand nationwide, Burger King turned to franchising in 1959. McLamore and Edgerton took a hands-off approach, allowing franchises to buy large territories and operate with autonomy. Although their technique spurred growth, it also created large service inconsistencies among Burger Kings across the US; this gaffe would haunt the company for years. Having grown to 274 stores in the US and abroad, Burger King was sold to Pillsbury in 1967.

During the early 1970s Burger King continued to add locations. The company did well during this time, launching its successful "Have It Your Way" campaign in 1974 and introducing drive-through service a year later. Yet parent Pillsbury had to fight to rein in large franchisees who argued they could run their Burger Kings better than a packaged-goods company could. In 1977 Pillsbury handed control of Burger King to Donald Smith, a McDonald's veteran, who soon silenced the insurrection. Smith tightened franchising regulations, created 10 regional management offices, and instituted annual visits.

Smith left for Pizza Hut in 1980, and by 1982 Burger King had reached the #2 hamburger chain plateau, trailing only McDonald's. The company struggled through the rest of the 1980s, hurt by high management turnover and a string of unsuccessful ad campaigns (such as the ill-fated 1986 NFL Super Bowl "Herb the Nerd" concept). Pillsbury became the target of a hostile takeover by UK-based Grand Metropolitan, and in 1988 Grand Met acquired Pillsbury along with its 5,500 Burger King restaurants.

Grand Met bolstered Burger King's foreign operations in 1990 by converting about 200 recently acquired UK-based Wimpy hamburger stores into Burger Kings. International expansion increased with new restaurants in Mexico (1991), Saudi Arabia (1993), and Paraguay (1995).

In 1997 Grand Met and Guinness combined their operations to form Diageo, making Burger King a subsidiary. That year Dennis Malamatinas left Grand Met's Asian beverage division to become Burger King's CEO. Malamatinas resigned as CEO and was replaced in 2001 by John Dasburg, former CEO of Northwest Airlines.

An investment group led by Texas Pacific Group (now TPG Capital) acquired Burger King for $1.5 billion in 2002. Earlier that year, Texas Pacific had agreed to pay $2.26 billion but renegotiated amid falling sales and a downturn in the burger market. Shortly after the purchase, Dasburg was

ousted and Brad Blum, vice chairman of Darden Restaurants, was named as his replacement.

After just 18 months on the job, Blum resigned his post as CEO in 2004, citing differences with the company's board. He was replaced by Greg Brenneman.

Burger King had consistent sales growth in 2004, and Brenneman's presence was a boost for the company. In addition, that year the company signed a deal (with rancher Luiz Eduardo Batalha) to develop about 50 restaurants in Brazil over a five-year period.

Disregarding the obesity trend in the US and health-officials' advice to citizens to cut down on fat intake, Burger King continues to offer ever-larger, ever-more-fat-laden menu items, such as the MEAT'NORMOUS OMELET SANDWICH, which it introduced in 2005. In 2006 the company ran advertising during the Super Bowl for the first time in 11 years. Brenneman resigned from Burger King that year, shortly before it went public; the company tapped president and CFO John Chidsey as his replacement. Burger King went public later that year.

EXECUTIVES

Chairman and CEO: John W. Chidsey, age 47, $5,457,773 total compensation
President, North America:
Charles M. (Chuck) Fallon Jr., age 46, $1,576,671 total compensation
President Europe, Middle East, and Africa: Kevin Higgins
President, Asia Pacific: Peter Tan, age 54
CFO: Ben K. Wells, age 56, $1,532,695 total compensation
EVP and Global Chief Marketing Officer: Natalia Franco
EVP: Peter Robinson, age 61
EVP Global Operations: Julio A. Ramirez, age 55
Chief Human Resources Officer: Peter C. (Pete) Smith, age 53
General Counsel, Chief Ethics and Compliance Officer, and Secretary: Anne Chwat, age 50
Chief Concept Officer: Denny Marie Post
SVP Operations, North America: Gladys H. DeClouet
SVP Global Product Marketing and Innovation: John Schaufelberger
SVP and CIO: Rajesh (Raj) Rawal
SVP Development and Franchising: Jonathan (John) Fitzpatrick
SVP Investor Relations and Global Communications: Amy E. Wagner, age 44
SVP Global Business Intelligence and Strategy: Michael (Mike) Kappitt
SVP Operations and Training, North America: David (Dave) Gagnon, age 62
SVP Global Operations Research and Development: John Reckert
Auditors: KPMG LLP

LOCATIONS

HQ: Burger King Holdings, Inc.
5505 Blue Lagoon Dr., Miami, FL 33126
Phone: 305-378-3000
Web: www.burgerking.com

2009 Sales

	$ mil.	% of total
US & Canada	1,743.0	69
Europe, Middle East & Asia/Pacific	687.4	27
Latin America	107.0	4
Total	**2,537.4**	**100**

2009 Locations

	No.
US & Canada	7,534
Europe, Middle East & Asia/Pacific	3,313
Latin America	1,078
Total	**11,925**

PRODUCTS/OPERATIONS

2009 Sales

	$ mil.	% of total
Restaurants	1,880.5	74
Franchising	543.4	21
Property	113.5	5
Total	**2,537.4**	**100**

2009 Locations

	No.
Franchised	10,496
Company-owned	1,429
Total	**11,925**

COMPETITORS

AFC Enterprises
Chick-fil-A
Chipotle
Church's Chicken
CKE Restaurants
Dairy Queen
Jack in the Box
McDonald's
Panda Restaurant Group
Panera Bread
Quiznos
Sonic Corp.
Subway
Wendy's/Arby's Group, Inc.
YUM!

HISTORICAL FINANCIALS

Company Type: Public

Income Statement

FYE: June 30

	REVENUE ($ mil.)	NET INCOME ($ mil.)	NET PROFIT MARGIN	EMPLOYEES
6/09	2,537	200	7.9%	41,320
6/08	2,455	190	7.7%	41,000
6/07	2,234	148	6.6%	39,000
6/06	2,048	27	1.3%	37,000
6/05	1,940	47	2.4%	30,300
Annual Growth	**6.9%**	**43.6%**	**—**	**8.1%**

2009 Year-End Financials

Debt ratio: 84.3%
Return on equity: 22.0%
Cash ($ mil.): 122
Current ratio: 0.77
Long-term debt ($ mil.): 821
No. of shares (mil.): 136
Dividends
  Yield: 1.4%
  Payout: 17.1%
Market value ($ mil.): 2,343

Stock History

NYSE: BKC

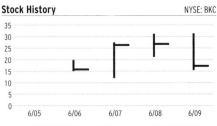

	STOCK PRICE ($) FY Close	P/E High/Low		PER SHARE ($) Earnings	Dividends	Book Value
6/09	17.27	21	11	1.46	0.25	7.18
6/08	26.79	22	16	1.38	0.25	6.23
6/07	26.34	25	11	1.08	0.13	5.28
6/06	15.75	81	64	0.24	—	4.18
Annual Growth	**3.1%**	**—**	**—**	**35.0%**	**38.7%**	**19.6%**

Burlington Northern Santa Fe

Over the years the number of major US railroads has dwindled, but Burlington Northern Santa Fe (BNSF) thrives as one of the survivors. Through its primary subsidiary, BNSF Railway, the company is one of the largest railroad operators in the US along with rival Union Pacific. BNSF makes tracks through 28 states in the West, Midwest, and SunBelt regions of the US and in two Canadian provinces. The company operates its trains over a system of about 32,000 route miles. Along with its rail operations, BNSF generates revenue from its BNSF Logistics unit, a provider of transportation management services. Already owning 23% of BNSF, Warren Buffett's Berkshire Hathaway bought the remaining 77% stake in February 2010.

Berkshire Hathaway's acquisition of BNSF was a sweeping move for the railway industry. The deal for buying the additional 77% of BNSF's shares, which was valued at $26 billion and also included $10 billion of BNSF debt, was Berkshire Hathaway's largest acquisition to date. For its part, BNSF is hoping that Buffett's potential long-term investment in the company signals a message that the freight industry (and the transportation services industry in general) is on the road to recovery.

BNSF's largest revenue generator is its consumer products business, which handles automotive products and containerized freight. Its industrial products business transports building and construction products, chemicals and plastics, food and beverages, and petroleum products.

Despite a strong year in 2008, BNSF was forced to cut 2,500 workers within the first quarter of 2009 and parked 700 locomotives and 35,000 rail cars due to slowing freight demand. Economic woes also prompted BNSF to put the brakes on some expansion projects including the planned 500-acre intermodal rail hub near Kansas City, Kansas, a vital point along its busy Chicago-Los Angeles corridor.

HISTORY

Burlington Northern (BN) was largely created by James Hill, who bought the St. Paul & Pacific Railroad in Minnesota in 1878. By 1893 Hill had completed the Great Northern Railway, extending from St. Paul to Seattle. The next year he gained control of Northern Pacific (chartered in 1864), which had been built between Minnesota and Washington. In 1901, with J.P. Morgan's help, Hill acquired the Chicago, Burlington & Quincy (Burlington), whose routes included Chicago-St. Paul and Billings, Montana-Denver-Fort Worth, Texas-Houston. The Spokane, Portland & Seattle Railway (SP&S), completed in 1908, gave Great Northern an entrance to Oregon.

Hill intended to merge Great Northern, Northern Pacific, SP&S, and Burlington under his Morgan-backed Northern Securities Company, but in 1904 the Supreme Court found that Northern Securities had violated the Sherman Antitrust Act. The holding company was dissolved, but Hill controlled the individual railroads until he died in 1916. Hill's railroads produced well-known passenger trains: Great Northern's Empire Builder began service in 1929, and in 1934 Burlington Zephyr was the nation's first streamlined passenger diesel.

After years of deliberation, the Interstate Commerce Commission allowed Great Northern and Northern Pacific to merge in 1970, along with jointly owned subsidiaries Burlington and SP&S. The new company, Burlington Northern (BN), acquired the St. Louis-San Francisco Railway in 1980, adding more than 4,650 miles to its rail network.

The company formed Burlington Motor Carriers (BMC) in 1985 to manage five trucking companies it had acquired. But to focus on its rail operations, BN sold BMC in 1988 and spun off Burlington Resources, a holding company for its other nonrailroad businesses.

A fiery collision between a BN freight train and one operated by Union Pacific in 1995 propelled the rivals to begin joint testing of global positioning satellites for use in guiding trains. Besides improving safety, the two hoped to end rail bottlenecks.

That year BN and Santa Fe Pacific (SFP), founded in 1859, formed Burlington Northern Santa Fe in a $4 billion merger. BN's strength lay in transporting manufacturing, agricultural, and natural resource commodities, and SFP specialized in intermodal shipping (combining train, truck, and ship). SFP (originally the Atchison, Topeka & Santa Fe) had taken the name Santa Fe Pacific in 1989 after its forced sale of Southern Pacific.

The new BNSF acquired Washington Central Railroad in 1996, adding a third connection between central Washington and the Pacific Coast. In 1997 customers protested when BNSF couldn't come up with enough cars and locomotives for grain shipping. A year later UP was in trouble with clogged rail lines: BNSF opened a joint dispatching center in Houston with UP to help unsnarl traffic. The effort proved successful, and in 1999 BNSF and UP began to combine dispatching in Southern California; the Kansas City, Missouri, area; and Wyoming's Powder River Basin.

In 1999 BNSF announced a $2.5 billion capital improvement program, but later decided to trim spending to $2.28 billion and cut 1,400 jobs.

Later that year BNSF agreed to merge with Canadian National Railway. The companies terminated the deal in 2000, however, after a US moratorium on rail mergers was upheld on appeal. Also in 2000 BNSF began offering intermodal service between the US and Monterrey, Queretaro, and Mexico City, Mexico, its first such US-Mexico service.

In 2001 BNSF became the first US railroad to use the Internet to purchase fuel (via the American Petroleum Exchange). Another milestone followed, albeit a more dubious one: To settle the first federal lawsuit against workplace genetic testing, BNSF agreed to drop its testing program. Without their knowledge, employees who had been diagnosed with carpal tunnel syndrome were tested for genetic defects.

In 2002 BNSF completed the construction of its BNSF Logistics Park in Chicago, designed to integrate direct rail, truck, intermodal, transload services, distribution, and warehousing in a single location.

Throughout 2007 and 2009, the company spent most of its efforts on cost cutting initiatives. In a huge move for the company's future, in February 2010 BNSF was acquired by Warren Buffett's Berkshire Hathaway for $36 billion.

EXECUTIVES

Chairman, President, and CEO, Burlington Northern Santa Fe Corporation and BNSF Railway:
Matthew K. (Matt) Rose, age 51,
$15,608,233 total compensation
EVP and COO: Carl R. Ice, age 53,
$3,700,325 total compensation
EVP Law and Secretary: Roger Nober, age 45,
$1,593,647 total compensation
EVP and Chief Marketing Officer: John P. Lanigan Jr.,
age 54, $3,369,870 total compensation
EVP and CFO: Thomas N. (Tom) Hund, age 56,
$3,239,362 total compensation
VP and Chief Sourcing Officer: Paul W. Bischler
VP and General Tax Counsel: Shelley J. Venick
VP Corporate Relations: John O. Ambler
VP Technology Services and CIO: Jo-ann M. Olsovsky
VP Corporate Audit Services: David W. Stropes
VP and General Counsel, Regulatory:
Richard E. (Rick) Weicher
VP Planning and Studies and Controller:
Julie A. Piggott
VP and General Counsel: Charles W. Shewmake
VP Government Affairs: Amy C. Hawkins
VP Network Strategy: Dean H. Wise, age 55
VP Human Resources and Medical:
Linda T. Longo-Kazanova, age 57
Auditors: PricewaterhouseCoopers LLP

LOCATIONS

HQ: Burlington Northern Santa Fe Corporation
2650 Lou Menk Dr., Fort Worth, TX 76131
Phone: 817-352-1000   **Fax:** 817-352-7171
Web: www.bnsf.com

PRODUCTS/OPERATIONS

2009 Sales

	$ mil.	% of total
Freight		
Consumer products	4,316	31
Coal	3,564	25
Industrial products	2,874	21
Agricultural products	2,834	20
Other	428	3
Total	**14,016**	**100**

COMPETITORS

American Commercial Lines
APL Logistics
Canadian National Railway
Canadian Pacific Railway
CSX
Hub Group
Ingram Industries
J.B. Hunt
Kansas City Southern
Kirby Corporation
Landstar System
Norfolk Southern
Pacer International
Schneider National
Union Pacific
Werner Enterprises

HISTORICAL FINANCIALS

Company Type: Subsidiary

Income Statement				FYE: December 31
	REVENUE ($ mil.)	NET INCOME ($ mil.)	NET PROFIT MARGIN	EMPLOYEES
12/09	14,016	1,721	12.3%	35,000
12/08	18,018	2,115	11.7%	40,000
12/07	15,802	1,829	11.6%	40,000
12/06	14,985	1,887	12.6%	41,000
12/05	12,987	1,531	11.8%	40,000
Annual Growth	**1.9%**	**3.0%**	**—**	**(3.3%)**

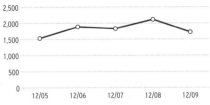
CA Technologies

CA wants to put your information technology under new management. One of the world's largest software companies, CA provides tools for managing networks, databases, applications, storage, security, and other systems. Its applications work across both mainframes and distributed computing environments, including cloud computing products. The company also offers consulting, implementation, and training services. It markets worldwide to businesses, government agencies, and schools. CA has actively used acquisitions to expand its product lines and grow its customer base.

A highly acquisitive company throughout its history, CA continues to expand its application portfolio with strategic purchases. Most recently it has looked to expand its security and IT asset management offerings. CA purchased some of Cassatt's data center automation assets in 2009, as well as buying IT management software provider NetQoS for $200 million in cash. In 2010 CA launched another deal to expand its IT asset management software line, buying Nimsoft for $350 million in cash. The Nimsoft purchase also strengthened CA's offerings for small and midsized clients, a newer area of focus for the company. Also that year the company agreed to sell its Information Governance business to Autonomy. Smaller deals included the purchases of 3Tera and Oblicore.

The company primarily focuses on large corporations with the resources to make substantial investments in hardware and software. Target industries include financial services and insurance, government, health care, manufacturing, retail, and technology.

The company's product strategy has included remaining focused on its core strengths in mainframe, application, and network management software while also expanding offerings for related areas such as IT asset management, security software, and cloud computing. CA offers many of its products under the Software-as-a-Service (SaaS) model, efforts the company plans to accelerate in the future.

Partners include systems integrators such as Accenture and PricewaterhouseCoopers, as well as managed services providers, including Hewlett-Packard and IBM. It also maintains technology partnerships to ensure the interoperability of its products with offerings from such companies as Microsoft, SAP, and VMware.

John Swainson retired as CEO in 2009 and was succeeded by William McCracken, chairman of the company's board and a retired IBM executive.

The company's largest individual shareholder is the 99-year-old Swiss billionaire Walter Haefner. He owns about a quarter of the company.

HISTORY

Boorn in Shanghai, Charles Wang fled Communist China with his family in 1952 and grew up in Queens, New York. After working in sales for software developer Standard Data, Wang started a joint venture in 1976 with Swiss-owned Computer Associates (CA) to sell software in the US. He started with four employees and one product, a file organizer for IBM storage systems. It was a great success, and in 1980 Wang bought out his Swiss partners. CA went public in 1981.

Wang realized that a far-flung distribution and service network (continuously fed by new products) was the key to success. Acquiring existing software (and its customers) reduced risky in-house development and moved products to market sooner.

The company expanded its offerings by buying the popular SuperCalc spreadsheet in 1984. The 1987 purchase of chief utilities rival UCCEL gave investor Walter Haefner what remains the largest individual stake in CA.

CA's purchases of mostly struggling software firms made it, in 1989, the first independent software company to reach $1 billion in sales. The $300 million acquisition of Cullinet that year added database and banking applications to CA's product line.

By the early 1990s, CA's acquisition methods had developed a reputation that were seen by some as ruthless — swoop in, gobble up, cut costs, and get rid of employees. As a new owner, CA strongly defended its licensing contracts — often in court.

In 1994 CA promoted EVP of operations Sanjay Kumar to president. Kumar's shift away from older systems to focus on network software was reflected by the acquisitions of ASK Group (1994), Legent (1995), and network management expert Cheyenne Software (1996). CA continued its practice of buying in cash to avoid diluting stock.

In 1999 CA bought database management software company PLATINUM technology for about $3.5 billion.

In 2000 CA acquired business software specialist Sterling Software in a deal valued at nearly $4 billion. Later that year the company began spinning off some of its promising software businesses; Wang stepped down as CEO to focus on new opportunities for CA as chairman. He handed the CEO reins to Kumar.

Alleging corporate mismanagement, in 2001 Sam Wyly (co-founder of Sterling Software) initiated a proxy fight designed to elect a new board of directors. Wyly's bid failed, however, as it was voted down by shareholders. He initiated a second proxy fight in 2002, but abandoned it after reaching a settlement with the company, which included a $10 million payment. Later in 2002, the board elected Kumar chairman after Wang retired.

An SEC investigation into the company's accounting practices led to the resignation of CA's CFO late in 2003. The investigation continued into 2004, resulting in additional executive resignations. Late in 2004 CA agreed to pay $225 million to shareholders in order to avoid criminal prosecution by the SEC and US Justice Department for fraudulently recording and reporting revenues. Shortly after the settlement was announced, former CEO Sanjay Kumar and former EVP Stephen Richards were indicted on charges of securities fraud, conspiracy, and obstruction of justice. Kumar resigned as chairman, president, and CEO that year (he left the company entirely after a brief stint as chief software architect). IBM veteran John Swainson was named CEO.

In 2005 it acquired network management specialist Concord Communications.

The company purchased application management specialist Wily Technology for $375 million early in 2006. Also in 2006, Computer Associates International officially changed its name to CA.

It acquired identity management software developer Eurekify in 2008 and data loss prevention specialist Orchestria in 2009.

EXECUTIVES

Chairman: Arthur F. Weinbach, age 66
Vice Chairman: Russell M. Artzt, age 63, $4,200,106 total compensation
CEO and Director: William E. (Bill) McCracken, age 67, $3,748,218 total compensation
EVP and CFO: Nancy E. Cooper, age 56, $3,707,331 total compensation
EVP and CTO: Donald Ferguson
EVP Enterprise Products and Solutions Business Line: Thomas W. (Tom) Kendra
EVP and General Counsel: Amy Fliegelman Olli, $3,027,752 total compensation
EVP; Group Executive, Customer Solutions Group: David Dobson, age 47
EVP Cloud Products and Solutions Business Line: Chris O'Malley, age 47
EVP: Donald R. (Don) Friedman, age 64
EVP Worldwide Human Resources: Andrew (Andy) Goodman, age 51
EVP Risk and Chief Administrative Officer: Phillip Harrington, age 53
EVP Strategy and Corporate Development: Jacob Lamm, age 45
EVP Growth and Emerging Markets: John Ruthven
EVP Worldwide Sales and General Manager; Managing Director, North America and Europe: Mark Thompson
EVP Technology and Development Group: Ajei S. Gopal, age 48
EVP Worldwide Sales and Marketing: George Fischer
SVP and CIO: Stephen Savage
Chief Communications Officer: William L. (Bill) Hughes
Chief Ethics Officer, Law Department: Joel Katz
Chief Marketing Officer: Marianne Budnik
Program Manager Investor Relations: Carol Lu
Auditors: KPMG LLP

LOCATIONS

HQ: CA, Inc.
1 CA Plaza, Islandia, NY 11749
Phone: 800-225-5224 **Fax:** 631-342-6800
Web: www.ca.com

2010 Sales

	$ mil.	% of total
US	2,414	55
Other countries	1,939	45
Total	**4,353**	**100**

PRODUCTS/OPERATIONS

2010 Sales

	$ mil.	% of total
Subscriptions & maintenance	3,887	88
Professional services	292	7
Software fees & other	174	5
Total	**4,353**	**100**

Selected Product Groups

Application development and databases
Application performance management
Database management
Infrastructure and operations management
IT service and asset management
Mainframe
Project, portfolio, and financial management
Security management
Storage and information governance

COMPETITORS

BMC Software
Check Point Software
Cisco Systems
Compuware
EMC
Hewlett-Packard
IBM
McAfee
Microsoft
Novell
Oracle
RSA Security
SAP
Symantec

HISTORICAL FINANCIALS

Company Type: Public

Income Statement

FYE: March 31

	REVENUE ($ mil.)	NET INCOME ($ mil.)	NET PROFIT MARGIN	EMPLOYEES
3/10	4,353	771	17.7%	13,800
3/09	4,271	694	16.2%	13,200
3/08	4,277	500	11.7%	13,700
3/07	3,943	118	3.0%	14,500
3/06	3,796	159	4.2%	16,000
Annual Growth	3.5%	48.4%	—	(3.6%)

2010 Year-End Financials

Debt ratio: 30.7%
Return on equity: 16.5%
Cash ($ mil.): 2,583
Current ratio: 1.11
Long-term debt ($ mil.): 1,530
No. of shares (mil.): 516
Dividends
Yield: 0.7%
Payout: 10.9%
Market value ($ mil.): 12,110

Stock History

NASDAQ (GS): CA

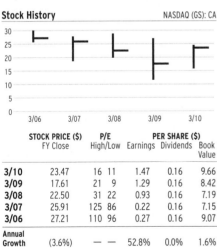

	STOCK PRICE ($) FY Close	P/E High/Low		PER SHARE ($) Earnings	Dividends	Book Value
3/10	23.47	16	11	1.47	0.16	9.66
3/09	17.61	21	9	1.29	0.16	8.42
3/08	22.50	31	22	0.93	0.16	7.19
3/07	25.91	125	86	0.22	0.16	7.15
3/06	27.21	110	96	0.27	0.16	9.07
Annual Growth	(3.6%)	—	—	52.8%	0.0%	1.6%

Cablevision Systems

There's no business like show business for Cablevision. Through its main operating subsidiary CSC Holdings, the company provides basic cable television to about 3 million customers in the New York City area. Another nearly 3 million viewers subscribe to its iO digital video service. Through subsidiary Lightpath, Cablevision serves about 2 million commercial broadband Internet users and another nearly 2 million VoIP telephony subscribers. Cablevision owns nationwide and regional cable programming networks through Rainbow Media. The family of founder and chairman Charles Dolan controls 70% of the company.

Cablevision is using divestitures and acquisitions to fine-tune its portfolio of media and entertainment holdings. The company spun off its Madison Square Garden business to its stockholders in 2010. The assets included in the spin-off were the Madison Square Garden and Radio City Music Hall venues, the Knicks and Rangers sports teams, and related broadcast and online media properties, such as the Fuse network. Also that year Cablevision agreed to acquire Bresnan Communications, a broadband telecommunications company with more than 320,000 subscribers in Colorado, Montana, Utah, and Wyoming, expanding its subscriber base beyond the New York metropolitan area. It will pay $1.36 billion for Bresnan.

Rainbow Media acquired the Sundance Channel from NBC Universal and Showtime Networks for $496 million the previous year. Also in 2008, Cablevision bought 97% of newspaper *Newsday* from Tribune Company for $650 million.

Other properties held by Rainbow Media include cable channels American Movie Classics (AMC), the Independent Film Channel (IFC), and WE: Women's Entertainment. The group also owns Clearview Cinemas, which operates about 50 New York-area movie theaters including Manhattan's famous Ziegfeld Theater. Its PVI Virtual Media Services unit provides real-time video insertion of computer-generated images to sporting events and other programming.

HISTORY

In 1954 Charles Dolan helped form Sterling Manhattan Cable, which won the cable TV franchise for Lower Manhattan in 1965. It began broadcasting pro basketball and hockey, courtesy of Madison Square Garden (MSG), in 1967. In 1970 Dolan started Home Box Office (HBO), the first nationwide pay-TV channel, and hired Gerald Levin to run it.

Dolan took the company public as Sterling Communications; its partner, media giant Time (now part of Time Warner), came to own 80% of Sterling. Costs mounted, however, and in 1973 Time liquidated Sterling (but kept HBO).

Dolan bought back the New York franchises and formed Long Island Cable Communications Development. He changed its name to Cablevision and expanded around New York and Chicago. In 1980 Cablevision formed Rainbow Programming, which soon included the American Movie Classics and Bravo channels; in 1983 it launched the popular SportsChannel (now Fox Sports New York). Cablevision went public in 1986. It bought two Connecticut cable systems that year and one in Massachusetts the next.

In 1989 Cablevision helped NBC launch the CNBC cable network but sold its interest to NBC in 1991. Cablevision began offering cable phone service to businesses on Long Island — two years before the Telecommunications Act of 1996 was passed. Subsidiary Cablevision Lightpath, a competitive local-exchange carrier, signed a groundbreaking co-carrier agreement with Baby Bell NYNEX (now part of Verizon) in 1995.

To get a grip on NYC entertainment, Cablevision partnered with ITT in 1995 to buy the MSG properties. Three years later Starwood acquired ITT. In late 1996 Charles' son James became CEO.

In 1997 Cablevision began dumping cable holdings, which were spread over 19 states, to focus on its New York City area operations and the upgrading of its cable infrastructure.

Cablevision sold 40% of Rainbow's regional sports business to Fox/Liberty (now Fox Sports Net, owned by News Corp.) to create a rival to Disney's ESPN. Fox/Liberty got 40% of MSG, and Cablevision got Fox Sports Net, a chain of 22 regional sports networks. In 1998 Cablevision sold cable systems in 10 states to Mediacom.

In 2001 MGM paid $825 million for a 20% stake in four of Rainbow's national networks. But the recession forced the company to take steps to improve operations, including the elimination of 5,000 jobs.

The next year, Cablevision battled with the Yankees Entertainment & Sports Network (YES Network) over the rights to broadcast New York Yankees games. The same year, the company sold its Bravo network to NBC, a subsidiary of GE.

Cablevision intended to shut down the financially challenged VOOM satellite service after a plan to spin off Rainbow Media fell apart in early 2005. Charles Dolan unsuccessfully tried to buy VOOM himself but son James, Cablevision's CEO, sided with the board of directors and favored shuttering the unit, resulting in a bit of a family feud. Charles responded to the decision by tossing three Cablevision directors and installing five new ones who were more aligned with his interests. The company gave him more time to come up with the money to make another bid for VOOM, yet the effort turned out to be futile and Cablevision eventually axed the service.

In a move that would have expanded the company's cable systems outside the New York City metro area, Cablevision in 2005 made a failed bid for troubled rival Adelphia's cable systems. The company also wanted to buy Adelphia in an effort to keep rivals Time Warner Cable and Comcast from growing bigger, but the two industry leaders eventually won the bidding war after all.

In 2005 the Dolan family abandoned an offer to take the company private for $7.9 billion, citing an overall decline of value in the communications sector. However, in October of the following year the Dolans made another offer to take the company private for the same amount. In 2007 their bid was raised to $8.9 billion. Both parties finally agreed on a deal worth $10.6 billion that would give the Dolans full control of the company. Shareholders rejected the bid in late 2007.

Also that year Cablevision restructured its Madison Square Garden partnership with News Corporation, resulting in Rainbow Media owning 100% of the sports and entertainment company. Cablevision also sold two regional sports networks to Comcast in 2007 for about $570 million. The deal included Cablevision's 60% stake in FSN Bay Area and its 50% stake in FSN New England.

EXECUTIVES

Chairman: Charles F. Dolan, age 83,
$1,099,631 total compensation
**Vice Chairman, Cablevision Systems and Rainbow
Media Holdings:** Hank J. Ratner, age 51,
$1,450,631 total compensation
President, CEO, and Director: James L. Dolan, age 54,
$1,159,092 total compensation
COO: Thomas M. (Tom) Rutledge, age 56,
$1,178,953 total compensation
EVP and CFO: Michael P. Huseby, age 55,
$344,925 total compensation
**EVP Strategy and Development, Office of the Chairman
and Director:** Thomas C. Dolan, age 57
EVP Communications and Community Relations:
Charles (Charlie) Schueler
EVP Government and Public Affairs: Lisa Rosenblum,
age 54
EVP: Gregg Seibert, age 54
EVP Product Management and Marketing:
Patricia Gottesmann
EVP and General Counsel: David Ellen, age 45
EVP Corporate Engineering and Technology:
James A. (Jim) Blackley
SVP, Deputy General Counsel, and Secretary:
Victoria D. Salhus, age 60
SVP and General Manager, Clearview Cinemas:
Douglas (Doug) Oines, age 55
SVP and Treasurer: Kevin Watson, age 43
SVP and Controller: Wm. Keith Harper, age 55
SVP Product Management: John Trierweiler
SVP Investor Relations: Patricia Armstrong
President, Local Media: Tad Smith, age 49
President, MSG Sports: Scott M. O'Neil, age 39
President, Cable and Communications:
John R. Bickham, age 58
President, Optimum Lightpath: Dave Pistacchio, age 49
President and CEO, Rainbow Media: Joshua W. Sapan
Director; President, News 12 Networks:
Patrick F. Dolan, age 58
Auditors: KPMG LLP

LOCATIONS

HQ: Cablevision Systems Corporation
1111 Stewart Ave., Bethpage, NY 11714
Phone: 516-803-2300   **Fax:** 516-803-3134
Web: www.cablevision.com

PRODUCTS/OPERATIONS

2009 Sales

	$ mil.	% of total
Telecommunications services	5,431.5	68
Madison Square Garden	1,062.4	14
Rainbow Media	1,043.4	13
Newsday	342.3	4
Other	82.1	1
Adjustments	(188.4)	—
Total	**7,773.3**	**100**

Selected Operations

Consumer Services
  Cable and Communications
    Video
    Consumer Modem
    Consumer Telephone
  Clearview Cinemas (movie theaters)
Business Services
  Cablevision Lightpath (integrated business
    communications systems)
Programming and Entertainment
  Rainbow Media Holdings
    American Movie Classics (classic films)
    The Independent Film Channel
    Mag Rack (video magazines video-on-demand,
      formerly Sterling Digital)
    News 12 Networks
    Sportskool (sports and fitness video on demand)
    VOOM HD Networks (80%, high-definition cable and
      satellite entertainment channels)
    WE: Women's Entertainment (entertainment and
      information for women)
    World Picks (foreign language video on demand
      programming)

COMPETITORS

A&E Networks
ABC, Inc.
AT&T
CBS
Charter Communications
Comcast
Cox Communications
DIRECTV
DISH Network
Disney
EchoStar
ESPN
FOX Broadcasting
Liberty Media
NBC
Qwest Communications
RCN Corporation
Time Warner Cable
Turner Broadcasting
Verizon
Viacom
Vonage

HISTORICAL FINANCIALS

Company Type: Public

Income Statement

FYE: December 31

	REVENUE ($ mil.)	NET INCOME ($ mil.)	NET PROFIT MARGIN	EMPLOYEES
12/09	7,773	285	3.7%	27,940
12/08	7,230	(228)	—	20,105
12/07	6,485	219	3.4%	22,935
12/06	5,928	(126)	—	22,075
12/05	5,176	94	1.8%	20,425
Annual Growth	**10.7%**	**31.9%**	**—**	**8.1%**

2009 Year-End Financials

Debt ratio: —
Return on equity: —
Cash ($ mil.): 355
Current ratio: 0.99
Long-term debt ($ mil.): 10,840

No. of shares (mil.): 305
Dividends
  Yield: 1.9%
  Payout: 41.7%
Market value ($ mil.): 6,497

Stock History

NYSE: CVC

	STOCK PRICE ($) FY Close	P/E High/Low		PER SHARE ($) Earnings	Dividends	Book Value
12/09	21.32	23	8	0.96	0.40	(16.92)
12/08	13.90	—	—	(0.78)	0.20	(17.59)
12/07	20.23	44	26	0.74	—	(16.73)
12/06	23.51	—	—	(0.45)	—	(17.52)
12/05	19.38	85	56	0.33	—	(8.10)
Annual Growth	**2.4%**	**—**	**—**	**30.6%**	**100.0%**	**—**

Cabot Corporation

Cabot may be an investor's dream — it's always in the black. The company is the world's #1 producer of carbon black, a reinforcing and pigmenting agent used in tires, inks, cables, and coatings. It has about 25% of the world market for the product. Cabot also holds its own as a maker of fumed metal oxides such as fumed silica and fumed alumina, which are used as anticaking, thickening, and reinforcing agents in adhesives and coatings. Other products include tantalum (used to make capacitors in electronics) and specialty fluids for gas and oil drilling. It operates in about 20 countries worldwide, with combined sales to China and Japan adding up to about a quarter of Cabot's total.

The company is among a small group of carbon black producers with a global presence. (Columbian Chemicals and Evonik Degussa also operate worldwide.) While the US is its single largest market, accounting for almost 20% of Cabot's total sales by itself, the company has focused on increasing its Chinese business; 2008 marked the first year that country crept past the 10% mark in terms of sales.

Much of its carbon black business is done with the top automobile tire makers. Goodyear Tire & Rubber is its largest customer, totaling more than 10% of its entire business.

Cabot moved to expand its portfolio of security technologies in 2010 by acquiring Oxonica Materials, a manufacturer of products used in anti-counterfeiting applications. Cabot's Security Business supplies covert tags and other markings for security applications added to inks, paper, films, and other materials that can only be detected with a specialized reader.

HISTORY

A descendant of two old-line Boston merchant families, Godfrey Lowell Cabot graduated from Harvard in 1882. His brother had a paint business in Pennsylvania that used coal tars to make black pigment, and the two decided that carbon black — an abundant waste product of the oil fields — would be their business. The brothers built a carbon black plant in Pennsylvania in 1882; five years later Godfrey bought his brother's share in the company. A carbon black glut and the increasing use of natural gas led Godfrey to drill his first gas well in 1888. He took advantage of the glut by buying distressed carbon black factories.

As the Pennsylvania oil fields dried up near the turn of the century, Godfrey moved operations to West Virginia, where he added to his gas holdings and, in 1914, built a natural gas extraction plant. Meanwhile, products such as high-speed printing presses increased the demand for carbon black. The reinforcing and stabilizing properties of the compound became widely known after its use in tires during WWI. The company was incorporated in 1922 as Godfrey L. Cabot, Inc.

The production of carbon black soon moved west, and by 1930 Cabot had eight plants in Texas and one in Oklahoma. Early that decade the company developed dustless carbon black pellets, which, along with gas profits, got Cabot through the Depression. In 1935 Cabot began drilling for oil and gas and processing natural gas in Texas. Soon natural gas accounted for more than half of sales.

WWII led to rubber shortages and temporary government control over the industry. It also led to the construction and improvement (with government assistance) of Cabot plants in Louisiana, Oklahoma, and Texas. The company was the #1 producer of carbon black in 1950 and began its fumed silica operations in 1952. The postwar economic boom allowed Cabot to open carbon black plants in Canada, France, Italy, and the UK by the end of the decade.

In 1960 the company's businesses were united under the Cabot Corporation name. Expansion continued into Argentina, Colombia, Germany, and Spain for the next decade. Godfrey Cabot died in 1962. The next year the company started producing titanium, sold a 12% stake in a public offering, and began experimenting with plastic polymers.

CEO Robert Sharpie used the cash derived from Cabot's chemical businesses during the 1970s for acquisitions — including Kawecki Berylco Industries (tantalum, 1978) and TUCO, Inc. (gas processing and pipeline, 1979) — while its chemical plants deteriorated. The oil crisis early in the decade resulted in the rapid growth of Cabot's energy business. However, when gas prices fell in the 1980s, Cabot's revenue base shrank and its liabilities didn't.

The Cabot family, which owned 30% of the company, replaced Sharpie with Samuel Bodman as CEO in 1987. Bodman invested in the plants and divested many of Cabot's noncore assets, including ceramics, metal manufacturing, and semiconductors. He also exited the energy production and exploration businesses.

In 1996 Cabot formed divisions to make pigment-based inks (ink jet colorants) and drilling fluids (Cabot Specialty Fluids) and sold TUCO. Two years later the company began field testing a drilling fluid (cesium formate) that would halve the drilling time in high-temperature, high-pressure wells. Cabot completed the second phase of its carbon black plant in China, a joint venture with a Chinese firm, in 1999. It also spun off 15% of its microelectronics materials business and sold Cabot LNG to Tractebel for around $680 million.

Cabot spun off its remaining stake (about 80%) in Cabot Microelectronics in 2000. The next year Kennett Burnes was named CEO and chairman after Bodman stepped down to become US deputy treasury secretary. (President Bush nominated Bodman to become secretary of energy for his second term, and Bodman was confirmed in early 2005.)

In 2002 Cabot purchased the remainder of Showa Cabot Supermetals (tantalum) from its joint venture partner, Showa Denko. However, the company experienced lower sales volumes of tantalum because of contract disagreements with some of its customers, including KEMET and AVX.

Cabot continued to develop and expand its newer businesses, including its growing ink jet colorants unit. In late 2002 it launched a new aerogels business (Nanogel), which produces materials for thermal and sound insulating purposes. Cabot sold its 40% stake in Aearo Corporation (maker of safety products such as eyewear; formerly called Cabot Safety Holding Corporation) in 2004.

The following year Cabot purchased Showa Denko's interest in another joint venture, Showa Cabot K.K., which marketed carbon black products in Japan.

Early in 2008 BASF executive Patrick Prevost took over the CEO post from Burnes.

EXECUTIVES

Chairman: John F. O'Brien, age 67
President, CEO, and Director: Patrick M. Prevost, age 54, $2,202,696 total compensation
EVP and CFO: Eduardo E. Cordeiro, age 42, $1,441,131 total compensation
EVP and General Manager, Core Segment and Americas Region: David A. Miller, age 50
VP and General Manager, Asia Pacific Region: Xinsheng Zhang
VP Research and Development: Yakov Kutsovsky
VP and CIO: Douglas A. Church
VP and General Manager, Europe, Middle East and Africa (EMEA) Region: Nick Cross
VP Tax: Peter M. Hunt
VP and Treasurer: Irene Sudac
VP and General Manager, Performance Segment: Sean Keohane, age 43, $816,999 total compensation
VP and General Counsel: Brian A. Berube, age 47, $1,065,023 total compensation
VP Human Resources: Robby D. Sisco
VP South America Rubber Blacks: Chang Loo Sih
VP Engineering: Helmut Lorat
VP Operations, Specialty Fluids Segment: James (Jim) Turner
VP and Controller: James P. (Jim) Kelly
VP Safety, Health, and Environmental Affairs: Martin O'Neill
Secretary: Jane A. Bell
Director Investor Relations: Susannah Robinson
Auditors: Deloitte & Touche LLP

LOCATIONS

HQ: Cabot Corporation
2 Seaport Ln., Ste. 1300, Boston, MA 02210
Phone: 617-345-0100 **Fax:** 617-342-6103
Web: www.cabot-corp.com

2009 Sales

	$ mil.	% of total
US	377	17
Japan	295	13
China	281	13
Other countries	1,290	57
Total	**2,243**	**100**

PRODUCTS/OPERATIONS

2009 Sales

	$ mil.	% of total
Core Segment		
Rubber blacks	1,286	57
Supermetals	140	6
Performance Segment	621	28
New Business Segment	67	3
Specialty Fluids Segment	59	3
Other	70	3
Total	**2,243**	**100**

Selected Products

Core Segment
 Rubber blacks (for tires and industrial products)
 Supermetals
  Niobium
  Tantalum
Performance Segment
 Performance products
  Specialty carbon blacks
  Thermoplastic concentrates
 Metal oxides
  Fumed alumina
  Fumed silica
New Business Segment
 Ink jet colorants
 Nanogel (insulative aerogel materials)
 Superior MicroPowders (business development)
Specialty fluids (cesium formate drilling fluids)

COMPETITORS

Aditya Birla Nuvo
Akzo Nobel
Allegheny Technologies
BASF SE
Clariant
Columbian Chemicals
Dow Chemical
Evonik Degussa
Flint Group
J.M. Huber
MacDermid
Mitsubishi Chemical
SABIC Innovative Plastics
Tokai Carbon
Wacker Chemie

HISTORICAL FINANCIALS

Company Type: Public

Income Statement

FYE: September 30

	REVENUE ($ mil.)	NET INCOME ($ mil.)	NET PROFIT MARGIN	EMPLOYEES
9/09	2,243	(77)	—	3,950
9/08	3,191	86	2.7%	4,300
9/07	2,616	129	4.9%	4,300
9/06	2,543	90	3.5%	4,300
9/05	2,125	(48)	—	4,400
Annual Growth	**1.4%**	**—**	**—**	**(2.7%)**

2009 Year-End Financials

Debt ratio: 54.9%
Return on equity: —
Cash ($ mil.): 304
Current ratio: 2.52
Long-term debt ($ mil.): 623
No. of shares (mil.): 65
Dividends
 Yield: 3.1%
 Payout: —
Market value ($ mil.): 1,511

Stock History

NYSE: CBT

	STOCK PRICE ($) FY Close	P/E High/Low		Earnings	PER SHARE ($) Dividends	Book Value
9/09	23.11	—	—	(1.23)	0.72	17.35
9/08	31.78	30	16	1.34	0.72	19.11
9/07	35.53	26	18	1.90	0.72	18.27
9/06	37.20	31	24	1.28	0.64	18.30
9/05	33.01	—	—	(0.84)	0.64	16.81
Annual Growth	**(8.5%)**	**—**	**—**	**—**	**3.0%**	**0.8%**

CACI International

CACI International doesn't need a lot of clients — just a few with deep pockets. As one of the largest government IT contractors, CACI derives most of its revenues from the US government. More than three-quarters of its sales come from the US Department of Defense (DOD). The company provides a wide range of technology services, including systems integration, network management, knowledge management, and engineering and simulation. Based in the UK, the company's European subsidiary, CACI Limited, accounts for all of its international sales and almost all of its commercial revenue.

In early 2010 the company purchased SystemWare, a manufacturer of signals acquisition and analysis systems that enable users to monitor and detect cybersecurity and physical security vulnerabilities.

The company's plan for securing more business with the DOD is based in part on acquiring companies that already serve the department. In 2007 CACI purchased the Institute for Quality Management, a performance management consultancy and provider of operational support services to the intelligence and homeland security community. It then bought government consulting company Wexford Group, giving it better access to contracts with the US Army. It also acquired government technical and engineering services provider Dragon Development in 2007, as well as Athena Innovative Solutions, a professional services firm serving US intelligence agencies.

CACI generates less than 5% of its revenues from international clients, but the company made small acquisitions to expand its overseas business. It purchased three UK-based businesses during fiscal 2008: Arete Software and Softsmart (software for local government education authorities), and Invocom (network support for telecom service providers).

While the Obama administration is increasing the Pentagon budget, it is shifting spending priorities for the Defense Department, focusing more on providing day-to-day operational support for air, ground, and naval forces around the world and less on R&D for futuristic military systems. That could benefit CACI and its capabilities in the years to come. As a government contractor, the company is subject to the General Services Administration and other federal agencies suspending its contracts on various grounds, or being debarred from certain contracts. Government contractors also are attracting more attention from Congressional oversight committees and audit scrutiny at the agency level due to controversies surrounding some contractors and their work in Iraq.

Certain government reports identified CACI employees as allegedly being involved in mistreatment of prisoners at the infamous Abu Ghraib prison in Iraq, where the company was providing interrogation services to the US Army. An internal company investigation failed to confirm the allegations, and no official charges were brought by the Army or the US Department of Justice in the case. In 2009 the US Court of Appeals for the DC Circuit upheld the dismissal of two lawsuits against CACI, ruling the company was exempt from tort claims by the Iraqi plaintiffs due to its role in assisting the US government in the prosecution of the Iraq war.

HISTORY

In 1962 Harry Markowitz (winner of the 1990 Nobel Memorial Prize in Economic Sciences) and Herb Karr formed California Analysis Center, which provided services related to the SIMSCRIPT programming language. The company went public in 1968 and four years later moved from Santa Monica, California, to the Washington, DC, area. Its name was changed to CACI in the late 1970s. J. P. (Jack) London, a 12-year company veteran, became CEO in 1984.

Through the 1980s and early 1990s, CACI's dependence on a struggling military sector hurt operations. The company got a big boost in 1991, however, when it won a US Department of Justice contract for litigation support services worth $130 million over five years. Profits were revived by 1995. The next year it won

a $66 million subcontract to provide information processing support to VGS, a software integration firm charged with building a federal information processing program.

In 1997 CACI gained a foothold in the government and commercial communications services segments when it acquired Infonet Services' Government Systems subsidiary. Also that year it bought AnaData (now CACI Ltd.), a UK-based database marketing software firm. In 1998 the company acquired QuesTech (now CACI Technologies), a computer services contractor to the military and national security segment; CACI began bundling products and services for availability over Internet-based networks.

In 2000 CACI acquired government services specialist XEN Corporation (systems engineering and IT services) and CENTECH (network services and e-commerce) as well as the network services and related assets (Federal Services Business) of net.com.

As part of its growth strategy, CACI acquired C-CUBED Corporation in 2003. C-CUBED provided specialized support services known as C4ISR (command, control, communications, computers, intelligence, surveillance, and reconnaissance) to clients in the Department of Defense, federal, and intelligence communities.

CACI also acquired intelligence contractor Premier Technology Group (PTG) in 2003. Prior to PTG, CACI purchased IT service providers Acton Burnell and Digital Systems International, the Government Solutions Division of Condor Technology Solutions, and Applied Technology Solutions of Northern VA.

The company purchased CMS Information Services in 2004. That year it also bought the Defense Intelligence Group of American Management Systems (AMS), which performed work for the Department of Defense and government intelligence agencies. The deal, valued at $415 million, happened in 2004 when CGI Group acquired the entirety of AMS, and then sold part of it to CACI.

CACI in 2006 acquired Falls Church, Virginia-based IT firm AlphaInsight. The deal expanded CACI's business with civilian agencies of the federal government, including the Department of State and the Justice Department, and provided additional contract opportunities with the Department of Homeland Security and the DOD. Also that year, CACI acquired Information Systems Support (ISS), a government systems integrator specializing in communications, IT, and logistics.

In 2007 US operations president Paul Cofoni was named company president and CEO, replacing London, who retained the title of chairman.

EXECUTIVES

Chairman: J. P. (Jack) London, age 72, $1,928,603 total compensation
President, CEO, and Director: Paul M. Cofoni, age 61, $6,494,416 total compensation
President, US Operations: William M. (Bill) Fairl, age 60, $2,512,267 total compensation
COO US Operations and Acting EVP Mission Systems Business Group: Randall C. (Randy) Fuerst, age 54, $1,714,666 total compensation
EVP, CFO, and Treasurer: Thomas A. (Tom) Mutryn, age 55, $1,539,515 total compensation
EVP and Chief Resources Officer: Robert B. Turner
EVP and Chief Human Resources Officer: H. Robert (Bob) Boehm
EVP Transformation Solutions Business Group: Gilbert B. (Gil) Guarino

EVP and Division Manager, Enterprise Technologies and Services Business Group: James McRoberts
EVP Mission Systems Group: Karl Johnson
EVP Corporate Business Development: Ronald A. (Ron) Schneider
EVP Enterprise Technologies and Services: Daniel E. Porter
EVP Security and Intelligence Integration: Albert M. (Bert) Calland III
EVP Business Development: Dale Luddeke
EVP and CTO: Deborah B. Dunie
EVP Government Business Operations: Steven H. Weiss
EVP Public Relations and Business Communications: Jody A. Brown
EVP National Solutions Group: Lowell E. (Jake) Jacoby
SVP Investor Relations: David Dragics
CEO CACI Limited and President, Information Solutions, United Kingdom: Gregory R. Bradford, age 60
Chief Scientist, Advanced Solutions: Stephen T. Makrinos
Auditors: Ernst & Young LLP

LOCATIONS

HQ: CACI International Inc
1100 N. Glebe Rd., Arlington, VA 22201
Phone: 703-841-7800   **Fax:** 703-841-7882
Web: www.caci.com

2009 Sales

	$ mil.	% of total
US	2,650.8	97
Other countries	79.4	3
Total	**2,730.2**	**100**

PRODUCTS/OPERATIONS

2009 Sales

	$ mil.	% of total
Department of Defense	2,078.4	76
Federal civilian agencies	542.1	20
Commercial	88.2	3
State & local government	21.5	1
Total	**2,730.2**	**100**

2009 Sales by Contract Type

	$ mil.	% of total
Time & materials	1,310.0	48
Cost reimbursable	875.7	32
Firm fixed-price	544.5	20
Total	**2,730.2**	**100**

Selected Services

Asset management
Automated procurement
Customer database management integration
Electronic commerce
Engineering support
Information management development
Intelligent document management integration
Knowledge management
Litigation support
Logistics support
Marketing and customer database management development
Networking support
Product data and supply-chain management integration
Records management development
Simulation and modeling languages
Software development
Systems integration and reengineering
Weapons systems/equipment configuration management integration

COMPETITORS

Affiliated Computer Services
Alion
Apptis
BAE SYSTEMS
Boeing
Booz Allen
CIBER
Computer Sciences Corp.
General Dynamics Information Technology
GTSI
HP Enterprise Services
IBM
Jacobs Engineering
L-3 Communications
Lockheed Martin
ManTech
Northrop Grumman
Perot Systems
QinetiQ
Raytheon
SAIC
SRA International
Unisys

HISTORICAL FINANCIALS

Company Type: Public

Income Statement

FYE: June 30

	REVENUE ($ mil.)	NET INCOME ($ mil.)	NET PROFIT MARGIN	EMPLOYEES
6/09	2,730	96	3.5%	12,400
6/08	2,421	83	3.4%	12,000
6/07	1,938	79	4.1%	10,400
6/06	1,755	85	4.8%	10,400
6/05	1,623	85	5.3%	9,600
Annual Growth	13.9%	2.9%	—	6.6%

2009 Year-End Financials

Debt ratio: 63.2%
Return on equity: 10.0%
Cash ($ mil.): 208
Current ratio: 2.28
Long-term debt ($ mil.): 628

No. of shares (mil.): 30
Dividends
  Yield: —
  Payout: —
Market value ($ mil.): 1,291

Stock History

NYSE: CACI

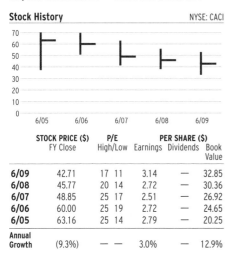

	STOCK PRICE ($) FY Close	P/E High/Low	PER SHARE ($) Earnings	Dividends	Book Value
6/09	42.71	17 11	3.14	—	32.85
6/08	45.77	20 14	2.72	—	30.36
6/07	48.85	25 17	2.51	—	26.92
6/06	60.00	25 19	2.72	—	24.65
6/05	63.16	25 14	2.79	—	20.25
Annual Growth	(9.3%)	— —	3.0%	—	12.9%

CalPERS

California's public-sector retirees already have a place in the sun; CalPERS gives them the money to enjoy it. CalPERS is the California Public Employees' Retirement System, the largest public pension system in the US. It manages retirement and health plans for nearly 2 million beneficiaries (employees, retirees, and their dependents) from more than 2,500 government agencies and school districts.

With some $200 billion in assets in its investment funds, CalPERS uses its clout to sway such corporate governance issues as company performance, executive compensation, and even social policy. CalPERS has often acted as a force for reform, urging companies to remove conflicts of interest and make themselves more accountable to shareholders, employees, and the public. CalPERS is also a powerful negotiator for such services as insurance; rates established by the system serve as benchmarks for employers throughout the nation.

Most of CalPERS' revenue comes from its enormous investment program: It has interests in US and foreign securities, oil and energy, real estate, and even hedge funds and venture capital activities. It owns stake in such prestigious entities as The Carlyle Group, Apollo Management, and Blackstone.

In 2010 CalPERS agreed to buy a 13% stake in London's Gatwick Airport from Global Infrastructure Partners.

Fred Buenrostro retired as CEO in 2008. Anne Stausboll, who'd been serving as CalPERS' interim chief investment officer, was named his successor. She is the fund's first female CEO.

Shortly after Buenrostro's retirement, CalPERS reported one of its worst performances in years, partly due to its investments in undeveloped land earlier in the decade.

Troubles continued in 2009. CalPERS had nearly a quarter of its assets wiped out due to the collapse of the market. In order to cover the losses, CalPERS proposed a plan to have cities and counties make higher contributions to the system. CalPERS also sued three credit rating agencies in 2009 — blaming them for a big chunk of its losses.

During the coming years CalPERS may be forced to sell assets, as it is expected to be hit with a wave of early retirements by middle-aged workers. The fund plans to sell some of its US stocks, which have been declining, in exchange for emerging markets such as India and China.

CalPERS' board consists of six elected, three appointed, and four designated members (the director of the state's Department of Personnel Administration, state controller, state treasurer, and a member of the State Personnel Board).

HISTORY

The state of California founded CalPERS in 1931 to administer a pension fund for state employees. By the 1940s the system was serving other public agencies and educational institutions on a contract basis.

When the Public Employees' Medical and Hospital Care Act was passed in 1962, CalPERS added health coverage. The fund was conservatively managed in-house, with little exposure to stocks. Despite slow growth, the state used the system's funds to meet its own cash shortfalls.

CalPERS became involved in corporate governance issues in the mid-1980s, when California treasurer Jesse Unruh became outraged by corporate greenmail schemes. In 1987 he hired as CEO Wisconsin pension board veteran Dale Hanson, who led the movement for corporate accountability to institutional investors.

In the late 1980s CalPERS moved into real estate and Japanese stocks. When both crashed around 1990, Hanson came under pressure. CalPERS was twice forced to take major writedowns for its real estate holdings and turned to expensive outside fund managers, but its investment performance deteriorated.

Legislation in 1990 enabled CalPERS to offer long-term health insurance. Governor Pete Wilson's 1991 attempt to use $1.6 billion from CalPERS to help meet a state budget shortfall resulted in legislation banning future raids. CalPERS made its first direct investment in 1993, an energy-related infrastructure partnership with Enron.

CalPERS suffered in the 1994 bond crash. That year Hanson resigned amid criticism that his focus on corporate governance had depressed fund performance. CalPERS eased its corporate relations stance, creating a separate office to handle investor issues and launching an International Corporate Governance Program. However, the next year CalPERS was uninvited from a KKR investment pool because of criticism of its fund management and fee structure.

In 2000 the system raised health care premiums almost 10% to keep up with rising care costs. It widened the scope of its direct investments with stakes in investment bank Thomas Weisel Partners and asset manager Arrowstreet Capital; it also moved into real estate development, buying Genstar Land Co. with Newland Communities. CalPERS said that year it would sell off more than $500 million in tobacco holdings; it then invested the same amount in five biotech funds, its first foray into the sector.

In 2001 California state controller and CalPERS board member Kathleen Connell successfully sued the system for not following state-sanctioned rules regarding pay increases. CalPERS was forced to cut salaries for investment managers, a move that prompted chief investment officer Daniel Szente to resign.

In 2003 CalPERS agreed to a record $250 million settlement relating to an age-discrimination suit brought by the Equal Employment Opportunity Commission. Also that year CalPERS clamored for (and got) the resignation of New York Stock Exchange (NYSE) chairman Richard Grasso. CalPERS and others claimed Grasso's pay of $140 million a year made it impossible for him to effectively monitor the exchange's member companies for corruption.

CalPERS in 2003 sued the NYSE and several specialist firms. The suit accused them of using the trading system for their own gain at the expense of investors. CalPERS found itself on the receiving end of a corporate governance issue in 2004 when a media group sued, demanding CalPERS make public the fees it pays to venture capital firms and hedge funds. It settled the suit by disclosing the fees.

Also in 2004 the president of CalPERS' board, Sean Harrigan, was ousted when the State Personnel Board voted to remove him as its representative. Harrigan had drawn the ire of the business community because of his labor ties and because, under his leadership, the board had withheld votes for directors of most of the companies in which CalPERS invests.

EXECUTIVES

CEO: Anne Stausboll, age 53
President, Board of Administration: Rob Feckner
Interim Chief Operating Investment Officer:
  Kenneth W. Marzion
Chief Investment Officer: Joseph A. Dear
Division Chief, Office of Public Affairs:
  Brad W. Pacheco
Chief Actuary: Ronald L. (Ron) Seeling
Information Officer: Wayne Davis
VP, Board of Administration: George Diehr
Deputy Executive Officer, Operations:
  Stephen W. (Steve) Kessler
Deputy Executive Officer, Benefits Administration:
  Kathleen Hamilton
**Assistant Executive Officer, Information Technology
  Services:** Teri Bennett
Assistant Executive Officer, Health Benefits:
  Robert P. David
**Assistant Executive Officer, Member and Benefit
  Services:** Donna Lum
General Counsel: Peter H. Mixon
Director, External Affairs: Patricia K. Macht
Auditors: Macias, Gini & Company LLP

LOCATIONS

HQ: California Public Employees' Retirement System
  Lincoln Plaza, 400 Q St., Sacramento, CA 95811
Phone: 916-795-3829   **Fax:** 916-795-4001
Web: www.calpers.ca.gov

PRODUCTS/OPERATIONS

Investment Portfolio by Type

	% of total
Domestic equity	31
Domestic debt securities	24
International equity	20
Alternative investments	10
Real estate	9
Inflation linked	2
Short-term investments	2
International debt securities	2
Total	**100**

COMPETITORS

AllianceBernstein
AXA Financial
Charles Schwab
Citigroup Global Markets
FMR
Franklin Resources
Janus Capital
Legg Mason
Merrill Lynch
MFS
Morgan Stanley
Nationwide Financial
Principal Financial
Putnam
Raymond James Financial
State Street
T. Rowe Price
TIAA-CREF
UBS Financial Services
USAA
VALIC
The Vanguard Group

HISTORICAL FINANCIALS

Company Type: Government-owned

Income Statement

FYE: June 30

	REVENUE ($ mil.)	NET INCOME ($ mil.)	NET PROFIT MARGIN	EMPLOYEES
6/09	3,882	—	—	2,315
6/08	3,514	—	—	2,300
6/07	3,263	—	—	2,154
6/06	3,103	—	—	1,924
6/05	2,886	—	—	1,924
Annual Growth	**7.7%**	**—**	**—**	**4.7%**

Revenue History

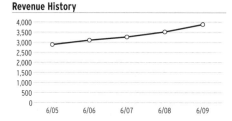

Calpine Corporation

Calpine may get hot, but it also knows how to blow off some steam. The independent power producer and marketer controls more than 24,800 MW of generating capacity through interests in about 80 primarily natural gas-fired power plants in 16 US states. Its fleet also includes 15 geothermal power plants in California. Calpine, the leading geothermal power producer in North America, owns 725 MW of capacity at the largest geothermal facility in the US (the Geysers in northern California), where electricity is produced from natural steam. The company's California and Texas operations account for the great majority of its business.

The global recession and slumping commodity prices depressed Calpine's sales in 2009.

Gearing up to grow the company's national footprint as the economy began to pick up in 2010, Calpine agreed to sell two of its gas-fired power plants to Xcel Energy for $739 million in order to generate cash. The two plants, located near Denver, already provide power to Public Service Company of Colorado, a Xcel subsidiary, under a contract agreement.

The company followed this up with a decision to buy 4,490 MW of power plants from Pepco Holdings for about $1.7 billion. This acquisition, which adds Conectiv Energy's power plants (18 operating and one under construction) to Calpine fleet, helps strengthen its market position in the Eastern US.

Although Calpine had scaled back on new plant development due to low demand — it has about 1,000 MW under construction — it is building a 775-megawatt power plant in Riverside County, California, for the Inland Empire Energy Center. The plant is based on General Electric's latest gas turbine technology.

Calpine sells electricity to utilities, wholesalers, and end-users, primarily through long-term contracts; the firm also trades power on the wholesale market. Other Calpine operations include construction, consulting, and management ser-

vices; turbine component manufacturing; and critical power provision for high-tech companies.

Calpine emerged from bankruptcy in 2008 (having filed for Chapter 11 protection in 2005). The company disposed of most of its natural gas reserves and gathering and transportation assets in order to focus on power generation.

EXECUTIVES

Chairman: William J. Patterson, age 48
President, CEO, and Director: Jack A. Fusco, age 47,
  $4,413,488 total compensation
EVP and CFO: Zamir Rauf, age 50,
  $1,246,885 total compensation
EVP, Chief Legal Officer, and Secretary:
  W. Thaddeus Miller, age 59,
  $2,422,289 total compensation
EVP and Chief Risk Officer: Gary M. Germeroth, age 51
EVP and Chief Commercial Officer:
  John B. (Thad) Hill III, age 42,
  $2,147,789 total compensation
SVP Government Affairs and Managing Counsel:
  Sarah Novosel
SVP Commercial Operations: Larry B. Leverett
SVP Geothermal Operations: Michael D. (Mike) Rogers,
  $4,592,447 total compensation
SVP Human Resources: Laura D. Guthrie
SVP Internal Audit and Chief Compliance Officer:
  Kevin G. McMahon, age 42
SVP Power Operations: John Adams
SVP and CIO: Dennis Fishback
SVP Government and Regulatory Affairs:
  Joseph E. (Joe) Ronan Jr.
VP Corporate Communications: Norma F. Dunn
VP, Controller, and Interim Chief Accounting Officer:
  Kenneth A. (Ken) Graves, age 45
VP Finance and Investor Relations: Andre K. Walker
Auditors: PricewaterhouseCoopers LLP

LOCATIONS

HQ: Calpine Corporation
  717 Texas Ave., Ste. 1000, Houston, TX 77002
Phone: 713-830-2000   **Fax:** 713-830-2001
Web: www.calpine.com

2009 Sales

	$ mil.	% of total
West	3,412	52
Texas	1,816	28
Southeast	778	12
North	558	8
Total	**6,564**	**100**

COMPETITORS

AEP	MidAmerican Energy
AES	Mirant
CMS Energy	PG&E Corporation
Covanta	PSEG Power
Duke Energy	RRI Energy
Edison International	Sempra Energy
Enel North America	

HISTORICAL FINANCIALS

Company Type: Public

Income Statement

FYE: December 31

	REVENUE ($ mil.)	NET INCOME ($ mil.)	NET PROFIT MARGIN	EMPLOYEES
12/09	6,564	145	2.2%	2,046
12/08	9,937	10	0.1%	2,049
12/07	7,970	2,693	33.8%	2,080
12/06	6,706	(1,765)	—	2,306
12/05	10,113	(9,939)	—	3,265
Annual Growth	**(10.2%)**	**—**	**—**	**(11.0%)**

2009 Year-End Financials

Debt ratio: 202.2% No. of shares (mil.): 445
Return on equity: 3.3% Dividends
Cash ($ mil.): 989 Yield: —
Current ratio: 1.49 Payout: —
Long-term debt ($ mil.): 8,996 Market value ($ mil.): 4,890

Stock History

NYSE: CPN

	STOCK PRICE ($) FY Close	P/E High/Low	PER SHARE ($) Earnings	Dividends	Book Value
12/09	11.00	48 15	0.31	—	10.00
12/08	7.28	1,168 318	0.02	—	9.83
Annual Growth	51.1%	—	—1,450.0%	—	1.8%

Campbell Soup

Soup means *M'm! M'm! Money!* for Campbell Soup. The company is the world's biggest soup maker; in the US its most popular selections are chicken noodle, tomato, and cream of mushroom. Campbell also makes meal kits, Franco-American canned pasta, Pace picante sauce, V8 beverages, and Pepperidge Farm baked goods (yes, it makes the Goldfish crackers you hide in your desk at work). Its Australian division produces snack foods and that Aussie favorite, Arnott's biscuits. The company has manufacturing facilities located throughout the world. In addition to North America, its principal markets are France, Germany, Belgium, and Australia; in all, Campbell's products are sold in more than 120 countries.

The company hopes to increase profits by focusing on three categories worldwide — simple meals, baked snacks, and healthy beverages. Campbell intends to increase product innovation and consumer marketing initiatives for products in the Campbell's, Swanson, Pace, Prego, Liebig Erasco, Pepperidge Farm, Goldfish, Arnott's, and V8 lines that fall under the three categories. Answering to changing consumer tastes, the company has been reducing the salt content of its foods and intends to continue to do so with some of its best-selling brands, including its iconic tomato soup, along with V8, Healthy Request, Chunky, and Goldfish products.

Challenged in quality and sales by General Mills' Progresso brand soups, Campbell has boosted the taste of its products — adding more veggies to its vegetable soup and making its cream soups creamier. The company's Away From Home unit is following customers out of the kitchen, selling soup and buns to cafeterias, fast-food restaurants, and harried consumers via the supermarket. It has also added microwaveable versions of its Chunky and Select soups.

Meanwhile, Campbell continued to expand its brand portfolio. In 2009 it acquired Ecce Panis,

a maker of artisan bread. It acquired the Wolfgang Puck soup label from Country Gourmet Foods in 2008.

In an effort to concentrate on its soup and snacks businesses, the company in 2008 sold its premium chocolate maker, Godiva, to Turkish food company Ülker. The company also sold some of its Australian salty snack brands including Cheezels, Thins, Tasty Jacks, French Fries, and Kettle Chips.

The descendants of John Dorrance, the inventor of condensed soup, own approximately 44% of Campbell.

HISTORY

Campbell Soup Company began in Camden, New Jersey, in 1869 as a canning and preserving business founded by icebox maker Abram Anderson and fruit merchant Joseph Campbell. Anderson left in 1876 and Arthur Dorrance took his place. The Dorrance family assumed control after Campbell retired in 1894.

Arthur's nephew, John Dorrance, joined Campbell in 1897. The young chemist soon found a way to condense soup by eliminating most of its water. Without the heavy bulk of water-filled cans, distribution was cheaper; Campbell products quickly spread.

In 1904 the firm introduced the Campbell Kids characters. Entering the California market in 1911, Campbell became one of the first US companies to achieve national distribution of a food brand. It bought Franco-American, the first American soup maker, in 1915.

The company's ubiquity in American kitchens made its soup can an American icon (consider Andy Warhol's celebrated 1960 print) and brought great wealth to the Dorrance family.

With a reputation for conservative management, Campbell began to diversify, acquiring V8 juice (1948), Swanson (1955), Pepperidge Farm (1961), Godiva Chocolatier (33% in 1966, full ownership in 1974), Vlasic pickles (1978), and Mrs. Paul's seafood (1982). It introduced Prego spaghetti sauce and LeMenu frozen dinners in the early 1980s.

Much of Campbell's sales growth in the 1990s came not from unit sales but from increasing its prices. John Sr.'s grandson, Bennett Dorrance, took up the role of vice chairman in 1993, becoming the first family member to take a senior executive position in 10 years.

Two years later Campbell paid $1.1 billion for Pace Foods (picante sauce) and acquired Fresh Start Bakeries (buns and muffins for McDonald's) and Homepride (popular cooking sauce in the UK).

As part of its international expansion, in 1996 the firm acquired Erasco, a top German soup maker, and Cheong Chan, a food manufacturer in Malaysia. However, back at home it sold Mrs. Paul's. In 1997 Campbell sold its Marie's salad dressing operations and bought Groupe Danone's Liebig (France's leading wet-soup brand). Also that year Dale Morrison, a relative newcomer to the firm, succeeded David Johnson as president and CEO. To reduce costs and focus on other core segments, in 1998 Campbell spun off Swanson frozen foods and Vlasic pickles into Vlasic Foods International. In 1999 Campbell redesigned its soup can labels, altering an American icon.

Morrison resigned abruptly as president and CEO in 2000; Johnson returned to the helm during the search for a permanent chief. In early 2001 Douglas Conant, previously of Nabisco Foods, joined Campbell as president and CEO.

A fresh plan was introduced to spend up to $600 million on marketing, product development, and quality upgrades (at the expense of shareholder dividends). In 2001 Campbell also bought the Batchelors, Royco, and Heisse Tasse brands of soup, as well as the OXO brand of stock cubes, from Unilever for about $900 million. The deal made Campbell the leading soup maker in Europe.

Campbell reorganized its North American business in 2004 into the following units: US Soup, Sauces, and Beverages; Campbell Away From Home, and Canada, Mexico, and Latin America; Pepperidge Farm; and Godiva Worldwide. (In response to dietary trends, the company announced that year that it was removing all trans-fatty acids from its Pepperidge Farm breads.) The company retired the Franco-American brand in 2004; products which carried the brand (most notably SpaghettiOs) now bear the Campbell brand. Also that year company chairman George M. Sherman retired and was replaced by Harvey Golub.

In 2006 Campbell sold its UK and Irish businesses to Premier Foods for about $870 million. Brands involved in the sale included Homepride sauces, OXO stock cubes, and Batchelors, McDonnells, and Erin soups.

EXECUTIVES

Chairman: Paul R. Charron, age 67
President, CEO, and Director:
Douglas R. (Doug) Conant, age 59,
$13,107,660 total compensation
SVP, CFO, and Chief Administrative Officer:
B. Craig Owens, age 55, $4,025,966 total compensation
SVP; President, North America Soup, Sauces, and Beverages: Denise M. Morrison, age 56,
$3,291,552 total compensation
SVP and Chief Strategy Officer: M. Carl Johnson III, age 61
SVP and Chief Human Resources and Communications Officer: Nancy A. Reardon, age 57
SVP Global Supply Chain: David R. White, age 54
SVP; President, Campbell International:
Larry S. McWilliams, age 54,
$3,971,862 total compensation
SVP and CIO: Joseph C. (Joe) Spagnoletti, age 45
SVP Law and Government Affairs: Ellen O. Kaden, age 57, $4,087,737 total compensation
SVP and Chief Customer Officer; President, North America Baking and Snacking: Mark Alexander, age 45
SVP Global Research and Development and Quality: George Dowdie
SVP Public Affairs: Jerry S. Buckley
VP Finance: Anthony P. DiSilvestro, age 51,
$1,942,036 total compensation
VP Investor Relations: Jennifer Driscoll, age 44
VP and Corporate Secretary: John J. Furey
President, Campbell USA: Sean Connolly, age 44
President, North America Foodservice:
Irene Chang Britt, age 46
President, Pepperidge Farm: Patrick J. (Pat) Callaghan
Senior Research Fellow External Scientific Affairs:
Chor San Khoo
Auditors: PricewaterhouseCoopers LLP

LOCATIONS

HQ: Campbell Soup Company
    1 Campbell Place, Camden, NJ 08103
Phone: 856-342-4800 **Fax:** 856-342-3878
Web: www.campbellsoup.com

2009 Sales

	$ mil.	% of total
US	5,548	73
Australia & Asia Pacific	816	11
Europe	608	8
Other	614	8
Total	**7,586**	**100**

PRODUCTS/OPERATIONS

2009 Sales

	$ mil.	% of total
US soup, sauces & beverages	3,784	50
Baking & snacking	1,846	24
International soup, sauces & beverages	1,357	18
North America foodservice	599	8
Total	**7,586**	**100**

Selected Brand Names

Domestic
  Campbell (condensed and ready-to-serve soups;
    canned pasta, gravies, and beans)
  Ecce Panis (par-baked artisan breads)
  Pace (Mexican sauces)
  Pepperidge Farm (cookies, crackers, bakery, and
    frozen products)
  Prego (pasta sauces)
  Stockpot (foodservice soups)
  Swanson (broths, stocks, and canned poultry)
  V8 and V8 Splash (juice and juice drinks)
  Wolfgang Puck (soups)
International
  Arnott's (biscuits, Australia and Asia/Pacific; salty
    snacks, Australia)
  Erasco (soups, Germany)
  Habitant (soups, Canada)
  Heisse Tasse (soups, Germany)
  Liebig (soups, France)
  Royco (soups, France)
  V8 Splash (beverages, Canada and Asia/Pacific)

Selected Subsidiaries

Arnott's Biscuits Limited (Australia)
Eugen Lacroix GmbH (Germany)
Grundstuecksverwaltungsgesellschaft GmbH (Germany)
Pepperidge Farm, Incorporated
Players Group Limited (Australia)
Royco Voedingsmiddelenfabrieken B.V. (Netherlands)
Sinalopasta S.A. de C.V. (Mexico)
Stockpot Inc.

COMPETITORS

Associated British Foods	Hormel
B&G Foods	Kellogg U.S. Snacks
Barbara's Bakery	Kraft Foods
Baxters	Lance Snacks
Bush Brothers	Morgan Foods
Canyon Creek Food	Mott's
ConAgra	Nestlé
Del Monte Foods	NORPAC
Faribault Foods	Ocean Spray
Frito-Lay	Pacific Coast Producers
General Mills	Red Gold
Golden Enterprises	Reily Foods
Hanover Foods	Renée's Gourmet Foods
Harry's Fresh Foods	Unilever
Heinz	Walkers Snack Foods

HISTORICAL FINANCIALS

Company Type: Public

Income Statement

FYE: Sunday nearest July 31

	REVENUE ($ mil.)	NET INCOME ($ mil.)	NET PROFIT MARGIN	EMPLOYEES
7/09	7,586	736	9.7%	18,700
7/08	7,998	1,165	14.6%	19,400
7/07	7,867	854	10.9%	22,500
7/06	7,343	766	10.4%	24,000
7/05	7,548	707	9.4%	24,000
Annual Growth	**0.1%**	**1.0%**	**—**	**(6.0%)**

2009 Year-End Financials

Debt ratio: 308.5%
Return on equity: 71.9%
Cash ($ mil.): 51
Current ratio: 0.95
Long-term debt ($ mil.): 2,246

No. of shares (mil.): 340
Dividends
  Yield: 3.2%
  Payout: 48.5%
Market value ($ mil.): 10,536

Stock History

NYSE: CPB

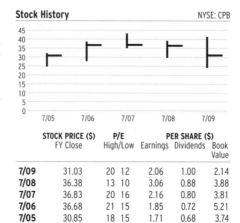

	STOCK PRICE ($) FY Close	P/E High/Low		PER SHARE ($) Earnings	Dividends	Book Value
7/09	31.03	20	12	2.06	1.00	2.14
7/08	36.38	13	10	3.06	0.88	3.88
7/07	36.83	20	16	2.16	0.80	3.81
7/06	36.68	21	15	1.85	0.72	5.21
7/05	30.85	18	15	1.71	0.68	3.74
Annual Growth	**0.1%**	**—**	**—**	**4.8%**	**10.1%**	**(13.0%)**

Capital One Financial

Capital One isn't just concerned with what's in your wallet; it's interested in your bank account as well. The company is best known as one of the largest issuers of Visa and MasterCard credit cards in the US, but it also boasts a banking network of approximately 1,000 branches, mainly in New York, New Jersey, Louisiana, and Texas; it expanded its franchise into the Washington, DC, market in 2009 by buying Chevy Chase Bank for some $475 million in cash and stock. Capital One, which serves approximately 45 million customers in the US, Canada, and the UK, also has units that offer auto financing, write home loans, sell insurance, and manage assets for institutional and high-net-worth clients.

Capital One works hard to keep the *custom* in customer. Cardholders can customize their cards' appearance, rates, and rewards. Products range from platinum and gold cards for preferred customers to secured cards for customers with poor or limited credit histories.

The company's foray into banking, which began in 2005, has allowed it to use deposits to fund its lending, rather than relying on capital markets. Though charge-off rates in Capital One's domestic credit card portfolio have hovered around 10%, the company's focus on consumer lending has shielded it somewhat from the downturn in commercial markets. Nonetheless, the company expects charge-offs in that segment to continue to increase as well. In response, Capital One has tightened underwriting standards and ramped up collections.

HISTORY

Capital One Financial is a descendant of the Bank of Virginia, which was formed in 1945. The company began issuing products similar to credit cards in 1953 and was MasterCard issuer #001. Acquisitions and mergers brought some 30 banks and several finance and mortgage companies under the bank's umbrella between 1962 and 1986, when Bank of Virginia became Signet Banking.

Signet's credit card operations had reached a million customers in 1988, when the bank hired consultants Richard Fairbank and Nigel Morris (Fairbank is now chairman and CEO) to implement their "Information-Based Strategy." Under the duo's leadership, the bank began using sophisticated data-collection methods to gather massive amounts of information on existing or prospective customers; it then used the information to design and mass-market customized products to the customer.

In 1991 — after creating an enormous database and developing sophisticated screening processes and direct-mail marketing tactics — Signet escalated the credit card wars, luring customers from its rivals with its innovative balance-transfer credit card. The card let customers of other companies transfer what they owed on higher-interest cards to a Signet card with a lower introductory rate.

The new card immediately drew imitators (by 1997 balance-transfer cards accounted for 85% of credit card solicitations). After skimming off the least risky customers, Fairbank and Morris began going after less desirable credit customers who could be charged higher rates. The result was what they call second-generation products — secured and unsecured cards with lower credit lines and higher annual percentage rates and fees for higher-risk customers.

The credit card business had grown to 5 million customers by 1994, but at a high cost to Signet, which had devoted most of its resources to finding and servicing credit card holders. That year Signet spun off its credit card business as Capital One to focus on banking. (Signet was later acquired by First Union.)

The company moved into Florida and Texas in 1995 and into Canada and the UK in 1996; that year it established its savings bank, mainly to offer products and services to its cardholders. In 1997 the company used this unit to move into deposit accounts, buying a deposit portfolio from J. C. Penney. In 1998 the company began marketing its products to such clients as immigrants and high school students (whose parents must co-sign for the card). The company also expanded in terms of products and geography, acquiring auto lender Summit Acceptance and opening a new office in Nottingham, England.

In 1999 the firm's growth continued. The company stepped up its marketing efforts and was rewarded with significant boosts to its noninterest income and customer base. The next year the company launched The Capital One Place, an Internet shopping site. In 2001 the company acquired AmeriFee, which provides loans for elective medical and dental surgery; and PeopleFirst, Inc., the nation's largest online provider of direct motor vehicle loans.

In response to industry-wide concern over subprime lending, Capital One agreed in 2002 to beef up reserves on its subprime portfolio. Also in 2002, the company's UK operations proved profitable for the first time.

The company expanded into banking in 2005 and 2006 with the acquisitions of Hibernia and North Fork Bancorporation, respectively. The deals gave it a boost in the banking sector, expanding its presence both geographically in the Northeast and in the South and turning the company into one of the top bank holding companies in the US. The $13.2 billion stock-and-cash North Fork deal gave the company more than 300 bank branches in New York, New Jersey, and Connecticut.

The 2005 purchase of New Orleans-based Hibernia was a stock-and-cash transaction valued at some $5 billion, nearly 10% less than the originally agreed-upon price. The transaction was delayed, then renegotiated, after Hurricane Katrina devastated Hibernia's home city. Hibernia, which relocated to Houston, adopted the Capital One moniker.

Capital One closed wholesale lender Green-Point Mortgage Funding, acquired as part of its acquisition of North Fork, in 2007. The unit suffered from the credit woes that have plagued the subprime mortgage industry.

EXECUTIVES

Chairman, President, and CEO:
Richard D. (Rich) Fairbank, age 59,
$6,087,365 total compensation
CFO: Gary L. Perlin, age 58,
$8,941,110 total compensation
Chief Risk Officer: Peter A. Schnall, age 46,
$6,352,862 total compensation
General Counsel and Corporate Secretary:
John G. Finneran Jr., age 60,
$6,479,013 total compensation
CIO: Robert M. Alexander, age 45
Chief Human Resources Officer: Jory A. Berson, age 39
EVP Consumer and Private Banking: Carolyn Drexel
EVP Commercial Real Estate Banking:
Richard (Rick) Lyon
EVP Brand Management: William J. (Bill) McDonald, age 53
EVP; President, Banking: J. Herbert (Herb) Boydstun, age 63
EVP and Chief Auditor: James R. Tietjen
EVP and Chief Commercial Credit Risk Officer:
Suzanne Hammett, age 54
EVP and Lead Banker, Commercial Real Estate:
William McCahill
President, Capital One Bank: Lynn A. Pike, age 53,
$7,778,797 total compensation
President, Financial Services: Sanjiv Yajnik, age 53
President, Card: Ryan Schneider, age 40
Head U.K. Business: Srinivasan Gopalan
Head Treasury Management and Merchant Services, Capital One Bank: Colleen J. Taylor
Head Capital Markets and Government Banking:
Mark Smith
Investor Relations: Jeff Norris
Treasurer: Steve Linehan
Public Relations: Diana Don
Auditors: Ernst & Young LLP

LOCATIONS

HQ: Capital One Financial Corporation
1680 Capital One Dr., McLean, VA 22102
Phone: 703-720-1000　　**Fax:** 703-720-2306
Web: www.capitalone.com

PRODUCTS/OPERATIONS

2009 Sales

	$ mil.	% of total
Interest		
Loans held for investment, including		
past-due fees	8,757.1	55
Securities available for sale	1,610.2	10
Other	297.3	2
Noninterest		
Servicing & securitizations	2,279.8	14
Service charges & other customer fees	1,997.0	13
Interchange	501.8	3
Other	507.5	3
Total	**15,950.7**	**100**

COMPETITORS

American Express	HSBC USA
AmeriCredit	JPMorgan Chase
Bank of America	PNC Financial
Citigroup	Regions Financial
Credit Acceptance	Wells Fargo
Discover	

HISTORICAL FINANCIALS

Company Type: Public

Income Statement

FYE: December 31

	ASSETS ($ mil.)	NET INCOME ($ mil.)	INCOME AS % OF ASSETS	EMPLOYEES
12/09	169,646	884	0.5%	28,000
12/08	165,914	(46)	—	25,800
12/07	150,590	1,570	1.0%	17,800
12/06	149,739	2,415	1.6%	31,800
12/05	88,701	1,809	2.0%	21,000
Annual Growth	**17.6%**	**(16.4%)**	**—**	**7.5%**

2009 Year-End Financials

Equity as % of assets: 15.7%
Return on assets: 0.5%
Return on equity: 3.5%
Long-term debt ($ mil.): 21,014
No. of shares (mil.): 457
Dividends
　Yield: 1.4%
　Payout: 70.3%
Market value ($ mil.): 17,513
Sales ($ mil.): 15,951

Stock History

NYSE: COF

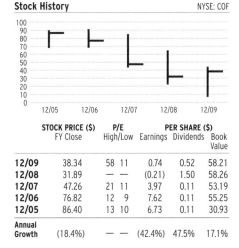

	STOCK PRICE ($) FY Close	P/E High/Low	PER SHARE ($) Earnings	Dividends	Book Value
12/09	38.34	58　11	0.74	0.52	58.21
12/08	31.89	—　—	(0.21)	1.50	58.26
12/07	47.26	21　11	3.97	0.11	53.19
12/06	76.82	12　9	7.62	0.11	55.25
12/05	86.40	13　10	6.73	0.11	30.93
Annual Growth	**(18.4%)**	**—　—**	**(42.4%)**	**47.5%**	**17.1%**

Cardinal Health

Cardinal Health seeks to deliver medicine to all points of the compass. The company is a top distributor of pharmaceuticals and other medical supplies and equipment in the US. Its pharmaceutical division provides supply chain services including prescription and over-the-counter drug distribution, while its medical division parcels out medical, laboratory, and surgical supplies. The divisions also provide logistics, consulting, and data management services. Customers include pharmacies, hospitals, doctor's offices, and other health care businesses. Cardinal Health spun off its medical equipment manufacturing and clinical technologies operations into CareFusion in 2009.

Cardinal Health completed the spinoff of about 81% of CareFusion to its shareholders in August 2009 to maximize shareholder and customer value for all of its businesses. Former Cardinal chairman and CEO Kerry Clark retired at the time of the spinoff, with George Barrett (the former leader of the distribution operations) taking over Clark's roles.

Pharmaceutical distribution has historically accounted for about 85% of Cardinal Health's sales, with pharmacies accounting for the largest chunk of Cardinal's customer revenues.

CVS and Walgreen each account for about 20% of the company's sales. The Cardinal Health Pharmaceutical division operates distribution facilities and nuclear pharmacy labs (for the distribution of medical imaging agents) across the US; it also has limited operations in Mexico (nuclear labs) and the UK (generic drugs). The division also includes the Cardinal Health Pharmacy Management business, the Medicine Shoppe retail pharmacy subsidiary, and a specialty pharmacy unit that distributes plasma and intensive care therapies.

The smaller Cardinal Health Medical distribution division offers branded and private-label supplies, including fluid collection devices, scientific laboratory equipment, and general hospital and physician practice supplies in Canada and the US. It also assembles procedure kits and makes exam gloves and surgical drapes.

Cardinal has expanded through acquisitions of companies and products within all of its operating segments. Since 1980 it has acquired more than 50 companies. In 2007 the company dropped about $1.5 billion on medical equipment manufacturer VIASYS Healthcare. The following year the company added to its infection prevention line by acquiring private health care firm Enturia, maker of the ChloraPrep brand line of skin disinfectant products.

In 2010 Cardinal bolstered its specialty pharmaceutical services by purchasing Healthcare Solutions Holding in a deal worth roughly $670 million. The company provides tools and services that include product data and claims management help for specialty care industry doctors, payers, and drug makers.

On the paring side Cardinal Health sold its Pharmaceutical Technologies and Services division, which offered drug delivery systems, packaging services, and development services, to The Blackstone Group for $3.3 billion in 2007.

HISTORY

Cardinal Health harks back to Cardinal Foods, a food wholesaler named for Ohio's state bird. In 1971 Robert Walter, then 26 and with the ink still fresh on his Harvard MBA, acquired Cardinal in a leveraged buyout. He hoped to grow Cardinal by acquisitions but was frustrated when he found that the food distribution industry was already highly consolidated.

In 1980 Cardinal moved into pharmaceuticals distribution with the acquisition of Zanesville. It went public in 1983 as Cardinal Distribution, and Walter began looking for more acquisitions. Cardinal soon expanded nationwide by swallowing other distributors. During the 1980s these purchases included two pharmaceuticals distributors headquartered in New York and a Massachusetts-based pharmaceuticals and food distributor. In 1988 Cardinal sold its food group, including Midland Grocery and Mr. Moneysworth, to Roundy's and narrowed its focus to pharmaceuticals.

Drug distributors joined the rest of the pharmaceutical industry in its rush toward consolidation during the 1990s. Cardinal's acquisitions in those years included Ohio Valley-Clarksburg (1990, the Mid-Atlantic), Chapman Drug Co. (1991, Tennessee), PRN Services (1993, Michigan), Solomons Co. (1993, Georgia), Humiston-Keeling (1994, Illinois), and Behrens (1994, Texas).

One of Cardinal's most important acquisitions during this period was its cash purchase of Whitmire Distribution in 1994. When Cardinal bought it, Whitmire was the US's #6 drug wholesaler;

the purchase bumped Cardinal up to #3. At that time the company changed its name to Cardinal Health and Melburn Whitmire became Cardinal's vice chairman.

In 1995 Cardinal made its biggest acquisition yet when it purchased St. Louis-based Medicine Shoppe International, the US's largest franchisor of independent retail pharmacies. Founded by two St. Louis obstetricians in 1970, the Medicine Shoppe had 987 US outlets and 107 abroad at the time of its purchase by Cardinal.

Over the next few years Cardinal continued to grow through acquisitions, including automatic drug-dispensing system maker Pyxis, pharmaceutical packaging company PCI Services, and pharmacy management services company Owen Healthcare (now Cardinal Health Pharmacy Management).

In 1998, however, plans to acquire Bergen Brunswig were blocked by the Federal Trade Commission, along with rival McKesson's bid to buy AmeriSource Health. (AmeriSource later became AmerisourceBergen after boosting itself into the top drug-distributor ranks by purchasing Bergen Brunswig.) This did not deter Cardinal from its strategy; it acquired surgical equipment distribution company Allegiance Healthcare about a year later.

In 2001 Cardinal purchased pharmaceuticals distributor Bindley Western, and it bought contract drug developer Magellan Labs the following year. The company made several acquisitions in 2003, including UK contract manufacturer Intercare Group, radiopharmaceuticals firm Syncor International, and pharmacy franchiser Medicap. It made a $2 billion purchase of IV medication safety products maker Alaris Medical Systems in 2004.

Founder Robert Walter stepped aside as CEO in 2006 to make room for Kerry Clark to take over the role; the following year Clark assumed the founder's chairman role as well. Also in 2006 the company acquired generic drug distributor ParMed Pharmaceuticals.

EXECUTIVES

Chairman, President, and CEO: George S. Barrett, age 55, $5,246,159 total compensation
CFO: Jeffrey W. (Jeff) Henderson, age 44, $3,774,474 total compensation
Chief Human Resources Officer: Carole S. Watkins, age 48
Chief Customer Officer: Mark Rosenbaum
EVP Strategy and Corporate Development: Mark Blake, age 38
EVP, General Counsel, and Secretary: Stephen T. (Steve) Falk, age 44
EVP and CIO: Patricia B. (Patty) Morrison, age 50
EVP Strategic Sourcing: Frank Segrave
EVP Operations, Pharmaceutical Segment: Jon Giacomin
EVP Operations, Medical Segment: Mike Duffy
EVP Corporate Affairs and Executive Communication: Shelley Bird
EVP Integrated Provider Sales: Anthony (Tony) Caprio
President, Medical Supply Chain Products and Services, Medical: Tom Kapfer
President and General Manager, Nuclear and Specialty Pharmacy: John Rademacher
President, Presource and Clinical Apparel, Patient Protection (CAPP): Steve Inacker
President, International: Rudy Mareel, age 47
CEO, Pharmaceutical Segment: Michael C. (Mike) Kaufmann, age 47
CEO, Medical Segment: Michael (Mike) Lynch
Auditors: Ernst & Young LLP

LOCATIONS

HQ: Cardinal Health, Inc.
7000 Cardinal Place, Dublin, OH 43017
Phone: 614-757-5000
Web: www.cardinal.com

2009 Sales

	$ mil.	% of total
US	97,849.1	98
International	1,663.3	2
Total	**99,512.4**	**100**

PRODUCTS/OPERATIONS

2009 Sales

	$ mil.	% of total
Healthcare Supply Chain Services	95,717.9	94
Clinical Technologies & Services	4,588.5	5
Other	1,018.3	1
Adjustments	(1,812.3)	—
Total	**99,512.4**	**100**

2009 Healthcare Supply Chain Sales

	% of total
Pharmaceutical distribution	91
Medical distribution	9
Total	**100**

Selected Subsidiaries and Divisions

Cardinal Health Medical (formerly Cardinal Healthcare Supply Chain Services — Medical; Endura, Presource, SP Lab)
Cardinal Health Pharmaceutical (formerly Cardinal Healthcare Supply Chain Services — Pharmaceutical)
Beckloff Associates, Inc.
Cardinal Health Pharmacy Management
Leader Drugstores, Inc.
SpecialtyScripts, LLC
Medicine Shoppe International, Inc.
Medicap Pharmacies Incorporated

COMPETITORS

AmerisourceBergen
CVS Caremark
Express Scripts
Franz Haniel
H. D. Smith Wholesale Drug
Henry Schein
McKesson
Medco Health
Medline Industries
Moore Medical
Omnicare
Owens & Minor
PharMerica
PSS World Medical
Quality King
Rite Aid
Thermo Fisher Scientific
Walgreen

HISTORICAL FINANCIALS

Company Type: Public

Income Statement

FYE: June 30

	REVENUE ($ mil.)	NET INCOME ($ mil.)	NET PROFIT MARGIN	EMPLOYEES
6/09	99,512	1,152	1.2%	29,600
6/08	91,091	1,301	1.4%	47,600
6/07	86,852	1,931	2.2%	43,500
6/06	81,364	1,000	1.2%	55,000
6/05	74,911	1,051	1.4%	55,000
Annual Growth	**7.4%**	**2.3%**	**—**	**(14.3%)**

2009 Year-End Financials

Debt ratio: 37.6%
Return on equity: 14.0%
Cash ($ mil.): 1,848
Current ratio: 1.39
Long-term debt ($ mil.): 3,280
No. of shares (mil.): 362
Dividends
  Yield: 2.6%
  Payout: 17.6%
Market value ($ mil.): 7,943

Stock History

NYSE: CAH

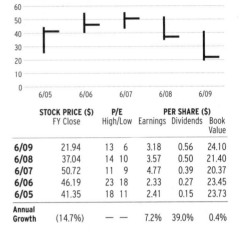

	STOCK PRICE ($) FY Close	P/E High/Low		PER SHARE ($) Earnings	Dividends	Book Value
6/09	21.94	13	6	3.18	0.56	24.10
6/08	37.04	14	10	3.57	0.50	21.40
6/07	50.72	11	9	4.77	0.39	20.37
6/06	46.19	23	18	2.33	0.27	23.45
6/05	41.35	18	11	2.41	0.15	23.73
Annual Growth	**(14.7%)**	**—**	**—**	**7.2%**	**39.0%**	**0.4%**

Cargill, Incorporated

Cargill may be private, but it's highly visible. The agribusiness giant, the US's largest private corporation, has operations in 70 countries. It has five main business segments — Agriculture Services; Food Ingredients and Applications; Industrial, Origination and Processing; Risk Management and Financial; and Industrial (salt, steel, and fertilizer). Cargill's customers include food, beverage, industrial, pharmaceutical, and personal care product makers, as well as farmers and foodservice providers.

Through its five segments, the company offers a plethora of diversified operations and products, including grain, cotton, sugar, petroleum, and financial trading; food processing; futures brokering; health and pharmaceutical products; animal feed and crop protection; and industrial products such as biofuels, oils and lubricants, starches, salt, and fertilizer for crop and livestock farmers. The company is one of the leading grain producers in the US, and its Excel unit (part of Cargill Meat Solutions) is one of the top US meatpackers. Cargill is also a global supplier of oils, syrups, flour, and other products used in food processing. Cargill's more familiar brands include Diamond Crystal (salt), Wilbur (cocoa and chocolate), Honeysuckle White (poultry), Sterling Silver (fresh pork), and Nutrena (dog and cat food). Cargill is also a major US supplier for McDonald's, providing the burger behemoth with eggs, oils, sauces, and beef products.

The company has a partnership with Coca-Cola to produce and market the sweetener Rebiana, which is said to sweeten without adding calories, while at the same time producing a natural flavor. It is made from the South American herb stevia. Rebiana received regulatory approval in the US for general use in food and beverages at the end of 2008.

Expanding its retail and foodservice meat products segment, Cargill acquired turkey processor Willow Brook Foods in 2008. The deal came a year after the company introduced Meadowlands Farms ground beef at food retailers throughout the US, Cargill's first product in the nationally branded hamburger market.

In 2009 Cargill founded a joint venture with Sugar Growers and Refiners and Imperial Sugar to construct and operate a new 3,100 ton-per-day cane-sugar refinery in Gramercy, Louisiana. The venture, called Louisiana Sugar Refining, is 33% owned by each partner.

Cargill is looking for additional growth opportunities in the world of bio-plastics. It reclaimed full control of its NatureWorks subsidiary in 2009, acquiring the 50% stake of former joint venture partner Teijin. NatureWorks makes commercial biopolymers, focusing on applications in eco-friendly products.

Cargill sold its Brazilian pork and poultry operation, Seara Alimentos, to one of Brazil's top beef companies, Marfrig, in 2009.

HISTORY

William W. Cargill founded Cargill in 1865 when he bought his first grain elevator in Conover, Iowa. He and his brother Sam bought grain elevators all along the Southern Minnesota Railroad in 1870, just as Minnesota was becoming an important shipping route. Sam and a third brother, James, expanded the elevator operations while William worked with the railroads to monopolize transport of grain to markets and coal to farmers.

Around the turn of the century, William's son William S. invested in a number of ill-fated projects. William W. found that his name had been used to finance the projects; shortly afterward, he died of pneumonia. Cargill's creditors pressed for repayment, which threatened to bankrupt the company. John MacMillan, William W.'s son-in-law, took control and rebuilt Cargill. It had recovered by 1916 but lost its holdings in Mexico and Canada. MacMillan opened offices in New York (1922) and Argentina (1929), expanding grain trading and transport operations.

In 1945 Cargill bought Nutrena Mills (animal feed) and entered soybean processing; corn processing began soon after and grew with the demand for corn sweeteners. In 1954 Cargill benefited when the US began making loans to help developing countries buy American grain. Subsidiary Tradax, established in 1955, became one of the largest grain traders in Europe. A decade later, Cargill began trading sugar by purchasing sugar and molasses in the Philippines and selling them abroad.

Cargill made its finances public in 1973 (as a requirement for its unsuccessful takeover bid of Missouri Portland Cement), revealing it to be one of the US's largest companies, with $5.2 billion in sales. In the 1970s it expanded into coal, steel, and waste disposal and became a major force in metals processing, beef, and salt production.

To placate family heirs who wanted to take Cargill public, CEO Whitney MacMillan, grandson of John, created an employee stock plan in 1991 that allowed shareholders to cash in their shares. He also boosted dividends and reorganized the board, reducing the family's control. MacMillan retired in 1995 and non-family member Ernest Micek became CEO and chairman.

The firm bought Akzo Nobel's North American salt operations in 1997, becoming the #2 US salt company. Micek resigned as CEO that year and was replaced by Warren Staley. Also in 1999 Cargill fessed up to misappropriating some ge-

netic seed material from rival Pioneer Hi-Bred, killing the $650 million sale of its North American seed assets to Germany's AgrEvo.

In 2004 the company announced the discovery of genetic markers in cattle that predict whether or not a specific steer will produce good-tasting meat. Also that year Cargill combined its crop-nutrition segment with phosphate fertilizer maker IMC Global to form a new, publicly traded company called Mosaic. Cargill owns about 66% of the company. This is the first time privately held Cargill has ventured into the public sector.

In 2005 Cargill acquired The Dow Chemical Company's interest in the two companies' 50-50 plastics business joint venture, Cargill Dow LLC, and renamed it NatureWorks. It also broke ground for its first oil refinery in Russia.

Cargill's Meadowlands Farms was forced to recall meat products twice in 2007 because of *E. coli* contamination. The first involved more than 800,000 pounds of frozen beef patties. More than 1 million pounds of fresh ground beef was involved in the second recall.

Longtime CEO Warren Staley retired in 2007. Cargill's board chose a 33-year company veteran, president and COO Gregory Page, to replace Staley. Page stated that he hopes to make Cargill, an historically tight-lipped company, more visible. Later that year Page was appointed chairman of the company.

EXECUTIVES

Chairman and CEO: Gregory R. (Greg) Page, age 58
SVP and CFO: David W. (Dave) MacLennan, age 51
SVP: Paul D. Conway
SVP: Richard D. Frasch, age 55
SVP: William A. (Bill) Buckner
Corporate VP, General Counsel, and Corporate Secretary: Steven C. Euller
Corporate VP and Treasurer: Jayme D. Olson
Corporate VP and Controller: Kimberly A. Lattu
Corporate VP, Corporate Affairs: Bonnie E. Raquet
Corporate VP and Controller: Galen G. Johnson, age 63
Corporate VP, Research and Development: Christopher P. (Chris) Mallett
Corporate VP and CIO: Rita J. Heise
Corporate VP, Operations: Tom Hayes
Corporate VP, Human Resources: Peter Vrijsen, age 55
President, Cargill Beef: John Keating
President, Cargill Meat Solutions and President, Cargill Case Ready Beef: Jody Horner
President, Cargill Energy, Transportation, and Industrial Group: Thomas (Tom) Intrator
Auditors: KPMG LLP

LOCATIONS

HQ: Cargill, Incorporated
   15407 McGinty Rd. West, Wayzata, MN 55391
Phone: 952-742-7575   **Fax:** 952-742-7393
Web: www.cargill.com

PRODUCTS/OPERATIONS

Selected Brands

Animal Nutrition
   ACCO Feeds (poultry and rabbit feed, US only)
   Loyall (pet food)
   Nutrena (animal feed)
   Purina (licensed from Nestlé Purina PetCare Company, non-US only)
   Right Now (minerals)
   Sportsman's Choice (deer, elk, game, and bird feed)
Business-to-Business Ingredients
   Clear Valley (canola oil)
   CoroWise (cholesterol reducer)
   GrainWise (wheat aleurone)
   MaizeWise (corn products)
   Progressive Baker (flours)
   Regenasure (glucosamine)
   Sunny Fresh (egg products)

Construction
   Agri-Pure Gold (vegetable oils)
   Oxi-Cure (low-VOC oils and coalescing agents)
   Prolia (soy flour)
Consumer Products
   Diamond Crystal (salt, US)
   Honeysuckle White (turkey, US)
   Sterling Silver (meats, US)
   Liza (oils and dressings, Brazil)
   Truvia (stevia-based sweetener, US)
   NatureFresh (cooking oil, India)
   Untdelemn Bunica (cooking oil, Romania)
   Empacadora Perry (meat, Guatemala)
Foam/Polyurethane Manufacturing
   BiOH (soy-based polyols)
Functional Fluids and Lubricants
   Agri-Pure (base oils)
   Agri-Pure Gold (vegetable oils)
Winter Road Maintenance
   AccuBrine (automated brine maker)
   CG90 (non-phosphate anti-corrosive deicer)
   CG-90 Original (anti-corrosive deicer)
   CG-90 Surface Saver (anti-corrosive deicer)
   ClearLane (enhanced deicer)
   Hydro Melt (liquid deicer)
   SafeLane (anti-icing surface overlay)

COMPETITORS

Abengoa Bioenergy	Kraft Foods
ADM	Lake Area Corn Processors
Ag Processing Inc.	Land O'Lakes
Amalgamated Sugar	Land O'Lakes Purina Feed
American Animal Health	Louis Dreyfus
American Steel	Commodities
Asia Food & Properties	Mars, Incorporated
Aventine	Mars Petcare
Badger State Ethanol	Merck
BASF SE	Merisant
Bayer Animal Health	Michigan Sugar Company
Beef Products	Monsanto Company
BioFuel Energy	Morton Salt
Blyth	Nippon Steel
Bunge Limited	Nisshin Oillio
Butterball	Nordzucker
C&H Sugar	North American Salt
Casco	Northern Growers
CGC	Nucor
Chaparral Energy	NutraSweet
CHS	Omega Protein
COFCO	Pacific Ethanol
Coleman Natural Foods	Palm Restaurants
Corn Products	Perdue Incorporated
International	Pfizer
CSM	Phibro Animal Health
Cumberland Packing	PPB Group
Danisco A/S	Raeford Farms
Del Monte Foods	Royal Canin
Dow Chemical	Royal Schouten Group
DuPont	Südzucker
DuPont Agriculture &	Sara Lee North American
Nutrition	Retail
Eight in One Pet Products	Sime Darby
Ellison Meat Company	SMBSC
Eurosugar	Smithfield Foods
Evialis	Sterling Sugars
Faultless Starch	Sugar Cane Growers
Florida Crystals	Cooperative of Florida
General Mills	Sugar Foods
Goodman Fielder	SYSCO
Hershey	Tate & Lyle
Hill's Pet Nutrition	Teva Pharmaceuticals
Holly Sugar	Tyson Foods
Iams	Tyson Fresh Meats
Imperial Sugar	United Salt
IOI Corporation	United States Steel
JBS	U.S. Sugar
Jennie-O	Viterra Inc.
J-OIL MILLS	Western Beef
King Arthur Flour	Western Sugar Cooperative
Koch Industries, Inc.	Yankee Candle

HISTORICAL FINANCIALS

Company Type: Private

Income Statement

FYE: May 31

	REVENUE ($ mil.)	NET INCOME ($ mil.)	NET PROFIT MARGIN	EMPLOYEES
5/09	116,579	3,334	2.9%	159,000
5/08	120,439	3,951	3.3%	160,000
5/07	88,266	2,343	2.7%	158,000
5/06	75,208	1,537	2.0%	149,000
5/05	71,066	2,103	3.0%	124,000
Annual Growth	13.2%	12.2%	—	6.4%

Net Income History

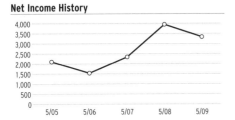

Carlisle Companies

Commercial manufacturing group Carlisle Companies is nothing if not diverse. Through dozens of subsidiaries, the company makes an array of products including roofing materials, specialty wheels and tires, truck trailers, foodservice equipment, and wire and cable assemblies for aerospace and industrial clients. Representing about half of the group's sales, the construction materials segment makes rubber roofing systems as well as rigid foam insulation, waterproofing, and protective coatings. Its next-largest segment, engineered transportation, makes tires, wheels, industrial brakes, and power transmission belts. Carlisle sells its products globally, but the US accounts for around 90% of sales.

The group has shuffled its operations in recent years to keep its competitive edge. Part of that shuffling has included winding down its heavy-duty braking system manufacturing business — a one-time sales staple for Carlisle that suffered from declines in sales due to industry forces. In 2009 the company exited the on-highway friction and brake shoe business and dissolved its Motion Control Industries subsidiary. It consolidated several of its manufacturing and distribution facilities and folded weaker operations into stronger ones. Carlisle sought a buyer for its power transmission belt business but instead combined those operations with its tire and wheel operations to create the new engineered transportation segment.

Carlisle is no stranger to adjusting its operations. The group has acquired more than 50 companies since 1990, and it continues to grow through bolt-on acquisitions and joint ventures. Carlisle typically focuses on niche markets where it can gain a leading market share, and constantly tweaks its mix of businesses to optimize value.

In 2008, for example, Carlisle acquired two more companies: Dinex International, which makes foodservice equipment used in the health care and other institutional industries; and Carlyle Incorporated, which provides aerospace and network interconnections equipment. The following year the company bought Jerrik, a maker of specialty filter connectors.

HISTORY

Charles Moomy founded Carlisle Tire and Rubber Company in Carlisle, Pennsylvania, in 1917 to make rubber inner tubes for auto tires. The company debuted its full-molded inner tube in 1926. Success followed until the stock market crash of 1929.

Carlisle limped through the Depression with help from the New Deal's Industrial Loan Act. However, Moomy was forced to turn his stock over to the Federal Reserve Bank of Philadelphia, which became Carlisle's biggest shareholder. Pharis Tire and Rubber Company acquired Carlisle from the Federal Reserve Bank in 1943. Upon Pharis' liquidation in 1949, Carlisle stock was distributed to Pharis stockholders and company officials. Carlisle Corporation was formed, and it bought Dart Truck (mining and construction trucks).

Carlisle continued to diversify. During the 1960s it added jar sealant rings, roofing materials, automotive accessories, and tires for recreational vehicles. It moved to Cincinnati in the 1970s and acquired foodservice product and computer peripherals companies.

In the 1980s, unable to compete with the big car tire makers, Carlisle focused on tires for smaller vehicles (motorcycles and snowblowers), and it sold car tires to the auto aftermarket. The company restructured in 1986 as Carlisle Companies Incorporated and moved to Syracuse, New York, the next year.

Carlisle bought Brookpark Plastics (plastic compression molding) and Off-Highway Braking Systems (from B.F. Goodrich Aerospace) in 1990, gaining factories in Europe and South America. After taking a hit in the early 1990s recession, Carlisle consolidated operations and sold its communications and electronics industries. With its 1993 purchase of Goodyear's roofing products business, Carlisle became the US's top maker of nonresidential roofing products.

Since the mid-1990s Carlisle has increased its acquisitions, buying Sparta Brush (specialty brushes and cleaning tools), Trail King Industries (specialized low-bed trailers), Ti-Brook (trailers and dump bodies), Walker Stainless (trailers and in-plant processing equipment), Intero (steel and aluminum wheel rims), and Unique Wheel (steel wheels). The company also bought the engineered plastics unit of Johnson Controls and Hartstone (ceramic tableware, cookware, and decorative products).

Carlisle acquired several small tire and wheel makers in 1997. The next year the company bought Vermont Electromagnetics and Quality Microwave Interconnects, both makers of specialty cable assemblies; Industrial Tire Products, an industrial and recreational vehicle tire distributor; and Hardcast Europe (adhesives and sealants, the Netherlands).

Carlisle stopped making refrigerated marine shipping containers in 1999, and its Carlisle Tire & Wheel Company subsidiary sold its surfacing products division. In 2000 Carlisle bought Damrow Denmark and Damrow USA (cheese-making equipment) and Red River Manufacturing (custom trailers and paving equipment).

In 2001 the company moved to North Carolina, and the deal-making continued apace with the acquisitions of Wincanton Engineering (food- and beverage-processing equipment) and EcoStar (roofing). Carlisle also bought Mark IV Industries' Dayco industrial power transmission business for about $150 million. Carlisle acquired the MiraDri division (waterproofing) from Nicolon Corporation in late 2002. The following year the group added Flo-Pac, a broom and cleaning tool manufacturer, to its General Industry segment.

In early 2003 it sold its European-based power transmission belt operations to Italy-based Megadyne and closed a plastic automotive parts plant in Erie-Bundy Park, Pennsylvania. Carlisle sold Carlisle Engineered Products to the Reserve Group in 2005.

It sold Carlisle Process Systems (cheese-making and food-processing equipment) to Tetra Laval subsidiary Tetra Pak in 2006.

The group was affected by economic trends, including the near-collapse of the US automotive industry and a widespread slowdown in construction. In 2007, the company closed facilities in Virginia and Wisconsin in the US and a third facility in Wales. It also began actively reducing its inventory. However, it boosted its construction materials segment — its biggest — with the $160 million acquisition of insulation company Insulfoam.

EXECUTIVES

Chairman, President, and CEO: David A. Roberts, age 62, $4,747,553 total compensation
VP, CFO, and Secretary: Steven J. Ford, age 50, $1,219,932 total compensation
VP, Corporate Development: Scott C. Selbach, age 54
VP, Carlisle Operating System: Michael D. Voigt
President, Construction Materials: John W. Altmeyer, age 50, $2,043,842 total compensation
President, Carlisle Interconnect Technologies: John E. Berlin
President, Trail King Industries: Carol P. Lowe, age 44, $1,166,096 total compensation
President, Engineered Transportation Solutions: Fred A. Sutter, age 49, $1,457,504 total compensation
President, Carlisle Industrial Brake and Friction: D. Christian (Chris) Koch, age 45, $1,401,156 total compensation
President, Asia-Pacific: Kevin G. Forster, age 56
President, Carlisle FoodService Products: David M. (Dave) Shannon
Auditors: Ernst & Young LLP

LOCATIONS

HQ: Carlisle Companies Incorporated
13925 Ballantyne Corporate Place, Ste. 400
Charlotte, NC 28277
Phone: 704-501-1100   **Fax:** 704-501-1190
Web: www.carlisle.com

2009 Sales

	$ mil.	% of total
US	2,086.5	88
Canada	108.1	4
Europe	92.2	4
Latin America	30.3	1
Asia	25.8	1
Middle East	22.1	1
Australia, Africa & other	14.5	1
Total	**2,379.5**	**100**

PRODUCTS/OPERATIONS

2009 Sales

	$ mil.	% of total
Construction materials	1,125.9	47
Engineered transportation	708.1	30
Foodservice products	243.6	10
Interconnect technologies	180.5	8
Specialty products	121.4	5
Total	**2,379.5**	**100**

Selected Products

Construction materials
  Roofing accessories
    Coatings
    Foam insulation panels
    Waterproofings
  Roofing systems
    Rubber (EPDM)
    TPO single-ply
Engineered transportation products
  Industrial brake and friction
    Off-highway braking systems
    On-highway brake actuation systems
    Power transmission belt products
    Specialty friction products
  Tires and wheels
    Assemblies
    Non-automotive rubber tires
    Roll-formed steel wheels
    Steel-belted radial trailer tires
Foodservice products
  Cookware
  Lighting equipment
  Table coverings
Interconnect technologies
  Cable assemblies
  Connectors
    Cable
    Fiber optic
    RF/microwave
    Specialty filter
    Wire
Specialty products
  Dump trailers
  Multi-unit trailers
  Open-deck trailers
  Refrigerated truck bodies

Selected Subsidiaries

Aztec Holdings (Denmark)
Carlisle Coatings & Waterproofing Incorporated
Carlisle Corporation
Carlisle Engineered Transportation Solutions, Inc.
  (formerly Carlisle Tire & Wheel Company)
Carlisle Europe BV (The Netherlands)
Carlisle Financial Services BV (The Netherlands)
Carlisle FoodService Products Incorporated
Carlisle Intangible Company
Carlisle Plastic Products (Changzhou) Co., Ltd.
Carlisle Roofing Systems, Inc.
Carlisle Shanghai Trading Co., Ltd
Carlyle Holding Inc. (dba Carlisle Interconnect
  Technologies, Inc.)
CFS Property, Inc.
Electronic Cable Specialists, Inc.
Hunter Panels, LLC
Trail King Industries, Inc.

COMPETITORS

Atlas Roofing	Johns Manville
Bridgestone	Michelin
CertainTeed	Pirelli
Dover Corp.	Southwire
Evergreen Marine	Sumitomo Electric
General Cable	Superior Essex
G-I Holdings	Wabash National
Harvey Industries	

HISTORICAL FINANCIALS
Company Type: Public

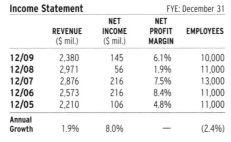

Income Statement
FYE: December 31

	REVENUE ($ mil.)	NET INCOME ($ mil.)	NET PROFIT MARGIN	EMPLOYEES
12/09	2,380	145	6.1%	10,000
12/08	2,971	56	1.9%	11,000
12/07	2,876	216	7.5%	13,000
12/06	2,573	216	8.4%	11,000
12/05	2,210	106	4.8%	11,000
Annual Growth	1.9%	8.0%	—	(2.4%)

2009 Year-End Financials

Debt ratio: 12.8%
Return on equity: 12.5%
Cash ($ mil.): 96
Current ratio: 2.66
Long-term debt ($ mil.): 156

No. of shares (mil.): 61
Dividends
  Yield: 1.8%
  Payout: 26.9%
Market value ($ mil.): 2,089

Stock History
NYSE: CSL

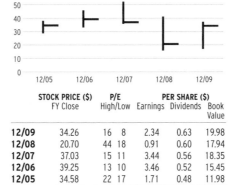

	STOCK PRICE ($) FY Close	P/E High	P/E Low	PER SHARE ($) Earnings	PER SHARE ($) Dividends	PER SHARE ($) Book Value
12/09	34.26	16	8	2.34	0.63	19.98
12/08	20.70	44	18	0.91	0.60	17.94
12/07	37.03	15	11	3.44	0.56	18.35
12/06	39.25	13	10	3.46	0.52	15.45
12/05	34.58	22	17	1.71	0.48	11.98
Annual Growth	(0.2%)	—	—	8.2%	7.0%	13.7%

CarMax, Inc.

To the greatest extent possible, CarMax helps drivers find late-model used autos. The US's largest specialty used-car retailer buys, reconditions, and sells cars and light trucks at about 100 superstores in 25 US states, mainly in the Southeast and Midwest; CarMax also operates several new-car franchises and sells older vehicles at in-store auctions at about 50 of its superstores. CarMax sells vehicles that are generally under six years old with less than 60,000 miles. CarMax also sells older cars and trucks with higher mileage through its ValuMax program. The company's website lets customers search CarMax outlets nationwide for a particular model. Its CarMax Auto Finance unit offers financing.

Its financing activities have been a profit center for the firm, which recently began offering loans to customers at rates of 9% or more. Also, with an average selling price of more than $17,000 for one of its late-model used vehicles, and its "no-haggle" pricing policy, CarMax realizes a hefty $2,000 gross profit on each sale. Despite sales of more than 350,000 vehicles a year, CarMax has just 2.5% of the late-model used-car market.

CarMax's used-vehicle niche has been a buffer for the firm during the deep recession and credit crisis, which have negatively impacted both new- and used-car sales. Sales of the company's used vehicles rebounded (up 9%) in 2009 vs. 2008, after falling 14% in the previous fiscal year. While the number of vehicles sold at auction also rose, new car sales declined in 2009 for the fourth consecutive year. Indeed, to make room for more used-car sales, which account for over 80% of the company's business, CarMax has divested half of its new-car franchises and may sell more. New vehicles account for only 2% of CarMax's retail vehicle unit sales.

Historically fast-growing CarMax, which increased its store count from 58 locations in 2005 to 100 in 2009, put the brakes on new superstore openings in late 2008 after a dramatic drop-off in sales. However, given the recent improvement in the economy, credit markets, and retail scene, the used-car dealer plans to begin growing again with three new locations slated to open in 2010, followed by between three and five stores in 2011, and as many as 10 new superstores in 2012. With a presence in only about 45 markets nationwide, CarMax feels it has plenty of room to grow. Also, in the wake of the worst financial crisis since the Great Depression, CarMax believes that many newly thrifty consumers will buy a used vehicle when the time comes to replace their current ride.

HISTORY

Looking for new retailing channels to conquer, in 1993 Circuit City Stores began test-driving the used-car concept when it opened its first CarMax outlet in Richmond, Virginia. Richard Sharp, who was named Circuit City's CEO in 1986, became the chairman and CEO for CarMax Group as well.

A pioneer in the car industry, CarMax offered computerized shopping, play areas for children, and no-haggle pricing. Competing car dealers criticized CarMax's TV ads, which tarred rivals with a stereotype of sleaze and greed. Some dealers disputed CarMax's low-price claims.

The company extended its geographical reach into North Carolina, Georgia, and Florida in 1995 and 1996. In 1996 CarMax began selling new cars at an Atlanta store.

No longer riding it as a test-drive, Circuit City spun off about 25% of CarMax to the public in 1997. The following year it moved into Illinois.

Also in 1998 CarMax bought a new-car Toyota dealership in Maryland and the multi-make Mauro Auto Mall of Wisconsin. It entered South Carolina that year and added a Georgia Mitsubishi dealership in early 1999. The company acquired two new-car franchises in the competitive Los Angeles market in mid-1999.

In mid-2001 Circuit City reduced its share in CarMax from 75% to about 65%, having sold some stock to help remodel the company's electronics stores. Circuit City then spun off CarMax as an independent company in October 2002. President Austin Ligon took the CEO title at that time (Sharp remained chairman).

CarMax opened five superstores, but sold four new-car dealerships in 2003.

Ligon retired as CEO in June 2006. He was succeeded by EVP Thomas J. Folliard, a 13-year company veteran, who was named president, CEO, and a director of the company.

EXECUTIVES

Chairman: William R. Tiefel, age 76
President, CEO, and Director:
Thomas J. (Tom) Folliard, age 45,
$5,304,112 total compensation
EVP and Chief Administrative Officer:
Michael K. (Mike) Dolan, age 60,
$2,599,517 total compensation
EVP, CFO, Corporate Secretary, and Director:
Keith D. Browning, age 57,
$2,874,577 total compensation
SVP Marketing and Strategy: Joseph S. Kunkel, age 47,
$1,914,271 total compensation
SVP, General Counsel, and Secretary: Eric M. Margolin,
age 56, $1,420,186 total compensation
SVP and CIO: Richard M. Smith, age 52,
$864,800 total compensation
SVP Sales: William C. (Cliff) Wood Jr., age 43
SVP Finance: Tom Reedy
SVP Merchandising: William D. (Bill) Nash
SVP CarMax Auto Finance: Angela Chattin
VP Investor Relations: Katherine Kenny
VP Construction and Facilities: Dan Bickett
VP Marketing: Rob Sorenson
VP Consumer Finance: Robert W. (Rob) Mitchell
VP Human Resources: Scott A. Rivas
VP Service Operations: Edwin J. (Ed) Hill
VP Store Administration: Fred Wilson
VP and Controller: Kim D. Orcutt
VP Information Technology: Barbara B. Harvill
VP Advertising: Laura R. Donahue
Manager Investor Relations: Celeste Gunter
Auditors: KPMG LLP

LOCATIONS

HQ: CarMax, Inc.
12800 Tuckahoe Creek Pkwy.
Richmond, VA 23238
Phone: 804-747-0422   **Fax:** 804-217-6819
Web: www.carmax.com

2010 Stores

	No.
California	13
Texas	12
Florida	10
North Carolina	8
Virginia	8
Illinois	6
Georgia	5
Maryland	4
Tennessee	4
Arizona	3
South Carolina	3
Wisconsin	3
Alabama	2
Connecticut	2
Indiana	2
Kansas	2
Nevada	2
Ohio	2
Oklahoma	2
Colorado	1
Kentucky	1
Mississippi	1
Missouri	1
Nebraska	1
New Mexico	1
Utah	1
Total	**100**

PRODUCTS/OPERATIONS

2010 Sales

	% of total
Used vehicles	83
Wholesale vehicles	11
New vehicles	3
Other	3
Total	**100**

COMPETITORS

Asbury Automotive	Holman Enterprises
AutoNation	Internet Brands
Brown Automotive	JM Family Enterprises
Danner Company	Manheim
DriveTime Automotive	McCombs Enterprises
Ed Morse Auto	Penske Automotive Group
Group 1 Automotive	Serra Automotive
Hendrick Automotive	Sonic Automotive

HISTORICAL FINANCIALS

Company Type: Public

Income Statement

FYE: February 28

	REVENUE ($ mil.)	NET INCOME ($ mil.)	NET PROFIT MARGIN	EMPLOYEES
2/10	7,470	282	3.8%	13,439
2/09	6,974	59	0.8%	13,035
2/08	8,200	182	2.2%	15,637
2/07	7,466	199	2.7%	13,736
2/06	6,260	148	2.4%	12,061
Annual Growth	**4.5%**	**17.4%**	**—**	**2.7%**

2010 Year-End Financials

Debt ratio: 1.4%	No. of shares (mil.): 224
Return on equity: 16.0%	Dividends
Cash ($ mil.): 18	Yield: —
Current ratio: 3.26	Payout: —
Long-term debt ($ mil.): 27	Market value ($ mil.): 4,517

Stock History

NYSE: KMX

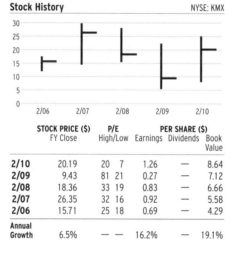

	STOCK PRICE ($) FY Close	P/E High/Low		Earnings	PER SHARE ($) Dividends	Book Value
2/10	20.19	20	7	1.26	—	8.64
2/09	9.43	81	21	0.27	—	7.12
2/08	18.36	33	19	0.83	—	6.66
2/07	26.35	32	16	0.92	—	5.58
2/06	15.71	25	18	0.69	—	4.29
Annual Growth	**6.5%**	**—**	**—**	**16.2%**	**—**	**19.1%**

Carnival Corporation

Carnival offers a boatload of fun. The company is the world's #1 cruise operator, boasting about a dozen cruise lines and 90-plus ships with a total passenger capacity of more than 180,000. Carnival operates in North America primarily through its Princess Cruise Line, Holland America, and Seabourn luxury cruise brand, as well as its flagship Carnival Cruise Lines unit. Brands such as AIDA, P&O Cruises, and Costa Cruises offer services to passengers in Europe, and the Cunard Line runs luxury trans-Atlantic liners. Carnival operates as a dual-listed company with UK-based Carnival plc, forming a single enterprise under a unified executive team.

Carnival maintains its top position in the industry by leveraging its cruise lines to penetrate

a number of different markets. Carnival Cruises, a leading brand in the US, and Princess both target families, retirees, and other upper middle class customers with competitively priced cruise packages. Its popular destinations include the Caribbean, the Mexican Riviera, and Alaska. P&O Cruises chases after a similar target customer in the UK with trips to the Mediterranean and Scandinavia. (P&O also operates out of Australia and New Zealand.) Holland America is known for its scenic getaways in New England, Canada, and along the Pacific coast. The company offers trips within the Asian market through its Costa Cruises. The line serves cruise-goers with Chinese-style food, mah-jongg tables in its casino, and luxury brands in its retail shops.

While Carnival has been known as the Fun Ship, the cruiser also attracts those looking for a fine ship. Carnival's Seabourn brand operates luxury cruises to upscale travelers and caters to them with fine food, personalized service, and exotic destinations worldwide. Similarly, its Swan Hellenic premium brand sails throughout Europe and Asia. Of course, luxury is the name of the game for Cunard, which provides a variety of cruises in addition to its liner services.

Despite fears of terrorism during the past few years and a wavering global economy, the company has been growing at full steam since its $5.4 billion acquisition of UK-based rival P&O Princess in 2003. The mega deal boosted Carnival's presence in the UK and throughout Europe and put it leagues ahead of rival cruising company Royal Caribbean. The cruise firm is counting on Europe, as well as Australia, New Zealand, Asia, and South America, for future growth, as it believes these markets are relatively untapped.

Fueled by optimism for the future, Carnival has orders in place for more than a dozen additional cruise ships, which it will integrate into its fleet by 2012.

Carnival continues to spend heavily on marketing its cruises, especially to consumers who have never taken to the high seas. While it relies on the traditional mediums, such as television and magazines, Carnival since 2009 has been shifting its efforts from print media to online and social media, utilizing Facebook, YouTube, Twitter, Flickr, and Podcasts. Also, the company has expanded its number of homeports to put cruising possibilities closer to customers.

CEO Micky Arison and his family own about 35% of Carnival Corporation and control a 27% voting stake in the combined entity that consists of Carnival Corporation and Carnival plc. Arison, one of the wealthiest people in Miami, also owns the Miami Heat basketball team.

HISTORY

Israeli emigrant Ted Arison got into the cruise business in the mid-1960s, forming Norwegian Caribbean Lines with shipping magnate Knut Kloster. After their partnership ended in 1971, Arison persuaded old friend Meshulam Riklis to bankroll his $6.5 million purchase of the *Empress of Canada* in 1972. Riklis owned (among other things) the Boston-based American International Travel Service (AITS). Arison set up Carnival Cruise Lines as an AITS subsidiary and renamed his ship the *Mardi Gras*. Unfortunately, she ran aground on her maiden voyage, sending Carnival into red ink for three years.

Arison bought out Riklis in 1974 for $1 and assumed Carnival's $5 million debt. He envisioned a cruise line that would offer affordable vacation packages to young, middle-class consumers, and invented a new type of cruise ship featuring live music, gambling, and other entertainment on board. Carnival was profitable within a month, and by the end of the following year, Arison had paid off Carnival's debt and bought its second ship. Arison's son, Micky, became CEO in 1979. Despite the rising costs of shipbuilding and fuel prices, Carnival continued to add to its fleet. The company grew to become the world's #1 cruise operator, and the Arisons took Carnival public in 1987.

The company acquired luxury cruise business Holland America Line in 1989 and formed a joint venture with Seabourn Cruise Lines in 1992. Carnival changed its name to Carnival Corporation in 1994 to reflect its diversifying operations, and it took a 50% stake in Seabourn the following year. Carnival stepped up its European expansion in 1996 by buying a stake in UK-based Airtours. The next year Carnival and Airtours jointly acquired an interest in European cruise giant Costa Crociere for about $275 million.

Carnival bought a majority interest in the prestigious Cunard Line (*Queen Elizabeth 2*) in 1998, merged it with Seabourn, and bought the remainder of the two cruise lines in 1999. An ugly lawsuit reared its head that year after a woman claimed to have been sexually assaulted while on a Carnival ship. Carnival acknowledged that it had received more than 100 similar complaints against its cruise employees dating back to 1995. (The suit was settled later that year.)

In 2000 Carnival acquired the remaining 50% of Costa Crociere from Airtours. The next year, Carnival sold its 25% stake in Airtours (now known as MyTravel Group).

In an effort to make the airfares sold in connection with cruise packages more competitive, the cruise line announced its plan in 2001 to cut travel agent commissions on the air-travel segment of cruise bookings. Also that year the company countered competitor Royal Caribbean's agreement to merge with P&O Princess Cruises with its own offer of £2.15 billion. P&O shareholders snubbed the offer but later softened and said it would consider a revised offer, leaving the door open for a bidding war between Carnival and Royal Caribbean. That same year, the company pleaded guilty to charges of polluting the ocean and falsifying oil-contaminated discharge records. It agreed to pay $18 million in fines and environmental costs, hire overseers to monitor its ships, and hire an environmental standards officer.

In 2003 Carnival succeeded in wooing P&O away from Royal Caribbean and the two corporations merged operations via a dual-listed company structure. Consequently, P&O changed its name to Carnival plc.

EXECUTIVES

Chairman and CEO: Micky Arison, age 60,
$9,541,563 total compensation
Vice Chairman and COO: Howard S. Frank, age 68,
$6,713,448 total compensation
SVP and CFO: David Bernstein, age 52,
$1,389,963 total compensation
SVP, General Counsel, and Secretary: Arnaldo Perez,
age 49
SVP Shared Services: Richard D. Ames
VP, Chief Accounting Officer, and Controller:
Larry Freedman, age 58
Senior Director, Marketing: Bill Harber
President, AIDA Cruises: Michael Thamm, age 44
President, Costa Crociere: Gianni Onorato
CEO, Carnival Australia: Ann C. Sherry

President and CEO, Holland America Line: Stein Kruse,
age 51
President and CEO, Princess Cruises:
Alan B. Buckelew, age 61
President and CEO, Carnival Cruise Lines:
Gerald R. (Gerry) Cahill, age 58,
$4,061,425 total compensation
President and CEO, Seabourn Cruise Lines:
Pamela C. Conover
Director; Chairman and CEO, Costa Crociere:
Pier Luigi Foschi, age 63,
$4,562,326 total compensation
CEO, Carnival UK: David K. Dingle, age 52
Director, Public Relations: Jennifer de la Cruz
Auditors: PricewaterhouseCoopers LLP

LOCATIONS

HQ: Carnival Corporation
3655 NW 87th Ave., Miami, FL 33178
Phone: 305-599-2600   **Fax:** 305-406-4700
Web: www.carnivalcorp.com

2009 Revenue

	% of total
North America	52
Europe	39
Other	9
Total	**100**

PRODUCTS/OPERATIONS

2009 Revenue

	% of total
Cruise	
Passenger tickets	76
Onboard & other	22
Other	2
Total	**100**

Selected Cruise Ships

AIDA
  AIDAaura (launched in 2003; 1,266 passengers)
  AIDAbella (2008; 2,050)
  AIDAcara (1996; 1,180)
  AIDAdiva (2007; 2,050)
  AIDAvita (2002; 1,266)
Carnival Cruise Lines
  Carnival Conquest (2002; 2,966)
  Carnival Destiny (1996; 2,634)
  Carnival Freedom (2007; 2,966)
  Carnival Glory (2003; 2,966)
  Carnival Legend (2002; 2,118)
  Carnival Liberty (2005; 2,966)
  Carnival Miracle (2004; 2,118)
  Carnival Pride (2001; 2,118)
  Carnival Spirit (2001; 2,118)
  Carnival Splendor (2008; 2,998)
  Carnival Triumph (1999; 2,750)
  Carnival Valor (2004; 2,966)
  Carnival Victory (2000; 2,750)
  Ecstasy (1991; 2,050)
  Elation (1998; 2,050)
  Fantasy (1990; 2,054)
  Fascination (1994; 2,050)
  Holiday (1985; 1,450)
  Imagination (1995; 2,050)
  Inspiration (1996; 2,050)
  Paradise (1998; 2,048)
  Sensation (1993; 2,050)
Costa Cruises
  Costa Allegra (1992; 784)
  Costa Atlantica (2000; 2,114)
  Costa Classica (1991; 1,302)
  Costa Concordia (2006; 2,978)
  Costa Europa (1986; 1,488)
  Costa Fortuna (2003; 2,702)
  Costa Magica (2004; 2,702)
  Costa Marina (1990; 762)
  Costa Mediterranea (2003; 2,114)
  Costa Romantica (1993; 1,344)
  Costa Serena (2007; 2,978)
  Costa Victoria (1996; 1,928)
Cunard Line
  Queen Mary 2 (2003; 2,592)

  Queen Victoria (2007; 1,980)
Holland America Line
  Amsterdam (2000; 1,380)
  Eurodam (2008; 2,104)
  Maasdam (1993; 1,258)
  Noordam (2006; 1,918)
  Oosterdam (2003; 1,848)
  Prinsendam (1988; 792)
  Rotterdam (1997; 1,316)
  Ryndam (1994; 1,260)
  Statendam (1993; 1,258)
  Veendam (1996; 1,258)
  Volendam (1999; 1,432)
  Westerdam (2004; 1,916)
  Zaandam (2000; 1,432)
  Zuiderdam (2002; 1,848)
Ibero Cruises
  Grand Celebration (1987; 1,494)
  Grand Mistral (1999; 1,244)
  Grand Voyager (2000; 834)
Ocean Village
  Ocean Village (1989; 1,578)
  Ocean Village Two (1990; 1,708)
P&O Cruises
  Arcadia (2005; 2,016)
  Artemis (1984; 1,200)
  Aurora (2000; 1,870)
  Oceana (2000; 2,016)
  Oriana (1995; 1,818)
  Ventura (2008; 3,078)
P&O Cruises Australia
  Pacific Dawn (1991; 1,596)
  Pacific Sun (1986; 1,480)
Princess Cruise Lines
  Caribbean Princess (2004; 3,100)
  Coral Princess (2002; 1,974)
  Crown Princess (2006; 3,080)
  Dawn Princess (1997; 1,998)
  Diamond Princess (2004; 2,678)
  Emerald Princess (2007; 3,080)
  Golden Princess (2001; 2,598)
  Grand Princess (1998; 2,592)
  Island Princess (2003; 1,974)
  Pacific Princess (1999; 676)
  Royal Princess (2001; 710)
  Ruby Princess (2008; 3,080)
  Sapphire Princess (2004; 2,678)
  Sea Princess (1998; 2,016)
  Star Princess (2002; 2,598)
  Sun Princess (1995; 2,022)
  Tahitian Princess (2000; 676)
Seabourn
  Seabourn Legend (1992; 208)
  Seabourn Pride (1988; 208)
  Seabourn Spirit (1989; 208)

COMPETITORS

Carlson Companies
Club Med
Disney
Fred. Olsen Energy
Genting Hong Kong
NCL
NYK Line
Royal Caribbean Cruises
Saga Group
TUI

HISTORICAL FINANCIALS

Company Type: Public

Income Statement			FYE: November 30	
	REVENUE ($ mil.)	NET INCOME ($ mil.)	NET PROFIT MARGIN	EMPLOYEES
11/09	13,157	1,790	13.6%	84,800
11/08	14,646	2,330	15.9%	85,900
11/07	13,033	2,408	18.5%	81,200
11/06	11,839	2,279	19.2%	74,700
11/05	11,087	2,257	20.4%	71,200
Annual Growth	**4.4%**	**(5.6%)**	**—**	**4.5%**

2009 Year-End Financials

Debt ratio: 41.3%	No. of shares (mil.): 826
Return on equity: 8.7%	Dividends
Cash ($ mil.): 538	Yield: 0.0%
Current ratio: 0.31	Payout: —
Long-term debt ($ mil.): 9,097	Market value ($ mil.): 26,453

Stock History NYSE: CCL

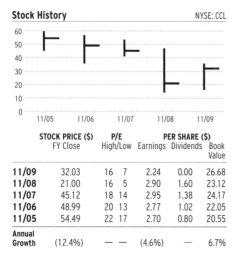

	STOCK PRICE ($) FY Close	P/E High/Low		PER SHARE ($) Earnings	Dividends	Book Value
11/09	32.03	16	7	2.24	0.00	26.68
11/08	21.00	16	5	2.90	1.60	23.12
11/07	45.12	18	14	2.95	1.38	24.17
11/06	48.99	20	13	2.77	1.02	22.05
11/05	54.49	22	17	2.70	0.80	20.55
Annual Growth	(12.4%)	—	—	(4.6%)	—	6.7%

Carpenter Technology

The Tin Man never would have rusted had he been built with metal from Carpenter Technology. The company makes a variety of corrosion-resistant materials; most of its sales come from stainless steel products and alloys that provide special heat- or wear-resistance or special magnetic or conductive properties. Finished products come in billet, bar, rod, wire, and other forms. Carpenter also makes titanium products, engineered ceramic products, and tool and other specialty steels. Customers include companies in the aerospace, automotive, medical, and industrial markets. The aerospace sector, Carpenter's largest market, accounts for more than 40% of its business.

The company's former Special Products unit, sold in 2005, now operates as Veridiam. Carpenter continues to supply alloys to Veridiam, which serves customers in the aerospace, medical device, and nuclear power generation businesses. In 2008 Carpenter also sold its ceramics businesses to Morgan Crucible Co. PLC for about $145 million.

William Wulfsohn was named president and CEO of Carpenter in 2010. Wulfsohn is a former senior vice president with PPG Industries. He replaces interim CEO Gregory Pratt, who will continue to serve as chairman of the board.

HISTORY

Engineer James Henry Carpenter founded Carpenter Steel in Pennsylvania in 1889. The company began making specialty steels after winning a US Navy contract to develop armor-piercing projectiles. Business declined after Carpenter's death in 1898, but former rival Robert Jennings took over and the company rebounded, thanks to marketing savvy and the development of new steel grades. Carpenter first produced stainless steel in 1917.

The company went public in 1937 and continued to grow. It made huge expansions in its production capacity to meet the demands spawned by WWII. The company changed its name to Carpenter Technology Corporation in 1968.

Carpenter survived the 1981-82 recession largely because of its lucrative niche in specialty steel. Another recession led to a 1991 reorganization. Robert Cardy, a 30-year company veteran, became chairman, president, and CEO the next year.

In 1994 Carpenter established a joint venture in Taiwan with Walsin-Lihwa (a Taiwanese maker of cable and wire). It also acquired Aceros Fortuna (Mexico's largest distributor of specialty steel) and purchased Certech (structural ceramics). In 1997 the company bought Dynamet, a producer of titanium bar and wire. It also purchased about 75% of diversified manufacturer Talley Industries for about $312 million, acquiring the remainder of Talley the next year. Carpenter formed a joint venture with Kalyani Steels in 1999 to make and distribute specialty steels in India.

High natural gas prices forced the company to increase prices for its nickel- and cobalt-based high-temperature alloys in 2001. The following year Carpenter's sales decreased due to lower stainless steel shipments and an overall weakness in the manufacturing industry.

In 2003 Carpenter's president Robert Torcolini was named to the added positions of chairman and CEO after chairman Dennis Draeger's retirement. Because of broad-based demand on its products, Carpenter raised prices primarily on its stainless bar, premium-metal alloys, and high-speed tool steel products in 2004.

The next year Carpenter sold its Special Products unit, a manufacturer of precision engineered metal components and assemblies, to investment firm WHI Capital Partners.

Three years after he took on the added roles of chairman and CEO, Torcolini announced his retirement. Carpenter went outside the company to find his replacement, tabbing Ford veteran Anne Stevens to take on all three titles.

EXECUTIVES

Chairman: Gregory A. Pratt, age 61
President and CEO: William A. Wulfsohn, age 47
EVP Advanced Metals and Premium Alloys Operations: Michael L. Shor, age 51, $2,440,259 total compensation
SVP Finance and CFO: K. Douglas (Doug) Ralph, age 49, $1,212,920 total compensation
SVP Organizational Effectiveness, Strategy, and Corporate Staffs: T. Kathleen Hanley, age 56, $1,278,290 total compensation
VP International, Carpenter Powder Products and Dynamet: Mark S. Kamon, age 56, $1,345,828 total compensation
VP Investor Relations and Business Development: David A. Christiansen, age 53
VP and Chief Accounting Officer: Thomas F. Cramsey, age 49
VP Research and Development: Timothy R. Armstrong
VP Advanced Engineering: Bernard M. Mara
VP, General Counsel, and Secretary: Oliver C. Mitchell Jr., age 55
VP and Treasurer: Michael A. (Mike) Hajost
VP Technology: David L. Strobel
VP Forged Bar and Billet Business Group: Russell E. Reber Jr.
VP Bar and Coil Products Business: Andrew T. Ziolkowski
VP and Chief Marketing Officer: Sanjay Guglani
VP Manufacturing: J. Michael Hom
VP Carpenter Powder Products and Dynamet: Williams B. Kent
Auditors: PricewaterhouseCoopers LLP

LOCATIONS

HQ: Carpenter Technology Corporation
2 Meridian Blvd., Wyomissing, PA 19610
Phone: 610-208-2000   **Fax:** 610-208-3716
Web: www.cartech.com

2009 Sales

	$ mil.	% of total
North America		
US	885.3	65
Mexico	72.0	5
Canada	34.2	3
Europe	261.5	19
Asia/Pacific	86.4	6
Other regions	22.9	2
Total	**1,362.3**	**100**

PRODUCTS/OPERATIONS

2009 Sales

	$ mil.	% of total
Special alloys	694.6	51
Stainless steel	460.1	34
Titanium products	141.4	10
Other materials	66.2	5
Total	**1,362.3**	**100**

2009 Sales

	$ mil.	% of total
Aerospace	579.3	42
Industrial	326.6	24
Energy	149.9	11
Medical	108.7	8
Consumer	103.4	8
Automotive	94.4	7
Total	**1,362.3**	**100**

COMPETITORS

AK Steel Holding Corporation
Allegheny Technologies
Dofasco
Earle M. Jorgensen
Essar Steel Algoma
Gerdau Ameristeel
JFE Holdings
Nucor
Precision Castparts
RTI International Metals
Titanium Metals
United States Steel

HISTORICAL FINANCIALS

Company Type: Public

Income Statement FYE: June 30

	REVENUE ($ mil.)	NET INCOME ($ mil.)	NET PROFIT MARGIN	EMPLOYEES
6/09	1,362	48	3.5%	3,200
6/08	1,954	278	14.2%	3,400
6/07	1,945	227	11.7%	4,152
6/06	1,568	212	13.5%	3,990
6/05	1,314	136	10.3%	4,003
Annual Growth	0.9%	(22.9%)	—	(5.4%)

2009 Year-End Financials

Debt ratio: 41.9%	No. of shares (mil.): 44
Return on equity: 6.6%	Dividends
Cash ($ mil.): 340	Yield: 3.5%
Current ratio: 3.78	Payout: 66.7%
Long-term debt ($ mil.): 259	Market value ($ mil.): 915

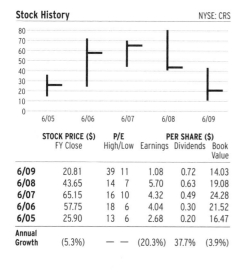

	STOCK PRICE ($) FY Close	P/E High/Low		PER SHARE ($) Earnings	Dividends	Book Value
6/09	20.81	39	11	1.08	0.72	14.03
6/08	43.65	14	7	5.70	0.63	19.08
6/07	65.15	16	10	4.32	0.49	24.28
6/06	57.75	18	6	4.04	0.30	21.52
6/05	25.90	13	6	2.68	0.20	16.47
Annual Growth	(5.3%)	—	—	(20.3%)	37.7%	(3.9%)

Casey's General Stores

Casey's General Stores makes sure that small towns in the Midwest get their fill of convenient shopping. It operates about 1,530 company-owned convenience stores (all sell gas), mostly in Illinois, Iowa, and Missouri, but also in about half a dozen other states in the Midwest, all within about 500 miles of its headquarters and distribution center. Towns with 5,000 people or fewer, where rent is low, are home to about 60% of the chain's stores. Casey's sells beverages, gasoline, groceries, and fresh prepared foods. The company also sells tobacco products, automotive goods, and other nonfood items, such as ammunition and photo supplies. Canada's Alimentation Couche-Tard in April 2010 offered to buy the company.

In July, Casey's announced that its board of directors unanimously recommends that shareholders reject Couche-Tard's revised bid of $36.75 per share (up from $36 initially), and announced a $500 million recapitalization plan designed to encourage them to do so. The board continues to assert that even the sweetened offer substantially undervalues the company. Couche-Tard, the largest independent convenience store operator in North America by number of company-operated stores, has been on an acquisition spree in 2010. The purchase of Casey's would expand its presence in the Midwest.

While sales were down about 1% in fiscal 2010 for Casey's, primarily due to a 7.5% decline in gas prices, an increase in grocery and prepared food sales helped to moderate the loss. Indeed, gasoline and gasohol, generally sold under the Casey's name, accounts for more than two-thirds of the company's sales. To fuel the body, nearly all Casey's outlets sell donuts as well as cookies, brownies, Danish pastries, cinnamon rolls, muffins, and pizza prepared on the premises. Prepared foods return a higher profit margin than fuel sales and so are an attractive and growing business for Casey's. Indeed, while prepared food and nongasoline items generate about 30% of total revenue, they account for about 75% of the chain's retail profits.

To make more room for food in its stores, in late 2008 the convenience store operator opened its first larger (about 3,800 sq. ft.) "O-shaped" store in Des Moines, Iowa. The new format devotes more space to food and beverages, offering plenty of beer, energy drinks, and other high-margin items. The cashier is located at the center of the store. About 15 such shops opened in fiscal 2009.

Casey's has been expanding in existing markets and broadening its presence by acquiring other Midwestern chains. In 2010 it acquired 10 Holiday convenience stores in Iowa and Nebraska. Previously, in 2009 the company purchased about 15 stores, including nine Bullseye locations in Missouri and the three-store Green Lantern chain in Kansas. Prior to those deals, Casey's acquired about a dozen convenience stores in fiscal 2008, and about 50 stores, including 30-plus HandiMart convenience stores and a truck stop in Iowa, in 2007.

In addition to Casey's General Stores, other banners operated by the chain include HandiMart and Just Diesel.

HISTORY

Donald Lamberti, who had run his family's grocery store, founded Casey's General Stores with Kurvin C. "K. C." Fish. The men converted a gas station into the first Casey's convenience store in 1968. To expand and build brand recognition, the company began franchising outlets two years later. By focusing on small towns, the company avoided competition and expensive building and property costs. A significant growth spurt in 1979 took Casey's from 119 stores to 226. Fish retired the following year.

The company went public in 1983 and began to curtail its franchising efforts in favor of more profitable company-owned stores (at the time there were about 190 company-owned stores and 215 franchised outlets; today only about 130 are franchised). Casey's introduced carryout pizza in 1984 and sandwiches two years later. Fueled by another stock offering in 1985, the company continued to grow quickly. It opened its 500th store that year and by 1990 had stores in eight states.

By 1996 Casey's had 1,000 stores, and it continued to add about 70 stores a year. After 30 years at the helm, in 1998 Lamberti retired as CEO; president Ronald Lamb took his place. In 2000 Casey's continued to expand at a rate of about 85 stores per year.

The company was accused of charging up to $5 a gallon for gas at 25 Casey's stores in Illinois on September 11, 2001, the day of terrorist attacks in New York City and Washington, DC. Casey's agreed the next month to pay $25,000 to the Red Cross and $5,000 to the state of Illinois. It also agreed to refund customers who were overcharged for gas. In fiscal 2002 the company opened more than 50 company-owned stores.

In fiscal 2003 the company built 15 new stores and purchased another. In April 2003 co-founder Lamberti retired from the company and Ronald Lamb added chairman to his title in May.

In early 2006 the company acquired 51 convenience stores in Nebraska from Gas 'N Shop for about $29 million. In June COO Robert Myers was named CEO of Casey's, succeeding Ronald Lamb, who held onto the chairman's title. In October the company acquired 33 HandiMart convenience stores in Iowa from Nordstrom Oil for about $63 million.

In March 2009 Casey's ended its franchising program begun in the 1970s. (At its peak, Casey's had a total of 230 franchised stores.) As a result, all of its convenience stores are and will be company owned going forward.

In April 2010, Canada's Couche-Tard launched an unsolicited takeover of Casey's. In August, Casey's completed a $569 million private placement financing plan designed to thwart Couche-Tard's advance.

EXECUTIVES

President, CEO, and Director: Robert J. (Bob) Myers, age 63, $1,543,107 total compensation
COO: Terry W. Handley, age 50, $618,971 total compensation
SVP and CFO: William J. (Bill) Walljasper, age 45, $520,250 total compensation
SVP Logistics and Acquisitions: Sam J. Billmeyer, age 53, $523,792 total compensation
VP Marketing: Michael R. (Mike) Richardson, $363,574 total compensation
VP and Corporate Counsel: Eli J. Wirtz
VP Store Operations: Robert C. Ford
VP Finance and Corporate Secretary: Brian J. Johnson
VP and Treasurer: Russell D. Sukut
VP Human Resources: Julie L. Jackowski
VP Transportation and Distribution: Jay F. Blair
VP Support Services: Hal D. Brown
VP Food Services: Darryl F. Bacon
Auditors: KPMG LLP

LOCATIONS

HQ: Casey's General Stores, Inc.
1 Convenience Blvd., Ankeny, IA 50021
Phone: 515-965-6100   **Fax:** 515-965-6160
Web: www.caseys.com

PRODUCTS/OPERATIONS

2010 Sales

	$ mil.	% of total
Gasoline	3,177.5	69
Grocery & other merchandise	1,073.5	23
Prepared food & fountain	365.8	8
Other	20.3	—
Total	**4,637.1**	**100**

Selected Merchandise

Ammunition
Automotive products
Beverages
Food
Gasoline (self-service)
Health and beauty aids
Housewares
Pet products
Photo supplies
School supplies
Tobacco products

COMPETITORS

7-Eleven
Chevron
CVS Caremark
Exxon Mobil
Holiday Companies
Hy-Vee
IGA
Krause Gentle
Kroger
Kwik Trip
Martin & Bayley
QuikTrip
Royal Dutch Shell
Walgreen

HISTORICAL FINANCIALS

Company Type: Public

Income Statement

FYE: April 30

	REVENUE ($ mil.)	NET INCOME ($ mil.)	NET PROFIT MARGIN	EMPLOYEES
4/10	4,637	117	2.5%	19,434
4/09	4,688	86	1.8%	18,780
4/08	4,827	85	1.8%	17,983
4/07	4,024	62	1.5%	17,136
4/06	3,515	62	1.8%	15,692
Annual Growth	7.2%	17.4%	—	5.5%

2010 Year-End Financials

Debt ratio: 18.8%
Return on equity: 15.1%
Cash ($ mil.): 152
Current ratio: 1.29
Long-term debt ($ mil.): 155

No. of shares (mil.): 51
Dividends
  Yield: 0.9%
  Payout: 14.8%
Market value ($ mil.): 1,968

Stock History

NASDAQ (GS): CASY

	STOCK PRICE ($) FY Close	P/E High/Low		PER SHARE ($) Earnings	Dividends	Book Value
4/10	38.63	17	10	2.29	0.34	16.18
4/09	26.61	19	11	1.68	0.30	14.15
4/08	22.13	19	12	1.67	0.26	12.71
4/07	25.15	22	17	1.22	0.20	11.23
4/06	21.39	23	14	1.19	0.18	10.27
Annual Growth	15.9%	—	—	17.8%	17.2%	12.0%

Caterpillar Inc.

Caterpillars are remarkable creatures; Caterpillar Inc. is a remarkable company — the world's #1 maker of earthmoving machinery and a big supplier of agricultural equipment. The company makes construction, mining, and logging machinery; diesel and natural gas engines; industrial gas turbines; and electrical power generation systems. Caterpillar operates plants worldwide and sells equipment via a network of 3,500 offices in some 180 countries. It provides rental services, too, through 1,600-plus outlets, and offers financing and insurance for dealers and customers. Cat Power Ventures invests in power projects that use Caterpillar power generation equipment. Caterpillar Logistics offers supply chain services.

Other Caterpillar businesses include Progress Rail Services, a unit that outsources maintenance and repair services to the railroad industry. Growing rail volumes coupled with the prospect of US stimulus money is spurring Caterpillar to expand the unit. In mid-2010 the company bought Electro-Motive Diesel (EMD), a diesel-electric locomotive manufacturer, from Berkshire Partners and Greenbriar Equity Group.

Despite the depth and breadth of its manufacturing reach, Caterpillar has been hampered by the decrease in infrastructure activity. The company offset the decline by squeezing manufacturing costs by approximately $2 billion.

Everyone at Caterpillar is shouldering the recessionary response. In December 2009 the company trimmed executive pay by half and salaried employee pay by as much as 15%. Workforce reductions included cuts in October at five plants in Illinois, Indiana, and Georgia, dropping 2,500 workers. Earlier in 2009 Caterpillar eliminated more than 22,000 workers from its payroll, a reduction in force of around 20%.

In July 2010 Caterpillar veteran Doug Oberhelman became vice chairman and CEO of the company; in October 2010 he will assume the chairman position in conjunction with outgoing board chairman and former CEO James Owens' retirement.

The company is investing heavily in China, where it intends to launch lower-priced equipment, with fewer frills and performance features, under an alternative brand. (Developing markets such as China, India, and Indonesia have shown weak interest in buying machinery carrying the pricier Cat label.)

Caterpillar and Navistar International formed a 50/50 joint venture in 2009 to manufacture and distribute on-highway commercial trucks outside North America. In North America, Navistar and Caterpillar are working together to produce Caterpillar-branded heavy-duty vocational trucks.

HISTORY

In 1904 in Stockton, California, combine maker Benjamin Holt modified the farming tractor by substituting a gas engine for steam and replacing iron wheels with crawler tracks. This improved the tractor's mobility over dirt.

The British adapted the "caterpillar" (Holt's nickname for the tractor) design to the armored tank in 1915. Following WWI, the US Army donated tanks to local governments for construction work. The caterpillar's efficiency spurred the development of earthmoving and construction equipment.

Holt merged with Best Tractor in 1925. The company, renamed Caterpillar (Cat), moved to Peoria, Illinois, in 1928. Cat expanded into foreign markets in the 1930s and phased out combine production to focus on construction and road-building equipment.

Sales volume more than tripled during WWII when Cat supplied the military with earthmoving equipment. Returning GIs touted Cat durability and quality, and high demand continued. Cat held a solid first place in the industry, far ahead of #2 International Harvester.

Moving beyond US borders, Cat established its first overseas plant in the UK (1951). In 1963 it entered a joint venture with Japanese industrial titan Mitsubishi. Cat bought Solar Turbines (gas turbine engines) in 1981. Fifty consecutive years of profits ended, however, when Cat ran up $953 million in losses between 1982 and 1984 as equipment demand fell and foreign competition intensified. Cat doubled its product line between 1984 and 1989 and shifted production toward smaller equipment.

In 1990 CEO Donald Fites reorganized Cat along product lines. The next year the company clashed with the UAW (United Auto Workers) over wage and health benefits. A strike resulted, and Cat reported its first annual loss since 1984. Most of the striking workers returned to work without a contract by mid-1992.

The firm completed a six-year, $1.8 billion modernization program in 1993 that automated many of its plants. That investment benefited the company when almost two-thirds of Cat's UAW employees at eight plants in Colorado, Illinois, and Pennsylvania went on strike in 1994. The company hired replacement workers and used its foreign factories to help fill orders. In 1995, after two years of record earnings at Cat, the UAW called off the strike. Cat set up a holding company, Caterpillar China Investment Co. Ltd., in 1996 for joint ventures in China.

In 1998 Cat and the UAW (with federal mediation) hammered out their first contract agreement in more than six years. That year Cat paid $1.33 billion for LucasVarity's UK-based Perkins Engines, expanding its capacity to produce small and midsize diesel engines.

Fites retired in 1999; vice chairman Glen Barton succeeded him. Cat cut back its workforce and production after slowdowns in the agricultural, mining, and oil exploration industries reduced machinery orders.

In 2003 the company inked a deal with diversified global resources company BHP Billiton to supply an estimated $1.5 billion in equipment and support to its operations.

In early 2004 Jim Owens became CEO. Later that year Caterpillar acquired Swiss industrial gas turbine packager Turbomach S.A. In the same year recreation vehicle manufacturer Fleetwood Enterprises announced that it would equip all of its diesel-powered vehicles with Caterpillar engines by the end of 2005.

In 2006 Caterpillar bought Progress Rail from One Equity Partners for about $1 billion. Also in 2006, Caterpillar agreed to acquire the rail and non-Cat engine component remanufacturing business of O.E.M. Remanufacturing Company, a subsidiary of Caterpillar distributor Finning.

In 2007 it completed the acquisition of French company Eurenov, which greatly enhanced the remanufacturing division's reach into the European market.

EXECUTIVES

Chairman: James W. (Jim) Owens, age 64, $8,749,785 total compensation
Vice Chairman and CEO:
Douglas R. (Doug) Oberhelman, age 57, $2,994,775 total compensation
Group President: Steven H. Wunning, age 58, $2,832,156 total compensation
Group President: Stuart L. Levenick, age 56, $2,948,268 total compensation
Group President: Gérard R. Vittecoq, age 61, $3,395,749 total compensation
Group President: Richard P. (Rich) Lavin, age 57, $2,483,454 total compensation
CFO: Edward J. (Ed) Rapp, age 52, $2,432,183 total compensation
VP and Chief Human Resources Officer:
Gregory S. (Greg) Folley, age 50
VP Product Development Center of Excellence and CTO: Tana L. Utley, age 46
VP; President, Global Mining: Christopher C. Curfman
VP Distribution Services Division, Caterpillar SARL:
Paolo Fellin
VP and CIO: John S. Heller
VP; President, Solar Turbines: Jim Umpleby
VP; President, Caterpillar Financial Services:
Kent M. Adams
VP; President, Caterpillar China: Jiming Zhu, age 48
VP, General Counsel, and Secretary:
James B. (Jim) Buda, age 62
Chief Accounting Officer: Jananne A. Copeland, age 47
President and CEO, Progress Rail Services:
William P. (Billy) Ainsworth, age 53
President, NC2 Global: Al Saltiel
Auditors: PricewaterhouseCoopers LLP

LOCATIONS

HQ: Caterpillar Inc.
100 NE Adams St., Peoria, IL 61629
Phone: 309-675-1000 **Fax:** 309-675-1182
Web: www.cat.com

2009 Sales

	$ mil.	% of total
US	10,560	33
Other countries	21,836	67
Total	**32,396**	**100**

PRODUCTS/OPERATIONS

2009 Sales

	$ mil.	% of total
Machinery	18,148	56
Engines	11,392	35
Financial products	2,856	9
Total	**32,396**	**100**

Selected Products

Machinery
    Articulated trucks
    Backhoe loaders
    Log loaders
    Log skidders
    Mining shovels
    Motor graders
    Off-highway trucks
    Paving products
    Pipelayers
    Related parts
    Skid steer loaders
    Telescopic handlers
    Track and wheel excavators
    Track and wheel loaders
    Track and wheel tractors
    Wheel tractor-scrapers
Engines
    Engines for Caterpillar machinery
    Engines for electric power generation systems
    Engines for marine, petroleum, construction,
        industrial, and agricultural applications
    Engines for on-highway trucks and locomotives
Financing and insurance services
    Financing to customers and dealers
    Insurance to customers and dealers

Selected Brands

Cat
Caterpillar
F.G. Wilson
MaK
Olympian
Perkins
Solar Turbines

COMPETITORS

AGCO	Komatsu
Charles Machine Works	Kubota
CIT Group	Mahindra
Citibank	MAN
CNH Global	Menlo Worldwide
Cummins	Mitsubishi Heavy
Daimler	Industries
Deere	Multiquip
Detroit Diesel	Navistar International
DHL	Rolls-Royce
Dongfeng Motor	Sandvik
Dresser, Inc.	Scania
GE	Siemens AG
GENCO Distribution	Sumitomo Heavy
Hitachi Construction	Industries
Machinery	Terex
Hyundai Heavy Industries	Toyota
Ingersoll-Rand	UPS
Isuzu	Volvo
J C Bamford Excavators	Volvo Financial Services
JLG Industries	Wells Fargo Equipment
John Deere Credit	Finance
John Deere Thibodaux	Woods Equipment
Kawasaki Heavy Industries	

HISTORICAL FINANCIALS

Company Type: Public

Income Statement

FYE: December 31

	REVENUE ($ mil.)	NET INCOME ($ mil.)	NET PROFIT MARGIN	EMPLOYEES
12/09	32,396	895	2.8%	93,813
12/08	51,324	3,557	6.9%	112,887
12/07	44,958	3,541	7.9%	101,333
12/06	41,517	3,537	8.5%	94,593
12/05	36,339	2,854	7.9%	85,116
Annual Growth	**(2.8%)**	**(25.2%)**	**—**	**2.5%**

2009 Year-End Financials

Debt ratio: 250.0%
Return on equity: 12.1%
Cash ($ mil.): —
Current ratio: 1.39
Long-term debt ($ mil.): 21,847
No. of shares (mil.): 630
Dividends
    Yield: 2.9%
    Payout: 117.5%
Market value ($ mil.): 35,931

Stock History

NYSE: CAT

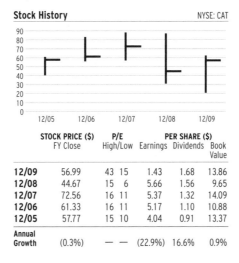

	STOCK PRICE ($) FY Close	P/E High/Low	PER SHARE ($) Earnings	Dividends	Book Value
12/09	56.99	43 15	1.43	1.68	13.86
12/08	44.67	15 6	5.66	1.56	9.65
12/07	72.56	16 11	5.37	1.32	14.09
12/06	61.33	16 11	5.17	1.10	10.88
12/05	57.77	15 10	4.04	0.91	13.37
Annual Growth	**(0.3%)**	**— —**	**(22.9%)**	**16.6%**	**0.9%**

CB Richard Ellis Group

CB Richard Ellis Group (CBRE) is all about location, location, location — not to mention *ubicación, l'emplacement, posizione,* and *Standort.* The world's largest commercial real estate services company and an international powerhouse, CBRE operates more than 300 offices in 30 countries. Services include property and facilities management, leasing, brokerage, valuation, asset management, financing, and market research. Subsidiary Trammell Crow provides property development services for corporate and institutional clients, primarily in the US. The company manages more than 1.1 billion sq. ft. of commercial space for third-party owners and occupants.

CBRE operates in three geographic segments: the Americas; Europe, the Middle East, and Africa (EMEA); and the Asia/Pacific region. The Americas division is its largest, accounting for more than half of all sales. CBRE continues to expand its geographic reach and broaden its service offerings. In 2008 it opened its first offices in Bahrain and joined forces with Vanke to provide residential property management services in China. The following year, CBRE expanded its existing UK-based investment banking business to the Americas; that division provides advisory and

restructuring services for real estate, hospitality, and gaming companies.

The company's acquisitions of Insignia Financial and Trammell Crow represent some of the largest transactions for CBRE to date. The additions deepened its outsourcing services, especially project and facilities management, for corporate and institutional clients in the US. The company regularly seeks fill-in acquisitions in regional markets that complement or expand existing operations, but CBRE has been cooling its heels somewhat as it awaits economic recovery. The company's sales fell in 2008 and 2009 as credit markets slowed down, property valuations declined, and real estate transactions around the world followed.

Private equity firm Blum Capital Partners owns about 10% of CBRE. Blum is headed by Richard Blum, who is also the chairman of CBRE.

HISTORY

Colbert Coldwell and Albert Tucker started real estate brokerage Tucker, Lynch, & Coldwell in 1906 in San Francisco. In 1922 the company expanded to Los Angeles, where it began developing real estate in 1933 with a 60-acre subdivision in the burgeoning city.

Having profited from California's rapid growth in the 1950s and 1960s, the firm expanded out of state. The partnership incorporated in 1962 as Coldwell Banker, which went public in 1968. Sears, Roebuck & Co. bought the company in 1981 for 80% above its market price. But by 1991 Sears had abandoned aims to become a financial services giant and sold Coldwell Banker's commercial operations to The Carlyle Group as CB Commercial Real Estate Services Group.

Free of Sears but $56 million in the red, the company didn't return to profitability until 1993. Two years later it embarked on a shopping spree in real estate services, buying tenant representatives Langon Rieder and Westmark Realty. In 1996 the company went public and bought mortgage banker L. J. Melody & Company (now named CBRE | Melody); it purchased Koll Real Estate Services in 1997.

In 1998 the company widened its global scope with the acquisition of REI Limited, the non-UK operations of Richard Ellis; it was renamed CB Richard Ellis Services. CB Richard Ellis also bought Hillier Parker May & Rowden (now operating in the UK as CB Hillier), a London-based provider of commercial property services.

CB Richard Ellis experienced a revenue crunch in 1999 and responded by restructuring its North American operations into three divisions (transaction, financial, and management services) and cutting management ranks by 30%. Growth continued in 1999 with the purchase of Pittsburgh-based Gold & Co., the addition of an office in Venezuela, and a fat contract to manage more than 1,100 locations for Prudential.

In 2000 the company committed significant resources to the Internet, inking a deal to offer the lease management services of MyContracts.com and investing in Canadian real estate transaction tracker RealNet Canada.

A group of investors including then-CEO Ray Wirta, chairman Richard Blum (and his BLUM Capital Partners), and Freeman Spogli took the company private in 2001. Blum Capital Partners bought the 60% of publicly traded CBRE that it did not already own, forming CBRE Holding. Three years later the company went public once again.

In 2003 CBRE merged with top commercial real estate broker and property manager Insignia Financial. The next year the company changed its name to CB Richard Ellis Group and went public. It bought rival Trammell Crow in 2006, as well as a dozen or so other companies as it sought to fill in its holdings.

CBRE spun off former subsidiary Realty Finance Corporation in 2008 after the real estate investment trust continued to post losses in a troubled credit market.

EXECUTIVES

Chairman: Richard C. Blum, age 74
CEO and Director: W. Brett White, age 50,
  $7,224,535 total compensation
EVP, General Counsel, Chief Compliance Officer, and
  Secretary: Laurence H. Midler, age 45
EVP Brokerage Services: Paul Muratore
EVP Brokerage Services: Peter C. Turchin
EVP Office and Commercial Properties: Jeffrey S. Pion
EVP and CFO: Gil Borok, age 42,
  $1,485,395 total compensation
Global Finance: Nicholas M. (Nick) Kormeluk
Global Chief Economist: Raymond Torto
Global Strategy and Chief Investment Officer:
  James R. (Jim) Groch
Global CIO: Donald B. (Don) Goldstein
Global Director Human Resources:
  J. Christopher (Chris) Kirk
Chief Accounting Officer; CFO, Trammell Crow:
  Arlin E. Gaffner, age 53
Chairman, Global Brokerage: Stephen B. (Steve) Siegel,
  age 65
Chairman, President, and CEO, Asia Pacific:
  Robert (Rob) Blain, age 54,
  $3,041,959 total compensation
Chairman, President, and CEO, EMEA:
  Michael J. (Mike) Strong, age 62,
  $3,147,995 total compensation
President; CEO, Trammell Crow Company:
  Robert E. (Bob) Sulentic, age 53,
  $4,319,467 total compensation
President, Global Corporate Services:
  William F. (Bill) Concannon, age 54
President, Global Services: Calvin W. (Cal) Frese Jr.,
  age 53, $4,009,330 total compensation
President, Investment Properties; COO, Capital
  Markets: Gregory S. (Greg) Vorwaller
Senior Managing Director Corporate Communications:
  Steven (Steve) Iaco
Auditors: KPMG LLP

LOCATIONS

HQ: CB Richard Ellis Group, Inc.
  11150 Santa Monica Blvd., Ste. 1600
  Los Angeles, CA 90025
Phone: 310-405-8900
Web: www.cbre.com

2009 Sales

	$ mil.	% of total
Americas	2,594.1	62
Europe, Middle East & Africa	818.1	20
Asia/Pacific	524.3	13
Global investment management	141.5	3
Development services	87.8	2
Total	**4,165.8**	**100**

PRODUCTS/OPERATIONS

Selected Subsidiaries

CB Richard Ellis, Inc.
CB Richard Ellis Real Estate Services, LLC
CB Richard Ellis Services, Inc
Insignia Financial Group, LLC
Relam Amsterdam Holdings B.V.
Trammell Crow Company

COMPETITORS

Colliers International	Jones Lang LaSalle
Cushman & Wakefield	Lincoln Property
DTZ	Mitsui Fudosan
FirstService	Realogy
Grubb & Ellis	Studley
Inland Group	

HISTORICAL FINANCIALS

Company Type: Public

Income Statement

FYE: December 31

	REVENUE ($ mil.)	NET INCOME ($ mil.)	NET PROFIT MARGIN	EMPLOYEES
12/09	4,166	(28)	—	29,000
12/08	5,129	(1,012)	—	30,000
12/07	6,034	391	6.5%	29,000
12/06	4,032	319	7.9%	24,000
12/05	2,911	217	7.5%	14,500
Annual Growth	**9.4%**	**—**	**—**	**18.9%**

2009 Year-End Financials

Debt ratio: 377.1%   No. of shares (mil.): 322
Return on equity: —   Dividends
Cash ($ mil.): 742   Yield: —
Current ratio: 1.39   Payout: —
Long-term debt ($ mil.): 2,372   Market value ($ mil.): 4,367

Stock History

NYSE: CBG

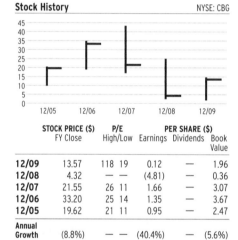

	STOCK PRICE ($) FY Close	P/E High/Low		PER SHARE ($) Earnings	Dividends	Book Value
12/09	13.57	118	19	0.12	—	1.96
12/08	4.32	—	—	(4.81)	—	0.36
12/07	21.55	26	11	1.66	—	3.07
12/06	33.20	25	14	1.35	—	3.67
12/05	19.62	21	11	0.95	—	2.47
Annual Growth	**(8.8%)**	**—**	**—**	**(40.4%)**	**—**	**(5.6%)**

CBS Corporation

You might say this company has a real eye for broadcasting. CBS Corporation is a leading media conglomerate with operations in television, radio, online content, and publishing. Its portfolio is anchored by CBS Broadcasting, which operates the #1 rated CBS television network, along with a group of local TV stations. CBS also produces and distributes TV programming through CBS Television Studios and CBS Television Distribution. Other operations include CBS Radio, CBS Interactive, and book publisher Simon & Schuster. In addition, the company's CBS Outdoor is a leading operator of billboards and other outdoor advertising. Chairman Sumner Redstone controls CBS Corporation through National Amusements.

Like rival media companies including Walt Disney and News Corporation, CBS Corporation focuses on the integration of its content production and distribution businesses in order to generate multiple streams of revenue. A television show created by CBS Television Studios, for example, can be broadcast by the CBS network and later syndicated to local stations and cable outlets. Programming can also be released to consumers on DVD by CBS Home Entertainment and turned into licensed apparel and other retail goods by its CBS Consumer Products division. CBS Corporation also uses its multiple outlets on TV, radio, and online to cross-promote its vast array of media properties.

CBS continues to draw the largest number of TV viewers among broadcast networks with hit crime shows (*CSI, NCIS*) and comedies (*Big Bang Theory, Two and a Half Men*). The network continues to invest in new programming to keep the hits coming, which has paid off in the form of such shows as *The Good Wife* and *The Mentalist*. CBS also makes significant investments in sports programming through broadcasting agreements with the National Football League and the NCAA, among other organizations.

In addition to its flagship network, CBS Corporation owns a 50% stake in The CW Network with joint venture partner Warner Bros. Entertainment (a unit of Time Warner). The upstart broadcast outlet launched in 2006 and has found its niche appealing mostly to young adults with such shows as *Gossip Girl, Smallville*, and *America's Next Top Model*.

Showtime is the crown jewel of the company's cable holdings. While still chasing market leader Home Box Office, the network has made significant inroads with the help of such original series programming as *Dexter* and *Weeds*.

The company does have a significant presence online with such leading websites as CNET (technology news and reviews), GameSpot (video game information), and Last.fm (social networking for music fans). Its CBS Interactive focuses on selling advertising across its vast collection of properties. CBS is also expanding its use of online video and other digital distribution channels for its television content. The company took a $1.8 billion gamble on the Internet when it acquired CNET Networks in 2008.

Like other publishers, Simon & Schuster is struggling to manage the long, slow decline in consumer book purchasing by focusing on cutting operating and production costs. Part of that effort has meant investing in new technologies to sell books to users of electronic readers, such as Amazon's Kindle and the iPad from Apple.

HISTORY

The company that would eventually become CBS Corporation began as Viacom in 1970. It was the result of numerous mergers and acquisitions dating back nearly 90 years, combining everything from a movie studio to a company that made car bumpers. CBS launched Viacom after the FCC ruled that TV networks could not own cable systems and TV stations in the same market. Viacom took over CBS's program syndication division and bought TV and radio stations in the late 1970s and early 1980s. In 1978 it co-founded pay-TV network Showtime. Viacom became full owner in 1982 and combined Showtime with The Movie Channel the following year to form Showtime Networks. Viacom also began producing TV series and bought MTV Networks in 1986.

After a bidding war with renowned financier Carl Icahn and a Viacom management group,

Sumner Redstone's National Amusements bought 83% of Viacom in 1987. Viacom bought King's Entertainment (theme parks) shortly thereafter and followed that with two mega-deals in 1994: it bought Paramount Communications for about $10 billion (which included Simon & Schuster) and Blockbuster for $8.4 billion (which included Spelling Entertainment). The next year, along with Chris-Craft, Viacom launched UPN (United Paramount Network), the fifth commercial-broadcast TV network in the US.

Chiseling away at a mountain of debt, Viacom dumped its radio stations and sold its share in USA Networks (now named IAC/InterActiveCorp) to Universal for $1.7 billion in 1997. In 1998 it sold the reference and education publishing divisions of Simon & Schuster to Pearson for $4.6 billion.

In 1999 it sold 18% of Blockbuster in an IPO and sold 10% of MTVi to TCI Music (later Liberty Digital) in exchange for the SonicNet websites.

Viacom's $45 billion merger with CBS went through (reuniting two companies split apart by the government 30 years ago) in 2000.

In 2001 Viacom bought the rest of Infinity Broadcasting that it didn't already own, as well as Black Entertainment Television (the media company targeting African-Americans) for $3 billion.

Two years later, Viacom finally sold its majority stake in Blockbuster, which never really fit in with Viacom's other media properties. The media firm also didn't want to deal with the new challenges facing Blockbuster, such as stiff competition from video on demand services, the cheap DVD market, and mail order video rental company Netflix.

In a move designed to simplify the firm's operations and re-focus the company on its core assets, in late 2005 Viacom split into two separately traded firms — one called CBS Corporation, consisting of traditional television and radio broadcasting operations and headed by former co-COO Les Moonves; and the other called the "new" Viacom, made up of cable television and film operations and headed by former co-COO Tom Freston. (Freston resigned in 2006.) Redstone retained his title as chairman of both firms, as well as his majority control.

Shortly after the split, CBS Corp. sold Paramount Parks to Cedar Fair for $1.2 billion. A newly formed network called The CW, a combination of UPN and The WB, debuted in 2006. CBS Corp. expanded its online publishing operations in 2008 with the $1.8 billion acquisition of CNET Networks.

EXECUTIVES

Executive Chairman: Sumner M. Redstone, age 86, $16,210,860 total compensation
Vice Chairman: Shari E. Redstone, age 56
President, CEO, and Director: Leslie (Les) Moonves, age 60, $43,238,876 total compensation
EVP and CFO: Joseph R. Ianniello, age 42, $5,758,981 total compensation
EVP Planning, Policy, and Government Relations: Martin D. Franks, age 59, $2,805,164 total compensation
EVP Investor Relations: Adam Townsend
EVP and Chief Communications Officer: Gil Schwartz, age 58
EVP Human Resources and Administration: Anthony G. Ambrosio, age 49
EVP and General Counsel: Louis J. Briskman, age 61, $7,440,298 total compensation

SVP, Controller, and Chief Accounting Officer: Thomas S. (Tom) Shilen Jr., age 50
SVP Strategic Development: Dan Harrison
SVP, Deputy General Counsel, and Secretary: Angeline C. Straka, age 64
Chairman and CEO, Showtime Networks: Matthew C. (Matt) Blank
Chairman and CEO, CBS Outdoor: Wally C. Kelly, age 54
President, CBS Television Stations: Peter Dunn
President and CEO, CBS Radio: Daniel R. (Dan) Mason
President, CBS Television Studios: David Stapf
President, CBS Entertainment: Nina Tassler
President, Entertainment, The CW: Dawn Ostroff
President and CEO, Simon & Schuster: Carolyn K. Reidy, age 60
Auditors: PricewaterhouseCoopers LLP

LOCATIONS

HQ: CBS Corporation
51 W. 52nd St., New York, NY 10019
Phone: 212-975-4321   **Fax:** 212-975-4516
Web: www.cbscorporation.com

2009 Sales

	$ mil.	% of total
US	11,154.0	86
International	1,860.6	14
Total	**13,014.6**	**100**

PRODUCTS/OPERATIONS

2009 Sales

	$ mil.	% of total
Advertising	8,171.4	63
Content	3,120.4	24
Affiliate fees & subscriptions	1,462.3	11
Other	260.5	2
Total	**13,014.6**	**100**

2009 Sales

	$ mil.	% of total
Entertainment	6,976.7	53
Local broadcasting	2,359.7	18
Outdoor advertising	1,722.6	13
Cable networks	1,347.2	10
Publishing	793.5	6
Adjustments	(185.1)	—
Total	**13,014.6**	**100**

Selected Operations

Entertainment
  CBS Films (motion picture production)
  CBS Interactive (online content)
    BNET
    CBS.com
    CBSSports.com
    CNET
    GameSpot
    TV.com
  CBS Studios International (international program syndication)
  CBS Television Distribution (domestic programming syndication)
  CBS Television Network (broadcast television network)
    CBS Entertainment
    CBS News
    CBS Sports
  CBS Television Studios (television production)
  The CW Network (50%, broadcast television network)
Local broadcasting
  CBS Radio
  CBS Television Stations
Outdoor advertising
  CBS Outdoor
Cable networks
  CBS College Sports Network
  Showtime (pay-TV service)
Publishing
  Simon & Schuster

COMPETITORS

AOL	NBC Universal
Citadel Broadcasting	News Corp.
Clear Channel	Random House
Cumulus Media	SIRIUS XM
Disney	Sony Pictures
JCDecaux	Time Warner
Lamar Advertising	Yahoo!

HISTORICAL FINANCIALS

Company Type: Public

Income Statement

FYE: December 31

	REVENUE ($ mil.)	NET INCOME ($ mil.)	NET PROFIT MARGIN	EMPLOYEES
12/09	13,015	227	1.7%	25,580
12/08	13,950	(11,673)	—	25,920
12/07	14,073	1,247	8.9%	23,970
12/06	14,320	1,661	11.6%	23,654
12/05	14,536	(7,089)	—	32,160
Annual Growth	**(2.7%)**	**—**	**—**	**(5.6%)**

2009 Year-End Financials

Debt ratio: 72.7%
Return on equity: 2.6%
Cash ($ mil.): 717
Current ratio: 1.19
Long-term debt ($ mil.): 6,553

No. of shares (mil.): 681
Dividends
  Yield: 1.4%
  Payout: 60.6%
Market value ($ mil.): 9,564

Stock History

NYSE: CBS

	STOCK PRICE ($) FY Close	P/E High/Low		PER SHARE ($) Earnings	Dividends	Book Value
12/09	14.05	44	9	0.33	0.20	13.25
12/08	8.19	—	—	(17.43)	1.06	12.63
12/07	27.25	21	15	1.73	0.94	31.54
12/06	31.18	15	11	2.15	0.74	34.55
12/05	24.05	—	—	(8.98)	0.56	31.93
Annual Growth	**(12.6%)**	**—**	**—**	**—**	**(22.7%)**	**(19.7%)**

CenterPoint Energy

CenterPoint Energy pivots around its core operations which include power and gas distribution utilities, and natural gas pipeline, gathering, and marketing operations. CenterPoint Energy's regulated utilities distribute natural gas to 3.2 million customers in six US states and electricity to more than 2.1 million customers on the Texas Gulf Coast. The company's main stomping ground is Texas, where it has regulated power distribution operations through subsidiary CenterPoint Energy Houston Electric. CenterPoint Energy also operates 8,200 miles of interstate gas pipeline, has 3,700 miles of gas gathering pipeline, and provides natural gas field services.

The company's natural gas distribution subsidiaries serve customers in Arkansas, Indiana,

Louisiana, Minnesota, Mississippi, Oklahoma, and Texas. CenterPoint Energy also markets natural gas and related services to 11,100 commercial, industrial, and wholesale customers located primarily in the eastern US. It also provides HVAC and other energy-related services through its gas division.

CenterPoint Energy's strategy is focused on enhancing and expanding existing core operations, while acquiring complementary and synergistic businesses. In 2008 the company expanded its presence in Indiana with the acquisition of Nordic Energy Services' commercial gas accounts.

CenterPoint Energy Houston's power infrastructure was badly affected by Hurricane Ike in 2008, which caused about $30 million worth of property damage. In addition, CenterPoint Energy's sales dropped dramatically in 2009 as the global recession prompted a slump in commodity prices which hurt the performance of its different energy segments.

HISTORY

CenterPoint Energy's earliest predecessor, Houston Electric Lighting and Power, was formed in 1882 by a group including Emanuel Raphael, cashier at Houston Savings Bank, and Mayor William Baker. In 1901 General Electric's financial arm, United Electric Securities Company, took control of the utility, which became Houston Lighting & Power (HL&P). United Electric sold HL&P five years later; by 1922 HL&P ended up in the arms of National Power & Light Company (NP&L), a subsidiary of Electric Bond & Share (a public utility holding company that had been spun off by General Electric).

In 1942 NP&L was forced to sell HL&P in order to comply with the 1935 Public Utility Holding Company Act. As the oil industry boomed in Houston after WWII, so did HL&P.

HL&P became the managing partner in a venture to build a nuclear plant on the Texas Gulf Coast in 1973. Construction on the South Texas Project, with partners Central Power and Light and the cities of Austin and San Antonio, began in 1975. In 1976 Houston Industries (HI) was formed as the holding company for HL&P.

By 1980 the nuke was four years behind schedule and over budget. HL&P and its partners sued construction firm Brown & Root in 1982 and received a $700 million settlement in 1985. (The City of Austin also sued HL&P for damages but lost.) The nuke was finally brought online in 1988, with the final cost estimated at $5.8 billion.

Meanwhile, HI diversified into cable TV in 1986 by creating Enrcom (later Paragon Communications) through a venture with Time Inc. Two years later it bought the US cable interests of Canada's Rogers Communications. HI left the cable business in 1995, selling out to Time Warner.

Developing Latin fever, HI joined a consortium that bought 51% of Argentinean electric company EDELAP in 1992. (However, in 1998 HI sold its stake to AES.) On a roll, HI acquired 90% of Argentina's electric utility EDESE (1995); joined a consortium that won a controlling stake in Light, a Brazilian electric utility (1996); bought a stake in Colombian electric utility EPSA (1997); and bought interests in three electric utilities in El Salvador (1998).

Back in the US, HI acquired gas dealer NorAm for $2.5 billion in 1997. The next year it bought five generating plants in California from Edison International and laid plans to build merchant plants in Arizona (near Phoenix), Illinois, Nevada

(near Las Vegas, in partnership with Sempra Energy), and Rhode Island.

In 1999 HI became Reliant Energy and HL&P became Reliant Energy HL&P. That year the company bought a 52% stake in Dutch power generation firm UNA; it bought the remaining 48% the next year. Also in 2000 Reliant Energy paid Sithe Energies (now a part of Dynegy) $2.1 billion for 21 power plants in the mid-Atlantic states. Reliant Energy also announced plans to spin off Reliant Resources that year.

Reliant Energy netted about $1.7 billion in 2001 from the sale to the public of nearly 20% of Reliant Resources. Later that year Reliant Resources announced that it would acquire US independent power producer Orion Power Holdings in a $4.7 billion deal; the deal was completed in 2002. Deregulation took effect in Texas that year, and Reliant Energy transferred its retail power supply business to Reliant Resources.

As the finances of wholesale energy companies came under scrutiny in 2002, the SEC issued a formal investigation into "round-trip" energy trades completed by Reliant Resources. These activities artificially inflated the firm's trading volumes and led it to restate its 1999, 2000, and 2001 financial results; it also reduced its energy marketing and trading workforce by about 35%.

Reliant Energy announced plans in 2001 to form a new holding company (CenterPoint Energy) for itself and Reliant Resources; it completed the name change in 2002.

In 2003 CenterPoint Energy spun off its 83% stake in Reliant Resources, a global independent power producer and energy marketer; the spin-off was completed later that year. (Reliant Resources changed its name to Reliant Energy in 2004.)

As part of its corporate reorganization, and in response to Texas' electricity deregulation (which took effect in 2002), CenterPoint Energy separated its Texas power generation and distribution operations. CenterPoint Energy sold Texas Genco to GC Power Acquisition (owned by investment firms The Blackstone Group, Hellman & Friedman, Kohlberg Kravis Roberts, and Texas Pacific Group) for $3.65 billion.

The company has also divested all of its international assets, including its Latin American utility interests.

In 2007 CenterPoint Energy Gas Transmission opened the 172-mile Carthage to Perryville pipeline, enabling the delivery of 1 billion cu. ft. of natural gas a day to pipelines serving end users in the Midwest, Northeast, and Southeast.

EXECUTIVES

Chairman: Milton Carroll, age 59
President, CEO, and Director: David M. McClanahan, age 60, $7,618,537 total compensation
Division President, CenterPoint Energy Gas Operations: Joseph B. McGoldrick, age 56
Division President, CenterPoint Energy Services: Wayne D. Stinnett Jr., age 59
EVP and CFO: Gary L. Whitlock, age 60, $1,828,645 total compensation
EVP, General Counsel, and Corporate Secretary: Scott E. Rozzell, age 60, $1,720,204 total compensation
SVP and Chief Accounting Officer: Walter L. Fitzgerald, age 52
SVP; Group President, Regulated Operations: Thomas R. (Tom) Standish, age 60, $2,449,786 total compensation
SVP Gas Operations and Engineering: Rick Zapalac
SVP; Group President, CenterPoint Energy Pipelines and Field Services: C. Gregory (Greg) Harper, age 45, $942,882 total compensation
SVP Strategic Planning and Business Development: Jim M. Dumler

VP Policy and Government Affairs: Clarence H. (Bud) Albright Jr.
VP Gas Operations, Louisiana and Mississippi: Walter Bryant
VP Gas Operations, Minnesota: Tal Centers
Auditors: Deloitte & Touche LLP

LOCATIONS

HQ: CenterPoint Energy, Inc.
1111 Louisiana St., Houston, TX 77002
Phone: 713-207-1111   **Fax:** 713-207-3169
Web: www.centerpointenergy.com

PRODUCTS/OPERATIONS

2009 Sales

	$ mil.	% of total
Natural gas distribution	3,374	41
Competitive natural gas sales & services	2,215	27
Electric transmission & distribution	2,013	24
Interstate pipelines	456	5
Field services	212	3
Other	11	—
Total	**8,281**	**100**

COMPETITORS

AEP
AEP Texas Central
AEP Texas North
Ameren
Avista
Cleco
CMS Energy
Constellation Energy Group
Dominion Resources
Duke Energy
El Paso Corporation
Energy Future
Entergy
Exelon
Koch Industries, Inc.
Mirant
Mississippi Power
OGE Energy
ONEOK
Progress Energy
Southern Company
Southwestern Electric Power
Southwestern Energy
Williams Companies
Xcel Energy

HISTORICAL FINANCIALS

Company Type: Public

Income Statement			FYE: December 31	
	REVENUE ($ mil.)	NET INCOME ($ mil.)	NET PROFIT MARGIN	EMPLOYEES
12/09	8,281	372	4.5%	8,810
12/08	11,322	447	3.9%	8,801
12/07	9,623	399	4.1%	8,568
12/06	9,319	432	4.6%	8,623
12/05	9,722	222	2.3%	9,001
Annual Growth	(3.9%)	13.8%	—	(0.5%)

2009 Year-End Financials

Debt ratio: 345.5%	No. of shares (mil.): 422
Return on equity: 15.9%	Dividends
Cash ($ mil.): 740	Yield: 5.2%
Current ratio: 0.96	Payout: 75.2%
Long-term debt ($ mil.): 9,119	Market value ($ mil.): 6,119

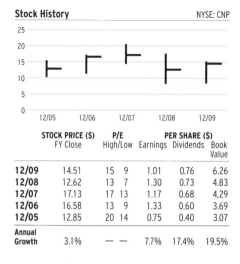

	STOCK PRICE ($) FY Close	P/E High/Low		PER SHARE ($) Earnings	Dividends	Book Value
12/09	14.51	15	9	1.01	0.76	6.26
12/08	12.62	13	7	1.30	0.73	4.83
12/07	17.13	17	13	1.17	0.68	4.29
12/06	16.58	13	9	1.33	0.60	3.69
12/05	12.85	20	14	0.75	0.40	3.07
Annual Growth	3.1%	—	—	7.7%	17.4%	19.5%

Central Garden & Pet

Central Garden & Pet is happy to help with both pets and pests. The company is among the largest US manufacturers and distributors of lawn, garden, and pet supplies, providing its products to pet supplies retailers, home improvement centers, nurseries, and mass merchandisers from approximately 40 manufacturing plants and another 30 distribution centers throughout the US; it also has sales offices in the UK. Central Garden & Pet's proprietary brand lines include AMDRO fire ant bait, Four Paws animal products, Kaytee bird seed, Nylabone dog chews, Norcal pottery, Pennington grass seed and bird seed products, and TFH pet books. Chairman and CEO William Brown controls not quite 50% of the company's voting rights.

As might be expected, Central Garden & Pet relies heavily on just a few national retailers for much of its sales. Wal-Mart accounts for about 20% of total sales and Lowe's 10%. Additionally, the company's Garden products segment sells a significant amount of its products through The Home Depot, and the Pets Products segment is reliant on both PetSmart and Petco.

Having built a sizable nationwide distribution network, the company has turned its focus to promoting its existing proprietary brands and adding new products (both through its own innovation and acquisitions). Until the mid-1990s Central Garden & Pet derived almost all of its sales from distributing other manufacturers' products; today that figure is just about 15% of total sales.

HISTORY

Central Garden & Pet Company's roots go back to 1955, when it was founded as a small California distributor of lawn and garden supplies. After nearly three decades of unremarkable growth, it was purchased in 1980 by William Brown, a former VP of finance at camera maker Vivitar. The company acquired small distributors but let them operate autonomously. By 1987 Central had sales of $25 million with distribution in California.

The company's first major acquisition was the result of a restructuring of forestry giant Weyerhaeuser, which had diversified into insurance, home building, and diapers, among other products, but was selling noncore divisions to focus solely on timber. It sold Weyerhaeuser Garden Supply to Central in 1990 for $32 million.

Overnight, Central became a national powerhouse with 25 distribution centers serving 38 states. In 1991 sales reached $280 million, of which acquired operations accounted for nearly 70%. The purchase also gave Central 10 high-volume customers — including Costco, Kmart, and Wal-Mart — which accounted for half of its business. That year the company also acquired a pet distributor, its first move into pet supplies.

To pay down debt associated with the Weyerhaeuser acquisition, the company (then officially known as Central Garden & Pet Company) went public in 1993 (a 1992 IPO was withdrawn when a warehouse fire damaged inventory). With the capital for growth, Central continued to acquire other distributors (from early 1993 to early 1994, it acquired six distributors with about $70 million in sales).

In 1994 the company's largest supplier, Solaris (then a unit of Monsanto and maker of Ortho and Roundup products), decided to bypass Central as its distributor and sell products directly. Solaris products accounted for nearly 40% of the company's sales, and revenues dipped in 1995. However, that year Solaris decided that self-distribution was too difficult and made Central its exclusive distributor. Total sales increased about 65% in 1996.

Broadening its pet supply distribution network, in 1996 Central paid $33 million for Kenlin Pet Supply, the East Coast's largest pet distributor, and Longhorn Pet Supply in Texas. The following year the company bought Four Paws Products and Sandoz Agro.

In 1997 Central paid $132 million for TFH Publications, one of the nation's largest producers of pet books and maker of Nylabone dog snacks, and Kaytee Products, a maker of bird seed. It added Pennington Seed, a maker of grass and bird seed, in 1998.

The company broadened its scope in 1999 with the purchase of Norcal Pottery Products. It also tried to buy Solaris, but that year Monsanto sold its Solaris unit to grass firm The Scotts Company (now Scotts Miracle-Gro). In a familiar refrain for Central, Scotts then decided to shift partially toward self-distribution, costing Central between $200 million and $250 million in annual sales; Scotts would completely sever distribution ties with Central the following year, leading to countering lawsuits.

Central said in early 2000 it would spin off its lawn and garden distribution business to shareholders, but the company abandoned the plan less than a year later. In March 2000 the company acquired AMDRO fire ant killer and IMAGE, a weed herbicide, from American Home Products (now Wyeth) for $28 million. Later that year Central purchased All-Glass Aquarium Company, a manufacturer and marketer of aquariums and related products.

As a result of no longer being the distributor of Scotts products, Central closed 13 of its distribution centers in 2001. Central announced the next year that it would restate its financial results for 1998 through 2002.

In 2004 the company completed a menagerie's worth of acquisitions: Kent Marine, an aquarium supplements maker; New England Pottery, which sells decorative pottery and Christmas items

(from Heritage Partners); Lawrence plc's pet products division, Interpet; KRB Seed, which does business as Budd Seed (Rebel and Palmer's Pride grass-seed brands); and Energy Savers Unlimited, which distributes aquarium lighting systems and related environmental controls and conditioners.

It continued along the same path throughout the rest of the decade, acquiring Gulfstream Home & Garden (garden products), Pets International (small animal and specialty pet supplies), Farnam Companies (animal health products), and the assets of family-owned pet food maker Breeder's Choice. The firm also increased its stakes in insect control products supplier Tech Pac (from 20% to 80%) and garden controls manufacturer Matson (from 50% to full ownership).

EXECUTIVES

Chairman and CEO: William E. Brown, age 68, $1,261,297 total compensation
CFO: Stuart W. Booth, age 59
EVP: Michael Reed, age 62, $617,521 total compensation
SVP Sales, Garden Group: Paul Duval
VP and CIO: John A. Casella
VP Investor Relations: Eileen VanEss
VP Product Development: Fredric W. Vogelgesang
VP, Treasurer, and Assistant Secretary: Paul J. Warburg
President, Pet Products: Glen Fleischer, $400,834 total compensation
President, Business Development: James V. (Jim) Heim, age 55, $566,132 total compensation
President, Aquatics: Mark S. Cavanaugh
President, Garden Décor: Bruce Cazenave
President, Four Paws Products: Allen J. Simon
President, Garden Distribution: Dean Morrison
President, Breeder's Choice: Rick S. Taylor
President, Farnam Companies: Eric N. Blomquist
President, Avian and Small Animal SBU: Chris Mings
President, Central Life Sciences: Kay M. Schwichtenberg
President, Distribution Pet Products: Jeff Sutherland
Auditors: Deloitte & Touche LLP

LOCATIONS

HQ: Central Garden & Pet Company
 1340 Treat Blvd., Ste. 600, Walnut Creek, CA 94597
Phone: 925-948-4000   **Fax:** 925-287-0601
Web: www.central.com

PRODUCTS/OPERATIONS

2009 Sales

	$ mil.	% of total
Pet products		
Bird feed	200.7	12
Other products	756.8	47
Garden products		
Garden chemicals & control products	270.5	17
Grass seed	174.5	11
Other products	211.8	13
Total	**1,614.3**	**100**

Selected Products and Brands

Pet products
 Aquatics (All-Glass Aquarium, ESU, Kent Marine, Oceanic)
 Bird and small animal (Canopy Scientific, Kaytee, Super Pet)
 Dog and cat (Four Paws, Interpet, Nylabone, Pet Select, TFH)
 Insect control and animal health (Pre-Strike, Wellmark, Zodiac)
Garden products
 Garden decor and pottery (GKI/Bethlehem Lighting, Matthews Four Seasons, New England Pottery, Norcal Pottery)
 Grass seed (Lofts Seed, Pennington, Rebel)
 Weed, insect, and pest control (AMDRO, Grant's, IMAGE, Lilly Miller, Over'n Out, Sevin)
 Wild bird (Cedar Works, Kaytee, and Pennington)

A.C. Graham
Bayer CropScience
Boss Holdings
Doskocil Manufacturing
Dow AgroSciences
Hartz Mountain

Meda Pharmaceuticals
Rollins, Inc.
Sara Lee
Scotts Miracle-Gro
Spectrum Brands
Virbac Corporation

HISTORICAL FINANCIALS

Company Type: Public

Income Statement				FYE: Last Saturday in September
	REVENUE ($ mil.)	NET INCOME ($ mil.)	NET PROFIT MARGIN	EMPLOYEES
9/09	1,614	66	4.1%	4,300
9/08	1,705	(267)	—	4,600
9/07	1,671	32	1.9%	4,860
9/06	1,622	66	4.0%	4,865
9/05	1,381	54	3.9%	4,800
Annual Growth	4.0%	5.2%	—	(2.7%)

2009 Year-End Financials

Debt ratio: 74.3%
Return on equity: 12.5%
Cash ($ mil.): 86
Current ratio: 3.20
Long-term debt ($ mil.): 405

No. of shares (mil.): 64
Dividends
  Yield: —
  Payout: —
Market value ($ mil.): 694

Stock History

NASDAQ (GS): CENTA

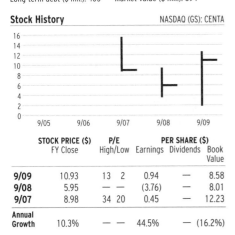

	STOCK PRICE ($) FY Close	P/E High/Low		PER SHARE ($) Earnings	Dividends	Book Value
9/09	10.93	13	2	0.94	—	8.58
9/08	5.95	—	—	(3.76)	—	8.01
9/07	8.98	34	20	0.45	—	12.23
Annual Growth	10.3%	—	—	44.5%	—	(16.2%)

CenturyTel, Inc.

Bright lights and big cities are not necessarily for CenturyTel. The company (which does business as CenturyLink) mainly provides local telephone services in rural areas, as well as network access to other carriers and businesses. It also offers long-distance and Internet access. CenturyTel serves about 7 million local voice lines and provides Internet access to about 2 million subscribers in 33 US states. The company's core service areas include Alabama, Arkansas, Missouri, Washington, and Wisconsin. Additionally, it provides paid television service to residential customers through a deal with DIRECTV. CenturyTel's other services include commercial printing, database management, and direct mail advertising.

CenturyTel paid $11.6 billion in stock and debt to buy Overland Park, Kansas-based local phone company Embarq. The deal resulted in the shareholders of Embarq owning two-thirds of the combined company, with CenturyTel investors controlling the remaining shares. CenturyTel chief Glen Post remained in the top executive spot.

The purchase gave CenturyTel greater access to the metropolitan and suburban markets where Embarq operated, but it also put the company up against stiffer competition from other carriers that also vie for customers in those areas. The name of the combined company is slated to be officially changed to CenturyLink pending shareholder approval in 2010.

CenturyTel announced an even bigger deal in 2010 with the agreement to buy Qwest Communications in an all-stock transaction valued at about $22.4 billion. If it is completed, the combined company will serve 17 million landline phone, 5 million broadband Internet, 1.4 million video, and 850,000 wireless accounts. The acquisition will bolster CenturyTel's position against industry leaders AT&T and Verizon and give it an operational advantage over regional players with smaller networks.

Looking ahead to new opportunities, CenturyTel paid about $150 million to the FCC in 2008 for wireless spectrum licenses slated for commercial availability during 2009. The company said it may develop wireless voice and data services to take advantage of these resources in the future.

HISTORY

Today's CenturyTel began in 1930 when Marie and William Clarke Williams bought the Oak Ridge Telephone Company in Oak Ridge, Louisiana. In 1946 they gave the 75-line company as a wedding present to their son, Clarke, who launched a course of growth by acquisition, buying the Marion, Louisiana, telephone exchange in 1950 (Clarke Williams remained active in the company until his death in 2002). The company was renamed Century Telephone Enterprises in 1971; it went public in 1978.

Century bought local-exchange and cellular networks, building regional clusters. States targeted during the early to mid-1990s included Louisiana, Michigan, Mississippi, Ohio, Tennessee, and Texas. Century's biggest purchase came in 1997: It bought Pacific Telecom, Inc. (PTI) from electric utility PacifiCorp for $2.2 billion. Century gained operations in 12 western and midwestern states and in Alaska, more than doubling its telephone customer base.

Also in 1997 Century merged its Metro Access Networks (MAN) subsidiary into Brooks Fiber and became Brooks' largest shareholder. Brooks' shares rose when WorldCom agreed to buy it, and Century sold 85% of its interest in Brooks.

The company rolled out the CenturyTel brand name in 1998 and bought Ameritech's local-exchange and directory operations in 21 Wisconsin communities. To help pay for the acquisition, the carrier sold its Alaska operations in 1999 to Alaska Communications Systems Holdings, a firm headed by former PTI executives. It also bought the Montana ISP DigiSys.

CenturyTel purchased nearly 500,000 access lines from GTE (which later became Verizon) in Arkansas, Missouri, and Wisconsin in 2000 and the next year sold its PCS licenses to Leap Wireless International.

ALLTEL offered to buy CenturyTel in 2001 for $6.1 billion in cash and stock and $3.3 billion in assumed debt. ALLTEL announced the offer to the public after being told by CenturyTel that the company was not for sale. CenturyTel subsequently sued ALLTEL for releasing information about the company's plans. Tensions eased, however, and in 2002 the two companies reached the agreement that sent CenturyTel's wireless operations, which served more than 800,000 customers in six states, to ALLTEL. The $1.6 billion cash deal enabled the company to expand its fixed-line business, including the acquisition that year of 675,000 switched phone lines in Alabama and Missouri from Verizon Communications for about $2.2 billion.

In 2003 CenturyTel acquired the regional fiber-optic business of bankrupt wholesale transport services provider Digital Teleport in a deal valued at $38 million. It also acquired fiber transport assets in Arkansas, Missouri, and Illinois, from Level 3 Communications in a deal valued at about $16 million.

The company further expanded its network operations with the 2005 acquisition of the fiber-optic network and customer base of KMC Telecom's operations in Monroe and Shreveport, Louisiana, as well as metro fiber networks in 16 additional markets for $75 million in cash.

In 2007 CenturyTel purchased Madison River Communications for $830 million. The acquisition added more than 160,000 rural access lines to its books and gave the company ownership of an additional 2,400 miles of fiber network.

EXECUTIVES

Chairman: William A. (Bill) Owens, age 69
Executive Vice Chairman, Regulatory and Governmental Affairs and Human Resources and Director: Thomas A. (Tom) Gerke, age 53, $1,466,544 total compensation
Vice Chairman: Harvey P. Perry, age 65
President and CEO: Glen F. Post III, age 57, $7,467,007 total compensation
EVP and COO: Karen A. Puckett, age 49, $3,270,978 total compensation
EVP, CFO, and Assistant Secretary: R. Stewart Ewing Jr., age 58, $2,877,465 total compensation
EVP, General Counsel, and Secretary: Stacey W. Goff, age 44, $1,808,821 total compensation
EVP Network and IT: Dennis G. Huber
SVP Operations Support: David D. Cole, age 52, $1,942,712 total compensation
VP Investor Relations: Tony Davis
President, Wholesale Operations: William E. (Bill) Cheek, age 54
Region President, Southern Region: Dana Chase
Region President, Western Region: Terry E. Beeler
Region President, Northeast Region: Duane Ring
Region President, Mid-Atlantic Region: Todd C. Schafer
Region President, South Central Region: Kenneth Wyatt
Auditors: KPMG LLP

LOCATIONS

HQ: CenturyTel, Inc.
  100 CenturyTel Dr., Monroe, LA 71201
Phone: 318-388-9000   **Fax:** 318-388-9064
Web: www.centurytel.com

PRODUCTS/OPERATIONS

2009 Sales

	$ mil.	% of total
Voice	1,827	37
Network access	1,269	26
Data	1,202	24
Fiber transport & CLEC	173	4
Other	503	10
Total	**4,974**	**100**

2009 Voice Lines by Market

	% of total
Residential	68
Business	32
Total	**100**

COMPETITORS

AT&T
Comcast
Cox Communications
Level 3 Communications
Nsight
NTELOS
Qwest Communications
Sprint Nextel
Telephone & Data Systems
Verizon

HISTORICAL FINANCIALS

Company Type: Public

Income Statement

FYE: December 31

	REVENUE ($ mil.)	NET INCOME ($ mil.)	NET PROFIT MARGIN	EMPLOYEES
12/09	4,974	511	10.3%	20,200
12/08	2,600	366	14.1%	6,500
12/07	2,656	418	15.8%	6,600
12/06	2,448	370	15.1%	6,400
12/05	2,479	335	13.5%	6,900
Annual Growth	**19.0%**	**11.2%**	**—**	**30.8%**

2009 Year-End Financials

Debt ratio: 76.7%
Return on equity: 8.1%
Cash ($ mil.): 162
Current ratio: 0.66
Long-term debt ($ mil.): 7,254

No. of shares (mil.): 301
Dividends
Yield: 7.7%
Payout: 86.7%
Market value ($ mil.): 10,915

Stock History

NYSE: CTL

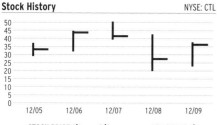

	STOCK PRICE ($) FY Close	P/E High/Low		PER SHARE ($) Earnings	Dividends	Book Value
12/09	36.21	12	7	3.23	2.80	31.39
12/08	27.33	12	6	3.56	1.53	10.49
12/07	41.46	13	11	3.72	0.26	11.31
12/06	43.66	14	11	3.07	0.25	10.59
12/05	33.16	15	12	2.49	0.24	12.00
Annual Growth	**2.2%**	**—**	**—**	**6.7%**	**84.8%**	**27.2%**

Cenveo, Inc.

Commercial printer Cenveo produces not only items that go inside envelopes, but also the envelopes themselves. The company's printing units churn out catalogs, journals, magazines, and marketing materials. Cenveo's envelopes and other packaging products are used for purposes such as billing, catalog distribution, and direct mail. The company also produces business forms and pressure-sensitive labels. Its envelopes, forms, and labels products are sold both directly to end users and through wholesalers. Cenveo operates production, fulfillment, and distribution facilities throughout the US and Canada. The company is growing rapidly as a result of an aggressive acquisition schedule.

To that end, Cenveo in February 2010 purchased Clixx Direct Marketing Services to boost its direct mail, data management, imaging, and fulfillment capabilities. It also acquired Nashua Corp. in a transaction valued at more than $40 million in September 2009. By buying Nashua, which makes specialty papers and prints labels, the firm strengthened its position in pharmaceutical labeling.

The company previously purchasesd Cadmus Communications, a leading printer of periodicals, in 2007 for about $430 million, including some $200 million in debt. The addition of Cadmus made Cenveo one of the largest printing companies in North America, behind giants such as R.R. Donnelley and Quebecor World. Besides bringing together the companies' complementary operations in printing and specialty packaging and benefiting from economies of scale in purchasing, Cenveo looks to build upon Cadmus' strength in the scientific, technical, and medical journal printing markets. It took a step in that direction in mid-2010, when it acquired Glyph International. Glyph has production expertise in the journal and book publishing markets, and the deal strengthened Cenveo's market presence in this area, in addition to enhancing its already productive Cadmus operations.

Cenveo has expanded its packaging printing operations through acquisitions, as well. It purchased Commercial Envelope Manufacturing Co. and PC Ink (known as Printegra), both specialists in printing business forms, labels, and envelopes. The company then shifted its focus to building up its commercial business, buying the West Coast-based Madison/Graham ColorGraphics in 2007. It also acquired Rex Corp. in an all-cash deal that closed in 2008. Rex, which had annual revenues of about $40 million prior to the purchase, helps to boost Cenveo's standing in the specialty packaging market for commercial customers.

After its 2007 and 2008 acquisitions, Cenveo began working to cut costs and focus on its strongest operations. As part of this initiative, the company reduced its workforce by about 10% and shuttered a commercial printing plant in 2008. Throughout 2009 the company continued to reduce its headcount, primarily through the elimination of redundancies associated with the Nashua acquisition toward the end of the year. Throughout the entire year Cenveo closed and consolidated nine manufacturing plants and cut 1,700 job positions. It continued the process of integrating Nashua's operations through the first half of 2010.

HISTORY

Mail-Well (later Cenveo) evolved from Denver's Rockmont Envelope, founded in 1921. The company was owned by paper mill Great Northern Nekoosa (GNN) until 1990 when GNN was acquired by Georgia-Pacific. Then in 1994, in an effort to get back to its roots in its core forest business, Georgia-Pacific sold Mail-Well to investment firm Sterling Group. Sterling merged the company with its Pavey Envelope business and initiated an aggressive acquisition strategy. Mail-Well went public in 1995. The company bought Canada's largest envelope printer, Supremex, that year.

Mail-Well's six acquisitions in 1997 were followed by 23 more in 1998. Among the company's purchases were Poser Business Forms, label maker Lawson Mardon Packaging, International Paper's label operation, and commercial printer Anderson Lithograph.

Mail-Well's 10 acquisitions in 1999 included UK-based label manufacturing firm Porter Chadburn. The company made its largest acquisition to date the next year when it bought American Business Products, a maker of office products and specialty packaging.

In 2001 Mail-Well closed a number of printing plants and cut about 1,200 jobs. The company sold its Curtis 1000 unit, which distributed printed office products, in 2002. Later that year the company sold Mail-Well Label for $75 million to real estate developer Gregory Mosher and Arsenal Capital Partners.

In 2003 the company sold off much of its digital graphics division to Group360. Mail-Well changed its corporate name to Cenveo in 2004, consolidating its operating companies, such as Anderson Lithograph, Color-Art, Graphic Arts Center, and Supremex, under the name, as well.

Cenveo spent the next three years streamlining its business. The company consolidated envelope operations by closing 15 envelope and printing facilities. In the early 2000s it sold off other divisions such as office products distribution, adhesive labels, and filing products. As a part of the process, the firm cut about 1,200 jobs. Turnaround specialist James Malone was named the company's new CEO and chairman in 2005. He resigned before the year was out, however, and Robert Burton took over as CEO in fall 2005.

As part of the streamlining effort, Cenveo spun off its Supremex unit to the public in 2006. Also that year the company bought Rx Label Technology, a maker of pressure-sensitive prescription labels for the retail pharmacy market in the US that generated about $40 million in annual sales.

In 2007 Cenveo purchased Cadmus Communications, Commercial Envelope Manufacturing Co., Madison/Graham ColorGraphics, and PC Ink (known as Printegra). To expand its specialty packaging expertise, Cenveo acquired Rex Corp. in 2008.

Extending its reach into label and specialty papers, Cenveo acquired Nashua in late 2009.

EXECUTIVES

Chairman and CEO: Robert G. Burton Sr., age 69, $4,203,940 total compensation
EVP and CFO: Mark S. Hiltwein, age 46, $979,883 total compensation
SVP Business Development, Envelope Group: Robert J. (Bob) Muma
VP Human Resources and Benefits: Gina Genuario
Treasurer: Michael (Mickey) Walsh
Corporate Controller: Scott J. Goodwin

President, Envelope Group: Dean E. Cherry, age 49, $806,134 total compensation
President, Commercial Print, Packaging, and Cadmus Publisher Services Group: Harry R. Vinson, age 49, $720,754 total compensation
Auditors: Ernst & Young LLP

LOCATIONS

HQ: Cenveo, Inc.
1 Canterbury Green, 201 Broad St.
Stamford, CT 06901
Phone: 203-595-3000   **Fax:** 203-595-3070
Web: www.cenveo.com

2009 Sales

	$ mil.	% of total
US	1,636.1	95
Other countries	78.5	5
Total	**1,714.6**	**100**

PRODUCTS/OPERATIONS

2009 Sales

	$ mil.	% of total
Commercial printing	895.2	52
Envelopes, forms & labels	819.4	48
Total	**1,714.6**	**100**

Selected Products and Services

Articles
Books
Business documents
Catalogs
Commercial envelopes
Commercial print
Custom envelopes
Directories
Journals
Labels
Magazines
Packaging
Promotional printing

COMPETITORS

Bowne
Consolidated Graphics
Merrill
National Envelope
Penn Lithographics
Quad/Graphics
R.R. Donnelley
Transcontinental Inc.
Vertis Inc

HISTORICAL FINANCIALS

Company Type: Public

Income Statement   FYE: December 31

	REVENUE ($ mil.)	NET INCOME ($ mil.)	NET PROFIT MARGIN	EMPLOYEES
12/09	1,715	(31)	—	8,700
12/08	2,099	(298)	—	9,700
12/07	2,047	41	2.0%	10,700
12/06	1,511	119	7.9%	6,600
12/05	1,749	(135)	—	8,000
Annual Growth	**(0.5%)**	**—**	**—**	**2.1%**

2009 Year-End Financials

Debt ratio: —
Return on equity: —
Cash ($ mil.): 11
Current ratio: 1.50
Long-term debt ($ mil.): 1,219

No. of shares (mil.): 62
Dividends
  Yield: —
  Payout: —
Market value ($ mil.): 545

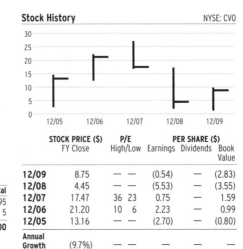

Stock History   NYSE: CVO

	STOCK PRICE ($) FY Close	P/E High/Low		PER SHARE ($) Earnings	Dividends	Book Value
12/09	8.75	—	—	(0.54)	—	(2.83)
12/08	4.45	—	—	(5.53)	—	(3.55)
12/07	17.47	36	23	0.75	—	1.59
12/06	21.20	10	6	2.23	—	0.99
12/05	13.16	—	—	(2.70)	—	(0.80)
Annual Growth	**(9.7%)**	**—**	**—**	**—**	**—**	**—**

Cephalon, Inc.

Cephalon isn't asleep at the wheel. The company sells PROVIGIL, a treatment for the sleep disorder narcolepsy, in the US and select countries around the world. The company's other top sellers are cancer pain medications ACTIQ and FENTORA, epilepsy treatment GABITRIL (licensed from Abbott Labs and Novo Nordisk), cancer drug TREANDA, and narcolepsy treatment NUVIGIL. It sells seven products in the US and has more than a dozen approved drugs on the market in Europe. Cephalon's drug research and development activities focus on central nervous system disorders, cancer, pain, and inflammatory disease.

Cephalon's two biggest sellers are PROVIGIL and NUVIGIL, which together comprise about half of the company's sales. Like most pharmaceutical companies, Cephalon depends on new products (and new applications for existing products) to fight off potential operating losses brought on by patent protection and regulatory hurdles. It adds to its product line through internal and collaborative development as well as acquisitions.

The company's clinical development focus is primarily on developing therapies for neurological disorders and cancer. It is developing potential treatments for hematological cancers, solid tumors, pain, fatigue, and Alzheimer's disease. Development partners include AstraZeneca and Merck.

One of Cephalon's treatments for chronic lymphocytic leukemia and non-Hodgkin's lymphoma, TREANDA, received approval from the FDA in 2008 and was successfully launched later that year. NUVIGIL was launched as a next-generation version of PROVIGIL. The company hopes sales of NUVIGIL will ward off competition when PROVIGIL loses its patent protection in 2012, and so far sales of the drug have not disappointed.

Cephalon maintains a steady acquisition pace to keep its pipeline flowing. In 2009 the company bought Australian biotech firm Arana Therapeutics, a developer of antibody-based drugs to address cancer and inflammatory diseases.

In early 2010 Cephalon expanded its development operations further when it exercised an option to acquire privately held Ception Therapeutics, which had candidates in clinical trials for esophagitis and asthma, for $250 million after Ception's lead pipeline candidate passed certain development milestones.

To broaden its product range and geographical footprint, the company also acquired Swiss generic drugmaker Mepha in 2010. Cephalon spent some $615 million on the deal to enter into the generics business and double the size of its international business.

The company has suffered some grief over its pain medication franchise. The active ingredient in cancer pain medication ACTIQ and its next-generation version FENTORA is fentanyl, which is 80 times stronger than morphine and can be highly addictive. The fentanyl drugs have not been approved for use in any context other than cancer pain, but the company has been under investigation for pushing ACTIQ and FENTORA for off-label uses, including use against migraines. Cephalon reached settlement agreements with several government agencies over the charges in 2007 and 2008.

HISTORY

A senior research biologist with DuPont, Dr. Frank Baldino formed Cephalon in 1987 to research neural degeneration. The company raised $500 million in venture capital and went public in 1991.

Cephalon in 1990 teamed with Schering-Plough to research Alzheimer's disease. By 1992 it had developed Myotrophin to treat amyotrophic lateral sclerosis (ALS, or Lou Gehrig's disease).

With optimism running high for Myotrophin, Cephalon in 1992 bought a drug plant (sold 1996). The next year it joined with SmithKline Beecham (now GlaxoSmithKline) to research neurodegenerative diseases. In 1995 the firm established a sales force. Word of promising Myotrophin trial results sent the stock soaring, but criticism of the trial brought it crashing back. A 1996 shareholder suit charging that Cephalon hid poor results was settled for $17 million in 1999.

Meanwhile, it bought rights to PROVIGIL from Group Lafon and shepherded it through the FDA approval process for the treatment of sleep disorder narcolepsy.

In 1997 the FDA rejected Myotrophin; Cephalon's research agreements with Schering-Plough and SmithKline Beecham ended too. The next year the FDA ruled Myotrophin "potentially approvable" and required more expensive trials. Better news came from Ireland and the UK, where PROVIGIL was approved for sale.

In 2000 PROVIGIL failed to treat attention deficit hyperactivity disorder in trials. Cephalon bounced back by boosting its pipeline with the purchase of pain drugmaker Anesta. The following year it bought Group Lafon to gain full control of PROVIGIL's marketing rights. Spooked by the on-the-sly partnerships that helped bring down Enron, Cephalon also acquired control of two joint ventures it had set up to market PROVIGIL and GABITRIL to avoid arousing suspicion among investors. It also bought back European rights to ACTIQ from Elan.

Cephalon received approval from the FDA in 2004 to market PROVIGIL as a therapy for other sleep disorders such as obstructive sleep apnea.

The company's 2004 purchase of CIMA allowed Cephalon to develop new versions of its existing drugs using CIMA's delivery technologies. But the acquisition didn't come without costs — in addition to the $515 million it paid for CIMA,

Cephalon agreed to give Barr Pharmaceuticals the right to license a generic version of ACTIQ to gain FDA approval.

Cephalon acquired drugmaker Zeneus Pharma in 2005. Zeneus added nearly 15 products to the company's portfolio, but more importantly Zeneus' 15 European operations greatly expanded Cephalon's presence across the pond. Also that year the company expanded its cancer pipeline with its purchase of Salmedix and of the TRISENOX franchise from Cell Therapeutics.

In 2006 lead drug candidate FENTORA (the next-generation version of ACTIQ) was approved for cancer pain. Sales of ACTIQ were cut in half in 2007 due to generic competition; however, the company took up some of the slack through increased sales of FENTORA and the launch of its own generic version of ACTIQ.

In 2007 the company sent a warning letter to doctors about several deaths related to FENTORA, which Cephalon primarily attributed to inappropriate prescribing of the drug. The FDA later issued a health advisory urging the use of caution when prescribing FENTORA.

EXECUTIVES

Chairman and CEO: Frank Baldino Jr., age 56, $11,149,392 total compensation
COO: J. Kevin Buchi, age 54, $2,738,972 total compensation
EVP and CFO: Wilco Groenhuysen
EVP and Chief Administrative Officer: Carl A. Savini, age 60, $3,387,820 total compensation
EVP, General Counsel and Secretary: Gerald J. (Jerry) Pappert, age 46, $2,732,616 total compensation
EVP Worldwide Technical Operations: Peter E. Grebow, age 63, $3,298,493 total compensation
EVP Worldwide Medical and Regulatory Operations and Chief Medical Officer: Lesley Russell Cooper, age 49, $2,589,205 total compensation
EVP; President, Cephalon Europe: Alain Aragues
EVP and Chief Scientific Officer: Jeffry L. Vaught, age 59
EVP and Chief Compliance Officer: Valli F. Baldassano, age 49
VP Intellectual Property and Chief Patent Counsel: Robert T. Hrubiec
VP Government and Corporate Affairs: Fritz Bittenbender
VP Strategic Planning and Business Development: Martin Reeves
VP Public Affairs: Sheryl L. Williams
Senior Director Product Communications: Candace Steele
Senior Director Investor Relations: Robert S. (Chip) Merritt, age 58
Auditors: PricewaterhouseCoopers LLP

LOCATIONS

HQ: Cephalon, Inc.
41 Moores Rd., Malvern, PA 19355
Phone: 610-344-0200
Web: www.cephalon.com

2009 Sales

	$ mil.	% of total
US	1,808.2	82
Europe	384.1	18
Total	**2,192.3**	**100**

PRODUCTS/OPERATIONS

2009 Sales

	$ mil.	% of total
CNS products		
PROVIGIL	1,024.7	47
NUVIGIL	73.4	3
GABITRIL	56.5	3
Pain products		
ACTIQ	146.9	7
FENTORA	140.7	6
Generic OTFC	83.0	4
AMRIX	114.4	5
Oncology products		
TREANDA	222.1	10
Other oncology	113.8	5
Other products	176.0	8
Other	40.8	2
Total	**2,192.3**	**100**

Selected Products

US
ACTIQ (cancer pain)
AMRIX (muscle spasms)
FENTORA (cancer pain)
GABITRIL (epilepsy)
NUVIGIL (narcolepsy, obstructive sleep apnea, shift work sleep disorder)
PROVIGIL (narcolepsy, obstructive sleep apnea, shift work sleep disorder)
TREANDA (chronic lymphocytic leukemia, indolent B-cell non-Hodgkin's lymphoma)
TRISENOX (promyelocytic leukemia)

Europe
Abelcet (antifungal)
ACTIQ
DILZEM (angina and mild to moderate hypertension)
GABITRIL
MYOCET (chemotherapy agent for breast cancer)
NAXY and MONO-NAXY (antibiotic)
PROVIGIL
SPASFON (bowel and urinary tract ailments)
TARGRETIN (T-cell lymphoma)

COMPETITORS

Allergan
Amgen
AstraZeneca
Athena Neurosciences
Bayer AG
Biogen Idec
Bristol-Myers Squibb
Ceregene
Cortex Pharmaceuticals
Dr. Reddy's
DRAXIS
Eli Lilly
Endo Pharmaceuticals
Genzyme
GlaxoSmithKline
Jazz Pharmaceuticals
Johnson & Johnson
King Pharmaceuticals
Millennium: The Takeda Oncology Company
Neurocrine Biosciences
Novartis
Pfizer
Purdue Pharma
Ranbaxy Laboratories
ResMed
Roche Holding
Sanofi-Aventis
Sepracor
Shire
Teva Pharmaceuticals

HISTORICAL FINANCIALS

Company Type: Public

Income Statement

FYE: December 31

	REVENUE ($ mil.)	NET INCOME ($ mil.)	NET PROFIT MARGIN	EMPLOYEES
12/09	2,192	343	15.6%	3,026
12/08	1,975	223	11.3%	2,780
12/07	1,773	(192)	—	2,796
12/06	1,764	145	8.2%	2,895
12/05	1,212	(175)	—	2,895
Annual Growth	**16.0%**	**—**	**—**	**1.1%**

2009 Year-End Financials

Debt ratio: 16.1%
Return on equity: 18.2%
Cash ($ mil.): 1,648
Current ratio: 1.92
Long-term debt ($ mil.): 364
No. of shares (mil.): 75
Dividends
  Yield: —
  Payout: —
Market value ($ mil.): 4,694

Stock History

NASDAQ (GS): CEPH

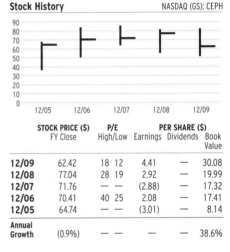

	STOCK PRICE ($) FY Close	P/E High/Low		PER SHARE ($) Earnings	Dividends	Book Value
12/09	62.42	18	12	4.41	—	30.08
12/08	77.04	28	19	2.92	—	19.99
12/07	71.76	—	—	(2.88)	—	17.32
12/06	70.41	40	25	2.08	—	17.41
12/05	64.74	—	—	(3.01)	—	8.14
Annual Growth	**(0.9%)**	—	—	—	**—**	**38.6%**

Cerner Corporation

Cerner provides the IV that pumps information through a health care organization's computer network. The company's products and services combine clinical, financial, and administrative information management applications, including tools for managing electronic medical records, patient care, and health information access. Cerner's clinical and administrative information systems link emergency rooms, pharmacies, and other health care departments. The company's service offerings include data migration, implementation, maintenance, and security compliance services. Cerner gets most of its sales in the US.

Targeting a US health care market which still relies heavily on paper documents and manual processes and is under increasing pressure to improve operating efficiency, Cerner appeals to customers looking to reduce waste and cut costs by automating processes and replacing paper with electronic information systems. The company also hopes to profit from broader efforts in the US — such as the passage of the American Recovery and Reinvestment Act (ARRA) in 2009 — that are designed to encourage health care providers to upgrade their IT infrastructures.

Cerner has grown rapidly by focusing both on enterprise software that organizes large health care systems and on specialized applications for individual departments within these systems. The company is expanding its product line and offering applications designed for specific markets such as nursing, pharmacies, and emergency medicine. Cerner has targeted services for future growth, including expanding its managed services offerings and introducing new services such as Cerner ITWorks and Cerner RevWorks.

HISTORY

Neal Patterson, Clifford Illig, and Paul Gorup, all former information systems consultants for Arthur Andersen, started Cerner in 1979. The name came from the Latin *cernere* — to sift or understand. They knew nothing about health care, but a stint consulting for a medical lab had tickled their entrepreneurial instincts. "The level of automation was low. The amount the market was willing to pay for automation was high," Illig once said.

Cerner introduced its first product, a laboratory information system called PathNet, in 1984. Cerner went public in 1986, and a year later began expanding its product line, creating systems for various medical specialties. Each component was built from the same foundation, so they could be combined to share information. Making the systems patient-driven rather than finance-driven appealed to an industry turning increasingly toward managed care and affordable services.

In a health care landscape of disparate departmental computer systems, Cerner poured research and development dollars into systems that integrated an organization's business and clinical sides. The purchase in 1993 of pharmacy information systems specialist Megasource edged Cerner into the smaller hospital market. In 1998 the company bought drug knowledge database supplier Multum Information Services. President Illig in 1999 took the more strategic vice chairman position.

In 2000 Cerner acquired smaller competitor CITATION Computer Systems, a maker of information management systems for health care providers. The next year Cerner acquired medical information technology firm Dynamic Healthcare Technologies.

Cerner moved into the home health care technology market in 2003 with its purchase of BeyondNow Technologies. The following year, working to build on its core customer base, Cerner paid about $100 million for rival VitalWorks' (now AMICAS) Medical Division, which provided practice management and electronic medical records software. In 2005 it acquired Axya, a French IT services company targeting the health care market.

EXECUTIVES

Chairman, Acting President, and CEO:
Neal L. Patterson, age 60,
$3,319,732 total compensation
Vice Chairman: Clifford W. (Cliff) Illig, age 59
EVP and COO: Michael G. (Mike) Valentine, age 41,
$1,196,476 total compensation
EVP and CFO: Marc G. Naughton, age 54,
$877,592 total compensation
EVP and Chief of Staff: Jeffrey A. (Jeff) Townsend,
age 46, $1,342,524 total compensation
EVP and Chief Engineering Officer: Michael R. Nill,
age 45, $1,199,444 total compensation

SVP PowerWorks: Shellee K. Spring
SVP Research Services: Richard J. (Dick) Flanigan Jr.,
age 50
SVP and Engineering Fellow: Douglas S. (Doug) McNair
SVP Client Organization, Cerner Pacific:
Michael C. (Mike) Neal
SVP Client Organization, Cerner Atlantic:
John T. Peterzalek, age 49
SVP Client Development: Jude G. Dieterman
SVP and Chief People Officer: Julia M. (Julie) Wilson,
age 47
VP and CIO: Kevin Smyth
VP, Chief Legal Officer, and Secretary: Randy D. Sims,
age 49
VP and Chief Quality Officer: Gay M. Johannes
VP LifeSciences: J. Randall (Randy) Nelson
VP IT and Medical Device Technologies:
Thomas Herzog
Chief Innovation: Paul N. Gorup
President, Cerner Canada: Robert J. Shave
Auditors: KPMG LLP

LOCATIONS

HQ: Cerner Corporation
2800 Rockcreek Pkwy., Kansas City, MO 64117
Phone: 816-201-1024   **Fax:** 816-474-1742
Web: www.cerner.com

2009 Sales

	$ mil.	% of total
US	1,398.7	84
Other countries	273.2	16
Total	**1,671.9**	**100**

PRODUCTS/OPERATIONS

2009 Sales

	$ mil.	% of total
Services	643.7	39
System sales	504.6	30
Support & maintenance	493.2	29
Reimbursed travel	30.4	2
Total	**1,671.9**	**100**

Selected Products

Cerner Millennium (platform architecture)
Clinical information management applications
  Cerner APACHE (clinical management system)
  Cerner Multum (drug information integration)
  Cerner Women's Health Information System
  Computerized Physician Order Entry System
  Critical Care INet (intensive care management system)
  CVNet (cardiology clinical information system)
  Discern Expert (decision support)
  Discern Explorer (decision support)
  FirstNet (emergency medicine information system)
  HealthSmart Medication Integration (medication
    information integration system)
  PathNet (laboratory information system)
  PharmNet (pharmacy information system)
  PowerChart Electronic Medical Record System
  PowerChart Oncology Information System
  PowerOrders (physician ordering system)
  ProVision (image management system)
  RadNet (radiology information system)
  SurgiNet (surgery and anesthesia information system)
  VantageRx (drug information delivery application)
Consumer applications
  IQHealth (networked health care customer
    relationship management application)
  SubscribeRx (Internet-based drug information)
Decision support and knowledge management
  applications
  APACHE (clinical decision support)
  HealthSentry (pharmacy, laboratory, and public health
    department connection application)
  PowerInsight (data collection and decision support
    applications)
  PowerVision (management process automation)

Enterprise and executive applications
  CapStone (enterprise access management system)
  Clinically Driven Workforce Management (supply
    chain automation application)
  ProFile (health information management system)
  ProFit (clinical and financial patient accounting
    system)
Financial and administrative applications
  HealthSmart Revenue Cycle Integration (revenue cycle
    management application)
Home health care information systems
  HomeWorks (home health care services management)
  RoadNotes (remote patient information access)
Nursing applications
  CareGuard (patient safety application)
  CareNet (acute care management system)
Repositories and foundations applications
  Open Agreement Foundation Data Repository (health
    plan database)
  Open Clinical Foundation Data Repository (patient
    database)
  Open Image Foundation (clinical and document
    imaging)
  Open Management Foundation Data Repository
    (management database)
  Open Research Foundation (repository storage of
    clinical and medical information)

Selected Services

Benefits realization
Education
Implementation
Maintenance
Technical support

COMPETITORS

3M HIS
Accenture
Allscripts
Capgemini US
CareFusion
Computer Sciences Corp.
CPSI
Deloitte LLP
Eclipsys
GE Healthcare
IBM Global Services
iSOFT Group
McKesson
MEDITECH
NextGen
Omnicell
Perot Systems
Precyse Solutions
QuadraMed
Quality Systems
Siemens Healthcare

HISTORICAL FINANCIALS

Company Type: Public

Income Statement		FYE: Saturday nearest December 31		
	REVENUE ($ mil.)	NET INCOME ($ mil.)	NET PROFIT MARGIN	EMPLOYEES
12/09	1,672	194	11.6%	7,600
12/08	1,676	189	11.3%	7,500
12/07	1,520	127	8.4%	7,873
12/06	1,378	110	8.0%	7,419
12/05	1,161	86	7.4%	6,830
Annual Growth	9.6%	22.4%	—	2.7%

2009 Year-End Financials

Debt ratio: 6.0%
Return on equity: 13.4%
Cash ($ mil.): 242
Current ratio: 3.20
Long-term debt ($ mil.): 96
No. of shares (mil.): 82
Dividends
  Yield: —
  Payout: —
Market value ($ mil.): 6,800

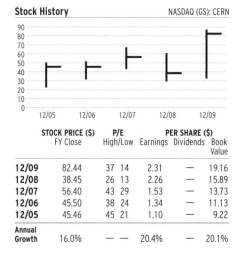

	STOCK PRICE ($) FY Close	P/E High/Low		PER SHARE ($) Earnings	Dividends	Book Value
12/09	82.44	37	14	2.31	—	19.16
12/08	38.45	26	13	2.26	—	15.89
12/07	56.40	43	29	1.53	—	13.73
12/06	45.50	38	24	1.34	—	11.13
12/05	45.46	45	21	1.10	—	9.22
Annual Growth	**16.0%**	**—**	**—**	**20.4%**	**—**	**20.1%**

C.H. Robinson Worldwide

C.H. Robinson Worldwide (CHRW) keeps merchandise moving. A third-party logistics provider, the company arranges freight transportation using trucks, trains, ships, and airplanes belonging to other companies. It contracts with some 47,000 carriers. CHRW handles about 7.5 million shipments per year for its 35,000-plus customers, which include companies in the food and beverage, manufacturing, and retail industries. Together with overseeing freight transportation for its customers, it offers supply chain management services through some 235 offices. In addition, CHRW buys, sells, and transports fresh produce throughout the US, and its T-Chek unit provides fuel purchasing management services for motor carriers.

Truckload services are CHRW's primary transportation offering (about 75% of sales), but the company is endeavoring to diversify by providing more less-than-truckload (LTL) and freight consolidation services. The company is also looking to sell more supply chain management services to its transportation customers.

Although CHRW does most of its business in the US, the company also has branch offices elsewhere in the Americas, Europe, the Middle East, and Asia. The company has been working to expand — especially outside North America — both through organic growth and acquisitions.

Along these lines, it purchased London-based Walker Logistics Overseas, an international freight forwarder, serving primarily the electronics, telecommunications, medical, sporting goods, and military industries. The 2009 acquisition expands its capabilities in Asia-to-Europe trade and brings two key distribution gateways — London and Amsterdam. That same year CHRW acquired certain assets of International Trade & Commerce (ITC), a US customs brokerage company that specializes in warehousing, distribution, and services between the US and Mexico.

Also in 2009 the company acquired produce marketing company Rosemont Farms, as well as Quality Logistics, which provides logistics for produce transportation; both companies are based in Florida. CHRW expanded its produce distribution business even further by opening a European-based produce sourcing company in France, which will focus on bringing fresh produce from France, Italy, and Spain to North and South America, Europe, Asia, and Middle Eastern countries.

In mid-2008 CHRW acquired Transera International Holdings, a project forwarding business based in Canada. Transera has office locations in Canada, Dubai, Singapore, and the US.

HISTORY

In the early 1900s Charles H. Robinson began a produce brokerage in Grand Forks, North Dakota. Robinson entered a partnership in 1905 with Nash Brothers, the leading wholesaler in North Dakota, and the company C.H. Robinson was born.

Robinson became president but soon relinquished control under mysterious circumstances (rumor had it he ran off with Annie Oakley). H. B. Finch took charge, and by 1913 a new company, Nash Finch, became C.H. Robinson's sole owner.

As a subsidiary, C.H. Robinson primarily procured produce for Nash Finch, which helped it expand into Illinois, Minnesota, Texas, and Wisconsin. To avoid FTC scrutiny over preferential treatment, Nash Finch split CHR into two operations: C.H. Robinson Co., owned by C.H. Robinson employees, which sold produce to Nash Finch warehouses; and C.H. Robinson, Inc., owned by Nash Finch.

After WWII the interstate highway system and refrigerated trucks changed the industry. No longer dependent on railroads, C.H. Robinson began charging for truck brokerage of perishables. The two companies formed by the 1940s split reunited under the C.H. Robinson name in the mid-1960s; Nash Finch kept a 25% stake in the company and sold the rest to employees. Not surprisingly, Nash Finch wanted to divert C.H. Robinson profits to its other businesses, so in 1976 C.H. Robinson employees bought out Nash Finch.

The next year D. R. "Sid" Verdoorn was named president and Looe Baker became chairman. They focused on increasing C.H. Robinson's data-processing capability and adding branch offices. In 1980 the Motor Carrier Act deregulated the transportation industry, and C.H. Robinson entered the freight-contracting business, acting as a middleman for all types of goods. The company grew rapidly, from about 30 offices in 1980 to more than 60 in 1990.

As part of its overall effort to become a full-service provider, C.H. Robinson formed its Intermodal Division (more than one mode of transport) in 1988. It also established an information services division (1991) and bought fruit juice concentrate distributor Daystar International (1993). By this time the company was working with more than 14,000 shippers and moving more than 500,000 shipments a year.

Meanwhile, C.H. Robinson had ventured overseas with the launch of its international division in 1989. It entered Mexico in 1990 and added air-freight operations and international freight forwarding through the 1992 purchase of C.S. Green International.

In 1997 the company went public and became C.H. Robinson Worldwide (CHRW); the next year Verdoorn, who was CEO, assumed the additional role of chairman.

The company acquired Argentina's Comexter transportation group in 1998 to gain market share in South America, and it expanded its European operation in 1999 through the purchase of Norminter, a French third-party logistics provider.

CHRW continued to expand in 2002 with the purchase of Miami-based Smith Terminal Transportation Services. Verdoorn stepped down as CEO that year, and company president John Wiehoff was promoted to replace him. Verdoorn retired at the end of 2006, and Wiehoff succeeded him as chairman.

The company acquired three US-based produce sourcing and marketing companies — FoodSource, Inc., FoodSource Procurement, and Epic Roots — in 2004. Also that year CHRW added seven offices in China by acquiring a Dalian-based freight forwarder. In 2005 CHRW bought US-based freight broker Payne, Lynch & Associates, as well as an India-based freight forwarder, Triune. The following year the company acquired US-based LXSI Services, a specialist in domestic airfreight and expedited ground transportation management.

EXECUTIVES

Chairman, President, and CEO: John P. Wiehoff, age 48, $3,321,677 total compensation
SVP: Scott A. Satterlee, age 41, $1,133,879 total compensation
SVP Transportation: Mark A. Walker, age 52, $1,453,912 total compensation
SVP: James E. (Jim) Butts, age 54, $1,138,556 total compensation
SVP Sourcing: James P. (Jim) Lemke, age 43, $1,176,398 total compensation
SVP and CFO: Chad M. Lindbloom, age 45, $1,128,982 total compensation
VP and CIO: Thomas K. (Tom) Mahlke, age 38
VP International Forwarding: Jeffrey W. Scovill, age 40
VP, General Counsel, and Secretary: Ben G. Campbell, age 44
VP Human Resources: Laura Gillund, age 49
President, T-Chek: Bryan D. Foe, age 42
VP Investor Relations and Public Affairs: Angela K. (Angie) Freeman, age 42
Treasurer and Assistant Secretary: Troy A. Renner, age 45
Director: David W. (Dave) MacLennan, age 51
Auditors: Deloitte & Touche LLP

LOCATIONS

HQ: C.H. Robinson Worldwide, Inc.
14701 Charlson Rd., Eden Prairie, MN 55347
Phone: 952-937-8500   **Fax:** 952-937-6714
Web: www.chrobinson.com

2009 Sales

	$ mil.	% of total
US	6,800.5	90
Other countries	776.7	10
Total	**7,577.2**	**100**

PRODUCTS/OPERATIONS

2009 Sales

	$ mil.	% of total
Transportation	5,976.1	79
Sourcing	1,555.3	20
Information services	45.8	1
Total	**7,577.2**	**100**

Selected Services

Air
Intermodal
Less-than-truckload
Ocean
Truckload

HISTORICAL FINANCIALS

Company Type: Public

Income Statement
FYE: December 31

	REVENUE ($ mil.)	NET INCOME ($ mil.)	NET PROFIT MARGIN	EMPLOYEES
12/09	7,577	361	4.8%	7,347
12/08	8,579	359	4.2%	7,961
12/07	7,316	324	4.4%	7,332
12/06	6,556	267	4.1%	6,768
12/05	5,689	203	3.6%	5,776
Annual Growth	7.4%	15.4%	—	6.2%

2009 Year-End Financials

Debt ratio: —
Return on equity: 33.0%
Cash ($ mil.): 337
Current ratio: 1.79
Long-term debt ($ mil.): —

No. of shares (mil.): 166
Dividends
 Yield: 1.7%
 Payout: 45.5%
Market value ($ mil.): 9,741

Stock History
NASDAQ (GS): CHRW

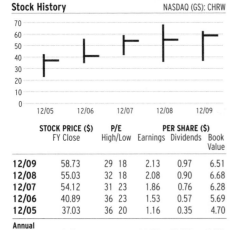

	STOCK PRICE ($) FY Close	P/E High/Low		PER SHARE ($) Earnings	Dividends	Book Value
12/09	58.73	29	18	2.13	0.97	6.51
12/08	55.03	32	18	2.08	0.90	6.68
12/07	54.12	31	23	1.86	0.76	6.28
12/06	40.89	36	23	1.53	0.57	5.69
12/05	37.03	36	20	1.16	0.35	4.70
Annual Growth	12.2%	—	—	16.4%	29.0%	8.5%

Charles Schwab

The once-rebellious Charles Schwab is all grown up. The discount broker now offers the same traditional brokerage services it shunned some three decades ago. Schwab manages more than $1.4 trillion in assets for nearly 10 million individual and institutional clients. Traders can access its services via telephone, wireless device, the Internet, and through more than 300 offices in some 45 states, plus London and Hong Kong. Besides discount brokerage, the firm offers financial research, advice, and planning; investment management; retirement plans; and proprietary Schwab and Laudus mutual funds, in addition to mortgages, CDs, and other banking products through its Charles Schwab Bank unit.

Schwab's primary business remains making trades for investors who make their own decisions. Its OneSource service offers investors access to more than 2,000 no-load funds. The company also provides access to nearly 28,000 bonds, bond funds, and other fixed-income investment products from more than 300 dealers.

Additional services include futures and commodities trading, access to IPOs, and educational investment material, including ratings of more than 3,000 stocks. Schwab provides trading and support services to independent investment advisors as well.

Through Charles Schwab Bank, the company remains in step with the industrywide movement toward one-stop shopping for financial services. Schwab also reduced its minimum investment requirement in its brokerage accounts and savings accounts, and instituted a simpler, less-expensive trading fee structure that recalls the company's discount roots.

As a result, Schwab's assets under management continue to balloon, though its revenue and income levels have sunk as clients make fewer equity trades due to the shaky investment environment. Historically low interest rates have also impacted the company's bottom line.

In 2010 portfolio manager AXA Rosenberg disclosed that it had discovered a coding glitch in its computer-driven investment models. The firm helped run funds for various asset managers and pension plans, including Charles Schwab's Laudus Rosenberg funds. Charles Schwab is liquidating the four mutual funds in the aftermath of the disclosure.

Charles Schwab owns approximately 17% of his namesake firm. He was succeeded as CEO of the company by president and COO Walter Bettinger in late 2008, but remained chairman.

HISTORY

During the 1960s Stanford graduate Charles Schwab founded First Commander Corp., which managed investments and published a newsletter. But he failed to properly register with the SEC, and after a hiatus, he returned to the business under the name Charles Schwab & Co. in 1971. Initially a full-service broker, Schwab moved into discount brokerage after the SEC outlawed fixed commissions in 1975. While most brokers defiantly raised commissions, Schwab cut its rates steeply.

From 1977 to 1983 Schwab's client list increased thirtyfold, and revenues grew from $4.6 million to $126.5 million, enabling the firm to automate its operations and develop cash-management account systems. To gain capital,

Charles sold the company to BankAmerica (now Bank of America) in 1983. Schwab grew, but federal regulations prevented expansion into such services as mutual funds and telephone trading. Charles bought his company back in 1987 and took it public. When the stock market crashed later that year, trading volume fell by nearly half, from 17,900 per day. Stung, Schwab diversified further, offering new fee-based services. Commission revenues fell from 64% of sales in 1987 to 39% in 1990, but by 1995 the long bull market had pushed commissions to more than 50%.

In 1989 Schwab introduced TeleBroker, a 24-hour Touch-Tone telephone trading service available in English, Spanish, Mandarin, or Cantonese.

Schwab continued to diversify, courting independent financial advisors. Other buys included Mayer & Schweitzer (1991, now Schwab Capital Markets), an OTC market maker that accounted for about 7% of all NASDAQ trades. In 1993 the firm opened its first overseas office in London, but traded only in dollar-denominated stocks until it bought Share-Link (later Charles Schwab Europe), the UK's largest discount brokerage, in 1995. It subsequently sold the British pound sterling brokerage business to Barclays PLC, although it has maintained its US dollar business in the UK.

During the next year Schwab made a concerted effort to build its retirement services by creating a 401(k) administration and investment services unit. In 1997 Schwab allied with J.P. Morgan, Hambrecht & Quist (now J.P. Morgan H&Q), and Credit Suisse First Boston (CSFB) to give its customers access to IPOs; the next year the relationship with CSFB deepened to give Schwab access to debt offerings. In late 1997 and early 1998 Schwab reorganized to reflect its new business lines. The firm also began recruiting talent rather than promoting from within.

Expansion was key at the turn of the century. In 1999 Schwab moved toward more broker-advised investing: It inked a deal (geared toward its retirement products customers) with online financial advice firm Financial Engines, and introduced Velocity, a desktop system designed to make trading easier for fiscally endowed investors. In 2000 Schwab bought online broker CyBerCorp (now CyberTrader), as well as U.S. Trust, which markets to affluent clients.

While Schwab's World Trade Center offices were destroyed by the September 11 terrorist attacks, the company did not lose any of its New York staff.

To pare expenses, Schwab reduced its workforce by about 35% between 2000 and 2003. Founder and chairman Charles Schwab relinquished his role of co-CEO in early 2003, only to move back into the driver's seat in mid-2004 when former CEO David Pottruck was asked to step down by the company's board.

Schwab acquired The 401(k) Companies from Nationwide Financial Services in 2007. The addition became part of the company's existing Charles Schwab Trust subsidiary, which serves as a trustee for employee benefit plans. Also that year Schwab sold U.S. Trust to Bank of America for some $3.3 billion in cash and shut down its CyberTrader day trading arm, merging the direct-access brokerage's business with its own.

EXECUTIVES

Chairman: Charles R. (Chuck) Schwab, age 72, $4,659,103 total compensation
President, CEO, and Director; CEO Charles Schwab Bank: Walter W. (Walt) Bettinger II, age 49, $10,029,410 total compensation
EVP and CFO: Joseph R. Martinetto, age 47, $2,212,814 total compensation
EVP Shared Support Services: Jan Hier-King, age 54
EVP and Chief Marketing Officer: Rebecca (Becky) Saeger, age 54, $3,218,103 total compensation
EVP, General Counsel, and Secretary: Carrie E. Dwyer, age 59, $4,121,198 total compensation
EVP Shared Strategic Services: John S. Clendening
EVP Investor Services: Benjamin L. Brigeman, age 47, $2,518,430 total compensation
EVP Institutional Services: James D. McCool, age 51, $2,652,666 total compensation
EVP Schwab Investor Development: Lisa K. Hunt
EVP Human Resources and Employee Services: Jay L. Allen, age 53
EVP Investment Management Services: Randall W. Merk, age 54
SVP Investor Relations: Richard G. Fowler
SVP Corporate Public Relations: Greg Gable
SVP Schwab Community Services, Charles Schwab and Company; President, Charles Schwab Foundation: Carrie Schwab-Pomerantz
SVP Schwab Equity Ratings: Greg Forsythe
SVP Corporate Brokerage Services: Trish Cox
SVP Advisor Services: Bernie Clark
SVP and Chief Investment Strategist, Charles Schwab and Company: Elizabeth Ann (Liz Ann) Sonders
President, Schwab Charitable: Kimberly Wright-Violich
Auditors: Deloitte & Touche LLP

LOCATIONS

HQ: The Charles Schwab Corporation
211 Main St., San Francisco, CA 94105
Phone: 415-636-7000   **Fax:** 415-636-9820
Web: www.schwab.com

PRODUCTS/OPERATIONS

2009 Sales

	$ mil.	% of total
Asset management & administration fees	1,875	42
Interest	1,428	32
Trading revenue	996	23
Other	115	3
Total	**4,414**	**100**

Selected Subsidiaries

Charles Schwab Bank
Charles Schwab Investment Management, Inc. (mutual fund investment adviser)
Schwab Holdings, Inc.
    Charles Schwab & Co., Inc. (securities broker-dealer)

COMPETITORS

Ameriprise
Bank of America
E*TRADE Financial
Edward Jones
FMR
Franklin Resources
John Hancock Financial Services
Legg Mason
Morgan Stanley
Principal Financial
Raymond James Financial
Scottrade
ShareBuilder
TD Ameritrade
The Vanguard Group

HISTORICAL FINANCIALS

Company Type: Public

Income Statement

	REVENUE ($ mil.)	NET INCOME ($ mil.)	NET PROFIT MARGIN	EMPLOYEES
12/09	4,414	787	17.8%	12,400
12/08	5,393	1,212	22.5%	13,400
12/07	5,617	2,407	42.9%	13,300
12/06	4,988	1,227	24.6%	12,400
12/05	5,151	725	14.1%	14,000
Annual Growth	**(3.8%)**	**2.1%**	**—**	**(3.0%)**

FYE: December 31

2009 Year-End Financials

Debt ratio: 29.8%
Return on equity: 17.2%
Cash ($ mil.): 26,614
Current ratio: —
Long-term debt ($ mil.): 1,512
No. of shares (mil.): 1,194
Dividends
   Yield: 1.3%
   Payout: 35.3%
Market value ($ mil.): 22,462

Stock History

NYSE: SCHW

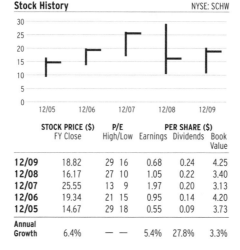

	STOCK PRICE ($) FY Close	P/E High/Low		Earnings	Dividends	Book Value
12/09	18.82	29	16	0.68	0.24	4.25
12/08	16.17	27	10	1.05	0.22	3.40
12/07	25.55	13	9	1.97	0.20	3.13
12/06	19.34	21	15	0.95	0.14	4.20
12/05	14.67	29	18	0.55	0.09	3.73
Annual Growth	**6.4%**	**—**	**—**	**5.4%**	**27.8%**	**3.3%**

Charming Shoppes

Charming Shoppes is big in women's plus-size clothing. The company runs more than 2,100 stores (and related websites) at three fashion chains that cater to the amply proportioned: about 860 Lane Bryant and Lane Bryant Outlet stores in 46 states; some 800 Fashion Bug stores that sell moderately priced apparel and accessories in girls, juniors, misses, and plus sizes; and about 460 Catherines Plus Size stores. The stores are primarily located in suburban areas and small towns across the US and court low- to middle-income women and teens who follow fashion styles rather than set them. The company's purchase of Lane Bryant from Limited Brands elevated Charming Shoppes to #1 in the plus-size market.

About half of American women wear size 14 or larger and Americans continue to gain weight, presenting Charming Shoppes with a growth market. (Indeed, plus-size apparel contributes more than 85% of the company's total sales.) Nevertheless, the recession and less-than-charming environment for women's apparel retailers contributed to a 17% decline in net sales in 2009 vs. 2008, during which time same-store sales at all three chains fell by double digits.

In response, Charming Shoppes is attempting to become fiscally fit by slimming down. After cutting jobs and shuttering about 280 stores since early 2008, Charming Shoppes has announced plans to close between 100 and 120 additional locations in 2010. Its restructuring is being led by turnaround specialist James Fogarty, who joined Charming Shoppes as president and CEO in April 2009. Under Fogarty, the retailer is focusing on its three core brands. To that end, in 2009 the company decided to close its Petite Sophisticate chain of stores and converted most to Catherines outlet locations. In early 2010 the company shut down its Lane Bryant Woman catalog operation to focus on its Lane Bryant retail business and also linked its four e-commerce sites — lanebryant.com, cacique.com, fashionbug.com, and catherines.com — on a common platform to encourage cross selling. (Cacique is the apparel retailer's private-label intimate apparel brand.)

HISTORY

Morris and Arthur Sidewater opened their first women's apparel store, called Charm Shoppes, in Philadelphia in 1940. Morris, a buyer with apparel company Associated Merchandising, and Arthur, who performed as a dancer on tour with Red Skelton, were challenged from the start: Legal notice came during their first week that the "Charm" name was already taken. The brothers responded by changing the name of the store to Charming Shoppes.

By the end of the 1940s, the brothers began taking on partners to add new stores, with the new partners becoming store managers of the outlets they opened. In 1951 the brothers formed what would become the most significant of their partnerships with a friend of Arthur's, David Wachs, and David's brother Ellis. That year the Sidewater and Wachs brothers opened a store in Norristown, Pennsylvania; later they added another store in Woodbury, New Jersey.

During the 1960s the pairs of brothers moved to follow the steady flight of consumers to malls and large shopping centers, opening new stores in those areas under the Fashion Bug name and renaming old stores. By 1971, the year the company went public, Charming Shoppes operated 21 stores and had a total of 18 partners. As rent at the mall climbed in the mid-1970s, the company began expanding into cheaper strip malls, where rents were less than half those in enclosed malls.

As it entered the 1980s, Charming Shoppes operated nearly 160 stores. That decade marked a period of rapid expansion for the company. Charming Shoppes began opening Fashion Bug Plus stores (and departments within existing stores), featuring sizes for larger women. By 1985 it had more than 500 stores (about 65% of which were located in strip malls). That year the company expanded its product line by adding fashions for preteens.

During the last half of the decade, Charming Shoppes began changing its selection from name brands to private brands. In 1988 David became CEO, replacing Morris, who had served as CEO since the company went public. Although sales had increased unabated for two decades, shrinking profits led the company to curtail expansion, but only slightly. By the end of 1989, it operated more than 900 outlets.

Charming Shoppes continued to grow and increase sales, adding menswear in the early 1990s. With more than 1,400 stores in 1995, the company named Dorrit Bern, a former group VP of apparel and home merchandise at Sears, as CEO.

That year Charming Shoppes reported its biggest loss of $139 million. Bern promptly laid off a third of the company's workforce. She closed nearly 300 poorly performing stores and revamped Charming Shoppes' merchandising strategy, stemming losses in 1996 and bringing the company back to profitability the next year.

In 1998 Charming Shoppes closed another 65 poorly performing stores, replacing them with about 65 new sites. Restructuring charges contributed to a loss for fiscal 1999. Charming Shoppes bought plus-sized chain Modern Woman and integrated the stores with its acquisition of 436-store Catherines Plus Size chain.

Charming Shoppes positioned itself as a leader in plus-size women's apparel in 2001 with the $335 million purchase of plus-size apparel chain Lane Bryant (with more than 650 stores) from retailer The Limited.

In a move to cut out its biggest drains on capital, the company closed its 80-store Added Dimensions and The Answer plus-size chains, closed 130 Fashion Bug stores, and converted about 45 of its Fashion Bug stores to the more successful Lane Bryant format in 2002. It also moved about 45 Fashion Bug stores under the Lane Bryant banner.

In June 2005 the plus-size chain acquired catalog retailer Crosstown Traders from JPMorgan Partners. Crosstown Traders sells women's apparel through its Old Pueblo Traders, Bedford Fair Lifestyles, Bedford Fair Shoestyles, Willow Ridge, Lew Magram, Brownstone Studio, Regalia, Intimate Appeal, Monterey Bay Clothing Company, and Coward Shoe catalog titles.

In July 2008 the board accepted CEO Dorrit Bern's resignation, with chairman Alan Rosskamm taking the helm in the interim.

In April 2009 turnaround specialist James Fogarty joined the company as CEO. In October the company sold its credit card business to Alliance Data Systems Corporation (ADS) to reduce debt.

EXECUTIVES

Chairman: Michael Goldstein, age 68
President, CEO, and Director: James P. (Jim) Fogarty, age 41, $5,212,682 total compensation
EVP and CFO: Eric M. Specter, age 52, $958,866 total compensation
EVP Supply Chain Management, Information Technology, and Shared Business Services: James G. (Jim) Bloise, age 66, $678,373 total compensation
EVP, General Counsel, and Secretary: Colin D. Stern, age 61, $850,681 total compensation
EVP Human Resources: Frederick B. (Fred) Lamster
EVP Global Sourcing and Business Transformation: Anthony M. (Tony) Romano, age 47
SVP Finance, Treasury, and Business Development: Steven R. Wishner, age 58
SVP and CIO: Denis F. Gingue
SVP General Merchandising, Fashion Bug: Rachel A. Ungaro
VP and Chief Accounting Officer: John Lee
VP Strategy: Jeffrey H. Liss
VP Real Estate Finance and Analysis: Andrew D. Galasso
VP Sourcing, Asia: Stephen Yeung
VP Investor Relations: Gayle M. Coolick
President, Charming Direct: Bill Bass
President, Catherines: Carol L. Williams, age 59
President, Lane Bryant: Brian P. Woolf, age 61, $1,031,034 total compensation
President, Fashion Bug: MaryEllen MacDowell
Auditors: Ernst & Young LLP

LOCATIONS

HQ: Charming Shoppes, Inc.
450 Winks Ln., Bensalem, PA 19020
Phone: 215-245-9100 **Fax:** 215-633-4640
Web: www.charmingshoppes.com

PRODUCTS/OPERATIONS

2010 Stores

	No.
Lane Bryant & Lane Bryant Outlet	860
Fashion Bug	801
Catherines Plus Sizes	460
Total	**2,121**

2010 Sales

	$ mil.	% of total
Retail	1,947.6	94
Direct-to-consumer	116.6	6
Other	0.4	—
Total	**2,064.6**	**100**

Selected Operations

Catalogs and e-commerce
  Figi's
  Lane Bryant Woman
Retail stores
  Catherines Plus Sizes
  Fashion Bug
  Lane Bryant
  Lane Bryant Outlet

COMPETITORS

Burlington Coat Factory	Kmart
Cato	Kohl's
Charlotte Russe Holding	Provide Commerce
Chico's FAS	Redcats USA
Claire's Stores	Ross Stores
Coldwater Creek	Sears
Deb Shops	Stage Stores
dELiA*s	Stein Mart
Dress Barn	Talbots
Foot Locker	Target
The Gap	TJX Companies
Harry and David	Tween Brands
Hot Topic	Wal-Mart
J. C. Penney	

HISTORICAL FINANCIALS

Company Type: Public

Income Statement

FYE: Saturday nearest January 31

	REVENUE ($ mil.)	NET INCOME ($ mil.)	NET PROFIT MARGIN	EMPLOYEES
1/10	2,065	(78)	—	27,000
1/09	2,475	(244)	—	28,700
1/08	3,010	(84)	—	30,200
1/07	3,068	109	3.6%	30,000
1/06	2,756	99	3.6%	28,000
Annual Growth	**(7.0%)**	**—**	**—**	**(0.9%)**

2010 Year-End Financials

Debt ratio: 36.9%
Return on equity: —
Cash ($ mil.): 187
Current ratio: 2.17
Long-term debt ($ mil.): 172

No. of shares (mil.): 116
Dividends
  Yield: 0.0%
  Payout: —
Market value ($ mil.): 673

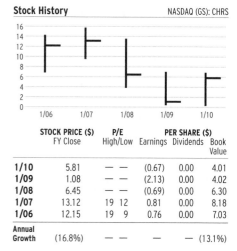

Stock History

NASDAQ (GS): CHRS

	STOCK PRICE ($) FY Close	P/E High/Low		Earnings	PER SHARE ($) Dividends	Book Value
1/10	5.81	—	—	(0.67)	0.00	4.01
1/09	1.08	—	—	(2.13)	0.00	4.02
1/08	6.45	—	—	(0.69)	0.00	6.30
1/07	13.12	19	12	0.81	0.00	8.18
1/06	12.15	19	9	0.76	0.00	7.03
Annual Growth	**(16.8%)**	**—**	**—**	**—**	**—**	**(13.1%)**

Charter Communications

Charter Communications is a cable television system operator with about 5 million residential and commercial subscribers in 27 US states, making it one of the top cable companies, behind Comcast, Time Warner Cable, and Cox Communications. Not just a leading cable TV player, Charter offers broadband Internet to 3 million customers and computer telephony services to another 1 million users. The company also derives a portion of its revenue from the sale of local advertising on such cable networks as MTV and CNN. Charter Communications, which skirted bankruptcy for years, completed a Chapter 11 bankruptcy reorganization in 2009.

Driven by dreams of creating a "wired world," chairman Paul Allen (a co-founder of Microsoft) reportedly poured more than $12 billion into Charter since 1998, and the billionaire saw most of that investment evaporate. After expanding through the purchase of a slew of small-town cable assets that needed extensive infrastructure upgrades, Charter experienced ongoing subscriber losses, financial losses, and a debt load in excess of $20 billion.

Faced with legal opposition from some of its lenders, the company's bankruptcy reorganization plan was intended to reduce its interest expenses, repay creditors, and free up funds to put back into the business. It eliminated about $8 billion of Allen's debt and left him controlling just about one-third of the company. Charter's lenders, led by JPMorgan Chase and Wells Fargo, argued that this would constitute a change in control of the company and put the reins in their hands, freeing them up to sell Charter in an effort to recoup their investment.

The company, however, is still pursuing its strategy and continues to tout its ability to provide voice, Internet access, and other data services as a complete package. Through an agreement with Oxygen Media, it offers an interactive TV service that allows viewers to access information related to programming via the Web. Charter has seen some success with its push to grow its cable telephony service, which now boasts about 1 million customers.

Coming out of Chapter 11, Charter raised around $1.6 billion in an equity rights offering. Paul Allen will name four directors of the reorganized company, while bondholders will name another four directors.

CEO Neil Smit resigned in 2010 to become president of Comcast Cable Communications. EVP/COO Michael Lovett was named Charter's president and CEO to succeed Smit.

HISTORY

Crown Media bought St. Louis-based Cencom Cable in 1992. Rather than relocate to Crown's Dallas home, Cencom CEO Howard Wood joined with fellow executives Barry Babcock and Jerry Kent to form Charter Communications as a cable acquisition and management company in St. Louis. With an investment from Crown, owned by Hallmark Cards, the trio partnered with LEB Communications in 1994 to manage Charter's growth. And grow it did.

In 1994 Charter paid about $900 million for a majority stake in Crown. Charter spent $3 billion on 15 cable acquisitions in its first four years. It had more than 1 million subscribers by early 1997 and began offering high-speed cable Internet access and paging services in some of its markets.

Charter went into acquisition overdrive in 1998 when Microsoft co-founder Paul Allen took control with his $4.5 billion investment. The deal closely followed Allen's $2.8 billion takeover of Dallas-based Marcus Cable; Marcus was merged with Charter. The combined company, based in St. Louis with Kent as CEO, was the #7 US cable business with 2.5 million subscribers. Also that year the company teamed up with Wink and WorldGate to offer TV Internet services with set-top boxes.

Before the ink was dry on the merger papers, Allen was at it again. The company's 1999 acquisitions included Falcon Communications (1 million cable subscribers) and Fanch Cablevision (more than 500,000); it also bought cable systems from Helicon, InterMedia Partners, Avalon Cable, InterLink Communications, Renaissance Media, and Rifkin. Charter said it would spend $3.5 billion upgrading its systems over three years after raising that amount in a major junk bond sale. Months later the company raised $3.2 billion in its IPO.

In 2000 Charter completed its purchase of Bresnan Communications (700,000 subscribers) and bought a system from Cablevision to form a major cluster in Michigan, Minnesota, and Wisconsin. The next year the company gained 554,000 subscribers by swapping noncore cable systems and $1.8 billion in cash to AT&T Broadband in exchange for systems serving the St. Louis area, parts of Alabama, and the Reno area of Nevada and California.

Also in 2001 Kent resigned from the company and its board of directors and was replaced as CEO by former Liberty Media executive Carl Vogel. Vogel stayed on the job until 2005, at which point he also retired. Former AOL executive Neil Smit replaced Vogel later that year. Several other executive departures followed and a subsequent securities investigation led to convictions against former COO Dave Barford (sentenced to one year in prison) and former CFO Kent Kalkwarf (14 months in prison).

The company in 2006 sold nearly $900 million in assets, including systems in Illinois and Kentucky to New Wave Communications and systems in West Virginia and Virginia to Cebridge Connections. Shedding more assets, Charter also sold cable TV systems serving nearly 70,000 customers in the western US to subsidiaries of Orange Broadband Holding Company.

EXECUTIVES

Chairman: Eric L. Zinterhofer, age 38
President, CEO, and Director: Michael J. (Mike) Lovett, age 48, $10,000,755 total compensation
EVP Operations and CTO: Marwan Fawaz, age 47, $4,494,462 total compensation
EVP Corporate Development and Strategy: Gregory S. Rigdon
EVP and General Counsel: Gregory L. (Greg) Doody, age 45, $4,468,230 total compensation
EVP and Chief Marketing Officer: Ted W. Schremp, age 38
SVP, Charter Business: Jim McGann
SVP Finance, Controller, Chief Accounting Officer, and Interim CFO: Kevin D. Howard, age 40
VP Investor Relations and Communications: Mary Jo Moehle
VP, Associate General Counsel, and Corporate Secretary: Richard R. Dykhouse
President, Charter Media: James M. (Jim) Heneghan
President, Operations: Steven E. Apodaca, age 43
Auditors: KPMG LLP

LOCATIONS

HQ: Charter Communications, Inc.
12405 Powerscourt Dr., Ste. 100
St. Louis, MO 63131
Phone: 314-965-0555   **Fax:** 314-965-9745
Web: www.charter.com

PRODUCTS/OPERATIONS

2009 Sales

	$ mil.	% of total
Video	3,468	51
High-speed Internet	1,476	22
Telephone	713	10
Commercial	446	7
Advertising sales	249	4
Other	403	6
Total	**6,755**	**100**

Selected Services

Broadband Internet access
Cable TV
Digital TV
High-definition TV
Interactive video programming
Pay-per-view
Telephony
Video-on-demand

COMPETITORS

AT&T
Cablevision Systems
Comcast
Cox Communications
DIRECTV
DISH Network
EarthLink
Insight Communications
LodgeNet
Mediacom Communications
RCN Corporation
Suddenlink Communications
Time Warner Cable
United Online
Verizon

HISTORICAL FINANCIALS

Company Type: Public

Income Statement

FYE: December 31

	REVENUE ($ mil.)	NET INCOME ($ mil.)	NET PROFIT MARGIN	EMPLOYEES
12/09	6,755	11,366	168.3%	16,700
12/08	6,479	(2,451)	—	16,600
12/07	6,002	(1,616)	—	16,500
12/06	5,504	(1,370)	—	15,500
12/05	5,254	(967)	—	17,200
Annual Growth	**6.5%**	—	—	**(0.7%)**

2009 Year-End Financials

Debt ratio: 692.0%
Return on equity: —
Cash ($ mil.): 709
Current ratio: 1.11
Long-term debt ($ mil.): 13,252

Net Income History   Pink Sheets: CCMM

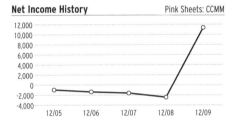

Cheesecake Factory

These restaurants have some industrial-strength menus for foodies. The Cheesecake Factory owns and operates about 150 casual-dining restaurants in 35 states that offer some 200 menu items ranging from sandwiches and salads to steaks and seafood. The highlight of the menu, of course, is cheesecake, which comes in about 40 varieties, including Chocolate Tuxedo Cream and Kahlua Cocoa Coffee. Each restaurant has a unique design, but all of them feature over-the-top opulence and Las Vegas-style glitz. In addition to its flagship concept, the company has more than a dozen upscale Grand Lux Cafes that offer a similar menu. The Cheesecake Factory also sells desserts to grocery stores and foodservice operators.

The company has succeeded in creating a unique brand within the themed dining segment by focusing on a few key aspects of the Cheesecake Factory dining experience, namely the chain's outsized menu and hallmark cheesecake. With a ridiculous number of choices, customers are able to satisfy almost any craving and, most importantly, they have more reasons to return to try something new. The company also delivers on the promise of its namesake dessert, which helps make The Cheesecake Factory a favorite destination for many families.

Another feature that makes The Cheesecake Factory different from its competitors is the enormous size of its restaurants, which typically feature seating for several hundred customers at a time. The company also targets areas near suburban retail and entertainment centers to make its restaurants convenient destinations. With very good return and word-of-mouth business, waiting times of two hours are not uncommon in some locations. All of these factors in turn help the company generate nearly

$10 million in annual sales per location, an industry-leading figure.

The economic slowdown, however, has taken its toll even on popular chains such as The Cheesecake Factory. In response to slower business at its restaurants, the company is focused primarily on containing food costs and other expenses. It has also slowed expansion efforts, opening just one new restaurant during 2009 compared to more than half a dozen openings the previous year.

The company is, however, experimenting with a new casual-dining concept to diversify into new customer markets. Called RockSugar Pan Asian Kitchen, the eatery offers foods inspired by the cuisine of Southeast Asia, including Indonesia, Malaysia, and Thailand. The Cheesecake Factory opened the first RockSugar location in Los Angeles during 2008. The company is also working to improve its Grand Lux Cafe concept with plans to expand the smaller chain into new markets.

HISTORY

For 25 years Evelyn Overton made cheesecakes in her basement for friends and bake sales. In 1972 she, her husband Oscar, and their son David founded The Cheesecake Factory in Los Angeles to make cheesecakes and other desserts for local restaurants. David opened a restaurant in Beverly Hills in 1978 to showcase the company's cheesecakes to restaurateurs. The first Cheesecake Factory, which served salads, sandwiches, and a few entrees, was a hit, and a second location was opened in Marina del Rey in 1983.

In the late 1980s the company opened two more outlets in Southern California, and a Washington, DC, location opened in 1991. After going public the next year, The Cheesecake Factory opened one or two restaurants a year (in California and Atlanta in 1993, Maryland in 1994, and Florida in 1994 and 1995). Evelyn Overton died in 1996.

In 1998 the company opened a new bakery/cafe concept called The Cheesecake Factory Express to serve the crowds at Walt Disney's indoor interactive theme park, DisneyQuest, in Orlando. In 1999 it tried another new concept called the Grand Lux Cafe, opening the first in Las Vegas Sands' Venetian Casino Resort.

Continued expansion in 1999 and 2000 helped drive growth in both sales and profits. The following year the company formed The Cheesecake Factory — Oscar and Evelyn Overton Charitable Foundation to help employees participate in local charitable programs and community services.

Despite a gloomy economic outlook, the company accelerated the pace of its expansion, opening nine new Cheesecake Factory locations in 2001. By 2005 the company had exceeded 100 restaurants.

EXECUTIVES

Chairman and CEO: David Overton, age 64, $3,611,812 total compensation
President: Michael E. (Mike) Jannini, age 57
COO: David Gordon
EVP and CFO: W. Douglas Benn, age 55, $1,819,235 total compensation
EVP, Secretary, and General Counsel: Debby R. Zurzolo, age 53, $914,808 total compensation

SVP Human Resources: Dina R. Barmasse-Gray
SVP Strategic Planning: Matthew E. Clark
SVP Operations Services: Russell S. Greene
SVP Kitchen Operations: Donald C. Moore
SVP Development: Brian MacKellar
SVP New Restaurant Openings and Operations: Lisa A. McDowell
SVP Information Technology and CIO: James D. Rasmussen
SVP and Chief Marketing Officer: Mark Mears
SVP Purchasing: Ronald S. (Ron) McArthur
SVP Bakery Operations: Keith T. Carango
VP, Controller, and Chief Accounting Officer: Cheryl M. Slomann, age 44, $387,587 total compensation
VP Information Technology: Robert T. West
VP Investor Relations: Jill S. Peters
President, The Cheesecake Factory Bakery: Max S. Byfuglin, age 64, $670,841 total compensation
Auditors: PricewaterhouseCoopers LLP

LOCATIONS

HQ: The Cheesecake Factory Incorporated
26901 Malibu Hills Rd., Calabasas Hills, CA 91301
Phone: 818-871-3000　　**Fax:** 818-871-3001
Web: www.thecheesecakefactory.com

2009 Locations

	No.
California	34
Florida	17
Texas	12
New York	9
Arizona	7
Massachusetts	7
Illinois	6
New Jersey	6
Ohio	6
Virginia	6
Maryland	5
Nevada	5
Colorado	4
Georgia	4
Pennsylvania	4
Missouri	3
North Carolina	3
Washington	3
Indiana	2
Oklahoma	2
Wisconsin	2
Alabama	1
Connecticut	1
Hawaii	1
Idaho	1
Iowa	1
Kansas	1
Kentucky	1
Minnesota	1
Nebraska	1
Oregon	1
Rhode Island	1
Tennessee	1
Utah	1
Washington, DC	1
Total	**161**

PRODUCTS/OPERATIONS

2009 Sales

	$ mil.	% of total
Restaurants	1,534.3	93
Bakery	118.4	7
Adjustments	(50.7)	—
Total	**1,602.0**	**100**

2009 Locations

	No.
The Cheesecake Factory	147
Grand Lux Cafe	13
RockSugar Pan Asian Kitchen	1
Total	**161**

COMPETITORS

Acapulco/El Torito Restaurants
Applebee's
Benihana
BJ's Restaurants
Brinker
California Pizza Kitchen
Carlson Restaurants
Claim Jumper Restaurants
Darden
Dave & Buster's
Fox Restaurant Concepts
Houlihan's
Ignite Restaurant Group
Islands Restaurants
Johnny Rockets
Landry's
Marie Callender
Mimi's Cafe
OSI Restaurant Partners
P.F. Chang's
Planet Hollywood
Red Robin
Ruby Tuesday

HISTORICAL FINANCIALS

Company Type: Public

Income Statement

	REVENUE ($ mil.)	NET INCOME ($ mil.)	NET PROFIT MARGIN	EMPLOYEES
FYE: Tuesday nearest December 31				
12/09	1,602	43	2.7%	30,000
12/08	1,606	52	3.3%	31,000
12/07	1,512	74	4.9%	29,400
12/06	1,315	81	6.2%	29,400
12/05	1,178	88	7.4%	24,700
Annual Growth	**8.0%**	**(16.4%)**	**—**	**5.0%**

2009 Year-End Financials

Debt ratio: 19.4%
Return on equity: 8.8%
Cash ($ mil.): 74
Current ratio: 0.86
Long-term debt ($ mil.): 100

No. of shares (mil.): 59
Dividends
　Yield: —
　Payout: —
Market value ($ mil.): 1,284

Stock History

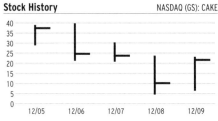

NASDAQ (GS): CAKE

	STOCK PRICE ($) FY Close	P/E High/Low		PER SHARE ($) Earnings	Dividends	Book Value
12/09	21.59	32	10	0.71	—	8.68
12/08	10.10	28	6	0.82	—	7.61
12/07	23.71	29	21	1.01	—	9.46
12/06	24.60	39	21	1.02	—	11.96
12/05	37.39	35	27	1.09	—	10.89
Annual Growth	**(12.8%)**	**—**	**—**	**(10.2%)**	**—**	**(5.5%)**

Chesapeake Energy

Chesapeake Energy knows the peaks and valleys of the oil and gas business, including the 2008-09 oil slump. The exploration and production company concentrates on building natural gas reserves through the acquisition and development of oil and gas assets across the US. The mid-continent region accounts for about a third of the company's estimated proved reserves of 13.5 trillion cu. ft. of natural gas equivalent, but Chesapeake also has assets along the Gulf Coast, in Appalachia, and the Ark-La-Tex region. In 2009 it owned or had stakes in 44,100 producing oil and natural gas wells that produced 2.5 billion cu. ft. of natural gas equivalent per day, 93% of which was natural gas.

A national leader in deep vertical and horizontal drilling, Chesapeake (which was named after the childhood Chesapeake Bay haunts of one of its founders) is concentrating on growing its proved reserves through acquisitions. It is also seeking to save costs by owning and operating its own equipment.

Chesapeake is one of the top drillers of natural gas wells in the US, with drilling projects in Arkansas, Kansas, Louisiana, New Mexico, Oklahoma, and Texas.

In 2007 Chesapeake began drilling at the Dallas/Fort Worth Airport, which sits above the productive Barnett Shale formation.

Facing a deepening economic valley as oil prices began to slump, in 2008 the company moved to cut the costs of exploiting its shale assets by selling some of these properties to joint venture partners. In this regard Chesapeake sold 90,000 net acres of natural gas assets in the Arkoma Basin Woodford Shale play for $1.7 billion to BP. It subsequently sold a 25% stake in its Fayetteville Shale assets in Arkansas to BP for $1.9 billion. In 2009 Chesapeake formed a joint venture with Global Infrastructure Partners to operate natural gas midstream assets. And in early 2010 it also sold 25% of Barnett Shale properties to TOTAL, forming a $2.25 billion joint venture with that company.

Chesapeake sold its assets in the Permian Basin of West Texas and southeast New Mexico to Riverstone Holdings in 2010. Riverstone manages a group of energy-focused private equity funds.

Chesapeake plans to shift its strategy in 2010 from capturing new drilling inventory to stepping up its program to convert what had been inactive fields into developed producing reserves. Utilizing horizontal drilling technology combined with hydraulic fracturing and 3-D seismic information, the company plans to increase production in wells that had previously thought to be tapped out.

HISTORY

Aubrey McClendon (who grew up near Maryland's Chesapeake Bay) and Tom Ward had been non-operating partners in about 600 wells in Oklahoma before forming their own company in 1989 to develop new fields in Texas and Oklahoma during the 1990s. The firm went public in 1993. In 1995 the company acquired oil and gas acreage in Louisiana, as well as Princeton Natural Gas, an Oklahoma City-based gas marketing firm.

Oil finds in Louisiana and strong production from its Texas and Oklahoma wells helped lift Chesapeake's sales in 1996. That year it acquired Amerada Hess' (later renamed Hess) half of their joint operations in two Oklahoma fields. In 1997 chairman McClendon and president Ward acquired control of Chesapeake.

The company's success was based on its "growth through the drillbit" strategy — developing new wells. But after a 1997 loss, Chesapeake modified its strategy and sought to grow by acquiring other companies. That year it bought energy company AnSon Production. Chesapeake subsequently bought oil and gas explorer-producer Hugoton Energy and energy company DLB Oil & Gas.

In 1998 the company acquired a 40% stake in Canadian oil producer Ranger Oil and paid Occidental Petroleum $105 million for natural gas reserves in the Texas Panhandle. Chesapeake then began to transform itself from a hotshot driller to an acquirer of natural gas properties, almost tripling its proved reserves. The company suffered a huge loss that year, in part from the acquisitions and continuing lower gas prices.

With gas prices soaring again, the company continued its buying spree into 2000, when it agreed to buy midcontinent natural gas producer Gothic Energy for $345 million in stock and assumed debt. The deal closed in 2001. The company also sold its Canadian assets that year, in order to focus on its core US properties.

In 2002 Chesapeake acquired oil and gas producer Canaan Energy for about $118 million. Later that year the company announced plans to sell or trade its Permian Basin assets.

Chesapeake acquired in 2003 a 25% stake in Pioneer Drilling (which it subsequently sold). In 2004 the company acquired Barnett Shale assets from Hallwood Energy for $292 million. That year it also bought privately owned Concho Resources for $420 million. The next year the company acquired privately held BRG Petroleum, which held assets of more than 450 wells with proved reserves of more than 275 billion cu. ft. of natural gas, for $325 million.

In 2005 Chesapeake acquired 20% of Gastar Exploration (reduced to 15% by 2007). That year, in a major move, the company acquired Columbia Natural Resources for $2.2 billion.

EXECUTIVES

Chairman and CEO: Aubrey K. McClendon, age 50, $18,551,296 total compensation
EVP Operations and Geosciences and COO: Steven C. (Steve) Dixon, age 51, $8,287,073 total compensation
EVP and CFO: Marcus C. (Marc) Rowland, age 57, $8,728,453 total compensation
EVP Acquisitions and Divestitures: Douglas J. Jacobson, age 56, $7,357,172 total compensation
SVP Accounting, Chief Accounting Officer, and Controller: Michael A. Johnson, age 44
SVP Information Technology and CIO: Cathlyn L. (Cathy) Tompkins, age 48
SVP Natural Gas Projects; CEO, Chesapeake Midstream Partners: J. Michael (Mike) Stice, age 51
SVP Drilling: Stephen W. Miller, age 53
SVP Investor Relations and Research: Jeffrey L. (Jeff) Mobley, age 41
SVP Corporate Development: Thomas S. (Tom) Price Jr., age 58
SVP Land and Legal and General Counsel: Henry J. Hood, age 49
SVP Human and Corporate Resources: Martha A. Burger, age 57
SVP, Secretary, and Treasurer: Jennifer M. Grigsby, age 41
SVP Energy Marketing: James C. Johnson, age 52
SVP Production: Jeffrey A. Fisher, age 50
Auditors: PricewaterhouseCoopers LLP

LOCATIONS

HQ: Chesapeake Energy Corporation
6100 N. Western Ave., Oklahoma City, OK 73118
Phone: 405-848-8000   **Fax:** 405-843-0573
Web: www.chk.com

2009 Proved Reserves

	% of total
Big 6 Shales	
Barnett Shale	24
Fayetteville Shale	15
Haynesville Shale	13
Marcellus Shale	2
Other	
Mid-Continent	29
Appalachian Basin	8
Permian & Delaware Basins	5
South Texas/Gulf Coast/Ark-La-Tex	4
Total	**100**

PRODUCTS/OPERATIONS

2009 Sales

	$ mil.	% of total
Exploration & production	5,049	66
Marketing	2,463	32
Service operations	190	2
Total	**7,702**	**100**

COMPETITORS

Adams Resources	ConocoPhillips
Anadarko Petroleum	Exxon Mobil
Apache	Koch Industries, Inc.
Ashland Inc.	Noble Energy
BP	Occidental Petroleum
Chevron	Pioneer Natural Resources

HISTORICAL FINANCIALS

Company Type: Public

Income Statement				FYE: December 31
	REVENUE ($ mil.)	NET INCOME ($ mil.)	NET PROFIT MARGIN	EMPLOYEES
12/09	7,702	(5,830)	—	8,200
12/08	11,629	723	6.2%	7,600
12/07	7,800	1,451	18.6%	6,200
12/06	7,326	2,003	27.3%	4,900
12/05	4,665	948	20.3%	2,885
Annual Growth	13.4%	—	—	29.8%

2009 Year-End Financials

Debt ratio: 112.0%
Return on equity: —
Cash ($ mil.): 307
Current ratio: 0.91
Long-term debt ($ mil.): 12,295

No. of shares (mil.): 654
Dividends
  Yield: 1.2%
  Payout: —
Market value ($ mil.): 16,934

Stock History

NYSE: CHK

	STOCK PRICE ($) FY Close	P/E High/Low		PER SHARE ($) Earnings	Dividends	Book Value
12/09	25.88	—	—	(9.57)	0.30	17.49
12/08	16.17	65	9	1.14	0.29	24.91
12/07	39.20	16	10	2.62	0.26	18.54
12/06	29.05	8	6	4.35	0.23	17.20
12/05	31.73	16	6	2.51	0.19	9.44
Annual Growth	(5.0%)	—	—	—	12.1%	16.7%

Chevron Corporation

Having added Texaco's star (and subsequently Unocal's authority) to its stripes, Chevron can pull rank on its rivals. Among the largest US integrated oil companies, along with Exxon Mobil and ConocoPhillips, it has proved reserves of 11.3 billion barrels of oil equivalent and a daily production of 2.7 million barrels of oil equivalent, and it also owns interests in chemicals, mining, pipelines, and power production businesses. The company, which is restructuring its refinery and retail businesses to cut costs, owns or has stakes in 9,600 gas stations in the US that operate under the Chevron and Texaco brands. Outside the US it owns or has stakes in 12,400 branded gas stations, which also use the Caltex brand.

Chevron owns a 50% stake in chemicals producer Chevron Phillips Chemical, a joint venture with ConocoPhillips. It produces coal and molybdenum through Chevron Mining.

The poor economy, low commodities prices, and weak demand for oil and gas caused the company's revenues to plummet in 2009, prompting Chevron to accelerate its strategy of selling some of its global fuel marketing businesses to reduce costs. Ultrapar acquired Chevron's Texaco-branded fuel distribution business in Brazil for $720 million in 2008, and the next year Chevron sold its Nigerian fuel marketing business. In 2010 the company announced plans to cut its US refining and marketing business staff by 20%.

A leading producer of viscous, heavy oil, in 2010 a Chevron-led consortium was awarded the rights to 40% of a heavy oil project in Venezuela's Orinoco Oil Belt. The company has also been growing its natural gas assets. In 2008 it announced plans to construct a $3.1 billion natural gas project in the Gulf of Thailand. The project will have the capacity to meet 14% of Thailand's natural gas needs.

In 2010, in the wake of the BP oil rig disaster in the Gulf of Mexico, Chevron announced it was forming a $1 billion joint venture with Exxon Mobil, Royal Dutch Shell, and ConocoPhillips to create a rapid-response system capable of capturing and containing up to 100,000 barrels of oil from an oil spill in water depths of 10,000 feet.

HISTORY

Thirty years after the California gold rush, a small firm began digging for a new product — oil. The crude came from wildcatter Frederick Taylor's well located north of Los Angeles. In 1879 Taylor and other oilmen formed Pacific Coast Oil, attracting the attention of John D. Rockefeller's Standard Oil. The two competed fiercely until Standard took over Pacific Coast in 1900.

When Standard Oil was broken up in 1911, its West Coast operations became the stand-alone Standard Oil Company (California), which was nicknamed Socal and sold Chevron-brand products. After winning drilling concessions in Bahrain and Saudi Arabia in the 1930s, Socal summoned Texaco to help, and they formed Caltex (California-Texas Oil Company) as equal partners. In 1948 Socony (later Mobil) and Jersey Standard (later Exxon) bought 40% of Caltex's Saudi operations, and the Saudi arm became Aramco (Arabian American Oil Company).

Socal exploration pushed into Louisiana and the Gulf of Mexico in the 1940s. In 1961 it bought Standard Oil Company of Kentucky (Kyso). The 1970s brought setbacks: Caltex holdings were nationalized during the OPEC-spawned upheaval, and the Saudi Arabian government claimed Aramco in 1980.

In 1984 Socal was renamed Chevron and doubled its reserves with its $13 billion purchase of Gulf Corp., which had origins in the 1901 Spindletop gusher in Texas. Gulf became an oil power by developing Kuwaiti concessions but was hobbled when those assets were nationalized in 1975. After Gulf was rocked by disclosures that it had an illegal political slush fund, Socal stepped in. The deal loaded the new company with debt, and it cut 20,000 jobs and sold billions in assets.

Chevron bought Tenneco's Gulf of Mexico properties in 1988 and in 1992 swapped fields valued at $1.1 billion for 15.7 million shares of Chevron stock owned by Pennzoil. It also moved into the North Sea in 1994.

The company sold 450 UK gas stations and a refinery to Shell in 1997, and it signed an onshore exploration contract in China that year. Poor economic conditions in Asia and slumping oil prices in 1998 forced Chevron to shed some US holdings, including California properties. Chevron trimmed about 10% of its workforce in 1999 and 2000 in an effort to cut costs. In 1999 CEO Ken Derr retired, and vice chairman Dave O'Reilly replaced him.

In 2000 Chevron formed a joint venture with Phillips Petroleum (later ConocoPhillips) that combined the companies' chemicals businesses as Chevron Phillips Chemical. That year Chevron agreed to acquire Texaco for about $35 billion in stock and about $8 billion in assumed debt. The deal, completed in 2001, formed ChevronTexaco.

Part of the 2001 deal to acquire Texaco required Chevron to sell exclusive rights to the Texaco brand for a period of three years. A division of Royal Dutch Shell owned rights to the Texaco brand until 2004 and changed the name of the service stations to Shell. Once Chevron regained the rights to the Texaco name, it revitalized the brand name by adding about 400 Texaco stations in the western US.

In 2002 ChevronTexaco divested its stakes in US downstream joint ventures Equilon (to Shell) and Motiva (to Shell and Saudi Aramco). It also sold part of a Gulf of Mexico pipeline and two natural gas plants in Louisiana to Duke Energy, and its 12.5% stake in a natural gas liquids fractionator to Enterprise Products Partners. In 2004 ChevronTexaco sold 150 US natural gas and oil properties to XTO Energy for $912 million. The company changed its name to Chevron Corporation in 2005.

In 2005 Chevron acquired Unocal for more than $16 billion, boosting its proved reserves by about 15%. Equally attractive to Chevron was the strategic position of Unocal's operations; at a time when industries are trying to get a foothold in China, the reserves in Southeast Asia could easily be transported not only there but also to a surging India as well. Unocal's other operations easily supplied the US (from the Gulf of Mexico) and Europe (Caspian Sea) with gas and oil. Chevron bought a 5% stake in Indian refiner Reliance Petroleum for about $300 million in 2006. That year a company-led group of exploration firms announced a new successful oil strike in the Gulf of Mexico.

EXECUTIVES

Chairman and CEO: John S. Watson, age 53, $8,792,691 total compensation
Vice Chairman; EVP Global Upstream and Gas: George L. Kirkland, age 59, $10,145,921 total compensation
EVP Technology and Services: John E. Bethancourt, age 58
EVP Global Downstream: Michael K. (Mike) Wirth, age 49
VP and CFO: Patricia E. (Pat) Yarrington, age 54, $6,345,878 total compensation
VP Policy, Government, and Public Affairs: Rhonda I. Zygocki, age 53
VP and CTO: John W. McDonald, age 58
VP Corporate Business Development: Jay R. Pryor, age 53
VP Strategic Planning: Paul K. Siegele
VP Health, Environment, and Safety: Charles A. (Chuck) Taylor, age 52
VP and Treasurer: Pierre R. Breber, age 45
VP and General Counsel: R. Hewitt (Hew) Pate, age 48
Corporate VP and Comptroller: Matthew J. (Matt) Foehr, age 52
Corporate VP Human Resources: Joe W. Laymon, age 56
Corporate Secretary and Chief Governance Officer: Lydia I. Beebe, age 57
Chief Procurement Officer: Leo G. Lonergan
General Tax Counsel: Thomas R. Schuttish, age 62
General Manager Public Affairs: David A. (Dave) Samson
CIO; President, Chevron Information Technology: Louis V. (Louie) Ehrlich
President, Chevron Energy Technology: Melody Meyer
President and CEO, Chevron Phillips Chemical Company: Greg C. Garland, age 52
President, Chevron Shipping: Michael L. (Mike) Carthew
President, Chevron Canada: Jeffrey K. Lehrmann
President, Chevron Global Manufacturing: Gary Yesavage
President, Global Marketing: S. Shariq Yosufzai
President, Asia Pacific Exploration and Production Co.: James R. Blackwell, age 47
President, Chevron Pipe Line Co.: Rebecca B. Roberts, age 55
General Manager Investor Relations: Jeanette Ourado
Auditors: PricewaterhouseCoopers LLP

LOCATIONS

HQ: Chevron Corporation
  6001 Bollinger Canyon Rd., San Ramon, CA 94583
Phone: 925-842-1000 **Fax:** 925-842-3530
Web: www.chevron.com

2009 Sales

	$ mil.	% of total
US	84,145	42
Other countries	113,631	58
Adjustments	(26,140)	—
Total	**171,636**	**100**

PRODUCTS/OPERATIONS

2009 Sales

	$ mil.	% of total
Downstream	142,854	72
Upstream	51,328	26
Chemicals	1,893	1
Other	1,701	1
Adjustments	(26,140)	—
Total	**171,636**	**100**

COMPETITORS

Anadarko Petroleum	Koch Industries, Inc.
BP	PEMEX
ConocoPhillips	PETROBRAS
Devon Energy	Petróleos de Venezuela
Eni	Repsol YPF
Exxon Mobil	Royal Dutch Shell
Hess Corporation	TOTAL
Imperial Oil	

HISTORICAL FINANCIALS

Company Type: Public

Income Statement

FYE: December 31

	REVENUE ($ mil.)	NET INCOME ($ mil.)	NET PROFIT MARGIN	EMPLOYEES
12/09	171,636	10,483	6.1%	95,500
12/08	273,005	23,931	8.8%	67,000
12/07	220,904	18,688	8.5%	65,000
12/06	210,118	17,138	8.2%	62,500
12/05	198,200	14,099	7.1%	59,000
Annual Growth	(3.5%)	(7.1%)	—	12.8%

2009 Year-End Financials

Debt ratio: 11.0%
Return on equity: 11.7%
Cash ($ mil.): 8,716
Current ratio: 1.42
Long-term debt ($ mil.): 10,130

No. of shares (mil.): 2,011
Dividends
Yield: 3.5%
Payout: 50.8%
Market value ($ mil.): 154,796

Stock History

NYSE: CVX

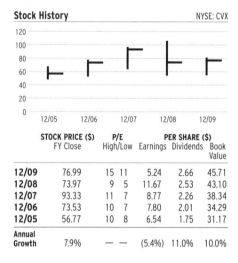

	STOCK PRICE ($) FY Close	P/E High/Low		PER SHARE ($) Earnings	Dividends	Book Value
12/09	76.99	15	11	5.24	2.66	45.71
12/08	73.97	9	5	11.67	2.53	43.10
12/07	93.33	11	7	8.77	2.26	38.34
12/06	73.53	10	7	7.80	2.01	34.29
12/05	56.77	10	8	6.54	1.75	31.17
Annual Growth	7.9%	—	—	(5.4%)	11.0%	10.0%

Chiquita Brands International

As one of the world's top banana producers, Chiquita Brands International deals in big bunches. The company grows, procures, markets, and sells bananas and other fresh fruits and vegetables under the Chiquita and other brand names. Bananas accounted for 56% of Chiquita's 2009 total sales. Its other offerings include whole citrus fruits, melons, grapes, apples, and tomatoes, as well as packaged fresh-cut items, juices, and processed fruit ingredients. With a 44% market share, the company's Fresh Express unit is the leading US seller of packaged ready-to-eat salads. Chiquita's products are sold in some 80 countries, mainly in North America and Europe.

Company-owned farms produce 30% of Chiquita's bananas. In order to meet demand, however, it also sources bananas from other growers in Colombia, Costa Rica, Ecuador, Guatemala, Honduras, Mexico, Nicaragua, Panama, and the Philippines. Chiquita also obtains all of its other produce from third-party growers.

The company's Fresh Express business supports Chiquita's strategy of providing more convenient, healthy-food options. The company shipped an average of 15 million ready-made salads in 2009.

To expand its menu of healthy products, as well as to establish a stronger European presence, in 2010 Chiquita formed a joint venture with France's Groupe Danone to market fruit beverages based on Chiquita's Just Fruit in a Bottle business in Europe.

Another of Chiquita's strategies involves expanding its product range so as to introduce its brands into new segments, categories, and geographies. To that end, in 2009 it introduced Gourmet Café, Chiquita to Go, Just Fruit in a Bottle, and Pineapple Bites to non-grocery venues, including convenience outlets, gas stations, club stores, and coffee shops.

HISTORY

Lorenzo Baker sailed into Jersey City, New Jersey, in 1870 with 160 bunches of Jamaican bananas. Baker arranged to sell bananas through Boston produce agent Andrew Preston and, with the support of Preston's partners, the two formed the Boston Fruit Company in 1885. In 1899 Boston Fruit merged with three other banana importers and incorporated as United Fruit Company. Soon the company was importing bananas from numerous Central American plantations for expanded distribution in the US.

United Fruit entered the Cuban sugar trade with the purchase of Nipe Bay (1907) and Saetia Sugar (1912). It bought Samuel Zemurray's Cuyamel Fruit Company in 1930, leaving Zemurray as the largest shareholder. Zemurray, who had masterminded the overthrow of the Honduran regime in 1905 to establish one favorable to his business, forcibly established himself as United Fruit's president in 1933.

In 1954, when Guatemalan president Jacobo Arbenz threatened to seize United Fruit's holdings, the company claimed he was a communist threat and provided ships to transport CIA-backed troops and ammunition, leading to his ultimate overthrow.

Diversifying in the 1960s, United Fruit purchased A&W (restaurants and root beer, 1966) and Baskin-Robbins (ice cream, 1967). Eli Black, founder of AMK (which included the Morrell meat company), bought United Fruit in 1970 and changed its name to United Brands. Through American Financial Group, Carl Lindner began acquiring large amounts of United Brands' stock in 1973; he became chairman of the company in 1984. During the 1970s and 1980s, United Brands sold many of its holdings, including Baskin-Robbins (1973) and A&W (restaurants, 1982; soft drinks, 1987).

The firm became Chiquita Brands International in 1990. Chiquita acquired Friday Canning two years later. It then began divesting its meat operations, and all were sold by 1995.

In 1993 the European Union (EU) set up trade barriers against banana imports from Latin America, favoring banana-producing former European colonies in the Caribbean. The preference system angered Chiquita, whose bananas come from non-favored countries, although it retained more than 20% of the European market. In 1997 the WTO ruled the EU's trade policy illegal; the battle continued, however, over just how open the market should be.

Chiquita bought vegetable canners Owatonna Canning (1997), American Fine Foods (1997), and Stokely USA (1998) and merged them with Friday Canning in 1998. Also that year Hurricane Mitch destroyed Chiquita plantations in Honduras and Guatemala, costing the company $74 million. Sales were not affected though, as Chiquita was able to turn to growers in Ecuador and Panama. In 2000 the company announced cost-cutting efforts that included job cuts and a reorganization of some divisions.

Beset by a weakened European currency and a banana glut, the company announced in January 2001 that it was unable to pay its public debt. Chiquita also sued the European Commission, demanding $525 million in damages, due to the EU banana trade policy. The EU and the US later reached an agreement modifying quotas and tariffs. In 2001 Chiquita filed for Chapter 11 bankruptcy. The plan was approved and the reorganization went into effect in mid-March of 2002, and the company began trading again on the NYSE. That same month, Chiquita announced the resignation of Steve Warshaw as the company president, CEO, and director. Cyrus Freidheim Jr. was named new chairman and CEO.

In a move to further concentrate on its fresh produce business, in 2003 the company sold its subsidiary, Chiquita Processed Foods (vegetable canning), to Seneca Foods. Fernando Aguirre took over the roles of chairman, president, and CEO during 2004.

After Chiquita voluntarily revealed in 2004 that one of its Colombian banana subsidiaries had made protection payments from 1997 though 2004 to terrorist groups, the Justice Department began a criminal investigation, examining the role and conduct of Chiquita and some of its officers in the criminal activity. Chiquita sold the subsidiary in 2004 but owned it at the time of the payments, admitting the payments were improper but that it was trying to ensure the safety of its employees. (In 2007 Chiquita agreed to pay $25 million to settle the case.)

Chiquita acquired Performance Food Group's Fresh Express unit for $855 million in 2005.

As an efficency move, in 2007 the company sold its fleet of 12 refrigerated cargo ships to Eastwind Maritime.

EXECUTIVES

Chairman, President, and CEO: Fernando G. Aguirre, age 52, $7,653,994 total compensation
SVP and Chief People Officer: Kevin R. Holland, age 48
SVP Product Supply Organization: Waheed Zaman, age 49
SVP and CFO: Michael Sims, age 50, $1,352,281 total compensation
SVP Government and International Affairs and Corporate Responsibility Officer: Manuel Rodriguez, age 60
SVP, General Counsel, and Secretary: James E. Thompson, age 49, $941,373 total compensation
VP and CIO: Manjit Singh, age 40
VP, Controller, and Chief Accounting Officer: Lori A. Ritchey, age 46
VP Taxation: Joseph W. Bradley
President, North America: Brian W. Kocher, age 40
President, Global Innovation and Emerging Markets and Chief Marketing Officer: Tanios E. Viviani, age 48, $1,942,090 total compensation
President, Europe and Middle East: Michel Loeb, age 55, $1,806,805 total compensation
Auditors: Ernst & Young LLP

LOCATIONS

HQ: Chiquita Brands International, Inc.
    250 E. 5th St., Cincinnati, OH 45202
Phone: 513-784-8000   **Fax:** 513-784-8030
Web: www.chiquita.com

2009 Sales

	$ mil.	% of total
US	1,944.0	56
International		
Italy	235.7	7
Germany	212.5	6
Other	1,078.2	31
Total	**3,470.4**	**100**

PRODUCTS/OPERATIONS

2009 Sales

	$ mil.	% of total
Bananas	2,081.5	60
Salads & healthy snacks	1,135.5	33
Other produce	253.4	7
Total	**3,470.4**	**100**

Selected Brands and Products

Fresh produce
  Bananas
  Other
    Fresh cut (packaged salads and fresh-cut fruits,
      including Fresh Express products)
    Fresh whole
      Apples
      Avocados
      Bell peppers
      Cherries
      Cucumbers
      Grapes
      Kiwi
      Melons
      Nectarines
      Peaches
      Pears
      Pineapples
      Plums
      Stone fruit
      Tomatoes
Fruit ingredients (concentrates, flakes, IQF, juice,
  natural essences, natural extracts, powders, purees,
  whole peeled)
  Mango
  Papaya
  Passion fruit
  Pineapple
Healthy snacks
  Just Fruit in a Bottle (fruit smoothies)
  Chiquita Frozen Fruit Smoothies
  Pineapple Bites

COMPETITORS

American Fruit & Produce	Kraft Foods
Bakkavor	National Grape Cooperative
BC Hot House Foods	Natural Selection Foods
Bonduelle	Naturipe Farms
Calavo Growers	Oceanside Produce
Campbell Soup	Orchard House Foods
C.H. Robinson Worldwide	Poupart
Coca-Cola	Premier Foods
Del Monte Foods	Ready Pac
Dole Food	Redbridge
Fresh Del Monte Produce	River Ranch Fresh Foods
Fyffes	Sunkist
Gentile Bros.	Tampico Beverages
Giumarra Companies	Taylor Fresh Foods
Global Pacific Produce	Tropicana
Hansen Natural	Village Farms International
Jamaica Producers Group	Wilkinson-Cooper Produce
J.G. Boswell Co.	Worldwide Fruit

HISTORICAL FINANCIALS

Company Type: Public

Income Statement

FYE: December 31

	REVENUE ($ mil.)	NET INCOME ($ mil.)	NET PROFIT MARGIN	EMPLOYEES
12/09	3,470	91	2.6%	21,000
12/08	3,609	(324)	—	23,000
12/07	4,663	(49)	—	24,000
12/06	4,499	(96)	—	25,000
12/05	3,904	131	3.4%	25,000
Annual Growth	**(2.9%)**	**(8.9%)**	**—**	**(4.3%)**

2009 Year-End Financials

Debt ratio: 96.7%
Return on equity: 16.3%
Cash ($ mil.): 121
Current ratio: 1.75
Long-term debt ($ mil.): 638
No. of shares (mil.): 45
Dividends
  Yield: 0.0%
  Payout: —
Market value ($ mil.): 810

Stock History

NYSE: CQB

	STOCK PRICE ($) FY Close	P/E High/Low		PER SHARE ($) Earnings	Dividends	Book Value
12/09	18.04	10	2	2.00	0.00	14.71
12/08	14.78	—	—	(7.40)	0.00	9.97
12/07	18.39	—	—	(1.22)	0.00	19.94
12/06	15.97	—	—	(2.28)	0.20	19.40
12/05	20.01	11	7	2.92	0.40	22.13
Annual Growth	**(2.6%)**	**—**	**—**	**(9.0%)**	**—**	**(9.7%)**

CHS Inc.

CHS goes with the grain. As one of the US's leading publicly traded, cooperative marketers of grain, oilseed and energy, it represents farmers, ranchers, and co-ops from the Great Lakes to the Pacific Northwest and from the Canadian border to Texas. CHS trades grain and sells farm supplies to members through its stores. It processes soybeans for use in food and animal feeds, and grinds wheat into flour used in pastas and bread. Through joint ventures, the company sells soybean oil and crop nutrient and protection products, and markets grain. CHS also provides insurance and financial and risk-management services, and operates petroleum refineries and sells Cenex brand fuels, lubricants, and energy products.

CHS's grain trading activities include buying, selling, and arranging for transport. The co-op operates wheat mills to produce flour for pasta and bread, and it provides supplies to its Cenex/Ampride stores; CHS also processes soybeans for use in margarine, salad dressings, and animal feed. Extending its reach beyond the US, the company formed a joint venture (Multigrain A.G.) with Brazilian agricultural commodities company Multigrain Comercio.

The company's energy division operates oil refineries, and the Country Energy subsidiary sells wholesale propane and other petroleum products. Joint ventures with United Grain Corporation (United Harvest) and Cargill (TEMPCO) operate grain terminals and export grain. CHS also provides ethanol and biodiesel fuel products.

In 2009 CHS acquired Winona River & Rail, including 90,000 tons of dry-fertilizer storage capacity, a dedicated river dock, and a 65-car railroad track capacity. The acquisition of the Minnesota operations bolstered the company's storage capacity and rail access in the midwestern and upper Mississippi River regions. Later that year, it formed a joint venture with Russia's farm operation Agrico Group (called ACG) in order to manage the export and worldwide marketing of its wheat and feed grains. In turn, it gave CHS access to the Russian grain market and improved its ability to serve its global customers.

Also that year, CHS joined with Nebraska's Central Valley Ag Cooperative (CVA) to form Advanced Energy Fuels to provide customers with an industry-leading fuel delivery system.

Recognizing the growing demand for soy-based food products and, in turn, to increase shareholder value, in 2008 the company acquired Legacy Foods, maker of Ultra Soy and TSP brands of textured soybean products for use by both human food and pet food manufacturers. Legacy's operations are overseen by CHS's oilseed processing division.

On the energy front, in 2008 CHS became the sole owner of Provista Renewable Fuels Marketing by purchasing US BioEnergy's 50% interest in the biofuels maker. (VeraSun Energy bought out US BioEnergy later that year.)

HISTORY

To help farmers through the Great Depression, the Farmers Union Terminal Association (a grain marketing association formed in 1926) created the Farmers Union Grain Terminal Association (GTA) in 1938. With loans from the Farmers Union Central Exchange (later known as CENEX) and the Farm Credit Association, the organization operated a grain elevator in St. Paul, Minnesota. By 1939 GTA had 250 grain-producing associations as members.

GTA leased terminals in Minneapolis and Washington and then built others in Wisconsin and Montana. It took over a Minnesota flour mill and created Amber Milling. GTA also began managing farming insurance provider Terminal Agency. In 1958 the association bought 57 elevators and feed plants from the McCabe Company.

Adding to its operations in 1960, GTA bought the Honeymead soybean plant. The next year the co-op acquired Minnesota Linseed Oil. In 1977 it acquired Jewett & Sherman (later Holsum Foods), which helped transform the company into a provider of jams, jellies, salad dressings, and syrups.

In 1983 GTA combined with North Pacific Grain Growers, a Pacific Northwest co-op incorporated in 1929, to form Harvest States Cooperatives. Harvest States grew in the early and mid-1990s by acquiring salad dressing makers Albert's Foods, Great American Foods, and Saffola Quality Foods; soup stock producer Private Brands; and margarine and dressings manufacturer and distributor Gregg Foods.

The company started a joint venture to operate the Ag States Agency agricultural insurance company in 1995. The next year the co-op's Holsum Foods division and Mitsui & Co.'s edible oils unit, Wilsey Foods, merged to form Ventura Foods, a distributor of margarines, oils, spreads, and other food products.

Harvest States merged in 1998 with Minnesota-based CENEX, a 16-state agricultural supply co-op that had been founded in 1931 as Farmers Union Central Exchange. (Among CENEX's major operations was a farm inputs, services, marketing, and processing joint venture with dairy cooperative Land O'Lakes formed in 1987.) CENEX CEO Noel Estenson took the helm of the resulting co-op, Cenex Harvest States Cooperatives, which soon formed a petroleum joint venture called Country Energy with Farmland Industries.

CHS members rejected a proposed merger with Farmland Industries in 1999. Also that year Cenex/Land O'Lakes Agronomy (it became Agriliance in 2000 when Farmland Industries joined the joint venture) bought Terra Industries' $1.7 billion distribution business (400 farm supply stores, seed and chemical distribution operations, partial ownership of two chemical plants).

CHS bought the wholesale propane marketing operations of Williams Companies in 2000. Additionally, Estenson retired that year and company president John Johnson took over as CEO.

In 2002 CHS acquired Agway's Grandin, North Dakota-based sunflower business and formed a wheat-milling joint venture (Horizon Milling) with Cargill. In 2003 the company changed its name from Cenex Harvest States Cooperatives to CHS Inc. and began trading on the NASDAQ.

In 2004 CHS purchased all of bankrupt Farmland Industries' ownership of Agriliance, thus giving CHS a 50% ownership of Agriliance (with Land O'Lakes owning the other 50%). With an eye to this growing energy sector, CHS acquired a 28% ownership of ethanol production and marketing company US BioEnergy Corporation in 2005. Also that year it sold off its Mexican foods business and sold 81% of its 20% ownership of crop-nutrient manufacturer CF Industries in an initial public offering. In 2008 it sold off all its remaining shares of CF.

EXECUTIVES

Chairman: Michael Toelle, age 47
First Vice Chairman: Robert Bass, age 55
President and CEO: John D. Johnson, age 62, $6,243,936 total compensation
EVP and COO, Ag Business: Mark Palmquist, age 52, $2,560,624 total compensation
EVP and COO, Processing: Jay D. Debertin, age 49, $2,128,530 total compensation
EVP and COO, Energy: Leon E. Westbrock, age 62, $3,967,605 total compensation
EVP and CFO: John Schmitz, age 59, $2,411,960 total compensation
EVP, Business Solutions: Thomas D. (Tom) Larson, age 61
EVP, Corporate Administration: Patrick (Pat) Kluempke, age 61
SVP, Grain Marketing: Rick Browne
SVP, and General Counsel: David (Dave) Kastelic
SVP, Oilseed Processing: Dennis Wendland
SVP, Energy Sales: Kevin L. Williams
VP, Information Technology: Beth Nordin
President and CEO, Ventura Foods, LLC: Christopher (Chris) Furman
President, CHS Foundation: William J. Nelson
General Manager and CEO, CHS Europe: Claudio Scarrozza
Secretary, Treasurer, and Director: Jerry Hasnedl, age 63
Director, Corporate Communications: Lani Jordan
Auditors: PricewaterhouseCoopers LLP

LOCATIONS

HQ: CHS Inc.
5500 Cenex Dr., Inver Grove Heights, MN 55077
Phone: 651-355-6000
Web: www.chsinc.com

PRODUCTS/OPERATIONS

2009 Sales

	% of total
Ag business	66
Energy	30
Processing	4
Total	**100**

Selected Operations

Convenience stores (Cenex)
Farm financing (Fin-Ag, Inc.)
Farm supplies (Agri-Service Centers)
  Crop-protection products
  Fertilizer
  Grain purchasing
  Seeds
Feed manufacturing
Futures and option services
Grain merchandising
Petroleum marketing
Soybean crushing (soybean conversion into animal feed and crude soybean oil)
Soybean refining (soybean oil conversion into margarine, salad dressings, and baked goods)
Wheat milling (semolina and durum wheat milling for flour)

COMPETITORS

ACH Food Companies
ADM
Ag Processing Inc.
Agrium
AmeriGas Partners
Andersons
Bartlett and Company
BP
Bunge Limited
Cargill
Central Soya
C.F. Sauer
CGC
CITGO
Columbia Grain
ConAgra
ConocoPhillips
Dakota Growers
ExxonMobil Chemical
Ferrellgas Partners
Flint Hills
GROWMARK
JR Simplot
Koch Industries, Inc.
Kraft Foods
Land O'Lakes Purina Feed
Louis Dreyfus Group
Marathon Petroleum
Marzetti
Mosaic Company
Nestlé
Riceland Foods
Ridley Inc.
Scoular
Shell Oil Products
Smucker
Terra Industries
Unilever NV
U.S. Oil
US Soy
Valero Energy
Western Petroleum
Whole Harvest Foods
Wilbur-Ellis

HISTORICAL FINANCIALS

Company Type: Public

Income Statement

FYE: August 31

	REVENUE ($ mil.)	NET INCOME ($ mil.)	NET PROFIT MARGIN	EMPLOYEES
8/09	25,730	381	1.5%	8,802
8/08	32,168	803	2.5%	8,099
8/07	17,216	750	4.4%	6,885
8/06	14,384	490	3.4%	6,540
8/05	11,941	250	2.1%	6,370
Annual Growth	**21.2%**	**11.1%**	**—**	**8.4%**

2009 Year-End Financials

Debt ratio: 32.0%
Return on equity: 12.6%
Cash ($ mil.): —
Current ratio: —
Long-term debt ($ mil.): 988

Net Income History

NASDAQ (GS): CHSCP

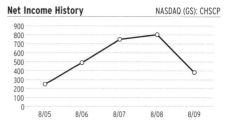

The Chubb Corporation

Here's the skinny on Chubb: The insurer is best known for comprehensive homeowners insurance for the demographic that owns yachts (the company insures those, too). Chubb also offers commercial property/casualty insurance including multiple peril, property and marine, and workers' compensation. Its specialty insurance arm offers professional liability policies for executives across a spectrum of industries and also provides construction and commercial surety bonds. Chubb distributes its products through 8,500 independent agents and brokers in 120 offices across the US and in more than 25 countries. The company began in 1882 when Thomas Chubb and his son began writing marine insurance in New York City.

Although the US accounts for more than three-fourths of Chubb's direct business, developing its presence in foreign markets through organic growth is an element of the company's strategy. It prefers to target small and midsized public and privately held companies, and has reduced the number of larger public companies in its customer list. It opened a reinsurance subsidiary in Brazil in 2008.

While much of the insurance industry was in spasm during the economic crisis of 2008 and 2009, Chubb only experienced a mild ache as its conservative investments temporarily lost some of their value. Meanwhile, the company created the largest private wildfire fighting force in the US when it engaged federal contractor Wildfire Defense Systems, of Montana, to protect customers' homes in 14 western states. Customers can enroll to use the service at no additional cost.

HISTORY

Thomas C. Chubb and his son Percy formed Chubb & Son in New York in 1882 to underwrite cargo and ship insurance. The company soon became the US manager for Sea Insurance Co. of England and co-founded New York Marine Underwriters (NYMU). In 1901 NYMU became Chubb's chief property/casualty affiliate, Federal Insurance Co.

Chubb expanded in the 1920s, opening a Chicago office (1923) and, just before the 1929 crash, organizing Associated Aviation Underwriters. Growth slowed during the Depression, but Chubb recovered enough by 1939 to buy Vigilant Insurance Co.

The company bought Colonial Life in 1959 and Pacific Indemnity in 1967. That year Chubb Corporation was formed as a holding company, with Chubb & Son designated the manager of the property/casualty insurance businesses. A 1969 takeover attempt by First National City Corp. (predecessor of Citigroup) was foiled by federal regulators.

Chubb acquired Bellemead Development in 1970 to expand its real estate portfolio. Following a strategy of offering specialized insurance, Chubb in the 1970s launched insurance packages for the entertainment industry, including films and Broadway shows. After the Tylenol poisonings of 1982, Chubb developed insurance against product tampering (which it no longer offers). During the 1980s Chubb focused on specialized property/casualty insurance lines; in 1985 it retreated from medical malpractice insurance.

The company combined three subsidiaries into Chubb Life Insurance Co. of America in 1991. The next year Chubb subsidiary Pacific Indemnity settled a suit over Fibreboard Corporation's asbestos liability (Fibreboard was later bought by Owens Corning); the company ultimately paid some $675 million in asbestos-related settlements.

Financial difficulties at Lloyd's of London caused that market to rethink and subsequently relax its rules about doing business with corporate insurance companies. Chubb took advantage of the opportunity and opened an office at Lloyd's in 1993. The next year Chubb's acquisitions included the personal lines business of Alexander & Alexander (now part of Aon Corporation).

Since the 1880s Chubb had maintained an alliance with UK-based Royal & Sun Alliance Insurance Group and its predecessors. Royal & Sun Alliance owned about 5% of Chubb, and Chubb held about 3% of Royal & Sun Alliance. In 1993 the US insurer formed a new joint venture with the British company, with the purpose of extending to the UK Chubb's insurance products targeting the affluent. But in 1996 a major client of Royal & Sun Alliance Insurance Group defected, and Chubb ended the agreement.

To focus on the property/casualty market, Chubb in 1997 sold its life and health insurance operations to Jefferson Pilot and parts of its Bellemead real estate business to Paine Webber and Morgan Stanley Dean Witter. (Chubb blamed the real estate market for its lower 1996 earnings.) The next year the commercial lines market tanked and was followed by a drop in Chubb's earnings.

With losses dragging down its otherwise profitable property/casualty segment, Chubb vowed to get tough — raising rates and getting out of unprofitable businesses. It also forged ahead with its overseas plans, buying Venezuelan insurer Italseguros Internacional and creating Chubb Re to offer international reinsurance. In

1999 Chubb bought corporate officer insurer Executive Risk (now with a Chubb prefix) to beef up its executive protection and financial services lines. The next year UK aviation insurer British Aviation Group bought Chubb's Associated Aviation Underwriters.

Severely affected by terrorist strikes on September 11, 2001, and the collapse of Enron, Chubb paid out almost $900 million in claims. In 2002 Chubb took a $700 million charge related to asbestos and toxic waste.

While other insurers were busily adding financial services to their offerings, Chubb went the other way. In 2003 it shuttered its Chubb Financial Solutions unit and put the existing business into run-off. To continue pruning its noncore operations, in 2004 the company sold its post-secondary educational subsidiary, The Chubb Institute.

EXECUTIVES

Chairman, President, and CEO; Chairman and CEO, Chubb & Son: John D. Finnegan, age 61, $19,161,232 total compensation
Vice Chairman and COO: John J. Degnan, age 65, $7,730,663 total compensation
EVP and CFO: Richard G. Spiro, age 45, $5,227,023 total compensation
EVP, General Counsel, and Chief Ethics Officer: Maureen A. Brundage, age 53
EVP and Chief Underwriting Officer: Paul J. Krump, age 50, $2,551,904 total compensation
EVP and Chief Global Field Officer: Harold L. Morrison Jr., age 52, $2,459,444 total compensation
EVP and Chief Investment Officer, Domestic Fixed Income Investments: Ned I. Gerstman
EVP, Chief Administrative Officer, and Chief Claim Officer: Dino E. Robusto, age 52, $2,372,298 total compensation
SVP and Chief Accounting Officer: John J. Kennedy, age 54
VP, Corporate Counsel, and Secretary: W. Andrew Macan
Chief Innovation Officer: Jon Bidwell
Chairman, President, and CEO, Chubb Insurance Company of Canada: Ellen J. Moore
President and CEO, Chubb Insurance Company of Europe SE: Michael J. Casella
Auditors: Ernst & Young LLP

LOCATIONS

HQ: The Chubb Corporation
　15 Mountain View Rd., Warren, NJ 07059
Phone: 908-903-2000　　Fax: 908-903-2027
Web: www.chubb.com

PRODUCTS/OPERATIONS

2009 Premiums Earned

	% of total
Commercial insurance	42
Personal insurance	32
Specialty insurance	25
Reinsurance	1
Total	**100**

Selected Subsidiaries

Bellemead Development Corporation
Chubb Atlantic Indemnity Ltd. (Bermuda)
　DHC Corporation
　　Chubb do Brasil Companhia de Seguros (99%, Brazil)
Federal Insurance Company
　Executive Risk Indemnity Inc.
　　Executive Risk Specialty Insurance Company
　Great Northern Insurance Company
　Pacific Indemnity Company
　　Northwestern Pacific Indemnity Company
　　Texas Pacific Indemnity Company
　Vigilant Insurance Company

COMPETITORS

AIG	CNA Financial
Allstate	The Hartford
Arch Capital	Liberty Mutual
AXA	Travelers Companies
Berkshire Hathaway	XL Group plc

HISTORICAL FINANCIALS

Company Type: Public

Income Statement

FYE: December 31

	ASSETS ($ mil.)	NET INCOME ($ mil.)	INCOME AS % OF ASSETS	EMPLOYEES
12/09	50,449	2,183	4.3%	10,200
12/08	48,429	1,804	3.7%	10,400
12/07	50,574	2,807	5.6%	10,600
12/06	50,277	2,528	5.0%	10,800
12/05	48,061	1,826	3.8%	10,800
Annual Growth	**1.2%**	**4.6%**	**—**	**(1.4%)**

2009 Year-End Financials

Equity as % of assets: 31.0%
Return on assets: 4.4%
Return on equity: 15.0%
Long-term debt ($ mil.): 3,975
No. of shares (mil.): 327
Dividends
　Yield: 2.8%
　Payout: 22.7%
Market value ($ mil.): 16,071
Sales ($ mil.): 13,016

Stock History

NYSE: CB

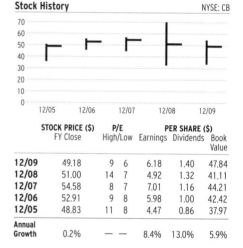

	STOCK PRICE ($) FY Close	P/E High/Low		PER SHARE ($) Earnings	Dividends	Book Value
12/09	49.18	9	6	6.18	1.40	47.84
12/08	51.00	14	7	4.92	1.32	41.11
12/07	54.58	8	7	7.01	1.16	44.21
12/06	52.91	9	8	5.98	1.00	42.42
12/05	48.83	11	8	4.47	0.86	37.97
Annual Growth	**0.2%**	**—**	**—**	**8.4%**	**13.0%**	**5.9%**

Church & Dwight

Whether you call it saleratus (aerated salt), sodium bicarbonate, or plain old baking soda, Church & Dwight is a top maker worldwide of the powder. Church & Dwight's ARM & HAMMER baking soda, first marketed in 1846, is used as leavening, a deodorizer, a cleaner, and a swimming pool pH stabilizer. While laundry detergent represents Church & Dwight's top consumer business by sales, the company also makes a variety of other products: bathroom cleaners, carpet deodorizer, air fresheners, toothpaste, antiperspirants, Trojan condoms, industrial-grade carbonates, cat litter, and animal nutrition. It operates in North America, as well as in Australia, Brazil, China, France, and the UK.

The company's business segments are divided into three groups: consumer domestic, consumer international, and specialty products. Church & Dwight's specialty products division, which logs some 10% of its sales, is what sets the firm apart from other consumer products companies. It manufactures antacid feed additives for cattle, industrial- and medical-grade sodium bicarbonate (used in kidney dialysis), potassium carbonate (used in video monitor glass), and industrial cleaning products. A small subsidiary in the UK produces specialty chemicals for European markets.

Despite a global economic downturn during the past couple of years, Church & Dwight has posted sales increases each year. Overall, the rise was generated from organic growth; the remaining came from a purchase in its oral care segment and the disposal of certain assets. The company points to its Orajel acquisition and sales of its Brotherton Specialty Products subsidiary and its consumer products unit in Spain for the boost, as well as generally higher volumes and higher selling prices. The recession and an aggressive marketing campaign have helped Church & Dwight steer consumers toward its value-priced brands.

Church & Dwight has been investing in its consumer business in the US, where it sells most of these products. The segment houses Church & Dwight's eight "power brands," or well-recognized brand names: ARM & HAMMER, Trojan, XTRA, Oxiclean, Nair, First Response, Orajel, and SpinBrush. The company also got an unexpected boost to its bottom line in September 2009 from a net gain of $20 million through a patent infringement lawsuit settlement with Abbott Laboratories. To expand its oral care products portfolio, it bought the pharmaceuticals business of Del Laboratories (maker of Orajel) in July 2008 from Coty for about $380 million.

To increase its manufacturing capacity and keep up with growth of its laundry segment, the firm in late 2009 completed the construction of a new integrated laundry detergent manufacturing plant and distribution center located in York County, Pennsylvania. The facility replaced its existing laundry detergent plant in North Brunswick, New Jersey. It has also expanded its distribution of ARM & HAMMER laundry and pet care products, as well as Oxiclean and Orange Glo, in North America. The firm took a step back in early 2010 by paring its products portfolio. It sold the well-known Brillo brand of scouring pads to Armaly Brands, a manufacturer of polyester sponge brand Estracell.

HISTORY

Chemistry enthusiast Dr. Austin Church and his marketing-driven brother-in-law, John Dwight, founded a company to make bicarbonate of soda for baking in 1846. The ARM & HAMMER trademark — representing Vulcan, the Roman god of fire, and originally used by Church's son James, owner of the Vulcan Spice Mills — was adopted in 1867.

After Church's retirement, his sons ran a separate company until 1896, when they formed Church & Dwight, which became known for direct marketing and distinctive packaging. Church & Dwight began preaching alternative uses for baking soda in the 1920s and accelerated the effort after WWII, when home baking declined.

Dwight Minton, the great-great-grandson of Church, was named CEO in 1968. Under his direction the company began appealing to "green" sentiments with new products such as nonphosphate laundry detergent (1970). Church & Dwight went public in 1977.

The Statue of Liberty's inner walls were cleaned with ARM & HAMMER baking soda in 1986 in preparation for its 100th anniversary. New product introductions intensified in the late 1980s and into the 1990s; offerings included toothpaste (1988), carpet deodorizer (1988), and deodorant and other products (1994). The product introductions were badly handled, and a large earnings drop ensued. Minton resigned in 1995 and was replaced by former marketing VP Robert Davies, the first CEO without ties to the founding family.

Broadening its household cleaning products base, the company bought the Brillo soap pad and five other brands from Dial in 1997 and folded Dial's Toss 'N Soft fabric softener business into its laundry basket in 1998. In 1999 it bought the Clean Shower brand (from Clean Shower L.P.) and the Scrub Free and Delicare brands (from Reckitt Benckiser), doubling its household cleaner business.

In 2000 Church & Dwight agreed to combine its laundry detergent business with value-brand cleaning products company USA Detergents. The two companies formed a joint venture, Armkel LLC, before Church & Dwight decided to buy all of USA Detergents in 2001. Several years later, in 2007, Church & Dwight sold USA Detergents to Tital Global Holdings.

Also in 2001 the company acquired Carter-Wallace's consumer products business (Arrid, Trojan, Nair) for $739 million. It bought the US antiperspirant and pet care businesses outright, but the larger part of the deal was made in partnership with private equity firm Kelso & Company. Church & Dwight purchased Unilever's oral care brands in the US and Canada in 2003. Products included in the deal were Mentadent toothpaste and toothbrushes, Pepsodent and Aim toothpaste, and exclusive licensing rights to Close-Up toothpaste. In early 2004 Church & Dwight bought the balance of Kelso & Company's stake for more than $250 million.

In July 2004 chairman and CEO Davies stepped down as CEO, retaining his title as chairman. Former president and CEO of Spalding Sports, James Craigie, took over as president and CEO. He added the title of chairman in mid-2007 when Davies retired.

EXECUTIVES

Chairman Emeritus: Dwight C. Minton
Chairman, President, and CEO: James R. (Jim) Craigie, age 56, $4,847,628 total compensation
EVP Finance and CFO: Matthew T. Farrell, age 53, $1,591,015 total compensation
EVP and Chief Marketing Officer: Bruce F. Fleming, age 52, $996,703 total compensation
EVP, General Counsel, and Secretary: Susan E. Goldy, age 55, $1,014,680 total compensation
EVP; President, International Consumer Products: Adrian J. Huns, age 61, $1,065,401 total compensation
EVP; President and COO, Specialty Products Division: Joseph A. Sipia Jr., age 61, $1,185,404 total compensation
EVP Domestic Consumer Sales: Louis H. (Lou) Tursi Jr., age 49, $996,074 total compensation
EVP Human Resources: Jacquelin J. (Jackie) Brova, age 56
EVP Global Research and Development: Paul A. Siracusa, age 53
EVP Global New Products Innovation: Steven P. Cugine, age 47
EVP Global Operations: Mark G. Conish, age 57, $1,106,525 total compensation
VP Investor Relations: Maureen K. Usifer
VP, Controller, and Chief Accounting Officer: Steven Katz, age 52
Auditors: Deloitte & Touche LLP

LOCATIONS

HQ: Church & Dwight Co., Inc.
    469 N. Harrison St., Princeton, NJ 08543
Phone: 609-683-5900   **Fax:** 609-497-7269
Web: www.churchdwight.com

PRODUCTS/OPERATIONS

2009 Sales

	$ mil.	% of total
Consumer domestic		
Household	1,196.5	47
Personal care	685.3	27
Consumer international	393.7	16
Specialty products	245.4	10
Total	**2,520.9**	**100**

Consumer Domestic Products

Household
  ARM & HAMMER
  Kaboom
  Nice 'N Fluffy
  Orange Glo
  Oxiclean
  Scrub Free
  Sno Bol
  Xtra
Personal care
  Aim
  Answer
  ARM & HAMMER
  Arrid
  Close-Up
  First Response
  Nair
  Orajel
  Spinbrush
  Trojan
Specialty products
  ARM & HAMMER feed-grade sodium bicarbonate
  ARM & HAMMER performance grade sodium bicarbonate
  ARM & HAMMER potassium carbonate and potassium bicarbonate
  ArmaKleen aqueous cleaner
  Armand potassium carbonate
  Armex blast media
  Bio-Chlor rumen fermentation enhancers
  Fermenten rumen fermentation enhancers
  MEGALAC rumen bypass fat (animal feed supplement)
  SQ-810 rumen buffer (animal feed supplement)

COMPETITORS

ADM
Ag Processing Inc.
Alere
Alticor
Ansell
Cargill
CHS
Clorox
Colgate-Palmolive
Dr. Bronner's
FMC
Henkel
Johnson & Johnson
Nestlé Purina PetCare
Oil-Dri
Procter & Gamble
Reckitt Benckiser
Sara Lee International Household and Body Care
S.C. Johnson
SSL International
Sun Products
Unilever

HISTORICAL FINANCIALS

Company Type: Public

Income Statement

FYE: December 31

	REVENUE ($ mil.)	NET INCOME ($ mil.)	NET PROFIT MARGIN	EMPLOYEES
12/09	2,521	244	9.7%	3,700
12/08	2,422	195	8.1%	3,500
12/07	2,221	169	7.6%	3,700
12/06	1,946	139	7.1%	3,700
12/05	1,737	123	7.1%	3,700
Annual Growth	9.8%	18.6%	—	0.0%

2009 Year-End Financials

Debt ratio: 37.3%
Return on equity: 16.6%
Cash ($ mil.): 447
Current ratio: 1.64
Long-term debt ($ mil.): 597

No. of shares (mil.): 71
Dividends
 Yield: 0.8%
 Payout: 13.5%
Market value ($ mil.): 4,293

Stock History

NYSE: CHD

	STOCK PRICE ($) FY Close	P/E High/Low	PER SHARE ($) Earnings	Dividends	Book Value
12/09	60.45	18 13	3.41	0.46	22.55
12/08	56.12	24 17	2.78	0.34	18.75
12/07	54.07	23 17	2.46	0.30	15.21
12/06	42.65	21 16	2.07	0.26	12.16
12/05	33.03	22 18	1.83	0.24	9.81
Annual Growth	16.3%	— —	16.8%	17.7%	23.1%

CIGNA Corporation

One of the top US health insurers, CIGNA covers nearly 12 million people with its various medical plans, which include PPO, HMO, point-of-service (POS), indemnity, and consumer-directed products. CIGNA also offers specialty health coverage in the form of dental, vision, pharmacy, and behavioral health plans, and it sells group accident, life, and disability insurance. Its customers include employers, government entities, unions, Medicare recipients, and other groups and individuals in the US and Canada. Internationally, the company sells life, accident, and health insurance in parts of Asia and the European Union, and it provides health coverage to expatriate employees of multinational companies.

CIGNA is trying to grow its health care segment by offering new and innovative products, particularly trendy consumer-directed programs such as health savings accounts (through its CIGNA Choice Fund line), health risk assessments, and online tools for comparing coverage options and making sound health care decisions. It also offers low-cost voluntary plans for small employer groups. In addition, CIGNA has jumped on the Medicare Part D bandwagon, offering a Medicare prescription drug benefit program jointly with distributor NationsHealth, and

has also been opening onsite health clinics for large employer groups.

The company's health care insurance operations manage care for its members through a network of some 5,000 hospitals and more than 600,000 physicians. The health care segment also includes more than 75,000 behavioral health providers, 48,000 vision centers, and 160,000 dentists, and it provides prescription benefits management services through a network of some 60,000 pharmacies.

CIGNA does much of its business with large employer groups, mainly through direct sales representatives and independent consultants, but it is working to expand its customer base to include more small and midsized businesses, government entities, individuals, and seniors. As part of this strategy, it acquired Great-West Healthcare, the health insurance division of Great-West Life & Annuity, in 2008.

CIGNA's disability and life insurance operations offer long- and short-term disability insurance, workers' compensation case management, group life insurance, and accident insurance, among other products. The company sells the policies to employer groups and other professional associations, primarily through brokers and consultants. It covers about 5 million lives with its group life insurance policies.

In addition to its domestic operations, CIGNA is one of the world's largest providers of expatriate health insurance, which covers the overseas employees of multinational corporations. CIGNA also sells international life, accident, and supplemental health insurance, primarily through independent distributors and consultants.

Chairman and CEO Edward Hanway retired at the end of 2009. President and COO David Cordani stepped into the role of CEO while director Isaiah Harris became chairman.

HISTORY

The Insurance Company of North America (INA) was founded in 1792 by Philadelphia businessmen. INA was the US's first stock insurance company and its first marine insurer. It later issued life insurance, fire insurance, and coverage for the contents of buildings. In 1808 it began using agents outside Pennsylvania. INA grew internationally in the late 1800s, appointing agents in Canada as well as in London and Vienna in Europe. It was the first US company to write insurance in China, beginning in Shanghai in 1897.

In 1942 INA provided both accident and health insurance for men working on the Manhattan Project, which developed the atomic bomb. It introduced the first widely available homeowner coverage in 1950. In 1978 INA bought HMO International, which was then the largest publicly owned health maintenance organization in the US. INA merged with Connecticut General in 1982 to form CIGNA.

Connecticut General began selling life insurance in 1865 and health insurance in 1912. It wrote its first group insurance (for the *Hartford Courant* newspaper) in 1913 and the first individual accident coverage for airline passengers in 1926. In the late 1930s Connecticut General was a leader in developing group medical coverage. The company offered the first group medical coverage for general use in 1952 and in 1964 added group dental insurance.

After the merger, CIGNA bought Crusader Insurance (UK, 1983; sold 1991) and AFIA (1984). To begin positioning itself as a provider of managed health care, the company sold its individual

insurance products division to InterContinental Life in 1988 and its Horace Mann Cos. (individual financial services) to an investor group in 1989. To further its goal, in 1990 CIGNA bought EQUICOR, an HMO started by Hospital Corporation of America (now part of HCA Inc.) and what is now AXA Equitable Life Insurance.

In the early 1990s it began to withdraw from the personal property/casualty business to focus on small and midsized commercial clients in the US, cutting sales overseas and combining them with life and health operations.

CIGNA expanded internationally in the mid-1990s, opening a Beijing office in 1993, 43 years after its departure from China.

Reeling from unforeseen environmental liabilities (chiefly related to asbestos), CIGNA in 1995 split its remaining property/casualty business between a healthy segment that continued to write new policies and one for run-off business. Four years later it finally sold these operations (including Cigna Insurance Co. of Europe) to ACE Limited in order to fund internal growth and acquisitions.

In 1997 the company expanded its group benefits operations to India, Brazil, and Poland; at home, it cut its payroll by 1,300 in the US to counter rising costs. It sold its domestic individual life insurance and annuity business in 1998 but began offering investment and pension products in Japan in 1999. In 2000 CIGNA settled a federal lawsuit over Medicare billing fraud. It also sold its reinsurance businesses that year to a subsidiary of Swiss Reinsurance Company.

In 2002 CIGNA formed a joint venture with SDZ, an affiliate of China Merchants Group, to sell life insurance in China. CIGNA sold its retirement division to Prudential in early 2004.

To expand its health care offerings, the company in 2006 bought UK-based vielife, which provides online health management and coaching services, and it acquired Star-HRG, a voluntary health coverage business offering low-cost plans to hourly and part-time workers.

EXECUTIVES

Chairman: Isaiah (Ike) Harris Jr., age 57
President, CEO, and Director: David M. Cordani, age 44, $6,593,921 total compensation
EVP and CFO: Annmarie T. Hagan, age 49, $1,729,993 total compensation
EVP Legal and Public Affairs and General Counsel: Carol Ann Petren, age 57, $4,275,112 total compensation
EVP and CIO: Michael D. Woeller, age 57, $3,529,085 total compensation
EVP Human Resources and Services: John M. Murabito, age 51, $1,951,088 total compensation
Chief Marketing Officer: Benjamin (Benjy) Karsch
Chief Medical Officer: Jeffrey L. Kang
SVP and Chief Investment Officer: Richard H. Forde
VP Corporate Communications: Christopher Curran
VP and Treasurer: Thomas McCarthy
VP Investor Relations: Edwin J. (Ted) Detrick
VP and Chief Accounting Officer: Mary T. Hoeltzel
President, CIGNA International: William L. (Bill) Atwell, age 59, $3,477,246 total compensation
President and CEO, CIGNA Behavioral Health: Keith Dixon
President, US Service, Clinical and Specialty: Matthew G. (Matt) Manders, age 48
President, CIGNA Pharmacy Management: C. Daniel (Dan) Haron
President, US Commercial: Bertram L. Scott
Auditors: PricewaterhouseCoopers LLP

LOCATIONS

HQ: CIGNA Corporation
2 Liberty Place, 1601 Chestnut St.
Philadelphia, PA 19192
Phone: 215-761-1000   **Fax:** 215-761-5515
Web: www.cigna.com

PRODUCTS/OPERATIONS

2009 Sales

	$ mil.	% of total
Insurance		
Health care	11,646	62
Disability & life	2,747	15
International	1,904	10
Run-off reinsurance	(254)	—
Corporate & other insurance	118	1
Mail order pharmacy	1,282	7
Net investment income	1,014	5
Realized investment gains (losses)	(43)	—
Total	**18,414**	**100**

Selected Products and Services

Health care
  Behavioral health care benefits
  CareAllies (disease management and health advocacy)
  CIGNA Choice Fund (consumer-directed products)
  CIGNA Tel-Drug (mail order pharmacy)
  Dental insurance
  Managed care health plans (HMO, PPO, POS)
  Medicare Part D prescription drug coverage)
  Prescription drug coverage
  Stop-loss coverage
  Voluntary plans
Life and disability
  Group disability insurance
  Group term life insurance
  Leave management services
  Workers' compensation case management
International
  Expatriate insurance
  Life, accident, and supplemental health insurance

COMPETITORS

AEGON
Aetna
AIG
Allianz
Allstate
AMERIGROUP
Aon
AXA
Blue Cross
BUPA
Catalyst Health Solutions
Centene
CNA Financial
Coventry Health Care
CVS Caremark
Express Scripts
The Hartford
Health Net
Highmark
Humana
ING
John Hancock Financial Services
Kaiser Foundation Health Plan
MassMutual
Medco Health
MetLife
Molina Healthcare
New York Life
Northwestern Mutual
Principal Financial
Prudential
UnitedHealth Group
Unum Group
WellCare Health Plans
WellPoint

HISTORICAL FINANCIALS

Company Type: Public

Income Statement

	REVENUE ($ mil.)	NET INCOME ($ mil.)	NET PROFIT MARGIN	EMPLOYEES
12/09	18,414	1,305	7.1%	29,300
12/08	19,101	292	1.5%	30,300
12/07	17,623	1,115	6.3%	26,600
12/06	16,547	1,155	7.0%	27,100
12/05	16,684	1,625	9.7%	32,700
Annual Growth	**2.5%**	**(5.3%)**	**—**	**(2.7%)**

FYE: December 31

2009 Year-End Financials

Debt ratio: 45.0%
Return on equity: 29.0%
Cash ($ mil.): 924
Current ratio: —
Long-term debt ($ mil.): 2,436
No. of shares (mil.): 277
Dividends
  Yield: 0.1%
  Payout: 0.8%
Market value ($ mil.): 9,758

Stock History

NYSE: CI

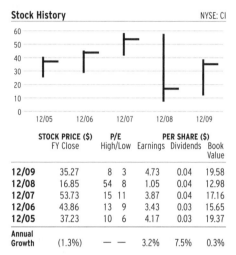

	STOCK PRICE ($) FY Close	P/E High	P/E Low	Earnings	Dividends	Book Value
12/09	35.27	8	3	4.73	0.04	19.58
12/08	16.85	54	8	1.05	0.04	12.98
12/07	53.73	15	11	3.87	0.04	17.16
12/06	43.86	13	9	3.43	0.03	15.65
12/05	37.23	10	6	4.17	0.03	19.37
Annual Growth	**(1.3%)**	**—**	**—**	**3.2%**	**7.5%**	**0.3%**

Cincinnati Bell

Cincinnati Bell rings for Bengals and Bearcats, Musketeers, and even the Reds. The company provides local phone services through its Cincinnati Bell Telephone subsidiary to residential and business customers in southwestern Ohio, northern Kentucky, and eastern Indiana. It has been the incumbent local-exchange carrier (ILEC) for greater Cincinnati since the 1870s, and it operates in other areas as a competitive local-exchange carrier (CLEC), providing voice and data services through its own networks, as well as through agreements with other carriers. Cincinnati Bell also offers data center services for businesses. More than 500,000 subscribers use wireless voice and data services provided by Cincinnati Bell Wireless.

Due to a gradual decline in demand for local and long distance services in the face of increased numbers of wireless and Internet phone suscribers, Cincinnati Bell has tried to cut expenses in its wireline division. At the same time, the company has invested heavily in its wireless and technology solutions businesses. It has also made improvements to its network and IT services arm by expanding its capacity in core markets through construction of new facilities.

In addition, the company is using acquisitions to expand its data center business. In 2010 it bought Texas-based CyrusOne for $525 million in cash. The deal enabled a push into the southwestern US market where CyrusOne operated seven data centers in Houston, Austin, and Dallas.

Cincinnati Bell additionally bought computer telephony and data communications services provider (and hometown rival) Cintech and Toronto-based software company Virtual Blocks in 2009. Both deals served to broaden and support Cincinnati Bell's managed IT services arm and its customer base.

Also that year, Cincinnati Bell sold nearly 200 wireless network towers to American Tower for about $100 million in cash. The company said that the deal was intended to improve liquidity. Cincinnati Bell will continue to use the towers as a tenant to enable its wireless network.

In addition to its core telephone offerings, the company operates a handful of subsidiaries that together provide customer premises equipment, data center collocation and managed services, and IT consulting. Its other noncore offerings include long-distance services in the greater Cincinnati and Dayton areas (through its Cincinnati Bell Any Distance unit); a surveillance hardware business (operated by its Cincinnati Bell Complete Protection unit); and Internet-based television programming (through its Cincinnati Bell Entertainment subsidiary).

HISTORY

Cincinnati Bell got its start in the 1870s after Charles Kilgour, injured and homebound, set up a telegraph wire to communicate with his office. Cincinnati manufacturer Andrew Erkenbrecher and other businessmen liked the idea, and the City and Suburban Telegraph Association was incorporated in 1873. For $300 a year, a customer could have a line (up to a mile long), and by 1877 the firm operated 50 lines.

In 1878 the company started selling the telephone under license from Bell Telephone of Boston. The exclusive agent for the Cincinnati area, it added "and Telephonic Exchange" to the end of its name. The next year it published its first phone directory, listing 500 customers. The company began to offer long-distance service through National Bell (which became AT&T) in 1882.

Floods in the 1880s damaged the firm's unwieldy network of overhead wires, and in 1891 it started combining wires into underground cables. In 1903 the company adopted the name Cincinnati and Suburban Bell Telephone.

The firm fell under state regulation in 1911 and soon bought Kentucky's Citizens Telephone, Indiana's Harrison Telephone, and several independent phone companies in Ohio. From 1930 to 1952 it converted its switchboards to dial service.

In 1971 the company became Cincinnati Bell and formed Cincinnati Bell Information Systems (CBIS) in 1983 to develop software. Largely deregulated after the 1984 Bell breakup, the company diversified and spent the late 1980s making acquisitions, including Auxton Computer and Vanguard Technologies. In 1989 Cincinnati Bell formed telemarketing subsidiary MATRIXX.

Technology and telemarketing acquisitions continued into the 1990s. But bad investments hurt profits, and the firm cut 550 jobs in 1991 and sold its equipment-leasing business to AT&T the next year. MATRIXX nearly doubled in size in 1993 with the purchase of telemarketer WATS Marketing. Two years later CBIS bought billing software developers for wireless phones (Europe) and cable TV (US).

Cincinnati Bell began offering Internet access in 1997 and the next year launched its digital mobile phone service in and around Cincinnati through a joint venture with AT&T.

In 1998 CBIS, now a major outsourcing firm for client-data and billing systems, acquired AT&T's Solutions Customer Care segment and became AT&T's preferred supplier of outsourced services. The status irked CBIS clients such as Sprint PCS, an AT&T rival. Cincinnati Bell resolved concerns by spinning off CBIS and MATRIXX into the independent Convergys. It also formed network integration and consulting unit EnterpriseWise IT Consulting.

CEO John LaMacchia retired in 1999 and was succeeded by COO Richard Ellenberger. In a dramatic move, the company that year bought Austin, Texas-based fiber-optic network operator IXC Communications in a $2.2 billion stock-and-debt deal, and Cincinnati Bell changed its name to Broadwing.

To continue the transformation, Broadwing in 2000 became one of the first to deploy all-optical networking equipment from Corvis on part of its network, which was completed the next year. Ellenberger resigned in 2002 and was replaced by COO Kevin Mooney; Jack Cassidy, who was serving as president, was named COO.

The company then began an ambitious restructuring in an effort to strengthen its Cincinnati Bell operations and reduce the losses of its Broadwing Communications unit. It sold its Bell Directory Business unit and in 2003, facing a glut of broadband capacity on the market and a lack of demand for the services, the company sold the Broadwing broadband business to C III Communications, a joint venture of Corvis and Cequel III, a venture capital firm backed by Jerry Kent, founder of cable company Charter Communications, for $129 million.

At the same time, the company changed its name back to Cincinnati Bell. Following the restructuring, Mooney stepped down and Cassidy was named CEO.

In 2006 the company acquired 20% of Cincinnati Bell Wireless, a former joint venture with AT&T Wireless Services following its venture partner's acquisition in 2004 by Cingular Wireless (now AT&T Mobility).

The following year Cincinnati Bell expanded its network infrastructure management business with the $20.3 million acquisition of South Bend, Indiana, data center services provider GramTel USA. It also pushed its voice and cable service area into Lebanon, Ohio, that same year.

The company extended its reach beyond the core service area of Cincinnati and the surrounding communities in 2008 when it bought Carmel, Indiana-based voice and data services provider eGix for about $18 million; eGix served small and midsized customers in Indiana and Illinois.

EXECUTIVES

Chairman: Phillip R. Cox, age 63
CFO: Gary J. Wojtaszek, age 43, $1,150,710 total compensation
SVP and Chief Marketing Officer: Tara L. Khoury, $1,250,955 total compensation
VP and Treasurer: Kimberly H. Sheehy, age 45
VP, General Counsel, and Secretary: Christopher J. (Chris) Wilson, age 44, $921,435 total compensation
President, CBTS: John P. Burns
VP Human Resources and Administration: Brian G. Keating, age 56, $800,239 total compensation

Director New Product Development and Value Added Services: Brian Duerring
Senior Manager Wireless Product and Supply Chain, Cincinnati Bell Wireless: Eric Bernard
VP, Controller, and Investor Relations: Kurt A. Freyberger, age 43
President, CEO, and Director: John F. (Jack) Cassidy, age 55, $4,985,633 total compensation
Auditors: Deloitte & Touche LLP

LOCATIONS

HQ: Cincinnati Bell Inc.
221 E. 4th St., Cincinnati, OH 45202
Phone: 513-397-9900   **Fax:** 513-397-5092
Web: www.cincinnatibell.com

PRODUCTS/OPERATIONS

2009 Sales

	$ mil.	% of total
Wireline	773.1	56
Wireless	307.0	23
Technology Solutions	293.1	21
Adjustments	(37.2)	—
Total	**1,336.0**	**100**

COMPETITORS

AT&T	Sprint Nextel
AT&T Mobility	Terremark Worldwide
Cellco	Time Warner Cable
DukeNet Communications	T-Mobile USA
Leap Wireless	tw telecom
Qwest Communications	Verizon

HISTORICAL FINANCIALS

Company Type: Public

Income Statement

FYE: December 31

	REVENUE ($ mil.)	NET INCOME ($ mil.)	NET PROFIT MARGIN	EMPLOYEES
12/09	1,336	90	6.7%	3,200
12/08	1,403	103	7.3%	3,300
12/07	1,349	73	5.4%	3,100
12/06	1,270	86	6.8%	2,950
12/05	1,210	(65)	—	2,900
Annual Growth	**2.5%**	**—**	**—**	**2.5%**

2009 Year-End Financials

Debt ratio: —
Return on equity: —
Cash ($ mil.): 23
Current ratio: 0.99
Long-term debt ($ mil.): 1,963
No. of shares (mil.): 201
Dividends
 Yield: 0.0%
 Payout: —
Market value ($ mil.): 694

Stock History

NYSE: CBB

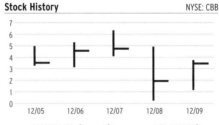

	STOCK PRICE ($) FY Close	P/E High/Low		PER SHARE ($) Earnings	Dividends	Book Value
12/09	3.45	10	3	0.37	0.00	(3.25)
12/08	1.93	13	1	0.38	0.00	(3.53)
12/07	4.75	26	17	0.24	0.00	(3.32)
12/06	4.57	17	11	0.30	0.00	(3.94)
12/05	3.51	—	—	(0.30)	0.00	(3.67)
Annual Growth	**(0.4%)**	**—**	**—**	**—**	**—**	**—**

Cincinnati Financial

At Skyline Chili in Cincinnati you can order your chili 3-way, 4-way, or 5-way; at Cincinnati Financial Corporation (CFC) you can order your insurance with plenty of extras as well. The company's flagship Cincinnati Insurance (operating through three subsidiaries) sells commercial property, liability, excess, surplus, auto, bond, and fire insurance; personal lines include homeowners, auto, and liability products. Cincinnati Life sells life, disability income, and annuities. The company's CFC Investment subsidiary provides commercial financing, leasing, and real estate services to its independent insurance agents.

CFC markets its policies in about 37 states through more than 1,000 independent agencies. The company writes more than 20% of its business in Ohio, and is strong in Illinois, Indiana, and Pennsylvania. Its commercial lines segment targets primarily small to midsized businesses. CFC has tied its growth to expanding the territories it markets in, and increasing the number of new agencies with which it strikes new relationships. Following that strategy it moved into Texas in late 2008 and Colorado and Wyoming in 2009, and began targeting Connecticut and Oregon in 2010.

New products are another means to growth for the company. In 2008 it created The Cincinnati Specialty Underwriters Insurance Company to offer excess and surplus lines of coverage. It then created a brokerage, CSU Producer Resources, to distribute the excess and surplus products to its existing network of independent agents.

For many years CFS held more than 10% of Fifth Third Bancorp and prior to the economic meltdown, it accounted for more than 25% of the company's stock holdings. During the meltdown, bank stock grew less reliable, prompting CFS to sell half of its holdings in Fifth Third for more than $450 million in 2008. As the general market sank, CFS offloaded the rest for $67 million in 2009.

The founding Schiff family, including brothers John and Thomas Schiff who serve as directors, owns about 14% of CFC.

HISTORY

Jack Schiff spent three years with the Travelers Company before he joined the Navy in WWII. He returned to Cincinnati to start his own independent insurance agency in 1946 and was joined by his younger brother Robert; both were Ohio State graduates whose affection for the Buckeyes led them in later years to close company banquets with the school fight song. The brothers incorporated Cincinnati Insurance with $200,000 from investors.

Under Harry Turner, the company's first president, the company offered property/casualty insurance to small businesses and homeowners through its network of agents. By 1956 the company had spread into neighboring Kentucky and Indiana. During the next decade Cincinnati Insurance expanded its products and network, adding auto, burglary, and commercial all-risk lines and enlisting agents throughout the Midwest.

In 1963 Turner took the chairman's seat and Jack Schiff became president, introducing a more aggressive leadership style. In 1969 the company reorganized and went public, forming Cincinnati Financial Corporation as a holding company for the insurance operation. CFC used the money to pay off debts and buy new businesses, forming two subsidiaries: CFC Investment Company, in 1970, to deal in commercial real estate and financing; and Queen City Indemnity (later named The Cincinnati Casualty Company), in 1972, to offer direct-bill personal policies.

By 1973 operations included The Life Insurance Company of Cincinnati, Queen City Indemnity, and fellow Cincinnati giant Inter-Ocean Insurance Company. That year Jack Schiff added CEO to his title.

CFC continued to grow throughout the 1970s with a new emphasis on independent investments. In 1982 Cincinnati Financial veteran Robert Morgan became president and CEO. The company's conservative roots and investment base helped it shake off the early-1980s recession and a string of natural disasters that left many other insurers dangling in the wind.

Also during the 1980s the company started to shift its focus from personal to commercial lines. In 1988 it reorganized its life insurance subsidiaries under the Cincinnati Life banner and formed The Cincinnati Indemnity Company to offer workers' compensation and personal insurance. In 1998 a string of storms (reminiscent of others earlier in the decade) dampened the company's earnings.

In 1999 Jack Schiff Jr. succeeded Morgan as president and CEO. The next year, 96-year-old Harry Turner died. After a 1999 decision by the Ohio Supreme Court that increased exposure on auto policies, CFC set up $110 million in reserves for uninsured motorists claims that year and the following year; the decision was overturned in 2003.

EXECUTIVES

Chairman: John J. Schiff Jr., age 66, $2,072,844 total compensation
Vice Chairman: James E. Benoski, age 71, $1,861,187 total compensation
President, CEO, and Director: Kenneth W. Stecher, age 63, $1,651,689 total compensation
SVP, CFO, Treasurer, and Secretary: Steven J. Johnston, age 47, $390,004 total compensation
SVP Operations: Timothy L. Timmel, age 61, $1,616,287 total compensation
SVP; President, Cincinnati Casualty Company: Thomas A. Joseph, age 54, $895,634 total compensation
SVP and CIO: John S. Kellington, age 48
CTO: Craig W. Forrester, age 51
President and COO, Cincinnati Life Insurance Company: David H. Popplewell, age 66, $985,903 total compensation
EVP Cincinnati Insurance Company: Jacob F. Scherer Jr., age 57, $1,053,078 total compensation
SVP Commercial Lines, Cincinnati Insurance Co.: Charles P. Stoneburner II
SVP Corporate Communications, Cincinnati Insurance Company: Joan O. Shevchik, age 58
SVP Excess & Surplus Lines, Cincinnati Insurance Co.: Donald J. Doyle Jr.
SVP and Chief Claims Officer, Cincinnati Insurance Co.: Martin J. Mullen
Investor Relations Officer: Dennis E. McDaniel
Auditors: Deloitte & Touche LLP

LOCATIONS

HQ: Cincinnati Financial Corporation
6200 S. Gilmore Rd., Fairfield, OH 45014
Phone: 513-870-2000   **Fax:** 513-870-2911
Web: www.cinfin.com

PRODUCTS/OPERATIONS

2009 Revenues

	$ mil.	% of total
Earned premiums		
Property/casualty	2,911	74
Life	143	4
Investment income	501	13
Net investment gains	336	9
Other income	12	—
Total	**3,903**	**100**

COMPETITORS

ALLIED Group
CNA Financial
Erie Indemnity
Farmers Group
Great American Insurance Company
The Hartford
Indiana Insurance
MetLife of Connecticut
Ohio Casualty
OneBeacon
Progressive Corporation
Selective Insurance
Travelers Companies
Westfield Group
Zurich American

HISTORICAL FINANCIALS
Company Type: Public

Income Statement
FYE: December 31

	ASSETS ($ mil.)	NET INCOME ($ mil.)	INCOME AS % OF ASSETS	EMPLOYEES
12/09	14,440	432	3.0%	4,170
12/08	13,369	429	3.2%	4,179
12/07	16,637	855	5.1%	4,087
12/06	17,222	930	5.4%	4,048
12/05	16,003	602	3.8%	3,983
Annual Growth	(2.5%)	(8.0%)	—	1.2%

2009 Year-End Financials

Equity as % of assets: 33.0%
Return on assets: 3.1%
Return on equity: 9.7%
Long-term debt ($ mil.): 839
No. of shares (mil.): 163
Dividends
Yield: 6.0%
Payout: 59.2%
Market value ($ mil.): 4,269
Sales ($ mil.): 3,903

Stock History
NASDAQ (GS): CINF

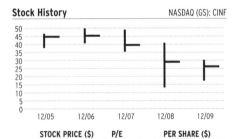

	STOCK PRICE ($) FY Close	P/E High/Low		PER SHARE ($) Earnings	Dividends	Book Value
12/09	26.24	11	7	2.65	1.57	29.26
12/08	29.07	15	5	2.62	1.56	25.71
12/07	39.54	10	7	4.97	1.42	36.45
12/06	45.31	9	8	5.30	1.34	41.85
12/05	44.68	14	11	3.40	1.21	37.41
Annual Growth	(12.5%)	—	—	(6.0%)	6.7%	(6.0%)

Cinemark Holdings

Cinemark Holdings has left its mark on the cinema landscape. The third-largest movie exhibitor in the US (following Regal Entertainment and AMC) has more than 4,800 screens in some 420 theatres in the US, Canada, and Latin America. Cinemark operates its multiplex theaters in smaller cities and suburban areas of major metropolitan markets. Some larger theaters operate under the Tinseltown name; others are "discount" theaters showing no first-run films. The company prefers to build new theaters in midsized markets or in suburbs of major cities where the Cinemark theater is the only game in town.

Despite an economic downturn, people still flocked to the movies, and 2009 hits such as the record-breaking *Avatar* were a boon for Cinemark. Other popular titles at the box office that year included *Harry Potter and the Half-Blood Prince*, *Up*, *Twilight Saga: New Moon*, *The Hangover*, and *Star Trek*. During 2009 the company continued its expansion by adding some 180 new screens to its holdings. It has commitments to build nearly 140 additional screens by 2012.

Cinemark focuses its efforts on being one of the most modern and technologically advanced movie chains. More than 80% of the company's first-run screens feature stadium seating. The company has also developed a large screen digital format, XD Extreme Digital Cinema, or XD. The format includes wall-to-wall and ceiling-to-floor screens, wrap-around sound, and can play any available digital print, including 3-D content. Cinemark has installed XD screens in about 15 theatres, and plans to install 30 to 40 more XD screens during 2010. The company is also capitalizing on the increased popularity of 3D, and at the close of 2009 Cinemark operated nearly 400 screens with digital 3D projection systems.

The company is able to finance many of its technological advancements by forming partnerships with the other major theater chains. National CineMedia, a joint venture with Regal Entertainment and AMC Entertainment, delivers digital advertising, pre-recorded concerts, meetings, sporting events, and other non-film entertainment content. In addition, it is continuing to roll-out digital cinema through its Digital Cinema Implementation Partners, another joint venture between Cinemark, Regal, and AMC.

In addition to its mainstream theaters, Cinemark operates seven art theaters, showing titles such as *The Hurt Locker* and *Precious*, under the CinéArts brand. Internationally, the company has been expanding in Latin America through construction of theaters in growing urban markets. All total, Cinemark operates some 130 theaters and 1,000 screens in about a dozen countries in Latin America.

The company is using net proceeds from its 2007 IPO to repay debt. The previous year Cinemark expanded significantly with the acquisition of Century Theatres, the eighth-largest movie-theater operator. The combination added more than 1,000 screens to Cinemark's operations and strengthened its foothold as the third-largest movie-theater operator.

Madison Dearborn Capital Partners owns about a third of Cinemark; Chairman and former CEO Lee Roy Mitchell and the Mitchell Special Trust collectively own about 11%. Members of the Syufy family, the founders of Century Theatres, hold a 5% stake.

HISTORY

Lee Roy Mitchell and partner Paul Broadhead founded Cinemark in 1985, and by the end of 1989, Cinemark had about 660 screens in 18 states. Mitchell set a company goal of 1,000 screens by 1992 and, in addition to constructing its own theaters, Cinemark made acquisitions to achieve its goal.

In 1992 Cinemark built its first megaplex, Hollywood USA — featuring 15 movie screens, a pizzeria, and an arcade. As the multiplex became one of its most profitable theaters, the company added more to its portfolio. Cinemark also started developing a Latin American presence in 1992, building theaters in Mexico and Chile.

The company formed a joint venture in 1995 to build theaters in Argentina, and in 1996 created three more joint ventures for theaters in Brazil, Ecuador, and Peru.

Meanwhile, Cinemark continued to add megaplexes; it opened 12 theaters with 165 screens (an average of about 14 screens per theater) in 1997. In the first half of 1998, the company added 223 more screens, including 64 in Latin America.

Later that year a group of wheelchair users sued the company, claiming the front-row spaces reserved for them in Cinemark's stadium-seating theaters were uncomfortably close to screens. A US Court of Appeals sided with the theater chain in 2000 and the US Supreme Court refused to hear the plaintiffs' appeal. The company later agreed to modify some theaters and build future theaters in compliance with a court-approved plan.

Cinemark, along with the rest of the movie-theater industry, struggled through the late 1990s as numerous bankruptcies abounded, thanks to overbuilding. The overall decline of the stock market forced the firm to postpone filing an IPO in 2002.

In 2001 Cinemark introduced the electronic gift card for movie ticket and concessions purchases. During 2002 Cinemark opened seven new theaters with 58 screens. The following year the company opened nine new theaters with 77 screens and added three screens to existing theaters.

In 2004 the company brought in investor Madison Dearborn rather than going public, and additional minority investors joined up in the next two years. The following year Cinemark joined Regal Entertainment and AMC Entertainment in National CineMedia, a joint venture that delivers ads and pre-movie entertainment to screens throughout the US and Canada via a private digital network.

In 2006 Cinemark continued its growth with the acquisition of Century Theatres. Also during 2006 the company grew by building 210 screens. In 2007 it again filed an IPO after a brighter year at the box office.

EXECUTIVES

Chairman: Lee Roy Mitchell, age 73, $1,985,417 total compensation
CEO: Alan W. Stock, age 49, $2,242,340 total compensation
President and COO: Timothy (Tim) Warner, age 65, $1,380,438 total compensation
EVP, CFO, Treasurer, and Assistant Secretary: Robert D. Copple, age 51, $1,301,748 total compensation

SVP Real Estate: Tom Owens, age 53
SVP Film Licensing: Steven (Steve) Bunnell, age 50
SVP, General Counsel, and Secretary: Michael D. Cavalier, age 43, $1,060,959 total compensation
SVP New Technology and Training: Robert F. Carmony, age 52
SVP Purchasing: Walter Hebert III, age 64
VP Marketing and Communications: James Meredith, age 41
VP Construction: Don Harton, age 52
VP and Director Theatre Operations: Steve Zuehlke, age 51
President, Cinemark International: Valmir Fernandes, age 49
Auditors: Deloitte & Touche LLP

LOCATIONS

HQ: Cinemark Holdings, Inc.
3900 Dallas Pkwy., Ste. 500, Plano, TX 75093
Phone: 972-665-1000   **Fax:** 972-665-1004
Web: www.cinemark.com

2009 US Locations

	Theaters	Screens
Texas	79	1,024
California	62	752
Ohio	20	223
Utah	13	169
Nevada	10	154
Illinois	9	128
Colorado	8	127
Arizona	7	106
Oregon	7	102
Kentucky	7	87
Pennsylvania	6	89
Oklahoma	6	67
Florida	5	98
Louisiana	5	74
Indiana	5	48
New Mexico	4	54
Virginia	4	52
North Carolina	4	41
Mississippi	3	41
Iowa	3	37
Arkansas	3	30
Washington	2	30
Georgia	2	27
New York	2	27
South Carolina	2	22
West Virginia	2	22
Maryland	1	24
Kansas	1	20
Michigan	1	16
Alaska	1	16
New Jersey	1	16
Missouri	1	15
South Dakota	1	14
Tennessee	1	14
Wisconsin	1	14
Massachusetts	1	12
Delaware	1	10
Minnesota	1	8
Montana	1	8
Total	**293**	**3,818**

2009 Foreign Locations

	Theaters	Screens
Brazil	46	388
Mexico	31	296
Central America (Costa Rica, El Salvador, Guatemala, Honduras, Nicaragua & Panama)	12	81
Chile	11	87
Colombia	11	64
Argentina	9	74
Peru	6	50
Ecuador	4	26
Canada	1	12
Total	**131**	**1,078**

2009 Sales

	$ mil.	% of total
US & Canada	1,558.7	79
Brazil	218.2	11
Mexico	65.2	3
Other countries	138.3	7
Adjustments	(3.9)	—
Total	**1,976.5**	**100**

PRODUCTS/OPERATIONS

2009 Sales

	$ mil.	% of total
Admissions	1,293.4	65
Concession	602.9	31
Other	80.2	4
Total	**1,976.5**	**100**

COMPETITORS

AMC Entertainment
Carmike Cinemas
Cineplex Galaxy
Clearview Cinemas
Hoyts Cinemas
Landmark Theatres
Marcus Corporation
National Amusements
Pacific Theatres
Rave Cinemas
Regal Entertainment

HISTORICAL FINANCIALS

Company Type: Public

Income Statement

	REVENUE ($ mil.)	NET INCOME ($ mil.)	NET PROFIT MARGIN	EMPLOYEES
12/09	1,977	97	4.9%	20,700
12/08	1,742	(48)	—	18,300
12/07	1,683	89	5.3%	12,300
12/06	1,221	1	0.1%	13,600
12/05	1,021	(25)	—	13,600
Annual Growth	18.0%	—	—	11.1%

FYE: December 31

2009 Year-End Financials

Debt ratio: 185.0%
Return on equity: 11.3%
Cash ($ mil.): 438
Current ratio: 1.81
Long-term debt ($ mil.): 1,665
No. of shares (mil.): 113
Dividends
 Yield: 5.0%
 Payout: 82.8%
Market value ($ mil.): 1,630

Stock History

NYSE: CNK

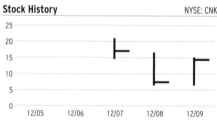

	STOCK PRICE ($) FY Close	P/E High/Low		PER SHARE ($) Earnings	Dividends	Book Value
12/09	14.37	17	8	0.87	0.72	7.93
12/08	7.43	—	—	(0.45)	0.72	7.15
12/07	17.00	24	17	0.85	0.31	8.99
Annual Growth	(8.1%)	—	—	1.2%	52.4%	(6.0%)

Cintas Corporation

If Cintas had its way, you'd never agonize over what to wear to work. The #1 uniform supplier in the US has about 800,000 clients (Delta Air Lines, DHL) and some 5 million people wear its garb each day. Cintas — which sells, leases, and rents uniforms — operates about 415 facilities across the US and Canada; it leases about half of them. Besides offering shirts, jackets, slacks, and footwear, the company provides clean-room apparel and flame-resistant clothing. Other products offered by Cintas include uniform cleaning, first-aid and safety products, clean-room supplies, and document handling and storage. CEO Scott Farmer owns about 10% of the firm. His father, Richard, founded the company in 1968.

Uniform rentals generate about 70% of Cintas' sales. The balance of its revenue is logged from uniform sales and its array of other products and services. Although it is the leading renter of corporate uniforms, the company still sees growth potential in this area of its business.

Cintas has been active in building its non-uniform operations, especially its document services unit, through acquisitions. In fiscal 2009 the company purchased about 10 document management businesses in North America. It also made its second acquisition in Europe: Munich, Germany-based Aktenmuehle, which had been the largest independently owned document destruction firm in the country. (Its first European deal was for Certo Information Management in the Netherlands in 2007.) The European acquisitions are in line with Cintas' plans to expand its service offerings in the region. Besides document management firms, Cintas is adding first-aid and fire protection businesses to its portfolio. It acquired three firms in this segment in fiscal 2009. Cintas was particularly active in fiscal 2008, buying up 20 document management services businesses, nine first-aid and fire protection businesses, and one uniform rental business.

Amid the global economic downturn, however, the company is slowing its acquisitive pace and restructuring its business. The US recession and accompanying job losses pushed Cintas in fiscal 2009 to reel in discretionary spending, shut down two manufacturing plants, initiate wage and hiring freezes, and lay off employees. (The firm has slashed more than 10% of its workforce between 2008 and 2009.) The cost-reduction moves saved Cintas about $60 million, but it also took an after-tax charge of about $50 million.

Despite the effects of the turbulent marketplace, Cintas is still recognized as a top company. It was named among the nation's "Most Admired Companies" by *Fortune* magazine for the ninth consecutive year in 2009. *Report on Business* magazine also ranked it among Canada's best employers. Cintas employees must wear a Cintas uniform or business suit to work.

HISTORY

In 1929 onetime animal trainer, boxer, and blacksmith Richard "Doc" Farmer started a business of salvaging old rags, cleaning them, and then selling them to factories. Farmer later began renting the rags to his customers. He would pick up the dirty rags, clean them, and return them to the factory. By 1936 the Acme Overall & Rag Laundry had established itself in Cincinnati with plans to convert an old bathhouse into a laundry. Farmer, along with his adopted son Herschell, suffered a setback from flood damage in 1937, but the family rebuilt and continued to grow the business.

Doc Farmer died in 1952, and Herschell assumed command of the company. Five years later Herschell turned the reins over to his 23-year-old son, Richard, who immediately moved Acme into the uniform rental market, and the company blossomed. Throughout the 1960s the company grew enormously, aided by Richard's innovative leadership. (Acme was the first to use a polyester-cotton blend that lasted twice as long as normal cotton work uniforms.) Through a holding company, Richard established a string of uniform plants in the Midwest, starting with a factory in Cleveland in 1968. Four years later the company changed its name to Cintas.

At this time the company began tapping into the new corporate identity market, pushing the idea that uniforms convey a sense of professionalism and present a cleaner, safer image. The company began to custom-design the uniforms, adding logos and distinctive colors. This aspect of the business compelled Cintas to expand to help accommodate its national clients; by 1972 the company had offices throughout Ohio and in Chicago, Detroit, and Washington, DC. By 1975 Cintas was operating in 13 states.

The company went public in 1983. For the rest of the 1980s, Cintas rode the wave of consolidation in the uniform rental industry, making a slew of acquisitions. The company also expanded from its blue-collar base into the service industry and began to supply uniforms to hotels, restaurants, and banks. By the early 1990s Cintas was a presence in most major US cities, and its share of the US market had climbed to about 10%. Farmer turned over the title of CEO to president Robert Kohlhepp in 1995. That year the company acquired Cadet Uniform Services, a Toronto uniform rental business, for $41 million.

Scott Farmer, Richard's 38-year-old son, was named president and COO in 1997. That year Cintas made a number of acquisitions, including Micron-Clean Uniform Service and Canadian firms Act One Uniform Rentals and DW King Services. The company also moved into the first aid supplies industry with its purchase of American First Aid, and added clean-room garments to its expanding list of uniform rentals. In 1998 Cintas acquired uniform rental company Apparelmaster, as well as Chicago-based Uniforms To You, a $150 million design and manufacturing company. In an effort to expand its corporate uniform business, the company acquired rival Unitog in 1999 for about $460 million.

As part of the integration of Unitog, in 2000 Cintas closed several of Unitog's uniform rental operations, distribution centers, and manufacturing plants. The company also established first aid supplies and safety equipment unit Xpect. In 2002 Cintas purchased Omni Services, marking its largest acquisition to date.

PRODUCTS/OPERATIONS

2010 Sales

	$ mil.	% of total
Rentals	2,569.4	72
Uniform direct sales	386.4	11
First aid, safety, & fire protection services	338.6	10
Document management services	253.9	7
Total	**3,547.3**	**100**

Selected Products and Services

Clean-room supplies
Document shredding and storage
Entrance mats
Fender covers
Fire protection
First aid and safety products and services
Linen products
Mops
Restroom supplies
Towels
Uniform cleaning
Uniform rental and sales

COMPETITORS

Alsco	Iron Mountain Inc
Angelica Corporation	NCH
ARAMARK	Superior Uniform Group
G&K Services	UniFirst

HISTORICAL FINANCIALS

Company Type: Public

Income Statement

	REVENUE ($ mil.)	NET INCOME ($ mil.)	NET PROFIT MARGIN	EMPLOYEES
				FYE: May 31
5/10	3,547	216	6.1%	30,000
5/09	3,775	226	6.0%	31,000
5/08	3,938	335	8.5%	34,000
5/07	3,707	335	9.0%	34,000
5/06	3,404	327	9.6%	32,000
Annual Growth	1.0%	(9.9%)	—	(1.6%)

2010 Year-End Financials

Debt ratio: 31.0%	No. of shares (mil.): 153
Return on equity: 8.8%	Dividends
Cash ($ mil.): 411	Yield: 1.8%
Current ratio: 3.97	Payout: 34.3%
Long-term debt ($ mil.): 785	Market value ($ mil.): 3,975

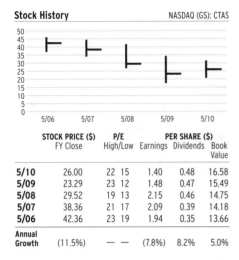

Stock History

NASDAQ (GS): CTAS

	STOCK PRICE ($) FY Close	P/E High/Low	PER SHARE ($) Earnings	Dividends	Book Value
5/10	26.00	22 15	1.40	0.48	16.58
5/09	23.29	23 12	1.48	0.47	15.49
5/08	29.52	19 13	2.15	0.46	14.75
5/07	38.36	21 17	2.09	0.39	14.18
5/06	42.36	23 19	1.94	0.35	13.66
Annual Growth	(11.5%)	— —	(7.8%)	8.2%	5.0%

Cisco Systems

Cisco Systems routes packets and routs competitors with equal efficiency. Dominating the market for Internet protocol-based networking equipment, the company provides routers and switches used to direct data, voice, and video traffic. Other products include remote access servers, IP telephony equipment, optical networking components, Internet conferencing systems, set-top boxes, and network service and security systems. It sells its products primarily to large enterprises and telecommunications service providers, but it also markets products designed for small businesses and consumers through its Consumer Business Group. Cisco gets about half of its sales in North America.

Cisco has used acquisitions — more than 120 since 1993 — to broaden its product lines and secure engineering talent in the highly competitive networking sector. Though Cisco remains committed to investments that insure the dominance of its core lines (switches and routers still account for about half of sales), many of the company's recent acquisitions have moved it into new markets.

With the global recession apparently on the wane, Cisco signaled it is back in the M&A game in a big way with its 2010 purchase of TANDBERG, a Norwegian competitor in the videoconferencing market. The $3.4 billion cash deal supplements Cisco's high-end TelePresence systems with TANDBERG's lower-end line, which ranges from PC-based conferencing capabilities to more sophisticated gear, less expensive than Cisco's offerings. Upon completion of the transaction, Cisco formed a TelePresence Technology Group, which is headed by SVP Fredrik Halvorsen, previously TANDBERG's CEO.

On a smaller scale, but potentially significant, Cisco bought CoreOptics, a German-American developer of integrated circuits and optical network transponders capable of delivering high-speed data transmission rates. The company paid about $99 million in cash and incentives to the shareholders of privately held CoreOptics. With global IP traffic projected to grow 40% per year due to high demand for cloud computing services, mobile data services, and video streaming,

Cisco could find plenty of applications for the CoreOptics technology. The deal also boosted Cisco's presence in Europe.

In 2009 Cisco acquired Starent Networks for about $2.9 billion in cash. Starent specialized in systems and software for wireless networks, helping satisfy global demand for more mobile access to the Internet.

Cisco unveiled a new line of hardware called the Unified Computing System in 2009. Designed to simplify the computing and networking resources in data centers, the product line — which includes blade servers — places Cisco in direct competition with traditional partners, such as Hewlett-Packard and IBM.

HISTORY

Cisco Systems was founded by Stanford University husband-and-wife team Leonard Bosack and Sandra Lerner and three colleagues in 1984. Bosack developed technology to link his computer lab's network with his wife's network in the graduate business school. Anticipating a market for networking devices, Bosack and Lerner mortgaged their house, bought a used mainframe, put it in their garage, and got friends and relatives to work for deferred pay. They sold their first network router in 1986. Originally targeting universities, the aerospace industry, and the government, the company in 1988 expanded its marketing to include large corporations. Short of cash, Cisco turned to venture capitalist Donald Valentine of Sequoia Capital, who bought a controlling stake and became chairman. He hired John Morgridge of laptop maker GRiD Systems as president and CEO.

Cisco, whose products had a proven track record, had a head start as the market for network routers opened up in the late 1980s. Sales leapt from $1.5 million in 1987 to $28 million in 1989.

The company went public in 1990. That year Morgridge fired Lerner, with whom he had clashed, and Bosack quit. The couple sold their stock for about $200 million, giving most to favorite causes, including animal charities and a Harvard professor looking for extraterrestrials.

With competition increasing, Cisco began expanding through acquisitions. Purchases included networking company Crescendo Communications (1993) and Ethernet switch maker Kalpana (1994). Cisco also surpassed the $1 billion revenue mark in 1994. In 1995 EVP John Chambers succeeded Morgridge as president and CEO; Morgridge became chairman (and Valentine vice chairman).

Cisco entered the service provider market in 1996, when it introduced a line of customer premises equipment (CPE) products. The following year the company broke into the *FORTUNE* 500.

In 1999 Cisco launched a new business line aimed at bringing high-speed Internet access to the consumer market. In its largest acquisition to date, Cisco bought Cerent (fiber-optic network equipment) for $7 billion.

The company's heavy investment in Internet Protocol-based telecommunications equipment proved costly when an industrywide downturn slowed spending among telecom service providers in 2001. Chambers guided Cisco through significant rebuilding measures, including job cuts and a reorganization that aligned its operations around core technologies rather than customer segments.

Key acquisitions over the next few years included home networking specialist Linksys

(2003), conferencing systems provider Latitude Communications (2004), and router developer Procket Networks (2004). In mid-2004 the company introduced the CRS-1, a new router designed to compete with high-end offerings from challengers such as Juniper. Featuring an overhauled version of Cisco's Internetwork Operating System (IOS), the CRS-1 resulted from four years of development and an investment of $500 million.

Cisco purchased wireless networking vendor Airespace in 2005. The acquisition provided Cisco with wireless LAN equipment for the enterprise and government sectors.

In 2006 Cisco's advanced technologies unit launched a video messaging product called the Cisco Digital Media System; the system was designed to let companies distribute video messages to employees and customers.

Cisco's 2007 acquisitions included conferencing systems provider WebEx Communications ($3.2 billion), and network security specialist IronPort Systems ($830 million).

Cisco purchased Pure Networks, a developer of management software for home networks, in 2008. It also acquired e-mail and calendar software maker PostPath.

EXECUTIVES

Chairman and CEO: John T. Chambers, age 60, $10,270,083 total compensation
Chairman Emeritus: John P. Morgridge
CTO: Padmasree Warrior, age 49
EVP Cisco Services and Chief Globalization Officer: Wim Elfrink, age 57, $7,484,734 total compensation
EVP Worldwide Operations and Business Development: Richard J. (Rick) Justice, age 59, $5,116,105 total compensation
EVP Operations, Processes, and Systems: Randy Pond, age 55, $4,979,477 total compensation
EVP Worldwide Operations: Robert Lloyd, $4,860,701 total compensation
EVP and CFO: Frank Calderoni, age 52, $3,745,157 total compensation
EVP and Chief Marketing Officer, Global Policy and Government Affairs: Susan L. (Sue) Bostrom, age 49
Chief Strategy Officer and SVP Consumer Business: Ned Hooper
SVP and CIO: Rebecca J. Jacoby
SVP, General Counsel, and Secretary: Mark Chandler, age 53
SVP, Office of the President: Howard S. Charney
SVP Research and Advanced Development: Gregory (Greg) Akers
SVP Human Resources: Brian (Skip) Schipper
SVP Corporate Communications: Blair Christie
President, Cisco Capital: Kristine A. (Kris) Snow, age 50
President, European Markets: Chris Dedicoat
President, Emerging Markets Theater: Paul Mountford
President, Asia/Pacific and Japan Theaters: Edzard J.C. Overbeek
Chairman and CEO, Cisco China: Jim Sherriff
Auditors: PricewaterhouseCoopers LLP

LOCATIONS

HQ: Cisco Systems, Inc.
170 W. Tasman Dr., Bldg. 10, San Jose, CA 95134
Phone: 408-526-4000   **Fax:** 408-526-4100
Web: www.cisco.com

2009 Sales

	$ mil.	% of total
US & Canada	19,345	54
Europe	7,683	21
Asia/Pacific		
Japan	1,372	4
Other countries	3,718	10
Emerging markets	3,999	11
Total	**36,117**	**100**

PRODUCTS/OPERATIONS

2009 Sales

	$ mil.	% of total
Products		
Switches	12,025	33
Advanced technologies	9,218	26
Routers	6,271	17
Other	1,617	5
Services	6,986	19
Total	**36,117**	**100**

Selected Products

Access servers
Blade servers
Cable modems
Cables and cords
Content delivery devices
Customer contact software
Digital video recorders
Ethernet concentrators, hubs, and transceivers
Interfaces and adapters
Network management software
Networked applications software
Optical platforms
Power supplies
Routers
Security components
Switches
Telephony access systems
Television set-top boxes
Video networking
Virtual private network (VPN) systems
Voice integration applications
Wireless networking

COMPETITORS

Alcatel-Lucent
ARRIS
Aruba Networks
Avaya
Belden
Belkin
Brocade Communications
CA Technologies
Check Point Software
Ciena
Citrix Systems
Dell
D-Link
ECI Telecom
Enterasys
Ericsson
Extreme Networks
F5 Networks
Force10
Fortinet
Fujitsu
Harris Corp.
Hewlett-Packard
Huawei Technologies
IBM
Juniper Networks
LogMeIn
Meru Networks
Microsoft
Motorola
MRV Communications
NEC
NETGEAR
Nokia Siemens Networks
Nortel Networks
Novell
Pace
Polycom
Riverbed Technology
Sycamore Networks
Symantec
Technicolor
Tellabs
UTStarcom
ZTE

HISTORICAL FINANCIALS

Company Type: Public

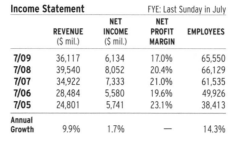

Income Statement

	REVENUE ($ mil.)	NET INCOME ($ mil.)	NET PROFIT MARGIN	EMPLOYEES
				FYE: Last Sunday in July
7/09	36,117	6,134	17.0%	65,550
7/08	39,540	8,052	20.4%	66,129
7/07	34,922	7,333	21.0%	61,535
7/06	28,484	5,580	19.6%	49,926
7/05	24,801	5,741	23.1%	38,413
Annual Growth	**9.9%**	**1.7%**	**—**	**14.3%**

2009 Year-End Financials

Debt ratio: 26.6%
Return on equity: 16.8%
Cash ($ mil.): 5,718
Current ratio: 3.24
Long-term debt ($ mil.): 10,295

No. of shares (mil.): 5,711
Dividends
  Yield: —
  Payout: —
Market value ($ mil.): 125,702

Stock History

NASDAQ (GS): CSCO

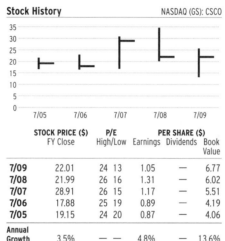

	STOCK PRICE ($) FY Close	P/E High/Low		PER SHARE ($) Earnings	Dividends	Book Value
7/09	22.01	24	13	1.05	—	6.77
7/08	21.99	26	16	1.31	—	6.02
7/07	28.91	26	15	1.17	—	5.51
7/06	17.88	25	19	0.89	—	4.19
7/05	19.15	24	20	0.87	—	4.06
Annual Growth	**3.5%**	**—**	**—**	**4.8%**	**—**	**13.6%**

CIT Group

If you haven't heard of CIT Group, then you're O-U-T of the proverbial loop. On the big-business landscape for about a century, CIT is a commercial bank holding company that offers lending, leasing, debt restructuring, equipment financing, and advisory services to small and midsized businesses and to more than half of the *FORTUNE* 1000 in such industries as energy, health care, retail, media, manufacturing, services, and transportation. Its real estate services include mortgage, mezzanine debt, and net lease financing. CIT has more than $60 billion in assets and serves clients in more than 50 countries around the world. The company is rebuilding itself after undergoing a brief stint in Chapter 11 in 2009.

CIT was hit hard in the economic recession, which nearly shut down the credit markets. The company struggled to stay afloat as liquidity levels sank (a situation exacerbated as nervous customers drew on their credit lines). It exited money-losing businesses, sold units, and secured $3 billion from company bondholders, including PIMCO and Oaktree Capital. The firm also converted to a bank holding company, enabling it to access government bailout funds. Still struggling, CIT filed for Chapter 11 in November

2009. The restructuring lasted six weeks and helped the company eliminate more than $10 billion in debt. None of CIT's operating subsidiaries were included in the bankruptcy.

CIT has renewed its focus on commercial lending after unsuccessfully branching into subprime mortgages and student loans, two segments that led the company's losses. In 2008 it sold its home loan unit to Lone Star Funds and its manufactured housing portfolio to Vanderbilt Mortgage and Finance. In the longer term, CIT intends to increase deposits by buying other banks.

Jeffrey Peek, who oversaw CIT's untimely expansion activities, stepped down as CEO in early 2010. He was succeeded by John Thain, who has also led Merrill Lynch and New York Stock Exchange. No stranger to turning ailing companies around, Thain is credited with bringing the NYSE into the modern era with electronic trading. He also merged NYSE with Euronext, establishing the first trans-Atlantic exchange.

CIT was working toward expanding its international business, with a goal of doubling its size. To that end, it acquired a UK banking license so it could make loans in the European Union and bought a portion of Barclays' vendor finance businesses in Germany and the UK. However, as part of its streamlining efforts, it exited its Canadian joint venture with CIBC and agreed to sell its Australian and New Zealand operations to Bank of Queensland.

In another deal, CIT sold M&A advisory firm Edgeview Partners to that firm's employees in 2010, just three years after buying the firm.

HISTORY

Henry Ittleson founded CIT Group as Commercial Credit and Investment Trust in St. Louis in 1908. Initially financing horse-drawn carriages, it moved to New York in 1915 as Commercial Investment Trust (CIT) to participate in one of the milestones of modern consumer debt: Its auto financing program, launched in collaboration with Studebaker, was the first of its kind.

CIT diversified into industrial financing during the 1920s and went public in 1924 on the NYSE. Cars remained a strong focus, though: When Ford Motor Co. ran into difficulties in 1933, it sold financing division Universal Credit Corp. to CIT. CIT continued to expand into industrial financing, incorporating its industrial business as CIT Financial Corp. in 1942.

During the post-WWII boom, CIT began financing manufactured home sales and offering small loans. In 1964 it consolidated factoring operations into Meinhard-Commercial Corp. By the end of the 1960s the firm started to retreat from auto financing, focusing instead on industrial leasing, factoring, and equipment financing.

In 1980 RCA bought CIT, seeking to buy financing to develop its other businesses. RCA found the debt from the purchase unwieldy, however, and sold CIT to Manufacturers Hanover Bank (Manny Hanny) in 1984. The bank bought CIT to expand outside its home state of New York: Though it could not open banks out of state, Manny Hanny could still offer financial services through CIT, which became The CIT Group in 1986.

Manny Hanny executives tried to bring aggressive management to staid, top-heavy CIT. The company sold its Inventory Finance division in 1987 and divested the consumer loan business in 1988. It consolidated the Meinhard-Commercial and Manufacturers Hanover factoring units in 1989. By then Manny Hanny was cash-strapped over losses incurred from foreign loans, so it sold a 60% stake in CIT to The Dai-Ichi Kangyo Bank of Japan.

CIT gave Dai-Ichi entrée into US financial services, and it began expanding CIT's range of services again, including equity investment (1990), credit finance (from its purchase of Fidelcor Business Credit in 1991), and venture capital (1992). CIT also reentered the consumer loan market (including home equity lending) with a new Consumer Finance group (1992).

In 1995 Chemical Bank (Manny Hanny's successor; now part of JPMorgan Chase) sold an additional 20% share to Dai-Ichi, bumping the Japanese bank's holdings to 80% and arranging to sell its remaining shares to Dai-Ichi. In 1997, instead of Dai-Ichi buying the rest of Chase's shares, CIT bought them and spun them off to the public. In 1998 Dai-Ichi reduced its stake.

In 1999 CIT bought Newcourt Credit Group, North America's #2 equipment finance and leasing firm; it also bought Heller Financial's commercial services unit.

Tyco International bought CIT in 2001, renaming the new subsidiary Tyco Capital. Under Tyco's umbrella, it sold its manufactured home loan portfolio to Lehman Brothers and recreational vehicle portfolio to Salomon Smith Barney in an effort to exit noncore businesses. Tyco, however, expanded too far too fast, and the next year announced an about-face on its financial services subsidiary, deciding to spin off the division and return it to its CIT identity.

Jeff Peek took the reins of the company from longtime chairman and CEO Al Gamper in 2004.

CIT Group's Student Loan Xpress unit was one of several companies in the student-lending industry that came under investigation for business practices in 2007. It discontinued its private student loans that year, and in 2008 it stopped originating government-guaranteed student loans.

Amid losses, the company also exited the consumer finance business to focus on commercial lending. The previous year, it sold its construction lending unit to Wells Fargo and its 30% stake in Dell Financial Services to Dell.

In 2010 Peek stepped down as CEO; he was succeeded by John Thain.

EXECUTIVES

Chairman and CEO: John A. Thain, age 54
EVP and CFO: Scott T. Parker, age 43
EVP, Chief Administrative Oficer, and Head, Strategy: Nelson J. Chai, age 44
EVP and Global CIO: Michael Baresich
EVP and Head, Communications, Marketing, and Government Relations: Margaret D. Tutwiler, age 59
EVP and Director Investor Relations: Kenneth A. (Ken) Brause
EVP Internal Audit: Michael E. Roemer, age 48
EVP Brand Marketing and Communications: Kelley J. Gipson, age 48
EVP, CIT Aerospace: Anthony (Tony) Diaz
EVP, General Counsel, and Secretary: Robert J. (Bob) Ingato, age 49, $569,031 total compensation
EVP and Global Head Human Resources: Lisa D. Zonino
EVP and Chief Credit Officer: Robert C. Rowe, age 49
EVP and Treasurer: Glenn A. Votek
EVP Corporate Sales and Strategy; President, Insurance Services: Paul G. Petrylak
Chief Risk Officer: Lisa K. Polsky, age 53
President, CIT Healthcare: Steven N. (Steve) Warden, age 54
President, CIT Rail: George D. Cashman
President, Vendor Finance: Ron G. Arrington, age 48, $828,328 total compensation

President, Transportation Finance: C. Jeffrey (Jeff) Knittel, age 51, $2,183,390 total compensation
President, CIT Small Business Lending: Christine L. (Chris) Reilly
Auditors: PricewaterhouseCoopers LLP

LOCATIONS

HQ: CIT Group Inc.
505 5th Ave., New York, NY 10017
Phone: 212-771-0505
Web: www.cit.com

PRODUCTS/OPERATIONS

Selected Subsidiaries

Aireal Technologies of Harrisburg, LLC
AlphaGen Power LLC
ATMOR Properties Inc.
Baffin Shipping Co., Inc.
Capita Colombia Holdings Corp.
Education Lending Services, Inc.
Education Loan Servicing Corporation
Equipment Acceptance Corporation
The Equipment Insurance Company
Flex Holdings, LLC
GFSC Aircraft Acquisition Financing Corporation
Graybar Financial Services, LLC
Snap-On Credit LLC
Waste to Energy II LLC
Western Star Finance, Inc. (50%)

COMPETITORS

Ally Financial
Citigroup
Deutsche Bank
GE Capital
ILFC
JPMorgan Chase
Merrill Lynch
ORIX

HISTORICAL FINANCIALS

Company Type: Public

Income Statement				FYE: December 31
	ASSETS ($ mil.)	NET INCOME ($ mil.)	INCOME AS % OF ASSETS	EMPLOYEES
12/09	60,029	183	0.3%	4,293
12/08	80,449	(2,800)	—	4,995
12/07	90,248	(81)	—	6,700
12/06	77,068	1,046	1.4%	7,345
12/05	63,387	949	1.5%	6,340
Annual Growth	(1.4%)	(33.7%)	—	(9.3%)

2009 Year-End Financials

Equity as % of assets: 14.0%
Return on assets: 0.3%
Return on equity: 2.7%
Long-term debt ($ mil.): 43,263
No. of shares (mil.): 200

Dividends
  Yield: —
  Payout: —
Market value ($ mil.): 5,523
Sales ($ mil.): 3,985

Stock History

NYSE: CIT

	STOCK PRICE ($) FY Close	P/E High/Low	PER SHARE ($) Earnings	Dividends	Book Value
12/09	27.61	— —	(0.01)	—	41.99

Citigroup Inc.

This is the Citi. One of the largest financial services firms known to man, Citigroup (also known as Citi) has some 200 million customer accounts and does business in more than 140 countries. Citigroup offers deposits and loans (mainly through Citibank), investment banking, brokerage, wealth management, and other financial services. Reeling from $90 billion in writedowns and losses on mortgage-related securities and other investments, Citigroup has restructured itself into two primary segments — the regional consumer and institutional banking units of Citicorp and the brokerage and consumer finance units of Citi Holdings. The major reorganization hives off its money-losing assets from its banking divisions.

Citigroup was one of the hardest-hit financial companies in the worldwide credit crisis of 2008. After years of assembling an international cache of assets involved in commercial and corporate banking, investment banking, wealth management, brokerage, and equity and alternative investments, the company faced several quarters of losses as a result of investments turned sour. To stay afloat, it raised money from private investors (including Saudi investor Prince Al-Waleed bin Talal, who owns some 5% of the company), began selling off noncore units, and cut its workforce by some 15% (approximately 55,000 jobs) in 2008. It slashed another 50,000 jobs the following year and cut still more in 2010.

The US government also came to the company's aid with a $45 billion cash injection and the backing of more than $300 billion in loans and securities. In exchange, the government took a 34% stake in Citigroup. The firm received approval to pay the funds back in 2009, and the government began reducing its ownership.

Irrespective of its myriad problems, few other banks, domestic or foreign, can equal Citigroup's global reach. The company owns stakes in regional banks in several countries (notably, KorAm Bank in South Korea, Taiwan's Bank of Overseas Chinese, Banco de Chile, and one of Mexico's largest banks, Banamex) in addition to its own offices, which include some 4,000 retail branches around the world. The group also has more 50 million Citi-branded credit card accounts in the Americas, Europe, Asia, the Middle East, and Africa.

As part of its restructuring plan, Citigroup has divested some 40 noncore units since 2008. In 2009 Citigroup sold its Diners Club North American franchise to Bank of Montreal's BMO Financial Group. Other sales include its $1.93 billion Canadian MasterCard portfolio (to CIBC), a $3.5 billion real estate loan portfolio (to JPMorgan Chase), and a $3.2 billion auto loan portfolio (to Santander).

HISTORY

Empire builder Sanford "Sandy" Weill, who helped build brokerage firm Shearson Loeb Rhoades, sold the company to American Express (AmEx) in 1981. Forced out of AmEx in 1985, Weill bounced back in 1986, buying Control Data's Commercial Credit unit.

Primerica caught Weill's eye next. Its predecessor, American Can, was founded in 1901 as a

New Jersey canning company; it eventually expanded into the paper and retail industries before turning to financial services in 1986. The firm was renamed Primerica in 1987 and bought brokerage Smith Barney, Harris Upham & Co.

Weill's Commercial Credit bought Primerica in 1988. In 1993 Primerica bought Shearson from AmEx, as well as Travelers, taking its name and logo. Weill set about trimming Travelers. He sold life subsidiaries and bought Aetna's property/casualty business in 1995. In 1996 he consolidated all property/casualty operations to form Travelers Property Casualty and took it public. In 1997 Travelers bought investment bank Salomon Brothers and formed Salomon Smith Barney Holdings (now Citigroup Global Markets).

Weill sold Citicorp chairman and CEO John Reed on the idea of a merger in 1998, in advance of the Gramm-Leach-Bliley act, which deregulated the financial services industry in the US. By the time the merger went through, a slowed US economy and foreign-market turmoil brought significant losses to both sides. The renamed Citigroup consolidated in 1998 and 1999, laying off more than 10,000 employees.

In 1999 former Treasury Secretary Robert Rubin joined Citigroup as a co-chairman. In 2000 Reed retired. That same year Citigroup bought subprime lender Associates First Capital for approximately $27 billion.

The company parlayed the $4 billion it netted from the 2002 spinoff of 20% of Travelers Property Casualty into a $5.8 billion purchase of California-based Golden State Bancorp, the parent of the then-third-largest thrift in the US, Cal Fed. Also that year Citigroup paid $215 million to settle federal allegations that Associates First Capital made customers unwittingly purchase credit insurance by automatically billing for it.

A landmark ruling by the SEC in 2003 implied that Citigroup issued favorable stock ratings to companies in exchange for investment banking contracts. As part of the ruling, erstwhile star analyst Jack Grubman agreed to pay some $15 million in fines for his overly rosy stock reports and accepted a lifetime ban from working in the securities industry. Citigroup forked over $400 million in fines, the largest portion of a total of some $1.4 billion levied against 10 brokerage firms regarding conflicts of interest between analysts and investment bankers.

Amid the investigations, Citigroup separated its stock-picking and corporate advisory businesses, creating a retail brokerage and equity research unit called Smith Barney. In the SEC's 2003 ruling, such a "Chinese Wall" between bankers and analysts was later made mandatory at all firms.

In 2004 the company — while admitting no wrongdoing — paid $2.65 billion to investors who were burned when WorldCom went bankrupt amid an accounting scandal. (Citigroup was one of the lead underwriters of WorldCom stocks and bonds.) The settlement was one of the largest ever for alleged securities fraud, and compelled Citigroup to set aside an additional $5 billion to cover legal fees for this case and others involving Enron and spinning. The company eventually paid $2 billion in mid-2005 to investors who lost money on publicly traded Enron stocks and bonds, again settling the matter while denying it broke any laws. Enron shareholders had argued that Citigroup helped Enron to set up offshore companies and shady partnerships to exaggerate the energy trader's cash flow.

Weill named investment bank head Chuck Prince as CEO in 2003. Weill retired as chairman in 2006, and Prince assumed that title as well. Prince resigned in 2007.

Prince was succeeded by Vikram Pandit, a Morgan Stanley veteran who came to Citigroup when it acquired hedge fund and private equity manager Old Lane Partners in 2007.

EXECUTIVES

Chairman: Richard D. (Dick) Parsons, age 61
Vice Chairman: Lewis B. (Lew) Kaden, age 66
Vice Chairman: Stephen R. Volk, age 74, $10,532,273 total compensation
Vice Chairman: Edward J. (Ned) Kelly III, age 56, $9,927,462 total compensation
CEO and Director: Vikram S. Pandit, age 53, $128,751 total compensation
CFO: John C. Gerspach, age 56, $5,063,817 total compensation
General Counsel and Corporate Secretary: Michael S. Helfer, age 64
Chief Compliance Officer: Cindy Armine
Chief Economist: Willem Buiter
Chief Tax Officer: Saul M. Rosen
Chief Administrative Officer: Don Callahan, age 53
Chief Risk Officer: Brian Leach, age 50
EVP Global Marketing and Corporate Affairs; Chairman and CEO, Women & Company: Lisa M. Caputo, age 46
EVP Global Government Affairs: Nicholas E. (Nick) Calio
EVP International Customer Franchise and CitiBusiness, Global Consumer Group: Vicky Bindra
EVP Global Public Affairs: Edward Skyler, age 36
Co-Head, Global Markets, Markets & Banking Institutional Clients Group: James A. (Jim) Forese, age 47, $12,855,072 total compensation
Co-Head Global Markets, Institutional Clients Group: Paco Ybarra
CEO, Consumer Banking for the Americas; Chairman, Global Consumer Council; Chairman and CEO, Latin America and Mexico: Manuel Medina-Mora, age 59, $10,400,007 total compensation
CEO, EMEA, Central and Eastern Europe and the Middle East: Alberto J. Verme, age 52, $7,802,494 total compensation
CEO, Institutional Clients Group: John P. Havens, age 53, $11,276,454 total compensation
CEO, Citi Holdings: Michael L. Corbat, age 49
CEO, Citi Cards: Paul Galant, age 42
Head Human Resources: Paul D. McKinnon, age 57
Auditors: KPMG LLP

LOCATIONS

HQ: Citigroup Inc.
399 Park Ave., New York, NY 10043
Phone: 212-559-1000
Web: www.citigroup.com

PRODUCTS/OPERATIONS

2009 Sales

	$ mil.	% of total
Interest		
Loans, including fees	47,457	43
Investments, including dividends	13,119	12
Trading account assets	10,723	9
Federal funds sold & securities purchased under resale agreements	3,084	3
Deposits with banks	1,478	1
Other	774	1
Noninterest		
Commissions & fees	17,116	15
Administration & other fiduciary fees	5,195	5
Principal transactions	3,932	3
Insurance premiums	3,020	3
Realized gains on sales of investments	1,996	2
Other	3,018	3
Adjustments	(2,906)	—
Total	**108,006**	**100**

2009 Assets

	$ mil.	% of total
Cash & equivalents	414,908	22
Brokerage receivables	33,634	2
Trading account	342,773	18
Treasury & agency securities	54,114	3
Mortgage-backed securities	29,068	2
Foreign government securities	102,519	5
Debt securities held to maturity	52,998	3
Loans		
Consumer	423,249	22
Corporate	169,721	9
Allowance for loan losses	(38,760)	—
Other	272,422	14
Total	**1,856,646**	**100**

COMPETITORS

American Express
Bank of America
Bank of New York Mellon
Barclays
Capital One
Deutsche Bank
FMR
GE
Goldman Sachs
HSBC
JPMorgan Chase
Mizuho Financial
UBS
U.S. Bancorp
USAA
Wells Fargo

HISTORICAL FINANCIALS

Company Type: Public

Income Statement

FYE: December 31

	ASSETS ($ mil.)	NET INCOME ($ mil.)	INCOME AS % OF ASSETS	EMPLOYEES
12/09	1,856,646	(1,511)	—	269,000
12/08	1,938,470	(27,684)	—	326,900
12/07	2,187,631	3,617	0.2%	387,000
12/06	1,884,318	21,538	1.1%	337,000
12/05	1,494,037	24,638	1.6%	307,000
Annual Growth	5.6%	—	—	(3.2%)

2009 Year-End Financials

Equity as % of assets: 8.2%
Return on assets: —
Return on equity: —
Long-term debt ($ mil.): 364,019
No. of shares (mil.): 28,974

Dividends
  Yield: 0.3%
  Payout: —
Market value ($ mil.): 95,902
Sales ($ mil.): 108,006

Stock History

NYSE: C

	STOCK PRICE ($) FY Close	P/E High/Low		PER SHARE ($) Earnings	Dividends	Book Value
12/09	3.31	—	—	(0.80)	0.01	5.27
12/08	6.71	—	—	(5.59)	1.12	4.89
12/07	29.44	77	40	0.72	2.16	3.92
12/06	55.70	13	10	4.31	1.96	4.13
12/05	48.53	11	9	4.75	1.76	3.88
Annual Growth	(48.9%)	—	—	—	(72.5%)	7.9%

Citrix Systems

Citrix Systems is taking connectivity to the next level. The company provides access infrastructure products that enable PCs, IP phones, and other devices to remotely and securely access applications across wired and wireless networks, freeing customers from facing the difficult task of installing and updating software on each piece of hardware. Its product line includes application virtualization software, VPN appliances, and password management tools, with most applications capable of being deployed in both Windows and UNIX-based computing environments. The company also offers online managed services for meetings and presentations, technical support, and remote desktop access.

In early 2010 the company announced it was launching an offering called GoToManage that targets the IT management market. Based on technology the company acquired when it purchased Paglo Labs, GoToManage provides a Web-based platform to monitor, control, and support IT assets such as desktops, mainframes, and servers.

Citrix's strategy has included using selective acquisitions to expand its product line and broaden its offerings into related fields. Purchases from 2005-2008 added expertise in areas such as WAN optimization, application traffic management, server and desktop virtualization, and quality of service capabilities. Citrix's expanded product line targets customers of all sizes, with its GoToMyPC remote-access product used by individuals and small businesses and its NetScaler Web applications and XenDesktop products licensed by IT departments and network engineers.

The company's key strategic partners include Microsoft and Intel, with Citrix working closely with each to ensure integration of its products. Citrix also has a host of other technology partners (more than 10,000) that provide products complementary to Citrix's offerings.

HISTORY

Citrix Systems was founded in 1989 by a crew of former IBM engineers that included Edward Iacobucci. It was Iacobucci who, as a Big Blue designer in 1984 working alongside Bill Gates and a cadre of engineers from IBM and the fledgling Microsoft, led the team that developed the OS/2 operating system. Iacobucci quit IBM in 1989 and turned down a technology officer position at Microsoft to start his own business.

Iacobucci licensed Microsoft's OS/2 source code to start the Citrus Company, quickly changing the company name when one venture capitalist mistook it for a fruit concern. Waiting for investment funds, Iacobucci wrote an OS/2 programmer's guide (featuring a foreword by Gates) that significantly boosted his credibility among the software elite.

By 1991 Citrix had developed an OS/2-based program that let users on separate terminals run software off a larger computer. The week the product shipped, IBM and Microsoft called off their OS/2 development partnership. With business publications sounding the death of OS/2, Citrix in 1992 regrouped its network vision around Windows. The changes contributed to losses for 1992 and 1993.

Through a partnership with network software specialist Novell, in 1993 Citrix introduced WinView, which let non-Windows PC users tap into Microsoft programs on a network of disparate systems. Novell's clout boosted the company's distribution capabilities, and sales ballooned. Citrix went public in 1995.

Microsoft in 1997 made plans to incorporate some features offered by Citrix into Windows. Knowing his company's future was on the line, Iacobucci flew to Microsoft headquarters in Washington in the wake of a Citrix stock drop and shareholder lawsuits and spent 11 weeks negotiating. Microsoft signed a $175 million deal to continue licensing Citrix software.

In a burst of international expansion, Citrix in 1998 opened offices across Europe. It formed an e-business unit in 1999 to help application service providers host Web-based applications. In 2000 Citrix acquired Internet consultancy Innovex.

Citrix continued to expand its product lines via acquisitions with the 2004 purchases of ExpertCity and Net6.

Citrix acquired NetScaler, a developer of application acceleration appliances, for $300 million in 2006, and expanded into virtualization management and software provisioning with the purchases of Ardence and XenSource in 2007.

EXECUTIVES

Chairman: Thomas F. (Tom) Bogan, age 58
President, CEO, and Director: Mark B. Templeton, age 57, $5,168,534 total compensation
SVP and CFO: David J. Henshall, age 42, $2,039,282 total compensation
SVP and General Manager, Datacenter and Cloud Division: Peter J. Levine, age 49, $15,069,392 total compensation
SVP and General Manager, Desktop Division: J. Gordon Payne, age 48, $1,616,273 total compensation
SVP Human Resources and General Counsel: David R. Friedman, age 48, $1,661,224 total compensation
SVP and Chief Marketing Officer: Wesley R. (Wes) Wasson, age 43
SVP Sales and Services: Alvaro J. (Al) Monserrat, age 42, $2,096,000 total compensation
Corporate VP Strategic Development: Michael Cristinziano, age 45
VP Business Development: Frank Artale, age 38
VP Corporate Marketing: Kim Woodward
Director Corporate Communications: Eric Armstrong
Director Investor Relations: Eduardo Fleites
Auditors: Ernst & Young LLP

LOCATIONS

HQ: Citrix Systems, Inc.
851 W. Cypress Creek Rd.
Fort Lauderdale, FL 33309
Phone: 954-267-3000 **Fax:** 954-267-9319
Web: www.citrix.com

2009 Sales

	$ mil.	% of total
Americas	696.2	43
Europe, Middle East & Africa	480.7	30
Citrix Online division	308.2	19
Asia/Pacific	129.0	8
Total	**1,614.1**	**100**

PRODUCTS/OPERATIONS

2009 Sales

	$ mil.	% of total
Desktop Solutions	1,046.0	65
Online Services	308.2	19
Datacenter & Cloud Solutions	241.2	15
Other	18.7	1
Total	**1,614.1**	**100**

2009 Sales

	$ mil.	% of total
License updates	605.0	38
Product licenses	539.0	33
Online services	308.2	19
Technical services	161.9	10
Total	**1,614.1**	**100**

Selected Products and Services

Citrix Access Infrastructure
  Citrix Gateway
    Access Gateway
    Application Gateway
  Citrix MetaFrame
    Conferencing Manager
    Presentation Server for Windows
    Presentation Server for UNIX
    Password Manager
    Secure Access Manager
  Citrix Online
    GoToAssist
    GoToMeeting
    GoToMyPC
Citrix Services
  Consulting
  Product training and certification
  Technical Support

COMPETITORS

Adobe Systems	IBM
Blue Coat	Juniper Networks
Cisco Systems	LogMeIn
EMC	Microsoft
F5 Networks	Oracle
GraphOn	Riverbed Technology
Hewlett-Packard	VMware

HISTORICAL FINANCIALS

Company Type: Public

Income Statement

FYE: December 31

	REVENUE ($ mil.)	NET INCOME ($ mil.)	NET PROFIT MARGIN	EMPLOYEES
12/09	1,614	191	11.8%	4,816
12/08	1,583	178	11.3%	5,040
12/07	1,392	215	15.4%	4,620
12/06	1,134	183	16.1%	3,742
12/05	909	166	18.3%	3,171
Annual Growth	**15.4%**	**3.5%**	**—**	**11.0%**

2009 Year-End Financials

Debt ratio: —
Return on equity: 9.3%
Cash ($ mil.): 261
Current ratio: 1.25
Long-term debt ($ mil.): —
No. of shares (mil.): 187
Dividends
  Yield: —
  Payout: —
Market value ($ mil.): 7,779

Stock History

NASDAQ (GS): CTXS

	STOCK PRICE ($) FY Close	P/E High/Low		PER SHARE ($) Earnings	Dividends	Book Value
12/09	41.61	43	19	1.03	—	11.71
12/08	23.57	39	20	0.96	—	10.26
12/07	38.01	39	24	1.14	—	9.83
12/06	27.05	47	27	0.97	—	7.83
12/05	28.73	32	22	0.93	—	6.44
Annual Growth	**9.7%**	**—**	**—**	**2.6%**	**—**	**16.1%**

Cliffs Natural Resources

Cliffs Natural Resources' favorite period in history? The Iron Age, hands down. The company produces iron ore pellets, a key component of steelmaking, and owns or holds stakes in six iron ore properties that represent almost half of North America's iron ore production. Cliffs' operations, including Northshore Mining and Empire Iron, produce more than 38 million tons of iron ore pellets annually. The company sells its ore primarily in North America but also in Europe and China. The company owns Australian iron properties that supply the Asia/Pacific region. It also has iron ore interests in Latin America, specifically Brazil.

As the North American steel industry struggled early in the 2000s, Cliffs began to increase its mine ownership by buying up stakes from its steel company partners. The company has continued to buy out the co-owners of the mines it operates even as demand and the greater economy have fluctuated. The latest such deal came in 2008 when it bought Chinese steelmaker Laiwu Steel Group's 30% ownership stake in United Taconite.

In addition, Cliffs has begun to look internationally for new iron ore properties to acquire in order to supply the Chinese steel industry's growing demand for raw materials. Following the 2005 acquisition of an 80% stake in Australian miner Portman, the company also bought a stake in a venture in Brazil and another in Australia. In the years since its original stake purchase, Cliffs continued to add to its holdings in Portman until it owned the company outright. In early 2009 Portman took on the Cliffs name and identity fully.

It raised its minority stake in iron ore producer Wabush Mines in 2010, buying out partners U.S. Steel Canada and Dofasco and spending $88 million to make Wabush wholly owned. Around that same time, Cliffs bought Freewest Resources for about C$240 million ($225 million US). Also that year, Cliffs entered a joint venture with Mariana Resources to explore iron oxide-copper-gold deposits in the SCM Mariana Area of north-central Chile. Cliffs is a 51% partner in the $2 million program.

Cliffs agreed to acquire Spider Resources in 2010 in order to gain control of the "Big Daddy" chromite project in Northern Ontario. Cliffs had pursued control of the project through the purchase of KWG Resources or Spider stock, who each owned about 26% of the project. Spider backed out of a merger agreement with KWG to accept a buyout offer from Cliffs. The deal will give Cliffs the majority stake it sought for the chromite project.

The company also acquired the West Virginia coal-mining operations of INR Energy LLC for $757 million in 2010. The operation produces both metallurgical coal used in steelmaking and thermal coal burned by power plants.

ArcelorMittal USA accounts for almost one-third of the total sales of Cliffs' North American iron ore pellets.

HISTORY

Samuel Mashers founded the Cleveland Iron Mining Co. in 1846, just five years after the discovery of iron ore in Michigan's Upper Peninsula. To compete in a consolidating market, the company merged with Iron Cliffs Mining in 1891 to form Cleveland-Cliffs. The company offset risks by forming joint ventures with steel companies to own and operate mines. It survived the Depression by selling all its steel and timber operations. The demands of WWII prompted Cleveland-Cliffs to invest in iron mines outside the US — in Canada, Chile, Colombia, Peru, and Venezuela (cut back after WWII to Canada and Australia).

In the 1960s the company rebuffed a takeover bid by Detroit Steel, and in the 1970s it diversified again, acquiring copper, shale oil, timber, and uranium assets. However, Cleveland-Cliffs stumbled financially and sold all its businesses not related to iron ore. The revival of the steel industry in the late 1980s and 1990s lifted Cleveland-Cliffs' sales, but the financial struggles of its major customers forced losses on the company.

In 1994 the company bought Cypress Ajax Mineral's Minnesota iron mine (Northshore). In 1996 Cleveland-Cliffs closed its exhausted Australian operations. That year the company formed a joint venture with LTV and Lurgi (of Germany) to make reduced-iron briquettes in Trinidad and Tobago.

Faced with a tide of steel imports from Asia, Brazil, and Russia, the company curtailed production and deferred plans to supply steel minimills with the iron ore pellets needed to produce iron in electric furnaces — the company's planned start-up of its ferrous metallics plant in Trinidad was delayed in 2000 due to mechanical problems. During late 2000 two of Cleveland-Cliffs' mine partners — LTV and Wheeling-Pittsburgh — filed for bankruptcy protection. Cleveland-Cliffs was able to up its stake in the Empire Iron mine, previously co-owned with Wheeling-Pittsburgh, to 35%.

Later that year Canada-based Algoma Steel, co-owner with Cleveland-Cliffs of the Tilden mine, filed for bankruptcy. Also in 2001 Cleveland-Cliffs began production at its ferrous metallics plant in Trinidad; that plant was idled later in the year. In late 2001 the company, along with ALLETE subsidiary Minnesota Power, acquired the iron ore mining and processing facilities of LTV Steel Mining Co., including a rail line and dock facility on Lake Superior. In 2001 Cleveland-Cliffs increased its stake in the Tilden mine to 85%.

In late 2001 the Empire Iron mine was temporarily closed and its operations restructured. The mine reopened in 2002; Cleveland-Cliffs took a $52.7 million charge related to the closure. The following year the company increased its stake in the Empire Iron mine to 79%. In 2003 United Taconite (70%-owned by Cleveland-Cliffs) was formed to hold the mining operations it purchased from bankrupt Eveleth Mines.

EXECUTIVES

Chairman, President, and CEO: Joseph A. Carrabba, age 57, $5,350,667 total compensation
President, North American Business Unit:
Donald J. Gallagher, age 57,
$1,396,056 total compensation
EVP and CFO: Laurie Brlas, age 52,
$1,206,550 total compensation
EVP Human and Technical Resources:
William A. Brake Jr., age 49,
$1,178,945 total compensation

EVP Legal, Government Affairs, and Sustainability: P. Kelly Tompkins, age 53
EVP Commercial, North American Iron Ore:
William R. Calfee, age 63,
$1,021,470 total compensation
SVP; President, Ferroalloys: William C. (Bill) Boor, age 44
SVP; President and CEO Asia/Pacific:
Richard R. Mehan, age 54
SVP North American Coal: Duke D. Vetor, age 51
SVP and Managing Director, Asia/Pacific Iron Ore: Duncan Price
SVP Operations, North American Iron Ore:
David B. Blake
General Counsel and Secretary: George W. Hawk Jr., age 53
CIO: Ronald K. Aderhold, age 47
VP, Corporate Controller, and Chief Accounting Officer: Terrance M. Paradie, age 41
Director, Investor Relations and Corporate Communications: Steven R. (Steve) Baisden
Auditors: Deloitte & Touche LLP

LOCATIONS

HQ: Cliffs Natural Resources Inc.
     200 Public Sq., Ste. 3300, Cleveland, OH 44114
Phone: 216-694-5700   **Fax:** 216-694-4880
Web: www.cliffsnaturalresources.com

2009 Sales

	$ mil.	% of total
US	1,049.5	45
China	711.5	30
Canada	236.6	10
Japan	157.4	7
Other countries	187.0	8
Total	**2,342.0**	**100**

PRODUCTS/OPERATIONS

2009 Sales

	$ mil.	% of total
North American operations		
Iron	1,447.8	62
Coal	207.2	9
Asian Iron	542.1	23
Other products	144.9	6
Total	**2,342.0**	**100**

Selected Operations

Michigan (Marquette Range)
  Empire Iron Mining Partnership (79%)
  Tilden Mine (85%)
Minnesota (Mesabi Range)
  Hibbing Taconite Company (23%)
  Northshore Mining Company
  United Taconite
Canada
  Wabush Mines (Newfoundland/Quebec)

COMPETITORS

Baffinland Iron Mines
BHP Billiton
CONSOL Energy
Dofasco
Ferrexpo
Great Northern Iron Ore
International Briquettes
Massey Energy
Peabody Energy
Rio Tinto Limited
United States Steel
Vale

HISTORICAL FINANCIALS
Company Type: Public

Income Statement
FYE: December 31

	REVENUE ($ mil.)	NET INCOME ($ mil.)	NET PROFIT MARGIN	EMPLOYEES
12/09	2,342	204	8.7%	5,404
12/08	3,609	516	14.3%	5,711
12/07	2,275	270	11.9%	5,298
12/06	1,922	280	14.6%	4,189
12/05	1,740	272	15.7%	4,085
Annual Growth	7.7%	(6.9%)	—	7.2%

2009 Year-End Financials

Debt ratio: 28.4%
Return on equity: 11.4%
Cash ($ mil.): 503
Current ratio: 2.04
Long-term debt ($ mil.): 525
No. of shares (mil.): 135
Dividends
Yield: 0.6%
Payout: 15.3%
Market value ($ mil.): 6,242

Stock History
NYSE: CLF

	STOCK PRICE ($) FY Close	P/E High/Low		PER SHARE ($) Earnings	Dividends	Book Value
12/09	46.09	30	7	1.63	0.25	18.77
12/08	25.61	26	3	4.76	0.35	12.92
12/07	50.40	21	9	2.57	0.25	8.59
12/06	24.22	11	6	2.60	0.24	5.51
12/05	22.14	10	5	2.49	0.15	4.81
Annual Growth	20.1%	—	—	(10.1%)	13.6%	40.6%

The Clorox Company

Bleach is the cornerstone of Clorox. The company's namesake household cleaning products are world leaders, but Clorox reaches far beyond bleach. While the firm makes and markets laundry and cleaning items (Formula 409, Pine-Sol, Tilex), its products portfolio also extends into dressings/sauces (Hidden Valley, KC Masterpiece), plastic wrap and containers (Glad), cat litters (Fresh Step, Scoop Away), car care products (Armor All, STP), the Brita water-filtration system (in North America), charcoal briquettes (Kingsford, Match Light), and natural personal-care products (Burt's Bees).

Clorox relies on three top product lines — liquid bleach, trash bags, and charcoal — for about 35% of its sales. Sales of bleach and other disinfecting products are benefiting as consumers stock up because of concerns about the flu.

With its namesake bleach being its biggest business, Clorox is looking to the future of its primary product to safeguard its sales. It's garnering accolades from environmental groups, such as Greenpeace, for implementing changes to its supply chain for bleach-making. In 2010 the firm will stop transporting chlorine in the US. While the transition stands to be a potentially costly one, Clorox is changing its manufacturing process, beginning with its Fairfield, California, factory outside San Francisco and rolling out the changes to its handful of bleach manufacturing facilities nationwide. Rather than buy chlorine and make bleach onsite at its factories, Clorox will be making a stronger bleach with a higher concentration of sodium hypochlorite, with no changes to quality, color, or smell.

The firm sells products in more than 100 countries and makes them in more than two dozen countries. Much of Clorox's foreign growth has been from Latin America and Canada. To secure its foothold there, Clorox bought Latin American and Canadian bleach brands (Javex, Agua Jane, Nevex) from Colgate-Palmolive Company in 2007. The company also teamed up with Sara Lee in 2009 to launch new air freshener products under Clorox's Poett and Mistolin brands in Argentina, Chile, Colombia, Peru, Uruguay, and Venezuela.

It's also inking deals with companies in niche markets to diversify and chase after growing sectors. Clorox purchased the Burt's Bees line of natural skin and hair-care products for $925 million in 2007. The deal has secured a spot for Clorox in the natural products marketplace. Also, in late 2006 Clorox unit The Armor All/STP Products Company signed a licensing agreement with Canada-based Recochem to make and market a line of antifreeze/coolants, windshield washing fluids, and de-icers for sale in North America.

The cleaning products company named Donald R. Knauss as its chairman and CEO in late 2006. Knauss came to Clorox with experience from consumer giant Procter & Gamble and Coca-Cola North America.

HISTORY

Known first as the Electro-Alkaline Company, The Clorox Company was founded in 1913 by five Oakland, California, investors to make bleach using water from salt ponds around San Francisco Bay. The next year the company registered the brand name Clorox (the name combines the bleach's two main ingredients, chlorine and sodium hydroxide). At first the company sold only industrial-strength bleach, but in 1916 it formulated a household solution.

With the establishment of a Philadelphia distributor in 1921, Clorox began national expansion. The company went public in 1928 and built plants in Illinois and New Jersey in the 1930s; it opened nine more US plants in the 1940s and 1950s. In 1957 Procter & Gamble (P&G) bought Clorox. The Federal Trade Commission raised antitrust questions, and litigation ensued over the next decade. P&G was ordered to divest Clorox, and in 1969 Clorox again became an independent company.

Following its split with P&G, the firm added household consumer goods and foods, acquiring the brands Liquid-Plumr (drain opener, 1969), Formula 409 (spray cleaner, 1970), Litter Green (cat litter, 1971), and Hidden Valley (salad dressings, 1972). Clorox entered the specialty food products business by purchasing Grocery Store Products (Kitchen Bouquet, 1971) and Kingsford (charcoal briquettes, 1973).

In 1974 Henkel, a large West German maker of cleansers and detergents, purchased 15% of Clorox's stock as part of an agreement to share research. Beginning in 1977, Clorox sold off subsidiaries and brands, such as Country Kitchen Foods (1979), to focus on household goods.

During the 1980s Clorox launched a variety of new products, including Match Light (instant-lighting charcoal, 1980), Tilex (mildew remover, 1981), and Fresh Step (cat litter, 1984). Clorox began marketing Brita water filtration systems in the US in 1988 (adding Canada in 1995). In 1990 it paid $465 million for American Cyanamid's household products group, including Pine-Sol cleaner and Combat insecticide. (It sold Combat and Soft Scrub to Henkel in 2004.)

In 1991 Clorox left the laundry detergent business (begun in 1988) after it was battered by heavyweights P&G and Unilever. Household products VP Craig Sullivan became CEO the next year (stepping down in December 2003).

A string of acquisitions brought the company into new markets as it built on existing brands. Clorox bought Black Flag and Lestoil in 1996 and car care product manufacturer Armor All in 1997. With its 1999 purchase of First Brands — for about $2 billion in stock and debt — Clorox added four more brands of cat litter and diversified into plastic products (Glad).

In 2002 Clorox announced that due to the difficult economic environment in the region, it was selling its Brazil business. In 2003 it jumpstarted a joint venture with Procter & Gamble to take advantage of P&G's manufacturing acumen to improve its Glad products. P&G received a 10% stake in Glad. In late 2004, though, P&G boosted its share in the joint venture from 10% to 20%.

Chemical giant Henkel once owned nearly 30% of Clorox, but Clorox bought it back in 2004 through an asset swap valued at $2.8 billion.

Also in 2004 Robert Matschullat, the company's nonexecutive chairman, replaced Sullivan upon his retirement. Matschullat stepped down as chairman in January 2005, passing the title to Jerry Johnston, and became a director. Matschullat reclaimed the titles of chairman and CEO on an interim basis when Johnston suffered a heart attack and retired in 2006. Former Coca-Cola executive Donald Knauss was named chairman and CEO in late 2006; Matschullat remained a director.

EXECUTIVES

Chairman and CEO: Donald R. (Don) Knauss, age 59, $8,165,546 total compensation
EVP and CFO: Daniel J. (Dan) Heinrich, age 54, $2,895,349 total compensation
EVP International and Natural Personal Care: Beth (Beth) Springer, age 45, $2,618,594 total compensation
EVP; COO Clorox North America: Lawrence S. (Larry) Peiros, age 55, $3,739,325 total compensation
EVP Strategy and Growth, Bags and Wraps and Away From Home: Frank A. Tataseo, age 56, $2,980,923 total compensation
SVP and Chief Product Supply Officer: James Foster, age 47
SVP and Chief Innovation Officer: Wayne L. Delker, age 56
SVP Human Resources and Corporate Affairs: Jacqueline P. (Jackie) Kane, age 58
SVP and Chief Customer Officer: Grant J. LaMontagne, age 54
SVP and General Manager Cleaning Division: Benno Dorer, age 46
SVP and General Counsel: Laura Stein, age 48
SVP and General Manager Specialty Division: George C. Roeth, age 49
SVP and Chief Marketing Officer: Thomas P. (Tom) Britanik, age 52
VP Investor Relations: Steve Austenfeld
VP Global Corporate Communications: Kathryn Caulfield
Auditors: Ernst & Young

LOCATIONS

HQ: The Clorox Company
1221 Broadway, Oakland, CA 94612
Phone: 510-271-7000   **Fax:** 510-832-1463
Web: www.thecloroxcompany.com

2009 Sales

	$ mil.	% of total
North America	4,375	80
International	1,075	20
Total	**5,450**	**100**

PRODUCTS/OPERATIONS

Selected Brands and Products

Food-Related
  Brita
  Glad
  Glad Press 'n Seal
  GladWare
  Hidden Valley
  K.C. Masterpiece
Household Cleaning
  Clorox
  Clorox 2
  Clorox Clean-Up
  Clorox Disinfecting Wipes
  Clorox FreshCare
  Clorox Oxi Magic
  Clorox ReadyMop
  Clorox Toilet Bowl Cleaner
  Formula 409
  Formula 409 Carpet Cleaner
  Handi-Wipes
  Lestoil
  Liquid-Plumr
  Pine-Sol
  S.O.S
  Stain Out
  Tilex
  ToiletWand
  Tuffy
  Ultra Clorox Bleach
International
  Agua Jane (bleach, Uruguay)
  Ant Rid (insecticides)
  Arela (waxes)
  Astra (disposable gloves)
  Bluebell (cleaners)
  Chux (cleaning tools)
  Clorisol (bleach)
  Clorox Gentle (color-safe bleach)
  Glad (containers)
  Glad-Lock (reclosable bags)
  Guard (shoe polish)
  Gumption (cleaners)
  Home Mat (insecticides)
  Home Keeper (insecticides)
  Javex (bleach, Canada)
  Mono (aluminum foil)
  Nevex (bleach, Venezuela)
  OSO (aluminum foil)
  Prestone (coolant)
  Selton (insecticides)
  S.O.S (cleaners)
  Super Globo (bleach)
  XLO (sponges)
  Yuhanrox (bleach)
Specialty
  Armor All
  BBQ Bag
  Burt's Bees
  EverClean
  EverFresh
  Fresh Step
  Fresh Step Scoop
  Kingsford
  Match Light
  Rain Dance
  Scoop Away
  Son of a Gun!
  STP
  Tuff Stuff

COMPETITORS

Alticor
Avalon Natural Cosmetics
Blistex
Bonne Bell
CalCedar
Campbell Soup
Church & Dwight
Colgate-Palmolive
ConAgra
Del Monte Foods
The Dial Corporation
Diversey
Dow Chemical
Dr. Bronner's
Estée Lauder
Forever Living
Kiehl's
Kiss My Face
Kraft Foods
McBride plc
Natural Health Trends
Nature's Sunshine
Newman's Own
Oil-Dri
Pactiv
Procter & Gamble
Reckitt Benckiser
S.C. Johnson
Seventh Generation
Tree of Life
Turtle Wax
Unilever

HISTORICAL FINANCIALS

Company Type: Public

Income Statement

FYE: June 30

	REVENUE ($ mil.)	NET INCOME ($ mil.)	NET PROFIT MARGIN	EMPLOYEES
6/09	5,450	537	9.9%	8,300
6/08	5,273	461	8.7%	8,300
6/07	4,847	501	10.3%	7,800
6/06	4,644	444	9.6%	7,600
6/05	4,388	1,096	25.0%	7,600
Annual Growth	**5.6%**	**(16.3%)**	**—**	**2.2%**

2009 Year-End Financials

Debt ratio: —
Return on equity: —
Cash ($ mil.): 206
Current ratio: 0.61
Long-term debt ($ mil.): 2,151

No. of shares (mil.): 141
Dividends
  Yield: 3.3%
  Payout: 48.3%
Market value ($ mil.): 7,863

Stock History

NYSE: CLX

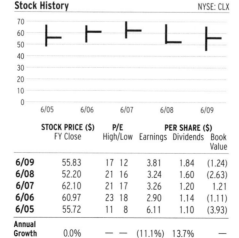

	STOCK PRICE ($) FY Close	P/E High/Low		PER SHARE ($) Earnings	Dividends	Book Value
6/09	55.83	17	12	3.81	1.84	(1.24)
6/08	52.20	21	16	3.24	1.60	(2.63)
6/07	62.10	21	17	3.26	1.20	1.21
6/06	60.97	23	18	2.90	1.14	(1.11)
6/05	55.72	11	8	6.11	1.10	(3.93)
Annual Growth	**0.0%**	**—**	**—**	**(11.1%)**	**13.7%**	**—**

CMS Energy

Michigan consumers rely on CMS Energy. The energy holding company's utility, Consumers Energy, has a generating capacity of more than 8,950 MW (primarily fossil-fueled) and distributes electricity and natural gas to 2.5 million customers (6.5 million end users) in Michigan. CMS Enterprises operates the non-utility businesses of CMS Energy, and is an operator of independent power generating plants; its independent power projects are primarily located in Michigan, but also in California and North Carolina, and have a gross capacity of 1,200 MW. Subsidiary EnerBank USA provides unsecured home improvement payment option programs for homeowners.

Having reined in its international and non-utility expansion strategy for something less financially risky, CMS Energy now focuses solely on the North American market. It has sold numerous assets, including its Latin American electric utilities, as well as its Australian generation and pipeline units and other international power plants and assets in Africa, India, and the Middle East. CMS Energy has also sold its oil and gas exploration and production units, as well as its domestic gas transportation assets.

Facing a tough economy in Michigan (particularly the downturn of the auto industry), CMS Energy is committed to investing in growing Consumers Energy's utility infrastructure and adding to its portfolio of green energy plants in order to meet stricter environmental regulations. In 2009 the company put its Exeter Connecticut scrap-tire-fueled independent power plant up for sale.

Consumers Energy veteran David Joos served briefly as president and CEO of CMS Energy in 2010, but retired in May to take the role of non-executive chairman. John G. Russell was named president and CEO. Russell previously was president and CEO of Consumers Energy.

HISTORY

In the late 1880s W. A. Foote and Samuel Jarvis formed hydroelectric company Jackson Electrical Light Works in Jackson, Michigan. After building plants in other Michigan towns, Foote formed utility holding company Consumers Power. In 1910 the firm merged with Michigan Light to create Commonwealth Power Railway and Light (CPR&L) and began building a statewide transmission system.

Foote died in 1915, and after nine years of acquisitions, successor Bernard Cobb sold the rail systems and split CPR&L into Commonwealth Power (CP) and Electric Railway Securities. In 1928 Cobb bought Southeastern Power & Light (SP&L) and merged CP with Penn-Ohio Edison to form Allied Power & Light. Commonwealth and Southern (C&S) was then created as the parent of Allied and SP&L.

In 1932 future GOP presidential nominee Wendell Willkie took the helm and became a national political figure by opposing the Public Utility Holding Company Act of 1935, which began 60 years of regulated monopolies. Consumers Power was divested from C&S after WWII.

Consumers brought a nuclear plant on line in 1962 and the next year began buying Michigan oil and gas fields. In 1967 it formed NOMECO (now CMS Oil and Gas) to guide its oil and gas efforts.

The completion of the Palisades nuke in 1971 began a 13-year run of chronic problems and lengthy shutdowns. Cost overruns and an environmental lawsuit killed the firm's third nuke (Midland) in 1984 — after $4.1 billion was spent.

A rate hike and new CEO William McCormick set the company on a new path in 1985. McCormick formed a subsidiary to develop and invest in independent power projects in 1986 and created holding company CMS (short for "Consumers") Energy the next year. CMS Gas Transmission was formed in 1989.

Midland Cogeneration Venture (CMS Energy and six partners) completed converting Midland to a natural gas-fueled cogeneration plant in 1990, and CMS Energy wrote off $657 million from its losses at the former nuke. It regained profitability in 1993.

McCormick split the utilities into electric and gas divisions in 1995 and also issued stock for its gas utility and transmission businesses, Consumers Gas Group. The next year CMS Energy formed an energy marketing arm.

In 1996 and 1997 CMS Energy invested in power plants in Morocco and Australia and bought a stake in a Brazilian electric utility. The next year it began developing a gas-fired plant in Ghana and won a bid to build a plant in India. CMS Energy also bought gas gathering and processing firms Continental Natural Gas and Heritage Gas Services in 1998.

Michigan's public service commission (PSC) issued utility restructuring orders in 1997 and 1998, but in 1999 the state Supreme Court ruled that the PSC lacked restructuring authority. Facing less-favorable proposed legislation, CMS Energy and DTE Energy moved to implement competition per the PSC's guidelines.

CMS Energy bought Panhandle Eastern Pipe Line from Duke Energy for $2.2 billion in 1999. It also grabbed a 77% stake in another Brazilian utility and began building its Powder River Basin gas pipeline. In 2000 the company partnered with Marathon Ashland Petroleum (now Marathon Petroleum) and TEPPCO to operate a pipeline transporting refined petroleum from the US Gulf Coast to Illinois.

CMS Energy agreed in 2001 to sell Consumers' high-voltage electric transmission assets to independent transmission operator Trans-Elect for about $290 million; the deal, which was the first of its kind in the US, was completed in 2002. That year the company sold its Equatorial Guinea (West Africa) oil and gas assets to Marathon Oil for about $1 billion. Also that year McCormick stepped down amid controversy over "round trip" power trades that artificially inflated the company's sales and trading volume; CMS Energy later announced that it would restate its 2000 and 2001 financial results to eliminate the effects of the trades.

In 2002 the company exited the exploration and production business. CMS Energy sold its CMS Panhandle companies, which together operated an 11,000-mile pipeline system, to Southern Union for $1.8 billion in 2003.

EXECUTIVES

Chairman: David W. Joos, age 57,
$7,781,355 total compensation
Presiding Director: Philip R. Lochner Jr., age 67
President, CEO, and Director: John G. Russell, age 52,
$2,954,210 total compensation
EVP and CFO, CMS Energy, Consumers Energy, and CMS Enterprises: Thomas J. (Tom) Webb, age 57,
$2,700,012 total compensation
SVP Governmental and Public Affairs and Chief Compliance Officer: David G. Mengebier, age 52
SVP and General Counsel: James E. Brunner, age 57,
$1,975,336 total compensation

SVP Human Resources and Administrative Services: John M. Butler, age 45, $1,054,994 total compensation
VP and CIO: Mamatha Chamarthi
VP and Secretary: Catherine M. Reynolds
VP, Controller, and Chief Accounting Officer: Glenn P. Barba, age 44
VP and Chief Tax Counsel: Theodore J. Vogel
VP Investor Relations and Treasurer: Laura L. Mountcastle
Director News and Information: Jeff Holyfield
Director Public Information: Dan Bishop
Auditors: PricewaterhouseCoopers LLP

LOCATIONS

HQ: CMS Energy Corporation
1 Energy Plaza, Jackson, MI 49201
Phone: 517-788-0550   **Fax:** 517-788-1859
Web: www.cmsenergy.com

PRODUCTS/OPERATIONS

2009 Sales

	$ mil.	% of total
Electric utility	3,407	55
Gas utility	2,556	41
Enterprises	216	4
Other	26	—
Total	**6,205**	**100**

Selected Subsidiaries

Consumers Energy Company (electric and gas utility)
CMS Capital
　EnerBank USA (banking services)
CMS Enterprises Company (nonutility holding company)

COMPETITORS

AEP
AES
Allegheny Energy
Alliant Energy
Calpine
CenterPoint Energy
Con Edison
DTE
Duke Energy
Dynegy
Edison International
Integrys Energy Group
NextEra Energy
ONEOK
SEMCO Energy
Sempra Energy
SUEZ-TRACTEBEL
Wisconsin Energy
Xcel Energy

HISTORICAL FINANCIALS

Company Type: Public

Income Statement

				FYE: December 31
	REVENUE ($ mil.)	NET INCOME ($ mil.)	NET PROFIT MARGIN	EMPLOYEES
12/09	6,205	240	3.9%	8,039
12/08	6,821	300	4.4%	7,970
12/07	6,464	(215)	—	7,898
12/06	6,810	(79)	—	8,640
12/05	6,288	(84)	—	8,713
Annual Growth	**(0.3%)**	**—**	**—**	**(2.0%)**

2009 Year-End Financials

Debt ratio: 214.4%
Return on equity: 9.0%
Cash ($ mil.): 90
Current ratio: 1.40
Long-term debt ($ mil.): 6,092

No. of shares (mil.): 230
Dividends
　Yield: 3.2%
　Payout: 54.9%
Market value ($ mil.): 3,605

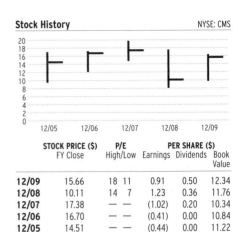

Stock History　　　　　　　　　　NYSE: CMS

	STOCK PRICE ($) FY Close	P/E High/Low		Earnings	PER SHARE ($) Dividends	Book Value
12/09	15.66	18	11	0.91	0.50	12.34
12/08	10.11	14	7	1.23	0.36	11.76
12/07	17.38	—	—	(1.02)	0.20	10.34
12/06	16.70	—	—	(0.41)	0.00	10.84
12/05	14.51	—	—	(0.44)	0.00	11.22
Annual Growth	**1.9%**	**—**	**—**	**—**	**—**	**2.4%**

CNA Financial

CNA Financial is the umbrella organization for a wide range of insurance providers, including Continental Casualty. The company primarily provides commercial coverage, with such standard offerings as workers' compensation, auto, general and professional liability, and other products for businesses and institutions. CNA also sells specialty insurance including professional liability for doctors, lawyers, and architects, and vehicle warranty service contracts. The company offers commercial surety bonds, risk and health care claims management, claims administration, and information services. Its products are sold by independent agents and brokers. Holding company Loews owns about 90% of CNA.

The company has pared back its operations to strictly commercial property/casualty, and is focused on strengthening its core operations through both enhanced customer retention efforts and new customer additions. Most of its non-core insurance products are in run-off, including a few remaining life, annuity, and pension products, as well as accident and health insurance.

Like most large insurers, CNA was pinched hard by investment losses and catastrophe losses during industry upheavals in 2008. However, unlike other insurance companies, it has the comfort of being held by a good old-fashioned conglomerate. In late 2008 Loews proactively committed up to $1.25 billion of capital injection to CNA to protect the insurer's base.

HISTORY

When merchant Henry Bowen could not find the type of fire insurance he wanted, he began Continental Insurance. Bowen assembled a group of investors and started with about $500,000 in capital. In 1882 Continental Insurance added marine and tornado insurance. Seven years later Francis Moore became president; he was developer of the Universal Mercantile Schedule, a system of assessing fire hazards in buildings.

About the time Continental Insurance was writing the book on fire insurance, several midwestern investors were having trouble assessing risk in their own insurance field — disability.

In 1897 this group founded Continental Casualty in Hammond, Indiana. In the early years its primary clients were railroads. Continental Casualty eventually merged with other companies in the field and by 1905 had branch offices in nine states and Hawaii and was writing business in 41 states and territories.

Both Continentals added new insurance lines in 1911: Continental Insurance went into personal auto, and Continental Casualty formed subsidiary Continental Assurance to sell life insurance. By 1915 Continental Insurance had four primary companies; spurred by growing prewar patriotism, they were called the America Fore Group. Both Continentals rose to the challenges presented by the World Wars and the Depression; they entered the 1950s ready for new growth.

In the 1960s the companies began to diversify. Continental Insurance added interests in Diners Club and Capital Financial Services; in 1968 it formed holding company Continental Corp. Meanwhile, Continental Assurance (which had formed its own holding company, CNA Financial) went even farther afield, adding mutual fund, consumer finance, nursing home, and residential construction companies.

By the early 1970s CNA was on the ropes because of the recession and setbacks in the housing business. In 1974 Robert and Laurence Tisch bought most of the company and cut costs ruthlessly. Continental had its own problems in the 1970s, including an Iranian joint venture that got caught up in the revolution.

Both companies suffered losses arising from Hurricane Andrew in 1992, but CNA, which did its housecleaning in the 1970s, was better able to deal with the blow than Continental, which entered the 1990s in need of restructuring.

Rising interest rates in 1994 hurt Continental, whose merger with CNA in 1995 made CNA one of the US's top 10 insurance companies. CNA consolidated the two operations, cutting about 5,000 jobs.

CNA bought Western National Warranty in 1995, followed by managed care provider CoreSource the next year. In 1997 the company spun off its surety business in a deal with Capsure Holdings and formed CNA Surety. Taking advantage of outsourcing trends, CNA created CNA UniSource (payroll and human resources services) and bought its payroll servicer, Interlogic Systems, the next year.

CNA pursued a global strategy, buying majority interests in an Argentine workers' compensation carrier and a British marine insurer, but with 1998 sales flat and earnings down the tube, the company did more slashing than accumulating. It cut 2,400 jobs and exited such lines as agriculture and entertainment insurance.

The company exited the personal insurance business to focus on the commercial market: It transferred its personal insurance lines, including its auto and homeowners coverage, to Allstate in 1999. Then, in 2000 CNA sold its life reinsurance operations to a subsidiary of Munich Re.

As part of a restructuring effort (the company reshuffled itself into three major segments: property/casualty, life, and group), CNA fired some 10% of its workforce in 2001. In 2002 CNA paid out more than $450 million in claims related to the attacks on the World Trade Center.

CNA Financial restated its earnings in 2002, after being questioned by the SEC over the accounting treatment of investment losses.

Freeing up some much needed capital, CNA sold its group benefits business to The Hartford

in 2003 for some $530 million. To better focus on its remaining property & casualty lines, the company sold its individual life insurance segment to Swiss Re Life & Health in 2004.

EXECUTIVES

Chairman and CEO: Thomas F. (Tom) Motamed, age 61, $10,431,113 total compensation
EVP, General Counsel, and Secretary:
Jonathan D. (Jon) Kantor, age 54,
$4,493,400 total compensation
EVP and CFO: D. Craig Mense, age 58,
$2,963,653 total compensation
EVP and Chief Actuary: Larry A. Haefner,
$1,556,598 total compensation
EVP and Chief Administration Officer:
Thomas (Tom) Pontarelli, age 60,
$1,941,551 total compensation
EVP Worldwide Property and Casualty Claim:
George R. Fay, age 61
SVP Warranty and Alternative Risks: Brian Loebach
SVP CNA Select Risk: John Angerami
SVP Commercial Segments: David Rutkowski
SVP and CIO: Ray Oral
SVP Business Insurance: Michael W. (Mike) Coyne
SVP Business Process Reengineering:
Robert (Bob) Jirgal
CEO Europe: John Hennessy
President and COO, CNA Specialty: Peter W. Wilson, age 50, $2,600,640 total compensation
President Worldwide Field Operations:
Timothy J. (Tim) Szerlong, age 57
President and COO, Commercial Lines:
Robert A. (Bob) Lindemann, age 56
Auditors: Deloitte & Touche LLP

LOCATIONS

HQ: CNA Financial Corporation
333 S. Wabash, Chicago, IL 60604
Phone: 312-822-5000   **Fax:** 312-822-6419
Web: www.cna.com

PRODUCTS/OPERATIONS

2009 Sales

	$ mil.	% of total
CNA Commercial	4,061	48
CNA Specialty	3,243	38
Life & Group	1,035	12
Corporate & other	136	2
Other	(3)	—
Total	**8,472**	**100**

Selected Subsidiaries

CNA Commercial
  Business insurance
  CNA Select Risk
  Commercial insurance
  International
CNA Specialty
  International
  Professional and management liability
  Surety
  Warranty and alternative risks
Life, Group, and other noncore
  CNA Re
  Health
  Life and annuity

COMPETITORS

AIG	State Farm
American Financial Group	Travelers Companies
Berkshire Hathaway	W. R. Berkley
Chubb Corp	White Mountains
The Hartford	Insurance Group
Liberty Mutual	Zurich Financial Services
Nationwide	

HISTORICAL FINANCIALS

Company Type: Public

Income Statement FYE: December 31

	ASSETS ($ mil.)	NET INCOME ($ mil.)	INCOME AS % OF ASSETS	EMPLOYEES
12/09	55,298	481	0.9%	8,900
12/08	51,688	(299)	—	9,000
12/07	56,732	851	1.5%	9,400
12/06	60,283	1,108	1.8%	9,800
12/05	58,786	264	0.4%	10,100
Annual Growth	**(1.5%)**	**16.2%**	**—**	**(3.1%)**

2009 Year-End Financials

Equity as % of assets: 17.5%
Return on assets: 0.9%
Return on equity: 6.3%
Long-term debt ($ mil.): 2,303
No. of shares (mil.): 269
Dividends
  Yield: 0.0%
  Payout: —
Market value ($ mil.): 6,458
Sales ($ mil.): 8,472

Stock History

NYSE: CNA

	STOCK PRICE ($) FY Close	P/E High/Low		PER SHARE ($) Earnings	Dividends	Book Value
12/09	24.00	24	6	1.10	0.00	39.62
12/08	16.44	—	—	(1.18)	0.45	25.71
12/07	33.72	17	10	3.13	0.35	37.72
12/06	40.32	10	7	4.05	—	36.30
12/05	32.73	46	34	0.76	—	33.26
Annual Growth	**(7.5%)**	**—**	**—**	**9.7%**	**—**	**4.5%**

CNO Financial Group

Have a modest but stable income? Graying at the temples? CNO Financial Group (formerly Conseco) finds that especially attractive, and has life insurance and related products targeted toward you and 4 million other customers. Its primary units include Bankers Life & Casualty, which provides Medicare supplement, life, annuities, and long-term care insurance sold through its own agents; Colonial Penn, which offers life insurance to consumers through direct selling; and Conseco Insurance, which offers specified disease insurance, accident insurance, life insurance, and annuities through its Washington National business and independent agents. CNO Financial Group operates nationwide.

The company also has a handful of smaller life and supplemental health insurance companies operating under the Conseco brand while its 40/86 Advisors subsidiary is a fixed income investment advisor.

The company changed its name in 2010 to reflect a broader brand identity outside of the Conseco name. The firm also sought to distance itself from historical financial instabilities associated with the brand.

In 2008 the company agreed to pay a fine of $6.3 million after an investigation determined that its long-term care insurance business Conseco Senior Health had wrongly denied claims and mishandled complaints. The investigation also determined that some sales and marketing practices at Banker's Life did not comply with industry standards.

Ready to be rid of its closed block of long-term care insurance, in late 2008 the firm spun off that portion of its business into a new company. The new entity was named Senior Health Insurance Company of Pennsylvania and consisted entirely of policies in run-off.

However, CNO Financial Group continued to struggle with accurate internal financial reporting. In 2009 the problems were confirmed by its auditors and the company moved to correct its internal controls. It made progress by the end of the year, and began paying down debt.

To conserve capital and reduce complexity, in 2009 it consolidated three of its insurance units. The then-named Conseco Insurance Company and Conseco Health Insurance Company were merged into the Washington National Insurance subsidiary. During 2010 the company will reshuffle these holdings one more time, move all active business under the Washington National segment, and place any closed blocks of business under the title of "Other CNO Business."

HISTORY

The company evolved from Security National, an Indiana insurance company formed in 1979 by Stephen Hilbert. The former encyclopedia salesman and Aetna executive believed most insurance companies were bloated and the industry itself overcrowded, as well as ripe for consolidation by a smart, lean organization.

In 1982 it began a growth-by-acquisition strategy with the purchase of Executive Income Life Insurance (renamed Security National Life Insurance). The next year it bought Consolidated National Life Insurance and renamed the expanded company Conseco.

The firm went public in 1985, using the proceeds to fund an acquisitions spree that included Lincoln American Life Insurance, Lincoln Income Life (sold 1990), Bankers National Life Insurance, Western National Life Insurance (sold 1994), and National Fidelity Life Insurance.

In 1990 the company formed Conseco Capital Partners (with General Electric and Bankers Trust) to finance acquisitions without seeming to burden the parent company with debt. This device financed the purchase of Great American Reserve and the 1991 acquisition of Beneficial Standard Life. The former Conseco bought Bankers Life Insurance in 1992, then sold 67% of it the next year. Also in 1993 the company formed the Private Capital Group to invest in noninsurance companies.

In 1994 the company tried to acquire the much larger Kemper Corp., but shied away from the debt load that the $2.6 billion deal would have entailed. The aborted deal cost $36 million in bank and accounting fees and spelled the end of the company's relationship with Merrill Lynch, which had underwritten the company's IPO, when a Merrill Lynch analyst downgraded its stock after the fiasco.

Meanwhile, Private Capital's success led the company to form Conseco Global Investments. Other investments included stakes in racetrack and riverboat gambling operations in Indiana.

In 1996 and 1997 the firm absorbed eight life, health, property/casualty, and specialty insurance companies and raised its interest in American Life Holdings to 100%.

Itching to move beyond insurance, in 1998 the company bought Green Tree Financial, the US's #1 mobile home financier. Charges of Green Tree's own fuzzy accounting practices helped torpedo the company's quest for a federal thrift charter. But the troubles had just begun. The mobile home finance industry took a dive as customers refinanced at lower rates and prepayments slammed Green Tree Financial, reducing Conseco's earnings.

The company tried to recoup in 1999 by launching an ad campaign portraying the company as the "Wal-Mart of financial services." It also continued the acquisition spree. But Green Tree Financial (renamed Conseco Finance that year) couldn't stanch the flow of red ink: Buyers grew wary of the quality of the finance unit's loan securities, and changes in accounting methods cost the parent company a $350 million charge against earnings for 1999.

In 2002, due to its financial woes, Gary Wendt stepped down as CEO, the NYSE suspended trading in the company, and its stock was moved to the OTC. The company also filed for Chapter 11 protection in 2002. As part of the reorganization agreement, it agreed to sell Conseco Finance. The company's insurance operations were not subject to the Chapter 11 agreement.

In 2003 it finally unloaded the Conseco Finance unit to CFN Investment Holdings LLC, an investor group, and General Electric Co.'s consumer finance unit for $1 billion. The company emerged from bankruptcy in September 2003.

EXECUTIVES

Chairman: R. Glenn Hilliard, age 67
CEO and Director: C. James (Jim) Prieur, age 59, $3,326,059 total compensation
EVP and CFO: Edward J. (Ed) Bonach, age 56, $1,507,504 total compensation
EVP Technology and Operations: Russell M. (Russ) Bostick, age 53
EVP Government Relations: William (Bill) Fritts
EVP Product Development; President, Other CNO Business: Christopher J. (Chris) Nickele, age 53
EVP and General Counsel: Matthew J. (Matt) Zimpfer, age 42
EVP Human Resources: Susan L. (Sue) Menzel, age 45
EVP Corporate Communications: Anthony B. (Tony) Zehnder, age 60
SVP and Chief Compliance Officer: W. Mark Johnson
SVP and Chief Accounting Officer: John R. Kline, age 52
SVP Financial Planning & Analysis: Thomas D. Barta
SVP Operations and Customer Support: Grace E.M. Cowan, age 50
SVP and Corporate Actuary: Timothy J. (Tim) Tongson
VP Investor Relations: Scott L. Galovic
President, Bankers Life and Casualty: Scott R. Perry, age 47, $1,543,677 total compensation
President, Washington National: Steven M. (Steve) Stecher, age 49, $1,188,942 total compensation
Secretary: Karl W. Kindig
Auditors: PricewaterhouseCoopers LLP

LOCATIONS

HQ: CNO Financial Group, Inc.
11825 N. Pennsylvania St., Carmel, IN 46032
Phone: 317-817-6100   **Fax:** 317-817-2847
Web: www.cnoinc.com

PRODUCTS/OPERATIONS

2009 Premiums Collected

	% of total
Supplemental health	56
Annuities	28
Life	16
Total	**100**

2009 Revenues

	$ mil.	% of total
Insurance policy income	3,093.6	70
Net investment income	1,292.7	30
Realized investment losses	(60.5)	—
Fee revenue & other income	15.6	—
Total	**4,341.4**	**100**

Selected Subsidiaries and Brands

40/86 Advisors, Inc.
Bankers Life
  Bankers Life and Casualty Company
Colonial Penn Life Insurance Company
Conseco Insurance Group
  Conseco Health Insurance Company
  Conseco Life Insurance Company
  Washington National

COMPETITORS

Aetna	Mutual of Omaha
Aflac	Northwestern Mutual
AIG American General	Protective Life
Colonial Life & Accident	Prudential
Lincoln Financial Group	Securian Financial
MassMutual	Torchmark
MetLife	Unum Group
Monumental Life	

HISTORICAL FINANCIALS

Company Type: Public

Income Statement

	ASSETS ($ mil.)	NET INCOME ($ mil.)	INCOME AS % OF ASSETS	EMPLOYEES
12/09	30,344	86	0.3%	3,500
12/08	28,770	(1,127)	—	3,700
12/07	33,515	(194)	—	3,950
12/06	32,717	59	0.2%	4,000
12/05	31,557	325	1.0%	4,000
Annual Growth	**(1.0%)**	**(28.3%)**	**—**	**(3.3%)**

FYE: December 31

2009 Year-End Financials

Equity as % of assets: 11.6%
Return on assets: 0.3%
Return on equity: 3.3%
Long-term debt ($ mil.): 684
No. of shares (mil.): 251
Dividends
  Yield: —
  Payout: —
Market value ($ mil.): 1,255
Sales ($ mil.): 4,341

Stock History

NYSE: CNO

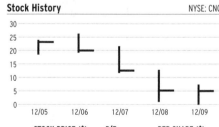

	STOCK PRICE ($) FY Close	P/E High/Low		Earnings	PER SHARE ($) Dividends	Book Value
12/09	5.00	16	1	0.45	—	14.08
12/08	5.18	—	—	(6.10)	—	6.45
12/07	12.56	—	—	(1.12)	—	16.88
12/06	19.98	68	51	0.38	—	18.78
12/05	23.17	13	11	1.76	—	18.01
Annual Growth	**(31.8%)**	**—**	**—**	**(28.9%)**	**—**	**(6.0%)**

Coca-Cola Bottling Co. Consolidated

Southerners like their drinks sweet and for Coca-Cola Bottling Co. Consolidated (CCBCC), there's nothing sweeter than a Coke. CCBCC produces, bottles, and distributes beverages, principally the products of The Coca-Cola Company. Its distribution area is mainly in the southeastern US. The company is the #2 Coke bottler in the US (behind Coca-Cola Enterprises), serving areas in 11 US states — home to about 20 million prospective and hopefully thirsty consumers. Coca-Cola products account for more than 88% of CCBCC's sales. The company does, however, handle other manufacturers' beverages and actually owns some brands, including the flavored and vitamin-enhanced Tum-E Yummies drink and Country Breeze bottled tea.

The company holds the bottling rights from Coca-Cola for the majority of North Carolina, South Carolina, and West Virginia, as well as parts of Alabama, Mississippi, Tennessee, Kentucky, Virginia, Pennsylvania, Georgia, and Florida. CCBCC has boasted that its territories have some of the highest per capita Coca-Cola consumption in the world. The company attributes this success in part to anticipating consumer needs and investing in multi-pack packaging, such as its 15-packs of 20-ounce bottles and 20-packs of 12-ounce cans.

Recognizing the continuing decline in demand for sugar-sweetened carbonated beverages, the company concentrates on adding to its roster of diet, sports-drink, bottled-water, and energy-beverage products, including Coke's FUZE and Energy Brands' vitaminwater, smartwater, and vitaminenergy beverages. It has a 20-year agreement (entered into in 2008) with Hansen Natural Corporation to distribute Hansen's Monster brand energy drinks. It is also the sole licensee of Cinnabon Premium Coffee Lattes and produces and markets Dr Pepper in some of its regions.

Wal-Mart is CCBCC's largest customer, accounting for 15% of its 2009 sales. Chairman and CEO Frank Harrison and his family control approximately 85% of CCBCC's voting stock; combined, The Coca-Cola Company owns some 27% of its common and Class B common stock.

HISTORY

North Carolina entrepreneurs J. B. Harrison, J. Luther Snyder, and J. P. Gibbons started the Greensboro Coca-Cola Bottling Company in 1902. They bottled Coca-Cola by hand, using refillable bottles, and sold it from horse-drawn carriages. With a loyal customer base, the company survived the Great Depression and the sugar rationing of two World Wars.

It went public in 1972 and in 1980 changed its name from Coca-Cola Bottling Company of Mid-Carolina to Coca-Cola Bottling Co. Consolidated (CCBCC).

In the 1980s CCBCC began expanding its territory with a string of acquisitions. In 1993 it formed Piedmont Coca-Cola Bottling Partnership (Piedmont CCBP), a 50-50 joint venture with The Coca-Cola Company to distribute and market soft drinks in the Carolinas. The next year, the bottler struck a 10-year deal to manage South Atlantic Canners, a manufacturing cooperative based in South Carolina. J. Frank Harrison III, great-grandson of a company founder, was named CEO in 1994 and chairman in 1996.

CCBCC bought Coca-Cola Southeast (Alabama) and St. Paul Coca-Cola (Virginia) in 1998. It added Carolina Coca-Cola Bottling Co. (South Carolina) and Lynchberg Coca-Cola Bottling (Virginia) in 1999. Also in 1999 CCBCC revealed that 4% of its stock had been acquired by #1 US Coke bottler Coca-Cola Enterprises (CCE), a company known for its aggressive growth. Harrison stated that CCBCC is not for sale. CCE upped its stake in CCBCC to almost 9% in 2000.

In an effort to streamline its operations, CCBCC in 2000 sold its Ohio and Kentucky sales territories to CCE and initiated a restructuring that included layoffs and a $3 million write-down.

In 2002 CCBCC raised its stake in Piedmont CCBP to nearly 55%; operations of Piedmont were then consolidated with those of CCBCC. The next year it bought 50% of Coca-Cola's remaining ownership of Piedmont, raising its stake to more than 77%.

EXECUTIVES

Chairman and CEO: J. Frank Harrison III, age 55, $5,235,296 total compensation
Vice Chairman: Henry W. Flint, age 55, $1,530,329 total compensation
President, COO, and Director: William B. (Bill) Elmore, age 54, $2,477,429 total compensation
EVP Operations and Systems: Steven D. Westphal, age 55, $1,227,416 total compensation
SVP and CFO: James E. (Jamie) Harris, age 47, $1,024,886 total compensation
SVP Sales: Robert G. Chambless, age 44
SVP and Chief Marketing and Customer Officer: Melvin F. Landis III, age 44
SVP Planning and Administration: Umesh M. Kasbekar, age 52
VP, Controller, and Chief Accounting Officer: William J. Billiard, age 43
VP Corporate Affairs: Lauren C. Steele, age 55
VP and Treasurer: Clifford M. Deal III, age 48
President, ByB Brands: Norman C. George, age 54
Auditors: PricewaterhouseCoopers LLP

LOCATIONS

HQ: Coca-Cola Bottling Co. Consolidated
4100 Coca-Cola Plaza, Charlotte, NC 28211
Phone: 704-557-4400   **Fax:** 704-551-4646
Web: www.cokeconsolidated.com

PRODUCTS/OPERATIONS

2009 Sales

	$ mil.	% of total
Bottles & cans		
Sparkling beverages	1,006	70
Still beverages	207	14
Other	230	16
Total	**1,443**	**100**

Selected Brands

Sparkling beverages
  Barqs Root Beer
  Coca-Cola Zero
  Coke Cherry
  Coke Zero Cherry
  Diet Coke
  Diet Coke Plus
  Diet Coke Splenda
  Diet Dr Pepper (licensed)
  Dr Pepper (licensed)
  Fanta Flavors
  Fresca
  Full Throttle
  Mello Yello
  Monster Energy (licensed)
  NOS
  Pibb Xtra
  Sprite
  Sprite Zero
  Sundrop (licensed)
  Tab
  Vault
Still beverages
  Country Breeze Tea (company-owned)
  Dasani
  Dasani Flavors
  Dasani Plus
  Diet Country Breeze Tea (company-owned)
  FUZE
  Gold Peak tea
  Minute Maid Adult Refreshments
  Minute Maid Juices To Go
  Nestea (licensed)
  POWERade
  POWERade Zero
  smartwater
  Tum-E Yummies (company-owned)
  V8 juice (licensed)
  vitaminenergy
  vitaminwater

COMPETITORS

Aquaterra Corporation
Big Red
Buffalo Rock
Carolina Beverage
Clearly Canadian
Coca-Cola Enterprises
Coke United
Cott
Crystal Rock Holdings
Danone Water
Dr Pepper Snapple Group
DS Waters
Eldorado Artesian Springs
Faygo
Georgia Crown
Hain Celestial
Hawaiian Springs
Honickman Group
Hornell Brewing
Impulse Energy USA
IZZE
Jones Soda
Monarch Beverage (GA)
Mountain Valley
Naked Juice
National Beverage
Nestlé Waters
Odwalla
Pepsi Americas Beverages
Pepsi Bottling of Knoxville
Pepsi Bottling Ventures
Polar Beverages
Red Bull
Reed's
Sunny Delight
Suntory Holdings
Sweet Leaf Tea
Welch's
Wet Planet Beverages
XELR8

HISTORICAL FINANCIALS

Company Type: Public

Income Statement

FYE: Sunday nearest December 31

	REVENUE ($ mil.)	NET INCOME ($ mil.)	NET PROFIT MARGIN	EMPLOYEES
12/09	1,443	38	2.6%	6,000
12/08	1,464	9	0.6%	6,200
12/07	1,436	20	1.4%	5,800
12/06	1,431	23	1.6%	5,700
12/05	1,380	23	1.7%	6,200
Annual Growth	1.1%	13.4%	—	(0.8%)

2009 Year-End Financials

Debt ratio: 513.5%
Return on equity: 39.6%
Cash ($ mil.): 18
Current ratio: 1.42
Long-term debt ($ mil.): 597

No. of shares (mil.): 9
Dividends
 Yield: 1.9%
 Payout: 29.8%
Market value ($ mil.): 496

Stock History

NASDAQ (GM): COKE

	STOCK PRICE ($) FY Close	P/E High/Low	PER SHARE ($) Earnings	Dividends	Book Value
12/09	54.01	17 11	3.36	1.00	12.66
12/08	45.96	63 32	0.99	1.00	8.31
12/07	58.88	31 23	2.17	1.00	13.12
12/06	68.43	27 17	2.55	1.00	10.23
12/05	43.00	23 17	2.53	1.00	8.18
Annual Growth	5.9%	— —	7.4%	0.0%	11.5%

The Coca-Cola Company

Coke *is* it — *it* being the world's #1 soft-drink company. The Coca-Cola Company (TCCC) owns four of the top five soft-drink brands (Coca-Cola, Diet Coke, Fanta, and Sprite). Its other brands include Minute Maid, Powerade, and Dasani water. In North America it sells Groupe Danone's Evian; it also sells brands from Dr Pepper Snapple Group (Crush, Dr Pepper, and Schweppes) outside Australia, Europe, and North America. The firm makes or licenses more than 3,000 drinks under 500 brand names in some 200 nations. Although it does no bottling itself, Coke owns 34% of the world's #1 Coke bottler Coca-Cola Enterprises (CCE), as well as 32% of Mexico's bottler Coca-Cola FEMSA, and 23% of European bottler Coca-Cola Hellenic Bottling.

In what it called a "substantially cashless transaction," TCCC announced in 2010 that it will acquire CCE's North American business, which includes 75% of the US product volume and almost 100% of Canadian product volume. When the deal becomes final, TCCC will have direct control over approximately 90% of the total North America volume of its popular beverages.

As a result of these agreements, a new company, which will retain the name Coca-Cola Enterprises Inc., will be created. It will remain headquartered in Atlanta and will continue to be traded on the NYSE; in addition, its management team will remain in place.

In a bid to partner with the another top-five soda supplier, TCCC in June 2010 announced that it has inked a 20-year deal with Dr Pepper Snapple Group valued at about $715 million. As part of the agreement, Coca-Cola will distribute the Dr Pepper brand in the US and Canada Dry in the Northeast. Also, the deal reaches to Canada, where TCCC plans to distribute Canada Dry, C'Plus, and Schweppes.

The company's plans to expand its juice operations in China hit a snag in 2009. It was forced to abandon its $2.5 billion offer to buy the Chinese juice company Huiyuan Juice Group after the Chinese government declined to approve the deal on the grounds that it would squeeze out local competition. Coke said that it would, instead, approach expansion in the Chinese market by growing its existing brands and introducing new products.

Neville Isdell, who came out of retirement in 2004 to help turn the company around, retired as chairman and CEO in 2008. Muhtar Kent, former company president and COO, succeeded Isdell as CEO and retained the title of president. Kent — who was born in New York City, holds dual US and Turkish citizenship, and is known as a skilled tactician — led Coke's 2007 acquisition of Energy Brands, the largest acquisition in company history.

Warren Buffett's Berkshire Hathaway owns 9% of Coca-Cola.

HISTORY

Atlanta pharmacist John Pemberton invented Coke in 1886. His bookkeeper, Frank Robinson, came up with the name based on two ingredients, coca leaves (later cleaned of narcotics) and kola nuts. By 1891 druggist Asa Candler had bought The Coca-Cola Company, and within four years the soda-fountain drink was available in all states; it was in Canada and Mexico by 1898.

Candler sold most US bottling rights in 1899 to Benjamin Thomas and John Whitehead of Chattanooga, Tennessee, for $1. The two designed a regional franchise bottling system that created more than 1,000 bottlers within 20 years. In 1916 Candler retired to become Atlanta's mayor; his family sold the company to Atlanta banker Ernest Woodruff for $25 million in 1919. Coca-Cola went public that year.

The firm expanded overseas and introduced the slogans "The Pause that Refreshes" (1929) and "It's the Real Thing" (1941). To keep WWII soldiers in Cokes at a nickel a pop, the government built 64 overseas bottling plants. Coca-Cola bought Minute Maid in 1960 and began launching new drinks — Fanta (1960), Sprite (1960), TAB (1963), and Diet Coke (1982).

In 1981 Roberto Goizueta became chairman. Four years later, with Coke slipping in market share, the firm changed its formula and introduced New Coke, which consumers soundly rejected (thus, Coca-Cola Classic was born). In 1986 it consolidated the US bottling operations it owned into Coca-Cola Enterprises and sold 51% of the new company to the public. Goizueta also engineered the purchase of Columbia Pictures in 1982. (Columbia earned Coke a $1 billion profit when it sold the studio to Sony in 1989.)

Goizueta died of lung cancer in 1997; while he was at the helm, the firm's value rose from $4 billion to $145 billion. Douglas Ivester, the architect of Coca-Cola's restructured bottling operations, succeeded him. Ivester resigned in 2000; president and COO Douglas Daft was named chairman and CEO. Coca-Cola began its largest cutbacks ever, slashing nearly 5,000 jobs, and later agreed to pay nearly $193 million to settle a race-discrimination suit filed by African-American workers.

Coca-Cola acquired Mad River Traders (teas, juices, sodas) and Odwalla (juices and smoothies) in 2001. As part of the restructuring initiated by Daft in 2000, another 1,000 employees (half in Atlanta) were laid off in 2003. The company laid off 2,800 employees worldwide in 2003.

Daft retired as Coca-Cola's chairman and CEO in 2004 and former Coca-Cola HBC CEO E. Neville Isdell replaced him. In 2005 Coke bought Danone's 49% stake in their North American bottled-water venture.

Bowing to the public's growing concern about childhood obesity, in 2006 Coke, along with Pepsi, Cadbury Schweppes (whose beverage operations later became Dr Pepper Snapple Group), and the American Beverage Association, agreed to sell only water, unsweetened juice, and low-fat milks to public elementary and middle schools in the US.

In 2006 Coke also joined with Coca-Cola FEMSA to buy top Brazilian juice maker, Jugos del Valle, for $440 million. Still concentrating on Brazil, the next year Coke bought Brazil's bottled tea and beverage maker, Leao Junior. The purchase added more than 60 new products to Coke's Brazilian portfolio.

The purchase of the maker of smartwater and vitaminwater, Energy Brands (also known as Glacéau), saw Coke forking over some $4 billion in cash in 2007. Another addition to its non-cola offerings took place in 2007, when the company acquired Fuze Beverage, an alternative juice and tea producer, for about $250 million. Coke also purchased the San Miguel Corporation's 63% share of Coca-Cola Bottlers Philippines for $590 million.

EXECUTIVES

Chairman and CEO: Muhtar Kent, age 57, $18,813,012 total compensation
COO: T. Krishnakumar
EVP and CFO: Gary P. Fayard, age 57, $5,755,536 total compensation
EVP and Chief Marketing and Commercial Officer: Joseph V. (Joe) Tripodi, age 54
EVP; President, Bottling Investments and Supply Chain: Irial Finan, age 52, $5,424,563 total compensation
EVP and Chief Administrative Officer: Alexander B. (Alex) Cummings Jr., age 53, $4,772,663 total compensation
EVP Business Transformation: Melody Justice
Chief Human Resources Officer: Carolyn Jackson
SVP Global Accounts Management: Bonnie P. Wurzbacher
SVP and Chief Customer and Commercial Officer: Jerry S. Wilson, age 55
SVP Integrated Marketing Communications and Capabilities: Wendy Clark
SVP and Chief People Officer: Ceree Eberly
SVP and General Counsel: Geoffrey J. (Geoff) Kelly, age 65
SVP and Treasurer: David M. Taggart
VP and Chief of Internal Audit: Connie D. McDaniel
VP and Director Investor Relations: Jackson Kelly
VP and Chief Scientific and Regulatory Officer: Rhona Applebaum
VP and CIO: Edmund R. (Ed) Steinike, age 51

President, Latin America Group: José Octavio Reyes, age 58, $6,617,527 total compensation
President, North America Group:
  J. Alexander M. (Sandy) Douglas Jr., age 48
President, Europe Group: Dominique Reiniche, age 54
President, Middle East Business Unit: Alexis Sacre, age 59
Chief Executive, Beverage Partners Worldwide:
  Beatrice Guillaume-Grabisch, age 45
Auditors: Ernst & Young LLP

LOCATIONS

HQ: The Coca-Cola Company
  1 Coca-Cola Plaza, Atlanta, GA 30313
Phone: 404-676-2121
Web: www.thecoca-colacompany.com

2009 Sales

	$ mil.	% of total
International	22,979	74
US	8,011	26
Total	30,990	100

PRODUCTS/OPERATIONS

2009 Sales

	% of total
Beverage concentrates, fountain syrups & finished products	74
Bottling investments	26
Total	100

Selected Brands

Aquarius
Bacardi (mixers and concentrate, licensed)
Barq's
Caffeine free Coca-Cola
Caffeine free Diet Coke
Canada Dry (licensed)
Cappy
Cherry Coke
Coca-Cola
Coca-Cola Light
Coca-Cola Zero
Coke Zero
Crush
Dasani
del Valle
Diet Cherry Coke
Diet Coke
Diet Coke with Lime
Diet Sprite/Sprite Zero/Sprite Light
Dr Pepper (licensed)
Eight O'Clock
Emerald Mountain Blend
Evian (licensed)
Fanta
Five Alive
Frestea (Beverage Partners Worldwide, joint venture with Nestlé SA)
Full Throttle
Fuze
Gold Peak
glacéau smartwater
glacéau vitaminwater
Gladiator
Hi-C
Java Monster (distribution in 21 US states, Canada, and six EU countries)
Lift
Lost Energy (distribution in 21 US states, Canada, and six EU countries)
Mello Yello
Minute Maid
Monster Energy (distribution in 21 US states, Canada, and six EU countries)
Mother
Nestea (Beverage Partners Worldwide, joint venture with Nestlé SA)
Odwalla
Pibb Xtra
Powerade

Rock Star
Schweppes (licensed)
Seagram's (mixers and sparkling beverages, licensed)
Simply Orange
Sprite
Tab
Thums Up

COMPETITORS

Alamance Foods
American Beverage
Aquaterra Corporation
Britvic
Chiquita Brands
Clearly Canadian
Clement Pappas
Cliffstar
Cott
Cranberries Limited
Danone
Danone Water
Del Monte Foods
Del Monte Pacific
Dole Food
Dr Pepper Snapple Group
Faygo
Fiji Water
Florida's Natural
Fresh Del Monte Produce
Freshco
Gatorade
Goya
Great Western Juice
Hansen Natural
Hawaiian Springs
Hornell Brewing
Impulse Energy USA
IZZE
Jamba
Jones Soda
Kirin Holdings Company
Kraft Foods
Leading Brands
Monarch Beverage (GA)
Mountain Valley
Naked Juice
National Beverage
National Grape Cooperative
Naumes
Nestlé
Nestlé Waters
Ocean Spray
Old Orchard
PepsiCo
Pernod Ricard
Red Bull
Silver Springs
South Beach Beverage
Southern Gardens Citrus
Sunny Delight
Sun-Rype
Suntory Holdings
Tree Top
Tropicana
Unilever
Welch's
Wet Planet Beverages
XELR8

HISTORICAL FINANCIALS

Company Type: Public

Income Statement

FYE: December 31

	REVENUE ($ mil.)	NET INCOME ($ mil.)	NET PROFIT MARGIN	EMPLOYEES
12/09	30,990	6,824	22.0%	92,800
12/08	31,944	5,807	18.2%	92,400
12/07	28,857	5,981	20.7%	90,500
12/06	24,088	5,080	21.1%	71,000
12/05	23,104	4,872	21.1%	55,000
Annual Growth	7.6%	8.8%	—	14.0%

2009 Year-End Financials

Debt ratio: 20.4%
Return on equity: 30.1%
Cash ($ mil.): 7,021
Current ratio: 1.28
Long-term debt ($ mil.): 5,059
No. of shares (mil.): 2,309
Dividends
  Yield: 2.9%
  Payout: 56.0%
Market value ($ mil.): 131,639

Stock History

NYSE: KO

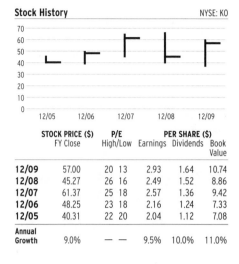

	STOCK PRICE ($) FY Close	P/E High/Low	Earnings	PER SHARE ($) Dividends	Book Value
12/09	57.00	20 13	2.93	1.64	10.74
12/08	45.27	26 16	2.49	1.52	8.86
12/07	61.37	25 18	2.57	1.36	9.42
12/06	48.25	23 18	2.16	1.24	7.33
12/05	40.31	22 20	2.04	1.12	7.08
Annual Growth	9.0%	— —	9.5%	10.0%	11.0%

Coca-Cola Enterprises

The scientists and the suits at The Coca-Cola Company (TCCC) concoct the secret syrup recipe and market the powerhouse brands, but Coca-Cola Enterprises (CCE) does much of the bottling and distribution of Coke's products. The world's #1 Coke bottler, CCE brings in 16% of worldwide sales of Coca-Cola beverages. CCE also bottles and distributes other beverages, including Canada Dry and Dr Pepper (both brands owned by Dr Pepper Snapple Group), Nestea (Nestlé), bottled waters, and juice. It sells soft drinks in 46 US states; Washington, DC; the US Virgin Islands; Canada; and six European countries. The company's territories consist of more than 420 million potential customers. The Coca-Cola Company owns 34% of CCE.

In 2010, in what it called a "substantially cash-less transaction," TCCC announced it will acquire CCE's North American business, which is made up of 75% of the US product volume and almost 100% of Canadian product volume. When the deal is final, TCCC will have direct control over approximately 90% of the total North America volume of its popular beverages. In addition, TCCC and CCE have agreed that CCE will buy TCCC's bottling operations in Norway and Sweden for $822 million and that CCE will have the right to acquire TCCC's 83% holding in its German bottling operations in the future.

As a result of these agreements, a new company, which will retain the name Coca-Cola Enterprises Inc., will be created. It will remain headquartered in Atlanta and will continue to be traded on the NYSE; in addition its management team will remain in place. The deals will strengthen TCCC's North American operations and expand CCE's business in Western Europe.

HISTORY

Coca-Cola Enterprises (CCE) was formed in 1986 when The Coca-Cola Company bought its two largest bottlers — JTL Corp. and BCI Holdings — and formed a single corporation. The company went public immediately, though Coca-Cola retained a significant interest in it.

CCE set about acquiring smaller bottling concerns across the US and by 1988 the company had become the #1 bottler in the world. The company centralized operations to boost its slim profit margin.

In 1991 CCE merged with the Johnston Coca-Cola Bottling Group, the #2 US Coca-Cola bottler. The acquisition cost the ailing CCE $125 million, and led a number of disaffected investors to protest. Johnston executives took control when Summerfield Johnston Jr. (whose grandfather had co-founded the first Coke bottling franchisee) assumed the post of CEO, and Henry Schimberg, a former RC Cola route salesman, became president and COO.

In 1992 the bottler was reorganized into 10 US operating regions to allow for better control of individual market dynamics. A $1.5 billion public debt offering occurred that year, and the following year the company began looking outward for growth, acquiring Nederland B.V. (the Coca-Cola bottler of the Netherlands) as well as two Tennessee bottlers. In 1994 CCE recorded its first profitable year since 1990.

CCE bought the 51% stake it didn't already own in Coca-Cola & Schweppes Beverages UK from Cadbury Schweppes for $2 billion in 1997, and it also purchased Coca-Cola's shares in Coca-Cola Beverages Ltd. (Canada's leading bottler) and The Coca-Cola Bottling Company of New York. A half-dozen deals in 1998 included the $1.1 billion purchase of Coke Southwest and other bottling acquisitions in the US and Luxembourg. Schimberg became CEO that year.

Also in 1998 the bottler expanded its vending-machine business, and many distributors and vending-machine owners (who use CCE as a supplier) complained that the firm was charging lower prices in its own machines than independent owners could for the same products.

Bad news came in 1999 when products bottled by CCE in Antwerp, Belgium, and Dunkirk, France, were contaminated by bad carbon dioxide and paint used on wooden pallets to prevent mold. Coca-Cola products were banned or recalled in Belgium, France, and a handful of other European countries for about two weeks, costing the company more than $100 million. Schimberg retired in 1999 and Johnston became CEO again.

In 1999 CCE acquired seven bottlers in the US and one in Europe. European Commission regulators raided various CCE offices in 1999 and 2000 as part of an investigation into anticompetitive marketing programs. In 2001 Johnston stepped down as CEO, but remained chairman. Vice chairman Lowry Kline was named CEO. That same year, the company bought bottlers Hondo and Herbco Enterprises (collectively known as Herb Coca-Cola, the #3 Coke bottler in the US) for about $1.4 billion. The company also announced plans to lay off 2,000 employees as a result of stagnant sales in North America. In 2002 Kline replaced Johnston as chairman.

Having held the position for just one year, president and CEO John Alm left the company in early 2006. Chairman (and former company CEO) Lowery Kline took over temporary leadership until John Brock was appointed president and CEO later in the year. (Brock was formerly CEO of InBev.) Kline continued as chairman.

The company was named (along with the Coca-Cola Company) in a suit brought by independent bottlers in 2006, seeking to bar the two companies from abandoning the tradition in which independent companies that put Coke beverages in bottles and cans also deliver the products to and stack them on the shelves of grocery stores. CCE reached a conditional settlement with Ozarks Coca-Cola and Dr. Pepper Bottling Company.

In addition, a group of shareholders filed a class-action suit against CCE, claiming that the company's practice of channel-stuffing (forcing extra product onto customers in order to boost revenue) affected CCE's financial condition.

The same day that The Coca-Cola Company announced the building of a $45 million plastic recycling plant in 2007, Coca-Cola Enterprises announced the formation of Coca-Cola Recycling. Based at CCE's Atlanta's corporate base, Coca-Cola Recycling will focus on recovering and recycling Coke packaging materials used in North America.

Boosting its tea offerings, Coca-Cola Enterprises struck an agreement to begin distributing new flavors of AriZona Iced Tea in 2007. That year it also began distributing Campbell fruit and vegetable juice beverages in the US and Canada under an agreement with TCCC.

EXECUTIVES

Chairman and CEO: John F. Brock, age 61, $15,551,862 total compensation
EVP and CFO: William W. (Bill) Douglas III, age 49, $3,834,748 total compensation
EVP; President, European Group: Hubert Patricot, age 50, $3,539,308 total compensation
EVP and President, North American Group: Steven A. Cahillane, age 45, $4,840,748 total compensation
SVP and General Counsel: John R. Parker Jr., age 58, $3,099,913 total compensation
SVP Human Resources: Pamela O. (Pam) Kimmet, age 51
SVP and CIO: Esat Sezer, age 48
VP, Controller, and Chief Accounting Officer: Suzanne D. Patterson, age 48
VP Finance Global Initiatives: Joseph D. Heinrich, age 54
VP Internal Audit: Keith Allen
VP Process Optimization and SAP Implementation: Bernard Bommier
VP and Treasurer: Joyce King-Lavinder
VP, Secretary, and Deputy General Counsel: William T. Plybon
Investor Relations: Thor Erickson
Auditors: Ernst & Young LLP

LOCATIONS

HQ: Coca-Cola Enterprises Inc.
2500 Windy Ridge Pkwy., Atlanta, GA 30339
Phone: 770-989-3000 **Fax:** 770-989-3790
Web: www.cokecce.com

2009 Sales

	$ mil.	% of total
North America	15,128	70
Europe	6,517	30
Total	**21,645**	**100**

PRODUCTS/OPERATIONS

2009 Sales

	% of total
Coca-Cola products	55
Sparkling flavors & energy products	24
Juices, isotonics & sport drinks	14
Other	7
Total	**100**

Selected Company Brands

North America
Coca-Cola Classic
Dasani
Diet Coke
POWERade
Sprite
smartwater
vitaminenergy
vitaminwater
Europe
Capri-Sun
Coca-Cola
Coca-Cola Light
Coca-Cola Zero
Diet Coke
Fanta

Selected Other Brands

North America
A&W
Ale 8 One
AriZona Tea
Big Red
Canada Dry
C'Plus
Dannon water
Dannon water with Flouride
Diet Ale 8 One
Diet Big Red
Diet Canada Dry
Diet Dr Pepper
Diet Eas Piranha
Diet Squirt
Dr Pepper
Eas Piranha
Mendota
Monster Energy
Nestea
Nestea Cool
Orangina
Pentric Akers
Rockstar
Schweppes
Spirit
Squirt
Vermont Pure
Yoohoo
Europe
Appletiser
Cadbury Schweppes
Capri-Sun
Evian
Fernandes
Monster Energy
Rosport
Viva

HISTORICAL FINANCIALS

Company Type: Public

Income Statement

FYE: December 31

	REVENUE ($ mil.)	NET INCOME ($ mil.)	NET PROFIT MARGIN	EMPLOYEES
12/09	21,645	731	3.4%	70,000
12/08	21,807	(4,394)	—	72,000
12/07	20,936	711	3.4%	73,000
12/06	19,804	(1,143)	—	74,000
12/05	18,706	514	2.7%	73,000
Annual Growth	3.7%	9.2%	—	(1.0%)

2009 Year-End Financials

Debt ratio: 918.6%
Return on equity: 176.6%
Cash ($ mil.): 1,036
Current ratio: 1.13
Long-term debt ($ mil.): 7,891

No. of shares (mil.): 503
Dividends
Yield: 1.4%
Payout: 20.3%
Market value ($ mil.): 10,655

Stock History

NYSE: CCE

	STOCK PRICE ($) FY Close	P/E High/Low		PER SHARE ($) Earnings	Dividends	Book Value
12/09	21.20	15	7	1.48	0.30	1.71
12/08	12.03	—	—	(9.05)	0.28	(0.06)
12/07	26.03	19	14	1.46	0.24	11.32
12/06	20.42	—	—	(2.41)	0.24	9.01
12/05	19.17	22	17	1.08	0.16	11.23
Annual Growth	2.5%	—	—	8.2%	17.0%	(37.5%)

Colgate-Palmolive

Colgate-Palmolive takes a bite out of grime. The company is a top global maker and marketer of toothpaste and other soap and cleaning products. Many of its oral care products fall under the Colgate brand and include toothbrushes, mouthwash, and dental floss. Its Tom's of Maine unit covers the natural toothpaste niche. Personal and home care items include Ajax brand household cleaner, Palmolive dishwashing liquid, Softsoap shower gel, and Speed Stick deodorant. Colgate-Palmolive also offers pet nutrition products through subsidiary Hill's Pet Nutrition, which makes Science Diet and Prescription Diet pet foods. The company boasts operations in 70-plus countries and sells its products in more than 200 countries. About 80% of Colgate-Palmolive's net sales come from markets outside of the US, with Latin America leading the way.

Its oral care business segment holds a growing share of the global toothpaste market and the manual toothbrush market worldwide. However, those core products face stiff competition from large multinational rivals, such as Procter & Gamble, which boasts a similar product portfolio, including brands Braun, Olay, Secret, Mr. Clean, and pet products under the Eukanuba and Iams names. Colgate-Palmolive additionally competes with discount and private-label brands sold at leading retail chains.

Although the company's growth in part depends on brand recognition and the continued success of its existing products, it is becoming increasingly aware of the necessity to develop and launch new products and line extensions. In recent years Colgate-Palmolive has been polishing up its portfolio by extending well-known brands into newer product areas, such as Colgate Simply White teeth whiteners, Motion battery-powered toothbrushes, and Palmolive aromatherapy dishwashing liquids.

The completion of a major four-year restructuring at the end of 2008 is allowing the company to support such new product development and also look toward a more streamlined future.

HISTORY

William Colgate founded The Colgate Company in Manhattan in 1806 to produce soap, candles, and starch. Colgate died in 1857, and the company was passed to his son Samuel, who renamed it Colgate and Company. In 1873 the company introduced toothpaste in jars, and in 1896 it began selling Colgate Dental Cream in tubes. By 1906 Colgate was making 160 kinds of soap, 625 perfumes, and 2,000 other products. The company went public in 1908.

In 1898 Milwaukee's B. J. Johnson Soap Company (founded 1864) introduced Palmolive, a soap made of palm and olive oils rather than smelly animal fats. It became so popular that the firm changed its name to The Palmolive Company in 1916. Ten years later Palmolive merged with Peet Brothers, a Kansas City-based soap maker founded in 1872. Palmolive-Peet merged with Colgate in 1928, forming Colgate-Palmolive-Peet (shortened to Colgate-Palmolive in 1953). The stock market crash of 1929 prevented a planned merger of the company with Hershey and Kraft.

During the 1930s the firm purchased French and German soap makers and opened branches in

Europe. Colgate-Palmolive-Peet introduced Fab detergent and Ajax cleanser in 1947; the brands soon became top sellers in Europe. The company expanded to Asia in the 1950s, and by 1961 foreign sales were 52% of the total.

Colgate-Palmolive introduced a host of products in the 1960s and 1970s, including Palmolive dishwashing liquid (1966), Ultra Brite toothpaste (1968), and Irish Spring soap (1972). During the same time, the company diversified by buying approximately 70 other businesses, including Kendall hospital and industrial supplies (1972), Helena Rubinstein cosmetics (1973), Ram Golf (1974), and Riviana Foods and Hill's Pet Products (1976). The strategy had mixed results, and most of these acquisitions were sold in the 1980s.

Reuben Mark became CEO of Colgate-Palmolive in 1984. The company bought 50% of Southeast Asia's leading toothpaste, Darkie, in 1985; it changed its name to Darlie in 1989 following protests of its minstrel-in-blackface trademark. Both Palmolive automatic dishwasher detergent and Colgate Tartar Control toothpaste were introduced in 1986. That year Colgate-Palmolive purchased the liquid soap lines of Minnetonka, the most popular of which is Softsoap. In 1992 the company bought Mennen, maker of Speed Stick (the leading US deodorant).

Increasing its share of the oral care market in Latin America to 79% in 1995, Colgate-Palmolive acquired Brazilian company Kolynos (from Wyeth for $1 billion) and 94% of Argentina's Odol Saic. The company also bought Ciba-Geigy's oral hygiene business in India, increasing its share of that toothpaste market. At home, however, sales and earnings in key segments were dismal, so in 1995 Colgate-Palmolive began a restructuring that included cutting more than 8% of its employees and closing or reconfiguring 24 factories in two years.

The company introduced a record 602 products in 1996 and continued to expand its operations in countries with emerging economies. In 1997 Colgate-Palmolive took the lead in the US toothpaste market for the first time in 35 years (displacing P&G).

In 1999 the company sold the rights to Baby Magic (shampoos, lotions, oils) in the US, Canada, and Puerto Rico to Playtex Products, retaining the rights in all other countries. Two years later the company sold its heavy-duty laundry detergent business in Mexico (primarily the Viva brand) to Henkel, one of Europe's leading detergent producers.

In 2002 Colgate-Palmolive introduced a teeth-whitening gel, Simply White, to compete with rival P&G's Crest Whitestrips. The company saw success that year when its Hill's Pet Nutrition subsidiary launched new specialty foods for cats and dogs; one of its dog foods reportedly slows brain aging in canines.

By selling its North American laundry detergent brands in 2005, Colgate-Palmolive began focusing on the high-margin pearly whites (with bite) of its portfolio — oral care and pet care. The company's purchase of natural oral-care products maker Tom's of Maine in 2006 marked its effort to target the natural niche.

Chairman and CEO Reuben Mark handed over the title of CEO to then-president and COO Ian Cook in July 2007 and the title of chairman to Cook in January 2009 as Mark retired at the end of 2008.

Colgate-Palmolive in early 2010 sold its Code 10 Malaysian hair-styling brand to Indian consumer goods maker Marico.

EXECUTIVES

Chairman, President, and CEO: Ian M. Cook, age 57,
$17,160,398 total compensation
Vice Chairman: Michael J. Tangney, age 65,
$6,341,723 total compensation
**COO Europe, Global Marketing, Customer
Development, Supply Chain and Technology:**
Fabian T. Garcia, age 50, $4,708,231 total compensation
COO Emerging Markets: Franck J. Moison, age 56,
$5,058,159 total compensation
CFO: Stephen C. Patrick, age 60,
$7,171,772 total compensation
VP and CIO: Tom Greene
VP and Chief Ethics and Compliance Officer:
Gregory P. (Greg) Woodson, age 58
SVP Global Human Resources: Daniel B. Marsili, age 49
SVP, General Counsel, and Secretary:
Andrew D. Hendry, age 62,
$4,165,930 total compensation
VP Global Research and Development:
Mary Beth Robles
VP Global Technology: Robert (Bob) Russo
VP and Controller: Dennis J. Hickey, age 61
VP Treasury: Hans L. Pohlschroeder
VP Office of the Chairman: John J. Huston, age 55
VP Investor Relations: Bina H. Thompson, age 60
VP Corporate Communications: Jan Guifarro
CEO Tom's of Maine: Tom O'Brien
President, Global Oral Care: Nigel B. Burton
President and CEO, Hill's Pet Nutrition:
Neil Thompson
**President, Colgate-North America and Global
Sustainability:** Noel R. Wallace
President, Global Customer Development: Antonio Caro
Auditors: PricewaterhouseCoopers LLP

LOCATIONS

HQ: Colgate-Palmolive Company
300 Park Ave., New York, NY 10022
Phone: 212-310-2000   **Fax:** 212-310-2475
Web: www.colgate.com

2009 Sales

	$ mil.	% of total
Oral, personal & home care		
Latin America	4,319	28
Europe/South Pacific	3,271	22
North America	2,950	19
Greater Asia/Africa	2,655	17
Pet nutrition	2,132	14
Total	**15,327**	**100**

PRODUCTS/OPERATIONS

2009 Sales

	$ mil.	% of total
Oral, personal & home care	13,195	86
Pet nutrition	2,132	14
Total	**15,327**	**100**

Selected Brands and Products

Home Care
   Ajax (dishwashing liquid and household cleaner)
   Fabuloso (household cleaner)
   Murphy (oil soap)
   Palmolive (dishwashing liquid)
   Suavitel (fabric softener)

Oral Care
   Colgate (oral rinse, toothbrush, toothpaste, and tooth
   whitener)

Personal Care
   Afta (aftershave)
   Irish Spring (body wash and bar soap)
   Skin Bracer (aftershave)
   Softsoap (body wash and liquid hand soap)
   Speed Stick (deodorant)

Pet Nutrition (for cats and dogs)
   Prescription Diet
   Science Diet

COMPETITORS

Alberto-Culver	L'Oréal USA
Amden	Mars Petcare
Avon	Nestlé
Church & Dwight	Nu Skin
Clorox	Philips Oral
Dr. Fresh	Procter & Gamble
GlaxoSmithKline	Reckitt Benckiser
Hain Celestial	S.C. Johnson
Henkel	Sun Products
Johnson & Johnson	Unilever
Kiss My Face	

HISTORICAL FINANCIALS

Company Type: Public

Income Statement

FYE: December 31

	REVENUE ($ mil.)	NET INCOME ($ mil.)	NET PROFIT MARGIN	EMPLOYEES
12/09	15,327	2,291	14.9%	38,100
12/08	15,330	1,957	12.8%	36,600
12/07	13,790	1,737	12.6%	36,000
12/06	12,238	1,353	11.1%	34,700
12/05	11,397	1,351	11.9%	35,800
Annual Growth	**7.7%**	**14.1%**	**—**	**1.6%**

2009 Year-End Financials

Debt ratio: 95.7%
Return on equity: 97.7%
Cash ($ mil.): 600
Current ratio: 1.06
Long-term debt ($ mil.): 2,821

No. of shares (mil.): 486
Dividends
   Yield: 2.1%
   Payout: 39.4%
Market value ($ mil.): 39,925

Stock History

NYSE: CL

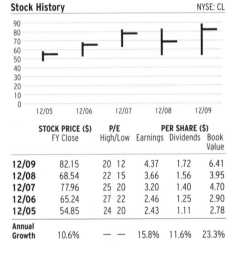

	STOCK PRICE ($) FY Close	P/E High/Low		PER SHARE ($) Earnings	Dividends	Book Value
12/09	82.15	20	12	4.37	1.72	6.41
12/08	68.54	22	15	3.66	1.56	3.95
12/07	77.96	25	20	3.20	1.40	4.70
12/06	65.24	27	22	2.46	1.25	2.90
12/05	54.85	24	20	2.43	1.11	2.78
Annual Growth	**10.6%**	**—**	**—**	**15.8%**	**11.6%**	**23.3%**

Collective Brands

Collective Brands is banking on its collective efforts in shoe making and retailing. The holding company boasts a portfolio of premium and moderate footwear and accessories through its Performance + Lifestyle Group (PLG), a wide reach of more than 4,400 Payless ShoeSource outlets in about 20 countries, and an established licensing and brand management unit in Collective Licensing. Collective Brands was formed in 2007, when powerhouse Payless ShoeSource acquired Stride Rite, which is primarily a wholesaler to department stores and operates leased departments at Macy's stores. With brands such as Keds and Saucony, the company operates in the US, Canada, the Caribbean, Central and South America, and Puerto Rico.

The deal to pair Payless ShoeSource with Stride Rite in Collective Brands' closet was valued at $800 million plus an estimated $100 million in debt. A joined Payless ShoeSource, Stride Rite (now under PLG umbrella), and Collective Licensing provides numerous competitive advantages for Collective Brands. These include the ability to target a variety of customers at a broader price-point range through multiple channels, such as wholesale, retail, licensing, and e-commerce. Not only did the deal make Collective Brands a top shoe seller worldwide, but it also gave the firm a foothold at the premium and moderate levels of children's shoes. In September 2009 Collective Brands announced that going forward its Stride Rite unit — which operates about 360 shoe stores — would do business under the name Collective Brands Performance + Lifestyle Group. The name change is designed to reflect the broad range of the company's brands, which include Sperry Top-Sider, Saucony, Keds, and the Stride Rite Children's Group.

Since its formation in 2007, Collective Brands has seen same-store sales at its shoe stores, average selling prices, and shoes sold per store decline. The company has closed more than 150 Payless outlets in the US since early 2008, while adding stores abroad.

Payless' 3,825 US stores account for about two-thirds of Collective Brands' sales. On the international front, in 2009 the company announced plans to expand in Russia through a franchising agreement with M.H. Alshaya. The first Payless stores in Russia and the Philippines are slated to debut in 2010. Alshaya is also Payless' franchise partner in the Middle East, where the shoe seller already operates stores in the UAE, Saudi Arabia, and Kuwait. Other countries in the region, including Bahrain, Egypt, and Lebanon, are on the list for expansion.

Denver-based Collective Licensing International (CLI), acquired in March 2007 for about $91 million, is a youth-oriented brand development, management, and licensing lifestyle business. CLI is planning to expand in 2010 through its January agreement to purchase the Above The Rim (ATR) brand from Reebok International. The move will allow CLI to extend its reach in youth lifestyle and athletic brands.

In 2008 a federal jury in Oregon awarded adidas AG $305 million for trademark violation of its three-stripe design by Collective Brands. In 2009 Collective Brands and adidas entered into a confidential settlement agreement to settle all pending litigation, with the two parties agreeing that the terms of the permanent injunction issued by the court would remain in place.

Matt Rubel, Payless' CEO, also serves as the holding company's top executive. Stride Rite CEO David Chamberlain stepped down as the firm's top executive at the completion of the deal.

EXECUTIVES

Chairman, President, and CEO:
Matthew E. (Matt) Rubel, age 52,
$6,456,055 total compensation
EVP and Chief Administrative Officer: Douglas J. Treff,
age 52, $1,530,148 total compensation
EVP Supply Chain: Darrel J. Pavelka, age 54,
$1,662,231 total compensation
Division SVP Corporate Strategy: Paul J. Fenaroli
Division SVP, CFO, and Treasurer:
Douglas G. (Doug) Boessen, age 47,
$689,349 total compensation
Division SVP Global Logistics: David W. Milton
Division SVP and CIO: Eric C. Gordon

Division SVP Product Development: Dan D. Park
SVP Human Resources: Betty J. Click, age 48
SVP Design, Product Development, and Global
Sourcing: Michael Jeppesen
SVP, General Counsel, and Secretary: Michael J. Massey,
age 45, $1,206,330 total compensation
President – Saucony, Performance + Lifestyle Group:
Richie Woodworth
President – Stride Rite Children's Group, Performance
+ Lifestyle Group: Sharon John
President – Sperry Top-Sider, Performance + Lifestyle
Group: Craig L. Reingold, age 54
President – Keds, Performance + Lifestyle Group:
Kristin Kohler Burrows
President and CEO, Performance + Lifestyle Group:
Gregg S. Ribatt, age 41
President and CEO, Payless ShoeSource: LuAnn Via,
$2,294,847 total compensation
President and CEO, Collective Licensing International:
Bruce Pettet
Auditors: Deloitte & Touche LLP

LOCATIONS

HQ: Collective Brands, Inc.
3231 SE 6th Ave., Topeka, KS 66607
Phone: 785-233-5171   Fax: 785-368-7510
Web: www.collectivebrands.com

2010 Sales

	$ mil.	% of total
US	2,781.8	84
International	526.1	16
Total	**3,307.9**	**100**

PRODUCTS/OPERATIONS

2010 Stores

	No.
Payless domestic	3,827
Payless international	643
Stride Rite retail	363
Total	**4,833**

2010 Sales

	$ mil.	% of total
Payless domestic	2,153.2	65
Payless international	422.4	13
PLG (Stride Rite) wholesale	513.9	16
PLG (Stride Rite) retail	218.4	6
Total	**3,307.9**	**100**

Selected Brands

Collective Licensing
  Airwalk
  Dukes
  genetic
  Lamar
  LDT
  Rage
  Sims
  Skate Attack
  Vision Street Wear
  Ultra-Wheels

Payless
  Abaeté for Payless
  ABT for Spotlights
  alice + olivis for Payless
  Airwalk
  American Eagle
  Champion
  Dexter
  Disney
  Dunkman
  Lela Rose for Payless

Stride Rite
  Hind
  Keds
  Pro-Keds
  Robeez
  Saucony
  Sperry Top-Sider
  Stride Rite

COMPETITORS

Aldo	Mizuno
ASICS	NIKE
Bata	Nine West
Birkenstock	Nordstrom
Brown Shoe	Rack Room Shoes
C&J Clark	Reebok
Cherokee Inc.	Ross Stores
The Children's Place	Sears
Converse	Sears Canada
Crocs	Shoe Carnival
Deckers Outdoor	Shoe Show
Dillard's	Skechers U.S.A.
DSW	Sports Authority
ECCO Sko	Target
Foot Locker	Timberland
The Gap	TJX Companies
Genesco	Vans
Gymboree	Wal-Mart
Iconix Brand Group	Weyco
J. C. Penney	Wolverine World Wide
Kohl's	Zappos.com
K-Swiss	Zellers
Macy's	

HISTORICAL FINANCIALS

Company Type: Public

Income Statement

FYE: Saturday nearest January 31

	REVENUE ($ mil.)	NET INCOME ($ mil.)	NET PROFIT MARGIN	EMPLOYEES
1/10	3,308	88	2.7%	30,000
1/09	3,442	(69)	—	31,000
1/08	3,035	43	1.4%	31,000
1/07	2,797	122	4.4%	31,000
1/06	2,667	71	2.6%	27,550
Annual Growth	**5.5%**	**5.8%**	**—**	**2.2%**

2010 Year-End Financials

Debt ratio: 114.6%
Return on equity: 13.0%
Cash ($ mil.): 394
Current ratio: 2.71
Long-term debt ($ mil.): 842
No. of shares (mil.): 65
Dividends
  Yield: —
  Payout: —
Market value ($ mil.): 1,277

Stock History

NYSE: PSS

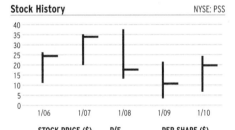

	STOCK PRICE ($) FY Close	P/E High/Low		PER SHARE ($) Earnings	Dividends	Book Value
1/10	19.68	19	6	1.28	—	11.33
1/09	10.67	—	—	(1.09)	—	9.59
1/08	17.62	57	21	0.65	—	10.83
1/07	33.95	19	11	1.82	—	10.79
1/06	24.36	26	12	0.98	—	10.05
Annual Growth	**(5.2%)**	**—**	**—**	**6.9%**	**—**	**3.0%**

Comcast Corporation

Commerce plus broadcasting equals Comcast. The company's core cable division is the largest provider in the US (ahead of #2 Time Warner Cable) with more than 24 million subscribers. Comcast derives the bulk of its revenue from television, Internet, and digital phone services offered in 39 states. It has about 16 million subscribers to its broadband Internet service, while its Comcast Digital Voice computer telephony service has more than 7 million customers. Comcast also has cable programming interests, such as G4, VERSUS, and The Golf Channel, and it owns entertainment channel E!. The company announced in late 2009 that it would form a joint venture with General Electric giving it a 51% interest in NBC Universal.

If approved by federal regulators, the transaction will leave GE with a 49% stake in a joint venture valued at approximately $30 billion. As part of the deal, Comcast will contribute assets and cash valued at about $14 billion. The company stands to control a portfolio of communications, media, and entertainment businesses with combined 2008 revenues of more than $50 billion. To its existing cable, phone service, and sports holdings the company would add the NBC television network, Spanish-language broadcaster Telemundo, Universal Studios, Focus Features, ten local NBC broadcast stations, and more than 20 cable channels. Other assets included in the deal are a long list of broadcast-related Internet media properties and the Universal theme parks in Orlando and Hollywood.

Universal's extensive catalog of feature films would be a compelling addition to Comcast's selection of video-on-demand content and enable better distribution of movies and television programming to consumers via cable and potentially mobile devices.

Comcast made an investment in its cable TV subscription business with the 2008 purchase of Insight Midwest for about $1.3 billion. The deal added about 700,000 subscribers in Illinois and Indiana. Additionally, Comcast bought the remaining 50% of New England Cable News (NECN) that it did not already own from The Hearst Corp. in 2009; NECN serves about 3 million subscribers in six New England states.

In 2010 the company agreed to buy wholesale VoIP telephony services provider New Global Telecom in another move to build out its digital phone services for small business customers, in particular.

Through majority-owned subsidiary Comcast Spectacor, the company owns Philadelphia's professional sports teams, the 76ers and the Flyers, and two arenas in that city.

One-third of Comcast's voting power is controlled by CEO Brian Roberts, son of founder and former chairman Ralph Roberts.

HISTORY

In 1963 Ralph Roberts, Daniel Aaron, and Julian Brodsky bought American Cable Systems in Tupelo, Mississippi. The company soon expanded throughout the state. In 1969 the company got a new name: Comcast, combining "communications" and "broadcast." Two years later Comcast acquired franchises in western Pennsylvania, and when it went public in 1972, it moved to Philadelphia.

Comcast bought up local operations nationwide through the early 1980s and gained its first foreign cable franchise in 1983 in London (it sold its affiliate there to NTL — now Virgin Media — in 1998). It took a 26% stake in the large Group W Cable in 1986. Roberts also lent financial support that year to a fledgling home-shopping channel called QVC — for "quality, value, and convenience."

A big step into telecommunications came in 1988 when Comcast bought American Cellular Network, with Delaware and New Jersey franchises. Two years later Roberts' son Brian — who had trained as a cable installer during a summer away from college — became Comcast's president.

In 1992 Comcast bought Metromedia's Philadelphia-area cellular operations and began investing in fiber-optic and wireless phone companies. By then the company was a major QVC shareholder. With an eye toward Comcast's programming needs, Brian persuaded FOX network head Barry Diller to become QVC's chairman. But when Diller tried to use QVC to take over CBS, Comcast bought control of QVC in 1994 to quash the bid, which went against cross-ownership bans. To pay for QVC, Comcast had to sell its 20% stake in cable firm Heritage Communications in 1995. Diller left the company (he now oversees InterActiveCorp, parent of QVC's archrival HSN). Also in 1995 Comcast funded former Disney executive Richard Frank to launch the C3 (Comcast Content and Communication) programming company.

The company agreed to acquire rival MediaOne in 1999, but soon after the $54 billion deal was struck, AT&T weighed in with a $58 billion offer. Comcast dropped its bid for MediaOne when AT&T offered to sell Comcast 2 million cable subscribers. More than a million of those subscribers came from Pennsylvania cable operator Lenfest Communications, which Comcast bought in 2000 from AT&T and the Lenfest family in a $7 billion deal.

In 2001 Comcast completed a systems swap with Adelphia Communications and completed the $2.75 billion purchase of systems in six states from AT&T. Also that year AT&T agreed to sell its cable unit to Comcast for $47 billion in stock and $25 billion in assumed debt. C. Michael Armstrong came from AT&T to Comcast, and was named chairman. Challenged with the task of absorbing AT&T Broadband's assets, Comcast struggled to meet its numbers. About 18 months after the AT&T Broadband deal, Comcast had reduced its headcount by 10,000 people. Also in 2001 Comcast sold its 57% stake in QVC to Liberty Media for about $7.7 billion.

When Armstrong stepped down as chairman in 2004, president and CEO Brian Roberts was named successor. The following year the company joined a consortium that bought film studio MGM.

In 2006 Comcast bought Disney's nearly 40% stake in E! Entertainment Television in a deal valued at nearly $1.25 billion (Comcast already owned 60%).

Comcast had owned a 21% stake in rival Time Warner Cable (TWC), which made for strange bedfellows, but the companies managed to unwind their relationship in mid-2006. The two rivals purchased all of troubled Adelphia Communications' cable television assets. Adelphia shareholders received about $9 billion from TWC and $3.5 billion in cash from Comcast, which also contributed its TWC stake to the deal. Comcast no longer owns any part of TWC.

EXECUTIVES

Chairman Emeritus: Ralph J. Roberts, age 90, $22,683,120 total compensation
Vice Chairman: Julian A. Brodsky, age 76
Chairman, President, and CEO: Brian L. Roberts, age 50, $27,246,368 total compensation
EVP and COO: Stephen B. (Steve) Burke, age 52, $33,988,056 total compensation
EVP and CFO: Michael J. Angelakis, age 45, $21,554,132 total compensation
EVP: David L. Cohen, age 54, $9,839,379 total compensation
EVP and CTO: Tony G. Werner
SVP Corporate Communications: D'Arcy F. Rudnay
SVP, General Counsel, and Secretary: Arthur R. Block, age 54, $6,151,593 total compensation
SVP Corporate Development: Robert S. Pick, age 53
SVP; President, Comcast Interactive Media: Amy L. Banse
SVP External Affairs and Public Policy Counsel: Joseph W. (Joe) Waz Jr.
SVP Investor Relations: Marlene S. Dooner
SVP Employee Engagement: Ron Phillips, age 44
SVP Human Performance: Tina Waters
SVP and Treasurer: William E. (Bill) Dordelman
SVP, Chief Accounting Officer, and Controller: Lawrence J. Salva, age 53
President and CEO, Comcast Entertainment Group: Ted Harbert, age 55
President, Comcast Cable Communications: Neil Smit, age 50
President, Comcast Network Advertising Sales, Comcast Content: David T. (Dave) Cassaro, age 57
Auditors: Deloitte & Touche LLP

LOCATIONS

HQ: Comcast Corporation
1 Comcast Center, Philadelphia, PA 19103
Phone: 215-286-1700
Web: www.comcast.com

PRODUCTS/OPERATIONS

2009 Sales

	$ mil.	% of total
Cable		
Video	19,377	54
High-speed Internet	7,757	22
Phone	3,262	9
Advertising	1,444	4
Franchise fees	948	3
Other	1,069	3
Programming	1,496	4
Other	403	1
Total	**35,756**	**100**

COMPETITORS

AT&T
Blockbuster Inc.
Cablevision Systems
Charter Communications
Cox Communications
DIRECTV
DISH Network
ESPN
FOX Sports
Insight Communications
Liberty Media
NBC Universal Cable
Netflix
RCN Corporation
Time Warner Cable
ValueVision Media
Verizon
Viacom
Xanadoo

HISTORICAL FINANCIALS

Company Type: Public

Income Statement

FYE: December 31

	REVENUE ($ mil.)	NET INCOME ($ mil.)	NET PROFIT MARGIN	EMPLOYEES
12/09	35,756	3,638	10.2%	107,000
12/08	34,256	2,547	7.4%	100,000
12/07	30,895	2,587	8.4%	100,000
12/06	24,966	2,533	10.1%	90,000
12/05	22,255	928	4.2%	80,000
Annual Growth	**12.6%**	**40.7%**	**—**	**7.5%**

2009 Year-End Financials

Debt ratio: 65.4%
Return on equity: 8.7%
Cash ($ mil.): 671
Current ratio: 0.44
Long-term debt ($ mil.): 27,940

No. of shares (mil.): 2,807
Dividends
　Yield: 1.8%
　Payout: 23.8%
Market value ($ mil.): 47,319

Stock History

NASDAQ (GS): CMCSA

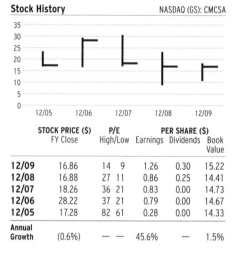

	STOCK PRICE ($) FY Close	P/E High/Low		PER SHARE ($) Earnings	Dividends	Book Value
12/09	16.86	14	9	1.26	0.30	15.22
12/08	16.88	27	11	0.86	0.25	14.41
12/07	18.26	36	21	0.83	0.00	14.73
12/06	28.22	37	21	0.79	0.00	14.67
12/05	17.28	82	61	0.28	0.00	14.33
Annual Growth	**(0.6%)**	**—**	**—**	**45.6%**	**—**	**1.5%**

Comerica Incorporated

If you have a cosigner, Comerica will be your copilot. The holding company owns Comerica Bank and is organized into three main segments: The Business Bank division is the largest, offering loans, deposits, and capital markets products to middle-market, large corporate, and government clients. The Retail Bank serves small businesses and consumers. Comerica's Wealth and Institutional Management arm provides private banking, investment management, financial advisory, investment banking, discount brokerage, insurance, and retirement services. Comerica has about 450 branches in about a dozen states across the US; Arizona, California, Florida, Michigan, and Texas are its primary markets.

Comerica has long been a leading commercial lender in the US, and more than half of the company's assets are wrapped up in commercial real estate and operating loans. However, as its core small and mid-market clientele has suffered during the economic downturn, so has Comerica, which has seen both its revenue and income decline in each of the last two fiscal years. While the company has increased its provisions for loan losses, it has tightened its lending standards to the energy, technology, and life sciences industries, and has reduced its exposure to the auto supply, commercial and residential construction, and Small Business Administration franchise sectors.

In 2009 Comerica sold its institutional retirement plan recordkeeping business, which served some 250 retirement plans, to Wells Fargo, signaling the company's move away from ancillary lines. The company is pursuing measured growth by opening about 10 new bank branches a year.

HISTORY

Comerica traces its history to 1849, when Michigan governor Epaphroditus Ransom tapped Elon Farnsworth to found the Detroit Savings Fund Institute. At that time Detroit was a major transit point for shipping between Lakes Huron and Erie, as well as between the US and Canada. The bank grew with the town and in 1871 became Detroit Savings Bank.

By 1899 Detroit was one of the top 10 US manufacturing centers and, thanks to a group of local tinkerers and mechanics that included Henry Ford, was on the brink of even greater growth. Detroit Savings grew also, fueled by the deposits of workers whom Ford paid up to $5 a day. Detroit Savings was not, however, the beneficiary of significant business with the auto makers; for corporate banking they turned first to eastern banks and then to large local banks in which they had an interest.

Detroit boomed during the 1920s as America went car-crazy, but after the 1929 crash Detroiters defaulted on mortgages by the thousands. By 1933 Michigan's banks were in such disarray that the governor shut them down three weeks prior to the federal bank holiday. Detroit Savings was one of only four Detroit banks to reopen. None of the major banks associated with auto companies survived.

A few months later Manufacturers National Bank, backed by a group of investors that included Edsel Ford (Henry's son), was founded. Although its start was rocky, Manufacturers National was on firm footing by 1936; around the same time, Detroit Savings Bank renamed itself the Detroit Bank to appeal to a more commercial clientele.

WWII and the postwar boom put Detroit back in gear. In the 1950s and 1960s, both banks thrived. In the 1970s statewide branching was permitted and both banks formed holding companies (DETROITBANK Corp. and Manufacturers National Corp.) and expanded throughout Michigan. As they grew, they added services; when Detroit's economy was hit by the oil shocks of the 1970s, these diversifications helped them through the lean years.

DETROITBANK opened a trust operation in Florida in 1982 to maintain its relationship with retired customers and renamed itself Comerica to be less area-specific. Manufacturers National also began operating in Florida (1983) and made acquisitions in the Chicago area (1987). Comerica went farther afield, buying banks in Texas (1988) and California (1991).

Following the national consolidation trend, in 1992 Comerica and Manufacturers National merged (retaining the Comerica name) but did not fully integrate until 1994, when the new entity began making more acquisitions. To increase sales and develop its consumer business, the company reorganized in 1996. It sold its Illinois bank and its Michigan customs brokerage business and acquired Fairlane Associates to expand its property/casualty insurance line.

As part of its strategy to have operations in all three NAFTA countries, Comerica opened a bank in Mexico in 1997 and one in Canada in 1998. That year it dropped $66 million for the naming rights to the Detroit Tigers' baseball stadium, which opened as Comerica Park in 2000. It also started a Web-based payment system for its international trade business.

To fortify its business lending operations in California, Comerica bought Imperial Bancorp in 2001. At the beginning of 2002, chairman Eugene Miller handed the CEO reins to Ralph Babb, who had been CFO. Later that year, Babb became chairman as well.

EXECUTIVES

Chairman, President, and CEO, Comerica Incorporated and Comerica Bank: Ralph W. Babb Jr., age 61, $4,266,395 total compensation
EVP and CFO, Comerica Incorporated and Comerica Bank: Elizabeth S. Acton, age 58, $1,266,847 total compensation
EVP The Retail Bank, Comerica Incorporated and Comerica Bank: Mary C. (Connie) Beck, age 64, $1,458,893 total compensation
EVP National Business Finance: Ronald P. Marcinelli
EVP Wealth and Institutional Management, Comerica Incorporated and Comerica Bank: Curtis C. Farmer, age 47, $1,197,240 total compensation
EVP and General Auditor, Comerica Incorporated and Comerica Bank: David E. Duprey, age 52
EVP; President, Michigan Market, Comerica Bank: Thomas D. Ogden, age 61
EVP Finance, Comerica Incorporated and Comerica Bank: Robert D. (Bob) McDermott, age 52
EVP and Chief Human Resources Officer, Comerica Incorporated and Comerica Bank: Megan D. Burkhart, age 38
EVP Business Bank: Dale E. Greene, age 63
EVP Corporate Planning, Development, and Risk Management: Michael H. Michalak, age 52
SVP and Chief Economist: Dana Johnson, age 59
SVP Corporate Marketing and Corporate Communications: Jim H. Weber
President, World Asset Management, Comerica Bank: Todd B. Johnson
Auditors: Ernst & Young LLP

LOCATIONS

HQ: Comerica Incorporated
Comerica Bank Tower, 1717 Main St.
Dallas, TX 75201
Phone: 800-925-2160
Web: www.comerica.com

Selected Markets

Arizona	Michigan
California	Nevada
Colorado	Ohio
Florida	Texas
Illinois	Washington

PRODUCTS/OPERATIONS

2009 Sales

	$ mil.	% of total
Interest		
Loans, including fees	1,767	56
Investments	338	11
Noninterest		
Net securities gains	243	8
Service charges on deposit accounts	228	7
Fiduciary income	161	5
Commercial lending fees	79	2
Letter of credit fees	69	2
Card fees	51	2
Other	219	7
Total	**3,155**	**100**

2009 Assets

	$ mil.	% of total
Cash & equivalents	5,755	10
Investment securities available for sale	7,416	12
Commercial loans	21,690	36
Real estate construction loans	3,461	6
Commercial mortgage loans	10,457	17
Residential mortgage loans	1,651	3
Consumer loans	2,511	4
Lease financing	1,139	2
International loans	1,252	2
Allowance for loan losses	(985)	—
Other	4,902	8
Total	**59,249**	**100**

Selected Subsidiaries

Comerica Bank
Comerica Bank & Trust, National Association
Comerica Capital Advisors Incorporated
Comerica Equities Incorporated
Comerica Financial Incorporated
Comerica Holdings Incorporated
Comerica Insurance Group, Inc.
Comerica Insurance Services, Inc.
Comerica Leasing Corporation
Comerica Merchant Services, Inc.
Wilson, Kemp & Associates, Inc.
World Asset Management, Inc.

COMPETITORS

Bank of America	SunTrust
Citigroup	SVB Financial
Cullen/Frost Bankers	TCF Financial
Fifth Third	UnionBanCal
Huntington Bancshares	U.S. Bancorp
JPMorgan Chase	Wells Fargo

HISTORICAL FINANCIALS

Company Type: Public

Income Statement

	ASSETS ($ mil.)	NET INCOME ($ mil.)	INCOME AS % OF ASSETS	EMPLOYEES
				FYE: December 31
12/09	59,249	17	0.0%	9,720
12/08	67,548	213	0.3%	10,639
12/07	62,331	686	1.1%	11,337
12/06	58,001	893	1.5%	11,270
12/05	53,013	861	1.6%	11,343
Annual Growth	**2.8%**	**(62.5%)**	**—**	**(3.8%)**

2009 Year-End Financials

Equity as % of assets: 8.2%	Dividends
Return on assets: 0.0%	Yield: 0.7%
Return on equity: 0.3%	Payout: —
Long-term debt ($ mil.): 11,060	Market value ($ mil.): 5,214
No. of shares (mil.): 176	Sales ($ mil.): 3,155

Stock History

NYSE: CMA

	STOCK PRICE ($) FY Close	P/E High/Low		Earnings	Dividends	Book Value
12/09	29.57	—	—	(0.79)	0.20	39.87
12/08	19.85	42	12	1.29	2.31	40.56
12/07	43.53	14	9	4.43	2.56	29.02
12/06	58.68	11	9	5.49	2.36	29.23
12/05	56.76	12	10	5.11	2.20	28.74
Annual Growth	**(15.0%)**	**—**	**—**	**—**	**(45.1%)**	**8.5%**

Commercial Metals

If companies have heart, Shakespeare might say Commercial Metals' is as true as steel. CMC manufactures, recycles, and sells steel. Its operations straddle five segments. CMC's Americas and international fabrication and distribution segments buy and sell primary and secondary metals, and fabricated and related metals. Fabrication includes a heat treating plant, producing fence posts, beams, and joists. CMC's Americas and international mills make steel products and copper tubing used in construction, energy, and transportation. A recycling segment runs 42 secondary metals processing plants that shred and pulverize scrap metal, for subsequent sale to steel mills. More than half of CMC's sales are in the US.

CMC's depth of operations along with a diversified portfolio and global footprint are helping the company to weather the worldwide economic recession and slow recovery in 2009. Despite reduced revenue across all business segments, the company maximized internal purchases, cut its workforce by 19%, and remained profitable.

CMC's domestic business, organized as the CMC Americas, does business through a broad network of manufacturing facilities and related support centers. These include steel mini-mills planted in Alabama, Arkansas, Texas, and South Carolina, with annual production capacity up to 150,000 tons. A copper tube mini-mill subsidiary, CMC Howell Metal, churns out some 80 million pounds. Fabrication capacity drives approximately 30,000 tons under CMC's heat treating facility.

Overseas, the company runs three rebar fabrication shops in Poland and Germany, as well as a wire mesh fabrication site in Poland. A marketing and trading segment operates through nearly 20 international trading offices. It brokers industrial products that include primary and secondary metals, fabricated metals, chemicals, and industrial minerals to customers in the steel, nonferrous metals, metal fabrication, chemical, refractory, and transportation industries.

CMC grew heavy with acquisitions in 2008. It acquired a group of companies — ABC Coating Company (of Texas and Colorado), Banner Rebar, Toltec Steel Services, and Rebar Trucking. The deal also scored a 50% stake in both ABC Coating of North Carolina and ABC Coating of Tennessee. All joined the CMC Americas Fabrication and Distribution business segment.

HISTORY

Russian immigrant Moses Feldman moved to Dallas in 1914 and founded scrap metal company American Iron & Metal the next year. In the 1920s Feldman suffered a heart attack, and his son Jake helped out with the business. Low metal prices hurt the company during the Depression. In 1932 Jake formed a two-man brokerage firm, Commercial Metals Company (CMC), which was combined as a partnership with his father's scrap metal operations. Moses Feldman died in 1937. CMC was incorporated in 1946 and began buying related businesses during the 1950s.

CMC was listed on the American Stock Exchange in 1960. It soon expanded geographically, buying a stake in Texas steelmaker Structural Metals (1963). In 1965 it formed Commercial Metals Europa (the Netherlands), its first overseas subsidiary, and Commonwealth Metal (New York).

By 1966 CMC was one of the world's top three scrap metal companies. It bought copper tube manufacturer Howell Metals (Virginia) in 1968, the remainder of Structural Metals, and major stakes in seven affiliated businesses. Over 10 years, CMC opened trading offices around the world. Business continued to grow throughout the 1970s. The company added a small minimill in Arkansas (1971) and certain assets of General Export Iron and Metal in Texas (1976).

CMC began trading on the New York Stock Exchange in 1982. The next year the company bought Connors Steel (Alabama), its third minimill. By the end of 1984 CMC was operating 20 metal recycling plants from Texas to Florida.

The company modernized its minimills in the 1990s. CMC acquired small scrap-metal operations and Shepler's, a concrete-related products business, in 1994. Also that year CEO Stanley Rabin completed the $50 million purchase of Owen Steel (a South Carolina minimill), which expanded CMC's reach into the Mid-Atlantic and Southeast. The company wrapped up a $30 million capital improvement program at its Alabama minimill in 1995 — just in time to ride a strong steel market to record profits.

Although a correction in the steel and metals industry depressed prices in 1996, CMC achieved record sales and profits that fiscal year. However, both dipped the next year, with lower steel and scrap prices widely attributed to an influx of foreign imports. CMC strengthened its vertical integration in 1997 by acquiring Allegheny Heat Treating (heat treatment services to steel mills) and two auto salvage plants in Florida.

During 1998 CMC moved into the Midwest, buying a metals recycling company in Missouri. It boosted global operations by purchasing a metals trading firm in Australia and entering a joint venture with Trinec, a Czech Republic steel mill, to sell steel products in Germany.

In 2000 CMC picked up three rebar fabricators — two in California (Fontana Steel and C&M Steel), and one in Florida (Suncoast Steel).

In late 2001 the company acquired Florida-based Allform, a maker of concrete-related forms and supplies. The following year Commercial Metals started manufacturing its corrosion-resistant stainless steel-clad products in its facilities in South Carolina.

Marvin Selig, founder and chairman of the company's steel group, retired in 2002 after working for more than 50 years in the steel industry.

In 2003 CMC purchased a 71% stake in Poland-based Huta Zawiercie S.A. for approximately $50 million. CMC purchased the assets of J. L. Davidson Company, a rebar fabricating operation based in California, in 2004.

In 2006 the company acquired Tucson-based concrete products supplier Brost Forming Supply, Inc., and almost all of the assets of Yonack Iron & Metal Co. and Metallic Resources, Inc. Later that year the company bought Cherokee Supply, a provider of tools and supplies for the construction, oilfield, and industrial sectors. The acquisition became part of CMC Construction Services division and operated under the CMC Cherokee name.

Quick on the heels of the Cherokee deal came CMC's purchase of Concrete Formtek Services, a renter of concrete forming and shoring equipment. Concrete Formtek Services was renamed CMC Formtek and became part of CMC Construction Services. In 2008 CMC reorganized its operations under two divisions, CMC Americas and CMC International.

EXECUTIVES

Chairman, President, and CEO: Murray R. McClean, age 61, $1,627,469 total compensation
EVP and COO: Joseph (Joe) Alvarado, age 57
EVP; President, CMC International: Hanns Zoellner, age 61, $944,112 total compensation
EVP and Division Manager, Howell Metal: James K. Forkovitch
SVP and CFO: William B. Larson, age 56, $713,318 total compensation
VP; President, CMC Americas: Tracy L. Porter
VP Human Resources: James (Jim) Alleman
VP, General Counsel, and Corporate Secretary: Ann J. Bruder
VP and Director Internal Audit: Manny Rosenfeld
VP and CIO: Malinda G. Passmore, age 51
VP and Treasurer: Louis A. Federle, age 61
VP Business Development: Devesh Sharma
VP and Controller: Leon K. Rusch, age 58
President, CMC Europe: Ludovit Gajdos
President, CMC Australia: Peter Muller
President, CMC Cometals: Eliezer Skornicki
Director Public Relations: Debbie L. Okle
Auditors: Deloitte & Touche LLP

LOCATIONS

HQ: Commercial Metals Company
6565 N. MacArthur Blvd., Ste. 800
Irving, TX 75039
Phone: 214-689-4300   **Fax:** 214-689-5886
Web: www.commercialmetals.com

2009 Sales

	$ mil.	% of total
US	4,059.2	60
Europe	1,272.6	19
Asia	727.7	10
Australia & New Zealand	533.5	8
Other regions	200.4	3
Total	**6,793.4**	**100**

PRODUCTS/OPERATIONS

2009 Sales

	$ mil.	% of total
Steel products	4,713.7	70
Industrial materials	885.3	13
Nonferrous scrap	411.5	6
Construction materials	288.7	4
Ferrous scrap	260.8	4
Nonferrous products	150.5	2
Other	82.9	1
Total	**6,793.4**	**100**

COMPETITORS

AK Steel Holding Corporation
BHP Billiton
Blue Tee
Connell LP
David J. Joseph
Gerdau Ameristeel
Indel
Keywell
Metals USA
Mueller Industries
Nucor
OmniSource
Quanex Building Products
Roanoke Bar Division
Ryerson
Schnitzer Steel
Severstal North America
Simec
Steel Dynamics
Tang Industries
Tube City IMS
United States Steel
Universal Forest Products
Worthington Industries

HISTORICAL FINANCIALS

Company Type: Public

Income Statement

FYE: August 31

	REVENUE ($ mil.)	NET INCOME ($ mil.)	NET PROFIT MARGIN	EMPLOYEES
8/09	6,793	21	0.3%	13,586
8/08	10,427	232	2.2%	15,276
8/07	8,329	355	4.3%	12,730
8/06	7,556	356	4.7%	11,734
8/05	6,593	286	4.3%	11,027
Annual Growth	0.8%	(48.1%)	—	5.4%

2009 Year-End Financials

Debt ratio: 77.3%
Return on equity: 1.3%
Cash ($ mil.): 406
Current ratio: 2.45
Long-term debt ($ mil.): 1,182

No. of shares (mil.): 114
Dividends
  Yield: 2.8%
  Payout: 266.7%
Market value ($ mil.): 1,935

Stock History

NYSE: CMC

	STOCK PRICE ($) FY Close	P/E High/Low	PER SHARE ($) Earnings	Dividends	Book Value
8/09	16.93	134 35	0.18	0.48	13.38
8/08	26.03	20 11	1.97	0.45	14.33
8/07	28.89	13 6	2.92	0.33	13.55
8/06	21.59	11 5	2.89	0.17	10.67
8/05	14.97	8 4	2.32	0.12	7.87
Annual Growth	3.1%	— —	(47.2%)	41.4%	14.2%

CommScope, Inc.

CommScope doesn't need to be coaxed into making cable. The company makes coaxial, fiber-optic, and other cable products for data, voice, and video transmission; including high-bandwidth cable that provides telephone, cable TV, and Internet access through a single line. It develops radio frequency subsystems for wireless networks through its Andrew Solutions brand/division. SYSTIMAX and Uniprise brands encompass CommScope's network infrastructure products, including cabinets, antennas, software, and network design services for business applications. Telecommunications service providers and OEMs such as Anixter, Alcatel-Lucent, and Comcast are customers. CommScope makes about half of its sales outside the US.

The company faced challenges in 2009, including having a limited number of key customers, distributors, and suppliers; relying on contract electronics manufacturers to make the company's products; and intense industry competition. Add to that the global recession and credit crisis, and you've got a rough year.

The global economic doldrums spurred CommScope to consolidate and reorganize its operations in order to trim costs and to focus on its growth. After the 2007 acquisition of Andrew,

the company reorganized its business to include four segments: Antenna, Cable, and Cabinets Group (ACCG); Enterprise; Broadband; and Wireless Network Solutions (WNS). It plans an additional reorganization in 2010 to break the company out into three new organizations across its existing segments to ensure global coverage of CommScope's commercial, supply, and technology areas. CommScope announced that it will close its Omaha, Nebraska, manufacturing facility, which houses its Connectivity Solutions Manufacturing (CSMI) subsidiary, by late 2011. Manufacturing will be relocated to other CommScope facilities in North America. The company also communicated its plans to consolidate its wireless network cable production in Newton, North Carolina, into its larger manufacturing facility in Illinois.

In 2009 the company closed its enterprise cabling operations in Australia. The year prior it pared down its microwave antenna operations in England to one facility, while in the Czech Republic the company plans to close its antenna operations. In Scotland it will consolidate its machine shop operations at two plants into one, located in Andrews.

Divestures have also played a part in the company's desire to remain profitable. CommScope exited its satellite communications (SatCom) product line in 2008, which had been part of the Andrew acquisition in 2007. The SatCom division was acquired by ASC Signal for $8.5 million in cash.

Concomitant to the closures, the company's Andrew Solutions division expanded its Suzhou, China, manufacturing and distribution center to serve local customers. The wireless telecommunications market is growing in this region and the Andrew brand is the only non-Chinese cable and antenna supplier that is approved by state-run China Telecom. To meet demand, Andrew has been continually expanding its manufacturing operations in all its China locations.

HISTORY

CommScope began as Hickory, North Carolina-based Superior Cable, a maker of telephone cables. The company initiated the CommScope product line of coaxial cables in 1964 and opened its Catawba, North Carolina, manufacturing site two years later.

When Continental Telephone purchased Superior Cable in 1967, CommScope became a division under the new company, Superior Continental. In 1967 Superior sold the CommScope division to a group of Hickory-area investors led by Frank Drendel, CommScope's current chairman and CEO.

In 1980 CommScope became a division of M/A-COM, a cable television equipment company based in Massachusetts. General Instrument, a leading maker of cable television equipment, acquired M/A-COM and CommScope in 1986. As a part of General Instrument's plan to split into three companies, CommScope was spun off in 1997.

In 1998 CommScope sold its aerospace cable business to French telecommunications giant Alcatel (now Alcatel-Lucent) for $13 million. It bought Alcatel's coaxial cable business in 1999.

Expanding into South America in 2000, CommScope purchased a manufacturing facility in Brazil from Motorola. The slowing US economy forced the company to cut about 500 positions — about 13% of its workforce — in 2001. Later that year CommScope acquired an 18%

stake in the US-based optical fiber and fiber cable manufacturer OFS BrightWave.

In 2002 the company signed a distribution deal with Hutton Communications to sell and distribute CommScope's wireless products. Not all news was good in 2002, as CommScope was forced to write off more than $20 million due to cable system operator Adelphia Communications' Chapter 11 bankruptcy.

In 2004 CommScope strengthened its core operations with the acquisition of Avaya's connectivity solutions business for $263 million. The acquisition included product groups Exchange-MAX (cable management systems), Integrated Cabinet Solutions (enclosures), and SYSTIMAX (end-to-end cabling solutions for phones, LANs, and workstations).

CommScope acquired Trilogy Communications' 75-ohm trunk and distribution cable television products business in 2006. The following year it bought rival Andrew Corporation for $2.65 billion in cash and stock. Andrew Corp. was rechristened Andrew Wireless Solutions following the acquisition and absorbed into CommScope.

EXECUTIVES

Chairman and CEO: Frank M. Drendel, age 65, $4,660,985 total compensation
President and COO: Marvin S. Edwards Jr., age 61, $488,731 total compensation
EVP and CFO: Jearld L. Leonhardt, age 61, $630,405 total compensation
EVP and Chief Supply Officer: Randall W. (Randy) Crenshaw, age 52, $504,648 total compensation
EVP and Chief Commercial Officer: Edward A. (Ted) Hally, age 60, $569,617 total compensation
SVP and CTO: Robert C. Suffern, age 49
SVP and CIO: Kap K. Kim
SVP Broadband: Ric Johnsen
SVP Broadband Sales: James R. (Jim) Hughes, age 49
SVP and Controller: Mark A. Olson, age 51
SVP Human Resources: James L. Wright
SVP Global Operations: Christopher A. Story, age 50
SVP, General Counsel, and Secretary: Frank B. Wyatt II, age 47
SVP Global Supply Chain: Carson Cato
SVP Corporate Finance: Philip M. Armstrong Jr., age 48
SVP Technology: Luc Adriaenssens
Director Corporate Communications: Rick Aspan
Auditors: Deloitte & Touche LLP

LOCATIONS

HQ: CommScope, Inc.
  1100 CommScope Place SE, Hickory, NC 28602
Phone: 828-324-2200   **Fax:** 828-328-3400
Web: www.commscope.com

2009 Sales

	$ mil.	% of total
US	1,557.7	52
Europe, Middle East & Africa	677.1	22
Asia/Pacific	568.9	19
Central & Latin America	158.2	5
Canada	63.0	2
Total	**3,024.9**	**100**

PRODUCTS/OPERATIONS

2009 Sales

	$ mil.	% of total
Antenna, Cable & Cabinets Group	1,276.4	42
Enterprise	660.6	22
Wireless Network Solutions	617.7	20
Broadband	472.9	16
Adjustments	(2.7)	—
Total	**3,024.9**	**100**

Selected Products and Services

Antennas
Bimetals (alternative to copper conductors)
Cabinets and enclosures
Cables
Conduit
Enterprise solutions
Equipment
FTTX equipment (BrightPath hybrid fiber coax architectures)
Remote cell site control and monitoring
Steel products
Subscriber drop products (amplifiers, splitters, grounding products)
Towers
Transmission line system
Wireless network solutions

COMPETITORS

ADC Telecommunications	Nexans
Agilent Technologies	OFS Fitel
Amphenol	Optical Cable
ARRIS	Ortronics
Belden	Panduit
Comarco	Powerwave Technologies
Comba Telecom	Prysmian
Corning	QUALCOMM
Draka Holding	Radio Frequency Systems
Emerson Electric	Sumitomo Electric
Ericsson	Superior Essex
General Cable	SWCC SHOWA
Huawei Technologies	TruePosition
HUBER + SUHNER	Tyco Electronics
KATHREIN-Werke	

HISTORICAL FINANCIALS

Company Type: Public

Income Statement

FYE: December 31

	REVENUE ($ mil.)	NET INCOME ($ mil.)	NET PROFIT MARGIN	EMPLOYEES
12/09	3,025	78	2.6%	12,500
12/08	4,017	(229)	—	15,000
12/07	1,931	205	10.6%	15,500
12/06	1,624	112	6.9%	4,550
12/05	1,337	50	3.7%	4,400
Annual Growth	22.6%	11.7%	—	29.8%

2009 Year-End Financials

Debt ratio: 90.6%
Return on equity: 6.1%
Cash ($ mil.): 662
Current ratio: 2.96
Long-term debt ($ mil.): 1,404

No. of shares (mil.): 95
Dividends
  Yield: —
  Payout: —
Market value ($ mil.): 2,513

Stock History

NYSE: CTV

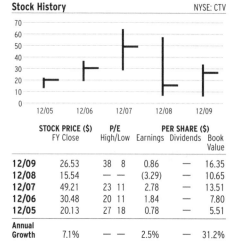

	STOCK PRICE ($) FY Close	P/E High	P/E Low	PER SHARE ($) Earnings	PER SHARE ($) Dividends	PER SHARE ($) Book Value
12/09	26.53	38	8	0.86	—	16.35
12/08	15.54	—	—	(3.29)	—	10.65
12/07	49.21	23	11	2.78	—	13.51
12/06	30.48	20	11	1.84	—	7.80
12/05	20.13	27	18	0.78	—	5.51
Annual Growth	7.1%	—	—	2.5%	—	31.2%

Computer Sciences Corporation

CSC has mastered the art and science of computer technology. One of the world's leading providers of systems integration and other technology services, Computer Sciences Corporation (CSC) provides application development, data center management, communications and networking development, and business consulting. It also offers business process outsourcing (BPO) services in such areas as billing and payment processing, customer relationship management (CRM), and human resources. A major government and defense contractor, CSC generates about 40% of its revenues from US federal agencies.

The company's government contracts include such tasks as helping the Federal Aviation Administration upgrade and modernize its air traffic control systems, and supporting multiple US Navy programs. CSC's long history of serving the US government (dating back to 1961) gives it an advantage over many competitors when bidding on contracts. The company serves a broad range of government clients, including most branches of the military as well as the Department of Homeland Security.

CSC divides its offerings into three main service lines: Managed Services Sector (MSS), North American Public Sector (NPS), and Business Solutions and Services (BS&S). MSS, which primarily handles large-scale outsourcing contracts, accounts for about 40% of CSC's revenues. NPS, its federal government business, also is responsible for about 40% sales. The remaining 20% of sales comes from BS&S, which provides industry-specific consulting and outsourcing services for clients in sectors such as chemicals, aerospace, financial services, manufacturing, and telecommunications.

CSC has benefited from an increased interest in outsourcing in the private sector. It has multiyear contracts with such corporations as insurance broker Aon, hospital system Ascension Health, transportation giant Bombardier, and diversified manufacturer Textron. Large contract wins in 2010 included deals with Zurich Financial, UTC, and Raytheon.

The company has been active on the acquisition front, including purchasing Covansys in a deal valued at $1.3 billion. Covansys specializes in outsourcing services in such industries as financial services, health care, manufacturing, retail, and technology. CSC also acquired First Consulting Group, an IT services firm focused on the health care sector, for $352 million. The acquisitions of Covansys and First Consulting were part of a strategy to expand its offshore capabilities. Covansys operated primarily from development centers in India, and First Consulting added operations in India and Vietnam.

CSC has also identified international expansion — particularly in Asia, Eastern Europe, and Latin America — as a growth driver. The company generated about 40% of its revenues outside the US in fiscal 2009.

HISTORY

Computer Sciences Corporation (CSC) was founded in Los Angeles in 1959 by Fletcher Jones and Roy Nutt to write software for manufacturers such as Honeywell. In 1963 CSC became the first software company to go public. Three years later it signed a $5.5 million contract to support NASA's computation laboratory. Annual sales had climbed to just over $53 million by 1968.

In 1969 CSC agreed to merge with Western Union, but the deal ultimately fell through. When Jones died in a plane crash in 1972, William Hoover, a former NASA executive who had come aboard eight years earlier, became chairman and CEO. Under Hoover, CSC began transforming itself into a systems integrator. In 1986, when federal contracts still accounted for 70% of sales, the company started diversifying into the commercial sector.

In 1991 CSC signed a 10-year, $3 billion contract with defense supplier General Dynamics. In 1995 Hoover, after more than three decades with CSC, stepped down as CEO (remaining chairman until 1997); he was succeeded by president and COO Van Honeycutt. Also that year CSC bought Germany's largest independent computer services company, Ploenzke. In 1996 CSC acquired insurance services provider Continuum Company for $1.5 billion.

In 1998 CSC found itself on the other side of the bargaining table with a $9.8 billion hostile takeover bid from software giant Computer Associates (now CA). After weeks of contentious battle, CA withdrew its bid. That same year the IRS chose CSC to head the PRIME Alliance team that includes IBM, Lucent, and Unisys in a multibillion-dollar project to update the agency's computer system.

That year CSC continued its acquisition spree, buying consulting firms in Europe including Informatica Group (Italy), KMPG Peat Marwick (France), Pergamon (Germany), and SYS-AID (the Netherlands). In 1999 CSC inked an 11-year, $1 billion deal to manage the back-office functions of energy trading giant Enron's energy services unit.

CSC in 2000 boosted its expertise in financial software and services with the cash acquisition of Mynd Corporation (formerly Policy Management Systems) for an estimated $570 million. Also that year CSC signed two large outsourcing contracts — a seven-year, $3 billion deal with telecom equipment maker Nortel Networks that arranged for Nortel to transfer 2,000 employees to CSC, and a $1 billion outsourcing and application development agreement with AT&T.

The company continued to make large deals in 2001, including contracts with the National Security Agency (NSA) and BAE SYSTEMS. The next year saw more of the same: CSC was contracted to operate a central data exchange for the US Environmental Protection Agency, and to collaborate on missile defense systems engineering for the US Army. CSC acquired Defense Department services contractor DynCorp for about $900 million in 2003, doubling the size of its federal services division. (The company sold off various DynCorp units two years later, recouping about $850 million.)

Also in 2003 it won a 10-year, $2.4 billion contract to provide a new network and voice, data, mobile, and Internet services to the UK's Royal

Mail. In 2006 CSC acquired Datatrac Information Services, a prime contractor for the US Department of Homeland Security and other federal agencies.

President and COO Michael Laphen assumed the CEO's chair in 2007, inheriting the position from Honeycutt. Laphen also became chairman that year.

EXECUTIVES

Chairman, President, and CEO:
Michael W. (Mike) Laphen, age 59,
$15,527,343 total compensation
VP and CFO: Michael J. Mancuso, age 67,
$3,077,924 total compensation
VP: Nathan G. (Gus) Siekierka, age 61,
$3,068,588 total compensation
VP Corporate Development: Randy E. Phillips, age 51,
$2,333,179 total compensation
VP, General Counsel, and Secretary:
William L. (Bill) Deckelman Jr., age 52,
$2,562,592 total compensation
VP and Controller: Donald G. DeBuck, age 52,
$1,521,310 total compensation
VP and CTO: John Glowacki
VP and CIO: David McCue
VP Human Resources: Denise M. Peppard, age 53
VP and Treasurer: Thomas R. Irvin, age 61
VP Corporate Responsibility and Analyst Relations:
Susan Pullin
VP and Senior Partner, Global Business Solutions:
Alex Martignago
VP Global Sales Operations: Michael (Mike) O'Donnell
VP Investor Relations: Bryan Brady
President, Global Sales and Marketing: Peter A. Allen, age 48
Director Office of Communications, North American Public Sector: Chuck Taylor
Auditors: Deloitte & Touche LLP

LOCATIONS

HQ: Computer Sciences Corporation
3170 Fairview Park Dr., Falls Church, VA 22042
Phone: 703-876-1000
Web: www.csc.com

2010 Sales

	$ mil.	% of total
US	10,192	63
Europe		
UK	1,923	12
Other countries	2,478	15
Other regions	1,535	9
Total	**16,128**	**100**

PRODUCTS/OPERATIONS

2010 Sales

	$ mil.	% of total
MSS	6,451	40
NPS	6,225	39
BSS	3,560	21
Corporate	17	—
Adjustments	(125)	—
Total	**16,128**	**100**

Selected Service Areas

Application outsourcing
Business process outsourcing
Credit services (consumer credit reporting)
Customer relationship management
Data hosting
Enterprise application integration
Knowledge management
Management consulting
Risk management
Security
Supply chain management

COMPETITORS

Accenture
ADP
Affiliated Computer Services
Atos Origin
Booz Allen
CACI International
Capgemini
CIBER
Cognizant Tech Solutions
Convergys
Deloitte Consulting
Getronics
Honeywell International
HP Enterprise Business
HP Enterprise Services
IBM Global Services
Infosys
Keane
L-3 Communications Titan
Lockheed Martin
Logica
Northrop Grumman
Perot Systems
Raytheon
SAIC
Satyam
Siemens AG
Tata Consultancy
Tech Mahindra
Unisys
Wipro Technologies

HISTORICAL FINANCIALS

Company Type: Public

Income Statement

FYE: Friday nearest March 31

	REVENUE ($ mil.)	NET INCOME ($ mil.)	NET PROFIT MARGIN	EMPLOYEES
3/10	16,128	817	5.1%	94,000
3/09	16,740	1,115	6.7%	92,000
3/08	16,500	545	3.3%	89,000
3/07	14,857	389	2.6%	79,000
3/06	14,616	638	4.4%	79,000
Annual Growth	**2.5%**	**6.4%**	**—**	**4.4%**

2010 Year-End Financials

Debt ratio: 56.9%
Return on equity: 13.7%
Cash ($ mil.): 2,784
Current ratio: 2.04
Long-term debt ($ mil.): 3,669
No. of shares (mil.): 154
Dividends
  Yield: —
  Payout: —
Market value ($ mil.): 8,405

Stock History

NYSE: CSC

	STOCK PRICE ($) FY Close	P/E High/Low		PER SHARE ($) Earnings	Dividends	Book Value
3/10	54.49	11	7	5.28	—	41.79
3/09	36.84	7	3	7.31	—	35.72
3/08	40.79	20	12	3.20	—	35.41
3/07	52.13	27	21	2.21	—	38.16
3/06	55.55	18	13	3.38	—	43.90
Annual Growth	**(0.5%)**	**—**	**—**	**11.8%**	**—**	**(1.2%)**

ConAgra Foods

ConAgra Foods fills Americans' refrigerators, freezers, and pantries and, ultimately, their tummies. The company is a top US food producer, offering name brand packaged and frozen foods. ConAgra's brands are a cornucopia of America's well-known foods, including Banquet, Chef Boyardee, Egg Beaters, Healthy Choice, Hunt's, Jiffy, Orville Redenbacher's, PAM, Slim Jim, and Van Camp's. It is also one of the country's largest foodservice and food manufacturing suppliers, offering them convenience foods and ingredients. The company has sold off its agricultural, meat, and commodity products operations, as well as a number of noncore brands to focus on branded and value-added packaged foods.

As part of its strategy to shed non-core brands, ConAgra Foods in 2010 sold its Gilroy Foods & Flavors business-to-business unit to Singapore-headquartered Olam International for $250 million. Also that year it sold off its noncore Luck's baked-bean brand. Previous sales of noncore assets included ConAgra's Mexican entree and appetizer Fernando's and El Extremo foodservice brands to Foster Poultry Farms in 2009.

The shedding of these nonfood-related businesses have allowed the company to better pay attention to its consumer-aimed brands, including Chef Boyardee, PAM, and others, as well as shelf-stable and frozen foods such as Banquet, Hunt's, Peter Pan, and Wesson. It also continued to add to its name-brand products. The 2010 takeover of American Pie, maker of Marie Callender's fruit pies, cobblers, and pie crusts, along with Claim Jumper brand frozen appetizers, dinners, and pot pies was an example of this, adding two more popular brands to the ConAgra roster.

HISTORY

Alva Kinney founded Nebraska Consolidated Mills in 1919 by combining the operations of four Nebraska grain mills. It did not expand outside Nebraska until it opened a mill and feed processing plant in Alabama in 1942.

Consolidated Mills developed Duncan Hines cake mix in the 1950s. But Duncan Hines failed to raise a large enough market share, and the company sold it to Procter & Gamble in 1956. Consolidated Mills used the proceeds to expand, opening a flour and feed mill in Puerto Rico the next year. In the 1960s, while competitors were moving into prepared foods, the firm expanded into animal feeds and poultry processing. By 1970 it had poultry processing plants in Alabama, Georgia, and Louisiana. In 1971 the company changed its name to ConAgra (Latin for "in partnership with the land"). During the 1970s it expanded into the fertilizer, catfish, and pet accessory businesses.

Poorly performing subsidiaries and commodity speculation caused ConAgra severe financial problems until 1974, when Mike Harper, a former Pillsbury executive, took over. Harper trimmed properties to reduce debt and had the company back on its feet by 1976. ConAgra stayed focused on the commodities side of the business, but was thus tied to volatile price cycles. In 1978 it bought United Agri Products (agricultural chemicals).

ConAgra moved into consumer food products in the 1980s. It bought Banquet (frozen food, 1980) and within six years had introduced almost 90 new products under that label. Other purchases included Singleton Seafood (1981), Armour Food Company (meats, dairy products, frozen food; 1983), and RJR Nabisco's frozen food business (1986). ConAgra became a major player in the red meat market with the 1987 purchases of E.A. Miller (boxed beef), Monfort (beef and lamb), and Swift Independent Packing.

ConAgra continued with acquisitions of consumer food makers, including Beatrice Foods (Orville Redenbacher's popcorn, Hunt's tomato products) in 1991. In 1997 it agreed to pay $8.3 million to settle federal charges of wire fraud and watering down grain. That year ConAgra named president Bruce Rohde as CEO; he became chairman in 1998.

In 2000 ConAgra acquired major brand holder International Home Foods from HM Capital Partners (known as Hicks, Muse, Tate & Furst at the time) for about $2.9 billion. The company then became ConAgra Foods. During 2001 the company drew SEC attention and was forced to restate earnings for the previous three years due to accounting no-nos in its United Agri Products division.

In 2002 the USDA forced ConAgra to recall 19 million pounds of ground beef because of possible *E. coli* contamination, making it the second-largest food recall in US history.

In 2003 ConAgra agreed to pay $1.5 million in cash and job offers to settle an EEOC lawsuit charging bias against disabled workers at the company's California-based Gilroy Foods plant. The agreement involved the largest disability settlement in the agriculture industry.

In 2005 Rhode retired. His replacement was former chairman and CEO of PepsiCo Beverages and Foods North America, Gary Rodkin. ConAgra agreed to pay a $14 million shareholder settlement in 2005 regarding a lawsuit claiming fictitious sales and mis-reported earnings at its former subsidiary United Agri Products.

In early 2007 salmonella was found in some of the company's Peter Pan and Great Value (a Wal-Mart product) brands of peanut butter, forcing a nationwide recall. Salmonella food poisoning was linked to some 600 people in 47 states. No deaths related to the peanut butter were confirmed.

Just two months later, the company voluntarily stopped production at the Missouri plant that makes its Banquet and generic brands of frozen turkey and chicken pot pies after learning that the were linked to some 140 cases of salmonella in 30 states. ConAgra did not recall the pies but offered mail-in refunds and store returns. The USDA began an investigation and advised consumers not to eat the pies.

ConAgra sold its trading and merchandising operations (ConAgra Trade Group) in 2008 to a group of investors that included the Ospraie Special Opportunities Fund for $2.8 billion. Saying it couldn't give the brand the attention it needs, in 2008 the company sold its Knott's Berry Farm jam and jelly business to J. M. Smucker.

In a tragedy that made the evening news, three ConAgra workers were killed and some 40 were injured in an explosion and fire at a company Slim Jim manufacturing plant in Garner, North Carolina, in June 2009. It was later determined that the blast was caused by a natural-gas leak. ConAgra partnered with the United Way, forming the Garner Plant Fund that raised money to assist the victims and their families. The company also continued to pay workers salaries while the plant remained closed for investigation. ConAgra was fined $106,000 by the government in 2010 and the plant was eventually closed.

EXECUTIVES

Chairman: Steven F. (Steve) Goldstone, age 64
President, CEO, and Director: Gary M. Rodkin, age 58, $8,830,972 total compensation
EVP and CFO: John F. Gehring, age 49, $1,645,615 total compensation
EVP, General Counsel, and Corporate Secretary: Colleen Batcheler, age 35
EVP External Affairs; President, Commercial Foods: Robert F. (Rob) Sharpe Jr., age 57, $3,470,715 total compensation
EVP and Chief Marketing Officer: Joan K. Chow, age 49
EVP Research, Quality, and Innovation: Albert D. (Al) Bolles, age 52
EVP Supply Chain: Gregory L. (Greg) Smith, age 45
SVP, Treasurer, and Assistant Corporate Secretary: Scott E. Messel, age 51, $1,172,391 total compensation
SVP and Corporate Controller: Patrick D. (Doug) Linehan, age 41
VP Corporate Communication: Teresa Paulsen
VP Corporate Real Estate and Facilities: James D. Doyle
VP Environment, Health, and Safety: James Lime
VP Government Affairs: Brent A. Baglien
VP Human Resources and Staffing: Tim Jones
VP Investor Relations: Christopher W. (Chris) Klinefelter, age 43
VP Corporate Affairs; President, ConAgra Foods Foundation: Chris Kircher
President, Consumer Foods: André J. Hawaux, age 50, $2,541,391 total compensation
President, ConAgra Foods, Lamb Weston: Jeffery J. (Jeff) DeLapp
Auditors: KPMG LLP

LOCATIONS

HQ: ConAgra Foods, Inc.
1 ConAgra Dr., Omaha, NE 68102
Phone: 402-240-4000   **Fax:** 402-240-4707
Web: www.conagrafoods.com

PRODUCTS/OPERATIONS

2010 Sales

	$ mil.	% of total
Consumer foods	8,001.9	66
Commercial foods	4,077.5	34
Total	**12,079.4**	**100**

Selected Brands

Foodservice and ingredient brands
  Angela Mia (tomato products)
  Award Cuisine (precooked entrees, breakfasts, and cheese sauces)
  ConAgra Mills (wheat flour, barley flour)
  J. Hungerford Smith (dessert toppings)
  J.M. Swank (food ingredients)
  Lamb Weston (frozen potato-based products)
  The Max (pizzeria products)
  Vogel Popcorn

Retail brands
  Act II (microwave popcorn)
  Alexia (organic breads, appetizers, and potato products)
  Andy Capp's (salty snacks)
  Banquet (frozen dinners and poultry)
  Banquet Brown 'N Serve Sausage
  Blue Bonnet Margarine
  Chef Boyardee (canned pasta)
  Crunch 'N Munch (snack mix)
  DAVID Seeds (salted sunflower seeds)
  Dennison's Chile
  Eagle Mills (multi-grain flour)
  Egg Beaters (frozen liquid egg substitute)
  Fiddle Faddle (popcorn and caramel snack mix)
  Fleischmann's Margarine
  Gilroy Foods & Flavors (seasonings and flavorings)
  Gulden's Mustard
  Healthy Choice (soups, frozen dinners, pasta sauce)
  Hebrew National (frankfurters)
  Hunt's (canned tomato products)
  Jiffy Pop Popcorn
  Kid Cuisine (frozen meals)
  La Choy (Asian sauces, canned chow mein noodles, canned vegetables, meals, and frozen egg rolls)
  Libby's (canned meats)
  Luck's Baked Beans
  Manwich Sloppy Joe Sauce
  Marie Callender's (frozen meals and desserts)
  Orville Redenbacher's Popcorn
  PAM (non-stick cooking spray)
  Parkay Margarine
  Patio (frozen dinners and burritos)
  Penrose Pickled Sausage
  Peter Pan Peanut Butter
  Poppycock Snack Mix
  Ranch Style Beans
  Reddi-Wip (aerosol whipped cream)
  Ro*Tel (canned processed tomatoes)
  Rosarita Refried Beans
  Slim Jim Beef Jerky
  Snack Pack (shelf-stable pudding)
  Swiss Miss (hot chocolate mix)
  Van Camp's Pork and Beans
  Wesson (cooking oil)
  Wolf Chili

COMPETITORS

American Pop Corn	Kraft Foods
B&G Foods	Link Snacks
Bush Brothers	Malt-O-Meal
Campbell Soup	Manischewitz
Clorox	McCain Foods
Del Monte Foods	McIlhenny
Eden Foods	Monterey Gourmet Foods
Frito-Lay	Mott's
General Mills	Nestlé
Gilster-Mary Lee	Newman's Own
Goya	NutriSystem
H. J. Heinz Limited	Pinnacle Foods
Hain Celestial	Ralcorp
Hanover Foods	Sara Lee
Heinz	Schwan's
Hormel	Seneca Foods
Inventure foods	Slim-Fast
Jenny Craig	smart balance
J-OIL MILLS	Smucker
JR Simplot	Snappy Popcorn
Kellogg	Weaver Popcorn Company

HISTORICAL FINANCIALS

Company Type: Public

Income Statement

	REVENUE ($ mil.)	NET INCOME ($ mil.)	NET PROFIT MARGIN	EMPLOYEES
			FYE: Last Sunday in May	
5/10	12,079	723	6.0%	24,400
5/09	12,731	978	7.7%	25,600
5/08	11,606	931	8.0%	25,000
5/07	12,028	765	6.4%	24,500
5/06	11,579	534	4.6%	33,000
Annual Growth	1.1%	7.9%	—	(7.3%)

Stock History

NYSE: CAG

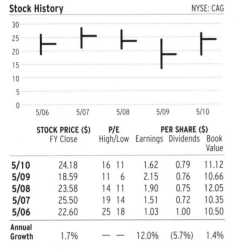

	STOCK PRICE ($) FY Close	P/E High/Low		PER SHARE ($) Earnings	Dividends	Book Value
5/10	24.18	16	11	1.62	0.79	11.12
5/09	18.59	11	6	2.15	0.76	10.66
5/08	23.58	14	11	1.90	0.75	12.05
5/07	25.50	19	14	1.51	0.72	10.35
5/06	22.60	25	18	1.03	1.00	10.50
Annual Growth	1.7%	—	—	12.0%	(5.7%)	1.4%

ConocoPhillips

Proudly combining two venerable names in the US oil industry, ConocoPhillips is the #2 integrated oil and gas company in the US, behind Exxon Mobil. The company explores for oil and gas in more than 30 countries and has proved reserves of 10 billion barrels of oil equivalent. It has a global refining capacity of more than 2.6 million barrels per day and sells petroleum at 8,500 retail outlets in the US under the 76, Conoco, and Phillips 66 brands, and at 1,225 gas stations in Europe. Other operations include chemicals, gas gathering, fuels technology, and power generation.

In 2008 ConocoPhillips acquired a 50% stake in TransCanada's Keystone Oil Pipeline, which plans to construct a 2,148¬mile Canadian-US crude oil pipeline. That year, in a move to further expand its energy sources, the company and Origin Energy in an $8 billion deal formed an Australasian natural gas business focused on coal bed methane production and liquefied natural gas processing and sales.

While the Conoco/Phillips merger proved to be of real value in terms of growing the company's refining capacity and market share, the slumping economy and the underperformance of its LUKOIL and Burlington Resources investments prompted the company to post a record loss for the fourth quarter of 2008. The largest impairment charge it took in Q4 was a $25.4 billion write-down of exploration and production assets, mainly relating to the $36 billion purchase of Burlington Resources. It was also forced to reduce the value of its stake in LUKOIL by $7.3 billion and lower the book value of two refineries by $537 million. The global economic slump hurt the bottom line in 2009 as well.

Subsequently, in 2010 ConocoPhillips sold its 9% stake in Canadian oil sands operator Syncrude to China Petroleum & Chemical Corp. for $4.6 billion. It also announced plans to sell its

stake in LUKOIL as part of larger program to dispose of $10 billion of assets in order to pay down debt.

In 2010, as a result of the BP oil rig disaster in the Gulf of Mexico, the company teamed with Exxon Mobil, Chevron, and Royal Dutch Shell to form a $1 billion rapid-response joint venture with the capabilities to manage and contain future deepwater oil spills.

HISTORY

The roots of ConocoPhillips go back more than a century and run deep into the history of the US oil industry.

Isaac Elder Blake, an Easterner who had lost everything on a bad investment, came to Ogden, Utah, and founded Continental Oil & Transportation (CO&T) in 1875. In 1885 CO&T merged with Standard Oil's operations in the Rockies and was reincorporated in Colorado as Continental Oil. Continental tightened its grip on the Rocky Mountain area and by 1906 had taken over 98% of the western market. Its monopoly ended in 1911 when the US Supreme Court ordered Standard to divest several holdings: Continental was one of 34 independent oil companies created in 1913.

Seeing opportunity in autos, Continental built a gas station in 1914. Two years later it got into oil production when it bought United Oil, and by 1924 it had become fully integrated by merging with Mutual Oil, which owned production, refining, and distribution assets. Continental's biggest merger came in 1929 when it merged with Marland Oil of Oklahoma.

Continental diversified in the 1960s, acquiring American Agricultural Chemicals in 1963 and Consolidation Coal (Consol) in 1966. Restructuring in the 1970s into Conoco Chemical, Consol, and two petroleum divisions, the company ramped up oil exploration and entered ventures to develop uranium. In 1979 it changed its name to Conoco.

In the late 1970s, Conoco began joint ventures with chemical titan DuPont. The companies worked together well, and in 1981 Conoco was acquired by DuPont to forestall hostile takeover attempts by Mobil and Seagram. DuPont sold off $1.5 billion of Conoco's assets and absorbed Conoco Chemical. In 1998, however, DuPont spun off Conoco in what was the US's largest-ever IPO at the time (DuPont had completely divested its 70% stake by the next year).

Conoco expanded its natural gas reserves in 2001 by buying Gulf Canada Resources for $4.3 billion in cash and $2 billion in assumed debt. Also that year Conoco agreed to merge with Phillips Petroleum.

The story of Phillips Petroleum begins with Frank Phillips, a prosperous Iowa barber who married a banker's daughter in 1897 and began selling bonds. When a missionary who worked with Native Americans in Oklahoma regaled him with stories about the oil patch, Phillips migrated to Bartlesville, Oklahoma, and established Anchor Oil in 1903.

Anchor's first two wells were dry, but the next one — the Anna Anderson No. 1 — was the first of a string of 81 successful wells. Phillips and his brother L. E., doubling as bankers in Bartlesville, transformed Anchor into Phillips Petroleum in 1917.

With continued success on Native American lands in Oklahoma, Phillips moved into refining and marketing. In 1927 the company opened its

first gas station in Wichita, Kansas. Frank Phillips retired after WWII and died in 1950.

During the 1980s Phillips became a target of takeover attempts. To fend off bids from corporate raiders T. Boone Pickens (1984) and Carl Icahn (1985), Phillips repurchased stock and ran its debt up to $9 billion. It then cut 8,300 jobs and sold billions of dollars' worth of assets; strong petrochemicals earnings kept it afloat.

As part of an industry trend to share costs of less-profitable operations, Phillips and Conoco flirted with the idea of merging their marketing and refining operations in 1996, but the talks failed. Discussions between Phillips and Ultramar Diamond Shamrock about merging the companies' North American oil refining and marketing operations broke down in 1999.

James Mulva took over as CEO in 1999, and Phillips decided to shift its focus to its upstream operations. The next year Phillips acquired ARCO's Alaska assets for $7 billion and merged its chemicals division with Chevron's.

In 2001 the company bought Tosco for about $9.3 billion. Big as it was, that deal was eclipsed the next year by the merger of Phillips and Conoco. In 2003 the company sold its Circle K gas station chain to Alimentation Couche-Tard.

In 2006, to boost its reserves base, ConocoPhlllips acquired Burlington Resources for about $36 billion. In 2007 under nationalization pressure from President Hugo Chavez, ConocoPhillips exited Venezuela.

EXECUTIVES

Chairman and CEO: James J. (Jim) Mulva, age 64, $14,388,661 total compensation
President and COO: John A. Carrig, age 58, $12,297,171 total compensation
SVP Finance and CFO: Sigmund L. (Sig) Cornelius, age 55, $4,388,521 total compensation
SVP and Chief Administrative Officer: Eugene L. (Gene) Batchelder, age 63
SVP Corporate Shared Services: Rand C. Berney, age 54, $2,827,862 total compensation
SVP Government Affairs: Red Cavaney
SVP Technology: Stephen R. Brand
SVP Exploration and Business Development: Larry E. Archibald
SVP Exploration and Production, Americas: Kevin O. Meyers, age 56, $4,417,830 total compensation
SVP Refining, Marketing, and Transportation: W.C. W. (Willie) Chiang, age 50
SVP Exploration and Production, International: Ryan M. Lance, age 47, $4,037,665 total compensation
SVP Project Development and Procurement: Luc J. Messier
SVP Commercial and Planning & Strategy: Jeff W. Sheets, age 52
SVP Legal, General Counsel, and Corporate Secretary: Janet Langford Kelly, age 52
VP Human Resources: Carin S. Knickel
VP and Treasurer: Frances M. Vallejo
President, Strategy, Integration and Specialty Businesses: Rex W. Bennett
President, Gas and Power: John W. Wright
President and CEO, Chevron Phillips Chemical Company: Greg C. Garland, age 52
President, Global Refining: Larry M. Ziemba
President, Europe Refining, Marketing and Transportation: Robert J. (Bob) Hassler, age 58
Auditors: Ernst & Young LLP

LOCATIONS

HQ: ConocoPhillips
  600 N. Dairy Ashford Rd., Houston, TX 77079
Phone: 281-293-1000
Web: www.conocophillips.com

2009 Sales

	% of total
US	65
UK	14
Canada	2
Australia	2
Norway	1
Other countries	16
Total	**100**

PRODUCTS/OPERATIONS

2009 Sales

	$ mil.	% of total
Refining, marketing & transportation	107,233	72
Exploration & production	37,097	25
Midstream	4,892	3
Emerging businesses	86	—
Chemicals	11	—
Adjustments	3,521	—
Total	**152,840**	**100**

COMPETITORS

Admiral Petroleum	George Warren
Arabian American	Hess Corporation
Development	Koch Industries, Inc.
BHP Billiton	Marathon Oil
BP	Occidental Permian
BW Gas	Occidental Petroleum
Chevron	Shell Oil Products
CITGO	Sinclair Oil
CVR	Sunoco
Eni	TOTAL
Exxon Mobil	Ultra Petroleum
Frontier Oil	Valero Energy

HISTORICAL FINANCIALS

Company Type: Public

Income Statement

FYE: December 31

	REVENUE ($ mil.)	NET INCOME ($ mil.)	NET PROFIT MARGIN	EMPLOYEES
12/09	152,840	4,858	3.2%	30,000
12/08	246,182	(16,998)	—	33,800
12/07	194,495	11,891	6.1%	32,600
12/06	167,578	15,550	9.3%	38,400
12/05	183,364	13,617	7.4%	35,600
Annual Growth	**(4.4%)**	**(22.7%)**	**—**	**(4.2%)**

2009 Year-End Financials

Debt ratio: 51.1%
Return on equity: 8.3%
Cash ($ mil.): 542
Current ratio: 0.89
Long-term debt ($ mil.): 31,934

No. of shares (mil.): 1,483
Dividends
  Yield: 3.7%
  Payout: 59.0%
Market value ($ mil.): 75,755

Stock History

NYSE: COP

	STOCK PRICE ($) FY Close	P/E High/Low		PER SHARE ($) Earnings	Dividends	Book Value
12/09	51.07	18	11	3.24	1.91	42.11
12/08	51.80	—	—	(11.16)	1.88	37.19
12/07	88.30	13	9	7.22	1.64	59.99
12/06	71.95	8	6	9.66	1.44	55.72
12/05	58.18	7	4	9.55	1.18	35.55
Annual Growth	**(3.2%)**	**—**	**—**	**(23.7%)**	**12.8%**	**4.3%**

CONSOL Energy

Consolation prizes don't interest CONSOL Energy. CONSOL is one of the US's largest coal mining companies, along with Peabody Energy and Arch Coal. The company has some 4.5 billion tons of proved reserves, mainly in northern and central Appalachia and the Illinois Basin, and produces about 59 million tons of coal annually. CONSOL primarily mines high BTU coal, which burns cleaner than lower grades. Customers include electric utilities and steel mills. CONSOL delivers coal using its own railroad cars, export terminals, and fleet of towboats and barges. The company also engages in natural gas exploration and production; its proved reserves total 1.9 trillion cu. ft.

Aware that most planned power plants will be gas-fired, CONSOL has diversified its energy holdings by acquiring additional natural gas reserves. In 2010 the company acquired Dominion Resources' Appalachian exploration and production assets for about $3.5 billion. The acquisiton doubles CONSOL's natural gas reserves to 3 million cu. ft.

Also in 2010, as a logical follow-up on the Dominion Resources deal, CONSOL acquired the remaining shares in CNX Gas that it did not already own (for about $965 million) in order to consolidate its natural gas holdings.

In addition to its coal and gas businesses, CONSOL distributes mining and industrial supplies through its Fairmont Supply unit. About 40% of Fairmont's business is with its parent company. CONSOL also runs about 25 towboats and 700 barges.

HISTORY

When Consolidation Coal was formed in Maryland in 1864, coal was just beginning to replace wood as the world's top industrial energy source. In the 1880s Consolidation Coal, like other large coal companies, began operations in the Appalachia region of the US. During the 1920s the company built the Kentucky mining city of Van Lear. (Country music superstar Loretta Lynn's father worked as a Consolidation Coal miner nearby.) In 1945 Consolidation Coal merged with Pittsburgh Coal, and the next year the combined company took over Hanna Coal.

In 1966 Continental Oil, founded in 1875 and later renamed Conoco, bought Consolidation Coal. Two years later 78 workers were killed in a Consolidation Coal mine explosion. Also in 1968 a federal jury found the United Mine Workers (UMW) and the company guilty of conspiring to put Kentucky's South East Coal out of business. In 1971 the UMW and Consolidation Coal paid South East almost $9 million in damages, court costs, and interest. Consolidation Coal became part of DuPont when that company bought Conoco in 1981.

Ten years later the mining unit of German conglomerate RWE, Rheinbraun, bought 50% of Consolidation Coal (later increased to 74%) from DuPont. That year Consolidation Coal and Conoco formed the Pocahontas Gas Partnership to recover coalbed methane gas.

A restructuring in 1992 created CONSOL Energy as a holding company for more than 60 subsidiaries, including principal operating subsidiary Consolidation Coal. The next year the UMW initiated a strike against CONSOL, which was using more and more nonunion workers in its mines.

CONSOL opened its ash disposal facility the next year and began developing ways to reuse its plant waste and by-products.

From 1994 to 1997 the company reduced its workforce by 20% and closed six of its mining complexes. By 1997 about one-third of CONSOL's coal came from nonunion mines. In 1998 the company filed to go public and bought Rochester & Pittsburgh Coal.

CONSOL completed its IPO in 1999. The depressed coal market halved CONSOL's sales that year, and the company scaled back production at some of its smaller, high-cost mines in Pennsylvania and West Virginia. During the winter of 2000 and in early 2001, coal prices improved by 36% and natural gas prices skyrocketed as cold temperatures and an energy crisis in California increased demand for energy sources. Despite the improvement in coal prices, the company continued to shut down high-cost mines.

In 2001 CONSOL acquired Conoco's half of the Pocahontas Gas joint venture. It also bought Windsor Coal, Southern Ohio Coal, and Central Ohio Coal from American Electric Power. In addition, CONSOL bought 50% of the Glennies Creek Mine, its first Australian property.

That year CONSOL contracted with Allegheny Energy Supply (an affiliate of largest customer Allegheny Energy) to build an 88-MW electric generating plant in Virginia to be fueled by coalbed methane gas produced by CONSOL.

CONSOL in 2003 sold its Canadian operations (Cardinal River and Line Creek Mines) to Fording. The next year CONSOL sold its Glennies Creek mine interest, thus exiting Australia. Also in 2004 RWE severed ties with CONSOL by selling its remaining 19% stake in the company.

The next year CONSOL created a new subsidiary, CNX Gas, to handle the company's gas operations. It then sold a minority stake in CNX Gas to a group of institutional investors in a private transaction, and in 2006 CNX Gas went public, with CONSOL retaining an 82% stake.

EXECUTIVES

Chairman, President, and CEO; Chairman and CEO, CNX Gas: J. Brett Harvey, age 59, $13,750,926 total compensation
Vice Chairman: John L. Whitmire, age 69
EVP Corporate Affairs and Chief Legal Officer, CONSOL Energy and CNX Gas Corporation: P. Jerome Richey, age 60, $1,545,646 total compensation
EVP and COO; President and COO, CNX Gas: Nicholas J. DeIuliis, age 41, $5,191,344 total compensation
EVP and CFO, CONSOL Energy and CNX Gas: William J. Lyons, age 61, $3,869,410 total compensation
EVP Energy Sales and Transportation Services, CONSOL Energy and CNX Gas; President, CONSOL Energy Sales: Robert F. Pusateri, age 59
EVP Business Advancement and Support Services, CONSOL Energy and CNX Gas: Robert P. King, age 57, $1,400,699 total compensation
COO, Coal: Bart J. Hyita, age 51
SVP Sales: James J. McCaffrey
SVP Operations Support: Albert A. Aloia
VP Investor and Public Relations: Brandon R. Elliott
Auditors: Ernst & Young LLP

LOCATIONS

HQ: CONSOL Energy Inc.
  CNX Center, 1000 CONSOL Energy Dr.
  Canonsburg, PA 15317
Phone: 724-485-4000
Web: www.consolenergy.com

2009 Sales

	$ mil.	% of total
US	4,026.6	87
Europe	298.3	6
South America	120.2	3
Canada	25.1	1
Other regions	151.7	3
Total	**4,621.9**	**100**

PRODUCTS/OPERATIONS

2009 Sales

	$ mil.	% of total
Coal		
Thermal	3,148.0	68
Metallurgical	223.0	5
Other coal	117.0	3
Gas		
Produced	629.0	14
Gas royalty	48.0	1
Industrial supplies	195.0	4
Freight revenue	148.0	3
Other	113.9	2
Total	**4,621.9**	**100**

COMPETITORS

Alliance Resource	Peabody Energy
Arch Coal	Penn Virginia
Devon Energy	RAG AG
EQT Corporation	Rio Tinto Limited
Massey Energy	SM Energy
Nippon Coke	Westmoreland Coal
& Engineering	

HISTORICAL FINANCIALS
Company Type: Public

Income Statement — FYE: December 31

	REVENUE ($ mil.)	NET INCOME ($ mil.)	NET PROFIT MARGIN	EMPLOYEES
12/09	4,622	540	11.7%	8,012
12/08	4,486	443	9.9%	8,176
12/07	3,762	268	7.1%	7,728
12/06	3,715	409	11.0%	7,253
12/05	3,810	581	15.2%	7,257
Annual Growth	**4.9%**	**(1.8%)**	**—**	**2.5%**

2009 Year-End Financials

Debt ratio: 23.7%
Return on equity: 33.2%
Cash ($ mil.): 66
Current ratio: 0.66
Long-term debt ($ mil.): 423
No. of shares (mil.): 226
Dividends
Yield: 0.8%
Payout: 13.6%
Market value ($ mil.): 11,245

Stock History
NYSE: CNX

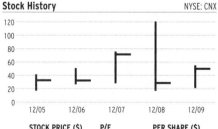

	STOCK PRICE ($) FY Close	P/E High	P/E Low	PER SHARE ($) Earnings	PER SHARE ($) Dividends	PER SHARE ($) Book Value
12/09	49.80	18	8	2.95	0.40	7.91
12/08	28.58	50	8	2.40	0.40	6.48
12/07	71.52	51	20	1.45	0.31	5.38
12/06	32.13	22	13	2.20	0.28	4.72
12/05	32.59	13	6	3.13	0.28	4.54
Annual Growth	**11.2%**	**—**	**—**	**(1.5%)**	**9.3%**	**14.9%**

Consolidated Edison

Utility holding company Consolidated Edison (Con Edison) is the night light for the city that never sleeps. Con Edison's main subsidiary, Consolidated Edison Company of New York, distributes electricity to 3.3 million residential and business customers in New York City; it also delivers natural gas to about 1.1 million customers. Subsidiary Orange and Rockland Utilities serves more than 400,000 electric and gas customers in three states. Con Edison's nonutility operations include retail and wholesale energy marketing, independent power production, and infrastructure project development.

Competitive energy businesses include subsidiary Consolidated Edison Solutions, which markets power and gas to retail customers and provides energy procurement and management services, and Consolidated Edison Energy, which markets and trades wholesale energy. Subsidiary Consolidated Edison Development has interests in power generation facilities.

The company seeks to balance growing its competitive operations (with an emphasis on green energy) with improving its regulated infrastructure assets.

In 2008, in order to raise cash to pay down debt and reinvest in core businesses, the company's Consolidated Edison Development unit sold its merchant generation portfolio (1,706 MW of fossil-fueled power generation projects) to investment group North American Energy Alliance, LLC for $1.5 billion. The move also allowed Consolidated Edison Development to reorient its operations toward developing wholesale renewable power, natural gas, and transmission infrastructure in the US, primarily in the Northeast.

Promoting green power sources, in 2010 Con Edison proposed to develop 25 MW of solar energy resources in New York City by 2015. The solar power would annually offset about 16,000 tons of carbon dioxide.

HISTORY

Several professionals, led by Timothy Dewey, formed The New York Gas Light Company in 1823 to illuminate part of Manhattan. In 1884 five other gas companies joined New York Gas Light to form the Consolidated Gas Company of New York.

Thomas Edison's incandescent lamp came on the scene in 1879, and The Edison Electric Illuminating Company of New York was formed in 1880 to build the world's first commercial electric power station (Pearl Street), financed by a group led by J.P. Morgan. Edison supervised the project, and in 1882 New York became the first major city with electric lighting.

Realizing electricity would replace gas, Consolidated Gas acquired electric companies, including Anthony Brady's New York Gas and Electric Light, Heat and Power Company (1900), which joined Edison's Illuminating Company in 1901 to form the New York Edison Company. More than 170 purchases followed, including that of the New York Steam Company (1930), a cheap source of steam for electric turbines.

The Public Utility Holding Company Act of 1935 ushered in the era of regulated, regional monopolies. The next year New York Edison combined its holdings to form the Consolidated Edison Company of New York (Con Ed).

Con Ed opened its first nuclear station in 1962. By then, Con Ed had a reputation for inefficiency and poor service, and shareholders were angry about its slow growth and low earnings. Environmentalists joined the grousers in 1963 when Con Ed began constructing a pumped-storage plant in Cornwall near the Hudson River. Charles Luce, a former undersecretary with the Department of Interior, was recruited to rescue Con Ed in 1967. He added power plants and beefed up customer service.

In the 1970s inflation and the energy crisis drove up oil prices (Con Ed's main fuel source), and in 1974 Luce withheld dividends for the first time since 1885. He persuaded the New York State Power Authority to buy two unfinished power plants, saving Con Ed $200 million. In 1980 Luce ended the Cornwall controversy and donated the land for park use. He retired in 1982.

The utility started buying power from various suppliers and in 1984 began a two-year price freeze, a boon to rate-hike-weary New Yorkers. The New York State Public Service Commission didn't approve another rate increase until 1992.

In 1997 Con Ed, government officials, consumer groups, and other energy firms outlined the company's deregulation plan, which included the formation of the Consolidated Edison, Inc., holding company (known as Con Edison) and a power marketing unit in 1998. The next year Con Edison sold New York City generating facilities to KeySpan, Northern States Power, and Orion Power for a total of $1.65 billion.

Also in 1999 Con Edison bought Orange and Rockland Utilities for $790 million to increase its New York base and expand into New Jersey and Pennsylvania. In an effort to push into New England, the company that year agreed to buy Northeast Utilities (NU) for $3.3 billion in cash and stock and $3.9 billion in assumed debt. But the deal broke down in 2001. NU accused Con Edison of improperly trying to renegotiate terms, while Con Edison accused NU of concealing information about unfavorable power supply contracts.

Con Edison's Indian Point Unit 2 nuclear plant was shut down temporarily in 2000 after a radioactive steam leak; later that year it agreed to sell Indian Point Units 1 and 2 to Entergy for $502 million. The sale was completed in 2001. That year Con Edison also incurred an estimated $400 million in costs related to emergency response and asset damage from the September 11 terrorist attacks on New York City.

After evaluating strategic alternatives for its telecommunications business due to losses at the unit, in 2006 the company sold its Con Edison Communications unit (now RCN Business Solutions) to RCN Corporation for $32 million.

EXECUTIVES

Chairman, President, and CEO; Chairman, CEO, and Trustee, Consolidated Edison of New York:
Kevin Burke, age 59, $7,899,301 total compensation
EVP, Consolidated Edison Company of New York:
John D. McMahon, age 58,
$3,833,271 total compensation
SVP Enterprise Shared Services, Consolidated Edison Company of New York: Luther Tai, age 61
SVP and CFO; SVP and CFO, Consolidated Edison of New York; and CFO and Controller, Orange and Rockland Utilities: Robert N. Hoglund, age 48,
$2,000,864 total compensation
General Counsel, Consolidated Edison and Consolidated Edison Company of New York:
Elizabeth D. Moore, age 55

VP and Controller, Consolidated Edison and Consolidated Edison Company of New York: Robert Muccilo, age 54
VP and Treasurer, Consolidated Edison and Consolidated Edison Company of New York: Scott L. Sanders, age 46
VP Strategic Planning: Gurudatta Nadkarni, age 44
Secretary: Carole Sobin
Director Investor Relations: Jan C. Childress
President, Consolidated Edison of New York: Craig S. Ivey, age 47
President and CEO, Orange and Rockland Utilities: William G. Longhi, age 56, $1,755,314 total compensation
SVP Electric Operations, Consolidated Edison Company of New York: John F. Miksad, age 50
SVP Customer Operations, Consolidated Edison Company of New York: Marilyn Caselli, age 55
SVP Public Affairs, Consolidated Edison Company of New York: Frances A. Resheske, age 49
SVP Business Shared Services, Consolidated Edison Company of New York: JoAnn F. Ryan, age 52
Auditors: PricewaterhouseCoopers LLP

LOCATIONS

HQ: Consolidated Edison, Inc.
4 Irving Place, New York, NY 10003
Phone: 212-460-4600   **Fax:** 212-982-7816
Web: www.conedison.com

PRODUCTS/OPERATIONS

2009 Sales

	$ mil.	% of total
Electricity	8,320	64
Gas	1,943	15
Steam	661	5
Other	2,108	16
Total	**13,032**	**100**

Selected Subsidiaries

Consolidated Edison Company of New York, Inc. (utility)
Consolidated Edison Development, Inc. (investments in power generation projects)
Consolidated Edison Energy, Inc. (wholesale energy marketing and trading)
Consolidated Edison Solutions, Inc. (retail energy marketing and services)
Orange and Rockland Utilities, Inc. (utility)

COMPETITORS

Accent Energy	National Grid USA
AEP	New York Power Authority
CH Energy	Northeast Utilities
CMS Energy	NSTAR
Delmarva Power	PPL Corporation
Duke Energy	Public Service Enterprise
Enbridge	Group
Green Mountain Energy	South Jersey Industries
Iberdrola USA	USPowerGen
National Fuel Gas	Viridis Energy Inc

HISTORICAL FINANCIALS

Company Type: Public

Income Statement

FYE: December 31

	REVENUE ($ mil.)	NET INCOME ($ mil.)	NET PROFIT MARGIN	EMPLOYEES
12/09	13,032	879	6.7%	15,541
12/08	13,583	1,196	8.8%	15,628
12/07	13,120	929	7.1%	15,214
12/06	12,137	737	6.1%	14,795
12/05	11,690	719	6.2%	14,537
Annual Growth	**2.8%**	**5.2%**	**—**	**1.7%**

2009 Year-End Financials

Debt ratio: 96.3%
Return on equity: 8.8%
Cash ($ mil.): —
Current ratio: 1.10
Long-term debt ($ mil.): 9,868
No. of shares (mil.): 282
Dividends
  Yield: 5.2%
  Payout: 75.2%
Market value ($ mil.): 12,810

Stock History

NYSE: ED

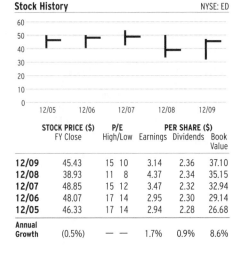

	STOCK PRICE ($) FY Close	P/E High/Low		PER SHARE ($) Earnings	Dividends	Book Value
12/09	45.43	15	10	3.14	2.36	37.10
12/08	38.93	11	8	4.37	2.34	35.15
12/07	48.85	15	12	3.47	2.32	32.94
12/06	48.07	17	14	2.95	2.30	29.14
12/05	46.33	17	14	2.94	2.28	26.68
Annual Growth	**(0.5%)**	**—**	**—**	**1.7%**	**0.9%**	**8.6%**

Constellation Brands

Thinking about alcohol makes this company starry-eyed. Constellation Brands is a leading beer, wine, and spirits maker. It offers more than 100 brands, which it sells in some 150 countries. Its wine division, anchored by its domestic winemaking subsidiary Constellation Wines U.S., is a global leader in wine production, offering brands such as Robert Mondavi and Vendange, as well as such premium labels as Ravenswood and Simi. Its Crown Imports joint venture with Grupo Modelo imports Corona and Tsingtao beer, among other beer brands. Constellation Brands also markets premium spirits, including Black Velvet whiskey and SVEDKA vodka.

Changes in the beverage industry over the past decade include an increase in global wine consumption — with sales of premium wines growing faster than value-priced wines — and a growing preference in the US for high-end and imported beers over domestic brands. In response, Constellation Brands has been tweaking its vast portfolio to focus more on wine and higher-growth, premium brands of beer and spirits. To that end, in 2010 it sold its UK assets (i.e., Gaymer Cider) to Ireland's C&C Group for €45 million ($74 million). The sale includes the Blackthorn, Olde English, and Gaymers brands. The divestment followed the 2009 sale of its value spirits brands to New Orleans-based Sazerac Company for about $331 million. Some of the brands included in the sale were Barton, Sköl, Mr. Boston, Fleischmann's, the 99 schnapps line, the di Amore line, Chi-Chi's pre-mixed cocktail line, and Montezuma Tequila.

The company's 2007 purchase of the Fortune Brands US wine business, which makes and sells super-premium and fine wines, such as Clos du Bois and Wild Horse, bolstered Constellation Wines' position as the leading purveyor of premium wine in the US. The company grows

grapes and makes its wine at about 50 wineries in the US, Canada, Australia, and New Zealand.

CEO Robert Sands and his family control about 65% of Constellation's voting power.

HISTORY

Marvin Sands, the son of winemaker Mordecai (Mack) Sands, exited the Navy in 1945 and entered distilling by purchasing an old sauerkraut factory in Canandaigua, New York. His business, Canandaigua Industries, struggled while making fruit wines in bulk for local bottlers in the East. Aiming at regional markets, the company began producing its own brands two years later. Marvin opened the Richards Wine Cellar in Petersburg, Virginia, in 1951 and put his father in charge of the unit. In 1954 Marvin developed his own brand of "fortified" wine — boosted by 190-proof brandy — and named it Richards Wild Irish Rose after his son Richard.

The company slowly expanded, buying a number of small wineries in the 1960s and 1970s. It went public in 1973, changing its name to Canandaigua Wine. A year later the company expanded to the West Coast, thus gaining access to the growing varietal market.

Canandaigua continued to grow through acquisitions and new product introductions in the early 1980s. In 1984, when wine coolers became popular, the company introduced Sun Country Coolers, doubling sales to $173 million by 1986.

The short-lived wine cooler fad made Canandaigua realize that its distribution network could handle more volume, so it began looking for additional brands. The company picked up Kosher winemaker Manischewitz and East Coast winemaker Widmer's Wine Cellars, both in 1987. The company made a major purchase in 1991 when it bought Guild Wineries & Distillers (Cook's champagne) for $60 million.

Richard Sands became CEO in 1993. Subsequent acquisitions included Barton (beer importing, branded spirits; 1993), Vintners International (Paul Masson and Taylor, 1993), Heublein's Almaden and Inglenook (1994), and 12 distilled spirits brands from United Distillers Glenmore (1995). The moves doubled Canandaigua's share of the spirits market, making it the #4 US spirits supplier. After the flurry of acquisitions, the company changed its name in 1997 to Canandaigua Brands.

In 1998 it bought Matthew Clark, a UK-based maker of cider, wine, and bottled water, for $359 million. Further stocking its cabinet, in 1999 Canandaigua bought several whiskey brands (including Black Velvet) and two Canadian production facilities from Diageo. Also in 1999 Canandaigua entered the premium wine business with the purchases of vintners Simi Winery and Franciscan Estates.

Founder Marvin Sands died in 1999. His son, Richard, who had been CEO since 1993, succeeded his father as chairman. In 2000 the firm changed its name to Constellation Brands.

In 2001 Constellation Brands acquired Turner Road Vintners, a division of Sebastiani Vineyards, including the Vendange, Talus, Heritage, Nathanson Creek, La Terre, and Farallon brands of wine, as well as two wineries in California.

Constellation Brands teamed with Australian vintner BRL Hardy in 2001 to form its Pacific Wine Partners joint venture, which targets the mid-priced wine market in the US. That year Constellation Brands also purchased Ravenswood Winery. In 2003 Constellation Brands acquired BRL Hardy. In 2004 the company completed its landmark acquisition of The Robert Mondavi Corporation, further adding to the company's dominance in the wine industry. Also that year Constellation Brands announced plans to buy 40% of Italy's Ruffino.

In 2005 the company acquired Rex Goliath from Hahn Estates and made a number of bids to take over Canada's Vincor International. Vincor's board rejected all offers until 2006, when it accepted an offer of C$1 billion dollars. As part of the integration of Vincor into the company, Constellation eliminated 230 Vincor jobs and renamed the company Vincor Canada.

Constellation Brands formed a 50-50 joint venture with Grupo Modelo in 2006 (Crown Imports) to import and market the Mexican brewer's beer in the US and Guam through a joint venture.

In 2007 Constellation added to its premium spirits line with the acquisition of the Swedish vodka label Svedka, along with its New York import operations, Spirits Marque One, for $384 million. In a major boost to its wine division, the company acquired the wine business of Fortune Brands (Beam Wine Estates) for $885 million in cash. The deal added such labels as Clos du Bois, Geyser Peak, and Wild Horse.

Top management changes also took place in 2007. CEO Richard Sands was replaced by Robert (Rob) Sands; Richard Sands remained as chairman. (The men are brothers.) In 2008 the company sold some of its wine assets to Sonoma Valley-based Eight Estates Fine Wines.

EXECUTIVES

Chairman: Richard Sands, age 59, $7,098,287 total compensation
President, CEO, and Director: Robert S. (Rob) Sands, age 51, $6,772,375 total compensation
EVP and CFO: Robert (Bob) Ryder, $2,333,259 total compensation
EVP and Chief Human Resources and Administrative Officer: W. Keith Wilson, age 60, $2,129,586 total compensation
EVP and General Counsel: Thomas J. (Tom) Mullin, age 58, $2,116,099 total compensation
EVP Business Development, Corporate Strategy, and International: F. Paul Hetterich, age 47
VP Investor Relations: Patty Yahn-Urlaub
President, Constellation Wines US, Constellation Wines North America, and Vincor Canada: John A. (Jay) Wright, age 52
President, Constellation Wines Australia Regional Estates: John Grant, age 50
VP Corporate Communications: Cheryl Gossin
Director Investor Relations: Bob Czudak
Auditors: KPMG LLP

LOCATIONS

HQ: Constellation Brands, Inc.
207 High Point Dr., Bldg. 100, Victor, NY 14564
Phone: 585-678-7100   **Fax:** 585-218-3601
Web: www.cbrands.com

2010 Sales

	$ mil.	% of total
US	1,981.4	59
UK	611.5	18
Canada	399.1	12
Australia & New Zealand	345.2	10
Other countries	27.6	1
Total	**3,364.8**	**100**

PRODUCTS/OPERATIONS

2010 Sales

	$ mil.	% of total
Branded wine	2,928.0	87
Spirits	223.9	7
Other	212.9	6
Total	**3,364.8**	**100**

Selected Subsidiaries and Operations

Constellation Spirits, Inc.
Constellation Wines U.S.
Crown Imports LLC (50%, joint venture with Grupo Modelo, S.A.B. de C.V., beer)
Matthew Clark (50%, joint venture with Punch Taverns plc, drinks wholesaler, UK)
Vincor International, Inc. (wine, Canada)

COMPETITORS

Andrew Peller	Heineken
Anheuser-Busch InBev	Jackson Family Wines
Bacardi	Korbel
Beam Global Spirits & Wine	LVMH
	MillerCoors
Boston Beer	Patrón Spirits
Bronco Wine Co.	Pernod Ricard
Brown-Forman	SABMiller
Carlsberg	Scheid Vineyards
Diageo	Sebastiani Vineyards
E. & J. Gallo	Taittinger
Fortune Brands	Terlato Wine
Foster's Americas	Trinchero Family Estates
Foster's Group	Willamette Valley
GIV	Vineyards
Halewood	Wine Group

HISTORICAL FINANCIALS

Company Type: Public

Income Statement

FYE: Last day in February

	REVENUE ($ mil.)	NET INCOME ($ mil.)	NET PROFIT MARGIN	EMPLOYEES
2/10	3,365	99	3.0%	6,000
2/09	3,655	(301)	—	6,600
2/08	3,773	(613)	—	8,200
2/07	5,216	332	6.4%	9,200
2/06	4,603	325	7.1%	7,900
Annual Growth	**(7.5%)**	**(25.7%)**	**—**	**(6.6%)**

2010 Year-End Financials

Debt ratio: 127.2%
Return on equity: 4.4%
Cash ($ mil.): 44
Current ratio: 1.89
Long-term debt ($ mil.): 3,277
No. of shares (mil.): 211
Dividends
  Yield: —
  Payout: —
Market value ($ mil.): 3,172

Stock History

NYSE: STZ

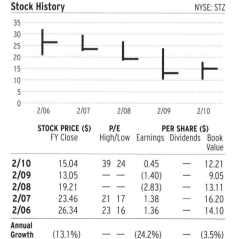

	STOCK PRICE ($) FY Close	P/E High/Low		PER SHARE ($) Earnings	Dividends	Book Value
2/10	15.04	39	24	0.45	—	12.21
2/09	13.05	—	—	(1.40)	—	9.05
2/08	19.21	—	—	(2.83)	—	13.11
2/07	23.46	21	17	1.38	—	16.20
2/06	26.34	23	16	1.36	—	14.10
Annual Growth	**(13.1%)**	**—**	**—**	**(24.2%)**	**—**	**(3.5%)**

Constellation Energy

Constellation Energy Group's leading light is still utility Baltimore Gas and Electric (BGE), which distributes electricity and natural gas in central Maryland. The company trades and markets wholesale energy through subsidiary Constellation Energy Commodities Group, which is one of the top power marketers in North America. Constellation Energy also operates independent power plants with more than 8,200 MW of generating capacity through its Constellation Generation unit, and it competes in retail energy supply through Constellation NewEnergy. Other operations include HVAC services, appliance sales; nuclear plant development; and energy consulting services.

In need of a major capital injection, in 2008 Constellation Energy agreed to be acquired by MidAmerican Energy Holdings, but the deal was terminated after EDF Development (a subsidiary of EDF) acquired 50% of Constellation Energy's Constellation Energy Nuclear Group for $4.5 billion in 2009. The well-funded nuclear group operates five reactors at three power stations in the US Northeast.

Overstretched by its rapid expansion in the early 2000s, the company has sold noncore assets, including its real estate investments and Latin American power projects. It also sold the Oleander power plant in Cocoa, Florida, to fellow utility provider Southern Company. In 2009 the company divested most of its international commodities business and its downstream natural gas unit. It also completed the sale of its Houston-based downstream gas unit as well as most of its London-based coal, freight, and international commodities business. In 2010 the company sold its district cooling system in Baltimore to Veolia Energy.

Exploiting an opportunity to grow its power plant assets in New England, in 2010 Constellation Energy agreed to buy bankrupt Boston Generating Company from USPowerGen for $1.1 billion. The deal will give the company a 2,950-MW gas-powered fleet.

Growing its green energy portfolio, Constellation acquired a Maryland-based wind power project from Clipper Windpower in 2010. The 70 MW project includes 28 2.5-MW wind turbines and will provide power to the Old Dominion Electric Cooperative in a 20-year power purchase deal. That same year it purchased two natural-gas-fired power facilities in Texas for $365 million from privately held Navasota Holdings.

HISTORY

In 1816, back when gas was made out of tar, Rembrandt Peale (an artist and son of painter Charles Willson Peale), William Lorman, and three others formed the US's first gas utility: Gas Light Company of Baltimore; Lorman was president until 1832. The firm soon ran out of money and issued stock to raise capital.

Baltimore's growth outstripped the firm's gas-main capacity, and by 1860 it had a fierce rival in the People's Gas Light Co. In 1871 the two firms divided the city up and then fought a price war with yet another rival. Finally, the three merged as the Consolidated Gas Company of Baltimore City in 1880.

The next year the Brush Electric Light Company and the United States Electric Light and Power Company were established. In 1906 their descendants merged with Consolidated Gas to form the Consolidated Gas Electric Light and Power Co.

As demand for electricity grew, the company turned from hydroelectric power to steam generators in the 1920s. Its revenues increased despite the Depression, and it later set records producing gas and electricity during WWII. Despite a postwar boom in sales, earnings fell as Consolidated spent money on new plants, shifting to natural gas and converting downtown Baltimore from DC to AC.

In 1955 Consolidated was renamed Baltimore Gas and Electric Company (BGE). BGE announced plans in 1967 for Maryland's first nuclear power plant; Calvert Cliffs Unit 1 went on line in 1975, and Unit 2 followed two years later.

BGE began adding to the Safe Harbor Hydroelectric Project in 1981. Over the next two years it sought to form a holding company in order to diversify, but state regulators rejected the request in 1983. Undaunted, the firm formed subsidiary Constellation Holdings in 1985 and began investing in nonutility businesses and pursuing independent power projects.

Both Calvert Cliffs nukes were shut down between 1989 and 1990 for repairs, and BGE had to spend $458 million on replacement power.

The Energy Policy Act fundamentally changed the electric utility industry in 1992 by allowing wholesale power competition in monopoly territories. BGE began expanding its gas division that year, and in 1995 it ventured into Latin America and took a stake in a Bolivian power firm.

BGE formed its power marketing arm that year with Goldman Sachs as its advisor. It teamed up with Goldman Sachs again in 1998 when the duo formed joint venture Orion Power Holdings to buy electric plants in the US and Canada. In 1999 Orion bought plants from Niagara Mohawk, Con Ed, and U.S. Generating.

Meanwhile, Maryland passed deregulation legislation in 1999, and Constellation Energy Group was formed in 1999 as the holding company for BGE and its nonregulated subsidiaries. Competition began in BGE's territory in 2000, and Constellation Energy separated BGE's generation assets from its distribution assets in accordance with the state's deregulation laws.

In 2001 Constellation Energy purchased the Nine Mile Point Nuclear Station Unit 1 and 82% of Unit 2 (most of the holdings were bought from Niagara Mohawk), and sold its Guatemalan power plants to Duke Energy. Constellation Energy reorganized its management and corporate structure in 2002; it also reduced its workforce by approximately 10%.

Constellation Energy purchased two retail supply and consulting units (Alliance Energy Services and Fellon-McCord) from Allegheny Energy in 2003. To further expand its nonregulated operations, the company purchased a New York nuclear plant for $408 million from Rochester Gas and Electric.

In late 2005 Constellation agreed to be acquired by FPL Group Inc. However, the companies called the deal off in 2006, citing uncertainty about regulatory approvals.

In 2006 Constellation Energy sold 3,145 MW of natural gas-fired generation assets to Tenaska's Tenaska Power Fund, L.P. unit.

In 2007 the company acquired Cornerstone Energy, creating one of the largest natural gas marketing companies in the US.

EXECUTIVES

Chairman, President, and CEO: Mayo A. Shattuck III, age 56, $10,910,105 total compensation
Vice Chairman, EVP, and COO:
  Michael J. (Mike) Wallace, age 62,
  $5,689,853 total compensation
EVP; President, CEO, and Chief Nuclear Officer, Constellation Energy Nuclear Group:
  Henry B. (Brew) Barron Jr., age 59,
  $2,714,692 total compensation
EVP Corporate Affairs, Public and Environmental Policy: James L. Connaughton, age 48
SVP Corporate Affairs and Chief Environmental Officer: Paul J. Allen, age 58
SVP and CFO: Jonathan W. (Jack) Thayer, age 38, $2,993,480 total compensation
SVP, General Counsel, and Corporate Secretary:
  Charles A. (Charlie) Berardesco, age 51
SVP; President and CEO, Baltimore Gas and Electric:
  Kenneth W. (Ken) DeFontes Jr., age 59
SVP; COO, Constellation Energy Resources:
  Kathleen W. (Kathi) Hyle, age 51,
  $2,430,817 total compensation
SVP and Chief Human Resources Officer:
  Shon J. Manasco, age 39
SVP and Chief Risk Officer: Brenda Boultwood, age 45
SVP Corporate Strategy and Development:
  Andrew L. Good, age 42
Managing Director and Chief Marketing Officer, Retail Energy: Bruce J. Stewart
VP Corporate Communications: Robert L. (Rob) Gould
VP, Controller, Chief Accounting Officer:
  Bryan P. Wright, age 43
Auditors: PricewaterhouseCoopers LLP

LOCATIONS

HQ: Constellation Energy Group, Inc.
  100 Constellation Way, Baltimore, MD 21202
Phone: 410-470-2800
Web: www.constellation.com

PRODUCTS/OPERATIONS

2009 Sales

	$ mil.	% of total
Nonregulated operations	12,024.3	77
Regulated electric business	2,820.7	18
Regulated gas business	753.8	5
Total	**15,598.8**	**100**

Selected Subsidiaries

Merchant Energy Operations
  Constellation Energy Commodities Group (formerly Constellation Power Source, wholesale power marketing and trading)
  Constellation Generation Group, LLC (holds former BGE generation assets, plus acquired assets)
  Constellation NewEnergy (formerly AES NewEnergy, competitive retail power supply to commercial and industrial customers)
Utility and Other Unregulated Operations
  Baltimore Gas and Electric Company (BGE, gas and electric utility)
  BGE Home Products & Services, Inc. (HVAC [heating, ventilation, and air-conditioning] and plumbing, appliances, home improvements, and retail gas marketing)
  Constellation Nuclear Services, Inc. (nuclear license renewal services)
  Constellation Real Estate Group, Inc. (commercial properties)

COMPETITORS

AEP
Allegheny Energy
CenterPoint Energy
Chesapeake Utilities
Dominion Resources
Duke Energy
Dynegy
Edison International
Entergy
Entergy Nuclear
Integrys Energy Services
New Jersey Resources
NiSource
Pepco Holdings
PG&E Corporation
PPL Corporation
Public Service Enterprise Group
Sempra Energy
Southern Company
WGL Holdings
Williams Companies

HISTORICAL FINANCIALS

Company Type: Public

Income Statement

FYE: December 31

	REVENUE ($ mil.)	NET INCOME ($ mil.)	NET PROFIT MARGIN	EMPLOYEES
12/09	15,599	4,503	28.9%	7,200
12/08	19,818	(1,314)	—	10,200
12/07	21,193	822	3.9%	10,200
12/06	19,285	936	4.9%	9,645
12/05	17,132	630	3.7%	9,850
Annual Growth	**(2.3%)**	**63.5%**	**—**	**(7.5%)**

2009 Year-End Financials

Debt ratio: 55.4%
Return on equity: 75.8%
Cash ($ mil.): 3,440
Current ratio: 1.85
Long-term debt ($ mil.): 4,814
No. of shares (mil.): 202
Dividends
  Yield: 2.7%
  Payout: 4.3%
Market value ($ mil.): 7,103

Stock History

NYSE: CEG

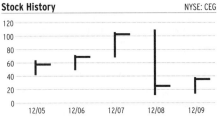

	STOCK PRICE ($) FY Close	P/E High/Low		Earnings	PER SHARE ($) Dividends	Book Value
12/09	35.17	2	1	22.19	0.96	44.00
12/08	25.09	—	—	(7.34)	1.91	16.69
12/07	102.53	23	15	4.50	1.74	27.38
12/06	68.87	14	10	5.16	1.51	23.76
12/05	57.60	18	12	3.47	1.34	25.28
Annual Growth	**(11.6%)**	**—**	**—**	**59.0%**	**(8.0%)**	**14.9%**

Con-way Inc.

Con-way (no relation to Twit-ty) provides trucking and logistics services. Con-way Freight, the company's less-than-truckload (LTL) unit, provides regional and inter-regional service throughout North America. (LTL carriers consolidate loads from multiple shippers into a single truckload.) Con-way Freight operates a fleet of about 8,300 tractors and some 25,000 trailers, utilizing five terminals. Con-way offers truckload transportation services through its Con-way Truckload subsidiary, which maintains a fleet of about 2,700 tractors and 8,100 trailers. Con-way's Menlo Worldwide Logistics unit provides contract logistics, freight brokerage, warehousing, and supply chain management services.

The company operates more than 400 locations across North America. It also has an international presence (through its logistics division) in 17 countries on five continents.

Feeling the pressure of record-high fuel prices followed by the economic downturn in 2008, Con-way cut positions, suspended bonuses, and slashed salaries and retirement benefits. The move came as Con-way and other shipping companies faced a freefall in freight demand.

It launched regional truckload services to handle mid-distance shipments of less than 600 miles and short-distance hauls of less than 100 miles; the new services complement the division's long-haul services. The deal opens up opportunities for Con-way Truckload to strengthen its "through-trailer" service into and out of Mexico through Texas, Arizona, and California. Through-trailer service eliminates the need for transfer and/or storage fees at the border, making delivery faster and reducing transportation costs.

Con-way Freight and Netherlands-based TNT entered into an alliance in 2009, offering intercontinental service. In 2010 the companies expanded that offering to include road pick-up and delivery of heavy shipments in the US and Europe, connected by air service. Con-way Truckload will pick up the US shipments, while TNT will manage customs clearance and European pick up.

Menlo Worldwide, which accounts for a little less than one-third of Con-way's sales, intends to grow by expanding its presence in the Asia/Pacific region. Menlo Worldwide has grown by absorbing supply chain management businesses that previously were part of Con-way Freight. In 2010 the subsidiary created an export logistics center for Caterpillar.

HISTORY

What is now Con-way got its start in 1929, when Leland James, co-owner of a bus company in Portland, Oregon, founded Consolidated Truck Lines to serve in the Pacific Northwest. Operations extended to San Francisco and Idaho by 1934 and to North Dakota by 1936. It adopted the name Consolidated Freightways (CF) in 1939.

James formed Freightways Manufacturing that year, making CF the only trucking company to design and build its own trucks (Freightliners). In the 1940s CF extended service to Chicago, Minneapolis, and Los Angeles.

CF went public in 1951 and moved to Menlo Park, California, in 1956. It continued to buy companies (52 between 1955 and 1960) and extended its reach throughout the US and Canada.

When an attempt to coordinate intermodal services with railroads and shipping lines failed in 1960, William White became president and exited intermodal operations to focus on less-than-truckload (LTL) shipping.

In 1966 CF formed CF AirFreight to offer air cargo services in the US. Three years later it bought Pacific Far East Lines, a San Francisco shipping line (now a part of Con-way).

CF sold Freightways Manufacturing to Daimler-Benz in 1981 and started the Con-Way carriers, its regional trucking businesses, in 1983 after the US trucking industry was deregulated. In the 1980s Con-Way moved back into intermodal rail, truck, and ocean shipping.

The company bought Emery Air Freight in 1989 and combined it with CF AirFreight to form Emery Worldwide. Founded in 1946, Emery Air Freight had expanded across the US and overseas, first by using extra cargo space on scheduled airline flights, then by chartering aircraft. Later operating its own air fleet, Emery began having troubles in the 1980s, including difficulties in integrating its 1987 acquisition, Purolator Courier. A 1988 takeover attempt by former FedEx president Arthur Bass further plagued Emery; fending off the takeover resulted in losses of about $100 million in 1989. That year Emery brought CF a deal with the US Postal Service (USPS) to handle its next-day express mail.

Amid the beginning of a three-year profit slump, CF formed Menlo Logistics in 1990 to provide its customers with a range of third-party logistics services. A Teamsters' strike in 1994 that halted union carriers nationwide boosted demand for Con-Way's services, as customers sought nonunion carriers to move their shipments. The next year Con-Way opened 40 service centers and bought another 3,300 tractors and trailers.

In 1996 CF spun off most of its long-haul transportation businesses and renamed the resulting entity Consolidated Freightways. CF then changed its own name to CNF Transportation.

CNF Transportation received a five-year, $1.7 billion contract from the USPS in 1997 to sort and transport two-day priority mail in the eastern US.

In 2000 CNF Transportation shortened its name to CNF and began renegotiating its money-losing second-day priority mail contract with USPS. (FedEx eventually got the job.) That year CNF formed Vector SCM, a supply chain management and logistics joint venture with General Motors. In 2001 CNF's Con-Way Transportation established Con-Way Air Express, an airfreight forwarder that serves the US and Puerto Rico.

Emery grounded its aircraft fleet in 2001 because of maintenance problems discovered by Federal Aviation Administration (FAA) inspectors. The company hired other carriers in order to continue its airfreight services. In a settlement with the FAA, Emery agreed to pay a $1 million civil fine.

To emphasize its focus on logistics, CNF combined the operations of Emery Worldwide, Menlo Logistics, and Vector SCM into a new company, Menlo Worldwide, in 2002.

As part of an effort to focus on its operating businesses, CNF renamed itself Con-way in 2006.

The company's truckload business expanded dramatically in 2007 when Con-way paid $750 million for CFI.

EXECUTIVES

Chairman: W. Keith Kennedy Jr., age 66
President, CEO, and Director: Douglas W. Stotlar, age 49, $3,443,735 total compensation
EVP, General Counsel, and Corporate Secretary: Jennifer W. Pileggi, age 45
EVP; President, Con-way Truckload: Herbert J. (Herb) Schmidt, age 54, $2,629,299 total compensation
EVP; President, Menlo Worldwide: Robert L. (Bob) Bianco Jr., age 45, $1,887,115 total compensation
EVP; President Con-way Freight: John G. Labrie, age 43, $1,355,531 total compensation
EVP and CFO: Stephen L. (Steve) Bruffett, age 45, $1,351,145 total compensation
SVP Human Resources: Leslie P. Lundberg, age 52
SVP and Corporate Controller: Kevin S. Coel, age 51
SVP and CIO: Jacquelyn A. (Jackie) Barretta, age 48
SVP and Treasurer: Mark C. Thickpenny, age 57
VP Strategic Planning: Richard J. (Rich) Lunardi
VP Operational Accounting: Kevin C. Schick, age 58, $1,199,388 total compensation
VP Government Relations and Public Affairs: C. Randal Mullett
VP Investor Relations: Patrick J. (Pat) Fossenier
VP Corporate Development: J. Craig Boretz
VP Communications and Chief Marketing Officer: Thomas (Tom) Nightingale
President, Road Systems: Lynn C. Reinbolt
Auditors: KPMG LLP

LOCATIONS

HQ: Con-way Inc.
  2855 Campus Dr., Ste. 300, San Mateo, CA 94403
Phone: 650-378-5200   **Fax:** 650-357-9160
Web: www.con-way.com

2009 Sales

	$ mil.	% of total
US	4,018.9	94
Canada	81.3	2
Other countries	169.0	4
Total	**4,269.2**	**100**

PRODUCTS/OPERATIONS

2009 Sales

	$ mil.	% of total
Freight	2,574.3	60
Logistics	1,326.0	31
Truckload	365.1	9
Other	3.8	—
Total	**4,269.2**	**100**

COMPETITORS

APL Logistics
Arkansas Best
Central Freight Lines
CEVA Logistics
C.H. Robinson Worldwide
DHL
Estes Express
Expeditors
FedEx Freight
J.B. Hunt
Landstar System
Old Dominion Freight
Pacer Transportation Solutions
Panalpina, Inc.
Ryder System
Saia
Schneider National
Swift Transportation
Transplace
UPS
UTi Worldwide
Werner Enterprises
YRC Worldwide

HISTORICAL FINANCIALS

Company Type: Public

Income Statement

FYE: December 31

	REVENUE ($ mil.)	NET INCOME ($ mil.)	NET PROFIT MARGIN	EMPLOYEES
12/09	4,269	(108)	—	27,400
12/08	5,037	74	1.5%	26,600
12/07	4,387	153	3.5%	27,100
12/06	4,222	270	6.4%	21,800
12/05	4,170	223	5.3%	21,800
Annual Growth	0.6%	—	—	5.9%

2009 Year-End Financials

Debt ratio: 110.8%
Return on equity: —
Cash ($ mil.): 477
Current ratio: 1.36
Long-term debt ($ mil.): 761

No. of shares (mil.): 54
Dividends
  Yield: 1.1%
  Payout: —
Market value ($ mil.): 1,901

Stock History

NYSE: CNW

	STOCK PRICE ($) FY Close	P/E High/Low		PER SHARE ($) Earnings	Dividends	Book Value
12/09	34.91	—	—	(2.33)	0.40	12.61
12/08	26.60	39	14	1.40	0.40	11.49
12/07	41.54	19	13	3.04	0.40	16.70
12/06	44.04	12	8	4.98	0.40	13.61
12/05	55.89	16	11	3.85	0.40	16.73
Annual Growth	(11.1%)	—	—	—	0.0%	(6.8%)

Cooper Industries

Cooper Industries likes to keep customers from blowing a fuse. The company's electrical products segment makes circuit protection equipment, as well as lighting fixtures, wiring devices, and other power management and distribution equipment for residential, commercial, and industrial use. Its other main business segment manufactures power tools for the industrial market and hand tools for the do-it-yourself and commercial markets. Major electrical product and tool brands include Buss fuses, Capri conduits, Crescent pliers and wrenches, EMSA power transformers, Plumb hammers, and Weller soldering supplies.

In 2010 the company formed a 50-50 joint venture with Danaher to combine their respective tools businesses. Cooper contributed its hand tools, power tools, and wireless technologies to meld with Danaher's line of hand tools for mechanics. The company noted the JV — named Apex Tool Group, LLC — will bring together two complementary product lines into a business with annual sales of more than $1.2 billion and a worldwide footprint. Tools represent about 10% of Cooper's sales.

Later in 2010 the company acquired Eka Systems, a provider of RF wireless networking technologies for smart grid applications. Eka Systems' products include radios, wireless repeaters, meter nodes, gateways, and data collection tools that utility providers use to handle tasks such as automated meter reading, power outage detection, and customer billing. Eka Systems will be integrated into Cooper's Energy Automation Solutions business unit.

In 2009 Cooper bought Illumination Management Solutions (IMS), a provider of specialized optics and system design for light-emitting diode (LED) fixtures. The LED tech deal complements previously acquired io Lighting and UK-based Clarity Lighting. Earlier, Cooper bought electronic instrument and protection equipment maker MTL Instruments for about £144 million (nearly $281 million).

HISTORY

In 1833 Charles Cooper sold a horse for $50 and borrowed additional money to open a foundry with his brother Elias in Mount Vernon, Ohio. Known as C. & E. Cooper, the company made plows, hog troughs, maple syrup kettles, stoves, and wagon boxes.

C. & E. Cooper began making steam engines in the 1840s for mill and farm use; it later adapted its engines for wood-burning locomotives. In 1868 the company built its first Corliss steam engine, and in 1875 it introduced the first steam-powered farm tractor. By 1900 C. & E. Cooper sold its steam engines in the US and overseas. The company debuted an internal combustion engine-compressor in 1909 for natural gas pipelines.

In the 1920s the company became the #1 seller of compression engines for oil and gas pipelines. A 1929 merger with Bessemer (small engines) created Cooper-Bessemer, which made diesel engines for power boats.

Diversification began in 1959 with the purchase of Rotor Tools. Cooper adopted its current name in 1965 and moved its headquarters to Houston in 1967. It went on to buy other firms, including Lufkin Rule (measuring tapes, 1967), Crescent (wrenches, 1968), and Weller (soldering tools, 1970).

Cooper's 1979 purchase of Gardner-Denver gave it a strong footing in oil-drilling and mining equipment, and the addition of Crouse-Hinds in 1981 was key to its diversification into electrical materials. The decline in oil prices in the early 1980s caused sales to drop, but Cooper stayed profitable due to its tools and electrical products.

Cooper's electrical segment expanded with the 1985 purchase of McGraw-Edison, a maker of consumer products (Buss fuses) and heavy transmission gear for electrical utilities. Growth continued as it added RTE (electrical equipment, 1988), Cameron Iron Works (oil-drilling equipment, 1989), and Ferramentas Belzer do Brasil (hand-tool maker, 1992).

Expanding into auto parts, Cooper bought Champion Spark Plug (1989) and Moog (auto replacement parts, 1992). From 1991 to 1993, the company divested 11 businesses and bought 13. In 1994 it spun off Gardner-Denver Industrial Machinery (now Gardner Denver), sold Cameron Forged Products, and added Abex Friction Products (brake materials) and Zanxx (lighting components) to its auto parts line.

Cooper spun off Cooper Cameron (petroleum equipment; now Cameron International) in 1995. The next year Cooper bought electrical fuse supplier Karp Electric, tool manufacturer Master Power, and electrical hub maker Myers Electric Products. Company veteran John Riley took over as chairman that year. Cooper added eight acquisitions in 1997, and some, such as Menvier-Swain Group (emergency lights and alarms, UK), helped to bolster its electrical segment. Despite its growth, the company trimmed its workforce by 30% that year.

Cooper completed 11 acquisitions in 1998 and 10 in 1999; among them were the tool business of Global Industrial Technologies (Quackenbush and Rotor Tool brands), Apparatebau Hundsbach (electronic sensors) and Metronix Elektronik (power tool controls), and several lighting firms. In the meantime, the company sold its automotive operations to Federal-Mogul.

In 2000 Cooper acquired B-Line Systems from Sigma-Aldrich for around $425 million. The next year toolmaker Danaher offered to acquire Cooper in a deal worth about $5.5 billion. Cooper rejected the initial offer, then Danaher lost interest when Cooper's former automotive unit (sold in 1998) was named in asbestos lawsuits. (Cooper recorded a charge of about $125 million for discontinued operations in 2003 for liability exposure relating to those claims.)

In 2002 the company reincorporated in Bermuda for tax reasons and changed its name from Cooper Industries, Inc., to Cooper Industries, Ltd.

In 2006 Cooper acquired electrical interconnect maker G&H Technology. In early 2007 the company acquired WPI Interconnect Products, a manufacturer of custom connectors and cable assemblies for commercial, industrial, and military applications.

EXECUTIVES

Chairman, President, and CEO: Kirk S. Hachigian, age 50, $10,756,244 total compensation
Vice Chairman: Terry A. Klebe, age 55, $2,769,211 total compensation
EVP Cooper Connection; President, Cooper Lighting: Neil A. Schrimsher, age 45, $1,495,751 total compensation
SVP and CFO: David A. Barta, age 48
SVP Business Development: C. Thomas (Tom) O'Grady, age 58, $1,718,129 total compensation
SVP, General Counsel, and Chief Compliance Officer: Bruce M. Taten, age 54, $1,481,611 total compensation
SVP Human Resources: James P. Williams, age 47
Chief Marketing Officer: Robert L. Taylor, age 45
VP and Treasurer: Tyler W. Johnson
VP Business Systems: Melissa Scheppele
VP Taxes: John B. Reed
VP Internal Audit: David T. Gunther
VP, Controller, and Chief Accounting Officer: Rick L. Johnson, age 57
VP Operations; President, Cooper Tools: Laura K. Ulz, age 47
Group President, Cooper Power Systems: Michael A. (Mike) Stoessl, age 46, $1,533,325 total compensation
Associate General Counsel and Secretary: Terrance V. Helz
Director Investor Relations: Mark Doheny
Auditors: Ernst & Young LLP

LOCATIONS

HQ: Cooper Industries plc
  600 Travis St., Ste. 5600, Houston, TX 77002
Phone: 713-209-8400   **Fax:** 713-209-8996
Web: www.cooperindustries.com

2009 Sales

	$ mil.	% of total
US	3,456.5	68
UK	290.2	6
Germany	239.7	5
Canada	224.2	4
China	181.6	4
Mexico	149.1	3
Other countries	528.3	10
Total	**5,069.6**	**100**

PRODUCTS/OPERATIONS

2009 Sales

	$ mil.	% of total
Electrical products	4,511.9	89
Tools	557.7	11
Total	**5,069.6**	**100**

Selected Products and Brands

Electrical Products
 Architectural recessed lighting (Portfolio)
 Architectural and landscape lighting (Lumiere)
 Aviation lighting products (Crouse-Hinds)
 Current-limiting fuses (Combined Technologies)
 Distribution switchgear (Kyle)
 Electric fuses (B&S, Edison, Karp, Mercury)
 Electrical connectors (Cam-Lok)
 Electrical construction materials (CEAG, Crouse-
  Hinds)
 Electrical hubs (Myers)
 Electrical outlet and switch boxes (Thepitt)
 Emergency alarm systems
 Emergency lighting and fire-detection systems (CEAG,
  JSB, Luminox, Menvier)
 Emergency lighting and power systems (Blessing,
  CSA, Pretronica, Univel)
 Enclosures (B-Line)
 Exit and emergency lighting (AtLite, Sure-Lites)
 Fire-detection systems (Fulleon, Nugelec, Transmould)
 Fluorescent lighting (Metalux)
 Fasteners (B-Line)
 Fuses (Buss, Kearney)
 High-abuse, clean room, and vandal-resistant lighting
  fixtures (Fail-Safe)
 Indoor and outdoor HID lighting (McGraw-Edison)
 Inductors and transformers (Coiltronics)
 Lighting systems (Iris)
 Lighting systems for hazardous and corrosive
  environments (Pauluhn)
 Modular wiring systems (MWS)
 Plugs and receptacles (Arktite)
 Public address systems
 Recessed and track-lighting fixtures (Halo)
 Relays (Edison and Edison Pro)
 Security equipment (Menvier, Scantronic)
 Terminal strips and disconnect blocks (Magnum)
 Transformer components, cable accessories, and fuses
  (McGraw-Edison, RTE)
 Transient voltage protection devices (TransX)
 Wiring devices (Arrow Hart)
Tools and Hardware
 Assembly equipment, assembly stations, and transport
  lines (Assembly Systems, Cooper Automation,
  DGD/Gardner-Denver, GardoTrans)
 Chain products (Campbell)
 Cutters and tweezers (Erem)
 Farrier tools (Diamond)
 Files and saws (Nicholson)
 Hammers (Plumb)
 Industrial power tools (Airetool, Buckeye, Cleco,
  Dotco, Quackenbush, Rotor Tool)
 Measuring and layout products (Lufkin)
 Scissors, shears, and snips (H.K. Porter and Wiss)
 Screwdrivers and nutdrivers (Xcelite)
 Sockets, screwdriver bits, extensions, and universal
  joints (Apex, Geta)
 Soldering equipment (Weller)
 Torque-measuring and control equipment (Utica)
 Wrenches and pliers (Crescent)

COMPETITORS

ABB
Acuity Brands
Bel Fuse
Danaher
Dover Corp.
Eaton
Emerson Electric
GE
Hubbell
Illinois Tool Works
Ingersoll-Rand
Legrand
Littelfuse
Makita
Milwaukee Electric Tool
Molex
Newell Rubbermaid
Philips Lighting North America
Powell Industries
Schneider Electric
Siemens AG
Simpson Manufacturing
SL Industries
Snap-on
Stanley Black and Decker
Techtronic
Thomas & Betts
Tyco

HISTORICAL FINANCIALS

Company Type: Public

Income Statement

FYE: December 31

	REVENUE ($ mil.)	NET INCOME ($ mil.)	NET PROFIT MARGIN	EMPLOYEES
12/09	5,070	439	8.7%	28,255
12/08	6,521	632	9.7%	31,202
12/07	5,903	692	11.7%	31,504
12/06	5,185	505	9.7%	30,561
12/05	4,730	164	3.5%	28,903
Annual Growth	1.7%	27.9%	—	(0.6%)

2009 Year-End Financials

Debt ratio: 31.1%
Return on equity: 15.8%
Cash ($ mil.): 382
Current ratio: 1.99
Long-term debt ($ mil.): 923
No. of shares (mil.): 168
Dividends
 Yield: 2.3%
 Payout: 38.3%
Market value ($ mil.): 7,143

Stock History

NYSE: CBE

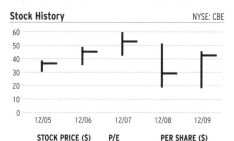

	STOCK PRICE ($) FY Close	P/E High/Low		PER SHARE ($) Earnings	Dividends	Book Value
12/09	42.64	17	7	2.61	1.00	17.69
12/08	29.23	14	5	3.60	1.00	15.56
12/07	52.88	16	12	3.73	0.84	16.96
12/06	45.22	19	15	2.47	0.74	14.78
12/05	36.50	44	36	0.87	0.74	13.16
Annual Growth	4.0%	—	—	31.6%	7.8%	7.7%

Cooper Tire & Rubber

Cooper Tire & Rubber is a real wheeler dealer. The company is the fourth-largest tire manufacturer in North America (behind the likes of Bridgestone, Michelin, and Goodyear). It makes and sells replacement tires mainly for passenger cars and light trucks but also for motorcycles, race cars, commercial, and off-road vehicles for North American and international markets. Cooper operates seven manufacturing facilities and over 35 distribution centers worldwide. Customers include tire dealers, wholesale distributors, and regional and national tire chains. Unlike some of its rivals, Cooper does not typically sell to automotive OEMs.

The company divested its tread rubber and retreading operations in 2007 to focus on the replacement tire business. A weak market started to rear its ugly head a year prior, and ultimately the company experienced a drastic loss in revenue for 2008 over 2007. Weak market conditions were exacerbated by high rubber costs and the global recession. Trying to secure its long-term financial health, Cooper closed manufacturing facilities in Georgia and New Jersey as part of a restructuring.

Demand for tires began returning, however, at the end of 2009 and into the new year. The company began to bounce back and expanded its production capacity at its Arkansas plant to a 24/7 schedule beginning in 2010 to match that demand. Cooper also announced plans to expand operations at its Mississippi, Ohio, and Mexico manufacturing facilities. In 2009 it finalized an agreement with Sears to supply passenger tires to its nationwide auto centers.

Cooper sought international markets in hopes that lower-cost regions, such as Asia and Mexico, would help offset rising raw material costs. Its international tire segment caters primarily to the replacement markets in the UK, continental Europe, and Scandinavia. This segment is composed of two main joint venture manufacturing facilities in China, including Cooper Chengshan and Cooper Kenda. As economic conditions improved, the company sought to increase its stake in its Chengshan joint venture. In March 2010 the company was given approval by the Chinese government to increase its stake in Cooper Chengshan Tire to 65% from 51%.

Cooper Tire is onboard for the war effort, which is helping to expand its market share. It entered into a joint venture with Resilient Technologies in late 2008 to produce an airless military tire prototype. Troops get stranded everyday due to flat tires caused by bad roads, bullets, or shrapnel. The two companies are employing polymer-based engineering to create a non-pneumatic tire (NPT) that will provide better mobility and reliability.

HISTORY

John Schaefer and Claude Hart (brothers-in-law) bought M and M Manufacturing of Akron, Ohio, in 1914. M and M made tire patches, cement, and repair kits. In 1915 the two bought The Giant Tire & Rubber Company (tire rebuilding). Two years later they moved their business to Findlay, Ohio.

Ira Cooper joined Giant's board in 1917 and soon formed his own company, The Cooper Corporation, which began making tires in 1920. The industry began consolidating in the 1920s, and in 1930 Cooper and Giant merged with Falls Rubber Company (a small tire maker), and Master Tire & Rubber Company was born.

Cooper died in 1941, but the company went on to supply the war effort with tires, pontoons, life jackets, and tank decoys. After WWII the company changed its name to Cooper Tire & Rubber Company. Cooper earned sales and loyalty from retailers and private-brand customers by promising not to open its own sales outlets — a policy continued to this day. The growth of the interstate system in the postwar years meant more cars, tires, and sales. Cooper went public in 1960. In 1964 it established Cooper Industrial Products to make industrial rubber products.

The 1970s brought the radial tire into widespread use. Radials had been around since the late 1940s, but the manufacturing process hadn't been cheap or easy enough to be practical. After undertaking its own research and development, Cooper rolled out its first radial in 1974. Around the same time, it bought a Bowling Green, Ohio, plant that made extruded rubber products and reinforced hose. The plant was quickly adapted to produce rubber parts for cars.

A tire glut in the 1980s (due in part to longer-lasting tires) led to rapid downsizing in the industry. As competitors exited the tire business, Cooper was buying plants and modernizing them for about a third of the cost of building new ones. The company made its first foray outside the US with the acquisition of Rio Grande Servaas (inner tubes, Mexico). Cooper also undertook several projects in the 1980s to upgrade its research capabilities and to improve distribution. By the mid-1980s it could warehouse more than 3 million tires. By the end of the decade Cooper's stock was 68 times its 1980 level. The success came from growth in the replacement market, which was three times the size of the original equipment market.

The benefits of Cooper's capital investments became clear in the 1990s. As the decade began, the company recorded the best margins in the industry (about 33%), and investment continued. It passed the billion-dollar sales mark in 1991 and spent $110 million in capital investments in 1992.

In 1996 Cooper opened an automotive hose plant in Kentucky. The next year it bought Avon Tyres Limited (UK), its first overseas purchase.

Cooper completed its acquisition of Kentucky-based Dean Tire in 1999, expanding its sales of replacement tires for cars and light trucks to 10 countries. Cooper entered joint ventures with Italy's Pirelli in which Cooper sells and distributes Pirelli passenger car and light truck replacement tires in North America, and Pirelli distributes and markets Cooper tires in South America. The company boosted its automotive sealing system business with the purchase of The Standard Products Company in a deal valued at about $750 million.

A class-action lawsuit was settled in 2002 stemming from claims that the tire maker did not disclose adhesion problems with its steel-belted radial tires; the decision, valued between $1 billion and $3 billion, gave an estimated 40 million consumers an extended warranty.

In 2003 Cooper purchased Max Trac Tire (better known as Mickey Thompson Performance Tires & Wheels). In 2004 the company completed the sale of its automotive unit, Cooper Standard Automotive, to Cypress Group and Goldman Sachs Capital Partners.

EXECUTIVES

Chairman, President, and CEO: Roy V. Armes, age 57, $3,957,915 total compensation
VP Global Technology: Churck Yurkovich
VP Manufacturing, North American Tire: John Bodart
VP and CFO: Bradley E. Hughes, age 47, $1,770,509 total compensation
VP, General Counsel, and Secretary: James E. Kline, age 68, $1,005,060 total compensation
VP; President, International Tire Division: Harold C. (Hal) Miller, age 57, $1,007,244 total compensation
VP, ERP Implementation: Ron Ranallo
VP Sales and Marketing: Phillip D. (Phil) Caris
VP Strategic Initiatives: James P. (Jim) Keller
VP and Chief Human Resources Officer: Brenda S. Harmon, age 58
VP and General Manager, Asian Operations: Allen Tsaur
VP Corporate Purchasing: Linda L. Rennels
VP Marketing, North American Tire: Hal Gardner
General Manager, Corporacion de Occidente: Jeffrey J. Schumaker
General Manager, Cooper Chengshan (Shandong) Tire: Steven Zhou
General Manager, China: Liak Sze (Alex) Koi
General Manager, Mickey Thompson Performance Tires & Wheels: Steve Kersh
Director Corporate Communications: Cathy Huffman
Director Information Technology Infrastructure: Loren Wagner
Director Investor Relations: Curtis Schneekloth
Auditors: Ernst & Young LLP

LOCATIONS

HQ: Cooper Tire & Rubber Company
701 Lima Ave., Findlay, OH 45840
Phone: 419-423-1321   **Fax:** 419-424-4212
Web: www.coopertire.com

2009 Sales

	$ mil.	% of total
North America	1,933.5	70
Asia	588.1	21
Europe	257.4	9
Total	**2,779.0**	**100**

PRODUCTS/OPERATIONS

2009 Sales

	$ mil.	% of total
North American Tire	2,006.2	67
International Tire	993.8	33
Adjustments	(221.0)	—
Total	**2,779.0**	**100**

Selected Products

Commercial tires
Light truck tires
Motorcycle tires
Off-road tires
Passenger car tires
Racing tires
Radial medium truck tires
Sport utility vehicle tires
Ultra high performance

COMPETITORS

Bridgestone
China Enterprises
Continental AG
Continental Tire the Americas
Falken Tire
Goodyear Dunlop Tires
Goodyear Tire & Rubber
Hankook Tire
Michelin
Sumitomo Rubber
Toyo Tire & Rubber
Yokohama Rubber

HISTORICAL FINANCIALS

Company Type: Public

Income Statement

FYE: December 31

	REVENUE ($ mil.)	NET INCOME ($ mil.)	NET PROFIT MARGIN	EMPLOYEES
12/09	2,779	84	3.0%	12,568
12/08	2,882	(219)	—	13,311
12/07	2,933	93	3.2%	13,355
12/06	2,676	(79)	—	13,361
12/05	2,155	(9)	—	8,762
Annual Growth	**6.6%**	**—**	**—**	**9.4%**

2009 Year-End Financials

Debt ratio: 95.8%
Return on equity: 26.1%
Cash ($ mil.): 427
Current ratio: 1.78
Long-term debt ($ mil.): 331

No. of shares (mil.): 61
Dividends
  Yield: 2.1%
  Payout: 49.4%
Market value ($ mil.): 1,228

Stock History

NYSE: CTB

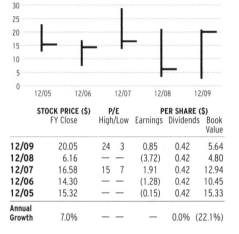

	STOCK PRICE ($) FY Close	P/E High/Low		PER SHARE ($) Earnings	Dividends	Book Value
12/09	20.05	24	3	0.85	0.42	5.64
12/08	6.16	—	—	(3.72)	0.42	4.80
12/07	16.58	15	7	1.91	0.42	12.94
12/06	14.30	—	—	(1.28)	0.42	10.45
12/05	15.32	—	—	(0.15)	0.42	15.33
Annual Growth	**7.0%**	**—**	**—**	**—**	**0.0%**	**(22.1%)**

Corning Incorporated

Corning is cookin' up some great technology. Once known mainly for its kitchenware and lab products, the company designs and produces material components for five industries: display technologies (flat-screen televisions, computer monitors, laptops), environmental technologies (mobile emission control systems), telecommunications (optical fiber, cable), life sciences (biosensors for drug research), and specialty materials (semiconductors, optical sensors for aerospace and defense).

Demand for Display Technologies products increased in 2009. Corning, which produces 60% of the world's glass substrates used in LCD televisions, jumped at the chance to step up manufacturing of LCD glass. The company, which derives about 45% of its sales from Display Technologies, invested approximately $552 million in this segment and plans to enlarge further its investment in China by pumping $400 million to $700 million into building a glass melting facility in that country. Its LCD products are also used in computers, cell phones, and digital camera displays.

The Telecommunications segment has a significant portfolio of patents relating to its products, technologies, and manufacturing processes. The

Environmental Technologies segment includes ceramic technologies and solutions for emissions and pollution control. Future emissions regulations coming into effect in the US, Europe, and Japan could create a demand for heavy-duty emissions controls by 2012.

Its Life Sciences segment produces laboratory products such as coated slides, cell culture dishes, and liquid-handling instruments, to name a few. In 2009 the company acquired California-based Axygen BioScience, a manufacturer and distributor of laboratory research plastic ware and bench-top equipment. Corning purchased the company and its subsidiaries from American Capital for about $400 million.

The company continues to focus on emerging technologies. Gorilla Glass, a damage-resistant cover glass, was introduced in 2008 for use in mobile phones, notebook computers, and for touchscreen technologies. The company's Green Laser technology rivals light-emitting diodes (LEDs) by offering improved images on mobile devices. The company is also in the early stages of creating a filter that will remove mercury released at coal-fired power plants.

In 2008 Corning created its fifth operating segment, Specialty Materials, which includes semiconductors and optical sensors for aerospace and defense.

HISTORY

Amory Houghton started Houghton Glass in Massachusetts in 1851 and moved it to Corning, New York, in 1868. By 1876 the company, renamed Corning Glass Works, was making several types of technical and pharmaceutical glass. In 1880 it supplied the glass for Thomas Edison's first lightbulb. Other early developments included the red-yellow-green traffic light system and borosilicate glass (which can withstand sudden temperature changes) for Pyrex oven and laboratory ware.

Joint ventures have been crucial to Corning's success. Early ones included Pittsburgh Corning (with Pittsburgh Plate Glass, 1937, glass construction blocks), Owens-Corning (with Owens-Illinois, 1938, fiberglass), and Dow Corning (with Dow Chemical, 1943, silicones).

By 1945 the company's laboratories had made it the undisputed leader in the manufacture of specialty glass. Applications for its glass technology included the first mass-produced television tubes, freezer-to-oven ceramic cookware (Pyroceram, Corning Ware), and car headlights.

After World War II Corning emphasized consumer product sales and expanded globally. In the 1970s the company pioneered the development of optical fiber and auto emission technology (now two of its principal products).

Seeing maturing markets for such established products as lightbulbs and television tubes, Corning began buying higher-growth laboratory services companies — MetPath in 1982, Hazleton in 1987, Enseco in 1989, and G.H. Besse-laar in 1989. Vice chairman James Houghton, the great-great-grandson of Corning's founder, was named chairman and CEO in 1983.

Corning established international joint ventures with Siemens, Mitsubishi, and Samsung. In 1988 the company bought Revere Ware (cookware). The next year Corning dropped Glass Works from its name.

Joint venture Dow Corning, under assault from thousands of women seeking damages because of leaking breast implants, entered Chapter 11 bankruptcy protection in 1995 (and exited Chapter 11 in 2004). The massive losses incurred by Dow Corning due to litigation and a downturn in Corning's lab products sales prompted the company to recast itself. Corning began selling off its well-known consumer brands and putting greater emphasis on its high-tech optical and display products through acquisitions and R&D.

Company veteran Roger Ackerman was named chairman and CEO in 1996, replacing Houghton. He moved quickly to transform the company from a disjointed conglomerate to a high-tech optics manufacturer.

In 1998 Corning sold a majority stake in the housewares unit to Kohlberg Kravis Roberts. In 2000 Corning made more than $5 billion worth of acquisitions to expand its optical fiber and hardware business. It acquired Siemens' optical cable and hardware operations and the remaining 50% of the companies' Siecor joint venture. Corning bought Oak Industries (optical components) for $1.8 billion and NetOptix (optical filters) for $2.15 billion, and purchased the 67% of microelectromechanical systems specialist IntelliSense it didn't already own.

Continuing its spending spree, the company bought part of Pirelli's fiber-optic telecom components business for about $3.6 billion; it also acquired Cisco's 10% stake in the business.

In the first half of 2001, Ackerman retired as chairman and CEO of the company. COO John Loose was named CEO, and Houghton was again appointed chairman.

Slowing demand prompted Corning to lay off about 25% of its staff, shut down plants, and discontinue its glass tubing operations that year. Houghton returned to the position of chief executive after Loose retired in 2002. That year the company made more layoffs, closed plants, and sold several noncore operations.

Corning president Wendell Weeks succeeded Houghton as CEO in 2005. Houghton remained chairman, and retired again in 2006, becoming non-executive chairman. Houghton became chairman emeritus in 2007 and remained on the board as a director. Weeks was elected chairman of the board.

EXECUTIVES

Chairman and CEO: Wendell P. Weeks, age 50, $12,050,391 total compensation
Vice Chairman and CFO: James B. Flaws, age 61, $6,183,318 total compensation
President, COO, and Director: Peter F. Volanakis, age 55, $8,449,583 total compensation
EVP and Chief Administrative Officer: Kirk P. Gregg, age 50, $5,177,013 total compensation
EVP and CTO: Joseph A. (Joe) Miller Jr., age 68, $4,714,855 total compensation
SVP and Director, New Business Development: Mark A. Newhouse
SVP and Controller: R. Tony Tripeny, age 51
SVP Science and Technology: Charles R. Craig
SVP and Treasurer: Mark S. Rogus, age 50
SVP and General Counsel: Vincent P. Hatton, age 59
SVP Corporate Product and Process Development: Jean-Pierre Mazeau
SVP, Life Sciences: Mark A. Beck
SVP, Environmental Technologies: Thomas R. Hinman
SVP Strategy and Corporate Development: Lawrence D. McRae, age 51
SVP Operations Chief of Staff: Pamela C. Schneider, age 55
SVP and Director Corporate Research: David L. Morse
SVP Photovoltaic Glass Technologies: Marc S. Giroux

VP and CIO: Kevin J. McManus
VP Human Resources: Christine M. Pambianchi
VP, Secretary, and Assistant General Counsel: Denise A. Hauselt
VP Investor Relations: Kenneth C. Sofio
President and CEO, Corning Gilbert: Steven W. Karaffa
President and CEO, Corning Cable Systems: Clark S. Kinlin
President, Display Technologies, Asia: James P. Clappin, age 52
Auditors: PricewaterhouseCoopers LLP

LOCATIONS

HQ: Corning Incorporated
1 Riverfront Plaza, Corning, NY 14831
Phone: 607-974-9000   **Fax:** 607-974-8091
Web: www.corning.com

2009 Sales

	$ mil.	% of total
Asia/Pacific		
Taiwan	1,735	32
China	638	12
Japan	630	12
South Korea	61	1
Other countries	105	2
North America		
US	1,314	24
Canada	112	2
Mexico	44	1
Europe		
Germany	190	3
UK	92	2
France	48	1
Other countries	264	5
Latin America	35	1
Other regions	127	2
Total	**5,395**	**100**

PRODUCTS/OPERATIONS

2009 Sales

	$ mil.	% of total
Display Technologies	2,426	45
Telecommunications	1,677	31
Environmental Technologies	590	11
Life Sciences	366	7
Specialty Materials	331	6
Other	5	—
Total	**5,395**	**100**

Selected Products

Display technologies
Liquid crystal displays

Environmental technologies
Industrial and stationary emissions products
Mobile emissions and automotive catalytic converter products

Life sciences
Genomics and laboratory equipment

Telecommunications
Optical fiber and cable
Optical networking components

Other
Polarized glass
Semiconductor materials

COMPETITORS

3M
ADC Telecommunications
Alcatel-Lucent
Amphenol
Asahi Glass
Becton, Dickinson
Belden
Carl-Zeiss-Stiftung
CommScope
Dai Nippon Printing
Draka Holding
Fujikura Ltd.
Furukawa Electric
General Cable
Gerresheimer Glass
Heraeus Holding
Hoya Corp.
IBIDEN
JDS Uniphase
NGK INSULATORS
Nippon Electric Glass
Nippon Sheet Glass
Nortel Networks
Oerlikon
Prysmian
Saint-Gobain
SCHOTT
Shin-Etsu Chemical
Sumitomo Electric
Superior Essex
SWCC SHOWA
Thermo Fisher Scientific
Thomas & Betts
Toppan Printing
Tyco Electronics

HISTORICAL FINANCIALS

Company Type: Public

Income Statement

FYE: December 31

	REVENUE ($ mil.)	NET INCOME ($ mil.)	NET PROFIT MARGIN	EMPLOYEES
12/09	5,395	2,008	37.2%	23,500
12/08	5,948	5,257	88.4%	27,000
12/07	5,860	2,150	36.7%	24,800
12/06	5,174	1,855	35.9%	24,500
12/05	4,579	585	12.8%	26,000
Annual Growth	4.2%	36.1%	—	(2.5%)

2009 Year-End Financials

Debt ratio: 12.4%
Return on equity: 13.9%
Cash ($ mil.): 2,541
Current ratio: 3.59
Long-term debt ($ mil.): 1,930

No. of shares (mil.): 1,562
Dividends
  Yield: 1.0%
  Payout: 15.6%
Market value ($ mil.): 30,155

Stock History

NYSE: GLW

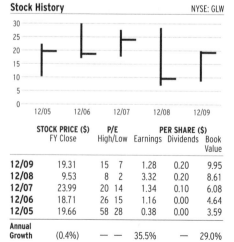

	STOCK PRICE ($) FY Close	P/E High/Low		PER SHARE ($) Earnings	Dividends	Book Value
12/09	19.31	15	7	1.28	0.20	9.95
12/08	9.53	8	2	3.32	0.20	8.61
12/07	23.99	20	14	1.34	0.10	6.08
12/06	18.71	26	15	1.16	0.00	4.64
12/05	19.66	58	28	0.38	0.00	3.59
Annual Growth	(0.4%)	—	—	35.5%	—	29.0%

Costco Wholesale

Wal-Mart isn't the biggest in *every* business. Costco Wholesale is the largest wholesale club operator in the US (ahead of Wal-Mart's SAM'S CLUB). The company operates about 565 membership warehouse stores serving some 56 million cardholders in some 40 US states and Puerto Rico, Canada, Japan, Mexico, South Korea, Taiwan, the UK, and Australia, primarily under the Costco Wholesale name. Stores offer discount prices on an average of about 4,000 products (many in bulk packaging), ranging from alcoholic beverages and appliances to fresh food, pharmaceuticals, and tires. Certain club memberships also offer products and services such as car and home insurance, mortgage and real estate services, and travel packages.

With more than 1,200 warehouse clubs across North America, competition is intense. Fierce competition and the deep recession in the US led Costco to book its first ever sales decline in fiscal 2009. Despite the weak sales environment, Costco is looking to increase its annual rate of new Costco openings to between 30 and 40 per year when economic conditions improve.

On the international front, Costco is looking to take advantage of opportunities for growth, especially in Asia. Key markets include Japan, Korea, and Taiwan. Also, the company opened its first location in Australia in mid-2009. Closer to home, through a joint venture with Mexico's Controladora Comercial Mexicana, Costco Mexico operates 30-plus warehouse stores south of the border.

To shop at Costco, customers must be members — a policy the company believes reinforces customer loyalty and provides a steady source of fee revenue. Facing competition from discounters, including Target, that don't charge a membership fee, as well as from rival SAM'S CLUB, Costco has been busy expanding and retrofitting its warehouses (which average about 142,000 sq. ft.) to accommodate fresh food sections and other ancillary units, such as gas stations, optical departments, pharmacies, and food courts. Costco's foray into grocery sales has been a success. Food and sundries account for more than half of Costco's total sales, making it the third-largest seller of groceries in the US behind Wal-Mart Supercenters and Kroger. Costco is expanding its premium private-label Kirkland Signature line of some 330 items (about 15% of sales) to 500 products by 2011. (It has even struck a deal with Martha Stewart Living Omnimedia for a new line of food products exclusive to Costco, launched in 2008.)

In what amounts to a black eye for Costco, which enjoys its image as a benevolent employer relative to other retailers (notably Wal-Mart), a federal judge has granted class-action status to a lawsuit filed on behalf of more than 700 female Costco managers. The suit claims the company has discriminated against women seeking promotions to store managers.

Davis Selected Advisers, L.P. owns about 10% of Costco's shares.

HISTORY

From 1954 to 1974 retailer Sol Price built his Fed-Mart discount chain into a $300 million behemoth selling general merchandise to government employees. Price sold the company to Hugo Mann in 1975 and the next year, with son

Robert, Rick Libenson, and Giles Bateman, opened the first Price Club warehouse, in San Diego, to sell in volume to small businesses at steep discounts.

Posting a large loss its first year prompted Price Club's decision to expand membership to include government, utility, and hospital employees, as well as credit union members. In 1978 it opened a second store, in Phoenix. With the help of his father, Sol's other son Laurence began a chain of tire-mounting stores (located adjacent to Price Club outlets on land leased from the company and using tires sold by the Price Clubs).

The company went public in 1980 with four stores in California and Arizona. Price Club moved into the eastern US with its 1984 opening of a store in Virginia and continued to expand, including a joint venture with Canadian retailer Steinberg in 1986 to operate stores in Canada; the first Canadian warehouse opened that year in Montreal.

Two years later Price Club acquired A. M. Lewis (grocery distributor, Southern California and Arizona), and the next year it opened two Price Club Furnishings, offering discounted home and office furniture.

Price Club bought out Steinberg's interest in the Canadian locations in 1990 and added stores on the East Coast and in California, Colorado, and British Columbia. However, competition in the East from ensconced rivals such as SAM'S CLUB and PACE forced the closure of two stores two years later. A 50-50 joint venture with retailer Controladora Comercial Mexicana led to the opening of two Price Clubs in Mexico City, one each in 1992 and 1993.

Price Club merged with Costco Wholesale in 1993. Founded in 1983 by Jeffrey Brotman and James Sinegal (a former EVP of Price Company), Costco Wholesale went public in 1985 and expanded into Canada.

In 1993 Price/Costco opened its first warehouse outside the Americas in a London suburb. Merger costs led to a loss the following year, and Price/Costco spun off its commercial real estate operations, as well as certain international operations as Price Enterprises (now Price Legacy). In 1995 the company launched its Kirkland Signature brand of private-label merchandise. Two years later the company changed its corporate name to Costco Companies.

Costco began online sales and struck a deal to buy two stores in South Korea in 1998 and opened its first store in Japan in 1999. Under industrywide pressure over the way members-only chains record fees, Costco took a $118 million charge for fiscal 1999 to change accounting practices. That year the company made yet another name change to Costco Wholesale (emphasizing its core warehouse operations).

In 2000 the company purchased private retailer Littlewoods' 20% stake in Costco UK, increasing Costco's ownership to 80%.

In 2002 the retailer opened its first home store — called Costco Home — in Kirkland, Washington, stocked with mostly high-end furniture. A second Costco Home store opened in Tempe, Arizona, in 2004.

In July 2009 Costco shuttered its two Costco Home stores. The retailer cited the weak economy and market for home furnishings, and the fact that the concept didn't fit with its expansion plans, for their closure. In August the company opened its first warehouse club in Australia.

EXECUTIVES

Chairman: Jeffrey H. (Jeff) Brotman, age 68, $3,351,794 total compensation
CEO and Director: James D. (Jim) Sinegal, age 74, $3,353,120 total compensation
President and COO: W. Craig Jelinek, age 58, $2,926,577 total compensation
EVP and COO, Eastern and Canadian Divisions: Joseph P. (Joe) Portera, age 56, $2,878,291 total compensation
EVP and COO, Southwest Division and Mexico: Dennis R. Zook, age 60, $2,012,155 total compensation
EVP and COO, Northern Division: John D. McKay
EVP, CFO, and Director: Richard A. Galanti, age 53, $2,923,413 total compensation
EVP Merchandising: Douglas W. (Doug) Schutt, age 50
EVP Real Estate Development: Paul G. Moulton, age 58
EVP Construction and Distribution: Thomas K. Walker, age 70
SVP Administration and Chief Legal Officer: Joel Benoliel
SVP Information Systems: Don Burdick
SVP Administration, Global Operations: Franz E. Lazarus
SVP and Corporate Controller: David S. Petterson
SV, Costco Wholesale Industries and Business Development: Richard C. Chavez
SVP Pharmacy: Charles V. Burnett
SVP Human Resources and Risk Management: John Matthews
SVP Construction: Ali Moayeri
VP Legal and General Counsel: Richard J. Olin
Auditors: KPMG LLP

LOCATIONS

HQ: Costco Wholesale Corporation
999 Lake Dr., Issaquah, WA 98027
Phone: 425-313-8100
Web: www.costco.com

2009 Locations

	No.
US & Puerto Rico	413
Canada	77
Mexico	32
UK	21
Japan	9
South Korea	7
Taiwan	6
Australia	1
Total	**566**

PRODUCTS/OPERATIONS

2009 Sales

	% of total
Sundries (including candy, snacks, beverages, cleaning products & tobacco)	23
Food (dry & institutionally packaged)	21
Hardlines (including major appliances, electronics, office & auto supplies)	19
Fresh food (meat, bakery, deli & produce)	12
Softlines (including apparel, books, cameras & jewelry)	10
Other (including pharmacy, optical, photo & gas stations)	15
Total	**100**

2009 Sales

	$ mil.	% of total
Sales	69,889	98
Membership fees	1,533	2
Total	**71,422**	**100**

Selected Products and Services

Alcoholic beverages
Apparel
Appliances
Automotive insurance products (tires, batteries)
Automobile sales
Baby products
Books
Cameras, film, and photofinishing
Candy
Caskets
CDs
Checks and form printing
Cleaning and institutional supplies
Collectibles
Computer hardware and software
Computer training services
Copying and printing services
Credit card processing
DVDs
Electronics
Eye exams
Flooring
Floral arrangements
Fresh foods (bakery, deli, meats, produce, seafood)
Furniture
Gasoline
Gifts
Glasses and contact lenses
Groceries and institutionally packaged foods
Hardware
Health and beauty aids
Hearing aids
Home insurance
Housewares
Insurance (automobile, small-business health, home)
Jewelry
Lighting supplies
Mortgage service
Office equipment and supplies
Outdoor living products
Payroll processing
Pet supplies
Pharmaceuticals
Plumbing supplies
Real estate services
Snack foods
Soft drinks
Sporting goods
Tobacco
Tools
Toys
Travel packages and other travel services
Video games and systems

Private Label

Kirkland Signature

COMPETITORS

ALDI
Amazon.com
Army and Air Force Exchange
Aurora Wholesalers
AutoZone
Barnes & Noble
Best Buy
Big Lots
BJ's Wholesale Club
Dollar General
Family Dollar Stores
Home Depot
Kmart
Kohl's
Kroger
Lowe's
Office Depot
PETCO
PetSmart
Safeway
Staples
Target
Toys "R" Us
Trader Joe's
Walgreen
Wal-Mart
Whole Foods

HISTORICAL FINANCIALS

Company Type: Public

Income Statement
FYE: Sunday nearest August 31

	REVENUE ($ mil.)	NET INCOME ($ mil.)	NET PROFIT MARGIN	EMPLOYEES
8/09	71,422	1,086	1.5%	142,000
8/08	72,483	1,283	1.8%	137,000
8/07	64,400	1,083	1.7%	127,000
8/06	60,151	1,103	1.8%	127,000
8/05	52,935	1,063	2.0%	118,000
Annual Growth	**7.8%**	**0.5%**	**—**	**4.7%**

2009 Year-End Financials

Debt ratio: 22.0%
Return on equity: 11.3%
Cash ($ mil.): 3,157
Current ratio: 1.11
Long-term debt ($ mil.): 2,206
No. of shares (mil.): 439
Dividends
  Yield: 1.3%
  Payout: 27.5%
Market value ($ mil.): 22,387

Stock History
NASDAQ (GS): COST

	STOCK PRICE ($) FY Close	P/E High/Low		PER SHARE ($) Earnings	Dividends	Book Value
8/09	50.98	29	12	2.47	0.68	22.81
8/08	67.06	26	19	2.89	0.61	20.93
8/07	61.75	28	20	2.37	0.55	19.64
8/06	46.79	25	18	2.30	0.49	20.82
8/05	43.40	23	18	2.18	0.43	20.22
Annual Growth	**4.1%**	**—**	**—**	**3.2%**	**12.1%**	**3.1%**

Covance Inc.

Behind every great big drug company stands a great big contract research organization (CRO), and Covance is one of the biggest. Covance helps pharmaceutical and biotech companies worldwide develop new drugs by providing preclinical testing services, as well as designing and carrying out human clinical trials to determine if the drugs are safe and effective. Services include toxicology studies, biostatistical analysis, clinical laboratory testing, and post-marketing studies. Among the company's customers are pharmaceutical, biotech, and medical device companies; Covance also offers laboratory testing services to companies in the chemical, agrochemical, and food industries.

Covance is capitalizing on the industry's trend toward more outsourcing of drug development activities, a practice which generally saves money for drug and medical device companies. Also, as clinical trials become increasingly complex, requiring sophisticated testing capabilities, drug companies are finding it more economical to outsource the development rather than invest in expensive lab and personnel upgrades. Additionally, Covance has been expanding its already extensive global presence in order to take advantage of other industry trends, including the increasing desire of drug companies to test compounds in multiple geographic markets simultaneously.

The company established new offices in Israel, the Ukraine, and Slovakia in 2009. Covance also beefed up its presence in South and Central America, adding or expanding offices in Argentina, Brazil, Chile, Mexico, and Peru.

Covance's growing Early Development segment provides preclinical toxicology and chemistry testing that determine a drug's effects on animals and chromosomes and whether its chemical makeup remains stable over time. The division also produces monoclonal antibodies and lab animals used in drug research, and provides early-stage clinical services such as pharmacology testing in humans.

Its Late-Stage Development services include central laboratory testing of urine, blood, and tissue samples from patients in drug trials; design and management of clinical trials; and commercialization services, including post-marketing studies and various marketing consulting services.

The company serves about 300 pharmaceutical and biotechnology customers. For its more limited chemical and food industry customers, Covance provides services such as testing pesticides for risks to humans and determining nutritional information for food labels.

Covance tends to grow its business by making selective acquisitions that fit with its long-term expansion plans. For example, Covance paid $50 million to acquire one of Eli Lilly's early stage drug development facilities in 2008. In return, Lilly awarded Covance with a ten-year, $1.6 billion contract for early and late-stage drug development services. The next year, Covance entered into a five-year, $145 million agreement to provide genomics analysis services to Merck. Covance acquired Merck's Seattle-based Gene Expression Laboratory, which had been part of Merck's broken-up Rosetta Inpharmatics group, as part of the deal. The addition of the lab expands Covance's genomic testing and personalized medicine capabilities.

HISTORY

Glassmaker Corning began collecting research organizations in 1987 when it decided to move into laboratory and clinical services. Over the next several years, Corning bought Hazleton (preclinical and clinical trials, 1987), G.H. Besselaar Associates (clinical trials, 1989), PACT (periapproval studies, 1990), and SciCor (clinical laboratory, 1991). It also acquired an interest in Bio-Imaging Technologies in 1994 and National Packaging Systems, a pharmaceutical packaging company, in 1995. Corning moved into health economics and outcomes in 1996 with the purchase of Health Technology Associates and added to its packaging operations with Swiss company Pacamed.

After attempts to sell its laboratory testing division failed, Corning divided the operations into Covance (clinical trials) and Quest Diagnostics (laboratory testing services) and spun them off in late 1996. In 1997 Covance formed an alliance with the China Innovation Center for Life Sciences to develop biopharmaceutical research facilities in China to train Chinese scientists in international research practices and conduct feasibility studies on potential drugs. The next year the firm created a unit to research psychiatric ailments and central nervous system disorders.

In 1999 Covance announced a merger with PAREXEL International, the #3 contract research organization, then canceled it after investors criticized the union.

After a dip in earnings, the firm announced plans to cut its workforce in 2000. It then sold its pharmaceutical packaging services business to Fisher Scientific (which later became Thermo Fisher) in 2001.

To expand its geographical reach, it launched operations in Eastern Europe in mid-2003.

During 2005 and 2006 the company expanded its early development segment by acquiring clinical pharmacology sites of GFI Clinical Services and Radiant Research. It also bought Signet Laboratories to boost its antibody production capabilities.

EXECUTIVES

Chairman and CEO: Joseph L. (Joe) Herring, age 54, $5,285,503 total compensation
EVP and COO: Wendel D. Barr, age 48, $1,678,670 total compensation
Corporate SVP, CFO, and Principal Accounting Officer: William E. Klitgaard, age 56, $1,567,271 total compensation
Corporate SVP; President, Global Central Laboratory and Discovery and Translational Services: Deborah L. Tanner, age 47, $1,411,112 total compensation
Corporate SVP; President, Clinical Development: Richard F. Cimino, age 50, $1,210,171 total compensation
Corporate SVP, General Counsel, and Secretary: James W. Lovett, age 45
Corporate SVP; President, Nonclinical Safety Assessment Services: Mike Lehmann, age 47
Auditors: Ernst & Young LLP

LOCATIONS

HQ: Covance Inc.
210 Carnegie Center, Princeton, NJ 08540
Phone: 609-452-4440 **Fax:** 609-452-9375
Web: www.covance.com

2009 Sales

	$ mil.	% of total
Customer revenue		
US	1,075.6	55
Switzerland	282.1	15
UK	204.0	14
Other countries	305.9	10
Other	95.0	6
Total	**1,962.6**	**100**

PRODUCTS/OPERATIONS

2009 Sales

	$ mil.	% of total
Late-Stage Development	1,075.8	55
Early Development	791.8	40
Other	95.0	5
Total	**1,962.6**	**100**

Selected Services

Early Development
 Preclinical Services
  Bioanalytical services
  Pharmaceutical and nutritional chemistry
  Research products
  Toxicology
 Clinical pharmacology services
Late-Stage Development
 Central laboratory services
 Clinical development services
 Clinical trial support services
 Commercialization services
  Periapproval services
  Market access services

COMPETITORS

Albany Molecular Research	Medpace
Bioanalytical Systems	Meridian Bioscience
Charles River Laboratories	MPI Research
Commonwealth	PAREXEL
Biotechnologies	Pharmaceutical Product
Harlan Laboratories	Development
ICON	PharmaNet Development
inVentiv Health	PRA International
Jackson Laboratory	Quest Diagnostics
Kendle	Quintiles Transnational
LabCorp	Taconic Farms
Life Sciences Research	WuXi PharmaTech
MDS	

HISTORICAL FINANCIALS

Company Type: Public

Income Statement

				FYE: December 31
	REVENUE ($ mil.)	NET INCOME ($ mil.)	NET PROFIT MARGIN	EMPLOYEES
12/09	1,963	176	9.0%	10,320
12/08	1,827	197	10.8%	9,600
12/07	1,632	176	10.8%	8,700
12/06	1,406	145	10.3%	8,100
12/05	1,251	120	9.6%	7,300
Annual Growth	**11.9%**	**10.1%**	**—**	**9.0%**

2009 Year-End Financials

Debt ratio: — No. of shares (mil.): 65
Return on equity: 13.5% Dividends
Cash ($ mil.): 289 Yield: —
Current ratio: 2.18 Payout: —
Long-term debt ($ mil.): — Market value ($ mil.): 3,534

Stock History

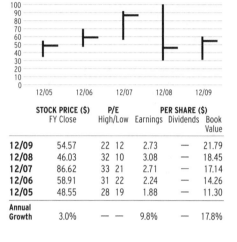

NYSE: CVD

	STOCK PRICE ($) FY Close	P/E High/Low		PER SHARE ($) Earnings	Dividends	Book Value
12/09	54.57	22	12	2.73	—	21.79
12/08	46.03	32	10	3.08	—	18.45
12/07	86.62	33	21	2.71	—	17.14
12/06	58.91	31	22	2.24	—	14.26
12/05	48.55	28	19	1.88	—	11.30
Annual Growth	**3.0%**	—	—	**9.8%**	—	**17.8%**

Cox Enterprises

Cox Enterprises is a family-owned holding company with operations spanning cable TV, broadcasting, publishing, and auctions. Its flagship subsidiary, Cox Communications, is the #3 cable system operator (behind Comcast and Time Warner Cable) serving more than 6 million customers with TV, Internet, and digital phone services. Its Manheim unit is the largest wholesale vehicle auction company in the US, with about 145 locations. Cox's media operations, overseen by Cox Media Group, include Cox Newspapers (eight daily papers), Cox Television (about 15 local stations), and Cox Radio (more than 80 stations). Cox also owns a majority stake in AutoTrader.com, an online used car listing service.

The family of founder James Cox, now led by grandson and chairman James Kennedy, has been able to diversify its fortune through Cox Enterprises into holdings that span the country. However, unlike highly integrated media conglomerates such as Time Warner and Walt Disney, Cox's operations do not benefit as much from multi-purposed content and cross-promotion. Its focus on technology and telecommunications, though, does put the company in a position to capitalize on the rapidly converging digital media world.

The company's Cox Communications unit has focused on expanding the number of different services it delivers to subscribers. The cable company has been heavily marketing bundled service packages that include digital phone and broadband Internet access. It has also expanded video on demand (VOD) offerings. Cox Communications has also built a mobile communications network to offer cellular phone service and wireless broadband Internet access to its customers.

The Cox organization has also invested heavily in digital media and services in conjunction with its telecommunications infrastructure. The company has more than 100 online properties, including websites for its newspapers, television stations, and radio stations.

Real world publishing, however, has not been so kind to the company. Its Cox Newspapers unit has struggled along with the rest of the newspaper industry with declining readership and advertising revenue. In response, Cox put all but three of its papers up for sale and plans to use the proceeds to pay down debt and to fund new business investments. Its remaining properties, including the *Atlanta Journal-Constitution*, the *Palm Beach Post* (Florida), and the *Dayton Daily News*, plan to boost their online publishing efforts to expand readership. Cox is also selling its Valpak direct mail advertising unit.

The company reorganized its media operations in early 2009, forming Cox Media Group to oversee its broadcasting and publishing businesses. Longtime newspaper chief Sandy Schwartz was named head of the new division.

Cox divested a portion of its cable programming business in 2009, selling a 65% stake in the Travel Channel to Scripps Networks Interactive.

Company veteran Jimmy Hayes replaced James Kennedy as CEO of Cox Enterprises in 2008. Kennedy, who remained chairman, had led the business since 1987.

HISTORY

James Middleton Cox, who dropped out of school in 1886 at 16, worked as a teacher, reporter, and congressional secretary before buying the *Dayton Daily News* in 1898. In 1905 he acquired the nearby *Springfield Press-Republican* and then took up politics, serving two terms in the US Congress (1909-1913) and three terms as Ohio governor (1913-1915; 1917-1921). He even ran for president in 1920 (his running mate was future President Franklin Roosevelt) but lost to rival Ohio publisher Warren G. Harding.

Once out of politics, Cox began building his media empire. He bought the *Miami Daily News* in 1923 and founded WHIO (Dayton, Ohio's first radio station). He bought Atlanta's WSB ("Welcome South, Brother"), the South's first radio station, in 1939 and added WSB-FM and WSB-TV, the South's first FM and TV stations, in 1948. Cox founded Dayton's first FM and TV stations (WHIO-FM and WHIO-TV) the next year, and *The Atlanta Constitution* joined his collection in 1950. Cox died in 1957.

The company continued to expand its broadcasting interests in the late 1950s and early 1960s. It was one of the first major broadcasting companies to expand into cable TV when it purchased a system in Lewistown, Pennsylvania, in 1962. The Cox family's broadcast properties were placed in publicly held Cox Broadcasting in 1964. Two years later its newspapers were placed into privately held Cox Enterprises, and the cable holdings became publicly held Cox Cable Communications. The broadcasting arm diversified,

buying Manheim Services (auto auctions, 1968), Kansas City Automobile Auction (1969), and TeleRep (TV ad sales, 1972).

Cox Cable had 500,000 subscribers in nine states when it rejoined Cox Broadcasting in 1977. Cox Broadcasting was renamed Cox Communications in 1982, and the Cox family took the company private again in 1985, combining it with Cox Enterprises. The company also invested in upstart cable broadcaster Discover Channel (now part of Discovery Communications) during the 1980s. James Kennedy, grandson of founder James Cox, became chairman and CEO in 1987.

Expansion became the keyword for Cox in the 1990s. The company merged its Manheim unit with the auto auction business of Ford Motor Credit and GE Capital in 1991. It also formed Sprint Spectrum in 1994, a partnership with Sprint, TCI (acquired by AT&T and later by Comcast), and Comcast to bundle telephone, cable TV, and other communications services (Sprint bought out Cox in 1999). Then, in one of its biggest transactions, Cox bought Times Mirror's cable TV operations for $2.3 billion in 1995 and combined them with its own cable system into a new, publicly traded company called Cox Communications.

To expand its online presence, the company formed Cox Interactive Media in 1996, establishing a series of city websites and making a host of investments in various Internet companies. Cox also applied the online strategy to its automobile auction businesses, establishing AutoTrader.com in 1998.

In 2002 Cox dropped plans to expand its local Internet city guide business nationwide. Two years later, fed up with the demands of running a publicly traded cable company, Cox bought the 38% of Cox Communications that it didn't already own for $8.5 billion.

The company in 2007 exchanged Cox Communications' 25% stake in Discovery Communications for $1.3 billion in cash. The deal also included cable broadcaster the Travel Channel.

EXECUTIVES

Chairman, Cox Enterprises, Cox Communications, and Cox Radio: James C. Kennedy, age 62
Vice Chairman: G. Dennis Berry, age 65
President, CEO, and Director: Jimmy W. Hayes, age 57
EVP and CFO: John M. Dyer, age 55
SVP Product Marketing, Cox Communications: David Pugliese
SVP Human Resources and Administration: Marybeth H. Leamer
SVP Strategic Investments and Real Estate Planning: R. Dale Hughes
VP Supply Chain Services and Chief Procurement Officer: Michael J. (Mike) Mannheimer
VP Public Policy and Regulatory Affairs: Alexandra M. Wilson
VP and CIO: Gregory B. (Greg) Morrison
VP Internal Audit: Alexander R. (Alex) Stickney
VP Corporate Communications and Public Affairs: Roberto I. Jimenez
VP Corporate Tax: Maria Friedman
VP Government Affairs: Joab M. (Joey) Lesesne III
VP Corporate Security: Robert R. (Bob) Brand
VP Development: Robert N. (Bob) Redella
VP Legal Affairs, General Counsel, and Corporate Secretary: Andrew A. (Andy) Merdek
President, Cox Media Group and Cox Auto Trader: Sanford H. (Sandy) Schwartz, age 57
President and CEO, Manheim Auctions: Dean H. Eisner
President and Co-Founder, Adify: Russ Fradin
President and CEO, AutoTrader.com: Chip Perry
President, Cox Communications: Patrick J. (Pat) Esser
Publisher, Atlanta Journal-Constitution: Michael Joseph

LOCATIONS

HQ: Cox Enterprises, Inc.
6205 Peachtree Dunwoody Rd., Atlanta, GA 30328
Phone: 678-645-0000　　**Fax:** 678-645-1079
Web: www.coxenterprises.com

PRODUCTS/OPERATIONS

2009 Sales

	% of total
Cox Communications	61
Manheim	23
Cox Media Group	12
Cox Auto Trader	4
Total	**100**

Selected Operations

Cox Communications (cable TV system operations)
Manheim (wholesale automotive auctions)
Cox Media Group
  Cox Newspapers
    The Atlanta Journal-Constitution
    Austin American-Statesman (Texas)
    Dayton Daily News (Ohio)
    JournalNews (Hamilton, OH)
    The Middletown Journal (Ohio)
    Palm Beach Daily News (Florida)
    The Palm Beach Post (Florida)
    Springfield News-Sun (Ohio)
  Cox Radio
  Cox Television
    KFOX (FOX; El Paso, TX)
    KICU (Ind.; San Jose, CA)
    KIRO (CBS, Seattle)
    KRXI (FOX; Reno, NV)
    KTVU (FOX; Oakland, CA)
    WFTV (ABC; Orlando, FL)
    WHIO (CBS; Dayton, OH)
    WJAC (NBC; Johnstown, PA)
    WPXI (NBC; Pittsburgh)
    WSB (ABC, Atlanta)
    WSOC (ABC; Charlotte, NC)
    WTOV (NBC; Steubenville, OH)
Cox Auto Trader (AutoTrader.com online used vehicle listings)

COMPETITORS

A. H. Belo	DIRECTV
Advance Publications	DISH Network
AT&T	eBay
CBS Corp	Entrade
Clear Channel	McClatchy Company
Columbus Fair Auto Auction	Pittsburgh Independent Auto Auction
Comcast	Ritchie Bros. Auctioneers
Cumulus Media	Verizon

HISTORICAL FINANCIALS

Company Type: Private

Income Statement

				FYE: December 31
	REVENUE ($ mil.)	NET INCOME ($ mil.)	NET PROFIT MARGIN	EMPLOYEES
12/09	14,829	—	—	66,000
12/08	15,400	—	—	77,000
12/07	15,033	—	—	81,693
12/06	13,200	—	—	80,000
12/05	12,000	—	—	77,000
Annual Growth	5.4%	—	—	(3.8%)

Revenue History

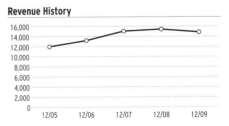

C. R. Bard, Inc.

C. R. Bard is no upstart in the world of medical devices. The company has been in the business for more than a century and introduced the Foley urological catheter (still one of its top sellers) in 1934. Its products fall into four general therapeutic categories: vascular, urology, oncology, and surgical specialties. Among other things, the company makes stents, catheters, and guidewires used in angioplasties and other vascular procedures; urology catheters and products used to treat urinary incontinence; and catheters for delivering chemotherapy treatments. Its line of specialty surgical tools, made by subsidiary Davol, includes devices used in laparoscopic and orthopedic procedures and for hernia repair.

While the US accounts for more than two-thirds of sales, Bard sells its products in more than 100 countries through numerous subsidiaries, joint ventures, and affiliated representatives. The company focuses marketing programs and expansion efforts on its four key product areas, seeking to provide a diverse and cutting-edge line of offerings to hospitals, doctors' offices, and other health care facilities.

Along with catheters, the urology segment includes sales of surgical slings used to treat incontinence, brachytherapy seeds for prostate cancer treatment, and urine monitoring and collection systems. In 2008 the company launched its Dignicare fecal incontinence line of products. Bard's urology catheter portfolio includes an infection-control catheter (the Bardex IC) that uses a silver coating technology to reduce the risk of urinary tract infection.

The company's vascular unit makes angioplasty catheters, peripheral vascular stents, biopsy devices, and electrode catheters (used to diagnose and treat heart arrhythmias). Bard bought the LifeStent line of peripheral vascular stents from Edwards Lifesciences in 2008. The same year, Bard acquired Specialized Health Products International, which already supplied subsidiary Bard Access Systems with infusion sets for its vascular access lines.

In addition to catheters for urological and vascular procedures, Bard makes catheters and ports used to deliver chemotherapy in cancer patients. Its oncology segment also includes ultrasound devices and enteral feeding tubes. In 2009 the company launched a new biopsy sample tool, the Finesse, which can take multiple samples at one time.

Bard further widened its oncology offerings in 2010 when it purchased breast cancer device manufacturer SenoRx for about $200 million. SenoRx's products include Contura, a catheter that delivers radiation to eliminate cancerous tumors and EnCor, which lets physicians collect multiple breast biopsy samples with a single probe insertion.

HISTORY

When visiting Europe at the turn of the century, silk importer Charles Russell Bard discovered that gomenol, a mixture of olive oil with a eucalyptus extract, offered him relief from urinary problems caused by tuberculosis. He brought gomenol to America and began distributing it.

In 1907 C. R. Bard began selling a ureteral catheter developed by French firm J. Eynard.

The company incorporated in 1923 with its present name. When Charles Bard's health declined in 1926, he sold the business to John Willits and Edson Outwin (his sales manager and accountant, respectively).

In 1934 Bard became the sole agent for Davol Rubber's new Foley catheter, which helped the company achieve $1 million in sales by 1948. During the 1950s sales increased more than 400% when the firm introduced its first pre-sterilized packaged product and expanded its product line to include disposable drainage tubes and an intravenous feeding device.

Bard went public in 1963. In the 1960s the firm expanded both vertically — boosting its manufacturing capabilities (it began making its own plastic tubing) — and through acquisitions. It also established joint ventures with Davol to manufacture and distribute hospital and surgical supplies internationally.

The company diversified into the cardiovascular, respiratory therapy, home care products, and kidney dialysis fields in the 1970s and manufactured the first angioplasty catheter, a nonsurgical device to clear blocked arteries, in 1979.

In 1984 Bard watched its urological business go limp. In response, the company began a buying spree to gain market share in a consolidating hospital products industry. It swallowed up around a dozen companies, including Davol (maker of its best-selling Foley catheter), garnering such products as catheters and other products for angioplasty, diagnostics, and urinary incontinence. In 1988 it faced increasing competition in the coronary catheter market from such giants as Eli Lilly and Pfizer. Bard struck back with innovative products, but it was too little too late — even though the company continued to struggle for 10 more years, it finally pulled out of the cardiovascular market.

Bard agreed in 1993 to pay a then-record $61 million for mislabeling and improperly testing angioplasty catheters blamed for the deaths of two people (and later taken off the market). However, a year later Bard's sales topped $1 billion for the first time, and it purchased catheter-related companies in Canada, France, and Germany.

Purchases in 1995 and 1996 included medical device manufacturers MedChem Products and the Cardiac Assist Division of St. Jude Medical. In 1996 Bard bought a majority stake in Italy-based X-Trode and acquired IMPRA, a leading supplier of vascular grafts (its largest deal ever). That year the ongoing catheter litigation snared three former Bard executives, who received 18-month prison sentences for conspiring to hide potentially fatal flaws in the products.

Beginning in 1998 Bard sold its cardiovascular line after deciding it was going to cost too much time and money to re-establish dominance in that field. It built its other fields through purchases, including ProSeed (radiation seed therapy, 1998) and Dymax (ultrasound catheter guidance systems, 1999).

In 2000 it obtained the Kugel Patch product line with the acquisition of Surgical Sense. In 2003 and 2004 it made several purchases, including a brachytherapy seeds business, a biopsy device, and several hernia repair products. The company added the StatLock line of catheter stabilization products to the urology division with the 2006 acquisition of Venetec International. In 2007 the company introduced a breathing tube (the Agento IC) using a silver coating technology to reduce the risk of infection. Bard also introduced the Dorado angioplasty catheter that year.

EXECUTIVES

Chairman and CEO: Timothy M. Ring, age 52, $9,683,341 total compensation
President, COO, and Director: John H. Weiland, age 54, $6,906,055 total compensation
SVP and CFO: Todd C. Schermerhorn, age 49, $4,187,106 total compensation
SVP Quality and Regulatory Affairs: Gary D. Dolch, age 62
SVP Science, Technology, and Clinical Affairs: John A. DeFord, age 48
Group VP: Sharon M. Alterio, age 47, $2,720,482 total compensation
Group VP: Brian P. Kelly, age 51, $2,189,139 total compensation
Group VP: Timothy P. (Tim) Collins, age 49
Group VP, Bard Access Systems and Bard Peripheral Vascular: Jim C. Beasley
VP and Controller: Frank Lupisella Jr., age 49
VP, General Counsel, and Secretary: Stephen J. Long, age 44
VP Investor Relations: Eric J. Shick
VP Human Resources: Bronwen K. Kelly, age 57
VP Strategic Planning and Business Development: Robert L. (Bob) Mellen, age 53
VP Quality, Environmental Services, and Safety: Christopher D. (Chris) Ganser, age 57
VP and Treasurer: Scott T. Lowry, age 43
VP Regulatory and Quality Systems Excellence: James M. Howard II
President, Asia and Americas: P. R. Curry
President, Bard Europe: P. J. Byloos
President, Davol: John P. (J.P.) Groetelaars
President, Bard Japan: Daniel W. (Dan) LaFever
Auditors: KPMG LLP

LOCATIONS

HQ: C. R. Bard, Inc.
   730 Central Ave., Murray Hill, NJ 07974
Phone: 908-277-8000   **Fax:** 908-277-8240
Web: www.crbard.com

2009 Sales

	$ mil.	% of total
US	1,759.2	69
Europe	471.7	19
Japan	126.5	5
Other regions	177.5	7
Total	**2,534.9**	**100**

PRODUCTS/OPERATIONS

2009 Sales

	$ mil.	% of total
Urology	700.3	28
Vascular	681.5	27
Oncology	678.7	27
Surgical specialties	387.8	15
Other	86.6	3
Total	**2,534.9**	**100**

Selected Brands and Products

Urology
   Agento IC (infection control endotracheal tube)
   Bardex IC Foley (infection control catheter)
   Contigen Bard Collagen (stress urinary incontinence implant)
   Criticore (urinary output monitor)
   Dignicare (fecal incontinence products)
   Simetry Brachytherapy Program (prostate cancer treatment products)
   StatLock (catheter stabilization products)

Oncology
   Hickman & Groshong (venous access catheter)
   PowerPICC (vascular access catheter)
   PowerPort (implanted IV port)
   Precisor Direct Bite (biopsy forceps)
   Site-Rite 6 Ultrasound System (for central venous access)

Vascular
 Atlas (angioplasty catheter)
 Conquest (angioplasty catheter)
 Dorado (angioplasty catheter)
 E-Luminexx (iliac stent)
 Flair (access stent graft)
 G2 and G2 Express (vena cava filter)
 LifeStent (peripheral vascular stent)
 Vacora (biopsy device)
Surgical specialties
 Allomax (hernia repair)
 Collamend (hernia repair)
 PerFex Plug (hernia repair)
 Permasorb (fixation device)
 Sepramesh (hernia repair)
 Ventrio Sperma (hernia repair)
 Ventralex (hernia repair)

COMPETITORS

Abbott Labs	Ethicon
American Medical Systems	Ethicon Endo-Surgery
AngioDynamics	HealthTronics
Angiotech Pharmaceuticals	Hologic
B. Braun Melsungen	I-Flow
Baxter International	Kimberly-Clark Health
Becton, Dickinson	Medtronic
Boston Scientific	Merit Medical Systems
CONMED Corporation	St. Jude Medical
Cook Group	Terumo
Covidien	

HISTORICAL FINANCIALS

Company Type: Public

Income Statement

FYE: December 31

	REVENUE ($ mil.)	NET INCOME ($ mil.)	NET PROFIT MARGIN	EMPLOYEES
12/09	2,535	460	18.2%	11,000
12/08	2,452	417	17.0%	11,000
12/07	2,202	406	18.5%	10,200
12/06	1,986	272	13.7%	9,400
12/05	1,771	337	19.0%	8,900
Annual Growth	9.4%	8.1%	—	5.4%

2009 Year-End Financials

Debt ratio: 6.8%	No. of shares (mil.): 94
Return on equity: 22.1%	Dividends
Cash ($ mil.): 674	Yield: 0.8%
Current ratio: 5.30	Payout: 14.3%
Long-term debt ($ mil.): 150	Market value ($ mil.): 7,295

Stock History

NYSE: BCR

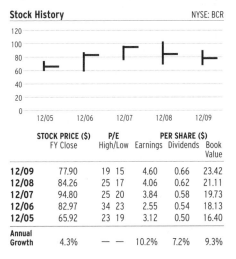

	STOCK PRICE ($) FY Close	P/E High/Low		PER SHARE ($) Earnings	Dividends	Book Value
12/09	77.90	19	15	4.60	0.66	23.42
12/08	84.26	25	17	4.06	0.62	21.11
12/07	94.80	25	20	3.84	0.58	19.73
12/06	82.97	34	23	2.55	0.54	18.13
12/05	65.92	23	19	3.12	0.50	16.40
Annual Growth	4.3%	—	—	10.2%	7.2%	9.3%

Cracker Barrel Old Country Store

This company has gotten ahead in the restaurant business by holding on to a bit of the past. Cracker Barrel Old Country Store owns and operates more than 590 of its flagship restaurants known for their country kitsch, rustic decor, and down-home cooking. The eateries, located in more than 40 states, offer mostly standard American fare, such as chicken, ham, and roast beef dishes, but they are most popular as breakfast spots. Each Cracker Barrel location features a retail area where patrons can buy hand-blown glassware, cast iron cookware, and woodcrafts, as well as jellies and old-fashioned candies. Most of the restaurants are found along interstate highways and target hungry travelers.

While most casual dining chains have developed around a theme in order to distinguish themselves from the crowd, few take it to the extreme like Cracker Barrel. Its restaurants are festooned with advertisements and product packaging harkening back to the early 1900s, its menu is an unabashed gallery of down-home comfort foods, and each eatery features a front porch complete with rocking chairs. That hardcore appeal to nostalgia has earned the chain a distinct presence in the family dining segment as well as a loyal following. Cracker Barrel has been able to maintain the look and feel of its restaurants thanks in part to the fact that it has not relied on franchising to expand its chain.

The company's commitment to delivering a familiar dining experience paid off during the economic downturn in 2008. High gasoline prices that summer did hurt business, but restaurant sales rebounded at a time when several of Cracker Barrel's rivals were starving for customers.

In 2008 it rechristened itself with a new corporate name. Previously known as CBRL Group, the company adopted the same moniker as its dining chain two years after the sale of its secondary steakhouse concept Logan's Roadhouse.

HISTORY

Dan Evins opened the first Cracker Barrel Old Country Store in Lebanon, Tennessee, in 1969. As a sales representative for Shell Oil, Evins believed he could sell more gas if he combined gas stations with restaurants. He also envisioned placing his new concept along what was then a relatively new enterprise — the interstate highway system. The company was incorporated in 1970.

Four years later Evins resigned from his job at Shell Oil to give full attention to his burgeoning restaurant chain, which had grown to a dozen locations. The oil embargo of the mid-1970s prompted the company to back away from the sale of gas, and it completely did away with gas pumps by the mid-1980s. Cracker Barrel went public in 1981.

Company sales slumped in 1985, when a plan to force its smaller stores to squeeze out large-store-scale revenue failed. The company rebounded by remodeling the smaller stores to the dimensions of the larger stores and by creating middle management positions to oversee real estate purchasing, gift shop merchandising, and human resource training. It also introduced an incentive program to reward store managers for curbing costs and increasing sales. Between

1980 and 1990, the company added 84 new restaurants to its rapidly expanding chain.

Controversy struck the company during the 1990s when its old country values clashed with present day reality. In 1991 the company issued a statement declaring that it would no longer employ "individuals whose sexual preferences fail to demonstrate normal heterosexual values." Believing that the sexual orientation of such individuals was not in line with the values of its customer base, the company fired more than a dozen employees. Cracker Barrel later rescinded the policy, but the incident deeply scarred the company's image and continued to haunt it throughout the decade. The controversy also spurred changes in SEC regulations — a protest by Cracker Barrel stockholders who opposed the policy eventually led to a 1998 decision permitting stockholders to propose resolutions on employment matters.

As the company expanded its chain of restaurants beyond the southern states, it also began adapting its menus and decor to the tastes and preferences of each region. Cracker Barrel acquired Carmine's Prime Meats (later Carmine Giardini's Gourmet Market), a chain of gourmet food stores, in 1998. With the addition of a second chain of stores, the company restructured into a holding company called CBRL Group the following year and later acquired the Logan's Roadhouse steakhouse chain (founded in 1991) for about $180 million.

A group of African-American employees filed a lawsuit against the company in 1999, claiming racial discrimination. Evins resigned his post as CEO in 2001 and was replaced by company veteran Michael Woodhouse.

Even as the racial discrimination suit was pending, the company was hit by a class action discrimination suit by 21 customers claiming that African-Americans were seated in segregated areas, denied service, and served food taken from the garbage. In 2002 a federal court in Georgia ruled against the plaintiffs, claiming that they'd failed to prove that a set of discriminatory circumstances existed to warrant a national class action suit.

That same year the US Justice Department began an investigation into the public accommodations policies of CBRL's Cracker Barrel division. As part of a 2004 settlement with the department, Cracker Barrel agreed to hire an independent auditor to monitor its race-bias policies. Despite this effort, new allegations were brought against the company in 2004 when 10 employees at three Illinois restaurants filed federal charges of sexual harassment and racial discrimination. Later that year CBRL settled a handful of lawsuits at once (while denying any wrongdoing), paying a total of $8.7 million in a variety of southern US courts.

The following year the company dealt with a lawsuit brought on by donations made to a political group called Texans for a Republican Majority, a political action group connected to former congressman Tom DeLay that was alleged to be involved in illegal campaign contributions. CBRL settled their involvement in the case by agreeing to donate money to fund a nonpartisan information program at the University of Texas LBJ School of Public Affairs.

In 2006 CBRL sold its Logan's steakhouse business to a group of private equity firms, including Bruckmann, Rosser, Sherrill & Co., for $486 million.

EXECUTIVES

Chairman, President, and CEO:
Michael A. (Mike) Woodhouse, age 64,
$4,736,509 total compensation
EVP and COO: Douglas E. (Doug) Barber, age 52,
$1,710,082 total compensation
EVP and CFO: Sandra B. (Sandy) Cochran, age 51,
$616,722 total compensation
SVP, Secretary, and Chief Legal Counsel:
N. B. Forrest Shoaf, age 59,
$1,177,776 total compensation
SVP Corporate Affairs: Diana S. Wynne, age 54
SVP Strategic Initiatives: Edward A. Greene, age 54,
$716,694 total compensation
SVP Human Resources: Robert J. Harig, age 59
SVP Retail Operations: Terry A. Maxwell, age 50,
$860,283 total compensation
SVP Finance: P. Doug Couvillion
VP Accounting and Tax and Chief Accounting Officer:
Patrick A. Scruggs, age 45
VP Restaurant Operations: Nicholas V. Flanagan
VP Compensation and Benefits: John W. Rains
VP Development: S. James Torcivia
VP Innovation: Joseph Larry Jones
VP, General Counsel, and Secretary: Michael J. Zylstra
VP Training and Management Development:
Thomas R. Pate
VP Information Services: Timothy W. (Tim) Mullen
VP Brand and Menu Strategy: Christopher A. Ciavarra
VP Marketing: Peter B. Keiser
VP Product Development and Quality Assurance:
Robert F. (Bob) Doyle
Investor Contact: Barbara A. Gould
Director Corporate Communications: Julie K. Davis
Auditors: Deloitte & Touche LLP

LOCATIONS

HQ: Cracker Barrel Old Country Store, Inc.
305 Hartmann Dr., Lebanon, TN 37087
Phone: 615-444-5533   **Fax:** 615-443-9476
Web: www.crackerbarrel.com

2009 Locations

	No.
Florida	59
Tennessee	50
Georgia	42
Texas	41
North Carolina	35
Ohio	31
Kentucky	30
Virginia	29
Alabama	28
Indiana	27
Illinois	22
South Carolina	22
Pennsylvania	21
Missouri	17
Michigan	16
Arizona	13
Arkansas	11
Mississippi	11
West Virginia	10
Louisiana	9
New York	8
Oklahoma	7
New Jersey	6
Maryland	5
Wisconsin	5
Colorado	4
Kansas	4
Massachusetts	4
New Mexico	4
Utah	4
Iowa	3
Connecticut	2
Montana	2
Nebraska	2
Other states	7
Total	**591**

PRODUCTS/OPERATIONS

2009 Sales

	$ mil.	% of total
Restaurant	1,875.7	79
Retail	491.6	21
Total	**2,367.3**	**100**

COMPETITORS

American Blue Ribbon Holdings
Biglari Holdings
Bob Evans
Brinker
Buffets Holdings
Carlson Restaurants
Darden
Denny's
DineEquity
Huddle House
O'Charley's
OSI Restaurant Partners
Perkins & Marie Callender's
Red Robin
Ruby Tuesday
Shoney's
Waffle House

HISTORICAL FINANCIALS

Company Type: Public

Income Statement

FYE: Friday nearest July 31

	REVENUE ($ mil.)	NET INCOME ($ mil.)	NET PROFIT MARGIN	EMPLOYEES
7/09	2,367	66	2.8%	66,000
7/08	2,385	66	2.8%	65,000
7/07	2,352	162	6.9%	64,000
7/06	2,643	116	4.4%	74,031
7/05	2,568	127	4.9%	75,029
Annual Growth	**(2.0%)**	**(15.1%)**	**—**	**(3.2%)**

2009 Year-End Financials

Debt ratio: 470.5%
Return on equity: 57.7%
Cash ($ mil.): 12
Current ratio: 0.75
Long-term debt ($ mil.): 638
No. of shares (mil.): 24
Dividends
  Yield: 2.8%
  Payout: 27.7%
Market value ($ mil.): 680

Stock History

NASDAQ (GS): CBRL

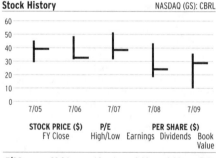

	STOCK PRICE ($) FY Close	P/E High	P/E Low	PER SHARE ($) Earnings	PER SHARE ($) Dividends	PER SHARE ($) Book Value
7/09	28.86	12	4	2.89	0.80	5.76
7/08	24.17	15	7	2.80	0.72	3.94
7/07	38.43	10	6	5.23	0.56	4.42
7/06	32.67	19	13	2.50	0.52	12.83
7/05	39.17	18	12	2.45	0.48	36.93
Annual Growth	**(7.4%)**	**—**	**—**	**4.2%**	**13.6%**	**(37.2%)**

Crane Co.

In many cultures the crane is a symbol of longevity, and this Crane, indeed, reflects such endurance. Founded in 1855, the company makes a wide variety of engineered industrial products through its five business segments: Aerospace & Electronics (sensing and control systems), Engineered Materials (plastic composites, substrates), Merchandising Systems (vending machines), Fluid Handling (valves and pumps), and Controls (diagnostic, measurement, and control devices). Crane products have applications in aerospace, military and defense, recreational vehicle, construction, transportation, automated merchandising, petrochemical, chemical, and power generation industries.

Albeit highly specialized, Crane's businesses are driven to play a dominant role in their global markets. Crane strives for growth through business acquisitions and divestitures that contribute to its activities, as well as through operational integration that delivers efficiencies coupled with strategic performance benchmarks.

Among the events also affecting the company's bottom line (settlements, lawsuits, restructuring costs, and environmental penalties), acquisitions and divestitures are notable. Targeting promising prospects in its Aerospace & Electronics business segment, one which represents more than 25% of consolidated sales, Crane purchased kingpin Merrimac Industries for about $52 million in February 2010. Merrimac sells a slew of RF microwave components, assemblies, and multi-function modules to core customers in the aerospace and military markets.

In December 2008 the company picked up all of Friedrich Krombach GmbH & Company KG Armaturenwerke and Krombach International GmbH. Krombach manufactures specialty valve flow solutions for the power, oil and gas, and chemical markets.

HISTORY

Crane was founded in 1855 by Richard Teller Crane as a small foundry in a lumberyard owned by his uncle, Martin Ryerson. Crane grew along with Chicago and its railroads. Its first big order was to supply parts to a maker of railroad cars. In 1872 the company began making passenger elevators through the Crane Elevator Company, which was sold in 1895 to a joint venture that became the Otis Elevator Company. Although it had made plumbing materials since 1886, Crane developed a broader line during the 1920s and became a household name. The company remained under the leadership of the Crane family until Thomas Mellon Evans was elected as chief executive in 1959. Evans diversified the company through acquisitions that included Huttig Sash & Door (1968) and CF&I Steel (1969). Crane also added basic materials with its purchase of Medusa (cement and aggregates) in 1979.

Evans' son, Robert, took over as Crane's chairman in 1984 and began restructuring the company. That year Crane sold its U.S. Plumbing division, and the next year it spun off CF&I Steel to its shareholders. The company then began buying manufacturing companies in the defense, aerospace, fluid controls, vending machine, fiberglass panel, and electronic components markets. Crane expanded its Ferguson Machine business with the purchase of PickOmatic Systems of Detroit (mechanical parts-handling equipment), then boosted its wood building distribution segment with the 1988 acquisitions of Pozzi-Renati Millwork Products and Palmer G. Lewis.

In 1990 Crane acquired Lear Romec (pumps for the aerospace industry) and Crown Pumps' diaphragm pump business. In the early 1990s the company continued its successful strategy of selective buying, adding Jenkins Canada (bronze and iron valves, 1992), Rondel's millwork distributions (1993), Burks Pumps (1993), and Mark Controls (valves, instruments, and controls, 1994).

Crane picked up Interpoint (DC-DC power converters) and Grenson Electronics (low-voltage power conversion components, UK) in 1996. The company's 1998 acquisitions included Environmental Products USA (water-purification systems), Consolidated Lumber Company (wholesale distributor of lumber and millwork products), and the plastic-lined piping products division of Dow Chemical.

In 1999 the company bought Stentorfield (beverage vending machines, UK). Late in the year Crane spun off its distribution subsidiary, Huttig Sash & Door. Huttig sold a 32% stake to UK-based Rugby Group in return for Rugby's US building products business.

In 2001 Crane acquired the industrial flow business of Alfa Laval, Ventech Controls (valve repair), and Laminated Profiles (fiberglass-reinforced panels, UK). In March 2001 the investment firm led by Mario Gabelli increased its stake in Crane to nearly 8%.

Crane continued to add complementary businesses in 2002, purchasing Lasco Composites LP, a manufacturer of fiberglass-reinforced plastic panels; the US-based valve and actuator distributor Corva Corporation; and General Technology Corporation, an electronics company geared for the defense industry.

The buying spree continued in 2003 when Crane acquired Signal Technology Corporation and the pipe couplings and fittings business of Etex Group S.A..

The next year had hardly begun when Crane acquired P.L. Porter, a maker of motion control products for airline seating. A few days later Crane bought the Hattersley valve brand from Hattersley Newman Hender Ltd., a subsidiary of Tomkins PLC. At 2004's close Crane announced it had sold the UK-based businesses and intellectual property of Victaulic (Victaulic was a subsidiary of Crane's U.K. subsidiary Crane Limited) to Euro-Victaulic B.V.B.A., a subsidiary of Victaulic Company of America, for $15.4 million.

The company focused on growing its merchandising segment in 2006. Early in the year, Crane acquired CashCode, a company that makes banknote validation, storage, and recycling devices used by the gaming industry as well as vending companies, for $86 million.

Later in 2006 Crane acquired most of the assets of Automatic Products International (APi), which made and distributed vending equipment, for more than $30 million, and it paid $46 million to buy vending-machine maker Dixie-Narco from Whirlpool.

In the fall of 2006 Crane acquired Noble Composites, which made composite panels used to construct RVs, for $72 million. Noble has been combined into the company's Engineered Materials segment. The following year Crane dropped nearly $40 million to acquire another composite panel manufacturer, Fabwel, from Owens Corning.

EXECUTIVES

Chairman: Robert S. Evans, age 65
President, CEO, and Director: Eric C. Fast, age 60, $4,119,403 total compensation
Group President, Aerospace: Michael (Mike) Romito
Group President, Electronics: David E. Bender, age 50, $810,663 total compensation
Group President, Merchandising Systems and VP, Crane Business System: Bradly L. (Brad) Ellis, age 41
Group President, Fluid Handling: Max H. Mitchell, age 45, $806,889 total compensation
Group President, Engineered Materials Group: Thomas J. (Jeff) Craney, age 54
VP and Treasurer: Andrew L. Krawitt, age 44
VP Taxes: Thomas M. Noonan, age 55
VP Corporate Strategy and Group President, Controls: Thomas J. Perlitz, age 41
VP Human Resources: Elise M. Kopczick, age 56
VP, General Counsel, and Secretary: Augustus I. duPont, age 58, $1,057,314 total compensation
VP Business Development: Curtis P. Robb, age 55
VP Environment, Health, and Safety: Anthony D. Pantaleoni, age 55
VP, Controller, and Chief Accounting Officer: Richard A. (Rich) Maue, age 40
Director Investor Relations and Corporate Communications: Richard E. Koch
Auditors: Deloitte & Touche LLP

LOCATIONS

HQ: Crane Co.
100 First Stamford Place, Stamford, CT 06902
Phone: 203-363-7300   **Fax:** 203-363-7295
Web: www.craneco.com

2009 Sales

	$ mil.	% of total
US	1,322.4	60
Europe	544.6	25
Canada	227.1	10
Other regions	102.2	5
Total	**2,196.3**	**100**

PRODUCTS/OPERATIONS

2009 Sales

	$ mil.	% of total
Fluid Handling	1,050.0	48
Aerospace & Electronics	590.1	27
Merchandising Systems	292.6	13
Engineered Materials	172.1	8
Controls	91.5	4
Total	**2,196.3**	**100**

Selected Business Segments and Subsidiaries

Aerospace and Electronics
  ELDEC Corporation (sensing and control systems for aircraft)
  Hydro-Aire, Inc. (anti-skid brake control systems)
  Interpoint Corporation (hybrid power converters)
  Lear Romec (lubrication and fuel pumps)
  Keltec (power solutions)
  Merrimac Industries, Inc. (microwave and radio-frequency components and subsystems)
  Olektron (microwave systems)
  P. L. Porter (motion control products for airline seating)
  Signal Technology Corporation (STC Microwave Systems, electronic radio frequency components)
Controls
  Azonix Corporation (measurement and control systems)
  Barksdale Inc. (pressure switches and transducers)
  Crane Wireless Monitoring Solutions
  Crane Environmental
  Dynalco Controls Corporation (monitoring, diagnostic, and control products)

Engineered Materials
  Crane Composites Inc. (Kemlite, fiberglass-reinforced plastic panels)
  Polyflon (specialty components, substrates for antennas)
Fluid Handling
  Building Services & Utilities Crane Fluid Systems
  Crane Chempharma Flow Solutions
  Crane Ltd. (commercial valves, UK)
  Crane Nuclear, Inc. (valve products for the nuclear power industry)
  Crane Pumps & Systems (pumps)
  Crane Supply (distribution)
  Crane Valve Group (valves, pipes, couplings, connectors, actuators)
Merchandising Systems
  Crane Merchandising Systems (Vending Solutions)
  Payment Solutions
    CashCode Co. Inc.
    National Rejectors, Inc. GmbH (coin changers, Germany)
    Telquip Corporation

COMPETITORS

AZKOYEN	KSB AG
Chori	Kubota
CIRCOR International	Legris Industries Group
Colfax	Meggitt Aircraft Braking
Curtiss-Wright	Systems
Dover Corp.	Parker Hannifin
Eaton	Precision Castparts
Emerson Electric	Standex
Flowserve	Swagelok
Goodrich Corp.	Tuthill
IMI plc	Tyco
Kohler	

HISTORICAL FINANCIALS

Company Type: Public

Income Statement

FYE: December 31

	REVENUE ($ mil.)	NET INCOME ($ mil.)	NET PROFIT MARGIN	EMPLOYEES
12/09	2,196	134	6.1%	10,000
12/08	2,604	135	5.2%	12,000
12/07	2,619	(62)	—	12,000
12/06	2,257	166	7.4%	11,870
12/05	2,061	136	6.6%	10,400
Annual Growth	1.6%	(0.4%)	—	(1.0%)

2009 Year-End Financials

Debt ratio: 126.4%
Return on equity: 16.5%
Cash ($ mil.): 373
Current ratio: 2.24
Long-term debt ($ mil.): 1,119

No. of shares (mil.): 59
Dividends
  Yield: 2.6%
  Payout: 35.1%
Market value ($ mil.): 1,802

Stock History

NYSE: CR

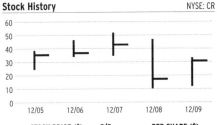

	STOCK PRICE ($) FY Close	P/E High/Low		PER SHARE ($) Earnings	Dividends	Book Value
12/09	30.62	14	5	2.28	0.80	15.05
12/08	17.24	21	5	2.24	0.76	12.54
12/07	42.90	—	—	(1.04)	0.66	15.03
12/06	36.64	17	13	2.67	0.55	15.61
12/05	35.27	17	11	2.25	0.45	12.80
Annual Growth	(3.5%)	—		0.3%	15.5%	4.1%

Crown Holdings

Crown Holdings knows how to keep a lid on profits. The company is a global manufacturer of consumer packaging; steel and aluminum food and beverage cans, and related packaging are Crown's primary lines. Its portfolio includes aerosol cans, and various metal closures marketed under brands Liftoff, SuperEnd, and Easylift, as well as specialty packaging, such as novelty containers and industrial cans. Crown also supplies can-making equipment and parts. Its roster of customers includes Coca-Cola, Cadberry Schweppes, Heinz, Nestlé, SC Johnson, Unilever, and Procter & Gamble.

Crown's performance is driven by an unwavering focus to build segment income worldwide. It is one of the world's largest packaging manufacturers, and successfully leads the market in making several products, such as food cans and metal vacuum closures, in addition to capturing the #3 spot in beverage can production.

Crown is fighting back with heavy investments in international markets, particularly those promising urban growth, including Latin America, Asia, and southern and central Europe.

Responding to a dent in net income in 2008 coupled with approximately $2.8 billion in debt, the company shored up its bottom line and boosted cash flow from operations in 2009 over 2008 by restructuring its business. Crown closed two Canadian food can plants and an aerosol plant, as well as reduced headcount both in Canada (pushed in 2008) and Europe.

Crown's facilities also recalibrated during 2009 with investments in capital amounting to $180 million to build new and existing production capacity. It plowed in some $22 million to buy a business in Vietnam, and $12 million to boost capacity in a Brazilian beverage can plant, picked up in 2008 for $44 million. The latter seeks to snatch up beer and soft drink demand fueled by the 2014 Football World Cup and the 2016 Summer Olympic Games held in Brazil. Across the Atlantic, in 2009 the company added $47 million to its ongoing construction of a new beverage can plant in eastern Slovakia. A new $32 million production line at its plant in Spain was installed in 2008. New facilities were also opened in 2008 in Africa, Cambodia, and the Middle East.

HISTORY

Formed as Crown Cork & Seal Co. (CC&S) of Baltimore in 1892, the company was consolidated into its present form in 1927 when it merged with New Process Cork and New York Patents. The next year CC&S expanded overseas and formed Crown Cork International. In 1936 CC&S acquired Acme Can and benefited from the movement at the time from home canning to processed canning. The company was the first to develop the aerosol can (1946).

By 1957 heavy debt had CC&S in trouble. Teetering on the brink of bankruptcy, the company hired John Connelly as president. Connelly immediately stopped can production (sending stockpiled inventory to customers), discontinued unprofitable product lines, and reduced costs (25% of employees were laid off in less than two years). He then directed CC&S to take advantage of new uses for aerosol cans (insecticides, hair spray, and bathroom cleaning supplies) and to expand overseas. CC&S obtained "pioneer rights" between 1955 and 1960 from

foreign countries that granted it the first crack at new closure and can businesses.

The introduction of the pull-tab pop-top in 1963 hit the can business like an exploding grenade. Connelly embraced pull tabs, but he rejected getting into the production of two-piece aluminum cans (first introduced in the mid-1970s), focusing instead on existing technology for three-piece cans. He also resisted the diversification trend then popular in the can-making industry, which later led to the declining performances of competitors Continental Can and American Can.

In 1970 CC&S moved into the printing end of the industry. It gained the ability to imprint color lithography on its bottle caps and cans after buying R. Hoe.

Connelly kept CC&S debt-free through most of the 1980s, using cash flow to buy back about half of CC&S's stock. In 1989 he picked Bill Avery to succeed him. With Connelly's blessing, Avery started a buying spree that included the purchase of the plants of Continental Can. Connelly died in 1990. Acquisitions continued throughout the 1990s. CC&S's purchases included CONSTAR International, the #1 maker of polyethylene terephthalate (PET) plastic containers (1992), can maker Van Dorn (1993), and the can-manufacturing unit of Tri Valley Growers (1994). California's Northridge earthquake in 1994 ruined the company's plant in Van Nuys.

CC&S bought French packaging company CarnaudMetalbox in 1996. The purchase united CC&S's efficient operations and strong presence in North America with the French company's state-of-the-art manufacturing technology and international marketing experience. That year strikes over contract disputes halted production at eight of the company's plants. In addition, CC&S acquired Polish packaging company Fabryka Opakowan Blaszanyck.

In 1997 CC&S bought a 96% stake in Golden Aluminum from ACX Technologies, but returned the aluminum recycler in 1999 at a cost of $10 million. Dropping sales and foreign currency fluctuations in 1998 forced the company to close seven factories and cut 7% of its workforce. CC&S closed more factories in 1999 and sold its composite can (paper cans with metal or plastic ends) business. That year the company increased its foreign presence with the purchase of two can manufacturers in Spain and Greece.

CC&S entered into a joint venture with Tempra Technology in 2000 to make and market a self-refrigerating can. The same year Avery announced his retirement; president and COO John Conway succeeded him as CEO in 2001. To reduce debt and move closer to profitability, CC&S sold three product divisions in 2001 and sold its fragrance pump unit to Rexam PLC for about $107 million in 2002. In March 2002 the company sold its Europe-based pharmaceutical packaging business. In May CC&S spun off its PET bottle subsidiary Constar in an IPO offering.

In 2003 the company completed a refinancing plan and formed a new public holding company, Crown Holdings, Inc.; the CC&S name was retained for the company's operating subsidiary. Crown sold its Global Plastic Closures business to PAI Partners for about $750 million in 2005.

Crown Holdings sold its plastics closures business for about $750 million. The company previously had sold several divisions and spun off its PET bottle subsidiary, Constar International. The company then sold its remaining North American and European plastics operations.

EXECUTIVES

Chairman, President, and CEO: John W. Conway, age 64, $15,659,135 total compensation
Vice Chairman: Alan W. Rutherford, age 66, $10,776,037 total compensation
EVP and CFO: Timothy J. Donahue, age 47, $3,480,491 total compensation
EVP Corporate Technology and Regulatory Affairs: Daniel A. Abramowicz
SVP Finance: Thomas A. Kelly, age 50
SVP, General Counsel, and Secretary: William T. Gallagher
VP and Corporate Controller: Kevin C. Clothier, age 41
VP Planning and Development: Torsten J. Kreider
VP Corporate Affairs and Public Relations: Michael F. Dunleavy
VP and Treasurer: Michael B. Burns
VP Corporate Risk Management: Karen E. Berigan
President, European Division: Christopher C. Homfray, age 52, $4,397,393 total compensation
President, Asia/Pacific: Jozef Salaerts, age 55, $2,144,660 total compensation
President, Americas Division: Raymond L. McGowan Jr., age 58, $3,303,422 total compensation
Auditors: PricewaterhouseCoopers LLP

LOCATIONS

HQ: Crown Holdings, Inc.
 1 Crown Way, Philadelphia, PA 19154
Phone: 215-698-5100
Web: www.crowncork.com

2009 Sales

	$ mil.	% of total
US	2,224	28
UK	729	9
France	686	9
Other regions	4,299	54
Total	**7,938**	**100**

PRODUCTS/OPERATIONS

2009 Sales

	$ mil.	% of total
Metal beverage cans & ends	3,777	47
Metal food cans & ends	2,698	34
Other metal packaging	1,336	17
Plastics packaging	54	1
Other products	73	1
Total	**7,938**	**100**

Selected Products

Metal packaging
 Aerosol cans
 Beverage cans
 Closures and caps
 Crowns
 Ends
 Food cans
Plastics packaging
Specialty packaging (unusual containers)
 Vacuum closures
Other products
 Canmaking equipment and spares

COMPETITORS

Alcoa
Amcor
AptarGroup
Ball Corp.
BWAY
Calmar
Metal Container Corporation
Owens-Illinois
Rexam
Silgan
Sonoco Products
Tetra Laval

HISTORICAL FINANCIALS

Company Type: Public

Income Statement

	REVENUE ($ mil.)	NET INCOME ($ mil.)	NET PROFIT MARGIN	EMPLOYEES
				FYE: December 31
12/09	7,938	334	4.2%	20,500
12/08	8,305	226	2.7%	21,300
12/07	7,727	528	6.8%	21,800
12/06	6,982	309	4.4%	21,700
12/05	6,908	(362)	—	24,000
Annual Growth	3.5%	—	—	(3.9%)

2009 Year-End Financials

Debt ratio: —
Return on equity: —
Cash ($ mil.): 459
Current ratio: 1.16
Long-term debt ($ mil.): 2,739

No. of shares (mil.): 162
Dividends
  Yield: 0.0%
  Payout: —
Market value ($ mil.): 4,144

Stock History

NYSE: CCK

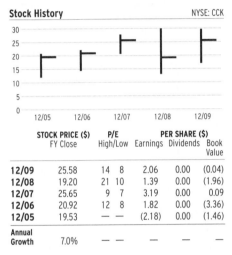

	STOCK PRICE ($) FY Close	P/E High/Low		PER SHARE ($) Earnings	Dividends	Book Value
12/09	25.58	14	8	2.06	0.00	(0.04)
12/08	19.20	21	10	1.39	0.00	(1.96)
12/07	25.65	9	7	3.19	0.00	0.09
12/06	20.92	12	8	1.82	0.00	(3.36)
12/05	19.53	—	—	(2.18)	0.00	(1.46)
Annual Growth	7.0%	—	—	—	—	—

CSX Corporation

CSX banks on the railway as the right way to make money. Its main subsidiary, CSX Transportation (CSXT), operates a major rail system (some 21,000 route miles) in the eastern US. The freight carrier links 23 states, 70 ports, the District of Columbia, and two Canadian provinces. Freight hauled by the company includes a wide variety of merchandise (food, chemicals, consumer goods), coal, automotive products, and intermodal containers. CSX's rail segment also includes units that operate motor vehicle distribution centers and bulk cargo terminals. Subsidiary CSX Intermodal arranges the transportation of freight by combinations of road and rail carriers.

CSXT operates with a fleet of more than 4,000 locomotives and around 84,000 railcars (gondolas, hoppers, and box/flat cars). To recover from the global financial train wreck of 2009 (the company's revenues were down 20% year-over-year), the company adjusted its workforce to coincide with decreased orders; it also concentrated on boosting efficiency and safety, as well as improving customer services and the rate of on-time performance.

Citing fuel prices and environmental efficiency, CSX Intermodal hopes to persuade more shippers to shift freight from trucks to trains, especially for cross-country journeys. CSX announced an $842 million project in 2008 called the National Gateway, which will enable double-stacked railcars to ride three tracks in the eastern US, thus doubling the amount of cargo carried on a single line. CSX has invested almost $400 million and is working with several states and the federal government to outfit tunnels, bridges, and overpasses to accommodate the taller railcars. Along with CSX's investment, sponsoring states have ponied up $189 million; and in March 2010, through the US Department of Transportation, the company was pledged enough grant money by the Transportation Investment Generating Economic Recovery (TIGER) fund to cover the remainder of the price tag.

CSX's other holdings include Total Distribution Services, a storage and distribution company for the automotive industry; Transflo Terminal Services, a logistics company for transferring shipments from rail to truck; and CSX Technology, which provides IT services to its parent company. Additionally, the company's subsidiary CSX Real Property handles real estate sales, leasing, acquisition, and management and development activities. In May 2009 CSX sold The Greenbrier Resort, which it had owned since 1910, to investor James Justice.

In 2008 the Children's Investment Fund Management (TCI) and 3G Capital Partners, leader of a group that owns about 9% of CSX, staged a proxy fight and sought to elect a slate of four directors to the company's board. Two directors from the group's slate were seated in July, and two more joined the board in September. In 2009 TCI sold all of its CSX shares, but Alexandre Behring, a company board member and managing director of 3G Capital Partners, owns over 4% of the company.

HISTORY

CSX Corporation was formed in 1980, when Chessie System and Seaboard Coast Line (SCL) merged in an effort to improve the efficiency of their railroads.

Chessie's oldest railroad, the Baltimore & Ohio (B&O), was chartered in 1827 to help Baltimore compete against New York and Philadelphia for freight traffic. By the late 1800s the railroad served Chicago, Cincinnati, New York City, St. Louis, and Washington, DC. Chesapeake & Ohio (C&O) acquired it in 1962.

C&O originated in Virginia with the Louisa Railroad in 1836. It gained access to Chicago, Cincinnati, and Washington, DC, and by the mid-1900s was a major coal carrier. After B&O and C&O acquired joint control of Baltimore-based Western Maryland Railway (1967), the three railroads became subsidiaries of newly formed Chessie System (1973).

One of SCL's two predecessors, Seaboard Air Line Railroad (SAL), grew out of Virginia's Portsmouth & Roanoke Rail Road of 1832. SCL's other predecessor, Atlantic Coast Line Railroad (ACL), took shape between 1869 and 1893 as William Walters acquired several southern railroads. In 1902 ACL bought the Plant System (railroads in Georgia, Florida, and other southern states) and the Louisville & Nashville (a north-south line connecting New Orleans and Chicago), giving ACL the basic form it was to retain until 1967, when it merged with SAL to form SCL.

After CSX inherited the Chessie System and SCL, it bought Texas Gas Resources (gas pipeline, 1983), American Commercial Lines (Texas Gas' river barge subsidiary, 1984), and Sea-Land Corporation (ocean container shipping, 1986). To improve its market value, CSX sold most of its oil and gas properties, its communications holdings (Lightnet, begun in 1983), and most of its resort properties (Rockresorts) in 1988 and 1989. American Commercial Lines acquired Valley Line in 1992.

Sea-Land struck a deal with Danish shipping company Maersk Line in 1996 to share vessels and terminals. That year CSX entered a takeover battle with rival Norfolk Southern for Conrail. Conrail decided to split its assets between the two; CSX paid $4.3 billion for 42%. (The division took place in 1999.)

In 1999 CSX sold Grand Teton Lodge to Vail Resorts for $50 million. It sold its international shipping business to Denmark's A.P. Møller (parent of Maersk Line) for $800 million.

Rail service disruptions stemming from the integration of Conrail assets were exacerbated by damage from Hurricane Floyd in 1999. The next year a federal audit found defects in CSX track. Service problems related to the Conrail takeover continued, and the company's rail unit underwent a management shake-up.

Later in 2000, CSX, looking to pay down debt, sold its CTI Logistx unit to TNT Post Group for $650 million.

In 2002 CSX established a CSXT office in Europe to focus on international freight and to create partnerships with European freight forwarders and ocean carriers.

CSX sold a controlling stake in its ocean container shipping unit to investment firm Carlyle Group in 2003. The former CSX Lines took the name Horizon Lines. In 2004 Carlyle sold its stake in Horizon Lines to another investment firm, Castle Harlan. The next year CSX sold its CSX World Terminals to Dubai Ports International (later DP World) for $1.14 billion.

In 2004 the two companies reorganized Conrail so that each railroad directly owned the Conrail assets that it operates. (Conrail continued to operate switching facilities and terminals used by both Norfolk Southern and CSX.)

EXECUTIVES

Chairman, President, and CEO; President and CEO, CSX Transportation: Michael J. Ward, age 58, $10,120,406 total compensation
EVP Sales and Marketing and Chief Commercial Officer, CSX Corporation and CSX Transportation: Clarence W. Gooden, age 57, $4,126,305 total compensation
EVP and CFO, CSX Corporation and CSX Transportation: Oscar Munoz, age 49, $2,984,966 total compensation
SVP Human Resources and Labor Relations: Lisa A. Mancini
SVP Law and Public Affairs, General Counsel, and Corporate Secretary, CSX Corporation and CSX Transportation: Ellen M. Fitzsimmons, age 49, $2,741,952 total compensation
VP and Controller, CSX Corporation and CSX Transportation: Carolyn T. Sizemore, age 45
VP Strategic Infrastructure Initiatives: Louis E. Renjel
VP Federal Regulation and General Counsel: Peter J. Shudtz, age 61
VP Strategic Planning: Lester M. Passa, age 56
VP Tax and Treasurer: David A. Boor, age 56
Assistant VP Treasury and Investor Relations: David H. Baggs, age 50
General Counsel, Transactions and Insurance: David Bowling
General Counsel, Corporate and Transportation Law: Nathan Goldman
President, CSX Technology Inc.: Frank A. Lonegro
President, CSX Real Property: Stephen A. Crosby
Auditors: Ernst & Young LLP

LOCATIONS

HQ: CSX Corporation
    500 Water St., 15th Fl., Jacksonville, FL 32202
Phone: 904-359-3200   **Fax:** 904-633-3450
Web: www.csx.com

PRODUCTS/OPERATIONS

2009 Sales

	$ mil.	% of total
Rail merchandise		
Coal	2,615	29
Chemicals	1,267	14
Agricultural products	960	11
Emerging markets (aggregates)	585	6
Forest products	547	6
Automotive	511	6
Metals	399	4
Phosphates & fertilizers	373	4
Food & consumer	233	3
Coke & iron ore	112	1
Other	235	3
Intermodal		
Domestic	831	9
International	353	4
Other	20	—
Total	**9,041**	**100**

Selected Services

Container/trailer shipping
Freight shipping by rail
Property/real estate (buying/leasing property for
    commercial or rail)
Salvage sales (distressed cargo sales)

COMPETITORS

APL Logistics
Burlington Northern Santa Fe
Canadian National Railway
Canadian Pacific Railway
Hub Group
J.B. Hunt
Norfolk Southern
Pacer International
Schneider National
Union Pacific

HISTORICAL FINANCIALS

Company Type: Public

Income Statement

FYE: Last Friday in December

	REVENUE ($ mil.)	NET INCOME ($ mil.)	NET PROFIT MARGIN	EMPLOYEES
12/09	9,041	1,152	12.7%	30,088
12/08	11,255	1,365	12.1%	34,000
12/07	10,030	1,336	13.3%	35,000
12/06	9,566	1,310	13.7%	36,000
12/05	8,618	1,145	13.3%	35,000
Annual Growth	**1.2%**	**0.2%**	**—**	**(3.7%)**

2009 Year-End Financials

Debt ratio: 89.2%
Return on equity: 13.6%
Cash ($ mil.): 1,029
Current ratio: 1.38
Long-term debt ($ mil.): 7,895

No. of shares (mil.): 380
Dividends
    Yield: 1.8%
    Payout: 30.2%
Market value ($ mil.): 18,409

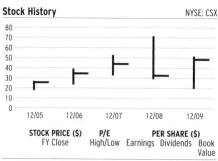
Cummins, Inc.

Cummins is in it for the long haul, on the road, rail, or river. The company is the world's leader in the manufacture of large diesel engines. Cummins engines also power school buses, medium-duty trucks, pickups (primarily Dodge Rams), and equipment for mining and construction. Cummins claims just under one-third of the North American market for heavy-duty truck engines. The company also makes power generation products such as its Onan generator sets and Stamford alternators. Other products and brands include Fleetguard (filtration), Kuss (fuel filters), and Holset (turbochargers). Among its customers are OEMs PACCAR, Daimler, Chrysler, Komatsu, and Case.

The company's global footprint is shaped in large part by the cyclical booms and busts of the on-highway, construction, and industrial markets. Its customers are particularly sensitive to the general economic climate, interest rates, and access to credit, as well as regulatory issues (environmental and emissions standards) and political shifts. In an effort to mitigate a slump in demand in any one market or region, Cummins is continuing to transform itself from a company concentrated in North America to one whose business is seizing up opportunities in developing countries. Following the US, China, Brazil, and India are Cummins' largest markets.

The economic meltdown of 2009, however, forced double-digit declines in sales across all Cummins business segment, collectively a 25% decrease. The company shored up its bottom line by trimming costs, including headcount and manufacturing capacity. Cummins also cut the salaries of its officers by 10% in 2009.

Despite the recession's corrosive effects, Cummins is not deterred from penetrating developing markets. In mid-2008 the company and China-based vehicle manufacturer Beiqi Foton entered into a 50-50 joint venture known as Beijing Foton Cummins Engine Co., to manufacture diesel engines for Beiqi Foton's Aumark light-duty trucks, as well as other vehicle models; production at the Beijing plant commenced in mid-2009.

Cummins is also investing in its distribution network. It has accumulated four overseas distribution partnerships, most notably with Komatsu America, which offers Cummins' full slate of products and services. In tandem with the joint ventures, Cummins has planted purchasing offices around the world. These offices are driving sales and service relationships with local manufacturers.

HISTORY

Chauffeur Clessie Cummins believed that Rudolph Diesel's cumbersome and smoky engine could be improved for use in transportation. Borrowing money and work space from his employer — Columbus, Indiana, banker W. G. Irwin — Cummins founded Cummins Engine in 1919. Irwin invested more than $2.5 million, and in the mid-1920s Cummins produced a mobile diesel engine. Truck manufacturers were reluctant to switch from gas to diesel, so Cummins used publicity stunts (such as racing in the Indianapolis 500) to advertise his engine.

The company was profitable by 1937, the year Irwin's grandnephew, J. Irwin Miller, took over. During WWII the Cummins engine was used in cargo trucks. Sales went from $20 million in 1946 to more than $100 million by 1956. That year Cummins started its first overseas plant in Scotland, and bought Atlas Crankshafts in 1958. By 1967 it had 50% of the diesel engine market.

Cummins diversified in 1970 by acquiring the K2 Ski Company (fiberglass skis) and Coot Industries (all-terrain vehicles), but sold them by 1976. It added turbochargers in 1973 with its acquisition of Holset Engineering. (Founded in 1948 and named for founders W.C. Holmes and Louis Croset, Holset became a subsidiary of BHD Engineering Limited Group in 1952; it first was acquired by Hanson Trust in 1973 and later that year by Cummins. Holset changed its name to Cummins Turbo Technologies in 2006.) In the early 1980s Cummins introduced a line of midrange engines developed in a joint venture with J.I. Case (then a subsidiary of Tenneco; now a part of Fiat-controlled CNH Global). To remain competitive, Cummins cut costs by 22%, doubled productivity in its US and UK plants, and spent $1.8 billion to retool its factories.

Having twice repelled unwelcome foreign suitors in 1989, Cummins sold 27% of its stock to Ford, Tenneco, and Kubota for $250 million in 1990. The move raised cash and protected Cummins from future takeover bids.

In 1993 Cummins established engine-making joint ventures with Tata Engineering & Locomotive, India's largest heavy vehicle maker, and Komatsu, a leading Japanese construction equipment maker. Also in 1993 Cummins introduced a natural-gas engine for school buses and formed a joint venture to produce turbochargers in India. The company began Cummins Wartsila, a joint venture with engineering company Wartsila NSD, to develop high-speed diesel and natural gas engines in France and the UK in 1995. It also began restructuring that year, selling plants and laying off workers.

Continuing its strategy of teaming with other manufacturers, Cummins agreed in 1996 to make small and midsize diesel engines with Fiat's Iveco and New Holland (now CNH Global) subsidiaries.

In 1997 subsidiary Cadec Systems signed a license to develop and sell Montreal-based Canadian Marconi's (now BAE SYSTEMS CANADA) fleet-tracking system, which uses satellites and computers. Cummins bought diesel exhaust and air filtration company Nelson Industries for $490 million in early 1998. The company also agreed, without admission of guilt, to pay a $25 million fine and contribute $35 million to environmental programs after the EPA accused Cummins of cheating on emissions tests.

Chairman and CEO James Henderson retired at the end of 1999 and was succeeded by Theodore Solso.

In 2001 the company announced that it had signed a long-term deal to supply PACCAR (Peterbilt and Kenworth trucks) with heavy-duty engines. Later in 2001 the company shortened its name to Cummins, Inc.

The following year Cummins and Mercury Marine formed a joint venture, Cummins MerCruiser Diesel Marine LLC, to provide diesel engines to the recreational and commercial marine markets.

In 2003 Cummins and Westport Innovations strengthened their joint venture ties by signing a technology partnership agreement that made it easier for the two companies to develop and share alternative fuel technologies.

EXECUTIVES

Chairman and CEO: Theodore M. (Tim) Solso, age 62, $8,430,337 total compensation
President, COO, and Director: N. Thomas (Tom) Linebarger, age 47, $4,446,580 total compensation
EVP Corporate Responsibility; CEO, Cummins Foundation: Jean S. Blackwell, age 55, $3,508,459 total compensation
VP and CFO: Patrick J. (Pat) Ward, age 46, $1,366,954 total compensation
VP and CTO: John C. Wall, age 58
VP; President, Engine Business: Richard J. (Rich) Freeland, age 52, $2,492,365 total compensation
VP; President, Cummins Fuel Systems: Ray J. Amlung, age 51
VP; President, Cummins Turbo Technologies: Jim Lyons
VP; President, Cummins Distribution Business: Pamela L. (Pam) Carter, age 60
VP; President, Cummins Filtration: Jihad (Joseph) Saoud
VP; President, Power Generation: Livingston L. Satterthwaite, age 50
VP and Chief Administrative Officer: Mark R. Gerstle, age 54
VP, General Counsel, and Corporate Secretary: Marya M. Rose, age 47
VP and Chief Investment Officer: Richard E. Harris, age 57
VP, Corporate Controller, and Principal Accounting Officer: Marsha L. Hunt, age 46
VP Research and Technology: Wayne Eckerle
Executive Director Corporate Communications: Mark D. Land
Director Investor Relations: Dean Cantrell
Auditors: PricewaterhouseCoopers LLP

LOCATIONS

HQ: Cummins Inc.
500 Jackson St., Columbus, IN 47201
Phone: 812-377-5000   **Fax:** 812-377-3334
Web: www.cummins.com

2009 Sales

	$ mil.	% of total
US	5,141	48
China	630	6
Brazil	596	5
India	592	5
UK	406	4
Canada	327	3
Mexico	240	2
Other countries	2,868	27
Total	**10,800**	**100**

PRODUCTS/OPERATIONS

2009 Sales

	$ mil.	% of total
Engines	5,582	52
Power generation	1,879	17
Distribution	1,777	16
Components	1,562	15
Total	**10,800**	**100**

Selected Products

Components business
  Emission solutions (catalytic exhaust systems)
  Filtration (heavy-duty air, fuel, hydraulic and lube filtration, chemicals and exhaust system technology products)
  Fuel systems (new fuel systems, remanufactured electronic control modules)
  Turbo technologies (turbochargers)
Engine business
  Bus engines
  Heavy- and medium-duty truck engines
  Industrial engines for construction, mining, agricultural, rail, and marine equipment
  Light, commercial vehicle engines
  Marine diesels (recreational and commercial)
Filtration business
  Air system
  Cooling system (crankcase ventilation)
  Diesel emission additives
  Exhaust system
  Fuel system (hydraulic)
  Lube system (transmission)
Fuel systems
  CELECT electronically controlled unit injection system
  Common rail pump
  Extreme pressure injection system
  High Pressure Injection (HPI) system
  Remanufactured products
Power generation business
  Diesel and alternative-fuel electrical generator sets (PowerCommand, Onan, Newage AVK SEG, G-Drive)
Turbo technologies, Holset (medium and heavy-duty diesel engines)

COMPETITORS

AAF-McQUAY
BorgWarner
Briggs & Stratton Power Products
Caterpillar
China Yuchai
CLARCOR
Daimler
Detroit Diesel
DEUTZ
Donaldson Company
Emerson Electric
Hino Motors
Honeywell International
Invensys
Isuzu
Kohler
Mack Trucks
MAN
Mitsubishi Heavy Industries
Navistar International
PACCAR
Regal Beloit
Renault
Robert Bosch
Scania
Tenneco
ThyssenKrupp
Tognum
UD Trucks
Volvo
Weichai Power

HISTORICAL FINANCIALS

Company Type: Public

Income Statement

FYE: December 31

	REVENUE ($ mil.)	NET INCOME ($ mil.)	NET PROFIT MARGIN	EMPLOYEES
12/09	10,800	428	4.0%	34,900
12/08	14,342	755	5.3%	39,800
12/07	13,048	739	5.7%	37,800
12/06	11,362	715	6.3%	34,600
12/05	9,918	550	5.5%	33,500
Annual Growth	**2.2%**	**(6.1%)**	**—**	**1.0%**

2009 Year-End Financials

Debt ratio: 16.9%   No. of shares (mil.): 199
Return on equity: 12.2%   Dividends
Cash ($ mil.): 930   Yield: 1.5%
Current ratio: 2.06   Payout: 32.4%
Long-term debt ($ mil.): 637   Market value ($ mil.): 9,116

Stock History

NYSE: CMI

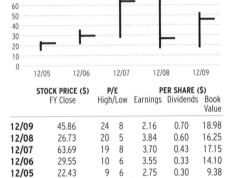

	STOCK PRICE ($) FY Close	P/E High	P/E Low	PER SHARE ($) Earnings	PER SHARE ($) Dividends	PER SHARE ($) Book Value
12/09	45.86	24	8	2.16	0.70	18.98
12/08	26.73	20	5	3.84	0.60	16.25
12/07	63.69	19	8	3.70	0.43	17.15
12/06	29.55	10	6	3.55	0.33	14.10
12/05	22.43	9	6	2.75	0.30	9.38
Annual Growth	**19.6%**	**—**	**—**	**(5.9%)**	**23.6%**	**19.3%**

CVS Caremark

Size matters to CVS Caremark (formerly CVS), the nation's second-largest drugstore chain and its third-largest pharmacy benefits manager. With about 7,090 retail and specialty drugstores under the CVS and Longs Drug banners, it trails archrival Walgreen by about 400 stores. CVS has grown rapidly through a string of acquisitions that included the Eckerd chain, stores from Albertsons, and most recently Longs Drug Stores (2008). In 2007 CVS purchased prescription benefits management (PBM) firm Caremark Rx for about $26.5 billion. Caremark was combined with CVS's PBM and specialty pharmacy unit PharmaCare Management Services to form Caremark Pharmacy Services.

CVS's active acquisition schedule has both greatly expanded the number of retail and specialty pharmacies it operates and the range of services it offers to customers, employers, insurance companies, unions, managed care organizations, and other clients. The company is betting that size will make it a more convenient and efficient operator and a preferred provider to health benefit plans attempting to better manage their health care costs. Indeed, acquisitions have increased both revenues and profits for the company.

While size has its advantages, it can also make a company a target. Indeed, the Federal Trade Commission (FTC), which approved the CVS-Caremark merger, in August 2009 reopened its investigation in response to lawmakers' pleas. In their letter to the FTC, a bipartisan group of eight US congressmen accused CVS Caremark of unfair and deceptive business practices, including arranging to have consumers' prescriptions filled only at CVS pharmacies. CVS is drawing fire from consumer groups and the attorneys general of two major states (California and New York) over the alleged sale of expired over-the-counter products in its stores. The attorney general of New York has also filed suit against the company.

The Caremark purchase positioned the company as a leading manager of pharmacy benefits in the US. The hard-won deal, launched in late 2006, led to a bidding war between CVS and Caremark rival Express Scripts that forced CVS to raise its offer several times. Combined, CVS and Caremark created an industry leader in pharmacy and specialty pharmacy sales, PBM enrollments, mail-order pharmacy sales, and retail-based clinics (through its MinuteClinic business).

CVS's MinuteClinic (acquired in 2006) runs about 570 health clinics in some 25 states, most of which are located within CVS stores.

Chairman and CEO Thomas Ryan, a 36-year veteran of CVS and its president for the past 16 years, plans to retire as chief executive in May 2011. Larry Merlo, president and COO of the firm, is expected to succeed him.

HISTORY

Brothers Stanley and Sid Goldstein, who ran health and beauty products distributor Mark Steven, branched out into retail in 1963 when they opened up their first Consumer Value Store in Lowell, Massachusetts, with partner Ralph Hoagland.

The chain grew rapidly, amassing 17 stores by the end of 1964 (the year the CVS name was first used) and 40 by 1969. That year the Goldsteins sold the chain to Melville Shoe to finance further expansion.

Melville had been founded in 1892 by shoe supplier Frank Melville. Melville's son, Ward, grew the company, creating the Thom McAn shoe store chain and later buying its supplier. By 1969 Melville had opened shoe shops in Kmart stores (through its Meldisco unit), launched one apparel chain (Chess King, sold in 1993), and purchased another (Foxwood Stores, renamed Foxmoor and sold in 1985).

In 1972 CVS bought the 84-store Clinton Drug and Discount, a Rochester, New York-based chain. Two years later, when sales hit $100 million, CVS had 232 stores — only 45 of which had pharmacies. The company bought New Jersey-based Mack Drug (36 stores) in 1977. By 1981 CVS had more than 400 stores.

CVS's sales hit $1 billion in 1985 as it continued to add pharmacies to many of its older stores. In 1987 Stanley's success was recognized companywide when he was named chairman and CEO of CVS's parent company, which by then had been renamed Melville.

CVS bought the 490-store Peoples Drug Stores chain from Imasco in 1990, giving it locations in Maryland, Pennsylvania, Virginia, West Virginia, and Washington, DC. CVS created PharmaCare Management Services in 1994 to take advantage of the growing market for pharmacy services and managed-care drug programs. Pharmacist Tom Ryan was named CEO that year.

With CVS outperforming Melville's other operations, in 1995 Melville decided to concentrate on the drugstore chain. By that time Melville's holdings had grown to include discount department store chain Marshalls and furniture chain This End Up, both sold in 1995; footwear chain Footaction, spun off as part of Footstar in 1996, along with Meldisco; the Linens 'n Things chain, spun off in 1996; and the Kay-Bee Toys chain, sold in 1996.

Melville was renamed CVS in late 1996. Amid major consolidation in the drugstore industry, in 1997 CVS — then with about 1,425 stores — paid $3.7 billion for Revco D.S., which had nearly 2,600 stores in 17 states, mainly in the Midwest and Southeast. The next year the company bought Arbor Drugs (200 stores in Michigan, later converted to the CVS banner) for nearly $1.5 billion. Stanley retired as chairman in 1999 and was succeeded by Ryan.

In June 2005 CVS agreed to pay $110 million to settle a shareholders' lawsuit filed in 2001 that alleged the company had made misleading statements to artificially raise its stock price and violated accounting practices. CVS denied the charges and said the settlement was "purely a business decision."

In June 2006 CVS completed the acquisition of some 700 stand-alone Sav-On and Osco drugstores from Albertsons. In March 2007 CVS changed its name to CVS Caremark Corporation. In November CEO Ryan added the chairman's title to his job description following the retirement of Mac Crawford.

In 2008 CVS settled a lawsuit regarding drug-switching allegations for $36.7 million. The company had been accused of switching Medicaid customers to a more expensive capsule form of Zantac from a tablet form; CVS denied the allegations.

In June 2009 CVS agreed to pay almost $1 million to settle allegations stemming from the sale of expired OTC medications, infant formula, and dairy products.

EXECUTIVES

Chairman and CEO: Thomas M. (Tom) Ryan, age 57, $30,429,112 total compensation
President and COO; President, CVS/pharmacy: Larry J. Merlo, age 54, $9,179,718 total compensation
EVP and CFO: David M. (Dave) Denton, age 44
EVP and Chief Legal Officer: Douglas A. Sgarro, age 50, $4,973,559 total compensation
EVP and Chief Medical Officer: Troyen A. Brennan, age 55, $2,918,977 total compensation
EVP; President, Caremark Pharmacy Services: Per G. H. Lofberg, age 62
EVP Rx Purchasing, Pricing, and Network Relations: Jonathan C. Roberts, age 54
EVP, CVS Caremark: Jack E. Bruner
EVP and Chief Marketing Officer: Helena B. Foulkes, age 45
SVP and CIO: Stuart M. McGuigan, age 51
SVP, Controller, and Chief Accounting Officer: Laird K. Daniels, age 40
SVP and Chief Human Resources Officer: Lisa Bisaccia, age 53
SVP Investor Relations: Nancy R. Christal
SVP and Associate Chief Medical Officer; President and COO, MinuteClinic: Andrew J. (Andy) Sussman
SVP and General Counsel: Sara J. Finley, age 49
SVP Merchandising and Supply Chain: Mike Bloom
SVP Internal Operations and Real Estate: Scott Baker
VP Corporate Communications: Carolyn Castel
Secretary: Zenon P. Lankowsky
President, TheraCom: Chip Phillips
President and CEO, Generation Health: Rick Schatzberg
Auditors: Ernst & Young LLP

LOCATIONS

HQ: CVS Caremark Corporation
1 CVS Dr., Woonsocket, RI 02895
Phone: 401-765-1500   Fax: 401-762-9227
Web: www.cvs.com

2009 Stores

	No.
California	825
Florida	697
Texas	512
New York	443
Pennsylvania	374
Massachusetts	352
Ohio	311
Georgia	304
North Carolina	299
Indiana	290
New Jersey	259
Illinois	253
Virginia	249
Michigan	243
South Carolina	194
Maryland	167
Alabama	151
Connecticut	137
Arizona	132
Tennessee	127
Louisiana	91
Nevada	85
Kentucky	58
Rhode Island	58
District of Columbia	57
West Virginia	50
Missouri	47
Hawaii	46
Minnesota	42
Mississippi	39
Oklahoma	36
New Hampshire	33
Kansas	31
Wisconsin	30
Maine	21
Other states	49
Total	**7,092**

PRODUCTS/OPERATIONS

2009 Sales

	% of total
Prescription drugs	68
Over-the-counter & personal care	11
Beauty/cosmetics	5
General merchandise & other	16
Total	**100**

COMPETITORS

A&P
Aetna
Ahold USA
BioScrip
CIGNA
Costco Wholesale
drugstore.com
Express Scripts
H-E-B
Kerr Drug
Kmart
Kroger
Medco Health
Prescription Solutions
Rite Aid
Target
UnitedHealth Group
Walgreen
Wal-Mart
WellPoint

HISTORICAL FINANCIALS

Company Type: Public

Income Statement

FYE: December 31

	REVENUE ($ mil.)	NET INCOME ($ mil.)	NET PROFIT MARGIN	EMPLOYEES
12/09	98,729	3,696	3.7%	295,000
12/08	87,472	3,212	3.7%	215,000
12/07	76,330	2,637	3.5%	200,000
12/06	43,814	1,369	3.1%	176,000
12/05	37,006	1,225	3.3%	148,000
Annual Growth	27.8%	31.8%	—	18.8%

2009 Year-End Financials

Debt ratio: 24.5%
Return on equity: 10.5%
Cash ($ mil.): 1,086
Current ratio: 1.43
Long-term debt ($ mil.): 8,756

No. of shares (mil.): 1,358
Dividends
  Yield: 0.9%
  Payout: 12.2%
Market value ($ mil.): 43,748

Stock History

NYSE: CVS

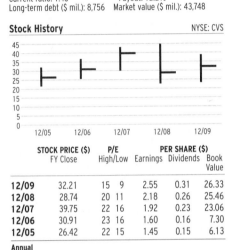

	STOCK PRICE ($) FY Close	P/E High/Low	PER SHARE ($) Earnings	Dividends	Book Value
12/09	32.21	15 9	2.55	0.31	26.33
12/08	28.74	20 11	2.18	0.26	25.46
12/07	39.75	22 16	1.92	0.23	23.06
12/06	30.91	23 16	1.60	0.16	7.30
12/05	26.42	22 15	1.45	0.15	6.13
Annual Growth	5.1%	— —	15.2%	19.9%	43.9%

Cytec Industries

Cytec Industries covers its business bases. The company produces the building-block chemicals from which it makes engineered materials (composites and adhesives for the aerospace industry), specialty chemicals (resins and coatings for metal, plastic, and wood), and additives used in industrial processes. Cytec also sells its building-block chemicals (acrylonitrile, melamine, and sulfuric acid) to third parties. Cytec Engineered Materials includes aerospace products such as advanced composites and structural adhesives. The Specialty Chemicals unit's products are used in mining, drilling, and the manufacture of pharmaceuticals. The unit combines Cytec's Performance Chemicals and Surface Specialties segments.

After a decrease in earnings in late 2008 due to the economic downturn, Cytec began a number of restructuring initiatives across the company to trim operating expenses, cutting 336 positions. The moves were felt mostly in the company's Strategic Chemical, Engineered Materials, and corporate services segments. The restructuring resulted in a significant ($76 million) increase in 2009 earnings, with similar savings expected in 2010.

Chairman and CEO David Lilley retired at the end of 2008. Cytec Specialty Chemicals president Shane Fleming took his place, having been with the company for a quarter of a century.

HISTORY

Cytec Industries was spun off of parent company American Cyanamid late in 1993. American Cyanamid had focused on agrichemical and pharmaceutical life sciences, while its specialty chemicals operations languished behind its competitors. Cytec was spun off to Cyanamid stockholders, and Darryl Fry, Cyanamid's head of agriculture, became CEO of Cytec. He dumped about $300 million worth of underperforming businesses. Fry overhauled the R&D process by dragging the engineers out of their labs and having them do field work with customers. Fry also encouraged research that focused on creating products with practical applications when he realized that the last breakthrough that translated into a usable product was super glue in the 1970s. The company focused on core areas in which Cytec had expertise. Rather than go for the blockbuster product, the company aimed for an array of smaller, less-profitable but more-accessible products.

By 1996 overseas sales accounted for about 40% of revenues, up from 28% in 1993. Also in 1996 Cytec sold its aluminum sulphate operations. Cost-reduction programs and the company's improved product mix were making themselves felt; though sales were flat between 1995 and 1996, earnings were up.

David Lilley (formerly of American Home Products/Wyeth) was named COO in 1997. That year Cytec completed the sale of its acrylic-fibers business to Sterling Chemicals Holdings. Cytec also acquired Fiberite (excluding its satellite-materials business). Fiberite, a composites maker, was merged with Cytec's advanced composites and aerospace adhesives line to form Cytec Fiberite (now Cytec Engineered Materials).

In 1998 Cytec began Dyno-Cytec, a European coatings joint venture (it bought its partner's stake later in the year). It also bought composite material maker American Materials & Technologies. That year COO Lilley was named CEO; the title of chairman was added in 1999. Also in 1999 Cytec bought Inspec Mining Chemical from the UK's Laporte PLC for $25 million and BIP (amino-coating resins) for $42 million. Later that year the company sold its interest in Fortier Methanol.

The company teamed up with GE Specialty Chemicals and Albemarle in 2000 to form an online B2B joint venture to streamline the companies' purchasing. Cytec sold its stake in Criterion Catalyst to its partner CRI International, a subsidiary of Royal Dutch Shell, for $60 million. That November Cytec sold most of its paper chemicals operations, including its sizing and strength business.

In 2001 Cytec added the carbon fiber business of BP and closed up shop on joint venture AC Molding Compounds, which manufactured melamine and urea molding compounds.

With chemical companies at their lowest levels of production in about a decade, Cytec undertook some cost-cutting efforts in 2001-02, including idling an ammonia plant and reducing its staff. Problems associated with the commercial airline industry also squeezed sales.

In June 2003 the company dissolved another of its partnerships, this one with Mitsui Chemicals

called Mitsui Cytec (water-treatment chemicals and melamine coating resins). Cytec kept the resins business, while Mitsui held on to the venture's water-treatment operations.

In 2006 the company sold its water treatment chemicals and acrylamide manufacturing operations to Kemira for about $240 million. The divestiture was designed to allow Cytec to pare down its operations and place its focus on core business lines.

David Lilley retired at the close of 2008.

EXECUTIVES

Chairman, President, and CEO: Shane D. Fleming, age 51, $2,756,968 total compensation
VP and CFO: David M. Drillock, age 52, $944,958 total compensation
VP Taxes: Richard T. Ferguson
VP Information Technology: Jeffrey C. Futterman
VP, General Counsel, and Secretary: Roy Smith, age 51, $743,451 total compensation
VP, Corporate and Business Development; President, Building Block Chemicals: William N. Avrin, age 54, $676,663 total compensation
VP Safety, Health, and Environment: Karen E. Koster
VP Human Resources: M. Regina Charles, age 52
President, Cytec Engineered Materials: William (Bill) Wood, age 48
President, Cytec Specialty Chemicals: Frank Aranzana, age 51, $1,031,936 total compensation
Corporate Controller: Jeffery P. Fitzgerald
Treasurer: Thomas P. Wozniak, age 56
Auditors: KPMG LLP

LOCATIONS

HQ: Cytec Industries Inc.
  5 Garret Mountain Plaza, West Paterson, NJ 07424
Phone: 973-357-3100   Fax: 973-357-3065
Web: www.cytec.com

2009 Sales

	$ mil.	% of total
Europe, Middle East & Africa	1,079.5	39
North America	1,061.4	38
Asia/Pacific	489.4	18
Latin America	159.2	6
Total	**2,789.5**	**100**

PRODUCTS/OPERATIONS

2009 Sales

	$ mil.	% of total
Coatings Resins	1,206.9	43
Engineered Materials	717.5	26
Building Block Chemicals	360.2	12
In Process Separation	265.8	10
Additive Technologies	239.1	9
Total	**2,789.5**	**100**

Selected Products

Cytec Surface Specialties
  Liquid coating resins (water- and solvent-borne resins, and amino resins)
  Powder coating resins (conventional and ultraviolet powders)
  Radcure resins (oligomers, monomers, and photo-initiators)
Cytec Engineered Materials
  Aerospace materials (structural adhesives and advanced composites)
Performance Chemicals
  Mining chemicals (reagents and polymers)
  Phosphine and phosphine derivatives
  Polymer additives (ultraviolet light absorbers and stabilizers, and antioxidants)
Building Block Chemicals
  Acrylamide
  Acrylonitrile
  Ammonia
  Melamine
  Sulfuric acid

COMPETITORS

Akzo Nobel	Hexcel
Arch Chemicals	Huntsman Corp
Ashland Inc.	Lubrizol
Dow Chemical	Lucite
DSM	Mitsubishi Chemical
DuPont	Rockwood Holdings
H.B. Fuller	

HISTORICAL FINANCIALS

Company Type: Public

Income Statement

FYE: December 31

	REVENUE ($ mil.)	NET INCOME ($ mil.)	NET PROFIT MARGIN	EMPLOYEES
12/09	2,790	(3)	—	5,800
12/08	3,640	(199)	—	6,700
12/07	3,504	207	5.9%	6,800
12/06	3,330	196	5.9%	6,700
12/05	2,926	59	2.0%	7,300
Annual Growth	(1.2%)	—	—	(5.6%)

2009 Year-End Financials

Debt ratio: 42.2%
Return on equity: —
Cash ($ mil.): 262
Current ratio: 1.98
Long-term debt ($ mil.): 658

No. of shares (mil.): 49
Dividends
  Yield: 0.4%
  Payout: —
Market value ($ mil.): 1,787

Stock History

NYSE: CYT

	STOCK PRICE ($) FY Close	P/E High/Low		PER SHARE ($) Earnings	Dividends	Book Value
12/09	36.42	—	—	(0.05)	0.16	31.78
12/08	21.22	—	—	(4.16)	0.50	30.06
12/07	61.58	18	13	4.20	0.40	39.34
12/06	56.51	16	11	4.01	0.40	32.01
12/05	47.63	43	31	1.27	0.40	25.24
Annual Growth	(6.5%)	—	—	—	(20.5%)	5.9%

Dana Holding

When it comes to building cars, it starts with the parts. Dana manufactures many of the parts carmakers use to piece together new vehicles. Its core products include axles and driveshafts, as well as sealing (gaskets, cover modules), thermal (cooling and heat transfer), and structural (frames, cradles, side rails) products. Among its largest customers are OEMs such as Ford, Toyota, Nissan, GM, and Hyundai. The company also supplies companies that make commercial and off-highway vehicles, such as PACCAR, Deere, Sandvik, and Navistar. Dana filed for Chapter 11 bankruptcy protection from creditors in 2006 and emerged in 2008.

The woes of the automotive industry weigh heavily on Dana, especially in the US, where new vehicle sales saw steep declines in 2009. The company has restructured and reduced the size of its operations in order to cut costs. During 2008 the company reduced its workforce by 6,000 people, a 17% cutback in employment. In 2009 the company slashed another 5,000 jobs, and announced that it expects to make additional workforce reductions in 2010. Dana has closed more than 25 facilities since 2007.

While the company has continued to shed operations, it is also looking to partnerships to expand. Dana agreed in early 2010 to form a joint venture with Bosch-Rexroth to develop and produce hydro-mechanical variable powersplit transmissions for off-highway vehicles. The 50-50 venture will be based in Italy, and brings together Dana's off-highway transmissions expertise with Bosch-Rexroth's experience in hydraulics systems.

Dana continues to sell product lines it considers noncore to operations. In March 2010 the company completed the sale of its Structural Products business — which included chassis, side rail, and other structural components — to Mexico-based structural components maker Metalsa, S.A. de C.V. (a subsidiary of Grupo Proeza). The transaction included operations in Argentina, Australia, Brazil, Canada, the US, and a UK joint venture. Throughout 2007 and 2008, Dana continued to unload product lines; divested operations included its trailer axle, engine hard parts, fluid products hose and tubing, and pump businesses.

Eaton executive James Sweetnam became Dana's president and CEO in mid-2009. His predecessor as CEO, John Devine, continued as executive chairman.

Centerbridge Capital Partners, a private equity firm, invested $790 million in Dana as part of the company's bankruptcy reorganization plan. The company owns all of Dana's Series A Preferred shares.

HISTORY

Clarence Spicer developed a universal joint and a driveshaft for autos while studying at Cornell University. Leaving Cornell in 1904, he patented his designs, founded Spicer Manufacturing in Plainfield, New Jersey, and marketed the product himself.

The company ran into financial trouble in 1913, and the following year New York attorney Charles Dana joined the firm, advancing Spicer money to refinance. Acquisitions after WWI strengthened Spicer's position in the growing truck industry. The business moved to Toledo, Ohio, in 1929 to be nearer the emerging Detroit automotive mecca. In 1946 the company was renamed in honor of Dana, who became chairman two years later. Sales topped $150 million in the 1950s.

The company entered the replacement-parts market in 1963, and Charles Dana retired that year. Continuing to expand its offerings, Dana acquired the Weatherhead Company (hoses, fittings, and couplings; 1977) and later branched into financial services. In 1989 Dana introduced a nine-speed, heavy-duty truck transmission (developed jointly with truckmaker Navistar), the first all-new design of its type in over 25 years.

Dana sold its mortgage banking business and some other financial services in 1992. It bought Delta Automotive and Krizman, both leading makers and distributors of automotive aftermarket parts. The next year Dana acquired the Reinz Group, a German gasket maker with worldwide operations. Purchases in 1994 included Sige (axles, Italy), Stieber Heidelberg (industrial components, Germany), Tece (auto parts distribution, the Netherlands), and Tremec (transmissions, Mexico).

Acquisitions in 1995 and 1996 included a number of rubber and plastics makers. The company bought Clark-Hurth Components (drivetrains) and the piston ring and cylinder liner operations of SPX Corporation in 1997; it also increased its shares in Wix Filtron (filtration products, Poland).

Dana sold some of its businesses in 1997 as well. These included its sheet-rubber and conveyor-belt business to Coltec Industries, its European warehouse distribution operations to Partco Group, and its Spicer clutch business to Eaton.

In 1998 Dana bought Eaton's heavy-axle and brake business and then paid $3.9 billion for Echlin. Dana then cut 3,500 jobs, or more than 4% of its workforce, and closed 15 plants, mostly former Echlin facilities. It paid $430 million in 1998 for the bearings, washers, and camshafts businesses of Federal-Mogul (auto parts).

In 2000 Dana sold Gresen's hydraulic business to Parker Hannifin and Warner Electric's industrial products business to Colfax. Anticipating a slowdown in North American car production, Dana closed five plants, downsized three, and terminated 1,280 employees.

On the buying side, Dana acquired the auto axle manufacturing and stamping operations of Invensys (UK) in 2000. Also that year president and CEO Joseph Magliochetti, a 33-year Dana veteran, became chairman. Late in 2000 the company announced it would cut 3,000 production jobs. In 2001 Dana announced 10,000 more job cuts through plant closings and consolidations.

Early in the summer of 2003, ArvinMeritor offered to acquire Dana for $15 per share or about $2.2 billion. By Thanksgiving 2003 the deal fell apart after Dana's board of directors rejected ArvinMeritor's sweetened deal of $2.67 billion. Within weeks of fending off ArvinMeritor, Dana announced it planned to sell all of its aftermarket parts businesses. The deal was finalized in November 2004.

As hard times hit the North American automotive market in 2005, Dana announced it would cut more costs by laying off workers, selling noncore operations, closing plants, and moving more of its manufacturing base to Mexico.

Dana filed for Chapter 11 bankruptcy early in 2006 and exited in 2008.

EXECUTIVES

Executive Chairman: John M. Devine, age 65, $2,588,489 total compensation
President, CEO, and Director: James E. Sweetnam, age 57, $4,345,033 total compensation
EVP and CFO: James A. (Jim) Yost, age 61, $982,702 total compensation
CTO: George T. Constand, age 51
Chief Administrative Officer: Robert H. Marcin, age 64, $836,382 total compensation
SVP Global Operations: Ernesto Gonzalez-Beltran, age 47
SVP Strategy and Business Development: Jacqueline A. Dedo, age 48
SVP, General Counsel, and Secretary: Marc S. Levin, age 55
VP Global Engineering and Business Development, Sealing and Thermal Product Groups: Ralf Goettel, age 43, $702,247 total compensation
VP and Chief Accounting Officer: Richard J. Dyer, age 54
VP and CIO: Doug S. Tracy, age 49
VP and Operations Controller: Kevin B. Biddle, age 55
VP Finance: Rodney R. Filcek, age 57

Treasurer: Ralph A. Than, age 49
President, Heavy Vehicle Group: Mark E. Wallace, age 43, $935,402 total compensation
President, Light Vehicle Driveline: Martin D. Bryant, age 40
President, Europe: Aziz Aghili
President, South American Operations: Harro Burmann
President, Asia/Pacific Operations: Ken J. Cao
Auditors: PricewaterhouseCoopers LLP

LOCATIONS

HQ: Dana Holding Corporation
3939 Technology Dr., Maumee, OH 43537
Phone: 419-887-3000
Web: www.dana.com

2009 Sales

	$ mil.	% of total
North America		
US	2,402	46
Canada	137	3
Mexico	120	2
Europe		
Italy	378	7
Germany	333	7
Other countries	479	9
South America		
Brazil	426	8
Other countries	372	7
Asia/Pacific		
Australia	157	3
Other countries	424	8
Total	**5,228**	**100**

PRODUCTS/OPERATIONS

2009 Sales

	$ mil.	% of total
Automotive		
Light vehicle driveline	2,021	39
Structures	592	11
Sealing	535	10
Thermal	179	4
Commercial vehicle	1,051	20
Off-highway	850	16
Total	**5,228**	**100**

Selected Products

Automotive
Axles
Cover modules
Cradles
Differentials
Driveshafts
Engine sealing products
Frames
Gaskets
Heat shields
Side rails
Thermal management products (cooling and heat transfer products)
Torque couplings

Commercial vehicle
Axles
Chassis and siderails
Driveshafts
Engine sealing products
Ride controls
Steering shafts
Thermal management products (cooling and heat transfer products)
Tire management systems
Thermal management products

Off-highway
Axles
Cooling and heat transfer products
Driveshafts
Electronic controls
Engine sealing products
Sealing products
Suspension components
Thermal management products (cooling and heat transfer products)
Transaxles
Transmissions

COMPETITORS

AISIN World Corp.
American Axle & Manufacturing
ArvinMeritor
BorgWarner
Capsonic
Carraro
Chrysler
Continental AG
Daimler
Delphi Automotive
DENSO
Eaton
Emerson Electric
Federal-Mogul
Ford Motor
Freudenberg-NOK
GKN
Honeywell International
Ingersoll-Rand
ITT Corp.
LEONI
Magna International
Mahle International
Mark IV
Martinrea International
Metaldyne
Modine Manufacturing
Prestolite Electric
Robert Bosch
Tower Automotive
TRW Automotive
Valeo
Visteon
Wanxiang
ZF Friedrichshafen

HISTORICAL FINANCIALS

Company Type: Public

Income Statement

FYE: December 31

	REVENUE ($ mil.)	NET INCOME ($ mil.)	NET PROFIT MARGIN	EMPLOYEES
12/09	5,228	(436)	—	24,000
12/08	8,095	18	0.2%	29,000
12/07	8,721	(551)	—	35,000
12/06	8,504	(739)	—	45,000
12/05	8,611	(1,609)	—	44,000
Annual Growth	**(11.7%)**	**—**	**—**	**(14.1%)**

2009 Year-End Financials

Debt ratio: 106.7%
Return on equity: —
Cash ($ mil.): 947
Current ratio: 2.23
Long-term debt ($ mil.): 969
No. of shares (mil.): 140
Dividends
　Yield: —
　Payout: —
Market value ($ mil.): 1,522

Stock History

NYSE: DAN

	STOCK PRICE ($) FY Close	P/E High/Low	PER SHARE ($) Earnings	Dividends	Book Value
12/09	10.84	— —	(4.19)	—	11.95
12/08	0.74	— —	(0.11)	—	14.34
Annual Growth	**1,364.9%**	**— —**	**—**	**—**	**(16.6%)**

Danaher Corporation

If you've ever used Craftsman hand tools or bought something with a bar code on it, then odds are you've been in touch with Danaher's business. Its Professional Instrumentation segment produces environmental and electronic testing technology; Industrial Technologies makes motion control equipment and devices that read bar codes; Medical Technologies makes dental products and medical instrumentation devices; and Danaher's Tools and Components manufactures hand and automotive specialty tools and accessories under brand names like Sears' Craftsman. The two Rales brothers, Steven (board chairman) and Mitchell (executive committee chairman), together own approximately 20% of the company.

Though the company makes a little more than half of its revenues in North America, it has operations in more than 40 countries where it designs, manufactures, and markets its products under various brand names. The company touts its diverse industry endeavors and vast geographic presence as mitigating factors in the event any one sector experiences a downturn. This strategy, however, did not make Danaher impervious to the financial crisis that befell businesses around the world in 2009.

While Danaher countered with additional restructuring efforts in low growth business segments, including more job cuts and plant closings to those announced earlier in the year, it kept up its aggressive acquisition of businesses, as well as formed joint ventures to augment its product offerings.

Danaher's Professional Instrumentation division, its largest, has two segments. Environmental makes water analysis and purification systems and petroleum monitoring equipment while Test and Measurement produces test and calibration tools for electrical applications. Customers in engineering, network operations, aerospace, semiconductors, and retail use the division's Fluke and Tektronix branded products.

The Medical Technologies division's dental products range from imaging systems to dental devices, while life science related products include acute care (blood gas measurement devices), pathology diagnostics (tissue embedding and chemical reagents), and life sciences instrumentation (microscopes).

In 2010, Danaher scooped up the MDS Analytical Technologies business (drug discovery and life sciences research instruments) of Canada-based MDS for about $580 million. The unit included MDS's interest in AB SCIEX (a joint venture with Life Technologies), which makes mass spectrometry instruments for medical researchers and clinicians. Danaher purchased the remaining shares of AB SCIEX from Life Technologies for about $450 million.

The Tools and Components division consists of several companies that do business as the Danaher Tool Group (DTG) and Matco Tools. These companies make manual and power tools, braking systems, truckboxes, vehicle lifts, and tire changers for the automotive, industrial, and do-it-yourself mechanics markets.

HISTORY

Danaher (from the Celtic word *dana* meaning "swift flowing") is named for a fishing stream off the Flat Head River in Montana. The term is also an appropriate description of the spotlight-averse Rales brothers. The two have proven to be fishers not only of trout but also of companies, buying underperforming companies with strong market shares and recognizable brand names.

Once dubbed "raiders in short pants" by *Forbes,* Steven and Mitchell Rales began making acquisitions in their 20s. In 1981 they bought their father's 50% stake in Master Shield, a maker of vinyl building products. The brothers bought tire manufacturer Mohawk Rubber the following year. In 1983 they acquired control of publicly traded DMG, a distressed Florida real-estate firm; the next year they sold DMG's real estate holdings and folded Mohawk and Master Shield into the company, which they renamed Danaher.

Danaher then began taking over low-profile industrial firms that weren't living up to their growth potential. Backed by junk bonds from Michael Milken, it had purchased 12 more companies within two years. Among these early acquisitions were makers of tools (Jacobs, Matco Tools), controls (Partlow, Qualitrol, Veeder-Root), precision components (Allen, maker of the namesake hexagonal wrench), and plastics (A.L. Hyde). With its purchases, Danaher proceeded to cut costs and pay down debt by unloading underperforming assets.

The Rales brothers' takeover efforts weren't always successful. They lost out to Warren Buffett when they tried to buy Scott Fetzer (encyclopedias, vacuum cleaners) in 1985 and INTERCO (furniture, shoes, apparel) in 1988. They did, however, make off with $75 million for their troubles, and INTERCO was driven into dismantlement and bankruptcy in the process.

In 1989 Danaher bought Easco Hand Tools, the main maker of tools for Sears, Roebuck and Co.'s Craftsman line. (The Raleses already controlled Easco Hand Tools; a private partnership they controlled had bought the company from its parent in 1985 and taken it public in 1987.) The deal established the tool division as Danaher's largest, and two years later Sears selected Danaher as the sole manufacturer of Craftsman mechanics' hand tools.

The brothers hired Black & Decker power tools executive George Sherman as president and CEO in 1990. Between 1991 and 1995 Danaher grew through purchases such as Delta Consolidated Industries and Armstrong Brothers Tool. The firm improved its international distribution channels by adding West Instruments (UK, 1993) and Hengstler (Germany, 1994).

Focusing on tools and controls, Danaher sold its automotive components business in 1995.

Danaher's 1997 purchases included Current Technology and GEMS Sensors. Danaher made its two largest purchases to date in 1998 when it bought Pacific Scientific (motion controls and safety equipment) for $460 million and Fluke (electronic tools) for $625 million.

In 2001 Lawrence Culp, formerly the company's COO, was named president and CEO.

In 2004 the company acquired dental imaging product manufacturer Gendex from Dentsply International. The following year it bought German optical systems maker Leica Microsystems for about $550 million.

The company acquired Tektronix in 2007 and incorporated it into its Professional Instrumentation division. Tektronix brought general purpose test products such as oscilloscopes and data analyzers, as well as network management systems and network diagnostic equipment and services for fixed and mobile telecommunications to Danaher's product portfolio.

EXECUTIVES

Chairman: Steven M. Rales, age 59
President, CEO, and Director:
 H. Lawrence (Larry) Culp Jr., age 47,
 $11,049,312 total compensation
EVP: William K. (Dan) Daniel II, age 45,
 $2,749,181 total compensation
EVP and CFO: Daniel L. Comas, age 46,
 $3,752,892 total compensation
EVP: James A. (Jim) Lico, age 44,
 $3,618,669 total compensation
EVP: Thomas P. Joyce Jr., age 49,
 $3,645,526 total compensation
SVP and Chief Accounting Officer: Robert S. Lutz,
 age 52
SVP Finance and Tax: James H. Ditkoff, age 63
SVP Corporate Development: Daniel A. Raskas, age 43
SVP and General Counsel: Jonathan P. Graham, age 49
VP and Treasurer: Frank T. McFaden
VP Strategic Development: William H. King
VP; President, Fluke Corporation: Barbara B. Hulit
VP Corporate Development: Laurence S. Smith
VP Investor Relations: Matt R. McGrew
VP Human Resources: Kevin A. Klau
VP Environmental Health and Safety: Stephen Evanoff
VP Corporate Development: Jonathan L. Schwarz
President, Leica Biosystems: Arnd Kaldowski
President, AB SCIEX; President, Molecular Devices:
 Andrew W. (Andy) Boorn
President, Thomson: Ronald N. Meyer
President, Matco Tools Corporation: Thomas N. Willis
President and CEO, Tektronix: Amir Aghdaei, age 51
Associate General Counsel and Secretary:
 James F. O'Reilly
Auditors: Ernst & Young LLP

LOCATIONS

HQ: Danaher Corporation
 2099 Pennsylvania Ave. NW, 12th Fl.
 Washington, DC 20006
Phone: 202-828-0850   **Fax:** 202-828-0860
Web: www.danaher.com

2009 Sales

	$ mil.	% of total
US	5,919.7	53
Germany	1,475.4	14
China	702.3	6
UK	379.0	3
Other countries	2,708.5	24
Total	**11,184.9**	**100**

PRODUCTS/OPERATIONS

2009 Sales

	$ mil.	% of total
Professional Instrumentation	4,330.7	39
Medical Technologies	3,141.9	28
Industrial Technologies	2,658.0	24
Tools & Components	1,054.3	9
Total	**11,184.9**	**100**

Selected Products

Professional Instrumentation
 Environmental
  Analytical instruments
  Fuel dispensers
  Monitoring and leak detection systems
  Submersible turbine pumps
  Ultraviolet disinfection systems
  Vapor recovery equipment
  Water treatment systems
 Test and Measurement
  Video test, measurement, and monitoring products
Medical Technologies
 Acute care
  Blood gas and immunochemistry instruments
   (Radiometer brand)
 Dental
  Digital imaging
  Implant systems
  Impression, bonding, and restorative materials
  Infection control products
  Orthodontic brackets and lab products
 Life sciences instrumentation
  Compound microscopes
  Laser scanning
 Pathology diagnostics
  Chemical and immuno-staining instruments
  Slide coverslipping
  Tissue embedding
Industrial Technologies
 Aerospace and defense
  Electrical power generation systems
  Electronic security systems
  Smoke detection and fire suppression
  Submarine periscopes and related sensors
 Motion
  Controls
  Drives
  Mechanical components (linear bearings, clutches/brakes, and linear actuators)
  Standard and custom motors
 Product identification equipment
 Sensors and controls
  Monitoring and control instruments (temperature, position, quantity, level, flow, and time)
Tools and Components
 Mechanics hand tools

COMPETITORS

ABB	Labfacility
Baldor Electric	Makita
Bosch Rexroth Corp.	Mettler-Toledo
Datamax-O'Neil	Parker Hannifin
Dresser Wayne	PerkinElmer
Eaton	Rockwell Automation
Emerson Electric	Schneider Electric
GE	Siemens Water
Goodrich Corp.	Technologies
Greenlee Textron	Snap-on
Hitachi	SPX
Johnson & Johnson	Stanley Black and Decker
Medical	Thales Air Defence
Johnson Controls	Thermo Fisher Scientific

HISTORICAL FINANCIALS

Company Type: Public

Income Statement

FYE: December 31

	REVENUE ($ mil.)	NET INCOME ($ mil.)	NET PROFIT MARGIN	EMPLOYEES
12/09	11,185	1,152	10.3%	46,600
12/08	12,698	1,318	10.4%	50,300
12/07	11,026	1,370	12.4%	50,000
12/06	9,596	1,122	11.7%	45,000
12/05	7,985	898	11.2%	40,000
Annual Growth	**8.8%**	**6.4%**	**—**	**3.9%**

2009 Year-End Financials

Debt ratio: 24.8% No. of shares (mil.): 653
Return on equity: 10.7% Dividends
Cash ($ mil.): 1,722 Yield: 0.2%
Current ratio: 1.89 Payout: 3.5%
Long-term debt ($ mil.): 2,889 Market value ($ mil.): 24,539

Stock History

NYSE: DHR

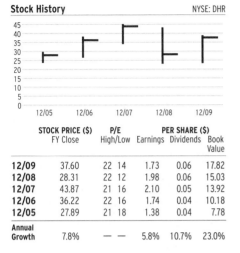

	STOCK PRICE ($)	P/E		PER SHARE ($)		
	FY Close	High/Low	Earnings	Dividends	Book Value
12/09	37.60	22 14	1.73	0.06	17.82
12/08	28.31	22 12	1.98	0.06	15.03
12/07	43.87	21 16	2.10	0.05	13.92
12/06	36.22	22 16	1.74	0.04	10.18
12/05	27.89	21 18	1.38	0.04	7.78
Annual Growth	7.8%	— —	5.8%	10.7%	23.0%

Darden Restaurants

This company has cornered not one but two dining markets: seafood and "Hospitaliano." Darden Restaurants is the #1 casual-dining operator (in terms of revenue), with about 1,825 restaurants in the US and Canada. Its flagship chains include seafood-segment leader Red Lobster and top Italian-themed concept Olive Garden. Both chains cater to families by offering mid-priced menu items, themed interiors, and primarily suburban locations. Darden also operates the LongHorn Steakhouse chain, with about 330 outlets. Other dining concepts include The Capital Grille (upscale steakhouse), Bahama Breeze (Caribbean food and drinks), and Seasons 52 (casual grill and wine bar).

Being at the forefront of the casual dining industry, Darden's flagship brands have come to epitomize the chain restaurant experience. Both Red Lobster and Olive Garden dominate the landscape of suburban America, offering a version of seafood and Italian cuisine designed for mass appeal and affordability. Darden spends heavily on research and development in order to roll out a succession of new menu items that are heavily promoted through television advertising. The chains also utilize discount pricing and special offers to win business against the competition, including Applebee's, Chili's (operated by Brinker International), and Outback Steakhouse (OSI Restaurant Partners).

Darden has built its dining empire without the aid of franchising, a strategy that allows the company the highest degree of control for maintaining food and service quality. The major downside, of course, is the cost of operating and maintaining all those restaurants. The company is constantly focused on improving margins by negotiating lower prices for food and other ingredients and by adjusting its workforce to reduce labor costs.

The recession during 2009 posed serious challenges for most casual dining operators, but Darden's chains fared better than some of the company's competitors thanks to intense customer loyalty. It was able to weather the downturn without heavy price discounting and managed to invest in expansion efforts that added more than 50 new locations. Most of the company's growth emphasis has been on its Olive Garden and LongHorn Steakhouse chains.

HISTORY

Nineteen-year-old Bill Darden entered the restaurant business in the late 1930s with a 25-seat luncheonette called the Green Frog in Waycross, Georgia. The restaurant, which featured the slogan "Service with a Hop," was a hit, and his dream was born. During the 1950s he owned a variety of restaurants, including several Howard Johnson's, Bonanza, and Kentucky Fried Chicken outlets.

Darden teamed with a group of investors in 1963 to buy an Orlando, Florida, restaurant, Gary's Duck Inn. The restaurant became the prototype for Darden's idea for a moderately priced, sit-down seafood chain. He decided to name the new chain Red Lobster, a takeoff on the old Green Frog.

The first Red Lobster opened in Lakeland, Florida, in 1968 with Joe Lee, who had worked in one of Darden's other restaurants, as its manager. It was such a success that within a month the restaurant had to be expanded. In 1970, when there were three Red Lobsters in operation and two under construction in Central Florida, Betty Crocker's boss, General Mills, bought the chain — keeping Darden on to run it.

Red Lobster was not General Mills' first foray into the restaurant business. The company opened Betty Crocker Tree House Restaurant in 1968 and acquired a fish-and-chips chain and a barbeque chain. But Red Lobster would be its first success. Rather than franchise the Red Lobster name, General Mills chose to develop the chain on its own. Lee was named president of Red Lobster in 1975, and Darden became chairman of General Mills Restaurants.

While General Mills continued to expand Red Lobster, it also sought another restaurant idea to complement the seafood chain. Among concepts tried and discarded were a steak house and Mexican and health-food restaurants. In 1980 the company decided on Italian. After two years of marketing questionnaires and recipe tests, General Mills opened a prototype Olive Garden in Orlando featuring moderately priced Italian food. General Mills began to add outlets in the mid-1980s, and Olive Garden became another success story of the casual-dining industry.

After testing a new Chinese restaurant concept, General Mills opened its first China Coast in Orlando in 1990. The chain grew rapidly, with more than 45 units opening in a single year. The Olive Garden drive began to cool off in 1993: Same-store sales slid as competitors added Italian items to their menus. The next year Olive Garden increased its advertising budget, introduced new menu items, and began testing new formats, including smaller cafes for malls.

General Mills decided to spin off the restaurant business as a public company in 1995 and focus on consumer foods. The restaurants were renamed Darden Restaurants in honor of Bill Darden (who had died in 1994, the same year that Joe Lee was appointed CEO). That year the company abandoned its China Coast chain.

Darden Restaurants tried again in 1997 with Bahama Breeze, opening a test restaurant in Orlando. Red Lobster's sales flagged in 1997, but the company initiated a turnaround in 1998, in part by revamping Red Lobster's menu. An ill-conceived all-you-can-eat offer at Red Lobster cost Darden in profits (and led to the ousting of chain president Edna Morris after just 18 months). The company dipped into the barbecue sauce in 1999 and opened its inaugural Smokey Bones in Orlando.

The following year Darden Restaurants began expanding its Smokey Bones concept nationally.

With financial results lagging at its Bahama Breeze chain, Darden slowed growth of the concept and expanded its operating hours to include lunch business. The company also promoted former development VP Laurie Burns to lead Bahama Breeze after the unexpected resignation of Gary Heckel in 2002. Clarence Otis Jr. was appointed CEO in 2004, succeeding Joe Lee; the following year Otis added chairman to his title.

The company expanded into the steakhouse market in 2007 with its $1.4 billion (including debt) acquisition of RARE Hospitality. The following year Darden sold its unprofitable Smokey Bones Barbeque & Grill chain to an affiliate of Sun Capital Partners for about $80 million.

EXECUTIVES

Chairman and CEO: Clarence Otis Jr., age 54, $5,013,601 total compensation
President, COO, and Director: Andrew H. (Drew) Madsen, age 54, $3,821,641 total compensation
SVP and CFO: C. Bradford (Brad) Richmond, age 51, $1,524,347 total compensation
SVP and Corporate Controller: Valerie K. (Val) Collins, age 51
SVP Development: Suk Singh
SVP Government and Community Affairs: Robert (Bob) McAdam, age 52
SVP; President, Red Lobster: Kim A. Lopdrup, age 52, $1,973,503 total compensation
SVP; President, Olive Garden: David T. (Dave) Pickens, age 55, $2,305,906 total compensation
SVP Human Resources: Daisy Ng, age 52
SVP Group Human Resources: Ronald (Ron) Bojalad
SVP Supply Chain: Barry B. Moullet, age 52
SVP, General Counsel, and Secretary: Paula J. Shives, age 59
SVP Business Development: James (J. J.) Buettgen, age 50
Chief Marketing Officer: John Caron
VP Information Technology: Jordan Lomas
VP Investor Relations: Matthew Stroud
President, The Capital Grille: John Martin
President, LongHorn Steakhouse: David C. (Dave) George, age 54
President, Specialty Restaurant Group: Eugene I. (Gene) Lee Jr., age 49
President, Seasons 52: Stephen Judge
Auditors: KPMG LLP

LOCATIONS

HQ: Darden Restaurants, Inc.
1000 Darden Center Dr., Orlando, FL 32837
Phone: 407-245-4000 **Fax:** 407-245-5389
Web: www.dardenrestaurants.com

2010 Locations

US	No.
Florida	204
Texas	136
Georgia	113
California	102
Ohio	101
Pennsylvania	87
Illinois	65
Michigan	58
Virginia	57
New York	56
North Carolina	53
Tennessee	51
Indiana	50
New Jersey	50
Missouri	45
Arizona	41
Alabama	39
Maryland	36
South Carolina	35
Colorado	32
Massachusetts	32
Washington	29
Minnesota	25
Kentucky	24
Oklahoma	21
Wisconsin	21
Kansas	18
Connecticut	17
Louisiana	17
Utah	17
Iowa	15
Mississippi	15
Arkansas	14
Nevada	14
Oregon	13
New Mexico	12
West Virginia	11
New Hampshire	10
Maine	9
Other states	45
Canada	34
Total	**1,824**

PRODUCTS/OPERATIONS

2010 Locations

	No.
Olive Garden	723
Red Lobster	694
LongHorn Steakhouse	331
The Capital Grille	40
Bahama Breeze	25
Seasons 52	11
Total	**1,824**

COMPETITORS

Bob Evans	DineEquity
Brinker	Hooters
Carlson Restaurants	OSI Restaurant Partners
Cheesecake Factory	Perkins & Marie
Cracker Barrel	Callender's
Denny's	Ruby Tuesday

HISTORICAL FINANCIALS

Company Type: Public

Income Statement

FYE: Last Sunday in May

	REVENUE ($ mil.)	NET INCOME ($ mil.)	NET PROFIT MARGIN	EMPLOYEES
5/10	7,113	405	5.7%	174,000
5/09	7,218	372	5.2%	179,000
5/08	6,627	377	5.7%	179,000
5/07	5,567	201	3.6%	157,000
5/06	5,721	338	5.9%	157,300
Annual Growth	5.6%	4.6%	—	2.6%

2010 Year-End Financials

Debt ratio: 77.4%	No. of shares (mil.): 141
Return on equity: 23.1%	Dividends
Cash ($ mil.): 249	Yield: 2.3%
Current ratio: 0.54	Payout: 35.2%
Long-term debt ($ mil.): 1,466	Market value ($ mil.): 6,033

Stock History

NYSE: DRI

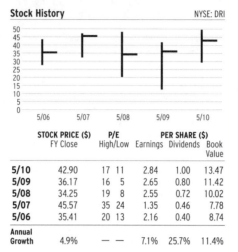

	STOCK PRICE ($) FY Close	P/E High/Low		PER SHARE ($) Earnings	Dividends	Book Value
5/10	42.90	17	11	2.84	1.00	13.47
5/09	36.17	16	5	2.65	0.80	11.42
5/08	34.25	19	8	2.55	0.72	10.02
5/07	45.57	35	24	1.35	0.46	7.78
5/06	35.41	20	13	2.16	0.40	8.74
Annual Growth	4.9%	—	—	7.1%	25.7%	11.4%

DaVita Inc.

DaVita — an Italian phrase that means "gives life" — provides life-sustaining dialysis treatments to patients suffering from end-stage renal disease (also known as chronic kidney failure). As one of the country's largest chains of outpatient dialysis centers, the company operates or provides administrative services to about 1,500 centers across the US. The firm also offers home-based dialysis services, as well as inpatient dialysis in some 700 hospitals. DaVita also operates clinical laboratories that specialize in routine testing of dialysis patients, and its DaVita Clinical Research business conducts research trials with dialysis patients.

Along with its dialysis-based revenue (which accounts for 95% of sales), DaVita offers other services related to kidney disease, including pharmacy services and the operation of chronic kidney disease management programs for employers and health plans. DaVita's Nephrology Partners business provides practice management and administrative services to physicians groups.

About 80% of the company's dialysis and lab-related income comes from Medicare and other government-sponsored programs, making DaVita particularly vulnerable to changes in government reimbursement rates (which are regularly under threat of being lowered by state and federal governments facing budget pressures). The company also receives income from commercial insurance payors.

DaVita expanded its health care offerings a couple of years ago by acquiring a majority stake in HomeChoice Partners, an infusion therapy provider with operations in the southeastern US. The company administers intravenous medications and enteral nutrition to patients with chronic or acute conditions, both in patients' homes and at ambulatory infusion sites.

The company also tends to grow by adding more outpatient dialysis centers to its operations. In 2009, for example, DaVita accumulated 80 more centers around the US. California, Florida, and Texas are home to about 30% of all DaVita's dialysis centers.

Nearly all of the outpatient dialysis centers are either wholly owned or majority-owned by DaVita. About 20 centers are owned by third parties, who pay DaVita for administrative services.

HISTORY

Hospital chain National Medical Enterprises (NME, now Tenet) formed Medical Ambulatory Care in 1979 to run its in-hospital dialysis centers. The unit bought other centers in NME's markets. In 1994 the subsidiary's management, backed by a Donaldson, Lufkin & Jenrette — now Credit Suisse First Boston (USA) — investment fund, bought the dialysis business and renamed it Total Renal Care (TRC).

To become a leader in its consolidating field, TRC began buying other centers and soon added clinical laboratory and dialysis-related pharmacy services and home dialysis programs. It went public in 1995.

The next year the firm added 66 facilities, 32 from its acquisition of Caremark International's dialysis business. In 1997 TRC expanded abroad, buying UK-based Open Access Sonography (vein care) and partnering with UK-based Priory Hospitals Group.

In 1998 TRC bought Renal Treatment Centers, nearly doubling its size. But the acquisition costs caused a loss that year and sparked shareholder lawsuits (settled in 2000) over alleged misleading statements. The firm also became embroiled in a reimbursement dispute with Florida's Medicare program. Problems continued into 1999 as the company struggled to meld operations. The company took a charge to cover a billing shortfall, and chairman and CEO Victor Chaltiel and COO/CFO John King resigned. New management began improving billing procedures and took other cost-cutting measures.

In 2000 the company changed its name to DaVita, an Italian phrase loosely translated as "he/she gives life." It also sold its international operations to competitor Fresenius.

In 2005 the company acquired Gambro's US dialysis operations for about $3 billion, adding some 565 dialysis clinics to its operations. To meet FTC requirements for the deal, DaVita sold about 70 clinics to RenalAmerica, a company founded by former Gambro Healthcare executive Michael Klein.

EXECUTIVES

Chairman and CEO: Kent J. Thiry, age 54, $11,672,142 total compensation
COO: Dennis L. Kogod, age 50, $6,059,867 total compensation
CFO: Luis Borgen, age 40
CIO: Anthony Gabriel
Chief Accounting Officer: James K. (Jim) Hilger, age 48
Chief Medical Officer: Allen R. Nissenson, age 63
Chief People Officer: Laura A. Mildenberger, age 51
SVP Federal Legislative Affairs: John Schaeffler
SVP: Javier J. Rodriguez, age 39, $2,096,220 total compensation
SVP: Thomas O. (Tom) Usilton Jr., age 58, $2,448,136 total compensation
SVP and Chief Compliance Officer: David T. Shapiro, age 40
SVP Operations: Scott Drake

VP Research: Mahesh Krishnan
VP Investor Relations: Jim Gustafson
VP Clinical Affairs Home Therapies: John Moran
VP Communications: Bill Myers
VP, General Counsel, and Secretary: Kim M. Rivera,
  age 41
Auditors: KPMG LLP

LOCATIONS

HQ: DaVita Inc.
  1551 Wewatta Street, Denver, CO 80202
Phone: 303-405-2100
Web: www.davita.com

2009 Locations

	No.
California	185
Florida	130
Texas	121
Georgia	97
Ohio	66
Pennsylvania	62
North Carolina	57
Virginia	55
Michigan	52
Maryland	49
Illinois	48
Minnesota	38
Alabama	37
Tennessee	36
Missouri	35
New York	33
Indiana	32
Oklahoma	30
Colorado	28
Kentucky	26
Louisiana	25
Arizona	23
New Jersey	23
South Carolina	22
Washington	20
Connecticut	19
Kansas	18
Nevada	16
Iowa	15
Oregon	15
Nebraska	13
Wisconsin	13
Massachusetts	12
Oregon	12
Arkansas	9
District of Columbia	9
Other states	29
Total	**1,510**

PRODUCTS/OPERATIONS

2009 Revenues by Payor

	% of total
Government-based programs	
Medicare & Medicare-assigned plans	57
Medicaid	6
Other government-based programs	2
Commercial	35
Total	**100**

2009 Dialysis Sales

	% of total
Outpatient hemodialysis centers	84
Peritoneal dialysis & home-based hemodialysis	11
Hospital inpatient hemodialysis	5
Total	**100**

COMPETITORS

Apria Healthcare	Gentiva
Dialysis Clinic Inc	LabCorp
Dialysis Corp.	National Renal
FMCNA	Quest Diagnostics
Fresenius Medical Care	Renal Advantage

HISTORICAL FINANCIALS

Company Type: Public

Income Statement

FYE: December 31

	REVENUE ($ mil.)	NET INCOME ($ mil.)	NET PROFIT MARGIN	EMPLOYEES
12/09	6,109	423	6.9%	32,500
12/08	5,660	374	6.6%	32,500
12/07	5,264	382	7.3%	31,000
12/06	4,881	290	5.9%	28,900
12/05	2,974	229	7.7%	28,000
Annual Growth	**19.7%**	**16.6%**	**—**	**3.8%**

2009 Year-End Financials

Debt ratio: 166.9%
Return on equity: 20.7%
Cash ($ mil.): 539
Current ratio: 2.20
Long-term debt ($ mil.): 3,563
No. of shares (mil.): 103
Dividends
  Yield: —
  Payout: —
Market value ($ mil.): 6,027

Stock History

NYSE: DVA

	STOCK PRICE ($) FY Close	P/E High/Low		PER SHARE ($) Earnings	Dividends	Book Value
12/09	58.74	15	10	4.06	—	20.81
12/08	49.57	17	12	3.53	—	19.03
12/07	56.35	19	14	3.55	—	16.88
12/06	56.88	22	17	2.74	—	12.14
12/05	50.64	25	18	2.20	—	8.29
Annual Growth	**3.8%**	**—**	**—**	**16.6%**	**—**	**25.9%**

Dean Foods

Dean Foods has become the king of milk by taking over other dairies' thrones. A leading US producer of fluid milk and other dairy products, Dean has grown and continues to grow through acquisitions. Its retail and foodservice dairy products are sold under more than 50 national, regional, and private-label brands, including Borden, Pet, Country Fresh, and Meadow Gold. In addition, the company manufactures coffee creamers (International Delight), dips and yogurt, ice cream, butter, cottage cheese, and specialty dairy products (lactose-free and organic milk, soy milk, and flavored milks). Dean owns and operates a number of smaller dairy companies, including Horizon Organic, Berkeley Farms, and Garelick Farms.

The company operates under two divisions — Fresh Dairy Direct, which manufactures conventional dairy products, including fluid milk, ice cream, juices, and teas; and its WhiteWave-Morningstar division, which makes organic and soy dairy-replacement products. In order to expand its holdings in the dairy-replacement sector, the company acquired the Alpro soy beverage and food operations of Belgium's Vandemoortele for

€325 million ($450 million) in 2009. Alpro, Europe's leading soy-based food and beverage business, was added to the WhiteWave-Morningstar division. The acquisition gave Dean a firm presence in Europe and a step up toward becoming a global brand. Answering customer demand, Dean's soy operations have largely switched to using non-GMO raw materials for manufacture of its products.

In 2008 Dean entered into a 50-50 joint venture with Swiss company Hero Group, a maker of international fruit and infant-nutrition products. The joint venture's first product, a chilled fruit snack called Fruit2Day, was introduced in 2009. Back in the US, Dean has an alliance with Land O'Lakes to market value-added dairy products, such as coffee creamer, and, through licensing agreements, it produces Hershey's flavored milks.

Adding to its retail brands, Dean acquired the milk-production plants of Baraboo, Wisconsin-based Foremost Farms in 2009. However, in January 2010 the US Department of Justice (DOJ) and the states of Illinois, Michigan, and Wisconsin filed a suit seeking to undo the Foremost acquisition, saying it resulted in a "substantial lessening of competition in Illinois, Michigan, and Wisconsin."

HISTORY

Investment banker Gregg Engles formed a holding company in 1988 with other investors, including dairy industry veteran Cletes Beshears, to buy the Reddy Ice unit of Dallas-based Southland (operator of the 7-Eleven chain). The company also bought Circle K's Sparkle Ice and combined it with Reddy Ice. By 1990 it had acquired about 15 ice plants.

The company changed its name to Suiza Foods when it bought Suiza Dairy in 1993 for $99 million. The Puerto Rican dairy was formed in 1942 by Hector Nevares Sr. and named for the Spanish word for "Swiss." By 1993 it was Puerto Rico's largest dairy, controlling about 60% of the island's milk market.

Suiza Foods bought Florida's Velda Farms, manufacturer and distributor of milk and dairy products, in 1994. The company went public in 1996, the same year it bought Swiss Dairy (dairy products, California and Nevada) and Garrido y Compañía (coffee products, Puerto Rico).

The company became one of the largest players in the North American dairy industry through its acquisitions in 1997. It paid $960 million for Morningstar (Lactaid brand lactose-free milk, Second Nature brand egg substitute), which — like Suiza Foods itself — was a Dallas-based company formed in 1988 through a Southland divestiture. The company entered the Midwest with its $98 million purchase of Country Fresh and the Northeast with the Bernon family's Massachusetts-based group of dairy and packaging companies, including Garelick Farms and Franklin Plastics (packaging).

Suiza Foods strengthened its presence in the southeastern US in 1998 with its $287 million acquisition of Land-O-Sun Dairies, operator of 13 fluid-dairy and ice-cream processing facilities. Also that year Suiza Foods purchased Continental Can (plastic packaging) for about $345 million and sold Reddy Ice to Packaged Ice for $172 million.

After settling an antitrust lawsuit brought by the US Department of Justice, in 1999 Suiza Foods bought dairy processors in Colorado,

Ohio, and Virginia. That year Suiza Foods combined its US packaging operations with Reid Plastics to form Consolidated Containers, retaining about 40% of the new company.

In 2001 Suiza Foods announced it had agreed to purchase rival Dean Foods for $1.5 billion and the assumption of $1 billion worth of debt. Dean Foods had begun as Dean Evaporated Milk, founded in 1925 by Sam Dean, a Chicago evaporated-milk broker. By the mid-1930s it had moved into the fresh milk industry. The company went public in 1961 and was renamed Dean Foods in 1963.

Suiza Foods completed the acquisition and took on the Dean Foods name later in 2001. The new Dean Foods bought out Dairy Farmers of America's interest in Suiza Dairy and merged it with the "old" Dean's fluid-dairy operations to create its internal division, Dean Dairy Group.

Along with the purchase of "old" Dean came a 36% ownership of soy milk maker WhiteWave, and in 2002 Dean Foods purchased the remaining 64%. By the end of the year, Dean had sold off some smaller businesses (boiled peanuts and contract hauling) and its Puerto Rico operations.

During 2003 Dean purchased Michigan milk processor Melody Farms, sold off its frozen non-dairy topping and creamer business to Rich Products, and renamed its Morningstar Foods division Dean Branded Products Group. With an eye on adding organic milk, Dean purchased 13% of Horizon Organic in 2003 and acquired the remainder of the company in 2004.

Dean purchased Milk Products of Alabama and Ross Swiss Dairies of California in 2004. Overseas, Dean acquired Tiger Foods, a dairy processing firm located in Spain.

The next year the company sold Dean's Dips and Marie's Dressings to Ventura Foods. The company also spun off its specialty foods group to its shareholders as TreeHouse Foods in 2005. TreeHouse makes private-label products such as pickles and non-dairy powdered coffee creamers and various regional brands.

Continuing its *modus operandi* of growth by purchasing regional dairies, in 2007 Dean acquired Friendship Dairies.

In July 2010, Dean sold Rachel's Dairy Limited (UK) business to France's Lactalis.

EXECUTIVES

Chairman and CEO: Gregg L. Engles, age 52, $10,262,423 total compensation
COO: Joseph E. (Joe) Scalzo, age 51, $3,882,787 total compensation
EVP and CFO: John F. (Jack) Callahan Jr., age 51, $2,722,251 total compensation
EVP and Chief Strategy and Transformation Officer: Gregory A. (Greg) McKelvey, age 36
EVP, General Counsel, and Secretary: Steven J. Kemps, age 46
EVP Research and Development: Kelly Duffin-Maxwell, age 45
EVP and Chief Supply Chain Officer: Gregg A. Tanner, age 53, $2,261,303 total compensation
EVP Human Resources: Paul T. Moskowitz, age 46
Chief Marketing Officer: Rick Zuroweste

SVP Business Optimization: Rick Fehr, age 58
SVP and CIO: Barbara D. Carlini, age 50
SVP and Chief Accounting Officer: Shaun P. Mara, age 45
SVP Innovation: Debra B. (Debbie) Carosella, age 53
VP Investor Relations: Barry Sievert
VP Corporate Communications: Marguerite Copel
President, Fresh Dairy Direct: Harrald F. Kroeker, age 52, $2,572,712 total compensation
President, Morningstar: Christopher (Chris) Sliva, age 46
President, WhiteWave Foods and Horizon Organic: Blaine E. McPeak, age 43
President, Horizon Organic Dairy: Mike Ferry
President, Garelick Farms: Alan J. Bernon, age 55
Auditors: Deloitte & Touche LLP

LOCATIONS

HQ: Dean Foods Company
    2515 McKinney Ave., Ste. 1200, Dallas, TX 75201
Phone: 214-303-3400   **Fax:** 214-303-3499
Web: www.deanfoods.com

2009 Sales

	% of total
Retailers	63
Foodservice	14
Convenience stores	7
Distributors	7
Other	9
Total	**100**

PRODUCTS/OPERATIONS

2009 Sales

	$ mil.	% of total
Fresh Dairy Direct	8,456.2	76
WhiteWave-Morningstar	2,702.2	24
Total	**11,158.4**	**100**

2009 Sales

	% of total
Fluid dairy	
Fresh milk	71
Ice cream	10
Other	8
Cultured dairy	5
Other beverages	5
Other	1
Total	**100**

2009 Sales

	% of total
Private-label brands	53
Company brands	47
Total	**100**

Selected Products

Bottled waters
Eggnog
Eggs
Cottage cheese
Half-and-half
Ice cream
Juice
Milk
Pudding
Sour cream
Soymilk
Whipping cream
Yogurt

COMPETITORS

American Milk Products
Associated Milk Producers
Aurora Organic Dairy
Bel Brands USA
BelGioioso Cheese
Ben & Jerry's
Blistex
Blue Bell
Brewster Dairy
California Dairies Inc.
ConAgra
Crystal Farms Refrigerated Distribution Company
Dairy Farmers of America
Dannon
Danone
Darigold, Inc.
Dreyer's
Ellsworth Cooperative
Farmland Dairies
Foster Dairy Farms
Friendly Ice Cream
Galaxy Nutritional Foods
Great Lakes Cheese
Grupo LALA
Hain Celestial
Hiland Dairy
HP Hood
Kemps, LLC
Kraft Foods
Lactalis
Leprino Foods
Lifeway Foods
Marathon Cheese
Maryland & Virginia Milk Producers
Mayfield Dairy Farms
Morinaga
National Dairy Holdings
Nestlé USA
Northwest Dairy
Organic Valley
Prairie Farms Dairy
Quality Chekd
Rockview Dairies
Saputo Cheese USA Inc.
Springfield Creamery
Stonyfield Farm
Tillamook County Creamery Association
Tofutti Brands
United Dairy Farmers
Vitasoy International

HISTORICAL FINANCIALS

Company Type: Public

Income Statement

FYE: December 31

	REVENUE ($ mil.)	NET INCOME ($ mil.)	NET PROFIT MARGIN	EMPLOYEES
12/09	11,158	228	2.0%	27,157
12/08	12,455	184	1.5%	25,820
12/07	11,822	131	1.1%	25,585
12/06	10,099	225	2.2%	26,348
12/05	10,506	329	3.1%	27,030
Annual Growth	1.5%	(8.8%)	—	0.1%

2009 Year-End Financials

Debt ratio: 294.4%
Return on equity: 23.9%
Cash ($ mil.): 48
Current ratio: 1.10
Long-term debt ($ mil.): 3,981

No. of shares (mil.): 182
Dividends
    Yield: 0.0%
    Payout: —
Market value ($ mil.): 3,275

Stock History

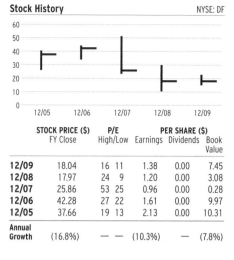

NYSE: DF

	STOCK PRICE ($) FY Close	P/E High/Low		PER SHARE ($)	
			Earnings	Dividends	Book Value
12/09	18.04	16 11	1.38	0.00	7.45
12/08	17.97	24 9	1.20	0.00	3.08
12/07	25.86	53 25	0.96	0.00	0.28
12/06	42.28	27 22	1.61	0.00	9.97
12/05	37.66	19 13	2.13	0.00	10.31
Annual Growth	(16.8%)	— —	(10.3%)	—	(7.8%)

Deere & Company

Deere & Company is interested in seeing its customers go to seed and grow. The company, one of the world's largest makers of farm equipment, is also a leading producer of construction, forestry, and commercial and residential lawn care equipment. Deere operates through three business segments: Agriculture & Turf and Construction & Forestry make up its Equipment Operations; the Credit division is part of Financial Services. Deere, which is famous for its "Nothing Runs Like A Deere" brand marketing campaign, operates factories and sales offices around the world.

Responding to the tough economic recession coupled with higher costs for basic materials and for transporting products, the company streamlined its activities in 2009. Deere combined the redundant processes and resources of its Commercial & Consumer Equipment division with its Agricultural Equipment division to form a new unit — Agriculture & Turf. This division manufactures utility, medium, and large tractors; loaders; combines; harvesters; irrigation equipment; mowers; and golf course equipment under brand names John Deere, as well as Frontier (mowers), SABO (scarifiers sold in Europe), and Benye (tractors sold in China); irrigation equipment is sold under the John Deere Water brand name.

Deere closed its plant in Ontario, Canada, in 2009 and transferred its Gator utility vehicle production and assembly to Mexico and to Horicon, Wisconsin. The company is concentrating on operating and expanding its manufacturing facilities in South America, the Middle East, Asia/Pacific, Western Europe, and even Eastern Europe, where it is building a new manufacturing facility near Moscow.

The Construction & Forestry division sells loaders, dozers, excavators, log skidders, and harvesters under the company and Waratah brand names. Through Bell Equipment, Deere designs articulated dump trucks for the Americas and Africa markets; Deere partners with Hitachi for the manufacture of hydraulic excavators and log

loaders for distribution in Central and South America, as well as in Finland and New Zealand.

In 2008 the company signed an agreement with Ashok Leyland to make backhoes and four-wheel-drive loaders in India, one of the largest markets for backhoes in the world. Also in 2008 the company took 50% ownership in Xuzhou Xuwa Excavator Machinery (XCG), the third-largest maker of excavator equipment in China.

In mid-2009 Deere named long-time company veteran Sam Allen to the position of president and CEO. He succeeds Robert Lane.

HISTORY

Vermont-born John Deere moved to Grand Detour, Illinois, in 1836 and set up a blacksmith shop. Deere and other pioneers had trouble with the rich, black soil of the Midwest sticking to iron plows designed for sandy eastern soils, so in 1837 Deere used a circular steel saw blade to create a self-scouring plow that moved so quickly, it was nicknamed the "whistling plow." He sold only three in 1838, but by 1842 he was making 25 a week.

Deere moved his enterprise to Moline in 1847. His son Charles joined the company in 1853, beginning a tradition of family management. (All five Deere presidents before 1982 were related by blood or marriage.) Charles set up an independent-dealership distribution system and added wagons, buggies, and corn planters to the product line.

Under Charles' son-in-law, William Butterworth (president, 1907-28), Deere bought agricultural equipment companies and developed harvesters and tractors with internal combustion engines. Butterworth's nephew, Charles Wiman, became president in 1928. He extended credit to farmers during the Depression and won customer loyalty. In 1931 Deere opened its first non-US plant in Canada.

William Hewitt, Wiman's son-in-law, became CEO in 1955. Deere passed International Harvester in 1958 to become the #1 US maker of farm equipment; by 1963 it led the world. Deere expanded into Argentina, France, Mexico, and Spain, and it used research and joint ventures abroad (Yanmar, small tractors, 1977; Hitachi, excavators, 1983) to diversify.

Robert Hanson became the first nonfamily CEO in 1982. He poured $2 billion into research and development during the 1980s. Despite an industry-wide sales slump resulting in losses totaling $328 million in 1986-87, Deere was the only major agricultural equipment maker to neither change ownership nor close factories during the 1980s. Instead, Deere cut its workforce 44% and improved efficiency.

In 1989 Deere acquired Funk Manufacturing (powertrain components), and Hans Becherer succeeded Hanson as CEO.

During the 1990s Deere expanded its lawn-care equipment business, mainly in Europe. In 1991 it bought a majority stake in Sabo-Maschinenfabrik (commercial lawn mowers, Germany). After spending most of the early 1990s in the doldrums because of recession and weak farm prices, Deere rebounded.

Deere signed a deal to sell combines in Ukraine (1996), and it formed a joint venture in 1997 to make combines in China. Fading demand for agricultural equipment at home and jeopardized sales contracts from failing economies in Asia, Brazil, and former Soviet states caused layoffs of about 2,400 workers in 1998 and production cutbacks in 1998-99.

In 2000 Deere purchased Finland-based Metso Corporation's Timberjack forestry-equipment business. President and COO Robert Lane succeeded Becherer as chairman and CEO. Deere bought McGinnis Farms — the US's largest horticultural products distributor — in 2001.

That year it cut production due to soft demand. Late in 2001 Deere said it would add to its previously announced job cuts, bringing the total to about 3,000 jobs. Deere also acquired Richton International Corporation; that deal included Richton's landscape irrigation-equipment distributor Century Supply (#1 in the US).

In 2004 Deere announced that it, along with iRobot, would develop a battlefield vehicle for the US Army. In 2006 Deere sold John Deere Health Care (now named UnitedHealthcare Services Company of the River Valley, Inc) to UnitedHealth Group for $500 million.

In 2007 Deere added to its barn-full of turf, lawn, and landscape products when it bought LESCO, Inc.

Looking to address demand for small tractors in a key global market, later in 2007 Deere acquired Ningbo Benye Tractor & Automobile Manufacture, based in southern China.

EXECUTIVES

Chairman, President, and CEO: Samuel R. (Sam) Allen, age 56, $4,050,604 total compensation
SVP and CFO: James M. Field, age 46, $2,882,913 total compensation
SVP Sale and Marketing, U.S. and Canada: Daniel C. McCabe
SVP Global Platform, Crop Harvesting Agriculture and Turf: Max A. Guinn
SVP, John Deere Intelligent Solutions Group: Bharat S. Vedak, age 62
SVP Global Platform, Tractor Agriculture and Turf: Bernard E. Haas
SVP Renewable Energy, Deere & Company: Martin L. Wilkinson
SVP and General Counsel: James R. Jenkins, age 64, $3,194,765 total compensation
SVP Credit and Operations, U.S. and Canada: Lawrence W. Sidwell
VP and Chief Compliance Officer: Linda E. Newborn
VP Human Resources: Mertroe B. (Mert) Hornbuckle
VP and CIO: Barry W. Schaffter
VP Corporate Communications and Brand Management: Frances B. Emerson
VP Advanced Technology and Engineering: Klaus G. Hoehn
VP and Comptroller: John J. Dalhoff
VP Investor Relations: Marie Z. Ziegler, age 52
President, John Deere Landscapes: David P. (Dave) Werning
President, Agriculture and Turf Division-North America, Asia, Australia, Sub-Saharan and South Africa, and Global Tractor and Turf Products: David C. Everitt, age 57, $3,651,935 total compensation
President, Worldwide Construction and Forestry Division: Michael J. Mack Jr., age 53
President, John Deere Credit: James A. Israel, age 53, $2,844,547 total compensation
President, Agriculture and Turf Division-Europe, CIS, Northern Africa, Middle East, Latin America, and Global Harvesting, Crop Care, Hay & Forage Products: Markwart von Pentz, age 46
Secretary and Associate General Counsel: Gregory R. Noe
Auditors: Deloitte & Touche LLP

LOCATIONS

HQ: Deere & Company
1 John Deere Place, Moline, IL 61265
Phone: 309-765-8000   **Fax:** 309-765-5671
Web: www.deere.com

2009 Sales

	$ mil.	% of total
US & Canada	14,823	64
Other countries	7,961	34
Other revenues	328	2
Total	**23,112**	**100**

PRODUCTS/OPERATIONS

2009 Sales

	$ mil.	% of total
Agricultural & turf	18,122	78
Construction & forestry	2,634	11
Credit	1,930	9
Other	426	2
Total	**23,112**	**100**

Selected Products and Services

Agricultural and Turf equipment
  Balers
  Combines
  Cotton harvesting equipment
  Cutters and shredders
  Golf course equipment
  Harvesters
  Hay and forage equipment
  Irrigation
  Landscape and nursery
  Loaders
  Material handling equipment
  Mowers (commercial, riding lawn equipment and
    walk-behind mowers)
  Planting and seeding equipment
  Power products (outdoor)
  Scrapers
  Seeding
  Sprayers
  Tillage
  Tractors (large, medium, and utility)
  Utility vehicles
Construction and Forestry equipment
  Articulated dump trucks
  Backhoe loaders
  Crawler dozers
  Crawler loaders
  Excavators
  Forestry harvesters
  Forklifts
  Landscape loaders
  Log skidders and loaders
  Motor graders
  Skid steers
Credit
  Leasing
  Retail and wholesale financing
Power systems
  Diesel and natural gas engines (marine, industrial,
    mining)
  Powertrain components
  Transmissions

COMPETITORS

AGCO
Buhler Industries
Caterpillar
CNH Global
Great Plains Manufacturing
Honda
Komatsu
Kubota
Mahindra
Navistar International
Terex
Toro Company
Uzel Makina Sanayi
Valmont Industries
Volvo
Woods Equipment

HISTORICAL FINANCIALS

Company Type: Public

Income Statement

FYE: October 31

	REVENUE ($ mil.)	NET INCOME ($ mil.)	NET PROFIT MARGIN	EMPLOYEES
10/09	23,112	874	3.8%	51,300
10/08	28,438	2,053	7.2%	56,700
10/07	24,082	1,822	7.6%	52,000
10/06	22,148	1,694	7.6%	46,500
10/05	21,931	1,447	6.6%	47,400
Annual Growth	**1.3%**	**(11.9%)**	**—**	**2.0%**

2009 Year-End Financials

Debt ratio: 360.9%
Return on equity: 15.4%
Cash ($ mil.): 4,652
Current ratio: 2.45
Long-term debt ($ mil.): 17,392

No. of shares (mil.): 425
Dividends
  Yield: 2.5%
  Payout: 54.4%
Market value ($ mil.): 19,351

Stock History

NYSE: DE

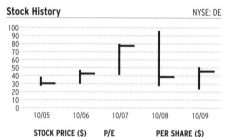

	STOCK PRICE ($) FY Close	P/E High/Low	PER SHARE ($) Earnings	Dividends	Book Value
10/09	45.55	24 12	2.06	1.12	11.34
10/08	38.56	20 6	4.70	1.06	15.38
10/07	77.45	20 11	4.00	0.91	16.84
10/06	42.56	13 9	3.59	0.78	17.63
10/05	30.34	13 10	2.93	0.61	16.13
Annual Growth	**10.7%**	**— —**	**(8.4%)**	**16.4%**	**(8.4%)**

Del Monte Foods

How does Del Monte's garden grow? Very well indeed. The company is one of the US's largest manufacturers of branded canned fruit, vegetables, soups, and broths. It owns no farms of its own but instead purchases fruits and veggies from growers in the US, Mexico, and Venezuela. Del Monte makes tomato-based foods such as ketchup and tomato sauce. Its retail brands include College Inn, Del Monte, and Contadina. The company helps pets grow too, with a stable of popular pet-food and -treat brands, including 9Lives, Gravy Train, Milk-Bone, and Meow Mix. It also makes private-label products as well as ingredients for other food manufacturers, and supplies products to foodservice operators, including the US military.

Del Monte's food operations purchases some 1.3 million tons of fresh fruit, vegetables and tomatoes a year, mostly from US growers, farmers, and agricultural cooperatives. It also procures fresh produce from about 400 growers in Mexico and Venezuela. In addition to the US, the company has food production facilities in Canada, Colombia, Ecuador, Mexico, Peru, and Venezuela. It also uses co-packers in Belgium, Chile, and the Philippines. It purchases commodities (soybean meal, corn, and wheat), as well as meat, meat by-products, vitamins, flavorings, flour and other ingredients for its pet food operations. Pet products are manufactured at five US production facilities; pet-food co-packers are used in the US, American Samoa, and Thailand. Del Monte's customers include pet, specialty, dollar, drug, and convenience stores; retail food outlets; foodservice providers; and other food manufacturers.

HISTORY

Fred Tillman adopted the name Del Monte (originally the name of a coffee blend made for the fancy Hotel Del Monte in Monterey, California) in 1891 for use at his newly formed Oakland Preserving Company. Brand-name labeling was becoming a significant marketing tool, and Del Monte ("of the mountain" in Spanish) became known for high value.

In 1899 Oakland Preserving merged into the California Fruit Canners Association (CFCA) with 17 other canneries (half of California's canning industry). The new company, the largest canner in the world, adopted Del Monte as its main brand name. CFCA merged with other California canneries in 1916 to form Calpak and created national demand for Del Monte products through mass advertising. The company's first ad appeared in the *Saturday Evening Post* in 1917.

Calpak expanded into the Midwest in 1925 by acquiring Rochelle Canneries (Illinois). That year it established British Sales Limited and Philippine Packing Corporation. In later years the company expanded into the Philippines. It weathered slow growth during the Depression, but WWII jump-started Calpak's operations — in 1942 about 40% of the company's products went to feed US troops — and the postwar boom kicked it into high gear.

The company bought control of Canadian Canners Limited, the world's second-largest canner, in 1956, gaining entry into the heavily protected British market. In the 1960s a venture into soft-drink products ended in failure. Calpak changed its name to Del Monte Foods in 1967.

RJR Industries bought Del Monte in 1979 as part of a diversification strategy. In 1989, after its buyout by Kohlberg Kravis Roberts, the newly named, debt-laden RJR Nabisco began selling assets, including Del Monte's Hawaiian Punch line in 1990 and its tropical fruit unit. Merrill Lynch and Del Monte executives bought Del Monte's domestic canning operations in 1990, but the transaction loaded the new company with debt.

To reduce debt, during the 1990s Del Monte sold its dried-fruit operations, its pudding division (to Kraft), and its Mexican subsidiary. Texas Pacific Group, an investment partnership known for recruiting specialists to revive companies, acquired a controlling interest in Del Monte in 1997. It installed Richard Wolford, former president of Dole Packaged Foods, as CEO. That year the company bought Contadina's canned tomato products from Nestlé (which kept the right to use the Contadina brand on refrigerated pasta and sauces).

Interested again in expanding in foreign markets, in 1998 it bought back from Nabisco the rights to the Del Monte brand in South America, and it purchased Nabisco's canned fruits and vegetables business in Venezuela. In 1999 the company completed its IPO. Later that year Del Monte purchased a vegetable processing plant from its competitor Birds Eye Foods and, like all food canners, enjoyed robust sales to Y2K-wary shoppers.

In 2000 Del Monte acquired the Sunfresh brand (citrus and tropical fruits) and a distribution center from The UniMark Group for more than $14 million. Del Monte acquired the S&W brand of canned fruits and vegetables, tomatoes, dry beans, and specialty sauces from bankrupted cooperative Tri Valley Growers for about $39 million in 2001.

Del Monte's 2002 acquisitions from Heinz shifted a mixed bag of stagnant and mature brands off Heinz's plate and more than doubled Del Monte's sales. In addition to StarKist tuna, the deal included Heinz's North American pet food business (9Lives, Kibbles 'n Bits), its US baby food business, and College Inn canned broths.

In 2004 Del Monte sold three of its pet-food brands (IVD, Medi-Cal, and Techni-Cal) to French pet-food company Royal Canin. That same year Del Monte acquired Industrias Citricolas de Montemorelos (ICMOSA), the Mexican subsidiary of The UniMark Group. ICMOSA is a processed tropical and citrus fruit producer and distributor.

The company sold private-label soup and baby food business Nature's Goodness to TreeHouse Foods for about $275 million in 2006. (The TreeHouse deal did not include College Inn broths.) Later that same year, it purchased the Milk-Bone pet product brand from Kraft for $580 million. In addition, it acquired privately held cat food maker Meow Mix Holdings, Inc., for $705 million. These moves were undertaken in the company's ongoing strategy to focus on its higher-margin branded products. The company sold its seafood operations, including StarKist, to South Korean fishery business Dongwon Industries in 2008 for approximately $359 million. The StarKist sale allowed Del Monte to plow even more money back into the company and to continue its focus on its faster-growing, value-added businesses.

EXECUTIVES

Chairman, President, and CEO: Richard G. Wolford, age 65, $7,324,207 total compensation
COO: Nils Lommerin, age 45, $2,387,534 total compensation
EVP Administration and CFO: David L. Meyers, age 64, $2,362,312 total compensation
EVP Sales: Timothy A. (Tim) Cole, age 53, $1,625,315 total compensation
EVP Operations: David W. (Dave) Allen, age 49, $1,518,962 total compensation
EVP Finance: Larry E. Bodner, age 47
SVP, Chief Accounting Officer, Treasurer, and Controller: Richard L. French, age 53
SVP and Chief Marketing Officer: William D. (Bill) Pearce, age 47
SVP and Chief Human Resources Officer: Richard W. Muto
SVP, General Counsel, and Secretary: James G. Potter, age 53
SVP Corporate Service Center and Chief Information Officer: Marc Brown, age 50
Investor Relations: Katherine Husseini
Auditors: KPMG LLP

LOCATIONS

HQ: Del Monte Foods Company
1 Market @ The Landmark
San Francisco, CA 94105
Phone: 415-247-3000 **Fax:** 415-247-3565
Web: www.delmonte.com

2010 Sales

	$ mil.	% of total
US	3,514.2	94
Other	225.6	6
Total	**3,739.8**	**100**

PRODUCTS/OPERATIONS

2010 Sales

	$ mil.	% of total
Consumer products	1,989.8	53
Pet products	1,750.0	47
Total	**3,739.8**	**100**

Selected Brand Names

Consumer products
  College Inn
  Contadina
  Del Monte
  S&W
Pet products
  9Lives
  Alley Cat
  Canine Carry-Outs
  Gravy Train
  Jerky Treats
  Kibbles 'n Bits
  Meaty Bone
  Meow Mix
  Milk-Bone
  Nature's Recipe
  Pounce
  Pup-Peroni
  Snausages
  Wagwells

Selected Products

Canned fruit (apricots, cherries, fruit cocktail, mandarin oranges, mixed and tropical mixed fruit, peaches, pears, pineapples)
Canned soup and broth
Canned tomatoes (chunky, crushed, diced, ketchup, stewed, paste, purée, sauce)
Canned vegetables (asparagus, carrots, corn, mixed and flavored vegetables, peas, potatoes, spinach, zucchini, and green, lima, and wax beans)
Pet food and treats
Sauces (pizza, spaghetti, sloppy Joe)

COMPETITORS

Bush Brothers
Campbell Soup
Chiquita Brands
Colgate-Palmolive
ConAgra
Dole Food
General Mills
Goya
Hanover Foods
Heinz
Hill's Pet Nutrition
Kraft Foods
Mars, Incorporated
Morgan Foods
Nestlé Purina PetCare
Pacific Coast Producers
Pictsweet
Procter & Gamble
Pro-Fac
Royal Canin
Seneca Foods
Simmons Foods
Unilever

HISTORICAL FINANCIALS

Company Type: Public

Income Statement

FYE: Sunday nearest April 30

	REVENUE ($ mil.)	NET INCOME ($ mil.)	NET PROFIT MARGIN	EMPLOYEES
4/10	3,740	244	6.5%	14,700
4/09	3,627	172	4.8%	14,800
4/08	3,737	133	3.6%	18,100
4/07	3,415	113	3.3%	18,200
4/06	2,999	170	5.7%	16,700
Annual Growth	**5.7%**	**9.5%**	**—**	**(3.1%)**

2010 Year-End Financials

Debt ratio: 68.7%
Return on equity: 14.2%
Cash ($ mil.): 54
Current ratio: 2.17
Long-term debt ($ mil.): 1,255
No. of shares (mil.): 200
Dividends
  Yield: 1.3%
  Payout: 16.7%
Market value ($ mil.): 2,984

Stock History

NYSE: DLM

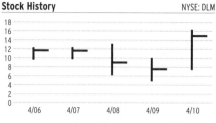

	STOCK PRICE ($) FY Close	P/E High/Low		PER SHARE ($) Earnings	Dividends	Book Value
4/10	14.94	13	6	1.20	0.20	9.15
4/09	7.55	11	6	0.87	0.16	8.04
4/08	9.02	20	10	0.66	0.16	7.51
4/07	11.60	22	18	0.55	0.16	7.27
4/06	11.66	15	12	0.83	0.08	6.58
Annual Growth	**6.4%**	**—**	**—**	**9.7%**	**25.7%**	**8.6%**

Dell Inc.

Dell wants its name to ring from the desktop to the data center. One of the world's top suppliers of personal computers, the company offers a broad range of technology products for the consumer, education, enterprise, and government sectors. In addition to a full line of desktop and notebook PCs, Dell offers network servers, data storage systems, printers, Ethernet switches, and peripherals such as displays and projectors. It also markets third-party software and hardware. Dell's growing services unit provides infrastructure consulting, systems integration, asset recovery, financing, support, and training.

Michael Dell pioneered the direct-sales model for computers and took the company from his dorm room to the top of the PC heap by keeping it focused on a simple formula: Eliminate the middleman and sell for less. Dell's built-to-order boxes allow for lower inventories, lower costs, and higher profit margins — elements that have served it well through PC price wars and IT spending recessions.

In 2009 Dell acquired Perot Systems for about $3.9 billion in cash. The transaction allows the company to deliver a broader range of IT services, particularly to clients in the US. Dell will be able to sell more computers to Perot clients through the combination.

Faced with slowing sales rates in the domestic PC market, Michael Dell has overseen an aggressive campaign to reposition the company for growth. Most significantly Dell has shifted its sales approach. Prior to 2007 Dell had practically no retail presence. Since then the company has partnered with stores such as Best Buy and Wal-Mart, as well as systems integrators, resellers, and distributors worldwide.

The company is looking to international revenue from developing markets such as Brazil, China, India, and Russia to supplant weak sales in the US. The company has also looked overseas to find operational cost-saving opportunities. Based in Singapore, Dell's Asia/Pacific segment includes manufacturing and distribution units in China, India, and Malaysia.

The company also provides servers, storage devices, and networking equipment. In June 2010 the company agreed to buy privately held Scalent Systems. Scalent makes software that is used to enhance scalability and efficiency in data center infrastructure, and Dell looks to combine the software with its servers, storage, and networking products. In August 2010 Dell moved to further expand its storage expertise when it announced plans to purchase 3PAR for about $1.13 billion. Shortly after 3PAR agreed to be acquired, HP stepped up with an unsolicited bid of $1.5 billion. Dell and HP then jockeyed back and forth with increasing bids, with HP coming out on top with a high bid of $1.88 billion.

The company's software and peripherals segment encompasses Dell-branded displays and printers, as well as third-party peripherals, consumer and enterprise software, digital cameras, printers, and televisions.

Michael Dell owns about 12% of the company.

HISTORY

At age 13 Michael Dell was already a successful businessman. From his parents' home in Houston, Dell ran a mail-order stamp trading business that, within a few months, grossed more than $2,000. At 16 he sold newspaper subscriptions and at 17 bought his first BMW. When Dell enrolled at the University of Texas in 1983, he was thoroughly bitten by the entrepreneurial bug.

Dell started college as a pre-med student but found time to establish a business selling random-access memory (RAM) chips and disk drives for IBM PCs. Dell bought products at cost from IBM dealers, who were required at the time to order from IBM large monthly quotas of PCs, which frequently exceeded demand. Dell resold his stock through newspapers and computer magazines at 10%-15% below retail.

By April 1984 Dell's dorm room computer-components business was grossing about $80,000 a month — enough to persuade him to drop out of college. Soon he started making and selling IBM clones under the brand name PC's Limited. Dell sold his machines directly to consumers rather than through retail outlets, as most manufacturers did. By eliminating the retail markup, Dell could sell PCs at about 40% of the price of an IBM.

The company was plagued by management changes during the mid-1980s. Renamed Dell Computer, it added international sales offices in 1987. In 1988 the company started selling to larger customers, including government agencies. That year Dell went public.

The company tripped in 1990, reporting a 64% drop in profits. Sales were growing — but so were costs, mostly because of efforts to design a PC using proprietary components and reduced instruction set computer (RISC) chips. Within a year Dell turned itself around by cutting inventories and introducing new products.

Dell entered the retail arena by letting Soft Warehouse (now CompUSA) in 1990 and office supply chain Staples in 1991 sell its PCs at mail-order prices, but the computer maker abandoned retail stores in 1994 to refocus on its mail-order origins. It also retooled its troubled notebook computer line and introduced servers.

In 1996 the company started selling PCs through its website. The next year Dell entered the market for workstations and strengthened its consumer business by separating it from its small-business unit and launching a leasing program for consumers. In 1998 the company stepped up manufacturing in the Americas and Europe and added a production and customer facility in China.

In 1999 the company made its first acquisition — storage area network equipment maker ConvergeNet. Faced with slumping PC sales in early 2001, the company eliminated 1,700 jobs — about 4% of its workforce. Late that year it expanded its storage offerings when it agreed to resell systems from EMC. Looking to grow its services unit, Dell acquired Microsoft software support specialist Plural in 2002.

The following year the company shortened its name to simply Dell Inc. Dell himself stepped down as CEO in mid-July 2004. Company president Kevin Rollins filled the position, but Dell remained chairman.

In 2007 Rollins resigned as CEO and as a member of the board of directors, and Dell reassumed the top role. Rollins' resignation came as the company struggled with a number of difficult issues, most notably disappointing earnings and an SEC investigation into its finances. (Dell restated several years of financial results after an audit revealed accounting irregularities.)

In mid-2007 the company announced plans to cut its workforce by 10% over the next year.

Early in 2008 Dell acquired storage systems provider EqualLogic for $1.4 billion.

EXECUTIVES

Chairman and CEO: Michael S. Dell, age 45, $963,623 total compensation
Vice Chairman Operations and Technology: Jeffrey W. (Jeff) Clarke, age 47
SVP and CFO: Brian T. Gladden, age 45, $5,120,111 total compensation
SVP and Chief Marketing Officer: Erin Nelson, age 40
SVP, General Counsel, and Secretary: Lawrence P. (Larry) Tu, age 55
SVP Consumer, Small, and Medium Business: Alexander (Alex) Gruzen, age 45
SVP Enterprise Product Group: Bradley R. (Brad) Anderson, age 50
SVP, Dell.com: Ronald V. (Ron) Rose, age 59
SVP Human Resources: Steve H. Price
VP Corporate Finance: Thomas W. Sweet, age 49
VP Finance; President, Dell Financial Services: Don Berman
VP and General Manager, Original Equipment Manufacturers: Rick Froehlich
President, Services: Peter A. Altabef, age 50, $17,258,084 total compensation
President, Communication Solutions: Ronald G. (Ron) Garriques, age 46, $8,393,132 total compensation
President, Large Enterprise: Stephen F. (Steve) Schuckenbrock, age 49, $10,665,312 total compensation
President, Consumer, Small and Medium Business: Stephen J. (Steve) Felice, age 52, $8,166,259 total compensation
President, Public: Paul D. Bell, age 49
Global Communications: Kelly McGinnis
Investor Relations: Robert Williams
Auditors: PricewaterhouseCoopers LLP

LOCATIONS

HQ: Dell Inc.
1 Dell Way, Round Rock, TX 78682
Phone: 512-338-4400   **Fax:** 512-283-6161
Web: www.dell.com

2010 Sales

	$ mil.	% of total
US	28,053	53
Other countries	24,849	47
Total	**52,902**	**100**

PRODUCTS/OPERATIONS

2010 Sales

	$ mil.	% of total
Products	43,697	83
Services & software	9,205	17
Total	**52,902**	**100**

2010 Sales

	$ mil.	% of total
Client		
Mobility	16,610	31
Desktop PCs	12,947	25
Software & peripherals	9,499	18
Services	5,622	11
Enterprise solutions		
Servers & networking	6,032	11
Storage	2,192	4
Total	**52,902**	**100**

2010 Sales by Market

	$ mil.	% of total
Public	14,484	27
Large enterprise	14,285	27
Small & medium business	12,079	23
Consumer	12,054	23
Total	**52,902**	**100**

Selected Products

Computers
 Desktop (Alienware, Dimension, OptiPlex, Studio, Vostro, XPS)
 Notebook (Adamo, Inspiron, Latitude, Vostro, XPS)
Enterprise systems
 Network servers (PowerEdge)
 Storage (EqualLogic, PowerVault)
 Workstations (Precision)
Ethernet switches (PowerConnect)
Point-of-sale systems
Printers
 Inkjet multifunction
 Laser
Projectors
Refurbished systems
Smartphones (Mini 3)
Third-party peripherals and software

COMPETITORS

Acer
Apple Inc.
ASUSTeK
BenQ
Brother Industries
Canon
CDW
Cisco Systems
EMC
Enterasys
Epson
Extreme Networks
Fujitsu Technology Solutions
HCL Infosystems
Hedy Holding
Hewlett-Packard
Hitachi
IBM
Insight Enterprises
Lenovo
NEC
Panasonic Corp
PC Connection
Positivo Informática
Sony
Tatung
Toshiba
Unisys

HISTORICAL FINANCIALS

Company Type: Public

Income Statement

FYE: Sunday nearest January 31

	REVENUE ($ mil.)	NET INCOME ($ mil.)	NET PROFIT MARGIN	EMPLOYEES
1/10	52,902	1,433	2.7%	96,000
1/09	61,101	2,478	4.1%	78,900
1/08	61,133	2,947	4.8%	88,200
1/07	57,420	2,583	4.5%	90,500
1/06	55,908	3,572	6.4%	66,100
Annual Growth	(1.4%)	(20.4%)	—	9.8%

2010 Year-End Financials

Debt ratio: 60.6%
Return on equity: 28.9%
Cash ($ mil.): 10,635
Current ratio: 1.28
Long-term debt ($ mil.): 3,417

No. of shares (mil.): 1,958
Dividends
  Yield: —
  Payout: —
Market value ($ mil.): 25,262

Stock History

NASDAQ (GS): DELL

	STOCK PRICE ($) FY Close	P/E High/Low	PER SHARE ($) Earnings	Dividends	Book Value
1/10	12.90	24 11	0.73	—	2.88
1/09	9.50	21 7	1.25	—	2.18
1/08	20.04	23 14	1.31	—	1.91
1/07	24.22	28 17	1.14	—	2.21
1/06	29.31	29 20	1.46	—	2.11
Annual Growth	(18.5%)	— —	(15.9%)	—	8.1%

Deloitte Touche Tohmatsu

This company is "deloitted" to make your acquaintance, particularly if you're a big business in need of accounting services. Deloitte Touche Tohmatsu (or Deloitte) is one of accounting's Big Four, along with Ernst & Young, KPMG, and PricewaterhouseCoopers. Deloitte operates through some 150 independent firms around the world, including US-based Deloitte LLP and its accounting arm, Deloitte & Touche LLP. Each independent member firm works in a specific geographic area offering audit, tax, consulting, risk management, and financial advisory services, in addition to human resources and technology services. Deloitte Touche Tohmatsu coordinates its member firms but does not provide services to clients.

The company was impacted by the global economic crisis and clients' ability to remain financially flexible during the downturn. Revenues from consulting remained strong during the recession, while tax and audit revenues were flat. Merger and acquisition activity languished during the recession and that was reflected in a drop in Deloitte's revenues from financial advisory services.

The company is looking to expand its presence in emerging markets such as China, India, Brazil, southeast Asia, and the Middle East. Deloitte has worked to establish new member firms in those regions and attract employees.

Deloitte also is keen on developing its capabilities in growing sectors of business. The company made a move in 2009 to increase its presence in the growing government services market with the purchase of North American public services practice of BearingPoint, which had filed for Chapter 11 bankruptcy protection. The $350 million deal helped position Deloitte as a top provider of professional services for the US government.

Deloitte made a rather unusual acquisition in 2010, acquiring Simulstrat, a scenario simulation program for public and private sector organizations, commonly known as war gaming. The program is a spinoff from the Department of War Studies at Kings College of London. Based on military methodology, Simulstrat helps organizations prepare for complex future political, economic, social, environmental, technological, legal, and regulatory events.

HISTORY

In 1845 William Deloitte opened an accounting office in London, at first soliciting business from bankrupts. The growth of joint stock companies and the development of stock markets in the mid-19th century created a need for standardized financial reporting and fueled the rise of auditing, and Deloitte moved into the new field. The Great Western Railway appointed him as its independent auditor (the first anywhere) in 1849.

In 1890 John Griffiths, who had become a partner in 1869, opened the company's first US office in New York City. Four decades later branches had opened throughout the US. In 1952 the firm partnered with Haskins & Sells, which operated 34 US offices.

Deloitte aimed to be "the Cadillac, not the Ford" of accounting. The firm, which became Deloitte Haskins & Sells in 1978, began shedding its conservatism as competition heated up; it was the first of the major accountancy firms to use aggressive ads.

The firm spent the 1980s and 1990s pursuing a strategy of using accountants and consultants in concert to provide seamless service in auditing, accounting, strategic planning, information technology, financial management, and productivity. In 1984 Deloitte Haskins & Sells tried to merge with Price Waterhouse, but the deal was dropped after Price Waterhouse's UK partners objected.

In 1989 Deloitte Haskins & Sells joined the flamboyant Touche Ross (founded 1899) to become Deloitte & Touche. Touche Ross's Japanese affiliate, Ross Tohmatsu (founded 1968) rounded out the current name. The merger was engineered by Deloitte's Michael Cook and Touche's Edward Kangas, in part to unite the former firm's US and European strengths with the latter's Asian presence. Cook continued to oversee US operations, with Kangas presiding over international operations. Many affiliates, particularly in the UK, rejected the merger and defected to competing firms.

As auditors were increasingly held accountable for the financial results of their clients, legal action soared. In the 1990s Deloitte was sued because of its actions relating to Drexel Burnham Lambert junk bond king Michael Milken, the failure of several savings and loans, and clients' bankruptcies.

Nevertheless, in 1995 the SEC chose Michael Sutton, the firm's national director of auditing and accounting practice, as its chief accountant. That year Deloitte formed Deloitte & Touche Consulting to consolidate its US and UK consulting operations; its Asian consulting operations were later added to facilitate regional expansion. Deloitte Consulting became Deloitte's fastest-growing line, offering strategic and management consulting in addition to information technology and human resources consulting services.

Increasingly, Deloitte and its peers came under fire for their combined accounting/consulting operations; regulators and observers wondered whether accountants could maintain objectivity when they were auditing clients for whom they also provided consulting services.

The Asian economic crisis hurt overseas expansion in 1998, but provided a boost in restructuring consulting. In 1999 Kangas stepped down as CEO to be succeeded by James Copeland.

In 2001 the SEC forced Deloitte & Touche to restate the financial results of Pre-Paid Legal Services. In an unusual move, Deloitte & Touche publicly disagreed with the SEC's findings.

The accountancy put some old trouble to bed in 2003 when it agreed to pay $23 million to settle claims it had been negligent in its auditing of failed Kentucky Life Insurance, a client in the 1980s. Later that year the UK's High Court found Deloitte negligent in audits related to the failed Barings Bank; however, the ruling was considered something of a victory for the accountancy because it essentially cleared Deloitte of the majority of charges against it and effectively limited its financial liability in the matter.

Copeland retired from the global CEO's office that year and handed the reins over to Bill Parrett, who had formerly served as managing director for the US and the Americas. Parrett was succeeded in 2007 by Jim Quigley, who'd served as CEO of Deloitte's US arm.

EXECUTIVES

Chairman: John P. Connolly
CEO: James H. (Jim) Quigley, age 58
CFO: Jeffrey P. (Jeff) Rohr
Chief Information Officer: Wolfgang Richter
Chief Knowledge Officer: Tracey Edwards
Global Managing Partner Consulting and Executive Member, US: Ainar D. Aijala Jr.
Global Managing Partner Strategic Client Program: Otmar Thoemmes
Global Managing Partner Financial Advisory Services and Executive Member, Canada: Frank Vettese
Global Managing Partner Tax: Dan Lange
Global Managing Partner Talent and Executive Member, United Kingdom: Vassi Naidoo
Global Managing Partner Audit and Executive Member, France: Alain Pons
Global Managing Partner Services and M&A and Executive Member, US: Jerry P. Leamon
Global Managing Partner Regulatory and Risk and Executive Member, US: Jeffrey K. (Jeff) Willemain
Global Brand and Marketing Director: Luis Gallardo
Global Middle Market Leader: Mike Owens
Human Resources Operations: Peter May
Chief Strategy Officer: Mumtaz Ahmed
General Counsel: Philip Rotner
Director Global PR and CEO Communications: Madonna Jarrett
EMEA Managing Partner: Jan Dalhuisen

LOCATIONS

HQ: Deloitte Touche Tohmatsu
  1633 Broadway, New York, NY 10019
Phone: 212-489-1600   **Fax:** 212-489-1687
Web: www.deloitte.com/global

2009 Sales by Region

	% of total
Americas	48
Europe/Middle East/Africa	39
Asia/Pacific	13
Total	**100**

PRODUCTS/OPERATIONS

2009 Sales

	% of total
Audit	46
Consulting	25
Tax	22
Financial advisory services	7
Total	**100**

2009 Sales by Industry

	% of total
Financial services	26
Consumer business & transportation	20
Manufacturing	14
Telecommunications, media & technology	11
Energy & resources	8
Public sector	8
Life sciences	7
Other	6
Total	**100**

Selected Products and Services

Audit
  Auditing services
  Global offerings services
  International financial reporting conversion services

Consulting
  Enterprise applications
  Human capital
  Outsourcing
  Strategy and operations
  Technology integration

Sustainability and Climate Change
  Assurance services
  Consulting
  Financial advisory
  Risk services
  Tax

Tax
  Corporate tax
  Global tax compliance
  Indirect tax
  International assignment services
  International tax
  M&A transaction services
  Research and development credits
  Tax publications
  Tax technologies
  Transfer pricing

Financial Advisory
  Corporate finance
  Forensic services
  Reorganization services
  Transaction services
  Valuation services

Other
  Enterprise Risk Services
    Capital markets
    Control assurance
    Corporate responsibility and sustainability
    Internal audit
    Regulatory consulting
    Security and privacy services

Merger and Acquisition Services

COMPETITORS

Accenture
BDO International
Booz Allen
Boston Consulting
Capgemini
Ernst & Young Global
Grant Thornton International
HP Enterprise Services
KPMG
Marsh & McLennan
McKinsey & Company
PricewaterhouseCoopers

HISTORICAL FINANCIALS

Company Type: Private

Income Statement

FYE: May 31

	REVENUE ($ mil.)	NET INCOME ($ mil.)	NET PROFIT MARGIN	EMPLOYEES
5/09	26,100	—	—	168,651
5/08	27,400	—	—	165,000
5/07	23,100	—	—	146,600
5/06	20,000	—	—	135,000
5/05	18,200	—	—	121,283
Annual Growth	9.4%	—	—	8.6%

Revenue History

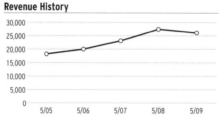

Delphi Financial Group

One doesn't need an oracle to see that Delphi Financial Group knows a thing or two about employee benefits and insurance. Through Reliance Standard Life and Safety National Casualty, Delphi sells life, disability, excess workers' compensation, and personal accident insurance to small and midsized businesses. Its Matrix Absence Management subsidiary provides disability and absence management services to larger employers. The company also offers asset accumulation products, mainly annuities, to individuals and groups. Delphi Financial products are sold through independent brokers and agents.

Delphi has grown by acquiring insurance and financial firms, as well as blocks of insurance business. Faced with a hard excess workers' compensation market, the company was able to raise prices and increase new production. Part of Delphi's strategy is to become firmly entrenched in niche insurance markets (such as absence management) where there is less competition.

The company has also introduced several new products over the past couple years, including a limited benefit health insurance product called RSL BasicCare and an equity indexed annuity product called Keystone.

Chairman and CEO Robert Rosenkranz owns all of the company's Class B stock, giving him control over 49.9% of the votes affecting the company. By agreement, Rosenkranz will never exercise any more than 49.9% control of Delphi.

HISTORY

Investment firm Rosencranz & Co. formed Delphi Financial Group predecessor RSL Holding in 1987 to acquire Reliance Standard Life (founded in 1907). Between 1988 and 1992 it made five block acquisitions of annuities (including nearly $1 billion in liabilities). The company went public in 1990.

In 1994 it bought the long-term-care insurance business of Blue Cross & Blue Shield of Connecticut. (Sales of long-term-care insurance slumped, so Delphi Financial discontinued the line in 1996 and sold it in 1997.) To avoid the heavy liability associated with acquired annuities, the company began marketing its own in 1995.

In the mid-1990s the company began to focus on employee benefits. In 1996 Delphi bought Safety National Casualty, one of the US's oldest writers of excess workers' compensation insurance. The purchase allowed Delphi to offer stop-loss coverage for self-insured companies. In 1997 it formed Delphi International to expand its services to self-insurers and provide reinsurance for its own policies, including Reliance Standard Life and Safety National. To hedge its workers' compensation operations, the firm acquired reinsurance pool Unicover Managers in 1998, then sold it in 1999 after discovering it had been selling workers' compensation policies too cheaply to cover future claims. In the wake of that debacle, the company in 2000 said it would look internally for growth, concentrating on integrated disability and absence management.

Delphi Financial Group capitalized on the hard workers' compensation market by raising prices in 2002, which helped grow the company's net income. Reliance Standard increased its group employee benefits business (primarily the small companies niche), which also helped grow revenues.

At the end of 2005 the company discontinued its property catastrophe reinsurance business due to the volatile nature of that segment.

EXECUTIVES

Chairman and CEO: Robert Rosenkranz, age 67, $4,388,477 total compensation
President, COO, and Director: Donald A. Sherman, age 59, $1,492,810 total compensation
EVP Business Development and Director: Harold F. Ilg, age 62
SVP, Secretary and General Counsel; SVP, General Counsel, and Assistant Secretary, Reliance Standard Life Insurance: Chad W. Coulter, age 47
VP and Treasurer; SVP and Treasurer, Reliance Standard Life Insurance: Thomas W. Burghart, age 51, $752,553 total compensation
VP Finance: Nita I. Savage
VP Investor Relations: Bernard J. Kilkelly
President and CEO, Reliance Standard Life Insurance: Lawrence E. Daurelle, age 58, $1,080,979 total compensation
President and COO, Matrix Absence Management: Ivars Zvirbulis
CEO, Safety National Casualty: Mark A. Wilhelm
Auditors: Ernst & Young LLP

LOCATIONS

HQ: Delphi Financial Group, Inc.
  1105 N. Market St., Ste. 1230
  Wilmington, DE 19899
Phone: 302-478-5142   **Fax:** 302-427-7663
Web: www.delphifin.com

Selected Subsidiaries

Matrix Absence Management
Reliance Standard Life Insurance Company
Safety National Casualty Corporation

PRODUCTS/OPERATIONS

2009 Sales

	% of total
Disability income	42
Life	29
Excess workers' compensation	21
Assumed workers' compensation & casualty reinsurance	2
Limited benefit health insurance	2
Accident & dental	4
Total	**100**

COMPETITORS

Accident Fund	New York Life
AIG	PMA Capital
CNA Financial	Prudential
GatesMcDonald	StanCorp Financial Group
Liberty Mutual	Unum Group
Meadowbrook Insurance	Zenith National

HISTORICAL FINANCIALS

Company Type: Public

Income Statement
FYE: December 31

	ASSETS ($ mil.)	NET INCOME ($ mil.)	INCOME AS % OF ASSETS	EMPLOYEES
12/09	6,921	99	1.4%	1,800
12/08	5,954	37	0.6%	1,700
12/07	6,095	165	2.7%	1,551
12/06	5,671	142	2.5%	1,410
12/05	5,276	113	2.1%	1,170
Annual Growth	7.0%	(3.3%)	—	11.4%

2009 Year-End Financials

Equity as % of assets: 19.6%	Dividends
Return on assets: 1.5%	Yield: 1.8%
Return on equity: 9.1%	Payout: 20.9%
Long-term debt ($ mil.): 596	Market value ($ mil.): 1,214
No. of shares (mil.): 54	Sales ($ mil.): 1,572

Stock History

NYSE: DFG

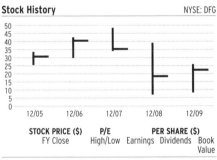

	STOCK PRICE ($) FY Close	P/E High/Low		PER SHARE ($) Earnings	Dividends	Book Value
12/09	22.37	13	5	1.91	0.40	25.04
12/08	18.44	51	10	0.75	0.39	15.12
12/07	35.28	15	11	3.19	0.35	21.03
12/06	40.46	15	11	2.79	0.31	21.65
12/05	30.67	15	12	2.25	0.24	19.04
Annual Growth	(7.6%)	—	—	(4.0%)	13.6%	7.1%

Delta Air Lines

Just as a delta is a symbol for change in math, Delta Air Lines symbolizes the changing mathematics of the airline industry. Delta became the world's largest airline by traffic after its $2.8 billion acquisition of Northwest Airlines in 2008. Through its regional carriers (including subsidiary Comair), the combined company serves more than 365 destinations in more than 65 countries, and it operates a mainline fleet of about 800 aircraft. Delta is a founding member of the SkyTeam marketing and code-sharing alliance (allowing airlines to sell tickets on one another's flights and thus extend their networks), which includes carriers such as Air France, KLM, and Alitalia.

Delta finished integrating Northwest's infrastructure, flight network, reservation systems, and brands with its own operations in early 2010. With is mainline operations bolstered, Delta shed two regional carriers that had been part of the Northwest deal, Mesaba Airlines and Compass Airlines.

The SkyTeam alliance extends Delta's reach to more than 900 destinations in almost 170 countries around the globe. Looking to become the preferred carrier in New York City, Delta announced in 2010 that it is adding about 30 flights between the Big Apple and key business markets, both domestic and international. Italy-based Alitalia joined SkyTeam in mid-2010.

Outside North America, Delta's international offerings are strongest in Europe and Latin America, which together account for some 30% of the company's sales. To expand its service in the Asia/Pacific region, Delta has joined other major airlines in applying for some of the limited number of nonstop routes available between the US and mainland China. Through its combination with Northwest, Delta launched nonstop flights between Seattle and Beijing and between Detroit and Shanghai in 2009.

Delta hopes to profit from a joint venture with Air France-KLM that covers the carriers' trans-Atlantic flights. The airlines will share revenue and split the cost of trans-Atlantic flights between the US, Canada, Mexico, Europe, the Mediterranean, Africa, the Middle East, India, and Latin America. In 2009 Delta announced a joint venture with Virgin Blue for flights on trans-Pacific routes between the US and Australia and the South Pacific.

Delta has gained ground since emerging from Chapter 11 bankruptcy protection in 2007, but an unprecedented surge in fuel prices in 2008 followed by a severe drop in travel demand caused the carrier to renew its efforts to control costs. In 2008 Delta offered buyout packages to about 30,000 of the company's 55,000 employees, and about 4,000 accepted — twice the number the company expected. The carrier also slashed international capacity by 15% and domestic capacity by 10%.

HISTORY

Delta Air Lines was founded in Macon, Georgia, in 1924 as the world's first crop-dusting service, Huff-Daland Dusters, to combat boll weevil infestation of cotton fields. It moved to Monroe, Louisiana, in 1925. In 1928 field manager C. E. Woolman and two partners bought the service and renamed it Delta Air Service after the Mississippi Delta region it served.

In 1929 Delta pioneered passenger service from Dallas to Jackson, Mississippi. Flying mail without a government subsidy, Delta finally got a US Postal Service contract in 1934 to fly from Fort Worth to Charleston via Atlanta. Delta relocated to Atlanta in 1941. Woolman became president in 1945 and managed the airline until he died in 1966.

Delta added more flights, including a direct route from Chicago to New Orleans with its 1952 purchase of Chicago and Southern Airlines. It offered its first transcontinental flight in 1961. In 1972 the airline bought Northeast Airlines and added service to New England and Canada; it offered service to the UK in 1978, the year that the US airline industry was deregulated.

In 1982 Delta's employees pledged $30 million to buy a Boeing 767 jet, christened *The Spirit of Delta*, as a token of appreciation. In fiscal 1983 the company succumbed to the weak US economy and posted its first loss ever; it quickly became profitable again in 1985. Delta began service to Asia in 1987, the year that longtime employee Ronald Allen became CEO. In 1990 Delta joined TWA and Northwest to form Worldspan, a computer reservation service.

Despite a slump in 1990 earnings, in 1991 Delta bought gates, planes, and Canadian routes from Eastern, as well as Pan Am's New York-Boston shuttle, European routes, and Frankfurt hub. The purchases elevated Delta from a domestic player to a top international carrier, but they also contributed to a $2 billion loss.

Allen began a cost-reduction plan in 1994 that cut many routes and 15,000 jobs over the next three years. However, it also drove down employee morale and Delta's customer service reputation. Allen was let go in 1997 and replaced by Leo Mullin, a former electric utility chief.

Delta bought regional carriers Atlantic Southeast Airlines and Comair. An 89-day pilots' strike led to flight cancellations at Comair in 2001.

In the wake of the September 11, 2001, terrorist attacks on New York and Washington, DC, and the resulting reduction in air travel, Delta cut back its flight schedule and reduced its workforce by about 15% (about 13,000 employees).

In 2003 CEO Leo Mullin resigned and was replaced by Gerald Grinstein, a Delta director. Also in 2003, the federal government approved the largest code-share agreement among US airlines, which included Delta as well as Continental and Northwest.

Delta cut costs significantly during 2005 in an effort to avoid bankruptcy. In a last-ditch bid to raise cash, the company sold its Atlantic Southeast Airlines unit to SkyWest for $425 million in September 2005. Days later, however, the combination of high fuel prices and a string of losses from operations dating back to 2001 finally forced Delta to file for Chapter 11 protection.

A milestone in Delta's journey back to solvency was reached in May 2006, when the company's pilots voted to accept a contract with changes in pay, benefits, and work rules designed to save Delta about $280 million a year. Delta exited Chapter 11 in April 2007 as an independent company.

Richard Anderson, the former CEO of Northwest Airlines, succeeded Grinstein as Delta's CEO in September 2007. A year later he steered the company through one of the airline industry's biggest mergers when Delta acquired Northwest Airlines for $2.8 billion in October 2008. The acquisition sent shockwaves throughout the industry and made Delta the #1 airline in the world by traffic.

EXECUTIVES

Chairman: Daniel A. (Dan) Carp, age 61
Vice Chairman: Roy J. Bostock, age 69
CEO and Director: Richard H. Anderson, age 54,
$8,375,332 total compensation
President and Director: Edward H. (Ed) Bastian, age 52,
$4,015,585 total compensation
EVP and COO: Stephen E. (Steve) Gorman, age 55,
$2,799,395 total compensation
EVP Network Planning and Revenue Management:
Glen W. Hauenstein, age 49,
$2,226,606 total compensation
SVP and CFO: Hank Halter, age 45,
$1,579,092 total compensation
EVP Human Resources and Labor Relations:
Michael H. (Mike) Campbell, age 61,
$5,004,133 total compensation
SVP International: Laura H. Liu
SVP Flight Operations: Stephen (Steve) Dickson
SVP Operations Control: Neil Stronach, age 44
SVP Finance and Treasurer: Paul A. Jacobson
SVP and CIO: Theresa Wise
SVP Human Resources: Elizabeth (Beth) Johnston
SVP Maintenance Operations: John Laughter, age 39
SVP and General Counsel: Richard B. (Ben) Hirst,
age 65
SVP Marketing: Tim Mapes
SVP Delta Connection: Donald T. (Don) Bornhorst,
age 45
SVP Global Sales and Distribution: Jim Cron
SVP Government Affairs: Andrea Fischer Newman
SVP Airport Customer Service: Gil West, age 49
SVP and Chief Communications Officer:
John E. (Ned) Walker, age 57
President, Comair: John N. Selvaggio, age 63
President and CEO, Delta Technology:
Shirley W. Bridges
President, Delta TechOps: Anthony N. (Tony) Charaf,
age 62
President, DAL Global Services: Cyril J. Turner, age 47
Auditors: Ernst & Young LLP

LOCATIONS

HQ: Delta Air Lines, Inc.
1030 Delta Blvd., Atlanta, GA 30320
Phone: 404-715-2600   **Fax:** 404-715-5042
Web: www.delta.com

2009 Sales

	$ mil.	% of total
North America	19,171	68
Atlantic	4,970	18
Pacific	2,485	9
Latin America	1,437	5
Total	**28,063**	**100**

PRODUCTS/OPERATIONS

2009 Sales

	$ mil.	% of total
Passenger		
Mainline	18,522	66
Regional affiliates	5,285	19
Cargo	788	3
Other	3,468	12
Total	**28,063**	**100**

COMPETITORS

ACE Aviation	Qantas
AirTran Holdings	SAS
AMR Corp.	Singapore Airlines
British Airways	Southwest Airlines
Cathay Pacific	UAL
Japan Airlines	US Airways
JetBlue	Virgin Atlantic Airways
Lufthansa	

HISTORICAL FINANCIALS

Company Type: Public

Income Statement

FYE: December 31

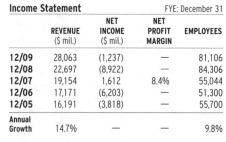

	REVENUE ($ mil.)	NET INCOME ($ mil.)	NET PROFIT MARGIN	EMPLOYEES
12/09	28,063	(1,237)	—	81,106
12/08	22,697	(8,922)	—	84,306
12/07	19,154	1,612	8.4%	55,044
12/06	17,171	(6,203)	—	51,300
12/05	16,191	(3,818)	—	55,700
Annual Growth	**14.7%**	**—**	**—**	**9.8%**

2009 Year-End Financials

Debt ratio: 6,393.9%   No. of shares (mil.): 789
Return on equity: —   Dividends
Cash ($ mil.): 4,607   Yield: —
Current ratio: 0.79   Payout: —
Long-term debt ($ mil.): 15,665   Market value ($ mil.): 8,977

Stock History

NYSE: DAL

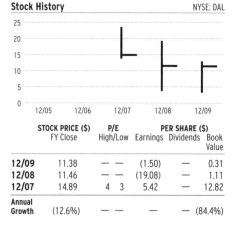

	STOCK PRICE ($) FY Close	P/E High	P/E Low	PER SHARE ($) Earnings	PER SHARE ($) Dividends	PER SHARE ($) Book Value
12/09	11.38	—	—	(1.50)	—	0.31
12/08	11.46	—	—	(19.08)	—	1.11
12/07	14.89	4	3	5.42	—	12.82
Annual Growth	**(12.6%)**	**—**	**—**	**—**	**—**	**(84.4%)**

Deluxe Corporation

When money can move at the speed of a mouse click, Deluxe wants to do more than keep its revenues in check. The company is a leading printer of checks in the US, serving the nation's banks, credit unions, and financial services companies. Checks and business forms account for the majority of Deluxe's sales; it sells checkbook covers and address labels, as well as stationery, greeting cards, stored-value gift cards, labels, and packaging supplies online. Deluxe also provides Web design services through its Hostopia.com unit. The company's Direct Checks division is the nation's #1 direct-to-consumer seller of personal and business checks under the brands Checks Unlimited and Designer Checks.

Check writing was already on the decline, due to the shift to electronic payment methods, when the recession in the US and turmoil in the financial services industry conspired to depress check volume even more. In a bid to drive down costs amid decreasing sales, in 2009 Deluxe closed call centers located in New Jersey and California and shut down seven manufacturing plants. The shutdowns come as the firm moves to expand its use of digital printing processes. The cost-cutting moves also come after the company was dethroned from the top position in the check printing industry as a result of the 2007 merger of its two primary competitors:

John H. Harland and Clarke American to form Harland Clarke.

In 2010 the company bought Custom Direct, Inc., a provider of checks based in Maryland, for $98 million. The deal enhanced Deluxe's toehold in the direct-to-consumer channel.

To diversify, Deluxe has been shifting its focus from checks to small business services with the aim of becoming a leading supplier of checks, business forms, Web services, marketing materials, and more to these clients.

In 2009 it obtained MerchEngines, a firm that helps small business owners to advertise directly using search engines like Google and Yahoo! MerchEngines automates the process of choosing keyword targets and creating ads, as well as tracking and reporting results.

Also that year, it bought Abacus America Inc., doing business as Aplus.net. The transaction gave Hostopia access to Aplus' 80,000 small business subscribers of shared Web hosting website management applications.

HISTORY

Deluxe Corporation began in 1915 with the determination of William Hotchkiss, a newspaper publisher turned chicken farmer, to produce one product "better, faster, and more economically than anyone else." From his office in St. Paul, Minnesota, Hotchkiss set out to provide banks with business checks within 48 hours of receiving the order. Deluxe Check Printers made just $23 that year. However, when a new Federal Reserve Bank was established in Minneapolis, the region soon became a major national banking center.

In the 1920s Hotchkiss introduced the most successful product in Deluxe's history: the Handy, a pocket-sized check. During the Depression the company cut employee hours and pay, but not jobs.

George McSweeney, a sales manager, created the Personalized Check Program in 1939 and was named president two years later. During WWII he stabilized the company by printing ration forms for banks. In the 1950s Deluxe was one of the first firms to implement the government's magnetic-ink character-recognition program.

By 1960 the company was selling its printing services to 99% of US commercial banks. Deluxe went public in 1965. The company integrated computers and advanced printing technology into production during the 1970s.

In the following decade Deluxe positioned itself to profit from the increasing automation of transactions, making acquisitions such as Chex-Systems (account verification, 1984), Colwell Systems (medical business forms, 1985), A. O. Smith Data Systems (banking software, 1986), and Current (mail-order greeting cards and checks, 1987). It established a UK base in 1992 with Stockforms Ltd. (computer forms). Deluxe closed about a fourth of its check-printing plants in 1993, the first layoffs in the firm's history.

When Gus Blanchard became president and CEO of Deluxe (the first outsider to do so) the following year, he began a major reorganization. In 1996 he initiated a plan to close more than 20 check-printing plants and eliminate 1,200 jobs (completed 1999). He pursued international business, including a joint venture to provide electronic financial services to India's banking system.

Deluxe bought Fusion Marketing Group (customized database marketing services) in 1997.

The next year, through a joint venture with Fair, Isaac and Company (now Fair Isaac Corporation) and Acxiom Corp., Deluxe developed FraudFinder, a computerized system to rate a merchant's risk in accepting an individual's check or debit card. Increasing its focus on financial services, the company sold off its greeting card, specialty paper, and marketing database businesses. Also in 1998 it began offering check ordering over the Internet and via voice-recognition technology.

The company bought eFunds, which provides the retail and financial sectors with electronic transaction and payment-protection technology. Deluxe also bought the remaining stake of its venture with HCL in 1999, renaming it iDLX and merging it into eFunds. Deluxe spun off the unit in 2000 to focus on paper payment systems.

Also in 2000 Deluxe bought Designer Checks. The next year Deluxe began offering Disney characters on checks, the first time Disney characters have been licensed to appear on personal checks. Also in 2001, Lawrence Mosner was named chairman and CEO of the company.

Looking to grow its small business customer roster, Deluxe purchased Massachusetts-based New England Business Service (NEBS), a provider of business forms and other products to North American small businesses, in 2004.

Mosner retired as chairman and CEO late in 2005. Company president Ronald Eilers succeeded Mosner as CEO on an interim basis; director Stephen Nachtsheim was named chairman. Lee Schram, previously at NCR Corporation, took over the CEO role in 2006. Soon after Schram took over, Deluxe announced cost-cutting measures designed to save the company some $150 million by the end of 2008. The cost-reduction initiatives included consolidating its call-center and check-fulfillment efforts, as well as more efficient manufacturing, supply chain, and shared services.

In 2008 Deluxe acquired Hostopia.com Inc., a provider of Web services to small businesses with an Internet presence, for about $96 million.

EXECUTIVES

Chairman: Stephen P. Nachtsheim, age 65
CEO and Director: Lee J. Schram, age 48, $2,124,041 total compensation
SVP and CIO: Malcolm J. McRoberts, age 45, $579,812 total compensation
SVP; President, Financial Services: Thomas L. (Tom) Morefield, age 47, $664,376 total compensation
SVP and CFO: Terry D. Peterson, age 45, $558,517 total compensation
SVP, General Counsel, and Secretary: Anthony C. Scarfone, age 48, $691,392 total compensation
SVP Human Resources: Julie M. Loosbrock, age 50
SVP Small Business Services: David M. Hemler, age 42
VP Enterprise Brand, Customer Experience, and Media Relations: Laura L. Radewald, age 49
VP Sales and Marketing, Direct-to-Consumer: Lynn R. Koldenhoven, age 43
VP Fulfillment: Pete J. Godich, age 45
Segment Leader Small Business Services: Joanne McGowan, age 23
Media Relations: Nicki Gibbs
Auditors: PricewaterhouseCoopers LLP

LOCATIONS

HQ: Deluxe Corporation
3680 Victoria St. North, Shoreview, MN 55126
Phone: 651-483-7111   **Fax:** 651-481-4163
Web: www.deluxe.com

2009 Sales

	$ mil.	% of total
US	1,275.9	95
Canada & other countries	68.3	5
Total	**1,344.2**	**100**

PRODUCTS/OPERATIONS

2009 Sales

	$ mil.	% of total
Small Business Services	785.1	59
Financial Services	396.4	29
Direct Checks	162.7	12
Total	**1,344.2**	**100**

2009 Sales

	$ mil.	% of total
Checks	851.5	63
Other printed products, including forms	293.2	22
Services, primarily business	90.9	7
Accessories & promotional products	89.2	7
Packaging supplies & other	19.4	1
Total	**1,344.2**	**100**

Selected Products and Services

Small Business Services (checks, forms, and related products; sold to small offices and home offices)
Financial Services
    Account conversion support
    Check merchandising
    Checks and related products
    Customized reporting
    File management
    Fraud prevention
Direct Checks (checks and related products; sold to consumers)

COMPETITORS

American Banknote
Cenveo
Checks In The Mail
Ennis
Harland Clarke
M & F Worldwide
MDC Partners
Northstar Computer Forms
R.R. Donnelley
Standard Register

HISTORICAL FINANCIALS

Company Type: Public

Income Statement
FYE: December 31

	REVENUE ($ mil.)	NET INCOME ($ mil.)	NET PROFIT MARGIN	EMPLOYEES
12/09	1,344	99	7.4%	6,089
12/08	1,469	102	6.9%	7,172
12/07	1,606	144	8.9%	7,991
12/06	1,640	101	6.2%	8,396
12/05	1,716	158	9.2%	8,310
Annual Growth	**(5.9%)**	**(10.9%)**	**—**	**(7.5%)**

2009 Year-End Financials

Debt ratio: 633.7%
Return on equity: 116.8%
Cash ($ mil.): 13
Current ratio: 0.66
Long-term debt ($ mil.): 743
No. of shares (mil.): 51
Dividends
    Yield: 6.8%
    Payout: 51.5%
Market value ($ mil.): 760

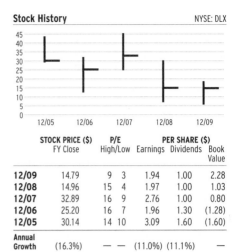

Stock History   NYSE: DLX

	STOCK PRICE ($) FY Close	P/E High/Low		PER SHARE ($) Earnings	Dividends	Book Value
12/09	14.79	9	3	1.94	1.00	2.28
12/08	14.96	15	4	1.97	1.00	1.03
12/07	32.89	16	9	2.76	1.00	0.80
12/06	25.20	16	7	1.96	1.30	(1.28)
12/05	30.14	14	10	3.09	1.60	(1.60)
Annual Growth	**(16.3%)**	**—**	**—**	**(11.0%)**	**(11.1%)**	**—**

Denny's Corporation

Feel like getting slammed for breakfast? The home of the Grand Slam Breakfast, Denny's is one of the leading full-service, family-style restaurant chains in the US, with about 1,550 of its signature eateries located across the country. Typically open 24 hours a day, the chain is best known for its menu of breakfast items, including eggs, pancakes, and combination plates carrying such names as All-American Slam, Lumberjack Slam, and the aforementioned Grand Slam Breakfast. Denny's also serves standard American fare (burgers, sandwiches, steak) for lunch and dinner. The company owns and operates about 230 of its restaurants, while the rest are franchised or operate under licensing agreements.

The company utilizes franchising as a means to oversee its wide-ranging chain of locations without the cost of owning and operating each of them. Local operators pay royalties or licensing fees in order to use the Denny's brand and other intellectual property. The company's relatively large number of corporate-run locations, meanwhile, accounts for about 80% of sales and gives the company a base from which it can control food and service quality.

With the restaurant industry struggling with weak consumer spending, Denny's is focused on reducing costs and improving margins. That effort includes an emphasis on expanding the number of franchised restaurants and selling some of its company-owned units to new and existing franchisees.

Chairman Debra Smithart-Oglesby took over as interim CEO following the resignation of Nelson Marchioli. The change in management came after dissident shareholders unhappy with Denny's direction tried unsuccessfully to remove both executives. Marchioli had served as CEO since 2001.

HISTORY

Denny's traces its roots to a Lockwood, California, doughnut stand called Danny's Donuts. Opened in 1953 by serial entrepreneur Harold Butler, Danny's was an instant hit and soon began offering coffee and sandwiches along with the doughnuts. Butler changed the name of his business to Danny's Coffee Shop the next year and began expanding. By the end of the decade, Butler had 20 shops in operation. He renamed the chain Denny's in 1959. Concentrated near major highways and freeway exits, Denny's expanded rapidly to more than 80 shops in seven western states. The company went public in 1966.

Denny's pushed eastward with its expansion, reaching about 200 locations by 1968. That year the company acquired other chains such as Sandy's Restaurants and Winchell's Donut Houses. Looking to expand his business into new markets, Butler made an offer to buy Parvin-Dohrmann, the company that owned Las Vegas' landmark Caesar's Palace. The deal soured, however, after government regulators charged Butler had privately sweetened the deal to certain shareholders. Denny's stock tumbled after the scandal and Butler left the company in 1971.

Doughnut mogul Verne Winchell took over as CEO and helped rebuild Denny's fortunes. With a focused expansion plan, the company grew to more than 1,300 outlets by 1977 — about half of them were Denny's Coffee Shops and the other half were Winchell's. That year Denny's introduced its Grand Slam Breakfast. With the addition of the El Pollo Loco grilled-chicken chain in 1983, Denny's operations had expanded to more than 2,000 restaurants, including 1,200 of its signature eateries.

A group led by then-president Vern Curtis took the company private for $750 million in 1985. The deal left Denny's saddled with hefty debt, however, and in 1987 the company spun off a 58% stake in its Winchell's business to the public to help raise cash. Later that year, however, Denny's was acquired by TW Services for $830 million in cash and assumed debt.

TW Services owned the hodgepodge of businesses left after Trans World Corporation had spun off its airline, TWA, in 1984. (TWA was later acquired by American Airlines parent AMR Corporation.) Its operations included the Hardee's and Quincy's Family Steakhouse chains, Canteen food and vending business, and American Medical Services. Corporate raider Coniston Partners bought TW Services for $1.7 billion in 1989 and immediately sold off the rest of Winchell's. The medical business was sold the next year. In 1992 Kohlberg Kravis Roberts bought a 47% stake in the remaining food services operations, which began doing business as Flagstar Companies the next year.

Flagstar's history got off to a rough start when patrons who claimed they were denied service because of race filed several lawsuits against its Denny's chain. Most notable was a suit filed by six African-American US Secret Service agents in Maryland. Denny's settled the suits for $54 million in 1994, one of the largest class-action settlements for a hospitality company.

In 1995 chairman and CEO Jerome Richardson stepped down from his executive position to devote more time to his new expansion football franchise, the Carolina Panthers. The company named former Burger King chief James Adamson as the new CEO. (Adamson also became chairman just four months later; in 1996 the NAACP named him Chief Executive of the Year.) It later bought the Coco's, Jojo's, and Carrows chains from Family Restaurants in 1996.

Soft sales and continued losses, however, forced the company to file for Chapter 11 bankruptcy protection in 1997. It emerged from bankruptcy the next year with a new name, Advantica Restaurant Group. That year the company sold its nearly 600 Hardee's fast-food units to CKE Restaurants, the Hardee's franchiser, and its Quincy's chain to Buckley Acquisition. In 1999 the company sold its El Pollo Loco chain to American Securities Capital Partners.

In 2000 Advantica refranchised nearly 150 restaurants that year, and in early 2001 Advantica sold another 28 restaurants to franchisees and added 40 new Denny's locations. Late that year James Adamson retired; director Charles Moran was named chairman and Nelson Marchioli, the former president of El Pollo Loco, was named CEO.

In 2002 Advantica sold its FRD Acquisition subsidiary (now Catalina Restaurant Group), the unit that oversaw Coco's and Carrows. Having shed all its other operations, the company changed its name to Denny's later that year. Moran died in 2004 and was replaced by Robert Marks. The following year Denny's closed several underperforming restaurants and began beefing up its franchising efforts. Debra Smithart-Oglesby was named chairman in 2006 when Marks retired.

EXECUTIVES

Chairman and Interim CEO: Debra Smithart-Oglesby, age 55
EVP, CFO, and Chief Administrative Officer, Denny's Corporation and Denny's, Inc.: F. Mark Wolfinger, age 54, $1,581,805 total compensation
EVP and Chief Marketing Officer: Frances Allen
SVP, General Counsel, and Chief Legal Officer, Denny's Corporation and Denny's Inc.: Timothy E. Flemming
VP Information Technology and CIO, Denny's Inc.: S. Alex Lewis
VP Sales, Denny's, Inc.: William H. Ruby
VP Concept Innovation, Denny's Inc.: Gregory P. Powell
VP Human Resources, Denny's Corporation and Denny's Inc.: Jill A. Van Pelt
VP Marketing, Denny's, Inc.: John W. Dillon
VP Procurement and Distribution, Denny's, Inc.: R. Gregory Linford
Director Franchise Development: Doug Wong
VP Brand Protection, Quality, and Regulatory Compliance, Denny's Inc.: Thomas M. (Mike) Starnes
VP Operations Strategy and Support, Denny's Inc.: Susan L. Mirdamadi
VP Development, Denny's Inc.: Steven (Steve) Dunn
VP, Corporate Controller, and Chief Accounting Officer, Denny's Corporation and Denny's Inc.: Jay C. Gilmore
VP Financial Planning and Analysis and Investor Relations, Denny's Inc.: Enrique N. Mayor-Mora
VP Tax and Treasurer, Denny's Corporation and Denny's Inc.: Ross B. Nell
Assistant General Counsel, Corporate Governance Officer, and Secretary; Assistant General Counsel and Secretary, Denny's, Inc.: J. Scott Melton
Auditors: KPMG LLP

LOCATIONS

HQ: Denny's Corporation
203 E. Main St., Spartanburg, SC 29319
Phone: 864-597-8000 **Fax:** 864-597-8780
Web: www.dennys.com

2009 Locations

	No.
US	
California	408
Texas	160
Florida	154
Arizona	76
Illinois	52
Washington	50
New York	43
Pennsylvania	36
Missouri	34
Indiana	33
Ohio	32
Nevada	30
Colorado	26
Virginia	25
New Mexico	24
Oregon	24
Maryland	23
Michigan	22
Utah	21
North Carolina	19
Wisconsin	17
Georgia	14
Minnesota	14
South Carolina	14
Oklahoma	13
Kentucky	12
New Jersey	10
Arkansas	9
Connecticut	8
Hawaii	8
Kansas	8
Idaho	7
Maine	6
Massachusetts	6
Other states	36
International	
Canada	49
Puerto Rico	11
Guam	2
Other countries	15
Total	**1,551**

PRODUCTS/OPERATIONS

2009 Sales

	$ mil.	% of total
Restaurants	488.9	80
Franchising & licensing	119.2	20
Total	**608.1**	**100**

2009 Locations

	No.
Franchised & licensed	1,318
Company-owned	233
Total	**1,551**

COMPETITORS

American Blue Ribbon Holdings
Biglari Holdings
Bob Evans
Brinker
Buffets Holdings
Carlson Restaurants
Cracker Barrel
Darden
DineEquity
Friendly Ice Cream
Golden Corral
Huddle House
OSI Restaurant Partners
Perkins & Marie Callender's
Ruby Tuesday
Waffle House

HISTORICAL FINANCIALS

Company Type: Public

Income Statement
FYE: December 31

	REVENUE ($ mil.)	NET INCOME ($ mil.)	NET PROFIT MARGIN	EMPLOYEES
12/09	608	42	6.8%	11,000
12/08	760	15	1.9%	15,000
12/07	939	35	3.7%	21,000
12/06	994	30	3.0%	27,000
12/05	979	(7)	—	27,000
Annual Growth	(11.2%)	—	—	(20.1%)

2009 Year-End Financials

Debt ratio: —
Return on equity: —
Cash ($ mil.): 27
Current ratio: 0.63
Long-term debt ($ mil.): 274

No. of shares (mil.): 100
Dividends
Yield: —
Payout: —
Market value ($ mil.): 218

Stock History

NASDAQ (CM): DENN

	STOCK PRICE ($) FY Close	P/E High/Low		PER SHARE ($) Earnings	Dividends	Book Value
12/09	2.19	7	3	0.42	—	(1.28)
12/08	1.99	27	8	0.15	—	(1.75)
12/07	3.75	16	10	0.35	—	(1.80)
12/06	4.71	17	8	0.31	—	(2.25)
12/05	4.03	—	—	(0.08)	—	(2.66)
Annual Growth	(14.1%)	—	—	—	—	—

DENTSPLY International

Open wider, please, so that DENTSPLY International can fit more of its products in your mouth. The company manufactures a range of dental goods, from anesthetics, pastes, and tooth whiteners to artificial teeth, crown and bridge materials, and implants. DENTSPLY also makes dental equipment, including root canal instruments, ultrasonic polishers, X-ray viewers, and other orthodontic appliances. The company manufactures its various products under more than 100 brand names. More than half of its products are sold through domestic and international distributors, but DENTSPLY also sells directly to dentists, dental labs, and dental schools in more than 120 countries.

The company's largest customer is distributor Henry Schein, which accounts for more than 10% of sales. The US is DENTSPLY's largest market, accounting for about 40% of sales.

The company's product offerings in various geographic regions reflect the demand of local markets. Developed markets, including the US, Canada, Japan, Australia, and Western Europe, require more technically advanced dental products used in preventive and cosmetic procedures. Less developed countries in Central and South America, Eastern Europe, Africa, and the Middle East typically call for more basic equipment used to fill cavities and finish bridgework. DENTSPLY is focused on supplying products to both ends of this spectrum.

To maintain a competitive edge, the company has invested in new product development through its own internal research centers and collaborations with research institutions and dental schools. DENTSPLY also cites acquisitions as a key part of its growth strategy. In 2008 and 2009 it acquired a handful of smaller dental companies to further build out its product portfolio, marketing network, technological capabilities, and geographic breadth.

HISTORY

DENTSPLY's roots go back to 1899 when dental business veterans Jacob Frantz, George Whiteley, Dean Osborne, and John Shepherd formed the Dentists' Supply Co. of New York. Facing a competitive market, the four bought a Pennsylvania porcelain teeth manufacturer. One of the company's first innovations was to make ceramic teeth. In 1914 Dentists' Supply introduced different-sized teeth to allow custom fitting for patients.

Between 1920 and 1950 the firm opened factories in Argentina, Australia, Brazil, Germany, Italy, Mexico, and the UK. Facing a mature denture market in the 1950s, Dentists' Supply began investing in other dental technologies. It collaborated with Dr. John Borden in the development of the Borden Airorotor, a high-speed dental drill that revolutionized dental practice. The firm changed its name to DENTSPLY in 1969.

In 1976 the company acquired its worldwide distributor, Amalgamated Dental; it purchased GE's dental X-ray division in 1983. During the 1980s and 1990s DENTSPLY opened operations in China, India, Japan, and Russia as part of its global expansion; it reorganized these operations in the late 1990s to achieve better efficiency. Moving into the information age, DENTSPLY purchased InfoSoft (dental office software). Following a protracted investigation, the Justice Department filed an antitrust suit against DENTSPLY in 1999.

In 2000 DENTSPLY decided to sell its InfoSoft LLC division. The following year, it acquired Friadent, one of Germany's leading makers of dental implants, and it also bought AstraZeneca's dental anesthetic business.

In mid-2006 DENTSPLY sold off its injectable anesthetic manufacturing facility in Chicago. Its supplier Pierrel S.p.A. of Italy agreed to pay $19.5 million for the facility and equipment, with $3 million settled at closing, and the balance to be paid through discounts on future products supplied by Pierrel. The company continued to have contracts with other companies to manufacture anesthetics.

EXECUTIVES

Chairman and CEO: Bret W. Wise, age 49, $4,156,934 total compensation
President and COO: Christopher T. (Chris) Clark, age 48, $1,972,595 total compensation
EVP: James G. (Jim) Mosch, age 52, $1,133,795 total compensation
SVP and CFO: William R. Jellison, age 52, $1,167,938 total compensation
SVP: Albert J. Sterkenburg, age 46, $977,830 total compensation
SVP: Robert J. (Bob) Size, age 51

VP and Treasurer: William E. Reardon
VP and Corporate Controller: Timothy S. Warady
VP, Secretary, and General Counsel: Brian M. Addison, age 55, $956,754 total compensation
VP Global Human Resources: Maureen J. MacInnis
VP Tax: Robert J. Winters, age 58
VP and Chief Clinical Officer: Linda C. Niessen
Auditors: PricewaterhouseCoopers LLP

LOCATIONS

HQ: DENTSPLY International Inc.
221 W. Philadelphia St., York, PA 17405
Phone: 717-845-7511   **Fax:** 717-849-4760
Web: www.dentsply.com

2009 Sales

	$ mil.	% of total
US	843.4	39
Germany	482.1	22
Other countries	834.4	39
Total	**2,159.9**	**100**

PRODUCTS/OPERATIONS

2009 Sales

	$ mil.	% of total
Dental specialty products	895.4	41
Dental consumable products	710.6	33
Dental laboratory products	500.2	23
Non-dental products	53.7	3
Total	**2,159.9**	**100**

Selected Products

Dental specialty products
  3D digital implantology
  Bone grafting materials
  Implants
  Orthodontic appliances and accessories
  Root canal instruments and materials
Dental consumable products
  Anesthetics
  High- and low-speed handpieces
  Impression materials
  Infection control materials
  Intraoral light systems
  Prophylaxis paste
  Restorative materials
  Sealants
  Tooth whiteners
  Topical fluoride
  Ultrasonic scalers and polishers
Dental laboratory products
  Computer-aided machining ceramic systems
  Crown and bridge materials
  Dental ceramics
  Precious metal dental alloys
  Prosthetics and artificial teeth
Non-dental products
  Casting materials (used in jewelry, golf club heads, and certain medical products)

COMPETITORS

AFP Imaging
Align Technology
Astra Tech
Astra Tech (Sweden)
BioHorizons
Den-Mat
DTI Dental Technologies
Glidewell Laboratories
Henry Schein
National Dentex
Nobel Biocare
Patterson Companies
Sirona
Straumann
Sybron Dental
Young Innovations

HISTORICAL FINANCIALS

Company Type: Public

Income Statement

FYE: December 31

	REVENUE ($ mil.)	NET INCOME ($ mil.)	NET PROFIT MARGIN	EMPLOYEES
12/09	2,160	274	12.7%	9,300
12/08	2,194	284	12.9%	9,400
12/07	2,010	260	12.9%	8,900
12/06	1,811	224	12.4%	8,500
12/05	1,715	45	2.6%	8,000
Annual Growth	5.9%	56.8%	—	3.8%

2009 Year-End Financials

Debt ratio: 21.1%
Return on equity: 16.0%
Cash ($ mil.): 450
Current ratio: 2.74
Long-term debt ($ mil.): 387

No. of shares (mil.): 143
Dividends
  Yield: 0.6%
  Payout: 10.9%
Market value ($ mil.): 5,023

Stock History

NASDAQ (GS): XRAY

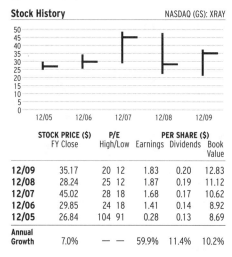

	STOCK PRICE ($) FY Close	P/E High/Low		PER SHARE ($) Earnings	Dividends	Book Value
12/09	35.17	20	12	1.83	0.20	12.83
12/08	28.24	25	12	1.87	0.19	11.12
12/07	45.02	28	18	1.68	0.17	10.62
12/06	29.85	24	18	1.41	0.14	8.92
12/05	26.84	104	91	0.28	0.13	8.69
Annual Growth	7.0%	—	—	59.9%	11.4%	10.2%

Devon Energy

Independent oil and gas producer Devon Energy puts its energy into oil and gas finds far from England's southern coast. It has exploration and production assets in North Texas, Oklahoma, Wyoming, and western Canada. In 2008 Devon Energy reported proved reserves of 429 million barrels of oil, 9.9 trillion cu. ft. of natural gas, and 325 million barrels of natural gas liquids. That year the company drilled a record 2,441 gross wells with an overall 98% rate of success. Devon Energy is the largest producer and largest lease holder in the Barnett Shale area of North Texas.

Once active in major oil patches worldwide such as Azerbaijan, Brazil, and China, the company has decided to focus on onshore exploration activity in North America. Consequently Devon has been pursuing an evolving strategy of selling its international assets. In 2007 Devon began to divest all of its assets in West Africa. It sold its oil and gas business in Egypt to Dana Petroleum for $375 million and its Gabon assets for $206 million. In 2008 it sold its oil and gas business in Côte d'Ivoire to Afren plc for $205 million and in Equatorial Guinea (to that country's national oil company, GE Petrol) for $2.2 billion.

In early 2010 it sold its stakes in the Cascade, Jack and St. Malo fields in the Gulf of Mexico

(about 200 million barrels of estimated recoverable reserves) to AP Moller-Maersk's oil unit for $1.3 billion. Later in 2010 it sold its most of its remaining international assets to BP for $7 billion. As part of this deal BP agreed to sell undeveloped oil sand leases in Canada to Devon for $500 million and form a joint venture with the company to exploit them. It also sold its remaining Gulf of Mexico shelf assets to Apache for $1 billion. The company also sold its Panyu field, offshore China, to China National Offshore Oil for $515 million.

Earlier in the decade Devon Energy had bought its way into the big leagues through a series of multibillion-dollar acquisitions of oil and gas producers, including Ocean Energy in 2003 for $3.5 billion and US-based Chief Holdings LLC in 2006 for $2.2 billion.

Devon Energy veteran John Richels was appointed CEO in 2010. Company cofounder Larry Nichols relinquished the CEO slot but retained the role of chairman.

HISTORY

Larry Nichols (a lawyer who clerked for US Supreme Court Chief Justice Earl Warren) and his father, John, founded Devon Energy in 1969. John Nichols was a partner in predecessor company Blackwood and Nichols, an oil partnership formed in 1946.

In 1981 the company bought a small stake in the Northeast Blanco Unit of New Mexico's San Juan Basin. To raise capital, Devon formed the limited partnership Devon Resource Investors and took it public in 1985. In 1988 Devon consolidated all of its units into a single, publicly traded company.

The firm increased its stake in Northeast Blanco in 1988 and again in 1989, ending up with about 25%. By 1990 Devon had drilled more than 100 wells in the area and had proved reserves of 58 billion cu. ft. of natural gas.

During the 1990s the company launched a major expansion program using a two-pronged strategy: acquiring producing properties and drilling wells in proven fields. In 1990 it bought an 88% interest in six Texas wells; two years later Devon snapped up the US properties of Hondo Oil & Gas. After its 1994 purchase of Alta Energy, which operated in New Mexico, Oklahoma, Texas, and Wyoming, Devon had proved reserves of more than 500 billion cu. ft. of gas.

Between 1992 and 1997 the company also drilled some 840 successful wells. Buoyed by new seismic techniques that raise the odds of finding oil, Devon devoted more resources to pioneering fields in regions where it already had expertise.

Continuing its buying spree, Devon bought Kerr-McGee's onshore assets in 1997. Two years later it bought Alberta, Canada-based Northstar for $775 million, creating a company with holdings divided almost evenly between oil and gas.

Also in 1999 Devon grabbed its biggest prize when it purchased PennzEnergy of Houston in a $2.3 billion stock-and-debt deal that analysts called a bargain. PennzEnergy, spun off from Pennzoil in 1998, dates back to the Texas oil boom after WWII. In addition to new US holdings, the deal gave Devon a number of international oil and gas assets in such places as Azerbaijan, Brazil, Egypt, Qatar, and Venezuela.

On a roll, Devon in 2000 bought Santa Fe Snyder for $2.35 billion in stock and $1 billion in assumed debt. The deal increased Devon's

proved reserves by nearly 400 million barrels of oil equivalent.

In 2001 the company agreed to a major deal to supply Indonesian natural gas to Singapore. It also made an unsuccessful bid for rival Barrett Resources that was trumped by a bid from Williams Companies. Undaunted, that year Devon acquired Anderson Exploration for $3.4 billion in cash and $1.2 billion in assumed debt. It also purchased Mitchell Energy & Development for $3.1 billion in cash and stock and $400 million in assumed debt.

As part of its strategy to refocus on core operations, in 2002 the company sold its Indonesian assets to PetroChina for $262 million. By mid-year the company had raised about $1.2 billion through the disposition of oil properties worldwide.

EXECUTIVES

Chairman: J. Larry Nichols, age 69, $16,202,560 total compensation
President, CEO, and Director: John Richels, age 59, $10,587,770 total compensation
EVP Public Affairs: William F. (Bill) Whitsitt
EVP and General Counsel: Lyndon C. Taylor, age 51
EVP Administration: R. Alan Marcum, age 43
EVP and CFO: Jeffrey A. (Jeff) Agosta, age 42
EVP Marketing and Midstream: Darryl G. Smette, age 62, $4,164,942 total compensation
EVP Exploration and Production:
David A. (Dave) Hager, age 53, $5,500,511 total compensation
EVP Human Resources: Frank W. Rudolph, age 53
SVP Accounting: Danny J. Heatly, age 54, $2,328,143 total compensation
SVP Corporate Finance and Treasurer: Jeff Ritenour, age 36
SVP Southern Division: Gregory T. Kelleher, age 55
SVP Central Division: Bradley A. Foster, age 52
SVP Offshore Division: Anthony D. (Tony) Vaughn, age 52
SVP Western Divisioin: Don D. DeCarlo, age 53
SVP Exploration: William A. (Bill) Van Wie, age 64
SVP Canadian Division, President, Devon Canada: Christopher R. (Chris) Seasons, age 49
SVP Investor Relations: Vincent W. White, age 52
VP Business Technology: Ben Williams
VP Corporate Governance and Secretary: Janice A. Dobbs, age 61
Director: Duane C. Radtke, age 61
Auditors: KPMG LLP

LOCATIONS

HQ: Devon Energy Corporation
20 N. Broadway, Oklahoma City, OK 73102
Phone: 405-235-3611   **Fax:** 405-552-4550
Web: www.devonenergy.com

2009 Sales

	$ mil.	% of total
US	5,838	73
Canada	2,177	27
Total	**8,015**	**100**

PRODUCTS/OPERATIONS

2009 Sales

	$ mil.	% of total
Oil, gas & natural gas liquids	6,097	76
Marketing & midstream	1,534	19
Other	384	5
Total	**8,015**	**100**

HISTORICAL FINANCIALS

Company Type: Public

Income Statement

FYE: December 31

	REVENUE ($ mil.)	NET INCOME ($ mil.)	NET PROFIT MARGIN	EMPLOYEES
12/09	8,015	(2,479)	—	5,400
12/08	15,211	(2,148)	—	5,500
12/07	11,362	3,606	31.7%	5,000
12/06	10,578	2,846	26.9%	4,600
12/05	10,741	2,930	27.3%	4,075
Annual Growth	(7.1%)	—	—	7.3%

2009 Year-End Financials

Debt ratio: 46.7%
Return on equity: —
Cash ($ mil.): 646
Current ratio: 0.79
Long-term debt ($ mil.): 7,265

No. of shares (mil.): 435
Dividends
  Yield: 0.9%
  Payout: —
Market value ($ mil.): 31,973

Stock History

NYSE: DVN

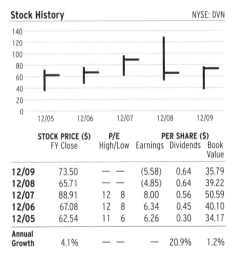

	STOCK PRICE ($) FY Close	P/E High/Low		PER SHARE ($) Earnings	Dividends	Book Value
12/09	73.50	—	—	(5.58)	0.64	35.79
12/08	65.71	—	—	(4.85)	0.64	39.22
12/07	88.91	12	8	8.00	0.56	50.59
12/06	67.08	12	8	6.34	0.45	40.10
12/05	62.54	11	6	6.26	0.30	34.17
Annual Growth	4.1%	—	—	—	20.9%	1.2%

DeVry Inc.

It isn't exactly Ivy League, but DeVry is in the big leagues of technical, health care, and business schools. The for-profit company offers professional, undergraduate, and graduate programs through several subsidiary schools. Flagship DeVry University, with about 100 US locations and one in Canada, specializes in business and technology education. Its Keller Graduate School of Management unit offers MBA and other graduate programs while its Ross University offers medical and veterinary school training. The company also offers health care education through Chamberlain College of Nursing and Carrington College. In all, DeVry has more than 70,000 students through campus and online enrollment.

The company's Becker Professional Education subsidiary offers professional exam review and continuing education courses in accounting, finance, and project management. It operates in the US and several international markets.

In addition to its business, health care, and technical education services, DeVry offers middle school and high school programs online through its Advanced Academics unit. It is also laying the groundwork to expand into elementary education through its K-12 program.

Internationally, the company operates DeVry Brasil and its Ross University programs are based in the West Indies. DeVry Brasil began as Fanor and was acquired in 2009. It offers offers business, law, and engineering programs from about a half-dozen campuses in Brazil. Ross students take academic coursework at the university campuses in the Caribbean, then complete their degrees with clinical training at US teaching hospitals and affiliated veterinary colleges.

DeVry University's student population is generally older than those at traditional colleges. More than half of its students are older than 25, and represent the school's fastest-growing demographic; many are working adults. The school boasts an enrollment of more than 55,000 undergraduate students and some 18,000 graduate students.

Acquisitions to add to or expand upon its offerings have been a key part of the company's growth strategy. DeVry added to its health care offerings in 2008 with the acquisition of U.S. Education Company, which included about 20 Apollo College and Western Career College locations in the western US. The locations were later renamed Carrington College.

DeVry enjoyed a boost in enrollments during the economic recession — many unemployed workers took the opportunity to seek new technical training, and at the same time federal student loan purse strings loosened up, giving those workers access to loans for tuition. However, the rapid growth in the entire private education industry, including DeVry, drew attention from lawmakers during 2010, who were concerned that people were adding to their debt with student loans but receiving incomplete or low-quality education services.

Company co-founder and former chairman Dennis Keller, now a director emeritus, owns about 10% of DeVry.

HISTORY

DeVry Institutes was founded in 1931 by Herman DeVry as an electronics repair school. It was later acquired by Bell & Howell (now Voyager Learning Company). While working at Bell & Howell, Dennis Keller, a Princeton graduate, met Ronald Taylor, who had degrees from Harvard and Stanford. In 1973 they created a private business school targeting working adults. In 1987 Keller and Taylor bought DeVry and combined it with their graduate business school under the DeVry name; the company went public in 1991.

The company acquired Becker CPA Review in 1996. With plans to increase the number of DeVry campuses to 40 by the next decade, the company opened DeVry Institutes in New York City and Fremont, California, in 1998. The following year it bought Denver Technical College, which later was integrated into DeVry University. Devry also began offering classes online.

The Becker Conviser Professional Review segment was bolstered in 2001 with the purchase of Argentum (which did business as Stalla Seminars), a firm engaged in the production of CFA (chartered financial analyst) test prep materials. DeVry Institutes and Keller Graduate School of Management merged to form DeVry University in 2002. DeVry acquired Ross University, a medical and veterinary school, in 2003.

In 2004 Keller turned over the CEO spot to fellow co-founder Ronald Taylor. He remained chairman for a couple of years before stepping down to become director emeritus.

Devry's medical credentials were expanded in 2005 with the acquisition of Deaconess College of Nursing, renamed Chamberlain College of Nursing. Also that year, the company acquired Gearty CPE, a provider of continuing education programs in accounting and finance operating in New York and New Jersey.

Ronald Taylor retired as CEO at the end of 2006. He was succeeded by company COO Daniel Hamburger.

Keller Graduate School expanded its degree offerings in 2007 with the addition of a master's degree in educational technology.

EXECUTIVES

Chairman: Harold T. Shapiro, age 75
President, CEO, and Director: Daniel M. Hamburger, age 45, $3,454,711 total compensation
EVP; President, Ross University: Thomas C. Shepherd, age 59, $714,688 total compensation
EVP; President, DeVry University:
David J. (Dave) Pauldine, age 52, $1,175,592 total compensation
SVP, CFO, and Treasurer: Richard M. (Rick) Gunst, age 53, $929,273 total compensation
SVP, General Counsel, and Secretary: Gregory S. Davis, age 47
SVP and CIO: Eric Dirst, age 42
SVP Government and Regulatory Affairs and Chief Compliance Officer: Sharon Thomas Parrott, age 59
SVP Business Development and International:
John P. Roselli, age 45
SVP Human Resources: Donna N. Jennings, age 47
SVP; President, Becker Professional Education:
Thomas J. Vucinic, age 62
President, DeVry Online Services:
Steven P. (Steve) Riehs, age 50, $714,688 total compensation
Director Investor Relations: Joan Bates
Auditors: PricewaterhouseCoopers LLP

LOCATIONS

HQ: DeVry Inc.
  3005 Highland Pkwy, Downers Grove, IL 60515
Phone: 630-571-7700
Web: www.devryinc.com

2009 Sales

	$ mil.	% of total
US	1,281.9	88
Dominica & St. Kitts/Nevis	161.4	11
Other countries	18.2	1
Total	**1,461.5**	**100**

PRODUCTS/OPERATIONS

2009 Sales by Segment

	$ mil.	% of total
Business, technology & management	989.5	68
Medical & healthcare	362.7	25
Professional education	84.2	6
Other educational services	25.1	1
Total	**1,461.5**	**100**

2009 Sales

	$ mil.	% of total
Tuition	1,354.9	93
Other	106.6	7
Total	**1,461.5**	**100**

Selected Fields of Study

Carrington College
- Dental assisting
- Diagnostic medical sonography
- Fitness training
- Medical assisting
- Medical laboratory technician
- Medical radiography
- Physical therapy assisting
- Practical nursing
- Respiratory care
- Veterinary assisting

Becker Professional Review
- CFA exam review
- CPA exam review

Chamberlain College of Nursing
- Nursing

DeVry University
- Accounting
- Biomedical engineering technology
- Business administration
- Computer engineering technology
- Computer information systems
- Electrical engineering
- Electronics and computer technology
- Electronics engineering technology
- Game and simulation programming
- Health information technology
- Network and communications management
- Network systems administration
- Technical management

DeVry Brasil
- Business management
- Engineering
- Law

Keller Graduate School of Management
- Accounting and finance
- Business administration
- Human resources
- Project management
- Public administration
- Technology management

Ross University
- Medicine
- Veterinary medicine

COMPETITORS

Apollo Group	Heald College
Bridgepoint Education	ITT Educational
Capella Education	Kaplan
Cardean Learning Group	Laureate Education
Career Education	Lincoln Educational
Concorde Colleges	Services
Corinthian Colleges	Strayer Education
Education Management	

HISTORICAL FINANCIALS

Company Type: Public

Income Statement

FYE: June 30

	REVENUE ($ mil.)	NET INCOME ($ mil.)	NET PROFIT MARGIN	EMPLOYEES
6/09	1,462	166	11.3%	10,200
6/08	1,092	126	11.5%	6,755
6/07	934	76	8.2%	5,400
6/06	843	43	5.1%	4,800
6/05	781	27	3.4%	5,700
Annual Growth	**16.9%**	**57.8%**	**—**	**15.7%**

2009 Year-End Financials

Debt ratio: 2.2%
Return on equity: 19.7%
Cash ($ mil.): 165
Current ratio: 0.98
Long-term debt ($ mil.): 20
No. of shares (mil.): 71
Dividends
  Yield: 0.3%
  Payout: 7.0%
Market value ($ mil.): 3,565

Stock History

NYSE: DV

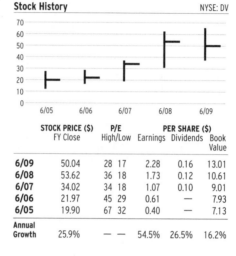

	STOCK PRICE ($) FY Close	P/E High/Low		PER SHARE ($) Earnings	Dividends	Book Value
6/09	50.04	28	17	2.28	0.16	13.01
6/08	53.62	36	18	1.73	0.12	10.61
6/07	34.02	34	18	1.07	0.10	9.01
6/06	21.97	45	29	0.61	—	7.93
6/05	19.90	67	32	0.40	—	7.13
Annual Growth	**25.9%**	**—**	**—**	**54.5%**	**26.5%**	**16.2%**

Diamond Offshore Drilling

This Diamond is an oiler's best friend. Diamond Offshore Drilling is a contract offshore oil and gas driller capable of descending the deep blue to depths of 10,000 feet. A leading US drilling contractor, Diamond Offshore has about 50 rigs, including 32 semisubmersibles, 13 jack-up rigs (mobile drilling platforms), and one drillship. Operating in waters off six of the world's continents, Diamond Offshore contracts with almost 50 oil and gas companies; Brazil's PETROBRAS is its major customer. The company also provides project management and other drilling-related services. Loews Corp. owns 50.4% of the company.

Although the majority of Diamond Offshore's vessels operate in the waters of the Gulf of Mexico, the company does have vessels operating in the North Sea and off the coasts of Africa, Australia, Brazil, Indonesia, New Zealand, Singapore, and Vietnam.

As oil majors increasingly pursue deepwater projects, Diamond Offshore is refitting its rigs for deepwater work and is installing advanced drilling systems. Diamond Offshore also plans to increase its fleet size by acquiring additional assets during oil and gas industry downturns. During 2009 the company acquired two new-build deepwater, semisubmersible, dynamically positioned drilling rigs, the *Ocean Courage* and the *Ocean Valor*.

A weak global economy depressed the day rates Diamond Offshore could charge in 2009. Nevertheless, the company was able to add new contracts in 2009 and enter 2010 with a contract backlog of $8.5 billion, and with improved revenues for 2009. To raise cash, in 2010 it sold a jack-up rig to Ensco for $186 million.

In 2008 long-term chairman and CEO James Tisch appointed company veteran Lawrence Dickerson as CEO. Tisch retained the chairman role and his position as Diamond Offshore's primary strategic decision maker.

HISTORY

Loews, a New York City-based holding company owned by billionaire brothers Larry and Bob Tisch, paid $48.5 million for offshore drilling rig operator Diamond M in 1989 during the depths of a major oil bust (the bust lasted from the mid-1980s through the mid-1990s). Few oil rigs were operating, and most of those were earning day rates of less than $30,000.

Diamond M was a Houston-based drilling firm that dated to the 1960s. Texas oilman and rancher Don McMahon had formed the company from several oil rigs in default when an oil bust was mirrored by a banking crisis. McMahon named the firm after his Houston area ranch, the Diamond M. (The logo used by Diamond M, and later Diamond Offshore, was styled after the ranch's brand.) At one point Diamond M was the world's largest barge drilling company, although it no longer operates drilling barges.

Kaneb Services, a Richardson, Texas-based oil pipeline and energy services company, bought Diamond M in 1978. After oil prices dropped and drilling activity slowed in the 1980s, Kaneb sold Diamond M to the Tisches, who through Loews have developed a reputation for buying companies in underperforming industries and waiting for an up cycle. Former Kaneb Services EVP Robert Rose headed Loews' new subsidiary.

With rig prices still low, Diamond M bought Odeco Drilling from Murphy Oil for $377 million in 1992. It was the first major consolidation in the offshore drilling industry; many more have followed. The Odeco acquisition gave Diamond M added deepwater capabilities and enough rigs to enter the international offshore drilling market.

In 1993 Loews' drilling interests were combined into a company named Diamond Offshore Drilling. When Loews spun off Diamond Offshore in 1995, it was operating 37 offshore rigs and 10 land rigs, all in South Texas. That year PETROBRAS contracted for several additional rigs off Brazil.

Diamond Offshore acquired deepwater rival Arethusa (Off-Shore) Limited in 1996 to add 11 oil rigs to its fleet. That year the company sold its land-based drilling operations in South Texas, Diamond M Onshore Inc., to DI Industries. By late 1996 day rates for deepwater rigs had rebounded to as high as $140,000. In 1997 Diamond Offshore acquired *Polyconfidence*, a semisubmersible accommodation vessel, and began converting it to an ultra-deepwater rig.

In 1998 Lawrence Dickerson, former SVP and CFO and a veteran of Diamond M, replaced Robert Rose as president; chairman James Tisch took over Rose's CEO duties. Also that year BP

Amoco (now BP), citing equipment problems, canceled a Gulf of Mexico drill rig project. Undeterred, Diamond Offshore won a three-year contract in 1999 for its *Ocean Clipper* drillship (idled by the collapse of the BP Amoco deal) to provide deepwater drilling services offshore Brazil.

The next year Diamond Offshore sold one of its older jack-up drilling rigs. It also won a three-year contract from PETROBRAS for the use of one of its most modern semisubmersibles, the *Ocean Alliance.*

Lower operating day-rate contracts and underutilization of semisubmersibles led the company to post lower revenues in 2000. However, early in 2001, buoyed by higher oil prices and increased exploration activity, the company reported much stronger sales for its semisubmersible unit.

In 2007 the company won four drilling contracts from PETROBRAS in Brazil for approximately $2.3 billion.

EXECUTIVES

Chairman: James S. Tisch, age 57,
$1,808,312 total compensation
President, CEO, and Director:
Lawrence R. (Larry) Dickerson, age 57,
$2,662,870 total compensation
EVP: John M. Vecchio, age 59,
$1,206,647 total compensation
SVP and CFO: Gary T. Krenek, age 51,
$1,043,694 total compensation
SVP Worldwide Operations: Lyndol I. Dew, age 55,
$1,045,186 total compensation
SVP Contracts and Marketing: Robert G. Blair, age 58
SVP, General Counsel, and Secretary: William C. Long, age 43, $1,102,997 total compensation
SVP, South America: Mark F. Baudoin, age 57
VP Engineering: Karl S. Sellers
VP Marketing: Bodley P. Thornton
VP Domestic Operations: Steven A. Nelson
VP Tax: Stephen G. Elwood
VP Human Resources: R. Lynn Charles
VP International Operations, Western Hemisphere:
Ronald L. James
VP International Operations, Eastern Hemisphere:
Robert N. Blank
VP Contracts and Marketing: Morrison R. Plaisance
Director Investor Relations: Lester F. (Les) Van Dyke
Controller and Chief Accounting Officer:
Beth G. Gordon, age 54
Auditors: Deloitte & Touche LLP

LOCATIONS

HQ: Diamond Offshore Drilling, Inc.
15415 Katy Fwy., Ste. 100, Houston, TX 77094
Phone: 281-492-5300   **Fax:** 281-492-5316
Web: www.diamondoffshore.com

2009 Sales

	$ mil.	% of total
North America		
US	1,232.9	34
Mexico	323.1	9
Australia/Asia/Middle East	717.6	20
South America	716.5	20
Europe/Africa/Mediterranean	641.2	17
Total	**3,631.3**	**100**

PRODUCTS/OPERATIONS

2009 Sales

	$ mil.	% of total
Contract drilling	3,536.6	97
Other	94.7	3
Total	**3,631.3**	**100**

2009 Sales

	$ mil.	% of total
Semisubmersibles		
Intermediate semisubmersibles	1,698.6	47
High-specification floaters	1,380.8	38
Jack-ups	457.2	12
Other	94.7	3
Total	**3,631.3**	**100**

Services

Contract offshore drilling
Drilling services
Drilling and completion operations
Extended well tests
Project management

COMPETITORS

Atwood Oceanics
Dolphin
Ensco
Fred. Olsen Energy
Halliburton
Helmerich & Payne
J. Ray McDermott
Nabors Industries
Noble
Parker Drilling
Pride International
Rowan Companies
Saipem
Siem Industries
Transocean
Weatherford International

HISTORICAL FINANCIALS

Company Type: Public

Income Statement

FYE: December 31

	REVENUE ($ mil.)	NET INCOME ($ mil.)	NET PROFIT MARGIN	EMPLOYEES
12/09	3,631	1,376	37.9%	5,500
12/08	3,544	1,311	37.0%	5,700
12/07	2,568	847	33.0%	5,400
12/06	2,053	707	34.4%	4,800
12/05	1,221	260	21.3%	4,500
Annual Growth	**31.3%**	**51.6%**	**—**	**5.1%**

2009 Year-End Financials

Debt ratio: 41.2%
Return on equity: 39.4%
Cash ($ mil.): 376
Current ratio: 4.17
Long-term debt ($ mil.): 1,495
No. of shares (mil.): 139
Dividends
Yield: 0.5%
Payout: 5.1%
Market value ($ mil.): 13,683

Stock History

NYSE: DO

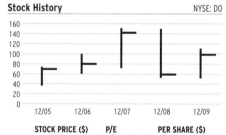

	STOCK PRICE ($) FY Close	P/E High/Low		PER SHARE ($) Earnings	Dividends	Book Value
12/09	98.42	11	5	9.89	0.50	26.11
12/08	58.94	16	6	9.43	0.50	24.09
12/07	142.00	24	12	6.12	0.50	20.69
12/06	79.94	19	12	5.12	0.50	16.68
12/05	69.56	38	20	1.91	0.38	13.33
Annual Growth	**9.1%**	**—**	**—**	**50.8%**	**7.1%**	**18.3%**

Diebold, Incorporated

Cash is king at Diebold. The company is one of the leading producers of automated teller machines (ATMs). In addition, Diebold offers remote teller systems, cash dispensers, and check cashing machines. Originally a manufacturer of safes, the company is still active in its original market, offering products that include vaults and security systems for financial institutions. Diebold also provides electronic voting machines through its Procomp Industria Eletronica subsidiary in Brazil. Its services range from product maintenance to installation consulting and plan design. Diebold, which has operations in about 90 countries, gets around three-quarters of its sales in the Americas.

Diebold's growth strategy also focused largely on becoming more service-oriented, and the company now generates more than half of its revenues from maintenance and other services supporting its self-service and security product lines. In addition to traditional maintenance services, Diebold offers outsourced and managed services, such as remote monitoring, transaction processing, and currency management.

Diebold took steps to become more efficient in its manufacturing, procurement and logistics, and product development, as part of a multiyear program aimed at reducing its costs. The company's efforts included consolidation of its manufacturing and distribution operations, as well as job cuts.

In 2009 Diebold sold its Premier Election Solutions subsidiary to Election Systems & Software. The company identified its US election systems business as a noncore line of business in 2006 and renamed it Premier Election Solutions the following year.

The US election systems business became an operating and political liability for Diebold as the company was sued by the State of California over alleged problems of reliability and security with its voting machines. Diebold settled the suit with a cash payment to the state. After Diebold entered the US voting machine market in 2002, controversy arose the following year when Walden O'Dell, then the company's chairman and CEO, raised money for the re-election of President Bush and urged other Republicans in Ohio (where Diebold makes its headquarters and where it supplied voting machines in some jurisdictions) to support the president's bid.

HISTORY

German immigrant Charles Diebold formed safe and vault maker Diebold Bahmann in Cincinnati in 1859. The Chicago Fire of 1871 gave the company an unexpected boost: All 878 of its safes in the area (and their contents) survived the inferno. The company relocated in 1872 to North Canton, Ohio, where it was incorporated in 1876. During the next two decades, it also made jails, trapdoors for gallows, and padded cells for asylums. In the 1930s Diebold helped develop a bank-lobby tear gas system, made in part to deter the notorious John Dillinger.

Compelled to diversify after the Great Depression, Diebold made seven major acquisitions between 1936 and 1947, including bank and office equipment firms and other safe makers. WWII government arms contracts helped boost the company's sales from about $3 million per year to $40 million in 1942. Two years later former

Prohibition G-man Eliot Ness (immortalized on television and in films in *The Untouchables*) joined Diebold's board, later becoming chairman and overseeing the 1946 takeover of York Safe, which had been the largest US safe maker before the war.

The 1947 acquisition of O.B. McClintock Co.'s bank equipment division moved Diebold into the drive-through teller-window business. Sales of the specialty windows and other bank equipment were stimulated by suburban growth in the 1950s. By 1957 business equipment represented about half of Diebold's sales.

Increased check use in the early 1960s led Diebold to enter check imprinting with the 1963 purchase of Consolidated Business Systems (business forms, magnetic imprinting ink for checks). Diebold went public the next year.

With security-equipment sales slowing in the early 1970s, CEO Raymond Koontz gambled on ATMs, investing heavily in R&D. In 1973 Diebold introduced its first ATM. Sales were helped by long-standing relationships with banks, and within five years Diebold had 45% of the US ATM market.

In 1990 Diebold formed InterBold, a joint venture with former rival IBM, to sell ATMs. Diebold acquired Griffin Technology, moving into the market for campus systems, in 1995. The company expanded its Asian presence in 1997 when it acquired Safetell International Security. The next year, after InterBold canceled its agreement with IBM, Diebold bought IBM's 30% interest in the venture, taking direct control over its global distribution.

In 1999 Emerson Electric executive Walden O'Dell became CEO. In 2000 Diebold furthered its global push by acquiring the financial self-service businesses of Amsterdam-based Getronics NV and Paris-based Bull.

Early in 2002 Diebold acquired voting-systems maker Global Election Systems and renamed the subsidiary Diebold Election Systems, then Premier Election Systems. The voting machine unit made headlines in 2004 when four counties in California banned the use of its terminals after a state advisory board raised concerns about security and reliability. Diebold later agreed to settle a civil action lawsuit brought by the state of California for $2.6 million.

Diebold bolstered its maintenance and support operations when it acquired TFE Technology Holdings in 2004. O'Dell resigned as chairman and CEO in 2005; president Thomas Swidarski replaced him as CEO, and director John Lauer was named chairman.

In 2006 the company augmented its Diebold Global Security division with the purchase of Actcom, a provider of security systems for government agencies including the US Department of Defense, in mid-2006.

An SEC investigation into Diebold's accounting practices caused the company to delay its annual filing for fiscal 2007. The investigation concerned the reporting of revenue for product shipments (versus delivery) and services.

Seeking to augment its UTC Fire & Security unit, United Technologies made an unsolicited offer to acquire Diebold for $2.6 billion in cash in 2008. Diebold's board of directors issued a statement rejecting the offer, as it had previous overtures from United Technologies. United Technologies later withdrew its offer.

In 2009 the company took a $25 million charge on an agreement in principle to settle civil charges planned by the SEC.

EXECUTIVES

Chairman: John N. Lauer, age 71
President, CEO, and Director: Thomas W. Swidarski, age 51, $4,594,850 total compensation
EVP and CFO: Bradley C. (Brad) Richardson, age 51, $1,176,005 total compensation
EVP International Operations: James L. M. Chen, age 49, $1,601,333 total compensation
EVP North America Operations:
Charles E. (Chuck) Ducey Jr., age 54, $1,102,582 total compensation
EVP Global Operations: George S. Mayes Jr., age 51, $1,079,830 total compensation
VP and CTO: Frank A. Natoli Jr.
VP and Chief Communications Officer: John D. Kristoff, age 42
VP and Chief Information Security Officer: Scott M. Angelo
VP and Chief Marketing Officer: John M. Deignan
VP and Chief Tax Officer: M. Scott Hunter, age 48
VP and Corporate Controller: Leslie A. Pierce, age 46, $607,625 total compensation
VP and Treasurer: Timothy J. McDannold, age 47
VP and General Counsel: Warren W. Dettinger, age 56
VP and Chief Human Resources Officer: Sheila M. Rutt, age 41
VP Security: Bradley J. (Brad) Stephenson
VP Integrated Services (IS), Global Software Development and Global Professional Services: Kumar Pavithran, age 47
President, Brazilian Division: Joao Abud Jr., age 53
Director Investor Relations: Christopher (Chris) Bast
Auditors: KPMG LLP

LOCATIONS

HQ: Diebold, Incorporated
5995 Mayfair Rd., North Canton, OH 44720
Phone: 330-490-4000   **Fax:** 330-490-3794
Web: www.diebold.com

2009 Sales

	$ mil.	% of total
Americas	1,985.0	73
Asia/Pacific	387.1	14
Europe, Middle East & Africa	346.2	13
Total	**2,718.3**	**100**

PRODUCTS/OPERATIONS

2009 Sales

	$ mil.	% of total
Financial self-service		
Services	1,083.9	40
Products	985.3	36
Security		
Services	396.1	15
Products	247.5	9
Lottery systems	5.5	—
Total	**2,718.3**	**100**

Selected Products

Alarm and monitoring systems
Automated teller machines (ATMs)
Cash dispensers and recyclers
Check imaging
Coin machines
Drive-up banking and pharmacy equipment
Lottery systems
Remote bank teller systems
Vaults, safe deposit boxes, locks, and safes

COMPETITORS

ACI Worldwide	NCR
ADT Security	Niscayah Group
De La Rue	Oki Electric
Election Systems &	Sequoia Voting
Software	Siemens AG
Fujitsu	Thales
Gemalto	Tranax Technologies
Hart InterCivic	Triton Systems
Itautec	Wincor Nixdorf

HISTORICAL FINANCIALS

Company Type: Public

Income Statement

FYE: December 31

	REVENUE ($ mil.)	NET INCOME ($ mil.)	NET PROFIT MARGIN	EMPLOYEES
12/09	2,718	32	1.2%	16,397
12/08	3,170	89	2.8%	16,658
12/07	2,965	40	1.3%	16,942
12/06	2,906	87	3.0%	15,451
12/05	2,587	97	3.7%	14,603
Annual Growth	**1.2%**	**(24.0%)**	**—**	**2.9%**

2009 Year-End Financials

Debt ratio: 51.6%
Return on equity: 3.2%
Cash ($ mil.): 328
Long-term debt ($ mil.): 540

No. of shares (mil.): 66
Dividends
  Yield: 3.7%
  Payout: 266.7%
Market value ($ mil.): 1,876

Stock History

NYSE: DBD

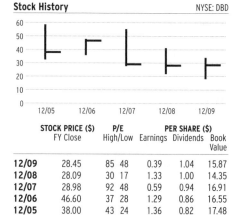

	STOCK PRICE ($) FY Close	P/E High/Low		PER SHARE ($) Earnings	Dividends	Book Value
12/09	28.45	85	48	0.39	1.04	15.87
12/08	28.09	30	17	1.33	1.00	14.35
12/07	28.98	92	48	0.59	0.94	16.91
12/06	46.60	37	28	1.29	0.86	16.55
12/05	38.00	43	24	1.36	0.82	17.48
Annual Growth	**(7.0%)**	**—**	**—**	**(26.8%)**	**6.1%**	**(2.4%)**

Dillard's, Inc.

Tradition is trying to catch up with the times at Dillard's. Sandwiched between retail giant Macy's and discount chains, such as Kohl's, Dillard's is rethinking its strategy and trimming its store count. The department store chain operates some 310 locations (down from 330 in 2005) in about 30 states, covering the Sun Belt and the central US. Its stores cater to middle- and upper-middle-income women, selling name-brand and private-label merchandise with a focus on apparel and home furnishings. Women's apparel and accessories account for more than a third of sales. Founded in 1938 by William Dillard, family members, through the W. D. Company, control nearly all of the company's voting shares and run the company.

Dillard's sales have been declining since 2006, and the company's store count has dipped as it shutters underperforming locations, including the last of its 16 home and furniture stores. Indeed, Dillard's schedule of store closings has accelerated in recent years as it attempts to reduce operating expenses in a recessionary environment.

Sales across all merchandise categories are falling. To remedy the situation, the department store chain is attempting to move upscale, positioning itself above Macy's and Belk and below high-end chains such as Nordstrom and Bloomingdale's. To attract more customers Dillard's is focusing on adding more fashion, much like J. C. Penney has done in recent years. The firm's new direction is inspired on the success of specialty stores with their edited displays or merchandise in boutique-like settings rather than an endless sea of apparel racks. New stores are smaller (averaging 170,000 sq. ft.) and located in open-air lifestyle centers rather than enclosed malls. Dillard's, which is averse to marking down merchandise but has been forced to discount by its lower-end competitors, hopes its move upmarket will stop the markdowns.

Despite these efforts to right itself, same-store sales have continued to decline and Dillard's has come under fire from disgruntled investors who are demanding the ouster of the family-led management team, including CEO Bill Dillard. The demand comes after Dillard's bowed to pressure from hedge funds Barington Capital Group and Clinton Group and appointed four new directors in April 2008 to avoid a proxy fight. (Both Barington and the Clinton Group has since substantially reduced their holdings in the company.)

HISTORY

At age 12 William Dillard began working in his father's general store in Mineral Springs, Arkansas. After he graduated from Columbia University in 1937, the third-generation retailer spent seven months in the Sears, Roebuck manager training program in Tulsa, Oklahoma.

With $8,000 borrowed from his father, William opened his first department store in Nashville, Arkansas, in 1938. Service was one of the most important things he had to offer, he said, and he insisted on quality — he personally inspected every item and would settle for nothing but the best. William sold the store in 1948 to finance a partnership in Wooten's Department Store in Texarkana, Arkansas; he bought out Wooten and established Dillard's the next year.

Throughout the 1950s and 1960s, the company became a strong regional retailer, developing its strategy of buying well-established downtown stores in small cities; acquisitions in those years included Mayer & Schmidt (Tyler, Texas; 1956) and Joseph Pfeifer (Little Rock, Arkansas; 1963). Dillard's moved its headquarters to Little Rock after buying Pfeifer. When it went public in 1969, it had 15 stores in three states.

During the early 1960s the company began computerizing operations to streamline inventory and information management. In 1970 Dillard's added computerized cash registers, which gave management hourly sales figures.

The chain continued acquiring outlets (more than 130 over the next three decades, including stores owned by Stix, Baer & Fuller, Macy's, Joske's, and Maison Blanche). In a 1988 joint venture with Edward J. DeBartolo, Dillard's bought a 50% interest in the 12 Higbee's stores in Ohio (buying the other 50% in 1992, shortly after Higbee's bought five former Horne's stores in Ohio).

In 1991 Vendamerica (subsidiary of Vendex International and the only major nonfamily holder of the company's stock) sold its 8.9 million shares of Class A stock (25% of the class) in an underwritten public offering.

A lawsuit filed by the FTC against Dillard's in 1994, claiming the company made it unreasonably difficult for its credit card holders to remove unauthorized charges from their bills, was dismissed the following year.

William retired in 1998 and William Dillard II took over the CEO position, while brother Alex became president. The company then paid $3.1 billion for Mercantile Stores, which operated 106 apparel and home design stores in the South and Midwest. To avoid redundancy in certain regions, Dillard's sold 26 of those stores and exchanged seven others for new Dillard's stores. The assimilation of Mercantile brought distribution problems that cut into earnings for fiscal 1999. In late 2000, with a slumping stock price and declining sales, Dillard's said it would de-emphasize its concentration on name-brand merchandise and offer deep discounts on branded items already in stock. Despite these efforts, sales and earnings continued to slide in 2001.

Founder and patriarch William Dillard (the company's guiding force) died in February 2002. Son William II became chairman of the company, which has been family-controlled for half a century.

In November 2004 Dillard's completed the sale of Dillard National Bank, the retailer's credit card portfolio, to GE Consumer Finance for about $1.1 billion (plus debt). Dillard's said it would use the proceeds to reduce debt, repurchase stock, and to achieve general corporate purposes.

In the spring of 2005 Dillard's shuttered the last of 16 home and furniture stores acquired when the department store chain acquired Mercantile Stores Co. in 1998. Hurricanes Katrina, Rita, and Wilma took a toll on Dillard's in 2005, interrupting business in about 60 of the company's stores at various times.

In August 2008 Dillard's purchased the 50% stake in the Arkansas-based construction firm CDI Contractors that it didn't already own for about $9.8 million. CDI is a general contactor that also builds stores for Dillard's. In November Dillard's announced 500 job cuts, including about 60 at headquarters.

EXECUTIVES

Chairman and CEO: William (Bill) Dillard II, age 65, $4,911,882 total compensation
President and Director: Alex Dillard, age 60, $4,825,146 total compensation
EVP and Director: Drue Corbusier, age 63, $3,086,998 total compensation
EVP and Director: Mike Dillard, age 58, $2,790,333 total compensation
EVP and Director: Drue Matheny, age 63, $1,043,822 total compensation
SVP, CFO, and Director: James I. Freeman, age 60, $2,178,358 total compensation
VP and CIO: William L. (Bill) Holder Jr.
VP Product Development: Les Chandler
VP and General Counsel: Paul J. Schroeder Jr., age 62
Director Investor Relations: Julie J. Bull
Auditors: Deloitte & Touche LLP

LOCATIONS

HQ: Dillard's, Inc.
  1600 Cantrell Rd., Little Rock, AR 72201
Phone: 501-376-5200   **Fax:** 501-399-7831
Web: www.dillards.com

2010 Stores

	No.
Texas	59
Florida	44
Arizona	16
North Carolina	15
Ohio	15
Louisiana	14
Georgia	12
Alabama	11
Oklahoma	11
Colorado	10
Missouri	10
Tennessee	10
Arkansas	8
South Carolina	8
Virginia	8
Kansas	7
Kentucky	6
Mississippi	6
New Mexico	6
Utah	6
Iowa	5
Nevada	4
California	3
Illinois	3
Indiana	3
Montana	3
Nebraska	3
Idaho	2
Wyoming	1
Total	**309**

PRODUCTS/OPERATIONS

2010 Sales

	% of total
Women's apparel & accessories	36
Men's apparel & accessories	17
Cosmetics	15
Shoes	14
Juniors' & children's apparel	8
Home & furniture	7
Construction segment	3
Total	**100**

COMPETITORS

Abercrombie & Fitch	Kohl's
American Eagle Outfitters	Lands' End
AnnTaylor	Macy's
Bed Bath & Beyond	Men's Wearhouse
Belk	Neiman Marcus
Bon-Ton Stores	Nordstrom
Brown Shoe	Saks
Burlington Coat Factory	Sears
Eddie Bauer llc	Stein Mart
Foot Locker	Talbots
The Gap	Target
J. C. Penney	TJX Companies
J. Crew	Tuesday Morning

HISTORICAL FINANCIALS

Company Type: Public

Income Statement			FYE: Saturday nearest January 31	
	REVENUE ($ mil.)	NET INCOME ($ mil.)	NET PROFIT MARGIN	EMPLOYEES
1/10	6,227	69	1.1%	41,300
1/09	6,988	(241)	—	49,000
1/08	7,371	54	0.7%	49,938
1/07	7,810	246	3.1%	51,385
1/06	7,708	122	1.6%	52,056
Annual Growth	(5.2%)	(13.3%)	—	(5.6%)

2010 Year-End Financials

Debt ratio: 42.1%   No. of shares (mil.): 69
Return on equity: 3.0%   Dividends
Cash ($ mil.): 342   Yield: 1.0%
Current ratio: 2.28   Payout: 17.2%
Long-term debt ($ mil.): 970   Market value ($ mil.): 1,135

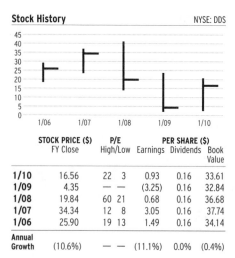

	STOCK PRICE ($) FY Close	P/E High/Low		PER SHARE ($) Earnings	Dividends	Book Value
1/10	16.56	22	3	0.93	0.16	33.61
1/09	4.35	—	—	(3.25)	0.16	32.84
1/08	19.84	60	21	0.68	0.16	36.68
1/07	34.34	12	8	3.05	0.16	37.74
1/06	25.90	19	13	1.49	0.16	34.14
Annual Growth	(10.6%)	—	—	(11.1%)	0.0%	(0.4%)

DineEquity, Inc.

This company shows an equal bias for breakfast, lunch, and dinner. DineEquity is one of the leading chain restaurant companies in the US with two flagship concepts, IHOP (the International House of Pancakes) and Applebee's Neighborhood Grill and Bar (operated through subsidiary Applebee's Services). The #3 family-style diner chain behind Denny's and Waffle House, IHOP has about 1,450 mostly franchised restaurants that are open 24 hours a day. The chain is best known for its breakfast menu, but it also offers standard family fare for lunch and dinner. Applebee's is the #1 casual-dining chain, with about 2,000 locations in the US and 20 other countries, offering a wide variety of appetizers and entrees.

Operationally, DineEquity is focused primarily on franchising to oversee its wide-ranging eatery chains. Licensing its brands and other intellectual property to local operators generates a steady stream of royalties and franchising fees and it helps insulate the company from the ebbs and flows of the dining business. Its IHOP chain includes just a dozen corporate-run locations used mostly for testing and training, but DineEquity still owns about 400 Applebee's restaurants that account for about 70% of sales. The company is slowly selling most of those units to new and existing franchisees with the goal of franchising 98% of its restaurants.

DineEquity is equally committed to maintaining a steady hand on its marketing and menu development efforts as it is to franchising. Like its rivals in the casual dining business, the company invests heavily in advertising to promote its chains as distinct options for families that are dining out, but it takes different marketing approaches for its two concepts. IHOP relies primarily on discounted value pricing and limited-time offers (such as its Free Pancake Giveaway) to drive traffic to its restaurants. Applebee's, meanwhile, focuses its efforts on new menu items and special price offers to attract attention away from such brands as Chili's (owned by Brinker International) and T.G.I. Friday's (Carlson Restaurants Worldwide).

CEO Julia Stewart plays a key role in efforts to promote both chains, championing new and improved food products to grab the attention of customers. Her efforts are largely focused on improving the Applebee's chain through menu development efforts. Stewart engineered IHOP's $2.1 billion acquisition of Applebee's in 2007. (Coincidentally, she had left Applebee's in 2002 to become CEO at IHOP.) A year following the buyout, IHOP changed its name to DineEquity to emphasize its new status as a multi-concept operator.

HISTORY

Al Lapin opened the first International House of Pancakes in Toluca Lake, California, in 1958. Taking inspiration from the Howard Johnson's chain (with its bright orange roof design), Lapin added a blue A-frame roof to the design of his restaurants in 1960. The company went public in 1961 and began acquiring other restaurant chains, and later expanded to businesses outside the restaurant segment. It changed its name to International Industries in 1963. The conglomerate eventually collected about 20 subsidiaries, including eateries such as Orange Julius, Love's Wood Pit Barbecue, and The Original House of Pies, as well as other businesses such as Michael's Artist & Engineering Supplies, Securities Supervisors, Shirt Gallery, and United Rent-All.

While the pancake house chain had grown quickly to more than 1,000 locations, its highly diversified parent ran into debt trouble in the early 1970s. Lapin left, and after a 1976 restructuring, the company was renamed IHOP Corp. and operated just three businesses: Copper Penny Restaurants, Love's Wood Pit Barbecue Restaurants, and International House of Pancakes. Still struggling, IHOP sold out to Swiss company Wienerwald Holding in 1979, and Richard Herzer was made president. After Wienerwald went bankrupt in 1982, creditors sold the Copper Penny and Love's chains. Herzer was named CEO in 1983.

IHOP's expansion remained stunted until 1987, when Herzer and a group of investors bought it, injecting money that allowed it to resume growth. IHOP went public in 1991 with about 500 restaurants and began opening about 65 new sites annually.

The company exceeded $1 billion in systemwide sales for the first time in 1998 and opened about 75 restaurants a year through 2000. In 2001 IHOP created a joint venture with the US Mint to change its Silver Dollar Pancakes to Golden Dollar Pancakes as part of a campaign connected to the release of the new dollar coins. Also that year the company developed 76 new restaurants, and its franchisees developed another 17.

Former Applebee's executive Julia Stewart took over as president and CEO in 2002, and early the next year Herzer retired as chairman (he died later that year). He was replaced by director Larry Kay. That year IHOP began its refranchising effort. The company developed 30 fewer restaurants in the full year, and the number of franchised restaurants increased by four. At the end of 2003 IHOP had 44 company-operated restaurants (compared to 76 at the end of 2002).

In 2004 the company announced that it would ultimately own only a handful of restaurants, franchising the rest. Later in the year IHOP opened its first franchised location in Harlem, New York City, and it quickly became one of the company's top earners. Founder Lapin died the same year.

Larry Kay stepped down as chairman in 2006, and Stewart was appointed to replace him. Kay remained as a board member. The following year the company acquired Applebee's International for about $2.1 billion. (The Applebee's Neighborhood Grill & Bar chain is now operated by Applebee's Services.) IHOP changed its name to DineEquity in 2008.

EXECUTIVES

Chairman and CEO: Julia A. Stewart, age 54, $2,572,012 total compensation
CFO: John F. (Jack) Tierney, age 57, $1,175,883 total compensation
SVP Human Resources: John Jakubek, age 57
SVP and Corporate Controller: Greggory (Gregg) Kalvin, age 50, $507,976 total compensation
President, IHOP's Business Unit: Jean M. Birch, age 50, $2,719,033 total compensation
President, Applebee's Business Unit: Michael J. (Mike) Archer, age 49, $1,518,458 total compensation
Executive Director Communications: Patrick J. Lenow
SVP Marketing, IHOP: Carolyn P. O'Keefe, age 53
SVP Operations, IHOP: Jim Peros
Director Investor Relations: Stacy Roughan
Auditors: Ernst & Young LLP

LOCATIONS

HQ: DineEquity, Inc.
450 N. Brand Blvd., 7th Fl., Glendale, CA 91203
Phone: 818-240-6055   **Fax:** 818-637-3131
Web: dineequity.com

2009 Locations

	No.
US	
California	340
Texas	274
Florida	254
New York	154
Georgia	143
Virginia	126
Ohio	125
Illinois	118
Michigan	104
North Carolina	97
New Jersey	95
Pennsylvania	94
Indiana	86
Missouri	85
Minnesota	70
Tennessee	70
Arizona	69
Washington	68
South Carolina	66
Wisconsin	60
Colorado	56
Maryland	56
Kansas	52
Massachusetts	48
Alabama	47
Oklahoma	44
Louisiana	42
Kentucky	40
Nevada	37
Iowa	36
Utah	35
New Mexico	30
Oregon	28
Mississippi	27
Arkansas	25
Nebraska	24
West Virginia	23
Idaho	21
New Hampshire	18
Delaware	17
Other states	97
International	163
Total	**3,464**

PRODUCTS/OPERATIONS

2009 Sales

	$ mil.	% of total
Restaurants	890.0	63
Franchising	372.2	26
Rent	133.9	10
Other	17.9	1
Total	**1,414.0**	**100**

2009 Locations

	No.
Franchised	3,052
Company-owned	412
Total	**3,464**

2009 Locations

	No.
Applebee's Neighborhood Grill & Bar	2,008
IHOP	1,456
Total	**3,464**

COMPETITORS

Bob Evans
Brinker
Carlson Restaurants
Cheesecake Factory
Cracker Barrel
Darden
Denny's
Hooters
OSI Restaurant Partners
Perkins & Marie Callender's
Ruby Tuesday
Waffle House

HISTORICAL FINANCIALS

Company Type: Public

Income Statement

FYE: December 31

	REVENUE ($ mil.)	NET INCOME ($ mil.)	NET PROFIT MARGIN	EMPLOYEES
12/09	1,414	31	2.2%	22,900
12/08	1,614	(155)	—	25,248
12/07	485	(1)	—	32,300
12/06	350	45	12.8%	972
12/05	348	44	12.6%	897
Annual Growth	**42.0%**	**(8.0%)**	**—**	**124.8%**

2009 Year-End Financials

Debt ratio: 6,933.0%
Return on equity: 175.8%
Cash ($ mil.): 82
Current ratio: 1.31
Long-term debt ($ mil.): 2,099
No. of shares (mil.): 18
Dividends
　Yield: 0.0%
　Payout: —
Market value ($ mil.): 435

Stock History

NYSE: DIN

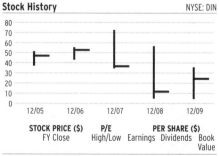

	STOCK PRICE ($) FY Close	P/E High/Low		PER SHARE ($) Earnings	Dividends	Book Value
12/09	24.29	63	10	0.55	0.00	3.90
12/08	11.56	—	—	(10.09)	1.00	2.39
12/07	36.58	—	—	(0.13)	1.00	11.68
12/06	52.70	22	18	2.43	1.00	16.13
12/05	46.91	23	17	2.24	1.00	16.39
Annual Growth	**(15.2%)**	**—**	**—**	**(29.6%)**	**—**	**(30.2%)**

The DIRECTV Group

DIRECTV takes television straight to the masses — no wires attached. The company (formerly the The DIRECTV Group) operates the largest direct broadcast satellite (DBS) service in the US, ahead of #2 DISH Network, and in direct competition with cable providers Comcast and Time Warner. In addition to its more than 18 million US customers, the company serves more than 6 million subscribers in Latin America under the DIRECTV and Sky brands. Phone companies such as Verizon bundle its video services with their own voice and Internet packages. Liberty Media owns 55% of DIRECTV's stock. The DIRECTV Group merged with Liberty Entertainment Inc. (LEI) in a series of transactions to form DIRECTV in 2009.

Also that year, Michael White took over as the company's president and CEO, six months after the resignation of Chase Carey, who left to take a new position at News Corporation. White retired as CEO of PepsiCo International and vice chairman of PepsiCo prior to accepting the job at DIRECTV.

Looking ahead, the company is betting on expanded service offerings to lure more subscribers. It is extending its US service area and boosting the number of HD channels the company can offer. DIRECTV made a move in 2008 to entice new customers and pull in additional revenue from existing subscribers with the launch of its DIRECTV-on-Demand video service and the expansion of its international programming options.

DIRECTV is also hoping that new distribution deals will draw in customers with a need for bundled video and communications services. The company in 2009 announced a partnership with AT&T that enables the telephone carrier to market bundled broadband Internet, digital telephone, and DIRECTV video programming to its customers in 22 US states.

One of DIRECTV's distinguishing points in terms of programming (relative to cable operators and satellite rival DISH Network) is its status as the only broadcaster authorized to sell NFL Sunday Ticket, which gives subscribers access to most of the Sunday professional football games.

Liberty Media in 2008 exchanged its 16% stake in News Corp. for that company's 41% share, held through Fox Entertainment Group, of DIRECTV. It increased its stake in a subsequent share purchase that year.

HISTORY

The DIRECTV Group's roots go back to 1932, when Hughes Aircraft was founded to build experimental airplanes for Howard Hughes, who set a number of world airspeed records with the company's H-1 racer. During WWII the company began building a mammoth flying boat to serve as a troop carrier, but the *Spruce Goose* wasn't completed until 1947, when Hughes piloted it for its only flight (to silence critics who claimed it couldn't fly). After WWII the company began moving into the growing defense electronics field. In 1953 it underwent a major shake-up when about 80 of its top engineers walked out, dissatisfied with Hughes, who was becoming distant and difficult.

The US Air Force threatened to cancel the company's contracts because of Hughes' erratic behavior, so he transferred the company's assets to the Howard Hughes Medical Institute (with himself as its sole trustee) and hired former Bendix Aviation executive Lawrence Hyland to run the company. Hyland rebuilt its research staff, and the institute produced the first beam of coherent laser light (1960) and placed the first communications satellite into geosynchronous orbit (1963). The Hughes-built Surveyor landed on the moon in 1966.

When Hughes died in 1976, a board of trustees was created to oversee the institute. In 1984 the Department of Defense canceled several missile contracts, and the firm found it difficult to fund R&D.

The next year the institute sold Hughes Aircraft to General Motors (GM) for $5.2 billion. GM teamed its Delco Electronics auto parts unit with Hughes to form GM Hughes Electronics (GMHE). GMHE acquired General Dynamics' missile business in 1992 and installed former IBM executive Michael Armstrong as CEO. He cut personnel by 25% and refocused the company on commercial electronics.

In 1995 GMHE became Hughes Electronics and launched its DIRECTV satellite service. Hughes bought a majority stake in satellite communications provider PanAmSat in 1996 (PanAmSat was acquired in 2006 by Intelsat).

In 1997 GM sold its defense electronics unit to Raytheon and merged Delco Electronics into GM subsidiary Delphi Automotive Systems. Armstrong left Hughes to head AT&T and was replaced by Michael Smith, whose brother John Smith was then GM's CEO.

In 1998 Hughes took a public relations hit when several of its satellites failed and temporarily halted most US pager activity. Hughes in 1999 bought United States Satellite Broadcasting and the satellite business of rival PRIMESTAR and folded the businesses into DIRECTV. America Online (now part of Time Warner) invested $1.5 billion in Hughes.

In early 2000 Hughes sold its satellite manufacturing market to Boeing in an effort to focus on its faster-growing communications services businesses. GM also issued a tracking stock for Hughes but retained ownership of all the company's assets. That same year, GM announced that it would try to sell Hughes.

Hughes bought Telocity (renamed DIRECTV Broadband), an ISP that uses DSL (digital subscriber line) technology, in 2001. Later that year Michael Smith retired abruptly amid reports of disputes over the sale of the company. GM's Harry Pearce took over as chairman of Hughes, and Jack Shaw was named CEO.

GM sold its 19.8% interest in Hughes Electronics to News Corp. in 2003. News Corp. acquired another 14.2% from common stockholders, amounting to a 34% stake.

In 2004 Hughes Electronics changed its name to The DIRECTV Group, declaring its focus and commitment to the DIRECTV brand and DTH satellite business. In 2005 the company sold its 80% stake in satellite network operator PanAmSat to a group of private equity firms (KKR, The Carlyle Group, and Providence Equity Partners) in a deal valued at $2.6 billion.

After selling a majority stake in its Mexico-based operations and making acquisitions in Brazil and other areas, DIRECTV restructured its Latin American unit in 2007 to include PanAmericana, Sky Brazil, and Sky Mexico. The segment came fully under DIRECTV's ownership in 2007 when it purchased Darlene Investment's 14% stake.

EXECUTIVES

Chairman, President, and CEO:
Michael D. (Mike) White, age 59
EVP and CTO: Romulo C. Pontual, age 50
EVP; President, New Ventures; President and CEO, DIRECTV Latin America: Bruce B. Churchill, age 52, $3,942,999 total compensation
EVP and CFO: Patrick T. (Pat) Doyle, age 54, $1,688,291 total compensation
EVP and General Counsel: Larry D. Hunter, age 59, $3,138,646 total compensation
EVP Operations: Michael W. (Mike) Palkovic, age 52, $2,986,982 total compensation
EVP and Chief Human Resources Officer: Joe Bosch
SVP Financial Planning and Investor Relations: Jonathan M. (Jon) Rubin
SVP Customer Care: Ellen Filipiak
SVP and Treasurer: J. William Little, age 41
SVP, Controller, and Chief Accounting Officer: John F. Murphy, age 41
VP and General Manager, The 101 Network: Patty Ishimoto
Media Contact: Darris Gringeri
Auditors: Deloitte & Touche LLP

LOCATIONS

HQ: DIRECTV
2230 E. Imperial Hwy., El Segundo, CA 90245
Phone: 310-964-5000   **Fax:** 310-535-5225
Web: www.directv.com

2009 Sales

	$ mil.	% of total
US	18,671	87
Latin America	2,878	13
Other	16	—
Total	**21,565**	**100**

COMPETITORS

Apple Inc.
AT&T
Brasil Telecom
Cablevision Systems
CenturyTel
Charter Communications
Comcast
Cox Communications
DISH Network
Hulu
Netflix
Telefónica
Telmex
Time Warner Cable
Verizon

HISTORICAL FINANCIALS

Company Type: Public

Income Statement

FYE: December 31

	REVENUE ($ mil.)	NET INCOME ($ mil.)	NET PROFIT MARGIN	EMPLOYEES
12/09	21,565	1,007	4.7%	23,300
12/08	19,693	1,521	7.7%	19,600
12/07	17,246	1,451	8.4%	12,300
12/06	14,756	1,420	9.6%	11,200
12/05	13,165	336	2.6%	9,200
Annual Growth	**13.1%**	**31.6%**	**—**	**26.2%**

2009 Year-End Financials

Debt ratio: 241.7%
Return on equity: 25.9%
Cash ($ mil.): 2,605
Current ratio: 0.89
Long-term debt ($ mil.): 7,037

No. of shares (mil.): 867
Dividends
  Yield: 0.0%
  Payout: —
Market value ($ mil.): 28,907

Stock History   NASDAQ (GS): DTV

	STOCK PRICE ($) FY Close	P/E High/Low		PER SHARE ($) Earnings	Dividends	Book Value
12/09	33.35	36	20	0.95	0.00	3.36
12/08	22.91	21	8	1.37	0.00	5.60
12/07	23.12	23	17	1.21	0.00	7.27
12/06	24.94	23	12	1.12	0.00	7.71
12/05	14.12	71	55	0.24	0.00	9.16
Annual Growth	**24.0%**	**—**	**—**	**41.1%**	**—**	**(22.2%)**

Discovery Communications

This company helps people discover nature and science programming right from their living rooms. Discovery Communications, Inc. (DCI) is a leading operator of cable channels focused primarily on such topics as history, natural and physical science, and technology. Its portfolio is anchored by the Discovery Channel, which reaches about 100 million US homes and is broadcast in more than 170 other countries. DCI also runs Animal Planet, the Military Channel, Science Channel, and TLC (The Learning Channel).

Like rival cable programmers such as Viacom and A&E Television Networks, DCI uses its portfolio of channels to segment its audience by programming each network around specific interests. Its TLC concentrates on personal interest shows (*Little People, Big World; What Not to Wear*) and Animal Planet highlights programming related to wildlife and pets (*Dogs 101, Whale Wars*), while the company's flagship Discovery Channel offers a mix of adventure, science, and history programming (*Deadliest Catch, Storm Chasers*).

The broadcaster has carved out its leading position in the television business by focusing on non-fiction and reality-based shows that mix entertainment and educational content. With its focus on attracting larger audiences, DCI is constantly developing or acquiring new programming to fit into its schedule. Its TLC plans to augment an already popular slate of programming with new shows such as *Sarah Palin's Alaska*, a reality-based show co-produced by Mark Burnett Productions and the former governor and vice-presidential candidate. Discovery Channel, meanwhile, has announced an ambitious project called *Curiosity: The Questions of Life*, a five-year series of specials each tackling different issues facing the world.

DCI is also working to expand its portfolio of cable channels in addition to maintaining its existing outlets. The company plans in 2011 to launch OWN: The Oprah Winfrey Network in

partnership with talk show host Oprah Winfrey (through her production company Harpo).

In addition to traditional TV programming, DCI is planning for the future of television content. The company joined with Sony Corporation of America and IMAX in 2010 to create a new programming service to provide a 24-hour schedule of 3-D TV content.

Media mogul John Malone, who controls various properties through his Liberty Media holding company, holds about 30% voting control in DCI. Advance/Newhouse, an affiliate of Advance Publications, has more than 25% voting control in the company.

HISTORY

John Hendricks, a history graduate who wanted to expand the presence of educational programming on TV, founded Cable Educational Network in 1982. Three years later he introduced the Discovery Channel. Devoted entirely to documentaries and nature shows, the channel premiered in 156,000 US homes. After dodging bankruptcy (it had $5,000 cash and $1 million in debt to the BBC), within a year the Discovery Channel had 7 million subscribers and a host of new investors, including Cox Cable Communications and TCI (now AT&T Broadband). It expanded its programming from 12 hours to 18 hours a day in 1987.

Discovery continued to attract subscribers, reaching more than 32 million by 1988. The next year it launched Discovery Channel Europe to more than 200,000 homes in the UK and Scandinavia. The company began selling home videos in 1990 and entered the Israeli market. The following year Discovery Communications, Inc. (DCI) was formed to house the company's operations, and it bought The Learning Channel (TLC, founded 1980). The company revamped TLC's programming and in 1992 introduced a daily six-hour commercial-free block of children's programs. The next year it introduced its first CD-ROM title, *In the Company of Whales,* based on the Discovery Channel documentary.

DCI increased its focus on international expansion in 1994, moving into Asia, Latin America, the Middle East, North Africa, Portugal, and Spain. The next year the company introduced its website and began selling company merchandise such as CD-ROMs and videos. DCI solidified its move into the retail sector in 1996 with the acquisition of The Nature Company and Scientific Revolution chains (renamed Discovery Channel Store). Also that year it launched its third major cable channel, Animal Planet.

The company continued expanding internationally throughout the mid-1990s, establishing operations in Australia, Canada, India, New Zealand, and South Korea (1995); Africa, Brazil, Germany, and Italy (1996); and Japan and Turkey (1997). DCI also added to its stable of cable channels with the purchase of 70% of the Travel Channel from Paxson Communications (now ION Media Networks) in 1997. (It acquired the remaining 30% interest in 1999.) The company's 1997 original production, "Titanic: Anatomy of a Disaster," attracted 3.2 million US households, setting a network ratings record.

The following year DCI and the BBC launched Animal Planet in Asia through a joint venture and agreed to market and distribute new cable channel BBC America. DCI spent $330 million launching its new health and fitness channel, Discovery Health, in 1999 and formed partnerships with high-speed online service Road Runner (to provide interactive information and services to Road Runner customers) and Rosen-bluth Travel (to provide vacation packages based on DCI programming).

In 2004 founder John Hendricks relinquished his CEO duties (he remained chairman). President Judy McHale replaced him.

DCI started off 2005 by rebranding its aviation-themed Discovery Wings channel as the Military Channel. Later that year former majority owner Liberty Media placed its stake in DCI into a new company called Discovery Holding, which it then spun off to Liberty shareholders.

Early in 2007 former NBC Universal Cable executive David Zaslav was named CEO, replacing McHale. DCI later bought out 25%-partner Cox Communications in exchange for $1.3 billion in cash, along with such assets as the Travel Channel and Antenna Audio. It also began shuttering its chain of Discovery Channel Stores as part of a cost-cutting effort.

Joint venture partners Discovery Holding and Advance/Newhouse (an affiliate of Advance Publications) combined their stakes in Discovery Communications in 2008, spinning off DCI as a public company.

EXECUTIVES

Chairman: John S. Hendricks, age 58, $17,297,508 total compensation
President, CEO, and Director: David M. Zaslav, age 50
SEVP and COO: Peter Liguori, age 50
SEVP and CFO: Bradley E. (Brad) Singer, age 44, $5,759,242 total compensation
SEVP Human Resources: Adria Alpert-Romm, age 55
SEVP, General Counsel, and Secretary:
Joseph A. (Joe) LaSala Jr., age 55, $1,207,773 total compensation
EVP and Chief Accounting Officer: Thomas R. Colan, age 55
EVP and CIO: David R. Kline
EVP and General Manager, Advertising Sales, Discovery Networks US: Scott McGraw
EVP Global Communications and Corporate Affairs: David C. Leavy
EVP and Managing Director, Discovery Networks, Europe, the Middle East, and Africa: Arthur Bastings
EVP Production and Chief Science Editor, National Geographic Channel: Steve Burns
EVP Media Technology, Production, and Operations: Glenn Oakley
EVP Business Affairs: Clara Kim
EVP Human Resources: Amy Girdwood
President and CEO, Discovery Networks International: Mark G. Hollinger, age 50, $6,089,977 total compensation
President, Digital Media and Corporate Development: Bruce L. Campbell, age 42, $3,063,161 total compensation
President and General Manager, Investigation Discovery, Military Channel, and HD Theater: Henry S. Schleiff, age 61
President and CEO, Hasbro-Discovery Communications Joint Venture: Margaret A. Loesch, age 61
CEO, OWN; The Oprah Winfrey Network: Christina Norman
President and CEO, Sony, Discovery Communications, and IMAX 3D Television Network: Tom Cosgrove
Auditors: PricewaterhouseCoopers LLP

LOCATIONS

HQ: Discovery Communications, Inc.
1 Discovery Place, Silver Spring, MD 20910
Phone: 240-662-2000 **Fax:** 240-662-1868
Web: corporate.discovery.com

2009 Sales

	$ mil.	% of total
US	2,311	66
International	1,205	34
Total	**3,516**	**100**

PRODUCTS/OPERATIONS

2009 Sales

	$ mil.	% of total
Distribution	1,713	49
Advertising	1,428	40
Other	375	11
Total	**3,516**	**100**

2009 Sales

	$ mil.	% of total
US networks	2,142	61
International networks	1,189	34
Commerce, education & other	176	5
Corporate	9	—
Total	**3,516**	**100**

Selected Operations

Cable channels
Animal Planet
Discovery Channel
Discovery Health
Discovery Kids
FitTV
HD Theater
Investigation Discovery
Military Channel
Planet Green
Science Channel
TLC (The Learning Channel)
Commerce and education
Discovery Education
DiscoveryStore.com

COMPETITORS

A&E Networks
CBS Corp
Disney
E! Entertainment Television
Fox Entertainment
NBC Universal
PBS
Rainbow Media
Scripps Networks
Turner Broadcasting
Viacom

HISTORICAL FINANCIALS

Company Type: Public

Income Statement

FYE: December 31

	REVENUE ($ mil.)	NET INCOME ($ mil.)	NET PROFIT MARGIN	EMPLOYEES
12/09	3,516	559	15.9%	4,400
12/08	3,443	317	9.2%	4,000
12/07	707	(68)	—	3,600
12/06	688	(46)	—	4,500
12/05	695	33	4.8%	3,800
Annual Growth	**50.0%**	**102.4%**	**—**	**3.7%**

2009 Year-End Financials

Debt ratio: 55.7%
Return on equity: —
Cash ($ mil.): 623
Current ratio: 2.13
Long-term debt ($ mil.): 3,457
No. of shares (mil.): 285
Dividends
Yield: —
Payout: —
Market value ($ mil.): 8,729

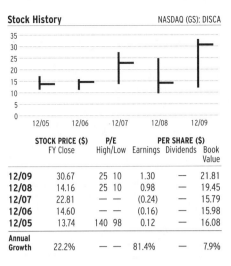

| Stock History | | | NASDAQ (GS): DISCA |

	STOCK PRICE ($) FY Close	P/E High/Low		PER SHARE ($) Earnings	Dividends	Book Value
12/09	30.67	25	10	1.30	—	21.81
12/08	14.16	25	10	0.98	—	19.45
12/07	22.81	—	—	(0.24)	—	15.79
12/06	14.60	—	—	(0.16)	—	15.98
12/05	13.74	140	98	0.12	—	16.08
Annual Growth	**22.2%**	**—**	**—**	**81.4%**	**—**	**7.9%**

DISH Network

DISH Network serves up fare intended to whet everyone's appetite for televised entertainment. The #2 provider of direct broadcast satellite TV service in the US (behind DIRECTV), the company serves about 14 million subscribers; customers include home viewers as well as business clients in such industries as hospitality, restaurant, and retail. DISH provides premium movies, SIRIUS satellite radio, and many local, international, and pay-per-view options in addition to basic video programming. It offers bundled voice and Internet services through partnerships with such voice and data communications providers as EarthLink and Qwest. Co-founder and CEO Charlie Ergen controls about 83% of the company's voting power.

As DISH works to build its subscriber base, the company faces the perpetual issue of keeping customer churn to a minimum. To keep existing subscribers interested, the company has tried to broaden the appeal of its brand by adding Sirius Satellite Radio music channels, more pay-per-view content, and local and national HD channels. Additionally, DISH paid $712 million to acquire wireless spectrum licenses granted to it by the FCC in February 2009; DISH plans to use the additional available spectrum to roll out more bandwidth intensive HD programming in the future.

To thwart increased competition from regional cable companies, DISH has deals with local TV affiliates; it offers about 2,500 local channels from markets in all 50 states.

Meanwhile, a distribution agreement with AT&T that brought in about 17% of DISH's annual gross subscriber additions in 2008, expired in January 2009. AT&T subsequently entered into a deal with chief rival DirecTV. The loss of this sales channel could make it more difficult for DISH to add new subscribers during 2010 and beyond.

HISTORY

Charlie Ergen, a former financial analyst for Frito-Lay, founded a Denver company called Echosphere, a retailer of large-dish, C-band satellite TV equipment, with his wife, Cantey, and James DeFranco in 1980. Echosphere evolved into a national manufacturer and distributor, which in 1987 began its move toward the new direct broadcast satellite (DBS) delivery system. It filed for a DBS license and set up subsidiary EchoStar Communications Corporation to build, launch, and operate DBS satellites. In 1992 the FCC granted the company an orbital slot.

By 1994 Echosphere was the US's largest distributor of conventional home satellite equipment, but the future clearly rested with DBS and EchoStar. A 1995 reorganization renamed the firm EchoStar Communications; the Echosphere distributor business became a subsidiary. EchoStar also created the DISH (Digital Sky Highway) Network brand, aiming for an easier-to-remember name than its rivals' "DSS" and "USSB."

The company launched the EchoStar I satellite in 1995, followed a year later by EchoStar II. Commencing DISH Network service in 1996, EchoStar competed against other DBS providers, including DIRECTV, to win 350,000 subscribers by year's end.

In 1997 Rupert Murdoch scrubbed a deal that called for News Corp. to buy half of EchoStar for $1 billion; Ergen sued for $5 billion in damages. EchoStar also went public in 1997 and reached the 1-million-customer mark.

The next year EchoStar tangled again with Murdoch, winning FCC approval to access programming from FX Networks (owned by News Corp. and the former TCI, now AT&T's cable unit), despite FX Networks' claims that it was locked up in exclusive programming agreements with cable companies. That issue and the 1997 lawsuit were put to rest in 1999 when News Corp. and MCI WorldCom (now WorldCom) traded DBS assets, including an orbital slot, for a combined 15% stake in EchoStar.

That year EchoStar and DIRECTV joined forces to successfully lobby for federal legislation allowing local TV signals to be delivered by satellites nationwide. The company entered the Internet business, providing WebTV Internet access via satellite to customers through an agreement with US software giant Microsoft. EchoStar also bought Media4 (now EchoStar Data Networks), which specializes in providing Internet and data transmission over satellite networks.

In 2000 the company reached an agreement to distribute two-way broadband Internet access using technology developed by the Israel-based Gilat Satellite Networks and Microsoft in a joint venture called StarBand Communications. In addition, EchoStar paid $50 million for a 13% stake in startup WildBlue Communications, which had planned to launch two geostationary satellites used to offer the two-way data services. EchoStar later backed out of those alliances.

When Hughes Electronics, at that time the parent of DIRECTV, was put up for sale in 2001, EchoStar expressed interest. After months of negotiations, EchoStar appeared to have given up but instead made an unsolicited offer. Hughes' parent, General Motors, agreed to sell the company to EchoStar after News Corp. dropped out of the bidding. Regulators rejected the deal in 2002, and the companies abandoned their merger plans.

As part of its attempt to compete with regional cable companies that have the capability to provide regional TV channels, DISH Network began offering local channels to towns in California, Idaho, Maryland, Montana, North Carolina, South Carolina, Virginia, and Wisconsin in 2003. The next year EchoStar announced it had made local channels available in markets in all 50 states.

In 2007 the company initiated a reorganization that resulted in the spinoff of its broadcast satellite receiver, antennae, and commercial satellite businesses as EchoStar Corporation. The remaining direct satellite subscription service operations became known as DISH Network Corporation. Also that year DISH bought video technology-maker Sling Media for $380 million in order to strengthen its technology development operations.

In a 2008 federal appeals court decision, a previous patent infringement ruling brought against DISH Network by digital video recorder maker TiVo was upheld. The company was ordered to pay millions in damages for violating a software patent held by TiVo that enables viewers to watch one program while recording others. The court agreed in 2010 to rehear the case at the request of DISH.

EXECUTIVES

Chairman, President, and CEO:
Charles W. (Charlie) Ergen, age 57,
$999,913 total compensation
EVP and COO: Bernard L. (Bernie) Han, age 46,
$1,713,423 total compensation
EVP and CFO: Robert E. Olson, age 51,
$1,057,485 total compensation
EVP Sales and Distribution and Director:
James DeFranco, age 57,
$1,133,979 total compensation
EVP and Chief Human Resources Officer:
Stephen W. Wood, age 51
EVP Operations: W. Erik Carlson, age 40
EVP, General Counsel, and Secretary:
R. Stanton Dodge, age 42,
$1,638,057 total compensation
EVP Programming, Sales, and Marketing:
Thomas A. (Tom) Cullen, age 50
EVP Advanced Technologies: Roger J. Lynch, age 47
EVP Commercial and Business Development:
Michael Kelly, age 48, $1,667,787 total compensation
SVP Programming: David (Dave) Shull
VP Ad Sales: Michael Finn
Chief Marketing Officer: Ira H. Bahr, age 47
Director and Senior Advisor: David K. Moskowitz, age 51
Auditors: KPMG LLP

LOCATIONS

HQ: DISH Network Corporation
9601 S. Meridian Blvd., Englewood, CO 80112
Phone: 303-723-1000   **Fax:** 303-723-1999
Web: www.dishnetwork.com

COMPETITORS

AT&T
Cablevision Systems
Charter Communications
Comcast
Cox Communications
DIRECTV
Grande Communications
Hulu
Netflix
Rainbow Media
RCN Corporation
Time Warner Cable
Verizon
Xanadoo

HISTORICAL FINANCIALS

Company Type: Public

Income Statement

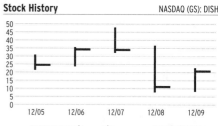

	REVENUE ($ mil.)	NET INCOME ($ mil.)	NET PROFIT MARGIN	EMPLOYEES
12/09	11,664	636	5.4%	24,500
12/08	11,617	903	7.8%	26,000
12/07	11,090	756	6.8%	23,000
12/06	9,819	608	6.2%	21,000
12/05	8,426	1,515	18.0%	21,000
Annual Growth	8.5%	(19.5%)	—	3.9%

FYE: December 31

2009 Year-End Financials

Debt ratio: —   No. of shares (mil.): 448
Return on equity: —   Dividends
Cash ($ mil.): 106   Yield: —
Current ratio: 1.06   Payout: —
Long-term debt ($ mil.): 6,470   Market value ($ mil.): 9,302

Stock History

NASDAQ (GS): DISH

	STOCK PRICE ($) FY Close	P/E High/Low		PER SHARE ($) Earnings	Dividends	Book Value
12/09	20.77	16	6	1.42	—	(4.67)
12/08	11.09	18	4	1.98	—	(4.35)
12/07	33.95	28	19	1.68	—	1.43
12/06	34.23	26	18	1.37	—	(0.49)
12/05	24.47	9	7	3.22	—	(1.94)
Annual Growth	(4.0%)	—	—	(18.5%)	—	—

Dole Food

Fans of bananas and other fresh fruit might find this company to be a-peel-ing. Dole Food is the world's largest producer of fresh fruit and vegetables, known best as a top grower of bananas, pineapples, and other tropical varieties of fruit. Some 200 products are sourced, grown, processed, marketed, and distributed in 90-plus countries, and it peddles its products to supermarkets, mass merchandisers, wholesalers, and foodservice operators worldwide. In addition to fresh fruits and vegetables, Dole produces sliced fruit, fresh salads, canned fruit, and frozen, bottled, and canned juices. The company traces its roots back to 1851, when James Dole founded a pineapple growing and canning company in Hawaii.

In North America Dole holds the #1 market share position in bananas, cauliflower, celery, iceberg lettuce, and packaged fruit products. It owns 122,000 acres of farms and other holdings, including 26,000 acres of farmland in Hawaii and approximately 2,600 acres of peach orchards in California. Worldwide, the company owns more than 1 million sq. ft. of vegetable processing facilities. In addition, its packaged food operation consists of 1.9 million sq. ft. of manufacturing facilities.

With the demand for convenient-to-use fruits and vegetables outstripping the demand for commodity fresh produce, Dole has been pursuing a strategy of shifting its product mix toward value-added products. It has successfully increased the sales percentage of its value-added sector, offering bagged vegetables and salads, ready-to-eat salads, and individual fruit servings packaged in plastic cups and bowls.

David Murdock, who has served as chairman of the company since 1985, took Dole private in 2003 through a $2.5 billion buyout that left the company saddled with substantial debt. Over time, Dole has been divesting some of its holdings in an effort to pay down that debt, including the sale of its fresh-cut flowers business and some real estate holdings. In 2009 the company went public in order to further repay its debt. Murdoch owns about 59% of the company.

In addition to Dole Food, Murdock controls interests in real estate and other businesses through holding company Castle & Cooke. The self-made billionaire is also known for his activities funding nutritional and medical research.

HISTORY

James Dole embarked on an unlikely career in a faraway land when he graduated from Harvard College in 1899 and sailed to Hawaii. He bought 61 acres of farmland for $4,000 in 1900 and the next year organized the Hawaiian Pineapple Company, announcing that the island's pineapples would eventually be in every US grocery store.

Others had tried and failed to sell fresh fruit to the mainland. Dole decided he would succeed by canning pineapples. He built his first cannery in 1903 and introduced a national magazine advertising campaign in 1908 designed to make consumers associate Hawaii with pineapples (then considered exotic fruits).

In 1922 Dole expanded his production by buying the island of Lanai, where he set up a pineapple plantation. He financed the purchase by selling a third interest in Hawaiian Pineapple to Waialua Agricultural Company, which was part of Castle & Cooke (C&C). Samuel Castle and Amos Cooke, missionaries to Hawaii, formed C&C in 1851 to manage their church's failing depository, which supplied outlying mission posts with staple goods. In 1858 they entered the sugar business and within 10 years served as agents for several Hawaiian sugar plantations and the ships that carried their cargoes.

C&C gained control of Hawaiian Pineapple in 1932 when it acquired an additional 21% interest in the business. The company began using the Dole name on packaging the next year. Dole became chairman of the board of the reorganized company in 1935 but pursued other business interests until he retired in 1948.

Hawaiian Pineapple was run separately until C&C bought the remainder in 1961. The company started pineapple and banana farms in the Philippines in 1963 to supply markets in East Asia. C&C began importing bananas when it purchased 55% of Standard Fruit of New Orleans in 1964. (It purchased the remainder four years later.)

Heavily in debt and limping from two hostile takeover attempts, C&C agreed in 1985 to merge with Flexi-Van, a container leasing company. The merger brought with it needed capital, Flexi-Van owner David Murdock (who became C&C's CEO), and a fleet of ships to transport produce. Murdock began trimming back, leaving C&C with its fruit and real estate operations. He then

decided to end all pineapple operations on Lanai to concentrate on tourist properties. (The company took a $168 million write-off on them in 1995, when it spun off its real estate and resort operations as Castle & Cooke.)

C&C became Dole Food in 1991. The company expanded at home and internationally, adding SAMICA (dried fruits and nuts, Europe, 1992), Dromedary (dates, US, 1994), Chiquita's New Zealand produce operations (1995), and SABA Trading (60%, produce importing and distribution, Sweden, 1998; Dole acquired 100% of SABA in 2005).

In 1995 Dole sold its juice business to Seagram's Tropicana Products division, keeping its pineapple juices and licensing the Dole name to Seagram. Dole entered the fresh-flower trade in 1998 by acquiring four major growers and marketers. It is now the world's largest producer of freshly cut flowers.

A worldwide banana glut, Hurricane Mitch, and severe freezes in California hit the company hard in late 1998. The next year Dole launched cost-cutting measures, which by early 2000 had ripened into better earnings. Nonetheless, cutbacks and disposals continued throughout 2001.

In 2002 Murdock made a takeover bid for the company worth about $2.5 billion. However, at least one minority shareholder was dissatisfied with the offer and filed a proposal calling for Murdock's resignation. After his offer was rejected, Murdock raised his bid, and the company agreed to the buyout the following year.

In 2004 Lawrence Kern, Dole's president and COO, left the company; chairman, CEO, and sole owner Murdock took over as president. In 2004 CFO Richard Dahl became president.

The company acquired fresh berry producer Coastal Berry Company (now Dole Berry Company) in 2004, making Dole a top North American strawberry producer. In 2006 Dole paid almost $42 million to Jamaica Producers Group for the remaining 65% that it did not already own of JP Fruit Distributors.

EXECUTIVES

Chairman: David H. Murdock, age 86, $2,108,377 total compensation
President, CEO, and Director: David A. DeLorenzo, age 62, $8,474,370 total compensation
EVP and CFO: Joseph S. Tesoriero, age 56, $2,086,366 total compensation
EVP and Chief of Staff: Roberta Wieman, age 64
EVP, General Counsel, Corporate Secretary, and Director: C. Michael Carter, age 66, $2,267,577 total compensation
EVP Corporate Development: Scott A. Griswold, age 56
SVP Worldwide Human Resources and Industrial Relations: Sue Hagen
VP, Corporate Controller, and Chief Accounting Officer: Yoon J. Hugh
VP and Director Worldwide Corporate Social Responsibility: Sylvain Cuperlier
VP and Director, Dole Nutrition Institute: Jennifer Grossman
VP New Products and Corporate Development and Director: Justin M. Murdock, age 37
Manager Corporate Social Responsibility: Roberto Vega
Auditors: Deloitte & Touche LLP

LOCATIONS

HQ: Dole Food Company, Inc.
1 Dole Dr., Westlake Village, CA 91362
Phone: 818-879-6600   **Fax:** 818-879-6615
Web: www.dole.com

2009 Sales

	$ mil.	% of total
North America		
US	2,831.3	42
Canada	311.0	4
Europe		
Sweden	456.4	6
Germany	447.9	6
UK	57.4	1
Other	743.9	11
Japan	793.9	12
Other	1,136.7	17
Total	**6,778.5**	**100**

PRODUCTS/OPERATIONS

2009 Sales

	$ mil.	% of total
Fresh fruit	4,711.0	70
Packaged foods	1,041.8	15
Fresh vegetables	1,024.5	15
Other	1.2	—
Total	**6,778.5**	**100**

COMPETITORS

A. Duda & Sons	Ocean Mist Farms
Bonduelle	Ocean Spray
Calavo Growers	Ready Pac
Chiquita Brands	Seneca Foods
Del Monte Foods	Sunkist
Fresh Del Monte Produce	Sunsweet Growers
Fresh Kist Produce	Tanimura & Antle
Fyffes	Taylor Fresh Foods
National Grape Cooperative	Tropicana
The Nunes Company	Worldwide Fruit

HISTORICAL FINANCIALS

Company Type: Public

Income Statement			FYE: Saturday nearest December 31	
	REVENUE ($ mil.)	NET INCOME ($ mil.)	NET PROFIT MARGIN	EMPLOYEES
12/09	6,779	88	1.3%	75,600
12/08	7,620	123	1.6%	75,800
12/07	6,931	(58)	—	87,000
12/06	6,172	(89)	—	75,000
12/05	5,871	44	0.8%	72,000
Annual Growth	3.7%	18.9%	—	1.2%

2009 Year-End Financials

Debt ratio: 185.1%	No. of shares (mil.): 88
Return on equity: 14.2%	Dividends
Cash ($ mil.): 120	Yield: —
Current ratio: 1.81	Payout: —
Long-term debt ($ mil.): 1,553	Market value ($ mil.): 1,095

Stock History

NYSE: DOLE

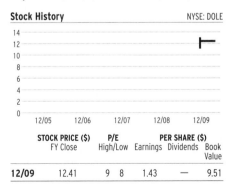

	STOCK PRICE ($) FY Close	P/E High/Low		PER SHARE ($) Earnings	Dividends	Book Value
12/09	12.41	9	8	1.43	—	9.51

Dollar General

Dollar General's at ease with living off the crumbs of Wal-Mart. The retailer commands a chain of more than 9,000 discount stores in 35 states, primarily in the southern and eastern US, the Midwest, and the Southwest. Offering basic household items, such as cleaning supplies and health and beauty aids, as well as some apparel and food, it targets low-, middle-, and fixed-income shoppers. Stores are generally located in small towns off the radar of giant discounters. Its big-city stores (about 30% of its total) are situated in lower-income neighborhoods. Some 25% of its merchandise is priced at $1 or less. Two years after being taken private by affiliates of KKR and Goldman Sachs, the chain went public in 2009.

Dollar General's IPO provided a rich payday for KKR and Goldman Sachs, which acquired the discount retailer in mid-2007 for about $7.3 billion. The company, KKR, and other owners, including Citigroup, sold a total of about $9.6 billion in stock. Post-IPO, a limited partnership controlled by KKR owns more than 85% of Dollar General's shares.

The timing of the IPO was fortuitous, as Dollar General has prospered during the recession, which proved to be very good for business at the discount chain. Cash-strapped consumers hunting for bargains flocked to Dollar General stores. (Over that difficult economic period, Dollar General's average sales per square foot increased to $195 in fiscal 2010 from $165 in 2007.)

CEO Rick Dreiling, who joined Dollar General following its acquisition by KKR, has focused on developing the chain's private-label business.

Because Dollar General's customers typically live in small towns, the company doesn't advertise. It only sends out direct mailings to announce new stores. Dollar General caters to customers who find shopping at its small-box, no-frills stores (typically 7,000 sq. ft.) easier and quicker than at super-sized competitors such as Wal-Mart (which are often much farther away). However, as Wal-Mart grows, its retail presence is being felt in more and more of Dollar General's markets.

In 2003 the company launched a new retail concept called Dollar General Market: larger stores (averaging 17,250 sq. ft.) that sell fresh produce and a range of refrigerated, frozen, and nonperishable foods in addition to core merchandise.

HISTORY

J. L. Turner was 11 when his father was killed during the 1890s in a Saturday night wrestling match. This forced J. L. to drop out of school and work on the family farm, which was weighted by a mortgage. By his 20s J. L., who never learned to read well, was running an area general store. Experiencing some success, he branched out and purchased two stores of his own. They failed, but J. L. rebounded, going to work for a wholesaler. With the onset of the Depression, J. L. found he could buy out the inventories of failing merchants for next to nothing, using short-term bank loans that were quickly repaid.

In 1939 J. L. was joined by his son Cal. The two each put up $5,000 to start a new Scottsville, Kentucky-based dry goods wholesaling operation called, not surprisingly, J.L. Turner & Son. It was not until 1945, when the company experienced a glut of women's underwear, that it expanded into retail. J.L. Turner & Son sold off the dainties in their first store, located in Albany, Kentucky. Within a decade the company was operating 35 stores. In 1956 J.L. Turner & Son introduced its first experimental Dollar General Store — all items priced less than a dollar — in Springfield, Kentucky. Like the company's first stores, the dollar store concept would grow: Dollar General Stores numbered 255 a decade later.

Cal Jr., J. L.'s 25-year-old grandson, joined the family business in 1965 and became a director in 1966. The company changed its name to Dollar General and went public two years later. In 1977 Cal Jr. was named president and CEO. That year Dollar General acquired Arkansas-based United Dollar Stores.

The early 1980s saw Dollar General continue its acquisition-powered growth. The company bought INTERCO's 280-store P.N. Hirsch chain and the 203-store Eagle Family Discount chain in 1983 and 1985, respectively. To cope with expanded distribution demands, Dollar General opened an additional distribution center in Homerville, Georgia, in 1986 to help out the original Scottsville facility. The acquisitions, led by Cal Jr.'s brother Steve, ended up costing the company dearly; Dollar General's 1987 stock price dropped nearly 85%. The next year they also cost Steve his job: He was forced out by the company's new chairman, Cal Jr. In addition to ousting Steve, Cal Jr. replaced more than half of Dollar General's executives in 1988. The retailer began moving toward everyday low pricing (à la Wal-Mart) in the late 1980s.

Growth from then on was powered by internal expansion. In 1990 the company operated nearly 1,400 stores; by 1995 it had more than 2,000. To accommodate the growth, Dollar General built a third distribution center in Ardmore, Oklahoma, in 1995 and another in South Boston, Virginia, in 1997. Cal Jr.'s CEO heir-apparent, former Circle K COO Bruce Krysiak, joined the company as president that January, only to resign in December, a casualty of differing corporate visions.

Dollar General opted to stop advertising in 1998. Cal Turner Sr. died in 2000.

Cal Jr. stepped down in 2002 amid a Securities and Exchange Commission investigation into accounting irregularities at the company launched in 2001. (Later the company restated its earnings for 1998 through 2000, saying it had overbooked earnings by about $100 million.) President and COO Donald Shaffer was named acting CEO in November 2002. In April 2003 former Reebok Brand president and CEO David Perdue joined Dollar General as its new chief executive. Perdue was elected chairman of the company in June 2003 when Turner stepped down.

In 2005 the company settled a Securities and Exchange Commission investigation into the circumstances that resulted in a $100 million earnings restatement for the years 1998 through 2000 with payment of a $10 million civil penalty.

In July 2007 Dollar General was taken private by Kohlberg Kravis & Roberts, GS Capital Partners (an affiliate of Goldman Sachs), and Citi Private Equity, an investment arm of Citigroup, in a deal valued at $7.3 billion. Concurrently, CEO David Perdue resigned.

In 2008 Richard Dreiling, formerly of drugstore chain Duane Reade and supermarket operator Safeway, was named CEO of the company.

The fast-growing chain opened its 9,000th store in late July 2010.

EXECUTIVES

Chairman and CEO: Richard W. (Rick) Dreiling, age 56, $4,421,325 total compensation
EVP and CFO: David M. Tehle, age 53, $1,790,455 total compensation
EVP and Chief People Officer: Robert D. (Bob) Ravener, age 51
EVP; Division President and Chief Merchandising Officer: Todd J. Vasos, age 48, $1,523,703 total compensation
EVP and General Counsel: Susan S. Lanigan, age 47
EVP Global Supply Chain: John W. Flanigan, age 58
EVP; Division President, Store Operations and Store Development: Kathleen R. Guion, age 58, $1,708,958 total compensation
SVP Store Operations: Thomas H. (Tom) Mitchell
SVP General Merchandise Manager: James W. (Jim) Thorpe
SVP and CIO: Ryan Boone
SVP Global Strategic Sourcing: Rod Birkins
SVP Real Estate and Store Development: Gayle Aertker
VP Internal Audit: Spencer Ferebee
VP Human Resources: Jeffrey R. (Jeff) Rice, age 42
VP Investor Relations and Public Relations: Mary Winn Gordon
Corporate Secretary and Chief Compliance Officer: Christine Connolly
Auditors: Ernst & Young LLP

LOCATIONS

HQ: Dollar General Corporation
100 Mission Ridge, Goodlettsville, TN 37072
Phone: 615-855-4000 **Fax:** 615-855-5252
Web: www.dollargeneral.com

2010 Stores

	No.
Texas	1,016
North Carolina	510
Georgia	502
Alabama	488
Ohio	486
Florida	456
Tennessee	455
Pennsylvania	409
Louisiana	353
South Carolina	353
Indiana	336
Missouri	336
Illinois	330
Kentucky	330
Oklahoma	289
Mississippi	286
Virginia	256
Michigan	250
Arkansas	246
New York	238
Iowa	170
Kansas	162
West Virginia	161
Wisconsin	89
Nebraska	80
Maryland	65
Arizona	54
New Mexico	45
New Jersey	34
Delaware	25
Colorado	22
Minnesota	16
Other states	29
Total	**8,877**

PRODUCTS/OPERATIONS

2010 Sales

	% of total
Consumables	71
Seasonal	15
Home products	7
Apparel	7
Total	**100**

Selected Merchandise

Basic apparel
Cleaning supplies
Dairy products
Frozen foods
Health and beauty aids
Housewares
Packaged foods
Seasonal goods
Stationery

COMPETITORS

99 Cents Only	Kmart
Big Lots	Rite Aid
Costco Wholesale	Target
CVS Caremark	TJX Companies
Dollar Tree	Variety Wholesalers
Family Dollar Stores	Walgreen
Fred's	Wal-Mart

HISTORICAL FINANCIALS

Company Type: Public

Income Statement

FYE: Friday nearest January 31

	REVENUE ($ mil.)	NET INCOME ($ mil.)	NET PROFIT MARGIN	EMPLOYEES
1/10	11,796	339	2.9%	79,800
1/09	10,458	108	1.0%	77,200
1/08	9,495	(13)	—	71,500
1/07	9,170	138	1.5%	69,500
1/06	8,582	350	4.1%	64,500
Annual Growth	8.3%	(0.8%)	—	5.5%

2010 Year-End Financials

Debt ratio: 100.3%
Return on equity: 10.9%
Cash ($ mil.): 222
Current ratio: 1.53
Long-term debt ($ mil.): 3,400

Net Income History

NYSE: DG

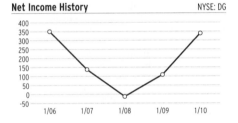

Dominion Resources

And darkness shall have no dominion, as far as Dominion Resources is concerned. Through its Dominion Virginia Power the company transmits and distributes electricity to 2.4 million customers and natural gas to 1.7 million customers in five states. Its Dominion Generation unit manages the company's regulated and non-regulated power plants (27,500 MW of owned or controlled capacity); subsidiary Dominion Energy trades and markets energy, oversees 12,000 miles of natural gas pipelines, and operates underground gas storage facilities (941 billion cu. ft. of capacity). Dominion is one of the largest producers and transporters of energy in the US.

The company has sold most of its exploration and production operations in recent years. In 2010 the company sold its remaining Appalachian exploration and production assets to CONSOL Energy for about $3.5 billion. The acquisition doubles CONSOL's natural gas reserves to 3 million cu. ft. (In 2007 Dominion sold the bulk of its oil and gas exploration and production assets — excluding its Appalachian operations, because at the time they offered less risk — for nearly $14 billion.)

Dominion agreed to sell The Peoples Natural Gas Company and Hope Gas, located in Pennsylvania and West Virginia, to investment firm SteelRiver Infrastructure Partners for $910 million. After receiving approval from Pennsylvania, the deal was rejected in late 2009 by West Virginia, saying the terms of the agreement were not in the public interest. The company then sold just Peoples Natural Gas to SteelRiver in 2010 for $780 million.

Dominion's divestments will allow it to concentrate its efforts in 2010 on its core businesses, distributing gas and electricity, along with its trading and marketing activities.

HISTORY

In 1781 the Virginia General Assembly established a group of trustees, including George Washington and James Madison, to promote navigation on the Appomattox River. The group (named the Appomattox Trustees) formed the Upper Appomattox Company in 1795 to secure its water rights. The company eventually began operating hydroelectric plants on the river, and by 1888 it had added a steam-powered plant to its portfolio.

The Virginia Railway and Power Company (VR&P), led by Frank Jay Gould, purchased the Upper Appomattox Company (which had changed its name) in 1909. The next year the firm acquired several electric and gas utilities, as well as some electric streetcar lines.

In 1925 New York engineering company Stone & Webster acquired VR&P. The company became known as Virginia Electric and Power Company (Virginia Power) and was placed under Engineers Public Service (EPS), a new holding company. Virginia Power purchased several North Carolina utilities following its acquisition.

During the 1930s the Depression (and the popularity of the automobile) led the company to exit the trolley business. The Public Utility Holding Company Act of 1935 (repealed in 2005), which ushered in an era of regulated utility monopolies, forced EPS to divest all of its operations except Virginia Power. However, the utility soon merged with the Virginia Public Service Company, thus doubling its service territory.

The company added new power plants to keep up with growing customer demand in the 1950s. Always an innovator, it also built an extra-high-voltage transmission system, the first in the world.

In the 1970s Virginia Power's first nuclear plants became operational. By 1980, however, the firm was near bankruptcy. That year William Berry, who had completed a 23-year rise through the ranks to become president, canceled two other nuclear units. He also became an early supporter of competition in the electric utility industry. In 1983 he formed Dominion Resources as a parent company for Virginia Power, and halted nearly all plant construction. Two additional subsidiaries were soon formed: Dominion Capital in 1985 and Dominion Energy in 1987.

In 1990, the year Thomas Capps took over as CEO, Dominion sold its natural gas distribution business, and in 1995 Dominion Energy began developing natural gas reserves through joint ventures and by purchasing three natural gas exploration and production companies.

The company acquired UK utility East Midlands Electricity in 1997. However, after it was hit by a hefty windfall tax by the newly elected Labour Party and its hopes for mergers with other UK utilities were dashed, it sold East Midlands to PowerGen just 18 months after acquiring it.

In 1999 Dominion prepared for energy deregulation through reorganization. It separated its electricity generation activities from its transmission and distribution operations. In 2000 Dominion bought Consolidated Natural Gas (CNG) for $9 billion, making it one of the largest fully integrated gas and electric power companies in the US; it then sold CNG's Virginia Natural Gas to AGL Resources and the two firms' combined Latin American assets to Duke Energy.

Virginia Power moved to head off state and federal lawsuits in 2000 by agreeing to spend $1.2 billion over 12 years to reduce pollution from coal-fired plants. The company also agreed to pay $1.3 billion for Northeast Utilities' Millstone nuclear power complex that year (the deal closed in 2001).

In 2001 Dominion bought exploration and production company Louis Dreyfus Natural Gas for about $1.8 billion in cash and stock and $500 million in assumed debt; the acquisition added 1.8 trillion cu. ft. of natural gas equivalent to Dominion's proved reserves.

Dominion began to prepare for power deregulation, implemented in most of its service territories, by expanding its nonregulated electric operations. The firm completed the acquisition of three fossil-fueled plants (2,800 MW) from USGen New England, a subsidiary of National Energy & Gas Transmission, for $656 million in 2005. That was the same year Dominion purchased the 550-MW Kewaunee nuclear plant from WPS Resources subsidiary Wisconsin Public Service and Alliant Energy subsidiary Wisconsin Power & Light for $220 million.

In 2007 Dominion began to dismantle its natural gas unit, selling its offshore operations in the Gulf of Mexico to Eni; its assets in Alabama, Michigan, and Texas to Loews Corp.; its Mid-Continent operations to Linn Energy; and operations in the Rocky Mountain and Gulf Coast regions to XTO Energy. Dominion Resources pocketed almost $14 billion from the sales.

EXECUTIVES

Chairman, President, and CEO; Chairman and CEO, Virginia Power: Thomas F. Farrell II, age 55, $11,973,541 total compensation
EVP and CFO, Dominion Resources and Virginia Power: Mark F. McGettrick, age 52, $5,117,226 total compensation
EVP; CEO Dominion Virginia Power: Paul D. Koonce, age 50, $2,537,983 total compensation
SVP and Chief Administrative Officer; President and Chief Administrative Officer, Dominion Resources Services: Steven A. Rogers, age 48
SVP Nuclear Operations: William R. Matthews
SVP Public Policy and Environment, Dominion Resources and Dominion Resources Services: Robert M. (Bob) Blue, age 42
SVP Regulation and Integrated Planning: James K. Martin, age 45
SVP Dominion Transmission: Paul E. Ruppert
SVP State Regulation: Thomas P. (Tom) Wohlfarth, age 49
SVP Fossil and Hydro: J. David Rives
SVP Tax and Treasurer: G. Scott Hetzer, age 53
SVP and General Counsel, Dominion Resources and Virginia Power: James F. Stutts, age 65, $2,835,993 total compensation

SVP and CIO: Margaret E. (Lyn) McDermid
SVP Alternative Energy Solutions: Mary C. Doswell, age 51
SVP Business Development and Generation Construction: Diane G. Leopold
VP and Chief Risk Officer: Christine M. Schwab
VP Human Resources: Roy Grier
VP Corporate Communications and Community Affairs: William C. (Bill) Hall Jr.
VP Financial Analysis and Investor Relations: Thomas E. (Tom) Hamlin
President and Chief Nuclear Officer, Dominion Nuclear: David A. Heacock, age 52
CEO, Dominion Energy: Gary L. Sypolt, age 56
CEO, Dominion Generation: David A. Christian, age 55, $3,198,354 total compensation
Auditors: Deloitte & Touche LLP

LOCATIONS

HQ: Dominion Resources, Inc.
120 Tredegar St., Richmond, VA 23219
Phone: 804-819-2000   **Fax:** 804-819-2233
Web: www.dom.com

PRODUCTS/OPERATIONS

2009 Sales

	$ mil.	% of total
Dominion Generation	8,751	53
Dominion Energy	3,810	23
Dominion Virginia Power	3,281	20
Corporate & other	653	4
Adjustments	(1,364)	—
Total	**15,131**	**100**

Selected Subsidiaries and Business Units

Dominion Generation Corporation (power plant management)
Dominion Virginia Power
  Consolidated Natural Gas
    Dominion East Ohio (or The East Ohio Gas Company, gas distribution)
    Dominion Hope (or Hope Gas, Inc., West Virginia gas distribution)
    Dominion North Carolina Power (or Virginia Electric and Power Company, electricity distribution)
  Dominion Retail, Inc. (retail energy marketing)
  Virginia Electric and Power Company (electricity distribution)
Dominion Energy (energy marketing, gas and power transmission)
  Dominion Transmission, Inc. (natural gas pipelines)

COMPETITORS

AEP
Allegheny Energy
CenterPoint Energy
Duke Energy
El Paso Corporation
Entergy
Exelon
Koch Industries, Inc.
NiSource
Piedmont Natural Gas

HISTORICAL FINANCIALS

Company Type: Public

Income Statement

FYE: December 31

	REVENUE ($ mil.)	NET INCOME ($ mil.)	NET PROFIT MARGIN	EMPLOYEES
12/09	15,131	1,304	8.6%	17,900
12/08	16,290	1,834	11.3%	18,000
12/07	15,674	2,697	17.2%	17,000
12/06	16,482	1,380	8.4%	17,500
12/05	18,041	1,039	5.8%	17,400
Annual Growth	**(4.3%)**	**5.8%**	**—**	**0.7%**

2009 Year-End Financials

Debt ratio: 138.4%
Return on equity: 12.3%
Cash ($ mil.): 48
Current ratio: 1.00
Long-term debt ($ mil.): 15,481
No. of shares (mil.): 589
Dividends
Yield: 4.5%
Payout: 80.6%
Market value ($ mil.): 22,929

Stock History

NYSE: D

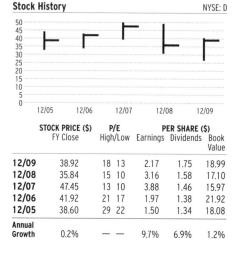

	STOCK PRICE ($) FY Close	P/E High	P/E Low	Earnings	Dividends	Book Value
12/09	38.92	18	13	2.17	1.75	18.99
12/08	35.84	15	10	3.16	1.58	17.10
12/07	47.45	13	10	3.88	1.46	15.97
12/06	41.92	21	17	1.97	1.38	21.92
12/05	38.60	29	22	1.50	1.34	18.08
Annual Growth	**0.2%**	**—**	**—**	**9.7%**	**6.9%**	**1.2%**

Domino's Pizza

This company knows the rules of the pizza delivery game. Domino's Pizza runs the world's #2 pizza chain (behind YUM! Brands' Pizza Hut division), with about 9,000 delivery locations in more than 60 countries. (The chain includes about 5,000 stores in the US.) Domino's menu features several different styles of pizza with a wide array of topping options, as well as additional items such as bread sticks, cheese bread, and chicken wings. Its stores are principally delivery locations and generally do not have any dine-in seating. The company owns and operates more than 450 locations in the US, while the rest are franchised. Private equity firm Bain Capital owns nearly 30% of the company.

Domino's relies heavily on franchising for both its dominant position in the pizza delivery market and the bulk of its revenue. Local operators, including #1 franchisee RPM Pizza, bear the cost of building and operating most of the company's far-flung network of eateries while paying royalties and fees in order to use the Domino's brand.

While rival Pizza Hut commands the largest portion of all quick-serve pizza sales, Domino's leads the pizza delivery segment with nearly 20% market share. The company has been able to expand rapidly thanks in large part to its delivery-store format with no dining area, which keeps startup and maintenance costs low for franchisees.

Domino's largely competes on price and the convenience of home delivery, but early in 2010 the company launched a new marketing campaign focused on a reformulated pizza recipe. While touting changes in how food is prepared is not so unusual in the cutthroat quick service restaurant industry, the campaign took the unexpected tact of admitting that consumers were unhappy with the taste of Domino's pizza. The effort to focus on food quality and taste was spearheaded by J. Patrick Doyle, who was promoted to CEO that year after leading the company's domestic operations. He replaced longtime chief David Brandon who stepped down as CEO while remaining chairman.

Responding to a harsh economy, the company has pulled back on its expansion efforts in the US. The company is making a big push to expand its international franchise network, however. More than 340 new Domino's locations were added to the chain outside the US during 2009.

HISTORY

Thomas Monaghan's early life was one of hardship. After growing up in an orphanage and numerous foster homes, Monaghan spent his young-adult life experimenting, trying everything from a Catholic seminary to a stint in the Marine Corps.

In 1960 Monaghan borrowed $500 and bought DomiNick's, a failed pizza parlor in Ypsilanti, Michigan, which he operated with the help of his brother James. In 1961 James traded his share in the restaurant to his brother for a Volkswagen Beetle, but Thomas pressed on, learning the pizza business largely by trial and error. After a brief partnership with an experienced restaurateur with whom he later had a falling out, Monaghan developed a strategy to sell only pizza and to locate stores near colleges and military bases. In 1965 the company changed its name to Domino's.

In the 1960s and 1970s, Monaghan endured setbacks that brought the company to the brink of bankruptcy. Among these were a 1968 fire that destroyed the Domino's headquarters and a 1975 lawsuit from Domino Sugar maker Amstar (now Tate & Lyle) for trademark infringement. But the company won the ensuing legal battles, and by 1978 it was operating 200 stores.

In the 1980s Domino's grew phenomenally. Between 1981 and 1983 the company doubled its number of US stores to 1,000; it went international in 1983, opening a store in Canada. The company's growth brought Monaghan a personal fortune. In 1983 he bought the Detroit Tigers baseball team and amassed one of the world's largest collections of Frank Lloyd Wright objects.

Domino's expansion continued in the mid-1980s with the help of a national advertising campaign featuring the red-suited Noid, an animated character meant to represent customers' concerns about pizza delivery ("Avoid the Noid"). With sales figures mounting, the company introduced pan pizza (its first new product) in 1989. That year Monaghan put Domino's up for sale, but his practice of linking his personal and professional finances had gotten both the founder and company into such dire fiscal straits that no one wanted to buy the chain. Monaghan installed a new management group and removed himself from day-to-day involvement.

Monaghan returned to the business in 1991 when its performance began to slide. Having experienced a religious rebirth, he sold off many of his private holdings (including his resort island and his baseball team, which went to cross-town pizza rival Michael Ilitch of Little Caesar). Monaghan also moved to reorganize management and reinvigorate the company. The next year Domino's introduced its first non-pizza menu item, bread sticks.

In 1993 a $79 million judgment was levied against the company resulting from a 1989 case in which a Domino's driver, trying to fulfill the company's 30-minute delivery guarantee, ran a red traffic light and collided with another car.

The incident prompted Domino's to drop its 30-minute delivery pledge and replace it with a satisfaction guarantee.

In 1998 Monaghan announced he would retire from the business he had guided for nearly 40 years in order to to devote more time to religious pursuits. He sold 93% of his stake in the company to investment firm Bain Capital for $1 billion. (The deal left Monaghan sizable voting control in the firm, however.) David Brandon, former CEO of sales promotion company Valassis Communications, replaced Monaghan as chairman and CEO.

Further restructuring efforts in 1999 eliminated about 100 corporate positions at Domino's.

In 2001 Domino's bought a majority stake in Dutch Pizza Beheer B.V., an operator of 52 Domino's restaurants in the Netherlands. The acquisition gave the company a base from which to manage future expansion in Europe.

Focusing in international expansion, the company added nearly 600 units between 2000 and 2003 in locations ranging from Iceland to Jamaica. The company went public in 2004.

Responding to an economic downturn in 2008, Domino's closed about 100 domestic locations, though it added more than 250 international restaurants.

EXECUTIVES

Chairman: David A. Brandon, age 58,
$4,207,131 total compensation
President, CEO, and Director: J. Patrick Doyle, age 46,
$1,784,361 total compensation
EVP Finance and CFO: Michael T. Lawton, age 51,
$727,390 total compensation
EVP Build the Brand and Chief Marketing Officer:
Russell J. Weiner, age 41,
$1,178,645 total compensation
EVP and CIO: Christopher K. McGlothlin, age 45
EVP Communications and Investor Relations:
Lynn M. Liddle, age 53
EVP Franchise Operations and Development:
Scott R. Hinshaw, age 47
EVP Supply Chain Services: John Macksood
EVP PeopleFirst: Patricia A. (Patti) Wilmot, age 61
EVP Franchise Relations: James G. Stansik, age 54
EVP, Domino's Team USA: Asi M. Sheikh, age 45
EVP and General Counsel: Kenneth B. (Ken) Rollin,
age 43
VP: William E. (Bill) Kapp, age 47,
$305,456 total compensation
VP and Corporate Controller: Steven Goda
VP Field Marketing: Lori Bohlen
VP Corporate Communications: Tim McIntyre
Director Treasury and Tax: Christian Dersidan
Director Franchise Recruiting and Sales: Mike Mettler
Auditors: PricewaterhouseCoopers LLP

LOCATIONS

HQ: Domino's Pizza, Inc.
30 Frank Lloyd Wright Dr., Ann Arbor, MI 48106
Phone: 734-930-3030
Web: www.dominos.com

PRODUCTS/OPERATIONS

2009 Sales

	$ mil.	% of total
Domestic foodservice distribution	763.7	54
Restaurants	335.8	24
Franchising	157.8	11
International	146.8	11
Total	**1,404.1**	**100**

2009 Locations

	No.
US	
Franchised	4,461
Company-owned	466
International	4,072
Total	**8,999**

COMPETITORS

Burger King
Godfather's Pizza
Jack in the Box
KFC
Little Caesar's
McDonald's
Noble Roman's
Papa John's
Papa Murphys
Pizza Hut
Quiznos
Round Table Pizza
Sbarro
Subway
Taco Bell
Wendy's/Arby's Group, Inc.

HISTORICAL FINANCIALS

Company Type: Public

Income Statement

	REVENUE ($ mil.)	NET INCOME ($ mil.)	NET PROFIT MARGIN	EMPLOYEES
12/09	1,404	80	5.7%	10,200
12/08	1,425	54	3.8%	10,500
12/07	1,463	38	2.6%	12,500
12/06	1,437	106	7.4%	13,300
12/05	1,512	108	7.2%	13,500
Annual Growth	**(1.8%)**	**(7.4%)**	**—**	**(6.8%)**

FYE: Sunday nearest December 31

2009 Year-End Financials

Debt ratio: —
Return on equity: —
Cash ($ mil.): 42
Current ratio: 1.27
Long-term debt ($ mil.): 1,538

No. of shares (mil.): 59
Dividends
  Yield: 0.0%
  Payout: —
Market value ($ mil.): 496

Stock History

NYSE: DPZ

	STOCK PRICE ($) FY Close	P/E High/Low	Earnings	PER SHARE ($) Dividends	Book Value
12/09	8.38	7 3	1.38	0.00	(22.31)
12/08	4.71	16 3	0.93	0.00	(24.06)
12/07	13.23	60 21	0.59	0.00	(24.49)
12/06	28.00	18 13	1.65	0.48	(9.54)
12/05	24.20	16 10	1.58	0.40	(8.63)
Annual Growth	**(23.3%)**	**— —**	**(3.3%)**	**—**	**—**

Donaldson Company

Grime fighter Donaldson is cleaning up the industrial world. The company makes filtration systems designed to remove contaminants from air and liquids. Donaldson's engine products business makes air intake and exhaust systems, liquid-filtration systems, and replacement parts; products are sold to manufacturers of construction, mining, and transportation equipment, as well as parts distributors and fleet operators. The company's industrial products include dust, fume, and mist collectors and air filtration systems used in industrial gas turbines, computer disk drives, and manufacturers' clean rooms. Donaldson has more than 100 locations worldwide, including 40 manufacturing plants.

Very much a global player, the company generated 58% of its revenues from outside the US in 2009.

It is pursuing a strategy of growth through the diversification of its products and technologies, and has acquired a number of companies to build its global brand base (30 major brands, including Duratek, Formix, PowerCore, Synteq, Tetratex, and Ultrafilter).

In particular, Donaldson is adding to its engine and industrial segment and its first fit-solutions and replacement filters businesses. Acquisitions have included AirCel Corporation, a privately held manufacturer of dryers and purification equipment (2006); Aerospace Filtration Systems, from Westar Aerospace and Defense Group (2007); and Western Filter Corp., a maker of liquid filtration systems and replacement filters (2008).

HISTORY

Frank Donaldson, a salesman for Bull Tractor, invented the first air filter for a combustion engine in 1915 after a tractor he had sold kept breaking down. Noticing a buildup of dirt in the intake manifold, he made a filter out of wire mesh and cloth. The tractor ran, but Donaldson lost his job: His boss did not appreciate his pointing out a defect in the company's products. Donaldson started his own company with his father and his brother Bob to make air filters for tractors. In 1941 the company won a contract to make air filters for US army tanks. Frank Donaldson died in 1945, and John Emblom became president. In 1951 Emblom and a group of senior managers tried to buy the company from the Donaldson family but were rebuffed. Emblom and his allies quit, and Frank Donaldson Jr. became president. The company went public in 1955.

Under Frank Jr. the company expanded, introducing new products (including the first paper filter for the heavy-duty air-cleaner industry) and buying other companies. In 1974 Donaldson bought Torit, which expanded the company into industrial dust collection. Frank Jr. retired as CEO in 1981.

During the 1990s Donaldson continued to expand its product line. In 1998 the company increased its ownership in PT Panata Jaya Mandiri, an Indonesian joint venture, to 30%. The next year it bought AirMaze (industrial compressor filters) and opened a manufacturing facility in China.

Donaldson acquired DCE (dust collection systems, UK) from Invensys in 2000. It then combined DCE with its Torit business to form Donaldson Dust Collection.

In 2002 Donaldson bought German-based ultrafilter international AG — maker of compress air purification components. The next year the company expanded its hydraulic filters business through the acquisition of LHA Industrial.

In 2004 Donaldson formed an aerospace and defense business unit, merging the operations of its aircraft and defense groups. The company also sold a manufacturing plant located in Stow, Ohio, to Falls Filtration Technology. Later that year Bill Van Dyke stepped down as president and CEO of the company, retaining his position as chairman. SVP Bill Cook was appointed president and CEO to replace him. (Cook was named chairman the next year after Van Dyke retired.) Donaldson closed out 2004 with the acquisition of Canadian liquid filter manufacturer Triboguard Company.

EXECUTIVES

Chairman, President, and CEO: William M. (Bill) Cook, age 56, $1,519,787 total compensation
SVP Industrial Products: Charles J. (Charlie) McMurray, age 56, $641,887 total compensation
SVP Engine Products: Jay L. Ward, age 45
VP and CFO: Thomas R. (Tom) VerHage, age 57, $604,230 total compensation
VP Human Resources and Communications: Sandra N. Joppa, age 44
VP Europe and Middle East: Tod E. Carpenter, age 51,
VP Global Operations: Joseph E. Lehman, age 55
VP Global Engine OEM Sales: Dennis D. Jandik, age 56
VP, Asia/Pacific: David W. Timm, age 56
VP Disk Drive and Microelectronic: Peggy A. Herrmann, age 54
VP and CTO: Debra L. (Deb) Wilfong, age 54
VP and CIO: Mary Lynne Perushek, age 51
VP, General Counsel, and Secretary: Norman C. Linnell, age 50
VP Global Engine Aftermarket: Franklin Cardenas, age 42
Chief Engineer: Don White
Director Investor Relations: Richard J. (Rich) Sheffer $792,648 total compensation
Auditors: PricewaterhouseCoopers LLP

LOCATIONS

HQ: Donaldson Company, Inc.
1400 W. 94th St., Minneapolis, MN 55431
Phone: 952-887-3131 **Fax:** 952-887-3155
Web: www.donaldson.com

2009 Sales

	$ mil.	% of total
US	779.0	42
Europe	567.1	30
Asia/Pacific	419.4	22
Other regions	103.1	6
Total	**1,868.6**	**100**

PRODUCTS/OPERATIONS

2009 Sales

	$ mil.	% of total
Engine products		
Aftermarket products	567.2	30
Off-road products	362.8	19
On-road products	71.9	4
Industrial products		
Industrial filtration products	503.6	27
Special application products	206.8	11
Gas turbine products	156.3	9
Total	**1,868.6**	**100**

COMPETITORS

AAF-McQUAY
Cummins
Merck Millipore
MFRI
Pall Corporation
Siemens Water Technologies
Williams Controls

HISTORICAL FINANCIALS

Company Type: Public

Income Statement

FYE: July 31

	REVENUE ($ mil.)	NET INCOME ($ mil.)	NET PROFIT MARGIN	EMPLOYEES
7/09	1,869	132	7.1%	10,600
7/08	2,233	172	7.7%	12,700
7/07	1,919	151	7.9%	12,000
7/06	1,694	132	7.8%	11,500
7/05	1,596	111	6.9%	11,180
Annual Growth	**4.0%**	**4.5%**	**—**	**(1.3%)**

2009 Year-End Financials

Debt ratio: 36.8%
Return on equity: 18.5%
Cash ($ mil.): 144
Current ratio: 2.26
Long-term debt ($ mil.): 254

No. of shares (mil.): 77
Dividends
  Yield: 1.2%
  Payout: 27.5%
Market value ($ mil.): 2,932

Stock History

NYSE: DCI

	STOCK PRICE ($) FY Close	P/E High/Low	PER SHARE ($) Earnings	Dividends	Book Value
7/09	38.01	29 13	1.67	0.46	8.93
7/08	45.11	25 16	2.12	0.42	9.59
7/07	36.39	21 17	1.83	0.36	8.10
7/06	32.89	23 18	1.55	0.32	7.09
7/05	32.58	27 20	1.27	0.23	6.80
Annual Growth	**3.9%**	**— —**	**7.1%**	**18.9%**	**7.0%**

Dover Corporation

The "D" in Dover could stand for diversity. Dover manages over 30 companies that make equipment ranging from car wash systems to aerospace components. Dover operates in four segments: Industrial Products (material handling and mobile equipment); Engineered Systems (product identification and refrigeration systems); Fluid Management (fluid and gas control, movement, measurement, and monitoring products); and Electronic Technologies (microcomponents for hearing aids and electronics, automated assembly and testing equipment, and RF/microwave filters). The company maintains a highly decentralized management culture, with a president for each division as well as for each subsidiary company.

The company continues to increase its expansion into international markets, including South America, Asia, and Eastern Europe. Most of its non-US subsidiaries and affiliates are based in Brazil, China, Europe, India, Malaysia, and Mexico. In 2009 it opened a regional headquarters in China, launching its shift to growing an Asian presence.

The company is focusing on acquisitions in such areas as product identification, energy and fluid solutions, refrigeration equipment, and electronic communication components.

Dover's largest segment, Engineered Systems, is composed of Engineered Products and Product Identification. Engineered products include refrigeration systems, air and ventilation systems, and food and beverage packaging machines for customers in the foodservice, consumer goods, and pharmaceutical industries. Product identification products handle industrial marking and bar coding systems.

Industrial Products is the company's second-largest segment. The material-handling equipment and mobile equipment manufactured by this segment's businesses include construction and demolition machinery attachments, four-wheel and all-wheel-drive power train systems, refuse truck bodies, tank trailers, car wash systems, and various aerospace components.

Its Fluid Management segment is split between energy and fluid applications. The businesses in this segment serve the fast-growing energy exploration and production markets, as well as the retail and commercial fueling industries by providing products used to transport, control, and dispense a wide variety of fluids.

Electronic Technologies is made up of seven companies that manufacture electronic components for hearing aid and consumer electronics, soldering equipment, microwave switches and filters, and automated assembly and test equipment.

HISTORY

George Ohrstrom, a New York stockbroker, formed Dover in 1955 and took it public that year. Originally headquartered in Washington, DC, Dover consisted of four companies: C. Lee Cook (compressor seals and piston rings), Peerless (space-venting heaters), Rotary Lift (automotive lifts), and W.C. Norris (components for oil wells). In 1958 Dover made the first of many acquisitions and entered the elevator industry by buying Shepard Warner Elevator.

Dover continued to diversify throughout the 1960s. Acquisitions included OPW (gas pump nozzles) in 1961 and De-Sta-Co (industrial clamps and valves) the next year. OPW head Thomas Sutton became Dover's president in 1964, and the company moved its headquarters to New York City. Dover acquired Groen Manufacturing (food industry products) in 1967 and Ronningen-Petter (filter-strainer units) the following year.

During the 1970s Dover expanded beyond its core industries (building materials, industrial components, and equipment). In 1975 it acquired Dieterich Standard, a maker of liquid-measurement instruments. Dieterich Standard's president, Gary Roubos, became Dover's president and COO in 1977 and its CEO in 1981. The company sold Peerless in 1977 and acquired electronics assembly equipment manufacturer Universal Instruments in 1979.

Electronics became an increasingly important part of Dover's business during the 1980s. The company bought K&L Microwave, a maker of microwave filters used in satellites and cable TV equipment (1983), Dielectric Laboratories (microwave filter parts, 1985), and NURAD (microwave antennas, 1986). Between 1985 and 1990 Dover bought some 25 companies, including Weldcraft Products (welding equipment, 1985), Wolfe Frostop (salad bars, 1987), Weaver Corp. (automotive lifts, 1987), General Elevator (1988), Texas Hydraulics (1988), Security Elevator (1990), and Marathon Equipment (waste-handling equipment, 1990).

The corporation spun off its DOVatron circuit board assembly subsidiary to shareholders in 1993 after finding that DOVatron was competing with important Dover customers. That year Dover acquired The Heil Company (garbage trucks).

President/COO Thomas Reece succeeded Gary Roubos as CEO in 1994. Dover purchased 10 companies that year, including Hill Phoenix (commercial refrigeration cases) and Koolrad Design & Manufacturing (radiators for transformers). In 1995 it bought France-based Imaje (ink-jet printers and specialty inks) for $200 million. It was the largest purchase in the company's history at the time.

In 1998 the company sold its Dover elevator unit — a popular brand, but a management headache — to German steel giant Thyssen (now ThyssenKrupp) for $1.1 billion.

Dover continued its acquisitive ways in 1999 and 2000, picking up 18 and 23 companies, respectively. Notable were Alphasem, which makes semiconductor manufacturing equipment, and Graphics Microsystems, which took Dover into the pressroom equipment market. Dover picked up Triton Systems, a maker of ATMs, in 2000.

Dover looked to Asia, and China in particular, as its best hope for near-term growth for its beleaguered telecommunications and electronic assembly businesses; Dover subsidiary Universal Instruments christened a major manufacturing plant in China early in 2003.

COO Ronald Hoffman took over as CEO at the outset of 2005. In 2005 the company aquired Knowles Electronics for $750 million. Knowles makes components for hearing aids and microphones for high-end cell phones.

The company sold Kurz-Kasch to Monomoy Capital Partners, a private equity firm, in early 2007. The following year Ronald Hoffman retired as CEO and was succeeded in that post by Robert Livingston, former president and CEO of Dover's Engineered Systems.

In 2009 subsidiary Hill Phoenix acquired Barker Company Limited (refrigerated, non-refrigerated, and hot display cases).

EXECUTIVES

Chairman: Robert W. Cremin, age 69
President, CEO, and Director:
Robert A. (Bob) Livingston, age 57,
$5,089,646 total compensation
VP Finance and CFO: Brad M. Cerepak, age 51,
$884,698 total compensation
VP, General Counsel, and Secretary: Joseph W. Schmidt, age 63
VP and Senior Advisor: Robert G. (Rob) Kuhbach,
age 63, $3,918,763 total compensation
VP; President and CEO, Dover Electronic Technologies: David R. Van Loan, age 61,
$4,599,855 total compensation
VP; President and CEO, Dover Fluid Management:
William W. (Bill) Spurgeon, age 51,
$3,061,919 total compensation
VP; President and CEO, Dover Engineered Systems:
Raymond (Ray) Hoglund, age 59,
$2,781,049 total compensation

VP; President and CEO, Dover Industrial Products:
Thomas (Tom) Giacomini, age 44,
$2,414,764 total compensation
VP; EVP, Dover Fluid Management; President, Fluid Solutions Platform:
Sivasankaran (Soma) Somasundaram, age 44
VP; Director, Dover Industrial Products:
Timothy J. (Tim) Sandker, age 61
VP Taxation: George Pompetzki, age 57
VP Corporate Development: Stephen R. Sellhausen,
age 51
VP Supply Chain and Global Sourcing: James H. Moyle,
age 57
VP and Controller: Raymond T. McKay Jr., age 56
VP Human Resources: Jay L. Kloosterboer, age 49
Treasurer and Director Investor Relations:
Paul E. Goldberg, age 46
Auditors: PricewaterhouseCoopers LLP

LOCATIONS

HQ: Dover Corporation
3005 Highland Pkwy., Ste. 200
Downers Grove, IL 60515
Phone: 630-541-1540   **Fax:** 630-743-2671
Web: www.dovercorporation.com

2009 Sales

	$ mil.	% of total
Americas		
US	3,257.1	56
Other countries	463.2	8
Europe	1,078.3	19
Asia	791.3	14
Other regions	185.8	3
Total	**5,775.7**	**100**

PRODUCTS/OPERATIONS

2009 Sales

	$ mil.	% of total
Engineered Systems	1,861.9	32
Industrial Products	1,621.8	28
Fluid Management	1,270.9	22
Electronic Technologies	1,027.0	18
Adjustments	(5.9)	—
Total	**5,775.7**	**100**

Selected Companies

Industrial Products
  Material Handling
    Crenlo, LLC
    DE-STA-CO Industries
    Paladin
    Texas Hydraulics
    Tulsa Winch
    Warn Industries
  Mobile Equipment
    Heil Environmental
    Heil Trailer International
    Marathon Equipment Co.
    PDQ Manufacturing
    Performance Motorsports
    Sargent
    Vehicle Service Group
Electronic Technologies
  Ceramics and microwave products
  DEK
  Everett Charles Technologies
  Knowles Electronics
  Microwave Products Group
  OK International
  Vectron International
Engineered Systems
  Engineered Products
    Belvac Production Machinery
    Hill PHOENIX
    SWEP
    Tipper Tie
    Unified Brands
  Product Identification
    Datamax-O'Neil
    Markem-Imaje

Fluid Management
  Energy
    Cook Compression
    Norris Production Solutions
    Quartzdyne
    US Synthetic
    Waukesha Bearings Corp.
  Fluid Solutions
    Colder Products Company
    Hydro Systems
    OPW Fluid Transfer Group
    OPW Fueling Components
    Pump Solutions Group

COMPETITORS

Carlisle Companies	Navistar
Cookson Group	Oshkosh Truck
Cooper Industries	Paul Mueller
Crane Co.	Sequa
Gardner Denver	Smith Bits
IDEX	Snap-on
Ingersoll-Rand	Swagelok
Kaydon	Tatung
KEMET	Thermador Groupe
KSB AG	Wastequip
Mark IV	Weatherford International
Middleby	Weston EU

HISTORICAL FINANCIALS

Company Type: Public

Income Statement

FYE: December 31

	REVENUE ($ mil.)	NET INCOME ($ mil.)	NET PROFIT MARGIN	EMPLOYEES
12/09	5,776	356	6.2%	29,300
12/08	7,569	591	7.8%	32,300
12/07	7,226	661	9.1%	33,400
12/06	6,512	562	8.6%	33,000
12/05	6,078	510	8.4%	31,650
Annual Growth	**(1.3%)**	**(8.6%)**	**—**	**(1.9%)**

2009 Year-End Financials

Debt ratio: 44.7%	No. of shares (mil.): 187
Return on equity: 9.0%	Dividends
Cash ($ mil.): 714	Yield: 2.5%
Current ratio: 2.60	Payout: 53.4%
Long-term debt ($ mil.): 1,825	Market value ($ mil.): 7,767

Stock History

NYSE: DOV

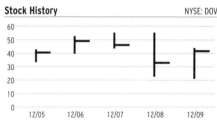

	STOCK PRICE ($) FY Close	P/E High/Low	PER SHARE ($) Earnings	Dividends	Book Value
12/09	41.61	23 11	1.91	1.02	21.88
12/08	32.92	17 7	3.12	0.90	20.32
12/07	46.09	17 14	3.26	0.77	21.14
12/06	49.02	19 15	2.73	0.71	20.42
12/05	40.49	17 14	2.50	0.66	17.84
Annual Growth	**0.7%**	**— —**	**(6.5%)**	**11.5%**	**5.2%**

Dow Chemical

Dow Chemical is a leader in the production of plastics, chemicals, hydrocarbons, and agrochemicals. The largest chemical company in the US and #2 worldwide (ahead of ExxonMobil and behind BASF), Dow also makes performance plastics (engineering plastics, polyurethanes, and materials for Dow Automotive). Other products include materials for packaging (such as its Styrofoam brand insulation), fibers, and films, as well as performance chemicals like acrylic acid. The company also manufactures commodity chemicals (chlor-alkalies and glycols) and agrochemicals. Its Hydrocarbons and Energy unit makes olefins and aromatics, raw materials for other chemicals. Dow also owns half of silicone products maker Dow Corning.

Good times for performance products (both performance chemicals and performance plastics) and advanced materials have led Dow to focus on growing those segments ahead of old reliables such as basic chemicals and basic plastics. (Increasingly high prices for the raw materials needed to make those latter products have also helped Dow make that decision.) While it still professes to believe in the US market for its basics, expansion in that sector will focus on Asia, and in particular China, and the Middle East.

Its major move in that direction came in 2009 when Dow spent more than $15 billion to buy specialty chemicals maker Rohm and Haas. Among the largest specialty chemicals makers in the world, Rohm and Haas produced coatings additives, electronics materials, acrylates, and salt products.

The deal encountered trouble, however, as Dow began to move more slowly as the closing date approached. The failure in 2008 to launch a proposed joint venture with the petrochemicals subsidiary of Kuwait Petroleum Corporation (KPC) took away much of the cash Dow had hoped to pay for Rohm and Haas with, and the general tightness of global credit markets made it that much tougher for the company. Rohm and Haas filed suit, trying to force Dow to close the acquisition. Eventually the companies were able to work it out, and the deal closed in the middle of 2009.

In 2010 Dow announced an agreement for a 50-50 joint venture with Mitsui & Co. to build and operate a new membrane chlor-alkali facility at Dow's Freeport, Texas, complex. The project would combine the two company's strengths in a modern chlor-alkali facility.

HISTORY

Herbert Dow founded Dow Chemical in 1897 after developing a process to extract bromides and chlorides from underground brine deposits around Midland, Michigan. Its first product was chlorine bleach. Dow eventually overcame British and German monopolies on bleach, bromides, and other chemicals.

In the mid-1920s Dow rejected a takeover by DuPont. By 1930, the year of Herbert Dow's death, sales had reached $15 million. Dow started building new plants around the country in the late 1930s.

Dow research yielded new plastics in the 1940s, such as Saran Wrap, the company's initial major consumer product. In 1952 Dow built a plant in Japan (Asahi-Dow), its first subsidiary outside North America. Plastics represented 32% of sales by 1957, compared with 2% in 1940. Strong sales of plastics and silicone products propelled the company into the top ranks of US firms. Dow entered the pharmaceutical field with the 1960 purchase of Allied Labs.

Dow suffered earnings drops from 1981 to 1983 from falling chemical prices. To limit the cyclical effect of chemicals on profits, the company expanded its interests in pharmaceuticals and consumer goods. In 1989 it merged its pharmaceutical division with Marion Labs to create Marion Merrell Dow (it sold its 71% stake to Hoechst in 1995). Also in 1989 it formed DowElanco, a joint venture with Eli Lilly to produce agricultural chemicals.

Following allegations that it had put a breast implant on the market without proper testing, Dow Corning (a joint venture with glassmaker Corning Inc.), the #1 producer of silicone breast implants, stopped making the devices in 1992. In 1995 a federal judge ordered Dow to pay a Nevada woman $14 million in damages — the first breast-implant verdict against the company as a sole defendant. Facing thousands of pending cases, Dow Corning filed for bankruptcy protection. (In 1998 Dow Corning agreed to pay $3.2 billion to settle most breast-implant claims.) Dow Corning finally climbed out of bankruptcy in 2004.

Dow entered the polypropylene and polyethylene terephthalate markets with the 1996 purchase of INCA International.

The company bought Eli Lilly's 40% stake in DowElanco (renamed Dow AgroSciences, 1998).

In 1998 Dow sold its DowBrands unit — maker of bathroom cleaner (Dow), plastic bags (Ziploc), and plastic wrap (Saran Wrap) — to S.C. Johnson & Son.

The company paid $600 million in 1999 to purchase ANGUS Chemical (specialty chemicals) from TransCanada PipeLines. Dow also announced it planned to buy rival Union Carbide for $9.3 billion; it completed the acquisition early in 2001 after agreeing to divest some polyethylene assets to satisfy regulatory concerns.

In 2000 Michael Parker succeeded William Stavropoulos as president and CEO (Stavropoulos remained chairman). Dow acquired Rohm and Haas' agricultural chemicals (fungicides, insecticides, herbicides) business for $1 billion in 2001.

A weakened economy, high raw material costs, and falling prices took a toll on Dow's sales and profits around the turn of the century. As a result of costs related to the Union Carbide takeover — such as the $830 million charge related to Union Carbide's exposure to asbestos claims — and the sputtering economy, Dow recorded its first annual loss in nearly 10 years in 2001, then reported another loss in 2002. Parker was let go and William Stavropoulos returned to his post as CEO. Stavropoulos went to work cutting jobs and closing plants in an effort to cut at least $1 billion in costs.

From 2002 to 2004 the company cut nearly 7,000 jobs or better than 13% of its entire workforce. By 2004 those moves, coupled with a rebounding chemicals market, had made Dow profitable again. Stavropoulos felt comfortable enough to relinquish the chief executive title and gave it to president and COO Andrew Liveris.

In the latter half of the decade, the company began to switch its focus to more downstream products like performance plastics and systems. It acquired Bayer company Wolff Walsrode in 2007 and then, more grandly, specialty chemicals company Rohm and Haas in 2009.

EXECUTIVES

Chairman, President, and CEO: Andrew N. Liveris, age 55, $18,279,792 total compensation

EVP and CFO: William H. (Bill) Weideman, age 55, $1,970,304 total compensation

EVP Business Services, Chief Sustainability Officer, and CIO: David E. (Dave) Kepler II, age 57

EVP Manufacturing and Engineering Operations: Michael R. (Mike) Gambrell, age 56, $6,110,482 total compensation

EVP; President, Dow Europe, Middle East, and Africa; Chairman, Dow Europe: Geoffery E. (Geoff) Merszei, age 58, $3,741,718 total compensation

EVP Law and Government Affairs, General Counsel, and Corporate Secretary: Charles J. Kalil, age 58, $7,307,492 total compensation

EVP Performance Systems: Heinz Haller, age 54, $4,986,738 total compensation

EVP Ventures, New Business Development, and Licensing and CTO: William F. (Bill) Banholzer, age 53, $6,570,308 total compensation

EVP Human Resources, Corporate Affairs, and Aviation: Gregory M. Freiwald, age 56

SVP Performance Products and Mega Projects: James D. (Jim) McIlvenny, age 52

SVP; CEO, Dow Advanced Materials: Jerome A. Peribere

SVP Corporate Development: James R. (Jim) Fitterling

SVP Basic Chemicals Division: Carol Dudley-Williams

SVP, Hydrocarbons & Energy, Basic Plastics, and Joint Ventures: Juan R. Luciano

Chief Tax Officer and Assistant Secretary: William L. Curry

Corporate VP and Treasurer: Fernando Ruiz, age 53

President and CEO, Dow Kokam LLC: Ravi Shanker

President and CEO, Dow AgroSciences: Antonio Galindez

President, Dow Automotive Systems: Steve Henderson

President, Middle East Region: Henry Roth

President, Eastern Europe/Russia Region: Kostas Katsoglou

President, Dow Greater China: Peter Sykes

President, Asia Pacific: Pat D. Dawson

Auditors: Deloitte & Touche LLP

LOCATIONS

HQ: The Dow Chemical Company
2030 Dow Center, Midland, MI 48674
Phone: 989-636-1000 **Fax:** 989-636-1830
Web: www.dow.com

2009 Sales

	$ mil.	% of total
Europe	15,069	33
US	14,145	32
Other regions	15,661	35
Total	**44,875**	**100**

PRODUCTS/OPERATIONS

2009 Sales

	$ mil.	% of total
Basic Plastics	9,925	22
Performance Products	8,996	20
Performance Systems	5,744	13
Health & Agricultural Sciences	4,522	10
Hydrocarbons & Energy	4,241	9
Coatings & Infrastructure	4,156	9
Electronic & Specialty Materials	4,119	9
Basic Chemicals	2,467	6
Corporate services	705	2
Total	**44,875**	**100**

Selected Products

Basic Plastics
Polyethylene (resins, including HDPE, LDPE, and LLDPE grades, and catalysts and process technology)
Polypropylene (resins and performance polymers)
Styrenics (resins and styrenic alloys)

Performance Products
Engineering plastics (thermoplastic resins and elastomers, advanced resins, and crystalline polymers)
Emulsion polymers (synthetic latex)
Epoxy products and intermediates (acetone, acrylic monomers, epoxy resins, glycerine, and phenol)
Polyurethanes (Great Stuff foam sealant, dispersions, carpet backings, polyurethane gloves, roof adhesives, and fiberboard products)

Performance Systems
Dow Automotive (resins, engineering plastic materials, fluids, adhesives, sealants, acoustical systems)
Industrial chemicals (biocides, surfactants, and deicing fluids)
Oxide derivatives (glycol ethers and amines)
Specialty polymers (acrylic acid/acrylic esters, epoxides, dispersants, vinyl resins, specialty monomers)
Wire and cable compounds (flame-retardant compounds, wire and cable insulation compounds)

Health and Agricultural Sciences
Fumigants
Fungicides
Herbicides
Insecticides

Hydrocarbons and Energy
Benzene
Butadiene
Butylene
Cumene
Ethylene
Propylene
Styrene

Coatings and Infrastructure
Adhesives and Functional Polymers
Dow Building and Construction
Fabricated products (plastic film, Styrofoam, and Weathermate house wrap)
Dow Coating Materials

Electronic and Specialty Materials
Electronic Materials
Antireflective coatings
CMP slurries
Immersion photoresists
Specialty Materials
Ion-exchange resins
Nitroparaffins and nitroparaffin-based specialty chemicals
Printing ink distillates
Scale inhibitors
UCAR emulsion systems (water-based emulsions)
Water-soluble resins

Basic Chemicals
Caustic soda
Chlorine
Ethylene glycol
Ethylene oxide
Vinyl chloride monomer

Other
Property and casualty insurance (Liana Limited)

COMPETITORS

Akzo Nobel	LANXESS
BASF SE	Lucite
Bayer AG	Mitsui Chemicals
Chevron Phillips Chemical	Monsanto Company
DuPont	Occidental Chemical
Eastman Chemical	Olin Chlor Alkali
Eni	PPG Industries
ExxonMobil Chemical	SABIC
FMC	Shell Chemicals
Formosa Plastics	Sunoco Chemicals
Honeywell International	Syngenta
INEOS	Wellman
Koch Industries, Inc.	

HISTORICAL FINANCIALS

Company Type: Public

Income Statement

FYE: December 31

	REVENUE ($ mil.)	NET INCOME ($ mil.)	NET PROFIT MARGIN	EMPLOYEES
12/09	44,875	676	1.5%	52,195
12/08	57,514	579	1.0%	46,102
12/07	53,513	2,887	5.4%	45,856
12/06	49,124	3,724	7.6%	42,578
12/05	46,307	4,535	9.8%	42,413
Annual Growth	(0.8%)	(37.9%)	—	5.3%

2009 Year-End Financials

Debt ratio: 115.7%
Return on equity: 4.5%
Cash ($ mil.): 2,846
Current ratio: 1.49
Long-term debt ($ mil.): 19,152

No. of shares (mil.): 1,160
Dividends
  Yield: 2.2%
  Payout: 187.5%
Market value ($ mil.): 32,047

Stock History

NYSE: DOW

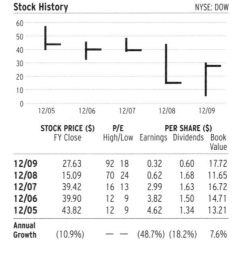

	STOCK PRICE ($) FY Close	P/E High/Low		PER SHARE ($) Earnings	Dividends	Book Value
12/09	27.63	92	18	0.32	0.60	17.72
12/08	15.09	70	24	0.62	1.68	11.65
12/07	39.42	16	13	2.99	1.63	16.72
12/06	39.90	12	9	3.82	1.50	14.71
12/05	43.82	12	9	4.62	1.34	13.21
Annual Growth	(10.9%)	—	—	(48.7%)	(18.2%)	7.6%

D.R. Horton

When this Horton heard a Who, it built the little guy a house. D.R. Horton builds single-family homes designed for the entry-level and move-up markets. Homes range from 1,000 sq. ft. to 5,000 sq. ft., with an average selling price of about $213,400; luxury homes cost up to $700,000. In fiscal 2009 the company sold some 16,700 homes, a 37% drop from the previous year. D.R. Horton operates in about 30 states and provides mortgage financing (through DHI Mortgage) as well as title services. One of the top homebuilders in the US, D.R. Horton has suffered along with its competitors as a result of the housing market bust, the subprime mortgage crisis, the global credit crunch, and years of industrywide overbuilding.

The housing market continued downward in 2009, and D.R. Horton sales continued to fall with it, losing its position as the largest homebuilder in the US. Economic indicators in the housing market, particularly unemployment, were the worst in 25 years. Demand for new homes was down 20% over 2008 and and more than 50% since 2007. D.R. Horton moved in 2009 to take advantage of the down market, strategically buying land at distressed prices to be prepared when conditions improve.

CEO Donald Tomnitz summed it up in 2007 when he said, "I don't want to be too sophisticated here, but '07 is going to suck, all 12 months of the calendar year." Indeed, the company suffered a loss that year and the next, when sales orders declined and cancellation rates rose due to tightened mortgage markets and severe liquidity shortages. Adding to homebuilders' difficulties, an influx of foreclosed homes on the market brought down the demand for new homes.

D.R. Horton responded to the downturn in 2008 by reducing land and housing inventory, controlling construction and inventory costs, and using its cash to reduce debt. Despite drops in many markets D.R. Horton saw improvements in its eastern market, where home affordability and employment has lead to a higher demand for new homes. In response D.R. Horton moved forward on opening new communities in the eastern US (the Carolinas in particular). However, that segment of D.R. Horton's business saw a 5% retreat in 2009.

Investment giant FMR owns a 15% stake in the company.

HISTORY

Donald R. Horton was selling homes in Fort Worth, Texas, when he hit upon a strategy for increasing sales — add options to a basic floor plan. In 1978 he borrowed $33,000 to build his first home, added a bay window for an additional charge, and sold the home for $44,000. Donald soon added floor plans and options that appealed to regional preferences.

The depressed Texas market drove the company to expand beyond the Dallas/Fort Worth area in 1987, when it entered the then-hot Phoenix market. It continued to expand into the Southeast, Mid-Atlantic, Midwest, and West in the late 1980s and early 1990s. By 1991 Horton and his family owned more than 25 companies that were combined as D.R. Horton, which went public in 1992.

D.R. Horton acquired six geographically diverse construction firms in 1994 and 1995. In 1996 the company started a mortgage services joint venture, expanded its title operations, and added three more firms.

In 1998 the company bought four builders, including Scottsdale, Arizona-based Continental Homes. Continental had been expanding beyond its Arizona and Southern California base and had entered the lucrative retirement community market. After the Continental purchase, Donald Horton stepped down as president, remaining chairman. Richard Beckwitt took over as president, and Donald Tomnitz became CEO. In 1999 the company acquired Century Title and Midwest builder Cambridge Properties.

D.R. Horton sold its St. Louis assets to McBride & Son Enterprises in 2000, after spending five years trying to break into the St. Louis homebuilding market. Tomnitz also took over the duties of president in 2000 when Beckwitt retired.

D.R. Horton gained homebuilding operations in Houston and Phoenix when it bought Emerald Builders in 2001. In February 2002 the company acquired Schuler Homes for $1.2 billion, including debt.

Sales continued to climb in fiscal 2003 and 2004. D.R. Horton experienced its 27th consecutive year of earnings and revenue growth in

2004 and broke records by being the first residential homebuilder to sell more than 45,000 homes in the US in a fiscal year; in fiscal 2005 the company closed 51,172 homes. By 2007, however, it was evident that the heady days were over with a rise in cancellations and a larger value of backlog orders.

EXECUTIVES

Chairman: Donald R. Horton, age 59,
$8,436,920 total compensation
Vice Chairman, President, and CEO:
Donald J. (Don) Tomnitz, age 61,
$6,821,439 total compensation
EVP, CFO, and Director: William W. (Bill) Wheat,
age 43, $912,872 total compensation
EVP Investor Relations and Treasurer: Stacey H. Dwyer,
age 42, $921,864 total compensation
VP and Director, National Accounts: Brad Conlon
VP and Assistant Secretary: Thomas Montano
Director Information Technology: Rick Rawlings
Chief Legal Officer: Ted I. Harbour
President, North Region: George W. Seagraves
President, East Region: David Auld
President, South Region: Rick Horton
President, West Region: Chris Chambers
President, Financial Services:
Randall C. (Randy) Present
Director Investor Relations: Jessica Hansen
Auditors: Ernst & Young LLP

LOCATIONS

HQ: D.R. Horton, Inc.
301 Commerce St., Ste. 500, Fort Worth, TX 76102
Phone: 817-390-8200 **Fax:** 817-390-1715
Web: www.drhorton.com

2009 Homes Closed

	Units	% of total
South Central	5,745	34
West	3,318	20
Southeast	2,921	17
Southwest	2,135	13
East	1,447	9
Midwest	1,137	7
Total	**16,703**	**100**

2009 Home Sales

	No.	% of total
South Central	6,074	36
West	3,287	19
Southeast	3,107	18
Southwest	1,849	11
East	1,519	9
Midwest	1,198	7
Total	**17,034**	**100**

PRODUCTS/OPERATIONS

2009 Sales

	$ mil.	% of total
Homebuilding		
Homes	3,563.6	97
Land/lots	40.3	1
Financial services	53.7	2
Total	**3,657.6**	**100**

Selected Subsidiaries

Austin Data, Inc.
C. Richard Dobson Builders, Inc. (dba Dobson Builders)
CH Investments of Texas, Inc.
CHTEX of Texas, Inc.
Continental Homes, Inc. (dba D.R. Horton —
Continental Series, D.R. Horton — Astanté Series,
Homestead by D.R. Horton — Continental Series,
Traditions, and Traditions — D.R. Horton)
Cypress Road, L.P. (dba D.R. Horton America's Builder)

DHI Mortgage Company, Ltd. (dba CH Mortgage
Company I, Ltd.; DHI Mortgage Company, Ltd. L.P.;
DHI Mortgage Limited Partnership; DHI Mortgage
Company Ltd. Limited Partnership; CH Mortgage
Company I, Ltd., L.P.; CH Mortgage Company I, Ltd.;
and CH Mortgage I, Ltd.)
D.R. Horton, Inc. — Louisville (dba Mareli Development
& Construction)
DRH Cambridge Homes, Inc. (dba Cambridge Homes)
DRH FS Mortgage Reinsurance, Ltd. (Turks & Caicos)
DRH Southwest Construction, Inc.
Golden Fox LLC
McQueen & Willis, LLC
Schuler Homes of California, Inc. (dba D.R. Horton
America's Builder)
Surprise Village North, LLC (dba Arizona Traditions)
Western Pacific Housing — Copper Canyon, LLC (D.R.
Horton America's Builder)
Western Pacific Housing — Poinsettia, L.P.
Western Pacific Housing — Windflower, L.P. (D.R.
Horton America's Builder)

COMPETITORS

Beazer Homes	M/I Homes
Century Homebuilders	NVR
David Weekley Homes	Orleans Homebuilders
Gehan Homes	Pardee Homes
Hovnanian Enterprises	PulteGroup
J.F. Shea	Ryan Building
KB Home	The Ryland Group
Lennar	Standard Pacific
M.D.C.	Toll Brothers
Mercedes Homes	Weyerhaeuser Real Estate
Meritage Homes	Woodbridge Holdings

HISTORICAL FINANCIALS

Company Type: Public

Income Statement

FYE: September 30

	REVENUE ($ mil.)	NET INCOME ($ mil.)	NET PROFIT MARGIN	EMPLOYEES
9/09	3,658	(545)	—	2,926
9/08	6,646	(2,634)	—	3,800
9/07	11,297	(713)	—	6,231
9/06	15,051	1,233	8.2%	8,772
9/05	13,864	1,471	10.6%	8,900
Annual Growth	**(28.3%)**	**—**		**(24.3%)**

2009 Year-End Financials

Debt ratio: —
Return on equity: —
Cash ($ mil.): 1,957
Current ratio: 1.33
Long-term debt ($ mil.): —
No. of shares (mil.): 318
Dividends
Yield: 1.0%
Payout: —
Market value ($ mil.): 3,632

Stock History

NYSE: DHI

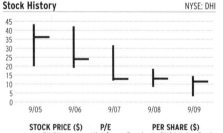

	STOCK PRICE ($) FY Close	P/E High/Low		PER SHARE ($) Earnings	Dividends	Book Value
9/09	11.41	—	—	(1.72)	0.11	7.10
9/08	13.02	—	—	(8.34)	0.45	8.90
9/07	12.81	—	—	(2.27)	0.60	17.55
9/06	23.95	11	5	3.90	0.44	20.27
9/05	36.22	9	4	4.62	0.31	16.84
Annual Growth	**(25.1%)**	**—**	**—**	**—**	**(22.8%)**	**(19.4%)**

Dress Barn

Although its name is evocative of *Green Acres,* The Dress Barn caters to women who have more to do and less to spend than Mrs. Douglas. The retailer operates more than 2,400 stores, including about 120 Dress Barn locations, 35 Dress Barn Woman shops, and 685 combined Dress Barn/Dress Barn Woman stores. It also has about 900 Justice shops and 720 Maurices locations. The retailer's Dress Barn, Dress Barn Woman (larger sizes), and combination stores sell in-season, moderate- to better-quality women's apparel and accessories at discount prices and cater to professional women in their mid-30s to mid-50s. The Dress Barn opened its doors in 1962. In November 2009 it acquired Tween Brands and its Justice banner.

The Dress Barn is hoping to repeat the success of its 2005 acquisition of Maurices with the purchase of Tween Brands, which targets girls ages 7 to 14. The acquisition, valued at about $160 million, significantly boosts Dress Barn's retail presence and expands its market from professional and younger women to the teeny-bopper set.

While The Dress Barn aims to grow its business through Tween Brands, the company is also working to right-size its current store network. Lower consumer spending and fierce competition in the retail apparel industry has encouraged the company to focus more of its growth efforts on existing markets with successful locations. It is also shuttering underperforming stores. In 2009 the company opened about 50 new Maurices locations and 30 new Dress Barn combo shops, which combine Dress Barn and Dress Barn Woman formats in a single location. The 80 new stores outnumbered the two dozen shops closed by the retailer. In 2010 Dress Barn plans to open about 50 new locations, consisting of 35 Maurices shops and 15 combo stores.

The founding Jaffe family owns about 30% of The Dress Barn. CEO David Jaffe holds the most significant share, with a nearly 10% stake.

HISTORY

Roslyn Jaffe started The Dress Barn in 1962. Focusing on career women in need of reasonably priced wardrobes, the store offered a 20%-50% discount from department store prices. By the mid-1970s Dress Barn had 18 stores and was expanding through acquisitions. It went public in 1983. The Dress Barn Woman division was introduced three years later. The company discontinued its casual apparel stores (SBX) in fiscal 1995.

The discount appeal of Dress Barn stores has been undermined in recent years by the increased use of moderately priced private-label brands by major department stores. Manufacturers such as Jones Apparel Group have also entered the retail market via factory outlets. In its rapid expansion during the 1990s, Dress Barn countered this trend by focusing on combination stores offering both regular and larger-size merchandise. These larger stores (8,000-9,000 sq. ft.) provide the company a greater presence in shopping center locations and have lower operating costs.

Dress Barn added shoe departments and petite sizes in 1996 and 1997 and stepped up closures of poorly performing stores. It continued doing so in fiscal 1998 and 1999, while opening new combo stores and converting existing stores to the combo format. Dress Barn introduced a mail-order catalog in the fall of 1999 and launched a website the following year. The Jaffes' son, David, was named CEO in early 2002; Roslyn's husband, Elliot, remains chairman.

Dress Barn's longtime search for acquisition opportunities was consummated in January 2005 with the purchase of specialty chain Maurices, which targets younger women (ages 17 to 34) in small to metro fringe markets with more fashion-forward merchandise.

In late 2009 Dress Barn tapped into the teen market again with its purchase of Tween Brands and the retailer's Justice stores.

EXECUTIVES

Chairman: Elliot S. Jaffe, age 84, $893,002 total compensation
President, CEO, and Director: David R. Jaffe, age 51, $1,932,613 total compensation
EVP and CFO: Armand Correia, age 64, $670,513 total compensation
EVP and Chief Merchandising Officer: Keith Fulsher, age 51
SVP and Chief Marketing Officer: Vivian Behrens, age 57, $824,446 total compensation
SVP Operations: Jeffrey C. (Jeff) Gerstel
SVP Real Estate: Elise Jaffe
SVP, General Counsel, and Assistant Secretary: Gene L. Wexler, age 55, $568,990 total compensation
VP Real Estate: Richard Sosnovy
VP Asset Protection: Arthur L. Senn
VP Human Resources: David Montieth
VP Merchandise Planning: Robin Gray
VP and CIO: Phillip Giusto
VP Merchandise Allocation: Tanzim Ahmad
VP Finance and Controller: Reid Hackney, age 52
Secretary and Treasurer: Roslyn S. Jaffe
Auditors: Deloitte & Touche LLP

LOCATIONS

HQ: The Dress Barn, Inc.
30 Dunnigan Dr., Suffern, NY 10901
Phone: 845-369-4500   **Fax:** 845-369-4829
Web: www.dressbarn.com

PRODUCTS/OPERATIONS

2009 Sales

	$ mil.	% of total
Dress Barn & Dress Barn Woman	906.2	61
Maurices	588.0	39
Total	**1,494.2**	**100**

2009 Stores

	No.
Maurices	721
Combination stores	684
Dress Barn	120
Dress Barn Woman	34
Total	**1,559**

COMPETITORS

Aéropostale	Limited Brands
American Eagle Outfitters	Macy's
Burlington Coat Factory	Old Navy
Charming Shoppes	Ross Stores
Christopher & Banks	Saks
Deb Shops	Sears
Dillard's	Stage Stores
Fashion Bug	Target
J. C. Penney	United Retail
Jones Apparel	Wal-Mart
Kohl's	

HISTORICAL FINANCIALS

Company Type: Public

Income Statement

FYE: Last Saturday in July

	REVENUE ($ mil.)	NET INCOME ($ mil.)	NET PROFIT MARGIN	EMPLOYEES
7/09	1,494	70	4.7%	14,100
7/08	1,444	74	5.1%	13,700
7/07	1,427	101	7.1%	13,200
7/06	1,300	79	6.1%	12,800
7/05	1,000	53	5.3%	12,000
Annual Growth	**10.6%**	**7.3%**	**—**	**4.1%**

2009 Year-End Financials

Debt ratio: 4.2%
Return on equity: 11.8%
Cash ($ mil.): 241
Current ratio: 1.57
Long-term debt ($ mil.): 26
No. of shares (mil.): 80
Dividends
  Yield: —
  Payout: —
Market value ($ mil.): 1,247

Stock History

NASDAQ (GS): DBRN

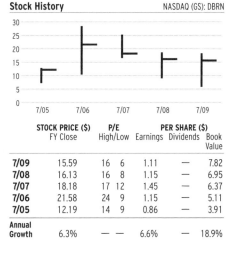

	STOCK PRICE ($) FY Close	P/E High/Low		PER SHARE ($) Earnings	Dividends	Book Value
7/09	15.59	16	6	1.11	—	7.82
7/08	16.13	16	8	1.15	—	6.95
7/07	18.18	17	12	1.45	—	6.37
7/06	21.58	24	9	1.15	—	5.11
7/05	12.19	14	9	0.86	—	3.91
Annual Growth	**6.3%**	**—**	**—**	**6.6%**	**—**	**18.9%**

DST Systems

The feeling is mutual at DST Systems. A leading provider of information processing software and services for the mutual fund industry, DST's Financial Services segment processes millions of mutual fund accounts and offers software, systems, and processing services for banks, investment firms, and insurance companies. The company's Output Solutions unit manages statement and bill mailings and customer communications. Its applications and services are used to address a wide range of tasks including business process management, investment management, customer care, and health care claims processing and administration. DST Systems gets most of its sales in the US.

The company has historically been very active on the acquisition front, using selective purchases to complement its product line and strategically expand into new geographic areas. While sales in the US account for a majority of its revenues, the company is eyeing expansion in areas such as Australia and Asia. DST has balanced its acquisition strategy by purchasing both complementary software and technology providers as well as service providers, with a particular emphasis on buying business process outsourcing and consulting firms.

Recent purchases have included BlueDoor Technologies (an Australia-based provider of funds and savings management software), TASS (shareowner subaccounting services provider), Mosiki (consulting services), and Amisys Synertech (enterprise software and business process outsourcing).

DST Systems bought the 50% of claims processing services and software joint venture Argus Health Systems that it did not already own from partner Financial Holding Corporation in 2009. The purchase was a bid by DST to build its presence in the health care market. Argus provides services and offers custom software to manage and automate such functions as claims processing, rebate administration, and clinical services administration primarily for pharmacy benefits purposes.

DST also is involved in real estate and equity investments in various companies, although that segment only accounted for about 3% of DST's overall revenues in fiscal 2009 (and much of that involved leasing real estate to other business units of the company).

HISTORY

After expanding into mutual funds during the early 1960s, Kansas City Southern Industries (KCSI) formed an electronic computer data processing unit to handle its mutual fund transactions, using technology designed originally for tracking railroad cars and their revenues.

In 1968 KCSI incorporated its data processing unit as DST Systems and began offering its services to the financial industry. To establish itself on the East Coast, in 1974 DST formed Boston Financial Data Services, a joint venture with State Street. Also during the 1970s DST entered the insurance market with a system for variable annuity policyholders.

In 1983 KCSI bought a majority stake in Janus Capital, a Denver-based mutual funds company. DST went public later that year; KCSI kept an 86% stake. Thomas McDonnell, president since the early 1970s, was named CEO in 1984.

By the early 1990s DST had a solid position in its markets, and it had begun to increase its service offerings and expand internationally into Canada and Europe. The company bought Vantage Computer to gain a foothold in the life and property insurance software industry, and it established joint ventures with Kemper Financial Services (now part of Zurich Financial Services) and State Street Boston, thereby pushing into portfolio accounting and stock transfer services.

In 1993 DST sold Vantage to insurance software maker Continuum, gaining a 19% stake in that company. It also bought 50% of client Argus Health Systems, as well as a stake in DBS Systems (by 1997 it owned 100%). By the end of 1993 DST was the leader in mutual fund third-party services. In 1995 KCSI sold 51% of DST to the public. Computer Sciences Corporation (CSC) acquired Continuum in 1996, leaving DST with a minority stake in CSC.

In 1998 DST, BankBoston, First Chicago Trust, and State Street formed EquiServe, the largest provider of corporate stock transfer services in the US. That year DST bought USCS International, a provider of customer management software and billing services, in an $824 million deal.

DST in 2000 took aim at fund supermarkets operated by Charles Schwab and FMR (Fidelity Investments) by launching a service that enabled independent commission-based financial advisers to research and trade funds over the

Internet. The company also purchased a controlling stake in EquiServe from the other partners in the joint venture.

In 2001 the company acquired the remainder of EquiServe, and it sold its portfolio accounting systems business to State Street for $75 million. The following year DST bought lock/line, a provider of administrative support services for providers of insurance for telecommunications equipment and event-based debt protection programs.

In 2003 Janus Capital Group sold most of its remaining stake in DST back to the company, in exchange for ownership of DST's commercial printing and graphics design unit; it sold the rest of its stake in 2004.

DST Systems sold its billing and customer management software and services business, including the operations of DST Innovis and DST Interactive, to Amdocs in 2005.

DST's Output Solutions segment, which operates primarily in the US through subsidiary DST Output, expanded its geographic reach through its purchase of DST International, a provider of customer communications and document management services in the UK.

In 2006 DST merged its lock/line unit (administrative services for telecom carriers) with customer contact and support services provider Asurion Corporation; in 2007 DST sold the majority of the 37% stake it received in Asurion as part of the transaction.

Also in 2006 the company acquired Amisys Synertech, a software developer and applications provider to the commercial health care industry in the US.

EXECUTIVES

CEO and Director: Thomas A. (Tom) McDonnell, age 64, $3,730,448 total compensation
EVP US Investment Recordkeeping Solutions:
  Robert L. Tritt, age 54
EVP, DST Health Solutions and Argus Health Systems:
  Jonathan J. Boehm, age 49, $1,685,332 total compensation
VP and Chief Accounting Officer: Gregg W. Givens, age 49
VP Automated Work Distributor: John C. Vaughn
VP, General Counsel, and Secretary: Randall D. Young, age 53
VP, CFO, and Treasurer: Kenneth V. Hager, age 59, $1,444,910 total compensation
President and CEO, Boston Financial Data Services:
  Terry L. Metzger
President and CEO, DST Output:
  Steven J. (Steve) Towle, age 52, $1,763,673 total compensation
President, DST Retirement Solutions: Jude C. Metcalfe
President and COO; Chairman, Boston Financial Data Services: Stephen C. Hooley, age 46, $4,099,530 total compensation
CEO, DST International: Thomas R. (Tom) Abraham, age 58, $2,359,232 total compensation
Auditors: PricewaterhouseCoopers LLP

LOCATIONS

HQ: DST Systems, Inc.
  333 W. 11th St., Kansas City, MO 64105
Phone: 816-435-1000   **Fax:** 816-435-8618
Web: www.dstsystems.com

2009 Sales

	$ mil.	% of total
US	2,032.9	92
UK	75.9	3
Canada	48.8	2
Australia	34.2	2
Other countries	26.1	1
Total	**2,217.9**	**100**

PRODUCTS/OPERATIONS

2009 Sales

	$ mil.	% of total
Financial Services	1,169.5	51
Output Solutions	1,053.8	46
Investments & other	60.1	3
Adjustments	(65.5)	—
Total	**2,217.9**	**100**

Selected Products and Services

DST Output
  Call center management support
  Direct Access (instantaneous online data monitoring)
  Exact View (customer statement replica viewing)
  Info Disc (customer document replica viewing)
  Package configuration and inventory management support
  Rapid Confirm (delivery service for trade confirmations)
  Rapid NetSale (lead management for prospective online brokerage customers)
Financial Services
  eLLITE (fund information access)
  Securities Transfer System (transfer agent support)
  TA2000 (mutual fund shareholder record keeping)
  TRAC-2000 (record keeping for defined contribution plans)
  Vision (Web-based mutual fund processing for independent financial advisers)

COMPETITORS

ACS International
ADP
Advent Software
Assurant
Bank of New York Mellon
Bowne
Cerner
CSG Systems International
CVS Caremark
Emdeon
Express Scripts
First Data
Fiserv
GE Healthcare
Greenway Medical Technologies
HealthPort
HP Enterprise Services
IBM
Lombardi Software
McKesson
Medco Health
Misys
Pegasystems
Perot Systems
RiskMetrics
R.R. Donnelley
Savvion
SS&C
State Street
SunGard
TIBCO Software
TMG Health
TriZetto

HISTORICAL FINANCIALS

Company Type: Public

Income Statement

				FYE: December 31
	REVENUE ($ mil.)	NET INCOME ($ mil.)	NET PROFIT MARGIN	EMPLOYEES
12/09	2,218	242	10.9%	11,200
12/08	2,285	243	10.6%	10,900
12/07	2,303	875	38.0%	11,000
12/06	2,236	273	12.2%	10,500
12/05	2,515	425	16.9%	10,500
Annual Growth	**(3.1%)**	**(13.1%)**	**—**	**1.6%**

2009 Year-End Financials

Debt ratio: 97.9%
Return on equity: 55.4%
Cash ($ mil.): 106
Current ratio: 0.53
Long-term debt ($ mil.): 621

No. of shares (mil.): 47
Dividends
  Yield: —
  Payout: —
Market value ($ mil.): 2,034

Stock History

NYSE: DST

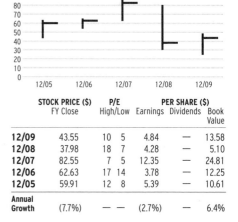

	STOCK PRICE ($) FY Close	P/E High/Low		PER SHARE ($) Earnings	Dividends	Book Value
12/09	43.55	10	5	4.84	—	13.58
12/08	37.98	18	7	4.28	—	5.10
12/07	82.55	7	5	12.35	—	24.81
12/06	62.63	17	14	3.78	—	12.25
12/05	59.91	12	8	5.39	—	10.61
Annual Growth	**(7.7%)**	**—**	**—**	**(2.7%)**	**—**	**6.4%**

DTE Energy

Detroit's economy may be lackluster, but DTE Energy still provides a reliable spark. The holding company's main subsidiary, Detroit Edison, distributes electricity to some 2.1 million customers in southeastern Michigan. The utility's power plants (mainly fossil-fueled) have a generating capacity of more than 11,060 MW. The company's Michigan Consolidated Gas (MichCon) unit distributes natural gas to 1.2 million customers. DTE Energy's nonregulated operations (in 25 US states) include energy marketing and trading; coal transportation and procurement; energy management services for commercial and industrial customers; independent and on-site power generation; and gas exploration, production, and processing.

DTE Energy, which is expanding its nonutility businesses to broaden its revenue base, has wholesale power, gas, and coal marketing operations in the Midwest and northeastern US and eastern Canada; it also has merchant generation facilities in Illinois, Indiana, and Michigan.

The global recession led to a decreased demand for power and gas that resulted in lower revenues in 2009.

As part of its commitment to reduce its carbon footprint to meet regulatory requirements, in 2008 DTE Energy began to convert its 800 diesel-fueled trucks and service vehicles to cleaner-burning biodiesel fuel. In 2009 the company had two biomass-fired electric generating plants under development. DTE Energy also offers appliance recycling and other conservation incentives to its utility customers.

Clearing out some noncore assets, in 2007 the company sold its Michigan Antrim Shale gas exploration and production assets to Atlas Energy Resources for about $1.3 billion. That year, due to the expiration of synthetic fuel production tax credits, DTE Energy exited the synfuels business.

HISTORY

DTE Energy's predecessor threw its first switch in 1886 when George Peck and local investors incorporated the Edison Illuminating Company of Detroit. Neighboring utility Peninsular Electric Light was formed in 1891, and both companies bought smaller utilities until they merged in 1903 to form Detroit Edison. A subsidiary of holding company North American Co., Detroit Edison was incorporated in New York to secure financing for power plants.

Detroit's growth in the 1920s and 1930s led the utility to build plants and buy others in outlying areas. Detroit Edison acquired Michigan Electric Power, which had been divested from its holding company under the Public Utility Holding Company Act of 1935, and was itself divested from North American in 1940.

The post-WWII boom prompted Detroit Edison to build more plants, most of them coal-fired. In 1953 it joined a consortium of 34 companies to build Fermi 1, a nuclear plant brought on line in 1963. Still strapped for power, Detroit Edison built the coal-fired Monroe plant, which began service in 1970. In 1972 Fermi 1 had a partial core meltdown and was taken off line.

Detroit Edison began shipping low-sulfur Montana coal through its Wisconsin terminal in 1974, which reduced the cost of obtaining the fuel. The next year it began building another nuke, Fermi 2. The nuke had cost more than $4.8 billion by the time it went on line in 1988. That year the utility began its landfill gas recovery operation (now DTE Biomass Energy).

A recession pounded automakers in the early 1990s, leading to cutbacks in electricity purchases. In 1992 Congress passed the Energy Policy Act, allowing wholesale power competition. In 1993 a fire shut down Fermi 2 for almost two years. Michigan's public service commission (PSC) approved retail customer-choice pilot programs for its utilities in 1994. Detroit Edison and rival Consumers Energy (now CMS Energy) took the PSC to court.

DTE Energy became Detroit Edison's holding company in 1996. The next year it formed DTE Energy Trading (to broker power) and DTE-CoEnergy (to provide energy-management services and sell power to large customers). It also formed Plug Power with Mechanical Technology to develop fuel cells that convert natural gas to power without combustion.

In 1997 and 1998 the PSC, bolstered by state court decisions, issued orders to restructure Michigan's utilities. The transition to retail competition began in 1998. That year DTE Energy and natural gas provider Michigan Consolidated Gas (MichCon) began collaborating on some operations, including billing and meter reading. DTE and GE formed a venture to sell and install Plug Power fuel cell systems.

A higher court shot down the PSC's restructuring orders in 1999, but DTE Energy and CMS Energy decided to implement customer choice using PSC guidelines. That year the US Department of Energy selected DTE Energy to install the world's first super power-cable, which could carry three times as much electricity as conventional copper. Also in 1999 DTE Energy agreed to acquire MCN Energy, MichCon's parent.

In 2000 DTE Energy formed subsidiary International Transmission (ITC) to hold Detroit Edison's transmission assets; the next year ITC joined the Midwest Independent System Operator, which began to manage ITC's network. It also completed its $4.3 billion purchase of MCN Energy in 2001. Full deregulation of Michigan's electricity market was completed in 2002. International Transmission was sold in 2003 to affiliates of Kohlberg Kravis Roberts and Trimaran Capital Partners for $610 million.

EXECUTIVES

President, COO, and Director: Gerard M. (Gerry) Anderson, age 52, $4,888,941 total compensation
EVP and CFO: David E. Meador, age 53, $2,894,071 total compensation
SVP and Assistant to Chairman: Harold Gardner, age 63
SVP and General Counsel: Bruce D. Peterson, age 53, $1,649,238 total compensation
SVP Major Enterprise Projects: Ron A. May, age 58
SVP Energy Resources: Knut Simonsen, age 46
SVP and CIO: Lynne Ellyn, age 59
SVP and Chief Nuclear Officer, Detroit Edison: Jack M. Davis, age 62
SVP Corporate Affairs: Paul C. Hillegonds, age 61
Corporate Secretary and Chief of Staff: Lisa Muschong
VP and Chief Tax Officer: JoAnn Chavez, age 45
VP Corporate Communications: Sandra K. (Sandy) Ennis, age 53
VP Corporate and Governmental Affairs: Frederick E. (Fred) Shell, age 58
VP Regulatory Affairs: Daniel G. (Dan) Brudzynski, age 49
VP and Treasurer: Nick A. Khouri, age 52
VP Human Resources: Larry E. Steward, age 57
VP, Controller, and Investor Relations: Peter B. Oleksiak, age 43
Chairman and CEO, DTE Energy and Detroit Edison: Anthony F. Earley Jr., age 60, $9,211,101 total compensation
President and COO, Michigan Consolidated Gas Company: Gerardo (Jerry) Norcia, age 47, $1,017,659 total compensation
President and COO, Detroit Edison: Steven E. Kurmas, age 54, $2,359,436 total compensation
President, DTE Biomass Energy: Mark Cousino, age 45
President, DTE Coal Services: Matt T. Paul, age 40
President, DTE Gas Resources: Steven H. Prelipp, age 43
President, Midwest Energy Resources: Fred L. Shusterich, age 55
President, DTE Gas Storage and DTE Pipeline: Peter Cianci, age 42
President, DTE Energy Trading: Steven (Steve) Mabry, age 48
Auditors: PricewaterhouseCoopers LLP

LOCATIONS

HQ: DTE Energy Company
1 Energy Plaza, Detroit, MI 48226
Phone: 313-235-4000   **Fax:** 313-235-8055
Web: www.dteenergy.com

PRODUCTS/OPERATIONS

2009 Sales

	$ mil.	% of total
Electric utility	4,714	58
Gas utility	1,788	22
Nonutility operations		
Energy trading	804	10
Power & industrial products	661	8
Gas storage & pipeline	82	1
Unconventional gas production	31	1
Adjustments	(66)	—
Total	**8,014**	**100**

COMPETITORS

AEP
CMS Energy
CMS Enterprises
Dairyland Power
DPL
Duke Energy
Dynegy
Exelon Energy
Integrys Energy Group
Nicor
Peabody Energy
PG&E Corporation
SEMCO Energy
Southern Company
Wisconsin Energy
Xcel Energy

HISTORICAL FINANCIALS

Company Type: Public

Income Statement
FYE: December 31

	REVENUE ($ mil.)	NET INCOME ($ mil.)	NET PROFIT MARGIN	EMPLOYEES
12/09	8,014	535	6.7%	10,244
12/08	9,329	546	5.9%	10,471
12/07	8,506	971	11.4%	10,262
12/06	9,022	432	4.8%	10,527
12/05	9,022	540	6.0%	11,410
Annual Growth	**(2.9%)**	**(0.2%)**	**—**	**(2.7%)**

2009 Year-End Financials

Debt ratio: 117.4%
Return on equity: 8.7%
Cash ($ mil.): 52
Current ratio: 1.09
Long-term debt ($ mil.): 7,370
No. of shares (mil.): 169
Dividends
  Yield: 4.9%
  Payout: 65.4%
Market value ($ mil.): 7,358

Stock History
NYSE: DTE

	STOCK PRICE ($) FY Close	P/E High/Low		PER SHARE ($) Earnings	Dividends	Book Value
12/09	43.59	14	7	3.24	2.12	37.19
12/08	35.67	13	8	3.36	2.12	35.52
12/07	43.96	10	8	5.70	2.12	34.68
12/06	48.41	20	16	2.43	2.08	34.65
12/05	43.19	16	14	3.05	2.06	34.18
Annual Growth	**0.2%**	**—**	**—**	**1.5%**	**0.7%**	**2.1%**

Duke Energy

Duke Energy is a John Wayne-sized power business. The company has 4 million electric customers and about 500,000 gas customers in the South and Midwest. Its US Franchised Electric and Gas unit operates primarily through its Duke Energy Carolinas, Duke Energy Ohio, Duke Energy Indiana and Duke Energy Kentucky regional businesses. The company has 35,000 MW of electric generating capacity in the Midwest and the Carolinas, including 7,550 MW of commercial power generation (not counting renewables). Duke Energy International has more than 4,000 MW of generation capacity, primarily in Latin America. While it is focused on energy operations, Duke also has stakes in insurance, real estate, and telecom businesses.

Pursuing its strategy to develop green energy sources (to shrink its carbon footprint) and expand its non-regulated power business, in 2009 the company agreed to build a second wind power project in Wyoming. In 2010 Duke had more than 730 MW of wind power in operation and another 5,000 MW in development in 14 US states. In 2010 the company acquired its first commercial-scale solar power project, from juwi solar. Under development in San Antonio, Blue Wing Solar Project will be capable of generating up to 16 MW of power. That year Duke Energy teamed up with Areva to build a $250 million biomass-fueled power plant in Shelton, in Washington state.

In 2008 Duke moved to strengthen its alternative energy assets by buying wind energy producer Catamount Energy for about $240 million plus assumed debt. Catamount had about 500 MW of renewable energy in operation.

In a major industry power move, in 2006 the company bought energy provider Cinergy in a $9 billion stock swap. Reorganizing its business lines to focus on its US power businesses, that year Duke Energy sold its commercial marketing and trading businesses to Fortis, and in 2007 it spun off its natural gas transmission business as Spectra Energy. The company also exited the European energy marketing business; it also left the proprietary (third-party) energy trading business in North America (primarily made up of Duke Energy North America or DENA, sold to LS Power Equity Partners for a reported $1.5 billion). Duke also wound down its energy-trading joint venture with Exxon Mobil.

HISTORY

Surgeon Gill Wylie founded Catawba Power Company in 1899; its first hydroelectric plant in South Carolina was on line by 1904. The next year Wylie and James "Buck" Duke (founder of the American Tobacco Company and Duke University's namesake) formed Southern Power Company with Wylie as president.

In 1910 Buck Duke became president of Southern Power and organized Mill-Power Supply to sell electric equipment and appliances. He also began investing in electricity-powered textile mills, which prospered as a result of the electric power, and continued to bring in customers. He formed the Southern Public Utility Company in 1913 to buy other Piedmont-region utilities. Wylie died in 1924, the same year the company was renamed Duke Power; Buck Duke died the next year.

Growing after WWII, the company went public in 1950 and moved to the NYSE in 1961. It also formed its real estate arm, Crescent Resources, in the 1960s. Insulating itself from the 1970s energy crises, Duke invested in coal mining and three nuclear plants, the first completed in 1974.

In 1988 Duke began to develop power projects outside its home region, and it also bought neighboring utility Nantahala Power and Light. The next year it formed a joint venture with Fluor's Fluor Daniel unit to provide engineering and construction services to power generators. Mill-Power Supply was sold in 1990.

By the 1990s Duke had moved into overseas markets, acquiring an Argentine power station in 1992. It also tried its hand at telecommunications, creating DukeNet Communications in 1994 to build fiber-optic systems, and in 1996 it joined oil giant Mobil to create a power trading and marketing business. As the US power industry traveled toward deregulation, Duke also sought natural gas operations. It targeted PanEnergy, which owned a major pipeline system in the eastern half of the US. Duke Power bought PanEnergy in 1997 to form Duke Energy Corporation.

Seeing an opportunity in 1998, Duke formed Duke Communication Services to provide antenna sites to the fast-growing wireless communications industry. It also acquired a 52% stake in Electroquil, an electric power generating company in Guayaquil, Ecuador. That year it bought three PG&E power plants to compete in California's deregulated electric utility marketplace.

Duke merged its pipeline business, Duke Energy Trading and Transport, with TEPPCO Partners and acquired gas processing operations from Union Pacific Resources. To further enhance natural gas operations in other regions, Duke bought El Paso's East Tennessee Natural Gas pipeline unit in 2000 and a 20% stake in Canadian 88 Energy; it also purchased $1.4 billion in South American generation assets, including assets from Dominion Resources, and the gas trading operations of Mobil (now Exxon Mobil) in the Netherlands. Also in 2000 Duke and Phillips Petroleum (now ConocoPhillips) merged their gas gathering and processing and NGL operations into Duke Energy Field Services.

In 2001 Duke announced the $8 billion acquisition of Westcoast Energy; the purchase, which was completed in 2002, added more than a million natural gas customers and 6,900 miles of gas pipeline in Canada.

In 2003 Duke sold its stake in Foothills Pipe Lines to TransCanada for $181 million, and it sold $300 million in renewable energy facilities to privately owned Highstar Renewable Fuels.

In 2004 the company sold an Indonesian power plant to Freeport-McMoRan in a $300 million deal, and it sold its 30% interest in the Vector Pipeline to Enbridge and DTE Energy for $145 million. It also sold the assets of its merchant finance business (Duke Capital Partners), and its stake in Canadian 88 Energy (now Esprit Exploration). Following this trend in 2005, Duke Energy sold its 620-MW Grays Harbor facility (Washington) to an affiliate of Invenergy for $21 million.

In 2006 Duke sold a 50% stake in its real estate subsidiary, Crescent Resources, to Morgan Stanley Real Estate. That year the company bought an 825-MW power plant in Rockingham County, North Carolina, from Dynegy for $195 million.

EXECUTIVES

Chairman, President, and CEO: James E. (Jim) Rogers, age 62, $6,927,663 total compensation
Group Executive and CFO: Lynn J. Good, age 50, $3,139,797 total compensation
Group Executive; President and COO, U.S. Franchised Electric and Gas: James L. (Jim) Turner, age 50, $4,352,268 total compensation
Group Executive, Chief Legal Officer, and Corporate Secretary: Marc E. Manly, age 57, $3,572,501 total compensation
Group Executive; President, Commercial Businesses: B. Keith Trent, age 50, $2,346,278 total compensation
Group Executive, Chief Generation Officer, and Chief Nuclear Officer: Dhiaa M. Jamil, age 53
SVP and Chief Customer Officer: Gianna M. Manes
SVP and Chief Communications Officer: Ginny Mackin
SVP and Chief Sustainability Officer: Roberta B. Bowman, age 55
SVP and Chief Human Resources Officer: Jennifer L. Weber, age 43
SVP Audit Services and Chief Ethics and Compliance Officer: Jeffery G. Browning
SVP and Controller: Steven K. Young, age 51
SVP Power Delivery, US Operations: Jim L. Stanley, age 55
SVP Financial Re-Engineering and Financial Information Technology: Sara S. (Sally) Whitney
SVP Investor Relations and Treasurer: Stephen G. De May, age 47
VP and CTO: David W. Mohler
President, Duke Energy South Carolina: Catherine Heigel
President, Duke Energy North Carolina: Brett C. Carter
President, Office Nuclear Development: Ellen T. Ruff, age 62
President, Duke Energy Ohio and Duke Energy Kentucky: Julia S. (Julie) Janson, age 45
President, Indiana Operations: Michael W. Reed
Auditors: Deloitte & Touche LLP

LOCATIONS

HQ: Duke Energy Corporation
526 S. Church St., Charlotte, NC 28202
Phone: 704-594-6200   **Fax:** 704-382-3814
Web: www.duke-energy.com

2009 Sales

	$ mil.	% of total
North America		
US	11,573	91
Latin America	1,158	9
Total	**12,731**	**100**

PRODUCTS/OPERATIONS

2009 Sales

	$ mil.	% of total
Regulated electric	10,033	79
Nonregulated electric, natural gas & other	2,050	16
Regulated natural gas	648	5
Total	**12,731**	**100**

Selected Operations

Commercial Power (unregulated power generation)
Duke Energy International (foreign asset development and marketing)
U.S. Franchised Electric and Gas (electric and gas utility)
Other
  Bison Insurance Company Limited
  Crescent Resources (50%, real estate)
  Dukenet Communications (50%, telecom)

HISTORICAL FINANCIALS

Company Type: Public

Income Statement				FYE: December 31
	REVENUE ($ mil.)	NET INCOME ($ mil.)	NET PROFIT MARGIN	EMPLOYEES
12/09	12,731	1,085	8.5%	18,680
12/08	13,207	1,295	9.8%	18,250
12/07	12,720	1,500	11.8%	17,800
12/06	15,184	1,863	12.3%	25,600
12/05	16,746	1,828	10.9%	20,400
Annual Growth	(6.6%)	(12.2%)	—	(2.2%)

2009 Year-End Financials

Debt ratio: 74.1%
Return on equity: 5.1%
Cash ($ mil.): 1,542
Current ratio: 1.41
Long-term debt ($ mil.): 16,113

No. of shares (mil.): 1,319
Dividends
  Yield: 5.5%
  Payout: 113.3%
Market value ($ mil.): 22,695

Stock History

NYSE: DUK

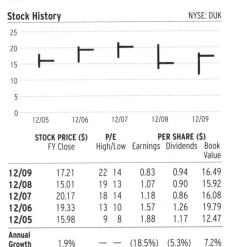

	STOCK PRICE ($) FY Close	P/E High/Low		PER SHARE ($) Earnings	Dividends	Book Value
12/09	17.21	22	14	0.83	0.94	16.49
12/08	15.01	19	13	1.07	0.90	15.92
12/07	20.17	18	14	1.18	0.86	16.08
12/06	19.33	13	10	1.57	1.26	19.79
12/05	15.98	9	8	1.88	1.17	12.47
Annual Growth	1.9%	—	—	(18.5%)	(5.3%)	7.2%

Dun & Bradstreet

For The Dun & Bradstreet Corporation, there's no business like "know" business. The company, known as D&B, is one of the world's leading suppliers of business information, services, and research. Its database contains statistics on more than 150 million companies in over 200 countries, including the largest volume of business-credit information in the world. The company's risk management segment (its largest) sells that information and integrates it into software products and Web-based applications. D&B also offers marketing information and purchasing-support services. The company acquired Hoover's, the publisher of this profile, in 2003.

D&B has invested heavily in technology, both to expand its online offerings and strengthen its operating platforms. In 2007 it acquired business information provider Allbusiness.com. It also bought First Research, a Web-based publisher of industry reports targeting sales people. Both became part of D&B's Internet Solutions segment, a key company focus.

The company is also making technology investments designed to expand its core businesses. It is improving its risk management data and delivering more predictive indicators about credit risks to its customers. In 2010 it established a partnership with consumer credit and information provider TransUnion to provide improved risk data on small and micro businesses. Additionally, D&B is focused on improving its sales and marketing segment, which supplies lists and related data to direct mail and marketing customers.

D&B conducts international operations on a market-by-market basis, conducting business through wholly owned subsidiaries, independent correspondents, and strategic partner relationships through its D&B Worldwide Network. As a result, the company offers more international company records to its customers around the world. In 2009 it acquired the UK and Irish operations of digital business provider Bisnode, certain assets of Quality Education Data, and a majority stake in Chinese marketing services firm RoadWay International. The following year D&B and its Middle East/North Africa partner expanded into Turkey, an emerging market for investors.

The company sold its North American Credit-on-Self unit for approximately $100 million in 2010. Steve Alesio retired as CEO at the end of 2009 and as chairman in mid-2010. Sara Mathew, who had been D&B's president and COO since 2005, took over in both capacities. Davis Selected Advisors owns about 16% of D&B.

HISTORY

D&B originated as Lewis Tappan's Mercantile Agency, established in 1841 in New York City. One of the first commercial credit-reporting agencies, the Mercantile supplied wholesalers and importers with reports on their customers' credit histories. The company's credit reporters included four future US presidents (Lincoln, Grant, Cleveland, and McKinley). In the 1840s it opened offices in Boston, Philadelphia, and Baltimore, and in 1857 it established operations in Montreal and London.

In 1859 Robert Dun took over the agency and renamed it R.G. Dun & Co. The first edition of the *Dun's Book* (1859) contained information on 20,268 businesses; by 1886 that number had risen to over a million. During this time Dun's was competing fiercely with the John M. Bradstreet Company, founded in 1849 by its namesake in Cincinnati. The rivalry continued until the Depression, when Dun's CEO Arthur Whiteside negotiated a merger of the two firms in 1933; the new company adopted the Dun & Bradstreet name in 1939.

In 1961 Dun & Bradstreet bought Reuben H. Donnelley Corp., a direct-mail advertiser and publisher of the Yellow Pages (first published 1886) and 10 trade magazines. In 1962 Moody's Investors Service (founded 1900) became part of Dun & Bradstreet. The company began computerizing its records in the 1960s and eventually developed the largest private business database in the world. Repackaging that information, the company began creating new products such as Dun's Financial Profiles, first published in 1979.

Dun & Bradstreet continued buying information and publishing companies during the 1970s and 1980s, including Technical Publishing (trade and professional publications, 1978), National CSS (computer services, 1979), and McCormack & Dodge (software, 1983). Later came ACNielsen (1984) and IMS International (pharmaceutical sales data, 1988).

Finding that not all information was equally profitable, Dun & Bradstreet sold its specialty industry and consumer database companies in the early 1990s. Still hoping to cash in on medical and technology information, the company formed D&B HealthCare Information and bought a majority interest in consulting firm Gartner Group. In 1993 the company consolidated its 27 worldwide data centers into four locations. The following year it settled a class-action suit involving overcharging customers for credit reports. After its second earnings decline in three years, management revamped the company in 1996, selling off ACNielsen and Cognizant (consisting of IMS Health and Nielsen Media Research). Volney Taylor was appointed chairman and CEO of Dun & Bradstreet. In 1998 it spun off R. H. Donnelley (now Dex One).

Under pressure from unhappy shareholders, Taylor resigned in late 1999. With director Clifford Alexander Jr. acting as interim CEO, Dun & Bradstreet announced plans to spin off its Moody's unit. After completing the spinoff the following year, Allan Loren took over as chairman and CEO of Dun & Bradstreet. Loren retired from the company in mid-2005 and president Steven Alesio became chairman and CEO.

In 2001 Dun & Bradstreet acquired Harris InfoSource, adding a database of US manufacturers to its coffers. The company made a major commitment to providing online data with its 2003 acquisition of Hoover's (the publisher of this profile). It then boosted its risk management and supply management businesses with the acquisitions of online credit management software provider LiveCapital and online risk management provider Open Ratings. The company also began making technology investments to expand its core business. In 2007 it acquired Purisma, a provider of data integration software.

D&B strengthened its online presence again in 2007 with the purchases of business information provider Allbusiness.com and First Research, a Web-based provider of editorial-based industry reports aimed at sales people.

EXECUTIVES

Chairman, President, and CEO: Sara S. Mathew, age 54, $4,089,398 total compensation
SVP and CFO: Anastasios G. (Tasos) Konidaris, age 43, $1,675,000 total compensation
SVP and Chief Data Officer: David Clarke
SVP Technology and CIO: Walter S. Hauck III, age 50
SVP, General Counsel, and Corporate Secretary: Jeffrey S. (Jeff) Hurwitz, age 49
SVP Strategic Solutions Channel and Government Solutions Business: Michael (Mike) Downing
SVP MaxCV Customer Leader: Stacy A. Cashman
SVP Commercial Customer Solutions: John Cucci
SVP Corporate Development, Strategy, and Global Reengineering: Richard H. (Rich) Veldran
Interim Chief Human Resources Officer: Patricia A. (Patti) Clifford, age 45
President, Purisma: Joseph M. (Joe) DiBartolomeo
President, D&B Asia/Pacific: David J. Emery
President, Europe, Latin America, and Partnerships: Emanuele A. Conti
President, Global Sales and Marketing Solutions: James H. (Jim) Delaney
President, Global Risk and Analytics: Byron C. Vielehr, age 46, $1,551,312 total compensation
President, North America and Internet Solutions: George I. Stoeckert, age 61, $1,824,915 total compensation
Leader, Government Solutions: Ethan Treese
Leader, Internet Solutions; President, Hoover's: Hyune Hand
Leader, CEO Communications: Susan Lawler
Leader, US Customer Operations: Steve Karl
Auditors: PricewaterhouseCoopers LLP

LOCATIONS

HQ: The Dun & Bradstreet Corporation
103 JFK Pkwy., Short Hills, NJ 07078
Phone: 973-921-5500   **Fax:** 973-921-6056
Web: www.dnb.com

2009 Sales

	$ mil.	% of total
North America	1,309.7	78
International	355.4	21
Divested businesses	21.9	1
Total	**1,687.0**	**100**

PRODUCTS/OPERATIONS

2009 Sales

	$ mil.	% of total
Risk management solutions	1,071.8	64
Sales & marketing solutions	474.6	28
Internet solutions	118.7	7
Divested businesses	21.9	1
Total	**1,687.0**	**100**

COMPETITORS

Acxiom
Coface
CreditRiskMonitor.com
Equifax
Experian
Fair Isaac
Harte-Hanks
infoGROUP
Kreller Business Information
Kroll Factual Data
Moody's
OneSource
S&P

HISTORICAL FINANCIALS

Company Type: Public

Income Statement

FYE: December 31

	REVENUE ($ mil.)	NET INCOME ($ mil.)	NET PROFIT MARGIN	EMPLOYEES
12/09	1,687	322	19.1%	5,000
12/08	1,726	311	18.0%	4,900
12/07	1,599	298	18.6%	4,900
12/06	1,531	241	15.7%	4,400
12/05	1,444	221	15.3%	4,350
Annual Growth	**4.0%**	**9.8%**	**—**	**3.5%**

2009 Year-End Financials

Debt ratio: —
Return on equity: —
Cash ($ mil.): 223
Current ratio: 0.88
Long-term debt ($ mil.): 962
No. of shares (mil.): 50
Dividends
  Yield: 1.6%
  Payout: 22.7%
Market value ($ mil.): 4,223

Stock History

NYSE: DNB

	STOCK PRICE ($) FY Close	P/E High/Low	PER SHARE ($) Earnings	Dividends	Book Value
12/09	84.37	14 12	5.99	1.36	(14.90)
12/08	77.20	18 11	5.60	1.20	(17.11)
12/07	88.63	22 16	4.99	1.00	(8.79)
12/06	82.79	23 18	3.70	—	(7.97)
12/05	66.96	21 17	3.19	—	1.55
Annual Growth	**5.9%**	**— —**	**17.1%**	**16.6%**	**—**

DuPont

E. I. du Pont de Nemours wants to cover your house, feed your crops, and coat your car. The #3 US chemical maker (behind Dow and ExxonMobil Chemicals) operates through six business units. These segments produce crop protection chemicals and genetically modified seeds, coatings (automotive finishes and coatings), electronic materials (LCDs and sensors), films and resins for packaging and other uses, performance chemicals (fluorine products and white pigments), and safety and security materials (under brand names like Tyvek, Kevlar, and Corian). In the last decade, the company slimmed down substantially, exiting the pharmaceutical and fibers businesses, and is now focusing on biotech and safety and protection.

At the end of 2009 the company re-configured its business segments, essentially creating the Performance Chemicals segment by fitting together the titanium dioxide business from the former Coatings & Technologies segment and the fluoro products unit from the Electronic Materials business. The re-org was designed to aid DuPont in its strategic priorities going forward: increasing food production; decreasing dependency on fossil fuels; protecting people, assets, and the environment; and growing its business

in emerging markets (such as Latin America, China, and India).

DuPont's Chemicals division agreed to enter a joint venture with Honeywell in 2010 to produce a new refrigerant for use in automotive air conditioning systems. The new product has 99.7 percent lower global warming potential than current refrigerants. DuPont and Honeywell will share financial and technological resources and will jointly design, construct, and operate a world-scale manufacturing facility. However, each company will market and sell the product separately.

Its Agriculture & Nutrition unit, which includes the biotech and seeds operations in addition to crop protection chemicals, is far and away DuPont's biggest business, accounting for about a third of total sales. The company operates 300 sites in more than 80 countries worldwide, getting almost two-thirds of its sales from outside the US.

HISTORY

Eleuthère Irénée du Pont de Nemours fled to America in 1800 after the French Revolution. Two years later he founded a gunpowder plant in Delaware. Within a decade the DuPont plant was the largest of its kind in the US. After Irénée's death in 1834, his sons Alfred and Henry took over. DuPont added dynamite and nitroglycerine in 1880, guncotton in 1892, and smokeless powder in 1894.

In 1902 three du Pont cousins bought DuPont. By 1906 the company controlled most of the US explosives market, but a 1912 antitrust decision forced it to sell part of the powder business. WWI profits were used to diversify into paints, plastics, and dyes.

DuPont acquired an interest in General Motors in 1917; the stake increased to 37% by 1922 (the company surrendered its stake in 1962 due to antitrust regulations). In the 1920s the firm bought and improved French cellophane technology and began producing rayon. DuPont's inventions include neoprene synthetic rubber (1931), Lucite (1937), nylon (1938), Teflon (1938), and Dacron. The last du Pont to head the company resigned as chairman in 1972. DuPont got into the energy business by acquiring Conoco for $7.6 billion in 1981.

In 1991 DuPont and Merck created DuPont Merck Pharmaceutical to focus on non-US markets. After record earnings in 1994, DuPont spent $8.8 billion the next year to buy back shares of the corporation from Seagram. In 1997 DuPont purchased Protein Technologies International (soy proteins) from Ralston Purina and Imperial Chemical's polyester-resins and intermediates operations (1997) and polyester-film business (1998).

DuPont president Chad Holliday became CEO in early 1998. That year DuPont purchased a 20% stake in Pioneer Hi-Bred International (corn seed) for $1.7 billion and Merck's 50% stake in DuPont Merck Pharmaceutical for $2.6 billion. DuPont's public offering of Conoco in 1998 raised $4.4 billion, the largest US IPO at the time.

In 1999 DuPont bought the Herberts paints and coatings unit from Hoechst. It also bought the remaining 80% of Pioneer Hi-Bred for $7.7 billion and biotechnology research firm CombiChem for $95 million. Making a clean break with its oil business, DuPont sold its remaining 70% stake in Conoco. In late 2001 Bristol-Myers Squibb bought DuPont's pharmaceutical operations (HIV, heart disease, nerve disorder, and cancer drugs) for $7.8 billion in cash.

In early 2002 DuPont initiated a restructuring that included the eventual spinoff of its fibers businesses (now called INVISTA) and the reorganization of its remaining business units into five segments: Electronics & Communication Technologies, Performance Materials, Coatings & Color Technologies, Safety & Protection, and Agriculture & Nutrition. Later that year DuPont acquired TOTAL's surface protection and fluoroadditives business to become the largest integrated fluorotelomer protectants maker in both Europe and North America.

Excluding the former pharmaceutical operations, DuPont wasn't profitable for the first few years of the new century. Much of its losses were due to employee severance costs and the writedown of assets. In 2003 the company took a large hit from the separation of INVISTA, among other costs. And so despite a 12% increase in sales, the company saw no real profit.

In 2003, in addition to workforce cuts and product consolidation, DuPont also began to shift its focus to emerging markets, by which it meant Asia. The company announced a substantial shift in management in January 2004 to follow up on the initiative, which included appointing a head of global sales for the first time and rearranging its leadership in Asia. The workforce cuts were announced in April; 3,500 jobs were lost in 2004, mostly in the US and Western Europe.

Preparing to separate INVISTA, DuPont reabsorbed DuPont Canada (which had been a separate, public company) into the fold. In early 2004 the company completed the sale of INVISTA; with that, DuPont was completely out of the fibers business.

In 2007 the company sold part of its fluorochemical products business to Huntsman. The unit sold provided fluoro-products for nonwovens to the textiles industry.

EXECUTIVES

Chairman and CEO: Ellen J. Kullman, age 54, $4,443,472 total compensation
President, DuPont Greater China: Douglas W. (Doug) Muzyka, age 55
EVP: Jeffrey L. Keefer, age 57, $4,286,206 total compensation
EVP, Production Agriculture Businesses: James C. Borel, age 54
EVP and CFO: Nicholas C. (Nick) Fanandakis, age 53
EVP and Chief Innovation Officer: Thomas M. (Tom) Connelly Jr., age 57, $3,638,016 total compensation
SVP Human Resources: W. Donald (Don) Johnson, age 62
SVP and Chief Science and Technology Officer: Uma Chowdhry, age 58
SVP Integrated Operations and Engineering: Jeffrey A. Coe, age 57
SVP Corporate Strategy: David G. Bills, age 48
SVP and General Counsel: Thomas L. Sager, age 60
VP Engineering, Facilities, and Real Estate and Chief Engineer: Jocelyn E. Scott
VP, Associate General Counsel, and Chief Intellectual Property Counsel: P. Michael Walker
VP Investor Relations: Karen A. Fletcher

President, Safety Resources: James R. Weigand, age 54
President, Protection Technologies: Thomas G. (Tom) Powell, age 50
President, Chemicals and Fluoroproducts: Gary W. Spitzer, age 52
President, Pioneer Hi-Bred: Paul E. Schickler, age 58
President, Crop Protection: James C. Collins Jr., age 47
President, Performance Polymers: Diane H. Gulyas, age 53
President, Electronics & Communications: David B. Miller, age 53
President, Packaging & Industrial Polymers: William J. (Bill) Harvey, age 59
President, Performance Coatings: Terry Caloghiris, age 59
President, Nutrition & Health and Applied BioSciences; Chairman, Solae: Craig F. Binetti, age 54
Secretary and Corporate Counsel: Mary E. Bowler
Auditors: PricewaterhouseCoopers LLP

LOCATIONS

HQ: E. I. du Pont de Nemours and Company
1007 Market St., Wilmington, DE 19898
Phone: 302-774-1000   **Fax:** 302-999-4399
Web: www.dupont.com

2009 Sales

	$ mil.	% of total
US	9,814	38
Europe/Middle East/Africa		
Germany	1,645	6
Other countries	5,520	21
Asia/Pacific		
China/Hong Kong	1,827	7
Japan	1,096	4
Other countries	2,266	9
Latin America		
Brazil	1,584	6
Other countries	1,598	6
Canada	759	3
Total	**26,109**	**100**

PRODUCTS/OPERATIONS

2009 Sales

	$ mil.	% of total
Agriculture & Nutrition	8,287	31
Performance Chemicals	4,819	19
Performance Materials	4,728	18
Performance Coatings	3,428	13
Safety & Protection	2,800	11
Electronics & Communications	1,898	7
Other	149	1
Total	**26,109**	**100**

Selected Operations

Agriculture and Nutrition
  DuPont Crop Protection
  DuPont Nutrition and Health
  DuPont Protein Technologies
  DuPont Qualicon
  Pioneer HiBred International
Performance Chemicals
  DuPont Fluoroproducts
  DuPont Titanium Technologies
Performance Materials
  DuPont Dow Elastomers
  DuPont Engineering Polymers
  DuPont Packaging and Industrial Polymers
  DuPont Teijin Films
Performance Coatings
  DuPont Performance Coatings
Safety and Protection
  DuPont Advanced Fiber Systems
  DuPont Chemical Solutions Enterprise
  DuPont Nonwovens
  DuPont Safety Resources
  DuPont Surfaces
Electronic and Communication Technologies
  DuPont Displays Technologies
  DuPont Electronic Technologies
  DuPont Imaging Technologies

COMPETITORS

3M
Ahlstrom
Akzo Nobel
Asahi Kasei
Ashland Inc.
BASF SE
Bayer AG
Cargill
Chevron Phillips Chemical
ConAgra
DIC Corporation
Dow Chemical
Eastman Chemical
Evonik Degussa
FMC
Formosa Plastics
Henkel
Honeywell International
Occidental Chemical
PPG Industries
Reliance Industries
Sherwin-Williams
Shin-Etsu Chemical
Syngenta
Wellman

HISTORICAL FINANCIALS

Company Type: Public

Income Statement

FYE: December 31

	REVENUE ($ mil.)	NET INCOME ($ mil.)	NET PROFIT MARGIN	EMPLOYEES
12/09	26,109	1,755	6.7%	58,000
12/08	30,529	2,007	6.6%	60,000
12/07	29,378	2,988	10.2%	60,000
12/06	28,982	3,148	10.9%	59,000
12/05	28,491	2,053	7.2%	60,000
Annual Growth	(2.2%)	(3.8%)	—	(0.8%)

2009 Year-End Financials

Debt ratio: 135.2%
Return on equity: 25.2%
Cash ($ mil.): 4,021
Current ratio: 1.84
Long-term debt ($ mil.): 9,528

No. of shares (mil.): 907
Dividends
  Yield: 4.9%
  Payout: 85.4%
Market value ($ mil.): 30,522

Stock History

NYSE: DD

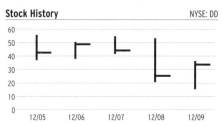

	STOCK PRICE ($) FY Close	P/E High/Low		PER SHARE ($) Earnings	Dividends	Book Value
12/09	33.67	19	8	1.92	1.64	7.96
12/08	25.30	24	10	2.20	1.64	7.86
12/07	44.09	17	13	3.22	1.52	12.28
12/06	48.71	15	11	3.38	1.48	10.39
12/05	42.50	27	18	2.07	1.46	9.83
Annual Growth	(5.7%)	—	—	(1.9%)	2.9%	(5.1%)

Dynegy Inc.

Power dynamo Dynegy (short for "dynamic energy") provides wholesale power, capacity, and ancillary services to a broad range of customers (utilities, cooperatives, municipalities and other energy operations) in 13 states, in the Midwest, the Northeast, and on the West Coast. The company's power generation portfolio consists of 18 power plants (in six states) fueled by coal, fuel oil, and natural gas, and have a generation capacity of 12,300 MW. Originally a natural gas trader, the company has refocused in recent years on the wholesale electricity market. In 2010 Dynegy agreed to be taken private by equity firm The Blackstone Group in a $4.7 billion transaction.

Dynegy has been endeavoring to find the right mix of assets to secure reliable and consistent financial returns. In 2007 the company paid approximately $2 billion in stock for LS Power's power generation facilities, acquiring ten power plants (roughly 8,000 MW) that are primarily natural gas-fired. The addition of these facilities nearly doubled Dynegy's generating capacity, providing it with a stronger foothold in the key western US region. Dynegy also acquired a 50% interest (alongside LS Power) in a development joint venture, whose focus was on high-return greenfield and brownfield development projects including natural gas, coal, and renewable options. However in 2009, citing an uncertain economy, the partners dissolved the joint venture, and Dynegy returned most of the plants to LS Power. The return of the eight facilities brought back to Dynegy $1 billion and lowered LS Group's holding in Dynegy from 40% to 15%.

The company has been selling other assets to pay down debt. In 2007 Dynegy sold its CoGen Lyondell power plant in Texas to a joint venture of PNM Resources and Cascade Investment.

That year it also sold the Rolling Hills Power Generation Facility in Ohio to an affiliate of Tenaska Capital Management for $368 million. In 2009 the company agreed to sell the Heard County Power Generation Facility in Georgia to Oglethorpe Power for $105 million.

HISTORY

Dynegy, originally Natural Gas Clearinghouse (NGC), emerged from the deregulation of the natural gas industry. In 1978 the Natural Gas Policy Act reduced interstate pipeline companies' control over the marketplace. Federal Energy Regulatory Commission (FERC) Order 380 (1984) made gas prices on the open market competitive with those of pipeline companies. NGC was founded in late 1984 to match gas buyers and sellers without taking title. Chuck Watson became president and CEO in 1985. The company grew dramatically as deregulation secured larger volumes of gas for independent marketers.

The company developed financial instruments (such as natural gas futures) to provide customers with a hedge against wide fluctuations in natural gas prices. By 1990 NGC was trading natural gas futures on NYMEX. It also branched out by buying gas gathering and processing facilities, and it formed NGC Oil Trading and Transportation to market crude oil.

FERC Order 636 (1992) required most interstate pipeline companies to offer merchant sales, transportation, and storage as separate services, on the same terms that their own affiliates received. With the low-price advantage taken away from pipeline companies, NGC began selling more to local gas utilities.

In 1994 NGC set up partnerships with Canada's NOVA (Novagas Clearinghouse, a natural gas marketer) and British Gas (Accord Energy, an energy marketer), which gave those firms sizable stakes (later reduced) in the company. It also set up an electric power marketing unit, Electric Clearinghouse.

The company changed its name to NGC and went public in 1995 after it bought Trident NGL, an integrated natural gas liquids company. The next year NGC bought Chevron's natural gas business, giving Chevron (which became ChevronTexaco in 2001 and then Chevron again in 2005) a stake in NGC.

In 1997 NGC acquired Destec Energy, a leading independent power producer. Taking the name Dynegy in 1998, the company allied with Florida Power to market wholesale electricity and gas. In 2000 Dynegy paid about $4 billion for utility holding company Illinova.

In November 2001 Dynegy announced an agreement to buy energy trading giant Enron for about $9 billion in stock and $13 billion in assumed debt. Later that month, after Enron's stock price continued to plunge, Dynegy canceled the deal and announced that it would exercise its option to buy Enron's Northern Natural Gas (NNG) pipeline for $1.5 billion. Enron then filed for Chapter 11 bankruptcy protection, and the two companies filed lawsuits against each other. In early 2002 Enron let Dynegy take control of the NNG pipeline, and Dynegy agreed to pay Enron $25 million to settle the suits. Dynegy sold the NNG pipeline to MidAmerican Energy Holdings later that year for $928 million plus $950 million in assumed debt.

Also in 2002 the SEC held a formal fraud investigation into how Dynegy accounted for a multi-year natural gas transaction called Project Alpha; the company later restated its 1999-2001 earnings to eliminate a tax benefit and other accounting improprieties related to the transaction. In addition, federal authorities sought information about Dynegy's participation in round-trip energy trades with CMS Energy, which artificially drove up the companies' trading volumes. The company reduced its workforce by 15% that year.

Amid the inquiries, Watson resigned as Dynegy's chairman and CEO. Dynegy later agreed to pay a $3 million fine in relation to the Project Alpha investigation, and in 2003 Jamie Olis was the first former Dynegy executive to be convicted on fraud charges over his involvement in the project. (Olis was sentenced to 24 years in prison in 2004; also that year Dynegy joint venture West Coast Power reached a $280 million settlement — $260 million in lost payments and $20 million in fines — with the FERC over charges of manipulating the California power market during its energy crisis in 2000-01.)

In 2002 and 2003 Dynegy sold its UK gas storage assets to Centrica and Scottish and Southern for a total of $700 million. In 2003 Dynegy sold the utility and its interest in the Joppa power generation facility to Ameren Corporation for $500 million in cash and $1.8 billion in debt in 2004. Dynegy sold off its energy trading unit and

its gas processing business in 2005 to Targa Resources for $2.5 billion.

In April 2007 Dynegy acquired LS Power; in return, the private equity fund became Dynegy's largest shareholder. Shortly thereafter, Chevron Corporation and Chevron U.S.A. sold off the remainder of their shares in Dynegy.

EXECUTIVES

Chairman, President, and CEO: Bruce A. Williamson, age 50, $8,181,452 total compensation
EVP and CFO: Holli C. Nichols, age 39, $2,533,551 total compensation
EVP Administration and General Counsel: J. Kevin Blodgett, age 38, $1,994,657 total compensation
EVP Commercial Operations and Market Analytics: Charles C. (Chuck) Cook, age 45, $1,876,511 total compensation
EVP Operations: Lynn A. Lednicky, age 49, $2,017,226 total compensation
SVP Commercial Management and Strategy: Eric Watts
SVP Technology and Administration and CIO: Biren Kumar
SVP and Treasurer: Carolyn J. Stone, age 37
SVP Gen Operations, Midwest: Keith McFarland
SVP and Deputy General Counsel: Kent R. Stephenson, age 59
SVP and Controller: Tracy A. McLauchlin, age 40
VP Tax: Amy Jolley
VP Fuels and Emissions: Mike Gray
VP Plant Operations: Sam Krueger
VP Procurement and Business Services: Mike Sanders
VP Human Resources: Julius Cox, age 36
VP and General Auditor: James (Jim) Horsch, age 52
VP Operations, West Region: Daniel P. Thompson
VP Commercial Strategy and Trading: Rudi Zipter
VP Strategic Planning and Corporate Business Development: Mario E. Alonso, age 39
VP Investor and Public Relations: Norelle V. Lundy, age 34
Auditors: PricewaterhouseCoopers LLP

LOCATIONS

HQ: Dynegy Inc.
1000 Louisiana St., Ste. 5800, Houston, TX 77002
Phone: 713-507-6400   **Fax:** 713-507-6808
Web: www.dynegy.com

2009 Sales

	$ mil.	% of total
Midwest	1,257	51
Northeast	834	34
West	380	15
Other	(3)	—
Total	**2,468**	**100**

COMPETITORS

AEP	Midwest Generation
AES	Mirant
Calpine	NRG Energy
Duke Energy	RRI Energy
Edison International	Sempra Energy
Exelon	Texas New Mexico Power

HISTORICAL FINANCIALS
Company Type: Public

Income Statement

FYE: December 31

	REVENUE ($ mil.)	NET INCOME ($ mil.)	NET PROFIT MARGIN	EMPLOYEES
12/09	2,468	(1,262)	—	2,800
12/08	3,549	174	4.9%	2,000
12/07	3,103	264	8.5%	1,800
12/06	2,017	(334)	—	1,339
12/05	2,313	108	4.7%	1,371
Annual Growth	**1.6%**	**—**	**—**	**19.5%**

2009 Year-End Financials

Debt ratio: 164.5%
Return on equity: —
Cash ($ mil.): 471
Current ratio: 1.10
Long-term debt ($ mil.): 4,775
No. of shares (mil.): 121
Dividends
  Yield: 0.0%
  Payout: —
Market value ($ mil.): 1,091

Stock History

NYSE: DYN

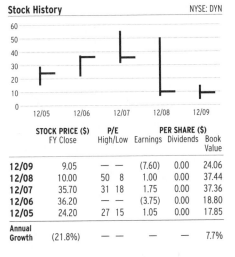

	STOCK PRICE ($) FY Close	P/E High/Low		PER SHARE ($) Earnings	Dividends	Book Value
12/09	9.05	—	—	(7.60)	0.00	24.06
12/08	10.00	50	8	1.00	0.00	37.44
12/07	35.70	31	18	1.75	0.00	37.36
12/06	36.20	—	—	(3.75)	0.00	18.80
12/05	24.20	27	15	1.05	0.00	17.85
Annual Growth	(21.8%)	—	—	—	—	7.7%

E. & J. Gallo Winery

E. & J. Gallo Winery brings merlot to the masses. The company is one of the world's largest winemakers, thanks in part to its low-end jug and box brands, including Carlo Rossi and Boone's Farm brands. The vintner owns seven wineries and some 15,000 acres of California vineyards; it also contracts with other growers to meet its supply demands. It is the leading US exporter of California wine, selling its some 60 brands in more than 90 countries across the globe. Among its premium wines and imports are those of Gallo Family Vineyards Sonoma Reserve and the Italian wine Ecco Domani. For those who prefer a little more kick to their imbibing, Gallo offers a number of distilled beverages, including brandy and gin.

Due to heavy government taxation, in 2010 the company began cutting back on its product offerings in the UK, reducing the number of wines it offers there to just five core brands. (The price of a bottle of wine has increased by 25% since Britain's Labour Party came to power in 1997; the duty on it has increased by 53%.) However, it continues to expand its geographical reach, entering the South African wine market the same year.

Gallo once only sold wine in the low-to-moderate price range, but now sells across a wide price range, from alcohol-added wines and wine coolers to upscale varietals that fetch more than $50 a bottle. It has successfully expanded premium wines such as Turning Leaf and Frei Brothers, which don't have the Gallo name on the label. It also imports wines from Argentina, Australia, France, Germany, Italy, New Zealand, South Africa, and Spain.

The company has tried new approaches to marketing its products, such as sponsoring pro volleyball tournaments and other events. It also rebranded its California wines as the "Gallo Family Vineyards" and removed the "Ernest & Julio" tag from its packaging and advertising. In 2008 it began producing wines under the MARTHA STEWART VINTAGE label. Offering three varieties — chardonnay, cabernet sauvignon, and merlot — the label is a limited-release product consisting of 15,000 cases.

Along with brewing wine and spirits, Gallo makes its own labels and bottles at its subsidiary, Gallo Glass Company. Founded in 1933, the company is still owned and operated by the Gallo family.

HISTORY

Giuseppe Gallo, the father of Ernest and Julio Gallo, was born in 1882 in the wine country of northwest Italy. Around 1900 he and his brother, Michelo (they called themselves Joe and Mike), traveled to America seeking fame and fortune in San Francisco. Both brothers became wealthy growing grapes and anticipating the growth of the market during Prohibition (homemade wine was legal and popular).

Giuseppe's eldest sons, Ernest and Julio, worked with their father from the beginning, but their relationship was strained. The father was reluctant to help his sons, particularly Ernest, in business. However, the mysterious murder-suicide that ended the lives of Giuseppe and his wife in 1933 eliminated that problem: The sons inherited the business their father had been unwilling to share.

From then on, Ernest ran the business end, assembling a large distribution network and building a national brand, while Julio made the wine and Joe Jr., the third, much younger, brother, worked for them. In the early 1940s Gallo opened bottling plants in Los Angeles and New Orleans, using screw-cap bottles, which then seemed more hygienic and modern than corks. Gallo lagged during WWII, when alcohol was diverted for the military. Under Julio's supervision, it upgraded its planting stock and refined its technology.

In an attempt to capitalize on the sweet wines popular in the 1950s, Gallo introduced Thunderbird, a fortified wine (its alcohol content boosted to 20%), in 1957. In the 1960s Gallo spurred its growth by heavily advertising and keeping prices low. It introduced Hearty Burgundy, a jug wine, in 1964, along with Ripple. Gallo introduced the carbonated, fruit-flavored Boone's Farm Apple Wine in 1969, creating short-term interest in "pop" wines.

The company introduced its first varietal wines in 1974. In the 1970s Gallo field workers switched unions, from the United Farm Workers to the Teamsters. Repercussions included protests and boycotts, but sales were largely unaffected. From 1976 to 1982 Gallo operated under an FTC order limiting its control over wholesalers. The order was lifted after the industry's competitive balance changed.

Through the 1970s and 1980s Gallo expanded its production of varietals; in 1988 it began adding vintage dates to labels. But it also kept a hand in the lower levels of the market, introducing Bartles & Jaymes wine coolers.

Gallo began a legal battle in 1986 with Joe, who had been eased out of the business, over the use of the Gallo name. In 1992 Joe lost the use of his name for commercial purposes. Julio died the next year when his Jeep overturned on a family ranch.

In 1996 rival Kendall-Jackson sued Gallo for trademark infringement over Gallo's new wine brand, Turning Leaf, claiming Gallo copied its Vintner's Reserve bottle and label. A jury ruled in Gallo's favor in 1997; a federal appeals court supported that decision in 1998.

In 2000 Gallo announced plans to promote wine-cooler market leader Bartles & Jaymes with a new advertising campaign, although the category continued to wane. The next year Gallo expanded the technological end of the wine business. Gallo's research team patented a number of tools licensed to winemakers around the world; one tool, for example, can diagnose a sick vine in a matter of hours, rather than years.

The purchase of Louis M. Martini Winery in Napa Valley in 2002 furthered Gallo's expansion into premium wines. It marked the first time Gallo bought an entire winery rather than land or wine labels. It invested about $1 million in capital improvements at the winery and ramped up production of cabernet under the Martini label.

In 2004 it bought the brand name and stocks of San Jose-based wine producer Mirassou Vineyards, one of the oldest wineries in California, and Santa Barbara company Bindlewood Weste Winery. In 2005 Gallo added Grape Links, Inc., maker of Barefoot Cellars, to its stable of holdings.

Ernest Gallo died in 2007 at the age of 97.

EXECUTIVES

Co-Chairman: Robert J. (Bob) Gallo, age 75
Co-Chairman: James E. (Jim) Coleman, age 75
President and CEO: Joseph E. (Joe) Gallo, age 66
EVP and General Counsel: Jack B. Owens
VP Operations: Steven (Steve) Kidd
VP Finance: Doug Vilas
VP Viticulture: Nick K. Dokoozlian
VP and CIO: Kent Kushar
VP North Coast Operations: Matt Gallo
VP, Gallo Glass: John Gallo, age 48
VP Supply Chain and Logistics: Ulli Thiersch
VP, Europe, Middle East, and Africa: George Marsden
VP Domestic Sales: Steve Sprinkle
VP National Sales: Gary Ippolito
VP Grower Relations: Gregory J. (Greg) Coleman, age 50
VP Strategic Planning and Corporate Communications: Susan Hensley
VP and General Manager: Peter Abate
Director Consumer Insights and Strategy: Christopher Bacon
Director Global Consumer Relations: Marie Shubin
Director Winemaking: Gina Gallo
Director Marketing: Stephanie Gallo, age 37
Director Marketing Communications: Michael J. Heintz

LOCATIONS

HQ: E. & J. Gallo Winery
  600 Yosemite Blvd., Modesto, CA 95354
Phone: 209-341-3111
Web: www.gallo.com

PRODUCTS/OPERATIONS

Selected Brands

Spirits
 E. & J. Cask & Cream
 E. & J. Cask & Cream Chocolate Temptation
 E. & J. VS Brandy
 E. & J. VSOP Brandy
 E. & J. XO Brandy
 New Amsterdam Gin

Wine
 Anapamu Cellars
 André
 Ballatore
 Barefoot Bubbly
 Bartles & Jaymes
 Bella Sera
 Black Swan
 Boone's Farm
 Bridlewood Estate Winery
 Burlwood
 Carlo Rossi
 Cask & Cream
 Clarendon Hills
 Copperidge
 Dancing Bull
 DaVinci
 Don Miguel Gascon
 Ecco Domani
 Frei Brothers Reserve
 Frutézia
 Gallo Family Vineyard Estate
 Gallo Family Vineyard Single Vineyard
 Gallo Family Vineyard Sonoma Reserve
 Gallo Family Vineyard Twin Valley
 Ghost Pines
 Gossamer Bay
 Hornsby's
 Indigo Hills
 Las Rocas
 Liberty Creek
 Livingston Cellars
 Louis M. Martini
 MacMurray Ranch
 Marcelina
 Martn Côdax
 Maso Canali
 Mattie's Perch
 McWilliam's Hanwood Estate
 Mirassou
 Napa Valley Vineyards
 Peter Vella
 Pölka Dot
 Rancho Zabaco
 Red Bicyclette
 Red Rock Winery
 Redwood Creek
 Sebeka
 Starborough
 Tisdale Vineyards
 Turning Leaf Costal Reserve
 Turning Leaf Sonoma Reserve
 Whitehaven
 Wild Vines
 William Hill Estate
 William Wycliff Vineyards

COMPETITORS

Asahi Breweries	Newton Vineyard
Bacardi	Pernod Ricard
Bacardi USA	Premier Pacific
Bronco Wine Co.	Ravenswood Winery
Brown-Forman	Robert Mondavi Winery
Concha y Toro	Scheid Vineyards
Constellation Wines	Sebastiani Vineyards
Diageo	Sunview Vineyards
Foster's Americas	Taittinger
Foster's Group	Terlato Wine
GIV	Trinchero Family Estates
Heaven Hill Distilleries	UST llc
Jackson Family Wines	Vincor
Kirin Holdings Company	Wine Group
LVMH	

HISTORICAL FINANCIALS

Company Type: Private

Income Statement

FYE: December 31

	ESTIMATED REVENUE ($ mil.)	NET INCOME ($ mil.)	NET PROFIT MARGIN	EMPLOYEES
12/08	2,000	—	—	5,000
12/07	3,150	—	—	5,000
12/06	2,700	—	—	4,600
12/05	2,700	—	—	4,400
12/04	3,000	—	—	—
Annual Growth	(9.6%)	—	—	4.4%

Revenue History

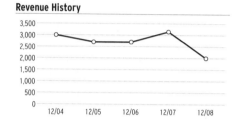

EarthLink, Inc.

Some of us spend way too much time online, and EarthLink is OK with that. The company provides Internet connections to more than 2 million consumer and business subscribers in the US. About two-thirds of those are broadband users. The company also offers such services as VoIP computer telephony and Web hosting. EarthLink provides broadband access over cable lines through agreements with network operators including Time Warner Cable, Bright House, and Comcast, while DSL connections are made possible over phone lines owned by AT&T and Verizon, among others. Subsidiary New Edge Networks implements and manages private data networks in addition to providing Internet access and Web hosting for businesses.

While EarthLink's revenue declined for the third consecutive year, its income increased in 2009, as it did in 2008 following a loss-making 2007. The company's shrinking sales are mainly the result of steadily decreasing consumer and business subscriber numbers, but fewer customers is translating to lower expenses in some areas as EarthLink works to bring down costs to improve profits through a variety of means.

The company renegotiated contracts with its network service providers to allow for its reduced bandwidth needs, and it brought down operational expenses partly by reducing staff, particularly in customer service and technical support roles. EarthLink also continued to cut back on sales and marketing activities, and staff, as it refocused on customer retention efforts as opposed to costly marketing campaigns aimed at bringing in large volumes of potential subscribers. The company has said that it does hope to add more new customers primarily through partnerships with other ISPs or via acquisitions.

HISTORY

After his first attempt to log onto the Internet took 80 hours in 1993, a frustrated 23-year-old Sky Dayton had an idea for a new business: an ISP focused on customer service. Dayton, who had already co-founded Los Angeles coffeehouse Cafe Mocha and graphics firm Dayton Walker Design, persuaded investors Reed Slatkin and Kevin O'Donnell to contribute $100,000. EarthLink Network was launched in Glendale, California, in 1994.

Dayton, an Ayn Rand fan who graduated from high school at 16 and never attended college, first tried to do everything — from sales to software — himself. He ultimately decided to concentrate on customer service, correctly betting that such elements as browser software and backbone networks would emerge from other providers. Offering phone help and a flat monthly rate of $19.95, EarthLink sold its first account by the end of 1994.

The next year EarthLink released TotalAccess, a package of leading Internet software that included the popular Netscape Navigator browser and QUALCOMM's Eudora, the oft-used e-mail program. Viacom's Macmillan Publishing agreed to sell TotalAccess disks in its Internet books. EarthLink was to gain similar deals with about 90 other partners.

By 1996 EarthLink had won 30,000 subscribers. The company signed a deal with PSINet giving EarthLink customers dial-up access through PSINet's more than 230 locations in the US and Canada. The next year EarthLink went public.

In 1998 EarthLink teamed with Sprint in a 10-year deal that combined the companies' Internet access services and gave Sprint 29.5% of the firm. As EarthLink passed the 1 million-subscriber mark in 1999, it agreed to offer a co-branded version of America Online's instant messaging service.

EarthLink Network agreed to merge with MindSpring in 1999 in a $1.4 billion deal (closed in 2000). The new company, EarthLink, Inc., moved to MindSpring's Atlanta headquarters. MindSpring founder Charles Brewer took over as chairman, and Dayton remained a director. Brewer left EarthLink later in 2000, however, and Dayton stepped back in as chairman.

Investments in EarthLink during 2000 included $200 million from Apple (which made EarthLink the default ISP on Macintoshes) and another $431 million from Sprint (which boosted its stake after heavy dilution from the MindSpring deal). That year, EarthLink gained 700,000 subscribers by buying OneMain.com, an ISP focused on small cities and rural communities, for $262 million.

EarthLink and Sprint stepped back from their co-branding arrangement in 2001, and Sprint sold about 40% of its stake in the company. That year EarthLink agreed to acquire Cidco, a California-based maker of personal e-mail appliances, in a $5 million deal (completed in 2002). Also in 2002 EarthLink acquired the assets of wireless Internet access provider OmniSky as well as PeoplePC, which used to sell computers with bundled Internet access and now sells value-priced narrowband Internet access (sans computer).

In 2005 Robert Kavner replaced Dayton as EarthLink's chairman of the board. Two years later the company tapped Mpower Communications chairman Rolla Huff as its new president and CEO.

Spurred by mounting costs and dwindling subscribers, Earthlink in 2007 initiated a restructuring plan that included the closure of four offices and workforce cuts of roughly half.

EXECUTIVES

Chairman and CEO: Rolla P. Huff, age 53, $3,873,929 total compensation
President and COO: Joseph M. (Joe) Wetzel, age 54, $1,539,831 total compensation
CFO: Bradley A. (Brad) Ferguson, age 39, $1,182,618 total compensation
General Counsel and Secretary: Samuel R. (Sam) DeSimone Jr., age 50, $820,525 total compensation
Chief People Officer: Stacie Hagan, age 43, $761,825 total compensation
VP Consumer Products and Service: Kevin F. Brand, age 51
President, New Edge Networks: Cardi Prinzi, age 53
Auditors: Ernst & Young LLP

LOCATIONS

HQ: EarthLink, Inc.
1375 Peachtree St., Atlanta, GA 30309
Phone: 404-815-0770   **Fax:** 404-892-7616
Web: www.earthlink.net

PRODUCTS/OPERATIONS

2009 Sales

	$ mil.	% of total
Consumer	575.4	80
Business	148.3	20
Total	**723.7**	**100**

COMPETITORS

AOL
Aplus.net
AT&T
Charter Communications
Comcast
Covad Communications Group
Cox Communications
Google
Internet America
Level 3 Communications
MegaPath
Microsoft
Qwest Communications
ReaLLinx
Sprint Nextel
Time Warner Cable
United Online
Verizon
Vonage
XO Holdings
Yahoo!

HISTORICAL FINANCIALS

Company Type: Public

Income Statement   FYE: December 31

	REVENUE ($ mil.)	NET INCOME ($ mil.)	NET PROFIT MARGIN	EMPLOYEES
12/09	724	287	39.7%	623
12/08	956	190	19.8%	754
12/07	1,216	(135)	—	998
12/06	1,301	5	0.4%	2,210
12/05	1,290	143	11.1%	1,732
Annual Growth	**(13.5%)**	**19.1%**	**—**	**(22.6%)**

2009 Year-End Financials

Debt ratio: 0.0%
Return on equity: 48.6%
Cash ($ mil.): 611
Current ratio: 2.42
Long-term debt ($ mil.): 0
No. of shares (mil.): 108
Dividends
  Yield: 3.4%
  Payout: 10.5%
Market value ($ mil.): 899

Stock History   NASDAQ (GS): ELNK

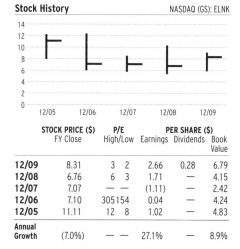

	STOCK PRICE ($) FY Close	P/E High	P/E Low	PER SHARE ($) Earnings	PER SHARE ($) Dividends	PER SHARE ($) Book Value
12/09	8.31	3	2	2.66	0.28	6.79
12/08	6.76	6	3	1.71	—	4.15
12/07	7.07	—	—	(1.11)	—	2.42
12/06	7.10	305	154	0.04	—	4.24
12/05	11.11	12	8	1.02	—	4.83
Annual Growth	**(7.0%)**	**—**	**—**	**27.1%**	**—**	**8.9%**

Eastman Chemical

Eastman Chemical can recall its past through photos — it was once part of film giant Eastman Kodak. The company has developed into a major producer of chemicals, fibers, and plastics. Among Eastman's operating segments are its CASPI (coatings, adhesives, specialty polymers, and inks), Specialty Plastics (engineering polymers), and Fibers (acetate tow and textile fibers) units. Its Performance Polymers segment is the #1 maker of polyethylene terephthalate (PET), a plastic used to make packaging for soft drinks, food, and water. The largest segment manufactures Performance Chemicals and Intermediates. Eastman's products go into such items as food and medical packaging, films, and toothbrushes.

Eastman Chemical has operations worldwide, with the US accounting for just more than half of sales. It's continually expanded internationally — even through the global recession of 2008-2009 — by building plants, acquiring businesses, and expanding existing facilities in Asia, Europe, and Latin America.

Eastman acquired Genovique Specialties Corporation, a global provider of benzoate plasticizers, from Arsenal Capital Partners in 2010. Chicago-based Genovique produces benzoic acid, sodium benzoate, and specialty plasticizers for the adhesives and sealants, coatings, and PVC markets, with operations in North America, Europe, and Asia.

In 2009 the company joined with SK Chemicals in a joint venture to construct a cellulose acetate tow facility in Ulsan, South Korea. Eastman owns 80% of the JV and operates the plant, which began production in 2010. It also bought a facility in China in 2010 that serves Eastman's CASPI segment. The previous year, Eastman had expanded an acetate tow facility it owns in the UK.

Chairman and CEO Brian Ferguson retired in 2009 after nearly seven years as CEO. James

Rogers, who had been president of the company and head of the chemicals and fibers group, is his successor, and Ferguson became executive chairman.

HISTORY

Eastman Chemical went public in 1994, but the company traces its roots to the 19th century. George Eastman, after developing a method for dry-plate photography, established the Eastman Dry Plate and Film Company in 1884 in Rochester, New York (the name was changed to Eastman Kodak in 1892).

In 1886 Eastman hired scientist Henry Reichenbach to help create and manufacture new photographic chemicals. As time passed, Reichenbach and the company's other scientists came up with chemicals that were either not directly related to photography or had uses in addition to photography.

Eastman bought a wood-distillation plant in Kingsport, Tennessee, in 1920 and formed the Tennessee Eastman Corporation to make methanol and acetone for the manufacture of photographic chemicals. The company, by this time called Kodak, introduced acetate yarn and Tenite, a cellulose ester plastic, in the early 1930s. During WWII the company formed Holston Defense to make explosives for the US armed forces.

Kodak began to vertically integrate Tennessee Eastman's operations during the 1950s, acquiring A. M. Tenney Associates, Tennessee Eastman's selling agent for its acetate yarn products, in 1950. It also established Texas Eastman, opening a plant in Longview to produce ethyl alcohol and aldehydes, raw materials used in fiber and film production. At the end of 1952, Kodak created Eastman Chemical Products to sell alcohols, plastics, and fibers made by Tennessee Eastman and Texas Eastman. Also that year Tennessee Eastman developed cellulose acetate filter tow for use in cigarette filters. In the late 1950s the company introduced Kodel polyester fiber.

Kodak created Carolina Eastman Company in 1968, opening a plant in Columbia, South Carolina, to produce Kodel and other polyester products. It also created Eastman Chemicals Division to handle its chemical operations.

In the late 1970s Eastman Chemicals Division introduced polyethylene terephthalate (PET) resin used to make containers. It acquired biological and molecular instrumentation manufacturer International Biotechnologies in 1987.

Eastman Chemicals Division became Eastman Chemical Company in 1990. In 1993 it exited the polyester fiber business. When Kodak spun off Eastman Chemical in early 1994, the new company was saddled with $1.8 billion in debt.

Eastman's 1996 earnings were reduced when oversupply lowered prices for PET. Eastman opened plants in Argentina, Malaysia, and the Netherlands in 1998.

Eastman added to its international locations in 1999 by opening a plant in Singapore and an office in Bangkok. It also bought Lawter International (specialty chemicals for ink and coatings) with locations in Belgium, China, and Ireland. In 2000 the company began restructuring into two business segments (chemicals and polymers) and acquired resin and colorant maker McWhorter Technologies.

In 2001 Eastman acquired most of Hercules' resins business. In November the company announced that it had postponed plans to split into two companies (one focusing on specialty chemicals and plastics, the other concentrating on polyethylene, plastics, and acetate fibers) until mid-2002 due to the weak economy. In early 2002 the company announced that it had cancelled those plans altogether and would operate the two as separate divisions.

The following year Eastman announced it would split off part of its coatings, adhesives, specialty polymers, and inks (CASPI) segment. Eastman sold a portion of CASPI to investment firm Apollo Management for $215 million. Businesses included in the sale were composites, inks and graphic arts raw materials, liquid and powder resins, and textile chemicals. (Apollo called the acquired businesses Resolution Specialty Materials, and then joined RSM with Resolution Performance Products and another of its chemical companies, Borden Chemical, to form the new Hexion Specialty Chemicals in 2005.)

It restructured its divisional alignment in 2006 in an attempt to group together related product groups and technologies. In the process, Eastman disbanded its former Voridian Division.

At the end of 2007, the company decided to divest its PET facilities in the UK and the Netherlands as well as its Dutch PTA plants. Eastman sold the facilities to Indorama for about $330 million.

EXECUTIVES

Chairman: J. Brian Ferguson, age 55,
$3,664,162 total compensation
President, CEO, and Director: James P. (Jim) Rogers,
age 58, $3,665,854 total compensation
EVP Specialty Polymers, Coatings, and Adhesives, and Chief Marketing Officer: Mark J. Costa, age 43,
$1,647,720 total compensation
EVP Performance Polymers and Chemical Intermediates: Ronald C. Lindsay, age 51,
$1,482,613 total compensation
SVP and CFO: Curtis E. Espeland, age 45,
$2,528,283 total compensation
SVP and CTO: Gregory W. (Greg) Nelson, age 47,
$2,241,499 total compensation
SVP, Chief Legal Officer, and Corporate Secretary:
Theresa K. Lee, age 57, $1,460,439 total compensation
SVP Fibers and Global Supply Chain:
Richard L. Johnson, age 60
SVP Manufacturing Support and Chief Administrative Officer: Norris P. Sneed, age 54
VP, Controller, and Chief Accounting Officer:
Scott V. King, age 41
Director Investors Relations: Gregory (Greg) Riddle
Auditors: PricewaterhouseCoopers LLP

LOCATIONS

HQ: Eastman Chemical Company
200 S. Wilcox Dr., Kingsport, TN 37662
Phone: 423-229-2000 **Fax:** 423-229-2145
Web: www.eastman.com

2009 Sales

	$ mil.	% of total
US	2,716	54
Other countries	2,331	46
Total	**5,047**	**100**

PRODUCTS/OPERATIONS

2009 Sales

	$ mil.	% of total
PCI	1,330	26
CASPI	1,217	24
Fibers	1,032	21
Specialty Plastics	749	15
Performance Polymers	719	14
Total	**5,047**	**100**

Selected Products

Chemicals
  Adhesives
    Agricultural chemicals
    Food and beverage ingredients
    Inks
    Performance chemicals (chemicals for agricultural products, fibers, food and beverage ingredients, photographic chemicals, pharmaceutical intermediates, polymer compounding)
  Specialty polymers and intermediates
Specialty Plastics
  Polymers
    Container plastics
    Specialty plastics
  Fibers
    Estron acetate tow
    Estron and Chromspun acetate yarns
    Estrobond triacetin plasticizers

COMPETITORS

Akzo Nobel
BASF SE
Bostik
Celanese
Clariant
DAK Americas
DIC Corporation
Dow Chemical
DSM
DuPont
ExxonMobil Chemical
Honeywell Specialty Materials
Huntsman Corp
Mitsubishi Rayon
Nan Ya Plastics
NatureWorks
Reliance Industries
Rhodia
SABIC Innovative Plastics
Sterling Chemicals
Teijin
Wellman

HISTORICAL FINANCIALS

Company Type: Public

Income Statement

FYE: December 31

	REVENUE ($ mil.)	NET INCOME ($ mil.)	NET PROFIT MARGIN	EMPLOYEES
12/09	5,047	136	2.7%	10,000
12/08	6,726	346	5.1%	10,500
12/07	6,830	300	4.4%	10,800
12/06	7,450	409	5.5%	11,000
12/05	7,059	557	7.9%	12,000
Annual Growth	**(8.0%)**	**(29.7%)**	**—**	**(4.5%)**

2009 Year-End Financials

Debt ratio: 106.0%
Return on equity: 8.9%
Cash ($ mil.): 793
Current ratio: 2.17
Long-term debt ($ mil.): 1,604
No. of shares (mil.): 72
Dividends
  Yield: 2.9%
  Payout: 95.1%
Market value ($ mil.): 4,352

Stock History

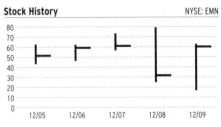

NYSE: EMN

	STOCK PRICE ($) FY Close	P/E High/Low		PER SHARE ($) Earnings	Dividends	Book Value
12/09	60.24	33	10	1.85	1.76	20.94
12/08	31.71	17	6	4.55	1.76	21.50
12/07	61.09	20	16	3.58	1.76	28.82
12/06	59.31	12	10	4.91	1.76	28.09
12/05	51.59	9	6	6.81	1.76	22.31
Annual Growth	**4.0%**	—	—	**(27.8%)**	**0.0%**	**(1.6%)**

Eastman Kodak

When Kodak made Brownies, folks began to say cheese. The inventor of the Brownie camera (1900), Kodak has retouched its image from a top maker of photographic film to a provider of imaging technology products and services to the photographic and graphic communications markets. The firm reorganized its business to focus less on film sales and more on sales of digital cameras and imaging systems. Kodak's multi-year shift to become a digital technology business spurred the company in 2009 to discontinue its iconic Kodachrome color film.

As part of the company's shift to digital, Kodak has purged some 30,000 employees. During 2009 the imaging firm shed 17% of its global workforce. More than half of those who received pink slips in 2009 were located in the US.

Kodak kicked off its restructuring efforts several years ago. The shakeup was intended to help the company retool its offerings and concentrate on digital products and services. The global recession has not helped Kodak's plans to turn its business around.

Its Consumer Digital Imaging segment is one of the top providers to consumers of digital still cameras, retail printing, and digital picture frames. The Kodak Imaging Network, with its 70 million Kodak Gallery members, is part of this business segment, along with the Kodak All-in-One Inkjet Printing System. The Film, Photofinishing, and Entertainment segment serves up traditional photographic products and services for consumers and professionals. The company's Graphic Communications segment offers software, media, and hardware products for prepress customers and those who do digital and traditional printing.

Kodak built the foundation for its growing Graphic Communications business several years ago when it purchased Canada's Creo Inc., the top provider worldwide of workflow software for commercial printers, for about $980 million in 2005. It also acquired Sun Chemical's 50% stake in Kodak Polychrome Graphics for about $817 million. In 2009 the company bought the scanner division of Böwe Bell + Howell to expand its assortment of scanners and complement its business products.

In an effort to streamline its film finishing business, Kodak in early 2010 sold the assets and operations of Laser Pacific Media, its Emmy Award-winning post-production subsidiary, to investment firm H.I.G. Capital.

Kodak and Motorola inked a 10-year global product, licensing, and marketing agreement in 2006 to co-develop camera phones with Kodak sensors. It also entered a licensing deal with Univision Technology (based in Taiwan) in 2006 to lend Kodak's passive-matrix OLED technology to be applied to Univision's flat panel displays.

Investment firm Legg Mason Capital Management owns about 20% of the company's common stock.

HISTORY

After developing a method for dry-plate photography, George Eastman established The Eastman Dry Plate and Film Company in 1884. In 1888 it introduced its first camera, a small, easy-to-use device that was loaded with enough film for 100 pictures. Owners mailed the camera back to the company, which returned it with the pictures and more film. The firm settled on the name Eastman Kodak in 1892, after Eastman tried many combinations of letters starting and ending with "k," which he thought was a "strong, incisive sort of letter." The user-friendly Brownie camera followed in 1900. Three years later Kodak introduced a home movie camera, projector, and film.

Ailing and convinced that his work was done, Eastman committed suicide in 1932. Kodak continued to dominate the photography industry with the introduction of color film (Kodachrome, 1935) and a handheld movie camera (1951). The company established US plants to produce the chemicals, plastics, and fibers used in its film production.

The Instamatic, introduced in 1963, became Kodak's biggest success. The camera's foolproof film cartridge eliminated the need for loading in the dark. By 1976 Kodak had sold an estimated 60 million Instamatics, 50 million more cameras than all its competitors combined. Subsequent introductions included the Kodak instant camera (1976) and the unsuccessful disc camera (1982).

In the 1980s Kodak diversified into electronic publishing, batteries, floppy disks (Verbatim, 1985, sold 1990), pharmaceuticals (Sterling Drug, sold 1994), and do-it-yourself and household products (L&F Products, sold 1994).

George Fisher, former chairman of Motorola, became Kodak's chairman and CEO in 1993. Fisher began cutting debt by selling noncore assets. Kodak spun off Eastman Chemical in 1994. Sales in 1996 included its money-losing copier sales and services business. Kodak acquired the medical imaging business of Imation in 1998, but it also unloaded more of its noncore operations, including its 450-store Fox Photo chain.

COO Daniel Carp replaced Fisher as CEO in early 2000. Further hits to the economy and Kodak's revenue prompted management in 2001 to eliminate regional divisions and realign the business along product lines. In 2003 the company announced it would cut as many as 6,000 jobs worldwide. This came after reducing as many as 2,200 jobs in the US and Western Europe earlier in the year and cutting as many as 7,000 jobs worldwide in 2002.

In 2004, on the heels of its announcement that it would stop selling film-based cameras in Western markets by year's end, Kodak said it would also stop global production of its Advantix Advanced Photo System (APS) cameras.

In 2005 Kodak said that it would phase out production of black-and-white photographic paper. The firm attributed its exit from the business to a move from chemical-based photography to digital imaging and a 25% decline in demand for black-and-white paper annually. The company continued a restructuring program that included consolidating color photographic paper manufacturing for North America, closing a Rochester operation that recycles waste to produce Estar polyester film base, and reducing capacity for the production of consumer film products at its Xiamen, China, plant.

Antonio Perez, who took over as president and CEO in mid-2005, added the title of chairman in 2006, when Dan Carp retired. Also that year, Kodak inked an agreement with now-defunct Fischer Imaging Corporation to provide postsale support (including repair and maintenance) for Fischer's mammography products (such as SenoScan and MammoTest) installed worldwide.

In December 2009 the company sold its organic light-emitting diode (OLED) business to LG Electronics. The technology was pioneered by Kodak in the 1970s.

EXECUTIVES

Chairman and CEO: Antonio M. Perez, age 64, $12,625,319 total compensation
President and COO; President, Graphic Communications Group: Philip J. (Phil) Faraci, age 54, $4,599,518 total compensation
EVP and CFO: Frank S. Sklarsky, age 53, $2,910,501 total compensation
SVP and General Counsel: Joyce P. Haag, age 59, $1,984,008 total compensation
SVP; President Film, Photofinishing and Entertainment Group: Brad W. Kruchten, age 49
SVP and Chief Human Resources Officer: Robert L. (Bob) Berman, age 52, $1,955,074 total compensation
Secretary and Chief Compliance Officer: Patrick M. Sheller, age 48
VP; President and General Manager, Entertainment Imaging, Film, Photofinishing, and Entertainment Group: Kimberly A. (Kim) Snyder, age 47
VP, Chief Diversity Officer, and Director Community Affairs: Essie L. Calhoun
VP and Director Investor Relations: Antoinette P. (Ann) McCorvey, age 52
VP and CTO: Terry R. Taber, age 55
VP and CIO: Kim E. VanGelder
Chief Accounting Officer and Controller: Eric Samuels, age 42
Manager Corporate Communications: Christopher (Chris) Veronda
Auditors: PricewaterhouseCoopers LLP

LOCATIONS

HQ: Eastman Kodak Company
343 State St., Rochester, NY 14650
Phone: 585-724-4000 **Fax:** 585-724-1089
Web: www.kodak.com

2009 Sales

	$ mil.	% of total
US	3,083	41
Europe, Middle East & Africa	2,358	31
Asia/Pacific	1,298	17
Canada & Latin America	867	11
Total	**7,606**	**100**

PRODUCTS/OPERATIONS

Selected Products and Services

Commercial inkjet printing systems
Commercial printing workflow software
Consumer and professional photographic film
Digital picture frames
Digital still cameras
Document scanners
Electrophotographic equipment
Inkjet printers
KODAK Gallery online imaging services
Origination and print films
Photographic paper
Prepress equipment
Processing chemicals
Retail printing kiosks, APEX drylab systems, and related media
Video cameras and related accessories
Wholesale photofinishing services

2009 Sales

	$ mil.	% of total
Graphic Communications Group	2,726	36
Consumer Digital Imaging Group	2,619	34
Film, Photofinishing & Entertainment Group	2,257	30
Other	4	—
Total	**7,606**	**100**

COMPETITORS

3M
Agfa
Canon
CASIO COMPUTER
Dell
FUJIFILM
Hewlett-Packard
Konica Minolta
Leica Camera
Lexmark
NEC
Nikon
Olympus
Panasonic Corp
Philips Electronics
Polaroid
Procter & Gamble
Ricoh Company
Sharp Corp.
Sony
Xerox

HISTORICAL FINANCIALS

Company Type: Public

Income Statement

FYE: December 31

	REVENUE ($ mil.)	NET INCOME ($ mil.)	NET PROFIT MARGIN	EMPLOYEES
12/09	7,606	(215)	—	20,250
12/08	9,416	(442)	—	24,400
12/07	10,301	676	6.6%	26,900
12/06	13,274	(601)	—	40,900
12/05	14,268	(1,314)	—	51,100
Annual Growth	**(14.6%)**	**—**	**—**	**(20.7%)**

2009 Year-End Financials

Debt ratio: —
Return on equity: —
Cash ($ mil.): 2,024
Current ratio: 1.49
Long-term debt ($ mil.): 1,129
No. of shares (mil.): 269
Dividends
  Yield: 0.0%
  Payout: —
Market value ($ mil.): 1,134

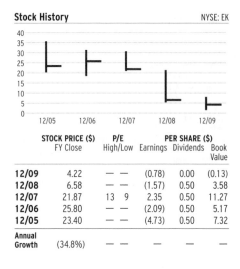

	STOCK PRICE ($) FY Close	P/E High/Low		PER SHARE ($) Earnings	Dividends	Book Value
12/09	4.22	—	—	(0.78)	0.00	(0.13)
12/08	6.58	—	—	(1.57)	0.50	3.58
12/07	21.87	13	9	2.35	0.50	11.27
12/06	25.80	—	—	(2.09)	0.50	5.17
12/05	23.40	—	—	(4.73)	0.50	7.32
Annual Growth	(34.8%)	—	—	—	—	—

Eaton Corporation

When it comes to diversification, Eaton favors an all-you-can-eat approach. The manufacturer has made dozens of acquisitions (as well as divestitures) in its long and storied history. The company's product lines include electrical power distribution and control equipment, hydraulic products for use in mobile and industrial applications, aerospace propulsion systems, and truck safety systems. It is also one of the world's largest manufacturers of grips for golf clubs. Electrical power management is its leading line of business these days, accounting for about half of Eaton's sales. Geographically, the company makes more than half of its sales within the US.

Eaton is looking to recover from the global economic downturn, which helped drive down its annual sales and reduced profits during 2009. Its Automotive and Truck segments continued to decline as the automotive industry weathered its worst slump since the Great Depression.

In order to get a better handle on its ever-shifting operations, the company reorganized in 2009, dividing itself between Electrical, Hydraulics (Eaton Hydraulics), Aerospace, Truck, and Automotive business segments. Electrical manufactures power distribution and protection equipment, such as circuit breakers, switchgear, panelboards, motor controls, and sensors and relays which are used in industrial, institutional, government, utility, and commercial markets. Sales in this segment are made through distributors and resellers.

Hydraulics makes related systems and components for use in mobile and industrial applications. The segment also includes Eaton's Filtration, Golf Grip, and Airflex Industrial clutch and brake businesses. Aerospace designs and manufactures hydraulic, fuel, motion control, and propulsion systems for commercial and military programs. The Truck segment delivers drivetrain and safety systems to fleet owners and freight companies. Automotive develops products to improve fuel economy, emissions, safety, and performance.

While adjusting its product mix, keeping a close eye on costs, and making targeted acquisitions, Eaton's other key focus for growth is innovation. The company worked with General Motors to develop a displacement-on-demand system that delivers increased fuel economy by shutting down half the engine in light load situations. These systems were created for Chevy TrailBlazer EXTs and GMC Envoy XLs.

HISTORY

In 1911 Joseph Eaton and Viggo Torbensen started the Torbensen Gear and Axle Company to make an internal-gear rear truck axle that Torbensen had patented in 1902. The company moved from Newark, New Jersey, to Cleveland in 1914. After Republic Motor Truck bought Torbensen (1917), Eaton formed the Eaton Axle Company (1919), repurchased Torbensen (1922), and by 1931 had bought 11 more auto parts businesses. In 1932 it became Eaton Manufacturing.

The Depression flattened auto sales, and Eaton's profits fell. WWII sparked demand that helped the company recover. Joseph Eaton died in 1949. During the 1950s and 1960s, Eaton diversified and expanded geographically. It bought Fuller Manufacturing (truck transmissions, 1958), Dole Valve (1963), and Yale & Towne Manufacturing (locks and forklifts, 1963). Eaton's international business grew, with foreign sales increasing from almost nil in 1961 to 20% of sales by 1966.

Eaton sold its lock business in 1978 and bought Cutler-Hammer (electronics), Kenway (automated storage and retrieval systems), and Samuel Moore (plastics and fluid power). Downturns in the truck and auto industries forced Eaton to close 30 plants and trim 23,000 jobs between 1979 and 1983. The company reported its first loss in 50 years in 1982 and decided to diversify into high technology and to expand operations overseas.

From 1984 to 1993 Eaton spent almost $4 billion in capital improvements and R&D. In 1986 it bought Consolidated Controls (precision instruments), Pacific-Sierra Research (computer and defense systems), and Singer Controls (valves and switches).

Eaton's acquisitions in the 1990s included Nordhauser Ventil (automotive engine valves, Germany), Control Displays (flight-deck equipment), Heinemann Electric (hydraulic-magnetic circuit breakers), and the automotive switch business of Illinois Tool Works. In 1994 Eaton tripled the size of its electrical power and controls operation with its $1.1 billion purchase of Westinghouse's electrical distribution and control business. The next year it bought Emwest Products (electrical switch gear and controls, Australia) and the IKU Group, a Dutch auto-controls firm. It purchased CAPCO Automotive Products (truck transmissions, Brazil) in 1996.

In its repositioning, the company in 1997 sold off its appliance-control business to Siebe PLC and a majority stake in its high-tech defense electronics subsidiary, AIL Systems, to management. Eaton closed and consolidated plants and laid off more than 1,000 workers in its microchip division in 1998.

The company increased its share of the hydraulics market in 1999 by spending $1.7 billion for Aeroquip-Vickers. In 2002 Eaton signed a deal with Volvo to manufacture heavy-duty transmissions for the company's South American

truck market. In 2004 Eaton acquired Powerware, an uninterruptible power supply and power management system manufacturer, from UK-based Invensys.

In 2006 Eaton continued its string of acquisitions when it purchased Synflex, a maker of thermoplastic tubing and hoses, from materials giant Saint-Gobain. Later that year Eaton bought almost all of China-based Senyuan International Holdings, which makes circuit breakers and other electrical components.

In 2007 Eaton acquired the aerospace business of Argo-Tech for $695 million, a move that complemented the fuel systems business picked up in the 2005 acquisition of Cobham Aerospace.

The company continued its international growth through acquisitions, as well. In 2008 it bought the Moeller Group, a German provider of electrical components and industrial controls, for $2.2 billion.

Throughout 2008 Eaton filled product gaps in its uninterruptible power supply (UPS) portfolio through joint ventures and acquisitions, spending in excess of $2 billion in the expansion.

The company expanded its automotive product line by acquiring Kirloskar Oil Engines (India) and by entering into a joint venture with Nittan Global Tech to manage the global design and production of engine valves.

EXECUTIVES

Chairman, President, and CEO: Alexander M. (Sandy) Cutler, age 58, $8,536,007 total compensation
Vice Chairman and COO Electrical Sector: Thomas S. Gross, age 55, $3,905,467 total compensation
Vice Chairman and COO Industrial Sector: Craig Arnold, age 49, $3,644,312 total compensation
Vice Chairman, CFO, and Chief Planning Officer: Richard H. Fearon, age 53, $3,579,123 total compensation
EVP Eaton Business System: Uday Yadav
EVP and General Counsel: Mark M. McGuire, age 52
EVP and Chief Human Resources Officer: James W. (Jim) McGill, age 54
SVP Sales and Marketing: Steve Boccadoro
SVP Supply Chain Management: Craig Reed
SVP Public and Community Affairs: William B. Doggett
SVP and Secretary: Thomas E. (Tom) Moran, age 45
SVP and CIO: William W. Blausey Jr.
SVP and Controller: Billie K. Rawot, age 58
SVP Corporate Development and Treasury: Kurt B. McMaken, age 40
SVP Environment, Health, and Safety: Joseph L. Wolfsberger
SVP Communications: Donald J. (Don) McGrath
SVP Investor Relations: William C. Hartman
SVP Internal Audit: Jack Matejka
President, Vehicle Group: Joseph P. Palchak, $2,443,216 total compensation
President, Hydraulics Group: William R. VanArsdale
President, Aerospace Group: Bradley J. Morton
President, Asia/Pacific Region: Curtis J. Hutchins
President, South America: Patrick Randrianarison
President, Europe, Middle East, and Africa Region: Yannis P. Tsavalas, age 53
Auditors: Ernst & Young LLP

LOCATIONS

HQ: Eaton Corporation
1111 Superior Ave. East, Eaton Center
Cleveland, OH 44114
Phone: 216-523-5000   **Fax:** 216-523-4787
Web: www.eaton.com

2009 Sales

	$ mil.	% of total
Americas		
US	6,767	53
Latin America	1,061	8
Canada	355	3
Europe	3,007	23
Asia/Pacific	1,642	13
Adjustments	(959)	—
Total	**11,873**	**100**

PRODUCTS/OPERATIONS

2009 Sales

	$ mil.	% of total
Electrical	5,893	50
Hydraulics	1,692	14
Aerospace	1,602	14
Truck	1,457	12
Automotive	1,229	10
Total	**11,873**	**100**

Selected Brand Names

Electrical
  Cutler-Hammer
  Holec
  MEM
  Powerware
Fluid Power
  Aeroquip
  Boston
  Char-Lynn
  Eaton
  Golf Pride
  Hydro-Line
  Vickers
  Weatherhead
Truck Components
  Eaton
  Fuller
  Roadranger
Automotive Components
  Aeroquip
  Eaton

COMPETITORS

Acushnet	Metaldyne
ArvinMeritor	Navistar International
BorgWarner	PACCAR
Callaway Golf	Parker Hannifin
Cooper Industries	Precision Castparts
Cummins	Raytheon
Dana Holding	Robert Bosch
Danaher	Rockwell Automation
Delphi Automotive	Sauer-Danfoss
Detroit Diesel	Schneider Electric
Emerson Electric	Siemens AG
Golfsmith	SPX
Honeywell International	Textron
Hubbell	Thomas & Betts
INTERMET	Trane Inc.
ITT Corp.	TRW Automotive
Johnson Controls	United Technologies
Lear Corp	Valeo
Legrand	Woodhead Industries
Magna International	ZF Friedrichshafen

HISTORICAL FINANCIALS

Company Type: Public

Income Statement

FYE: December 31

	REVENUE ($ mil.)	NET INCOME ($ mil.)	NET PROFIT MARGIN	EMPLOYEES
12/09	11,873	385	3.2%	70,000
12/08	15,376	1,058	6.9%	75,000
12/07	13,033	994	7.6%	64,000
12/06	12,370	950	7.7%	60,000
12/05	11,115	805	7.2%	59,000
Annual Growth	**1.7%**	**(16.8%)**	**—**	**4.4%**

2009 Year-End Financials

Debt ratio: 49.4%
Return on equity: 5.9%
Cash ($ mil.): 340
Current ratio: 1.68
Long-term debt ($ mil.): 3,349
No. of shares (mil.): 168
Dividends
  Yield: 3.1%
  Payout: 88.1%
Market value ($ mil.): 10,675

Stock History

NYSE: ETN

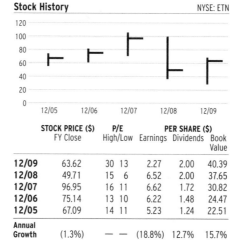

	STOCK PRICE ($) FY Close	P/E High/Low		PER SHARE ($) Earnings	Dividends	Book Value
12/09	63.62	30	13	2.27	2.00	40.39
12/08	49.71	15	6	6.52	2.00	37.65
12/07	96.95	16	11	6.62	1.72	30.82
12/06	75.14	13	10	6.22	1.48	24.47
12/05	67.09	14	11	5.23	1.24	22.51
Annual Growth	**(1.3%)**	**—**	**—**	**(18.8%)**	**12.7%**	**15.7%**

eBay Inc.

"I got it on eBay" is barreling its way into the lexicon of the new millennium and placing a cyber-grin on the corporate face of online auctioneer extraordinaire eBay. Trading $2,000 worth of goods every second, the company offers an online forum for selling merchandise worldwide, from fine antiques to the latest video games. eBay, which generates revenue through listing and selling fees and through advertising, boasts more than 90 million active users. It also sees gains from its online payments division, comprising PayPal and Bill Me Later, and other e-commerce platforms, including StubHub and Half.com. In 2009 eBay sold a 70% stake in its Skype Internet phone service to private-equity firm Silver Lake for about $2 billion.

Aiming to strengthen its international operations, eBay in June 2009 paid about $1 billion for a majority stake (99.2%) in Gmarket, a leading online marketplace in South Korea. To secure its foothold in the region, the auction giant plans to combine Gmarket's operations with Internet Auction Company, another South Korea-based e-commerce firm that eBay acquired in 2001. eBay's practice of aligning itself with local companies through partnerships and acquisitions when breaking into international markets has been key to its success.

In addition to competition abroad, eBay faces rivals from US-based online powerhouses such as Amazon.com and smaller competitors like Overstock.com. To encourage further growth in its auctions, the company reduced fees and rolled out an improved matching feature in 2008. It is also working to speed up the payment process. eBay has seen the most growth, however, from its fixed-price format sites, including Half.com.

Amid the global economic downturn, eBay in late 2008 began laying off about 10% of its workforce worldwide.

Consumers' use of online payment systems has risen as they have increasingly moved to the Internet for shopping. To get in on the action, eBay expanded its payments department in 2008 with the purchase of Bill Me Later, a firm that processes deferred payments. The deal was valued at about $900 million.

eBay is appealing a French court's ruling that ordered it to pay more than $60 million in damages to the French luxury goods firm LVMH over the sale of counterfeit goods on the Internet. (While eBay polices its site for counterfeit merchandise, the court said it was not doing enough to prevent counterfeit sales.) Just two weeks after the French court ruling, however, a federal judge in New York came to the opposite conclusion in a case over counterfeit goods with jeweler Tiffany & Co. The court ruled in July 2008 that eBay has fulfilled its legal obligation and took adequate precautions to prevent the sale of fake Tiffany jewelry on its site.

Meg Whitman, who led eBay for a decade, stepped down as CEO in 2008. She was succeeded by John Donahoe, who previously led the company's highest revenue-producing unit, eBay marketplaces. Although Whitman remained on the company's board after moving out of the chief executive's office, she eventually left in 2009 to consider a bid as California governor. eBay chairman and founder Pierre Omidyar owns about 12% of the company.

HISTORY

Pierre Omidyar created a flea market in cyberspace when he launched online auction service Auction Web on Labor Day weekend in 1995. Making a name for itself largely through word of mouth, the company incorporated in 1996, the same year it began to charge a fee to auction items online. That year it enhanced its service with Feedback Forum (buyer and seller ratings).

The company changed the name to eBay in 1997 and began promoting itself through advertising. By the middle of that year, eBay was boasting nearly 800,000 auctions each day and Benchmark Capital came on board as a significant financial backer.

Margaret ("Meg") Whitman, a former Hasbro executive, replaced Omidyar as CEO in early 1998. eBay made a blockbuster debut as a public company later that year. The company moved closer to household name status in 1998 by launching a national ad campaign and inking alliance deals with America Online (now Time Warner) and WebTV.

A bit of the bloom came off the rose in 1999 when online service interruptions (one "brownout" in June persisted for 22 hours) revealed a chink in eBay's armor. The company called its top 10,000 users to convey its apologies and pledged to improve its website's performance.

In 2000 the US Department of Justice began an investigation to determine if eBay had violated antitrust laws in its dealings with competitors. In other legal news, a class-action lawsuit was filed against the company claiming that eBay is an auctioneer and therefore must authenticate the items on its site. (A trial court dismissed the case in early 2001.) Also in 2000 the company expanded into Japan through eBay Japan, with computer firm NEC acquiring 30% of the Japanese subsidiary and eBay owning the rest; it also launched Canadian and Austrian sites.

eBay strengthened its European position in 2001 through the purchase of French Internet auction firm iBazar. It also launched sites in Ireland, New Zealand, and Switzerland. It shuttered its eBay Japan operations in 2002 after its dismal performance in that market.

In 2004 eBay took several steps toward diversifying its business. It expanded its international presence through acquisitions in China and India. The company purchased about a 25% stake in online classifieds provider craigslist and announced plans to offer a music downloading service. In 2005 eBay acquired Internet listing site Rent.com. Also that year eBay acquired Shopping.com — a provider of online comparison shopping and consumer reviews with sites in France, the UK, and the US. In mid-October eBay announced it had completed the acquisition of Internet-based telephone services firm Skype, for about $2.6 billion. In November eBay acquired VeriSign's payment gateway business.

In 2008 eBay settled its long-running patent dispute with MercExchange, agreeing to buy the three MercExchange patents it had been accused of violating. MercExchange had sued eBay in 2001, claiming that eBay's "Buy It Now" option infringed on its patent technology.

In June 2008 eBay acquired the California-based visual media company VUVOX Network to further develop rich media capabilities in the eBay marketplace.

EXECUTIVES

Chairman: Pierre M. Omidyar, age 42
President and CEO: John J. Donahoe, $10,132,748 total compensation
SVP Technology: Mark T. Carges, age 48, $3,463,752 total compensation
SVP Finance and CFO: Robert H. (Bob) Swan, $5,900,390 total compensation
SVP Human Resources: Elizabeth L. (Beth) Axelrod, age 47, $4,342,825 total compensation
SVP Legal Affairs, General Counsel, and Secretary: Michael R. Jacobson, age 55
SVP Corporate Communications: Alan Marks, age 47
VP and Deputy General Counsel for Government Relations: Tod Cohen
President, eBay Marketplaces: Lorrie M. Norrington, age 50, $3,184,136 total compensation
President, Skype: Josh Silverman
President, PayPal: Scott Thompson, age 52, $3,217,606 total compensation
Country Manager, eBay Canada: Andrea Stairs
Senior Director, U.S. Vehicles, eBay Motors: Nicolas Franchet
Senior Counsel: Braden Dong
Director, eBay Green Team: Amy Skoczlas Cole
General Manager, eBay Fashion: Miriam Lahage
Auditors: PricewaterhouseCoopers LLP

LOCATIONS

HQ: eBay Inc.
2145 Hamilton Ave., San Jose, CA 95125
Phone: 408-376-7400   **Fax:** 408-516-8811
Web: www.ebay.com

2009 Sales

	$ mil.	% of total
US	3,985.1	46
Germany	1,140.2	13
UK	1,054.7	12
Other countries	2,547.4	29
Total	**8,727.4**	**100**

PRODUCTS/OPERATIONS

2009 Sales

	$ mil.	% of total
Marketplaces	5,311.0	61
Payments	2,796.0	32
Communications	620.4	7
Total	**8,727.4**	**100**

Selected Auction Categories

Antiques
Automobiles
Books
Coins and paper money
Collectibles
Computers
Electronics
Dolls and bears
DVDs and movies
Jewelry and watches
Pottery and glass
Real estate
Sports memorabilia
Toys and hobbies

COMPETITORS

Alibaba.com
Amazon.com
Buy.com
Christie's
Collectors Universe
Costco UK
Costco Wholesale
Costco Wholesale Canada
Enable Holdings
First Data
Gallery of History
Google
Half Price Books
HSN
J. C. Penney
K-tel
MasterCard
Microsoft
MSN
NexTag
Office Depot
OfficeMax
OnlineAuction
Overstock.com
PriceGrabber.com
QVC
QVC UK
Rbid
Royal Bank of Scotland
Sam's Club
Sears
Shopzilla
Sotheby's
Spectrum Group
Staples
Target
Tickets.com
Visa Inc
Walmart.com
Yahoo!

HISTORICAL FINANCIALS

Company Type: Public

Income Statement

FYE: December 31

	REVENUE ($ mil.)	NET INCOME ($ mil.)	NET PROFIT MARGIN	EMPLOYEES
12/09	8,727	2,389	27.4%	16,400
12/08	8,541	1,780	20.8%	16,200
12/07	7,672	348	4.5%	15,000
12/06	5,970	1,126	18.9%	13,200
12/05	4,552	1,082	23.8%	12,600
Annual Growth	**17.7%**	**21.9%**	**—**	**6.8%**

2009 Year-End Financials

Debt ratio: —
Return on equity: 19.2%
Cash ($ mil.): 4,000
Current ratio: 2.32
Long-term debt ($ mil.): —
No. of shares (mil.): 1,312
Dividends
  Yield: —
  Payout: —
Market value ($ mil.): 30,875

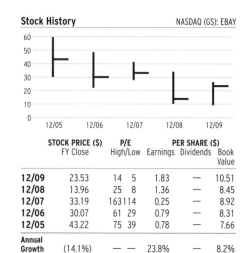

Stock History				NASDAQ (GS): EBAY

	STOCK PRICE ($) FY Close	P/E High/Low		Earnings	PER SHARE ($) Dividends	Book Value
12/09	23.53	14	5	1.83	—	10.51
12/08	13.96	25	8	1.36	—	8.45
12/07	33.19	163	114	0.25	—	8.92
12/06	30.07	61	29	0.79	—	8.31
12/05	43.22	75	39	0.78	—	7.66
Annual Growth	**(14.1%)**	**—**	**—**	**23.8%**	**—**	**8.2%**

Ecolab Inc.

Ecolab cleans up by cleaning up. The company offers cleaning, sanitation, pest-elimination, and maintenance products and services to hospitality, institutional, and industrial customers. Its institutional division is its largest, accounting for half of sales, and serves hotels, health care facilities, schools, and commercial and institutional laundries. Other divisions focus on products for textile care, water care, food and beverage, and pest control; its Kay unit provides cleaning supplies to quickservice restaurants. Ecolab makes most of its products, although it does sell some products made by other manufacturers. It does about half of its business outside the US, operating in more than 75 countries.

The company has grown through several acquisitions over the years, which have granted Ecolab access to geographic areas as well as business sectors it previously did not have. In 2009 it bought a pesticides business in the UK and a surgical products business as well.

German consumer products and adhesives giant Henkel had owned more than 25% of Ecolab until it sold that stake through a public offering in 2008. Ecolab itself paid Henkel $300 million for a portion of its stake.

HISTORY

Salesman Merritt Osborn founded Economics Laboratory in 1924 as a specialty chemical maker; its first product was a rug cleaner for hotels. It added industrial and institutional cleaners and consumer detergents in the 1950s. The company went public in 1957. By 1973 it had been organized into five divisions: industrial (cleaners and specialty chemical formulas), institutional (dishwasher products, sanitation formulas), consumer (dishwasher detergent and laundry aids, coffee filters, floor cleaners), food-processing (detergents), and international (run by future CEO Fred Lanners Jr.).

At the time, household dishwasher detergent was Economics Laboratory's top seller, second to Procter & Gamble in the US and #1 overseas. The company began offering services and products as packages in the early 1970s, including on-premise laundry services for hotels and hospitals and sanitation and cleaning services for the food industry.

E. B. Osborn, son of the founder, retired in 1978, and Lanners became the company's first CEO outside the Osborn family. Sales of dishwashing detergent had fallen, while the institutional cleaning business had become its primary segment, quadrupling in sales between 1970 and 1980. International sales were growing rapidly. In 1979 the company bought Apollo Technologies (chemicals and pollution-control equipment) to improve its share of the industrial market.

A depressed industrial sector caused Apollo's sales to drop in early 1980. The man expected to save Apollo, Richard Ashley, succeeded Lanners in 1982 but died in a car crash that year. Pierson "Sandy" Grieve became CEO in 1983 and shut down Apollo. Meanwhile, debt was up, the institutional market had shrunk, and the company was slipping in the dishwashing-detergent market. Grieve sold the firm's coffee-filters unit and several plants, laid off employees, and began new packaging processes. The company changed its name to Ecolab in 1986, and in 1987 it sold its dishwashing-detergent unit and bought lawn-service provider ChemLawn. (ChemLawn was sold in 1992.)

As 1990 neared, Grieve introduced what's now known as "Circle the Customer — Circle the Globe," the aim being to become a worldwide leader in core businesses and broaden product offerings. The company concentrated on building its presence in Africa, the Asia/Pacific region, Latin America, and the Middle East. In 1991 Ecolab also began a highly successful joint venture, Henkel-Ecolab, with German consumer-products company Henkel to better exploit European markets.

Ecolab acquired Kay Chemical (cleaning and sanitation products for the fast-food industry, 1994), Monarch (cleaning and sanitation products for food processing, 1996), Huntington Laboratories (janitorial products, 1996), and Australia-based Gibson (cleaning and sanitation products, 1997). In 1995 Grieve stepped down, and president Allan Schuman became CEO. Adding a few more degrees to its circle of services, in 1998 Ecolab bought GCS Service (commercial kitchen equipment repair).

The company further secured footholds in Asia and South America in 2000 by acquiring industrial and institutional cleaning firms Dong Woo Deterpan (South Korea), Spartan de Chile, and Spartan de Argentina. At home, it bought kitchen-equipment companies ARR/CRS and Southwest Sanitary Distributing. Late in 2000 Ecolab sold its Johnson dish machines unit to Endonis and announced a restructuring that was soon followed by the departure of several top executives, including president and COO Bruno Deschamps.

In 2001 Ecolab purchased the 50% of Henkel-Ecolab that it didn't own from Henkel for about $435 million; the move greatly expanded the company's international business.

In mid-2004 Schuman stepped down as CEO (retaining the chairman's role); president Doug Baker took over and became a director in addition to his role as president and CEO. Two years later Allan Schuman retired as chairman, ending his 49-year tenure with Ecolab. The company named Baker to replace Schuman.

In 2007 Ecolab made an acquisition to expand its operations in the health care field, buying Microtek Medical Holdings, which makes infection control products for health care facilities, for about $275 million. The next year it paid $210 million for Ecovation, a company that treats wastewater, solid waste, and air pollution primarily for food and beverage companies.

EXECUTIVES

Chairman, President, and CEO:
Douglas M. (Doug) Baker Jr., age 51, $8,774,567 total compensation
CFO: Steven L. Fritze, age 55, $3,389,426 total compensation
EVP, Service Sector: Michael A. Hickey, age 48
EVP, Institutional Sector, North America: Christophe Beck, age 42
EVP and General Manager, Food and Beverage and Water Care, North America: Thomas W. Schnack
General Counsel and Secretary: Lawrence T. Bell, age 61, $2,783,010 total compensation
SVP and CTO: Larry L. Berger, age 49
SVP Institutional Global and Corporate Accounts: Robert J. Sherwood
SVP Institutional Field Sales: Derrick A. Johns
SVP and General Manager, Food and Beverage, North America: Timothy Mulhere
SVP Human Resources: Michael L. Meyer, age 52
SVP and General Manager, Institutional North America, Hospitality, Healthcare, and Commercial Business: Tracy J. Crocker
SVP and General Manager, Institutional Foodservice Division: James W. Chamberlain
VP and Treasurer: Ching-Meng Chew
VP and Corporate Controller: John J. Corkrean, age 44
VP and CIO: Robert P. Tabb, age 59
President, Specialty, Industrial, and Services: James A. Miller, age 53, $2,126,980 total compensation
President, EMEA Sector: James H. White, age 45
President, Global Healthcare Sector: Susan K. Nestegard, age 49
President, Global Food and Beverage: Thomas W. Handley, age 55, $1,938,501 total compensation
President, International Sector: Phillip J. Mason, age 59
Auditors: PricewaterhouseCoopers LLP

LOCATIONS

HQ: Ecolab Inc.
370 Wabasha St. North, St. Paul, MN 55102
Phone: 651-293-2233　　**Fax:** 651-293-2092
Web: www.ecolab.com

PRODUCTS/OPERATIONS

2009 Sales

	$ mil.	% of total
United States		
Cleaning & Sanitizing	2,663.3	45
Other services	449.4	8
International	2,674.9	45
Other	113.0	2
Total	**5,900.6**	**100**

COMPETITORS

3M Health Care
ABM Industries
Chemed
CPAC
Diversey
Healthcare Services
ISS A/S
Medline Industries
Reckitt Benckiser (US)
Rentokil Initial
Rollins, Inc.
ServiceMaster
STERIS
Tranzonic
UGL Unicco
Unilever
Unisource
Zep Inc.

HISTORICAL FINANCIALS

Company Type: Public

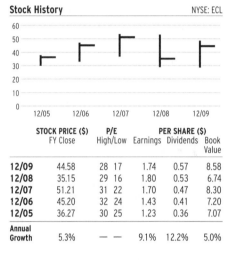

Income Statement

FYE: December 31

	REVENUE ($ mil.)	NET INCOME ($ mil.)	NET PROFIT MARGIN	EMPLOYEES
12/09	5,901	417	7.1%	25,931
12/08	6,138	448	7.3%	26,568
12/07	5,470	427	7.8%	26,052
12/06	4,896	369	7.5%	23,130
12/05	4,535	320	7.0%	22,404
Annual Growth	**6.8%**	**6.9%**	**—**	**3.7%**

2009 Year-End Financials

Debt ratio: 43.4%
Return on equity: 23.4%
Cash ($ mil.): 74
Current ratio: 1.45
Long-term debt ($ mil.): 869
No. of shares (mil.): 233
Dividends
　Yield: 1.3%
　Payout: 32.8%
Market value ($ mil.): 10,401

Stock History

NYSE: ECL

	STOCK PRICE ($) FY Close	P/E High/Low		PER SHARE ($) Earnings	Dividends	Book Value
12/09	44.58	28	17	1.74	0.57	8.58
12/08	35.15	29	16	1.80	0.53	6.74
12/07	51.21	31	22	1.70	0.47	8.30
12/06	45.20	32	24	1.43	0.41	7.20
12/05	36.27	30	25	1.23	0.36	7.07
Annual Growth	**5.3%**	**—**	**—**	**9.1%**	**12.2%**	**5.0%**

Edison International

Although Edison International has been around the world, but the company's largest subsidiary is Southern California Edison (SCE), which distributes electricity to a population of more than 13 million people in central, coastal, and southern California; it is the leading purchaser of renewable energy in the US. The utility's system consists of about 12,000 circuit miles of transmission lines and more than 113,500 circuit miles of distribution lines. SCE also has 5,500 MW of generating capacity from interests in nuclear, hydroelectric, and fossil-fueled power plants. Edison created an international portfolio through Edison Mission Energy (EME), but it has pulled back on almost all of its non-US operations.

The pullback the result of Edison International's strategy to focus on the financially more secure US power market. After having sold plants in Asia and Europe, EME now markets energy in only the US and Turkey. The company has interests in more than 40 power plants in the US and one in Turkey (Doga project) that give it a net physical generating capacity of more than 10,400 MW.

The economic downturn hurt Edison's revenues in 2009; however, SCE reported a spike in earnings, thanks to an increase in the rates it could pass on to customers.

Edition is investing in upgrading its traditional power infrastructure and expanding its portfolio of solar and wind energy projects, to make the company compliant with increasingly stringent state and federal carbon emission requirements.

Edison also provides consulting, management, and maintenance services for energy projects.

HISTORY

In 1896 a group including Elmer Peck and George Baker organized West Side Lighting to provide electricity in Los Angeles. The next year Baker became president, and the company merged with Los Angeles Edison Electric, which owned the rights to the Edison name and patents in the region. Edison Electric installed the first DC-power underground conduits in the Southwest.

John Barnes Miller took over the top spot in 1901. During his 31-year reign the firm bought many neighboring utilities and built several power plants. In 1909 it took the name Southern California Edison (SCE).

SCE doubled its assets by buying Southern California electric interests from rival Pacific Light & Power in 1917. However, in 1912 the City of Los Angeles had decided to develop its own power distribution system, and by 1922 SCE's authority in the city had ended. A 1925 earthquake and the 1928 collapse of the St. Francis Dam severely damaged SCE's facilities.

SCE built 11 fossil-fueled power stations (1948-1973) and moved into nuclear power in 1963, when it broke ground on the San Onofre plant with San Diego Gas & Electric (brought online in 1968). It finished consolidating its service territory with the 1964 purchase of California Electric Power. In the late 1970s SCE began to build solar, geothermal, and wind power facilities.

Edison Mission Energy (EME) was founded in 1986 to develop, buy, and operate power plants around the world. The next year investment arm Edison Capital was formed, as well as a holding company for the entire group, SCEcorp. EME began to build its portfolio in 1992 when it snagged a 51% stake in an Australian plant and bought hydroelectric facilities in Spain. In 1995 it bought UK hydroelectric company First Hydro; it also began building plants in Italy, Turkey, and Indonesia.

The 1994 Northridge earthquake that cut power to a million SCE customers was nothing compared to the industry's seismic shifts. In 1996 SCEcorp became the more worldly Edison International. California's electricity market opened to competition in 1998, and the utility began divesting SCE's generation assets; it sold 12 gas-fired plants. Overseas EME picked up 25% of a power plant being built in Thailand and a 50% stake in a cogeneration facility in Puerto Rico.

SCE got regulatory approval to offer telecom services in its utility territory in 1999. That year EME snapped up several plants in the Midwest from Unicom for $5 billion. Overseas it purchased two UK coal-fired plants from PowerGen (which it sold to American Electric Power in 2001 for $960 million). The next year EME CEO Edward Muller (who had held the post since 1994) abruptly resigned, and Edison bought Citizens Power from the Peabody Group.

In 2000 SCE got caught in a price squeeze brought on in part by deregulation. Prices on the wholesale power market soared, but the utility was unable to pass along the increase to customers because of a rate freeze. The company gained some prospect of relief in 2001 when California's governor signed legislation to allow a state agency to buy power from wholesalers under long-term contracts. In addition, the California Public Utilities Commission (CPUC) approved a substantial increase in retail electricity rates, and the Federal Energy Regulatory Commission approved a plan to limit wholesale energy prices during periods of severe shortage in 11 western states.

To reduce debt, Edison International agreed to sell its transmission grid to the state for $2.8 billion. While the California legislature debated the agreement, however, the CPUC announced a settlement in which SCE would be allowed to keep its current high rates in place until its debts are paid off. The settlement, which was approved in 2002, eliminated the need for the sale of the company's transmission grid.

Also in 2001, the company sold most of its Edison Enterprises businesses, including home security services unit Edison Select, which was sold to ADT Security Services.

In 2004 Edison International committed to taking a lead position in developing comprehensive national programs to reduce greenhouse gas emissions, primarily carbon dioxide.

In 2006 SCE signed the largest wind energy deal ever completed by a US utility, providing for 1,500 MW of wind power from plants in the Tehachapi area of California.

EXECUTIVES

Chairman, President, and CEO:
Theodore F. (Ted) Craver Jr., age 58, $6,770,345 total compensation
EVP, CFO, and Treasurer: W. James (Jim) Scilacci Jr., age 54, $2,170,029 total compensation
EVP and General Counsel: Robert L. Adler, age 62, $1,983,271 total compensation
EVP Southern California Edison: Pedro J. Pizzarro, $1,463,298 total compensation
EVP Public Affairs: Polly L. Gault, age 56, $1,447,067 total compensation
SVP Human Resources: Daryl D. David, age 54
SVP Corporate Communications: Barbara J. Parsky, age 62
VP, Associate General Counsel, Chief Governance Officer, and Corporate Secretary; VP, Associate General Counsel, Chief Governance Officer, and Corporate Secretary, Southern California Edison: Barbara E. Mathews
VP and Controller: Mark C. Clarke, age 53
VP Investor Relations: Scott S. Cunningham
VP and General Auditor; VP and General Auditor, Southern California Edison: Megan E. Scott-Kakures
VP Tax: Jeffrey L. (Jeff) Barnett
Chairman, President, and CEO, Edison Mission Group and Edison Mission Energy: Ronald L. Litzinger, $1,977,454 total compensation
Director; Chairman and CEO, Southern California Edison: Alan J. Fohrer, age 59, $3,258,043 total compensation
President, Southern California Edison: John R. Fielder, age 64, $1,526,590 total compensation
SVP and CFO, Southern California Edison: Linda G. Sullivan, age 46, $972,802 total compensation
SVP and General Counsel, Southern California Edison: Stephen E. Pickett, age 59, $1,390,362 total compensation
SVP Business Integration and CIO, Southern California Edison: Mahvash Yazdi, age 58, $1,379,017 total compensation
Auditors: PricewaterhouseCoopers LLP

LOCATIONS

HQ: Edison International
2244 Walnut Grove Ave., Rosemead, CA 91770
Phone: 626-302-2222 **Fax:** 626-302-2517
Web: www.edison.com

PRODUCTS/OPERATIONS

2009 Sales

	$ mil.	% of total
Electric utility	9,959	81
Nonutility power generation	2,374	19
Financial services & other	28	—
Total	**12,361**	**100**

Selected Subsidiaries

Edison Mission Group (unregulated activities)
Edison Mission Energy (power generation, energy trading and marketing)
Southern California Edison Company (SCE, electric utility)

COMPETITORS

AES	MidAmerican Energy
Avista	Mirant
Calpine	NextEra Energy
CMS Energy	NRG Energy
Constellation Energy	NV Energy
Dynegy	PacifiCorp
Electricité de France	PG&E Corporation
Endesa S.A.	Portland General Electric
Enel	RRI Energy
Entergy	Sacramento Municipal
IBERDROLA	Utility
Los Angeles Water and Power	Sempra Energy

HISTORICAL FINANCIALS

Company Type: Public

Income Statement

FYE: December 31

	REVENUE ($ mil.)	NET INCOME ($ mil.)	NET PROFIT MARGIN	EMPLOYEES
12/09	12,361	945	7.6%	19,244
12/08	14,112	1,215	8.6%	18,291
12/07	13,113	1,098	8.4%	17,275
12/06	12,622	1,180	9.3%	16,139
12/05	11,852	1,138	9.6%	15,838
Annual Growth	1.1%	(4.5%)	—	5.0%

2009 Year-End Financials

Debt ratio: 106.1%	No. of shares (mil.): 326
Return on equity: 9.8%	Dividends
Cash ($ mil.): 1,673	Yield: 3.6%
Current ratio: 1.17	Payout: 48.4%
Long-term debt ($ mil.): 10,437	Market value ($ mil.): 11,332

Stock History

NYSE: EIX

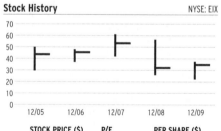

	STOCK PRICE ($) FY Close	P/E High/Low		PER SHARE ($) Earnings	Dividends	Book Value
12/09	34.78	14	9	2.58	1.25	32.99
12/08	32.12	15	7	3.68	1.23	31.99
12/07	53.37	18	13	3.31	1.17	28.73
12/06	45.48	13	11	3.57	1.10	26.47
12/05	43.61	14	9	3.43	1.02	22.51
Annual Growth	(5.5%)	—	—	(6.9%)	5.2%	10.0%

El Paso Corporation

Out in the West Texas town of El Paso, this company fell in love with the natural gas industry. Founded in 1928 in its namesake city, El Paso Corp. is primarily engaged in gas transportation and storage, oil and gas exploration and production, and gas gathering and processing. Operator of the largest gas transportation system in the US, El Paso has interests in 42,000 miles of interstate pipeline. The company also has interests in global energy projects and markets wholesale energy commodities. Subsidiary El Paso Exploration and Production has estimated proved reserves of 2.3 trillion cu. ft. of natural gas equivalent in Brazil, Egypt, and the US.

As part of an ongoing sale of noncore assets and eventual divestiture of all of its international power plant operations, in 2009 the company sold its stake in the Porto Velho thermoelectric power plant in Brazil's Rondonia state for about $175 million. In 2010 it sold its Mexican pipeline and compression interests to a unit of Sempra Energy for $300 million.

Boosting its domestic exploration and production assets, in 2009 El Paso agreed to acquire Flying J Oil & Gas, which owns exploration units with 200 wells in the Rockies, from the Pilot Flying J company, for $103.5 million.

In 2008 El Paso acquired a 50% stake in the Gulf LNG Clean Energy Project, a planned liquefied natural gas terminal in Mississippi.

In 2010 El Paso plans some $2.9 billion in capital spending, putting three new projects in place by the end of the year. The largest portion of El Paso's capital program is the anticipated construction of its Ruby pipeline project, which consists of some 680 miles of 42-inch pipeline and multiple compressor stations.

HISTORY

In 1928 Paul Kayser, a Houston attorney, started the El Paso Natural Gas Company and got the rights to sell natural gas to that West Texas town a year later. Despite the 1929 stock market crash, the company built a 200-mile pipeline, first connecting El Paso, Texas, with natural gas wells in Jal, New Mexico. In 1931 it laid pipe again to reach the copper mines of Arizona and Mexico, and three years later expanded to Phoenix and Tucson.

After World War II the company began a 700-mile pipeline to bring natural gas from Texas' Permian Basin to California. As the Golden State's population exploded, sales soared. El Paso also ventured into new business areas, first chemicals and later textiles, mining, land development, and insurance.

In 1974 the Supreme Court ruled that El Paso had to divest its pipeline holdings north of New Mexico and Arizona. Federal regulators had granted the company the right to buy the holdings two decades earlier but later rescinded. Other operations, such as fiber manufacturing, were posting losses, so the company jettisoned some nongas businesses. El Paso received a boost in 1978 when the Natural Gas Policy Act allowed it more freedom to purchase its own reserves, but later weak demand, coupled with oversupply brought on by the 1970s spike in energy prices, cut into its business by 1982.

Conglomerate Burlington Northern acquired El Paso Natural Gas in 1983. Many of El Paso's operations were spun off when federal regulations required pipeline companies to break apart their sales and transportation businesses and open up interstate pipelines to third parties. El Paso became mainly a gas transportation company.

The company became independent again when Burlington spun it off in 1992. It entered the big leagues in 1996 by buying Tenneco Energy for $4 billion. With some 16,000 miles of pipeline, Tenneco more than doubled El Paso's transportation capacity and gave it the only coast-to-coast natural gas pipeline in the US. El Paso Natural Gas began using the name El Paso Energy and moved from its namesake town to Houston, Tenneco's headquarters. In 1997 it sold Tenneco's oil and gas exploration unit to help pay off debt and bought a 29% stake in Capsa, an Argentine energy concern.

In 1999 El Paso bought Sonat, a natural gas transportation and marketing firm that also had an exploration and production unit, in a $6 billion deal. To gain regulators' approval of the Sonat deal, El Paso sold three pipeline systems in 2000, including East Tennessee Natural Gas (to Duke Energy) and Sea Robin Pipeline (to CMS Energy).

El Paso bought PG&E's natural gas and natural gas liquids businesses for about $900 million in 2000. Also that year the company agreed to buy diversified energy company Coastal in a $24 billion deal, which closed early in 2001. The acquisition helped boost the company's proved reserves to more than 6 trillion cu. ft. of natural gas equivalent. The company changed its name from El Paso Energy to El Paso that year.

Following the collapse of #1 energy trader Enron in 2001, El Paso, along with many other wholesale energy companies, fell under financial scrutiny from investors and regulators. As a result, the company scaled back operations at its El Paso Marketing unit (formerly named El Paso Merchant Energy).

To raise cash to help offset its heavy debt load, the company began selling noncore assets in 2002, including the $782 million sale of midstream oil and gas assets in the Southwest to 27%-owned El Paso Energy Partners (now GulfTerra Energy Partners). The company sold a total of nearly $4 billion in assets in 2002.

In 2003 El Paso was engaged in an unsuccessful proxy contest with dissident shareholders who attempted to replace the company's board of directors. The company reached a $1.7 billion settlement agreement with the California government and the Federal Energy Regulatory Commission over charges of withholding natural gas supplies from the troubled California market in 2000 and 2001, although it admitted no wrongdoing. In addition, the SEC launched an investigation into El Paso's accounting methods for power plant contracts that it restructured in 2002. El Paso sold more than $3 billion in assets that year to further pay down debt, including $500 million in mid-continent gas reserves to Chesapeake Energy; it also sold a 900-MW power plant in New Jersey to The Goldman Sachs Group for $450 million.

The following year, the company sold its Aruba refinery to Valero Energy in a $627 million deal. El Paso also sold its Canadian exploration and production assets to BG Group for $346 million. El Paso purchased two natural gas exploration and production facilities, which boosted the company's proven reserves by 124 billion cu. ft. and 29 million cu. ft. per day, in East and South Texas, respectively.

In 2005 El Paso acquired Denver-based Medicine Bow Energy Corporation for $814 million.

EXECUTIVES

Chairman, President, and CEO:
Douglas L. (Doug) Foshee, age 50,
$6,306,902 total compensation
EVP and CFO: John R. (J. R.) Sult, age 50,
$1,039,970 total compensation
EVP and Chief Administrative Officer:
Susan B. (Sue) Ortenstone, age 53
EVP and General Counsel: Robert W. Baker, age 53,
$1,752,238 total compensation
**EVP Pipeline Group; Chairman and President,
Tenneco Gas Pipeline; Chairman, El Paso Natural
Gas; President, CEO, and Director, El Paso Pipeline
GP Company:** James C. (Jim) Yardley, age 58,
$2,529,781 total compensation
EVP; President, Midstream: D. Mark (Mark) Leland,
age 48, $2,094,362 total compensation
**EVP; President, El Paso Exploration and Production
Company:** Brent J. Smolik, age 48,
$2,545,754 total compensation
SVP Operations, Pipeline: Daniel B. (Dan) Martin,
age 53
SVP Strategy and Enterprise Business Development:
Dane E. Whitehead, age 48
VP Investor and Public Relations: Bruce L. Connery
VP and Corporate Secretary:
Marguerite Woung-Chapman
**President, Western Pipeline Group; SVP El Paso
Pipeline GP Company:** James J. Cleary, age 55
**President, Southern Natural Gas and Tennessee Gas
Pipeline; SVP El Paso Pipeline Partners:**
Norman G. Holmes, age 54
Director, Environmental Health and Safety, Pipelines:
Thomas D. Hutchins
Director, Environmental Health and Safety:
Mike Frampton
Manager, Investor Relations: Bill Baerg
Auditors: Ernst & Young LLP

LOCATIONS

HQ: El Paso Corporation
El Paso Bldg., 1001 Louisiana St.
Houston, TX 77002
Phone: 713-420-2600   **Fax:** 713-420-4417
Web: www.elpaso.com

PRODUCTS/OPERATIONS

2009 Sales

	$ mil.	% of total
Pipelines	2,767	60
Exploration & production	1,828	39
Marketing & other	36	1
Total	**4,631**	**100**

COMPETITORS

Apache
BP
CenterPoint Energy
DCP Midstream Partners
Dominion Resources
Dynegy
Enbridge
Enron
Enterprise Products
EOG
EQT Corporation
Exxon Mobil
Kinder Morgan
Southern Union
Williams Companies

HISTORICAL FINANCIALS

Company Type: Public

Income Statement

FYE: December 31

	REVENUE ($ mil.)	NET INCOME ($ mil.)	NET PROFIT MARGIN	EMPLOYEES
12/09	4,631	(474)	—	4,991
12/08	5,363	(823)	—	5,344
12/07	4,648	1,110	23.9%	4,992
12/06	4,281	475	11.1%	5,050
12/05	4,017	(602)	—	5,700
Annual Growth	3.6%	—	—	(3.3%)

2009 Year-End Financials

Debt ratio: 545.2%
Return on equity: —
Cash ($ mil.): 635
Current ratio: 0.75
Long-term debt ($ mil.): 13,391

No. of shares (mil.): 704
Dividends
Yield: 1.6%
Payout: —
Market value ($ mil.): 6,918

Stock History

NYSE: EP

	STOCK PRICE ($) FY Close	P/E High/Low		PER SHARE ($) Earnings	Dividends	Book Value
12/09	9.83	—	—	(0.83)	0.16	4.56
12/08	7.83	—	—	(1.24)	0.18	5.73
12/07	17.24	12	9	1.53	0.16	7.50
12/06	15.28	26	18	0.64	0.16	5.95
12/05	12.16	—	—	(0.98)	0.16	4.82
Annual Growth	(5.2%)	—	—	—	0.0%	(1.4%)

Electronic Arts

To armchair quarterbacks and those with trigger finger, Electronic Arts (EA) is their Picasso. EA is a leading video game publisher with popular titles such as *Madden NFL, The Sims, FIFA 10, Spore,* and *Medal of Honor.* It also distributes titles for third-party labels (including *Rock Band*) and publishes games based on Hollywood franchises such as *The Lord of the Rings, The Godfather, Harry Potter,* and *Batman.* EA develops its games for PCs and console systems and portable devices from Sony, Nintendo, and Microsoft. It sells its games in more than 35 countries. In 2008 the company offered $2 billion to purchase Take-Two Interactive, publisher of the *Grand Theft Auto* franchise; Take-Two rejected the offer.

In 2009 the company implemented a cost-reduction plan to narrow its product portfolio, reduce its workforce by about 11%, and close 10 facilities. As part of that push EA consolidated its operations into three operating labels: EA Games, EA SPORTS, and EA Play. Its EA Interactive division includes online and mobile games offered through the websites Pogo and Playfish, and its publishing segment distributes games from other companies, such as MTV Games'

Rock Band franchise and the Valve Software title *Left 4 Dead.*

EA Games includes wholly owned games (*Need for Speed, Spore, Dead Space,* and *Battlefield*) that it develops at its own studios. EA SPORTS titles are based on intellectual property that it licenses (*Madden NFL, FIFA Soccer,* and *Tiger Woods PGA Tour*), while EA Play games have a simple format to appeal to a wider audience, such as *Harry Potter, Hasbro,* and *The Sims.*

EA has expanded its target markets to include titles and ringtones for cellular phones and smart phones, including Apple's iPhone. This is part of a broader strategic push of the company into the arena of online delivery of game content and services, a trend that is occurring across the broader video game market as more and more games include multiplayer options over the Internet. As part of this strategic push in late 2009, EA bought social networking game developer Playfish in a deal worth up to $400 million.

Looking to cash in on the massively multiplayer online role-playing games (MMORPG) market, the company has developed its *Warhammer Online* and *Star Wars: the Old Republic* franchises, which compete with *World of Warcraft* and *EverQuest* in that genre.

Revenue dipped in 2010 for the first time in years; however, net loss was not as severe, primarily due to restructuring efforts. In 2009 EA announced it would shutter Pandemic Studios, a company it bought in 2007 along with BioWare for $775 million.

HISTORY

After four years with Apple, video game pioneer Trip Hawkins left in 1982, raised $5 million, and founded Electronic Arts to explore the entertainment potential of PCs. The company went public in 1989, and sales exploded the next year when EA began designing games for SEGA's Genesis video game system. Hawkins stepped down as CEO in 1991 and was replaced by president Larry Probst. (Hawkins remained chairman until 1994; he left to devote time to another game company, 3DO, which later went bankrupt.) The company bought game developer ORIGIN Systems in 1992 and began marketing its games in Japan with partner JVC. By 1995 more than 40% of EA's sales were from outside the US. That year Sony introduced its PlayStation game system in the US.

In 1997 the company bought US publisher Maxis (*SimCity*) for about $215 million. That year ORIGIN introduced *Ultima Online,* an online fantasy game in which players interact with each other. In 1998 EA bought Westwood Studios for $122 million. The next year it established EA.com, an Internet division to develop games for online players. It also agreed to pay America Online (now AOL) about $80 million to operate AOL's game channel.

In 2000 the company bought DreamWorks Interactive, a joint venture between Microsoft and DreamWorks. It also launched EA.com's website, released six titles for Sony's PlayStation 2, and agreed to develop titles for Microsoft's Xbox game system. In 2001 EA bought online gaming site pogo.com and launched *Majestic* (an interactive, subscription-based game played online), only to terminate the game in 2002 because of its failure to catch on with fans.

EA was banking on the success of the Internet incarnation of its popular Sims franchise, *The Sims Online,* which charged players a monthly subscription fee. The game was launched in 2002;

the response — including negative reviews and sluggish sales — was a letdown. In 2003 EA consolidated its money-losing online unit (EA.com) into its core operations. However, the company continued to experiment with online gaming; it made some of its titles available for online play via the PlayStation 2 and Xbox systems.

John Riccitiello stepped down as president and COO in 2004 to start his own private equity business (He returned as CEO in 2007). Also that year EA moved the operations of ORIGIN Systems from Austin, Texas, to Redwood City, California, as part of a larger move toward consolidation of development in California and British Columbia.

When EA suffered a challenge to its popular *Madden NFL* franchise from Take-Two and SEGA (which had joined up to create a set of low-priced, ESPN-branded sports titles), it fired back by procuring a five-year exclusive license to use NFL players and teams in its games, as well as acquiring the exclusive rights to the ESPN trademark in 2006. Take-Two retaliated to these challenges with a two-year exclusive license to use MLB teams in its games, essentially putting an end to any new versions of EA's blockbuster hit *MVP Baseball* during that time.

Hardcore video game fans don't just love the company's games, they love the music heard in the games as well. In recognition of this, EA teamed with Nettwerk Music Group in 2005 in the creation of EA Recordings, a digital-only record label that distributes music from EA's games to popular digital music-downloading services, such as Apple's iTunes.

In its most aggressive move to snatch up a portion of the mobile gaming market, the company acquired mobile gaming leader JAMDAT Mobile in 2006 and created a new division, EA Mobile. The next year it bought Mythic Entertainment, an MMORPG developer and publisher. Later that year it purchased VG Holding Corp., the owner of BioWare and Pandemic Studios.

EXECUTIVES

Chairman: Lawrence F. (Larry) Probst III, age 60
CEO and Director: John S. Riccitiello, age 50, $9,845,212 total compensation
COO: John Schappert, age 38, $10,282,621 total compensation
EVP EA Play Label: Rodney (Rod) Humble, age 44
EVP Western World Publishing: Gerhard Florin, age 51, $6,089,619 total compensation
EVP Business and Legal Affairs: Joel Linzner, age 58
EVP Human Resources: Gabrielle Toledano, age 43
EVP and CFO: Eric F. Brown, age 44, $3,120,685 total compensation
SVP, General Counsel, and Corporate Secretary: Stephen G. Bene, age 46
SVP and Chief Accounting Officer: Kenneth A. (Ken) Barker, age 43
VP Business Development and Strategic Partnerships, Interactive: Sebastien de Halleux
VP; General Manager, Playfish: Kristian Segerstråle, age 32
VP; Chief Technical Officer, Playfish: Sami Lababidi
President, EA Games Label: Frank D. Gibeau, age 41, $3,636,119 total compensation
President, EA SPORTS: Peter R. Moore, age 55, $3,634,119 total compensation
Marketing Director, EA Sports: Nathan Stewart
Director Public Relations, EA Sports: David Tinson
Director Communications, Europe: Tiffany Steckler
Director Communications, US: Holly Rockwood
Auditors: KPMG LLP

LOCATIONS

HQ: Electronic Arts Inc.
209 Redwood Shores Pkwy.
Redwood City, CA 94065
Phone: 650-628-1500   **Fax:** 650-628-1422
Web: www.ea.com

2010 Sales

	$ mil.	% of total
North America	2,025	55
Europe	1,433	39
Asia	196	6
Total	**3,654**	**100**

PRODUCTS/OPERATIONS

2010 Sales

	$ mil.	% of total
Consoles	2,342	64
PC	687	19
Mobile	472	13
Licensing & other	153	4
Total	**3,654**	**100**

Selected Game Titles

Battlefield
Dante's Inferno
Dead Space
FIFA Soccer
Madden NFL
Mass Effect
Medal of Honor
Need for Speed
NHL
Shank
Skate 3
Spore
Stygian Abyss
The Saboteur
The Sims

COMPETITORS

Activision Blizzard
Atari
Big Fish Games
Capcom
eGames
Eidos
Gameloft
Glu Mobile
Konami
Lucasfilm Entertainment
Microsoft
Namco Limited
NCsoft
Nintendo
SEGA
Sony Online Entertainment
Square Enix
Take-Two
THQ
Ubisoft
Valve Corporation

HISTORICAL FINANCIALS

Company Type: Public

Income Statement

	REVENUE ($ mil.)	NET INCOME ($ mil.)	NET PROFIT MARGIN	EMPLOYEES
3/10	3,654	(677)	—	7,800
3/09	4,212	(1,088)	—	9,100
3/08	3,665	(454)	—	9,000
3/07	3,091	76	2.5%	7,900
3/06	2,951	236	8.0%	7,200
Annual Growth	**5.5%**	**—**	**—**	**2.0%**

FYE: March 31

2010 Year-End Financials

Debt ratio: —   No. of shares (mil.): 330
Return on equity: —   Dividends
Cash ($ mil.): 1,273   Yield: —
Current ratio: 1.64   Payout: —
Long-term debt ($ mil.): —   Market value ($ mil.): 6,163

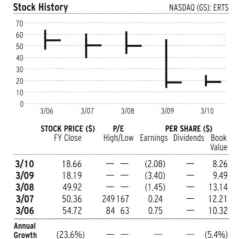

Stock History

NASDAQ (GS): ERTS

	STOCK PRICE ($) FY Close	P/E High/Low	PER SHARE ($) Earnings	Dividends	Book Value
3/10	18.66	— —	(2.08)	—	8.26
3/09	18.19	— —	(3.40)	—	9.49
3/08	49.92	— —	(1.45)	—	13.14
3/07	50.36	249 167	0.24	—	12.21
3/06	54.72	84 63	0.75	—	10.32
Annual Growth	(23.6%)	— —	—	—	(5.4%)

Eli Lilly

Eli Lilly hopes everything will come up roses for you, healthwise. Although best known for its popular antidepressant Prozac, the company develops medicines for a wide variety of ailments. Its top drugs include neurological therapies Zyprexa (schizophrenia and bipolar disorder) and Cymbalta (depression), cancer treatments Gemzar and Alimta, and endocrinology (hormone-related) products such as Humalog insulin and osteoporosis medication Evista. The company also makes cardiovascular therapies and anti-infective agents, as well as animal health products (Elanco Animal Health).

Eli Lilly knows the value of drug patents: After the company lost its lucrative patent protection for Prozac in August 2001, it saw sales drop dramatically. Lilly's current bestseller Zyprexa, which accounts for about 20% of annual sales, will have patent protection until October 2011, but Eli Lilly is avidly seeking new potential blockbusters and has started making "knockoff" versions of its own drugs so it will be less susceptible to generic competition.

The company has some 60 drug candidates in development stages, including treatments for cancer, diabetes, rheumatoid arthritis, depression, atherosclerosis (arterial plaque), and Alzheimer's disease. Its programs are conducted both independently and in concert with research partners. Biotechnology is increasingly important; the firm completed a $1 billion biotech research facility in Indianapolis in 2008.

Lilly received FDA approval on a top pipeline candidate, blood thinner Effient (or prasugrel, developed with Daiichi Sankyo), in 2009, though the drug will carry heavy warning labels due to fatal bleeding risks. Another promising development candidate is a once-a-week version of diabetes treatment Byetta; the drug is being co-developed with Amylin and Alkermes. In 2009 the FDA approved Zyprexa Relprevv, a

long-acting injectable version of Zyprexa, and bipolar therapy Symbyax was expanded for treatment-resistant depression indications.

The company gave its biotech ambitions a big boost through the 2008 acquisition of biotech firm ImClone for about $6.5 billion. ImClone has one approved blockbuster therapy, Erbitux for colorectal and head/neck cancers, and is developing numerous other cancer therapy candidates.

In 2010 Lilly further diversified its product offerings by acquiring Alnara Pharmaceuticals. The privately held biotechnology company is focused on developing protein therapies to treat metabolic diseases.

On the slimming-down side, in 2009 Lilly announced a reorganization plan to cut $1 billion in costs by 2011; the plan includes a 14% workforce reduction.

The power of bestseller Zyprexa has been somewhat diminished due to consumer lawsuits alleging that the drug causes side-effects including diabetes, weight gain, and high cholesterol. In early 2007 Lilly agreed to settle with a large group of patients; total settlement figures have since reached $1.2 billion. In addition, the company agreed in 2009 to pay an additional $1.4 billion in government fines to settle allegations over its marketing tactics for Zyprexa.

The Lilly Endowment, a charitable foundation created by the company and the Lilly family in the 1930s, owns 12% of the company.

HISTORY

Colonel Eli Lilly, pharmacist and Union officer in the Civil War, started Eli Lilly and Company in 1876 with $1,300. His process of gelatin-coating pills led to sales of nearly $82,000 in 1881. Later, the company made gelatin capsules, which it still sells. Lilly died in 1898, and his son and two grandsons ran the business until 1953.

Eli Lilly began extracting insulin from the pancreases of hogs and cattle in 1923; 6,000 cattle glands or 24,000 hog glands made one ounce of the substance. Other products created in the 1920s and 1930s included antiseptic Merthiolate, sedative Seconal, and treatments for pernicious anemia and heart disease. In 1947 the company began selling diethylstilbestrol (DES), a drug to prevent miscarriages. Eli Lilly researchers isolated the antibiotic erythromycin from a species of mold found in the Philippines in 1952. Lilly was also the major supplier of Salk polio vaccine.

The company enjoyed a 70% share of the DES market by 1971, when researchers noticed that a rare form of cervical cancer afflicted many of the daughters of women who had taken the drug. The FDA restricted the drug's use and Lilly found itself on the receiving (and frequently losing) end of a number of trailblazing product-liability suits that stretched into the 1990s.

The firm diversified in the 1970s, buying Elizabeth Arden (cosmetics, 1971; sold 1987) and IVAC (medical instruments, 1977). It launched such products as analgesic Darvon and antibiotic Ceclor. Lilly's 1982 launch of Humulin, a synthetic insulin developed by Genentech, made it the first company to market a genetically engineered product. In 1986 Lilly introduced Prozac.

In 1995 the firm and developer Centocor introduced ReoPro, a blood-clot inhibitor used in angioplasties. The next year it launched antipsychotic Zyprexa, Humalog, and Gemzar, and Prozac was approved to treat bulimia nervosa.

In 1999 a US federal judge found that the firm illegally promoted osteoporosis drug

Evista as a breast cancer preventative similar to AstraZeneca's Nolvadex. Lilly halted tests on its variation of heart drug Moxonidine after 53 patients died. Also that year Zyprexa was approved to treat bipolar disorder.

In 2000 the firm began marketing Prozac under the Sarafem name for severe premenstrual syndrome. A federal appeals court knocked more than two years off Prozac's patent, reducing the expected 2003 expiration date to 2001.

While the firm fretted over Prozac and its patents, it continued work to find its next blockbuster. In 2000 Lilly and partner ICOS announced favorable results from a study of erectile dysfunction treatment Cialis, which was approved in Europe in 2002 and in the US in 2004.

In 2002 the company settled with eight states in an infringement-of-privacy case involving the company's accidental disclosure of e-mail addresses for more than 600 Prozac patients.

In late 2004 Lilly announced its attention-deficit disorder drug Strattera had been linked to rare liver problems. The company agreed to add warning labels about the potential side effects to the drug's packaging and advertisements.

After a lengthy lawsuit regarding its patents for its top seller, Zyprexa, a federal judge ruled in Lilly's favor against generic manufacturers IVAX, Dr. Reddy's Laboratories, and Teva Pharmaceutical Industries. Federal courts ruled that the drug's patents would remain valid until October 2011.

EXECUTIVES

Chairman, President, and CEO: John C. Lechleiter, age 56, $20,927,648 total compensation
EVP and CFO: Derica W. Rice, age 45, $7,646,019 total compensation
EVP and President, Lilly Bio-Medicines: Bryce D. Carmine, $8,660,955 total compensation
SVP Global Quality: Fionnuala Walsh
SVP and General Counsel: Robert A. Armitage, age 60, $5,746,032 total compensation
SVP; President, Oncology Business Unit: John H. Johnson, age 51
SVP; President, Emerging Markets: Jacques Tapiero
SVP; President, Diabetes Business Unit: Enrique A. Conterno
SVP Drug Product Manufacturing, Americas: Maria Crowe
SVP and Controller: Elizabeth G. O'Farrell
SVP Product Research and Development: William F. Heath Jr.
SVP Human Resources: Susan (Sue) Mahony
SVP Compliance and Enterprise Risk Management and Chief Compliance Officer: Anne Nobles, age 53
Chief Medical Officer; SVP, Development Center of Excellence: Timothy J. (Tim) Garnett
SVP Corporate Affairs and Communications: Bart Peterson
SVP and Treasurer: Thomas W. Grein, age 58
SVP Corporate Strategy and Business Development: Gino Santini, age 53
SVP Information Technology and CIO: Michael C. (Mike) Heim, age 55
President and General Manager, Lilly Japan: Alfonso G. (Chito) Zulueta
President, European Operations: Karim Bitar
President, Elanco Animal Health: Jeffrey N. (Jeff) Simmons
President, Manufacturing: Frank M. Deane, age 60
Auditors: Ernst & Young LLP

LOCATIONS

HQ: Eli Lilly and Company
Lilly Corporate Center, 893 S. Delaware
Indianapolis, IN 46285
Phone: 317-276-2000   **Fax:** 317-276-4878
Web: www.lilly.com

2009 Sales

	$ mil.	% of total
US	12,294.4	56
Europe	5,227.2	24
Other regions	4,314.4	20
Total	**21,836.0**	**100**

PRODUCTS/OPERATIONS

2009 Sales

	$ mil.	% of total
Neurosciences	8,976.4	41
Endocrinology	5,677.4	26
Oncology	3,161.7	14
Cardiovascular	1,971.1	9
Animal health	1,207.2	6
Other pharmaceuticals	177.7	1
Collaboration & other	664.5	3
Total	**21,836.0**	**100**

2009 Sales

	$ mil.	% of total
Zyprexa	4,915.7	22
Cymbalta	3,074.7	14
Humalog	1,959.0	9
Alimta	1,706.0	8
Cialis	1,559.1	7
Gemzar	1,363.2	6
Animal health products	1,207.2	5
Evista	1,030.4	5
Humulin	1,022.0	5
Forteo	816.7	4
Strattera	609.4	3
Other pharmaceuticals	1,908.1	9
Collaboration & other	664.5	3
Total	**21,836.0**	**100**

Selected Products

Neuroscience
Cymbalta (duloxetine hydrocholoride; depression, anxiety, pain)
Prozac (fluoxetine hydrochloride; depression, panic disorder, obsessive-compulsive disorder)
Strattera (atomoxetine hydrochloride, ADHD)
Symbyax (olanzapine and fluoxetine hydrochloride, bipolar and treatment-resistant depression)
Zyprexa (olanzapine, schizophrenia and bipolar)
Zyprexa Relprevv/Zypadhera (long-acting injectable Zyprexa)
Endocrinology (including diabetes)
Actos (pioglitazone hydrochloride, type 2 diabetes)
Byetta (exenatide injection, type 2 diabetes)
Evista (raloxifene hydrochloride, osteoporosis and breast cancer prevention in postmenopausal women)
Forteo (osteoporosis)
Humatrope (somatropin for injection, rDNA origin; growth disorders)
Humulin (human insulin, rDNA origin; diabetes)
Humalog (insulin lispro injection, rDNA origin; diabetes)
Humalog Mix75/25 (75% Insulin lispro protamine suspension, 25% insulin lispro injection, rDNA origin; diabetes)
Humalog Mix50/50 (50% Insulin lispro protamine suspension, 50% insulin lispro injection, rDNA origin; diabetes)
Humalog Pen (insulin lispro, rDNA origin; diabetes)
Humulin Pen (human insulin, rDNA origin; diabetes)
Oncology (cancer)
Alimta (pemetrexed, non-small cell lung cancer and malignant pleural mesothelioma)
Erbitux (colorectal, head and neck cancers; from ImClone)
Gemzar (gemcitabine hydrochloride; pancreatic, breast, lung, bladder, and ovarian cancers)

Cardiovascular
Cialis (tadalafil, erectile dysfunction)
Efient/Effient (atherothrombotic events)
ReoPro (percutaneous coronary intervention)
Xigris (activated drotrecogin alfa, severe sepsis)
Animal Health
Apralan (antibiotic)
Coban, Monteban, and Maxiban (anticoccidal)
Comfortis (flea prevention)
Elector (parasiticide)
Micotil, Pulmotil, and Pulmotil AC (antibiotics)
Paylean, Optaflexx (performance enhancers)
Posilac (protein supplement)
Reconcile (separation anxiety)
Rumensin (feed additive)
Surmax/Maxus (performance enhancer)
Tylan (antibiotic)
Other pharmaceuticals
Ceclor (bacterial infections)
Vancocin (staphylococcal infections)

COMPETITORS

Abbott Labs	Merck KGaA
Amgen	Mylan
AstraZeneca	Myriad Genetics
Baxter International	Novartis
Bayer AG	Novo Nordisk
Boehringer Ingelheim	Pfizer
Bristol-Myers Squibb	Ranbaxy Laboratories
Dr. Reddy's	Roche Holding
Elan	Sanofi-Aventis
Forest Labs	Shire
GlaxoSmithKline	Takeda Pharmaceutical
Johnson & Johnson	Teva Pharmaceuticals
Merck	

HISTORICAL FINANCIALS

Company Type: Public

Income Statement

FYE: December 31

	REVENUE ($ mil.)	NET INCOME ($ mil.)	NET PROFIT MARGIN	EMPLOYEES
12/09	21,836	4,329	19.8%	40,360
12/08	20,378	(2,072)	—	40,500
12/07	18,634	2,953	15.8%	40,600
12/06	15,691	2,663	17.0%	41,500
12/05	14,645	2,002	13.7%	42,600
Annual Growth	**10.5%**	**21.3%**	**—**	**(1.3%)**

2009 Year-End Financials

Debt ratio: 81.1%
Return on equity: 53.2%
Cash ($ mil.): 4,463
Current ratio: 1.90
Long-term debt ($ mil.): 7,723

No. of shares (mil.): 1,153
Dividends
  Yield: 5.5%
  Payout: 49.7%
Market value ($ mil.): 41,179

Stock History

NYSE: LLY

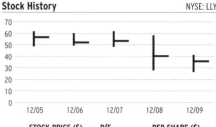

	STOCK PRICE ($) FY Close	P/E High/Low		PER SHARE ($) Earnings	Dividends	Book Value
12/09	35.71	10	7	3.94	1.96	8.26
12/08	40.27	—	—	(1.89)	1.88	5.84
12/07	53.39	23	18	2.71	1.70	11.85
12/06	52.10	24	20	2.45	1.60	9.52
12/05	56.59	34	27	1.81	1.52	9.36
Annual Growth	**(10.9%)**	**—**	**—**	**21.5%**	**6.6%**	**(3.1%)**

EMC Corporation

EMC bytes data storage problems and swallows every bit. The company is a leading provider of RAID (redundant array of independent disks) storage systems. Banks, government agencies, ISPs, manufacturers, and retailers use EMC's systems to store and retrieve massive amounts of information. It also markets a line of network attached storage (NAS) file servers, and a wide array of software designed to manage, protect, and share data. EMC is the majority owner of virtualization specialist VMware, and its RSA division provides security software.

Essentially a pure-play storage company, EMC competes against larger companies, such as Fujitsu, Hewlett-Packard, and IBM, that can offer storage systems as part of a package that includes servers and other hardware. The company also competes with fellow storage specialists Hitachi Data Systems and NetApp.

EMC is at the forefront of the movement away from direct-attached storage configurations, with products optimized for use in storage area networks (SANs). The company has pursued an open-system strategy that encourages greater interoperability with competitors' products. In addition to its relationship with Dell (its biggest partner), EMC has international alliances with such companies as NEC and Wipro.

EMC is also looking to gain a foothold in the booming data warehousing market. In mid-2010 the company agreed to acquire privately held Greenplum, which specializes in storing and analyzing large amounts of data from multiple sources. EMC plans to grow the unit by making additional acquisitions in the data warehousing market, similar to the way the company built its security division around RSA.

EMC built its storage empire with refrigerator-sized systems used to store data for huge mainframe computers. While the company's high-end Symmetrix and mid-size CLARiiON storage arrays are still EMC's bread and butter, its hardware portfolio has expanded into complementary NAS devices (Celerra). The company's Centera content-addressed storage systems are designed to manage huge archives of fixed data.

CEO Joe Tucci has led an aggressive, multiyear effort to broaden EMC's product portfolio, largely through acquisitions. Much of the company's product expansion has focused on software, and its offerings now encompass a wide range of information lifecycle management applications for storing, managing, protecting, and sharing data.

In 2009 EMC acquired Configuresoft, a developer of software that manages server configuration, updates, and compliance issues. Also in 2009 the company acquired Kazeon Systems, a developer of e-discovery software for law firms, corporations, and government agencies.

In 2009, after a two-month bidding war with rival NetApp, EMC won its bid to acquire Data Domain for $2.4 billion in cash, trumping NetApp's $1.9 billion cash and stock offer.

HISTORY

Former Intel executive Dick Egan and his college roommate, Roger Marino, founded EMC in 1979. (Their initials gave the company its name.) Egan, a feisty entrepreneur whose first job was shining shoes, served as a Marine in Korea and later worked at MIT on the computer system for NASA's Apollo program. Egan also helped found Cambridge Memory Systems (later Cambex).

EMC was started with no business plan, only the idea that Egan and Marino would be better off working for themselves. At first, they sold office furniture, which in short order led to contacts at technology companies and recognition of the niche market for add-on memory boards for minicomputers.

EMC grew steadily throughout the early 1980s and went public in 1986. Two years later Michael Ruettgers, a former COO of high-tech publishing and research company Technical Financial Services, joined the company as EVP of operations. Ruettgers spent his first year and a half at EMC dealing with a crisis that almost ruined the company: Defective disk drives in some of its products were losing customers' files. Ruettgers stepped up quality control and guided EMC through the crisis period. In 1989 he became the company's president and COO.

In the late 1980s EMC expanded into data storage, developing a system that employed small hard disks rather than larger, more expensive disks and tapes used in IBM mainframes. EMC then separated itself from competitors by providing systems with a large cache — a temporary storage area used for quicker data retrieval.

In 1990 EMC pioneered redundant array of independent disks (RAID) storage and eliminated nearly a dozen major product lines, focusing on storage for large IBM computers in a bid to beat Big Blue by undercutting prices. The company introduced its original Symmetrix system, based on the new integrated cached disk array technology that held data from a variety of computer types. Marino left the company in 1990.

Ruettgers became CEO in 1992. The next year the company acquired Epoch Systems, a provider of data management software, and in 1994 it bought storage products company Array Technology and Magna Computer, a leader in tape storage technology for IBM computers. EMC also introduced its first storage product for open systems, the Centriplex series, and its sales passed the $1 billion mark.

EMC increased its presence in this fast-growing data switching and computer connection market with the 1995 acquisition of McDATA. The next year it launched a digital video storage and retrieval system for the TV and film industry and introduced software that let its systems work on networks instead of requiring file servers for data storage management.

EMC bought data storage software provider SOFTWORKS in early 2000. In early 2001 Joe Tucci, who had joined EMC in 2000 as president, added CEO to his title. Ruettgers became chairman and Egan was named chairman emeritus. (Tucci suceeded Ruettgers as chairman at the end of 2005.)

EMC began a major push to expand its software offerings in 2003. It acquired LEGATO Software for $1.3 billion, and Documentum for approximately $1.5 billion. The following year it purchased server software maker VMware for approximately $625 million. EMC acquired System Management ARTS (SMARTS) for about $260 million in 2005. In 2006 EMC acquired RSA Security for about $2.1 billion.

It bought network configuration and change management specialist Voyence, as well as Berkeley Data Systems, the provider of an online backup and recovery service called Mozy, in 2007.

Co-founder Dick Egan died in 2009, after serving as the US ambassador to Ireland for a brief tenure under President George W. Bush.

EXECUTIVES

Chairman, President, and CEO: Joseph M. (Joe) Tucci, age 62, $9,047,763 total compensation
Vice Chairman: William J. (Bill) Teuber Jr., age 58, $3,752,112 total compensation
EVP Office of the Chairman: Harry L. You, age 50, $3,923,629 total compensation
EVP and CFO: David I. Goulden, age 50, $3,421,278 total compensation
EVP; President and COO, EMC Information Infrastructure and Cloud Services: Howard D. Elias, age 52, $3,398,447 total compensation
EVP Human Resources: John T. (Jack) Mollen, age 59
EVP, General Counsel, and Assistant Secretary: Paul T. Dacier, age 52
EVP; President, RSA Security: Arthur W. (Art) Coviello Jr., age 56
EVP and Chief Marketing Officer: Jeremy Burton, age 42
EVP Global Marketing and Customer Quality: Frank M. Hauck, age 50
EVP Americas and Global Sales Programs: Bill Scannell
SVP and Chief Accounting Officer: Mark A. Link
SVP and CIO: Sanjay Mirchandani, age 45
SVP and CTO: Jeffrey M. (Jeff) Nick
President and COO, EMC Information Infrastructure Products: Patrick P. (Pat) Gelsinger, age 48, $11,709,822 total compensation
President, Europe, Middle East, and Africa: Rainer Erlat
President, EMC India and South Asian Association for Regional Cooperation (SAARC): Manoj Chugh
President, EMC Australia and New Zealand: David Webster
President, Cloud Infrastructure Business: Harel Kodesh, age 52
President, EMC Information Intelligence Group: Mark S. Lewis, age 47
President, Asia/Pacific and Japan: Steven (Steve) Leonard
Secretary: Thomas J. Dougherty
Senior Director Public Relations: Michael J. Gallant
Auditors: PricewaterhouseCoopers LLP

LOCATIONS

HQ: EMC Corporation
176 South St., Hopkinton, MA 01748
Phone: 508-435-1000   **Fax:** 508-555-1212
Web: www.emc.com

2009 Sales

	$ mil.	% of total
US	7,384.3	53
Europe, Middle East & Africa	4,290.3	31
Asia/Pacific	1,603.1	11
Latin America, Mexico & Canada	748.2	5
Total	**14,025.9**	**100**

PRODUCTS/OPERATIONS

2009 Sales

	$ mil.	% of total
Products	8,828.1	63
Services	5,197.8	37
Total	**14,025.9**	**100**

2009 Sales

	$ mil.	% of total
Information storage	10,659.4	76
VMware Virtual Infrastructure	2,021.0	15
Content management & archiving	739.6	5
RSA Information Security	605.9	4
Total	**14,025.9**	**100**

Selected Products and Services

Information Storage Products
Storage systems
Content-addressed storage (Centera)
Data storage arrays (CLARiiON, Symmetrix)
Fibre Channel switches and directors (Connectrix)
Network file and media servers (Celerra)
EMC platform-based software (networked storage system management)

Services
  Customer education
  Customer service
  Technology solutions
Multi-platform Software
  Backup and archive
  Content management
  Resource management
VMware

COMPETITORS

CA Technologies
Citrix Systems
Dell
Fujitsu
Hewlett-Packard
Hitachi Data Systems
IBM
LSI Corp.
McAfee
Microsoft
NetApp
Oracle
Quantum Corporation
Symantec
Teradata
Western Digital
Xyratex

HISTORICAL FINANCIALS

Company Type: Public

Income Statement

FYE: December 31

	REVENUE ($ mil.)	NET INCOME ($ mil.)	NET PROFIT MARGIN	EMPLOYEES
12/09	14,026	1,088	7.8%	43,200
12/08	14,876	1,346	9.0%	42,100
12/07	13,230	1,666	12.6%	37,700
12/06	11,155	1,227	11.0%	31,100
12/05	9,664	1,133	11.7%	26,500
Annual Growth	9.8%	(1.0%)	—	13.0%

2009 Year-End Financials

Debt ratio: 19.9%
Return on equity: 7.6%
Cash ($ mil.): 6,302
Current ratio: 2.05
Long-term debt ($ mil.): 3,100

No. of shares (mil.): 2,056
Dividends
  Yield: —
  Payout: —
Market value ($ mil.): 35,911

Stock History

NYSE: EMC

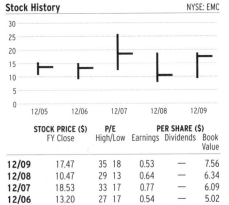

	STOCK PRICE ($) FY Close	P/E High/Low	PER SHARE ($) Earnings	Dividends	Book Value
12/09	17.47	35 18	0.53	—	7.56
12/08	10.47	29 13	0.64	—	6.34
12/07	18.53	33 17	0.77	—	6.09
12/06	13.20	27 17	0.54	—	5.02
12/05	13.62	32 24	0.47	—	5.87
Annual Growth	6.4%	— —	3.0%	—	6.5%

EMCOR Group

The core of EMCOR Group is electrical and mechanical construction. One of the world's largest specialty construction firms, EMCOR designs, installs, operates, and maintains complex mechanical and electrical systems. These include systems for power generation and distribution, lighting, voice and data communications, fire protection, plumbing, and heating, ventilation, and air-conditioning (HVAC). It also provides facilities services, including management and maintenance support. Through about 75 subsidiaries and joint ventures, the company serves various commercial, industrial, institutional, and utility customers.

EMCOR's mechanical and electrical construction services account for the lion's share of its business. Of this business, more than half of revenues are related to new construction. The remainder is derived from renovation or retrofit projects.

Some of EMCOR's largest institutional, industrial, and commercial projects include water treatment plants, hospitals, correctional facilities, research labs, manufacturing plants, oil refineries, data centers, hotels, shopping malls, and office buildings. Clients include Microsoft, the US Department of Veteran Affairs, and Hard Rock Hotel & Casino in Las Vegas.

Although demand for construction services (especially in the US commercial and hospitality markets) has declined as a result of the economic downturn, the company continues to grow and has a strategy to weather the current economic situation by diversifying its services and expanding geographically. It added to its industrial services operations by acquiring South Carolina-based facilities maintenance provider MOR PPM in 2008. During the past several years EMCOR expanded its US mechanical construction and facilities services operations through several acquisitions of fire protection systems businesses. In 2009 the company bought LT Mechanical of North Carolina, a leading plumbing and mechanical contractor. The following year it bought Pennsylvania-based engineering and facilities services firm Scalise Industries.

In efforts to reduce costs and match demand, EMCOR shed nearly 4,000 jobs (or some 14% of its workforce) between 2008 and 2010. The company is one of the largest union employers, with nearly 65% of its 25,000 employees belonging to various unions.

HISTORY

EMCOR's forerunner, Jamaica Water Supply Co., was incorporated in 1887 to supply water to some residents of Queens and Nassau Counties in New York. In 1902 it bought Jamaica Township Water Co., and by 1906 it was generating revenue — reaching $1.6 million by 1932. Over the next 35 years, the company kept pace with the population of its service area.

In 1966 the enterprise was acquired by Jamaica Water and Utilities, which then bought Sea Cliff Water Co. In 1969 and 1970 it acquired Welsbach (electrical contractors) and A to Z Equipment (construction trailer suppliers); it briefly changed its name in 1974 to Welsbach Corp. before becoming Jamaica Water Properties in 1976.

Diversification proved unprofitable, however, and in 1977 Martin Dwyer and his son Andrew took over the management of the struggling firm. Despite posting million-dollar losses in 1979, it was profitable by 1980.

The Dwyers acquired companies in the electrical and mechanical contracting, security, telecommunications, computer, energy, and environmental businesses. In 1985 Andrew Dwyer became president, and the firm changed its name the next year to JWP.

Between 1986 and 1990 JWP acquired more than a dozen companies, including Extel (1986), Gibson Electric (1987), Dynalectric (1988), Drake & Scull (1989), NEECO and Compumat (1990), and Comstock Canada (1990).

In 1991 JWP capped its strategy of buying up US computer systems resellers by acquiring Businessland. It then bought French microelectronics distributor SIVEA. Later that year JWP bought a 34% stake in Resource Recycling Technologies (a solid-waste recycler).

JWP's shopping spree extended the firm's reach, but the company began to struggle when several sectors turned sour. A price war in the information services business and a weak construction market led to a loss of more than $600 million in 1992. That year president David Sokol resigned after questioning JWP's accounting practices. He turned over to the SEC a report that claimed inflated profits.

Cutting itself to about half its former size, the company sold JWP Information Services in 1993. (JWP Information Services later became ENTEX Information Services, which was acquired by Siemens in 2000.) However, JWP continued to struggle, and in early 1994 it filed for bankruptcy. Emerging from Chapter 11 protection in December 1994, the reorganized company took the name EMCOR. That year Frank MacInnis, former CEO of electrical contractor Comstock Group, stepped in to lead EMCOR.

In 1995 the SEC, using Sokol's information, charged several former JWP executives with accounting fraud, claiming they had overstated profits to boost the value of their company stock and their bonuses. EMCOR later reached a nonmonetary settlement with the SEC. The company sold Jamaica Water Supply and Sea Cliff in 1996; it also achieved profitability that year.

Focusing on external growth, EMCOR acquired a number of firms in 1998 and 1999, including Marelich Mechanical Co. and Mesa Energy Systems, BALCO, Inc., and the Poole & Kent group of mechanical contracting companies based in Baltimore and Miami.

That year, about six years after emerging from bankruptcy, EMCOR began trading on the New York Stock Exchange. In 2002 EMCOR bought 19 subsidiaries from its financially troubled rival, Comfort Systems USA, including its largest unit, Shambaugh & Son. Later that year it expanded its facilities services operations with the acquisition of Consolidated Engineering Services (CES), an Archstone-Smith subsidiary that operated in 20 states.

EMCOR broadened its facilities services operations by acquiring the US facility management services unit of Siemens Building Technologies in 2003; in 2005 it added Fluidics, Inc., a mechanical services company based in Philadelphia.

In 2007 EMCOR acquired FR X Ohmstede Acquisitions Co., a leading provider of aftermarket maintenance and repair services, and replacement parts for oil refinery equipment.

EXECUTIVES

Chairman and CEO: Frank T. MacInnis, age 63, $6,089,625 total compensation
President, COO, and Director: Anthony J. (Tony) Guzzi, age 45, $3,539,428 total compensation
EVP Shared Services: R. Kevin Matz, age 51, $1,997,261 total compensation
EVP and CFO: Mark A. Pompa, age 45, $2,154,944 total compensation
EVP, Secretary, and General Counsel:
Sheldon I. (Shelly) Cammaker, age 70, $2,359,660 total compensation
SVP Operations, Government Services:
Michael L. Rodgers
VP Finance and Controller: William E. Feher
VP Risk Management: Rex C. Thrasher
VP Integrated Services: Anthony R. Triano
VP Marketing and Communications: Mava K. Heffler
VP and CIO: Joseph A. (Joe) Puglisi
VP Safety and Quality Management: David Copley
Chairman, Government Services:
Michael W. (Mike) Shelton
President, EMCOR Energy Services:
Arthur L. Strenkert
President, EMCOR Facilities Services: Mike Viox
President, Government Services: Joseph M. Gleeson
President and CEO, EMCOR Construction Services:
Michael J. (Mike) Parry, age 61
President, Mechanical Services: Michael P. Bordes
CEO, Emcor UK: Keith Chanter, age 51
CEO, Comstock Canada: Geoff W. Birkbeck
Treasurer: Joseph A. Serino
Auditors: Ernst & Young LLP

LOCATIONS

HQ: EMCOR Group, Inc.
301 Merritt Seven, 6th Fl., Norwalk, CT 06851
Phone: 203-849-7800   **Fax:** 203-849-7900
Web: www.emcorgroup.com

PRODUCTS/OPERATIONS

2009 Sales

	$ mil.	% of total
US mechanical construction & facilities services	2,027.2	37
US facilities services	1,426.3	26
US electrical construction & facilities services	1,273.7	23
UK construction & facilities services	500.5	9
Canada construction & facilities services	320.2	5
Total	**5,547.9**	**100**

Selected Operations

Mechanical and Electrical Construction
    Building plant and lighting systems
    Data communications systems
    Electrical power distribution systems
    Energy recovery
    Heating, ventilation, and air-conditioning (HVAC) systems
    Lighting systems
    Low-voltage systems (alarm, security, communications)
    Piping and plumbing systems
    Refrigeration systems
    Voice communications systems
Facilities Services
    Facilities management
    Installation and support for building systems
    Mobile maintenance and service
    Program development and management for energy systems
    Remote monitoring
    Site-based operations and maintenance
    Small modification and retrofit projects
    Technical consulting and diagnostic services

COMPETITORS

ABM Industries
APi Group
Carrier
CB Richard Ellis
Comfort Systems USA
Dycom
Fluor
Hoffman Corporation
Honeywell International
InfrastruX
Integrated Electrical Services
Jacobs Technology
Johnson Controls
Jones Lang LaSalle
Limbach Facility Services
Linc Facility Services
MasTec
MYR Group
Quanta Services
Schneider Electric
Siemens AG
SteelFab
Trane Inc.
UGL Unicco
URS

HISTORICAL FINANCIALS

Company Type: Public

Income Statement

FYE: December 31

	REVENUE ($ mil.)	NET INCOME ($ mil.)	NET PROFIT MARGIN	EMPLOYEES
12/09	5,548	163	2.9%	25,000
12/08	6,785	182	2.7%	28,000
12/07	5,927	127	2.1%	29,000
12/06	5,021	87	1.7%	27,000
12/05	4,715	60	1.3%	26,000
Annual Growth	**4.2%**	**28.4%**	**—**	**(1.0%)**

2009 Year-End Financials

Debt ratio: 12.3%
Return on equity: 14.4%
Cash ($ mil.): 727
Current ratio: 1.48
Long-term debt ($ mil.): 150
No. of shares (mil.): 66
Dividends
    Yield: —
    Payout: —
Market value ($ mil.): 1,785

Stock History

NYSE: EME

	STOCK PRICE ($) FY Close	P/E High/Low		PER SHARE ($) Earnings	Dividends	Book Value
12/09	26.90	12	6	2.38	—	18.36
12/08	22.43	13	4	2.71	—	15.73
12/07	23.63	20	12	1.90	—	13.34
12/06	28.42	24	13	1.33	—	10.71
12/05	16.88	19	11	0.94	—	9.28
Annual Growth	**12.4%**	**—**	**—**	**26.1%**	**—**	**18.6%**

Emerson Electric

Ralph Waldo Emerson once said, "Make yourself necessary to somebody," and Emerson Electric follows that adage. The company, generally known as just Emerson, makes a host of electrical, electromechanical, and electronic products, many of which are used to control gases, liquids, and electricity. Emerson pursues an active, aggressive acquisition strategy (with select divestitures along the way) in building up its global business with dozens of subsidiaries. The company gathers its 60-plus business units and divisions under eight Emerson Brands. It has more than 250 manufacturing locations, with about 165 locations outside of the US. Foreign operations make up more than half of Emerson's sales.

Despite the breadth of markets served, the company's sales and profits have eroded under the ongoing impact of the worldwide recession. In response, in mid-2010, the company inked an agreement to sell its Commercial and Industrial Motors and Emerson Appliance Motors and Controls to Nidec.

Moving forward, Emerson is targeting a diverse group of opportunities, including infrastructure projects in developing geographies, alternative energy and energy-efficient products, power generation and distribution, and network and data center management operations. The company's Network Power division acquired UK-based Chloride Group for $1.5 billion in mid-2010. Chloride Group's product line of power backup systems ensures uninterrupted power in nuclear, data center, emergency, and hospital applications. In developing regions, such as China and India, Emerson is working to boost its sales from about one-third to 40%. To this end, the company raised its stake in ABB India from 52% to 75% in 2010.

Emerson's earlier efforts to realign its operations with the turbulent business environment included cutting its workforce by about 10%, reducing inventory levels, and closing or consolidating about 25 plants. At the same time, Emerson took advantage of the historic low period; it invested about $1 billion to strengthen its core operations via the acquisition of several small businesses. In a larger move, Emerson acquired Avocent Corp., a network equipment technology provider, for about $1.2 billion.

Emerson Process Management also bolstered its oil and gas recovery and flow management business with the purchase of Roxar, a Norway-based maker of measurement instruments and software for offshore oil platforms. Emerson Industrial Automation bought Trident Power, an India-based maker of power generating alternators, and System Plast, a maker of belts and conveyer components based in Italy. In addition, Emerson added to its manufacturing plant capacity in Brazil, thereby supporting growth in its petrochemicals, telecommunications, and offshore oil and gas operations.

HISTORY

Emerson Electric was founded in 1890 in St. Louis by brothers Alexander and Charles Meston, inventors who developed uses for the alternating-current electric motor, which was new at the time. The company was named after former Missouri judge and US marshal John Emerson, who financed the enterprise and became its first president. Emerson's best-known product was an electric fan introduced in 1892. Between 1910 and 1920 the company helped develop the first forced-air circulating systems.

The Depression and labor problems in the 1930s brought Emerson close to bankruptcy, but new products, including a hermetic motor for refrigerators, revived it. The company's electric motors were adapted for additional uses during WWII, including powering the gun turrets in B-24 bombers.

Emerson suffered in postwar years, having grown dependent on military business. Wallace Persons took over as president in 1954 and reorganized the company's commercial product line, seeking to bring in customers from outside the consumer appliance market.

In the early 1960s the company bought a number of smaller companies to produce thermostats and gas controls, power transmission products, and welding and cutting tools. Emerson's sales increased from $56 million in 1954 to $800 million in 1973. Persons retired in 1974, and Chuck Knight became CEO. Knight took the company into high-tech fields and expanded its hardware segment with six acquisitions between 1976 and 1986.

In 1989 Emerson expanded its electrical offerings by acquiring a 45% stake in Hong Kong-based Astec (power supplies). The company spun off its defense systems, electronics, and other businesses in 1990 as ESCO Electronics.

Emerson bought Fisher Controls International in 1992 and formed S-B Power Tool with Robert Bosch. It also acquired Buehler International (destructive testing equipment). From 1993 through 1995 Emerson expanded globally by targeting the Asia/Pacific market, setting up operations in China and Eastern Europe, and forming joint ventures in China and India.

Bosch bought out Emerson's interest in S-B Power Tool (now Robert Bosch Tool) in 1996. In 1998 Emerson bought CBS Corporation's Westinghouse Process Control division.

Early in 2000 Emerson acquired the telecom products division of Jordan Industries for about $980 million and later bought European telecommunications power provider Ericsson Energy Systems from Ericsson for $725 million. Later that year the company dropped "Electric" from its everyday name to reflect its diverse product line.

Also in 2000 Emerson executive David Farr replaced long-time CEO Chuck Knight. In 2004 Farr also assumed the chairmanship as Knight retired and was named chairman emeritus.

Emerson acquired Metran Industrial, a provider of flow products and services in Russia and Eastern Europe, in 2004. Emerson also acquired the US-based outside plant and power systems businesses of Marconi (now telent) for $375 million.

Emerson acquired process measurement and control equipment maker Solartron Mobrey from the Roxboro Group in 2005. The following year Emerson purchased Knurr, a German manufacturer of racks and enclosures for data centers. It acquired power conversion equipment maker Artesyn Technologies. Emerson sold the wireline test systems business of Emerson Network Power to Tollgrade Communications in 2006. It then acquired Bristol Babcock, a unit of British diversified manufacturer FKI.

In 2008 Emerson acquired the Embedded Communications Computing (ECC) business of Motorola for $350 million in cash. The purchase extended Emerson's product portfolio in embedded computing, a niche key to telecommunications industry customers, among others.

EXECUTIVES

Chairman, President, and CEO: David N. Farr, age 55, $12,050,745 total compensation
Vice Chairman: Walter J. Galvin, age 63, $6,027,183 total compensation
COO: Edward L. Monser, age 59, $3,232,649 total compensation
SEVP and Director: Charles A. Peters, age 55, $3,697,494 total compensation
EVP Planning and Development: Craig W. Ashmore, age 47
SVP and CFO: Frank J. Dellaquila, age 53
CIO: Kathleen (Kathy) McElligott
SVP and CTO: Randall D. Ledford, age 60
SVP, Secretary, and General Counsel: Frank L. Steeves, age 56, $2,156,816 total compensation
SVP Administration: Robert M. Cox Jr.
SVP Organization Planning: Paul E. McKnight
SVP Human Resources: M.G. Rohret
VP and Chief Accounting Officer: Richard J. Schlueter, age 56
VP and Chief Marketing Officer: Katherine Button Bell
Chairman, Emerson Climate Technologies:
Thomas E. Bettcher
Chairman, Emerson Process Management:
John M. Berra, age 62
Chairman, Leroy Somer: C. Henry
President, Emerson Network Power:
Stephen C. (Steve) Hassell
President, Emerson Asia/Pacific: S. Y. Bosco
President, Emerson Canada: C. F. Eagleson
President, Emerson Latin America: L. A. Rodriguez
President, Emerson Middle East and Africa:
S. L. Nicholls
President, Emerson India: Pradipta Sen
Assistant Treasurer and Director Investor Relations:
L. M. Maxeiner
Auditors: KPMG LLP

LOCATIONS

HQ: Emerson Electric Co.
8000 W. Florissant Ave., St. Louis, MO 63136
Phone: 314-553-2000 **Fax:** 314-553-3527
Web: www.emerson.com

2009 Sales

	$ mil.	% of total
US	9,359.0	45
Asia/Pacific		
China	2,335.0	11
Other countries	2,017.0	10
Europe	4,346.0	21
Latin America	1,065.0	5
Other regions	1,793.0	8
Total	**20,915.0**	**100**

PRODUCTS/OPERATIONS

2009 Sales

	$ mil.	% of total
Process management	6,233.0	29
Network power	5,359.0	25
Industrial automation	3,698.0	17
Climate technologies	3,197.0	15
Appliances & tools	3,029.0	14
Adjustments	(601.0)	—
Total	**20,915.0**	**100**

Selected Products and Services

Process Management
  Measurement and analytical
  Software, services, and systems
  Valves and regulators
Network Power
  AC power systems
  Connectivity
  DC power systems
  Inbound power
  Information technology infrastructure management products
  OEM power
  Precision air
  Service

Industrial Automation
  Alternators
  Fluid control
  Industrial equipment
  Mechanical power transmission
  Modular belts and custom conveyor components
  Motors and drives
  Power generating alternators
  Power distribution
Climate Technologies
  Compressors
  Flow controls
  Terminal assemblies
  Thermal controls
  Thermostats and valve controls
Appliance and Tools
  Appliance controls
  Hand/power tools and wet/dry vacuums
  Motors
  Plumbing products and disposers

COMPETITORS

ABB
AMETEK
Cooper Industries
Cummins
Dana Holding
Danaher
Dresser, Inc.
Eaton
Endress + Hauser
GE
Hitachi
Honeywell International
Illinois Tool Works
Ingersoll-Rand
Interpump
Invensys
Johnson Controls
Kinetek
Lennox
Mark IV
McDermott
NEC
Power-One
Raytheon
Rexnord
Rockwell Automation
Rolls-Royce
Siemens AG
Sino-American Electronic
Snap-on
SPX
Stanley Black and Decker
Tecumseh Products
Toshiba
Trippe Manufacturing
Tyco Electronics
United Technologies

HISTORICAL FINANCIALS

Company Type: Public

Income Statement

FYE: September 30

	REVENUE ($ mil.)	NET INCOME ($ mil.)	NET PROFIT MARGIN	EMPLOYEES
9/09	20,915	1,724	8.2%	129,000
9/08	24,807	2,412	9.7%	140,700
9/07	22,572	2,136	9.5%	137,700
9/06	20,133	1,845	9.2%	127,800
9/05	17,305	1,422	8.2%	114,200
Annual Growth	**4.9%**	**4.9%**	**—**	**3.1%**

2009 Year-End Financials

Debt ratio: 46.7%
Return on equity: 19.5%
Cash ($ mil.): 1,560
Current ratio: 1.54
Long-term debt ($ mil.): 3,998
No. of shares (mil.): 752
Dividends
  Yield: 3.3%
  Payout: 58.1%
Market value ($ mil.): 30,157

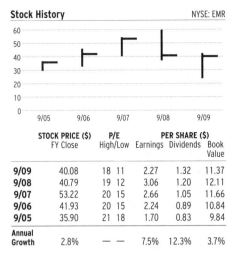

	STOCK PRICE ($) FY Close	P/E High/Low		PER SHARE ($) Earnings	Dividends	Book Value
9/09	40.08	18	11	2.27	1.32	11.37
9/08	40.79	19	12	3.06	1.20	12.11
9/07	53.22	20	15	2.66	1.05	11.66
9/06	41.93	20	15	2.24	0.89	10.84
9/05	35.90	21	18	1.70	0.83	9.84
Annual Growth	2.8%	—	—	7.5%	12.3%	3.7%

Energen Corporation

Energen's natural gas distribution business puts the energy out in Dixie, but the company also takes it in through gas and oil exploration operations that extend into the Southwest. The diversified energy company generates more than half of its sales from its regulated utility, Alabama Gas Corporation (Alagasco), which distributes natural gas to approximately 413,150 residential and more than 33,900 commercial and industrial customers. Energen has oil and gas exploration and production operations in the Southwest through subsidiary Energen Resources; the unit has estimated proved reserves of 1.6 trillion cu. ft. of natural gas equivalent.

Alagasco distributes gas in 184 central and northern Alabama communities (including Birmingham and Montgomery). The utility also uses its 22,100 miles of main and service lines to transport gas for commercial and industrial customers that buy from other suppliers.

Energen is pouring money into its oil and gas wells. Energen Resources has boosted its proved reserves through property acquisitions and developments. The unit sells most of its oil, gas, and natural gas liquids (NGL) to third parties.

In 2007 Energen Resources acquired 30 billion cu. ft. of proved and probable natural gas reserves in Carracas Canyon in the San Juan Basin from Dominion Resources.

Boosting its Permian assets, in 2009 the company bought Range Resources' stake (13,000 net acres) in the Fuhrman-Mascho Field in the Permian Basin for $182 million.

HISTORY

Alagasco was formed in 1948 through the merger of two utilities (Alabama Gas Company and Birmingham Gas Company) that trace their origins to the late 1800s. Alagasco went public

in 1953. By the late 1970s Alagasco was a mature utility in a slow-growing market. To increase profits, it formed the Energen holding company in 1978 and moved into the nonregulated business of oil and gas exploration and production.

In addition to acquiring oil and gas properties in the southern and southwestern US, Energen's Taurus Exploration unit specialized in coalbed methane development, for which the federal government gave tax credits. By 1990 Taurus Exploration was a leading developer of coalbed methane in Alabama's Black Warrior Basin. In 1994 Energen teamed with Conoco in a five-year program to develop coalbed methane projects.

In 1995 Energen launched an acquisition drive to expand its oil and gas operations. The company spent $72 million in 1997 to acquire 107 billion cu. ft. of coalbed methane reserves from Amoco. The following year Taurus Exploration changed its name to Energen Resources and traded the bulk of its Gulf of Mexico operations for the Permian Basin properties of EEX Corp. It also purchased Total Minatome from Total American Holdings for $192 million, then immediately sold 31% of its Minatome stock to Westport Oil & Gas. It sold the remainder of its Gulf of Mexico operations in 1999.

Its Energen Resources subsidiary announced an agreement with natural gas company Southwestern Energy in 2001 to jointly explore the New Mexico portion of the Permian Basin. Also that year Energen changed its fiscal year-end from September to December.

In 2002 Energen purchased about 43 million barrels of oil equivalent reserves in West Texas from oil and gas production firm First Permian for about $182 million.

In 2004 Energen Resources paid $263 million for coal bed methane properties in the San Juan Basin that have proved reserves of about 240 billion cu. ft. of natural gas equivalent. In 2005 the company acquired Permian Basin oil properties from a private company for $168 million.

EXECUTIVES

Chairman and CEO: James T. McManus II, age 51, $3,108,487 total compensation
SVP Operations: D. Paul Sparks Jr.
VP, CFO, and Treasurer: Charles W. (Chuck) Porter Jr., age 45, $896,631 total compensation
VP Corporate Development; General Counsel and Secretary: J. David Woodruff Jr., age 53, $830,299 total compensation
VP Human Resources: William K. (Bill) Bibb
VP Investor Relations: Julie S. Ryland
VP Audit and Compliance: Marvell (Chip) Bivins Jr., age 47
VP and Controller, Energen Resources: Cindy Rayburn
VP and Controller: Russell E. Lynch Jr., age 36
VP and CIO: L. Brunson White, age 53
VP External Affairs: Robert (Sid) McAnnally
VP Marketing and Administration, Energen Resources: Holley S. LaGrone, age 49
President, Alabama Gas: Dudley C. Reynolds, age 57, $1,001,684 total compensation
President and COO, Energen Resources: John S. Richardson, age 52, $1,386,172 total compensation
Investor Relations Coordinator: Michelle A. Speed
Auditors: PricewaterhouseCoopers LLP

LOCATIONS

HQ: Energen Corporation
605 Richard Arrington Jr. Blvd. North
Birmingham, AL 35203
Phone: 205-326-2700   **Fax:** 205-326-2704
Web: www.energen.com

PRODUCTS/OPERATIONS

2009 Sales

	$ mil.	% of total
Oil & gas operations	822.5	57
Natural gas distribution	617.9	43
Total	**1,440.4**	**100**

Subsidiaries

Alabama Gas Corporation (Alagasco)
Energen Resources Corporation

COMPETITORS

Apache
Atmos Energy
Chesapeake Energy
Duke Energy
Entergy
Pioneer Natural Resources
Sempra Energy
Southern Company
Southwestern Energy

HISTORICAL FINANCIALS

Company Type: Public

Income Statement				FYE: December 31
	REVENUE ($ mil.)	NET INCOME ($ mil.)	NET PROFIT MARGIN	EMPLOYEES
12/09	1,440	256	17.8%	1,515
12/08	1,569	322	20.5%	1,530
12/07	1,435	309	21.5%	1,542
12/06	1,394	274	19.6%	1,530
12/05	1,128	173	15.3%	1,500
Annual Growth	6.3%	10.3%	—	0.2%

2009 Year-End Financials

Debt ratio: 20.7%	No. of shares (mil.): 72
Return on equity: 13.1%	Dividends
Cash ($ mil.): 76	Yield: 1.1%
Current ratio: 0.99	Payout: 14.0%
Long-term debt ($ mil.): 411	Market value ($ mil.): 3,364

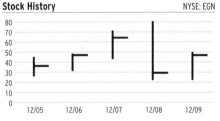

	STOCK PRICE ($) FY Close	P/E High/Low		PER SHARE ($) Earnings	Dividends	Book Value
12/09	46.80	14	6	3.57	0.50	27.66
12/08	29.33	18	5	4.47	0.48	26.62
12/07	64.23	16	10	4.28	0.46	19.18
12/06	46.94	13	9	3.73	0.44	16.72
12/05	36.32	19	12	2.35	0.40	12.42
Annual Growth	6.5%	—	—	11.0%	5.7%	22.2%

Entergy Corporation

If Entergy had an Entergizer bunny for a mascot, it would stay fully charged (with a safe, radioactive glow). The integrated utility holding company's subsidiaries distribute electricity to 2.7 million customers in four southern states (Arkansas, Louisiana, Mississippi, and Texas) and provide natural gas to 189,000 customers in Louisiana. Entergy operates more than 15,500 miles of high-voltage transmission lines and 1,550 transmission substations. In addition, the company has interests in regulated and nonregulated power plants in North America that have a combined generating capacity of about 30,000 MW. An advocate of nuclear power, Entergy is one of the largest nuclear power generators in the US.

To generate shareholder return, in 2009 Entergy was pursuing a spinoff of its non-utility nuclear businesses from its regulated utility nuclear segment. However, it received a major setback in 2010 when the New York Public Service Commission rejected the plan, concerned at the debt load of the proposed new company.

Despite a dip in revenues prompted by weakened demand in the wake of the global recession, Entergy managed to post an increase in operating income in 2009, due in part to lower commodity prices and cost-cutting measures.

The company is increasing its generating capacity (to support its utilities and its marketing and trading operations) through domestic nuclear plant acquisitions. In 2007 Entergy acquired Consumers Energy's 798 MW Palisades Nuclear Plant in Michigan for $380 million.

Entergy has also been focused on new plant construction. In 2007 it received one of the first early site permits in the US from the US Nuclear Regulatory Commission for a possible new nuclear unit at the Grand Gulf site in Mississippi. It was also the first company to submit (in 2008) two combined Construction and Operating Licenses for new nuclear plants at two different sites — at Grand Gulf and at River Bend Station near St. Francisville, Louisiana.

HISTORY

Arkansas Power & Light (AP&L, founded in 1913) consolidated operations with three other Arkansas utilities in 1926. Also that year, New Orleans Public Service Inc. (NOPSI, founded in 1922) merged with two other Big Easy electric companies. Louisiana Power & Light (LP&L) and Mississippi Power & Light (MP&L) were both formed in 1927, also through consolidation of regional utilities.

AP&L, LP&L, MP&L, NOPSI, and other utilities were combined into a Maine holding company, Electric Power and Light, which was dissolved in 1949. A new holding company, Middle South Utilities, emerged that year to take over the four utilities' assets.

In 1971 the company bought Arkansas-Missouri Power. In 1974 it brought its first nuclear plant on line and formed Middle South Energy (now System Energy Resources) to develop two more nuclear facilities, Grand Gulf 1 and 2. Unfortunately, Grand Gulf 1 was completed behind schedule and about 400% over budget. When Middle South tried to pass on the costs to customers, controversy ensued. Construction of Grand Gulf 2 was halted, and the CFO, Edwin Lupberger, took charge in 1985. Two years later, nuke-related losses took the company to the brink of bankruptcy.

The company moved to settle the disputes by absorbing a $900 million loss on Grand Gulf 2 in 1989. To distance itself from the controversy, Middle South changed its name to Entergy. In 1991 NOPSI settled with the City of New Orleans over Grand Gulf 1 costs.

That year Entergy, anticipating deregulation, branched out into nonregulated industries and looked abroad for growth opportunities. In 1993 a consortium including Entergy acquired a 51% interest in Edesur, a Buenos Aires electric utility. In 1995 Entergy agreed to buy a 20% stake in a power plant under construction in India, but the state government soon halted the project, accusing the participating US companies of exploiting India.

Entergy completed its acquisition of CitiPower, an Australian electric distributor, in 1996, and the next year it bought the UK's London Electricity.

But diversification had drained funds. Lupberger resigned in 1998, and a new management team began selling noncore businesses, such as CitiPower and London Electricity. It contracted out construction on two UK power plants, to be owned by Entergy, and moved into Eastern Europe through a joint venture with Bulgaria's National Electricity Company. NYMEX began trading electricity futures in 1998, using Entergy and Cinergy as contract-delivery points.

In 1999 Wayne Leonard, Cinergy's former CFO, stepped in as Entergy's CEO. The company bought the Pilgrim nuclear reactor in Massachusetts, its first plant outside its utility territory, from BEC Energy (now NSTAR); it also contracted to operate the Nine Mile Point nuclear plants in New York. Entergy sold its security monitoring business and its interest in a telecom joint venture to partner Adelphia Business Solutions.

Entergy continued its push into the Northeast by buying two nuclear plants — Indian Point 3 and James Fitzpatrick — from the New York Power Authority for $967 million in 2000, and it announced that it would purchase Indian Point 1 and 2 from Consolidated Edison (completed in 2001). In 2001 the company agreed to buy the Vermont Yankee nuclear plant from a group of New England utilities; the deal was completed in 2002 for $180 million.

Entergy agreed to merge with FPL Group in 2000, but the deal was called off the next year. The company also moved to expand through joint ventures. In 2000 Entergy and The Shaw Group, a piping systems fabricator, formed Entergy-Shaw, which designs and builds power plants. Entergy announced an agreement with Framatome to create a nuclear operations company, and in 2001 Entergy and Koch Industries formed an energy marketing and trading joint venture.

Entergy and Koch Industries exited their Entergy-Koch's joint venture in 2004 through the sale of the unit's marketing operations to Merrill Lynch for an undisclosed amount and the sale of its gas transportation and storage assets to TGT Pipeline, a subsidiary of Loews, for approximately $1.1 billion.

As a result of Hurricane Katrina, more than 1 million of Entergy's customers in Mississippi and Louisiana lost power; not all have been able to return to their homes. Lost customers and extensive storm damage led to Entergy New Orleans filing for Chapter 11 bankruptcy in 2005; it emerged from bankruptcy in 2007.

EXECUTIVES

Chairman and CEO: J. Wayne Leonard, age 59, $15,166,209 total compensation
EVP and COO: Mark T. Savoff, age 53, $2,168,118 total compensation
EVP and Chief Adminstrative Officer: Roderick K. (Rod) West, age 41, $1,005,487 total compensation
EVP and CFO: Leo P. Denault, age 50, $2,968,713 total compensation
EVP, Secretary, and General Counsel: Robert D. Sloan, age 62
EVP Human Resources and Administration: E. Renae Conley, age 52
Chief Nuclear Officer; President and CEO, Nuclear Operations: John T. Herron, age 56
SVP, Chief Accounting Officer, and Acting Principal Financial Officer: Theodore H. Bunting Jr., age 51, $1,401,645 total compensation
SVP Federal Policy, Regulatory, and Government Affairs: Kimberly Despeaux
VP Finance and Risk: Barrett Green
VP Planning and Financial Communications: Michele Lopiccolo
VP Investor Relations: Paula Waters
President, Wholesale Commodity: Richard J. (Rick) Smith, age 58, $2,875,755 total compensation
President and CEO, Entergy Texas: Joe Domino
President and CEO, Entergy Louisiana and Entergy Gulf States Louisiana: Bill Mohl
President and CEO, Entergy New Orleans: Charles Rice
Group President, Utility Operations: Gary J. Taylor, age 56, $2,680,664 total compensation
President and CEO, Entergy Mississippi: Haley R. Fisackerly, $660,581 total compensation
President and CEO, Entergy Arkansas: Hugh T. McDonald, age 51, $890,488 total compensation
Auditors: Deloitte & Touche LLP

LOCATIONS

HQ: Entergy Corporation
639 Loyola Ave., New Orleans, LA 70113
Phone: 504-576-4000   **Fax:** 504-576-4428
Web: www.entergy.com

PRODUCTS/OPERATIONS

2009 Sales

	$ mil.	% of total
Electric	7,880.0	73
Competitive businesses	2,693.4	25
Natural gas	172.2	2
Total	**10,745.6**	**100**

Selected Subsidiaries

Entergy Arkansas, Inc. (electric utility)
Entergy Gulf States, Inc. (electric and gas utility)
Entergy Louisiana, LLC. (electric utility)
Entergy Mississippi, Inc. (electric utility)
Entergy New Orleans, Inc. (electric and gas utility)
Entergy Nuclear, Inc. (nuclear plant operation)
Entergy Operations, Inc. (plant management and maintenance for Entergy utilities)
Entergy Services, Inc. (management services for Entergy utilities)
System Energy Resources, Inc. (plant management and supply to Entergy utilities)
System Fuels, Inc. (fuel storage and delivery to Entergy utilities)

COMPETITORS

AEP
AES
Atmos Energy
Avista
Brazos Electric
CenterPoint Energy
Cleco
Constellation Energy Group
Dominion Resources
Duke Energy
Edison International
El Paso Electric
Energy Future
Exelon
MidAmerican Energy
Mirant
NextEra Energy
OGE Energy
Peabody Energy
PG&E Corporation
Progress Energy
RRI Energy
Sempra Energy
Southern Company
TVA
Williams Companies
Xcel Energy

HISTORICAL FINANCIALS

Company Type: Public

Income Statement

FYE: December 31

	REVENUE ($ mil.)	NET INCOME ($ mil.)	NET PROFIT MARGIN	EMPLOYEES
12/09	10,746	1,251	11.6%	15,000
12/08	13,094	1,241	9.5%	14,669
12/07	11,484	1,135	9.9%	14,322
12/06	10,932	1,133	10.4%	13,800
12/05	10,106	924	9.1%	14,100
Annual Growth	1.5%	7.9%	—	1.6%

2009 Year-End Financials

Debt ratio: 127.0%
Return on equity: 15.0%
Cash ($ mil.): 1,710
Current ratio: 1.42
Long-term debt ($ mil.): 11,060

No. of shares (mil.): 189
Dividends
  Yield: 3.7%
  Payout: 47.6%
Market value ($ mil.): 15,490

Stock History

NYSE: ETR

	STOCK PRICE ($) FY Close	P/E High/Low	PER SHARE ($) Earnings	Dividends	Book Value
12/09	81.84	14 10	6.30	3.00	46.01
12/08	83.13	21 10	6.20	3.00	43.73
12/07	119.52	22 16	5.60	2.58	43.19
12/06	92.32	18 12	5.36	2.16	45.14
12/05	68.65	19 15	4.19	2.16	43.26
Annual Growth	4.5%	— —	10.7%	8.6%	1.5%

Enterprise Products Partners

Both enterprising and productive, Enterprise Products Partners is the leading player in the North American natural gas, natural gas liquids (NGL), and crude oil industries, with a range of processing, transportation, and storage services. Operations include natural gas processing, NGL fractionation, petrochemical services, and crude oil transportation. The hub of the company's business is Houston's Mont Belvieu refinery complex. In a major expansion move, in 2009 the company acquired rival TEPPCO Partners L.P. As a result, Enterprise has 48,000 miles of pipelines, and 200 million of crude oil, refined products, and NGL storage capacity. Chairman Dan Duncan holds a 34.5% stake in Enterprise.

Enterprise's strategy is focused on building and managing an integrated network of midstream energy assets (including salt domes, and fractionation and natural gas processing plants) to take advantage of growing US market demand for natural gas, NGLs, crude oil and refined products. The TEPPCO Partners purchase made the company the largest publicly traded energy partnership in the US. The expanded company's assets include 60 liquid storage terminals, 25 natural gas storage facilities, 17 fractionation facilities, and six offshore hub platforms.

In 2010, in a move to increase its footprint in the lucrative Haynesville/Bossier Shale play, Enterprise acquired two natural gas gathering and treating systems in Northwest Louisiana and East Texas from M2 Midstream LLC for $1.2 billion.

In 2008 Enterprise acquired from BP the remaining quarter stake in Dixie Pipeline and Dixie Terminals and Storage Company it had not already owned. Dixie operates a pipeline system that serves seven states throughout the southeastern US. That year the company formed the Texas Offshore Port System project, a joint venture with TEPPCO Partners and Oiltanking Holding Americas, to own and operate a new offshore crude oil port and pipeline system in Texas.

In 2008, to raise cash, Enterprise sold to Duncan Energy 51% of Enterprise Texas Pipeline LLC, 51% of Enterprise Intrastate LP, and 66% of Enterprise GC, LP. These companies own assets in Texas, including more than 8,000 miles of natural gas pipelines, a leased natural gas storage facility with 4.4 billion cu. ft. of storage capacity, more than 1,000 miles of NGL pipelines, and 18 million barrels of leased NGL storage capacity.

EXECUTIVES

President, CEO, and Director: Michael A. Creel, age 56, $2,522,291 total compensation
EVP and COO: William (Bill) Ordemann, age 50
EVP and CFO: W. Randall Fowler, age 53, $802,931 total compensation
EVP, Chief Commercial Officer, and Director: A. J. (Jim) Teague, age 63, $2,343,299 total compensation
EVP, Chief Legal Officer, and Secretary: Richard H. Bachmann, age 57, $1,496,832 total compensation

SVP Enterprise General Partner: Terry L. Hurlburt
SVP Enterprise General Partner: James A. (Jim) Cisarik
SVP Enterprise General Partner: Lynn L. Bourdon III
SVP Distribution: Rudy Nix
SVP Natural Gas Processing: Gil H. Radtke, age 48
SVP, Controller, and Principal Accounting Officer: Michael J. Knesek, age 55
SVP Engineering: Leonard W. Mallett, age 51
SVP Natural Gas Services and Marketing Group: Christopher R. (Chris) Skoog, age 46
SVP Enterprise GP and EPCO: Thomas M. Zulim, age 52
VP and Treasurer: Bryan F. Bulawa
VP Investor Relations: John R. (Randy) Burkhalter
VP Petrochemical Services: G. R. (Jerry) Cardillo, age 52
Director Public Relations: Rick Rainey
Auditors: Deloitte & Touche LLP

LOCATIONS

HQ: Enterprise Products Partners L.P.
  1100 Louisiana St., 10th Fl., Houston, TX 77002
Phone: 713-381-6500   **Fax:** 713-381-8200
Web: www.epplp.com

PRODUCTS/OPERATIONS

2009 Sales

	$ mil.	% of total
NGL pipelines & services	19,174.5	57
Onshore crude oil pipelines & services	7,238.6	22
Onshore natural gas pipelines & services	3,665.2	11
Petrochemical services	3,133.4	9
Offshore pipeline & services	341.2	1
Adjustments, eliminations	(8,042.0)	—
Total	**25,510.9**	**100**

Selected Subsidiaries

Baton Rouge Fractionators LLC (32%)
Baton Rouge Propylene Concentrator, LLC (30%)
Belle Rose NGL Pipeline LLC (42%)
Belvieu Environmental Fuels GP, LLC
K/D/S Promix, LLC (50%)
Mid-America Pipeline
Seminole Pipeline (90%)
Tri-States NGL Pipeline LLC (50%)
Wilprise Pipeline Co., LLC (75%)

COMPETITORS

Dynegy
Equistar Chemicals
Exxon Mobil
Huntsman International
Occidental Petroleum
Quicksilver Gas Services
Spectra Energy
Williams Companies

HISTORICAL FINANCIALS

Company Type: Public

Income Statement

FYE: December 31

	REVENUE ($ mil.)	NET INCOME ($ mil.)	NET PROFIT MARGIN	EMPLOYEES
12/09	25,511	1,031	4.0%	4,800
12/08	21,906	954	4.4%	3,500
12/07	16,950	534	3.1%	3,200
12/06	13,991	600	4.3%	3,000
12/05	12,257	424	3.5%	2,600
Annual Growth	20.1%	24.9%	—	16.6%

2009 Year-End Financials

Debt ratio: 113.0%
Return on equity: 12.8%
Cash ($ mil.): 55
Current ratio: 0.94
Long-term debt ($ mil.): 11,346

No. of shares (mil.): 639
Dividends
  Yield: 6.9%
  Payout: 124.9%
Market value ($ mil.): 20,080

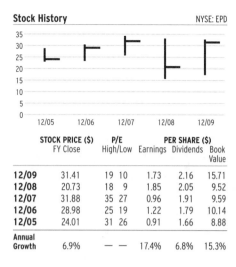

	STOCK PRICE ($) FY Close	P/E High/Low		PER SHARE ($) Earnings	Dividends	Book Value
12/09	31.41	19	10	1.73	2.16	15.71
12/08	20.73	18	9	1.85	2.05	9.52
12/07	31.88	35	27	0.96	1.91	9.59
12/06	28.98	25	19	1.22	1.79	10.14
12/05	24.01	31	26	0.91	1.66	8.88
Annual Growth	6.9%	—	—	17.4%	6.8%	15.3%

EOG Resources

EOG Resources hogs a resource — natural gas. The independent oil and gas company is engaged in exploring for natural gas and crude oil and developing, producing, and marketing those resources. In 2009 EOG, an independent offspring of the once powerful Enron, reported estimated proved reserves of 10.8 trillion cu. ft. equivalent, including 8.9 trillion cu. ft. of natural gas reserves and 313 million barrels of crude oil, condensate, and natural gas liquid (NGL) reserves. The company operates in major production basins in Canada, offshore Trinidad, the US, the UK sector of the North Sea, and in China (Sichuan basin).

EOG's strategy is to focus on growth through internal generation (such as developing its major shale plays — the Barnett Shale in North Texas and the Bakken Formation in North Dakota) and through strategic acquisitions of properties in North America and internationally. In 2009 the company drilled 116 net gas wells in the Barnett Shale and produced a daily rate of 400 million cu. ft. per day.

That year EOG saw its revenues slump in the wake of low commodity prices and oil and gas demand caused by the global recession.

In 2010 the company announced significant oil finds in Texas, North Dakota, and Colorado and targeted double-digit growth in its organic production through 2012.

Expanding its energy portfolio, in 2010 EOG Resources Canada agreed to buy Galveston LNG, giving it a 24.5% stake in Pacific Trail Pipelines Limited Partnership and a 49% share of Kitimat LNG, a planned liquefied natural gas export terminal in British Columbia.

Boosting its Trinidad assets, in 2008 EOG acquired an 80% working interest in the exploration and production license covering the Pelican field and its related facilities from Trinidad and Tobago Marine Petroleum Company Limited.

Moving into a new exploration area, that year EOG acquired rights from ConocoPhillips in a Petroleum Contract covering the Chuanzhong Block exploration area (approximately 130,000

acres) in China's Sichuan Basin. It subsequently acquired more acreage. In 2008 the company sold its assets in California and Appalachia in order to raise cash and focus on its core areas.

HISTORY

In 1987 Enron formed Enron Oil & Gas from its existing InterNorth and Houston Natural Gas operations to concentrate on exploration for oil and natural gas and their production. Enron maintained full ownership until 1989, when it spun off 16% of Enron Oil & Gas to the public, raising about $200 million. Later offerings reduced its holdings to just over 50%.

Enron Oil & Gas in 1992 was awarded a 95% working interest in three fields off Trinidad that previously had been held by government-owned companies. Two years later the company assumed the operations of three drilling blocks off Bombay (including the Tapti field), as well as a 30% interest in them. Natural gas prices fell in the winter of 1994, causing Enron Oil & Gas to focus its 1995 drilling on crude oil exploitation and the enhancement of its natural gas reserves. Natural gas prices rebounded in 1996. That year Enron Oil & Gas was awarded a 90% interest in an offshore area of Venezuela. In 1997 the company inked a 30-year production contract with China. The company made a major discovery of natural gas in offshore Trinidad in 1998. That year Mark Papa succeeded Forrest Hoglund as CEO (Papa became chairman in 1999).

In 1999 Enron traded most of its remaining stake in Enron Oil & Gas to the company in exchange for Enron Oil & Gas' operations and assets in India and China. Consequently, the company changed its name from Enron Oil & Gas to EOG Resources.

The next year EOG won contracts to develop properties in Canada's Northwest Territories. It also moved into the Appalachian Basin in 2000, through the acquisition of Somerset Oil & Gas. Buoyed by a strong performance that year, the company increased its capital spending on North American exploration by more than 30%, and in 2001 it bought Energy Search, a small natural gas exploration and production company that operated in the Appalachian Basin.

EXECUTIVES

Chairman and CEO: Mark G. Papa, age 63, $12,713,702 total compensation
SEVP Exploration: Loren M. Leiker, age 56, $5,464,794 total compensation
SEVP Operations: Gary L. Thomas, age 60, $5,462,631 total compensation
EVP and General Manager, San Antonio: Robert K. Garrison, age 57, $1,654,824 total compensation
EVP and General Manager, Fort Worth: William R. Thomas
EVP and General Manager, Denver: Kurt D. Doerr
SVP and General Counsel: Frederick J. (Rick) Plaeger II, age 56
VP and CFO: Timothy K. Driggers, age 48, $1,293,607 total compensation
VP and Treasurer: Helen Y. Lim
VP and CIO: Sandeep Bhakhri
VP Human Resources, Administration: Patricia L. Edwards
VP Investor Relations: Maire A. Baldwin
Director Investor Relations: Elizabeth M. Ivers
Corporate Secretary: Michael P. Donaldson
Auditors: Deloitte & Touche LLP

LOCATIONS

HQ: EOG Resources, Inc.
1111 Bagby, Sky Lobby 2, Houston, TX 77002
Phone: 713-651-7000   **Fax:** 713-651-6995
Web: www.eogresources.com

2009 Sales

	$ mil.	% of total
US	4,115.9	86
Canada	414.1	9
Trinidad	233.2	5
Other countries	23.8	—
Total	**4,787.0**	**100**

PRODUCTS/OPERATIONS

2009 Sales

	$ mil.	% of total
Natural gas	2,051.0	43
Crude oil, condensate & natural gas liquids	1,348.5	28
Gains of property disposition	535.4	11
Gains on Mark-to-Market commodity derivatives	431.8	9
Gathering, processing & marketing	407.1	9
Other	13.2	—
Total	**4,787.0**	**100**

COMPETITORS

Adams Resources	Exxon Mobil
Anadarko Petroleum	Murphy Oil
Apache	Occidental Petroleum
BP	Pioneer Natural Resources
Cabot Oil & Gas	Royal Dutch Shell
Chevron	Sonde Resources Corp.
El Paso Corporation	Talisman Energy

HISTORICAL FINANCIALS

Company Type: Public

Income Statement   FYE: December 31

	REVENUE ($ mil.)	NET INCOME ($ mil.)	NET PROFIT MARGIN	EMPLOYEES
12/09	4,787	547	11.4%	2,100
12/08	6,387	2,437	38.2%	2,100
12/07	4,039	1,090	27.0%	1,800
12/06	3,904	1,300	33.3%	1,570
12/05	3,607	1,260	34.9%	1,400
Annual Growth	7.3%	(18.8%)	—	10.7%

2009 Year-End Financials

Debt ratio: 27.6%
Return on equity: 5.7%
Cash ($ mil.): 686
Current ratio: 1.37
Long-term debt ($ mil.): 2,760

No. of shares (mil.): 253
Dividends
  Yield: 0.6%
  Payout: 26.3%
Market value ($ mil.): 24,662

Stock History   NYSE: EOG

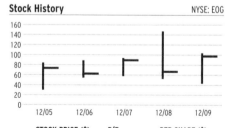

	STOCK PRICE ($) FY Close	P/E High/Low		PER SHARE ($) Earnings	Dividends	Book Value
12/09	97.30	47	21	2.17	0.57	39.44
12/08	66.58	15	6	9.72	0.47	35.56
12/07	89.25	21	14	4.37	0.33	27.58
12/06	62.45	17	11	5.24	0.22	22.09
12/05	73.37	16	6	5.13	0.15	17.03
Annual Growth	7.3%	—	—	(19.4%)	39.6%	23.4%

Equifax Inc.

Ever get the feeling you're being watched? You could be feeling the gaze of Equifax. One of the country's big three credit bureaus (Experian and TransUnion are the others), Equifax provides credit scores, history information, and risk analysis. The company also provides credit card marketing and fraud detection services, and offers database marketing and credit-scoring software. Subsidiary TALX provides outsourced payroll and human resources services in the US. Equifax's customers include financial institutions, retailers, automotive dealers, and mortgage companies. The group operates in North America, Latin America, and Europe, but the majority of its revenues come from the US.

Equifax has targeted such emerging markets as Latin America, where fast-growing economies have a need for its offerings but the infrastructure for consumer credit reporting is nascent. It acquired a Peruvian credit reporting agency in 2007.

Other target markets for growth include India, Russia, and China. In 2010 Equifax won clearance to begin operating a credit reporting business in India through joint ventures with six Indian banks. In Russia, Equifax owns a minority stake in Global Payments Credit Services.

In the mature US market, Equifax's strategy for growth includes buying firms that are active in other areas. Through such deals, the company has entered direct marketing, business process outsourcing, risk management, and other auxiliary businesses. In 2009 the company acquired consumer wealth and asset management data collector IXI Corporation. The deal expanded Equifax's pool of data to include deeper information about consumer wealth, credit, and spending.

In 2010 Equifax sold its direct marketing services unit to Alliance Data Systems for $117 million. The division provided consumer demographic information and database services.

HISTORY

Brothers Cator and Guy Woolford started Retail Credit Co. in Atlanta in 1899. They compiled credit records of local residents into their Merchants Guide, which they sold to retailers for $25 a year. The brothers extended their services to the insurance industry in 1901, investigating applicants' backgrounds. The company grew steadily and by 1920 had offices across the US and Canada. After several decades, Retail Credit branched into other information sectors, partly through acquisitions of regional credit reporters.

The company came under scrutiny in 1973 when the FTC filed an antimonopoly suit (dropped in 1982) against its consumer credit division and a complaint against its investigative practices (Retail Credit used field investigators to probe people's backgrounds). In 1976 the company became Equifax, short for "equitability in the gathering and presentation of facts."

In the 1980s and 1990s Equifax continued to buy small businesses in the US and Europe. As the Information Age matured, businesses clamored for its services. By the end of the 1980s, Equifax had passed TRW (now part of Experian) as the largest provider of consumer information.

Receptive to consumer concerns in the late 1980s, the company ended list sales to US direct marketers and scrapped Marketplace, a 1991 joint venture with Lotus Development to compile a database of the shopping habits of 100 million Americans.

During the 1990s Equifax acquired regional credit and collection firms in Florida, Georgia, and Texas. It restructured in 1992, merging its US and Canadian operations, closing field offices, and expanding its international operations.

In 1992 and 1993 it settled cases with several states over intrusive and inaccurate credit and job reference reports. The California State Lottery ended its scratch ticket terminal contract with an Equifax unit, claiming the subsidiary ran substandard operations. The contract was reinstated in 1995 after Equifax threatened to sue, but the lottery business left a bad impression on Equifax. In 1996 it subcontracted most of its contract obligations to GTECH.

Also in 1996 Equifax exited the health care information business; the next year it spun off its insurance services business as Choicepoint. As part of this effort it reassigned CDB Infotek (acquired 1996) to ChoicePoint. After CDB was alleged to have improperly sold voter registration and Social Security number lists, shareholders wondered whether Equifax's management had been unaware of the supposed activities, or if it had bought CDB knowing that it could be assuming legal responsibility for them. Equifax spokespeople gave contradictory explanations. At least partially in response to these woes, Equifax helped launch a self-policing initiative for the industry.

Equifax turned to building its Latin American business, buying the remaining 50% of South American credit company DICOM in 1997. It also bought 80% of Brazil's largest credit information firm, Segurança ao Crédito e Informações (1998), Chilean card processing firm Procard (2000), and one of Uruguay's largest credit information providers, Clearing de Informes (2001).

In 1999 the company entered the UK credit card market with a card-processing contract with IKANO Financial Services. The next year it expanded its direct marketing prowess with its acquisition of R.L. Polk's consumer information database. Also in 2000 the company agreed to pay $500,000 to the FTC for blocking or not responding promptly enough to consumers' phone calls.

In 2001 the company spun off credit-card processing and check-management unit Centegy (since acquired by Fidelity National Information Services) to shareholders, sold its city directory business (acquired in the R.L. Polk acquisition) to infoUSA (now infoGROUP), and underwent a restructuring that included cutting some 700 jobs, primarily outside the US.

In 2005 Equifax acquired APPRO Systems, a provider of automated credit risk management and financial technologies, for approximately $92 million. That year, Richard F. Smith (former COO of GE Insurance Solutions) succeeded Thomas F. Chapman as CEO of the company. Smith also took on the role of chairman when Chapman retired from the firm.

In 2006 Equifax purchased Austin-Tetra, which offers business-to-business data management services. Other acquisitions that added to its service offerings included the 2007 acquisition of human resources outsourcing firm TALX, direct-marketing firm Naviant (renamed Equifax eMarketing Solutions), and marketing technology firm BeNOW.

The company expanded its operations in Peru in 2007 with the acquisition of a rival credit reporting agency.

EXECUTIVES

Chairman and CEO: Richard F. (Rick) Smith, age 50, $9,634,759 total compensation
SVP Corporate Development: John T. Hartman, age 52
SVP Global Operations: Andy S. Bodea
SVP and Controller: Nuala M. King, age 56
SVP Investor Relations: Jeffrey L. (Jeff) Dodge, age 58
CIO: David C. (Dave) Webb, age 54
VP and CFO: Lee Adrean, age 58, $1,862,534 total compensation
VP and Chief Legal Officer: Kent E. Mast, age 66, $1,542,860 total compensation
VP and Chief Human Resources Officer: Coretha M. Rushing, age 53, $1,552,782 total compensation
VP and Chief Marketing Officer: Paul J. Springman, age 64
VP Public Relations: Tim Klein
President, U.S. Consumer Information Solutions: J. Dann Adams, age 52
President, Commercial Information Solutions: Alex Gonzalez
President, North America Personal Solutions: Joseph M. (Trey) Loughran III, age 42
President, Technology and Analytical Services: Rajib Roy, age 43
President, International: Rodolfo M. (Rudy) Ploder, age 49
Auditors: Ernst & Young LLP

LOCATIONS

HQ: Equifax Inc.
1550 Peachtree St. NW, Atlanta, GA 30309
Phone: 404-885-8000   **Fax:** 404-885-8988
Web: www.equifax.com

2009 Sales

	$ mil.	% of total
US	1,363.1	75
Canada	122.6	7
UK	104.9	6
Brazil	82.3	4
Other countries	151.6	8
Total	**1,824.5**	**100**

PRODUCTS/OPERATIONS

2009 Sales

	$ mil.	% of total
US consumer information solutions	820.7	45
International	438.6	24
TALX	346.4	19
North America personal solutions	149.0	8
North America commercial solutions	69.8	4
Total	**1,824.5**	**100**

Selected Subsidiaries and Affiliates

Acrofax Inc. (Canada)
Alphafax Properties Limited Partnership
Austin Consolidated Holdings, Inc.
Clearing de Informes S.A. (Uruguay)
Compliance Data Center LLC
Computer Ventures, Inc.
Credit Bureau Services, Inc.
Inversiones Equifax de Chile S.A.
IXI Corporation
Management Insight Incentives, LLC
Opt-Out Services LLC
Performance Assessment Network, Inc.
Propago S.A. (Chile)
TBT Enterprises, Incorporated
TALX Corporation
UI Advantage, Inc.
Verdad Informatica de Costa Rica, S.A.

COMPETITORS

Acxiom	Harte-Hanks
ADP	infoGROUP
Aon	Marmon Group
Ceridian	Moody's
Ceridian UK	Paychex
D&B	Right Management
Elavon	SHL Group
Experian	Total System Services
Fair Isaac	TransUnion LLC
First Data	

HISTORICAL FINANCIALS

Company Type: Public

Income Statement

FYE: December 31

	REVENUE ($ mil.)	NET INCOME ($ mil.)	NET PROFIT MARGIN	EMPLOYEES
12/09	1,825	234	12.8%	6,600
12/08	1,936	273	14.1%	6,500
12/07	1,843	273	14.8%	7,000
12/06	1,546	275	17.8%	4,960
12/05	1,443	247	17.1%	4,600
Annual Growth	6.0%	(1.3%)	—	9.4%

2009 Year-End Financials

Debt ratio: 61.9%
Return on equity: 16.1%
Cash ($ mil.): 103
Current ratio: 0.85
Long-term debt ($ mil.): 991

No. of shares (mil.): 125
Dividends
  Yield: 0.5%
  Payout: 8.7%
Market value ($ mil.): 3,862

Stock History

NYSE: EFX

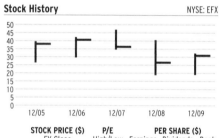

	STOCK PRICE ($) FY Close	P/E High/Low	PER SHARE ($) Earnings	Dividends	Book Value
12/09	30.89	17 11	1.83	0.16	12.81
12/08	26.52	19 9	2.09	0.16	10.50
12/07	36.36	23 17	2.02	0.16	11.19
12/06	40.60	20 14	2.12	0.16	6.70
12/05	38.02	21 14	1.86	0.15	6.56
Annual Growth	(5.1%)	— —	(0.4%)	1.6%	18.2%

Equity Residential

The "Grave Dancer" is also the lord of the rents. Sam Zell (whose moniker springs from his buying and turning around moribund properties) is at the head of the conga line at Equity Residential, the nation's #1 apartment owner by sales and units. (The company bypassed rival AIMCO in terms of units owned in 2009.) Equity Residential wholly or partially owns some 550 communities with about 140,000 units, comprising garden units, mid- and high rises, and military housing. A real estate investment trust (REIT), Equity Residential also provides property leasing, development, management, financial, and other support operations. The company focuses on growth regions throughout the US.

Equity Residential owns properties in several large markets in the Southwest, Northwest, Southeast, and Northeast. Top locations include Seattle, Phoenix, Boston, and Los Angeles — typically cities with high demand and a scarcity of developable land. The REIT sells assets in slower or exit markets, using funds from the sales to build up its portfolio in target areas.

However, the company has been affected by the turmoil in the credit and housing markets. Its revenues have fallen, particularly in markets where unemployment rates have risen the highest. To keep its turnover rates down, Equity Residential has offered lower rates on certain renewals. The REIT has also slowed down its acquisition and development activities during the economic downturn. Setting itself in place for expected recovery, Equity Residential sold some 60 properties in 2009 for approximately $1 billion.

HISTORY

Sam Zell founded Equity Residential Properties in Chicago in 1969.

When property prices plunged in the early 1990s, Zell earned his "Grave Dancer" nickname: He formed "vulture funds" with Merrill Lynch to buy distressed real estate cheaply. In 1993 Zell created a national apartment company with about 22,000 apartment units, called it Equity Residential Properties Trust, and took it public. Public offerings provided a steady flow of new capital (Equity Residential has had about 15 follow-up offerings since its IPO).

Equity Residential carried on Zell's traditional practice of buying undervalued assets and making them profitable. The REIT began expanding its regional management offices almost immediately. Initially it sought apartment properties or small portfolios, but its appetite grew for ever larger bites, including the acquisitions of entire real estate companies. In 1997 it spent $1 billion each for Wellsford Residential Property Trust and Evans Withycombe Residential, and overall added more than 70,000 units to its portfolio for the year.

The next year Equity Residential went even higher, buying Merry Land & Investment and its nearly 120 properties in the Southeast for $2.2 billion. Expansion continued in 1999, as Equity Residential bought Lexford Housing Trust, bringing Zell's empire to more than 1,000 apartment complexes.

In 2000 the company branched out with the purchase of Globe Business Resources (residential and office furniture) but also kept buying more apartments — this time Grove Property Trust (New England apartments). After taking a loss in the furniture business in 2001, it dumped that venture in 2002, but hung on to Globe's short-term furnished housing business, renaming it Equity Corporate Housing.

In 2005 Equity Residential bought land in the Lefrak waterfront development in Newport, New Jersey, across from Manhattan. The REIT found the area a hot market with a high housing demand. The following year, the company sold its Lexford Housing Division to Empire Group Holdings for $1.09 billion. Through the sale, which reduced its apartment holdings by a third, Equity Residential jettisoned around 300 apartment buildings in slower markets. It acquired around 40 such apartment buildings in target markets over the next year.

EXECUTIVES

Chairman: Samuel (Sam) Zell, age 68
Vice Chairman: Gerald A. (Gerry) Spector, age 64
President, CEO, and Trustee: David J. Neithercut, age 54, $3,652,749 total compensation
EVP and Chief Investment Officer: Alan W. George, age 52, $1,748,859 total compensation
EVP and CFO: Mark J. Parrell, age 43, $1,377,536 total compensation
EVP Human Resources: John Powers, age 62
EVP Operations: David Santee, age 51, $1,321,445 total compensation
EVP; President, Property Management: Frederick C. Tuomi, age 55, $1,759,354 total compensation
EVP Development: Mark N. Tennison, age 49
EVP and General Counsel: Bruce C. Strohm, age 55, $1,304,570 total compensation
SVP Dispositions, San Francisco, Washington DC, Boston, Hartford, and New York: Matt Wakenight
SVP, Associate General Counsel, and Secretary: Yasmina Duwe
SVP Acquisitions, Los Angeles, Orange County, Inland Empire, San Diego, and Phoenix: Anthony (Tony) Duplisse
SVP Acquisitions, Atlanta, Orlando, Tampa, Jacksonville, and South Florida: Barry Altshuler
SVP Acquisitions, Seattle, Tacoma, San Francisco, Denver, and Portland: Jim Alexander
SVP Development, East Coast: Richard Boales
SVP Acquisitions, Boston, New England, New York, New Jersey, and Washington DC: Alec Brackenridge
Investor Relations Contact: Marty McKenna
Auditors: Ernst & Young LLP

LOCATIONS

HQ: Equity Residential
  2 N. Riverside Plaza, Chicago, IL 60606
Phone: 312-474-1300   **Fax:** 312-454-8703
Web: www.equityapartments.com

2009 Sales

	% of total
Northeast	31
Southwest	24
Southeast	21
Northwest	20
Other	4
Total	**100**

2009 Properties by Market

	No.
Seattle/Tacoma, WA	47
Phoenix	41
South Florida	39
Boston	36
Los Angeles	36
San Francisco Bay	33
Washington, DC/Northern Virginia	27
Orlando, FL	26
Atlanta	23
Denver	23
New York Metro area	23
Suburban Maryland	22
New England (excluding Boston)	19
Inland Empire, CA	14
San Diego	14
Jacksonville	12
Orange County, CA	10
Portland, OR	10
Tampa	9
Raleigh/Durham, NC	6
Central Valley, CA	5
Dallas/Ft. Worth, TX	4
Other	16
Total	**495**

PRODUCTS/OPERATIONS

2009 Sales

	$ mil.	% of total
Rental income	1,933.4	99
Fees & asset management	10.3	1
Total	**1,943.7**	**100**

2009 Properties

	No. of properties	No. of units
Garden	413	112,961
Mid/high-rise	80	19,451
Military housing	2	4,595
Total	**495**	**137,007**

COMPETITORS

AMLI Residential
Apartment Investment and Management
Archstone
Associated Estates Realty
AvalonBay
BRE Properties
Camden Property
Essex Property Trust
Gables Residential Services
Home Properties
Irvine Apartment Communities
Lend Lease
Lincoln Property
Mid-America Apartment Communities
Milestone Management
Post Properties
UDR

HISTORICAL FINANCIALS

Company Type: Public

Income Statement

FYE: December 31

	REVENUE ($ mil.)	NET INCOME ($ mil.)	NET PROFIT MARGIN	EMPLOYEES
12/09	1,944	382	19.7%	4,100
12/08	2,103	420	20.0%	4,700
12/07	2,038	990	48.6%	4,800
12/06	1,990	1,073	53.9%	5,200
12/05	1,955	862	44.1%	6,000
Annual Growth	**(0.1%)**	**(18.4%)**	**—**	**(9.1%)**

2009 Year-End Financials

Debt ratio: 194.1%
Return on equity: 7.9%
Cash ($ mil.): 193
Current ratio: 1.40
Long-term debt ($ mil.): 9,393

No. of shares (mil.): 283
Dividends
  Yield: 4.9%
  Payout: 129.1%
Market value ($ mil.): 9,575

Stock History

NYSE: EQR

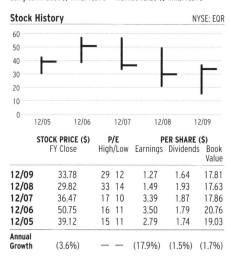

	STOCK PRICE ($) FY Close	P/E High/Low		PER SHARE ($) Earnings	Dividends	Book Value
12/09	33.78	29	12	1.27	1.64	17.81
12/08	29.82	33	14	1.49	1.93	17.63
12/07	36.47	17	10	3.39	1.87	17.86
12/06	50.75	16	11	3.50	1.79	20.76
12/05	39.12	15	11	2.79	1.74	19.03
Annual Growth	**(3.6%)**	**—**	**—**	**(17.9%)**	**(1.5%)**	**(1.7%)**

Ernst & Young Global

Accounting may actually be the *second*-oldest profession, and Ernst & Young is one of the oldest practitioners. Ernst & Young is also one of the world's Big Four accounting firms (third in revenue behind PricewaterhouseCoopers and Deloitte Touche Tohmatsu, ahead of KPMG). It has some 700 offices providing auditing and accounting services in 140 countries. The firm also provides legal services and advisory services relating to emerging growth companies, human resources issues, and corporate transactions (mergers and acquisitions, public offerings, and the like). Ernst & Young has one of the world's largest tax practices, serving multinational clients that have to comply with multiple local tax laws.

Ernst & Young offers its services to companies in a vast range of industries, including asset management, life sciences, mining, media and entertainment, retail, technology, and hotel and leisure. The company's financial reporting segment offers an IFRS/GAAP comparison so companies can compare and contrast the international and US accounting standards. Ernst & Young's tax business has grown as the economy has become increasingly globalized and companies face more complicated international compliance issues.

The group is organized in five geographic areas, with divisions covering Europe, Middle East, India, and Africa; the Americas (Ernst & Young LLP); Oceania; Japan; and the Far East. The structure allows the company to develop and strengthen its cross-country operations within integrated regions.

Ernst & Young hands out an Entrepreneur of the Year award annually. Past recipients include CEO of Rosetta Stone Tom Adams, Dr. Jean-Paul Clozel, founder of Swiss pharmaceuticals company Actelion, and Cirque du Soleil founder Guy Laliberté.

HISTORY

In 1494 Luca Pacioli's *Summa di Arithmetica* became the first published text on double-entry bookkeeping, but it was almost 400 years before accounting became a profession.

In 1849 Frederick Whinney joined the UK firm of Harding & Pullein. His ledgers were so clear that he was advised to take up accounting, which was a growth field as stock companies proliferated. Whinney became a name partner in 1859 and his sons followed him into the business. The firm became Whinney, Smith & Whinney (WS&W) in 1894.

After WWII, WS&W formed an alliance with Ernst & Ernst (founded in Cleveland in 1903 by brothers Alwin and Theodore Ernst), with each firm operating on the other's behalf across the Atlantic. Whinney merged with Brown, Fleming & Murray in 1965 to become Whinney Murray. In 1979 Whinney Murray, Turquands Barton Mayhew (also a UK firm), and Ernst & Ernst merged to form Ernst & Whinney.

But Ernst & Whinney wasn't done merging. Ten years later, when it was the fourth-largest accounting firm, it merged with #5 Arthur Young, which had been founded by Scotsman Arthur Young in 1895 in Kansas City. Long known as "old reliable," Arthur Young fell on hard times in the 1980s because its audit relationships with

failed S&Ls led to expensive litigation (settled in 1992 for $400 million).

Thus the new firm of Ernst & Young faced a rocky start. In 1990 it fended off rumors of collapse. The next year it slashed payroll, even thinning its partner roster. Exhausted by the S&L wars, in 1994 the firm replaced its pugnacious general counsel, Carl Riggio, with the more cost-conscious Kathryn Oberly.

In the mid-1990s Ernst & Young concentrated on consulting, particularly in software applications, and grew through acquisitions. In 1996 the firm bought Houston-based Wright Killen & Co., a petroleum and petrochemicals consulting firm, to form Ernst & Young Wright Killen. It also entered new alliances that year, including ones with Washington-based ISD/Shaw, which provided banking industry consulting, and India's Tata Consulting.

In 1997 Ernst & Young was sued for a record $4 billion for its alleged failure to effectively handle the 1993 restructuring of the defunct Merry-Go-Round Enterprises retail chain (it settled for $185 million in 1999). On the heels of a merger deal between Coopers & Lybrand and Price Waterhouse, Ernst & Young agreed in 1997 to merge with KPMG International. But Ernst & Young called off the negotiations in 1998, citing the uncertain regulatory process they faced.

The firm reached a settlement in 1999 in lawsuits regarding accounting errors at Informix and Avis Budget Group and sold its UK and southern African trust and fiduciary businesses to Royal Bank of Canada (now RBC Financial Group).

In 2000 Ernst & Young became the first of the (then) Big Five firms to sell its consultancy, dealing it to France's Cap Gemini Group for about $11 billion. The following year the UK accountancy watchdog group announced it would investigate Ernst & Young for its handling of the accounts of UK-based The Equitable Life Assurance Society. The insurer was forced to close to new business in 2000 because of massive financial difficulties.

Ernst & Young made headlines and gave competitors plenty to talk about in 2002 when closely held financial records were made public during a divorce case involving executive Rick Bobrow (who in 2003 abruptly retired as global CEO after just a year on the job).

Also in 2002 the firm allied with former New York City mayor Rudy Giuliani to launch a business consultancy bearing the Giuliani name. Ernst & Young later helped the venture to build its investment banking capabilities by selling its corporate finance unit (as well as its stake in Giuliani Partners) to that firm in 2004.

With the collapse of rival Andersen in 2002, Ernst & Young boosted its legal services, assembling some 2,000 lawyers in dozens of countries.

But the firm faced Andersen-style trouble of its own as client suits against auditors became more common in the wake of corporate scandals at Enron and other troubled companies. Both Avis Budget Group, Inc. (formerly Cendant) and HealthSouth sued Ernst & Young in connection with alleged accounting missteps in 2004.

In 2005 Ernst & Young's UK arm emerged victorious from a torrid legal battle with insurer Equitable Life, which in 2003 had sued the accountancy for professional negligence related to work performed when Ernst & Young was its auditor. Another highlight for that year was the fee bonanza fueled by changes in international accounting standards required by the Sarbanes-Oxley Act in the US.

EXECUTIVES

Chairman and CEO: James S. (Jim) Turley, age 54
Global Vice Chair, Advisory: Norman Lonergan
Global Vice Chair Assurance: Christian Mouillon
Global Vice Chair Tax: Mark A. Weinberger
Global Vice Chair Transaction Advisory Services (TAS):
  Pip McCrostie
Global COO: John Ferraro
Global Managing Partner, Operations and Finance:
  Jeffrey H. (Jeff) Dworken
**Global Managing Partner, Quality and Risk
  Management:** Victoria Cochrane
Global Managing Partner Markets: John Murphy
Global Managing Partner People: Sam Fouad
Global Managing Partner EMEIA Integration:
  Patrick Gounelle
Global Director, Automotive: Michael S. (Mike) Hanley
Managing Partner, Assurance, Canada: Rob Scullion
Managing Partner, New Zealand: Rob McLeod
**Managing Partner, Europe, Middle East, India, and
  Africa:** Mark Otty
Co-Area Managing Partner, Far East:
  James A. (Jim) Hassett
Co-Area Managing Partner, Far East: David Sun
Area Managing Partner, Americas: Steve Howe
Area Managing Partner, Oceania: James Millar
Managing Partner, Asia/Pacific: Lou P. Pagnutti
Managing Partner, Japan Area: Yoshitaka Kato
Chairman and CEO, Canada: Trent Henry

LOCATIONS

HQ: Ernst & Young Global Limited
  5 Times Square, New York, NY 10036
Phone: 212-773-3000   **Fax:** 212-773-6350
Web: www.ey.com

2009 Sales

	$ mil.	% of total
Europe, Middle East, India, Africa	9,636	45
Americas	8,647	41
Japan	1,196	6
Far East	1,144	5
Oceania	817	3
Total	**21,440**	**100**

PRODUCTS/OPERATIONS

2009 Sales by Service Line

	$ mil.	% of total
Assurance	10,141	47
Tax	5,822	27
Advisory	3,589	17
Transaction Advisory Services	1,888	9
Total	**21,440**	**100**

Industry Specializations

Asset management
Automotive
Banking and capital markets
Consumer products
Government and public sector
Insurance
Life sciences
Media and entertainment
Mining and metals
Oil and gas
Power and utilities
Provider care
Real estate
Retail and wholesale
Technology
Telecommunications

Selected Services

Assurance and Advisory
  Actuarial services
  Audits
  Accounting advisory
  Business risk services
  Internal audit
  Real estate advisory services
  Technology and security risk services
Emerging Growth Companies
  Corporate finance services
  Mergers and acquisitions advisory
  Operational consulting
  Strategic advisory
  Transactions advisory
Human Capital
  Compensation and benefits consulting
  Cost optimization and risk management
  Transaction support services
Law
  Corporate and M&A
  Employment
  Finance
  Information technology services
  Intellectual property
  International trade and anti-trust
  Litigation and arbitration
  Real estate
Tax
  Global tax operations
  Indirect tax
  International tax
Transactions
  Capital management
  Corporate development advisory
  Financial and business modeling
  M&A advisory
  Post-deal advisory
  Strategic finance
  Transaction management
  Valuation

COMPETITORS

Baker Tilly International
BDO International
Crowe Horwath International
Deloitte
Grant Thornton International
KPMG
Moore Stephens International
PKF International
PricewaterhouseCoopers

HISTORICAL FINANCIALS

Company Type: Private

Income Statement

FYE: June 30

	REVENUE ($ mil.)	NET INCOME ($ mil.)	NET PROFIT MARGIN	EMPLOYEES
6/09	21,440	—	—	144,441
6/08	24,500	—	—	135,000
6/07	21,160	—	—	121,000
6/06	18,400	—	—	114,000
6/05	16,902	—	—	106,650
Annual Growth	**6.1%**	**—**	**—**	**7.9%**

Revenue History

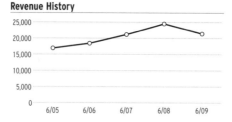

Estée Lauder

The firm's Estée and Bobbi are counted among some of the closest friends to women worldwide. Estée Lauder sells cosmetics, fragrances, and skin care products, with brands including upscale Estée Lauder and Clinique, professional Bobbi Brown *essentials,* and luxurious Tom Ford Collection. Its lines are sold in department stores, company stores, and by specialty retailers, as well as online. The firm operates a chain of freestanding retail stores (primarily for its M.A.C, Origins, and Aveda brands). The founding Lauder family controls about 75% of its voting shares. CEO Fabrizio Freda, a veteran of Procter & Gamble, joined the firm in 2008.

Freda, who'd been serving as president and COO of Estée Lauder, took over the chief executive's office in July 2009. He succeeded William Lauder, who became executive chairman of the cosmetics maker, completing a succession plan announced in 2007. Previously, Freda was president of global snacks at P&G and logged more than 20 years at the consumer products company. During half of his tenure there, he worked in P&G's health and beauty care division and had a two-year stint heading up marketing and strategy for Gucci SpA in the late 1980s.

With its products available in more than 140 countries, Estée Lauder is a world leader in upscale personal care products. It captures nearly half of all US prestige cosmetics sales. Nevertheless, the downturn in consumer spending spurred the beauty company in early 2009 to announce a four-year turnaround plan, which will eliminate 2,000 jobs by 2011.

Despite its ranking and market share, Estée Lauder and the Lauder family have been working to breathe new life into the company's flagship brand. In 2005 the company partnered with former Gucci Group creative director and fashion talent Tom Ford to develop a Tom Ford-inspired Estée Lauder line.

The company has expanded its customer base to include younger shoppers by peddling the M.A.C and Clinique cosmetics lines. It aims to attract additional clientele through its 2010 acquisition of Los Angeles-based Smashbox Beauty Cosmetics. Founded by the great-grandsons of legendary makeup artist Max Factor, Smashbox offers studio-inspired prestige cosmetics that are sold in high-end and specialty retail outlets.

Estée Lauder and Sean John, the private company formed by Sean "Diddy" Combs, co-developed a line of fragrances under the Sean John name.

The firm has been gradually shifting business from department stores to its own stores and other outlets. Estée Lauder now has more than 660 free-standing retail stores.

Estée Lauder is also jockeying for position in the doctor-based skin care arena. The firm operates the Clinique Skin Wellness Center through a partnership with Weill Cornell Medical College. The beauty company boasts The Estée Lauder Companies Innovation Institute located in Shanghai, China. The purpose of the institute is to study topical botanicals and synthetic materials for safety and efficacy, as well as study human skin in relation to the environment.

HISTORY

Estée Lauder (then Josephine Esther Mentzer) started her beauty career by selling skin care products formulated by her Hungarian uncle, John Schotz, during the 1930s. Eventually she packaged and peddled her variations of his formulas, which included face cream and a cleansing oil.

With the help of her husband, Joseph Lauder, she set up her first office in Queens, New York, in 1944, and added lipstick, eye shadow, and face powder to the line. Joseph oversaw production, and Estée sold her wares to beauty salons and department stores, using samples and gifts to win customers. Throughout the 1950s Estée traveled cross-country, at first to sell her line to high-profile department stores such as Neiman Marcus, I. Magnin, and Saks, and later to train saleswomen in these stores.

Estée Lauder created her first fragrance, Youth Dew perfume and bath oil, in 1953. In the late 1950s US cosmetics firms introduced European skin care lines with scientific names and supposedly advanced skin repair properties. Estée Lauder's contribution was Re-Nutriv cream, which sold for $115 a pound in 1960. The cream's advertising campaign established the sophisticated "Lauder look" — an image that Estée herself cultivated.

In 1964 Estée Lauder introduced Aramis, a fragrance for men, and in 1968, with the help of a *Vogue* editor, it launched Clinique, a hypoallergenic skin care line. In 1972 Estée's son Leonard became president; Estée remained CEO.

Estée Lauder created the Prescriptives skin care and makeup line for young professional women in 1979. Leonard was named CEO in 1983. By 1988 the company had captured a third of the US market in prestige cosmetics.

Estée Lauder unveiled its Origins botanical cosmetics line in 1990. The company launched the All Skins cosmetics line in 1991 and in 1994 bought a controlling stake in hip Make-Up Art Cosmetics (M.A.C).

Leonard became chairman in 1995. The company's IPO that year was structured to allow Estée and her son Ronald (previously an unsuccessful candidate for mayor of New York) to avoid a potential $95 million tax bill (inspiring a 1997 revision of the federal tax law). Filling out a busy year, Estée Lauder acquired the Bobbi Brown *essentials* line of cosmetics, bought botanical beauty products concern Aveda for $300 million (broadening its distribution into hair salons), and entered the mass market with its purchase of Sassaby (*jane* cosmetics, which was sold in early 2004).

In 1999 Estée Lauder bought rapidly growing Jo Malone Limited, a London-based seller of some 200 skin care and fragrance products. Company president Fred Langhammer succeeded Leonard Lauder as CEO in 2000; Leonard remained chairman. Also in 2000 Estée Lauder bought a majority interest in Bumble and bumble, a hair salon and products company.

In 2002 Estée Lauder restructured by outsourcing gloss.com and closing some distribution channels, including the remaining in-store Tommy Hilfiger shops.

Estée Lauder bought Paris-based Laboratories Darphin in 2003, adding the high-end Darphin skin care line to its portfolio. Also in 2003 Estée

Lauder acquired the Rodan + Fields skin care line, bringing with it the Proactiv skin care line. It sold the line back to its owners in 2007.

Langhammer retired and assumed the role of chairman of global affairs in July 2004, when William Lauder was promoted to CEO. Also that year company founder Estée Lauder died of a heart attack at the age of 97.

EXECUTIVES

Chairman: William P. Lauder, age 49, $6,060,811 total compensation
Chairman Emeritus: Leonard A. Lauder, age 77
President, CEO, and Director: Fabrizio Freda, age 52, $5,628,390 total compensation
EVP Global Human Resources: Amy DiGeso, age 58
EVP and CFO: Richard W. Kunes, age 57, $2,530,360 total compensation
EVP and General Counsel: Sara E. Moss, age 63
SVP Corporate Marketing and Diversity: Susan Akkad
EVP Global Supply Chain: Gregory (Greg) Polcer, age 55
EVP Global Research, Development and Product Innovation: Harvey Gedeon, age 67
EVP Global Communications: Alexandra C. Trower, age 46
SVP: Evelyn H. Lauder, age 74
SVP Creative Development, Estée Lauder: Donald Robertson
SVP Global Communications: Marianne Diorio
SVP Global Strategic Modernization Initiative (SMI): Christopher Wood, age 45
SVP Global Creative Directions and Director: Aerin Lauder, age 39
SVP Global Product Innovation: Anne Carullo
SVP Research and Development, Estée Lauder Worldwide: Daniel H. Maes
SVP, Deputy General Counsel, and Secretary: Spencer G. Smul
SVP Corporate Marketing: Georgia Garinois-Melenikiotou
SVP Corporate Administration: Deborah Krulewitch
Executive Director, Investor Relations: Eleanor F. Powell
Group President, International: Cedric Prouvé, age 49, $3,554,399 total compensation
Director; Global President and General Manager, Origins and Ojon: Jane Lauder, age 37
Chairman, Clinique Laboratories: Ronald S. Lauder, age 66
Auditors: KPMG LLP

LOCATIONS

HQ: The Estée Lauder Companies Inc.
767 5th Ave., New York, NY 10153
Phone: 212-572-4200
Web: www.elcompanies.com

2009 Sales

	$ mil.	% of total
Americas	3,421.2	47
Europe, Middle East & Africa	2,611.3	35
Asia/Pacific	1,299.4	18
Adjustments	(8.1)	—
Total	**7,323.8**	**100**

PRODUCTS/OPERATIONS

2009 Sales

	$ mil.	% of total
Skin care	2,886.0	38
Makeup	2,830.9	38
Fragrance	1,150.9	18
Hair care	402.4	5
Other	61.7	1
Adjustments	(8.1)	—
Total	**7,323.8**	**100**

Selected Brands

Aramis
Aveda
Beyond Paradise
Bobbi Brown
Bumble and bumble
Clinique
Darphin
DKNY
Donna Karan (licensed)
Estée Lauder
Jo Malone
La Mer
M.A.C
Michael Kors Fragrances
Origins
pleasures
Prescriptives
Rare Harvest
Smashbox
Tawaka
Tommy Hilfiger (licensed)

COMPETITORS

Alberto-Culver
Alliance Boots
Alticor
Avon
Bare Escentuals
BeautiControl
Beiersdorf
BeneFit Cosmetics
Body Shop
Bristol-Myers Squibb
Canderm Pharma
Chanel
Clarins
Coty Inc.
Dana Classic Fragrances
DFS Group
Elizabeth Arden Inc
The Gap
Helen of Troy
Hydron
Inter Parfums
Joh. A. Benckiser
Johnson & Johnson
Kao
Kiehl's
Limited Brands
L'Oréal
LVMH
Mary Kay
Neiman Marcus
Nu Skin
Perfumania Holdings
PPR SA
Procter & Gamble
Revlon
Sephora USA
Shiseido
Starwood Hotels & Resorts

HISTORICAL FINANCIALS

Company Type: Public

Income Statement

				FYE: June 30
	REVENUE ($ mil.)	NET INCOME ($ mil.)	NET PROFIT MARGIN	EMPLOYEES
6/09	7,324	218	3.0%	31,300
6/08	7,911	474	6.0%	32,000
6/07	7,038	449	6.4%	28,500
6/06	6,464	244	3.8%	26,200
6/05	6,336	406	6.4%	23,700
Annual Growth	**3.7%**	**(14.4%)**	**—**	**7.2%**

2009 Year-End Financials

Debt ratio: 84.6%
Return on equity: 13.3%
Cash ($ mil.): 865
Current ratio: 2.00
Long-term debt ($ mil.): 1,388

No. of shares (mil.): 199
Dividends
  Yield: 1.7%
  Payout: 50.0%
Market value ($ mil.): 6,502

Stock History

NYSE: EL

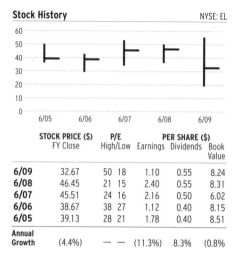

	STOCK PRICE ($) FY Close	P/E High/Low		PER SHARE ($) Earnings	Dividends	Book Value
6/09	32.67	50	18	1.10	0.55	8.24
6/08	46.45	21	15	2.40	0.55	8.31
6/07	45.51	24	16	2.16	0.50	6.02
6/06	38.67	38	27	1.12	0.40	8.15
6/05	39.13	28	21	1.78	0.40	8.51
Annual Growth	(4.4%)	—	—	(11.3%)	8.3%	(0.8%)

Esterline Technologies

Esterline Technologies has a trio of aerospace, defense, and commercial business segments: Avionics & Controls, Sensors & Systems, and Advanced Materials. Avionics & Controls makes interface systems (switches, indicators, keyboards, displays, GPS systems) for aircraft and military vehicles, communications systems, and medical equipment. Sensors & Systems operations include temperature and pressure sensors, as well as power switching, data communications, and fluid control devices. Advanced Materials makes elastomer products and, through the defense group, ordnance and military countermeasures. Esterline Technologies also offers aftermarket parts and service, which have higher sales margins than OEM sales.

The company took advantage of the global economic recession by enacting cost-saving measures to generate more operational efficiency in preparation for the market turnaround. After spending higher-than-industry-average on research and technology from 2005 to 2008, which resulted in Esterline's prominent foothold in high-profile programs, the company reduced that expenditure in 2009 and is continuing the reduction through 2010.

Some of the high-profile programs include the use of Esterline's avionics systems on the Joint Strike Fighter, the Hawker Beechcraft T-6B Texan Trainer (avionics computer and upfront panel), the Trent XWB (30 separate components and sensors package), the Boeing 787 Dreamliner (pilot controls and cockpit environmental sensors), the Airbus A-350, and the UH-60 Black Hawk (cockpit retrofit program). Esterline's Avionics & Controls division provides components to every Boeing commercial aircraft currently in production.

Additionally, Esterline increased production capacity during 2009 by upgrading several of its US operations and making strategic acquisitions

that positively impacted the year's results. In 2009 the company purchased UK-based Racal Acoustics for about $172 million; Racal makes ruggedized communications equipment such as protective headphones for military applications. In 2008 Esterline picked up Nylon Molding Corporation (NMC) Group, which brought specialized fasteners for aviation applications to Esterline's product portfolio. CMC Electronics (aerospace and defense avionics), a $335 million acquisition in 2007, yielded a dynamic financial performance in 2009.

Part of the company's strategy also included divesting some noncore assets. It sold Traxsys Input Products (sensors), as well as UK motion technology maker Muirhead Aerospace in 2008. Muirhead was sold to AMETEK, an electrical motor and monitoring equipment firm.

The company has manufacturing plants in Canada, China, France, Germany, Mexico, and the UK; there are 12 facilities in the US. Esterline gets about 30% of sales from the US government and the US Department of Defense.

HISTORY

Esterline Technologies Corporation was formed in 1967 as Boyar-Schultz. The company adopted its current name later that year after it merged with Esterline Angus Instrument. Esterline went public in 1968.

Esterline soon began a major period of expansion through acquisitions, including Federal Products (industrial automation, 1969), Auxitrol (precision measuring devices, 1972), and Excellon Automation (drilling systems, 1977). By the end of 1986, Esterline had acquired some 20 companies.

In 1987 Esterline turned over its operations to a management team from aerospace company Criton Technologies (the two shared a major investor, Dyson-Kissner-Moran, or DKM). The new management moved Esterline's headquarters from Darien, Connecticut, to Bellevue, Washington. Esterline bought back DKM's shares in its business in 1989. That year Wendell Hurlbut was named president and CEO.

Esterline encompassed 22 subsidiaries in six countries by 1990. Following a 1993 restructuring, the company began selling its smaller businesses, including Republic Electronics. It sold its Angus Electronics subsidiary to Thermo Instruments in 1997; later that year it made three strategic acquisitions, including hydraulic controls manufacturer Fluid Regulators, to bolster its aircraft offerings.

The company continued to expand through acquisitions in 1998. Among its seven purchases made that year were Kirkhill Rubber (aerospace components), Memtron Technologies (membrane switches used in instrumentation), and Korry Electronics (lighted switches and panels for the aerospace market).

Robert Cremin, a 22-year Esterline veteran, succeeded Hurlbut as CEO in 1999; Hurlbut remained chairman. That year the company opened an office in Hong Kong to boost sales in Asia. Esterline sold its Federal Products (automotive metrology technology) subsidiary, and later in 1999 it acquired privately held Advanced Input Devices (custom keyboards and multifunction data-input subsystems) and UK-based Muirhead Aerospace (motion-control devices, sold in 2008).

In 2001 Esterline received a contract potentially worth $40 million to produce combustible cases for US Army 155mm artillery rounds. The next year the company paid about $68 million

for BAE SYSTEMS' Electronic Warfare Passive Expendables Division, a maker of defensive countermeasures such as chaff. Chaff confuses radar and flares, which draw off heat-seeking weapons. In 2003 Esterline acquired Weston Group (speed, temperature, and rotational sensors) and BVR Aero Precision Corporation (gears and data concentrators).

Esterline in 2004 acquired Leach Holding Company, a maker of relays, power distribution assemblies, and switching devices, in a deal worth about $145 million. Acquisitions continued in 2005 with the addition of secure military communication product manufacturer Palomar Products, Inc., which enhanced the company's Avionics & Controls segment.

In 2005 the company paid about $120 million for UK-based Darchem, a maker of thermally engineered components such as insulation for jet exhaust ducting, nacelle and thrust reverser units, as well as environmental control ducting and heat shields. Darchem, which had annual sales of about $70 million, became part of Esterline's Advanced Materials segment.

The company bought UK-based Wallop Defense Systems for about $59 million in 2006. Wallop, a maker of military countermeasure flares, became part of the Esterline Defense Group.

EXECUTIVES

Chairman: Robert W. Cremin, age 69,
$6,731,506 total compensation
President, CEO, and Director:
R. Bradley (Brad) Lawrence, age 62,
$1,142,672 total compensation
SVP: Frank E. Houston, age 58,
$1,380,675 total compensation
Group VP: Albert S. Yost, age 44
VP Strategy and Technology: Stephen R. Larson, age 65,
$2,339,473 total compensation
VP, CFO, Secretary, and Treasurer: Robert D. George,
age 53, $1,915,641 total compensation
VP Human Resources: Marcia J. Mason, age 58
President, Esterline Communications Systems and Palomar Products: Kevin Moschetti
President, CMC Electronics: Gregory A. (Greg) Yeldon
Director Corporate Communications: Brian D. Keogh
Auditors: Ernst & Young LLP

LOCATIONS

HQ: Esterline Technologies Corporation
   500 108th Ave. NE, Ste. 1500, Bellevue, WA 98004
Phone: 425-453-9400   **Fax:** 425-453-2916
Web: www.esterline.com

2009 Sales

	$ mil.	% of total
US	809.4	57
UK	242.8	17
Canada	222.3	16
France	175.6	12
Other countries	32.0	2
Adjustments	(56.7)	(4)
Total	**1,425.4**	**100**

PRODUCTS/OPERATIONS

2009 Sales

	$ mil.	% of total
Avionics & Controls	672.8	47
Advanced Materials	412.9	29
Sensors & Systems	339.7	24
Total	**1,425.4**	**100**

2009 Sales by Sector

	% of total
Aerospace/defense	45
Commercial	40
Industrial	15
Total	**100**

Selected Products

Advanced Materials
Chaff
Combustible ammunition components
Elastomer products
Flares
Igniter tubes
Molded fiber cartridge cases (120mm tank rounds and 60mm, 81mm, and 120mm mortar rounds)
Mortar increments
Thermal insulation

Avionics & Controls
Electronic flight management systems
Enhanced vision systems
Global positioning systems
Head-up displays
Keyboards
Lighted indicators
Lighted push-button and rotary switches
Panels and displays

Sensors & Systems
Fluid control components
Micro-motors
Motion-control sensors
Pressure-sensing devices
Temperature-sensing devices

Selected Brands

Advanced Materials
Armtec
Darchem
Hytek
Kirkhill-TA
NMC Aerospace
Wallop

Avionics & Controls
Advanced Input Systems
Avista
BVR
CMC Electronics
Korry
LRE Medical
Mason
Memtron
Palomar
Racal Acoustics

Sensors & Systems
Auxitrol
Leach
Norwich Aero
Pressure Systems
Weston

COMPETITORS

AMETEK	Israel Aerospace Industries
BNS Holding	L. S. Starrett
Bose	Labfacility
Chemring	Meggitt
Doncasters	Renishaw
Ducommun	Rockwell Collins
Eaton	Sypris Solutions
Electro Scientific	Telephonics
Industries	Thales
EMS Technologies	Tyco
GE Aviation	Ultra Electronics
Goodrich Corp.	Universal Avionics
Honeywell Aerospace	Yokogawa Electric

HISTORICAL FINANCIALS

Company Type: Public

Income Statement

FYE: October 31

	REVENUE ($ mil.)	NET INCOME ($ mil.)	NET PROFIT MARGIN	EMPLOYEES
10/09	1,425	120	8.4%	8,901
10/08	1,483	121	8.1%	9,699
10/07	1,267	92	7.3%	9,361
10/06	972	56	5.7%	8,150
10/05	835	58	6.9%	6,700
Annual Growth	**14.3%**	**19.9%**	**—**	**7.4%**

2009 Year-End Financials

Debt ratio: 41.5%
Return on equity: 10.5%
Cash ($ mil.): 177
Current ratio: 2.71
Long-term debt ($ mil.): 520

No. of shares (mil.): 30
Dividends
  Yield: 0.0%
  Payout: —
Market value ($ mil.): 1,264

Stock History

NYSE: ESL

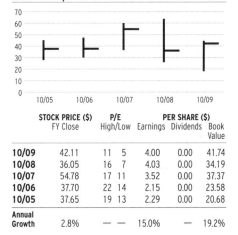

	STOCK PRICE ($) FY Close	P/E High/Low		PER SHARE ($) Earnings	Dividends	Book Value
10/09	42.11	11	5	4.00	0.00	41.74
10/08	36.05	16	7	4.03	0.00	34.19
10/07	54.78	17	11	3.52	0.00	37.37
10/06	37.70	22	14	2.15	0.00	23.58
10/05	37.65	19	13	2.29	0.00	20.68
Annual Growth	**2.8%**	**—**	**—**	**15.0%**	**—**	**19.2%**

E*TRADE Financial

E*TRADE wants you to use its services for E*VERYTHING financial. A top online brokerage, the company has more than 2.5 million retail account holders who can trade stock over the Internet (the majority of transactions) and by phone. It also offers mutual funds, options, fixed income products, exchange-traded funds, and portfolio management services. For corporate clients, the company performs market making, trade clearing, and employee stock option plan administration services. Subsidiary E*TRADE Bank offers deposits, savings, and credit cards online, as well as at some 30 financial centers in major US cities; customers can transfer funds between their banking and brokerage accounts in real-time.

E*TRADE's decision to move more strongly into banking — it aimed to triple its loan business — could not have come at a worse time, as the subprime credit crisis struck down banks and lenders around the world. As a result, in 2007 an affiliate of Citadel Investment Group provided E*TRADE with a $2.5 billion cash pick-me-up. The company reshuffled its senior management team as well. But E*TRADE suffered considerable losses tied to its home loan portfolio.

The company refocused its efforts on its retail customer business and has shed noncore operations. It is hoarding reserves to counter loan losses and exited both its wholesale lending and direct lending operations. The company also shuttered its institutional brokerage business. To raise additional cash it sold its Canadian operations to Scotiabank for more than $440 million in 2008. The following year it raised some $733 million in three separate stock offerings and exchanged another $1.7 billion in debt for convertible debentures.

E*TRADE also decided to exit its international channels focusing on local trades and instead concentrate on providing cross-border trades of US securities. It arranged to sell its local German, Nordic, and UK operations. The company currently maintains about a dozen retail brokerage websites in Europe, the Middle East, and the Pacific Rim, in addition to the US.

Donald Layton retired as chairman and CEO at the end of 2009. Director Robert Druskin succeeded Layton as chairman, and Steven Freiberg became CEO. Freiberg was formerly a co-CEO of Citigroup's global consumer group.

HISTORY

In 1982 physicist William Porter created Trade Plus, an electronic brokerage service for stockbrokers; clients included Charles Schwab & Co. and Fidelity Brokerage Services. A decade later subsidiary E*TRADE Securities became CompuServe's first online securities trader.

In 1996 E*TRADE moved from the institutional side to retail when it launched its website. Christos Cotsakos (a Vietnam and FedEx veteran) became CEO and took the firm public. But there were problems: E*TRADE covered $1.7 million in customer losses and added backup systems after computer failure stymied user access. In 1997 it formed alliances with America Online and BANK ONE and ended the year with 225,000 accounts.

The firm began to position itself globally in 1997 and 1998, opening sites for Australian, Canadian, German, Israeli, and Japanese customers. It offered its first IPO (Sportline USA) in 1997. Volume grew as Internet trading increased, but technical glitches dogged E*TRADE. In 1999 day trading became fashionable and the company began running ads promoting prudent trading to counter criticism that online trading fosters a get-rich-quick mentality.

The company also continued to add services. In 1999 it teamed with Garage.com to offer affluent clients venture capital investments in young companies and launched online investment bank E*OFFERING with former Robertson Stephens & Co. chairman Sanford Robertson. (E*TRADE sold its stake in the bank to Wit Soundview — which later became SoundView Technology Group — the next year.) It also bought TIR Holdings, which executes and settles multi-currency securities transactions.

Retail banking was a major focus in 2000. The company bought Telebanc Financial (now E*TRADE Financial), owner of Telebank, an online bank with more than 100,000 depositors, and started E*TRADE Bank, which offers retail banking products on the E*TRADE website. To provide clients with "real-world" access to their money, it bought Card Capture Services, an operator of more than 9,000 ATMs across the US.

Continuing to expand its global reach, E*TRADE bought the part of its E*TRADE UK joint venture it didn't already own; acquired Canadian firm VERSUS Technologies, a provider of electronic trading services; and teamed with UBS Warburg to allow non-US investors to buy US securities without needing to trade in dollars. Later its E*Trade International Capital announced plans to offer IPOs to European investors.

In 2001 E*TRADE entered consumer lending when it bought online mortgage originator LoansDirect (now E*TRADE Mortgage). Also that year the company bought online brokerage Web Street, and moved to the NYSE. In late 2002 E*TRADE Bank purchased Ganis Credit Corp. (a US-based unit of Germany's Deutsche Bank) to boost its consumer finance business.

E*TRADE purchased the online trading operations of Tradescape in mid-2002. The deal, which cost E*TRADE $280 million, was hashed out the previous April — just days after rival Ameritrade announced its acquisition of online brokerage Datek.

Cotsakos resigned in early 2003, days after the company issued a gloomy forecast (he also had been criticized for his 2001 pay of $80 million, although he subsequently gave up about $20 million). He was replaced by company president Mitch Caplan, who had been viewed as instrumental in the company's effort to integrate brokerage and banking operations.

In 2005 E*TRADE bought US-based online brokerage Harris*direct* from Bank of Montreal, as well as the former J.P. Morgan Invest unit BrownCo, which served experienced online traders. The acquisitions expanded its client base and helped the company to keep pace with TD Ameritrade (the result of the 2006 merger of rivals Ameritrade and TD Waterhouse).

E*TRADE built its wealth management operations in 2005 and 2006 by purchasing several money managers, including Boston-area investment advisory firm Kobren Insight Management.

After E*TRADE got snared in the subprime mortgage crisis in 2007, Caplan stepped down. He was replaced in 2008 by former JPMorgan exec Donald Layton.

EXECUTIVES

Chairman: Robert A. (Bob) Druskin, age 62
CEO and Director: Steven J. Freiberg, age 53
EVP and CFO: Bruce P. Nolop, age 59,
$2,296,475 total compensation
EVP and Chief Risk Officer: Paul Brandow
EVP and Chief Human Resource Officer: Karen Wall
EVP and Chief Marketing Officer:
Nicholas A. (Nick) Utton, age 53,
$3,196,635 total compensation
EVP; President, E*TRADE Bank:
Robert V. (Bob) Burton
EVP and CIO: Gregory (Greg) Framke, age 50,
$3,574,289 total compensation
EVP; President, E*TRADE Securities:
Michael J. Curcio, age 48,
$4,044,599 total compensation
EVP International: Mathias Helleu
EVP, Secretary, and General Counsel: Karl A. Roessner
VP Interactive and Alliance Marketing:
Alison Mittelstadt
Chairman, E*TRADE Futures: John F. (Jack) Sandner, age 68
Auditors: Deloitte & Touche LLP

LOCATIONS

HQ: E*TRADE Financial Corporation
135 E. 57th St., New York, NY 10022
Phone: 646-521-4300   **Fax:** 212-826-2803
Web: www.etrade.com

PRODUCTS/OPERATIONS

2009 Sales

	$ mil.	% of total
Operating interest income		
Balance sheet management	1,623.6	44
Traditional investing	1,007.3	28
Eliminations	(798.3)	—
Commissions	548.0	15
Service charges & fees	192.5	5
Net gains on loans & securities	169.1	5
Principal transactions	88.1	2
Net impairment	(89.1)	—
Other	47.8	1
Total	**2,789.0**	**100**

COMPETITORS

Charles Schwab
FMR
Morgan Stanley
Scottrade
ShareBuilder
Siebert Financial
TD Ameritrade
UBS Financial Services

HISTORICAL FINANCIALS

Company Type: Public

Income Statement

FYE: December 31

	REVENUE ($ mil.)	NET INCOME ($ mil.)	NET PROFIT MARGIN	EMPLOYEES
12/09	2,789	(1,298)	—	3,100
12/08	3,149	(512)	—	3,249
12/07	2,441	(1,442)	—	3,800
12/06	3,922	629	16.0%	4,100
12/05	2,637	429	16.3%	3,400
Annual Growth	**1.4%**	**—**	**—**	**(2.3%)**

2009 Year-End Financials

Debt ratio: 138.8%
Return on equity: —
Cash ($ mil.): 3,483
Current ratio: —
Long-term debt ($ mil.): 5,206

No. of shares (mil.): 221
Dividends
  Yield: —
  Payout: —
Market value ($ mil.): 3,885

Stock History

NASDAQ (GS): ETFC

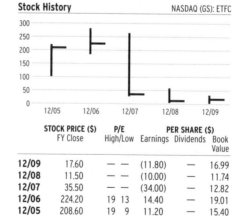

	STOCK PRICE ($) FY Close	P/E High/Low		PER SHARE ($) Earnings	Dividends	Book Value
12/09	17.60	— —		(11.80)	—	16.99
12/08	11.50	— —		(10.00)	—	11.74
12/07	35.50	— —		(34.00)	—	12.82
12/06	224.20	19	13	14.40	—	19.01
12/05	208.60	19	9	11.20	—	15.40
Annual Growth	**(46.1%)**	— —		**—**	**—**	**2.5%**

E. W. Scripps

You might say this media company tries to be appealing to both newspaper readers and television viewers. The E. W. Scripps Company is a venerable newspaper publisher with a portfolio of more than 15 dailies, including *The Commercial Appeal* (Memphis, Tennessee), the *Knoxville News Sentinel* (Tennessee), and the *Ventura County Star* (California). Scripps also owns 10 local TV stations, most of which are affiliated with broadcast networks ABC and NBC. In addition, subsidiaries Scripps Howard News Service and United Media distribute syndicated news and other content, including columnists, editorial cartoons, and such comic strips as *Dilbert* and *Peanuts*. The Scripps family controls the company through various trusts.

Like other ad-supported media businesses, E. W. Scripps struggled during the recession as advertisers reined in their spending. Its newspapers, meanwhile, are losing readers in parallel with that industry's long, slow decline. In response, the company has had to take difficult actions to cut expenses, including wage and staff reductions at its papers.

E. W. Scripps has also disposed of some business in order to focus on its core media operations. In 2010 the company sold its United Media Licensing division to Iconix Brand Group for about $175 million. The deal included such properties as the *Peanuts* characters, Dilbert, and Fancy Nancy. The United Media unit licensed the characters for apparel and other products; United Media continues to syndicate the *Peanuts* comic strip.

The sale of the licensing business comes a year after E. W. Scripps was forced to shut down some of its newspapers. It ceased publication of the *Rocky Mountain News*, which had been operated through joint venture Denver Newspaper Agency (DNA). Scripps later sold its 50% stake in DNA to *Denver Post* owner MediaNews Group. Other papers that fell victim to the harsh economics included *The Albuquerque Tribune* (New Mexico) and the *Cincinnati Post*.

E. W. Scripps was previously involved in the cable television business until 2008 when it spun off Scripps Networks Interactive as a separate, publicly-traded company. Scripps Networks oversees such channels as Home & Garden Television (HGTV) and the Food Network (70%-owned). Scripps Networks had accounted for more than half the company's revenue.

HISTORY

Edward Willis "E. W." Scripps launched a newspaper empire in 1878 with his creation of *The Penny Press* in Cleveland. While adding to his string of inexpensive newspapers, Scripps demonstrated his fondness for economy by shunning "extras" such as toilet paper and pencils for his employees.

In 1907 Scripps gave the Associated Press a new rival, combining three wire services to form United Press. E. W. Scripps' health began deteriorating in the 1920s, and Roy Howard was named chairman. Howard's contribution to the burgeoning media enterprise soon was acknowledged when the company's name was changed to the Scripps Howard League. E. W. Scripps died in 1926, leaving a newspaper chain second in size only to Hearst.

In the 1930s Scripps made a foray into radio, buying WCPO (Cincinnati) and KNOX (Knoxville, Tennessee). Roy Howard placed his son Jack in charge of Scripps' radio holdings; under Jack's leadership, Scripps branched into TV. Its first TV station, Cleveland's WEWS, began broadcasting in 1947. Scripps also made Charlie Brown a household name when it launched the *Peanuts* comic strip in 1950. By the time Charles Scripps (E. W. Scripps' grandson) became chairman and Jack Howard was appointed president in 1953, the company had amassed 19 newspapers and a handful of radio and TV stations.

United Press merged with Hearst's International News Service in 1958 to become United Press International (UPI). In 1963 Scripps took its broadcasting holdings public as Scripps Howard Broadcasting Company (Scripps retained controlling interest). Scripps Howard Broadcasting expanded its TV station portfolio in the 1970s and 1980s, buying KJRH (Tulsa, Oklahoma; 1971), KSHB (Kansas City; 1977), KNXV (Phoenix; 1985), WFTS (Tampa; 1986), and WXYZ (Detroit; 1986).

With UPI facing mounting losses, Scripps sold the news service in 1982. Under leadership of chief executive Lawrence Leser, Scripps began streamlining, jettisoning extraneous investments and refocusing on its core business lines. In 1988 after decades of family ownership, the company went public as The E. W. Scripps Company (the Scripps family retained a controlling interest).

In 1994 Scripps Howard Broadcasting merged back into E. W. Scripps Company. That year Scripps branched into cable TV when its Home & Garden Television network went on the air. Former newspaper editor William Burleigh became CEO in 1996. Scripps' 1997 purchase of the newspaper and broadcast operations of Harte-Hanks marked the largest acquisition in its history. Scripps promptly traded Harte-Hanks' broadcasting operations for a controlling interest in the Food Network.

Scripps sold television production unit Scripps Howard Productions in 1998. The company sold its Dallas Community Newspaper Group in 1999. In 2000 Scripps' financially struggling *Rocky Mountain News* entered into a joint operating agreement with rival *The Denver Post* (owned by MediaNews). The Justice Department approved the agreement in 2001. Scripps launched cable channel Fine Living in 2002 aimed at affluent households. (Fine Living was rebranded as the Cooking Channel in 2010.)

In late 2002 the company bought a 70% stake in home shopping network company Summit America Television (owner of the Shop At Home cable network) for $49 million. It bought the remaining 30% of the company in 2004.

Scripps made a foray into online shopping when it acquired comparison shopping site Shopzilla in 2005. The following year Scripps bought UK-based shopping site uSwitch.

The Shop At Home network came to an end in 2006 when Scripps shut down the network after several years of nothing but losses at the channel. Scripps later sold its five Shop At Home affiliate television stations to Multicultural Television Broadcasting for $170 million.

Former chairman Charles Scripps died in 2007. At the end of that year, the company shuttered the *Cincinnati Post*, and the following year it ceased publication of *The Albuquerque Tribune*. It shuttered the *Rocky Mountain News* early in 2009 after attempts to sell the money-losing paper failed.

EXECUTIVES

Chairwoman: Nackey E. Scagliotti, age 64
President, CEO, and Director:
 Richard A. (Rich) Boehne, age 53,
 $2,164,983 total compensation
SVP, CFO, and Corporate Treasurer:
 Timothy E. (Tim) Stautberg, age 47,
 $830,148 total compensation
SVP Newspapers: Mark G. Contreras, age 48,
 $905,925 total compensation
SVP Television: Brian G. Lawlor, age 42
SVP and Chief Legal Officer: William (Bill) Appleton,
 age 61, $762,131 total compensation
SVP Human Resources: Lisa A. Knutson, age 44,
 $717,709 total compensation
VP Content, Scripps Newspaper: Chris Doyle
VP and CIO: Robert A. (Bob) Carson, age 54
VP and Controller: Douglas F. Lyons, age 52
VP Strategic Planning and Development:
 Robin A. Davis, age 41
VP Audit and Compliance: Michael T. Hales, age 45
**VP, Chief Compliance and Ethics Officer, and
 Secretary:** Mary Denise Kuprionis, age 54
VP Corporate Communications and Investor Relations:
 Timothy (Tim) King, age 45
President and CEO, United Media: Douglas R. Stern
President and CEO, The Denver Newspaper Agency:
 Harry M. Whipple, age 60
**President, Scripps Howard Supply; President and CEO,
 Media Procurement Services:** Sharon Hite
Auditors: Deloitte & Touche LLP

LOCATIONS

HQ: The E. W. Scripps Company
 312 Walnut St., Cincinnati, OH 45202
Phone: 513-977-3000   **Fax:** 513-977-3721
Web: www.scripps.com

PRODUCTS/OPERATIONS

2009 Sales

	$ mil.	% of total
Advertising	565.7	71
Circulation	115.9	14
Licensing	69.9	9
Other	50.9	6
Total	**802.4**	**100**

2009 Sales

	$ mil.	% of total
Newspapers	455.2	57
Television	255.2	32
Licensing & other	92.0	11
Total	**802.4**	**100**

Selected Operations

Newspapers
 Abilene Reporter-News (Texas)
 Anderson Independent-Mail (South Carolina)
 Corpus Christi Caller-Times (Texas)
 Evansville Courier & Press (Indiana)
 Ft. Pierce Tribune (Florida)
 Henderson Gleaner (Kentucky)
 Kitsap Sun (Washington)
 Knoxville News Sentinel (Tennessee)
 Memphis Commercial Appeal (Tennessee)
 Naples Daily News (Florida)
 Redding Record-Searchlight (California)
 San Angelo Standard-Times (Texas)
 Stuart News (Florida)
 Ventura County Star (California)
 Wichita Falls Times Record News (Texas)

Television stations
 KJRH (NBC; Tulsa, OK)
 KMCI (Ind; Lawrence, KS)
 KNXV (ABC, Phoenix)
 KSHB (NBC, Kansas City)
 WCPO (ABC, Cincinnati)
 WEWS (ABC, Cleveland)
 WFTS (ABC, Tampa)
 WMAR (ABC, Baltimore)
 WPTV (NBC; West Palm Beach, FL)
 WXYZ (ABC, Detroit)

COMPETITORS

A. H. Belo	Media General
Andrews McMeel Universal	Meredith Corporation
CBS	New York Times
Fox Entertainment	Newport Television
Freedom Communications	Raycom Media
Gannett	Sinclair Broadcast Group
Hearst Corporation	Times Publishing Co.
Local TV	Tribune Company
McClatchy Company	Washington Post

HISTORICAL FINANCIALS

Company Type: Public

Income Statement

FYE: December 31

	REVENUE ($ mil.)	NET INCOME ($ mil.)	NET PROFIT MARGIN	EMPLOYEES
12/09	802	(210)	—	5,000
12/08	1,002	(477)	—	6,000
12/07	2,517	(2)	—	8,500
12/06	2,498	353	14.1%	9,000
12/05	2,514	249	9.9%	9,600
Annual Growth	**(24.8%)**	**—**	**—**	**(15.0%)**

2009 Year-End Financials

Debt ratio: 8.4%
Return on equity: —
Cash ($ mil.): 14
Current ratio: 1.91
Long-term debt ($ mil.): 36
No. of shares (mil.): 57
Dividends
 Yield: 0.0%
 Payout: —
Market value ($ mil.): 396

Stock History

NYSE: SSP

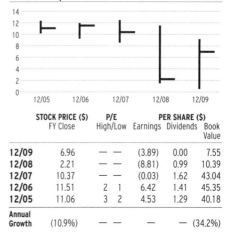

	STOCK PRICE ($) FY Close	P/E High/Low		PER SHARE ($) Earnings	Dividends	Book Value
12/09	6.96	—	—	(3.89)	0.00	7.55
12/08	2.21	—	—	(8.81)	0.99	10.39
12/07	10.37	—	—	(0.03)	1.62	43.04
12/06	11.51	2	1	6.42	1.41	45.35
12/05	11.06	3	2	4.53	1.29	40.18
Annual Growth	**(10.9%)**	**—**	**—**	**—**	**—**	**(34.2%)**

Exelon Corporation

The City of Brotherly Love meets the Windy City in utility holding company Exelon. The company distributes electricity to 5.4 million customers in northern Illinois (including Chicago) and southeastern Pennsylvania (including Philadelphia) through subsidiaries Commonwealth Edison (ComEd) and PECO Energy. PECO also distributes natural gas to 485,000 customers. Subsidiary Exelon Generation holds the company's power plants, whose production capacity is just about 25,000 MW. About two-thirds of Generation's power is nuclear. Exelon Power Team is a top wholesale energy marketer, and Exelon Energy markets retail power and offers other energy-related services.

In 2008, in a move to expand its geographic reach, Exelon made a $6.2 billion bid to buy NRG Energy. Though the offer to buy NRG met with resistance, Exelon had kept up its pursuit of the company. Toward the end of 2008 it announced an exchange offer for NRG's shares. By the expiration date of the offer early the next year, it had acquired just more than 50% of those shares. In addition to announcing another extension of the offer, Exelon said it hoped NRG's Board would allow it to do due diligence and begin negotiations for an acquisition. But an NRG proxy vote rejection in 2009 led Exelon to terminate its offer.

Exelon was formed in 2000 when Philadelphia-based PECO Energy bought Chicago-based Unicom. Both PECO and Unicom were leading nuclear plant operators, and in 2007 Exelon selected Victoria County as its site in southeast Texas for a federal license application that would allow construction and operation of a new nuclear plant should the company decide to build one. In 2009 Exelon began the process of upgrading capacity at its existing nuclear facilities that will give the company up to 1,500 MW greater capacity.

HISTORY

Thomas Dolan and local investors formed the Brush Electric Light Company of Philadelphia in 1881 to provide street and commercial lighting. Competitors sprang up, and in 1885 Brush merged with the United States Electric Lighting Company of Pennsylvania to form a secret "electric trust," or holding company. Dolan became president in 1886 and bought four other utilities.

In 1895 Martin Maloney formed Pennsylvania Heat Light and Power to consolidate the city's electric companies. By the next year it had acquired, among other businesses, Columbia Electric Light, Philadelphia Edison, and the electric trust. In 1899 a new firm, National Electric, challenged Maloney by acquiring neighboring rival Southern Electric Light. Before retiring, Maloney negotiated the merger of the two firms, forming Philadelphia Electric in 1902.

Demand rose rapidly into the 1920s, fueled in part by the company's promotion of electric appliances. In 1928, the year after it completed the Conowingo Hydroelectric Station, Philadelphia Electric was absorbed by the much larger United Gas Improvement. United Gas avoided large layoffs during the Depression, but passage of the Public Utility Holding Company Act (PUHCA) in 1935 sounded its death knell. (PUHCA was repealed in 2005.) In 1943 the SEC forced United Gas to divest Philadelphia Electric.

Philadelphia Electric built several plants in the 1950s and 1960s in response to a postwar electricity boom. A small experimental nuclear reactor was completed at Peach Bottom, Pennsylvania, in 1967, and in 1974 the company placed two nuclear units in service at the plant. The Salem (New Jersey) nuke (Unit 1) followed in 1977. The company relied on these plants during the OPEC oil crisis. Another one, Limerick Unit 1, began operations in 1986, and Unit 2 went on line in 1990, but the Peach Bottom plant was shut down from 1989 to 1991 because of management problems (later resolved).

The company began reorganizing in 1993 and changed its name the next year to PECO Energy Company. It also sold Maryland retail subsidiary Conowingo Power, retaining the hydroelectric plant. In 1995 rival PP&L rejected PECO's acquisition bid, citing PECO's nuclear liabilities.

A year later PECO teamed with AT&T Wireless to offer PCS in Philadelphia (service was launched in 1997). EnergyOne, a national venture formed in 1997 by PECO, UtiliCorp United (now Aquila), and AT&T, offered consumers a package of power, phone, and Internet services on one bill. However, the slow deregulation process caused the venture to fail.

PECO also joined with British Energy in 1997 to form AmerGen, hoping to buy nukes at rock-bottom prices from utilities eager to unload them. AmerGen purchased three nuclear facilities in 1999 and 2000: Unit 1 of the Three Mile Island (Pennsylvania) facility; a plant in Clinton, Illinois; and an Oyster Creek (New Jersey) location.

In 1999 PECO announced plans to acquire Chicago's Unicom, the parent company of Commonwealth Edison (ComEd). After the deal was completed in 2000, the combined company took the name Exelon and established its headquarters in Chicago.

Pennsylvania's utility markets were fully deregulated in 2000. To expand its power generation business, Exelon that year bought 49.9% of Sithe Energies for $682 million. In 2001 Exelon agreed to buy two gas-fired power plants (2,300 MW) in Texas from TXU for $443 million; the deal was completed in 2002.

Also in 2002 Exelon purchased Sithe Energies' stakes in six New England power plants with 2,000 MW of capacity (plus 2,400 MW under construction) for $543 million plus the assumption of $1.15 billion in debt. The company also sold its Philadelphia PCS venture interest to former partner AT&T Wireless Services (now part of AT&T Mobility). Sithe Energies was sold to Dynegy in 2005 for $135 million.

To focus on core utility operations, the company sold its infrastructure construction business, InfraSource, and its facility and infrastructure management business, Exelon Solutions. Exelon then completed the sale of its interest in telecommunications joint venture PECO TelCove, which provides voice and data services, to its partner TelCove, and sold its district heating and cooling division (Thermal Chicago) to Macquarie Bank. The company plans to sell additional noncore assets.

EXECUTIVES

Chairman and CEO; Chairman, Generation and PECO:
John W. Rowe, age 64, $6,350,158 total compensation
President and COO; President, Exelon Generation:
Christopher M. (Chris) Crane, age 51,
$3,178,930 total compensation
EVP; President and CEO PECO Energy:
Denis P. O'Brien, age 49
EVP and Chief Administrative and Diversity Officer; President, Exelon Business Services:
Ruth Ann M. Gillis, age 55
EVP Finance and Legal: William A. (Bill) Von Hoene Jr., age 56
SVP and CFO, Exelon and Exelon Generation:
Matthew F. Hilzinger, age 46,
$1,096,281 total compensation
SVP and General Counsel: Darryl M. Bradford, age 54
SVP; President, Power Team, Generation:
Kenneth W. (Ken) Cornew, age 44
SVP Federal Regulatory Affairs and Public Policy:
Joseph Dominguez
SVP Federal Government Affairs and Public Policy:
David C. Brown
VP Investor Relations: Stacie Frank
VP and Controller: Duane M. DesParte, age 46
VP Federal Regulatory Affairs and Policy:
Kathleen Barrón
VP and Director Federal Regulatory Affairs and Policy:
Karen Hill
VP Wholesale Market Development: Steve Naumann
VP and Assistant Corporate Controller; Chief Accounting Officer, Generation: Matthew R. Galvanoni, age 37
Chairman and CEO, Commonwealth Edison:
Frank M. Clark Jr., age 64,
$3,197,323 total compensation
President and Chief Nuclear Officer, Exelon Nuclear:
Michael Pacilio
Auditors: PricewaterhouseCoopers LLP

LOCATIONS

HQ: Exelon Corporation
10 S. Dearborn St., 52nd Fl., Chicago, IL 60603
Phone: 312-394-7398   **Fax:** 312-394-8941
Web: www.exeloncorp.com

PRODUCTS/OPERATIONS

2009 Sales

	$ mil.	% of total
Generation	9,703	45
ComEd	5,774	27
PECO	5,311	25
Other	757	3
Adjustments	(4,227)	—
Total	**17,318**	**100**

Major Operating Units, Subsidiaries, and Affiliates

Exelon Energy Delivery
    Commonweath Edison Company (ComEd, electric utility)
    PECO Energy Company (PECO, electric and gas utility)
Exelon Generation Company, LLC
    AmerGen Energy Company, LLC (independent power producer)
    Exelon Energy (nonregulated retail power sales)
    Exelon Nuclear (nuclear power generation)

COMPETITORS

AES	Dynegy
Allegheny Energy	Entergy
Alliant Energy	FirstEnergy
Ameren	Green Mountain Energy
American Transmission	Integrys Energy Group
CenterPoint Energy	NextEra Energy
Delmarva Power	Nicor
Dominion Resources	PPL Corporation
Duke Energy	RRI Energy
Duquesne Light Holdings	UGI

HISTORICAL FINANCIALS

Company Type: Public

Income Statement

FYE: December 31

	REVENUE ($ mil.)	NET INCOME ($ mil.)	NET PROFIT MARGIN	EMPLOYEES
12/09	17,318	2,707	15.6%	19,329
12/08	18,859	2,737	14.5%	19,610
12/07	18,916	2,736	14.5%	17,800
12/06	15,655	1,592	10.2%	17,200
12/05	15,357	965	6.3%	17,200
Annual Growth	**3.0%**	**29.4%**	**—**	**3.0%**

2009 Year-End Financials

Debt ratio: 90.1%
Return on equity: 22.9%
Cash ($ mil.): 2,010
Current ratio: 1.28
Long-term debt ($ mil.): 11,385

No. of shares (mil.): 661
Dividends
    Yield: 4.3%
    Payout: 51.3%
Market value ($ mil.): 32,303

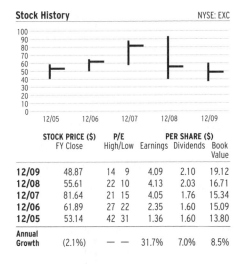

	STOCK PRICE ($) FY Close	P/E High/Low		PER SHARE ($) Earnings	Dividends	Book Value
12/09	48.87	14	9	4.09	2.10	19.12
12/08	55.61	22	10	4.13	2.03	16.71
12/07	81.64	21	15	4.05	1.76	15.34
12/06	61.89	27	22	2.35	1.60	15.09
12/05	53.14	42	31	1.36	1.60	13.80
Annual Growth	(2.1%)	—	—	31.7%	7.0%	8.5%

Exide Technologies

Exide Technologies hopes you'll get a charge out of its products. The company makes and recycles automotive and industrial batteries for retailers and transportation manufacturers, including Wal-Mart and NAPA, and Fiat and Toyota, respectively. The company also makes batteries for boats, farm equipment, golf carts, hybrid vehicles, and wheelchairs. Industrial applications include computer, locomotive, photovoltaic (solar power), power plant, and telecommunications systems. Classic, Marathon, NASCAR Extreme, Sunlyte, and Super Crank make up some of the company's brand names. Operations outside the US account for nearly two-thirds of sales.

Exide came through the global recession and credit crisis a bit battered, leading the company to reduce its workforce by around 14%. In addition Wal-Mart announced it was phasing out its aftermarket business with Exide.

CEO Gordon Ulsh retired in 2010. Exide named James Bolch to suceed him. Bolch was formerly president of Ingersoll-Rand's Industrial Technologies Sector.

Though Exide finally eked out a profit in fiscal 2008 (after 11 years of net losses), it went back into the red for the next two years, spurring continuation of restructuring plans, headcount reductions, and reorganization of corporate and divisional functions. It plans to sell nonstrategic assets and businesses and improve efficiencies in the manufacturing and distribution of its brand products.

In addition to its internal efforts to improve revenues, Exide is pursuing collaborative partnerships and acquisitions to expand its advanced battery technology and product offerings, as well as its global market share. In 2009 Exide acquired the principal assets of Mountain Power, a British Columbia firm that makes rechargeable lithium-ion batteries. Also that year Exide received $34 million from the federal government to develop affordable lead-acid batteries incorporating advanced carbon technology.

India is an investment focus for Exide. It acquired a controlling interest in Leadage Alloys

India, and it expanded capacity at its transportation manufacturing facility in Gujarat.

Tontine Capital Management owns more than 31% of Exide Technologies.

HISTORY

Exide got its start in 1888 when Thomas Edison founded The Electric Storage Battery Company (ESB) in Gloucester, New Jersey, to develop a backup battery for steam engines and dynamos. By 1890 ESB had installed the first practical battery backup in a Philadelphia utility, and that year it also provided batteries for the US's first streetcars. Sales picked up as the versatility of the battery was recognized, and in 1898 ESB batteries powered the US Navy's first submarine. The company was soon the world's top battery maker.

The Exide brand name (short for "excellent oxide") debuted in 1900, and the firsts kept coming: the first automobile ignition battery (1903), the batteries used in the first transcontinental telephone services (1915), and the batteries used for the first air-conditioned train (1931).

WWII saw the beginning of ESB's vertical integration, with the purchases of a maker of battery chargers and testers (1938) and a maker of battery containers (1946). ESB also developed battery-powered torpedoes used in WWII.

In 1951 Exide batteries assured the continuous operation of many Bell Systems relay stations for the first coast-to-coast wireless telephone network. In 1957 it entered the dry-cell battery business by acquiring the Ray-O-Vac Company. NASA used Exide batteries throughout the Apollo missions of the 1960s and 1970s, including the 1969 moon landing.

Inco Limited of Toronto purchased ESB in 1974. Management reorganized ESB in 1978 as a holding company, ESB Ray-O-Vac. The Exide brand stagnated, losing market share. In 1980 ESB Ray-O-Vac became INCO Electro Energy, with Exide as a subsidiary.

Investors led by the Spectrum Group and First Chicago Investment rescued Exide's North American operations in 1983. In 1985 the company hired ITT executive Arthur Hawkins as CEO and began a turnaround. Exide bought General Battery in 1987 to become #1 in the US auto battery market. The company acquired Speedclip Manufacturing (battery cables, terminals, and accessories; 1989) and Shadwood Industries (automotive battery chargers; fully acquired 1991) and went public in 1993.

Exide expanded into Europe in the mid-1990s, buying firms in France, Spain, and the UK, including two of the continent's largest battery makers. In 1997 it completed its European expansion by buying three battery-making units from Germany's CEAG AG.

Despite market dominance, Exide lost about 75% of its share value from 1996 to 1998. Some shareholders sued management, alleging misrepresentation, and the Florida attorney general and the SEC launched probes into whether the company sold used batteries as new. (In 1999 Exide settled with Florida without admitting wrongdoing, and it also settled with shareholders.) In 1998 management clumsily announced a recapitalization attempt and then changed its mind. Amid these problems, Hawkins resigned as chairman and CEO and former Chrysler exec Robert Lutz replaced him.

In 2001 Exide agreed to a plea deal with federal prosecutors whereby the company would pay out $27.5 million in fines over five years. It

admitted to making defective batteries, covering up the defects, and bribing a Sears, Roebuck buyer. Burdened with heavy debt, Exide also announced in 2001 that it planned to issue 20 million new shares in a debt-for-equity deal. That year the company changed its name from Exide Corporation to Exide Technologies.

Early in 2002 Exide filed Chapter 11 bankruptcy as a result of its acquisitions bender and poor conditions in the automotive sector.

Arthur Hawkins, the former CEO of Exide, was convicted in 2002 of fraudulently selling defective batteries to Sears Automotive Marketing Services, a subsidiary of Sears, Roebuck. He was sentenced to 10 years in federal prison; the sentence was upheld in 2005. Three other Exide executives were convicted of various federal charges.

When Exide emerged from Chapter 11 bankruptcy in 2004, the company had cut its debt by a reported 70%. While Exide exited Chapter 11, it still experienced corporate pain — the company continued to lose money, and it shut down its lead-acid battery manufacturing plant in Shreveport, Louisiana, in mid-2006. The Shreveport factory had been operating since 1968.

EXECUTIVES

Chairman: John P. Reilly, age 66
President, CEO, and Director: James R. (Jim) Bolch, age 52
EVP and CFO: Phillip A. Damaska, age 55, $727,031 total compensation
EVP and General Counsel: Barbara A. Hatcher, age 55, $716,160 total compensation
EVP Human Resources and Communications: George S. Jones Jr., age 57
VP US Aftermarket Sales and Branch System: Jeff Barna
VP Global Procurement: Douglas Gillespie
VP and Treasurer: Nicholas J. Iuanow
VP, Chief Accounting Officer, and Controller: Louis E. (Lou) Martinez, age 44
VP and CIO: Erach S. Balsara
VP Strategic Planning and Business Development; VP and General Manager, ReStore Energy Systems: Gary Reinert
VP Global Environment, Health, and Safety: Mark W. Cummings
VP Global Engineering and Research: Paul G. Cheeseman, age 49
President, Exide Europe and Interim President, Industrial Energy Europe: Michael Ostermann, age 44
President, Asia Pacific: Luke Lu
President, Transportation Americas: Bruce A. Cole, age 47
President, Industrial Energy Americas: Mitchell S. Bregman, age 56, $800,476 total compensation
Senior Director Investor Relations: Carol Knies
Auditors: PricewaterhouseCoopers LLP

LOCATIONS

HQ: Exide Technologies
13000 Deerfield Pkwy., Bldg. 200, Milton, GA 30004
Phone: 678-566-9000   **Fax:** 678-566-9188
Web: www.exide.com

2010 Sales

	$ mil.	% of total
US	1,028.3	38
Germany	297.7	11
Spain	242.1	9
Italy	183.5	7
France	180.2	7
Poland	109.7	4
Other countries	644.3	24
Total	**2,685.8**	**100**

PRODUCTS/OPERATIONS

2010 Sales

	$ mil.	% of total
Transportation	1,746.8	65
Industrial Energy	939.0	35
Total	**2,685.8**	**100**

Selected Products

Automotive batteries (for agricultural equipment, buses, commercial trucks, construction equipment, and emergency and passenger vehicles)
Industrial batteries
Motive power batteries (for forklifts, golf carts, and wheelchairs)
Network power batteries (for telecommunication, industrial, and military applications)
Standby/backup batteries (for hospitals, security systems, traffic control, and elevators)

COMPETITORS

C&D Technologies
Crown Battery
Eagle-Picher
East Penn Manufacturing
EnerSys
GS Yuasa
Hitachi
Interstate Batteries
Johnson Controls
Micro Power Electronics
SAFT
Valence Technology

HISTORICAL FINANCIALS

Company Type: Public

Income Statement FYE: March 31

	REVENUE ($ mil.)	NET INCOME ($ mil.)	NET PROFIT MARGIN	EMPLOYEES
3/10	2,686	(12)	—	10,349
3/09	3,322	(70)	—	12,081
3/08	3,697	32	0.9%	13,027
3/07	2,940	(106)	—	13,862
3/06	2,820	(173)	—	13,982
Annual Growth	(1.2%)	—	—	(7.2%)

2010 Year-End Financials

Debt ratio: 194.6%
Return on equity: —
Cash ($ mil.): 90
Current ratio: 1.70
Long-term debt ($ mil.): 647
No. of shares (mil.): 76
Dividends
  Yield: —
  Payout: —
Market value ($ mil.): 437

Stock History NASDAQ (GM): XIDE

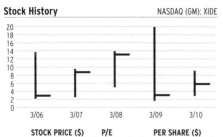

	STOCK PRICE ($) FY Close	P/E High/Low	PER SHARE ($) Earnings	Dividends	Book Value
3/10	5.76	— —	(0.16)	—	4.38
3/09	3.00	— —	(0.92)	—	4.30
3/08	13.10	30 11	0.46	—	7.18
3/07	8.72	— —	(2.39)	—	4.36
3/06	2.86	— —	(6.91)	—	2.96
Annual Growth	19.1%	— —	—	—	10.3%

Expeditors International

Need your goods moved expeditiously? Freight forwarder Expeditors International of Washington can help. As a freight forwarder, the company purchases air and ocean cargo space on a volume basis and resells that space to its customers at lower rates than they could obtain directly from the carriers. The company also acts as a customs broker for air and ocean freight shipped by its customers and offers supply chain management services. Expeditors operates from more than 250 facilities in more than 50 countries worldwide. Approximately half of the company's sales come from Asia. Customers include global businesses engaged in retailing/wholesaling, electronics, and manufacturing.

In its rapid development, Expeditors has favored internal growth over expansion by acquisition, and the company continues to open new offices and to invest in its information technology infrastructure. According to Expeditors, this philosophy enables it to stay outside the "trends of consolidation" in order to cope with regional economic downturns. The company's 2009 performance illustrates this. Suffering the backlash of the economic crisis, the company posted its revenues showing an almost 27% drop from 2008; the greatest drop occurred in the earlier part of the year. Rather than resorting to immediate layoffs, the company maintained a cool head, using its available financial resources to ensure customer retention and expand its market share. When the peak season arrived at the end of the year, Expeditors was able to manage it.

Construction began in mid-2009 for Expeditors' multimillion-dollar data center in Spokane, Washington. The facility's services will include coordination of warehousing, distribution, and shipping of industrial and mining equipment and materials, as well as providing shipping insurance and customs coordination.

Expeditors got its start in 1979. It began with one location in Seattle that focused on airfreight shipments primarily from Taiwan, Singapore, and Hong Kong to the US.

HISTORY

After leaving the freight forwarding company that became Circle International (later acquired by EGL), Peter Rose used $55,000 in seed money to start his own company, Expeditors International of Washington, in 1979. Two years later Rose met with several fellow shipping veterans to implement their idea of combining freight forwarding and customs clearing services.

Expeditors soon had people beating a path to its door. It grew quickly to become a leading importer of goods made in Asia. Expeditors added export services in 1982 and went public in 1984. The next year it added ocean freight services to its offerings, and in 1986 it entered the European market. As the 1980s ended, the company had offices in 42 countries. Expeditors expanded into the Middle East in 1991 and, despite the economic doldrums of the early 1990s, opened 14 offices in 1992.

Expeditors also diversified with services such as long-term customs brokerage contracts and distribution. In 1997 it added truck and rail border brokerage services for the US, Mexico, and Canada. Expeditors continued to expand rapidly: In 1997 it added 22 offices and in 1999 opened still more, including five in Turkey and others in Greece, Lebanon, and the UK.

In 2000 Expeditors and other freight forwarders urged the US Department of Transportation to allow more dedicated air freighter service for the US-China market.

EXECUTIVES

Chairman, CEO, and Director: Peter J. Rose, age 66, $4,782,892 total compensation
President, COO, and Director: R. Jordan Gates, age 54, $3,622,533 total compensation
Principal Financial and Accounting Officer: Bradley S. (Brad) Powell, age 49, $1,462,239 total compensation
EVP, North America: Eugene K. Alger, age 49
EVP, North America: Philip M. Coughlin, age 49
EVP and CIO: Jeffrey S. Musser, age 44
EVP Global Customs: Rosanne Esposito, age 58
SVP Ocean Services: Daniel R. Wall, age 41
SVP, Asia: David Hsieh
SVP and Regional Director, South East Asia: Andrew Goh
SVP Air Cargo: Roger A. Idiart, age 56
SVP, Australasia: Jean Claude Carcaillet, age 64
SVP and Corporate Controller: Charles J. Lynch, age 49
President, Europe, Africa, Near/Middle East, and Indian Subcontinent: Rommel C. Saber, age 52, $3,487,312 total compensation
President, Global Sales and Marketing: Timothy C. Barber, age 50
President, Asia and Director: James L. K. Wang, age 62, $4,462,745 total compensation
President, The Americas: Robert L. Villanueva, age 57, $3,487,312 total compensation
Auditors: KPMG LLP

LOCATIONS

HQ: Expeditors International of Washington, Inc.
1015 3rd Ave., 12th Fl., Seattle, WA 98104
Phone: 206-674-3400 **Fax:** 206-682-9777
Web: www.expeditors.com

2009 Sales

	$ mil.	% of total
Asia	2,035.6	50
North America		
US	982.1	24
Other countries	129.3	3
Europe & Africa	582.7	14
Middle East & India	232.8	6
Australasia	65.7	2
Latin America	64.1	1
Total	**4,092.3**	**100**

PRODUCTS/OPERATIONS

2009 Sales

	$ mil.	% of total
Airfreight	1,831.3	45
Ocean freight & ocean services	1,297.7	32
Customs brokerage & other services	963.3	23
Total	**4,092.3**	**100**

Selected Products and Services

Air consolidation and forwarding
Customs
Distribution
Domestic cargo
Insurance
Ocean shipment
Order management
Project cargo transportation
Tradeflow software (supply chain)
US/Canada border services

APL Logistics	Mitsui-Soko
CEVA Logistics	Nippon Express
C.H. Robinson Worldwide	Panalpina
DHL	Schenker
FedEx Trade Networks	Sinotrans
Kintetsu World Express	UPS
Kuehne + Nagel	UTi Worldwide

HISTORICAL FINANCIALS
Company Type: Public

Income Statement
FYE: December 31

	REVENUE ($ mil.)	NET INCOME ($ mil.)	NET PROFIT MARGIN	EMPLOYEES
12/09	4,092	240	5.9%	12,010
12/08	5,634	301	5.3%	12,580
12/07	5,235	269	5.1%	12,310
12/06	4,626	235	5.1%	11,600
12/05	3,902	219	5.6%	10,600
Annual Growth	1.2%	2.4%	—	3.2%

2009 Year-End Financials

Debt ratio: —	No. of shares (mil.): 213
Return on equity: 16.5%	Dividends
Cash ($ mil.): 926	Yield: 1.1%
Current ratio: 2.52	Payout: 34.2%
Long-term debt ($ mil.): —	Market value ($ mil.): 7,402

Stock History
NASDAQ (GS): EXPD

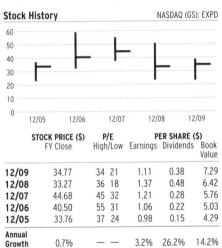

	STOCK PRICE ($) FY Close	P/E High/Low	PER SHARE ($) Earnings	Dividends	Book Value
12/09	34.77	34 21	1.11	0.38	7.29
12/08	33.27	36 18	1.37	0.48	6.42
12/07	44.68	45 32	1.21	0.28	5.76
12/06	40.50	55 31	1.06	0.22	5.03
12/05	33.76	37 24	0.98	0.15	4.29
Annual Growth	0.7%	— —	3.2%	26.2%	14.2%

Express Scripts

Express Scripts knows that its customers like their drugs fast. One of the largest pharmacy benefits management (PBM) companies in North America, Express Scripts administers the prescription drug benefits of millions of health plan members in the US and Canada. Members have access to a network of about 60,000 retail pharmacies, as well as the company's own mail-order pharmacies. Express Scripts processes claims for about 750 million prescriptions per year, designs drug plans, and offers such services as disease management programs and consumer drug data analysis. Clients include HMOs and other health insurers, self-insured businesses, and union benefit plans.

Express Scripts is one of the top three players in the PBM industry, the other two being Medco and Caremark Pharmacy Services. The company and the industry have grown rapidly, as the PBMs strive to save money for their customers by negotiating good deals for prescription drugs with networks of retail pharmacies, as well as by encouraging the use of cheaper generic drugs and home-delivered medications.

The company grew substantially in 2009 with the acquisition of NextRx, the PBM business of Blue Cross Blue Shield (BCBS) licensee WellPoint, for about $4.7 billion. As part of the acquisition, the company has a 10-year contract to provide PBM services to WellPoint, the nation's largest health insurer. The purchase launched Express Scripts closer to its top two rivals by increasing its claims processing load from 500 million to more than 750 million prescriptions per year. It also enhanced the company's online, generic drug, and mail delivery service offerings.

Express Scripts had previously expanded its PBM operations in 2008 by purchasing the pharmacy services division of Medical Services Company for $251 million. The acquired business specialized in managing pharmacy benefits for workers' compensation insurers. In addition, Express Scripts opened a new pharmacy fulfillment center in St. Louis in 2010. The center supports the company's growing home delivery business, which is experiencing increased demand from clients and patients seeking to cut costs on traditional maintenance medications through the use of mail-order services.

Another element of Express Scripts' PBM business that is experiencing higher consumer demand is specialty pharmacy subsidiary CuraScript. Through its primary operating unit, CuraScript Specialty Pharmacy (or CuraScript SP), the subsidiary provides home distribution of specialty prescriptions (primarily injectable biotech drugs that require special packaging and handling); the unit also delivers to doctors' offices and other health care providers. To focus on its core distribution operations, the company divested its CuraScript Infusion Pharmacy business, which operated infusion therapy centers in six states, to Walgreen's Option Care subsidiary in 2008.

In 2009 Express Scripts expanded the scope of its contract with the US Department of Defense, adding a number of services beyond its existing management of the pharmacy network of the TRICARE military health care program. The contract now includes home delivery, specialty pharmacy, claims management, and other integrated offerings.

While its PBM operations account for the lion's share of Express Script's revenues, the company has also been looking to expand into new high-growth fields of managed care through its Emerging Markets segment. It has added such services as group purchasing for doctors and clinics (through CuraScript Specialty Distribution, or CuraScript SD), fertility drug packaging and delivery (Freedom FP), and third-party administration of consumer-driven health plans (ConnectYourCare). In addition, Express Scripts assists pharmaceutical and biotech companies with activities such as delivering marketing samples to doctors and providing customized packaging and logistics services through its HealthBridge division.

HISTORY

In 1986 St. Louis-based drugstore chain Medicare-Glaser and HMO Sanus joined forces to create Express Scripts, which would manage the HMO's prescription program. Express Scripts began managing third-party programs in 1988 and later developed other operations: mail-order prescription, infusion therapy, and vision services. New York Life bought Sanus and picked up the rest of Express Scripts in 1989 when Medicare-Glaser went into bankruptcy.

In 1992 Express Scripts went public. The next year the company formed subsidiary Practice Patterns Science to begin profiling providers and tracking treatment outcomes.

In the late 1990s the company continued to expand, adding customers in Canada (1996) and building operations — with varying success. A 1996 expansion of its eye care management services was abandoned in 1998. Express Scripts has traditionally grown through big-ticket contracts, such as its 1997 pact with RightCHOICE Managed Care, and through acquisitions. For example, it boosted its PBM operations with its 1998 acquisition of Columbia/HCA's (now HCA) ValueRx unit and its 1999 purchase of Smith-Kline Beecham's Diversified Pharmaceutical Services (DPS); however, it lost DPS's largest customer when United Healthcare began moving its more than 8 million enrollees to Merck-Medco in 2000.

The company suffered another setback in 2000 when it wrote down its 20% interest in online pharmacy PlanetRx. It had bought into the company in 1999, when dot-coms were soaring, transferring its own Internet pharmacy operations (YourPharmacy.com) into the fledgling company. In 2001 Express Scripts joined rivals AdvancePCS and Merck-Medco (now Medco Health Solutions) to form RxHub to create technology to allow physicians to file prescriptions electronically.

In 2001 the firm began a bit of an acquisition spree. That year, it bought Phoenix Marketing Group, one of the biggest prescription drug sample fulfillment companies in the US. National Prescription Administrators, a top private pharmacy benefits management company in the US, joined the family in 2002. Express Scripts expanded its specialty pharmacy capabilities with the purchases of CuraScript, a leading specialty pharmacy in 2004, and biopharmaceutical pharmacy and distributor Priority Healthcare in 2005.

In 2007 it acquired ConnectYourCare, a third-party administrator of consumer-directed health plans, which link a high-deductible plan with tax-sheltered savings accounts.

EXECUTIVES

Chairman, President, and CEO: George Paz, age 54, $10,627,774 total compensation
EVP and CFO: Jeffrey L. Hall, age 42, $3,072,367 total compensation
EVP Sales and Marketing: Edward (Ed) Ignaczak, age 44, $2,717,580 total compensation
EVP Operations and Technology: Patrick (Pat) McNamee, age 50, $2,748,372 total compensation
EVP Strategy, Human Capital, and Emerging Markets: Michael R. Holmes, age 51, $2,682,745 total compensation
EVP, General Counsel, and Secretary: Keith J. Ebling, age 41, $2,787,672 total compensation

SVP and Chief Medical Officer: Steven (Steve) Miller
SVP Marketing and Corporate Communications:
  Larry Zarin, age 56
VP, Chief Accouting Officer, and Controller:
  Kelley Elliott, age 37
VP Investor Relations: David Myers
Chief Scientist: Bob Nease
Director Public Affairs: Maria C. Palumbo
President, International Operations: Agnes Rey-Giraud,
  age 45
Auditors: PricewaterhouseCoopers LLP

LOCATIONS

HQ: Express Scripts, Inc.
  1 Express Way, St. Louis, MO 63121
Phone: 314-996-0900
Web: www.express-scripts.com

PRODUCTS/OPERATIONS

2009 Sales

	$ mil.	% of total
Pharmacy Benefits Management (PBM)		
PBM products		
Network	15,019.3	61
Home delivery & specialty	8,099.0	33
Other PBM products	83.9	—
PBM services	264.7	1
Emerging Markets (EM)		
EM products	1,244.1	5
EM services	37.9	—
Total	**24,748.9**	**100**

Selected Products and Services

Pharmacy Benefits Management (PBM)
  Benefit design consultation
  Compliance management programs for members
  Drug formulary management
  Drug utilization review
  Electronic claims processing
  Home delivery pharmacy services
  Information analysis services
  Rebate and low income programs
  Retail drug card programs
  Retail network pharmacy management
  Specialty pharmacy services (CuraScript)
Emerging Markets (EM)
  Drug distribution to clinics
  Fertility drug distribution (specialty
    handling/packaging)
  Practitioner licensure verification
  Sample distribution to physicians
  Third-party administration of consumer-directed
    health plans

COMPETITORS

Aetna
Argus
BioScrip
Caremark Pharmacy Services
Catalyst Health Solutions
CIGNA
First Health Group
HealthTrans
Humana
Medco Health
MedImpact
NationsHealth
Omnicare
PharMerica
Prescription Solutions
Prime Therapeutics
Rite Aid
SXC
Walgreen
Wal-Mart

HISTORICAL FINANCIALS

Company Type: Public

Income Statement

FYE: December 31

	REVENUE ($ mil.)	NET INCOME ($ mil.)	NET PROFIT MARGIN	EMPLOYEES
12/09	24,749	828	3.3%	14,270
12/08	21,978	776	3.5%	10,820
12/07	18,274	568	3.1%	11,820
12/06	17,660	474	2.7%	11,300
12/05	16,266	400	2.5%	11,100
Annual Growth	**11.1%**	**19.9%**	**—**	**6.5%**

2009 Year-End Financials

Debt ratio: 70.2%
Return on equity: 35.7%
Cash ($ mil.): 1,070
Current ratio: 0.76
Long-term debt ($ mil.): 2,493
No. of shares (mil.): 542
Dividends
  Yield: —
  Payout: —
Market value ($ mil.): 23,438

Stock History

NASDAQ (GS): ESRX

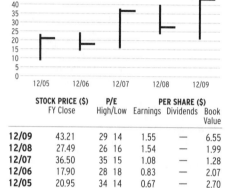

	STOCK PRICE ($) FY Close	P/E High/Low	PER SHARE ($) Earnings	Dividends	Book Value
12/09	43.21	29 14	1.55	—	6.55
12/08	27.49	26 16	1.54	—	1.99
12/07	36.50	35 15	1.08	—	1.28
12/06	17.90	28 18	0.83	—	2.07
12/05	20.95	34 14	0.67	—	2.70
Annual Growth	**19.8%**	**— —**	**23.3%**	**—**	**24.8%**

Exxon Mobil

It's not necessarily the oil standard, but Exxon Mobil is the world's largest integrated oil company (ahead of Royal Dutch Shell and BP). Exxon Mobil engages in oil and gas exploration, production, supply, transportation, and marketing worldwide. In 2009 it reported proved reserves of 23 billion barrels of oil equivalent, as well as major holdings in oil sands through Imperial Oil. Exxon Mobil's 37 refineries in 20 countries have a throughput capacity of 6.3 million barrels per day. It supplies refined products to almost 28,000 gas stations in 100 countries. Exxon Mobil is also a major petrochemical producer.

Through ExxonMobil Chemical, the company develops and sells petrochemicals (including ethylene, propylene, and their derivatives, which make up the base of most other petrochemicals and plastics). Another unit mines coal and other minerals. Exxon Mobil also has stakes in electric power plants in China.

In a move to grow its upstream assets, in 2010 the company acquired XTO Energy. The $41 billion all stock deal adds XTO Energy's unconventional natural gas production assets (45 trillion cu. ft. equivalent of shale gas, tight gas, coal bed methane, and shale oil).

With significant oil and gas holdings in Europe, the US, and eastern Canada, the company is looking for new opportunities in West Africa, both onshore and off; in the former Soviet Union; and in South America. (In 2007 President Hugo Chavez expropriated Exxon Mobil's Venezuelan assets, leading to intense international litigation, which remained unresolved in 2010.)

It is also investing heavily in deepwater exploration (in water depths greater than 1,350 feet). In 2010, in response to the BP oil rig disaster in the Gulf of Mexico, Exxon Mobil announced it was joining forces with Chevron, Royal Dutch Shell, and ConocoPhillips to create a $1 billion rapid-response joint venture capable of capturing and containing some 100,000 barrels of oil in water depths of 10,000 feet.

In response to market demand for cleaner fuels, in late 2008 Exxon Mobil announced it will invest more than $1 billion to increase the supply of cleaner burning diesel by about six million gallons per day. In 2009 it made its first major investment in developing biofuels, agreeing to spend $600 million in an algae-to-fuel project with biotech firm Synthetic Genomics.

In 2009 the company signed up to partner with TransCanada to jointly develop the $26 billion Alaska Pipeline Project. A long-term project, if and when built, the pipeline will deliver natural gas from Alaska's North Slope to US markets.

HISTORY

Exxon's 1999 acquisition of Mobil reunited two descendants of John D. Rockefeller's Standard Oil Company. Rockefeller, a commodity trader, started his first oil refinery in 1863 in Cleveland. Realizing that the price of oil at the well would shrink with each new strike, Rockefeller chose to monopolize oil refining and transportation. In 1870 he formed Standard Oil, and in 1882 he created the Standard Oil Trust, which allowed him to set up new, ostensibly independent, companies, including the Standard Oil Company of New Jersey (Jersey Standard); Rochester, New York-based Vacuum Oil; and Standard Oil of New York (nicknamed Socony).

Initially capitalized at $70 million, the Standard Oil Trust controlled 90% of the petroleum industry. In 1911, after two decades of political and legal wrangling, the Supreme Court broke up the trust into 34 companies, the largest of which was Jersey Standard.

Walter Teagle, who became president of Jersey Standard in 1917, secretly bought half of Humble Oil of Texas (1919) and expanded operations into South America. In 1928 Jersey Standard joined in the Red Line Agreement, which reserved most Middle East oil for a few companies. Teagle resigned in 1942 after the company was criticized for a prewar research pact with German chemical giant I.G. Farben.

The 1948 purchase of a 40% stake in Arabian American Oil Company, combined with a 7% share of Iranian production bought in 1954, made Jersey Standard the world's #1 oil company at that time.

Meanwhile, Vacuum Oil and Socony reunited in 1931 as Socony-Vacuum, and the company adopted the Flying Red Horse (Pegasus — representing speed and power) as a trademark. The fast-growing, diversifying company changed its name to Socony Mobil Oil in 1955 and became Mobil in 1976.

Other US companies, still using the Standard Oil name, objected to Jersey Standard's marketing in their territories as Esso (derived from the initials for Standard Oil). To end the confusion, in 1972 Jersey Standard became Exxon, a name change that cost $100 million.

Nationalization of oil assets by producing countries reduced Exxon's access to oil during the 1970s. Though it increased exploration that decade and the next, Exxon's reserves shrank.

Oil tanker *Exxon Valdez* spilled some 11 million gallons of oil into Alaska's Prince William Sound in 1989. Exxon spent billions on the cleanup, and in 1994 a federal jury in Alaska ordered the company to pay $5.3 billion in punitive damages to fishermen and others affected by the spill. (Exxon appealed, and in 2001 the jury award was reduced to $2.5 billion, and in 2008 to $507.5 million.)

With the oil industry consolidating, Exxon merged its worldwide oil and fuel additives business with that of Royal Dutch/Shell in 1996. The next year, under FTC pressure, Exxon agreed to run ads refuting claims that its premium gas enabled car engines to run more efficiently. Another PR disaster followed in 1998 when CEO Lee Raymond upset environmentalists by publicly questioning the global warming theory.

Still, Exxon was unstoppable. It acquired Mobil for $81 billion in 1999; the new company had Raymond at the helm and Mobil's Lucio Noto as vice chairman. (Noto retired in 2001.) To get the deal done, Exxon Mobil had to divest $4 billion in assets. It agreed to end its European gasoline and lubricants joint venture with BP and to sell more than 2,400 gas stations in the US. It sold 1,740 East Coast gas stations to Tosco and a California refinery and 340 gas stations to Valero Energy for about $1 billion.

In 2001 Exxon Mobil also announced that it was proceeding with a $12 billion project (with Japanese, Indian, and Russian partners) to develop oil fields in the Russian Far East.

Exxon Mobil sold its 3.7% stake in China Petroleum & Chemical Corp. (Sinopec) in 2005. Later that year the company was ordered to pay $1.3 billion to about 10,000 gas station owners for overcharges dating back to 1983. In 2008 the company began to sell to distributors its remaining 820 company-owned US gas stations.

EXECUTIVES

Chairman and CEO: Rex W. Tillerson, age 57,
$27,168,316 total compensation
SVP: Andrew P. (Andy) Swiger, age 53
SVP and Treasurer: Donald D. (Don) Humphreys,
age 62, $11,870,594 total compensation
SVP: Michael J. (Mike) Dolan, age 56,
$9,694,797 total compensation
SVP: Mark W. Albers, age 53
VP Safety, Security, Health, and Environment:
O. K. Owen
VP and General Counsel: S.J. Balagia, age 58
VP Human Resources: Lucille J. Cavanaugh
VP Public Affairs: Kenneth P. (Ken) Cohen
VP Environmental Policy and Planning:
Sherri K. Stuewer
VP Investor Relations and Secretary:
David S. Rosenthal, age 53
VP; President, ExxonMobil Chemical:
Stephen D. (Steve) Pryor, age 60,
$10,556,536 total compensation
VP; President, ExxonMobil Fuels Marketing:
Harold R. (Hal) Cramer, age 59,
$10,362,631 total compensation
VP; President, ExxonMobil Production:
R. M. (Rich) Kruger, age 50
**VP; President, ExxonMobil Lubricants and Petroleum
Specialties:** Allan J. Kelly, age 52
VP; President, ExxonMobil Exploration:
A. Timothy (Tim) Cejka, age 58
VP; President, ExxonMobil Upstream Ventures:
R. S. Franklin, age 52

VP; President, ExxonMobil Gas and Power Marketing:
T.R. (Tom) Walters, age 55
VP; President, ExxonMobil Refining and Supply:
Sherman J. Glass Jr., age 62
President, ExxonMobil Upstream Research:
Sara N. Ortwein
President, ExxonMobil Upstream Research:
Steve S. M. Greenlee
President, ExxonMobil Development Company:
Neil W. Duffin, age 53
President, XTO Energy: Jack Williams
President, ExxonMobil Research and Engineering:
Richard V. (Rich) Pisarczyk
President, ExxonMobil Global Services:
Neil A. Chapman
Auditors: PricewaterhouseCoopers LLP

LOCATIONS

HQ: Exxon Mobil Corporation
5959 Las Colinas Blvd., Irving, TX 75039
Phone: 972-444-1000   **Fax:** 972-444-1350
Web: www.exxon.mobil.com

2009 Sales

	% of total
US	30
Japan	7
Canada	7
UK	7
Belgium	6
Germany	5
Italy	4
France	4
Singapore	3
Other countries	27
Total	**100**

PRODUCTS/OPERATIONS

2009 Sales

	% of total
Downstream	83
Chemicals	9
Upstream	8
Total	**100**

Selected Subsidiaries and Affiliates

Aera Energy, LLC (48%)
Al-Jubail Petrochemical Company (50%)
Esso Petroleum Company, Limited (UK)
ExxonMobil Chemical Company
ExxonMobil Pipeline Company
Imperial Oil Limited (69.6%, Canada)

COMPETITORS

7-Eleven
Ashland Inc.
BHP Billiton
BP
Chevron
ConocoPhillips
Costco Wholesale
Dow Chemical
DuPont
Eastman Chemical
Eni
Hess Corporation
Huntsman International
JX Holdings
Koch Industries, Inc.
Marathon Oil
Norsk Hydro ASA
Occidental Petroleum
PEMEX
PETROBRAS
Petróleos de Venezuela
Racetrac Petroleum
Repsol YPF
Royal Dutch Shell
Saudi Aramco
Sunoco
TOTAL
Valero Energy

HISTORICAL FINANCIALS

Company Type: Public

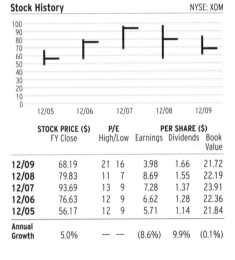

Income Statement				FYE: December 31
	REVENUE ($ mil.)	NET INCOME ($ mil.)	NET PROFIT MARGIN	EMPLOYEES
12/09	310,586	19,280	6.2%	80,700
12/08	477,359	45,220	9.5%	79,900
12/07	404,552	40,610	10.0%	80,800
12/06	377,635	39,500	10.5%	82,100
12/05	370,680	36,130	9.7%	83,700
Annual Growth	**(4.3%)**	**(14.5%)**	**—**	**(0.9%)**

2009 Year-End Financials

Debt ratio: 6.4%
Return on equity: 17.3%
Cash ($ mil.): 10,693
Current ratio: 1.06
Long-term debt ($ mil.): 7,129
No. of shares (mil.): 5,092
Dividends
  Yield: 2.4%
  Payout: 41.7%
Market value ($ mil.): 347,210

Stock History

NYSE: XOM

	STOCK PRICE ($) FY Close	P/E High/Low		PER SHARE ($) Earnings	Dividends	Book Value
12/09	68.19	21	16	3.98	1.66	21.72
12/08	79.83	11	7	8.69	1.55	22.19
12/07	93.69	13	9	7.28	1.37	23.91
12/06	76.63	12	9	6.62	1.28	22.36
12/05	56.17	12	9	5.71	1.14	21.84
Annual Growth	**5.0%**	—	—	**(8.6%)**	**9.9%**	**(0.1%)**

Family Dollar Stores

Penny-pinching moms are important to Family Dollar Stores. The nation's #2 dollar store (behind Dollar General) targets women shopping for a family earning less than $40,000 a year. It operates about 6,665 stores in some 45 states and the District of Columbia. Consumables (food, health and beauty aids, and household items) account for more than 60% of sales; the stores also sell apparel, shoes, and linens. Family Dollar emphasizes small-format neighborhood stores near its low- and middle-income customers in rural and urban areas. Most merchandise (national brands, Family Dollar private labels, and unbranded items) costs less than $10. Family Dollar was founded in 1959 by the father of CEO Howard Levine.

Rapidly rising unemployment and a decrease in the number of hours worked have hit Family Dollar's low-income customers hard in recent years. They responded by increasing purchases of lower-margin consumables and avoiding higher priced merchandise. The chain answered by devoting more retail space to consumable items and by controlling costs. Indeed, consumables have grown to account for about 65% of Family Dollar's sales (up from about 59% in fiscal 2007). Both the chain and its customers got a boost from certain government stimulus programs. Also, Family Dollar experienced more visits from middle-income shoppers seeking to save money on basic necessities.

In the face of increased competition from mass discounters, such as Wal-Mart, the company has shifted to an everyday-low-pricing strategy (as opposed to short-lived promotional advertising), while increasing the number of brand-name goods it carries. It announced in April 2009 that it will roll out some 250 new food items (including Triscuits and Double Stuf Oreos) at its stores to compete head to head with its rivals. Family Dollar Stores is also expanding its food offering to include milk and other perishables, as well as more quick-prep and ready-to-eat products. To keep food fresh, Family Dollar has installed refrigerated coolers in most stores. In addition to selling more groceries, the dollar chain has begun accepting food stamps to attract more low-income customers.

While Family Dollar has been aggressively expanding its retail footprint — adding more than 4,000 new stores in the last 10 years — the pace of new store openings has cooled more recently.

HISTORY

Leon Levine came from a retailing family. His father, who founded The Hub, a general store-style department store in Rockingham, North Carolina, in 1908, died when Levine was 13. Leon and his older brother Al helped their mother run the store. (Al went on to found the Pic 'n Pay self-service shoe stores in 1957.) In 1959, when he was 25, Levine (with his cousin Bernie) opened his own store in Charlotte, with nothing priced over a dollar, targeting low- and middle-income families. The concept of low prices and small neighborhood stores was immediately popular, and Levine began adding stores. By 1970, when he took Family Dollar Stores public, it had 100 stores in five states. That year Levine brought his cousin Lewis into the business.

Family Dollar's profits plummeted in the mid-1970s as the chain's low-income customers, hit by recession, cut back on spending — even though all merchandise was priced at $3 or less. Such pricing made for tight margins, so the company dropped the policy. Family Dollar also improved inventory controls to make operations more efficient and began moving into other states. Sales picked up, topping $100 million in 1977, and the next year the firm bought the 40-store Top Dollar chain from Sav-A-Stop.

As the 1980s began, Family Dollar had nearly 400 stores in eight southern states; rapidly expanding, it was adding more than 100 stores a year. But in an effort to boost margins, the company had lost its pricing edge to a new threat — Wal-Mart's truckload prices and quick domination of the southern discount retailing market.

After Family Dollar sales were flat in 1986 and dropped 10% in 1987, Levine finally took action. He found his prices were sometimes as much as 10% higher than Wal-Mart's and his stores were often insufficiently stocked with advertised products. He lowered prices, declaring that Family Dollar would not be undersold, and again instituted new inventory controls. But the action had not come quickly enough, argued president and COO Lewis, who left the company in 1987. (He was also upset over a huge salary disparity: Leon — noted for being a hard bargainer with suppliers — was making $1.8 million a year, compared to Lewis' $260,000.) Leon's son Howard, who

joined the firm in 1981, also left; he returned to the fold in 1996 and became CEO in 1998.

Family Dollar picked up momentum in the 1990s. It implemented a major renovation of stores and phased out low-margin items such as motor oil and tools in favor of such high-margin items as toys and electronics. The company also accelerated its growth plans, opening stores in a number of new markets and setting up a second distribution center, in Arkansas, in 1994 to support its westward expansion. Also that year Family Dollar began offering everyday low prices and scaled back its sales promotions.

The pace of expansion was steady during the late 1990s, as the company opened hundreds of new stores and more distribution centers and closed underperforming locations. Family Dollar added 165 stores in fiscal 1996, 186 in fiscal 1997, 250 in fiscal 1998, and 366 in fiscal 1999 (its largest single-year increase in stores). It continued adding stores in 2000 and 2001 (although the rate of growth began slowing) and it began emphasizing food, household products, and gift and seasonal items rather than clothing.

Family Dollar increased its presence in urban areas by locating 40% of the 475 stores added in 2002 in cities. Historically about 25% of its stores have been placed in urban markets.

Founder Leon Levine retired in January 2003, 43 years after starting the company. His son Howard (CEO) succeeded him as chairman. In 2003 Family Dollar Stores opened its seventh distribution center and 475 new stores, including its first outlets in Wyoming and North Dakota. In 2004 the chain opened an additional 500 outlets, increasing its store count by about 10%.

In 2006 an Alabama jury found Family Dollar guilty of violating the Federal Labor Standards Act by misclassifying hourly employees as salaried managers to avoid paying overtime. As a result the company was fined $16.6 million.

EXECUTIVES

Chairman and CEO: Howard R. Levine, age 50, $5,948,612 total compensation
President and COO: R. James (Jim) Kelly, $4,044,902 total compensation
EVP and Chief Merchandising Officer: Dorlisa K. Flur, age 44, $1,134,198 total compensation
EVP Supply Chain: Charles S. Gibson Jr., age 48, $1,300,824 total compensation
EVP Store Operations: Barry W. Sullivan, age 45
SVP and CFO: Kenneth T. (Ken) Smith, age 48, $716,058 total compensation
SVP and CIO: Joshua R. (Josh) Jewett, age 39
SVP Human Resources: Bryan E. Venberg, age 41
SVP General Counsel, and Secretary: Janet G. Kelley, age 54
SVP Store Construction and Facility Management: Keith M. Gehl, age 48
SVP Hardlines and Marketing: John J. Scanlon, age 59
SVP Planning, Allocation, and Replenishment: Bryan P. Causey
SVP General Counsel, and Secretary: James C. (Jim) Snyder Jr., age 46
SVP Global Sourcing: Kevin Boyanowski
SVP Customer Marketing: Don Hamblen
SVP Finance: C. Martin Sowers, age 51
SVP New Stores: Thomas M. (Tom) Nash
SVP Global Sourcing: Wook Lee
VP Marketing: Donald G. Smith
VP Replenishment: Jeff Thomas
VP Investor Relations and Communications: Kiley F. Rawlins
Auditors: PricewaterhouseCoopers LLP

LOCATIONS

HQ: Family Dollar Stores, Inc.
10401 Monroe Rd., Matthews, NC 28105
Phone: 704-847-6961 **Fax:** 704-847-0189
Web: www.familydollar.com

2009 Stores

	No.
Texas	841
Ohio	413
Florida	391
North Carolina	370
Michigan	349
Georgia	313
New York	291
Pennsylvania	273
Louisiana	228
Illinois	223
Virginia	215
Tennessee	205
South Carolina	203
Indiana	195
Kentucky	188
Alabama	144
Wisconsin	136
Arizona	135
Oklahoma	128
Mississippi	119
West Virginia	117
Colorado	105
Massachusetts	104
Arkansas	101
Missouri	95
New Mexico	94
Maryland	91
New Jersey	78
Minnesota	70
Utah	59
Maine	51
Connecticut	49
Kansas	35
Iowa	32
Idaho	31
Nebraska	31
Nevada	26
South Dakota	23
New Hampshire	22
Rhode Island	22
Other states	56
Total	**6,664**

PRODUCTS/OPERATIONS

2009 Sales

	% of total
Consumables	65
Home products	13
Apparel & accessories	11
Seasonal & electronics	11
Total	**100**

2009 Sales

	% of total
Nationally advertised brands	52
Family Dollar brands	19
Other labels	29
Total	**100**

Selected Products

Hardlines
Automotive supplies
Candy, snacks, and other foods
Electronics
Gifts
Hardware
Health and beauty aids
Household chemical products
Household paper products
Housewares
Seasonal goods
Stationery and school supplies
Toys

Soft goods
  Apparel (men's, women's, children's, and infants')
  Domestics (blankets, sheets, and towels)
  Shoes

COMPETITORS

7-Eleven
Big Lots
BJ's Wholesale Club
Costco Wholesale
CVS Caremark
Dollar General
Dollar Tree
Duckwall-ALCO
Food Lion
Fred's
J. C. Penney
Kmart
Kroger
Meijer
Old Navy
Pamida Stores
The Pantry
Retail Ventures
Rite Aid
Sears
ShopKo Stores
Simply Amazing
SUPERVALU
Target
Toys "R" Us
Variety Wholesalers
Walgreen
Wal-Mart

HISTORICAL FINANCIALS

Company Type: Public

Income Statement

FYE: Saturday nearest August 31

	REVENUE ($ mil.)	NET INCOME ($ mil.)	NET PROFIT MARGIN	EMPLOYEES
8/09	7,401	291	3.9%	47,000
8/08	6,984	233	3.3%	44,000
8/07	6,834	243	3.6%	44,000
8/06	6,395	195	3.1%	44,000
8/05	5,825	218	3.7%	42,000
Annual Growth	6.2%	7.6%	—	2.9%

2009 Year-End Financials

Debt ratio: 17.4%
Return on equity: 21.6%
Cash ($ mil.): 439
Current ratio: 1.51
Long-term debt ($ mil.): 250

No. of shares (mil.): 133
Dividends
  Yield: 1.7%
  Payout: 25.1%
Market value ($ mil.): 4,016

Stock History

NYSE: FDO

	STOCK PRICE ($) FY Close	P/E High/Low	PER SHARE ($) Earnings	Dividends	Book Value
8/09	30.28	17 10	2.07	0.52	10.86
8/08	24.92	18 9	1.66	0.48	9.45
8/07	29.28	22 15	1.62	0.44	8.86
8/06	25.57	22 15	1.26	0.40	9.11
8/05	19.88	27 15	1.30	0.36	10.77
Annual Growth	11.1%	— —	12.3%	9.6%	0.2%

Fastenal Company

Some might say it has a screw loose, but things are really pretty snug at Fastenal. The company operates more than 2,360 stores in all 50 US states as well as in Canada, Mexico, Puerto Rico, Asia, and Europe. Its stores stock about 690,000 products in about a dozen categories, including threaded fasteners (such as screws, nuts, and bolts). Other sales come from fluid-transfer parts for hydraulic and pneumatic power; janitorial, electrical, and welding supplies; material handling items; metal-cutting tool blades; and power tools. Its customers are typically construction, manufacturing, and other industrial professionals. Fastenal Company was founded by its chairman Bob Kierlin in 1967 and went public in 1987.

Fastenal has been one of the fastest-growing companies in the US, adding upwards of 150 stores annually over the past several years, yet its growth has slowed amid slumping revenues and tough economic conditions worldwide. In 2008 Fastenal's sales peaked at $2.3 billion, and it opened about 160 new locations worldwide. The following year, however, sales fell to $1.9 billion, a more than 15% drop. The company also reduced its store openings to about 70 new outlets. (Among these were new locations in China, Malaysia, and Hungary.) Compounding the revenue drop, Fastenal's profits fell by more than 30%, from nearly $280 million to $184 million, in 2009. Still, Fastenal sees growth in its future. It is adding bigger stores with larger staffs, in hopes of boosting revenues, albeit at a slower rate than in previous years. The company is optimistic that when the economy bounces back, North America can support at least 3,500 of its stores in small, midsized, and large markets. (It currently has about 2,350 locations in North America.) Fastenal also looks to continue growing in Asia. Nearly 10% of its revenue is generated outside the US.

Products manufactured by other companies account for about 95% of total sales, and the remainder comes from items custom-made or modified by Fastenal. Threaded fasteners typically bring in about 45% of revenue while the balance is generated by sales of various nonfastener products, such as material handling, electrical, and janitorial supplies. In a bid to boost fastener sales, the company acquired the inventory and assets of Holo-Krome, a Connecticut-based maker of socket head fasteners, for $5 million in late 2009. The deal included the rights to Holo-Krome's brand.

Fastenal stores have been moving away from their traditional focus on wholesaling. The company's "expected inventory" format tailors stores' product offerings to demands in their specific geographic areas with the goal of being the best industrial and construction supplier in their local markets. Stores are supplied by more than a dozen distribution centers throughout North America.

HISTORY

Peace Corps veteran Robert Kierlin led four friends and Winona Cotter High School classmates in founding Fastenal in 1967 as a distributor of threaded fasteners. (Kierlin's inspiration was customers' inquiries at his father's auto parts store.) The company and its lone store lost money its first two years, but it was able to open

another store by 1970. Fastenal then changed its retail focus from regular consumers to contractors and professionals.

The company expanded, locating stores on the outskirts of small and medium-sized cities where real estate and operating costs are lower. By 1987 it had 58 stores. Fastenal went public that year, using some 40% of the IPO proceeds to establish the Hiawatha Education Foundation to support private high school education, especially the founders' financially troubled alma mater.

Fastenal grew quickly during the early 1990s, from about 100 stores in 1990 to nearly 400 stores in small and large US cities in 1995. It added tool-sharpening services to its stores the next year. The firm also added new product lines as it expanded, including FastTool tools and safety supplies (1993), SharpCut blades and PowerFlow fluid-transfer components (1996), and FastArc welding supplies (1997). In 1997 Fastenal opened its first store in Puerto Rico.

In 1998 the company printed its first catalog and formed a subsidiary to sell its products in Mexico. Fastenal started selling online in 1999. In 2000 the company opened about 90 stores, and the next year opened more than 125, including one in Singapore. In 2002 the company made a move into the retail market through its purchase of the retail fastener and related hardware business of two Textron subsidiaries. The company sold that business, however, to Hillman Companies later that year.

In 2004 Fastenal opened 219 stores (including its first in the Netherlands) compared to 151 new outlets in 2003. In 2005 the company opened its first store in China and added, overall, about 220 stores. 2006 saw the opening of 225 additional stores.

EXECUTIVES

Chairman: Robert A. (Bob) Kierlin, age 70
President, CEO, and Director:
  Willard D. (Will) Oberton, age 51,
  $945,092 total compensation
EVP Operations: James C. (Cory) Jansen, age 39,
  $675,799 total compensation
EVP and CFO: Daniel L. (Dan) Florness, age 47,
  $365,562 total compensation
EVP Sales: Nicholas J. (Nick) Lundquist, age 52,
  $688,312 total compensation
EVP Human Resources and Director:
  Reyne K. Wisecup, age 47
EVP Sales: Steven A. (Steve) Rucinski, age 53,
  $322,443 total compensation
EVP Sales: Leland J. (Lee) Hein, age 49,
  $338,202 total compensation
Auditors: KPMG LLP

LOCATIONS

HQ: Fastenal Company
  2001 Theurer Blvd., Winona, MN 55987
Phone: 507-454-5374   **Fax:** 507-453-8049
Web: www.fastenal.com

2009 Stores

	No.
US	2,153
Canada	169
Mexico	32
Puerto Rico	9
China	2
Hungary	1
Malaysia	1
Netherlands	1
Singapore	1
Total	**2,369**

2009 Sales

	$ mil.	% of total
US	1,769.9	92
Canada	115.3	6
Other countries	45.1	2
Total	**1,930.3**	**100**

PRODUCTS/OPERATIONS

Selected Brands, Products, and Services

Blackstone (welding supplies and cutting tools)
Bodyguard (safety supplies)
Caliber (material handling and storage products)
Clean Choice (janitorial supplies)
Dynaflo (hydraulics and pneumatics)
EquipRite (material handling and storage products)
Fastenal (fasteners, tools, hydraulics and pneumatics, safety supplies, and metals)
FMT (cutting tools)
FNL G9 (fasteners)
Holo-Krome (fasteners)
PowerPhase (electrical supplies)
Profitter (hydraulics and pneumatics)
Rock River (fasteners and tools)
Tritan (cutting tools)

COMPETITORS

359Ace Hardware	MSC Industrial Direct
Anixter Aerospace	Noland
Applied Industrial Technologies	Park-Ohio Holdings
	PennEngineering
HD Supply	Production Tool Supply
Home Depot	Snap-on
Lawson Products	True Value
Lowe's	WinWholesale
Menard	W.W. Grainger

HISTORICAL FINANCIALS

Company Type: Public

Income Statement

FYE: December 31

	REVENUE ($ mil.)	NET INCOME ($ mil.)	NET PROFIT MARGIN	EMPLOYEES
12/09	1,930	184	9.6%	12,045
12/08	2,340	280	12.0%	13,634
12/07	2,062	233	11.3%	12,013
12/06	1,809	199	11.0%	10,415
12/05	1,523	167	10.9%	9,306
Annual Growth	**6.1%**	**2.5%**	**—**	**6.7%**

2009 Year-End Financials

Debt ratio: —
Return on equity: 15.8%
Cash ($ mil.): 165
Current ratio: 8.22
Long-term debt ($ mil.): —

No. of shares (mil.): 147
Dividends
  Yield: 1.7%
  Payout: 58.1%
Market value ($ mil.): 6,139

Stock History

NASDAQ (GS): FAST

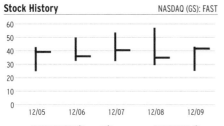

	STOCK PRICE ($) FY Close	P/E High/Low		PER SHARE ($) Earnings	Dividends	Book Value
12/09	41.64	34 21		1.24	0.72	8.08
12/08	34.85	30 16		1.88	0.52	7.75
12/07	40.42	34 21		1.55	0.44	6.85
12/06	35.88	37 25		1.32	0.40	6.25
12/05	39.13	38 23		1.10	0.31	5.31
Annual Growth	**1.6%**	**— —**		**3.0%**	**23.5%**	**11.0%**

Federal-Mogul

For Federal-Mogul, the sum of the parts is greater than the whole. The company makes components used in cars, trucks, and commercial vehicles, as well as in energy, industrial, and other transportation equipment. Its products include pistons, spark plugs, ignition coils, bearings, gaskets, seals, and brake pads sold under brand names such as Champion, Federal-Mogul, FelPro, Glyco, and Moog. Federal-Mogul has manufacturing and distribution facilities in 33 countries worldwide; customers include global automakers such as BMW, General Motors, Ford, and Volkswagen. Federal-Mogul also distributes its own and others' auto parts to aftermarket customers.

Using joint ventures and alliances, Federal-Mogul has expanded its geographic reach into emerging markets, including China, India, South Korea, Russia, and Turkey. These partnerships allow the company to develop and extend its product lines, lower manufacturing costs, broaden its customer base, and provide additional opportunities to grow its business with Asian and other OEMs operating in the BRIC (Brazil, Russia, India, China) growth regions.

While the company has worked to rebuild its health after a rough decade, the automotive market is still feeling the ill effects of decreased demand. To maintain flexibility and reduce its dependence on cars, trucks, and commercial vehicles, Federal-Mogul has applied its core products in other areas. It has expanded into the aerospace (brake products for airplanes), railroad (piston rings for locomotives), and off-shore and marine markets (large bore rings and seals). Its push into power generation (large bearings for windmills) includes a mid-2010 acquisition of piston ring supplier Daros Group, which expands Federal-Mogul's presence in commercial engines and wind energy.

The company is also streamlining its operations. It closed two powertrain plants in the US and two others in Western Europe, transferring the operations to Poland, Turkey, and Mexico. The company also mothballed distribution centers in the US, Canada, and Europe. Through 2009, Federal-Mogul cut its workforce by about 8,600 people, a 20% reduction.

After filing Chapter 11 six years earlier, Federal-Mogul emerged from bankruptcy in 2007. While out of bankruptcy reorganization, Federal-Mogul is carrying about $3 billion in debt, a factor that could become critical if the worldwide credit crisis continues and the company needs to refinance its debt.

Billionaire investor and chairman Carl Icahn previously owned about 25% of the company, after buying more than $1 billion worth of Federal-Mogul's debt. In 2008 he exercised his options to buy an additional 50.1 million shares in the company; as a result, Icahn now owns some 76% of Federal-Mogul.

HISTORY

In 1899 J. Howard Muzzy and Edward Lyon formed the Muzzy-Lyon Company, and later, subsidiary Mogul Metal Company. The two modified a printer's typecasting machine and developed a process for making die-cast engine bearings. Their first big order came in 1910, when Buick ordered 10,000 connecting rod bearings for the Buick 10. In 1924 Mogul Metal

merged with Federal Bearing and Bushing to become Federal-Mogul Corporation.

In 1941 Federal-Mogul had about 50 factories dedicated to the war effort, and by 1945 sales had doubled from prewar levels. In 1955 the company acquired Bower Roller Bearing Company and changed its name to Federal-Mogul-Bower Bearings, Inc. By the late 1950s it had nearly 100 distribution centers and sales had quadrupled in 10 years.

The company began investing in foreign manufacturing plants during the 1960s to safeguard against lower US car exports as more foreign cars entered the global market. It changed its name back to Federal-Mogul in 1965 and moved its headquarters from Detroit to Southfield, Michigan, the following year. Following a recession in the mid-1970s, Federal-Mogul realized that it was too dependent on the big automakers and began diversifying. It acquired the Mather Company, a maker of high-performance sealing products, in 1985. The next year it bought Carter Automotive (fuel pumps) and Signal-Stat (lighting and safety components).

In 1989 Dennis Gormley became CEO. He continued the diversification strategy and led the company into the automotive aftermarket. Gormley proposed a push into retail in 1992, and that year Federal-Mogul bought the aftermarket business of TRW Inc. In its effort to become the Pep Boys of the third world, the company sold parts of its manufacturing business to finance its retail ventures. By 1996 it owned about 130 retail stores, primarily in Latin America. The company lost money, and that year Gormley resigned. His successor, Dick Snell, put an immediate end to the retail fiasco.

By 1998 Federal-Mogul had sold all of its retail holdings and was concentrating on providing parts for entire engine systems. That year it made two major acquisitions: Fel-Pro, a domestic maker of gaskets and other sealing products, and T&N plc, a British maker of bearings, pistons, and brake pads, and Europe's largest asbestos maker during the 1980s. T&N was picked up on the cheap, as its stock was depressed by looming asbestos lawsuits. The decision would prove a grave one for Federal-Mogul.

Driving further into the aftermarket, Federal-Mogul paid $1.9 billion for the automotive business of Cooper Industries (Champion spark plugs, windshield wipers, steering and suspension parts, brake parts).

In 2000 Federal-Mogul announced plans to close 22 North American replacement parts warehouses and consolidate 18 manufacturing plants in Europe and Asia. CEO Richard Snell stepped down that year. Federal-Mogul director Robert Miller replaced Snell as chairman and became the interim CEO.

Early in 2001 Frank Macher, a former Ford and ITT Automotive executive, was named CEO. Not long after, in the midst of the economic slowdown, Federal-Mogul announced that it would cut its salaried workforce by almost 9%.

After an ill-advised acquisitions bender, which more than tripled the size of the company, and reeling from the costs of T&N asbestos claims, Federal-Mogul was forced into bankruptcy in 2001.

In 2005 the company named José Maria Alapont as CEO. Carl Icahn was appointed chairman in 2008 after acquiring an additional 50% stake in Federal-Mogul.

Following six years in bankruptcy, in 2007 Federal-Mogul emerged from Chapter 11.

EXECUTIVES

Chairman: Carl C. Icahn, age 74
President, CEO, and Director: José Maria Alapont, age 59, $3,314,205 total compensation
SVP and CFO: Alan Haughie, age 46
SVP Business and Operations Strategy: Jean Brunol, age 57, $1,298,761 total compensation
SVP Sales and Marketing: William (Steve) Bowers, age 57, $856,693 total compensation
SVP General Counsel, and Secretary: Robert L. (Bobby) Katz, age 47
SVP Powertrain Energy: Rainer Jueckstock, age 50
SVP Global Purchasing: Markus Wermers, age 45
SVP Customer Satisfaction and Global Manufacturing: Eric McAlexander, age 53
SVP Customer Satisfaction, Global Engineering, and Manufacturing: René L.F. Dalleur, age 56, $1,031,400 total compensation
SVP Vehicle Safety and Protection: Ramzi Y. Hermiz, age 44
SVP Powertrain Bearings and Sealings: Gérard Chochoy, age 56, $1,041,956 total compensation
SVP Global Aftermarket: James (Jay) Burkhart, age 52
SVP Global Human Resources and Organization: Pascal Goachet, age 59
VP Corporate Communications and Government Relations: Steven K. Gaut, age 48
VP Investor Relations: David Pouliot
VP and CIO: Alston German, age 45
Director Corporate Communications: Jim Burke
Investor Relations Representative: Kathy Fauls
Auditors: Ernst & Young LLP

LOCATIONS

HQ: Federal-Mogul Corporation
26555 Northwestern Hwy., Southfield, MI 48033
Phone: 248-354-7700   **Fax:** 248-354-8950
Web: www.federalmogul.com

2009 Sales

	$ mil.	% of total
US	2,131	40
Germany	880	16
France	427	8
Italy	263	5
UK	221	4
Mexico	193	4
Other countries	1,215	23
Total	**5,330**	**100**

PRODUCTS/OPERATIONS

2009 Sales

	$ mil.	% of total
Global aftermarket	2,326	44
Powertrain energy	1,413	27
Powertrain sealing & bearings	819	15
Vehicle safety & protection	772	14
Total	**5,330**	**100**

Selected Products

Global Aftermarket
- Bearings and seals
- Camshafts
- Chassis
- Driveline
- Engine bearings
- Filters
- Friction products (brake drums, linings, pads, and rotors)
- Fuel pumps
- Gaskets
- Ignition products
- Lighting products
- Oil pumps
- Performance additives
- Piston rings
- Pistons
- Spark plugs
- Steering and suspension products
- Timing components
- Valvetrain components
- Wipers

Powertrain Energy
- Camshafts
- Connecting rods
- Cylinder liners
- Engine pistons
- Ignition products
- Piston pins
- Piston rings
- Valve seats and guides

Powertrain Sealing and Bearings
- Aluminum engine bearings
- Bonded piston seals
- Bronze engine bearings
- Bushings and washers
- Combustion and exhaust gaskets
- Dynamic seals
- Engine bearings
- Heat shields
- Metallic filters
- Sintered engine and transmission components
- Static gaskets and seals
- Transmission components

Vehicle Safety and Protection
- Brake disc pads
- Brake linings and blocks
- Brake shoes
- Chassis parts (ball joints, tie rod ends, sway bar links, idler arms, and pitman arms)
- Element resistant sleeving systems (protection products for wires, hoses, sensors, and mechanical components)
- Fuel pumps
- Lighting (interior and exterior lighting components)
- Railway brake blocks
- Railway disc pads
- Windshield wipers

COMPETITORS

Affinia Group
Aisin Seiki
Akebono Brake
American Trim
ArvinMeritor
ATC Technology
Bendix Commercial Vehicle Systems
Continental AG
Cooper-Standard Automotive
Daido Steel
Dana Holding
Delphi Automotive
Edelbrock
EnPro
Freudenberg-NOK
GE
GKN
Hastings Manufacturing
Honeywell International
Kolbenschmidt Pierburg
Linamar Corp.
Mahle International
MAN
Miba
NGK SPARK PLUG
Nippon Piston Ring
Remy International
Robert Bosch
SPX
Stanadyne
Standard Motor Products
Stant Manufacturing
Sumitomo Metal Industries
Trico Products
TRW Automotive
Universal Manufacturing
Valeo
Visteon

HISTORICAL FINANCIALS

Company Type: Public

Income Statement

FYE: December 31

	REVENUE ($ mil.)	NET INCOME ($ mil.)	NET PROFIT MARGIN	EMPLOYEES
12/09	5,330	(45)	—	39,000
12/08	6,866	(468)	—	43,400
12/07	6,914	1,412	20.4%	50,000
12/06	6,326	(550)	—	43,100
12/05	6,286	(334)	—	41,700
Annual Growth	**(4.0%)**	**—**	**—**	**(1.7%)**

2009 Year-End Financials

Debt ratio: 269.8%
Return on equity: —
Cash ($ mil.): 1,034
Current ratio: 2.37
Long-term debt ($ mil.): 2,760
No. of shares (mil.): 99
Dividends
  Yield: 0.0%
  Payout: —
Market value ($ mil.): 1,711

Stock History

NASDAQ (GS): FDML

	STOCK PRICE ($) FY Close	P/E High/Low	PER SHARE ($) Earnings	Dividends	Book Value
12/09	17.30	— —	(0.46)	0.00	10.34
12/08	4.23	— —	(4.69)	0.00	9.62
Annual Growth	**309.0%**	**— —**	**—**	**—**	**7.6%**

FedEx Corporation

Holding company FedEx hopes its package of subsidiaries will keep delivering significant market share. Its FedEx Express unit is the world's #1 express transportation provider, delivering about 3.5 million packages daily to more than 220 countries and territories. It maintains a fleet of more than 665 aircraft and more than 41,000 motor vehicles and trailers. To complement the express delivery business, FedEx Ground provides small-package ground delivery in North America, and less-than-truckload (LTL) carrier FedEx Freight hauls larger shipments. FedEx Office stores offer a variety of document-related and other business services and serve as retail hubs for other FedEx units.

FedEx Express added a transpacific delivery in the spring of 2010 to accommodate the capacity from Asia to the US. In June 2009 the company cinched a deal with OfficeMax to provide express and ground shipping services at all US OfficeMax retail stores (more than 900 locations).

As part of its 2008 worldwide expansion plan, Fedex Express continues to grow outside the US, particularly in China, India, and Europe, and it has purchased six additional Boeing 777 air freighters for its fleet. The express unit opened several offices in Europe and the Middle East in mid-2010, responding to preferences by consumers to have a physical company presence in their region.

In the US, FedEx has been building out the networks of both FedEx Ground and FedEx Freight, which have been the company's fastest-growing units.

FedEx Office (formerly FedEx Kinko's) leads the company's FedEx Services segment, which also provides support services related to sales, marketing, and other functions, mainly for FedEx Express and FedEx Ground. Overall, FedEx Office has about 2,000 stores, primarily in the US. The holding company hopes to sell more air and ground shipping services from the stores, even as demand for copying and printing slows.

Like the rest of the industry, FedEx experienced high fuel costs at the beginning of 2008, which transitioned to lower consumer demand for its express services during the end of the year. Coping with the crisis, at the end of 2008 FedEx implemented a hiring freeze, suspended 401K contributions, and decreased pay for salaried personnel by 5%. The company shed some 10,000 workers by 2009 — still only about 3% of its total workforce.

HISTORY

From his undergraduate classes at Yale and his experience as a charter airplane pilot, Fred Smith got the idea that increased automation of business processes would create the need for a reliable overnight delivery service, and he presented his case in a term paper in 1965. After serving in the Marine Corps in Vietnam, Smith began raising money to develop the overnight delivery idea. He founded Federal Express in 1971 with $4 million inherited from his father and $80 million from investors. Overnight and second-day delivery to two dozen US cities began in 1973.

Several factors contributed to FedEx's early success: Airlines turned their focus from parcels to passengers; United Parcel Service (UPS) union workers went on strike in 1974; and competitor REA Express went bankrupt. FedEx went public in 1978.

Spotting e-mail's threat to express delivery during the early 1980s, FedEx invested heavily in satellite-based system ZapMail. However, the humble fax machine blindsided FedEx, and it lost over $300 million in 1986 on the short-lived service. The 1987 launch of PowerShip, which processed shipments electronically, was more successful.

FedEx expanded internationally in the late 1980s, buying Italy's SAMIMA and three Japanese freight carriers in 1988 and Tiger International (Flying Tigers line) in 1989.

In 1991 FedEx introduced EXPRESSfreighter, an international air-express cargo service, but suffered a setback when its loss-making European delivery service was scrapped the next year. However, FedEx was back on its feet in 1995 when it created Latin American and Caribbean divisions and became the first US express carrier with direct flights to China.

The 1997 UPS strike put an extra 850,000 packages a day into FedEx's hands. Turning the screws on UPS, FedEx bought ground carrier Caliber System in 1998 and reorganized into holding company FDX. FedEx pilots (unionized in 1993) threatened to strike during the 1998 holiday season, prompting FedEx to outsource more of its flight operations. Nevertheless, the pilots ratified a five-year contract in 1999.

In 2000 FDX changed its name to FedEx. In a landmark deal with the United States Postal Service, FedEx Express began transporting mail

shipments (but not making deliveries) in 2001, and FedEx drop boxes were placed in post offices.

The company acquired less-than-truckload (LTL) carrier American Freightways in 2001, and FedEx Freight was created to operate American Freightways and Viking Freight, which the company had acquired in the Caliber deal.

FedEx, which already operated service counters in more than 130 Kinko's locations, gained more than 1,000 additional outlets in 2004 by buying the document services and copying company. The $2.4 billion cash deal followed UPS's 2001 acquisition of Mail Boxes Etc. and its retail locations, most of which have been rebranded as The UPS Store.

In 2006 FedEx bought UK-based express transportation company ANC Holdings for about $240 million, gaining a fleet of 2,200 vehicles and a network of 80 offices. (ANC was rebranded as FedEx UK.)

To boost FedEx Freight's long-haul capabilities, FedEx in 2006 paid about $790 million for LTL carrier Watkins Motor Lines and the assets of Watkins' Canadian unit, Watkins Canada Express. They were renamed FedEx National LTL and FedEx Freight Canada, respectively.

In 2007 FedEx Express spent about $430 million to buy out DTW Group (its joint venture partner in China) and acquire DTW Group's domestic delivery network. It also acquired PAFEX, which had provided express delivery service in India under contract with FedEx since 2002, for about $30 million.

EXECUTIVES

Chairman, President, and CEO; Chairman, FedEx Express: Frederick W. (Fred) Smith, age 66, $8,479,584 total compensation
EVP, Market Development and Corporate Communications; President and CEO, FedEx Services: T. Michael Glenn, age 54, $3,296,959 total compensation
EVP and CFO: Alan B. Graf Jr., age 56, $3,843,005 total compensation
EVP, General Counsel, and Secretary: Christine P. Richards, age 55, $2,989,708 total compensation
CIO; EVP, FedEx Information Services: Robert B. (Rob) Carter, age 51
SVP, FedEx Solutions: Tom Schmitt
Corporate VP and Principal Accounting Officer: John L. Merino
SVP, Global Communications and Investor Relations: William G. Margaritis
VP, US Marketing: Karen Rogers
VP, Investor Relations: Mickey Foster
President and CEO, FedEx Trade Networks: Fred Schardt
President and CEO, FedEx Freight Corporation: William J. Logue, age 52
President and CEO, FedEx Ground: David F. (Dave) Rebholz, age 57
President and CEO, FedEx Office and Print Services: Brian D. Philips, age 42
President and CEO, FedEx Express: David J. Bronczek, age 55, $4,711,722 total compensation
President and CEO, FedEx SupplyChain: Craig M. Simon
Director Advertising: Steve Pacheco
Auditors: Ernst & Young LLP

LOCATIONS

HQ: FedEx Corporation
 942 S. Shady Grove Rd., Memphis, TN 38120
Phone: 901-818-7500   **Fax:** 901-395-2000
Web: www.fedex.com

2010 Sales

	$ in mil.	% of total
US	24,852	72
Other countries	9,882	28
Total	**34,734**	**100**

PRODUCTS/OPERATIONS

2010 Sales

	$ mil.	% of total
FedEx Express	21,555	62
FedEx Ground	7,439	21
FedEx Freight	4,321	12
FedEx Services	1,770	5
Adjustments	(351)	—
Total	**34,734**	**100**

COMPETITORS

Allegra Network
AlphaGraphics
Arkansas Best
Canada Post
Con-way Inc.
DHL
IKON
Japan Post
Mail Boxes Etc.
Nippon Express
Office Depot
Pitney Bowes
Ryder System
TNT
UPS
US Postal Service
Xerox
YRC Worldwide

HISTORICAL FINANCIALS

Company Type: Public

Income Statement

FYE: May 31

	REVENUE ($ mil.)	NET INCOME ($ mil.)	NET PROFIT MARGIN	EMPLOYEES
5/10	34,734	1,184	3.4%	141,000
5/09	35,497	98	0.3%	140,000
5/08	37,953	1,125	3.0%	290,000
5/07	35,214	2,016	5.7%	280,000
5/06	32,294	1,806	5.6%	260,000
Annual Growth	**1.8%**	**(10.0%)**	**—**	**(14.2%)**

2010 Year-End Financials

Debt ratio: 12.1% No. of shares (mil.): 315
Return on equity: 8.6% Dividends
Cash ($ mil.): 1,952   Yield: 0.5%
Current ratio: 1.57   Payout: 11.7%
Long-term debt ($ mil.): 1,668 Market value ($ mil.): 26,261

Stock History

NYSE: FDX

	STOCK PRICE ($) FY Close	P/E High/Low	PER SHARE ($) Earnings	Dividends	Book Value
5/10	83.49	26 13	3.76	0.44	43.91
5/09	55.43	313 110	0.31	0.44	43.32
5/08	91.71	33 22	3.60	0.30	46.18
5/07	111.62	19 15	6.48	0.46	40.24
5/06	109.27	21 13	5.83	0.32	36.60
Annual Growth	**(6.5%)**	**— —**	**(10.4%)**	**8.3%**	**4.7%**

Ferrellgas Partners

Ferrellgas Partners' flame is burning brightly as the second-largest US retail marketer of propane, behind AmeriGas. The company sells about 875 million gallons of propane a year to 1 million industrial, commercial, and agricultural customers in all 50 states. It operates about 1,000 distribution locations, and its delivery fleet includes about 4,300 trucks and trailers. The Blue Rhino unit operates a propane cylinder-exchange business throughout the US. Ferrellgas also trades propane and natural gas, markets wholesale propane, provides liquid natural gas storage, and markets chemical feedstock. About 30% of the company's stock is held in trust for employees.

Ferrellgas, a consolidator in a fragmented industry, has ferreted out a way to become a leader in the US retail propane business: Buy up the competition. It has acquired about 180 businesses since 1986, including Crow's LP Gas located in Granger, Iowa, and Hilltop Supply located in Guatay, California. It has also acquired ProAm, the propane operations of DQE, and Louisiana-based Aeropres Propane. In 2006 and 2007 Ferrellgas acquired propane companies in Washington and Massachusetts, including Puget Sound Propane and Yankee Gas. The next year it added assets in California and Texas.

The company is focusing its acquisition activities in strategic geographical areas in an effort to expand its current operations. It has acquired Suburban Propane's retail propane operations located in Kansas, Missouri, Oklahoma, and Texas. In 2009 the company acquired propane operations in eastern Kansas that added more than 1,700 customers, boosting its presence in one of Ferrellgas' core Midwest markets. It also bought Vanson LLC, which has 29,000 customers in Michigan, Indiana, and Illinois.

HISTORY

A. C. Ferrell began the company in 1939 as a single retail propane outlet in Atchison, Kansas. It was incorporated in 1954. When Ferrell retired in 1965, his son, current chairman and CEO James Ferrell, took over the business. Ferrellgas grew by acquiring small propane dealers in rural areas of Iowa, Kansas, Minnesota, Missouri, South Dakota, and Texas.

In 1984 Ferrellgas bought propane operations with annual retail sales volume of 33 million gallons, then followed that up in 1986 with another major buy that added 395 million gallons per year. Ferrellgas acquired more than 100 smaller independent propane retailers in the next 12 years, including Vision Energy Resources (1994) and Skelgas Propane (1996).

The company formed a limited partnership in 1994, Ferrellgas Partners, to acquire and manage the operations of Ferrellgas, Inc. Ferrellgas Partners went public that year. The company created trading and marketing subsidiary Ferrell Resources in 1996. In 1998 Ferrellgas implemented an employee stock ownership plan that placed a majority of the company's stock in a trust for its employees.

Ferrellgas acquired #5 retail propane distributor ThermoGas from energy and communications giant Williams Companies for $432.5 million in 1999, making it one of the largest propane retailers in the US. (Rival AmeriGas kept pace in 2001, however, with a major acquisition of its own.)

In 2000 the company ventured into a new direction by launching Bluebuzz.com, an ISP that serves rural communities, where few services offer local dial-up phone numbers, forcing users to pay long-distance charges to connect to the Internet. In 2001 Ferrellgas sold this ISP to Wisconsin-based network service provider Network Innovations.

In November 2002 the company expanded its operations geographically by acquiring Northstar Propane of Reno, Nevada, and the Des Moines, Iowa, branch of Cenex Propane Partners. Later that year, Ferrellgas acquired ProAm from DQE.

In 2003 Ferrellgas acquired Bud's Propane Service and Louisiana-based Aeropres Propane, representing its 63rd and 64th acquisitions since 1994. In 2004 Ferrellgas acquired an additional 11 customer service centers from Suburban Propane. Later that year the company acquired a 71% stake in Blue Rhino.

EXECUTIVES

Chairman: James E. Ferrell, age 69,
$894,307 total compensation
CEO and Director: Stephen L. (Steve) Wambold, age 41,
$1,478,367 total compensation
SVP, CFO, and Treasurer: J. Ryan VanWinkle, age 36,
$908,612 total compensation
SVP; President, Ferrell North America:
George L. Koloroutis, age 48,
$1,009,171 total compensation
SVP Sales and Marketing; President, Blue Rhino:
Tod D. Brown, age 46, $957,618 total compensation
VP Information Technology: Jennifer A. Boren, age 40
Media Relations: Jim Saladin
Investor Relations: Tom Colvin
Auditors: Deloitte & Touche LLP

LOCATIONS

HQ: Ferrellgas Partners, L.P.
7500 College Blvd., Ste. 1000
Overland Park, KS 66210
Phone: 913-661-1500   **Fax:** 816-792-7985
Web: www.ferrellgas.com

PRODUCTS/OPERATIONS

2009 Sales

	$ mil.	% of total
Propane & other gas liquids	1,829.6	88
Other	239.9	12
Total	**2,069.5**	**100**

COMPETITORS

AmeriGas Partners	RGC Resources
Energy Transfer	Star Gas Partners
Energy West	Suburban Propane
MDU Resources	Transammonia

HISTORICAL FINANCIALS

Company Type: Public

Income Statement

FYE: July 31

	REVENUE ($ mil.)	NET INCOME ($ mil.)	NET PROFIT MARGIN	EMPLOYEES
7/09	2,070	52	2.5%	3,637
7/08	2,291	25	1.1%	3,508
7/07	1,992	35	1.7%	3,564
7/06	1,896	25	1.3%	3,669
7/05	1,754	89	5.1%	3,704
Annual Growth	**4.2%**	**(12.5%)**	**—**	**(0.5%)**

2009 Year-End Financials

Debt ratio: —	No. of shares (mil.): 70
Return on equity: —	Dividends
Cash ($ mil.): 7	Yield: 10.9%
Current ratio: 1.15	Payout: 253.2%
Long-term debt ($ mil.): 1,010	Market value ($ mil.): 1,277

Stock History   NYSE: FGP

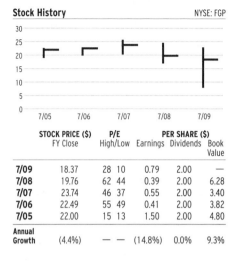

	STOCK PRICE ($) FY Close	P/E High/Low		PER SHARE ($) Earnings	Dividends	Book Value
7/09	18.37	28	10	0.79	2.00	—
7/08	19.76	62	44	0.39	2.00	6.28
7/07	23.74	46	37	0.55	2.00	3.40
7/06	22.49	55	49	0.41	2.00	3.82
7/05	22.00	15	13	1.50	2.00	4.80
Annual Growth	**(4.4%)**	**—**	**—**	**(14.8%)**	**0.0%**	**9.3%**

Fifth Third Bancorp

Fifth Third Bancorp wants to be first in the hearts and minds of its customers. The holding company operates more than 1,200 Fifth Third Bank branches in the Midwest and Southeast. It operates through five segments: branch banking, commercial banking, processing solutions, consumer lending, and investment advisors. It provides consumer and business banking (including deposit accounts, loans, and credit cards); investment advisory services (mutual funds, private banking, and securities brokerage); and ATM and merchant transaction processing. The company also runs the Jeanie ATM network.

In 2008 Fifth Third entered the North Carolina market with its purchase of First Charter and some 60 branch offices. Late that year it sold First Charter to insurance and employee benefits agency Ascension Insurance, which was seeking to grow its own network in that market.

Fifth Third had already begun expansion in the Southeast with the 2007 purchase of R-G Crown Bank from R&G Financial. That move added some 30 branches in Florida, in addition to branches in Georgia. The company also bought about 10 Atlanta-area bank branches from First Horizon National; the First Charter acquisition added a couple of Atlanta branches to its holdings. In late 2008 Fifth Third took over some $250 million in deposits from Florida's Freedom Bank, which was declared insolvent and placed into receivership by the FDIC earlier that year. The acquisition increases Fifth Third's reach in Florida by adding four branches.

The company is eyeing the sale of some of its noncore operations to help it weather rising mortgage defaults.

Fifth Third operates on an affiliate model, dividing its business operations into separate geographic regions. Each affiliate has considerable autonomy, on the grounds that local executives can make better business decisions applicable to their regions. To simplify its operations, particularly as banking regulations have grown in complexity, the holding company consolidated all of its separate bank charters: It went from having 13 separate charters in 1991 to having a single Ohio charter in 2009.

Also in 2009 Fifth Third sold a 51% stake in its processing division to Advent International for $561 million; it retained 49% ownership in Fifth Third Processing Solutions.

Fifth Third traces its unusual name to the 1908 merger of Cincinnati's Fifth National Bank and Third National Bank. Another financial services firm from the company's hometown, insurer Cincinnati Financial Corporation, was once Fifth Third's largest shareholder. CFC sold its entire Fifth Third stake in 2009.

HISTORY

In 1863 a group of Cincinnati businessmen opened the Third National Bank inside a Masonic temple to serve the Ohio River trade. Acquiring the Bank of the Ohio Valley (founded 1858) in 1871, the firm progressed until the panic of 1907. Third National survived, and in 1908 consolidated with Fifth National, forming the Fifth Third National Bank of Cincinnati. The newly organized bank acquired two local banks in 1910.

A second bank consolidation, in 1919, resulted in Fifth Third's affiliation with Union Savings Bank and Trust Company, permitting the bank to establish branches, theretofore forbidden by regulators. The company acquired the assets and offices of five more banks and thrifts that year, operating them as branches.

In 1927 the bank merged its operations with the Union Trust Company, forming the Fifth Third Union Trust. With its combined strength, it weathered the Great Depression and acquired three more banks between 1930 and 1933. However, the Depression also brought massive banking regulations to the industry, limiting Fifth Third's acquisitions.

In the postwar years and during the 1950s and 1960s, the bank expanded its consumer banking services, offering traveler's checks. Under CEO Bill Rowe, son of former CEO John Rowe, the firm emphasized the convenience of its locations and increased hours of operations.

In the 1970s Fifth Third shifted its lending program's emphasis from commercial loans to consumer credit and launched its ATM and telephone banking services. Aware that the bank was technologically unprepared for the onslaught of electronic information, Fifth Third expanded its data processing and information services resources, forming the basis for its Midwest Payment Systems division.

The company formed Fifth Third Bancorp, a holding company, and began to branch within Ohio (branching had previously been limited to the home county) in 1975. Ten years later, more deregulation allowed the bank to move into contiguous states. Focused on consumer banking, and with cautious underwriting policies, Fifth Third weathered the real estate bust and leveraged-buyout problems of the 1980s and acquired new outlets cheaply by buying several small banks, as well as branches from larger banks. It acquired the American National Bank in Kentucky and moved further afield with its purchase of the Sovereign Savings Bank in Palm Harbor, Florida, in 1991.

The company continued to expand, buying several banks and thrifts in Ohio in 1997 and 1998. In 1999 Fifth Third moved into Indiana in a big way with its purchase of CNB Bancshares, then solidified its position in the state with the acquisition of Peoples Bank of Indianapolis. Fifth Third also moved into new business areas, buying mortgage banker W. Lyman Case, broker-dealer The Ohio Company (1998), and Cincinnati-based commercial mortgage banker Vanguard Financial (1999). The company began to offer online foreign exchange via its FX Internet Trading Web in 2000.

In 2001 Fifth Third bought money manager Maxus Investments and added some 300 bank branches with its purchase of Capital Holdings (Ohio and Michigan) and Old Kent Financial (Michigan, Indiana, and Illinois), its largest-ever acquisition.

Fifth Third exited the property/casualty insurance brokerage business in 2002, selling its operations to Hub International. Also that year, Fifth Third arranged to enter Tennessee via its planned purchase of Franklin Financial. But the deal was stalled as industry regulators investigated Fifth Third's risk management procedures and internal controls. A moratorium on acquisitions was placed on the bank during the investigation. It was lifted in 2004, and the purchase of Franklin was completed not long afterwards. That opened the door for Fifth Third's acquisition of First National Bankshares of Florida in 2005.

EXECUTIVES

Chairman: William M. Isaac, age 66
President and CEO, Fifth Third Bancorp and Fifth Third Bank: Kevin T. Kabat, age 53, $5,215,692 total compensation
SEVP; President and CEO, Fifth Third Bank, Cincinnati: Robert A. (Bob) Sullivan, age 54, $1,618,130 total compensation
EVP and COO: Greg D. Carmichael, age 48, $2,147,704 total compensation
EVP and CFO: Daniel T. (Dan) Poston, age 51, $937,763 total compensation
EVP and Regional President; President and CEO, Fifth Third Bank, Chicago: Terry E. Zink, age 58, $1,592,581 total compensation
EVP and Chief Risk Officer: Mary E. Tuuk, age 45
EVP, Secretary, and CAO: Paul L. Reynolds, age 48
EVP Consumer Lending and Mortgage: Steve Alonso
EVP and Auditor: Robert Shaffer
EVP and Chief Human Resources Officer: Teresa J. Tanner
EVP and CIO: Joseph Robinson
SVP and Controller: Mark D. Hazel, age 44
SVP and Head of Investment Advisors: Philip R. McHugh
SVP and Chief Marketing Officer: Larry S. Magnesen, age 52
VP Corporate Communications: Debra DeCourcy
Director Investor Relations and Corporate Analysis: Jeff Richardson, age 45
Chairman, Fifth Third Bank, Tennessee: Gordon E. Inman
Chairman, Fifth Third Bank, Northwestern Ohio: John S. Szuch
Chairman, Fifth Third Bancorp, Central Florida: Charlie W. Brinkley Jr., age 55
Chairman, Fifth Third Bank, Central Ohio: Donald B. Shackelford, age 74
Chairman, Fifth Third Bank, Southern Indiana: H. Lee Cooper III
Auditors: Deloitte & Touche LLP

LOCATIONS

HQ: Fifth Third Bancorp
38 Fountain Sq. Plaza, Fifth Third Center
Cincinnati, OH 45263
Phone: 513-579-5300   **Fax:** 513-534-0629
Web: www.53.com

PRODUCTS/OPERATIONS

Selected Subsidiaries
Fifth Third Financial Corporation
  Fifth Third Bank (Ohio)
    Card Management Corporation
    Fifth Third Asset Management, Inc.
    The Fifth Third Company
    Fifth Third Holdings, LLC
    Fifth Third Insurance Agency, Inc.
    Fifth Third International Company
      Fifth Third Trade Services Limited (Hong Kong)
    The Fifth Third Leasing Company
      The Fifth Third Auto Leasing Trust
      Fifth Third Foreign Lease Management, LLC
    Fifth Third Mortgage Company
      Fifth Third Real Estate Investment Trust, Inc.
    Fifth Third Mortgage Reinsurance Company
    Fifth Third Real Estate Capital Markets Company
    Fifth Third Securities, Inc.
  Fifth Third Bank (Michigan)
    Community Financial Services, Inc.
    Fifth Third Auto Funding, LLC
    Fifth Third Funding, LLC
    GNB Management, LLC
      FNB Investment Company, Inc.
      GNB Realty, LLC
    Home Equity of America, Inc.
    Old Kent Mortgage Services, Inc.
  Fifth Third Bank, National Association
  Fifth Third Community Development Corporation
    Fifth Third New Markets Development Co., LLC
  Fifth Third Investment Company
  Fifth Third Reinsurance Company, LTD (Turks and Caicos Islands)
  Fountain Square Life Reinsurance Company, Ltd. (Turks and Caicos Islands)
  Vista Settlement Services, LLC

COMPETITORS

Bank of America
Cat Financial
Citigroup
Comerica
First Data
FirstMerit
Harris Bankcorp
Huntington Bancshares
JPMorgan Chase
KeyCorp
Marshall & Ilsley
Northern Trust
PNC Financial
U.S. Bancorp
Wells Fargo

HISTORICAL FINANCIALS

Company Type: Public

Income Statement				FYE: December 31
	ASSETS ($ mil.)	NET INCOME ($ mil.)	INCOME AS % OF ASSETS	EMPLOYEES
12/09	113,380	737	0.7%	21,901
12/08	119,764	(2,113)	—	22,423
12/07	110,962	1,076	1.0%	22,678
12/06	100,669	1,184	1.2%	21,362
12/05	105,225	1,548	1.5%	22,901
Annual Growth	1.9%	(16.9%)	—	(1.1%)

2009 Year-End Financials

Equity as % of assets: 8.7%
Return on assets: 0.6%
Return on equity: 8.3%
Long-term debt ($ mil.): 10,507
No. of shares (mil.): 796
Dividends
  Yield: 0.4%
  Payout: 6.0%
Market value ($ mil.): 7,764
Sales ($ mil.): 9,450

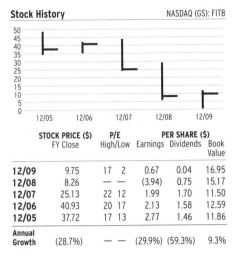

	STOCK PRICE ($) FY Close	P/E High/Low		PER SHARE ($) Earnings	Dividends	Book Value
12/09	9.75	17	2	0.67	0.04	16.95
12/08	8.26	—	—	(3.94)	0.75	15.17
12/07	25.13	22	12	1.99	1.70	11.50
12/06	40.93	20	17	2.13	1.58	12.59
12/05	37.72	17	13	2.77	1.46	11.86
Annual Growth	(28.7%)	—	—	(29.9%)	(59.3%)	9.3%

First American Financial

First American Financial knows that when you're buying real estate you'll probably want some insurance to go along with it. In addition to good old title insurance from its First American Title subsidiary, the company's financial services arm also provides specialty property/casualty insurance and home warranties through its First American Home Buyers Protection business. Its First American Trust offers banking and trust services to the escrow and real estate industries. Previously known as First American Corporation, the company spun off its real estate information services business and moved its remaining operations into its First American Financial business.

As First American Corporation the company executed a spinning-split in 2010: Its title insurance and specialty insurance operations were moved into its subsidiary First American Financial Corporation (and handed the existing trading ticker symbol), while its real estate information database operations were spun out into Core-Logic. CoreLogic's business provides real estate tax monitoring, flood-zone certification, appraisal services, and credit-reporting services for buyers and lenders. CoreLogic also took with it First Advantage, the company's screening and credit reporting business. Existing shareholders received equal shares in both companies.

The new CoreLogic business was built upon First American Corelogic, a provider of real estate transaction data. First American previously held a majority stake in First American Corelogic and in 2010 purchased the remaining shares from partner Experian.

The split was a response to the pressures from the weakened US real estate market, as the company makes most of its money whenever property is bought or sold.

First American Financial makes the majority of its money in the US (the company is the second-largest US title insurer after Fidelity National), and it provides title insurance in more than 60 countries and territories around the world. It has applied sales efforts in British Commonwealth countries, including Australia, Canada, and the UK. It is moving carefully into other regions through acquisitions (partial and total) of existing businesses. In 2009 the company moved into Russia; it already had secured a toehold in Croatia, Serbia, and — through a 38% holding in FU Gayrimenkul Danmanlk —Turkey.

Chairman Parker Kennedy is a descendant of the founder of the company, C. E. Parker. Immediately following the split, Kennedy stepped aside as CEO and COO Dennis Gilmore was named to that position.

HISTORY

In 1889, when Los Angeles was on its way to becoming a real city, the more countrified residents to the south (including the Irvine Company's founding family) formed Orange County, a peaceful realm of citrus groves where land transactions were assisted by title companies Orange County Abstract and Santa Ana Abstract. In 1894 the firms merged under the leadership of local businessman C. E. Parker. For three decades, the resulting Orange County Title limited its business to title searches.

In 1924, as real estate transactions became more complex (in part because of mineral-rights issues related to Southern California's oil boom), Orange County Title began offering title insurance and escrow services. The company remained under Parker family management until 1930, when H. A. Gardner took over and guided it through the Depression. In 1943 the company returned to Parker family control.

In 1957 the company began a major expansion beyond Orange County. The new First American Title Insurance and Trust name acknowledged the firm's expansion into trust and custody operations. Donald Kennedy (C. E. Parker's grandson) took over in 1963 and took the company public the next year.

In 1968 First American Financial was formed as a holding company for subsidiaries First American Title Insurance and First American Trust. This structure facilitated growth as the firm began opening new offices and buying all or parts of other title companies, including Title Guaranty Co. of Wyoming, Security Title & Trust (San Antonio), and Ticore, Inc. (Portland, Oregon), all purchased in 1968.

The 1970s were a quiet time for the company, but it began growing again in the 1980s, as savings and loan deregulation jump-started the commercial real estate market in Southern California. First American diversified into home warranty and real estate tax services. In 1988, on the brink of the California meltdown, the company bought an industrial loan corporation to make commercial real estate loans.

Reduced property sales during California's early 1990s real estate crash and recession rocked company results. Fluctuating interest rates didn't help the tremulous bottom lines. In 1994 Donald Kennedy became chairman; his son Parker became president.

As part of its expansion effort, First American bought CREDCO (mortgage credit reporting) and Flood Data Services (flood zone certification) in 1995. A year later it acquired Ward Associates, a property inspection and preservation service provider. In 1997 the company merged its real estate information subsidiaries with those of the Experian Information Solutions, a leading supplier of real estate data; it also bought Strategic Mortgage Services (mortgage information and document preparation), whose software formed the core of software operations for First American's title division.

Earnings jumped in 1998's hot real estate market. That year and the next, First American's acquisitions brought into the company's fold resident-screening services and providers of mortgage loan and loan default management software. In 1999 American Financial and Wells Fargo teamed to provide title insurance and appraisal services nationwide.

In 2000 the company bought National Information Group, a provider of tax service, flood certification, and insurance tracking for the mortgage industry. That year the company partnered with Transamerica to create the US's largest property database.

Following a Colorado Division of Insurance investigation into the company's First American Title Insurance subsidiary's alleged practice of offering kickbacks in exchange for business, First American reached a settlement in 2005 to pay $24 million back to US consumers affected by such practices, which it has since discontinued.

EXECUTIVES

Chairman, The First American Financial Corporation and CoreLogic: Parker S. Kennedy, age 62, $1,972,928 total compensation
CEO: Dennis J. Gilmore, age 51, $3,155,352 total compensation
CFO, Information Solutions Group: Anthony S. (Buddy) Piszel, age 55
CTO: Evan H. Jafa
SVP and Chief Accounting Officer: Max O. Valdes, age 55, $1,137,212 total compensation
SVP, General Counsel, and Interim Secretary: Kenneth D. (Ken) DeGiorgio, age 39
SVP and National Litigation Counsel: Timothy P. Sullivan
SVP Outsourcing and Technology Solutions Division: Scott Brinkley
SVP Investor Relations, Information Solutions: Dan Smith
SVP and General Manager, First American Flood Data Services: Vicki L. Chenault
SVP Corporate Communications: Jo Etta Bandy
VP and Chief Diversity Officer: Karen J. Collins
VP and Director Corporate Real Estate: Elise Luckham
VP Global Outsourcing: Russ Watts
VP and Chief Marketing Officer: Sandra Bell
President, Information and Outsourcing Solutions Segment: Barry M. Sando, age 50, $1,998,036 total compensation
President, Data and Analytic Solutions Segment; CEO, First American CoreLogic: George S. Livermore
CEO, MarketLinx: Ben Graboske
CEO, CoreLogic: Anand K. Nallathambi, age 48
CEO, United Kingdom, First Title Insurance: Phillip Oldcorn
Chief Actuary: David L. Ruhm
Chief Economist, First American CoreLogic: Mark Fleming
Auditors: PricewaterhouseCoopers LLP

LOCATIONS

HQ: The First American Financial Corporation
1 First American Way, Santa Ana, CA 92707
Phone: 714-250-3000
Web: www.firstam.com

PRODUCTS/OPERATIONS

2009 Revenues

	$ mil.	% of total
Title insurance	3,672.4	60
Information & outsourcing solutions	904.2	15
Risk mitigation & business solutions	705.4	12
Data & analytic solutions	532.4	9
Specialty insurance	277.5	4
Corporate	3.9	—
Adjustments	(123.1)	—
Total	**5,972.7**	**100**

COMPETITORS

American Home Shield
Commerce Title Company
Fidelity National Financial
Home Buyers Warranty
Investors Title
North American Title
Old Republic
Stewart Information Services
Ticor Title Co.

HISTORICAL FINANCIALS

Company Type: Public

Income Statement

FYE: December 31

	ASSETS ($ mil.)	NET INCOME ($ mil.)	INCOME AS % OF ASSETS	EMPLOYEES
12/09	8,723	200	2.3%	30,922
12/08	8,730	(26)	—	31,411
12/07	8,648	(3)	—	37,354
12/06	8,224	288	3.5%	39,670
12/05	7,599	485	6.4%	35,444
Annual Growth	3.5%	(19.9%)	—	(3.4%)

2009 Year-End Financials

Equity as % of assets: 36.2%
Return on assets: 2.3%
Return on equity: 6.8%
Long-term debt ($ mil.): 891
No. of shares (mil.): 117
Dividends
　Yield: 4.7%
　Payout: 42.1%
Market value ($ mil.): 2,211
Sales ($ mil.): 5,973

Stock History

NYSE: FAF

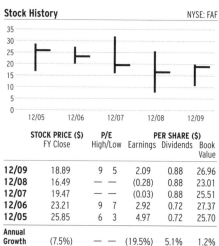

	STOCK PRICE ($) FY Close	P/E High	P/E Low	PER SHARE ($) Earnings	PER SHARE ($) Dividends	PER SHARE ($) Book Value
12/09	18.89	9	5	2.09	0.88	26.96
12/08	16.49	—	—	(0.28)	0.88	23.01
12/07	19.47	—	—	(0.03)	0.88	25.51
12/06	23.21	9	7	2.92	0.72	27.37
12/05	25.85	6	3	4.97	0.72	25.70
Annual Growth	(7.5%)	—	—	(19.5%)	5.1%	1.2%

FirstEnergy Corp.

FirstEnergy's first goal is to deliver power, but its second goal is to survive deregulation. Its utilities provide electricity to 4.5 million customers in Ohio, Pennsylvania, and New Jersey, three states that are ushering in power-industry competition. Its domestic power plants have a total generating capacity of more than 14,000 MW, most generated by coal-fired plants. Subsidiary FirstEnergy Solutions trades energy commodities in deregulated US markets and has more than 120,000 accounts. FirstEnergy's other non-regulated operations include electrical and mechanical contracting and energy planning and procurement. In 2010 the company agreed to acquire Allegheny Energy in a $8.5 billion deal.

The acquisition will increase FirstEnergy's power generation capacity by 70% (to 24,000 MW) and its customer base by 35%, dramatically boosting its position as a leading regional energy provider. The company will also have 2,200 MW of renewable energy.

As states push to reduce carbon emissions, FirstEnergy has been expanding its renewable energy operations. In 2009 FirstEnergy began to reengineer units 4 and 5 at its R.E. Burger Plant in Shadyside, Ohio, to generate electricity primarily with biomass, a move that boosted First-Energy's portfolio of renewable energy to more than 1,100 MW, including 451 MW of pumped-storage hydro and 376 MW of wind power. In 2010 the comapny sold a fossil-fueled generation facility in Michigan to Wolverine Power Supply, as it was no longer a strategic fit with the company's new direction.

HISTORY

FirstEnergy came to light in 1893 as the Akron Electric Light and Power Company. After several mergers, the business went bankrupt and was sold in 1899 to Akron Traction and Electric Company, which became Northern Ohio Power and Light (NOP&L).

In 1930 Commonwealth and Southern (C&S) bought NOP&L and merged it with four other Ohio utility holding companies to form Ohio Edison. The new firm increased sales during the Depression by selling electric appliances.

The Public Utility Holding Company Act of 1935 (passed to rein in uncontrolled utilities) caught up with C&S in 1949, forcing it to divest Ohio Edison. Rival Ohio Public Service was also divested from its holding company, and in 1950 Ohio Edison bought it.

In 1967, after two decades of expansion, Ohio Edison and three other Ohio and Pennsylvania utilities formed the Central Area Power Coordination Group (CAPCO) to share new power-plant costs, including the construction of the Beaver Valley nuclear plant (1970-76). Although the CAPCO partners agreed in 1980 to cancel four planned nukes, in 1985 Ohio Edison took part in building the Perry Unit 1 and Beaver Valley Unit 2 nuclear plants.

The federal Energy Policy Act of 1992 allowed wholesale power competition, and to satisfy new federal requirements, Ohio Edison formed a six-state transmission alliance in 1996 with fellow utilities Centerior Energy, Allegheny Power System, and Dominion Resources' Virginia Power to coordinate their grids.

Ohio Edison paid about $1.5 billion in 1997 for Centerior Energy, formed in 1986 as a holding company for Toledo Edison and Cleveland Electric. Ohio Edison and Centerior, both burdened by high-cost generating plants, merged to cut costs, and the expanded energy concern was renamed FirstEnergy Corp.

Looking toward deregulation, FirstEnergy began buying mechanical construction, contracting, and energy management companies in 1997, including Roth Bros. and RPC Mechanical. In 1998 it added nine more.

Power marketers Federal Energy Sales and the Power Co. of America couldn't deliver the juice to FirstEnergy during the summer of 1998's hottest days. FirstEnergy later sued Federal Energy for $25 million in damages. The next year it bought electricity outage insurance.

Pennsylvania began large-scale electric power competition in 1999, when Ohio lawmakers passed deregulation legislation. To comply with state regulation, FirstEnergy agreed to trade power plants, including Beaver Valley, with DQE (now Duquesne Light Holdings). That year brought trouble when the EPA named First-Energy and six other utilities in a suit that charged the utility with noncompliance with the Clean Air Act.

In 2000 FirstEnergy agreed to acquire New Jersey-based electric utility GPU in an $11.9 billion deal; it became one of the largest US utilities in 2001 when it completed the acquisition, which added three utilities (Jersey Central Power & Light, Metropolitan Edison, and Pennsylvania Electric) serving 2.1 million electricity customers.

Following the acquisition, FirstEnergy agreed to sell an 80% stake in GPU's UK utility, Midlands Electricity, to UtiliCorp (later Aquila) in a $2 billion deal, completed in 2002. It also agreed to sell four Ohio coal-fired plants (2,500 MW) to NRG Energy for $1.5 billion; however, the deal was later canceled. To focus on its domestic operations, FirstEnergy sold the international energy assets gained through the acquisition of GPU, including Australian utility GasNet and UK utility Midlands Electricity. It also exited its Argentine utility business (Emdersa).

The US-Canada Power System Outage Task Force, which investigated the massive August 14, 2003, blackout that affected eight states and a Canadian province, released its interim report that November and a final report the following year. The initial report found that FirstEnergy violated four voluntary standards set by the North American Electric Reliability Council and stated that the blackout was largely caused by FirstEnergy's failure to set up proper communication and monitoring procedures for its transmission assets. The report also cited the company's failure to trim trees, which caused several major transmission lines in its service territory to short-circuit during the incident.

FirstEnergy paid a total of $90 million to settle federal lawsuits over its involvement in the blackout, as well as other securities and derivative issues, without admitting any wrongdoing. FirstEnergy faced a formal SEC investigation into financial restatements (in 2003) and an extended nuclear power plant outage (2002-04); the investigation was not related to the blackout and was an extension of an informal SEC inquiry.

To settle with the US Environmental Protection Agency, FirstEnergy agreed in 2005 to pay an estimated $1.1 billion in fines and for anti-pollution devices to be installed at its coal-burning plants in Ohio and Pennsylvania.

EXECUTIVES

Chairman: George M. Smart, age 64
President, CEO, and Director, FirstEnergy Corp. and FirstEnergy Service: Anthony J. Alexander, age 58, $13,448,986 total compensation
EVP and CFO, FirstEnergy, FirstEnergy Service, and FirstEnergy Solutions: Mark T. Clark, age 59, $3,639,120 total compensation
EVP and General Counsel, FirstEnergy, FirstEnergy Service, and FirstEnergy Solutions: Leila L. Vespoli, age 50, $3,201,082 total compensation
EVP; President, FirstEnergy Generation: Gary R. Leidich, age 59, $4,741,210 total compensation
SVP; President, FirstEnergy Utilities: Charles E. (Chuck) Jones, age 54
VP, Controller, and Chief Accounting Officer; VP and Controller, FirstEnergy Service and FirstEnergy Solutions: Harvey L. Wagner, age 57
VP External Affairs: Michael J. Dowling
VP and Treasurer, FirstEnergy, FirstEnergy Service, and FirstEnergy Solutions: James F. Pearson, age 55
VP Federal Energy Regulatory Commission (FERC) Policy and Chief FERC Compliance Officer, FirstEnergy Service: Stanley F. Szwed
Investor Relations Principal: Rey Y. Jimenez Jr.
President, Jersey Central Power & Light: Donald M. Lynch
President and Chief Nuclear Officer, FirstEnergy Nuclear Operating Company: James H. (Jim) Lash
President, FirstEnergy Solutions: Donald R. (Donny) Schneider, age 48
SVP Human Resources, FirstEnergy Service: Lynn M. Cavalier, age 58
SVP Governmental Affairs, FirstEnergy Service: David C. Luff, age 62
VP Corporate Risk and Chief Risk Officer, FirstEnergy Service: William D. Byrd, age 55
Corporate Secretary, FirstEnergy and FirstEnergy Solutions; VP, Corporate Secretary, and Chief Ethics Officer, FirstEnergy Service: Rhonda S. Ferguson
VP Sales and Marketing, FirstEnergy Solutions: Arthur W. Yuan
Auditors: PricewaterhouseCoopers LLP

LOCATIONS

HQ: FirstEnergy Corp.
76 S. Main St., Akron, OH 44308
Phone: 800-633-4766   **Fax:** 330-384-3866
Web: www.firstenergycorp.com

PRODUCTS/OPERATIONS

2009 Sales

	$ mil.	% of total
Energy delivery services	11,144	70
Competitive energy services	4,731	30
Adjustments	(2,908)	—
Total	**12,967**	**100**

Electric Utility Subsidiaries

American Transmission Systems, Inc.
The Cleveland Electric Illuminating Company (The Illuminating Company)
Jersey Central Power & Light Company (JCP&L)
Metropolitan Edison Company (Met-Ed)
Ohio Edison Company
Pennsylvania Electric Company (Penelec)
Pennsylvania Power Company (Penn Power)
The Toledo Edison Company

Selected Unregulated Subsidiaries

FirstEnergy Nuclear Operating Co. (nuclear generation facilities)
FirstEnergy Properties, Inc.
FirstEnergy Securities Transfer Company
FirstEnergy Service Company
FirstEnergy Solutions Corp. (retail and wholesale energy marketing and management services)
FirstEnergy Ventures Corp.
GPU Diversified Holdings, LLC
GPU Nuclear, Inc. (nuclear plant management and decommissioning)

COMPETITORS

AEP
Allegheny Energy
Delmarva Power
Dominion Resources
DPL
Duke Energy
Duquesne Light
Duquesne Light Holdings
Dynegy
EnergySolve
Exelon
Exelon Energy
Integrys Energy Group
Peabody Energy
PG&E Corporation
PPL Corporation
PSEG Energy Holdings
Public Service Enterprise Group
Southern Company
Vectren

HISTORICAL FINANCIALS

Company Type: Public

Income Statement

FYE: December 31

	REVENUE ($ mil.)	NET INCOME ($ mil.)	NET PROFIT MARGIN	EMPLOYEES
12/09	12,967	1,006	7.8%	13,379
12/08	13,627	1,342	9.8%	14,698
12/07	12,802	1,309	10.2%	14,534
12/06	11,501	1,254	10.9%	13,739
12/05	11,989	891	7.4%	14,586
Annual Growth	**2.0%**	**3.1%**	**—**	**(2.1%)**

2009 Year-End Financials

Debt ratio: 139.1%
Return on equity: 11.9%
Cash ($ mil.): 874
Current ratio: 0.63
Long-term debt ($ mil.): 11,908
No. of shares (mil.): 305
Dividends
Yield: 4.7%
Payout: 66.9%
Market value ($ mil.): 14,160

Stock History

NYSE: FE

	STOCK PRICE ($) FY Close	P/E High/Low		PER SHARE ($) Earnings	Dividends	Book Value
12/09	46.45	16	11	3.29	2.20	28.08
12/08	48.58	19	9	4.38	2.20	27.17
12/07	72.34	18	14	4.22	2.00	29.45
12/06	60.30	16	13	3.81	1.80	29.64
12/05	48.99	20	14	2.61	1.67	30.14
Annual Growth	**(1.3%)**	**—**	**—**	**6.0%**	**7.1%**	**(1.8%)**

Fiserv, Inc.

It's 10:30, America. Do you know where your money is? Fiserv does. The company provides information management and electronic commerce services including transaction processing, electronic billing and payments, and business process outsourcing. Its clients include banks, lenders, credit unions, insurance firms, merchants, government agencies, and leasing companies. Fiserv operates in two primary business segments — financial institution services and payments and industry products (via its CheckFree business, acquired in 2007). It sold the bulk of its insurance services business in 2009. The company primarily operates in the US but has offices in about 20 other countries.

Fiserv hopes to capitalize on an increasing reliance on transaction-oriented, fee-based services, which typically demand a large data-processing capability. The company paid more than $4 billion for CheckFree, a leader in electronic bill payment services. That transaction was the largest in Fiserv's history and allowed the company to serve a broader market. In a smaller deal, it bought payment processor i_Tech from First Interstate BancSystem in 2008. Fiserv entered the front office side of operations when it acquired AdviceAmerica, which provides desktop technology for financial advisers. The unit will become part of Fiserv's Investment Services arm.

As it added new operations, the company in 2009 introduced a new marketing strategy to unify its brands under the Fiserv banner. And though highly acquisitive, the company is not averse to jettisoning businesses that are no longer central to its core operations.

In 2008 it sold most of its health business to UnitedHealth for some $480 million. The sale included Fiserv Health Plan Administration, Fiserv Health Plan Management, Innoviant Pharmacy, Avidyn Health, and other health businesses. Not included were WorkingRx (workers' compensation) and CareGain (technology), which remain with Fiserv.

The company also sold the bulk of its Fiserv Investment Support Services business, including advisor services and institutional retirement services, to TD AMERITRADE. In a separate transaction, the newly formed Trust Institution Bank (headed by former Fiserv ISS management) acquired most of the company's investment administration services business.

Fiserv sold a majority stake in StoneRiver (formerly Fiserv Insurance Services) to private equity firm Stone Point Capital for some $540 million. Fiserv retained a 49% stake in the unit, which changed its name to StoneRiver in 2009. Also that year Fiserv sold Loan Fulfillment Solutions, a provider of outsourced mortgage-related services including settlement and title certification, to ISGN.

HISTORY

When First Bank System of Minneapolis bought Milwaukee-based Midland Bank in 1984, the head of Midland's data processing operation, George Dalton, bought the unit and then merged that operation with Sunshine State Systems, a newly independent Florida processing company headed by Leslie Muma. Christened Fiserv, the company went public in 1986. It grew by providing outsourcing services to small banks and thrifts.

In the 1990s, Fiserv began targeting larger clients. But industry consolidation sometimes hurt the company, as when the 12-year term of a 1995 contract with Chase Manhattan was reduced to three after Chase and Chemical Bank merged in 1996.

As banks moved into new areas, Fiserv went along. In the late 1990s it acquired BHC Financial and Hanifen, Imhoff Holdings (securities transaction processing). Other purchases that broadened its service list included Automated Financial Technology (credit union software) and Network Data Processing (administrative software for insurance companies). The push into software continued with 1999 purchases in the field of workers' compensation systems.

Also in 1999 Fiserv bolstered its client list by buying QuestPoint's check servicing business. It moved into retirement plan administration with the purchase of a unit from what is now AIG Retirement Services. In 2000 a deal announced a year earlier to provide back-office services for American Express' online Membership Banking unit fell apart, but Fiserv recovered its momentum with enhanced mortgage servicing offerings and an agreement to provide technology services to cahoot, the online banking unit of the UK's Abbey National.

Fiserv continued its acquisitive activities the next year, buying Benefit Planners (a leading employee benefit program administrator with operations in Europe, the Middle East, South America, and the US), Facilities and Services Corporation (a California-based insurance software maker), NCSI (information and services targeting the flood insurance industry), and the bank processing operations of NCR Corporation. The company that year also sold its Human Resources Information Services unit to buyout firm Gores Technology Group.

Fiserv boosted its ATM and EFT (electronic funds transfer) business with the 2002 purchase of the Consumer Network Services unit of Electronic Data Systems (now HP Enterprise Services). The company sold its securities clearing operations to a unit of FMR in 2005.

EXECUTIVES

Chairman: Donald F. (Don) Dillon, age 70
President, CEO, and Director: Jeffery W. (Jeff) Yabuki, age 49, $5,757,685 total compensation
EVP, CFO, Treasurer, and Assistant Secretary: Thomas J. Hirsch, age 46, $1,365,281 total compensation
EVP; President, Digital Payments Group: Stephen (Steve) Olsen, age 50, $1,304,578 total compensation
EVP, Chief Administrative Officer, General Counsel, and Secretary: Charles W. Sprague, age 60
EVP and Chief Sales Officer: Thomas W. Warsop III, age 44, $1,124,898 total compensation
EVP Corporate Development: James W. Cox, age 47
EVP and CIO: Maryann Goebel
EVP and Chief Marketing Officer: Donald J. (Don) MacDonald, age 48
EVP Corporate Development: James W. Cox, age 47
EVP Human Resources and Shared Services: Lance F. Drummond, age 56
SVP Strategic Marketing and Business Development, Investment Services: Cheryl Nash
VP Corporate Communications: Judy DeRango Wicks
Group President, Financial Institutions Group: Michael (Mike) Gianoni, age 49
President, Investment Services: Sean Gallagher
President, Depository Institution Services Group: Steven (Steve) Tait, age 51
Chief Economist: David Stiff
Auditors: Deloitte & Touche LLP

LOCATIONS

HQ: Fiserv, Inc.
255 Fiserv Dr., Brookfield, WI 53045
Phone: 262-879-5000   **Fax:** 262-879-5013
Web: www.fiserv.com

PRODUCTS/OPERATIONS

2009 Sales

	$ mil.	% of total
Payments		
Processing & services	1,579	38
Products	581	14
Financial		
Processing & services	1,747	43
Products	195	5
Adjustments	(25)	—
Total	**4,077**	**100**

Selected Subsidiaries

BillMatrix Corporation
CheckFree Corporation
CheckFreePay Corporation
Data-Link Systems, LLC
Fiserv Automotive Solutions, Inc.
Fiserv CIR, Inc.
Information Technology, Inc.
ITI of Nebraska, Inc.
USERS Incorporated

COMPETITORS

Accenture
Banc of America Merchant Services
CGI Group
Computer Sciences Corp.
DST Systems
Fidelity National Information Services
First Data
IBM
Jack Henry
Open Solutions
Perot Systems
State Street
SunGard
Total System Services

HISTORICAL FINANCIALS

Company Type: Public

Income Statement

FYE: December 31

	REVENUE ($ mil.)	NET INCOME ($ mil.)	NET PROFIT MARGIN	EMPLOYEES
12/09	4,077	476	11.7%	20,000
12/08	4,739	569	12.0%	20,000
12/07	3,922	439	11.2%	25,000
12/06	4,544	450	9.9%	23,000
12/05	4,060	516	12.7%	22,000
Annual Growth	0.1%	(2.0%)	—	(2.4%)

2009 Year-End Financials

Debt ratio: 111.8%
Return on equity: 16.9%
Cash ($ mil.): 363
Current ratio: 1.10
Long-term debt ($ mil.): 3,382

No. of shares (mil.): 150
Dividends
  Yield: —
  Payout: —
Market value ($ mil.): 7,277

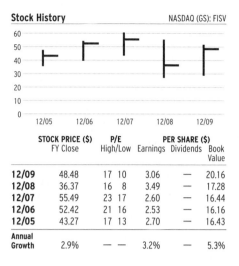
	STOCK PRICE ($) FY Close	P/E High/Low		PER SHARE ($) Earnings	Dividends	Book Value
12/09	48.48	17	10	3.06	—	20.16
12/08	36.37	16	8	3.49	—	17.28
12/07	55.49	23	17	2.60	—	16.44
12/06	52.42	21	16	2.53	—	16.16
12/05	43.27	17	13	2.70	—	16.43
Annual Growth	2.9%	—	—	3.2%	—	5.3%

Flowers Foods

Look for Flowers Foods in your breadbox, not your garden — the company is one of the largest wholesale bakeries in the US. It produces, markets, and distributes fresh breads, buns, rolls, corn and flour tortillas, and sweet bakery goodies to retail food and foodservice customers throughout the southeastern, southwestern, and mid-Atlantic sections of the US, as well as in selected areas of California and Nevada. The company's brand names include BlueBird, Cobblestone Mill, and Nature's Own. Flowers Foods makes snack cakes, pastry, donuts, and frozen bread products for retail, vending, and co-pack customers nationwide. It also rolls out hamburger buns for large national fast-food restaurant chains.

Flowers Bakeries makes private-label breads for food retailers. Wal-Mart is the company's largest customer, representing about 21% of its 2010 sales.

Continuing its long-term acquisition strategy, it acquired Holsum Bakers in 2008. Holsum operates two bakeries in the Phoenix area and supplies both retail and foodservice customers with fresh baked goods. The acquisition brought the Holsum, Aunt Hattie's, and Roman Meal brands to the fold. Flowers also acquired Lakeland, Florida-based ButterKrust Bakery in 2008. ButterKrust sells its baked goods under the ButterKrust, Country Hearth, Rich Harvest, and Sunbeam labels.

The company moved into a new food-product area in 2009 with the purchase of Leo's Foods, a Fort Worth, Texas-based tortilla maker. The acquisition of Leo's enabled the company to supply both retail and foodservice customers with corn and flour tortillas — new products for Flowers. The company did some of its own product innovating that year as well, introducing banana pudding cupcakes and cinnamon coffee cakes under the BlueBird and Mrs. Freshley's brands. Nature's Own-branded Sandwich Rounds and Thin Sliced Bagels were introduced in 2010. The acquisitions and new products reflect the Flowers strategies of investing in "bolt-on" baking businesses and developing new products in order to increase both its sales and geographic footprint.

Board member J.V. Shields Jr. owns approximately 7% of the company.

HISTORY

Georgia native William Flowers and his brother Joseph opened the Flowers Ice Cream Co. in the winter resort town of Thomasville, Georgia, in 1914 to serve wealthy visitors from the North. Seeing that there was no bakery in the town (the nearest bakery was more than 200 miles away), the brothers opened Flowers Baking Co. in 1919. During the 1920s William took charge of the bakery, while Joseph continued to run the ice-cream operation. In 1928 Flowers moved into the production of sweet rolls and cakes. As its reputation for high-quality baked goods spread, the firm established a regional network of customers. William died in 1934, and his 20-year-old son, Bill, took over.

Amidst the difficult Depression years, Bill led the company in its first acquisition, a bakery in Florida. Flowers operated its bakeries around the clock during WWII to supply military bases in the Southeast. Bill's brother Langdon joined the firm after the war and helped take the company on a major expansion drive in the 1950s and 1960s.

Flowers acquired additional southeastern bakers in the mid-1960s and bought the Atlanta Baking Co. in 1967. The next year the company changed its name to Flowers Industries and went public.

In 1976 the company diversified, entering the frozen-food business by acquiring Stilwell Foods (frozen fruits, battered vegetables) in Oklahoma and its subsidiary, Rio Grande Foods, in Texas. The firm also expanded its fresh bread line, including the Nature's Own brand of variety breads (1978).

During the 1970s and 1980s, the company expanded beyond its southeastern regional base by acquiring bakeries in the Southwest and Midwest. Company veteran Amos McMullian became CEO in 1981 and chairman in 1985, when both Bill and Langdon retired. (Langdon died in 2007 at the age of 85.) In 1989 Flowers bought out Winn-Dixie's bakery operations.

The company launched a $377 million, six-year capital investment program in 1991 to upgrade and automate its bakeries. Flowers began a major expansion strategy with the 1996 acquisition of Mrs. Smith's, the US's top frozen-pie brand, from J.M. Smucker. Later that year, Flowers and joint venture partners Artal Luxembourg and Benmore acquired cookie maker Keebler Foods (which it sold to Kellogg in 2001). In 1997 the company acquired Allied Bakery Products, a baker of frozen bread and rolls for foodservice customers in the Northeast US. When Keebler went public in 1998, Flowers increased its controlling stake to 55%.

Further acquisitions included Home Baking Company (foodservice buns, 1999) and Kroger's bakery operations in Memphis (2000). Weakened by equipment glitches in newly upgraded Mrs. Smith's facilities, earnings suffered at the end of 1999. Flowers snubbed an acquisition inquiry by Sara Lee in early 2000, but as other mega-food company acquisitions dominoed around it, Flowers agreed to sell Keebler to Kellogg in 2000.

Upon completion of the Keebler/Kellogg deal in 2001, Flowers Industries recreated itself, spinning off its Flowers Bakeries and Mrs. Smith's Bakeries businesses under the Flowers Foods name; it kept the same FLO stock ticker.

To better control costs, the company cut jobs at Mrs. Smith's in 2002 and initiated a restructuring of its operating units.

In 2003 Flowers sold the frozen dessert segment of Mrs. Smith's to The Schwan Food Company for $240 million. Flowers retained the frozen bread and roll dough portion of Mrs. Smith's. That same year, it also introduced a line of snack cakes under the names Tesoritos and Pan Dulce de Mi Casa, aimed at the Latino and Hispanic markets.

In 2004 the company acquired the Houston operations of the Sara Lee Bakery Group. The company in 2005 disclosed the settlement of a million-dollar class-action lawsuit brought against the company for producing non-kosher food items on a kosher pie shell line at its production facility in Pembroke, North Carolina. To settle, the company apologized for failing to notify the Orthodox Union for occasions when the error occurred and agreed to donate more than $2 million in cash and bread products to charitable groups.

In 2005 Flowers Foods acquired bankrupt snack maker Royal Cake. In order to broaden its product line, in 2007 the company began offering flour under its Nature's Own brand.

EXECUTIVES

Chairman and CEO: George E. Deese, age 64, $4,828,840 total compensation
President: Allen L. Shiver, age 54, $1,226,351 total compensation
EVP and COO: Gene D. Lord, age 63, $1,382,228 total compensation
EVP and CFO: R. Steve Kinsey, age 49, $859,456 total compensation
EVP Corporate Relations: Marta Jones Turner, age 56
EVP, Secretary, and General Counsel: Stephen R. (Steve) Avera, age 53, $1,096,478 total compensation
EVP Supply Chain: Michael A. (Mike) Beaty, age 59
SVP Human Resources: Donald A. Thriffiley Jr., age 56
SVP and CIO: Vyto F. Razminas, age 52
SVP and Chief Accounting Officer: Karyl H. Lauder, age 53
VP and Corporate Controller: Vandy T. Davis
VP Communications and Corporate Responsibility: Mary A. Krier
VP and Treasurer: Kirk L. Tolbert
Managing Director Communications: D. Keith Hancock
President, Flowers Bakeries: Bradley K. (Brad) Alexander, age 51
Auditors: PricewaterhouseCoopers LLP

LOCATIONS

HQ: Flowers Foods, Inc.
1919 Flowers Cir., Thomasville, GA 31757
Phone: 229-226-9110   **Fax:** 229-225-3806
Web: www.flowersfoods.com

PRODUCTS/OPERATIONS

2009 Sales

	% of total
Branded retail	52
Store-brand retail	16
Foodservice & other	32
Total	**100**

2009 Sales

	% of total
DSD	82
Warehouse delivery	18
Total	**100**

Selected Brands

DSD
　BlueBird
　ButterKrust
　Captain John Derst
　Cobblestone Mill
　Dandee
　Evangeline Maid
　Flowers
　Ideal
　Mary Jane
　Nature's Own
　Whitewheat
Regional franchised
　Aunt Hattie's
　Bunny
　Country Hearth
　Holsum
　Roman Meal
　Sunbeam
Warehouse delivery
　Broad Street Bakery
　European Bakers
　Juarez
　Leo's
　Mrs. Freshley's
　Snack Away

COMPETITORS

Alpha Baking	Kraft North America
Atlanta Bread	Lance Snacks
Azteca Foods	Lewis Bakeries
Bob's Red Mill Natural Foods	Manischewitz Company
Campagna Turano Bakery	McKee Foods
Campbell Soup	Olé Mexican Foods
Frito-Lay	Organic Milling
General Mills	Otis Spunkmeyer
George Weston	Panera Bread
Gruma Corporation	Ralcorp
Grupo Bimbo	Rich Products
Heinemann's Bakeries	Sara Lee
Hostess Brands	Silver Lake Cookie
Kellogg U.S. Snacks	Sterling Foods
King's Hawaiian	Tasty Baking
Kraft Foods	United States Bakery
	Voortman Cookies

HISTORICAL FINANCIALS

Company Type: Public

Income Statement				FYE: Saturday nearest December 31
	REVENUE ($ mil.)	NET INCOME ($ mil.)	NET PROFIT MARGIN	EMPLOYEES
12/09	2,601	130	5.0%	8,800
12/08	2,415	119	4.9%	8,800
12/07	2,037	95	4.6%	7,800
12/06	1,889	82	4.3%	7,800
12/05	1,716	61	3.6%	7,500
Annual Growth	11.0%	20.8%	—	4.1%

2009 Year-End Financials

Debt ratio: 31.6%
Return on equity: 19.3%
Cash ($ mil.): 19
Current ratio: 1.53
Long-term debt ($ mil.): 226

No. of shares (mil.): 92
Dividends
　Yield: 2.8%
　Payout: 48.2%
Market value ($ mil.): 2,180

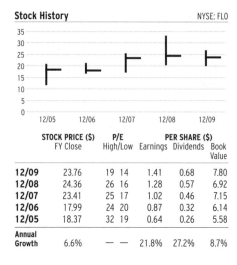

	STOCK PRICE ($)	P/E		PER SHARE ($)		
	FY Close	High/Low	Earnings	Dividends	Book Value
12/09	23.76	19 14	1.41	0.68	7.80
12/08	24.36	26 16	1.28	0.57	6.92
12/07	23.41	25 17	1.02	0.46	7.15
12/06	17.99	24 20	0.87	0.32	6.14
12/05	18.37	32 19	0.64	0.26	5.58
Annual Growth	6.6%	— —	21.8%	27.2%	8.7%

Fluor Corporation

Fluor Corporation is one of the world's largest international design, engineering, and contracting firms. The company provides engineering, procurement, construction, maintenance, and project management services for a variety of industrial sectors around the world. Its projects include manufacturing facilities, refineries, pharmaceutical facilities, health care buildings, power plants, and telecommunications and transportation infrastructure. The oil and gas industry accounts for more than half of Fluor's sales. The company also provides operations and maintenance services for its projects, as well as administrative and support services to the US government.

Fluor's oil and gas segment provides design, engineering, and construction and project management services to markets including upstream oil and gas producers, refiners, petrochemical manufacturers, and producers of specialty and fine chemicals. The unit provides oversight of other contractors and procurement of labor, equipment, and materials. Fluor's oil and gas segment has traditionally been the primary driver for growth in the company. It has generally benefited from increased global demand for oil. However, falling oil prices, the global recession, and the widespread credit crisis have impacted some projects. In late 2008 the company formed Fluor Offshore Solutions, which is dedicated to global oil and gas clients in the offshore market.

The company's industrial and infrastructure segment provides design, engineering, procurement, and construction services for pharmaceutical and biotechnology facilities, commercial and institutional buildings, and mining, telecommunications, wind power, and transportation projects. The unit participates in public/private partnerships to oversee financing and management of roadway and railway projects. One ongoing project is the world's largest offshore wind farm development off the coast of the UK. The project is expected to help produce 25 gigawatts of wind energy by 2020.

Fluor jumped into the growing outsourcing services market with its global services segment, which provides operations and maintenance support, temporary staffing (through TRS Staffing Solutions), and asset management. Fluor also provides construction equipment, tools, and fleet outsourcing for construction projects and plant sites worldwide through subsidiary American Equipment Company (AMECO).

Fluor's government services segment offers project management primarily to the US Departments of Energy, Defense, and Homeland Security. It provides environmental restoration, engineering and construction, and operations and maintenance services for two former nuclear weapons complexes that are now DOE cleanup sites: the Savannah River site in South Carolina and the Hanford Environmental Management Project in Richland, Washington. Subsidiary Del-Jen provides military base operations and maintenance services and other logistical and infrastructure services around the world.

HISTORY

Fluor's history began in 1890 when three Fluor brothers, immigrants from Switzerland, opened a Wisconsin lumber mill under the name Rudolph Fluor & Brothers. In 1912 John Simon Fluor formed a construction firm in Santa Ana, California. Fluor's company soon began a relationship with Southern California Gas, which led it to specialize in oil and gas construction. The company, incorporated as Fluor Construction in 1924, later began making engine mufflers. In 1930 it expanded outside of California with a contract to build Texas pipelines.

After WWII, Middle East oil reserves were aggressively developed by Western companies. Fluor cashed in on the stampede, winning major contracts in Saudi Arabia. During the early 1960s it continued to emphasize oil and gas work, establishing a contract drilling unit, and in the 1970s it began work on giant energy projects.

In 1977 Fluor made its biggest purchase: Daniel International, a South Carolina engineering and construction firm with more than $1 billion in annual revenues. The contracting firm, founded by Charles Daniel in 1934, initially did construction work for the textile industry, then later worked for the chemical, pharmaceutical, metal, and power industries.

Flush with cash, Fluor bought St. Joe Minerals in 1981. A drop in oil prices in the 1980s killed demand for the big projects that were its bread and butter. As metal prices fell, St. Joe didn't help the bottom line either. John Robert Fluor, the last of the founding family to head the firm, died in 1984.

When David Tappan stepped in as CEO, he faced a $573 million loss the first year. The white-haired son of missionaries to China, Tappan — known as the Ice Man — dumped subsidiaries and halved the payroll. In 1986 he merged Daniel into Fluor's engineering unit, forming Fluor Daniel.

Leslie McCraw succeeded Tappan as CEO in 1991. McCraw saw Fluor as overly conservative, and three years later he began setting up offices around the world while decentralizing Fluor's structure and adding new business such as temporary staffing and equipment leasing. Fluor also shed some of its commodity companies, including its lead business in 1994. In 1996 Fluor's environmental services unit merged with Groundwater Technology and was spun off as a public company, Fluor Daniel GTI.

Ill with cancer, McCraw stepped down in 1998, and Philip Carroll, who had overhauled Shell Oil, took over as CEO.

Fluor in 1999 cut 5,000 jobs, further streamlined operations, and shifted its focus to growth industries such as biotechnology and telecommunications. The next year the company split its construction and coal mining operations into two separate publicly traded companies, one to concentrate on engineering and construction and one on coal mining. Former Fluor subsidiary A. T. Massey Coal was spun off as Massey Energy.

Carroll, his restructuring job complete, announced in December 2001 that he would retire the following February. Alan Boeckmann, who had been president and COO, succeeded Carroll in 2002.

The next year Fluor acquired Del-Jen, a provider of outsourced services to US military bases and to the US Department of Labor. It also picked up five specialty operations and maintenance business groups from Philip Services. And in 2003 the company decided to dissolve its Duke/Fluor Daniel joint venture.

Fluor moved its headquarters from California to Dallas in 2006. The move resulted in the elimination of about 100 jobs. That year the company entered the health care construction market.

EXECUTIVES

Chairman and CEO: Alan L. Boeckmann, age 61, $10,006,619 total compensation
COO: David T. Seaton, age 48, $2,242,260 total compensation
SVP and CFO: D. Michael (Mike) Steuert, age 61, $3,719,727 total compensation
SVP Business Development and Strategy, Infrastructure Group: Robert (Bob) Prieto
SVP Health, Safety, and Environmental (HSE) and Corporate Security; President and CEO, Savannah River Nuclear Solutions (SRNS): Garry W. Flowers, age 58
SVP Environmental/Nuclear Business Line: J. Gregory (Greg) Meyer
SVP Government Relations: David (Dave) Marventano
SVP Human Resources and Administration: Glenn C. Gilkey, age 51
Chief Legal Officer and Corporate Secretary: Carlos M. Hernandez, age 55
VP and CIO: Ray F. Barnard, age 51
VP Corporate Finance and Investor Relations: Kenneth H. (Ken) Lockwood
VP and Treasurer: Joanna M. Oliva
Senior Group President, Industrial and Infrastructure, and Global Services: Stephen B. Dobbs, age 53, $2,017,555 total compensation
Group Executive Corporate Development: John L. Hopkins, age 56, $2,183,258 total compensation
Group President, Global Services: Kirk D. Grimes, age 52, $2,267,646 total compensation
Group President, Power: David R. (Dave) Dunning, age 58
Group President, Energy and Chemicals: Peter W. B. Oosterveer
Group President, Government: Bruce A. Stanski, age 48
Group President, Project Operations: David E. Constable, age 48
Manager Investor Relations: Jason Landkamer
Auditors: Ernst & Young LLP

LOCATIONS

HQ: Fluor Corporation
6700 Las Colinas Blvd., Irving, TX 75039
Phone: 469-398-7000   **Fax:** 469-398-7255
Web: www.fluor.com

2009 Sales

	$ mil.	% of total
US	10,792.6	49
Europe	3,910.5	18
Asia/Pacific	2,898.4	13
Middle East & Africa	2,300.3	11
Central & South America	1,379.5	6
Canada	709.0	3
Total	**21,990.3**	**100**

PRODUCTS/OPERATIONS

2009 Sales by Segment

	$ mil.	% of total
Oil & Gas	11,826.9	54
Industrial & Infrastructure	4,820.6	22
Global Services	2,069.0	9
Government	1,983.2	9
Power	1,290.6	6
Total	**21,990.3**	**100**

Selected Services

Construction management
Design
Engineering, procurement, and construction (EPC)
Operations and maintenance
Program management
Project development and finance
Project management
Staffing

Selected Industries Served

Biotechnology
Chemicals and petrochemicals
Commercial and institutional
Equipment
Gas processing
Government
Manufacturing
Mining
Oil and gas production
Petroleum refining
Pharmaceuticals
Power generation
Telecommunications
Transportation

Selected Subsidiaries

American Equipment Company, Inc.
  American Construction Equipment Company, Inc.
Fluor Constructors International, Inc.
Fluor Enterprises, Inc.
  Daniel International Corporation
  Del-Jen, Inc.
  Fluor Daniel Mexico S.A.
    ICA-Fluor Daniel, S. de R.L. de C.V. (49%, Mexico)
Fluor Holding Company LLC
TRS Staffing Solutions, Inc.

COMPETITORS

ARCADIS
Balfour Construction
Bechtel
Bilfinger Berger
Black & Veatch
Bouygues
CH2M HILL
Foster Wheeler
Hitachi
Jacobs Engineering
KBR
McDermott
Parsons Corporation
POSCO
Raytheon
Shaw Group
Technip
Tetra Tech
URS
WorleyParsons Corp.

HISTORICAL FINANCIALS

Company Type: Public

Income Statement

FYE: December 31

	REVENUE ($ mil.)	NET INCOME ($ mil.)	NET PROFIT MARGIN	EMPLOYEES
12/09	21,990	685	3.1%	36,152
12/08	22,326	721	3.2%	42,119
12/07	16,691	533	3.2%	41,260
12/06	14,079	264	1.9%	37,560
12/05	13,161	227	1.7%	34,836
Annual Growth	**13.7%**	**31.8%**	**—**	**0.9%**

2009 Year-End Financials

Debt ratio: 0.5%
Return on equity: 22.9%
Cash ($ mil.): 1,687
Current ratio: 1.55
Long-term debt ($ mil.): 18
No. of shares (mil.): 179
Dividends
  Yield: 1.1%
  Payout: 13.3%
Market value ($ mil.): 8,051

Stock History

NYSE: FLR

	STOCK PRICE ($) FY Close	P/E High/Low		PER SHARE ($) Earnings	Dividends	Book Value
12/09	45.04	16	8	3.75	0.50	18.49
12/08	44.87	26	7	3.93	0.50	14.94
12/07	72.86	29	13	2.92	0.40	12.72
12/06	40.83	35	25	1.48	0.40	9.68
12/05	38.63	30	19	1.31	0.32	9.12
Annual Growth	**3.9%**	**—**	**—**	**30.1%**	**11.8%**	**19.3%**

FMC Corporation

E may = mc^2, but FMC = chemicals. Once in areas as diverse as oil field equipment and food machinery, FMC Corporation now focuses on industrial, specialty, and agricultural chemicals. The company's industrial chemicals include soda ash (it's one of the largest producers), hydrogen peroxide, and phosphorus chemicals. The rest of its sales come from agricultural products (insecticides, herbicides, and fungicides) and specialty chemicals (food and pharmaceutical additives). FMC's equation lately has improved after a few years' effort to increase its efficiency, profitability, and credit rating. The company cut costs across the board, including closing plants, refocusing on growth areas such as specialty chemicals.

The food and pharmaceutical additives product groups are the areas of choice where FMC sees a real opportunity to improve its fortunes. Product development has been concentrated on specialty chemicals product areas such as energy storage (lithium products for batteries) and agricultural products (home and garden pesticides).

To that last point, the company acquired the CB Professional Products line of insecticides from Waterbury Companies in 2009. CB Professional Products makes an array of aerosol sprays as well as foggers, baits, and other insect control products. FMC also bought a line of fungicides from Italian company Isagro.

In 2010 FMC acquired the herbicide fluthiacet-methyl from Kumiai Chemical Industry Co. and Ihara Chemical Industry Co., both based in Tokyo. FMC was already distributing fluthiacet-methyl in the US under the brand Cadet herbicide. Going forward, it will develop and market the product globally.

Chairman and CEO William Walter stepped down as chief executive in 2010 and was replaced by Pierre Brondeau, who was also named to the Board of Directors. Brondeau had been the long-time CEO of Rohm and Haas before its acquisition by Dow Chemical, for which he worked briefly.

HISTORY

After retiring to California, inventor John Bean developed a pump to deliver a continuous spray of insecticide in 1884. This invention led to the Bean Spray Pump Company in 1904. In 1928 Bean Spray Pump went public and bought Anderson-Barngrover (food-growing and -processing equipment). The company became Food Machinery Corporation the next year. It bought Peerless Pump (agricultural and industrial pumps) in 1933.

During WWII the company began making military equipment. It entered the agricultural chemical field when it bought Niagara Sprayer & Chemical (1943). After the war it added Westvaco Chemical (1948) and changed its name to Food Machinery & Chemical.

The Bean family ran the company until 1956, when John Bean's grandson, John Crummey, retired as chairman. The company extended its product line, buying Oil Center Tool (wellhead equipment, 1957), Sunland Industries (fertilizer and insecticides, 1959), and Barrett Equipment (automotive brake equipment, 1961).

In light of its growing diversification, the company changed its name to FMC Corporation in 1961. Major purchases in the 1960s included American Viscose (rayon and cellophane, 1963) and Link-Belt (equipment for power transmission and for bulk-material handling, 1967).

To be centrally located, FMC moved its headquarters from San Jose to Chicago in 1972. Through the 1970s and early 1980s, the company sold several slow-growing businesses, including its pump and fiber divisions (1976), semiconductor division (1979), industrial packaging division (1980), Niagara Seed Operation (1980), and Power Transmission Group (1981).

It moved into other markets just as quickly. These included a Nevada gold mine (through a 1979 joint venture with Freeport Minerals), Bradley armored personnel carriers (through an early-1980s contract with the US Army), and lithium (by acquiring Lithium Corp. of America, 1985). In a 1986 antitakeover move, FMC gave employees a larger stake in the company.

FMC bought Ciba-Geigy's flame-retardant and water-treatment businesses in 1992 and combined its defense operations with Harsco as United Defense. FMC's 1994 acquisitions included Abex's Jetway Systems Division (aircraft support systems) and Caterpillar's Automated Vehicle Systems group. FMC formed a joint venture with Nippon Sheet Glass and Sumitomo Corporation in 1995 to mine for soda ash.

FMC made a deal with DuPont in 1996 to commercialize new herbicides. The company debuted its composite (nonmetallic) prototype armored vehicle in 1997. In the long shadow of reduced defense budgets, FMC and Harsco sold their stagnant defense operation for $850 million to The Carlyle Group investment firm.

The sale of its defense division didn't protect FMC from a $310 million damage award in a whistleblower suit against the company in 1998. A federal jury found that FMC had misled the Army about the safety of the Bradley armored infantry vehicle. The court later lowered the penalty to about $90 million.

In 1999 the company agreed to combine its phosphorus operations with Solutia to form a joint venture called Astaris. That year FMC sold its process-additives unit to Great Lakes Chemical (now called Chemtura).

FMC bought Northfield Freezing Systems (food processing) in 2000. The following year the company split into separate chemical and machinery companies by spinning off its machinery business as FMC Technologies; FMC Corporation then moved its headquarters from Chicago to Philadelphia. In early 2002 FMC sold its sodium cyanide business to Cyanco Company, a joint venture between Degussa Corporation and Winnemucca Chemicals (a subsidiary of Nevada Chemicals).

In 2005 FMC and Solutia sold Astaris (now called ICL Performance Products) to Israel Chemicals Limited for $255 million.

EXECUTIVES

Chairman: William G. (Bill) Walter, age 64, $6,870,119 total compensation
President, CEO, and Director: Pierre Brondeau, age 52
SVP and CFO: W. Kim Foster, age 61, $2,225,412 total compensation
VP and General Manager, Industrial Chemicals: D. Michael Wilson, age 46, $1,566,433 total compensation
VP and General Manager, Specialty Chemicals: Theodore H. (Ted) Butz, age 51, $1,488,356 total compensation
VP and General Manager, Agricultural Products: Milton Steele, age 61, $2,027,103 total compensation
VP, Secretary, and General Counsel: Andrea E. Utecht, age 61
VP Government and Public Affairs: Gerald R. (Jerry) Prout, age 55
VP and Corporate Controller: Graham R. Wood, age 56
VP and Treasurer: Thomas C. Deas Jr., age 59
VP Human Resources and Communications: Kenneth R. Garrett
Director, FMC Professional Solutions: Amy G. O'Shea
Auditors: KPMG LLP

LOCATIONS

HQ: FMC Corporation
1735 Market St., Philadelphia, PA 19103
Phone: 215-299-6000   **Fax:** 215-299-5998
Web: www.fmc.com

2009 Sales

	$ mil.	% of total
North America		
US	984.3	35
Other countries	60.6	2
Europe/Middle East/Africa	716.4	25
Latin America		
Brazil	470.8	17
Other countries	227.0	8
Asia/Pacific	367.1	13
Total	**2,826.2**	**100**

PRODUCTS/OPERATIONS

2009 Sales

	$ mil.	% of total
Agricultural Chemicals	1,051.6	37
Industrial Chemicals	1,026.7	36
Specialty Chemicals	753.1	27
Adjustments	(5.2)	—
Total	**2,826.2**	**100**

Selected Products

Agricultural products
  Herbicides
  Pesticides
Industrial chemicals
  Hydrogen peroxide
  Phosphorus chemicals
  Soda ash
  Sodium bicarbonate
  Sodium sesquicarbonate
Specialty chemicals
  Cellulose (alginate, carrageenan, and microcrystalline)
  Lithium

COMPETITORS

Agrium	Dow Chemical
Akzo Nobel	DuPont
Arkema	Evonik Degussa
Asahi Glass	PPG Industries
Asahi Kasei	Solvay
BASF SE	SQM
Bayer CropScience	Sumitomo Chemical
Cargill	Syngenta
CP Kelco	Terra Industries

HISTORICAL FINANCIALS

Company Type: Public

Income Statement
FYE: December 31

	REVENUE ($ mil.)	NET INCOME ($ mil.)	NET PROFIT MARGIN	EMPLOYEES
12/09	2,826	239	8.4%	4,800
12/08	3,115	305	9.8%	5,000
12/07	2,633	132	5.0%	5,000
12/06	2,347	132	5.6%	5,000
12/05	2,150	117	5.4%	5,000
Annual Growth	7.1%	19.5%	—	(1.0%)

2009 Year-End Financials

Debt ratio: 54.6%
Return on equity: 24.1%
Cash ($ mil.): 77
Current ratio: 2.10
Long-term debt ($ mil.): 588
No. of shares (mil.): 72
Dividends
  Yield: 0.9%
  Payout: 16.0%
Market value ($ mil.): 4,042

Stock History
NYSE: FMC

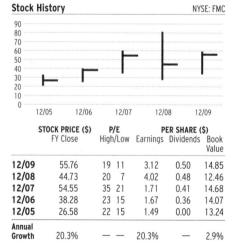

	STOCK PRICE ($) FY Close	P/E High/Low		PER SHARE ($) Earnings	Dividends	Book Value
12/09	55.76	19	11	3.12	0.50	14.85
12/08	44.73	20	7	4.02	0.48	12.46
12/07	54.55	35	21	1.71	0.41	14.68
12/06	38.28	23	15	1.67	0.36	14.07
12/05	26.58	22	15	1.49	0.00	13.24
Annual Growth	20.3%	—	—	20.3%	—	2.9%

FMR LLC

FMR is *semper fidelis* (ever faithful) to its core business. The financial services conglomerate, better known as Fidelity Investments, is one of the world's largest mutual fund firms. Serving more than 20 million individual and institutional clients, Fidelity manages almost 500 funds and has more than $1.5 trillion of assets under management. It also operates a leading online discount brokerage and has more than 100 investor centers in the US and Canada, as well as locations in Europe and Asia. The founding Johnson family controls FMR; Abigail Johnson, CEO Ned Johnson's daughter and perhaps his successor (not to mention one of the richest women in America), is the company's largest single shareholder.

Fidelity's nonfund offerings include life insurance, trust services, securities clearing, and retirement services. It is one of the largest administrators of 401(k) plans, and the firm continues to grow this segment, which includes other services related to benefits outsourcing. The company had been reluctant to give direct investment advice to 401(k) plan participants, but under pressure from customers struck a formal agreement with Financial Engines, which now provides those services to Fidelity's clients.

The company has private equity investments in telecommunications firm COLT Group and transportation company BostonCoach, among others. Like many institutional investors, Fidelity uses its clout to sway the boards of companies in which it has significant holdings.

In 2010 the firm's US venture capital arm, Fidelity Ventures, ceased operations after members of its management team left to form their own independent investment company. Fidelity continues to be active in venture capital through its Fidelity Growth Partners unit in Europe and Asia and through Fidelity Biosciences in the US.

Also that year Fidelity created two new organizations to run its asset management business. The vice president of BNY Mellon, Ronald O'Hanley, along with Abigail Johnson were chosen to head up the organizations. Both could be candidates to replace Ned Johnson.

FMR also holds about a 15% stake in venerable British investment bank Lazard, which it acquired in 2005.

HISTORY

Boston money management firm Anderson & Cromwell formed Fidelity Fund in 1930. Edward Johnson became president of the fund in 1943, when it had $3 million invested in Treasury bills. Johnson diversified into stocks, and by 1945 the fund had grown to $10 million. In 1946 he established Fidelity Management and Research to act as its investment adviser.

In the early 1950s Johnson hired Gerry Tsai, a young immigrant from Shanghai, to analyze stocks. He put Tsai in charge of Fidelity Capital Fund in 1957. Tsai's brash, go-go investment strategy in such speculative stocks as Xerox and Polaroid paid off; by the time he left to form his own fund in 1965, he was managing more than $1 billion.

The Magellan Fund started in 1962. The company entered the corporate pension plans market (FMR Investment Management) in 1964, and the self-employed individual retirement market (Fidelity Keogh Plan) in 1967. It began serving investors outside the US (Fidelity International) in 1968.

Holding company FMR was formed in 1972, the same year Johnson gave control of Fidelity to his son Ned, who vertically integrated FMR by selling directly to customers rather than through brokers. In 1973 he formed Fidelity Daily Income Trust, the first money market fund to offer check writing.

Peter Lynch was hired as manager of the Magellan Fund in 1977. During his 13-year tenure, Magellan grew from $20 million to $12 billion in assets and outperformed all other mutual funds. Fidelity started Fidelity Brokerage Services in 1978, becoming the first mutual fund company to offer discount brokerage.

In 1980 the company launched a nationwide branch network and in 1986 entered the credit card business. The Wall Street crash of 1987 forced its Magellan Fund to liquidate almost $1 billion in stock in a single day. That year FMR moved into insurance by offering variable life, single premium, and deferred annuity policies. In 1989 the company introduced the low-expense Spartan Fund, targeted toward large, less-active investors.

Magellan's performance faded in the early 1990s, dropping from #1 performer to #3. Most of Fidelity's best performers were from its 36 select funds, which focus on narrow industry segments. FMR founded London-based COLT Telecom (later named COLT Group) in 1993. In 1994 Johnson gave his daughter and possible heir apparent, Abigail, a 25% stake in FMR. She reportedly sold a significant portion of the stake in 2005.

Jeffrey Vinik resigned as manager of Magellan in 1996, one of more than a dozen fund managers to leave the firm that year and the next. Robert Stansky took the helm of the $56 billion fund, which FMR decided to close to new investors in 1997. Fidelity had a first that year when it went with an outside fund manager, hiring Bankers Trust (now part of Deutsche Bank) to manage its index funds.

FMR did some housecleaning in the late 1990s. It sold its Wentworth art galleries (1997) and *Worth* magazine (1998). Despite continued management turnover, it entered Japan and expanded its presence in Canada.

In 1999 the firm teamed with Internet portal Lycos (now part of Terra Networks) to develop its online brokerage. FMR opened savings and loan Fidelity Personal Trust Co. in 2000.

In 2006 the company announced that it would pay $42 million into its mutual funds after an internal investigation showed that some of its traders had allegedly guided business to brokers who had given the traders gifts. The SEC later slapped FMR with an $8 million fine.

In 2007 the company's Fidelity Equity Partners arm launched a $500 million buyout fund targeting middle-market firms involved in media, software, health care, and service industries in North America and Europe. Two years later, Fidelity shut the fund down after it had backed four companies total. It cited the economic downturn and the lack of available credit for the move.

HISTORICAL FINANCIALS

Company Type: Private

Income Statement

FYE: December 31

	REVENUE ($ mil.)	NET INCOME ($ mil.)	NET PROFIT MARGIN	EMPLOYEES
12/08	12,937	—	—	40,000
12/07	14,900	—	—	46,400
12/06	12,870	—	—	41,900
Annual Growth	0.3%	—	—	(2.3%)

Revenue History

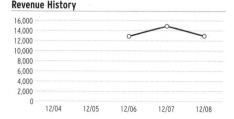

Foot Locker

Foot Locker leads the pack in the race to capture the biggest share of the athletic footwear market. The company is a leading retailer of athletic shoes and apparel, with about 3,500 specialty stores in more than 20 countries in North America and Europe, as well as Australia and New Zealand. Its 1,900-plus store namesake Foot Locker chain is the #1 seller of name-brand (NIKE) athletic footwear in the US. The company also operates stores under the Lady Foot Locker, Kids Foot Locker, Footaction, Champs Sports, and CCS banners. In addition to its bricks-and-mortar business, Foot Locker markets sports gear through its direct-to-customer unit, which consists of catalog retailer Eastbay and Footlocker.com.

Under the leadership of chairman and CEO Ken Hicks, who joined the business in mid-2009 from J. C. Penney, Foot Locker unveiled a new strategic plan in March 2010. The deep recession in the US and declining consumer confidence caused Foot Locker to stumble, hurting the firm's US operations, while the overseas business fared better.

Longer-term goals include expanding Foot Locker's footwear and apparel offering to court a more-diverse customer base and growing the business internationally. (Foot Locker is heavily dependent on athletic-shoe-giant NIKE, which supplies about two-thirds of its merchandise.) Hicks wants Foot Locker to become the leading global retailer of athletic shoes and apparel. Already more than a quarter of Foot Locker's revenue is earned outside the US and that share is growing. In addition to more than 500 stores throughout Europe, the company, through franchises, also has 20-plus stores in the Middle East and South Korea. Foot Locker is expanding in Europe, while continuing to reduce its US store count due to declining footwear sales here.

While the retail store side of the business is limping along, Foot Locker's direct-to-consumer business is enjoying healthy growth in online sales but experiencing a steep decline in sales from catalogs. To boost its online presence, in 2008 the company acquired CCS, a direct marketer of skateboard and snowboard equipment, apparel, and footwear that targets teenage boys. It opened the first CCS retail stores in California and New Jersey in 2009. Foot Locker has shuttered about 285 stores since 2007.

HISTORY

With the idea of selling merchandise priced at no more than five cents, Frank Woolworth opened the Great Five Cent Store in Utica, New York, in 1879; it failed. That year he moved to Lancaster, Pennsylvania, and created the first five-and-dime. Woolworth moved his headquarters to New York City (1886) and spent the rest of the century acquiring other dime-store chains. He later expanded to Canada (1897), England (1909), France (1922), and Germany (1927).

The 120-store chain, with $10 million in sales, incorporated as F.W. Woolworth & Company in 1905, with Woolworth as president. In 1912 the company merged with five rival chains and went public with 596 stores, making $52 million in sales the first year. The next year, paying $13.5 million in cash, Woolworth finished construction of the Woolworth Building, then the world's tallest building (792 feet). When he died in 1919, the chain had 1,081 stores, with sales of $119 million.

Woolworth became more competitive after WWII by advertising, establishing revolving credit and self-service, moving stores to suburbs, and expanding merchandise selections. In 1962 it opened Woolco, a US and Canadian discount chain.

From the 1960s through the 1980s, the company grew by acquiring and expanding in the US and abroad. It picked up Kinney (shoes, 1963), Richman Brothers (men's clothing, 1969), Holtzman's Little Folk Shop (children's clothing, 1983), Champs Sports (sporting goods, 1987), and Mathers (shoes, Australia, 1988).

The company introduced Foot Locker, the athletic shoe chain, in 1974, later developing Lady Foot Locker (1982) and Kids Foot Locker (1987). In 1993 Woolworth launched an ambitious restructuring plan, focusing on specialty stores (mostly apparel and shoes). It also closed 400 US stores and sold 122 Canadian Woolco stores to Wal-Mart that year. Former Macy's president Roger Farah became CEO in 1994. Farah eliminated 16 divisions and dozens of executives.

A year later the firm sold its Kids Mart/Little Folks children's wear chain. In 1996 Woolworth began a major remodeling program that included removing its venerable lunch counters. (Another alleged renovation at the Woolworth chain — the firing of older workers, who were replaced by teenagers — led to an Equal Employment Opportunity Commission lawsuit against the company in 1999.) The changes failed, and the next year the company closed its US Woolworth stores and bought athletic-products catalog company Eastbay.

In 1998 Woolworth changed its name to Venator Group and sold the Woolworth Building, a national landmark (headquarters remained in the building). The company then shed itself of more than 1,400 stores, including Kinney shoes and Footquarters (both closed).

Venator came out the champ in a proxy fight against investment group Greenway Partners in July 1999. Shortly thereafter, Farah was replaced as CEO (he remained chairman) by president Dale Hilpert.

In 2000 Venator slashed 7% of its workforce in the US and Canada (a small part of the planned 30% cut) and closed 465 stores. COO Matt Serra became president, and Hilpert became chairman when Farah resigned later that year.

In 2001 Hilpert resigned, replaced by Carter Bacot as chairman, and Serra added CEO to his title. Venator later sold its Canadian Northern Group unit to investment firm York Management Services and closed its Northern Reflections stores in the US. Venator changed its name to Foot Locker in November.

In 2004 chairman Bacot became lead director, and president and CEO Serra added chairman to his title. Also that year Foot Locker, capitalizing on the Chapter 11 filing of Footstar, purchased from the company 350 of its Footaction stores.

In 2007 Foot Locker made an unsolicited $1.2 billion bid for rival Genesco that was rejected by Genesco's board. In 2008 Foot Locker acquired the CCS brand from dELia*s. The CCS brand includes skateboarding and snowboarding equipment, apparel, and footwear targeting primarily teenage boys.

J.C. Penney executive Kenneth Hicks was recruited to succeed Serra as president and CEO in August 2009. Serra retained the chairman's title until his retirement in January 2010. At that time, Hicks became chairman.

EXECUTIVES

Chairman, President, and CEO:
Kenneth C. (Ken) Hicks, age 57,
$8,595,665 total compensation
SVP and Chief Accounting Officer: Giovanna Cipriano, age 40
SVP, CIO, and Investor Relations: Peter D. Brown, age 55
SVP, General Counsel, and Secretary: Gary M. Bahler, age 58, $1,228,292 total compensation
SVP Human Resources: Laurie J. Petrucci, age 51, $1,649,217 total compensation
SVP Strategic Planning: Lauren B. Peters, age 48
SVP and CFO: Robert W. McHugh, age 51, $1,151,115 total compensation
SVP Real Estate: Jeffrey L. Berk, age 54
VP Human Resources: Patricia A. Peck
President and CEO, Foot Locker U.S., Footaction, Kids Foot Locker, and Lady Foot Locker:
Richard A. (Dick) Johnson,
$2,126,894 total compensation
President and CEO Foot Locker, Inc. International:
Ronald J. Halls, age 56, $2,383,216 total compensation
President and CEO, Foot Locker Europe:
Lewis P. Kimble
President and CEO, Champs Sports: Stephen D. Jacobs
President and CEO, Footlocker.com/Eastbay/CCS:
Dowe S. Tillema
Auditors: KPMG LLP

LOCATIONS

HQ: Foot Locker, Inc.
112 W. 34th St., New York, NY 10120
Phone: 212-720-3700   **Fax:** 212-720-4397
Web: www.footlocker-inc.com

2010 Sales

	$ mil.	% of total
US	3,425	71
International	1,429	29
Total	**4,854**	**100**

2010 Foot Locker Stores

	No.
US, Puerto Rico, Guam & US Virgin Islands	1,171
Europe	518
Canada	129
Australia & New Zealand	93
Total	**1,911**

PRODUCTS/OPERATIONS

2010 Stores

	No.
Foot Locker	1,911
Champs Sports	552
Lady Foot Locker	415
Footaction	319
Kids Foot Locker	301
CCS	2
Total	**3,500**

2010 Sales

	$ mil.	% of total
Athletic stores	4,448	92
Direct-to-consumer	406	8
Total	**4,854**	**100**

COMPETITORS

Academy Sports	L.L. Bean
Brown Shoe	Macy's
Dick's Sporting Goods	Modell's
Dillard's	Pacific Sunwear
DSW	Quiksilver
Finish Line	Sears
Forzani Group	Shoe Carnival
The Gap	shoebuy.com
Genesco	Sports Authority
Hibbett Sports	Target
J. C. Penney	TJX Companies
Kmart	Wal-Mart

HISTORICAL FINANCIALS

Company Type: Public

Income Statement

FYE: Saturday nearest January 31

	REVENUE ($ mil.)	NET INCOME ($ mil.)	NET PROFIT MARGIN	EMPLOYEES
1/10	4,854	48	1.0%	38,764
1/09	5,237	(80)	—	39,758
1/08	5,437	51	0.9%	44,415
1/07	5,750	250	4.3%	45,406
1/06	5,653	264	4.7%	44,276
Annual Growth	**(3.7%)**	**(34.7%)**	**—**	**(3.3%)**

2010 Year-End Financials

Debt ratio: 7.1%
Return on equity: 2.5%
Cash ($ mil.): 582
Current ratio: 4.09
Long-term debt ($ mil.): 138
No. of shares (mil.): 156
Dividends
  Yield: 5.3%
  Payout: 200.0%
Market value ($ mil.): 1,764

Stock History

NYSE: FL

	STOCK PRICE ($) FY Close	P/E High/Low		PER SHARE ($) Earnings	Dividends	Book Value
1/10	11.29	43	24	0.30	0.60	12.47
1/09	7.36	—	—	(0.52)	0.60	12.32
1/08	13.69	75	27	0.33	0.50	14.54
1/07	22.44	17	13	1.60	0.40	14.69
1/06	22.72	18	11	1.68	0.31	12.98
Annual Growth	**(16.0%)**	**—**	**—**	**(35.0%)**	**17.9%**	**(1.0%)**

Ford Motor

Ford Motor began a manufacturing revolution with mass production assembly lines in the early 20th century. One of the world's largest auto makers, Ford brands include Ford, Lincoln, and Mercury — the latter to be dropped in late 2010. Among its successes are the redesigned Ford Mustang, the F-Series pickup, and the fuel-efficient Focus. Finance unit Ford Motor Credit is one of the US's leading auto finance companies. Ford owns a small stake in Mazda but has sold Volvo to Zhejiang Geely Holding, parent of Geely Automobile, for about $1.3 billion cash and other monetary consideration.

Ford was the only American carmaker to make it through the economic crisis without filing for bankruptcy; however, it still faced struggles with more than $27 billion in debt. The company made the decision to sell Volvo in order to focus on its North American and European businesses.

Geely, China's largest privately owned car maker, acquired Ford's Volvo unit in mid-2010. Volvo's headquarters and manufacturing operations will remain in Sweden and Belgium, with Stefan Jacoby (former CEO of Volkswagen Group of America) in the position of president and CEO of Volvo Cars. Ford will not retain any ownership in Volvo, but will provide engineering support and access to tooling for some components; Ford will also supply powertrains, stampings, and other components for a period of time.

The global economic downturn hit the auto industry particularly hard, especially in North America, one of its largest markets. Although Ford didn't seek loans from the US government or go through bankruptcy as Chrysler and General Motors did, it took a huge hit to its bottom line in 2008, after a couple of years of lackluster results. However, Ford responded more quickly than its peers to changing consumer demands, and restructured its production facilities to be more flexible, able to shift with consumer preferences as well as produce various combinations of transmissions and engines.

Ford reduced its North American salaried personnel by roughly 20% from 2008 through the end of 2009, and cut back on production. The company also reduced its 33% stake in Mazda to 11%, effectively ceding control back to the Japanese.

After clearing all of the antitrust and labor hurdles, Ford sold Land Rover and Jaguar to India-based Tata Motors for about $2.3 billion in 2008. (Ironically, one of the other firms bidding for the two car companies was One Equity Partners, an entity led by former Ford CEO Jacques Nasser. It was Nasser that oversaw the creation of Ford's Premier Automotive Group, which included both Jaguar and Land Rover.) Ford agreed to deposit some $600 million into the Jaguar and Land Rover pension funds.

The Ford family owns about 55% of the company's Class B stock.

HISTORY

Henry Ford started the Ford Motor Company in 1903 in Dearborn, Michigan. In 1908 Ford introduced the Model T, produced on a moving assembly line that revolutionized both carmaking and manufacturing. By 1920 some 60% of all vehicles on the road were Fords.

After Ford omitted its usual dividend in 1916, stockholders sued. Ford responded by buying back all of its outstanding shares in 1919 and didn't allow outside ownership again until 1956.

Ford bought Lincoln in 1922 and discontinued the Model T in 1927. Its replacement, the Model A, came in 1932. With Henry Ford's health failing, his son Edsel became president that year. Despite the debut of the Mercury (1938), market share slipped behind GM and Chrysler. After Edsel's death in 1943, his son, Henry II, took over and decentralized Ford, following the GM model. In 1950 the carmaker recaptured second place. Ford rolled out the infamous Edsel in 1958 and launched the Mustang in 1964.

Hurt by the oil crisis of the 1970s, Ford cut its workforce and closed plants during the 1980s. It also diversified into agricultural equipment by purchasing New Holland (1986) and Versatile (1987). Ford added luxury sports cars in 1987 by buying 75% of Aston Martin (it bought the rest in 1994). The 1988 introduction of the Taurus and Sable spurred Ford to its largest share of the US car market (21.7%) in 10 years. In 1989 it bought Associates First Capital (financial services) and Jaguar (luxury cars).

Ford acquired Hertz in 1994 and two years later bought #3 rental agency Budget Rent a Car (sold 1997). Also in 1996 it increased its stake in

Mazda to one-third. Ford began building a minibus line in China in 1997, beating GM in the race to produce vehicles for the Chinese market. Henry Ford's great-grandson, William Clay Ford Jr., became chairman in 1998. Company veteran Jacques Nasser became president and CEO in early 1999.

Ford bought Volvo's carmaking operations for $6.45 billion in 1999 and bought BMW's Land Rover SUV operations for about $2.7 billion in 2000. In 2001 Ford recalled some 300,000 cars, including 1995-96 Ford Contour and Mercury Mystique sedans, which posed possible fire danger linked to engine overheating problems.

Citing a study showing that the tires failed three times more frequently than the industry average, in May 2001 Ford announced that it would take a $2.1 billion charge to cover the replacement of up to 13 million Firestone Wilderness AT tires already on its vehicles.

In late 2001 Nasser resigned and was replaced as CEO by chairman Willam Clay Ford Jr. A week or so into 2002, Ford announced far-reaching cost-cutting measures, including 35,000 worldwide job cuts (22,000 in North America), and the closure of three North American assembly plants.

In 2005 Ford took full control of its operations in India with the purchase of a nearly 16% stake from its Indian partner, Mahindra & Mahindra Ltd. Also that year Ford sold its Hertz car rental business to a private equity group made up of Clayton Dubilier & Rice, The Carlyle Group, and Merrill Lynch Global Private Equity.

Former Boeing executive Alan Mulally was named president and CEO of Ford in September 2006. Bill Ford remained executive chairman.

In 2007 Ford sold Aston Martin to a group including British race-shop owner David Richards, Aston Martin racing backer John Sinders, and two Kuwaiti investment firms.

In 2007, Ford of Europe invested $88 million to acquire a Romanian car manufacturing plant owned by the government. Early in 2008, Ford took over the plant and invested around $1 billion in upgrades and expansions. Ford also invested some $3 billion in manufacturing facilities based in Mexico.

EXECUTIVES

Chairman: William C. (Bill) Ford Jr., age 52, $16,834,274 total compensation
President, CEO, and Director: Alan R. Mulally, age 64, $17,916,654 total compensation
EVP and CFO: Lewis W.K. Booth, age 61, $3,826,187 total compensation
EVP Global Manufacturing and Labor Affairs: John Fleming, age 59, $3,852,418 total compensation
EVP; President, The Americas: Mark Fields, age 49, $3,981,253 total compensation
EVP; Chairman and CEO, Ford Motor Credit Company: Michael E. (Mike) Bannister, age 60
Group VP Global Product Development: Derrick M. Kuzak, age 58
Group VP and General Counsel: David G. Leitch, age 49, $3,197,225 total compensation
Group VP; President, Asia/Pacific and Africa: Joseph R. (Joe) Hinrichs, age 43
Group VP Design and Chief Creative Officer: J. C. Mays, age 55
Group VP Quality: Bennie W. Fowler II, age 53
Group VP Purchasing: Thomas K. (Tony) Brown, age 53
Group VP Sustainability, Environment, and Safety Engineering: Susan M. (Sue) Cischke, age 55
Group VP and CIO: Nicholas J. (Nick) Smither, age 51
Group VP Human Resources and Corporate Services: Felicia J. Fields, age 44
Group VP Government and Community Relations: Ziad S. Ojakli, age 42

VP; Global Leader Marketing, Sales, and Service: James D. (Jim) Farley, age 48, $2,648,398 total compensation
VP Research and Advanced Engineering and CTO: Gerhard Schmidt, age 63
VP; Chairman and CEO, Ford Europe: Stephen T. Odell, age 55
Secretary: Peter J. Sherry Jr.
President, Ford Motor Company of Canada: David Mondragon, age 48
Chairman and CEO, Ford Motor China: Robert J. (Bob) Graziano, age 49
Director Global Corporate Communications: Mark Truby
Auditors: PricewaterhouseCoopers LLP

LOCATIONS

HQ: Ford Motor Company
1 American Rd., Dearborn, MI 48126
Phone: 313-322-3000   **Fax:** 313-845-6073
Web: www.ford.com

2009 Sales

	$ mil.	% of total
North America		
US	54,377	46
Canada	7,974	7
Mexico & other	1,336	1
Europe		
UK	8,448	7
Germany	7,843	7
Italy	4,529	4
France	3,102	3
Spain	2,174	2
Russia	1,573	1
Belgium	1,460	1
Other countries	8,976	7
Other regions	16,516	14
Total	**118,308**	**100**

PRODUCTS/OPERATIONS

2009 Sales

	$ mil.	% of total
Automotive		
Ford North America	50,514	43
Ford Europe	29,454	25
Volvo	12,447	10
Ford South America	7,947	7
Ford Asia/Pacific & Africa	5,531	5
Ford Credit & other financial services	12,415	10
Total	**118,308**	**100**

2009 US Sales by Vehicle Type

	% of total
Cars	
Small	24
Medium	16
Premium	7
Large	5
Trucks	
Crossover & sport utility vehicles	27
Full-size pickup	11
Bus/van	6
Compact pickup	3
Medium/heavy	1
Total	**100**

Selected Auto Brands

Ford
Lincoln
Mercury

HISTORICAL FINANCIALS

Company Type: Public

Income Statement				FYE: December 31
	REVENUE ($ mil.)	NET INCOME ($ mil.)	NET PROFIT MARGIN	EMPLOYEES
12/09	118,308	2,962	2.5%	198,000
12/08	146,277	(14,672)	—	213,000
12/07	172,455	(2,723)	—	246,000
12/06	160,123	(12,613)	—	283,000
12/05	177,089	2,275	1.3%	300,000
Annual Growth	(9.6%)	6.8%	—	(9.9%)

2009 Year-End Financials

Debt ratio: —
Return on equity: —
Cash ($ mil.): 21,441
Current ratio: 2.45
Long-term debt ($ mil.): 132,441

No. of shares (mil.): 3,439
Dividends
  Yield: 0.0%
  Payout: —
Market value ($ mil.): 34,393

Stock History

NYSE: F

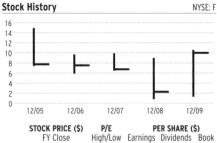

	STOCK PRICE ($) FY Close	P/E High/Low		PER SHARE ($) Earnings	Dividends	Book Value
12/09	10.00	12	2	0.86	0.00	(2.27)
12/08	2.29	—	—	(6.46)	0.00	(5.03)
12/07	6.73	—	—	(1.38)	0.00	1.64
12/06	7.51	—	—	(6.72)	0.25	(1.01)
12/05	7.72	14	7	1.05	0.40	3.77
Annual Growth	6.7%	—	—	(4.9%)	—	—

Forest Laboratories

Forest Laboratories doesn't just blend in with the trees. The company develops and manufactures name-brand as well as generic prescription and over-the-counter pharmaceutical products. The company's central nervous system (CNS) pharmaceutical line includes antidepressants Celexa and Lexapro, as well as Namenda, which treats Alzheimer's disease. Other products include treatments for hypertension, thyroid disease, respiratory ailments, and pain. Forest Laboratories markets directly to doctors, hospitals, drugstore chains, managed care organizations, and distributors through its own sales force in the US; it also has affiliated and independent sales representatives in the UK and Ireland.

Subsidiary Inwood Laboratories promotes the company's generic products in the US, while over-the-counter products are sold through UK and Irish subsidiaries. Nearly 90% of the company's sales revenues come from large pharmaceutical distributors McKesson, Cardinal Health, and AmerisourceBergen, which deliver Forest's products to customers on a wholesale basis in the US and abroad.

Despite fierce competition from other established brands, Forest Laboratories has found a niche in the antidepressant market. With Celexa's recent conversion to generic status, however, the company has become more dependent on sales of Lexapro, which accounts for around 60% of the company's revenues. In 2009 Lexapro received FDA approval for use to treat depression in adolescents, neatly extending the brand's potential profitability. Namenda is another top seller in the CNS field, accounting for about 30% of Forest's sales.

The firm is working to develop and release new drug candidates that it hopes will make up for any decline in sales seen from generic competition. Recent releases include Bystolic for hypertension treatment in 2008 and Savella for fibromyalgia in 2009. Its pipeline includes potential drugs to treat neuropathic pain, gastrointestinal disorders, asthma, and schizophrenia; many of the company's development programs are collaborative efforts with other pharmaceutical companies including Geodon Richter and AstraZeneca. In 2009 the company expanded its pipeline by partnering with Nycomed on a candidate for chronic obstructive pulmonary disease (COPD).

To bolster its biopharmaceutical research capabilities, Forest Laboratories purchased private biotech firm Cerexa for about $494 million in early 2007. Cerexa brought with it a series of injectable antibiotics under development to combat bacterial infections including MRSA (methicillin-resistant *Staphylococcus aureus*).

The company ended a co-promotion agreement with Daiichi Sankyo in 2008 for the hypertension drug Axor to focus on sales efforts for its other commercial products. The two companies have historically marketed antihypertensive drug Benicar together; Forest continues to receive royalties from the agreement but has stopped actively marketing the drug.

HISTORY

Forest Laboratories began as a drug research and development firm in 1956. The company diversified into the food business, but when company attorney Howard Solomon took charge in 1977, he sold the food holdings and moved from drug development to drug commercialization. It acquired drugs from other companies and improved them through its proprietary Synchron continuous-release drug-delivery technology.

In 1984 Forest bought scandal-ridden drug company O'Neal, Jones, & Feldman to grow its sales force. The next year it bought headache formula ESGIC (later pulled because it qualified as a new drug needing FDA approval). In 1986 it acquired Aerobid from Schering-Plough.

The company continued to grow through acquisitions, buying UAD Laboratories and its analgesic Lorcet in 1989, Pharmasciences' labor-induction agent Cervidil, and other drugs. Although the firm had mostly successes, one of its failures was Micturin, an incontinence treatment whose dangerous side effects led the company to discontinue it in 1991.

In 1998 the FDA approved antidepressant citalopram (Celexa). Celexa was to be marketed by Warner-Lambert, but when that firm was acquired by Pfizer (which makes rival antidepressant Prozac), Forest Labs bought its way out of the deal and grew its own sales force. Celexa proved worthy of such effort, becoming Forest Labs' biggest seller. The following year the company entered into an alliance with 3M's pharmaceutical unit to make asthma treatment Aerospan. In 2000 the company expanded its research facilities and licensed drugs to treat hypertension, dementia, and irritable bowel syndrome.

In 2002 the company launched hypertension drug Benicar through an alliance with Sankyo and failed to win FDA approval for alcohol dependence treatment acamprosate (licensed from Merck KGaA).

The company received FDA approval and launched pain treatment Combunox in 2004. Campral (acamprosate) for alcohol abstinence was finally approved in 2005.

EXECUTIVES

Chairman and CEO: Howard Solomon, age 82, $8,267,236 total compensation
President, COO, and Director: Lawrence S. Olanoff, age 58, $5,388,183 total compensation
EVP Global Marketing: Raymond Stafford
SVP Marketing and Chief Commercial Officer: Elaine Hochberg, age 53, $3,599,287 total compensation
SVP Finance and CFO: Francis I. Perier Jr., age 50, $3,011,375 total compensation
VP Research and Development: Marco Taglietti, age 50, $2,532,535 total compensation
VP, General Counsel, and Secretary: Herschel S. Weinstein
VP Investor Relations: Frank J. Murdolo
VP and Controller: Rita Weinberger
VP Marketing: William J. Meury
VP Information Systems and Manufacturing Operations: Kevin Walsh
VP Business Development and Strategic Planning: David F. Solomon
VP Corporate Tax and Treasury: Ralph Kleinman
VP Human Resources: Bernard J. McGovern
President, Cerexa: Dirk A. Thye
President, Forest Pharmaceuticals: Terrill J. Howell
Auditors: BDO Seidman, LLP

LOCATIONS

HQ: Forest Laboratories, Inc.
909 3rd Ave., New York, NY 10022
Phone: 212-421-7850   **Fax:** 212-750-9152
Web: www.frx.com

2010 Product Sales

	% of total
US	98
UK & Ireland	2
Total	**100**

PRODUCTS/OPERATIONS

2010 Sales

	$ mil.	% of total
Products		
Central nervous system	3,455.7	82
Cardiovascular	218.4	5
Other drugs	229.4	6
Contract revenue	208.5	5
Interest income	35.5	1
Other income	45.4	1
Total	**4,192.9**	**100**

Selected Products

Central Nervous System
  Campral (alcohol dependence)
  Celexa (antidepressant)
  Lexapro (antidepressant)
  Namenda (Alzheimer's disease)
  Savella (fibromyalgia)
Cardiovascular
  Benicar (antihypertensive)
  Bystolic (antihypertensive)
  Tiazac (antihypertensive)
Other drugs
  Aerobid (asthma)
  Armour Thyroid (endocrinology)
  Cervidil (labor induction)
  Citalopram (antidepressant)
  Combunox (pain)
  Infasurf (respiratory)
  Levothroid (endocrinology)
  Lorcet (pain)
  Thyrolar (endocrinology)

Selected Subsidiaries

Cerexa, Inc.
Cerexa UK Ltd.
Forest Laboratories Ireland Ltd.
Forest Laboratories UK Ltd.
Forest Pharmaceuticals, Inc.
Forest Tosara Ltd. (Ireland)
Inwood Laboratories, Inc. (generics)
Pharmax Healthcare Ltd. (UK)

COMPETITORS

AstraZeneca
Biovail
Bristol-Myers Squibb
Daiichi Sankyo
Eisai Inc.
Eli Lilly
GlaxoSmithKline
Hi-Tech Pharmacal
Johnson & Johnson
King Pharmaceuticals
Merck
Mylan Pharmaceuticals
Novartis
Par Pharmaceutical Companies
Pfizer
Ranbaxy Laboratories
Sepracor
Sun Pharmaceutical
Teva Pharmaceuticals
Watson Pharmaceuticals

HISTORICAL FINANCIALS

Company Type: Public

Income Statement

FYE: March 31

	REVENUE ($ mil.)	NET INCOME ($ mil.)	NET PROFIT MARGIN	EMPLOYEES
3/10	4,193	682	16.3%	5,200
3/09	3,923	768	19.6%	5,225
3/08	3,836	968	25.2%	5,211
3/07	3,442	454	13.2%	5,126
3/06	2,912	709	24.3%	5,050
Annual Growth	**9.5%**	**(0.9%)**	**—**	**0.7%**

2010 Year-End Financials

Debt ratio: —
Return on equity: 15.2%
Cash ($ mil.): 1,863
Current ratio: 4.67
Long-term debt ($ mil.): —
No. of shares (mil.): 286
Dividends
  Yield: —
  Payout: —
Market value ($ mil.): 8,955

Stock History

NYSE: FRX

	STOCK PRICE ($) FY Close	P/E High/Low		PER SHARE ($) Earnings	Dividends	Book Value
3/10	31.36	15	9	2.25	—	17.12
3/09	21.96	16	7	2.52	—	14.41
3/08	40.01	19	11	3.06	—	13.01
3/07	51.44	41	26	1.41	—	10.59
3/06	44.63	23	16	2.08	—	9.45
Annual Growth	**(8.4%)**	**—**	**—**	**2.0%**	**—**	**16.0%**

Fortune Brands

Execs at Fortune Brands have good reason to meet over a game of golf and a glass of bourbon. The holding company is a leading US producer and distributor of distilled spirits such as Jim Beam, Sauza, DeKuyper, Canadian Club, and Maker's Mark. Its golf equipment company, Acushnet, manufactures and markets brands such as Titleist, FootJoy, and Pinnacle. However, Fortune's largest segment is home products and hardware, where its holdings include Moen faucets, MasterBrand Cabinets, Master Lock padlocks, and Therma-Tru doors. All of Fortune Brands' products are sold primarily in Europe, Australia, and throughout North America.

Fortune Brands' home and hardware division suffered from the downturn in the US home products market. In order to weather the downturn, Fortune has reduced its number of manufacturing facilities by a third and cut jobs at all levels.

For the past few years, Fortune has been retooling its spirits division. The company shifted its focus to liquor in 2007 and sold its US wine holdings to Constellation Brands for nearly $900 million. Divested brands included Clos du Bois, Geyser Peak, and Wild Horse.

The following year, Fortune became embroiled in a lawsuit over the 10% stake in Beam Global Spirits & Wine that it didn't already own. Sweden's V&S Group owned the stake and wanted to transfer it to the Swedish government as part of its 2008 sale to Pernod Ricard. However, Fortune wanted to buy the stake back. After some legal wrangling and negotiating, Fortune repurchased the minority stake for some $455 million.

Also that year, Fortune acquired Cruzan, one of the fastest-growing brands of rum in the US, from Pernod Ricard. Fortune Brands continued to stock the bar when it bought the Holland-based vodka brand EFFEN from Sazerac in 2009. As part of the deal, Fortune sold its Old Taylor whiskey brand to Sazerac.

In 2010 Fortune Brand sold its Cobra golf brand to Puma. The sale will allow Fortune to focus on its Titleist and FootJoy brands, which represent its most popular and successful segments in the golf business.

HISTORY

Fortune Brands began in 1864 as W. Duke and Sons, a small tobacco company started by North Carolina farmer Washington Duke. James Buchanan Duke joined his father's business at age 14, and by age 25 was its president. James advertised to expanding markets, bought rival tobacco firms, and by 1904 controlled the industry. That year he merged all the competitive groups as American Tobacco Company. In a 1911 antitrust suit, the US Supreme Court dissolved American Tobacco into its original constituents, ordering them to operate independently.

James left American Tobacco the next year. He established a $100 million trust fund composed mainly of holdings in his power company, Duke Power and Light (now Duke Energy Corporation), for Trinity College. The school became Duke University in 1924.

George Washington Hill became president of American Tobacco in 1925. For the next 19 years until his death, George proved himself a consummate adman, pushing Lucky Strike, Pall Mall, and Tareyton cigarettes to top sales.

Smokers began switching to filter-tipped cigarettes in the 1950s because of health concerns. American Tobacco, however, ignored the trend and continued to rely on its popular filterless brands until the mid-1960s. In 1962 the firm sold J. Wix and Sons (Kensitas cigarettes) to UK tobacco firm Gallaher Group for a stake in Gallaher.

The company remained solely in the tobacco business until 1966, when it purchased Sunshine Biscuits (sold 1988) and Jim Beam Distillery. Reflecting its increasing diversity, the firm became American Brands in 1969. The next year it added Swingline (office supplies) and Master Lock. Meanwhile, American Brands increased its stake in Gallaher, controlling 100% by 1975. In 1976 the company bought Acushnet (Titleist and Bulls Eye); it added FootJoy in 1986.

Threatened with a takeover by E-II Holdings (a conglomerate of brands split from Beatrice), American Brands bought E-II in 1988. It kept five of E-II's companies — Day-Timers, Aristokraft (cabinets), Waterloo (tool boxes), Twentieth Century (plumbing supplies), and Vogel Peterson (office partitions; sold 1995) — and sold the rest (Culligan, Samsonite) to Riklis Family Corporation. Acquisitions in 1990 included Moen (faucets) and Whyte & Mackay (distillers). The company bought seven liquor brands in 1991 from Seagram.

American Brands sold its American Tobacco subsidiary, including the Pall Mall and Lucky

Strike brands, to onetime subsidiary B.A.T Industries in 1994. The firm acquired publicly held Cobra Golf in 1996.

The following year American Brands changed its name to Fortune Brands and completed the spinoff of its Gallaher tobacco subsidiary. In 1998 Fortune bought kitchen and bathroom cabinetmaker Schrock from Electrolux, doubling its sales in that category.

Seeking to trim costs, Fortune relocated its headquarters to Lincolnshire, Illinois, in 1999 (the company moved again in 2006, this time to Deerfield, Illinois). Also in 1999 Norman Wesley was named chairman and CEO. That year Fortune formed Maxxium Worldwide (a non-US wine/spirits sales and distribution joint venture) with Rémy Cointreau and Highland Distillers, and it bought Boone International (presentation products) and NHB Group, a manufacturer of ready-to-assemble kitchen and bath cabinetry.

Fortune bought The Omega Group, a manufacturer of kitchen and bath cabinetry, for $538 million in 2002.

About 20,000 barrels of Fortune's Jim Beam bourbon went up in smoke during a warehouse fire in the summer of 2003. The Bardstown, Kentucky, facility was believed to be the victim of a lightning strike from a passing thunderstorm. Also that year the company expanded its home and hardware division by acquiring privately held doormaker Therma-Tru.

Fortune Brands merged its holdings in General Binding Corporation and office products company ACCO World (Day-Timers, Swingline, Apollo, Kensington) in 2005. It spun off the resulting firm, ACCO Brands Corporation, in order to focus on its Home and Hardware, Spirits, and Golf segments.

That year Fortune spent about $5 billion to acquire more than 20 wine and liquor brands formerly owned by Allied Domecq. First, Pernod Ricard acquired Allied Domecq with Fortune's monetary help; Pernod Ricard then began transferring a group of assets — including Sauza tequila, Canadian Club whiskey, Courvoisier Cognac, Laphroaig single-malt Scotch, and Clos du Bois wines — to Fortune.

Fortune sold its US wine holdings in 2007. Wesley retired in 2008, and was replaced by Bruce Carbonari.

EXECUTIVES

Chairman and CEO: Bruce A. Carbonari, age 54, $10,735,904 total compensation
SVP Strategy and Corporate Development: Patrick J. Koley, age 45, $1,922,120 total compensation
SVP Finance and Treasurer: Mark Hausberg, age 60, $1,618,811 total compensation
SVP, General Counsel, and Secretary: Mark A. Roche, age 55, $3,226,753 total compensation
SVP and CFO: Craig P. Omtvedt, age 59, $4,658,423 total compensation
VP and Chief Internal Auditor: Gary L. Tobison
VP Human Resources: Elizabeth R. Lane
VP Taxes: Charles J. Ryan
VP Public Affairs: Matt Stanton
VP Corporate Communications and Public Affairs: C. Clarkson Hine
VP Investor Relations: Anthony J. (Tony) Diaz
VP and Corporate Controller: Edward A. Wiertel, age 40
VP Business Development: Allan J. Snape
President and CEO, Fortune Brands Home & Security: Christopher J. (Chris) Klein, age 46, $1,252,659 total compensation
SVP Operations and Supply Chain, Beam Global Spirits & Wine: Ian Gourlay
Auditors: PricewaterhouseCoopers LLP

LOCATIONS

HQ: Fortune Brands, Inc.
520 Lake Cook Rd., Deerfield, IL 60015
Phone: 847-484-4400   **Fax:** 847-478-0073
Web: www.fortunebrands.com

2009 Sales

	$ mil.	% of total
US	4,601.4	69
Canada	483.7	7
Australia	276.8	4
UK	239.2	3
Spain	178.9	3
Other countries	914.7	14
Total	**6,694.7**	**100**

PRODUCTS/OPERATIONS

2009 Sales

	$ mil.	% of total
Home & hardware	3,006.8	45
Spirits	2,469.6	37
Golf	1,218.3	18
Total	**6,694.7**	**100**

Selected Brands

Home and Hardware
  Aristokraft (cabinets)
  Master Lock (padlocks)
  MasterBrand (cabinets)
  Moen (faucets)
  Omega (cabinets)
  Schrock (cabinets)
  Waterloo (toolboxes)
Spirits
  Blended Whisky/Whiskey
    Alberta Premium   Lord Calvert
    Calvert Extra   Old Overholt
    Canadian Club   Tangle Ridge
    Furst Bismarck   Teacher's
    Jim Beam Rye   Whisky DYC
    Kessler   Windsor
  Bourbon
    Baker's   Knob Creek
    Basil Hayden's   Maker's Mark
    Booker's   Old Grand-Dad
    Jim Beam   Old Crow
    Jim Beam Black
  Brandy, Port, and Sherry
    Fundador
    Terry Centenario
    Tres Cepas
  Cognac
    Courvoisier
    Salignac
  Cordials and Liqueurs
    After Shock   Kuemmerling
    Castellana   Leroux
    DeKuyper   Sourz
    Kamora
  Gin
    Calvert
    Gilbey's
    Larios
  Pre-Mixed Cocktails
    Beam & Cola
    Beam Black & Cola
    Jim Beam Choice & Dry
  Rum
    Cruzan
    Ronrico
  Single Malt Scotch
    Ardmore
    Laphroaig
  Tequila
    El Tesoro   Sauza Blanco
    Hornitos   Sauza Gold
  Vodka
    EFFEN
    Gilbey's
    Kamchatka
    VOXWolfschmidt

Golf
  FootJoy (shoes and gloves)
  Pinnacle (balls)
  Scotty Cameron (putters)
  Titleist (balls, clubs, bags, and accessories)

COMPETITORS

American Woodmark
Armstrong World Industries
Atrium Companies
Bacardi USA
Bridgestone Sports
Brown-Forman
Brunswick Corp.
Callaway Golf
Cleveland Golf
Constellation Brands
Diageo
Grohe
Hampton Affiliates
JELD-WEN
Kohler
Kwikset Corporation
Masco
Masonite
Milgard Manufacturing
Newell Rubbermaid
NIKE
Pernod Ricard
Reebok
Rémy Cointreau
Skyy
Snap-on
Stanley Black and Decker
TaylorMade-adidas Golf
Trane Inc.
V&S
Waxman

HISTORICAL FINANCIALS

Company Type: Public

Income Statement

FYE: December 31

	REVENUE ($ mil.)	NET INCOME ($ mil.)	NET PROFIT MARGIN	EMPLOYEES
12/09	6,695	243	3.6%	24,248
12/08	7,609	311	4.1%	27,100
12/07	8,052	763	9.5%	31,027
12/06	8,255	830	10.1%	36,251
12/05	6,735	621	9.2%	30,298
Annual Growth	(0.1%)	(20.9%)	—	(5.4%)

2009 Year-End Financials

Debt ratio: 86.8%
Return on equity: 5.0%
Cash ($ mil.): 417
Current ratio: 2.65
Long-term debt ($ mil.): 4,413
No. of shares (mil.): 152
Dividends
  Yield: 2.3%
  Payout: 63.1%
Market value ($ mil.): 6,582

Stock History

NYSE: FO

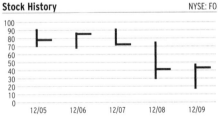

	STOCK PRICE ($) FY Close	P/E High/Low		PER SHARE ($) Earnings	Dividends	Book Value
12/09	43.20	29	11	1.60	1.01	33.42
12/08	41.28	37	15	2.02	1.72	30.76
12/07	72.36	19	15	4.87	1.62	37.32
12/06	85.39	16	13	5.42	1.50	31.03
12/05	78.02	22	17	4.13	1.38	23.93
Annual Growth	(13.7%)	—	—	(21.1%)	(7.5%)	8.7%

Fossil, Inc.

Fossil digs the watch business while unearthing a place in the accessories and apparel niches. A leading mid-priced watchmaker in the US, it generates most of its sales from watches. Brands include its Fossil and Relic watches, as well as licensed names Armani, Michael Kors, adidas, Burberry, and Marc Jacobs, and private-label watches for Target and Wal-Mart. Fossil also distributes fashion accessories, such as leather goods, sunglasses, and apparel. The firm sells through department stores and specialty shops in more than 100 countries and in the US through some 200 company-owned stores, as well as through its own catalog and website. Its products are also sold in gift shops on cruise ships and in airports.

Like rivals Swatch and Guess?, Fossil has typically targeted those in their teens, 20s, and 30s, i.e., those hip to the latest trends. But Fossil's target audience has become broader to include those who will drop some big green for some bling. Fossil entered the luxury products niche when it acquired Tempus International, which does business as Michele Watches, for about $50 million. The subsidiary launched Michele Jewelry, a collection of 18-karat gold pieces that are sold at Neiman Marcus stores nationwide. More recently, Fossil launched a vintage-inspired summer clothing collection — called Vintage Expedition — in stores in Germany and the UK. The 2010 launch was the first time Fossil made a full collection of its apparel available outside the US.

Fossil has been expanding its store base in recent years. Of its more than 300 company-owned stores worldwide, most operate under the Fossil banner. In 2010 the company plans to open up to 50 additional Fossil-branded stores worldwide (after opening about that number in the previous year). Fossil is focusing its efforts outside the US to peddle its full-price accessories. Building on the Fossil brand name, the company also markets wallets, handbags, and belts. The company's wholesale business represented about three-quarters of its 2009 revenue, while its direct-to-consumer segment generated the rest.

Fossil has inked several deals that have given the company traction for long-term growth. Fossil has a licensing agreement with Diesel through 2010 and holds the exclusive rights to manufacture, market, and distribute a Diesel jewelry collection. In a move that has placed Fossil at a noteworthy advantage is its deal with retailing behemoth Wal-Mart to design, make, and distribute watches for the retailer's private-label brand George. The company's mass market watch business increased about 40% soon thereafter, more or less attributable to this partnership. Sales of Burberry licensed products and the launch of both Marc by Marc Jacobs and adidas items have helped to boost Fossil's licensing revenue as well.

As a result, Fossil is watching the clock on its licensing agreements. Its DKNY watch license was slated to expire at the end of 2009, but was extended while the parties negotiate a new long-term contract. Its agreements with Diesel and Marc Jacobs wind down at the end of 2010. The Kartsotis brothers, former chairman Tom and CEO Kosta, own about 20% of the company.

HISTORY

Tom Kartsotis founded a Dallas area import-export company, originally called Overseas Products International, in 1984. He was only 24, and Swatch was the hot watch brand. His brother, Kosta Kartsotis, a department store executive, had told him about high profits from Asian imports. With Lynne Stafford (whom Tom later married) as designer, the company gave its Asian-made Fossil watches a retro image, and sales took off. In 1988 Kosta joined the firm to woo department stores.

Between 1987 and 1989 sales rose from $2 million to $20 million. In 1990 a less-expensive line of watches, Relic, was created for stores such as JCPenney and Sears. Tom renamed the company Fossil in 1992 and took it public in 1993. Its product line then included women's accessories (such as belts) and small leather goods for men. Two years later Fossil introduced sunglasses.

The company opened its first US retail outlets in 1996. The next year Fossil signed licensing agreements with Giorgio Armani for the Emporio Armani Orologi watch line and with London Fog to make Fossil outerwear. Through a joint venture with Netherlands-based Capstan Bay, the firm opened its first European store in 1998 in Amsterdam.

In 1999 Fossil entered a joint venture with the American subsidiary of Japanese watchmaker Seiko to produce and market Lorus and Disney character watches. The following year Fossil launched its own Fossil-brand jeans and apparel line to be sold at its approximately 12 new Fossil apparel stores. Fossil acquired UK-based The Avia Watch Company, maker of Avia-brand watches, in mid-2001 to grow its business in the UK, as well as 80% of its Australian distributor FSLA. In November 2001 the company acquired three Swiss watchmakers, Montres Antima SA, Meliga Habillement Horloger SA, and Synergies Horlogères SA. The next year Fossil acquired No-Time (its Swiss distributor) and X-Time (a retailer with three stores in Switzerland).

In 2003 Fossil gave nerds a watch to celebrate. The company developed the Wrist PDA, a line of watches that incorporates a Palm personal digital assistant that synchronizes with a Windows-based PC. The year 2004 brought a refined version of the Wrist PDA: In a joint effort with Citizen Watch, the companies began production of wrist watches capable of receiving news, weather, and other information, through a subscription-based service provided by Microsoft.

Founder Tom Kartsotis retired as chairman of Fossil in April 2010. He had served as chairman since 1991.

EXECUTIVES

Chairman and CEO: Kosta N. Kartsotis, age 56, $4,266 total compensation
Vice Chairman: Mark D. Quick, age 61, $971,001 total compensation
President and COO: Michael W. Barnes, age 49, $1,431,046 total compensation
EVP: Livio Galanti, age 42
EVP, CFO, and Treasurer: Mike L. Kovar, age 48, $400,549 total compensation
President, Retail Division: Jennifer Pritchard, age 51, $706,579 total compensation
Auditors: Deloitte & Touche LLP

LOCATIONS

HQ: Fossil, Inc.
2280 N. Greenville Ave., Richardson, TX 75082
Phone: 972-234-2525   **Fax:** 972-234-4669
Web: www.fossil.com

2009 Sales

	$ mil.	% of total
US wholesale	471.1	30
Europe wholesale	460.3	30
Direct to consumer	376.1	24
Other international wholesale	240.6	16
Total	**1,548.1**	**100**

PRODUCTS/OPERATIONS

2009 Sales

	$ mil.	% of total
Wholesale	1,172.0	76
Direct to consumer	376.1	24
Total	**1,548.1**	**100**

Selected Proprietary and Licensed Products

Watch brands
  adidas
  Burberry
  Diesel
  DKNY
  Emporio Armani
  Fossil
  Michele
  Relic
  Zodiac
Fashion accessories
  Apparel
  Jewelry
  Leather goods
  Sunglasses

COMPETITORS

Abercrombie & Fitch	Liz Claiborne
American Eagle Outfitters	LVMH
Armitron	Movado Group
Calvin Klein	Nine West
CASIO COMPUTER	Oakley
Citizen	Seiko
Coach, Inc.	Swank
Donna Karan	Swatch
Dooney & Bourke	TAG Heuer
The Gap	Tandy Brands
Gucci	Tandy Leather
Guess?	Timex
Jones Apparel	Tommy Hilfiger
Kenneth Cole	Victorinox Swiss Army

HISTORICAL FINANCIALS

Company Type: Public

Income Statement

FYE: December 31

	REVENUE ($ mil.)	NET INCOME ($ mil.)	NET PROFIT MARGIN	EMPLOYEES
12/09	1,548	139	9.0%	7,900
12/08	1,583	138	8.7%	7,355
12/07	1,433	123	8.6%	6,000
12/06	1,214	78	6.4%	7,400
12/05	1,041	78	7.5%	7,160
Annual Growth	**10.4%**	**15.5%**	**—**	**2.5%**

2009 Year-End Financials

Debt ratio: 0.5%	No. of shares (mil.): 67
Return on equity: 15.8%	Dividends
Cash ($ mil.): 405	Yield: —
Current ratio: 3.86	Payout: —
Long-term debt ($ mil.): 5	Market value ($ mil.): 2,253

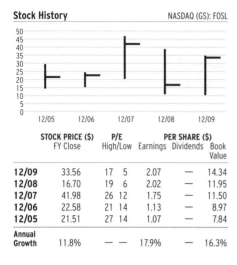

	STOCK PRICE ($)	P/E		PER SHARE ($)		
	FY Close	High/Low		Earnings	Dividends	Book Value
12/09	33.56	17	5	2.07	—	14.34
12/08	16.70	19	6	2.02	—	11.95
12/07	41.98	26	12	1.75	—	11.50
12/06	22.58	21	14	1.13	—	8.97
12/05	21.51	27	14	1.07	—	7.84
Annual Growth	11.8%	—	—	17.9%	—	16.3%

Fox Entertainment

This Fox has cunning ways to keep TV and movie fans entertained. Fox Entertainment Group (FEG) oversees a broad collection of film and TV entertainment assets owned by media giant News Corporation. Its Fox Filmed Entertainment (FFE) division is a leading producer of movies for theatrical and home entertainment release through such studios as Fox 2000, Fox Searchlight, and its flagship Twentieth Century Fox imprint. FEG also oversees the FOX television network, the upstart MyNetworkTV, and more than 25 company-owned TV broadcasting stations. In addition, it runs a portfolio of cable channels, including FOX News, FX, and the regional sports networks of Fox Sports Net.

FEG's film and TV units play an important role in the success of News Corporation as a whole. Financially, the entertainment group accounts for more than 50% of its parent's revenue, but more importantly the production and distribution of content is central to News Corporation's strategy as an integrated media conglomerate. By redistributing content through multiple channels, even a modest film or television program can provide a significant stream of revenue for the company.

FFE has been producing a string of winners at the box office, and none more successful than the science fiction epic *Avatar*. Released in late 2009, the film from *Titanic* director James Cameron broke all records as the top grossing picture of all time. The 3-D blockbuster followed on a successful summer season that included such hits as *X-Men Origins: Wolverine* and the animated *Ice Age: Dawn of the Dinosaurs*. Fox Filmed Entertainment continues to struggle with slow DVD sales, however.

Cable television has become a lucrative area of business for FEG, especially the company's popular FOX News channel. Garnering higher ratings than either CNN (owned by Time Warner)

or MSNBC (NBC Universal), the network has become one of the most watched ad-supported channels on television thanks largely to its primetime talks shows anchored by Bill O'Reilly and Sean Hannity. Its FX network, meanwhile, has won critical acclaim and higher ratings thanks to such original programming as *Damages, Nip/Tuck*, and *Rescue Me*.

The FOX television network continues to lead all broadcasters in attracting viewers in the all-important 18-49 demographic thanks to a schedule of popular shows led by *American Idol, House*, and the high school comedy *Glee*. Despite high ratings, the network struggles to generate revenue due largely to the economic downturn which has depressed spending by advertisers.

MyNetworkTV, Fox's smaller broadcast network, has struggled to find an audience. Originally launched with a schedule heavy on campy, telenovela-style shows, the network announced plans to remake itself as a programming service that relies mostly on syndicated programming and second-run movies.

The filmed entertainment and television operations of FEG were reorganized early in 2009 following the resignation of Peter Chernin, who served as president and COO of News Corporation and head of FEG. Chase Carey, previously CEO of DIRECTV, was named as Chernin's replacement. A longtime Murdoch lieutenant, Carey had served as co-COO with Chernin before taking over the direct satellite service in 2003.

HISTORY

Fox Entertainment Group traces its roots to Hungarian-born immigrant William Fox (originally Wilhelm Fried) who purchased a New York City nickelodeon for $1,600 in 1904. He transformed the failing operation into a success and soon owned (with two partners) 25 theaters across the city. The partners opened a film exchange, The Greater New York Rental Company, and in 1913 began making movies through the Box Office Attraction Company.

Fox became the first to combine film production, leasing, and exhibition when he founded the Fox Film Corporation in 1915. Soon after, he moved the studio to California. One of the first to recognize the value of individual actors, Fox is credited with developing Hollywood's "star system." Fox Film continued to grow through the 1920s, but the company began experiencing trouble in 1927 and by 1930 William Fox was forced out.

In 1935 the company was merged with Twentieth Century Pictures, a studio started two years earlier by Darryl Zanuck, former head of production at Warner Brothers. Under Zanuck's leadership, the studio flourished in the 1930s and 1940s, producing such films as *The Grapes of Wrath* and *All About Eve*. By the early 1950s, however, TV was dulling some of Hollywood's shine. Zanuck left the studio in 1956, only to return in 1962 to help it recover from the disastrously over-budget *Cleopatra*.

The 1960s brought both good (*The Sound of Music*) and bad (*Tora! Tora! Tora!*). By 1971 infighting between Darryl Zanuck and his son Richard, who had been president of the studio, resulted in the resignation of both men. The studio prospered during the 1970s, culminating in

1977 with the release of *Star Wars*, the biggest box office hit in history at that time.

Oilman Marvin Davis bought Twentieth Century Fox for $722 million in 1981. In 1985 the studio changed hands again when it was purchased by Rupert Murdoch. The next year Murdoch bought six TV stations from Metromedia and launched the FOX Broadcasting Company.

Murdoch became CEO in 1995. In 1996 and 1997, respectively, Murdoch created the Fox News Channel and purchased Pat Robertson's International Family Entertainment. The company also joined Liberty Media in 1996 to create a rival to Walt Disney's ESPN sports network.

Fox Entertainment Group went public in 1998, raising $2.8 billion — one of the largest offerings in American history. In 1999 News Corp. bought the 50% of the Fox/Liberty Networks business that it didn't already own from Liberty Media and transferred ownership to Fox (renamed FOX Sports Net). The deal gave Liberty Media an 8% stake in News Corp.

In 2001 Fox and partner Saban sold the Fox Family Channel, which they jointly owned, to Walt Disney for about $5.2 billion. It also gained an additional 10 TV stations, when parent News Corp. bought Chris-Craft. In 2003 News Corp. bought 34% of DIRECTV owner Hughes Electronics from General Motors.

In the early part of 2005, News Corp. purchased the rest of Fox Entertainment that it didn't already own for about $6.2 billion. At that time Murdoch passed Fox's top post to president Peter Chernin.

In 2008 News Corp. swapped its 40% stake in DIRECTV, along with three regional sports networks and $625 million in cash, for Liberty Media's 19% stake in News Corp.

EXECUTIVES

Deputy Chairman, President, and COO, News Corporation: Chase Carey, age 56
General Manager and COO: Beth-Ann Eason
SEVP and CFO: David F. DeVoe, age 63
EVP Strategic Planning: Preston Beckman
EVP Human Resources: Linda Johns
SVP Diversity Development: Mitsy Wilson
Chairman and CEO, Fox Networks: Anthony J. (Tony) Vinciquerra, age 55
Chairman and CEO, Fox Filmed Entertainment: Thomas E. (Tom) Rothman
Chairman and CEO, FOX Sports: David Hill
Chairman, Entertainment, Fox Broadcasting: Peter Rice
CEO, Fox Television Stations Group: Jack Abernethy
President, Twentieth Century Fox Animation: Vanessa Morrison
President, Fox Baseball Holdings: Frank McCourt Jr.
President, Twentieth Television: Rick Jacobson
President, FOX Sports: Eric Shanks, age 38
President and Editor Chief, Beliefnet.com: Steve Waldman
President, 20th Century Fox Films: Jim Gianopoulos
President, FOX News Channel: Roger Ailes, age 70
President, MyNetworkTV: Greg Meidel
President, Fox National Cable Networks: Richard (Rich) Battista, age 45
President, Engineering: Andrew G. (Andy) Setos
President, Fox Sports Net: Randy Freer
President, Sales, Fox Broadcasting: Jon Nesvig
Auditors: Ernst & Young LLP

LOCATIONS

HQ: Fox Entertainment Group, Inc.
   10201 W. Pico Blvd., Bldg. 100, Ste. 3220
   Los Angeles, CA 90035
Phone: 310-369-1000   **Fax:** 310-969-3300
Web: www.fox.com

PRODUCTS/OPERATIONS

Selected Operations

Cable network programming
  Big Ten Network (49%)
  Fox Business Network
  Fox College Sports
  Fox International Channels
    LAPTV (55%, Latin American pay television)
  Fox Movie Channel
  FOX News Channel
  Fox Pan American Sports (33%)
    Fox Sports en Español
    Fox Sports Latin America
  Fox Soccer Channel
  Fox Sports Net
  FUEL TV
  FX
  National Geographic Channel (67%)
  SPEED
Filmed entertainment
  Feature film production and distribution
    Fox Filmed Entertainment
      Fox 2000
      Fox Atomic
      Fox Searchlight Pictures
      Twentieth Century Fox
      Twentieth Century Fox Animation
      Twentieth Century Fox Home Entertainment
  Television production and distribution
    Fox Television Studios
    Twentieth Century Fox Television
    Twentieth Television
Television
  FOX Broadcasting
  Fox Television Stations
    KCOP (MyNetworkTV, Los Angeles)
    KDFI (FOX, Dallas)
    KDFW (FOX, Dallas)
    KMSP (FOX, Minneapolis)
    KRIV (FOX, Houston)
    KSAZ (FOX, Phoenix)
    KTBC (FOX, Austin, TX)
    KTTV (FOX, Los Angeles)
    KTXH (MyNetworkTV, Houston)
    KUTP (MyNetworkTV, Phoenix)
    WAGA (FOX, Atlanta)
    WDCA (MyNetworkTV; Washington, DC)
    WFLD (FOX, Chicago)
    WFTC (MyNetworkTV, Minneapolis)
    WFXT (FOX, Boston)
    WHBQ (FOX, Memphis)
    WJBK (FOX, Detroit)
    WNYW (FOX, New York City)
    WOFL (FOX; Orlando, FL)
    WOGX (FOX; Gainesville, FL)
    WPWR (MyNetworkTV, Chicago)
    WTTG (FOX; Washington, DC)
    WTVT (FOX, Tampa)
    WTXF (FOX, Philadelphia)
    WUTB (MyNetworkTV, Baltimore)
    WWOR (MyNetworkTV, New York City)
  MyNetworkTV

COMPETITORS

CBS Corp
Discovery Communications
Disney
Lionsgate
MGM
NBC Universal
Sony Pictures Entertainment
Time Warner
Univision
Viacom

Franklin Resources

Franklin Resources believes a penny saved is a penny lost — if it's not wisely invested. Operating as Franklin Templeton Investments, the firm manages a family of more than 300 mutual funds that invest in international and domestic stocks; taxable and tax-exempt money market instruments; and corporate, municipal, and US government bonds. The investment products are sold under the Franklin, Templeton, Mutual Series, Bissett, Darby, and Fiduciary banners. Franklin Resources also offers separately managed accounts and insurance product funds. The company has more than $520 billion in assets under management and 21 million shareholder accounts.

In addition to its core business, Franklin Resources also provides shareholder services and manages investments for pension plans, trusts, and other institutions. Through banking subsidiaries, it offers such services as lending and deposit accounts. Retail banking, private banking, consumer lending, auto-loan securitization, and trust services are offered through Franklin Templeton Bank & Trust, Franklin Capital, Fiduciary Trust Company International, and other subsidiaries.

The company continues to expand its product portfolio and strengthen its geographic reach. It operates mainly in North America and Europe, but is adding assets under management in South America, Asia, and the Middle East. All told, Franklin Resources has offices in some 30 countries and offers its products in more than 150.

Descendants of founder Rupert Johnson Sr. and their families own more than a third of Franklin Resources.

HISTORY

Rupert Johnson Sr. founded Franklin Distributors (capitalizing on Benjamin Franklin's reputation for thrift) in New York in 1947; it launched its first fund, Franklin Custodian, in 1948. Custodian grew into five funds, including conservatively managed equity and bond funds. In 1968 Johnson's son Charles (who had joined the firm in 1957) became president and CEO. The company went public in 1971 as Franklin Resources.

In 1973 Franklin bought San Mateo-based investment firm Winfield & Co. and relocated to the Golden State. The buy provided additional products, including the Franklin Gold Fund (made possible by the end of the prohibition in the US against private interests owning commodity gold). With interest rate spikes in the late 1970s and early 1980s, money drained from savings accounts was poured into more lucrative money market mutual funds.

The Franklin Money Fund, launched in 1975, fueled the firm's tremendous asset growth in the 1980s. In 1981 the Franklin Tax-Free Income Fund (introduced in 1977) began investing solely in California municipal bonds. The fund's success led Franklin to introduce 43 tax-free income funds in later years.

In 1985 Franklin bought Pacific Union Bank and Trust (now Franklin Bank), allowing it to offer consumers such services as credit cards and to compete with financial services supermarkets, such as Merrill Lynch. It also bought real estate firm Property Resources (now Franklin Properties).

The 1987 stock crash and the California real estate slump forced Franklin to focus on its funds businesses. In 1992 it bought Bahamas-based Templeton, Galbraith & Hansberger, the manager of Templeton Funds, a major international funds business. The Templeton deal added an aggressive investment management unit to complement the conservatively managed Franklin funds.

In 1940 Sir John Templeton gained control of investment company Templeton, Dobbrow and Vance (TDV). TDV launched Templeton Growth Fund in 1954. In 1969 Templeton sold his interest in TDV but continued to manage the Templeton Growth Fund. John Galbraith became president of Securities Fund Investors (SFI), the distribution company for Templeton Growth Fund, in 1974. In 1977 Galbraith bought SFI from Templeton and began building the Templeton funds broker-dealer network in the US. The Templeton World Fund was formed in 1978. Templeton Investment Counsel was launched to provide investment advice in 1979. In 1986 these companies were combined to form Templeton, Galbraith & Hansberger Ltd.

In 1996 Franklin bought Heine Securities, previous investment adviser to Mutual Series Fund Inc. Max Heine, a leading investor, had established Mutual Shares Corp. in 1949. Heine Securities was formed in 1975. Following the acquisition, Franklin set up a subsidiary, Franklin Mutual Advisers, to be the investment adviser to the Mutual Series Fund.

In 1997 the weak Asian economy hurt Templeton's international funds, prompting liquidation of a Japanese stocks-based fund. Franklin cut jobs and shuffled management in 1999; the restructuring acknowledged the clash between the firm's value-investing style and investors' bull-market optimism.

In 2000 the firm gained a foothold in Canada with its purchase of Bissett & Associates Investment Management. Franklin's purchase of Fiduciary Trust the following year gave the firm greater access to institutional investors and affluent individuals.

Franklin Resources boosted its alternative investment offerings with the 2003 acquisition of Darby Overseas, which focuses on private equity, mezzanine, and fixed-income investment products, and specializes in Asian and Latin American fixed-income securities.

Chairman Charles Johnson retired from the CEO's office in 2004, turning the reins over to a new generation; his son Gregory was named CEO. Also that year Franklin Resources agreed to pay $50 million to settle market-timing allegations and reached a $20 million settlement with the SEC and an $18 million settlement with the state of California over commissions paid to brokers for mutual fund sales.

The company continued its international growth with the acquisitions of stakes in Dubai's Algebra Capital (in 2007) and Brazilian asset manager Bradesco Templeton (in 2006), since renamed Franklin Templeton Investimentos (Brasil).

EXECUTIVES

Chairman: Charles B. (Charlie) Johnson, age 76
Vice Chairman: Rupert H. Johnson Jr., age 69
President, CEO, and Director:
Gregory E. (Greg) Johnson, age 48,
$6,289,140 total compensation
EVP and COO: Jennifer J. (Jenny) Bolt, age 45,
$1,614,721 total compensation
EVP and CFO: Kenneth A. Lewis, age 48,
$1,408,777 total compensation
EVP Investment Management: John M. Lusk, age 51
EVP Alternative Investment Strategies: William Y. Yun,
age 50, $1,562,458 total compensation
EVP and General Counsel: Craig S. Tyle, age 49
EVP Global Advisory Services: Vijay C. Advani, age 49,
$2,473,600 total compensation
SVP and Chief Administrative Officer:
Norman R. (Rick) Frisbie Jr., age 42
SVP: Leslie M. Kratter, age 64
VP Human Resources, US: Penelope S. Alexander,
age 50
**VP Corporate Communications and Corporate
Citizenship:** Holly E. Gibson, age 43
VP Human Resources, International: Donna S. Ikeda,
age 53
Secretary: Maria Gray
**CEO and President, Fiduciary Trust Company
International:** Henry P. Johnson
President, Indian Asset Management: Harshendu Bindal
Auditors: PricewaterhouseCoopers LLP

LOCATIONS

HQ: Franklin Resources, Inc.
1 Franklin Pkwy., Bldg. 970, 1st Fl.
San Mateo, CA 94403
Phone: 650-312-2000   **Fax:** 650-312-5606
Web: www.franklintempleton.com

2009 Sales

	$ mil.	% of total
North America		
US	2,917.7	70
Bahamas	488.7	12
Canada	233.1	5
Asia/Pacific, Australia & Latin America	356.3	8
Europe, Middle East & Africa	198.3	5
Total	**4,194.1**	**100**

PRODUCTS/OPERATIONS

2009 Sales

	$ mil.	% of total
Investment management fees	2,503.2	60
Underwriting & distribution fees	1,408.2	34
Shareholder servicing fees	267.3	6
Other	15.4	—
Total	**4,194.1**	**100**

2009 Assets under Management

	% of total
Equity	47
Fixed-income	33
Hybrid	19
Money market & similar funds	1
Total	**100**

COMPETITORS

AllianceBernstein	Nationwide Financial
American Century	New York Life
AXA Financial	Old Mutual (US)
BlackRock	PIMCO
Capital Group	Pioneer Investment
Citigroup	Management
FMR	Principal Financial
Invesco	Putnam
John Hancock Financial	T. Rowe Price
Services	Torchmark
JPMorgan Chase	USAA
Morgan Stanley	The Vanguard Group

HISTORICAL FINANCIALS

Company Type: Public

Income Statement

FYE: September 30

	ASSETS ($ mil.)	NET INCOME ($ mil.)	INCOME AS % OF ASSETS	EMPLOYEES
9/09	9,469	897	9.5%	7,700
9/08	9,177	1,588	17.3%	8,800
9/07	9,943	1,773	17.8%	8,700
9/06	9,500	1,268	13.3%	8,000
9/05	8,894	1,058	11.9%	7,200
Annual Growth	**1.6%**	**(4.0%)**	**—**	**1.7%**

2009 Year-End Financials

Equity as % of assets: 80.6%
Return on assets: 9.6%
Return on equity: 12.2%
Long-term debt ($ mil.): 0
No. of shares (mil.): 225

Dividends
Yield: 0.8%
Payout: 21.7%
Market value ($ mil.): 22,644
Sales ($ mil.): 4,194

Stock History

NYSE: BEN

	STOCK PRICE ($) FY Close	P/E High/Low	PER SHARE ($) Earnings	Dividends	Book Value
9/09	100.60	27 10	3.87	0.84	33.91
9/08	88.13	21 12	6.67	0.80	31.43
9/07	127.50	21 15	7.03	0.60	32.57
9/06	105.75	22 16	4.86	0.48	29.70
9/05	83.96	21 14	4.06	0.40	25.25
Annual Growth	**4.6%**	**— —**	**(1.2%)**	**20.4%**	**7.6%**

Freeport-McMoRan Copper & Gold

Freeport-McMoRan Copper & Gold (FCX) really digs its profits. Its 91%-owned subsidiary, PT Freeport Indonesia (PT-FI), operates the vast open-pit Grasberg gold, copper, and silver mine in Indonesia, while the government owns the other 9%. FCX controls proved and probable reserves of about 50 million tons of copper, 47 million ounces of gold, and 1.3 million tons of molybdenum. Copper, in the form of concentrates and in refined products such as cathodes and anodes, accounts for most of FCX's sales. It's the world's #2 copper company behind Codelco. FCX is also engaged in smelting and refining through PT-FI's 25% stake in PT Smelting, which operates a copper smelter and refinery in Indonesia.

Other FCX units include PT Irja Eastern Minerals, which explores for minerals in Indonesia, and Atlantic Copper, which operates a copper smelter in Spain.

The $26 billion acquisition of Phelps Dodge in 2007 brought that company's global copper, gold, and molybdenum business into the fold. The deal placed FCX in a position to thrive as a global competitor in the rank just below metals

and mining giants such as BHP Billiton, Rio Tinto, and Vale. A year later FCX sold the wire and cable business it acquired in the Phelps Dodge deal to General Cable Corporation for $735 million.

Following the acquisition — and benefiting from high copper prices and a good business climate — the company began to invest in its development projects. It was also able to retire a sizable portion of its debt, much of it accumulated from the Phelps Dodge acquisition. Toward the end of 2008 and through 2009 FCX was forced to halt development activities due to low copper prices and a generally poor global economy; it also slowed production at many of its mines and processing facilities. By 2010 the company was able to return its focus back toward development.

Political and environmental controversy in Indonesia has been a problem for FCX since its major protector, former President Suharto, was forced to resign in 1998 after more than 30 years in power. Sectarian violence in Indonesia, where FCX is one of the largest employers, also makes the company vulnerable to work stoppages. Anglo-Australian mining giant Rio Tinto is jointly involved with FCX in developing mineral properties in Indonesia's politically and environmentally sensitive Papua region. The company's Tenke Fungume copper and gold mine named Too is located in the Democratic Republic of Congo, which also can be an unstable environment in which to do business. Tenke Fungume is jointly owned with Lundin Mining and the Congolese government. It began production in 2009.

Moving only peripherally into the oil and gas business, FCX agreed in 2010 to make a $500 million investment in sister company McMoRan Exploration (MMR) to finance that operations's proposed acquisition of properties from Plains Exploration & Production Company. A group of instutitional investors also agreed to invest another $400 million with MMR as a part of the deal. The investment and subsequent acquisition will allow MMR to expand its exploration, development, and production of oil and gas in the lucrative shallow water region of the Gulf of Mexico's Continental Shelf.

HISTORY

The Freeport Sulfur Company was formed in Texas in 1912 by Francis Pemberton, banker Eric Swenson, and several investors to develop a sulfur field. The next year Freeport Texas was formed as a holding company for Freeport Sulfur and other enterprises.

During the 1930s the company diversified. In 1936 Freeport pioneered a process to remove hydrocarbons from sulfur. The company joined Consolidated Coal in 1955 to establish the National Potash Company. In 1956 Freeport formed an oil and gas subsidiary, Freeport Oil.

Internationally, Freeport formed an Australian minerals subsidiary in 1964 and a copper-mining subsidiary in Indonesia in 1967. The company changed its name to Freeport Minerals in 1971 and merged with Utah-based McMoRan Oil & Gas (formerly McMoRan Explorations) in 1982.

McMoRan Explorations had been formed in 1969 by William McWilliams, Jim Bob Moffett, and Byron Rankin. In 1973 McMoRan formed an exploration and drilling alliance with Dow Chemical and signed a deal with Indonesia to mine in the remote Irian Jaya region. McMoRan went public in 1978.

Moffett became chairman and CEO of Freeport-McMoRan in 1984. The company formed

Freeport-McMoRan Copper in 1987 to manage its Indonesian operations. The unit assumed the Freeport-McMoRan Copper & Gold name in 1991. Two years later Freeport-McMoRan acquired Rio Tinto Minera, a copper-smelting business with operations in Spain.

To support expansion in Indonesia, Freeport-McMoRan spun off its copper and gold division in 1994. In 1995 Freeport-McMoRan Copper & Gold (FCX) formed an alliance with the UK's RTZ Corporation to develop its Indonesian mineral reserves. Local riots that year closed the Grasberg Mine, and FCX's political risk insurance was canceled. Despite these setbacks, higher metal prices and growing sales in 1995 helped the company double its operating income.

An Indonesian tribal leader filed a $6 billion lawsuit in 1996 charging FCX with environmental, human rights, and social and cultural violations. The company called the suit baseless but offered to set aside 1% of its annual revenues, or about $15 million, to help local tribes. Tribal leaders rejected the offer, and in 1997 a judge dismissed the lawsuit.

In 1997 FCX pulled out of Bre-X Minerals' Busang gold mine project, which independent tests later proved to be a fraud of historic proportions. Amid widespread rioting, Indonesia's embattled president Suharto was forced out of office in 1998. The new government investigated charges of cronyism involving FCX.

FCX received permission from the Indonesian government in 1999 to expand the Grasberg Mine and increase ore output up to 300,000 metric tons per day. However, the next year an overflow accident killed four workers in Grasberg and, as a result of the accident, the Indonesian government ordered FCX to reduce its production at the mine by up to 30%. Normal production at the mine resumed in early 2001.

FM Services (administrative, legal, and financial services) was added as a subsidiary in 2002. In 2003 FCX bought an 86% stake in PT Puncakjaya Power, a supplier of power to PT-FI.

The $26 billion acquisition of Phelps Dodge in 2007 brought that company's global copper, gold, and molybdenum business into the fold. The deal placed Freeport in a position to thrive as a global competitor in the rank just below such metals and mining giants like BHP Billiton, Rio Tinto, and Vale.

A year later Freeport sold the wire and cable business it had acquired in the Phelps Dodge deal, selling the unit to General Cable Corporation for $735 million.

EXECUTIVES

Chairman: James R. (Jim Bob) Moffett, age 71, $21,477,084 total compensation
President, CEO, and Director: Richard C. Adkerson, age 63, $27,622,332 total compensation
Vice Chairman: B. M. Rankin Jr., age 80
EVP, CFO, and Treasurer: Kathleen L. Quirk, age 46, $5,389,129 total compensation
EVP and Chief Administrative Officer: Michael J. Arnold, age 57, $4,485,354 total compensation
SVP and General Counsel: L. Richards (Rick) McMillan II, age 62
SVP International Relations and Federal Government Affairs: W. Russell King

VP and Controller, Financial Reporting: C. Donald Whitmire Jr.
VP Communications: William L. (Bill) Collier III
President, Freeport-McMoRan Sales Company; VP, FCX (Cathode and Rod): Stephen T. Higgins
President, Freeport-McMoRan Indonesia: Mark J. Johnson, age 50
President, Climax Molybdenum: David H. (Dave) Thornton
President, Mining: Richard E. Coleman
President, Atlantic Copper; SVP, FCX (Concentrates): Javier Targhetta
President Director, PT Freeport Indonesia: Armando Mahler, age 54
President, Africa: Phillip S. (Phil) Brumit
President, Americas: Harry M. (Red) Conger, age 77
Secretary: Douglas N. Currault II
Director External Communications: Eric Kinneberg
Manager Investor Relations: David Joint
Auditors: Ernst & Young LLP

LOCATIONS

HQ: Freeport-McMoRan Copper & Gold Inc.
333 N. Central Ave., Phoenix, AZ 85004
Phone: 602-366-8100
Web: www.fcx.com

2009 Sales by Destination

	$ mil.	% of total
US	4,890	32
Japan	3,093	21
Indonesia	1,937	13
Spain	986	7
India	566	4
Chile	563	4
China	496	3
South Korea	475	3
Other countries	2,034	13
Total	**15,040**	**100**

PRODUCTS/OPERATIONS

2009 Sales

	$ mil.	% of total
Refined copper products	6,563	44
Copper in concentrates	4,763	32
Gold	2,591	17
Molybdenum	792	5
Other products	331	2
Total	**15,040**	**100**

Selected Subsidiaries and Affiliates

Atlantic Copper Holding, SA (smelting and refining, Spain)
Chino Mines Company
Climax Molybdenum Company
FM Service Company (administrative and financial services)
Missouri Lead Smelting Company
PT Freeport Indonesia Co. (91%, mining)
　PT Smelting (Gresik) Co. (25%, smelting, Indonesia)
PT Irja Eastern Minerals Corp. (mining, Indonesia)
PT Puncakjaya Power (86%, supplies power to PT Freeport Indonesia)

COMPETITORS

Antofagasta
Barrick Gold
BHP Billiton
Centromin
Chevron Mining
Codelco
Newmont Mining
Rio Tinto Limited
Southern Copper
Vale Limited

HISTORICAL FINANCIALS

Company Type: Public

Income Statement

	REVENUE ($ mil.)	NET INCOME ($ mil.)	NET PROFIT MARGIN	EMPLOYEES
12/09	15,040	3,534	23.5%	28,400
12/08	17,796	(11,067)	—	29,300
12/07	16,939	2,977	17.6%	25,400
12/06	5,791	1,457	25.2%	7,000
12/05	4,179	995	23.8%	26,938
Annual Growth	**37.7%**	**37.3%**	**—**	**1.3%**

2009 Year-End Financials

Debt ratio: 133.1%　　No. of shares (mil.): 470
Return on equity: 85.1%　Dividends
Cash ($ mil.): 2,656　　　Yield: 0.0%
Current ratio: 2.48　　　　Payout: —
Long-term debt ($ mil.): 8,311　Market value ($ mil.): 37,771

Stock History

NYSE: FCX

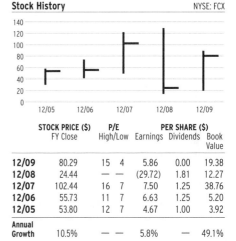

	STOCK PRICE ($) FY Close	P/E High/Low		PER SHARE ($) Earnings	Dividends	Book Value
12/09	80.29	15	4	5.86	0.00	19.38
12/08	24.44	—	—	(29.72)	1.81	12.27
12/07	102.44	16	7	7.50	1.25	38.76
12/06	55.73	11	7	6.63	1.25	5.20
12/05	53.80	12	7	4.67	1.00	3.92
Annual Growth	**10.5%**	**—**	**—**	**5.8%**	**—**	**49.1%**

Frontier Communications

Serving city dwellers and country folk alike, Frontier Communications provides local, long-distance, and digital phone services, as well as Internet access to about 3 million primarily residential subscribers in 24 states. The company is active mostly in rural and small to mid-sized markets, where it is the incumbent local-exchange carrier (ILEC) operating under the Frontier Residential brand. Other offerings include satellite television services (enabled through a partnership with DISH Network), as well as data, Internet, and telephone packages and equipment for business clients. The company was formerly known as Citizens Communication, but it adopted its longstanding brand, Frontier, as the corporate name in 2008.

The company has been expanding its horizons largely through acquisitions. It bought about 5 million telephone and broadband access lines in 14 states from Verizon Communications for about $8.6 billion in cash and stock. The deal roughly tripled Frontier's size and gave it a healthy boost against other rural communications carriers. The transaction met with opposition from labor unions and legislators in Illinois, in particular, but was completed in mid-2010. Verizon, which initiated the sale to meet regulatory requirements for its 2009 purchase of wireless carrier Alltel, took a more than two-thirds stake in Frontier as part of the deal.

Frontier Communications offers service in Arizona, California, Idaho, Illinois, Indiana, Michigan, Minnesota, Montana, Nebraska, Nevada, New Mexico, New York, North Carolina, North Dakota, Ohio, Oregon, Pennsylvania, South Carolina, Tennessee, Utah, Washington, West Virginia, and Wisconsin.

HISTORY

Frontier Communications was formed in 1935 as Citizens Utilities Company to acquire Public Utilities Consolidated Corporation, a Minneapolis-based company with interests in electric, gas, water, and telephone utilities throughout the US. From 1950 to 1970 the company bought utilities in rural and suburban areas of Arizona, California, Hawaii, Illinois, Indiana, Ohio, and Pennsylvania. A major acquisition was Hawaii's Kauai Electric Company, in 1969. By the mid-1970s, electric power brought in 40% of the company's revenues.

Leonard Tow, head of Century Communications, was brought on board in 1989 and elected chairman the next year, remaining in that position until 2004. Expanding Citizens through more electric, water, and natural gas acquisitions, he tripled the company's revenues in less than 10 years.

In 1993 Citizens acquired a majority stake in Electric Lightwave, the first competitive local-exchange carrier (CLEC) west of the Mississippi River. Citizens started its long-distance telephone service in 1994. It also acquired 500,000 local access lines in nine states from GTE, quadrupling the size of its operations. By 1995 the telecom group was the fastest-growing segment of the company.

After the Telecommunications Act was passed in 1996, Citizens acquired another 110,000 local access lines and cable systems with more than 7,000 customers from ALLTEL and bought three Southern California cable systems with Century Communications. Citizens aggressively marketed local phone service in neighboring areas to its service territories, but the company didn't see the return it expected and by 1997 had to cut its workforce and tighten cost controls. In light of the cutbacks, bookkeeping troubles, and 1996 threats from Vermont to revoke Citizens' license there for accounting and permit problems, the board voted Tow a pay cut.

The company sold a minority stake in Electric Lightwave to the public in 1997 (Citizens reacquired the stake in 2002 and Electric Lightwave became a wholly owned subsidiary). Citizens continued its buying spree with telecom and gas firms in New York and Hawaii, and a local phone company in Pennsylvania, in 1998.

The next year, Citizens began turning itself into a pure telecom company through a series of transactions. It agreed to pay about $2.8 billion for 900,000 local phone lines owned by U S WEST and GTE. It also sold its cable TV interests and agreed to sell its water and wastewater operations (for $835 million).

Citizens bought more than 1 million local phone lines in 2001 from Global Crossing for about $3.5 billion. Later that year the company canceled its pending acquisition agreements with Qwest, U S WEST's successor, amid a dispute over how much revenue the local lines were producing. The terminated deals, valued at $1.7 billion, would have given Citizens another 540,000 local lines. It later pulled out of a deal to buy an additional 63,000 access lines in Arizona and California from Verizon Communications.

The company also sold part of its natural gas business for $375 million in 2001, the same year it changed its name to Citizens Communications. Although an earlier deal to sell its electric properties fell through, the company completed the sale of its Kauai Electric division in 2002 for $215 million to the Kauai Island Utility Cooperative. That year it also reached an agreement to sell its Hawaiian gas division in a deal valued at $115 million and completed the following year.

In November 2002 two executives of the company's public utilities division were dismissed after an SEC investigation into $7.8 million in payments for services the company did not receive.

Citizens sold its competitive local-exchange carrier (CLEC), Electric Lightwave, to Integra Telecom in mid-2006 in a deal that was valued at $247 million. The next year it acquired Commonwealth Telephone, effectively expanding its access to the Pennsylvania market. Later that year the company then spent $62 million to purchase Global Valley Networks, a provider of telephone and Internet services in California, in a move to expand its service area in the Western US.

In 2008 the company took its brand name, Frontier, as its corporate name.

EXECUTIVES

Chairman, President, and CEO:
 Mary Agnes (Maggie) Wilderotter, age 55, $4,819,134 total compensation
EVP and COO: Daniel J. McCarthy, age 45, $1,155,976 total compensation
EVP and CFO: Donald R. (Don) Shassian, age 54, $1,801,231 total compensation
EVP Human Resources and Call Center Sales and Service: Cecilia K. McKenney, age 47, $948,173 total compensation
EVP Regulatory and Government Affairs and Chief Legal Officer: Kathleen Q. Abernathy, age 53
EVP Commercial Sales: Peter B. (Pete) Hayes, age 52, $1,018,966 total compensation
EVP and General Manager, Marketing and New Business Operations: Melinda M. White, age 50
SVP, General Counsel, and Secretary:
 Hilary E. Glassman, age 47
SVP and Chief Accounting Officer: Robert J. Larson, age 50
SVP and General Manager West Virginia:
 Dana E. Waldo, age 58
SVP and Treasurer: David R. Whitehouse
SVP Government and Regulatory Affairs:
 Steven C. (Steve) Crosby
Assistant VP Corporate Communications: Brigid Smith
Director Investor Relations: Gregory H. Lundberg
President and General Manager, Southeast Region:
 Ken Arndt
Auditors: KPMG LLP

LOCATIONS

HQ: Frontier Communications Corporation
 3 High Ridge Park, Stamford, CT 06905
Phone: 203-614-5600   **Fax:** 203-614-4602
Web: www.frontier.com

PRODUCTS/OPERATIONS

Selected Subsidiaries

Commonwealth Telephone Company
CTE Telecom
Evans Telephone Holdings
Frontier InfoServices Inc.
Frontier Subsidiary Telco LLC
Frontier Telephone of Rochester, Inc.
Mohave Cellular Limited Partnership
Navajo Communications Company
NCC Systems, Inc.
Ogden Telephone Company
Phone Trends, Inc.
Rhinelander Telecommunications, Inc.

COMPETITORS

AT&T
CenturyTel
FairPoint Communications, Inc.
Integra Telecom
Iowa Telecommunications
Qwest Communications
tw telecom
Verizon
Vonage
XO Holdings

HISTORICAL FINANCIALS

Company Type: Public

Income Statement

FYE: December 31

	REVENUE ($ mil.)	NET INCOME ($ mil.)	NET PROFIT MARGIN	EMPLOYEES
12/09	2,118	121	5.7%	5,400
12/08	2,237	183	8.2%	5,671
12/07	2,288	215	9.4%	5,900
12/06	2,025	345	17.0%	5,446
12/05	2,163	202	9.4%	6,103
Annual Growth	(0.5%)	(12.1%)	—	(3.0%)

2009 Year-End Financials

Debt ratio: 1,463.4%
Return on equity: 28.5%
Cash ($ mil.): 359
Current ratio: 1.73
Long-term debt ($ mil.): 4,794

No. of shares (mil.): 992
Dividends
 Yield: 12.8%
 Payout: 263.2%
Market value ($ mil.): 7,748

Stock History

NYSE: FTR

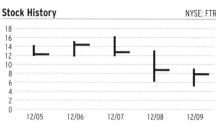

	STOCK PRICE ($) FY Close	P/E High/Low		PER SHARE ($) Earnings	Dividends	Book Value
12/09	7.81	23	14	0.38	1.00	0.33
12/08	8.74	23	11	0.57	1.00	0.52
12/07	12.73	25	19	0.65	1.00	1.01
12/06	14.37	14	11	1.06	1.00	1.07
12/05	12.23	23	20	0.60	1.00	1.05
Annual Growth	(10.6%)	—	—	(10.8%)	0.0%	(25.1%)

Furniture Brands International

Furniture Brands International runs a furniture-making empire. The company ranks as one of the top US makers of residential furniture. Furniture Brands' subsidiaries offer a lineup of nationally recognized brands, including Broyhill, Lane, Thomasville, and Drexel Heritage, among others. Broyhill makes mid-priced furniture for the bedroom and dining room, as well as other home furnishings. Laneventure (outdoor wicker and teak collections) and Henredon (wood and upholstered pieces) target the premium-priced furniture market. Furniture Brands distributes its products through a network of furniture centers, independent dealers, national and local chains, and department stores.

Since 2008, Furniture Brands has seen its sales decline as it weathers the recession. Several factors have contributed to the decrease, such as fewer customers with discretionary income to purchase furniture, the depressed housing market, and reduced access to consumer credit, among other factors.

Furniture Brands in 2008 laid off some 15% of its domestic workforce, amounting to about 1,400 jobs, which included both management and hourly employees. It made further cuts in 2009 by laying off 250 plant workers. The cuts have primarily affected manufacturing centers in North Carolina and Mississippi.

Furniture Brands also is refocusing its distribution efforts. Thomasville and Drexel Heritage are expanding their network of branded stores, both company- and dealer-owned, while Broyhill and Lane are focusing on distributing to traditional furniture retailers and mass merchants.

To tap the lucrative (more recession-proof) high-end market and sell directly to designers, Furniture Brands created the Designer Group, comprising several of the company's high-end lines, including Henredon, Maitland-Smith, Laneventure, Hickory Chair, and Pearson, to be marketed primarily through designers.

Due in part to the residential furniture industry trend of shifting to offshore sourcing (primarily to Asia), Thomasville has reorganized its domestic manufacturing operations. The company has closed or announced the closing of more than 35 domestic manufacturing facilities since 2001, and it has boosted its manufacturing capacity in Indonesia to capitalize on the low manufacturing costs.

Former CEO Mickey Holliman stepped down in 2008. His replacement —gum and candy supplier executive Ralph Scozzafava — serves as both chairman and CEO. Samson Holding holds a 15% stake in Furniture Brands and has indicated that it may seek control of the company or board representation.

HISTORY

Although already a diversified firm, INTERCO's purchase of Ethan Allen in 1980 took the company in a direction that would eventually become its only business. INTERCO (now Furniture Brands International) traces its roots back to the pairing of two shoe manufacturers and made a name for itself by running men's shoemaker and retailer Florsheim, which it acquired in 1953. It added other operations, including department stores and apparel, beginning in the 1960s. The Ethan Allen purchase gave INTERCO 24 furniture factories and 300 retail outlets.

The company grew its furniture business later in 1980 by purchasing Broyhill Furniture Industries, which was founded by J. E. Broyhill as Lenoir Chair Company in 1926. The Broyhill line first became popular during the 1930s. The Broyhill family built the company into the largest privately owned furniture makers, with 20 manufacturing facilities, when INTERCO bought it.

In 1986, after acquiring furniture maker Highland House (Hickory), INTERCO made its largest acquisition in the home furnishings and furniture market when it gained control of the Lane Company for approximately $500 million. Founded in 1912 by Ed Lane to make cedar chests, Virginia-based Lane had grown into a full-line maker of furniture with about 15 plants in operation. The acquisition of Lane lifted furniture and furnishings to 33% of INTERCO's total sales in 1987.

Meanwhile, INTERCO hadn't neglected its shoe business, adding Converse in 1986. Richard Loynd, the Converse CEO, served as INTERCO's CEO from 1989 to 1996. In 1988, under a takeover threat by the Rales brothers of Washington, DC, the company retained the investment banking firm of Wasserstein Perella, which advised payment of a special dividend, for which INTERCO borrowed $1.8 billion via junk bonds. To repay the debt, the firm began selling off assets, including its apparel businesses and Ethan Allen. However, the sales yielded low prices and some businesses failed to attract buyers.

After fighting off the hostile takeover, INTERCO filed bankruptcy in 1991 — one of the largest bankruptcy cases in US history. It also filed a malpractice suit against Wasserstein Perella when it emerged from Chapter 11; the suit was settled the following year, and Apollo Investment Fund acquired a large stake in the firm.

INTERCO sold the last of its 80-year-old shoe-making business with the spinoff of its Florsheim and Converse units in 1994. The company acquired Thomasville Furniture from Armstrong World Industries for about $330 million in 1993, a purchase that made it the leading shaker in residential furniture. Founded in 1904, the Finch brothers had run Thomasville until Armstrong acquired it in 1968.

W. G. "Mickey" Holliman became CEO in 1996, and INTERCO's board decided to change the company's name to Furniture Brands International. In 1997 Apollo Investment Fund, its largest shareholder, sold its nearly 40% stake. The next year Furniture Brands and retailer Haverty Furniture signed a deal (terminated in 2003) whereby Haverty's would allocate up to half its retail space for Furniture Brands' items.

In 2000 the company started selling kitchen and bathroom cabinets under the Thomasville brand in Home Depot. In 2001 Furniture Brands bought Drexel Heritage, Henredon, and Maitland-Smith units from LifeStyle Furnishings for $275 million. Overall economic pressures, as well as the residential furniture industry's shift to offshore sourcing, led Thomasville to shut down 21 domestic manufacturing facilities in 2003.

Holliman left the company and was replaced by Ralph Scozzafava in January 2008. Scozzafava, who had been an executive at Wm. Wrigley Jr. Co., was elected chairman of the board of Furniture Brands in May.

EXECUTIVES

Chairman and CEO: Ralph P. Scozzafava, age 51, $842,544 total compensation
SVP and CFO: Steven G. (Steve) Rolls, age 55, $644,110 total compensation
SVP Human Resources: Mary E. Sweetman, age 46, $1,604,323 total compensation
SVP Global Supply Chain: Raymond J. (Ray) Johnson, age 54, $808,242 total compensation
SVP, General Counsel, and Secretary: Jon D. Botsford, age 55, $413,016 total compensation
SVP Growth and Transformation: Vance C. Johnston
Controller and Chief Accounting Officer: Richard R. (Rick) Isaak, age 42, $715,518 total compensation
Chief Marketing Officer: James (Jim) Brenner
VP Strategy and Business Development: Daniel J. (Dan) Stone
VP Communications and Investor Relations: John S. Hastings
President, Broyhill Furniture Industries: Jeffrey L. (Jeff) Cook, age 54, $2,321,381 total compensation
President, Designer Brands Group: Daniel R. (Dan) Bradley, age 53
President, Special Markets: George Knobloch
President, Lane Furniture Industries: Gregory P. (Greg) Roy
President, Thomasville and Drexel Heritage: Edward D. (Ed) Teplitz, age 48, $430,722 total compensation
President, Canada: Mark Wiltshire
Auditors: KPMG LLP

LOCATIONS

HQ: Furniture Brands International, Inc.
101 S. Hanley Rd., St. Louis, MO 63105
Phone: 314-863-1100   **Fax:** 314-863-5306
Web: www.furniturebrands.com

PRODUCTS/OPERATIONS

Subsidiaries
Broyhill
Drexel Heritage
Henredon
Lane
Laneventure
MaitlandSmith
Pearson
Thomasville

Selected Products
Case goods furniture
  Bedroom
  Dining room
  Living room

Occasional furniture
  Accent items
  Freestanding home entertainment centers
  Home office items
  Wood tables

Stationary upholstery products
  Chairs
  Love seats
  Sectionals
  Sofas

Other
  Motion furniture
  Recliners
  Sleep sofas

HISTORICAL FINANCIALS

Company Type: Public

Income Statement

FYE: December 31

	REVENUE ($ mil.)	NET INCOME ($ mil.)	NET PROFIT MARGIN	EMPLOYEES
12/09	1,224	(109)	—	8,500
12/08	1,743	(386)	—	8,100
12/07	2,082	(46)	—	11,900
12/06	2,418	55	2.3%	13,800
12/05	2,387	61	2.6%	15,150
Annual Growth	(15.4%)	—	—	(13.5%)

2009 Year-End Financials

Debt ratio: 29.7%
Return on equity: —
Cash ($ mil.): 84
Current ratio: 2.85
Long-term debt ($ mil.): 78

No. of shares (mil.): 51
Dividends
  Yield: 0.0%
  Payout: —
Market value ($ mil.): 278

Stock History

NYSE: FBN

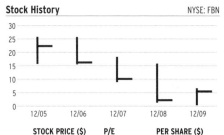

	STOCK PRICE ($) FY Close	P/E High/Low	PER SHARE ($) Earnings	Dividends	Book Value
12/09	5.46	— —	(2.25)	0.00	5.17
12/08	2.21	— —	(7.92)	0.12	7.21
12/07	10.06	— —	(0.94)	0.64	16.61
12/06	16.23	22 14	1.13	0.64	17.91
12/05	22.33	22 14	1.18	0.60	17.78
Annual Growth	(29.7%)	— —	—	—	(26.6%)

GameStop Corp.

GameStop holds the top score in the video game retailing industry. The company is the largest retailer of new and used games, hardware, entertainment software, and accessories. GameStop boasts more than 6,400 stores located in the US, Canada, Australia, and Europe. A majority of the company's revenue is generated by sales of new and used video games. Stores branded as GameStop and EB Games carry an average of 1,000 new titles and 3,500 used ones. The company also operates e-commerce websites (GameStop.com, ebgames.com), publishes *Game Informer*, a video game magazine that reaches some 4 million subscribers, and offers GameStop TV in many of its locations.

Used games have become an important segment for GameStop as more consumers turn to buying used rather than new games. Used game products is the company's most profitable segment, with profit margins of 47%.

GameStop has continued to expand its operations in the US and overseas, but most of its recent sales growth has come from outside the US. The company's international expansion was primarily driven by a pair of acquisitions inked in 2008. The largest of those was its $629 million purchase of video game retailer Micromania, which brought with it some 330 stores in France. South of the equator, GameStop acquired The Gamesman, the largest independent gaming retailer in New Zealand.

To maintain its foothold in new and used gaming, GameStop plans to continue to target hardcore gamers as well as those niche customers who purchase games as gifts during the holidays. The company considers itself a destination location for gamers. It develops a relationship with video game enthusiasts by allowing them to trade in used video games for store credits on future purchases.

Catering to a community of core gamers, GameStop secured a digital platform in mid-2010 when it acquired Kongregate, a gaming site launched in 2007 for social gaming that attracts some 10 million users a month. As part of the deal, Kongregate operates as a wholly owned subsidiary of GameStop and maintains its headquarters in San Francisco.

To further attract gamers and keep them in GameStop stores longer to boost same-store sales, the company in 2009 completed a yearlong launch of an in-store video network called GameStop TV. The effort is the result of a partnership with CBS Outernet and Reflect Systems. The in-store programming features product promotions, game previews, developer interviews, and other customized content.

In June 2010 Daniel DeMatteo was named executive chairman of GameStop, while Paul Raines was promoted from COO to CEO of the retailer.

HISTORY

NeoStar Retail Group resulted from the 1994 combination of software retailers Babbage's and Software Etc. Babbage's had been founded by James McCurry and Gary Kusin in 1983. Named for 19th-century mathematician Charles Babbage (considered the father of the computer), it went public in 1988.

Software Etc. began as a division of B. Dalton Bookseller in 1984. Bookstore chain Barnes & Noble and Dutch retailer Vendex acquired

B. Dalton two years later. Software Etc. went public in 1992.

Both companies focused on mall retailing: Babbage's on game software, and Software Etc. on a broader variety of PC software. Both saw growth spurred by the rising popularity of Nintendo and Sega game systems and by falling PC prices. The two merged in 1994 in an effort to stave off growing competition from big retail chains such as Best Buy and Wal-Mart. NeoStar opened 122 stores in 1995.

Amid flat sales the following year, several senior executives left. Also in 1996 NeoStar lost its contract to operate software departments at 136 Barnes & Noble sites, and it soon filed for Chapter 11. Late that year a group led by Barnes & Noble's head honcho Leonard Riggio purchased about 460 of NeoStar's 650 stores for $58.5 million and renamed the company Babbage's, Etc. Former Software Etc. chief Dick Fontaine was named CEO.

By 1997 the company began concentrating on popular games and software, and in 1999 it formed its e-commerce site GameStop.com. In late 1999 Barnes & Noble paid Riggio's group $210 million for Babbage's Etc. In June 2000 the company fortified its position and became the #1 US video game retailer with the purchase of rival game retailer Funco (about 400 stores) for $161.5 million. The company changed its name to GameStop in August 2001 and filed to go public, which it accomplished in February 2002. Though public, it was still under the majority control of Barnes & Noble until 2004 when GameStop bought back its shares.

GameStop bought rival Electronics Boutique in 2005, doubling its size from 2,000 to more than 4,500 stores. Steven R. Morgan, a former executive with Electronics Boutique, became president of GameStop later that year.

A new CEO took the controls at GameStop in 2008 — its first CEO change since the company's inception in 1996. Dick Fontaine gave up the title of chief executive to Daniel DeMatteo, who had served as COO since 1996 and vice chairman of the company since 2004. Also, Paul Raines, formerly with Home Depot, joined the company as COO in September 2008. Fontaine retained the chairman's title and focused on international operations and acquisitions.

In June 2010 DeMatteo was promoted to executive chairman of the company, while Raines was named CEO.

EXECUTIVES

Chairman, International: R. Richard (Dick) Fontaine, age 68, $7,008,496 total compensation
Chairman: Daniel A. (Dan) DeMatteo, age 62, $4,313,153 total compensation
CEO: J. Paul (Paul) Raines, age 45, $1,713,684 total compensation
President: Tony D. Bartel, age 46, $1,544,098 total compensation
EVP and CFO: Robert A. (Rob) Lloyd, age 48
EVP GameStop International: Michael (Mike) Mauler, age 49
EVP Finance and Assistant Secretary: David W. Carlson
SVP and General Manager, Digital Business: Shawn D. Freeman
SVP Supply Chain and Refurbishment: Bruce Kulp
SVP and Chief Accounting Officer: Tony W. Crawford, age 42
Director Investor Relations: Matt Hodges
General Manager Digital Media: Chris Petrovic
Auditors: BDO Seidman, LLP

LOCATIONS

HQ: GameStop Corp.
625 Westport Pkwy., Grapevine, TX 76051
Phone: 817-424-2000   **Fax:** 817-424-2002
Web: www.gamestop.com

2010 Sales

	$ mil.	% of total
US	6,275.0	69
Europe	1,781.4	20
Canada	530.2	6
Australia	491.4	5
Total	**9,078.0**	**100**

2010 Stores

	No.
US	4,429
Europe	1,296
Australia	388
Canada	337
Total	**6,450**

PRODUCTS/OPERATIONS

2010 Sales

	$ mil.	% of total
New video game software	3,730.9	41
Used video game products	2,394.1	27
New video game hardware	1,756.5	19
Other	1,196.5	13
Total	**9,078.0**	**100**

Selected Merchandise

Accessories
    PC entertainment accessories (video cards, joysticks, mice)
    Video game accessories (controllers, memory cards, add-ons)
    Other (strategy guides, magazines, action figures, trading cards)
PC entertainment software and other software
Used video games
Video game hardware
Video game software

COMPETITORS

Amazon.com
Best Buy
Blockbuster Inc.
Borders Group
Buy.com
CompUSA
Costco Wholesale
eBay
Fry's Electronics
GAME Group
GameFly
Hollywood Entertainment
Kmart
Movie Gallery
RadioShack
Target
Toys "R" Us
Wal-Mart
Zones

HISTORICAL FINANCIALS

Company Type: Public

Income Statement

FYE: Saturday nearest January 31

	REVENUE ($ mil.)	NET INCOME ($ mil.)	NET PROFIT MARGIN	EMPLOYEES
1/10	9,078	377	4.2%	59,000
1/09	8,806	398	4.5%	41,000
1/08	7,094	288	4.1%	43,000
1/07	5,319	158	3.0%	32,000
1/06	3,092	101	3.3%	42,000
Annual Growth	**30.9%**	**39.1%**	**—**	**8.9%**

2010 Year-End Financials

Debt ratio: 16.4%
Return on equity: 15.0%
Cash ($ mil.): 905
Current ratio: 1.28
Long-term debt ($ mil.): 447
No. of shares (mil.): 152
Dividends
    Yield: —
    Payout: —
Market value ($ mil.): 2,996

Stock History

NYSE: GME

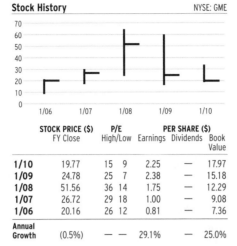

	STOCK PRICE ($) FY Close	P/E High	Low	PER SHARE ($) Earnings	Dividends	Book Value
1/10	19.77	15	9	2.25	—	17.97
1/09	24.78	25	7	2.38	—	15.18
1/08	51.56	36	14	1.75	—	12.29
1/07	26.72	29	18	1.00	—	9.08
1/06	20.16	26	12	0.81	—	7.36
Annual Growth	**(0.5%)**	**—**	**—**	**29.1%**	**—**	**25.0%**

Gannett Co.

Gannett satisfies news junkies with a stash of daily US papers. The company is the top newspaper publisher in the US with about 85 daily papers boasting a total circulation of about 5.7 million. Its flagship *USA TODAY*, with a circulation of 1.8 million, is the nation's second-largest newspaper (behind the *Wall Street Journal*). Other papers in Gannett's holdings include *The Arizona Republic* and the *Detroit Free Press*. The company also owns about 650 non-daily publications, as well as more than 200 papers in the UK through Newsquest. In addition, Gannett owns 23 television stations in about 20 markets, publishes periodicals and inserts (including *USA WEEKEND*), and operates websites for many of its papers.

Like other newspaper publishers, Gannett relies on both advertising and circulation revenue for the bulk of its sales. The entire industry is struggling through a long and slow decline, however, as readers migrate away from print publications as their principle news source. Gannett's flagship newspaper, meanwhile, has suffered deep declines in revenue due to lower levels of spending on print ads by national advertisers. *USA TODAY* also lost its top circulation ranking among US papers during 2009. With its wide-ranging portfolio of mastheads, Gannett ranks ahead of newspaper giants such as McClatchy and Tribune.

The company is largely focused on managing that decline and cutting costs in order to prop up its bottom line. Gannett cut about 1,400 positions from its workforce during 2009, mostly from its community newspaper operations. In addition to layoffs, the company is trying to increase efficiencies through consolidation. Many of its newsrooms have become digital media hubs that create and distribute content to both print and digital media products, resulting in smaller printed editions augmented by more stories appearing online. Some of the company's papers have scaled back print production and delivery even further. Detroit Media Partnership, a joint operating agency (JOA) that oversees the company's *Free Press* and its rival *Detroit News* (owned by MediaNews Group), cut home delivery of the papers to three times a week in 2009.

Largely as a result of its cost containment efforts, Gannett has been able to stabilize its profits even though newspaper revenue continues to decline. Its financial picture has also been helped by improvements in company's broadcasting operations, which account for about 10% of sales. Gannett is also counting on investments in digital media to start to pay off when a general recovery in the economy brings increased spending by advertisers. The company owns several online businesses, including comparison shopping site ShopLocal and online advertising company PointRoll, and it has investments in CareerBuilder (50%), Classified Ventures (24%), and Topix (33%).

HISTORY

In 1906 Frank Gannett started a newspaper empire when he and his associates purchased a stake in New York's *Elmira Gazette*. In 1923 Gannett bought out his associates' interests and formed the Gannett Company. The company's history of technical innovation dates to the 1920s, when Frank Gannett invested in the development of the Teletypesetter; some of his newspapers were printing in color by 1938. The company continued to buy small and midsized dailies in the Northeast, and by Gannett's death in 1957, it had accumulated 30 newspapers.

In the 1960s Gannett expanded nationally through acquisitions. It was not until 1966, however, that it started its own paper, *TODAY* (now *FLORIDA TODAY*), in Cocoa Beach, Florida. Gannett went public in 1967.

The company's greatest period of growth came during the 1970s and 1980s under the direction of Allen Neuharth (CEO from 1973 to 1986). Gannett captured national attention in 1979 when it merged with Phoenix-based Combined Communications Corporation (CCC), whose holdings included TV and radio stations, an outdoor advertising business, and pollster Louis Harris & Associates.

In 1982 Gannett started *USA TODAY,* a national newspaper whose splashy format and mini-stories made it an industry novelty. Critics branded it "McPaper," but circulation passed a million copies a day by the end of 1983. (It wasn't profitable until 1993, however.)

In 1990 declines in newspaper advertising, primarily among US retailers, broke the company's string of 89 consecutive quarters of positive earnings. USA TODAY-On-Demand, a fax news service, began in 1992. Gannett bought Multimedia Inc., a newspaper, TV, cable, and program syndication company, for about $2.3 billion in 1995. Website *USA TODAY Online* debuted in 1995. In 1996 Gannett sold Louis Harris & Associates and its outdoor advertising operations and traded six radio stations to Jacor Communications for one Tampa TV station.

Gannett exited the radio industry in 1998 by selling its last five stations. It also sold its Multimedia Security Service. Gannett's integrity took a blow in 1998 when a reporter for one of its newspapers (*The Cincinnati Enquirer*) illegally obtained information for a report accusing Chiquita Brands International of unscrupulous business practices. Gannett retracted the story and settled with Chiquita to the tune of about $14 million.

The company broke new ground in 1999 when Karen Jurgensen was named editor of *USA TODAY* (she was the first woman to head a national newspaper). In early 2000 Gannett sold its cable operations to Cox Communications for $2.7 billion. The company also formed TV and Web venture USA Today Live to produce news stories for its TV stations. Later that year chairman John Curley passed the title of CEO to president Douglas McCorkindale (McCorkindale would become chair the next year).

Also in 2000 Gannett made a slew of acquisitions, including a purchase of the UK's News Communications & Media, *Arizona Republic* publisher Central Newspapers, and 21 newspapers from Thomson Corp. (now Thomson Reuters). The company moved its headquarters in 2001 from Arlington to McLean, Virginia.

In 2004 Gannett purchased more than 30 newspapers and specialty publications from Brown County Publishing in Wisconsin. Jurgensen stepped down as editor of *USA Today* in the fallout of a scandal involving reporter Jack Kelley. Broadcasting chief Craig Dubow took over as CEO in 2005. In late 2005 Gannett acquired a TV station in Denver (KTVD-TV).

In 2006 McCorkindale retired and Dubow added chairman to his title. Later that year, the company acquired WATL-TV in Atlanta from the Tribune Company for $180 million.

EXECUTIVES

Chairman and CEO: Craig A. Dubow, age 55, $4,698,692 total compensation
President, COO, and Interim CFO: Gracia C. Martore, age 58, $4,018,194 total compensation
SVP Human Resources: Roxanne V. Horning, age 60
SVP Labor Relations: William A. Behan
SVP, General Counsel, and Secretary: Todd A. Mayman
VP and Senior Associate General Counsel: Barbara W. Wall
VP and Treasurer: Michael A. Hart
VP ContentOne: Tara J. Connell
VP Internal Audit: Jane Ann Wimbush
VP Taxes: Sally K. Clurman
VP Digital Content, Digital: Jennifer Carroll
VP and Controller: George R. Gavagan, age 63
VP Sales: Andy Jacobson
VP Planning and Development: Daniel S. Ehrman Jr., age 63
VP Corporate Communications: Robin Pence
President and Publisher, USA TODAY: David L. (Dave) Hunke, age 57, $1,287,497 total compensation
President, US Community Publishing: Robert J. Dickey, age 52, $1,936,591 total compensation
President, Gannett Broadcasting: David (Dave) Lougee, age 51, $1,100,969 total compensation
Director Investor Relations: Jeffrey Heinz
Auditors: Ernst & Young LLP

LOCATIONS

HQ: Gannett Co., Inc.
7950 Jones Branch Dr., McLean, VA 22107
Phone: 703-854-6000   **Fax:** 703-854-2053
Web: www.gannett.com

PRODUCTS/OPERATIONS

2009 Sales

	$ mil.	% of total
Newspapers		
Advertising	2,966.3	53
Circulation	1,167.0	21
Broadcasting	631.1	11
Digital media	586.2	10
Other	262.4	5
Total	**5,613.0**	**100**

Selected Operations

Newspapers
The Arizona Republic (Phoenix)
Asbury Park Press (New Jersey)
The Cincinnati Enquirer
The Courier-Journal (Louisville, KY)
The Des Moines Register (Iowa)
Detroit Free Press
The Indianapolis Star
Rochester Democrat and Chronicle (New York)
The Tennessean (Nashville)
USA TODAY (McLean, VA)
Broadcasting
KARE (NBC, Minneapolis)
KNAZ (NBC; Flagstaff, AZ)
KPNX (NBC, Phoenix)
KSDK (NBC, St. Louis)
KTHV (CBS; Little Rock, AR)
KTVD (MyNetworkTV, Denver)
KUSA (NBC, Denver)
KXTV (ABC; Sacramento, CA)
WATL (MyNetworkTV, Atlanta)
WBIR (NBC, Knoxville, TN)
WCSH (NBC; Portland, ME)
WFMY (CBS; Greensboro, NC)
WGRZ (NBC; Buffalo, NY)
WJXX (ABC; Jacksonville)
WKYC (NBC, Cleveland)
WLBZ (NBC; Bangor, ME)
WLTX (CBS; Columbia, SC)
WMAZ (CBS; Macon, GA)
WTLV (NBC, Jacksonville)
WTSP (CBS, Tampa)
WUSA (CBS; Washington, DC)
WXIA (NBC, Atlanta)
WZZM (ABC; Grand Rapids, MI)
Other holdings and investments
Army Times Publishing Company (newspapers)
California Newspapers Partnership (19%, community newspapers)
Captivate Network (display advertising)
CareerBuilder (51%, online job recruitment)
Classified Ventures (24%, online content publishing)
Clipper Magazine (direct mail advertising)
Gannett Healthcare Group (periodical publishing)
Gannett Media Technologies International (publishing software)
Gannett Offset (commercial printing)
Metromix (51%, local information Web sites)
Newsquest Media Group (newspaper publishing, UK)
Planet Discover (Internet search and advertising)
PointRoll (digital media marketing services)
Ponderay Newsprint (13%)
QuadrantONE (25%, online advertising)
ShopLocal.com (online shopping portal)
Texas-New Mexico Newspapers Partnership (41%, community newspapers)
Topix (34%, online news aggregation)
USA WEEKEND (weekly newspaper insert)

COMPETITORS

Advance Publications	MediaNews
CBS	New York Times
E. W. Scripps	News Corp.
Google	Philadelphia Media
Hearst Corporation	Raycom Media
Lee Enterprises	Sinclair Broadcast Group
Local TV	Tribune Company
McClatchy Company	Washington Post
Media General	Yahoo!

HISTORICAL FINANCIALS

Company Type: Public

Income Statement

FYE: Last Sunday in December

	REVENUE ($ mil.)	NET INCOME ($ mil.)	NET PROFIT MARGIN	EMPLOYEES
12/09	5,613	355	6.3%	35,000
12/08	6,768	(6,648)	—	41,500
12/07	7,440	982	13.2%	46,100
12/06	8,033	1,161	14.4%	49,675
12/05	7,599	1,226	16.1%	52,600
Annual Growth	**(7.3%)**	**(26.6%)**	**—**	**(9.7%)**

2009 Year-End Financials

Debt ratio: 190.9%
Return on equity: 26.7%
Cash ($ mil.): 99
Current ratio: 1.17
Long-term debt ($ mil.): 3,062
No. of shares (mil.): 239
Dividends
  Yield: 1.1%
  Payout: 10.6%
Market value ($ mil.): 3,543

Stock History

NYSE: GCI

	STOCK PRICE ($) FY Close	P/E High/Low	PER SHARE ($) Earnings	Dividends	Book Value
12/09	14.85	11 1	1.51	0.16	6.72
12/08	8.00	— —	(29.11)	1.60	4.43
12/07	39.00	14 8	4.52	1.42	37.80
12/06	60.46	13 11	4.90	1.20	35.14
12/05	60.57	16 12	5.05	1.12	31.73
Annual Growth	**(29.6%)**	**— —**	**(26.1%)**	**(38.5%)**	**(32.2%)**

The Gap

The ubiquitous clothing retailer Gap has been filling closets with jeans and khakis, T-shirts, and poplin since the Woodstock era. The firm, which operates about 3,100 stores worldwide, built its iconic casual brand on basics for men, women, and children, but over the years has expanded through the urban chic chain Banana Republic, budgeteer Old Navy, online-only retailer Piperlime, and Athleta, a purveyor of activewear via catalog. Other brand extensions include GapBody, GapKids, and babyGap; each also has its own online incarnation. All Gap clothing is private-label merchandise made exclusively for the company. From the design board to store displays, Gap controls all aspects of its trademark casual look.

After five consecutive years of declining sales, failed turnaround attempts, and fashion missteps, the nation's largest specialty apparel retailer is struggling to reverse the trend in a hostile retail environment. Under the leadership of CEO Glenn Murphy, who joined Gap in 2007 from the Canadian drugstore chain Shoppers Drug Mart, Gap has reduced its US store count while expanding cautiously in Europe and Asia.

A bright spot for Gap has been the improved performance of Old Navy. Indeed, Old Navy outsold the company's namesake Gap chain in 2009 posting sales of $5.8 billion vs. $5.6 billion at The Gap. Apparently, Old Navy's focus on value-priced family clothing is striking the right cord among budget-conscious shoppers.

In a bid to regain its merchandising edge, the company has made revamping its Gap-brand women's apparel collection a top priority. To that end, in fall 2008 the company acquired 10-year-old Athleta, a direct-marketer of women's active wear. Gap purchased Athleta as part of its strategy to diversify its brand offerings and upgrade women's apparel. Gap sells Athleta's merchandise online as the fifth brand in its e-commerce portfolio, which includes its namesake brand, Old Navy, Banana Republic, and Piperlime. Gap has also replaced its chief designer for Gap brand clothing, added petite and tall sizes, and redesigned its Spartan look-alike stores in an attempt to win back shoppers with a more homey atmosphere.

On the international front, the company plans to open its first Gap store in China, as well as adjacent Gap and Banana Republic locations in Milan's main shopping district in 2010. After opening stores in Paris and London, the chain has chosen Italy as the next focus of its European expansion, with stores slated to open in other Italian cities (including Rome in 2011). Closer to home, Gap in 2009 began opening stores inside Mexico's leading department store chain, Distribuidora Liverpool, via a franchise agreement.

The founding Fisher family owns about a third of Gap Inc.

HISTORY

Donald Fisher and his wife, Doris, opened a small store in 1969 near what is now San Francisco State University. The couple named their store The Gap (after "the generation gap") and concentrated on selling Levi's jeans. The couple opened a second store in San Jose, California, eight months later, and by the end of 1970 there were six Gap stores. The Gap went public six years later.

In the beginning the Fishers catered almost exclusively to teenagers, but in the 1970s they expanded into activewear that would appeal to a larger spectrum of customers. Nevertheless, by the early 1980s The Gap — which had grown to about 500 stores — was still dependent upon its largely teenage customer base. However, it was less dependent on Levi's (about 35% of sales), thanks to its growing stable of private labels.

In a 1983 effort to revamp the company's image, Donald hired Mickey Drexler, a former president of AnnTaylor with a spotless apparel industry track record, as The Gap's new president. Drexler immediately overhauled the motley clothing lines to concentrate on sturdy, brightly colored cotton clothing. He also consolidated the stores' many private clothing labels into the Gap brand.

Also in 1983 The Gap bought Banana Republic, a unique chain of jungle-themed stores that sold safari clothing. The company expanded the chain, which enjoyed tremendous success in the mid-1980s but slumped after the novelty of the stores wore off late in the decade. In response, Drexler introduced a broader range of clothes (including higher-priced leather items) and dumped the safari lines in 1988. By 1990 Banana Republic was again profitable.

The first GapKids opened in 1985 after Drexler couldn't find clothing that he liked for his son. During the late 1980s and early 1990s, the company grew rapidly, opening its first stores in Canada and the UK. In 1990 it introduced baby-Gap in 25 GapKids stores, featuring miniature versions of its GapKids line. The Gap announced in 1991 it would no longer sell Levi's (which had fallen to less than 2% of total sales) and would sell nothing but private-label items.

In 1994 the company launched Old Navy Clothing Co., named after a bar Drexler saw in Paris. Banana Republic opened its first two stores outside the US, both in Canada, in 1995.

Robert Fisher (the founders' son) became the new president of the Gap division (including babyGap and GapKids) in 1997 and was charged with reversing the segment's sales decline. The company refocused its Gap chain on basics (jeans, T-shirts, and khakis) and helped boost its performance with a high-profile advertising campaign focusing on those wares. Later in 1997 the Gap opened an online Gap store.

In late 1999, amid sluggish Gap division sales, Robert Fisher resigned and Drexler took over his duties. Gap misjudged fashion trends in 2000, which resulted in two years of disappointing earnings. After a 10% reduction in its workforce, the company returned to a more conservative fashion approach.

In 2002 Drexler retired and was replaced by Paul Pressler, a veteran of The Walt Disney Company. In 2006 Gap entered into a 10-year non-exclusive services agreement with International Business Machines valued at $1.1 billion.

Stung by allegations in the British press of forced child labor in India being used in the manufacture of apparel for its Gap Kids chain, Gap in 2007 announced a package of measures intended to strengthen its commitment to eradicating the exploitation of children in the garment industry. In 2008 Gap acquired Athleta, a direct-marketer of women's active wear.

Don Fisher, Gap co-founder, died in September 2009 at the age of 81.

EXECUTIVES

Chairman and CEO: Glenn K. Murphy, age 48, $5,037,290 total compensation
EVP and CFO: Sabrina Simmons, age 46, $4,378,005 total compensation
EVP and CIO: John T. (Tom) Keiser, age 44
EVP, Gap Kids and Baby: Mark Breitbard, age 41
EVP Design, Gap Adult and Body: Patrick Robinson
EVP Global Human Resources and Corporate Affairs: Eva Sage-Gavin, age 51
EVP Strategy and Operations; President, Gap Inc. Outlet: Arthur (Art) Peck, age 54, $3,906,098 total compensation
Chief Creative Officer and EVP New Business Development, Old Navy: Nancy Green, age 47
SVP, General Counsel, Secretary, and Chief Compliance Officer: Michelle Banks, age 46
SVP Global Responsibility: Dan Henkle
SVP Marketing, Old Navy: Amy Curtis-McIntyre
SVP Global Sourcing: Stanley P. (Stan) Raggio, age 52
SVP Global Real Estate: C. David Zoba, age 58
President, Old Navy: John T. (Tom) Wyatt, age 54, $3,717,683 total compensation
President, Gap North America: Marka Hansen, age 55, $3,843,591 total compensation
President, Gap Inc. Direct: Toby Lenk
President, Europe and International Strategic Alliances: Stephen (Steve) Sunnucks
President, Banana Republic: Jack Calhoun, age 45
President, Asia/Pacific: John Ermatinger
Chief Foundation Officer, Gap Foundation: Roberta H. (Bobbi) Silten, age 47
Investor Relations: Aina Konold
Auditors: Deloitte & Touche LLP

LOCATIONS

HQ: The Gap, Inc.
2 Folsom St., San Francisco, CA 94105
Phone: 650-952-4400
Web: www.gap.com

2010 Sales

	$ mil.	% of total
Retail		
US	10,491	74
Asia	928	7
Canada	860	6
Europe	743	5
Other regions	57	—
Direct (US only)	1,118	8
Total	**14,197**	**100**

2010 Stores

	No.
North America	2,767
Europe	181
Asia	147
Total	**3,095**

PRODUCTS/OPERATIONS

2010 Stores

	No.
Gap North America	1,152
Old Navy North America	1,039
Banana Republic North America	576
Gap Europe	178
Gap Asia	120
Banana Republic Asia	27
Banana Republic Europe	3
Total	**3,095**

2010 Sales

	$ mil.	% of total
Old Navy	5,808	41
Gap	5,601	40
Banana Republic	2,460	17
Other	328	2
Total	**14,197**	**100**

Selected Stores and Brands

Athleta (women's activewear)
babyGap (clothing for infants and toddlers)
Banana Republic (upscale clothing and accessories)
Gap (casual and active clothing and body care products)
GapBody (intimate apparel)
GapKids (clothing for children)
Old Navy (lower-priced family clothing)
Piperlime (online shoes)

COMPETITORS

Abercrombie & Fitch	Lands' End
Aéropostale	Levi Strauss
American Eagle Outfitters	L.L. Bean
AnnTaylor	Macy's
Arcadia	Marks & Spencer
Babies "R" Us	Nautica Apparel
Benetton	NIKE
Calvin Klein	Nordstrom
The Children's Place	OshKosh B'Gosh
Dillard's	Phillips-Van Heusen
Express LLC	Polo Ralph Lauren
Fast Retailing	Reebok
Foot Locker	REI
Fruit of the Loom	Retail Brand Alliance
Guess?	Ross Stores
Gymboree	Saks
H&M	Sears
HSN	Talbots
Inditex	Target
J. C. Penney	TJX Companies
J. Crew	VF
Juicy Couture	Wal-Mart
Kohl's	Zappos.com

HISTORICAL FINANCIALS

Company Type: Public

Income Statement

FYE: Saturday nearest January 31

	REVENUE ($ mil.)	NET INCOME ($ mil.)	NET PROFIT MARGIN	EMPLOYEES
1/10	14,197	1,102	7.8%	135,000
1/09	14,526	967	6.7%	134,000
1/08	15,763	833	5.3%	150,000
1/07	15,943	778	4.9%	154,000
1/06	16,023	1,113	6.9%	153,000
Annual Growth	(3.0%)	(0.2%)	—	(3.1%)

2010 Year-End Financials

Debt ratio: —
Return on equity: 23.8%
Cash ($ mil.): 2,348
Current ratio: 2.19
Long-term debt ($ mil.): —
No. of shares (mil.): 651
Dividends
 Yield: 1.8%
 Payout: 21.5%
Market value ($ mil.): 12,413

Stock History

NYSE: GPS

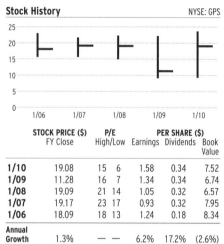

	STOCK PRICE ($) FY Close	P/E High/Low		PER SHARE ($) Earnings	Dividends	Book Value
1/10	19.08	15	6	1.58	0.34	7.52
1/09	11.28	16	7	1.34	0.34	6.74
1/08	19.09	21	14	1.05	0.32	6.57
1/07	19.17	23	17	0.93	0.32	7.95
1/06	18.09	18	13	1.24	0.18	8.34
Annual Growth	1.3%	—	—	6.2%	17.2%	(2.6%)

General Cable

With General Cable, you can keep the lights on and call if the power goes out. The company makes a comprehensive line of aluminum, copper, and fiber-optic wire and cable products, primarily sold to OEMs and distributors in the communications, construction, electric utility, and electrical infrastructure markets. Commercial and industrial applications include electrical distribution and transmission, voice and data communications, and power generation. Brand names include BICC, Carol, and NextGen. The company also makes flexible cords for temporary power and custom wire harnesses for any industry using wires and connectors.

Local customer bases around the world are handled through regional operations in three geographic segments: North America, Europe and North Africa, and Rest of World (consisting of Latin America, Asia/Pacific, sub-Saharan Africa, and the Middle East). The company sees long-term growth opportunities in emerging markets. Countries such as Brazil, South Africa, and Thailand are investing heavily in electrical infrastructure, electric utility development, and residential and non-residential construction projects.

General Cable is keeping an eye out for acquisitions: cash-strapped companies with limited access to capital are targets for a company looking for opportunities to expand. In early 2010 General Cable bought BERU SAS, a subsidiary of BorgWarner in France. BERU SAS, now operating as General Cable Automotive Europe, makes ignition wire harnesses for European automakers. The purchase supports General Cable's strategy to expand geographically in the increasingly global market for automotive components. In 2009 General Cable acquired cable products and systems provider Gepco International and the specialty electronic cable business of Isotec.

General Cable has also continued to expand in Sub-Saharan Africa. In 2010 the company acquired about 90% of South Africa-based Phoenix Power Cables, a maker of low and medium voltage power cables and overhead energy transmission and distribution cables. The company also owns a majority interest in National Cables, one of South Africa's biggest cable distributors.

HISTORY

General Cable originated from some of the oldest names in the wiring business: Standard Underground Cable (founded by George Westinghouse) and Phillips Wire and Safety Cable Company, both founded in the 1800s. The companies supplied wire for historic events such as Samuel Morse's first telegram between Baltimore and Washington, DC, in 1844, the lighting the Statue of Liberty in 1886, and the first Chicago World's Fair in 1892.

The company's best-known brand of nonmetallic sheathed cable, Romex, was invented at the company's Rome, New York, facility in 1922. Five years later, Phillips Wire and Standard Underground Cable joined to form General Cable Corporation. In 1935 the company's cables were used for power lines connecting the Hoover Dam to Los Angeles.

In the early 1980s the company was purchased by Penn Central Corporation (now known as American Premier Underwriters, part of American Financial Group). Later that decade Penn Central added the Carol brand when it purchased the Carol Cable Company (1989) and bought other wiring companies. The construction industry declined in the early 1990s, leaving wire inventories overstocked. In 1992 Penn Central spun off General Cable to shareholders, but the Lindner family (which owned Penn Central) continued to control most of the stock. The company also made news in 1992 when it moved its corporate headquarters from Cincinnati to northern Kentucky, representing a win in the battle for companies being waged between the bordering states. That year General Cable also sold its equipment-making subsidiary, Marathon LeTourneau, because it was not directly tied to the wire and cable business.

In 1994 Wassall, a British holding company, bought General Cable, which had lost more than $130 million in the previous two years. (Wassall sold its interest in 1997.) Soon afterward the company hired a new CEO, Stephen Rabinowitz, who had been president of General Electric's electrical distribution and control unit and president of the braking-systems business of AlliedSignal (now Honeywell International). He began integrating the company's many units, which previously had been run separately. He also consolidated the company's distribution sites and closed five manufacturing plants.

General Cable went public in 1997. That year it formed a joint venture with glass company Spectran Corporation (since acquired by Lucent) to create fiber-optic cable under the name General Photonics. In 1999 General Cable bought the energy cable businesses of BICC Plc for $440 million. The deal made General Cable one of the largest makers of wire and cable in the world. (The company briefly operated under the BICCGeneral name.)

When its energy cable businesses in Europe, Africa, and Asia failed to perform up to expectations, General Cable agreed to sell some of those businesses (in the UK, Italy, Africa, and Asia) to Italy-based Pirelli for $216 million in 2000. Fearing Pirelli's dominant position, the European Commission opened an in-depth investigation of the takeover, but the deal was approved and completed later that year.

In 2002 General Cable acquired the New Zealand-based data cable manufacturer Brand-Rex from Novar plc. Later that same year General Cable sold its building wire operations to Southwire Company.

In Europe it bought Silec in late 2005, which had been the wire and cable business of SAFRAN. The following year the company acquired French power cable maker E.C.N. Cable Group.

The company expanded into China in 2007 with the acquisition of Jiangyin Huaming Specialty Cable, which makes automotive and industrial cables.

As part of its global expansion into energy and electrical infrastructure markets, the company acquired Phelps Dodge International Corporation, the cable and wire operations of Freeport-McMoRan Copper & Gold Inc., for about $740 million in 2007. The acquisition gave it a significant foothold in emerging markets, including China, India, and parts of Africa.

The company continued to expand its geographic presence in 2008 when it partnered with the Algerian government to acquire a majority stake in Enica Biskra, a cable manufacturer previously run by the state. Adding to its interest for growing business in Southeast Asia, General Cable upped its stake in Phelps Dodge Philippines from 40% to 60% the same year.

EXECUTIVES

Chairman: John E. Welsh III, age 59
President, CEO, and Director: Gregory B. Kenny, age 57, $3,822,998 total compensation
EVP, CFO, and Treasurer: Brian J. Robinson, age 41, $1,288,970 total compensation
EVP, General Counsel, and Secretary: Robert J. Siverd, age 61, $1,340,300 total compensation
EVP Global Sales and Business Development: Roderick (Roddy) Macdonald, age 61, $1,046,956 total compensation
EVP General Cable Rest of World; President and CEO, Phelps Dodge International Corporation: Mathias F. Sandoval, age 49, $1,335,672 total compensation
EVP and Managing Director, Grupo General Sistemas, SA: Domingo Goenaga, age 68, $2,061,028 total compensation
EVP; President and CEO, General Cable North America: Gregory J. (Greg) Lampert, age 42, $1,279,862 total compensation
EVP; CEO and President, Europe and Mediterranean Region: Emmanuel Sabonnadiere
VP Finance, Investor Relations, and Corporate Development: Michael P. Dickerson
Auditors: Deloitte & Touche LLP

LOCATIONS

HQ: General Cable Corporation
 4 Tesseneer Dr., Highland Heights, KY 41076
Phone: 859-572-8000   **Fax:** 859-572-8458
Web: www.generalcable.com

2009 Sales

	$ mil.	% of total
Europe & North Africa	1,562.7	36
North America	1,484.6	34
Other regions	1,337.9	30
Total	**4,385.2**	**100**

PRODUCTS/OPERATIONS

2009 Sales

	$ mil.	% of total
Electric utility	1,494.4	34
Electrical infrastructure	1,095.2	25
Construction	1,008.5	23
Communications	626.1	14
Rod Mill products	161.0	4
Total	**4,385.2**	**100**

Selected Products and Brands

Automotive ignition wire and battery starter cables
Cord, cordsets, and portable power cables (Carol)
Data communications cables (GenSPEED)
Electric utility cables (BICC)
Electronic cables for audio/video, computers, microphones, and security and fire systems (Carol)
Fiber-optic cables for voice, video, and data networks (NextGen)
Industrial instrumentation, power, and control cables (FREP, UniShield, VNTC)
Military power, control, signal, and communications cable (Brand Rex)
Mining cables (Anaconda)
Nuclear cables (Brand Rex)
Office switchboard and digital transmission cables
Offshore and marine shipboard wire and cables
Telecommunications cables
Transit cables
Wire harnesses and assemblies

COMPETITORS

Belden
Coleman Cable
CommScope
Corning
Encore Wire
Hubbell
Kalas Manufacturing
LEONI
Nexans
Owl Wire & Cable
Quabbin Wire
Southwire
Sumitomo Electric
Superior Essex
Volex

HISTORICAL FINANCIALS

Company Type: Public

Income Statement

FYE: December 31

	REVENUE ($ mil.)	NET INCOME ($ mil.)	NET PROFIT MARGIN	EMPLOYEES
12/09	4,385	109	2.5%	11,300
12/08	6,230	217	3.5%	13,000
12/07	4,615	209	4.5%	11,800
12/06	3,665	135	3.7%	7,700
12/05	2,381	39	1.6%	7,300
Annual Growth	**16.5%**	**29.0%**	**—**	**11.5%**

2009 Year-End Financials

Debt ratio: 68.6%
Return on equity: 11.0%
Cash ($ mil.): 499
Current ratio: 2.08
Long-term debt ($ mil.): 869

No. of shares (mil.): 52
Dividends
  Yield: 0.0%
  Payout: —
Market value ($ mil.): 1,533

Stock History

NYSE: BGC

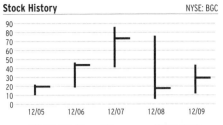

	STOCK PRICE ($) FY Close	P/E High/Low		PER SHARE ($) Earnings	Dividends	Book Value
12/09	29.42	21	6	2.06	0.00	24.38
12/08	17.69	18	2	4.07	0.00	13.60
12/07	73.28	22	11	3.82	0.00	12.50
12/06	43.71	17	8	2.60	0.00	8.34
12/05	19.70	51	27	0.41	0.00	5.63
Annual Growth	**10.5%**	**—**	**—**	**49.7%**	**—**	**44.3%**

General Dynamics

General Dynamics brings it on — by land, air, and sea. The company is a prime military contractor to the Pentagon (the US government accounts for more than 70% of sales). General Dynamics' military operations include Information Systems & Technology (information technology and collection, and command control systems); Marine Systems (warships, commercial tankers, and nuclear submarines); and Combat Systems (tanks, amphibious assault vehicles, munitions, ammunition/ordnance, and chemical/biohazard detection products). Its Aerospace unit, which is composed of Gulfstream Aerospace, Jet Aviation, and General Dynamics Aviation Services, designs, manufactures, and refurbishes business jets primarily for civilian customers.

Though the war in Iraq is starting to wind down, the conflict in Afghanistan is heating up, and the US Department of Defense (DoD) is appropriating its budgetary support accordingly. Allocations for combat warfare equipment are being cut; however, advanced sensors, communications, cyber security, logistics, unmanned reconnaissance vehicles, and other high-tech systems — which increase the flexibility, speed, and precision of the military — are getting increased funding.

General Dynamics manufactures both combat systems and high-tech systems — each side buffering the other in times of market downturn. The company's Combat Systems group realized a 15% increase in 2009 revenues year-over-year, but it was the Information Systems and Technology (IS&T) unit that generated the most revenue. In fact, all of the company's military segments showed an increase in sales. The global economic recession had a negative impact on the company's Aerospace division, which caters primarily to a non-military clientele; however, revenues from aircraft services in 2010 are expected to experience a slight increase due to the addition of Jet Aviation Management's maintenance and repair activities, fixed based operations, and aircraft management services.

Switzerland-based Jet Aviation Management was acquired for more than $2 billion in late 2008. Jet Aviation, which provides aviation services such as repairs, overhauls, and fixed base operations, maintains facilities in 20 locations worldwide, including Asia, Europe, the Middle East, and the US.

The Combat Systems division is composed of Armament and Technical Products, European Land Systems, and Land Systems. In 2010 a fourth unit, Ordnance and Tactical Systems acquired EBV Explosives Environmental, a company that disposes of munitions and explosives. EBV, which is based in Missouri, will be known as General Dynamics Ordnance and Tactical Systems – Munition Services.

Executing a major coup for its Combat Systems group, General Dynamics UK's division won the £500 million (almost $800 million) UK Ministry of Defense (MoD) contract in mid-2010 to develop a medium-weight armored fighting vehicle for the British Army.

Combat Systems provides logistics support to the US in its Middle East operations, as well as armor and weapons-systems, such as the M2 heavy machine gun and the MK19 and MK47 grenade launchers, 120mm mortars, and conventional bomb structures. It also outfits US fighter aircraft with high-speed Gatling guns. The division produces the Stryker wheeled combat vehicle and the Abrams battle tank and is the primary contractor for the maintenance and repair of the vehicles. Additionally, the division has a contract to design and test the Expeditionary Fighting Vehicle for the Marine Corps and expects to deliver prototypes in 2010.

The Marine Systems group is one of two primary shipbuilders for the US Navy, and it provides MRO (maintenance, repair, and overhaul) services to keep those vessels ship-shape. Marine Systems manufactures the Virginia-class nuclear-powered submarine, the Arleigh Burke-class guided-missile destroyer, and the Lewis and Clark-class dry cargo/ammunition combat-logistics ship. Subsidiary Electric Boat builds nuclear submarines (Seawolf, Ohio, and Los Angeles classes), while Bath Iron Works builds DDG 51 destroyers and LPD 17 landing craft. In 2009 the company's subsidiary Electric Boat was awarded an $18 million contract by the Naval Sea System Command for reactor plant services to support nuclear-powered submarines.

The company's IS&T business unit provides cyber security, fixed/mobile radio/satellite communications systems, ruggedized computers (for use in harsh environments, such as those with strong vibrations, extreme temperatures, and wet or dusty conditions), and antennas to customers in the DoD, the Department of Homeland Security, the intelligence community, federal civilian agencies, and international customers. In late 2009 the unit snagged a five-year $140 million order to provide information technology support services to the US Coast Guard's Telecommunication Information Systems Command. The acquisition in 2009 of Axsys Technologies (for $643 million) brings surveillance and imaging systems that gives General Dynamics an entrée into the government infrared sector. The IS&T unit expanded its geographic scope in mid-2010 with the acquisition of Klymar, a UK-based sensor and optical surveillances system manufacturer.

HISTORY

In 1899 John Holland founded Electric Boat Company, a New Jersey ship and submarine builder. The company built ships, PT boats, and submarines during WWII, but faced with waning postwar orders, CEO John Jay Hopkins diversified with the 1947 purchase of aircraft builder Canadair. Hopkins formed General Dynamics in 1952, merging Electric Boat and Canadair and buying Consolidated Vultee Aircraft (Convair), a major producer of military and civilian aircraft, in 1954.

Electric Boat launched the first nuclear submarine, the *Nautilus*, in the mid-1950s. In 1955, at the urging of Howard Hughes, Convair began designing its first commercial jetliners. Weakened by the planes' production costs, General Dynamics merged with building-materials supplier Material Service Corporation (1959). Nuclear subs became a mainstay for the company, and it abandoned jetliners in 1961 after losses on the planes reached the staggering sum of $425 million.

During the 1960s General Dynamics developed the controversial F-111 fighter. Despite numerous problems, the aircraft proved financially and militarily successful (F-111s participated in the 1986 US bombing raid on Libya).

In the following years the company won contracts for the US Navy's 688-class attack submarine (1971), liquefied natural gas tankers for Burmah Oil Company (1972), the Trident ballistic-missile submarine (1974), and the F-16 lightweight fighter aircraft (1975). The company sold Canadair in 1976 and bought Chrysler Defense, which had a contract to build the US Army's new M1 tank, in 1982.

The company bought Cessna Aircraft in 1986. The next year it won a contract to design and build the upper stage of the Titan IV space-launch rocket. Facing defense cuts, General Dynamics sold off pieces of the company: In 1992 it sold Cessna Aircraft to Textron and sold its missile operations to Hughes Aircraft; its electronics business was sold to The Carlyle Group in 1993. The company sold its space-systems business to Martin Marietta in 1994.

The next year General Dynamics began a buying spree with the purchase of shipbuilder Bath Iron Works. In 1996 it added Teledyne's combat vehicle unit, followed in 1997 by Lockheed Martin's Defense Systems and Armament Systems units and defense electronics units from Ceridian and Lucent. Also that year Nicholas Chabraja, director of Ceridian and former general counsel for General Dynamics, became CEO.

In 1999 General Dynamics bought business-jet maker Gulfstream Aerospace. In 2001 it bought Galaxy Aerospace, adding midsize aircraft to its Gulfstream lineup. Additionally, General Dynamics acquired Empresa Nacional Santa Bárbara de Industrias Militares (ENSB) of Spain.

General Dynamics sold its space propulsion and fire suppression operations to Aerojet-General in 2002. The next year it acquired General Motors' armored vehicle operations (for about $1.1 billion) and Austria's Steyr Spezialfahrzeug, maker of the Pandur line of wheeled armored vehicles. General Dynamics also acquired government security and intelligence specialist Veridian for about $1.5 billion in 2003.

In 2005 General Dynamics sold its aeronautics services business, which provides aeronautic testing, engineering, and support services, to Wyle Laboratories. Late in 2005 subsidiary Electric Boat said it would cut 2,400 jobs.

In 2006 General Dynamics also acquired IT specialist Anteon International for $2.1 billion. In 2008 it purchased AxleTech International, a Carlyle Group-owned manufacturer of axles and other suspension components used in military and off-road heavy vehicles.

EXECUTIVES

Chairman and CEO: Jay L. Johnson, age 64, $12,779,796 total compensation
EVP Information Systems and Technology: Gerard J. (Jerry) DeMuro, age 54, $4,447,202 total compensation
EVP Marine Systems: Phebe N. Novakovic, age 52
EVP Combat Systems: David K. Heebner, age 65
EVP Aerospace; President, Gulfstream Aerospace: Joseph T. (Joe) Lombardo, age 62
SVP and CFO: L. Hugh Redd, age 52, $4,727,966 total compensation
SVP Planning and Development: Robert W. Helm, age 58
SVP, General Counsel, and Corporate Secretary: Gregory S. (Greg) Gallopoulos, age 50
SVP Human Resources and Administration: Walter M. Oliver, age 64
VP; President, Advanced Information Systems: Lewis A. Von Thaer, age 49
VP; President, Bath Iron Works: Jeffrey S. Geiger, age 48
VP; President, General Dynamics C4 Systems: Christopher (Chris) Marzilli, age 50
VP; President, European Land Systems: John C. Ulrich
VP; President, Electric Boat: John P. Casey, age 55
VP; President, National Steel and Shipbuilding Company: Frederick J. (Fred) Harris, age 63
VP; President, General Dynamics Land Systems: Mark C. Roualet, age 51
VP; President, Armament and Technical Products: Michael J. Mulligan, age 45
VP; President, Ordnance and Tactical Systems: Michael S. Wilson, age 60
VP; President, General Dynamics Information Technology: S. Daniel (Dan) Johnson, age 62
VP Strategic Planning: Marion T. (Tom) Davis
Staff VP Investor Relations: Amy Gilliland
Staff VP Communications: Rob Doolittle
President, American Overseas Marine: Capt. Thomas W. Merrell
Auditors: KPMG LLP

LOCATIONS

HQ: General Dynamics Corporation
2941 Fairview Park Dr., Ste. 100
Falls Church, VA 22042
Phone: 703-876-3000   **Fax:** 703-876-3125
Web: www.gendyn.com

2009 Sales

	$ mil.	% of total
North America		
US	26,017	81
Canada	760	2
Other countries	33	—
Europe		
Switzerland	748	2
UK	614	2
Spain	529	2
Other countries	1,226	4
Asia/Pacific	1,154	4
Africa/Middle East	637	2
South America	263	1
Total	**31,981**	**100**

PRODUCTS/OPERATIONS

2009 Sales

	$ mil.	% of total
Information systems & technology	10,802	34
Combat systems	9,645	30
Marine systems	6,363	20
Aerospace	5,171	16
Total	**31,981**	**100**

2009 Sales

	% of total
US government	71
US commercial	10
International commercial	10
International defense	9
Total	**100**

Selected Operations

Aerospace
  Gulfstream Aerospace
    G150 (Midsize, range of 2,950 nautical miles, 4 passengers)
    G200 (Large-cabin, range of 3,400 nautical miles, 4 passengers)
    G350 (Large-cabin, range of 3,800 nautical miles, 8 passengers)
    G450 (Large-cabin, range of 4,350 nautical miles, 8 passengers)
    G500 (Large-cabin, range of 5,800 nautical miles, 8 passengers)
    G550 (Large-cabin, range of 6,750 nautical miles, 8 passengers)
Combat systems
  Armament Systems
    Advanced materials (composites)
    Detection systems (biological and chemical detection systems)
    Guns and munitions systems
    Hydra 70 2.75" air-to-ground rocket
  Land systems
    Advanced Amphibious Assault Vehicle (AAAV)
    M1A1 and M1A2 Abrams Main Battle Tank
    Pandur 6x6 and 8x8 wheeled armored vehicles
    Stryker Mobile Gun System
  Ordnance and tactical systems
    Electronic products
    Munitions
    Propellants
    Satellite propulsion systems
Information systems and technology
  Actionable intelligence, surveillance, and reconnaissance
  Homeland security
  Information assurance
  Integrated space systems
  Maritime combat systems
Marine systems
  American Overseas Marine (ship-management services)
  Bath Iron Works Corp.
    Arleigh Burke class DDG 51 destroyer
    Class DD 21 land attack destroyer
    Class LPD 17 amphibious assault transport
  Electric Boat Corp.
    New Attack submarine (Virginia class)
    Seawolf attack submarine
  General Dynamics Defense Systems, Inc.
  National Steel and Shipbuilding Company

COMPETITORS

Airbus	ITT Corp.
Alliant Techsystems	L-3 Communications
BAE SYSTEMS	Lockheed Martin
Boeing	Navistar International
Bombardier	Northrop Grumman
Dassault Aviation	Peugeot
Day & Zimmerman	Raytheon
DRS Technologies	Renco
FLIR Systems	Rockwell Collins
Goodrich Corp.	SAIC
Harris Corp.	Textron
Herley Industries	United Technologies
HP Enterprise Services	

HISTORICAL FINANCIALS

Company Type: Public

Income Statement

FYE: December 31

	REVENUE ($ mil.)	NET INCOME ($ mil.)	NET PROFIT MARGIN	EMPLOYEES
12/09	31,981	2,394	7.5%	91,700
12/08	29,300	2,459	8.4%	92,300
12/07	27,240	2,072	7.6%	83,500
12/06	24,063	1,856	7.7%	81,000
12/05	21,244	1,461	6.9%	72,200
Annual Growth	10.8%	13.1%	—	6.2%

2009 Year-End Financials

Debt ratio: 25.4%
Return on equity: 21.3%
Cash ($ mil.): 2,263
Current ratio: 1.28
Long-term debt ($ mil.): 3,159

No. of shares (mil.): 380
Dividends
  Yield: 2.2%
  Payout: 24.1%
Market value ($ mil.): 25,930

Stock History

NYSE: GD

	STOCK PRICE ($) FY Close	P/E High/Low		PER SHARE ($) Earnings	Dividends	Book Value
12/09	68.17	11	6	6.17	1.49	32.66
12/08	57.59	15	8	6.17	1.34	26.43
12/07	88.99	19	14	5.08	1.10	30.94
12/06	74.35	17	12	4.56	0.89	25.84
12/05	57.03	17	14	3.61	0.78	21.41
Annual Growth	4.6%	—	—	14.3%	17.6%	11.1%

General Electric

From turbines to TV, from household appliances to power plants, General Electric (GE) is plugged in to businesses that have shaped the modern world. The company produces — take a deep breath — aircraft engines, locomotives and other transportation equipment, kitchen and laundry appliances, lighting, electric distribution and control equipment, generators and turbines, and medical imaging equipment. GE is also one of the US's pre-eminent financial services providers. GE Capital, comprising commercial finance, commercial aircraft leasing, real estate, and energy financial services, is its largest segment. GE's other segments are Energy, Technology Infrastructure, NBC Universal, and GE Home & Business Solutions.

The company's financial services businesses took the largest hit in 2009. Amid uncertainty in the markets, GE plans to reduce its reliance on its riskier financial businesses and make further acquisitions in its infrastructure and health care sectors. It also intends to tighten lending practices to cut costs. In 2010 GE reorganized, recommitting to its appliances and lighting businesses with the creation of the Home & Business Solutions segment.

Further narrowing its focus on its industrial and manufacturing businesses, GE sold its security business to United Technologies Corporation (UTC) in 2010 and has arranged to sell a controlling stake of NBC Universal to cable systems operator Comcast. If the latter deal is approved, GE and Comcast will form a media group joint venture combining the NBC Universal businesses and Comcast's cable and regional sports networks. The venture will be 51% owned by Comcast and 49% owned by GE. (French media and telecom group Vivendi will sell its 20% interest in NBC Universal to GE to facilitate the transaction.)

In 2010 GE agreed to pay nearly $24 million to settle Securities and Exchange Commission charges. The SEC alleged that GE subsidiaries paid kickbacks in the early 2000s in order to receive special contracts for work in Iraq.

On the health care front, GE is partnering with Intel to develop products that will lower costs for at-home and assisted-living care. The venture will focus on chronic-disease management and independent living technologies.

CEO Jeff Immelt is obviously not shy about making sweeping changes. He has emerged from the considerable shadow of his predecessor, Jack Welch, by diverging somewhat from Welch's slavish obsession with the bottom line and encouraging managers to innovate and take more risks. As a result, GE has been growing in such areas as biotech, renewable energy, nanotechnology, and digital technology. In response to the poor performance of the financial segment, he didn't take a cash bonus for the years 2008 and 2009.

HISTORY

General Electric (GE) was established in 1892 in New York, the result of a merger between Thomson-Houston and Edison General Electric. Charles Coffin was GE's first president, and Thomas Edison, who left the company in 1894, was one of the directors.

GE's financial strength (backed by the Morgan banking house) and its research focus contributed to its initial success. Early products included such Edison legacies as light bulbs, elevators, motors, toasters, and other appliances under the GE and Hotpoint labels. In the 1920s GE joined AT&T and Westinghouse in a radio broadcasting venture, Radio Corporation of America (RCA), but GE sold off its RCA holdings in 1930 because of an antitrust ruling.

By 1980 GE had reached $25 billion in revenues from plastics, consumer electronics, nuclear reactors, and jet engines. But it had become rigid and bureaucratic. Jack Welch became president in 1981 and shook up the company. He decentralized operations and adopted a strategy of pursuing only high-achieving ventures and dumping those that didn't perform. GE shed air-conditioning (1982), housewares (1984), and semiconductors (1988), and with the proceeds acquired Employers Reinsurance (1984); RCA, including NBC (1986, but sold RCA in 1987); CGR medical equipment (1987); and investment banker Kidder, Peabody (1990).

In the early 1990s GE grew its lighting business. It bought mutual fund wholesaler GNA in 1993, and GE Investment Management (now GE Financial Network) began selling mutual funds to the public.

GE sold scandal-plagued Kidder, Peabody to Paine Webber in 1994. General Electric Capital Services (GECS) expanded its lines, buying

Amex Life Insurance (Aon's Union Fidelity unit) and Life Insurance Co. of Virginia in 1995 and First Colony the next year. The company sold its struggling GEnie online service in 1996 and formed an NBC and Microsoft venture, the MSNBC cable news channel. In 1997 GE Engine Services bought aircraft engine maintenance firms Greenwich Air Services and UNC. In 1998 GECS became the first foreign company to enter Japan's life insurance market when it bought assets from Toho Mutual Life Insurance and set up GE Edison Life.

In 1999 GECS bought the 53% of Montgomery Ward it didn't already own, along with the retailer's direct-marketing arm, as Montgomery Ward emerged from bankruptcy.

In 2000 the company announced its biggest acquisition of the Welch era. Moving in at the last minute, GE trumped a rival bid from United Technologies and agreed to pay $45 billion in stock for manufacturing giant Honeywell International and to assume $3.4 billion in Honeywell debt.

Welch, by then viewed as one of the best corporate leaders in the US, had agreed to postpone his retirement from April 2001 until the end of that year in order to oversee the completion of the Honeywell acquisition. But European regulators, concerned about the potential strength of the combined GE-Honeywell aircraft-related businesses, blocked the Honeywell deal that summer. Welch then stepped down, and Jeff Immelt, formerly CEO of GE Medical Systems, succeeded him in 2001.

Also in 2001 GE Capital expanded by buying commercial lender Heller Financial for $5.3 billion. The next year former business segment GE Industrial Systems acquired electronic security company Interlogix for $777 million.

Citing rising commodities costs, GE sold its advanced materials unit, which produced silicone, quartz, and ceramics products, to Apollo Management, and sold its GE Plastics unit (now SABIC Innovative Plastics) to SABIC for more than $11 billion in 2007. Also that year GE shut down the operations of wholesale subprime lender WMC Mortgage.

EXECUTIVES

Chairman and CEO: Jeffrey R. (Jeff) Immelt, age 54, $9,885,240 total compensation
Vice Chairman; Chairman and CEO, GE Capital: Michael A. (Mike) Neal, age 56, $15,195,888 total compensation
Vice Chairman and CFO: Keith S. Sherin, age 51, $13,955,956 total compensation
Vice Chairman; President and CEO, Technology Infrastructure: John G. Rice, age 53, $15,385,754 total compensation
Vice Chairman; President and CEO, GE Energy: John Krenicki Jr., age 47, $13,102,851 total compensation
SVP, General Counsel, and Secretary: Brackett B. Denniston III, age 62, $12,257,605 total compensation
SVP; President and CEO, GE Healthcare Systems: Omar S. Ishrak, age 54
SVP and CIO: Gary M. Reiner, age 55
SVP Human Resources: John F. Lynch, age 57
SVP; President and CEO, GE Appliances and Lighting: James P. (Jim) Campbell
SVP and Chief Marketing Officer: Elizabeth J. (Beth) Comstock, age 50
SVP; President and CEO, GE Aviation: David L. Joyce, age 53
VP and Chief Diversity Officer: Deborah (Deb) Elam, age 46
VP and Chief Risk Officer: Mark J. Krakowiak
VP Corporate Investor Communications: Trevor A. Schauenberg, age 41

President and CEO, GE Healthcare: John M. Dineen, age 47
Chairman, NBC Universal Sports and Olympics, NBC Universal: Dick Ebersol
President and CEO, NBC Universal:
Jeffrey A. (Jeff) Zucker, age 44
President and COO, Universal Studios, NBC Universal: Ron Meyer
Director Corporate Investor Communications:
JoAnna H. Morris
Auditors: KPMG LLP

LOCATIONS

HQ: General Electric Company
3135 Easton Tpke., Fairfield, CT 06828
Phone: 203-373-2211   **Fax:** 203-373-3131
Web: www.ge.com

2009 Sales

	% of total
US	46
Europe	24
Pacific Basin	13
Americas	8
Middle East & Africa	6
Other	3
Total	**100**

PRODUCTS/OPERATIONS

2009 Sales

	$ mil.	% of total
Sales of goods	65,068	41
GE Capital Services	52,000	33
Sales of services	38,709	25
Other	1,006	1
Total	**156,783**	**100**

2009 Sales by Segment

	$ mil.	% of total
Capital Finance	50,622	32
Technology Infrastructure	42,474	27
Energy Infrastructure	37,134	24
NBC Universal	15,436	10
Consumer & Industrial	9,703	6
Corporate items & eliminations	1,414	1
Total	**156,783**	**100**

COMPETITORS

Agilent Technologies
ALSTOM
Bank of America
Capital One
Caterpillar
CBS Corp
CIGNA
CIT Group
Citigroup
Cooper Industries
Deutsche Bank
Electrolux
General Re
Hitachi
HSBC
ITT Corp.
Jacuzzi Brands
Johnson Controls
JPMorgan Chase
News Corp.
Panasonic Corp
Philips Electronics
Polaroid
Raytheon
Rockwell Automation
Rolls-Royce
Siemens AG
Sony
Textron
ThyssenKrupp
Toshiba
United Technologies
Whirlpool

HISTORICAL FINANCIALS
Company Type: Public

Income Statement   FYE: December 31

	ASSETS ($ mil.)	NET INCOME ($ mil.)	INCOME AS % OF ASSETS	EMPLOYEES
12/09	781,818	11,241	1.4%	304,000
12/08	797,769	17,410	2.2%	323,000
12/07	795,337	22,208	2.8%	327,000
12/06	697,239	20,829	3.0%	319,000
12/05	673,342	16,353	2.4%	316,000
Annual Growth	**3.8%**	**(8.9%)**	**—**	**(1.0%)**

2009 Year-End Financials

Equity as % of assets: 15.0%
Return on assets: 1.4%
Return on equity: 10.1%
Long-term debt ($ mil.): 338,215
No. of shares (mil.): 10,691
Dividends
Yield: 4.0%
Payout: 60.4%
Market value ($ mil.): 161,758
Sales ($ mil.): 156,783

Stock History   NYSE: GE

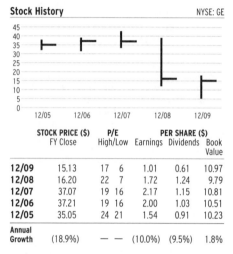

	STOCK PRICE ($) FY Close	P/E High/Low	PER SHARE ($) Earnings	Dividends	Book Value
12/09	15.13	17 6	1.01	0.61	10.97
12/08	16.20	22 7	1.72	1.24	9.79
12/07	37.07	19 16	2.17	1.15	10.81
12/06	37.21	19 16	2.00	1.03	10.51
12/05	35.05	24 21	1.54	0.91	10.23
Annual Growth	**(18.9%)**	**— —**	**(10.0%)**	**(9.5%)**	**1.8%**

General Mills

General Mills gets its Kix trying to grab the biggest-bowl prize as the US's #1 breakfast cereal maker (wrangling for the top spot every year with *über*-rival Kellogg). But #1 or not, the company has supermarket aisles full of kid-friendly morning-meal products. Its Big G Cereals include the well-known brands Cheerios, Chex, and Wheaties. But breakfast isn't the last meal on the menu at General Mills. The company makes yogurt (Yoplait), ice cream (Häagen-Dazs), canned soup (Progresso), and frozen dough products (Pillsbury and its poke-in-the-tummy Doughboy).

It other products include such familiar brands as Gold Medal flour, Betty Crocker and Bisquick baking mixes, Hamburger Helper dinner mixes, and Fruit Roll-Ups snacks, as well as "*ho, ho, ho*" Green Giant canned and frozen vegetables. Wal-Mart, which accounted for 35% of the company's sales in 2010, is General Mills' largest customer.

While most of its brands are found in supermarket chains, General Mills is a player in the natural foods niche with its Small Planet operation, which makes natural foods brands Muir Glen (canned tomato products) and Cascadian

Farms (frozen fruits and vegetables). It also operates about 600 Häagen-Dazs-branded ice cream parlors outside of the US and Canada as part of its international segment.

In 2008 the company sold its Pop-Secret operations to Diamond Foods for some $190 million in cash. While General Mills said it is concentrating its efforts on increasing the sales of its more lucrative core brands, the high price of corn most probably also figured into the decision to jettison Pop-Secret. It made no divestures in 2009 but in 2010 the company ceased making Perfect Portions refrigerated biscuits and exited the kids' refrigerated yogurt beverage and microwave soup segments in its US retail operations.

General Mills has two significant joint ventures — Cereal Partners Worldwide with Nestlé, which, along with the Big G cereals, sells breakfast brands such as Chocapic, Nesquick, Shreddies, and Uncle Toby's; and Häagen-Dazs Japan, which operates ice cream cafés in the Land of the Rising Sun.

HISTORY

Cadwallader Washburn built his first flour mill in 1866 in Minneapolis, which eventually became the Washburn Crosby Company. After winning a gold medal for flour at an 1880 exposition, the company changed the name of its best flour to Gold Medal Flour.

In 1921 advertising manager Sam Gale created fictional spokeswoman Betty Crocker so that correspondence to housewives could go out with her signature. The firm introduced Wheaties cereal in 1924. James Bell, named president in 1925, consolidated the company with other US mills in 1928 to form General Mills, the world's largest miller. The companies operated independently of one another, with corporate headquarters coordinating advertising and merchandising.

General Mills began introducing convenience foods such as Bisquick (1931) and Cheerios (1941). During WWII it produced war goods such as ordnance equipment and developed chemical and electronics divisions.

When Edwin Rawlings became CEO in 1961, he closed half of the flour mills and divested such unprofitable lines as electronics. This cost $200 million in annual sales but freed resources for such acquisitions as Kenner Products (toys, 1967) and Parker Brothers (board games, 1968), which made General Mills the world's largest toy company.

Through the next 20 years the company made many acquisitions, including Gorton's (frozen seafood, 1968), Monet (jewelry, 1968), Eddie Bauer (outerwear, 1971), and The Talbots (women's clothing, 1973). It bought Red Lobster in 1970 and acquired the US rights to Yoplait yogurt in 1977. When the toy and fashion divisions' profits fell in 1984, they were spun off as Kenner Parker Toys and Crystal Brands (1985). Reemphasizing food in 1989, the firm sold many businesses, including Eddie Bauer and Talbots.

To expand into Europe, General Mills struck two important joint ventures: Cereal Partners Worldwide (with Nestlé in 1989) and Snack Ventures Europe (with PepsiCo in 1992).

As part of a cereal price war, in 1994 the company cut coupon promotion costs by $175 million and lowered prices on many cereals. But some retailers did not pass on the price cuts to consumers due to shortages that developed after the FDA found an unauthorized pesticide in some cereals. General Mills destroyed 55 million boxes of cereal at a cost of $140 million. Stephen Sanger became CEO in 1995. That year the company sold Gorton's to Unilever and spun off its restaurant businesses as Darden Restaurants.

Focused on a food-only future, in the late 1990s the company picked up several smaller businesses, including Ralcorp Holdings' Chex snack and cereal lines and Gardetto's snack mixes, as well as the North American rights to Olibra, an appetite suppressant food additive made by Scotia Holdings.

Big changes came in 2001 when General Mills became the #1 cereal maker in the US, overtaking Kellogg for the first time since 1906. The company then completed its $10.5 billion purchase of Pillsbury from Diageo in October 2001. A month later General Mills sold competing product lines to International Multifoods. While busily integrating Pillsbury, in 2002 General Mills saw its income fall and watched as Kellogg regained the lead in the cereal market.

In 2004 Diageo sold part of its approximately 20% stake in General Mills. General Mills, in turn, sold an $835 million stake to an affiliate of Lehman Brothers Holding and used $750 million to buy back the Diageo shares and $85 million to pay down debt. Also in 2004 the company sold its US Häagen-Dazs ice cream shop franchise business to Dreyer's Grand Ice Cream. In 2005 it sold its stake in Snack Ventures Europe joint venture to PepsiCo for $750 million.

After more than 10 years of being ignored, the Jolly Green Giant came out of retirement in 2005 as part of a multi-million dollar marketing campaign by General Mills to up its veggie sales.

In order to develop healthier products, in 2006 the company entered a supply agreement for DHA (an omega-3 fatty acid said to play a role in mental and cardiovascular health) with Martek Biosciences, maker of DHA (which is already widely used in infant formula).

Also in 2007 CEO Sanger stepped down. President and COO Ken Powell replaced him. The following year, General Mills and DuPont sold their soy-milk joint venture, 8th Continent, to Stremicks Heritage Foods.

EXECUTIVES

Chairman, President, and CEO: Kendall J. (Ken) Powell, age 56, $13,378,603 total compensation
EVP and COO, U.S. Retail: Ian R. Friendly, age 49, $3,038,519 total compensation
EVP and COO, International: Christopher D. O'Leary, age 51, $2,818,285 total compensation
EVP and CFO: Donal L. (Don) Mulligan, age 49, $2,126,468 total compensation
EVP Human Resources and Business Services: Michael A. (Mike) Peel, age 60
EVP Worldwide Health, Brand, and New Business Development: Y. Marc Belton, age 51
EVP, General Counsel, Chief Corporate and Risk Management Officer, and Secretary: Roderick A. (Rick) Palmore, age 58
SVP Innovation, Technology, and Quality: Peter C. Erickson, age 49
SVP Supply Chain: John R. Church, age 44
SVP International Marketing and Sales: Peter J. Capell
SVP Global Human Resources: Michael L. Davis, age 54
SVP External Relations; President, General Mills Foundation: Christina L. (Chris) Shea, age 57

SVP; President, Greater China: Gary Chu
SVP and Chief Marketing Officer: Mark W. Addicks
SVP; President, Snacks Unlimited: Kimberly A. (Kim) Nelson
SVP; President, Europe, Latin America, and Africa: Giuseppe A. D'Angelo
SVP; President, Pillsbury USA: Juliana L. Chugg, age 42
SVP; President, Big G Cereals: Jeffrey L. Harmening
SVP; President, Consumer Foods Sales: Shawn P. O'Grady
SVP; President, Bakeries and Foodservice: John T. Machuzick
VP Investor Relations: Kristen S. Wenker
Auditors: KPMG LLP

LOCATIONS

HQ: General Mills, Inc.
1 General Mills Blvd., Minneapolis, MN 55426
Phone: 763-764-7600   **Fax:** 763-764-7384
Web: www.generalmills.com

2010 Sales

	$ mil.	% of total
US	12,077.6	82
Other	2,718.9	18
Total	**14,796.5**	**100**

PRODUCTS/OPERATIONS

2010 Sales

	$ mil.	% of total
US retail	10,323.5	70
International	2,702.5	18
Bakeries & foodservice	1,770.5	12
Total	**14,796.5**	**100**

Selected Brands

Dessert and baking mixes
 Betty Crocker
 Bisquick
 Gold Medal
 Warm Delights
Dry dinners and shelf stable and frozen vegetable products
 Bac*O's
 Betty Crocker
 Chicken Helper
 Green Giant
 Hamburger Helper
 Old El Paso
 Potato Buds
 Simply Steam
 Suddenly Salad
 Tuna Helper
 Wanchai Ferry
Frozen pizza and pizza snacks
 Jeno's
 Party Pizza
 Pillsbury Pizza Minis
 Pillsbury Pizza Pops
 Pizza Rolls
 Totino's
Grain, fruit, and savory snacks
 Bugles
 Chex Mix
 Fiber One
 Fruit By The Foot
 Fruit Roll-Ups
 Lärabar
 Nature Valley
Ice cream and frozen desserts
 Häagen-Dazs
Organic products
 Cascadian Farm
 Muir Glen

Ready-to-eat cereals
 Basic 4
 Cheerios
 Chex
 Cinnamon Toast Crunch
 Cocoa Puffs
 Cookie Crisp
 Fiber One
 Golden Grahams
 Kix
 Lucky Charms
 Reese's Puffs
 Total
 Trix
 Wheaties
Ready-to-serve soup
 Progresso
Refrigerated and frozen dough products
 Golden Layers
 Grands!
 Latina
 Pillsbury
 Savorings
 Toaster Scrambles
 Toaster Strudel
Refrigerated yogurt
 Go-GURT
 Fiber One
 Trix
 Yoplait
 Yoplait Kids
 YoPlus

COMPETITORS

B&G Foods	Hanover Foods
Barbara's Bakery	Heinz
Bay State Milling	Kellogg
Ben & Jerry's	King Arthur Flour
Birds Eye	Kraft Foods
Blue Bell	Lakeside Foods
Bob's Red Mill Natural	Malt-O-Meal
Foods	Manischewitz Company
Campbell Soup	McKee Foods
Carvel	Mrs. Fields
Chelsea Milling	Nature's Path
Cold Stone Creamery	Nestlé
ConAgra	NexCen Brands
Dairy Queen	Pinnacle Foods
Danone	Procter & Gamble
Del Monte Foods	Pro-Fac
Dole Food	Ralcorp
Dreyer's	Ralston Food
Freshēns	Seneca Foods
Friendly Ice Cream	Stonyfield Farm
Frito-Lay	Unilever
Gilster-Mary Lee	Victoria Packing
Hain Celestial	YoCream

HISTORICAL FINANCIALS

Company Type: Public

Income Statement

	REVENUE ($ mil.)	NET INCOME ($ mil.)	NET PROFIT MARGIN	EMPLOYEES
5/10	14,797	1,531	10.3%	33,000
5/09	14,691	1,304	8.9%	30,000
5/08	13,652	1,295	9.5%	29,500
5/07	12,442	1,144	9.2%	28,500
5/06	11,640	1,090	9.4%	28,100
Annual Growth	**6.2%**	**8.9%**	**—**	**4.1%**

FYE: Last Sunday in May

2010 Year-End Financials

Debt ratio: 97.5%
Return on equity: 28.9%
Cash ($ mil.): 673
Current ratio: 0.92
Long-term debt ($ mil.): 5,269
No. of shares (mil.): 651
Dividends
 Yield: 2.7%
 Payout: 42.9%
Market value ($ mil.): 23,193

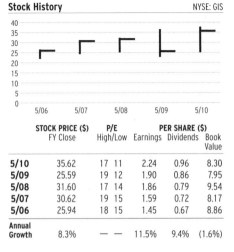

	STOCK PRICE ($) FY Close	P/E High/Low		PER SHARE ($) Earnings	Dividends	Book Value
5/10	35.62	17	11	2.24	0.96	8.30
5/09	25.59	19	12	1.90	0.86	7.95
5/08	31.60	17	14	1.86	0.79	9.54
5/07	30.62	19	15	1.59	0.72	8.17
5/06	25.94	18	15	1.45	0.67	8.86
Annual Growth	8.3%	—	—	11.5%	9.4%	(1.6%)

General Motors

General Motors (GM) makes a wide portfolio of cars and trucks, with brands such as Buick, Cadillac, Chevrolet, and GMC. GM also builds cars through its GM Daewoo, Opel, Vauxhall, and Holden units. Financing and insurance activities are conducted by Ally Financial (formerly known as GMAC), of which GM owns about a 10% stake. In recent years the century-old GM has experienced historic financial hurdles that threatened its viability. As a result, GM received billions of dollars in loans from the Canadian and US governments, negotiated concessions with labor unions, and jettisoned brands. The auto giant went through a brief Chapter 11 bankruptcy reorganization in 2009. About a year later, it filed to again go public.

The IPO signals the restructured company's desire to open the way for the US and Canadian governments to sell their stakes. The US government holds about 61% of GM's common shares; the Canadian federal government and the Ontario provincial government together hold another 12%. The remainder is held by a United Auto Workers retiree health care trust, and by unsecured bondholders. GM will not receive any money from the sale of common stock. Instead, it looks to distance itself from the negative nickname the automaker has been saddled with since the bailout, "Government Motors," by allowing its government owners to reduce (and eventually eliminate) their stakes in the company through gradual sales to private investors.

It bolstered investor and car dealer confidence in mid-2010 by announcing its proposed acquisition of auto finance company AmeriCredit. The $3.5 billion purchase creates a wholly owned lending arm, an advantage that GM has not had since it sold the majority of GMAC (now Ally Financial) in 2006.

GM's other big focus is to raise the quality of its cars and trucks, long a source of criticism for the company. To this end, the company is concentrating its resources on the Buick, Cadillac, Chevrolet, Opel, and GMC brands; HUMMER, Pontiac, and Saturn brands were discontinued. The smaller portfolio is also forcing a 40% reduction in US dealerships.

GM's efforts to improve its products include developing energy-saving technologies using biofuels, fuel cells, hybrid vehicles, and extended-range electric vehicles, as well as building batteries for its vehicles.

GM's fortunes are also leaning on the world's largest pool of potential drivers; China's automotive market is experiencing explosive growth and GM plans to spend $3 billion over the next couple of years in order to keep up with demand there.

CEO Edward Whitacre — the long-time CEO of AT&T until his retirement in 2007 — assumed the post in December 2009. He announced his plans to step down in late 2010. His replacement, Daniel Akerson is a former telecommunications executive with private equity firm The Carlyle Group.

HISTORY

In the early years of the auto industry, hundreds of carmakers each produced a few models. William Durant, who bought a failing Buick Motors in 1904, reasoned that manufacturers could benefit from banding together and formed the General Motors Company in Flint, Michigan, in 1908.

Durant bought 17 companies (including Oldsmobile, Cadillac, and Pontiac) by 1910, the year a bankers' syndicate forced him to step down. In 1915 he regained control when he formed a company with race car driver Louis Chevrolet. They soon formed GM Acceptance Corporation (GMAC, financing) and bought businesses including Frigidaire (sold in 1979) and Hyatt Roller Bearing.

With Hyatt came Alfred Sloan (president, 1923-37), who built GM into a corporate colossus via a decentralized management system. Unlike Ford — which offered cars in any color you liked as long as it was black — GM offered a range of models and colors; by 1927 it was the industry leader. It bought Vauxhall Motors (UK, 1925), merged with Adam Opel (Germany, 1931), added defense products for WWII, and diversified into home appliances and locomotives.

GM expanded with the nation in the post-war boom years; the good times rolled until Japanese automakers became established in the 1970s. GM spent much of the decade trying to emulate the Japanese while making its cars meet federal pollution-control mandates. CEO Roger Smith laid off thousands of workers.

GM bought Electronic Data Systems (1984), Hughes Aircraft (1986), and 50% of Saab Automobile (1989). GM launched the Saturn car in 1990; that year Robert Stempel became CEO. In 1992 GM made what was then the largest stock offering in US history ($2.2 billion), and Jack Smith replaced Stempel as CEO.

GM spun off Electronic Data Systems in 1996. In 1997 it sold the defense electronics business of Hughes Electronics to Raytheon. UAW walkouts at two Michigan GM parts plants in 1998 forced the shutdown of virtually all of the company's North American production lines. In 1999 GM spun off Delphi. The next year GM acquired the 50% of Saab Automobile that it didn't already own (from Investor AB).

President Rick Wagoner replaced Smith as CEO in June 2000. In 2001 GM doubled its stake in Suzuki to 20%. The following year GM took a 42% stake in South Korea's bankrupt Daewoo Motor (later increased to 51%).

In early 2006 GM's finance arm, GMAC, sold a 78% equity stake in its commercial mortgage business to a private equity consortium for about $9 billion. GM then sold a 51% stake in GMAC to a consortium of investors led by Cerberus Capital Management for $14 billion.

GM sold its Allison Transmission commercial and military business to The Carlyle Group and Onex Corp. for about $5.6 billion in 2007.

The company dodged a bullet in 2007 when the UAW, fighting for health care for retirees, ended a two-day strike — the first nationwide UAW strike against GM in more than 35 years. The two hammered out a deal creating a $50 billion independent health care trust (with GM ponying up most of the trust's funding).

For 2007 GM reported the largest annual loss in the history of the automotive industry — $38.7 billion.

The reporting of the record loss was accompanied by a fresh round of employee buyouts. The plan offered buyouts to as many as 74,000 US hourly workers. In addition, GM cut 7% of its white-collar positions, or about 2,500 jobs.

GM made merger overtures to Chrysler and Ford in 2008. Rebuffed by Ford, GM entered merger talks with Chrysler. Those talks were abandoned, however, as GM warned in 2008 that it might run out of cash by the end of the year.

EXECUTIVES

Chairman and CEO: Edward E. (Ed) Whitacre Jr., age 68, $181,308 total compensation
Director: Daniel F. (Dan) Akerson, age 61
Vice Chairman Global Product Operations: Thomas G. Stephens, age 61
Vice Chairman, Corporate Strategy and Business Development: Stephen J. (Steve) Girsky, age 48
Vice Chairman and CFO: Christopher P. (Chris) Liddell, age 52
VP Information Systems and Services and CIO: Terry S. Kline, age 48
VP International Operations: Ray G. Young, age 48
VP Manufacturing and Labor Relations: Diana D. Tremblay, age 48
VP US Sales Operations: Stephen K. (Steve) Carlisle, age 48
VP Communications: Selim Bingol, age 50
VP and General Counsel: Michael P. Millikin, age 61
VP, Controller, and Chief Accounting Officer: Nicholas S. (Nick) Cyprus, age 57
VP Finance and Treasurer: Daniel (Dan) Ammann, age 38
VP US Marketing: Joel Ewanick, age 50
VP Global Vehicle Engineering: Karl-Friedrich Stracke, age 54
VP Global Vehicle Program Management: Terry J. Woychowski, age 54
VP Global Powertrain Engineering: Daniel M. (Dan) Hancock, age 60
VP Global Vehicle Design: Edward T. (Ed) Welburn Jr., age 59
VP Global Purchasing and Supply Chain: Robert E. (Bob) Socia, age 55
VP Global Product Planning: Jonathan J. (Jon) Lauckner, age 52
VP Global Human Resources: Mary T. Barra, age 48
VP Global Manufacturing Engineering: Eric R. Stevens, age 54
President, GM International Operations: Timothy E. (Tim) Lee, age 59
President, GM North America: Mark L. Reuss, age 46
Corporate Secretary: Anne T. Larin
Auditors: Deloitte & Touche LLP

LOCATIONS

HQ: General Motors Company
300 Renaissance Center, Detroit, MI 48265
Phone: 313-556-5000
Web: www.gm.com

2009 Sales

	$ mil.	% of total
North America		
US	49,159	47
Canada & Mexico	8,168	8
Europe		
Germany	6,668	6
UK	5,280	5
Italy	2,340	2
France	1,947	2
Spain	1,471	1
Russia	676	1
Sweden & other countries	5,394	5
International Operations		
Brazil	8,257	8
South Korea	5,058	5
Australia	2,854	3
Venezuela	1,831	2
Thailand & other countries	4,304	4
Other regions	1,182	1
Total	**104,589**	**100**

PRODUCTS/OPERATIONS

2009 Sales

	$ mil.	% of total
Automotive		
GM North America	54,944	53
GM Europe	23,759	23
GM International Operations	25,413	24
Other	473	—
Total	**104,589**	**100**

Selected Brands

Buick
Cadillac
Chevrolet
GMC
Holden
Isuzu
Opel
Vauxhall

Selected Operations

Adam Opel GmbH (Germany)
Ally Financial, Inc. (formerly General Motors Acceptance Corp., "GMAC," 10%)
GM Automotive
GM Daewoo Auto & Technology Company

COMPETITORS

BMW	Mitsubishi Motors
Chrysler	Navistar International
Daimler	Nissan
Fiat	Peugeot
Ford Motor	Renault
Fuji Heavy Industries	Suzuki Motor
Honda	Tata Motors
Hyundai Motor	Toyota
Kia Motors	Volkswagen
Land Rover	Volvo Car Corp.
Mazda	

HISTORICAL FINANCIALS

Company Type: Private

Income Statement

FYE: December 31

	REVENUE ($ mil.)	NET INCOME ($ mil.)	NET PROFIT MARGIN	EMPLOYEES
12/09	104,589	105,217	100.6%	217,000
12/08	148,979	(30,860)	—	243,000
12/07	181,122	(38,732)	—	266,000
12/06	207,349	(1,978)	—	280,000
12/05	192,604	(10,458)	—	335,000
Annual Growth	(14.2%)	—	—	(10.3%)

2009 Year-End Financials

Debt ratio: 26.2%
Return on equity: —
Cash ($ mil.): 22,679
Current ratio: 1.13
Long-term debt ($ mil.): 5,562

Net Income History

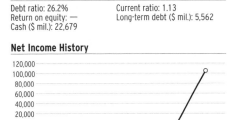

Genesco Inc.

Genesco's sole concern is nicely capped off, to boot (so to speak). It sells casual and dress shoes and headgear — primarily for men and boys — through some 2,275 footwear and headwear stores in the US, Puerto Rico, and Canada. Genesco operates through four footwear segments and one for headwear. Shoe operations include Journeys, Underground Station (with Jarman, targeting young urban men), Johnston & Murphy, and Licensed Brands (Levi Strauss' Dockers footwear). Its Hat World Group (acquired in 2004) consists of the Hat World, Lids, Hat Shack, Hat Zone, Head Quarters, Cap Connection, and Lids Locker Room retail stores. Founded in 1924 as a shoe retailer, Genesco has diversified by adding hats and apparel.

Disappointing financial results in recent years led to two ultimately unsuccessful takeover bids (from rivals Finish Line and Foot Locker) and plenty of legal wrangling for the company. Indeed, Genesco has met with more success buying companies than with selling itself. In late 2009 it acquired the 37-store Sports Fan-Attic chain of college and pro sports licensed apparel. Sports Fan-Attic joins the company's Hat World unit, and takes the company beyond hats by adding jerseys and other sports-related clothing and memorabilia. More recently, Hat World agreed to acquire the assets of Sports Avenue, which operates about 45 retail stores and e-commerce sites across the US that sell licensed pro sports headwear and apparel. (The deal is slated to close in late 2010.) The recent acquisitions are in line with Genesco's long-term strategy to grow organically and through acquisitions and suggest that the company may have put its financial woes behind it.

But the outlook for Genesco's financial health is far from clear. While the company posted a modest 1.5% increase in net sales in fiscal 2010 (ended January) — driven primarily by a 15% increase in sales by its Hat World Group — all of its other business segments saw their sales decrease. Also, net earnings plunged by about 80%.

Going forward, Genesco plans to open about 70 new stores and shutter about 60 in fiscal 2011. Banners catering to urban populations are targeted for closure, including Jarman (which is being phased out) and Underground Station. The company's Hat World Group will add about 25 locations in fiscal 2011, while its Johnston & Murphy chain will add another five shops.

In the shoe world, Genesco has been expanding its Journeys brand, which includes the Journeys, Journeys Kidz, and Shi by Journeys retail formats that number more than 1,000 stores across the US. In 2010 Journeys dipped its toe in the Canadian market with the opening of three stores there. (Genesco already operates about 60 stores in Canada as a result of its acquisition of Cap Connection.) To reach younger customers, the brand operates some 150 Journeys Kidz — shoe stores aimed at 5- to 12-year-olds — and about 55 Shi stores target fashion-conscious young women.

At the other end of the brand spectrum, the company has licensed its upmarket Johnston & Murphy brand for use in the coats niche, as well as apparel, luggage, leather goods and accessories; Johnston & Murphy is also expanding into women's footwear.

Adding to its retail operations, Genesco is also a wholesale distributor of branded footwear, including the Dockers brand licensed from Levi Strauss & Co. and its own Johnston & Murphy brand to department stores. The company's shoes are made by third parties overseas.

Robert Dennis, who joined Genesco from Hat World in 2005 as COO, was promoted to CEO in 2008 and added the chairman's title in April 2010.

HISTORY

James Jarman started the Jarman Shoe Company in 1924 and was soon joined in the business by his son Maxey, who dropped out of MIT to help. By 1933 Maxey (then 29) was company president, and after changing the company's name to General Shoe, he pushed for growth. Despite the Great Depression, Maxey opened four stores and stressed vertical integration; even the company's shoeboxes were produced in-house. With the success of the Jarman name, other retailers began stocking the company's shoes. General Shoe went public in 1939.

After WWII, General Shoe prospered. It started buying other shoe companies, including 100-year-old shoemaker Johnston & Murphy in 1951. By 1955 General Shoe's success drew the scrutiny of the Justice Department, which filed antitrust charges. After agreeing not to make any acquisitions in the shoe industry for five years, General Shoe diversified into apparel, renaming itself Genesco in 1959 to reflect the change. It bought interests in a host of men's and women's clothiers. By 1968 the company had more than $1 billion in sales. Maxey retired one year later.

Genesco overextended itself in the 1970s and 1980s. In 1994 David Chamberlain was named CEO and the following year oversaw a restructuring in which Genesco divested its apparel, soccer, and children's shoe businesses to focus on men's footwear. By 1996 sales began to rise again; Chamberlain passed the CEO baton to Ben Harris the next year.

In 1998 Genesco started a new chain, Underground Station, offering shoes and clothes to young urban men. The company also sold its slumping western boot business, including the Laredo Boot division and 26 Boot Factory stores, to Texas Boot that year. In 1999 Chamberlain left Genesco to become CEO of Stride Rite, and Harris became chairman. Genesco sold its leather finishing Volunteer Leather business to Minnesota-based S.B. Foot Tanning in 2000. Also that year the company closed its discount General Shoe Warehouse units. Genesco ended its license to sell Nautica branded footwear in 2001.

The following year the company said it would close its Nashville, Tennessee, plant that manufactures its Johnston & Murphy shoes.

Genesco and rival Finish Line, which offered to acquire the firm for about $1.5 billion in 2007, terminated the deal in 2008. (Previously, Genesco's board unanimously rejected a $1.3 billion unsolicited takeover bid from Foot Locker.) In August 2008 company executive Robert Dennis, who joined Genesco as its EVP and COO, became CEO of the firm. (He added the chairman's title in April 2010.)

In November 2009 Genesco's Hat World subsidiary acquired Tampa, Florida-based Sports Fan-Attic, a seller of licensed sports headwear, apparel, accessories, and novelties with about three dozen stores in seven states.

EXECUTIVES

Chairman, President, and CEO: Robert J. (Bob) Dennis, age 56, $2,674,409 total compensation
SVP; President, Hat World: Kenneth J. (Ken) Kocher, age 44, $1,119,456 total compensation
SVP, Secretary, and General Counsel: Roger G. Sisson, age 46
SVP Strategy and Shared Services: Mimi E. Vaughn, age 43
SVP; CEO, Branded Group; President, Johnston & Murphy: Jonathan D. (Jon) Caplan, age 56, $894,587 total compensation
SVP; President and CEO, Genesco Retail: James C. Estepa, age 58, $1,205,208 total compensation
SVP Finance, CFO, and Treasurer: James S. Gulmi, age 64, $1,208,987 total compensation
Chief Information and Logistics Officer: Jeff Orton
VP and Chief Accounting Officer: Paul D. Williams, age 55
VP Information Systems: Dennis Harris
Director Corporate Relations: Claire S. McCall
Auditors: Ernst & Young LLP

LOCATIONS

HQ: Genesco Inc.
Genesco Park, 1415 Murfreesboro Rd.
Nashville, TN 37217
Phone: 615-367-7000 **Fax:** 615-367-8278
Web: www.genesco.com

PRODUCTS/OPERATIONS

2010 Sales

	$ mil.	% of total
Journeys Group	749.2	48
Hat World Group	465.8	29
Johnston & Murphy Group	166.1	10
Underground Station Group	99.5	7
Licensed Brands	93.2	6
Corporate & other	0.6	—
Total	**1,574.4**	**100**

2010 Stores

	No.
Journeys Group	1,025
Hat World Group	921
Underground Station Group	170
Johnston & Murphy Group	160
Total	**2,276**

Selected Retail Store Concepts

Journeys Group
Journeys (casual footwear for guys ages 13 to 22)
Journeys Kidz (casual footwear for children ages 5 to 12)
Shi by Journeys (footwear and accessories for women ages 20-35)

Underground Station Group (footwear and apparel for urban men ages 18 to 35)
Jarman
Underground Station

Hat World Group
Cap Connection (headwear for youth ages 13-25)
Hat Shack (headwear for youth ages 13-25)
Hat World (headwear for youth ages 13-25)
Hat Zone (headwear for youth ages 13-25)
Head Quarters (headwear for youth ages 13-25)
Lids (headwear for youth ages 13-25)
Lids Locker Room

Johnston & Murphy Group (dress and casual footwear for men ages 25 to 54)

Selected Footwear Brands

Dockers (licensed)
Johnston & Murphy

COMPETITORS

Allen-Edmonds	Mainland Headwear
Bally	New Era Cap
Berkshire Hathaway	Nine West
Brown Shoe	Phillips-Van Heusen
C&J Clark	R. Griggs
Coach, Inc.	Red Wing Shoe
Collective Brands	Reebok
Concept One Accessories	Shoe Carnival
Deckers Outdoor	Sports Authority
Dick's Sporting Goods	Target
Finish Line	Timberland
Foot Locker	Vans
J. C. Penney	Wal-Mart
Kenneth Cole	Weyco
Liz Claiborne	Wolverine World Wide
L.L. Bean	

HISTORICAL FINANCIALS

Company Type: Public

Income Statement

FYE: Saturday nearest January 31

	REVENUE ($ mil.)	NET INCOME ($ mil.)	NET PROFIT MARGIN	EMPLOYEES
1/10	1,574	29	1.8%	13,900
1/09	1,552	153	9.8%	14,125
1/08	1,502	7	0.5%	13,950
1/07	1,461	68	4.6%	12,750
1/06	1,284	63	4.9%	11,100
Annual Growth	**5.2%**	**(17.7%)**	**—**	**5.8%**

2010 Year-End Financials

Debt ratio: 0.0%	No. of shares (mil.): 24
Return on equity: 5.7%	Dividends
Cash ($ mil.): 82	Yield: —
Current ratio: 2.65	Payout: —
Long-term debt ($ mil.): 0	Market value ($ mil.): 567

Stock History

NYSE: GCO

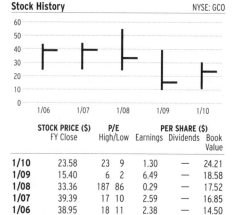

	STOCK PRICE ($) FY Close	P/E High	P/E Low	PER SHARE ($) Earnings	PER SHARE ($) Dividends	PER SHARE ($) Book Value
1/10	23.58	23	9	1.30	—	24.21
1/09	15.40	6	2	6.49	—	18.58
1/08	33.36	187	86	0.29	—	17.52
1/07	39.39	17	10	2.59	—	16.85
1/06	38.95	18	11	2.38	—	14.50
Annual Growth	**(11.8%)**	**—**	**—**	**(14.0%)**	**—**	**13.7%**

Genuine Parts

What do spark plugs, hydraulic hoses, note pads, and magnet wire have in common? They're all Genuine Parts. The diversified company is the largest member and majority owner of National Automotive Parts Association (NAPA), a voluntary trade association that distributes auto parts nationwide. Genuine Parts Company (GPC) operates about 1,100 NAPA Auto Parts stores in more than 40 US states. North of the border, NAPA Canada runs some 600 auto parts and TRACTION stores, supplied by UAP. GPC's Auto Todo unit runs four auto parts stores and four tire centers in Mexico. Other subsidiaries include auto parts distributor Balkamp, industrial parts supplier Motion Industries, and office products distributor S.P. Richards.

As a supplier of automotive and industrial replacement parts, office supplies, and electrical and electronic manufacturing materials, GPC maintains a presence in multiple markets. The company has not been entirely insulated from the effects of the economic downturn, however. Since hitting a high point in sales of $11 billion in 2008, GPC saw its revenues drop by about 10% the following year. The firm pointed to lower levels of industrial production, higher unemployment, and sluggish consumer spending as the reasons behind the decline. The slump followed years of steady growth and strategic planning to boost revenues; GPC had made advances through acquisitions, added and expanded product lines, entered new geographic areas, and enhanced marketing programs.

Despite the gloomy results, the company continues to pursue acquisition opportunities. GPC is building upon its hard-hit industrial parts business and hardy automotive group amid signs that certain areas of the US economy are recovering. To this end, Motion Industries in early 2010 acquired Canada's BC Bearing, a distributor of bearing and power transmission components. In 2009 GPC added eight companies to its industrial and automotive operations for about $70 million and snapped up the remaining 11% interest in Balkamp that it did not already control for some $60 million.

The automotive business is GPC's largest division, generating about half of total sales. In recent years it has suffered only a slight downturn in demand, also making it the company's most resistant.

HISTORY

Genuine Parts Company (GPC) got its start in Atlanta in 1928 when Carlyle Fraser bought a small auto parts store. That year GPC had the only loss in its history. Three years earlier a group that included Fraser had founded the National Automotive Parts Association (NAPA), an organization of automotive manufacturers, remanufacturers, distributors, and retailers.

The Depression was a boon for GPC because fewer new-car sales meant more sales of replacement parts. During the 1930s GPC's sales rose from less than $350,000 to more than $3 million. One tool it developed to spur sales during the Depression was its monthly magazine, *Parts Pups*, which featured pretty girls and corny jokes (discontinued in the 1990s). GPC acquired auto parts rebuilder Rayloc in 1931 and established parts distributor Balkamp in 1936.

WWII boosted sales at GPC because carmakers were producing for the war effort, but scarce resources limited auto parts companies to producing functional parts. GPC went public in 1948.

The postwar boom in car sales boosted GPC's sales in the 1950s and 1960s. It expanded during this period with new distribution centers across the country. GPC bought Colyear Motor Sales (NAPA's West Coast distributor) in 1965 and introduced a line of filters and batteries in 1966 that were the first parts to carry the NAPA name.

GPC moved into Canada in 1972 when it bought Corbetts, a Calgary-based parts distributor. That acquisition included Oliver Industrial Supply. During the mid-1970s GPC began to broaden its distribution businesses, adding S. P. Richards (office products, 1975) and Motion Industries (industrial replacement parts, 1976). In the late 1970s GPC acquired Bearing Specialty and Michigan Bearing as part of Motion Industries.

In 1982 the company introduced its now familiar blue-and-yellow NAPA logo. Canadian parts distributor UAP (formerly United Auto Parts) and GPC formed a joint venture, UAP/NAPA, in 1988, with GPC acquiring a 20% stake in UAP.

During the 1990s GPC diversified its product lines and its geographic reach. Its 1993 acquisition of Berry Bearing made the company a leading distributor of industrial parts. The next year GPC formed a joint venture with Grupo Auto Todo of Mexico.

NAPA formed an agreement in 1995 with Penske Corporation to be the exclusive supplier of auto parts to nearly 900 Penske Auto Centers. GPC purchased Horizon USA Data Supplies that year, adding computer supplies to S. P. Richards' product mix.

A string of acquisitions in the late 1990s increased GPC's industrial distribution business.

GPC paid $200 million in 1998 for EIS, a leading wholesale distributor of materials and supplies to the electrical and electronics industries. Late in 1998, after a 10-year joint venture, it bought the remaining 80% of UAP it didn't already own. GPC continued to expand its auto parts distribution network in 1999, acquiring Johnson Industries, an independent distributor of auto supplies for large fleets and car dealers. GPC also acquired Oklahoma City-based Brittain Brothers, a NAPA distributor that serves about 190 auto supply stores in Arkansas, Missouri, Oklahoma, and Texas.

GPC acquired NAPA Hawaii, which serves more than 30 independently owned NAPA stores and four company-owned ones in Hawaii and Samoa, in 2003.

President Thomas Gallagher became the company's fourth CEO in more than 75 years when he was named to the position in 2004. Former CEO Larry Prince remained chairman until early 2005 when Gallagher was elected chairman.

GPC subsidiary Motion Industries in mid-2006 acquired Lewis Supply Co., a provider of casters, cutting tools, machinery accessories and other general mill supplies.

In early 2008 the company sold its Johnson Industries subsidiary, which provided automotive supplies to fleets and new car dealers. In October GPC's S. P. Richards unit acquired ActionEmco's business assets in the midwestern US, including its Grand Rapids, Michigan, distribution center.

EXECUTIVES

Chairman, President, and CEO:
Thomas C. (Tom) Gallagher, age 62, $3,030,703 total compensation
Vice Chairman, EVP Finance, and CFO: Jerry W. Nix, age 64, $1,449,641 total compensation
EVP U.S. Automotive Parts Group: Lee A. Maher
EVP: Robert J. Susor, age 64, $944,122 total compensation
EVP and President, U.S. Automotive Parts Group:
Paul D. Donahue, age 53, $864,548 total compensation
SVP Human Resources: R. Bruce Clayton, age 62, $696,308 total compensation
SVP and Corporate Counsel: Scott C. Smith
SVP Technology and Process Improvement:
Charles A. Chesnutt, age 50
SVP Finance and Corporate Secretary: Carol B. Yancey
SVP and Treasurer: Frank M. Howard
VP Information Technolgy: Eric Sundby
VP Investor Relations: Sidney G. (Sid) Jones
President and CEO, EIS: Robert W. Thomas
President and COO, S. P. Richards: Richard T. Toppin
President, Rayloc: John Mosteller
President, Balkamp, Inc.: D. Tip Tollison
President and CEO, Motion Industries:
William J. (Bill) Stevens
President, Heavy Vehicle Parts Group: D. Gary Silva
President, Altrom America, Altrom Import Parts Group: Scott S. Mountford
President and CEO, Grupo Auto Todo, Mexico:
Juan Lujambio
Director; Chairman, NAPA Canada/UAP Inc.:
Jean Douville, age 66
Auditors: Ernst & Young LLP

LOCATIONS

HQ: Genuine Parts Company
2999 Circle 75 Pkwy., Atlanta, GA 30339
Phone: 770-953-1700   **Fax:** 770-956-2211
Web: www.genpt.com

PRODUCTS/OPERATIONS

2009 Sales

	% of total
Automotive	52
Industrial	29
Office products	16
Electrical/electronic materials	3
Total	**100**

Selected Operations

Automotive Parts Group
  Altrom Canada Corp. (distribution of import automotive parts, Canada)
  Balkamp (majority-owned subsidiary; distribution of replacement parts and accessories for cars, heavy-duty vehicles, motorcycles, and farm equipment)
  UAP Inc. (auto parts distribution, Canada)
Industrial Parts Group
  Motion Industries (Canada), Inc.
  Motion Industries, Inc.
Office Products Group
  S. P. Richards Company
Electrical/Electronic Materials Group
  EIS, Inc. (products for electrical and electronic equipment, including adhesives, copper foil, and thermal management materials)

COMPETITORS

Advance Auto Parts	General Motors
Applied Industrial	General Parts
Technologies	Graybar Electric
Arrow Electronics	Hahn Automotive
AutoZone	Ingersoll-Rand
Avnet	Office Depot
CARQUEST	OfficeMax
Coast Distribution	O'Reilly Automotive
D&H Distributing	Staples
Ford Motor	United Stationers

HISTORICAL FINANCIALS

Company Type: Public

Income Statement

FYE: December 31

	REVENUE ($ mil.)	NET INCOME ($ mil.)	NET PROFIT MARGIN	EMPLOYEES
12/09	10,058	400	4.0%	29,000
12/08	11,015	475	4.3%	30,300
12/07	10,843	506	4.7%	32,000
12/06	10,458	475	4.5%	32,000
12/05	9,783	437	4.5%	31,700
Annual Growth	**0.7%**	**(2.2%)**	**—**	**(2.2%)**

2009 Year-End Financials

Debt ratio: 19.1%
Return on equity: 16.2%
Cash ($ mil.): 337
Current ratio: 2.86
Long-term debt ($ mil.): 500
No. of shares (mil.): 158
Dividends
  Yield: 4.2%
  Payout: 64.0%
Market value ($ mil.): 5,983

Stock History

NYSE: GPC

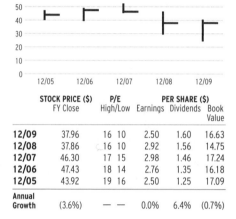

	STOCK PRICE ($) FY Close	P/E High/Low	PER SHARE ($) Earnings	Dividends	Book Value
12/09	37.96	16 10	2.50	1.60	16.63
12/08	37.86	16 10	2.92	1.56	14.75
12/07	46.30	17 15	2.98	1.46	17.24
12/06	47.43	18 14	2.76	1.35	16.18
12/05	43.92	19 16	2.50	1.25	17.09
Annual Growth	**(3.6%)**	**— —**	**0.0%**	**6.4%**	**(0.7%)**

Genzyme Corporation

Genzyme makes big money off uncommon diseases. The company's product portfolio focuses on treatments for rare genetic disorders, as well as kidney disease and cancer. One of its main products, Cerezyme, is a leading (and pricey) treatment for Gaucher's disease, a rare enzyme-deficiency condition. Founded in 1981, Genzyme also is involved in drug development, genetic testing, and other services. In addition, the company develops gene-based cancer diagnosis and treatment products, renal care and immunological therapies, and orthopedic biosurgery products.

Cerezyme, the first FDA approved biotech treatment for Gaucher's disease, is one of the most expensive drugs in the world and is Genzyme's top-selling product, accounting for about 20% of global sales in 2009. Genzyme is avidly working to diversify its product line to reduce dependence on the radical therapy, in case competition increases or other factors cause the drug to decrease in profitability over the long term.

The company's fears were realized in 2009 when a rash of difficulties at one of the company's main US manufacturing plants in Allston, Massachusetts, caused a shortage in Cerezyme, crimping annual sales of the drug and making room for competitors to elbow their way into the market. Genetic disorder drug Fabrazyme for Fabry disease, which accounts for 10% of sales, is also experiencing supply constraints due to the plant troubles. Genzyme is working to reverse the shortage by moving some manufacturing operations to its Ireland facility and correcting contamination issues at the plant. In 2010 the company also struck a deal with Hospira to outsource some of its manufacturing functions.

The company had already been working to expand capacity at its manufacturing facilities in Belgium and Ireland. In addition, it is nearing completion on a new biotech plant in Framingham, Massachusetts, scheduled to open in 2011.

In 2008 the company received approval for Mozobil, a treatment for cancer patients undergoing stem cell transplants, and in 2009 it launched Synvisc-One, an enhanced version of the Biosurgery division's osteoarthritis treatment, in the US market. Genzyme has also been expanding its cancer testing and treatment products in recent years, primarily through acquisitions; in 2009 it acquired full development and commercialization rights for leukemia drug Campath from former partner Bayer.

The company's development pipeline includes therapies for the treatment of multiple sclerosis, cystic fibrosis, and cancer tumors, as well as new rare disease treatments. Genzyme is collaborating with Isis Pharmaceuticals on cholesterol treatment mipomersen and with Osiris Therapeutics on cell therapeutics for cardiovascular, inflammatory, and orthopedic ailments. It is also developing a next-generation version of Myozyme (called Lumizyme) and is working to expand indications for drugs including Campath and pediatric leukemia treatment Clolar.

HISTORY

From little oaks, mighty biotech companies may grow. In 1981 Tufts professor Henry Blair (now a board member) teamed up with Sherman Snyder and Oak Venture Partners to buy biotech businesses. (The first purchase was an English company that made diagnostic enzymes and had an agreement with the National Institutes of Health to make an enzyme for Gaucher's disease patients.) Armed both with a good therapeutic candidate and a salable product to help fund its development, Genzyme became profitable in 1984 and went public in 1986.

Genzyme diversified through purchases, adding fine chemicals (for use in clinical chemistry testing; exited 1997), diagnostics (such as cholesterol testing), and biotherapeutics. In 1989 the firm bought prenatal testing company Integrated Genetics, which had molecular biology capabilities, and took it public in 1991. Genzyme's development efforts paid off that year when Ceredase was approved to treat Gaucher's disease. The product's protected orphan drug status quickly made it a cash cow. The company later made purchases in such areas as tissue repair (1995), surgical specialties (1996), and cancer treatments (1997).

In 1998 it began selling newly approved Renagel kidney disease treatment (developed with GelTex Pharmaceuticals, which it bought in

2000), as well as Biogen's AVONEX multiple sclerosis drug in Japan. In 1999 the company increased its niche focus by buying Peptimmune, which developed drugs for rare genetic disorders.

In 2000 Genzyme bought Biomatrix and combined it with Genzyme Tissue Repair and Genzyme Surgical Products to form Genzyme Biosurgery. The next year it bought a private Brazilian pharmaceutical company to regain Renagel distribution rights in that key market. In August 2001 its Fabry disease drug Fabrazyme won European approval, marking the firm's entrance into a niche market.

Looking to capitalize on some R&D, the firm in 2002 created subsidiary Peptimmune to create new therapies for autoimmune and allergy disorders. That year the company settled a 1991 suit with Genentech disputing royalty rights to Genentech's TNKase; Genzyme's buy of Integrated Genetics gave it patents the company alleged were key to TNKase. The FDA helped the company in 2003 expand its product portfolio: The agency approved Fabrazyme and Aldurazyme, another niche drug co-developed with BioMarin.

As part of plans to simplify its structure, Genzyme consolidated its tracking stocks under its primary GENZ ticker in 2003. (However, the consolidation resulted in a $64 million class action lawsuit settlement in 2009 for former Genzyme Biosurgery stockholders over alleged market price manipulations.)

With the 2004 purchase of ILEX Oncology, valued at $1 billion, Genzyme aimed to augment its oncology pipeline with two late-stage products. The next year it bought Verigen, which had developed a cartilage repair cell therapy available in Europe and Australia.

To further expand its oncology operations, Genzyme in 2006 acquired AnorMED, which was developing a treatment for cancer patients undergoing stem cell transplants (Mozobil, approved by the FDA in 2008). Genzyme also brought to market a new non-small cell lung cancer test for the KRAS gene (and mutations thereof) designed to help doctors determine therapy regimens.

In 2007 it acquired Bioenvision for $345 million, mostly to gain worldwide rights to Bioenvision's acute lymphoblastic leukemia treatment for pediatric patients, clofarabine (Clolar), which the two companies developed collaboratively.

EXECUTIVES

Chairman, President, and CEO: Henri A. Termeer, age 63, $13,773,782 total compensation
COO: David P. Meeker, age 55
EVP Finance and CFO: Michael S. Wyzga, age 54, $3,019,202 total compensation
EVP; President, International Group: Sandford D. (Sandy) Smith, age 62, $2,903,746 total compensation
EVP; President, Global Manufacturing and Corporate Operations: Scott A. Canute, age 49
EVP Legal and Corporate Development, and Secretary: Peter Wirth, age 59, $3,246,359 total compensation
SVP; President, Cardiometabolic and Renal: John P. Butler
SVP and Chief Human Resources Officer: Zoltan A. Csimma, age 68
SVP, General Counsel, and Chief Legal Officer: Thomas J. DesRosier, age 55
SVP Research and Chief Scientific Officer: Alan E. Smith, age 64
SVP Clinical Research: Andrew Lee
SVP and Head, Biologics Research and Development: John M. McPherson
SVP Global Medical Affairs: Ulrich Goldmann

SVP; Global Head Regulatory Affairs and Corporate Quality Compliance: Pamela Williamson-Joyce
SVP Genzyme Diagnostics: David D. Fleming
SVP Corporate Development: Richard H. Douglas, age 57
SVP Biomedical and Regulatory Affairs and Chief Medical Officer: Richard A. Moscicki, age 57
SVP Finance, Controller, and Chief Accounting Officer: Jason A. Amello
VP; President, Diagnostic Products: Donald E. (Don) Pogorzelski
Associate Director Corporate Communications: John Lacey
Investor Relations: Patrick Flanigan
Auditors: PricewaterhouseCoopers LLP

LOCATIONS

HQ: Genzyme Corporation
500 Kendall St., Cambridge, MA 02142
Phone: 617-252-7500   **Fax:** 617-252-7600
Web: www.genzyme.com

2009 Sales

	$ mil.	% of total
US	2,375.5	52
Europe	1,388.4	31
Other regions	751.6	17
Total	**4,515.5**	**100**

PRODUCTS/OPERATIONS

2009 Sales

	$ mil.	% of total
Genetic diseases	1,774.6	39
Cardiometabolic & renal	1,011.3	22
Biosurgery	561.8	13
Hematologic oncology	300.4	7
Corporate & other	867.4	19
Total	**4,515.5**	**100**

Selected Products

Genetic diseases (lysosomal storage disorders)
  Aldurazyme (Mucopolysaccharidosis I)
  Cerezyme (Gaucher's disease)
  Elaprase (Mucopolysaccharidosis II, with Shire)
  Fabrazyme (Fabry disease)
  Myozyme (Pompe disease)
Cardiometabolic and renal
  Hectorol (kidney disease)
  Renagel/Renvela (kidney disease)
  Thyrogen (adjunctive diagnostic for thyroid cancer)
Biosurgery
  Carticel (cartilage damage treatment)
  Epicel (severe burn treatment)
  Matrix-induced Autologous Chondrocyte Implantation (MACI, cartilage repair)
  Sepra products (wound healing biomaterials including Seprafilm adhesion barrier)
  Synvisc/Synvisc-One/Jonexa (osteoarthritis pain)
Oncology
  Campath/MabCampath (B-cell chronic lymphocytic leukemia)
  Clolar (clofarabine, acute lymphoblastic leukemia)
  Fludara (B-cell chronic lymphocytic leukemia, marketed as Oforta by Sanofi-Aventis in the US)
  Leukine (acute myelogenous leukemia)
  Mozobil (stem cell transplant therapy for non-Hodgkin's lymphoma and multiple myeloma)
Other
  Diagnostic products (infectious disease and cholesterol testing)
  Thymoglobulin (organ rejection)
  WelChol (cholesterol reduction)

HISTORICAL FINANCIALS

Company Type: Public

Income Statement

FYE: December 31

	REVENUE ($ mil.)	NET INCOME ($ mil.)	NET PROFIT MARGIN	EMPLOYEES
12/09	4,516	422	9.4%	12,000
12/08	4,605	421	9.1%	11,000
12/07	3,814	480	12.6%	10,000
12/06	3,187	(17)	—	9,000
12/05	2,735	442	16.1%	8,200
Annual Growth	13.4%	(1.1%)	—	10.0%

2009 Year-End Financials

Debt ratio: 12.6%
Return on equity: 5.6%
Cash ($ mil.): 742
Current ratio: 2.59
Long-term debt ($ mil.): 970
No. of shares (mil.): 267
Dividends
Yield: —
Payout: —
Market value ($ mil.): 13,079

Stock History

NASDAQ (GS): GENZ

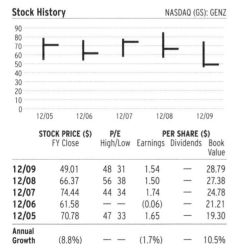

	STOCK PRICE ($) FY Close	P/E High/Low		PER SHARE ($) Earnings	Dividends	Book Value
12/09	49.01	48	31	1.54	—	28.79
12/08	66.37	56	38	1.50	—	27.38
12/07	74.44	44	34	1.74	—	24.78
12/06	61.58	—	—	(0.06)	—	21.21
12/05	70.78	47	33	1.65	—	19.30
Annual Growth	(8.8%)	—	—	(1.7%)	—	10.5%

Gilead Sciences

Gilead Sciences has biotech balms for infectious diseases, including hepatitis, HIV, and infections related to AIDS. The company's HIV franchise includes blockbuster Truvada, a combination of two of its other drugs, Viread and Emtriva. It co-promotes another HIV treatment, called Atripla, in the US and Europe with Bristol-Myers Squibb. Other products on the market include AmBisome, used to treat systemic fungal infections such as those that accompany AIDS; Vistide, for AIDS-related eye infections; and hepatitis B antiviral Hepsera. Outside of the infectious disease realm, Gilead markets Letairis, a treatment for pulmonary arterial hypertension (PAH), or high pulmonary blood pressure.

The FDA approval of Letairis was the first big payoff from Gilead's foray into areas outside of infectious disease. Letairis was gained through the acquisition of Myogen, which also contributed Flolan, an FDA-approved treatment for primary pulmonary hypertension that Gilead now markets in the US under license from GlaxoSmithKline. In 2008 Gilead acquired another potential PAH drug called cicletanine from Navitas Assets.

In further matters of the heart, Gilead acquired CV Therapeutics (and renamed it Gilead Palo Alto), which developed and marketed therapies for chronic angina (chest pain) and other cardiovascular ailments, as well as cardiac imaging agents. The $1.4 billion acquisition was completed in April 2009 after CV Therapeutics fended off a hostile takeover attempt from marketing partner Astellas Pharma.

Despite its expansion into the areas of cardiovascular and pulmonary diseases, Gilead's main source of revenue continues to be its HIV franchise, which contributes about 85% of sales.

Increasing international commercialization of Atripla is a major focus area for Gilead. The drug is an antiretroviral therapy that combines Bristol-Myers Squibb's Sustiva with Gilead's Truvada and the two companies are ramping up marketing activities for Truvada throughout the European territories.

Along with growing international sales, Gilead has to be ever-vigilant about protecting itself against patent expirations. Some of its big sellers (including Tamiflu and Hepsera) are set to lost patent exclusivity in the next few years. As generics of those same medications begin to flood the market, Gilead will have to launch new or next generation products to keep the money coming in.

Additionally, Gilead Sciences receives royalties on influenza treatment Tamiflu, which it developed with Roche, and on Macugen, an ophthalmologic drug developed by OSI Pharmaceuticals using technology licensed from Gilead.

As yet another way of fending off losses from patent expirations, Gilead Sciences has begun to diversify its product line through acquisitions. In 2010 the company announced it would acquire CGI Pharmaceuticals for up to $120 million. CGI gives Gilead a portfolio of small molecule kinase inhibitors that have a range of applications including the treatment of serious inflammatory diseases, such as rheumatoid arthritis.

HISTORY

Dr. Michael Riordan started Gilead Sciences in 1987, backed by venture capital firm Menlo Ventures. The name was derived from the Biblical phrase "Is there no balm in Gilead?" In 1990 Glaxo Wellcome (now GlaxoSmithKline) agreed to fund Gilead's research into code-blocking treatments for cancer. Gilead went public in 1992.

In 1994 the company formed an alliance with American Home Products' Storz Instruments (now part of Bausch & Lomb) to develop and market a topical treatment for an ophthalmic virus. Two years later Gilead joined forces with Roche to develop treatments for influenza.

Vistide was approved in the US in 1996 and in Europe in 1997. But more-effective HIV therapies brought declining demand for Vistide.

The company bounced back with Tamiflu (the fruit of its Roche partnership), which was approved in 1999. Sales were brisk during that flu season. Also that year Gilead expanded its pipeline and geographic reach with the $550 million, all-stock acquisition of NeXstar Pharmaceuticals, which focused on antifungals, antibiotics, and cancer treatments.

In 2000 Gilead sought approval for Tamiflu in Japan and Europe (it withdrew the European application after regulators there asked for more information) and also sought approval for pediatric uses for the drug, which was granted. The following year it resubmitted Tamiflu for approval in Europe.

Chairman Donald Rumsfeld resigned in 2001 to become US secretary of defense and was replaced by retired Sears, Roebuck executive James Denny. Perhaps the Defense connection helped: Vistide became one of the drugs that researchers began studying as possible alternatives to vaccines should a smallpox bio-attack occur in the US.

Also in 2001 Gilead sold its oncology pipeline to OSI Pharmaceuticals to focus on infection-control products and its hepatitis B lead drug candidate. The sale was a smart move — the FDA approved Hepsera less than a year later.

To help alleviate the AIDS epidemic, in 2003 the company announced plans to sell Viread at cost to all African nations and some 15 other impoverished countries stricken by the disease. That year Gilead won FDA approval for another weapon to battle AIDS: antiretroviral Emtriva.

To acquire new ammo in its battle against HIV, the firm bought Triangle Pharmaceuticals in 2003. Gilead sparred with its Tamiflu partner Roche in 2005, claiming Roche had not put forth enough effort to make the antiviral a blockbuster. The two reached a new agreement late that year, with Roche agreeing to a one-time $62.5 million payment and increased royalties.

The 2006 acquisition of Corus Pharma expanded the company's pipeline of investigational drugs outside its core area of infectious disease. Corus Pharma brought a focus on respiratory diseases, adding a late-stage compound that aims to fight cystic fibrosis-related infections.

It also completed a $2.4 billion acquisition of Myogen, which had development programs in the area of cardiovascular disease, including Letairis (approved in 2007).

Gilead Sciences shored up its manufacturing capabilities with a couple of acquisitions in 2006 and 2007. It bought Raylo Chemicals, formerly a Canada-based subsidiary of Degussa (now Evonik Degussa); Raylo is a manufacturer of active pharmaceutical ingredients and other chemicals used in drug development. It also purchased a manufacturing plant in Ireland in 2007.

EXECUTIVES

Chairman and CEO: John C. Martin, age 58, $14,675,231 total compensation
President and COO: John F. Milligan, age 49, $6,942,759 total compensation
EVP Research and Development and Chief Scientific Officer: Norbert W. Bischofberger, age 54, $4,201,572 total compensation
EVP Corporate and Medical Affairs: Gregg H. Alton, age 44, $2,682,789 total compensation
EVP Commercial Operations: Kevin Young, age 52, $4,568,146 total compensation
SVP and CFO: Robin L. Washington, age 47, $3,526,459 total compensation
SVP Pharmaceutical Development and Manufacturing: Taiyin Yang, age 56
SVP Liver Disease Therapeutics: John G. McHutchison
SVP Human Resources: Kristen M. Metza, age 50
SVP Development Operations: Andrew Cheng
SVP Respiratory Therapeutics: A. Bruce Montgomery
SVP Research: William A. Lee, age 54
SVP Manufacturing and Operations: Anthony D. Caracciolo, age 55
SVP Corporate Development: John J. Toole, age 56
SVP Commercial Operations, North America: James R. Meyers, age 45
SVP International Commercial Operations: Paul Carter
VP Investor Relations: Susan Hubbard
Auditors: Ernst & Young LLP

LOCATIONS

HQ: Gilead Sciences, Inc.
333 Lakeside Dr., Foster City, CA 94404
Phone: 650-574-3000   **Fax:** 650-578-9264
Web: www.gilead.com

2009 Sales

	$ mil.	% of total
US	3,599.3	51
Europe		
France	468.3	7
Spain	451.1	6
Switzerland	448.2	6
UK	393.0	6
Italy	323.7	5
Germany	293.1	4
Other European countries	603.1	9
Other countries	431.5	6
Total	**7,011.3**	**100**

PRODUCTS/OPERATIONS

2009 Sales

	$ mil.	% of total
Antiviral product sales		
Truvada	2,489.6	36
Atripla	2,382.1	34
Viread	667.5	10
Hepsera	271.6	4
Emtriva	27.9	—
Other product sales		
AmBisome	298.6	4
Letaris	184.0	3
Ranexa	131.1	2
Other	16.8	—
Royalties	491.8	7
Contract & other	50.3	—
Total	**7,011.3**	**100**

Selected Products

Approved
AmBisome (antifungal)
Atripla (HIV, with Bristol-Myers Squibb)
Cayston (cystic fibrosis)
Emtriva (HIV)
Flolan (pulmonary hypertension)
Hepsera (hepatitis B)
Letairis (pulmonary arterial hypertension)
Lexiscan (cardiovascular)
Ranexa (chronic angina)
Tamiflu (flu treatment)
Truvada (fixed-dose combination of Viread and Emtriva for HIV)
Viread (HIV)
Vistide (AIDS-related cytomegalovirus retinitis)

In development
Ambrisentan (idiopathic pulmonary fibrosis)
Aztreonam (cystic fibrosis)
Cobicistate (HIV/AIDS)
Elvitegravir (HIV)

COMPETITORS

Abbott Labs
Actelion
AstraZeneca
Bausch & Lomb
BioCryst Pharmaceuticals
Boehringer Ingelheim
Bristol-Myers Squibb
CIBA VISION
Enzon
Genentech
GlaxoSmithKline
Idenix Pharmaceuticals
InterMune
Merck
Novartis
Pfizer
Roche Holding
Shire
Three Rivers Pharmaceuticals
Valeant

HISTORICAL FINANCIALS

Company Type: Public

Income Statement

FYE: December 31

	REVENUE ($ mil.)	NET INCOME ($ mil.)	NET PROFIT MARGIN	EMPLOYEES
12/09	7,011	2,636	37.6%	3,852
12/08	5,336	2,011	37.7%	3,441
12/07	4,230	1,615	38.2%	2,979
12/06	3,026	(1,190)	—	2,515
12/05	2,028	814	40.1%	1,900
Annual Growth	**36.4%**	**34.1%**	**—**	**19.3%**

2009 Year-End Financials

Debt ratio: 19.5%
Return on equity: 50.1%
Cash ($ mil.): 1,273
Current ratio: 2.57
Long-term debt ($ mil.): 1,243
No. of shares (mil.): 839
Dividends
  Yield: —
  Payout: —
Market value ($ mil.): 36,288

Stock History

NASDAQ (GS): GILD

	STOCK PRICE ($) FY Close	P/E High/Low		PER SHARE ($) Earnings	Dividends	Book Value
12/09	43.27	19	14	2.82	—	7.59
12/08	51.14	27	17	2.10	—	4.95
12/07	46.01	29	19	1.68	—	4.13
12/06	32.47	—	—	(1.29)	—	2.17
12/05	26.28	33	18	0.86	—	3.61
Annual Growth	**13.3%**	**—**	**—**	**34.6%**	**—**	**20.4%**

Goldman Sachs

Goldman Sachs has traditionally possessed the Midas touch in the investment banking world. A global leader in mergers and acquisitions advice and securities underwriting, Goldman offers a gamut of investment banking and asset management services to corporate and government clients worldwide, as well as institutional and individual investors. It owns Goldman Sachs Execution & Clearing, one of the largest market makers on the NYSE and a leading market maker for fixed income products, currencies, and commodities. Through affiliates GS Capital Partners, GS Mezzanine Partners, and others, Goldman Sachs is also one of the largest private equity investors in the world.

In 2008 Goldman Sachs converted to a bank holding company and formed subsidiary Goldman Sachs Bank USA (GS Bank USA), now in charge of bank loan trading, mortgage originations, and other activities. The Federal Reserve mandated the change for Goldman Sachs and fellow investment bank Morgan Stanley. The shift marked a monumental change on Wall Street, as it put an end to the independent brokerage firm model that had been a mainstay in the US since reform measures were implemented during the Great Depression. Rivals Merrill Lynch, Lehman Brothers, and Bear Stearns, which were plagued by debt and credit problems, either merged with larger banks or filed for bankruptcy earlier in 2008. The bank holding company structure brings increased regulation, but allows Goldman Sachs to acquire commercial banks — all in an effort to shore up the company's balance sheet.

In the days following the Federal Reserve announcement, Warren Buffett's Berkshire Hathaway invested $5 billion in Goldman Sachs and acquired an option to assume $5 billion more of the company's common shares. Goldman Sachs made an additional $5 billion worth of stock available in a public offering. Additionally, the US government stepped in with funding for Goldman Sachs in late 2008, when it announced an economic stimulus plan to buy some $250 billion worth of preferred shares of the nation's top banks; approximately $10 billion went to Goldman Sachs.

The capital infusions helped, but didn't completely shield Goldman Sachs from the financial crisis, the effects of which were felt worldwide. To cut costs, the firm trimmed some 10% of its workforce. It eventually returned to profitability in 2009 and paid back the money it received from the government, but still drew ire from politicians over what have been perceived to be extravagant pay packages for its top employees.

In 2010 the Securities and Exchange Commission filed a lawsuit against the company accusing it of fraud. The SEC alleged that Goldman Sachs misled its clients about the structuring and marketing of a risky financial product related to subprime mortgages. As the value of the mortgage product plunged due to the housing bust, Goldman Sachs allowed one of its hedge fund clients (who heavily influenced the makeup of the product) to bet against the market. As a result, that client reaped billions of dollars. The SEC said it was a major conflict of interest. Though it denied any wrongdoing, Goldman Sachs paid some $550 million to settle a civil suit related to the fraud case.

HISTORY

German immigrant-cum-Philadelphia retailer Marcus Goldman moved to New York in 1869 and began buying customers' promissory notes from jewelers to resell to banks. Goldman's son-in-law came aboard in 1882, and the firm became Goldman, Sachs & Co. in 1885.

Two years later Goldman Sachs began offering US-UK foreign exchange and currency services. To serve such clients as Sears, Roebuck, it expanded to Chicago and St. Louis. In 1896 it joined the NYSE.

While the firm increased its European contracts, Goldman's son Henry made it a major source of financing for US industry. In 1906 it co-managed its first public offering, United Cigar Manufacturers (later General Cigar). By 1920 it had underwritten IPOs for Sears, B.F. Goodrich, and Merck.

Sidney Weinberg made partner in 1927 and stayed until his death in 1969. In the 1930s Goldman Sachs entered securities dealing and sales. After WWII it became a leader in investment banking, co-managing Ford's 1956 IPO. In the 1970s it pioneered buying blocks of stock for resale.

Under Weinberg's son John, Goldman Sachs became a leader in mergers and acquisitions. The 1981 purchase of J. Aron gave the firm a significant commodities presence and helped it grow in South America.

Seeking capital after 1987's market crash, Goldman Sachs raised more than $500 million from Sumitomo for a 12% nonvoting interest in the firm (since reduced to 3%). The Kamehameha Schools/Bishop Estate of Hawaii, an educational trust, also invested.

The 1994 bond crash and a decline in new debt issues led Goldman Sachs to cut staffing for the first time since the 1980s. But problems went deeper. Partners began leaving and taking their equity. Cost cuts, a stronger bond market, and the long bull market helped the firm rebound; firm members sought protection through limited liability partnership status. The firm also extended the period during which partners can cash out (slowing the cash drain) and limited the number of people entitled to a share of profits. Overseas growth in 1996 and 1997 focused on the UK and Asia.

After three decades of resistance, the partners in 1998 voted to sell the public a minority stake in the firm, but market volatility led to postponement. Goldman Sachs also suffered from involvement with Long-Term Capital Management, ultimately contributing $300 million to its bailout.

In 1999 Jon Corzine, then co-chairman and co-CEO, announced that he would leave the group after seeing it through its IPO, and Goldman Sachs finally went public that year in an offering valued at close to $4 billion. In 2000 Corzine was elected to a US Senate seat. The New Jersey Democrat spent more than $64 million on his campaign (a record), nearly $61 million of it from his own personal wealth (also a record). Corzine went on to win New Jersey's gubernatorial race in 2005.

In early 2004, Goldman president and COO John Thain left the firm to assume the helm of the New York Stock Exchange. Lloyd Blankfein was named his successor and became chairman and CEO in 2006 when his predecessor Henry "Hank" Paulson was named secretary of the US Treasury.

EXECUTIVES

Chairman and CEO: Lloyd C. Blankfein, age 55, $862,657 total compensation
Vice Chairman; Chairman, Goldman Sachs Asia: J. Michael (Mike) Evans, age 52, $1,624,448 total compensation
Vice Chairman; Co-Head, Global Investment Banking Division: John S. Weinberg, age 52, $732,540 total compensation
Vice Chairman; Co-CEO, Goldman Sachs International: Michael S. Sherwood, age 44
President, COO, and Director: Gary D. Cohn, age 49, $825,156 total compensation
EVP and CFO: David A. Viniar, age 54, $837,365 total compensation
EVP, General Counsel, and Co-Head Legal: Gregory K. Palm, age 61
EVP, General Counsel, and Co-Head Legal: Esta E. Stecher, age 52
EVP and Global Head Compliance: Alan M. Cohen, age 59
Global Head Recruiting and Managing Director: Edith Hunt
Managing Director and Co-CEO, Goldman Sachs Asset Management South Korea: Terence Lim
Managing Director, India Securities: Rohit Narang
Managing Director and Global Head, Corporate Credit, Goldman Sachs Asset Management.: Gregg Felton
Managing Director, India Securities: Vijay Karnani
Managing Director and Head, Greater China Securities: Alan Zhang
Managing Director, Controller, and Chief Accounting Officer, Korea: Sarah E. Smith
Co-Head, Global Investment Banking Division: David M. Solomon
Head, US Investment-Grade Syndicate Desk: Jonathan Fine
COO, Investment Banking Division: James Esposito
Senior Investment Strategist; President, Global Markets Institute: Abby Joseph Cohen
Secretary: John F. W. Rogers
Auditors: PricewaterhouseCoopers LLP

LOCATIONS

HQ: The Goldman Sachs Group, Inc.
85 Broad St., New York, NY 10004
Phone: 212-902-1000　　**Fax:** 212-902-3000
Web: www.goldmansachs.com

PRODUCTS/OPERATIONS

2009 Sales

	$ mil.	% of total
Trading & principal investments	28,879	56
Interest income	13,907	27
Investment banking	4,797	9
Asset management & securities services	4,090	8
Total	**51,673**	**100**

Selected Subsidiaries

Goldman, Sachs & Co.
Goldman Sachs Bank (Europe) PLC (Ireland)
Goldman Sachs Bank USA
　William Street Funding Corporation
Goldman Sachs Credit Partners L.P. (Bermuda)
Goldman Sachs Financial Markets, L.P.
Goldman Sachs International (UK)
Goldman Sachs International Bank (UK)
Goldman Sachs Japan Co., Ltd.
Goldman Sachs Mortgage Company
GS Mortgage Securities Corp.
GSTM LLC
　Goldman Sachs Execution & Clearing, L.P.
J. Aron & Company

COMPETITORS

Banc of America Securities
BMO Capital Markets
CIBC World Markets
Citigroup Global Markets
Credit Suisse (USA)
Deutsche Bank Securities (USA)
FMR
JPMorgan Chase
Lazard
Merrill Lynch
Morgan Stanley
Nomura Securities
RBC Capital Markets
Scotia Capital
UBS

HISTORICAL FINANCIALS

Company Type: Public

Income Statement

				FYE: December 31
	REVENUE ($ mil.)	NET INCOME ($ mil.)	NET PROFIT MARGIN	EMPLOYEES
12/09*	51,673	13,385	25.9%	32,500
11/08	53,579	2,322	4.3%	30,067
11/07	87,968	11,599	13.2%	30,522
11/06	69,353	9,537	13.8%	26,467
11/05	43,391	5,626	13.0%	31,005
Annual Growth	**4.5%**	**24.2%**	**—**	**1.2%**

*Fiscal year change

2009 Year-End Financials

Debt ratio: 290.3%　　No. of shares (mil.): 516
Return on equity: 24.0%　　Dividends
Cash ($ mil.): 74,954　　　Yield: 0.9%
Current ratio: —　　　　　Payout: 6.9%
Long-term debt ($ mil.): 185,085　Market value ($ mil.): 87,057

Stock History

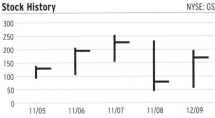

NYSE: GS

	STOCK PRICE ($) FY Close	P/E High/Low		Earnings	PER SHARE ($) Dividends	Book Value
12/09*	168.84	9	3	22.13	1.52	137.14
11/08	78.99	51	11	4.47	1.40	124.84
11/07	226.64	10	6	24.73	1.40	83.01
11/06	194.80	10	5	19.69	1.30	69.40
11/05	128.96	12	8	11.21	1.00	54.31
Annual Growth	**7.0%**	**—**	**—**	**18.5%**	**11.0%**	**26.1%**

*Fiscal year change

Goodrich Corporation

Goodrich is a tireless leader in aerospace systems. The company serves regional/business aircraft, original equipment and aftermarket, helicopters, military, and space markets through its three aerospace divisions. Goodrich's largest unit, Actuation and Landing Systems, makes fuel systems, aircraft wheels, brakes, landing gear, and flight control systems. Nacelles and Interior Systems offers MRO services and makes aerostructures (pylons and thrust reversers), as well as aircraft seats, and cargo and lighting systems. Finally, the Electronic Systems division makes fuel and engine controls, flight management systems, and reconnaissance and surveillance systems. The US government accounts for about 22% of sales.

In regard to defense spending, the White House has altered the budget to support items that will increase the military's speed, flexibility, and precision — as opposed to combat warfare equipment — such as unmanned aerial vehicles (UAV) and systems (UAS), advanced sensors, and other high-tech systems that support ongoing operations in Afghanistan and Iraq. The company's Electronic Systems division, which includes sensor and ISR systems (intelligence, surveillance, and reconnaissance), answers the call. ISR Systems has shown significant growth in international defense programs. In May 2009 the company acquired Cloud Cap Technology, a company that makes stabilized camera microgimbals (a pivoting device that allows rotation of an object) for UAS applications.

In mid-2010 it purchased Crompton Technology Group, a UK-based designer and manufacturer of carbon fiber composite products used in aerospace, defense, and energy applications. In 2009 Goodrich acquired AIS Global Holdings LLC (better known as Atlantic Inertial Systems) from J.H. Lehman & Company.

Later that year Goodrich bought TEAC Aerospace Holdings from private equity firm Thayer Hidden Creek Partners. TEAC is a provider of airborne mission data and video recording and debriefing equipment for defense customers. The company also offers cabin video systems for commercial airlines.

As the business jet market recovers, the company is taking the opportunity to build on its commercial jet business and has signed an agreement in mid-2010 to acquire the Cabin Management assets of DeCrane. Goodrich will spend approximately $280 million to acquire DeCrane's business jet interior systems.

Recognizing Turkey as a fast-growing region, the company agreed to form a joint venture with Turkish Technic in 2010 to provide MRO services in Istanbul. In 2009 it announced a 50/50 joint venture with Rolls-Royce plc, the world's second-largest airplane engine maker (BMW owns the car operations), to produce engine controls for Rolls-Royce aircraft. It partnered with China-based Xi'an Aircraft International to form two joint venture companies for the production of landing gear and engine nacelle components for the Chinese aerospace market.

HISTORY

Orphan, doctor, Civil War veteran, and entrepreneur Benjamin Franklin Goodrich bought stock in the Hudson River Rubber Co. in 1869 and moved the firm to Akron, Ohio, in 1870. Its rubber products included fire hoses, bottle stoppers, rubber rings for canning jars, and billiard cushions. After the depression of the mid-1870s, the company reorganized as B.F. Goodrich & Co (BFG).

BFG's new uses for rubber galvanized the industry, but it was the advent of rubber tires that secured the company's future. In 1896 bicycle maker Alexander Winton asked BFG to make tires for his "horseless carriage." (A British company named Silvertown had invented the pneumatic tire, and BFG acquired the patent.) As the automobile's popularity grew, BFG continued to improve its tires. It added fabric cords and carbon black to make tires tougher and give them black coloring.

BFG introduced the first rubber sponge in 1902 and began making aircraft tires in 1909 (standard on WWI airplanes). In the 1920s the company added sliding fasteners made by Universal Fastener to its rubber galoshes and began calling the boots "zippers." In 1926 BFG scientists formulated polyvinyl chloride (PVC). The following year the company supplied tires for Charles Lindbergh's *Spirit of St. Louis,* and in the 1930s BFG introduced the first commercial aircraft de-icer.

BFG was at the forefront of the effort to make synthetic rubber, especially after Japan cut the US's supply of natural rubber during WWII. Its chemicals division was organized in 1943. During the war BFG introduced continuous rubber tracks for tanks, as well as the technology used in pilots' "Mae West" life vests.

The company began selling tubeless tires in 1947, and by the mid-1950s new cars came equipped with the safer tires. In 1956 it formed its aerospace division. A few years later the company provided the space suit worn by Alan Shepard, the first American in space. BFG also made P-F Flyers, sneakers popular with children in the 1960s.

John Ong became chairman in 1979 and reduced the company's dependence on tires. In 1986 BFG and Uniroyal formed the Uniroyal Goodrich Tire Co. When Michelin bought the unit in 1990, BFG was out of the tire business.

Acquisitions during the 1990s include Hercules Aircraft and Electronics Group (1990), Eastern Airlines Avionics (test equipment, 1991), GE Specialty Heating and Avionics Power (heated and electrical components, 1994), and Rohr (commercial airline engine nacelles, 1997). David Burner, an executive at BFG since 1983, replaced Ong as chairman in 1997.

In 1999 BFG acquired Coltec Industries and moved its headquarters from Richfield, Ohio, to Coltec's home — Charlotte, North Carolina.

Early in 2001 BFG sold its performance materials operations (industrial plastics and additives) to an investor group for $1.4 billion. In June 2001 the company changed its name to Goodrich Corporation. In October Goodrich announced that it was closing 16 plants and cutting its workforce by about 10% because of the slowdown in the aircraft manufacturing business.

Late in 2002 Goodrich paid $1.5 billion in cash for TRW's Aeronautical Systems unit (flight controls, cargo systems, engine control systems, power/utility systems, missile actuation).

In 2004 Goodrich won a deal to supply Boeing with thrust reversers, engine coverings, wheels, brake systems, lighting, and cargo handling systems for its upcoming 787 airplane. In 2007 it sold its Goodrich Aviation Technical Services (ATS) subsidiary to Macquarie Bank Limited.

EXECUTIVES

Chairman, President, and CEO: Marshall O. Larsen, age 61, $8,703,163 total compensation
EVP and CFO: Scott E. Kuechle, age 50, $2,786,908 total compensation
EVP Administration and General Counsel: Terrence G. (Terry) Linnert, age 63, $2,705,878 total compensation
EVP Operational Excellence and Technology: Gerald T. (Jerry) Witowski, age 62
SVP Human Resources: Jennifer Pollino, age 45
VP; Segment President, Actuation and Landing Systems: John J. (Jack) Carmola, age 54, $2,742,788 total compensation
VP; Segment President, Nacelles and Interior Systems: Cynthia M. (Cindy) Egnotovich, age 52, $2,786,079 total compensation
VP Corporate Communications: Lisa Bottle
VP Investor Relations: Paul S. Gifford
President, Customer Services: Paul Snyder
President, Engine Components: Daphne Falletti
President, ISR Systems: Tom Bergeron
President, Sensor and Integrated Systems: Brian Gora
President, Aerostructures: Marc A. Duvall
President, Aircraft Wheels and Brakes: Brian Brandewie
President, Landing Gear: Mike Brand
President, Engine Control and Electrical Power Systems: Bob Yancey
President, Actuation Systems: Mike Gardiner
President, Interiors: Tom Mepham
President, China Activities: Michael Barbalas
Auditors: Ernst & Young LLP

LOCATIONS

HQ: Goodrich Corporation
Four Coliseum Centre, 2730 W. Tyvola Rd.
Charlotte, NC 28217
Phone: 704-423-7000 **Fax:** 704-423-7002
Web: www.goodrich.com

2009 Sales

	$ mil.	% of total
North America		
US	3,298.7	49
Canada	236.1	4
Europe	2,281.3	34
Asia/Pacific	510.6	8
Other regions	358.9	5
Total	**6,685.6**	**100**

PRODUCTS/OPERATIONS

2009 Sales by Product Group

	$ mil.	% of total
Engine products & services	2,438.9	36
Landing system products & services	1,471.1	22
Electrical & optical products & services	1,288.7	19
Airframe products & services	856.9	13
Safety products & services	509.9	8
Other	120.1	2
Total	**6,685.6**	**100**

2009 Sales by Business Segment

	$ mil.	% of total
Actuation & landing systems	2,524.3	38
Nacelles & interior systems	2,322.6	35
Electronic systems	1,838.7	27
Total	**6,685.6**	**100**

Selected Products and Markets

Actuation systems (hydraulic, fly-by-wire, and power-by-wire; markets: commercial, regional, helicopter, military)
Aircraft wheels and brakes
Engine components
  Aerospace gas turbine components
  Airfoils and rotating components
  Drive shafts and couplings
Landing gear (aircraft: large commercial, military, and regional/business)

Electronic Systems
  Engine control and electrical power systems
  ISR systems (intelligence, surveillance, and
    reconnaissance)
    Airborne
    Force protection (laser warning systems, precision
      optics for tanks, terahertz sensing systems for
      biological and chemical weapon detection)
    Industrial
    Space
  Sensor systems
    Cockpit information sensors
    Engine control system sensors
    Flight control sensors
Nacelles and Interiors Systems
  Aerostructures (engineered polymer products)
  Aftermarket components and parts, asset
    lease/exchange, and maintenance, repair, and
    overhaul
  GRID-LOCK (technology for joining structural
    components)
  Interiors
    Cargo
    Evacuation
    Lighting
    Propulsion
    Specialty seating
  Nacelle systems (aerodynamic structure that
    surrounds jet engine)
  Pylons (struts that connect propulsion system to
    aircraft)

COMPETITORS

AAR Corp.
Alcoa
Argo-Tech
Astronics
BAE SYSTEMS
BAE Systems Inc.
Banner Aerospace
BE Aerospace
Breeze-Eastern
Chemring
Crane Co.
Danaher
Ducommun
EADS
Esterline
Finmeccanica
GE
General Dynamics
Hamilton Sundstrand
Héroux-Devtek
Honeywell International
Hydro-Aire
ITT Corp.
Kaman Aerospace
L-3 Vertex
LSI Industries
Martin-Baker Aircraft
Meggitt
Moog
Northrop Grumman
Parker Hannifin
Precision Castparts
Raytheon
Rexnord
SAFRAN
Samsung Group
Singapore Technologies Engineering
Spirit AeroSystems
Teleflex
Thales
Triumph Aerostructures — Vought Aircraft Division
Triumph Group
Turbine Engine Components Technologies
United Technologies
Woodward Governor
Zodiac Aerospace

HISTORICAL FINANCIALS

Company Type: Public

Income Statement

FYE: December 31

	REVENUE ($ mil.)	NET INCOME ($ mil.)	NET PROFIT MARGIN	EMPLOYEES
12/09	6,686	611	9.1%	24,000
12/08	7,062	681	9.6%	25,000
12/07	6,392	483	7.5%	23,400
12/06	5,878	482	8.2%	23,400
12/05	5,397	264	4.9%	22,600
Annual Growth	5.5%	23.4%	—	1.5%

2009 Year-End Financials

Debt ratio: 68.7%
Return on equity: 24.4%
Cash ($ mil.): 811
Current ratio: 2.74
Long-term debt ($ mil.): 2,008
No. of shares (mil.): 125
Dividends
  Yield: 1.6%
  Payout: 21.7%
Market value ($ mil.): 8,049

Stock History

NYSE: GR

	STOCK PRICE ($) FY Close	P/E High	P/E Low	PER SHARE ($) Earnings	PER SHARE ($) Dividends	PER SHARE ($) Book Value
12/09	64.25	14	6	4.70	1.02	23.32
12/08	37.02	13	5	5.39	0.93	16.69
12/07	70.61	20	12	3.78	0.82	20.59
12/06	45.55	12	10	3.81	0.80	15.78
12/05	41.10	22	14	2.13	0.80	11.76
Annual Growth	11.8%	—	—	21.9%	6.3%	18.7%

Goodyear Tire & Rubber

With a worldwide alliance with Sumitomo Rubber Industries designed to dominate the tire industry, The Goodyear Tire & Rubber Company remains a leading tire maker, trailing rivals Bridgestone and Michelin. The company primarily sells tires under the Goodyear, Dunlop, Kelly, Fulda, Debica, and Sava brands for the replacement market as well as to the world's automakers. In addition to its own brand of tires, Goodyear makes Dunlop tires for sale in North America and Europe through its alliance with Japan's Sumitomo. The company operates about 57 plants worldwide, and has around 1,500 retail tire and auto repair centers. More than 60% of sales come from outside the US.

At the same time the company is trying to restore profitability to its North American division, Goodyear welcomed a new president and CEO. Former COO Richard Kramer, who has been an advocate of cutting costs, pushing innovation, and expanding into Asian markets, stepped into the head position in mid-April. Predecessor Robert Keegan continues to serve as the company's executive chairman.

The auto industry — a major driver of Goodyear's business — was hit hard by the 2008-2009 global economic downturn, as demand plummeted for high-ticket items like cars, trucks, and industrial machinery. As manufacturers reduced production, sales to the small but steady new car market fell. Even replacement tire sales, which make up a significant portion of Goodyear's business, were down as commercial and retail customers cut back on spending.

The company responded with cost-saving measures, including cutting about 5,700 jobs, eliminating all non-discretionary spending, and reducing its inventory levels. Goodyear is looking to sell non-core assets such as its farm tire business in Europe and Latin America. It also plans to reduce its global tire production capacity by between 15 million and 25 million tires a year by 2011; in 2009 the company discontinued consumer tire manufacturing at a facility in Amiens, France, and closed its Las Pinas, Philippines, plant. Goodyear also liquidated subsidiaries in Guatemala and Jamaica.

Simultaneously, Goodyear is courting customers by ramping up new product releases such as the Assurance Fuel Max tire in the US, which is currently used on commercial vehicles, but will soon appear on passenger cars and light-duty trucks.

For promotional purposes, Goodyear continues to operate three blimps in North America, from bases in California, Florida, and Ohio. Although a number of other companies have emulated Goodyear's blimp marketing, Goodyear's fleet of lighter-than-air-ships is recognized as the first. They have been featured in the company's TV commercials since 1925.

HISTORY

In 1898 Frank and Charles Seiberling founded a tire and rubber company in Akron, Ohio, and named it after Charles Goodyear (inventor of the vulcanization process, 1839). The debut of the Quick Detachable tire and the Universal Rim (1903) made Goodyear the world's largest tire maker by 1916.

Goodyear began manufacturing in Canada in 1910, and over the next two decades it expanded into Argentina, Australia, and the Dutch East Indies. The company established its own rubber plantations in Sumatra (now part of Indonesia) in 1916.

Financial woes led to reorganization in 1921, and investment bankers forced the Seiberlings out. Succeeding caretaker management, Paul Litchfield began three decades as CEO in 1926, a time in which Goodyear emerged to become the world's largest rubber company.

Goodyear blimps served as floating billboards nationwide by the 1930s. During that decade Goodyear opened company stores, acquired tire maker Kelly-Springfield (1935), and began producing tires made from synthetic rubber (1937). After WWII Goodyear was an innovative leader in technologies such as polyester tire cord (1962) and the bias-belted tire (1967).

By 1980 Goodyear had introduced radial tire brands such as the all-weather Tiempo, the Eagle, and the Arriva, as it led the US market.

Thwarting British financier Sir James Goldsmith's takeover attempt in 1986, CEO Robert Mercer raised $1.7 billion by selling the company's non-tire businesses (Motor Wheel, Goodyear Aerospace) and by borrowing heavily.

Recession, overcapacity, and price-cutting in 1990 led to hard times for tire makers. After suffering through 1990, its first money-losing year since the Depression, Goodyear lured Stanley Gault out of retirement. He ceased marketing tires exclusively through Goodyear's dealer network by selling tires through Wal-Mart, Kmart, and Sears. Gault also cut costs through layoffs, plant closures, and spending reductions and returned Goodyear to profitability in 1991.

The company increased its presence in the US retail market in 1995 when it began selling tires through 860 Penske Auto Centers and 300 Montgomery Ward auto centers. President Samir Gibara succeeded chairman Gault as CEO in 1996. That year Goodyear bought Poland's leading tire maker, T C Debica, and a 60% stake in South African tire maker Contred (acquiring the rest in 1998).

The company acquired Sumitomo Rubber Industries' North American and European Dunlop tire businesses in 1999. The acquisition returned Goodyear to its #1 position in the tire-making industry. Despite record sales in 2000, the company's profits hit some hard road, prompting Goodyear to lay off 10% of its workforce and implement other cost-cutting efforts.

Early in 2001 the company announced that it would close its Mexican tire plant. That same year the company agreed to replace Firestone Wilderness AT tires with Goodyear tires for Ford owners as part of Ford's big Firestone tire recall.

In 2002 the tire maker became embroiled in an age discrimination lawsuit claiming unfair job evaluations for the company's older employees. Blaming a slow US economy, Goodyear announced plans to cut 450 jobs at its Union City, Tennessee, manufacturing plant.

In 2003, as the company was embroiled in a lengthy debate with the United Steelworkers union, it was announced that the Huntsville, Alabama, tire manufacturing plant would be closed. Goodyear also announced that it would cut 500 nonunion salaried employees in North America.

The company announced more job cuts in the non-tire sector in 2004, affecting Goodyear's engineered products and chemical units.

The company struck a deal for The Carlyle Group in 2007 to buy its Engineered Products division for about $1.5 billion.

EXECUTIVES

Chairman: Robert J. (Bob) Keegan, age 62, $17,196,460 total compensation
President, CEO, and Director: Richard J. (Rich) Kramer, age 46, $5,553,042 total compensation
EVP and CFO: Darren R. Wells, age 44, $2,453,960 total compensation
SVP, General Counsel, and Secretary: David L. (Dave) Bialosky, age 52, $2,956,244 total compensation
SVP and CTO: Jean-Claude Kihn, age 50
SVP Global Communications: Charles L. (Chuck) Sinclair, age 58
SVP Global Operations: John D. (Jack) Fish, age 52
SVP Finance, Asia Pacific: Damon J. Audia, age 39
SVP Human Resources: Joseph B. (Joe) Ruocco, age 50
VP, Controller, and CIO: Thomas A. (Tom) Connell, age 61
VP Supply Chain: Kevin Olifiers
VP and Chief Procurement Officer: Mark Purtilar, age 49
VP Business Development: Laura K. Thompson, age 45
VP and Treasurer: Scott Honnold, age 45
President, Europe, Middle East, and Africa: Arthur de Bok, age 47, $3,379,946 total compensation
President, North American Tire: Curt J. Andersson, age 48
President, Latin American Region: Eduardo A. Fortunato, age 56
President, Asia Pacific Tire: Pierre E. Cohade, age 48
Director Investor Relations: Patrick (Pat) Stobb
Director Corporate Communications: Rob Whitehouse
Auditors: PricewaterhouseCoopers LLP

LOCATIONS

HQ: The Goodyear Tire & Rubber Company
1144 E. Market St., Akron, OH 44316
Phone: 330-796-2121   **Fax:** 330-796-2222
Web: www.goodyear.com

2009 Sales

	$ mil.	% of total
US	5,953	36
Germany	1,927	12
Other countries	8,421	52
Total	**16,301**	**100**

PRODUCTS/OPERATIONS

2009 Sales

	$ mil.	% of total
North American Tire	6,977	43
Europe, Middle East & Africa Tire	5,801	36
Latin American Tire	1,814	11
Asia/Pacific Tire	1,709	10
Total	**16,301**	**100**

Selected Products

Automotive repair services
Chemical products
Natural rubber
Tires
  Automotive
  Aviation
  Buses
  Construction
  Farm
  Mining
  Motorcycles
  Trucks
Tread rubber
Wholesale tires

COMPETITORS

Bridgestone
Continental AG
Cooper Tire & Rubber
Hankook Tire
Kumho Tire
Marangoni
Michelin
Midas
Pep Boys
Pirelli
Sime Darby
Titan International
Toyo Tire & Rubber
Yokohama Rubber
Zeon

HISTORICAL FINANCIALS

Company Type: Public

Income Statement

FYE: December 31

	REVENUE ($ mil.)	NET INCOME ($ mil.)	NET PROFIT MARGIN	EMPLOYEES
12/09	16,301	(364)	—	69,000
12/08	19,488	(77)	—	74,700
12/07	19,644	602	3.1%	72,000
12/06	20,258	(330)	—	77,000
12/05	19,723	239	1.2%	80,000
Annual Growth	**(4.7%)**	**—**	**—**	**(3.6%)**

2009 Year-End Financials

Debt ratio: 569.0%
Return on equity: —
Cash ($ mil.): 1,922
Current ratio: 1.76
Long-term debt ($ mil.): 4,182
No. of shares (mil.): 243
Dividends
  Yield: 0.0%
  Payout: —
Market value ($ mil.): 3,425

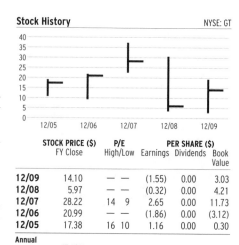

Stock History   NYSE: GT

	STOCK PRICE ($) FY Close	P/E High/Low		PER SHARE ($) Earnings	Dividends	Book Value
12/09	14.10	— —		(1.55)	0.00	3.03
12/08	5.97	— —		(0.32)	0.00	4.21
12/07	28.22	14 9		2.65	0.00	11.73
12/06	20.99	— —		(1.86)	0.00	(3.12)
12/05	17.38	16 10		1.16	0.00	0.30
Annual Growth	**(5.1%)**	**— —**		**—**	**—**	**78.1%**

Google Inc.

If you've never Googled, you probably aren't finding what you want online. Google operates the leading Internet search engine, offering targeted search results from billions of Web pages. Results are based on a proprietary algorithm — Google's technology for ranking Web pages is called PageRank. The company generates nearly all of its revenue through ad sales. Advertisers can deliver relevant ads targeted to search queries or Web content. The Google Network is a network of third-party customers that use Google's ad programs to deliver relevant ads to their own websites. Google subsidiaries include YouTube and DoubleClick. Founders Sergey Brin and Larry Page each have nearly 30% voting control of the firm.

Fueling Google's lead in the Internet search business is its advertising system, comprised of its AdWords and AdSense products. Customers of Google AdWords bid on keywords and have their ads appear as links on the right-hand column of Google's search results page under the sponsored links heading. With Google's AdSense for Content, Google automatically delivers ads to a publisher's website that are precisely targeted to the content on the publisher's site, and the publisher shares in the revenue generated when readers click on the ads.

The technology industry demands constant innovation, however, and Google has been nothing short of relentless in its efforts to develop or acquire new services and products in order to stay ahead of such rivals as Yahoo! and Microsoft. The company provides Web portal services such as Webmail (Gmail), blogging (Blogger), and photo sharing (Picasa). Other tools Google offers to help its users make the most of their digital life include an online image library (Google Images), general news stories (Google News), financial news (Google Finance), interactive maps (Google Maps), and comparison shopping services (Google Product Search).

In 2010 the company unveiled its own smart phone called Nexus One (manufactured by partner HTC) with which it hopes to compete with Apple's iPhone, Research in Motion's BlackBerry, and Palm's Pre. The Nexus One operates on the Android operating system, an open source mobile computing system Google acquired in 2005. Google is also engaged in the Web browser business with its Google Chrome, and it has in the works a PC operating system to directly compete with Microsoft's Windows system.

In a move to compete with rivals such as Facebook and Twitter, in 2010 Google purchased Aardvark, a social search engine firm that provides customized answers sent directly from real-life friends or friends of friends in real time. Later that year Google bought mobile advertising network AdMob for $750 million.

Google entered China, where Baidu.com is the market leader, in 2006. Google initially made a controversial agreement with the Chinese government to censor search results when it began doing business in that country. (The Chinese government controls what its citizens can read and discuss online.) After feuding with the Chinese government over these censorship issues, in 2010 Google and China reached a compromise, and Google began publishing a link on its government approved ".cn" domain (Google.cn) to an uncensored website based in Hong Kong (Google.com.hk).

Chairman and CEO Eric Schmidt has about 10% voting control.

HISTORY

Google is the product of two computer science grad students, Sergey Brin and Larry Page, who met in 1995 at Stanford University where they studied methods of searching and organizing large datasets. They discovered a formula to rank the order of random search results by relevancy, and in 1997 they adopted the name Google to their findings.

In 1998 the two presented their discovery at the World Wide Web Conference, and by 1999 they had raised almost $30 million in funding from private investors, venture capital firms, and Stanford University. Later that year the Google site was launched.

Brin and Page hired tech industry veteran Eric Schmidt (former CTO at Sun Microsystems and former CEO of Novell) in 2001 as Google's CEO. Brin, previously the company's chairman, adopted the role of president of technology, and Page, previously CEO of Google, became president of product. Also in 2001 Google launched AdWords, its search-based advertising service. The following year the company launched another advertising service, the context-based AdSense.

In 2004 the company entered the social networking sphere with the launch of its Orkut product, which allows users (by invitation only) to search and connect with one another through online networks of friends.

Later in 2004, the once highly secretive company went public in one of the most anticipated IPOs ever, raising $1.6 billion. In 2005 it invested $1 billion for a 5% stake in AOL, gaining ad distribution throughout the content portal's network of sites. In 2006 Google made the most expensive purchase in its history with the $1.65 billion acquisition of online video-sharing site YouTube. Also that year Google entered China.

The company further broadened distribution options for advertisers with the 2006 purchase of dMarc Broadcasting (audio ads). Also in 2006 the company made high-profile agreements with News Corp.'s News Corp. Digital Media (then called Fox Interactive Media) and Viacom's MTV Networks. News Corp. Digital Media selected

Google as the $900 million high bidder for providing search on MySpace.com and other Fox properties in a multiyear search agreement, and in the Viacom deal, Google distributed MTV video (shows such as *Laguna Beach* and *Sponge Bob Square Pants*) to a variety of sites.

Other smaller acquisitions include the 2007 purchase of e-mail security company Postini for $625 million in cash, a deal that furthers Google's push into business software. Also that year Google bought mobile social network firm Zingku, as well as Adscape Media, a technology company focused on placing advertising within videogames. It next purchased Jaiku, a Finnish startup that also specializes in mobile and Web-based instant messaging.

Google acquired digital ad firm DoubleClick for $3.2 billion in 2008. The following year the company sold its a 5% stake in AOL for more than $280 million. Also in 2008 and 2009 the company cut some 300 jobs. The following year Google acquired mobile advertising firm AdMob for $750 million.

EXECUTIVES

Chairman and CEO: Eric E. Schmidt, age 54, $245,322 total compensation
Director; President, Technology: Sergey Brin, age 36, $1,661 total compensation
Director; President, Products: Larry E. Page, age 37, $2,300 total compensation
President, Global Sales and Business Development: Nikesh Arora, age 42, $26,319,684 total compensation
President, Enterprise: David J. (Dave) Girouard
SVP Corporate Development, Chief Legal Officer, and Secretary: David C. Drummond, age 46, $5,118,884 total compensation
SVP Engineering: Jeffrey T. (Jeff) Huber, age 42
SVP Operations and Google Fellow: Urs Hölzle
SVP Product Management: Jonathan J. Rosenberg, age 48, $15,165,735 total compensation
SVP and CFO: Patrick Pichette, age 47, $24,686,744 total compensation
SVP Engineering: William M. (Bill) Coughran Jr.
SVP Engineering and Research: R. Alan Eustace, age 53, $15,166,263 total compensation
SVP Business Operations: Shona L. Brown, age 44
CIO: Ben Fried
VP Finance and Chief Accountant: Mark Fuchs
VP Product Management: Susan Wojcicki
VP Global Ad Operations: John Herlihy
VP Global Online Sales: Claire H. Johnson
VP Search Partnerships: Sanjay Kapoor
VP Business Operations: Kristen Gil
VP and General Counsel: Kent Walker
VP and Chief Internet Evangelist: Vinton G. (Vint) Cerf, age 67
VP Public Policy and Communications: Rachel Whetstone
Corporate Communications Chief: Jill Hazelbaker
Senior Advisor, Office of the CEO and Founders: Omid Kordestani, age 46
Investor Relations: Maria Shim
Auditors: Ernst & Young LLP

LOCATIONS

HQ: Google Inc.
1600 Amphitheatre Pkwy.
Mountain View, CA 94043
Phone: 650-253-0000   **Fax:** 650-253-0001
Web: www.google.com

2009 Sales

	$ mil.	% of total
US	11,194	47
UK	2,986	13
Other countries	9,471	40
Total	**23,651**	**100**

PRODUCTS/OPERATIONS

2009 Sales

	$ mil.	% of total
Advertising		
Google sites	15,723	67
Google networks	7,166	30
Licensing & other	762	3
Total	**23,651**	**100**

Selected Operations and Products

Advertising programs
AdSense (network ad program for online publishers)
AdWords (text-based ad placement for advertisers)
DoubleClick (digital marketing technology and services)
Internet search and content
Google Alerts (news and search e-mail alerts)
Google Answers (fee-based expert help)
Google Catalogs (searchable mail-order catalogs)
Google Earth (3-D satellite imagery)
Google Groups (message boards)
Google Image Search
Google Labs (online services research and development)
Google Local (localized search)
Google Mobile (wireless device content)
Google News
Google Product Search (comparison shopping)
Google Scholar (academic materials search)
Google Video
Google Web Directory
Google Web Search
YouTube
Tools and applications
Android (mobile operating system)
Blogger (blogging tools)
Gmail (Web-based e-mail)
Google Analytics (Web traffic measurement)
Google Chrome (Web browser)
Google Desktop Search
Google Language Tools (translation tools)
Google Talk (instant messaging)
Google Toolbar (browser plug-in application)
Nexus One (smart phone)
Picasa (digital photo organization and sharing)

COMPETITORS

24/7 Real Media	MSN
Acxiom Digital	MySpace
AOL	NetEase.com
Ask.com	Responsys
Baidu	Shopping.com
CityGrid Media	Shopzilla
craigslist	SINA
Daum Communications	Sohu.com
Facebook	ValueClick
InfoSpace	Vertro
LiveJournal	Yahoo!
LookSmart	

HISTORICAL FINANCIALS

Company Type: Public

Income Statement

FYE: December 31

	REVENUE ($ mil.)	NET INCOME ($ mil.)	NET PROFIT MARGIN	EMPLOYEES
12/09	23,651	6,520	27.6%	19,835
12/08	21,796	4,227	19.4%	20,222
12/07	16,594	4,204	25.3%	16,805
12/06	10,605	3,077	29.0%	10,674
12/05	6,139	1,465	23.9%	5,680
Annual Growth	**40.1%**	**45.2%**	**—**	**36.7%**

2009 Year-End Financials

Debt ratio: —
Return on equity: 20.3%
Cash ($ mil.): 10,198
Current ratio: 10.62
Long-term debt ($ mil.): —
No. of shares (mil.): 319
Dividends
  Yield: —
  Payout: —
Market value ($ mil.): 197,591

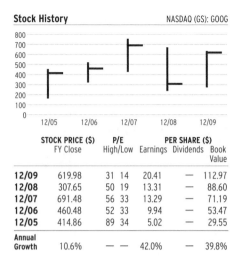
	STOCK PRICE ($) FY Close	P/E High/Low		PER SHARE ($) Earnings	Dividends	Book Value
12/09	619.98	31	14	20.41	—	112.97
12/08	307.65	50	19	13.31	—	88.60
12/07	691.48	56	33	13.29	—	71.19
12/06	460.48	52	33	9.94	—	53.47
12/05	414.86	89	34	5.02	—	29.55
Annual Growth	10.6%	—	—	42.0%	—	39.8%

Green Bay Packers

On the frozen tundra of Lambeau Field, the Green Bay Packers battle for pride in the National Football League. The not-for-profit corporation owns and operates the storied Packers football franchise, which was founded in 1919 by Earl "Curly" Lambeau and joined the NFL in 1921. Home to such icons as Bart Starr, Ray Nitschke, and legendary coach Vince Lombardi, Green Bay boasts a record 12 championship titles, including three Super Bowl victories (its last in Super Bowl XXXI after the 1996 season). The team is also the only community-owned franchise in American professional sports with more than 112,000 shareholders. The shares do not increase in value nor pay dividends, and can only be sold back to the team.

Despite being in the smallest market of any team in the NFL, Green Bay has managed to thrive primarily because of its tight association with the community and rabid fan base. Regular season games have been sold out since 1960 and the waiting list for season tickets boasts about 81,000 names. The team has also benefited from NFL revenue sharing agreements that distribute revenue from national TV broadcasting deals to all the franchises in the league.

After a long, stable, and successful run that began in the early 1990s, Green Bay is adjusting to a new leadership in the front office and on the field. Mark Murphy replaced Bob Harlan as CEO at the beginning of 2008. Harlan had led the franchise for nearly 20 years before retiring, spearheading efforts during his tenure to upgrade and expand Lambeau Field. A former NFL player and NFL Players Association executive, Murphy previously served as athletic director at Northwestern University.

On the field, the Packers lost one of its biggest stars of recent history in 2008 when three-time MVP quarterback Brett Favre was traded to the New York Jets after retiring early that year and then attempting a comeback. He had led the team to a 13-3 regular season record the previous year, though a bid for the Super Bowl ended with a loss to the New York Giants in the NFC

Championship game. Favre had played for Green Bay since 1992, winning one championship title and earning nearly every meaningful NFL passing record.

HISTORY

In 1919 Earl "Curly" Lambeau helped organize a professional football team in Green Bay, Wisconsin, with the help of George Calhoun, the sports editor of the *Green Bay Press-Gazette*. At 20 years old, Lambeau was elected team captain and convinced the Indian Packing Company to back the team, giving the squad its original name, the Indians. The local paper, however, nicknamed the team the Packers and the name stuck. Playing on an open field at Hagemeister Park, the team collected fees by passing the hat among the fans. In 1921 the franchise was admitted into the American Professional Football Association (later called the National Football League), which had been organized the year before.

The Packers went bankrupt after a poor showing its first season in the league and Lambeau and Calhoun bought the team for $250. With debts continuing to mount, *Press-Gazette* general manager Andrew Turnbull helped reorganize the team as the not-for-profit Green Bay Football Corporation and sold stock at $5 a share. Despite winning three straight championships from 1929-31, the team again teetered on the brink of bankruptcy, forcing another stock sale in 1935. With fortunes on and off the field dwindling, Lambeau retired in 1950 after leading the team to six NFL championships. A third stock sale was called for that year, raising $118,000. City Stadium (renamed Lambeau Field in 1965) was opened in 1957. In 1959 the team hired New York Giants assistant Vince Lombardi as head coach.

Under Lombardi, the Packers dominated football in the 1960s, winning five NFL titles with such players as Bart Starr and Ray Nitschke. The team defeated the Kansas City Chiefs in the first Super Bowl after the 1966 season. Lombardi resigned after leading Green Bay to victory over the Oakland Raiders in Super Bowl II. (Following his death in 1970, NFL commissioner Pete Rozelle named the league's championship trophy the Vince Lombardi trophy.)

The team again fell into mediocrity following the departure of Lombardi. Former MVP Starr was called upon to coach in 1974 but couldn't turn the tide before he was released in 1983. Forrest Gregg, another former Packer great, took over but was also unsuccessful in four seasons at the helm.

Bob Harlan, who had joined the Packers as assistant general manager in 1971, became president and CEO in 1989. He hired Ron Wolf as general manager in 1991, who in turn hired Mike Holmgren as head coach early the next year. With a roster including Brett Favre, Reggie White, and Robert Brooks, the Packers posted six straight playoff appearances and won its third Super Bowl (and 12th NFL title) in 1997. A fourth stock sale (preceded by a 1,000:1 stock split) netted the team more than $24 million.

After Holmgren resigned in 1999 (he left to coach the Seattle Seahawks), former Philadelphia Eagles coach Ray Rhodes tried to lead the team but lasted only one dismal season. In 2000 Mike Sherman, a former Holmgren assistant, was named the team's 13th head coach. Prompted by falling revenue, the team announced plans to renovate Lambeau Field, and

voters in Brown County later approved a sales tax increase to help finance the $295 million project. (The work was completed in 2003.) The next year Wolf retired and coach Sherman added general manager to his title. The team also signed quarterback Favre to a 10-year, $100 million contract extension.

While Sherman managed to lead the team to the playoffs in four of his first five seasons, the Packers were a disappointing 2-4 in postseason play. The team hired Ted Thompson from Seattle in 2005 to take over the general manager duties. That season turned out to be one of the worst in recent team history, however, and Sherman was replaced as head coach by San Francisco 49ers assistant coach Mike McCarthy in 2006.

The Packers rebounded during the 2007 season, reaching the NFC Championship game. (Green Bay lost to the New York Giants.) That off-season in 2008, the Packers underwent a change in the front office as Harlan retired as CEO and was replaced by Mark Murphy, a former NFL player and athletic director at Northwestern University. Favre announced his retirement that same year but attempted a comeback during the summer; he was later traded to the New York Jets.

EXECUTIVES

Chairman Emeritus: Robert E. (Bob) Harlan, age 73
President, CEO, and Director: Mark H. Murphy, age 55
EVP, General Manager, and Director Football Operations: Ted Thompson, age 57
VP Administration and Player Finance: Russ Ball, age 51
VP Finance: Paul Baniel, age 48
VP Administration and General Counsel: Jason Wied, age 38
VP Organizational and Staff Development: Betsy Mitchell
Secretary and Director: Peter M. Platten III, age 70
Head Coach: Michael (Mike) McCarthy
Pro Personnel Coordinator: Autumn Thomas-Beenenga
Treasurer and Director: Larry L. Weyers, age 64
Director Information Technology: Wayne Wichlacz
Director Public Relations: Jeff Blumb
Director Research and Development: Mike Eayrs, age 59
Director Marketing and Corporate Sales: Craig A. Benzel
Director Football Operations: Reggie McKenzie, age 47
Director College Scouting: John Dorsey, age 49
Director Player Development: Rob Davis, age 40
Director Football Administration and Communications: Mark Schiefelbein
Manager Human Resources: Nicole Ledvina
Auditors: Wipfli Ullrich Bertelson LLP

LOCATIONS

HQ: The Green Bay Packers, Inc.
Lambeau Field Atrium, 1265 Lombardi Ave.
Green Bay, WI 54304
Phone: 920-569-7500   **Fax:** 920-569-7301
Web: www.packers.com

The Green Bay Packers play at 72,928-seat capacity Lambeau Field in Green Bay, Wisconsin.

PRODUCTS/OPERATIONS

Championship Titles

Super Bowl Championships
Super Bowl XXXI (1997)
Super Bowl II (1968)
Super Bowl I (1967)
NFL Championships (1929-31, 1936, 1939, 1944, 1961-62, 1965-67)
NFC Championships (1996-97)
NFC North Division (2002-04, 2007)
NFC Central Division (1972, 1995-97)
NFL Western Conference (1936, 1938-39, 1944, 1960-62, 1965-67)

HISTORICAL FINANCIALS

Company Type: Not-for-profit

Income Statement
FYE: March 31

	REVENUE ($ mil.)	NET INCOME ($ mil.)	NET PROFIT MARGIN	EMPLOYEES
3/10	258	—	—	252
3/09	248	—	—	268
3/08	241	—	—	189
3/07	218	—	—	200
3/06	208	—	—	150
Annual Growth	5.5%	—	—	13.8%

Revenue History

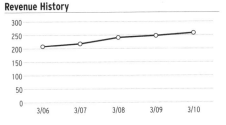

Greif, Inc.

Unlike a box of chocolates, with Greif (rhymes with "life") you know what you're going to get. The company produces containers and containerboard, mainly for bulk shippers in chemical, food, petroleum, and pharmaceutical industries. Greif's lineup includes shipping drums and drum closure systems, as well as water bottles. It also makes containerboard, corrugated sheets and containers, and multiwall packaging for specialized markets. Greif's multiwall bag products are used to ship industrial and consumer products, from chemicals to flour, pet foods, seed, and sugar. It manages timber properties in the US and Canada too. Manufacturing plants dot 45-plus countries, largely supporting sales in North America.

Greif's performance is underpinned by an international manufacturing and marketing footprint, as well as a broad product lineup. The company's competencies mitigate the cyclical and competitive risks inherent in the packing industry. A Shanghai, China, steel drum plant and headquarters, established in 2007, targets particularly promising growth markets in China, as well as Australia, Malaysia, New Zealand, the Philippines, and Singapore. Through subsidiary Delta Companies Group, the company moved ahead in 2009 with construction of an industrial packaging-service complex neighboring its Asia/Pacific headquarters. The facility is planned as a logistical service hub, along with manufacturing capacity for drums, pails, and totes used in shipping a diversity of oil-based and specialty chemical products. Greif also inked a deal with a China-based maker of intermediate bulk containers (IBCs), Zibo Jielin Plastic Pipe Manufacture Co., Ltd. Greif scores the exclusive right to pedal the Jielin IBCs worldwide.

Late in 2009, Greif gained global ground and enhanced its product offerings by acquiring Hannells Industrier. Hannells, which continues under the Greif nameplate, manufactures plastic and steel drums and pails, as well as bulk containers for use in chemical, paint, and petrochemical applications. Its factories are located in Sweden, Denmark, and Norway.

Simultaneously, Greif's sales have shrunk with the worldwide economic downturn. The company squeezed operating costs in 2009 by shuttering 19 facilities in its Industrial Packaging segment and slashing more than 10% of its workforce. In 2008 six facilities in Industrial Packaging and four in its Paper Packaging segment were closed.

Grief is also responding to US legislative, customer, and consumer pressure for sustainable paper fiber manufacturing practices of its products. Its mills in Virginia and Ohio achieved a slew of certifications in late 2009, including Sustainable Forestry Initiative (SFI), Forest Stewardship Council (FSC) and the Program for the Endorsement of Forest Certification (PEFC).

Prior to his death in 2009, Michael Dempsey, the son of former chairman John C. "Jack" Dempsey (not the boxer), owned nearly 56% of Greif. Michael Dempsey served as a director of the company. The family's majority ownership is retained through Judith Hook and Virginia Ragan, sisters of Michael Dempsey.

HISTORY

Charles Greif co-founded Vanderwyst and Greif, a Cleveland-based maker of casks, kegs, and barrels, in 1877. The next year his brothers William, Louis, and Thomas joined the company, which was renamed Greif Bros. to reflect the sibling involvement. The thriving company bought timberland as a source for raw materials and in 1926 went public as Greif Bros. Cooperage. In 1946 Jack Dempsey became chairman (his wife and mother-in-law owned minority stakes) and acquired a controlling interest. Dempsey moved Greif beyond barrels and kegs into fiber containers and steel drums. The company relocated to Delaware, Ohio, in 1951.

Greif entered the multiwall bag and corrugated packaging businesses in the 1960s and cut "Cooperage" from its name in 1969. In the early 1970s, it began making plastic containers. Greif teamed with Robert Macauley to form Virginia Fibre in 1974 and bought the supplier outright in 1992. In 1994, after 48 years at the helm, Dempsey was succeeded by COO Michael Gasser.

Greif bought three corrugated container firms and a pair of steel drum makers during 1997. Low paper prices and excess capacity dropped containerboard prices to a 19-year low in 1997. Jack Dempsey died that year. In 1998 Greif bought the industrial container business of Sonoco Products for $225 million in a deal that gave Greif control of two-thirds of the US fiber drum market. The company then announced a restructuring plan that would close plants and lay off workers. Greif joined with RDJ Holdings in a corrugated sheet joint venture, CorrChoice. In 1999 Greif bought Sonoco's intermediate bulk containers business and box maker Great Lakes Corrugated.

Late in 2000 Greif agreed to buy Finland-based Huhtamäki's industrial packaging operations. The deal, worth about $555 million, closed in 2001.

In 2003 the company changed its name to Greif, Inc. The company felt that Greif Bros. was

a regional-sounding name unworthy of a global industrial giant.

In 2006 Greif expanded further when it acquired Delta Petroleum Company, which blended and packaged lubricants and other chemical mixtures. Later that year, Greif spent $270 million to buy the European and Asian steel drum manufacturing business of Blagden Packaging Group.

EXECUTIVES

Chairman and CEO: Michael J. Gasser, age 59, $5,801,580 total compensation
President and COO: David B. Fischer, age 47, $2,095,031 total compensation
EVP and CFO: Donald S. (Don) Huml, age 63, $2,116,650 total compensation
EVP and General Counsel; President, Soterra LLC: Gary R. Martz, age 52, $1,534,646 total compensation
SVP Strategic Projects: Ronald L. Brown, age 62, $1,816,067 total compensation
SVP and Divisional President, Industrial Packaging and Services, Europe, Middle East and Africa: Ivan Signorelli, age 57
SVP People Services and Talent Development: Karen P. Lane, age 61
VP, CIO, and Controller: Kenneth B. (Ken) Andre III, age 44
VP Global Sourcing and Supply Chain; VP, Greif Business System (GBS) Worldwide: Brian Janki, age 37
VP Communications: Debra (Deb) Strohmaier
VP and Treasurer: John K. Dieker, age 46
VP Rigid Industrial Packaging and Services North America: Addison Kilibarda, age 46
Assistant Secretary: Sharon R. Maxwell, age 60
Auditors: Ernst & Young LLP

LOCATIONS

HQ: Greif, Inc.
425 Winter Rd., Delaware, OH 43015
Phone: 740-549-6000   **Fax:** 740-549-6100
Web: www.greif.com

2009 Sales

	$ mil.	% of total
North America	1,530.4	55
Europe, the Middle East, & Africa	835.1	30
Other regions	426.7	15
Total	**2,792.2**	**100**

PRODUCTS/OPERATIONS

2009 Sales

	$ mil.	% of total
Industrial Packaging	2,266.9	81
Paper Packaging	504.7	18
Land Management	20.6	1
Total	**2,792.2**	**100**

Selected Products

Industrial packaging
  Container closure systems
  Fibre drums
  Intermediate bulk containers
  Plastic drums
  Steel containers
  Water bottles
Paper packaging
  Containerboard
  Corrugated containers
  Multiwall packaging

COMPETITORS

Cascades SA	Sonoco Products
Georgia-Pacific	Tegrant
Longview Fibre	Temple-Inland
Pactiv	TriMas
Smurfit-Stone Container	Weyerhaeuser

HISTORICAL FINANCIALS

Company Type: Public

Income Statement

FYE: October 31

	REVENUE ($ mil.)	NET INCOME ($ mil.)	NET PROFIT MARGIN	EMPLOYEES
10/09	2,792	132	4.7%	8,200
10/08	3,777	234	6.2%	9,600
10/07	3,322	156	4.7%	10,300
10/06	2,629	142	5.4%	9,025
10/05	2,424	105	4.3%	9,100
Annual Growth	3.6%	6.0%	—	(2.6%)

2009 Year-End Financials

Debt ratio: 66.0%
Return on equity: 12.3%
Cash ($ mil.): 112
Current ratio: 1.48
Long-term debt ($ mil.): 721

No. of shares (mil.): 47
Dividends
 Yield: 2.8%
 Payout: 54.1%
Market value ($ mil.): 2,522

Stock History

NYSE: GEF

	STOCK PRICE ($) FY Close	P/E High/Low		PER SHARE ($) Earnings	Dividends	Book Value
10/09	53.52	21	9	2.81	1.52	23.19
10/08	40.58	15	7	4.97	1.32	22.41
10/07	63.60	24	18	2.65	0.92	21.22
10/06	46.85	20	12	2.41	0.60	17.91
10/05	30.41	22	12	1.78	0.40	15.51
Annual Growth	15.2%	—	—	12.1%	39.6%	10.6%

Guess?, Inc.

Guess? wants you to get in its pants. Founded as a designer jeans maker, the company makes trendy, upscale apparel and accessories for men, women, and children under brand names GUESS, GUESS Kids, Baby GUESS, and GUESS by MARCIANO, among others. Its trademark sexy ads, featuring the likes of Claudia Schiffer and Drew Barrymore, are designed in-house. Guess? sells its lines through a website, some 430 retail locations in the US and Canada, and about 140 stores in Europe, Asia, and Mexico. Guess? licenses its name for accessories (eyewear, footwear, jewelry, watches). Chairman Maurice Marciano and his brother Paul (CEO) run the company founded by their father. Together they own more than a third of its shares.

The company's retail operations account for more than 45% of its net revenue. To diversify its operations, Guess? has been looking at making its business more global, in turn, reducing its risk in any one market, particularly during the economic downturn.

Guess? is focused on international expansion, particularly in Asia and Europe. To that end, in recent years the company has acquired its licensee of children's apparel, BARN S.r.l.; a majority stake in Italy's Focus Europe; and Maco, one of its Italian licensees. As a result of these acquisitions, the company has taken its kids and adult apparel businesses in Europe in-house.

In 2009 the company opened about 125 new international stores, primarily through licensees and distributors. In North America, where the deep recession has battered retail sales, Guess? scaled back plans to about a dozen store openings. In addition to about 190 Guess? full-price retail stores, the company operates 100-plus factory outlet stores in the US and Canada, which sell discounted merchandise.

It is also growing its e-commerce business and is sniffing out opportunities in perfume, with a licensing an agreement with Parlux Fragrances to distribute fragrances under the Guess? trademark. The Guess? brand accounted for 30% of sales for its partner Parlux.

The company has been exploring other markets in recent years — particularly the upscale and accessories business with the introduction of some 35 Guess? Accessories stores. It also reached for a more upscale customer by rebranding its Guess? Collection as MARCIANO and by rolling it out in 50-plus namesake Guess by MARCIANO-exclusive stores. The line is sold in the company's retail locations in the US and Canada.

Guess? is also a wholesaler to major department stores, including Macy's and Dillard's, specialty shops, and upscale boutiques.

HISTORY

Guess? grew out of a jeans boutique owned by Georges Marciano in St. Tropez, France, during the 1970s. After moving to Los Angeles with brothers Maurice and Armand, he launched the new company in 1981. A fourth brother, Paul, joined the firm that year and started the lush marketing campaign, which eventually featured supermodels Claudia Schiffer and Naomi Campbell. The trademark sexy style catapulted the company's jeans into major brand status.

In 1983 the company sold 50% of Guess? to the Nakash brothers, who owned Jordache. The following year the Marcianos sued the Nakashes, claiming they had stolen Guess? designs. After more than five years of wrangling, the parties settled out of court and the Marcianos resumed ownership of the business.

The company began licensing the Guess? name in 1990 when it allowed Revlon to use it for a perfume. Licenses for other products, including eyewear and footwear, soon followed. In 1993, when the Marciano brothers disagreed on the company's future (Georges wanted to target the mass market, but the others wanted to remain upscale), Georges left Guess?, selling his 40% stake to his brothers (he went on to own rival jeans company Yes Clothing).

Guess? went public in 1996. A fizzled expansion effort overseas and competition from hot brands like Tommy Hilfiger hurt earnings in 1997 and 1998. To correct the decline, Guess? began streamlining operations, revamping stores and product lines, and bringing apparel licenses in-house in 1999. In 2001 Guess? launched a higher-end line of clothing in 2001 under the G Brand label; G Brand denim is priced between $88 and $148 compared to the Guess? collection range of $48 and $98. It sells exclusively in New York City.

Alleging that Guess? misrepresented the security of its website, the Federal Trade Commission made a settlement in 2003 with the company that includes a requirement to improve the website's security. The settlement also prohibits Guess? from misrepresenting the security of consumer information on its website.

European expansion was brought back to the table in 2004, thanks to a revamped license agreement. Guess? got back a Florence-based jeanswear licensee that could add an extra $100 million in wholesale revenue to the company's European business.

In January 2007 Paul Marciano was named vice chairman and CEO of the company, while his brother Maurice was named chairman.

EXECUTIVES

Chairman: Maurice Marciano, age 61, $5,631,860 total compensation
Vice Chairman and CEO: Paul Marciano, age 58, $9,799,620 total compensation
SVP and CFO: Dennis R. Secor, age 47, $1,174,231 total compensation
SVP and CIO: Michael (Mike) Relich, age 49, $1,312,774 total compensation
President, Guess? Asia: Kitty Yung
Auditors: Ernst & Young LLP

LOCATIONS

HQ: Guess?, Inc.
 1444 S. Alameda St., Los Angeles, CA 90021
Phone: 213-765-3100 **Fax:** 213-744-7838
Web: www.guess.com

2010 Sales

	$ mil.	% of total
US	908.1	43
Italy	366.6	17
Canada	252.5	12
Other foreign countries	601.3	28
Total	**2,128.5**	**100**

PRODUCTS/OPERATIONS

2010 Sales

	$ mil.	% of total
Products		
Retail	983.9	46
Wholesale	747.2	35
European operations	300.0	14
Licensing	97.4	5
Total	**2,128.5**	**100**

2010 North American Stores

	No.
Guess?	191
Guess? Outlet	107
Guess? by MARCIANO	52
G by Guess	44
Guess? Accessories	38
Total	**432**

Licensed GUESS? Products

Apparel (kids' and infants')
Eyewear
Fashion accessories
Footwear
Fragrance
Handbags
Jewelry
Leather apparel
Swimwear
Watches

COMPETITORS

HISTORICAL FINANCIALS

Company Type: Public

Income Statement

FYE: Saturday nearest January 31

	REVENUE ($ mil.)	NET INCOME ($ mil.)	NET PROFIT MARGIN	EMPLOYEES
1/10	2,129	243	11.4%	12,700
1/09	2,093	214	10.2%	10,800
1/08	1,750	187	10.7%	9,900
1/07*	1,750	187	10.7%	9,900
12/06	1,185	123	10.4%	8,800
Annual Growth	15.8%	18.5%	—	9.6%

*Fiscal year change

2010 Year-End Financials

Debt ratio: 1.4%
Return on equity: 27.0%
Cash ($ mil.): 502
Current ratio: 3.29
Long-term debt ($ mil.): 14
No. of shares (mil.): 93
Dividends
　Yield: 1.1%
　Payout: 17.2%
Market value ($ mil.): 3,702

Stock History

NYSE: GES

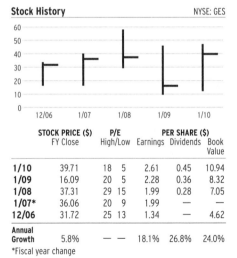

	STOCK PRICE ($) FY Close	P/E High/Low		PER SHARE ($) Earnings	Dividends	Book Value
1/10	39.71	18	5	2.61	0.45	10.94
1/09	16.09	20	5	2.28	0.36	8.32
1/08	37.31	29	15	1.99	0.28	7.05
1/07*	36.06	20	9	1.99	—	—
12/06	31.72	25	13	1.34	—	4.62
Annual Growth	5.8%	—	—	18.1%	26.8%	24.0%

*Fiscal year change

Halliburton Company

One of the largest oilfield services companies in the world, Halliburton serves the upstream oil and gas industry with a complete range of services, from the location of hydrocarbons to the production of oil and gas. It operates in two segments: Drilling and Evaluation and Completion and Production. Services include providing production optimization, drilling evaluation, fluid services, and oilfield drilling software and consulting. It combines tried-and-true well drilling and optimization techniques with high-tech analysis and modeling software and services. Halliburton works in established oilfields from the North Sea to the Middle East as well as in newer sites in Southeast Asia and Africa.

Establishing a new product service line (intervention services and pressure control) in 2010 the company agreed to acquire well control specialist and industry innovator Boots & Coots. Halliburton will combine its global hydraulic workover and coiled tubing deployed technologies with Boots & Coots' operations to provide customers with a wider range of services to help increase well production.

In 2010 the company was involved in cementing operations of a well on a BP rig in the Gulf of Mexico that exploded and sank, spewing oil into the Gulf. A board of inquiry was set up to find out the cause of the disaster.

The company has shifted its focus from exploiting difficult reserves in the Western Hemisphere to focusing on easier-to-access and underdeveloped targets in the Eastern Hemisphere. As part of this shift, in 2007 it opened a corporate headquarters in the United Arab Emirates and relocated CEO David Lesar to Dubai.

Halliburton became a lot lighter by divesting its KBR engineering and military contracts division. Halliburton took KBR public in 2006 by offering a 20% stake in an IPO and later divested the rest, cutting all ties with the company in 2007. However, revenues dropped significantly in 2009 (as it did for all oil services firms) primarily due to the global recession and the slump in drilling demand.

HISTORY

Erle Halliburton began his oil career in 1916 at Perkins Oil Well Cementing. He moved to oil boomtown Burkburnett, Texas, to start his Better Method Oil Well Cementing Company in 1919. Halliburton used cement to hold a steel pipe in a well, which kept oil out of the water table, strengthened well walls, and reduced the risk of explosions. Though the contribution would later be praised, his technique was considered useless at the time.

In 1920 Halliburton moved to Oklahoma. Incorporating Halliburton Oil Well Cementing Company in 1924, he patented its products and services, forcing oil companies to employ his firm if they wanted to cement wells.

Erle died in 1957, and his company grew through acquisitions between the 1950s and the 1970s. In 1962 it bought Houston construction giant Brown & Root, an expert in offshore platforms. After the 1973 Arab oil embargo Halliburton benefited from the surge in global oil exploration, and later, as drilling costs surged, it became a leader in well stimulation.

When the oil industry slumped in 1982, the firm halved its workforce. Three years later a suffering Brown & Root coughed up $750 million to settle charges of mismanagement at the South Texas Nuclear Project.

In the 1990s Halliburton expanded abroad, entering Russia in 1991 and China in 1993. The next year Brown & Root was named contractor for a pipeline stretching from Qatar to Pakistan. Halliburton drilled the world's deepest horizontal well (18,860 ft.) in Germany in 1995.

Also in 1995 Dick Cheney, a former US defense secretary, became CEO. Brown & Root began providing engineering and logistics services to US Army peacekeeping troops in the Balkans in 1995 and won a major contract to develop an offshore Canadian oil field the next year.

The company nearly doubled in size in 1998 with its $7.7 billion acquisition of oil field equipment manufacturer Dresser Industries. The purchase, coupled with falling oil prices in 1998 and 1999, prompted Halliburton to ax more than 9,000 workers.

Cheney resigned as chairman and CEO that year after he was chosen as George W. Bush's vice presidential running mate. President and COO David Lesar was named to succeed him.

In 2001 a group consisting of investment firms First Reserve and Odyssey Investment Partners and Dresser managers paid $1.55 billion for Dresser Equipment Group. That year a number of multimillion dollar verdicts against Halliburton in asbestos cases sparked rumors that the company was going to file for bankruptcy (flatly denied by Halliburton) and caused the firm's stock price to tumble.

In 2002, in part to protect the company's assets from the unresolved asbestos claims issue, Lesar announced plans to restructure Halliburton into two independent subsidiaries, separating the Energy Services Group from Halliburton's KBR engineering and construction operations.

Halliburton placed its subsidiaries, Dresser Industries and Kellogg Brown & Root, under Chapter 11 bankruptcy protection. Later that year, in an effort to boost its newly formed Energy Services unit, Halliburton purchased Pruett Industries, a fiber optic sensor technology company.

In 2003 Halliburton announced plans to divest its noncore assets in an effort to return its focus to its main operating divisions. In 2004 the company's KBR subsidiary was awarded nearly $1.4 billion worth of contracts to aid in the repair and restoration of Iraq's oil fields during the US-led invasion of Iraq. The US Army Corps of Engineers later withdrew the contracts after allegations that they were awarded to the subsidiary due to Halliburton's relationship to Cheney.

KBR also came under fire when the Pentagon claimed the company overcharged US taxpayers $61 million to supply fuel to Iraq. After an investigation by the US Army Corp of Engineers, Halliburton was cleared of any wrongdoing. The investigation was picked up by the Pentagon's criminal investigative unit and the US State Department. Following an internal audit, Halliburton repaid $6 million after discovering an overcharge from one of its subcontractors.

The company agreed to pay more than $4 billion in cash and stock to settle more than 300,000 asbestos and silica-related personal injury lawsuits filed against its DII Industries and KBR subsidiaries. DII and KBR emerged from Chapter 11 bankruptcy protection in 2005.

In 2006 Halliburton was awarded a multimillion-dollar contract by Saudi Aramco as part of the Khurais oilfield development project, the largest in the region since the 1950s.

EXECUTIVES

Chairman, President, and CEO: David J. (Dave) Lesar, age 56, $12,434,666 total compensation
EVP and CFO: Mark A. McCollum, age 51, $2,974,801 total compensation
EVP and General Counsel: Albert O. (Bert) Cornelison Jr., age 60, $3,597,014 total compensation
EVP Administration and Chief Human Resources Officer: Lawrence J. Pope, age 41
SVP and Corporate Secretary: Sherry D. Williams
SVP and Treasurer: Craig W. Nunez, age 48
SVP and Chief Ethics and Compliance Officer: Susan Ponce
VP, Corporate Controller, and Principal Accounting Officer: Evelyn M. Angelle, age 42
VP Investor Relations: Christian A. Garcia
VP Middle East Region: Gasser El-Badrashini
VP, Scandinavia: Jorunn Saetre
President, Eastern Hemisphere: Ahmed H.M. Lotfy, age 55
President, Global Business Lines and Corporate Development; Chief Health, Safety, and Environment Officer: Timothy J. (Tim) Probert, age 58, $2,990,573 total compensation
President, Completion and Production Division: David S. King, age 53
President, Western Hemisphere: James S. (Jim) Brown, age 55, $3,313,015 total compensation
Senior Manager Public Relations: Diana Gabriel
Auditors: KPMG LLP

LOCATIONS

HQ: Halliburton Company
3000 N. Sam Houston Parkway E.
Houston, TX 77032
Phone: 281-575-3000
Web: www.halliburton.com

2009 Sales

	$ mil.	% of total
North America	5,662	38
Europe/Africa/CIS	3,948	27
Middle East/Asia	2,884	20
Latin America	2,181	15
Total	**14,675**	**100**

PRODUCTS/OPERATIONS

2009 Sales

	$ mil.	% of total
Completion & production	7,419	51
Drilling & evaluation	7,256	49
Total	**14,675**	**100**

COMPETITORS

Baker Hughes
Saipem
Schlumberger
Technip
Transocean
Weatherford International

HISTORICAL FINANCIALS

Company Type: Public

Income Statement

FYE: December 31

	REVENUE ($ mil.)	NET INCOME ($ mil.)	NET PROFIT MARGIN	EMPLOYEES
12/09	14,675	1,155	7.9%	51,000
12/08	18,279	1,778	9.7%	57,000
12/07	15,264	3,499	22.9%	51,000
12/06	22,504	2,348	10.4%	104,000
12/05	21,007	2,358	11.2%	106,000
Annual Growth	**(8.6%)**	**(16.3%)**	**—**	**(16.7%)**

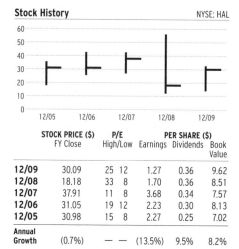

2009 Year-End Financials

Debt ratio: 43.8%
Return on equity: 14.0%
Cash ($ mil.): 2,082
Current ratio: 2.99
Long-term debt ($ mil.): 3,824
No. of shares (mil.): 907
Dividends
Yield: 1.2%
Payout: 28.3%
Market value ($ mil.): 27,305

Stock History

NYSE: HAL

	STOCK PRICE ($) FY Close	P/E High/Low		PER SHARE ($) Earnings	Dividends	Book Value
12/09	30.09	25	12	1.27	0.36	9.62
12/08	18.18	33	8	1.70	0.36	8.51
12/07	37.91	11	8	3.68	0.34	7.57
12/06	31.05	19	12	2.23	0.30	8.13
12/05	30.98	15	8	2.27	0.25	7.02
Annual Growth	**(0.7%)**	**—**	**—**	**(13.5%)**	**9.5%**	**8.2%**

Hallmark Cards

As the #1 producer of warm fuzzies, Hallmark Cards is the Goliath of greeting cards. The company's cards are sold under brand names such as Hallmark, Shoebox, and Ambassador and can be found in more than 41,000 US retail stores. (About 3,300 stores bear the Hallmark Gold Crown name; the majority of these stores are independently owned.) Hallmark also offers electronic greeting cards, gifts, and flowers through its website. In addition to greeting cards, the company owns crayon manufacturer Crayola (formerly Binney & Smith), a majority of cable broadcaster Crown Media, and Kansas City's Crown Center real estate development firm. Members of the founding Hall family own two-thirds of Hallmark.

While Hallmark has risen to the top tier in the industry, changes in the ways that people interact and communicate have created new challenges for the company. Sales have been fairly stagnant the past few years, leading Hallmark to continue to downsize its workforce as part of a cost-saving effort. In 2009 the company shuttered *Hallmark Magazine*, a women's lifestyle periodical launched in 2006. In 2008 it consolidated production at two printing plants in Kansas, eliminating several jobs at plants in Arkansas, Ontario, and at its Sunrise Publications subsidiary in Indiana.

Product development has been key for its traditional card business. Hallmark has had success with a line of musical cards (Cards With Sound) and now offers cards via cell phone at Hallmark Mobile Greetings. In 2009 the company teamed with Disney to launch Disney E-cards on Hallmark.com. The premium cards feature original scenes from Disney movies, and are 99-cents each. Hallmark also sells annual subscriptions that offer unlimited premium e-cards for about $10.

The Hallmark brand can additionally be found on television through Hallmark Hall of Fame original movies, and via cable's Hallmark Channel (operated by Crown Media). Internationally, Hallmark publishes products in more than 30 languages and distributes them in 100 countries across the globe. Global subsidiaries are located in Australia, Belgium, Japan, the Netherlands, New Zealand, and the UK.

HISTORY

Eighteen-year-old Joyce Hall started selling picture postcards from two shoe boxes in his room at the Kansas City, Missouri, YMCA in 1910. His brother Rollie joined him the next year, and the two added greeting cards to their line in 1912. The brothers opened Hall Brothers, a store that sold postcards, gifts, books, and stationery, but it was destroyed in a 1915 fire. The Halls got a loan, bought an engraving company, and produced their first original cards in time for Christmas.

In 1921 a third brother, William, joined the firm, which started stamping the backs of its cards with the phrase "A Hallmark Card." By 1922 Hall Brothers had salespeople in all 48 states. The firm began selling internationally in 1931.

Hall Brothers patented the "Eye-Vision" display case for greeting cards in 1936 and sold it to retailers across the country. The company aired its first radio ad in 1938. The next year it introduced a friendship card, displaying a cart filled with purple pansies. The card became the company's best-seller. During WWII Joyce Hall persuaded the government not to curtail paper supplies, arguing that his greeting cards were essential to the nation's morale.

The company opened its first retail store in 1950. The following year marked the first production of *Hallmark Hall of Fame*, TV's longest-running dramatic series and winner of more Emmy awards than any other program. Hall Brothers changed its name to Hallmark Cards in 1954 and introduced its Ambassador line of cards five years later.

Hallmark introduced paper party products and started putting *Peanuts* characters on cards in 1960. Donald Hall, Joyce Hall's son, was appointed CEO in 1966. Two years later Hallmark opened Crown Center, which surrounded company headquarters in Kansas City. Disaster struck in 1981 when two walkways collapsed at Crown Center's Hyatt Regency hotel, killing 114 and injuring 225.

Joyce Hall died in 1982, and Donald Hall became both chairman and CEO. Hallmark acquired Crayola Crayon maker Binney & Smith in 1984. It introduced Shoebox Greetings, a line of nontraditional cards, in 1986. Irvine Hockaday replaced Donald Hall as CEO the same year (Hall continued as chairman).

The company joined with Information Storage Devices in 1993 to market recordable greeting cards. The following year it acquired film production company RHI Entertainment, renaming the unit Hallmark Entertainment. Hallmark unveiled its website, Hallmark.com, in 1996 and began offering electronic greeting cards.

Hallmark's 1998 acquisition of UK-based Creative Publications boosted the company into the top spot in the British greeting card market. That same year it purchased Sunrise Publications. The following year the company acquired portrait studio chain The Picture People (sold in 2005) and Christian greeting card maker DaySpring Cards. It also acquired a stake in cable channel Odyssey, which was later renamed the Hallmark Channel (now operated by Crown Media).

The company began testing overnight flower delivery in the US just in time for Valentine's Day 2000. Hockaday retired as president and CEO at the end of 2001; vice chairman Donald Hall Jr. took the additional title of CEO in early 2002.

Hallmark decided to move some of its IT operations in 2004 to Affiliated Computer Services in a seven-year deal worth $230 million; the Dallas-based company opened a center near the Hallmark headquarters to handle the work. Binney & Smith subsidiary changed its name to Crayola in 2007.

EXECUTIVES

Chairman: Donald J. Hall, age 81
Vice Chairman, President, and CEO:
 Donald J. (Don) Hall Jr., age 54
EVP and General Counsel: Brian E. Gardner, age 57
SVP Public Affairs and Communication: Steve Doyal, age 61
SVP Information Technology:
 Michael W. (Mike) Goodwin
SVP Supply Chain and Business Enablement:
 Pete Burney
SVP Creative: Teri Ann Drake
SVP Marketing: Lisa H. Macpherson
SVP Strategic Planning and Finance, North America:
 Steve Hawn
VP Hallmark Licensing: Jodi Schade
VP Marketing Strategy: Jay Dittmann
VP Logistics Solutions: Daniel S. (Dan) Krouse
VP and Treasurer: Jeff McMillen
VP Business Development: Vince G. Burke
VP and General Manager, Hallmark Digital: Paul Barker
President and CEO, Crayola: Mike Perry
President, Hallmark Gold Crown: Jack E. Moore Jr., age 54
President, Hallmark North America: David E. Hall, age 47
Director Public Relations, Public Affairs, and Communications: Julie O'Dell

LOCATIONS

HQ: Hallmark Cards, Incorporated
 2501 McGee Trafficway, Kansas City, MO 64108
Phone: 816-274-5111   **Fax:** 816-274-5061
Web: www.hallmark.com

PRODUCTS/OPERATIONS

Selected Brands

Keepsake (holiday ornaments and other collectibles)
Mahogany (products celebrating African-American heritage)
Nature's Sketchbook (cards and gifts)
Shoebox (greeting cards)
Sinceramente (Spanish-language greeting cards)
Tree of Life (products celebrating Jewish heritage)

Selected Subsidiaries

Crayola (crayons and markers)
Crown Center Redevelopment (retail complex)
Crown Media Holdings (pay television channels, 95%)
DaySpring Cards (Christian greeting cards)
Hallmark Insights (business and consumer gift certificates)
Halls Merchandising (department store)
Image Arts (discount greeting card distribution)
Irresistible Ink (handwriting and marketing service)
Litho-Krome (lithography)
William Arthur (invitations, stationery)

COMPETITORS

1-800-FLOWERS	Dixon Ticonderoga
123Greetings	Enesco
American Greetings	Faber-Castell
Amscan	International Greetings
Andrews McMeel Universal	iParty
BIC	MEGA Brands
Blyth	NobleWorks
Build-A-Bear	Party City
Clinton Cards	SPS Studios
CSS Industries	Taylor Corporation

HISTORICAL FINANCIALS

Company Type: Private

Income Statement

	REVENUE ($ mil.)	NET INCOME ($ mil.)	NET PROFIT MARGIN	EMPLOYEES
12/09	4,000	—	—	13,400
12/08	4,300	—	—	15,500
12/07	4,400	—	—	15,900
12/06	4,100	—	—	16,000
12/05	4,200	—	—	18,000
Annual Growth	(1.2%)	—	—	(7.1%)

FYE: December 31

Revenue History

H&R Block

Only two things are certain in this life, and H&R Block has a handle on one of them. The company is one of the largest tax return preparers in the US, where it has approximately 11,500 retail locations (many of which are franchised). It has another 1,600 locations in Canada and Australia and serves approximately 23 million tax customers in all. The company also owns RSM McGladrey, which performs accounting, consulting, tax planning, and other services for midsized companies. One of the largest accounting firms in the US, the unit accounts for about one-quarter of H&R Block's sales. The company provides retail banking through H&R Block Bank and publishes a line of do-it-yourself tax-preparation software.

Throughout its history H&R Block has teetered between being focused on tax preparation services and providing a more diverse line of service offerings, including securities brokerage, mortgage lending, and business advisory. After losing a proxy battle with hedge fund Breeden Partners in 2007, the company has narrowed its focus back on its core tax offerings. It sold H&R Block Financial Advisors and Option One Mortgage and Mark Ernst was replaced as CEO by former McDonald's executive Russ Smyth.

The company acquired the franchise operator of its Arkansas, Oklahoma, and Texas stores for some $278 million in 2008. The deal included more than 600 offices, about two-thirds of which

became company-owned locations. H&R Block scaled back its holdings, selling or closing more than 2,000 offices within two years. Its licensing agreement with Wal-Mart expired in 2009, and the company closed more than 1,000 "shared" offices located within Wal-Mart stores. It sold about 350 locations to franchisees, as well.

In 2010 Russ Smyth resigned as CEO. He was succeeded by director Alan Bennett, who had served an interim term as H&R Block's CEO prior to Smyth's tenure.

HISTORY

Brothers Henry and Richard Bloch opened the United Business Co. in Kansas City, Missouri, in 1946 to provide accounting services. As tax preparation monopolized their time, a client suggested they specialize in taxes. The Blochs bought two ads, which brought a stampede of customers.

In 1955 the company became H&R Block (the Blochs didn't want customers to read the name as "blotch"). Basing charges on the number and complexity of tax forms resulted in a low-fee, high-volume business. The first tax season was a success, and the next year the brothers successfully tested their formula in New York City. But neither brother wanted to move to New York, so they worked out a franchise-like agreement with local CPAs. It was the first step toward becoming a nationwide chain.

As the chain grew, H&R Block began training preparers at H&R Block Income Tax Schools. By 1969, when Richard retired, the company had more than 3,000 offices in the US and Canada.

Henry began appearing in company ads in the 1970s; his reassuring manner inspired confidence and aided expansion. Fearing saturation of the tax preparer market, he pushed the company into new areas. H&R Block bought Personnel Pool of America in 1978 (taken public in 1994 as part of Interim Services) and two years later bought 80% of law office chain Hyatt Legal Services (sold in 1987).

In 1980 the firm bought CompuServe, which evolved from a computer time-share firm to a major online service by the 1990s. H&R Block sought to integrate its two operating areas in hopes that electronic filing and banking would increase its tax business.

In 1992 Henry was succeeded as president by his son, Thomas, who built on the nontax side of the business to try for more even revenue distribution. The next year the company bought MECA Software (personal finance software), mistakenly believing MECA's relationships with banks, based on its refund-anticipation loan program, would help it develop online banking services. It sold MECA in 1994, and Thomas stepped down.

In an effort to build a national accounting practice in 1996, it formed HRB Business Services with the purchase of Kansas City accounting firm Donnelly Meiners Jordan Kline and six other regional accounting firms. Frank Salizzoni became CEO in 1996.

After selling 20% of CompuServe in a 1996 IPO, H&R Block sold its remaining interest in the company two years later. In 1999 the firm sold its credit card operations and bought the non-consulting assets of the #7 US accounting firm, McGladrey & Pullen.

The McGladrey & Pullen deal didn't please everyone. In May 1999 a group of franchisees sued H&R Block to ensure that they receive their fair share of royalties from any sales generated in their territories by both the accounting group and H&R Block's tax software.

In 2000 co-founder Henry Bloch became honorary chairman, ceding the chairman slot to Salizzoni. Mark Ernst became CEO in 2001 and was named chairman in 2002, when Salizzoni retired. In July 2005 the company bought San Diego-based TaxNet Inc., a privately held online tax program company, for an undisclosed sum.

Company co-founder Richard Bloch, who retired from the business in 1969, died in 2004.

The company in 2004 was charged by the NASD with defrauding investors by selling them Enron bonds in the weeks leading up to that company's collapse.

In February 2006 the tax preparer announced that it had gotten its own taxes wrong in recent years. As a result, H&R Block had to restate results for fiscal years 2004 and 2005 and parts of 2006.

The company's expansion efforts served to lessen its reliance on tax services. The strategy didn't please all shareholders, and H&R Block lost a proxy battle with Connecticut hedge fund Breeden Partners in 2007. Headed up by former SEC chairman Richard Breeden, the fund accused H&R Block management of losing more than $4 billion in potential profits with poor decisions. Breeden Partners won three seats on the company's board of directors.

Shortly after, with the company facing mounting losses related to subprime mortgage lending activities (mainly thanks to wholesale mortgage lender Option One Mortgage), Mark Ernst resigned his post as chairman and CEO. Richard Breeden took over as chairman, and former Aetna CFO Alan Bennett took on the CEO duties on an interim basis. He was replaced with former McDonald's executive Russ Smyth in 2008.

In 2008 H&R Block returned its focus to providing tax services. It sold its H&R Block Financial Advisors brokerage unit to Ameriprise Financial for $300 million, and sold Option One Mortgage to an affiliate of W.L. Ross for over $1 billion.

EXECUTIVES

Chairman: Richard C. Breeden, age 59
President, CEO, and Director: Alan M. Bennett, age 59, $1,706,441 total compensation
Interim CFO: Jeffrey T. (Jeff) Brown, age 50
SVP and CIO: Richard (Rich) Agar
SVP and Chief Marketing Officer: Robert Turtledove
SVP Human Resources: Tammy S. Serati, age 51, $594,049 total compensation
SVP and General Counsel: Brian J. Woram, age 49
SVP and Chief Staff: Joan K. Cohen
SVP Government Relations and Public Policy: Kathryn (Kate) Fulton
SVP Tax Services Support: Phil Mazzini
SVP Franchise Development: Ken Treat
VP Marketing: Kathy Collins
VP Multi-Cultural Business Development: Luis Altuve
President, RSM McGladrey: Charles E. (C. E.) Andrews, age 58
Chief Tax Network Officer: Sabrina Wiewel
Auditors: Deloitte & Touche LLP

LOCATIONS

HQ: H&R Block, Inc.
1 H&R Block Way, Kansas City, MO 64105
Phone: 816-854-3000 **Fax:** 816-854-8500
Web: www.hrblock.com

2010 Offices

	No.
US	
Company-owned	7,191
Franchised	4,315
Canada	1,269
Australia	374
Total	**13,149**

PRODUCTS/OPERATIONS

2010 Sales

	$ mil.	% of total
Services	3,231.5	83
Interest	122.4	3
Product & other	520.4	14
Total	**3,874.3**	**100**

Selected Subsidiaries

Aculink Mortgage Solutions, LLC
Ada Services Corporation
Birchtree Insurance Agency, Inc.
Companion Insurance, Ltd.
Financial Marketing Services, Inc.
H&R Block Bank

COMPETITORS

BDO International
Deloitte
Ernst & Young Global
Gilman Ciocia
Grant Thornton International
Intuit
Jackson Hewitt
KPMG
Liberty Tax Service
PricewaterhouseCoopers
Universal Tax

HISTORICAL FINANCIALS

Company Type: Public

Income Statement

FYE: April 30

	REVENUE ($ mil.)	NET INCOME ($ mil.)	NET PROFIT MARGIN	EMPLOYEES
4/10	3,874	479	12.4%	110,400
4/09	4,084	486	11.9%	133,700
4/08	4,404	(309)	—	137,200
4/07	4,021	(434)	—	136,600
4/06	4,873	490	10.1%	134,500
Annual Growth	**(5.6%)**	**(0.6%)**	**—**	**(4.8%)**

2010 Year-End Financials

Debt ratio: 73.6%
Return on equity: 33.7%
Cash ($ mil.): 1,804
Current ratio: 1.14
Long-term debt ($ mil.): 1,060
No. of shares (mil.): 323
Dividends
  Yield: 3.3%
  Payout: 42.0%
Market value ($ mil.): 5,920

Stock History

NYSE: HRB

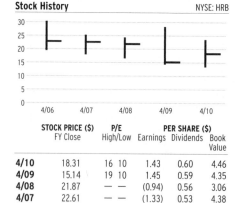

	STOCK PRICE ($) FY Close	P/E High/Low		PER SHARE ($) Earnings	Dividends	Book Value
4/10	18.31	16	10	1.43	0.60	4.46
4/09	15.14	19	10	1.45	0.59	4.35
4/08	21.87	—	—	(0.94)	0.56	3.06
4/07	22.61	—	—	(1.33)	0.53	4.38
4/06	22.83	20	13	1.47	0.49	6.64
Annual Growth	**(5.4%)**	**—**	**—**	**(0.7%)**	**5.2%**	**(9.5%)**

Hanover Insurance

The Hanover Insurance Group is an all-around property/casualty insurance holding company. Through its Hanover Insurance Company, it provides personal and commercial automobile, homeowners, workers' compensation, and commercial multiple-peril insurance and professional liability coverage. In Michigan, it operates as Citizens Insurance Company. The group sells its products through a network of 2,000 independent agents in the midwestern, northeastern, and southeastern US, but Michigan and Massachusetts account for more than a third of its business. Its Opus Investment Management subsidiary provides institutional investment management services.

Hanover's written premiums are split more or less evenly between its personal and commercial products, but competition is fierce in personal insurance, so the company has placed more emphasis on expanding its commercial offerings.

Wriggling into a niche is one method of expanding, which explains the company's 2007 acquisition of Professionals Direct, a provider of professional liability insurance for small and midsized law firms. To prove that it's a strategy and not a whim, in early 2008 the company spent $29 million to acquire privately held Verlan Holdings. Verlan brought with it Verlan Fire Insurance Company and Coatings Industry Services, which provide property/casualty and liability insurance to chemical companies. Hanover now markets these as Hanover Specialty Industrial.

Continuing its build up of specialty products, in 2010 the company acquired Benchmark Professional Insurance Services (insurance for the design industry, including architects and engineers) and Campania Group (liability coverage for the health care industry).

Hanover has also expanded its less specialized commercial offerings. To that end, the company purchased AIX Holdings in 2008. The acquired company offers specialty property/casualty products including workers' compensation, property, general liability, and auto insurance.

At the end of 2009 Hanover secured the renewal rights to a block of small and middle-market non-specialty commercial business worth $400 million from OneBeacon. The deal helped build up its business in that area just as it was also expanding geographically with new offices opening in the western US.

HISTORY

In 1842 a group of Worcester, Massachusetts, businessmen tried to form a mutual life insurance company. After a failed first attempt, they succeeded with the help of lobbyist Benjamin Balch. In 1844 the State Mutual Life Assurance Co. of Worcester set up business in the back room of secretary Clarendon Harris' bookstore. The first president was John Davis, a US senator. The company issued its first policy in 1845.

In the early years State Mutual reduced risk by issuing policies only for residents of such "civilized" areas as New England, New Jersey, New York, Pennsylvania, and Ohio. It also restricted movement, requiring policyholders to get permission for travel outside those areas. By the 1850s the company had begun issuing policies in the Midwest (with a 25% premium surcharge), the South (for 30% extra), and

California (for a pricey extra $25 per $1,000), with a maximum coverage of $5,000.

The Civil War was a problem for many insurers, who had to decide what to do about Southern policyholders and payment on war-related claims. State Mutual chose to pay out its Northern policyholders' benefits, despite the extra cost. In 1896 the firm began offering installment pay-out plans for policyholders concerned that their beneficiaries would fritter away the whole payment.

The first 30 years of the 20th century were, for the company, a time of growth that was stopped short by the Depression. But despite a great increase in the number of policy loans and surrenders for cash value, State Mutual's financial footing remained solid.

After WWII the company entered group insurance and began offering individual sickness and accident coverage. In 1957 it was renamed State Mutual Life Assurance Co. of America. The firm added property/casualty insurance in the late 1950s through alliances with such firms as Worcester Mutual Fire Insurance. During the 1960s State Mutual continued to develop property/casualty, buying interests in Hanover Insurance and Citizens Corp.

The firm followed the industrywide shift into financial services in the 1970s, adding mutual funds, a real estate investment trust, and an investment management firm. This trend accelerated in the 1980s, and State Mutual began offering financial planning services, as well as administrative and other services for the insurance and mutual fund industries (the mutual fund administration operations were sold in 1995). Managing this growth was another story: Its acquisitions left it bloated and disorganized. Technical systems were in disarray by the early 1990s, and the agency force had grown to more than 1,400. In response, the company began a five-year effort to upgrade systems, cut fat, and reduce sales positions.

In view of its shifting focus, State Mutual became Allmerica Financial in 1992. Three years later it demutualized. In 1997 it bought the 40% of Allmerica Property & Casualty it didn't already own. The next year heavy spring storms hammered Allmerica's bottom line, and the company incurred $15 million in catastrophe losses. Also in 1998 it bought the portion of Citizens it didn't previously own.

In 1999 Allmerica announced plans to sell its group life and health insurance operations to concentrate on its core businesses; Great-West Assurance bought them the next year. Its purchase that year of Advantage Insurance Network, a group of affiliated life insurance agencies, grew its distribution channels. In 2000 the firm reduced its workforce by 5% (some 6,000 employees) in an efficiency move. In 2001 Allmerica sold its 401(k) business to Minnesota Life.

Raising some much-needed capital, the company sold a large chunk of its life insurance and annuities operations in 2002. Deep in the red, the company in 2003 sold its fixed universal life insurance operations to John Hancock.

The company changed its name from Allmerica Financial Corporation to The Hanover Insurance Group in late 2005.

To better focus on its property/casualty lines, in 2008 the company sold its last remaining life insurance business to Goldman Sachs and its commercial-property finance company, Amgro, to Premium Financing Specialists.

EXECUTIVES

Chairman: Michael P. Angelini, age 67
President, CEO, and Director:
Frederick H. (Fred) Eppinger, age 51,
$3,825,811 total compensation
President, Specialty Lines and Chief Underwriting Officer, Commercial Lines: Antonio Z. dePadua, age 57
EVP and CFO: Steven J. (Steve) Bensinger, age 55
EVP; President, Property and Casualty Companies, The Hanover Insurance Group and The Hanover Insurance Company: Marita Zuraitis, age 49,
$1,888,663 total compensation
SVP, CIO, and Corporate Operations Officer, The Hanover Insurance Group and The Hanover Insurance Company: Gregory D. Tranter, age 53,
$1,021,794 total compensation
SVP, General Counsel, and Assistant Secretary, The Hanover Insurance Group and The Hanover Insurance Company: J. Kendall Huber, age 55,
$1,074,732 total compensation
SVP Corporate Development and Strategy; President, Specialty Casualty: Andrew S. Robinson, age 44
VP and Chief Human Resources Officer, The Hanover Insurance Group and The Hanover Insurance Company: Bryan D. Allen, age 42
VP and Secretary: Charles F. Cronin
VP; President, Business Insurance Group: John C. (Jack) Roche, age 46
VP; President, Personal Lines: Mark R. Desrochers, age 41
VP; President, Commercial Lines, The Hanover Insurance Group and The Hanover Insurance Company: David J. Firstenberg
VP Corporate Finance and Treasurer: John (JR) Reilly
Investor Relations: Robert P. Myron, age 42
Auditors: PricewaterhouseCoopers LLP

LOCATIONS

HQ: The Hanover Insurance Group, Inc.
440 Lincoln St., Worcester, MA 01653
Phone: 508-855-1000   **Fax:** 508-853-6332
Web: www.hanover.com

PRODUCTS/OPERATIONS

2009 Sales

	$ mil.	% of total
Premiums	2,546.4	90
Net investment income	252.1	9
Fees & other income	34.2	1
Net realized investment gains	1.4	—
Total	**2,834.1**	**100**

Selected Subsidiaries

Opus Investment Management, Inc.
 Citizens Insurance Company of Illinois
 The Hanover Insurance Company
  AIX Holdings, Inc.
  Citizens Insurance Company of America
  Hanover Texas Insurance Management Company, Inc.
  Massachusetts Bay Insurance Company
  Professionals Direct, Inc.
  Verlan Fire Insurance Company

COMPETITORS

Allstate
American Automobile Association (AAA)
American Financial Group
Auto-Owners Insurance
GEICO
Liberty Mutual
Markel Insurance
Nationwide
Progressive Corporation
State Farm
Travelers Companies
USAA

HISTORICAL FINANCIALS

Company Type: Public

Income Statement

	ASSETS ($ mil.)	NET INCOME ($ mil.)	INCOME AS % OF ASSETS	EMPLOYEES
12/09	8,043	197	2.5%	4,100
12/08	9,230	21	0.2%	4,000
12/07	9,816	253	2.6%	3,900
12/06	9,857	170	1.7%	4,000
12/05	10,634	(325)	—	4,100
Annual Growth	(6.7%)	—	—	0.0%

FYE: December 31

2009 Year-End Financials

Equity as % of assets: 29.3%
Return on assets: 2.3%
Return on equity: 9.3%
Long-term debt ($ mil.): 434
No. of shares (mil.): 45
Dividends
 Yield: 1.7%
 Payout: 19.4%
Market value ($ mil.): 1,992
Sales ($ mil.): 2,834

Stock History

NYSE: THG

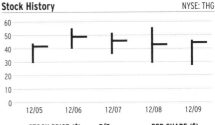

	STOCK PRICE ($) FY Close	P/E High	P/E Low	Earnings	Dividends	Book Value
12/09	44.43	12	7	3.86	0.75	52.59
12/08	42.97	137	74	0.40	0.45	42.08
12/07	45.80	11	8	4.83	0.40	51.27
12/06	48.80	17	12	3.27	0.30	44.58
12/05	41.77	—	—	(6.02)	0.25	43.51
Annual Growth	1.6%	—	—	—	31.6%	4.9%

Harley-Davidson

"Put your a** on some class," reads one (not necessarily official) Harley-Davidson T-shirt. Harley-Davidson is a major US maker of motorcycles and the nation's #1 seller of heavyweight cruisers. The company offers more than 30 models of touring and custom Harleys through a worldwide network of more than 1,500 dealers. Harley models include the Electra Glide, the Sportster, and the Fat Boy. The company also makes motorcycles under the MV Agusta and Cagiva nameplates. Harley-Davidson sells attitude with its brand-name products, which include a line of clothing and accessories (MotorClothes). Harley-Davidson Financial Services offers financing to dealers and consumers in the US and Canada.

The company experienced a 40% drop in sales in 2009 over 2008. Harley-Davidson put its wheels in motion to restructure its operations and adopt a single brand strategy for the long haul. It made a number of cutbacks, closing and consolidating several facilities in the US. After much deliberation, the company decided in late 2009 to keep its York, Pennsylvania, manufacturing plant open, rather than moving operations to a "cheaper plant," but it signed a labor agreement involving job cuts to a tune of almost 50%.

In the two years prior, the company lowered its headcount by approximately 1,100, a 12% reduction in force.

Along with the consolidations and closures in the US, the company is also shuttering certain international operations in Germany, Switzerland, and Italy. On the flipside, Harley-Davidson opened dealerships in India to market 12 models in that country starting in 2010.

Harley-Davidson is returning to its core business of making cruisers and announced in October 2009 that it is closing down its Buell line of sports bikes. In mid-2010 it sold MV Agusta, which it only just acquired a year earlier, to Claudio Castiglioni and his holding company, MV Agusta Motor Holding.

For the first time in the history of the company, a top executive from outside of Harley-Davidson was hired. In 2009 Keith Wandell, the former president and COO of auto parts supplier Johnson Controls, succeeded the retiring James Ziemer, a 40-year veteran of the company, as the president and CEO. Though he does not own a motorcycle, Wandell promised that he is buying a Harley as one of his first executive decisions.

HISTORY

In 1903 William Harley and the Davidson brothers (Walter, William, and Arthur) of Milwaukee sold their first Harley-Davidson motorcycles, which essentially were motor-assisted bicycles that required pedaling uphill. Demand was high, and most sold before leaving the factory. Six years later the company debuted its trademark two-cylinder, V-twin engine. By 1913 it had 150 competitors.

WWI created a demand for US motorcycles overseas that made foreign sales important. During the 1920s Harley-Davidson was a leader in innovative engineering, introducing models with a front brake and the "teardrop" gas tank that became part of the Harley look.

The Depression took a heavy toll on the motorcycle industry. As one of only two remaining companies, Harley-Davidson survived through exports and sales to the police and military. To improve sales, the company added styling features such as art deco decals and three-tone paint. The 1936 EL model, with its "knucklehead" engine (named for the shape of its valve covers), was a forerunner of today's models.

During WWII Harley-Davidson prospered from military orders. It introduced new models after the war to cater to a growing recreational market of consumers with money to spend: the K-model (1952), Sportster "superbike" (1957), and Duo-Glide (1958). Ever since competitor Indian Motorcycle Company gave up the ghost in the 1950s, Harley-Davidson has been the US's only major motorcycle manufacturer. (Indian Motorcycle was revived in 1998, however.)

The company began making golf carts (since discontinued) in the early 1960s. It went public in 1965, and American Machine and Foundry (AMF) bought the company in 1969. But by the late 1970s, sales and quality were slipping. Certain that Harley-Davidson would lose to Japanese bikes flooding the market, AMF put the company up for sale. There was no buyer until 1981, when Vaughn Beals and other AMF executives purchased it. Minutes away from bankruptcy in 1985, then-CFO Richard Teerlink convinced lenders to accept a restructuring plan.

Facing falling demand and increasing imports, Harley-Davidson made one of the greatest comebacks in US automotive history (helped in part by a punitive tariff targeting Japanese imports). Using Japanese management principles, it updated manufacturing methods, improved quality, and expanded the model line. Harley-Davidson again went public in 1986, and by the next year it had control of 25% of the US heavyweight-motorcycle market, up from 16% in 1985.

In 1993 the company acquired a 49% stake in Eagle Credit (financing, insurance, and credit cards for dealers and customers; it bought the rest in 1995) and a 49% share of Wisconsin-based Buell Motorcycle, gaining a niche in the performance market. (Harley-Davidson bought most of Buell's remaining stock in 1998.)

Jeffrey Bleustein, who had headed Harley-Davidson's manufacturing unit, was named the company's chairman and CEO in 1997. Two years later the company began production at its new assembly plant in Brazil, with an eye on increasing sales in Latin America. Harley-Davidson bested Honda in the US in 1999 for the first time in 30 years.

In 2000 Harley-Davidson's production increased by more than 15% over 1999, reaching just over 200,000 bikes. In 2001 Harley introduced the V-Rod, which drew design inspiration from Harley's legendary drag racing heritage.

Harley-Davidson marked its 100th year in operation in 2002. To celebrate, all 2003 model Harleys were designated 100th anniversary models. Harley-Davidson introduced two new lines of Buell motorcycles in 2003, the Firebolt and the Lightning.

Jeffrey Bleustein retired as president and CEO in 2005; he remained chairman. VP/CFO James Ziemer was promoted to succeed him.

In 2006 the company opened its first Chinese Harley dealership in Beijing. The move looked to protect the Harley brand in China against counterfeiting, as well as snag a toehold in the developing country. In 2006 Harley also acquired its Australian supplier of wheels and hubs, Castalloy.

After 40 years of service, Ziemer retired in 2009, and Keith Wandell took the driver's seat. Wandell, a veteran of Johnson Controls, is the first CEO hired from outside of the company.

EXECUTIVES

Chairman: Barry K. Allen, age 61
President, CEO, and Director: Keith E. Wandell, age 60, $6,363,579 total compensation
President and COO, Harley-Davidson Financial Services: Lawrence G. Hund, age 54
President and COO, Harley-Davidson Motor Company: Matthew S. (Matt) Levatich, age 45
EVP and Chief Organizational Transformation Officer: William B. (Bill) Dannehl, age 51
SVP and CFO, Harley-Davidson and Harley-Davidson Motor Company: John A. Olin, age 48, $933,809 total compensation
SVP and Chief Styling Officer, Harley-Davidson Motor Company: William G. Davidson
SVP and Chief Marketing Officer, Harley-Davidson Motor Company: Mark Hans Richer, age 43
SVP Manufacturing, Harley-Davidson Motor Company: Karl M. Eberle, age 61
Chief Accounting Officer: Mark Kornetzke
VP and Treasurer: Perry A. Glassgow
VP Communications: Susan Henderson, age 57
VP and General Manager, North American Sales, Harley-Davidson Motor Company: Jeffrey A. Merten
VP and CIO, Harley-Davidson Motor Company: James E. Haney
VP and Managing Director, Latin America: Mark Van Genderen

VP, Harley-Davidson Museum and Factory Tours: Bill Davidson
VP and General Counsel: Edward W. Krishok
VP Communications: Joanne M. Bischmann
Director Investor Relations: Amy S. Giuffre
Auditors: Ernst & Young LLP

LOCATIONS

HQ: Harley-Davidson, Inc.
 3700 W. Juneau Ave., Milwaukee, WI 53208
Phone: 414-342-4680   **Fax:** 414-343-8230
Web: www.harley-davidson.com

2009 Motorcycle Sales

	$ mil.	% of total
US	2,910.1	69
Europe	700.9	16
Japan	255.9	6
Canada	175.9	4
Australia	137.6	3
Other regions	106.7	2
Total	**4,287.1**	**100**

PRODUCTS/OPERATIONS

2009 Sales and Financial Services

	$ mil.	% of total
Motorcycles	4,287.1	90
Financial services	494.8	10
Total	**4,781.9**	**100**

2009 Unit Shipments

	Units
Harley-Davidson	
Custom motorcycles	91,650
Touring motorcycles	84,104
Sportster motorcycles	47,269
Total	**223,023**

Selected Motorcycles

Harley-Davidson
 CVO
  Fat Bob
  Softail Convertible
 Dyna
  Fat Bob
  Low Rider
  Street Bob
  Super Glide (and Custom)
  Wide Glide
 Softail
  Cross Bones
  Fat Boy
  Heritage Softail Classic
  Night Train
  Rocker & Rocker C
  Softail (Custom and Deluxe)
 Sportster
  883 (Low and Custom)
  1200 (Custom and Roadster)
  Forty Eight
  Iron 883
  Nightster
  XR1200
 Touring
  Electra Glide (Standard, Classic, and Ultra Classic)
  Road Glide
  Road King (and Classic)
  Street Glide
  Tri Glide Ultra Classic
 Trike
  Street Glide Trike
  Tri Glide Ultra Classic
 VRSC
  Night Rod Special
  V-Rod (and V-Rod Muscle)

Selected Operations

Motorcycles
 Harley-Davidson Motor Company
Financial services
 Harley-Davidson Financial Services, Inc.
  Harley-Davidson Credit
  Harley-Davidson Insurance

COMPETITORS

BMW	Polaris Industries
Ducati	Triumph Motorcycles
Honda	Ultra Motorcycle
Indian Motorcycle	Viper Motorcycle

HISTORICAL FINANCIALS
Company Type: Public

Income Statement
FYE: December 31

	REVENUE ($ mil.)	NET INCOME ($ mil.)	NET PROFIT MARGIN	EMPLOYEES
12/09	4,782	(55)	—	7,300
12/08	5,594	655	11.7%	10,100
12/07	5,727	934	16.3%	9,775
12/06	6,186	1,043	16.9%	9,704
12/05	5,342	960	18.0%	9,700
Annual Growth	(2.7%)	—	—	(6.9%)

2009 Year-End Financials

Debt ratio: 195.2%
Return on equity: —
Cash ($ mil.): 1,630
Current ratio: 1.91
Long-term debt ($ mil.): 4,114

No. of shares (mil.): 235
Dividends
  Yield: 1.6%
  Payout: —
Market value ($ mil.): 5,935

Stock History
NYSE: HOG

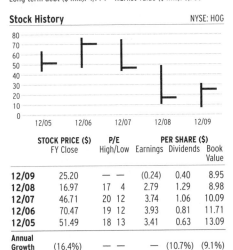

	STOCK PRICE ($) FY Close	P/E High/Low		PER SHARE ($) Earnings	Dividends	Book Value
12/09	25.20	—	—	(0.24)	0.40	8.95
12/08	16.97	17	4	2.79	1.29	8.98
12/07	46.71	20	12	3.74	1.06	10.09
12/06	70.47	19	12	3.93	0.81	11.71
12/05	51.49	18	13	3.41	0.63	13.09
Annual Growth	(16.4%)	—	—	—	(10.7%)	(9.1%)

Harman International

Harman International Industries is loud and clear. It makes high-end stereo and audio equipment for consumer and professional markets. Its consumer group makes loudspeakers, CD and DVD players, CD recorders, and amplifiers under such brands as Harman/Kardon, Infinity, Becker, Logic 7, JBL, Mark Levinson, and others. Harman's auto unit sells branded audio systems through several carmakers, including Toyota and General Motors. Its professional unit makes audio equipment, such as monitors, amplifiers, microphones, and mixing consoles for recording studios, cinemas, touring performers, and others. In addition, Harman offers computer software and development tools to the automotive, energy, medical, and telecom industries.

The company is taking a closer look at its operations as a result of declining revenues, reducing its footprint in high-cost countries while growing in low-cost regions. To that end, Harman sold its Canada-based QNX Software Systems business, which makes software for the automotive market, to Research In Motion for $200 million in 2010.

Since 2008 Harman has shuttered manufacturing centers in California, Indiana, Massachusetts, and New York, as well as a facility in South Africa. It has been focused on expanding throughout the Asia/Pacific region and parts of Europe, opening manufacturing and research and development centers in China in 2009. It also received a grant from the Hungarian government to help build a new plant, and in 2008 partnered with Wipro Technologies (of Wipro Limited) to open an engineering center in India. Besides these countries, Harman is also looking to grow in Russia.

Harman's shift to right-size its operations and strengthen its presence in developing markets is part of a restructuring plan that was rolled out in 2006 but accelerated because of the ailing economy. The plant closures combined with other moves in the company's restructuring has led to layoffs, especially in the US, the UK, Germany, and Austria. In 2009 alone Harman laid off about 2,000 employees, or nearly 20% of its workforce. The turnaround is expected to be completed by 2011 and save about $400 million.

Turbulent financial markets wreaked havoc in late 2007, when KKR & Co. and Goldman Sachs abandoned an $8 billion leveraged buyout of Harman. But amid a tightening credit market, KKR and Goldman Sachs said that unacceptable financial conditions at the stereo maker triggered a material adverse change that allows them to walk away from the deal. (Harman disagrees that a material adverse change had occurred or that it has breached the merger agreement.)

Feisty namesake and chairman Sidney Harman, the backbone of the company for half a century, has been considered a legend in the audio industry. He owns about 5% of Harman.

Just shy of his 90th birthday, Harman retired from his post as chairman in late 2008. Dinesh C. Paliwal was tapped to take over the position, in addition to continuing his duties as CEO.

HISTORY

Sidney Harman and his partner, Bernard Kardon, left their engineering jobs at a public address system company to found Harman/Kardon in 1953. The two marketed their home audio components to the general public instead of to the traditional audio buff. Their novel concept was to package amplifiers and a tuner in a single unit (called a receiver) that appealed to average consumers.

Kardon cashed out in a 1956 IPO that left Harman with about 33% of the firm. Harman/Kardon acquired the respected JBL speaker business in 1969.

Harman was also interested in internal growth. He introduced new management techniques emphasizing workers' quality of life, allowing employees to redesign their jobs and leave work after meeting production quotas. His projects, which had varying degrees of success, attracted the attention of President Carter's administration, which brought Harman on board as undersecretary of commerce in 1977. Harman sold the company to Beatrice Foods that year to avoid a conflict of interest. The company did poorly under the conglomerate, and Harman bought much of it back in 1980, taking it private.

He then changed the name to Harman International Industries.

Through acquisitions, he quickly expanded the business into the auto OEM market, acquiring Essex Loudspeaker from United Technologies (1981), then moving into the professional audio equipment market with his purchase of Infinity (1983). In the mid-1980s Harman signed exclusive deals to supply JBL speakers to Ford and Chrysler, and in 1985 it bought back the Harman/Kardon trade name (Beatrice Foods had sold it to Japanese company Shin Shirasuna). The company went public again the next year.

In 1991 Harman went into a tailspin (laying off 500) caused by a worldwide recession, poor auto sales, and four soured acquisitions. President Donald Esters quit in 1992, and Harman set about reorganizing the firm.

The company bought AKG, a leading Austrian microphone maker, in 1993. Signaling its interest in the new digital age, Harman created a new business unit, Harman Interactive, the following year to focus on PC and home theater systems.

In 1997 it boosted its car audio business with new agreements to supply audio systems to certain models of BMW, Toyota, Hyundai, and Peugeot, and it purchased two car loudspeaker makers (Oxford International and Audio Electronic Systems).

In the late 1990s Harman trimmed its consumer product lines from 2,000 to 200. With its sales to Asia down and European sales ailing as well, it closed plants and laid off workers in 1998. That year president Bernard Girod succeeded Harman as CEO. Harman sold its Orban broadcasting-products business in 1999, and replaced it with Crown International (maker of high-powered amplifiers) in 2000.

In 2001 Harman sold its Allen & Heath subsidiary, a maker of mixing consoles, to a group consisting of the company's top management.

Longtime CEO Bernard Girod, who took the reins from Sidney Harman in 1998, retired at the end of 2006. Earlier that year Douglas Pertz took over as CEO, but resigned from the company midyear after a short stint.

In 2007 Dinesh C. Paliwal joined the company as CEO and vice chairman. He was tapped to take over the position of chairman in late 2008, succeeding the retiring Sidney Harman.

In 2010 Harman expanded to Brazil with the purchase of Eletronica Selenium. The firm makes and sells professional loudspeakers primarily in Latin America.

EXECUTIVES

Chairman, President, and CEO: Dinesh C. Paliwal, age 52, $9,349,545 total compensation
EVP and CFO: Herbert K. Parker, age 51, $2,921,593 total compensation
CTO: Sachin Lawande
VP Human Resources and Chief Human Resources Officer: John Stacey, age 45
VP Operational Excellence: David Karch, age 49, $1,061,111 total compensation
VP Corporate Communications: Brad A. Hoffman
VP Corporate Development; President, Audio Division: David J. Slump
VP and Chief Accounting Officer: Jennifer Peter, age 37
VP, General Counsel, and Secretary: Todd A. Suko, age 43
VP Marketing Services: Eric M. Plaskonos
VP and Treasurer: Robert C. Ryan
VP Investor Relations: Robert V. Lardon

CEO, Automotive Division: Klaus Blickle, age 55, $1,756,922 total compensation
President, Harman Professional Group:
Blake Augsburger, age 47, $1,368,505 total compensation
President and Country Manager, China and North East Asia: David Jin
Country Manager, Japan; President, Harman Japan: Ken Yasuda
Director Corporate Communications: Darrin Shewchuk
Auditors: KPMG LLP

LOCATIONS

HQ: Harman International Industries, Incorporated
400 Atlantic St., 15th Fl., Stamford, CT 06901
Phone: 203-328-3500
Web: www.harman.com

2010 Sales

	$ mil.	% of total
Europe		
Germany	1,380.2	41
Other countries	623.2	19
US	678.4	20
Other regions	682.6	20
Total	**3,364.4**	**100**

PRODUCTS/OPERATIONS

2010 Sales

	$ mil.	% of total
Automotive	2,468.0	73
Professional	522.7	16
Consumer	373.0	11
Other	0.7	—
Total	**3,364.4**	**100**

Selected Products

Automotive
  Audio systems
  Information and entertainment systems
Professional
  Audio amplifiers
  Audio headphones
  Broadcasting studio equipment
  Cinema audio systems
  Digital audio workstations
  Equalizers
  Loudspeakers
  Microphones
  Mixing consoles
  Signal processing systems
  Sound reinforcement systems
  Special effects units
  Surround sound systems
Consumer
  Audio amplifiers
  Audio and video receivers
  CD players
  Digital signal processors
  DVD players
  Home theater systems
  Loudspeakers
  PC audio systems

Selected Brands

AKG
BSS
Crown
dbx
DigiTech
Harman/Kardon
Infinity
JBL
JBL Professional
Lexicon
Mark Levinson
Revel
Soundcraft
Studer

COMPETITORS

Aisin Seiki
Altec Lansing
Audio Research
Avid Technology
Bosch Communications
Bose
Boston Acoustics
Bosch und Siemens
Creative Technology
D&M
Delphi Automotive
Denon Electronics
DENSO
Digidesign
Fender Musical
  Instruments
Foster Electric (U.S.A.)
Harris Corp.
JVC KENWOOD
Klipsch
Krell
Logitech
LOUD Technologies
Macintosh Retail Group
Marshall Amplification
Meyer Sound
Mitsubishi Electric
Onkyo
Panasonic
Peavey Electronics
Pioneer Corporation
Polk Audio
QSC Audio
Sennheiser
Shure
Sony
TASCAM
TomTom
Visteon
Yamaha

HISTORICAL FINANCIALS

Company Type: Public

Income Statement

FYE: June 30

	REVENUE ($ mil.)	NET INCOME ($ mil.)	NET PROFIT MARGIN	EMPLOYEES
6/10	3,364	164	4.9%	9,816
6/09	2,891	(423)	—	9,482
6/08	4,113	108	2.6%	11,694
6/07	3,551	314	8.8%	11,688
6/06	3,248	255	7.9%	11,246
Annual Growth	**0.9%**	**(10.5%)**	**—**	**(3.3%)**

2010 Year-End Financials

Debt ratio: 32.1%
Return on equity: 15.6%
Cash ($ mil.): 646
Current ratio: 1.94
Long-term debt ($ mil.): 364
No. of shares (mil.): 70
Dividends
  Yield: 0.0%
  Payout: —
Market value ($ mil.): 2,079

Stock History

NYSE: HAR

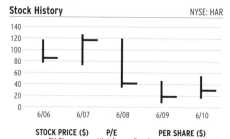

	STOCK PRICE ($) FY Close	P/E High/Low		PER SHARE ($) Earnings	Dividends	Book Value
6/10	29.89	24	8	2.25	0.00	16.32
6/09	18.80	—	—	(7.19)	0.04	14.00
6/08	41.39	68	21	1.73	0.05	19.27
6/07	116.80	27	16	4.72	0.05	21.48
6/06	85.37	31	21	3.75	0.05	17.66
Annual Growth	**(23.1%)**	**—**	**—**	**(12.0%)**	**—**	**(2.0%)**

Harris Corporation

Hail Harris for a high-flying, high-tech hookup. The company, which develops communications products for government and commercial customers worldwide, makes microwave, satellite, and other wireless network transmission equipment; air traffic control systems; mobile radio systems; and digital network broadcasting and management systems. Among its largest customers are the US government, prime contractors, and foreign militaries, which together account for more than three-quarters of sales. Harris' commercial clients are construction companies, oil producers, radio and TV broadcasters, and utilities, including Clear Channel Communications, Lockheed Martin, and Sony. Harris makes most of its sales in the US.

Harris continues to build its line of communications products with acquisitions and to adapt technologies created for its government customers to other markets. The company has drawn on its expertise in broadcast, high-frequency, and radio-frequency (RF) transmission to build up a portfolio of wireless broadband communications systems in an ongoing effort to expand into commercial markets. Harris' government and RF communications segments still account for most of its revenues.

The company in 2010 paid $525 million in cash to buy CapRock Communications, a provider of managed satellite communications services. The deal added a range of remote communication and support services for the oil exploration and drilling, military, maritime, mining industries to Harris' portfolio, and provided the company with new customers for its satellite equipment. It also marked the company's entry into the energy market and expands its geographic reach.

Harris acquired the wireless systems business of Tyco Electronics for $675 million in cash in 2009. The company combined Tyco Electronics, which makes wireless communications systems for law enforcement and other public service organizations, with its RF Communications unit. It also bought the air traffic control business of SolaCom Technologies that year. The deal included voice and data communications equipment for air traffic control facilities, along with radio systems for communication between air traffic control and in-flight airplanes.

HISTORY

Harris was founded in Niles, Ohio, in 1895 by brothers Alfred and Charles Harris, both jewelers and inventors. Among their inventions was a printing press that became Harris Automatic Press Company's flagship product.

Harris remained a small, family-run company until 1944, when engineer George Dively was hired as general manager. Under Dively the company began manufacturing bindery, typesetting, and paper converting equipment while remaining a leading supplier of printing presses. In 1957 Harris merged with typesetter maker Intertype and became known as Harris-Intertype Corporation.

During the 1960s and 1970s Harris-Intertype grew through acquisitions. In 1967 it bought electronics and data processing equipment maker Radiation, a company heavily dependent on government contracts, and relocated to Radiation's headquarters in Melbourne, Florida. The company also bought RF Communications (two-way radios, 1969), General Electric's broadcast equipment line (1972), and UCC-Communications Systems (data processing equipment, 1972).

The company changed its name to Harris Corporation in 1974. In 1980 Harris bought Farinon, a manufacturer of microwave radio systems, and Lanier Business Products, the leading maker of dictating equipment. In 1983 it sold its printing equipment business.

Harris formed a joint venture with 3M, called Harris/3M Document Products, in 1986 to market copiers and fax machines, and in 1989 it acquired the entire operation, which became Lanier Worldwide. Other 1980s acquisitions included Scientific Calculations, a CAD software developer (1986), and GE's Solid State semiconductor group (1988).

Harris won a contract with the FAA in 1992 to modernize voice communications between airports and airplanes. Later that year Harris acquired Westronic, a supplier of automated control systems for electric utilities. In 1994 Harris began installing the world's largest private digital telephone network along Russia's gas pipeline, and it spun off its computer products division as Harris Computer Systems.

In 1996 Harris became the first company to demonstrate a digital TV transmitter. That year it acquired NovAtel, a maker of cellular and wireless local-loop systems for rural areas, and it bought a stake in the Chile-based phone company Compañia de Teléfonos. In 1997 it purchased digital broadcasting specialist Innovation Telecommunications Image and Sound.

The company in 1998 purchased German chemical manufacturer Bayer's Agfa-Gevaert photocopier business, which doubled Lanier's share of the European office equipment market. Hurt by a tough semiconductor market that year, Harris laid off about 8% of its workforce.

Shifting toward a strictly communications-related operation in 1999, Harris sold its semiconductor operations (which now does business as Intersil) in a deal valued at about $600 million and spun off Lanier to shareholders. It also sold its photomask manufacturing unit to Align-Rite.

In 2000 Harris expanded its broadcasting and wireless transmission product lines with the acquisitions of Louth Automation and Wavtrace. That year the company began outsourcing the assembly of its commercial printed circuit boards and folded its telephone switching and alarm management product lines.

The company broadened its communications product portfolio in 2001 with the acquisitions of Exigent, a provider of satellite tracking and control software, and Hirschmann, a maker of digital broadcasting radio transmitters and cable systems.

In 2004 the company bought Encoda, a developer of software and services to customers in the broadcast media industry, for $340 million.

The company invested in broadcast communications with the acquisition of broadcast video systems maker Leitch Technology in 2006. The buy gave Harris a stake in the transition to high-definition digital TV services. The company also purchased broadcast management software maker Optimal Solutions and the digital video business of Aastra Technologies that year. Harris acquired Multimax — a provider of government IT and communication services — for $400 million in 2007.

EXECUTIVES

Chairman, President, and CEO: Howard L. Lance, age 54, $8,598,322 total compensation
EVP and COO: Daniel R. (Dan) Pearson, age 58, $1,807,251 total compensation
SVP and CFO: Gary L. McArthur, age 49, $2,294,283 total compensation
VP and General Counsel: Eugene S. (Gene) Cavallucci, age 62
VP, Associate General Counsel, and Corporate Secretary: Scott T. Mikuen, age 47
VP and Principal Accounting Officer: Lewis A. Schwartz, age 46
VP Engineering and CTO: R. Kent Buchanan, age 59
VP Internal Audit and Compliance: Terry L. Feiser, age 54
VP Strategy and Chief Growth Officer: Wesley B. (Wes) Covell
VP Investor Relations and Corporate Communications: Pamela (Pam) Padgett
VP Corporate Communications: Jim Burke
VP Information Services and CIO: William H. Miller Jr.
VP Tax and Treasurer: Charles J. (Chuck) Greene, age 55
VP Human Resources and Corporate Relations: Jeffrey S. (Jeff) Shuman, age 55
Group President, Government Communications Systems: Sheldon J. Fox, age 51
President, Broadcast Communications: P. Harris Morris
President, International Tactical Radio Communications: Andy Start
President, Technical Services: Paul T. (Ted) Hengst
President, Information Technology Services Business: John Heller, age 48
President, Public Safety and Professional Communications Business: Stephen (Steve) Shanck
President, RF Communications: Dana A. Mehnert, age 47
President, Maritime Communication Services, Government Communications Systems Division: Richard P. (Rick) Simonian
Auditors: Ernst & Young LLP

LOCATIONS

HQ: Harris Corporation
1025 W. NASA Blvd., Melbourne, FL 32919
Phone: 321-727-9100 **Fax:** 321-674-4740
Web: www.harris.com

2009 Sales

	$ mil.	% of total
US	4,754.4	95
Other countries	250.6	5
Total	**5,005.0**	**100**

PRODUCTS/OPERATIONS

2009 Sales

	$ mil.	% of total
Government Communications Systems	2,709.6	54
RF Communications	1,760.6	35
Broadcast Communications	583.6	11
Adjustments	(48.8)	—
Total	**5,005.0**	**100**

2009 Sales

	$ mil.	% of total
Products	3,915.3	78
Services	1,089.7	22
Total	**5,005.0**	**100**

Selected Business Groups

Government Communications Systems
  Civil programs
  IT services
  National intelligence programs
Radio-frequency (RF) Communications
  Antennas and accessories
  Information assurance
  Public safety
  Tactical radio communications

Broadcast Communications
  Advertising software
  Digital asset management
  Digital signage
  Infrastructure and networking
  Television and radio transmission systems

COMPETITORS

Alcatel-Lucent
Avid Technology
BAE Systems Inc.
Boeing
CACI International
Ceragon Networks
Chyron
Cisco Systems
Computer Sciences Corp.
EADS
Ericsson
General Dynamics
GTSI
Harmonic
ITT Defense
L-3 Communications
Lockheed Martin
ManTech
NCI
NEC
Nera
Nokia Siemens Networks
Nortel Networks
Northrop Grumman
Omneon
Pilat Media Global
Raytheon
Rockwell Collins
Rohde & Schwarz
SAIC
SELEX SI
Sony
SRA International
Stanley, Inc.
Technicolor
Tektronix
Thales
Vizrt
WideOrbit

HISTORICAL FINANCIALS

Company Type: Public

Income Statement

FYE: Friday nearest June 30

	REVENUE ($ mil.)	NET INCOME ($ mil.)	NET PROFIT MARGIN	EMPLOYEES
6/09	5,005	38	0.8%	15,400
6/08	5,311	444	8.4%	16,500
6/07	4,243	480	11.3%	16,000
6/06	3,475	238	6.8%	13,900
6/05	3,001	202	6.7%	12,600
Annual Growth	**13.6%**	**(34.2%)**	**—**	**5.1%**

2009 Year-End Financials

Debt ratio: 63.0%
Return on equity: 1.8%
Cash ($ mil.): 281
Current ratio: 1.68
Long-term debt ($ mil.): 1,177
No. of shares (mil.): 130
Dividends
  Yield: 2.8%
  Payout: 285.7%
Market value ($ mil.): 3,682

Stock History

NYSE: HRS

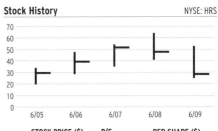

	STOCK PRICE ($) FY Close	P/E High/Low		PER SHARE ($) Earnings	Dividends	Book Value
6/09	28.36	186	92	0.28	0.80	14.40
6/08	47.80	19	13	3.26	0.60	17.51
6/07	51.64	16	10	3.43	0.44	14.66
6/06	39.30	28	17	1.71	0.32	12.80
6/05	29.54	23	14	1.46	0.24	11.08
Annual Growth	**(1.0%)**	**—**	**—**	**(33.8%)**	**35.1%**	**6.8%**

Hartford Financial Services

Despite its name, at its heart The Hartford Financial Services Group is an insurer with a range of personal and commercial life and property/casualty insurance products. Through its Hartford Life subsidiary, the company offers individual and group life insurance and annuities, as well as the financial services mentioned in its name (asset management, retirement plans, and mutual funds). Its property/casualty operations include both personal (homeowners, auto) and business coverage (workers' compensation) and specialty commercial coverage for large companies. The Hartford, in business since 1810, sells its products through about 11,000 independent agencies and more than 100,000 registered broker-dealers.

As the baby-boomer generation ages, Hartford Life is targeting the retirement savings market and seeking marketing alliances. The Hartford's property/casualty segment already enjoys such an arrangement with an exclusive agreement to provide auto and homeowners polices to members of AARP (the American Association of Retired Persons).

In 2008 European insurer Allianz made a capital investment of about $2.5 billion in The Hartford, in a deal intended to shore up its liquidity position and prevent a ratings downgrade. Allianz bought up both stock and debt (giving it 10% of the company) and warrants that allow it to acquire up to 20% of the company.

The Hartford's troubles stemmed from losses attributed to its investment holdings in Fannie Mae, Freddie Mac, and Lehman Brothers — all of them casualties of the 2008 financial crisis. In mid-2009 the US Treasury stepped in and offered The Hartford and other major life insurers access to its Troubled Asset Relief Program (TARP). The Hartford borrowed $3.4 billion to shore up its capital reserves. As the company and the economy stabilized, the loan was repaid by early 2010, including an additional $21.7 million dividend payment.

The company has exited virtually all of its international property/casualty operations and is pulling back on its international life insurance to better focus on its domestic businesses. It ended sales of variable annuities in Japan and the UK, is divesting its Brazilian joint venture, and reversed earlier plans to begin selling annuities in Germany.

Chairman and CEO Ramani Ayer had planned on retiring at the end of 2008, but agreed to stay at the helm through 2009. His final year was marked by efforts to stem the company's losses. Former head of consumer banking at Bank of America, Liam McGee, was appointed as the company's new CEO in late 2009.

HISTORY

In 1810 a group of Hartford, Connecticut, businessmen led by Walter Mitchell and Henry Terry founded the Hartford Fire Insurance Co. Frequent fires in America's wooden cities and executive ignorance of risk assessment and premium-setting often left the firm on the edge of insolvency. (In 1835 stockholders staged a coup and threw management out.) Still, each urban conflagration — including the Great Chicago Fire of 1871 — gave The Hartford an opportunity to seek out and pay all its policyholders, thus teaching the company to underwrite under fire, as it were, and to use such disasters to refine its rates.

The company's stag logo was initially a little deer, as shown on a policy sold to Abraham Lincoln in 1861. A few years later, however, Hartford began using the majestic creature (from a Landseer painting) now familiar to customers. By the 1880s Hartford operated nationwide, as well as in Canada and Hawaii.

The company survived both world wars and the Depression but emerged in the 1950s in need of organization. It set up new regional offices and added life insurance, buying Columbian National Life (founded 1902), which became Hartford Life Insurance Co.

In 1969 Hartford was bought by ITT (formerly International Telephone and Telegraph), whose CEO, Harold Geneen, was an avid conglomerateur. Consumer advocate Ralph Nader strongly opposed the acquisition — he fought the merger in court for years and felt vindicated when ITT spun off Hartford in 1995. Others opposed it, too, because ITT had engineered the merger based on an IRS ruling (later revoked) that Hartford stockholders wouldn't have to pay capital gains taxes on the purchase price of their stock.

Insurance operations consolidated under the Hartford Life Insurance banner in 1978. Through the 1980s, Hartford Life remained one of ITT's strongest operations. A conservative investment policy kept Hartford safe from the junk bond and real estate manias of the 1980s.

Hartford reorganized its property/casualty operations along three lines in 1986, and in 1992 it organized its reinsurance business into one unit. The company faced some liability in relation to Dow Corning's breast-implant litigation, but underwriting standards after 1985 reduced long-term risk. In 1994 the company began selling insurance products to AARP members under an exclusive agreement. In 1996 the company finished its spinoff from ITT, which was acquired by Starwood Hotels & Resorts two years later.

To grow its reinsurance operation, Hartford acquired the reinsurance business of Orion Capital (now Royal & SunAlliance USA) in 1996. It posted a loss of $99 million, due in large part to asbestos and pollution liabilities. Late that year the firm changed its name to The Hartford Financial Services Group.

To shore up reserves and fund growth, in 1997 the company spun off 19% of Hartford Life. The Hartford expanded into nonstandard auto insurance in 1998 by buying Omni Insurance Group (since sold in 2006). The company also sold its London & Edinburgh Insurance Group in 1998 to Norwich Union (now part of Aviva, formerly CGNU). In 1999 The Hartford acquired the reinsurance business of Vesta Fire Insurance, a subsidiary of Vesta Insurance Group.

In 2000 Hartford bought back the part of Hartford Life it had spun off. The Hartford also bought the financial products and excess and surplus specialty insurance lines of Reliance Group Holdings. Assurances Générales de France bought the company's Dutch subsidiary, Zwolsche Algemeene. In 2001 the company bought Fortis Financial, a US subsidiary of Belgian insurer Fortis, and sold Hartford Seguros, its Spanish subsidiary, to Liberty Mutual.

EXECUTIVES

Chairman, President, and CEO: Liam E. McGee, age 55, $361,450 total compensation
EVP and CFO: Christopher J. Swift, age 49
EVP and General Counsel: Alan J. Kreczko, age 58, $2,489,549 total compensation
EVP and Chief Investment Officer; President Hartford Investment Management Co.: Greg McGreevey, age 47, $3,648,950 total compensation
EVP Personal and Small Business Insurance: Jonathan R. Bennett
EVP; President and COO, Property and Casualty Operations: Juan C. Andrade, age 44
EVP and Chief Risk Officer: Lizabeth H. (Liz) Zlatkus, age 51, $4,639,196 total compensation
EVP and Sector Head of Municipal Finance, Hartford Investment Management Co.: Joseph Darcy
EVP: Neal S. Wolin, age 48, $3,447,039 total compensation
EVP Hartford Life Distributors: Kevin Connor, age 49
EVP Group Benefits Division: Ronald R. Gendreau
EVP Human Resources: Eileen G. Whelley, age 56
SVP and Head, Hartford Financial Products: Michael Dandini
SVP and Controller: Beth A. Bombara, age 42
SVP and CIO: Brian O'Connell
SVP and Secretary: Ricardo A. Anzaldua
President, Wealth Management: David N. Levenson
President, Heritage Holdings, Inc.: Andrew J. Pinkes
President, Consumer Markets: Andy Napoli, age 45
President and CEO, Woodbury Financial Services: Patrick McEvoy
President and Chief Executive, Hartford Life Insurance KK (Japan): Victor Chang
Senior Managing Director: Robert J. (Bob) Froehlich
Auditors: Deloitte & Touche LLP

LOCATIONS

HQ: The Hartford Financial Services Group, Inc.
One Hartford Plaza, Hartford, CT 06155
Phone: 860-547-5000 **Fax:** 860-547-2680
Web: www.thehartford.com

2009 Sales

	$ mil.	% of total
US	20,429	83
Japan	3,816	15
Other	456	2
Total	**24,701**	**100**

PRODUCTS/OPERATIONS

2009 Sales

	$ mil.	% of total
Life	13,729	55
Property/casualty	11,165	45
Corporate	(193)	—
Total	**24,701**	**100**

COMPETITORS

AEGON USA
AIG
Allstate
Berkshire Hathaway
CNA Financial
ING
Liberty Mutual
MetLife
Nationwide
New York Life
Northwestern Mutual
Prudential
State Farm
TIAA-CREF
Travelers Companies
Zurich Financial Services

HISTORICAL FINANCIALS

Company Type: Public

Income Statement
FYE: December 31

	ASSETS ($ mil.)	NET INCOME ($ mil.)	INCOME AS % OF ASSETS	EMPLOYEES
12/09	307,717	(887)	—	28,000
12/08	287,583	(2,749)	—	31,000
12/07	360,361	2,949	0.8%	31,000
12/06	326,710	2,745	0.8%	31,000
12/05	285,557	2,274	0.8%	30,000
Annual Growth	1.9%	—	—	(1.7%)

2009 Year-End Financials

Equity as % of assets: 4.8%
Return on assets: —
Return on equity: —
Long-term debt ($ mil.): 6,632
No. of shares (mil.): 444

Dividends
Yield: 0.9%
Payout: —
Market value ($ mil.): 10,335
Sales ($ mil.): 24,701

Stock History

NYSE: HIG

	STOCK PRICE ($) FY Close	P/E High/Low		PER SHARE ($) Earnings	Dividends	Book Value
12/09	23.26	—	—	(2.93)	0.20	40.21
12/08	16.42	—	—	(8.99)	1.91	20.86
12/07	87.19	11	9	9.24	2.03	43.22
12/06	93.31	11	9	8.69	1.70	42.48
12/05	85.89	12	9	7.44	1.17	34.49
Annual Growth	(27.9%)	—	—	—	(35.7%)	3.9%

Hasbro, Inc.

It's all fun and games at Hasbro, the #2 toy maker in the US (after Mattel) and the producer of such childhood favorites as G.I. Joe, Play-Doh, Tonka toys, Nerf balls, and My Little Pony. Besides toys, Hasbro makes board games under its Milton Bradley (*Scrabble, Candy Land*), Cranium, and Parker Brothers (*Monopoly, Trivial Pursuit*) brands, as well as trading cards such as *Magic: The Gathering* (through its Wizards of the Coast unit) and *Dungeons & Dragons*. Hasbro also makes *Star Wars* action figures; the company's the licensee of action figures and games for the prequels. Besides Disney and Disney's Marvel Entertainment, Hasbro licenses popular names and characters for toys and games.

Hasbro has been busy enlisting more superheroes to bring rival Mattel and its Barbie down a notch. The toy maker has access to some 5,000-odd Marvel characters (such as Fantastic Four, X-Men, Captain America, and Ghost Rider) thanks to a licensing agreement with Marvel for the sale of Marvel-branded toys and games through 2017. The company has logged spikes in boys' toy sales (at the tune of 36% of its 2009 revenue) that coincided with the movie releases of *Ironman, Indiana Jones and the Kingdom of the Crystal Skull, G.I. Joe: Rise of the Cobra*, and

Transformers: Revenge of the Fallen. Its Star Wars, Spider-Man, and Transformers offerings were also bolstered by the animated TV series.

Leaving a lucrative licensing agreement for competitor Mattel after nearly a decade, Sesame Workshop in late 2009 inked a deal with Hasbro to make *Sesame Street* toys and games. Boasting the rights to the Elmo, Big Bird, and Cookie Monster names, Hasbro plans to roll out new products beginning in 2011 from the Playskool unit.

Hasbro's long-term strategy involves extending its brands into the digital world. Hasbro teamed up with Electronic Arts (EA) to create video game versions of some of its classic board games, such as *Monopoly, Scrabble*, and *Yahtzee*. Titles are available for major platforms, including gaming consoles, mobile phones, and PCs.

The company hasn't forgotten about girls' toys, digital or otherwise, which generate 19% of its revenue. In 2008 Hasbro introduced the *Littlest Pet Shop* video game series, in accordance with its EA deal. It also grew the brand through a website that allows users to digitally customize their pets and interact with others. The toy maker saw increased revenues from the redesign of its classic Easy-Bake oven.

In keeping with creative partnerships, Hasbro teamed up with cable programming giant Discovery Communications in 2009 to form a joint venture for its children's TV channel, The Hub. The network plans to offer family and educational programming based on Hasbro's brands, including G.I. Joe, My Little Pony, and Scrabble, beginning in 2010.

Former chairman Alan Hassenfeld, the third generation of Hassenfelds to control the company, owns about 10% of Hasbro. Hassenfeld stepped down in May 2008 to make way for Al Verrecchia to become chairman. Brian Goldner, Hasbro's COO, succeeded Verrecchia as chief executive. Hassenfeld remains a director of the company.

HISTORY

Henry and Helal Hassenfeld formed Hassenfeld Brothers in Pawtucket, Rhode Island, in 1923 to distribute fabric remnants. By 1926 the company was manufacturing fabric-covered pencil boxes and shortly thereafter, pencils.

Hassenfeld Brothers branched into the toy industry during the 1940s by introducing toy nurse and doctor kits. The company's toy division was the first to use TV to promote a toy product (Mr. Potato Head in 1952).

Expansion continued in the mid-1960s with the introduction of the G.I. Joe doll, which quickly became its primary toy line. Hassenfeld Brothers went public in 1968 and changed its name to Hasbro Industries. It bought Romper Room (TV productions) the next year.

In the 1970s the toy and pencil divisions, led by different family members, disagreed over the company's finances, future direction, and leadership. The dispute caused the company to split in 1980. The toy division continued to operate under the Hasbro name; the pencil division (Empire Pencil Corporation in Shelbyville, Tennessee, led by Harold Hassenfeld) became a separate corporation.

Hasbro expanded rapidly in the 1980s under new CEO Stephen Hassenfeld. He reduced the number of products by one-third to concentrate on developing a line of toys aimed at specific markets. During that decade the firm released a number of successful toys, including a smaller version of G.I. Joe (1982) and Transformers (small vehicles that transform into robots, 1984).

Hasbro acquired Milton Bradley, a major producer of board games (*Chutes and Ladders, Candy Land*), puzzles, and preschool toys (Playskool) in 1984.

The company acquired Cabbage Patch Kids, *Scrabble, Parcheesi*, and other product lines in 1989. Stephen died that year. His brother Alan, who had spearheaded Hasbro's international sales growth in the late 1980s, became CEO.

Hasbro bought Tonka (including the Kenner and Parker Brothers brands) in 1991 and established operations in Greece, Mexico, and Hungary. Hasbro blocked a $5.2 billion hostile takeover attempt by Mattel in 1996, and in 1997 it began cutting about 2,500 jobs (20% of Hasbro's employees) that year.

Expanding in the high-tech toys niche, in 1998 Hasbro made several acquisitions, including Tiger Electronics (Giga Pets), the rights to some 75 Atari home console game titles (*Missile Command, Centipede*), MicroProse (3-D video games for PCs), and Galoob Toys, a fellow *Star Wars* prequel licensee and maker of Micro Machines and Pound Puppies. Tiger Electronics had the hit of the 1998 holiday season: a chattering interactive doll called Furby.

In 1999 Hasbro bought game maker and retailer Wizards of the Coast (maker of *Pokémon* trading cards). In late 1999 the company announced it would can another 19% of its workforce (2,200 jobs), and close two plants in Mexico and the UK. Another 750 job cuts followed in late 2000.

In 2003 Hasbro announced it would close its manufacturing plant in Valencia, Spain, and shift operations to China and Ireland, affecting about 500 employees. In 2004 Hasbro laid off about 125 employees across several departments.

In 2008 Hasbro picked up the intellectual property rights to the Trivial Pursuit brand for $80 million from Horn Abbot Ltd. and Horn Abbot International Ltd.

EXECUTIVES

Chairman: Alfred J. (Al) Verrecchia, age 67, $15,018,011 total compensation
President, CEO, and Director: Brian Goldner, age 47, $7,887,902 total compensation
COO: David D. R. Hargreaves, age 57, $4,823,029 total compensation
SVP and CFO: Deborah (Deb) Thomas, age 46, $1,221,433 total compensation
SVP, Chief Legal Officer, and Secretary: Barry Nagler, age 53, $1,814,869 total compensation
Global Chief Development Officer: Duncan Billing, age 51, $1,664,500 total compensation
Global Chief Marketing Officer: Johnathan (John) Frascotti, age 49, $1,578,315 total compensation
SVP and Treasurer: Martin R. Trueb, age 57
SVP and Global Brand Leader, Worldwide Preschool Business: Jerry Perez
SVP Corporate Communications: Wayne S. Charness
SVP Human Resources: Dolph Johnson
SVP Global Licensing: Simon Waters
SVP Marketing: Ira Hernowitz
VP Investor Relations: Debbie Hancock
President and CEO, Hub: Margaret A. Loesch, age 61
President, Hasbro Properties: Jane Ritson Parsons
Director Corporate Communications: Julie Duffy
Auditors: KPMG LLP

LOCATIONS

HQ: Hasbro, Inc.
1027 Newport Ave., Pawtucket, RI 02862
Phone: 401-431-8697   **Fax:** 401-431-8535
Web: www.hasbro.com

2009 Sales

	$ mil.	% of total
US & Canada	2,447.9	60
International	1,459.5	36
Entertainment & licensing	155.0	4
Global operations	5.5	—
Total	**4,067.9**	**100**

PRODUCTS/OPERATIONS

2009 Sales

	$ mil.	% of total
Boys' toys	1,470.9	36
Games & puzzles	1,340.9	33
Girls' toys	790.8	19
Preschool toys	451.4	11
Other	13.9	1
Total	**4,067.9**	**100**

Selected Brands and Products

Electronics
  Tiger Electronics
    Furby
    FurReal Friends
    Giga Pets
    Hitclips (micro music systems)
    Luv Cubs
    VideoNow (personal video player)
Games and Puzzles
  Avalon Hill
    Acquire
    Axis & Allies
    Diplomacy
    History of the World
    Risk 2210 A.D.
    Stratego Legends
  Milton Bradley
    Battleship
    Candy Land
    Chutes and Ladders
    Connect Four
    The Game of Life
    Hungry Hungry Hippos
    Jenga
    Mousetrap
    Operation
    Scattergories
    Scrabble
  Tiger Games
    Trouble
    Twister
    Yahtzee
  Parker Brothers
    Boggle
    Clue
    Monopoly
    Ouija
    Risk
    Sorry!
    Trivial Pursuit
  Wizards of the Coast
    Dungeons and Dragons
    Harry Potter trading cards
    Magic: The Gathering
    Magic: The Gathering Online
    Pokémon
Boys' Toys
  BTR (Built To Rule action building sets)
  Engine Gear spinning tops
  G.I. Joe action figures
  Micro Machines
  NakNak (stacking battle figures)
  Star Wars action figures
  Tonka (toy trucks)
  Transformers (small vehicles that transform into robots)

Preschool Toys
  2-in-1 Tummy Time Gym
  Bob the Builder toys
  Busy Ball Popper
  First Starts (role-playing products)
  Go-Bots
  Kick Start Gym
  Major Powers (action figure)
  Mr. Potato Head
  Playskool
  Sesame Street
  Silly Sports (action games)
  Sit 'N Spin
  Speedstars (race cars and track sets)
  Weebles
Creative Play
  Easy-Bake Oven
  Lite-Brite
  Lite-Brite Cube
  Play-Doh
  Spirograph
  Tinkertoys
Girls' Toys
  e-kera (handheld karaoke system)
  My Little Pony
  Raggedy Ann and Raggedy Andy dolls
  TwinkleTwirls Dance Studio
Other
  Nerf (soft play toys)
  Super Soaker water products
  Wheels on the Bus

COMPETITORS

Build-A-Bear
Enesco
Graco Children's Products
JAKKS Pacific
LeapFrog
LEGO
Marvel Entertainment
Mattel
MGA Entertainment
Nakajima USA
Namco Bandai
Ohio Art
Playmates Toys Limited
Playmobil
Poof-Slinky
Radio Flyer
RC2 Corporation
Sanrio
Simba Dickie Group
Smoby
Spin Master
TakaraTomy
Toy Quest
Ty
VTech Holdings
WHAM-O

HISTORICAL FINANCIALS

Company Type: Public

Income Statement

FYE: Last Sunday in December

	REVENUE ($ mil.)	NET INCOME ($ mil.)	NET PROFIT MARGIN	EMPLOYEES
12/09	4,068	375	9.2%	5,800
12/08	4,022	307	7.6%	5,900
12/07	3,838	333	8.7%	5,900
12/06	3,152	230	7.3%	5,800
12/05	3,088	212	6.9%	5,900
Annual Growth	**7.1%**	**15.3%**	**—**	**(0.4%)**

2009 Year-End Financials

Debt ratio: 71.0%
Return on equity: 25.1%
Cash ($ mil.): 636
Current ratio: 2.51
Long-term debt ($ mil.): 1,132
No. of shares (mil.): 140
Dividends
  Yield: 2.5%
  Payout: 32.3%
Market value ($ mil.): 4,483

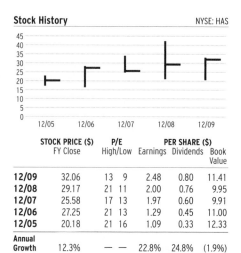

Stock History

NYSE: HAS

	STOCK PRICE ($) FY Close	P/E High/Low		PER SHARE ($) Earnings	Dividends	Book Value
12/09	32.06	13	9	2.48	0.80	11.41
12/08	29.17	21	11	2.00	0.76	9.95
12/07	25.58	17	13	1.97	0.60	9.91
12/06	27.25	21	13	1.29	0.45	11.00
12/05	20.18	21	16	1.09	0.33	12.33
Annual Growth	**12.3%**	**—**	**—**	**22.8%**	**24.8%**	**(1.9%)**

HCA Inc.

As the largest for-profit hospital operator in the US, "HCA" could stand for Health Care for America. HCA (AKA Hospital Corporation of America) operates roughly 170 acute care, psychiatric, and rehabilitation hospitals in the US and England. It also runs about 100 ambulatory surgery centers, as well as cancer treatment and outpatient rehab centers that form health care networks in many of the communities it serves. HCA has facilities in 20 states; about three-quarters of its hospitals are in the southern US (approximately 70 are in Florida and Texas). The hospital giant's HCA International operates its hospitals and clinics in the UK. HCA is planning to go public through a $4.6 billion initial public offering.

The private investor group that currently owns HCA includes co-founder Thomas Frist Jr. (the largest shareholder), as well as Bain Capital, Kohlberg Kravis Roberts, the private equity arm of Merrill Lynch, and other members of HCA management. The group bought HCA in 2006 in a $21 billion leveraged buyout.

Most of HCA's hospitals are in high-growth urban and suburban markets, and the vast majority are general acute care hospitals that offer a full range of services to accommodate medical specialties such as internal medicine, general surgery, cardiology, oncology, neurosurgery, orthopedics, and obstetrics. HCA also operates five psychiatric facilities and one rehabilitation hospital. The company expands in its selected markets by acquiring hospitals and by luring patients to its existing facilities by providing a broad range of services. It is particularly interested in bolstering its outpatient offerings, as well as specialty services in high-margin fields such as orthopedics and cardiology.

Thirty-year company veteran Jack Bovender Jr. retired as CEO at the end of 2008; he was succeeded by president and COO Richard Bracken. Bovender remained chairman of the board through 2009. Founder Frist relinquished his seat on the board to son William Frist shortly after Bovender announced his retirement.

HISTORY

In 1987 Dallas lawyer Rick Scott and Fort Worth, Texas, financier Richard Rainwater founded Columbia Hospital Corp. to buy two hospitals in El Paso, Texas. The partners eventually sold 40% of the hospitals to local doctors, hoping that ownership would motivate physicians to increase productivity and efficiency.

The company entered the Miami market the next year and by 1990 had four hospitals. After merging with Smith Laboratories that year, Columbia went public and then acquired Sutter Laboratories (orthopedic products). By the end of 1990 it had 11 hospitals.

Columbia moved into Florida in 1992, purchasing several hospitals and other facilities. The next year it acquired Galen Health Care, which operated 73 hospitals and had been spun off from health plan operator Humana earlier in the year. The merger thrust the hospital chain into about 15 new markets.

Columbia bought Hospital Corporation of America (HCA) in 1994. Thomas Frist, his son Thomas Frist Jr., and Jack Massey (former owner of Kentucky Fried Chicken, now part of TRICON) founded HCA in Nashville, Tennessee, in 1968. By 1973 the company had grown to 50 hospitals.

Meanwhile, the medical industry was changing — insurers, Medicare, and Medicaid began scrutinizing payment procedures, while the growth of HMOs (which aimed to restrict hospital admissions) cut hospital occupancy rates. HCA began paring operations in the late 1980s, selling more than 100 hospitals. In 1989 the younger Frist led a $5.1 billion leveraged buyout of the company. He sold more assets and in 1992 took HCA public again, but losses and a tumbling stock price made it a takeover target.

Later in 1994 the newly christened Columbia/HCA acquired the US's largest operator of outpatient surgery centers, Dallas-based Medical Care America. A year later it bought 117-hospital HealthTrust, a 1987 offshoot of HCA. Columbia/HCA was unstoppable in 1996, with some 150 acquisitions.

In 1997 the government began investigating the company's business practices. After executive indictments, the company fired Scott and several other top officers. Frist Jr. became chairman and CEO, pledging to shrink the company and tone down its aggressive approach. Columbia/HCA sold its home care business, more than 100 of its less-desirable hospitals, and almost all the operations of Value Health, a pharmacy benefits and behavioral health care management firm it had recently bought.

The trimming continued in 1998: The company sold nearly three dozen outpatient surgery centers and more than a dozen hospitals. That year Columbia/HCA sued former financial executive Samuel Greco and several vendors, accusing them of defrauding the company of several million dollars. In 1999 it spun off regional operators LifePoint Hospitals (23 facilities) and Triad Hospitals (34) to trim its holdings. The next year it sold some 120 medical buildings to MedCap Properties, a joint venture formed with First Union Capital Partners.

During 2000 the company bought out partner Sun Life and Provincial Holdings' (now AXA UK) interest in several London hospitals and bought three hospitals there from St. Martins Healthcare. It also renamed itself HCA – The Healthcare Company. While continuing a strategy of consolidating and streamlining operations, (and resolving remaining legal matters), in 2001 the company streamlined its name even further to simply HCA Inc.

By 2002 HCA began shaking off its past. Profits stabilized, allowing it to reinvest millions into modernizing facilities and equipment at its hospitals and surgery centers.

During 2003 the company finally closed the books on the numerous government investigations launched in 1997 into its business practices. In the five years leading up to 2003, HCA paid out some $2 billion in settlements for Medicare fraud and other claims. These settlements took their toll on the firm's bottom line.

In 2005 the firm acquired Tampa, Florida's Total I Imaging and its five centers that offer diagnostic services.

The devastating hurricane season of 2005 took a toll on HCA's operations, concentrated as they are in the southern US. When Hurricane Katrina hit, the devastation caused HCA to evacuate its Tulane University Hospital and Clinic (it reopened in early 2006). Hurricane Rita spurred HCA to evacuate three Houston-area hospitals (Mainland Medical Center in Texas City, East Houston Regional Medical Center in Houston, and Clear Lake Regional Medical Center in Webster) and partially evacuate two others.

EXECUTIVES

Chairman and CEO: Richard M. Bracken, age 57, $12,252,891 total compensation
EVP, CFO, and Director: R. Milton Johnson, age 53, $6,780,461 total compensation
SVP and Chief Ethics and Compliance Officer: Alan R. Yuspeh, age 60
SVP Finance and Treasurer: David G. Anderson, age 62
SVP: Victor L. Campbell, age 63
SVP and CIO: Noel Brown Williams, age 54
SVP and Controller: Donald W. (Don) Stinnett, age 54
SVP Development: V. Carl George, age 65
SVP Internal Audit Services: Joseph N. (Joe) Steakley, age 55
SVP and Chief Development Officer: Joseph A. Sowell III
SVP, General Counsel, and Chief Labor Relations Officer: Robert A. (Bob) Waterman, age 56
SVP Human Resources: John M. Steele, age 54
VP Investor Relations: Mark Kimbrough
VP Litigation: Cheryl White Mason, age 55
VP and Corporate Secretary: John M. Franck II
Chief Medical Officer; President, Clinical Services Group: Jonathan B. (Jon) Perlin, age 49
President, Western Group: Samuel N. (Sam) Hazen, age 49, $4,569,414 total compensation
President, Central Group: W. Paul (Paul) Rutledge, age 55, $4,090,328 total compensation
President, HCA International: Michael T. Neeb
President, Outpatient Services Group: A. Bruce Moore Jr., age 50
President, Shared Services Group: Beverly B. Wallace, age 59, $4,685,325 total compensation
Auditors: Ernst & Young LLP

LOCATIONS

HQ: HCA Inc.
1 Park Plaza, Nashville, TN 37203
Phone: 615-344-9551   **Fax:** 615-344-2266
Web: www.hcahealthcare.com

2009 Sales

	$ mil.	% of total
Western Group	13,140	44
Eastern Group	8,807	29
Central Group	7,225	24
Corporate & other	880	3
Total	**30,052**	**100**

2009 Locations

	No.
US	
Florida	38
Texas	35
Tennessee	12
Georgia	11
Virginia	9
Colorado	7
Louisiana	7
Missouri	6
Utah	6
California	5
Kansas	4
Nevada	3
South Carolina	3
Idaho	2
Kentucky	2
New Hampshire	2
Oklahoma	2
Alaska	1
Indiana	1
Mississippi	1
UK	6
Total	**163**

PRODUCTS/OPERATIONS

2009 Sales

	% of total
Managed care & other insurers	52
Medicare	23
Uninsured	8
Managed Medicare	7
Medicaid	6
Managed Medicaid	4
Total	**100**

COMPETITORS

Adventist Health	Health Management
Ascension Health	Associates
Banner Health	HealthSouth
Baptist Hospital	Kaiser Permanente
Baylor Health	Psychiatric Solutions
Catholic Health Initiatives	SSM Health Care
Catholic Healthcare West	Sutter Health
Children's Medical Center	Tenet Healthcare
of Dallas	Trinity Health (Novi)
CHRISTUS Health	Universal Health Services
Community Health	University Health Services
Systems	WellStar Health System

HISTORICAL FINANCIALS

Company Type: Private

Income Statement

FYE: December 31

	REVENUE ($ mil.)	NET INCOME ($ mil.)	NET PROFIT MARGIN	EMPLOYEES
12/09	30,052	1,054	3.5%	192,000
12/08	28,374	673	2.4%	191,000
12/07	26,858	874	3.3%	186,000
12/06	25,477	1,036	4.1%	186,000
Annual Growth	**5.7%**	**0.6%**	**—**	**1.1%**

2009 Year-End Financials

Debt ratio: —   Current ratio: —
Return on equity: —   Long-term debt ($ mil.): 24,824
Cash ($ mil.): —

Net Income History

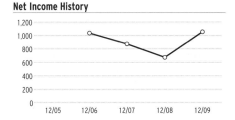

Health Management Associates

William Schoen, chairman of Health Management Associates (HMA), once described his company as the "Wal-Mart of the hospital business" because, like Sam Walton's empire, HMA thrives in small-town America. The company operates a network of about 60 acute care and psychiatric hospitals in 15 mainly southern states (although it also has facilities in Washington and Pennsylvania). Combined, the facilities have about 8,000 beds. HMA's hospitals provide general medical and surgical care, along with outpatient and emergency room services and specialty care in some areas such as cancer care and obstetrics. It also operates about a dozen rural health clinics and outpatient surgery centers.

Because of the smaller markets they serve, HMA's facilities aren't large research hospitals offering highly specialized care (like organ transplants, for instance). However, the company is interested in upgrading its hospitals and broadening the services they offer in order to prevent local populations from having to travel to urban medical centers for treatment. To that end, HMA focuses much of its energy on recruiting and retaining qualified primary care doctors and specialists to practice in its communities and affiliate with its hospitals.

HMA has built its portfolio through numerous acquisitions of hospitals that serve as the primary source of health care in their regions (basically ensuring a loyal patient base). It has typically looked for underperforming hospitals in nevertheless attractive markets and then worked to upgrade facilities and equipment and increase patient volumes and efficiency.

Historically, HMA bought several hospitals each year; however, it has slowed its acquisition activity (making only one purchase in 2009), choosing to focus instead on improving quality and efficiency at its existing facilities as a way to attract patients and the doctors who care for them. In mid-2010 HMA made another acquisition move when it agreed to purchase Wuesthoff Health System, a 400-bed hospital system to expand its care network in eastern Florida.

The health system is also increasingly entering into joint ventures with physicians in some of its markets, allowing doctors to own a minority stake in the hospitals they serve. It has instituted several such arrangements over the past few years, and in 2010 the company arranged to buy 60% stakes in three smaller hospitals owned by Shands HealthCare. While Shands will still own 40%, HMA will operate the community hospitals. As of the end of 2009, about two dozen of the company's hospitals were being run under similar joint venture agreements.

One reason for the interest in joint ventures is HMA's need to reduce its long-term debt and offload some underperforming facilities. It has divested or closed several such facilities: In 2008 it closed Mississippi's Gulf Coast Medical Center, which had failed to recover financially from the effects of 2005's devastating Hurricane Katrina; it also shut down a women's specialty hospital in Texas due to financial losses.

The company is led by CEO Gary Newsome, a former executive who returned to the company in 2008 after a 10-year stint at Community Health Systems.

HISTORY

From its founding in 1977 by Joseph Greene until 1985, Health Management Associates (HMA) owned only a handful of hospitals, mostly in urban areas. In 1983 CEO Greene brought aboard William Schoen, an ex-Marine who ran a beer company in New York before founding a bank in Florida. Schoen became president and COO that year, took a co-CEO position in 1985, and assumed full leadership in 1986 when Greene retired.

Schoen sold the urban hospitals and refocused on small-town hospitals in underserved, mainly southern communities with growing populations. To finance acquisitions and hospital overhauls, HMA went public in 1986. Two years later Schoen took it private, but it went public again in 1991. In the early 1990s it had a growth spurt, adding 10 hospitals.

HMA continued buying, adding two facilities in 1996, another two in 1997, and five in 1998 (three in Mississippi and two in Florida). The acquisitions continued in 1999 as Medicare cutbacks and costly Y2K computer fixes forced many small hospitals to seek buyers; the company bought facilities in Florida, Mississippi (two), and Pennsylvania. In 2000 HMA continued to be acquisitive, buying three medical centers (in Florida, North Carolina, and Pennsylvania), although it shut down its treatment center for at-risk youth in Kansas due to security concerns. In 2001 HMA bought some hospitals from the financially troubled Clarent Hospital.

Also in 2001 William Schoen resigned as CEO and was replaced by Joseph Vumbacco. Schoen remained as chairman.

In 2003 HMA acquired five hospitals from Tenet and expanded into the US Northwest by purchasing two hospitals in Washington. The next year, the company bought Chester County Hospital in South Carolina. In 2005 HMA acquired five hospitals in Florida, Mississippi, and Virginia.

HMA's 2006 acquisitions included Gulf Coast Medical Center in Mississippi (which it later closed) from Tenet Healthcare; Cleveland Clinic — Naples Hospital in Florida; and Barrow Community Hospital in Georgia. The same year, it sold off two psychiatric hospitals in Florida to Psychiatric Solutions.

EXECUTIVES

Chairman: William J. Schoen, age 74
President, CEO, and Director: Gary D. Newsome, age 52, $4,306,064 total compensation
EVP and CFO: Kelly E. Curry, age 55, $2,449,845 total compensation
SVP and Corporate Treasurer: Joseph C. Meek, $647,769 total compensation
SVP Finance: Robert E. Farnham, age 54, $1,350,852 total compensation
SVP, General Counsel, and Corporate Secretary: Timothy R. Parry, age 55, $1,148,271 total compensation
CIO: Ken Chatfield
VP Health Development Operations and Government Relations: Alan Levine
President, Division 4: J. Dale Armour
President, Divison 5: Joshua S. Putter
President, Division 2: Ann M. Barnhart
President, Division 1: Britt Reynolds
Chief Medical Officer: Ronald N. Riner
Auditors: Ernst & Young LLP

LOCATIONS

HQ: Health Management Associates, Inc.
5811 Pelican Bay Blvd., Ste. 500, Naples, FL 34108
Phone: 239-598-3131   **Fax:** 239-598-2705
Web: www.hma-corp.com

PRODUCTS/OPERATIONS

2009 Revenue by Source

	% of total
Commercial insurance & other	49
Medicare	32
Medicaid	9
Self-pay	10
Total	**100**

COMPETITORS

Ascension Health
Baptist Health Care
Baptist Memorial Health Care
Baylor Health
Catholic Health East
Catholic Health Initiatives
CHRISTUS Health
Community Health Corporation
Community Health Systems
FirstHealth of the Carolinas
Greenville Hospital System
HCA
Lee Memorial
LifePoint Hospitals
Methodist Healthcare
SSM Health Care
SunLink Health Systems
Tenet Healthcare
Texas Health Resources
Universal Health Services
University Health Services
WellStar Health System

HISTORICAL FINANCIALS

Company Type: Public

Income Statement

FYE: December 31

	REVENUE ($ mil.)	NET INCOME ($ mil.)	NET PROFIT MARGIN	EMPLOYEES
12/09	4,617	164	3.5%	33,700
12/08	4,452	167	3.8%	32,700
12/07	4,392	120	2.7%	35,645
12/06*	4,057	183	4.5%	34,500
9/05	3,589	353	9.8%	31,000
Annual Growth	6.5%	(17.5%)	—	2.1%

*Fiscal year change

2009 Year-End Financials

Debt ratio: 846.0%
Return on equity: 64.3%
Cash ($ mil.): 106
Current ratio: 2.04
Long-term debt ($ mil.): 3,005

No. of shares (mil.): 251
Dividends
  Yield: 0.0%
  Payout: —
Market value ($ mil.): 1,822

Stock History

NYSE: HMA

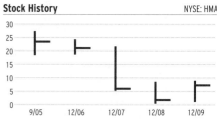

	STOCK PRICE ($) FY Close	P/E High/Low		PER SHARE ($) Earnings	Dividends	Book Value
12/09	7.27	15	3	0.56	0.00	1.42
12/08	1.79	12	1	0.68	0.00	0.62
12/07	5.98	44	11	0.49	0.00	0.32
12/06*	21.11	32	25	0.75	0.24	9.60
9/05	23.47	19	13	1.42	0.16	9.14
Annual Growth	(25.4%)	—	—	(20.8%)	—	(37.2%)

*Fiscal year change

Health Net

Health Net is not another website trying to give you health advice, but it is a web of health services. The company provides managed health care medical coverage to millions of members across the US. The company's health plan services unit offers HMO, PPO, Medicare, and Medicaid plans, as well as vision, dental care, and pharmacy benefit programs. The Managed Health Network subsidiary provides behavioral health and employee assistance to about 7 million individuals, including traditional health plan customers.

The company's managed care units focus on providing health plans to about 4 million members (including Medicare and Medicaid recipients) across the US. California comprises Health Net's largest health plan market. HN California, Health Net's California HMO, is part of the State Children's Health Insurance Program and insures some 130,000 children. Other key states include Arizona and Oregon. Some services, such as Medicare Part D and mental health provisions, are offered in all 50 states.

The company sold its Northeast subsidiaries (offering HMO, commercial, and Medicaid plans in Connecticut, New Jersey, and New York) to national provider UnitedHealth in 2009 in a deal worth close to $630 million.

In 2009 the company's cash flow took a major hit when it lost some valuable government contracts to provide health care coverage for some 3 million military and other government personnel and their dependents through TRICARE. It had held TRICARE contracts in more than 20 states in the Northeast and Midwest, as well as other Department of Defense and Veterans Affairs contracts.

In fact, 2009 was a rough year all-around for the company, which agreed to settle a lawsuit by paying as much as $14 million to former policyholders whose coverage was cancelled after submitting large medical bills. During the suits it was determined that Health Net had made 1,600 rescissions (dropping customers with large claims) to save some $35.5 million. The payments to customers, combined with other fines and fees will eventually cost the company more than $40 million.

To diversify its customer base and spread around some of the financial risk related to providing health care services, Health Net is focusing growth efforts within its commercial health plan segment toward adding new small employer (2 to 50 employees) and mid-market customers. It also acquired partner Guardian Life's stake in former joint venture HealthCare Solutions in a move designed to allow Health Net to increase small business enrollment in the Northeast.

Wellington Management, Barclays Global Investors, and Jana Partners hold a combined stake of nearly 25% of the company.

HISTORY

Foundation Health started as the not-for-profit Foundation Community Health Plan in the 1960s. In 1984 it was bought by AmeriCare Health, which had HMOs in six states. The acquisition was a coup: Foundation Health soon accounted for the bulk of AmeriCare's sales.

AmeriCare went public in 1985. The next year it lost to another firm the rights to that name. Redubbed Foundation Health, it expanded into new states and unrelated businesses: commercial real estate, silk flowers, and furniture.

In late 1986 senior management led a $140 million LBO that left Foundation Health hobbled with debt when the industry started to slide. A 1988 Department of Defense (DOD) CHAMPUS contract brightened prospects, but the five-year, $3 billion contract to provide health care to 860,000 military retirees and dependents in California and Hawaii provided little short-term relief against the effects of high debt and rapid growth: The company lost money again.

The CEO slot had been vacant a year when Dan Crowley, a trained accountant with a good turnaround record, came aboard in 1989. He cut staff, slashed budgets, sold unrelated and non-performing units, and kicked off a huge sales effort. To satisfy bankers and the DOD, which was threatening to rescind its contract, Crowley refinanced Foundation's debt. In a little over a year, Foundation Health recorded its best results ever. In 1990 the company went public.

Back on solid ground, the company expanded its services and markets, buying such firms as Western Universal Life Insurance (renamed Foundation Health Benefit Life Insurance, 1991), Occupational Health Services (employee assistance and substance abuse programs, 1992), and California Compensation Insurance (workers' compensation insurance, 1993).

Foundation Health lost the DOD Hawaii/California contract (almost half its revenues) in 1993, but managed to cope until it regained the business — by then worth $2.5 billion — two years later. Also that year Foundation Health won DOD's five-year, $1.8 billion managed-care contract for Oklahoma and parts of Arkansas, Louisiana, and Texas.

In 1996 the company added behavioral health and employee assistance programs with the purchase of Managed Health Network.

Renewed discussions with Health Systems International resulted in the companies merging to become Foundation Health Systems in 1997. Crowley — whose aggressive style garnered profits but was denounced as brutal by some critics — resigned after the merger.

In 1998 the company pushed into the Northeast, buying Connecticut-based HMO Physicians Health Services. Chairman Malik Hasan (founder of Health Systems' nucleus, QualMed) resigned that year, partly because president Jay Gellert planned to focus on Arizona and California health plans, CHAMPUS, and behavioral health and pharmacy benefit management.

The financial aftershocks of the companies' merger continued, and FHS pruned its operations in 1999 and 2000, exiting such states as Colorado, New Mexico, and Texas; trimming its Medicare operations; and selling certain noncore administrative business lines. In 2000 the California Medical Association sued the company under RICO statutes, claiming it coerced doctors and interfered in doctor-patient relationships. Later that year the company changed its name to Health Net.

In an effort to further expand its business in the Golden State, the company acquired the health plan assets of Universal Care in 2006, adding another 20,000 Medi-Cal and Healthy Families members to its ranks. Also that year the company exited its health plan operations in the Pennsylvania market (while continuing to offer TRICARE services in the state) in an effort to divest noncore businesses.

EXECUTIVES

Chairman: Roger F. Greaves, age 72
President, CEO, and Director: Jay M. Gellert, age 56, $3,643,342 total compensation
EVP and COO: James E. (Jim) Woys, age 51, $3,052,146 total compensation
EVP and CFO: Joseph C. Capezza, age 54, $1,713,037 total compensation
SVP, General Counsel, and Secretary: Angelee F. Bouchard, age 41, $1,458,133 total compensation
SVP and Chief Regulatory and External Relations Officer: Patricia T. (Pat) Clarey, age 56
SVP Organization Effectiveness: Karin D. Mayhew, age 59
CIO: Duncan Rose
Chief Medical Officer: Jonathan Scheff, age 55
Chief Medical Officer, MHN: Ian Shaffer
Chief Actuarial Officer: Joyce Li
Chief Quality Officer: Ray Nan Berry
Chief Government Programs Officer: Scott R. Kelly
VP External Communications: Margita Thompson
President, Health Net Health Plan of Oregon: Chris Ellertson, age 41
President, Health Net Arizona: Bret A. Morris
President, MHN: Juanell Hefner
President, Government Programs: Steven D. Tough, age 59, $1,505,543 total compensation
President, Regional Health Plans, Health Net of the Northeast: Linda V. Tiano, age 52
President, Western Region Health Plan: Steven (Steve) Sell, age 43
Manager Investor Relations: Lori A. Hillman
Auditors: Deloitte & Touche LLP

LOCATIONS

HQ: Health Net, Inc.
21650 Oxnard St., Woodland Hills, CA 91367
Phone: 818-676-6000   **Fax:** 818-676-8591
Web: www.healthnet.com

PRODUCTS/OPERATIONS

2009 Sales

	$ mil.	% of total
Health plan services	12,440.6	79
Government contracts	3,104.7	20
Net investment income	105.9	1
Administrative services fees & other	62.0	—
Total	**15,713.2**	**100**

Selected Subsidiaries

FH Surgery Centers, Inc.
FH Surgery Limited, Inc.
Foundation Health Facilities, Inc.
Health Net Federal Services, Inc.
Health Net of Arizona, Inc
Health Net of California, Inc.
Health Net of the Northeast, Inc.
Health Net of Pennsylvania, Inc.
Health Net One Payment Services, Inc.
Health Net Pharmaceutical Services
Health Net Services, Inc.
HSI Advantage Health Holdings, Inc.
Managed Health Network, Inc.
National Pharmacy Services, Inc.
QualMed, Inc.
   Health Net Health Plan of Oregon, Inc.
   QualMed Plans for Health of Colorado, Inc.

HISTORICAL FINANCIALS

Company Type: Public

Income Statement

FYE: December 31

	REVENUE ($ mil.)	NET INCOME ($ mil.)	NET PROFIT MARGIN	EMPLOYEES
12/09	15,713	(49)	—	8,922
12/08	15,367	95	0.6%	9,646
12/07	14,108	194	1.4%	9,910
12/06	12,908	329	2.6%	10,068
12/05	11,941	230	1.9%	9,286
Annual Growth	7.1%	—	—	(1.0%)

2009 Year-End Financials

Debt ratio: 29.4%
Return on equity: —
Cash ($ mil.): 683
Current ratio: 1.68
Long-term debt ($ mil.): 498

No. of shares (mil.): 97
Dividends
 Yield: —
 Payout: —
Market value ($ mil.): 2,269

Stock History

NYSE: HNT

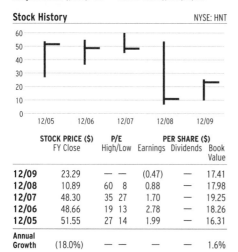

	STOCK PRICE ($) FY Close	P/E High/Low		PER SHARE ($) Earnings	Dividends	Book Value
12/09	23.29	—	—	(0.47)	—	17.41
12/08	10.89	60	8	0.88	—	17.98
12/07	48.30	35	27	1.70	—	19.25
12/06	48.66	19	13	2.78	—	18.26
12/05	51.55	27	14	1.99	—	16.31
Annual Growth	(18.0%)	—	—	—	—	1.6%

HealthSouth Corporation

Don't let the name fool you — HealthSouth doesn't just operate down South, it is one of the nation's largest rehabilitation services providers. Its facilities include rehabilitation hospitals, outpatient centers, home health, and long-term acute care facilities that provide nursing and therapy to patients who have experienced significant disabilities as a result of stroke, spinal cord injury, neuromuscular disease, or other conditions. Operating in more than two dozen states and Puerto Rico, HealthSouth owns or leases about 100 facilities with roughly 6,500 beds. Most of HealthSouth's income is derived from its inpatient operations, which are concentrated in Texas, Pennsylvania, and Florida.

The company spent 2007 undergoing a massive restructuring, selling off three of its major divisions in order to pay down debt and refocus as a pure-play inpatient rehab provider. It took its first step by selling its outpatient rehabilitation division — which comprised more than 550 facilities in about 35 states — to privately owned Select Medical. It sold its outpatient surgery unit, consisting of more than 135 surgery centers and three surgical hospitals, to private investment firm TPG. And later in the year, it offloaded its diagnostics unit (which provided MRI and other diagnostic imaging services) to private equity firm The Gores Group.

With its restructuring largely complete, HealthSouth is focused on providing post-acute care, primarily inpatient rehabilitative services. The company grows its business by building or acquiring new hospitals and expanding capacity at its existing facilities.

HealthSouth's development efforts in 2009 and early 2010 included opening a 40-bed freestanding inpatient rehabilitation hospital in Arizona and commencing construction on a 40-bed inpatient rehabilitation hospital in Virginia. The company also formed a joint venture with Wellmont Health System to open a 25-bed inpatient rehabilitation hospital, also in Virginia. Along with all of the new construction, HealthSouth also acquired an inpatient rehabilitation unit in Pennsylvania and acquired a 23-bed inpatient rehabilitation unit in Arkansas.

HISTORY

A one-time service station worker (when he was a 17-year-old married man with a baby on the way), Richard Scrushy got into the health care industry by working in respiratory therapy; he earned a degree in the subject in 1974. Recruited for a job with a Texas health care management firm, Scrushy saw the convergence of several trends: lowered reimbursements for medical care; a new emphasis on rehabilitation as a way to reduce the need for surgery and get employees back to work faster; and a dearth of brand names in health care. Scrushy decided to establish a national health care brand of rehabilitation hospitals, and in 1984 he and four of his co-workers founded Amcare and built its first outpatient center in Birmingham, Alabama.

From the beginning, Scrushy wanted to make his rehabilitation centers less like hospitals and more like upscale health clubs. He also sought

workers' compensation and rehabilitation contracts from self-insured companies and managed care operations. The strategies worked. The company had revenues of $5 million in 1985, the year it became HealthSouth. Other strategies included specializing in specific ailments, such as back problems and sports injuries, and using the same floor plan and furnishings for all HealthSouth locations to save money. The company went public in 1986.

By 1988 HealthSouth had nearly 40 facilities in 15 states and kept shopping for more. A merger with its biggest rival, Continental Medical Systems, fell through in 1992, but HealthSouth became the #1 provider of rehabilitative services the next year with its acquisition of most of the rehabilitation services of National Medical Enterprises (now Tenet Healthcare). (Scrushy and other officers formed MedPartners, a physician management company, in 1993.) Additional acquisitions included the inpatient rehabilitation hospitals of ReLife (1994) and NovaCare (now NAHC) and Caremark's rehabilitation services (1995). HealthSouth became the #1 operator of outpatient surgery centers with its acquisition of Surgical Care Affiliates in 1995. The $1.1 billion stock swap was the company's largest acquisition ever.

In 1997 HealthSouth acquired Horizon/CMS Healthcare, the US's largest provider of specialty health care. After completing the Horizon/CMS deal, HealthSouth sold Horizon's 139 long-term-care facilities, 12 specialty hospitals, and 35 institutional pharmacies to Integrated Health Services; it kept about 30 inpatient and 275 outpatient rehabilitation facilities.

In the late 1990s HealthSouth built its outpatient operations through acquisitions, buying nearly three dozen outpatient centers from what is now HCA — The Healthcare Company; it also bought National Surgery Centers, adding another 40 locations in 1998.

In 2003 the SEC initiated an investigation of HealthSouth's accounting practices which led to the firing of chairman and CEO Richard Scrushy, removal of the company's auditor, and delisting of its stock by the NYSE. Scrushy was brought to trial and eventually acquitted of any wrongdoing. However, several other executives at the company ended up in jail over the scandal, a $2.7 billion, seven-year run of accounting fraud aimed at inflating the company's profits. The scandal and its aftermath brought HealthSouth to the brink of bankruptcy.

Former HCA executive Jay Grinney was appointed CEO of HealthSouth in 2004. The company began selling off operations to pay down debt from earlier acquisitions and to pay SEC and Justice Department fines from the accounting scandal.

The company divested its last international facility, Australia's Cedar Court Rehabilitation Hospital, late in 2006.

HealthSouth's 2007 restructuring efforts came as the company was fighting to regain its footing after accounting scandals led the company to the brink of bankruptcy beginning in 2003. It ended up paying $3 million to avoid criminal prosecution by the Justice Department for the accounting fraud. Under terms of the federal agreement, the company accepted responsibility for crimes committed by its executives and is enacting more strict internal controls; it was on probation until 2009. It has also paid out millions in civil litigation settlements with the SEC and stockholders.

EXECUTIVES

Chairman: Jon F. Hanson, age 73
President, CEO, and Director: Jay Grinney, age 59, $6,038,344 total compensation
EVP and CFO: Douglas E. (Doug) Coltharp, age 48
EVP, General Counsel, and Corporate Secretary: John P. Whittington, age 62, $1,698,145 total compensation
EVP Operations: Mark J. Tarr, age 47, $1,646,972 total compensation
SVP and Chief Medical Officer: Dexanne B. Clohan, age 60, $796,271 total compensation
SVP Government and Regulatory Affairs: Justin Hunter
SVP Operations: David Klementz
SVP and Chief Accounting Officer: Andrew L. (Andy) Price, age 43
SVP and CIO: Randy Carpenter
SVP and Treasurer: Edmund M. (Ed) Fay, age 43, $692,613 total compensation
SVP Internal Audit and Controls and Inspector General: Sandra K. (Sandy) Vollman, age 52
SVP Reimbursement: Rob Wisner
Chief Human Resources Officer: Cheryl Levy
Chief Development Officer: Stephen L. (Steve) Royal
Chief Investor Relations Officer: Mary Ann Arico
Chief Real Estate Officer: Art Wilson
Auditors: PricewaterhouseCoopers LLP

LOCATIONS

HQ: HealthSouth Corporation
3660 Grandview Pkwy., Ste. 200
Birmingham, AL 35243
Phone: 205-967-7116   **Fax:** 205-969-3543
Web: www.healthsouth.com

PRODUCTS/OPERATIONS

2009 Sales

	$ mil.	% of total
Inpatient	1,743.4	91
Outpatient & other	167.7	9
Total	**1,911.1**	**100**

2009 Revenue Sources

	% of total
Medicare	68
Managed care & other discount plans	23
Other third-party payers	3
Workers' compensation	2
Medicaid	2
Patients	1
Other income	1
Total	**100**

COMPETITORS

Ascension Health
Burke Rehabilitation Hospital
Genesis HealthCare
HCA
Kindred Healthcare
Manor Care
RehabCare
Select Medical
Skilled Healthcare Group
Tenet Healthcare

HISTORICAL FINANCIALS

Company Type: Public

Income Statement

FYE: December 31

	REVENUE ($ mil.)	NET INCOME ($ mil.)	NET PROFIT MARGIN	EMPLOYEES
12/09	1,911	129	6.7%	22,000
12/08	1,842	252	13.7%	22,000
12/07	1,753	653	37.3%	22,000
12/06	3,000	(625)	—	33,000
12/05	3,208	(446)	—	37,000
Annual Growth	**(12.1%)**	**—**	**—**	**(12.2%)**

2009 Year-End Financials

Debt ratio: —
Return on equity: —
Cash ($ mil.): 81
Current ratio: 1.09
Long-term debt ($ mil.): 1,641
No. of shares (mil.): 93
Dividends
Yield: —
Payout: —
Market value ($ mil.): 1,754

Stock History

NYSE: HLS

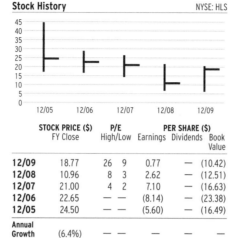

	STOCK PRICE ($) FY Close	P/E High/Low		PER SHARE ($) Earnings	Dividends	Book Value
12/09	18.77	26	9	0.77	—	(10.42)
12/08	10.96	8	3	2.62	—	(12.51)
12/07	21.00	4	2	7.10	—	(16.63)
12/06	22.65	—	—	(8.14)	—	(23.38)
12/05	24.50	—	—	(5.60)	—	(16.49)
Annual Growth	**(6.4%)**	**—**	**—**	**—**	**—**	**—**

Hearst Corporation

Like founder William Randolph Hearst's castle, The Hearst Corporation is sprawling. Through Hearst Newspapers, the company owns some 15 daily newspapers (such as the *San Francisco Chronicle* and the *Houston Chronicle*) and 50 weekly newspapers. Its Hearst Magazines publishes some 15 US consumer magazines (*Cosmopolitan, Esquire*) with nearly 200 international editions. Hearst has broadcasting operations through its Hearst Television subsidiary. Its Hearst Entertainment & Syndication unit includes syndication service King Features, newspaper production service Reed Brennan, and stakes in cable networks (A&E, ESPN). The Hearst Corporation is owned by the Hearst family, but managed by a board of trustees.

Hearst publishes information for automotive, electronic, pharmaceutical, and finance industries through its Hearst Business Media segment. Through its Hearst Interactive Media unit, the company makes strategic investments in online properties such as drugstore.com and Pandora Media, and operates entertainment network UGO Entertainment. Hearst's top magazine title, *Cosmopolitan*, is published in about 35 languages and sold in more than 100 countries, making it the largest magazine franchise in the world. In 2010 it sold its 50% stake in SmartMoney to Dow Jones (the financial news publisher had previously been a joint venture between Hearst and Dow Jones).

In a tough economic climate, especially for the print media world, Hearst has experienced a massive decline in newspaper and magazine advertising and newsstand sales. In 2009 the company published the last print edition of its *Seattle Post-Intelligencer*; it now operates a Web-only version, and is the largest American newspaper to make the leap from print to the exclusively digital format.

Through its investment in competitor MediaNews Group, Hearst has interests in more than 50 daily and 100 non-daily newspapers owned by MediaNews (including the *Denver Post* and *Salt Lake Tribune*). In 2010 Affiliated Media, the parent company of MediaNews, filed for Chapter 11. Hearst's investment will likely be wiped out by the bankruptcy.

Hearst is also working hard to offset its challenges by making progress on the digital media front and diversifying into marketing services. In 2010 it acquired iCrossing, one of the world's biggest independent digital marketing services providers, for about $325 million.

The company is also boosting its involvement in television broadcasting; in 2009 it acquired the remaining shares it didn't already own in Hearst Television (formerly Hearst-Argyle). The business operates about 30 TV stations in about two dozen markets. Also in 2009 Hearst's A&E expanded when it acquired cable network Lifetime Entertainment Services.

Former president and CEO Victor F. Ganzi resigned from his position in 2008. Vice chairman (and previous company head) Frank A. Bennack Jr. reassumed the role of CEO.

Upon his death, William Randolph Hearst left 99% of the company's common stock to two charitable trusts controlled by a 13-member board that includes five family and eight non-family members. The will includes a clause that allows the trustees to disinherit any heir who contests the will.

HISTORY

William Randolph Hearst, son of a California mining magnate, started as a reporter — after being expelled from Harvard in 1884 for playing jokes on professors. In 1887 he became editor of the *San Francisco Examiner*, which his father had obtained as payment for a gambling debt. In 1895 he bought the *New York Morning Journal* and competed against Joseph Pulitzer's *New York World*. The "yellow journalism" resulting from that rivalry characterized American-style reporting at the turn of the century.

Hearst branched into magazines (1903), film (1913), and radio (1928). Also during this time it created the Hearst International News Service (it was sold to E.W. Scripps' United Press in 1958 to form United Press International). By 1935 Hearst was at its peak, with newspapers in 19 cities, the largest syndicate (King Features), international news and photo services, 13 magazines, eight radio stations, and two motion picture companies. Two years later Hearst relinquished control of the company to avoid bankruptcy, selling movie companies, radio stations, magazines, and, later, most of his San Simeon estate. (Hearst's rise and fall inspired the 1941 film *Citizen Kane*.)

In 1948 Hearst became the owner of one of the US's first TV stations, WBAL-TV in Baltimore. When Hearst died in 1951, company veteran Richard Berlin became CEO. Berlin sold off failing newspapers, moved into television, and acquired more magazines.

Frank Bennack, CEO since 1979, expanded the company, acquiring newspapers, publishing firms (notably William Morrow, 1981), TV stations, magazines (*Redbook*, 1982; *Esquire*, 1986), and 20% of cable sports network ESPN (1991). Hearst branched into video via a joint venture with Capital Cities/ABC (1981) and helped launch the Lifetime and Arts & Entertainment cable channels (1984).

In 1992 Hearst brought on board former Federal Communications Commission chairman Alfred Sikes, who quickly moved the company onto the Internet. In 1996 Randolph A. Hearst passed the title of chairman to nephew George Hearst (the last surviving son of the founder, Randolph died in 2000).

The company sold its book publishing operations to News Corp.'s HarperCollins unit in 1999. It also agreed to buy the *San Francisco Chronicle* from rival Chronicle Publishing. That deal was called into question over concerns that the *San Francisco Examiner* would not survive and the city would be left with one major paper. To resolve the issue, the next year Hearst sold the *Examiner* to ExIn (a group of investors affiliated with the Ted Fang family and other owners of the *San Francisco Independent*).

In mid-2002 Victor Ganzi took over as CEO and president following Bennack's retirement from these positions.

Hearst further expanded its potent stable of magazines in 2003 by purchasing *Seventeen* magazine from PRIMEDIA. Hearst also became a major player in yellow page publishing with its 2004 purchase of White Directory Publishers, one of the largest telephone directory companies in the US.

In 2006 Hearst backed MediaNews when that company paid $1 billion to acquire four newspapers (including the *San Jose Mercury News*, the *Contra Costa Times*, and the *St. Paul Pioneer Press*) from McClatchy. The following year Hearst purchased a 31% interest in 47 daily and 37 non-daily newspapers of MediaNews Group.

EXECUTIVES

Chairman: George R. Hearst Jr., age 82
Vice Chairman and CEO: Frank A. Bennack Jr., age 77
CFO: Mitchell Scherzer, age 47
SVP Finance and Administration: Ronald J. Doerfler, age 68
SVP and Director; President, Entertainment & Syndication: Scott M. Sassa, age 50
SVP, Hearst Television Inc.: Frank Biancuzzo
SVP Corporate Innovation, Hearst Interactive Media: Beth Polish
SVP Finance, Hearst Newspapers: John M. (Jack) Condon
SVP Europe, Hearst Magazines International: Jay McGill
SVP and Director; President, Hearst Newspapers: Steven R. Swartz, age 47
SVP, Chief Legal and Development Officer, and Director: James M. Asher
VP and CTO, Hearst Interactive Media: Michael (Mike) Dunn
VP and Director Human Resources, Hearst Magazines: Scherri Roberts
Executive Director Corporate Communications; VP Communications, Hearst Magazines: Paul Luthringer
President, San Francisco Chronicle and SFGate.com: Mark Adkins
President, Hearst Business Media: Richard P. Malloch
President, Hearst Interactive Media: Kenneth A. Bronfin, age 50
Chairman, Hearst Magazines: Cathleen P. (Cathie) Black, age 65
President, Hearst Magazines: David Carey
President and CEO, Hearst Television: David J. Barrett, age 62
President and CEO, Hearst Magazines International: Duncan Edwards

LOCATIONS

HQ: The Hearst Corporation
300 W. 57th St., New York, NY 10019
Phone: 212-649-2000 **Fax:** 212-649-2108
Web: www.hearst.com

PRODUCTS/OPERATIONS

Selected Operations

Hearst Broadcasting
 Hearst Television
Hearst Business Media
 Black Book
 Diversion
 Electronic Products
 First DataBank
 MOTOR Magazine
Hearst Entertainment and Syndication
 A&E Television Networks (joint venture with ABC and NBC)
  A&E
  The Biography Channel
  The History Channel
  History Channel International
 ESPN (20%)
 King Features Syndicate
 Hearst Entertainment (content library and production operations)
 Lifetime Entertainment Services (with Walt Disney Company)
  Lifetime Movie Network
  Lifetime Online
  Lifetime Television
 Reed Brennan Media Associates (production services for newspapers)
Hearst Interactive Media
 Circles (online loyalty marketing programs)
 drugstore.com (online pharmacy site)
 Gather (social networking)
 Hire.com (job site)
Hearst Magazines
 Cosmopolitan
 Country Living
 Esquire
 Good Housekeeping
 Harper's BAZAAR
 House Beautiful
 Marie Claire
 O, The Oprah Magazine (with Harpo)
 Popular Mechanics
 Quick & Simple
 Redbook
 Seventeen
 Teen
 Weekend
Hearst Newspapers
 Albany Times Union (New York)
 Houston Chronicle
 Huron Daily Tribune (Michigan)
 Laredo Morning Times (Texas)
 Midland Daily News (Michigan)
 San Antonio Express-News
 San Francisco Chronicle
Other Operations
 Real estate

COMPETITORS

Advance Publications	Liberty Media
Andrews McMeel Universal	McClatchy Company
Bauer Publishing (UK)	McGraw-Hill
Belo Corp.	Meredith Corporation
Bertelsmann	New York Times
Bloomberg L.P.	News Corp.
Cox Enterprises	Reader's Digest
Dennis Publishing	Reed Elsevier Group
Disney	Rodale
E. W. Scripps	Time Warner
Freedom Communications	Tribune Company
Gannett	Viacom
IPC Group	Washington Post
Lagardère	Yellow Book USA

HISTORICAL FINANCIALS

Company Type: Private

Income Statement

FYE: December 31

	ESTIMATED REVENUE ($ mil.)	NET INCOME ($ mil.)	NET PROFIT MARGIN	EMPLOYEES
12/08	4,810	—	—	20,000
12/07	4,380	—	—	17,070
12/06	4,520	—	—	17,062
12/05	4,550	—	—	17,016
12/04	4,000	—	—	16,667
Annual Growth	4.7%	—	—	4.7%

Revenue History

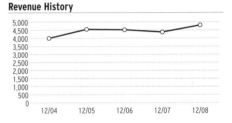

Helmerich & Payne

In the oil and gas industry, Helmerich & Payne knows the drill: The contract driller operates 244 land and nine offshore platform rigs, mostly for industry giants such as BP, Occidental Petroleum, and Devon Energy. Its US contract drilling operations are conducted mainly in Louisiana, Oklahoma, Texas, and Wyoming, as well as offshore California, in the Gulf of Mexico, in South America, and in North and West Africa. Helmerich & Payne operates 140 FlexRigs (drilling rigs equipped with new technologies, environmental and safety design, and the capability of simultaneous crew activity). The company also has real estate operations, including a shopping center and office buildings in Tulsa.

The bulk of Helmerich & Payne's international contract work is conducted in Argentina, Colombia, Ecuador, Equatorial Guinea, Mexico, Trinidad, Tunisia, and Venezuela.

In order to complement technology used by its FlexRig fleet, in 2008 Helmerich & Payne acquired TerraVici Drilling Solutions, which developed proprietary rotary steerable technology to improve horizontal and directional drilling operations. Through integrating this technology the company helps customers improve drilling productivity and reduce costs.

In 2009 Helmerich & Payne ceased operations on its 11 rigs in Venezuela as PDVSA failed to make good on its back payments. That year the company began operating six FlexRigs in Mexico under a Schlumberger contract.

The company has grown through the addition of new equipment and the enhancement of its current drilling fleet. In 2005 it launched a program to build 127 new FlexRigs.

In 2007 Helmerich & Payne lost a FlexRig in a well blowout fire.

HISTORY

H&P was founded in 1920 by Walt Helmerich and William Payne. The company expanded rapidly over the next two decades. Payne left in 1936 to form his own business, Big Chief Oil. Helmerich's son Walt III joined H&P in the late 1940s. The firm began international operations in Venezuela in 1957 and purchased chemical firm Natural Gas Odorizing in 1960.

Emerging from the 1980s oil slump, H&P focused on offshore drilling in Venezuela, Trinidad, and Papua New Guinea. In 1992 the company landed its largest contract ever, drilling for oil in Colombia for British Petroleum.

In 1995 Shell hired H&P to build two rigs for the deepwater Mars field in the Gulf of Mexico. Refocusing on its core oil and gas businesses, the company sold Natural Gas Odorizing in 1996 to Occidental Petroleum. The next year H&P started to increase its US land rig fleet by about 25%, but in 1998, as petroleum prices dropped, H&P sold a number of its oil and gas properties.

In 1999 H&P expanded its South American presence by placing two rigs in Argentina for contract work. The company also won a contract to manage Exxon Mobil's Jade offshore platform in Equatorial Guinea in 2000, and in 2001 it secured a contract with BP to drill in the Rockies for the first time since 1986.

In 2002 the company spun off its oil and gas exploration and production division and merged it with Key Production to form Cimarex Energy.

EXECUTIVES

Chairman: Walter H. Helmerich III, age 87
President, CEO, and Director: Hans Helmerich, age 51, $1,878,772 total compensation
EVP, General Counsel, and Secretary: Steven R. Mackey, age 58, $961,900 total compensation
EVP, US and International Operations, Helmerich and Payne International Drilling: John W. Lindsay, age 48, $1,177,711 total compensation
VP and CFO: Juan P. Tardio, age 44
VP and Chief Engineer, Helmerich & Payne International Drilling Co: Rob Stauder, age 47
VP and Controller: Gordon K. Helm, age 56
Media Contact: Mike Drickamer
Auditors: Ernst & Young LLP

LOCATIONS

HQ: Helmerich & Payne, Inc.
1437 S. Boulder Ave., Tulsa, OK 74119
Phone: 918-742-5531   **Fax:** 918-742-0237
Web: www.hpinc.com

2009 Sales

	$ mil.	% of total
US	1,613.9	85
Colombia	77.3	4
Ecuador	52.3	3
Venezuela	50.3	3
Argentina	42.1	2
Other countries	58.1	3
Total	**1,894.0**	**100**

PRODUCTS/OPERATIONS

2009 Sales

	$ mil.	% of total
Contract drilling		
US land	1,441.1	76
International land	237.4	12
US offshore platform	204.7	11
Real estate & other	10.8	1
Total	**1,894.0**	**100**

Selected Subsidiaries

Helmerich & Payne International Drilling Co.
  Helmerich & Payne (Africa) Drilling Co.
  Helmerich & Payne (Argentina) Drilling Co.
  Helmerich & Payne (Australia) Drilling Co.
  Helmerich & Payne (Boulder) Drilling Co.
  Helmerich & Payne (Colombia) Drilling Co.
  Helmerich & Payne de Venezuela, C.A.
  Helmerich & Payne del Ecuador, Inc.
  Helmerich & Payne Drilling (Bolivia) S.A.
  Helmerich & Payne (Gabon) Drilling Co.
  Helmerich & Payne Rasco, Inc.
  H&P Finco
  H&P Invest
Helmerich & Payne Properties, Inc.
  The Space Center, Inc.
  Utica Square Shopping Center, Inc.
    Fishercorp, Inc.

COMPETITORS

Diamond Offshore
Ensco
Nabors Industries
Noble
Parker Drilling
Patterson-UTI Energy
Pride International
Rowan Companies
Transocean

HISTORICAL FINANCIALS

Company Type: Public

Income Statement

FYE: September 30

	REVENUE ($ mil.)	NET INCOME ($ mil.)	NET PROFIT MARGIN	EMPLOYEES
9/09	1,894	354	18.7%	5,384
9/08	2,037	462	22.7%	6,198
9/07	1,630	449	27.6%	6,456
9/06	1,225	294	24.0%	5,705
9/05	801	128	15.9%	4,801
Annual Growth	**24.0%**	**29.0%**	**—**	**2.9%**

2009 Year-End Financials

Debt ratio: 15.7%
Return on equity: 14.3%
Cash ($ mil.): 141
Current ratio: 1.73
Long-term debt ($ mil.): 420
No. of shares (mil.): 106
Dividends
  Yield: 0.5%
  Payout: 6.0%
Market value ($ mil.): 4,183

Stock History

NYSE: HP

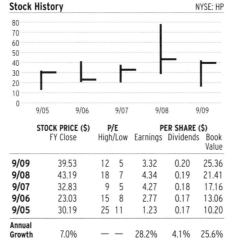

	STOCK PRICE ($) FY Close	P/E High	P/E Low	PER SHARE ($) Earnings	PER SHARE ($) Dividends	PER SHARE ($) Book Value
9/09	39.53	12	5	3.32	0.20	25.36
9/08	43.19	18	7	4.34	0.19	21.41
9/07	32.83	9	5	4.27	0.18	17.16
9/06	23.03	15	8	2.77	0.17	13.06
9/05	30.19	25	11	1.23	0.17	10.20
Annual Growth	**7.0%**	**—**	**—**	**28.2%**	**4.1%**	**25.6%**

Henry Schein

Whether you're in Poughkeepsie or Prague, Henry Schein will help your dentist get those sparkly whites to shine. The company is a leading global distributor of dental supplies and equipment, with operations in North America, Europe, and Australia. Henry Schein provides such items as impression materials, X-ray equipment, and anesthetics. But the company isn't only interested in teeth: It also supplies doctors' offices, veterinarians, and other office-based health care providers with diagnostic kits, surgical tools, drugs, vaccines, and animal health products. Additionally, its technology division offers practice management software and other services to dental, medical, and veterinary offices.

Not content with its more than half a million customers worldwide (and a particularly strong presence in North America), the company aggressively pursues acquisitions to further build its business. Henry Schein's purchases have expanded its array of products and its geographic reach. It also operates through affiliates in the Middle East and Iceland. Henry Schein has nine US distribution centers, three in Europe, and one in Canada. It sells its products via direct mail and an inside sales force.

In 2008 the company picked up European veterinary, medical, and dental firms Noviko of the Czech Republic, Medka of Germany, Minerva Dental Limited of the UK, and DNA Anthos Impianti of Italy. The following year it acquired Ortho Organizers, an orthodontic device manufacturer and distributor.

Previously, Henry Schein had bought a New Zealand-based developer of dental practice management software (Software of Excellence International) in order to add to its technology-related offerings. It also boosted its veterinarian offerings with the purchase of the UK's W&J Dunlop.

Henry Schein is counting on an aging US population and the migration from acute care settings to physician offices to fuel its sales. The company expects that over the next decade the 45-and-older population will grow by about 15%.

HISTORY

For more than 50 years, Henry Schein distributed drugs made by Schein Pharmaceuticals. In 1992 management spun off the drug business and, led by former accountant Stanley Bergman, began acquiring other dental supply companies at a terrific rate: 34 between 1994 and 1996 alone.

The company went public in 1995 and bought more than a dozen businesses. These purchases, which included product marketer Vertex Corporation's distribution unit, moved Henry Schein into the medical and veterinary supply fields. The purchase of Schein Dental Equipment (founded by Marvin Schein) boosted per-customer sales by adding big-ticket merchandise to the product mix.

Acquisitions continued hot and heavy as the company boosted operations abroad. The purchases hit the bottom line; Schein avoided bloat by restructuring operations, closing facilities, and developing new systems. The company consolidated 13 distribution centers into five in

1997. The following year the firm expanded into Canada, and bought a controlling stake in UK direct marketer Porter Nash.

To boost profits, the company announced in 2000 that it would cut 5% of its workforce. It also shut down some facilities and sold its software development business as part of its overall restructuring plan. In 2001 the firm resumed its acquisitions when it bought the dental supply business of drugmaker Zila.

EXECUTIVES

Chairman, President, and CEO: Stanley M. Bergman, age 60, $4,268,925 total compensation
President, COO, and Director: James P. Breslawski, age 56, $1,948,468 total compensation
EVP, CFO, and Director: Steven Paladino, age 53, $1,733,987 total compensation
EVP, Chief Administrative Officer, and Director: Gerald A. Benjamin, age 57
EVP Corporate Business Development and Director: Mark E. Mlotek, age 54, $1,663,416 total compensation
SVP and Chief Compliance Officer: Leonard A. David, age 61
SVP and General Counsel: Michael S. Ettinger
SVP and CTO: James A. (Jim) Harding, age 54
SVP and Chief Merchandising Officer: Michael Racioppi, age 55
VP Corporate Communications: Susan Vassallo
President, International Group: Michael Zack, age 57
President, Global Healthcare Specialties Group: Lonnie Shoff, age 51
VP Investor Relations: Neal Goldner
Senior Advisor: Stanley Komaroff, age 74, $1,708,244 total compensation
Auditors: BDO Seidman, LLP

LOCATIONS

HQ: Henry Schein, Inc.
135 Duryea Rd., Melville, NY 11747
Phone: 631-843-5500   **Fax:** 631-843-5658
Web: www.henryschein.com

2009 Sales

	$ mil.	% of total
US	3,902.4	60
Germany	699.3	11
Other countries	1,936.6	29
Total	**6,538.3**	**100**

PRODUCTS/OPERATIONS

2009 Sales

	$ mil.	% of total
Health care distribution		
Dental (US & Canadian dental markets)	2,509.9	38
International (non-US dental, medical & animal health markets)	2,398.1	37
Medical (US medical & animal health markets)	1,457.1	22
Technology	173.2	3
Total	**6,538.3**	**100**

Selected Products

Dental products
  Acrylics
  Alloys
  Anesthetics
  Articulators
  Bridges
  Composites
  Crowns
  Gypsum
  Impression materials
  Preventatives
  Surgical equipment
  X-ray equipment

Medical products
  Diagnostic kits
  Office equipment
  Pharmaceuticals (generic and brand-name)
  Surgical tools
  Vitamins
Technology
  Dental practice management software
Veterinary products
  Dental equipment
  Pharmaceuticals
  Surgical tools

COMPETITORS

Allscripts
athenahealth
Benco Dental
Cardinal Health
Darby Dental
IDEXX Labs
McKesson
Moore Medical
MWI Veterinary Supply
NextGen
Omega Pharma
Owens & Minor
Patterson Companies
PSS World Medical
Sybron Dental

HISTORICAL FINANCIALS

Company Type: Public

Income Statement

FYE: Last Saturday in December

	REVENUE ($ mil.)	NET INCOME ($ mil.)	NET PROFIT MARGIN	EMPLOYEES
12/09	6,538	333	5.1%	12,500
12/08	6,395	243	3.8%	12,500
12/07	5,920	215	3.6%	12,000
12/06	5,153	164	3.2%	11,000
12/05	4,636	151	3.3%	11,000
Annual Growth	**9.0%**	**21.8%**	**—**	**3.2%**

2009 Year-End Financials

Debt ratio: 11.3%
Return on equity: 16.3%
Cash ($ mil.): 471
Current ratio: 2.05
Long-term debt ($ mil.): 243
No. of shares (mil.): 92
Dividends
  Yield: —
  Payout: —
Market value ($ mil.): 4,814

Stock History

NASDAQ (GS): HSIC

	STOCK PRICE ($) FY Close	P/E High/Low		PER SHARE ($) Earnings	Dividends	Book Value
12/09	52.60	17	10	3.44	—	23.62
12/08	36.69	24	12	2.67	—	21.11
12/07	61.40	27	19	2.36	—	19.45
12/06	48.98	30	24	1.82	—	16.07
12/05	43.64	27	19	1.70	—	13.44
Annual Growth	**4.8%**	**—**	**—**	**19.3%**	**—**	**15.1%**

Herman Miller

Desk jockeys can ride Herman Miller's products all the way up the corporate ladder and home again. A top US maker of office furniture, it's known for developing designs for corporate, government, home office, leisure, and health care environments. Herman Miller's products include ergonomic devices, filing and storage systems, free-standing furniture, lighting, seating, textiles, and wooden casegoods. It makes products in the UK and the US and sells them worldwide through its sales staff and dealer network, as well as through independent dealers and the Internet. Columbia Wanger Asset Management and Ariel Capital Management each own about a 10% stake in the firm.

Looking to give its health care business a shot in the arm and cater to the sturdy health care construction sector, Herman Miller in June 2009 bought furnishings leader Nemschoff. While Nemschoff's expertise is in making soft seating and furniture for patient care environments, the company also provides complementary products for commercial office and education markets, adding depth to niche markets where Herman Miller already operates.

Herman Miller kick-started its strategy of chasing after the hospital furniture market with its Nala patient chair (at $1,800 apiece) in 2008. The chair is made by Brandrud, a Seattle-based health care furnishings manufacturer acquired by Herman Miller in early 2008. The company sees more of a future in health care than any other sector.

The furnishings maker is also growing through its Geiger International subsidiary. In early 2009 the commercial furnishings unit acquired North Carolina-based Ruskin Industries, which specializes in making seating, tables, and casegoods for the contract furniture markets. Ruskin has produced carved wood pieces for piano manufacturer Steinway and chair frames for contract furnishings makers HBF and Cabot Wrenn.

Herman Miller hopes to see profits from its expanding international customer base, especially in the Asia/Pacific region. In 2008 the company negotiated an international alliance with Hong Kong-based POSH Office Systems, a designer and manufacturer of modern work centers.

In addition to its investments in furniture manufacturing, Herman Miller has also developed an interest in energy management. Its Convia subsidiary offers programmable electrical distribution components. In 2009 Wiremold, a leading producer of electrical wiring systems, penned an agreement to have Convia's controls used in its units.

The company's furniture is known for its contemporary designs and upscale prices. Collectors still seek pieces designed and manufactured in the 1940s and 1950s.

HISTORY

In 1923 Herman Miller lent his son-in-law, D. J. De Pree, enough money to buy Star Furniture, started in 1905 in Zeeland, Michigan. (De Pree renamed the furniture maker after Miller.) Designer Gilbert Rohde led Herman Miller's transformation from traditional to more modern styles in the 1930s.

Rohde designed the company's first office component line, the Executive Office Group (introduced in 1942). Rohde died two years later, and in 1946 George Nelson was named Herman

Miller's design director. Nelson brought in a number of notable designers, including Charles Eames and Isamu Noguchi.

Throughout its history, the company has maintained a reputation for being open to suggestions and comments from its workers. This policy dates back to De Pree's learning that one of his millwrights who had died had also been a poet; De Pree began to value his employees for their innate talents rather than just for the work they did for him.

Herman Miller grew, largely unimpeded by national competitors, except for neighboring Steelcase. In 1950 the company adopted the Scanlon plan, an employee participation plan that included bonuses based on helpful participation, such as cost-cutting suggestions.

De Pree retired in 1962 and was succeeded by his son, Hugh. Two years later Herman Miller introduced the Action Office, a collection of panels, work surfaces, and storage units that could be moved about to create custom-designed work spaces within an open-plan office; this line has been the company mainstay ever since.

The firm, which went public in 1970, introduced its Ergon ergonomic chair in 1976. Hugh retired in 1980 and was succeeded by his brother Max, who capped executive salaries at 20 times the average wage of factory-line workers. Max became chairman in 1988 and resigned from day-to-day management duties to pursue teaching opportunities.

Max's successor, 33-year company veteran Richard Ruch, began restructuring to sharpen Herman Miller's focus. Then the commercial real estate market collapsed and, with it, the need for new office furnishings. Earnings tumbled in 1991 and 1992. Ruch retired in 1992 to become vice chairman and was succeeded by first-ever company outsider Kermit Campbell.

In 1994 Herman Miller acquired German furniture company Geneal. Earnings plummeted in 1995 and chairman Campbell was forced out. Despite his commitment to its traditionally employee-friendly corporate culture, CEO Michael Volkema led Herman Miller in a shakeup, cutting 180 jobs and closing underperforming plants. The company introduced its cubicle systems office furniture unit, Miller SQA ("simple, quick, and affordable"), in 1995.

Herman Miller and leading carpet tile maker Interface formed a joint venture in 1997 to provide integrated office furniture and carpeting systems for commercial clients. The next year the company became the first major office furniture maker to target customers over the Internet. Herman Miller acquired wood furniture maker Geiger Brickel in 1999. The company launched a low-cost line of office furniture, dubbed RED, aimed at fledgling Internet-oriented firms in late 2000, shortly before the bubble burst for Web startups.

A slowdown in the US economy prompted cut after cut in 2001; by March 2002 the company had eliminated some 3,900 positions (or 37% of its workforce). The company also phased out its SQA and RED lines that year amidst slowing sales; in 2003 it consolidated two of its manufacturing sites (Holland, Michigan and Canton, Georgia) into existing facilities. President and COO Brian Walker succeeded Volkema as CEO in July 2004. Volkema remains as chairman.

EXECUTIVES

Chairman: Michael A. Volkema, age 54
President, CEO, and Director: Brian C. Walker, age 48, $1,833,516 total compensation
EVP and CFO: Gregory J. (Greg) Bylsma, age 45, $239,968 total compensation
EVP Research, Design, and Development: Donald D. Goeman, age 53, $399,749 total compensation
EVP and Chief Administrative Officer: Andrew J. (Andy) Lock, age 56, $464,480 total compensation
EVP; President, Herman Miller Healthcare: Elizabeth A. (Beth) Nickels, age 48, $536,406 total compensation
EVP Operations: Kenneth L. Goodson Jr., age 58
EVP; President, North American Office and Learning Environments: Curt Pullen
Chief Development Officer: Gary S. Miller, age 60
SVP Marketing: Kathy Koch
SVP Legal Services and Secretary: James E. Christenson, age 63
President, Geiger International and Herman Miller for the Home: Steve Gane
President, Herman Miller International: John P. Portlock, age 64
Auditors: Ernst & Young LLP

LOCATIONS

HQ: Herman Miller, Inc.
855 E. Main Ave., Zeeland, MI 49464
Phone: 616-654-3000   **Fax:** 616-654-5234
Web: www.hermanmiller.com

2010 Sales

	$ mil.	% of total
US	1,028.7	78
Other countries	290.1	22
Total	**1,318.8**	**100**

PRODUCTS/OPERATIONS

2010 Sales

	$ mil.	% of total
Systems	349.3	26
Seating	329.7	25
International	290.1	22
Freestanding & storage	246.2	19
Other	103.5	8
Total	**1,318.8**	**100**

Selected Products and Brands

Accessories (Accents, Aalto, Eames)
Free-standing furniture (Passage, Aalto, Abak, Burdick, Eames, Arrio, Kiva)
Health care systems (Ethospace)
Modular systems (Action Office, Ethospace, Q System, Resolve, Vivo Interiors)
Screens (Eames)
Seating (Aeron, Ambi, Equa, Ergon, Mirra, Reaction)
Storage and filing (Meridian, Eames)
Textiles (Ituri, Meinecke)
Wooden casegoods (Geiger)

COMPETITORS

American of Martinsville	Knoll, Inc.
CFGroup	MITY
Flexsteel	Neutral Posture
Haworth, Inc.	Reconditioned Systems
HMU, LLC	Shelby Williams
HNI	Steelcase
Inscape corp	TAB Products
Kewaunee Scientific	Teknion
KI	Virco Mfg.
Kimball International	

HISTORICAL FINANCIALS

Company Type: Public

Income Statement

FYE: Saturday nearest May 31

	REVENUE ($ mil.)	NET INCOME ($ mil.)	NET PROFIT MARGIN	EMPLOYEES
5/10	1,319	28	2.1%	5,635
5/09	1,630	68	4.2%	5,229
5/08	2,012	152	7.6%	6,478
5/07	1,919	129	6.7%	6,574
5/06	1,737	99	5.7%	6,242
Annual Growth	(6.7%)	(26.9%)	—	(2.5%)

2010 Year-End Financials

Debt ratio: 251.2%	No. of shares (mil.): 57
Return on equity: 64.2%	Dividends
Cash ($ mil.): 135	Yield: 0.5%
Current ratio: 1.26	Payout: 20.9%
Long-term debt ($ mil.): 201	Market value ($ mil.): 1,097

Stock History

NASDAQ (GS): MLHR

	STOCK PRICE ($) FY Close	P/E High/Low		PER SHARE ($) Earnings	Dividends	Book Value
5/10	19.23	52	31	0.43	0.09	1.40
5/09	14.23	24	6	1.25	0.29	0.14
5/08	24.80	14	9	2.56	0.35	0.41
5/07	36.00	21	13	1.98	0.33	2.72
5/06	29.22	23	18	1.45	0.31	2.43
Annual Growth	(9.9%)	—	—	(26.2%)	(26.6%)	(12.8%)

The Hershey Company

The Hershey Company will cover you in Kisses and bring you Almond Joy. The company makes such well-known chocolate and candy brands as Hershey's Kisses, Reese's peanut butter cups, Twizzlers licorice, Mounds, York Peppermint Patty, and Kit Kat (licensed from Nestlé). Hershey also makes grocery goods such as baking chocolate, ice-cream toppings, chocolate syrup, cocoa mix, cookies, snack nuts, hard candies, and lollipops. Its products are sold throughout North America and exported overseas. The Hershey Trust — which benefits the Milton Hershey School for disadvantaged children — controls 80% of Hershey's voting power.

While it was rumored during 2009 that the company might have been interested in acquiring UK confectioner Cadbury, it remained mum about any deal until it was clear that Kraft Foods was intent upon purchasing the UK confectioner. Hershey issued a statement in January 2010, saying it did not intend to make an offer for Cadbury and Kraft ultimately succeeded in taking over the Dairy Milk maker. While it may have been a good fit to merge the two giant chocolate candy makers, Hershey, as always, was answerable to the trust, which, it was generally believed, opposed buying Cadbury.

In February 2009 the trust forced the resignation of the company's non-executive board chairman, Kenneth L. Wolf, and indicated that it wanted one of its members to serve as Hershey's chairman. The board then announced the unanimous election of trust member (and board member), James E. Nevels, as chairman.

Hershey did, however, make an acquisition in 2009. It purchased Van Houten Singapore from Switzerland-based producer of cocoa, chocolate, and confectionery products Barry Callebaut. Part of Barry Callebaut's divestiture plan, the acquisition gave Hershey a stronger presence in the growing Asian confectionery market.

Chocolate may be the name of the game at Hershey but the company is also a growing presence in the hard- and non-chocolate candy markets, offering such brands as Good & Plenty and Jolly Rancher. The company is expanding its products with new versions of old favorites, such as Jolly Rancher lollipops and bite-sized bits of its popular chocolate bars. It introduced sugar-free chocolate and expanded the snack-food and Hispanic markets, as well as producing packaged cookies whose flavors are based on the flavors of its Almond Joy, Reese's, and York products.

HISTORY

The Hershey Company is the legacy of Milton Hershey, of Pennsylvania Dutch origin. Apprenticed in 1872 at age 15 to a candy maker, Hershey started Lancaster Caramel Company at age 30. In 1893, at the Chicago Exposition, he saw a new chocolate-making machine, and in 1900 he sold the caramel operations for $1 million to start a chocolate factory.

The factory was completed in 1905 in Derry Church, Pennsylvania, and renamed Hershey Foods the next year. Chocolate Kisses, individually hand-wrapped in silver foil, were introduced in 1907. Two years later the candy man founded the Milton Hershey School, an orphanage; the company was donated to a trust in 1918 and for years existed solely to fund the school. Although Hershey went public in 1927, the school still controls the majority of shareholder votes.

The candy firm pioneered mass-production techniques for chocolates and developed much of the machinery for making and packaging its products. At one time Hershey supplied its own sugar cane from Cuba and enlarged the world's almond supply sixfold through nut farm ownership. The Hershey bar became so universally familiar that it was used overseas during WWII as currency. Milton refused to advertise, believing that quality would speak for itself. Even after his death in 1945, the company continued his policy. Then, in 1970, facing a sluggish candy market and a diet-conscious public, the company lost share to Mars and management relented.

During the 1960s and 1970s, Hershey diversified in order to stabilize the effects of changing commodity prices. The company got into the pasta business with its 1966 purchase of San Giorgio Macaroni, and it bought the Friendly Ice Cream chain in 1979 (sold 1988). It expanded candy operations by bringing out large-sized bars (1980) and buying Cadbury's US candy business (Peter Paul, Cadbury, Caramello; 1988).

Kenneth Wolfe was named chairman and CEO in 1994. In 1999 the company sold its pasta business to New World Pasta for $450 million and a 6% interest in that company. Also that year the Hershey Trust, wanting to diversify its holdings, sold $100 million of its stock to Hershey.

In 2001 Nabisco veteran Rick Lenny replaced Wolfe as CEO. Hershey established a manufacturing presence in South America that year by acquiring the chocolate and confectionery business of Brazilian company Visagis. It also cut about 400 salaried positions and closed three plants and a distribution facility.

In 2002 Wolfe retired as chairman and Lenny was selected to replace him. Also that year Hershey settled a bitter six-week factory-worker strike, the longest in company history.

Also in 2002 the Hershey Trust said that to diversify its holdings, it wanted to sell its 77% interest in Hershey. However, the sale was temporarily blocked while the state of Pennsylvania reviewed the impact it would have on the community. Despite the injunction against the sale, the trust continued to look for a buyer and was considering a $12.5 billion offer from chewing gum giant Wm. Wrigley Jr. and a $10.5 billion joint offer from Nestlé and Cadbury Schweppes (now Cadbury).

Amid the community outcry and legal wrangling, the sale was finally called off later in 2002, after 10 of the trust's 17 members changed their minds. Due to the uproar surrounding the proposed sale, the trust board promised to restructure itself. Among the outgoing board members was William Lepley, president and chief executive of the Milton Hershey School.

To expand its sales in the Hispanic market, in 2004 Hershey announced a new line of Latin-inspired candies, including those with chili-based flavors and *dulce de leche* fillings.

The company changed its name to The Hershey Company in 2005, dropping the "Foods" from its name to reflect the company's move away from coffee, pasta, and restaurant businesses and the concentration on confectionery.

In 2006 the company purchased organic chocolate confectioner, Dagoba.

President and CEO Richard Lenny left the company in 2007. CFO David West was named as his successor.

EXECUTIVES

Chairman: James E. Nevels, age 58
President, CEO, and Director: David J. (Dave) West, age 46, $8,004,029 total compensation
SVP and CFO: Humberto P. (Bert) Alfonso, age 52, $2,213,636 total compensation
SVP and Chief People Officer: Charlene H. Binder
SVP and CIO: George F. Davis, age 61
SVP Global Operations: Terence L. O'Day, age 59, $1,684,245 total compensation
SVP; President, Hershey North America:
John P. (J.P.) Bilbrey, age 53, $3,108,794 total compensation
SVP; President, Hershey International:
Thaddeus J. (Ted) Jastrzebski, age 48
SVP Strategy and Business Development:
Javier H. Idrovo
SVP and Global Chief Marketing Officer:
Michele G. Buck, age 48, $1,430,421 total compensation
VP Global Research and Development: C. Daniel Azzara, age 55
Public Relations: Kirk Saville
Auditors: KPMG LLP

LOCATIONS

HQ: The Hershey Company
100 Crystal A Dr., Hershey, PA 17033
Phone: 717-534-4200
Web: www.thehersheycompany.com

2009 Sales

	% of total
US	86
Other countries	14
Total	**100**

PRODUCTS/OPERATIONS

Selected Brands

Confectionery
 Hershey's
  Bliss
  Cookies N' Crème
  Hershey's Milk Chocolate
  Hugs
  Kisses
  Nuggets
  Sticks
 Reese's
  Fast Break
  Nutrageous
  Peanut Butter Cups
  Pieces
  Reesesticks
  Whipps
 Other
  5th Avenue
  Almond Joy (worldwide license from Cadbury)
  Cacao Reserve
  Caramello (USA license from Cadbury)
  Chipits (Canada)
  Dagoba
  Eat More (Canada)
  Glosette (Canada)
  Godrej (India)
  Good & Plenty (worldwide license from Huhtamäki)
  Heath (worldwide license from Huhtamäki)
  Jolly Rancher (worldwide license from Huhtamäki)
  Kit Kat (US license from Nestlé)
  Milk Duds (worldwide license from Huhtamäki)
  Mounds (worldwide license from Cadbury)
  Mr. Goodbar
  Payday (worldwide license from Huhtamäki)
  Pelón Pelo Rico (Mexico)
  Pot Of Gold
  Rolo (US license from Nestlé)
  Scharffen Berger
  Skor
  Special Dark
  Symphony
  Take5
  Twizzlers
  Whatchamacallit
  Whoppers (worldwide license from Huhtamäki)
  York (worldwide license from Cadbury)
  Zagnut
  Zero

Food and beverage enhancers
 Bake Shoppe
 Goodnight Hugs
 Goodnight Kisses
 Granola Bars
 Toppings

Refreshment products
 Breath Savers
 Bubble Yum
 Ice Breakers
 York

Snack products
 Almond Joy Cookies
 Hershey's Cookies
 Hershey's Granola Bars
 Mauna Loa Macadamia Snack Nuts and Cookies
 Reese's Cookies
 Reese's Granola Bars
 Snacksters Snack Mix
 York Cookies

COMPETITORS

Annabelle Candy	Kraft Foods
Anthony-Thomas Candy	Laura Secord
Asher's Chocolates	Lindt & Sprüngli
Betsy Ann Candies	Mars, Incorporated
Chase General	Nestlé
Chocolates à la Carte	Otis Spunkmeyer
Chupa Chups	Perfetti Van Melle
Endangered Species	Purdy's Chocolates
Chocolate	Rocky Mountain Chocolate
Enstrom	Russell Stover
Farley's & Sathers	See's Candies
Fazer Konfektyr	Smucker
Ferrero	Spangler Candy
Ghirardelli Chocolate	Sweet Shop USA
Godiva Chocolatier	Tasty Baking
Goetze's Candy	Tootsie Roll
Guittard	Warrell Corporation
Harry London Candies	World's Finest Chocolate
Hostess Brands	Wrigley
Jelly Belly Candy	Zachary Confections
Kellogg	

HISTORICAL FINANCIALS

Company Type: Public

Income Statement

FYE: December 31

	REVENUE ($ mil.)	NET INCOME ($ mil.)	NET PROFIT MARGIN	EMPLOYEES
12/09	5,299	436	8.2%	13,700
12/08	5,133	311	6.1%	14,400
12/07	4,947	214	4.3%	12,800
12/06	4,944	559	11.3%	15,000
12/05	4,836	493	10.2%	13,750
Annual Growth	2.3%	(3.0%)	—	(0.1%)

2009 Year-End Financials

Debt ratio: 208.6%	No. of shares (mil.): 227
Return on equity: 84.0%	Dividends
Cash ($ mil.): 254	Yield: 3.3%
Current ratio: 1.52	Payout: 62.6%
Long-term debt ($ mil.): 1,503	Market value ($ mil.): 8,129

Stock History

NYSE: HSY

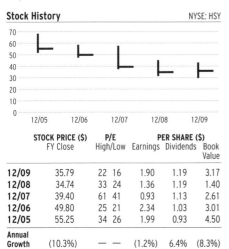

	STOCK PRICE ($) FY Close	P/E High/Low	PER SHARE ($) Earnings	Dividends	Book Value
12/09	35.79	22 16	1.90	1.19	3.17
12/08	34.74	33 24	1.36	1.19	1.40
12/07	39.40	61 41	0.93	1.13	2.61
12/06	49.80	25 21	2.34	1.03	3.01
12/05	55.25	34 26	1.99	0.93	4.50
Annual Growth	(10.3%)	— —	(1.2%)	6.4%	(8.3%)

Hertz Global Holdings

If you've ever said, "Don't worry about it, it's just a rental," guess who hurts: Hertz, a world leader in car rental. On its own and through agents and licensees, Hertz operates some 8,100 rental locations in more than 145 countries worldwide, including about 500 at US airports. Its fleet includes approximately 444,000 cars from Ford, General Motors, Toyota, and other manufacturers. Car rental accounts for more than 80% of its sales. Hertz also rents a variety of heavy equipment through 322 locations in North America, Europe, and China.

Hertz's proposed $1.2 billion purchase of Dollar Thrifty Automotive Group in 2010 didn't sit well with its rival Avis Budget Group (ABG), which reacted to Hertz's April announcment by saying it would beat Hertz's offer. The purchase is part of Hertz's strategy to move into the mid-tier car rental segment. It shifts it away from airport rentals — its traditional focus — and puts it in more direct competition with its chief rival and still off-airport-dominant Enterprise.

The recession in the US (and consequent decline in air travel) has led to declining sales at Hertz's airport locations. To lessen its dependence on the volatile air travel industry, the company has increased the number of off-airport locations it operates by 7% since 2006 to about 1,700 locations. To that end, in April 2009 Hertz acquired the assets of Texas-based Advantage Rent A Car for about $33 million. Advantage, which filed for bankruptcy in 2008, operates locations in key US leisure travel markets, including California, Florida, and Hawaii.

Hertz, which rings up about two-thirds of its revenue in the US, is attempting to also expand geographically through acquisitions and joint ventures. An example is its acquisition of UK-based car-rental firm Autotravel. The acquisition increased the number of Hertz's U.K. locations by more than 25%.

The company invested in its Connect by Hertz business by acquiring Paris-based Eileo S.A. also in 2009. Eileo specializes in car-sharing technology and buying the company boosted Hertz's operations in London, New York City, and Paris, where it uses its Connect by Hertz service.

To strengthen its fleet sales, in April 2010 the firm acquired the New Jersey-based Automoti Group, which created an online marketplace for used vehicles. Hertz hopes the purchase will help expand its Rent2Buy program, which allows customers to rent a vehicle for up to three days before purchase.

Hertz Equipment Rental Corporation (HERC), a subsidiary, is a supplier of industrial and construction equipment, mostly in the US and Canada, but also in France, Spain, and now China. HERC's inventory includes earthmoving equipment, material-handling equipment, and aerial and electrical equipment. Unlike the airport car rental industry, where several national brands dominate, the US equipment-rental market is fragmented, and Hertz sees opportunities for its unit to gain market share.

HISTORY

In 1918, 22-year-old John Jacobs opened a Chicago car rental business with 12 Model T Fords that he had repaired. By 1923, when Yellow Cab entrepreneur John Hertz bought Jacobs'

business, it had revenues of about $1 million. Jacobs continued as top executive of the company, renamed Hertz Drive-Ur-Self System. Three years later General Motors acquired the company when it bought Yellow Truck from John Hertz. Hertz introduced the first car rental charge card in 1926, opened its first airport location at Chicago's Midway Airport in 1932, and initiated the first one-way (rent-it-here/leave-it-there) plan in 1933. The company expanded into Canada in 1938 and Europe in 1950.

Omnibus bought Hertz from GM in 1953, sold its bus interests, and focused on vehicle leasing and renting. The next year Omnibus changed its name to The Hertz Corporation and was listed on the NYSE. Also in 1954 the company purchased Metropolitan Distributors, a New York-based truck leasing firm. In 1961 Hertz began operations in South America.

The company formed its Hertz Equipment Rental subsidiary in 1965. RCA bought Hertz two years later but allowed the company to maintain its board of directors and management. In 1972 it introduced the first frequent traveler's club, the #1 Club, which allowed the rental location to prepare a rental agreement before the customer arrived at the counter. Three years later Hertz began defining the company's image through TV commercials featuring football star/celebrity O. J. Simpson running through airports. (Hertz canceled Simpson's contract in 1994 after his arrest on murder charges — the TV ads had stopped in 1992.) Frank Olson became CEO in 1977 after serving in the same position at United Airlines.

United Airlines bought Hertz from RCA in 1985, then sold it in 1987 for $1.3 billion to Park Ridge, which had been formed by Hertz management and Ford Motor specifically for the purchase. (Hertz was Ford's largest customer.) In 1988 Ford, which held 80% of Park Ridge, sold 20% to Volvo North America for $100 million. (Ford later reduced its stake to 49% when it sold shares to Volvo.)

Ford bought all the shares of Hertz it didn't already own in 1994. Taking advantage of heightened investor interest in rental car companies, Ford sold 17% of Hertz to the public in 1997.

Hertz acquired several equipment rental companies in 1998, including the Boireau Group (France) and Matthews Equipment (Canada). In 1999 the company's European acquisitions included French car rental franchise SST and German van rental company Yellow Truck.

Olson retired as CEO in 1999, and president Craig Koch was named his successor. Lackluster performance of Hertz stock in 2001 prompted Ford to buy back shares held by the public — once again making the car rental company a wholly owned Ford subsidiary.

As part of an effort to strengthen its balance sheet and focus on its core automotive manufacturing operations, Ford sold Hertz to a group of investment firms — Clayton Dubilier & Rice, The Carlyle Group, and Merrill Lynch Global Private Equity — in December 2005 for $5.6 billion and nearly $10 billion in assumed debt. The firms spun Hertz off to the public in 2006.

Koch stepped down as CEO in 2006 because of a family medical issue. He was named chairman, and Tenneco's Mark Frissora was hired to be CEO. Frissora became chairman upon Koch's retirement in 2007. In July 2007 Hertz acquired Autotravel, a UK-based car-rental business.

In April 2009 HERC acquired Spain's Rent One, a leading power generation company serving event and media companies throughout Spain.

EXECUTIVES

Chairman and CEO; Chairman and CEO, Hertz:
Mark P. Frissora, age 54, $9,217,890 total compensation
EVP; President, Car Rental and Leasing, The Americas:
Scott P. Sider
EVP; President, International: Michel Taride, age 53,
$2,487,312 total compensation
EVP; President, HERC: Gerald A. Plescia, age 54,
$2,011,165 total compensation
EVP and CFO; EVP and CFO, Hertz: Elyse Douglas,
age 53, $2,018,046 total compensation
**EVP Supply Chain Management; EVP Supply Chain
Management, Hertz:** John A. Thomas, age 45
**SVP Corporate Affairs and Communications; SVP
Corporate Affairs and Communications, Hertz:**
Richard D. Broome, age 51
**SVP, General Counsel, and Secretary; SVP, General
Counsel, and Secretary, Hertz:** J. Jeffrey Zimmerman,
age 50, $1,474,560 total compensation
**SVP Finance and Corporate Controller; SVP Finance
and Corporate Controller, Hertz:** Jatindar S. Kapur,
age 51
**SVP and Chief Human Resources Officer; SVP and
Chief Human Resources Officer, Hertz:**
LeighAnne G. Baker, age 51
**SVP and Chief Marketing Officer; SVP and Chief
Marketing Officer, Hertz:** Michael P. (Mike) Senackerib,
age 44
SVP and CIO; SVP and CIO, Hertz:
Joseph F. (Joe) Eckroth Jr., age 51
**SVP Process Improvement and Project Management;
SVP Process Improvement and Project Management,
Hertz:** Lois I. Boyd, age 56
SVP Global Sales; SVP Global Sales, Hertz:
Robert J. Stuart, age 48
VP Global Tax: Anthony Fiore
VP Investor Relations: Leslie Hunziker
President, Off-Airport Operations: Kenneth Seavey
Auditors: PricewaterhouseCoopers LLP

LOCATIONS

HQ: Hertz Global Holdings, Inc.
225 Brae Blvd., Park Ridge, NJ 07656
Phone: 201-307-2000   **Fax:** 201-307-2644
Web: www.hertz.com

2009 Sales

	$ mil.	% of total
US	4,675.9	66
Other countries	2,425.6	34
Total	**7,101.5**	**100**

2009 Sales by Point of Rental

	% of total
Airport	73
Off-airport	27
Total	**100**

PRODUCTS/OPERATIONS

2009 Sales

	$ mil.	% of total
Car rental	5,872.9	83
Equipment rental	1,110.2	16
Other	118.4	1
Total	**7,101.5**	**100**

2009 Sales by Customer

	% of total
Leisure	57
Business	43
Total	**100**

COMPETITORS

Avis Budget	NES Rentals
Avis Europe	RSC Equipment Rental
Caterpillar	Sixt
Enterprise Rent-A-Car	Sunbelt Rentals
HD Supply	United Rentals
Neff	Zipcar

HISTORICAL FINANCIALS

Company Type: Public

Income Statement

FYE: December 31

	REVENUE ($ mil.)	NET INCOME ($ mil.)	NET PROFIT MARGIN	EMPLOYEES
12/09	7,102	(126)	—	23,050
12/08	8,525	(1,207)	—	24,900
12/07	8,686	265	3.0%	29,350
12/06	8,058	116	1.4%	31,500
12/05	7,469	350	4.7%	32,200
Annual Growth	**(1.3%)**	**—**	**—**	**(8.0%)**

2009 Year-End Financials

Debt ratio: 511.6%
Return on equity: —
Cash ($ mil.): 986
Current ratio: 1.71
Long-term debt ($ mil.): 10,642

No. of shares (mil.): 412
Dividends
Yield: —
Payout: —
Market value ($ mil.): 4,908

Stock History

NYSE: HTZ

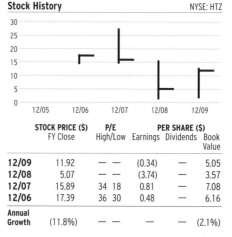

	STOCK PRICE ($) FY Close	P/E High/Low		Earnings	PER SHARE ($) Dividends	Book Value
12/09	11.92	—	—	(0.34)	—	5.05
12/08	5.07	—	—	(3.74)	—	3.57
12/07	15.89	34	18	0.81	—	7.08
12/06	17.39	36	30	0.48	—	6.16
Annual Growth	**(11.8%)**	**—**	**—**	**—**	**—**	**(2.1%)**

Hess Corporation

Hess Corporation (formerly Amerada Hess) has what it takes. The integrated oil and gas company conducts exploration and production primarily in Algeria, Australia, Azerbaijan, Brazil, Denmark, Egypt, Equatorial Guinea, Gabon, Ghana, Indonesia, Libya, Malaysia, Norway, Peru, Russia, Thailand, the UK, and the US. In 2009 Hess reported proved reserves totaling more than 1.4 billion barrels of oil equivalent. It operates a 50%-owned refinery (HOVENSA) in the US Virgin Islands and a smaller one in New Jersey, and it markets gasoline through about 1,360 HESS gas stations in 16 US states, chiefly in the eastern US. It also provides power to customers in the Northeast and Mid-Atlantic.

On the downstream side, Hess' refinery in the US Virgin Islands is operated as a joint venture with Venezuela's state oil company Petróleos de Venezuela S.A (PDVSA).

Hess' European properties account for more than 30% of its total proved oil and gas reserves. In 2009 it boosted its European assets further, swapping some noncore properties with Royal Dutch Shell in return for major stakes in two Norwegian offshore fields. The company is also seeking to exploit attractive properties in Algeria, Australia, Azerbaijan, and Latin America, as well as Asia (particularly in Malaysia and Thailand) to boost its reserves.

The company is also looking to grow its position in the lucrative Bakken oil shale play in North Dakota. In 2010 the company agreed to acquire Bakken player American Oil and Gas in a $450 million stock deal that will add 85,000 net acres to Hess' holdings in the Bakken play.

Although the exploration and production segment is the engine of growth for Hess (despite a slump in demand and revenues in 2009 due to the global recession), the company also seeks opportunities on the refining and marketing side of the business. In late 2008 Hess expanded its electricity marketing business in its core US retail market, acquiring power assets in the northeastern US from RRI Energy.

HISTORY

In 1919 British oil entrepreneur Lord Cowdray formed Amerada Corporation to explore for oil in North America. Cowdray soon hired geophysicist Everette DeGolyer, a pioneer in oil geology research. DeGolyer's systematic methods helped Amerada not only find oil deposits faster but also pick up fields missed by competitors. DeGolyer became president of Amerada in 1929 but left in 1932 to work independently.

After WWII Amerada began exploring overseas and during the 1950s entered pipelining and refining. It continued its overseas exploration through Oasis, a consortium formed in 1964 with Marathon, Shell, and Continental to explore in Libya.

Leon Hess began to buy stock in Amerada in 1966. The son of immigrants, he had entered the oil business during the Depression, selling "resid" — thick refining leftovers that refineries discarded — from a 1929 Dodge truck in New Jersey. He bought the resid cheap and sold it as heating fuel to hotels. Hess also speculated, buying oil at low prices in the summer and selling it for a profit in the winter. He later bought more trucks, a transportation network, refineries, and gas stations and went into oil exploration. Expansion pushed up debt, so in 1962 Leon's company went public as Hess Oil and Chemical after merging with Cletrac Corporation.

Hess acquired Amerada in 1969, after an ownership battle with Phillips Petroleum. During the Arab oil embargo of the 1970s, Amerada Hess began drilling on Alaska's North Slope. Oilman T. Boone Pickens bought up a chunk of Amerada Hess stock during the 1980s, spurring takeover rumors. They proved premature.

Amerada Hess completed a pipeline in 1993 to carry natural gas from the North Sea to the UK. In 1995 Leon Hess stepped down as CEO (he died in 1999), and his son John took the position. Amerada Hess sold its 81% interest in the Northstar oil field in Alaska to BP, and the next year Petro-Canada bought the company's Canadian operations. In 1996 the company acquired a 25% stake (sold in 2002) in UK-based Premier Oil.

The company teamed with Dixons Stores Group in 1997 to market gas in the UK. It also purchased 66 Pick Wick convenience store/service stations.

In 1998 Amerada Hess signed production-sharing contracts with a Malaysian oil firm as part of its strategy to move into Southeast Asia and began to sell natural gas to retail customers in the UK.

To offset losses brought on by depressed oil prices, Amerada Hess sold assets worth more than $300 million in 1999, including its southeastern pipeline network, gas stations in Georgia and South Carolina, and Gulf Coast terminals. It also moved into Latin America, acquiring stakes in fields in offshore Brazil.

In 2000 Amerada Hess acquired Statoil Energy Services, which markets natural gas and electricity to industrial and commercial customers in the northeastern US. It also announced its intention to buy LASMO, a UK-based exploration and production company, before Italy's Eni topped the Amerada Hess offer.

Undeterred, in 2001 the company bought Dallas-based exploration and production company Triton Energy for $2.7 billion in cash and $500 million in assumed debt. Amerada Hess also acquired the Gulf of Mexico assets of LLOG Exploration Company for $750 million. That year, however, stiff competition prompted Amerada Hess to put its UK gas and electricity supply business on the auction block. The unit was sold to TXU (now Energy Future Holdings) in 2002.

In 2003 Amerada Hess sold 26 oil and gas fields in the Gulf of Mexico to Anadarko Petroleum. Amerada Hess was granted permission by the Equatorial Guinea government in 2004 to develop 29 new wells in that country. That year Amerada Hess acquired a 65% stake in Trabant Holdings International, a Russia-based production and exploration company.

The company re-entered its former oil and gas production operations in the Waha concessions in Libya in 2006. Also that year it changed its name to Hess Corporation.

EXECUTIVES

Chairman and CEO: John B. Hess, age 55,
$18,950,608 total compensation
EVP and Director; President, Marketing and Refining:
F. Borden Walker, age 56,
$5,876,599 total compensation
EVP and Director; President, Worldwide Exploration and Production: Gregory P. Hill, age 48,
$10,641,553 total compensation
SVP and CFO: John P. Rielly, age 47,
$4,180,627 total compensation
SVP Global New Business Development: Howard Paver, age 59
SVP Global Production: George F. Sandison, age 53
SVP Terminals and Refining: Lori J. Ryerkerk, age 47
SVP Energy Marketing: John A. Gartman, age 62
SVP and General Counsel: Timothy B. Goodell, age 52,
$4,861,459 total compensation
SVP Terminals and Refining: Darius Sweet
SVP; CEO, Hess LNG: R. Gordon Shearer, age 55
SVP Retail and Energy Marketing: Christopher Baldwin
SVP Global Developments: Gary Boubel, age 55
SVP Global Exploration and New Ventures:
William (Bill) Drennen, age 59
SVP Marketing and Refining, Supply and Financial Controls: Lawrence H. Ornstein, age 58
SVP Finance and Corporate Development:
John J. Scelfo, age 52
SVP Global Production and Technology: Scott M. Heck, age 52
SVP Global Production: John V. Simon, age 56
VP and Chief Risk Officer: J. C. Stein
VP Corporate Communications: Jon L. Pepper
VP Investor Relations: Jay R. Wilson
VP, Secretary, and Deputy General Counsel:
George C. Barry
VP and CIO: Jeff L. Steinhorn
Auditors: Ernst & Young LLP

LOCATIONS

HQ: Hess Corporation
1185 Avenue of the Americas, New York, NY 10036
Phone: 212-997-8500   **Fax:** 212-536-8593
Web: www.hess.com

2009 Sales

	$ mil.	% of total
US	24,611	83
Africa	1,898	6
Europe	1,771	6
Asia & other regions	1,334	5
Adjustments	(45)	—
Total	**29,569**	**100**

PRODUCTS/OPERATIONS

2009 Sales

	$ mil.	% of total
Refined petroleum products	12,931	44
Natural gas	5,894	20
Crude oil & natural gas liquids	5,665	19
Electricity	3,408	11
Convenience stores & other	1,716	6
Adjustments	(45)	—
Total	**29,569**	**100**

COMPETITORS

BP
CAMAC International
Chevron
CMA CGM
ConocoPhillips
Constellation Energy Group
Continental Energy
Desire Petroleum
Devon Energy
Dominion Resources
Eni
Eni Lasmo
ERHC
Exxon Mobil
Getty Petroleum Marketing
Gulf Oil
Koch Industries, Inc.
Marathon Oil
Marathon Petroleum
Norsk Hydro ASA
Occidental Petroleum
PEMEX
PETROBRAS
Petróleos de Venezuela
Royal Dutch Shell
Serica Energy
Sinclair Oil
Sunoco
TOTAL
United Refining

HISTORICAL FINANCIALS

Company Type: Public

Income Statement

FYE: December 31

	REVENUE ($ mil.)	NET INCOME ($ mil.)	NET PROFIT MARGIN	EMPLOYEES
12/09	29,569	740	2.5%	13,300
12/08	41,165	2,360	5.7%	13,500
12/07	31,647	1,832	5.8%	13,300
12/06	28,067	1,916	6.8%	13,700
12/05	23,255	1,242	5.3%	11,610
Annual Growth	**6.2%**	**(12.1%)**	**—**	**3.5%**

2009 Year-End Financials

Debt ratio: 32.3%
Return on equity: 5.8%
Cash ($ mil.): 1,362
Current ratio: 1.17
Long-term debt ($ mil.): 4,319
No. of shares (mil.): 328
Dividends
  Yield: 0.7%
  Payout: 17.6%
Market value ($ mil.): 19,869

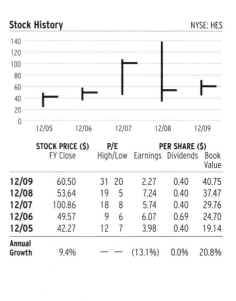

Stock History

NYSE: HES

	STOCK PRICE ($) FY Close	P/E High/Low		PER SHARE ($) Earnings	Dividends	Book Value
12/09	60.50	31	20	2.27	0.40	40.75
12/08	53.64	19	5	7.24	0.40	37.47
12/07	100.86	18	8	5.74	0.40	29.76
12/06	49.57	9	6	6.07	0.69	24.70
12/05	42.27	12	7	3.98	0.40	19.14
Annual Growth	**9.4%**	**—**	**—**	**(13.1%)**	**0.0%**	**20.8%**

Hewitt Associates

If any of a company's resources are human, chances are it'll need the assistance of Hewitt Associates. As one of the primary leaders in its industry, the company provides a variety of HR-related services including payroll, organizational change management, talent and reward consulting, and the largest portion of the company's business — benefits outsourcing. Hewitt administers medical, 401(k), and pension plans on an outsourced basis for larger companies with complex benefit programs. Hewitt was founded by Ted Hewitt in 1940 and has about 105 offices worldwide. In mid-2010 it agreed to be acquired by insurance brokerage giant Aon Corporation, which plans to integrate Hewitt with its Aon Consulting subsidiary.

Soon to be rebranded as Aon Hewitt, the combined entity will boast revenues of $4.3 billion, capable of serving clients in more than 120 countries around the globe. The deal will bolster Aon Consulting's expertise in benefits outsourcing and HR business process outsourcing, while Hewitt will see a boost in its risk services product portfolio. Aon Corporation is paying $4.9 billion in cash and stock to obtain Hewitt.

Hewitt's outsourcing services account for about 50% of its total revenue. The company has expanded its operations internationally through a number of acquisitions over the years. In 2008 Hewitt obtained New Bridge Street Consultants (specialist compensation consultancy in the UK) and CSi — The Remuneration Specialists (a provider of data, analytics, and compensation consulting in Australia and New Zealand). In July 2009 Hewitt took its stake in Germany-based BodeHewitt to full ownership. The acquisition beefed up Hewitt's offerings in pension administration and investment consulting in Germany, which it considers a key market.

A year later Hewitt bought two businesses in the health care and insurance fields. It purchased Senior Educators Ltd., a Web-based medical insurance platform supplying helpful information and advice to retirees. Hewitt plans for the deal to help it build a better portfolio of products serving the broader retiree customer base. It later acquired HRAdvance, a benefits dependent audit services firm. HR Advance's software products help companies save money by identifying ineligible dependents. The deal will augment Hewitt's existing dependent audit capabilities.

While the company does look to acquisitions for potential growth, it largely depends on its strong client retention rate, which in any given year typically exceeds 95%.

HISTORY

Edwin "Ted" Hewitt founded Hewitt Associates in 1940 to offer personal estate property and financial services. In the 1950s it became one of the first to measure defined-plan investment performance and offer personalized benefit statements. Hewitt also worked for the government, designing forms for the Welfare and Pension Plans Disclosure Act and serving on the Federal Interagency Task Force from 1964 to 1968.

Hewitt Associates developed the first flexible benefit plans and the Benefit Index (for measuring the competitive value between benefit plans) in the 1970s. It also established its investment consultancy, Hewitt Investment Group, in 1974. The company developed computerized employee benefit program systems and benefits software packages in the 1980s for integrated compensation management, defined contribution administration, pension management, and retirement plan simulation. Hewitt Technologies, its information technology division, became part of the firm in 1988.

In 1992 it created the Defined Contribution Alliance to bundle communication, investment management, record keeping, and trustee services for 401(k) plans. The company's new benefits management center opened near Orlando, Florida, in 1997. The following year Hewitt Associates teamed with online investment adviser Financial Engines to offer its clients Internet-based investment advice. In 2000 the company arranged with investment consulting firm James P. Marshall to establish a new Hewitt venture in Canada. Later that year, the company announced a merger with UK consulting firm Bacon & Woodrow.

After nearly 60 years as a privately held company, the company registered to trade on the New York Stock Exchange in 2002. Over the course of the next few years, Hewitt Associates acquired several additional human resources and consulting firms as a means for achieving growth.

In early 2007 Hewitt looked toward the mid-sized health and welfare benefits market when it acquired RealLife HR. A few months later, Hewitt divested its Cyborg operations (licensed HR and payroll software services) in order to streamline its HR outsourcing offerings. (Cyborg's software was not core to Hewitt's central outsourcing strategy.)

In a sweeping historical move, Hewitt agreed to be acquired for $4.9 billion by insurance brokerage firm Aon Corporation during the summer of 2010. Hewitt is being integrated with rival Aon Consulting and will be rebranded as Aon Hewitt.

EXECUTIVES

Chairman and CEO: Russell P. (Russ) Fradin, age 54, $7,739,592 total compensation
CFO: Robert A. (Rob) Schriesheim, age 49
CIO: David B. Baruch, age 43
Chief Diversity Officer: Andres Tapia
Chief Client Officer: Julie S. Gordon, age 52
SVP Large Market Benefits Outsourcing:
Kristi A. Savacool, age 50,
$1,783,257 total compensation
SVP Corporate Development and Strategy:
Matthew C. (Matt) Levin, age 36,
$1,573,891 total compensation
SVP Human Resources: Tracy Keogh, age 48
SVP Middle Market Benefits Outsourcing:
Craig Maloney
SVP Point Solutions, Outsourcing: Mike Rogalski
SVP Outsourcing Sales: Mike Wright
SVP, General Counsel, and Corporate Secretary:
Steven J. Kyono, age 48
SVP Global Business Services and New Products and Markets: Vince Coppola
President, Consulting: Yvan Legris, age 47
President, Consulting: Eric C. Fiedler, age 43
President, Global Benefits Outsourcing: Jay C. Rising, age 53, $2,146,414 total compensation
President, HR Business Process Outsourcing:
James R. Konieczny, age 48
Global COO, Consulting: Mark Stach
Corporate Controller and Principal Accounting Officer:
Joseph A. Tautges, age 34
Investor Relations Leader: Sean McHugh
Auditors: Ernst & Young LLP

LOCATIONS

HQ: Hewitt Associates, Inc.
100 Half Day Rd., Lincolnshire, IL 60069
Phone: 847-295-5000   **Fax:** 847-295-7634
Web: www.hewittassociates.com

2009 Sales

	$ mil.	% of total
US	2,383.2	78
UK	321.4	10
Other countries	369.0	12
Total	**3,073.6**	**100**

PRODUCTS/OPERATIONS

2009 Sales

	% of total
Benefits outsourcing	51
Consulting	33
HR business process outsourcing	16
Total	**100**

Selected Products and Services

Health care
HR, payroll, and benefits outsourcing
Retirement and financial management
Talent and organizational change

COMPETITORS

Accenture
Administaff
ADP
Affiliated Computer Services
Aon Consulting
Ceridian
Convergys
Envestnet
GatesMcDonald
HP Enterprise Services
IBM
Marsh & McLennan
Mercer
Right Management
Schloss & Co.
T. Rowe Price
Towers Watson
The Vanguard Group
Workscape

HISTORICAL FINANCIALS

Company Type: Public

Income Statement

FYE: September 30

	REVENUE ($ mil.)	NET INCOME ($ mil.)	NET PROFIT MARGIN	EMPLOYEES
9/09	3,074	265	8.6%	23,000
9/08	3,228	188	5.8%	23,000
9/07	2,990	(175)	—	23,000
9/06	2,857	(116)	—	24,000
9/05	2,898	135	4.6%	22,000
Annual Growth	1.5%	18.4%	—	1.1%

2009 Year-End Financials

Debt ratio: 71.9%
Return on equity: 35.1%
Cash ($ mil.): 582
Current ratio: 1.69
Long-term debt ($ mil.): 619

No. of shares (mil.): 92
Dividends
Yield: —
Payout: —
Market value ($ mil.): 3,350

Stock History

NYSE: HEW

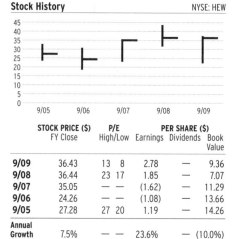

	STOCK PRICE ($) FY Close	P/E High/Low		PER SHARE ($) Earnings	Dividends	Book Value
9/09	36.43	13	8	2.78	—	9.36
9/08	36.44	23	17	1.85	—	7.07
9/07	35.05	—	—	(1.62)	—	11.29
9/06	24.26	—	—	(1.08)	—	13.66
9/05	27.28	27	20	1.19	—	14.26
Annual Growth	7.5%	—	—	23.6%	—	(10.0%)

Hewlett-Packard

HP wants to be "it" when it comes to IT. Hewlett-Packard provides one of the tech world's most comprehensive portfolios of hardware, software, and services. Its products include PCs, servers, storage devices, printers, and networking equipment. The company's services unit provides IT and business process outsourcing, application development and management, consulting, systems integration, and other technology services. HP's software products include enterprise IT management, information management, business intelligence, and carrier-grade communications applications.

In August 2010 CEO Mark Hurd resigned following an investigation into allegations of sexual harassment brought by a former HP contractor. The probe revealed no violation of sexual harassment policy, but turned up evidence of other workplace misconduct. Company CFO Cathie Lesjak was appointed as interim chief. Hurd oversaw a growth strategy emphasizing software and services, which are typically more profitable areas than the company's traditional focus on PCs. While PCs still account for about one-third of HP's sales, profit margins for that line of business have dwindled in recent years.

The company's Enterprise Business encompasses HP's services, enterprise storage and servers, and software segments. HP, which already boasted an IT services organization that was among the world's largest, acquired Electronic Data Systems (EDS) for about $13.9 billion in cash in 2008.

In 2010 HP acquired 3Com for about $3.15 billion in cash. The 3Com product portfolio complemented the company's ProCurve networking line. Later that year HP bought smartphone maker Palm, the creator of the iconic Palm Pilot PDA, for about $1.2 billion.

HP's software offerings include a collection of IT management tools it markets as the HP Business Technology Optimization (BTO) suite. Its BTO applications include tools for automating tasks associated with data center and client computer management. HP gave its BTO portfolio a boost when it purchased Opsware, a developer of data center automation software, for about $1.6 billion in 2007. Other major software groups include network services, as well as information management and business intelligence. HP's Personal Systems Group (PSG) markets desktop and notebook PCs under both HP and Compaq brand names. PSG also provides handheld computers, calculators, televisions, and digital media centers.

Imaging and Printing Group (IPG) provides inkjet, laser, and large-format printers. Its comprehensive line also includes copiers, digital presses, scanners, multifunction devices, software, and supplies. In addition to printing and imaging giants ranging from Canon to Xerox, HP clashes with its PC nemesis in the printer market as well; Dell sells branded printers made by Lexmark and others. IPG also oversees HP's digital photo printers and online photo services.

HISTORY

Encouraged by professor Frederick Terman (considered the founder of Silicon Valley), in 1938 Stanford engineers Bill Hewlett and David Packard started Hewlett-Packard (HP) in a garage in Palo Alto, California, with $538. Hewlett was the idea man, while Packard served as manager; the two were so low-key that the company's first official meeting ended with no decision on exactly what to manufacture. Finding good people took priority over finding something to sell. The first product ended up being an audio oscillator. Walt Disney Studios, one of HP's first customers, bought eight to use in the making of *Fantasia*.

Demand for HP's electronic testing equipment during WWII spurred sales growth from $34,000 in 1940 to nearly $1 million just three years later. HP went public in 1957. The company expanded beyond the US during 1959, establishing a marketing organization in Switzerland and a manufacturing plant in West Germany. HP entered the medical field in 1961 by acquiring Sanborn, and the analytical instrumentation business in 1965 with the purchase of F&M Scientific. Chairman Packard in 1969 began serving two years as deputy defense secretary.

In 1972 the company pioneered personal computing with the world's first handheld scientific calculator. Under the leadership of John Young, the founders' chosen successor (named CEO in 1978), HP introduced its first PCs, the first desktop mainframe, and the LaserJet printer. Its initial PCs were known for their rugged build, tailored for factory operations. They were also

more expensive than rival versions and, consequently, didn't enjoy strong sales.

By 1986 a five-year, $250 million R&D project — the company's largest to date — had produced a family of HP computers based on the reduced instruction set computing (RISC) architecture. Hewlett retired in 1987 (he died in 2001); sons of both Hewlett and Packard were named that year to the company's board of directors. HP became a leader in workstations with the 1989 purchase of market pioneer Apollo Computer.

In 1992 Lewis Platt, an EVP since 1987, was named president and CEO. Packard retired in 1993 (he died in 1996). In 1999 HP formed Agilent Technologies for its test and measurement and other noncomputer operations, and spun off 15% of the company to the public. (HP distributed to its shareholders its remaining 85% in mid-2000.) Also in 1999 Platt retired and HP — one of the first major US corporations to be headed by a woman — appointed Lucent executive Carly Fiorina president and CEO. She was named chairman the following year.

In 2001 HP agreed to pay $400 million to Pitney Bowes to settle a 1995 patent-infringement case related to printer technology. HP said in mid-2002 that it was cutting about 6,000 jobs.

Next came the announcement of a blockbuster deal: HP agreed to buy rival Compaq in a stock transaction initially valued at about $25 billion. The highly contentious deal eventually met with shareholder approval in early 2002. At the time of closing, the deal was valued at approximately $19 billion. Integration efforts included a workforce reduction of roughly 10%, as the company eliminated redundant product groups.

Fiorina's differences with HP's board over strategic direction finally came to a head in 2005, and she stepped down. CFO Robert Wayman was named interim CEO, and director Patricia Dunn took over as chairman. Mark Hurd, formerly CEO of NCR, was soon named to lead HP.

HP's leadership experienced another shakeup the following year prompted by tactics used in an investigation of boardroom leaks. HP's board came under fire after it was revealed that third-party investigators employed by the company impersonated board members and journalists to obtain their phone records.

Dunn was asked to resign from the board in September 2006, and Hurd replaced her as chairman. HP settled a related dispute with the California Attorney General later that year, agreeing to pay $14.5 million.

EXECUTIVES

Interim CEO and CFO: Catherine A. (Cathie) Lesjak, age 51, $7,585,775 total compensation
EVP and Chief Strategy and Technology Officer: Shane V. Robison, age 56
EVP HP Enterprise Business: Ann M. Livermore, age 51, $13,424,406 total compensation
EVP Imaging and Printing Group: Vyomesh (V.J.) Joshi, age 56, $11,644,691 total compensation
EVP Personal Systems Group: Todd Bradley, age 51, $12,538,329 total compensation
EVP Software and Solutions Business: Bill Veghte
EVP Enterprise Servers, Storage, and Networking: David A. Donatelli, age 44
EVP and Chief Administrative Officer: Peter J. (Pete) Bocian, age 55
EVP, General Counsel, and Secretary: Michael J. (Mike) Holston, age 47
EVP Enterprise Sales, Marketing, and Strategy: Thomas E. (Tom) Hogan, age 50
EVP Human Resources: Marcela Perez de Alonso, age 55
EVP Emerging Markets: Francesco Serafini

EVP and CIO: Randall D. (Randy) Mott, age 53
SVP and Chief Sales Officer: Donald C. (Don) Grantham, age 52
SVP and Chief Marketing Officer: Michael Mendenhall, age 48
SVP Global Information Technology: Linda M. Dillman, age 53
SVP, Controller, and Principal Accounting Officer: Jim Murrin, age 49
SVP Corporate Growth Initiatives, Office of Strategy and Technology: Joe Eazor, age 47
VP Investor Relations: James (Jim) Burns
Auditors: Ernst & Young LLP

LOCATIONS

HQ: Hewlett-Packard Company
3000 Hanover St., Palo Alto, CA 94304
Phone: 650-857-1501   **Fax:** 650-857-5518
Web: www.hp.com

2009 Sales

	$ mil.	% of total
US	41,314	36
Other countries	73,238	64
Total	**114,552**	**100**

PRODUCTS/OPERATIONS

2009 Sales

	$ mil.	% of total
Products	74,051	65
Services	40,124	35
Financing	377	—
Total	**114,552**	**100**

2009 Sales

	$ mil.	% of total
Enterprise Business		
Services	34,693	30
Enterprise storage & servers	15,359	13
Software	3,572	3
Personal Systems Group	35,305	30
Imaging & Printing Group	24,011	21
HP Financial Services	2,673	2
Investments	768	1
Adjustments	(1,829)	—
Total	**114,552**	**100**

Selected Products and Services

Enterprise Systems
  Business technology optimization software
  Networking equipment
  Servers (Linux, Unix, Windows)
    Blade
    Carrier-grade
    Rack-optimized
    Server appliances
    Super-scalable
    Tower
  Storage
    Disks and disk arrays
    Network-attached storage (NAS) devices
    Optical disk drives
    Storage area network (SAN) systems
    Tape drives and libraries
Services
  Consulting
  Design and installation
  Education
  Financing
  Outsourcing
  Printing
  Support and maintenance
  Web hosting
Personal Systems
  Calculators
  Desktop PCs
  Digital entertainment centers
  DVD writers
  Handheld computers
  Notebook computers
  Televisions (LCD, plasma)
  Workstations

Imaging and Printing
Commercial printing
Digital presses
Printers
Digital imaging
Projectors
Scanners
Personal printing
All-in-ones (copier, fax, printer, scanner)
Ink jet printers
Laser printers
Shared printing
Networked inkjet, laser, and multifunction printers
Office all-in-ones
Services

COMPETITORS

Accenture	Hewitt Associates
Acer	Hitachi
ADP	IBM
Affiliated Computer	Infosys
Services	Konica Minolta
Apple Inc.	Lenovo
ASUSTeK	Lexmark
BMC Software	Microsoft
Brother Industries	NCR
CA Technologies	NEC
CACI International	NetApp
Canon	Océ
Capgemini	Oki Electric
CGI Group	Oracle
Cisco Systems	Palm, Inc.
Computer Sciences Corp.	Panasonic Corp
Convergys	Ricoh Company
Dell	Samsung Electronics
Eastman Kodak	SAP
EMC	Sharp Corp.
Epson	Sony
First Data	Symantec
Fiserv	Tata Consultancy
Fuji Xerox	Teradata
Fujitsu	Toshiba
Fujitsu Technology	Unisys
Solutions	Wipro Technologies
Heidelberger	Xerox
Druckmaschinen	

HISTORICAL FINANCIALS

Company Type: Public

Income Statement

FYE: October 31

	REVENUE ($ mil.)	NET INCOME ($ mil.)	NET PROFIT MARGIN	EMPLOYEES
10/09	114,552	7,660	6.7%	304,000
10/08	118,364	8,329	7.0%	321,000
10/07	104,286	7,264	7.0%	172,000
10/06	91,658	6,198	6.8%	156,000
10/05	86,696	2,398	2.8%	150,000
Annual Growth	7.2%	33.7%	—	19.3%

2009 Year-End Financials

Debt ratio: 34.5%
Return on equity: 19.3%
Cash ($ mil.): 13,279
Current ratio: 1.22
Long-term debt ($ mil.): 13,980

No. of shares (mil.): 2,334
Dividends
 Yield: 0.7%
 Payout: 10.2%
Market value ($ mil.): 110,795

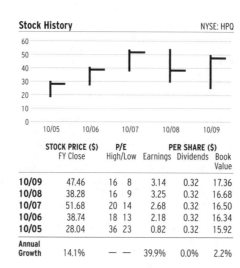

Stock History

NYSE: HPQ

	STOCK PRICE ($) FY Close	P/E High/Low		PER SHARE ($) Earnings	Dividends	Book Value
10/09	47.46	16	8	3.14	0.32	17.36
10/08	38.28	16	9	3.25	0.32	16.68
10/07	51.68	20	14	2.68	0.32	16.50
10/06	38.74	18	13	2.18	0.32	16.34
10/05	28.04	36	23	0.82	0.32	15.92
Annual Growth	14.1%	—	—	39.9%	0.0%	2.2%

Highmark Inc.

Highmark has staked its claim as the largest health insurer in the Keystone state. A licensee of the Blue Cross and Blue Shield Association, the not-for-profit firm covers some 3.9 million people in central and western Pennsylvania, as well as the Lehigh Valley. It serves another 800,000 customers in West Virginia and other areas of Pennsylvania through affiliations and partnerships with other insurers, and it provides administrative and network-access services nationally. In addition, Highmark sells Medicare Advantage and prescription drug plans to seniors in both states. Other subsidiaries (not operating under the BCBS license) provide dental insurance, vision care, and other products and services nationwide.

The company's core Pennsylvania service areas are served through wholly owned subsidiaries Highmark Blue Cross Blue Shield, Keystone Health Plan West, and Highmark Blue Shield. Medicare Advantage services are provided in Pennsylvania and West Virginia through its Keystone Health Plan West and Highmark Health Insurance units. Highmark also manages the health benefits of self-insured employers, provides third-party administrative and claims processing services to other BCBS plans, and offers services in adjacent regions through partnerships with nearby insurance providers.

For instance, it has a collaboration agreement to co-market Blue-branded coverage in southeastern Pennsylvania with its Philadelphia-based neighbor Independence Blue Cross (IBC). Highmark operates similarly in the northeastern part of the state through a partnership with Blue Cross of Northeastern Pennsylvania. It works through affiliate Mountain State Blue Cross Blue Shield (in which it owns a controlling stake) to offer health plans in West Virginia.

Highmark and IBC had hoped to strengthen their relationship, but the companies cancelled plans to merge in early 2009, citing concerns that the deal would not receive regulatory approval. The merger would have created a massive health insurer covering more than half of Pennsylvania's population and was the subject of harsh criticism from Pennsylvania politicians,

regulators, and other parties concerned that such a mega-company would stifle competition.

Since the deal fell through, Highmark has been focusing on expanding its health insurance operations by strengthening partnerships with other insurance companies and by increasing involvement in government health programs such as Medicare. It is also increasing its health plan offerings for individual consumers. To improve customer care, Highmark opened a handful of retail stores in 2009 and 2010; the stores provide health assessment services, coverage and billing assistance, and wellness classes. The company is experiencing strong growth in its dental and vision care businesses, as well.

Highmark provides an array of specialty services through its non-Blue subsidiaries. In the optical arena, subsidiaries include managed vision care organization Davis Vision, the Eye Care Centers of America chain of retail vision care centers, and eyewear manufacturer Viva. HM Insurance Group offers employer health risk solutions, such as stop-loss insurance and a limited benefit medical plan, while United Concordia Companies provides dental coverage to around 8 million members across the US.

HISTORY

Highmark was created from the merger of Blue Cross of Western Pennsylvania (founded in 1937) and Pennsylvania Blue Shield, created in 1964 when the Medical Service Association of Pennsylvania (MSAP) adopted the Blue Shield name.

The Pennsylvania Medical Society, in conjunction with the state of Pennsylvania, had formed MSAP to provide medical insurance to the poor and indigent. MSAP borrowed $25,000 from the Pennsylvania Medical Society to help set up its operations, and Chauncey Palmer (who had originally proposed the organization) was named president. Individuals paid 35 cents per month, and families paid $1.75 each month to join MSAP, which initially covered mainly obstetrical and surgical procedures.

In 1945 Arthur Daugherty replaced Palmer as president (he served until his death in 1968) and helped MSAP recruit major new accounts, including the United Mine Workers and the Congress of Industrial Organizations. MSAP in 1946 became a chapter of the national Blue Shield association, which was started that year by the medical societies of several states to provide prepaid health insurance plans.

In 1951 MSAP signed up the 150,000 employees of United States Steel, bringing its total enrollment to more than 1.6 million. Growth did not lead to prosperity, though, as the organization had trouble keeping up with payments to its doctors. This shortfall in funds led MSAP to raise its premiums in 1961, at which point the state reminded the association of its social mission and suggested it concentrate on controlling costs instead of raising rates.

MSAP changed its name to Pennsylvania Blue Shield in 1964. Two years later the association began managing the state's Medicare plan and started the 65-Special plan to supplement Medicare coverage. In the 1970s Pennsylvania Blue Shield again could not keep up with the cost of paying its doctors, which led to more rate increases and closer scrutiny of its expenses. Competition increased in the 1980s as HMOs cropped up around the state. Pennsylvania Blue Shield fought back by creating its own HMO plans — some of which it owned jointly with Blue Cross of Western Pennsylvania — in the 1980s.

After years of slowly collecting noninsurance businesses, Blue Cross of Western Pennsylvania changed its name to Veritus in 1991 to reflect the growing importance of its for-profit operations.

In 1996 Pennsylvania Blue Shield overcame physicians' protests and state regulators' concerns to merge with Veritus. The company adopted the name Highmark to represent its standards for high quality; it took a loss as it failed to meet cost-cutting goals and suffered early-retirement costs related to the merger consolidation. To gain support for the merger, Highmark sold for-profit subsidiary Keystone Health Plan East to Independence Blue Cross in 1997.

In 1999 Highmark teamed with Mountain State Blue Cross Blue Shield to become West Virginia's primary licensee.

As a result of some belt-tightening in 2004, the company shut down its Alliance Ventures (administrative and information services) and Lifestyle Advantage subsidiaries. Highmark sold its Medmark specialty pharmacy unit to Walgreens in 2006, and its HM Insurance subsidiary sold its life and disability insurance operations to Fort Dearborn Life Insurance. The company also acquired Eye Care Centers of America in 2006.

EXECUTIVES

Chairman: J. Robert Baum
President, CEO, and Director: Kenneth R. (Ken) Melani
EVP, Chief Marketing Officer, and Chief Strategy Officer: Thomas W. Kerr
EVP and Chief Medical Officer, HVHC, Inc.: Jeff Smith
EVP, CFO, Chief Administrative Officer, and Treasurer: Nanette P. (Nan) DeTurk
EVP Health Services: Deborah Rice
EVP Government Services: David M. O'Brien
EVP Subsidiary Business: Daniel J. (Dan) Lebish
SVP, Corporate Secretary, and General Counsel: Gary R. Truitt
SVP Community Affairs: Evan Frazier
SVP and Chief Audit Executive: Elizabeth A. Farbacher
President Operations, Mountain State Blue Cross Blue Shield: J. Fred Earley II
President and CEO, HVHC, Inc. and Chairman and CEO, Eye Care Centers of America: David L. Holmberg, age 51
Auditors: PricewaterhouseCoopers LLP

LOCATIONS

HQ: Highmark Inc.
Fifth Avenue Place, 120 Fifth Ave.
Pittsburgh, PA 15222
Phone: 412-544-7000   **Fax:** 412-544-8368
Web: www.highmark.com/hmk2

PRODUCTS/OPERATIONS

2009 Revenue

	$ mil.	% of total
Premiums	11,540.8	84
Vision revenue	1,126.3	8
Management services	653.4	5
Net investment income & other	373.7	3
Total	**13,694.2**	**100**

Selected Subsidiaries and Affiliates

Blue Cross Blue Shield Licensee Companies
Highmark Blue Cross Blue Shield (health care plans, western Pennsylvania)
Highmark Blue Shield (health care plans, central Pennsylvania and the Lehigh Valley; also operates through partnerships in northeastern and southeastern Pennsylvania)
Highmark Health Insurance Company (Medicare Advantage plans, West Virginia)
Highmark Senior Resources, Inc. (Medicare Part D prescription drug plans, Pennsylvania and West Virginia)
Keystone Health Plan West, Inc. (HMO and Medicare Advantage plans, western Pennsylvania)
Mountain State Blue Cross & Blue Shield (controlled affiliate; health care plans, West Virginia)
Other Subsidiaries
Davis Vision, Inc. (vision insurance and ophthalmic laboratories)
Eye Care Centers of America, Inc. (retail vision care centers)
Gateway Health Plan (Medical aAssistance coverage)
Highmark Foundation (community health charitable organization)
Highmark Medicare Services, Inc. (Medicare claims administration and financial management)
HM Insurance Group (stop-loss insurance, HMO reinsurance, and other health risk solutions)
Industrial Medical Consultants (physician workforce productivity services)
United Concordia Companies, Inc. (dental insurance)
Viva International Group (eyewear manufacturing)

COMPETITORS

Aetna	Geisinger Health System
American United Mutual	Genworth Financial
AmeriChoice of	HealthAmerica
Pennsylvania	Humana
Blue Cross of Northeastern	Independence Blue Cross
Pennsylvania	Independence Holding
Capital BlueCross	LensCrafters
CIGNA	National Vision
DeCare Dental	Pearle Vision
Delta Dental Plans	UPMC
Dental Benefit Providers	U.S. Vision
DentaQuest	Wal-Mart
Emerging Vision	

HISTORICAL FINANCIALS

Company Type: Not-for-profit

Income Statement

FYE: December 31

	REVENUE ($ mil.)	NET INCOME ($ mil.)	NET PROFIT MARGIN	EMPLOYEES
12/09	13,694	188	1.4%	20,000
12/08	13,002	94	0.7%	19,000
12/07	12,353	375	3.0%	18,500
12/06	11,084	398	3.6%	18,500
12/05	9,847	342	3.5%	12,000
Annual Growth	**8.6%**	**(13.9%)**	**—**	**13.6%**

Net Income History

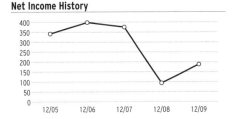

Hill-Rom Holdings

Hill-Rom Holdings holds Hill-Rom, which, in turn, holds hospital patients safe and secure. Hill-Rom makes, sells, and rents hospital beds and other patient-room furniture and equipment, along with stretchers, surgical table accessories, and other equipment for lifting and transporting patients. The company also sells non-invasive therapeutic products and surfaces for the care of pulmonary, bariatric, and circulatory conditions and wounds. Hill-Rom also provides information technology products, namely communication and software used in health care settings.

Hill-Rom Holdings, (formerly Hillenbrand Industries) used to operate in between the quick and the dead, until it cast its lot with the living. In 2008 the holding company spun off its funeral services business Batesville Casket into a separate entity owned by newly created holding company with an old name: Hillenbrand. That separation left Hill-Rom Holdings focused on its remaining operating unit, Hill-Rom.

The plans to split apart its two operating units were hatched in 2007 to increase value for shareholders and tighten industry focus for each unit. Leading up to the split, the company boosted its sales force effectiveness. It also focused on product improvements to reduce the side effects of long hospital stays, such as bed sores and infections; it established an ongoing collaboration with Ascension Health to address these issues. Additionally, it kick-started its rental business by cutting costs, improving efficiency, and investing in its out-of-date truck fleet.

Hill-Rom Holdings sees room for future growth in the post-acute care market (long-term care facilities and home care) and in some international markets. It has been expanding the post-acute care business via new product launches, distribution agreements, and acquisitions. It acquired Swedish firm Liko, which makes slings and other devices used to move mobility-impaired patients from one surface to another, in 2008, and it expanded into Australia with the 2006 acquisition of Medicraft, a maker of hospital beds.

A new area for growth may yet come from the sale of products direct to consumers who are seeking hospital beds for home care settings.

Rolf Classon was the first leader of the company outside the Hillenbrand family when he took on the role of chairman in 2006. At the same time, Peter Soderberg was appointed CEO and the two men oversaw the major shifts in the company's focus. Soderberg retired in 2010 and was replaced by John Greisch.

HISTORY

In 1906 John A. Hillenbrand, a banker, newspaperman, and general store owner in Batesville, Indiana, bought the ailing Batesville Casket Company (founded 1884) to save it from bankruptcy. Under Hillenbrand, and later his four sons (John W., who succeeded his father as president of the company; William; George; and Daniel), the casket company flourished.

In 1929 William Hillenbrand established the Hill-Rom Company in Batesville to make hospital furniture. Hill-Rom made its furniture out of wood instead of tubular steel and quickly became a leader in innovative hospital furnishings.

During the following decades George Hillenbrand created several patented products for both Batesville Casket and Hill-Rom. By the 1940s, for example, the company had developed corrosion-, air-, and water-resistant metal caskets. George constantly sought ways to improve manufacturing techniques and product quality, giving the company a competitive edge in sales and productivity.

Daniel, the youngest son, became president of Batesville Casket in 1964 and consolidated Batesville Casket and Hill-Rom into Hillenbrand Industries five years later. Hoping to make the company more competitive nationally (and eventually globally), Daniel took Hillenbrand public in 1971.

The company acquired Dominion Metalware Industries (1972) and luggage maker American Tourister (1978; sold to Astrum International, maker of Samsonite luggage, in 1993). In 1984 it bought Medeco Security Locks (sold 1998) and a year later purchased Support Systems International (SSI), provider of specialty rental mattresses for critically ill and immobile patients. (In 1994 SSI was integrated into Hill-Rom.)

Hillenbrand founded the Forethought Group in 1985 to provide special life insurance to cover prearranged funerals. In 1991 it entered the European market by acquiring Le Couviour, a French maker of hospital beds. The company also bought Block Medical, a maker of home infusion-therapy products, that year. August Hillenbrand, nephew of Daniel, became CEO in 1989.

In 1992 Batesville Casket set out to consolidate its market, buying casket producer Cormier & Gaudet (Canada). It then bought Bridge Casket (New Jersey), Lincoln Casket (Hamtramck, Michigan); and Industrias Arga (Mexico City), all in 1993. That year Hillenbrand also purchased L & C Arnold, one of the biggest and oldest hospital furniture makers in Germany.

With the casket market flat in the mid-1990s, Hillenbrand grew its business by going after market share in cremation products.

As the 20th century drew to a close, Medicare reimbursement cutbacks bit into Hill-Rom's sales. The company cut jobs in both 2000 and 2001. Those years also brought the retirement of both August and Daniel Hillenbrand. Frederick Rockwood became president and CEO in 2000; Ray Hillenbrand (nephew of Daniel) was named chairman in 2001.

Hillenbrand sold its piped medical gas unit (to Beacon Medical Products in late 2003) and the Air-Shields infant care products business of Hill-Rom, since those operations were not key to Hill-Rom's success. It acquired Advanced Respiratory, a maker of airway management equipment, in 2003 and MEDIQ, a company that provides medical equipment outsourcing, asset management, and rentals to the health care industry, in 2004.

To focus on Hill-Rom and Batesville, Hillenbrand sold its Forethought Financial Services subsidiary in July 2004. As its name suggests, Forethought offered funeral prepayment products and services.

Rockwood retired in 2005; Peter Soderberg replaced him the following year.

In 2008, following a review of strategic alternatives, the company split itself in two, spinning off Batesville Casket into a separately, publicly traded company.

EXECUTIVES

Chairman: Rolf A. Classon, age 63
Vice Chairperson: Joanne C. Smith, age 49
President, CEO, and Director: John J. Greisch, age 54
SVP and CFO, Hillenbrand Industries and Hill-Rom: Gregory N. Miller, age 46, $897,126 total compensation
SVP; President, North America: Martha G. Aronson, age 42
SVP; President, International: Alejandro Infante
SVP Global Marketing and Chief Marketing Officer: Phillip Settimi
SVP and Chief Human Resources Officer: Perry Stuckey
SVP Corporate Affairs and Chief Legal Officer: Susan R. Lichtenstein, age 53
SVP North America Post-Acute Care and Information Technology, Hill-Rom: Kimberly K. Dennis, age 42
SVP, General Counsel, and Secretary: Patrick D. de Maynadier, age 49, $940,133 total compensation
SVP Global Supply Chain: Mark D. Baron, age 53
SVP Human Resources, Hillenbrand Industries and Hill-Rom: John H. Dickey, age 55
Group VP Care Continuum Services: Earl DeCarli, age 53
VP Global Product Platforms and CTO: Abel Ang, age 36
VP, Controller, and Chief Accounting Officer, Hillenbrand Industries and Hill-Rom: Richard G. Keller, age 48
VP Business Development and Strategy, Hillenbrand Industries and Hill-Rom: Michael J. Grippo, age 40
VP Investor Relations, Communications, and Global Brand Development, Hillenbrand Industries and Hill-Rom: Blair A. (Andy) Rieth Jr., age 52
Auditors: PricewaterhouseCoopers LLP

LOCATIONS

HQ: Hill-Rom Holdings, Inc.
1069 State Rte. 46 East, Batesville, IN 47006
Phone: 812-934-7777   **Fax:** 812-934-8189
Web: www.hill-rom.com/usa

2009 Sales

	$ mil.	% of total
US	1,067.7	77
Other countries	319.2	23
Total	**1,386.9**	**100**

PRODUCTS/OPERATIONS

2009 Sales

	$ mil.	% of total
North America acute care	791.6	57
International & surgical	398.8	29
North America post-acute care	200.8	14
Adjustments	(4.3)	—
Total	**1,386.9**	**100**

Selected Products and Services

Patient surfaces
  Hospital beds (TotalCare, TotalCare Bariatric)
  Surgical beds (VersaCare, CareAssist, AvantGuard, Evolution156)
  ER and transport beds
  Labor and delivery beds (Affinity)
  Long-term care beds (Hill-Rom, AvantGuard)
Health care information technology
  Clinical communication software (NaviCare)
  Maternal and fetal monitoring software (WatchChild)
Medical equipment management services (equipment rental and asset management)
Patient mobilization products
  Patient lifts (Liko)

Therapeutic products
  Airway clearance (The Vest)
  Pressure redistribution products (Acucair, Flexicair Eclipse, Silkair Overlay)
  Treatments for pressure sores and burns (Clinitron Rite Hite Air Fluidized Therapy System)
  Wound prevention products (Primeaire, AccuMax, Thermo Contour)

COMPETITORS

BGI (California)
Dukane Corporation
Freedom Medical
Gaymar
Getinge
Invacare
Joerns
Kinetic Concepts
Medline Industries
Rauland-Borg
SimplexGrinnell
Span-America Medical
Stryker
Sunrise Medical
Universal Hospital

HISTORICAL FINANCIALS

Company Type: Public

Income Statement

FYE: September 30

	REVENUE ($ mil.)	NET INCOME ($ mil.)	NET PROFIT MARGIN	EMPLOYEES
9/09	1,387	(405)	—	6,500
9/08	1,508	116	7.7%	6,800
9/07	2,024	191	9.4%	9,900
9/06	1,963	221	11.3%	9,300
9/05	1,938	(94)	—	9,800
Annual Growth	**(8.0%)**	**—**	**—**	**(9.8%)**

2009 Year-End Financials

Debt ratio: 16.4%
Return on equity: —
Cash ($ mil.): 171
Current ratio: 2.02
Long-term debt ($ mil.): 100
No. of shares (mil.): 63
Dividends
  Yield: 1.9%
  Payout: —
Market value ($ mil.): 1,383

Stock History

NYSE: HRC

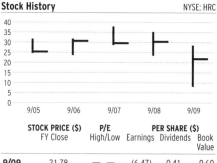

	STOCK PRICE ($) FY Close	P/E High/Low		PER SHARE ($) Earnings	Dividends	Book Value
9/09	21.78	—	—	(6.47)	0.41	9.60
9/08	30.31	19	13	1.85	0.67	17.05
9/07	29.58	12	9	3.07	1.14	20.12
9/06	30.64	9	7	3.59	1.13	17.82
9/05	25.30	—	—	(1.52)	1.12	15.18
Annual Growth	**(3.7%)**	**—**	**—**	**—**	**(22.2%)**	**(10.8%)**

Hilton Worldwide

If you need a bed for the night, Hilton Worldwide (formerly Hilton Hotels) has a few hundred thousand of them. The company is one of the world's largest hoteliers with a lodging empire that includes about 3,500 hotels and resorts in nearly 80 countries operating under such names as Doubletree, Embassy Suites, and Hampton, as well as its flagship Hilton brand. Many of its hotels serve the mid-market segment, though its Hilton and Conrad hotels offer full-service, upscale lodging. In addition, its Homewood Suites chain offers extended-stay services. The company franchises many of its hotels; it owns the Waldorf-Astoria and the New York Hilton. Hilton is owned by private equity firm The Blackstone Group.

With its extensive portfolio of brands, Hilton seeks to serve multiple segments within the lodging sector. Its largest chains, Hampton Inn and Hampton Inn & Suites, include about 1,600 locations and target mid-market travelers with moderately priced rooms and limited amenities. Nearly all its Hampton hotels are operated by franchisees or by the company under management contracts with third-party owners. At the other end of the scale, the company's Hilton and Conrad chains offer luxury services and distinctive locations, while its Waldorf-Astoria Collection is a prestigious collection of hotels inspired by the New York landmark. The company's Hilton Grand Vacations subsidiary operates about 50 time-share vacation resorts, with a concentration located in Florida.

Despite a challenging economic environment, the company is in the middle of a growth period as the global markets begin to improve. It has signed or approved some 280 hotel deals with more than 46,000 rooms, while its total pipeline includes more than 900 hotels with more than 129,000 rooms scheduled to open in the coming years.

Hilton has delayed the launch of another new brand, Denizen Hotels. The brand is designed to cater to globally conscious modern travelers, and the company had planned to operate Denizen as part of the company's Luxury & Lifestyle portfolio, which also includes the Waldorf Astoria, the Waldorf Astoria Collection, and Conrad Hotels & Resorts. However, development on Denizen Hotels hit a snag in 2009 following a lawsuit from rival Starwood Hotels & Resorts. The suit charges that Hilton stole confidential and proprietary documents and used that information to help create Denizen. Until a ruling is reached, the fate of Denizen remains unclear.

Another 2009 event for the company was the relocation of its corporate headquarters from Beverly Hills, California, to the Washington, DC, area. The move was prompted by a desire to tap into local real estate and hospitality expertise. (The DC area is also home to rival Marriott, as well as smaller players such as Choice Hotels International, Host Hotels & Resorts, and Interstate Hotels & Resorts.) Following the relocation, the company changed its name to Hilton Worldwide to better reflect its global operations.

Blackstone took the company private in 2007 through a $26 billion buyout that included about $6 billion in assumed debt. It was the largest private equity buyout in the hotel industry.

HISTORY

Conrad Hilton got his start in hotel management by renting out rooms in his family's New Mexico home. He served as a state legislator and started a bank before leaving for Texas in 1919, hoping to make his fortune in banking. Hilton was unable to shoulder the cost of purchasing a bank, however, but recognized a high demand for hotel rooms and made a quick change in strategy, buying his first hotel in Cisco, Texas. Over the next decade he bought seven more Texas hotels.

Hilton lost several properties during the Depression, but began rebuilding his empire soon thereafter through the purchase of hotels in California (1938), New Mexico (1939), and Mexico (1942). He even married starlet Zsa Zsa Gabor in 1942 (they later divorced, of course). Hilton Hotels Corporation was formed in 1946 and went public. The company bought New York's Waldorf-Astoria in 1949 (a hotel Hilton called "the greatest of them all") and opened its first European hotel in Madrid in 1953. Hilton paid $111 million for the 10-hotel Statler chain the following year.

Hilton took his company out of the overseas hotel business in 1964 by spinning off Hilton International and began franchising the following year to capitalize on the well-known Hilton name. Barron Hilton, Conrad's son, was appointed president in 1966 (he became chairman upon Conrad Hilton's death in 1979). Hilton bought two Las Vegas hotels (the Las Vegas Hilton and the Flamingo Hilton) in 1970 and launched its gaming division. The company returned to the international hotel business with Conrad International Hotels in 1982 and opened its first suite-only Hilton Suites hotel in 1989.

Hilton expanded its gaming operations in the 1990s, buying Bally's Casino Resort in Reno in 1992 and launching its first riverboat casino, the Hilton Queen of New Orleans, in 1994. Two years later it acquired all of Bally Entertainment, making it the largest gaming company in the world. Also that year, Stephen Bollenbach, the former Walt Disney CFO who had negotiated the $19 billion acquisition of Capital Cities/ABC, was named CEO — becoming the first nonfamily-member to run the company.

Hilton formed an alliance with Ladbroke Group in 1997 (later Hilton Group, owner of Hilton International and the rights to the Hilton name outside the US) to promote the Hilton brand worldwide. With a downturn in the gambling industry translating into sluggish results in Hilton's gaming segment, the company spun off its gaming interests as Park Place Entertainment (later Caesars Entertainment, now owned by Harrah's) later that year.

In 1999 Hilton made a massive acquisition with the $3.7 billion purchase of Promus Hotel Corp. In 2002 the company sold two Doubletree hotels and all 41 Red Lion locations to WestCoast Hospitality (now Red Lion Hotels).

Following an extended downturn in the hospitality business brought on by recession and post-9/11 fears about terrorism, Hilton began to invest in refurbishments for many of its properties and added about 150 locations in 2004.

Two years later the company re-unified the Hilton Hotels brand internationally by acquiring Hilton International from Hilton Group (now Ladbrokes) for about $5.7 billion.

In 2007 the company was acquired by The Blackstone Group, and Christopher J. Nassetta replaced Bollenbach as CEO. Hilton Hotels was renamed Hilton Worldwide in 2009.

EXECUTIVES

President and CEO: Christopher J. (Chris) Nassetta, age 47
EVP and CFO: Thomas C. (Tom) Kennedy, age 43
EVP; CEO, Americas and Global Brands: Thomas L. (Tom) Keltner, age 63
EVP and General Counsel: Richard M. (Rich) Lucas, age 45
EVP and Chief Human Resources Officer: Matthew W. (Matt) Schuyler, age 44
SVP Global Head Talent Management: Dottie Brienza
SVP Corporate Strategy and Treasurer: Kevin J. Jacobs
SVP Operations, East Region: Ted Ratcliff
SVP Government Affairs: Jonas E. Neihardt
SVP Global Corporate Communications: Ellen D. Gonda
SVP Global Online Services: Chuck Sullivan, age 54
VP Corporate Chef, Americas: Steven Peterson
VP Food and Beverage, Americas: Doug Zeif
VP Global Corporate Communications: Aaron C. Radelet
CIO: Robert J. (Rob) Webb, age 40
Global Head, Luxury and Lifestyle Brands: John T. A. Vanderslice, age 49
Global Head Architecture, Design, and Construction; Interim Head of Real Estate: Matthew L. Richardson
President, Hilton Grand Vacations: Mark Wang
President, Global Brands and Commercial Services: Paul Brown
President, Global Operations; Interim Head Development: Ian R. Carter, age 48
Auditors: Ernst & Young LLP

LOCATIONS

HQ: Hilton Worldwide
  7930 Jones Branch Dr., Ste. 1100
  McLean, VA 22102
Phone: 703-883-1000
Web: www.hiltonworldwide.com

PRODUCTS/OPERATIONS

Selected Brands

Conrad Hotels & Resorts
Doubletree
Embassy Suites Hotels
Hampton Inn
Hampton Inn & Suites
Hilton
Hilton Garden Inn
Hilton Grand Vacations Club
Homewood Suites by Hilton

Selected Owned Hotels

Chicago's Palmer House Hilton
The Hilton Hawaiian Village on Waikiki Beach
Hilton San Francisco on Union Square
The New York Hilton
The Waldorf Astoria

COMPETITORS

Accor
Best Western
Carlson Hotels
Choice Hotels
Fairmont Raffles
Four Seasons Hotels
Hyatt
InterContinental Hotels
Interstate Hotels
Loews
Marriott
Omni Hotels
Red Lion Hotels
Ritz-Carlton
Starwood Hotels & Resorts
Wyndham Worldwide

HISTORICAL FINANCIALS

Company Type: Private

Income Statement

FYE: December 31

	ESTIMATED REVENUE ($ mil.)	NET INCOME ($ mil.)	NET PROFIT MARGIN	EMPLOYEES
12/08	7,770	—	—	130,000
12/07	8,090	—	—	135,000
Annual Growth	(4.0%)	—	—	(3.7%)

Revenue History

```
9,000
8,000
7,000
6,000
5,000
4,000
3,000
2,000
1,000
   0
     12/04   12/05   12/06   12/07   12/08
```

H. J. Heinz Company

Forget those original 57 varieties. H. J. Heinz now has thousands of products. One of the world's largest food companies, Heinz produces ketchup and other condiments, soups, sauces, frozen foods, beans, pasta meals, infant food, and other processed food products. Its flagship product is ketchup, of course, and the company dominates the US ketchup market. Heinz's customers include food retailers, the foodservice industry, and the US military. Its leading brands include the aforementioned ketchup, Lea & Perrins Worcestershire sauce, Classico pasta sauces, Ore-Ida frozen potatoes, and its Boston Market, T.G.I. Friday's, and Weight Watchers frozen foods.

Heinz's products are in mature markets in the US. However, it continues to see success with its name-brand food products. The company's top 15 brands each bring in more that $100 million in yearly sales. Wal-Mart is largest customer, representing 11% of company sales in 2010.

And, as always, Heinz pursues acquisitions. The company announced in 2010 that it is scouting for baby-food purchases in emerging markets, including China and India. In another emerging-market move, in 2010 the company agreed to acquire Chinese soy-sauce maker Foodstar from private-equity firm Transpac Industrial Holding.

In 2009 it took full ownership of Egyptian condiments and sauces maker Cairo Food Industries, strengthening its operations in Egypt and the Middle East. During 2008 it acquired the license to the Cottee's and Rose's branded jams, jellies and toppings business in Australia and New Zealand. It also bought the remaining interest in its Shanghai LongFong Foods operation. The company added the Wyko sauce business in the Netherlands in 2008 as well. Later that year it purchased Benedicta, a French manufacturer of table-top sauces, mayonnaises, and salad dressings. It also acquired Golden Circle, Australian maker of canned foods, juices, and baby food that year. In the UK it sold its noncore private-label frozen dessert operations to Polestar Foods. The sale included the Heinz, Ross, American Dream, and Devonshire brands and a co-packing agreement to produce Weight Watchers desserts in the UK. It also sold off frozen hors d'oeuvres unit, Appetizers And.

Capital Research and Management Company owns 11% of the company; billionaire financier and corporate raider Nelson Peltz's Trian Fund owns almost 6%.

HISTORY

In 1852, 8-year-old Henry J. Heinz started selling produce from the family garden to neighbors in Sharpsburg, Pennsylvania. The young entrepreneur formed a partnership with his friend L. C. Noble in 1869, bottling horseradish sauce in clear glass, but the business went bankrupt in 1875. The following year, with the help of his brother John and his cousin Frederick, Heinz created F. & J. Heinz; the enterprise developed ketchup (1876) and sweet pickles (1880). He gained financial control of the firm in 1888 and changed the name to the H. J. Heinz Company.

Heinz developed a reputation as an advertising and marketing genius. He introduced pickle pins, a popular promotion at the 1893 Chicago World's Fair; coined the catchy "57 Varieties" slogan in 1897 (despite already having 60 products); and in 1900 raised New York City's first large electric advertising sign (a 40-ft. pickle). By 1905 Heinz was manufacturing food products in the UK.

After Heinz's death in 1919 the business, under the direction of his son and later his grandson, continued to rely on its traditional product lines for the next four decades, although some new ones were introduced, such as baby food in 1931. The company went public in 1946.

Heinz changed its strategy in 1958 when it made its first acquisition, a Dutch food processor. Major purchases that followed included Star-Kist (tuna and pet food, 1963) and Ore-Ida (potatoes, 1965). In 1966 Burt Gookin became CEO, the first nonfamily-member to hold that position.

The company bought Weight Watchers in 1978. The next year former rugby star Anthony O'Reilly became the company's fifth CEO. He intensified the focus on international expansion and presided over a string of acquisitions throughout the 1980s. O'Reilly became chairman in 1987.

Acquisitions in the 1990s included Wattie's Limited (New Zealand, 1992); Borden's foodservice business (1994); and pet food divisions from Quaker Oats (1995). However, faced with weak sales growth in its stable markets, in 1997 Heinz began shedding domestic units as it made global acquisitions. It sold its Ore-Ida foodservice operations (to McCain Foods, 1997) and its bakery products division (to Pillsbury, 1998).

William Johnson, who had turned around stagnant brands such as 9-Lives, succeeded O'Reilly as CEO in 1998. In 1999 Heinz announced a restructuring intended to eliminate jobs and close or sell about 20 factories over several years. Heinz sold the diet business of Weight Watchers that year.

In 2000 O'Reilly retired and Johnson was named chairman. In an effort to focus on its core food products (sauces, ketchup, frozen foods), Heinz spun off a number of its North American businesses to Del Monte Foods in 2002. The all-stock transaction included the company's pet food (Kibbles 'n Bits) and snacks, tuna (StarKist), private-label soup, and infant feeding (Nature's Goodness) businesses.

Heinz acquired the HP Foods Group from Groupe Danone in 2005. The HP group (for which Heinz paid $820 million in cash) included Lea & Perrins, HP, and Amoy Asian sauces.

In 2006 Heinz sold its European seafood business to Lehman Brothers Merchant Banking for $506 million. Continuing to shed noncore operations, Heinz sold its UK chilled prepared foods business (including the Linda McCartney brand of frozen vegetarian entrees) to Hain Celestial.

Heinz announced changes in 2006 to its corporate governance policy as a result of its proxy battle with dissident shareholders led by Peltz's Trian Fund. The changes, which Heinz disclosed after discussions with CalPERS and other large Heinz shareholders, included adding two independent board members and the adoption of a majority voting process with regard to the election of directors.

After many Heinz and Trian press-release statements back and forth and much press surrounding the bitter struggle between Peltz and Heinz leadership, it was announced that Heinz's board elected to add two of Trian's five nominees to its board: Peltz and Michael Weinstein.

In 2007 the company acquired Canadian maker of dressings and sauces Renée's Gourmet Foods.

EXECUTIVES

Chairman, President, and CEO:
William R. (Bill) Johnson, age 61,
$24,398,056 total compensation

EVP and CFO: Arthur B. (Art) Winkleblack, age 53,
$4,059,293 total compensation

EVP; President and CEO, Heinz Europe:
David C. (Dave) Moran, age 52,
$4,507,163 total compensation

EVP; President and CEO, Heinz North America:
C. Scott O'Hara, age 50, $4,014,829 total compensation

EVP Rest of World, Global Enterprise Risk Management, and Global Infant/Nutrition:
Michael D. (Mike) Milone, age 54,
$3,901,815 total compensation

EVP and General Counsel: Theodore N. (Ted) Bobby,
age 59

EVP, Asia/Pacific: Christopher (Chris) Warmoth, age 51

SVP and Chief Supply Chain Officer:
Robert (Bob) Ostryniec

SVP Finance and Corporate Controller:
Edward J. (Ed) McMenamin, age 54

SVP, CIO, and Global Program Management Officer:
Karen L. Alber, age 46

SVP Corporate Audit: Diane B. Owen, age 54

SVP Business Development: Mitchell A. (Mitch) Ring,
age 58

SVP Investor Relations: Margaret R. (Meg) Nollen
VP and Chief Strategy Officer: Daniel G. (Dan) Milich
VP and Chief People Officer: Steve Clark, age 42
VP Corporate Governance, Compliance, Ethics:
John Kraus

VP Corporate and Government Affairs: Michael Mullen,
age 41

President, US Foodservice: Brendan Foley
President, Global Infant/Nutrition: Stefano Clini
Global Processes and Business Enablement Officer:
Tony Cassavechia

Corporate Secretary: Rene Biedzinski
Senior Manager Public Relations: Jessica Jackson
Auditors: PricewaterhouseCoopers LLP

LOCATIONS

HQ: H. J. Heinz Company
  1 PPG Place, Ste. 3100, Pittsburgh, PA 15222
Phone: 412-456-5700   **Fax:** 412-456-6128
Web: www.heinz.com

2010 Sales

	$ mil.	% of total
US	3,993.7	38
UK	1,519.3	14
Other	4,982.0	48
Total	**10,495.0**	**100**

PRODUCTS/OPERATIONS

2010 Sales

	$ mil.	% of total
Ketchups & sauces	4,446.9	42
Meals & snacks	4,290.0	41
Infant/nutrition	1,158.0	11
Other	600.1	6
Total	**10,495.0**	**100**

Selected North American Brands

Alden Merrell
Arthur's Fresh
Bagel Bites
Bella Rossa
Boston Market (licensed)
Bravo
Catelli (licensed)
Chef Francisco
Classico
Delimex
Diana
Dianne's
Escalon
Heinz Bell 'Orto
Heinz
HP
Jack Daniel's (licensed)
Lea & Perrins
Nancy's
Ore-Ida
Poppers
PPI
Quality Chef Foods
Renee's Gourmet
Tater Tots
T.G.I. Friday's (licensed)
Todd's
Truesoups
Weight Watchers (licensed)
Wyler's

COMPETITORS

Associated British Foods	Kraft Foods
B&G Foods	La Doria
Babylicious	Lance Snacks
Barilla	McIlhenny
Beech-Nut	Nestlé
Bellisio Foods	New Dragon
Campbell Soup	NutriSystem
COFCO	Otis Spunkmeyer
ConAgra	Pepperidge Farm
Del Monte Foods	PepsiCo
Frito-Lay	Ralcorp
Gerber Products	Sara Lee
Hain Celestial	Slim-Fast
Indofood	Smucker
J & J Snack Foods	Uni-President
Jenny Craig	URC
John Sanfilippo & Son	

HISTORICAL FINANCIALS

Company Type: Public

Income Statement

FYE: Wednesday nearest April 30

	REVENUE ($ mil.)	NET INCOME ($ mil.)	NET PROFIT MARGIN	EMPLOYEES
4/10	10,495	882	8.4%	29,600
4/09	10,148	923	9.1%	32,500
4/08	10,071	845	8.4%	32,500
4/07	9,002	786	8.7%	33,000
4/06	8,643	646	7.5%	36,000
Annual Growth	**5.0%**	**8.1%**	**—**	**(4.8%)**

2010 Year-End Financials

Debt ratio: 241.1%
Return on equity: 56.7%
Cash ($ mil.): 483
Current ratio: 1.40
Long-term debt ($ mil.): 4,559
No. of shares (mil.): 318
Dividends
Yield: 3.6%
Payout: 62.0%
Market value ($ mil.): 14,907

Stock History

NYSE: HNZ

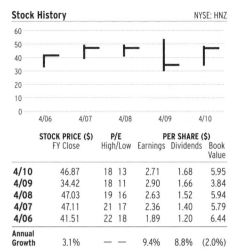

	STOCK PRICE ($) FY Close	P/E High/Low		PER SHARE ($) Earnings	Dividends	Book Value
4/10	46.87	18	13	2.71	1.68	5.95
4/09	34.42	18	11	2.90	1.66	3.84
4/08	47.03	19	16	2.63	1.52	5.94
4/07	47.11	21	17	2.36	1.40	5.79
4/06	41.51	22	18	1.89	1.20	6.44
Annual Growth	**3.1%**	**—**	**—**	**9.4%**	**8.8%**	**(2.0%)**

HNI Corporation

Tired of your office furniture? HNI can supply you with replacements, along with a fireplace to burn the old set. The company is a leading manufacturer of office furniture in the US, and its brand portfolio includes HON, Allsteel, Gunlocke, Maxon, Paoli, and HBF, among others. Products are marketed to furniture dealers, wholesalers, and retail superstores, including OfficeMax, Office Depot, and Staples. (The furniture division generates about 80% of sales.) HNI's Hearth & Home Technologies unit is one of the largest US makers of wood- and gas-burning fireplaces for the home. The company has distribution partners in more than 50 countries, but the majority of its products are sold in Canada and the US.

Along with a tough economic climate worldwide, HNI in recent years has been hit by a decline in demand for furniture as a result of rising office vacancies and corporate downsizing. Revenues have been on a downward path since reaching their peak of nearly $2.7 billion in 2006.

To compensate for the decline in business, HNI has been restructuring its operations and selling off properties. In 2009 the company transferred production from its plant in Iowa to other existing hearth products manufacturing plants; it then closed several distribution centers and shifted their work to the Iowa facility. Also that year HNI sold a facility in Minnesota and a corporate airplane. In 2008 the firm sold a manufacturing center in Virginia. The sales in 2008 and 2009 yielded about $10 million in proceeds, which HNI used to pay down its debt. Going forward, the company plans to continue reducing its cost structure as it works to grow through the introduction of new products and focus on customer satisfaction.

Before interest in its offerings took a dip, HNI had been expanding its operations through acquisitions. In 2008 it acquired Hickory Business Furniture (HBF) from Furniture Brands International. HBF's brand recognition among interior designers and emphasis on new products has strengthened HNI's contract business amid volatile economic conditions.

State Farm Insurance Companies owns more than 15% of the company.

HISTORY

Friends Maxwell Stanley, Clement Hanson, and Wood Miller founded The Home-O-Nize Co. (a name that suggested "modernize" and "economize") in 1944, planning to make home freezers and steel kitchen cabinets. These two products were never made, however, because of a steel shortage.

The first Home-O-Nize product was an aluminum hood used in the installation of natural gas systems. More important than the aluminum hood was the aluminum scrap left behind, which the company made into beverage coasters. These coasters, which could be imprinted with a company's name, were sold to businesses to give out as gifts. Home-O-Nize also transformed the aluminum scraps into boxes for file cards and, due to favorable response, decided to plunge into the office products business.

The move began in earnest in 1951, in an effort dramatically labeled "Operation Independence Home-O-Nize." The program was successful, and in 1952 the company started an unbroken string of profitable years. Helping this streak were such products as Unifile, a file cabinet that featured a single key that would lock all drawers simultaneously (1953). Home-O-Nize added cabinets, coat racks, and desks to its product line during this time and began marking all its products with the "H-O-N" label. Miller retired in 1958.

Home-O-Nize grew during the 1960s under the control of Stanley Howe, a Home-O-Nize employee since 1948. Howe had been appointed president in 1964 and made the company a national manufacturer by purchasing a plant in Georgia in 1967. The firm changed its name to HON INDUSTRIES the next year. Hanson left the company in 1969.

HON INDUSTRIES continued its expansion by purchasing California-based Holga Metal Products in 1971. Acquiring facilities in Pennsylvania and the opening of a plant in Virginia the next year gave HON INDUSTRIES a considerable presence on both US coasts. Howe replaced founder Maxwell Stanley as CEO in 1979.

In 1981 HON INDUSTRIES moved into the fireplace market by acquiring Heatilator, a leading brand of prefabricated fireplaces. By 1987, four decades after shipping its first product, HON INDUSTRIES had become a *FORTUNE* 500 company that many regarded as the most efficient in the making of office furniture. (It could produce a desk a minute and a chair every 20 seconds.) HON INDUSTRIES acquired Gunlocke, a maker of wooden office furniture, in 1989.

The rise of the office products superstore at the start of the 1990s did not go unnoticed by the company, which quickly positioned itself as a supplier to these businesses. Yet no action could spare HON INDUSTRIES from the office supply bust that occurred soon afterward, as oversupply and a lagging national economy dragged the industry downward.

Jack Michaels became the new CEO in 1991 as the company's sales dropped for the first time in decades. It adapted by investing in new products, and by 1992 sales were climbing again. In 1996 HON INDUSTRIES acquired rival fireplace maker Heat-N-Glo, which it merged with Heatilator to form Hearth Technologies. The next year it acquired three furniture makers, including Allsteel. In 1999 HON INDUSTRIES closed three plants to cut costs.

The company acquired hearth products distributors American Fireplace Company and the Allied Group in 2000, and wood case goods manufacturer Paoli (2004).

HON INDUSTRIES has been recognized repeatedly for its excellence; it was twice named as one of the "400 Best Big Companies in America" by *Forbes* magazine (2000, 2001) and was honored as the most admired company in the furniture industry by *FORTUNE* magazine (2003).

In 2004 the company changed its name to HNI in an attempt to reduce confusion between itself (HON INDUSTRIES Inc.) and its largest subsidiary (The HON Company). Its 2004 purchases included Paoli (wood case goods and seating, from Klaussner Furniture), Edward George (fireplace and stone products), and Omni Remanufacturing (panel systems).

Early in 2006 the company acquired Lamex, a Chinese office furniture manufacturer. Other acquisitions in 2006 included an office furniture services company, an office furniture dealer, and a manufacturer of fireplace facings.

Since 2007 the company has sold a corporate airplane and office furniture manufacturing centers in Virginia and Mexico.

EXECUTIVES

Chairman, President, and CEO:
Stanley A. (Stan) Askren, age 49,
$2,846,663 total compensation
EVP; President, Hearth and Home Technologies:
Bradley D. (Brad) Determan, age 48,
$874,472 total compensation
EVP; President, HNI International: Marco V. Molinari,
age 50, $978,793 total compensation
EVP; President, The HON Company:
Jerald K. (Jerry) Dittmer, age 52,
$1,230,901 total compensation
VP and CFO: Kurt A. Tjaden, age 46,
$1,056,866 total compensation
VP Investor Relations and Treasurer: Kelly J. McGriff
VP, General Counsel, and Secretary: Steven M. Bradford
VP and CIO: Douglas L. Jones, age 51
VP Corporate Marketing and E-Commerce:
Jean M. Reynolds, age 52
VP Manufacturing, Seating, and Woodcase Goods:
Timothy R. Summers, age 44
VP Member and Community Relations: Gary L. Carlson,
age 59
VP Financial Reporting: Tamara S. Feldman, age 49
President, HBF: Charlie Bell
President, Maxon Furniture:
Redus Woodrow (Woody) Brooks
President, Allsteel: Jeffrey D. Lorenger, age 42
President, The Gunlocke Company:
Donald T. (Don) Mead
President, Paoli: Brandon Sieben
President, Omni Workspace Company:
Timothy J. Anderson
Auditors: PricewaterhouseCoopers LLP

LOCATIONS

HQ: HNI Corporation
408 E. 2nd St., Muscatine, IA 52761
Phone: 563-272-7400   **Fax:** 563-272-7655
Web: www.hnicorp.com

PRODUCTS/OPERATIONS

2009 Sales

	$ mil.	% of total
Office furniture	1,370.2	83
Hearth products	286.1	17
Total	**1,656.3**	**100**

Selected Products

Office furniture
  Desks and related products (tables, bookcases, and credenzas)
  Office systems (modular and moveable workspaces)
  Seating (task, executive, conference/training, and side chairs)
  Storage (filing cabinets and pedestals)

Hearth products
  Accessories
  Fireplace inserts
  Fireplaces and stoves (wood, electric, gas and pellet)
  Gas logs

Selected Subsidiaries

Allsteel Inc. (office furniture)
Maxon Furniture Inc. (panel systems products and specialized services)
The Gunlocke Company (high-quality wood office furniture)
Hearth & Home Technologies Inc. (fireplaces and other hearth products)
Hickory Business Furniture (upholstered seating and other office furniture)
The HON Company (value-priced office furniture)
Omni Workspace Company (manufacturing services)
Paoli Inc. (wood case goods, modular desks, conference products, seating)

COMPETITORS

ABCO Office Furniture
Chromcraft Revington
Global Group
Haworth, Inc.
Herman Miller
KI
Kimball International
Knoll, Inc.
Lennox
Steelcase
Teknion
Virco Mfg.

HISTORICAL FINANCIALS

Company Type: Public

Income Statement			FYE: Saturday nearest December 31	
	REVENUE ($ mil.)	NET INCOME ($ mil.)	NET PROFIT MARGIN	EMPLOYEES
12/09	1,656	(6)	—	8,700
12/08	2,478	46	1.8%	12,200
12/07	2,571	120	4.7%	13,300
12/06	2,680	123	4.6%	14,200
12/05	2,451	137	5.6%	11,304
Annual Growth	**(9.3%)**	**—**	**—**	**(6.3%)**

2009 Year-End Financials

Debt ratio: 47.7%
Return on equity: —
Cash ($ mil.): 87
Current ratio: 1.20
Long-term debt ($ mil.): 200
No. of shares (mil.): 45
Dividends
  Yield: 3.1%
  Payout: —
Market value ($ mil.): 1,244

Stock History

NYSE: HNI

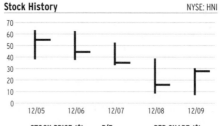

	STOCK PRICE ($) FY Close	P/E High/Low		PER SHARE ($) Earnings	Dividends	Book Value
12/09	27.63	—	—	(0.14)	0.86	9.31
12/08	15.84	37	9	1.02	0.86	9.97
12/07	35.06	20	13	2.57	0.78	10.19
12/06	44.41	25	16	2.45	0.72	11.01
12/05	54.93	25	16	2.50	0.62	13.19
Annual Growth	**(15.8%)**	**—**	**—**	**—**	**8.5%**	**(8.3%)**

Holly Corporation

Holly Corporation refines crude oil to produce gasoline, diesel fuel, and jet fuel, which it sells in the southwestern US, northern Mexico, and Montana. Subsidiary Navajo Refining (New Mexico) has a refining capacity of 100,000 barrels a day; Holly's Woods Cross refinery in Utah, 31,000 barrels; and its Tulsa refinery, 125,000 barrels. It owns a 34% stake in Holly Energy Partners, which has 960 miles of crude oil pipelines located primarily in West Texas and New Mexico, and 2,500 miles of petroleum product pipelines. Holly also owns and operates Holly Asphalt Company, which manufactures and markets asphalt products from various terminals in Arizona and New Mexico.

Holly Corporation buys crude from independents or on the spot market. Its growth strategy includes refinery expansion and selective acquisitions of complementary assets.

Expanding its refining assets to increase market share, in 2009 the company bought Sunoco's 85,000-barrels-per-day Tulsa refinery. Building the largest refinery complex in the Midcontinent, in 2009 the company acquired Sinclair Oil's 75,000-barrels-per-day Tulsa refinery for $128.5 million.

Despite increased oil production, the global recession and low commodity prices resulted in a downturn in Holly's revenues in 2009.

To free up cash, in 2008 it sold 136 miles of crude oil trunk lines and some tankage assets to Holly Energy Partners for $180 million.

HISTORY

Holly was founded in 1947 as General Appliance Corp. to process other companies' crude oil; the current name was adopted in 1952. Holly grew with the number of gas-guzzling cars in the 1950s and 1960s, and in the 1970s it developed its Navajo refinery in New Mexico. In 1981 Holly began producing higher-grade gasoline and started an asphalt company at Navajo.

In 1984 Holly became a partner in Montana Refining and later bought the entire business. It upgraded the Navajo refinery in the early 1990s to meet the demand for unleaded gasoline. In 1995 Amoco, Mapco, and Holly formed a joint venture, the 265-mile Rio Grande Pipeline (completed in 1997), to transport natural gas liquids to Mexico.

Also in 1997 FINA and Holly allied to expand and use Holly's pipelines in the southwestern US. A proposed merger with another southwestern refiner, Giant Industries, died in 1998 because of federal antitrust concerns and a billion-dollar lawsuit filed against Holly by Longhorn Partners Pipeline. Court papers revealed in 2000 that Holly had paid $4 million to fight Longhorn's request for a permit to transport gasoline in its Houston-to-El Paso pipeline. The permit, if approved, would compete with Holly's own interests in western Texas.

Later in 2000 Holly cut its workforce by about 10%, mostly at Navajo Refining. The following year Navajo Refining secured a $122 million contract to provide JP-8 jet fuel to the Defense Department.

In a move to expand its production capacity, in 2003 Holly acquired ConocoPhillips' Woods Cross refinery and related assets for $25 million. Holly agreed to be acquired by Frontier Oil for about $450 million that year, but the companies terminated the agreement, and litigation between the parties resulted.

In 2004 the company spun off its Navajo refinery-related refined petroleum pipeline and other distribution assets as Holly Energy Partners, L.P.; it retained a 45% interest.

In 2005 the Delaware Chancery Court ruled that Frontier Oil had not proved that Holly had repudiated the merger agreement, and awarded Frontier Oil only $1 in damages. Also that year, Holly acquired the remaining 51% of NK Asphalt Producers that it did not already own. The company sold its intermediate feedstock pipelines connecting two refining facilities in Lovington and Artesia, New Mexico, to Holly Energy Partners for $81.5 million.

EXECUTIVES

Chairman and CEO, Holly Corporation, Holly Logistic Services, and Holly Refining & Marketing:
Matthew P. (Matt) Clifton, age 58,
$4,990,342 total compensation
President, Holly Corporation and Holly Refining & Marketing: David L. Lamp, age 52,
$2,141,750 total compensation
President, Holly Energy Partners and Holly Logistic Services: David G. Blair, age 51
SVP and CFO, Holly Corporation, Holly Logistic Services, and Holly Refining & Marketing:
Bruce R. Shaw, age 42, $817,372 total compensation
SVP Refinery Operations, Holly Corporation and Holly Refining & Marketing: Gary B. Fuller
SVP Supply and Marketing, Holly Corporation and Holly Refining & Marketing: George J. Damiris, age 50,
$940,077 total compensation
VP, General Counsel, and Secretary, Holly Corporation, Holly Refining & Marketing Company, and Holly Logistic Services: Denise C. McWatters, age 50,
$649,964 total compensation
VP Information Technology: Nellson D. Burns
VP and Treasurer, Holly Corporation, Holly Logistic Services, and Holly Refining & Marketing:
Stephen D. Wise
VP Investor Relations, Holly Corporation and Holly Logistic Services: M. Neale Hickerson, age 57
VP Human Resources, Holly Corporation, Holly Refining & Marketing, and Holly Logistic Services:
Nancy F. Hartmann
Auditors: Ernst & Young LLP

LOCATIONS

HQ: Holly Corporation
100 Crescent Ct., Ste. 1600, Dallas, TX 75201
Phone: 214-871-3555   **Fax:** 214-871-3560
Web: www.hollycorp.com

PRODUCTS/OPERATIONS

2009 Sales

	$ mil.	% of total
Refining	4,786.9	97
HEP	146.6	3
Corporate & other	2.3	—
Adjustments	(101.5)	—
Total	**4,834.3**	**100**

Selected Subsidiaries

Black Eagle, Inc.
Holly Logistics
    Holly Energy Partners, L.P (34%)
Holly Petroleum, Inc.
Navajo Corp.
Navajo Holdings, Inc.
Navajo Pipeline Co.
    Navajo Southern, Inc.
Navajo Refining Co.
    Lorefco, Inc.
        Lea Refining Co.
    Navajo Northern, Inc.
    Navajo Western Asphalt Co.
Woods Cross Refining Co., L.L.C.

COMPETITORS

BP	Sunoco
Crown Central	Tesoro
Exxon Mobil	Valero Energy
George Warren	Western Refining, Inc.
Marathon Petroleum	Williams Companies

HISTORICAL FINANCIALS

Company Type: Public

Income Statement

	REVENUE ($ mil.)	NET INCOME ($ mil.)	NET PROFIT MARGIN	EMPLOYEES
12/09	4,834	53	1.1%	1,632
12/08	5,868	121	2.1%	978
12/07	4,792	334	7.0%	909
12/06	4,023	267	6.6%	859
12/05	3,213	167	5.2%	881
Annual Growth	**10.8%**	**(24.8%)**	**—**	**16.7%**

FYE: December 31

2009 Year-End Financials

Debt ratio: 114.3%   No. of shares (mil.): 53
Return on equity: 9.2%   Dividends
Cash ($ mil.): 125   Yield: 2.3%
Current ratio: 1.25   Payout: 153.8%
Long-term debt ($ mil.): 707 Market value ($ mil.): 1,364

Stock History

NYSE: HOC

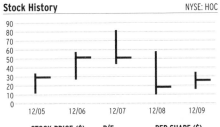

	STOCK PRICE ($) FY Close	P/E High/Low		PER SHARE ($) Earnings	Dividends	Book Value
12/09	25.63	86	43	0.39	0.60	11.63
12/08	18.23	24	5	2.38	0.60	10.18
12/07	50.89	13	8	5.98	0.46	11.16
12/06	51.40	12	6	4.58	0.29	8.76
12/05	29.43	12	5	2.65	0.19	7.09
Annual Growth	**(3.4%)**	**—**	**—**	**(38.1%)**	**33.3%**	**13.2%**

Hologic, Inc.

With its mammography and breast biopsy systems, Hologic puts the squeeze on women to help save their lives. Its mammography products include film-based and digital systems, as well as the workstations and computer-aided detection systems that interpret the images. Additional products include X-ray and ultrasound bone densitometers, which detect and monitor osteoporosis, and breast biopsy collection systems (branded ATEC) sold by its Suros division. Hologic's non-imaging products include tests to screen for cervical cancer. The company markets its products to hospitals and clinical labs.

Hologic's lead products include the Selenia breast imaging system, the Discovery and Explorer bone imaging systems, and the ThinPrep cervical cancer screening system, which is marketed as a better alternative to the conventional

Pap smear. Other women's health products include the NovaSure System to treat excessive menstrual bleeding, as well as a preterm birth diagnostic called the FullTerm Fetal Fibronectin Test.

To further build up its breast imaging product line, the company acquired Toronto-based Sentinelle Medical in 2010. The deal brought with it Sentinelle's magnetic resonance imaging technology used in detecting breast cancer.

Hologic's biggest jump in growth came when it paid more than $6 billion in 2007 to purchase its larger neighbor Cytyc. The two companies had discussed a tie-up off and on for a number of years; when they finally joined forces it created a women's health care behemoth.

Along with expanding its product lines, Hologic made the acquisition to take advantage of cross-selling opportunities that arose from combining the two companies' complementary product lines. Cytyc added products in the areas of cervical cancer screening, prenatal diagnostics, and breast cancer treatment to Hologic's existing portfolio of breast health and osteoporosis products.

In a boost to its gynecological surgical products line, in 2009 the company unveiled its FDA-approved Adiana system for permanent contraception for women. Introduced as an alternative to tubal ligation, the system allows doctors to perform the procedure with only local anesthesia.

In addition to its women's health line, Hologic manufactures and sells photoconductor materials used in electrophotographic devices and small fluoroscopic imaging systems used by orthopedic surgeons on extremities such as hands, feet, and knees. The company is also the US distributor of Esaote's MRI systems designed for use on extremities.

In mid-2008 the company further expanded its diagnostic operations by acquiring Third Wave Technologies for $580 million. The purchase of Third Wave added diagnostics for conditions such as hepatitis C and cystic fibrosis; it also contributed women's health tests for cervical cancer and human papillomavirus (HPV) that bolster Hologic's core product offerings.

HISTORY

In 1981 S. David Ellenbogen and Jay Stein founded Diagnostic Technology (DTI) and developed a digital angiography product. A Squibb subsidiary bought DTI in 1982, and three years later, Ellenbogen and Stein founded Hologic.

The firm shipped its first bone scanner in 1987 and went public in 1990. Increased global focus on women's health fueled Hologic's growth in 1994. That year it penetrated the Latin American and Japanese markets, and Medicare patients started receiving reimbursement for bone density examinations. Also in 1994 Hologic partnered with Serex to develop a test to monitor biochemical indicators of bone loss (Ostex International joined the effort in 1996).

Targeting private practices requiring less-expensive equipment, Hologic bought Walker Magnetic Group's ultrasound bone analyzer business and that of European rival Sophia Medical Systems in 1995. That year it purchased FluoroScan Imaging Systems, a maker of X-ray equipment.

In 1998 the company introduced its Sahara Clinical Bone Sonometer in the US. In 1999 Hologic acquired Direct Radiography, another X-ray equipment maker. That year Fleet Business Credit, which had an agreement with Hologic

445

through which it purchased bone densitometers and then leased them to physicians, pulled out of the partnership; sales sank, and Hologic filed a lawsuit against Fleet to recoup losses. Also in 1999 Hologic sold its Medical Data Management division to focus on core operations.

In 2000 the company bought the US operations of medical imaging company Trex Medical Corporation. This acquisition added the Lorad-brand line of mammography and breast biopsy systems, to Hologic's operations. The acquisition was costly, and, to recover, Hologic implemented a restructuring plan in 2001 that led to a reduction of the workforce, a reduction of operating expenses, and phasing out unprofitable units. The company closed its conventional X-ray equipment manufacturing facility in Littleton, Massachusetts, and relocated some of the product lines and personnel to Bedford, Massachusetts.

With a renewed appetite for growth, in 2005 Hologic resumed its acquisition strategy, starting with the purchase of Fischer Imaging's SenoScan digital mammography and MammoTest stereotactic breast biopsy systems for $32 million. The following year it acquired R2 Technology for $220 million to gain that company's computer-aided detection (CAD) technology. Also in 2006 it acquired breast biopsy and tissue excision device producer Suros Surgical Systems for $240 million.

EXECUTIVES

Chairman: John W. (Jack) Cumming, age 64, $8,176,095 total compensation
Chairman Emeritus, SVP, and CTO: Jay A. Stein, age 67, $1,590,098 total compensation
CEO and Director: Robert A. (Rob) Cascella, age 55, $4,586,431 total compensation
EVP Finance and Administration, CFO, Treasurer, Secretary, and Director: Glenn P. Muir, age 50, $2,691,518 total compensation
SVP and Chief Accounting Officer: Robert H. Lavallee
SVP Business Development: Thomas Umbel
SVP Human Resources: David J. Brady, age 50
SVP Customer Service: Roger D. Mills
SVP and CIO: David M. Rudzinsky
SVP Skeletal Health: William Healy
SVP Sales and Strategic Accounts: John R. Pekarsky, age 56
SVP Diagnostics & GYN Surgical International Products: Douglas Ikeda
SVP and General Manager, International: David P. Harding
SVP and and General Manager, GYN Surgical Products: Steven Williamson, age 37
SVP GYN Surgical: Stuart A. (Tony) Kingsley, age 46
SVP International Sales: Mark A. Duerst
SVP and and General Manager, Breast Health: Peter K. Soltani, age 49
SVP, General Counsel, and Secretary: Mark J. Casey, age 46
VP and Corporate Controller: Karleen Oberton
VP Investor Relations: Deborah R. Gordon
Auditors: Ernst & Young LLP

LOCATIONS

HQ: Hologic, Inc.
35 Crosby Dr., Bedford, MA 01730
Phone: 781-999-7300   **Fax:** 781-280-0669
Web: www.hologic.com

2009 Sales

	% of total
US	80
Europe	12
Asia	4
Other regions	4
Total	**100**

PRODUCTS/OPERATIONS

2009 Sales

	$ mil.	% of total
Breast Health	728.8	44
Diagnostics	547.9	34
GYN Surgical	264.9	16
Skeletal Health	95.4	6
Total	**1,637.0**	**100**

Selected Products

Breast Health
ATEC (Automated Tissue Excision and Collection, breast biopsy system)
Lorad Affinity (mammography system)
Lorad M-IV (mammography system)
MammoPad (mammography breast cushion)
MammoSite (breast cancer radiation therapy system)
Selenia (full field digital mammography system)
StereoLoc (stereotactic breast biopsy systems)
Diagnostic Products
FullTerm Fetal Fibronectin Test (preterm birth risk assessment)
Invader molecular diagnostic tests
ThinPrep System (cervical cancer screening)
GYN Surgical Products
NovaSure (treatment system for menorrhagia)
Skeletal Health Products
InSight fluoroscan imaging systems (mini c-arm X-ray imaging devices)
QDR X-Ray Bone Densitometers (osteoporosis diagnostic devices)
Sahara Clinical Bone Sonometers (portable ultrasound bone analyzers)
QDR series bone densitometer
Sahara Bone Sonometer (ultrasound-based densitometer)

COMPETITORS

Abbott Labs
American Medical Systems
Bard
Becton, Dickinson
Boston Scientific
Cardinal Health
Carestream Health
Celera
Ethicon
FUJIFILM
GE Healthcare
Gen-Probe
iCAD
Innogenetics
Intact Medical Corporation
Johnson & Johnson
Life Technologies Corporation
Luminex
Philips Healthcare
QIAGEN
Roche Diagnostics
Sectra
SenoRx
Siemens Healthcare
Toshiba

HISTORICAL FINANCIALS

Company Type: Public

Income Statement

FYE: Last Saturday in September

	REVENUE ($ mil.)	NET INCOME ($ mil.)	NET PROFIT MARGIN	EMPLOYEES
9/09	1,637	(2,176)	—	3,959
9/08	1,675	(386)	—	3,933
9/07	738	95	12.8%	3,580
9/06	463	27	5.9%	1,617
9/05	288	28	9.8%	870
Annual Growth	**54.4%**	**—**	**—**	**46.1%**

2009 Year-End Financials

Debt ratio: 74.2%
Return on equity: —
Cash ($ mil.): 293
Current ratio: 2.49
Long-term debt ($ mil.): 1,865
No. of shares (mil.): 259
Dividends
Yield: —
Payout: —
Market value ($ mil.): 4,235

Stock History

NASDAQ (GS): HOLX

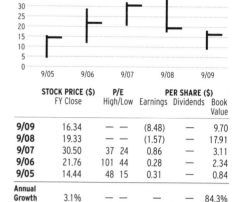

	STOCK PRICE ($) FY Close	P/E High/Low		PER SHARE ($) Earnings	Dividends	Book Value
9/09	16.34	—	—	(8.48)	—	9.70
9/08	19.33	—	—	(1.57)	—	17.91
9/07	30.50	37	24	0.86	—	3.11
9/06	21.76	101	44	0.28	—	2.34
9/05	14.44	48	15	0.31	—	0.84
Annual Growth	**3.1%**	**—**	**—**	**—**	**—**	**84.3%**

Home Depot

When embarking on household projects, many start their journey at The Home Depot. As the world's largest home improvement chain and second-largest US retailer after Wal-Mart, the firm operates about 2,200 stores across North America, Puerto Rico, and China, as well as an e-commerce site. It targets the do-it-yourself and professional markets with its selection of some 40,000 items, including lumber, flooring, plumbing supplies, garden products, tools, paint, and appliances. Home Depot also offers installation services for carpeting, cabinetry, and other products. Since shuttering its unprofitable EXPO, THD Design Center, and Yardbirds stores in 2009, the retailer has focused on boosting its revenue.

The exit, part of a move to satisfy investors calling for a more robust stock price, came amid the deepening economic downturn and a battered housing market. The EXPO, THD Design Center, and Yardbirds stores were part of Home Depot's upscale group of home design and hardware stores aimed at those remodeling their homes. Yet with decreased demand in the home improvement and construction markets, the retailer saw its revenue fall by 7% for the second straight year in 2010. (Sales dropped by $5 billion in 2010 and $6 billion in 2009.) Home Depot has suffered losses since hitting its high point in 2007, when it recorded some $90 billion in revenue.

Despite the challenging retail environment, the company is aiming to regain its balance through its core Home Depot chain. In 2009, shortly after shedding its EXPO, THD Design Center, and Yardbirds units, Home Depot began streamlining its operations. It eliminated about 7,000 jobs and is slashing another 2,000 non-store positions, as well as freezing the pay of its officers. The company also curtailed its growth plan by about 50 stores, opening just a dozen new locations in the

US, Mexico, and Canada that year. The cost-cutting measures turn up as the retailer repositions itself as a bargain-priced DIY chain. To spur sales along, Home Depot has slashed prices on its best-selling items, cleaned up stores to attract female customers, retrained employees in customer service, and rolled out technology improvements (including new supply chain and merchandising tools). While it does not expect to see results from this approach in the near-term, the retailer hopes its sales will rebound with the economy and housing market in the years following.

As the US's #2 retailer works to boost sales at home, it is also aiming to leverage itself in international markets. About 10% of The Home Depot's stores are located in Canada, China, and Mexico. The company operates about 180 locations in Canada and 10 stores in China. Home Depot Mexico is the country's #1 do-it-yourself operator with some 80 stores.

HISTORY

Bernard Marcus and Arthur Blank founded The Home Depot in 1978 after they were fired (under disputed circumstances) from Handy Dan Home Improvement Centers. They joined Handy Dan co-worker Ronald Brill to launch a "new and improved" home center for the do-it-yourselfer (DIY). In 1979 they opened three stores in the fast-growing Atlanta area and expanded to four stores in 1980.

Home Depot went public, opened four stores in South Florida, and posted sales of $50 million in 1981. The chain entered Louisiana and Arizona next. By 1983 sales were more than $250 million.

In 1984 Home Depot's stock was listed on the NYSE and the company acquired nine Bowater Home Centers in the South. Through subsequent stock and debenture offerings, Home Depot continued to grow, entering California (Handy Dan's home turf) with six new stores in 1985.

Back on track in 1986, sales exceeded $1 billion in the firm's 60 stores. Home Depot began the current policy of "low day-in, day-out pricing" the following year, achieving Marcus' dream of eliminating sales events. The company entered the competitive northeastern market with stores in Long Island, New York, in 1988 and opened its first EXPO Design Center in San Diego.

Home Depot's sales continued to rise during the 1990-92 recession and the retailer kept opening stores. It entered Canada in 1994 when it acquired a 75% interest in Aikenhead's, a DIY chain that it converted to the Home Depot name (it bought the remaining 25% in 1998).

A series of gender-bias lawsuits plagued the company in 1994 as female workers claimed they were not treated on an equal basis with male employees. Home Depot reached a $65 million out-of-court settlement in 1997, but not before the company was ordered to pay another female employee $1.7 million in a case in California.

In 1997 Blank succeeded Marcus as the company's CEO; Marcus remained chairman. In 2000 the company named General Electric executive Robert Nardelli as its president and CEO. Marcus and Blank were named co-chairmen, but Marcus was named chairman in 2001 after Blank stepped down. Later in the year Marcus retired and Nardelli became chairman.

In mid-2005 Home Depot acquired National Waterworks Holdings (now National Waterworks, Inc.) and Williams Bros. Lumber of Georgia, and folded them both into its The Home Depot Supply business (renamed HD Supply).

The company's direct-to-consumer division launched a pair of high-end catalogs in 2005: 10 Crescent Lane and Paces Trading Company. However, the catalogs, which featured home furnishings and lighting products, were discontinued in 2006 and selected products were folded back into the main Home Depot store catalog and website.

In January 2006 Home Depot acquired carpet and upholstery cleaning franchisor Chem-Dry, which it will add to its At-Home Services division. (Chem-Dry has nearly 4,000 franchises worldwide, including 2,500 in the US.) In March the company completed its largest acquisition to date: the construction, repair, and maintenance products distributor Hughes Supply Inc., for $3.2 billion. That purchase was followed in May by the acquisition of Cox Lumber Co., a Tampa-based provider of trusses, doors, and lumber-related products.

In early 2007 Nardelli left the company and vice chairman and EVP Frank Blake took the top spot. Home Depot decided to close its handful of flooring-only stores that year. It also closed a call center in Texas, affecting 550 employees.

The company sold its HD Supply business in 2007 to Bain Capital, Carlyle Group, and Clayton Dubilier & Rice.

EXECUTIVES

Chairman and CEO: Francis S. (Frank) Blake, age 60, $9,927,573 total compensation
EVP Corporate Services and CFO: Carol B. Tomé, age 53, $5,242,167 total compensation
EVP Merchandising: Craig A. Menear, age 52, $3,422,482 total compensation
EVP US Stores: Marvin R. Ellison, age 45, $3,294,707 total compensation
EVP, General Counsel, and Corporate Secretary: Jack A. VanWoerkom, age 56
EVP and CIO: Matt Carey
EVP Human Resources: Timothy M. (Tim) Crow, age 54
SVP Merchandising Services: Kevin Scott
SVP Retail Finance: Edward P. (Ted) Decker
SVP IT Store, Field and Corporate Support: Cara D. Kinzey, age 43
SVP Operations: Marc D. Powers
SVP and Chief Marketing Officer: Frank P. Bifulco Jr.
SVP Global Supply Chain: Mark Holifield
VP Corporate Communications and External Affairs: Brad Shaw
President, Home Depot Canada and Asia: Annette M. Verschuren, age 53, $3,170,164 total compensation
President, Western Division: Joseph (Joe) McFarland III, age 41
President, Southern Division: Ann-Marie Campbell
President, Northern Division: Jim Kane
President, Mexico: Ricardo E. Saldivar, age 57
President, Online: Hal Lawton
Auditors: KPMG LLP

LOCATIONS

HQ: The Home Depot, Inc.
2455 Paces Ferry Rd. NW, Atlanta, GA 30339
Phone: 770-433-8211   **Fax:** 770-384-2356
Web: www.homedepot.com

2010 Locations

	No.
US	1,976
Canada	179
Mexico	79
China	10
Total	**2,244**

PRODUCTS/OPERATIONS

2010 Sales

	% of total
Plumbing, electrical & kitchen	30
Hardware & seasonal	29
Building materials, lumber & millwork	22
Paint & flooring	19
Total	**100**

Selected Private Labels and Proprietary Brands

Behr Premium Plus (paint)
Glacier Bay (fixtures)
Hampton Bay (lighting)
Husky (hand tools)
Mill's Pride (cabinets)
Vigoro (lawn care products)

COMPETITORS

84 Lumber
Abbey Carpet
Ace Hardware
Amazon.com
B&Q
Best Buy
BMC Select
CCA Global
Costco Wholesale
Do it Best
F.W. Webb
Guardian Building Products Distribution
Improvement Direct
Kelly-Moore
Lowe's
Menard
Northern Tool
Pacific Coast Building Products
RONA
Sears Holdings
Sherwin-Williams
Stock Building Supply
Sutherland Lumber
Target
Tractor Supply
True Value
Wal-Mart
W.E. Aubuchon
WinWholesale
Wolseley

HISTORICAL FINANCIALS

Company Type: Public

Income Statement			FYE: Sunday nearest January 31	
	REVENUE ($ mil.)	NET INCOME ($ mil.)	NET PROFIT MARGIN	EMPLOYEES
1/10	66,176	2,661	4.0%	317,000
1/09	71,288	2,260	3.2%	322,000
1/08	77,349	4,395	5.7%	331,000
1/07	90,837	5,761	6.3%	364,000
1/06	81,511	5,838	7.2%	345,000
Annual Growth	(5.1%)	(17.8%)	—	(2.1%)

2010 Year-End Financials

Debt ratio: 44.7%
Return on equity: 14.3%
Cash ($ mil.): 1,421
Current ratio: 1.34
Long-term debt ($ mil.): 8,662
No. of shares (mil.): 1,680
Dividends
  Yield: 3.2%
  Payout: 57.3%
Market value ($ mil.): 47,067

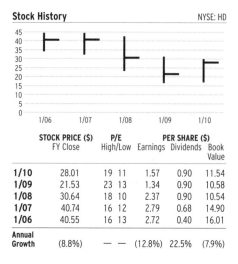

	STOCK PRICE ($) FY Close	P/E High/Low	PER SHARE ($) Earnings	Dividends	Book Value
1/10	28.01	19 11	1.57	0.90	11.54
1/09	21.53	23 13	1.34	0.90	10.58
1/08	30.64	18 10	2.37	0.90	10.54
1/07	40.74	16 12	2.79	0.68	14.90
1/06	40.55	16 13	2.72	0.40	16.01
Annual Growth	(8.8%)	— —	(12.8%)	22.5%	(7.9%)

Honeywell International

Jet engines and thermostats seem worlds apart, but they're Honeywell International's bread and butter. More than a century old, the company is a diverse industrial conglomerate, with four segments; the largest include Automation and Control (HVAC and manufacturing process products) and Aerospace (turbo engines, and flight safety and landing systems). Additional segments include Honeywell Specialty Materials (thermal interconnects, fibers, and chemicals) and Transportation Systems (engine boosting systems, brake materials, car care products). Sales to the US government account for about 15% of its revenues (primarily in Aerospace).

Given the international nature of the company, as well as its businesses in the automotive and commercial aircraft industries, it took a decided one-two punch in 2008 and 2009. Global demand for commercial air travel was down, which meant fewer jet deliveries. This decrease impacted the new and aftermarket demand for aircraft parts, maintenance, and repair services. With the gravity of the automotive financial crisis, the company's Transportation Systems segment experienced the biggest drop in sales for the company. Honeywell is expanding its operations and sales in international locations, and continuing to design innovative and technologically forward equipment across its industries.

In the fall of 2010 the company purchased protective gear maker Sperian Protection. The $1.4 billion offer outdid a previous bid made by European buyout firm Cinven by 63%.

The company purchased Matrikon in mid-2010, enhancing Honeywell's industrial lineup for monitoring and improving the performance and safety of oil and gas wells and mining equipment. It also purchased Germany-based RMG Group in 2009 for $416 million. RMG makes regulating and safety systems, metering and shut-off for natural gas businesses.

The company acquired Metrologic Instruments in 2008, bringing data capture and collection hardware and software for inclusion in Honeywell's Automation and Control products portfolio. In May of that year it picked up Norcross Safety Products for over $1 billion.

The company sold its Consumable Solutions segment to BE Aerospace for $1.15 billion in 2008. Consumable Solutions distributed aerospace fasteners and hardware.

HISTORY

During WWI Germany controlled much of the world's chemical industry, causing dye and drug shortages. In response, *Washington Post* publisher Eugene Meyer and scientist William Nichols organized the Allied Chemical & Dye Corporation in 1920.

Allied opened a synthetic ammonia plant in 1928 near Hopewell, Virginia, and became the world's leading producer of ammonia. After WWII Allied began making nylon, refrigerants, and other products. The company became Allied Chemical Corporation in 1958.

Seeking a supplier of raw materials for its chemical products, in 1962 Allied bought Union Texas Natural Gas. In the early 1970s CEO John Connor sold many of the firm's unprofitable businesses and invested in oil and gas exploration. By 1979, when Edward Hennessy became CEO, Union Texas produced 80% of Allied's income.

Hennessy led the company into the electronics and technical markets. Under a new name, Allied Corporation (1981), it bought the Bendix Corporation, an aerospace and automotive company, in 1983. In 1985 Allied merged with Signal Companies (founded by Sam Mosher in 1922) to form AlliedSignal. The company spun off more than 40 unprofitable chemical and engineering businesses over the next two years.

Larry Bossidy, hired from General Electric in 1991 as the new CEO, began to cut waste and buy growth businesses. Late in 1999 the company acquired Honeywell in a deal valued at $15 billion and changed its name to Honeywell International. Honeywell, after trying to make a go of it in the computer and telecommunications industries, had refocused on its core product lines — thermostats, security systems, and other automation equipment. The chairman and CEO of the original Honeywell, Michael Bonsignore, took the same titles in the combined company.

In 2000 Honeywell picked up building security and fire systems company Pittway for $2 billion. Then, amid lower-than-expected earnings, the company announced plans to cut an additional 6,000 jobs on top of the 11,000 cuts already planned.

Late in the year Honeywell was reportedly close to inking a deal to be acquired by United Technologies, but the talks ended when industrial behemoth GE made a better offer. Honeywell then agreed to be acquired by GE in a stock deal worth about $45 billion. However, the deal collapsed in 2001 when GE — which had offered to sell assets that generate about $2.2 billion a year — balked at demands from European Union regulators that it sell virtually all of Honeywell's avionics operations. The EU formally rejected the acquisition in July, and Honeywell ousted CEO Bonsignore, replacing him with Bossidy.

In September the company said that it would take cost-cutting measures with charges of almost $1 billion and increased the total of previously announced layoffs, cutting about 16,000 jobs (about 13% of its workforce) by year's end.

In December Honeywell agreed to pay Northrop Grumman $440 million to settle an antitrust and patent infringement lawsuit filed against it by Litton (now a part of Northrop) in 1990.

In 2002 David Cote (like Bossidy, a former GE executive), the former chairman, president, and CEO of TRW, was named president and CEO of Honeywell, replacing Bossidy (Cote also replaced Bossidy as chairman in July 2002).

Early in 2005 Honeywell acquired UK-based Novar plc for about $1.7 billion. Novar's operations include aluminum products, building control and security systems, and checkbook printing. Late in 2005 Honeywell sold its US nylon fibers business to Shaw Industries and its Clarke American Checks (check printing) business to M&F Worldwide for $800 million. It also bought Dow Chemical's 50% stake in UOP, their energy refining joint venture, for $825 million.

Honeywell sold Novar's Indalex Aluminum Solutions operations to Sun Capital Partners for $425 million early in 2006. Not long after, Honeywell completed the acquisition of First Technology PLC, a maker of gas sensing, automotive, and safety equipment, for $718 million.

In late 2007 Honeywell bought Hand Held Products Inc., a maker of automatic identification and data collection (AIDC) equipment.

EXECUTIVES

Chairman and CEO: David M. (Dave) Cote, age 57, $13,223,161 total compensation
SVP Human Resources and Communications: Mark R. James, age 48
SVP and CFO: David J. (Dave) Anderson, age 60, $6,523,166 total compensation
SVP and General Counsel: Katherine L. (Kate) Adams, age 45
SVP Engineering and Operations; President, Technology Solutions: Krishna Mikkilineni
CIO and Global Security Organization and Functional Transformation: Bask Iyer
VP Investor Relations: Elena Doom
VP and Controller: Kathleen A. Winters, age 42
VP External Communications: Robert C. (Rob) Ferris
VP, Secretary, and Deputy Corporate Counsel: Thomas F. Larkins
VP Strategy and Business Development: Rhonda G. Germany
President and CEO, Automation and Control Solutions: Roger Fradin, age 56, $4,818,244 total compensation
President and CEO, Specialty Materials: Andreas Kramvis, age 57, $2,731,983 total compensation
President and CEO, Aerospace: Timothy O. (Tim) Mahoney, age 53
President and CEO, Transportation Business: Alexandre (Alex) Ismail, age 45
CEO, Honeywell China and India: Shane Tedjarati
Auditors: PricewaterhouseCoopers LLP

LOCATIONS

HQ: Honeywell International Inc.
101 Columbia Rd., Morristown, NJ 07962
Phone: 973-455-2000   **Fax:** 973-455-4807
Web: www.honeywell.com

2009 Sales

	$ mil.	% of total
US	18,742	61
Europe	7,632	25
Other regions	4,534	14
Total	**30,908**	**100**

PRODUCTS/OPERATIONS

2009 Sales

	$ mil.	% of total
Automation & Control Solutions	12,611	41
Aerospace	10,763	35
Specialty Materials	4,144	13
Transportation Systems	3,389	11
Other	1	—
Total	**30,908**	**100**

COMPETITORS

3M	Kyocera
ABB AG	L-3 Communications
Air Products	Lockheed Martin
Akebono Brake	Lonza
Arkema	LSI Industries
Asahi Glass	Merck KGaA
Astronautics	Mexichem
Avecia	Mine Safety Appliances
BAE Systems Inc.	Modine Manufacturing
Ball Aerospace	Motorola
BASF SE	NavCom Technology
Bechtel	NGK SPARK PLUG
Boeing	Northrop Grumman
BorgWarner	Old World Industries
Clariant	Parker Hannifin
Computer Sciences Corp.	Pelco
Daikin	Raytheon
Dow Chemical	Riken Corporation
DSM	Robert Bosch
DuPont	Rockwell Automation
DynCorp International	Rolls-Royce
Eastman Chemical	SAFRAN
Eaton	SAIC
Emerson Electric	Sauer-Danfoss
Endress + Hauser	Schneider Electric
Exxon Mobil	Shinko Electric
Federal-Mogul	Siemens AG
Foxconn International	Sigma-Aldrich
Garmin	Solvay
GE	TAT Group
Goodrich Corp.	Teijin
Hella	Thales
INEOS	Thermo Fisher Scientific
Ingersoll-Rand	Trimble Navigation
Intermec	Tyco
Invensys	United Technologies
ITT Corp.	Unitika
Jeppesen Sanderson	Universal Avionics
Johnson Controls	Valeo
KVH Industries	Yokogawa Electric

HISTORICAL FINANCIALS

Company Type: Public

Income Statement

FYE: December 31

	REVENUE ($ mil.)	NET INCOME ($ mil.)	NET PROFIT MARGIN	EMPLOYEES
12/09	30,908	2,153	7.0%	122,000
12/08	36,556	2,792	7.6%	128,000
12/07	34,589	2,444	7.1%	122,000
12/06	31,367	2,083	6.6%	118,000
12/05	27,653	1,676	6.1%	116,000
Annual Growth	**2.8%**	**6.5%**	**—**	**1.3%**

2009 Year-End Financials

Debt ratio: 70.6%	No. of shares (mil.): 772
Return on equity: 26.9%	Dividends
Cash ($ mil.): 2,801	Yield: 3.1%
Current ratio: 1.25	Payout: 42.5%
Long-term debt ($ mil.): 6,246	Market value ($ mil.): 30,271

Stock History

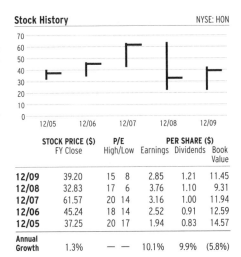

NYSE: HON

	STOCK PRICE ($) FY Close	P/E High/Low		PER SHARE ($) Earnings	Dividends	Book Value
12/09	39.20	15	8	2.85	1.21	11.45
12/08	32.83	17	6	3.76	1.10	9.31
12/07	61.57	20	14	3.16	1.00	11.94
12/06	45.24	18	14	2.52	0.91	12.59
12/05	37.25	20	17	1.94	0.83	14.57
Annual Growth	**1.3%**	**—**	**—**	**10.1%**	**9.9%**	**(5.8%)**

Hormel Foods

Now that Hormel Foods has stocked its pantry with ethnic convenience foods, can we look forward to SPAM soufflé, SPAM enchiladas, or SPAM curry? Along with its famous canned "spiced ham," SPAM, the company has branched out into convenience, ethnic, and frozen foods, offering brands such as Chi-Chi's Mexican, Marrakesh Express, and House of Tsang Asian products. Its other offerings include canned Stagg chili and Dinty Moore beef stews. In addition, Hormel is a top US turkey processor and a major pork processor, making Jennie-O turkey products, Cure 81 hams, and Always Tender fresh pork. Thirty-four Hormel brands are ranked #1 or #2 in their respective markets.

Say "Spam" and everyone has a story about the canned meat. Say "Dinty Moore . . ." and everyone will finish with "beef stew." "Hormel" is synonymous with chili. Home to highly recognizable brand names, Hormel is successful in its strategy of providing high-quality products with strong brand recognition.

Although 95% of its sales come from the US, Hormel has operations and/or joint ventures across the globe, including in Australia, Canada, China (the world's biggest market for pork), Japan, and the Philippines. In 2009 it formed another joint venture, this time with Herdez Del Fuerte to market Mexican foods in the US.

Hormel acquired the Shedd's Country Crock chilled side-dish business in the US from Unilever in 2010. The addition of Country Crock allows Hormel to expand its offerings in both the convenient-meals and side-dish areas.

Hormel's specialty foods segment packages and sells various sugar and sugar-substitute products, salt and pepper, liquid-portion products, dessert mixes, ready-to-drink products, gelatin products, and private-label canned meats to retail and foodservice customers. The segment also makes nutritional food products and supplements for hospitals, nursing homes, and other marketers of nutritional products.

The Hormel Foundation, a charitable trust formed during WWII, owns approximately 48% of the company's stock.

HISTORY

George Hormel opened his Austin, Minnesota, slaughterhouse in an abandoned creamery in 1891. By 1900 Hormel had modernized his facilities to compete with larger meat processors. In 1903 the enterprise introduced its first brand name (Dairy Brand) and a year later began opening distribution centers nationwide. The scandal that ensued after the discovery in 1921 that an assistant controller had embezzled over $1 million almost broke the company, causing Hormel to initiate tighter controls. By 1924 it was processing more than a million hogs annually. Hormel introduced canned ham two years later.

Jay Hormel, George's son, became president in 1929; under his guidance Hormel introduced Dinty Moore beef stew (1936) and SPAM (1937). A Hormel executive won a contest, and $100, by submitting the name, a contraction of "spiced ham." During WWII the US government bought over half of Hormel's output; it supplied SPAM to GIs and Allied forces.

In 1959 Hormel introduced its Little Sizzlers pork sausage and sold its billionth can of SPAM. New products rolled out in the 1960s included Hormel's Cure 81 ham (1963). By the mid-1970s the firm had more than 750 products.

The company survived a violent, nationally publicized strike triggered by a pay cut in 1985. In the end only 500 of the original 1,500 strikers returned to accept lower pay scales.

Sensing the consumer shift toward poultry, Hormel purchased Jennie-O Foods in 1986. Later acquisitions included the House of Tsang and Oriental Deli (1992), Dubuque (processed pork, 1993), and Herb-Ox (bouillon and dry soup mix, 1993). After more than a century as Geo. A. Hormel & Co., the company began calling itself Hormel Foods in 1993 to reflect its expansion into non-pork foods. Former General Foods executive Joel Johnson was named president and CEO that year (and chairman two years later).

Hormel proved it could take a joke with the 1994 debut of its tongue-in-cheek SPAM catalog, featuring dozens of SPAM-related products. But when a 1996 Muppets movie featured a porcine character named Spa'am, Hormel sued Jim Henson Productions; a federal court gave Spa'am the go-ahead.

Earnings fell in 1996, due in part to soaring hog prices. The company was hit hard again in 1998 when production contracts with hog growers meant it wound up paying premium rates, despite a market glut. In 1998 the Smithsonian Institution accepted two cans of SPAM (one from 1937, the other an updated 1997 version) for its History of Technology collection.

SPAM sales soared in 1999 as nervous consumers stockpiled provisions for the millennium. To build its growing HealthLabs division, Hormel acquired Cliffdale Farms (2000) and Diamond Crystal Brands nutritional products (a division of Imperial Sugar) in 2001 — boosting its share of the market for easy-to-swallow foods sold to hospitals and nursing homes.

In early 2001 Hormel acquired family-owned The Turkey Store for approximately $334 million and folded it into its Jennie-O division. Hormel produced its 6 billionth can of SPAM in 2002.

To further diversify, in 2003 Hormel acquired food manufacturer Century Foods International (whey-based protein powders, beverages, and nutrition bars) and added it to its burgeoning specialty foods group. In 2004 Hormel bought Southern California's Clougherty Packing for about $186 million.

Responding to the growing trend of the US population to dine out, Hormel expanded its foodservice segment (which it refers to as its specialty foods business) with the 2005 purchase of foodservice food manufacturer and distributor Mark-Lynn Foods.

Johnson retired in 2006; company veteran Jeffrey Ettinger was tapped to be the new chairman and CEO.

Adding to its grocery product offerings, in 2006 the company acquired canned, ready-to-eat chicken producer Valley Fresh Foods for $78 million. It also bought pepperoni and pasta maker Provena Foods, and sausage and sliced meat maker Saag's Products.

It added another to its list of countries in which it has joint ventures in 2006, when it formed a JV with San Miguel to raise and market hogs and animal feed in Vietnam. The JV is 49%-owned by Hormel.

Hormel acquired Burke Corporation, a maker of pizza toppings and other fully cooked meat items in 2007 for $115 million in cash.

EXECUTIVES

Chairman, President, and CEO: Jeffrey M. Ettinger, age 51, $7,344,599 total compensation
EVP Grocery Products and Corporate Development; Mergers and Acquisitions: Ronald W. Fielding, age 56, $1,598,086 total compensation
SVP, CFO, and Director: Jody H. Feragen, age 53, $1,647,165 total compensation
SVP Supply Chain: William F. Snyder, age 52
SVP Foodservice: Thomas R. Day, age 51
SVP External Affairs and General Counsel: James W. Cavanaugh, age 59
Group VP Refrigerated Products: Steven G. Binder, age 52, $1,753,959 total compensation
Group VP Specialty Foods: Michael D. (Mike) Tolbert, age 53
Group VP Consumer Products Sales: Larry L. Vorpahl, age 46
Group VP; President, Hormel Foods International: Richard A. Bross, age 58
Group Product Manager, Associated Brands: Swen Neufeldt
VP; SVP Consumer Products Sales: Douglas R. Reetz, age 55
VP; SVP Consumer Products Sales: Kurt F. Mueller, age 53
VP Human Resources: David P. Juhlke, age 50
VP Corporate Communications: Julie H. Craven, age 54
VP Engineering: James Schroeder
VP Consumer Product Sales: Donald H. (Don) Kremin, age 49
Corporate Secretary and Senior Attorney: Brian D. Johnson, age 49
Director Investor Relations: Kevin C. Jones
Auditors: Ernst & Young LLP

LOCATIONS

HQ: Hormel Foods Corporation
1 Hormel Place, Austin, MN 55912
Phone: 507-437-5611   **Fax:** 507-437-5129
Web: www.hormelfoods.com

2009 Sales

	$ mil.	% of total
US	6,198.8	95
Other	334.9	5
Total	**6,533.7**	**100**

PRODUCTS/OPERATIONS

2009 Sales

	$ mil.	% of total
Refrigerated foods	3,436.3	53
Jennie-O Turkey Store	1,227.7	18
Grocery products	924.7	14
Specialty foods	708.7	11
Other	236.3	4
Total	**6,533.7**	**100**

Selected Retail Brands

Refrigerated
  Country Crock Side Dishes
  Hormel
    Hormel Always Tender flavored pork and beef products
    Hormel Black Label and Microwave Ready bacon
    Hormel Cure 81 Ham
    Hormel dried beef
    Hormel Fresh Pantry meats
    Hormel Little Sizzlers pork sausage
    Hormel Pepperoni
    Hormel refrigerated entrees
    Hormel Wranglers franks
    Hormel Snac*Cups
  Lloyd's Barbeque products
Jennie-O Turkey Store
  Bratwursts and dinner sausages
  Deli
    Di Lusso Deli Meats
    Farmer John Deli Meats
    Hormel Deli beef, dry sausage, ham, and turkey)
    Hormel Party Trays
  Ground turkey
  So-Easy Entrees
  Turkey burgers and franks
Grocery products
  Dinty Moore Beef Stew
  Herb-Ox bouillon
  Herdez Salsa
  Hormel
    Hormel bacon toppings
    Hormel Chili Master
    Hormel Compleats microwave meals
    Hormel Kid's Kitchen microwave cups
    Hormel Mary Kitchen hash
  Not-So-Sloppy-Joe
  SPAM products (original, low-sodium, spread, singles, and oven-roasted turkey)
  Stagg chili
  Valley Fresh chunk meats and broths
Specialty Foods
  Century Foods International (dairy and vegetable proteins, nutraceuticals)
  Diamond Crystal Brands (salts, sugar substitutes)
  Hormel Foods Ingredients (sauces, powders, broths, oils, Omega-3 additives)
  Private Label products (canned meats, prepared foods and desserts, bouillon, sweeteners, salts, seasonings)
Other
  MegaMex Mexican brands
    Bufalo hot sauces
    CHI-CHI'S Mexican hot sauces, taco tubs, dips, seasoning mixes, and tortillas
    Doña María Authentic Mexican products
    El Torito sauces, dressings, and corn cakes
    Herdez imported salsas
  World Food ethnic brands
    House of Tsang oils
    Marrakesh Express Moroccan products (couscous, risotto)
    Peloponnese olives

COMPETITORS

B&G Foods
Boar's Head
Bob Evans
Bridgford Foods
Bush Brothers
Butterball
Campbell Soup
Cargill
ConAgra
Cooper Farms
The Dial Corporation
Eberly Poultry
Foster Farms
General Mills
Gusto Packing
H. J. Heinz Limited
JBS USA
Kraft Foods
Perdue Incorporated
Pilgrim's Pride
Pinnacle Foods
Plainville Farms
Sanderson Farms
Sara Lee
Seaboard
Smithfield Foods
Tyson Foods

HISTORICAL FINANCIALS

Company Type: Public

Income Statement

FYE: Last Saturday in October

	REVENUE ($ mil.)	NET INCOME ($ mil.)	NET PROFIT MARGIN	EMPLOYEES
10/09	6,534	343	5.2%	18,600
10/08	6,755	286	4.2%	19,100
10/07	6,193	302	4.9%	18,500
10/06	5,746	286	5.0%	18,100
10/05	5,414	254	4.7%	17,600
Annual Growth	**4.8%**	**7.8%**	**—**	**1.4%**

2009 Year-End Financials

Debt ratio: 16.5%
Return on equity: 16.6%
Cash ($ mil.): 385
Current ratio: 2.30
Long-term debt ($ mil.): 350
No. of shares (mil.): 133
Dividends
  Yield: 2.1%
  Payout: 30.0%
Market value ($ mil.): 4,858

Stock History

NYSE: HRL

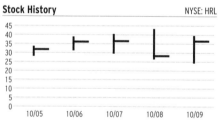

	STOCK PRICE ($) FY Close	P/E High/Low		PER SHARE ($) Earnings	Dividends	Book Value
10/09	36.46	15	10	2.53	0.76	15.94
10/08	28.26	21	13	2.08	0.74	15.07
10/07	36.48	18	14	2.17	0.60	14.15
10/06	36.11	19	15	2.05	0.56	13.53
10/05	31.80	18	16	1.82	0.52	11.82
Annual Growth	**3.5%**	**—**	**—**	**8.6%**	**10.0%**	**7.8%**

Hovnanian Enterprises

Gimme shelter. Hovnanian Enterprises designs, builds, and markets single-family detached homes, condominiums, and townhomes for first-time, move-up, and luxury buyers as well as for empty-nesters and active adults. Hovnanian delivered about 5,300 homes in fiscal 2009 (down from more than 20,000 in 2006), with base prices ranging from $36,000 to $1.8 million and averaging about $280,000. The company operates in some 180 communities in about 20 states, primarily operating along the East Coast and in the Midwest, California, and Texas. Its K. Hovnanian American Mortgage unit offers mortgage financing and title services. Members of the Hovnanian family control more than 90% of Hovnanian Enterprises.

The company builds homes under the K. Hovnanian, Brighton, CraftBuilt, Matzel and Mumford, Oster, Parkwood Builders, and Town and Country names, among others.

Like its peers, Hovnanian has been hit hard by the housing downturn and credit crunch, resulting in its building fewer homes, declines in sales, and increased cancellations. An influx of foreclosed homes on the market has also decreased demand for new housing. The company reduced its workforce some 60% between 2006 and 2008.

Hovnanian continued to operate in a difficult market in 2009, and further reduced its general and administrative expenses. However, the firm did begin seeing opportunities to purchase land at prices that made economic sense given the sale price of homes, and continued to seek those opportunities into 2010.

Also in 2009, Hovnanian entered into a joint agreement with GoldenTree InSite Partners (now GTIS Partners) to design, build, and sell homes across 11 communities in the greater Chicago and Palm Beach County, Florida, markets. Hovnanian owns a 20% stake in the venture, which it paid for with stock.

HISTORY

After fleeing revolution in his home of Iraq in the 1950s, Kevork Hovnanian came to America and began building homes in New Jersey in 1959 with his three brothers (including brother Vahak, later to become founder of Internet service provider SPEEDUS.COM). His firm incorporated as K. Hovnanian Enterprises in 1967, and Kevork's son Ara came on board in 1979. (Ara became president in 1988 and CEO in 1997.) The company's 1983 IPO helped Hovnanian take advantage of New Jersey's strong housing market, which peaked in 1986. However, the boom had declined dramatically by 1990, and Hovnanian landed in the red.

Responding to the setback, Hovnanian expanded geographically in the 1990s. It moved into the Washington, DC, area in 1992 and into Southern California in 1994. But the new markets did not add much to the bottom line, thanks to a slowdown in North Carolina and a recession in California.

Hovnanian crews traveled to Armenia in 1988 to help rebuild the country after devastating earthquakes wreaked havoc. The trip convinced Kevork, an Armenian who grew up in Iraq, to expand Hovnanian operations into the emerging economies of Eastern Europe. Because of its relatively more advanced real estate and mortgage

laws, Poland was chosen, and Hovnanian began constructing townhouses there in 1996.

In 1997 Hovnanian began to divest itself of commercial holdings to focus on housing; by 1998 the company had exited the investment properties business.

With cash to plow into homebuilding, Hovnanian strengthened its Washington, DC, operations in 1998 by acquiring Virginia's P.C. Homes. The next year the builder purchased New Jersey luxury homebuilder Matzel & Mumford and entered Texas with the purchase of Dallas-based Goodman Family of Builders. In 2001 Hovnanian bought Washington Homes, which operated primarily in North Carolina and the Washington, DC, metropolitan area.

In early 2002 Hovnanian acquired the homebuilding assets of The Forecast Group, increasing Hovnanian's presence in California. The company was listed that year as one of the 100 fastest-growing companies in the US by *FORTUNE* magazine. Also that year Hovnanian expanded its presence in Texas, entering the Houston homebuilding market with its purchase of Parkside Homes.

Hovnanian initiated plans in 2003 to stop selling homes in Poland and to liquidate some of its homebuilding operations in portions of the southern US. On the expansion side, the company acquired Brighton Homes to strengthen its position in the Houston area. It also acquired Great Western Homes, expanding its market into the Phoenix area and the Southwest, and Tampa, Florida-based Windward Homes, expanding its southeastern US market into Florida. In 2004 Hovnanian expanded its metro DC presence by acquiring the homebuilding assets of McLean, Virginia-based Rocky Gorge Homes for an undisclosed amount.

In 2005 Hovnanian entered the Chicago market by acquiring homebuilder Town and Country Homes. It also entered the Orlando market and expanded its operations in Florida and Minnesota by acquiring Cambridge Homes. Hovnanian also acquired Oster Homes (Ohio) and First Home Builders (Florida) in 2005.

EXECUTIVES

Chairman, President, and CEO: Ara K. Hovnanian, age 52, $3,439,121 total compensation
COO: Thomas J. Pellerito, age 62
EVP, CFO, and Director: J. Larry Sorsby, age 54, $1,164,622 total compensation
SVP Human Resources: Robyn T. Mingle
SVP and General Counsel: Peter S. Reinhart, age 59, $533,596 total compensation
SVP and Chief Accounting Officer: Paul W. Buchanan, age 59, $502,623 total compensation
VP Finance and Treasurer: David G Valiaveedan, age 43, $404,381 total compensation
Director Investor Relations: Jeffrey T. (Jeff) O'Keefe
Auditors: Deloitte & Touche LLP

LOCATIONS

HQ: Hovnanian Enterprises, Inc.
110 W. Front St., Red Bank, NJ 07701
Phone: 732-747-7800 **Fax:** 732-747-6835
Web: www.khov.com

2009 Home Building Sales

	% of total
Southwest	27
Northeast	23
Mid-Atlantic	19
West	15
Southeast	8
Midwest	8
Total	**100**

2009 Homes Delivered

	No.	% of total
Southwest	1,867	33
West	875	15
Northeast	823	15
Mid-Atlantic	788	14
Midwest	520	9
Southeast	489	9
Joint ventures	297	5
Total	**5,659**	**100**

PRODUCTS/OPERATIONS

2009 Sales

	$ mil.	% of total
Homebuilding		
Sale of homes	1,522.5	96
Land sales & other	38.3	2
Financial services	35.5	2
Total	**1,596.3**	**100**

Selected Trade Names

Brighton Homes
CraftBuilt Homes
Forecast Homes
K. Hovnanian Homes
K. Hovnanian Homes Built On Your Lot
K. Hovnanian Homes Metro Living
K. Hovnanian's Four Seasons (active-adult communities)
Matzel and Mumford
Oster Homes
Parkwood Builders
Town and Country Homes
Windward Homes

COMPETITORS

Beazer Homes
D.R. Horton
KB Home
Lennar
M/I Homes
NVR
Orleans Homebuilders
PulteGroup
Rottlund
The Ryland Group
Toll Brothers
Weyerhaeuser Real Estate

HISTORICAL FINANCIALS

Company Type: Public

Income Statement

FYE: October 31

	REVENUE ($ mil.)	NET INCOME ($ mil.)	NET PROFIT MARGIN	EMPLOYEES
10/09	1,596	(717)	—	1,750
10/08	3,308	(1,125)	—	2,816
10/07	4,799	(627)	—	4,318
10/06	6,148	150	2.4%	6,239
10/05	5,348	472	8.8%	6,084
Annual Growth	(26.1%)	—	—	(26.8%)

2009 Year-End Financials

Debt ratio: —
Return on equity: —
Cash ($ mil.): 420
Current ratio: 3.35
Long-term debt ($ mil.): 1,752
No. of shares (mil.): 78
Dividends
  Yield: —
  Payout: —
Market value ($ mil.): 304

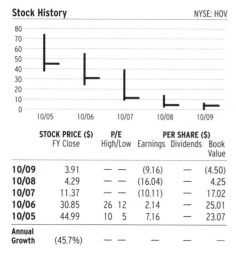

Stock History
NYSE: HOV

	STOCK PRICE ($) FY Close	P/E High/Low		PER SHARE ($) Earnings	Dividends	Book Value
10/09	3.91	—	—	(9.16)	—	(4.50)
10/08	4.29	—	—	(16.04)	—	4.25
10/07	11.37	—	—	(10.11)	—	17.02
10/06	30.85	26	12	2.14	—	25.01
10/05	44.99	10	5	7.16	—	23.07
Annual Growth	(45.7%)	—	—	—	—	—

HSN, Inc.

There's no need to worry about normal business hours when shopping from this retailer. HSN (known to night owls and from-the-couch shoppers as Home Shopping Network) operates a home shopping television network, which reaches more than 94 million US homes, and a related website, HSN.com. HSN sells apparel and accessories, jewelry, electronics, housewares, health, beauty, and fitness products, and more. Its Cornerstone Brands business is a catalog and Internet retailer. Titles include Garnet Hill, Smith+Noble, and TravelSmith, among others. It also operates about 25 retail outlets.

The recession in the US made for a rocky retailing environment for HSN in recent years. The firm operates through two segments: HSN and Cornerstone. Its HSN business, which generates about three-fourths of the company's sales, boasts a flexible business model that enables the retailer to quickly change its merchandise mix to meet customer demand. The company's Cornerstone segment houses its home and lifestyle brands, such as Frontgate, Smith+Noble, and Improvements. The business distributes some 200 million catalogs each year.

The company's focus on marketing HSN-exclusive items is a marketing strategy that has worked well. Under former NIKE executive Mindy Grossman, who joined HSN in 2006 as its CEO, the company has boosted sales by ditching hour-long programs that focus on one product —such as a treadmill — and paring down its celebrity-driven product pitches.

HSN's sales are increasingly coming from its website, as well. HSN.com accounts for about a third of the company's sales.

HSN was a subsidiry of Barry Diller's IAC/InterActiveCorp until 2008, when it was spun off. HSN, which accounted for about half of IAC's revenue prior to the separation, was one of four businesses spunoff by Diller so that the companies could trade and operate as separate entities.

Following the spinoff, Liberty Media Corporation (an investor in HSN's former parent IAC) owns about 32% of HSN's shares. Liberty opposed the spinoff, arguing that it diluted Liberty's control. In return for ultimately agreeing to the spinoff of HSN (and other IAC companies), Liberty was awarded representation on HSN's board of directors.

HISTORY

Lowell Paxson, who had spent years working in radio, owned an AM radio station in Clearwater, Florida, in the mid-1970s that began losing listeners to its FM competitors. Paxson began selling merchandise over the air in 1977. He bought distressed and overstocked merchandise from local merchants and sold it on his Suncoast Bargaineers program. The show was a hit, and Paxson began giving it more airtime.

By the early 1980s the Clearwater area was wired for cable, and Paxson teamed with Roy Speer, a Florida assistant attorney general, to found the Home Shopping Club in 1982. They soon expanded to other cable services in the Tampa Bay area. In 1985 the jump was made to become a national network. The company's name was changed to Home Shopping Network, which offered live 24-hour shopping on cable services across the nation.

The network was a success, as viewers embraced the bargain-basement prices coupled with game-show-type entertainment. Products were displayed one at a time, for 2-10 minutes, and could be bought only while on screen. Shoppers never knew what was going to come up next, so some of the more rabid fans stayed riveted for hours just to see what would come up for sale. The network's rotating collection of hosts gained cult followings.

Home Shopping Network went public in 1986 in one of the hottest IPOs of the year. That year the company moved into broadcast TV, paying $226 million for 12 UHF stations. The deal gave it broadcast and cable programming in several major markets, including New York, Los Angeles, and Boston.

The luster began to wear off when a host of competitors entered the TV retail fray. The network's competitors were given a boost when the Home Shopping Network's phone system became overloaded in 1987. Home Shopping Network sued GTE for $1.5 billion, claiming it lost half of its incoming calls because of the phone problems.

The company, led by CEO Speer, made unsuccessful attempts to diversify into other businesses, including financial services and mail-order pharmaceuticals, but in 1989 decided to focus solely on electronic retailing. That year the network lost its case against GTE, and it was forced to pay $4.5 million in legal fees and damages from a countersuit for libel.

Despite these setbacks, its core shopping business continued to grow, and by 1990 it reached $1 billion in sales. Also that year Paxson retired as president. Then in 1992, Home Shopping Network spun off its television stations unit, HSN. Speer sold his controlling interest in the company the next year to Liberty Media. He left the company amid allegations of corruption, including vendor kickbacks, but the investigation was dropped in 1994.

In 1995 Hollywood mogul Barry Diller acquired HSN. Diller (who built the Fox network) and TCI chief John Malone were named that year to the company's board. Also in 1995 the network and Sumitomo Corp., one of Japan's largest trading companies, agreed to start a television shopping business in Japan. That company, Silver King Communications, changed its name to HSN, Inc. in 1996, after buying the much larger Home Shopping Network and Savoy Pictures Entertainment.

In 1998 HSN formed a 50-50 joint venture with Scandinavian Broadcast System to operate a home shopping network (HSN-SBS) in Italy. HSN changed its name to USA Networks Inc. Also that year it purchased Ticketmaster.

In 2002 USA Networks sold all of its entertainment assets to Vivendi Universal and became a holding company, USA Interactive (now IAC/InterActiveCorp), with HSN as its strong arm.

IAC acquired catalog retailer Cornerstone Brands in 2005 for about $720 million. IAC later merged HSN's catalog operations into the acquired business. As a benefit from the deal, HSN began to offer many of Cornerstone's upscale lifestyle products through its television and Web operations. Mindy Grossman was named CEO of IAC Retailing, which oversees HSN, in 2006.

In April 2007, citing increasing cable and satellite distribution costs, HSN shut down America's Store, a home shopping network that reached about 14.3 million households in 2006. In May the company laid off 60 workers, primarily in operations at its St. Petersburg TV production and customer service campus. In June the company sold Home Shopping Europe.

EXECUTIVES

Chairman: Arthur C. Martinez, age 70
President, CEO, and Director: Mindy Grossman, age 52, $3,238,665 total compensation
EVP and CFO: Judy Schmeling, $1,852,671 total compensation
EVP Programming, Advanced Services, Marketing, and Business Development: Bill Brand
EVP Human Resources: Lisa Letizio
EVP Television and Executive Creative Director, HSN: Andrew Sheldon
EVP HSN Affiliate Relations Group: Peter Ruben
EVP Merchandising: Barbara Lynne Ronon
EVP HSN.com and Advanced Services: Brian S. Bradley, age 39
EVP, General Counsel, and Secretary: Gregory J. (Greg) Henchel, age 42
SVP Apparel: June Saltzman
SVP Customer Care: Rob Solomon
SVP Beauty Merchandising: Michael Henry
SVP Investor Relations and Strategy: Felise Glantz Kissell
SVP Merchandising, Apparel: Chuck Anderson
CEO, Cornerstone: Mark Ethier, $1,775,423 total compensation
Director Technology: Gerard Johnson
Director Public Relations and Events: Brad Bohnert
Auditors: Ernst & Young LLP

LOCATIONS

HQ: HSN, Inc.
1 HSN Dr., St. Petersburg, FL 33729
Phone: 727-872-1000
Web: www.hsn.com

PRODUCTS/OPERATIONS

2009 Sales

	$ mil.	% of total
HSN	2,007.9	73
Cornerstone Brands	741.7	27
Total	**2,749.6**	**100**

HISTORICAL FINANCIALS

Company Type: Public

Income Statement

FYE: December 31

	REVENUE ($ mil.)	NET INCOME ($ mil.)	NET PROFIT MARGIN	EMPLOYEES
12/09	2,750	73	2.6%	5,807
12/08	2,824	(2,391)	—	5,973
12/07	2,908	165	5.7%	6,600
12/06	2,878	123	4.3%	—
12/05	2,671	223	8.4%	—
Annual Growth	0.7%	(24.5%)	—	(6.2%)

2009 Year-End Financials

Debt ratio: 97.1%	No. of shares (mil.): 58
Return on equity: —	Dividends
Cash ($ mil.): 270	Yield: —
Current ratio: 1.74	Payout: —
Long-term debt ($ mil.): 334	Market value ($ mil.): 1,162

Stock History

NASDAQ (GS): HSNI

	STOCK PRICE ($) FY Close	P/E High/Low	PER SHARE ($) Earnings	Dividends	Book Value
12/09	20.19	17 3	1.26	—	5.98
12/08	7.27	— —	(42.54)	—	4.49
Annual Growth	177.7%	— —	—	—	33.2%

Hub Group

Hub Group helps its clients by handling the hubbub of freight movement throughout North America. An intermodal marketing company, Hub Group specializes in arranging the transportation of freight by a combination of rail and truck. A customer's freight is loaded into a container or trailer and transported by rail from one Hub Group operating center to another, then taken to its destination by a local trucking company, which in some cases is operated by a Hub Group unit. The company also provides truck brokerage and logistics services. It operates from about 20 main offices, each located near one or more railheads. The family of the company's late founder, Phillip Yeager, owns a controlling stake in Hub Group.

As part of its intermodal business, the company provides drayage (local trucking) services in key markets through subsidiary Comtrak Logistics, which primarily contracts with local trucking companies, but also operates its own fleet of about 300 tractors and 550 trailers.

Hub's flexibility, however, comes from its access to dedicated containers and trailers owned by railroads and leasing companies. The company has access to a rail fleet of more than 150,000 containers and trailers; it has dedicated access to around a total of 8,700 rail-owned containers on the Union Pacific, Norfolk Southern, and Burlington Northern Santa Fe rail lines.

Hub Group's truck brokerage business, known as Hub Highway Services, matches shippers' loads with carriers' capacity. The unit manages the transportation of refrigerated and other specialty cargo, as well as standard dry freight. As part of its brokerage service, Hub negotiates rates, tracks shipments, and handles freight loss and damage claims for customers.

To spur the growth of its logistics unit, Unyson, Hub Group has invested in technology and enhanced its online presence. Unyson arranges the transportation of cargo not handled by other Hub Group units, such as parcels, freight requiring expedited delivery, and less-than-truckload freight. Companies such as Big Lots, General Mills, and Pfizer are among its logistics customers.

Hub Group markets its services to customers in a wide range of industries, including consumer products, durable goods, and retail. Much of the company's business comes from long-term clients, but it is also considering acquisitions that would add to its mix of services as a key to its growth prospects.

HISTORY

Phillip Yeager and his wife, Joyce, founded the first Hub City Terminal in 1971. At the time, intermodal transport was neither efficient nor widely used, and the enterprise grew slowly. The deregulation of the trucking and rail industries in the early 1980s and the passage of the GATT and NAFTA trade agreements in the early 1990s spurred intermodal growth.

Hub Group launched Hub Group International in 1994 to market intermodal services to shippers, forwarders, and shipping lines moving international cargo. The company was incorporated as Hub Group in 1995; it went public the next year. At the time, the 26 existing hubs were separately held corporations; the money from the IPO was used to buy out hubs and purchase a controlling interest in the logistics arm (Hub Group Distribution Services, or HGDS), whose ownership had been shared by the individual hubs.

In 1997, while struggling with the railroads' congestion problems, the company continued buying the remaining interests in its Los Angeles, New Orleans, and San Francisco hubs. The next year Hub Group bought Quality Intermodal (intermodal and truck brokerage service), and in 1999 the company teamed up with Norfolk Southern to serve the rail company's customers in the eastern and southeastern US. Norfolk Southern had acquired more than half of Conrail, but problems resulting from the split-up of Conrail and integration of its assets caused some of Hub Group's intermodal customers to switch from rail to truck.

The company's HGDS unit began offering home delivery services in 2000 for Internet retailers. Hub Group came under fire from investors in 2002 when it announced it had overstated $3.4 million of HGDS revenues for 1999 and 2000. Later that year the company said it had received proposals from potential purchasers but had declined to pursue any of them.

Also in 2002 the company bought out the remaining 35% partnership interest in HGDS to assume full ownership. In 2004 HGDS transferred its pharmaceutical-sample delivery business to the parent company. Two years later the group sold the remaining assets of HGDS to that unit's president.

Hub Group reorganized in 2004 in an effort to recover market share that had been lost to trucking companies, many of which had begun providing intermodal services. Each hub had been managed essentially as a stand-alone business while Hub Group oversaw railroad relations, financial services, and information systems support. Under the new system, responsibility for key sales functions was centralized at company headquarters, along with the other administrative functions.

The company expanded its drayage operations in March 2006 when it paid about $40 million for Memphis-based Comtrak, which was renamed Comtrak Logistics.

Founder and chairman Phillip Yeager died in 2008 at age 80.

EXECUTIVES

Chairman and CEO: David P. Yeager, age 56, $1,318,483 total compensation
Vice Chairman, President, and COO: Mark A. Yeager, age 45, $1,011,380 total compensation
Chief Marketing Officer: David L. Marsh, age 42, $631,478 total compensation
Chief Intermodal Officer: Christopher R. (Chris) Kravas, age 44, $579,797 total compensation
EVP, CFO, and Treasurer: Terri A. Pizzuto, age 51, $650,291 total compensation
EVP Information Services: Dennis R. Polsen, age 56
EVP Highway: Dwight C. Nixon, age 47
EVP Customer Service: Stephen P. Cosgrove, age 50
EVP Sales: James B. (Jim) Gaw, age 59
EVP Logistics: Donald G. Maltby, age 55
VP, Secretary, and General Counsel: David C. Zeilstra, age 40
Auditors: Ernst & Young LLP

LOCATIONS

HQ: Hub Group, Inc.
3050 Highland Pkwy., Ste. 100
Downers Grove, IL 60515
Phone: 630-271-3600   **Fax:** 630-964-6475
Web: www.hubgroup.com

PRODUCTS/OPERATIONS

2009 Sales

	$ mil.	% of total
Intermodal	1,054.9	70
Brokerage	292.6	19
Logistics	163.5	11
Total	**1,511.0**	**100**

COMPETITORS

APL Logistics
C.H. Robinson Worldwide
CSX
J.B. Hunt
Landstar System
Menlo Worldwide
Pacer International
Transplace
UPS Supply Chain Solutions

HISTORICAL FINANCIALS

Company Type: Public

Income Statement

FYE: December 31

	REVENUE ($ mil.)	NET INCOME ($ mil.)	NET PROFIT MARGIN	EMPLOYEES
12/09	1,511	34	2.3%	1,329
12/08	1,861	59	3.2%	1,420
12/07	1,658	60	3.6%	1,412
12/06	1,610	49	3.0%	1,513
12/05	1,532	33	2.1%	1,184
Annual Growth	**(0.3%)**	**1.0%**	**—**	**2.9%**

2009 Year-End Financials

Debt ratio: —
Return on equity: 10.3%
Cash ($ mil.): 127
Current ratio: 2.02
Long-term debt ($ mil.): —
No. of shares (mil.): 38
Dividends
  Yield: —
  Payout: —
Market value ($ mil.): 1,009

Stock History

NASDAQ (GS): HUBG

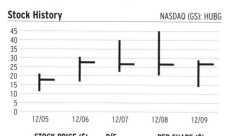

	STOCK PRICE ($) FY Close	P/E High/Low		PER SHARE ($) Earnings	Dividends	Book Value
12/09	26.79	31	16	0.91	—	9.39
12/08	26.53	28	13	1.58	—	8.36
12/07	26.58	26	15	1.53	—	6.66
12/06	27.55	25	15	1.19	—	6.87
12/05	17.67	26	15	0.80	—	6.42
Annual Growth	**11.0%**	**—**	**—**	**3.3%**	**—**	**10.0%**

Humana Inc.

Medicare has made Humana a big-time player in the health insurance game. One of the country's largest Medicare providers and a top health insurer, Humana provides Medicare Advantage plans and prescription drug coverage to more than 3.4 million members throughout the US. It also administers managed care plans for other government programs, including Medicaid plans in Florida and Puerto Rico and TRICARE (a program for military personnel) in 10 southern states. Additionally, Humana offers traditional health plans and some specialty products (group life and disability insurance, for example) to commercial employers and individuals. All told, it covers more than 10 million health plan members in the US.

The company has been aggressive in signing up Medicare recipients for its Medicare Advantage plans, which include HMO, PPO, and private fee-for-service (PFFS) plans, as well as prescription drug coverage under the Medicare Part D program. It has also been expanding its geographic reach, and now has at least one Medicare product available in every state in the US.

In addition to organic growth efforts, the company regularly pursues acquisitions that will bolster its government insurance operations. In 2008 it acquired about 25,000 Medicare Advantage members in Nevada from UnitedHealth. And later that year it acquired Florida-based Medicare Advantage provider Metcare Health Plans from Metropolitan Health Networks.

More than two-thirds of Humana's sales come from government program premiums, and more than half come from Medicare-related premiums alone. The company's reliance on its government business has brought it significant growth, but also leaves it vulnerable to cuts in reimbursement rates. And as financial pressure on the government grows, Congress has noted the cost-cutting potential in rate reductions for Medicare Advantage programs, which are more costly than traditional government-run Medicare plans.

Humana is also working to bolster its commercial business, which offers health coverage to employer groups on a fully-insured basis or with an "administrative services only" model to self-funded groups. Its products include HMO and PPO plans, as well as consumer-directed products such as health savings accounts.

In 2008 the company acquired OSF Health-Plans, an Illinois-based managed care company belonging to OSF Healthcare. The deal, worth about $90 million, gave Humana another 60,000 commercial members, as well as some new Medicare customers, in Illinois. The company had already wrapped up its acquisition of Tennessee-based PHP Companies (which does business as Cariten Healthcare) from Covenant Health. Humana spent $250 million in late 2008 to gain Cariten's managed care operations in East Tennessee, adding 70,000 commercial customers and 45,000 Medicare members.

HISTORY

In 1961 Louisville, Kentucky, lawyers David Jones and Wendell Cherry bought a nursing home as a real estate investment. Within six years their company, Extendicare, was the largest nursing home chain in the US (with only eight homes).

Faced with a glutted nursing home market, the partners noticed that hospitals received more money per patient per day than nursing homes, so they took their company public in 1968 to finance hospital purchases (one per month from 1968 to 1971). The company then sold its 40 nursing homes. Sales rose 13 times over in the next five years, and in 1973 the firm changed its name to Humana.

By 1975 Humana had built 27 hospitals in the South and Southwest. It targeted young, privately insured patients and kept its charity caseload and bad-debt expenses low. Three years later #3 for-profit hospital operator Humana moved up a notch when it bought #2 American Medicorp.

In 1983 the government began reimbursing Medicare payments based on fixed rates. Counting on its high hospital occupancy, in 1984 the company launched Humana Health Care Plans, rewarding doctors and patients who used Humana hospitals. However, hospital occupancy dropped, and the company closed several clinics. When its net income fell 75% in 1986, the firm responded by lowering premiums to attract employers.

In 1991 co-founder Cherry died. With hospital profits down, in 1993 Jones spun off Humana's 76 hospitals as Galen Healthcare, which formed the nucleus of what is now HCA — The Healthcare Company. The next year Humana added 1.3 million members when it bought EMPHESYS, and the company's income, which had stagnated since the salad days of the late 1980s and early 1990s, seemed headed in the right direction.

In the mid-1990s cutthroat premiums failed to cover rising health care costs as members' hospital use soared out of control, particularly in the company's new Washington, DC, market. Profits dropped 94%, and Humana's already tense relationship with doctors and members worsened. President and COO Wayne Smith and CFO Roger Drury resigned as part of a management shake-up, and newly appointed president Gregory Wolf offered to drop the company's gag clause after the Florida Physicians Association threatened to sue.

A reorganized Humana rebounded in 1997. The company pulled out of 13 unprofitable markets, including Alabama (though it did not drop TRICARE, its military health coverage program, in that state) and Washington, DC. Refocusing on core markets in the Midwest and Southeast, Humana bought Physician Corp. of America (PCA) and ChoiceCare, a Cincinnati HMO. Wolf replaced Jones as CEO in 1997.

Humana did everything *but* party in 1999. The company faced RICO charges for allegedly overcharging members for co-insurance; it agreed to repay $15 million in Medicare overpayments to the government; and it became the first health insurance firm to be slapped with a class-action suit over its physician incentives and other coverage policies.

Humana sold PCA in 2000, saying that it had paid too much for the company. That year Humana also sold its underperforming Florida Medicaid HMO to Well Care HMO, and agreed to pay more than $14 million to the government for submitting false Medicare payment information.

Humana acquired Louisiana's Ochsner Health Plan in 2004. It further grew its product line with the 2007 acquisition of Atlanta-based CompBenefits, a provider of dental and vision benefits to nearly 5 million members. Later that year the company bought KMG America, a life and health insurer and third-party administrator for more than 1 million members.

EXECUTIVES

Chairman: David A. Jones Jr., age 52
President, CEO, and Director:
  Michael B. (Mike) McCallister, age 57,
  $6,509,452 total compensation
COO: James E. (Jim) Murray, age 56,
  $3,135,790 total compensation
SVP, CFO, and Treasurer: James H. (Jim) Bloem,
  age 59, $2,325,967 total compensation
SVP and Chief Service and Information Officer:
  Bruce J. Goodman, age 68,
  $1,588,048 total compensation
SVP and Chief Strategy Officer: Paul B. Kusserow,
  $2,808,334 total compensation
SVP and Chief Innovation and Marketing Officer:
  Venkata Raja Rajamannar Madabhushi
SVP and Chief Human Resources Officer:
  Bonita C. (Bonnie) Hathcock, age 61
SVP Government Relations: Heidi S. Margulis, age 56
SVP Senior Products: Thomas J. (Tom) Liston, age 48
SVP and General Counsel: Christopher M. Todoroff,
  age 47
VP, Controller, and Principal Accounting Officer:
  Steven E. McCulley, age 48
**President Commercial Market Operations, Nevada,
  Arizona, and Utah:** Curt Howell
Corporate Communications: Doug Bennett
Auditors: PricewaterhouseCoopers LLP

LOCATIONS

HQ: Humana Inc.
  500 W. Main St., Louisville, KY 40202
Phone: 502-580-1000   **Fax:** 502-580-3677
Web: www.humana.com

PRODUCTS/OPERATIONS

2009 Premiums

	% of total
Government	
Medicare Advantage	55
Military services	11
Medicare prescription plans	8
Medicaid	2
Commercial	
PPO	11
HMO	10
Specialty	3
Total	**100**

2009 Membership

	No.
Government	
Medicare stand-alone PDP	1,927,900
Medicare Advantage	1,508,500
Military services	1,756,000
Military administrative services only (ASO)	1,278,400
Medicaid	401,700
Commercial	
ASO	1,571,300
PPO	1,053,200
HMO	786,300
Total	**10,283,300**

Selected Products and Services

Government
  Medicaid managed care plans
  Medicare Advantage plans
  Medicare prescription drug plans
  TRICARE (military personnel)

Commercial
  Administrative services only
  Health care spending accounts
  HMO plans
  Humana Classic (traditional indemnity plan)
  HumanaOne (individual insurance)
  POS (point-of-service) plans
  PPO plans
  Specialty products
    Dental insurance
    Life insurance
    Short-term disability insurance

COMPETITORS

Aetna
AMERIGROUP
Assurant
Blue Cross
Caremark Pharmacy Services
Centene
CIGNA
Coventry Health Care
Express Scripts
First Health Group
HCSC
Health Net
HealthSpring
Highmark
Kaiser Foundation Health Plan
Medco Health
Molina Healthcare
UnitedHealth Group
Universal American
WellCare Health Plans
WellPoint

HISTORICAL FINANCIALS

Company Type: Public

Income Statement

FYE: December 31

	REVENUE ($ mil.)	NET INCOME ($ mil.)	NET PROFIT MARGIN	EMPLOYEES
12/09	30,960	1,040	3.4%	28,100
12/08	28,946	647	2.2%	28,900
12/07	25,290	834	3.3%	25,000
12/06	21,417	487	2.3%	22,300
12/05	14,418	309	2.1%	18,700
Annual Growth	**21.1%**	**35.5%**	**—**	**10.7%**

2009 Year-End Financials

Debt ratio: 29.1%
Return on equity: 20.3%
Cash ($ mil.): 1,614
Current ratio: —
Long-term debt ($ mil.): 1,678

No. of shares (mil.): 169
Dividends
  Yield: —
  Payout: —
Market value ($ mil.): 7,428

Stock History

NYSE: HUM

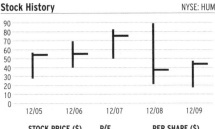

	STOCK PRICE ($) FY Close	P/E High/Low		PER SHARE ($) Earnings	Dividends	Book Value
12/09	43.89	8	3	6.15	—	34.13
12/08	37.28	23	6	3.83	—	26.34
12/07	75.31	17	10	4.91	—	23.81
12/06	55.31	24	14	2.90	—	18.05
12/05	54.33	30	15	1.87	—	14.62
Annual Growth	**(5.2%)**	**—**	**—**	**34.7%**	**—**	**23.6%**

Huntington Bancshares

Huntington Bancshares is the holding company for The Huntington National Bank, which operates more than 600 branches in Indiana, Kentucky, Michigan, Ohio, Pennsylvania, and West Virginia. The bank offers commercial and consumer banking, and mortgage services. The company's Auto Finance and Dealer Services Group offers auto loans and provides commercial loans to car dealerships throughout the Midwest and other states. Huntington's Private Financial and Capital Markets Group provides asset management, private banking, and brokerage services to wealthy customers. Huntington Bancshares also offers trust and insurance services and has international offices in the Cayman Islands and Hong Kong.

Huntington survived the downturn in the economy but did post losses in 2008 and 2009. Much of the company's losses were attributed to credit losses due to nonperforming assets and value losses tied to past acquisitions. The company tried to curb losses by focusing on growing revenue and increasing deposits. Also, early in 2009, management announced a plan to eliminate bonuses and other incentive programs for all employees, and initiated additional cost-cutting measures designed to save one-time expenses.

Despite the challenges, Huntington is looking to grow and has made moves to better position itself as the country emerges from the recession. The bank hired new staff with the aim of increasing revenues. In particular, it doubled the size of its commercial banking staff, who will target lending to small businesses. Huntington also is looking to expand its Midwest franchise by acquiring failed banks. It made one such acquisition in 2009, when it took over the deposits and six branches of Warren Bank in Michigan. Subsidiary Huntington Investment Company also has plans to expand in central Ohio. It is opening two new offices and hiring staff.

Thomas Hoaglin retired as chairman, president, and CEO in 2009 after serving eight years in those positions. Former Citizens Financial Group CEO Stephen Steinour was named Hoaglin's successor.

HISTORY

Pelatiah Webster (P. W.) Huntington, descendant of both a Revolutionary War leader and a Declaration of Independence signer, went to work at sea in 1850 at age 14. He returned to go into banking, and in 1866 founded what would become Huntington National Bank of Columbus. As the business grew, he conscripted four of his five sons. The bank took a national charter in 1905 and became The Huntington National Bank of Columbus. It survived the hard times of 1907 and 1912 through the Huntington philosophy of sitting on piles of cash.

P. W. died in 1918 and his son Francis became president. Francis expanded the company into trust services. Unlike many bankers in the 1920s, he refused to make speculative loans based on the stock market. Francis died in 1928 and was succeeded by brother Theodore. By 1930 Huntington's trust assets accounted for more than half of the total. The family's conservative philosophy helped the bank sail through the 1933 bank holiday, although when it reopened the amount of cash it could pay out was restricted to 10% of deposits.

P. W.'s son Gwynne chaired the bank during its post-WWII expansion. His death in 1958 ended the Huntington family reign. The bank began opening branches and adding new services, such as mortgage and consumer loans. In 1966, in order to expand statewide, the bank formed a holding company, Huntington Bancshares. In the 1960s and 1970s, the corporation added new operations, including mortgage and leasing companies and an international division to help clients with foreign exchange.

In 1979 the company consolidated its 15 affiliates into The Huntington National Bank. Three years later the company bit off more than it could chew with the acquisitions of Reeves Banking and Trust Company of Dover and Union Commerce Corporation of Cleveland. The latter purchase loaded the company with debt. Nevertheless, it continued to expand, particularly after 1985 when banking regulations were changed to permit interstate branch banking, and it soon had operations in Florida, Indiana, Kentucky, Michigan, and West Virginia.

Huntington Bancshares was largely insulated from the real estate problems of the late 1980s and early 1990s, thanks to its continuing conservative lending policies. But the company was at risk from the nationwide consolidation of the banking industry, which made it a potential takeover target. It increased its service offerings and bolstered its place in the market through acquisitions. In 1996 Huntington Bancshares bought life insurance agency Tice & Associates and began cross-selling bank and insurance products. Important banking acquisitions in 1997 included First Michigan Bank and several Florida companies.

Also in 1997 the company took advantage of deregulation to consolidate its interstate operations (except for The Huntington State Bank) into a single operating company. In 1998 Huntington Bancshares continued to build its Huntington insurance services unit with the acquisition of Pollock & Pollock. In 1999 the bank launched a mortgage program aimed at wealthy clients and sold its credit card receivables portfolio to Chase Manhattan (now JPMorgan Chase & Co.). In 2000 the company bought Michigan's Empire Banc Corporation.

Former BANK ONE executive Thomas Hoaglin was named president and CEO in 2001. Later that year he became chairman when Frank Wobst retired after leading the company for 20 years.

In 2002 the company consolidated some branches in the Midwest to cut costs and exited the retail banking market in Florida, selling some 140 retail branches there to SunTrust. After the mid-2007 acquisition of Sky Financial, Sky's CEO Marty Adams became president and COO of Huntington Bancshares. He retired at the end of 2007, and Hoaglin resumed the president's role until his own retirement in 2009; Stephen Steinour then took the helm.

EXECUTIVES

Chairman, President, and CEO:
Stephen D. (Steve) Steinour, age 51,
$1,968,566 total compensation
SEVP and CFO: Donald R. Kimble, age 50,
$758,067 total compensation
**SEVP and Director Strategy and Segment
Performance:** Mark E. Thompson,
$745,906 total compensation
SEVP and Head Auto Finance and Dealer Services:
Nicholas G. (Nick) Stanutz, age 55,
$745,993 total compensation

SEVP and Senior Trust Officer:
Daniel B. (Dan) Benhase, age 50,
$629,441 total compensation
SEVP and Chief Risk Officer: Kevin M. Blakely, age 58
SEVP and Director Commercial Real Estate:
Randy G. Stickler
**SEVP and Director Commercial Banking; Regional
President, West Michigan:** James S. (Jim) Dunlap,
age 57
EVP and CIO: Zahid Afzal
EVP and Chief Auditor: Eric N. Sutphin
EVP and Director Payments and Channels:
Mark W. Sheehan
EVP and Chief Customer and Marketing Officer:
David B. Clifton, age 60
SVP and Director Investor Relations: Jay S. Gould
**General Counsel and Secretary; EVP, General Counsel,
Secretary, and Cashier, The Huntington National
Bank:** Richard A. Cheap, age 58
Auditors: Deloitte & Touche LLP

LOCATIONS

HQ: Huntington Bancshares Incorporated
Huntington Center, 41 S. High St.
Columbus, OH 43287
Phone: 614-480-8300   **Fax:** 614-480-5284
Web: www.huntington.com

PRODUCTS/OPERATIONS

2009 Sales

	$ mil.	% of total
Interest		
Loans & leases	1,944.3	60
Investment securities	258.8	8
Other	35.1	1
Noninterest		
Service charges on deposit accounts	302.8	9
Brokerage & insurance income	138.2	4
Mortgage banking income	112.3	3
Trust services	103.6	3
Electronic banking	100.2	3
Bank-owned life insurance	54.8	2
Automobile operating lease income	51.8	2
Net gains on sales of investment securities	48.8	2
Other	93.1	3
Total	**3,243.8**	**100**

2009 Assets

	$ mil.	% of total
Cash & equivalents	1,840.7	4
Loans held for sale	461.6	1
Investment securities	8,587.9	17
Net loans & leases	35,308.2	68
Other	5,356.3	10
Total	**51,554.7**	**100**

COMPETITORS

Bank of America
Bank of Kentucky Financial
Citigroup
Comerica
Fifth Third
FirstMerit
JPMorgan Chase
KeyCorp
NorthWest Indiana Bancorp
Ohio Valley Banc
PNC Financial
Regions Financial
U.S. Bancorp

HISTORICAL FINANCIALS

Company Type: Public

Income Statement

FYE: December 31

	ASSETS ($ mil.)	NET INCOME ($ mil.)	INCOME AS % OF ASSETS	EMPLOYEES
12/09	51,555	(3,094)	—	10,272
12/08	54,353	(114)	—	10,951
12/07	54,698	75	0.1%	11,925
12/06	35,329	461	1.3%	8,081
12/05	32,765	412	1.3%	7,602
Annual Growth	**12.0%**	**—**	**—**	**7.8%**

2009 Year-End Financials

Equity as % of assets: 7.1%
Return on assets: —
Return on equity: —
Long-term debt ($ mil.): 3,803
No. of shares (mil.): 717
Dividends
  Yield: 1.1%
  Payout: —
Market value ($ mil.): 2,617
Sales ($ mil.): 3,244

Stock History

NASDAQ (GS): HBAN

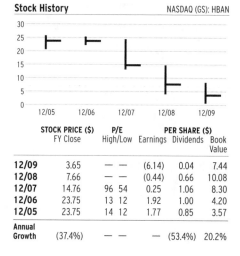

	STOCK PRICE ($) FY Close	P/E High/Low		PER SHARE ($) Earnings	Dividends	Book Value
12/09	3.65	—	—	(6.14)	0.04	7.44
12/08	7.66	—	—	(0.44)	0.66	10.08
12/07	14.76	96	54	0.25	1.06	8.30
12/06	23.75	13	12	1.92	1.00	4.20
12/05	23.75	14	12	1.77	0.85	3.57
Annual Growth	**(37.4%)**	**—**	**—**	**—**	**(53.4%)**	**20.2%**

Hyatt Hotels Corporation

Travelers interested in luxury lodgings can check in for the Hyatt touch. The company is one of the world's top operators of full-service luxury hotels and resorts with more than 420 managed, franchised, and owned properties in some 45 countries. Its core Hyatt Regency brand offers hospitality services targeted primarily to business travelers and upscale vacationers. The firm also operates properties under six additional brands: Grand Hyatt, Park Hyatt, Hyatt Place, Hyatt Summerfield Suites, Hyatt Resorts, and Andaz. It is majority-owned by the wealthy Pritzker family of Chicago. In 2009 the company filed an IPO.

With revenues declining in 2009, the timing of the public offering was questionable, given the weak economy and a hotel industry suffering from decreased occupancy levels. However, Hyatt's IPO had been years in the making as a way for the Pritzker family to raise cash. (The family is splitting up its assets among 11 adult cousins.)

Hyatt's operations had, in the past, been hindered by feuds within the Pritzker family. Though the Pritzkers remain in control, the IPO gave several family members the chance to cash out, allowing for an end to the feuds and paving the way for changes at the company.

In an effort to focus on its luxury hotel businesses and international expansion, the company is opening several properties in key growth markets. These include China (Grand Hyatt Shenzhen), India (Hyatt Regency Pune and Park Hyatt Hyderabad), Mexico (Park Hyatt Mexico City), and the United Arab Emirates (Park Hyatt Abu Dhabi). Hyatt also sold its U.S. Franchise Systems subsidiary in 2008 to Wyndham Worldwide in order to focus on its global growth and luxury brands. The unit, acquired in 2000, operated the smaller Hawthorn Suites and Microtel Inns & Suites chains.

Hyatt Hotels has additionally been busy investing in its newer brands, including its two select service offerings: Hyatt Place and Hyatt Summerfield Suites. The select service hotels have limited food and beverage offerings, and do not offer full business or banquet facilities; instead they cater to smaller business meetings. Despite the more limited offerings, the brands still emphasize higher-quality amenities. Hyatt Place is designed to attract younger travelers with wireless Internet access, flat screen televisions, and contemporary interiors. The chain was rebranded from AmeriSuites, a brand Hyatt acquired in 2005 from Prime Hospitality. Hyatt Summerfield Suites is an upscale all-suite/extended-stay brand previously known as Summerfield Suites.

As part of an ongoing effort to restructure H Group Holding, the holding company that oversees the Pritzker's various business enterprises, Hyatt Hotels was formed to consolidate the family's hospitality interests. The reorganization brought together the operations of Hyatt Hotels Corporation (domestic hotels), Hyatt International (international hotels), Hyatt Equities (hotel ownership), and Hyatt Vacation Ownership (timeshares) under one umbrella.

The Pritzkers control 78% of the company's total voting power.

HISTORY

Nicholas Pritzker left Kiev for Chicago in 1881, where his family's ascent to the ranks of America's wealthiest families began. His son A. N. left the family law practice in the 1930s and began investing in a variety of businesses. He turned a 1942 investment (Cory Corporation) worth $25,000 into $23 million by 1967. A. N.'s son Jay followed in his father's wheeling-and-dealing footsteps. In 1953, with the help of his father's banking connections, Jay purchased Colson Company and recruited his brother Bob, an industrial engineer, to restructure a company that made tricycles and US Navy rockets. By 1990 Jay and Bob had added 60 industrial companies, with annual sales exceeding $3 billion, to the entity they called The Marmon Group.

The family's connection to Hyatt hotels was established in 1957 when Jay Pritzker bought a hotel called Hyatt House, located near the Los Angeles airport, from Hyatt von Dehn. Jay added five locations by 1961 and hired his gregarious youngest brother, Donald, to manage the hotel company. Hyatt went public in 1967, but the move that opened new vistas for the hotel chain was the purchase that year of an 800-room hotel in Atlanta that both Hilton and Marriott had turned down. John Portman's design, incorporating a 21-story atrium, a large fountain, and a revolving rooftop restaurant, became a Hyatt trademark.

The Pritzkers formed Hyatt International in 1969 to operate hotels overseas, and the company grew rapidly in the US and abroad during the 1970s. Donald Pritzker died in 1972, and Jay assumed control of Hyatt. The family decided to take the company private in 1979. Much of Hyatt's growth in the 1970s came from contracts to manage Hyatt hotels built by other investors. When Hyatt's earnings on those contracts shrank in the 1980s, the company launched its own hotel and resort developments under Nick Pritzker, a cousin to Jay and Bob. In 1988, with US and Japanese partners, it built the Hyatt Regency Waikoloa on Hawaii's Big Island for $360 million — a record at the time for a hotel.

The Pritzkers took a side-venture into air travel in 1983 when they bought bedraggled Braniff Airlines through Hyatt subsidiaries as it emerged from bankruptcy. After a failed 1987 attempt to merge the airline with Pan Am, the Pritzkers sold Braniff in 1988.

Hyatt opened Classic Residence by Hyatt, a group of upscale retirement communities, in 1989. The company joined Circus Circus (now part of MGM MIRAGE) in 1994 to launch the *Grand Victoria*, the nation's largest cruising gaming vessel.

President Thomas Pritzker, Jay's son, took over as Hyatt chairman and CEO following his father's death in early 1999. In 2000 the Pritzker family led a buyout of U.S. Franchise Systems (sold to Wyndham Worldwide in 2008).

In 2004 the Pritzker family consolidated its hospitality holdings to form Global Hyatt Corporation. The following year the company bought the AmeriSuites limited-service hotel chain from Prime Hospitality.

Mark Hoplamazian, president of The Pritzker Organization, a merchant-banking firm serving the family's business activities, took over as president and CEO in 2006; Thomas Pritzker remained chairman.

In 2009 the company changed its name from Global Hyatt Corporation to Hyatt Hotels Corporation. Later that year it filed an IPO.

EXECUTIVES

Executive Chairman: Thomas J. (Tom) Pritzker, age 59, $587,889 total compensation
President, CEO, and Director: Mark S. Hoplamazian, age 46, $3,670,913 total compensation
COO North America: H. Charles (Chuck) Floyd, age 50, $3,921,986 total compensation
COO International Operations: Rakesh K. Sarna, age 53, $3,292,629 total compensation
CFO: Harmit J. Singh, age 47, $2,295,630 total compensation
EVP Global Real Estate and Development: Stephen G. (Steve) Haggerty, age 42, $1,997,806 total compensation
VP Corporate Communications: Farley Kern
Global Head Marketing and Brand Strategy: John Wallis, age 57
General Counsel and Secretary: Rena H. Reiss
Chief Human Resources Officer: Robert W. K. Webb, age 54
Auditors: Deloitte & Touche LLP

LOCATIONS

HQ: Hyatt Hotels Corporation
71 S. Wacker Dr., 12th Fl., Chicago, IL 60606
Phone: 312-750-1234
Web: www.hyatt.com

2009 Sales

	$ mil.	% of total
US	2,678	80
International	654	20
Total	**3,332**	**100**

PRODUCTS/OPERATIONS

2009 Sales

	$ mil.	% of total
Owned & leased hotels	1,782	52
North American management & franchising	1,382	41
International management & franchising	181	5
Corporate & other	67	2
Eliminations	(80)	—
Total	**3,332**	**100**

2009 Properties by Type

	No. of properties
Managed	162
Franchised	109
Owned & leased	102
Vacation ownership	15
Residential properties	10
Total	**424**

Selected Brands

Andaz (simple, sophisticated luxury hotels)
Grand Hyatt Hotels (large-scale luxury format)
Hyatt Regency Hotels (core hotel format)
Hyatt Resorts (local culture, including spas and cuisine)
Hyatt Summerfield Suites (extended stay)
Hyatt Vacation Ownership (timeshares)
Park Hyatt Hotels (smaller-scale luxury hotels)

Selected Properties

Andaz West Hollywood
Grand Hyatt New York
Grand Hyatt San Antonio
Grand Hyatt San Francisco
Grand Hyatt Seattle
Grand Hyatt Tampa Bay
Hyatt Place Atlanta/Perimeter Center
Hyatt Place Baltimore/Owings Mills
Hyatt Place Birmingham/Inverness
Hyatt Place Boise/Towne Square
Hyatt Place Charlotte Airport/Tyvola Road
Hyatt Place Chicago/Hoffman Estates
Hyatt Place Chicago/Itasca
Hyatt Place Chicago/Lombard/Oak Brook
Hyatt Place Cincinnati Northeast
Hyatt Regency Atlanta
Hyatt Regency Baltimore
Hyatt Regency Bellevue
Hyatt Regency Boston
Hyatt Regency Buffalo
Hyatt Regency Cincinnati
Hyatt Regency Cleveland at The Arcade
Hyatt Regency Coconut Point Resort & Spa
Hyatt Summerfield Suites Boston/Waltham
Hyatt Summerfield Suites Denver Tech Center
Hyatt Summerfield Suites Miami Airport
Hyatt Summerfield Suites Morristown
Hyatt Summerfield Suites Parsippany/Whippany
Park Hyatt Chicago
Park Hyatt Philadelphia at Bellevue
Park Hyatt Toronto
Park Hyatt Washington

COMPETITORS

Accor
Carlson Hotels
Club Med
Four Seasons Hotels
Hilton Worldwide
InterContinental Hotels
LXR Luxury Resorts
Marriott
Millennium & Copthorne Hotels
Sonesta International Hotels
Starwood Hotels & Resorts
Wyndham Worldwide

HISTORICAL FINANCIALS

Company Type: Public

Income Statement

	REVENUE ($ mil.)	NET INCOME ($ mil.)	NET PROFIT MARGIN	EMPLOYEES
12/09	3,332	(46)	—	45,000
12/08	3,837	170	4.4%	125,000
12/07*	3,738	271	7.2%	90,000
1/06	3,471	329	9.5%	85,000
1/05	3,200	—	—	70,000
Annual Growth	1.0%	—	—	(10.5%)

*Fiscal year change

2009 Year-End Financials

Debt ratio: 32.3%
Return on equity: —
Cash ($ mil.): 1,327
Current ratio: 4.02
Long-term debt ($ mil.): 1,620

No. of shares (mil.): 174
Dividends
  Yield: —
  Payout: —
Market value ($ mil.): 5,185

Stock History

NYSE: H

	STOCK PRICE ($) FY Close	P/E High/Low	PER SHARE ($) Earnings	Dividends	Book Value
12/09	29.81	— —	(0.28)	—	28.84

IAC/InterActiveCorp

IAC/InterActiveCorp (IAC) satisfies inquisitive minds who want to use the Web to explore local hot spots, meet the right partner, find a contractor, and maybe even host a party or two. The Internet conglomerate owns more than 50 brands, including search engine Ask.com, local guide Citysearch (part of advertising network CityGrid Media), dating site Match.com, home service provider network ServiceMagic, and online-invitation firm Evite. Other IAC holdings include shoe site Shoebuy.com, current affairs Web magazine Daily Beast, and a majority stake in Connected Ventures, the parent company of racy college entertainment site CollegeHumor.com. IAC is controlled by CEO Barry Diller.

Ask.com (formerly Ask Jeeves) is the company's flagship search engine that falls under its Search segment. The unit has an advertising partnership with Google — worth an estimated $3.5 billion — that expires in 2012. The deal grants Google the right to sell ads on Ask.com and other IAC sites. Google accounts for some 40% of revenues. The Search business took a huge loss in 2009 (some $1 billion) as a result of a weak advertising market and a down economy.

Online local city guide Citysearch had also been classified as part of IAC's Search segment. In 2010 the parent company changed the name of the subsidiary; Citysearch became CityGrid Media. The new name reflects that business's evolution to a local advertising and content network that also houses Urbanspoon (online restaurant guide acquired in 2009) and Insider Pages (consumer reviews of local businesses, purchased in 2007). CityGrid Media still operates Citysearch as its flagship website that covers approximately 18 million business listings with information and reviews.

While Search is the largest portion of the business, the company has been especially focused on building up its Match segment, which earns revenues through subscription fees. In 2009, it acquired PeopleMedia, an operator of targeted dating sites such as BlackPeopleMeet, SingleParentMeet, and SeniorPeopleMeet. Also that year it sold the European operations of Match.com to Meetic, a European online dating company, in exchange for a 27% interest in Meetic and €5 million (or about $6.7 million). In 2010 IAC announced the formation of a joint venture between Match.com and Meetic, through which it intends to provide personals services in certain countries in Latin America.

Formerly a jumble of disparate assets that included cable-TV networks, travel services, and mortgage lending, IAC slimmed down considerably to focus on the online search and content market in 2008, when Diller spun off HSN, Ticketmaster, Tree.com, and Interval Leisure Group. The spinoff undid years of acquisitions by IAC that positioned it as a big player in e-commerce, but also created a complex corporate structure that confused investors.

John Malone's Liberty Interactive Group owns a stake in IAC. Malone had been against the 2008 corporate breakup, but eventually dropped his opposition in exchange for a voting agreement with Diller; in exchange, Liberty was given the power to appoint board members to the spinoff companies.

HISTORY

TV networks aren't built in a day; but if anyone could do it, it's probably Barry Diller. Since dropping out of UCLA in 1958 to work in the mailroom at the William Morris talent agency (he was promoted to agent in 1961), Diller has been all over Tinseltown. He got into television in 1968 as the VP of programming for ABC, where he developed the concepts of the miniseries and the made-for-TV movie. Diller's next step took him into movies as chairman of Paramount Pictures in 1974. His 10-year Paramount stint produced films including *Raiders of the Lost Ark*. But Diller's biggest claim to fame is his tenure at FOX. Beginning in 1984, Diller led the brash television network from joke to jewel. After a scrape with FOX boss Rupert Murdoch in 1992, he moved on to home shopping as head of QVC in 1993.

Diller built a company of his own in 1995 after leaving QVC. With financial backing from TCI (later bought by AT&T Broadband), Diller took over the Home Shopping Network (now HSN) and its separately traded distribution unit, Silver King Communications. In 1997 HSN bought Microsoft co-founder Paul Allen's 47% interest in Ticketmaster. Diller followed that up with the $4 billion purchase of USA Networks in 1998.

USA Networks dates back to 1977, when Kay Koplovitz founded the all-sports Madison Square Garden Network cable channel. In 1980 she sold the channel (now USA Network) to Time, MCA, and Paramount. By 1988 Paramount (later bought by Viacom) and MCA had become equal owners in USA. (Universal bought out Viacom's interest in 1997.)

Diller bought USA Networks and Vivendi UNIVERSAL Entertainment's TV production and US distribution business as well. The deal gave Seagram a 45% stake in HSN, which changed its name to USA Networks. USA Networks bought the remainder of Ticketmaster in 1998, then purchased online entertainment guide publisher Citysearch, merging it with Ticketmaster Online.

In 1999 Diller bought parts of PolyGram Filmed Entertainment and independent film companies Gramercy and October from Seagram, renaming them Focus. In 2000 French utility and media firm Vivendi (now Vivendi UNIVERSAL) bought Seagram, gaining Seagram's 43% stake in USA Networks.

In 2001 USA Networks agreed to sell its TV stations to Univision for $1.1 billion. At the end of 2001 Diller decided to shift USA Interactive's focus entirely to retailing. He agreed to sell USA Networks' entertainment assets to Vivendi UNIVERSAL for $10.3 billion. The deal was completed in 2002, and the company changed its name to USA Interactive with Diller retaining his voting control of the firm.

In 2003 the company completed its acquisition of the outstanding shares of Hotels.com and Expedia that it didn't already own. The same day of the Expedia deal, IAC completed its acquisition of online financial services company LendingTree (now Tree.com).

In 2004 the company changed its name to IAC/InterActiveCorp. In 2005 it completed the acquisition of Cornerstone Brands, a portfolio of leading print catalogs and online retailing sites. Later that year IAC completed the spinoff to IAC shareholders of its travel businesses.

In 2007 IAC sold its German TV and Internet retailer, HSE Germany. In 2007 IAC struck a deal with online video syndication firm Brightcove to create and distribute video for IAC's brands.

EXECUTIVES

Chairman and CEO: Barry Diller, age 68, $19,781,414 total compensation
Vice Chairman: Victor A. Kaufman, age 66, $6,213,285 total compensation
EVP and CFO: Thomas J. (Tom) McInerney, age 45, $9,414,810 total compensation
SVP and Chief Administrative Officer: Jason Stewart
SVP Mobile: Dinesh Moorjani
SVP and General Counsel: Gregg Winiarski
SVP and Controller: Michael H. Schwerdtman
SVP Tax: Greg Morrow
SVP Mergers and Acquisitions and Strategy: Shana Fisher
SVP Corporate Development; Chief Strategy Officer, Mindspark: Mark J. Stein
VP Investor Relations and Treasurer: Nick Stoumpas
VP Corporate Communications: Stacy Simpson
CEO, Match.com: Gregory R. (Greg) Blatt, age 41, $7,464,789 total compensation
CEO, Citysearch: Jay Herratti
CEO, ServiceMagic: Craig Smith
CEO, Mindspark Interactive Network: Joey Levin
Editor-in-Chief, Connected Ventures; CEO, Notional: Ricky Van Veen
CEO, Shoebuy.com: Scott Savitz
President, Connected Ventures: Josh D. Abramson, age 28
President, Ask Networks: Scott B. Garell, age 44
President, IAC Advertising: Greg Stevens
President, Evite: Hans Woolley
Senior Advisor: Michael Jackson
Auditors: Ernst & Young LLP

LOCATIONS

HQ: IAC/InterActiveCorp
555 West 18th St., New York, NY 10011
Phone: 212-314-7300
Web: www.iac.com

2009 Sales

	$ mil.	% of total
US	1,167.7	85
Other countries	208.1	15
Total	**1,375.8**	**100**

PRODUCTS/OPERATIONS

2009 Sales

	$ mil.	% of total
Search	688.2	50
Match	342.6	25
Service Magic	155.8	11
Media & other	197.8	14
Adjustments	(8.6)	—
Total	**1,375.8**	**100**

Selected Properties

Ask.com
Citysearch
CollegeHumor.com
The Daily Beast
Evite
FiLife.com
Gifts.com
InstantAction.com
Match.com
Pronto.com
RushmoreDrive.com
ServiceMagic
Shoebuy
UrbanSpoon
VeryShortList.com

COMPETITORS

AOL
CBS Interactive
CND
Cox Enterprises
craigslist
Facebook
Google
Hearst Interactive Media
MSN
MSNBC.com
News Corp. Digital Media
Vertro
Yahoo!

HISTORICAL FINANCIALS

Company Type: Public

Income Statement

FYE: December 31

	REVENUE ($ mil.)	NET INCOME ($ mil.)	NET PROFIT MARGIN	EMPLOYEES
12/09	1,376	(980)	—	3,200
12/08	1,445	(156)	—	3,200
12/07	6,373	(144)	—	21,000
12/06	6,278	193	3.1%	20,000
12/05	5,754	806	14.0%	28,000
Annual Growth	**(30.1%)**	**—**	**—**	**(41.9%)**

2009 Year-End Financials

Debt ratio: 3.1%
Return on equity: —
Cash ($ mil.): 1,246
Current ratio: 6.89
Long-term debt ($ mil.): 96

No. of shares (mil.): 105
Dividends
 Yield: —
 Payout: —
Market value ($ mil.): 2,142

Stock History

NASDAQ (GS): IACI

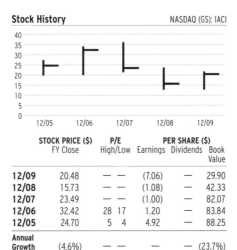

	STOCK PRICE ($) FY Close	P/E High/Low		PER SHARE ($) Earnings	Dividends	Book Value
12/09	20.48	—	—	(7.06)	—	29.90
12/08	15.73	—	—	(1.08)	—	42.33
12/07	23.49	—	—	(1.00)	—	82.07
12/06	32.42	28	17	1.20	—	83.84
12/05	24.70	5	4	4.92	—	88.25
Annual Growth	**(4.6%)**	—	—	—	—	**(23.7%)**

IDEX Corporation

The big idea at IDEX is to dispense with inefficiencies and pump up profits. The company is a major manufacturer of pumps, dispensing equipment, and other engineered industrial products. It operates through four segments. A fluid and metering segment makes pumps, meters, and injectors used in the movement and treatment of industrial chemicals, gases, and water. Its dispensing unit specializes in paint dispersal and mixing tools, sold by US and European home centers and other retailers. A health and science unit produces fluidics components for medical instruments and implantable devices. IDEX's fire and safety equipment unit manufactures clamps, firefighting pumps, and rescue tools, such as the Jaws of Life.

Despite weakened demand from industrial customers hit by the economic recession, the company is persevering in developing its product portfolio to broaden its market opportunities. IDEX fluid and metering technologies, which accounts for about half of the company's sales, expanded with offerings for wastewater management, fresh water monitoring, power generation, and fuel production and distribution. In 2009 IDEX's bundle of leak detection products and services helped the company win work in the Middle East for monitoring and preventing water loss.

An aggressive acquisition strategy has helped build the IDEX lineup and global footprint. The acquisition of Seals, Ltd. in April 2010 brings IDEX the opportunity to expand into significant new markets including clean room, food processing, and pharmaceutical research. Seals has two divisions: Polymer Engineering (seals used in hazardous applications) and Perlast (seals for instrumentation, electronics, and food applications). IDEX paid £35 million (about $54 million) in cash for the company, which will become part of its Health and Science Technologies segment. Italy-based OBL joined IDEX's water and wastewater group in 2010, and brought with it a stronger presence in both Europe and Asia, regions where the pump manufacturing company has made inroads in recent years.

Acquisitions in late 2008 (Richter, Integrated Environmental Technology Group, and iPEK) gave IDEX additional water distribution and sewer management products and services, as well as wastewater infrastructure inspection capabilities. These deals followed IDEX's move to pick up ADS, a provider of metering technology and flow monitoring services.

IDEX's health and science technologies segment received an infusion in late 2008. Semrock, a supplier of optical filters, was acquired. The deal widens IDEX's access to health and life science OEMs specializing in biotechnology and analytical instrumentation.

HISTORY

IDEX is the successor of Houdaille (pronounced "WHO-dye") Industries, which took its name from Maurice Houdaille, the French inventor of recoilless artillery used in WWI. After the war a US firm bought the name and the rights to Houdaille's patented rotary shock absorber. By the 1930s Houdaille was the #1 maker of shock absorbers in the US. During WWII it was involved in building the atomic bomb. With the trend toward in-house manufacture by the auto giants in the 1950s, the company diversified into industrial and construction products, pumps, and machine tools. Facing difficult economic conditions, Phil Reilly (Houdaille's then CEO-nominee) and investors Kohlberg Kravis Roberts took the company private in 1979 in the first leveraged buyout of any company worth more than $100 million.

In 1987 IDEX (an acronym for "innovation, diversity, and excellence") was formed to buy back six units Houdaille had sold to the British TI Group earlier that year. In 1989 IDEX went public. Following the IPO, the company pursued an aggressive acquisition strategy. Purchases included Corken (1991), Devjo's Pump Group (now Viking Pump, 1992), and Hale Products (1994).

The company acquired Micropump (small magnetically driven pumps) for $33 million in 1995. The following year it paid $135 million for Fluid Management, a top maker of color-formulation equipment for paints, coatings, inks, and dyes.

In 1998 IDEX acquired Gast Manufacturing, which makes vacuum pumps, air motors, and compressors, for about $118 million. The following year it gained a foothold in Italy when it paid $62 million for FAST (refinishing and color-formulation equipment). In 2000 IDEX acquired Trebor International, maker of high purity fluid handling products for the microelectronics industry.

In 2001 IDEX acquired displacement flow meter and process control systems maker Liquid Controls LLC. Acquisitions in 2003 included Sponsler Co. (turbine meters) and Classic Engineering (industrial pumps). In early 2004 Idex acquired Manfred Vetter, a Germany-based rescue equipment (pneumatic lifting and sealing bags) manufacturer. IDEX acquired Systec, a vacuum degassing product manufacturer, in 2004. Later in the year IDEX completed the acquisition of Scivex, Inc., a pump and valve manufacturer that serves medical companies.

In 2006 it acquired Banjo Corporation, which makes specialized pumps and related hardware for handling fluids in agricultural and industrial applications.

The company expanded its sanitary control operations with the 2007 purchase of Quadro Engineering, which provides particle handling products to the pharmaceutical laboratory market. Quadro operates as a unit of IDEX's fluid and metering segment. That same year it picked up Isolation Technologies, which makes analytical chemistry instruments. IDEX paid about $30 million for the company.

EXECUTIVES

Chairman, President, and CEO:
Lawrence D. (Larry) Kingsley, age 47, $3,636,943 total compensation
VP and CFO: Dominic A. Romeo, age 50, $1,315,549 total compensation
VP Process Technology: John L. McMurray, age 59, $1,284,324 total compensation
VP Corporate Finance: Heath A. Mitts
VP Strategy and Business Development:
Daniel J. Salliotte, age 43
VP Health and Science Technologies and Global Dispensing: Andrew K. Silvernail, age 38
VP Tax and International Finance:
Gerald F. (Jerry) Carter
VP and Chief Accounting Officer: Michael J. Yates, age 44
VP Human Resources: Harold Morgan, age 53
VP Fluid and Metering Technologies:
Kevin G. Hostetler, age 41
CIO: Divakar (Dave) Kamath, age 59
Auditors: Deloitte & Touche LLP

LOCATIONS

HQ: IDEX Corporation
630 Dundee Rd., Ste. 400, Northbrook, IL 60062
Phone: 847-498-7070   **Fax:** 847-498-3940
Web: www.idexcorp.com

2009 Sales

	$ mil.	% of total
US	698.8	53
Europe	361.8	27
Other countries	269.0	20
Total	**1,329.6**	**100**

PRODUCTS/OPERATIONS

2009 Sales

	$ mil.	% of total
Fluid & metering technologies	640.2	48
Health & science technologies	299.3	22
Fire & safety/diversified products	262.8	20
Dispensing equipment	127.3	10
Total	**1,329.6**	**100**

Selected Products and Business Units

Dispensing Equipment
FAST (tinting, mixing, dispensing, and measuring equipment)
Fluid Management (dispensing, metering, and mixing equipment)
Fire & Safety/Diversified Products
BAND-IT (stainless-steel bands, buckles, and clamping systems)
Hale-Fire Suppression and Hale-Hydraulic Equipment (fire pumps and rescue tool systems)
HURST Jaws of Life/LUKAS/Dinglee/Vetter (hydraulic rescue tools, re-railing equipment, lifting and position devices)

Fluid & Metering Technologies
ADS (metering and flow monitoring equipment)
Air operated double diaphragm pumps (air-operated and motor-driven double diaphragm pumps)
Banjo (severe-duty pumps, valves, fittings, and systems)
iPEK (remote-controlled infrastructure inspection equipment)
Liquid controls (flow meters and electronic controls)
Pulsafeeder (rotary pumps, metering pumps, peristaltic pumps, electronic controls, and dispensing equipment)
Richter (corrosion-resistant lined pumps, valves, and controls)
Viking Pump (gear pumps, strainers and reducers, and controls)
Health & Science Technologies
Gast Manufacturing (air motors, blowers, compressors, vacuum generators, and vacuum pumps)
HST Core (valves, fitting, injectors, medical tubing assemblies, optical filters, filter sensors, nano-fluidic components, and engineered plastics)
Micropump (rotary gear, piston, and centrifugal pumps)
Seals, Ltd. (seals for analytical instrumentation, clean room environments, food processing, hazardous applications, and pharmaceutical research)

COMPETITORS

American Cast Iron Pipe
Dover Corp.
Dresser, Inc.
Flowserve
Gardner Denver
Gardner Denver Thomas
Gorman-Rupp
Graco
Graham Corp.
Illinois Tool Works
ITT Corp.
Oilgear
Pentair
Robbins & Myers
Roper Industries
Tuthill
United Technologies
Weir Group
Wilden Pump & Engineering

HISTORICAL FINANCIALS

Company Type: Public

Income Statement

FYE: December 31

	REVENUE ($ mil.)	NET INCOME ($ mil.)	NET PROFIT MARGIN	EMPLOYEES
12/09	1,330	113	8.5%	5,300
12/08	1,490	131	8.8%	5,813
12/07	1,359	155	11.4%	5,009
12/06	1,155	147	12.7%	4,863
12/05	1,043	110	10.5%	4,300
Annual Growth	**6.3%**	**0.8%**	**—**	**5.4%**

2009 Year-End Financials

Debt ratio: 30.9%
Return on equity: 9.3%
Cash ($ mil.): 74
Current ratio: 2.38
Long-term debt ($ mil.): 392

No. of shares (mil.): 81
Dividends
  Yield: 1.5%
  Payout: 34.3%
Market value ($ mil.): 2,538

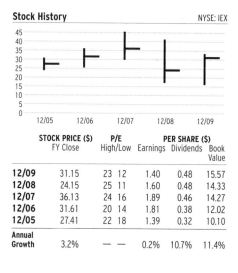

Stock History   NYSE: IEX

	STOCK PRICE ($) FY Close	P/E High/Low		PER SHARE ($) Earnings	Dividends	Book Value
12/09	31.15	23	12	1.40	0.48	15.57
12/08	24.15	25	11	1.60	0.48	14.33
12/07	36.13	24	16	1.89	0.46	14.27
12/06	31.61	20	14	1.81	0.38	12.02
12/05	27.41	22	18	1.39	0.32	10.10
Annual Growth	**3.2%**	**—**	**—**	**0.2%**	**10.7%**	**11.4%**

IDT Corporation

IDT keeps a corporate finger in several pies. The company makes most of its money through IDT Telecom, which provides retail domestic and international long-distance access mainly in the US, as well as wholesale voice and data services. IDT also offers wireless service and pre-paid calling cards. The company's international business consists of calling card sales to customers primarily in Europe. IDT's other operations include an energy services unit that resells natural gas and electric power in New York state and alternative energy operations in the US and Israel. The company had been involved in the debt collection business through its IDT Carmel division but sold those operations in late 2009.

IDT pioneered international callback technology, sometimes known as call reorigination, which allows international phone callers to bypass overseas carriers (and their high rates) by rerouting calls through less expensive US exchanges. IDT now operates a network that includes switches in Europe and the US to connect callers around the globe. The company leases additional capacity from other carriers, including undersea fiber-optic cables that connect to the facilities of IDT's partners in Asia, Europe, and Latin America.

In 2008 the company bought a stake in EGL Oil Shale in a move to expand its energy sector holdings. EGL holds leases from the US Bureau of Land Management to explore for oil shale in western Colorado. The business was later renamed American Shale Oil Corporation (AMSO), which IDT holds a 50% interest in. IDT also owns a stake in Israeli Energy Initiatives, Ltd.

The following year IDT spun off CTM Media Holdings as a stock dividend to its shareholders. CTM Media Holdings, previously known as IDT Capital, encompasses CTM Media Group, a distributor of print and online advertising and information in North America; IDW Publishing, a publisher of books and comics; and an AM radio station in the Washington, DC, metropolitan area. It also sold its European prepaid payment services operations, which had offered prepaid MasterCards under the Prime brand.

Founder and chairman Howard Jonas controls IDT with 40% ownership. CEO Jim Courter stepped down from the chief executive's post in 2009; he remained nonexecutive vice chairman. Jonas re-assumed the position of CEO as a result.

HISTORY

Howard Jonas started a trade publishing business in 1978; when he ran up an $8,000 phone bill establishing a sales office in Israel, the 33-year-old entrepreneur bought $300 worth of components and rigged up a callback device. That feat of ingenuity led Jonas to start International Discount Telecommunications (IDT) in 1990. The next year the company began selling its international call reorigination services, which took advantage of cheaper US rates. By 1993 it had more than 1,000 customers in some 60 countries and had begun reselling long-distance services to its US customers.

In 1994 IDT added Internet access to its service portfolio. Jonas renamed the company IDT Corporation in 1995. That year IDT took advantage of the volume of callers that used its callback services and began reselling to other long-distance carriers. The company went public the next year and also acquired the Genie online service. Continuing to experiment with telephony services, IDT formed Net2Phone in 1997 to provide long-distance phone service over the Internet.

IDT dropped its rates in 1998, offering long-distance rates of five cents per minute in some markets. It introduced Net2Fax, which routes faxes over the Internet, and Click2Talk, which connects Web-surfing customers directly to live customer service representatives. Also in 1998 it acquired InterExchange, a debit card company that complemented its own calling card services.

The next year IDT spun off Net2Phone, then sold a stake in the former subsidiary to AT&T. It formed a joint venture with Spain's Terra Networks (spun off from Telefónica) to provide Internet products and services to the US Hispanic population. Also in 1999 Chattle, IDT's wholly owned subsidiary, joined with Westmintech to provide high-speed voice and data services, cable TV, and Internet access worldwide.

In 2000 IDT reorganized into two divisions: IDT Telecom, with its international retail and wholesale telecom services, and IDT Ventures and Investments, to pursue other opportunities, including branded wireless services using the Sprint PCS network. That year Liberty Media bought a stake in IDT. In addition, the company raised $1.1 billion by selling most of its remaining stake in Net2Phone to AT&T.

When its joint venture with Terra Networks crumbled in 2001, IDT launched a lawsuit. That year the company bought the debit card business of PT-1 Communications (part of STAR Telecommunications) and invested $1.2 million in STAR. Still flush with cash, IDT traded some of its own stock to Liberty Media for stakes in struggling competitive local-exchange carriers ICG and Teligent. It regained control of its Net2Phone spinoff that year when it took the lead in a consortium with AT&T and Liberty Media that holds a 49% stake in Net2Phone and controls about 64% of the voting power (AT&T later sold its stake to the other two).

IDT could, at times, stand for "Invest in Distressed Telecom" companies: It has pieced together remnants of struggling competitive carriers Teligent, ICG Communications, and long-distance firm STAR Telecommunications. It

once offered to buy parts of WorldCom (MCI). But the company's investments have sometimes provided mixed results. It hoped to repeat the success of Net2Phone with the spinoff of IDT Spectrum, but it discontinued IDT Spectrum instead in 2006.

The company in 2006 sold operating subsidiaries Winstar Communications, Winstar Government Solutions, and Winstar Wireless, entities that provide telecom services under US government contracts, to GVC Networks.

In 2006 the company acquired the remaining 60% of Net2Phone that it did not already own. Net2Phone, which was a leading provider of global hosted VoIP services for service providers, is a success story in IDT's telecom industry investment strategy. The acquired company became a privately held subsidiary of IDT.

In 2007 the company sold its IDT Entertainment unit, now known as Starz Media, to Liberty Media. In the deal, IDT received all of Liberty Media's shareholdings in IDT, including a 5% stake in IDT Telecom, plus $186 million. IDT Entertainment included animation and live-action production studios and a home entertainment distribution business.

EXECUTIVES

Chairman and CEO: Howard S. Jonas, age 53, $1,754,544 total compensation
Vice Chairman: James A. (Jim) Courter, age 68, $1,526,022 total compensation
President: Ira A. Greenstein, age 49
COO: Shmuel (Samuel) Jonas
CFO and Treasurer: Bill Pereira, age 44, $910,483 total compensation
EVP: Claude Pupkin, age 47
EVP: Liore Alroy, age 41
EVP, General Counsel, and Secretary: Joyce J. Mason, age 50
Controller and Chief Accounting Officer: Mitch Silberman, age 41
Chairman, Israel Energy Initiatives, Genie Energy: Michael Steinhardt
Chairman, Genie Energy: Wes Perry
CEO, IDT Internet Mobile Group: Morris Berger
Investor Relations: Bill Ulrey
Auditors: Ernst & Young LLP

LOCATIONS

HQ: IDT Corporation
520 Broad St., Newark, NJ 07102
Phone: 973-438-1000   **Fax:** 973-482-3971
Web: www.idt.net

PRODUCTS/OPERATIONS

2009 Sales

	$ mil.	% of total
IDT Telecom	1,234	80
IDT Energy	265	17
Other	40	3
Total	**1,539**	**100**

COMPETITORS

Arbinet	Orange & Rockland
AT&T	Utilities
Blackhawk Network	Qwest Communications
Coinstar	Rochester Gas and Electric
Con Edison	Royal Dutch Shell
Exxon Mobil	Skype
France Telecom	Sprint Nextel
KDDI	Telefónica
National Fuel Gas	Valero Energy
National Grid	Verizon

HISTORICAL FINANCIALS

Company Type: Public

Income Statement

FYE: July 31

	REVENUE ($ mil.)	NET INCOME ($ mil.)	NET PROFIT MARGIN	EMPLOYEES
7/09	1,539	(154)	—	1,400
7/08	1,878	(224)	—	1,850
7/07	2,013	59	2.9%	2,360
7/06	2,226	(179)	—	3,000
7/05	2,469	(44)	—	5,951
Annual Growth	**(11.1%)**	**—**	**—**	**(30.4%)**

2009 Year-End Financials

Debt ratio: 27.8%
Return on equity: —
Cash ($ mil.): 111
Current ratio: 1.20
Long-term debt ($ mil.): 49

No. of shares (mil.): 23
Dividends
  Yield: 0.0%
  Payout: —
Market value ($ mil.): 59

Stock History

NYSE: IDT

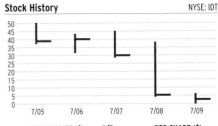

	STOCK PRICE ($) FY Close	P/E High/Low	PER SHARE ($) Earnings	Dividends	Book Value
7/09	2.60	— —	(6.90)	0.00	7.79
7/08	5.31	— —	(8.85)	0.00	15.13
7/07	29.94	21 14	2.13	1.13	27.86
7/06	40.14	— —	(5.58)	—	35.51
7/05	38.97	— —	(1.35)	—	45.90
Annual Growth	**(49.2%)**	**— —**	**—**	**—**	**(35.8%)**

IGA, Inc.

IGA grocers are independent, but not alone. The world's largest voluntary supermarket network, IGA has 6,200 stores in more than 35 countries worldwide, including about 1,350 in the US. Collectively, its members are among North America's leaders in terms of supermarket sales. IGA (which stands for either International or Independent Grocers Alliance, the company says) is owned by about 35 worldwide distribution companies, including SUPERVALU. Members can sell IGA-brand private-label products (over 2,300 items) and take advantage of joint operations and services, such as advertising and volume buying. Some stores in the IGA alliance, which primarily caters to smaller towns, also sell gas.

About two-thirds of IGA's total stores are located outside the US. As the first US grocer in China and Singapore, the company has plans for some 1,000 IGA-affiliated stores in China. IGA is also present in Europe, with operations in Poland and Spain. In 2008 it entered Russia followed by the opening of the first IGA on the island of Guam in 2009.

In 2010 Thomas Haggai stepped down as president and CEO of IGA, Inc. and IGA Global, but remained chairman of the two organizations. He was succeeded by Mark Batenic, who added international responsibilities to his role as president and CEO of IGA USA. (In 2006 the company reorganized by splitting itself into three companies: IGA USA, IGA Global, and the IGA Coca-Cola Institute. All three operate under IGA, Inc. Previously, IGA realigned its corporate structure in 2001.)

By separating IGA's domestic stores from its stores overseas, the company hopes to improve communications among IGA's US retailers.

IGA claims that it doesn't try to fight large chains such as Wal-Mart and Publix, instead preferring to keep the focus on its own niche of hometown and family-owned grocery stores.

HISTORY

IGA was founded in Chicago in 1926 by a group led by accountant Frank Grimes. During the 1920s chains began to dominate the grocery store industry. Grimes, an accountant for many grocery wholesalers, saw an opportunity to develop a network of independent grocers that could compete with the burgeoning chains. Grimes and five associates — Gene Flack, Louis Groebe, W. K. Hunter, H. V. Swenson, and William Thompson — created IGA.

Their idea was to "level the playing field" for independent grocers and chain stores by taking advantage of volume buying and mass marketing. IGA originally acted as a purchasing agent for its wholesalers but eventually passed that duty to the wholesalers. The group's first members were Poughkeepsie, New York-based grocery distributor W. T. Reynolds Company and the 69 grocery stores it serviced.

IGA focused on adding distributors and retailers, and it soon added wholesaler Fleming-Wilson (now Fleming Companies) and Winston & Newell (now SUPERVALU). In 1930 it hired Babe Ruth as a spokesman; other celebrity endorsers during the period included Jackie Cooper, Jack Dempsey, and Popeye. IGA also sponsored a radio program called the *IGA Home Town Hour.*

In 1945 the company introduced the Foodliner format, a design for stores larger than 4,000 sq. ft. The next year IGA introduced the 30-ft.-by-100-ft. Precision Store — designed so customers had to pass all the other merchandise in the store to get to the dairy and bread sections.

Grimes retired as president in 1951. He was succeeded by his son, Don, who continued to expand the company. Don was succeeded in 1968 by Richard Jones, head of IGA member J. M. Jones Co.

Thomas Haggai was named chairman of the company in 1976. A Baptist minister, radio commentator, and former CIA employee, Haggai had come to the attention of Grimes in 1960 when he praised Christian Scientists in one of his radio broadcasts. Grimes, a Christian Scientist, asked Haggai to speak at an IGA convention and eventually asked him to join the IGA board. Haggai, who became CEO in 1986, tightened the restrictions for IGA members, weeding out many of the smaller, low-volume mom-and-pop stores making up much of the group's network.

Haggai also began a push for international expansion. In 1988 the organization signed a deal with Japanese food company C. Itoh (now ITOCHU) to open a distribution outlet in Tokyo.

The 1990s saw expansion into Australia, Papua New Guinea, the Caribbean, China, Singapore, South Africa, and Brazil. IGA also expanded outside the continental US when it entered Hawaii. In 1993 IGA began an international television advertising campaign, a first for the supermarket industry. The next year the company launched its first line of private-label products for an ethnic food market, introducing several Mexican food products. In 1998 the group developed a new format for its stores that included on-site gas pumps.

SUPERVALU signed 54 independent grocery stores (primarily in Mississippi and Arkansas, and Trinidad in the Caribbean) to the IGA banner in August 1999.

With more than 60% of sales from international operations, IGA realigned its corporate structure in 2001, setting up IGA North America, IGA Southern Hemisphere/Europe/Caribbean, and IGA Asia, each with its own president.

IGA suffered the loss of Fleming (one of the grocery chain's principal wholesale distributors) and 300 stores in 2003. On the plus side, four Julian's Supermarkets on the Caribbean island of St. Lucia converted to IGA, giving IGA a presence in 45 countries worldwide.

The company's 2006 reorganization resulted in a three-way split that formed three separate companies (IGA USA, IGA Global, and the IGA Coca-Cola Institute) operating under the IGA, Inc. name. In 2008 IGA expanded into Russia.

EXECUTIVES

Chairman and CEO: Thomas S. Haggai
SVP Procurement and Private Brands: David S. Bennett
SVP Retail and Business Development: Doug Fritsch
VP Finance and CFO: John Collins
VP Information Technology: Nick Liakopulos
VP Communications and Events: Barbara G. Wiest
Senior Director Marketing, Branding, and Business Development, IGA USA: Jim Walz
New Area Director, Western US: Terry Carr
Director Private Brands: Wayne Altschul
Manager Marketing and Retail Programs: Heidi Huff
National Accounts Manager: Jim Collins
President, IGA Coca-Cola Institute: Paulo Goelzer
CEO, IGA USA: Mark K. Batenic
Liaison: Richard Lukeman

LOCATIONS

HQ: IGA, Inc.
 8745 W. Higgins Rd., Ste. 350, Chicago, IL 60631
Phone: 773-693-4520   **Fax:** 773-693-4533
Web: www.iga.com

PRODUCTS/OPERATIONS

Selected Joint Operations and Services

Advertising
Community service programs
Equipment purchase
IGA Brand (private-label products)
IGA Grocergram (in-house magazine)
Internet services
Marketing
Merchandising
Red Oval Family (manufacturer/IGA collaboration on sales, marketing, and other activities)
Volume buying

COMPETITORS

A&P	Hannaford Bros.
Albertsons	H-E-B
Associated Wholesale Grocers	Ito-Yokado
	Kroger
BJ's Wholesale Club	Meijer
C&S Wholesale	Publix
Carrefour	Roundy's Supermarkets
Casino Guichard	Royal Ahold
Coles Group	Safeway
Daiei	Spartan Stores
Dairy Farm International	Wakefern Food
Delhaize	Wal-Mart
George Weston	Winn-Dixie

HISTORICAL FINANCIALS

Company Type: Holding company

Income Statement				FYE: December 31
	REVENUE ($ mil.)	**NET INCOME** ($ mil.)	**NET PROFIT MARGIN**	**EMPLOYEES**
12/08	21,000	—	—	92,000
12/07	21,000	—	—	92,000
12/06	21,000	—	—	92,000
Annual Growth	0.0%	—	—	0.0%

Revenue History

Illinois Tool Works

Don't let the name fool you — Illinois Tool Works (ITW) hammers out more than just tools, and it operates well beyond the Land of Lincoln. With 840 separate operations in 57 countries, ITW manufactures and services equipment used in the automotive, construction, electronics, food and beverage, packaging, power system, and pharmaceutical industries. The company groups its work into eight segments. The largest, transportation, plies fasteners, anchors, and other binding tools for concrete, wood, and metal applications. Second in sales, an industrial packaging arm churns out metal jacketing, stretch film, and paper and plastic products to protect shipped goods.

The multinational manufacturer often buys small, niche companies that expand the applications of its existing portfolio and offer potential to drive more efficient production processes. In early 2010 ITW bought Slime, a maker of tire care products and accessories, from private-equity firm Friend Skoler & Co. Slime brings a strong brand, including its flagship green Slime tire sealants, that ITW will continue to expand in the global tire care markets.

In late 2009 ITW acquired the assets of South Carolina-based Hartness International, a manufacturer of conveyor systems and line automation for the beverage and food industries. The acquisition complements ITW's packaging business in a lower cost geography. Given ITW's decentralized business structure, Hartness is integrated as a separate business unit and preserves its own brand name.

ITW is also intent upon freeing its operations from businesses holding dim opportunities for growth. The company divested its Click Commerce, a business with a buffet of industrial software applications in mid-2009 to private equity Marlin Equity Partners. Marlin bought three software divisions from Requisite Technology (formerly Click Commerce), and raked away Service Network Solutions, Research and Healthcare Solutions, and Contract Service and Management operations, as well as the Click Commerce nameplate.

ITW also pushed to unload an automotive components business, on the sale rack since 2007. The business was reclassified, instead, as discontinued, along with an automotive machinery business, and two consumer packaging businesses. Its consumer products holdings (appliances and cookware, exercise equipment, and ceramic tile acquired with Premark International) were also curbed. (In a surprise move, ITW's decorative surfaces segment, which could not find a buyer, was revived in 2009 as a continuing business.)

HISTORY

In the early years of the 20th century, Byron Smith, founder of Chicago's Northern Trust Company, recognized that rapid industrialization was outgrowing the capacity of small shops to supply machine tools. Smith encouraged two of his four sons to launch Illinois Tool Works (ITW) in 1912. Harold C. Smith became president of ITW in 1915 and expanded its product line into automotive parts.

ITW developed the Shakeproof fastener, the first twisted-tooth lock washer, in 1923. When Harold C. died in 1936, the torch passed to his son Harold B., who decentralized the company and exhorted salesmen to learn customers' businesses so they could develop solutions even before the customers recognized the problems. Smith plowed profits back into research as WWII spurred demand.

In the 1950s the company began exploring plastics and combination metal and plastic fasteners, as well as electrical controls and instruments, to become a leader in miniaturization. Its major breakthrough came in the early 1960s with the development of flexible plastic collars to hold six-packs of beverage cans. This item, under a new division called Hi-Cone, was ITW's most-profitable offering.

Silas Cathcart became CEO in 1970. Smith's son, another Harold B., was president and COO until 1981 (he remained on the board of directors and served as chairman of the board's executive committee). By the early 1980s ITW had become bureaucratic and susceptible to foreign competition. It was forced to lower prices to hold on to customers. Wary after the 1982 recession, ITW hired John Nichols as CEO.

Nichols broadened the company's product line, introduced more effective production methods, and doubled ITW's size by buying 27 companies, the largest being Signode Industries, bought for $524 million (1986). Nichols broke Signode into smaller units to speed development of 20 new products.

ITW purchased Ransburg Corporation (electrostatic finishing systems, 1989) and the DeVilbiss division of Eagle Industries (1990) and merged the two to form its Finishing Systems and Products division. Through a stock swap, ITW acquired ownership of the Miller Group (arc welding equipment and related systems) in 1993.

In 1995 ITW named president James Farrell as CEO. He replaced Nichols as chairman in 1996. ITW acquired Hobart Brothers (welding products) and Medalists Industries (industrial fasteners) in 1996 and made 28 acquisitions and joint ventures in 1997.

In 1999 ITW paid $3.5 billion for Premark International (consumer products, which it began selling off in 2002). Early in 2001 the company added to its welding operations by buying four welding component businesses from Dover Corporation. In early 2002 the company's board of directors gave its stamp of approval for the divestiture of ITW's consumer products segment. That decision led to the sale of its Precor fitness equipment business to Finland's Amer Sports.

Farrell retired as CEO, though he remained chairman, in 2005; he was replaced by president David Speer. Farrell retired as chairman in 2006 and was succeeded by Speer in that post.

In early 2005 ITW purchased the Wynn Oil segment of industrial products maker Parker Hannifin. Wynn Oil manufactures chemical car care products and maintenance technology for the auto industry.

In early 2006 ITW bought Alpine Engineered Products, a maker of connectors, design software, and related machinery from Stonebridge Partners. In mid-2006 ITW bought BagCo (plastic recloseable packaging) and Kester (solder and related materials). In late 2006 ITW purchased Speedline Technologies, a manufacturer of printed circuit board assembly and semiconductor packaging equipment.

In 2007 ITW acquired the assets of Avery Berkel, a venerable manufacturer of retail scales and other food processing equipment, from Avery Weigh-Tronix. The company bought the rest of Avery Weigh-Tronix in 2008.

EXECUTIVES

Chairman and CEO: David B. Speer, age 58, $10,484,381 total compensation
Vice Chairman: E. Scott Santi, age 48, $3,435,037 total compensation
Vice Chairman: Thomas J. (Tom) Hansen, age 61, $4,606,959 total compensation
EVP Global Welding: Sundaram (Naga) Nagarajan, age 47
EVP: David C. Parry, age 56
EVP: Craig A. Hindman, age 55
EVP: Juan Valls, age 48
EVP: Robert E. Brunner, age 52
EVP: Steven L. (Steve) Martindale, age 53
EVP: Philip M. (Phil) Gresh Jr., age 61
EVP: Jane L. Warner, age 63
EVP: Roland M. Martel, age 55
EVP: Timothy J. Gardner, age 55
SVP and CFO: Ronald D. (Ron) Kropp, age 44, $1,871,342 total compensation
SVP Human Resources: Sharon M. Brady, age 59
SVP Taxes and Investments: Allan C. (Al) Sutherland, age 46
SVP, General Counsel, and Secretary: James H. Wooten Jr., age 61
VP and Chief Accounting Officer: Randall J. (Randy) Scheuneman, age 42
VP Intellectual Property: Mark W. Croll
VP Research and Development: Lei Z. Schlitz
VP Investor Relations: John L. Brooklier
Manager Corporate Communications: Alison Donnelly
Auditors: Deloitte & Touche LLP

LOCATIONS

HQ: Illinois Tool Works Inc.
3600 W. Lake Ave., Glenview, IL 60026
Phone: 847-724-7500 **Fax:** 847-657-4261
Web: www.itw.com

2009 Sales

	$ mil.	% of total
North America		
US	5,901.4	42
Other countries	827.2	6
Europe	4,574.2	33
Asia	1,366.7	10
Australia & New Zealand	690.9	5
Other regions	516.7	4
Total	**13,877.1**	**100**

PRODUCTS/OPERATIONS

2009 Sales

	$ mil.	% of total
Transportation	2,070.9	15
Industrial Packaging	1,895.7	14
Food Equipment	1,859.3	13
Power Systems & Electronics	1,614.5	12
Construction Products	1,529.5	11
Polymers & Fluids	1,155.8	8
Decorative Surfaces	998.2	7
Other	2,786.7	20
Adjustments	(33.5)	—
Total	**13,877.1**	**100**

COMPETITORS

3M
BASF SE
Cooper Industries
DuPont
Emerson Electric
Entegris
ESAB
Federal Screw Works
GE
Graco
IBIDEN
Ingersoll-Rand
Koch Enterprises
Lincoln Electric
Manitowoc
Marmon Group
NCH
Nordson
Park-Ohio Holdings
PennEngineering
Snap-on
Stanley Black and Decker
Textron
Thermadyne
TriMas
TRW Automotive
Tyco
W. R. Grace

HISTORICAL FINANCIALS

Company Type: Public

Income Statement

FYE: December 31

	REVENUE ($ mil.)	NET INCOME ($ mil.)	NET PROFIT MARGIN	EMPLOYEES
12/09	13,877	947	6.8%	59,000
12/08	15,869	1,519	9.6%	65,000
12/07	16,171	1,870	11.6%	60,000
12/06	14,055	1,718	12.2%	55,000
12/05	12,922	1,495	11.6%	50,000
Annual Growth	**1.8%**	**(10.8%)**	**—**	**4.2%**

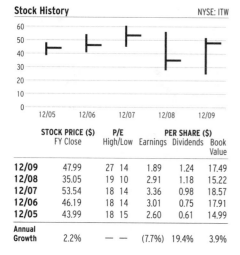

Stock History   NYSE: ITW

	STOCK PRICE ($) FY Close	P/E High/Low		PER SHARE ($) Earnings	Dividends	Book Value
12/09	47.99	27	14	1.89	1.24	17.49
12/08	35.05	19	10	2.91	1.18	15.22
12/07	53.54	18	14	3.36	0.98	18.57
12/06	46.19	18	14	3.01	0.75	17.91
12/05	43.99	18	15	2.60	0.61	14.99
Annual Growth	**2.2%**	—	—	**(7.7%)**	**19.4%**	**3.9%**

Imation Corp.

Imation wants to start fresh with a blank disk. The company is one of the world's top makers of media used to capture, process, store, and distribute information on computers and other electronic devices. Its removable data storage media products include optical disks (CD-R, CD-RW, DVD) and magnetic storage tapes. It also offers flash memory drives. Imation sells its products directly and through distributors to customers ranging from PC owners to large corporations. Imation has used acquisitions to dramatically expand its recording media product lines. More than half of Imation's sales are to customers outside the US.

2009 was a bad year for consumer electronics in general, due to the global recession. It's not surprising, then, that anything relating to consumer electronics suffered, as well. Imation saw its sales drop almost one-quarter during the year, because of the general economic conditions, and it marked its third consecutive year in the red. To help reduce costs, the company trimmed its workforce by around 23%.

In 2007 Imation acquired TDK's brand and recording media sales operations for $300 million in cash and stock. (TDK owns about 20% of Imation.) The company then acquired the assets of Memcorp, a manufacturer of Memorex-branded electronics. The Memcorp purchase included products such as LCD televisions, iPod accessories, and digital cameras.

Imation has traditionally been a leader in magnetic diskettes, but in recent years the company has turned its focus to optical media. Optical products now make up nearly half of Imation's sales. Magnetic media products accounts for about 30% of revenues. The company's long-term strategy has three main elements: optimize the magnetic tape business; grow the data storage media business, offering products under

multiple brands; and extend certain brands across multiple product categories.

Vice chairman and CEO Frank Russomanno retired in 2010. Imation's board designated Mark Lucas, president and COO, as his successor in the CEO's post. In 1973 Russomanno began his career with 3M, which spun off Imation in 1996.

HISTORY

Imation's ancestry stretches back to 1902, when five businessmen founded Minnesota Mining and Manufacturing (3M) in Two Harbors, Minnesota, to sell corundum to manufacturers for grinding wheels. Faced with stiff competition and the realization that its mining holdings contained the nearly worthless igneous rock anorthosite instead of corundum, the company shifted gears and began making sandpaper and abrasive wheels.

In a research-fueled corporate culture, 3M's engineers thrived, launching a long line of culturally implanted products including Scotch masking tape, the dry-printing photocopy process, Post-it adhesive notepads, and, in 1947, the first commercially viable magnetic recording tape. This ancestor of the cassette tape would mark 3M's leap into the business that later helped make Imation.

The genesis of Imation's other lines continued in the 1950s and 1960s when 3M ventured into photographic products. It jumped into color proofing systems and X-ray and other medical imaging technologies in the 1970s. When its diskette manufacturing business faced intense global competition in the 1980s, 3M expanded its efforts in the data storage products market.

Imation — a name taken from the words "imaging" and "information" — was born in 1996 when 3M spun off its low-performing data storage, imaging, and printing businesses. The move was part of a broader 3M reorganization that saw it retain its industrial and consumer and life science units, while discontinuing its audio- and videotape business. About 75% of 3M's data storage and medical imaging employees made the move; the rest opted for early retirement. That year William Monahan, who began his career in the early 1970s selling 3M data storage products on Wall Street and rose to serve as VP of the company's Electro and Communication Group, was named chairman and CEO.

In 1996 Imation also unveiled the LS-120 diskette for a drive that used both standard floppy disks (1.44 MB) and 120-MB, 3.5-in. disks. Hitachi, Panasonic, and Mitsubishi made products based on the technology. Also that year the company bought Seattle-based pre-press software company Luminous Corp., and was awarded its first non-3M patent for a minicartridge design.

While Imation struggled in an intensely competitive market with plummeting product prices, industry watchers questioned the company's commitment to new technology. Imation intensified restructuring efforts to pare operations and sharpen its focus. In 1997 it stepped up a new technology push by acquiring digital medical imaging specialist Cemax-Icon, as well as Internet service provider Imaginet, resulting in the creation of Imation Internet Studio. (The unit was sold in 1999 to Gage Marketing Group when its strategies conflicted with Imation's.)

More losses piled up in 1997 despite a slew of new products and features. So in 1998 Imation

tried to turn around its financial results by slashing 3,400 jobs. The company also sold its CD-ROM services unit to optical media company Metatec and its medical imaging systems to Eastman Kodak for about $520 million, partly to settle an intellectual-property lawsuit. In 1999 Imation sold its Photo Color Systems business (photographic film, single-use cameras) to Schroder plc affiliate Schroder Ventures.

In 2000 Imation introduced Verifi — technology that let online shoppers verify the accuracy of colors on their monitors. The following year the company agreed to sell its color proofing and color software businesses to Kodak Polychrome Graphics (a joint venture between Kodak and Dainippon Ink and Chemicals subsidiary Sun Chemical); the deal closed in 2002. Later that year Imation sold its North American Digital Solutions and Services (DSS) operations to DecisionOne, and closed DSS operations outside of North America.

Monahan retired from Imation in 2004. Bruce Henderson, a former chief executive for Invensys Control Systems, replaced him.

In 2005 the company sold its specialty papers business, which generated about 4% of its sales, to Nekoosa Coated Products for $17 million, plus possible future consideration. Nekoosa was a company formed by Dunsirn Partners and PS Capital Partners, two investment firms.

Imation purchased rival Memorex for $329 million in 2006.

Henderson resigned due to health reasons in 2007. President Frank Russomanno, who served as acting CEO since 2006, replaced him.

EXECUTIVES

Chairman: Linda W. Hart, age 69
President, CEO, and Director: Mark E. Lucas, age 55, $2,861,604 total compensation
SVP and CFO: Paul R. Zeller, age 49, $1,087,308 total compensation
SVP Global Commercial Business and CTO: Subodh K. Kulkarni, age 45, $609,163 total compensation
SVP, Secretary, and General Counsel: John L. Sullivan, age 55, $922,531 total compensation
VP Strategy and Mergers and Acquisitions: James C. Ellis, age 52, $622,594 total compensation
VP Global Supply Chain Operations: Carl M. Thielk
VP North Asia Region: Kuniyoshi Matsui
VP and Corporate Controller: Scott J. Robinson, age 43
VP Americas Region: Gregory J. Bosler
VP South Asia Region: Brian J. Plummer
VP Global Human Resources: Patricia A. (Patty) Hamm
VP Europe Region: Peter A. Koehn, age 49
Director Corporate Communications and Public Relations: Mary Rawlings-Taylor
Director Investor Relations: Timothy J. (Tim) Gallaher, age 42
Auditors: PricewaterhouseCoopers LLP

LOCATIONS

HQ: Imation Corp.
  1 Imation Way, Oakdale, MN 55128
Phone: 651-704-4000   **Fax:** 651-704-4200
Web: www.imation.com

2009 Sales

	$ mil.	% of total
US	726.9	44
Other countries	922.6	56
Total	**1,649.5**	**100**

PRODUCTS/OPERATIONS

2009 Sales

	$ mil.	% of total
Optical	738.0	45
Magnetic	474.2	29
Flash	90.0	5
Other	347.3	21
Total	**1,649.5**	**100**

Selected Products

Optical
  CD-R
  CD-RW
  DVD

Magnetic
  Audio and video tape
  Data storage tape media
  Floppy diskettes

Flash (primarily Memorex)
  Flash cards
  USB flash drives

Other
  CD and DVD cleaning, labeling, and storing products
  Electronic products (primarily Memcorp consumer electronics)

COMPETITORS

Altec Lansing
FUJIFILM
Griffin Technology
Hewlett-Packard
Iomega
Kingston Technology
LaCie
Lexar
LG Electronics
Maxell
Philips Electronics
PNY Technologies
Quantum Corporation
Samsung Electronics
SanDisk
SDI Technologies
Seagate Technology
Sony
Technicolor
Toshiba
Verbatim Corp.
VIZIO
Western Digital

HISTORICAL FINANCIALS

Company Type: Public

Income Statement

FYE: December 31

	REVENUE ($ mil.)	NET INCOME ($ mil.)	NET PROFIT MARGIN	EMPLOYEES
12/09	1,650	(42)	—	1,210
12/08	2,155	(33)	—	1,570
12/07	2,062	(50)	—	2,250
12/06	1,585	76	4.8%	2,070
12/05	1,258	88	7.0%	2,100
Annual Growth	**7.0%**	**—**	**—**	**(12.9%)**

2009 Year-End Financials

Debt ratio: —	No. of shares (mil.): 39
Return on equity: —	Dividends
Cash ($ mil.): 163	Yield: 0.0%
Current ratio: 2.36	Payout: —
Long-term debt ($ mil.): —	Market value ($ mil.): 337

Stock History

NYSE: IMN

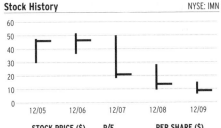

	STOCK PRICE ($) FY Close	P/E High/Low		PER SHARE ($) Earnings	Dividends	Book Value
12/09	8.72	—	—	(1.13)	0.00	23.98
12/08	13.57	—	—	(0.89)	0.56	24.43
12/07	21.00	—	—	(1.36)	0.62	27.26
12/06	46.43	23	17	2.17	0.54	24.48
12/05	46.07	18	12	2.54	0.46	22.12
Annual Growth	**(34.0%)**	**—**	**—**	**—**	**—**	**2.0%**

Ingram Micro

There's nothing micro about Ingram. Ingram Micro is the world's largest wholesale distributor of computer products. It provides thousands of products — desktop and notebook PCs, servers, storage devices, monitors, printers, and software — to more than 180,000 reseller customers around the globe. The company also provides a wide range of services for its resellers and suppliers, including contract manufacturing and warehousing, customer care, financing, logistics, outsourcing management, and enterprise network support services. Customers include resellers such as Wal-Mart.com, Staples, and Office Depot. Ingram Micro generates about 60% of its sales outside North America.

In 2010 it bought Asiasoft Hong Kong, which distributes business software from companies such as Adobe Systems and Symantec, in order to expand its sales in Asia.

Ingram Micro was not unique among companies that saw their sales contract during the global recession. The company was able to generate a profit, however, albeit at its traditional razor-thin margin.

In 2009 Ingram Micro bought certain assets of Computacenter Distribution (CCD), a wholesale distributor of server, storage, and networking equipment in the UK. Ingram Micro bought Barcelona-based Albora Soluciones the following year. The purchases were made to bolster the company's business in Europe.

Though it remains primarily focused on computer-related products, Ingram Micro has expanded into such markets as automatic identification and data capture (AIDC), point-of-sale (POS) systems, and consumer electronics. The company cites the breadth of its product offerings as some protection against demand volatility.

The company also continues to expand its managed and professional services. Its Ingram Micro Services Division offers managed services such as network security, application hosting, and remote monitoring under the Seismic brand. The unit's professional services include consulting and staffing, and it also provides warranty contract management. Another division, Ingram Micro Logistics, handles fulfillment, order management, transportation, and warehousing.

HISTORY

Micro D was founded in Fountain Valley, California, in 1979 by husband-and-wife entrepreneurs Geza Csige and Lorraine Mecca. As the company grew, Mecca sought to merge the computer distributor with a partner that could take over daily operations. She relinquished control of Micro D to Linwood "Chip" Lacy in 1986 and sold her 51% share of the company to minority shareholder Ingram Distribution Group.

Sales bottomed out for Micro D that year. Lacy tightened Micro D's belt and took huge charges for outdated inventory it sold at a discount and overdue payments from customers that had gone bankrupt.

At the same time, Ingram Industries was busy merging recently acquired Ingram Software Distribution Services of Buffalo, New York, with Compton, California-based Softeam. The merger made the company one of the nation's largest wholesale distributors of computer software. Lacy saw Ingram's purchase of Micro D shares as a conflict of interest, but he was too busy returning Micro D to profitability — centralizing its marketing and distribution functions, cutting costs, and expanding its market to include more small retailers, which provided higher margins. Micro D went from the fourth-largest distributor of microcomputer products to #1 in just one year.

The surging PC market in the late 1980s fueled Micro D's growth. By 1988 the firm had expanded outside the US for the first time, acquiring Canadian company Frantek Computer Products.

Ingram Industries offered to acquire the 41% of outstanding Micro D stock it did not own in 1988, but Lacy resisted, preferring to let Ingram wait. Though Ingram owned a majority of Micro D stock, it only controlled three of seven seats on the board. Ingram was forced to play Lacy's game and finally acquired the company at a higher cost in 1989. The new company, which controlled 20% of the computer distribution market, was called Ingram Micro D. The merger was anything but smooth, and several Micro D executives jumped ship.

As the PC took hold in the US in the 1990s, Ingram Micro D became the dominant industry player, but relations between Lacy and the Ingram family never improved. The company shortened its name to Ingram Micro in 1991, and two years later, as it was hitting stride, Lacy announced plans to leave. To keep him, Ingram Industries CEO Bronson Ingram (much to his distaste) promised to let Lacy take the company public.

Bronson Ingram died in 1995, and the next year his widow, Martha, forced Lacy's resignation. Lacy was replaced by Jerre Stead, formerly CEO of software maker LEGENT (bought by CA), who devised a compensation package for himself consisting solely of stock options (no salary) and listed "Head Coach" on his business card. Ingram went public a few months after Stead took over.

In 1998 Ingram Micro forged a distribution alliance with Japanese computer giant SOFTBANK and bought a majority stake in German computer products distributor Macrotron. It also expanded into build-to-order PC manufacturing. Amid softer PC sales industrywide, Ingram Micro in 1999 terminated nearly 600 employees as part of a worldwide realignment and signed a deal (worth an estimated $10 billion) with CompUSA to be its primary PC manufacturer and distributor.

Later in 1999 Stead — with Ingram Micro's sales slipping and its stock slumping — made plans to step down as CEO. The search ended in 2000 when the company named GTE veteran Kent Foster to the post.

Ingram Micro expanded its portfolio of services for enterprises and began offering more extensive network and product support services. Ingram Micro continued to expand international operations that year, acquiring the 49% of a Singapore exporter it did not previously own, and purchasing operations in Belgium and the Netherlands. In a move to expand its presence in the Asia/Pacific region, Ingram acquired Australian distributor Tech Pacific in 2004.

Company president Greg Spierkel replaced Foster as CEO in 2005. The following year it expanded its reach in Northern Europe when it purchased the assets of SymTech Nordic.

Ingram purchased consumer electronics distributor DBL Distributing in 2007.

EXECUTIVES

Chairman: Dale R. Laurance, age 64
CEO and Director: Gregory M.E. (Greg) Spierkel, age 53, $7,917,273 total compensation
President and COO: Alain Monié, age 59, $3,902,912 total compensation
SEVP and CFO: William D. Humes, age 45, $2,232,713 total compensation
SEVP; President, North America: Keith W. F. Bradley, age 46, $1,224,746 total compensation
SEVP; President, Europe, Middle East, and Africa: Alain Maquet, age 58, $2,821,354 total compensation
SEVP; President, Asia/Pacific: Shailendra Gupta, age 47, $2,821,354 total compensation
EVP, General Counsel, and Secretary: Larry C. Boyd, age 57
EVP and CIO: Mario F. Leone, age 54
EVP Human Resources: Lynn Jolliffe, age 57
EVP; President, Latin America: Eduardo Araujo, age 53
EVP North America: Paul Bay
EVP Global Logistics: Robert K. Gifford, age 52
SVP Strategy and Communications: Ria Marie Carlson, age 48
Senior Director Investor Relations: Kay Leyba
Auditors: PricewaterhouseCoopers LLP

LOCATIONS

HQ: Ingram Micro Inc.
1600 E. St. Andrew Place, Santa Ana, CA 92705
Phone: 714-566-1000 **Fax:** 714-566-7900
Web: www.ingrammicro.com

2009 Sales

	$ mil.	% of total
North America	12,326.6	42
Europe, Middle East & Africa	9,483.3	32
Asia/Pacific	6,243.4	21
Latin America	1,462.1	5
Total	**29,515.4**	**100**

PRODUCTS/OPERATIONS

Selected Products

IT Peripheral/CE/AIDC/POS/Mobility and Others
  Barcode/card printers
  Cell phones
  Components
  Digital cameras
  Digital signage products
  Digital video disc players
  Game consoles
  Mass storage
  Printers
  Projectors
  Scanners
  Supplies and accessories
  Televisions
Networking
  Network interface cards
  Storage
  Switches, hubs, and routers
  Wireless local area networks
Software
  Business application software
  Developer software tools
  Entertainment software
  Middleware
  Operating system software
  Security software
  Storage software
Systems
  Desktops
  Personal digital assistants
  Portable personal computers
  Rack, tower, and blade servers

COMPETITORS

Agilysys	Menlo Worldwide
Arrow Electronics	New Age Electronics
ASI Computer	Redington Group
Technologies	ScanSource
Avnet	Schindler Holding
Black Box	SED International
Computacenter	Softmart
D&H Distributing	Software House
DHL	Supercom
Digiland	SYNNEX
Digital China	Tech Data
Dimension Data	United Stationers
Flextronics	UPS
GTSI	Westcon
Intcomex	

HISTORICAL FINANCIALS

Company Type: Public

Income Statement

FYE: Saturday nearest December 31

	REVENUE ($ mil.)	NET INCOME ($ mil.)	NET PROFIT MARGIN	EMPLOYEES
12/09	29,515	202	0.7%	13,750
12/08	34,362	(395)	—	14,500
12/07	35,047	276	0.8%	15,000
12/06	31,358	266	0.8%	13,700
12/05	28,808	217	0.8%	13,000
Annual Growth	**0.6%**	**(1.8%)**	**—**	**1.4%**

2009 Year-End Financials

Debt ratio: 10.0%
Return on equity: 7.1%
Cash ($ mil.): 911
Current ratio: 1.62
Long-term debt ($ mil.): 302
No. of shares (mil.): 157
Dividends
  Yield: —
  Payout: —
Market value ($ mil.): 2,734

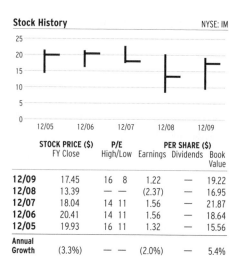

Stock History NYSE: IM

	STOCK PRICE ($) FY Close	P/E High/Low		PER SHARE ($) Earnings	Dividends	Book Value
12/09	17.45	16	8	1.22	—	19.22
12/08	13.39	—	—	(2.37)	—	16.95
12/07	18.04	14	11	1.56	—	21.87
12/06	20.41	14	11	1.56	—	18.64
12/05	19.93	16	11	1.32	—	15.56
Annual Growth	**(3.3%)**	**—**	**—**	**(2.0%)**	**—**	**5.4%**

Insight Enterprises

With this firm around, the end of your technology woes could be in sight. Insight Enterprises is a top distributor of computer hardware and software in North America, carrying thousands of products from major manufacturers, such as Hewlett-Packard, IBM, and Microsoft. It uses direct telesales, field sales agents, and an e-commerce site to reach clients in the public sector and at small and midsized businesses. Outside North America, the firm serves customers in about 190 countries across Europe, the Middle East, Africa, and the Asia/Pacific region. In recent years it has focused on networking and communications services, acquiring Calence (a leading Cisco provider in the US) and UK-based MINX.

North America accounts for about 70% of Insight's revenue, and the company provides this market with its full line of products and services. The UK also gets the hardware, software, and services treatment while other markets have been limited to software and related services. The purchases of Calence and MINX, both completed in 2008, are part of Insight's strategy to stay ahead of the competition through broadened revenue streams. By growing its technology services business (which accounts for about 5% of sales), the company has been able to capture more of its existing clients' IT spending and strengthen its status as a trusted provider globally. Sales of hardware and software remain at the center of Insight's growth strategy, however.

Expanding its services division, Insight Enterprises in April 2008 purchased Arizona-based Calence, one of the largest Cisco providers in the US. The purchase of Calence, at $125 million (plus $35 million through 2012 if Calence hits set performance targets), gave the company a leg up in several US regions (including the Southwest, Northwest, and Midwest) and strategic states (New York, Texas, and North Carolina). Insight Enterprises also added Calence's managed services, security, and technological expertise to its menu of services. As part of the deal, the company retained Calence CEO Michael Fong. Complementing the Calence deal across the Atlantic, Insight acquired MINX, a Cisco-accredited network integrator in the UK, for more than $1 million and the assumption of nearly $4 million in debt.

The deep recession in the US and tough economic conditions abroad have slowed technology purchases by businesses and put the squeeze on Insight's operations. To control expenses in a difficult environment, the company cut more than 500 jobs (more than 10% of its workforce) in 2008 and 2009. Also in early 2009 Insight combined the management of its North American businesses with its corporate headquarters.

As it moves to reduce spending, Insight is moving to expand internationally. The company in 2010 is introducing hardware sales to customers in key markets throughout Europe (outside the UK) and has plans to grow its partner network in the UK and Canada. Insight has operations in about 20 countries outside North America.

HISTORY

Eric Crown worked for a small computer retail chain in the mid-1980s before leaving to market PCs. In 1986 he and his brother, Tim, pooled $2,000 from credit cards and $1,300 in savings and, anticipating a drop in hard drive prices, placed an ad for low-cost hard drives in a computer magazine. The ad pulled in $20,000 worth of sales and, since costs did indeed drop, the profit was enough to start a new company, Hard Drives International. In 1988 they changed the name to Insight Enterprises; by 1991 the Crowns also sold Insight-branded PCs, software, and peripherals (discontinued in 1995). The company passed the $100 million revenue mark in 1992.

Insight shifted its marketing focus to catalogs in 1993 and had a circulation of more than 7 million by 1995. The company went public that year and entered an alliance with Computer City (acquired by CompUSA in 1998) to handle its mail-order fulfillment. It also launched its website. The next year subsidiary Insight Direct began to offer on-site service warranties, and in 1997 retailing subsidiary Direct Alliance was chosen to provide product fulfillment for Internet software firm Geo Publishing. That year the company began sponsoring the Copper Bowl, a college football game played in Arizona, which was renamed the Insight.com Bowl (and later the Insight Bowl).

Looking beyond the US, in 1998 Insight established operations in Canada and acquired direct marketers Choice Peripherals (UK) and Computerprofis Computersysteme (Germany). At home it added direct marketer Treasure Chest Computers. Sales passed the billion-dollar mark that year.

The company formed an alliance with Daisytek International in 1999 that expanded its product line by more than 10,000. Soon thereafter, Insight walked away from a merger with UK-based computer wholesaler Action Computer Supplies when Action's profits slumped.

Insight withdrew its planned IPO and spinoff of Direct Alliance in 2001 due to poor market conditions. Also that month Eric became chairman and Tim became CEO (they had previously shared the title of co-CEO). Insight ended up buying Action Computer Supplies in 2001. It also shut down its German operations and acquired computer direct marketers in both the UK and Canada in late 2001.

In April 2002 Insight acquired Comark, a leading private reseller of computers, peripherals, and computer supplies in the US, and began integrating its operations into Insight North America's existing operational structure.

Tim stepped down as president and CEO and became chairman in late 2004, while Eric assumed the title of chairman emeritus. The company appointed IBM veteran Richard Fennessy to the position of president and CEO. That year Insight spun off its UK-based Internet service provider PlusNet.

In 2006 Insight Enterprises bought software and mobile solutions firm Software Spectrum.

To fund its expansion into the services sector, Insight Enterprises has been offloading other units. Insight Enterprises in 2006 also sold its business process outsourcing (BPO) division, Direct Alliance, to TeleTech Holdings for $46 million. The company sold the PC Wholesale division (acquired in 2002) of its subsidiary Insight Direct USA to Synnex Corp. in 2007 for about $10 million, plus approximately $20 million for net assets acquired.

In early 2008 Insight Enterprises purchased Calence to extend its reach into the services sector once again. Soon after that purchase the company realigned its US sales organization and in November laid off some 240 employees.

EXECUTIVES

Chairman: Timothy A. (Tim) Crown, age 46
President, CEO, and Director:
 Kenneth T. (Ken) Lamneck, age 55
COO and CIO: Stephen A. Speidel, age 45
CFO: Glynis A. Bryan, age 51,
 $1,021,351 total compensation
SVP, Corporate Controller, and Principal Accounting Officer: David C. Olsen, age 48
SVP Investor Relations and Treasurer:
 Helen K. Johnson, age 41
SVP Strategic Partnerships and Marketing: Dave Casillo
Chief Administrative Officer, General Counsel, and Secretary: Steven R. (Steve) Andrews, age 57
Senior Manager Corporate Communications:
 Amy Kweder
Senior Manager Marketing: Shana Diana
Investor Relations Contact: Rosalind Berkley
President, Insight EMEA and APAC: Stuart A. Fenton, age 41, $1,211,000 total compensation
Auditors: KPMG LLP

LOCATIONS

HQ: Insight Enterprises, Inc.
 6820 S. Harl Ave., Tempe, AZ 85283
Phone: 480-902-1001   **Fax:** 480-902-1157
Web: www.insight.com

2009 Sales

	$ mil.	% of total
North America	2,840.8	69
Europe, Middle East & Africa	1,151.7	28
Asia/Pacific	144.4	3
Total	**4,136.9**	**100**

PRODUCTS/OPERATIONS

Selected Products

Computer memory and processors
Desktop computers
Displays
Laptop computers
Networking equipment
Servers
Software
Storage devices

Selected Services

Business process outsourcing
 Collections
 Credit card processing
 Customer support
 Direct marketing
 Fulfillment
 Inbound and outbound call handling
 Supply chain management
Information technology
 Consulting
 Help desk support
 Maintenance
 Managed services
 Network administration
 Project management
 Security
 Systems integration

COMPETITORS

Amazon.com
Best Buy
Buy.com
CDW
CompuCom
Convergys
Dell
Digital River
DSG International
Fry's Electronics
Gateway, Inc.
Hewlett-Packard
HP Enterprise Services
IBM
Lenovo
Micro Electronics
Microsoft
ModusLink
Office Depot
OfficeMax
PC Connection
PC Mall
PFSweb
RadioShack
Softchoice
Software House International
Staples
Symantec
Systemax
Zones

HISTORICAL FINANCIALS

Company Type: Public

Income Statement

FYE: December 31

	REVENUE ($ mil.)	NET INCOME ($ mil.)	NET PROFIT MARGIN	EMPLOYEES
12/09	4,137	34	0.8%	4,898
12/08	4,826	(240)	—	4,763
12/07	4,800	78	1.6%	4,763
12/06	3,817	77	2.0%	4,568
12/05	3,261	55	1.7%	3,967
Annual Growth	**6.1%**	**(11.7%)**	**—**	**5.4%**

2009 Year-End Financials

Debt ratio: 31.9%
Return on equity: 7.6%
Cash ($ mil.): 68
Current ratio: 1.31
Long-term debt ($ mil.): 149

No. of shares (mil.): 46
Dividends
 Yield: —
 Payout: —
Market value ($ mil.): 528

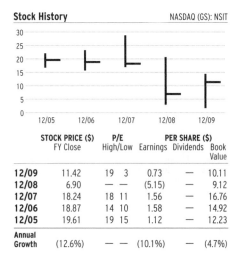

	STOCK PRICE ($) FY Close	P/E High/Low		PER SHARE ($) Earnings	Dividends	Book Value
12/09	11.42	19	3	0.73	—	10.11
12/08	6.90	—	—	(5.15)	—	9.12
12/07	18.24	18	11	1.56	—	16.76
12/06	18.87	14	10	1.58	—	14.92
12/05	19.61	19	15	1.12	—	12.23
Annual Growth	(12.6%)	—	—	(10.1%)	—	(4.7%)

Intel Corporation

The intelligence inside your computer could very well be Intel. The company — which holds about 80% of the market share for microprocessors that go into desktop and notebook computers, and also into computer servers — is still #1 in semiconductors. Archrival AMD ate into Intel's market share for a time, but the big guy fought back with faster processors and advanced manufacturing technology. Intel also makes embedded semiconductors for the industrial, medical, and in-vehicle infotainment markets. While most computer makers use Intel processors, PC giants Dell and Hewlett-Packard are the company's largest customers.

The world's largest semiconductor manufacturer was humbled by a series of events, including slumping demand for PCs, lawsuits, and unsuccessful forays into niche markets. The global financial crisis hasn't helped. In response, Intel closed older plants in China, Malaysia, and the Philippines, along with plants in Oregon and California. Intel has refocused on what it does best — developing and producing advanced microprocessors — and narrowed its focus by identifying several key end market applications.

In mid-2010 Intel agreed to acquire Texas Instruments' Puma cable modem product lines, which it will use to develop set top boxes, residential gateway, and other products for the cable industry. Just days after announcing the deal to acquire the Puma cable modem line, Intel announced an even bigger purchase, agreeing to purchase security software provider McAfee for about $7.68 billion.

Intel works to have its architecture used as the platform in embedded applications, and is bulking up its software programming offerings in order to provide a complete product. Another area of focus is developing products that allow handheld devices and consumer electronics linked through the home to deliver content and the Internet in new ways.

AMD's antitrust suit against Intel, alleging that its rival used improper subsidies and coercion to secure sales, was settled in 2009 in AMD's favor. Intel agreed to pay $1.25 billion in damages and to implement new business sales practices.

Also in 2009 the European Commission levied a record fine against Intel — more than €1 billion or about $1.44 billion. The antitrust regulators alleged that Intel paid hidden rebates to PC manufacturers to only use Intel's microprocessors in their computers. Intel is appealing the ruling and fine, stating it took "strong exception" to the decision and denying that consumers were harmed by its business practices.

Additionally, New York Attorney General Andrew Cuomo filed an additional antitrust lawsuit against Intel in 2009. This suit once again centers on Intel's questionable payments to PC makers to use Intel products. The Federal Trade Commission upgraded an informal inquiry on Intel's practices in the microprocessor market to a formal investigation that same year.

In 2009 the company acquired Wind River Systems, a supplier of software for embedded electronics, for about $884 million in cash.

Paul Otellini is only the fifth CEO in the company's four-decade history, and the first nonengineer. His predecessor, Craig Barrett, retired as chairman in 2009.

HISTORY

In 1968 three engineers from Fairchild Semiconductor created Intel in Mountain View, California, to develop technology for silicon-based chips. ("Intel" is a contraction of "integrated electronics.") The trio consisted of Robert Noyce (who co-invented the integrated circuit, or IC, in 1958), Gordon Moore, and Andy Grove.

Intel initially provided computer memory chips such as DRAMs (1970) and EPROMs (1971). These successes funded the microprocessor designs that revolutionized the electronics industry. In 1971 Intel introduced the 4004 microprocessor, promoted as "a microprogrammable computer on a chip."

In 1979 Moore became Intel's chairman and Grove its president. (Grove became CEO in 1987.) When Intel's 8088 chip was chosen for IBM's PC in 1981, Intel secured its place as the microcomputer standard-setter.

Cutthroat pricing by Japanese competitors forced Intel out of the DRAM market in 1985; in a breathtaking strategy shift that became the subject of countless business school studies, the company refocused on microprocessors. It licensed its 286 chip technology to Advanced Micro Devices (AMD) and others in an effort to create an industry standard. Reacting to AMD's escalating market share (which stood at more than half by 1990), Intel fiercely protected the technology of its 386 (1985) and 486 (1989) chips; AMD sued for breach of contract.

Grove handed the CEO reins to president Craig Barrett in 1998; Grove replaced Moore as chairman, while Moore became chairman emeritus. (Thanks to a mandatory retirement age he helped set, Moore retired from Intel's board in 2001.) Also in 1998 Intel unveiled its low-end Celeron chip. Late in 1999 the company began shipping prototypes of its Itanium 64-bit processor; Itanium's general release was delayed repeatedly, ultimately into mid-2001.

A string of other problems beset Intel in 2000. The company recalled hundreds of thousands of its motherboards that were distributed with a defective chip, and later cancelled development of a low-cost microprocessor for budget PCs.

In 2005 Grove retired from the board, Barrett retired as CEO and succeeded Grove as chairman, and Otellini succeeded Barrett as CEO.

Intel announced in 2005 that it would join with Micron Technology to form a new company devoted to NAND flash memory. Each contributed roughly $1.3 billion to create IM Flash Technologies, which manufactures memory exclusively for Micron and Intel.

Responding to reports of lost market share and other problems, Intel in 2006 cut 1,000 management jobs to trim costs in the face of stiff competition and lower demand for PCs.

In 2006 Intel sold its communications and application processor line to Marvell Technology for $600 million in cash.

EXECUTIVES

Chairman: Jane E. Shaw, age 71
President, CEO, and Director: Paul S. Otellini, age 59, $14,581,900 total compensation
EVP; President, Intel Capital: Arvind Sodhani, age 56
EVP; Co-General Manager, Intel Architecture Group: Sean M. Maloney, age 53, $6,393,900 total compensation
EVP Technology, Manufacturing, and Enterprise Services, and Chief Administrative Officer: Andy D. Bryant, age 59, $6,393,100 total compensation
EVP; Co-General Manager, Intel Architecture Group: David (Dadi) Perlmutter, age 56, $6,399,900 total compensation
SVP and CFO: Stacy J. Smith, age 47, $4,937,500 total compensation
SVP and General Counsel: Douglas (Doug) Melamed, age 63
SVP; General Manager, Sales and Marketing Group: Thomas M. (Tom) Kilroy, age 52
SVP and Director, Human Resources: Patricia Murray
SVP; General Manager, Manufacturing and Supply Chain: Brian M. Krzanich, age 49
SVP; General Manager, Ultra Mobility Group: Anand Chandrasekher, age 47
SVP; Co-General Manager, Technology and Manufacturing Group: Robert J. (Bob) Baker, age 54
SVP; Co-General Manager, Technology and Manufacturing Group: William M. (Bill) Holt, age 57
SVP; General Manager, Software and Services Group: Renee J. James, age 45
VP and Chief Marketing Officer: Deborah S. Conrad, age 48
VP and CTO; Director, Intel Labs; Senior Fellow: Justin R. Rattner, age 60
VP and Director, Human Resources: Richard G. A. Taylor
VP and Treasurer: Ravi Jacob, age 57
VP Finance and Corporate Controller: James G. Campbell, age 54
Auditors: Ernst & Young LLP

LOCATIONS

HQ: Intel Corporation
2200 Mission College Blvd., Santa Clara, CA 95054
Phone: 408-765-8080   **Fax:** 408-765-3804
Web: www.intel.com

2009 Sales

	$ mil.	% of total
Asia/Pacific		
Taiwan	10,574	30
China (including Hong Kong)	5,835	17
Japan	3,389	10
Other countries	2,933	8
Americas		
US	5,280	15
Other countries	1,838	5
Europe	5,278	15
Total	**35,127**	**100**

PRODUCTS/OPERATIONS

2009 Sales

	$ mil.	% of total
PC Client Group		
Microprocessors	19,914	57
Chipset, motherboard & other	6,261	18
Data Center Group		
Microprocessors	5,301	15
Chipset, motherboard & other	1,149	3
Other architecture	1,402	4
Other	970	3
Corporate	130	—
Total	**35,127**	**100**

Selected Products

Chipsets (consumer electronics, desktop, embedded, laptop, modem, server, workstation)
Communication infrastructure components
   Network processors
   Networked storage products
Flash memory (embedded, wireless)
Microprocessors (control plane, desktop, embedded, laptop, network, server, wireless, workstation)
   Celeron
   Core Duo
   Core Quad
   Itanium
   Pentium
   Xeon
Motherboards
Wired and wireless connectivity components

COMPETITORS

AMD
Analog Devices
Applied Micro Circuits
ARM Holdings
Atmel
Broadcom
Centaur Technology
Cisco Systems
Conexant Systems
Creative Technology
Freescale Semiconductor
Fujitsu Semiconductor
IBM Microelectronics
Infineon Technologies
Integrated Device Technology
Intersil
LSI Corp.
Marvell Technology
Maxim Integrated Products
Microchip Technology
MIPS Technologies
Mitsubishi Electric
National Semiconductor
NVIDIA
NXP Semiconductors
Opnext
PMC-Sierra
QUALCOMM
Samsung Electronics
SANYO Semiconductor
Seagate Technology
Silicon Integrated Systems
STMicroelectronics
Texas Instruments
Toshiba Semiconductor
VIA Technologies

HISTORICAL FINANCIALS

Company Type: Public

Income Statement

FYE: Last Saturday in December

	REVENUE ($ mil.)	NET INCOME ($ mil.)	NET PROFIT MARGIN	EMPLOYEES
12/09	35,127	4,369	12.4%	79,800
12/08	37,586	5,292	14.1%	83,900
12/07	38,334	6,976	18.2%	86,300
12/06	35,382	5,044	14.3%	94,100
12/05	38,826	8,664	22.3%	99,900
Annual Growth	**(2.5%)**	**(15.7%)**	**—**	**(5.5%)**

2009 Year-End Financials

Debt ratio: 4.9%
Return on equity: 10.8%
Cash ($ mil.): 3,987
Current ratio: 2.79
Long-term debt ($ mil.): 2,049
No. of shares (mil.): 5,568
Dividends
  Yield: 2.7%
  Payout: 72.7%
Market value ($ mil.): 113,587

Stock History

NASDAQ (GS): INTC

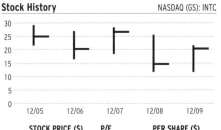

	STOCK PRICE ($) FY Close	P/E High/Low		Earnings	PER SHARE ($) Dividends	Book Value
12/09	20.40	28	16	0.77	0.56	7.49
12/08	14.66	27	13	0.92	0.55	7.02
12/07	26.66	24	16	1.18	0.45	7.68
12/06	20.25	31	19	0.86	0.40	6.60
12/05	24.96	21	16	1.40	0.32	6.50
Annual Growth	**(4.9%)**	**—**	**—**	**(13.9%)**	**15.0%**	**3.6%**

International Business Machines

Big Blue? Try Huge Blue. International Business Machines (IBM) is the world's top provider of computer products and services. Among the leaders in almost every market in which it competes, the company focuses primarily on its growing services business, which accounts for well over half of sales. Though perhaps still best known for its hardware, its IT and business services units are among the largest in the world and serve customers across most industries. IBM is also one of the largest providers of both business software and semiconductors. The company's computing hardware legacy lives on in the form of its industry-leading enterprise server and storage products lines.

IBM continues to use acquisitions to augment its own R&D into better business software and services, while shrinking its lower margin hardware operations with divestitures and organizational changes. The company steadily buys small firms with technology or expertise that complement or expand its product lines and service selection. It made more than 100 acquisitions in the first decade of the 2000s.

IBM paid about $5 billion for software developer Cognos in a bid to increase its portfolio of business process optimization applications.

In 2010 it bought business process management software maker Lombardi, it agreed to acquire the Sterling Commerce subsidiary of AT&T for about $1.4 billion in cash, and it agreed to buy security software developer BigFix to expand its corporate security products lineup.

The company is positioning itself to offer a wide array of enterprise software tools and processes to better harness and analyze the rapidly expanding volumes of data generated by the global growth in digital communications and commerce. Sterling Commerce will add to IBM's portfolio of middleware, the code that connects software components and applications.

Meanwhile the company in 2010 sold its declining product lifecycle management software business to Dassault Systèmes for $600 million.

Another area of focus is the development of applications and services to support cloud computing. In other words, IBM is designing tools for managing and optimizing access to corporate information stored at data center facilities by the growing number of businesses looking to outsource or enhance their network and data management efforts.

IBM's international business has become increasingly important to the bottom line. With clients in about 170 countries, overseas sales account for a growing portion of total revenues. The company's businesses in Brazil, China, India, and Russia have been particularly active.

HISTORY

In 1914 National Cash Register's star salesman, Thomas Watson, left to rescue the flagging Computing-Tabulating-Recording (C-T-R) Company, the pioneer in US punch card processing that had been incorporated in 1911. Watson aggressively marketed C-T-R's tabulators, supplying them to the US government during WWI and tripling company revenues to almost $15 million by 1920. The company became International Business Machines (IBM) in 1924 and soon dominated the global market for tabulators, time clocks, and electric typewriters. It was the US's largest office machine maker by 1940.

IBM perfected electromechanical calculation (the Harvard Mark I, 1944) but initially dismissed the potential of computers. When Remington Rand's UNIVAC computer (1951) began replacing IBM machines, IBM quickly responded.

The company unveiled its first computer in 1952. With its superior research and development and marketing, IBM built a market share near 80% in the 1960s and 1970s. Its innovations included the STRETCH systems, which eliminated vacuum tubes (1960), and the first compatible family of computers, the System/360 (1964). IBM also developed floppy disks (1971) and the first laser printer for computers (1975). The introduction of the IBM PC in 1981 ignited the personal computer industry, sparking a barrage of PC clones. Through it all IBM was the subject of a 12-year government antitrust investigation that ended in 1982.

The shift to smaller, open systems, along with greater competition in all of IBM's segments, caused wrenching change. Instead of responding to the market need for cheap PCs and practical business applications, IBM stubbornly stuck with mainframes, and rivals began capitalizing on Big Blue's technology. After posting profits of $6.6 billion in 1984, the company began a slow slide. It sold many noncomputer businesses, including its copier division to Kodak in 1988 and its Lexmark typewriter business in 1991. Closing the book on its heritage, IBM shuttered the last of its punch card plants that year.

In 1993 CEO John Akers was replaced by Louis Gerstner, the first outsider to run IBM. He began to turn the ailing, antiquated company around by slashing costs and nonstrategic divisions, cutting the workforce, shaking up entrenched management, and pushing services. His $1 billion R&D budget cut caused an exodus of IBM scientists and created an operation geared more toward quick turnaround than lengthy research. In 1994 Big Blue reported its first profit in four years. It also began making computer chips that year.

A pioneer in server operating system software, IBM made an early move into messaging and network management software with its acquisitions of spreadsheet pioneer Lotus Development in 1995. Hoping to turn around its ailing PC business, IBM in 1999 axed manufacturing staff and halted sales of its PCs through US retailers.

In a move intended to bolster its data management division, IBM in 2001 purchased the database software unit of Informix for $1 billion.

IBM acquired PricewaterhouseCoopers' consulting and IT services unit, PwC Consulting, for an estimated $3.5 billion in 2002. While presenting IBM with a significant integration challenge, the transaction served the dual purpose of augmenting IBM's standard array of outsourcing, maintenance, and integration services, while moving the company into high-end management consulting. COO Samuel Palmisano succeeded Gerstner as CEO that year.

In 2003 IBM acquired development tool maker Rational Software for $2.1 billion. The company in 2005 sold its PC business to Lenovo. Also in 2005 it acquired Ascential Software for about $1.1 billion. In 2006 IBM bought FileNet, a maker of content management software, for $1.6 billion. One of IBM's most notable acquisitions in 2008 was the $885 million purchase of business process optimization and embedded systems software specialist Telelogic.

EXECUTIVES

Chairman, President, and CEO: Samuel J. Palmisano, age 58, $2,431,379 total compensation
SVP and CFO: Mark Loughridge, age 56, $6,461,973 total compensation
SVP Software Group: Steven A. (Steve) Mills, age 58, $5,757,942 total compensation
SVP Global Technology Services:
Michael E. (Mike) Daniels, age 55, $5,460,525 total compensation
SVP Global Business Sales and Distribution:
Virginia M. (Ginni) Rometty, age 51, $5,179,731 total compensation
SVP Systems and Technology: Rodney C. (Rod) Adkins, age 51
SVP Legal and Regulatory Affairs and General Counsel:
Robert C. Weber, age 59
SVP Application Management Services:
Colleen F. Arnold, age 53
SVP Services Delivery: Timothy S. Shaughnessy, age 52
SVP Human Resources: J. Randall (Randy) MacDonald, age 61
SVP Software Solutions Group:
Michael D. (Mike) Rhodin, age 49

SVP Software Middleware Group: Robert J. LeBlanc, age 51
SVP Global Business Services: R. Franklin Kern, age 56
SVP Marketing and Communications: Jon C. Iwata, age 47
SVP Research and Intellectual Property:
John E. Kelly III, age 56
SVP Enterprise Transformation: Linda S. Sanford, age 57
Chief Scientist, Entity Analytic Solutions, Software Group, and Distinguished Engineer: Jeff Jonas
VP and CIO: Pat Toole
VP, Assistant General Counsel, and Secretary:
Andrew Bonzani
VP Deep Computing: Dave Turek
VP Investor Relations: Patricia Murphy
Auditors: PricewaterhouseCoopers LLP

LOCATIONS

HQ: International Business Machines Corporation
1 New Orchard Rd., Armonk, NY 10504
Phone: 914-499-1900   **Fax:** 800-314-1092
Web: www.ibm.com

2009 Sales

	$ mil.	% of total
Americas	40,184	42
Europe, Middle East & Africa	32,583	34
Asia/Pacific	20,710	22
OEM	2,281	2
Total	**95,758**	**100**

PRODUCTS/OPERATIONS

2009 Sales

	$ mil.	% of total
Services	55,127	58
Sales	38,300	40
Financing	2,331	2
Total	**95,758**	**100**

2009 Sales

	$ mil.	% of total
Global technology services	37,348	39
Software	21,396	22
Global business services	17,653	19
Systems & technology	16,190	17
Global financing	2,302	2
Other	869	1
Total	**95,758**	**100**

Selected Services

Business services
  Application management
  E-business
  Strategic consulting
  Systems integration
Financing
Technology services
  Business process outsourcing
  Infrastructure
  Maintenance
  Outsourcing
  Software integration
  Systems management
  Web hosting
Training

Selected Products

Microelectronics
  Application-specific integrated circuits (ASICs)
  Foundry services
  Memory chips
  Microprocessors and embedded processors
  Packaging and interconnect products and services
Printing systems
Servers

Software
  Application development
  Database and data management
  E-commerce
  Graphics and multimedia
  Groupware
  Networking and communication
  Operating systems
  Product life cycle management
  Security
  Speech recognition
  System management
  Transaction system
  Web application servers
Storage
  Hard drive systems
  Optical libraries
  Storage networking
  Tape drives, systems, and libraries

COMPETITORS

Accenture
Alcatel-Lucent
BMC Software
CA Technologies
Capgemini
Computer Sciences Corp.
Dell
Deloitte Consulting
EMC
Epson
Ericsson
Fujitsu
GE
HCL Technologies
Hewlett-Packard
Hitachi
HP Enterprise Services
Infosys
Intel
Lexmark
Microsoft
Motorola
NEC
Novell
NTT DATA
Oracle
Panasonic Corp
Ricoh Company
SAP
Sony
Tata Consultancy
Texas Instruments
Toshiba
TSMC
Unisys
Wipro Technologies

HISTORICAL FINANCIALS

Company Type: Public

Income Statement

FYE: December 31

	REVENUE ($ mil.)	NET INCOME ($ mil.)	NET PROFIT MARGIN	EMPLOYEES
12/09	95,758	13,425	14.0%	399,409
12/08	103,630	12,334	11.9%	398,455
12/07	98,786	10,418	10.5%	426,969
12/06	91,424	9,492	10.4%	355,766
12/05	91,134	7,970	8.7%	366,345
Annual Growth	1.2%	13.9%	—	2.2%

2009 Year-End Financials

Debt ratio: 96.9%
Return on equity: 74.4%
Cash ($ mil.): 12,183
Current ratio: 1.36
Long-term debt ($ mil.): 21,932

No. of shares (mil.): 1,261
Dividends
  Yield: 1.6%
  Payout: 21.5%
Market value ($ mil.): 165,101

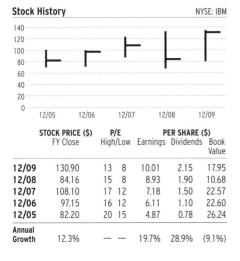

STOCK PRICE ($)		P/E		PER SHARE ($)		
	FY Close	High/Low		Earnings	Dividends	Book Value
12/09	130.90	13	8	10.01	2.15	17.95
12/08	84.16	15	8	8.93	1.90	10.68
12/07	108.10	17	12	7.18	1.50	22.57
12/06	97.15	16	12	6.11	1.10	22.60
12/05	82.20	20	15	4.87	0.78	26.24
Annual Growth	12.3%	—	—	19.7%	28.9%	(9.1%)

International Flavors & Fragrances

If you've got a taste for the sweet and the salty, then International Flavors & Fragrances (IFF) is your kind of company. One of the world's leading creators and manufacturers of artificial and natural aromas and flavors, IFF produces fragrances used in the manufacture of perfumes, cosmetics, soaps, and other personal care and household products. The company has more than 15% of the world market. IFF sells its flavors principally to makers of prepared foods, dairy foods, beverages, confections, and pharmaceuticals. The company sells its fragrances and flavors in solid and liquid forms in amounts that range from a few pounds to several tons.

The company has manufacturing, sales, and distribution facilities in more than 30 countries. Sales outside North America account for nearly 70% of revenues. The compounds used in IFF's products are made both synthetically and from natural ingredients such as flowers and fruits.

It operates about 30 fragrance and flavor laboratories, called Creative Center, in more than 20 countries. While IFF's flavor products represent 60% of the total production volume, fragrances contribute more than half of the company's sales. The company most recently opened Creative Centers in Shanghai, China, and Sao Paulo, Brazil.

IFF continues to introduce new products and to invest heavily in product development. One of its newest products is a plastic imbued with fragrance, allowing the manufacture of odor-resistant trash bags and similar products. R&D spending at IFF amounts to about 10% of sales.

Douglas Tough was named IFF's CEO in 2010. He replaced chairman and CEO Robert Amen, who resigned in 2009. Tough was formerly the CEO of Ansell Limited.

HISTORY

International Flavors & Fragrances (IFF) began in 1929 when Dutch immigrant and perfumer A. L. van Ameringen (who originally came to the US to work for an agent of the Dutch firm Polak & Schwarz, later leaving to form his own business) and William Haebler formed a fragrance company, van Ameringen-Haebler, in New York City.

The company produced the fragrance for Youth Dew, Estée Lauder's first big cosmetics hit, in 1953. One biographer of Estée Lauder linked her romantically with van Ameringen after her 1939 divorce (she later remarried Joseph Lauder). The business association with van Ameringen's company endured, and by the late 1980s it had produced an estimated 90% of Estée Lauder's fragrances.

In 1958 the company changed its name to International Flavors & Fragrances after it bought Polak & Schwarz. The US market for fragrances grew as consumers bought items such as air fresheners, and manufacturers began adding fragrances to household cleaning items.

Henry Walter, who became CEO when van Ameringen retired in 1963, expanded IFF's presence overseas. Walter boasted, "Most of the great soap fragrances have been ours." So have many famous French perfumes, but most perfume companies wanted to cultivate product mystique, preventing IFF from taking credit for its scents.

Most of IFF's products were made for manufacturers of consumer goods. But under Walter's direction in the 1970s, IFF's R&D team experimented to find scents for museum exhibits and participated in Masters & Johnson research on the connection between sex and smell. Said Walter, "Our business is sex and hunger."

During the early 1980s IFF conducted fragrance research for relieving stress, lowering blood pressure, and alleviating depression. In 1982 IFF researchers developed a way to bind odors to plastic, a process used by makers of garbage bags and toys.

Walter retired in 1985 and Eugene Grisanti became CEO. After a three-year slump in new creations, IFF developed fragrances for several prestigious perfumes (Eternity and Halston) in 1988. IFF enhanced its position in dairy flavors with its 1991 purchase of Wisconsin-based Auro Tech. In 1993 IFF's Living Flower process successfully synthesized the fragrance of growing flowers for perfumes.

IFF inaugurated its flavor and fragrance facility in China (Guangzhou) and formed a joint venture with China's Hangzhou Xin'anjiang Perfumery Factory. The company reasserted its leadership in the US fragrance market in 1996 with the launch of two IFF-developed fragrances: Elizabeth Taylor's Black Pearls and Escada's Jardin de Soleil.

Sales and profits dipped in 1997, prompting IFF to consolidate production. Asia's economic crisis and turmoil in Russia continued to hurt profits in 1998, and in 1999 IFF was hit by the devaluation of Brazil's currency, weak demand for aroma chemicals, and the US dollar's strength against the euro.

In 2000 Unilever executive Richard Goldstein was appointed chairman and CEO. Boosting its natural ingredients operations, IFF bought Laboratoire Monique Remy (France). The same year IFF acquired rival fragrance and flavor maker Bush Boake Allen in a deal worth about $1 billion. The acquisition led to a company-wide reorganization, including the closing of some manufacturing, distribution, and sales facilities worldwide.

In 2001 the company sold its US and Brazilian formulated fruit and vegetable preparation businesses and its aroma chemicals business in the UK. Continuing its product development strategy, in 2003 IFF launched a high-intensity cooling technology (CoolTek) for use in the food, beverage, and pharmaceutical industries that does not use the traditional mint-based technology. The following year it opened a new culinary and baking center to support customers' product development programs.

IFF sold its fruit preparations operations in Switzerland and Germany in August 2004 to Israel's Frutarom. The deal was for $36.5 million. Later that year, it sold the remainder of its fruit preparations business (located in France) to Frutarom. It also closed its Canadian manufacturing facility and its plant in Dijon, France.

Chairman and CEO Goldstein retired in 2006. Former Sears chairman and CEO Arthur Martinez, an IFF director, took over on an interim basis until International Paper's Robert Amen was named chairman and CEO. He left in 2009.

EXECUTIVES

Chairman and CEO: Douglas D. Tough, age 60
Group President, Fragrances: Nicolas Mirzayantz, age 47, $1,775,120 total compensation
Group President, Flavors: Hernan Vaisman, age 51, $1,754,883 total compensation
EVP and CFO: Kevin C. Berryman, age 51
EVP and Head Supply Chain: Beth E. Ford, age 45, $1,657,864 total compensation
SVP Human Resources: Angelica T. Cantlon, age 58, $522,199 total compensation
SVP, General Counsel, and Secretary: Dennis M. Meany, age 62, $1,500,326 total compensation
VP and Controller: Richard A. (Rich) O'Leary, age 50, $932,281 total compensation
Auditors: PricewaterhouseCoopers LLP

LOCATIONS

HQ: International Flavors & Fragrances Inc.
521 W. 57th St., New York, NY 10019
Phone: 212-765-5500   **Fax:** 212-708-7132
Web: www.iff.com

2009 Sales

	$ mil.	% of total
Europe, Africa & Middle East	808	35
North America	600	26
Greater Asia	575	25
Latin America	343	14
Total	**2,326**	**100**

PRODUCTS/OPERATIONS

2009 Sales

	$ mil.	% of total
Fragrances	1,245	54
Flavors	1,081	46
Total	**2,326**	**100**

Selected Applications for IFF's Products

Fragrance chemical uses
Aftershave lotions
Air fresheners
All-purpose cleaners
Colognes
Cosmetic creams
Deodorants
Detergents
Hair care products
Lipsticks
Lotions
Perfumes
Powders
Soaps

Flavor chemical uses
  Alcoholic beverages
  Baked goods
  Candies
  Dairy products
  Desserts
  Diet foods
  Drink powders
  Pharmaceuticals
  Prepared foods
  Snacks
  Soft drinks

COMPETITORS

Ajinomoto
BASF SE
Bayer AG
Danisco A/S
Firmenich
Frutarom
Givaudan
Henkel
Human Pheromone Sciences
International Specialty Products
Kerry Group
M & F Worldwide
McCormick & Company
Newly Weds Foods
PCAS
Robertet
Sensient
Symrise
Takasago International
Wrigley

HISTORICAL FINANCIALS

Company Type: Public

Income Statement

FYE: December 31

	REVENUE ($ mil.)	NET INCOME ($ mil.)	NET PROFIT MARGIN	EMPLOYEES
12/09	2,326	196	8.4%	5,400
12/08	2,389	230	9.6%	5,300
12/07	2,277	247	10.9%	5,315
12/06	2,095	227	10.8%	5,087
12/05	1,993	193	9.7%	5,160
Annual Growth	3.9%	0.3%	—	1.1%

2009 Year-End Financials

Debt ratio: 121.6%
Return on equity: 29.1%
Cash ($ mil.): 80
Current ratio: 2.33
Long-term debt ($ mil.): 935

No. of shares (mil.): 80
Dividends
  Yield: 2.4%
  Payout: 40.7%
Market value ($ mil.): 3,285

Stock History

NYSE: IFF

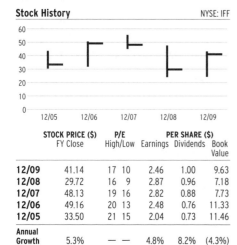

	STOCK PRICE ($) FY Close	P/E High/Low		PER SHARE ($) Earnings	Dividends	Book Value
12/09	41.14	17	10	2.46	1.00	9.63
12/08	29.72	16	9	2.87	0.96	7.18
12/07	48.13	19	16	2.82	0.88	7.73
12/06	49.16	20	13	2.48	0.76	11.33
12/05	33.50	21	15	2.04	0.73	11.46
Annual Growth	5.3%	—	—	4.8%	8.2%	(4.3%)

International Game Technology

International Game Technology (IGT) has hit the jackpot in the casino gaming business. The company is the world's largest gaming machine manufacturer, with a product portfolio that includes traditional reel slot machines, video slots and video poker, and progressive payout machines. IGT also makes casino management software systems for tracking activity on the casino floor, as well as multiplayer game software and customer relationship management (CRM) systems. It sells products mostly in North America, but it also serves international customers in about 10 other countries.

IGT generates just over 50% of its revenue through product sales and service agreements under which the company collects recurring fees, some of which are based on the amount of money wagered on its machines. The rest of its business comes from more traditional sales and service contracts. IGT is working to increase the number of customers paying under recurring revenue contracts.

A key strategic initiative of IGT is to invest heavily in product development to make games that will attract attention on the crowded casino floor. It has about 1,000 different game themes designed to appeal to game players, including several based on licensed brands and entertainment properties such as popular game shows *Wheel of Fortune* and *The Price Is Right*. IGT has also introduced a multigame slot system (MultiPLAY) that allows gamblers to play up to four slot games at once with progressive payouts. In addition, the company is putting emphasis on developing and expanding its casino information management systems and server-based gaming platforms that help operate multiple gaming machines.

To help maintain its leadership in the industry, IGT has made several strategic acquisitions and investments in other gaming machine companies. In 2009 the company acquired the global operations of Progressive Gaming International. Complementing its current technology, the acquisition increased IGT's system-install base, providing the company with a more complete product offering.

IGT appointed Patti Hart to replace T.J. Matthews as CEO in 2009. The move was prompted by Matthews' resignation that year. Hart previously served as CEO of software maker Pinnacle Systems.

HISTORY

International Game Technology (IGT) was formed in 1980 by William "Si" Redd, a veteran of the slot machine industry. Lady Luck was good to Redd for five years before turning fickle. Rather than fold, Redd dealt himself a king (hiring Charles Mathewson, a retired top executive from investment firm Jefferies & Co.). Mathewson flushed top management, cinched IGT's belt, and dealt new managers a fresh hand (stock options rather than cash). IGT developed its Telnaes patent-based slot machine — a reel-type slot with higher payouts and higher odds — featuring flashy themes, fewer breakdowns, and improved reporting systems. Slots went from a nickel-and-dime game to a major source of casino revenue.

In 1997 IGT debuted Mega$ports, which accepts unique wagers on sports (such as which quarterback will throw the most yards in a game). That year IGT's vast new headquarters became fully operational (five plants and seven warehouses were moved under one roof). In 1998 IGT beefed up its Australian operations with the $114 million acquisition of Olympic Amusements, a Melbourne-based supplier of gaming equipment and services. IGT also bought the UK-based Barcrest gaming machine business from Bass (which later split into Mitchells & Butlers and InterContinental Hotels) for $70 million.

In 1999 the company acquired Sodak Gaming, a supplier of gaming machines to Native American casinos and other clients. In 2001 IGT bought rivals Silicon Gaming (for about $45 million) and Anchor Gaming. The latter buy was part of the company's strategy of expanding into the lottery business. The following year it created a new division, IGT Lottery, to house its lottery operations, including the former Anchor companies AWI, United Tote, and VLC, and its own Oregon lottery route operations and SAMS lottery system.

IGT purchased gaming software development company Acres Gaming for $130 million in 2003. The company also sold its online lottery operations to Scientific Games for $143 million. That same year, Thomas (T.J.) Matthews was named CEO. In late 2004 IGT created its IGT-Canada unit with the acquisition of Canadian gaming equipment provider Hi-Tech Gaming. It also expanded into online gaming that same year through the purchase of WagerWorks.

Acquisitions continued in 2007 when IGT purchased a stake in electronic table game maker DigiDeal. It also expanded into the Chinese gaming market by investing in Hong Kong-based LotSynergy. Former Pinnacle Systems chief Patti Hart replaced Matthews as CEO in 2009.

EXECUTIVES

Chairman: Philip G. (Phil) Satre, age 61
President, CEO, and Director: Patti S. Hart, age 53, $3,048,471 total compensation
President, International: Paulus Karskens, age 57, $2,136,154 total compensation
COO: Eric P. Tom, age 52
EVP, CFO, and Treasurer: Patrick W. (Pat) Cavanaugh, age 49, $853,817 total compensation
EVP Global Operations: Anthony Ciorciari, age 62, $1,103,576 total compensation
EVP New Media: Gideon Bierer
EVP Research and Development and CTO: Christopher J. (Chris) Satchell, age 37
SVP Government Affairs and Business Development: Charles (Chuck) Brooke
SVP North American Sales: Ron Rivera
General Counsel: Neil Friedman
Chief of Staff and Head of Corporate Development: Craig Billings
Chief Marketing Officer: Susan Macke
Corporate Secretary and Chief Legal Officer: Robert C. Melendres, age 45
VP Native American Development: Knute Knudson
VP Network Systems: Javier Saenz
VP Compliance: Michelle Chatigny
VP Corporate Law and Assistant Secretary: J. Kenneth Creighton
VP Human Resources: Tami Corbin
VP Core Products: Harold Zeitz
Managing Director, IGT Europe: James Boje
Auditors: Deloitte & Touche LLP

LOCATIONS

HQ: International Game Technology
9295 Prototype Dr., Reno, NV 89521
Phone: 775-448-7777   **Fax:** 775-448-0719
Web: www.igt.com

2009 Sales

	$ mil.	% of total
North America	1,631	77
International	483	23
Total	**2,114**	**100**

PRODUCTS/OPERATIONS

2009 Sales

	$ mil.	% of total
Gaming	1,179	56
Products	935	44
Total	**2,114**	**100**

Selected Products

Amusement with prize machines (limited-payout skill games)
Casino gaming machines
  Progressive payout machines
  Reel and video slot machines
  Video poker
Casino information systems
  Customer relationship management (CRM) software
  Electronic table games
  Multiplayer game management systems
Electronic bingo games
Pachisuro (slot-style gaming machines in Japan)
Video lottery terminal

COMPETITORS

Aristocrat Leisure
Bally Technologies
John Huxley
Konami Gaming
Lottomatica
Multimedia Games
Novomatic
Scientific Games
Shuffle Master
Universal Entertainment
WMS Industries

HISTORICAL FINANCIALS

Company Type: Public

Income Statement

FYE: September 30

	REVENUE ($ mil.)	NET INCOME ($ mil.)	NET PROFIT MARGIN	EMPLOYEES
9/09	2,114	149	7.0%	5,100
9/08	2,529	343	13.5%	5,900
9/07	2,621	508	19.4%	5,400
9/06	2,512	474	18.9%	5,200
9/05	2,379	437	18.3%	5,000
Annual Growth	**(2.9%)**	**(23.6%)**	**—**	**0.5%**

2009 Year-End Financials

Debt ratio: 224.3%
Return on equity: 15.9%
Cash ($ mil.): 147
Current ratio: 1.98
Long-term debt ($ mil.): 2,170

No. of shares (mil.): 298
Dividends
  Yield: 1.5%
  Payout: 62.7%
Market value ($ mil.): 6,403

Stock History

NYSE: IGT

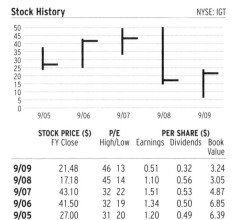

	STOCK PRICE ($) FY Close	P/E High/Low		PER SHARE ($) Earnings	Dividends	Book Value
9/09	21.48	46	13	0.51	0.32	3.24
9/08	17.18	45	14	1.10	0.56	3.05
9/07	43.10	32	22	1.51	0.53	4.87
9/06	41.50	32	19	1.34	0.50	6.85
9/05	27.00	31	20	1.20	0.49	6.39
Annual Growth	**(5.6%)**	**—**	**—**	**(19.3%)**	**(10.1%)**	**(15.6%)**

International Paper

For International Paper (IP), business is a paper chase. It is one of the world's largest manufacturers of printing papers. Products include uncoated paper used in printers, market pulp for making towel and tissue goods, and coated paper and uncoated bristols (heavyweight art paper). In the US, IP is #1 in containerboard production, 70% of which is used in industrial corrugated boxes. A consumer packaging arm churns out board to box cosmetics and food, or print lottery tickets. IP's distribution subsidiary, xpedx, plies products and supply chain services to markets in North America. IP owns forestland in the US and Brazil, and a pulp and paper business in Russia, through a 50-50 venture with Ilim Holding.

IP is adding lower-cost paper mills, which expand the company's uncoated free sheet production capacity, shrinking marginal costs, as well as open the door to serving local developing markets. One of the company's goals is to capture rising demand for consumer packaging in Asia. In 2010 IP purchased Svenska Cellulosa's Asian packaging business. The acquisition promises to deepen the company's geographic footprint with 13 corrugated box plants and two specialty packaging facilities established in China, Singapore, Malaysia, and Indonesia.

The company formed a joint venture in mid-2010 with Natural Resource Partners (NRP), a Houston-based mineral reserve property manager. IP will hold 49% to NRP's 51% stake in a venture that will manage current leases and develop IP's more than 7 million acres of mineral holdings, such as oil and gas, coal bed methane, and precious metals.

The company's direction includes right-sizing production with customer demand, eroded by the global recession. It earmarked a Louisiana mill to convert to lower-cost 100% pulp production. With the $10 million conversion complete, the mill had softwood pulp capacity of 450,000 tons per year. But declining pulp demand coupled with a weak economy, and the mill was permanently shuttered in 2009. Mills in Oregon, Virginia, Oklahoma, France, and Scotland were also closed or curbed. As a result IP's headcount fell by nearly 10%.

A year earlier, IP had made a transformational decision that propelled the company to the top spot in the North American containerboard industry. It purchased the containerboard, packaging, and recycling business of rival Weyerhaeuser for $6 billion. The new operations included 10 specialty packaging plants, and four kraft bag and sack locations, as well as 19 recycling facilities.

HISTORY

In 1898, 18 northeastern pulp and paper firms consolidated to lower costs. The resulting International Paper had 20 mills in Maine, Massachusetts, New Hampshire, New York, and Vermont. The mills relied on forests in New England and Canada for wood pulp. When Canada enacted legislation to stop the export of pulpwood in 1919, International Paper formed Canadian International Paper.

In the 1920s International Paper built a hydroelectric plant on the Hudson River. Between 1928 and 1941 the company called itself International Paper & Power. It entered the market for kraft paper (paper sacks) in 1925 with the purchase of Bastrop Pulp & Paper (Louisiana).

During the 1940s and 1950s, the company bought Agar Manufacturing (shipping containers, 1940), Single Service Containers (Pure-Pak milk containers, 1946), and Lord Baltimore Press (folding cartons, 1958). It diversified in the 1960s and 1970s, buying Davol (hospital products, 1968; sold to C. R. Bard, 1980), American Central (land development, 1968; sold to developers, 1974), and General Crude Oil (gas and oil, 1975; sold to Mobil Oil, 1979).

In the 1980s International Paper modernized its plants to focus on less-cyclical products. After selling Canadian International Paper in 1981, the company bought Hammermill Paper (office paper, 1986), Arvey (paper manufacturing and distribution, 1987), and Masonite (composite wood products, 1988). International Paper entered the European paper market in 1989 by buying Aussedat Rey (France), Ilford Group (UK), and Zanders (West Germany). In 1990 it bought Dixon Paper (distributor of paper and graphic arts supplies), Nevamar (laminates), and the UK's Cookson Group (printing plates).

International Paper expanded in the early 1990s with acquisitions such as Scaldia Papier (the Netherlands, 1991) and Western Paper (1992) and through investments in Carter Holt Harvey (New Zealand) and Scitex (Israel), a leading maker of electronic prepress systems. In 1994 International Paper formed a Chinese packaging joint venture and bought two Mexican paper-distributing companies.

After recording a loss in 1997, International Paper began downsizing: It sold $1 billion in marginal assets and cut its workforce by 10%. Branching its US box-making operations into the South and Midwest, International Paper bought Weston Paper & Manufacturing in 1998; it also bought Mead's distribution business. Then the company announced that it would close 25 plants in the combined enterprise.

International Paper paid $7.9 billion in 1999 for rival Union Camp, and it acquired Champion for about $9.6 billion. In 2001 International Paper sold its Masonite operations to Premdor for $500 million. The company also began cutting 10% (3,000 jobs) of its US workforce as part of a restructuring program.

International Paper closed its mill in Natchez, Mississippi, and exited the Chemical Cellulose pulp business in 2003. Layoffs affected about 600 workers, or 6% of IP's workforce.

At the close of 2004 International Paper completed the sale of its Weldwood of Canada, Ltd., subsidiary to West Fraser Timber Co. Ltd. of Vancouver, Canada, for about $950 million.

The company also sold its 50.5% stake in Carter Holt Harvey for $1.14 billion.

Other divestitures between 2000 and 2006 included its retail and flexible packaging operations, its Zanders European coated papers business, its oriented strand board business, its decorative products business, and more than 5 million acres of forestland.

IP followed with a joint-venture deal with Ilim Pulp through Ilim Holding. IP bought in 2007 50% of Ilim Holding for about $650 million. The JV, Ilim Group, will operate pulp and paper mills in the European and Siberian regions of Russia with partnering companies investing around $1.5 billion over five years in Ilim Group's four mills.

In Brazil in 2007, IP exchanged an in-progress pulp mill project and certain forestland operations for Votorantim Celulose e Papel's (VCP) Luiz Antonio uncoated paper and pulp mill plus forestlands in the state of São Paulo.

EXECUTIVES

Chairman and CEO: John V. Faraci Jr., age 60, $12,163,797 total compensation
SVP and CFO: Timothy S. (Tim) Nicholls, age 49, $2,456,475 total compensation
SVP Industrial Packaging: Carol L. Roberts, age 50, $2,867,959 total compensation
SVP Printing and Communications Papers, Americas: Mark S. Sutton, age 48
SVP Human Resources and Communications: Paul J. Karre, age 57
SVP Manufacturing and Technology, EHS&S and Global Supply Chain Sourcing: Tommy S. Joseph, age 50
SVP Consumer Packaging and IP Asia: Thomas G. (Tom) Kadien, age 54
SVP; President, xpedx: Mary A. Laschinger, age 49
SVP, General Counsel, and Secretary: Maura Abeln Smith, age 54, $2,129,752 total compensation
SVP and CIO: John N. Balboni, age 61
SVP and President, IP Europe, Middle East, Africa, and Russia: Maximo Pacheco, age 57
SVP Corporate Development: C. Cato Ealy, age 53
VP Finance, Coded Paper Board, and Customer Packaging: Terri L. Herrington, age 54
VP Commercial Printing: Teri Shanahan
VP Finance and Controller: Robert J. Grillet, age 54
VP Environment, Health, Safety and Sustainability: David (Dave) Kiser
VP Investor Relations: Thomas A. Cleves, age 48
Senior Communications Manager: Amy J. Sawyer
Auditors: Deloitte & Touche LLP

LOCATIONS

HQ: International Paper Company
6400 Poplar Ave., Memphis, TN 38197
Phone: 901-419-9000 **Fax:** 901-214-9682
Web: www.ipaper.com

2009 Sales

	$ mil.	% of total
Americas		
US	18,355	79
Other countries	1,293	5
Europe	2,716	12
Pacific Rim	1,002	4
Total	**23,366**	**100**

PRODUCTS/OPERATIONS

2009 Sales

	$ mil.	% of total
Industrial packaging	8,890	37
Distribution	6,525	27
Printing papers	5,680	23
Consumer packaging	3,060	13
Forest products	45	—
Adjustments	(834)	—
Total	**23,366**	**100**

Selected Operations and Products

Consumer Packaging
  Cold cups and lids
  Consumer-ready packaging (Shorewood Packaging folding carton, set-up box)
  Folding carton board
  Food buckets and lids
  Hot cups and lids
  Milk container and lids
  Starcote tobacco board
Industrial Packaging
  Automotive packaging
  Corrugated pallet
  Die-cut package
  Flapless
  Kraft linerboard
  Laminated bulk bin
  Liquid bulk
  Litho lamination
  Medium paper
  Retail displays
  Saturating draft
  Slotted container
  White top liner
Papers
  HP (Hewlett-Packard) home and commercial papers
  Office papers
Pulp
  Fluff pulp
  Paper and tissue pulp
Recycling products
  Old corrugated containers and kraft corrugated cuttings
  Old newspaper
Distribution (xpedx)
  Building services and away-from-home markets with facility supplies
  Commercial printers with printing papers and graphic pre-press
  Manufacturers with packaging supplies and equipment
  Printing presses and post-press equipment
  Warehousing and delivery services

COMPETITORS

Alcoa
Amcor
Cascades Inc.
Domtar
ENCE
Environmental Mill & Supply
Georgia-Pacific
Louisiana-Pacific
McFarland Cascade
MeadWestvaco
Myllykoski Paper
NewPage
Nippon Paper
OfficeMax
Packaging Corp. of America
Potlatch
Pratt Industries USA
Sappi
Smurfit-Stone Container
Temple-Inland
UPM-Kymmene
Weyerhaeuser

HISTORICAL FINANCIALS

Company Type: Public

Income Statement

FYE: December 31

	REVENUE ($ mil.)	NET INCOME ($ mil.)	NET PROFIT MARGIN	EMPLOYEES
12/09	23,366	681	2.9%	56,100
12/08	24,829	(1,282)	—	61,700
12/07	21,890	1,168	5.3%	51,500
12/06	21,995	1,050	4.8%	60,600
12/05	24,097	1,100	4.6%	68,700
Annual Growth	**(0.8%)**	**(11.3%)**	**—**	**(4.9%)**

2009 Year-End Financials

Debt ratio: 144.9%
Return on equity: 13.4%
Cash ($ mil.): —
Current ratio: 1.88
Long-term debt ($ mil.): 8,729
No. of shares (mil.): 437
Dividends
  Yield: 1.2%
  Payout: 20.6%
Market value ($ mil.): 11,704

Stock History

NYSE: IP

	STOCK PRICE ($) FY Close	P/E High/Low	Earnings	PER SHARE ($) Dividends	Book Value
12/09	26.78	18 3	1.55	0.32	13.78
12/08	11.80	— —	(3.05)	1.00	9.54
12/07	32.38	15 11	2.70	1.00	19.84
12/06	34.10	17 14	2.18	1.00	18.22
12/05	33.61	19 12	2.21	1.00	19.11
Annual Growth	**(5.5%)**	**— —**	**(8.5%)**	**(24.8%)**	**(7.8%)**

Interpublic Group

Subsidiaries of this company come between brands and the general public. The Interpublic Group of Companies is one of the world's largest advertising and marketing services conglomerates, operating through offices in more than 100 countries. Its flagship creative agencies include McCann Worldgroup, DraftFCB, and Lowe & Partners, while such firms as Campbell-Ewald, Deutsch, and Hill, Holliday are leaders in the US advertising business. Interpublic also offers direct marketing, media services, and public relations through such agencies as Initiative and Weber Shandwick. Its largest clients include General Motors, Johnson & Johnson, Microsoft, and Unilever.

As with most global companies in the advertising industry, Interpublic has seen a lower demand for its products and services amid the recession. It primarily attributes this decrease to spending declines and lost accounts within the technology and telecommunications sectors, two of the largest it serves. It also lost businesses within the auto, transportation, and financial services sectors — three industries hit the hardest during the economic downturn.

Over the years Interpublic's growth strategy has involved acquiring controlling stakes in emerging markets. Looking to India, in mid-2007 Interpublic bought all the shares of FCB Ulka, a top-five ad agency in the country that operated from six offices. Interpublic integrated the Indian agency with its DraftFCB operations. At the same time, it acquired the remaining 51% stake it didn't hold in Lintas India Private Limited at a cost of $50 million in cash, and integrated it into its Lowe Worldwide network. In 2008 Interpublic upped its stake to 51% in Middle East Communication Networks, a marketing services company headquartered in Dubai, operating out of 60 offices across almost 15 countries.

In 2010 Interpublic gained ground in the largest country in South America when it acquired CUBOCC, a creative advertising strategy firm well-versed in all forms of digital media. Based in Brazil, CUBOCC works with multinational clients such as Unilever. A few months later, Interpublic snatched up London-based marketing agency Delaney Lund Knox Warren & Partners (DLKW).

HISTORY

Standard Oil advertising executive Harrison McCann opened the H. K. McCann Company in 1911 and signed Standard Oil of New Jersey (later Exxon) as his first client. McCann's ad business boomed as the automobile became an integral part of American life. His firm merged with Alfred Erickson's agency (created 1902) in 1930, forming the McCann-Erickson Company. At the end of the decade, the firm hired Marion Harper, a top Yale graduate, as a mailroom clerk. Harper became president in 1948.

Harper began acquiring other ad agencies, and by 1961 controlled more than 20 companies. That year he unveiled a plan to create a holding company that would let the ad firms operate separately, allowing them to work on accounts for competing products, but giving them the parent firm's financial and information resources. He named the company Interpublic Inc. after a German research company owned by the former H. K. McCann Co. The conglomerate continued expanding and was renamed The Interpublic Group of Companies in 1964. Harper's management capabilities weren't up to the task, however, and the company soon faced bankruptcy. In 1967 the board replaced him with Robert Healy, who saved Interpublic and returned it to profitability. The company went public in 1971.

The 1970s were fruitful years for Interpublic; its ad teams created memorable campaigns for Coke ("It's the Real Thing" and "Have a Coke and a Smile") and Miller Beer ("Miller Time" and Miller Lite ads). After Philip Geier became chairman in 1980, the company gained a stake in Lowe Howard-Spink (1983; it later became The Lowe Group) and bought Lintas International (1987). Interpublic bought the rest of The Lowe Group in 1990.

Interpublic bought Western International Media (now known as Initiative) and Ammirati & Puris (which was merged with Lintas to form Ammirati Puris Lintas) in 1994. As industry consolidation picked up in 1996, Interpublic kept pace with acquisitions of PR company Weber Group and DraftWorldwide. Interpublic bought a majority stake in artist management and film production company Addis-Wechsler & Associates (now Industry Entertainment) in 1997 and later formed sports marketing and management group Octagon.

Interpublic acquired US agencies Carmichael Lynch and Hill, Holliday, Connors, Cosmopulos in

1998. It also boosted its PR presence with its purchase of International Public Relations (UK), the parent company of public relations networks Shandwick and Golin/Harris. Interpublic strengthened its online position in 1999 when it bought 20% of Stockholm-based Internet services company Icon Medialab International.

Interpublic bought market research firm NFO Worldwide for $580 million in 2000 and merged Weber Public Relations with Shandwick International to form Weber Shandwick Worldwide, one of the world's largest PR firms. Later that year the company bought ad agency Deutsch for about $250 million. John Dooner took the position of chairman and CEO at the end of the year after Geier resigned. His first move proved a big one: Interpublic acquired True North Communications for $2.1 billion in stock in 2001.

The honeymoon was short lived; facing a recession, the mounting debt from its buying spree, and with the revelation of accounting discrepancies at McCann-Erickson WorldGroup (renamed McCann Worldgroup in 2004), Dooner stepped aside as chairman and CEO in 2003. Interpublic chose vice chairman David Bell (former CEO of True North) as Dooner's replacement. After almost two years of work to improve Interpublic's balance sheet, Bell was replaced by former MONY Group chief Michael Roth.

In 2005 Roth was tasked with straightening out Interpublic's financial controls and improving its balance sheet. Later that year, the company revealed extensive bookkeeping problems, primarily in its overseas operations, leading to a financial restatement going back to 2000.

In order to simplify its operating structure, in 2006 Interpublic integrated direct marketer Draft, Inc., with advertising agency Foote, Cone & Belding (forming DraftFCB). A year later it restructured its network of media brands to report under a single management structure (Mediabrands).

EXECUTIVES

Chairman and CEO: Michael I. Roth, age 64, $10,843,080 total compensation
EVP and CFO: Frank Mergenthaler, age 49, $4,520,687 total compensation
EVP and Chief Human Resources Officer: Timothy A. Sompolski, age 57, $2,231,678 total compensation
EVP Strategy and Corporate Relations: Philippe Krakowsky, age 47, $2,568,175 total compensation
EVP Emeritus: Barry R. Linsky
SVP Audit and Chief Risk Officer: Julie M. Connors, age 38
SVP Finance and Development: Jonathan B. (Jon) Burleigh
SVP Global Taxation: Anthony G. (Tony) Alexandrou
SVP and Chief Diversity and Inclusion Officer: Heide Gardner
SVP and Managing Director: Peter Leinroth
SVP and Treasurer: Ellen T. Johnson
SVP Corporate Services: Richard J. Haray
SVP Business Development: David L. Weiss
SVP and CIO: Joseph W. (Joe) Farrelly, age 65
SVP, General Counsel, and Secretary: Nicholas J. (Nick) Camera, age 63
SVP and Managing Director: Terry D. Peigh
SVP Leadership and Organizational Development: Frank Guglielmo
SVP Investor Relations: Jerome J. (Jerry) Leshne
VP Corporate Communications: Tom Cunningham
Controller and Chief Accounting Officer: Christopher F. Carroll, age 43
CEO Worldwide: Richard Beaven
Auditors: PricewaterhouseCoopers LLP

LOCATIONS

HQ: The Interpublic Group of Companies, Inc.
1114 Avenue of the Americas, New York, NY 10036
Phone: 212-704-1200   **Fax:** 212-704-1201
Web: www.interpublic.com

2009 Sales

	$ mil.	% of total
US	3,372.3	56
Europe		
UK	458.5	8
Other countries	922.2	15
Asia/Pacific	575.4	10
Latin America	307.3	5
Other regions	391.9	6
Total	**6,027.6**	**100**

PRODUCTS/OPERATIONS

2009 Sales

	$ mil.	% of total
Integrated Agency Network	5,112.5	85
Constituency Management Group	915.1	15
Total	**6,027.6**	**100**

Selected Operations

Advertising and marketing services
  Advertising agencies
    Austin-Kelly
    Avrett Free Ginsberg
    Campbell-Ewald
    Campbell Mithun
    Carmichael Lynch
    Dailey & Associates
    Deutsch
    Gotham
    Hill, Holiday
    Jay Advertising
    Lowe & Partners (UK)
    The Martin Agency
    McCann Erickson Worldwide
    Mullen
    Tierney Communications
    TM Advertising
  Marketing agencies
    DraftFCB
    The Hacker Group
    MRM Partners
    Momentum
    Rivet
    Translation Consulting + Brand Imaging
  Media services
    Initiative Media
    MAGNA Global
    Universal McCann
Public relations and corporate communications
  DeVries Public Relations
  MWW Group
  Weber Shandwick

COMPETITORS

Aegis Group
Dentsu
Hakuhodo
Havas
Omnicom
Publicis Groupe
WPP

HISTORICAL FINANCIALS

Company Type: Public

Income Statement

FYE: December 31

	REVENUE ($ mil.)	NET INCOME ($ mil.)	NET PROFIT MARGIN	EMPLOYEES
12/09	6,028	121	2.0%	40,000
12/08	6,963	295	4.2%	45,000
12/07	6,554	168	2.6%	43,000
12/06	6,191	(32)	—	42,000
12/05	6,274	(263)	—	43,000
Annual Growth	(1.0%)	—	—	(1.8%)

2009 Year-End Financials

Debt ratio: 83.0%
Return on equity: 6.2%
Cash ($ mil.): 2,495
Current ratio: 1.11
Long-term debt ($ mil.): 1,638
No. of shares (mil.): 489
Dividends
Yield: 0.0%
Payout: —
Market value ($ mil.): 3,607

Stock History

NYSE: IPG

	STOCK PRICE ($) FY Close	P/E High/Low	PER SHARE ($) Earnings	Dividends	Book Value
12/09	7.38	41 16	0.19	0.00	5.11
12/08	3.96	20 5	0.52	0.00	5.06
12/07	8.11	54 30	0.26	0.00	4.77
12/06	12.24	— —	(0.19)	0.00	3.97
12/05	9.65	— —	(0.68)	0.00	3.98
Annual Growth	(6.5%)	— —	—	—	6.4%

Intuit Inc.

Intuit knows that good accounting takes more than a pocket calculator. The company is a leading provider of personal finance (Quicken), small business accounting (QuickBooks), and consumer tax preparation (TurboTax) software for consumers, accountants, and small businesses; Intuit claims more than 50 million users for its products and services. Other software offerings include industry-specific accounting and management applications for construction, real estate, retail, and wholesale distribution organizations. Intuit also provides payroll services, financial supplies, and software for professional tax preparation, as well as products and services geared toward financial institutions.

Intuit used a string of acquisitions to expand its product lines and services beyond the consumer finance and accounting markets, adding offerings for small and midsized businesses and industry-specific accounting and management applications.

Acquisitions to further that strategy include its 2009 purchase of PayCycle (online payroll services) for $170 million, as well as the 2008 purchase of Electronic Clearing House (ECHO), a provider of transaction processing services, for about $131 million. In 2009 Intuit acquired Mint.com for about $170 million; the deal boosted Intuit's Web-based personal finance offerings and added a well-known consumer brand to its product catalog.

Intuit has also used purchases to expand into the health care industry, where it feels it can extend its core strength and expertise in software products for individuals and small and midsized businesses. In May 2010 Intuit purchased Medfusion. Medfusion provides software tools and services that improve communication between patients and health care providers, including applications for patients to schedule appointments, access patient information online, and to settle and track health care expenses.

Aside from acquisitions, the company's internal product strategy has revolved around what it calls its "Connected Services strategy." Unveiled in 2008, the plan involves ensuring that Intuit products and services are all accessible online and can be accessed via desktops, laptops, and handheld devices, as well as through social communities such as online forums and social media sites.

In 2010 the company sold its Intuit Real Estate Solutions subsidiary (a company formerly called Management Reports, acquired by Intuit in 2002) to Vista Equity Partners for about $128 million in cash. Although the business, known as IRES, has more than 1,700 customers, Intuit stated that it was no longer a strategic, long-term fit for the company as part of the Connected Services strategy.

Intuit believes the ease of use of its products give it a competitive edge over rivals, especially for its consumer-oriented offerings, such as TurboTax and QuickBooks. The ubiquity of its products in prominent retail locations also gives the company an edge in the consumer space that competitors such as H&R Block, Sage, and Microsoft struggle to match.

HISTORY

After earning his MBA from Harvard, Scott Cook spent three years in marketing at Procter & Gamble and four years with consultancy Bain & Company before founding Intuit in 1983. Research showed that consumers wanted an easy-to-use personal finance software package. Quicken was introduced in 1984.

Intuit was near collapse in 1986 when it received its first big order from software retailer Egghead.com. Intuit released QuickBooks in 1992 and went public in 1993. The next year Intuit acquired a number of firms, including tax preparation software developer ChipSoft, which brought TurboTax onboard.

In 1995 Microsoft's $2 billion bid to buy Intuit was halted by a Justice Department antitrust lawsuit. Also in 1995 Intuit launched an online banking service and forged its first ties with the Web by bundling a browser and free Internet access with Quicken.

Intuit sold its online banking and bill presentation business to CheckFree in 1997. In 1998 the company bought Lacerte Software, a provider of software and services to tax professionals.

In 1999 Intuit bought Computing Resources, which had been providing the company's online payroll services, for about $200 million. The company also purchased Rock Financial, an online consumer mortgage company, for about $370 million and renamed it Quicken Loans.

Stephen Bennett, a former GE Financial Services executive, replaced Campbell as CEO in 2000. Later that year Intuit sold its Quicken-Insurance business to InsWeb, an online insurance service. Intuit also bought small business services provider EmployeeMatters for $39 million in stock from FrontLine Capital Group.

Moving to boost its small business offerings, in 2001 the company expanded its QuickBooks software to include industry-specific versions designed for retailers and accountants, and it acquired OMware, a provider of business management software for the construction industry.

In 2002 the company completed a string of acquisitions, purchasing American Fundware (public-sector accounting software), Management Reports (property management software), Eclipse (business management software), CBS Payroll (outsourced payroll services), and Blue Ocean Software (information technology asset management software).

In 2002 the company sold its Quicken Loans mortgage operation, followed by the sale of its Japanese subsidiary Intuit KK in 2003.

Intuit continued to pare down its product line over the next few years in order to focus on its core products, selling its Intuit Public Sector Solutions and Intuit Information Technology Solutions businesses in 2005, as well as its Master Builder operations in 2006.

Deals in 2007-2008 included the acquisitions of online banking software provider Digital Insight for about $1.35 billion and e-commerce and website software maker Homestead Technologies for about $170 million.

EXECUTIVES

Founder, Chairman of the Executive Committee, and Director: Scott D. Cook, age 57
Chairman: William V. (Bill) Campbell, age 69
President and CEO: Brad D. Smith, age 45, $4,814,826 total compensation
EVP and General Manager, Small Business: Kiran M. Patel, age 61, $3,396,833 total compensation
SVP and CFO: R. Neil Williams, age 56, $1,940,106 total compensation
SVP; President, Digital Insight: Sasan K. Goodarzi, age 41, $1,887,021 total compensation
SVP Global Business Division: Alexander M. (Alex) Lintner, age 47, $1,637,848 total compensation
SVP and CTO: Tayloe Stansbury
SVP Product Development, Small Business Division: Richard W. (Bill) Ihrie, age 59
SVP and CIO: Ginny Lee
SVP, General Counsel, and Corporate Secretary: Laura A. Fennell, age 48
SVP; General Manager, Consumer Group: Daniel R. (Dan) Maurer, age 53
SVP Human Resources: Sherry Whiteley
SVP Sales: Caroline F. Donahue, age 47
SVP and General Manager Global Tax: Rick W. Jensen, age 50
SVP and General Manager, Employee Management Solutions: Nora M. Denzel, age 47
SVP; General Manager, Quicken Health Group: Peter J. Karpas, age 40
Chief Innovation Officer: Per-Kristian (Kris) Halvorsen, age 58
Chief Communications Officer and Marketing Leader: Harry Pforzheimer
Auditors: Ernst & Young LLP

LOCATIONS

HQ: Intuit Inc.
2700 Coast Ave., Mountain View, CA 94043
Phone: 650-944-6000   **Fax:** 650-944-3699
Web: www.intuit.com

PRODUCTS/OPERATIONS

2009 Sales

	$ mil.	% of total
Consumer Tax	996	31
Financial Management Solutions (QuickBooks)	579	18
Employee Management Solutions (Payroll)	365	12
Accounting Professionals	352	11
Financial Institutions	311	10
Payments Solutions	291	9
Other businesses	289	9
Total	**3,183**	**100**

2009 Sales

	$ mil.	% of total
Services	1,799	51
Products	1,384	49
Total	**3,183**	**100**

Selected Software and Services

Small Business
  Check forms, tax forms, and other supplies
  QuickBooks (accounting software)
    QuickBooks Basic
    QuickBooks Credit Check Services (for access to
      credit reports)
    QuickBooks Enterprise Solutions Business
      Management Software (for businesses with up to
      250 employees)
    QuickBooks Merchant Account Service (for enabling
      credit card payments)
    QuickBooks Online Billing (for enabling electronic
      billing and customer payments)
    QuickBooks Point of Sale (for retail businesses)
    QuickBooks Premier (for small businesses)
    QuickBooks Premier: Accountant Edition (for
      professional accountants)
    QuickBooks Pro (for up to five simultaneous users)
Consumer Tax
  TurboTax (desktop tax preparation software for
    individuals and small businesses)
  TurboTax for the Web (Internet-based tax preparation
    and filing service)
  TurboTax Premier (tax preparation software for
    investors and rental property owners)
Professional Accounting Solutions
  EasyACCT Professional Accounting Series (software for
    helping accountants prepare financial statements
    and tax forms)
  IntuitAdvisor (subscription-based information and
    tools for accounting business growth)
  Lacerte (professional tax preparation software)
  Lacerte Tax Planner (tax planning service software for
    accountants)
  ProSeries (professional tax preparation software)
Personal Finance
  Quicken (desktop personal finance software)
  Quicken Brokerage (online and phone-based securities
    brokerage service powered by Siebert)
  Quicken Financial Planner (retirement planning)
  Quicken Lite
  Quicken Premier (Quicken with added investment and
    tax planning tools)
  Quicken.com (online personal finance information and
    tools)

COMPETITORS

ADP	Jackson Hewitt
Bank of America	JPMorgan Chase
CA Technologies	Microsoft Dynamics
CCH Incorporated	MYOB
Deluxe Corporation	NetSuite
Elavon	Online Resources
Fidelity National	Paychex
Information Services	S1 Corp.
First Data	Sage Group
Fiserv	SAP
Global Payments	Thomson Reuters
H&R Block	Wells Fargo
Jack Henry	

HISTORICAL FINANCIALS

Company Type: Public

Income Statement

FYE: July 31

	REVENUE ($ mil.)	NET INCOME ($ mil.)	NET PROFIT MARGIN	EMPLOYEES
7/09	3,183	447	14.0%	7,800
7/08	3,075	477	15.5%	8,200
7/07	2,673	440	16.5%	8,200
7/06	2,342	417	17.8%	7,500
7/05	2,038	382	18.7%	7,000
Annual Growth	**11.8%**	**4.0%**	**—**	**2.7%**

2009 Year-End Financials

Debt ratio: 46.4%
Return on equity: 19.3%
Cash ($ mil.): 679
Current ratio: 1.82
Long-term debt ($ mil.): 1,185
No. of shares (mil.): 314
Dividends
  Yield: —
  Payout: —
Market value ($ mil.): 9,329

Stock History

NASDAQ (GS): INTU

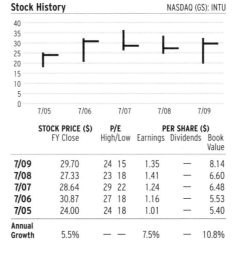

	STOCK PRICE ($) FY Close	P/E High/Low	Earnings	PER SHARE ($) Dividends	Book Value
7/09	29.70	24 15	1.35	—	8.14
7/08	27.33	23 18	1.41	—	6.60
7/07	28.64	29 22	1.24	—	6.48
7/06	30.87	27 18	1.16	—	5.53
7/05	24.00	24 18	1.01	—	5.40
Annual Growth	**5.5%**	**— —**	**7.5%**	**—**	**10.8%**

Invacare Corporation

Invacare allows wheelchair users to set their own pace. Invacare is a leading maker of wheelchairs — including manual, powered, custom-made, and the ultra zippy chairs used by athletes. It also makes other medical equipment including crutches, bed systems, respiratory devices, and motorized scooters. It manufactures and sells its own products to home health care and medical equipment dealers in North America, Europe, and the Asia/Pacific region, as well as to government agencies and distributors. Invacare's Supply Group distributes other companies' medical equipment and disposable products, such as home diabetic and wound care items.

Invacare makes other home care durables such as bathing equipment, cushions, and slings. Its institutional products group manufactures health care furnishings including recliners used during dialysis, patient handling equipment, and beds for the non-acute and long-term care facility market.

Invacare continues to benefit from a population that is getting older and living longer, as well as from an increase in home care provision. However, the company also faces lower-cost overseas competitors and ongoing reimbursement challenges from public and private health care insurers. During the economic recession, the company pulled back some of its product development activities and sought to reduce its manufacturing costs. A combination of product line simplification, shaving distribution costs, shuttering some manufacturing and distribution facilities, and shifting some manufacturing to its facilities in China have helped the company reduce costs.

The company does look toward a future of fresh organic growth, and has plans to put resources into research and development, bolster its presence in new international markets, and take on new product areas such as wound care and support surfaces (high-tech hospital beds).

Chairman Malachi Mixon owns 20% of the company. Joseph Richey, a company executive and board member, owns 10%.

HISTORY

Invacare traces its roots to the Worthington Company, which began making vehicles for the disabled in 1885. Worthington's successor, Invacare, became a subsidiary of medical equipment maker Technicare in 1971. When Johnson & Johnson bought Technicare in 1978, it put Invacare up for sale; a group led by A. Malachi Mixon, then Technicare's VP of marketing, bought the company. Mixon cut unprofitable lines and pushed product innovation. In 1982 Invacare put out the first motorized wheelchair with computer controls. The company went public in 1984 and entered the European market by purchasing a UK firm. Invacare introduced some 50 new products in 1990, and in 1991 began selling directly to consumers.

In the 1990s Invacare focused on acquisitions, such as makers of personal care products, beds and patient-room furniture, and bathing equipment and lifts. Profits dipped in 1997 as many of its larger customers reduced orders in response to federally legislated Medicare reimbursement cuts. In 1998 it acquired medical supplies wholesaler Suburban Ostomy Supply; in 1999 it bought medical supplies maker Scandinavian Mobility International.

To enhance consumer brand recognition, in 1999 Invacare began a retail merchandising program and brought its acquired products under the Invacare brand name.

After integration with Invacare, Suburban Ostomy Supply was renamed Invacare Supply Group in 2000. Invacare bought Carroll Healthcare, a maker of beds and furniture for the long-term care market, in 2003. In 2004 the company acquired Domus, a manufacturer of complementary products such as bath lifts and walking aids. Invacare bought Medical Support Systems Holdings Limited in 2005.

EXECUTIVES

Chairman: A. Malachi Mixon III, age 70,
$4,843,901 total compensation
Interim CEO and Director: Gerald B. Blouch, age 63,
$2,564,202 total compensation
CIO: Dave Mewes

SVP Electronic and Design Engineering and Director; President, Invacare Technologies: Joseph B. Richey II, age 73, $1,128,720 total compensation
SVP Global Market Development: Louis F. J. (Lou) Slangen, age 62, $1,184,618 total compensation
SVP Human Resources: Patricia A. Stumpp, age 47
SVP, CFO, and Treasurer: Robert K. (Rob) Gudbranson, age 46, $1,312,024 total compensation
SVP, General Counsel, and Secretary: Anthony C. LaPlaca, age 51
Auditors: Ernst & Young LLP

LOCATIONS

HQ: Invacare Corporation
1 Invacare Way, Elyria, OH 44036
Phone: 440-329-6000   **Fax:** 440-366-9008
Web: www.invacare.com

PRODUCTS/OPERATIONS

2009 Sales

	$ mil.	% of total
North America/Home Medical Equipment	748.4	44
Europe	503.1	30
Invacare Supply Group	280.3	17
Institutional Products Group	89.4	5
Asia/Pacific	71.9	4
Total	**1,693.1**	**100**

Selected Subsidiaries

Adaptive Switch Laboratories, Inc.
Dynamic Controls Ltd. (New Zealand)
Garden City Medical, Inc.
Kuschall AG (Switzerland)
Morris Surgical Pty Ltd. (Australia)
Scandinavian Mobility International ApS (Denmark)
SCI Des Hautes Roches (France)

COMPETITORS

Amigo Mobility
Bruno Independent Living Aids
Electric Mobility Corporation
Getinge
Golden Technologies
Graham-Field Health Products
Hill-Rom
Joerns
Kinetic Concepts
Medline Industries
Otto Bock Healthcare (UK)
Pride Mobility Products
Respironics
Span-America Medical
Sunrise Medical
Vital Signs

HISTORICAL FINANCIALS

Company Type: Public

Income Statement

FYE: December 31

	REVENUE ($ mil.)	NET INCOME ($ mil.)	NET PROFIT MARGIN	EMPLOYEES
12/09	1,693	41	2.4%	5,900
12/08	1,756	39	2.2%	6,100
12/07	1,602	1	0.1%	5,700
12/06	1,498	(318)	—	6,000
12/05	1,530	49	3.2%	6,100
Annual Growth	**2.6%**	**(4.2%)**	**—**	**(0.8%)**

2009 Year-End Financials

Debt ratio: 38.8%
Return on equity: 7.0%
Cash ($ mil.): 38
Current ratio: 1.82
Long-term debt ($ mil.): 272
No. of shares (mil.): 31
Dividends
  Yield: 0.2%
  Payout: 3.9%
Market value ($ mil.): 780

Stock History   NYSE: IVC

	STOCK PRICE ($) FY Close	P/E High/Low		PER SHARE ($) Earnings	Dividends	Book Value
12/09	24.94	20	11	1.29	0.05	22.41
12/08	15.52	22	11	1.21	0.05	15.36
12/07	25.20	694	431	0.04	0.05	17.71
12/06	24.55	—	—	(10.00)	0.05	15.51
12/05	31.49	32	20	1.51	0.05	24.06
Annual Growth	**(5.7%)**	**—**	**—**	**(3.9%)**	**0.0%**	**(1.8%)**

Iron Mountain

You think you have a mountain of paperwork to deal with? Iron Mountain is one of the largest records storage and information management companies in the world. The company stores paper and digital documents, computer disks, tapes, microfilm and microfiche, audio and videotapes, film, X-rays, and blueprints for more than 140,000 corporate customers. It provides such services as records filing, digital conversion, database management, packing, transportation, disaster recovery, and information destruction. Its COMAC unit stores, builds, and mails information packets for companies. Iron Mountain traces its paper trail back to when it was established — in 1951.

The company sees acquisitions and joint ventures as a key business strategy when it comes to expansion. In 2010 Iron Mountain expanded its content archiving solutions by purchasing Mimosa Systems, based in California, for some $112 million in cash. The deal strengthened Iron Mountain's product portfolio as Mimosa offers NearPoint, an archiving platform used for several database applications, from retention and disposition to compliance supervision and recovery. In 2008 Iron Mountain acquired Colorado-based DocuVault Group, the owner of five records management firms. It also bought the remaining interest of its Brazilian partner that year.

The company has pushed into digital markets and has plans to expand its business overseas. By offering customers its secure shredding, online back-up, and electronic discovery services, Iron Mountain looks to strengthen its position in Germany, Japan, and the Middle East. Each year, about one-third of the company's revenue comes from regions outside the US.

The company also looks to capitalize on the transition to electronic records in the healthcare industry. In 2008 Iron Mountain introduced a medical records management tool and a digital file storage system for X-rays, CT scans, and other medical images.

Richard Reese stepped down as CEO in 2008, and he was succeeded by Bob Brennan, who joined the company in 2004 as president of North American operations.

HISTORY

Leo W. Pierce founded L.W. Pierce in 1957. Based in Philadelphia, the company sold filing systems and other storage equipment. In 1969 Pierce made the move into document storage, keeping other companies' records in his basement. Off-site document storage caught on during the 1980s, when a depressed economy forced managers to find creative ways to reduce costs.

The company doubled its size in 1990 by paying $36 million to buy Leahy Business Archives. The first corporate records storage firm, Leahy was founded in the 1950s in New York City. Pierce Leahy went public in 1997.

Pierce Leahy's sales increased in the mid-1990s, aided by acquisitions. The company was intent on consolidating the records management market, grabbing up as many smaller firms as it could. Pierce Leahy bought two more data storage companies, Archive (Canada) and Amodio (Connecticut), in 1998. The company made several acquisitions in 1999, including Datavault, a UK records management company, and ImageMax, a digital imaging company.

In early 2000 Pierce Leahy was acquired by its primary competitor, Iron Mountain, for $1.2 billion. Pierce Leahy was the surviving entity of the reverse merger, taking the Iron Mountain name. Richard Reese, chairman of the former Iron Mountain, became chairman and CEO of the new company. The company acquired Canadian record management company FACS Records Centre in late 2000.

In 2004 Iron Mountain created a new business unit — Iron Mountain Intellectual Property Management — by combining its DSI Technology Escrow and Arcemus subsidiaries. The new unit extended the Iron Mountain brand name to services such as online trademark protection, management of domain name records, and technology escrow. Iron Mountain also purchased Mentmore's interest in joint venture Iron Mountain Europe in 2004, making the company a wholly owned subsidiary. That year Iron Mountain acquired Connected Corp., a maker of data storage and recovery software. The next year the company bought Pickfords Records Management, the Australian and New Zealand operations of SIRVA, for $87 million.

In 2006 Iron Mountain cast its eye on the Pacific Rim when it bought Australia-based DigiGuard, an off-site data storage provider. It also expanded its Asia/Pacific presence later that year when it entered a joint venture with Transnational Company, a provider of information storage services headquartered in Singapore.

In November 2007 Iron Mountain expanded its film and sound archive services business with the purchase of Xepa Digital, a converter of analog and outmoded digital audio and video tapes to high-resolution digital file formats for archiving and distribution. Other domestic acquisitions that year included ArchivesOne, a smaller rival serving more than 8,500 customers; Michigan-based RMS Services USA, which it will integrate into its health information services unit; and Stratify, a software developer and electronic document services provider, for about $160 million.

EXECUTIVES

Chairman: C. Richard Reese, age 64,
$2,473,171 total compensation
President, CEO, and Director: Robert T. (Bob) Brennan,
age 50, $1,676,456 total compensation
EVP and CFO: Brian P. McKeon, age 48,
$811,123 total compensation
EVP Human Resources: Annie Drapeau
SVP and Chief Security Officer: Joseph DeSalvo
SVP Records Management: Richard Wilder
SVP and CIO: William (Bill) Brown, age 54
SVP, General Counsel, and Secretary:
  Ernest W. Cloutier, age 36
SVP Digital Healthcare Solutions: Ken Rubin
VP Strategic Alliances: Todd Koopersmith
VP Document Management Solutions: Chris Churchill
VP Investor Relations: Stephen P. Golden
President, Iron Mountain Digital: Ramana Venkata,
age 45, $2,074,642 total compensation
President, North America:
  Harold E. (Harry) Ebbighausen, age 55,
  $692,406 total compensation
President, Iron Mountain International: Marc A. Duale,
age 58, $984,084 total compensation
**Group President, Latin America; President, Iron
  Mountain Fulfillment Services:** Ross Engelman
Director Corporate Communications: Dan O'Neill
Auditors: Deloitte & Touche LLP

LOCATIONS

HQ: Iron Mountain Incorporated
  745 Atlantic Ave., Boston, MA 02111
Phone: 617-535-4766   **Fax:** 617-350-7881
Web: www.ironmountain.com

2009 Sales

	$ mil.	% of total
US	2,116.5	70
UK	292.7	10
Canada	196.3	6
Other countries	408.1	14
Total	**3,013.6**	**100**

PRODUCTS/OPERATIONS

2009 Sales

	$ mil.	% of total
Records management	2,155.7	72
Data protection & discovery	606.6	20
Information destruction	251.3	8
Total	**3,013.6**	**100**

Selected Services

Archiving
Consulting
Conversion
Database management
Disaster recovery
Electronic vaulting
Fulfillment
Information destruction
Packing
Shredding
Transportation

COMPETITORS

Administaff
Anacomp
Cintas
DataBank IMX
IPSA
Recall Corporation
Shred-it International
SOURCECORP
TAB Products
Venyu
Xerox

HISTORICAL FINANCIALS

Company Type: Public

Income Statement

FYE: December 31

	REVENUE ($ mil.)	NET INCOME ($ mil.)	NET PROFIT MARGIN	EMPLOYEES
12/09	3,014	221	7.3%	10,500
12/08	3,055	82	2.7%	21,000
12/07	2,730	153	5.6%	20,100
12/06	2,350	129	5.5%	18,600
12/05	2,078	117	5.6%	15,800
Annual Growth	**9.7%**	**17.3%**	**—**	**(9.7%)**

2009 Year-End Financials

Debt ratio: 150.0%
Return on equity: 11.2%
Cash ($ mil.): 447
Current ratio: 1.49
Long-term debt ($ mil.): 3,211

No. of shares (mil.): 203
Dividends
  Yield: —
  Payout: —
Market value ($ mil.): 4,627

Stock History

NYSE: IRM

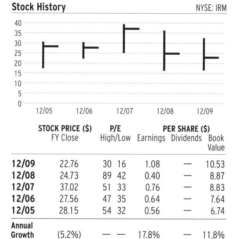

	STOCK PRICE ($) FY Close	P/E High/Low		PER SHARE ($) Earnings	Dividends	Book Value
12/09	22.76	30	16	1.08	—	10.53
12/08	24.73	89	42	0.40	—	8.87
12/07	37.02	51	33	0.76	—	8.83
12/06	27.56	47	35	0.64	—	7.64
12/05	28.15	54	32	0.56	—	6.74
Annual Growth	**(5.2%)**	**—**	**—**	**17.8%**	**—**	**11.8%**

Itron, Inc.

Itron aims to make meter-reading a desk job. The company is a global supplier of wireless data acquisition and communication products for electric, gas, and water utilities. Itron makes radio- and telephone-based automatic meter-reading (AMR) systems, handheld meter-reading computers, and meter data acquisition and analysis software. Its systems are installed at more than 2,000 utilities worldwide — many using more than one Itron product. The company also provides consulting, project management, and outsourcing services. Customers include BC Hydro, Electrabel, Ford, Old Dominion Electric Cooperative, and Progress Energy. Europe is Itron's biggest market, closely followed by North America.

Itron targets the electric utility, water and public power, and natural gas markets. Among the company's challenges in 2009 were the global recession, long and unpredictable sales cycles in the utility industry, the assimilation of acquisitions, the availability and regulation of radio spectrum (some of its products use radio frequencies for communication), and increasing competition. Itron continues to grow by acquisitions, acquiring nine companies in the past decade.

In 2007 the company acquired Luxembourg-based Actaris Metering Systems for €800 million in cash, plus the assumption of about €445 million in debt, valuing the transaction at about $1.7 billion. Actaris was profitable on 2006 sales of around $1 billion. A former division of Schlumberger that went through a leveraged buyout in 2001, Actaris primarily operated in Europe, offering AMR equipment and related services. It has operations in Africa, the Asia/Pacific region, Australia, and South America.

President and COO Malcolm Unsworth in 2009 succeeded LeRoy Nosbaum as CEO of Itron. Nosbaum remained on the board and served as its executive chairman until the end of 2009. Unsworth's promotion was part of a leadership succession plan that the board developed.

Itron has facilities around the world. The company has more than 55 assembly, distribution, manufacturing, and service facilities, and 85 administration and sales offices.

HISTORY

Itron was formed by a group of engineers in 1977 with financial backing from utility Washington Water Power (now Avista). In 1992 Itron acquired EnScan, a maker of mobile automatic meter reading (AMR) systems. The company went public in 1993. During 1994 and 1995 it installed the largest AMR system in the world for the Public Service Company of Colorado (now New Century Energies).

Itron in 1996 won a major contract from Pittsburgh-based Duquesne Light Co. Itron acquired Utility Translation Services (commercial and industrial AMR systems) that year and Design Concepts (outage detection, quality monitoring, and AMR systems that communicate over telephone lines) in 1997. Also that year Itron and UK Data Collections Services (meter reading services) formed joint venture STAR Data Services to provide meter reading and billing services.

Restructuring charges related to cost-cutting efforts contributed to a loss in 1998. The next year Itron won an 11-year pact to provide meter reading services for Southern California Edison's 350,000 customers — a deal worth at least $20 million. During 1999 new CEO Michael Chesser led another restructuring — including layoffs and factory closures. Charges led to a loss for the year.

In 2000 Itron spun off part of its manufacturing operations as contract electronics manufacturer Servatron. That year COO LeRoy Nosbaum replaced Chesser as CEO, and was later named chairman.

In 2002 Itron bolstered its energy consulting and software business through the acquisition of several privately held companies: LineSoft (consulting and software for utility transmission and distribution systems) for about $42 million, Regional Economic Research (energy consulting and software) for $14 million, and eMobile Data Corporation (wireless utility workforce management software) for about $6 million. The following year Itron acquired Silicon Energy (enterprise energy management software) for about $71 million.

In 2004 Itron acquired the Electricity Metering business unit of Schlumberger for $256 million. Schlumberger Electricity Metering became the company's Electricity Metering business. A major restructuring that year — including the replacement of leading executives and the layoff of 15% of its workforce — repositioned Itron to take advantage of new technologies and industry deregulation. Itron reorganized its market segments from five business units to two main segments: hardware and software. Within the hardware segment, the business was broken down into two lines of business: meter data collection and electricity metering.

In 2006 the company expanded into South America's biggest market with the acquisition of ELO Sistemas e Tecnologia, a Brazilian firm that was distributing Itron products since 2004 and manufacturing Itron's CENTRON meters since 2005. ELO Tecnologia had offices and a manufacturing assembly facility in Campinas and São Paulo, Brazil, and in Chile, employing about 80 people. Itron paid about $2 million in cash for the Brazilian firm.

Purchases during 2006 included Flow Metrix, a manufacturer of leak detection systems for underground pipelines, and Quantum Consulting, an energy consulting firm.

EXECUTIVES

Chairman: Jon E. Eliassen, age 63
President, CEO, and Director: Malcolm Unsworth, age 60, $2,506,496 total compensation
SVP and COO, North America: Philip C. Mezey, age 50, $417,372 total compensation
SVP and CFO: Steven M. (Steve) Helmbrecht, age 47, $416,311 total compensation
SVP, General Counsel, and Corporate Secretary: John W. Holleran, age 55, $362,921 total compensation
SVP and COO, Itron International: Marcel Regnier, age 52
VP Marketing: Russell E. (Russ) Vanos
VP Software Solutions: Julie Hance
VP Water Sales and Marketing: Lou Gust
VP Canadian Sales: Scott Owen
VP Information Technology and CIO: Chuck McAtee
VP Competitive Resources: Jared P. Serff, age 42
VP Investor Relations: Ranny Dwiggins
Director Marketing and Communications: Sharelynn Moore
Auditors: Ernst & Young LLP

LOCATIONS

HQ: Itron, Inc.
2111 N. Molter Rd., Liberty Lake, WA 99019
Phone: 509-924-9900   **Fax:** 509-891-3355
Web: www.itron.com

2009 Sales

	$ mil.	% of total
Europe	806.5	48
North America	606.5	36
Other regions	274.4	16
Total	**1,687.4**	**100**

PRODUCTS/OPERATIONS

2009 Sales

	$ mil.	% of total
Itron International	1,071.7	64
Itron North America	615.7	36
Total	**1,687.4**	**100**

Selected Products

Automatic meter reading (AMR) systems and products
  Meter modules (utility meter attachments that transmit data to remote receivers)
  Mobile AMR (transportable systems for mounting on vehicles)
  Network AMR (utility-automated meter readers)
  Off-site meter reading units (remote reading of radio-equipped meters)
  Telephone-based technology (programmable modules for data collection over telephone lines)

Commercial and industrial meters
Forecasting, research, and analysis software
Handheld systems and products (electronic meter reading — EMR — handheld systems)
Surveying software
Workforce automation software (Service-Link)

Services

Engineering consulting
Forecasting services
Installation
Outsourcing
Project management
System design and installation
Training

COMPETITORS

Badger Meter	E-MON
Bentley Systems	EnerNOC
Cooper Industries	Equitrac
DeltaTRAK	ESCO Technologies
Diehl Stiftung	GE
Dresser, Inc.	Honeywell International
Echelon Corporation	Invensys
El Sewedy Cables	Oracle
Electric & Gas Technology	Pointer Telocation
Electro Industries	PowerSecure International
Elster American Meter	Roper Industries
Emerson Electric	Schneider Electric
eMeter	Telvent

HISTORICAL FINANCIALS

Company Type: Public

Income Statement

FYE: December 31

	REVENUE ($ mil.)	NET INCOME ($ mil.)	NET PROFIT MARGIN	EMPLOYEES
12/09	1,687	(2)	—	9,000
12/08	1,910	28	1.5%	8,700
12/07	1,464	(16)	—	8,400
12/06	644	34	5.2%	2,400
12/05	553	33	6.0%	2,000
Annual Growth	**32.2%**	**—**	**—**	**45.6%**

2009 Year-End Financials

Debt ratio: 55.0%
Return on equity: —
Cash ($ mil.): 122
Current ratio: 1.64
Long-term debt ($ mil.): 771
No. of shares (mil.): 40
Dividends
  Yield: —
  Payout: —
Market value ($ mil.): 2,728

Stock History

NASDAQ (GS): ITRI

	STOCK PRICE ($) FY Close	P/E High/Low		PER SHARE ($) Earnings	Dividends	Book Value
12/09	67.57	—	—	(0.06)	—	34.69
12/08	63.74	133	43	0.80	—	25.64
12/07	95.97	—	—	(0.55)	—	18.79
12/06	51.84	58	31	1.28	—	9.68
12/05	40.04	41	16	1.33	—	7.86
Annual Growth	**14.0%**	**—**	**—**	**—**	**—**	**44.9%**

ITT Corporation

ITT doesn't get defensive when you associate its name with fluid motion. The company has three primary segments: defense (offering broadly, combat radios, night vision devices, airborne electronic warfare systems), fluid technology (pumps, mixers, heat exchangers, valves, and analytical instruments for water and wastewater systems), and fluid & motion control (connectors, boat pumps, shock absorbers, friction pads for communication and transportation applications). ITT traces its corporate roots back nearly 90 years to the old ITT phone empire; it continues to provide repair and maintenance services for the products it manufactures. The company garners about two-thirds of its sales in the US.

Although ITT's footprint is primarily red, white, and blue, its businesses operate in more than 62 countries. More than 40% of its workforce is employed outside of the US, serving customers in China, the Middle East, and India.

The company's performance relies heavily on its defense segment, which accounts for more than half of sales. Moreover, US government prime and sub-contractors represent more than 90% of the defense segment's revenue. Thus, as the Obama administration takes a closer look at the Pentagon budget, ITT risks a considerable loss in business if certain military programs are reduced or eliminated. The company is responding by rolling out a reorganization of its defense segment. ITT has agreed to sell the defense segment's systems-engineering and technical-assistance unit, CAS, Inc., to Wyle, Inc. (part of Wyle Laboratories) for $235 million.

In the meantime, ITT is making selective acquisitions with an eye toward opportunities in such non-defense sectors as sustainable resource practices, aging infrastructure, rising middle-income populations, and maintaining security. In 2010 ITT acquired Godwin Pumps for $585 million. Godwin, which joins ITT's water and wastewater business, rents automatic self-priming pumps. Its fleet numbers more than 6,000.

On its heels, ITT bought a manufacturer of analytical instruments, Nova Analytics Corporation, for approximately $390 million. Nova's product lineup — laboratory, portable, and on-line analytical instruments — are used in food and beverage, water and wastewater, medical, and environmental applications. Moreover, the acquisition carries a slew of brands (Aanderaa, Bellingham + Stanley, ebro, Global Water, SI Analytics, and WTW) that, when integrated with ITT's $4.7 billion fluid, and motion and flow segments, give ITT one of the industry's broadest sensor and instrument portfolios for monitoring and controlling wastewater and other commercial plant operations.

HISTORY

Colonel Sosthenes Behn founded International Telephone and Telegraph (ITT) in 1920 to build a global telephone company. After three small acquisitions, Behn bought International Western Electric (renamed International Standard Electric, or ISE) from AT&T in 1925, making ITT an international maker of phone equipment. In the late 1920s ITT bought Mackay, a US company that made telegraph, cable, radio, and other equipment.

In the 1930s sales outside the US made up two-thirds of revenues. To increase US opportunities during WWII, Behn arranged for a Mackay subsidiary, Federal AT&T Telegraph (later Federal Electric), to become part of ITT. Behn took charge of Federal and created Federal Telephone & Radio Laboratories. Meanwhile, ISE scientists who fled war-torn Europe gravitated to ITT's research and development operations and laid the foundation for its high-tech electronics business.

ITT became a diverse and unwieldy collection of companies by the 1950s. In mid-decade ISE, its biggest unit, developed advanced telephone-switching equipment.

During the 1960s and 1970s ITT added auto-part makers such as Teves (brakes, West Germany), Ulma (trim, Italy), and Altissimo (lights and accessories, Italy). ITT's electronics acquisitions included Cannon Electric (electrical connectors) and National Computer Products (satellite communications). It also bought Bell & Gossett (the US's #1 maker of commercial and industrial pumps). When ITT bought Sheraton's hotel chain in 1968, it also got auto-parts supplier Thompson Industries. By 1977 its Engineered Products division consisted of nearly 80 automotive and electrical companies. In 1979 ITT began selling all or part of 250 companies, including the last of its telecom operations.

In the 1980s ITT became a major supplier of antilock brakes and, with the 1988 purchase of the Allis-Chalmers pump business, a global force in fluid technology. Its Defense & Electronics unit earned contracts to make equipment used in the Gulf War. In 1994 ITT Automotive purchases solidified its position as the world's top maker of electric motors and wiper systems.

ITT split into three independent companies in 1995: ITT Corporation (hospitality, entertainment, and information services; now part of Starwood Hotels & Resorts), ITT Hartford (insurance; now Hartford Financial Services), and ITT Industries (auto parts, defense and electric systems, and fluid-control products).

In 1997 ITT Industries acquired Goulds Pumps, establishing it as the world's largest pump maker. After the $815 million takeover, that year the company sold its automotive electrical systems unit to Valeo for $1.7 billion and its brake and chassis unit to Germany's Continental for about $1.9 billion.

In 2004 ITT acquired the Remote Sensing Systems business of Eastman Kodak Company for $725 million. The acquisition of WEDECO through 2004 and 2005 share purchases gave ITT the world's largest manufacturer of ultraviolet disinfection and ozone oxidation systems.

Early in 2006 ITT exited the automotive tubing (steel and plastic tubing for fuel and brake lines) business by selling those operations to Cooper-Standard Automotive for $205 million.

In mid-2006 the company changed its name from ITT Industries to ITT Corporation.

The company was fined $100 million in 2007 for illegally providing classified night vision equipment to foreign countries, including China. ITT pleaded guilty to felony charges under the Arms Export Control Act after an extensive investigation by the US Departments of Defense and Justice.

Building on its defense electronics business, ITT bought EDO Corporation during 2007 in a deal valued at about $1.7 billion. EDO is a provider of a wide range of aerospace and defense products, including electronic warfare systems, sonar systems, reconnaissance and surveillance systems, and flight line products.

EXECUTIVES

Chairman, President, and CEO: Steven R. Loranger, age 58, $13,844,981 total compensation
SVP; President, Fluid and Motion Control: Gretchen W. McClain, age 47, $3,919,837 total compensation
SVP; President, ITT Defense and Information Solutions: Lt. Gen. David F. Melcher, age 55, $1,629,771 total compensation
SVP and CFO: Denise L. Ramos, age 53, $2,328,032 total compensation
SVP and Chief Communications Officer: Angela A. Buonocore, age 51
SVP and Director Corporate Strategy and Development: Aris C. Chicles, age 48
VP and Treasurer: Colleen Ostrowski, age 36
VP and CIO: Carol J. Zierhoffer, age 49
VP and Chief Learning Officer: Nancy Lewis, age 57
VP and Secretary: Burt M. Fealing
VP and General Counsel: Frank R. Jimenez, age 45
VP Finance: Robert J. (Bob) Pagano Jr., age 47
VP Corporate Responsibility: Ann D. Davidson, age 57
VP, Chief Accounting Officer, and Assistant Secretary: Janice M. Klettner, age 49
Chief Inclusion and Diversity Officer: Robert Ellis, age 58
President, Residential and Commercial Water, Fluid Technology: John P. Williamson, age 49
President, Space Systems Division: Chris Young
President, Interconnect Solutions: William E. Taylor, age 56
Contact, Investor Relations: Thomas (Tom) Scalera
Auditors: Deloitte & Touche LLP

LOCATIONS

HQ: ITT Corporation
1133 Westchester Ave., White Plains, NY 10604
Phone: 914-641-2000   **Fax:** 914-696-2950
Web: www.itt.com

2009 Sales

	$ mil.	% of total
US	7,592.3	70
Western Europe	1,814.0	17
Asia/Pacific	576.8	5
Other regions	921.4	8
Total	**10,904.5**	**100**

PRODUCTS/OPERATIONS

2009 Sales

	$ mil.	% of total
Defense Electronics & Services	6,296.8	58
Fluid Technology	3,363.3	31
Motion & Flow Control	1,253.0	11
Adjustments	(8.6)	—
Total	**10,904.5**	**100**

2009 Sales by Type

	$ mil.	% of total
Products	8,243.5	76
Services	2,661.0	24
Total	**10,904.5**	**100**

Selected Products

Defense Electronics
  Aircraft armament systems
  Electronic warfare systems
  Imaging and navigation systems
  Night vision devices
  Tactical communications equipment
Fluid Technology
  Analytical instruments (water and wastewater, environmental, industrial, food and beverage, pharmaceutical, and medical)
  Heat exchangers (industrial process)
  Pumps (water and wastewater, industrial process, residential and commercial water)
  Treatment systems (water and wastewater)
  Steam and boiler products (residential and commercial water)
  Valves (industrial process)

Motion and Flow Control
  Brake pads
  Connectors and interconnects
  Electro-mechanical actuators
  Friction materials
  Fuel systems
  Motion controls
  Pneumatic automation components
  Pump systems
  Servomotors
  Shock absorbers
  Suspension systems
  Valve actuation controls

COMPETITORS

Alliant Techsystems	KSB AG
BAE SYSTEMS	L-3 Communications
Dana Holding	Lockheed Martin
Delphi Automotive	Marmon Group
DENSO	Molex
Dresser, Inc.	Northrop Grumman
DynCorp International	Oilgear
Eaton	Parker Hannifin
Ebara	Raytheon
Flowserve	Robert Bosch
GE	Roper Industries
GenCorp	Siemens AG
General Dynamics	SPX
Goodrich Corp.	Swagelok
Harris Corp.	Thomas & Betts
Honeywell International	Tyco
IDEX	Watts Water Technologies
Ingersoll-Rand	Woodward Governor
Interpump	

HISTORICAL FINANCIALS

Company Type: Public

Income Statement

FYE: December 31

	REVENUE ($ mil.)	NET INCOME ($ mil.)	NET PROFIT MARGIN	EMPLOYEES
12/09	10,905	644	5.9%	40,200
12/08	11,695	795	6.8%	40,800
12/07	9,003	742	8.2%	39,700
12/06	7,808	581	7.4%	37,500
12/05	7,427	366	4.9%	40,900
Annual Growth	**10.1%**	**15.2%**	**—**	**(0.4%)**

2009 Year-End Financials

Debt ratio: 36.9%
Return on equity: 18.6%
Cash ($ mil.): 1,216
Current ratio: 1.63
Long-term debt ($ mil.): 1,431
No. of shares (mil.): 183
Dividends
  Yield: 1.7%
  Payout: 24.3%
Market value ($ mil.): 9,122

Stock History

NYSE: ITT

	STOCK PRICE ($) FY Close	P/E High/Low		PER SHARE ($) Earnings	Dividends	Book Value
12/09	49.74	16	9	3.50	0.85	21.15
12/08	45.99	16	8	4.33	0.70	16.68
12/07	66.04	18	14	4.03	0.56	21.51
12/06	56.82	19	15	3.10	0.44	15.62
12/05	51.41	30	21	1.91	0.36	14.85
Annual Growth	**(0.8%)**	**—**	**—**	**16.3%**	**24.0%**	**9.2%**

J. Crew Group

The crews depicted in the polished catalogs of the J. Crew Group are far from motley. The retailer is known for its preppy fashions, including jeans, khakis, and other basic (but pricey) items sold to young professionals through its catalogs, websites, and some 320 retail and outlet stores in the US under the J. Crew, crewcuts (for kids), and Madewell banners. Madewell, launched in 2006, is a women's-only collection of hip, casual clothes. Asian contractors produce about 80% of the company's merchandise. Chief executive Millard "Mickey" Drexler, recruited in 2003 from The Gap to revive J. Crew's ailing fortunes, has led a retail renaissance at the firm, marked by taking the company public in 2006.

Shrugging off the recession, J. Crew has enjoyed strong sales growth. The company credited its on-target fashion sense and lean inventories for its strong performance. (Of course, having the First Lady Michelle Obama sport its fashions probably didn't hurt either.) Sales also got a boost from the expansion of the Madewell and crewcuts formats (both launched in 2006). Madewell offers women's apparel, including a new line of suits, that is priced 20% to 30% lower than J. Crew merchandise.

Buoyed by its recent strong performance at home, the US retailer has targeted the UK for expansion, with the proposed launch of an online retail operation there as soon as 2011.

More than two-thirds of J. Crew's sales come from its retail locations, which include more than 75 outlet stores. Hemmed by the stagnant growth of its catalog operations, the New York City-based company has sold or closed two of its noncore catalog businesses, Popular Club Plan and Clifford & Wills, leaving it with only its namesake operations.

CEO Drexler owns about 12% of the company's shares; mutual fund firm FMR owns almost 15%.

HISTORY

Although the J. Crew Group started in 1983, the Cinader family's participation in the mail-order catalog business extends back to 1947, when Arthur Cinader's father, Mitchell, along with Saul Charles, founded the Popular Club Plan, a mail-order catalog selling ladies' apparel, furniture, and kitchen supplies.

After inheriting the Popular Club Plan, Arthur observed the remarkable growth in the early 1980s of The Talbots, L.L. Bean, and other clothing catalogs. In 1983 he established his own classic apparel catalog as J. Crew, a name that connoted casual, collegiate clothing. First-year sales were about $3 million.

The following year Arthur offered a job to his eldest daughter, Emily, a recent college graduate. Her first decision was to ban polyester from all J. Crew clothes. Although early catalogs included clothing from a number of manufacturers, Emily, as the company's chief designer, moved the company to selling its own brand exclusively. J. Crew's early unisex styles were shaped by her desire to wear some of the same clothes she wore while growing up, such as her brother's chinos. Also in 1984 Arthur started the Clifford & Wills catalog operation (low-priced women's clothing). J. Crew catalog sales grew rapidly during the mid-1980s.

In 1989 Emily, then 28, became president of the J. Crew catalog division and launched a risky expansion into retail, with its first store in New York City. Later in 1989 J. Crew unveiled an ambitious store-opening plan (50 stores in five years). However, a weakened economy and sharp competition slowed growth. In 1993 J. Crew signed an agreement with ITOCHU, permitting the Japanese retailer to distribute its clothes in that country.

High executive turnover also stunted growth, possibly attributable to the rough-edged style of Arthur. President and COO Arnold Cohen stepped down in 1993. His replacement, Robert Bernard, resigned in 1996, and Arthur took on his duties.

In an effort to recapitalize the struggling company, the Texas Pacific Group bought its stake in J. Crew the following year, with an eye on taking it public when its performance improved. At that time Arthur retired and Emily succeeded her father as J. Crew's chair (Emily retired from the board in late 2006). In 1998 J. Crew attributed a loss of $27 million to disappointing mail-order sales caused by the USPS strike and a warm fall and winter. The company dismissed 10% of its workforce to reduce overhead costs that year. Also that year J. Crew sold its Popular Club Plan to catalog firm Fingerhut.

Speaking of losing popularity, CEO Howard Socol fell out of favor and left the company in early 1999 after less than a year on the job. Mark Sarvary, former president of Nestlé Frozen Foods, succeeded him. Also in 1999 J. Crew ceased its Clifford & Wills catalog and sold its trademarks and mailing list to Spiegel. In summer 2000 the company launched a bath and body line called So J. Crew, which included soap, lotion, mouthwash, and candles.

In 2001 J. Crew announced plans to launch a complete line of children's wear for boys and girls ages 6 to 12. Then the company laid off about 30 workers at its headquarters after recording disappointing sales.

The years 2002 and 2003 brought a bit of management turmoil for the company: Mark Sarvary left in May 2002, and in August was replaced by former Gap executive Ken Pilot. Pilot, however, did not last long and was replaced the following January by another Gap executive, Millard "Micky" Drexler, who recruited yet another Gap exec, Jeff Pfeifle, to join him in efforts to strengthen the J. Crew brand the way he'd already successfully done at The Gap. (Pfeifle, second in line behind Mickey Drexler since 2003, left the company in February 2008.)

Just in time for Fashion Week in 2004, Drexler led J. Crew down the wedding aisle by introducing an abbreviated collection of wedding ensembles for men and women. The success of the wedding line prompted the company to launch bridal-only catalog "J. Crew Wedding" in April 2005. Also in 2005 the company brought its J. Crew factory business to the Internet with the launch of jcrewfactory.com.

In 2006 the company expanded into the children's apparel market with a new collection called crewcuts for kids ages two through 10. In June, J. Crew finally went public. Also that year it launched Madewell, a new retail concept, in Dallas. In 2008 the company opened a small men's shop in downtown Manhattan where it plans to work on fine tuning its men's apparel business in preparation for the launch of stand-alone J. Crew men's stores. It also opened its first store in Hawaii.

EXECUTIVES

Chairman and CEO: Millard S. (Mickey) Drexler, age 65, $5,842,881 total compensation
President and Executive Creative Director: Jenna Lyons, age 42, $4,266,703 total compensation
EVP Human Resources: Linda Markoe, age 43
SVP Marketing and Public Relations: Margot Fooshee
President, Retail and Direct: Tracy Gardner, age 46, $3,017,903 total compensation
EVP Retail & Factory: Libby Wadle, age 37, $2,055,053 total compensation
CFO and Chief Administrative Officer: James S. Scully, age 45, $2,071,803 total compensation
SVP and General Counsel: Arlene S. Hong
EVP Direct Channel: Trish Donnelly
SVP Madewell Retail Channel: Laura Willensky
Auditors: KPMG LLP

LOCATIONS

HQ: J. Crew Group, Inc.
  770 Broadway, New York, NY 10003
Phone: 212-209-2500 **Fax:** 212-209-2666
Web: www.jcrew.com

2010 Stores

	No.
California	40
New York	29
Florida	22
New Jersey	19
Texas	19
Pennsylvania	16
Connecticut	14
Massachusetts	14
Georgia	10
Illinois	10
North Carolina	10
Michigan	9
Virginia	9
Maryland	8
Ohio	8
Colorado	7
South Carolina	6
Arizona	5
Minnesota	5
Missouri	5
Washington	5
Alabama	4
Nevada	4
Oregon	4
Tennessee	4
Wisconsin	4
Indiana	3
New Hampshire	3
Utah	3
Other states	21
Total	**321**

PRODUCTS/OPERATIONS

2010 Sales

	$ mil.	% of total
Stores	1,110.9	70
Direct	428.2	27
Other	38.9	3
Total	**1,578.0**	**100**

2010 Sales

	% of total
Apparel	
Women's	65
Men's	19
Children's	4
Accessories	12
Total	**100**

2010 Stores

	No.
J. Crew	217
J. Crew factory	78
Madewell	17
crewcuts	9
Total	**321**

HISTORICAL FINANCIALS

Company Type: Public

Income Statement

FYE: Saturday nearest January 31

	REVENUE ($ mil.)	NET INCOME ($ mil.)	NET PROFIT MARGIN	EMPLOYEES
1/10	1,578	123	7.8%	12,000
1/09	1,428	54	3.8%	10,900
1/08	1,335	97	7.3%	8,700
1/07	1,152	78	6.8%	7,600
1/06	953	4	0.4%	6,800
Annual Growth	13.4%	138.7%	—	15.3%

2010 Year-End Financials

Debt ratio: 13.1%
Return on equity: 41.1%
Cash ($ mil.): 298
Current ratio: 2.21
Long-term debt ($ mil.): 49
No. of shares (mil.): 64
Dividends
  Yield: —
  Payout: —
Market value ($ mil.): 2,502

Stock History

NYSE: JCG

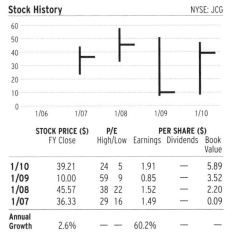

	STOCK PRICE ($) FY Close	P/E High/Low		PER SHARE ($) Earnings	Dividends	Book Value
1/10	39.21	24	5	1.91	—	5.89
1/09	10.00	59	9	0.85	—	3.52
1/08	45.57	38	22	1.52	—	2.20
1/07	36.33	29	16	1.49	—	0.09
Annual Growth	2.6%	—	—	60.2%	—	—

Jabil Circuit

Jabil Circuit takes more than a jab at contract electronics manufacturing. The company is one of the leading providers of electronics manufacturing services (EMS) in the world. Parts made by Jabil on a contract basis are used in communications products, medical instruments, computers and networking gear, and automobiles. Services range from product design and component procurement to product testing, order fulfillment, and supply chain management. Top customers include Cisco Systems, Research in Motion, Hewlett-Packard, EchoStar, and Nokia.

The 2008-09 economic recession, and the company's shift to developing countries for manufacturing, has squeezed operations in the US. In 2009 Jabil began shutting down a Massachusetts plant, laying off more than 300 workers. In addition to competing with other contract manufacturers, Jabil has seen competition with its customers increase during the economic downturn. Some customers have moved production in-house to make use of excess manufacturing capacity, rather than outsourcing production to EMS providers such as Jabil.

Bringing a more specialized approach to its customer base, Jabil reorganized two of its divisions: Consumer Electronics and EMS. Consumer Electronics makes cell phones and other mobile electronic products, TVs, set-top boxes, and computer peripherals. The EMS division essentially manufactures everything else, from electronic components to printed circuit boards, serving both traditional and emerging markets including aerospace, automotive, industrial instrumentation, medical, solar, storage, and telecommunications.

To compete in a rapidly consolidating industry, Jabil provides global parallel production and uses a "workcell" approach, in which semiautonomous business units are dedicated to individual customers. The company continues to add services and to expand globally through acquisitions, including deals to acquire manufacturing operations from customers looking to reduce costs through outsourcing. Jabil has acquired or established manufacturing facilities in regions with lower operating costs, including Brazil, China, Hungary, India, Malaysia, Mexico, Poland, Turkey, Ukraine, and Vietnam.

Jabil cooperated with the SEC and the US Department of Justice in probing stock option practices of the past. The inquiries were initiated after the company conducted an internal review of its processes in granting stock options, as did dozens of publicly held companies in the US. The SEC notified Jabil in late 2008 that its Division of Enforcement concluded its investigation and would not recommend any enforcement action against the company.

Chairman William Morean and his family own about 13% of Jabil Circuit.

HISTORY

Jabil Circuit was named for founders James Golden and Bill Morean. The duo, who originally ran an excavation business, started Jabil in suburban Detroit in 1966 to provide assembly and reworking services to electronics manufacturers. Jabil incorporated in 1969 and began making printed circuit boards for Control Data Corporation (later renamed Control Data Systems) that year.

William D. Morean, the founder's son who had worked summers at Jabil while in high school, joined the company in 1977. The next year the younger Morean took over Jabil's day-to-day operations. The company entered the automotive electronics business in 1976 through a $12 million contract with General Motors.

During the 1980s Jabil began building computer components, adding such customers as Dell, NEC, Sun Microsystems, and Toshiba. Jabil moved its headquarters to St. Petersburg, Florida, in 1983. William Morean became Jabil's chairman and CEO in 1988.

Production design accounted for most of Jabil's sales for the first time in 1992. The next year the company went public and also opened a factory in Scotland. A major laptop computer manufacturing contract from Epson soured when, in 1995, cracks appeared in the casings of the laptops, and Epson balked at paying its tab.

By 1997 Jabil had successfully diversified beyond low-margin PC manufacturing, becoming one of the top US circuit board manufacturers, while adding higher-margin products such as networking hardware.

In 1999 the company expanded into China when it acquired electronics manufacturing services provider GET Manufacturing. The next year William Morean stepped down as CEO (he remained chairman); he was succeeded by president Timothy Main.

In 2001 Jabil announced it would cut about 3,000 jobs, or about 10% of its staff. Also in 2001 it signed an agreement with chip titan Intel under which Jabil would acquire an Intel plant in Malaysia and supply Intel with parts for three years.

In 2002 Jabil acquired most of the assets of Lucent Technologies of Shanghai, a joint venture among Lucent (now Alcatel-Lucent) and three Chinese partners. Also that year the company bought Philips Contract Manufacturing Services, an arm of the Dutch electronics giant, for around $210 million.

In late 2004 Jabil began expanding its manufacturing capacity in Asia by breaking ground on new plants in India and China. The facilities represented the company's second plant in India and its fourth in China.

In early 2005 the company paid about $195 million to acquire the contract manufacturing business of Varian, Inc., the instrument vendor. Together with Carl Zeiss, Jabil created a joint venture in early 2006 to manufacture optical modules for computer displays and other applications.

In 2006 Jabil exercised a purchase option to acquire Celetronix International, an India-based electronics manufacturer, which had operations in India, the UK, and the US.

Late in the year Jabil started building a new facility in Uzhgorod, Ukraine. The plant was its second in the former Soviet republic and joined other Eastern European facilities in Hungary and Poland.

In 2007 Jabil acquired Taiwan Green Point Enterprises, a contract manufacturer with plants in China, Malaysia, and Taiwan. Green Point specialized in plastic parts for cell phones and other portable electronics products. Jabil planned to operate Green Point as an autonomous subsidiary, hiring about 30,000 employees and keeping the company's management in place.

Further expanding into Asian markets, Jabil opened a facility in Vietnam in mid-2007.

EXECUTIVES

Chairman: William D. Morean, age 54
Vice Chairman: Thomas A. Sansone, age 60
President, CEO, and Director: Timothy L. Main, age 52, $4,134,740 total compensation
COO: Mark T. Mondello, age 45, $2,455,151 total compensation
CFO: Forbes I. J. Alexander, age 49, $1,664,871 total compensation
CIO: David Couch
General Counsel and Secretary: Robert L. Paver, age 53
EVP; CEO EMS Division: William D. (Bill) Muir Jr., age 41, $1,749,828 total compensation
EVP; CEO Consumer Division: John P. Lovato, age 49, $3,203,969 total compensation
SVP Strategic Planning and Development: Joseph A. (Joe) McGee, age 47
SVP Aftermarket Services: Hartmut Liebel
SVP Global Business Units, EMS Division: Courtney J. Ryan, age 40
SVP Worldwide Operations, EMS Division: Teck Ping Yuen, age 54
SVP Worldwide Operations, EMS Division: Michael J. Matthes
SVP Consumer Division: Hai Hwai (HH) Chiang
SVP Human Development: William E. (Bill) Peters, age 46
VP Investor Relations and Communications: Beth A. Walters, age 49
VP Tax: Thomas R. Blythe
Senior Legal Counsel and Assistant Corporate Secretary: Susan Allan
Chairman and CEO, Jabil Japan: Isamu Kamata
Treasurer: Sergio A. Cadavid, age 53
Auditors: KPMG LLP

LOCATIONS

HQ: Jabil Circuit, Inc.
10560 Dr. Martin Luther King Jr. St. North
St. Petersburg, FL 33716
Phone: 727-577-9749   **Fax:** 727-579-8529
Web: www.jabil.com

2009 Sales

	$ mil.	% of total
Mexico	2,704.7	23
China	2,444.3	21
US	1,887.8	16
Hungary	1,005.1	9
Malaysia	814.4	7
Brazil	510.1	4
Poland	478.4	4
Other countries	1,839.7	16
Total	**11,684.5**	**100**

PRODUCTS/OPERATIONS

2009 Sales

	$ mil.	% of total
Electronics manufacturing services	6,802.4	58
Consumer electronics	4,160.1	36
Aftermarket services	722.0	6
Total	**11,684.5**	**100**

2009 Sales by Market

	% of total
Electronics manufacturing services	
Instrumentation & medical	19
Networking	17
Computing & storage	11
Telecommunications	6
Automotive	3
Other	2
Consumer electronics	
Mobility	20
Peripherals	12
Display	4
Aftermarket services	6
Total	**100**

Services

Component selection, sourcing, and procurement
Design and prototyping
Engineering
Order fulfillment
Printed circuit board and backplane assembly
Product testing
Repair and warranty
Systems assembly
Test development
Tooling design (molds and dies)

COMPETITORS

ASUSTeK
Benchmark Electronics
BenQ
Celestica
Compal Electronics
CTS Corp.
Elcoteq
Flextronics
Hon Hai
Inventec
Key Tronic
LaBarge
Nam Tai
Plexus
Sanmina-SCI
SMTC Corp.
Sparton
Suntron
SYNNEX
Universal Scientific
Venture Corp.
Viasystems
Wistron

HISTORICAL FINANCIALS

Company Type: Public

Income Statement

FYE: August 31

	REVENUE ($ mil.)	NET INCOME ($ mil.)	NET PROFIT MARGIN	EMPLOYEES
8/09	11,685	(1,165)	—	61,000
8/08	12,780	134	1.0%	61,000
8/07	12,291	73	0.6%	61,000
8/06	10,265	165	1.6%	49,000
8/05	7,524	232	3.1%	40,000
Annual Growth	**11.6%**	**—**	**—**	**11.1%**

2009 Year-End Financials

Debt ratio: 72.2%
Return on equity: —
Cash ($ mil.): 876
Current ratio: 1.37
Long-term debt ($ mil.): 1,037
No. of shares (mil.): 217
Dividends
  Yield: 2.6%
  Payout: —
Market value ($ mil.): 2,381

Stock History

NYSE: JBL

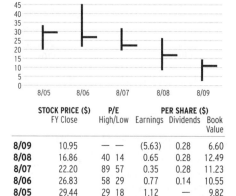

	STOCK PRICE ($) FY Close	P/E High/Low		PER SHARE ($) Earnings	Dividends	Book Value
8/09	10.95	—	—	(5.63)	0.28	6.60
8/08	16.86	40	14	0.65	0.28	12.49
8/07	22.20	89	57	0.35	0.28	11.23
8/06	26.83	58	29	0.77	0.14	10.55
8/05	29.44	29	18	1.12	—	9.82
Annual Growth	**(21.9%)**	—	—	**—**	**26.0%**	**(9.5%)**

Jack in the Box

Led by an affable "CEO" with a Ping-Pong ball for a head, Jack in the Box is among the leading quick-service restaurant businesses in the US. The company operates and franchises more than 2,200 of its flagship hamburger outlets in California, Texas, and about 15 other states. Jack in the Box offers such standard fast-food fare as burgers, fries, and soft drinks, as well as salads, tacos, and breakfast items. About 1,200 locations are company-owned, while the rest are franchised. In addition to its mainstay burger business, the company runs a chain of more than 500 Qdoba Mexican Grill fast-casual eateries through its Qdoba Restaurant subsidiary.

Unlike some of its fast-food rivals, Jack in the Box has traditionally had a large number of corporate locations compared to its franchised outlets. The company-owned units account for the bulk of the company's revenue and give it an increased amount of control over local operations, but building and operating that chain involves a great deal of capital while exposing Jack in the Box to the sometimes uneven ebb and flow of the restaurant business.

Looking to reduce costs and provide for a more steady stream of revenue, the company has been focused on its franchising operations in part through selling its corporate-run eateries to franchisees. It refranchised almost 200 Jack in the Box locations during fiscal 2009. In addition to royalties and other franchising fees, the company also supplies many of its franchisees with equipment and other goods.

Jack in the Box leans on quirky marketing efforts and an almost constant stream of new menu items to help compete with such larger rivals as McDonald's and Burger King. Its advertising campaign featuring the company's fictional CEO, Jack, strikes a balance somewhere between the family-friendly image of the Golden Arches and the marketing efforts of Burger King, which skews more toward the young male demographic. (During 2009 Jack was hit by a bus and put into a coma. He emerged several weeks later with the announcement of a new corporate logo.) On its menu, the Jack in the Box chain added such items as Mini Sirloin Burgers and several value-priced items. Meanwhile, Jack in the Box is working to upgrade many of its outlets with modern interior designs, complete with flat-screen televisions and ceramic tile floors.

Jack in the Box sold its 61-unit Quick Stuff convenience store chain during 2009. The disposal was part of an effort to focus on the company's core dining business.

HISTORY

Robert Peterson founded his first restaurant, Topsy's Drive-In, in 1941 in San Diego. He soon renamed it Oscar's (his middle name) and began to expand the restaurant. By 1950 he had four Oscar's drive-in restaurants. That year he changed the name again to Jack in the Box and in 1951 opened one of the country's first drive-through restaurants, which featured a speaker mounted in the chain's signature clown's head.

The drive-through concept took off, and by the late 1960s the company, renamed Foodmaker, operated about 300 Jack in the Box restaurants. In 1968 Peterson sold Foodmaker to Ralston Purina (now Nestlé Purina PetCare). To differentiate itself from competitors, Foodmaker added new food items, including the first breakfast sandwich (1969). The company continued to expand during the 1970s, and by 1979 it had more than 1,000 restaurants. That year it decided to concentrate on the western and southwestern US, selling 232 restaurants in the East and Midwest.

To attract more adult customers, in 1980 Foodmaker began remodeling its stores and adding menu items geared toward adult tastes. The company ran a series of TV ads showing its trademark clown logo being blown up. The ads were meant to show that Jack in the Box was not just for children anymore, but they drew protests from parents worried about the violence in the advertisements.

In 1985 Foodmaker's management acquired the company in a $450 million LBO. The company went public in 1987, but management took it private again the next year. Led by then-CEO Jack Goodall, Foodmaker expanded its number of franchises. (Unlike most of its competitors, the company had previously owned almost all of its restaurants.) By 1987 about 30% of the company's 900 stores were owned by franchisees.

The next year Foodmaker paid about $230 million for the Chi-Chi's chain of 200 Mexican restaurants. It made its first move outside the US in 1991, opening restaurants in Mexico and Hong Kong. The company went public again the following year.

In 1993 four people died, and more than 700 became ill, after eating E. coli-tainted hamburgers from Jack in the Box restaurants in several states, the largest such contamination in US history. Customers, shareholders, and franchisees sued Foodmaker, which in turn sued meat supplier and supermarket chain Vons and Vons's suppliers. Foodmaker's stock and profits plummeted, and the company subsequently enacted a stringent food safety program, which became a model for the fast-food industry and won kudos from the FDA.

Foodmaker sold its Chi-Chi's chain to Family Restaurants in 1994. In 1996 Goodall retired as CEO, and Robert Nugent succeeded him. The next year Foodmaker announced a major expansion to add 200 Jack in the Box restaurants, primarily in the western US.

Foodmaker put the E. coli episode farther behind it in 1998 when it accepted a $58.5 million settlement from Vons and others. In 1999 the company began building units in selected southeastern markets. Also that year Foodmaker dropped its generic moniker and renamed the firm Jack in the Box. The following year it got a nice break from Uncle Sam in the form of a nearly $23 million tax benefit related to the 1995 selling of its stake in Family Restaurants Inc. The company also opened 120 new stores, many in the southeastern US.

In 2001 Goodall stepped down from the board and was replaced by Nugent as chairman. With same-store sales down amidst a sagging economy and fewer tourist dollars, the company scaled down its expansion plans. In 2002 it built 100 new locations (down from 126 the previous year), including about 30 in the Southeast.

Following the lead of its competitors, Jack in the Box acquired fast-casual restaurant operator Qdoba Restaurant Corporation in 2003.

In 2004 the company announced it would restate earnings dating back to 2002 as a result of adjustments in its accounting practices. The next year Nugent retired from Jack in the Box and was replaced by company president Linda Lang.

EXECUTIVES

Chairman, President, and CEO: Linda A. Lang, age 51, $7,107,658 total compensation
EVP and CFO: Jerry P. Rebel, age 52, $2,436,599 total compensation
SVP and COO: Leonard A. Comma
SVP and Chief Marketing Officer: Terri Funk Graham, age 44, $1,376,915 total compensation
SVP and Chief Development Officer: Charles E. Watson, age 54, $1,414,705 total compensation
SVP, General Counsel, and Secretary: Phillip H. (Phil) Rudolph, age 51
VP Investor Relations and Corporate Communications: Carol A. DiRaimo, age 48
VP Operations, Initiatives: Elana M. (Lani) Hobson
VP Human Resources and Operational Services: Mark H. Blankenship, age 48
VP Franchising: Michael Bamrick
Division VP Corporate Communications: Brian Luscomb
Division VP Menu Marketing and Promotions: Tammy Bailey
Division VP Food and Safety: Ann Marie McNamara
President and CEO Qdoba Restaurant Corporation: Gary J. Beisler, age 53
Director Menu Marketing and Promotions: Teka O'Rourke
Auditors: KPMG LLP

LOCATIONS

HQ: Jack in the Box Inc.
9330 Balboa Ave., San Diego, CA 92123
Phone: 858-571-2121 **Fax:** 858-571-2101
Web: www.jackinthebox.com

PRODUCTS/OPERATIONS

2009 Sales

	$ mil.	% of total
Restaurants	1,975.9	80
Foodservice distribution	302.1	12
Franchising	193.1	8
Total	**2,471.1**	**100**

2009 Sales

	$ mil.	% of total
Dining chains		
Jack in the Box	2,025.8	82
Qdoba Mexican Grill	143.2	6
Foodservice distribution	302.1	12
Total	**2,471.1**	**100**

2009 Locations

	No.
Franchised	1,375
Company-owned	1,347
Total	**2,722**

2009 Locations

	No.
Jack in the Box	2,212
Qdoba Mexican Grill	510
Total	**2,722**

COMPETITORS

AFC Enterprises	Fresh Enterprises
American Dairy Queen	In-N-Out Burgers
Burger King	McDonald's
Checkers Drive-In	Quiznos
Chick-fil-A	Sonic Corp.
Chipotle	Subway
Church's Chicken	Wendy's/Arby's Group, Inc.
CKE Restaurants	Whataburger
Del Taco	YUM!
FOCUS Brands	

HISTORICAL FINANCIALS

Company Type: Public

Income Statement

FYE: Sunday nearest September 30

	REVENUE ($ mil.)	NET INCOME ($ mil.)	NET PROFIT MARGIN	EMPLOYEES
9/09	2,471	118	4.8%	35,700
9/08	2,540	119	4.7%	42,700
9/07	2,876	126	4.4%	42,500
9/06	2,766	109	3.9%	44,300
9/05	2,507	92	3.6%	44,600
Annual Growth	**(0.4%)**	**6.7%**	**—**	**(5.4%)**

2009 Year-End Financials

Debt ratio: 68.1%
Return on equity: 24.1%
Cash ($ mil.): 53
Current ratio: 0.89
Long-term debt ($ mil.): 357
No. of shares (mil.): 55
Dividends
Yield: —
Payout: —
Market value ($ mil.): 1,129

Stock History

NASDAQ (GS): JACK

	STOCK PRICE ($) FY Close	P/E High/Low		PER SHARE ($) Earnings	Dividends	Book Value
9/09	20.49	14	6	2.05	—	9.52
9/08	21.10	17	9	2.01	—	8.30
9/07	32.42	21	14	1.88	—	7.52
9/06	26.09	18	9	1.50	—	12.90
9/05	14.95	17	11	1.24	—	10.26
Annual Growth	**8.2%**	**—**	**—**	**13.4%**	**—**	**(1.9%)**

Jacobs Engineering

Jacobs climbs the ladder of success by keeping it professional. Jacobs Engineering Group provides professional, technical, and construction services for the industrial, commercial, and government sectors. It provides a wide range of services, including project design and engineering, construction, operations and maintenance, and scientific consultation. Engineering and construction projects for the chemical, petroleum, and pharmaceutical and biotech industries generate much of the group's revenues. US government contracts, chiefly for aerospace and defense, also add to Jacobs' bottom line.

Projects have included buildings, process plants, manufacturing facilities, and paper and pulp plants. The company also works on roads, highways, railways, ports, and other infrastructure projects.

Jacobs Engineering Group gets jobs and keeps jobs for the long term. Its main strategy is to build on long-standing client relationships — some that have spanned nearly 60 years.

For example, US government agencies involved in defense and aerospace programs have been pivotal to the company's growth. The Air Force's Arnold Engineering Development Center

(AEDC) has been a key client for 50 years. Another long-term client is NASA, for which the company has a 40-year history of contract work. Overseas Jacobs U.K. works on several projects for the Ministry of Defense and the Nuclear Decommissioning Authority.

The group also participates in the environmental restoration of former weapons production and defense sites. Jacobs' strategy to speed up environmental cleanup at the Department of Energy's Oak Ridge site has earned it contracts to help accelerate cleanup at other major DOE facilities. The company has also been providing services for the Air Force Center for Environmental Excellence (AFCEE) to help the agency with its environmental cleanup goals since 1991.

Acquisitions also are key to Jacobs' strategy. The company grows by entering new markets and services lines via strategic mergers and acquisitions, allowing it to offer one-stop services. Over the years the company has made key acquisitions that either added to its service lines or expanded its geographic footprint. Recent examples include the acquisitions of Carter & Burgess and transportation specialist Edwards and Kelcey. Both deals added to the group's infrastructure business. In 2010 Jacobs bought Jordan Jones and Goulding. The deal significantly expanded Jacobs' North American position in the wastewater market. It also broadened the company's global aviation, transit, and transportation business.

Jacobs acquired TYBRIN Corporation, a professional services firm headquartered in Fort Walton Beach, Florida, in 2009. TYBRIN supplied mission planning solutions, systems engineering, software development, modeling, combat environment simulations, and other services to the Department of Defense, NASA, and other government clients.

HISTORY

Joseph Jacobs graduated from the Polytechnic Institute of Brooklyn in 1942 with a doctorate in engineering. He went to work for Merck, designing processes for pharmaceutical production. Later he moved to Chemurgic Corp. near San Francisco, where he worked until 1947, when he founded Jacobs Engineering as a consulting firm. Jacobs also sold industrial equipment, avoiding any apparent conflict of interest by simply telling his consulting clients.

When equipment sales outstripped consulting work by 1954, Jacobs hired four salesmen and engineer Stan Krugman, who became his right-hand man. Two years later the company got its first big chemical design job for Kaiser Aluminum. Jacobs incorporated his sole proprietorship in 1957.

In 1960 the firm won its first construction contract to design and build a potash flotation plant, and Jacobs Engineering became an integrated design and construction firm. In 1967 it opened its first regional office but kept management decentralized to replicate the small size and hard-hitting qualities of its home office. Three years later Jacobs Engineering went public.

The firm merged with Houston-based Pace Companies, which specialized in petrochemical engineering design, in 1974. Also that year the firm became Jacobs Engineering Group and began building its first major overseas chemical plant in Ireland.

By 1977 sales had reached $250 million. A decade of lobbying paid off that year when the firm won a contract for the Arab Potash complex in Jordan. Jacobs began to withdraw from his firm's operations in the early 1980s, but the 1982-83 recession and poor management decisions pounded earnings. Jacobs returned from retirement in 1985, fired 14 VPs, cut staff in half, and pushed the firm to pursue smaller process-plant jobs and specialty construction.

After abandoning a 1986 attempt to take the company private, Jacobs began making acquisitions to improve the firm's construction expertise. In 1992 he relinquished his role as CEO to president Noel Watson. The next year the company expanded its international holdings by acquiring the UK's H&G Process Contracting and H&G Contractors.

The firm's $38 million purchase of CRS Sirrine Engineers and CRSS Constructors in 1994 was the company's largest buy to that point and added new markets in the paper and semiconductor industries. By 1995 Jacobs Engineering was working on a record backlog.

Continuing its acquisition drive, the company bought a 49% interest in European engineering specialist Serete Group in 1996; it bought the rest the next year. Also in 1997 it gained control of Indian engineering affiliate Humphreys & Glasgow (now Jacobs H&G), increasing its 40% stake to 70%, and bought CPR Engineering, a pulp and paper processing specialist.

After being accused of overcharging the US government, the company settled a whistle-blower lawsuit (for $35 million) in 2000 while continuing to deny the allegations. However, the next year Jacobs continued to receive federal contracts, including contracts for boosting security at the US Capitol complex and providing logistics to the US Special Operations Command.

The company airport bought consulting firm Leigh Fisher Associates in 2003. In 2004 the group's founder and chairman died at the age of 88. He was succeeded as chairman by Watson, who retained the CEO post until 2005. Former president Craig Martin was named CEO the following year. Jacobs expanded its Middle East operations in 2008 by acquiring a 60% interest in the Saudi Arabia-based Zamel & Turbag Consulting Engineers.

EXECUTIVES

Chairman: Noel G. Watson, age 73, $4,221,402 total compensation
President, CEO, and Director: Craig L. Martin, age 61, $4,674,603 total compensation
EVP Finance and Administration and Treasurer: John W. Prosser Jr., age 64, $2,249,273 total compensation
EVP Operations: George A. Kunberger Jr., age 57, $2,412,570 total compensation
EVP Operations: Thomas R. (Tom) Hammond, age 58, $3,077,409 total compensation
EVP Operations: Gregory J. Landry, age 61
SVP Global Human Resources: Patricia H. Summers, age 52
SVP and General Counsel: William C. Markley III, age 64
SVP Acquisitions and Strategy: John McLachlan, age 63
SVP Information Technology: Cora L. Carmody, age 52
SVP and Controller: Nazim G. Thawerbhoy, age 62
SVP Global Sales: Andrew F. (Andy) Kremer, age 52
SVP Public Sector Sales: William J. Birkhofer, age 62
SVP Quality and Safety: Robert G. Norfleet, age 46
President, Jacobs Technology: Rogers F. Starr, age 67
Auditors: Ernst & Young LLP

LOCATIONS

HQ: Jacobs Engineering Group Inc.
1111 S. Arroyo Pkwy., Pasadena, CA 91105
Phone: 626-578-3500   **Fax:** 626-568-7144
Web: www.jacobs.com

2009 Sales

	$ mil.	% of total
US	7,362.7	64
Europe	2,204.5	19
Canada	1,597.6	14
Asia	253.7	2
Other regions	48.9	1
Total	**11,467.4**	**100**

PRODUCTS/OPERATIONS

2009 Sales by Industry

	$ mil.	% of total
Downstream energy & refining	4,047.8	35
National government programs	2,424.6	21
Chemicals & polymers	1,210.0	11
Infrastructure	933.5	8
Upstream oil & gas	895.3	8
Pharmaceuticals & biotechnology	875.0	7
Buildings	517.1	5
Industrial & other	564.1	5
Total	**11,467.4**	**100**

2009 Sales by Segment

	$ mil.	% of total
Construction	4,763.7	42
Project services	4,644.0	40
Operations & maintenance	1,165.3	10
Process, scientific & systems consulting	894.4	8
Total	**11,467.4**	**100**

COMPETITORS

AECOM	KBR
Aker Solutions	Lockheed Martin
AMEC	Louis Berger
Babcock & Wilcox	Parsons Brinckerhoff
BE&K	Parsons Corporation
Bechtel	Peter Kiewit Sons'
CH2M HILL	Raytheon
Computer Sciences Corp.	SAIC
Day & Zimmermann	Shaw Group
Fluor	Technip
Foster Wheeler	Tetra Tech
HDR	Turner Construction
HNTB Companies	URS
HOK	Weston Solutions
Honeywell International	

HISTORICAL FINANCIALS

Company Type: Public

Income Statement

FYE: September 30

	REVENUE ($ mil.)	NET INCOME ($ mil.)	NET PROFIT MARGIN	EMPLOYEES
9/09	11,467	400	3.5%	38,900
9/08	11,252	421	3.7%	43,700
9/07	8,474	287	3.4%	36,400
9/06	7,421	197	2.7%	31,700
9/05	5,635	151	2.7%	38,600
Annual Growth	**19.4%**	**27.6%**	**—**	**0.2%**

2009 Year-End Financials

Debt ratio: 0.0%	No. of shares (mil.): 126
Return on equity: 16.4%	Dividends
Cash ($ mil.): 1,034	Yield: —
Current ratio: 2.17	Payout: —
Long-term debt ($ mil.): 1	Market value ($ mil.): 5,777

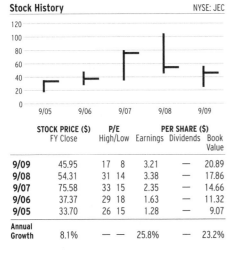

	STOCK PRICE ($) FY Close	P/E High/Low		PER SHARE ($) Earnings	Dividends	Book Value
9/09	45.95	17	8	3.21	—	20.89
9/08	54.31	31	14	3.38	—	17.86
9/07	75.58	33	15	2.35	—	14.66
9/06	37.37	29	18	1.63	—	11.32
9/05	33.70	26	15	1.28	—	9.07
Annual Growth	8.1%	—	—	25.8%	—	23.2%

J.B. Hunt Transport Services

When it comes to hauling freight, J.B. Hunt Transport Services is a leader of the pack. Its intermodal unit, the company's largest, maintains some 2,200 tractors and 40,000 containers and moves customers' cargo by combinations of truck and train. J.B. Hunt's dedicated contract services unit supplies customers with drivers and equipment; it operates about 4,000 company-controlled trucks. The company's truckload transportation unit, which has a fleet of about 1,700 tractors, provides dry van freight transportation service in the US, Canada, and Mexico. A fourth business segment, integrated capacity solutions (ICS), manages freight transportation via third-party carriers as well as J.B. Hunt equipment.

Formerly part of J.B. Hunt's truckload transportation segment, ICS began to have its results reported separately in 2007. The business often arranges specialty trucking services, such as transporting freight that requires the use of flatbed or refrigerated trailers. ICS had strong sales growth in 2009 (up 24% over 2008) as load volumes increased, but the increase was offset in part by higher personnel and technology costs related to investments in the business. J.B. Hunt was also engaged in transportation management through its 37% stake in Transplace, a company formed from the logistics units of several truckload carriers. However, an investment firm acquired all the shares of Transplace in late 2009 and J.B. Hunt relinquished its stake.

J.B. Hunt hopes to grow by concentrating on its operating segments as separate, but overlapping, businesses and by selling more value-added services to its customers. It has continued to expand its intermodal unit, which has agreements with major North American railroads, including Burlington Northern Santa Fe and Norfolk Southern railways. In 2009 the company expanded its network in the eastern region of the US, a market traditionally served by truck service, through an agreement with Norfolk Southern. To emphasize higher-margin offerings, J.B.

Hunt has been shifting resources away from truckload transportation and reducing its overall equipment fleet.

Freight transported by J.B. Hunt includes automotive parts, building materials, chemicals, food and beverages, forest and paper products, and general merchandise. One of the company's top customers is its Arkansas neighbor, Wal-Mart.

The family of founder J.B. Hunt, who retired as senior chairman in 2004 and died in 2006, owns about 22% of the company. His son, Bryan Hunt, is a board member. Company chairman Wayne Garrison holds a 4% stake.

HISTORY

Johnnie Bryan (J.B.) Hunt's life was a classic tale of rolling from rags to riches — with a little help from a Rockefeller.

Hunt grew up in a family of sharecroppers during the Depression, and he left school at age 12 to work for his uncle's Arkansas sawmill. In the late 1950s, after driving trucks for more than nine years, Hunt noticed that the rice mills along his eastern Arkansas route were burning rice hulls. Believing the hulls could be used as poultry litter, Hunt got a contract to haul away the hulls and began selling them to chicken farmers.

In 1961 he began the J.B. Hunt Company with help from future Arkansas governor Winthrop Rockefeller, who owned Winrock grass company, where Hunt bought sod for one of his side businesses. Hunt developed a machine to compress the rice hulls, which made their transportation profitable, and within a few years the company was the world's largest producer of rice hulls for poultry litter.

Still looking for new opportunities, Hunt bought some used trucks and refrigerated trailers in 1969, though the company continued to focus on its original business. In the 1970s it found that the ground rice hulls made a good base for livestock vitamins and medications. Buyers of the ground hulls included Pfizer and Eli Lilly. J.B. Hunt, with Pfizer's backing, soon began selling a vitamin premix to feed companies.

In the 1980s J.B. Hunt's trucking division grew dramatically and became lucrative as the trucking industry was being deregulated. In 1981-82 the Hunt trucking business had higher margins than most trucking firms. In 1983, when J.B. Hunt Transport Services went public, Hunt sold the rice hull business to concentrate on trucking.

By 1986 J.B. Hunt was the US's third-largest irregular-route trucking company. The time was ripe to expand, and it began trucking in Canada (1988) and Mexico (1989). It also formed an alliance in 1989 with Santa Fe Pacific Railroad (now Burlington Northern Santa Fe) to provide intermodal services between the West Coast and the Midwest.

The company began adding computers to its trucks in 1992 to improve data exchange and communication on the road. J.B. Hunt also formed a joint venture with Latin America's largest transportation company, Transportación Marítima Mexicana. Founder Hunt retired in 1995 and became senior chairman.

J.B. Hunt tried hauling automobiles in 1996 but abandoned the idea when it found that cars were easily dented on intermodal trailers. More in line with the trucking company's long-term goals was an effort to stabilize its roster of drivers. It raised wages by one-third in 1997 to counteract driver shortages and high turnover. That

year J.B. Hunt sold its underperforming flatbed-trucking unit (renamed Charger Inc.).

In 1998 the company reaped the benefits of greater profits from its efforts to retain drivers. The next year it began testing a satellite system from ORBCOMM Global to track empty trailers.

The company combined its J.B. Logistics (JBL) unit with the logistics businesses of five other truckers in 2000 to form Transplace.com (later known as Transplace). Also that year J.B. Hunt inked a $100 million deal with Wal-Mart to increase its full-truckload services to the retailer by 50%. In 2002 J.B. Hunt bought a 10% stake in Transplace from Werner Enterprises, increasing its stake in the logistics company to 37%.

Founder Hunt stepped down from the company's board in 2004. He died in 2006.

In late 2009 J.B. Hunt sold its stake in Transplace to an affiliate of investment firm CI Capital Partners LLC.

EXECUTIVES

Chairman: Wayne Garrison, age 57, $564,710 total compensation
President, CEO, and Director: Kirk Thompson, age 56, $3,166,995 total compensation
EVP and COO: Craig Harper, age 52, $922,200 total compensation
EVP Finance and Administration, CFO, and Corporate Secretary: David G. Mee, age 49, $1,135,535 total compensation
EVP and Chief Marketing Officer; President, Intermodal: Paul R. Bergant, age 63, $901,277 total compensation
EVP; President, Integrated Capacity Solutions: Shelley Simpson, age 38
EVP; President, Dedicated Contract Services: John N. Roberts III, age 45
EVP and CIO: Kay Johnson Palmer, age 46
EVP Equipment and Properties: Bob D. Ralston, age 63
EVP Sales and Marketing, Truck and Intermodal: Terrence D. Matthews, age 51
SVP, Controller, and Chief Accounting Officer: Donald G. Cope, age 59
Auditors: Ernst & Young LLP

LOCATIONS

HQ: J.B. Hunt Transport Services, Inc.
615 J.B. Hunt Corporate Dr., Lowell, AR 72745
Phone: 479-820-0000 **Fax:** 479-820-3418
Web: www.jbhunt.com

PRODUCTS/OPERATIONS

2009 Sales

	$ mil.	% of total
Intermodal	1,764	55
Dedicated contract services	757	23
Trucking	447	14
Integrated capacity solutions	259	8
Adjustments	(24)	—
Total	**3,203**	**100**

COMPETITORS

APL Logistics
Canadian National Railway
Con-way Inc.
CSX
Hub Group
Kansas City Southern
Landstar System
Pacer International
Ryder System
Schneider National
Swift Transportation
Union Pacific
U.S. Xpress
Werner Enterprises
YRC Worldwide

HISTORICAL FINANCIALS
Company Type: Public

Income Statement
FYE: December 31

	REVENUE ($ mil.)	NET INCOME ($ mil.)	NET PROFIT MARGIN	EMPLOYEES
12/09	3,203	136	4.3%	14,171
12/08	3,732	201	5.4%	14,667
12/07	3,490	213	6.1%	15,795
12/06	3,328	220	6.6%	5,916
12/05	3,128	207	6.6%	16,367
Annual Growth	0.6%	(9.9%)	—	(3.5%)

2009 Year-End Financials

Debt ratio: 87.8%
Return on equity: 23.3%
Cash ($ mil.): 8
Current ratio: 1.46
Long-term debt ($ mil.): 565

No. of shares (mil.): 123
Dividends
  Yield: 1.4%
  Payout: 41.9%
Market value ($ mil.): 3,979

Stock History
NASDAQ (GS): JBHT

	STOCK PRICE ($) FY Close	P/E High/Low	PER SHARE ($) Earnings	Dividends	Book Value
12/09	32.27	33 17	1.05	0.44	5.22
12/08	26.27	26 13	1.56	0.40	4.29
12/07	27.55	21 14	1.55	0.36	2.78
12/06	20.77	18 13	1.44	0.32	6.16
12/05	22.64	20 14	1.28	0.24	6.63
Annual Growth	9.3%	— —	(4.8%)	16.4%	(5.8%)

J. C. Penney

An old name in retailing, J. C. Penney has been busy reinventing itself to bring style to Middle America's department store shoppers. The company's chain of more than 1,100 JCPenney department stores in the US and Puerto Rico has found itself squeezed between upscale competitors and major discounters (Kohls, Target, Wal-Mart). The firm runs one of the top catalog operations in the US. J. C. Penney Corporation is a wholly owned subsidiary of holding company J. C. Penney Company (created in 2002), which is the publicly traded entity.

CEO Myron Ullman, an experienced retail veteran and former chief executive of archrival Macy's, has focused on affordable, high-quality fashion in his attempt to reshape Penney. Ullman has been aggressively expanding Penney's stable of private-label and exclusive brand offerings as a way to draw customers and foster brand loyalty. Ullman's latest move is an agreement with Liz Claiborne to make his store the exclusive department store retailer for Liz Claiborne-branded merchandise (other than footwear and beauty products) beginning in fall 2010.

Penney's American Living collection — developed exclusively for Penney by Polo Ralph Lauren's Global Brands Concepts — launched in 2008. It has emerged as the chain's largest exclusive brand by volume, offering men's, women's, and children's clothing; shoes; handbags; bedding; towels; window treatments; luggage; furniture; and swimwear. Cindy Crawford's newest collaboration with Penney, a jewelry line called One Kiss, launched in April 2010. Other big names in Penney's stable include Nicole Miller, Joseph Abboud, and the Olsen twins. All have exclusive deals with Penney.

In a bid to attract younger and more affluent shoppers, Penney has teamed up with beauty purveyor Sephora USA, which operates about 200 Sephora ministores inside Penney's department stores. Other innovations to drive sales include a tie-in with the celebrity-focused magazine *People StyleWatch*. Penney's "must have" fashion items will be showcased in its pages, as well as in Penney stores and online.

Like Macy's, which aims to be the department store brand of choice for Middle America, J.C. Penney is also doing its best to recapture the middle ground between discount chains and more upscale department stores. But instead of expanding through acquisitions — as Macy's did with its purchase of May Department Stores — Penney is doing it through new store openings and relocations.

HISTORY

In 1902 James Cash Penney and two former employers opened the Golden Rule, a dry goods store, in Kemmerer, Wyoming. Penney bought out his partners in 1907 and opened stores that sold soft goods in small towns. Basing his customer service policy on his Baptist heritage, he held employees (called "associates") to a high moral code.

The firm incorporated in Utah in 1913 as the J. C. Penney Company, with headquarters in Salt Lake City, but it moved to New York City the next year to improve buying and financial operations. It expanded to nearly 1,400 stores in the 1920s and went public in 1929. The company grew during the Depression with its reputation for high quality and low prices.

J. C. Penney rode the postwar boom, and by 1951 sales had surpassed $1 billion. It introduced credit plans in 1958 and entered catalog retailing in 1962 with its purchase of General Merchandise Co. The next year the stores added hard goods, which allowed them to compete with Sears and Montgomery Ward.

The company formed J. C. Penney Insurance in the mid-1960s and bought Thrift Drug in 1969. The chain continued to grow, and in 1973, two years after Penney's death, there were 2,053 stores. Also in the 1970s J. C. Penney began its ill-fated foray overseas by buying chains in Belgium and Italy in hopes of duplicating its US formula — giant department stores.

It bought Delaware-based First National Bank in 1983 (renamed J. C. Penney National Bank in 1984) to issue MasterCard and Visa cards. Stores refocused on soft goods during the 1980s and stopped selling automotive services, appliances, paint, hardware, and fabrics in 1983. It discontinued sporting goods, consumer electronics, and photographic equipment in 1987.

The next year J. C. Penney Telemarketing was formed to take catalog phone orders and provide telemarketing services for other companies. Also in 1988 the company moved its headquarters to Plano, Texas. J. C. Penney tried to move upmarket in the 1980s, enlisting fashion designer Halston. The line failed, however, so the company developed its own brands.

James Oesterreicher was named CEO in 1995. Facing a slow-growing department store business back home, the company then bought 272 drugstores from Fay's Inc. and 200 more from Rite Aid. In 1997 it acquired Eckerd (nearly 1,750 stores) for $3.3 billion, converting its other drugstores to the Eckerd name. The company also sold its $740 million credit card portfolio of J. C. Penney National Bank to Associates First Capital in 1997.

With its stock value falling, J. C. Penney announced in 1999 it would sell 20% of Eckerd in the form of a tracking stock, but it postponed the IPO three times. That year it also sold its private-label credit card operations to GE Capital and sold its store in Chile to department store chain Almacenas Paris.

In 2000 Oesterreicher retired and was replaced by Allen Questrom, who was hired because of the work he did turning around Federated Department Stores and Barneys New York.

In 2001 the company shuttered about 50 more department stores and drugstores. Also that year Dutch insurer AEGON acquired J. C. Penney's Direct Marketing Services (DMS) unit, including its life insurance subsidiaries, for $1.3 billion. The company changed its name to J. C. Penney Corporation in January 2002 and formed a holding company under its former name.

Despite a major initiative to remodel hundreds of Eckerd stores and centralize the drugstore chain's distribution and merchandising systems, sales gains continued to lag behind rivals. Ultimately J.C. Penney sold its drugstores operations to The Jean Coutu Group and CVS for $4.5 billion in cash in August 2004.

In 2004 Questrom stepped down and was succeeded by Myron E. "Mike" Ullman III.

In 2005 J. C. Penney's Brazilian subsidiary sold its controlling stake in the 60-store Brazilian department store chain through an IPO, which generated net proceeds of about $260 million.

In 2008 Penney unveiled its first Manhattan store just down 6th Avenue from Macy's flagship store on Herald Square.

EXECUTIVES

Chairman and CEO: Myron E. (Mike) Ullman III, age 63, $7,985,615 total compensation
EVP and CFO: Robert B. Cavanaugh, age 58, $1,982,449 total compensation
EVP and Chief Marketing Officer: Michael J. (Mike) Boylson
EVP and Senior General Merchandise Manager, Women's Apparel, Accessories, Handbags, Shoes, Fine Jewelry, Juniors, and Sephora: Elizabeth H. (Liz) Sweney, age 55
EVP, Chief Human Resources and Administration Officer: Michael T. Theilmann, age 45, $2,267,817 total compensation
EVP Product Development and Sourcing: Peter M. McGrath
EVP and Director Planning and Allocation: Clarence Kelley
EVP and Senior General Merchandise Manager, Men's, Home, and Children's: Steven (Steve) Lawrence, age 42
EVP and CIO: Thomas M. Nealon, age 49
EVP and Director, JCPenney Stores: Michael W. Taxter
EVP, General Counsel, and Secretary: Janet L. Dhillon, age 48

SVP Property Development: Thomas A. (Tom) Clerkin
SVP and General Merchandise Manager, Children's:
  Clark McNaught
SVP Corporate Strategy and Investor Relations:
  James (Jim) Kenney
SVP and Controller: Dennis P. Miller, age 57
SVP and Director Brand Marketing: Ruby Anik, age 52
SVP and Director Supply Chain Management; President
  JCP Logistics LP: Marie Lacertosa
VP Corporate Communications and Community
  Relations: Darcie M. Brossart
VP and Director Investor Relations:
  Phillip (Phil) Sanchez, age 49
Auditors: KPMG LLP

LOCATIONS

HQ: J. C. Penney Corporation, Inc.
  6501 Legacy Dr., Plano, TX 75024
Phone: 972-431-1000   Fax: 972-431-1362
Web: www.jcpenney.net

2010 Stores

	No.
Texas	93
California	80
Florida	60
Ohio	47
Michigan	44
New York	43
Illinois	42
Pennsylvania	41
North Carolina	36
Georgia	31
Indiana	30
Virginia	28
Minnesota	26
Missouri	26
Tennessee	26
Wisconsin	26
Arizona	23
Washington	23
Colorado	22
Kentucky	22
Alabama	21
Iowa	20
Oklahoma	19
Kansas	18
Mississippi	18
South Carolina	18
Maryland	17
New Jersey	17
Arkansas	16
Louisiana	16
Oregon	14
Massachusetts	13
Nebraska	12
Connecticut	10
New Hampshire	10
New Mexico	10
Puerto Rico	7
Other states	83
Total	**1,108**

PRODUCTS/OPERATIONS

2010 Sales

	% of total
Women's apparel	24
Home	19
Men's apparel & accessories	19
Children's apparel	11
Women's accessories, including Sephora	11
Family footwear	7
Fine jewelry	4
Services & other	5
Total	**100**

Major Product Lines

Accessories
Family apparel
Home furnishings
Jewelry
Shoes

Selected Private and Exclusive Labels

Ambrielle (intimate apparel)
American Living (apparel and home furnishings)
a.n.a. (casual women's apparel)
Arizona
Bisou Bisou
Cindy Crawford
Crazy Horse by Liz Claiborne (exclusive third-party
  brand)
Decree
east5th
Every Day Matters
Hunt Club
J. Ferrar
Jacqueline Ferrar
JCPenney Home Collection (bedding, furniture, window
  coverings)
Linden Street
Liz & Co.
nicole by Nicole Miller
Okie Dokie
Olsenboye
St. John's Bay
Sephora
Stafford
The Chris Madden for JCPenney Home
Worthington

COMPETITORS

Bed Bath & Beyond	Lands' End
Belk	Macy's
Bon-Ton Stores	Nine West
Brown Shoe	Nordstrom
Costco Wholesale	Otto GmbH & Co KG
Dillard's	Ross Stores
Dress Barn	Saks
Eddie Bauer llc	Sears
Foot Locker	Signet
The Gap	Stage Stores
J. Crew	Target
J. Jill Group	TJX Companies
Kmart	Wal-Mart
Kohl's	Zale

HISTORICAL FINANCIALS

Company Type: Subsidiary

Income Statement

FYE: Saturday nearest January 31

	REVENUE ($ mil.)	NET INCOME ($ mil.)	NET PROFIT MARGIN	EMPLOYEES
1/10	17,556	251	1.4%	154,000
1/09	18,486	572	3.1%	147,000
1/08	19,860	1,111	5.6%	155,000
1/07	19,903	1,153	5.8%	155,000
1/06	18,781	1,088	5.8%	151,000
Annual Growth	(1.7%)	(30.7%)	—	0.5%

2010 Year-End Financials

Debt ratio: 62.8%   Current ratio: —
Return on equity: —   Long-term debt ($ mil.): 2,999
Cash ($ mil.): —

Net Income History

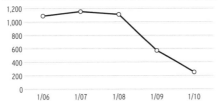

JDS Uniphase

JDS Uniphase (JDSU) is drawn to the warming glow of optical networks. Its Communications Test and Measurement division makes instruments and test tools used in optical and data networks, DSL services, cable networks, and digital video broadcast equipment. Its Communications and Commercial Optical Communications unit produces optical transmission and transport products, lasers, and photovoltaic cells and receivers sold to makers of network and other equipment. Advanced Optical Technologies makes optical coating and holographic technologies to protect documents, transaction cards, and consumer electronics against counterfeiting. JDSU sells to the networking, communications, medical, aerospace, and defense markets.

JDSU sold its factory in Shenzhen, China, to Sanmina-SCI in 2009. The transfer allowed the company to shed about 2,000 workers from its payroll. Sanmina-SCI will provide electronics manufacturing services to JDSU. The company also is planning to cut its research and development sites down from 19 to 12.

JDSU is contracting out more of its production, shifting several facilities to contract manufacturer Fabrinet and adding Benchmark Electronics as a manufacturing contractor during 2009 and 2010. The acquisitive company continues to make select acquisitions that complement or add to its product lines and markets.

In 2010 the company purchased the Network Solutions business of Agilent Technologies for $165 million in cash. The acquisition brings network protocol test and drive test products to the company and gives JDSU a market lead in wireless test instruments and systems.

In 2009 JDSU bought the Network Tools business of archrival Finisar, a maker of fiber-optic subsystems; the business added storage area network test tools and software, and became the storage network test unit in JDSU's Communications Test and Measurement business.

In 2008 JDSU acquired American Bank Note Holographics (ABNH) for about $138 million in cash and stock. The purchase strengthens its position in security products for brand protection and expands its position into security products for transaction card-based commerce.

The company has tried to shift its primary focus from the telecommunications market in order to reduce its dependence on a few customers and tap new revenue streams. JDSU turned to the storage networking and enterprise data communications markets to seek new customers for optical components. Meanwhile, communications test equipment emerged as the company's leading line of business.

HISTORY

Engineer Dale Crane was already making helium neon lasers in his garage when he left laser developer Spectra-Physics in 1979 to start Uniphase. Initially the company developed and marketed gas laser subsystems to manufacturers of biomedical, industrial process control, and printing equipment.

In 1992 Demax Software executive Kevin Kalkhoven became CEO, and Uniphase formed Ultrapointe, introducing the Ultrapointe laser imaging system for semiconductor production the following year. Expenses related to a gas laser subsystem patent-infringement suit filed by Spectra-Physics caused losses in 1993, the year Uniphase went public.

In the mid-1990s Uniphase began to use acquisitions to expand its market share and consolidate product lines. In 1995 the company bought optical components supplier United Technologies Photonics from United Technologies, entering the telecom market.

In 1997 it bought IBM's laser business and Australia-based Indx, a maker of reflection filters used to increase the carrying capacity of a fiber-optic strand. Uniphase's 1998 acquisitions included Philips Optoelectronics (semiconductor lasers) and Broadband Communications Products (fiber-optic transmitters and receivers). The company sold its Ultrapointe unit to chip equipment maker KLA-Tencor late that year. The acquisition spree contributed to losses for fiscal 1997 and 1998.

In 1999 Uniphase merged with JDS FITEL, a Canada-based maker of fiber-optic communications gear, in a $7 billion deal. JDS FITEL, founded in 1981 by four Nortel engineers, focused on making so-called "passive" fiber-optic components that route and manipulate optical signals. It was a complementary fit to Uniphase's "active" gear that generates and transmits signals. The combined company named itself JDS Uniphase. Both JDS FITEL and Uniphase aggressively pursued acquisitions prior to the merger, and JDS Uniphase continued shopping.

In fiscal 2000, following a huge run-up in its share price, JDS Uniphase made 10 acquisitions, including EPITAXX (optical detectors and receivers) and Optical Coating Laboratory. Its largest acquisition was of rival E-Tek Dynamics (for $20.4 billion), which JDSU used to further increase its capacity to produce passive components such as amplifiers and better equip itself to offer customers complete optical systems. That year Kalkhoven retired, and co-chairman Jozef Straus (former CEO of JDS FITEL) was named as his replacement.

In 2001 JDSU bought rival SDL, a maker of equipment that lets customers send multiple light signals over a single fiber, in a $17 billion stock deal. JDS Uniphase faced a sharp drop in sales following the spending spree it used to build a presence in the optical telecommunications equipment market. In 2001 the company began a monumental restructuring program intended to offset massive losses of more than $56 billion brought on by a collapse of the global telecom market. JDSU subsequently cut its workforce by nearly three-quarters and shut down redundant operations and non-essential facilities. It closed more than 50 facilities worldwide, most of them in North America.

Straus stepped down as CEO in 2003; director Kevin Kennedy took over as chief. Also that year, JDSU sold its MEMS (microelectromechanical systems) for about $4 million; JDSU paid 140 times that amount for the technology in 2000.

In 2005 JDSU purchased network test and management systems provider Acterna for approximately $760 million. In 2007 the company acquired Picolight, which makes optical pluggable transceivers.

Kevin Kennedy resigned as president and CEO in 2008, after the perennially unprofitable company reported yet another quarterly loss. While quitting his executive posts at the end of the year, following five years as chief executive, Kennedy remained on the JDSU board as vice chairman. He left to become president and CEO of Avaya.

EXECUTIVES

Chairman: Martin A. (Marty) Kaplan, age 72
Vice Chairman: Kevin J. Kennedy, age 54, $5,945,954 total compensation
President, CEO, and Director: Thomas H. (Tom) Waechter, age 57, $2,155,167 total compensation
Head Executive Operations: Judith Kay
EVP; President, Communications Test and Measurement Group: David (Dave) Holly, age 44, $1,157,630 total compensation
EVP and CFO: David W. Vellequette, age 53, $1,395,230 total compensation
EVP; President, Communications & Commercial Optical Products: Alan S. Lowe, age 47, $1,974,078 total compensation
SVP Information Technology: John Rough
SVP Sales, Communications Test and Measurement Business: Bart Freedman
SVP Corporate Development and Marketing: Sharad Rastogi, age 42
SVP Advanced Optical Technologies Product Group: Roy W. Bie, age 52, $959,044 total compensation
VP and Senior Advisor, Optical Technologies: David Gudmundson, age 45
VP and Senior Advisor: Alan (Al) Etterman, age 59
VP Communications Test and Measurement Business: Jerry Gentile
VP and General Manager, Communications Test and Measurement Business: Lars Friedrich
VP and General Manager, Solutions Division, Communcations Test and Measurement Business: Tom Smith
VP and General Manager, Communications Test and Measurement Business: Jim Nerschook
VP Global Services, Communications Test and Measurement Business: David Opsahl
Investor Relations: Michelle Levine
Human Resources: Brett Hooper, age 47
Auditors: Ernst & Young LLP

LOCATIONS

HQ: JDS Uniphase Corporation
430 N. McCarthy Blvd., Milpitas, CA 95035
Phone: 408-546-5000   **Fax:** 408-546-4300
Web: www.jdsu.com

2009 Sales

	$ mil.	% of total
Americas	591.6	46
Europe	402.1	31
Asia/Pacific	300.7	23
Total	**1,294.4**	**100**

PRODUCTS/OPERATIONS

2009 Sales

	$ mil.	% of total
Communications Test & Measurement	606.2	47
Communications & Commercial Optical Products	481.1	37
Advanced Optical Technologies	208.4	16
Adjustments	(1.3)	—
Total	**1,294.4**	**100**

Selected Products

Optical Communications
  Components
    High-power pump lasers
    Modulators
    Switches and attenuators
    Wavelength division multiplexing couplers, filters, isolators, and circulators
  Modules and subsystems
    Agile optical amplifiers
    Agile optical switches
    Agile transmission modules
    Optical channel monitors
    Optical layer subsystems
    Transceivers and transponders
    Transmitters

Communications Test and Measurement
  Communications test and monitoring instruments
  Network test and management systems
Advanced Optical Technologies
  Custom optics
  Decorative products
  Document authentication and brand protection
Lasers
  Argon ion lasers
  Diode-pumped solid-state lasers
  Fiber lasers
  Helium-neon lasers
  Industrial diode lasers
  Photonic power products

COMPETITORS

Anritsu	MRV Communications
Apogee Enterprises	New Focus
Asahi Glass	Newport Corp.
Avago Technologies	Nikon
BASF SE	Nitto Denko
Coherent, Inc.	Oclaro
Cymer	Oplink Communications
Deposition Sciences	Opnext
DiCon Fiberoptics	ROFIN-SINAR
EMCORE	Spectra-Physics
EXFO	Spirent
Finisar	Sumitomo Electric
FUJIFILM	Sunrise Telecom
Fujitsu	Sycamore Networks
Furukawa Electric	Tektronix
Harmonic	Tollgrade Communications
IPG Photonics	Toppan Printing
Merck KGaA	Toray Industries
Mitsubishi Electric	

HISTORICAL FINANCIALS

Company Type: Public

Income Statement

FYE: June 30

	REVENUE ($ mil.)	NET INCOME ($ mil.)	NET PROFIT MARGIN	EMPLOYEES
6/09	1,294	(866)	—	4,000
6/08	1,530	(22)	—	7,100
6/07	1,397	(26)	—	7,000
6/06	1,204	(151)	—	7,099
6/05	712	(261)	—	5,022
Annual Growth	**16.1%**	**—**		**(5.5%)**

2009 Year-End Financials

Debt ratio: 37.8%
Return on equity: —
Cash ($ mil.): 287
Current ratio: 3.58
Long-term debt ($ mil.): 325

No. of shares (mil.): 220
Dividends
  Yield: —
  Payout: —
Market value ($ mil.): 1,260

Stock History

NASDAQ (GS): JDSU

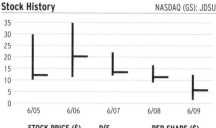

				35
				30
				25
				20
				15
				10
				5
				0
6/05	6/06	6/07	6/08	6/09

	STOCK PRICE ($) FY Close	P/E High/Low	PER SHARE ($) Earnings	Dividends	Book Value
6/09	5.72	— —	(4.02)	—	3.91
6/08	11.36	— —	(0.10)	—	8.25
6/07	13.43	— —	(0.12)	—	7.78
6/06	20.24	— —	(0.72)	—	7.19
6/05	12.08	— —	(1.44)	—	6.04
Annual Growth	**(17.0%)**	— —		—	**(10.3%)**

Jefferies Group

Because smaller companies need hostile-takeover advice, too. Jefferies Group (along with its main subsidiary Jefferies & Company) raises capital, performs securities trading and research, and provides advisory services for small and mid-sized companies in the US. Serving about 2,500 institutional clients worldwide, the company also trades derivatives and commodities and makes markets for some 5,000 US and international equities. Jefferies Group also oversees more than $3 billion on behalf of investors and private clients. Jefferies made a move into the municipal business in 2009 and now serves national and local governments. The company has about 25 offices in North America, Europe, and Asia.

Despite some initial apprehension in light of the economic downturn, Jefferies Group was able to quickly regain momentum and it actually enhanced its capabilities, grew its staff, and diversified its business.

Jefferies Group was impacted by the uncertainty in the global markets in 2008 and struggled with declining revenue. The company, which had been focused on expanding into Latin America and the Middle East, put the brakes on some of its expansion plans. It also announced in late 2008 that it would cut more than 10% of its workforce and close offices in Dubai, Singapore, and Tokyo. But the pendulum quickly swung back in the other direction. After financial markets regained momentum, Jefferies rebounded and was able to post record operating results in 2009, thanks in part to its broad success in the fixed income business. The company then began expanding its team once again in Asia, Latin America, and other emerging markets. Also, in late 2009, Jefferies launched a European government bond sales and trading platform in London.

In addition to serving government clients Jefferies has a long tradition of serving markets such as aerospace and defense, consumer energy, financial services, gaming and leisure, health care, industrial, maritime, media, and technology.

Leucadia National Corporation owns nearly 30% of Jefferies. Chairman Richard Handler owns about 6% of the company.

HISTORY

Former cowboy and stock exchange clerk Boyd Jefferies founded Jefferies & Company in 1962. The firm referred customers to brokers in exchange for cuts of their commissions. In 1969 mutual fund giant Investors Diversified Services (IDS) acquired the upstart. Because IDS was not a broker, Jefferies was kicked off the NYSE and increased its off-exchange activities.

Boyd Jefferies bought back his company in 1973 and took it public in 1983. Because the SEC had less control over off-exchange trades, Jefferies was a popular stop for greenmailers amassing stock for hostile takeovers. By 1986 the firm was in Japan, Switzerland, and the UK.

After 1987's "Black Monday" stock crash it was revealed that Jefferies had illegally "parked" stocks for Ivan Boesky. Boyd Jefferies pleaded guilty to SEC rules violations, resigned, and sold his interest in the company. New CEO Frank Baxter launched subsidiary Investment Technology Group (ITG). When Michael Milken's Drexel Burnham Lambert failed in 1990, Baxter hired scores of former Drexelites.

During the 1990s ITG grew along with demand for off-exchange trading. In 1999 Jefferies merged ITG into a separate company, spinning off its other operations as the new Jefferies Group. Jefferies formed an alliance with Crédit Lyonnais' US brokerage subsidiary and bought a stake in online bond trading system LIMITrader.com, which had mostly ceased operations by 2001.

At the end of 2000 Baxter retired as CEO but stayed on as chairman until 2002. He was succeeded in both capacities by Jefferies Group veteran Richard Handler. Also in 2000, Jefferies bought The Europe Company to boost its international operations.

The company's Helfant Group subsidiary (which was renamed Jefferies Execution Services in 2004) was created from the 2002 merger of Lawrence Helfant and W&D Securities.

Jefferies Group enhanced its capital-raising capabilities by acquiring Helix Associates, a UK-based private equity fund placement firm, in 2005. Jefferies & Company was fined $5.5 million by the NASD and $4.2 million by the SEC in 2006 for giving nearly $2 million worth of improper gifts to equity traders at Fidelity.

Jefferies Group acquired the financial services investment banking business of Putnam Lovell from National Bank of Canada in 2007. Two years later it acquired First Albany Securities, which specializes in municipal capital markets, from DEPFA.

EXECUTIVES

Chairman and CEO; President and CEO, Jefferies & Company: Richard B. Handler, age 48, $7,145,270 total compensation
Vice Chairman and Co-Head of Investment Banking, Jefferies & Company: Andrew R. Whittaker, age 46
EVP and Co-Head of Investment Banking: Chris M. Kanoff, age 51
EVP and CFO: Peregrine C. de M. (Peg) Broadbent, age 45, $3,004,515 total compensation
EVP, General Counsel, and Secretary: Lloyd H. Feller, age 67, $2,906,219 total compensation
SVP MBS and ABS Sales, Chicago: Elizabeth Harper
SVP Par Loan Trading: John Gally
SVP and Global Head of Compliance: Robert J. (Bob) Albano
SVP Private Client Services Department, Jefferies & Company: Michael W. Hyde
SVP Investment Banking Technology, Jefferies & Company: Omer Soykan
SVP and Chief Strategist, Emerging Markets Sales and Trading, Jefferies & Company: Eric Ollom, age 47
SVP Prime Brokerage Services, Jefferies & Company: Robin H. Fink
Treasurer: Charles J. (Chuck) Hendrickson, age 59, $901,267 total compensation
SVP Prime Brokerage Services, Jefferies & Company: Jeffrey M. McCarthy
Chairman, Randall & Dewey: Ralph Eads III
Co-Head Investment Banking: Alec L. Ellison, age 46
President International and Co-Head Investment Banking: David Weaver
Global Head Investment Banking and Capital Markets, Jefferies & Company, Inc.: Benjamin D. (Ben) Lorello
Global Head Equity Research, Jefferies & Company: Steven R. Black
Auditors: KPMG LLP

LOCATIONS

HQ: Jefferies Group, Inc.
520 Madison Ave., 10th Fl., New York, NY 10022
Phone: 212-284-2300   **Fax:** 212-284-2111
Web: www.jefco.com

PRODUCTS/OPERATIONS

2009 Sales

	$ mil.	% of total
Principal transactions	843.9	34
Interest	567.4	23
Commissions	512.3	21
Investment banking	474.3	19
Other	74.8	3
Total	**2,472.7**	**100**

Selected Subsidiaries

Jefferies & Company, Inc.
Jefferies Asset Management LLC
Jefferies Execution Services, Inc.
Jefferies Finance, LLC
Jefferies Financial Products, LLC
Jefferies High Yield Holdings, LLC
Jefferies High Yield Trading, LLC
Jefferies International Limited (UK)
Jefferies International (Holdings) Limited (UK)
Jefferies Investment Management Limited (UK)

COMPETITORS

Arlington Asset Investment	Lehman Brothers
Banc of America Securities	Lincoln International
Collins Stewart (US)	Merrill Lynch
Cowen Group	N M Rothschild & Sons
Deutsche Bank Alex.	Piper Jaffray
Brown	RBC Wealth Management
Goldman Sachs	Robert W. Baird & Co.
Houlihan Lokey	Thomas Weisel Partners
JPMorgan Chase	UBS Financial Services
KBW	Wedbush Morgan
Lazard	WR Hambrecht

HISTORICAL FINANCIALS

Company Type: Public

Income Statement

FYE: December 31

	REVENUE ($ mil.)	NET INCOME ($ mil.)	NET PROFIT MARGIN	EMPLOYEES
12/09	2,473	280	11.3%	2,628
12/08	1,683	(536)	—	2,270
12/07	2,719	145	5.3%	2,568
12/06	1,963	204	10.4%	2,254
12/05	1,498	157	10.5%	2,045
Annual Growth	13.4%	15.5%	—	6.5%

2009 Year-End Financials

Debt ratio: 133.9%
Return on equity: 12.6%
Cash ($ mil.): 1,853
Current ratio: —
Long-term debt ($ mil.): 3,092
No. of shares (mil.): 172
Dividends
　Yield: 0.0%
　Payout: —
Market value ($ mil.): 4,074

Stock History

NYSE: JEF

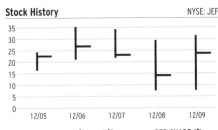

	STOCK PRICE ($) FY Close	P/E High/Low		PER SHARE ($) Earnings	Dividends	Book Value
12/09	23.73	22	6	1.38	0.00	13.45
12/08	14.06	—	—	(3.23)	0.25	12.36
12/07	23.05	35	23	0.97	0.50	10.26
12/06	26.82	25	15	1.42	0.45	9.21
12/05	22.49	21	14	1.16	0.25	7.50
Annual Growth	1.4%	—	—	4.4%	—	15.7%

The J. M. Smucker Company

The J. M. Smucker Company is best known for sweet and sticky fruity stuff, but coffee also fattens its bottom line. The #1 US producer of jams, jellies, and preserves also makes dessert toppings, juices, and specialty fruit spreads under names such as Smucker's, Laura Scudder's, and Knott's Berry Farm. The company is home to the #1 coffee brand in the US — Folgers. Many of its brands, including Folgers, Smucker's, Jif, and Crisco, are US market leaders. Smucker's roster also includes baking-goods brands Hungry Jack, Pillsbury, and Eagle, Carnation, and PET evaporated milk products. The company has manufacturing and processing facilities in the US and Canada.

As a result of the Folger purchase the company is undergoing restructuring and now operates four segments — US retail coffee market (Folgers, Millstone, and Dunkin' Donuts coffees); US retail consumer market (Smucker's, Jif, and Hungry Jack brands); US retail oils and baking market (Crisco, Eagle Brand, Martha White, Pillsbury, and White Lily brands); and special markets (sales in the foodservice and health and natural foods stores sectors).

In 2010 Smucker sold the Hungry Jack and Idaho Spuds frozen potato brands to Basic American Foods, which had already been co-packing the products for Smucker. The divestiture was part of a product and resource realignment by Smucker. The Hungry Jack pancake mix and syrup products were not part of the transaction.

In a major acquisition, the company purchased The Folger Coffee Company from Procter & Gamble in 2008. The all-stock transaction was valued at some $3 billion. As part of the Folgers deal, the company gained operations in Cincinnati, New Orleans, Kansas City, and Sherman, Texas, as well as some 1,250 employees (its pre-deal employee number was about 3,500). The Folgers coffee deal rocketed the company to the top tier of US coffee purveyors.

Never forgetting the spread on the bread of its bottom line, in 2008 Smucker also acquired the jam and jelly business, Knott's Berry Farm, from ConAgra. Both the Knott's and Folger deals were in line with the company's strategy to offer top name brands. To this end (and in addition to the Dunkin' Donuts agreement), Smucker has royalty-free licensing agreements with General Mills, National Dairy Holdings, and Nestlé to make and sell, consecutively, Pillsbury flour and baking mixes, Borden canned milk and eggnog, and Carnation canned milk.

Wal-Mart accounted for about 27% of the company's sales for its 2010 fiscal year.

HISTORY

Jerome Smucker began operating a steam-powered cider mill in 1897 for farmers in Orrville, Ohio, but he found that his biggest business was selling apple butter made using a secret Smucker family recipe. By the 1920s The J. M. Smucker Company had begun producing a full line of preserves and jellies, and in 1935 it acquired its first fruit-processing operations.

Under Jerome's grandson, Paul Smucker, the company gained widespread national distribution by the mid-1960s. Tim Smucker succeeded his father, Paul, as president in 1981, then as chairman in 1987, when his brother Richard became president.

The company's growth has been enhanced through the development of its industrial fruit fillings business and acquisitions of domestic natural juice and peanut butter companies, including Knudsen & Sons (1984), After the Fall (1994), and Laura Scudder's (from National Grape Co-op, 1994). It has gradually expanded internationally through acquisitions. In 1993 it acquired the jam, preserves, and pie-filling unit of Canada's Culinar. In a 1998 deal Smucker purchased Australia's Allowrie jam and Lackersteens marmalade lines.

Smucker sold its flagging Mrs. Smith's frozen pie business to Flowers in 1997, less than two years after buying the unit from Kellogg. It bought Kraft's domestic fruit spread unit in 1997 and in 1999 purchased the northwestern Adams peanut butter business from Pro-Fac Cooperative. Smucker kept the Adams name but shifted packaging to its Pennsylvania peanut butter plant.

Spreading into retail, the company opened a store in 1999 in its hometown of Orrville and then launched online and catalog sales. Also that year Smucker bought a fruit filling plant in Brazil from Groupe Danone, a major customer. During 2000 the company's Henry Jones Foods subsidiary (Australia) purchased Taylor Foods (sauces, marinades).

Smucker acquired International Flavors & Fragrances' formulated fruit and vegetable preparation businesses in 2001. Moving beyond its stronghold in natural peanut butter brands, the next year Smucker purchased the Jif peanut butter and Crisco cooking oil and shortening brands from Procter & Gamble. The $670 million purchase price for Jif and Crisco included shifting 53% of Smucker stock into the hands of P&G shareholders.

A decision to concentrate on North America led to the $37 million sale of Australian subsidiary Henry Jones Foods in 2004. Also that year, Smucker sold its operations in Brazil to Cargill and closed down two fruit processing plants in California and Oregon. Its purchase of International Multifoods that year added an array of US brands to the Smucker family, including Pillsbury flour, baking mixes, and ready-to-spread frostings; Hungry Jack pancake mixes, syrup, and potato side dishes; Martha White baking mixes and ingredients; and PET evaporated milk brands. Canadian brands included Robin Hood flour and baking mixes, Bick's pickles and condiments, and Golden Temple flour and rice.

To further its strategy of concentrating on its core retail brands, in 2005 Smucker sold its US foodservice and bakery business and the Canadian operations of Gourmet Baker (all part of its International Multifoods acquisition) to Value Creation Partners. The following year, the company sold its Canadian grain-based foodservice operations and industrial businesses to Cargill and CHS Inc. The operations were integrated into leading US flour miller Horizon Milling (which is jointly owned by Cargill and CHS). Adding to its name-brand offerings in 2006, Smucker acquired the White Lily brand of flours, baking mixes, and frozen biscuits from C.H. Guenther.

The company extended its baking offerings with the 2007 acquisition of sweetened condensed and evaporated milk producer Eagle Family Foods Holdings.

EXECUTIVES

Executive Chairman, President, and Co-CEO:
Richard K. Smucker, age 62,
$7,977,283 total compensation
Chairman and Co-CEO: Timothy P. (Tim) Smucker,
age 66, $6,830,263 total compensation
SVP and CFO: Mark R. Belgya, age 49,
$1,856,506 total compensation
SVP Corporate and Organization Development:
Barry C. Dunaway, age 47,
$1,767,515 total compensation
SVP Logistics and Operations: Dennis J. Armstrong,
age 55
VP and Controller: John W. Denman, age 53
VP Information Services and CIO: Andrew G. Platt,
age 54
VP Alternate Channels: Kenneth A. Miller, age 61
VP, Deputy General Counsel, and Corporate Secretary:
Jeannette L. Knudsen, age 40
VP US Grocery Sales: James A. Brown, age 49
VP and General Counsel: M. Ann Harlan, age 50
VP and General Manager, Smucker Natural Foods:
Julia L. Sabin, age 50
VP Marketing Communications:
Christopher R. Resweber, age 48
VP Industry and Government Affairs: Albert W. Yeagley,
age 62
VP Sales, Grocery Market: John F. Mayer, age 54
Treasurer: Debra A. Marthey
Director; President, US Retail, Coffee: Vincent C. Byrd,
age 55, $3,108,168 total compensation
President, US Retail, Smucker's, Jif, and Hungry Jack:
Steven T. Oakland, age 49,
$2,039,409 total compensation
Director; President, Special Markets: Mark T. Smucker,
age 40
Director; President, US Retail, Oils and Baking:
Paul Smucker Wagstaff, age 40
Auditors: Ernst & Young LLP

LOCATIONS

HQ: The J. M. Smucker Company
1 Strawberry Ln., Orrville, OH 44667
Phone: 330-682-3000   **Fax:** 330-684-6410
Web: www.smucker.com

PRODUCTS/OPERATIONS

2010 Sales

	$ mil.	% of total
US retail coffee market	1,700.5	37
US retail consumer market	1,125.3	24
US retail oils & baking market	905.7	20
Special markets	873.8	19
Total	**4,605.3**	**100**

Selected Products

Baking ingredients
Baking mixes
Coffee
Condiments
Dessert toppings
Edible oils
Evaporated milk
Frozen sandwiches
Fruit and vegetable juices
Fruit spreads
Jams
Jellies
Juice beverages
Peanut butter
Pickles
Preserves
Ready-to-spread frostings
Shortening
Sweetened, condensed milk
Syrups

Selected Brands

Adams (peanut butter)
After The Fall (juice beverages)
Bick's (pickles and condiments, Canada)
Crisco (cooking oils, shortening)
Crosse & Blackwell (chutneys, jellies, relishes, meat and seafood sauces)
Dickinson's (fruit spreads)
Double Fruit (fruit spreads, Canada)
Eagle Brand (canned milk products, dessert kits)
Europe's Best (frozen fruits and vegetables, Canada)
Folgers (coffee)
Golden Temple (flour and rice)
Hungry Jack (pancake mixes and syrups)
Jif (peanut butter)
Knott's Berry Farm (jams, jellies, preserves)
Laura Scudder's (peanut butter)
Martha White (baking mixes and ingredients)
Magnolia (sweetened condensed milk)
Millstone (coffee)
PET (canned milk products)
Pillsbury (flour, frostings, and refrigerated doughs)
Red River (hot cereal mix, Canada)
Rocket Juice (juice beverages)
Robin Hood (flour and baking mixes, Canada)
R.W. Knudsen (juice beverages)
Santa Cruz Organic (juice beverages)
Smucker's (dessert topping, jam, jelly, preserves, peanut butter)
Smucker's Goober (peanut butter)
Smucker's Simply Fruit (fruit spreads)
Smucker's Uncrustables (frozen peanut-butter-and-jelly sandwiches)
White Lily (flour)

COMPETITORS

B&G Foods	Hansen Natural
Boyd Coffee	Hershey
Caribou Coffee	Kraft Foods
Chiquita Brands	National Grape Cooperative
Coca-Cola	Nestlé
Coca-Cola North America	Ocean Spray
Community Coffee	PepsiCo
ConAgra	Pinnacle Foods
Cranberries Limited	Ralcorp
Darigold, Inc.	Rowland Coffee Roasters
Dean Foods	Sara Lee
Diedrich Coffee	Spectrum Organic
Dole Food	Starbucks
E.D. Smith	Tata Tea
General Mills	Tree Top
Glanbia Foods	Tropicana
Goya	Unilever
Green Mountain Coffee	Welch's
H. J. Heinz Limited	

HISTORICAL FINANCIALS

Company Type: Public

Income Statement

FYE: April 30

	REVENUE ($ mil.)	NET INCOME ($ mil.)	NET PROFIT MARGIN	EMPLOYEES
4/10	4,605	494	10.7%	4,850
4/09	3,758	266	7.1%	4,700
4/08	2,525	170	6.7%	3,250
4/07	2,148	157	7.3%	3,025
4/06	2,155	143	6.7%	3,500
Annual Growth	20.9%	36.2%	—	8.5%

2010 Year-End Financials

Debt ratio: 16.9%
Return on equity: 9.6%
Cash ($ mil.): 284
Current ratio: 2.56
Long-term debt ($ mil.): 900

No. of shares (mil.): 119
Dividends
  Yield: 2.3%
  Payout: 33.7%
Market value ($ mil.): 7,296

Stock History

NYSE: SJM

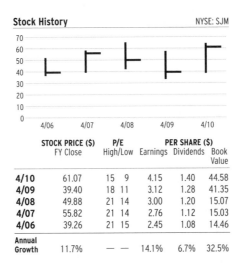

	STOCK PRICE ($) FY Close	P/E High/Low		PER SHARE ($) Earnings	Dividends	Book Value
4/10	61.07	15	9	4.15	1.40	44.58
4/09	39.40	18	11	3.12	1.28	41.35
4/08	49.88	21	14	3.00	1.20	15.07
4/07	55.82	21	14	2.76	1.12	15.03
4/06	39.26	21	15	2.45	1.08	14.46
Annual Growth	11.7%	—	—	14.1%	6.7%	32.5%

Jo-Ann Stores

Jo-Ann Stores has sewn up the leadership of the fabric store market. The company is the #1 fabric retailer in the US (ahead of Hancock Fabrics), with about 745 Jo-Ann Fabric and Craft and Jo-Ann stores in 48 states. The stores sell fabrics and sewing supplies, craft materials, frames, home decorations, artificial floral items, and seasonal goods. Most of the company's small-format stores (about 14,700 sq. ft.) are located in strip shopping centers and operate under the Jo-Ann Fabrics and Crafts name. The company also operates a growing number of more than 225 large-format (36,500 sq. ft.) Jo-Ann superstores and an e-commerce site, Joann.com. The company traces its roots back to the 1940s.

The recession in the US may bode well for the company's business, which saw a small uptick in sales of sewing products in 2009 and 2008 and a modest increase in its sales overall. Changes in consumer behavior, including families spending more time together and making their own gifts and clothes, should help Jo-Ann Stores in the long run.

Over the past few years the company's growth strategy has focused on its larger Jo-Ann superstores, which offer an expanded and more complete assortment of products than the smaller stores. In 2009 it opened 20 stores (15 large format and five small format) and remodeled another 30 locations. In 2010, 30 stores are slated to open, with the number of new store openings expected to increase by at least 10 stores in each of the following four years. However, in 2010 and beyond the average size of standard new stores will measure only about 22,000 sq. ft., with an even smaller footprint (15,000 sq. ft.) in urban areas.

The retailer is also partnering with celebrities, most recently Christie Brinkley, to raise its profile and spur sales. In spring 2009 the company launched the Christie Brinkley Home collection of organic cotton and other ecologically friendly fabrics.

HISTORY

Jo-Ann Stores' predecessor began in 1943 when the German immigrant Rohrbach family started Cleveland Fabric with the help of fellow immigrants, the Reichs. Alma, daughter of the Rohrbachs, worked at the store and was joined by Betty Reich in 1947.

Betty's and Alma's respective husbands, Martin Rosskamm and Freddy Zimmerman, also joined the company. At the urging of Martin (who eventually became chairman), Cleveland Fabric opened more stores, mainly in malls. As it moved beyond Cleveland, it adopted a new store name — Jo-Ann — devised from the names of Alma and Freddy's daughter Joan and Betty and Martin's daughter Jackie Ann. It changed its name to Fabri-Centers of America in 1968 and went public the following year.

The very postwar boom that brought Alma and Betty into the workforce worked against the company in the 1970s, as women tucked away their sewing baskets in favor of jobs outside their homes. As department stores responded to the trend and stopped offering sewing supplies, specialty fabric stores found a niche. But they soon faced competition from fabric superstores and heavily discounted ready-made clothing.

Martin and Betty's son Alan took over as president and CEO in 1985 and began to modernize the company and the stores. Trained in real estate law, he began focusing on opening larger stores in strip shopping centers, which offered cheaper leases than malls. The company had about 625 stores by mid-1989.

As its industry consolidated, Fabri-Centers held on, despite missteps such as its 1984 launch of the Cargo Express housewares chain (the money-losing venture, with about 40 stores at its peak, ended in 1994). The firm became the nation's #1 fabrics and crafts chain in 1994 when it bought 300-plus Cloth World stores. At the close of that deal, Fabri-Centers had nearly 1,000 stores, with locations in every state except Hawaii.

In 1995 Fabri-Centers opened a store on its home turf in Hudson, Ohio, that offered not only a range of fabric and craft items, but also home decorating merchandise, furniture, craft classes, and day care. At three times the size of its other stores, the Jo-Ann etc superstore helped the company pull in non-sewers looking for art supplies, picture frames, and decorating ideas. Jo-Ann etc became the focus of its growth.

Fabri-Centers paid $3.8 million in 1997 to settle SEC charges that it had overstated its profits during a 1992 debt offering. In 1998 it paid nearly $100 million for ailing Los Angeles-based fabric and craft company House of Fabrics, adding about 260 locations and strengthening its West Coast presence. Fabri-Centers then renamed itself Jo-Ann Stores and began placing all of its stores under the Jo-Ann name.

Jo-Ann continued relocating traditional stores and opening new shops while snipping underperforming locations. In 1999 the company signed a pact with Martha Stewart Living Omnimedia to sell fancy decorating fabrics under the Martha Stewart Home name. (As of 2003 the company no longer offers Martha Stewart's fabrics.)

Jo-Ann invested in and partnered with Idea Forest, an Internet-based arts and crafts retailer, in 2000 to run Jo-Ann's e-commerce site. In 2001 the company reported a $13.2 million loss (only the second in its history), in part because of inventory and distribution problems. As a result, Jo-Ann closed more than 90 underperforming stores and reduced the number of items carried in the shops.

In 2003 Jo-Ann Stores bought three stores in the Dallas-Fort Worth area from bankrupt MJDesigns. Those stores had a combined revenue of $16 million during the last fiscal year they operated under the former name.

In September 2005 CFO Brian P. Carney left the firm to join supermarket operator BI-LO.

In January 2006 Jo-Ann Stores eliminated 75 administrative jobs. In April the company completed construction of its new 700,000-sq.-ft. distribution center in Opelika, Alabama; the facility was designed to support growth in the South, specifically in Florida, Georgia, and Texas. Jo-Ann Stores operates two other distribution centers in California and Ohio. In July, Alan Rosskamm stepped down as chairman, president, and CEO (although he remains a director of the company) when Darrell Webb, formerly with Fred Meyer, was appointed as chairman and CEO. James Kerr became CFO in August. Previously, Kerr was the retailer's VP, controller, and chief accounting officer.

EXECUTIVES

Chairman and CEO: Darrell D. Webb, age 52, $7,484,533 total compensation
President and COO: Travis Smith, age 37, $2,061,654 total compensation
EVP and CFO: James C. Kerr, age 47, $1,252,119 total compensation
SVP, General Counsel and Secretary: David B. Goldston
EVP Store Operations: Kenneth (Ken) Haverkost, age 53, $1,345,231 total compensation
Auditors: Ernst & Young LLP

LOCATIONS

HQ: Jo-Ann Stores, Inc.
5555 Darrow Rd., Hudson, OH 44236
Phone: 330-656-2600   **Fax:** 330-463-6675
Web: www.joann.com

2010 Stores

	No.
California	81
Ohio	52
Florida	49
Pennsylvania	42
Michigan	41
New York	36
Texas	36
Illinois	33
Washington	28
Indiana	26
Oregon	24
Massachusetts	23
Virginia	23
Minnesota	20
Wisconsin	19
Maryland	16
Colorado	14
Arizona	13
Georgia	12
New Jersey	12
Missouri	11
Connecticut	10
Iowa	10
Utah	10
Other states	105
Total	**746**

PRODUCTS/OPERATIONS

2010 Sales

	% of total
Sewing products	52
Non-sewing products	48
Total	**100**

Selected Products

Softlines
  Fabrics
    Apparel fabrics used in the construction of garments (cottons, linens, wools, fleece, and outerwear)
    Craft fabrics (for quilting, craft, and holiday projects)
    Home-decorating fabrics (for window treatments, furniture, and bed coverings)
    Printed fabrics (juvenile designs, seasonal designs, National Football League logo prints, and proprietary print designs)
    Special-occasion fabrics (satins, metallics, and other fabrics for evening wear and bridal gowns)
  Patterns
  Sewing machines
  Sewing notions
    Buttons
    Cutting implements
    Elastics
    Pins
    Ribbons
  Tapes
  Threads
  Trims
  Zippers
Hardlines
  Accessories for arranging flowers and making wreaths
  Craft materials (for making stencils, dolls, jewelry, wood projects, wall décor, rubber stamps, memory books, and plaster)
  Custom floral arrangements
  Decorations
  Fine art materials
    Brushes
    Canvas
    Easels
    Paints (pastels, water colors, oils, and acrylics)
  Floral products line
  Framed art
  Full-service framing
  Gifts
  Hobby items
  Holiday supplies
  Home accessories
    Baskets
    Candles
    Potpourri
  Needlecraft items
  Needles
  Paint-by-number kits
  Paper
  Photo albums
  Picture-framing materials (custom frames, mat boards, glass, and backing materials)
  Plastic model kits and supplies
  Ready-made frames
  Seasonal products
  Silk, dried, and artificial flowers
  Wooden model kits and supplies
  Yarns and threads (for knitting, needlepoint, embroidery, cross-stitching, crocheting, and other stitchery)

COMPETITORS

A.C. Moore
Burnes Home Accents
Garden Ridge
Hancock Fabrics
Hobby Lobby
Kirkland's
Kmart
Martha Stewart Living
Michaels Stores
Pier 1 Imports
Target
Wal-Mart

HISTORICAL FINANCIALS

Company Type: Public

Income Statement

FYE: Saturday nearest January 31

	REVENUE ($ mil.)	NET INCOME ($ mil.)	NET PROFIT MARGIN	EMPLOYEES
1/10	1,991	67	3.3%	21,135
1/09	1,901	22	1.2%	21,708
1/08	1,879	15	0.8%	21,707
1/07	1,851	(3)	—	22,280
1/06	1,883	(23)	—	24,060
Annual Growth	**1.4%**	**—**	**—**	**(3.2%)**

2010 Year-End Financials

Debt ratio: 18.6%
Return on equity: 12.8%
Cash ($ mil.): 217
Current ratio: 2.10
Long-term debt ($ mil.): 105
No. of shares (mil.): 27
Dividends
  Yield: —
  Payout: —
Market value ($ mil.): 956

Stock History

NYSE: JAS

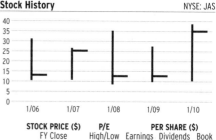

	STOCK PRICE ($) FY Close	P/E High/Low		PER SHARE ($) Earnings	Dividends	Book Value
1/10	35.02	15	4	2.51	—	20.71
1/09	12.77	31	12	0.86	—	17.49
1/08	12.69	56	15	0.62	—	16.11
1/07	25.28	—	—	(0.08)	—	15.01
1/06	13.13	—	—	(1.01)	—	14.63
Annual Growth	**27.8%**	**—**	**—**	**—**	**—**	**9.1%**

John Wiley & Sons

John Wiley & Sons might not adorn its books with shirtless hunks, but with such titles as *Patty's Industrial Hygiene and Toxicology,* who needs Fabio? The company publishes scientific, technical, and medical works, including journals and reference works such as *Current Protocols* and *Kirk-Othmer Encyclopedia of Chemical Technology*. In total, it publishes more than 1,600 journal titles. It also produces professional and nonfiction trade books, and is a publisher of college textbooks. The firm publishes the *For Dummies* how-to series, the travel guide brand *Frommer's*, and *CliffsNotes* study guides, as well. Wiley has publishing, marketing, and distribution centers in North America, Europe, Asia, and Australia.

In addition to acquiring (and divesting) companies, Wiley's corporate strategy relies heavily on forming partnerships. The company also focues on investing in new technology, such as the 2010 launch of the Wiley Online Library. The offering hosts a multidisciplinary collection of online resources covering a broad range of academic subjects.

Wiley's core business is its Scientific, Technical, Medical and Scholarly (STMS) division, which accounts for nearly 60% of sales. The company significantly boosted this holding with the acquisition of Blackwell Publishing for $1 billion in 2007, the largest purchase in the company's history. Blackwell subsequently became Wiley-Blackwell, a part of STMS; the unit is a leading publisher of journals and books for the academic, research, and professional markets focused on science, technology, medicine, social sciences, and humanities.

The company's second-largest revenue generator is its Professional/Trade division (about 25% of sales), which includes titles published under the *For Dummies*, *Frommer's*, *Betty Crocker*, *Weight Watchers*, *CliffsNotes*, and *Webster's New World* brands. Several books in the Professional/Trade division are released through partnerships with other media firms. In 2010 Wiley was named the exclusive global publisher of Bloomberg and Bloomberg Businessweek branded books, to be marketed as "BLOOMBERG PRESS, a Wiley imprint." In addition, the division publishes Meredith books in the lifestyles, pets, and education categories.

In addition to STMS and Professional/Trade units, Wiley operates a Higher Education division, which publishes textbooks and other educational materials. The division expanded in 2009, when it acquired the rights to publish a list of business and modern language textbooks from Cengage Learning. The purchase reflects the company's growth strategy of making acquisitions that complement its existing businesses, as the Cengage titles complement Wiley's existing programs in business and modern language.

The Wiley family controls the majority of voting stock through a trust.

HISTORY

Charles Wiley founded a bookstore when he was 25 years old in 1807 and began printing and marketing books for local authors in return for a share of the profits. Soon, prominent writers began meeting in the store's back room (known as "The Den"), which attracted more attention to the business. By the end of the Civil War, the firm (renamed John Wiley & Sons, after Charles' son) had become an established publisher of books on science and technology. Wiley pioneered technical textbooks that became industry standards. In 1899 it published Charles Davenport's *Statistical Methods* and in 1947 Hans Liepmann's *Aerodynamics of a Compressible Fluid,* among others. The company went public in 1962.

In 1989, Wiley acquired Alan R. Liss, a publisher of scientific journals. Four years later Bradford Wiley II took over as chairman of the company. Wiley sold its Canadian high school and Australian primary school textbook subsidiaries the next year and bought the professional computer book line of QED Information Services and UK-based science publisher Belhaven. Wiley teamed with publisher Adweek Magazines in 1995 to print media and marketing books under the name Adweek Books. Also that year the company purchased the publishing operations of Executive Enterprises.

In 1996 Wiley acquired a 90% stake in Germany's VCH Publishing Group, boosting the company's presence in the scientific and technical journal markets. The company increased its Teutonic knowledge base in 1998 by buying German scientific book publisher Huthig Publishing. In addition, it bought the publishing business of Chronimed (which included about 80 titles), a provider of health care products and pharmacy services. Also that year Wiley started

working with various online publishers on interactive quizzes in accounting and other educational fields.

In 1999 the company bought a number of college textbook titles from Pearson for $58 million, and later bought San Francisco-based business publisher Jossey-Bass from the same UK company for $82 million.

In 2001 the company bought Hungry Minds, publisher of the *For Dummies* series of how-to books, for about $185 million. The acquisition was the largest in the company's history at that time. It also bought Frank J. Fabozzi Publishing, a finance title publisher based in Pennsylvania. In 2002 the company moved its headquarters from New York to Hoboken, New Jersey. That year the company acquired 250 teacher education titles from Prentice Hall Direct, part of Pearson Education, for $6.5 million.

In 2005 the company sold Chronimed to MIM Corporation (now BioScrip). Wiley expanded in 2007 with the acquisition of Blackwell Publishing, which became Wiley-Blackwell.

EXECUTIVES

Chairman: Peter Booth Wiley, age 67
President, CEO, and Director: William J. (Will) Pesce, age 59, $7,209,914 total compensation
EVP and COO: Stephen M. (Steve) Smith, age 55
EVP; President, Professional and Trade Publishing: Mark Allin
EVP, CFO, and Operations Officer: Ellis E. Cousens, age 58, $2,305,612 total compensation
SVP Scientific, Technical, Medical, and Scholarly: Eric A. Swanson, age 62, $3,154,770 total compensation
SVP Scientific, Technical, Medical, and Scholarly: Steve Miron
SVP Information Technology and CIO: Warren C. Fristensky
SVP Corporate Communications: Deborah E. Wiley, age 64
SVP Human Resources: William J. Arlington, age 61
SVP and General Counsel: Gary M. Rinck, age 58
SVP Planning and Development: Timothy B. King, age 70
SVP Customer Service and Distribution: Clifford Kline
VP, Corporate Controller, and Chief Accounting Officer: Edward J. Melando, age 54
VP and Treasurer: Vincent Marzano, age 47
VP and Corporate Secretary: Josephine A. Bacchi-Mourtziou, age 63
VP and COO, Global HE: Joe Heider
COO, John Wiley & Sons Canada: Bill Zerter
Managing Director, John Wiley & Sons Australia, Ltd.: Heather Linaker
Auditors: KPMG LLP

LOCATIONS

HQ: John Wiley & Sons, Inc.
111 River St., Ste. 2000, Hoboken, NJ 07030
Phone: 201-748-6000 **Fax:** 201-748-6088
Web: www.wiley.com

2010 Sales

	$ mil.	% of total
US	866	51
Asia	234	14
UK	121	7
Germany	92	5
Australia	79	5
Canada	71	4
Other regions	236	14
Total	**1,699**	**100**

PRODUCTS/OPERATIONS

2010 Sales

	$ mil.	% of total
STMS	987	58
Professional trade	430	25
Higher education	282	17
Total	**1,699**	**100**

Selected Products

Educational textbooks
Electronic publications
Instructional materials
Online content
Professional books
Scientific, technical, and medical titles
Trade books

Selected Imprints

Betty Crocker
Capstone
CliffsNotes
Current Protocols
For Dummies
Frommer's
InfoPOEMs
Interscience
Jacaranda
J.K. Lasser
Jossey-Bass
Pfeiffer
Webster's New World
Weight Watchers
Wiley
WileyPLUS
Wiley-Blackwell
Wiley Online Library

COMPETITORS

Flat World Knowledge
Goodheart-Willcox
HarperCollins
IHS
Lonely Planet
McGraw-Hill
National Academies Press
O'Reilly Media
Pearson plc
Random House
Reader's Digest
Reed Elsevier Group
Scholastic
Simon & Schuster
Sterling Publishing
Thomson Reuters
Time Inc.
Wolters Kluwer
W.W. Norton

HISTORICAL FINANCIALS

Company Type: Public

Income Statement

	REVENUE ($ mil.)	NET INCOME ($ mil.)	NET PROFIT MARGIN	EMPLOYEES
				FYE: April 30
4/10	1,699	144	8.4%	5,100
4/09	1,611	128	8.0%	5,100
4/08	1,674	148	8.8%	4,800
4/07	1,235	100	8.1%	4,800
4/06	1,044	110	10.6%	3,600
Annual Growth	**12.9%**	**6.8%**	**—**	**9.1%**

2010 Year-End Financials

Debt ratio: 77.4%
Return on equity: 23.2%
Cash ($ mil.): 154
Current ratio: 0.72
Long-term debt ($ mil.): 559

No. of shares (mil.): 60
Dividends
  Yield: 1.3%
  Payout: 23.2%
Market value ($ mil.): 2,541

Stock History   NYSE: JW.A

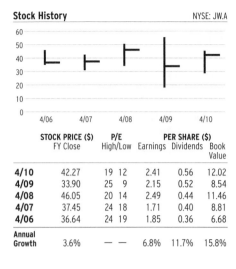

	STOCK PRICE ($) FY Close	P/E High/Low		PER SHARE ($) Earnings	Dividends	Book Value
4/10	42.27	19	12	2.41	0.56	12.02
4/09	33.90	25	9	2.15	0.52	8.54
4/08	46.05	20	14	2.49	0.44	11.46
4/07	37.45	24	18	1.71	0.40	8.81
4/06	36.64	24	19	1.85	0.36	6.68
Annual Growth	3.6%	—	—	6.8%	11.7%	15.8%

Johnson & Johnson

It's nearly impossible to get well without Johnson & Johnson (J&J). The diversified health care giant operates in three segments through more than 250 operating companies located in some 60 countries. Its Pharmaceuticals division makes drugs for an array of ailments, such as neurological conditions, blood disorders, autoimmune diseases, and pain. Top sellers are psoriasis drug Remicade and schizophrenia medication Risperdal. J&J's Medical Devices and Diagnostics division offers surgical equipment, monitoring devices, orthopedic products, and contact lenses, among other things. Its Consumer segment makes over-the-counter drugs and products for baby, skin, and oral care, as well as first aid and women's health.

Along with Risperdal and Remicade (which treats Crohn's disease and rheumatoid arthritis in addition to psoriasis), key drugs are anemia treatment Procrit (sold internationally as Eprex), attention deficit drug Concerta, anti-infectives Floxin and Levaquin, and epilepsy medicine Topamax. Its dermatological division offers acne treatment Retin-A, sun damage treatment Renova, and wound care gel Biafine.

The company's push for R&D growth is driven by the drug industry's biggest challenge: patent expiration. Global blockbusters Risperdal and Topamax lost patent protection in 2008 and 2009, respectively, and thus face competition from cheaper generics. The company still has market exclusivity for Risperdal Consta, a long-acting injectable version of the drug that is increasing its market penetration; Risperdal Consta received approval for the expanded application of bipolar disorder treatment in 2009.

Safety concerns and bad publicity have inflicted wounds on a couple of other J&J brands. Its anemia drug Procrit, which is prescribed for dialysis and chemotherapy patients, has been under fire after some studies indicated that patients on the drug were at higher risk for cardiovascular events, as well as possible worsening of their cancer. Another product, contraceptive patch Ortho Evra, is facing lawsuits over claims that the product creates a greater risk for blood clots than do birth control pills.

In its ever-expanding Medical Devices and Diagnostics division, many operating companies — including surgical supplies companies Ethicon and Ethicon Endo-Surgery, orthopedics device maker DePuy, vision care subsidiary Vistakon, and diagnostics unit Ortho-Clinical Diagnostics — have experienced strong sales growth. However, Cordis, a maker of cardiology products such as the Cypher drug-coated stent, has experienced declining sales due to increased competition and safety concerns over blood clotting in the stent market.

In 2009 J&J paid about $1.1 billion for Mentor Corporation, a maker of devices for aesthetic procedures. In 2010 Ethicon expanded through the acquisition of ear, nose, and throat device maker Acclarent for $785 million. In addition, J&J bought Cougar Biotechnology, an oncology research and development firm with a promising prostate cancer candidate, for about $1 billion.

Another bright spot for J&J has been its growing Consumer segment, which has also expanded through acquisitions over the years. Offerings include consumer brands Benadryl, Listerine, Lubriderm, Neutrogena, Rolaids, Splenda, Sudafed, Tylenol, and (of course) Johnson's.

HISTORY

Brothers James and Edward Mead Johnson founded their medical products company in 1885 in New Brunswick, New Jersey. In 1886 Robert joined his brothers to make the antiseptic surgical dressings he developed. The company bought gauze maker Chicopee Manufacturing in 1916. In 1921 it introduced two of its classic products, the Band-Aid and Johnson's Baby Cream.

Robert Jr. became chairman in 1932 and served until 1963. A WWII Army general, he believed in decentralization; managers were given substantial freedom, a principle still used today. Product lines in the 1940s included Ortho (birth control products) and Ethicon (sutures). In 1959 Johnson & Johnson bought McNeil Labs, which launched Tylenol (acetaminophen) as an OTC drug the next year. Foreign acquisitions included Switzerland's Cilag-Chemie (1959) and Belgium's Janssen (1961). The company focused on consumer products in the 1970s, gaining half the feminine protection market and making Tylenol the top-selling painkiller.

J&J bought Iolab, a developer of intraocular lenses used in cataract surgery, in 1980. Trouble struck in 1982 when someone laced Tylenol capsules with cyanide, killing eight people. The company's response is now a damage-control classic: It immediately recalled 31 million bottles and totally redesigned its packaging to prevent future tampering. The move cost $240 million but saved the Tylenol brand. The next year prescription painkiller Zomax was linked to five deaths and was pulled.

New products in the 1980s included ACUVUE disposable contact lenses and Retin-A. The company bought LifeScan (blood-monitoring products for diabetics) in 1986. In 1989 it began a joint venture with Merck to sell Mylanta and other drugs bought from ICI Americas.

The firm continued its acquisition and diversification strategy in the 1990s. After introducing the first daily-wear, disposable contact lenses in 1993, it bought skin-care product maker Neutrogena (1994) to enhance its consumer lines. To diversify its medical products and better compete for hospital business, it bought Mitek Surgical Products (1995) and heart disease product maker Cordis (1996).

In 1997 J&J bought the OTC rights to Motrin from Pharmacia (now Pfizer). In response to numerous negative events in 1998 — several drugs in late development fell through, rights to an anemia drug were lost, and the company's share of the coronary stent market fell — the firm cut jobs and consolidated plants worldwide to control inventory and improve service.

After more than 80 deaths were linked to its use, J&J pulled heartburn drug Propulsid from the US market in 2000. The company made headlines in 2002 with its INDEPENDENCE iBOT, a robotic wheelchair capable of climbing staircases and traversing rough terrain, made by subsidiary Independence Technology.

In 2006 the company paid $16.6 billion to acquire Pfizer's consumer products business, which added about 40 brands to J&J's offerings. In order to clear some FTC hurdles, J&J sold US marketing rights for Pfizer's Zantac to Boehringer Ingelheim Pharmaceuticals. J&J also sold five brands (Act mouthwash, Unisom sleep aid, Cortizone anti-itch treatment, Kaopectate anti-diarrhea medication, and Balmex for diaper rash) to Chattem.

In 2009 J&J bought an 18% stake in Dutch biotech firm Crucell and formed a collaboration with Crucell to develop influenza therapies.

EXECUTIVES

Chairman and CEO: William C. (Bill) Weldon, age 61, $30,813,844 total compensation
VP Finance and CFO: Dominic J. Caruso, age 52, $5,220,350 total compensation
VP Human Resources and General Counsel: Russell C. Deyo, age 60, $8,631,394 total compensation
VP Public Affairs and Corporate Communications: Raymond C. Jordan
VP and CIO: Laverne H. Council
VP Corporate Media Relations: Jeffrey J. Leebaw
VP Investor Relations: Louise Mehrotra
VP Corporate Affairs: Brian D. Perkins, age 56
Worldwide Chairman, Pharmaceuticals Group: Sherilyn S. McCoy, age 51, $5,780,034 total compensation
Worldwide Chairman, Consumer Group: Colleen A. Goggins, age 55, $8,316,896 total compensation
Worldwide Chairman, Medical Devices and Diagnostics Group: Alex Gorsky, age 49
Treasurer: John A. Papa
Senior Director Investor Relations: Stanley (Stan) Panasewicz
Associate General Counsel and Secretary: Steven M. Rosenberg
Corporate Controller: Stephen J. Cosgrove
Auditors: PricewaterhouseCoopers LLP

LOCATIONS

HQ: Johnson & Johnson
1 Johnson & Johnson Plaza
New Brunswick, NJ 08933
Phone: 732-524-0400   **Fax:** 732-214-0332
Web: www.jnj.com

2009 Sales

	$ mil.	% of total
US	30,889	50
Europe	15,934	26
Asia/Pacific & Africa	9,918	16
Western Hemisphere, excluding US	5,156	8
Total	**61,897**	**100**

PRODUCTS/OPERATIONS

2009 Sales

	$ mil.	% of total
Medical Devices & Diagnostics		
DePuy	5,372	9
Ethicon Endo-Surgery	4,492	7
Ethicon	4,122	7
Cordis	2,679	4
Vision care (Vistakon)	2,506	4
Diabetes care (LifeScan)	2,440	4
Ortho-Clinical Diagnostics	1,963	3
Pharmaceuticals		
Remicade	4,304	7
Procrit/Eprex	2,245	4
Levaquin/Floxin	1,550	3
Risperdal Consta	1,425	2
Concerta	1,326	2
Topamax	1,151	2
Aciphex/Pariet	1,096	2
Risperdal	899	1
Duragesic/Fentanyl transdermal	888	1
Other	7,636	12
Consumer		
OTC pharmaceuticals & nutritionals	5,630	9
Skin care	3,467	6
Baby care	2,115	3
Women's health	1,895	3
Oral care	1,569	3
Wound care & other	1,127	2
Total	**61,897**	**100**

COMPETITORS

3M	Eli Lilly
Abbott Labs	Forest Labs
Alberto-Culver	Genzyme
Alcon	GlaxoSmithKline
Allergan	Kimberly-Clark
Amgen	L'Oréal USA
ArthroCare	Medtronic
AstraZeneca	Mentholatum Company
Bard	Merck
Bausch & Lomb	Mylan
Baxter International	Novartis
Bayer AG	NutraSweet
Beckman Coulter	Perrigo
Becton, Dickinson	Pfizer
Biogen Idec	Procter & Gamble
Boehringer Ingelheim	Roche Holding
Boston Scientific	Sanofi-Aventis
Bristol-Myers Squibb	Shire
Chattem	Smith & Nephew
Colgate-Palmolive	St. Jude Medical
Cook Incorporated	Terumo
Covidien	Teva Pharmaceuticals
The Dial Corporation	UCB
Dr. Reddy's	Unilever
Edwards Lifesciences	Watson Pharmaceuticals
Elan	

HISTORICAL FINANCIALS

Company Type: Public

Income Statement

FYE: Sunday nearest December 31

	REVENUE ($ mil.)	NET INCOME ($ mil.)	NET PROFIT MARGIN	EMPLOYEES
12/09	61,897	12,266	19.8%	115,500
12/08	63,747	12,949	20.3%	118,700
12/07	61,095	10,576	17.3%	119,200
12/06	53,324	11,053	20.7%	122,200
12/05	50,514	10,411	20.6%	115,600
Annual Growth	**5.2%**	**4.2%**	**—**	**(0.0%)**

2009 Year-End Financials

Debt ratio: 16.3%
Return on equity: 26.4%
Cash ($ mil.): 15,810
Current ratio: 1.82
Long-term debt ($ mil.): 8,223

No. of shares (mil.): 2,754
Dividends
  Yield: 3.0%
  Payout: 43.9%
Market value ($ mil.): 177,414

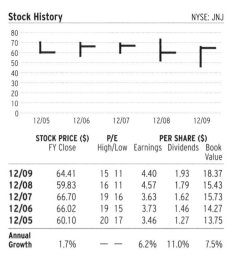

Stock History

NYSE: JNJ

	STOCK PRICE ($) FY Close	P/E High/Low		PER SHARE ($) Earnings	Dividends	Book Value
12/09	64.41	15	11	4.40	1.93	18.37
12/08	59.83	16	11	4.57	1.79	15.43
12/07	66.70	19	16	3.63	1.62	15.73
12/06	66.02	19	15	3.73	1.46	14.27
12/05	60.10	20	17	3.46	1.27	13.75
Annual Growth	**1.7%**	**—**	**—**	**6.2%**	**11.0%**	**7.5%**

Johnson Controls

Johnson Controls (JCI) wants to put you in the driver's seat — an environmentally conscious one. The company makes car batteries and interior parts for passenger and hybrid electric vehicles, as well as energy-efficient HVAC systems for commercial buildings. Car interior products include seating, instrument panels, and electronics. The battery unit makes car batteries. The building efficiency division makes, installs, and services mechanical equipment that controls HVAC, lighting, security, and fire systems in commercial buildings. The unit also offers onsite facility management.

The Automotive Experience business provides seating, interior electronics, overhead systems, and cockpits. JCI is focused on beefing up its automotive presence in China. Since opening its first Chinese factory in 1997, JCI has added 10 more, and expanded capacity at a Shanghai seat plant, to command the largest share of the Chinese seating market.

In the meantime, JCI is responding to lower vehicle production levels in Europe and North America; the company is expected to close 10 low-production plants, resulting in a sharply reduced workforce. JCI began restructuring its businesses in late 2008. In 2009 JCI made an additional round of cuts.

The company's Power Solutions business claims it is the largest lead-acid automotive battery producer in the world. Its 50 manufacturing and assembly facilities are located in over 20 countries and produce lead-acid batteries as well as AGM, nickel-metal-hydride, and lithium-ion batteries used in hybrid vehicles. This segment is increasing its footprint in Asia, particularly in China where it purchased Delphi's global auto battery operations. The deal was valued at over $200 million and is tied to a long-term, global contract to supply GM with batteries.

In Europe, Johnson Controls-Saft, the joint venture between JCI and France's SAFT, set plans in 2009 to build a plant for making lithium-ion hybrid batteries in Holland, Michigan. The timing is strategic as other battery suppliers are planning advanced manufacturing facilities in Michigan for the automotive industry.

Also in partnership with Saft, JCI opened the world's first lithium-ion hybrid vehicle battery production facility in 2008. The operation is supplying batteries for a test fleet of Ford Escape plug-in hybrid vehicles, in Nersac, France.

The Building Efficiency segment designs control systems, mechanical equipment, and provides services for non-residential properties. Almost half of this segment's sales come from HVAC products and control systems for construction and retrofit markets. Branded products include Metasys control systems monitors and York chillers, among others.

JCI is also expanding its lighting services from solely school, health care, and government applications to retail, commercial, and industrial markets through its acquisition of National Energy Services (NES) in 2010.

HISTORY

Professor Warren Johnson developed the electric telethermoscope in 1880 so that janitors at Whitewater, Wisconsin's State Normal School could regulate room temperatures without disturbing classrooms. His device, the thermostat, used mercury to move a heat element that opened and shut a circuit. Milwaukee hotelier William Plankinton believed in the invention and invested $150,000 to start production.

The two men formed Johnson Electric Service Company in 1885. They sold the marketing, installation, and service rights to concentrate on manufacturing. Johnson also invented other devices such as tower clocks, and he experimented with the telegraph before becoming intrigued with the automobile and beginning production of steam-powered cars. He won the US Postal Service's first automotive contract, but never gained support within his own company. Johnson continued to look elsewhere for financing until his death in 1911.

The renamed Johnson Services regained full rights to its thermostats in 1912 and sold its other businesses. During the Depression it produced economy systems that regulated building temperatures. Johnson Services became a public company in 1940. During WWII it aided the war effort, building weather-data gatherers and test radar sets.

In the 1960s Johnson Services began developing centralized control systems for temperature, fire alarm, lighting, and security regulation. The company was renamed Johnson Controls in 1974; it acquired automotive battery maker Globe-Union in 1978.

Johnson Controls bought auto seat makers Hoover Universal and Ferro Manufacturing in 1985. It expanded its controls business through the purchases of ITT's European controls group (1982) and Pan Am World Services (1989).

The company sold its car-door components business in 1990 and bought battery maker Varta's Canadian plant. The next year Johnson Controls purchased several car-seat component makers in Europe, and in 1992 it bought a Welsh plastics manufacturer and a Czech seat-cover producer.

The battery unit faced a major setback in 1994, when Sears dropped the company as its battery maker. Two years later, however, the battery business was recharged by an exclusive supply contract with Target stores.

In 1996 Johnson Controls bought most of Roth Frères (auto components) and Prince Automotive (interior systems), becoming a major interior-systems integrator.

Late in 2000 the company bought a 15% stake in Donnelly Corporation (automotive components). In 2001 Johnson Controls paid $435 million in cash for the automotive electronics business of France's Sagem (now SAFRAN). It added the automotive battery operations of Varta AG (Germany) in 2002 and Borg Instruments (automotive electronics) in 2003.

In 2005 Johnson Controls sold its engine electronics division (engine management systems and components) to France's Valeo. Later that year it acquired York International, the US's third-largest supplier of heating, ventilation, air-conditioning, and refrigeration equipment for $3.2 billion.

In 2006 Johnson Controls bought Environmental Technologies Inc., a supplier of HVAC equipment. In mid-2006 Johnson Controls began a restructuring aimed at reducing costs at its automotive interiors and facilities management businesses. The plan included the cutting of 5,000 jobs and the closure of 16 plants over one year.

Johnson Controls bought financially strapped Plastech Engineered Products' automotive interiors operations in 2008.

EXECUTIVES

Chairman, President, and CEO: Stephen A. Roell, age 59, $12,924,421 total compensation
EVP, CFO and Principal Financial Officer: R. Bruce McDonald, age 49, $3,501,149 total compensation
EVP Human Resources: Susan F. Davis, age 56
VP; President, Building Efficiency: C. David (Dave) Myers, age 46, $3,004,705 total compensation
VP and President, Automotive Experience: Beda-Helmut Bolzenius, age 53, $2,969,981 total compensation
VP; President, Power Solutions: Alex A. Molinaroli, age 50, $3,188,295 total compensation
VP and General Manager, Asia, Building Efficiency: Wilson Sun
VP and General Manager, Hybrid Systems; CEO, Johnson Controls-Saft Advanced Power Solutions: Mary Ann Wright
VP and General Manager, Global WorkPlace Solutions: Guy Holden
VP; Group VP and General Manager, Japan and Asia/Pacific, Automotive Group: Jeffrey S. Edwards, age 47
VP Diversity and Public Affairs: Charles A. Harvey, age 57
VP, Secretary, and General Counsel: Jerome D. Okarma, age 57
VP Information Technology and CIO: Colin Boyd, age 50
VP Government Affairs: Mark Wagner
VP and Managing Director, Middle East: Magdy A. Mekky
VP; VP Finance, Building Efficiency: Jeffrey G. Augustin, age 47
VP and Treasurer: Frank A. Voltolina, age 49
VP Communication: Jacqueline F. Strayer, age 55
Group VP and General Manager, North America: Jeff Williams
Executive Director Investor Relations: Glen Ponczak
Auditors: PricewaterhouseCoopers LLP

LOCATIONS

HQ: Johnson Controls, Inc.
5757 N. Green Bay Ave., Milwaukee, WI 53209
Phone: 414-524-1200   **Fax:** 414-524-2077
Web: www.johnsoncontrols.com

2009 Sales

	$ mil.	% of total
US	11,099	39
Europe		
Germany	2,877	10
Other countries	7,330	26
Other regions	7,191	25
Total	**28,497**	**100**

PRODUCTS/OPERATIONS

2009 Sales

	$ mil.	% of total
Building efficiency	12,493	44
Automotive experience	12,016	42
Power solutions	3,988	14
Total	**28,497**	**100**

Selected Products

Automotive experience
  Electronics
    Body electronics
    Driver information
    Energy management
    Infotainment and connectivity
  Interiors
    Cockpits and instrument panels
    Door panels and systems
    Floor consoles
    Overhead systems and modules
  Seating
    Climate systems
    Foam
    Front seats
    Metal structures and mechanisms
    Rear seats
    Safety systems
    Trim
Building efficiency
  Building automation and control systems
  Fire life safety products
  HVAC products
  Refrigeration
  Safety and security products
  Snowmaking equipment
  York equipment
Power solutions
  Batteries (passenger cars, commercial, agricultural, motorcycles, golf carts, wheelchairs, marine, solar energy, snowmobiles, etc.)
  Plastic battery containers

COMPETITORS

A123 Systems
Addison
Building Technologies
Carrier
Comfort Systems USA
Delphi Automotive
DENSO
Eagle-Picher
East Penn Manufacturing
Eaton
Emerson Electric
Exide
Faurecia
General Motors
Goodman Global
GS Yuasa
Honeywell International
Invensys
Lear Corp
Lennox
Magna International
Paloma Co.
Rieter Automotive North America
Robert Bosch
SPX
Trane Inc.
Valeo
Visteon
Yazaki North America

HISTORICAL FINANCIALS

Company Type: Public

Income Statement

FYE: September 30

	REVENUE ($ mil.)	NET INCOME ($ mil.)	NET PROFIT MARGIN	EMPLOYEES
9/09	28,497	(338)	—	130,000
9/08	38,062	979	2.6%	140,000
9/07	34,624	1,252	3.6%	140,000
9/06	32,235	1,035	3.2%	136,000
9/05	27,479	909	3.3%	114,000
Annual Growth	**0.9%**	**—**	**—**	**3.3%**

2009 Year-End Financials

Debt ratio: 34.7%
Return on equity: —
Cash ($ mil.): 761
Current ratio: 1.13
Long-term debt ($ mil.): 3,168
No. of shares (mil.): 673
Dividends
  Yield: 2.0%
  Payout: —
Market value ($ mil.): 17,210

Stock History

NYSE: JCI

	STOCK PRICE ($) FY Close	P/E High/Low		PER SHARE ($) Earnings	Dividends	Book Value
9/09	25.56	—	—	(0.57)	0.52	13.57
9/08	30.33	27	16	1.63	0.52	14.00
9/07	39.37	21	11	2.09	0.44	13.23
9/06	23.91	17	11	1.74	0.37	10.92
9/05	20.68	14	11	1.56	0.33	9.00
Annual Growth	**5.4%**	**—**	**—**	**—**	**12.0%**	**10.8%**

Jones Apparel

While some are busy keeping up with the Joneses, Jones Apparel Group is too busy taking stock in its own brand portfolio to take notice. The company provides a wide range of clothing, shoes, and accessories for men, women, and children. Its brands include Anne Klein, Jones New York, Gloria Vanderbilt, Kasper, Evan-Picone, and l.e.i., among many others. Subsidiary Nine West Group designs apparel and shoes under the names Easy Spirit, Enzo Angiolini, Bandolino, and Nine West. Through licensing agreements, Jones also supplies Givenchy jewelry, Rachel Roy designer apparel, Dockers footwear, and Jessica Simpson jeanswear. The firm operates about 940 outlet and specialty stores, as well as branded e-commerce sites.

In recent years Jones has faced declining sales as consumers slash spending on their wardrobes and retailers pare their inventory levels to match the falloff in business because of the economic downturn. The firm has been working to turn its fortunes around by freshening up its mainstay labels, adding new ones that are poised for growth, and marketing exclusive collections through select retailers. The company has also been shrinking the size of its brick-and-mortar store network and focusing on e-tailing.

Along with other apparel wholesalers, Jones has struggled as department stores have cut back on inventory amid the economic downturn. To boost demand for its offerings, Jones has been inking exclusive brand distribution deals with select retailers. In 2010 it launched the Rachel Roy collection as an exclusive Macy's line and began providing GLO Jeans casualwear exclusively to Kmart.

Jones acquired Moda Nicola International, the owner of the Robert Rodriguez Collection of contemporary womenswear in 2010. It also purchased a 55% interest in high-end women's shoes and accessory maker Stuart Weitzman Holdings in 2010.

Licensing deals also remain key to Jones' business. In 2010 the company announced plans to design, manufacture, and distribute Jessica Simpson brand jeanswear.

Richard Dickson, formerly of toymaker Mattel where he ran the resurgent Barbie business, joined the company in February 2010 as president and CEO of branded businesses. As a result, Wesley Card relinquished the title of president but remained as CEO.

HISTORY

When diversifying chemical firm W. R. Grace & Co. began a brief foray into the fashion world in 1970, it hired Sidney Kimmel to run the show. Kimmel had worked in a knitting mill in the 1950s and served as president of women's sportswear maker Villager in the 1960s. He and his companion, designer Rena Rowan, created Grace's fashionable but moderately priced Jones New York line.

Kimmel and Grace's accountant, Gerard Rubin, bought Grace's fashion division in 1975, incorporating it as Jones Apparel Group. Jones expanded quickly by bringing out new labels and licensing others, such as Christian Dior. Talks to sell the company to underwear maker Warnaco fell through in 1981.

Tapping into two trends of the early 1980s, Jones Apparel offered the sweatsuit fashions of Norma Kamali and in 1984 acquired the license for the Gloria Vanderbilt line from Murjani. Swan-adorned Gloria Vanderbilt jeans had been must-haves early in the decade, but the deal turned into an ugly duckling as costs beyond Jones Apparel's control pushed the company into the red. (Meanwhile, Kimmel produced the films *9 1/2 Weeks* and *Clan of the Cave Bear* and led a group that briefly controlled the Famous Amos Cookie Co.)

Creditors forced Jones Apparel to unload most of its brands — all but Jones New York, Saville, and Christian Dior — and cut jobs, and by 1988 it was profitable again. Kimmel bought Rubin's interest in the company in 1989 and took it public in 1991, retaining about half of the stock.

In the early 1990s, as recession-minded shoppers looked for bargains and the American workplace became more casual, Jones again took off. The company expanded with new lines, such as Rena Rowan (inexpensive suits) and Jones & Co. (career casuals). Jones Apparel moved into women's accessories with the 1993 purchase of the Evan-Picone brand name.

Two years later the company struck its first licensing agreement with Polo Ralph Lauren, for the Lauren by Ralph Lauren line of women's sportswear. Propelled by the new line, Jones reached $1 billion in sales in 1996. The company ended its long-held licensing agreement with Christian Dior the next year.

Jones Apparel licensed Ralph by Ralph Lauren, a lower-priced juniors' line, in 1998. That year it purchased Sun Apparel, picking up the rights to Todd Oldham and Polo jeans, and in 1999 it bought the remaining clothing, footwear, cosmetics, and apparel rights to the youth-oriented Oldham name.

The firm then made its biggest acquisition by far when it paid $1.4 billion for shoe designer and retailer Nine West Group (Easy Spirit, Enzo Angiolini, Bandolino, Amalfi). With the Nine West purchase, Jones Apparel inherited an FTC investigation into the footwear designer's pricing policies. The company closed several Nine West facilities in 1999, cutting about 1,900 jobs, followed by the sale of its retail operations in Canada (1999), Asia (2000), and the UK (2001).

President Peter Boneparth was named CEO in 2002 after Kimmel stepped down. Jones Apparel bought RSV Sport, maker of l.e.i. jeanswear for girls, in that year.

On the spending side, Jones Apparel acquired Kasper, maker of Anne Klein, in 2003, and in 2004 launched a successful hostile takeover of shoemaker Maxwell Shoe. Jones also acquired Barneys New York for about $400 million.

The company had held the exclusive license to produce Lauren-branded apparel in Canada, Mexico, and the US for the Polo Ralph Lauren Corp. The deal, however, spurred litigation over control of the brand. In 2006 Jones and Polo Ralph Lauren agreed to a settlement. Polo Ralph Lauren paid Jones some $355 million for the Jones Sun Apparel subsidiary that operates the brand as well as a controlling ownership of the brand in the US.

Veteran executive Peter Boneparth, who joined Jones when it acquired McNaughton in 1997, stepped down in July 2007. Wesley Card, the company's president and COO, was appointed as the firm's CEO.

In 2007 Jones Apparel sold Barneys New York to an affiliate of the Dubai-based private equity firm Istithmar for about $945 million.

EXECUTIVES

Chairman: Sidney Kimmel, age 82, $1,329,225 total compensation
CEO and Director: Wesley R. Card, $5,482,687 total compensation
CFO: John T. McClain, age 48, $1,437,496 total compensation
Chief Marketing Officer: Stacy Lastrina
EVP, General Counsel, and Secretary: Ira M. Dansky, age 64, $1,169,163 total compensation
EVP, Chief Accounting Officer, and Controller: Christopher R. Cade, age 42
SVP Corporate Taxation and Risk Management and Treasurer: Joseph Donnalley
SVP Product Development, Jeanswear: Mehmet Tangoren
CEO, Wholesale Footwear and Accessories: Andrew (Andy) Cohen, age 60, $2,201,834 total compensation
President and CEO, Branded Businesses: Richard Dickson, age 41
CEO, Denim and Junior Businesses: Jack Gross
Auditors: BDO Seidman, LLP

LOCATIONS

HQ: Jones Apparel Group, Inc.
1411 Broadway, New York, NY 10018
Phone: 212-642-3860   **Fax:** 215-785-1795
Web: www.jny.com

2009 Sales

	$ mil.	% of total
US	3,033.6	91
International	293.8	9
Total	**3,327.4**	**100**

PRODUCTS/OPERATIONS

2009 Sales

	$ mil.	% of total
Wholesale better apparel	922.8	28
Wholesale footwear & accessories	839.6	25
Wholesale jeanswear	828.9	25
Retail	689.3	21
Licensing & other	46.8	1
Total	**3,327.4**	**100**

2009 Sales

	$ mil.	% of total
Net sales	3,279.7	99
Licensing	46.8	1
Service & other revenues	0.9	—
Total	**3,327.4**	**100**

2009 Stores

	No.
Outlet	617
Specialty retail	321
Total	**938**

Selected Brand Affiliates

Jones New York
Nine West
Anne Klein
Gloria Vanderbilt
Kasper
Bandolino
Easy Spirit
Evan-Picone
l.e.i.
Energie
Enzo Angiolini
Joan & David
Mootsies Tootsies
Sam & Libby
Napier
Judith Jack
Le Suit
Givenchy (costume jewelry licensed from Givenchy Corporation)
Dockers Women (footwear licensed from Levi Strauss & Co.)

COMPETITORS

AnnTaylor
Bally
bebe stores
Berkshire Hathaway
Bernard Chaus
Bill Blass
Brand Matter
Brown Shoe
Caché
Calvin Klein
Chico's FAS
Coach, Inc.
Coldwater Creek
Collective Brands
Etienne Aigner Group
Gucci
Hampshire Group
Iconix Brand Group
IT Holding
J. Jill Group
Kenneth Cole
Levi Strauss
Liz Claiborne
LVMH
Nordstrom
Phillips-Van Heusen
Polo Ralph Lauren
Salvatore Ferragamo
Skechers U.S.A.
St. John Knits
Steven Madden
Talbots
VF

HISTORICAL FINANCIALS

Company Type: Public

Income Statement

FYE: December 31

	REVENUE ($ mil.)	NET INCOME ($ mil.)	NET PROFIT MARGIN	EMPLOYEES
12/09	3,327	(86)	—	11,535
12/08	3,616	(765)	—	7,925
12/07	3,849	311	8.1%	8,450
12/06	4,743	(146)	—	16,485
12/05	5,074	274	5.4%	18,430
Annual Growth	(10.0%)	—	—	(11.1%)

2009 Year-End Financials

Debt ratio: 48.2%
Return on equity: —
Cash ($ mil.): 333
Current ratio: 3.29
Long-term debt ($ mil.): 526

No. of shares (mil.): 87
Dividends
  Yield: 1.2%
  Payout: —
Market value ($ mil.): 1,399

Stock History

NYSE: JNY

	STOCK PRICE ($) FY Close	P/E High/Low		PER SHARE ($) Earnings	Dividends	Book Value
12/09	16.06	—	—	(1.02)	0.20	12.54
12/08	5.86	—	—	(9.23)	0.56	13.57
12/07	15.99	12	5	3.07	0.56	22.92
12/06	33.43	—	—	(1.30)	0.50	25.39
12/05	30.72	16	12	2.30	0.44	30.61
Annual Growth	(15.0%)	—	—	—	(17.9%)	(20.0%)

Jones Lang LaSalle

Borders mean little to Jones Lang LaSalle. The company provides commercial real estate brokerage, management, advisory, and financing services in some 60 countries around the world. Its offerings include property management and leasing, sales and dispositions, tenant representation, valuations, development services, and real estate investment banking. The company has expertise in a wide variety of commercial real estate, including office, retail, hotel, health care, industrial, cultural, and multi-family residential properties. Jones Lang LaSalle has some $40 billion in assets under management and a total portfolio of 1.6 billion sq. ft. worldwide.

The company has grown by opening new offices and by buying up others; during the past half-dozen years it has completed more than 35 acquisitions around the world. The company broadened its presence in key North American markets when it acquired The Staubach Company in 2008. Jones Lang LaSalle paid $613 million for the rival real estate services firm, which was founded by football legend and former Dallas Cowboys quarterback Roger Staubach.

In the tumultous real estate market, though, Jones Lang LaSalle has been seeking alternative ways to expand beyond outright acquisitions. To better compete with regional or local firms that provide complementary property services, the company is also seeking to form new alliances with other firms. In 2009 Jones Lang LaSalle teamed up with Real Estate Disposition to begin offering online auction sales, a product to help customers quickly sell commercial property and other distressed assets.

In another deal, Jones Lang LaSalle acquired the third-party leasing and management duties of General Growth Properties in 2010 as part of the mall owner's restructuring efforts. The deal added about 20 shopping centers to the company's management portfolio.

HISTORY

Jones Lang Wootton had roots in London's Paternoster Row auction houses in 1783. LaSalle Partners, originally known as IDC Real Estate, was founded in El Paso, Texas, in 1968. The two companies could not have started out in a more disparate fashion, yet their combined force is now one of the largest real estate services firms in the world.

Richard Winstanley opened an auction house in 1783, and his son James joined him in that business in 1806. In 1840 the Joneses entered the picture — the Winstanleys created a partnership with one James Jones. The business moved to King Street (in the Guildhall section of London) in 1860 and remained in that location for some 100 years in various incarnations — James' son Frederick took over the business, renaming it Frederick Jones and Co. When James retired in 1872, the firm was again renamed, to Jones Lang and Co., and was controlled by C. A. Lang. Jones Lang merged with Wootton and Son in 1939, becoming Jones Lang Wootton and Sons.

Jones Lang Wootton was active in redrawing the property lines in London after the Blitz. In 1945 the firm began contacting small landowners and by combining small parcels of land, secured development, leasing, and/or purchase contracts. When the rebuilding of London began in 1954, Jones Lang Wootton was in a secure place to be right at the forefront of that new development. The firm began engaging in speculative development in the West End and in the City of London.

The year 1958 saw the expansion of Jones Lang Wootton into Australia; the firm had offices throughout the Asia/Pacific region by 1968. Further expansion took place closer to home in Scotland (1962) and Ireland (1965), and the first continental European office in Brussels (also 1965). The firm moved into the Manhattan market in 1975.

On the other side of the story, IDC Real Estate (the name change to LaSalle Partners came in 1977) was a group of partnerships, initially focused on investment banking, investment management, and land. The firm began offering development management services in 1975; it moved into property management, leasing, and tenant representation in 1978 and facility management operations in 1980.

It built market share by buying other firms, including Kleinwort Benson Realty Advisors Corp. (1994) and UK-based investment adviser CIN Property Management (1996).

The firm leveraged its experience and long-term client base to pursue an acquisition strategy, taking advantage of trends shaping commercial real estate — globalization, consolidation, and merchant banking. LaSalle went public in 1997,
amalgamating the Galbreath Company (a property and development management firm with which it merged that year) with its other partnerships and becoming a corporation.

In 1998 it acquired the project management business of Satulah Group and two retail management business units from Lend Lease, and took real estate investment trust LaSalle Hotel Properties public. In 1999 the firm strengthened its world position by merging with Jones Lang Wootton; the company was renamed Jones Lang LaSalle.

The merger with Jones Lang Wootton combined Wootton's strength in Asia and Europe with LaSalle Partners' large presence in North America to create a worldwide real estate services firm. In 2006 the company acquired Spaulding & Slye, strengthening operations in the Mid-Atlantic and New England. Also that year it opened an office in Dubai and acquired RSP Group, which operates in North Africa and the Middle East. The year 2007 saw Jones Lang LaSalle buying German property advisory firm Kemper's Holding and taking a stake in the former Trammell Crow Meghraj, one of the largest private real estate companies in India.

EXECUTIVES

Chairman: Sheila A. Penrose, age 64
President, CEO, and Director: Colin Dyer, age 57, $1,979,657 total compensation
EVP and Chief Human Resources Officer: Nazneen Razi, age 57
EVP, COO, CFO, and Director: Lauralee E. Martin, age 59, $1,901,654 total compensation
EVP and Manager, Global Finance Operations: Stanley (Stan) Stec, age 51
EVP, Global General Counsel, and Corporate Secretary: Mark J. Ohringer, age 51
SVP, Property Management: Daniel Ozelius
SVP, Marketing: Nicholas Spadavecchia, age 44
SVP and National Director, Brokerage: Christopher Ostop
Chief Marketing and Communications Officer: Charles J. Doyle, age 50
CEO, Americas: Peter C. Roberts, age 49, $1,930,115 total compensation
CEO, LaSalle Investment Management: Jeff A. Jacobson, age 48, $2,082,944 total compensation
CEO, Europe, Middle East, and Africa: Christian Ulbrich, age 43, $1,221,811 total compensation
Chairman, Asia/Pacific and Jones Lang LaSalle Hotels: Peter A. Barge, age 60, $2,505,088 total compensation
CEO, Asia/Pacific: Alastair Hughes, age 44, $1,949,048 total compensation
CEO, Public Institutions: Herman E. Bulls, age 54
CEO, Brokerage, Americas: Gregory P. (Greg) O'Brien
Global CEO, Jones Lang LaSalle Hotels: Arthur de Haast
President and CEO, Retail, Americas: Greg Maloney
CEO, Latin America: Pedro Azcue
Director; Executive Chairman, Americas: Roger T. Staubach, age 68
CIO: David A. Johnson
Auditors: KPMG

LOCATIONS

HQ: Jones Lang LaSalle Incorporated
  200 E. Randolph Dr., Chicago, IL 60601
Phone: 312-782-5800   **Fax:** 312-782-4339
Web: www.joneslanglasalle.com

PRODUCTS/OPERATIONS

2009 Sales

	% of total
Investor & occupier services	
Americas	43
Europe, Middle East & Africa	27
Asia/Pacific	22
Investment management	8
Total	**100**

Selected Services

Investor services
  Agency leasing
  Property management
  Valuations and consulting
Occupier services
  Facilities management
  Project and development services
  Tenant representation
Construction management
Capital markets
Energy and sustainability services
Hotel advisory
Money management
Strategic consulting

COMPETITORS

CB Richard Ellis	Lend Lease
Colliers International	Realogy
Cushman & Wakefield	Shorenstein
Grubb & Ellis	Studley
Hines	Trammell Crow Company
Inland Group	

HISTORICAL FINANCIALS

Company Type: Public

Income Statement

FYE: December 31

	REVENUE ($ mil.)	NET INCOME ($ mil.)	NET PROFIT MARGIN	EMPLOYEES
12/09	2,481	(4)	—	36,600
12/08	2,698	85	3.1%	36,200
12/07	2,652	258	9.7%	32,700
12/06	2,014	175	8.7%	25,500
12/05	1,367	103	7.6%	22,000
Annual Growth	**16.1%**	**—**	**—**	**13.6%**

2009 Year-End Financials

Debt ratio: 12.7%
Return on equity: —
Cash ($ mil.): 69
Current ratio: 0.86
Long-term debt ($ mil.): 175

No. of shares (mil.): 43
Dividends
  Yield: 0.3%
  Payout: —
Market value ($ mil.): 2,575

Stock History

NYSE: JLL

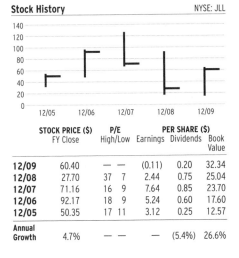

	STOCK PRICE ($) FY Close	P/E High/Low		PER SHARE ($) Earnings	Dividends	Book Value
12/09	60.40	—	—	(0.11)	0.20	32.34
12/08	27.70	37	7	2.44	0.75	25.04
12/07	71.16	16	9	7.64	0.85	23.70
12/06	92.17	18	9	5.24	0.60	17.60
12/05	50.35	17	11	3.12	0.25	12.57
Annual Growth	**4.7%**	**—**	**—**	**—**	**(5.4%)**	**26.6%**

Joy Global

Joy Global is pretty happy for a company that builds equipment destined to spend the majority of its life down in a hole. The company makes heavy equipment for the mining industry through two subsidiaries. Its Joy Mining Machinery subsidiary makes underground coal-mining equipment that includes armored face conveyors, roof supports, longwall shearers, and shuttle cars. Subsidiary P&H Mining Equipment makes electric mining shovels, rotary blasthole drills, and other equipment used in open-pit mining; it also provides parts and service through its P&H MinePro Services group. Joy Global, which operates manufacturing and service facilities worldwide, gets about half of its sales from outside the US.

In response to industry fluctuations, Joy Global depends to some extent on aftermarket sales and service (about 55% of sales) which extends the life of the expensive machinery through spare parts and repair services. The company also looks to emerging markets — specifically China and India, which import commodities to support growing construction and energy needs — to create more stable worldwide demand and encourage spending for capital equipment. While Joy Global experienced cancellations and drops in new orders throughout most of 2009, its backlog had started to recover towards the end of the year.

Joy Global continues to grow globally through acquisitions and by expanding its sales and service operations. The company gained a foothold in the domestic equipment manufacturing sector of China when it acquired Wuxi Shengda, a China-based firm that makes longwall shearing machines, in 2008. The following year the company introduced remote equipment monitoring systems, allowing maintenance personnel to check machines for reliability and safety, fleet status, productivity, and other performance related issues using wireless technology.

HISTORY

In the mid-1880s German immigrant Henry Harnischfeger and partner Alonzo Pawling started Pawling and Harnischfeger (P&H), a small machine and pattern shop, in Milwaukee. The company shipped its first overhead electric crane in 1888. After a fire destroyed its main shop in 1903, P&H built a new plant in West Milwaukee the following year that became the world's leading manufacturer of overhead cranes. The company became Harnischfeger Corporation after Pawling died in 1914. In remembrance of Pawling, Harnischfeger kept its P&H trademark.

The highly cyclical heavy-equipment industry encountered a big upswing with WWI. After the war, Harnischfeger began selling excavating and mining equipment to help weather downturns in the industry. Harnischfeger died in 1930, and his son Walter became president. The Depression was hard for the company, as it lost money every year from 1931 to 1939. Harnischfeger diversified into welding equipment, diesel engines, and prefabricated houses during the 1930s and 1940s.

WWII and the postwar period boosted the company, and Harnischfeger was listed on the AMEX in 1956. Walter became chairman in 1959, and his son Henry became president. Harnischfeger streamlined operations in the 1960s, keeping its construction and mining division and its industrial and electrical division.

Harnischfeger was listed on the NYSE in 1971. After the 1973 oil embargo, its machinery sales increased with the opening of coal reserves and the construction of oil pipelines and mass transit systems. By the end of the 1970s, however, recession and high interest rates took their toll on the company.

On the verge of bankruptcy in the early 1980s, Harnischfeger revived itself by trimming down, diversifying, and making key acquisitions. It formed Harnischfeger Engineering in 1984 (sold in the early 1990s), and in 1986 the company bought Beloit (papermaking equipment) and formed Harnischfeger Industries as a holding company.

Harnischfeger began moving away from systems handling in the early 1990s. It bought underground mining equipment maker Joy Technologies (now Joy Mining Machinery) in 1994 and Longwall International (through the acquisition of Dobson Park Industries) in 1995. The next year Harnischfeger bought Ingersoll-Rand's pulp machinery division. In 1997 the company's $631 million bid for Giddings & Lewis (machine tools) was thwarted when Giddings & Lewis agreed to be acquired by Thyssen (now ThyssenKrupp AG).

After the Asian economic crisis and other factors weakened demand for its papermaking and mining equipment, Harnischfeger announced in 1998 it would be laying off about 20% of its workforce — about 3,100 jobs. It also sold an 80% stake in P&H Material Handling to Chartwell Investments for $340 million that year.

In 1999 CEO Jeffery Grade, also chairman since 1993, stepped down. Grade spearheaded the company's aggressive growth strategy, which was stymied by slips in demand for the company's machinery due to weak prices for metal and paper. President John Hanson succeeded Grade as CEO. Unable to keep up with its debt, the company filed for Chapter 11 bankruptcy protection.

Creditors accepted a $160 million offer from Metso Corporation in 2000 to buy Beloit's assets, including its roll cover division, paper machine aftermarket assets, and related paper machine technology. Harnischfeger emerged from bankruptcy and changed its name to Joy Global Inc. in 2001.

Orders for new equipment were soft in 2002, although limited sales were offset by paced revenue growth through the company's operations in China. In 2003 Joy Global completed the purchase of the remaining 25% interest in P&H-Australia (surface mining equipment) that it didn't already own.

P&H sold its subsidiary The Horsburgh & Scott Co., a manufacturer of industrial gears and mechanical gear drives, in 2005. The following year Joy Global purchased the Stamler business of Oldenburg Group, Inc. for $118 million. Stamler's products, used in underground and surface coal mining, included feeder breakers, battery haulers, and continuous haulage systems.

Also in 2006 EVP Michael Sutherlin succeeded John Hanson as president and CEO; Hanson remained chairman.

In 2008 Joy Global acquired Continental Global Group, a maker of conveyor systems and material-handling machinery used in mining and other industrial applications. Also in 2008 it acquired Wuxi Shengda, a China-based firm that makes longwall shearing machines.

EXECUTIVES

Chairman: John N. Hanson, age 68
President, CEO, and Director: Michael W. Sutherlin, age 63, $5,523,176 total compensation
EVP; President and COO, Joy Mining Machinery: Edward L. (Ted) Doheny II, age 48, $1,998,841 total compensation
EVP; President and COO, P&H Mining Equipment: Randal W. (Randy) Baker, age 46
EVP, CFO, and Treasurer: Michael S. (Mike) Olsen, age 58, $2,932,639 total compensation
EVP Human Resources: Dennis R. Winkleman, age 59, $1,645,312 total compensation
EVP, General Counsel, and Secretary: Sean D. Major, age 45, $1,454,909 total compensation
VP, Controller, and Chief Accounting Officer: Ricky T. Dillon, age 39
VP Investor Relations and Corporate Communications: Sara Leuchter Wilkins, age 55
Executive Assistant: Sandra L. McKenzie
President and COO, Continental Crushing & Conveying and EVP, Joy Global Inc.: Terry Nicola
Auditors: Ernst & Young LLP

LOCATIONS

HQ: Joy Global Inc.
100 E. Wisconsin Ave., Ste. 2780
Milwaukee, WI 53202
Phone: 414-319-8500   **Fax:** 414-319-8520
Web: www.joyglobal.com

2009 Sales

	$ mil.	% of total
US	2,333.6	52
Australia	579.2	13
Europe	520.0	11
Other regions	1,071.3	24
Adjustments	(905.8)	—
Total	**3,598.3**	**100**

PRODUCTS/OPERATIONS

2009 Sales

	$ mil.	% of total
Undergroung mining machinery	1,930.5	54
Surface mining equipment	1,347.0	37
Crushing & conveying	320.8	9
Total	**3,598.3**	**100**

2009 Sales

	$ mil.	% of total
Aftermarket	1,969.9	55
Original equipment	1,628.4	45
Total	**3,598.3**	**100**

Selected Products

Underground mining machinery
  Armored face conveyors
  Complete longwall mining systems
  Continuous chain haulage systems
  Continuous miners
  Feeder breakers
  Flexible conveyor trains
  Longwall shearers
  Roof bolters
  Roof supports
  Shuttle cars
Surface mining equipment
  Electric mining shovels
  Rotary blasthole drills
  Walking draglines

COMPETITORS

Bucyrus	Marmon Group
Caterpillar	Metso
Hitachi	Multi-Shifter
Howle Holdings	Rowan Companies
Ingersoll-Rand	Sandvik
Jervis B. Webb	Sime Darby
Komatsu	Terex

HISTORICAL FINANCIALS

Company Type: Public

Income Statement

FYE: Saturday nearest October 31

	REVENUE ($ mil.)	NET INCOME ($ mil.)	NET PROFIT MARGIN	EMPLOYEES
10/09	3,598	455	12.6%	11,300
10/08	3,419	374	10.9%	11,800
10/07	2,547	280	11.0%	9,200
10/06	2,402	415	17.3%	8,900
10/05	1,928	148	7.7%	7,900
Annual Growth	**16.9%**	**32.4%**	**—**	**9.4%**

2009 Year-End Financials

Debt ratio: 64.4%
Return on equity: 67.5%
Cash ($ mil.): 472
Current ratio: 2.10
Long-term debt ($ mil.): 524
No. of shares (mil.): 103
Dividends
  Yield: 1.4%
  Payout: 15.9%
Market value ($ mil.): 5,201

Stock History

NASDAQ (GS): JOYG

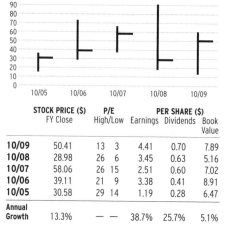

	STOCK PRICE ($) FY Close	P/E High/Low		PER SHARE ($) Earnings	Dividends	Book Value
10/09	50.41	13	3	4.41	0.70	7.89
10/08	28.98	26	6	3.45	0.63	5.16
10/07	58.06	26	15	2.51	0.60	7.02
10/06	39.11	21	9	3.38	0.41	8.91
10/05	30.58	29	14	1.19	0.28	6.47
Annual Growth	**13.3%**	**—**	**—**	**38.7%**	**25.7%**	**5.1%**

JPMorgan Chase

JPMorgan Chase was born with a silver spoon in its mouth but that hasn't stopped it. One of the largest financial services firms in the US, the company has more than 5,100 bank branches in some two dozen states (and counting) and is also among the nation's top mortgage lenders and credit card issuers. Active in some 60 countries, it also boasts formidable investment banking and asset management operations. Its subsidiaries include JPMorgan Private Bank and institutional investment manager JPMorgan Asset Management (with some $1.7 trillion in assets under supervision).

JPMorgan Chase made a bargain-basement offer of $270 million for the struggling rival Bear Stearns, although it later raised its offer to $1.2 billion. The high-profile deal came after the Fed extended a $30 billion lifeline to Bear Stearns, which had been drowning in subprime mortgage investment debt.

It also stepped in to buy WaMu when that bank failed and was seized by regulators later in the year. JPMorgan paid $1.9 billion for the bank's operations and assumed some $31 billion in losses. JPMorgan began integrating WaMu's branches with its own retail network, but announced plans to close about 10% of the total 5,400 branches. Shortly after the acquisition,

JPMorgan cut 9,200 WaMu jobs — about 20% of its workforce.

As part of a plan to stimulate the economy, the US government invested in JPMorgan Chase and other banks. The bank got $25 billion of the $700 billion taxpayer-funded bailout package that was approved in late 2008, with the stipulation that the banks use the money and not hoard it. The investment came with restrictions on executive pay and other rules, and JPMorgan returned the money the following year, saying it was doing just fine without it.

Among other operations, JPMorgan Chase owns private equity firm One Equity Partners and 42% of mutual fund company American Century. In 2008 it assumed full ownership of payments processor Chase Paymentech Solutions, which had been a joint venture with First Data. First Data assumed 49% of Chase Paymentech's assets and clients in the deal.

In 2009 JPMorgan Chase acquired full ownership of hedge fund Highbridge Capital Management, which has some $21 billion in assets under management.

In 2010 JPMorgan acquired the European and Asian segments of RBS Sempra Commodities, the energy trading joint venture between Royal Bank of Scotland and Sempra Energy.

JPMorgan also put its money behind the struggling newspaper industry in 2010 with the acquisition of 10% of Gannett, which publishes USA Today and other newspapers. JPMorgan is now Gannett's largest stakeholder.

HISTORY

JPMorgan Chase & Co.'s roots are in The Manhattan Company, created in 1799 to bring water to New York City. A provision buried in its incorporation documents let the company provide banking services; investor and future US Vice President Aaron Burr brought the company (eventually the Bank of Manhattan) into competition with The Bank of New York, founded by Burr's political rival Alexander Hamilton. JPMorgan Chase still owns the pistols from the notorious 1804 duel in which Burr mortally wounded Hamilton.

In 1877 John Thompson formed Chase National, naming it for Salmon Chase, Abraham Lincoln's secretary of the treasury and the architect of the national bank system. Chase National merged with John D. Rockefeller's Equitable Trust in 1930, becoming the world's largest bank and beginning a long relationship with the Rockefellers. Chase National continued growing after WWII, and in 1955 it merged with the Bank of Manhattan. Christened Chase Manhattan, the bank remained the US's largest into the 1960s.

When soaring 1970s oil prices made energy loans attractive, Chase invested in Penn Square, an obscure oil-patch bank in Oklahoma and the first notable bank failure of the 1980s. (The legal aftereffects of Penn Square's 1982 failure dragged on until 1993.) Losses following the 1987 foreign loan crisis hit the company hard, as did the real estate crash. In 1995 the bank went looking for a partner. After talks with Bank of America, it settled on Chemical Bank.

Chemical Bank opened in 1824 and was one of the US's largest banks by 1900. As with Chase, Chemical Bank began as an unrelated business (New York Chemical Manufacturing) in 1823, largely in order to open a bank (it dropped its chemical operations in 1844). Chemical would merge with Manufacturers Hanover in 1991.

After its 1996 merger with Chase, Chemical Bank was the surviving entity but assumed Chase's more prestigious name. In 1997 Chase acquired the credit business of The Bank of New York and the corporate trustee business of Mellon Financial.

In 2001 it closed its $30 billion buy of J.P. Morgan and renamed itself JPMorgan Chase & Co. The new firm eliminated some 10% of its combined workforce as a result of the merger. Chairman Sandy Warner (who ran J.P. Morgan) retired at year-end and was replaced by former Chase Manhattan leader CEO William Harrison.

JPMorgan Chase had more than $1 billion in exposure to Enron, but in 2003 recovered some $600 million after a court battle with the failed energy trader's insurers.

In 2004 JPMorgan Chase and its investment banking arm, JPMorgan Securities, avoided a trial by paying some $2 billion to settle claims from investors who lost money on bonds that the firm underwrote in 2000 and 2001 for scandal-ridden WorldCom (now MCI). JPMorgan Chase aquired BANK ONE in 2004.

Enron continued to haunt the company: In 2005 it forked over $2.2 billion to settle part of an investor class-action suit over fraud charges related to the Enron debacle and paid another $350 million to the infamous energy trading firm, which asserted that JPMorgan Chase and about 10 other banks aided and abetted the company's collapse. However, the next year the company got some good news when the class action suit against it was dismissed.

In 2006 the bank was quick to settle its part of a class-action lawsuit brought by investors claiming they were cheated in the dot-com IPO boom. JPMorgan Chase paid $425 million to settle that case. William Harrison retired as chairman at the end of 2006; he was succeeded by president and CEO Jamie Dimon (former CEO of BANK ONE).

As one of the largest mortgage and home equity providers in the country, JPMorgan Chase was hurt by the subprime mortgage crisis and subsequent fall in home values in 2007.

EXECUTIVES

Chairman, President, and CEO: James (Jamie) Dimon, age 54, $8,952,400 total compensation
Vice Chairman, Mergers and Acquisitions:
William Rifkin
CFO: Douglas L. (Doug) Braunstein
CIO: Guy Chiarello
Chief Administrative Officer: Frank J. Bisignano, age 50, $10,192,946 total compensation
CEO, Asset Management: Mary C. Erdoes, age 42, $8,012,900 total compensation
CEO, Retail Financial Services:
Charles W. (Charlie) Scharf, age 44, $13,031,844 total compensation
CEO, Treasury and Securities Services:
Michael J. (Mike) Cavanagh, age 43, $5,806,500 total compensation
CEO, Investment Bank: James E. (Jes) Staley, age 53, $7,674,100 total compensation
CEO, Retail Affluent and Investment Services:
Barry Sommers
Executive Committee Member, Card Services:
Gordon A. Smith, age 51, $12,232,483 total compensation
Executive Committee Member, Global Government Relations and Public Policy: Peter L. Scher
Executive Committee Member, Investment Bank and Risk Management: John J. Hogan
Executive Committee Member, Treasury and Securities Services: Conrad J. Kozak

Executive Committee Member, Corporate Communications: Joseph M. Evangelisti
Executive Committee Member, Treasury Services:
Melissa J. Moore
General Counsel: Stephen M. (Steve) Cutler, age 48
Chief Investment Officer: Ina R. Drew, age 53
Chief Risk Officer: Barry L. Zubrow, age 57
Head, Strategy and Business Development:
Jay Mandelbaum, age 47
Director, Human Resources: John L. Donnelly, age 53
Auditors: PricewaterhouseCoopers LLP

LOCATIONS

HQ: JPMorgan Chase & Co.
270 Park Ave., New York, NY 10017
Phone: 212-270-6000   **Fax:** 212-270-1648
Web: www.jpmorganchase.com

PRODUCTS/OPERATIONS

2009 Sales

	$ mil.	% of total
Interest income		
Loans	38,704	34
Securities	12,377	11
Trading assets	12,098	10
Other	3,171	3
Noninterest income		
Asset management, administration & commissions	12,540	11
Principal transactions	9,796	8
Credit cards	7,110	6
Investment banking fees	7,087	6
Lending & deposit-related fees	7,045	6
Mortgage fees & related income	3,678	3
Other	2,026	2
Total	**115,632**	**100**

2009 Assets

	$ mil.	% of total
Cash & equivalents	284,840	14
Securities borrowed	119,630	6
Trading assets	411,128	20
Securities	360,390	18
Net loans	601,856	30
Other	254,145	12
Total	**2,031,989**	**100**

COMPETITORS

American Express
Bank of America
Barclays
Capital One
CIBC
Citigroup
Citigroup Global Markets
Credit Suisse (USA)
Deutsche Bank
Goldman Sachs
HSBC
Morgan Stanley
RBC Financial Group
UBS
Wells Fargo

HISTORICAL FINANCIALS

Company Type: Public

Income Statement

FYE: December 31

	ASSETS ($ mil.)	NET INCOME ($ mil.)	INCOME AS % OF ASSETS	EMPLOYEES
12/09	2,031,989	11,652	0.6%	222,316
12/08	2,175,052	3,699	0.2%	224,961
12/07	1,562,147	15,365	1.0%	180,667
12/06	1,351,520	14,444	1.1%	174,360
12/05	1,198,942	8,483	0.7%	168,847
Annual Growth	**14.1%**	**8.3%**	**—**	**7.1%**

2009 Year-End Financials

Equity as % of assets: 7.7%
Return on assets: 0.6%
Return on equity: 8.0%
Long-term debt ($ mil.): 266,318
No. of shares (mil.): 3,979
Dividends
Yield: 0.5%
Payout: 8.8%
Market value ($ mil.): 165,792
Sales ($ mil.): 115,632

Stock History

NYSE: JPM

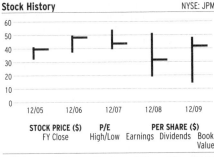

	STOCK PRICE ($) FY Close	P/E High/Low		PER SHARE ($) Earnings	Dividends	Book Value
12/09	41.67	21	7	2.26	0.20	41.56
12/08	31.53	37	14	1.37	1.52	41.94
12/07	43.65	12	9	4.38	1.48	30.97
12/06	48.30	12	9	4.04	1.36	29.10
12/05	39.69	17	14	2.38	1.36	26.95
Annual Growth	**1.2%**	**—**	**—**	**(1.3%)**	**(38.1%)**	**11.4%**

Kaiser Foundation Health Plan

Kaiser Foundation Health Plan aims to be the emperor of the HMO universe. With more than 8.6 million members in nine states and the District of Columbia, it is one of the largest not-for-profit managed health care companies in the US. Kaiser has an integrated care model, offering both hospital and physician care through a network of hospitals and physician practices operating under the Kaiser Permanente name. Members of Kaiser health plans have access to hospitals and hundreds of other health care facilities operated by Kaiser Foundation Hospitals and Permanente Medical Groups; these associations consist of about 14,000 doctors.

California is the company's largest market, accounting for more than 75% of its members. It also operates in Colorado, Georgia, Hawaii, Maryland, Ohio, Oregon, Virginia, Washington, and the District of Columbia.

Kaiser's strategy for growth and profitability consists of strengthening its integrated care model via increased use of technology and construction of new health care facilities, particularly in markets that are not already saturated with competition.

HISTORY

Henry Kaiser — shipbuilder, war profiteer, builder of the Hoover and Grand Coulee dams, and founder of Kaiser Aluminum — was a bootstrap capitalist who did well by doing good. A high school dropout from upstate New York, Kaiser moved to Spokane, Washington, in 1906 and went into road construction. During the Depression, he headed the consortium that built the great WPA dams.

It was in building the Grand Coulee Dam that, in 1938, Kaiser teamed with Dr. Sidney Garfield, who earlier had devised a prepayment health plan for workers on California public works projects. As Kaiser moved into steelmaking and shipbuilding during WWII (turning out some 1,400 bare-bones Liberty ships — one per day at peak production), Kaiser decided healthy workers produce more than sick ones, and he called on Garfield to set up on-site clinics funded by the US government as part of operating expenses. Garfield was released from military service by President Roosevelt for the purpose.

After the war, the clinics became war surplus. Kaiser and his wife bought them — at a 99% discount — through the new Kaiser Hospital Foundation. His vision was to provide the public with low-cost, prepaid medical care. He created the health plan — the self-supporting entity that would administer the system — and the group medical organization, Permanente (named after Kaiser's first cement plant site). He then endowed the health plan with $200,000. This health plan, the classic HMO model, was criticized by the medical establishment as socialized medicine performed by "employee" doctors.

But the plan flourished, becoming California's #1 medical system. In 1958 Kaiser retired to Hawaii and started his health plan there. But physician resistance limited national growth; HMOs were illegal in some states well into the 1970s. As health care costs rose, Congress legalized HMOs in all states. Kaiser expanded in the 1980s; as it moved outside its traditional geographic areas, the company contracted for space in hospitals rather than build them. Growth slowed as competition increased.

Some health care costs in California fell in the early 1990s as more medical procedures were performed on an outpatient basis. Specialists flooded the state, and as price competition among doctors and hospitals heated up, many HMOs landed advantageous contracts. Kaiser, with its own highly paid doctors, was unable to realize the same savings and was no longer the best deal in town. Its membership stalled.

To boost membership and control expenses, Kaiser instituted a controversial program in 1996 in which nurses earned bonuses for cost-cutting. Critics said the program could lead to a decrease in care quality; Kaiser later became the focus of investigations into wrongful death suits linked to cost-cutting in California (where it has since beefed up staffing and programs) and Texas (where it has agreed to pay $1 million in fines).

In 1997 Kaiser and Washington-based Group Health Cooperative of Puget Sound formed Kaiser/Group Health to handle administrative services in the Northwest. Kaiser also tried to boost membership by lowering premiums, but the strategy proved *too* effective: Costs linked to an unwieldy 20% enrollment surge brought a loss in 1997 — Kaiser's first annual loss ever.

A second year in the red in 1998 prompted Kaiser to sell its Texas operations to Sierra Health Services. It also entered the Florida market via an alliance with Miami-based AvMed Health Plan. In 1999 Kaiser announced plans to sell its unprofitable North Carolina operations (it closed the deal the following year).

In 2000 Kaiser announced plans to charge premiums for its Medicare HMO, Medicare Advantage, to offset the shortfall in federal reimbursements. Kaiser also responded to rising costs

by selling its unprofitable operations in North Carolina (2000) and Kansas (2001). In 2001 the company's hospital division bought the technology and assets of defunct Internet grocer Webvan in an effort to increase its distribution activity. Also that year the son of a deceased anthrax victim sued a Kaiser facility for failing to recognize and treat his father's symptoms.

EXECUTIVES

Chairman and CEO: George C. Halvorson
EVP and CFO: Kathy Lancaster
EVP, Health Plan Operations: Arthur M. Southam
EVP, Health Plan and Hospital Operations: Bernard J. Tyson
SVP and Chief Information Officer: Philip (Phil) Fasano
SVP, Brand Strategy, Communications, and Public Relations: Diane Gage Lofgren
SVP, Research and Policy Development: Robert M. Crane
SVP, Government Relations: Anthony A. (Tony) Barrueta
SVP and Chief Human Resources Officer: Chuck Columbus
SVP, Community Benefit, Research, and Health Policy; CEO, KP Cal: Raymond J. (Ray) Baxter
SVP and General Counsel: Mark S. Zemelman
SVP, Quality and Care Delivery Excellence: Jed Weissberg
Auditors: KPMG LLP

LOCATIONS

HQ: Kaiser Foundation Health Plan, Inc.
1 Kaiser Plaza, Oakland, CA 94612
Phone: 510-271-5800   **Fax:** 510-271-6493
Web: www.kaiserpermanente.org

2008 Membership

	No. of members
Northern California	3,285,068
Southern California	3,281,915
Mid-Atlantic States (Virginia, Maryland & Washington, DC)	485,401
Colorado	479,980
Northwest (Oregon & Washington)	472,555
Georgia	269,802
Hawaii	222,594
Ohio	137,669
Total	**8,634,984**

COMPETITORS

Aetna
AMERIGROUP
Assurant Health
Blue Shield Of California
CareFirst
CIGNA
Community Health Plan of Washington
Coventry Health Care
First Choice Health
Group Health Cooperative (Puget Sound)
Hawaii Medical Service Association
Health Net
Humana
Molina Healthcare
Oregon Dental
PacificSource
Premera Blue Cross
Regence
Sharp Health Plan
UnitedHealth Group
WellCare Health Plans
WellPoint

Kansas City Southern

Kansas City Southern (KCS) rides the rails of a 6,000-mile network that stretches from Missouri to Mexico. The company's Kansas City Southern Railway (KCSR) owns and operates more than 3,200 miles of track in the midwestern and southern US. KCS offers rail freight service in Mexico through Kansas City Southern de México (KCSM, formerly TFM), which maintains more than 2,600 miles of track and serves three major ports. Another KCS unit, Texas Mexican Railway, connects the KCSR and KCSM systems. The KCS railroads transport such freight as industrial and consumer products, agricultural and mineral products, and chemical and petroleum products.

Through its own system and marketing agreements with other railroads, KCS can arrange to have its customers' freight carried throughout much of Canada, Mexico, and the US, thus capitalizing on business generated by the North American Free Trade Agreement (NAFTA).

KCS sees traffic at the Port of Lázaro Cárdenas, on Mexico's Pacific coast, as a key source of new business. The railroad is building intermodal hubs in Lázaro Cárdenas; Mexico City; Rosenberg, Texas (southeast of Houston); and Kansas City, Missouri. In early 2010, KCS solidified its position in Mexico even further when it acquired a Puerta Mexico intermodal facility at Toluca (located in the state of Mexico).

KCS picks up intermodal containers arriving from Asia at the port in Mexico and hauls them into the US through Texas, offering Asian shippers an alternative to busier ports in California. In order to optimize its route network and clamp down on costs, in 2009 KCS opened a new rail line from Rosenberg to Victoria, Texas.

Within the US, KCS is working with railroad operator Norfolk Southern to boost capacity on the Meridian Speedway, a 320-mile line between Shreveport, Louisiana, and Meridian, Mississippi, that has become a key rail link between the southeastern and southwestern US. The Mexican port of Lázaro Cárdenas and the southern US rail lines are central to the KCS strategy of promoting rail as an alternative to hauling freight by truck.

In addition to its main rail system, KCS owns a 50% stake in the Panama Canal Railway Company, which transports passengers and cargo over a 48-mile railroad between the Atlantic and Pacific oceans. KCS also owns a bulk material-handling facility on the Gulf of Mexico, which enables the company to transfer cargo from railcars to ships.

KCS has a railcar and locomotive leasing business with GATX Rail called Southern Capital Corporation LLC. The partnership company leases more than 2,800 railcars and about 300 locomotives to KCSR.

HISTORY

Arthur Edward Stilwell founded the Kansas City Southern Railway (KCSR) in 1887 to transport commodities for local meatpackers and granaries. By 1891 Stilwell had expanded the line southward to Fort Smith, Arkansas. Two years later he extended the line to the Gulf of Mexico to give the heartland's agricultural producers an outlet to the sea. Stilwell decided to route his lines to Lake Sabine, Texas, seven miles inland from the Gulf and relatively protected from hurricanes. He built a port on the lake and then dredged a canal to the Gulf. Subsequently named Port Arthur, the site became the second-largest grain port after New York.

In the 1920s and 1930s Leonore Loree, Stilwell's successor, guided the company through the Depression and beyond with sound financial management. In 1939 KCSR bought the Louisiana and Arkansas Railways to extend its lines to New Orleans and Dallas. That year General Motors chose the railroad to test its first passenger-service diesel-electric locomotive.

Kansas businessmen wrested control of the company from its eastern owners in 1944 and appointed William Deramus as president. With a new leader and operating strategy in place, the railroad focused on expanding its business into territories that were experiencing a post-WWII industrial boom.

In the 1950s KCSR developed a computerized data-processing system for its businesses. During the mid-1950s Deramus and his son, William Deramus III (then president of the Chicago Great Western and Katy Railway), were heavily involved in building the Mid-America Pipeline (MAPCO) along their railroads' rights-of-way, though KCSR's interest ended by the early 1980s.

In 1961 William Deramus III joined his father in senior management at the company. Kansas City Southern Industries (KCSI) was incorporated as a holding company for the purpose of diversification in the face of growing competition from airlines and the trucking industry. As the company's data-processing and information management needs increased, KCSI capitalized on its early data-processing experience by forming DST Systems.

Growth during the 1980s resulted from an increase in coal transport and additional freight traffic. In 1983 KCSI bought a majority stake in Janus Capital, a Denver-based mutual funds company. By the late 1980s the company's transportation and financial management divisions were prospering because of higher coal volume and the growth of the mutual funds industry.

KCSI increased its mutual funds holdings by buying Berger and Associates in 1992. In 1997 the company formed Kansas City Southern Lines, a holding company for its transportation segments, to streamline its corporate structure and refocus on its core businesses.

The next year KCSI created FAM Holding Company to house its financial asset management subsidiaries, including Janus Capital, Berger Associates, and DST Systems. Also in 1998, with partner Mi-Jack Products (a maker of intermodal equipment), KCSI was awarded the Panama Canal railroad concession by the government of Panama.

In 1999 KSCI announced plans to spin off its financial services businesses to shareholders as a new company, Stilwell Financial (renamed Janus Capital Group in 2003).

KCSI completed reconstruction of the Panama Canal Railway in 2001 and reopened the railroad for freight and passenger transport. Two years after the Stilwell spinoff, KCSI shortened its name to Kansas City Southern (KCS) to reflect its renewed focus on transportation.

KCS completed its purchase of Grupo TMM's stake in Grupo TFM in 2005. Later in 2005 the settlement of a tax dispute that involved KCS, TFM, Grupo TFM, Grupo TMM, and the Mexican government resulted in KCS receiving the 20% stake in TFM held by the government and thus gaining full ownership of the railroad.

EXECUTIVES

Chairman: Michael R. (Mike) Haverty, age 65, $3,504,351 total compensation
President and CEO: David L. Starling, age 60
EVP and CFO: Michael W. (Mike) Upchurch, age 48, $645,846 total compensation
EVP and Assistant to the Chairman: Larry M. Lawrence, age 47
EVP Corporate Affairs: Warren K. Erdman, age 51
EVP Sales and Marketing: Patrick J. (Pat) Ottensmeyer, age 52, $1,344,692 total compensation
SVP Operations; EVP and COO, Kansas City Southern Railway Company: David R. (Dave) Ebbrecht
SVP Intermodal and Automotive: Brian Bowers
SVP and Chief Legal Officer: W. James (Jim) Wochner, age 62
SVP Human Resources: John E. Derry, age 42
SVP International Engineering: Jerry W. Heavin
SVP, Finance and Treasurer, Kansas City Northern and Kansas City Southern Railway: Paul J. Weyandt, age 56
SVP and Chief Accounting Officer: Mary K. Stadler, age 50
SVP Sales and Marketing and Asset Management: David Eaton
VP and Chief Engineer: John S. Jacobsen
VP Investor Relations: William (Bill) Galligan
VP and Chief Mechanical Officer: John Foster
Assistant VP Corporate Communications and Community Affairs: C. Doniele Kane
President and Director General, Panama Canal Railway Company: Thomas H. (Tom) Kenna
President and Executive Representative, Mexico: Jose G. Zozaya Delano
Head Corporate Affairs: Edgar Guillaumin
Auditors: KPMG LLP

LOCATIONS

HQ: Kansas City Southern
427 W. 12th St., Kansas City, MO 64105
Phone: 816-983-1303   **Fax:** 816-983-1108
Web: www.kcsi.com

2009 Sales

	$ mil.	% of total
US	864.2	58
Mexico	616.0	42
Total	**1,480.2**	**100**

PRODUCTS/OPERATIONS

2009 Sales

	$ mil.	% of total
Agriculture & minerals	360.0	24
Industrial & consumer products	344.4	23
Chemical & petroleum	323.4	22
Coal	187.2	13
Intermodal	143.4	10
Automotive	52.9	3
Other	68.9	5
Total	**1,480.2**	**100**

COMPETITORS

American Commercial Lines
Burlington Northern Santa Fe
Canadian National Railway
Canadian Pacific Railway
Crowley Maritime
CSX
Grupo Carso
Grupo México
Ingram Industries
J.B. Hunt
Kirby Corporation
Norfolk Southern
Schneider National
Union Pacific
Werner Enterprises

HISTORICAL FINANCIALS

Company Type: Public

Income Statement

FYE: December 31

	REVENUE ($ mil.)	NET INCOME ($ mil.)	NET PROFIT MARGIN	EMPLOYEES
12/09	1,480	57	3.9%	6,100
12/08	1,852	169	9.1%	6,400
12/07	1,743	154	8.8%	6,485
12/06	1,660	109	6.6%	6,470
12/05	1,352	101	7.5%	3,060
Annual Growth	**2.3%**	**(13.3%)**	**—**	**18.8%**

2009 Year-End Financials

Debt ratio: 93.1%
Return on equity: 2.9%
Cash ($ mil.): 118
Current ratio: 1.49
Long-term debt ($ mil.): 1,912

No. of shares (mil.): 103
Dividends
  Yield: 0.0%
  Payout: —
Market value ($ mil.): 3,414

Stock History

NYSE: KSU

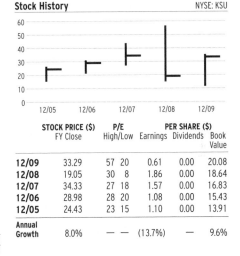

	STOCK PRICE ($) FY Close	P/E High/Low		PER SHARE ($) Earnings	Dividends	Book Value
12/09	33.29	57	20	0.61	0.00	20.08
12/08	19.05	30	8	1.86	0.00	18.64
12/07	34.33	27	18	1.57	0.00	16.83
12/06	28.98	28	20	1.08	0.00	15.43
12/05	24.43	23	15	1.10	0.00	13.91
Annual Growth	**8.0%**	**—**	**—**	**(13.7%)**	**—**	**9.6%**

KB Home

For a dwelling done your way, you might turn to KB Home. KB builds houses mainly for first-time, trade-up, and active adult buyers primarily in the West, Southwest, and along the East Coast. The company markets houses under its Built to Order brand, which allows buyers to customize their homes by choosing a floor plan as well as exterior and interior features. The average selling price of a KB home is around $207,000. KB offers attached and detached single-family homes, in addition to townhomes and condos. It offers financing, mortgage assistance, title, and insurance through its KB Home Mortgage, a joint venture with Bank of America. KB has built more than a half a million homes since it was founded in 1957.

However, those numbers have been slower to grow in the past few years. The economic recession has led to declining revenues and fewer home starts for KB since 2008. The company has delivered fewer homes with lower average selling prices since the slump. The downtrend is due to the glut of housing made available by high foreclosure rates, coupled with overbuilding and tight credit. At the same time demand has decreased due to rising unemployment and declining consumer confidence.

The company has reduced costs by cutting staff, abandoning non-performing markets such as Detroit, shedding assets such as its international subsidiary in 2007, and working to move products to generate cash flow and manage debt.

Another key to its strategy for surviving the downturn is the company's ability to turn out cheaper and smaller houses (something customers are hungry for). In 2009 KB announced a product line called "Open Series" that allows homebuyers to control such specifications as square footage or how many rooms they want.

Among its design options are special packages and that are carry branding by Stewart and the Walt Disney Company. Other available features include the My Home My Earth environmental program, which features energy-efficient appliances and other earth-friendly options.

HISTORY

Kaufman and Broad Building Co. was founded in Detroit in 1957 by Eli Broad and Donald Kaufman. Broad, an accountant, parlayed an initial $25,000 investment into sales of $250,000 on the first weekend of business. By the end of its first year, Kaufman and Broad was posting revenues of $1.7 million.

The company expanded rapidly and went public in 1961. A year later it was the first homebuilder to be listed on the NYSE. Kaufman and Broad moved into California in 1963. Through acquisitions, it rapidly became a top US homebuilder, expanding into New York, San Francisco, and Chicago. In 1965 it formed a mortgage subsidiary to arrange loans for its customers.

In the early 1970s the firm entered Europe and Canada. Sales passed the $100 million mark in 1971 and the company diversified, buying Sun Life Insurance. Housing operations were renamed Kaufman and Broad Development Group (KBDG).

In 1980 the flamboyant Bruce Karatz, who had joined the firm in 1972, was appointed president. Karatz steered the company through the recession of the early 1980s, focusing on California, France, and Canada. KBDG acquired Bati-Service, a major French developer of affordable homes, in 1985.

The company was renamed Kaufman and Broad Home Corporation in 1986. In 1989 it reorganized into two separate billion-dollar companies: Broad Inc. (now SunAmerica), an insurance firm with Eli Broad as its chairman and CEO; and Kaufman and Broad Home, with Karatz as CEO (and later chairman), which was spun off to shareholders in 1989.

When the California real estate market crashed in 1990, earnings plummeted. Karatz diversified by buying up strong regional builders. Kaufman and Broad entered Arizona, Colorado, and Nevada in 1993 and Utah in 1994. Profits dropped in 1995-96 because of weakness in the California and Paris markets and the company's winding down of Canadian operations. But expansion continued, including the acquisition of Rayco, a Texas builder, in 1996.

Borrowing from the methods of Rayco, Kaufman and Broad began surveying homebuyers for suggestions to incorporate into new designs. In 1998 the company began to build its New Home Showrooms. The corporation continued its expansion drive that year when it paid about $165 million for Dover/Ideal, PrideMark, and Estes, privately held builders based in Houston, Denver, and Tucson, respectively. In 1999 Kaufman and Broad bought Lewis Homes, a major

California builder and the #1 builder in Las Vegas, for about $545 million.

In 2001 the company changed its name again, shortening it to KB Home.

KB Home launched a division in Tampa and expanded operations into Central Florida in 2002 by acquiring Orlando-based American Heritage Homes for about $74 million. It also expanded in other markets, which included Tucson (by acquiring assets of New World Homes, gaining more than 1,600 lots in 12 new home communities there) and the Rio Grande Valley of Texas (by opening a division in the fast-growing McAllen region, about four miles from the Mexican border).

KB Home continued to build its empire in 2003 by acquiring Atlanta-based Colony Homes, one of the Southeast's largest privately owned homebuilders, with principal operations in Atlanta, Raleigh, and Charlotte. The company also moved into the Midwest with the purchase of privately held homebuilder Zale Homes (Chicago). KB Home also added to its French holdings by acquiring Euro Immobilier.

In 2004 KB Home expanded its operations in the Southeast by acquiring South Carolina-based Palmetto Traditional Homes, which builds in the state's largest metropolitan areas: Charleston, Columbia, and Greenville-Spartanburg-Anderson. It also acquired Indianapolis builder Dura Builders and two French builders, Groupe Avantis and Foncier Investissement.

KB Home sold its KB Home Mortgage subsidiary to Countrywide Home Loans in 2005, and then formed its Countrywide KB Home Loans joint venture to serve KB customers.

When charges of fraud surrounding company stock options were leveled against Karatz in 2006, the chairman and president retired from KB Home; former COO Jeff Mezger was then named president and CEO.

In 2007 KB sold its 49% stake in its French subsidiary Kaufman & Broad to PAI Partners for about $800 million, thus exiting all international operations.

EXECUTIVES

Chairman: Stephen F. Bollenbach, age 67
President, CEO, and Director: Jeffrey T. (Jeff) Mezger, age 54, $9,028,489 total compensation
EVP and CFO: Jeff Kaminski, age 48
EVP, General Counsel, and Corporate Secretary: Wendy C. Shiba, age 59, $1,350,430 total compensation
SVP Human Resources: Thomas F. (Tom) Norton, age 39
SVP Sales, Marketing, and Communications: Wendy L. Marlett, $1,168,631 total compensation
SVP KBnxt Group: Glen Barnard, age 65, $887,060 total compensation
SVP Studios: Lisa M. Kalmbach
SVP Tax: Cory C. Cohen
SVP and Chief Accounting Officer: William R. (Bill) Hollinger, age 51, $1,403,795 total compensation
VP Land Acquisition, Washington, D.C.: Mark Boastfield
Auditors: Ernst & Young LLP

LOCATIONS

HQ: KB Home
10990 Wilshire Blvd., Los Angeles, CA 90024
Phone: 310-231-4000   **Fax:** 310-231-4222
Web: www.kbhome.com

2009 Sales

	$ mil.	% of total
West Coast	812.2	45
Central	434.4	24
Southeast	351.7	19
Southwest	218.1	12
Financial services	8.4	—
Total	**1,824.8**	**100**

PRODUCTS/OPERATIONS

2009 Sales

	$ mil.	% of total
Homebuilding	1,816.4	99
Financial Services	8.4	1
Total	**1,824.8**	**100**

COMPETITORS

Beazer Homes
Capital Pacific
David Weekley Homes
D.R. Horton
Highland Homes
Hovnanian Enterprises
Lennar
M.D.C.
Mercedes Homes
Meritage Homes
NVR
PulteGroup
The Ryland Group
Shapell Industries
Standard Pacific
Toll Brothers
Weyerhaeuser Real Estate
William Lyon Homes

HISTORICAL FINANCIALS

Company Type: Public

Income Statement

	REVENUE ($ mil.)	NET INCOME ($ mil.)	NET PROFIT MARGIN	EMPLOYEES
			FYE: November 30	
11/09	1,825	(102)	—	1,400
11/08	3,034	(976)	—	1,600
11/07	6,417	(929)	—	3,100
11/06	11,004	482	4.4%	5,100
11/05	9,442	842	8.9%	6,700
Annual Growth	**(33.7%)**	**—**	**—**	**(32.4%)**

2009 Year-End Financials

Debt ratio: —	No. of shares (mil.): 88
Return on equity: —	Dividends
Cash ($ mil.): 1,175	Yield: 1.8%
Current ratio: 1.15	Payout: —
Long-term debt ($ mil.): —	Market value ($ mil.): 1,193

Stock History

NYSE: KBH

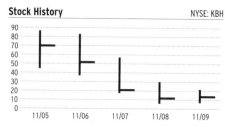

	STOCK PRICE ($) FY Close	P/E High/Low		PER SHARE ($) Earnings	Dividends	Book Value
11/09	13.55	—	—	(1.33)	0.25	8.03
11/08	11.63	—	—	(12.59)	0.81	9.43
11/07	20.89	—	—	(12.04)	1.00	21.02
11/06	51.69	14	7	5.82	1.00	33.20
11/05	69.77	9	5	9.53	0.75	32.39
Annual Growth	**(33.6%)**	**—**	**—**	**—**	**(24.0%)**	**(29.4%)**

Kellogg Company

Location as irony — Battle Creek, Michigan-based Kellogg is in a constant battle for the #1 spot in the US cereal market with its main rival, General Mills. Kellogg's boasts many a familiar brand name, including Kellogg's Corn Flakes, Frosted Flakes, Corn Pops, and Rice Krispies. And while the company fills many a cereal bowl every morning, it puffs up its bottom line with snacks and cookies (Keebler, Cheez-It, and Famous Amos), along with convenience foods such as Eggo waffles and Nutri-Grain and Bear Naked cereal bars. Its products are sold in more than 180 countries worldwide.

And although Kellogg may have snapped under the pressure of its ongoing cereal war with General Mills, it also crackled under fierce competition from private-label breakfast cereal maker Ralcorp, which acquired the Post cereal operations of Kraft Foods in 2008. However, Kellogg pops with continued pursuit of new markets, one acquisition being Worthington Foods, owner of the Morningstar Farms brand of meat alternatives.

Expanding its international presence, in 2008 the company acquired Chinese cookie and cracker manufacturer Zhenghang Food Company (dba Navigable Foods). Also that year Kellogg acquired The United Bakers Group, a top cracker, biscuit, and breakfast cereal manufacturer in Russia, as well as Specialty Cereals, an Australian cereal manufacturer. The company wrapped up 2008 in a sweet fashion a little closer to home with the purchase of the recipes and trademarks from the bankrupt Mother's Cake & Cookie Co., adding suchs brands as Chips Deluxe, Fudge Shoppe, and Sandies.

The company's largest customer is Wal-Mart, which accounted for about 21% of Kellogg's 2009 sales.

The private charity the W. K. Kellogg Foundation owns about 23% of the company; philanthropist George Gund III owns 9%; and financial services firm KeyCorp owns 8%.

HISTORY

Will Keith (W. K.) Kellogg first made wheat flakes in 1894 while working for his brother, Dr. John Kellogg, at Battle Creek, Michigan's famed homeopathic sanitarium. While doing an experiment with grains (for patients' diets), the two men were interrupted; by the time they returned to the dough, it had absorbed water. They rolled it anyway, toasted the result, and accidentally created the first flaked cereal. John sold the flakes via mail order (1899) in a partnership that W. K. managed. In 1906 W. K. started his own firm to produce corn flakes.

As head of the Battle Creek Toasted Corn Flake Company, W. K. competed against 42 cereal companies in Battle Creek (one run by former patient C. W. Post) and roared to the head of the pack with his innovative marketing ideas. A 1906 *Ladies' Home Journal* ad helped increase demand from 33 cases a day earlier that year to 2,900 a day by year-end. W. K. soon introduced Bran Flakes (1915), All-Bran (1916), and Rice Krispies (1928). International expansion began in Canada (1914) and followed in Australia (1924) and England (1938). Diversifying a little, the company introduced the Pop-Tart in 1964

and acquired Eggo waffles in the 1970s. By the early 1980s Kellogg's US market share dipped, due to strong competition from General Mills and other rivals. The company pitched new cereals to adults and aggressively pursued the fast-growing European market.

Kellogg spent the mid-1990s reengineering itself, creating the USA Convenience Foods Division and selling such noncore assets as its carton container and Argentine snack-food makers (1993). It teamed with ConAgra in 1994 to create a cereal line sold under the latter's popular Healthy Choice label.

In 1997-98 the company expanded operations in Australia, the UK, Asia, and Latin America, and it slashed about 25% of its salaried North American workforce and hiked prices on about two-thirds of its cereals. Several top officers left in 1998-99, and Cuban-born president and COO Carlos Gutierrez became CEO.

The company sold the disappointing Lender's division to Aurora Foods in 1999 for just $275 million. (Aurora later merged with Pinnacle Foods to become Pinnacle Foods Group — now Pinnacle Foods Finance and owned by Blackstone.) Kellogg took another crack at non-breakfast foods when it bought Worthington Foods (Morningstar Farms meat alternatives, Harvest Burgers) for $307 million.

By the beginning of 2000, cereal competitor General Mills had closed the gap with Kellogg in US market share (in 2001 it passed Kellogg as the #1 cereal maker). In 2001 Kellogg bulked up its snacks portfolio by acquiring Keebler Foods for $4.5 billion. In the aftermath of the acquisition, the company trimmed jobs at Keebler and its own headquarters.

To boost enthusiasm among kids for breakfast, in 2002 Kellogg launched new cereals featuring Disney characters Buzz Lightyear, Mickey Mouse, and Winnie the Pooh — the first such alliance for The Walt Disney Company. That move, combined with better marketing and General Mills being distracted by its purchase of Pillsbury, helped Kellogg grab back the top spot in the US.

In 2004 Kellogg reached an agreement with then New York Attorney General Eliot Spitzer to stop using promotional toys identified as a possible environmental risk in its cereal products. In addition, the company agreed to phase out the sale or distribution of promotional products containing mercury by the end of 2004, recycle mercury batteries returned by consumers, and educate consumers as to the need to dispose of mercury properly.

In 2005 Gutierrez resigned from Kellogg to become secretary of the Department of Commerce in the George W. Bush administration. He was succeeded at the cereal behemoth by advertising executive and Kellogg board member James Jenness. In 2006 David Mackay was appointed Kellogg's CEO, replacing Jenness who remained as chairman.

The company began using oils derived from genetically modified soybeans in some of its products in 2006 in order to lower their fat content. It added to its meatless menu with its 2007 acquisition of Wholesome & Hearty Foods, the maker of Gardenburger. It also acquired Bear Naked, a small seller of natural granola, in 2007.

In 2009 Kellogg voluntarily recalled selected products that contained peanut butter ingredients supplied by the now defunct Peanut Corporation of America, whose products were found to contain salmonella.

EXECUTIVES

Chairman: James M. (Jim) Jenness, age 64
President, CEO, and Director: A. D. David Mackay, age 55, $11,419,447 total compensation
EVP, COO, and Director: John A. Bryant, age 44, $4,726,262 total compensation
CFO: Ronald L. (Ron) Dissinger, age 51
SVP; President, Kellogg North America: Bradford J. (Brad) Davidson, age 49, $4,275,174 total compensation
SVP; President, Kellogg International: Paul Norman, age 45, $3,390,589 total compensation
SVP; EVP, Kellogg International; President, Kellogg Europe: Timothy P. Mobsby, age 55, $4,096,450 total compensation
SVP; President, U.S. Morning Foods: Juan P. Villalobos, age 44
SVP; President, Kellogg Specialty Channels: David J. (Dave) Pfanzelter, age 56
SVP and CIO: Brian S. Rice, age 47
SVP Global Human Resources: Dennis W. Shuler, age 55
SVP Global Nutrition and Corporate Affairs and Chief Sustainability Officer: Celeste A. Clark, age 56
SVP Corporate Development, General Counsel, and Secretary: Gary H. Pilnick, age 45
VP Corporate Social Responsibility: Tim Knowlton
VP and Corporate Controller: Alan R. Andrews, age 54
VP; President, Kellogg U.S. Snacks: Todd Penegor, age 45
VP and Global Chief Marketing Officer: Mark R. Baynes, age 49
VP Investor Relations: Kathryn C. Koessel, age 47
Auditors: PricewaterhouseCoopers LLP

LOCATIONS

HQ: Kellogg Company
1 Kellogg Sq., Battle Creek, MI 49016
Phone: 269-961-2000 **Fax:** 269-961-2871
Web: www.kelloggcompany.com

2009 Sales

	$ mil.	% of total
North America	8,510	68
Europe	2,361	19
Latin America	963	7
Asia/Pacific	741	6
Total	**12,575**	**100**

PRODUCTS/OPERATIONS

2009 Sales

	$ mil.	% of total
Cereal	6,406	51
Snacks	4,012	32
Frozen & specialty foods	1,418	11
Convenience foods	739	6
Total	**12,575**	**100**

Selected US Cereal Brands

All-Bran	Frosted Mini-Wheats
Apple Jacks	Just Right
Bran Buds	Kellogg's Corn Flakes
Cinnamon Crunch	Kellogg's Frosted Flakes
Cocoa Krispies	Kellogg's Low-Fat Granola
Complete Bran Flakes	Kellogg's Raisin Bran
Complete Wheat Flakes	Mueslix
Corn Pops	Pops
Cracklin' Oat Bran	Product 19
Crispix	Raisin Bran
Crunch	Rice Krispies
Cruncheroos	Smacks/Honey Smacks
Froot Loops	Smart Start
Frosted Krispies	Special K

Selected Other US Brands

Cereal Bars and Granola
All-Bran
Bear Naked
GoLean
Kashi

Convenience Foods
Austin
Cheez-It
Chips Deluxe
Club
Croutettes Croutons
E. L. Fudge
Famous Amos
Fudge Shoppe
Hi-Ho
Keebler
Krispy Munch'Ems
Pop-Tarts
Ready Crust
Rice Krispies Squares
Rice Krispies Treats
Right Bites
Sandies
Soft Batch
Sunshine

Frozen Waffles and Pancakes
Eggo
Froot Loops
Nutri-Grain
Special K

Water and Water Mixes
Special K
Special K2O

Meat and Egg Alternatives
Gardenburger
Loma Linda
Morningstar Farms
Natural Touch
Worthington

COMPETITORS

Amy's Kitchen	Jordans & Ryvita
Barbara's Bakery	Kraft Foods
Bob's Red Mill Natural	Lance Snacks
Foods	Malt-O-Meal
Boca Foods	McKee Foods
Campbell Soup	Nestlé
ConAgra	Patty King
Frito-Lay	PepsiCo
General Mills	Pinnacle Foods
Gilster-Mary Lee	PowerBar
Goodman Fielder	Ralcorp
granoVita	Ralston Food
Hain Celestial	Weetabix
Hostess Brands	Wellness Foods
J & J Snack Foods	Wessanen

HISTORICAL FINANCIALS

Company Type: Public

Income Statement

FYE: December 31

	REVENUE ($ mil.)	NET INCOME ($ mil.)	NET PROFIT MARGIN	EMPLOYEES
12/09	12,575	1,212	9.6%	30,900
12/08	12,822	1,148	9.0%	32,400
12/07	11,776	1,103	9.4%	26,000
12/06	10,907	1,004	9.2%	26,000
12/05	10,177	980	9.6%	25,600
Annual Growth	5.4%	5.4%	—	4.8%

2009 Year-End Financials

Debt ratio: 212.8%
Return on equity: 65.2%
Cash ($ mil.): 334
Current ratio: 1.12
Long-term debt ($ mil.): 4,835

No. of shares (mil.): 378
Dividends
  Yield: 2.7%
  Payout: 45.3%
Market value ($ mil.): 20,097

Stock History

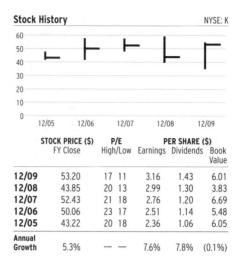

NYSE: K

	STOCK PRICE ($) FY Close	P/E High/Low	PER SHARE ($) Earnings	Dividends	Book Value
12/09	53.20	17 11	3.16	1.43	6.01
12/08	43.85	20 13	2.99	1.30	3.83
12/07	52.43	21 18	2.76	1.20	6.69
12/06	50.06	23 17	2.51	1.14	5.48
12/05	43.22	20 18	2.36	1.06	6.05
Annual Growth	5.3%	— —	7.6%	7.8%	(0.1%)

Kelly Services

These days a lot of "Kelly Girls" are men. Once a business that supplied only female clerical help, Kelly Services has expanded to include male and female temporary employees in light industrial, technical, and professional sectors, including information technology specialists, engineers, and accountants. It also places lawyers (Kelly Law Registry), scientists (Kelly Scientific Resources), substitute teachers (Kelly Educational Staffing), nurses and other medical staff (Kelly Healthcare Resources), and teleservices personnel (KellyConnect). Kelly Services assigns some 480,000 temporary employees each year. Chairman Terence Adderley owns a controlling stake in the company.

The company provides additional personnel in areas such as electronics (Kelly Electronic Assembly Services), merchandising (Kelly Marketing Services), and catering (Kelly Catering and Hospitality). It also offers career transition, outplacement, and human resources consulting services through its Ayers Group division.

As demand for staffing services plummeted in 2009, Kelly Services was forced to launch cost-saving initiatives. These moves resulted in the reduction of its global workforce by 1,900 employees. The company also shut down 240 branch locations. To sidestep the widening weak economy, Kelly plans to focus on contracting with large corporate clients to provide temporary workers.

Before the recession, the company pursued a strategy of growth in specialized industry sectors through the use of acquisitions. In 2008 the company entered a new market with the acquisition of all the Portuguese subsidiaries of global staffing powerhouse Randstad Holding for about $13 million in cash. Kelly also expanded its expertise in specialized accounting and finance recruiting by purchasing UK-based Toner Graham for $9 million that year.

HISTORY

William Russell Kelly, a college dropout and former car salesman, went to Detroit after WWII to seek his fortune. An owner of modern business equipment, he set up Russell Kelly Office Service in 1946 to provide copying, typing, and inventory services for other businesses; first-year sales from 12 customers totaled $848.

Although companies began to acquire their own machines, Kelly knew that they still needed people to work at their offices. He reincorporated his rapidly expanding business as Personnel Service in 1952 and opened the company's first branch office in Louisville, Kentucky, in 1955; by the end of that year, he had 35 offices throughout the US. In 1957 the company was renamed Kelly Girl Service to reflect its all-female workforce.

In the 1960s Kelly ventured beyond office services and began placing convention hostesses, blue-collar workers, data processors, door-to-door marketers, and drafters, among others. Kelly Girl went public in 1962, boasting 148 branches at the time. In 1966 the company adopted the name Kelly Services. It opened its first non-US office in Toronto in 1968, and one in Paris followed in 1972.

A tough US economy in the 1970s saw a surge in corporate interest in temporary employees. Employers saw the benefits of hiring "Kelly Girls" to meet seasonal needs and special projects. In 1976 Kelly Services acquired a modest health care services company and used it to form Kelly Home Care. In the 1980s this division abandoned the Medicaid and Medicare markets and shifted to private-sector care. Renamed Kelly Assisted Living Services in 1984 (and later known as Kelly Home Care Services), the unit offered aides to perform household duties and nurses to conduct home visits for the elderly and disabled. Also in the 1980s Kelly Services began hiring retired people as part of its ENCORE Program.

In 1988 Kelly began a program of international expansion that would see the company add operations in the Asia/Pacific region and in Europe.

The company developed specialty services in the US in the 1990s. It acquired ComTrain (testing and training software products) and Your Staff (an employee-leasing firm providing companies with entire human resources departments, including benefits and payroll services) in 1994. The following year it bought the Wallace Law Registry (renamed Kelly Law Registry), a provider of lawyers, paralegals, and clerks. Kelly also established Kelly Scientific Resources to place science professionals. In 1996 that subsidiary acquired Oak Ridge Research Institute, which provided scientists to the defense and energy industries.

William Kelly died at the age of 92 in 1998, and the company named president and CEO Terence Adderley, his adopted son, to replace him as chairman. (Adderley relinquished the title of president in late 2001.) The next year the company made four additions to its staffing services: Kelly Healthcare Resources, Kelly Financial Resources, Kelly Educational Staffing (substitute teachers), and KellyConnect (teleservices).

In 2000 the company made three acquisitions: Extra ETT in Spain (automotive staffing), ProStaff Group in the US (general staffing), and Business Trends Group in Singapore (general staffing). Kelly Services continued with its acquisition strategy the following year, purchasing the engineering services business of Compuware, among others. In 2002 the company opened new offices in the US, Europe, and Canada. In 2003

Kelly Services launched Kelly FedSecure, which provides professionals with security clearances to companies and government contractors.

Citing medical reasons, Adderley stepped down as chairman and CEO in 2006. President and COO Carl Camden took over as CEO, but by May 2006, Adderley had recovered and was named chairman again.

In order to augment its portfolio of career transition services and business effectiveness consulting, Kelly Services bought New York-based The Ayers Group. It also expanded its reach to the Czech Republic and Poland with the buyout of executive search firm Talents Technology in 2007. Also that year its presence in Japan grew when it acquired all the shares of former joint venture Tempstaff Kelly. Looking to China, Hong Kong, and Singapore, Kelly Services acquired executive search and HR outsourcing services firm P-Serv.

At the same time, the company shed some non-core operations. Kelly Services sold its Home Care Services unit to Res-Care in 2007 and sold its staff leasing operations to Oasis Outsourcing Holdings the year before. Kelly Services also closed 22 underperforming branches in the UK.

EXECUTIVES

Chairman: Terence E. (Terry) Adderley, age 76
President, CEO, and Director: Carl T. Camden, age 55, $957,565 total compensation
EVP and COO: George S. Corona, age 51, $894,733 total compensation
EVP and CFO: Patricia Little, age 50, $655,927 total compensation
EVP and General Manager, Americas:
  Michael S. (Mike) Webster, age 54, $725,878 total compensation
EVP and Chief Administrative Officer:
  Michael L. Durik, age 61, $636,587 total compensation
SVP and CIO: Joseph Drouin
SVP, General Counsel, and Corporate Secretary:
  Daniel T. Lis, age 63
SVP, Controller, and Chief Accounting Officer:
  Michael E. Debs, age 52, $500,635 total compensation
SVP Outsourcing and Consulting Group:
  Rolf E. Kleiner, age 55
SVP Global Service: Teresa S. Carroll
SVP Global Client Relationships: Peter W. Quigley
SVP Global Human Resources:
  Antonina M. (Nina) Ramsey, age 55
SVP and General Manager, KellyConnect:
  Jonathan D. Means
SVP Global Marketing: Michael S. Morrow
SVP Global Solutions and Services: Pamela M. Berklich
SVP Technical Services Group: Steve S. Armstrong
Senior Director Investor and Public Relations:
  James M. (Jim) Polehna
Auditors: PricewaterhouseCoopers LLP

LOCATIONS

HQ: Kelly Services, Inc.
  999 W. Big Beaver Rd., Troy, MI 48084
Phone: 248-362-4444
Web: www.kellyservices.com

PRODUCTS/OPERATIONS

2009 Sales

	$ mil.	% of total
Americas		
Commercial	2,006.1	44
Professional & Technical	793.4	18
International		
Commercial	1,283.5	29
Professional & Technical	180.0	4
Other	222.3	5
Adjustments	(170.5)	—
Total	**4,314.8**	**100**

Selected Services

CGR/seven (creative services staffing)
Kelly Catering and Hospitality (chefs, porters)
Kelly Educational Staffing (substitute teachers)
Kelly Electronic Assembly Services
Kelly Engineering Resources (engineers)
Kelly Financial Resources (accounting, analysts)
Kelly Government Solutions (US federal government staffing)
Kelly Healthcare Resources (nurses, medical technicians)
Kelly Information Technology Resources
Kelly Law Registry
Kelly Light Industrial
Kelly Marketing Services
Kelly Office Services (clerical staffing)
Kelly Scientific Resources (science staffing)
KellyConnect (call center staffing)
KellyDirect (permanent placement service)
KellySelect (temporary-to-hire service)

COMPETITORS

Adecco
Administaff
Allegis Group
ATC Healthcare
Manpower
On Assignment
Randstad Holding
Robert Half
SFN Group
TAC Worldwide
TrueBlue
Volt Information

HISTORICAL FINANCIALS

Company Type: Public

Income Statement

FYE: Sunday nearest December 31

	REVENUE ($ mil.)	NET INCOME ($ mil.)	NET PROFIT MARGIN	EMPLOYEES
12/09	4,315	(105)	—	487,900
12/08	5,517	(82)	—	660,100
12/07	5,668	61	1.1%	760,000
12/06	5,606	64	1.1%	750,000
12/05	5,290	39	0.7%	708,600
Annual Growth	**(5.0%)**	**—**	**—**	**(8.9%)**

2009 Year-End Financials

Debt ratio: 10.2%
Return on equity: —
Cash ($ mil.): 89
Current ratio: 1.67
Long-term debt ($ mil.): 58

No. of shares (mil.): 37
Dividends
  Yield: 0.0%
  Payout: —
Market value ($ mil.): 438

Stock History

NASDAQ (GS): KELYA

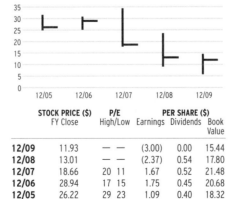

	STOCK PRICE ($) FY Close	P/E High/Low		PER SHARE ($) Earnings	Dividends	Book Value
12/09	11.93	—	—	(3.00)	0.00	15.44
12/08	13.01	—	—	(2.37)	0.54	17.80
12/07	18.66	20	11	1.67	0.52	21.48
12/06	28.94	17	15	1.75	0.45	20.68
12/05	26.22	29	23	1.09	0.40	18.32
Annual Growth	**(17.9%)**	**—**	**—**	**—**	**—**	**(4.2%)**

Kennametal Inc.

Kennametal welcomes your cutting-edge remarks. The company offers a host of metal-cutting tools and tooling systems for machining steel, equipment for mining and highway construction, and engineering services for production processes, across two business divisions: Metalworking Solutions and Services, and Advanced Materials Solutions. Its multi-trademark lineup includes cutting, milling, and drilling tools used in metalworking; drums, bits, and accessories used in mining; and bits, grader blades, and snowplow blades used in construction. Kennametal and its subsidiaries sell products and services worldwide, directly and through a distributor network. More than half of sales come from outside of North America.

The diversity and strength of Kennametal's end use markets, product and service lineup, and breadth of geographic operations has traditionally fueled the company's growth. Although still true, in 2009 Kennametal's bottom line has been exposed to weakening business activity, particularly in industrial metals, and oil and gas industries, agricultural markets, as well as slumping global economic conditions. Shoring up performance, the company has reshaped its business portfolio around competitive technologies, as well as rationalized its manufacturing footprint by reducing its salaried workforce and consolidating eight North American warehouses to a single, central location near Cleveland. In addition, Kennametal exited its high speed steel drills business in 2009, selling the product lines and assets to Top-Eastern Drills. The transaction involved four sites in North America, employing about 400 people.

Aiming to boost sales through an enhanced array of offerings, and further diversify its customer base, Kennametal is pushing its Advanced Materials Solutions Group (AMSG) into a revenue leading position. To that end, it rolled out a shrink-fit toolholding system in 2009 for machining centers and multi-purpose equipment. Kennametal also purchased Tricon Metals & Services, Inc. in 2008. Tricon supplies specialized steels for surface and underground mining businesses, and offers greater economies of scale for the group's operations. Tricon was renamed Kennametal Tricon Metals & Services.

Also in 2008 Kennametal acquired the metal-cutting tool business of Federal Signal. The business comprised Manchester Tool Company, ClappDiCO Corporation, and OTM.

HISTORY

In 1832 Irish immigrant and coppersmith Robert McKenna came to Pittsburgh and opened a copper works. His three sons took over the business after he died in 1852. In 1900 Robert's grandson, A. G. McKenna, developed a revolutionary cutting tool made of steel and tungsten (and later, of vanadium). The family set up Vanadium Alloys Steel Co. in 1910.

In 1938 Philip McKenna, A. G.'s son, formed a new business called Kennametal, based on a tungsten-titanium carbide alloy for cutting tools. The family incorporated the company as Kennametal in 1943. WWII and the Korean War brought strong US military demand for the company's products. Kennametal expanded overseas during the 1960s and 1970s and went public in 1977. During the 1980s Kennametal bought

Bristol Erickson (UK), as well as companies in Belgium, Canada, France, and the Netherlands.

The company was accused of illegally selling equipment to an Iraqi-controlled firm in the UK in 1991, in violation of a trade embargo imposed by the first Bush Administration in 1990. While the US Department of Justice ultimately concluded that no export laws had been broken by Kennametal, the company settled the case in 1997 by paying a fine of $13,457, without admitting any wrongdoing.

The firm bought J & L Industrial Supply, a Detroit-based catalog supplier of metalwork tools, in 1991, and continued to grow by buying a majority stake in German toolmaker Hertel (1993) and by forming a marketing alliance with industrial supplies distributor W.W. Grainger (1994). During fiscal 1995 Kennametal invested in Asia, Mexico, and Poland. The next year William Newlin became the first outsider to become chairman. He succeeded Quentin McKenna, a nephew of Philip McKenna, who had been chairman for 13 years.

Kennametal added JLK Direct Distribution to its supply operations in 1997 and then spun off the unit, retaining about 80% ownership. It also bought rival toolmaker Greenfield Industries. Weak product demand caused by slumps in the oil and paper industries and Asian economic woes contributed to Kennametal's job cuts (about 5% of its workforce) and its plans for plant closures in 1998 and 1999.

Markos Tambakeras succeeded Robert McGeehan as president and CEO in mid-1999. McGeehan had served 10 years as president of Kennametal, and was the first person outside the McKenna family to hold that post.

In 2001 Kennametal announced that it would cut between 6% and 8% of its salaried workforce. Newlin stepped down as chairman, remaining on the board as lead director, and was succeeded by Tambakeras as chairman in 2002.

In 2003 the company named its global technology center in Latrobe the Quentin C. McKenna Technology Center, after its former chief executive, who died that year at the age of 76. After being named president of Kennametal in 1978 and CEO a year later, Quentin McKenna built the company from a regional toolmaker into a *FORTUNE* 500 company.

In early 2005 Kennametal added Pennsylvania-based Extrude Hone, which provides engineered component process technologies to a variety of industries, in a deal valued at $137 million.

In 2006 the company made a move to narrow its focus, selling its distribution subsidiary, J & L Industrial Supply, to MSC Industrial Direct for about $350 million. With the closing of the J & L sale, Kennametal exited the distribution business completely.

EVP/COO Carlos Cardoso was promoted to president and CEO at the outset of 2006, after one year as chief of manufacturing operations. Markos Tambakeras remained as executive chairman following the management transition.

In mid-2006 the company acquired Sintec Group of Germany, a manufacturer of ceramic engineered components for the aerospace, medical, and metalizing markets. Tambakeras served one year as executive chairman before leaving the board at the end of 2006. Larry Yost, the former chairman and CEO of ArvinMeritor and a Kennametal director since 1987, was elected to succeed Tambakeras as chairman.

In late 2007 the board selected president/CEO Carlos Cardoso to serve in the additional post of chairman. Larry Yost was picked to serve as the board's lead director.

EXECUTIVES

Chairman, President, and CEO: Carlos M. Cardoso, age 52, $3,042,373 total compensation
VP and CFO: Frank P. Simpkins, age 47, $1,186,521 total compensation
VP and Chief Marketing Officer: John H. Jacko Jr., age 53, $809,682 total compensation
VP; President, Business Groups: Gary W. Weismann, age 55, $781,348 total compensation
VP and Chief Human Resources Officer: Kevin R. Walling, age 45
VP and CTO: John R. Tucker
VP and CIO: Steven R. (Steve) Hanna
VP, Secretary, and General Counsel: Kevin G. Nowe, age 55
VP and Treasurer: Lawrence J. Lanza, age 61
VP Finance and Corporate Controller: Martha A. Bailey, age 35
VP Integrated Supply Chain and Logistics: Philip H. Weihl, age 54
VP Mergers and Acquisitions: James E. Morrison, age 59
VP Corporate Strategic Initiatives: Wayne D. Moser, age 57
Investor Relations: Quynh McGuire
Auditors: PricewaterhouseCoopers LLP

LOCATIONS

HQ: Kennametal Inc.
1600 Technology Way, Latrobe, PA 15650
Phone: 724-539-5000   **Fax:** 724-539-6657
Web: www.kennametal.com

2010 Sales

	$ mil.	% of total
North America		
US	839.2	45
Canada	44.5	2
Europe		
Germany	313.9	17
UK	52.1	3
Asia	311.6	16
Other regions	322.7	17
Total	**1,884.0**	**100**

PRODUCTS/OPERATIONS

2010 Sales

	$ mil.	% of total
Metalworking Solutions & Services	1,098.8	58
Advanced Materials Solutions	785.2	42
Total	**1,884.0**	**100**

Selected Products

Metalworking Tools
  Boring tools
  Combination tools
  Metal-cutting inserts
  Milling kits
  Tool management software
Mining, Construction, and Other Equipment
  Agricultural implements
  Auger tooling and drilling products
  Face and roof augers
  Motor grader blades
  Pining-rod systems
  Scraper and grader blades
  Snowplow blades
  Soil stabilization tooling
  Two-prong bits
Industrial Supply
  Bandsaws
  Boring bars
  Calipers
  Dies
  Drills and drill bits
  Lathes
  Milling cutters
  Reamers
  Safety wear and equipment
  Taps

Selected Brand Names

Block Style K	Kenna-LOK
Chicago Latrobe	KennaMAX
Circle	Kennametal
Cleveland	Kennametal Hertel
Conforma Clad	Kentip
Drill-Fix	KM
Ecogrind	KM Micro
Erickson	Kyon
Extrude Hone	Mill1
Fix-Perfect	RTW
Greenfield	Surftran
Heinlein	ToolBoss
Hertel	Top Notch
K	Widia
Kendex	Widia Heinlein
Kenloc	Widma

COMPETITORS

Actuant
Allegheny Technologies
Atlas Copco
Flow International
GILDEMEISTER
Hardinge
Jore
L. S. Starrett
MAG Giddings & Lewis
Sandvik
Seco Tools
WALTER

HISTORICAL FINANCIALS

Company Type: Public

Income Statement

FYE: June 30

	REVENUE ($ mil.)	NET INCOME ($ mil.)	NET PROFIT MARGIN	EMPLOYEES
6/10	1,884	48	2.6%	11,000
6/09	2,000	(120)	—	11,600
6/08	2,705	168	6.2%	13,673
6/07	2,386	174	7.3%	13,947
6/06	2,330	256	11.0%	13,300
Annual Growth	**(5.2%)**	**(34.1%)**	**—**	**(4.6%)**

2010 Year-End Financials

Debt ratio: 23.9%	No. of shares (mil.): 82
Return on equity: 3.8%	Dividends
Cash ($ mil.): 118	Yield: 1.9%
Current ratio: 2.33	Payout: 84.2%
Long-term debt ($ mil.): 315	Market value ($ mil.): 2,084

Stock History

NYSE: KMT

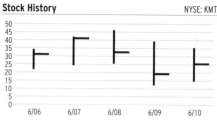

	STOCK PRICE ($) FY Close	P/E High/Low		PER SHARE ($) Earnings	Dividends	Book Value
6/10	25.43	61	27	0.57	0.48	16.05
6/09	19.18	—	—	(1.64)	0.48	15.22
6/08	32.55	21	12	2.15	0.47	20.11
6/07	41.01	19	11	2.22	0.41	18.12
6/06	31.13	10	7	3.24	0.38	15.81
Annual Growth	**(4.9%)**	**—**	**—**	**(35.2%)**	**6.0%**	**0.4%**

Key Energy Services

Energy is the key to growth for Key Energy Services, one of the US's largest well-servicing and workover companies. The company provides maintenance, workover, and recompletion of wells, primarily for onshore drilling. It also provides services such as contract drilling, well completion and abandonment, oil field fluid transportation, production testing, and storage and disposal services to major and independent oil companies. Key Energy Services has a fleet of 924 well service rigs, which operate primarily in the US, as well as in Argentina, Canada, and Mexico. It also has minority stakes in a Canada-based drilling and production services company and a Russia-based drilling and workover services firm.

Key Energy Services is active in major onshore oil and gas regions of the US, including the Four Corners area, the Gulf Coast, the mid-continent area, the Rocky Mountains, and the Appalachian, Permian, and San Joaquin basins.

To complement its core drilling contracting business, the company makes strategic acquisitions to expand its product lines and geographic coverage. In 2007 it acquired well services company Moncla Companies. In 2008 the company expanded its shale play assets in the US through the acquisition of Leader Energy Services Ltd. for $34.6 million. That year it also acquired drilling and services firms Tri-Energy Services, Western Drilling, and Hydra-Walk.

Expanding into the Middle East, in 2010 Key Energy Services formed a joint venture in Dubai with AlMansoori Specialized Engineering, a top regional oilfield services provider. Also that year it agreed to sell a package of pressure pumping and wireline assets to Patterson-UTI Energy for some $238 million.

HISTORY

Yankee Oil & Gas was formed by Paul Montle in 1977 to run a mix of energy and financial businesses. By 1987 it was fighting for its financial life. Steep dips in oil and gas prices devastated its energy businesses (including flagship Yale E. Key), and its Yankee Bank for Finance and Savings went into receivership in 1988.

The company restructured around its oil and gas businesses while acquiring an asbestos-abatement firm, a sludge treatment unit, and Toxic Clean up Systems. After Montle stepped down as CEO in 1989, Francis John took over as the company struggled to stay afloat. The firm sold its environmental services unit and declared bankruptcy in 1992. It also adopted the name Key Energy Group that year.

Buoyed by an oil industry recovery, John turned the company (which he had pared down to a small West Texas oil and gas well service firm) into a major consolidator in the highly fragmented industry. In 1993 Key Energy Group acquired Odessa Exploration (which it subsequently sold) and picked up Clint Hurt Drilling in 1995. That year it also acquired a 58% stake in Orbitron, a firm with 24 gas wells in West Texas, and added 58 well service rigs in 1996 by buying WellTech.

Key Energy Group acquired or agreed to acquire more than two dozen companies in 1997, including two well service operations with more than 100 rigs from Nabors Industries. In 1998 it bought Dawson Production Services, nearly doubling its assets, and changed its name to Key Energy Services, amid a major reorganization. Rising oil prices in 1999 stimulated exploration, prompting increased demand for Key Energy's services.

In 2000 Key Energy added three rigs to the seven it is operating in Argentina. The company expanded its domestic well service operations in 2002 by buying closely held Q Services.

Financial discrepancies forced the company to delay its 2003, 2004, and 2005 annual SEC filings, and to write down assets. In 2005 it sold US land drilling operations (35 rigs) to Patterson-UTI.

EXECUTIVES

Chairman, President, and CEO: Richard J. (Dick) Alario, age 55, $2,420,366 total compensation
SVP and CFO: T.M. (Trey) Whichard III, age 51, $939,168 total compensation
EVP and COO: Newton W. (Trey) Wilson III, age 59, $1,082,147 total compensation
SVP Production Services: Don D. Weinheimer, age 51, $1,092,019 total compensation
SVP Administration and Chief People Officer: Kim B. Clarke, age 54, $1,409,429 total compensation
SVP, General Counsel, and Secretary: Kimberly R. (Kim) Frye, age 41, $594,862 total compensation
SVP Industry Relations: Thomas R. (Tommy) Pipes, age 54
SVP Fluid Management Services: Dennis C. Douglas, age 56
SVP Rig Services: Jeff Skelly
SVP Marketplace Business Development: F. Doug McDonald, age 56
VP and Treasurer: J. Marshall Dodson, age 39, $522,538 total compensation
VP and Controller: Ike C. Smith, age 35
VP Investor Relations: Gary L. Russell
Auditors: Grant Thornton LLP

LOCATIONS

HQ: Key Energy Services, Inc.
  1301 McKinney St., Ste. 1800, Houston, TX 77010
Phone: 713-651-4300   **Fax:** 713-652-4005
Web: www.keyenergy.com

2009 Sales

	$ mil.	% of total
US	881.3	82
Mexico	118.7	11
Argentina	68.6	6
Other countries	10.1	1
Total	**1,078.7**	**100**

PRODUCTS/OPERATIONS

2009 Sales

	$ mil.	% of total
Well servicing	859.8	80
Production services	218.9	20
Total	**1,078.7**	**100**

COMPETITORS

Allis-Chalmers
Basic Energy
Halliburton
Helmerich & Payne
Nabors Industries
Pride International
Schlumberger
Weatherford International

HISTORICAL FINANCIALS

Company Type: Public

Income Statement

FYE: December 31

	REVENUE ($ mil.)	NET INCOME ($ mil.)	NET PROFIT MARGIN	EMPLOYEES
12/09	1,079	(156)	—	8,100
12/08	1,972	84	4.3%	8,582
12/07	1,662	169	10.2%	9,820
12/06	1,546	171	11.1%	9,400
12/05	1,190	46	3.8%	9,400
Annual Growth	**(2.4%)**	**—**	**—**	**(3.7%)**

2009 Year-End Financials

Debt ratio: 74.1%
Return on equity: —
Cash ($ mil.): 37
Current ratio: 2.02
Long-term debt ($ mil.): 524
No. of shares (mil.): 126
Dividends
  Yield: —
  Payout: —
Market value ($ mil.): 1,105

Stock History

NYSE: KEG

	STOCK PRICE ($) FY Close	P/E High/Low		PER SHARE ($) Earnings	Dividends	Book Value
12/09	8.79	—	—	(1.29)	—	5.63
12/08	4.41	31	5	0.67	—	6.85
12/07	14.39	16	10	1.27	—	7.07
12/06	15.65	15	10	1.28	—	5.81
Annual Growth	**(17.5%)**	**—**	**—**	**—**	**—**	**6.3%**

KeyCorp

Financial services giant KeyCorp has the clout of mean Henry Potter of Bedford Falls, but wants to be the sweet George Bailey of bankers. With a focus on retail operations, flagship subsidiary KeyBank operates about 1,000 branches in more than a dozen states scattered throughout the Northeast, the Midwest, the Rocky Mountains, and the Pacific Northwest (including Alaska). Its operations are divided into two groups: community banking offers traditional services such as deposits, loans, and financial planning, while national banking provides real estate capital, equipment financing, and capital markets services to large corporate clients nationwide.

Like many of its peers, KeyCorp has been hit by the economic downturn, resulting in lower revenues and billions of dollars in losses. In response, the company more than doubled its allowance for loan losses from 2008 to 2009 and curbed risky lending. For instance, it no longer offers student loans, recreational vehicle loans, financing for commercial vehicle fleets, and office products leasing. (The company was a bit ahead of the curve in exiting the subprime mortgage business, selling off the operations of Champion Mortgage in 2006 and 2007.) KeyCorp has also wound down noncore businesses, such as hedge fund manager Austin Capital Management, to focus on consumer and corporate banking.

The company's community banking group continues to grow, despite the economic turmoil. It bought New York-based U.S.B. Holding Co. and its Union State Bank subsidiary for some $550 million in early 2008. The deal added more than 30 branches, nearly doubling KeyCorp's presence in the Hudson River Valley region. The company has also been opening about 40 new branches a year and plans to continue to do so.

HISTORY

KeyCorp predecessor Commercial Bank of Albany was chartered in 1825. In 1865 it joined the new national banking system and became National Commercial Bank of Albany. After WWI National Commercial consolidated with Union National Bank & Trust as National Commercial Bank and Trust, which then merged with First Trust and Deposit in 1971.

In 1973 Victor Riley became president and CEO. Under Riley, National Commercial grew during the 1970s and 1980s through acquisitions. Riley sought to make the company a regional powerhouse but was thwarted when several New England states passed legislation barring New York banks from buying banks in the region.

As a result, the company, renamed Key Bank in 1979, turned west, targeting small towns with less competition. Thus situated, it prospered, despite entering Alaska just in time for the 1986 oil price collapse. Its folksy image and small-town success earned it a reputation as the "Wal-Mart of banking."

Meanwhile, in Cleveland, Society for Savings followed a different path. Founded as a mutual savings bank in 1849, the institution succeeded from the start. It survived the Civil War and postwar economic turmoil and built Cleveland's first skyscraper in 1890. It continued to grow even during the Depression and became the largest savings bank outside the Northeast in 1949.

In 1955 the bank formed a holding company, Society National. Society grew through the acquisitions of smaller banks in Ohio until 1979, when Ohio allowed branch banking in contiguous counties. Thereafter, Society National opened branches, as well. In the mid-1980s and the early 1990s, the renamed Society Corporation began consolidating its operations and continued growing.

A 1994 merger of National Commercial with Society more than doubled assets for the surviving KeyCorp; compatibility of the two companies' systems and software simplified consolidation. KeyCorp sold its mortgage-servicing unit to NationsBank (now Bank of America) in 1995 and over the next year bought investment management, finance, and investment banking firms.

In 1997 KeyCorp began trimming its branch network, divesting 200 offices, including its 28-branch KeyBank Wyoming subsidiary. It expanded its consumer lending business that year by buying Champion Mortgage. In cooperation with USF&G (now part of The St. Paul Travelers Companies) and three HMOs, KeyCorp began offering health insurance to the underserved small-business market.

In 1998 the company bought Leasetec, which leases computer storage systems globally through its StorageTek subsidiary; it also bought McDonald & Company Investments (now McDonald Investments; sold in 2007), with an eye toward reaching its goal of earning half of its revenues from fees. Also in 1998 KeyCorp began offering business lines of credit to customers of Costco Wholesale, the nation's largest wholesale club.

As part of a restructuring effort, KeyCorp sold 28 Long Island, New York, branches to Dime Bancorp in 1999. The next year the company sold its credit card portfolio to Associates First Capital (now part of Citigroup) and bought National Realty Funding, a securitizer of commercial mortgages. In 2001 it acquired Denver-based investment bank The Wallach Company.

The company expanded further in the Denver area with its 2002 purchase of Union Bankshares. Two years later KeyCorp bought Seattle-area bank EverTrust Financial Group.

In 2007 the company acquired Tuition Management Systems, which provides outsourced tuition billing, accounting, and counseling services for schools and colleges; the unit was later merged into its Key Education Resources operations. Also that year KeyCorp sold investment bank and brokerage McDonald Investments to UBS Financial Services.

EXECUTIVES

Chairman, President, and CEO: Henry L. Meyer III, age 60, $8,152,386 total compensation
Vice Chairman and Chief Administrative Officer: Thomas C. (Tom) Stevens, age 60, $2,440,060 total compensation
Vice Chairman and Head Key Community Banking: Beth E. Mooney, age 54, $2,377,527 total compensation
SEVP and CFO: Jeffrey B. Weeden, age 53, $2,359,684 total compensation
SEVP and Head National Banking: Christopher M. (Chris) Gorman, age 49
Chief Marketing and Communications Officer: Karen R. Haefling
Chief Accounting Officer: Robert L. Morris, age 57
EVP, Chief Risk Review Officer, and General Auditor: Kevin T. Ryan
EVP and Chief Human Resources Officer: Thomas E. (Tom) Helfrich, age 57
EVP and and Chief Credit Officer: William L. (Bill) Hartmann
EVP and Chief Risk Officer: Charles S. (Chuck) Hyle, age 58
EVP Investor Relations: Vernon L. (Vern) Patterson
EVP Corporate Development and Strategic Planning: Andrew R. (Andy) Tyson
EVP and Head Credit Portfolio Management: Jeffery J. (Jeff) Weaver
EVP and Treasurer: Joseph M. Vayda
EVP and Director, Call Center Sales and Service: Dean Kontul
EVP and Director Corporate Diversity and Philanthropy: Margot J. Copeland
EVP, General Counsel, and Secretary: Paul N. Harris, age 51
EVP, Group Head Real Estate and Corporate Banking Services, Key National Banking: E.J. Burke
Auditors: Ernst & Young LLP

LOCATIONS

HQ: KeyCorp
127 Public Sq., Cleveland, OH 44114
Phone: 216-689-6300   **Fax:** 216-689-0519
Web: www.key.com

PRODUCTS/OPERATIONS

2009 Sales

	$ mil.	% of total
Interest		
Loans	3,223	55
Securities	462	8
Other investments	110	2
Noninterest		
Trust & investment services	459	8
Service charges on deposits	330	6
Operating lease income	227	4
Letter of credit & loan fees	180	3
Other	839	14
Total	**5,830**	**100**

COMPETITORS

Bank of America
Citigroup
Citizens Financial Group
Comerica
Fifth Third
Flagstar Bancorp
HSBC USA
Huntington Bancshares
JPMorgan Chase
M&T Bank
Northern Trust
PNC Financial
Sovereign Bank
U.S. Bancorp
Wells Fargo

HISTORICAL FINANCIALS

Company Type: Public

Income Statement

FYE: December 31

	ASSETS ($ mil.)	NET INCOME ($ mil.)	INCOME AS % OF ASSETS	EMPLOYEES
12/09	93,287	(1,311)	—	16,698
12/08	104,531	(1,468)	—	18,095
12/07	99,983	919	0.9%	18,934
12/06	92,337	1,050	1.1%	20,006
12/05	93,126	1,129	1.2%	19,485
Annual Growth	**0.0%**	**—**	**—**	**(3.8%)**

2009 Year-End Financials

Equity as % of assets: 8.5%
Return on assets: —
Return on equity: —
Long-term debt ($ mil.): 11,558
No. of shares (mil.): 880
Dividends
 Yield: 1.7%
 Payout: —
Market value ($ mil.): 4,886
Sales ($ mil.): 5,830

Stock History

NYSE: KEY

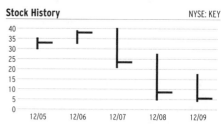

	STOCK PRICE ($) FY Close	P/E High/Low		PER SHARE ($) Earnings	Dividends	Book Value
12/09	5.55	—	—	(2.34)	0.09	12.11
12/08	8.52	—	—	(3.36)	1.00	11.91
12/07	23.45	17	9	2.32	1.46	8.80
12/06	38.03	15	13	2.57	1.38	8.75
12/05	32.93	13	11	2.73	1.30	8.63
Annual Growth	**(35.9%)**	**—**	**—**	**—**	**(48.7%)**	**8.8%**

Kimberly-Clark

Nobody knows noses and diapering babies better than Kimberly-Clark, the world's top maker of personal paper products. The company operates through four business segments: personal care, consumer tissue, K-C Professional, and health care. Kimberly-Clark's largest unit, personal care, makes products such as diapers (Huggies, Pull-Ups), feminine care items (Kotex), and incontinence care products (Poise, Depend). Through its consumer tissue segment, the manufacturer offers facial and bathroom tissues, paper towels, and other household items under the names Cottonelle, Kleenex, Viva, and Scott. Kimberly-Clark's professional unit makes WypAll commercial wipes, among other items. The company operates its paper, pulp, and timber business under the spunoff Neenah Paper company.

Until the economy fully rebounds, Kimberly-Clark is working to improve profit margins by cutting costs and raising prices. Additionally, the paper products company is looking to grow its business in Asia, Latin America, the Middle East, Eastern Europe, and Africa as it continues to concentrate on its health care business.

The company purged about 10% of its employees, or some 6,000 people globally, in late 2008 followed by another 1,600 salaried positions during 2009. While it shed staff, Kimberly-Clark also shuttered or sold more than 20 manufacturing facilities (representing about 17% of its plants).

Kimberly-Clark still maintains a broad global presence. It boasts manufacturing facilities in some 35 countries and sells its products in more than 150 countries. Its products enjoy the #1 or #2 position in 80 countries, as well.

The company has been expanding into high-margin medical products and is now a leading US maker of disposable medical goods. It produces sterilization wrap, face masks, surgical drapes and gowns, and closed-suction respiratory products. Kimberly-Clark also has been purchasing products tailored to the health care market. In 2009 the company acquired Baylis Medical's pain management business, which focuses on chronic spinal pain. Also, in late 2009 it acquired I-Flow, a leading developer and marketer of low-cost drug-delivery systems for post-surgical pain relief and surgical site care.

The manufacturer is looking to overseas markets to help it diversify its revenue streams and lessen its risk in the US as the economy rebounds. In 2009 the company acquired the remaining 31% of its Bogota, Colombia-based subsidiary Colombiana Kimberly Colpapel (CKC). The transaction boosted the firm's business in the developing markets of Bolivia, Colombia, Ecuador, Peru, and Venezuela. Kimberly-Clark also purchased the remaining stake (about 50%) in its Kimberly-Clark of South Africa unit in 2008 from The Lion Match Company. Kimberly-Clark and other companies have operated the South African joint venture since 1955.

HISTORY

John Kimberly, Charles Clark, Havilah Babcock, and Frank Shattuck founded Kimberly, Clark & Company in Neenah, Wisconsin, in 1872 to manufacture newsprint from rags. The company incorporated as Kimberly & Clark Company in 1880 and built a pulp and paper plant on the Fox River in 1889.

In 1914 the company developed cellu-cotton, a cotton substitute used by the US Army as surgical cotton during WWI. Army nurses used cellu-cotton pads as disposable sanitary napkins, and six years later the company introduced Kotex, the first disposable feminine hygiene product. Kleenex, the first throwaway handkerchief, followed in 1924. Kimberly & Clark joined with The New York Times Company in 1926 to build a newsprint mill (Spruce Falls Power and Paper) in Ontario, Canada. Two years later the company went public as Kimberly-Clark.

The firm expanded internationally during the 1950s, opening plants in Mexico, Germany, and the UK. It began operations in 17 more foreign locations in the 1960s.

CEO Guy Minard, who retired in 1971, sold the four mills that handled Kimberly-Clark's unprofitable coated-paper business and entered the paper towel and disposable diaper markets. Minard's successor, Darwin Smith, introduced Kimbies diapers in 1968, but they leaked and were withdrawn from the market. An improved version came out in 1976, followed by Huggies, a premium-priced diaper with elastic leg bands, two years later.

The company formed Midwest Express Airlines from its corporate flight department in 1984 (a business it exited in 1996). Smith moved Kimberly-Clark's headquarters from Neenah to Irving, Texas, the following year.

In 1991 Kimberly-Clark and The New York Times Company sold Spruce Falls Power and Paper. Smith retired as chairman in 1992 and was succeeded by Wayne Sanders, who was largely responsible for designing Huggies Pull-Ups (introduced in 1989). Kimberly-Clark entered a joint venture to make personal care products in Argentina in 1994 and also bought the feminine hygiene units of VP-Schickedanz (Germany) and Handan Comfort and Beauty Group (China).

Kimberly-Clark bought Scott Paper in 1995 for $9.4 billion. The move boosted its market share in bathroom tissue from 5% to 31% and its share in paper towels from 6% to 18%, but led to some headaches as the company absorbed Scott's operations.

In 1997 Kimberly-Clark sold its 50% stake in Canada's Scott Paper to forest products company Kruger and bought diaper operations in Spain and Portugal and disposable surgical face masks maker Tecnol Medical Products. A tissue price war in Europe bruised the company's bottom line that year and it began massive job cuts. (By the end of 1999, nearly 4,000 jobs, mostly in the tissue-based businesses, had been axed.)

In part to focus on its health care business, which it entered in 1997, the company in 1999 sold some of its timber interests and its timber fleet to Cooper/T. Smith Corp. Adding to its lineup of medical products, the company bought Ballard Medical Products in 1999 for $744 million and examination glove maker Safeskin in 2000 for about $800 million.

Also in 2000 the company bought virtually all of Taiwan's S-K Corporation; the move made Kimberly-Clark one of the largest manufacturers of consumer packaged goods in Taiwan and set the stage for expanded distribution in the Asia/Pacific region. In 2002 Kimberly-Clark purchased paper-packaging rival Amcor's stake in their Kimberly-Clark Australia joint venture.

Its 2005 acquisition of Microcuff extended Kimberly-Clark's reach into medical devices and catheter technology.

EXECUTIVES

Chairman, President, and CEO: Thomas J. (Tom) Falk, age 52, $11,387,428 total compensation
Group President, International: Robert W. (Bob) Black, age 50, $2,347,398 total compensation
Group President, North Atlantic Consumer Products: Robert E. Abernathy, age 54, $4,133,895 total compensation
SVP and CFO: Mark A. Buthman, age 49, $3,138,526 total compensation
SVP and Chief Marketing Officer: Anthony J. Palmer, age 50, $1,894,972 total compensation
SVP and Chief Human Resources Officer: Lizanne C. (Liz) Gottung, age 53
SVP and Chief Strategy Officer: Elane Stock, age 46
SVP Law, Government Affairs, and Chief Compliance Officer: Thomas J. (Tom) Mielke, age 51
VP and Controller: Michael T. Azbell, age 45
VP Investor Relations: Paul J. Alexander
CEO, Kimberly-Clark UK: Kim Underhill
President, Global Health Care and President and CEO, I-Flow: Joanne B. Bauer, age 54
President, Global K-C Professional: Jan B. Spencer, age 54
Auditors: Deloitte & Touche LLP

LOCATIONS

HQ: Kimberly-Clark Corporation
351 Phelps Dr., Irving, TX 75038
Phone: 972-281-1200   **Fax:** 972-281-1490
Web: www.kimberly-clark.com

2009 Sales

	$ mil.	% of total
US	10,146	51
Asia, Latin America & other	6,124	30
Europe	3,220	16
Canada	596	3
Adjustments	(971)	—
Total	**19,115**	**100**

PRODUCTS/OPERATIONS

2009 Sales

	$ mil.	% of total
Personal care products	8,365	44
Consumer tissue	6,409	34
K-C Professional & other	3,007	16
Health care	1,371	6
Corporate & other	53	—
Adjustments	(90)	—
Total	**19,115**	**100**

Selected Products and Brands

Medical
  Closed-suction respiratory products
  Examination gloves (Safeskin)
  Face masks
  Infection-control products
  Scrub suits and apparel
  Sterile wrap (Kimguard)
  Surgical drapes and gowns

Personal Care
   Baby wipes (Huggies)
   Disposable diapers (Huggies, Pull-Ups)
   Feminine hygiene products (Kotex, New Freedom,
      Lightdays)
   Incontinence products (Depend, Poise)
   Swimpants (Little Swimmers)
Tissue-Based
   Bathroom tissue (Cottonelle, Scott)
   Commercial wipes (Kimwipes, WypAll)
   Facial tissue (Kleenex)
   Paper napkins (Scott)
   Paper towels (Kleenex, Scott, Viva)

COMPETITORS

3M
Ansell
Becton, Dickinson
Bristol-Myers Squibb
Cardinal Health Medical
CCA Industries
DSG International Ltd
Energizer Holdings
Georgia-Pacific
Johnson & Johnson
Medline Industries
Nice-Pak Products
Potlatch
Procter & Gamble
SSI Surgical Services

HISTORICAL FINANCIALS

Company Type: Public

Income Statement

FYE: December 31

	REVENUE ($ mil.)	NET INCOME ($ mil.)	NET PROFIT MARGIN	EMPLOYEES
12/09	19,115	1,994	10.4%	56,000
12/08	19,415	1,698	8.7%	53,000
12/07	18,266	1,823	10.0%	53,000
12/06	16,747	1,500	9.0%	55,000
12/05	15,903	1,581	9.9%	57,000
Annual Growth	4.7%	6.0%	—	(0.4%)

2009 Year-End Financials

Debt ratio: 88.6%
Return on equity: 43.0%
Cash ($ mil.): 987
Current ratio: 1.19
Long-term debt ($ mil.): 4,792

No. of shares (mil.): 409
Dividends
   Yield: 3.8%
   Payout: 53.1%
Market value ($ mil.): 26,077

Stock History

NYSE: KMB

	STOCK PRICE ($) FY Close	P/E High/Low	PER SHARE ($) Earnings	PER SHARE ($) Dividends	PER SHARE ($) Book Value
12/09	63.71	15 10	4.52	2.40	13.21
12/08	52.74	17 12	4.04	2.32	9.47
12/07	69.34	18 16	4.09	2.12	12.76
12/06	67.95	21 17	3.25	1.96	14.90
12/05	59.65	21 17	3.28	1.80	13.58
Annual Growth	1.7%	— —	8.3%	7.5%	(0.7%)

Kindred Healthcare

Kindred Healthcare is one of the largest long-term health care providers in the US. Kindred operates some 220 nursing homes and more than 80 long-term acute care hospitals located in about 35 states. Its facilities have a combined capacity of about 34,000 beds. The company owns some of its facilities, but operates most of them under lease agreements with Ventas and other third parties. Kindred also operates a contract rehabilitation therapy business, which serves its own and other long-term care facilities, through its People*first* Rehabilitation division.

Kindred's health services division, which accounts for nearly half of sales, operates nursing home facilities and provides specialized treatment for certain diseases such as Alzheimer's. It also provides rehabilitative care, often through contracts with Kindred's People*first* division.

The company's hospital division includes both free-standing hospitals and "hospitals-within-hospitals," which are co-located with short-term acute care facilities and sometimes receive patients as they are discharged from the host facility. Providing high quality care, increasing patient volumes through sales and marketing initiatives, recruiting qualified medical personnel, and improving operating efficiencies are key to Kindred's strategy across all its divisions. The company also wants to capitalize on marketing opportunities within "cluster markets" where it has multiple facilities.

Medicare and Medicaid reimbursements make up nearly three-fourths of Kindred's revenue. As health care laws change in the US market, the company is looking for ways to increase admissions (particularly in its hospital division) of patients with commercial insurance, which reimburses at higher rates.

Kindred tries to manage its portfolio of facilities to rid itself of underperforming assets. It divested or closed about 30 unprofitable nursing homes and several long-term acute care hospitals from 2007 through 2009.

Looking to add more profitable facilities, in 2010 the company purchased a 100-bed nursing home in Ohio, which it plans to expand into a transitional-care rehabilitation center. In addition, Kindred has a handful of new freestanding hospital facilities under development. It completed construction of a 60-bed hospital in Florida in 2009, and it opened a new long-term care hospital to replace an aging facility in Houston in 2010; the older Houston facility will be converted into a rehabilitation facility.

HISTORY

After a stint as Kentucky's commerce secretary in the 1980s, Bruce Lunsford was approached by respiratory therapist Michael Barr with the idea of establishing long-term hospitals for ventilator-dependent patients. Barr said these hospitals would be cheaper to run than full-service facilities, which require additional equipment. Lunsford (who became chairman, president, and CEO) and Barr (who was COO) founded Vencare in 1983 with backing from Gene Smith (a wealthy political associate of Lunsford). They bought a money-losing, 62-bed Indiana hospital and soon turned the operation around.

Vencare expanded into Florida and Texas and, by the end of the 1980s, operated more than 420 beds in seven facilities. Revenues jumped from

less than $1 million in 1985 to $54 million by 1989, the year it changed its name to Vencor.

During the early 1990s Vencor added facilities in Arizona, California, Colorado, Georgia, and Missouri. Vencor ran 29 facilities by the end of 1993, the same year it launched its Vencare respiratory care program.

Vencor acquisitions in 1995 included hospital respiratory and cardiopulmonary departments in seven states. Later that year it bought the much-larger Hillhaven, the US's #2 nursing home operator at that time. (In 1990 Hillhaven had been spun off from what is now Tenet Healthcare.) When Vencor bought it, Hillhaven owned 310 nursing homes, 60 pharmacies, and 23 retirement communities. The buy furthered Lunsford's vision of creating a network of long-term-care facilities and services. Vencor also debuted VenTouch, an electronic-pad-based record-keeping system for its facilities, in 1995.

In 1996 Vencor spun off its assisted and independent living properties as Atria Communities; as part of the Hillhaven assimilation, it also consolidated its MediSave pharmacy unit into its hospital operations and sold 34 nursing homes to Lennox Healthcare.

Vencor's 1997 buys included TheraTx (216 rehabilitation centers, 28 nursing centers, 16 occupational health clinics), and Transitional Hospitals (long-term acute care hospitals). That year Vencor formed an alliance with insurer CNA to develop an insurance product for long-term care.

In 1998 the company split into Ventas (real estate) and Vencor (operations). It also sold most of its remaining interest in an assisted living company (now called Atria Senior Quarters) it had spun off in 1996. To attract wealthier residents, it also launched a program in 1998 to turn away — and turn out — Medicaid patients. Vencor soon abandoned the plan amid heated attacks from advocacy groups. (Welcoming back the evictees didn't stop Florida regulators from fining Vencor.) Several other states and the federal government also began probing Vencor's practices; in 1999 the affair prompted Congressional action designed to protect Medicaid patients. Lunsford and Barr were ousted in the turmoil. The government also demanded that Vencor return $90 million in overpayments over 60 months ($2 million a month) or risk losing Medicare payments.

The company filed for Chapter 11 bankruptcy later in 1999. Despite bankruptcy protection, the Justice Department in 2000 filed claims for more than $1 billion from Vencor for Medicare fraud since 1992. Vencor settled the majority of these claims the next year. The company emerged from bankruptcy in April 2001 and changed its name to Kindred Healthcare. In 2003 the company sold all of its Texas and Florida nursing center operations.

In 2006 the company bought the long-term care operations of Commonwealth Communities Holdings, gaining six long-term acute care hospitals and 11 nursing homes in Massachusetts. The company entered lease agreements for eight nursing homes in San Francisco in 2007.

In 2007 Kindred spun off its Kindred Pharmacy Services unit, which distributed drugs to long-term care facilities. The unit was combined with the institutional pharmacy unit of AmerisourceBergen to form a new entity named PharMerica. The deal created the #2 institutional pharmacy nationwide (behind Omnicare).

EXECUTIVES

Chairman: Edward L. (Eddie) Kuntz, age 65,
$1,904,045 total compensation
President, CEO, and Director: Paul J. Diaz, age 48,
$4,745,504 total compensation
COO: Frank J. Battafarano, age 59,
$2,190,583 total compensation
EVP and CFO: Richard A. (Rich) Lechleiter, age 51,
$1,611,873 total compensation
EVP; President, Hospital Division: Benjamin A. Breier,
age 38, $1,735,393 total compensation
EVP; President, Health Services Division:
Lane M. Bowen, age 59, $1,473,093 total compensation
EVP, CIO, and Chief Administrative Officer:
Richard E. Chapman, age 61
EVP, Central Region, Hospital Division:
Steven L. (Steve) Monaghan
SVP and Chief Compliance Officer: Kim Martin
SVP Corporate Legal Affairs and Corporate Secretary:
Joseph L. Landenwich, age 45
SVP and General Counsel: M. Suzanne Riedman, age 58
SVP Finance and Corporate Controller:
John J. Lucchese
**SVP Operational Reimbursement, Health Services
Division:** Dennis J. Hansen
SVP Corporate Development and Financial Planning:
Gregory C. (Greg) Miller, age 40
**SVP Clinical and Residential Services, Health Services
Division:** Barbara L. Baylis
SVP Strategy and Public Policy: William M. Altman,
age 50
VP Communications: Susan E. Moss
President, Peoplefirst Rehabilitation Division:
Christopher M. (Chris) Bird, age 45
Auditors: PricewaterhouseCoopers LLP

LOCATIONS

HQ: Kindred Healthcare, Inc.
680 S. 4th St., Louisville, KY 40202
Phone: 502-596-7300   **Fax:** 502-596-4170
Web: www.kindredhealthcare.com

2009 Nursing Home Locations

	No.
Massachusetts	41
Indiana	24
California	21
North Carolina	19
Kentucky	13
Ohio	13
Wisconsin	12
Maine	8
Idaho	8
Tennessee	8
Washington	7
Connecticut	5
Arizona	4
Utah	4
Georgia	4
Colorado	4
Virginia	4
Wyoming	4
Alabama	3
New Hampshire	3
Missouri	2
Montana	2
Nevada	2
Oregon	2
Rhode Island	2
Vermont	2
Pennsylvania	1
Total	**222**

2009 Hospital Locations

	No.
Texas	11
California	10
Florida	10
Massachusetts	7
Pennsylvania	7
Illinois	5
Arizona	4
Missouri	3
Nevada	3
New Jersey	3
Ohio	3
Indiana	2
Kentucky	2
Oklahoma	2
Tennessee	2
Colorado	1
Georgia	1
Louisiana	1
New Mexico	1
North Carolina	1
South Carolina	1
Virginia	1
Washington	1
Wisconsin	1
Total	**83**

PRODUCTS/OPERATIONS

2009 Sales

	$ mil.	% of motal
Health services division	2,150.4	47
Hospital division	1,932.9	42
Rehabilitation division	475.0	11
Adjustments	(288.3)	—
Total	**4,270.0**	**100**

2009 Sales by Payor

	$ mil.	% of total
Medicare	1,811.2	40
Medicaid	1,086.5	24
Medicare Advantage	321.4	7
Other payors	1,339.2	29
Adjustments	(288.3)	—
Total	**4,270.0**	**100**

COMPETITORS

Ascension Health	Manor Care
Catholic Healthcare	National HealthCare
Partners	Paradigm Management
Covenant Care	Physiotherapy Associates
Emeritus Corporation	RehabCare
Ensign Group	SavaSeniorCare
Extendicare REIT	Select Medical
Five Star Quality Care	Skilled Healthcare Group
Genesis HealthCare	Sun Healthcare
Golden Horizons	Sunrise Senior Living
HCA	Tenet Healthcare
HealthSouth	U.S. Physical Therapy
Life Care Centers	

HISTORICAL FINANCIALS

Company Type: Public

Income Statement

FYE: December 31

	REVENUE ($ mil.)	NET INCOME ($ mil.)	NET PROFIT MARGIN	EMPLOYEES
12/09	4,270	40	0.9%	54,100
12/08	4,151	36	0.9%	53,700
12/07	4,220	(47)	—	38,200
12/06	4,267	146	3.4%	55,000
12/05	3,924	145	3.7%	51,600
Annual Growth	**2.1%**	**(27.5%)**	**—**	**1.2%**

2009 Year-End Financials

Debt ratio: 15.3%	No. of shares (mil.): 39
Return on equity: 4.3%	Dividends
Cash ($ mil.): 16	Yield: —
Current ratio: 1.40	Payout: —
Long-term debt ($ mil.): 148	Market value ($ mil.): 729

Stock History

NYSE: KND

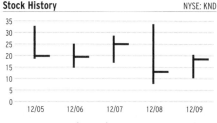

	STOCK PRICE ($) FY Close	P/E High/Low	PER SHARE ($) Earnings	Dividends	Book Value
12/09	18.46	20 10	1.02	—	24.48
12/08	13.02	36 9	0.93	—	23.17
12/07	24.98	— —	(1.17)	—	21.84
12/06	19.47	13 8	1.92	—	25.22
12/05	19.86	10 6	3.20	—	22.05
Annual Growth	**(1.8%)**	**— —**	**(24.9%)**	**—**	**2.7%**

Kinetic Concepts

Kinetic Concepts has made its bed and has no problems lying in it. The company's "therapeutic surfaces" (commonly known as hospital beds and specialized mattresses) treat and prevent complications associated with patient immobility, such as pressure sores and buildup of fluid in the lungs. The company also makes vacuum-assisted wound care systems and critical care therapy systems, which rotate immobilized patients to reduce the incidence of pulmonary complications and pressure sores. Its LifeCell business develops tissue regeneration products used in surgical procedures. Customers include acute and long-term care facilities, home health agencies, wound care clinics, and individuals in the US and abroad.

The company's bariatric care products include surfaces (tables, beds, wheelchairs) which can accommodate patients weighing between 300 and 1,000 pounds. Such specialized products help health care workers move and treat such patients with a reduced risk of injury to themselves and the patients.

Kinetic Concepts markets and distributes its products through its own sales force in the US. The company also maintains an in-house team of some 200 specialists who help customers negotiate the paperwork of Medicare and private insurance. Internationally, the company distributes its products directly, and through local distributors in some 20 countries. In addition to individual hospitals and long-term care facilities, its customers include group purchasing organizations such as Novation, which accounts for 10% of revenue.

The company acquired regenerative tissue maker LifeCell Corporation in 2008 for $1.7 billion to create a new biosurgery division. LifeCell's products are primarily marketed in the US for general surgical and periodontal surgical applications.

Kinetic Concepts is adapting its negative-pressure wound care technology for use during surgery and to assist with regenerative medicine. As part of that strategy, the company in 2009 acquired the patents and intellectual property rights of Hill-Rom's negative wound pressure therapy business. The deal included both US and foreign patents.

Growth overseas has come slowly, but in 2009 Kinetic Concepts entered into the Japanese market with approval for its vacuum-assisted closure (V.A.C.) systems. In other countries, the company is working to build up its distribution networks and launching new products for its geographic expansion. As it is back home, much of the company's international growth is dependent upon securing reimbursement agreements from private and public insurers.

Founder and chairman emeritus James Leininger holds 12% of the company's shares.

HISTORY

As a doctor, James Leininger was disturbed to see patients survive intense physical trauma only to die from complications caused by immobility. In 1975 he and his wife bought a troubled hospital bed maker, renaming it Kinetic Concepts (KCI). Leininger bought the rights to the RotoRest, which KCI began renting and selling. The firm's first decade was marked by slow, painful growth; its 1984 introduction of the KinAir bed boosted sales and put the company on firm fiscal ground. KCI went public in 1988.

In 1992 KCI sued its biggest rival Hillenbrand (now Hill-Rom Holdings) for patent infringement on its rotating bed. Two years later Hillenbrand settled with KCI for $84.8 million. In 1995 KCI sued Hillenbrand again, this time filing an antitrust suit for more than $200 million.

KCI went on a binge in 1997, buying five medical equipment firms. Among them was Colorado's RIK Medical, which made non-electric beds that could be used in prisons and psychiatric wards. In 1998 KCI was taken private again when two investment concerns, Richard C. Blum & Associates and Fremont Partners, offered it a deal worth about $850 million. Legal woes also surfaced that year when the company was sued over injuries allegedly caused by one of its beds. In 1999 KCI formed Wound Works, a wound management joint venture, with Georgia company Coloplast.

With a broader base of products and solid growth record, Kinetic Concepts was taken public again in 2004.

EXECUTIVES

Chairman: Ronald W. (Ron) Dollens, age 63
President, CEO, and Director:
Catherine M. (Cathy) Burzik, age 59,
$4,388,090 total compensation
EVP, Japan and Office of CEO: Lynne D. Sly, age 49,
$1,322,064 total compensation
EVP and CFO: Martin J. (Marty) Landon, age 50,
$1,633,558 total compensation
SVP Advanced Research and Technology:
David McQuillan
SVP and CIO: David H. Ramsey, age 40
SVP Quality, Regulatory, Safety, and Compliance:
Jason Cone
SVP, U.S. and Latin America Sales and Marketing, Active Healing Solutions:
Michael J. (Mike) DelVacchio Jr., age 42
SVP Human Resources and Corporate Communications: R. James (Jim) Cravens, age 46
SVP Global Operations: Michael G. Schneider, age 60
VP Corporate Communications: Kevin Belgrade

VP Global Marketing, Active Healing Solutions:
Kien Nguyen
VP Business Development and Investor Relations:
Adam J. Rodriguez
Global President, Therapeutic Support Systems and General Counsel: Stephen D. Seidel, age 53,
$1,748,792 total compensation
Global President, Active Healing Solutions:
Michael C. (Mike) Genau, age 50,
$3,553,211 total compensation
President, LifeCell: Lisa N. Colleran, age 52,
$1,976,446 total compensation
President, Active Healing Solutions, Europe, Middle East, and Africa: TLV Kumar, age 55
Auditors: Ernst & Young LLP

LOCATIONS

HQ: Kinetic Concepts, Inc.
8023 Vantage Dr., San Antonio, TX 78230
Phone: 210-524-9000   **Fax:** 210-255-6998
Web: www.kci1.com

2009 Revenues

	$ mil.	% of total
Wound healing systems		
North America	1,066.1	54
Other	340.4	17
Regenerative medicine		
North America	284.1	14
Other	1.8	—
Therapeutic support systems		
North America	196.4	10
Other	103.8	5
Total	**1,992.6**	**100**

PRODUCTS/OPERATIONS

2009 Revenues

	$ mil.	% of total
Rental	1,178.1	59
Sales	814.5	41
Total	**1,992.6**	**100**

2009 Revenue

	$ mil.	% of total
Wound healing systems	1,406.6	71
Therapeutic support systems	300.1	15
Regenerative medicine	285.9	14
Total	**1,992.6**	**100**

Selected Products

Regenerative medicine
  AlloCraft DBM (bone grafting material)
  AlloDerm (plastic and periodontal regenerative material)
  GraftJacket (orthopedic surgery)
  Repliform (urogynecologic surgery)
  Strattice (reconstructive surgery)
Therapeutic support systems
  BariAir Therapy System (convertible hospital bed/cardiac chair for obese patients)
  BariMaxx II (hospital bed for obese patients)
  KinAir MedSurg (pressure sore prevention overlay)
  RotoProne Therapy System (rotating bed)
  TheraPulse (wound care beds)
  TriaDyne Proventa Therapy System (rotating bed)
Wound healing systems
  ABThera (open abdominal vacuum-assisted closure)
  V.A.C. Freedom System (negative pressure portable wound healing system)
  V.A.C. Instill System (wound therapy equipment)

COMPETITORS

Bard	Medela
ConvaTec	Osteotech
Cook Incorporated	RTI Biologics
Covidien	Smith & Nephew
Gaymar	Span-America Medical
Getinge	Stryker
Hill-Rom	Synovis Life Technologies
Integra LifeSciences	W.L. Gore
Johnson & Johnson	Wright Medical Group

HISTORICAL FINANCIALS

Company Type: Public

Income Statement

FYE: December 31

	REVENUE ($ mil.)	NET INCOME ($ mil.)	NET PROFIT MARGIN	EMPLOYEES
12/09	1,993	229	11.5%	6,800
12/08	1,878	174	9.3%	6,900
12/07	1,610	237	14.7%	6,400
12/06	1,372	196	14.3%	6,300
12/05	1,209	122	10.1%	5,735
Annual Growth	**13.3%**	**17.0%**	**—**	**4.4%**

2009 Year-End Financials

Debt ratio: 99.7%	No. of shares (mil.): 72
Return on equity: 23.0%	Dividends
Cash ($ mil.): 263	Yield: —
Current ratio: 1.95	Payout: —
Long-term debt ($ mil.): 1,174	Market value ($ mil.): 2,705

Stock History

NYSE: KCI

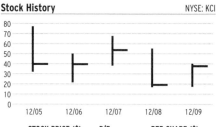

	STOCK PRICE ($) FY Close	P/E High/Low		PER SHARE ($) Earnings	Dividends	Book Value
12/09	37.65	12	6	3.24	—	16.39
12/08	19.18	22	7	2.42	—	11.29
12/07	53.56	20	12	3.31	—	9.42
12/06	39.55	18	8	2.69	—	4.96
12/05	39.76	46	20	1.67	—	2.67
Annual Growth	**(1.4%)**	**—**	**—**	**18.0%**	**—**	**57.5%**

King Ranch

Meanwhile, back at the ranch . . . the sprawling King Ranch, to be exact. Founded in 1853, King Ranch's operations extend beyond its original 825,000 Texan cattle-raising acres. The ranch is still home to cattle and horses, of course. However, King Ranch oversees considerable farming interests in its home state and elsewhere (cotton, sorghum, sod, citrus, pecans, vegetables, and cane sugar). It also has varied retail operations (hardware, designer saddles and other leather goods, publishing and printing). In addition, King Ranch also beefs up revenues with tourist dollars from birdwatchers, hunters, and sightseers who visit its Texas ranch lands. The descendants of founder Richard King own King Ranch.

Considered the birthplace of the American ranching industry, King Ranch introduced the highly fertile breed of beef cattle, the King Ranch Santa Cruz, which is one-fourth Gelbvieh, one-fourth Red Angus, and one-half Santa Gertrudis. Raising animals isn't the only thing King Ranch cottons to — this sprawl of four noncontiguous ranches is also one of the US's largest cotton producers and a significant producer of shelled pecans. In addition to its cattle, King Ranch has about 300 quarter horses. Its quarter horse and thoroughbred programs can be traced back to Richard King and his son-in-law, Robert Kleberg Sr.

The company owns the Kingsville Publishing Company, which offers printing services and publishes several local newspapers, including the *Kingsville Record* and *Bishop News*. It also owns the Robstown Hardware Company.

According to CEO Jack Hunt, King sought a company in the nut sector for acquisition because the nut industry isn't involved in farm subsidy programs and the sector also has little or no competition from foreign markets.

The company's operations are managed from its Houston corporate headquarters.

HISTORY

King Ranch was founded in 1853 by former steamboat captain Richard King and his wife Henrietta, the daughter of a Brownsville, Texas, missionary. On the advice of his friend Robert E. Lee, King used his steamboating profits and occasional strong-arm tactics to buy land — miles of flat, brush-filled coastal plain and desert south of Corpus Christi, Texas, valued at pennies an acre.

The next year King relocated the residents of an entire drought-ravaged village to the ranch and employed them as ranch hands, known ever after as *kineños* ("King's men"). The Kings built their homestead in 1858 at a site recommended by Lee.

King Ranch endured attacks from Union guerrillas during the Civil War and Mexican bandits after the war. Times were tough, but King was up to the challenge, always traveling armed and with outriders.

In 1867 the ranch used its famed Running W brand for the first time. After King's death in 1885, Robert Kleberg, who married King's daughter Alice, managed the 1.2 million-acre ranch for his mother-in-law. Henrietta died in 1925 and left three-fourths of the ranch to Alice. Before Robert's death in 1932, control of the ranch passed to sons Richard and Bob. In 1933 Bob negotiated an exclusive oil and gas lease with Houston-based Humble Oil, which later became part of Exxon.

While Richard served in Congress, Bob ran the ranch. He developed the Santa Gertrudis, the first breed of cattle ever created in the US, by crossing British shorthorn cattle with Indian Brahmas. The new breed was better suited to the hot, dry South Texas climate.

Bob made King Ranch a leading breeder of quarter horses, which worked cattle, and Thoroughbreds, which he raced. He bought Kentucky Derby winner Bold Venture in 1936 and a Kentucky breeding farm in 1946; that year a King Ranch horse, Assault, won racing's Triple Crown.

When Bob died in 1974, the family asked James Clement, husband of one of the founders' great-granddaughters, to become CEO and bypassed Robert Shelton, a King relative and orphan whom Bob had raised as his own son. Shelton severed ties with the ranch in 1977 over a lawsuit he filed against Exxon, and partially won, alleging underpayment of royalties.

Under Clement, King Ranch became a multinational corporation. In 1980 it formed King Ranch Oil and Gas (also called King Ranch Energy) to explore for and produce oil and gas in five states and the Gulf of Mexico. In 1988 Clement retired, and Kimberly-Clark executive Darwin Smith became the first CEO not related to the founders. Smith left after one year, and the reins passed to petroleum geologist Roger Jarvis

and then to Jack Hunt in 1995. With the help of scientists, in the early 1990s the company developed a leaner, more fertile breed of the Santa Gertrudis called the Santa Cruz.

In 1998 Stephen "Tio" Kleberg, the only King descendant still actively working the ranch, was pushed from the saddle of daily operations to a seat on the board. King Ranch sold its Kentucky horse farm in 1998 and teamed up with Collier Enterprises that year to purchase citrus grower Turner Foods from utility holding company FPL Group. In 2000 King Ranch sold King Ranch Energy to St. Mary Land and Exploration Co. for $60 million.

Like a good western movie, some things ride into the sunset at King Ranch. By 2000 the company had sold its 670-acre Kentucky Thoroughbred breeding and racing farm, most of its foreign ranches, and its primary oil and gas subsidiary.

In order to expand and diversify its agricultural operations, in 2006 King acquired North Carolina's Young Pecan Company. Young Pecan grows no nut crops of its own but, with state-of-the-art laser operations, it is one of the world's largest pecan shellers, selling its products to food manufacturers as ingredients as well as to retail food purveyors as snacks and for baking.

EXECUTIVES

President and CEO: Jack Hunt, age 65
Chief Wildlife Biologist: Mickey W. Hellickson
Director Security and Wildlife: Butch Thompson
Recreational Hunting Leases and Guided Hunts, Deer and Quail: Mary Crowell
King Ranch Wildlife Biologist: Justin Feild
King Ranch Wildlife Biologist: Marc Bartoskewitz
King Ranch Wildlife Biologist: Oscar Cortez
Cattle Feeding: Willie Pakebusch
Registered and Composite Seedstock: Robert Silguero
Stockers and Feeders: Mike Mayo
Quarter Horses: Jared Lee

LOCATIONS

HQ: King Ranch, Inc.
   3 River Way, Ste. 1600, Houston, TX 77056
Phone: 832-681-5700
Web: www.king-ranch.com

Selected Farming Operations

Florida
   3,100 acres (St. Augustine sod)
   12,000 acres (sugar cane)
   40,000 acres (orange and grapefruit groves)
Texas
   60,000 acres (cotton and grain)
   825,000 acres (cattle)

PRODUCTS/OPERATIONS

Selected Operations

Caesar Kleberg Wildlife Research Institute
Consolidated Citrus L.P.
Kingsville Publishing
King Ranch — Florida
King Ranch — Texas
King Ranch Cattle
King Ranch Citrus
King Ranch Feeding
King Ranch Institute of Ranch Management
King Ranch Museum
King Ranch Nature Tour Program
King Ranch Quarter Horses
King Ranch Saddle Shop
King Ranch Sod
King Ranch Sugar Cane
Robstown Hardware Company
Young Pecan Company

COMPETITORS

A. Duda & Sons
Ace Hardware
Alico, Inc.
AzTx Cattle
Bartlett and Company
Blue Diamond Growers
Cactus Feeders
CGC
Chiquita Brands
Coleman Natural Foods
Dakota Beef
Diamond Foods
Dole Food
Golden Peanut
Golden West Nuts
Green Valley Pecan
Home Depot
King Nut Companies
Laura's Lean Beef Co.
Lowe's
Lykes Bros.
M. A. Patout
Maverick Ranch
Meridian Nut Growers
ML Macadamia Orchards
Niman Ranch
Organic Valley
Pederson's
SMBSC
Southern States
Sugar Cane Growers Cooperative of Florida
Sun Growers
Sun-Maid
Texoma Peanut

KLA-Tencor

KLA-Tencor is hard-core when it comes to hunting down flaws in chips. The company — one of the world's largest makers of semiconductor equipment — offers yield management systems that monitor and analyze wafers at various stages of chip production, inspecting reticles (which make circuit patterns) and measuring crucial microscopic layers. The systems' feedback allows flaws to be corrected before they can ruin the costly wafers. KLA-Tencor has long dominated the market for equipment that inspects semiconductor photomasks and reticles.

KLA-Tencor is the undisputed leader in its niche; it tries to position itself as a one-stop shop for its customers' yield management needs, particularly by complementing its technology offerings with consulting services and software. The company's software includes products for factorywide yield management and for test floor automation and control.

As chip makers generally stopped buying capital equipment in the worldwide financial meltdown, in 2008 KLA-Tencor initiated a cost reduction program that included a 15% reduction in workforce and more than $660 million a year through additional cost-cutting measures.

Seeing no improvement in business conditions the following year, KLA-Tencor said it would lay off another 10% of its global workforce, consolidate facilities, schedule more forced time off, and reduce employee stock purchase plan benefits.

KLA-Tencor uses selective acquisitions as well as intensive R&D to keep up with advances in chip fabrication. The company collaborates with customers to develop process recipes through its Technology Engagement Services segment.

Late in 2008 KLA-Tencor acquired the Micro-electronic Inspection Equipment (MIE) business unit of Vistec Semiconductor Systems. Based in Germany, MIE provides semiconductor photomask and wafer manufacturing systems.

In mid-2008 the company acquired ICOS Vision Systems, a leading supplier of inspection equipment for semiconductor packaging and interconnects, photovoltaic solar cells, and light-emitting diodes (LEDs).

Entities affiliated with The Capital Group Companies own more than 44% of KLA-Tencor.

HISTORY

In the semiconductor industry's early years, chip defects rendered about half of some product runs unusable. Silicon Valley entrepreneurs Kenneth Levy — who helped develop image processing equipment pioneer Computervision (later merged into Parametric Technology) — and Robert Anderson founded KLA Instruments in 1975. ("KLA" originally stood for Kenneth Levy Associates.) Their goal was to develop inspection equipment to improve semiconductor factory yields. In 1978 KLA introduced a first-of-its-kind inspection system that employed advanced optical and image processing technology to test the templates used to etch circuit designs onto silicon wafers. It cut inspection time from eight hours to about 15 minutes.

KLA went public in 1980; within two years it had introduced wafer inspection and wafer metrology systems. As chip yields jumped, so did KLA's sales, shooting past $60 million by mid-decade. When increased competition left US demand faltering, Levy began targeting markets in Europe and Asia. By 1987, 40% of KLA's sales came from those two regions.

Levy named former Hewlett-Packard executive Kenneth Schroeder president in 1991 to take more day-to-day control of the company. Anderson by then had given up his executive duties; he retired in 1994.

Seeking an edge in an increasingly splintered market, the company merged with Tencor Instruments (and changed its name to KLA-Tencor) in 1997. The $1.3 billion deal created a company with the broadest line of wafer inspection equipment, film measurement systems, and yield management software in the industry.

Czechoslovakian Karel Urbanek had started Tencor in 1976 to make semiconductor measurement and test instruments. Tencor's first product was the Alpha-Step, a film layer profiler, but the company became known for a system that detected and analyzed wafer defects measuring as small as 1/100,000th the width of a human hair. Tencor went public in 1993.

Following the merger, Levy gave up his CEO duties (he remained chairman) to top Tencor executive Jon Tompkins. The two switched titles in 1998 to better reflect their strengths.

Tompkins retired as chairman in 1999 but remained on the board. Levy resumed the chairmanship, and Schroeder became CEO.

Kenneth Schroeder retired as CEO at the end of 2005 and became a special advisor to the company. His successor, COO Richard Wallace, had joined KLA in 1988.

KLA-Tencor in 2006 acquired competitor ADE Corporation. Following a special board committee's review of historical practices in granting stock options, co-founder Ken Levy retired from the board in late 2006 and was named chairman emeritus. Edward Barnholt, a director since

1995 and the former CEO of Agilent Technologies, was named non-executive chairman to succeed Levy. The company repriced all outstanding retroactively priced stock options held by Levy and other executives following the probe, which resulted in KLA-Tencor restating financial results from mid-1997 to mid-2002 and taking a non-cash charge of $370 million for stock-based compensation expenses.

KLA-Tencor also "terminated all aspects of its employment relationship" with former CEO and director Kenneth Schroeder after the conclusion of the options probe and canceled all options held by Schroeder. The former CEO contested the company's actions. Stuart Nichols, the company's general counsel for six years, resigned his post. Other top executives were exonerated of wrongdoing by the board committee. Former chairman and CEO Jon Tompkins resigned from the board just before the end of 2006.

KLA-Tencor nearly put an end to the stock-options mess in mid-2007, reaching a settlement with the SEC. The company consented to a permanent injunction against violations of federal securities laws on books and records, internal controls, and reporting. KLA-Tencor wasn't required to pay any fine, penalty, or monetary damages to settle the case.

Kenneth Schroeder didn't get off as easy, however; the SEC charged him with fraud, accusing the former CEO of backdating more than $200 million worth of stock options.

In early 2008 the company agreed to pay $65 million in cash to settle a class-action shareholder lawsuit over backdated stock-option grants, brought by the City of Philadelphia Board of Pensions and other plaintiffs.

EXECUTIVES

Chairman: Edward W. (Ned) Barnholt, age 66
President, CEO, and Director:
Richard P. (Rick) Wallace, age 49,
$4,806,663 total compensation
EVP and CFO: Mark P. Dentinger, age 46,
$443,904 total compensation
EVP Corporate Alliances and CTO:
Bin-ming Benjamin (Ben) Tsai, age 51
SVP, General Counsel, and Corporate Secretary:
Brian M. Martin, age 48, $921,033 total compensation
SVP and Chief Accounting Officer:
Virendra A. Kirloskar, age 46,
$785,770 total compensation
Chief Engineer and Group VP, PSG, Rapid, and Ebeam:
Zain Saidin
Senior Director Investor Relations: Ed Lockwood
Senior Director Corporation Communications:
Meggan Powers
Auditors: PricewaterhouseCoopers LLP

LOCATIONS

HQ: KLA-Tencor Corporation
1 Technology Dr., Milpitas, CA 95035
Phone: 408-875-3000   **Fax:** 408-875-4144
Web: www.kla-tencor.com

2010 Sales

	$ mil.	% of total
Asia/Pacific		
Taiwan	688.1	38
Japan	239.4	13
South Korea	151.2	8
Other countries	289.5	16
US	341.1	19
Europe & Israel	111.5	6
Total	**1,820.8**	**100**

PRODUCTS/OPERATIONS

2010 Sales

	$ mil.	% of total
Defect inspection	1,016.4	56
Service	489.8	27
Metrology	262.7	14
Other	51.9	3
Total	**1,820.8**	**100**

Selected Products

Metrology systems
  Critical dimension scanning electron microscopes (SEMs)
  Film and film stress measurement
  Optical overlay measurement
  Surface profiling
Reticle (circuit pattern mask) inspection systems
Wafer inspection systems
  Automated defect classification
  Defect analysis software
  In-line monitoring
  Optical and SEM defect review
  Process tool performance monitoring
Yield management software
  Factorywide yield management software
  Test floor automation/control software

COMPETITORS

Applied Materials	Keithley Instruments
Camtek	Nanometrics
Carl Zeiss	Nova Measuring
Cascade Microtech	Orbotech
Cognex	PDF Solutions
Dainippon Screen	Rudolph Technologies
EG Systems	Veeco Instruments
FEI	Zygo
Hitachi High-Technologies	

HISTORICAL FINANCIALS

Company Type: Public

Income Statement

FYE: June 30

	REVENUE ($ mil.)	NET INCOME ($ mil.)	NET PROFIT MARGIN	EMPLOYEES
6/10	1,821	212	11.7%	5,000
6/09	1,520	(523)	—	4,900
6/08	2,522	359	14.2%	6,000
6/07	2,731	528	19.3%	6,000
6/06	2,071	381	18.4%	5,900
Annual Growth	**(3.2%)**	**(13.6%)**	**—**	**(4.1%)**

2010 Year-End Financials

Debt ratio: 35.6%
Return on equity: 9.6%
Cash ($ mil.): 530
Current ratio: 3.67
Long-term debt ($ mil.): 799
No. of shares (mil.): 168
Dividends
  Yield: 2.2%
  Payout: 48.8%
Market value ($ mil.): 4,679

Stock History

NASDAQ (GS): KLAC

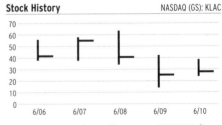

	STOCK PRICE ($) FY Close	P/E High/Low		PER SHARE ($) Earnings	Dividends	Book Value
6/10	27.88	31	20	1.23	0.60	13.39
6/09	25.25	—	—	(3.07)	0.60	13.02
6/08	40.71	32	18	1.95	0.60	17.77
6/07	54.95	22	15	2.61	0.48	21.15
6/06	41.57	30	21	1.86	0.48	21.26
Annual Growth	**(9.5%)**	**—**	**—**	**(9.8%)**	**5.7%**	**(10.9%)**

Kmart Corporation

Attention Kmart shoppers: Kmart is the #3 discount retailer in the US, behind Wal-Mart and Target. It sells name-brand and private-label goods (including its Joe Boxer and Jaclyn Smith labels), mostly to low- and mid-income families. It runs about 1,300 off-mall stores (including 35 Supercenters) in 49 US states, Puerto Rico, Guam, and the US Virgin Islands. About 275 Kmart stores sell home appliances (including Sears' Kenmore brand) and more than 1,020 locations house in-store pharmacies. The company also operates the kmart.com website, which includes merchandise from sister company Sears. Kmart is a subsidiary of Sears Holdings Corp., formed by the 2005 combination of ailing Sears, Roebuck and Kmart.

The combination of Sears and Kmart was intended to leverage the strengths of both chains and to make their products, brands, and services available through more locations and customer distribution channels. Sears, which has long sought a way to diversify away from the shopping mall, was attracted to Kmart's off-mall locations. But so far the combination has proved disappointing. Both retailers are suffering from falling same-store sales as they fail to attract customers. Indeed, 21 Kmart stores closed in early 2010, following the shutdown of about another 55 Kmart stores since 2007. Kmart's total sales have fallen more than 8% since 2007.

To cater to customers in tough economic times, Kmart revived its layaway program in 2008 and it has experienced double-digit growth. The program allows customers to purchase items using an eight-week payment plan.

Sears has indeed taken advantage of cross-selling opportunities by offering proprietary Sears brands, including Craftsman, Diehard, and Kenmore products, in Kmart stores. The sale of Kenmore brand appliances is meant to help Kmart differentiate itself from its larger rivals, Wal-Mart and Target, which stock a more limited range of appliances. There are also about 20 Sears Auto Centers operating in Kmart stores.

HISTORY

Sebastian Kresge and John McCrorey opened five-and-dime stores in Memphis and Detroit in 1897. When the partners split two years later, Kresge got Detroit and McCrorey took Memphis. By the time Kresge incorporated as S. S. Kresge Company in 1912, it had become the second-largest dime store chain in the US, with 85 stores. Kresge expanded rapidly in the next several decades, forming S. S. Kresge, Ltd., in 1929 to operate stores in Canada. In the late 1920s and 1930s, the company opened stores in suburban shopping centers. By the 1950s Kresge was one of the largest general merchandise retailers in the US.

A marketing study prompted management to enter discount retailing in 1958, and three unprofitable locations were transformed into Jupiter Discount stores in 1961. The company judged this a success and opened the first Kmart discount store in Detroit in 1962; by 1966 the company had more than 160 Kmart stores. Kresge formed a joint venture with G. J. Coles & Coy (later Coles Myer) to operate Kmart stores in Australia (1968; sold in 1994). The company expanded the Kmart format swiftly in the 1970s, opening more than

270 stores in 1976 alone. With about 95% of its sales coming from Kmart stores, the company changed its name to Kmart in 1977.

Kmart diversified during the 1980s and early 1990s, adding various retailers, including Walden Book Company, then the #1 US bookstore chain, and Builders Square (formerly Home Centers of America) in 1984; PayLess Drug Stores Northwest in 1985; PACE Membership Warehouse in 1989; The Sports Authority in 1990; a 90% stake in OfficeMax by 1991; and the Borders bookstore chain in 1992.

In 1994 and 1995, amid falling earnings, the company began shedding operations, spinning off or selling OfficeMax, The Sports Authority, PACE, its US automotive service centers (to Penske, which still runs them), and Borders. In 1995 CEO Joseph Antonini — architect of the diversification strategy — was replaced by Floyd Hall. More than 200 US stores were closed.

The company then sold Kmart Mexico, a joint venture with El Puerto de Liverpool, and an 87.5% stake in Kmart Canada in 1997 (it sold the rest in 1998). Also in 1997 it unveiled the new Big Kmart format. The company also sold woebegone 162-store Builders Square to Leonard Green & Partners (owners of the Hechinger chain) for a mere $10 million, but retained a $761 million liability for the stores' lease obligations. (Hechinger filed for bankruptcy in 1999, and Kmart assumed the obligations of 115 stores.)

In May 2000 Hall was replaced by former CVS president and COO Charles Conaway. In July 2001 Kmart said it would close 72 stores (in about 30 states) in locations that did not fit with expansion plans.

In a management shake-up that followed downgrades in Kmart's credit rating in January 2002, director James Adamson replaced Conaway as chairman. Soon after, key vendors suspended shipments to the troubled discounter saying Kmart failed to make regular weekly payments. Kmart filed for Chapter 11 bankruptcy protection that month. Soon after, Adamson was also named CEO. After filing for bankruptcy, Kmart closed 283 stores, resulting in 22,000 job losses. It announced additional job cuts, including about 400 corporate positions, in August. Nearly a year after filing for bankruptcy, Kmart's shares were delisted in December after 84 years on the New York Stock Exchange.

In January 2003 Adamson was succeeded as CEO by Julian Day, president and COO of Kmart. Later in the month Kmart won final approval from the bankruptcy court to close another 316 stores and proceed with a $2 billion exit financing package. In May 2003, 15 months after filing Chapter 11, Kmart emerged from bankruptcy protection with the help of its largest shareholder, ESL Investments.

Aylwin Lewis, a 13-year veteran of YUM! Brands, succeeded Day as president and CEO of Kmart Holding Corp. in 2004. In 2005 two former Kmart executives (Conaway and ex-CFO John McDonald) were accused by the SEC of misleading investors about the company's finances prior to its 2002 bankruptcy filing. (Conaway was fined more than $10 million in 2010.)

The company settled a class-action lawsuit regarding disabled-shopper access for $13 million in 2006. The $13 million awarded $8 million in cash and $5 million in gift cards to the plaintiffs.

In 2008 CEO Aylwin Lewis stepped down and was replaced on an interim basis by EVP W. Bruce Johnson.

EXECUTIVES

Interim President and Interim CEO: W. Bruce Johnson, age 58
EVP; President, Retail Services: James H. (Jim) Haworth, age 47
EVP Operating and Support Businesses: Scott J. Freidheim, age 44
EVP Apparel and Home: John D. Goodman, age 44
SVP and CFO: Michael D. (Mike) Collins, age 46
SVP, Controller, and Chief Accounting Officer: William K. Phelan, age 47
SVP, General Counsel, and Corporate Secretary: Dane A. Drobny
SVP Supply Chain and Operations: James P. (Jim) Mixon, age 65
SVP Marketing: Richard Gerstein
SVP; President, Kmart Apparel: Tara Poseley, age 43
SVP and General Manager, Kmart Retail: Donald J. Germano
Auditors: Deloitte & Touche LLP

LOCATIONS

HQ: Kmart Corporation
3333 Beverly Rd., Hoffman Estates, IL 60179
Phone: 847-286-2500   **Fax:** 847-286-5500
Web: www.kmartcorp.com

PRODUCTS/OPERATIONS

2010 Stores

	No.
Kmart discount stores	1,292
Kmart Supercenters	35
Total	**1,327**

Selected Private Labels

Cannon (bed and bath)
Craftsman (tools)
DieHard (car batteries)
Jaclyn Smith (ladies' apparel)
Joe Boxer (men's and women's apparel)
Kenmore (appliances)
Martha Stewart Everyday (bed and bath)
Route 66 (casual wear and shoes)

Retail Divisions

Kmart discount store (general merchandise/small grocery section)
Kmart Supercenter (general merchandise/supermarkets)

COMPETITORS

Bed Bath & Beyond
Best Buy
Big Lots
BJ's Wholesale Club
Costco Wholesale
CVS Caremark
Dollar General
Family Dollar Stores
Home Depot
J. C. Penney
Kohl's
Kroger
Lowe's
Office Depot
PETCO
Rite Aid
Ross Stores
ShopKo Stores
Staples
Target
TJX Companies
Toys "R" Us
Walgreen
Wal-Mart

HISTORICAL FINANCIALS

Company Type: Subsidiary

Income Statement

FYE: Last Wednesday in January

	REVENUE ($ mil.)	NET INCOME ($ mil.)	NET PROFIT MARGIN	EMPLOYEES
1/09	16,219	—	—	133,000
1/08	17,256	—	—	133,000
1/07	18,647	—	—	133,000
1/06	19,094	—	—	133,000
1/05	19,701	—	—	133,000
Annual Growth	(4.7%)	—	—	0.0%

Revenue History

Koch Industries

Koch (pronounced "coke") Industries is the *real thing*, one of the largest (if not the largest) private companies in the US. Koch's operations are diverse, including refining and chemicals, process and pollution control equipment, and technologies; fibers and polymers; commodity and financial trading; and forest and consumer products (led by Georgia-Pacific LLC). Its Flint Hills Resources subsidiary owns three refineries that process more than 800,000 barrels of crude oil daily. Koch operates crude gathering systems and pipelines across North America as well as cattle ranches with a total of 15,000 head of cattle in Kansas, Montana, and Texas. Brothers Charles and David Koch control the company.

Koch has a presence in almost 60 countries. Among other assets, the company owns a 3% stake in the Trans Alaska Pipeline System, 4,000 miles of oil and products pipelines in the US, an 80,000-barrels-per-day refinery in Rotterdam.

Koch's numerous subsidiary companies leverage capabilities such as its proprietary Market Based Management system, and a high level of operational, trading, transaction, and public sector skills, to create long-term value for its customers. The company has pursued a strategy of reinvesting about 90% of its earnings into acquisitions and investments (some $32 billion over the past five years, including the $21 billion purchase of forest products giant Georgia-Pacific.

Expanding its product line, in 2010 Georgia-Pacific agreed to buy oriented strand board manufacturer Grant Forest Products for $400 million.

Charles Koch released a book in 2007, *THE SCIENCE OF SUCCESS: How Market-Based Management Built the World's Largest Private Company*, outlining the company's philosophy for business growth.

HISTORY

Fred Koch grew up poor in Texas and worked his way through MIT. In 1928 Koch developed a process to refine more gasoline from crude oil, but when he tried to market his invention, the major oil companies sued him for patent infringement. Koch eventually won the lawsuits (after 15 years in court), but the controversy made it tough to attract many US customers. In 1929 Koch took his process to the Soviet Union, but he grew disenchanted with Stalinism and returned home to become a founding member of the anticommunist John Birch Society.

Koch launched Wood River Oil & Refining in Illinois (1940) and bought the Rock Island refinery in Oklahoma (1947). He folded the remaining purchasing and gathering network into Rock Island Oil & Refining (though he later sold the refineries).

After Koch's death in 1967, his 32-year-old son Charles took the helm and renamed the company Koch Industries. He began a series of acquisitions, adding petrochemical and oil trading service operations.

During the 1980s Koch was thrust into various arenas, legal and political. Charles' brother David, also a Koch Industries executive, ran for US vice president on the Libertarian ticket in 1980. That year the other two Koch brothers, Frederick and William (David's fraternal twin), launched a takeover attempt, but Charles retained control, and William was fired from his job as VP.

In a 1983 settlement Charles and David bought out the dissident family members for just over $1 billion. William and Frederick continued to challenge their brothers in court, claiming they had been shortchanged in the deal (the two estranged brothers eventually lost their case in 1998, and their appeals were rejected in 2000).

Despite this legal wrangling, Koch Industries continued to expand, purchasing a Corpus Christi, Texas, refinery in 1981. It expanded its pipeline system, buying Bigheart Pipe Line in Oklahoma (1986) and two systems from Santa Fe Southern Pacific (1988).

In 1991 Koch purchased the Corpus Christi marine terminal, pipelines, and gathering systems of Scurlock Permian (a unit of Ashland Oil). In 1992 the company bought United Gas Pipe Line (renamed Koch Gateway Pipeline) and its pipeline system extending from Texas to Florida.

To strengthen its engineering services presence worldwide, Koch acquired Glitsch International (a maker of separation equipment) from engineering giant Foster Wheeler in 1997. It also acquired USX-Delhi Group, a natural gas processor and transporter.

In 1998 Koch bought Purina Mills, the largest US producer of animal feed, and formed the KoSa joint venture with Mexico's Saba family to buy Hoechst's Trevira polyester unit. (Koch acquired the Saba family's stake in KoSa in 2001.) Lethargic energy and livestock prices in 1998 and 1999, however, led Koch to lay off several hundred employees, sell its feedlots, and divest portions of its natural gas gathering and pipeline systems. Purina Mills filed for bankruptcy protection in 1999 (later, it emerged from bankruptcy and held an IPO in 2000, and was acquired by #2 US dairy co-op Land O'Lakes in 2001).

William Koch sued Koch Industries in 1990, claiming the company had underreported the amount of oil purchased on US government and Native Americans lands. A jury found for William, but he, Charles, and David agreed to settle the case in 2001 — and sat down to dinner together for the first time in 20 years.

In other legal matters, in 2000 Koch agreed to pay a $30 million civil fine and contribute $5 million toward environmental projects to settle complaints over oil spills from its pipelines in the 1990s. The company agreed to pay $20 million in 2001 to settle a separate environmental case concerning a Texas refinery.

The company acquired INVISTA in 2004 for $4.2 billion and merged it with its KoSa unit. In 2005 SemGroup acquired all of Koch Materials Company's US and Mexico asphalt operations and ONEOK, Inc. acquired the natural gas liquids businesses owned by several Koch companies.

In 2005 a Koch subsidiary completed the $21 billion acquisition of Georgia-Pacific.

EXECUTIVES

Chairman and CEO: Charles G. Koch, age 74
Vice-Chairman: Joseph W. (Joe) Moeller, age 67
President, COO, and Director:
David L. (Dave) Robertson, age 48
CFO and Director: Steve Feilmeier
EVP Operations and Director: James L. (Jim) Mahoney
EVP and Director: Richard Fink
EVP and Director: David H. Koch, age 70
SVP Corporate Strategy: John C. Pittenger
SVP and General Counsel: Mark Holden
VP Business Development: Ron Vaupel
VP Federal Affairs: Brian Henneberry
President, Koch Pipeline Company: Kim Penner
President, Koch Fertilizer: Steve Packebush
President, Koch Carbon: Steve Tatum
President and COO, Koch Chemical Technology Group:
Robert (Bob) DiFulgentiz
President, Koch Supply & Trading: Steve Mawer
Treasurer: David May
President and COO, Flint Hills Resources:
Bradley J. (Brad) Razook
Director Corporate Compliance and Environmental, Health, and Safety: Tom Butz
Director Communication: Melissa Cohlmia
Corporate Controller: Richard Dinkel

LOCATIONS

HQ: Koch Industries, Inc.
4111 E. 37th St. North, Wichita, KS 67220
Phone: 316-828-5500   **Fax:** 316-828-5739
Web: www.kochind.com

PRODUCTS/OPERATIONS

Selected Operations

Refining & Chemicals
Flint Hills Resources (formerly Koch Petroleum, crude oil, petrochemicals, and refined products)
Koch Pipeline Co. LP

Process & Pollution Control Equipment & Technologies (specialty equipment and services for refining and chemical industry)
Iris Power Engineering, Inc.
The John Zink Company
Koch-Glitsch, Inc.
Koch Heat Transfer Group (formerly Brown Fintube Company)
Koch Membrane Systems Inc.

Minerals
Koch Mineral Services
Koch Carbon LLC.
Koch Exploration Company, LLC.
Fertilizers
Koch Nitrogen Company
Fibers & Polymers
INVISTA B.V.
Commodity & Financial Trading & Services
Koch Financial Corp.
Koch Supply & Trading
Forest & Consumer Products
Georgia-Pacific LLC
Ranching
Matador Cattle Co.
Business Development
Koch Genesis Company (investment in noncore businesses)

COMPETITORS

AbitibiBowater
ADM
AEP
Ashland Inc.
Avista
BP
Cargill
CenterPoint Energy
CGC
Chevron
ConocoPhillips
Duke Energy
Dynegy
Exxon Mobil
Gypsum Products
Imperial Oil
International Paper
Kimberly-Clark
King Ranch
Marathon Oil
Motiva Enterprises
Occidental Petroleum
OfficeMax
Packaging Corp. of America
Peabody Energy
PEMEX
PG&E Corporation
Royal Dutch Shell
Shell Oil Products
Smurfit-Stone Container
Southern Company
SUEZ-TRACTEBEL
Sunoco
Weyerhaeuser
Williams Companies

HISTORICAL FINANCIALS
Company Type: Private

Income Statement

FYE: December 31

	REVENUE ($ mil.)	NET INCOME ($ mil.)	NET PROFIT MARGIN	EMPLOYEES
12/08	100,000	—	—	80,000
12/07	98,000	—	—	80,000
12/06	90,000	—	—	80,000
12/05	80,000	—	—	80,000
12/04	40,000	—	—	30,000
Annual Growth	25.7%	—	—	27.8%

Revenue History

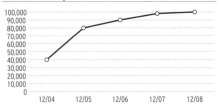

Kohl's Corporation

Kohl's wants to be easy on shoppers and tough on competition. It operates 1,050-plus discount department stores in 49 states. More than a quarter of its stores are in the Midwest, where Kohl's continues to grow while rapidly expanding into other markets. Moderately priced name-brand and private-label apparel, shoes, accessories, and housewares are sold through centrally located cash registers, designed to expedite checkout and keep staff costs down. Merchandising relationships allow Kohl's to carry top brands (NIKE, Levi's, OshKosh B'Gosh) not typically available to discounters.

To ride out the recession and capitalize on the woes of other retailers, Kohl's is focusing on controlling expenses while it continues to expand. Continuing its expansion in the western US, Kohl's opened its first store in Alaska in 2009, expanding its presence to 49 states. In 2010 the chain announced plans to open 30 stores.

Brands — both Kohl's own and big-name national brands — are key to Kohl's merchandising strategy. In a bid to emulate its "cheap chic" rival Target and JCPenney, Kohl's has been busy enlisting big-name designers to produce merchandise exclusively for its stores. Indeed, private-label and exclusive brands accounted for 44% of sales (up from 25% in 2004). To build its "Available Only at Kohl's" business the discounter signed designer Vera Wang to produce a low-cost collection, named Simply Vera, which debuted in Kohl's stores and on its website in the fall of 2007. The collection comprises women's apparel, intimate apparel, handbags, leather accessories, footwear, jewelry, linens, and towels. In 2008 Kohl's signed a licensing agreement with Liz Claiborne naming Kohl's as the exclusive US retailer for the Dana Buchman line of women's apparel and accessories, which debuted in Kohl's stores in early 2009. Kohl's also is the exclusive US retailer for MUDD-branded apparel, accessories, jewelry, and domestics through a multi-year licensing deal it inked in December 2008 with Iconix Brand Group. It also partnered with the Canadian pop singer Avril Lavigne to bring a juniors' brand called Abbey Dawn to market in 2008. The brand mirrors Lavigne's personal style, which mixes a rock style with a feminine touch.

Private-label offerings are another leg in Kohl's growth strategy. The discount retailer has signed a licensing agreement with Lagardère Active, the company that publishes *ELLE* magazine, to develop an *ELLE*-branded line of women's clothing. (The line debuted in the spring of 2008.) Also, Kohl's has licensing agreements with sportswear maker Quicksilver to gain exclusive rights to skateboarder Tony Hawk's brand of boys and young men's fashions, as well as with American Brand Holdings for its Hang Ten brand of young California lifestyle wear. Other private-label lines include the Genuine Sonoma and Croft & Barrow brands.

In August 2008 Kohl's appointed company-veteran Kevin Mansell to the position of president and CEO. Mansell has served as president since 1999. He added the chairman's title in September 2009 when Larry Montgomery retired.

HISTORY

Max Kohl (father of Sen. Herbert Kohl of Wisconsin) opened his first grocery store in Milwaukee in the late 1920s. Over the years he and his three sons developed it into a chain and in 1938 Kohl's incorporated.

Kohl opened a department store (half apparel, half hard goods) in 1962 next door to a Kohl's grocery. In the mid-1960s he hired William Kellogg, a twentysomething buyer in the basement discount department at Milwaukee's Boston Store, for his expertise in budget retailing. Kellogg came from a retailing family (his father was VP of merchandising at Boston Store; the younger Kellogg had joined that firm out of high school). Kohl and Kellogg began developing the pattern for the store, carving out a niche between upscale department stores and discounters (offering department store quality at discount store prices).

The Kohl family entered real estate development in 1970, building the largest shopping center in the Milwaukee area. By 1972 the family's 65 food stores and five department stores were generating about $90 million in yearly sales. That year the Kohls sold 80% of the two operations to British American Tobacco's Brown & Williamson Industries division (later called BATUS), the first in a string of department store acquisitions that would eventually include Marshall Field's and Saks Fifth Avenue.

BATUS bought the rest of Kohl's in 1978. Herb and Allen Kohl left the business to concentrate on real estate and politics, and Kellogg was named president and CEO. The next year BATUS separated the food and department store operations and eventually sold the food store chain to A&P in 1983.

Kohl's discount image did not fit in with BATUS's other retail operations, so it decided to sell the department store chain. In 1986 Kellogg and two other executives, with the backing of mall developers Herbert and Melvin Simon, led an LBO to acquire the chain's 40 stores and a distribution center.

Two years later Kohl's acquired 26 Main Street department stores from Federated Department Stores (now Macy's), moving the company into new cities such as Chicago and Detroit. When Kohl's went public in 1992, it had 81 stores in six states, and sales topped $1 billion.

In 1996 Kohl's began its mid-Atlantic expansion by opening stores in North Carolina. Kohl's continued its expansion in 1998, entering Tennessee and building its mid-Atlantic presence. In early 1999 Kohl's named Larry Montgomery as CEO. The company also bought 30 stores from bankrupt Caldor (mostly in the New York City area) and reopened them as Kohl's in 2000.

Montgomery was named chairman of Kohl's in February 2003, succeeding Kellogg, who retired after 34 years with the company. Kohl's, which had become one of the fastest-growing and most successful US department store chains in the last decade, hit some serious bumps in 2003, including excess inventory (built up based on previous years of strong sales).

In 2004 Kohl's launched a new private label, Apt. 9, which was designed to compete with the likes of Banana Republic, Liz Claiborne, and Perry Ellis. It entered the Florida market in 2005. In 2006 Kohl's sold its private-label credit card business to JPMorgan Chase for about $1.6 billion.

In late 2007 Kohl's partnered with Fila in a multiyear licensing agreement to be Fila's exclusive US retailer of the FILA SPORT collection. Having debuted in fall 2008, the collection consists of apparel, footwear, and accessories for women, men, and children.

EXECUTIVES

Chairman, President, and CEO: Kevin B. Mansell, age 57, $9,037,962 total compensation
EVP and CFO: Wesley S. (Wes) McDonald, age 47, $2,687,944 total compensation
SVP Corporate Governance: Brian F. Miller
SEVP: John M. Worthington, age 46, $4,540,451 total compensation
SEVP: Donald A. (Don) Brennan, age 49, $4,523,797 total compensation
Auditors: Ernst & Young LLP

LOCATIONS

HQ: Kohl's Corporation
N56 W17000 Ridgewood Dr.
Menomonee Falls, WI 53051
Phone: 262-703-7000   **Fax:** 262-703-6143
Web: www.kohlscorporation.com

2010 Stores

	No.
California	121
Texas	80
Illinois	61
Ohio	56
Florida	48
Michigan	45
New York	45
Pennsylvania	43
Wisconsin	39
New Jersey	38
Indiana	37
Georgia	33
North Carolina	27
Arizona	26
Virginia	26
Minnesota	25
Colorado	23
Missouri	23
Massachusetts	21
Tennessee	19
Connecticut	18
Maryland	17
Washington	15
Kentucky	15
Iowa	14
South Carolina	12
Utah	12
Nevada	11
Alabama	10
Kansas	10
New Hampshire	9
Oklahoma	9
Oregon	9
Arkansas	8
Nebraska	7
West Virginia	7
Other states	39
Total	**1,058**

PRODUCTS/OPERATIONS

2010 Sales

	% of total
Women's	32
Men's	19
Home	18
Children's	13
Accessories	10
Footwear	8
Total	**100**

COMPETITORS

Bed Bath & Beyond
Belk
BJ's Wholesale Club
Dillard's
Fashion Bug
J. C. Penney
Kmart
Macy's
Men's Wearhouse
Old Navy
Ross Stores
Saks
Sears
ShopKo Stores
Syms
Target
TJX Companies
Wal-Mart

HISTORICAL FINANCIALS

Company Type: Public

Income Statement

FYE: Saturday nearest January 31

	REVENUE ($ mil.)	NET INCOME ($ mil.)	NET PROFIT MARGIN	EMPLOYEES
1/10	17,178	991	5.8%	133,000
1/09	16,389	885	5.4%	126,000
1/08	16,474	1,084	6.6%	125,000
1/07	15,544	1,109	7.1%	125,000
1/06	13,402	842	6.3%	107,000
Annual Growth	**6.4%**	**4.2%**	**—**	**5.6%**

2010 Year-End Financials

Debt ratio: 26.1%
Return on equity: 13.6%
Cash ($ mil.): 2,267
Current ratio: 2.29
Long-term debt ($ mil.): 2,052
No. of shares (mil.): 308
Dividends
  Yield: —
  Payout: —
Market value ($ mil.): 15,510

Stock History

NYSE: KSS

	STOCK PRICE ($) FY Close	P/E High/Low		PER SHARE ($) Earnings	Dividends	Book Value
1/10	50.37	19	10	3.23	—	25.50
1/09	36.71	19	8	2.89	—	21.89
1/08	45.53	23	11	3.39	—	19.82
1/07	70.91	23	13	3.31	—	18.20
1/06	44.39	24	18	2.43	—	19.35
Annual Growth	**3.2%**	**—**	**—**	**7.4%**	**—**	**7.2%**

KPMG International

Businesses all over the world count on KPMG for accounting. KPMG is the smallest, yet one of the most geographically dispersed of accounting's Big Four firms, which also include Deloitte Touche Tohmatsu, Ernst & Young, and PricewaterhouseCoopers. KPMG, a cooperative that operates as an umbrella organization for its global network of member firms, has organized its structure into three operating regions: the Americas (which includes KPMG L.L.P.); Australia and Asia/Pacific; and Europe, the Middle East, South Asia, and Africa. Member firms' offerings include audit, tax, and advisory services. KPMG focuses on clients in such industries as financial services, consumer products, and government.

KPMG, which operates in more than 145 countries worldwide, is focusing its growth in the Middle East and the BRIC countries (Brazil, Russia, India, and China. Growth in those markets helped make up for losses elsewhere, which were a result of the global economic recession.

As the global economy stabilizes KMPG is looking for new opportunities. Increased spending on infrastructure has the company ramping up its advisory capabilities around the world. KPMG plans to tap its experience in building public-private partnerships in order to help finance future infrastructure projects. The company also is looking to meet an increased demand for risk management as businesses deal with new regulations and look to properly align themselves after the recession.

Another key issue KPMG is tackling is global accounting standards. The firm is a big proponent of International Financial Reporting Standards (IFRS). The set of global accounting practices have been adopted by more than 110 countries around the world, but KPMG would like to see that number grow. As countries make the shift, KPMG firms offer guidance and training.

HISTORY

Peat Marwick was founded in 1911, when William Peat, a London accountant, met James Marwick during an Atlantic crossing. University of Glasgow alumni Marwick and Roger Mitchell had formed Marwick, Mitchell & Company in New York in 1897. Peat and Marwick agreed to ally their firms temporarily, and in 1925 they merged as Peat, Marwick, Mitchell, & Copartners.

In 1947 William Black became senior partner, a position he held until 1965. He guided the firm's 1950 merger with Barrow, Wade, Guthrie, one of the US's oldest firms, and built its consulting practice. Peat Marwick restructured its international practice as PMM&Co. (International) in 1972 (renamed Peat Marwick International in 1978).

The next year several European accounting firms led by Klynveld Kraayenhoff (the Netherlands) and Deutsche Treuhand (Germany) began forming an international accounting federation. Needing an American member, the European firms encouraged the merger of two American firms founded around the turn of the century, Main Lafrentz and Hurdman Cranstoun. Main Hurdman & Cranstoun joined the Europeans to form Klynveld Main Goerdeler (KMG), named after two of the member firms and the chairman of Deutsche Treuhand, Reinhard Goerdeler. Other members were C. Jespersen (Denmark), Thorne Riddel (Canada), Thomson McLintok (UK), and Fides Revision (Switzerland).

Peat Marwick merged with KMG in 1987 to form Klynveld Peat Marwick Goerdeler (KPMG). KPMG lost 10% of its business as competing client companies departed. Professional staff departures followed in 1990 when, as part of a consolidation, the firm trimmed its partnership rolls.

In the 1990s the then-Big Six accounting firms all faced lawsuits arising from an evolving standard holding auditors responsible for the substance, rather than merely the form, of clients' accounts. KPMG was hit by suits stemming from its audits of defunct S&Ls and litigation relating to the bankruptcy of Orange County, California (settled for $75 million in 1998). Nevertheless, KPMG kept growing; it expanded its consulting division with the acquisition of banking consultancy Barefoot, Marrinan & Associates in 1996.

In 1997, after Price Waterhouse and Coopers & Lybrand announced their merger, KPMG and Ernst & Young announced one of their own. But they called it quits the next year, fearing that regulatory approval of the deal would be too onerous.

The creation of PricewaterhouseCoopers (PwC) and increasing competition in the consulting sides of all of the Big Five brought a realignment of loyalties in their national practices. KPMG Consulting's Belgian group moved to PwC and its French group to Computer Sciences Corporation. Andersen nearly wooed away KPMG's Canadian consulting group, but the plan was foiled by the ever-sullen Andersen Consulting group (now Accenture) and by KPMG's promises of more money. Against this background, KPMG sold 20% of its consulting operations to Cisco Systems for $1 billion. In addition to the cash infusion, the deal allowed KPMG to provide installation and system management to Cisco's customers.

Even while KPMG worked on the IPO of its consulting group (which took place in 2001), it continued to rail against the SEC as it called for relationships between consulting and auditing organizations to be severed. In 2002 KPMG sold its British and Dutch consultancy units to France's Atos Origin.

In 2003 the SEC charged US member firm KPMG L.L.P. and four partners with fraud in connection with alleged profit inflation at former client Xerox in the late 1990s. (In April 2005 the accounting firm paid almost $22.5 million, including a $10 million civil penalty, to settle the charges.)

KPMG exited various businesses around the globe during fiscal 2004, including full-scope legal services and certain advisory services, to focus on higher-demand services.

EXECUTIVES

Chairman: Timothy P. (Tim) Flynn, age 53
Chairman, Americas Region; Chairman and CEO, KPMG LLP: John B. Veihmeyer, age 54
Deputy Chairman and COO, KPMG LLP: Henry Keizer, age 53
Deputy Chairman: John B. Harrison, age 53
COO: Brian Ambrose
Global Head, Healthcare: Alan Downey
Global Head, Insurance: Frank Ellenbuerger
Global Head, People, Performance, and Culture: Rachel Campbell
Global Head Performance and Technology: Aidan Brennan
Global Head, Advisory: Alan Buckle
Global Head, Tax: Loughlin Hickey
Global Head, Markets: Neil D. Austin, age 58
Global Chair, Automotive: Dieter Becker
Global Chair, Information, Communications and Entertainment: Gary Matuszak
Global Chair, Communications and Media: Sean Collins

Chairman, High Growth Market Practice: Ian Gomes
Chairman, Global Financial Services Practice: Jeremy Anderson
Chairman, Asia-Pacific and Chairman, China and Hong Kong: Carlson Tong, age 54
Chairman, EMA and Global Board Member: John Griffith-Jones
CEO, Switzerland and Global Board Member: Hubert Achermann

LOCATIONS

HQ: KPMG International
Burgemeester Rijnderslaan 10
1185 MC Amstelveen, The Netherlands
Phone: 31-20-656-7890   **Fax:** 31-20-656-7700
US HQ: 3 Chestnut Ridge Road, Montvale, NJ 07645
US Phone: 201-307-7000   **US Fax:** 201-830-8617
Web: www.kpmg.com

2009 Sales

	% of total
Europe, Middle East & Africa	54
Americas	31
Asia/Pacific	15
Total	**100**

PRODUCTS/OPERATIONS

2009 Sales

	% of total
Audit	50
Advisory	30
Tax	20
Total	**100**

2009 Sales by Industry

	% of total
Financial services	26
Industrial	25
Consumer	12
Infrastructure, Government & Healthcare	19
Information, Communication & Entertainment	18
Total	**100**

Selected Services

Audit services
  Attestation services
  Financial statement audit
Advisory services
  Audit support services
  Performance and technology
  Risk and compliance
  Transactions and restructuring
Tax services
  Corporate and business tax
  Global tax
  Global transfer pricing services
  Indirect tax
  International corporate tax
  International executive services
  Mergers and acquisitions

COMPETITORS

Bain & Company
Baker Tilly International
BDO International
Booz Allen
Deloitte
Ernst & Young Global
Grant Thornton International
H&R Block
Hewitt Associates
Marsh & McLennan
McKinsey & Company
PricewaterhouseCoopers

HISTORICAL FINANCIALS

Company Type: Partnership

Income Statement

FYE: September 30

	REVENUE ($ mil.)	NET INCOME ($ mil.)	NET PROFIT MARGIN	EMPLOYEES
9/09	20,110	—	—	140,235
9/08	22,690	—	—	136,896
9/07	19,810	—	—	123,322
9/06	16,880	—	—	112,795
9/05	15,690	—	—	103,621
Annual Growth	**6.4%**	**—**	**—**	**7.9%**

Revenue History

Kraft Foods

Mac & cheese if you please, and a Crème Egg for dessert. Kraft Foods is the #1 US food company and #2 worldwide (after Nestlé). Its North America unit boasts the world's largest-selling cheese brand (Kraft); cookie and cracker baker (Nabisco); and the milk-dunking favorite, Oreos. Its international business unit offers many of the same brands plus national favorites. The Oscar Mayer, Kraft, Philadelphia, Maxwell House, Nabisco, Oreo, Jacobs, Milka, and LU brands all have revenues of at least $1 billion; more than 50 of its brands regularly hit the $100 million mark. Kraft paid $19 billion to acquire Cadbury in 2010.

Kraft's original unsolicited 2009 offer for Cadbury was immediately rejected. Cadbury said the €10.2 billion ($16.7 billion) cash and stock offer undervalued the company. Kraft then announced it would issue more stock in order to improve its Cadbury bid. Subsequently and in a rare occurrence, the usually reticent Warren Buffett came out against any issuing of shares, saying that Kraft should not take on debt and overpay for the candy company. (After Kraft purchased Cadbury, Buffett reduced Berkshire Hathaway's holdings, selling off shares worth almost $1 billion. However, Berkshire Hathaway still owns some 6% of the company.)

The union of the #1 US food company and the 200-plus-year-old UK confectioner bumped Kraft up into the top spot of confectionery makers by revenue, unseating long-time champ Mars. Kraft now has 40 confectionery brands that each have annual sales of more than $100 million. Kraft already had Oreo, LU, and Toblerone; Cadbury's top brands included Dairy Milk bars, Roses chocolates, Trident gum, Halls cough drops, and the ever-popular Crème Eggs.

The purchase also made Kraft the #2 chewing gum maker by revenue, just behind Wrigley.

To help fund the acquistion, in 2010 Kraft sold its frozen pizza business in the US and Canada to Nestlé for $3.7 billion. The sale included the DiGiorno, Tombstone, California Pizza Kitchen, Jack's, and Delissio brands. (It also made Nestlé the largest maker of frozen pizza in the world.)

HISTORY

The Kraft tale began in 1903 when James L. Kraft began delivering cheese to Chicago grocers. His four brothers joined in, forming the J.L. Kraft & Bros. Company, in 1909. By 1914 the company had opened a cheese factory and was selling cheese across the US. Kraft developed its first blended, pasteurized cheese the following year.

Kraft went public in 1924; four years later it merged with Philadelphia cream-cheese maker, Phoenix, and also created Velveeta cheese spread. In 1930 Kraft was bought by National Dairy, but its operations were kept separate. New and notable products included Miracle Whip salad dressing (1933), macaroni and cheese dinners (1937), and Parkay margarine (1940). In the decades that followed, Kraft expanded into foreign markets.

National Dairy became Kraftco in 1969 and Kraft in 1976, hoping to benefit from its internationally known trademark. To diversify, Kraft merged with Dart Industries in 1980; Dart's subsidiaries (including Duracell batteries) and Kraft kept separate operations. With non-food sales sagging, Dart & Kraft split up in 1986. Kraft kept its original lines and added Duracell (sold 1988); the rest became Premark International. Tobacco giant Philip Morris Companies bought Kraft in 1988 for $12.9 billion. The next year Philip Morris joined Kraft with another unit, General Foods.

General Foods began when Charles Post, who marketed a wheat/bran health beverage, established the Postum Cereal Co. in 1896; he expanded the firm with such cereals as Grape-Nuts and Post Toasties. The company went public in 1922. Postum bought the makers of Jell-O (1925), Baker's chocolate (1927), Log Cabin syrup (1927), and Maxwell House coffee (1928), and in 1929 it acquired control of General Foods (owned by frozen vegetable pioneer Clarence Birdseye) and changed its own name to General Foods.

Its later purchases included Perkins Products (Kool-Aid, 1953) and Kohner Brothers (toys, 1970). Most of its non-food lines proved unsuccessful and were sold throughout the years. General Foods bought Oscar Mayer, the US's #1 hot dog maker, in 1981. Philip Morris bought General Foods for $5.6 billion in 1985.

The 1989 combination of Kraft and General Foods (the units still ran independently) created the largest US food maker, Kraft General Foods. To streamline management, Philip Morris integrated Kraft and General Foods in 1995.

In 2000 parent Philip Morris (which renamed itself the Altria Group in 2003) outbid Danone and Cadbury Schweppes (later Cadbury) and agreed to buy Nabisco Holdings. It completed the deal that December for $18.9 billion and began integrating those operations into Kraft Foods and Kraft Foods International. Then Philip Morris created a holding company for the newly combined food operations under the Kraft Foods Inc. name in 2001. The original Kraft Foods was renamed Kraft Foods North America.

Kraft Foods International CEO Roger Deromedi was appointed co-CEO of the new holding company, along with Betsy Holden. Kraft Foods Inc. was spun off by Altria in 2001 in what was the US's second-largest IPO ever at the time. Kraft cut 7,500 jobs in 2002 as a result of the integration of Nabisco operations.

Deromedi was named sole CEO in 2003. As part of his plan to refashion Kraft's product lineup, in 2005 the company sold its Altoids breath mints, LifeSavers and CremeSavers candies brands. Wm. Wrigley Jr. Company paid about $1.4 billion for the popular brands.

Despite his best efforts to improve the bottom line, Deromedi was shown the door in 2006. He was replaced by Frito-Lay's CEO Irene Rosenfeld (a former top Kraft executive who was instrumental in the company's acquisition and integration of Nabisco). She returned to Kraft after being head of Pepsico's Frito-Lay from 2004 to 2006.

Kraft extricated itself from the haze of secondhand tobacco smoke when it was spun off from Altria in 2007.

Kraft expanded its foreign operations with its 2007 purchase of the cookie/biscuit business of Groupe Danone for some $7.6 billion. The purchase gave the company brands such as LU, Petit Ecolier, and Crème Roulee, and made biscuits (cookies to us Yanks) the company's largest global business.

Kraft's 2008 sale of its slow-growing Post (Shredded Wheat, Raisin Bran, Honeycomb, Grape-Nuts, Pebbles and others) to Ralcorp, a maker of private-label cereals and other foods, is part of Kraft's strategy to pare down its brand offerings and concentrate on high-yield products. Ralcorp paid some $1.6 billion in stock for the acquisition.

EXECUTIVES

Chairman and CEO: Irene B. Rosenfeld, age 56, $26,345,200 total compensation
EVP; President, Kraft North America: W. Anthony (Tony) Vernon, age 54
EVP; President, Kraft Foods Europe: Michael A. (Mike) Clarke, age 45, $4,847,022 total compensation
EVP; President, Developing Markets and Global Categories: Sanjay Khosla, age 58, $5,788,013 total compensation
EVP and CFO: Timothy R. (Tim) McLevish, age 54, $5,405,878 total compensation
EVP Corporate and Legal Affairs and General Counsel: Marc S. Firestone, age 50, $5,214,377 total compensation
EVP Strategy: Michael Osanloo, age 43
EVP Global Human Resources: Karen J. May, age 52
EVP Operations and Business Services: David A. (Dave) Brearton, age 49
EVP Research, Development, and Quality: Jean E. Spence, age 52
EVP and Chief Marketing Officer: Mary Beth West, age 47
SVP Global Research and Technology Strategy: Todd Abraham
SVP Sales, International Commercial: Franco Suardi
SVP Corporate Affairs: Perry Yeatman
SVP and Controller: Pamela E. King, age 47
SVP Health and Wellness and Sustainability: Lance Friedmann
VP Finance and Investor Relations: Christopher M. (Chris) Jakubik
Senior Director Corporate External Communications: Michael Mitchell
Auditors: PricewaterhouseCoopers LLP

LOCATIONS

HQ: Kraft Foods Inc.
3 Lakes Dr., Northfield, IL 60093
Phone: 847-646-2000   **Fax:** 847-646-6005
Web: www.kraft.com

2009 Sales

	$ mil.	% of total
North America	23,662	58
Europe	8,768	22
Other	7,956	20
Total	**40,386**	**100**

PRODUCTS/OPERATIONS

2009 Sales

	$ mil.	% of total
Snacks	15,042	37
Beverages	8,029	20
Cheese	6,796	17
Convenient meals	6,448	16
Grocery	4,071	10
Total	**40,386**	**100**

Selected Brands

North America
  Snacks
    Cadbury
    Cheese Nips
    Chips Ahoy!
    Honey Maid Grahams
    Newtons
    Nilla
    Nutter Butter
    Oreo
    Planters
    Ritz
    SnackWell's
    Teddy Grahams
    Toblerone
    Triscuit
    Wheat Thins
  Beverages
    Country Time
    Crystal Light
    General Foods International
    Gevalia
    Kool-Aid
    Maxwell House
    Sanka
    Tang
  Cheese
    Cheez Whiz
    Cracker Barrel
    Deli Deluxe
    Kraft
    Philadelphia
    Velveeta
  Convenient Meals
    Deli Creations
    Louis Rich
    Lunchables
    Oscar Mayer
    Stove Top
  Grocery
    Cool Whip
    Easy Cheese
    Grey Poupon
    Jell-O
    Miracle Whip
    Shake N' Bake

HISTORICAL FINANCIALS

Company Type: Public

Income Statement
FYE: December 31

	REVENUE ($ mil.)	NET INCOME ($ mil.)	NET PROFIT MARGIN	EMPLOYEES
12/09	40,386	3,028	7.5%	97,000
12/08	42,201	2,901	6.9%	98,000
12/07	37,241	2,590	7.0%	103,000
12/06	34,356	3,060	8.9%	90,000
12/05	34,113	2,632	7.7%	94,000
Annual Growth	4.3%	3.6%	—	0.8%

2009 Year-End Financials

Debt ratio: 69.7%	No. of shares (mil.): 1,744
Return on equity: 12.6%	Dividends
Cash ($ mil.): 2,101	Yield: 4.3%
Current ratio: 1.08	Payout: 57.1%
Long-term debt ($ mil.): 18,024	Market value ($ mil.): 47,403

Stock History
NYSE: KFT

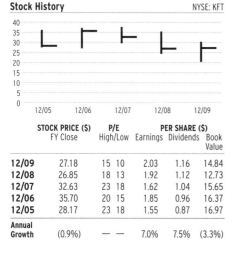

	STOCK PRICE ($) FY Close	P/E High/Low		PER SHARE ($) Earnings	Dividends	Book Value
12/09	27.18	15	10	2.03	1.16	14.84
12/08	26.85	18	13	1.92	1.12	12.73
12/07	32.63	23	18	1.62	1.04	15.65
12/06	35.70	20	15	1.85	0.96	16.37
12/05	28.17	23	18	1.55	0.87	16.97
Annual Growth	(0.9%)	—	—	7.0%	7.5%	(3.3%)

The Kroger Co.

Kroger is the nation's #1 pure grocery chain, but it still must watch out for falling prices; Wal-Mart has overtaken Kroger as the largest seller of groceries in the US. While Kroger has diversified through acquisitions, adding jewelry and general merchandise to its mix, food stores still account for about 85% of sales. The company operates about 3,620 stores, including some 2,465 supermarkets and multidepartment stores, under two dozen banners, in about 30 states. It also runs 775 convenience stores under names such as Quik Stop and Kwik Shop. Kroger's Fred Meyer Stores subsidiary (acquired in 1999) operates about 125 supercenters, which offer groceries, general merchandise, and jewelry, in the western US.

In response to intense price competition and aggressive supercenter expansion from non-traditional grocery sellers, such as Wal-Mart Supercenters and Costco Wholesale (the #1 and #3 sellers of groceries in the US, respectively), Kroger has been cutting prices while improving service and product selection to hang on to customers, with some success. The difficult retail environment, price competition, and food price deflation were to blame for the missed goal.

Private-label products help to differentiate supermarket chains from their competitors and foster customer loyalty. They are a pillar of Kroger's merchandising strategy. To keep its shelves stocked with its own store brands, Kroger operates 40 food processing plants, including 18 dairies and 10 deli or bakery plants, that supply its supermarkets with a growing stable of some 14,000 private-label products (accounting for about 25% of its grocery sales), including Naturally Preferred, Kroger's own brand of natural and organic products. Digging deeper into the organics market, Kroger has launched a second line of some 60 organic items (including pasta, tea, waffles, peanut butter, snacks, and milk) called "Organics for Everyone." The new line, which targets mainstream consumers, is priced lower than Kroger's Naturally Preferred brand.

Kroger is also a major pharmacy operator, with pharmacies in about 80% of its food stores. Kroger pharmacies, as well as those in Ralphs, Fred Meyer, QFC, City Market, and King Soopers stores, offer a $4 generic prescription drug program (as does archrival Wal-Mart). The grocer is also adding drive-through pharmacies to some of its convenience stores. To complement its pharmacy operation, Kroger runs about 115 walk-in medical clinics through its Little Clinic subsidiary. In 2010 the clinic company pared down its network by 30 locations (exiting such markets as Houston, Indianapolis, and Detroit) as part of a restructuring; it plans to re-evaluate clinic expansion in 2011.

HISTORY

Bernard Kroger was 22 when he started the Great Western Tea Company in 1883 in Cincinnati. Kroger lowered prices by cutting out middlemen, sometimes by making products such as bread. Growing to 40 stores in Cincinnati and northern Kentucky, the company became Kroger Grocery and Baking Company in 1902. It expanded into St. Louis in 1912 and grew rapidly during the 1910s and 1920s by purchasing smaller, cash-strapped companies. Kroger sold his holdings in the company for $28 million in 1928, the year before the stock market crash, and retired.

The company acquired Piggly Wiggly stores in the late 1920s and bought most of Piggly Wiggly's corporate stock, which it held until the early 1940s. The chain reached its largest number of stores — a whopping 5,575 — in 1929. (The Depression later trimmed that total.) A year later Kroger manager Michael Cullen suggested opening self-service, low-price supermarkets, but company executives demurred. Cullen left Kroger and began King Kullen, the first supermarket. If he was ahead of his time at Kroger, it wasn't by much; within five years, the company had 50 supermarkets.

During the 1950s Kroger acquired companies with stores in Texas, Georgia, and Washington, DC. It added New Jersey-based Sav-on drugstores in 1960 and it opened its first SupeRx drugstore in 1961. The company began opening larger supermarkets in 1971; between 1970 and 1980 Kroger's store count grew just 5%, but its selling space nearly doubled.

In 1983 the grocer bought Kansas-based Dillons Food Stores (supermarkets and convenience stores) and Kwik Shop convenience stores. Kroger sold most of its interests in the Hook and SupeRx drug chains (which became Hook-SupeRx) in 1987 and focused on its food-and-drugstores. (It sold its remaining stake to Revco in 1994.) The next year it faced two separate takeover bids from the Herbert Haft family and from Kohlberg Kravis Roberts. The company warded off the raiders by borrowing $4.1 billion to pay a special dividend to shareholders and to buy shares for an employee stock plan.

Joseph Pichler became CEO in 1990. Kroger sold its Time Saver Stores in 1995. In 1999 Kroger acquired Fred Meyer, operator of about 800 stores mainly in the West, in a $13 billion deal.

In late 2001 Kroger said it would cut 1,500 jobs. Kroger acquired 17 supermarkets (16 in the Houston area) from Albertson's (now Albertsons LLC) and another seven stores from Winn-Dixie in the Dallas/Fort Worth area in 2002.

In June, Pichler stepped down as CEO (but remained chairman) and was succeeded by David B. Dillon.

A four-and-a-half-month-long strike by grocery workers at Kroger's Ralphs chain in Southern California ended in March 2004. The dispute pitted workers' demands for continued generous health care benefits against management's call to control costs in the face of increasing non-union competition.

Pichler retired as chairman in June 2004 and was succeeded by Dillon.

In August 2006 Kroger sold 11 Cala Foods and Bell Markets in the San Francisco Bay area to DeLano Retail Partners, headed by Hartley DeLano, the former president of the Cala chain, for an undisclosed sum.

In July 2007 Kroger bought 20 Farmer Jack stores in the Detroit area from A&P. Also in 2007 the firm purchased 18 Scott's Food & Pharmacy stores in Indiana from rival SUPERVALU for an undisclosed amount. Kroger retained the Scott's banner and incorporated the business into its Indianapolis-based Central division.

In February 2010 Kroger made in-store walk-in medical chain The Little Clinic a wholly owned subsidiary. (Kroger first acquired a majority stake in the chain in mid-2008.)

EXECUTIVES

Chairman and CEO: David B. Dillon, age 59,
$10,339,393 total compensation
President, COO, and Director: W. Rodney McMullen,
age 49, $5,857,111 total compensation
EVP, Secretary, and General Counsel: Paul W. Heldman,
age 58, $3,098,218 total compensation
EVP: Donald E. Becker, age 61,
$3,512,418 total compensation
SVP and CFO: J. Michael Schlotman, age 52,
$2,211,360 total compensation
SVP Human Resources: Kathleen S. (Katy) Barclay,
age 54
SVP Retail Operations: Paul J. Scutt, age 61
SVP: M. Marnette Perry, age 58
SVP and CIO: Christopher T. (Chris) Hjelm, age 48
SVP: R. Pete Williams, age 55
Chief Diversity Officer: Carver L. Johnson, age 60
Group VP Human Resources: Della Wall, age 58
Group VP Corporate Affairs: Lynn Marmer, age 57
Group VP; President, Manufacturing:
Calvin J. Kaufman, age 47
Group VP Logistics: Kevin M. Dougherty, age 57
VP Pharmacy Operations: Lincoln Lutz
VP and Treasurer: Scott M. Henderson, age 54
VP and Controller: M. Elizabeth Van Oflen, age 52
Director Corporate Communications: Meghan Glynn
Director Investor Relations: Carin Fike
Auditors: PricewaterhouseCoopers LLP

LOCATIONS

HQ: The Kroger Co.
1014 Vine St., Cincinnati, OH 45202
Phone: 513-762-4000   **Fax:** 513-762-1160
Web: www.kroger.com

PRODUCTS/OPERATIONS

2010 Stores

	No.
Supermarkets & multidepartment stores	2,468
Convenience stores	777
Jewelry	374
Total	**3,619**

2010 Grocery Stores

	No.
Combo stores	2,143
Price-impact warehouse stores	147
Multidepartment stores	125
Marketplace stores	53
Total	**2,468**

2010 Sales

	$ mil.	% of total
Food stores	65,649	85
Food store fuel sales	6,671	9
Other stores & manufacturing	4,413	6
Total	**76,733**	**100**

Selected Kroger Stores

Multidepartment Stores
  Fred Meyer

Supermarkets
  Baker's
  City Market Food & Pharmacy
  Dillon Food Stores
  Fry's Food & Drug Stores
  Gerbes Supermarkets
  Hilander Food Stores
  Jay C Food Stores
  King Soopers
  Kroger
  Kroger Fresh Fare
  Owen's
  Pay Less Super Markets
  Quality Food Centers (QFC)
  Ralphs
  Scott's Food & Pharmacy
  Smith's Food & Drug Centers

Warehouse Stores
  Food 4 Less
  FoodsCo
Convenience Stores
  Kwik Shop
  Loaf 'N Jug
  Quik Stop Markets
  Tom Thumb Food Stores
  Turkey Hill Minit Markets
Jewelry Stores
  Barclay Jewelers
  Fox's Jewelers
  Fred Meyer Jewelers
  Littman Jewelers

Food Production

Bread and other baked goods
Cheese
Coffee
Crackers
Cultured products (cottage cheese, yogurt)
Deli products
Fruit juices and fruit drinks
Ice cream
Juice
Meat
Milk
Nuts
Oatmeal
Peanut butter
Snacks
Soft drinks
Spaghetti sauce
Water

COMPETITORS

7-Eleven	Publix
99 Cents Only	Raley's
A&P	Randall's
Ahold USA	Rite Aid
Albertsons	Safeway
Costco Wholesale	Save Mart
CVS Caremark	Stater Bros.
Delhaize America	Sterling Jewelers
Dollar General	SUPERVALU
Family Dollar Stores	Target
Giant Eagle	Walgreen
H-E-B	Wal-Mart
Hy-Vee	Wegmans
IGA	Whole Foods
Kmart	Winn-Dixie
Marsh Supermarkets	Zale
Meijer	

HISTORICAL FINANCIALS

Company Type: Public

Income Statement

FYE: Saturday nearest January 31

	REVENUE ($ mil.)	NET INCOME ($ mil.)	NET PROFIT MARGIN	EMPLOYEES
1/10	76,733	70	0.1%	334,000
1/09	76,000	1,249	1.6%	326,000
1/08	70,235	1,181	1.7%	323,000
1/07	66,111	1,115	1.7%	310,000
1/06	60,553	958	1.6%	290,000
Annual Growth	**6.1%**	**(48.0%)**	**—**	**3.6%**

2010 Year-End Financials

Debt ratio: 154.7%
Return on equity: 1.4%
Cash ($ mil.): 1,078
Current ratio: 0.97
Long-term debt ($ mil.): 7,477
No. of shares (mil.): 642
Dividends
  Yield: 1.7%
  Payout: 336.4%
Market value ($ mil.): 13,760

Stock History

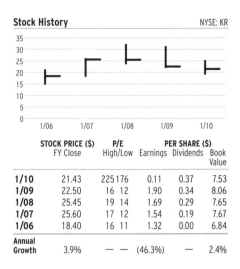

NYSE: KR

	STOCK PRICE ($) FY Close	P/E High/Low	PER SHARE ($) Earnings	Dividends	Book Value
1/10	21.43	225 176	0.11	0.37	7.53
1/09	22.50	16 12	1.90	0.34	8.06
1/08	25.45	19 14	1.69	0.29	7.65
1/07	25.60	17 12	1.54	0.19	7.67
1/06	18.40	16 11	1.32	0.00	6.84
Annual Growth	**3.9%**	**— —**	**(46.3%)**	**—**	**2.4%**

L-3 Communications

L-3's good defense is its best commercial offense. L-3 Communications Holdings makes secure and specialized systems for satellite, avionics, security, and marine communications. It also provides engineering and intelligence, surveillance, and reconnaissance products and services. The US government (primarily the Department of Defense) accounts for more than 80% of the company's business, but L-3 is using acquisitions to expand its commercial offerings. As a government contractor, the company is subject to the priorities of the Pentagon and other government agencies and faces potential cuts in military programs as defense priorities change.

L-3 uses acquisitions to grow its business and add new products, services, technologies, programs, and customers, positioning the company to benefit from changes in DoD and other government agency funding. The current focus on security systems, information technology (IT) and cyber security, intelligence reconnaissance, and defense electronics bodes well for L-3.

In mid-2010 L-3 purchased Airborne Technologies (ATI), an aeronautical engineering firm that specializes in unmanned aircraft systems (UAS) manufacture and operations support. The deal builds L-3's portfolio of UAS offerings, particularly in precision-guided unmanned systems. Earlier in the year L-3 acquired Insight Technology, a maker of night vision goggles, thermal imaging systems, and laser aiming and illumination devices, for about $613 million.

In 2009 L-3 acquired Chesapeake Sciences Corp. (CSC), a manufacturer of anti-submarine warfare systems. Renamed L-3 CSC, it became part of the Marine and Power Systems Group.

L-3's acquisitions leave the company with a substantial debt load of $4.15 billion, a figure that may grow difficult to manage if the credit crisis continues. On the positive side, L-3 was awarded in spring 2010 a five-year contract worth $152 million to provide IT and operational support to the US Air Forces Central Command (USAFCENT) through its STRATIS division. Earlier, the company's WESCAM subsidiary won a contract worth $110 million to provide the US

Air Force with electro-optic/infrared imaging turrets, along with training courses and services.

Commercial products and services — which make up around 10% of sales — include flight recorders (black boxes), display systems, and aircraft modification and maintenance services.

HISTORY

In the early 1970s Frank Lanza caught defense giant Lockheed's eye by building Loral Corporation into an aerospace industry contender through acquisitions of smaller defense technology firms. Lockheed (now Lockheed Martin) eventually bought Loral in 1996 and made Lanza the head of defense electronics. Looking for more action, Lanza formed L-3 Communications Holdings in 1997 by convincing Lockheed Martin's CEO to spin off a group of 10 communications technology units and put him at the helm. The operations were units from General Electric and Loral acquired by Lockheed Martin in 1993 and 1996, respectively.

In charge were two of the L's in the L-3 name: 20-year Loral executives Lanza (chairman and CEO, by then old enough to retire) and Robert LaPenta (president and CFO). The third L stood for major backer Lehman Brothers. The company embarked on an acquisition binge (just as Loral had originally done) in 1997. L-3 targeted strapped independent companies and the potential noncore operations resulting from large corporate mergers.

Much as he had during his tenure at Loral, Lanza remained a hands-off executive, a surprising approach in a red tape-wrapped industry. As a result, L-3's divisions developed an entrepreneurial freedom. In 1998, the year L-3 went public, it purchased the Ocean Systems unit of AlliedSignal (now Honeywell International; sonar products), ILEX Systems (information technology and support for the US government), SPD Technologies (electronics and power products), and the satellite transmission systems unit of California Microwave.

In 2000 L-3 sold its network security software division to Symantec. The next year L-3 sued Raytheon for not disclosing material liabilities before the sale of the division. The company later dropped the lawsuit, saying it intended to improve its relations with Raytheon to benefit the Defense Department following September 11.

In 2002 L-3 made its largest acquisition to date, buying Raytheon's Aircraft Integration Systems unit for $1.13 billion in cash.

L-3 acquired Vertex Aerospace, a company that provides technical services for government agencies, for about $650 million in 2003.

The acquisition roll continued in 2005 as L-3 acquired the Marine Controls division (shipboard control systems) of CAE, the Propulsion Systems business unit (transmissions, engines, suspensions, and turret drives) of General Dynamics, and most of Boeing's Electron Dynamic Devices, Inc. business, including the space and military traveling wave tubes, traveling wave tube amplifiers, passive microwave devices, and electric propulsion operations.

Early in 2006 L-3 completed its $150 million acquisition of SAM Electronics, a German naval electronics company. Not long afterwards it added CyTerra Corp.(military and homeland security sensors) and SafeView Inc. (security systems).

Later that year the company acquired Germany's Magnet-Motor GmbH, a maker of high-tech electric and energy systems for propulsion of commercial and combat vehicles, and marine vessels. The company was renamed L-3 Communications Magnet-Motor; terms of the deal were not disclosed.

L-3 then kept the 2006 acquisitions spree going with the agreement to purchase Crestview Aerospace Corporation (airframe assemblies and military aircraft modifications) for $135 million. Crestview became part of L-3's Aircraft Modernization and Maintenance division when the transaction closed in late 2006. L-3 also bought SSG Precision Optronics, a maker of optics, telescopes, and optical subsystems for government, defense, and commercial customers.

In June 2006 Lanza died suddenly. Shortly after Lanza's death, L-3 completed its acquisition of Nautronix Defence Group, a provider of mine warfare and anti-submarine systems.

Within days of Lanza's death L-3 CFO Michael Strianese was named interim CEO. Board member Robert Millard was named chairman.

In 2007 L-3 acquired Global Communications Solutions, a maker of portable satellite communications equipment, for $152 million.

EXECUTIVES

Chairman, President, and CEO: Michael T. Strianese, age 54, $15,178,729 total compensation
EVP Corporate Strategy and Development: Curtis Brunson, age 62, $3,033,711 total compensation
SVP; President, Products Group: Charles J. Schafer, age 62
SVP; President, Sensors and Simulation Group: James W. Dunn, age 66, $3,084,342 total compensation
SVP and Senior Counsel: Kathleen E. Karelis, age 49
SVP and CFO: Ralph G. D'Ambrosio, age 42, $2,837,901 total compensation
SVP; President, Integrated Systems Group: John C. McNellis, age 57
SVP: Robert W. RisCassi, age 74
SVP, Corporate Secretary, and General Counsel: Steven M. (Steve) Post, age 57
SVP and General Counsel Mergers and Acquisitions: Christopher C. Cambria
Corporate VP International Programs: Lt. Gen. James J. (Jim) Lovelace
VP; President, Marine and Power Systems: Robert E. (Bob) Leskow
VP; President, Microwave Group: John S. Mega
VP; President, Communications Systems Group: Susan D. Opp
VP, Controller, and Principal Accounting Officer: Dan Azmon, age 46
VP and Chief Technology Officer: A. Michael Andrews II
VP and Chief Information Officer: Vincent T. Taylor
VP Business Development: Jill J. Wittels
VP Corporate Communications: Karen C. Tripp
VP Human Resources: John Hill
President, Homeland Security Group: Craig P. Coy
President, Displays Group: Robert J. (Bob) McGill, age 49
President, Services: Steven (Steve) Kantor, age 65
Auditors: PricewaterhouseCoopers LLP

LOCATIONS

HQ: L-3 Communications Holdings, Inc.
600 3rd Ave., New York, NY 10016
Phone: 212-697-1111   **Fax:** 212-805-5477
Web: www.l-3com.com

2009 Sales

	$ mil.	% of total
US	13,666	87
Canada	283	2
Germany	276	2
Australia	176	1
UK	173	1
South Korea	132	1
Other countries	909	6
Total	**15,615**	**100**

PRODUCTS/OPERATIONS

2009 Sales

	$ mil.	% of total
Electronic systems	5,538	35
Government services	4,155	27
Command, control & communications, intelligence, surveillance & reconnaissance (C3ISR)	3,095	20
Aircraft modernization & maintenance	2,827	18
Total	**15,615**	**100**

2009 Sales by Customer

	$ mil.	% of total
US Government		
US Department of Defense		
Army	4,107	26
Air Force	3,721	24
Navy & Marines	2,544	16
Other defense agencies	1,560	10
Other US government	1,127	7
Allied foreign governments	1,082	7
Commercial		
Foreign commercial	867	6
Domestic commercial	607	4
Total	**15,615**	**100**

Selected Operations

Aircraft Modernization & Maintenance (AM&M)
  Aircraft maintenance and modification services
  Airborne traffic and collision avoidance systems
  Ruggedization of displays, computers, and electronics
  Voice recorders, flight data recorders, and maritime hardened voyage recorders
Command, Control & Communications & Intelligence, Surveillance, and Reconnaissance (C3ISR)
  Fleet management of special mission aircraft
  Ground-based satellite communications terminals and payloads
  Prime mission systems integration, sensor development, and operations and support
  Satellite command and control sustainment and support
  Satellite communication and tracking systems
  Secure communication terminals and equipment, and secure network encryption products
  Shipboard communications
Electronic Systems
  Display solutions
    Active Matrix Liquid Crystal Display (AMLCD)
    Light Emitting Diode (LED)
  Ground vehicle electronic solutions
  Repair and overhaul
    24/7 Aircraft On Ground (AOG) emergency service
    Field support
    Ground support
    Maintenance and operation manuals
    Personnel training
  Systems engineering
    Equipment engineering
    Program management
    System design
    System test
  Value-added manufacturing
  Weapon systems management (Avionics life-cycle support)
    Automated testing equipment
    Maintenance planning
    Repair and overhaul
    Technical documentaiton/publication revisions
    Training
Government Services
  Battlefield and weapon simulation
  Communication software support
  Information management and IT systems support and software design, development, and systems integration
  Information technology systems
  Linguistic interpretation, translation, and analysis services
  Surveillance systems and products, installation, logistics, and support
  Systems engineering, operations analysis, research and technical analysis
  Weapons training

HISTORICAL FINANCIALS

Company Type: Public

Income Statement

FYE: December 31

	REVENUE ($ mil.)	NET INCOME ($ mil.)	NET PROFIT MARGIN	EMPLOYEES
12/09	15,615	911	5.8%	67,000
12/08	14,901	929	6.2%	65,000
12/07	13,961	756	5.4%	64,600
12/06	12,477	526	4.2%	63,700
12/05	9,445	509	5.4%	59,500
Annual Growth	13.4%	15.7%	—	3.0%

2009 Year-End Financials

Debt ratio: 62.6%
Return on equity: 14.7%
Cash ($ mil.): 1,016
Current ratio: 2.08
Long-term debt ($ mil.): 4,112

No. of shares (mil.): 114
Dividends
  Yield: 1.6%
  Payout: 18.4%
Market value ($ mil.): 9,953

Stock History

NYSE: LLL

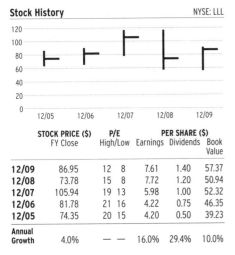

	STOCK PRICE ($) FY Close	P/E High/Low		PER SHARE ($) Earnings	Dividends	Book Value
12/09	86.95	12	8	7.61	1.40	57.37
12/08	73.78	15	8	7.72	1.20	50.94
12/07	105.94	19	13	5.98	1.00	52.32
12/06	81.78	21	16	4.22	0.75	46.35
12/05	74.35	20	15	4.20	0.50	39.23
Annual Growth	4.0%	—	—	16.0%	29.4%	10.0%

Lam Research

It's not uncommon for chip makers in need of critical manufacturing equipment to go on the Lam. Lam Research is a top maker of semiconductor processing equipment. The company's products address two key steps in the chip-making process. Its plasma etch machines are used to create tiny circuitry patterns on silicon wafers. Lam also makes cleaning equipment that keeps unwanted particles from contaminating processed wafers. The company's customers include many large chip makers, such as Hynix Semiconductor, Samsung Electronics, STMicroelectronics, and Toshiba. Most of the company's sales are to customers outside of the US, primarily in the Asia/Pacific region.

Lam has staked a claim on its niche markets, and showed itself quick to introduce equipment designed to process the latest-generation wafers. The company has been hurt, however, by the trend toward joint ventures and partnership in the semiconductor manufacturing industry, as chip makers look to reduce the amount they spend on new equipment. On the other hand, as the market improves, chip makers that have combined manufacturing operations are better able to afford the newest wafer processing technologies, which often come with a very high price.

Confronting poor business conditions in 2008, due to the credit crisis and the subsequent global financial meltdown, Lam reacted as many other suppliers of semiconductor equipment did. It kicked off a corporate restructuring that included the layoff of about 600 people, a 15% reduction in force.

With business worsening in 2009, the company laid off another 375 employees, a 10% reduction, and planned to close some facilities. The majority of the layoffs were in North America.

HISTORY

Chinese immigrant David Lam started Lam Research in 1980 to use plasma chemistry to improve processes for making semiconductors. The company introduced its first product, AutoEtch, in 1982 and went public in 1984. David Lam left the company in 1985. Roger Emerick became Lam Research's CEO in 1982 and continued in that post until 1997, presiding over the company's growth into an industry leader.

Lam Research introduced its Rainbow line of dry-etch equipment in 1987 and its Transformer Coupled Plasma technology in 1992. The company signed a development agreement in 1994 with the U.S. Display Consortium to develop equipment for making advanced circuits for flat-panel displays. Lam posted its first "gigabuck" year, with annual revenues of $1.25 billion, in fiscal 1996. Since then, the company's revenues have yo-yoed up and down in response to cyclicality in the semiconductor equipment industry.

In 1997 Lam acquired OnTrak Systems, a maker of chemical mechanical planarization (CMP) wafer cleaning equipment. OnTrak's chairman and CEO, James Bagley, a former Applied Materials executive, became Lam's CEO and, in 1998, the company's chairman.

In 1998 Lam formed a pact with National Semiconductor to develop aluminum etch systems. That year a steep downturn in the global semiconductor industry, fed by the Asian economic crisis, led the company to close plants and cut its workforce by more than a quarter.

Lam also exited the market for deposition equipment (which applies thin layers of material onto silicon wafers), and shuttered its flat-panel display operations.

With the chip industry rebounding in 1999, Lam won major orders from big chip makers, including AMD and STMicroelectronics. Lam posted strong profits in 2000 after three years of losses.

In 2001 the chip industry braked sharply. Lam responded with various cost-cutting measures, including two rounds of layoffs.

As the company (and the chip industry) rebounded in 2004, Lam discontinued its line of chemical mechanical planarization (CMP) products to focus on its offerings of etching and cleaning equipment.

In mid-2005 Bagley was succeeded as CEO by Stephen Newberry, who had been Lam's COO since 1997. Bagley remained as executive chairman. Like Bagley, Newberry had a long tenure at Applied Materials before joining Lam.

In late 2006 Lam acquired the silicon-growing and fabrication assets of Bullen Ultrasonics, a manufacturer of precision machined components, for approximately $175 million in cash. Bullen had been a supplier to Lam since 1991, providing silicon materials used in the process chambers of Lam's etching equipment. The business was renamed Bullen Semiconductor, a division of Lam.

In 2008 Lam acquired the SEZ Group, a maker of wafer cleaning equipment, for about $568 million in cash. Lam combined the Swiss company with its own wafer cleaning products to form its Clean Product division.

EXECUTIVES

Chairman: James W. (Jim) Bagley, age 71
President, CEO, and Director:
Stephen G. (Steve) Newberry, age 56,
$2,635,170 total compensation
EVP and COO: Martin B. Anstice, age 43,
$1,308,708 total compensation
SVP and CFO: Ernest E. Maddock, age 51,
$1,242,407 total compensation
Group VP; General Manager, Etch Products:
Richard A. (Rick) Gottscho, age 58,
$1,661,408 total compensation
Group VP Global Operations: Abdi Hariri, age 47,
$912,176 total compensation
Group VP Human Resources and Chief Legal Officer:
Sarah A. O'Dowd, age 59
VP, General Counsel, and Secretary:
George M. Schisler Jr.
VP; General Manager, Global Clean Business Group:
Jeffery Marks
VP and General Manager, Sales and Marketing:
Thomas J. Bondur, age 42
Managing Director Corporate Communications:
Lisa Garber
Investor Relations: Shauna O'Boyle
Auditors: Ernst & Young LLP

LOCATIONS

HQ: Lam Research Corporation
4650 Cushing Pkwy., Fremont, CA 94538
Phone: 510-572-0200   **Fax:** 510-572-2935
Web: www.lamrc.com

2009 Sales

	$ mil.	% of total
Asia/Pacific		
South Korea	239.9	21
Japan	234.1	21
Taiwan	208.0	19
Other countries	141.4	13
US	171.4	15
Europe	121.2	11
Total	**1,116.0**	**100**

PRODUCTS/OPERATIONS

Selected Products

Plasma ("dry") wafer-etching equipment
Plasma-based bevel clean system
Single-wafer spin and linear clean products
Transformer Coupled Plasma (TCP) silicon etch
  equipment

COMPETITORS

Applied Materials
Dainippon Screen
Ebara
Hitachi High-Technologies
Hitachi Kokusai Electric
Intevac
Mattson Technology
Novellus
Plasma Etch
Semitool
Suss MicroTec
Tegal
Tokyo Electron
ULVAC
Veeco Instruments

HISTORICAL FINANCIALS

Company Type: Public

Income Statement

FYE: Last Sunday in June

	REVENUE ($ mil.)	NET INCOME ($ mil.)	NET PROFIT MARGIN	EMPLOYEES
6/09	1,116	(302)	—	2,711
6/08	2,475	439	17.8%	3,800
6/07	2,567	686	26.7%	3,000
6/06	1,642	336	20.4%	2,430
6/05	1,503	299	19.9%	2,200
Annual Growth	(7.2%)	—	—	5.4%

2009 Year-End Financials

Debt ratio: 2.8%
Return on equity: —
Cash ($ mil.): 374
Current ratio: 3.51
Long-term debt ($ mil.): 41

No. of shares (mil.): 127
Dividends
  Yield: —
  Payout: —
Market value ($ mil.): 3,290

Stock History

NASDAQ (GS): LRCX

	STOCK PRICE ($) FY Close	P/E High/Low		PER SHARE ($) Earnings	Dividends	Book Value
6/09	26.00	—	—	(2.41)	—	11.48
6/08	36.15	18	10	3.47	—	14.06
6/07	51.40	12	8	4.85	—	9.30
6/06	46.72	23	12	2.34	—	11.03
6/05	28.94	15	9	2.10	—	8.43
Annual Growth	(2.6%)	—	—	—	—	8.0%

Land O'Lakes

The people at Land O'Lakes cooperate in order to butter up customers. Owned by and serving more than 4,600 dairy farmer/members and some 980 smaller community cooperatives, Land O'Lakes is one of the largest dairy co-ops in the US. It provides its member/farmers with crop nutrient and protection products, seed, and animal feed. Its oldest and best known product, LAND O' LAKES butter, is the top butter brand in the US. The co-op offers more than 300 dairy-based food products from the 12.7 billion pounds of milk its member supply annually. Land O'Lakes operates 10 dairy product production sites in the US. Its Land O'Lakes Purina Feed division is a leading animal feed and pet food maker.

The cooperative reordered its business segments in 2009. What had been two separate segments — seed and agronomy — were combined into one segment called Crop Inputs. That, along with Dairy Foods, Feeds, and Layers now make up the four segments of Land O'Lake's business operations. In line with its strategy to concentrate on its crop-protection products, in 2009 the company sold nine Agriliance retail stores to Agri-AFC and 11 more to the Tennessee Farmers Cooperative. (Agriliance is a retail agronomy joint venture that Land O'Lakes has with Minnesota grain cooperative CHS.)

In addition to Agriliance, Land O'Lakes has any number of other foreign and domestic joint ventures, the most recent of which, Superior Feed Solutions, was formed with Indiana-based co-op Ceres Solutions in 2009. Also in 2009 it formed another feed joint venture, DaLOL BioNutrition, this time in conjunction with China's Hwabei Agri Corporation. On the seed side of things, in 2008 it acquired a native grass seed company for $1.7 million.

The co-op owns egg producer MoArk, which supplies shell eggs under the LAND O'LAKES All-Natural Farm Fresh Eggs and Eggland's Best brand names. In addition, the co-op's subsidiary, Land O'Lakes Finance, provides financing services its members.

HISTORY

In the old days, grocers sold butter from communal tubs and it often went bad. Widespread distribution of dairy products had to await the invention of fast, reliable transportation. By 1921 the necessary transportation was available. That year about 320 dairy farmers in Minnesota formed the Minnesota Cooperative Creameries Association and launched a membership drive with $1,375, mostly borrowed from the US Farm Bureau.

The co-op arranged joint shipments for members, imposed strict hygiene and quality standards, and aggressively marketed its sweet cream butter nationwide, packaged for the first time in the familiar box of four quarter-pound sticks. A month after the co-op's New York sales office opened, it was ordering 80 shipments a week.

Minnesota Cooperative Creameries, as part of its promotional campaigns, ran a contest in 1924 to name that butter. Two contestants offered the winning name — Land O'Lakes. The distinctive Indian Maiden logo first appeared about the same time, and in 1926 the co-op changed its name to Land O'Lakes Creameries. By 1929, when it began supplying feed, its market share approached 50%.

During WWII civilian consumption dropped, but the co-op increased production of dried milk to provide food for soldiers and newly liberated concentration camp victims.

In the 1950s and 1960s, Land O'Lakes added ice cream and yogurt producers to its membership and fought margarine makers, yet butter's market share continued to melt. The co-op diversified in 1970 through acquisitions, adding feeds and agricultural chemicals. Two years later Land O'Lakes threw in the towel and came out with its own margarine. Despite the decreasing use of butter nationally, the co-op's market share grew.

Land O'Lakes formed a marketing joint venture, Cenex/Land O'Lakes Agronomy, with fellow co-op Cenex in 1987. As health consciousness bloomed in the 1980s, Land O'Lakes launched reduced-fat dairy products. It also purchased a California cheese plant, doubling its capacity. Land O'Lakes began ramping up its international projects at the same time: It built a feed mill in Taiwan, introduced feed products in Mexico, and established feed and cheese operations in Poland.

In 1997 the co-op bought low-fat cheese maker Alpine Lace Brands. Land O'Lakes took on the eastern US when it merged with the 3,600-member Atlantic Dairy Cooperative (1997), and it bulked up on the West Coast when California-based Dairyman's Cooperative Creamery Association joined its fold (1998).

During 2000 the co-op sold five plants to Dean Foods with an agreement to continue supplying the plants with raw milk. Also in 2000 Land O'Lakes combined its feed business with those of Farmland Industries to create Land O'Lakes Farmland Feed, LLC, with a 69% ownership. That same year, Land O'Lakes and CHS joined their agronomy operations to create a 50-50 joint venture, Agriliance LLC.

In late 2001 the company spent $359 million to acquire Purina Mills (pet and livestock feeds). Purina Mills was folded into Land O'Lakes Farmland Feed and, as part of the purchase, Land O'Lakes increased its ownership of the feed business to 92%. In 2004 it purchased the remaining 8%.

To take advantage of its nationally recognized brand, Land O'Lakes formed an alliance with Dean Foods in 2002 to develop and market value-added dairy products.

Exiting the meat business, Land O'Lakes sold its swine operations in 2005 to private pork producer Maschhoff West LLC for an undisclosed sum. That same year, it sold its interest in fertilizer manufacturer CF Industries. Long-time president and CEO Jack Gherty retired that year; he was replaced by Chris Policinski. In 2006 the company acquired 100% ownership of MoArk.

In 2007 the company sold its international cheese and protein operations (known as CPI) to Saputo Cheese USA for about $216 million. The sale included the Golden Valley Dairy Products cheese manufacturing and cut-and-wrap operations. The deal also included a long-term milks agreement, such that Land O'Lakes is the sole milk supplier for CPI.

Also in 2007 Land O'Lakes and CHS realigned the businesses of their 50-50 joint venture Agriliance, with CHS acquiring its crop-nutrients wholesale-products business and Land O'Lakes acquiring the crop-protection products business. The following year, Canadian ag cooperative La Coop fédérée, purchased Agriliance's remaining retail agronomy operation.

EXECUTIVES

Chairman: Peter (Pete) Kappelman, age 47
First Vice Chairman: Ronnie Mohr, age 61
Second Vice Chair: Larry Kulp, age 67
President and CEO: Christopher J. (Chris) Policinski, age 51, $6,737,200 total compensation
EVP Operations and Supply Chain: Fernando J. Palacios, age 50, $2,226,173 total compensation
EVP; COO, Crop Protection Products: Rodney (Rod) Schroeder, age 54
EVP; COO, Seed Division: Mike Vande Logt, age 55
EVP; COO Retail Foods: Steve Dunphy, age 52
EVP; COO Purina Feed: David R. (Dave) Hoogmoed, age 44
EVP; COO Industrial Foods: Jerry Kaminski
SVP and CFO: Daniel E. (Dan) Knutson, age 53, $3,576,245 total compensation
SVP and General Counsel: Peter S. Janzen, age 50, $1,837,233 total compensation
SVP Corporate Marketing and Communications: Barry C. Wolfish, age 53, $1,809,881 total compensation
SVP Human Resources: Karen Grabow, age 60
SVP Member Affairs and Business Development: James D. (Jim) Fife, age 60
SVP Corporate Strategy and Business Development: Jean-Paul (JP) Ruiz-Funes, age 52
VP Quality Assurance and Regulatory Affairs: Sara Mortimore
Director Corporate Communications: Jeanne Forbis
Director Government Relations: Steven Krikava
Director Environment, Health and Safety: Vic Hammer
Director; Secretary: Douglas (Doug) Reimer, age 59
Auditors: KPMG LLP

LOCATIONS

HQ: Land O'Lakes, Inc.
4001 Lexington Ave., North, Arden Hills, MN 55112
Phone: 651-481-2222   **Fax:** 651-481-2000
Web: www.landolakesinc.com

PRODUCTS/OPERATIONS

2009 Sales

	$ mil.	% of total
Feed	3,441	33
Crop inputs	3,284	31
Dairy foods	3,208	31
Layers	523	5
Adjustments	(47)	—
Total	**10,409**	**100**

Selected Dairy Foods

Butter
  Blends
  Flavored
  Light
  Salted
  Spreadable
  Whipped
  With Canola Oil
  Unsalted
Canola oil
Cheese
  American
  Cheddar
  Monterey Jack
  Mozzarella
  Parmesan
  Provolone
  Romano
Chicken eggs
  All-natural
  Cage-free
  Nutritionally enhanced
  Organic
  Regular
Industrial ingredients
  Nonfat dry milk
  Whey
Spreads
  Butter blends
  Margarine

COMPETITORS

ADM	Kraft Foods
Agrium	Latham Seed Company
Associated Milk Producers	Mars, Incorporated
Barkley Seed	Mars Petcare
Blue Seal Feeds	Michael Foods, Inc.
Breeder's Choice	Milk Specialties Company
California Dairies Inc.	Monsanto Company
Cal-Maine Foods	National Dairy Holdings
Cargill	NC Hybrids
ConAgra	Nestlé Purina PetCare
Dairy Farmers of America	Nestlé USA
Darigold, Inc.	Northwest Dairy
Dean Foods	Pfister Hybrid Corn
Del Monte Foods	Pioneer Hi-Bred
Fonterra	Prairie Farms Dairy
Foremost Farms	Rose Acre Farms
Frontier Agriculture	Royal Canin
Harris Moran	Sakata Seed
Hartz Mountain	Saputo
Hill's Pet Nutrition	Sargento
HP Hood	Schreiber Foods
Iams	Syngenta Seeds
Keller's Creamery	Unilever
Kent Feeds	Wilbur-Ellis

HISTORICAL FINANCIALS

Company Type: Cooperative

Income Statement

FYE: December 31

	REVENUE ($ mil.)	NET INCOME ($ mil.)	NET PROFIT MARGIN	EMPLOYEES
12/09	10,409	209	2.0%	9,000
12/08	12,039	160	1.3%	9,100
12/07	8,925	164	1.8%	8,700
12/06	7,275	89	1.2%	8,500
12/05	7,557	129	1.7%	7,500
Annual Growth	**8.3%**	**12.8%**	**—**	**4.7%**

Net Income History

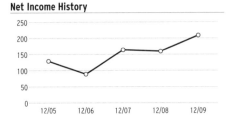

La-Z-Boy

The kickback that La-Z-Boy gives its customers is perfectly legal. A top US maker of upholstered furniture, La-Z-Boy sells its ubiquitous recliners, plus chairs, sofas, tables, and modular seating units. One recliner boasts a drink cooler, phone, and massage and heat system. Its brands include La-Z-Boy, Bauhaus USA, Hammary, American Drew/Lea, and Kincaid. La-Z-Boy sells its products through about 70 company-owned stores, some 240 independent La-Z-Boy Furniture Galleries, and about 510 Comfort Studios (about 5,000 sq. ft. of dedicated La-Z-Boy space hosted by an independent retailer). La-Z-Boy also makes wood desks and bedroom items and licenses its name for use on furniture for the health care industry.

The company's upholstered items account for 77% of its sales. La-Z-Boy was able to reach healthy revenues of upholstered items, but held steady overall in 2010 as it saw declines among its casegoods operations. To ensure it didn't face further declines, La-Z-Boy implemented changes in this segment to spur growth for these higher-priced items. During the fourth quarter of fiscal 2010, the furniture maker consolidated its American Drew/Lea and Hammary operations and transferred some 90% of its domestic fabric cut-and-sew operations to its facility in Mexico; the rest of the transfer and a transition of its leather cut-and-sew operation to the same facility are slated for fiscal 2011.

La-Z-Boy's effort to streamline its manufacturing operations started in late 2008, at the early signs of an economic downturn. It began to consolidate all its cutting and sewing operations at a handful of US plants into one centralized facility in Mexico. (The firm began production in Mexico in January 2009 and hired about 1,200 employees to staff the plant there.) Also, in mid-2009 the firm combined two of its hardwood furniture plants in North Carolina.

Besides the recession, a few other factors have made life for La-Z-Boy a little less laid back in recent years. An influx of cost-conscious competitors, such as Costco, IKEA, and Home Depot, has eroded La-Z-Boy's revenue. The weakening US housing market also led to a decline in sales at the furniture maker, particularly through its upholstered products segment. Compounding the problem, IKEA's and Costco's alternative distribution and rivals that offer online furniture shopping lured some customers away from traditional furniture retail outlets and brick-and-mortar shopping.

In response to the increased pressure, La-Z-Boy reduced its overall workforce by about 10%. Also, it shuttered some 20 mostly dealer-owned La-Z-Boy Furniture Galleries stores.

HISTORY

Carpenter Edward Knabusch repaired and built furniture in his family's garage in Monroe, Michigan, in the early 1920s. When people began clamoring for Knabusch's repair expertise, he quit his job, hired his cousin, Edwin Shoemaker, and in 1927 formed Floral City Furniture.

The duo specialized in new designs, including a telephone stand with seat that they dubbed "the Gossiper." Their first recliner, a wooden porch chair that shaped itself to body contours, was developed in 1928. Positive response prompted family and friends to raise money (Shoemaker's dad mortgaged the farm) for a manufacturing plant. At a customer's urging, the pair upholstered the chair, and Knabusch drummed up even more interest with a contest to name the new piece. Entries included Slack-Back, Sit-N-Snooze, and the moniker that would help define an industry, La-Z-Boy.

In the midst of the Depression, the company thrived, turning the bottom factory floor into a showroom and offering entertainment and circus tents stuffed with merchandise to attract out-of-state visitors. The cousins amassed a petting zoo of farm animals collected, instead of money, from cash-strapped customers.

To separate manufacturing and a burgeoning retail operation, La-Z-Boy Chair was incorporated in 1941. Production stopped during WWII while Knabusch and Shoemaker made tank seats and crash pads.

Its one-of-a-kind product styles helped to distinguish the company through the 1950s and 1960s. Its reputation grew, thanks to products such as a love seat fashioned in the form of a car seat, replete with lights, horns, fins, and tires (1959), and a chair that both rocked and reclined (1961). La-Z-Boy also began what would become a long-lived marketing campaign by using such celebrity spokesmen as football player Joe Namath and talk-show host Johnny Carson.

Sales reached nearly $53 million in 1971, and La-Z-Boy went public the next year. It diversified through the late 1970s into sleeper sofas (1977) and other products. Knabusch's adopted son Charles became chairman in 1985 and vowed to increase female clientele. La-Z-Boy also began making business furniture and began a continuing buying binge, including table maker Hammary Furniture (1986) and dining room and bedroom furniture specialist Kincaid Furniture (1988). Knabusch died in 1988, and the company's largest investor, Prescott Investors, made a failed takeover bid in 1989. That year La-Z-Boy opened its first superstore gallery.

The company changed its name to La-Z-Boy in 1996. Charles Knabusch, Edward's son and company CEO, died in 1997; COO Gerald Kiser was made president. (He was later named CEO in July 2001.) The next year co-founder Shoemaker, who still held the EVP of engineering and VC titles, died in his recliner at the age of 90. Acquisitions continued, including mid-priced furniture maker Bauhaus USA (1999) and LADD Furniture (2000).

In 2003 three casegoods manufacturing facilities were shut down, resulting in the elimination of an additional 400 positions. That year Kiser stepped down, and La-Z-Boy veteran Kurt Darrow became president and CEO. In 2004 production facilities in Pennsylvania, North Carolina, and Mississippi were shut down, putting about 650 La-Z-Boy employees out of work.

The company exited the office furniture manufacturing industry in mid-2005 so it could focus on the home furnishings business. In a move that further emphasized the company's realignment to the consumer market, it sold its La-Z-Boy Contract Unit, which manufactured furnishings used in commercial and health care settings, to the owners of Best Home Furnishings in 2005.

In July 2006 the company sold American of Martinsville, a maker of furniture for the hospitality industry, to private equity firm Hancock Park Associates for an undisclosed sum.

As it re-evaluated its products portfolio, La-Z-Boy sold off its Sam Moore Furniture unit to Hooker Furniture in May 2007. The La-Z-Boy unit specialized in making upscale fabric-to-frame occasional chairs. Having acquired Sam Moore in 1998, La-Z-Boy chose to refocus on functional upholstered furniture.

EXECUTIVES

Chairman: James W. Johnston, age 71
President, CEO, and Director: Kurt L. Darrow, age 55, $1,807,884 total compensation
SVP and CFO: Louis M. (Mike) Riccio Jr., age 47, $517,473 total compensation
SVP and Chief Retail Officer: Mark S. Bacon Sr., age 46, $216,407 total compensation
SVP; President, Casegoods Product and Kincaid Furniture Company: Steven M. (Steve) Kincaid, age 61, $584,888 total compensation
SVP; President, Non-Branded Upholstery Product and England: Otis S. Sawyer, age 52, $485,076 total compensation

Chief Marketing Officer: J. Doug Collier, age 42
CIO: Daniel F. DeLand, age 48
VP and Treasurer: Greg A. Brinks, age 52
VP, Real Estate Development: David Baratta
VP Corporate Human Resources: Steven P. (Steve) Rindskopf, age 47
VP and Corporate Controller: Margaret L. (Peg) Mueller, age 41
President, American Drew and Lea Industries: R. Jack Richardson Jr.
President, Bauhaus USA: James (Al) Wiygul, age 60
President, Hammary Furniture: John V. Labarowski
Secretary and General Counsel: James P. Klarr
Director Investor Relations and Corporate Communications: Kathy Liebmann
Auditors: PricewaterhouseCoopers LLP

LOCATIONS

HQ: La-Z-Boy Incorporated
  1284 N. Telegraph Rd., Monroe, MI 48162
Phone: 734-242-1444   **Fax:** 734-457-2005
Web: www.lazboy.com

2010 Sales

	% of total
US	88
Canada & other countries	12
Total	**100**

PRODUCTS/OPERATIONS

2010 Sales

	$ mil.	% of total
Upholstery	904.8	72
Retail	153.6	12
Casegoods	146.7	12
Variable Interest Entities (VIEs)	53.2	4
Corporate & other	4.6	—
Adjustments	(83.7)	—
Total	**1,179.2**	**100**

Selected Products

Bedroom furniture
Chairs
Dining room furniture
Entertainment units
Leather furniture
Love seats
Modular seating groups
Recliners
Reclining sofas
Sleep sofas
Sofas
Tables
Wall systems
Youth furniture

Divisions and Brands

Upholstery Group
  Bauhaus USA (upholstered furniture, convertible sofas)
  England (mid-priced upholstered and motion furniture for living, family rooms)
  La-Z-Boy (residential and health care furniture)
Casegoods Group
  American Drew (wood furniture for bedroom, dining room, occasional use)
  Hammary (tables, entertainment units, wall units, and upholstered furniture for living, family rooms)
  Kincaid (wood furniture)
  Lea (bedroom furniture)

COMPETITORS

Art Van Furniture
Ashley Furniture
Bassett Furniture
Berkline BenchCraft
Bernhardt Furniture
Brown Jordan International
Chromcraft Revington
Costco Wholesale
DFS Furniture
Ethan Allen
Flexsteel
Furniture Brands International
Herman Miller
HNI
Home Depot
Home Meridian
Hooker Furniture
IKEA
KI
Kimball International
Klaussner Furniture
Natuzzi
Palliser Furniture
Rooms To Go
Rowe Fine Furniture
Sam's Club
Shelby Williams
Stanley Furniture
Steelcase
Target
Thomasville Furniture
Universal Furniture
W. S. Badcock
Wal-Mart

HISTORICAL FINANCIALS

Company Type: Public

Income Statement

FYE: Last Saturday in April

	REVENUE ($ mil.)	NET INCOME ($ mil.)	NET PROFIT MARGIN	EMPLOYEES
4/10	1,179	33	2.8%	8,290
4/09	1,227	(121)	—	7,730
4/08	1,451	(14)	—	10,057
4/07	1,617	4	0.3%	11,729
4/06	1,917	(3)	—	13,404
Annual Growth	(11.4%)	—	—	(11.3%)

2010 Year-End Financials

Debt ratio: 13.7%
Return on equity: 10.0%
Cash ($ mil.): 108
Current ratio: 2.91
Long-term debt ($ mil.): 47
No. of shares (mil.): 52
Dividends
  Yield: 0.0%
  Payout: —
Market value ($ mil.): 675

Stock History

NYSE: LZB

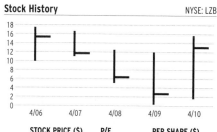

	STOCK PRICE ($) FY Close	P/E High/Low		PER SHARE ($) Earnings	Dividends	Book Value
4/10	13.04	25	3	0.62	0.00	6.61
4/09	2.66	—	—	(2.36)	0.10	5.90
4/08	6.37	—	—	(0.26)	0.40	8.70
4/07	11.69	205	141	0.08	0.48	9.37
4/06	15.32	—	—	(0.06)	0.44	9.86
Annual Growth	(3.9%)	—	—	—	—	(9.5%)

Lear Corporation

Lear doesn't take a back seat to anyone when it comes to manufacturing automotive seats. The company is a leader in the global market for car seat systems and a supplier of automotive electronics. In addition to seating systems and their components, Lear manufactures wire harnesses, junction boxes, terminals and connectors, and body control modules. It has some 200 facilities in 35 countries and sells to automakers such as BMW, Fiat, Ford, General Motors, Renault, Nissan, and VW. Lear gets about 70% of its sales outside North America. Struggling with debt and the effects of the global automotive industry downturn, Lear filed for Chapter 11 bankruptcy protection in July 2009 and emerged that November.

The company came out of bankruptcy with more than $1 billion in working capital and it reduced its debt obligations by $2.8 billion. Lear received debtor-in-possession financing of about $500 million from secured lenders led by J.P. Morgan and Citigroup, allowing it to continue to operate during reorganization.

Like many companies in the sector, Lear felt the pinch as the woes of its North American customers — primarily GM and Ford, and to a lesser extent Chrysler — trickled down the supply chain. Automakers worldwide, faced with sluggish demand and rising inventory levels, slashed production, closed factories, and implemented extended work stoppages.

To cope, Lear closed factories, reduced headcount, and eliminated all non-essential spending. The company also scaled back on new investments, although it has continued to transfer some manufacturing to regions with lower labor and materials costs, including China and Eastern Europe. Since 2005, Lear has relocated more than half of all its facilities and about three-quarters of its employees to 20 countries where production costs are lower.

Lear is also focused on increasing sales outside of the North American market, particularly in regions where production volume has increased (China) or remained stable (India and Brazil). It invests heavily in Asia, primarily through joint ventures. In addition, Lear is expanding manufacturing capacity in other regions, primarily Mexico, Eastern Europe, and Africa.

While seating and related components remain a significant product line (about 80% of sales), Lear sees opportunity for growth in its electrical power management products. Lear is focused on the trend of increasing electronic equipment in vehicles; the company's research indicates that by 2010, electronic components will account for up to 35% of a car's total value. To take advantage of the trend, Lear is developing safety, communications, and information/entertainment electronics products and increasing its vertical integration in certain components. Lear also offers a portfolio of electronics products used in hybrid vehicles.

HISTORY

Lear dates back to 1917, when American Metal Products began supplying seats to Detroit's fledgling car industry. The seat maker incorporated in 1928 and grew during the 1950s and 1960s by buying other auto parts makers.

Siegler Heating, an industrial conglomerate with interests in the aerospace, auto parts, and manufacturing industries, was founded in 1950 as a maker of climate-control equipment. Entrepreneur John Brooks and a group of associates bought the company (renamed Siegler Corporation) in 1954 and led it through a series of acquisitions, including that of aerospace firm Lear in 1962. The company then became Lear Siegler.

Lear Siegler acquired American Metal Products in 1966. Beset by project delays, the company's aerospace unit sputtered in the 1970s, but the seat business did well. By 1985 metal seat frames had become Lear Siegler's major auto parts revenue producer. Spurred by growing competition with Japanese carmakers, the company built a plant near a General Motors factory in Michigan to allow for swift delivery of its car seats.

In 1986 Forstmann Little bought the financially troubled Lear Siegler and began selling off the parts. Two years later the investment firm offered Lear Seating to its management (including Ken Way, who had been with the company since 1966). Way took the company private in a $500 million LBO, with the help of Kidder, Peabody, and the company's name was changed to Lear Seating. Kidder sold its stake in Lear Seating to Lehman Brothers in 1991.

Lear Seating bought a slice of Ford's North American automotive and trim operation and manufacturing factory in Ciudad Juárez, Mexico, in 1993. As a result of the purchase, the company entered into a long-term supply agreement with Ford. In another strategic buy of a customer's seat business, Lear Seating acquired Fiat's seat operations in 1994. This purchase encompassed Sepi Poland, Sepi S.p.A. (Italy), and a 35% stake in a Turkish joint venture, giving Lear Seating a presence in those countries. The purchase also made the company Europe's largest seat maker and gave it access to Fiat's 5% of the global automotive market. That year Lear Seating went public.

In 1995 Lear Seating bought Automotive Industries and inked a contract to provide seats for Brazil's top-selling car, the Volkswagen Gol. To reflect the broader scope of its business, the company dropped "Seating" from its name and became Lear Corporation in 1996. That year the company acquired Pennsylvania-based Masland for $475 million and formed a joint venture with China's Jiangling Motors to make seats and interior trim for Ford and Isuzu vehicles.

In 1998 Lear bought the automotive seating unit of GM's Delphi Automotive Systems subsidiary (now the independent Delphi), giving it a bigger chunk of GM's business. To cut costs, the company announced that it would shut down 18 plants and cut 2,800 jobs in the US, Europe, and South America.

The company paid $2.3 billion for United Technologies' auto unit to complete its instrument panel offerings in 1999. Lear also bought Hyundai Motor's seat business to boost Pacific Rim sales. Early in 2002 Lear announced it would cut 6,500 more jobs and close 21 manufacturing facilities.

In 2006 Lear sold $200 million in common stock to activist investor Carl Icahn, whose funds already held 5% of the company. The sale gave Icahn a combined 16% stake in Lear. Early in 2007 Icahn offered to buy the entire company in a deal valued at $2.8 billion. However, shareholders voted to reject the offer. Icahn then sold two-thirds of his Lear holdings in late 2008, bringing his ownership stake back down to about 5%.

EXECUTIVES

Chairman: Henry D. G. Wallace, age 64
President, CEO, and Director: Robert E. (Bob) Rossiter, age 64, $9,464,890 total compensation
SVP and CFO: Matthew J. (Matt) Simoncini, age 49, $3,026,702 total compensation
SVP; President, Global Seating Systems: Louis R. Salvatore, age 55, $3,023,441 total compensation
SVP, General Counsel, and Corporate Secretary: Terrence B. (Terry) Larkin, age 55, $2,611,357 total compensation
SVP; President, Global Electrical Power Management Operations: Raymond E. Scott, age 44, $3,042,309 total compensation
SVP Communications, Corporate Relations, and Human Resources: Melvin L. (Mel) Stephens, age 54
VP Electrical Power Management, Business Development and Strategy: Jeneanne Hanley
VP Information Technology: James L. Murawski
VP Health, Safety, and Environmental: Barbara Boroughf
VP and Treasurer: Shari L. Burgess, age 51
VP Business Planning and Financial Analysis: John Trythall
VP Sales and Marketing: Dave Mullin
VP Corporate Development: Eric Rasmussen
VP and Corporate Controller: Wendy L. Foss, age 52
VP China: Tom Tang
VP Corporate Human Resources and Diversity: Marianne Churchwell
Director: Jonathan F. (Jon) Foster, age 49
Deputy General Counsel and Chief Compliance Officer: Liam E. Hart
Auditors: Ernst & Young LLP

LOCATIONS

HQ: Lear Corporation
21557 Telegraph Rd., Southfield, MI 48033
Phone: 248-447-1500   **Fax:** 248-447-1772
Web: www.lear.com

2009 Sales

	$ mil.	% of total
North America		
US	1,595.2	16
Mexico	1,030.5	11
Canada	238.6	3
Germany	1,937.5	20
China	903.5	9
Other countries	4,034.3	41
Total	**9,739.6**	**100**

PRODUCTS/OPERATIONS

2009 Sales

	$ mil.	% of total
Seating	7,812.9	80
Electrical power management	1,926.7	20
Total	**9,739.6**	**100**

2009 Sales by Customer

	% of total
General Motors	20
Ford	19
BMW	12
Others	49
Total	**100**

Selected Products

Seating
- Automotive seats
- Head restraints
- Seat foam
- Trim covers

Electrical power management
- Electrical distribution and power management systems
  - Fuse boxes
  - Junction boxes
  - Terminals and connectors
  - Wire harness assemblies
- High-power electrical systems
- Hybrid electrical systems
- Specialty electronics
  - In-vehicle television tuner module
  - Lighting control module
  - Media console
  - Radio amplifiers
  - Sound systems
- Wireless systems
  - Keyless entry systems
  - Passive entry systems
  - Tire pressure monitoring systems

COMPETITORS

Alps Automotive	Robert Bosch
Delphi Automotive	Stoneridge
DENSO	Tokai Rika
Faurecia	Toyota Boshoku
Johnson Controls	TRW Automotive
LEONI	Valeo
Magna International	Visteon
Methode Electronics	Yazaki
Mitsubishi Electric	

HISTORICAL FINANCIALS

Company Type: Public

Income Statement

FYE: December 31

	REVENUE ($ mil.)	NET INCOME ($ mil.)	NET PROFIT MARGIN	EMPLOYEES
12/09	9,740	814	8.4%	75,000
12/08	13,571	(690)	—	80,000
12/07	15,995	242	1.5%	91,000
12/06	17,839	(710)	—	104,000
12/05	17,089	(1,382)	—	115,000
Annual Growth	(13.1%)	—	—	(10.1%)

2009 Year-End Financials

Debt ratio: 55.2%
Return on equity: 86.6%
Cash ($ mil.): 1,554
Current ratio: 1.58
Long-term debt ($ mil.): 927

Net Income History

NYSE: LEA

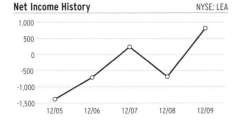

Legg Mason

Legg Mason's feats include wealth management and mutual fund management. The financial services firm has several subsidiaries that offer asset management, trust services, and annuities to retail and institutional investors. The company manages about 140 mutual funds under the Legg Mason, Western Asset, and The Royce Funds banners. Other offerings include closed-end funds and separately managed accounts. Legg Mason distributes its products through its own offices, retirement plans, and financial intermediaries, as well as through an agreement with Morgan Stanley Smith Barney. The company operates primarily in North America and the UK, but also has offices in about 15 other countries.

The Legg Mason Funds comprise equity, income, investment-grade, and municipal securities funds, while the Royce Funds concentrate on small- and micro-cap stocks. Western Asset Management markets its funds to retirement plans and other institutional investors.

Legg Mason also manages assets for institutional and high-net-worth clients through several subsidiaries, including Cincinnati-based Bartlett & Co., Philadelphia's Brandywine Global Investment Management, and Private Capital Management in Naples, Florida. Boston-based Batterymarch Fininical Management uses quantative strategies to manage portfolios of US and international equities for institutional investors; Legg Mason Investment Counsel & Trust performs trust services for individual and employee benefits plans.

Legg Mason has approximately $680 million of client assets under management, about a quarter less than it had as recently as 2008. More than half of that figure is invested in fixed-income products. The rocky economy prompted many clients to pull out large amounts of money from their mutual funds, leading to losses for the company in fiscal 2009. Recovery in the financial markets had a hand in Legg Mason returning to profitability the following year, despite a decline in revenues of more than 20%. Cost-cutting and restructuring measures enacted by the company helped too.

In 2008 Legg Mason named Mark Fetting, who had led the company's mutual fund and managed account business, as chairman and CEO, succeeding founder Raymond "Chip" Mason, who had been the only chief executive in the company's history. Also that year the company cut jobs at its Baltimore headquarters and at its money-management subsidiaries by about one-third.

HISTORY

In 1899 George Mackubin and G. Clem Goodrich established brokerage firm Mackubin & Goodrich. The next year John Legg joined the company as a "board boy," employed to chalk stock prices on a small blackboard.

The 1904 Baltimore fire destroyed the firm's offices, and it temporarily had to move to two rooms owned by Legg's dentist until it could rebuild. Legg became a partner in 1905. The firm was hit hard by the halt in trading due to WWI and was reduced to brokering mortgages for a local homebuilder. In 1925 the company started what may have been the first real estate investment trust, National Union Mortgage Company. The company established a new department in 1930 devoted exclusively to women investors and hired A. Catherine Overbeck to run it.

The 1929 stock market crash and Depression devastated the firm, and in 1930 the partners liquidated their own portfolios to inject cash into the company. After Goodrich died in 1932, the firm was renamed Mackubin, Legg & Co. It lost its other founder in 1942 when Mackubin argued with Legg and left to join a competitor. The firm became John C. Legg & Co.

The company flourished in the postwar boom. In 1962 Raymond "Chip" Mason founded his own brokerage in Virginia and eight years later merged it with Legg to form Legg Mason & Co. In 1973 the firm acquired New York broker-dealer Wood Walker & Co. and became Legg Mason Wood Walker.

The company introduced a money market mutual fund in 1979 and its first equity fund in 1982. Between those two events, it established Legg Mason, Inc., as a holding company for its growing list of subsidiaries; it went public in 1983. During the 1980s and 1990s, the firm added to its straight brokerage business by buying a string of asset management companies.

Targeting wealthy individuals, in 1999 the company obtained a national thrift charter, allowing it to take on trust business outside Maryland. Expanding outside the US at century's end, it bought UK investment firm Johnson Fry Holdings and Canadian pension fund manager Perigee; both acquisitions were ultimately rebranded under the Legg Mason name.

Legg Mason bought New York-based investment manager Barrett Associates in 2000 and purchased Private Capital Management and Royce & Associates the following year.

In 2004 Legg Mason was one of several companies that settled NASD and SEC charges of failing to pay mutual fund customers discounts to which they were entitled.

Legg Mason swapped its brokerage and capital markets operations for most of the mutual fund and asset management business of Citigroup in a $3.7 billion deal in 2005. The company also bought 80% of The Permal Group, a large funds-of-hedge-funds administrator.

Legg Mason announced the latter agreement the same day it unveiled the unusual Citigroup transaction. The two significant deals allowed Legg Mason to focus solely on asset management and made it one of the largest such companies in the US. The acquisitions also significantly increased the company's assets under management overseas.

In 2006 Legg Mason changed the name of the former Citigroup Asset Management US Equity Group to ClearBridge Advisors. The Smith Barney funds, also acquired in the Citi deal, were renamed Legg Mason Partners Funds; the Legg Mason Partners Funds were merged into the Legg Mason Funds in 2009.

EXECUTIVES

Chairman, President, and CEO: Mark R. Fetting, age 55, $4,613,374 total compensation
Interim CFO: Terrence J. Murphy
SEVP and Chief Administrative Officer: Joseph A. Sullivan, age 52, $3,562,850 total compensation
SEVP; Senior Managing Director and Head, International Asset Management: Ronald R. (Ron) Dewhurst, age 57, $3,128,172 total compensation
SEVP and Head, Americas: David R. Odenath, age 53, $5,541,516 total compensation
EVP and Head Specialized Managers: Jeffrey A. Nattans, age 43

SVP and General Counsel: Thomas P. Lemke
President and CEO, ClearBridge Advisors:
Peter E. Sundman, age 51
CEO, Legg Mason Capital Management:
Jennifer Murphy
CEO, Batterymarch: William L. (Bill) Elcock
Chairman and CEO, Permal Asset Management:
Isaac R. Souede
Chairman, Chief Investment Officer, and Portfolio Manager, Legg Mason Capital Management:
William H. (Bill) Miller III, age 61
Chairman and CEO, Private Capital Management:
Gregg J. Powers
Chairman, Investment Policy Committee and Portfolio Manager, Legg Mason Capital Management':
David E. Nelson
Managing Director, Chief Investment Officer, and Senior Portfolio Manager, ClearBridge Advisors:
Harry D. (Hersh) Cohen
Director Investor Relations and Corporate Communications: Alan F. Magleby, age 54
Secretary: Thomas C. Merchant
Auditors: PricewaterhouseCoopers LLP

LOCATIONS

HQ: Legg Mason, Inc.
100 International Dr., Baltimore, MD 21202
Phone: 410-539-0000
Web: www.leggmason.com

2010 Sales

	$ mil.	% of total
Americas	1,866.9	71
International	768.0	29
Total	**2,634.9**	**100**

PRODUCTS/OPERATIONS

2010 Sales

	$ mil.	% of total
Investment advisory fees		
Funds	1,367.3	52
Separate accounts	814.8	31
Performance fees	71.5	3
Distribution & service fees	375.3	14
Other	6.0	—
Total	**2,634.9**	**100**

COMPETITORS

AllianceBernstein
BlackRock
Capital Group
Charles Schwab
Edward Jones
FMR
Franklin Resources
PIMCO
Principal Financial
Raymond James Financial
T. Rowe Price
The Vanguard Group

HISTORICAL FINANCIALS

Company Type: Public

Income Statement

FYE: March 31

	ASSETS ($ mil.)	NET INCOME ($ mil.)	INCOME AS % OF ASSETS	EMPLOYEES
3/10	8,614	204	2.4%	3,550
3/09	9,321	(1,948)	—	3,890
3/08	11,830	268	2.3%	4,220
3/07	9,605	647	6.7%	4,030
3/06	9,303	1,144	12.3%	3,800
Annual Growth	**(1.9%)**	**(35.0%)**	**—**	**(1.7%)**

2010 Year-End Financials

Equity as % of assets: 67.8%	Dividends
Return on assets: 2.3%	Yield: 0.4%
Return on equity: 4.0%	Payout: 9.1%
Long-term debt ($ mil.): 1,165	Market value ($ mil.): 4,434
No. of shares (mil.): 155	Sales ($ mil.): 2,635

Stock History

NYSE: LM

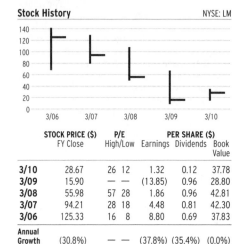

	STOCK PRICE ($) FY Close	P/E High/Low		PER SHARE ($) Earnings	Dividends	Book Value
3/10	28.67	26	12	1.32	0.12	37.78
3/09	15.90	—	—	(13.85)	0.96	28.80
3/08	55.98	57	28	1.86	0.96	42.81
3/07	94.21	28	18	4.48	0.81	42.30
3/06	125.33	16	8	8.80	0.69	37.83
Annual Growth	**(30.8%)**	**—**	**—**	**(37.8%)**	**(35.4%)**	**(0.0%)**

Leggett & Platt

That spring in your step after a good night's sleep may be there courtesy of Leggett & Platt (L&P) — the pioneer of coiled bedsprings. Primarily using aluminum and steel, the company makes residential furnishings (such as innersprings and bed frames) and commercial fixtures (store displays, shelves, furniture components). It also produces industrial materials (wire, steel tubing) and specialized items (quilting machines, automotive seating, docking stations for electronic devices). Customers include furniture retailers, telecommunications firms, and makers of automobiles, construction products, bedding, and lawn gear. The firm operates production, distribution, and warehousing facilities in about 20 countries.

In an effort to boost shareholder returns, L&P has narrowed the focus of its business, only operating in areas where it can be a market leader and emphasizing cost controls. The profit-centered strategy, introduced in 2007, marked a turning point for the manufacturer, which had acquired more than 100 companies since 1996 and previously was more focused on revenue growth.

As part of the plan, the company is shedding its least-profitable business units, which account for about 20% of its revenue base. Its die-cast aluminum products segment constituted its largest sale. Disposed of in 2008, the die-cast segment generated nearly $500 million in revenue in 2007. L&P in 2008 also sold its divisions in wood products and fibers, plastics, and the dealer portion of commercial vehicle products; it sold its coated fabrics unit in 2009. The disposals have yielded some $420 million in proceeds and have helped L&P in the repurchase of more than 25 million stock shares in 2008 and 2009.

Feeling the squeeze from the global economic downturn, the company focused on curbing expenses further in 2009. L&P reduced its workforce, consolidated facilities, and exercised

discipline with regard to pricing. The moves led to improved profits that year, despite lower revenues. L&P in 2010 remains focused on boosting its margins.

HISTORY

Carthage, Missouri, resident J. P. Leggett, an inventor with several patents, took his coiled bedspring to his businessman/manufacturer brother-in-law, C. B. Platt, in 1883. The two formed a partnership and began selling bedsprings (patented in 1885) to retailers that incorporated them into their mattresses (previous mattresses were made of cotton, horsehair, or feathers). They had two plants when they incorporated as Leggett & Platt Spring Bed & Manufacturing in 1901.

Leggett was president until 1921, when Platt took over. Leggett's son got the nod in 1929, and though he headed the company for only three years, he initiated the production of both innerspring mattress springs (the original coiled spring had been the company's sole product) and coiled springs for upholstered furniture.

By this time L&P was selling to manufacturers rather than retailers, and sales and profits took off along with the innerspring market, though the conservative company didn't open another plant until 1942. Another plant opening in 1947 was its last expansion until 1960. That year CEO Harry Cornell (grandson of J. P. Leggett), who joined the company in 1950, took the reins. By then L&P had three plants and nearly $10 million in annual sales.

Cornell envisioned the company as a national low-cost supplier of furnishings components. He acquired a woodworking plant in 1960, giving the firm the ability to make wooden bed frames. Acquisitions steadily increased the company's range of products and its geographic scope, and by the early 1970s (the company went public in 1967) L&P had nearly 20 plants and annual sales of around $50 million. The increasing size of the company, along with vertical integration (it began making its own wire in 1970), gave it economies of scale and cost advantages in the fragmented industry.

In 1970 bedding components accounted for about 70% of sales; just four years later — as L&P focused on finished furniture and furniture components — they accounted for about 45%. The company also made investments in new plants, equipment, and products. By 1980 it had about 60 plants and sales of more than $250 million. L&P introduced its continuous coil innerspring — which contributed to the company's good performance in an otherwise slumping industry — around the middle of the decade.

The recession at the beginning of the 1990s hurt the company's sales, but L&P bounced back with the economy and had more than $1 billion in sales in 1992. The next year the company added to its 135 plants with the acquisitions of Hanes Holding Company and VWR Textiles & Supplies (bedding and furniture fabrics).

About 75% of the company's 1995 sales increase resulted from acquisitions. The following year L&P acquired almost 15 companies, including Pace Holdings (aluminum die-cast components). Cornell's nearly 50-year-old strategy continued through 1998 as the company purchased more than 40 businesses (about 30 furnishings-related) with aggregate annual sales of about $560 million.

President Felix Wright added CEO to his duties in 1999, and Cornell remained chairman.

Throughout 1999 L&P bought 29 companies with a combined revenue of about $480 million. In 2000 the company kept up its buying habit, purchasing about 20 companies. By 2001, however, the firm began to reverse that trend, closing or selling off facilities it deemed unprofitable.

In 2005 L&P bought the assets of Ikex; the membership interests of Jarex Distribution, a Jiajiang, China, furniture mechanism facility; Toronto-based Westex International; and Mississippi's Everwood Products. It also purchased a Shanghai, China, fixtures facility.

L&P's acquisition of America's Body Company (ABC) in 2005 gave the company a leg up in the commercial truck equipment segment of the industry and spurred the firm to restructure its operations. ABC makes bodies for vans, flatbed trucks, utility work vehicles, and dump trucks, as well as interiors for vans and equipment for snow and ice control.

Cornell became chairman emeritus in May 2006, when Wright resigned as CEO and took the title of chairman. President David Haffner became CEO as part of the succession.

Following a restructuring announced in 2007, L&P sold its Pace business of aluminum products for some $300 million. It also sold its L&P Plastics unit (a maker of components for the furniture, medical device, power tool, and automotive industries) to Monomoy Capital Partners in September 2008.

Wright retired in 2008; he was succeeded by Richard Fisher.

EXECUTIVES

Chairman: Richard T. Fisher, age 71
President, CEO, and Director: David S. (Dave) Haffner, age 57, $7,277,916 total compensation
EVP, COO, and Director: Karl G. Glassman, age 51, $4,545,332 total compensation
SVP, CFO, and Director: Matthew C. (Matt) Flanigan, age 48, $2,721,222 total compensation
SVP; President, Industrial Materials:
Joseph D. Downes Jr., age 65, $1,099,433 total compensation
SVP; President, Residential Furnishings:
Paul R. Hauser, age 58, $1,134,898 total compensation
SVP; President, Commercial Fixturing and Components: Dennis S. Park, age 55
SVP; President, Specialized Products: Jack D. Crusa, age 55
SVP, General Counsel, and Secretary: Ernest C. Jett, age 64
Chief Procurement Officer: Peter W. Connelly
VP, Corporate Controller, and Chief Accounting Officer: William S. Weil, age 51
VP, Chief Legal and Human Resources Officer, and Secretary: John G. Moore, age 49
VP Information Technology: Michael Blinzler
VP Strategy and Investor Relations:
David M. (Dave) DeSonier, age 53
VP Tax: Kenneth W. (Ken) Purser
VP and Treasurer: Sheri L. Mossbeck
VP Commercial Vehicle Products: Elliott J. Lyons, age 43
VP Engineering and Technology: Vincent S. Lyons
VP Global Systems and Machinery: John A. Garrett
VP Public Affairs and Government Relations:
Lance G. Beshore
Auditors: PricewaterhouseCoopers LLP

LOCATIONS

HQ: Leggett & Platt, Incorporated
No. 1 Leggett Rd., Carthage, MO 64836
Phone: 417-358-8131   **Fax:** 417-358-5840
Web: www.leggett.com

2009 Sales

	$ mil.	% of total
North America		
US	2,289.1	75
Canada	170.1	6
Mexico	41.8	1
Europe	278.1	9
China	233.1	8
Other regions	42.9	1
Total	**3,055.1**	**100**

PRODUCTS/OPERATIONS

2009 Sales

	$ mil.	% of total
Residential furnishings	1,684.8	55
Commercial fixturing & components	487.1	16
Specialized products	445.6	15
Industrial materials	437.6	14
Total	**3,055.1**	**100**

Selected Products

Residential Furnishings
Finished products
Adjustable electric beds
Bed frames
Bunk beds
Carpet underlay
Daybeds
Fashion beds
Headboards
Non-slip products
Innerspring and box spring units
Springs and seating suspensions (chairs, sofas)
Steel mechanisms and hardware (reclining chairs, sleeper sofas)
Commercial Furnishings
Finished products
Point-of-purchase displays
Storage products
Store counters, carts, fixtures, and shelving
Specialized Products
Quilting machinery
Seating suspension, lumbar support, and control cable systems (automobile industry)
Industrial Materials
Drawn steel wire
Steel tubing

Selected Trademarks

Gribetz and Porter (quilting and sewing machines)
Hanes (fiber materials)
Lifestyles, S-cape, and Adjustables by Leggett & Platt (adjustable electric beds)
Mira-Coil, VertiCoil, Lura-Flex, and Superlastic (mattress innersprings)
No-Sag (wire forms used in seating)
Quietflex and Masterack (equipment and accessories for vans and trucks)
Schukra, Pullmaflex, and Flex-O-Lator (automotive seating products)
Semi-Flex (boxspring components and foundations)
Spuhl (mattress innerspring manufacturing machines)
Super Sagless (motion and sofa sleeper mechanisms)
Tack & Jump and Pattern Link (quilting machines)
Wall Hugger (reclining chairs)

COMPETITORS

Advance Auto Parts
Alcoa
AutoZone
Diam International
Flexsteel
Foamex International
Genuine Parts
Holophane
Keystone Consolidated
Knape & Vogt
Load King Manufacturing
Louisville Bedding
Lozier
Marmon Group
Wal-Mart

HISTORICAL FINANCIALS

Company Type: Public

Income Statement

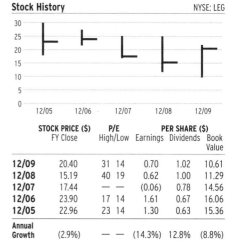

	REVENUE ($ mil.)	NET INCOME ($ mil.)	NET PROFIT MARGIN	EMPLOYEES	FYE: December 31
12/09	3,055	115	3.8%	18,500	
12/08	4,076	104	2.6%	20,600	
12/07	4,306	(11)	—	24,000	
12/06	5,505	300	5.5%	32,828	
12/05	5,299	251	4.7%	33,000	
Annual Growth	**(12.9%)**	**(17.8%)**	**—**	**(13.5%)**	

2009 Year-End Financials

Debt ratio: 50.8%
Return on equity: 7.2%
Cash ($ mil.): 261
Current ratio: 2.27
Long-term debt ($ mil.): 789
No. of shares (mil.): 146
Dividends
  Yield: 5.0%
  Payout: 145.7%
Market value ($ mil.): 2,987

Stock History

NYSE: LEG

	STOCK PRICE ($) FY Close	P/E High/Low		PER SHARE ($) Earnings	Dividends	Book Value
12/09	20.40	31	14	0.70	1.02	10.61
12/08	15.19	40	19	0.62	1.00	11.29
12/07	17.44	—	—	(0.06)	0.78	14.56
12/06	23.90	17	14	1.61	0.67	16.06
12/05	22.96	23	14	1.30	0.63	15.36
Annual Growth	**(2.9%)**	**—**	**—**	**(14.3%)**	**12.8%**	**(8.8%)**

Lennar Corporation

Lennar is one of the largest homebuilding, land-owning, loan-making leviathans in the US, along with D.R. Horton and Pulte Homes. The company builds single-family attached and detached homes in 14 states under brand names including Lennar, Cambridge, NuHome, and Greystone. Lennar targets first-time, move-up, and active adult buyers and markets its homes as "everything included." The company also provides financial services including mortgage financing, title, and closing services. CEO Stuart Miller controls 46% of the company.

Along with the rest of the homebuilding industry, Lennar started to see trouble in 2006 as interest rates rose and years of overbuilding began taking their toll. Fallout from the subprime mortgage crisis and global credit crunch further unraveled the market. Lennar's average price per home has fallen by $40,000 and the number of homes delivered fell by approximately 40,000. In addition to lowering home prices, Lennar responded to the market downturn by buying fewer homesites. It also reduced its workforce by some 40% and tightened its lending standards to reduce its exposure to loan defaults. It continued to lower prices, further focusing on the first-time buyer and limiting the number of home plans offered. However, taking advantage of a rise in distressed sales opportunities, Lennar began picking up more land for development.

In another sign of possible recovery, the company introduced its PowerSmart line of energy-efficient homes in early 2010. Initially available in the Minnesota region, the homes are designed to save residents up to 40% on energy bills.

In early 2007 Lennar and its spun-off investment unit LNR Properties reduced their stakes in LandSource, a joint venture that invests in raw land (among the riskiest of real estate investments, particularly vulnerable to market downturns). MW Housing Partners, an investment vehicle of the California Public Employees' Retirement System, bought 68% of LandSource for $900 million in cash and property; Lennar lowered its stake from 50% to 16%. The sale proved to be fortuitous for Lennar: Not only did it bring the company much-needed cash, but it also reduced Lennar's exposure to the debt-laden LandSource, which filed for Chapter 11 bankruptcy protection one year later. LandSource emerged from bankruptcy as the debt-free Newhall Land Development.

HISTORY

Lennar is the creation of Leonard Miller and Arnold Rosen, and the name of the company is a combination of their given names. Rosen, a Miami homebuilder, formed F&R Builders in 1954. A year later Miller graduated from Harvard with no firm career plans. Having worked summers in Florida, Miller decided it would be a good place to make his fortune, and the 23-year-old began selling real estate there.

With $10,000 earned from commissions, Miller bought 42 lots and in 1956 entered a joint venture with Rosen to build homes on the lots. They worked well together, and Miller soon joined F&R. The operation grew, emphasizing marketing and concentrating on low- and medium-priced single-family homes for first-time buyers and retirees.

After expanding into commercial real estate in the late 1960s, the duo folded F&R into a new company — Lennar Corporation — in 1971 and went public. During the 1970s and 1980s, the company hawked Jacuzzi tubs and designer homes (such as the Calvin and the Liz) and promised customers "$10,000 worth of extras" free at Midnight Madness shopping mall sales. Lennar also began expanding, acquiring land and builders in the Phoenix area in 1973. Rosen retired in 1977.

Spurred by a recession, Lennar began to offer mortgage services nationwide in 1981, keeping the potentially lucrative servicing for itself and selling its mortgages to Fannie Mae, Ginnie Mae, and Freddie Mac, among others. In 1984 it dissolved its construction operations and began subbing out its work (a practice that it continues today). Lennar was relatively unscathed by the recession of the late 1980s, in part because Miller had foreseen a slump and had cut corporate debt and overhead. When other builders were overextending themselves by buying land in good times, Miller had used profit to pay down debt so he would have the resources to buy land cheap when bad times arrived.

During the 1990s Lennar targeted other Sun Belt markets and began buying portfolios of distressed property in partnership with heavy hitters like Morgan Stanley. Although Miller had looked at Texas as a development site since 1987,

it was not until 1991 that Lennar entered the state, beginning in Dallas.

The company bought up the secured debt of Bramalea Homes in Southern California in 1995 and entered Northern California with its acquisition of Renaissance Homes. Lennar's acquisition of Village Homes and Exxon's Friendswood Development in 1996 made it Houston's top home builder.

In 1997 Stuart Miller became president and CEO (Leonard, his father, remained chairman). That year Lennar also spun off its commercial real estate operations as LNR Property.

The following year the company strengthened its position in the western US, acquiring three California homebuilders: Winncrest Homes (Sacramento), ColRich Communities (San Diego), and Polygon Communities (Southern California and Sacramento).

In 2000 Lennar bought fellow builder U.S. Home for about $1.1 billion in a deal that expanded its operations into 13 states. The company acquired the North and South Carolina operations of The Fortress Group in late 2001.

In July 2002 Leonard Miller died of liver cancer. Stuart Miller continued to lead the company as its president and CEO.

Lennar continued to acquire in 2003, adding Seppala Homes and Coleman Homes, expanding its positions, respectively, in South Carolina and the Central Valley of California.

In mid-2003 an entity jointly owned by Lennar and LNR Property Corporation (real estate investment, finance, and management) agreed to acquire The Newhall Land and Farming Company (California master-planned communities) for about $1 billion.

Lennar continued to acquire regional builders, mortgage operations, and title and closing businesses. During 2005 Lennar entered the Boston, New York City, and Reno markets; it also expanded its Jacksonville operations by acquiring Admiral Homes. The condo and apartment buildings in New York and Boston were valued at more than $2 billion.

EXECUTIVES

President, CEO, and Director: Stuart A. Miller, age 52, $4,416,430 total compensation
EVP, Lennar Financial Services and President, North American Title Group: Linda L. Reed
EVP: Richard Beckwitt, age 50, $4,166,364 total compensation
VP and COO: Jonathan M. (Jon) Jaffe, age 50, $3,917,840 total compensation
VP and CFO: Bruce E. Gross, age 51, $3,160,509 total compensation
VP Investor Relations: Marshall H. Ames, age 65
VP and Treasurer: Diane J. Bessette, age 49, $1,677,789 total compensation
CIO: John R. Nygard III
Secretary and General Counsel: Mark Sustana, age 48
President, Eagle Home Mortgage: Gary E. Carlson
Regional President, Lennar Land and Homebuilding: Sam Sparks
President, Universal American Mortgage Company: James T. Timmons
Regional President, Lennar Land and Homebuilding: Jeff Roos
Regional President, Lennar Land and Homebuilding: Fred Rothman
President, Lennar Ventures: David J. Kaiserman
Regional President, Lennar Land and Homebuilding: Don Luke
Director Communications: Kay L. Howard
Controller: David M. Collins, age 40
Auditors: Deloitte & Touche LLP

LOCATIONS

HQ: Lennar Corporation
700 NW 107th Ave., Miami, FL 33172
Phone: 305-559-4000   **Fax:** 305-228-8383
Web: www.lennar.com

2009 Homes Delivered

	Units (No.)	% of total
East (FL, MD, NJ & VA)	3,817	33
West (CA & NV)	2,480	21
Houston	2,150	19
Central (AZ, CO & other TX)	1,796	16
Other (IL; MN, NY, NC & SC)	1,235	11
Total	**11,478**	**100**

PRODUCTS/OPERATIONS

2009 Sales

	$ mil.	% of total
Homebuilding		
Home sales	2,776.9	89
Land sales	57.4	2
Financial services	285.1	9
Total	**3,119.4**	**100**

COMPETITORS

Beazer Homes	PulteGroup
D.R. Horton	The Ryland Group
Hovnanian Enterprises	Standard Pacific
KB Home	Toll Brothers
M.D.C.	Weyerhaeuser Real Estate
NVR	

HISTORICAL FINANCIALS

Company Type: Public

Income Statement

FYE: November 30

	REVENUE ($ mil.)	NET INCOME ($ mil.)	NET PROFIT MARGIN	EMPLOYEES
11/09	3,119	(417)	—	3,835
11/08	4,575	(1,109)	—	4,704
11/07	10,187	(1,941)	—	6,934
11/06	16,267	594	3.7%	12,605
11/05	13,867	1,355	9.8%	13,687
Annual Growth	**(31.1%)**	**—**	**—**	**(27.2%)**

2009 Year-End Financials

Debt ratio: —	No. of shares (mil.): 185
Return on equity: —	Dividends
Cash ($ mil.): 1,331	Yield: 1.3%
Current ratio: 1.71	Payout: —
Long-term debt ($ mil.): —	Market value ($ mil.): 2,343

Stock History

NYSE: LEN

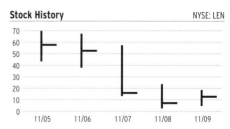

	STOCK PRICE ($) FY Close	P/E High/Low		PER SHARE ($) Earnings	Dividends	Book Value
11/09	12.67	—	—	(2.45)	0.16	13.21
11/08	7.11	—	—	(7.00)	0.52	14.18
11/07	15.84	—	—	(12.31)	0.64	20.67
11/06	52.50	18	10	3.69	0.64	30.83
11/05	57.68	8	5	8.23	0.57	28.39
Annual Growth	**(31.5%)**	**—**	**—**	**—**	**(27.2%)**	**(17.4%)**

Lennox International

Lennox International makes sure the temperature is just right. The company makes climate control equipment such as heating, ventilation, air conditioning, and refrigeration units for residential and commercial uses. It sells furnaces, heat pumps, fireplaces, and air conditioners under such brands as Lennox, Armstrong Air, and Aire-Flo; chillers and condensing units are sold under the Bohn and Larkin names. Products are sold to some 7,000 dealers in the US and Canada. Lennox also owns and operates 100 service and installation centers. The company has operations in Asia, Australia, Europe, and South America. Named after inventor Dave Lennox, the company was acquired in 1904 by newspaper publisher D.W. Norris.

Lennox has felt the ripple effects of the residential construction downturn, which has softened demand for home heating and cooling appliances. Company revenue was down nearly 20% in 2009 (compared to the previous year).

In response, the company has adopted lean manufacturing practices and has worked to improve efficiency at certain facilities in order to reduce waste. Lennox also has divested and consolidated some operations. During 2008 and 2009 Lennox reduced its number of factories from 28 to 18. The company transferred its Iowa-based air conditioning operations to a new manufacturing facility it opened in Mexico so that it may more effectively compete, particularly in the Sun Belt region. Lennox also closed a commercial refrigeration manufacturing plant in Illinois, an HVAC plant in South Carolina, and a fireplace manufacturing plant in California, resulting in hundreds of employee layoffs.

At the same time Lennox is focusing on the long term by investing in innovative products such as solar-powered heating and cooling systems. Lennox also is working to double the number of its distribution locations in North America in order to drive customer service and gain market share. Internationally, Lennox is expanding its geographic footprint, especially in developing markets such as China. The company is increasing the size of its manufacturing facilities there in anticipation of growth in the cold storage market.

HISTORY

Inventors Ernest Bryant and Ezra Smith developed and patented a riveted-steel sheet metal coal furnace in Marshalltown, Iowa, in the 1890s. The cast iron furnaces in use at the time tended to warp with usage; their sheet metal furnace did not. The inventors hired machine shop operator Dave Lennox to build the manufacturing equipment necessary to produce the new furnace. They were underfunded, however, and Lennox took over the patents in lieu of payment and redesigned the furnace. Lennox didn't warm to the furnace business and sold out to D. W. Norris, the local newspaper publisher, and three other people for $40,000 in 1904.

Norris, the company's first president, incorporated the business as Lennox Furnace Company and sold about 600 units the first year. Norris soon established the company's method of selling and delivering directly to authorized dealers.

Lennox built a manufacturing plant in New York in 1925 and acquired Armstrong Furnace, a steel coal furnace plant in Ohio, in 1927. That year John Norris, D. W.'s son, joined the company after graduating from MIT. The younger Norris pushed for new innovations such as oil burners, gas furnaces, and blowers. He set up a research department in the 1930s and soon developed a line of gas- and oil-burning furnaces. The company opened another Ohio plant in 1940 and bought a machine shop there in 1942 to make bomb and aircraft parts for WWII. John Norris became president after the death of his father in 1949.

The company established Lennox Industries (Canada) Ltd. in 1952. Norris began developing an air conditioner the same year, after shopping the idea around to his dealers. Soon the company was turning out residential, commercial, and industrial air conditioners and compressors. In 1955 the company's name was changed to Lennox Industries Inc. to reflect its broader product range. The international division was created in 1962. Soon manufacturing facilities were established outside London and other offices were opened in the Netherlands and West Germany.

Lennox acquired Heatcraft, a maker of heating and cooling components, in 1973. Headquarters were moved to Dallas in 1978; in 1980 John Norris Jr. was named CEO. Lennox International Inc. (LII) was formed as the parent company for Heatcraft and Lennox Industries in 1986. The company reacquired Armstrong Air Conditioning (which it had owned in the 1920s and sold in the mid-1950s) in 1988.

LII underwent restructuring in 1989 and 1991, leading to the consolidation of production to four locations and the grouping of the sales, management, product ordering, and marketing teams at its headquarters in Dallas. In 1995 the company formed Lennox Global and rededicated itself to international expansion through joint ventures with foreign companies. LII formed HCF-Lennox, a joint venture with France's Brancher group, in 1996. The company agreed in 1998 to pay $6.2 million to settle an age bias lawsuit filed by 11 former employees. LII went public in 1999 and began buying HVAC dealers.

In 2000 the company more than doubled its number of owned retail outlets with the $300 million acquisition of Service Experts, an HVAC installation and sales business with 120 locations. However, the acquisition disappointed, and some of the locations were later closed.

COO Robert Schjerven succeeded John W. Norris Jr. as CEO in early 2001; Norris remained as chairman. Every operating segment but its commercial segment saw significant sales declines in 2001. The company restructured its service experts operations and some of its manufacturing and distribution operations that year. LII closed plants in Canada and Australia and closed retail centers to cut costs.

In 2002 LII continued restructuring its noncore heat transfer engineering business and made moves to focus on its core operations. That year it formed a joint venture with Outokumpu Oyj (Finland), selling 55% of its former heat transfer business segment in the US and Europe to Outokumpu. (In 2005 Outokumpu exercised its option to buy the remainder of the venture, however.) LII also sold its 50% interest in its underperforming commercial HVAC joint venture in Argentina. Sales overall continued to decline, although slight increases were made in the residential heating and cooling segment and in the refrigeration segment.

Norris retired as chairman in 2006; he was succeeded by Rich Thompson. Schjerven retired in 2007, passing the CEO title to United Technologies veteran Todd Bluedorn.

EXECUTIVES

Chairman: Richard L. (Rich) Thompson, age 70
CEO and Director: Todd M. Bluedorn, age 47, $5,232,110 total compensation
EVP and CFO: Robert W. (Bob) Hau, age 44, $1,805,439 total compensation
EVP and Chief Human Resources Officer: Daniel M. Sessa, age 45, $1,243,258 total compensation
EVP; President and COO, LII Worldwide Refrigeration: David W. Moon, age 48
EVP; President and COO, LII Commercial Heating & Cooling: Harry J. Bizios, age 60
EVP; President and COO, LII Residential Heating & Cooling: Douglas L. (Doug) Young, age 47, $1,778,165 total compensation
EVP; President and COO, Service Experts: Michael J. Blatz, age 44
EVP, Chief Legal Officer, and Secretary: John D. Torres, age 51, $1,924,798 total compensation
EVP and CTO: Prakash Bedapudi, age 43
VP, Controller, and Chief Accounting Officer: Roy A. Rumbough Jr., age 54, $726,350 total compensation
VP Operations: James Borzi
VP and Treasurer: Richard A. (Rick) Pelini, age 51
VP Investor Relations: Steve L. Harrison
Director Communications and Public Relations: Ozzie Buckler
Auditors: KPMG LLP

LOCATIONS

HQ: Lennox International Inc.
2140 Lake Park Blvd., Richardson, TX 75080
Phone: 972-497-5000   **Fax:** 972-497-5292
Web: www.lennoxinternational.com

2009 Sales

	$ mil.	% of total
US	2,033.1	72
Canada	327.0	11
Other countries	487.4	17
Total	**2,847.5**	**100**

PRODUCTS/OPERATIONS

2009 Sales

	$ mil.	% of total
Residential heating & cooling	1,293.5	44
Commercial heating & cooling	594.6	20
Service experts	535.4	19
Refrigeration	512.7	17
Adjustments	(88.7)	—
Total	**2,847.5**	**100**

Selected Products and Brand Names

Heating and cooling
  Residential products
    Air conditioners
    Free-standing stoves
    Furnaces
    Heat pumps
    Indoor air quality equipment
    Packaged heating and cooling systems
    Prefabricated fireplaces
  Brand names
    Advanced Distributor Products (ADP)
    AireEase
    Aire-Flo
    Armstrong Air
    Concord
    Country Stoves
    Ducane
    Lennox
    Magic-Pak
    Security Chimneys
    Superior
    Whitfield
  Commercial products
    Unitary heating and air conditioning equipment and
      applied systems
  Brand names
    Allied Commercial
    Lennox
Service experts
  Installation
  Maintenance
  Repair
Refrigeration
  Products
    Air-cooled condensers
    Air handlers
    Chillers
    Condensing units
    Fluid coolers
    Unit coolers
  Brand names
    Bohn
    Chandler Refrigeration
    Climate Control
    Friga-Bohn
    Frigus-Bohn
    Heatcraft Worldwide Refrigeration
    HK Refrigeration
    Kirby
    Larkin
    Lovelocks

COMPETITORS

AAON
Airwell-Fedders
Alfa Laval Inc.
Bard Manufacturing
Comfort Systems USA
Daikin
Electrolux
Emerson Electric
GEA Group
Goodman Global
Goodman Manufacturing
HNI
Hong Leong Asia
Hussmann International
Ingersoll-Rand Climate Control
Johnson Controls
Mestek
Nordyne
Paloma Co.
Tecumseh Products
Trane Inc.
United Electric Company
United Technologies
Watsco
Whirlpool
Yazaki Energy Systems

HISTORICAL FINANCIALS
Company Type: Public

Income Statement
FYE: December 31

	REVENUE ($ mil.)	NET INCOME ($ mil.)	NET PROFIT MARGIN	EMPLOYEES
12/09	2,848	51	1.8%	11,600
12/08	3,481	123	3.5%	13,500
12/07	3,750	169	4.5%	15,000
12/06	3,671	166	4.5%	16,000
12/05	3,366	151	4.5%	16,000
Annual Growth	(4.1%)	(23.7%)	—	(7.7%)

2009 Year-End Financials

Debt ratio: 32.1%
Return on equity: 9.6%
Cash ($ mil.): 124
Current ratio: 1.40
Long-term debt ($ mil.): 194

No. of shares (mil.): 54
Dividends
  Yield: 1.4%
  Payout: 62.2%
Market value ($ mil.): 2,125

Stock History
NYSE: LII

	STOCK PRICE ($) FY Close	P/E High/Low		PER SHARE ($) Earnings	Dividends	Book Value
12/09	39.04	46	26	0.90	0.56	11.10
12/08	32.29	20	9	2.11	0.56	8.42
12/07	41.42	17	12	2.43	0.53	14.85
12/06	30.61	15	9	2.26	0.46	14.78
12/05	28.20	15	9	2.11	0.41	14.59
Annual Growth	8.5%	—	—	(19.2%)	8.1%	(6.6%)

Level 3 Communications

Level 3 Communications owns a piece of the communications networking market. The company operates one of the world's largest Internet protocol (IP)-based fiber-optic networks, connecting customers in 22 countries. Its services include broadband Internet access, wholesale voice origination and termination, enterprise voice, content distribution, broadband transport, and colocation. Level 3's wholesale customers include ISPs, telecom carriers, cable TV operators, wireless providers, and the US government.

Level 3's core network services include transport and infrastructure, IP and data services, and local and enterprise voice services, primarily for clients in North America and Europe. Its transport and infrastructure group encompasses point-to-point connections of fixed bandwidth, dark fiber leasing, colocation sites, and transatlantic cable transport. The company's IP and data services include high-speed Internet access, dedicated Internet access, ATM and frame relay, VPN, and content delivery services.

The company's ongoing expansion efforts included the addition of network miles and resources in California, Florida, Ohio, and Texas during 2010. Internationally, it invested in its infrastructure in Poland and along the US-Mexico border in Texas in 2009. Level 3 also continues to expand its portfolio of services to include more bundled options for clients looking to add support for wireless broadband connectivity (Clearwire) and managed video networking services (FOX Broadcasting).

Due to declining revenues from transport services for audio and video programming, Level 3 sold the advertising portion of it Vyvx content distribution unit to DG FastChannel for $129 million in 2008.

Besides its communications network, Level 3 owns a coal-mining company, KCP, that holds a 50% stake in two mines in Montana and Wyoming. The company's mining operations accounts for less than 5% of sales.

HISTORY

Thoroughly modern Level 3 Communications was the brainchild of an Omaha, Nebraska, construction company that traces its roots to 1884 — the multinational Peter Kiewit Sons'. With cash to invest in the 1980s, Kiewit acquired Metropolitan Fiber Systems, which built fiber-optic networks for phone companies. In 1986 Kiewit executive James Crowe convinced CEO Walter Scott that Kiewit should build some phone circuits of its own, and by 1987 Kiewit had created MFS Communications, headed by Crowe, to build networks in business districts. Kiewit slated $500 million for the project in 1989.

By 1995 MFS had gone public and was the biggest of the competitive local-exchange carriers (CLECs). That year Crowe and Scott heard Bill Gates speak on the power of the Internet to destroy traditional phone traffic. MFS launched "Project Silver" to decide how to respond. The answer: buy UUNET. In 1996 MFS acquired the giant ISP and Internet backbone operator, and in the process made itself an acquisition target. WorldCom bought MFS for $14 billion by year's end.

Within a month Crowe walked away from WorldCom (with several MFS execs in tow) to head Kiewit Diversified Group, with holdings in telecommunications, technology, and energy.

In 1998 Kiewit split into the Peter Kiewit Sons' construction group, headed by Ken Stinson, and a diversified company called Level 3 Communications, headed by Crowe. Level 3 kept stakes in telecom companies RCN and C-TEC (now Commonwealth Telephone Enterprises). The Level 3 name came from the seven-layer Open Systems Interconnect (OSI) network model: the company saw its field of play in the bottom three levels — the physical plant, data link, and network layers.

Kiewit provided Crowe with a $2.5 billion grubstake; Level 3 went public and sold its oil interests and Michigan cable TV operation. It retained its coal-mining and toll-road interests to help fund the buildout of a new fiber-optic network to be based on Internet protocol (IP) technology instead of the old circuit-switching system.

Level 3 secured rights-of-way from Burlington Northern and Union Pacific. The company found a new angel in Craig McCaw, whose INTERNEXT agreed to plunge $700 million into the Level 3 network in return for capacity. By year's end the company had begun local networks in 25 US cities and had completed gateway sites in 17.

In 1999 Level 3 moved from Omaha to Broomfield, Colorado, deciding that it could grow faster in the Rockies. Level 3 hired Tyco International to develop an Atlantic undersea cable and agreed to participate in the building of the Japan-US Cable Network across the Pacific.

Fellow fiber baron Global Crossing agreed to buy a 50% interest in the transatlantic cable in 2000. In early 2001 the company announced the completion of its network construction and said it would expand its European network to eight additional markets despite cutting about 6% of its workforce.

For Level 3, as for many of its rivals, demand for bandwidth capacity and services failed to reach expected levels and the company in 2001 scaled back its revenue estimates and cut almost 25% of its workforce. It also sold its Asian operations, including its Tiger network and its capacity on a Japan-US submarine cable and backhaul network, to Reach, the wholesale carrier partnership of Telstra and PCCW.

In 2002 Level 3 acquired Massachusetts-based software distributor CorpSoft and Software Spectrum, a business software distributor based in Texas. The companies were combined and Level 3 soon derived much of its revenues from software distribution, which provided relief from the telecom sector's hard times.

In 2003 the company teamed up with PanAmSat, combining the two companies' network capabilities to form a hybrid fiber-optic and satellite delivery system for entertainment content and information to cable and TV broadcasters, ISPs, and others (PanAmSat was acquired in 2006 by Intelsat). In a separate deal, Level 3 agreed to provide Internet access through its satellite platform to the 500,000 Internet access customers of Hughes Electronics' DIRECTV unit. Vyvx was acquired in 2005 when Level 3 bought WilTel Communications Group from Leucadia National.

The company acquired Broadwing, a provider of voice and data communications services, for $254 million in early 2007. Level 3 also completed its purchase of SAVVIS's content delivery network (CDN) services business for approximately $132 million, and it bought online video management firm Servecast for $45 million.

EXECUTIVES

Chairman: J. Walter (Walter) Scott Jr., age 78
Vice Chairman: Charles C. (Buddy) Miller III, age 57, $2,260,171 total compensation
President and COO: Jeffrey K. (Jeff) Storey, age 49
CEO and Director: James Q. (Jim) Crowe, age 60, $5,819,886 total compensation
EVP and CFO: Sunit S. Patel, age 49, $2,482,057 total compensation
EVP, Chief Legal Officer. and Secretary: Thomas C. (Tom) Stortz, age 58, $2,829,116 total compensation
SVP Content Markets: peter Neill
SVP and Corporate Treasurer: Robin Grey
SVP Corporate Communications: Jeff Battcher, age 48
CIO: Mark Martinet
Chief Marketing Officer: Sureel A. Choksi, age 37
Chief Human Resources: Anthony Fogel
VP Strategy, Business Development and Marketing European Markets: Daniel Sjoberg
VP Corporate Communications: Skip Thurman
CTO and President, Global Network Services: John F. (Jack) Waters Jr., age 45
President, Wholesale Markets: Andrew Crouch, age 39
President, Business Markets: Jeff Tench, age 37
President, European Markets: James Heard, age 47
Auditors: KPMG LLP

LOCATIONS

HQ: Level 3 Communications, Inc.
1025 Eldorado Blvd., Broomfield, CO 80021
Phone: 720-888-1000 **Fax:** 720-888-5085
Web: www.level3.com

2009 Sales

	$ mil.	% of total
North America	3,436	91
Europe		
UK	134	4
Germany	73	2
Other	119	3
Total	**3,762**	**100**

PRODUCTS/OPERATIONS

2009 Sales

	$ mil.	% of total
Communications		
Core network services	2,843	76
Wholesale services	660	17
Other	192	5
Coal mining	67	2
Total	**3,762**	**100**

Selected Services

Communications services
  Transport and infrastructure
    Colocation
    Dark fiber
    Metropolitan and intercity wavelengths
    Private line
    Professional services
    Transoceanic
  Voice
    Enterprise
    Wholesale voice origination and termination
    Wholesale VoIP component services
  IP and data
    ATM and frame relay
    Content delivery network (CDN) services
    Dedicated Internet access
    High-speed Internet access
    VPNs
  Managed modem (dial-up Internet access)
  Level 3 Vyvx (audio and video program broadcasting)
  Reciprocal compensation (interconnection agreements with carriers)
  Managed IP (low-speed services, primarily from Genuity acquisition)
SBC contract services
Coal mining

COMPETITORS

AboveNet
Akamai
AT&T
Belgacom
Cogent Communications
COLT Group
Deutsche Telekom
Equinix
France Telecom
Global Crossing
Internap Network Services
KPN
Limelight
PAETEC
Qwest Communications
SAVVIS
Switch and Data Facilities
TeleCity
TeliaSonera
tw telecom
Verizon Business
XO Holdings

HISTORICAL FINANCIALS

Company Type: Public

Income Statement

FYE: December 31

	REVENUE ($ mil.)	NET INCOME ($ mil.)	NET PROFIT MARGIN	EMPLOYEES
12/09	3,762	(618)	—	5,200
12/08	4,301	(290)	—	5,300
12/07	4,269	(1,114)	—	6,680
12/06	3,378	(744)	—	7,400
12/05	3,613	(638)	—	4,800
Annual Growth	**1.0%**	**—**	**—**	**2.0%**

2009 Year-End Financials

Debt ratio: 1,172.1%
Return on equity: —
Cash ($ mil.): 836
Current ratio: 0.83
Long-term debt ($ mil.): 5,755
No. of shares (mil.): 1,665
Dividends
  Yield: —
  Payout: —
Market value ($ mil.): 2,547

Stock History

NASDAQ (GS): LVLT

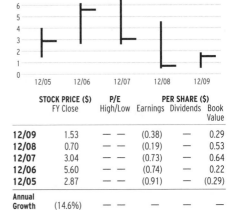

	STOCK PRICE ($) FY Close	P/E High/Low	PER SHARE ($) Earnings	Dividends	Book Value
12/09	1.53	— —	(0.38)	—	0.29
12/08	0.70	— —	(0.19)	—	0.53
12/07	3.04	— —	(0.73)	—	0.64
12/06	5.60	— —	(0.74)	—	0.22
12/05	2.87	— —	(0.91)	—	(0.29)
Annual Growth	**(14.6%)**	**— —**	**—**	**—**	**—**

Levi Strauss

Levi Strauss & Co. (LS&CO.) strives to provide the world's casual workday wardrobe, inside and out. LS&CO., a top manufacturer of brand-name clothing globally, sells jeans and sportswear under the Levi's, Dockers, and Levi Strauss Signature names in more than 110 countries. It also markets men's and women's underwear and loungewear. Levi's jeans — department store staples — were once the uniform of American youth, but LS&CO. has been working to reconnect with the niche and expand outside the US. It has transformed its products portfolio to include wrinkle-free and stain-resistant fabrics used in making some of its Levi's and Dockers slacks. The Haas family (relatives of founder Levi Strauss) owns LS&CO.

While Levi's is marketed as an authentically American brand, about 50% of the company's net revenues come from outside the US. LS&CO. operates in mature markets in the Americas, Europe, and the Asia/Pacific region. Sales in North America, Japan, and Western Europe have suffered in recent years from the downturn in the global economy, demographic changes, and increased competition from trendy lower-priced apparel offerings. For growth, the company is looking to developing markets, including Brazil, China, India, and Russia.

Also, like many other apparel makers, which have traditionally relied on department and specialty stores to distribute their products, LS&CO. is developing its own retail network to increase the availability and visibility of the Levi's brand. Currently, it operates about 1,900 company-owned and franchised stores and sells apparel online. Still, increased sales from its expanding retail network have failed to make up for declines in the company's wholesale business.

Part of the decline in sales is attributable to growing competitive pressure. Through increased spending on advertising and selling as well as its store expansion, LS&CO hopes to regain some of the market share lost to rival VF Corporation (maker of Lee and Wrangler brand jeans and apparel) and others over the past decade. It has also been squeezed by makers of pricey, premium denim (True Religion, Diesel SpA) on the high-end, and purveyors of trendy, low-priced denim (Wal-Mart Stores and JCPenney) on the low end. In response, the jeans maker created the Signature by Levi Strauss brand for the mass market, but with lackluster results to date.

Despite the increased competition, LS&CO. has had to rely more heavily on its core Levi's label and less on its other brands. In an effort to revitalize the Dockers brand, the company launched its "Wear the Pants" global marketing campaign designed to emphasize the masculinity of Dockers apparel.

HISTORY

Levi Strauss arrived in New York City from Bavaria in 1847. In 1853 he joined his brother-in-law, David Stern, in San Francisco selling dry goods to the gold rushers. Shortly after, a prospector told Strauss of miners' problems in finding sturdy pants. Strauss made a pair out of canvas for the prospector; word of the rugged pants spread quickly.

Strauss continued his dry-goods business in the 1860s. During this time he switched the pants' fabric to a durable French cloth called serge de Nimes, soon known as denim. He colored the fabric with indigo dye and adopted the idea from Nevada tailor Jacob Davis of reinforcing the pants with copper rivets. In 1873 Strauss and Davis produced their first pair of waist-high overalls (later known as jeans). The pants soon became de rigueur for lumberjacks, cowboys, railroad workers, oil drillers, and farmers.

Strauss continued to build his pants and wholesaling business until he died in 1902. Levi Strauss & Co. passed to four Stern nephews who carried on their uncle's jeans business while maintaining the company's philanthropic reputation.

After WWII Walter Haas and Peter Haas (a fourth-generation Strauss family member) assumed leadership of LS&CO. In 1948 they ended the company's wholesaling business to concentrate on Levi's clothing. In the 1950s Levi's jeans ceased to be merely functional garments for workers: They became the uniform of American youth. In the 1960s LS&CO. added women's attire and expanded overseas.

The company went public in 1971. That year it added a women's career line and bought Koret sportswear (sold in 1984). By the mid-1980s profits declined. Peace Corps-veteran-turned-McKinsey-consultant Robert Haas (Walter's son) grabbed the reins of LS&CO. in 1984 and took the company private the next year (he became

chairman in 1989). He also instilled a touchy-feely corporate culture often at odds with the bottom line.

In 1986 LS&CO. introduced Dockers casual pants. The company's sales began rising in 1991 as consumers forsook the designer duds of the 1980s for more practical clothes. LS&CO. says seven out of every 10 American men own a pair of Dockers. However, LS&CO. missed out on the birth of another trend: the split between the fashion sense of US adolescents and their Levi's-loving, baby boomer parents.

In 1996 LS&CO. bought back nearly one-third of its stock from family and employees for $4.3 billion. Grappling with slipping sales and debt from the buyout, in 1997 LS&CO. closed 11 of its 37 North American plants, laying off 6,400 workers and 1,000 salaried employees; it granted generous severance packages even to those earning minimum wage.

In 1998, citing improved labor conditions in China, LS&CO. announced it would step up its use of Chinese subcontractors. Further restructuring added a third of its European plants to the closures list that year. LS&CO.'s sales fell 13% in fiscal 1998. Also that year Haas handed his CEO title to Pepsi executive Philip Marineau; Haas remained chairman.

LS&CO. closed 11 of 22 remaining North American plants. in 1999. It also unleashed several new jeans brands that eschewed the company's one-style-fits-all approach of old. In 2002 LS&CO. announced it would close six of its last eight US plants and cut 20% of its worldwide staff (3,300 workers). In 2003 it cut another 5% of its global staff (650 workers).

Marineau retired at the end of 2006. John Anderson, president of LS&CO.'s Asia/Pacific division, replaced him. In 2007 Levi Strauss chairman Robert Haas announced plans to retire after 18 years in that role. His successor was Dryer's ice cream executive T. Gary Rogers, who became the first leader in the company's history who was not a descendant of the founder.

Looking to gain a more active role in its store business, LS&CO. in July 2009 bought the operating rights for more than 70 Levi's and Dockers Outlet locations from store operator Anchor Blue Retail Group, which had filed for bankruptcy, for $72 million.

Rogers retired in late 2009, and Richard Kauffman became chairman.

EXECUTIVES

Chairman Emeritus: Robert D. (Bob) Haas, age 67
Chairman: Richard L. Kauffman, age 55
President, CEO, and Director: R. John Anderson, age 58
EVP and CFO: Blake J. Jorgensen, age 50
SVP and Chief Supply Chain Officer: David Love, age 47
SVP Global Human Resources: Cathleen L. Unruh, age 61
SVP and General Manager, Signature by Levi Strauss & Co.(TM)Brand, US: Susan Brennan
SVP and CIO: Tom Peck
SVP and Chief Marketing Officer: Jaime C. Szulc, age 47
SVP Strategy, Business Development, and Chief Strategy Officer: Lawrence W. (Larry) Ruff, age 53
SVP and President, Levi Strauss Americas: Robert L. Hanson, age 46
SVP and President, Levi Strauss Asia/Pacific: Beng Keong (Aaron) Boey, age 48
SVP; President, Levi Strauss Europe: Armin Broger, age 48

VP, Controller, and Principal Accounting Officer: Heidi L. Manes, age 38
VP: Mary Jane Luck
President, Dockers Brand: Jim Calhoun
Executive Director and Secretary: Ann Ure
Investor Relations: Roger Fleischman
Director Corporate Communications: E.J. Bernacki
Auditors: PricewaterhouseCoopers LLP

LOCATIONS

HQ: Levi Strauss & Co.
 1155 Battery St., San Francisco, CA 94111
Phone: 415-501-6000   **Fax:** 415-501-7112
Web: www.levistrauss.com

PRODUCTS/OPERATIONS

2009 Sales

	% of total
Levi's brand	79
Dockers brand	16
Levi Strauss Signature brand	5
Total	**100**

COMPETITORS

Abercrombie & Fitch	Lands' End
adidas	Liz Claiborne
American Eagle Outfitters	Macy's
Benetton	Nautica Apparel
Calvin Klein	NIKE
Diesel SpA	OshKosh B'Gosh
Fast Retailing	Oxford Industries
Fruit of the Loom	Perry Ellis International
FUBU	Phillips-Van Heusen
The Gap	Polo Ralph Lauren
Guess?	Sean John
Haggar	Sears
Hugo Boss	Target
Inditex	True Religion Apparel
J. C. Penney	Under Armour
J. Crew	VF
Jockey International	Victoria's Secret Stores
Joe's Jeans	Wacoal
Jones Apparel	Wal-Mart
Kmart	Warnaco Group
Kohl's	

HISTORICAL FINANCIALS

Company Type: Private

Income Statement				FYE: Last Sunday in November
	REVENUE ($ mil.)	NET INCOME ($ mil.)	NET PROFIT MARGIN	EMPLOYEES
11/09	4,023	152	3.8%	11,800
11/08	4,303	229	5.3%	11,400
11/07	4,266	460	10.8%	11,550
11/06	4,107	239	5.8%	10,680
11/05	4,125	156	3.8%	9,635
Annual Growth	(0.6%)	(0.6%)	—	5.2%

Net Income History

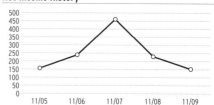

Lexmark International

Lexmark International attacks printing with a host of jets and lasers. A leading maker of printers and related supplies, the company provides color, monochrome, and multifunction laser printers; color and multifunction ink jet printers; dot matrix printers; and ink cartridges. Lexmark markets to customers ranging from individual consumers to large organizations in the financial services, government, health care, manufacturing, and retail sectors.

In 2010 Lexmark acquired Perceptive Software, a supplier of enterprise content management software and services, for $280 million in cash. The transaction allows the company to build on its existing document workflow products and its managed print services. Perceptive, which makes most of its sales in the US, benefits from Lexmark's global infrastructure and sales channels. Perceptive represents a fast-growing software business that has significant experience in the health care, higher education, and government segments.

Under the pressure of the global recession and credit crisis, Lexmark's net income plummeted. Among other cost-cutting measures, such as the planned closing of its ink jet cartridge manufacturing plant in Juarez, Mexico, the company reduced its workforce by 15%.

The highly competitive nature of Lexmark's industry is driving down prices for products on a regular basis, particularly in ink jet and laser printers. In 2009 Lexmark rolled out a new line of all-in-one ink jet printers targeted at small and midsized businesses, part of the company's transition to higher-usage segments of the ink jet printer market.

Under an agreement with Dell, Lexmark manufactures printers that the PC maker sells under its own brand. Dell accounts for approximately 13% of Lexmark's revenues. The companies expanded their business relationship in 2009, extending the number of printer models involved and related aftermarket cartridges.

One area it is targeting for growth is managed print services, with Lexmark taking over the maintenance and replenishment of a customer's printing and imaging equipment infrastructure.

Unlike many of its competitors, Lexmark develops and manufactures its own devices, thereby speeding product cycles. It points to its singular focus on printing products as an advantage it holds in a sector that features diverse players, such as market leader Hewlett-Packard. Lexmark is concentrating its manufacturing and support functions in China and the Philippines to gain a cost advantage on competitors.

The company continues to grow its printer supplies business, which accounts for about 70% of its revenues. However, Lexmark is shifting the focus of its Imaging Solutions Division to higher-end products designed for greater volume usage.

HISTORY

During the late 1980s, as a horde of Davids took aim at Goliath IBM, the computer giant began downsizing to become more competitive. IBM cut its workforce by 100,000 between 1986 and 1992 and began to sell off its peripherals businesses. One of these was Lexmark ("Lex" as in "lexicon" and "mark" as in "marks on paper").

In 1991 IBM sold Lexmark to a group led by investment firm Clayton, Dubilier & Rice for $1.5 billion. Martin Dubilier, who helped found the firm in 1978, learned the leveraged buyout (LBO) ropes as a turnaround expert for Jerome Kohlberg, founder of investment firm Kohlberg Kravis Roberts (now KKR), during the 1970s. Clayton, Dubilier's LBO of Lexmark was financed primarily with bank loans, leaving the new company over $1 billion in debt. Marvin Mann, a 32-year IBM veteran, was appointed Lexmark's chairman.

Mann took a cue from his former bosses and did some downsizing of his own at Lexmark, cutting the number of employees from 5,000 to 3,000. Mann also put more of the responsibility for running the company in the hands of his line managers, allowing them to come up with their own goals and business plans rather than take strategy from above.

Although many employees were given their walking papers, Mann put up a "Help Wanted" sign in his sales department. As an IBM subsidiary, Lexmark relied on Big Blue's general sales force and Mann now needed to create one from scratch. By the end of 1991, staff rose to 4,000.

As another sign of Lexmark's break from IBM, where it sometimes got lost in the shuffle, Mann reorganized the company into four operating groups and made each group's financial information available to everyone in the company.

Lexmark began to flex its muscles as an independent in 1992, when it introduced the first products (IBM PC-compatible keyboards) bearing its own name rather than the IBM logo. That year Lexmark's first color printer debuted. Lexmark's operating profits doubled in 1992, its second year of operation. Using the additional cash flow, the company reduced its debt ahead of schedule, to about $750 million. In 1993 it made its first acquisition when it bought Australian printer maker Gestetner Lasers; the purchase increased Lexmark's presence in the Pacific Rim.

Lexmark began removing the IBM logo from its printers in 1994 and kicked off retail distribution of its own brand of ink jet printers and low-end laser printers. In 1995 the company went public and introduced its first color laser printer. In 1996 Lexmark doubled the number of its manufacturing facilities, opening ink jet plants in the US, Mexico, and the UK to help keep up with rising demand and put its products closer to burgeoning markets.

In continuing efforts to swipe market share from Hewlett-Packard, Lexmark in 1997 revamped its line of office and home printers. Clayton, Dubilier & Rice sold its remaining 23% stake in Lexmark in 1998. COO Paul Curlander, who developed IBM's first laser printer, replaced Mann as CEO that year and as chairman the next.

Lexmark in 2000 opened an ink jet plant in the Philippines and a second such plant in Mexico. Later that year the company announced it would move some manufacturing operations to Mexico and China and cut about 900 jobs. In 2001 the company announced further jobs cuts — about 1,600 — and the closure of one of its plants in Mexico.

Sales and profits peaked in 2004 and began a gradual decline in following years, as Lexmark was pressured by a wide number of competitors around the world.

EXECUTIVES

Chairman and CEO: Paul J. Curlander, age 57, $2,449,277 total compensation
EVP; President, Imaging Solutions Division: Paul A. Rooke, age 52, $3,631,812 total compensation
EVP and CFO: John W. Gamble Jr., age 47, $2,733,642 total compensation
VP; President, Printing Solutions and Services Division: Martin S. (Marty) Canning, age 47, $2,878,080 total compensation
VP, General Counsel, and Secretary: Robert J. (Bob) Patton, age 49
VP Human Resources: Jeri L. Isbell, age 52, $946,266 total compensation
VP PSSD and Corporate Finance: Gary D. Stromquist, age 54
VP, Asia Pacific and Latin America: Ronaldo M. Foresti, age 57, $1,655,647 total compensation
VP Corporate Communications: Barbara Leary
Enterprise Sales and Services Director, Latin America: Mario Pedreros
Country Manager, Australia and New Zealand: Jan Parker
Auditors: PricewaterhouseCoopers LLP

LOCATIONS

HQ: Lexmark International, Inc.
  740 W. New Circle Rd., Lexington, KY 40550
Phone: 859-232-2000   **Fax:** 859-232-2403
Web: www.lexmark.com

2009 Sales

	$ mil.	% of total
US	1,672.1	43
Europe, Middle East & Africa	1,453.9	38
Other regions	753.9	19
Total	**3,879.9**	**100**

PRODUCTS/OPERATIONS

2009 Sales

	$ mil.	% of total
Supplies	2,751.8	71
Printers	938.8	24
Other	189.3	5
Total	**3,879.9**	**100**

2009 Sales

	$ mil.	% of total
Printing Solutions & Services	2,624.9	68
Imaging Solutions	1,255.0	32
Total	**3,879.9**	**100**

Selected Products

Printers
  Dot matrix
  Ink jet
  Laser
  Multifunction
  Refurbished
  Wide-format
Software
  Drivers
  Network management
Supplies
  Labels
  Paper
  Print cartridges

COMPETITORS

Brother Industries	NEC
Canon	Oki Data
Eastman Kodak	Ricoh Company
Epson	Samsung Electronics
Hewlett-Packard	Sharp Corp.
Konica Minolta	Static Control Components
Kyocera Mita	Xerox

HISTORICAL FINANCIALS

Company Type: Public

Income Statement

FYE: December 31

	REVENUE ($ mil.)	NET INCOME ($ mil.)	NET PROFIT MARGIN	EMPLOYEES
12/09	3,880	146	3.8%	11,900
12/08	4,528	240	5.3%	14,000
12/07	4,974	301	6.0%	13,800
12/06	5,108	338	6.6%	14,900
12/05	5,222	356	6.8%	13,600
Annual Growth	(7.2%)	(20.0%)	—	(3.3%)

2009 Year-End Financials

Debt ratio: 64.0%
Return on equity: 16.0%
Cash ($ mil.): 459
Current ratio: 1.80
Long-term debt ($ mil.): 649

No. of shares (mil.): 79
Dividends
  Yield: —
  Payout: —
Market value ($ mil.): 2,039

Stock History

NYSE: LXK

	STOCK PRICE ($) FY Close	P/E High/Low		PER SHARE ($) Earnings	Dividends	Book Value
12/09	25.98	16	8	1.86	—	12.91
12/08	26.90	14	8	2.69	—	10.34
12/07	34.86	23	10	3.14	—	16.28
12/06	73.20	23	13	3.27	—	13.19
12/05	44.83	30	14	2.91	—	18.20
Annual Growth	(12.7%)	—	—	(10.6%)	—	(8.2%)

Liberty Mutual

Boston boasts of baked beans, the Red Sox, and the Liberty Mutual Group. Liberty Mutual Holding is the parent company for the Liberty Mutual Group and its operating subsidiaries. Liberty Mutual is one of the top property/casualty insurers in the US and among the top 10 providers of automobile insurance. The company also offers homeowners' insurance and commercial lines for small to large companies. Liberty Mutual Group operates through four business divisions: Personal Markets, Commercial Markets, Agency Markets, and Liberty International. It distributes its products through a diversified blend of independent and exclusive agents, brokers, and direct sales.

True to its name, the company's Personal Market division offers personal lines property/casualty insurance including private auto and homeowners' insurance. Personal Markets uses a multichannel distribution model including direct online sales, call centers, and sales through affinity groups such as credit unions, employers, and professional and alumni associations. The Commercial Markets division provides commercial property/casualty products.

The Agency Markets division serves a balanced mix of small and midsized employers and individuals. It operates through smaller regional businesses, including Peerless Insurance and America First Insurance, while its specialty commercial products are sold through Liberty Mutual Surety and Liberty Agency Underwriters. To extend the division's geographical reach, Liberty Mutual acquired property/casualty insurer Ohio Casualty for $2.6 billion in 2007 and spent $6.3 billion to acquire Safeco in 2008. That deal gave the company a greater share of the West Coast markets, and it turned the Safeco brand into a new line of personal insurance distributed nationally.

To gain access to public equity, while maintaining its status as a mutual insurer, Liberty Mutual has announced plans to spin off its Agency Markets' business through an initial public offering. The company will retain 80% of the new company, Liberty Mutual Agency Corporation.

Liberty's International division has grown in importance as part of a planned long-term expansion outside of the US. The International division includes operations that offer personal and commercial insurance to local markets in more than a dozen countries and Liberty International Underwriters, which provides specialty commercial lines worldwide. To establish a presence in new markets, the company relies on both acquisitions of existing local businesses as well as start-ups of new businesses.

The company's distribution strategy has shifted away from an in-house sales force, and into a blend of independent and exclusive agents, brokers, direct-response call centers, and the Internet. To that end, in early 2009 Liberty Mutual sold off its direct distribution business and Wausau agency brand to three brokers: Arthur J. Gallagher, Hub International, and USI Holdings. Simultaneously, Liberty Mutual retired its Wausau Insurance brand, and merged those operations into a newly formed Middle Market unit of its Commercial division.

HISTORY

The need for financial aid to workers injured on the job was recognized in Europe in the late 19th century but did not make its way to the US until a workers' compensation law for federal employees was passed in 1908. Massachusetts was one of the first states to enact similar legislation. Liberty Mutual was founded in Boston in 1912 to fill this newly recognized niche.

Liberty Mutual followed the fire insurance practice of taking an active part in loss prevention. It evaluated clients' premises and procedures and recommended ways to prevent accidents. The company rejected the budding industry practice of limiting medical fees, instead studying the most effective ways to reduce the long-term cost of a claim by getting the injured party back to work.

In 1942 the company acquired the United Mutual Fire Insurance Company (founded 1908, renamed Liberty Mutual Fire Insurance Company in 1949). The next year it founded a rehabilitation center in Boston to treat injured workers and to test treatments.

In the 1960s and 1970s Liberty Mutual expanded its line to include life insurance (1963), group pensions (1970), and IRAs (1975).

Seeking to increase its national presence, the company formed Liberty Northwest Insurance Corporation in 1983. It continued expanding its offerings, with new subsidiaries in commercial, personal, and excess lines and, in 1986, by moving into financial services by buying Stein Roe & Farnham (founded 1958).

Liberty Mutual restructured in 1994, withdrawing from the group health business and reorganizing claims operations into two units: Personal Markets and Business Markets. The next year it gained a foothold in the UK when it received permission to invest in a Lloyd's of London syndicate management company.

The company expanded its financial services operations in 1995 and 1996, merging its Liberty Financial subsidiary with the already public Colonial Group; it also acquired American Asset Management and Newport Pacific Management.

In 1999 the company bought Guardian Royal Exchange's US operations. In a new international initiative that year, Liberty Mutual bought 70% of Singapore-based insurer Citystate Holdings as its foothold in Asia. Also in 1999 Liberty Mutual strengthened its US business insurance lineup by adding the Wausau Companies.

After failing to find a buyer, asset management subsidiary Liberty Financial in 2001 began liquidating assets. Canadian insurer Sun Life acquired Keyport Life Insurance and mutual fund distributor Independent Financial Marketing Group. Liberty Financial's investment management segment (including subsidiaries Crabbe Huston, Stein Roe & Farnham, and Liberty Wanger Asset Management) was snapped up by FleetBoston (now part of the Bank of America empire). Liberty Mutual then bought the nearly 30% of Liberty Financial it did not already own and merged the remains into its subsidiary operations.

The company's diversification efforts included Liberty International, which expanded operations in such countries as Canada, Japan, Mexico, Singapore, and the UK. The company also grew its international presence in areas such as China and southern Europe.

Slumping property/casualty lines and the events of September 11 hit Liberty Mutual in 2001 (the company paid out some $500 million in claims). In 2001 and 2002 the company reorganized into a mutual holding company structure with three principal operating companies (Liberty Mutual Insurance, Liberty Mutual Fire Insurance, and Employers Insurance Company of Wausau) and Liberty Mutual Holding Company as the parent.

The company rebounded nicely in 2002-03, thanks to the rebounding stock market and strategic acquisitions worldwide. Strengthening its personal lines business, Liberty Mutual in 2003 bought Prudential's domestic property/casualty operations. The deal included some 1,400 Prudential agents which were added to the company's distribution mix.

Hurricane-related losses totaled $1.5 billion in 2005, but were offset by nice returns from the company's investments that same year.

EXECUTIVES

Chairman and CEO: Edmund F. (Ted) Kelly, age 64
President, Liberty Mutual and Liberty International: David H. Long, age 50
SVP and CIO: James M. McGlennon
EVP and Chief Investment Officer: A. Alexander Fontanes, age 55
SVP and General Counsel: Christopher C. Mansfield, age 60
SVP Communications Services: Stephen G. Sullivan
SVP and CFO: Dennis J. Langwell, age 51
SVP and General Manager Technology Infrastructure: Baron Thrower
SVP Human Resources and Administration: Helen E. R. Sayles, age 59

VP and Treasurer: Laurance H. S. Yahia
VP and Comptroller: John D. Doyle
VP and Secretary: Dexter R. Legg
VP and Manager External Relations: John Cusolito
**CEO, Liberty International Underwriters, Liberty
  Mutual Group:** Daniel T. N. (Danny) Forsythe
**President and CEO, America First Insurance, Liberty
  Mutual Group:** Philip J. Broughton
Auditors: Ernst & Young LLP

LOCATIONS

HQ: Liberty Mutual Holding Company Inc.
  175 Berkeley St., Boston, MA 02116
Phone: 617-357-9500   **Fax:** 617-350-7648
Web: www.libertymutual.com

PRODUCTS/OPERATIONS

2009 Revenues

	$ mil.	% of total
Agency markets	11,928	37
International	7,589	23
Personal markets	7,001	21
Commercial markets	6,028	19
Other	(1,452)	—
Total	**31,094**	**100**

Selected Subsidiaries and Affiliates

Liberty International
  Liberty ART SA (Argentina)
  Liberty Direct (Poland)
  Liberty Insurance Pte.Ltd. (Singapore)
  Liberty International Underwriters (LIU)
  Liberty Seguros (Brazil)
  Liberty Seguros SA (Colombia)
  Seguros Caracas de Liberty Mutual C.A. (Venezuela)
  Seker Sigorta A.S. (Turkey)

Domestic and Regional Companies
  America First Insurance
  Colorado Casualty
  Golden Eagle Insurance
  Indiana Insurance
  Liberty Northwest
  Montgomery Insurance
  Ohio Casualty
  Peerless Insurance
  Safeco Insurance
  Summit

COMPETITORS

ACE Limited
AIG
Allianz
Allstate
Chubb Corp
CNA Financial
Hanover Insurance
The Hartford
Progressive Corporation
State Farm
Travelers Companies
W. R. Berkley
White Mountains Insurance Group
Zurich Financial Services

HISTORICAL FINANCIALS

Company Type: Mutual company

Income Statement

	ASSETS ($ mil.)	NET INCOME ($ mil.)	INCOME AS % OF ASSETS	FYE: December 31 EMPLOYEES
12/09	109,475	1,023	0.9%	100,000
12/08	104,300	1,140	1.1%	45,000
12/07	94,679	1,518	1.6%	41,000
12/06	85,498	1,626	1.9%	39,000
12/05	78,824	1,027	1.3%	39,000
Annual Growth	8.6%	(0.1%)	—	26.5%

2009 Year-End Financials
Equity as % of assets: 13.3%   Long-term debt ($ mil.): 6,535
Return on assets: 1.0%   Sales ($ mil.): 31,094
Return on equity: —

Net Income History

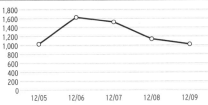

Limited Brands

Limited Brands is as much of a shopping-mall mainstay as food courts and teenagers. The company operates about 2,970 stores throughout North America under the Victoria's Secret, Bath & Body Works (BBW), and La Senza (in Canada) banners, as well as corresponding websites and catalogs. Originally focused on apparel, Limited Brands sold its ailing Limited Stores and Express chains — leaving the company free to focus on two core businesses: Victoria's Secret and BBW. Limited Brands also owns apparel importer MAST Industries, luxe department store operator Henri Bendel, and The White Barn Candle Co. Limited Brands was founded in 1963 by its chairman Leslie Wexner.

Wexner's goal is for Victoria's Secret to blossom into a $10 billion brand, but the global financial crisis and decline in consumer confidence have thwarted his growth strategy for the bra-and-panty business.

With company-owned stores in Canada and independently owned La Senza stores in some 45 countries, the $600-million purchase of La Senza is key to Wexner's goal of becoming an international player in lingerie. (The Canadian retailer operates under the banners La Senza, La Senza Express, and La Senza Spirit, after exiting the La Senza Girl business.) To build its business in Canada, in April 2010 Limited Brands created Limited Brands Canada, a Montreal-based company that will support all of its retail stores — including La Senza, BBW, Victoria's Secret Pink, and Victoria's Secret — and expansion there. Victoria's Secret Pink, the retailer's youth-oriented feeder brand, opened its first four shops in Ontario in 2009; Victoria's Secret opened a store each in Alberta and Ontario the next year. Overall, Limited Brands plans to open about 50 stores in 2010, primarily in Canada.

Beyond North America, the company has formed a partnership with M.H. Alshaya (a popular franchise partner for many American retailers, including American Eagle Outfitters and Pottery Barn) to operate stores in the Middle East.

The retail picture was a bit brighter at BBW, Limited Brands' other core business. BBW is expanding in Canada. Limited Brands is also expanding Henri Bendel, which operates about a dozen specialty stores that feature fashion and accessories, and cosmetics.

Wexner owns about 18% of the company.

HISTORY

After a disagreement with his father in 1963 over the operation of the family store (Leslie's), Leslie Wexner, then 26, opened the first Limited store in Columbus, Ohio, with $5,000 borrowed from his aunt. The company was named from Wexner's desire to do one product line well — moderately priced fashionable attire for teenagers and young women.

When The Limited went public in 1969, it had only five stores, but the rapid development of large, covered malls spurred growth to 100 stores by 1976. Two years later The Limited acquired MAST Industries, an international apparel purchasing and importing company. The company opened Express in 1980 to serve the teen market.

The Limited grew with acquisitions, including the 1982 purchases of Lane Bryant (large sizes) and Victoria's Secret (lingerie). That year it formed the Brylane fashion catalog division and acquired Roaman's, a bricks-and-mortar and catalog merchandiser of plus sizes.

Wexner bought The Lerner Stores (budget women's apparel) and Henri Bendel (high fashion) in 1985, sportswear retailer Abercrombie & Fitch (A&F) in 1988, and London-based perfumer Penhaligon's in 1990 (sold in 1997). The Limited introduced several in-store shops, including Cacique (French lingerie) in 1988 and Limited Too (girls' fashions), which were later expanded into stand-alone stores. It also launched Structure (men's sportswear) in 1989 and Bath & Body Works shops in 1990. All of these stores were in malls, often strategically clustered together.

The company closed many The Limited and Lerner stores in 1993 and sold 60% of its Brylane catalog unit to Freeman Spogli (Brylane went public in 1997). It opened four Bath & Body Works stores in the UK (its first non-US stores) to compete with British rival The Body Shop.

The company began spinning off its businesses while keeping controlling stakes; it spun off Intimate Brands (Victoria's Secret, Cacique, and Bath & Body Works) in 1995 and A&F in 1996. (The Limited sold its remaining 84% in A&F in 1998.)

The Limited closed more than 100 of its women's apparel stores in 1997 and Intimate Brands shuttered the Cacique chain; the next year The Limited closed nearly 300 more stores companywide (excluding the Intimate Brands chains) and the majority of its Henri Bendel stores. In 1999 the company spun off Limited Too, its most successful chain, as Too, Inc.

In 2001 The Limited sold its Lane Bryant unit to Charming Shoppes for $335 million. The Limited bought back the remaining shares of Intimate Brands it did not already own in March 2002. In May 2002 the company changed its name to Limited Brands from The Limited. Later that year Limited Brands sold off its remaining stake in Lerner New York.

Limited Brands in 2004 sold 1.6 million shares of the plus-size United Retail Group Inc. and it acquired New York-based Slatkin & Co. (a prestige home fragrance company). Later that year Limited Brands laid off 25% of the headquarters workforce of its Express division — including managers and support personnel, but not store employees or warehouse workers — in the face of slipping earnings.

In January 2007 Limited Brands completed its acquisition of lingerie maker and retailer La Senza, based in Montreal, for about $600 million. La Senza is a specialty retailer offering lingerie and sleepwear for women age 18 to 35, as well as apparel for girls in the 7 to 14 age group. In July

Limited Brands sold a 75% interest in its Express chain to affiliates of Golden Gate Capital for about $425 million. In a similar transaction completed in August, Limited Brands sold a 75% stake in its 251-store Limited Stores business to Sun Capital Partners.

Former vice chairman and COO Len Schlesinger retired in September 2007 after eight years with the firm. Wexner and administrative executive Martyn Redgrave took over Schlesinger's responsibilities.

In 2008 BBW opened its first stores in Canada. In 2009 Limited Brands closed 53 La Senza Girl stores, exiting that business. The company in mid-2010 sold off the remaining 25% stake it held in Limited Stores LLC, which operates The Limited retail locations.

EXECUTIVES

Chairman and CEO: Leslie H. Wexner, age 72, $10,821,970 total compensation
President and Chief Marketing Officer, Brand and Creative Services: Edward G. Razek
EVP and CFO: Stuart B. Burgdoerfer, age 47, $2,769,963 total compensation
EVP and Chief Administrative Officer: Martyn R. Redgrave, age 57, $4,253,246 total compensation
EVP Retail Real Estate: Jamie Bersani
EVP Human Resources: Jane L. Ramsey, age 52
SVP Law, Policy, and Governance and Secretary: Samuel P. Fried
SVP and General Merchandise Manager Fashion, Henri Bendel: Scott Schramm
SVP and General Counsel: Douglas L. Williams
VP Government Affairs: Ted Adams
VP Investor Relations: Amie Preston
VP Treasury, Mergers, and Acquisitions: Timothy J. Faber, age 48
VP External Communication: Tammy Roberts Myers
President and CEO, Victoria's Secret: Sharen J. Turney, age 53, $7,639,594 total compensation
CEO, Bath & Body Works: Diane L. Neal, age 53, $3,885,297 total compensation
CEO, Victoria's Secret Stores: Lori Greeley
CEO, Henri Bendel: Edward (Ed) Bucciarelli, age 50
President Brand Development, Bath & Body Works: Camille McDonald
President & CEO, Victoria's Secret PINK: Denise Landman
President, La Senza and Limited Brands Canada: Joanne Nemeroff
President, International: Martin Waters
Auditors: Ernst & Young LLP

LOCATIONS

HQ: Limited Brands, Inc.
3 Limited Pkwy., Columbus, OH 43216
Phone: 614-415-7000 **Fax:** 614-415-7440
Web: www.limitedbrands.com

PRODUCTS/OPERATIONS

2010 Stores

	No.
Victoria's Secret	
Victoria's Secret Stores	1,040
La Senza	258
Victoria's Secret PINK Canada	4
Bath & Body Works US	1,627
Bath & Body Works Canada	31
Henri Bendel	11
Total	**2,971**

2010 Sales

	$ mil.	% of total
Victoria's Secret Stores	3,496	40
Victoria's Secret Direct	1,388	16
La Senza	423	5
Bath & Body Works	2,383	28
Other (includes Henri Bendel, Mast & BBW Canada)	942	11
Total	**8,632**	**100**

Selected Retail Brands

Bath & Body Works
C.O. Bigelow
Henri Bendel
La Senza
Pink
The White Barn Candle Company
Victoria's Secret

COMPETITORS

Abercrombie & Fitch	Kiehl's
American Eagle Outfitters	Macy's
Avon	Mary Kay
Bergdorf Goodman	Natori
Body Shop	Nordstrom
CVS Caremark	Revlon
Dillard's	Saks
Estée Lauder	Sephora USA
Frederick's of Hollywood	Shiseido Americas
Fruit of the Loom	Target
The Gap	Ulta
Hanesbrands	VF
J. C. Penney	Wal-Mart
Jockey International	Warnaco Group

HISTORICAL FINANCIALS

Company Type: Public

Income Statement

	REVENUE ($ mil.)	NET INCOME ($ mil.)	NET PROFIT MARGIN	EMPLOYEES
1/10	8,632	448	5.2%	92,100
1/09	9,043	220	2.4%	90,900
1/08	10,134	718	7.1%	97,500
1/07	10,671	675	6.3%	125,500
1/06	9,699	666	6.9%	110,000
Annual Growth	(2.9%)	(9.4%)	—	(4.3%)

FYE: Saturday nearest January 31

2010 Year-End Financials

Debt ratio: 124.7%
Return on equity: 22.1%
Cash ($ mil.): 1,804
Current ratio: 2.46
Long-term debt ($ mil.): 2,723
No. of shares (mil.): 325
Dividends
  Yield: 3.2%
  Payout: 43.8%
Market value ($ mil.): 6,185

Stock History

NYSE: LTD

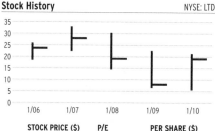

	STOCK PRICE ($) FY Close	P/E High/Low		PER SHARE ($) Earnings	Dividends	Book Value
1/10	19.02	15	4	1.37	0.60	6.71
1/09	7.92	34	11	0.65	0.60	5.76
1/08	19.07	16	8	1.89	0.60	6.82
1/07	27.94	19	14	1.68	0.60	9.09
1/06	23.66	15	11	1.66	0.60	7.60
Annual Growth	(5.3%)	—	—	(4.7%)	0.0%	(3.1%)

Lincare Holdings

Lincare Holdings doesn't take breathing for granted. With more than 1,000 offices across the US, the company helps some 750,000 patients with chronic obstructive pulmonary diseases (including emphysema and severe asthma) by providing oxygen therapy services. Through its local service centers, Lincare delivers oxygen equipment to patients in their homes, and it trains them and monitors their use of the equipment. The company offers positive airway pressure machines for patients with sleep apnea and supplies other home medical equipment. In some markets the company also provides home infusion services, such as chemotherapy, pain management, parenteral nutrition, and other procedures.

Lincare's oxygen and respiratory therapy services account for more than 90% of sales; the company derives more than half of its sales from Medicare and Medicaid reimbursements. A series of changes to Medicare rules have lowered reimbursement rates for many of the company's services, including some inhalation drug therapies and oxygen equipment.

Despite those changes, the company has so far managed to expand its customer base and geographic reach through selective acquisitions and internal growth. Lincare prefers to acquire smaller regional home respiratory service providers to enter into new markets and increase its market share in existing geographic markets.

Lincare also depends on referrals from physicians and hospital discharge planners to keep its business operating at full capacity. The company then supplies its referred patients with information regarding medical and insurance coverage and coordinates the delivery of care.

In 2010, Lincare made a larger-than-usual acquisition when it purchased the respiratory, infusion, and home medical equipment division of Gentiva Health Services for an undisclosed amount. The acquired business added about 40 agency locations in seven states.

Lincare's acquisition strategy, though somewhat conservative, did cause a drop off in revenue in 2009. Combined with that was a nearly 20% negative impact from Medicare price reductions and payment changes. Like any other health care company that is dependent upon government reimbursements for its income, Lincare is particularly vulnerable to those changes.

FMR LLC and BlackRock hold about 30% of the company's shares.

HISTORY

Linde Homecare Medical Systems was formed in 1972 as part of Union Carbide's industrial gases division (now Praxair). Under threat of a hostile takeover bid, Union Carbide in 1987 decided to raise cash by spinning off Linde Homecare's operations as Lincare Inc. In 1990 investors helped the spinoff's management buy out the company, renamed Lincare Holdings.

The company went public that year. Flush with cash from the IPO, Lincare Holdings went on an acquisition spree, spreading by targeting existing companies in new markets. It also benefited from new regulations; in 1993 the government set up an expensive and complicated claims process that forced out smaller competitors. In 1994 the company bought Wyoming-based Home Oxygen Plus Equipment and Colorado-based Meridian Medical. A merger attempt the following year between Lincare Holdings and competitor Coram Healthcare failed.

The buying frenzy, however, continued in 1996, when the company inhaled 17 competitors, and again in 1997, when it acquired 24 more. In 1998 Lincare Holdings received government warnings about inadequate testing of liquid medical oxygen at several manufacturing plants. Expansion continued in 1999 and 2000, with purchases of home nursing services firm Healthcor Holdings and of home respiratory provider United Medical. In 2001 Lincare acquired 18 competitors. The company's legal woes also continued: The federal Department of Health and Human Services subpoenaed Medicare billing records for certain local operations in 1999 and a federal grand jury launched an investigation in 2000. One part of the investigations focused on possible inappropriate gifts given to doctors, while other parts focused on whether Lincare sought inappropriate reimbursement from Medicare.

Lincare settled the investigations in 2006 with a $12 million payment to the government and signed a corporate integrity agreement with the Office of Inspector General.

EXECUTIVES

Chairman and CEO: John P. Byrnes, age 51, $19,754,002 total compensation
President and COO: Shawn S. Schabel, age 45, $13,249,899 total compensation
CFO and Secretary: Paul G. Gabos, age 45, $10,141,428 total compensation
Compliance Officer: Jenna Pedersen
Marketing and Development: Mickey McKenzie
Auditors: KPMG LLP

LOCATIONS

HQ: Lincare Holdings Inc.
19387 US 19 North, Clearwater, FL 33764
Phone: 727-530-7700   **Fax:** 727-532-9692
Web: www.lincare.com

PRODUCTS/OPERATIONS

2009 Sales

	$ mil.	% of total
Oxygen & other respiratory therapy	1,398.2	90
Home medical equipment & other	152.3	10
Total	**1,550.5**	**100**

2009 Sales by Payer

	% of total
Medicare & Medicaid	60
Private insurance	33
Direct payment	7
Total	**100**

Selected Subsidiaries

Alpha Respiratory Inc.
Caring Responders LLC
ConvaCare Services Inc.
Health Care Solutions at Home Inc.
Home-Care Equipment Network Inc.
Healthlink Medical Equipment LLC
Lincare Pharmacy Services Inc.
Med4Home Inc.
PulmoRehab LLC

COMPETITORS

Accredo Health	DaVita
Addus HomeCare	Gentiva
Amedisys	National Home Health
American HomePatient	Option Care
Apria Healthcare	Rotech Healthcare
BioScrip	Trinity HomeCare
Critical Homecare	

HISTORICAL FINANCIALS
Company Type: Public

Income Statement
FYE: December 31

	REVENUE ($ mil.)	NET INCOME ($ mil.)	NET PROFIT MARGIN	EMPLOYEES
12/09	1,551	136	8.8%	9,867
12/08	1,665	237	14.2%	9,957
12/07	1,596	226	14.2%	9,450
12/06	1,410	213	15.1%	9,070
12/05	1,267	214	16.9%	8,258
Annual Growth	**5.2%**	**(10.7%)**	**—**	**4.6%**

2009 Year-End Financials

Debt ratio: 53.5%
Return on equity: 14.5%
Cash ($ mil.): 20
Current ratio: 1.74
Long-term debt ($ mil.): 482

No. of shares (mil.): 98
Dividends
  Yield: —
  Payout: —
Market value ($ mil.): 2,428

Stock History
NASDAQ (GS): LNCR

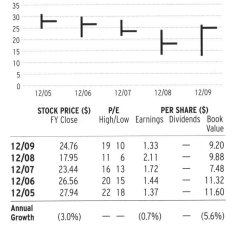

	STOCK PRICE ($) FY Close	P/E High/Low	PER SHARE ($) Earnings	Dividends	Book Value
12/09	24.76	19 10	1.33	—	9.20
12/08	17.95	11 6	2.11	—	9.88
12/07	23.44	16 13	1.72	—	7.48
12/06	26.56	20 15	1.44	—	11.32
12/05	27.94	22 18	1.37	—	11.60
Annual Growth	**(3.0%)**	**— —**	**(0.7%)**	**—**	**(5.6%)**

Lincoln Electric Holdings

With this thing, I thee weld. Lincoln Electric, the world's largest manufacturer of arc welders and welding gear by sales, is a global manufacturer of welding and cutting products, including arc welding power sources, consumable electrodes, fluxes, fume extraction equipment, robotic welding systems, and wire feeders; other welding products include regulators and torches. In North America, which geographically accounts for more than 40% of its sales, products are sold primarily through a network of industrial distributors. Outside of North America, the company has manufacturing facilities and an international sales organization that serve customers in Asia/Pacific, Europe, and South America.

Lincoln Electric is expanding geographically through acquisitions and has completed several deals in South America and China to expand its product base and local manufacturing capabilities, thereby enabling it to reach customers directly in those regions. Its Asian subsidiary, Lincoln Electric Company (Asia/Pacific) Pte.,

Ltd., improved its welding consumables business in China by penning a deal in early 2009 with Jinzhou Jin Tai Welding and Metal Co., a welding wire business, to make Jin Tai a wholly owned subsidiary of Lincoln Electric.

Just a few months prior in 2008, the severity of global economic conditions forced the company to initiate a series of cost-cutting moves, including a reduction in its worldwide workforce of more than 10%, salary cuts for executives, lower bonuses, and a hiring freeze. But even with the economy short-circuiting, the company boosted its brazing product offerings in 2008 by acquiring a 90% interest in a Brazilian manufacturer in cash and assumed debt; the company operates as Harris Soldas Especiais. It also picked up the stock of Electro-Arco, a Portugal-based manufacturer of welding equipment.

HISTORY

John Lincoln founded The Lincoln Electric Company in 1895 to make and repair electric motors. By the time his younger brother James joined Lincoln as a salesman in 1907, John had expanded into rechargeable batteries and had also begun researching arc welding. John dedicated himself to research and left James to handle management. In the workplace, James formed an advisory board made up of elected employee representatives from each department. Its twice-monthly meetings became a cornerstone of the company's Incentive Management System, which Lincoln based on six tenets: people as assets, Christian ethics, principles, simplicity, competition, and customer satisfaction.

As part of the management system, piecework pay and group life insurance (unusual at the time) were begun in 1915. Meanwhile, John perfected the electric arc welding machine that soon became the company's chief product, and in 1917 he formed The Lincoln Electric Welding School.

In 1934 workers offered to work longer hours during the Depression in exchange for a share of the company's profits; that year bonuses averaged 30% of pay. By the 1940s Lincoln was the world's #1 maker of arc-welding equipment, with subsidiaries in Australia, Canada, and the UK and licensees in Argentina, Brazil, Canada, and Mexico. Lincoln added a pension plan and an internal promotion program during WWII as ship manufacturing fueled demand for its products.

William Irrgang, a German engineer with 26 years at the company, succeeded James Lincoln as president in 1954 (James became chairman). Under Irrgang and Lincoln the company practiced conservative policies: It prohibited capital spending projects with paybacks lasting more than one year. Irrgang became chairman in 1965 and was named CEO (a new title) in 1972, the same year George Willis, a Harvard MBA and devotee of the Incentive Management System, became president. Willis was constrained by Irrgang's conservatism and the economic woes of the early 1980s. Sales dropped and though Lincoln's policy of not laying off workers was strained, workers shifted jobs into maintenance or sales work.

Irrgang died in 1986, leaving Willis in control. Willis quickly expanded product lines and geographic coverage. Soon the company's offerings included robotic and gas-based welding products. When he retired the next year, Willis left a legacy of expansion and debt. Though sales had doubled and the company's international presence had grown to 15 countries, debt had risen from about $18 million in 1988 to

$222 million in 1993. Lincoln also had trouble exporting its incentive system to other countries. It returned to profitability in 1994, cutting jobs and closing factories in Europe and Latin America and adding jobs in the US.

Anthony Massaro became CEO in 1996. He looked overseas for opportunities, including deals in China, Indonesia, and Italy. In 1997 Lincoln consolidated production at its European plants and agreed to settle some of the lawsuits alleging that a type of its welding wire contributed to building damage in California's 1994 Northridge earthquake.

In 1998 the company acquired Indalco, a Canada-based maker of aluminum welding wire, and Germany-based Uhrhan & Schwill, which made pipe-welding systems. It also obtained a 50% stake in Turkish welding company AS Kaynak and opened a distribution center near Johannesburg, South Africa.

In 2000 Lincoln bought a 35% stake in Kuang Tai Metal Industrial, a Taiwan-based company that made mild and stainless-steel welding wires. It then went after UK-based welding-equipment maker Charter plc, but was unable to complete the transaction after the US Federal Trade Commission ruled it would require Lincoln to divest certain operations if it acquired Charter. In 2001 the company opened a new research facility in Cleveland; the next year it acquired 85% of Polish welding equipment maker Bester S.A.

In 2004 John Stropki replaced Massaro as president and CEO of Lincoln Electric. Stropki also became chairman when Massaro retired near the end of 2004.

In 2006 the company purchased Metrode Products, a UK-based firm that made specialty consumables for the process and power generation industries. Aiming to advance into key energy and infrastructure markets, Lincoln Electric acquired pipe-cutting equipment maker Vernon Tool Company in late 2007.

EXECUTIVES

Chairman, President, and CEO: John M. Stropki Jr., age 60, $4,604,784 total compensation
SVP; President, Lincoln Electric International: David M. LeBlanc, age 45, $1,486,649 total compensation
SVP, CFO, and Treasurer: Vincent K. Petrella, age 49, $1,419,349 total compensation
SVP; President, Lincoln Electric North America: George D. Blankenship, age 47, $1,045,514 total compensation
SVP Global Marketing and Product Development: Richard J. Seif
SVP Human Resources and Compliance: Gretchen A. Farrell, age 47
SVP, General Counsel, and Secretary: Frederick G. Stueber, age 56, $1,463,294 total compensation
VP; President, Lincoln Electric Asia/Pacific: Thomas A. (Tom) Flohn, age 49, $1,270,260 total compensation
VP; President, Lincoln Electric Canada: Joseph G. Doria
VP; Group President, Brazing, Cutting, and Retail Subsidiaries: David J. (Dave) Nangle
VP Internal Audit: Anthony Battle
VP Strategy and Business Development: Steven B. Hedlund
VP Corporate Tax: Michele R. Kuhrt
VP and Controller: Gabriel Bruno
VP Mergers, Acquisitions, and Investor Relations: Earl L. Ward, age 57
VP Sales, North America: Michael S. Mintun
Auditors: Ernst & Young LLP

LOCATIONS

HQ: Lincoln Electric Holdings, Inc.
22801 St. Clair Ave., Cleveland, OH 44117
Phone: 216-481-8100   **Fax:** 216-486-1751
Web: www.lincolnelectric.com

2009 Sales

	$ mil.	% of total
United States	722.7	42
Other regions	1,006.6	58
Total	**1,729.3**	**100**

PRODUCTS/OPERATIONS

2009 Sales

	$ mil.	% of total
North America Welding	858.2	50
Europe Welding	346.4	20
The Harris Products Group	217.2	12
Asia/Pacific Welding	208.3	12
South America Welding	99.2	6
Total	**1,729.3**	**100**

Selected Products

Robotics and automation
    Fixed table systems
    Lincoln Automation/FANUC
    Positioning systems
    Power sources
    Wire feeders
Welding and cutting equipment
    Advanced process welders
    Engine driven welders
    Environmental systems
    Guns & torches
    MIG/flux-cored welders
    Multi-operator welders
    Multi-process welders
    Retail welding products
    Semiautomatic wire feeders
    Stick welders
    Subarc welders
    Subarc wire feeders
    TIG welders
    Welding helmets
Welding consumables (welding wire, flux, and rods)
    Aluminum MIG (GMAW) wires
    Cast Iron/non-ferrous stick electrodes
    Cut length consumables
    Flux-cored wires — gas shielded
    Flux-cored wires — self shielded
    Hardfacing consumables
    Metal-cored wires — gas shielded
    MIG (GMAW) wires
    Murex consumables
    Pipeliner consumables
    Stainless nickel and high alloy
    Stick Electrodes — mild and low alloy steels
    Submerged arc consumables

COMPETITORS

Airgas	Kobe Steel
Charter International	KUKA
ESAB	Schumacher Electric
Illinois Tool Works	Thermadyne
Indel	

HISTORICAL FINANCIALS

Company Type: Public

Income Statement

FYE: December 31

	REVENUE ($ mil.)	NET INCOME ($ mil.)	NET PROFIT MARGIN	EMPLOYEES
12/09	1,729	49	2.8%	8,950
12/08	2,479	212	8.6%	9,329
12/07	2,281	203	8.9%	8,992
12/06	1,972	175	8.9%	8,430
12/05	1,601	122	7.6%	7,485
Annual Growth	**1.9%**	**(20.6%)**	**—**	**4.6%**

2009 Year-End Financials

Debt ratio: 8.2%
Return on equity: 4.7%
Cash ($ mil.): 388
Current ratio: 3.44
Long-term debt ($ mil.): 88
No. of shares (mil.): 43
Dividends
Yield: 2.0%
Payout: 95.6%
Market value ($ mil.): 2,277

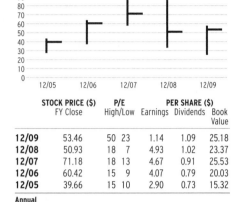

Stock History   NASDAQ (GS): LECO

	STOCK PRICE ($) FY Close	P/E High/Low	PER SHARE ($) Earnings	Dividends	Book Value
12/09	53.46	50 23	1.14	1.09	25.18
12/08	50.93	18 7	4.93	1.02	23.37
12/07	71.18	18 13	4.67	0.91	25.53
12/06	60.42	15 9	4.07	0.79	20.03
12/05	39.66	15 10	2.90	0.73	15.32
Annual Growth	**7.8%**	**— —**	**(20.8%)**	**10.5%**	**13.2%**

Lincoln National

Who better to trust with your nest egg than the company that took its name from Honest Abe? Lincoln National, which operates as Lincoln Financial Group, provides retirement planning and life insurance to individuals and employers in the form of annuities, 401(k) savings plans, and a variety of life, dental, and disability insurance products. It does business through such subsidiaries as Lincoln National Life Insurance and Lincoln Life & Annuity Company of New York. The company is also active in the investment management business, offering individual and institutional clients such financial services as pension plans, trusts, and mutual funds through its subsidiaries.

Historically, Lincoln's investment income has accounted for more of its revenues than its insurance premiums or fees. This was pretty sweet when the market was high, but as investments lost their luster beginning in 2007, Lincoln's net income suffered.

When the economic waters turned murky and cold in 2008 Lincoln Financial sought relief under the US Treasury's TARP program. As the TARP was originally structured to assist banks, Lincoln's earliest efforts were focused on making itself more eligible by acquiring regional banking company Newton Country Loan & Savings of Goodland, Indiana. The Office of Thrift Supervision now technically recognizes the company as a savings and loan holding company. However, while Lincoln Financial was still waiting for approval to participate in the Capital Purchase Programs as a bank, in 2009 the feds instead decided to extend its funds to major life insurers, including Lincoln Financial. It received approval for up to $2.5 billion of TARP funds to shore up its capital but only issued some $2.1 billion in equity, debt, and preferred stock to the Treasury.

Having secured itself to a life raft, Lincoln Financial chose to jettison several businesses in

2009 to lighten its load. To better focus on the US markets, it sold its UK retirement products and financial services subsidiary Lincoln National (UK) to Canada-based Sun Life Financial for about $300 million. It then sold its asset management subsidiary, Delaware Management Holdings, to Australian financial services firm Macquarie Group for nearly $430 million.

Its subsidiary Lincoln Financial Media owns and operates more than 10 radio stations — a legacy from its 2006 acquisition of Jefferson-Pilot. However, Lincoln's main activity is insurance and it is gradually exiting the media business by selling off assets.

HISTORY

Wilbur Wynant, a sort of Johnny Appleseed of shady fraternal benefits societies, arrived in Fort Wayne, Indiana, in 1902. He persuaded several respected businessmen and professionals to help him found the Fraternal Assurance Society of America, an assessable mutual organization in which surviving members contributed to the death benefits of deceased members. Wynant absconded within a couple of years, and the local organizers restructured the society's remains as a stock company in 1905. To clean up the organization's reputation, they obtained permission from Abraham Lincoln's son Robert to use his father's name and image.

In 1905, when the company wrote its first policy, it had three agents, including its leading executive, Arthur Hall. By 1911 the company had 106 agents. Careful risk assessment was an early hallmark of the company and allowed it to accept business that other companies rejected based on more superficial analysis.

From a very early period, the company grew through acquisitions. WWI increased claims, but not as much as the global flu epidemic that followed the war. Organic growth continued in the 1920s.

Death and disability claims increased abnormally during the Depression, and the company's underwriting became more stringent. Lincoln National used the financial turmoil of the period to buy other troubled insurers. Reinsurance became the firm's primary line until after WWII.

The company bought up other firms in the 1950s and 1960s, and in 1968 it formed holding company Lincoln National. Soon it began diversifying, buying Chicago Title and Trust (1969; sold 1985) as well as more life and reinsurance companies. Lincoln National also went into the health benefits business, setting up its own HMO and investing in EMPHESYS (which it took public in 1994, divesting the remainder of its stock in 1995).

The collapse of the real estate market in many areas nicked results in the late 1980s, and in 1990 the company accepted an infusion of cash from Dai-Ichi Mutual Life Insurance. Property/casualty results were hurt in the early 1990s by an unprecedented string of natural disasters.

With the growth of retirement savings from baby boomers hitting their 50s, the company shifted gears into wealth management. In 1995 Lincoln National expanded its investment management capacities by purchasing Delaware Management Holdings and Laurentian Financial Group. In 1997 it bought Voyageur Fund Managers, a tax-free-bond fund business. It sold its 83% interest in property/casualty firm American States Financial in 1996.

Lincoln National bought CIGNA's annuity and individual life insurance business and Aetna's

US individual life insurance operations in 1998. It reorganized that year to help it absorb these businesses, causing earnings to take a substantial hit.

In 1999, after nearly a century in the heartland, Lincoln National moved its headquarters to Philadelphia. Other transformations included the sale of its individual disability income business in 1999. In 2001 it sold its reinsurance operations to Swiss Re to re-focus on wealth and asset accumulation products and services. The reshaping continued in 2002 when the company acquired employee benefits record-keeping firm The Administrative Management Group.

Lincoln National completed a merger/acquisition of Jefferson-Pilot in early 2006. The $7.5 billion deal combined the Lincoln Financial Group with the Jefferson Pilot Financial group (the operating brand for Jefferson-Pilot Corporation) and created a new company, operating as Lincoln Financial Group. Led by management from both former organizations, the new group expanded insurance and financial products offerings and national retail and wholesale distribution platforms.

The Jefferson-Pilot purchase came with several media businesses which Lincoln National promptly deemed to be noncore. In 2008 the company sold off three television stations and a sports syndication business to Raycom Media, and it sold three radio stations to Greater Media.

EXECUTIVES

Chairman: William H. Cunningham, age 65
President, CEO, and Director; President, Lincoln National Life Insurance: Dennis R. Glass, age 60, $6,996,596 total compensation
EVP and CFO: Frederick J. (Fred) Crawford, age 46, $2,435,536 total compensation
SVP and Chief Human Resources Officer: Lisa M. Buckingham, age 44
SVP and Chief Marketing Officer: Heather C. Dzielak, age 41
SVP and General Counsel: Nicole S. Jones
VP Investor Relations: Jim Sjoreen
VP and Treasurer: Duane L. Bernt
VP and Head of IRA Strategies, Retirement Solutions: Tom McGirr
VP Profitability and Risk Management, Individual Annuity Life Insurance and Group Protection Businesses: Jeff Coutts
VP Corporate Development: Lisa Marie DeSimone
President and CEO, Lincoln Financial Distributors: Wilford H. (Will) Fuller, age 39, $4,970,315 total compensation
President, Retirement and Insurance Solutions: Mark E. Konen, age 50, $3,776,255 total compensation
President, Lincoln National Investment Company, Inc. and Delaware Management Holdings, Inc: Patrick P. (Pat) Coyne, age 46, $3,645,212 total compensation
President and CEO, Lincoln Financial Advisors: Robert W. (Bob) Dineen, age 60, $2,248,881 total compensation
President, Defined Contribution: Charles C. (Chuck) Cornelio, age 50
President and Managing Director, Lincoln National (UK): Michael Tallett-Williams, age 56
Auditors: Ernst & Young LLP

LOCATIONS

HQ: Lincoln National Corporation
150 N. Radnor Chester Rd., Radnor, PA 19807
Phone: 484-583-1400   **Fax:** 484-583-1421
Web: www.lfg.com

PRODUCTS/OPERATIONS

2009 Revenues

	$ mil.	% of total
Insurance		
Life insurance	4,293	44
Group protection	1,713	18
Retirement		
Annuities	2,301	24
Defined Contribution	926	9
Other operations	470	5
Realized losses	(1,204)	—
Total	**8,499**	**100**

2009 Revenues

	$ mil.	% of total
Net investment income	4,178	43
Insurance fees	2,922	30
Insurance premiums	2,064	22
Realized losses	(1,146)	—
Other revenues & fees	481	5
Total	**8,499**	**100**

COMPETITORS

AEGON	MetLife
AIG	Nationwide Financial
American Equity	New York Life
Investment	Northwestern Mutual
AXA	Pacific Mutual
Guardian Life	Principal Financial
The Hartford	Prudential
Hartford Life	TIAA-CREF
ING	Torchmark
John Hancock Financial	Unum Group
MassMutual	

HISTORICAL FINANCIALS

Company Type: Public

Income Statement

	ASSETS ($ mil.)	NET INCOME ($ mil.)	INCOME AS % OF ASSETS	EMPLOYEES
				FYE: December 31
12/09	177,433	(485)	—	8,208
12/08	163,136	57	0.0%	9,696
12/07	191,435	1,215	0.6%	10,870
12/06	178,494	1,316	0.7%	10,744
12/05	124,788	831	0.7%	5,259
Annual Growth	**9.2%**	**—**	**—**	**11.8%**

2009 Year-End Financials

Equity as % of assets: 6.1%	Dividends
Return on assets: —	Yield: 0.2%
Return on equity: —	Payout: —
Long-term debt ($ mil.): 5,050	Market value ($ mil.): 7,880
No. of shares (mil.): 317	Sales ($ mil.): 8,499

Stock History

NYSE: LNC

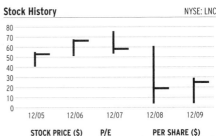

	STOCK PRICE ($) FY Close	P/E High/Low		PER SHARE ($) Earnings	Dividends	Book Value
12/09	24.88	—	—	(1.85)	0.04	36.94
12/08	18.84	273	22	0.22	1.87	25.19
12/07	58.22	17	12	4.43	1.58	37.00
12/06	66.40	13	10	5.13	1.14	38.52
12/05	53.03	12	9	4.72	1.48	20.16
Annual Growth	**(17.2%)**	**—**	**—**	**—**	**(59.5%)**	**16.4%**

Lions Gate Entertainment

Independent films are the cat's meow at Lions Gate Entertainment. The firm, which operates as Lionsgate, is the leading producer and distributor of independent films — such as the Academy Award-nominated *Precious* and the horror title *Saw IV*. It produces TV programming (including *Nurse Jackie* for Showtime Networks) through Lionsgate Television. Lionsgate also releases films under the Trimark brand and owns a library of more than 8,000 movie and 4,000 TV titles. In addition, it owns production studio Roadside Attractions. Lionsgate's significant 2003 purchase of rival Artisan Entertainment for $160 million created the industry's largest indie studio.

Lionsgate has historically released about 15 movies a year. However, during its 2010 fiscal year it scaled back by releasing approximately 10 titles due to a crowded marketplace and a desire to focus on its TV output. The company is continuing to release movies with lower production budgets that appeal to specific audiences (such as genre pictures). Its productions typically have budgets of $20 million or less. The company also spends relatively little on marketing campaigns and focuses on its home video library.

The company's 2009 film *Precious* was the subject of considerable buzz (as well as several Academy Award nominations) after Oprah Winfrey praised the film; and the company's *Saw* series is the leading horror franchise in DVD history. Despite these successes, the company is suffering losses, experiencing an overall decline in DVD sales as a result of a weakening economy, and in 2009 it cut some 8% of its workforce.

In the television market, Lionsgate produces nearly 80 hours of programming a year, which includes a variety of one-hour dramas, miniseries, and made-for-TV movies. Recent TV hits include the hour-long drama *Mad Men*, airing on AMC, and the Showtime series *Weeds*. The company in 2009 formed a joint venture with Viacom and Metro-Goldwyn-Mayer to launch a pay-TV network called EPIX to directly compete with Showtime, HBO, and Starz. And in 2010 it partnered with Saban Capital Group to manage Tiger Gate, an operator of pay TV channels and a distributor of TV programming and action and horror films across Asia.

In 2009 Lionsgate boosted its Media Network holdings when it acquired the TV Guide Network and TV Guide Online (TVGuide.com) from Macrovision Solutions Corp. for $255 million. However, later that year Lionsgate sold a 49% stake in the TV Guide Network and TV Guide Online to One Equity Partners (the private equity investment arm of JPMorgan Chase) and media entrepreneur Allen Shapiro.

In 2010 Carl Icahn became the company's largest shareholder, raising his stake from about 18% to more than 30%, in order to exert more control over the studio.

HISTORY

Investment banker Frank Giustra founded Lions Gate Entertainment in 1997, naming the company after a landmark Vancouver bridge. He wasted little time bringing the fledgling film company up to speed. By year's end Giustra had acquired 30-year-old Canadian film producer and distributor Cinepix Film Properties (CFP), TV production unit Mandalay Television, and studio complex North Shore Studios (renamed Lions Gate Studios), and had taken Lions Gate public on the Toronto Stock Exchange.

CFP was renamed Lions Gate Films the following year. The company also took its 45% stake in Mandalay Pictures in 1998 (the deal that requires Lions Gate to absorb 100% of Mandalay's losses) and acquired its stake in Montreal-based animation house CinéGroupe. In 1999 Lions Gate bought the rights to *Affliction* and *Gods and Monsters* for US distribution; the two films received a total of five Oscar nominations and put the company on the map as a player in independent cinema.

Mandalay chairman Peter Guber reacquired Mandalay Television from Lions Gate in 1999 (the company has since established its own TV unit). The following year Giustra stepped down as CEO (he remained as chairman) and was replaced by former Sony Pictures executive Jon Feltheimer, who focused on assembling a library of film and TV titles. Lions Gate Entertainment acquired Trimark Holdings for $50 million in 2000, giving the studio titles such as *Beautiful People* and *Rules of Attraction*, as well as the licensing rights to *Saturday Night Live*.

In 2001 the company bought a 75% equity stake in Christal Films Distribution, a distributor of French and English films. That year Lions Gate Entertainment declined a buyout offer from Artisan Entertainment. The two companies then joined together to acquire distribution rights to the TV and film library of troubled Kushner-Locke. Also that year Lions Gate's *Monster's Ball* earned Halle Barry an Oscar for best actress.

Giustra sold his share of the company in 2002, and Lions Gate operations expanded from Canada to the Los Angeles area. The following year company president Andre Link added the chairman title to his name, replacing Giustra.

In 2003 the company dramatically increased the size of its film and TV library with purchase of Artisan Entertainment, adding an extensive 6,000-title library to its holdings and creating the industry's last remaining truly independent studio (not owned by a major media conglomerate like Time Warner or Disney). It announced 150 job cuts the day after closing the Artisan acquisition.

Lions Gate won big in 2004 when it stepped up to help distribute Michael Moore's lucrative Bush-bashing film *Fahrenheit 9/11* after Disney refused to release the controversial Miramax documentary. (Lions Gate released the film in conjunction with IFC Entertainment and Bob and Harvey Weinstein.)

In 2005 the company announced that it would begin operating under the new name, Lionsgate, meant to represent a unified media company. Its official legal name remains unchanged. Also that year the studio scored another hit with *Crash*, which won the Academy Award for Best Picture.

Jon Feltheimer, CEO since 2000, took on the co-chairman mantle in 2005. The following year the company sold Lions Gate Studios, its Vancouver studios facilities, which included eight sound stages occupying nearly 14 acres. In 2007 it sold its 19% stake in Image Entertainment as part of a $130 million buyout of that company by a group led by film financier David Bergstein. Also that year Lionsgate acquired independent film producer, financier, and distributor Mandate Pictures.

EXECUTIVES

Co-Chairman and CEO: Jon Feltheimer, age 58, $4,116,666 total compensation
Co-Chairman: Harald H. Ludwig, age 55
Vice Chairman: Michael Burns, age 51, $3,621,298 total compensation
President and Co-COO: Steven (Steve) Beeks, age 53, $2,048,159 total compensation
Co-COO; President, Motion Picture Group; CEO, Mandate Pictures: Joseph (Joe) Drake, age 49, $1,708,167 total compensation
CFO and Principal Accounting Officer: James (Jim) Keegan, age 52, $659,086 total compensation
EVP Corporate Operations and General Counsel: Wayne Levin, age 47
EVP and General Sales Manager, Theatrical Domestic Distribution: David Spitz
EVP Motion Picture Production: Lisa Ellzey
EVP Family Home Entertainment and Marketing: Anne Parducci
EVP Post Production and Delivery Services: Bob Wenokur
EVP Original Programming and Development, EPIX: Laverne McKinnon
EVP Corporate Development: Marni Wieshofer, age 47
EVP Business and Legal Affairs: Jim Gladstone
EVP Family Entertainment: Ken Katsumoto
EVP Television and Distribution: Jon Ferro
SVP Motion Picture Production: John Sacchi
SVP Marketing, Home Entertainment: Michael Rathauser
SVP Television Marketing: Priscilla Pesci
SVP Investor Relations and Executive Communications: Peter D. Wilkes
Co-President, Theatrical Marketing: Tim Palen
Co-President, Theatrical Marketing: Sarah Greenberg
President, International Film Sales: Stephanie Denton
President, Theatrical Distribution: Steve Rothenberg
President, TV Programming and Production: Kevin Beggs
President, Music and Publishing: Jay Faires
Auditors: Ernst & Young LLP

LOCATIONS

HQ: Lions Gate Entertainment Corp.
2700 Colorado Ave., Santa Monica, CA 90404
Phone: 310-449-9200   **Fax:** 310-255-3870
Web: www.lionsgatefilms.com

2010 Sales

	$ mil.	% of total
US	1,265.4	80
Canada	71.4	5
Other countries	246.9	15
Total	**1,583.7**	**100**

PRODUCTS/OPERATIONS

2010 Sales

	$ mil.	% of total
Motion Pictures	1,119.2	71
Television Production	350.9	22
Media Networks	113.6	7
Total	**1,583.7**	**100**

HISTORICAL FINANCIALS

Company Type: Public

Income Statement

FYE: March 31

	REVENUE ($ mil.)	NET INCOME ($ mil.)	NET PROFIT MARGIN	EMPLOYEES
3/10	1,584	(20)	—	497
3/09	1,466	(163)	—	802
3/08	1,361	(74)	—	444
3/07	977	28	2.8%	400
3/06	951	6	0.6%	354
Annual Growth	13.6%	—	—	8.9%

2010 Year-End Financials

Debt ratio: 825.9%
Return on equity: —
Cash ($ mil.): 91
Current ratio: 0.44
Long-term debt ($ mil.): 445

No. of shares (mil.): 136
Dividends
  Yield: —
  Payout: —
Market value ($ mil.): 850

Stock History

NYSE: LGF

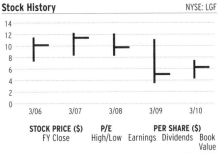

	STOCK PRICE ($) FY Close	P/E High/Low	PER SHARE ($) Earnings	Dividends	Book Value
3/10	6.24	— —	(0.17)	—	0.40
3/09	5.05	— —	(1.40)	—	(0.06)
3/08	9.75	— —	(0.62)	—	1.38
3/07	11.42	48 34	0.25	—	1.82
3/06	10.15	189 124	0.06	—	1.10
Annual Growth	(11.5%)	— —	—	—	(22.5%)

Live Nation Entertainment

Live Nation Entertainment holds center stage as the world's largest ticket seller and promoter of live entertainment. In 2010 the company significantly expanded its ticketing services with the purchase of Ticketmaster Entertainment. The deal created a powerful live-music conglomerate. The firm also owns or operates more than 140 venues in North America and Europe. Annually, more than 52 million people attend some 22,000 Live Nation events. Live Nation also owns House of Blues venues through HOB Entertainment. In addition, through deals with pop stars such as Madonna and U2, Live Nation owns a stake in various artists' music, including albums, tours, and merchandise.

The combination of Live Nation and Ticketmaster established a giant in the music industry that controls concert promotion, ticketing services, and artist management, all under one roof. In order to address concerns that the deal would inhibit competition, the two companies waited for months to get clearance from the Justice Department's antitrust division. They did so only after agreeing to three major demands. First,

Live Nation Entertainment agreed to divest a subsidiary called Paciolan that provides software for venue operators to sell their own tickets. Next, Live Nation agreed to license its ticketing software to Anschutz Company subsidiary Anschutz Entertainment for five years. The licensing deal allows Anschutz's AEG Live, a rival concert promoter, to create a competing ticket service. Finally, Live Nation agreed not to retaliate against venue owners who leave the company to sign up with rival services.

Despite these concessions, critics remain apprehensive that major artists, such as the Eagles, Christina Aguilera, Guns N Roses, and Aerosmith, could have their merchandising, ticketing, and management under the control of the same company that owns the venues they perform in. The purchase of Ticketmaster creates an even more dominant force in the concert business, as ticket sales remain strong even as record sales continue to decline, and Live Nation promotes shows or tours for approximately 2,000 artists globally.

The company had already begun expanding beyond staging live events when it lured away Madonna from her deal with traditional record label Warner Bros. Records in 2007. The 10-year pact stunned the music business, giving Madonna a mix of cash and stock worth some $120 million in exchange for the rights to sell three studio albums, produce and promote concert tours, sell merchandise, and license her image. Live Nation in 2008 signed similar deals with Irish rock band U2 and hip-hop star Jay-Z. Live Nation's strategy to grow the music business also included the purchase of concert T-shirt seller Signatures Network, as well as the acquisitions of UltraStar Entertainment and MusicToday, which run fan-club and e-commerce websites for musicians.

HISTORY

Robert Sillerman began his career teaching advertisers how to reach young consumers. He started investing in radio and TV stations and founded SFX Broadcasting (named for a scrambling of his initials) in 1992. In early 1997 the firm entered the live entertainment field with the formation of SFX Concerts and the purchase of concert promoter Delsener/Slater.

When SFX Broadcasting agreed to be bought in 1997 by Capstar Broadcasting, 87% controlled by investment firm Hicks, Muse, Tate & Furst (now HM Capital), SFX Entertainment was formed to house the live entertainment operations (it was spun off in 1998). In 1998 the company continued its rapid acquisition rate with the purchases of sports marketing and management team FAME, New England concert promoter Don Law, and national concert producer PACE Entertainment.

In 1999 the company bought concert promoter The Cellar Door Companies (which almost doubled SFX's size), sports marketing firm Integrated Sports International, sporting event management company The Marquee Group, sports talent agency Hendricks Management, 50% of urban-music producer A.H. Enterprises, and troubled theatrical producer Livent. SFX also made its first foray abroad through its purchase of Apollo Leisure, a UK-based live entertainment firm. The company rolled all of its sports talent and marketing businesses into a new division, SFX Sports Group, that year.

In 2000 SFX jumped on the other side of the acquisition train when it was bought by radio station owner Clear Channel Communications for about $4 billion. Sillerman stepped down as chairman and CEO and was replaced by Clear Channel EVP Brian Becker. Later that year SFX acquired Philadelphia-based concert promoter and venue operator Electric Factory Concerts; Core Audience Entertainment, Canada's second-largest concert promoter and events marketer; and the Cotter Group, a North Carolina-based motorsports marketing agency.

In 2001 SFX acquired a majority interest in the International Hot Rod Association. It also bought professional golf talent agency Signature Sports Group. Later that year the company changed its name to Clear Channel Entertainment.

While operating as Clear Channel Entertainment, Live Nation spent nearly $2 billion on acquisitions (Pace Entertainment, Livent), almost single-handedly consolidating the live entertainment industry.

Before being spun off in 2005, the company changed its name to Live Nation. Also that year Randall Mays became chairman and Michael Rapino replaced Becker as CEO. As part of the Clear Channel spinoff, the company relocated from Houston to headquarters in tony Beverly Hills. It trimmed the fat by shutting down operating divisions such as museum exhibitions and music publishing (and laying off about 400 employees in the process).

In 2006 the company acquired rival HOB Entertainment. Live Nation used the acquisition to expand its presence in the midsized venue business and fill in geographic gaps in its existing amphitheater network. As part of the deal, it gained high-profile House of Blues-branded music venues such as San Francisco's Fillmore Auditorium, Jones Beach in New York, and London's Apollo Theatre and Wembley Arena.

In 2008 the company divested itself of its North American theatrical assets. Later that year the company signed pacts with U2 and Jay-Z. Michael Cohl, chairman and Live Nation Artists chief who spearheaded the deals, later resigned over conflicts with CEO Rapino.

EXECUTIVES

Chairman: Barry Diller, age 68
Executive Chairman: Irving Azoff, age 61
President, CEO, and Director: Michael (Mike) Rapino, age 44, $6,676,223 total compensation
EVP and CFO: Kathy Willard, age 43, $1,133,330 total compensation
EVP and General Manager, LiveNation.com: Noah T. Maffitt
EVP, Mergers and Acquisitions and Strategic Finance: John Hopmans, age 51
EVP, Business Development and Strategy, Ticketing: Greg Bettinelli
SVP, Touring: Bruce Kapp
General Counsel and Secretary: Michael G. Rowles, age 44, $1,067,475 total compensation
Chief Accounting Officer: Brian Capo, age 43
CEO, Global Music: Jason Garner, age 37, $2,658,074 total compensation
CEO, International Music: Alan Ridgeway, age 43, $636,352 total compensation
CEO, TicketsNow.com and Ticketmaster: Ronald (Ron) Bension
CEO, Ticketing: Nathan Hubbard, age 34
CEO, Global Touring; Chairman, Global Music: Arthur Fogel, age 56
President, Touring, Live Nation International Music: Phil Bowdery
President, Talent, Live Nation International Music: Shane Bourbonnais

President, Arenas: Michael R. (Mike) Evans
President, Music Sales, North America: Maureen Ford
President, North American Alliances: Russell Wallach
President, Marketing, Artist Marketing Products: Faisel Durrani, age 44
President and Chief Creative Officer, Merchandising; CEO and Creative Director, TRUNK: Brad Beckerman
Auditors: Ernst & Young LLP

LOCATIONS

HQ: Live Nation Entertainment, Inc.
9348 Civic Center Dr., Beverly Hills, CA 90210
Phone: 310-867-7000   **Fax:** 310-867-7001
Web: www.livenation.com

PRODUCTS/OPERATIONS

2009 Sales

	$ mil.	% of total
North American Music	2,568	61
International Music	1,534	37
Ticketing & other	79	2
Total	**4,181**	**100**

Selected Artist Rights Agreements
U2
Jay-Z
Madonna
Nickelback
Shakira

Selected Concerts
Aerosmith
Jimmy Buffett
Cher
Kenny Chesney
Dave Matthews Band
Genesis
Josh Groban
Toby Keith
Linkin Park
Madonna
Bette Midler
The Police
The Rolling Stones
Barbra Streisand
Sting
Van Halen
The Who

Selected Music Venues
Cynthia Woods Mitchell Pavilion (Houston)
Electric Factory (Philadelphia)
House of Blues Chicago
The Fillmore (San Francisco)
The Fillmore Detroit
Roseland Ballroom (New York)
Verizon Wireless Amphitheatre (Los Angeles)

COMPETITORS

Anschutz Entertainment
Brillstein
CAA
Dodger Properties
Feld Entertainment
Gaylord Entertainment
IMG
International Creative Management
Jujamcyn Theaters
Madison Square Garden
Nederlander Producing Company
Octagon
On Stage Entertainment
Palace Sports & Entertainment
Shubert Organization
SMG Management
TBA Global
United Talent
Universal Music Group
Warner Music
Westwood One
William Morris Endeavor Entertainment

HISTORICAL FINANCIALS

Company Type: Public

Income Statement

FYE: December 31

	REVENUE ($ mil.)	NET INCOME ($ mil.)	NET PROFIT MARGIN	EMPLOYEES
12/09	4,181	(50)	—	4,300
12/08	4,167	(232)	—	4,700
12/07	4,185	(12)	—	4,700
12/06	3,692	(31)	—	4,400
12/05	2,937	(131)	—	3,000
Annual Growth	**9.2%**	**—**	**—**	**9.4%**

2009 Year-End Financials

Debt ratio: 107.2%
Return on equity: —
Cash ($ mil.): 237
Current ratio: 0.95
Long-term debt ($ mil.): 699

No. of shares (mil.): 173
Dividends
  Yield: —
  Payout: —
Market value ($ mil.): 1,471

Stock History

NYSE: LYV

	STOCK PRICE ($) FY Close	P/E High/Low		Earnings	PER SHARE ($) Dividends	Book Value
12/09	8.51	—	—	(0.73)	—	3.77
12/08	5.74	—	—	(3.04)	—	3.60
12/07	14.52	—	—	(0.17)	—	5.02
12/06	22.40	—	—	(0.48)	—	3.69
12/05	13.10	—	—	(1.96)	—	3.68
Annual Growth	**(10.2%)**	**—**	**—**	**—**	**—**	**0.6%**

Liz Claiborne

Liz Claiborne is dressed for success as a leading US seller of clothes and accessories for women. It markets its products as designer items but prices them for a broader market. Its brands — including Liz & Co., Concepts by Claiborne, kate spade, Juicy Couture, and Lucky — are sold worldwide in department stores, more than 450 specialty stores, about 360 outlets, and more than a handful of branded websites. Liz Claiborne also makes men's clothing and licenses its name for shoes, sunglasses, swimwear, formalwear, home furnishings, and stationery.

The company in 2010 rolled out a new distribution strategy for a handful of its collections, limiting availability of the Liz Claiborne and Claiborne brands to J. C. Penney stores and the New York label to the QVC network. To reduce costs, the apparel firm has shuttered eight distribution centers since 2007. Liz Claiborne has also agreed to sell 38 of its retail stores across Canada to Laura Canada in 2010.

In an additional move, in 2010 the company announced its exit from its 87 Liz Claiborne-branded outlet stores in the US and Puerto Rico. The stores were originally designed to handle clearance for many of its brands. The company feels this is an outdated venue given the changes it has made in its portfolio and business strategy.

In 2008 the company cut jobs, repurposed its stores, and began catering to its top brands. The move involved purging some 8% of its global workforce, or 700 positions, as well as shuttering or rebranding about 20 retail locations. Most staff reductions involved senior-level positions.

Liz Claiborne has been pulling the plug on retail formats that don't have the potential to support a minimum of 100 stores and trimming its stable of brands. The company sold eight of its 16 brands, including Ellen Tracy and prAna men's and women's lines. Other brands sold include Laundry By Design and C&C California, which was acquired by Perry Ellis International in February 2008. The company also closed its remaining 54 Sigrid Olsen stores in 2008.

In a major move to revitalize its name, the company hired high-fashion designer Isaac Mizrahi to design and market Liz Claiborne apparel and accessories. His Liz products hit stores in early 2009.

The firm has a history of increasing its product offerings by licensing or acquiring new brands. In December 2006 the apparel giant acquired handbag and accessories maker kate spade from Neiman Marcus for some $124 million. The purchase gave Liz Claiborne a strong foothold in the handbag business, which is one of the hottest segments of the accessories sector.

The top job at the company was assumed by drug industry veteran William McComb, formerly with Johnson & Johnson, who succeeded retiring CEO Paul Charron in November 2006.

HISTORY

In 1975 Liz Claiborne, a dress designer in Jonathan Logan's Youth Guild division, had a vision of stylish, sporty, affordable clothes for working women. Unable to sell the concept to her employer, Claiborne quit and, with husband Arthur Ortenberg and partners Jerome Chazen and Leonard Boxer, founded Liz Claiborne in 1976 with $250,000.

Born just as women were beginning to flood the workforce, Liz Claiborne became an immediate success by rescuing them from drab business suits. Making money its first year, Liz Claiborne remained the fastest-growing, most profitable US apparel maker in the 1980s. In 1981 it went public and by 1986 had made the *FORTUNE* 500, with sales topping $800 million.

The company expanded into men's clothing (Claiborne, 1985), cosmetics (Liz Claiborne, a 1986 joint venture with Avon; in 1988 it acquired full rights to the line), women's plus sizes (Elisabeth, 1989), and knit sportswear (Liz & Co., 1989). Higher-priced sportswear by in-house designer Dana Buchman was introduced in 1987. Liz Claiborne moved into retailing the following year, opening First Issue boutiques.

Claiborne and Ortenberg began withdrawing from the business side in 1989 and left the board the next year. About this time the retail business began to slow down as a recession loomed. In addition, baby boomers' clothing tastes began to shift toward comfort and versatility.

Liz Claiborne acquired the Crazy Horse, Russ Togs, Villager, and Red Horse brand names in 1992 and took over 16 outlet stores from bankrupt Russ Togs.

In response to slow sales, Liz Claiborne brought in VF veteran Paul Charron as COO. Named CEO in 1995, Charron closed the First Issue stores and moved production from US union plants to foreign factories. In 1996, as sales picked up, the company began selling its repositioned First Issue line through Sears. It launched Emma James (moderately priced career separates) in 1997.

In response to sagging sales, the company took a $27 million charge in 1998 to close 30 retail stores and cut 400 jobs.

Charron set out to give Liz Claiborne a broader appeal. In 1999 the company bought trendy Laundry (women's sportswear and dresses), an 85% stake in women's sportswear firm Segrets (Sigrid Olsen), teen-targeted Lucky Brand Dungarees, and a minority stake in Kenneth Cole Productions.

By 2000 about 20% of Liz Claiborne's sales came from non-Liz lines. Increasing that percentage even further, the company bought fashion jeweler Monet Group for about $40 million.

In 2003 the company bought Travis Jeans (now named Juicy Couture), maker of Juicy Couture upscale casualwear and jeans.

In 2005 and 2006 the firm extended its reach across North America. It acquired California-inspired men's and women's apparel maker C&C California. In 2006 Liz Claiborne picked up Vancouver, Canada-based Westcoast Contempo Fashions Limited and Mac and Jac Holdings Limited.

Company namesake Liz Claiborne died at the age of 78 in mid-2007.

Trimming its stable of brands, Liz Claiborne sold the Laundry By Design and C&C California labels to Perry Ellis International in February 2008. It also sold prAna to that company's management in April 2008.

In 2008 the company sold the Enyce brand to Sean "Diddy" Combs, the music artist and fashion designer who runs Sean John Clothing.

EXECUTIVES

Chairman: Kay Koplovitz, age 66
CEO and Director: William L. McComb, age 47, $3,487,322 total compensation
EVP and CFO: Andrew C. (Andy) Warren, age 43, $1,589,109 total compensation
SVP, Chief Legal Officer, General Counsel, and Secretary: Nicholas Rubino, age 48, $829,055 total compensation
SVP Global Sourcing and Operations: Peter Warner, $1,207,755 total compensation
SVP and Chief Human Resources Officer: Lisa Piovano Machacek
SVP Real Estate and Construction: Trent Merrill
SVP and CIO: Evon L. Jones, age 46
SVP Corporate Communications and Brand Services: Jane Randel
Chief Creative Officer: Timothy (Tim) Gunn
VP, Corporate Controller, and Chief Accounting Officer: Elaine H. Goodell
CEO, Liz Claiborne Canada: Walter LaMothe
CEO, Lucky Brand Jeans: David M. (Dave) DeMattei, age 53
CEO, Mexx Worldwide: Thomas J. Grote, age 47
Co-President and Creative Director, Kate Spade: Deborah J. Lloyd
Co-President and COO, Kate Spade: Craig Leavitt
President, Special Sales: Mary Lee Gallagher
President, Juicy Couture: Edgar O. Huber
Director, Investor Relations: Elizabeth Schwartz
Auditors: Deloitte & Touche LLP

LOCATIONS

HQ: Liz Claiborne, Inc.
1441 Broadway, New York, NY 10018
Phone: 212-354-4900   **Fax:** 212-626-3416
Web: www.lizclaiborneinc.com

2009 Sales

	$ mil.	% of total
Domestic-based direct brands	1,120.7	37
Partnered brands	1,059.3	35
International-based direct brands	831.9	28
Total	**3,011.9**	**100**

2009 Sales

	$ mil.	% of total
Domestic	2,018.1	67
International	993.8	33
Total	**3,011.9**	**100**

PRODUCTS/OPERATIONS

2009 US Specialty Retail Stores

	No.
Lucky Brand Jeans	182
Juicy Couture	65
kate spade	36
Jack Spade	2
Total	**285**

2009 Foreign Specialty Retail Stores

	No.
Mexx Europe	118
Mexx Canada	39
Lucky Brand Canada	12
Monet Europe	3
Juicy Couture Europe	1
Total	**173**

2009 US Outlet Stores

	No.
Liz Claiborne	92
Lucky Brand	46
Juicy Couture	33
kate spade	29
DKNY Jeans	14
Kensie	1
Total	**215**

2009 Foreign Outlet Stores

	No.
Mexx Canada	58
Liz Claiborne Canada	47
Mexx Europe	43
Total	**148**

2009 Foreign Concession Stores

	No.
Mexx Jewelry	270
Mexx Europe	206
Liz Claiborne Apparel	90
Total	**566**

COMPETITORS

AnnTaylor	Jones Apparel
BCBG Max Azria Group	Lands' End
bebe stores	Limited Brands
Benetton	Marc Jacobs International
Bernard Chaus	michael kors
Calvin Klein	Nautica Apparel
Chico's FAS	NEXT plc
Coach, Inc.	Polo Ralph Lauren
Cole Haan	Roc Apparel
Diesel SpA	Sean John
Donna Karan	St. John Knits
Esprit Holdings	Talbots
French Connection	Tommy Hilfiger
The Gap	Tory Burch
Guess?	True Religion Apparel
H&M	Urban Outfitters
Inditex	Warnaco Group
J. Crew	Zara
J. Jill Group	

HISTORICAL FINANCIALS

Company Type: Public

Income Statement
FYE: Saturday nearest December 31

	REVENUE ($ mil.)	NET INCOME ($ mil.)	NET PROFIT MARGIN	EMPLOYEES
12/09	3,012	(306)	—	11,500
12/08	3,985	(952)	—	15,000
12/07	4,577	(373)	—	16,500
12/06	4,994	255	5.1%	17,000
12/05	4,848	317	6.5%	15,400
Annual Growth	(11.2%)	—	—	(7.0%)

2009 Year-End Financials

Debt ratio: 238.4%
Return on equity: —
Cash ($ mil.): 20
Current ratio: 1.38
Long-term debt ($ mil.): 516

No. of shares (mil.): 94
Dividends
Yield: 0.0%
Payout: —
Market value ($ mil.): 532

Stock History
NYSE: LIZ

	STOCK PRICE ($) FY Close	P/E High/Low	PER SHARE ($) Earnings	Dividends	Book Value
12/09	5.63	— —	(3.26)	0.00	2.29
12/08	2.60	— —	(10.17)	0.23	5.33
12/07	20.35	— —	(3.74)	0.23	16.04
12/06	43.46	18 14	2.46	0.23	22.54
12/05	35.82	15 11	2.94	0.23	21.20
Annual Growth	(37.0%)	— —	—	—	(42.7%)

Lockheed Martin

Lockheed Martin takes flight in times of crisis — the company is one of the world's top military contractors (along with Boeing and Northrop Grumman). Lockheed is firmly on the defense/government side of the aerospace industry; in fact, the US government accounts for about 85% of sales. This reliance on the US government is a double-edged sword: Lockheed can largely avoid turbulence in the commercial aerospace sector, but the company is vulnerable to military spending cuts. The Electronic Systems and Information Systems & Global Services segments account for more than half of Lockheed's sales.

Its business segments include Aeronautics, which makes the F-16 and F-22 fighters, the F-35 Joint Strike Fighter (Lightning II), and the C-130 family of tactical airlifters; Electronic Systems, encompassing everything from missiles and submarine warfare systems to homeland security systems, radar, and postal automation systems; Space Systems, which supplies satellites, strategic and defensive missiles, and space transportation systems (including the Space Shuttle); and Information Systems & Global Services, which

provides IT services, mission systems, surveillance systems, and command, control, and communication systems.

The conflicts in Afghanistan and Iraq, along with increased spending on homeland security, have buoyed the company's sales, but looming cuts in some defense programs may affect some of Lockheed's largest programs. A spending freeze called for in the budget could impact IT and other managed services that the company provides to non-DoD government agencies, such as the Social Security Administration, the National Archives, the Library of Congress, and the Departments of Energy, Justice, Health and Human Services, and Transportation.

The company announced plans in 2010 to team up with Sikorsky to build an upgraded version of the UH-60 Black Hawk for the US Air Force. Sikorsky would act as the primary contractor for the project and Lockheed Martin would integrate combat equipment and mission systems.

During 2009 the DoD terminated two significant Lockheed programs: the VH-71 Presidential Helicopter Replacement and the Transformational Communications Satellite (TSAT) and TSAT Mission Operations System contracts. While DoD priorities may change Lockheed priorities to some extent, the company's strategy is to focus on aligning its businesses with what it considers to be enduring national security and critical mission initiatives.

Lockheed is the prime contractor for the US military's two most recent jet fighters, the $200 billion F-35 Lightning II (formerly called the Joint Strike Fighter) program and the F-22 Raptor. The Raptor program will be discontinued after delivery of the 187 aircraft on order, estimated to be completed in 2012.

The company teamed up with rivals Northrop Grumman and Alliant Techsystems in 2008 to develop multi-role weapons for Lockheed's F-22 Raptor and F-35 Lightning II. The partnership is intended to address a void the companies see in the weapons market for the aircraft. They plan to pool their weapons technologies in order to stave off potential competitors.

HISTORY

Brothers Allan and Malcolm Loughead (pronounced "Lockheed") joined Fred Keeler in 1926 to form Lockheed Aircraft. John Northrop (who later founded Northrop Corporation) designed Lockheed's first airplane, the Vega (flown by Amelia Earhart).

Robert Gross, Carl Squier, and Lloyd Stearman bought Lockheed in 1932. The company produced such aviation classics as the P-38 Lightning fighter, the U-2 spy plane, and the SR-71 Blackbird spy plane. It also produced submarine-launched ballistic missiles (Polaris, 1958), military transports (C-5 Galaxy, 1968), and the L-1011 TriStar airliner (1971).

Lockheed suffered from the cancellation of its Cheyenne attack helicopter, the C-5A cost-overrun scandal, and financial problems with the L-1011. Government loans saved the firm from bankruptcy in 1971.

In the late 1970s Lockheed was at the center of a corporate bribery scandal that overturned governments in Japan and Italy and led to tougher US anti-bribery laws. During the 1970s

and 1980s, Lockheed developed the Hubble Space Telescope and the F-117A stealth fighter. Lockheed merged with Martin Marietta in 1995 to form Lockheed Martin.

Glenn Martin started Martin Marietta in 1917. Martin Marietta made the first US-built bombers, as well as military and commercial flying boats. During the 1950s Martin Marietta made missiles, electronics, and nuclear systems. In 1961 it merged with American-Marietta Company (construction materials and chemical products).

In 1996 Lockheed Martin sold its Defense Systems and Armament Systems units to General Dynamics and bought most of Loral Corporation (advanced electronics). In 1997 it partly spun off 10 noncore technology units as L-3 Communications Holdings. In 1999 it acquired a 49% stake in COMSAT, a satellite network company that is the centerpiece of Lockheed Martin's communications business.

A series of launch failures in 1999 destroyed about $4 billion in rockets and payloads and led to an inquiry that blamed poor management oversight and quality-control problems.

In 2000 the Pentagon bailed out Lockheed Martin by agreeing to buy 24 C-130J transports. The company also won a $3.97 billion contract from the Pentagon to develop the Theater High-Altitude Area Defense (THAAD) anti-missile defense system. Lockheed sold some defense electronics units, including its Sanders unit (aerial electronic warfare and countermeasure systems), to UK-based BAE SYSTEMS for around $1.67 billion; in a separate deal it also sold its Lockheed Martin Control Systems unit to BAE. That year Lockheed Martin purchased the 51% of COMSAT it didn't already own.

In 2001 Lockheed Martin (along with TRW) was awarded a $2.7 billion contract for the US military's next-generation communications satellite system. In 2002 the company was awarded a $12.7 billion US defense contract (spread out over 23 years) to provide support work for single-seat F-16s flown by 16 different countries.

In 2005 the US Navy selected Lockheed (prime contractor) and AgustaWestland to build a new fleet of 23 Presidential Marine One helicopters in a deal worth about $6.1 billion. In 2006 NASA awarded the company with the coveted Orion manned lunar spaceship contract. Orion was slated to be NASA's next generation of manned spacecraft and to eventually replace the space shuttle.

EXECUTIVES

Chairman and CEO: Robert J. Stevens, age 58, $22,996,764 total compensation
President and COO: Christopher E. Kubasik, age 48, $9,053,587 total compensation
EVP and CFO: Bruce L. Tanner, age 50, $6,998,254 total compensation
EVP Electronic Systems: Marillyn A. Hewson, age 56
EVP Aeronautics: Ralph D. Heath, age 61, $7,698,190 total compensation
EVP Information Systems and Global Services: Linda R. Gooden, age 56, $5,454,383 total compensation
EVP Space Systems: Joanne M. Maguire, age 55
Deputy EVP Information Systems and Global Services: William L. Graham, age 59
SVP and General Counsel: Maryanne R. Lavan, age 51
SVP Human Resources: John T. Lucas, age 49
SVP and CTO: Ray O. Johnson
VP Mergers and Acquisitions: Jeffery D. MacLauchlan
VP Solar Energy Programs: Chris Myers
VP Accounting: Mark R. Bostic, age 53
VP and Controller: Christopher (Chris) Gregoire, age 40

President, Information Systems and Global Solutions–Defense: Gerry Fasano
President, Maritime Systems and Sensors (MS2): Orlando P. Carvalho, age 51
President, PAE: Dell L. Dailey
President, Simulation, Training and Support: Dale Bennett
Chief Executive, United Arab Emirates: Charles (Willy) Moore
CEO Lockheed Martin UK Holdings: Stephen R. Ball
Auditors: Ernst & Young LLP

LOCATIONS

HQ: Lockheed Martin Corporation
6801 Rockledge Dr., Bethesda, MD 20817
Phone: 301-897-6000   **Fax:** 301-897-6704
Web: www.lockheedmartin.com

2009 Sales

	$ mil.	% of total
US	38,689	86
Other countries	6,500	14
Total	**45,189**	**100**

PRODUCTS/OPERATIONS

2009 Sales

	$ mil.	% of total
Electronic Systems	12,204	27
Aeronautics	12,201	27
Information Systems & Global Services	12,130	27
Space Systems	8,654	19
Total	**45,189**	**100**

2009 Sales by Customer

	$ mil.	% of total
US government	38,414	85
Foreign governments	5,841	13
Commercial & other	934	2
Total	**45,189**	**100**

Selected Products and Services

Electronic Systems
Advanced aviation management
Air and theater missile defense systems
Anti-submarine and undersea warfare systems
Avionics and ground combat vehicle integration
Homeland security systems
Missiles and fire control systems
Platform integration systems
Postal automation systems
Radars
Security and information technology solutions
Simulation and training systems
Surface ship and submarine combat systems
Surveillance and reconnaissance systems

Aeronautics
C-5 (strategic airlift aircraft)
C-130J (tactical airlift aircraft)
F-2 (Japanese combat aircraft)
F-16 (multi-role fighter)
F-22 (air-superiority fighter)
F-35 Joint Strike Fighter (next-generation multi-role fighter)
Special mission and reconaissance aircraft (S-3 Viking, U-2, P-3 Orion)
T-50 (Korean advanced trainer)

Information Systems & Global Services
Aircraft and engine maintenance and modification services
Application development
Command, control, and communication systems
Computer system design and service
Engineering, science, and information services for NASA
Engineering, science, and technology services
Enterprise solutions
Government technology services
Information technology integration and management
Intelligence
Launch, mission, and analysis services for military, classified, and commercial satellites
Nuclear operations and materials management (Oak Ridge, Tennessee, and other locations)
Operation, maintenance, training, and logistics support for military, homeland security, and civilian systems
Surveillance
Space Systems
Airborne defense systems
Defensive missiles
Missile launch vehicles
Satellites (for commercial and government use)
Satellite launch services
Strategic missiles

COMPETITORS

Alliant Techsystems
Arianespace
BAE SYSTEMS
Boeing
CACI International
DynCorp International
EADS
Finmeccanica
General Dynamics
Goodrich Corp.
Herley Industries
Honeywell International
ITT Corp.
L-3 Communications
Northrop Grumman
Orbital Sciences
Raytheon
Saab AB
SAFRAN
SAIC
Textron
Thales
United Technologies
URS

HISTORICAL FINANCIALS

Company Type: Public

Income Statement

FYE: December 31

	REVENUE ($ mil.)	NET INCOME ($ mil.)	NET PROFIT MARGIN	EMPLOYEES
12/09	45,189	3,024	6.7%	140,000
12/08	42,731	3,217	7.5%	146,000
12/07	41,862	3,033	7.2%	140,000
12/06	39,620	2,529	6.4%	140,000
12/05	37,213	1,825	4.9%	135,000
Annual Growth	**5.0%**	**13.5%**	**—**	**0.9%**

2009 Year-End Financials

Debt ratio: 122.4%
Return on equity: 86.5%
Cash ($ mil.): 2,391
Current ratio: 1.17
Long-term debt ($ mil.): 5,052
No. of shares (mil.): 362
Dividends
  Yield: 3.1%
  Payout: 30.1%
Market value ($ mil.): 27,314

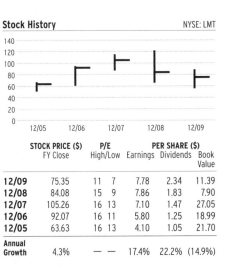

Stock History   NYSE: LMT

	STOCK PRICE ($) FY Close	P/E High/Low	Earnings	Dividends	Book Value
12/09	75.35	11 7	7.78	2.34	11.39
12/08	84.08	15 9	7.86	1.83	7.90
12/07	105.26	16 13	7.10	1.47	27.05
12/06	92.07	16 11	5.80	1.25	18.99
12/05	63.63	16 13	4.10	1.05	21.70
Annual Growth	**4.3%**	**— —**	**17.4%**	**22.2%**	**(14.9%)**

Loews Corporation

When it comes to diversification, Loews definitely has the low-down. The holding company's main interest is insurance through publicly traded subsidiary CNA Financial, which offers commercial property/casualty coverage. Other wholly owned and partially owned holdings include hotels in the US and Canada through its Loews Hotels subsidiary. Its energy holdings include contract oil-drilling operator Diamond Offshore Drilling (which operates roughly 50 offshore oil rigs), interstate natural gas transmission pipeline systems operator Boardwalk Pipelines, and HighMount Exploration & Production (also natural gas).

Despite Loews' eclectic collection of businesses, its flagship unit CNA Financial still accounts for more than half of the corporation's revenues. CNA's affiliates include The Continental Insurance Company and Continental Assurance Company.

While commercial insurance is generally stable stuff, CNA has been faced with the same investment losses most big insurers have seen over the past couple of years. To make sure CNA would have enough cash on hand to pay any claims that might arise, Loews committed to inject up to $1.25 billion. Shortly thereafter, the company announced it would invest up to $500 million in Boardwalk Pipeline to help it complete pipeline expansion projects.

Tobacco was long a staple in Loews' portfolio until the company kicked the habit. Prior to quitting, the company kept its 62% ownership of Lorillard rolled up as Carolina Group and traded it as a tracking subsidiary. Lorillard, which included the Kent, Newport, and True US cigarette brands, accounted for more than 20% of Loews' revenues. However, after a steady stream of tobacco-related litigation, the company spun Lorillard off into an independent public company, eliminating the Carolina Group, and exiting the industry.

That disposition was fully in keeping with the Loews strategy of acquiring what can be turned around, letting go of what can't be turned around, and the wisdom to know the difference. The company spent $4 billion to acquire oil and gas exploration operator HighMount Exploration & Production. And, while accessories make the outfit, in 2008 Loews slipped its Bulova subsidiary off of its wrist and handed it to competitor Citizen Watch for $250 million.

Members of the Tisch family, including cochairmen cousins Andrew and Jonathan Tisch, CEO James Tisch, and their mothers, control more than 20% of the company's stock.

HISTORY

In 1946 Larry Tisch, who earned a business degree from New York University at age 18, dropped out of Harvard Law to run his parents' New Jersey resort. Younger brother Bob joined him in creating a new entity, Tisch Hotels. The company bought two Atlantic City hotels in 1952, quickly making them profitable. Later Tisch purchased such illustrious hotels as the Mark Hopkins, The Drake, the Belmont Plaza, and the Regency.

Moving beyond hotels, the brothers bought money-losing companies with poor management. Discarding the management along with underperforming divisions, they tightened operational control and eliminated such frills as fancy offices, company planes, and even memos.

In 1960 Tisch Hotels gained control of MGM's ailing Loew's Theaters to take advantage of their desirable city locations. The company then began demolishing more than 50 stately movie palaces and selling the land to developers. In 1968 the company bought Lorillard, the oldest US tobacco company; it shed Lorillard's unprofitable pet food and candy operations and reversed its slipping tobacco market share.

Taking the Loews name in 1971, the company bought CNA Financial in 1974. The Tisch method turned losses of more than $200 million to profits of more than $100 million the very next year. It bought Bulova Watch in 1979, and guided by Larry's son Andrew, it gradually returned to profitability.

In the early 1980s Loews entered the energy business by investing in oil supertankers. The company sold its last movie theaters in 1985. Then in 1987 Loews helped CBS fend off a takeover attempt by Ted Turner and ended up with about 25% of the company. Larry became president of the broadcaster.

In 1989 Loews acquired Diamond M Offshore, a Texas drilling company, and with the acquisition of Odeco Drilling in 1992, the company amassed the world's largest fleet of offshore rigs. The next year Loews grouped its drilling interests as Diamond Offshore Drilling.

In 1994 CNA expanded its insurance empire, buying The Continental Corp. The next year Loews sold its interest in CBS, and the following year Diamond Offshore Drilling merged with Arethusa (Off-Shore) Limited.

As deft as the Tisch brothers had been in accumulating their riches, Larry's bearish investment strategy (short-selling stocks) cost Loews in the late 1990s (more than $900 million alone during 1997's bull market). Larry and Bob retired as co-CEOs at the end of 1998; Larry's son James, already president and COO, became CEO.

That year Lorillard signed on to the 46-state tobacco lawsuit settlement; the first payment cost the company $325 million (payments continue until 2025). Facing a softened insurance market, CNA sold unprofitable lines to focus on commercial insurance; in 1999 it transferred its

auto and homeowners lines to Allstate (it continues writing and renewing these policies) and put its life and life reinsurance units up for sale in 2000. Also that year Lorillard was hit with $16 billion of a record-breaking $144 billion punitive damage award in a smokers' class-action suit in Florida. CNA Financial paid out over $450 million in 2001-02 for claims related to the attacks on the World Trade Center.

In 2004 the company continued to expand its natural resource offerings when its subsidiary Boardwalk Pipelines (formerly known as TGT Pipeline) acquired Gulf South Pipeline, which operates natural gas pipeline and gathering systems in Texas, Louisiana, Mississippi, Alabama, and Florida, including several major supply hubs. Loews had acquired gas pipeline operator Texas Gas Transmission in 2003. Texas Gas operates natural gas pipeline systems reaching from the Louisiana Gulf Coast and East Texas north through Louisiana, Arkansas, Mississippi, Tennessee, Kentucky, Indiana, and into Ohio and Illinois.

Larry Tisch died at the age of 80 in 2003. Chairman Bob Tisch died of cancer in late 2005. Tisch also was co-owner of the New York Giants of the National Football League.

EXECUTIVES

Co-Chairman and Office of the President; Chairman and CEO, Loews Hotels: Jonathan M. Tisch, age 56, $7,360,935 total compensation
Co-Chairman, Office of the President, and Chairman, Executive Committee: Andrew H. Tisch, age 60, $7,019,098 total compensation
President, CEO, Office of the President, and Director: James S. Tisch, age 57, $8,477,742 total compensation
SVP, General Counsel, and Secretary: Gary W. Garson, age 63
SVP and CFO: Peter W. Keegan, age 65, $3,549,288 total compensation
SVP: Herbert C. Hofmann, age 67
SVP: David B. Edelson, age 50, $4,250,432 total compensation
SVP: Kenneth I. Siegel, age 52
VP and CIO: Robert D. Fields
VP Internal Audit: Robert F. Crook
VP and Chief Investment Officer: Richard W. Scott, age 56
VP Risk Management: Audrey A. Rampinelli
VP Human Resources: Alan Momeyer
VP Tax: Susan Becker
VP Corporate Development: Jonathan Nathanson
Treasurer: John J. Kenny
Public Affairs: Candace Leeds
Investor Relations: Darren Daugherty
Auditors: Deloitte & Touche LLP

LOCATIONS

HQ: Loews Corporation
667 Madison Ave., New York, NY 10065
Phone: 212-521-2000   **Fax:** 212-521-2525
Web: www.loews.com

PRODUCTS/OPERATIONS

2009 Sales

	$ mil.	% of total
Insurance premiums	6,721	48
Contract drilling revenues	3,537	25
Net investment income	2,499	18
Other	1,360	9
Total	**14,117**	**100**

2009 Sales

	$ mil.	% of total
CNA Financial	8,472	60
Diamond Offshore	3,653	26
Boardwalk Partners	910	6
HighMount	620	4
Loews Hotels	284	2
Corporate & other	187	2
Total	**14,117**	**100**

Selected Subsidiaries

Boardwalk Pipeline Partners, LP (66%)
CNA Financial Corporation (90%)
  The Continental Corporation
    Continental Casualty Company
Diamond Offshore Drilling, Inc. (50%)
HighMount Exploration & Production LLC
Loews Hotels Holding Corporation

COMPETITORS

ACE Limited	Hyatt
AIG	Marriott
American Financial Group	Ritz-Carlton
Apache	Safeco
Berkshire Hathaway	Starwood Hotels & Resorts
Chubb Corp	Statoil
Cincinnati Financial	Travelers Companies
Four Seasons Hotels	Wyndham Worldwide
The Hartford	XL Group plc
Hilton Worldwide	

HISTORICAL FINANCIALS

Company Type: Public

Income Statement

FYE: December 31

	ASSETS ($ mil.)	NET INCOME ($ mil.)	INCOME AS % OF ASSETS	EMPLOYEES
12/09	74,070	1,383	1.9%	18,500
12/08	69,857	4,530	6.5%	19,100
12/07	76,079	2,489	3.3%	21,700
12/06	76,881	2,491	3.2%	21,600
12/05	70,676	1,212	1.7%	21,600
Annual Growth	**1.2%**	**3.4%**	**—**	**(3.8%)**

2009 Year-End Financials

Equity as % of assets: 22.8%
Return on assets: 1.9%
Return on equity: 9.2%
Long-term debt ($ mil.): 9,475
No. of shares (mil.): 418
Dividends
  Yield: 0.7%
  Payout: 19.2%
Market value ($ mil.): 15,203
Sales ($ mil.): 14,117

Stock History

NYSE: L

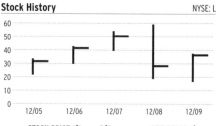

	STOCK PRICE ($) FY Close	P/E High/Low		PER SHARE ($) Earnings	Dividends	Book Value
12/09	36.35	28	13	1.30	0.25	40.40
12/08	28.25	6	2	9.05	0.25	31.38
12/07	50.34	15	11	3.65	0.25	42.06
12/06	41.47	11	8	3.75	0.24	39.45
12/05	31.62	19	13	1.72	0.20	31.30
Annual Growth	**3.5%**	**—**	**—**	**(6.8%)**	**5.7%**	**6.6%**

Lowe's Companies

No longer a low-profile company, Lowe's Companies has evolved from a regional hardware store operator into a nationwide chain of home improvement superstores bent on international expansion. The #2 US home improvement chain (after The Home Depot), Lowe's has about 1,700 superstores in 50 states and more than 15 locations in Canada and Mexico, as well as an e-commerce site. Its stores sell some 40,000 products for do-it-yourselfers and professionals for home improvement and repair projects, such as lumber, paint, plumbing and electrical supplies, tools, and gardening products, as well as appliances, lighting, and furniture. Lowe's is the #2 US home appliance retailer after Sears.

Ever-expanding Lowe's has grown its store base by more than 50% since 2005, when it operated fewer than 1,100 locations. The company typically concentrates on small and midsized markets, but it also targets large metropolitan areas (with populations of 500,000 or more). Lowe's sees potential in the North American market for up to 2,500 locations, but the economic downturn has slowed its progress on making that a reality. Falling home prices, tightened credit markets, and rising unemployment have dampened growth prospects for the retailer, which has also seen slightly lower revenues. In response, Lowe's refined its plans, opening 115 new outlets in 2008 and about 60 in 2009, including its first location in Monterrey, Mexico. (Home Depot is Mexico's #1 DIY operator with some 80 stores there.)

In partnership with Australia's top retailer, Woolworths Ltd., Lowe's expects to begin opening its big-box hardware stores in Australia in 2011. Woolworths will own two-thirds of the joint venture, which plans to launch more than 150 locations over five years.

The home improvement chain expanded its distribution footprint in 2008. It opened a regional distribution center in Pittston, Pennsylvania, and a flatbed distribution center in Purvis, Mississippi, boosting its total count to about 30 distribution facilities.

Lowe's is also trying to attract more female customers, who, the company claims, call the shots on about 80% of home improvement decisions. To make its big-box stores appealing, the company makes effective use of lighting and signage and caters to women and baby boomers with an attractive store layout. In addition, Lowe's has been increasing exclusive product arrangements with suppliers. Like Home Depot, Lowe's is putting more emphasis on services, offering installation service in more than 40 categories, such as flooring and cabinet products.

HISTORY

Lowe's Companies was founded in 1921 as Mr. L. S. Lowe's North Wilkesboro Hardware in North Wilkesboro, North Carolina. A family operation by 1945, Mr. Lowe's store (which also sold groceries, snuff, and harnesses) was run by his son Jim and his son-in-law H. Carl Buchan. Buchan bought Lowe's share of the company in 1956 and incorporated as Lowe's North Wilkesboro Hardware; he wanted Lowe's as part of the company name because he liked the slogan "Lowe's Low Prices." The chain expanded from North Carolina into Tennessee, Virginia, and West Virginia. By 1960 Buchan had 15 stores and sales of $31 million — up $4 million from a decade before.

Buchan planned to create a profit-sharing plan for Lowe's employees, but in 1960 he died of a heart attack at age 44. In 1961 Lowe's management and the executors of Buchan's estate established the Lowe's Employees Profit Sharing and Trust, which bought Buchan's 89% of the company (later renamed Lowe's Companies). That year they financed the transaction through a public offering, which diluted the employees' stock. Lowe's was listed on the NYSE in 1979.

Robert Strickland, who had joined the company in 1957, became chairman in 1978. Revenues increased from $170 million in 1971 to more than $900 million, with a net income of $25 million, in 1979. Traditionally, the majority of Lowe's business was in sales to professional homebuilders, but in 1980 housing starts fell, and company profits dropped. Concurrently, The Home Depot introduced its low-price warehouse concept. Instead of building warehouse stores of its own, Strickland changed the stores' layouts and by 1982 had redesigned half of the 229 stores to be more oriented toward do-it-yourself (DIY) consumers. The new designs featured softer lighting and displays of entire room layouts to appeal to women, who made up over half of all DIY customers. In 1982 Lowe's made more than half of its sales to consumers for the first time in its history.

Although Lowe's had more than 300 stores by 1988, its outlets were only about 20,000 sq. ft. (one-fifth the size of Home Depot's warehouse stores). By 1989 Lowe's, which had continued to target contractors as well as DIYers, was overtaken by Home Depot as the US's #1 home retail chain. Since 1989 the company has focused on building larger stores. In 1993 Lowe's opened 57 large stores (half were replacements for existing stores), almost doubling its total floor space.

The retailer opened 29 new stores in 1995. During 1996 Lowe's added a net of 37 stores, and in 1997 it opened 42 stores in new markets. Also that year president and CEO Leonard Herring retired and was replaced by former COO Robert Tillman, who also took the post of chairman when Strickland stepped down in 1998.

Also in 1998 the company entered a joint venture to sell an exclusive line of Kobalt-brand professional mechanics' tools produced by Snap-on and, to better serve commercial customers, began allowing them to special order items not stocked in stores. In addition, Lowe's announced it would spend $1.5 billion over the next several years on a 100-store push into the western US. Lowe's westward expansion was fueled when it purchased Washington-based, 38-store Eagle Hardware & Garden in 1999 in a stock swap deal worth $1.3 billion.

In 2001 the company earmarked $2.4 billion of its $2.7 billion capital budget for store expansions and new distribution centers. Lowe's opened more than 100 new stores that year and more than 110 new stores in 2002.

Robert Niblock was promoted from CFO to president in 2003. Lowe's sold its some 30 outlets operating as The Contractor Yard to The Strober Organization in 2004. Also in 2004 it opened its first predominantly urban-oriented store, suited to the needs of city dwellers and building superintendents, in Brooklyn. Chairman and CEO Robert Tillman retired in 2005 and was succeeded by Niblock.

Lowe's entered the Canadian market in 2007.

HISTORICAL FINANCIALS

Company Type: Public

Income Statement

	REVENUE ($ mil.)	NET INCOME ($ mil.)	NET PROFIT MARGIN	EMPLOYEES
1/10	47,220	1,783	3.8%	239,000
1/09	48,230	2,195	4.6%	229,000
1/08	48,283	2,809	5.8%	216,000
1/07	46,927	3,105	6.6%	210,000
1/06	43,243	2,771	6.4%	185,000
Annual Growth	2.2%	(10.4%)	—	6.6%

FYE: Friday nearest January 31

2010 Year-End Financials

Debt ratio: 23.7%
Return on equity: 9.6%
Cash ($ mil.): 632
Current ratio: 1.32
Long-term debt ($ mil.): 4,528
No. of shares (mil.): 1,429
Dividends
Yield: 1.6%
Payout: 28.9%
Market value ($ mil.): 30,942

Stock History

NYSE: LOW

	STOCK PRICE ($) FY Close	P/E High/Low		PER SHARE ($) Earnings	Dividends	Book Value
1/10	21.65	20	11	1.21	0.35	13.34
1/09	18.27	19	11	1.49	0.34	12.63
1/08	26.43	19	11	1.86	0.29	11.26
1/07	33.71	18	13	1.99	0.18	11.00
1/06	31.77	20	15	1.73	0.11	10.03
Annual Growth	(9.1%)	—	—	(8.5%)	33.6%	7.4%

LSI Corporation

LSI can show you around the circuit. The fabless semiconductor developer provides standard integrated circuits (ICs) and custom-designed application-specific ICs (ASICs), focusing on broadband and wireless communications, data storage, and networking markets. LSI was a pioneer of system-on-a-chip (SoC) devices, which combine elements of an electronic system — essentially a microprocessor, memory, and logic — onto a single chip. Its top customers include Hewlett-Packard, IBM (about 19% of sales), and Seagate (around 15%). LSI also provides hardware and software for storage area networks. The Asia/Pacific region accounts for approximately half of the company's sales.

LSI not only contends with the highly cyclical nature of the semiconductor industry, but — like other chip makers — it faced a downturn in sales of electronic products, and consequently semiconductors, pushed by the worldwide economic crisis.

In the past decade, LSI has regularly struggled with profitability — partly due to industry cyclicality and partly because it digested a series of acquisitions. One challenge for the company is its limited customer base; its top 10 clients account for about two-thirds of sales. LSI must

also contend with using outside contractors for its manufacturing, which carries the potential risks of higher costs, production delays, and other problems with those contractors. The company primarily outsources production of its chips to Taiwan Semiconductor Manufacturing Company (TSMC), and also to IBM Microelectronics and to Singapore-based Silicon Manufacturing Partners, a joint venture between GLOBALFOUNDRIES and LSI. The company also uses third-party contractors to assemble and test its data storage systems products.

The company has reframed its product portfolio through a series of acquisitions and divestitures. In 2008 Infineon Technologies sold the assets of its hard-disk drive (HDD) semiconductor business to LSI. Customers for the HDD chip line include Hitachi Global Storage Technologies. The following year LSI acquired the 3ware RAID adapter business of Applied Micro Circuits; the 3ware business joined the LSI Engenio Storage Group. LSI's lineup of network-attached and unified storage systems was further expanded in 2009 when the company acquired ONStor, a provider of clustered network-attached storage (NAS) tools, enabling enterprises to consolidate, protect, and manage unstructured data.

HISTORY

Wilfred (Wilf) Corrigan, an engineer and former CEO of Fairchild Camera & Instrument (the original parent company of Fairchild Semiconductor), founded LSI Logic in 1981. (Its name is the acronym for large-scale integration, describing a chip that has up to 100,000 transistors.) LSI Logic went public in 1983 with a $152 million IPO, a record for its time. That year the company introduced regional design centers — where customers could design chips using LSI Logic equipment and facilities — in Massachusetts and the UK. It established affiliates in Japan and Germany in 1984.

By 1985 LSI Logic had won big military and aerospace customers and, with sales of $140 million, was the US's leading application-specific integrated circuit (ASIC) maker. By the end of the 1980s, however, LSI Logic was foundering after heavy investment in factories (it had geared up for a boom that failed to materialize). In 1992 the company began developing its CoreWare mix-and-match standardization technology.

A trimmer, smarter LSI Logic emerged in 1993 — the year it introduced the 0.5-micron CMOS ASIC chip. Also that year LSI Logic penned 10-year technology sharing agreements with electronic design automation leaders Synopsys and Cadence Design Systems. LSI Logic passed the $1 billion sales mark in 1995.

LSI Logic paid $804 million to acquire Symbios, a US electronics subsidiary of cash-strapped Hyundai, in 1998. It also entered a DVD development joint venture with SANYO.

In 1999 the company bought SEEQ Technology, a maker of data communications semiconductor products. That year LSI Logic won a lucrative contract to make chips for Sony's PlayStation consoles, and teamed up with Hitachi to develop embedded hybrid chips.

In 2001 the company purchased C-Cube Microsystems (chips for digital set-top boxes and DVDs) in a deal valued at about $850 million. Also in 2001 LSI Logic bought a business unit of American Megatrends that makes hardware and software for redundant array of independent disks (RAID) systems used in networking and storage applications. Early in 2002 the company

shed two product lines and cut 1,400 positions in an effort to return to profitability.

Intel veteran Abhi Talwalkar succeeded Wilf Corrigan as CEO in 2005. Corrigan remained chairman of the board. In 2006, however, LSI Logic's founder retired from the board of directors, officially ending his 25-year association with the company. James Keyes, the former CEO of Johnson Controls and an LSI Logic director since 1983, succeeded Corrigan as non-executive chairman.

Late in 2005 the company announced plans to sell its Oregon-based manufacturing facility and transition to a fabless model, under which the company contracted out its manufacturing chores. In 2006 LSI sold the Oregon fab to ON Semiconductor for about $105 million in cash.

In late 2006 LSI acquired StoreAge Networking Technologies, a developer of network storage management and data protection software.

In early 2007 LSI Logic completed its $4 billion acquisition of rival Agere Systems and changed its name to LSI Corporation. Also that year Gregorio Reyes became non-executive chairman.

Softness in business during the first half of 2007 led LSI to eliminate approximately 900 jobs, a 10% reduction for the combined Agere-LSI workforce. As part of a general corporate restructuring in 2007, LSI sold its consumer products business to Magnum Semiconductor, a venture-funded chip company. Later that year, LSI sold its division that made semiconductors and software for mobile telephones to Infineon Technologies for $450 million. LSI phased out assembly and test operations in Singapore and Wichita, Kansas, in 2008, turning over those facilities to contract manufacturers.

EXECUTIVES

Chairman: Gregorio Reyes, age 69
President, CEO, and Director:
Abhijit Y. (Abhi) Talwalkar, age 46,
$3,483,779 total compensation
EVP, CFO, and Chief Administrative Officer:
Bryon Look, age 56, $1,250,997 total compensation
EVP and General Manager, Semiconductor Solutions Group: D. Jeffrey (Jeff) Richardson, age 45,
$1,398,593 total compensation
EVP, General Counsel, and Secretary: Jean F. Rankin,
age 51
EVP and General Manager, Engenio Storage Group:
Philip W. (Phil) Bullinger, age 45,
$1,192,664 total compensation
SVP Human Resources: Gautam Srivastava
SVP Corporate Planning and Marketing:
Philip G. Brace, age 39
SVP Worldwide Manufacturing and Operations:
Hayden Thomas
Auditors: PricewaterhouseCoopers LLP

LOCATIONS

HQ: LSI Corporation
1621 Barber Ln., Milpitas, CA 95035
Phone: 408-433-8000 **Fax:** 408-954-3220
Web: www.lsi.com

2009 Sales

	$ mil.	% of total
Asia/Pacific	1,126.0	51
Europe & Middle East	574.0	26
North America	519.2	23
Total	**2,219.2**	**100**

PRODUCTS/OPERATIONS

2009 Sales

	$ mil.	% of total
Semiconductors	1,421.5	64
Storage systems	797.7	36
Total	**2,219.2**	**100**

Selected Semiconductor Products and Markets

Broadband and wireless networking (analog and digital chip cores, ASICs, and baseband processors)
Wide-area network (WAN) equipment
Wireless local-area network (LAN) equipment

Broadband entertainment (analog and digital chip cores, ASICs, and software)
Digital set-top boxes
DVD players
Home video games
Satellite and terrestrial television broadcasting

Networking infrastructure
Analog equipment (Ethernet physical-layer devices)
Digital equipment (ARM- and MIPS-based microprocessors, Ethernet controllers, and high-speed content-addressable memory)

Storage components (ASICs, software, and standard input/output components)
Fibre Channel (host adapters and adapter boards, physical-layer components, protocol controllers, SAN switches, and transceivers)
Hard disk drives and tape peripherals (controllers)

COMPETITORS

3PAR	Integrated Device
Adaptec	Technology
Altera	Isilon Systems
Applied Micro Circuits	Marvell Technology
Atmel	MediaTek
Avago Technologies	NetApp
Broadcom	NetLogic Microsystems
Cirrus Logic	NXP Semiconductors
Compellent Technologies	PMC-Sierra
Conexant Systems	Promise Technology
Dell	QLogic
Dot Hill	Samsung Electronics
EMC	Silicon Labs
Emulex	STMicroelectronics
Epson	Texas Instruments
Freescale Semiconductor	Xilinx
Fujitsu Semiconductor	Xiotech
Hitachi Data Systems	Xyratex
IBM Microelectronics	

HISTORICAL FINANCIALS

Company Type: Public

Income Statement

FYE: December 31

	REVENUE ($ mil.)	NET INCOME ($ mil.)	NET PROFIT MARGIN	EMPLOYEES
12/09	2,219	(48)	—	5,397
12/08	2,677	(622)	—	5,488
12/07	2,604	(2,487)	—	6,193
12/06	1,982	170	8.6%	4,010
12/05	1,919	(6)	—	4,322
Annual Growth	**3.7%**	**—**	**—**	**5.7%**

2009 Year-End Financials

Debt ratio: 0.0%	No. of shares (mil.): 642
Return on equity: —	Dividends
Cash ($ mil.): 778	Yield: 0.0%
Current ratio: 1.86	Payout: —
Long-term debt ($ mil.): 0	Market value ($ mil.): 3,857

Stock History

NYSE: LSI

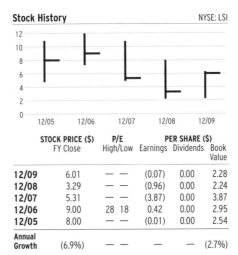

	STOCK PRICE ($) FY Close	P/E High/Low	Earnings	PER SHARE ($) Dividends	Book Value
12/09	6.01	— —	(0.07)	0.00	2.28
12/08	3.29	— —	(0.96)	0.00	2.24
12/07	5.31	— —	(3.87)	0.00	3.87
12/06	9.00	28 18	0.42	0.00	2.95
12/05	8.00	— —	(0.01)	0.00	2.54
Annual Growth	**(6.9%)**	**— —**	**—**	**—**	**(2.7%)**

The Lubrizol Corporation

Lubrizol is a smooth operator — the company is the world's #1 maker of additives for lubricants and fuels. Its Lubrizol Additives segment includes engine oil additives that fight sludge buildup, viscosity breakdown, and component wear; fuel additives designed to control deposits and improve combustion; and additives for paints, inks, greases, metalworking, and other markets. Lubrizol's Advanced Materials segment (performance coatings and chemicals) delivers its products to the personal care and rubber and plastics markets. The company markets nearly 3,000 products in more than 100 countries; operates research facilities and testing labs in Europe, Asia, and North America; and has plants in 17 countries.

After a few years in which Lubrizol concentrated on slimming down and developing its core operations, by 2007 the company was in the mood to build its business back up a bit. Toward the end of the year, it acquired Croda's refrigeration lubricants operations. Then, at the end of 2008, the company bought DuPont's thermoplastic polyurethane business, which it merged into its Lubrizol's Estane Engineered Polymers unit.

However, the global recession produced a sharp slump in demand that hurt the company's sales in 2009 as clients reduced their inventories. Lubrizol countered with cost reductions and an organizational restructuring.

As part of the restructuring of its Performance Coatings segment to focus on fewer, higher-value products, Lubrizol has closed a number of business lines, including an acrylic emulsions production line at its Avon Lake, Ohio, plant and a styrene butadiene latex line at its Gastonia, North Carolina, plant (both in 2008) and the Chagrin Falls, Ohio, overprint coatings manufacturing plant (in 2010).

HISTORY

The company that eventually became Lubrizol was founded in 1928 by the Smith (Kelvin, Kevin, and Vincent) and Nason (Alex and Frank) brothers, along with their friend, Thomas James. Chemistry was in the Smiths' blood; all three had worked at Dow Chemical, a company their chemist father helped start. Known originally as The Graphite Oil Products Company, Lubrizol's first product, Lubri-graph, was a suspended graphite and oil product designed to keep car springs quiet. Following the success of their anti-squeak product, the principals turned their attention to the gunk that built up from the mineral oil used in car engines. Cars of the era overheated often and pistons frequently became stuck from excessive heat or sludge build-up. Graphite Oil chemists discovered that the addition of chlorine to lubricants solved the overheating problem. The new product (and later the company) was named Lubrizol.

Alex Nason went to Detroit in 1935 and convinced General Motors to add Lubrizol to its list of recommended products. Following that success Lubrizol was used extensively during WWII by the military, which established performance standards. During the war the company stopped producing lubricants and concentrated solely on additives, including rust inhibitors, detergents, and chemicals to slow oil breakdown.

After WWII performance standards for cars were set, and Lubrizol cleaned up, having patented many ingredients and processes used to manufacture lubricants. By the 1950s the privately held corporation was the #1 petroleum additive company in the world. It was during this time that the company made its first acquisition, R.O. Hull Company, a rustproofing chemicals manufacturer (it has since been sold). Lubrizol went public in 1960.

The company benefited as environmental regulations grew, since unleaded gas and catalytic converters required new additives. Lubrizol also benefited from the oil crisis in the early 1970s because the more fuel-efficient cars that resulted required new transmission fluids, fuel additives, and gear lubricants. Even the recession helped the slippery firm, as industrial companies relied more on quality lubricants and additives to protect costly machinery.

Lubrizol purchased lithium battery maker Althus Corporation in 1979 and moved into biotechnology soon afterward. In 1985 the firm bought Agrigenetics Corporation and focused its biotechnology efforts on genetically altered plants. Biotechnology seemed to offer vast patent potential, whereas additives had become so effective that growth opportunities there seemed limited in comparison. However, after seven costly years, Lubrizol sold a controlling interest in Agrigenetics, which had become the sixth-largest seed company in the US, to Mycogen (acquired by Dow Chemical in 1998).

Lubrizol continued divesting noncore interests, and by 1996 it was back to being an additives company. Despite the turmoil in Asia, the company formed two joint ventures in China in 1997. The next year Lubrizol acquired the Adibis unit of BP Chemicals (now called BP Petrochemicals) and five other companies, adding a few additional percentage points to its share of the additives market. Shrinking profits caused the company to cut production by approximately 20% and its workforce by 11% between 1999 and 2000.

In 2000 Lubrizol bought RPM's Alox metalworking additive business. The next year it acquired ROSS Chem, a privately held maker of antifoam and defoaming agents used by the coatings, inks, textile, food, and metalworking industries. The company's 2002 acquisitions included Kabo International (defoaming products), Chemron (specialty surfactants), and Lambent Technologies (silicone defoamers).

Lubrizol bought the additives business of Avecia in 2004. The former Avecia unit makes pigment and color dispersants for inks and coatings under the brand names Solsperse, Solplus, and Solthix. Later that year it bought up the formerly private company Noveon, which had announced its intention to go public. Noveon makes polymers and additives used in food and pharmaceuticals. The total price Lubrizol paid for the company was $1.85 billion.

In the summer of 2005 the company announced its intention to divest noncore operations. The first move came later that year with the sale of Lubrizol Performance Systems to the Dutch medical and industrial technology company Delft Instruments. The following year brought the sale of Noveon's consumer specialties line of chemical products to Sun Capital Partners. The unit provided chemicals and performance materials to the food and beverage, personal care, and textiles industries.

EXECUTIVES

Chairman, President, and CEO: James L. Hambrick, age 54, $7,973,810 total compensation
SVP and COO: Stephen F. (Steve) Kirk, age 60, $2,498,382 total compensation
SVP, CFO, and Treasurer: Charles P. Cooley, age 54, $2,373,484 total compensation
VP and General Counsel: Joseph W. Bauer, age 56, $1,526,863 total compensation
VP; President, Lubrizol Additives: Daniel L. Sheets, age 52, $1,022,203 total compensation
VP; President, Lubrizol Advanced Materials: Eric R. Schnur, age 43
VP Driveline and Specialty Additives: Val A. Pakis
VP Information Systems and Business Processes: Patrick H. Saunier, age 54
VP Finance, Lubricant Additives: Gregory P. Lieb, age 55
VP Operations: Larry D. Norwood, age 59
VP Corporate Planning, Development, and Communications: Gregory D. Taylor, age 51
VP Human Resources: C. Lawrence Miller, age 53
VP Research and Development: Robert T. Graf, age 51
VP Global Risk Management and Chief Ethics Officer: Gregory R. (Greg) Lewis, age 51
Corporate Secretary and Counsel: Leslie M. Reynolds, age 49
Chief Tax Officer; President and Treasurer, Lubrizol Inter-Americas: Jeffrey A. Vavruska, age 49
Director Investor Relations and Corporate Communications: Mark Sutherland
Auditors: Deloitte & Touche LLP

LOCATIONS

HQ: The Lubrizol Corporation
29400 Lakeland Blvd., Wickliffe, OH 44092
Phone: 440-943-4200   **Fax:** 440-943-5337
Web: www.lubrizol.com

2009 Sales

	$ mil.	% of total
North America		
US	1,528.6	33
Canada	150.8	3
Europe	1,332.4	29
Asia/Pacific & Middle East	1,227.3	27
Latin America	347.2	8
Total	**4,586.3**	**100**

PRODUCTS/OPERATIONS

2009 Sales

	$ mil.	% of total
Lubrizol Additives	3,283.9	72
Lubrizol Advanced Materials	1,302.4	28
Total	**4,586.3**	**100**

Selected Products and Services

Lubrizol Additives
  Compression lubricants
  Corrosion control products
  Fuel additives
    E-diesel products (non-petroleum based)
  Lubricant additives
    Engine oils
    Driveline lubricants
    Industrial lubricants
    Viscosity modifiers
  Metalworking additives
  Refinery and oilfield products
  Specialty surfactants
  Terminals
  Toll manufacturing
  Warehousing
Lubrizol Advanced Materials
  Engineered Polymers
    Chlorinated polyvinyl chloride (TempRite)
    Foam control additives
    Reactive liquid polymers (Hycar)
    Specialty monomers
    Thermoplastic polyurethane (Estane)
  Performance Coatings
    Acrylic-based coatings for textiles
    Dye thickeners and binders
    Emulsions for specialty paper
    Glyoxal and glyoxal resins
    Ink additives
      Dispersants
      Ink vehicles
      Waxes
      Paints and coatings
      Polymers for inks and packaging
  Consumer Specialties
    Food and Beverage
      Benzoates (sodium and potassium)
      Flavor and fragrance enhancers
      Intermediates (phenol, benzaldehyde, benzyl alcohol, and benzoic acid)
      Natural colors and pigments
    Personal care and pharmaceuticals
      Acrylic thickener (Carbopol)
      Advanced intermediates
      Amino acid-based actives
      Cassia gum
      Colorants
      Polymeric emulsifier (Pemulen)
      Polymers for cosmetics and skin care products (Avalure)
      Resins for hair styling (Fixate)
      Specialty silicones

COMPETITORS

Afton Chemical
Avecia
BASF SE
Bayer MaterialScience
Chevron Oronite
Cognis
CP Kelco
Dow Chemical
DSM
FUCHS
Infineum
Reichhold
Rhodia
Symrise

HISTORICAL FINANCIALS

Company Type: Public

Income Statement

FYE: December 31

	REVENUE ($ mil.)	NET INCOME ($ mil.)	NET PROFIT MARGIN	EMPLOYEES
12/09	4,586	501	10.9%	6,700
12/08	5,028	(66)	—	6,970
12/07	4,499	283	6.3%	6,900
12/06	4,041	106	2.6%	6,700
12/05	4,043	189	4.7%	7,500
Annual Growth	**3.2%**	**27.5%**	**—**	**(2.8%)**

2009 Year-End Financials

Debt ratio: 67.5%
Return on equity: 27.9%
Cash ($ mil.): 991
Current ratio: 3.68
Long-term debt ($ mil.): 1,390

No. of shares (mil.): 68
Dividends
  Yield: 1.7%
  Payout: 17.1%
Market value ($ mil.): 4,924

Stock History

NYSE: LZ

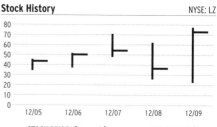

	STOCK PRICE ($) FY Close	P/E High/Low		PER SHARE ($) Earnings	Dividends	Book Value
12/09	72.95	11	3	7.26	1.24	30.53
12/08	36.39	—	—	(0.97)	1.23	22.57
12/07	54.16	17	12	4.05	1.16	28.91
12/06	50.13	33	25	1.52	1.04	25.29
12/05	43.43	16	13	2.75	1.04	23.22
Annual Growth	**13.8%**	**—**	**—**	**27.5%**	**4.5%**	**7.1%**

MacAndrews & Forbes

Through MacAndrews & Forbes Holdings, financier Ron Perelman is focused on cosmetics and cash. The holding company has investments in an array of public and private firms, most notably cosmetics giant Revlon and M&F Worldwide, which deals in licorice flavors and financial products. It also has an influential role in entertainment, with significant stakes in Panavision, the top provider of cameras for movies and TV shows, and Deluxe Entertainment Services Group, the largest processor of motion picture film. MacAndrews & Forbes' other holdings include biotech firm SIGA Technologies, lottery system and gaming developer Scientific Games, and AM General, maker of Humvee and HUMMER vehicles.

Perelman is intent on reversing the fortunes of Revlon, which he has controlled since 1985. The company in 2009 boosted its holding in the cosmetics maker from about 60% to 80%.

Adding more companies to the mix, MacAndrews & Forbes acquired the data management business of Pearson for $225 million in 2008. As part of the agreement, the business is operated by MacAndrews & Forbes' Scantron testing unit. The data management business deal follows the company's 2007 acquisition of John

H. Harland for nearly $2 billion, which was paired with its Clarke American unit.

Also in 2008 MacAndrews and Forbes unloaded its security services assets. It struck a deal with private equity firm Blackstone Group to take over its Allied Security business for $750 million.

HISTORY

Ron Perelman grew up working in his father's Philadelphia-based conglomerate, Belmont Industries, but he left at the age of 35 to seek his fortune in New York. In 1978 he bought 40% of jewelry store operator Cohen-Hatfield Industries. The next year Cohen-Hatfield bought a minority stake in MacAndrews & Forbes (licorice flavoring). Cohen-Hatfield acquired MacAndrews & Forbes in 1980.

In 1984 Perelman reshuffled his assets to create MacAndrews & Forbes Holdings, which acquired control of Pantry Pride, a Florida-based supermarket chain, in 1985. Pantry Pride then bought Revlon for $1.8 billion with the help of (convicted felon) Michael Milken. After Perelman acquired Revlon, he added several other cosmetics vendors, including Max Factor and Yves Saint Laurent's fragrance and cosmetic lines.

In 1988 MacAndrews & Forbes agreed to invest $315 million in five failing Texas savings and loans (S&Ls), which Perelman combined and named First Gibraltar (sold to BankAmerica, now Bank of America, in 1993). The next year MacAndrews & Forbes bought The Coleman Company, a maker of outdoor equipment.

With a growing reputation for buying struggling companies, revamping them, and then selling them at a higher price, Perelman bought Marvel Entertainment Group (Marvel Comics) in 1989 and took it public in 1991. That year he sold Revlon's Max Factor and Betrix units to Procter & Gamble for more than $1 billion.

MacAndrews & Forbes acquired 38% of TV infomercial producer Guthy-Renker and SCI Television's seven stations and merged them to create New World Television. That company was combined with TV syndicator Genesis Entertainment and TV production house New World Entertainment to create New World Communications Group, which Perelman took public in 1994. That year MacAndrews & Forbes and partner Gerald J. Ford bought Ford Motor's First Nationwide, the US's fifth-largest S&L at that time.

Subsidiaries Mafco Worldwide and Consolidated Cigar Holdings merged with Abex (aircraft parts) to create Mafco Consolidated Group in 1995. Following diminishing comic sales, Perelman placed Marvel in bankruptcy in 1996 and subsequently lost control of the company.

In 1997 First Nationwide bought California thrift Cal Fed Bancorp for $1.2 billion. In addition, Perelman sold New World to Rupert Murdoch's News Corp.

The next year Perelman orchestrated a $1.8 billion deal in which First Nationwide merged with Golden State Bancorp to form the US's third-largest thrift. Sunbeam Corp. (now American Household) bought Perelman's stake in Coleman that year, making Perelman a major American Household shareholder. Also in 1998 MacAndrews & Forbes bought a 72% stake in Panavision (movie camera maker, later increased to 91%), invested in WeddingChannel.com, and sold its 64% stake in Consolidated Cigar to French tobacco giant Seita (netting Perelman a smoking $350 million profit).

Still burdened by debt, Revlon sold its professional products business in 2000.

Perelman's stock in American Household was rendered worthless when the company initiated bankruptcy proceedings in February 2001. (It would emerge from bankruptcy, however, in December 2002.) He also was sued by angry shareholders after the board of M&F Worldwide, the licorice company he controls, bought Perelman's stock in Panavision at more than five times its market value. In order to settle the litigation surrounding the purchase, in 2002 M&F agreed to return Perelman's 83% stake in Panavision to Mafco. Golden State Bancorp also left the MacAndrews fold in 2002 when it was acquired by Citigroup.

MacAndrews & Forbes Holdings acquired Allied Security, the largest independent provider of contract security services and products in the US, from Gryphon Investors in February 2003 for an undisclosed sum.

Perelman's sale of The Coleman Company — in the late 1990s — helped the investor improve his cash flow later on. In his suit against Morgan Stanley, Perelman alleged that the investment bank withheld its knowledge of Sunbeam's accounting fraud when Perelman sold The Coleman Company to Sunbeam in 1998 for about $1.5 billion. Perelman's investment (he held 14.1 million shares of Sunbeam stock as part of the sale) later tanked as news broke of the accounting irregularities. Despite an attempt to settle the dispute with Morgan Stanley in 2003 for $20 million, Perelman took the bank to court and was awarded more than $1.5 billion in damages by a Florida jury in mid-2005.

It bought Deluxe Entertainment Services Group from The Rank Group in 2006. The purchase complements its majority stake in Panavision, the top provider of cameras for shooting movies and TV shows. Also in 2006, around the time of his public breakup with wife #4, actress Ellen Barkin, Perelman's MacAndrews & Forbes sold WeddingChannel.com to The Knot.

EXECUTIVES

Chairman and CEO: Ronald O. (Ron) Perelman, age 67
Executive Vice Chairman and Chief Administrative Officer: Barry F. Schwartz, age 61
SEVP: David L. Kennedy, age 63
EVP and CFO: Paul G. Savas
EVP Life Sciences; CEO, SIGA Technologies: Eric Rose
SVP Corporate Communications: Christine Taylor
CEO, Revlon: Alan T. Ennis, age 39
CEO, Mafco Worldwide: Stephen Taub
CEO, Faneuil: Joseph (Joe) Ahearn
CEO, Harland Clarke: Charles T. (Chuck) Dawson, age 61
CEO, Deluxe Entertainment Services Group: Cyril Drabinsky
President, Harland Financial Solutions: Raju M. (Raj) Shivdasani
President and COO, AM General: Paul J. Kern, age 64
President, Scantron: William D. (Bill) Hansen, age 50
President and CEO, Panavision: William C. (Bill) Bevins, age 64
President and CEO, TransTech Pharma: Adnan M. Mjalli, age 46
President and CEO, Scientific Games: Michael R. Chambrello, age 52

LOCATIONS

HQ: MacAndrews & Forbes Holdings Inc.
35 E. 62nd St., New York, NY 10065
Phone: 212-572-8600
Web: www.macandrewsandforbes.com

PRODUCTS/OPERATIONS

Selected Holdings

AM General (majority stake, multipurpose and military vehicles)
Deluxe Entertainment Services Group (film processing)
M&F Worldwide (minority stake, licorice extract and financial products)
Revlon (majority stake, cosmetics and personal care products)

COMPETITORS

Alberto-Culver
Alticor
Avon
BAE Systems Land & Armaments
Body Shop
Boeing
Chattem
Colgate-Palmolive
The Dial Corporation
Estée Lauder
General Dynamics
iRobot
Johnson & Johnson
Kellwood
Lockheed Martin
L'Oréal USA
LVMH
Mary Kay
Procter & Gamble
Ulta
Unilever

Macy's, Inc.

The nation's #1 department store chain has adopted the name of its most famous brand and cash cow: Macy's. Macy's, Inc., operates about 850 stores in 45 states, the District of Columbia, Guam, and Puerto Rico under the Macy's and Bloomingdale's banners that ring up some $25 billion in annual sales. The stores sell men's, women's, and children's apparel and accessories, cosmetics, and home furnishings, among other things. It also operates macys.com and bloomingdales.com. Macy's flagship store in Manhattan's Herald Square is the world's largest. The Macy's Thanksgiving Day Parade, started in 1924, is an annual rite. Macy's (formerly Federated Department Stores) began as a dry goods store more than 150 years ago.

The road to success has been a bumpy one for Macy's since its 2005 purchase of May Department Stores. Indeed, sales have been on the decline since 2006, with the deep recession and retail slump in the US making matters worse.

In 2009 the company restructured around its "My Macy's" localization initiative. (The initiative is designed to grow sales by doing a better job of focusing on local markets and reducing expenses.) The restructuring resulted in the elimination of some 7,000 jobs across the company.

Macy's is exploring opportunities for international expansion of both the Bloomingdale's and Macy's brands. To that end, the first Bloomingdale's store outside the US opened in Dubai, United Arab Emirates, in early 2010. That store will serve as a laboratory of sorts for Macy's, which hopes to gain some insight as to how its brands translate internationally. (The Dubai operation is managed and operated by Al Tayer Insignia, a company of Al Tayer Group, under a licensing agreement.)

The difficult retail climate has hampered the company's charismatic chairman's mission to reinvent the American department store by making it more relevant to younger consumers, who increasingly tend to shop elsewhere. The four key elements in chairman and CEO Terry Lundgren's plan include strengthening private-label brands (already about 20% of sales), simplifying pricing, catering to the local audience, and increasing its offering of exclusive merchandise. With sales of its 15 private-label brands outperforming national brands at Macy's stores, the importance of building its private-label business can't be underestimated. The company has also worked to increase its offering of exclusive merchandise, signing exclusive deals with big names, such as the domestic diva Martha Stewart and designer Tommy Hilfiger. (Macy's also has exclusive deals with designers Elie Tahari and Oscar de la Renta.)

HISTORY

In 1929 Fred Lazarus, who controlled Columbus, Ohio's giant F&R Lazarus department store and the John Shillito Company (the oldest department store west of the Alleghenies; 1830), met with three other great retailers on a yacht in Long Island Sound: Walter Rothschild of Brooklyn-based Abraham & Straus; Louis Kirstein of Boston-based Filene's; and Samuel Bloomingdale, head of Manhattan's Bloomingdale's. Lazarus, Rothschild, and Kirstein agreed to merge their stores into a loose federation. Bloomingdale joined the next year.

Though Federated set up headquarters in Cincinnati in 1945, it continued to be run by powerful merchants in each city where it operated. Under Lazarus' leadership, it was among the first to see the coming growth of the Sunbelt, acquiring Foley's (Houston, 1945), Burdines (Miami, 1956), Sanger's (Dallas, 1958), Bullock's and I. Magnin (California, 1964), and Rich's (Atlanta, 1976).

Federated's growth stalled after Lazarus' son Ralph stepped down in 1981. The company faced stiffer competition from rival department store operators and chains, including May Department Stores, Nordstrom, and Dillard's. By 1989 Federated was no longer a leader, although it was still financially strong.

Years before, when Federated was leader of the department store industry, Allied Stores was #2. Allied was made up mostly of stores that were in small towns or were #2 in their market, with a few leaders (Maas Brothers, The Bon Marché, Jordan Marsh). It had a mediocre track record until Thomas Macioce took the helm in 1971. He closed unprofitable stores, downsized others, and went on an acquisition spree (Brooks Brothers, Ann Taylor).

Campeau Corporation bought Allied and Federated in 1988. Saddled with more than $8 billion in debt from the purchase, both companies declared bankruptcy in 1990. Allen Questrom became Federated's CEO, and in 1992 the companies emerged from bankruptcy as Federated Department Stores.

The next year, after being rebuffed in a bid to merge with Macy's, Federated purchased 50% of Macy's unsecured debt, setting the stage for Federated's 1994 acquisition of the respected department store.

Rowland Macy opened a store under his name in Manhattan in 1858. After Macy's death, the Strauses, a New York china merchant family, bought the department store in 1896 and expanded it across the US. In 1986 chairman Edward Finkelstein led a $3.5 billion buyout of Macy's and took it private. Its debt load increased into the early 1990s, and Macy's entered bankruptcy proceedings in 1992.

Questrom quit (under longstanding tensions with Federated) in 1997, succeeded by president James Zimmerman.

In July 2002 Federated sold $1.2 billion in Fingerhut credit card receivables to credit card company CompuCredit and other Fingerhut assets to FAC Acquisitions, of which former Fingerhut CEO Thomas Fedders and business partner Theodore Deikel were principals.

In 2003 COO Terry J. Lundgren succeeded Zimmerman as CEO of the company. Lundgren took on the chairman title in 2004. On August 30, 2005, Federated completed its $11 billion acquisition of rival May Department Stores.

In 2006 Federated completed the first of two transactions in its sale of the May Company's credit card receivables to Citigroup, for about $753 million. The second transaction was completed in mid-July for $1 billion. In October Federated completed the sale of its 48-store Lord & Taylor department store chain to NRDC Equity Partners LLC for nearly $1.1 billion.

Adopting the name of its most famous brand, Federated changed its corporate name to Macy's, Inc., in June 2007.

Macy's celebrated its 150th birthday in October 2008. To mark the occasion, the company renamed the address of its flagship Herald Square store in New York City R.H. Macy Way to honor its founder.

EXECUTIVES

Chairman, President, and CEO: Terry J. Lundgren, age 58, $16,092,487 total compensation
Vice Chair, Department Store Divisions: Susan D. Kronick, age 58, $6,974,659 total compensation
Vice Chair, Merchandising, Private Brand and Product Development; Chairman and CEO, Federated Merchandising Group: Janet E. Grove, age 59, $2,283,700 total compensation
Vice Chair, Legal, Human Resources, Internal Audit and External Affairs: Thomas G. Cody, age 68
CFO: Karen M. Hoguet, age 53, $5,095,425 total compensation
Chief Administrative Officer: Thomas L. (Tom) Cole, age 61, $2,319,433 total compensation
Chief Stores Officer: Ronald (Ron) Klein, age 60, $6,642,478 total compensation
Chief Merchandise Planning Officer: Julie Greiner, age 56, $5,887,724 total compensation
Chief Marketing Officer; Chairman and CEO, macys.com: Peter R. Sachse, age 52
Chairman and CEO, Bloomingdale's: Michael (Mike) Gould
SVP Government and Consumer Affairs, Diversity Vendor Development, Macy's East: Ed Goldberg
SVP Diversity Strategies and Legal Affairs: William L. (Bill) Hawthorne III, age 50
SVP Corporate Communications and External Affairs: James A. (Jim) Sluzewski, age 50
President, Stores: Mark S. Cosby, age 51
General Counsel and Secretary: Dennis J. Broderick, age 61
Treasury and Risk Management: Felicia Williams, age 40
Auditors: KPMG LLP

LOCATIONS

HQ: Macy's, Inc.
7 W. 7th St., Cincinnati, OH 45202
Phone: 513-579-7000   **Fax:** 513-579-7555
Web: www.macysinc.com

2010 Stores

	No.
Northwest	139
Southwest	131
Southeast	119
Northeast	118
Mid-Atlantic	106
Midwest	105
North	67
South Central	65
Total	**850**

PRODUCTS/OPERATIONS

2010 Sales

	% of total
Women's accessories, intimate apparel, shoes & cosmetics	36
Women's apparel	26
Men's & children's	22
Home & miscellaneous	16
Total	**100**

2010 Stores

	No.
Macy's	810
Bloomingdale's	40
Total	**850**

Store Chains

Bloomingdale's
Macy's

Other Selected Operations

bloomingdales.com
macys.com

Selected Private Labels

Alfani (women's and men's apparel)
American Rag Cie. (casual sportswear for juniors and young men)
The Cellar (housewares and related home merchandise)
Charter Club (women's and men's apparel, home furnishings)
First Impressions (infant and layette apparel)
Greendog (children's apparel)
Hotel Collection (sheets, towels, tabletop, and barware)
I.N.C. (casual and career fashions for men and women)
ML/Material London (men's sportswear, suits, shoes)
Style & Co. (sportswear & casual apparel)
Tasso Elba (menswear)
Tools of the Trade (cookware, bakeware, cutlery, and kitchen gadgets)

COMPETITORS

AnnTaylor	Limited Brands
Bed Bath & Beyond	Lord & Taylor
Belk	Men's Wearhouse
Bon-Ton Stores	Neiman Marcus
Brown Shoe	Nine West
Burlington Coat Factory	Nordstrom
Dillard's	Polo Ralph Lauren
Eddie Bauer LLC	Saks
Foot Locker	Sears
The Gap	Stage Stores
J. C. Penney	Talbots
J. Crew	Target
Jos. A. Bank	TJX Companies
Kohl's	Wal-Mart
Lands' End	Zale

HISTORICAL FINANCIALS

Company Type: Public

Income Statement

	REVENUE ($ mil.)	NET INCOME ($ mil.)	NET PROFIT MARGIN	EMPLOYEES
			FYE: Saturday nearest January 31	
1/10	23,489	350	1.5%	161,000
1/09	24,892	(4,803)	—	167,000
1/08	26,313	893	3.4%	182,000
1/07	26,970	995	3.7%	188,000
1/06	22,390	1,406	6.3%	232,000
Annual Growth	1.2%	(29.4%)	—	(8.7%)

2010 Year-End Financials

Debt ratio: 179.9%
Return on equity: 7.5%
Cash ($ mil.): 1,686
Current ratio: 1.55
Long-term debt ($ mil.): 8,456

No. of shares (mil.): 422
Dividends
  Yield: 1.3%
  Payout: 24.1%
Market value ($ mil.): 6,724

Stock History

NYSE: M

	STOCK PRICE ($) FY Close	P/E High/Low		PER SHARE ($) Earnings	Dividends	Book Value
1/10	15.93	25	8	0.83	0.20	11.14
1/09	8.95	—	—	(11.40)	0.53	11.01
1/08	27.62	24	11	1.97	0.52	23.47
1/07	41.49	25	18	1.81	0.51	29.03
1/06	33.31	12	8	3.23	0.38	32.03
Annual Growth	(16.8%)	—	—	(28.8%)	(14.8%)	(23.2%)

Magellan Health Services

Magellan Health Services has charted its course to become one of the largest managed behavioral health care companies in the nation. The company manages mental health plan, employee assistance, and work/life programs through its nationwide third-party provider network that consists of about 70,000 behavioral health professionals. Magellan also provides specialty pharmaceutical management and radiology benefits management. Overall, the company serves some 60 million members through contracts with federal and local government agencies, insurance companies, and employers. Its services include administration, billing, claims handling, technology programs, and coordination of care.

Magellan's managed care operations for public sector programs make up more than half of the company's sales. These programs generally provide behavioral health benefits to Medicaid recipients through contracts with state and local authorities.

The firm is expanding by developing new products and purchasing other companies. Through acquisitions Magellan entered new service categories, radiology benefits management and specialty pharmaceutical management, which have grown to account for about 20% of the company's sales. These services are provided through subsidiaries National Imaging Associates (NIA), which manages benefits for diagnostic imaging facilities, and ICORE Healthcare, which manages coverage of specialty drugs to treat cancer and other serious diseases.

Magellan intends to keep growing its radiology benefits management sector through cross-selling to its other specialty segments' customer base and broadening its focus to new market segments.

In addition to growing its existing operations, the company is diversifying into specialty areas in order to provide a one-stop shopping point for outsourced managed care services. To that end, Magellan paid $110 million in 2009 to acquire First Health Services from Coventry Health Care. The acquisition marked Magellan's entry into the pharmacy benefits management market, and also expanded its breadth of Medicaid offerings.

HISTORY

William Fickling, once a star basketball player at Auburn University, started his career in his father's real estate office in Georgia. In 1969 Fickling founded Charter Medical as a holding company for the family's six nursing homes and one hospital. The company went public in 1971 as an owner/manager of general acute care hospitals. By the mid-1980s it had focused on psychiatric facilities and was adding addiction treatment centers to its portfolio. Charter had 63 psychiatric and 13 acute care hospitals by 1987, when Fickling engineered a $1.4 billion LBO, largely funded by the company's employee stock ownership plan (ESOP), which ended up owning 68% of the company, with Fickling owning the rest.

By 1989 Charter was in trouble. Not only was it dogged by Medicare and Medicaid fraud probes, but Fickling was accused of cheating the ESOP, which had purchased another 13% of the company from him at allegedly inflated prices. (A month after that sale, Fickling announced accounting errors that cut operating income by $26 million and the ESOP's stake plummeted.) In 1992 the Medicare fraud charges were settled for $1.9 million; a suit related to the ESOP stock sale was settled for $82 million.

But Charter's problems ran deeper — the industry itself was in flux. New treatments and managed care restrictions reduced the average stay for psychiatric patients from 26 days to 20 by 1991. Stories of abuses in the psychiatric industry surfaced, and payers were demanding fewer hospitalizations and more outpatient care. Undaunted, but deeply in debt, Charter continued to build inpatient facilities, bringing losses.

The company went into Chapter 11 in 1991, emerging in 1992 with a plan to focus on behavioral health care; it also went public again. The next year Fickling left Charter and was eventually replaced by E. Mac Crawford. As part of its plan, Charter sold its general hospitals and bought 40 psychiatric hospitals from National Medical Enterprises (now Tenet Healthcare) in 1994; it also began offering outpatient and home care services. That year Charter relocated to Atlanta.

As part of its reorganization, Charter in 1995 bought Magellan Health Services and took that name. It also bought 51% of Green Spring Health Services, a managed care company specializing in mental health and substance abuse. (It bought the rest in 1998.)

Reorganization costs and corporate cutbacks on mental health benefits brought losses until 1996, when it posted its only profit of the decade amid the increasing privatization of government psychiatric care. Seeing fast growth in managed care, Magellan sold its psychiatric hospitals to Crescent Operating in 1997, using the money to buy two more managed behavioral care companies. Magellan and Crescent created joint venture Charter Behavioral Health Systems (CBHS) to run the psychiatric facilities under the Charter name.

In 1998 Crawford was succeeded by Henry Harbin, a founder of Green Spring. In 1999 Magellan sold its European operations, and relocated to Columbia, Maryland. With CBHS flailing, Magellan gave Crescent all but 10% of the hospital firm, which filed for bankruptcy in 2000. While making plans to sell its specialty managed health care segment, Magellan also agreed to sell human services segment National Mentor, which offered at-home care for sufferers of chronic disorders, in a management buyout. The National Mentor sale closed in 2001, when Magellan also began its exit from its stake in CBHS. The company then became engaged in the managed behavioral health care business only.

In 2003 weak earnings and high debt prompted Magellan to file for Chapter 11 bankruptcy. In January 2004 Magellan emerged from Chapter 11.

The company expanded through the acquisition of National Imaging Associates (NIA), a provider of radiology benefits management services, in 2006. Specialty pharmaceutical management firm ICORE Healthcare was also added to the fold that year.

EXECUTIVES

Chairman and CEO: René Lerer, age 54, $5,862,853 total compensation
President: Karen S. Rohan, age 47, $1,531,554 total compensation
CFO: Jonathan N. (Jon) Rubin, age 47, $1,620,014 total compensation
CIO: Gary D. Anderson
Chief Medical Officer, Magellan Behavioral Health: Gary M. Henschen
Chief Corporate Development Officer: Prakash R. Patel
Chief Operations Finance Officer: Edward J. Christie
Chief Human Resources Officer: Caskie Lewis-Clapper, age 45, $1,111,999 total compensation
Chief Medical Officer: Anthony M. (Tony) Kotin, age 56
General Counsel and Secretary: Daniel N. Gregoire, age 54, $1,105,828 total compensation
SVP Public Sector Behavioral Health: Anne M. McCabe
SVP Commercial Behavioral Health: Suzanne Kunis
VP Service Operations: Jan Williams
Senior Director Corporate Communications: Tami Schmidt
CEO National Imaging Associates: Tina M. Blasi, age 52, $1,310,314 total compensation
President, ICORE Healthcare: Alan M. Lotvin, age 48
President, First Health Services: Timothy P. (Tim) Nolan, age 48
Auditors: Ernst & Young LLP

LOCATIONS

HQ: Magellan Health Services, Inc.
  55 Nod Rd., Avon, CT 06001
Phone: 860-507-1900   **Fax:** 860-507-1990
Web: www.magellanhealth.com

PRODUCTS/OPERATIONS

2009 Sales

	$ mil.	% of total
Public sector	1,362.4	52
Commercial	650.1	25
Radiology benefits management	305.3	12
Specialty pharmaceutical management	259.7	10
Medicaid administration	64.3	1
Total	**2,641.8**	**100**

COMPETITORS

American Imaging Management
APS Healthcare
CareCore
Caremark Pharmacy Services
CIGNA Behavioral Health
Comprehensive Care
ComPsych
Express Scripts
FHC Health Systems
First Health Group
Horizon Health
HSG Health Systems
Medco Health
Mental Health Network
Psychiatric Solutions
Schaller Anderson Inc
UBH
US Oncology

HISTORICAL FINANCIALS

Company Type: Public

Income Statement

FYE: December 31

	REVENUE ($ mil.)	NET INCOME ($ mil.)	NET PROFIT MARGIN	EMPLOYEES
12/09	2,642	107	4.0%	5,200
12/08	2,625	86	3.3%	5,200
12/07	2,156	94	4.4%	5,600
12/06	1,690	86	5.1%	3,900
12/05	1,808	131	7.2%	3,900
Annual Growth	9.9%	(4.9%)	—	7.5%

2009 Year-End Financials

Debt ratio: —
Return on equity: 11.5%
Cash ($ mil.): 197
Current ratio: 2.04
Long-term debt ($ mil.): —

No. of shares (mil.): 33
Dividends
 Yield: —
 Payout: —
Market value ($ mil.): 1,360

Stock History

NASDAQ (GS): MGLN

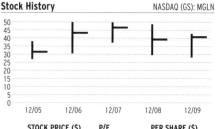

	STOCK PRICE ($) FY Close	P/E High/Low	PER SHARE ($) Earnings	Dividends	Book Value
12/09	40.73	14 10	3.01	—	28.47
12/08	39.16	22 14	2.16	—	27.20
12/07	46.63	21 16	2.36	—	27.21
12/06	43.22	22 14	2.23	—	22.87
12/05	31.45	11 8	3.46	—	18.96
Annual Growth	6.7%	— —	(3.4%)	—	10.7%

Manitowoc Company

Be it hoisting a steel column or a frosty mug, The Manitowoc Company plays a leading role. Manitowoc manufactures an array of cranes and related parts, as well as a variety of foodservice equipment. Its lifting equipment includes tower cranes, mobile telescopic cranes, and boom trucks, prevalent in construction and mining operations. Catering to commercial kitchens in restaurants, hotels, health care, and institutions, Manitowoc supplies a slate of ice-making and beverage-dispensing machines, and food prep and warming equipment. In 2008 the company bought foodservice equipment maker Enodis for $2.7 billion — Manitowoc's largest acquisition and one that launched it on the world's stage of foodservice products.

Among its strategies for growth, Manitowoc aggressively pursues acquisitions that competitively position the company within its two business segments. Enodis was acquired through a bidding war between Manitowoc and Illinois Tool Works (ITW); Manitowoc topped ITW's offer by about 5% and won the auction. The deal expands Manitowoc's offerings, enabling it to equip entire commercial kitchens.

As part of the Enodis acquisition, Manitowoc agreed with the European Commission and the US Department of Justice to divest most of Enodis' ice machine business to satisfy anticompetition concerns. In 2009 the company unloaded the ice business to an affiliate of Warburg Pincus for $160 million. The transaction included the Barline, Ice-O-Matic, Scotsman, Simag, and other ice machine brand names. Manitowoc also axed two of its foodservice product lines.

The up-tick in food service equipment sales, spurred by Enodis, however, was not enough to offset the slump in Manitowoc's crane business. Both business segments were restructured, including shuttering two facilities within the foodservice business.

Manitowoc also jockeys for growth outside the US. Since 2007 international sales have accounted for more than 50% of the company's net revenue. Enodis gave Manitowoc 22 facilities, four of which are in Europe and two in Asia.

The company is also buffering its exposure to North American demand, as well as gaining a foothold in the promising Asian market, by pursuing joint ventures. Manitowoc holds a 50% joint venture with China-based TaiAn Dongyue Heavy Machinery. The venture, begun in 2008, builds mobile and truck-mounted hydraulic cranes.

HISTORY

Manitowoc began in 1902 when naval architect Charles West and shipbuilder Elias Gunnell bought a shipyard. The company grew during WWI, but the government canceled its contracts at war's end. After feuding with Gunnell, West bought Manitowoc (he would run it until his death in 1957) and diversified into industrial equipment. Crane manufacturing helped Manitowoc survive the Depression. During WWII Manitowoc built submarines and landing craft. After the war the company branched out into freezers and dry-cleaning machines.

A recession and oil-patch bust in the 1980s caused Manitowoc's sales to plummet. By the decade's end, aging product lines had stalled earnings growth. CEO Fred Butler ended the company's shipbuilding operations and focused it on repairing vessels instead. It also modernized its cranes and broadened its product line through acquisitions in 1990. From 1994 to 1998 the company grew six-fold, largely through acquisitions.

In 1998 Manitowoc improved earnings by buying boom truck and forklift maker Powerscreen USC and by expanding into Europe with a 50% stake in Italy-based ice-machine maker F.A.G. That year Butler retired and Terry Growcock, president of subsidiary Manitowoc Ice, became CEO.

Manitowoc bought Purchasing Support Group, a beverage equipment distributor with broad US regional reach, in 1999. The next year Manitowoc boosted its cranes and related equipment business by acquiring Pioneer Holdings (hydraulic boom trucks). It also acquired Harford Duracool, a maker of walk-in refrigerators and freezers in the eastern US, and Marinette Marine, a Great Lakes shipyard (which added a significant shipbuilding business to its marine repair operations).

In 2001 the company bought Legris Industries' Potain tower crane unit. Manitowoc then added mobile cranes to its crane business in 2002 by acquiring Grove Worldwide for about $270 million. In 2002 Terry Growcock, the company's CEO, was also named as chairman, a post that had been vacant for 10 years.

Manitowoc sold its Manitowoc Boom Trucks unit to Quantum Heavy Equipment in early 2003. The company sold this unit to satisfy an order set by the Justice Department to complete the acquisition of Grove Worldwide.

In 2004 the company sold its Delta Manlift subsidiary to JLG Industries, exiting the aerial platform business. The following year it sold its Diversified Refrigeration, Inc. (DRI) subsidiary to a subsidiary of GE.

Manitowoc attempted in 2006 to make a $1.8 billion bid for the UK commercial foodservice concern Enodis; the offer was rebuffed. Enodis then warmed to the idea after Manitowoc said informally that any future bid would be higher. Enodis granted Manitowoc duediligence access to its books, but after a period of looking more closely at each other's operations, the two companies walked away from discussions. In 2008 Illinois Tool Works (ITW) made an offer to buy Enodis for about $2 billion in cash, an offer initially accepted by the Enodis board. Manitowoc answered by bumping up its bid, topping the ITW offer by about 5% and valuing Enodis at around $2.1 billion. The Enodis board recommended the higher Manitowoc offer to shareholders.

Meanwhile, in 2007 Manitowoc picked up the Carrydeck line of mobile industrial cranes from privately held Marine Travelift. The move enhanced Manitowoc's position in industrial cranes with the addition of six models. Later in 2007 the company bolstered its international presence with the purchase of India's Shirke Construction Equipments, a maker of tower cranes.

At the end of 2008 Manitowoc sold its original line of business, building and repairing ships, to Fincantieri Cantieri Navali Italiani to focus on its businesses in construction machinery and foodservice equipment.

EXECUTIVES

Chairman, President, and CEO: Glen E. Tellock, age 49, $2,033,174 total compensation
SVP; President, Crane Group: Eric P. Etchart, age 53, $678,721 total compensation
SVP; President, Foodservice Segment: Mike Kachmer, age 51
SVP, CFO, and Treasurer: Carl J. Laurino, age 48, $633,285 total compensation
SVP, Secretary, and General Counsel: Maurice D. Jones, age 50, $680,260 total compensation
SVP Human Resources and Administration:
  Thomas G. Musial, age 58, $928,738 total compensation
VP Finance and Treasurer: Dean J. Nolden, age 41
Director Investor Relations and Corporate
  Communications: Steven C. (Steve) Khail
Auditors: PricewaterhouseCoopers LLP

LOCATIONS

HQ: The Manitowoc Company, Inc.
  2400 S. 44th St., Manitowoc, WI 54221
Phone: 920-684-4410   **Fax:** 920-652-9778
Web: www.manitowoc.com

2009 Sales

	$ mil.	% of total
North America		
US	1,862.6	49
Other countries	177.3	5
Europe	824.8	22
Asia	279.1	8
Middle East	274.6	7
Central & South America	155.0	4
Africa	88.9	2
Australia	88.1	2
South Pacific & Caribbean	32.2	1
Total	**3,782.6**	**100**

PRODUCTS/OPERATIONS

2009 Sales

	$ mil.	% of total
Cranes & Related Products	2,285.0	60
Foodservice Equipment	1,497.6	40
Total	**3,782.6**	**100**

Selected Products

Cranes and Related Products
  Boom trucks (telescopic and articulated)
  Lattice-boom cranes (crawler and truck mounted; crawler crane attachments)
  Mobile telescopic cranes (rough terrain, all-terrain, truck mounted and industrial)
  Parts and service (replacement parts, product services, rebuilding and remanufacturing)
  Tower cranes (top slewing luffing jib, topless and self-erecting)
Foodservice Equipment
  Beverage dispensers and related products
  Ice-cube machines, ice flaker machines, and storage bins
  Food preparation equipment
  Primary cooking and warming equipment
  Refrigerator and freezer equipment
  Servicing and storage equipment
  Warewashing equipment

COMPETITORS

Aga Rangemaster	Ingersoll-Rand
Altec Industries	Instant UpRight
American Panel	Kobelco Construction
Caterpillar	Machinery America
CLARK Material Handling	Komatsu
Deere-Hitachi	Lancer
Delfield	Scotsman Group
Furukawa	Terex
Hitachi	Vulcan-Hart

HISTORICAL FINANCIALS

Company Type: Public

Income Statement

FYE: December 31

	REVENUE ($ mil.)	NET INCOME ($ mil.)	NET PROFIT MARGIN	EMPLOYEES
12/09	3,783	(707)	—	13,100
12/08	4,503	(11)	—	18,400
12/07	4,005	337	8.4%	10,500
12/06	2,933	166	5.7%	9,500
12/05	2,254	66	2.9%	8,000
Annual Growth	**13.8%**	**—**	**—**	**13.1%**

2009 Year-End Financials

Debt ratio: 333.5%
Return on equity: —
Cash ($ mil.): 106
Current ratio: 1.10
Long-term debt ($ mil.): 2,028
No. of shares (mil.): 131
Dividends
  Yield: 0.8%
  Payout: —
Market value ($ mil.): 1,309

Stock History

NYSE: MTW

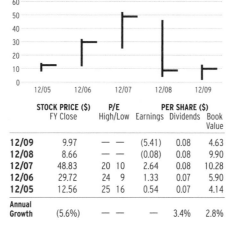

	STOCK PRICE ($) FY Close	P/E High/Low		PER SHARE ($) Earnings	Dividends	Book Value
12/09	9.97	—	—	(5.41)	0.08	4.63
12/08	8.66	—	—	(0.08)	0.08	9.90
12/07	48.83	20	10	2.64	0.08	10.28
12/06	29.72	24	9	1.33	0.07	5.90
12/05	12.56	25	16	0.54	0.07	4.14
Annual Growth	**(5.6%)**	**—**	**—**	**—**	**3.4%**	**2.8%**

Manpower Inc.

Millions of men (and women) have helped power this firm to the upper echelon of the staffing industry. Manpower is one of the world's largest providers of temporary employees, placing about 4 million people in office, industrial, and professional positions every year. It offers services through five different brands, including Manpower, Manpower Professional (accounting, finance, and engineering positions), Elan (technology professionals), and Jefferson Wells (accounting and finance). The company's Right Management unit provides management consulting services focused on leadership development and assessment. Manpower has some 4,000 owned or franchised offices in 80 countries and territories.

Supplying temporary employees to businesses on an as-needed basis accounts for the bulk of the company's business, with most of its sales coming from from office and light-industrial placements. Manpower is focused on its professional services division, however, which has been its fastest-growing segment. Operations outside the US, including Manpower UK, account for about 90% of Manpower's sales.

In keeping with its strategic focus on professional staffing services, Manpower acquired

COMSYS IT Partners in 2010 for about $375 million. The Houston-based firm provides information technology staffing through more than 50 offices in the US, Canada, and the UK. Manpower plans to integrate the new staffing operations into its Manpower Professional and Elan brands.

The deal to acquire COMSYS IT followed a relatively quiet period for the normally acquisitive Manpower. During 2009 the company focused primarily on reducing expenses in light of the economic downturn. Before the recession, though, Manpower had completed several deals during 2008 to expand both its professional services offerings and its geographic reach. It purchased professional recruitment provider Clarendon Parker Middle East, which gave Manpower its own operations in Bahrain, Kuwait, Qatar, Saudi Arabia, and the United Arab Emirates. The company also acquired Los Angeles-based business process outsourcer CRI and Dutch professional recruitment provider Vitae that year.

HISTORY

Milwaukee lawyers Elmer Winter and Aaron Scheinfeld founded Manpower in 1948. It originally concentrated on supplying temporary help to industry during the first few years of the post-war boom. In the next few years the company expanded, and in 1956 it began franchising. During the 1960s Manpower opened franchises in Europe, Asia, and South America. Unlike many of its competitors, however, it continued to emphasize blue-collar placements.

Manpower embarked on a series of acquisitions in the 1970s and began to shift its emphasis from industrial to clerical placements. It was Mitchell Fromstein, Manpower's advertising account executive in the 1960s, who orchestrated the company's growth into a powerhouse. Fromstein joined the board in 1971 and became president and CEO in 1976.

Mid-decade, with Scheinfeld deceased and Winter eager to sell, the Parker Pen Company came along. Parker Pen, also based in Wisconsin, was trying to re-energize its fading fortunes after the arrival of the disposable pen. Parker Pen bought Manpower in 1976, sold the pen business 10 years later, and became Manpower Inc. Fromstein continued as president and CEO, with a 20% interest in the company.

In the late 1970s Manpower entered the computer age, instituting a computer training program for its temporary employees. The company grew as the character of employment in the US changed from career-long employment with one company to a series of shorter-term jobs with many employers. In addition to providing short-term workers, Manpower began offering hiring and training services for permanent employees, thus saving companies in-house recruitment and training costs.

Blue Arrow, a temporary-employment agency based in the UK, acquired the firm in 1987. The combined companies operated as Manpower, and almost immediately tensions arose between Fromstein and his new boss, Antony Berry, who accused Fromstein of obstructing efforts to unite the two companies. Fromstein was fired in 1988.

Manpower's worldwide franchisees revolted against Berry, and the UK began an investigation of how the acquisition of Manpower was financed — a $1.5 billion stock sale by UK bank NatWest (now Royal Bank of Scotland Group). Berry was ousted in 1989, and Fromstein regained control.

A push by US interests changed the US composition of the company's ownership during that year from just 9% in January to over 60% by the end of the year. This gave Fromstein the support he needed to move Manpower back to Wisconsin in 1991.

Fromstein then worked to disentangle the two companies by selling off all Blue Arrow holdings not related to employment. During the mid-1990s the company opened hundreds of new offices in the US and abroad. It spent more than $15 million in 1995 to upgrade its computerized worker-to-job matching system. An alliance with Drake Beam Morin the following year gave the company access to more than 200,000 new clients.

Manpower began two pilot programs in 1997 — one to place inner-city welfare recipients in the workforce, and one offering free technology-related training to company applicants via the Internet. In 1998 the company acquired Australia's Kirby Contract Labour, which added 15 branches to the 55 already operating in Australia and New Zealand. The following year Fromstein retired after leading Manpower for 23 years. Jeffrey Joerres took over as CEO (and added chairman to his title in 2001).

Later in 1999 Manpower changed the name of its Manpower Technical division to Manpower Professional to better indicate the variety of disciplines it supported and compete in an increasingly tight market for professional workers. In 2001 the company bought financial services provider Jefferson Wells International. In 2003 the company launched its Business Resource Center, which offers online human resources information for small and midsized businesses.

Manpower was awarded a temporary staffing business license in China in 2007, making it the first global staffing company to be allowed to offer those services in that market. The company made several acquisitions the following year, including Clarendon Parker Middle East, a professional recruitment provider with operations in Bahrain, Kuwait, Qatar, Saudi Arabia, and the United Arab Emirates.

EXECUTIVES

Chairman, President, and CEO: Jeffrey A. (Jeff) Joerres, age 50, $5,358,568 total compensation
EVP and CFO: Michael J. (Mike) Van Handel, age 50, $2,163,543 total compensation
EVP; CEO Right Management Consultants and Jefferson Wells International: Owen J. Sullivan, age 52, $1,347,068 total compensation
EVP; President, Europe, Middle East, and Africa: Barbara J. Beck, age 49, $1,646,056 total compensation
EVP; President, The Americas: Jonas Prising, age 44, $1,393,013 total compensation
EVP; President, France: Françoise Gri, age 52, $1,534,499 total compensation
EVP; President, Asia/Pacific and Middle East Operations: Darryl E. Green, age 49, $1,397,942 total compensation
EVP Global Strategy and Talent: Mara E. Swan, age 50
SVP Global Workforce Strategy: Tammy Johns
SVP, General Counsel, and Secretary: Kenneth C. Hunt, age 60
SVP Marketing: Emma van Rooyen
VP and U.S. Managing Partner, Manpower Public Sector: Andrew Jones
VP and Global Chief Information Officer: Denis Edwards
VP Operations, Staffing Services, Manpower Canada: Lori Rogers
Director, Global Strategic Communications: Britt Zarling
President, Corporate and Government Affairs: David Arkless
Auditors: Deloitte & Touche LLP

LOCATIONS

HQ: Manpower Inc.
100 Manpower Place, Milwaukee, WI 53212
Phone: 414-961-1000
Web: www.manpower.com

PRODUCTS/OPERATIONS

2009 Sales

	$ mil.	% of total
France	4,675.5	29
Italy	950.8	6
Other Europe, Middle East & Africa	5,371.7	34
Americas		
US	1,593.7	10
Other	967.3	6
Asia/Pacific	1,728.0	11
Right Management	559.4	3
Jefferson Wells	192.3	1
Total	**16,038.7**	**100**

Selected Services

Staffing
Industrial trades
Manpower Professional
  Engineering
  Finance
  Information technology
  Telecommunications
Office and clerical

Other Services

Brook Street (office and light industrial staffing in the UK)
Elan Group (IT staffing in UK)
Global Learning Center (online employee testing and training)
Jefferson Wells (financial services)
Right Management Consultants (career consulting)

COMPETITORS

Adecco
Kelly Services
Korn/Ferry
Michael Page
Randstad Holding
Robert Half
SFN Group
TrueBlue
Volt Information

HISTORICAL FINANCIALS

Company Type: Public

Income Statement

FYE: December 31

	REVENUE ($ mil.)	NET INCOME ($ mil.)	NET PROFIT MARGIN	EMPLOYEES
12/09	16,039	(9)	—	3,028,000
12/08	21,553	219	1.0%	4,033,000
12/07	20,500	485	2.4%	5,033,000
12/06	17,563	398	2.3%	4,030,000
12/05	16,080	260	1.6%	4,027,000
Annual Growth	**(0.1%)**	**—**	**—**	**(6.9%)**

2009 Year-End Financials

Debt ratio: 28.2%
Return on equity: —
Cash ($ mil.): 1,015
Current ratio: 1.66
Long-term debt ($ mil.): 716
No. of shares (mil.): 82
Dividends
  Yield: 1.4%
  Payout: —
Market value ($ mil.): 4,488

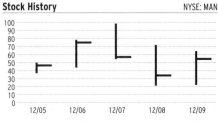
Marathon Oil

In the long-running competition for profits in the oil and gas industry, Marathon Oil is keeping up a steady pace. Through its Marathon Oil Company subsidiary, the company explores for and produces oil and gas primarily in Angola, Canada, Equatorial Guinea, Libya, Norway, Indonesia, the UK, and the US. In 2009 it reported proved reserves of 1.7 billion barrels of oil equivalent including 600 million barrels of synthetic oil from oil sands. Marathon Oil's Marathon Petroleum operates seven refineries with a total capacity of 1.2 million barrels of crude oil a day. Marathon Petroleum supplies about 4,600 Marathon-branded US retail gas outlets. Marathon Oil also services 1,600 Speedway SuperAmerica gas stations.

In a move to focus on its core businesses the company is selling $2 billion–$4 billion in non-core assets. In 2009 Marathon Oil sold its 50% stake in truck stop chain Pilot Travel Centers LLC to the joint venture's partner, Pilot Corp., for $700 million. It also sold its Irish exploration and production subsidiary for $180 million. In 2009 the company agreed to sell 20% of its 30% stake in its Angola-based oil and gas operations to CNOOC and Sinopec in order to raise about $1.3 billion.

In late 2008 Marathon Oil was looking at splitting the company's two main business units into separate public entities. Its Houston operations would retain the exploration, oil-sands mining, and natural gas businesses, while the Findlay, Ohio, operations would keep the marketing, refining, pipeline, and transportation functions. However, the global depression and slump in commodity prices and demand hurt the company's bottom line in 2009, and put separation plans on hold.

As a way to expand its hydrocarbon asset base, the company has been investing heavily in non-conventional exploration and production areas. In 2006, as part of a five-year $1.5 billion investment, the company announced plans to drill as many as 225 new wells in western North Dakota in the Bakken Oil Formation (tight shale layers) over a five-year period. The following year Marathon Oil expanded into the Canadian oil sands market through the acquisition of Western Oil Sands for about $5.8 billion.

HISTORY

Marathon Oil was founded in 1887 in Lima, Ohio, as The Ohio Oil Company by 14 independent oil producers to compete with Standard Oil. Within two years Ohio Oil was the largest producer in the state. This success did not go unnoticed by Standard Oil, which proceeded to buy Ohio Oil in 1889. In 1905 the company moved to Findlay, Ohio, where it remained until it relocated to Houston in 1990.

When the US Supreme Court broke up Standard Oil in 1911, Ohio Oil became independent once again and expanded its exploration activities to Kansas, Louisiana, Texas, and Wyoming.

In a 1924 attempt to drill three wells west of the Pecos River in Texas, Ohio Oil mistakenly drilled three dry holes to the east. The company was on the verge of abandoning the project until a geologist reported the error. Ohio Oil drilled in the right area and the wells flowed. That year the company bought Lincoln Oil Refining — its first venture outside crude oil production.

Ohio Oil continued its expansion into refining and marketing operations in 1927. After WWII the company began international exploration. Through Conorada Petroleum (later Oasis), a partnership with Continental Oil (later Conoco and then ConocoPhillips) and Amerada Hess, the company explored in Africa and South and Central America. Conorada's biggest overseas deal came in 1955, when it acquired concessions on more than 60 million acres in Libya.

In 1962 the company acquired Plymouth Oil and changed its name to Marathon Oil Company; it had been using the Marathon name in its marketing activities since the late 1930s. Marathon added a 200,000-barrel-a-day refinery in Louisiana to its operations in 1976 when it acquired ECOL Ltd.

After a battle with Mobil, U.S. Steel acquired Marathon in 1982 for $6.5 billion. U.S. Steel changed its name to USX in 1986 and acquired Texas Oil & Gas. That year the US government introduced economic sanctions against Libya, putting Marathon's Libyan holdings in suspension.

USX consolidated Texas Oil and Marathon in 1990. After a protracted struggle with corporate raider Carl Icahn, USX split Marathon and U.S. Steel into two separate stock classes in 1991. A third offering, USX-Delhi Group (the pipeline operator division), followed the next year. (Koch Industries bought USX-Delhi in 1997.)

A consortium led by USX-Marathon signed an agreement with the Russian government in 1994 to develop oil and gas fields off Sakhalin Island (although USX-Marathon sold its stake in the project in 2000). In 1996 Marathon formed a venture, ElectroGen International, with East Coast utility DQE to develop power generation projects in the Asia/Pacific region.

In 1998 Marathon and Ashland merged their refining and retail operations, creating Marathon Ashland Petroleum (MAP), with Marathon owning 62%. That year Marathon, in a deal that boosted its reserves by 18%, acquired Calgary-based Tarragon Oil and Gas.

As part of a restructuring drive, in 1999 MAP sold its crude oil gathering business, Scurlock Permian, to Plains All American Pipeline. With oil prices rebounding, Marathon ramped up its oil exploration in 2000, buying more deepwater leases in the Gulf of Mexico and acquiring an interest in an oil and gas play offshore the Republic of Congo.

The company bought Pennaco Energy, a Colorado-based producer of coalbed methane gas, for about $500 million in 2001, and it agreed to buy CMS Energy's Equatorial Guinea (West Africa) oil and gas assets in a $993 million deal that was completed in 2002. At the end of 2001, USX spun off U.S. Steel and changed the name of the remaining company to Marathon Oil Corporation. In 2002 Marathon acquired Globex Energy, a privately held exploration and production company with assets in West Africa.

In 2005 Ashland sold its 38% stake in Marathon Ashland to Marathon Oil for about $3.7 billion. In addition to acquiring MAP, Marathon Oil also obtained Ashland's maleic anhydride business, a share of its Valvoline Instant Oil Change business in Michigan and Ohio, and other assets.

In 2006 the company sold its oil and gas assets in the Khanty-Mansiysk autonomous region of western Siberia to LUKOIL for $787 million. That year Marathon Oil announced a plan to spend $3.2 billion to expand the crude oil refining capacity of its refinery in Garyville, Louisiana.

EXECUTIVES

Chairman: Thomas J. Usher, age 67
President, CEO, and Director: Clarence P. Cazalot Jr., age 59, $9,029,606 total compensation
EVP and CFO: Janet F. Clark, age 55, $3,269,151 total compensation
EVP Down Stream: Gary R. Heminger, age 56, $7,032,252 total compensation
EVP Upstream: David E. (Dave) Roberts Jr., age 49, $3,562,622 total compensation
CIO: Thomas K. Sneed
SVP Exploration: Annell R. Bay
VP Strategic Planning and Portfolio Management: Robert E. Estill
VP Natural Gas and Crude Oil Sales: Patrick J. Kuntz
VP Investor Relations and Public Affairs: Howard J. Thill, age 51
VP and General Counsel: Sylvia J. Kerrigan, age 45
VP Technology Services: Timothy N. Tipton
VP Accounting and Controller: Michael K. Stewart, age 52
VP Emerging Technology: Linda A. Capuano
VP Public Policy: Eileen M. Campbell, age 48
VP Health, Environment, Safety and Security: R. Douglas Rogers
VP Finance and Treasurer: Paul C. Reinbolt, age 54
VP Human Resources: Robert L. Sovine
VP Tax: Stephen J. Landry
VP Corporate Compliance and Ethics: Daniel J. Sullenbarger, age 54
Auditors: PricewaterhouseCoopers LLP

LOCATIONS

HQ: Marathon Oil Corporation
5555 San Felipe Rd., Houston, TX 77056
Phone: 713-629-6600   **Fax:** 713-296-2952
Web: www.marathon.com

2009 Sales

	$ mil.	% of total
US	47,293	88
Other countries	6,177	12
Adjustments	669	—
Total	**54,139**	**100**

PRODUCTS/OPERATIONS

2009 Sales

	$ mil.	% of total
Refined products	40,518	76
Liquid hydrocarbons	8,253	15
Merchandise	3,308	6
Natural gas	1,265	3
Other products & services	126	—
Adjustments	669	—
Total	**54,139**	**100**

COMPETITORS

7-Eleven
BP
Chevron
ConocoPhillips
Ergon
Exxon Mobil
Hess Corporation
J.M. Huber
Koch Industries, Inc.
Norsk Hydro ASA
Occidental Petroleum
PEMEX
Petróleos de Venezuela
Royal Dutch Shell
Sibir Energy
Sinclair Oil
Sunoco
TransCanada

HISTORICAL FINANCIALS

Company Type: Public

Income Statement				FYE: December 31
	REVENUE ($ mil.)	NET INCOME ($ mil.)	NET PROFIT MARGIN	EMPLOYEES
12/09	54,139	1,463	2.7%	28,855
12/08	78,569	3,528	4.5%	30,360
12/07	59,389	3,956	6.7%	29,524
12/06	64,896	5,234	8.1%	28,195
12/05	58,958	3,051	5.2%	27,756
Annual Growth	**(2.1%)**	**(16.8%)**	**—**	**1.0%**

2009 Year-End Financials

Debt ratio: 38.5%	No. of shares (mil.): 710
Return on equity: 6.8%	Dividends
Cash ($ mil.): 2,057	Yield: 3.1%
Current ratio: 1.17	Payout: 46.6%
Long-term debt ($ mil.): 8,436	Market value ($ mil.): 22,156

Stock History

NYSE: MRO

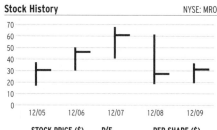

	STOCK PRICE ($) FY Close	P/E High/Low		PER SHARE ($) Earnings	Dividends	Book Value
12/09	31.22	17	10	2.06	0.96	30.87
12/08	27.36	12	4	4.95	0.96	30.17
12/07	60.86	12	7	5.69	0.92	27.09
12/06	46.25	7	4	7.25	0.76	20.58
12/05	30.49	9	4	4.22	0.61	16.49
Annual Growth	**0.6%**	**—**	**—**	**(16.4%)**	**12.0%**	**17.0%**

Markel Corporation

Have you ever thought about who insures the manicurist or an antique motorcycle? Specialty insurer Markel Corporation takes on the risks other insurers won't touch, from amusement parks to thoroughbred horses and summer camps. Coverage is also available for one-time events, such as golf tournaments and auto races. Markel's commercial excess and surplus products include a wide range of liabilities (professional, pollution) while its specialty admitted segment covers businesses ranging from martial arts schools to dude ranches. Markel International provides specialty insurance internationally from its base in the UK. The company's products are distributed through independent agents and brokers.

Excess insurance kicks in when a company's regular insurance fizzles out. For example, a regular policy might pay up to $100,000 on claims, but the excess policy could then pay any amounts over $100,000 and up to $1 million. Surplus insurance is coverage that no regular insurance company can offer and typically comes with a higher level of risk and higher-priced premiums.

Higher premium volume (primarily in its excess and surplus segment) and improved results by its previously struggling international business have helped to increase Markel's underwriting profits. Rather than sit on its hands while its investment portfolio tanked during 2008, Markel chose to sell off portions of its investments and took substantial write-downs that year. By 2010 its investment arm Markel Ventures had stabilized enough to resume investing in new non-insurance businesses, ranging from food processing equipment manufacturers to manufactured housing communities.

Unlike standard insurers (whose rates are generally regulated), specialty insurers can charge the rates they consider reasonable. To that end, after taking significant losses from the 2005 hurricane season (Katrina, Rita, Wilma), and additional hits from the 2008 season (Gustav, Ike), the company decided to raise the rates on its catastrophe-exposed businesses.

Markel moved to expand its international specialty property/casualty operations in 2009 by acquiring Elliott Special Risks, a Canadian general agent providing underwriting services for nonstandard policies, for $70 million. Elliot Special Risks was then housed within Markel International. In 2010 Markel added workers' compensation to its roster of insurance offerings when it agreed to acquire Aspen Holdings, which does business as FirstComp Insurance, for at least $135 million (plus stock option value). Following the buy, FirstComp will operate as a separate business unit of Markel.

Cousins and co-vice chairmen Anthony Markel and Steven Markel control about 6% of the company.

HISTORY

In the 1920s Sam Markel formed a mutual insurance company for "jitneys" (passenger cars refurbished as public transportation buses). In 1930 he founded Markel Service to expand nationally. To keep up with industry growth, the company revamped itself as a managing general agent and independent claims service organization in the late 1950s. In 1978 Markel began covering taverns, restaurants, and vacant buildings. It created excess and surplus lines underwriter Essex Insurance in 1980.

Markel went public in 1986. The next year it invested in Shand Morahan and Evanston Insurance (specialty coverage, including architects, engineers, and lawyers professional liability; officers and directors insurance; errors and omissions; and medical malpractice). It bought summer camp insurer Rhulen Agency in 1989.

In the 1990s Markel began buying insurers with their own offbeat niches. In 1990 it bought the rest of Shand Morahan and Evanston Insurance. In 1995 it bought Lincoln Insurance (excess and surplus lines) from media giant Thomson (now Thomson Reuters). The next year the company bought Investors Insurance Holding (excess and surplus lines). Markel, which already owned nearly 10% of Gryphon Holdings (commercial property/casualty), bought the rest in 1999.

Expanding internationally, Markel bought Bermuda-based Terra Nova Holdings, a reinsurer and a Lloyd's managing agency, in 2000. The company experienced heavy losses in 2001, not only related to the events of September 11 but also to its slumping international business (the company took a $100 million charge).

EXECUTIVES

Chairman and CEO: Alan I. Kirshner, age 74, $1,021,709 total compensation
Vice Chairman: Steven A. Markel, age 61, $986,685 total compensation
Vice Chairman: Anthony F. (Tony) Markel, age 68, $689,671 total compensation
President and Co-COO: Richard R. Whitt III, age 46, $855,658 total compensation
President and Co-COO: F. Michael (Mike) Crowley, age 58, $1,265,046 total compensation
President and Chief Investment Officer; President, Markel-Gayner Asset Management: Thomas S. Gayner, age 48, $815,231 total compensation
EVP and Chief Underwriting Officer: Gerard Albanese Jr., age 58, $1,206,617 total compensation
VP, CFO, and Treasurer: Anne G. Waleski, age 43
VP Investor Relations: Bruce A. Kay
Chief Accounting Officer and Controller: Nora N. Crouch, age 50
Chief Administrative Officer: Britton L. (Britt) Glisson, age 53
Secretary: D. Michael Jones
Auditors: KPMG LLP

LOCATIONS

HQ: Markel Corporation
4521 Highwoods Pkwy., Glen Allen, VA 23060
Phone: 804-747-0136   **Fax:** 804-965-1600
Web: www.markelcorp.com

PRODUCTS/OPERATIONS

2009 Revenues

	$ mil.	% of total
Earned premiums		
Excess & surplus lines	940.1	43
London insurance market	572.4	27
Specialty admitted	303.9	14
Net investment income	259.8	12
Net realized investment losses & other losses	(96.7)	—
Other revenues	89.8	4
Total	**2,069.3**	**100**

COMPETITORS

Assurant
Chubb Corp
CNA Financial
Fireman's Fund Insurance
Great American Insurance Company
HCC Insurance
Liberty International Underwriters
Meadowbrook Insurance
Medical Liability Mutual Insurance
National Indemnity Company
Nationwide
NYMAGIC
Penn-America
Philadelphia Insurance Companies
RLI
Travelers Companies
United States Liability Insurance Group
XL Group plc

HISTORICAL FINANCIALS

Company Type: Public

Income Statement

FYE: December 31

	ASSETS ($ mil.)	NET INCOME ($ mil.)	INCOME AS % OF ASSETS	EMPLOYEES
12/09	10,242	202	2.0%	2,800
12/08	9,478	(59)	—	2,000
12/07	10,134	406	4.0%	2,000
12/06	10,088	393	3.9%	1,897
12/05	9,814	148	1.5%	1,866
Annual Growth	**1.1%**	**8.1%**	**—**	**10.7%**

2009 Year-End Financials

Equity as % of assets: 27.1%
Return on assets: 2.0%
Return on equity: 8.1%
Long-term debt ($ mil.): —
No. of shares (mil.): 10
Dividends
  Yield: —
  Payout: —
Market value ($ mil.): 3,322
Sales ($ mil.): 2,069

Stock History

NYSE: MKL

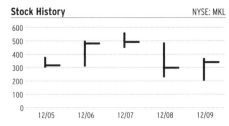

	STOCK PRICE ($) FY Close	P/E High/Low	Earnings	PER SHARE ($) Dividends	Book Value
12/09	340.00	18 10	20.52	—	283.96
12/08	299.00	— —	(5.95)	—	223.20
12/07	491.10	14 11	40.64	—	270.33
12/06	480.10	13 8	39.40	—	235.04
12/05	317.05	25 21	14.80	—	174.56
Annual Growth	**1.8%**	**— —**	**8.5%**	**—**	**12.9%**

Marriott International

Marriott International signs in at the top of the lodging industry. The company is one of the world's leading hoteliers with some 3,400 operated or franchised properties in more than 65 countries. Marriott's hotels include such full-service brands as Renaissance Hotels and its flagship Marriott Hotels & Resorts, as well as select-service and extended-stay brands Courtyard and Fairfield Inn. It also owns the Ritz-Carlton luxury chain and resort, and time-share properties operated by Marriott Vacation Club International. Marriott additionally provides more than 2,000 rental units for corporate housing and manages 40 golf courses. The Marriott family, including CEO J. W. Marriott Jr., owns about 30% of the firm.

Marriott operates more than 1,000 of its hotels and gets most of its revenue through lease agreements and management fees collected from property owners. It has more than 2,000 franchised hotels that pay the company fees and royalties as well as a percentage of their food and beverage revenue. (Marriott owns fewer than 10 of its properties.) While the bulk of its hotels are located in the US, about 15% of its properties are international. The company has long-term management agreements with properties that are owned or leased by Host Hotels & Resorts, a major customer that accounts for about 20% of Marriott's sales.

In response to the declining economy, Marriott eliminated more than 1,000 jobs in 2009. It has additionally cut costs by modifying menus and restaurant hours, adjusting room amenities and relaxing some brand standards, and restructuring its time-share business to reduce prices and halt new development. It is also engaging in tactics to reward and retain loyal customers and to attract new guests. Such activities include new sales promotions, using social media such as Facebook and Twitter to communicate with customers, and enhancing its Marriott Rewards loyalty program offerings. In addition, the company redesigned its Marriott.com website to enhance its functionality and update its look.

The company is also developing a boutique chain (small, upscale, stylish hotels in prime locations) called Edition, designed by Ian Schrager, the hotelier behind hip properties such as Manhattan's Morgans Hotel. The first Edition hotel is expected to open later in 2010. Other expansion plans include its acquisition of The Greenbrier, a resort in White Sulpher Springs, West Virginia. The Greenbrier's roots go back to the 18th century. However, in recent years The Greenbrier has posted losses, and Marriott is buying the resort — a National Historic landmark — just as it announced it is filing for bankruptcy.

HISTORY

The company began in 1927 as a Washington, DC, root beer stand operated by John and Alice Marriott. Later they added hot food and named their business the Hot Shoppe. In 1929 they incorporated and began building a regional chain.

Hot Shoppes opened its first hotel, the Twin Bridges Marriott Motor Hotel, in Arlington, Virginia, in 1957. When the Marriotts' son Bill became president in 1964 (CEO in 1972, chairman in 1985), he focused on expanding the hotel business. The company changed its name to Marriott Corp. in 1967. With the rise in airline travel, Marriott built several airport hotels during the 1970s. By 1977 sales had topped $1 billion.

Marriott became the #1 operator of airport food, beverage, and merchandise facilities in the US with its 1982 acquisition of Host International, and it introduced moderately priced Courtyard hotels in 1983. Acquisitions in the 1980s included a time-share business, foodservice companies, and competitor Howard Johnson. (Marriott later sold the hotels but kept the restaurants and turnpike units.)

The company entered three new market segments in 1987: Marriott Suites (full-service suites), Residence Inn (moderately priced suites), and Fairfield Inn (economy hotels). It also began developing "life-care" communities, which provide apartments, meals, and limited nursing care to the elderly, in 1988.

Marriott split its operations into two companies in 1993: Host Marriott to own hotels, and Marriott International primarily to manage them. However, Marriott International still owned some of the properties, and in 1995 it bought 49% of the Ritz-Carlton luxury hotel group.

Marriott introduced its Marriott Executive Residences in 1997. Also that year the firm expanded overseas operations with its purchase of the 150-unit Hong Kong-based Renaissance Hotel Group, a deal that included branding rights to the Ramada chain.

In 1998, after the division of its lodging and food distribution services, the new Marriott International then began trading as a separate company. That year Marriott also acquired the rest of Ritz-Carlton.

Marriott entered the corporate housing business in 1999 through its acquisition of ExecuStay Corporation (renamed ExecuStay by Marriott), which provides fully furnished and accessorized apartments for stays of 30 days or more. The following year the company set up a $3.7 billion investment fund with Ripplewood Holdings (Marriott owns about 20%) that would buy Japanese hotels to operate under Marriott management. It also agreed to pay $400 million to settle a lawsuit brought by stockholders who contended the company defrauded them.

Marriott refocused its operations on the lodging market in 2003 when it exited both the senior living and distribution services businesses. It sold Marriott Distribution Services (food and beverage distribution) to Services Group of America, and sold Marriott Senior Living Services to Sunrise Assisted Living (the management business) and CNL Retirement Properties (nine communities). The following year Marriott sold the international branding rights to the Ramada and Days Inn chains to Cendant (now Avis Budget Group) for about $200 million.

In 2005 Marriott acquired about 30 properties from CTF Holdings (an affiliate of Hong Kong-based New World Development) for nearly $1.5 billion. It sold 14 properties immediately to Sunstone Hotel Investors and Walton Street Capital. The deal put an end to an ongoing legal battle between Marriott and CTF Holdings, which alleged that the hotelier had pocketed kickbacks and fees from outside vendors.

It invested about $200 million in 2005 to upgrade its hotel beds with higher thread-count sheets and triple-sheeted tops, and it renovated and upgraded many of its Courtyard and Residence Inn locations during 2006.

EXECUTIVES

Chairman and CEO: J. W. (Bill) Marriott Jr., age 78, $1,579,599 total compensation
Vice Chairman: John W. Marriott III, age 49
Vice Chairman: William J. (Bill) Shaw, age 64, $4,916,139 total compensation
President and COO: Arne M. Sorenson, age 51, $4,280,311 total compensation
Group President, The Americas and Global Lodging Services: Robert J. (Bob) McCarthy, age 56, $2,381,421 total compensation
EVP and CFO: Carl T. Berquist, age 59, $1,088,662 total compensation
EVP and CIO: Carl Wilson
EVP Architecture and Construction:
A. Bradford (Brad) Bryan Jr.
EVP Global Development: Anthony G. (Tony) Capuano, age 44
EVP Global Human Resources: David A. Rodriguez, age 51
EVP Development, Planning, and Feasibility:
Scott E. Melby
EVP and General Counsel: Edward A. (Ed) Ryan, age 56
EVP Mergers, Acquisitions, and Business Development: Richard S. Hoffman
EVP Brand Management and Operations:
Donald J. Semmler
EVP Global Communications and Public Affairs:
Kathleen Matthews
SVP Investor Relations: Laura E. Paugh
VP, Senior Counsel, and Corporate Secretary:
Bancroft S. Gordon
President and Managing Director, Europe:
Amy C. McPherson, age 48
President, The Americas Division: David J. Grissen, age 52
President and Managing Director, Marriott Lodging, International Operations: Edwin D. (Ed) Fuller, age 64
President, Marriott Vacation Club International:
Stephen P. (Steve) Weisz, age 59
President and Managing Director, Asia/Pacific:
Simon F. Cooper, age 64
Auditors: Ernst & Young LLP

LOCATIONS

HQ: Marriott International, Inc.
10400 Fernwood Rd., Bethesda, MD 20817
Phone: 301-380-3000   **Fax:** 301-380-3969
Web: www.marriott.com

2009 Locations

	No.
Americas	
US	2,969
Other countries	125
Europe	
UK & Ireland	61
Other countries	108
Asia	114
Middle East & Africa	35
Australia	8
Total	**3,420**

PRODUCTS/OPERATIONS

2009 Sales

	$ mil.	% of total
Lodging		
North American full-service	4,848	44
North American limited-service	1,986	18
Timeshare	1,439	13
Luxury	1,413	13
International	1,145	11
Other	77	1
Total	**10,908**	**100**

COMPETITORS

Accor
Best Western
Carlson Hotels
Choice Hotels
Club Med
Fairmont Raffles
Four Seasons Hotels
Hilton Worldwide
HVM
Hyatt
InterContinental Hotels
Loews Hotels
LXR Luxury Resorts
Starwood Hotels & Resorts

HISTORICAL FINANCIALS

Company Type: Public

Income Statement — FYE: Friday nearest December 31

	REVENUE ($ mil.)	NET INCOME ($ mil.)	NET PROFIT MARGIN	EMPLOYEES
12/09	10,908	(353)	—	137,000
12/08	12,879	362	2.8%	146,000
12/07	12,990	696	5.4%	151,000
12/06	12,160	717	5.9%	150,600
12/05	11,550	669	5.8%	143,000
Annual Growth	(1.4%)	—	—	(1.1%)

2009 Year-End Financials

Debt ratio: 195.6%
Return on equity: —
Cash ($ mil.): 115
Current ratio: 1.25
Long-term debt ($ mil.): 2,234

No. of shares (mil.): 363
Dividends
  Yield: 0.3%
  Payout: —
Market value ($ mil.): 9,887

Stock History — NYSE: MAR

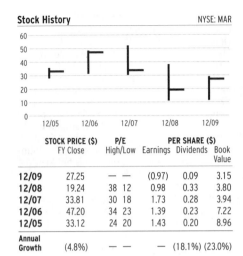

	STOCK PRICE ($) FY Close	P/E High/Low		PER SHARE ($) Earnings	Dividends	Book Value
12/09	27.25	—	—	(0.97)	0.09	3.15
12/08	19.24	38	12	0.98	0.33	3.80
12/07	33.81	30	18	1.73	0.28	3.94
12/06	47.20	34	23	1.39	0.23	7.22
12/05	33.12	24	20	1.43	0.20	8.96
Annual Growth	(4.8%)	—	—	—	(18.1%)	(23.0%)

Mars, Incorporated

Mars knows chocolate sales are nothing to snicker at. The company makes such worldwide favorites as M&M's, Snickers, and the Mars bar. Its other confections include 3 Musketeers, Dove, Milky Way, Skittles, Twix, and Starburst candy; Combos and Kudos snacks; Uncle Ben's rice; and pet food under the names Pedigree, Sheba, and Whiskas. It also owns the world's largest chewing gum maker, the Wm. Wrigley Jr. Company. The Mars family (including siblings and retired company CEO Forrest Mars Jr., chairman John Franklyn Mars, and VP Jacqueline Badger Mars) owns the highly secretive firm, making the family one of the richest in the US.

Sweet deals are the name of the game in the confectionery sector, and Mars' 2008 takeover of chewing gum giant Wrigley (valued at some $23 billion) brought together two iconic US companies, both of which already had a substantial worldwide presence. Mars acquired such well-known brands as Altoids, Life Savers, and Creme Savers, along with the best-selling chewing gum brands Spearmint, Juicy Fruit, Doublemint, and a host of others. Together, the companies benefited from greater global marketing and distribution muscle, as well as cost-savings in manufacturing and raw materials.

Despite promises not to interfere with Wrigley, a mere two weeks after the acquisition was final, Mars yanked its CEO and president, William Perez, and replaced him with a Mars 19-year veteran, Dushan "Duke" Petrovich. Petrovich was given the title of president, Mars having eliminated the CEO position at its newest acquisition.

In addition to a vast array of chocolate candy (including salty M&M's), Mars also makes nonchocolate foods, including breath mints such as AquaDrops, and snack foods like Combos and Kudos. It swallows a large bite of the pet food market with its Royal Canin, Pedigree, and Whiskas brands. In order to reassure dog owners as to the lineage of their canine companions, Pedigree makes a product called Wisdom Panel, which is a DNA test kit for dogs that determines the pet's breed mix. Turning back to the people menu, Mars' other food brands include Uncle Ben's rice, Seeds of Change organic food, and the Klix and Flavia Beverage Systems.

Mars stays virtually debt-free and uses its profits for expansion. It has 135 factories in 68 countries and sells its products worldwide.

HISTORY

Frank Mars invented the Milky Way candy bar in 1923 after his previous three efforts at the candy business left him bankrupt. After his estranged son, Forrest, graduated from Yale, Mars hired him to work at his candy operation. When Forrest demanded one-third control of the company and Frank refused, Forrest moved to England with the foreign rights to Milky Way and started his own company (Food Manufacturers) in the 1930s. He made a sweeter version of Milky Way for the UK, calling it a Mars bar. Forrest also ventured into pet food with the 1934 purchase of Chappel Brothers (renamed Pedigree). At one point he controlled 55% of the British pet food market.

During WWII Forrest returned to the US and introduced Uncle Ben's rice (the world's first brand-name raw commodity) and M&M's (a joint venture between Forrest and Bruce Murrie, son of Hershey's then-president). The idea for M&M's was borrowed from British Smarties, for which Forrest obtained rights (from Rowntree Mackintosh) by relinquishing similar rights to the Snickers bar in some foreign markets. The ad slogan "Melts in your mouth, not in your hand" (and the candy's success in non-air-conditioned stores and war zones) made the company an industry leader. Mars introduced M&M's Peanut in 1954. It was one of the first candy companies to sponsor a television show — Howdy Doody in the 1950s.

Forrest merged his firm with his deceased father's company in 1964, after buying his dying half-sister's controlling interest. (He renamed the business Mars at her request.) The merger was the end of an alliance with Hershey, who had supplied Frank with chocolate since his Milky Way inception.

In 1968 Mars bought Kal Kan. In 1973 Forrest, then 69 years old, delegated his company responsibilities to sons Forrest Jr. and John. Five years later the brothers, looking for snacks to offset dwindling candy sales resulting from a more diet-conscious America, bought the Twix chocolate-covered cookie brand. During the late 1980s they bought ice-cream bar maker Dove Bar International and Ethel-M Chocolates, producer of liqueur-flavored chocolates, a business their father had begun in his retirement.

Hershey in 1988 surpassed Mars as the largest candy maker in the US when it acquired Mounds, Almond Joy, and other US brands from Cadbury Schweppes (now Cadbury). In response to the success of Hershey's Symphony Bar, Mars introduced its dark-chocolate Dove bar in 1991.

The company entered the huge confectionery market of India in 1989 by building a $10 million factory there. In 1996 the company opened a confectionery processing plant in Brazil.

Forrest Sr. died in 1999, spurring rumors that Mars would go public or be sold. Instead, the company dismantled most of its sales force, opting to use less-costly food brokers. Forrest Jr. retired the same year, leaving brother John Franklyn as president and CEO.

In 2000 the company established a subsidiary, Effem India, to market Mars' products in India. In 2003 Mars acquired French pet food producer Royal Canin. That year its Mexican subsidiary, Effem México SA de CV, merged with Mexican confectioner Grupo Matre to form a partnership to produce candy for Hispanic markets.

In 2004 the company appointed Peter Cheney and Paul Michaels co-presidents, leaving John Franklyn Mars as chairman. Cheney retired in 2005.

The company sold off its payment-processing subsidiary, MEI Conlux (which has headquarters in Pennsylvania and Japan), in 2006 to investment firms Bain Capital and Advantage Partners for more than $500 million.

Adding to its fast-growing pet-products sector, in 2006 Mars purchased dog-treat manufacturer S&M Nu Tec. Still barking up the pet-product tree, Mars acquired private-label dry pet food manufacturer Doane Pet Care Company that year as well. Doane's products are sold in the US and Europe.

The company discontinued brands in 2006, including Pop'ables and Cookies &, for an estimated $300 million savings, which it invested in advertising. The company introduced new Dove varieties and a dark chocolate version of M&Ms that year as well.

EXECUTIVES

Chairman: John F. Mars
President and CEO: Paul S. Michaels
EVP and CFO: Olivier Goudet
Chief Science Officer: Harold Schmitz
Global Chief Marketing Officer: Bruce McColl
Corporate Ombudsman: Victoria Mars
VP Technology: Richard Ware
VP, Secretary, General Counsel: Alberto Mora
VP Personnel and Organization: Aileen Richards
VP Research and Development, Mars Foods US: Mike Wilson
VP Procurement: Andy Parton
VP Global Sustainability: Julia Tuthill Mulligan
President, Mars Chocolate North America: Todd R. Lachman
President, Chocolate: Grant Reid
President, Food: Brian Camastral
President, Mars Drinks and Developing Petcare: Martin Radvan
President, Wrigley Gum and Confections: Dushan (Duke) Petrovich, age 56
President, Symbioscience: Frank Mars
President, Snackfoods, Masterfoods Europe: Andy Weston-Webb
President, Mars Nutrition for Health and Well-Being: James (Jamie) Mattikow
Global President, Mars Petcare: Pierre Laubies

LOCATIONS

HQ: Mars, Incorporated
6885 Elm St., McLean, VA 22101
Phone: 703-821-4900 **Fax:** 703-448-9678
Web: www.mars.com

PRODUCTS/OPERATIONS

Selected Products and Brands
Mars Candy and Snacks
3 Musketeers
Bounty
Combos
Dove
Galaxy
Generation Max
Kudos
M&M's
Mars
Milky Way
Munch
Skittles
Snickers
Starburst
Twix
Mars Drinks
Flavia
Klix
Mars Food
Castellari
Dolmio
Ebly
Masterfoods
Seeds of Change
Suzi Wan
Thomas
Uncle Ben's
Mars Pet Care
Advance
Catsan
Cesar
Champ
Dentabone
Dentastix
Dine
Exelpet
Frolic
Gourmania
KalKan
Kitbits
KiteKat
Max
Miss Cat
My Dog
Natural Choice
Nutro
Optimum
Oral Fresh Biscuit
Pal
Pedigree
Perfect Fit
Pockets
Rodeo
Sheba
Temptations
Trill
Ultra
Whiskas
Mars Symbioscience
CirkuHealth
Cocoapro
Seramis
Wisdom Panel
Wrigley
Altoids
Aquadrops
Big League Chew
Crème Savers
Doublemint
Eclipse
Extra
Freedent
Hubba Bubba
Juicy Fruit
Life Savers
Orbit
Spearmint
Winterfresh

COMPETITORS

American Italian Pasta
Barilla
Barry Callebaut
Breeder's Choice
Caribou Coffee
Chupa Chups
Colgate-Palmolive
ConAgra
Ezaki Glico
Farley's & Sathers
Fazer Konfektyr
Ferrara Pan Candy
Ferrero
General Mills
Ghirardelli Chocolate
Godiva Chocolatier
Green Mountain Coffee
Guittard
HARIBO
Harry London Candies
Heinz
Hershey
Hill's Pet Nutrition
Iams
Jelly Belly Candy
Kraft Foods
Lindt & Sprüngli
Meiji Holdings
Nestlé
Nestlé Purina PetCare
Perfetti Van Melle
PETCO
Riviana Foods
Rocky Mountain Chocolate
Royal Cup Coffee
Russell Stover
S&D Coffee
Sara Lee
Smucker
Starbucks
SweetWorks
Tootsie Roll
Topps
Unilever
Upper Deck

HISTORICAL FINANCIALS
Company Type: Private

Income Statement

	REVENUE ($ mil.)	NET INCOME ($ mil.)	NET PROFIT MARGIN	EMPLOYEES
12/08	30,000	—	—	70,000
12/07	25,000	—	—	48,000
12/06	21,000	—	—	40,000
12/05	18,000	—	—	40,500
12/04	18,000	—	—	39,000
Annual Growth	13.6%	—	—	15.7%

FYE: December 31

Revenue History

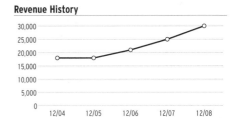

Marsh & McLennan

Marsh & McLennan Companies is the ultimate middleman. The company is one of the world's largest insurance brokers. Through core insurance subsidiary Marsh, the company provides a broad array of insurance and risk management services; its reinsurance business is handled by subsidiary Guy Carpenter. Kroll is Marsh & McLennan's risk consulting and technology services arm. The company also owns Mercer, which provides human resources and financial consulting services to customers worldwide, and Oliver Wyman, which provides management consulting services.

Citing such high-profile natural disasters as tsunamis and hurricanes as well as international terrorism, Marsh & McLennan plans to expand its role as a risk consultant; its paring of other operations is part of a greater plan to focus on this business sector.

The company's Marsh insurance subsidiary has been steadily branching out from its straight brokerage operations. It now offers risk consulting and has launched a commercial insurance agency. Nonetheless, like its leading US competitors, Marsh's most basic strategy for growth through the years has been to buy up regional brokerages large and small. It has kept up a steady pace of acquisitions, including the 2009 and 2010 purchases of regional brokerage firms The NIA Group and Rutherfoord.

Brian Duperreault, formerly of ACE Limited, was tapped as CEO in 2007. He replaced Michael Cherkasky, who had shepherded the company through a legal crisis with the New York state attorney general's office.

In 2008 Duperreault announced that the company would seek to divest certain underperforming portions of its Kroll business. Later that year, MMC divested Kroll's Corporate Advisory and Restructuring division, and in 2009 it sold the Kroll Government Services business. In early 2010 Kroll sold its Laboratory Specialists division, which conducts drugs-of-abuse testing, to diagnostic firm Inverness for $110 million. In mid-2010 MMC finally sold off all of Kroll to private-equity firm Providence Equity Partners' Altegrity for just over $1 billion.

In early 2009 the company announced plans to grow Mercer's investment consulting division by acquiring rival Callan Associates. The acquisition will boost Mercer's consulting position in the US market.

HISTORY

Marsh & McLennan Companies dates back to the Dan H. Bomar Company, founded in 1871 after the Great Chicago Fire. In 1885 a plucky Harvard dropout named Henry Marsh joined the company, then known as R.A. Waller and Company. When Robert Waller died in 1889, Marsh and fellow employee Herbert Ulmann bought a controlling stake and renamed the company Marsh Ulmann & Co. Marsh pioneered insurance brokering and in 1901 set up U.S. Steel's self-insurance program.

In 1904 different directors at Burlington Northern Railroad promised their account to Marsh Ulmann, as well as Manley-McLennan of Duluth (railroad insurance), and D.W. Burrows (a small Chicago-based railroad insurance firm). Rather than fight over it, the firms joined forces to form the world's largest insurance brokerage.

When Burrows retired in 1906, the firm became Marsh & McLennan.

In the early 20th century, Marsh won AT&T's business and McLennan landed the account of Armour Meat Packing.

In 1923 Marsh & McLennan became a closely held corporation. Marsh sold out to McLennan in 1935. The company weathered the Depression without major layoffs by cutting pay and branching into life insurance and employee-benefits consulting after passage of the Social Security Act (1935).

The firm grew through acquisitions in the 1950s, went public in 1962, and in 1969 formed a holding company that became Marsh & McLennan Companies. In the 1970s it diversified, buying Putnam Management (investment management). It set up subsidiary William M. Mercer's employee-benefits consulting business in 1975, and in 1980 it acquired a foothold in the UK with C.T. Bowring Reinsurance. In 1982 Marsh & McLennan formed Seabury & Smith to manage its insurance group programs.

As the insurance business slowed in the 1980s, financial and consulting fields grew. In 1992 the firm formed Mercer Consulting Group as an umbrella for its various consulting companies.

In 1995 Marsh & McLennan opened global brokering centers to centralize its insurance placement services to mid-market businesses. In 1998 the company bought Sedgwick Group, a UK-based insurance services firm.

The next year the firm named Jeffrey Greenberg, the son of AIG chairman Hank Greenberg, to replace chairman and CEO A. J. C. Smith.

With offices in the World Trade Center, the company lost some 300 employees in the September 11 terrorist attacks. Following the attacks on the World Trade Center, Marsh & McLennan launched a new subsidiary (AXIS Specialty) to deal with the capacity shortage in the insurance industry.

Two major Marsh & McLennan units came under legal fire in probes of the mutual fund and insurance brokerage industries, respectively. In 2003 Putnam agreed to settle securities fraud charges with the SEC and reimburse investors; many of Putnam's top officers were replaced and its compliance procedures were restructured.

The following year, Marsh found itself at the center of a price-fixing investigation that involved several insurance companies, including AIG and ACE Limited. At least nine employees of Marsh and AIG pled guilty to criminal charges. Jeffery Greenberg, the son of outspoken AIG CEO Maurice Greenberg, who had served as Marsh & McLennan's chairman and CEO, resigned in 2004 as a result of the allegations.

Strengthening its risk management operations, Marsh & McLennan acquired risk consulting company Kroll for about $2 billion in 2004.

Michael Cherkasky was named as Greenberg's successor. Before entering the insurance industry, Cherkasky had headed the investigations unit of the New York County district attorney's office. Cherkasky guided the company during Marsh's alleged bid-rigging investigation, which ended with an $850 million settlement agreement in early 2005. Following the settlement, the company slashed its dividends and cut jobs.

As part of an effort to relieve possible conflicts of interest following the investigation, MMC divested its US-based wholesale insurance brokerage Crump Group in late 2005.

In 2007 the company sold its money management operation, Putnam Investments, to Power Financial Corporation subsidiary Great-West Lifeco for $3.9 billion.

EXECUTIVES

Director: Rt. Hon. Lord Lang of Monkton, age 69
Chairman: Stephen R. Hardis, age 74
Vice Chairman, Office of the CEO: David A. Nadler, age 61
President, CEO, and Director: Brian Duperreault, age 62, $14,081,039 total compensation
EVP and CFO: Vanessa A. Wittman, age 42, $3,897,438 total compensation
EVP and General Counsel: Peter J. Beshar, age 48, $4,298,290 total compensation
SVP and Chief Compliance Officer: E. Scott Gilbert, age 54
SVP and Chief Human Resources Officer: Orlando D. Ashford, age 41
SVP International and Client Development: David R. Frediani
SVP and CIO: William P. (Bill) Krivoshik
VP and Director Government Relations: Erick Gustafson
Chairman and CEO, Marsh: Daniel S. (Dan) Glaser, age 49, $8,615,234 total compensation
Chairman and CEO, Mercer: M. Michele Burns, age 51, $4,790,944 total compensation
President and CEO, Guy Carpenter: Peter Zaffino, age 43
President and CEO, Oliver Wyman: John P. Drzik, age 47
Chief Diversity Officer: Kathryn Komsa
Auditors: Deloitte & Touche LLP

LOCATIONS

HQ: Marsh & McLennan Companies, Inc.
1166 Avenue of the Americas, New York, NY 10036
Phone: 212-345-5000 **Fax:** 212-345-4808
Web: www.marshmac.com

2009 Revenues

	$ mil.	% of total
US	4,965	47
UK	1,759	17
Continental Europe	1,843	17
Other	1,994	19
Adjustments	(68)	—
Total	**10,493**	**100**

PRODUCTS/OPERATIONS

2009 Revenues

	$ mil.	% of total
Risk & insurance services		
Marsh	4,319	41
Guy Carpenter	911	9
Consulting		
Mercer	3,327	32
Oliver Wyman Group	1,282	12
Risk consulting & technology		
Kroll	667	6
Adjustments	(13)	—
Total	**10,493**	**100**

COMPETITORS

Accenture
ADP Screening and Selection
Anthony Clark International Insurance Brokers
Aon
Arthur Gallagher
Bain & Company
Brown & Brown
FTI Consulting
Hewitt Associates
Hub International
ING
Jardine Lloyd
Lloyd's
McKinsey & Company
THB Group
USI
Wells Fargo Insurance Services
Willis Group Holdings

HISTORICAL FINANCIALS
Company Type: Public

Income Statement
FYE: December 31

	REVENUE ($ mil.)	NET INCOME ($ mil.)	NET PROFIT MARGIN	EMPLOYEES
12/09	10,493	242	2.3%	52,000
12/08	11,587	(73)	—	54,400
12/07	11,350	2,475	21.8%	56,000
12/06	11,921	990	8.3%	55,200
12/05	11,652	404	3.5%	55,000
Annual Growth	(2.6%)	(12.0%)	—	(1.4%)

2009 Year-End Financials

Debt ratio: 52.1%
Return on equity: 4.2%
Cash ($ mil.): 1,777
Current ratio: 1.33
Long-term debt ($ mil.): 3,034

No. of shares (mil.): 542
Dividends
  Yield: 3.6%
  Payout: 190.5%
Market value ($ mil.): 11,978

Stock History
NYSE: MMC

	STOCK PRICE ($) FY Close	P/E High/Low	PER SHARE ($) Earnings	Dividends	Book Value
12/09	22.08	61 41	0.42	0.80	10.74
12/08	24.27	— —	(0.14)	0.80	10.55
12/07	26.47	7 5	4.53	0.76	14.42
12/06	30.66	19 14	1.76	0.51	10.73
12/05	31.76	46 36	0.74	0.85	9.88
Annual Growth	(8.7%)	— —	(13.2%)	(1.5%)	2.1%

Martha Stewart Living

If anyone could turn a stay in jail into a good thing, it's legendary lifestyle maven Martha Stewart. Following the completion of her sentence on federal criminal charges related to insider trading, Stewart has not shied away from the limelight. Rather, she and her company, Martha Stewart Living Omnimedia (MSLO), have embraced the spotlight. The company has its fingers in many money-making pies: publishing (magazines and books), broadcasting (TV programs, satellite radio), Internet, and merchandising. Stewart controls about 50% of MSLO's stock and about 90% of voting stock.

Her recipe: Mix equal parts Julia Child, Miss America, and P. T. Barnum; stir in liberal amounts of ambition and chutzpah; and serve with a flourish to a public hungry for a more gracious existence. Topics covered by the media empire include cooking, entertainment, home, craft, holidays, weddings, organizing, and gardening. Magazines such as Martha Stewart Living, Everyday Food, and Martha Stewart Weddings, and a library of more than 80 books (Entertaining, Martha Stewart's Christmas) illustrate MSLO's reach into publishing (more than half of sales).

In recent years the company has suffered — along with the rest of the media world — from declines in its publishing business, a direct result of the down economy. The company decided to discontinue its Blueprint magazine only a year after the title had launched; the "how-to" lifestyle magazine ceased publication in 2008.

In the broadcasting arena, MSLO's daytime show The Martha Stewart Show in 2010 signed a deal with Crown Media to air on The Hallmark Channel. As part of the deal, MSLO is developing a new original series for the cable network. Another TV series, this one based on MSLO's Everyday Food magazine, airs on PBS. The company purchased the media and licensed properties of popular TV chef Emeril Lagasse. Included in the deal are rights to the TV show The Essence of Emeril, syndicated episodes of the Emeril Live show on the Food Network, and a dozen cookbooks, as well as Emeril-branded food products.

Retail partnerships with companies such as The Home Depot, Macy's, and 1-800-Flowers.com fall into MSLO's merchandising division. In 2009 The Martha Stewart Everyday Home collection at Kmart accounted for nearly half of the company's merchandising revenues, and some 10% of total revenues; however, the partnership ended in 2010.

Stewart's current title is founder, a non-officer position. She was forced to resign from the board of directors after the scandal around her sale of ImClone stock, allegedly based on an insider trading tip, briefly rocked Stewart's seemingly perfect world. She was subsequently convicted for lying to investigators and obstruction of justice, and her persona (which had been her most successful recipe to date) suffered a hit. While serving less than six months in jail, she saw her company struggle: its stock price dropped, her TV show was put on hold, and for a time executives carefully tried to de-emphasize the "Martha-ness" of its products. The star's jail and home confinement sentence ended in 2005, and her reputation has since recovered. As part of her settlement with the SEC, in 2006 Stewart agreed to a five-year bar from serving as a director of MSLO (and any other public company) and paid a $5 million fine.

HISTORY

A former model and stockbroker, Martha Stewart's entry into the commerce of gracious living can be traced to 1972 when she launched a catering business in Westport, Connecticut. Culling her experiences as a caterer, Stewart published her first book, Entertaining, in 1982.

The resounding success of Entertaining (the book has gone into 30 printings) propelled Stewart into the public spotlight. Kmart appointed Stewart as its lifestyle consultant in 1987, and in 1991 her notoriety led media giant Time Inc. to begin publishing the Martha Stewart Living magazine. Though beautiful to look at, the publication was expensive to produce; it did not achieve profitability until 1996.

Stewart rode the coattails of her magazine's success into a variety of other ventures. Dipping a toe into merchandising, she teamed with Sherwin Williams in 1992 to create a line of paints. Her syndicated TV show, Martha Stewart Living, debuted the following year. Expanding further into merchandising, Stewart introduced Martha by Mail, a direct-mail catalog business, in 1995.

Frustrated with what she perceived as Time's inability to keep pace with the growth of her burgeoning empire and desirous of a hefty equity stake in her collection of companies, Stewart

wrested her operation (then called Martha Stewart Enterprises) away from Time in 1997. Her friend Sharon Patrick negotiated a buyout valuing the company at about $53 million.

Christening her new undertaking Martha Stewart Living Omnimedia (MSLO), Stewart wasted no time in expanding the company. MSLO soon entered into an alliance with Kmart to market the Martha Stewart Everyday line of merchandise.

When MSLO went public in 1999, Stewart greeted harried Wall Street traders with a breakfast of brioches stuffed with scrambled eggs.

Stewart resigned as CEO and chairman in 2003 after being indicted on insider trading charges related to a biotech stock. She remained on the board and was given a new title, chief creative officer. Stewart was replaced by COO and president Sharon Patrick as CEO, and managing partner of ValueAct Capital Partners Jeffrey Ubben as chairman.

Stewart was found guilty on all charges in 2004. Shortly after her conviction, Stewart stepped down as chief creative officer and director. Patrick stepped down in 2004 and was replaced by director Susan Lyne, a former ABC television executive. Ubben served as chairman until July 2004 when board member Thomas Siekman was named as his replacement. Charles Koppelman took over as chairman in 2005.

Stewart completed her prison sentence in March 2005 and then served another five months of house arrest. That year the company announced a four-year deal with Sirius Satellite Radio (later SIRIUS XM Radio) to create a 24-hour radio channel featuring cooking, gardening, and entertainment shows aimed at women.

MSLO piled on another deal in 2005, announcing several television programs in development with Discovery Communications. The company also that year began working on a new brand not starring Stewart, called "Petkeeping with Marc Marrone." Marrone has a TV show and other plans include a magazine, newspaper columns, and merchandising.

Lyne left the company in 2008. MSLO tapped president of merchandising Robin Marino to the position of co-CEO. Millard left the company in 2009; Marino remains as sole CEO.

EXECUTIVES

Founder: Martha Stewart, age 68, $9,743,331 total compensation
Chairman: Charles A. Koppelman, age 70, $2,122,062 total compensation
Director; President and CEO, Merchandising: Robin Marino, age 55, $1,418,510 total compensation
EVP and CFO: Kelli Turner, age 39, $779,754 total compensation
EVP, General Counsel, and Secretary: Peter A. Hurwitz, age 50, $424,434 total compensation
EVP Media Sales and Marketing: Janet Balis
EVP Merchandising: Patsy Pollack
EVP and General Manager, Broadcasting: Bernie Young
Editorial Director: Gael Towey, age 58, $652,737 total compensation
SVP Broadcasting and Omnimedia Content Strategy: Liz Aiello
SVP Digital Advertising Sales: Christine Cook
SVP Compensation: Rita Christiansen
SVP Integrated Marketing: Lee Heffernan, age 47
SVP Human Resources: Tanya Saffadi
SVP Broadcast Sales: Orlando Reece
SVP Consumer Marketing: Richard P. Fontaine
SVP and Group Publisher: Sally Preston
SVP Digital Programming and Strategy: Gail Horwood
VP, Controller, and Principal Financial Officer: Allison Jacques, age 45, $396,209 total compensation
Director, Corporate Technology: Steve Rollins
Auditors: Ernst & Young LLP

LOCATIONS

HQ: Martha Stewart Living Omnimedia, Inc.
601 W. 26th St., New York, NY 10001
Phone: 212-827-8000 **Fax:** 212-827-8204
Web: www.marthastewart.com

PRODUCTS/OPERATIONS

2009 Sales

	$ mil.	% of total
Publishing	129.0	53
Merchandising	52.6	21
Broadcasting	46.1	19
Internet	17.1	7
Total	**244.8**	**100**

Selected Operations

Publishing
Everyday Food (magazine)
Martha Stewart's Baking Handbook (book)
Martha Stewart Living (magazine)
Martha Stewart Weddings (magazine)
Martha Stewart's Homekeeping Handbook: The Essential Guide to Caring for Everything in Your Home (book)
Whole Living (healthy living magazine)

Merchandising
Martha Stewart Collection at Macy's
Martha Stewart Flowers with 1-800-Flowers
Martha Stewart Living at Home Depot

Broadcasting
Everyday Food
Everyday Baking from Everyday Food
Martha Stewart Living Radio (on SIRIUS XM Radio)
The Martha Stewart Show

Internet
MarthaStewart.com

COMPETITORS

Bertelsmann
Condé Nast
DailyCandy
Dwell, LLC
Harpo
Hearst Magazines
iVillage
The Knot
Lagardère Active
Lifetime
Meredith Corporation
News Corp.
Oxygen Media
Reader's Digest
Time Warner

HISTORICAL FINANCIALS

Company Type: Public

Income Statement

FYE: December 31

	REVENUE ($ mil.)	NET INCOME ($ mil.)	NET PROFIT MARGIN	EMPLOYEES
12/09	245	(15)	—	620
12/08	284	(16)	—	645
12/07	328	10	3.1%	760
12/06	288	(17)	—	755
12/05	210	(76)	—	656
Annual Growth	**4.0%**	**—**	**—**	**(1.4%)**

2009 Year-End Financials

Debt ratio: 9.4%
Return on equity: —
Cash ($ mil.): 25
Current ratio: 1.90
Long-term debt ($ mil.): 14
No. of shares (mil.): 55
Dividends
 Yield: —
 Payout: —
Market value ($ mil.): 272

Stock History

NYSE: MSO

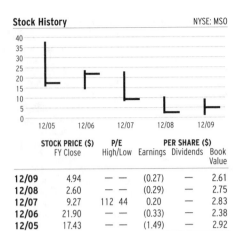

	STOCK PRICE ($) FY Close	P/E High/Low		PER SHARE ($) Earnings	Dividends	Book Value
12/09	4.94	—	—	(0.27)	—	2.61
12/08	2.60	—	—	(0.29)	—	2.75
12/07	9.27	112	44	0.20	—	2.83
12/06	21.90	—	—	(0.33)	—	2.38
12/05	17.43	—	—	(1.49)	—	2.92
Annual Growth	**(27.0%)**	**—**	**—**	**—**	**—**	**(2.7%)**

Martin Marietta Materials

Martin Marietta Materials (MMM) is a rock star. The company is the #2 US producer (behind Vulcan Materials) of aggregates for highway, infrastructure, commercial, and residential construction. Its Martin Marietta Aggregates division (representing 90% of sales) produces more than 120 million tons of granite, gravel, limestone, and sand annually. Magnesia Specialties produces magnesia-based chemicals for industrial, environmental, and agricultural uses, as well as fiber-reinforced composite materials used for transportation and military applications. MMM serves customers in 30 countries through about 300 quarries, plants, mines, and distribution facilities in the US, Canada, and the Bahamas.

Infrastructure sales represent more than half of the group's business. As a result of the American Recovery and Reinvestment Act that was passed in 2009, infrastructure projects have increased throughout the nation. The company expects to see a boost in infrastructure sales, especially in the coming several months as stimulus projects reach their construction stage.

On the other hand, a slowdown in residential and commercial construction has softened demand for building projects nationwide. MMM's business is concentrated in certain states, including Georgia, Iowa, Louisiana, North Carolina, and Texas (which combined account for about 60% of all sales). When those states suffer economic downturns, MMM's sales are similarly affected.

To wait out the troubled economy, MMM has slowed down its expansion activities and focused on keeping costs down. When the economic climate improves, the company plans to pick up its acquisitions, primarily in the Southeast and Southwest (where winter weather has less impact on construction than in the northern regions). MMM spent several years prior to the downturn expanding into new areas, focusing on businesses near rail facilities or navigable waterways for economic shipping.

While the company made strategic expansions, it also shuttered or sold underperforming operations, including its its road-paving businesses in Arkansas and Louisiana, its specialty products refractories business, and its composite materials segment. MMM continues to keep an eye on potential divestitures that could provide the group with capital.

In 2010 Stephen Zelnak retired after 27 years as CEO of the company, but remained chairman. He was succeeded by president Howard Nye.

HISTORY

Aerospace giant Martin Marietta Corporation kept its aggregates business out of the fray during the industry's acquisition binge of the 1980s, during which quarry prices became inflated. When recession hit at the beginning of the 1990s, the company was able to pick up quarries at fire-sale prices before spinning off the group as Martin Marietta Materials (MMM) in 1993. An initial public offering of 19% was completed in 1994.

The next year the company acquired Dravo Corporation's aggregates business for about $121 million, a move that added production and distribution operations in nine states and the Bahamas, as well as new distribution methods (by barge) and nonconstruction markets. Lockheed Martin Corporation (formed by the merger of Martin Marietta and Lockheed in 1995) owned 81% of the company until 1996, when it spun off its stake to shareholders.

In 1997 MMM shelled out $242 million for American Aggregates Corporation to add distribution and production facilities in Indiana and Ohio. The company extended its reach to Arkansas, Louisiana, and Texas the next year with the acquisition of Hot Springs, Arkansas-based Mid-State Construction & Materials. It also acquired Texas-based Redland Stone Products for $272 million from France's Lafarge. Other 1998 purchases included a 14% interest in Meridian Aggregates Company.

Rival Vulcan Materials sued MMM in 1999; Vulcan claimed it had rights to some of the leased reserves MMM had acquired in its purchase of Redland Stone Products. (The suit was dropped in 2000.) Also in 1999 MMM bought another Texas aggregates company, Marock.

In 2000 MMM completed four deals that added three asphalt plants and an aggregate company in Texas, as well as limestone operations in Ohio and West Virginia. The next year MMM bought Brauntex Materials, a limestone facility in Texas, and the part of Meridian Aggregates Company it didn't already own. Also in 2001 MMM sold its Magnesia Specialties refractories business to Minerals Technologies.

From 2002 to 2005, while continuing to pursue strategic acquisitions, the company divested several noncore and underperforming operations, as well as two nonstrategic magnesia business lines. In 2002 MMM began selling noncore aggregates businesses; it also made acquisitions in key markets, including quarries in Texas and North Carolina and an asphalt plant in Texas. It sold facilities in Illinois, Iowa, Ohio, Oklahoma, Tennessee, and Virginia.

The company continued selling noncore assets over the next several years, including underperforming asphalt operations and aggregates plants.

EXECUTIVES

Chairman: Stephen P. (Steve) Zelnak Jr., age 65, $5,808,927 total compensation
President, CEO, and Director; President and CEO, Martin Marietta Aggregates: C. Howard (Ward) Nye, age 47, $2,707,817 total compensation
EVP; President, Martin Marietta Materials West: Bruce A. Vaio, age 49, $1,825,836 total compensation
EVP, CFO, and Treasurer: Anne H. Lloyd, age 48, $1,830,487 total compensation
EVP; CEO, Magnesia Specialties; Interim President, Carolina Division: Daniel G. (Dan) Shephard, age 51, $2,084,285 total compensation
SVP, General Counsel, and Corporate Secretary: Roselyn R. Bar, age 51
SVP Human Resources: Jonathan T. (Jon) Stewart, age 61
VP, Controller, and Chief Accounting Officer: Dana F. Guzzo
VP Finance and Assistant Controller: Beth Michael
President, Western Division, Martin Marietta Aggregates: Tom Jones
President, Southeast Division, Martin Marietta Aggregates: Tony DiRico
President, Southwest Division, Martin Marietta Aggregates: Larry J. Roberts
President, Martin Marietta Magnesia Specialties: John R. Harman
President, Mideast Division, Martin Marietta Aggregates: John Tiberi
President, South Central Division, Martin Marietta Aggregates: Jay Moreau
President, Midwest Division, Martin Marietta Aggregates: William Gahan
Auditors: Ernst & Young LLP

LOCATIONS

HQ: Martin Marietta Materials, Inc.
2710 Wycliff Rd., Raleigh, NC 27607
Phone: 919-781-4550   **Fax:** 919-783-4695
Web: www.martinmarietta.com

PRODUCTS/OPERATIONS

2009 Sales by Segment

	$ mil.	% of total
Aggregates		
West	651.6	38
Mideast	467.0	28
Southeast	424.1	25
Specialty Products	159.9	9
Total	**1,702.6**	**100**

2009 Sales by Product Line

	$ mil.	% of total
Aggregates		
Aggregates	1,426.3	84
Asphalt	59.9	3
Ready-mixed concrete	26.3	2
Road paving	13.5	1
Other	16.7	1
Specialty products		
Magnesia-based chemicals	109.7	6
Dolomitic lime	48.6	3
Other	1.6	—
Total	**1,702.6**	**100**

Selected Operations

Aggregates Division
    Aggregates (granite, gravel, limestone, and sand)
    Asphalt
    Ready-mixed concrete
    Road paving
Specialty Products Division
    Magnesia Specialties (dolomitic lime, magnesia-based chemicals)
    Structural Composite Products (fiber-reinforced polymer composites)

COMPETITORS

Aggregate Industries
Ashland Inc.
BPB
Carmeuse Lime & Stone Inc.
CEMEX
Cookson Group
CRH
CSR Limited
Eagle Materials
Giant Cement
Holcim
Lafarge North America
Lehigh Hanson
Lhoist North America
MDU Resources
Minerals Technologies
Ready Mix USA
Rogers Group
ShengdaTech
Trinity Industries
TXI
Vulcan Materials

HISTORICAL FINANCIALS

Company Type: Public

Income Statement

FYE: December 31

	REVENUE ($ mil.)	NET INCOME ($ mil.)	NET PROFIT MARGIN	EMPLOYEES
12/09	1,703	88	5.2%	4,554
12/08	2,120	176	8.3%	4,860
12/07	2,207	263	11.9%	5,255
12/06	2,206	245	11.1%	5,500
12/05	2,004	193	9.6%	5,754
Annual Growth	**(4.0%)**	**(17.7%)**	**—**	**(5.7%)**

2009 Year-End Financials

Debt ratio: 75.0%
Return on equity: 7.4%
Cash ($ mil.): 264
Current ratio: 2.29
Long-term debt ($ mil.): 1,023
No. of shares (mil.): 46
Dividends
    Yield: 1.8%
    Payout: 83.8%
Market value ($ mil.): 4,070

Stock History

NYSE: MLM

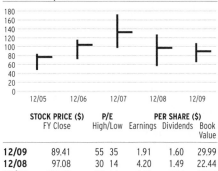

	STOCK PRICE ($) FY Close	P/E High/Low		PER SHARE ($) Earnings	Dividends	Book Value
12/09	89.41	55	35	1.91	1.60	29.99
12/08	97.08	30	14	4.20	1.49	22.44
12/07	132.60	28	16	6.06	1.24	20.78
12/06	103.91	21	14	5.29	1.01	27.55
12/05	76.72	20	12	4.08	0.86	25.78
Annual Growth	**3.9%**	**—**	**—**	**(17.3%)**	**16.8%**	**3.9%**

Masco Corporation

Masco's ideal customer is a home improvement junkie with a thing for cabinets — and a hand-washing fetish. The company is a leading manufacturer of a variety of home improvement and building products. Its cabinet and plumbing products businesses account for more than half its sales. Cabinet brands include KraftMaid, Quality Cabinets, and Merillat in the US and The Moores Group and Tvilum-Scanbirk in Europe. Faucets and bath and shower accessories are sold under the Delta and Peerless brands in the US and as Hansgrohe in Europe. Masco also makes BEHR paints and stains, windows, doors, staple guns, locksets, and HVAC products. If you're more comfortable on the couch, Masco also provides installation services.

Masco's products and services are offered through home builders, retail chains, and wholesale outlets. It has capitalized on the popularity of home-center retail chains such as The Home Depot and Lowe's by offering a single source for a wide range of home improvement products that range in style and price point. The Home Depot alone accounts for about 25% of Masco's sales.

The downturn in home building and home improvement has forced Masco to shutter several cabinet and window plants and cut jobs. The company also has shut more than 90 locations that were operated by its installations business. Masco is now focused on lean manufacturing principals and product innovation.

In addition to other cost-cutting measures Masco has consolidated some of its operations. The company retooled its cabinet business within the past couple of years. In 2008 the company merged its Mill's Price brand with KraftMaid to form the Masco Retail Cabinet Group. It also merged Merillat and Quality Cabinets to form Masco Builder Cabinet Group. Masco then announced the combination of its two cabinet divisions to form one new organization, Masco Cabinetry. The division is working to manufacture a common base cabinet that can be used for a variety of applications.

HISTORY

Masco founder Alex Manoogian moved to the US at age 19 in 1920. He wound up in Detroit, and with partners Harry Adjemian and Charles Saunders, he started Masco (the first letters of their last names plus "co" for "company") Screw Products Company eight days before the crash of 1929. Manoogian's partners left within the year.

Largely reliant on Detroit's auto industry, Masco grew slowly during the Depression, making custom parts for Chrysler, Ford, and others. With sales of $200,000 by 1937, it went public on the Detroit Stock Exchange. During WWII Masco focused on defense, and in 1942 sales passed $1 million. A new plant opened in 1948 in Dearborn, Michigan, as Masco resumed peacetime business, mainly in the auto industry.

In 1954 Masco began selling Manoogian's one-handle kitchen faucet (Delta). Sales of faucets passed $1 million by 1958, and Masco opened a new faucet factory in Indiana.

Under Manoogian's son Richard — whose dinner was often delayed while his father used the stove to test the heat tolerance of new faucet parts — Masco Corporation (so renamed in 1961) diversified. From 1964 to 1980 it bought more than 50 companies, concentrating on tool and metal casting, energy exploration, and air compressors. In 1984 the firm split. Masco Corporation pursued the course set by its successful faucet sales, expanding its interests in home improvement and furnishings. The industrial products business was spun off as Masco Industries, a separate public corporation (later Metaldyne) in which Masco maintained a sizable stake.

Masco Corporation became the #1 US furniture maker in the late 1980s by buying Lexington Furniture (1987) and Universal Furniture (1989), both of North Carolina. In 1990 Masco acquired KraftMaid cabinets.

Two years later the company sold its interests in Mechanical Technology, Payless Cashways, and Emco Limited of Canada (Masco bought back 40% of Emco in 1997). Masco reduced its stake in Metaldyne from 47% to 35% in 1993.

Masco sought to establish itself in Europe, and in 1994 it bought a German cabinetmaker and a UK producer of handheld showers. In 1996 founder Manoogian died, but the company flowed on. It added a UK cabinetmaker, a German shower manufacturer, and a German insulation firm. The same year Masco sold its troubled furniture unit to a group of investors and executives (who renamed the unit LifeStyle Furnishings International) for about $1 billion and further reduced its stake in Metaldyne to less than 20% (and later sold it all).

Masco made 13 acquisitions from 1999 through early 2000, including Heritage Bathrooms (bathroom equipment, UK), Faucet Queens (plumbing and hardware supply), BEHR Process (coatings), and Mill's Pride (cabinets).

In late 2000 and early 2001 it acquired two US-based installation services companies, Davenport Insulation Group and BSI Holdings, respectively.

During 2002 Masco acquired home improvement products and service companies that included Bristan Ltd. (kitchen and bath faucets and shower and bath accessories), Cambrian Windows Ltd. (vinyl window frames), Duraflex Ltd. (extruded vinyl frame components), SCE Unlimited (siding, shutters, gutters; Illinois), IDI Group (fireplaces, garage doors, shower enclosures; Atlanta), and Service Partners LLC (insulation and other building products, Virginia).

In 2003 the company established Color Solutions Centers in more than 1,500 Home Depot stores throughout the US. Acquisitions in 2003 included PowerShot Tool Company, Inc. (fastening products, New Jersey) and several small installation service companies for a combined $63 million.

In 2004 Masco sold its Jung Pumpen (pumps), The Alvic Group (kitchen cabinets), Alma Kuchen (kitchen cabinets), E. Missel (acoustic insulation), and SKS Group (shutters and ventilation systems) businesses for $199 million. Masco continued its business review in 2005, selling two operating companies that made and distributed cabinets, vanities, medicine cabinets, shower rods, and bath accessories.

After reorganizing its European business operations, Masco sold off several of its operating units, including Gebhardt Consolidated (HVAC), The Heating Group (radiators), and GMU Group (cabinets). The company also disposed of North American businesses that were not core to its long-term growth strategy, which included Computerized Security Systems (CSS) and Zenith Products (bathroom storage).

EXECUTIVES

Chairman: Richard A. Manoogian, age 73, $3,625,312 total compensation
President, CEO, and Director: Timothy (Tim) Wadhams, age 61, $11,342,878 total compensation
EVP and COO: Donald J. DeMarie Jr., age 47, $5,361,387 total compensation
Chief Design Officer: Charles L. Jones
VP, CFO, and Treasurer: John G. Sznewajs, age 42, $2,301,708 total compensation
VP and Controller: William T. Anderson, age 62, $2,255,913 total compensation
VP Human Resources: Charles F. Greenwood, age 62, $1,050,229 total compensation
VP and CIO: Timothy J. Monteith
VP Innovation and Sustainability: Gary L. Yezbick
VP Finance, North America Builder: Timothy J. LaRouere
VP Sales and Marketing: Karen R. Mendelsohn
VP Corporate Affairs: Sharon J. Rothwell
VP, General Counsel, and Secretary: Gregory D. Wittrock
VP and Controller, Corporate Accounting: John P. Lindow
VP Finance, Retail and Wholesale, North America: Jai Shah
VP Investor Relations and Communications: Maria C. Duey
Group President, North America Builder: W. Timothy (Tim) Yaggi
Group President, Retail and Wholesale, North America: Jerry Volas
President, Masco Europe: Thomas Voss
Auditors: PricewaterhouseCoopers LLP

LOCATIONS

HQ: Masco Corporation
   21001 Van Born Rd., Taylor, MI 48180
Phone: 313-274-7400   **Fax:** 313-792-6135
Web: www.masco.com

2009 Sales

	$ mil.	% of total
North America	6,135	79
Europe & other regions	1,657	21
Total	**7,792**	**100**

PRODUCTS/OPERATIONS

2009 Sales

	$ mil.	% of total
Plumbing products	2,564	33
Decorative architectural products	1,714	22
Cabinets & related products	1,674	22
Installation & other services	1,256	16
Other specialty products	584	7
Total	**7,792**	**100**

Selected Brand Names

Plumbing products
   Alsons
   American Shower & Bath
   Aqua Glass
   Axor
   BrassCraft
   Brasstech
   Breuer
   Bristan
   Brizo
   Caldera
   Damixa
   Delta
   Glass
   Hansgrohe
   Heritage
   Hot Spring
   HÜPPE
   BrassCraft
   Mirolin
   Newport Brass
   Peerless
   Pharo
   Plumb Shop

Cabinets and related products
   KraftMaid
   Merillat
   Moores
   Quality Cabinets
   Tvilum-Scanbirk
   Woodgate
Decorative architectural products
   BEHR
   Decor Bathware
   Expressions
   Franklin Brass
   Kilz
   Liberty
Other specialty products
   Arrow
   Brugman
   Cambrian
   Duraflex
   Griffin
   Milgard Windows
   Powershot
   Premier
   Superia
   Thermic
   Vasco

COMPETITORS

Akzo Nobel Paints
American Woodmark
Armstrong World Industries
Benjamin Moore
Columbia Pipe
Elkay Manufacturing
Fortune Brands
Furniture Brands International
Gerber Plumbing Fixtures
Grohe
Helen of Troy
Ingersoll-Rand Security Technologies
Jacuzzi Brands
Jones-Blair
Kohler
Marmon Group
Master Lock
MasterBrand Cabinets
Moen
Nordyne
Nortek
Omega Cabinets
PPG Industries
Price Pfister
Republic National Cabinet
Richelieu Hardware
RSI Home Products
Sherwin-Williams
Simpson Manufacturing
Simpson Strong-Tie
Spear & Jackson
Stanley Black and Decker
Trane Inc.
US Home Systems
Valspar
Waxman

HISTORICAL FINANCIALS
Company Type: Public

Income Statement

	REVENUE ($ mil.)	NET INCOME ($ mil.)	NET PROFIT MARGIN	EMPLOYEES
12/09	7,792	(145)	—	35,400
12/08	9,600	(391)	—	39,000
12/07	11,770	386	3.3%	52,000
12/06	12,778	491	3.8%	57,000
12/05	12,642	940	7.4%	62,000
Annual Growth	(11.4%)	—	—	(13.1%)

FYE: December 31

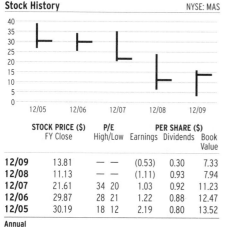
MasTec, Inc.

MasTec digs the trenches, lays the cable, and builds the towers for communication. The contractor provides telecommunications and energy infrastructure construction to telecom vendors, wireless providers, cable TV operators, and energy companies. In addition to internal and external network construction — from digging ditches to erecting radio towers and installing digital wiring — MasTec designs communications infrastructure and builds cable TV networks. It offers engineering, installation, and maintenance of internal and external networks for clients such as Verizon, EMBARQ, and AT&T; however, its largest customer, DIRECTV, accounts for about a third of revenue. Chairman Jorge Mas and his family own 28% of MasTec.

Communications services make up more than half of MasTec's revenue, but the company is seeing green in the alternative energy market. Three wind farm companies, including Iberdrola Renewables, are part of its top 10 customers. In 2009 MasTec bought North Dakota-based Wanzek Construction for about $200 million. Wanzek derives most of its revenue from building wind farms. MasTec is also expecting a windfall of federal dollars from the American Recovery and Reinvestment Act in 2010, which earmarks investment dollars for energy infrastructure and wireless networks.

In 2010 MasTec appointed Ray Harris as president (José Mas remains vice chairman and CEO). Harris is the former president and CEO of Mesa Power Group, T. Boone Pickens' privately held renewable energy company.

As utility companies move toward natural gas usage, which is believed to be more clean-burning than fossil fuels, MasTec has responded with acquisitions to boost its energy offerings. It bought Precision Pipeline, a company that lays oils and gas pipeline, for $132 million in 2009. The previous year MasTec acquired oil and gas

pipeline construction firm Pumpco and certain assets of wireless design and construction company Nsoro. One of its largest projects, beginning in late 2010, is the construction of the Ruby Pipeline, a 680-mile natural gas line that stretches from Oregon to Wyoming. Currently, utility companies account for about 40% of MasTec's business.

While most other industries suffered during the economic crisis that began in 2008, MasTec actually began recording net revenues that year. The company works because it doesn't have a lot of overhead — it rents much of its equipment from fellow Florida company Neff Corp and its customers supply the necessary materials and supplies for its projects.

HISTORY

MasTec was formed by the merger of Burnup & Sims (B&S) and Church & Tower (C&T). B&S was founded in 1929 to provide construction and maintenance services to the phone and utilities industries. C&T began in 1968 building phone networks in Miami and Puerto Rico. Jorge Mas Canosa was brought on board in 1969 and given half the company in exchange for managing it. By 1971 he had succeeded in turning C&T around and had bought the remainder.

In 1994 C&T and B&S merged; B&S became MasTec and C&T became a subsidiary. Mas was named chairman, and his son, who had been at C&T since 1980, was named president and CEO. The company began a program of acquisitions and started building a presence in Latin America.

MasTec doubled its size in 1996 by acquiring Sintel, a telecom infrastructure construction firm operating in South America and Spain, from Teléfonica. MasTec continued to grow through acquisitions, buying 10 more companies the next year. Mas died in 1997 and his son, Jorge Jr., succeeded him. It sold a near-bankrupt Sintel and began to refocus on domestic operations.

In 2000 MasTec acquired GMR Telecom, a telecommunication systems engineering and design company. In 2004 the company exited Brazil and sold its Network Services division. Two years later it entered the market for the installation of residential and commercial satellite and security services with the acquisition of Digital Satellite Services, Inc. (DSSI), which operated as Ron's Digital Satellite and Ron's TV, for $18.5 million.

MasTec took the exit ramp for its highways business in 2007 after selling its Department of Transportation (DOT) Service Business, which provided specialty contracting services to state DOTs and local transportation authorities, to an investor group led by private equity firm LEÓN, MAYER & Co.

EXECUTIVES

Chairman: Jorge Mas Jr., age 47
CEO: José R. Mas, age 38,
  $1,073,637 total compensation
COO: Robert E. (Bob) Apple, age 60,
  $720,412 total compensation
President: Ray E. Harris, age 53
EVP, General Counsel, and Secretary:
  Alberto de Cardenas, age 41,
  $499,439 total compensation
EVP Mergers and Acquisitions: Pablo A. Alvarez
EVP and CFO: C. Robert (Bob) Campbell, age 65,
  $933,282 total compensation
SVP Business Development: Oscar Primelles

VP Government Services: Larry Burch
VP Investor Relations: J. Marc Lewis, age 48
VP Business Development, Electric Utility:
  Barry J. Batson
VP, Central Office, EF&I: John E. Brewer
Group President, Wireless: Darrell Mays
Group President, Communications: Bryan Westerman
Group President, Satellite Services: Zach McGuire
Director Human Resources, South and West Regions:
  Sandi Adler Cornelius
Director Human Resources, East Region: Ani de Varona
Auditors: BDO Seidman, LLP

LOCATIONS

HQ: MasTec, Inc.
  800 S. Douglas Rd., 12th Fl.
  Coral Gables, FL 33134
Phone: 305-599-1800   **Fax:** 305-406-1960
Web: www.mastec.com

PRODUCTS/OPERATIONS

2009 Sales

	$ mil.	% of total
Communications	940.1	58
Utilities	614.1	38
Government	69.3	4
Total	**1,623.5**	**100**

Selected Services

Broadband networks
  Aerial and underground construction
  Bonding/grounding
  Engineering and design
  FCC testing
  Modem installation
  Optical fiber splicing, activation, and testing
  Warehouse and inventory management
Telecommunications
  Aerial construction
  Copper/coaxial cable systems
  Directional drilling
  Engineering
  Fiber-optic cable systems
  Fiber-to-the-premises (FTTP) deployment
  Splicing and testing
  Underground construction
Utilities
  Design and engineering
  Gas distribution construction and maintenance
  Storm restoration
  Submarine cable installation
  Substation construction
  Transmission line construction
  Trench construction

COMPETITORS

Bechtel	MYR Group
Dycom	Pike Electric Corporation
EMCOR	Quanta Services
Goldfield	Sabre Industries
Henkels & McCoy	Sirti
Lexent	SteelFab
M. A. Mortenson	Tetra Tech
MDU Construction	

HISTORICAL FINANCIALS

Company Type: Public

Income Statement

FYE: December 31

	REVENUE ($ mil.)	NET INCOME ($ mil.)	NET PROFIT MARGIN	EMPLOYEES
12/09	1,624	71	4.4%	8,600
12/08	1,379	66	4.8%	8,400
12/07	1,038	(7)	—	8,240
12/06	946	(50)	—	9,260
12/05	848	(15)	—	7,700
Annual Growth	17.6%	—	—	2.8%

2009 Year-End Financials

Debt ratio: 77.6%
Return on equity: 14.6%
Cash ($ mil.): 89
Current ratio: 1.63
Long-term debt ($ mil.): 410

No. of shares (mil.): 76
Dividends
Yield: —
Payout: —
Market value ($ mil.): 951

Stock History

NYSE: MTZ

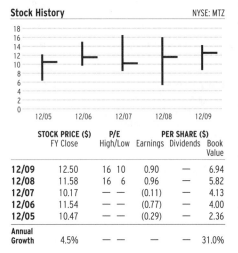

	STOCK PRICE ($)	P/E		PER SHARE ($)		
	FY Close	High/Low		Earnings	Dividends	Book Value
12/09	12.50	16	10	0.90	—	6.94
12/08	11.58	16	6	0.96	—	5.82
12/07	10.17	—	—	(0.11)	—	4.13
12/06	11.54	—	—	(0.77)	—	4.00
12/05	10.47	—	—	(0.29)	—	2.36
Annual Growth	4.5%	—	—	—	—	31.0%

MasterCard Incorporated

Surpassing Visa in market share — now *that* would be priceless. Serving approximately 23,000 member financial institutions worldwide, MasterCard is the #2 payment system in the US. The company does not issue credit or its namesake cards; rather, it markets the MasterCard (credit and debit cards) and Maestro (debit cards, mainly in Europe) brands, provides a transaction authorization network, establishes guidelines for use, and collects fees from members. The company provides its services in more than 210 countries and territories. MasterCard also operates the Cirrus ATM network.

While not entirely recession-proof, MasterCard has proven to be resilient during the economic downturn, as consumers increasingly conduct fewer paper-based (check and cash) transactions and migrate to card-based ones. Though the number of MasterCard-branded cards in circulation has declined along with the number of financial institutions that issue them, the company's transaction volume, not to mention the corresponding processing fees it collects from them, has increased. With the US market virtually saturated, MasterCard has been focusing its expansion efforts overseas.

MasterCard offers computer chip-enabled cards in several markets, including Europe, Latin America and the Caribbean, and the Asia/Pacific region. US consumers have been slower to adopt this technology, but not for the company's lack of trying. One "smart" product, however, that's showing signs of success stateside is the company's MasterCard PayPass, which allows customers to quickly tap or swipe their payment cards at specially equipped merchant terminals.

MasterCard continued its international expansion in 2010 when it announced the acquisition of British payment services provider DataCash Group. The $520 million deal will expand MasterCard's e-commerce business and increase the company's ability to process payments online, especially in Europe. Also in 2010 MasterCard promoted COO Ajay Banga to CEO. He succeeded Robert Selander, who remains with MasterCard as executive vice chairman.

After some 40 years as a private entity, MasterCard went public in 2006 in one of the largest IPOs in recent history. Following the offering, the approximately 1,400 financial institutions that wholly owned MasterCard before the offering retained a stake of more than 40%. Two of the top three US banks (Citigroup and JPMorgan Chase) are among MasterCard's largest shareholders.

Some of the proceeds from the company's IPO were used to fight antitrust lawsuits from such rivals as American Express and Discover, as well as other payment processors. In 2008 the company agreed to a $1.8 billion settlement with American Express, which had claimed that MasterCard and others tried to stop financial institutions from issuing its AmEx cards. Later that year MasterCard settled the Discover lawsuit, agreeing to pay $862.5 million.

HISTORY

A group of bankers formed The Interbank Card Association (ICA) in 1966 to establish authorization, clearing, and settlement procedures for bank credit card transactions. This was particularly important to banks left out of the rapidly growing BankAmericard (later Visa) network sponsored by Bank of America.

By 1969 ICA was issuing the Master Charge card throughout the US and had formed alliances in Europe and Japan. In the mid-1970s ICA modernized its system, replacing telephone transaction authorization with a computerized magnetic strip system. ICA had members in Africa, Australia, and Europe by 1979. That year the organization changed its name (and the card's) to MasterCard.

In 1980 Russell Hogg became president when John Reynolds resigned after disagreeing with the board over company performance and direction. Hogg made major organizational changes and consolidated data processing in St. Louis. MasterCard began offering debit cards in 1980 and traveler's checks in 1981.

MasterCard issued the first credit cards in China in 1987. The next year it bought Cirrus, then the world's largest ATM network. It also secured a pact with Belgium-based card company Eurocard (which later became Europay) to supervise MasterCard's European operations and help build the brand.

Hogg resigned in 1988 after disagreements with the board and was succeeded by Alex Hart. In 1991 the Maestro debit card was unveiled.

The 1990s were marked by trouble in Europe: The pact with Europay hadn't resulted in the boom MasterCard had hoped for, customer service was below par, and competition was keen. Alex Hart retired in 1994 and was succeeded by Eugene Lockhart, who tackled the European woes. Lockhart considered ending the relationship but eventually worked things out with Europay. By the end of the decade, Europay was locked in a vicious battle to undercut Visa's market share through lower fees.

In October 1996 a group of merchants, including Wal-Mart and Sears, filed class-action lawsuits against both MasterCard and Visa, challenging the "honor all cards" rule. Because usage fees are higher, merchants balked at accepting consumers' MasterCard- or Visa-branded offline, or signature-based debit cards, and claimed the card issuers violated antitrust laws by tying acceptance of debit to that of credit. Minutes before the trial was set to begin in 2003, MasterCard announced a settlement (it was required to pay $125 million in 2003 and $100 million annually from 2004 through 2012).

Just months later, armed with the lawsuit's settlement which also freed merchants to pick which credit and debit card services they use, Wal-Mart (along with a handful of others) stopped accepting signature debit cards issued by MasterCard.

Lockhart resigned in 1997 and was succeeded by former head of overseas operations Robert Selander. Yet another management upheaval began in 1999 as the company moved to streamline its organizational structure and shift away from geographical divisions.

In 2002 MasterCard merged with Europay, with which it already had close ties. As part of the transaction, holding company MasterCard Incorporated was formed; MasterCard International become the company's main subsidiary and MasterCard Europe (formerly Europay) became its European subsidiary.

EXECUTIVES

Chairman: Richard N. Haythornthwaite, age 53
Executive Vice Chairman: Robert W. (Bob) Selander, age 59, $10,331,575 total compensation
President, CEO, and Director: Ajaypal (Ajay) Banga, age 50, $11,347,105 total compensation
CFO, MasterCard Incorporated and MasterCard International Incorporated: Martina Hund-Mejean, age 49, $2,272,744 total compensation
General Counsel, Chief Payment System Integrity and Compliance Officer, and Corporate Secretary, MasterCard Incorporated and MasterCard International: Noah J. Hanft, age 57, $3,163,243 total compensation
Chief Marketing Officer: Alfredo Gangotena
Chief Emerging Payments Officer: Ed McLaughlin
Chief Human Resources Officer, MasterCard Incorporated and MasterCard International: Stephanie E. Voquer, age 58
Controller and Principal Accounting Officer: Melissa J. Ballenger, age 38
President, US Markets, MasterCard Incorporated and MasterCard International: Christopher A. (Chris) McWilton, age 51, $2,752,830 total compensation
President, Asia/Pacific, Middle East, and Africa, MasterCard Worldwide: Vicky S. Bindra, age 45
President, Global Products and Solutions: Gary J. Flood, age 51, $2,463,654 total compensation
President, Core Products: Timothy H. (Tim) Murphy, age 42
President, Innovative Platforms, MasterCard Worldwide: Joshua L. Peirez, age 38
President, International Markets, MasterCard Incorporated and MasterCard International: Walter M. (Walt) Macnee, age 55
President, MasterCard Technologies: Robert (Rob) Reeg, age 54
CEO, MasterCard Mobile Payments Gateway: Tara Nathan
Corporate Public Relations and President, US Markets: Chris Monteiro
Corporate Treasurer: Sachin J. Mehra, age 39
Investor Relations Contact: Barbara Gasper
Auditors: PricewaterhouseCoopers LLP

LOCATIONS

HQ: MasterCard Incorporated
2000 Purchase St., Purchase, NY 10577
Phone: 914-249-2000   **Fax:** 914-249-4206
Web: www.mastercard.com

2009 Sales

	% of total
International	54
US	46
Total	**100**

PRODUCTS/OPERATIONS

2009 Sales

	$ mil.	% of total
Domestic assessments	2,382	35
Transaction processing fees	2,042	30
Cross-border volume fees	1,509	23
Other	784	12
Rebates & incentives	(1,618)	—
Total	**5,099**	**100**

COMPETITORS

American Express
Discover
Fifth Third
First Data
JCB International
NYCE Payments Network
PULSE Network
Total System Services
Visa Inc
Visa International

HISTORICAL FINANCIALS

Company Type: Public

Income Statement

FYE: December 31

	REVENUE ($ mil.)	NET INCOME ($ mil.)	NET PROFIT MARGIN	EMPLOYEES
12/09	5,099	1,463	28.7%	5,100
12/08	4,992	(254)	—	5,500
12/07	4,068	1,086	26.7%	5,000
12/06	3,326	50	1.5%	4,600
12/05	2,938	267	9.1%	4,300
Annual Growth	**14.8%**	**53.0%**	**—**	**4.4%**

2009 Year-End Financials

Debt ratio: 0.6%
Return on equity: 53.9%
Cash ($ mil.): 2,055
Current ratio: 1.58
Long-term debt ($ mil.): 22

No. of shares (mil.): 131
Dividends
  Yield: 0.2%
  Payout: 4.0%
Market value ($ mil.): 33,497

Stock History

NYSE: MA

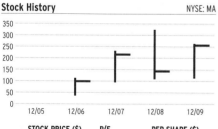

	STOCK PRICE ($) FY Close	P/E High/Low		PER SHARE ($) Earnings	Dividends	Book Value
12/09	255.98	23	10	11.16	0.45	26.78
12/08	142.93	—	—	(1.95)	0.75	14.73
12/07	215.20	28	12	8.00	0.54	23.13
12/06	98.49	294	109	0.37	0.09	18.07
Annual Growth	**37.5%**	**—**	**—**	**43.0%**	**71.0%**	**31.6%**

Mattel, Inc.

Barbie is the platinum blonde in power at Mattel, the #1 toy maker in the world. Its products include Barbie dolls, Fisher-Price toys, Hot Wheels and Matchbox cars, American Girl dolls and books, and various *Barney*, Ferrari, and other licensed items. Mattel also produces action figures and toys based on Walt Disney movies. To satisfy techie kids, Mattel has accessorized Barbie with interactive games, software, and a line of Barbie MP3 players. The company has even licensed the Barbie name for eyewear. Just three customers (Wal-Mart, Toys "R" Us, and Target) account for about 40% of Mattel's sales.

Mattel is capitalizing on its core brands, particularly with licensing deals. REM Eyewear developed a line of Barbie eyewear for girls. Other licensing deals include a plethora of purple playthings featuring TV's Barney character for its littlest customers; toys based on Warner Bros. characters, including Looney Tunes, Batman, and Superman; and Innovo Group adult apparel and accessories under the Hot Wheels brand. After pumping out *Sesame Street* products, including the once sought-after Tickle Me Elmo, under license with Sesame Workshop for nearly a decade, Mattel lost the licensing rights to rival Hasbro in late 2009.

Mattel is pursing additional licensing agreements to expand its offerings outside the realm of traditional toys. Another top priority for the company includes reinvigorating the Barbie brand. Universal Pictures in 2009 acquired the movie rights to the Barbie brand, making it the fashion doll's first live-action picture deal.

Mattel continues a long-running legal battle against Bratz doll maker MGA Entertainment. In 2005 MGA filed a lawsuit against Mattel, alleging that Mattel engaged in unfair competition by copying the Bratz dolls' design with its "My Scene" version of Barbie. The following year Mattel said it had legal claim to Bratz because it employed the designer and freelancer (Carter Bryant) at the time he developed and sold the concept for the doll. In 2008 a federal jury awarded Mattel $100 million in damages in the dispute, and the judge on the case further ordered that MGA turn over the entire Bratz franchise and name. The decision was later suspended, and in mid-2010 it was thrown out on appeal.

A spate of recalls in 2007, spurred by Chinese-made products considered harmful, were expensive both for Mattel's pocketbook (it estimates its losses at nearly $50 million in product returns and related expenses) and its image. The company had to recall over 2 million Chinese-made toys in 2007, after learning that they may contain hazardous levels of lead paint. Mattel also recalled more than 18 million toys due to potentially hazardous small magnets.

In December 2008 the company agreed to pay $12 million to 39 states to settle an investigation into lead-tainted toys and to lower acceptable levels of lead in imported toys. A class-action suit related to the recalls has also been filed against Mattel on behalf of parents who bought the toys.

In response to hard economic times, Mattel in late 2008 cut 1,000 jobs (less than 5% of its worldwide workforce), thus reducing its professional and management ranks by nearly 10%.

Janus Capital Management and Franklin Mutual Advisors each maintain about a 5% stake in the company.

HISTORY

A small California toy manufacturer began operating out of a converted garage in 1945, producing dollhouse furniture. Harold Matson and Elliot Handler named their new company Mattel, using letters from their last and first names. Matson soon sold his share to Handler and his wife, Ruth, who incorporated the business in 1948.

By 1952 the company's toy line had expanded to include burp guns and musical toys, and sales exceeded $5 million. Sponsorship of Walt Disney's *Mickey Mouse Club* (debuted 1955), a first in toy advertising, was a shrewd marketing step for Mattel, providing direct, year-round access to millions of young potential customers.

In 1959 Mattel introduced the Barbie doll, named after the Handlers' daughter, Barbara, and later introduced Ken, named after their son. Barbie, with her fashionable wardrobe and extensive line of accessories, was an instant hit and eventually became the most successful brand-name toy ever sold.

Mattel went public in 1960, and within two years sales had jumped from $25 million to $75 million. It launched the popular Hot Wheels miniature cars line in 1968.

The Handlers were ousted from management in 1974 after an investigation by the SEC found irregularities in reports of the company's profits. The new management moved into non-toy businesses, adding Western Publishing (Golden Books) and the Ringling Brothers-Barnum & Bailey Combined Shows circus in 1979.

By the 1980s Mattel was a high-volume business with heavy overhead expenses and high development costs. By 1984, in an effort to recapitalize, the company had sold all its non-toy assets. Sales were more than $1 billion in 1987, but Mattel lost $93 million. Toying with bankruptcy, newly appointed chairman John Amerman cut Mattel's manufacturing capacity by 40% and fired 22% of its corporate staff.

The early 1990s saw several acquisitions — Fisher-Price (toys for preschoolers), and Kransco (battery-powered ride-on vehicles).

Amerman relinquished his roles as chairman and CEO in 1997 and was replaced by COO Jill Barad, who had enlivened the Barbie brand. Also in 1997 the company bought #3 US toy maker Tyco Toys (Tickle Me Elmo and Matchbox cars).

Barad started restructuring Mattel in 1999, closing plants and laying off 3,000 workers.

The company entered unfamiliar territory in 1999, paying $3.6 billion for leading educational software maker The Learning Company in a deal that would be Barad's downfall. Losses followed, and Barad left in 2000. Mattel named Kraft Foods veteran Bob Eckert chairman and CEO.

Co-founder Ruth Handler, credited with the creation of the Barbie doll, died in April 2002.

Mattel and two former employees agreed in December 2002 to pay $477,000 in fines for making political donations in other people's names, the third-largest fine imposed by the Federal

Election Commission. Also that year the company closed its Kentucky manufacturing and distribution facilities and in early 2003 consolidated two of its manufacturing facilities in Mexico.

Looking to further its presence in the electronic toys business, Mattel acquired Hong Kong-based Radica Games for $230 million in 2006. The products appeal to children older than Mattel's typical consumer, as well as adults. Also that year Mattel selected Activision Blizzard in a multiyear deal to be the exclusive worldwide distributor for Barbie-branded video games.

EXECUTIVES

Chairman and CEO: Robert A. Eckert, age 55, $11,430,584 total compensation
CFO: Kevin M. Farr, age 52, $4,634,975 total compensation
EVP Worldwide Operations: Thomas A. Debrowski, age 59, $3,741,067 total compensation
EVP; President, American Girl: Ellen L. Brothers, age 54
SVP Product Integrity and Chief Regulatory Officer: Jim Walter
SVP and CIO: Paul Rasmusson
SVP and General Manager, Mattel Brands: Tim Kilpin
SVP Human Resources: Alan Kaye, age 56
SVP Corporate Responsibility: Geoff Massingberd, age 52
SVP and Corporate Controller: H. Scott Topham, age 49
SVP, General Counsel, and Secretary: Robert (Bob) Normile, age 50
SVP Design, Barbie Brand: Evelyn Viohl
SVP Marketing, Barbie: Stephanie Cota
SVP Mattel Brands: Jerry Bossick
SVP Investor Relations and Treasurer: Dianne Douglas, age 53
VP Marketing: Doug Wadleigh
VP PR and Brand Communications: Sara Rosales
President, Mattel Brands: Neil B. Friedman, age 62, $6,135,494 total compensation
President, International: Bryan G. Stockton, age 56, $4,662,595 total compensation
Auditors: PricewaterhouseCoopers LLP

LOCATIONS

HQ: Mattel, Inc.
  333 Continental Blvd., El Segundo, CA 90245
Phone: 310-252-2000   **Fax:** 310-252-2179
Web: www.mattel.com

2009 Sales

	$ mil.	% of total
US	3,176.0	58
Europe	1,442.5	27
Latin America	860.5	16
Asia/Pacific	267.4	5
Other regions	187.9	3
Adjustments	(503.5)	(9)
Total	**5,430.8**	**100**

PRODUCTS/OPERATIONS

2009 Sales

	$ mil.	% of total
Domestic		
Mattel Girls & Boys Brands US	1,402.2	26
Fisher-Price Brands US	1,310.9	24
American Girl Brands	462.9	8
International	2,758.3	51
Adjustments	(503.5)	(9)
Total	**5,430.8**	**100**

Selected Brands

Boys
  Batman
  DC Universe
  Hot Wheels
  Kung Fu Panda
  Magic 8 Ball
  Masters of the Universe
  Matchbox
  Mattel
  Max Steel
  Nickelodeon *Rugrats*
  Radica
  Scrabble (International)
  Speed Racer
  Tyco Radio Control
  Yu-Gi-Oh!
Girls
  American Girl
  Barbie
  Bitty Baby
  Boom-O
  Cabbage Patch Kids
  Coconut
  Disney
  Diva Starz
  ello
  Fashion Avenue
  Flavas
  High School Musical
  Just Like You
  Little Mommy
  Polly Pocket!
Infant and preschool
  BabyGear
  Barney
  Blue's Clues
  Disney
  Dora the Explorer
  Fisher-Price
  Geo Trax
  Go-Diego-Go!
  Little People
  Matchbox Kids
  Mickey Mouse
  Pixter
  Power Wheels
  See 'n Say
  UNO
  View-Master
  Winnie the Pooh

COMPETITORS

Electronic Arts	Playmobil
Hasbro	Radio Flyer
JAKKS Pacific	RC2 Corporation
LeapFrog	Sanrio
LEGO	Simba Dickie Group
Marvel Entertainment	TakaraTomy
MGA Entertainment	Toy Quest
Motorsports Authentics	Ty
Namco Bandai	VTech Holdings
Ohio Art	

HISTORICAL FINANCIALS

Company Type: Public

Income Statement

FYE: December 31

	REVENUE ($ mil.)	NET INCOME ($ mil.)	NET PROFIT MARGIN	EMPLOYEES
12/09	5,431	529	9.7%	27,000
12/08	5,918	380	6.4%	29,000
12/07	5,970	600	10.1%	31,000
12/06	5,650	593	10.5%	32,000
12/05	5,179	417	8.1%	26,000
Annual Growth	**1.2%**	**6.1%**	**—**	**0.9%**

2009 Year-End Financials

Debt ratio: 27.7%
Return on equity: 22.7%
Cash ($ mil.): 1,117
Current ratio: 2.41
Long-term debt ($ mil.): 700
No. of shares (mil.): 360
Dividends
Yield: 3.8%
Payout: 51.7%
Market value ($ mil.): 7,187

Stock History

NASDAQ (GS): MAT

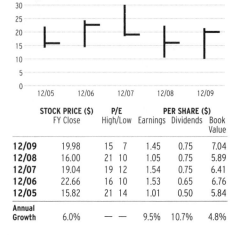

	STOCK PRICE ($) FY Close	P/E High/Low		PER SHARE ($) Earnings	Dividends	Book Value
12/09	19.98	15	7	1.45	0.75	7.04
12/08	16.00	21	10	1.05	0.75	5.89
12/07	19.04	19	12	1.54	0.75	6.41
12/06	22.66	16	10	1.53	0.65	6.76
12/05	15.82	21	14	1.01	0.50	5.84
Annual Growth	**6.0%**	**—**	**—**	**9.5%**	**10.7%**	**4.8%**

Maxim Integrated Products

Maxim's maxim? Invent! Maxim Integrated Products makes more than 6,000 kinds of analog and mixed-signal integrated circuits (ICs); more than 80% were invented by the company. Maxim's chips — which include amplifiers, data converters, transceivers, and switching ICs — translate physical data such as temperature, pressure, and sound into digital signals for electronic processing. The company's ICs are used by thousands of electronics manufacturers in products including computers and peripherals, appliances, telecommunications and networking gear, automobiles, medical devices, instruments, and utility meters.

In response to the global economic downturn, Maxim restructured its operations in order to cut costs. The company transferred production from its San Jose, California, plant to Japan; closed its wafer fab in Dallas; outsourced testing operations to contract manufacturers in Asia; consolidated global corporate functions; combined some product lines and discontinued others; and reduced its workforce.

Even during the notorious roller-coaster ups and downs of the chip industry, Maxim backs up its emphasis on invention by reinvesting a substantial chunk of sales (typically between about 20%-30% a year) in R&D, and by rolling out hundreds of new products each year.

More closely targeting the energy measurement and "smart meter" market, Maxim in 2010 acquired Teridian Semiconductor for about $315 million in cash. Teridian holds 50% of the system-on-a-chip energy measurement market. It is a supplier to three of the top four utility meter manufacturers in the US and to more than 50 meter makers around the world.

In 2009 Maxim acquired the hardware portion of ZiLOG's Wireless Control business, which included microcontroller product lines and related intellectual property. On its own, Maxim bought ZiLOG's Secure Transaction product line, with its Zatara line of 32-bit MCUs used in consumer payment terminals. The acquisition dovetails with Maxim's earlier purchase of a French firm, Innova Card, in providing chips for the financial transaction terminal market.

Later that year Maxim spun out its radio-frequency (RF) division — consisting of designs, intellectual property, and an engineering team — to Intelleflex in exchange for equity ownership in that company and an agreement to partner on future product marketing.

The company has discontinued development of certain stand-alone, high-speed, high-resolution analog-to-digital converters. While Maxim concluded there was a limited market for these parts, it cut the converters in part to avoid an intellectual property dispute with rival Analog Devices over the devices. Jettisoning the products helped the company settle the case with ADI rather than going to trial.

HISTORY

Jack Gifford, a former UCLA baseball star who began his career at Fairchild Semiconductor and later headed the Intersil subsidiary (later divested) of General Electric, founded Maxim in 1983. Gifford focused on analog chips, which were less vulnerable to Japanese competition than digital integrated circuits (ICs), had a longer product life, and cost less to make. Maxim went public in 1988.

From the beginning, Maxim emphasized research and development: Gifford's 1983 business plan set the ambitious goal of developing at least 15 new products each quarter. The company developed 479 new products between 1993 and 1996.

In 1994 Maxim bought Tektronix's IC business, and the two companies formed the Maxtek joint venture, a maker of multichip modules and hybrid circuits. For the rest of the decade Maxim focused on expanding and modernizing its manufacturing. It opened offices in Hong Kong, South Korea, and Singapore in 1996, and added factories in the Philippines and California in 1997.

Maxim released 250 new products in fiscal 1998, including breakthrough chips for portable computers, flat-panel displays, and paging. Maxim sold its half of Maxtek to Tektronix in 2000. That year it also introduced a record 383 products, and broke ground for a testing facility in Thailand.

In 2001 Maxim acquired specialty IC maker Dallas Semiconductor for about $2.5 billion. It also continued its "product proliferation" strategy as it topped itself once again by introducing 500 new products. Fiscal 2001 also saw the company expand its facilities in California, Thailand, and the Philippines.

Maxim bought a Texas chip fabrication plant from Philips Semiconductors (now NXP) in 2003.

For health reasons, Jack Gifford retired as CEO at the end of 2006; he also left the board of directors. Tunc Doluca, a group president and 22-year veteran of Maxim, was named president and CEO effective at the beginning of 2007. Director B. Kipling Hagopian, a member of the board since 1997, was elected interim chairman to succeed Gifford.

Gifford's sudden departure came while the company was still investigating its past practices in granting stock options, a subject that came to dominate his last year with Maxim. A shareholder derivative lawsuit challenging Maxim's practices in stock-option grants was filed in May 2006. While the company publicly dismissed the complaint as without merit, the SEC soon after opened an informal inquiry on the subject.

The board's special committee wrapped up its review in early 2007, concluding that there were instances from 2000 to 2006 where the recorded price of certain stock-option grants did not reflect the fair market value of the shares on the actual measurement dates. As a result, Jack Gifford retired from his part-time advisory position and CFO Carl Jasper resigned from the company.

Near the end of 2007 Maxim reached a settlement with the SEC on options backdating, agreeing to a permanent injunction against violations of federal securities laws and anti-fraud statutes. The SEC didn't assess any fines or penalties against the company under the settlement. The regulators brought civil charges against Gifford and Jasper for their roles in backdating options.

Gifford settled his case with the SEC, agreeing to return more than $650,000 in bonuses and to pay a penalty of $150,000. Jasper contested the charges, however.

In 2008 the company settled the shareholder derivative lawsuit over the misdated stock options for $28.5 million.

Gifford died in early 2009 at the age of 67.

EXECUTIVES

Chairman: B. Kipling (Kip) Hagopian, age 68
President, CEO, and Director: Tunc Doluca, age 51, $2,774,291 total compensation
Group President and CTO: Pirooz Parvarandeh, age 49, $2,529,027 total compensation
Group President: Vijay Ullal, age 50, $2,489,625 total compensation
SVP and CFO: Bruce E. Kiddoo, age 49, $1,503,607 total compensation
SVP Administration and General Counsel: Charles G. Rigg, age 65, $1,816,829 total compensation
SVP Manufacturing Operations: Vivek Jain, age 49
Division VP: Christopher J. (Chris) Neil, age 43
VP and Principal Accounting Officer: Dave Caron, age 50
VP and Senior Counsel: Edwin Medlin, age 53
VP Worldwide Sales: Matthew J. Murphy, age 36
Senior Public Relations Specialist: Drew Ehrlich
Auditors: Deloitte & Touche LLP

LOCATIONS

HQ: Maxim Integrated Products, Inc.
120 San Gabriel Dr., Sunnyvale, CA 94086
Phone: 408-737-7600   **Fax:** 408-737-7194
Web: www.maxim-ic.com

2010 Sales

	$ mil.	% of total
Asia/Pacific		
China	685.9	34
South Korea	311.9	16
Japan	131.5	7
Other countries	223.8	11
US	291.5	15
Europe	288.7	14
Other regions	64.3	3
Total	**1,997.6**	**100**

PRODUCTS/OPERATIONS

Selected Products

Amplifiers and comparators
  Audio amplifiers
  Operational amplifiers
Analog switches and multiplexers
Data converters, sample-and-hold devices, and voltage references
Digital potentiometers
Fiber and communications devices
  Circuits for fiber and cable data transmission
  Framers
  Transceivers
Filters
High-frequency application-specific integrated circuits (ASICs)
Hot-swap and power switching circuits
Interface and interconnect devices
LED lighting and LCD display devices
Memories
  Electrically erasable programmable read-only memories (EEPROMs)
  Erasable programmable read-only memories (EPROMs)
  Non-volatile static random-access memories (SRAMs)
  Non-volatile timekeeping RAMs
Microcontrollers
Microprocessor supervisors and non-volatile RAM controllers
Multiplexers
Optoelectronic devices
Power supplies and battery management devices
  DC-to-DC power supplies
  Low-dropout linear regulators
  Power metal oxide semiconductor field-effect transistor (MOSFET) drivers
Protection and isolation circuits
Sensors, sensor conditioners, and thermal management devices
Storage products
Timing devices
  Counters and timers
  Oscillators and waveform generators
  Real-time clocks (RTCs)
Wireless and radio-frequency (RF) products
  Amplifiers
  Receivers
  Transmitters and transceivers
Video amplifiers, processors, and switches
Voltage monitors

COMPETITORS

Advanced Analogic Technologies	Mitsui
Altera	Monolithic Power Systems
Analog Devices	National Semiconductor
Applied Micro Circuits	NXP Semiconductors
Atmel	O2Micro
Conexant Systems	ON Semiconductor
Exar	PMC-Sierra
Fairchild Semiconductor	QUALCOMM
Freescale Semiconductor	RF Micro Devices
Fujitsu Microelectronics America	Ricoh Company
	ROHM
Infineon Technologies	Seiko
Intel	Semtech
International Rectifier	Silicon Labs
Intersil	Siliconix
Linear Technology	Skyworks
Marvell Technology	STMicroelectronics
Micrel	Texas Instruments
Microchip Technology	Vishay Intertechnology
Mindspeed	Vitesse Semiconductor
Mitsubishi Corp.	Volterra Semiconductor

HISTORICAL FINANCIALS

Company Type: Public

Income Statement

FYE: Last Saturday in June

	REVENUE ($ mil.)	NET INCOME ($ mil.)	NET PROFIT MARGIN	EMPLOYEES
6/10	1,998	125	6.3%	9,200
6/09	1,646	11	0.6%	8,765
6/08	2,053	318	15.5%	9,810
6/07	2,009	286	14.2%	10,136
6/06	1,857	388	20.9%	9,096
Annual Growth	1.8%	(24.6%)	—	0.3%

2010 Year-End Financials

Debt ratio: 18.4%
Return on equity: 5.1%
Cash ($ mil.): 827
Current ratio: 3.20
Long-term debt ($ mil.): 432

No. of shares (mil.): 298
Dividends
  Yield: 4.8%
  Payout: 200.0%
Market value ($ mil.): 4,991

Stock History

NASDAQ (GS): MXIM

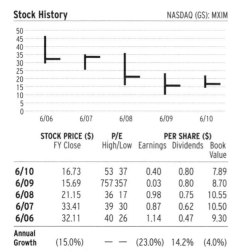

	STOCK PRICE ($) FY Close	P/E High/Low	PER SHARE ($) Earnings	Dividends	Book Value
6/10	16.73	53 37	0.40	0.80	7.89
6/09	15.69	757 357	0.03	0.80	8.70
6/08	21.15	36 17	0.98	0.75	10.55
6/07	33.41	39 30	0.87	0.62	10.50
6/06	32.11	40 26	1.14	0.47	9.30
Annual Growth	(15.0%)	— —	(23.0%)	14.2%	(4.0%)

MBIA Inc.

MBIA will make sure that bonds get paid, no matter what. Its independent subsidiary, National Public Finance Guarantee Corporation, is a leading provider of insurance for municipal bonds and stable corporate bonds (such as utility bonds) in the US. Separately, its MBIA Insurance Corporation provides global structured finance products and non-US public financial guarantees. MBIA's Cutwater business manages assets for public-sector clients. Other lines of business include tax compliance services and buying and servicing municipal real estate tax liens.

That MBIA is still standing is remarkable. As one of the largest providers of insurance to asset- and mortgage-based securities, MBIA was among the most vulnerable companies when the US housing market imploded in 2007. The company posted losses of $2.3 billion the last quarter of 2007, a result of its investments in subprime mortgage-backed securities. In response, MBIA escorted its CEO Gary Dunton to the door and welcomed back his predecessor, Joseph Brown.

MBIA and its similarly afflicted competitors, FGIC and Ambac Financial, struggled to tread water in a maelstrom. MBIA laid out a plan to

split apart its public, structured, and asset management businesses to separate the stable from the unstable. It first set in place some drastic changes to reduce its exposure to any single risk: in 2008 the company stopped writing structured finance for six months and quit insuring credit derivative transactions. Other firms didn't fare as well that year, and MBIA was able to pick up a block of US public finance business from FGIC as that company foundered.

The big change came in early 2009: MBIA split its municipal bond insurance business off into an independent subsidiary named National Public Finance Guarantee Corporation. It receives a credit rating separate from the rest of MBIA's riskier structured-finance businesses. However, regulators have not quite made peace with the strategy and have challenged National's existence, hampering its ability to write new business.

After the big split, smaller ones followed: MBIA continued to sort its units into clearly separate businesses. In 2010 it restructured its fixed-income asset management business into a stand-alone operation under its new name, Cutwater Asset Management.

Before the meltdown, MBIA had expanded internationally for long-term growth, while still writing more than 60% of its business in the US. The company's international business consists primarily of guarantees on privately issued bonds for public projects.

Private equity firm Warburg Pincus owns about a third of the company and holds two seats on the board of directors.

HISTORY

In 1974 such insurers as Aetna, CIGNA, Fireman's Fund (now part of Allianz), and Continental (now part of CNA) formed consortium Municipal Bond Insurance Association. The insurance was intended to reduce investor risk and to boost ratings and cut costs for bond issuers. Holding company MBIA was incorporated and went public in 1986. Three years later it absorbed rival Bond Investors Group.

As bond insurance gained wide acceptance, MBIA moved into coverage of investment-grade corporate bonds, and asset- and mortgage-backed bonds. It also began offering institutional brokerage services and money market funds to municipal customers. But with acceptance came competition, forcing MBIA to take on riskier bond issues. It joined forces with Ambac Indemnity in 1995 to offer bond insurance abroad; the decision pricked MBIA three years later when a Thai company defaulted.

It began investing in real estate tax lien and tax compliance companies in 1996 and picked up asset-backed bond insurer CapMAC Holdings in 1998, despite that company's exposure in Asia. The same year MBIA formed an alliance with Japan's Mitsui Marine & Fire (now Mitsui Sumitomo Insurance) and bought 1838 Investment Advisors, which oversees assets of $6 billion.

The following year the company inked a deal to be the exclusive insurer of municipal bonds on Trading Edge's BondLink trading service. MBIA also sold its bond administration and consulting firm, MBIA MuniFinancial, saying it no longer fit with company strategy.

In 2000 MBIA's venture with Trading Edge opened for online business. That year the company exited its alliance with Mitsui Sumitomo Insurance. Due to its decision to discontinue equity

advisory services operations, MBIA sold subsidiary 1838 Investment Advisors to that company's management in 2004; MBIA then focused its advisory services on fixed-income asset management.

EXECUTIVES

Chairman: Daniel P. Kearney, age 70
CEO and Director: Joseph W. (Jay) Brown, age 61, $5,167,360 total compensation
President, CFO, and Chief Administrative Officer; Vice Chairman and CFO, MBIA Insurance; President, CEO, and Chief Administrative Officer, Optinuity Alliance Resources: C. Edward (Chuck) Chaplin, age 53, $3,859,748 total compensation
EVP and Chief Portfolio Officer: Mitchell I. Sonkin, age 57, $4,266,979 total compensation
EVP, Chief Legal Officer, and Secretary: Ram D. Wertheim, age 55, $2,281,503 total compensation
VP: Elizabeth James
Chief Marketing and Communications Officer: Willard I. Hill Jr.
Managing Director, International Infrastructure Finance, London: Paul David
Managing Director, International, Australia: Graham Metcalf
Managing Director, International Infrastructure Finance, London: Deborah Zurkow
Managing Director, Fixed-Income Investor Relations, Europe: Iain Barbour
Managing Director, International and New Business Development: Eugenio Mendoza
Managing Director and Head of International: Christopher E. (Chris) Weeks, age 49
Managing Director, Investor Relations: Greg Diamond
Director, Corporate Communications: Kevin Brown
President and COO, MBIA Inc. and MBIA Insurance: William C. (Bill) Fallon, age 50, $3,661,679 total compensation
President and Chief Investment Officer, Cutwater Asset Management: Clifford D. Corso, age 48, $3,154,548 total compensation
President and CEO, National Public Finance Guarantee: Thomas G. (Tom) McLoughlin, age 49
Auditors: PricewaterhouseCoopers LLP

LOCATIONS

HQ: MBIA Inc.
113 King St., Armonk, NY 10504
Phone: 914-273-4545   **Fax:** 914-765-3163
Web: www.mbia.com

PRODUCTS/OPERATIONS

2009 Revenues

	$ mil.	% of total
Insurance		
Structured finance & international	2,213	67
US public finance	819	25
Eliminations	(271)	—
Investment management services	280	8
Corporate & eliminations	(87)	—
Total	**2,954**	**100**

COMPETITORS

Ambac
Assured Guaranty
FGIC
Primus Guaranty
Radian Asset Assurance
Radian Group
Syncora Holdings

HISTORICAL FINANCIALS

Company Type: Public

Income Statement

FYE: December 31

	ASSETS ($ mil.)	NET INCOME ($ mil.)	INCOME AS % OF ASSETS	EMPLOYEES
12/09	25,685	634	2.5%	416
12/08	29,657	(2,673)	—	420
12/07	47,415	(1,922)	—	486
12/06	39,763	819	2.1%	492
12/05	34,561	711	2.1%	626
Annual Growth	(7.2%)	(2.8%)	—	(9.7%)

2009 Year-End Financials

Equity as % of assets: 10.1%	Dividends
Return on assets: 2.3%	Yield: 0.0%
Return on equity: 35.4%	Payout: —
Long-term debt ($ mil.): 8,113	Market value ($ mil.): 798
No. of shares (mil.): 200	Sales ($ mil.): 2,954

Stock History

NYSE: MBI

	STOCK PRICE ($) FY Close	P/E High/Low	PER SHARE ($) Earnings	PER SHARE ($) Dividends	PER SHARE ($) Book Value
12/09	3.98	24 1	2.99	0.00	13.01
12/08	4.07	— —	(12.29)	0.00	4.96
12/07	18.63	— —	(15.17)	1.36	18.24
12/06	73.06	12 9	5.99	1.24	35.95
12/05	60.16	12 9	5.18	1.12	32.89
Annual Growth	(49.3%)	— —	(12.8%)	—	(20.7%)

McAfee, Inc.

McAfee puts a virtual padlock on IT resources. The company provides security products that protect computers, networks, and mobile devices. Its software and hardware protect users from viruses, spam, and spyware. Other offerings include data loss prevention, mobile security, host intrusion prevention, encryption, and e-mail security tools. McAfee also provides consulting, support, and training services. The company sells its products directly and through resellers and distributors to consumers, corporate clients, service providers, and government agencies worldwide. In August 2010 the company agreed to be acquired by chip giant Intel for about $7.68 billion.

While Intel has been expanding its software offerings through acquisitions in recent years, the McAfee deal would be by far its largest foray into software. Intel's interest in McAfee included expanding its security expertise in areas such as mobile computing, ATMs, and Internet-connected devices, as well as fueling its broader strategic push to provide a secure package of hardware, software, and services to clients. McAfee would become a wholly owned subsidiary that would report to Intel's software and services group.

McAfee's products span the spectrum from PC products targeted at individual consumers to enterprise-grade network security offerings. The company has actively used acquisitions to expand its product line, strategically adding new technologies and capabilities that address the increasingly complex security threats that networks and computers face.

Recent deals have included purchases of ScanAlert (creators of the HACKER SAFE Web site security certification service) and data loss prevention specialist Reconnex. McAfee also significantly expanded with the $465 million acquisition of network security gateway provider Secure Computing. The purchase of Secure Computing made McAfee one of the world's largest network security software providers and enabled it to offer a comprehensive security product for both individual PCs and networks.

McAfee also acquired IT infrastructure protection specialist Solidcore in June 2009. Solidcore's products prevent the installation of unauthorized applications on servers and workstations. The purchase gives McAfee a foothold in new markets, as Solidcore's products are also used in such devices as ATMs, point-of-sale systems, and multifunction printers. Later that year the company purchased MX Logic for $140 million; MX Logic provides e-mail and Web security services.

In 2010 it announced plans to purchase ten-Cube, a provider of mobile security services. tenCube's WaveSecure service is used by consumers to remotely control and manage data on smart phones and other mobile devices. The deal will boost McAfee's mobile security product line and broaden its potential markets to include security for smart phones.

McAfee has also focused on internal product development as well, releasing Web-based versions of many of its products, upgrading its consumer security software lines, and developing new complementary services such as its McAfee Online Backup data protection service.

HISTORY

John McAfee, a former systems consultant for Lockheed (now part of Lockheed Martin), started McAfee Associates in 1989 to sell his antivirus software. Normal retail channels were too difficult for a small entrepreneur to crack, so he marketed his product on computer bulletin boards as shareware, depending on the honesty of users to pay for the product if they found it useful. Enough of them did, and the success was compounded as satisfied individual users recommended it for their companies' systems.

McAfee Associates went public in 1992. The next year former Apple and Sun Microsystems marketer William Larson became CEO. He built a suite of products through more than a dozen acquisitions, bundled them to reap higher returns, and stretched the company's sales and marketing efforts.

From 1994 to 1997 sales grew to more than $600 million. Following a failed bid to acquire Cheyenne Software in 1996, McAfee bought network management specialist Network General in 1997 and changed its name to Network Associates. It also bought software encryption company Pretty Good Privacy (now PGP) that year.

The company continued to pursue acquisitions in 1998, seeking to convert the company from an antivirus leader into a network security and desktop management specialist rivaling CA. (Larson chose the company's Santa Clara headquarters partly because its offices towered over CA's across

the highway.) Network Associates moved into firewalls (Trusted Information Systems), intrusion detection (Secure Networks), more antivirus technology (UK-based Dr Solomon's), and diagnostic software (CyberMedia).

That year the SEC began examining the large amount of acquisition-related charges Network Associates had written off. In 1999 Network Associates was forced to restate its 1998 results, resulting in a number of shareholder lawsuits. Also that year Network Associates sold a 15% stake in McAfee.com to the public.

In 2000 a surprise earnings warning was followed by the departure of several top executives, including Larson. In 2001 Network Associates named George Samenuk, former head of online exchange company Tradeout, CEO and chairman. In 2002 the company sold its firewall security unit to Secure Computing. Network Associates also repurchased the publicly traded shares of McAfee.com, as part of a broad effort to streamline its product lines.

In 2003 Network Associates entered the intrusion detection market with the acquisitions of Entercept Security Technologies and IntruVert Networks. The company also restated its financial results for fiscal years 1998-2000 after investigations by the SEC and Department of Justice.

The company purchased vulnerability management software provider Foundstone for about $86 million in 2004. Later that year it sold its Sniffer product line to Silver Lake Partners and Texas Pacific Group (now TPG Capital) for $235 million and changed its name to McAfee.

It acquired security software maker Wireless Security in 2005. The following year it purchased website test and rating specialist SiteAdvisor, as well as data protection service provider Onigma.

In 2007 McAfee acquired SafeBoot, a developer of security software for mobile devices, for $350 million.

EXECUTIVES

Chairman: Charles J. (Chuck) Robel, age 60
President, CEO, and Director: David G. (Dave) DeWalt, age 45, $8,072,610 total compensation
EVP and CFO: Jonathan Chadwick, age 44
EVP and Worldwide CTO: George Kurtz
EVP Worldwide Sales Operations: Michael P. DeCesare, age 45, $3,068,575 total compensation
EVP Worldwide Strategy and Business Development; General Manager, Data Protection: Gerhard Watzinger, age 49, $1,924,908 total compensation
EVP, Chief Legal Officer, and General Counsel: Mark D. Cochran, age 51, $1,663,130 total compensation
EVP and Chief Marketing Officer: David B. Milam, age 54
EVP Product Operations: Bryan R. Barney
EVP and General Manager, Consumer, Mobile, and Small Business: Todd W. Gebhart, age 55
EVP Human Resources: Joseph P. (Joe) Gabbert, age 58
SVP Finance and Chief Accounting Officer: Keith S. Krzeminski, age 48, $831,181 total compensation
SVP Worldwide Technical Support and Customer Service: Barry McPherson
SVP and General Manager, Content and Cloud Security: Marc Olesen
SVP Global Strategic Alliances: Dave Scholtz
SVP; Chairman, Japan: Takahiro Kato
VP and Chief Technology Evangelist: Carl E. Banzhof, age 40
VP and Corporate Controller: Kandis Thompson
VP Investor Relations: Kate Scolnick
Director, Investor Relations: Brandie Claborn
President, Europe, Middle East, and Africa: David Quantrell
Auditors: Deloitte & Touche LLP

LOCATIONS

HQ: McAfee, Inc.
3965 Freedom Cir., Santa Clara, CA 95054
Phone: 408-988-3832   **Fax:** 408-970-9727
Web: www.mcafee.com

2009 Sales

	$ mil.	% of total
North America	1,091.8	57
Europe, Middle East & Africa	531.8	28
Asia/Pacific		
Japan	138.6	7
Other countries	96.3	5
Latin America	68.8	3
Total	**1,927.3**	**100**

PRODUCTS/OPERATIONS

2009 Sales

	$ mil.	% of total
Service, support & subscriptions	1,739.1	90
Products	188.2	10
Total	**1,927.3**	**100**

COMPETITORS

Barracuda Networks
BigFix
Blue Coat
CA Technologies
Check Point Software
Cisco Systems
Comodo
EMC
Fortinet
F-Secure
Google
Hauri
IBM Internet Security Systems
Juniper Networks
Kaspersky Lab
Lumension
Microsoft
nCircle
Novell
Panda Security
Qualys
SonicWALL
Sophos
Sourcefire
Symantec
Trend Micro
Tripwire
Websense

HISTORICAL FINANCIALS

Company Type: Public

Income Statement

FYE: December 31

	REVENUE ($ mil.)	NET INCOME ($ mil.)	NET PROFIT MARGIN	EMPLOYEES
12/09	1,927	173	9.0%	6,100
12/08	1,600	172	10.8%	5,600
12/07	1,308	167	12.8%	4,250
12/06	1,145	138	12.0%	3,700
12/05	987	139	14.1%	3,290
Annual Growth	**18.2%**	**5.7%**	**—**	**16.7%**

2009 Year-End Financials

Debt ratio: —
Return on equity: 9.0%
Cash ($ mil.): 677
Current ratio: 1.23
Long-term debt ($ mil.): —
No. of shares (mil.): 152
Dividends
  Yield: —
  Payout: —
Market value ($ mil.): 6,164

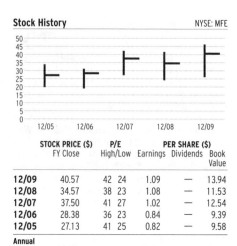
McClatchy Company

This company has gotten its clutches on quite a few newspapers. The McClatchy Company is the #3 newspaper business in the US (behind *USA TODAY* publisher Gannett and Tribune Company) with 30 daily papers boasting a combined circulation of about 2.3 million. Its portfolio includes *The Kansas City Star, The Miami Herald, The Sacramento Bee* (California), and the *Star-Telegram* (Fort Worth, Texas). McClatchy also publishes more than 40 nondaily newspapers in eight states and operates online news sites in conjunction with many of its papers. In addition, it has a 49% stake in The Seattle Times Company. The McClatchy family controls the company.

Smaller in stature than some of its rivals, McClatchy is also one of the few big newspaper companies that has not diversified into other forms of media. Both Gannett and Tribune, for example, own several television stations, while Advance Publications and The Washington Post Company have diversified into magazines and education publishing, respectively. Wholly reliant on newspaper advertising and subscriptions for the bulk of its sales, McClatchy offers a portrait of the industry's downward spiral caused by readers migrating away from print publications for their news.

The company has tried to manage that decline primarily through cost cuts to make up for lost revenue, and a large part of that effort has included layoffs that reduced McClatchy's workforce by about a third from 2008 through 2009. Early in 2010 it announced additional staff cuts at *The Kansas City Star* and *Sacramento Bee*. At the same time that it is working to reduce expenses, the company is focused on paying down its mountain of debt accumulated as a result of acquisitions. McClatchy refinanced part of that debt early in 2010 through a debt tender.

While downsizing and refinancing have helped keep creditors at bay, McClatchy is still working to boost revenue by transforming itself into a mixed-media news business. It continues to invest in Internet publishing operations to reach readers online and build new followings for its mastheads. McClatchy also has investments in several digital media companies, including CareerBuilder (about a 15% stake) and Classified Ventures (25%). Online advertising accounts for more than 10% of sales.

HISTORY

In the 1840s James McClatchy was a reporter for Horace Greeley's *New York Tribune*. When Greeley exhorted young men to go west, McClatchy went. He worked for several newspapers in Sacramento before co-founding *The Bee* (named to liken reporters to industrious insects) in 1857. The paper gained a reputation as a crusader and was known for its antislavery stance. During the 1920s the company expanded with sister *Bees* in Fresno and Modesto, California.

The McClatchy family bought out the other owners, and the company grew under its watch. Granddaughter Eleanor McClatchy ran the company from 1936 until 1978. It went public in 1988.

McClatchy bought three South Carolina dailies from The News and Observer Publishing Co. in 1990. Five years later it bought the Raleigh-based publisher — giving it a toehold in North Carolina's fast-growing Research Triangle area — as well as Nando.net (renamed Nando Media in 1998), its Internet publishing company. In 1996 and 1997 the company sold five of its community newspapers. Also in 1996 Gary Pruitt, who joined the company in 1984, was named CEO.

In 1997 McClatchy became the surprise winner in the bidding for Cowles Media Company (*Star Tribune*), for which it paid $1.4 billion. In 1998 the company sold Cowles' magazine and book publishing divisions. The company also changed its name from McClatchy Newspapers to The McClatchy Company.

The company made several Web-related investments in 2000; it took equity stakes in StreamSearch.com (a now defunct online audio and video search engine) and BrightStreet.com (online loyalty programs). McClatchy continued to focus on the Internet in 2001 even as it cut costs to combat a slump in ad spending.

In 2003 the company sold its Newspaper Network unit in two parts to news service Associated Press and ad services company Vertis (now called Vertis Communications). The McClatchy Company acquired six California newspapers, including the *Merced Sun-Star*, for $41 million in early 2004. The following year Nando changed its name once again when it became McClatchy Interactive.

Former chairman and patriarch of the family James McClatchy, great-grandson of the company's founder, died in 2006 at the age of 85. McClatchy briefly became the second-largest newspaper publisher in the US that year after it purchased rival Knight-Ridder for $4.5 billion in cash and the assumption of $2 billion in debt. Following the deal, the company sold several of the newly acquired newspapers, as well as the *Star Tribune* (now owned by Star Tribune Media Company).

With newspaper revenue declining industry-wide, McClatchy moved to pay down debt in 2008. The company sold its stake in SP Newsprint to Brant Industries as part of a $350 million disposal along with former partners Cox Enterprises and Media General. It also sold the online directory Real Cities Network (purchased as part of the Knight-Ridder acquisition) to online media buyer Centro.

EXECUTIVES

Chairman, President, and CEO: Gary B. Pruitt, age 52, $3,753,229 total compensation
VP, General Counsel, and Corporate Secretary: Karole Morgan-Prager, age 47
VP Advertising: Stephen Bernard
VP Human Resources: Heather L. Fagundes, age 41
VP Finance and CFO: Patrick J. (Pat) Talamantes, age 45, $1,020,461 total compensation
VP Operations: Frank R. J. Whittaker, age 60, $1,449,987 total compensation
VP Interactive Media: Christian A. Hendricks, age 47, $874,076 total compensation
VP Operations: Robert J. (Bob) Weil, age 59, $1,328,189 total compensation
Treasurer: R. Elaine Lintecum
Controller: Hai V. Nguyen, age 39
Director Communications: Peter Tira
Auditors: Deloitte & Touche LLP

LOCATIONS

HQ: The McClatchy Company
2100 Q St., Sacramento, CA 95816
Phone: 916-321-1846   **Fax:** 916-321-1964
Web: www.mcclatchy.com

PRODUCTS/OPERATIONS

2009 Sales

	$ mil.	% of total
Advertising	1,143.1	78
Circulation	278.3	19
Other	50.2	3
Total	**1,471.6**	**100**

Selected Newspapers

Anchorage Daily News (Alaska)
The Beaufort Gazette (South Carolina)
Belleville News-Democrat (Illinois)
The Bellingham Herald (Washington)
The Bradenton Herald (Florida)
Centre Daily Times (Pennsylvania)
Charlotte Observer (North Carolina)
El Nuevo Herald (Spanish-language, Miami)
The Fresno Bee (California)
The Herald (Rock Hill, SC)
Idaho Statesman (Boise)
The Island Packet (Hilton Head, SC)
The Kansas City Star
Ledger-Enquirer (Columbus, GA)
Lexington Herald-Leader (Kentucky)
Merced Sun-Star (California)
The Miami Herald
The Modesto Bee (California)
The News & Observer (Raleigh, NC)
The News Tribune (Tacoma, WA)
The Olympian (Olympia, WA)
The Sacramento Bee (California)
Star-Telegram (Fort Worth, TX)
The State (Columbia, SC)
Sun Herald (Biloxi, MS)
The Sun News (Myrtle Beach, SC)
The Telegraph (Macon, GA)
Tri-City Herald (Kennewick, WA)
The Tribune (San Luis Obispo, CA)
The Wichita Eagle (Kansas)

COMPETITORS

A. H. Belo
Dow Jones
Gannett
Hearst Newspapers
Lee Enterprises
Media General
Morris Publishing
New York Times
Paxton Media
Tribune Company
Washington Post

HISTORICAL FINANCIALS

Company Type: Public

Income Statement

FYE: Sunday nearest December 31

	REVENUE ($ mil.)	NET INCOME ($ mil.)	NET PROFIT MARGIN	EMPLOYEES
12/09	1,472	54	3.7%	9,600
12/08	1,901	(4)	—	12,100
12/07	2,260	(2,736)	—	15,748
12/06	1,675	(156)	—	16,791
12/05	1,186	161	13.5%	8,948
Annual Growth	**5.5%**	**(23.8%)**	**—**	**1.8%**

2009 Year-End Financials

Debt ratio: 1,114.3%
Return on equity: 48.6%
Cash ($ mil.): 6
Current ratio: 1.22
Long-term debt ($ mil.): 1,896
No. of shares (mil.): 85
Dividends
　Yield: 2.5%
　Payout: 13.8%
Market value ($ mil.): 300

Stock History

NYSE: MNI

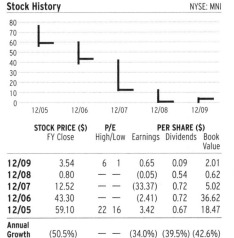

	STOCK PRICE ($) FY Close	P/E High/Low		PER SHARE ($) Earnings	Dividends	Book Value
12/09	3.54	6	1	0.65	0.09	2.01
12/08	0.80	—	—	(0.05)	0.54	0.62
12/07	12.52	—	—	(33.37)	0.72	5.02
12/06	43.30	—	—	(2.41)	0.72	36.62
12/05	59.10	22	16	3.42	0.67	18.47
Annual Growth	**(50.5%)**	**—**	**—**	**(34.0%)**	**(39.5%)**	**(42.6%)**

McCormick & Company

This company offers more than just the flavor of the month. It has more than enough flavors for not only the month, but for the day, the hour, and the minute. As the world's #1 spice maker, McCormick & Company offers a tasty assortment of herbs, spices, seasonings, marinades, flavorings, sauces, and extracts. The company distributes its own products, which are sold to consumers under brands including Club House, Ducros, McCormick, and Schwartz, as well as private labels. Its customers include food retailers, the foodservice industry, and industrial food-processors worldwide.

With product innovation as one of its main strategies, the company employs some 400 researchers. In 2009 McCormick introduced a new consumer product line of seasoning blends called Perfect Pinch. It also introduced Recipe Inspirations, which feature a packet of premeasured spices and a recipe card. Both are designed to help the customer explore new flavors.

Another part of the company's strategy is to grow through acquisitions. Expanding its well-known brand roster, McCormick acquired the Lawry's brand of marinades and spice blends

from Unilever for $605 million in 2008 (its largest acquisition ever). In order to buy Lawry's, the company was required by the FTC to sell its Season-All business, which it did — to Morton International. Continuing its brand-name acquisition strategy, the company also purchased Canada's largest honey business, Billy Bee Honey Products, in 2008. McCormick paid $75 million for the name-brand honey producer.

Robert Lawless retired as CEO in 2008, after 11 years in the position. COO and president Alan Wilson, who oversaw a $50 million cost-saving restructuring program at the company, was named his replacement. In 2009 Lawless stepped down as chairman and Wilson succeeded him.

An employee profit-sharing plan owns about 24% of McCormick; Lawless holds about 10%.

McCormick is known for scenting its annual reports with one of its more aromatic products, such as vanilla or Chinese five-spice. For 2008 the scent was cinnamon; the 2009 annual report had the aroma of pumpkin pie spice.

HISTORY

McCormick & Company was founded in 1889 by 25-year-old Willoughby McCormick, who crafted fruit syrups, root beer, and nerve and bone liniment in his Baltimore home. He employed three assistants to hawk his wares door-to-door. His company soon expanded its product line to include food coloring, cream of tartar, and blood purifier. By 1894 McCormick was exporting, and two years later it acquired the F.G. Emmett Spice Company of Philadelphia, firmly committing itself to the spice industry. By the turn of the century, McCormick was trading around the world.

Willoughby's nephew, Charles McCormick, joined the company as a part-time shipping clerk in 1912. When Willoughby died in 1932, Charles succeeded him as CEO. He increased employee wages, shortened the workweek, and established the Multiple Management system (still an integral part of the company's management structure), which solicited employee input. By 1933 McCormick was on a growth track that continued unabated through the 1930s. In 1938 Charles wrote a book expounding his participative management philosophy.

The company opened its first international office in 1940 and achieved coast-to-coast distribution seven years later with the acquisition of A. Schilling & Co., producers of spices and extracts. In 1959 McCormick purchased Gorman Eckert & Co., Canada's largest spice business and the precursor to Club House Foods. It acquired Gilroy Foods in 1961 and rival Baker Extract in 1962. From 1962 until its sale in 1988 McCormick ran a real estate subsidiary, Maryland Properties (renamed McCormick Properties, 1979).

Charles died in 1970. Though the years following his death were characterized by acquisitions and joint venture agreements in the US and abroad, profits slumped until his son, Charles "Buzz" McCormick, took over as CEO in 1987.

In 1989 Australia's Burns, Philp began challenging McCormick by buying up spice companies in the US and Europe, including the Spice Islands and Durkee French brands. Buzz — succeeded twice as CEO in the mid-1990s, only to return when one successor died and the other left for health reasons — responded with a bruising battle for shelf space that led to Burns, Philp's near-collapse in 1997. The company also sold garlic and onion processing subsidiary Gilroy Foods, Minipack Systems (UK), and several smaller, non-core operations. In 1997 Buzz yielded the CEO's post — for good — to Robert Lawless.

The company's earnings were erratic in the 1990s, partly because of a price war with then-rival Burns, Philp, but also due to the decline of home cooking in the US. McCormick countered with increased advertising and a growing emphasis on industrial sales to flavor the foods eaten outside the home. McCormick also has been expanding internationally through its Decors spice business and operations in China.

Economic woes in Venezuela caused McCormick to cease manufacturing operations there in 1998. In 1999 Lawless succeeded Buzz as chairman. In June 1999 the company announced it would cut costs by eliminating 300 jobs (mostly overseas) and closing a British plant.

McCormick's sweet victory over Burns, Philp was soured by an FTC investigation into its alleged practice of offering some grocery chains low prices in exchange for up to 90% of their shelf space for spices. The investigation brought scrutiny on a common supermarket practice known as slotting fees. McCormick settled with the FTC in 2000, agreeing not to illegally discriminate against retailers in its pricing. Also that year the company bought France-based Ducros (spices, herbs, dessert aid products) from Béghin-Say for about $380 million.

In 2003 McCormick's UK subsidiary acquired condiment maker Uniqsauces, adding the Beswicks and Hammonds, as well as the licensed Newman's Own brands to its European product line. Acquisitions continued in 2004 with McCormick's purchase of C.M. van Sillevoldt B.V. and its Silvo brand of spices, herbs, and seasonings, which is sold in the Netherlands and Belgium.

Continuing its expansion via acquisitions, the company purchased Dessert Products International (DPI) in 2006. DPI markets the Vahine brand dessert toppings in Europe. It also purchased Simply Asia Foods that year for $97.6 million in cash. Simply Asia manufactures products under the Thai Kitchen and Simply Asia brands; its products include noodle and soup bowls, meal kits, coconut milk, and sauces and pastes.

EXECUTIVES

Chairman, President, and CEO: Alan D. Wilson, age 52, $4,844,732 total compensation
EVP and CFO: Gordon M. Stetz Jr., age 49, $1,312,521 total compensation
SVP Finance and Treasurer: Paul C. Beard, age 55
SVP and Controller: Kenneth A. Kelly Jr., age 55
VP Corporate Operations: James Radin
VP Investor Relations: Joyce L. Brooks
VP Tax: Paul Nolan
VP Human Resources: Cecile K. Perich, age 58
VP Supply Chain and CIO: Jeryl (Jerry) Wolfe
VP Strategic Sourcing: Stephen J. Donohue
VP, General Counsel, and Secretary: W. Geoffrey (Geoff) Carpenter, age 57
VP Research and Development: Hamed Faridi
VP International Marketing and Innovation: Angela (Angie) Francolini
VP Corporate Communications and Community Relations: John G. McCormick

President, North American Consumer Foods: Mark T. Timbie, age 55, $2,699,907 total compensation
President, International: Lawrence E. Kurzius, age 52, $1,312,521 total compensation
President, U.S. Industrial Group: Charles T. (Chuck) Langmead, age 52, $1,622,717 total compensation
President, US Consumer Products Division: Ken Stickevers
President and CEO, McCormick Canada: Keith Gibbons
President, Europe, the Middle East, and Africa: Malcolm Swift
Director Consumer Communications: Laurie Harrsen
Director Investor Relations: Dorothy Powe
Auditors: Ernst & Young LLP

LOCATIONS

HQ: McCormick & Company, Incorporated
18 Loveton Circle, Sparks, MD 21152
Phone: 410-771-7301 **Fax:** 410-771-7462
Web: www.mccormick.com

2009 Sales

	$ mil.	% of total
US	1,981.5	62
Europe	671.0	21
Other countries	539.6	17
Total	**3,192.1**	**100**

PRODUCTS/OPERATIONS

2009 Sales

	$ mil.	% of total
Consumer products	1,911.2	60
Industrial & foodservice products	1,280.9	40
Total	**3,192.1**	**100**

Selected Brands

Billy Bee
Club House
Ducros
Lawry's
McCormick
Schwartz
Silvo
Simply Asia
Thai Kitchen
Vahine
Zatarain's

Selected Products

Coating systems
 Batters
 Breaders
 Glazes
 Marinades
 Rubs
Compound flavors
 Beverage flavors
 Confectionery flavors
 Dairy flavors
Condiments
 Flavored oils
 Jams and jellies
 Ketchup
 Mustards
 Salad dressings
 Sandwich sauces
 Seafood cocktail sauces
Ingredients
 Extracts
 Essential oils and oleoresins
 Fruit and vegetable powders
 Honey
 Spices and herbs
 Tomato powder
Processed flavors
 Meat flavors
 Savory flavors
Seasonings
 Sauces and gravies
 Salty snack seasonings
 Seasoning blends
 Side dish seasonings

COMPETITORS

A.A. Sayia
ACH Food Companies
Adams Extract & Spice
Alberto-Culver
Associated British Foods
B&G Foods
Bolner's Fiesta Products
D. D. Williamson
Danisco A/S
Denali Flavors
First Spice Mixing
Flavormatic Industries
Flayco Products
Givaudan
Goya
The Great Spice Company
Heinz
International Flavors
Kerry Group
La Flor
M & F Worldwide
Magic Seasoning Blends
Main Street Ingredients
Newly Weds Foods
Nielsen-Massey
Ottens Flavors
Penzeys
RFI Ingredients
Sensient
Sterling Extract

HISTORICAL FINANCIALS

Company Type: Public

Income Statement

FYE: November 30

	REVENUE ($ mil.)	NET INCOME ($ mil.)	NET PROFIT MARGIN	EMPLOYEES
11/09	3,192	300	9.4%	7,500
11/08	3,177	237	7.5%	7,500
11/07	2,916	230	7.9%	7,500
11/06	2,716	202	7.4%	7,500
11/05	2,592	215	8.3%	8,000
Annual Growth	**5.3%**	**8.7%**	**—**	**(1.6%)**

2009 Year-End Financials

Debt ratio: 65.6%
Return on equity: 25.1%
Cash ($ mil.): 40
Current ratio: 1.19
Long-term debt ($ mil.): 875
No. of shares (mil.): 133
Dividends
 Yield: 2.7%
 Payout: 42.3%
Market value ($ mil.): 4,754

Stock History

NYSE: MKC

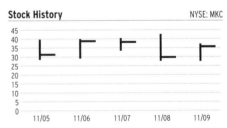

	STOCK PRICE ($) FY Close	P/E High/Low		PER SHARE ($) Earnings	Dividends	Book Value
11/09	35.68	16	12	2.27	0.96	10.02
11/08	29.77	22	15	1.94	0.88	7.92
11/07	38.21	23	20	1.73	0.80	8.14
11/06	38.72	26	20	1.50	0.72	7.00
11/05	31.22	25	19	1.56	0.64	6.00
Annual Growth	**3.4%**	**—**	**—**	**9.8%**	**10.7%**	**13.7%**

McDermott International

Whether you are in deep water or all fired up, it's all in a day's work for McDermott International, a global engineering and construction firm focused on offshore oil and gas construction. The company's offshore business segment includes subsidiary J. Ray McDermott, which builds deepwater and subsea oil and gas production and distribution facilities. Customers include major energy companies. McDermott has operations in more than 20 countries around the world. It operates a fleet of marine vessels and has several fabrication and manufacturing facilities in Canada, Indonesia, Mexico, the United Arab Emirates, and the US.

In 2010 McDermott spun off its power generation systems and government operations subsidiaries Babcock & Wilcox (B&W) and B&W NPG. The deal was completed through the distribution of shares of Babcock & Wilcox to McDermott shareholders. As a result, Babcock & Wilcox became an independent, publicly traded company. The separation allows McDermott to focus on its engineering, procurement, and construction and installation work. New federal regulations regarding government contracts prompted the split. However, the separation is also expected to accelerate growth and create a more efficient flow of capital for each company.

The company's management went through a shuffle in preparation for the spinoff, including the resignation of John Fees as CEO. Stephen Johnson, subsidiary J. Ray McDermott's CEO, was named to lead McDermott International.

Meanwhile, McDermott's two main growth initiatives are focused on the development of floating oil and gas production faculties located in deep waters and subsea infrastructure. J. Ray, along with the company's joint ventures in China and Mexico, plan to expand their capabilities to provide solutions for floating facilities through the expansion and development of deepwater fabrication facilities. McDermott also recently formed a subsea infrastructure, umbilical, riser and flowline systems division (or SURF). The division handles engineering, procurement, installations, and construction of subsea pipelines and other projects. McDermott hopes to expand its SURF division into new, growing markets such as the Atlantic Basin and Brazil.

HISTORY

When Thomas McDermott won a contract to supply drilling rigs to a Texas wildcatter in 1923, he started J. Ray McDermott & Co., named after his father. Following the oil industry's expansion into Louisiana, J. Ray McDermott made New Orleans its headquarters in the 1930s. When the company incorporated in 1946, it supplied services for oil and natural gas production.

After WWII McDermott became a pioneer in the construction of offshore drilling platforms. Spurred by increased demand for oil in the 1960s and by price inflation in the 1970s, the company's offshore business boomed. McDermott supplied the US Navy and the salvage and subsea markets.

In 1978 McDermott diversified. That year it bought Babcock & Wilcox (B&W), which had been founded as a boilermaker in 1867, then later focused on nuclear energy and built the reactor for the first nuclear-powered merchant ship. It made major contributions to the US Navy's nuclear program during the 1950s.

J. Ray McDermott became McDermott Inc. in 1980, and in 1983, McDermott International, Inc. Unprepared for industry changes of the 1980s, McDermott had to shrink its workforce 57% by selling its insulation, controls, trading, and seamless-tube operations.

In a sweeping reorganization, McDermott consolidated its marine construction operations into a subsidiary, J. Ray McDermott, which in 1995 merged with Offshore Pipeline; McDermott owned a majority stake in the resulting company. A consortium including McDermott won a $275 million power plant contract with Huaneng International Power Development, the largest independent power producer in China, in 1996.

In 1997 Roger Tetrault became chairman and CEO as McDermott swallowed about $123 million in charges, including $72 million in asbestos claims. It also sold its interests in Sakhalin Energy Investment and Unifab International. Under government pressure, the company dissolved its joint ventures with Heerema Offshore in 1997 (an employee of the JV was later fined after pleading guilty to criminal charges) and ETPM in 1998 (amid allegations of anti-competitive activity in the marine construction business).

As oil prices (and McDermott's profits) slumped during fiscal 1999, the company sought ways to cut costs. In 1999 the company paid $513 million for the remainder of oil platform installer J. Ray McDermott and consolidated its management. Also that year, plans to build a 650-kilometer underwater natural gas pipeline from gas fields in the South China Sea to Singapore came under scrutiny by the Indonesian government. A committee recommended the contract be voided because of McDermott's connections to Mohammed Hasan, an 18% owner of McDermott Indonesia and close friend of Indonesia's former president Suharto. The project was later approved by the country's minister of mines and energy.

Babcock & Wilcox, weighed down by 20 years of asbestos liability claims (and having paid $1.6 billion), filed for Chapter 11 bankruptcy protection early in 2000. With the company's marine construction division suffering losses, Bruce Wilkinson replaced Roger Tetrault as chairman and CEO the same year. In 2002 a judge ruled that McDermott didn't have to return the $622 million that Babcock & Wilcox transferred to it in 1998. (The ruling suggested that McDermott might be able to limit the claims to its subsidiary.) Later that year McDermott discontinued its Hudson Products subsidiary.

Babcock & Wilcox emerged from bankruptcy in 2006. The company then restructured the Babcock & Wilcox unit in 2007, rolling into it the operations of Babcock & Wilcox Nuclear Power Generation (B&W NPG).

McDermott spun off Babcock & Wilcox in 2010.

EXECUTIVES

Chairman: Ronald C. Cambre, age 71
President, CEO, and Director; President and CEO, J. Ray McDermott, S.A.: Stephen M. (Steve) Johnson, age 58, $5,877,788 total compensation
EVP and COO: John T. Nesser III, age 61, $2,248,800 total compensation
SVP and CFO; CFO, J. Ray McDermott, S.A.: Perry L. Elders, age 48
SVP, General Counsel, and Corporate Secretary: Liane K. Hinrichs, age 52
SVP and Chief Human Resources Officer: Gary L. Carlson
SVP Operations, Atlantic Region; SVP Operations, J. Ray McDermott: David P. (Dave) Roquemore
SVP Operations, Asia/Pacific, Middle East, and Caspian; SVP Operations, J. Ray McDermott: John T. (Jack) McCormack
VP Engineering: William L. (Bill) Soester
VP Litigation, Claims, and Disputes: Claire P. Hunter
VP Finance, Operations: Jeff J. Hightower
VP Business Development and Operational Strategy: Steven W. Roll
VP, Chief Risk Officer, and Associate General Counsel - Corporate and Compliance: J. Timothy (Tim) Woodard
VP Business Development: Peter A. Marler
VP Treasury and Investor Relations: John E. (Jay) Roueche III
VP and Corporate Compliance Officer: Thomas A. Henzler, age 52
Director Investor Relations and Corporate Communications: Robby Bellamy
President and CEO, Babcock & Wilcox: Brandon C. Bethards, age 62, $2,874,059 total compensation
Auditors: Deloitte & Touche LLP

LOCATIONS

HQ: McDermott International, Inc.
777 N. Eldridge Pkwy., Houston, TX 77079
Phone: 281-870-5901
Web: www.mcdermott.com

2009 Sales

	$ mil.	% of total
US	2,431.7	39
Qatar	1,293.8	21
Saudi Arabia	658.7	11
Canada	312.2	5
Brazil	245.4	4
Thailand	227.7	4
Australia	187.0	3
Vietnam	166.6	3
Malaysia	98.7	1
Indonesia	85.7	1
Russia	62.3	1
Mexico	60.0	1
China	55.1	1
Trinidad	43.8	1
Other countries	264.4	4
Total	**6,193.1**	**100**

PRODUCTS/OPERATIONS

2009 Sales

	$ mil.	% of total
Offshore oil & gas construction	3,338.5	54
Power generation systems	1,825.1	29
Government operations	1,032.0	17
Adjustments	(2.5)	—
Total	**6,193.1**	**100**

Selected Products and Services

Offshore oil and gas construction
  Fabrication
  Offshore operations
  Procurement
  Project services and engineering

HISTORICAL FINANCIALS

Company Type: Public

Income Statement

FYE: December 31

	REVENUE ($ mil.)	NET INCOME ($ mil.)	NET PROFIT MARGIN	EMPLOYEES
12/09	6,193	387	6.3%	29,000
12/08	6,572	429	6.5%	26,400
12/07	5,632	608	10.8%	28,400
12/06	4,120	342	8.3%	27,800
12/05	1,856	198	10.7%	14,200
Annual Growth	35.1%	18.2%	—	19.5%

2009 Year-End Financials

Debt ratio: 3.1%
Return on equity: 24.8%
Cash ($ mil.): 899
Current ratio: 1.17
Long-term debt ($ mil.): 57

No. of shares (mil.): 232
Dividends
　Yield: 0.0%
　Payout: —
Market value ($ mil.): 2,878

Stock History

NYSE: MDR

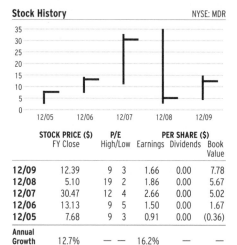

	STOCK PRICE ($) FY Close	P/E High/Low		PER SHARE ($) Earnings	Dividends	Book Value
12/09	12.39	9	3	1.66	0.00	7.78
12/08	5.10	19	2	1.86	0.00	5.67
12/07	30.47	12	4	2.66	0.00	5.02
12/06	13.13	9	5	1.50	0.00	1.67
12/05	7.68	9	3	0.91	0.00	(0.36)
Annual Growth	12.7%	—	—	16.2%	—	—

McDonald's Corporation

Serving billions of hamburgers has put a shine on these arches. McDonald's is the world's #1 fast-food company by sales, with more than 32,400 restaurants serving burgers and fries in more than 100 countries. (There are nearly 14,000 Golden Arches locations in the US.) The popular chain is well-known for its Big Macs, Quarter Pounders, and Chicken McNuggets. Most of the outlets are free-standing units offering dine-in and drive-through service, but McDonald's also has many eateries located in airports, retail areas, and other high-traffic locations. About 80% of the restaurants are run by franchisees or affiliates.

McDonald's has come to dominate the fast-food dining industry largely through its effective franchising efforts, its focus on consistent food quality, and its successful marketing campaigns. The company's far-flung network of franchise operators are all controlled by agreements meant to ensure that a Big Mac purchased in Pittsburgh tastes the same as one bought in Beijing. Each restaurant gets its food and packaging from approved suppliers that are held to high standards.

The company focuses its advertising efforts primarily at families with children, touting its kid-friendly Family Meals and budget-minded Value Menu. McDonald's is also continuously developing new menu items in order to strike a chord with consumers. Looking to steal business from Starbucks, the company is heavily promoting a line of espresso coffee drinks under the banner McCafé, and is moving in on Jamba Juice's market by offering fruit smoothie drinks. The chain also employs some limited-time menu items, including the McRib sandwich, which has been sold on-and-off many times since its introduction in 1981.

The recession that hurt many in the restaurant industry during 2009 looked like a boon for McDonald's as consumers looked to less expensive alternatives for feeding their families. Higher unemployment and tighter consumer budgets, though, have led to increased price competition from rivals such as Burger King, the #2 burger chain, and the various chains under the YUM! Brands umbrella. In response, McDonald's is leaning heavily on its value-priced menu items. Stagnant sales have not stopped the company from expanding its chain, particularly in emerging markets such as China.

McDonald's continues to be a target for critics who charge the company's food lacks nutritional value and may be contributing to increasing rates of obesity, especially among children. In response, McDonald's has introduced healthier menu items and shifted its marketing toward children to show a more active Ronald McDonald. (The effort has also meant the demise of other McDonaldland characters such as Grimace and the Hamburglar.)

HISTORY

The first McDonald's opened in 1948 in San Bernardino, California. In 1954 owners Dick and Mac McDonald signed a franchise agreement with 52-year-old Ray Kroc (a malt machine salesman), and a year later Kroc opened his first restaurant

in Des Plaines, Illinois. By 1957 Kroc was operating 14 McDonald's restaurants in Illinois, Indiana, and California. In 1961 Kroc bought out the McDonald brothers for $2.7 million.

In 1962 the now-ubiquitous Golden Arches appeared for the first time, and the company sold its billionth burger. Ronald McDonald made his debut the following year, and the company introduced its first new menu item — the Filet-O-Fish. Two years later McDonald's went public and ran its first TV ads. The company opened its first stores outside the US (in Canada) in 1967, and the next year it added the Big Mac to the menu and opened its 1,000th restaurant.

During the 1970s McDonald's grew at the rate of about 500 restaurants per year, and the first Ronald McDonald House (a temporary residence for families of hospitalized children) opened in 1974. The drive-through window appeared in 1975.

McDonald's introduced Chicken McNuggets in 1983. Kroc, who had become senior chairman in the 1970s, died the next year. Growing competition slowed the company's US sales growth to about 5% per year at the end of the 1980s. In response, McDonald's added specially priced "value menu" items.

In 1990 the company made history and headlines when it opened the first McDonald's in Moscow. In 1997 US division CEO Edward Rensi retired and was replaced by division chairman Jack Greenberg. The next year Greenberg launched the Made For You food preparation system, designed to reduce waste and produce a better tasting burger. He was named CEO later that year. McDonald's also made its first investment in another restaurant concept in 1998 when it bought a stake in Chipotle Mexican Grill, a Denver-based chain of Mexican food restaurants. That same year saw the death of co-founder Dick McDonald, who died at age 89.

The company's biggest deal came in 2000 when it purchased the Boston Market chain from struggling Boston Chicken.

Following three quarters of declining profits, in 2001 McDonald's announced a major restructuring of its US operations, cutting about 700 corporate jobs

Business failed to improve, however, and in 2002 it laid off approximately 600 corporate employees and closed about 175 underperforming units. At the end of 2002, after the company posted its first quarterly loss in history, vice chairman and president Jim Cantalupo, a veteran of McDonald's international operation, replaced Jack Greenberg as chairman and CEO.

McDonald's business began to improve during 2003 with the introduction of healthier menu fare. Cantalupo died in 2004. Director Andrew McKenna was named chairman and president. Charlie Bell became CEO. Diagnosed with cancer and undergoing surgery a month later, he eventually stepped down near the end of 2004. (Bell died early the next year.) Vice chairman Jim Skinner assumed the mantle of CEO, becoming the company's third chief executive in seven months.

The Venezuelan government ordered all 80 of the country's McDonald's restaurants closed for three days in 2005 as punishment for not following its tax laws. McDonald's sold a 35% stake in Chipotle through an IPO in 2006 and disposed of its remaining holdings later that year. It sold Boston Market to private equity firm Sun Capital Partners for $250 million the following year and in 2008 McDonald's cashed out its stake in Pret A Manger as part of a $670 million buyout by private equity firm Bridgepoint Capital.

EXECUTIVES

Chairman: Andrew J. (Andy) McKenna Sr., age 80
Honorary Chairman: Fred L. Turner, age 77
Vice Chairman and CEO: James A. (Jim) Skinner, age 65, $17,574,124 total compensation
President and COO: Donald (Don) Thompson, age 46
EVP and CFO: Peter J (Pete) Bensen, age 47, $4,981,715 total compensation
EVP and Chief Restaurant Officer: Jeffrey P. (Jeff) Stratton, age 54
EVP, General Counsel, and Secretary: Gloria Santona, age 59
EVP and Chief Human Resources Officer: Richard R. (Rich) Floersch, age 52
CIO, McDonald's USA: David Grooms
Global Chief Diversity Officer: Patricia (Pat) Harris, age 61
Corporate SVP and Controller: Kevin M. Ozan, age 46
Corporate VP, Associate General Counsel, and Assistant Secretary: Denise A. Horne
VP and Chief Creative Officer: Marlena Peleo-Lazar
US Division President, Central: Michael (Mike) Andres
US Division President, East: Karen King
President, McDonald's Europe: Denis Hennequin, age 51, $5,678,020 total compensation
President, McDonald's Asia/Pacific, Middle East, and Africa: Timothy J. (Tim) Fenton, age 52, $6,129,118 total compensation
CEO, McDonald's China: Kenneth Chan
President, McDonald's USA: Janice L. (Jan) Fields, age 54
EVP and COO, McDonald's USA: James (Jim) Johannesen, age 56
SVP North America Supply Chain Management, McDonald's USA: Dan Gorsky
VP Communications, McDonald's USA: William (Bill) Whitman Jr.
Chief Marketing Officer, McDonald's USA: Neil Golden
Director Nutrition, McDonald's USA: Cynthia M. Goody
Auditors: Ernst & Young LLP

LOCATIONS

HQ: McDonald's Corporation
1 McDonald's Plaza, Oak Brook, IL 60523
Phone: 630-623-3000   **Fax:** 630-623-5004
Web: www.mcdonalds.com

2009 Sales

	$ mil.	% of total
Europe	9,274	41
US	7,944	35
Asia/Pacific, Middle East & Africa	4,337	19
Other regions	1,190	5
Total	**22,745**	**100**

2009 Locations

	No.
US	13,980
Asia/Pacific, Middle East & Africa	8,488
Europe	6,785
Other regions	3,225
Total	**32,478**

PRODUCTS/OPERATIONS

2009 Sales

	$ mil.	% of total
Restaurants	15,459	68
Franchising	7,286	32
Total	**22,745**	**100**

2009 Locations

	No.
Franchised	26,216
Company-owned	6,262
Total	**32,478**

COMPETITORS

AFC Enterprises	Quiznos
Burger King	Sonic Corp.
Chick-fil-A	Starbucks
Church's Chicken	Subway
CKE Restaurants	Tim Hortons
Dairy Queen	Wendy's/Arby's Group, Inc.
Jack in the Box	YUM!
Panda Restaurant Group	

HISTORICAL FINANCIALS

Company Type: Public

Income Statement

FYE: December 31

	REVENUE ($ mil.)	NET INCOME ($ mil.)	NET PROFIT MARGIN	EMPLOYEES
12/09	22,745	4,551	20.0%	385,000
12/08	23,522	4,313	18.3%	400,000
12/07	22,787	2,395	10.5%	390,000
12/06	21,586	3,544	16.4%	465,000
12/05	20,460	2,602	12.7%	447,000
Annual Growth	**2.7%**	**15.0%**	**—**	**(3.7%)**

2009 Year-End Financials

Debt ratio: 75.2%
Return on equity: 33.2%
Cash ($ mil.): 1,796
Current ratio: 1.14
Long-term debt ($ mil.): 10,560
No. of shares (mil.): 1,064
Dividends
  Yield: 3.3%
  Payout: 49.9%
Market value ($ mil.): 66,457

Stock History

NYSE: MCD

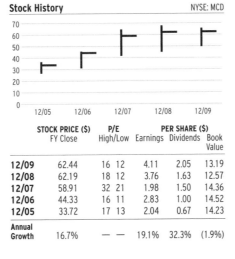

	STOCK PRICE ($) FY Close	P/E High/Low		PER SHARE ($) Earnings	Dividends	Book Value
12/09	62.44	16	12	4.11	2.05	13.19
12/08	62.19	18	12	3.76	1.63	12.57
12/07	58.91	32	21	1.98	1.50	14.36
12/06	44.33	16	11	2.83	1.00	14.52
12/05	33.72	17	13	2.04	0.67	14.23
Annual Growth	**16.7%**	**—**	**—**	**19.1%**	**32.3%**	**(1.9%)**

McGraw-Hill

As a successful publishing operation, McGraw-Hill is a textbook case. The company is one of the world's largest producers of textbooks, tests, and related materials, serving the elementary, secondary, and higher education markets through its McGraw-Hill Education unit. Its McGraw-Hill Financial Services unit is a leading supplier of financial and business information services, providing indexes and ratings for both domestic and overseas markets through Standard & Poor's. A third unit, McGraw-Hill Information & Media, publishes trade journals and other industry content (such as *Aviation Week*). The company also operates nine TV stations (including four ABC affiliates).

In 2009 McGraw-Hill sold its unprofitable *BusinessWeek* magazine and related Business-Week operations, which had been experiencing a steep decline in advertising revenue, to financial information provider Bloomberg. Bloomberg made the acquisition in order to boost its content and grow its audience. The title was since renamed *Bloomberg BusinessWeek*. The sale follows a reorganization at McGraw-Hill to cut costs. All total, in 2009 the company eliminated about 550 jobs across the business.

While making these cuts, McGraw-Hill Education is also expanding its digital learning products and services. It is focused on individualized online tutoring, a service that gives students access to course lectures, and assessment placement tools that help schools determine appropriate courses for new students.

The McGraw-Hill Financial Services unit operates under the Standard & Poor's (S&P) brand and provides global credit ratings, indices, risk evaluation, and investment research and data to investors, corporations, governments, financial institutions, and investment managers. In 2009 McGraw-Hill sold the unit's Vista Research business (information for institutional money managers) in order to focus on its core business of providing independent research, ratings, data indices, and portfolio services. The recent weak economy and credit crunch has S&P suffering from lost business and regulatory inquiries about the independence of its ratings. The company has taken steps to improve the brand's reputation, including making adjustments to its analysis and appointing an ombudsman for S&P.

McGraw-Hill Information & Media provides energy information to the global oil, natural gas, electricity, and commodity markets through its Platts service; and its Broadcasting Group includes ABC-affiliated television stations in the markets of Bakersfield (KERO), Denver (KMGH), Indianapolis (WRTV), and San Diego (KGTV), as well as five Spanish-language stations affiliated with Azteca America in California and Colorado. In addition, McGraw-Hill Information & Media oversees J.D. Power and Associates, a company that offers automobile ratings.

McGraw-Hill is expanding in China, where it sees an opportunity to meet demand for an increase in economic and financial literacy as the country's economy develops. In 2009 McGraw-Hill announced a partnership with the Chinese vocational-training firm Ambow Education to develop digital products for teaching English.

Chairman, president, and CEO Harold "Terry" McGraw III is the great-grandson of the company's founder James H. McGraw. Terry's father, former CEO Harold W. McGraw Jr., died in 2010.

HISTORY

Sir James H. McGraw bought his first industry journal, *American Journal of Railway Appliances,* in 1888 and incorporated The McGraw Publishing Company in 1899. Journal editor John Hill started The Hill Publishing Company (*American Machinist, Locomotive Engineer*) in 1902. The two men merged their book publishing operations into the McGraw-Hill Book Company in 1909. The rest of the companies merged as the McGraw-Hill Publishing Company in 1917 following Hill's death the previous year. In 1929, two months before the stock market crash, McGraw-Hill launched *BusinessWeek,* which bucked popular opinion in its first issue with concerns about the economy's health. The company also went public that year. James McGraw retired as chairman in 1935; he was succeeded by his son, Jay.

During the 1930s and 1940s, McGraw-Hill produced trade journals for aviation, health care, and atomic energy. In 1947 its trade division published *Betty Crocker's Picture Cook Book,* which sold 2.3 million copies its first two years. The company's textbook operations began printing for the elementary and secondary school markets to capitalize on booming enrollment in the 1950s and 1960s. In 1966 it bought Standard & Poor's financial services and bought four TV stations from Time in 1972. Harold McGraw, grandson of founder James, became president in 1974 and successfully fended off a takeover attempt by American Express in 1979.

Harold retired as CEO in 1983 (he remained chairman until 1988) and was replaced by Joseph Dionne. During the 1980s the company expanded its electronic information services and sold its trade books division in 1989. That year McGraw-Hill started textbook and educational software joint venture Macmillan/McGraw-Hill School Publishing. (McGraw-Hill bought Macmillan's share in 1993 after Macmillan's parent, Maxwell Communications, went bankrupt.)

Its financial services unit expanded with the purchases of J.J. Kenny (municipal securities information) in 1990 and 25% of Liberty Brokerage in 1993, giving McGraw-Hill access to US Treasury securities pricing information. In 1995 it rechristened itself The McGraw-Hill Companies.

When Dionne retired in 1998, the company named Harold McGraw III (the founder's great-grandson) CEO. McGraw-Hill expanded its presence in the educational publishing market with its acquisition of Tribune Education in 2000.

After a belt-tightening period in the early 2000s that included a restructuring as well as layoffs of nearly 1,000 employees, the company rebounded by refocusing on its core markets — education and financial — and reducing its stakes in e-commerce and emerging technology firms.

The federal "No Child Left Behind" act, passed in 2001, was a boost for the company as the law opened up additional federal funds for education and created additional testing and assessment opportunities. In early 2002 the company closed its Lifetime Learning unit as part of a restructuring, letting go 100 employees.

McGraw-Hill sold its financial data provider, S&P ComStock, to Interactive Data Corp. in 2003. In 2005 the company acquired J.D. Power and Associates, a provider of automobile ratings.

In 2006 the company bought a stake in social networking site Gather Inc. Also in 2006 the company took some cost-cutting measures when it announced 500 layoffs, mainly from its educational testing and *BusinessWeek* divisions.

EXECUTIVES

Chairman, President, and CEO:
Harold W. (Terry) McGraw III, age 61,
$7,168,335 total compensation
EVP and CFO: Robert J. (Bob) Bahash, age 64,
EVP Global Strategy: Charles L. Teschner Jr., age 49,
$2,353,490 total compensation
EVP and CIO: Bruce D. Marcus, age 61,
$874,000 total compensation
EVP Corporate Affairs and Executive Assistant to the Chairman, President, and CEO:
D. Edward I. (Ted) Smyth, age 61,
$1,480,557 total compensation
EVP and General Counsel: Kenneth M. (Ken) Vittor,
age 60, $987,180 total compensation
EVP Human Resources: David L. Murphy, age 64,
$2,028,690 total compensation
SVP Investor Relations: Donald S. Rubin

SVP Global Sustainability Business Development:
Vickie A. Tillman
SVP McGraw-Hill School Education Group, Literacy and Humanities Center: Stephen Mico
SVP and Corporate Controller: Emmanuel N. Korakis
President, McGraw-Hill Education:
Peter C. (Pete) Davis, age 55,
$855,163 total compensation
President, McGraw-Hill School Solutions Group:
Steven McClung
President, McGraw-Hill Learning Group: Daniel Caton
President, McGraw-Hill Broadcasting: Darrell K. Brown,
age 54
President, Platts: Lawrence P. (Larry) Neal, age 48
President, Information & Media: Glenn S. Goldberg,
age 51
President, J.D. Power and Associates:
Finbarr J. (Fin) O'Neill, age 57
President, McGraw-Hill Construction: Keith Fox, age 45
President, Standard & Poor's: Deven Sharma, age 54
Senior Director Marketing Communications, McGraw-Hill Construction: Kathy Malangone
$3,514,986 total compensation
Senior Director Corporate Communications:
Frank Briamonte
Auditors: Ernst & Young LLP

LOCATIONS

HQ: The McGraw-Hill Companies, Inc.
1221 Avenue of the Americas, New York, NY 10020
Phone: 212-512-2000   **Fax:** 212-512-3840
Web: www.mcgraw-hill.com

2009 Sales

	$ mil.	% of total
US	4,226	71
Europe	964	16
Asia	468	8
Other regions	294	5
Total	**5,952**	**100**

PRODUCTS/OPERATIONS

2009 Sales

	$ mil.	% of total
Financial services	2,610	44
Education	2,388	40
Information & media services	954	16
Total	**5,952**	**100**

Selected Financial Services Holdings

Credit Market Services
Investment Services
Standard & Poor's
    Ubria

Selected McGraw-Hill Education Holdings

Higher Education
    McGraw-Hill Dushkin
    McGraw-Hill/Irwin
    McGraw-Hill/Primis Custom Publishing
    McGraw-Hill Science, Engineering & Mathematics
    McGraw-Hill Social Sciences and World Languages
School Education Group
    Glencoe/McGraw-Hill
    Macmillan/McGraw-Hill
    McGraw-Hill Digital Learning
    McGraw-Hill Professional Development
    SRA/McGraw-Hill
    Wright Group/McGraw-Hill

Selected Information and Media Services Holdings

Aviation Week Group
    AviationNow.com
    Conferences & Exhibitions
    Custom Media
    Education
    Magazines
    Newsletters
    References & Directories
    Television & Video

Broadcasting Group
    KERO-TV (Bakersfield, CA)
    KGTV (San Diego)
    KMGH-TV (Denver)
    WRTV (Indianapolis)
J.D. Power and Associates (marketing information provider)
McGraw-Hill Construction
    Architectural Record
    Construction.com
    Design-Build
    Engineering News-Record
    F.W. Dodge
Platts
    Coal
    Electric Power
    Energy Information Technology
    Energy Policy
    Engineering
    Metals
    Natural Gas
    Nuclear
    Oil
    Petrochemicals
    Utility Data Institute

COMPETITORS

Cengage Learning	John Wiley
CME	Media General
Crain Communications	Moody's
Educational Development	Pearson plc
ETS	Reed Elsevier Group
FactSet	Scholastic
Flat World Knowledge	Thomson Reuters
Hanley Wood	W.W. Norton
Houghton Mifflin Harcourt	

HISTORICAL FINANCIALS

Company Type: Public

Income Statement

FYE: December 31

	REVENUE ($ mil.)	NET INCOME ($ mil.)	NET PROFIT MARGIN	EMPLOYEES
12/09	5,952	731	12.3%	21,077
12/08	6,355	800	12.6%	21,649
12/07	6,772	1,014	15.0%	21,171
12/06	6,255	882	14.1%	20,214
12/05	6,004	844	14.1%	19,600
Annual Growth	**(0.2%)**	**(3.6%)**	**—**	**1.8%**

2009 Year-End Financials

Debt ratio: 64.8%
Return on equity: 46.7%
Cash ($ mil.): 1,210
Current ratio: 1.20
Long-term debt ($ mil.): 1,198

No. of shares (mil.): 309
Dividends
    Yield: 2.7%
    Payout: 38.6%
Market value ($ mil.): 10,358

Stock History

NYSE: MHP

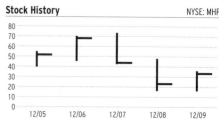

	STOCK PRICE ($) FY Close	P/E High/Low		PER SHARE ($) Earnings	Dividends	Book Value
12/09	33.51	15	7	2.33	0.90	5.98
12/08	23.19	19	7	2.51	0.88	4.15
12/07	43.81	25	15	2.94	0.82	5.20
12/06	68.02	29	19	2.40	0.73	8.67
12/05	51.63	24	18	2.21	0.66	10.07
Annual Growth	**(10.2%)**	**—**	**—**	**1.3%**	**8.1%**	**(12.2%)**

McKesson Corporation

McKesson moves medicine. The largest pharmaceuticals distributor in North America, McKesson delivers prescription and generic drugs, as well as health and beauty care products, to more than 40,000 retail and institutional pharmacies throughout the US and Canada. The company is also a major medical supplies wholesaler, providing medical and surgical equipment to alternate health care sites, such as doctors' offices, surgery centers, and long-term care facilities. In addition to distribution services, McKesson offers software and technical services that help pharmacies, health care providers, and insurers manage supply chain, clinical, administrative, and financial operations.

McKesson's distribution operations bring in most of the company's money. The McKesson Distribution Solutions division primarily provides prescription and over-the-counter pharmaceuticals and other health care items to retailers and health care institutions in the US; it also is a wholesaler of drugs in Canada and owns about half of Nadro, a Mexican pharma distributor. The distribution division also supplies medical equipment and beauty care items, and it provides consulting and inventory management services. Major US pharmacy operators CVS Caremark and Rite Aid are among the company's key clients, each accounting for more than 10% of sales.

Outside of its traditional retail and institutional distribution operations, McKesson provides disease management programs that serve health providers, drug manufacturers, insurers, and employers. Its specialty pharmacy solutions unit coordinates the delivery of complex medicines directly to physicians. Additionally, the company supplies automated pharmacy dispensing systems through its minority stake in North Carolina-based Parata Systems, and it provides first aid kits and workplace safety training through subsidiary ZEE Medical. McKesson launched a new Plasma and BioLogics division in 2008; the unit delivers plasma and plasma-related products to hospital pharmacies.

Strategic acquisitions have been important to the growth of the company, both in its core distribution operations and its smaller but growing Technology Solutions (software and data management) division. The company regularly purchases small to midsized regional distributors and distribution support companies, including the 2008 purchase of Midwest pharmacy distributor McQueary Brothers for $190 million.

The company has also trimmed some operations to focus on core drug distribution and technology initiatives. It sold specialty pharmacy unit ivpcare to Walgreen in 2008.

HISTORY

John McKesson opened a Manhattan drugstore in 1833, and Daniel Robbins joined him as a partner in 1840. McKesson-Robbins soon expanded into chemical and drug production, and the enterprise grew steadily. In 1926, after differences arose between the McKesson and Robbins heirs, the company was sold to Donald Coster.

Coster was actually convicted felon Philip Musica, who purchased McKesson-Robbins with fraudulently obtained bank loans. For more than a decade his real identity remained secret from all but one blackmailer. By 1930 McKesson-Robbins had wholesale drug operations in 33 states. The company appeared to be growing, but a treasurer discovered a Musica-orchestrated accounting scam and a cash shortfall of $3 million. Faced with exposure, Musica killed himself in 1939; company bankruptcy followed. McKesson-Robbins emerged from bankruptcy in 1941.

In a hostile takeover in 1967, San Francisco-based Foremost Dairies bought McKesson-Robbins to form Foremost-McKesson. Over the next 20 years, the company bought liquor, chemical, and software wholesalers, as well as several bottled-water companies. It sold Foremost Dairies in 1983 to focus on distribution, changed its name to McKesson the next year, and continued to build its drug wholesaling business through acquisitions. By 1985 it was the US's largest distributor of drugs and medical equipment, wine and liquor, bottled water, and car waxes and polishes.

In 1986 McKesson narrowed its focus to the health industry by selling its liquor and chemical distributors. It acquired Canadian drug distributor Medis by halves in 1990 and 1991, and a 23% stake in Mexican drug distributor Nadro in 1993.

McKesson sold PCS, the US's #1 prescription claims processor (acquired in 1970), to Eli Lilly in 1994. In 1996 the firm bought bankrupt distributor FoxMeyer Drug and sold its stake in Armor All (auto and home cleaning products) to Clorox.

In 1997 the company purchased General Medical, the US's largest distributor of medical surgical supplies, for about $775 million. McKesson began to focus on health care, selling its Millbrook Distribution Services unit (health and beauty products, general merchandise, and specialty foods).

Under new CEO Mark Pulido, it agreed to buy drug wholesaler AmeriSource Health (now AmerisourceBergen), but withdrew the offer in 1998, facing FTC opposition. Instead, McKesson moved into information systems, paying $14 billion for health care information top dog HBO & Company and forming McKesson HBOC. HBO, a high-flyer in the high-growth health information systems segment, balanced its rather dowdy drug and medical distribution operations.

But just months after the deal closed, accounting inconsistencies at HBO prompted McKesson to restate fourth-quarter results for fiscal 1999 twice, triggering shareholder lawsuits and a housecleaning of top brass. Five ex-HBO executives, including McKesson HBOC chairman Charlie McCall (who was later indicted for securities fraud), were canned for using improper accounting methods. McKesson's veteran CEO Pulido and CFO Richard Hawkins were forced to resign for not seeing the problems coming.

The company changed its name to McKesson Corporation in 2001. The National Health Services Information Authority entered into an agreement with McKesson to develop a human resources and payroll system for use at the over 600 NHS locations throughout the UK.

To catch former #1 pharmaceutical distributor Cardinal Health, McKesson built up its core areas in 2003 and 2004, while trimming away some of the dead weight (Abaton.com, Amysis Managed Care Systems, and ProDental Corp.). The company bought PMO, a specialty mail order prescription business. It also acquired Canadian firm A.L.I. Technologies, which provided systems for managing medical images.

In 2007 McKesson acquired Oncology Therapeutics Network, a specialty pharmaceuticals distributor, for $519 million.

EXECUTIVES

Chairman, President, and CEO: John H. Hammergren, age 51, $54,584,020 total compensation
EVP and Group President; President, McKesson Supply Solutions: Paul C. Julian, age 54, $23,003,300 total compensation
EVP and CFO: Jeffrey C. (Jeff) Campbell, age 50, $13,677,863 total compensation
EVP, General Counsel, and Chief Compliance Officer: Laureen E. Seeger, age 49, $8,748,928 total compensation
EVP Corporate Strategy and Business Development: Marc E. Owen, age 51, $8,747,704 total compensation
EVP, CIO, and CTO: Randall N. (Randy) Spratt, age 59
EVP; Group President, McKesson Technology Solutions: Patrick (Pat) Blake, age 46
EVP Human Resources: Jorge L. Figueredo
SVP and President, Health Mart: Tim Canning
SVP Strategy, Product Management and Marketing, Pharmacy Systems: Brenton Burns
VP and Treasurer: Nicholas A. Loiacono
VP Investor Relations: Ana Schrank
VP and Controller: Nigel A. Rees
Group President, International Operations Group: Patrick Carter
President, McKesson Provider Technologies: David A. Souerwine
President, Specialty Care Solutions: Mark Walchirk
President, Pharmacy Systems: Stanton McComb
President, McKesson Health Solutions: Emad Rizk
President, U.S. Pharmaceutical Distribution: John Figueroa
President, McKesson Canada: Domenic Pilla
Corporate Communications: Kris Fortner
Secretary: Willie C. Bogan
Auditors: Deloitte & Touche LLP

LOCATIONS

HQ: McKesson Corporation
1 Post St., San Francisco, CA 94104
Phone: 415-983-8300   **Fax:** 415-983-7160
Web: www.mckesson.com

2010 Sales

	$ mil.	% of total
US	99,387	91
Other countries	9,315	9
Total	**108,702**	**100**

PRODUCTS/OPERATIONS

2010 Sales

	$ mil.	% of total
Distribution Solutions		
US pharmaceutical distribution	93,645	86
Canada pharmaceutical distribution & services	9,072	8
Medical-surgical distribution & services	2,861	3
Technology Solutions		
Services	2,439	2
Software & software systems	571	1
Hardware	114	—
Total	**108,702**	**100**

Selected Services

Distribution Solutions
  Ethical and proprietary drug distribution
  Health and beauty care products distribution
  Institutional pharmacy services (consulting, inventory
    management, cost control, SKY Packaging)
  McKesson Canada (drug distribution)
  McKesson Medical-Surgical (supplies and equipment
    distribution, includes ZEE Medical and Moore
    Medical)
  McKesson Pharmacy Systems (financial, operational,
    and clinical solutions for retail and institutional
    pharmacies)
  McKesson Specialty Care Solutions (specialty
    pharmaceutical solutions for biotech and
    pharmaceutical manufacturers)
  Nadro, S.A. de C.V. (49%, drug distribution, Mexico)
  Parata Systems, LLC (39%, automated pharmacy and
    supply management systems and services)
  Retail pharmacy services (franchising, consulting, data
    and claims management, cost control, inventory
    management, value brands, redistribution,
    repackaging, refilling)
Technology Solutions
  Automation
  Clinical management (data and care management,
    procurement and planning)
  Connectivity (RelayHealth vendor neutral health
    information exchange)
  Enterprise imaging and information management
  Financial management (accounting and cost control)
  InterQual claims payment
  Outsourcing
  Pharmacy automation for hospitals
  Physician practice solutions
  Remote hosting and management
  Resource management
  Software
  Technology infrastructure

COMPETITORS

AmerisourceBergen
Apothecary Products
athenahealth
BioScrip
Cardinal Health
CuraScript
FFF Enterprises
Franz Haniel
GE Healthcare
Grifols
H. D. Smith Wholesale Drug
The Harvard Drug Group
Henry Schein
Imperial Distributors
Kinray
Medco Health
Medline Industries
Omnicare
Owens & Minor
Perot Systems
PharMerica
PSS World Medical
Quality King
Siemens Healthcare
Surgical Express

HISTORICAL FINANCIALS

Company Type: Public

Income Statement

FYE: March 31

	REVENUE ($ mil.)	NET INCOME ($ mil.)	NET PROFIT MARGIN	EMPLOYEES
3/10	108,702	1,263	1.2%	32,500
3/09	106,632	823	0.8%	32,500
3/08	101,703	990	1.0%	32,900
3/07	92,977	913	1.0%	31,800
3/06	88,050	751	0.9%	26,400
Annual Growth	5.4%	13.9%	—	5.3%

2010 Year-End Financials

Debt ratio: 30.4%
Return on equity: 18.4%
Cash ($ mil.): 3,731
Current ratio: 1.26
Long-term debt ($ mil.): 2,293

No. of shares (mil.): 261
Dividends
  Yield: 0.7%
  Payout: 10.4%
Market value ($ mil.): 17,183

Stock History

NYSE: MCK

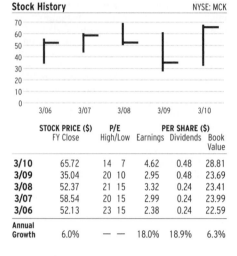

	STOCK PRICE ($) FY Close	P/E High/Low		PER SHARE ($) Earnings	Dividends	Book Value
3/10	65.72	14	7	4.62	0.48	28.81
3/09	35.04	20	10	2.95	0.48	23.69
3/08	52.37	21	15	3.32	0.24	23.41
3/07	58.54	20	15	2.99	0.24	23.99
3/06	52.13	23	15	2.38	0.24	22.59
Annual Growth	6.0%	—	—	18.0%	18.9%	6.3%

McKinsey & Company

McKinsey & Company is one of the world's top management consulting firms. With roughly 90 offices in more than 50 countries around the globe, it serves three of the world's five largest companies and about two-thirds of the *FORTUNE* 1000. The company advises corporate enterprises, as well as government agencies, institutions, and foundations on a number of business practices. They include business technology, corporate finance, marketing and sales, operations, organization, risk, and strategy. McKinsey's consulting services focus on more than a dozen different industries, from automotive and banking to pharmaceuticals and telecommunications. Founded by James McKinsey in 1926, the firm is owned by its partners.

McKinsey takes advantage of its global reach to gain business from multinational companies that want help in harmonizing their diverse operations. Toward that end, the firm aims to work collaboratively across its own organization, bringing together the work of multiple offices and practices on behalf of a single client.

In addition to being one of the oldest consulting firms, McKinsey is considered one of the most prestigious (along with Boston Consulting Group and Bain) as measured in surveys of aspiring consultants. Contributing to McKinsey's allure as an employer is the firm's network of more than 21,000 alumni, many of whom have been tapped for C-level jobs during the course of their careers. Alumni running companies, in turn, represent a potential source of business for the firm.

Among the firm's major achievements are the designing of the initial setup of NASA, advising the Vatican in setting up its banking system, and developing of the Universal Product Code. As part of a special, cross-industry initiative, McKinsey is also involved in advising global clients on the business impact of climate change.

It specifically provides analytical tools to help companies and governments become more cost, energy, land, and water efficient for a more sustainable future.

In 2009 managing director Ian Davis stepped down as Dominic Barton, the firm's regional leader in Asia, was elected to the post by McKinsey's 400 or so senior partners. Davis served in the slot for two terms, the maximum allowed under McKinsey's policy.

HISTORY

McKinsey & Company was founded in Chicago in 1926 by University of Chicago accounting professor James McKinsey. The company evolved from an auditing practice of McKinsey and his partners, Marvin Bower and A. T. Kearney, who began analyzing business and industry and offering advice. McKinsey died in 1937; two years later Bower, who headed the New York office, and Kearney, in Chicago, split the firm. Kearney renamed the Chicago office A.T. Kearney & Co. (later acquired by Electronic Data Systems), and Bower kept the McKinsey name and built up a practice structured like a law firm.

Bower focused on the big picture instead of on specific operating problems, helping boost billings to $2 million by 1950. He hired staff straight out of prestigious business schools, reinforcing the firm's theoretical bent. Bower implemented a competitive up-or-out policy requiring employees who are not continually promoted to leave the firm.

The firm's prestige continued to grow during the booming 1950s along with demand for consulting services. Before becoming president in 1953, Dwight Eisenhower asked McKinsey to find out exactly what the government did. By 1959 Bower had opened an office in London, followed by others in Amsterdam; Düsseldorf, Germany; Melbourne; Paris; and Zurich.

In 1964 the company founded management journal *The McKinsey Quarterly*. When Bower retired in 1967, sales were $20 million and McKinsey was the #1 management consulting firm. During the 1970s it faced competition from firms with newer approaches and lost market share. In response, then-managing director Ronald Daniel started specialty practices and expanded foreign operations.

The consulting boom of the 1980s was spurred by mergers and buyouts. By 1988 the firm had 1,800 consultants, sales were $620 million, and 50% of billings came from overseas.

The recession of the early 1990s hit white-collar workers, including consultants. McKinsey, scrambling to upgrade its technical side, bought Information Consulting Group (ICG), its first acquisition. But the corporate cultures did not meld, and most ICG people left by 1993.

In 1994 the company elected its first managing director of non-European descent, Indian-born Rajat Gupta. Two years later the traditionally hush-hush firm found itself at the center of that most public 1990s arena, the sexual discrimination lawsuit. A female ex-consultant in Texas sued, claiming McKinsey had sabotaged her career (the case was dismissed).

McKinsey partnered in 1998 with Northwestern University and the University of Pennsylvania to establish a business school in India. The following year graduating seniors surveyed in Europe and the US named the company as their ideal employer.

Also in 1999 the company created McKinsey to help "accelerate" Internet startups. The next year it increased salaries and offered incentives to better compete with Internet firms for employees. In 2001 the company expanded its branding business with the acquisition of Envision, a Chicago-based brand consultant.

Like its rivals in the consulting industry, McKinsey took a hit from the dot-com bust and the economic downturn of 2001 and 2002, as many companies were slower to sign up for costly long-term strategy consulting engagements, and mergers and acquisitions work dried up.

In 2003 Ian Davis was elected as managing director of the firm, succeeding Gupta, who had served as McKinsey's top executive for nine years. Davis had previously served as the head of the firm's UK office. Davis stepped down in 2009 to make way for Dominic Barton, who was the firm's regional leader in Asia.

EXECUTIVES

Global Managing Director: Dominic Barton, age 47
Chairman, Americas: Vik Malhotra
Chairman, Asia: Gordon Orr
Chairman, Europe, Middle East, and Africa:
 Michael Halbye
Director External Relations, Europe, Middle East, and Africa: Andrew (Andy) Whitehouse
Director External Relations, UK:
 Andrea Minton Beddoes
Director External Relations, Germany: Kai Peter Rath
Manager External Relations, The McKinsey Global Institute: Rebeca Robboy
Manager Media Relations, North America:
 Yolande Daeninck
Global Director Communications: Michael Stewart

LOCATIONS

HQ: McKinsey & Company, Inc.
 55 E. 52nd St., 21st Fl., New York, NY 10022
Phone: 212-446-7000   **Fax:** 212-446-8575
Web: www.mckinsey.com

PRODUCTS/OPERATIONS

Selected Industry Practices

Automotive and assembly
Chemicals
Consumer packaged goods
Electric power and natural gas
Financial services
Health care payor and provider
High tech
Media and entertainment
Metals and mining
Oil and gas
Pharmaceuticals and medical products
Private equity
Public sector
Pulp and paper/forest products
Retail
Social sector
Telecommunications
Travel infrastructure logistics

COMPETITORS

Accenture	HP Enterprise Services
A.T. Kearney	IBM
Bain & Company	Mercer
Booz	Monitor Group
Booz Allen	Oliver Wyman
Boston Consulting	PA Consulting
Capgemini	Perot Systems
Computer Sciences Corp.	PRTM Management
Deloitte Consulting	Roland Berger
ESource	

HISTORICAL FINANCIALS

Company Type: Private

Income Statement

FYE: December 31

	ESTIMATED REVENUE ($ mil.)	NET INCOME ($ mil.)	NET PROFIT MARGIN	EMPLOYEES
12/08	6,000	—	—	16,500
12/07	5,330	—	—	15,600
12/06	4,370	—	—	14,190
12/05	3,800	—	—	12,900
12/04	3,150	—	—	12,100
Annual Growth	17.5%	—	—	8.1%

Revenue History

MeadWestvaco

MeadWestvaco (MWV) might say that most things' covers are judged by their package. MWV's packaging business — folding cartons, corrugated boxes, and printed plastics — serves many of the world's major brands. MWV wraps up health care, personal and beauty care, food, and tobacco, as well as home and garden goods. It makes school supplies, too, branded Mead, Five Star, and Trapper Keeper; consumer office products; AT-A-GLANCE and Cambridge labels; and specialty chemicals (activated carbons, and compounds for applications ranging from asphalt paving to printing inks). The lineup is produced in the Americas, Europe, and Asia. MWV also packages pharmaceuticals, and manufactures packaging equipment for dairy and beverage OEMs.

Despite the breadth of activities, MWV's sales are dipping under the weight of the global economic downturn, coupled with weak volumes in consumer and office products, as well as the paperboard producer's move to drop less profitable packaging products. Changes in pricing, offerings, and packaging market targets, along with divestitures, production cuts, and workforce reductions all figure in MWV's strategy to gain an uptick in net income.

Packaging (both resource and consumer applications) and specialty chemicals businesses are receiving a makeover. In March 2010 MWV sold its visual packaging brand, Klearfold, to the North American affiliate of Hip Lik Packaging Products (Hong Kong), HLP Packaging, for an undisclosed price. MWV sold its Web-based branding and packaging business, Paxonix, in fall 2009 to Persistent Systems. MWV also closed or restructured 16 factories, and cut about 3,000 jobs, or 13% of its worldwide work force.

MWV has found success in the health care and personal care markets; with its Shellpak branded unit-dose medication packages and MWV dispensers — used in packaging liquid soaps and antibacterial lotions. In its eroded specialty chemicals business, MWV regained its footing in

pine chemicals targeting oilfield and adhesive end uses, in addition to asphalt solutions and carbon technologies for water and food purification industries.

Chipping away its forest products business, MWV is selling off large tracts of timber. The company reached deals to sell 59,700 acres for $118 million in 2009. In 2008, 21,200 acres were axed for $57 million.

In 2008 MWV sold its kraft paper mill in North Charleston, South Carolina, to KapStone Paper and Packaging for $485 million. MWV's packaging plant in Warrington, Pennsylvania, was shuttered, as well, and its specialty paper mill in Potsdam, New York, sold to newly formed Potsdam Specialty Paper.

More promising markets have since beckoned; MWV partnered with pharmaceutical-packaging company Bilcare to acquire pharmaceutical package-maker International Labs for an undisclosed amount. In 2008 MWV also formed a joint venture with Wadco Packaging, an Indian manufacturer of corrugated boxes. The venture, of which MWV owns 51%, churns out packaging to protect fresh produce in transit from field to market. At the same time, MWV's Specialty Chemicals division grew by acquiring Eastman Chemical Company's pine chemical products.

HISTORY

Late in August 2001 Mead agreed to merge with Westvaco to form MeadWestvaco. Together, the two companies had combined annual sales of about $7 billion and a market capitalization of some $6 billion; their combined debt tallied to $4.4 billion. The combined company — 50.2%-owned by former Mead shareholders — had an equally split board. Westvaco executives occupied the new CEO, CFO, and transition officer positions, while the new corporate headquarters were Westvaco's Connecticut offices. The two companies merged as MeadWestvaco Corporation in January 2002.

To quickly expand its production capability in Europe, MeadWestvaco also bought Kartoncraft Limited, near Dublin, Ireland, a leading pharmaceutical packaging producer. In July 2002 the company reported that it had eliminated 2,100 jobs of the 2,500 it expected to cut by the end of the year. As part of its plan to divest 950,000 nonstrategic acres, the company sold 95,500 acres of forest land in West Virginia for $50 million; the purchase was made through The Forestland Group LLC for Heartwood Forestland Fund IV Limited Partnership in December 2002.

In 2003 the company bought AMCAL, a maker of stationery products including journals, notepads, decorative calendars, and holiday cards.

Sticking with its consolidation and realignment strategy, in mid-2004 MeadWestvaco eliminated some 600 jobs by closing both its Garland, Texas, and St. Joseph, Missouri, facilities. Also in 2004 MeadWestvaco acquired Brazilian-based Tilibra S.A. Produtos de Papelaria, a maker of office products.

In 2005 MWV decided it would rather box than shuffle paper; it sold its Papers business — which made labels, book/catalog/magazine papers, and business forms — to Cerberus Capital Management. The decision marked a particularly strategic step toward global leadership in premium packaging. Papers accounted for a little less than 30% of MWV's sales prior to the deal, but the segment had consistently struggled in the red. (Cerberus set up the divested business as an independent company, NewPage Group Inc.) The deal included mills in Kentucky, Maine, Maryland, Michigan, and Ohio and about 900,000 acres of forest land in Illinois, Kentucky, Michigan, Missouri, Ohio, and Tennessee.

Striving to play a larger role in its customers' packaging process rather than just as a supplier, the company established a packaging research facility in collaboration with North Carolina State University in Raleigh and moved its headquarters to Richmond, Virginia, in 2006. MWV realigned operations, as well, by launching into packaging made from materials other than paperboard. The company burned through $714 million to acquire Saint-Gobain Calmar (now MeadWestvaco Calmar) from Compagnie de Saint-Gobain. The French packager specializes in plastic dispensing and spraying systems for personal and health care products.

MWV also snatched up Netherlands-based Keltec Dispensing Systems and California-based Hayes Products.

EXECUTIVES

Chairman and CEO: John A. Luke Jr., age 61, $6,108,446 total compensation
President: James A. Buzzard, age 55, $3,087,607 total compensation
SVP and CFO: E. Mark Rajkowski, age 51, $1,917,888 total compensation
SVP MWV Packaging: Mark S. Cross, age 53, $1,517,837 total compensation
SVP, General Counsel, and Secretary: Wendell L. Willkie II, age 58, $1,728,200 total compensation
SVP Emerging Markets and Innovation: Bruce V. Thomas, age 53
SVP: Linda V. Schreiner, age 50
SVP; President, Community Development and Land Management Group: Kenneth T. Seeger, age 59
SVP Technology: Mark T. Watkins, age 56
VP and Controller: John E. Banu, age 63
VP Communications: Donna O. Cox, age 46
President, Consumer & Office Products Group: Neil A. McLachlan, age 53
President, Personal & Beauty Care and Home & Garden: Thomas Jonas, age 40
President, MWV Healthcare: Ted Lithgow, age 56
President, Global Business Services: Mark V. Gulling, age 56
President, Primary Plastics Operations: John Taylor, age 47
President, Specialty Chemicals Division: Edward Rose, age 48
President, Beverage, Media, and Entertainment Folding Carton Operations: Stephen R. Scherger, age 45
President, Tobacco, Paperboard SBUs, and Operations: Robert A. (Bob) Feeser, age 47
Treasurer: Robert E. Birkenholz, age 49
Director Public Relations: Alison von Puschendorf
Auditors: PricewaterhouseCoopers LLP

LOCATIONS

HQ: MeadWestvaco Corporation
501 S. 5th St., Richmond, VA 23219
Phone: 804-327-5200
Web: www.meadwestvaco.com

2009 Sales

	$ mil.	% of total
Sales from inside of the US	3,267	54
Export sales from US operations	786	13
Sales from foreign operations	1,996	33
Total	**6,049**	**100**

PRODUCTS/OPERATIONS

2009 Sales

	$ mil.	% of total
Packaging		
Consumer solutions	2,248	37
Packaging resources	2,058	34
Consumer & office products	1,006	17
Specialty chemicals	499	8
Community development & land management	189	3
Corporate & other	49	1
Total	**6,049**	**100**

Selected Products

Consumer and office products
  Envelopes
  School and office products
  Time management products
Community development and land management
  Forestry operations (growing and harvesting softwood and hardwood)
  Leasing activities (third-party fees for mineral extraction, recreations leases)
  Real estate development (selling noncore forestlands, joint ventures, master planning)
Packaging
  Packaging resources
    Bleached paperboard (packaging pharmaceuticals, personal care, beauty, tobacco, beverage, food service)
    Coated Natural Kraftpaperboard (multipack beverage packaging)
    Linerboard (corrugated boxes)
  Consumer solutions
    Multipack cartons and packaging systems (beverages and tobacco)
    Packaging for media products (DVDs, CDs, video games, software)
    Packaging equipment for beverage and dairy products
    Pharmaceutical packaging contract with mass-merchant
    Plastic dispensing and spraying systems (personal care, beauty, health care, fragrance, and home and garden)
    Printed plastic packaging and injection-molded products (personal care, beauty, pharmaceutical products)
Specialty chemicals
  Activated carbon (automobile and truck emission control systems, water and food purification)
  Performance chemicals (printing inks, asphalt paving, adhesives, lubricants)

COMPETITORS

3M
ACCO Brands
Alcoa
Amcor
Anglo American
Ball Corp.
Bemis
Boise Cascade
Cascades Inc.
Disc Graphics
Georgia-Pacific
Graphic Packaging Holding
Iggesund Paperboard
International Paper
Pratt Industries USA
Smurfit-Stone Container
Sonoco Products
Temple-Inland
UPM-Kymmene
Weyerhaeuser

HISTORICAL FINANCIALS

Company Type: Public

Income Statement

FYE: December 31

	REVENUE ($ mil.)	NET INCOME ($ mil.)	NET PROFIT MARGIN	EMPLOYEES
12/09	6,049	225	3.7%	20,000
12/08	6,637	90	1.4%	22,000
12/07	6,906	285	4.1%	24,000
12/06	6,530	93	1.4%	24,000
12/05	6,170	28	0.5%	22,200
Annual Growth	**(0.5%)**	**68.4%**	**—**	**(2.6%)**

2009 Year-End Financials

Debt ratio: 63.2%
Return on equity: 7.1%
Cash ($ mil.): 850
Current ratio: 2.03
Long-term debt ($ mil.): 2,153
No. of shares (mil.): 171
Dividends
  Yield: 3.2%
  Payout: 70.8%
Market value ($ mil.): 4,890

Stock History

NYSE: MWV

	STOCK PRICE ($) FY Close	P/E High/Low	PER SHARE ($) Earnings	Dividends	Book Value
12/09	28.63	23 6	1.30	0.92	19.94
12/08	11.19	58 18	0.52	0.92	17.37
12/07	31.30	23 18	1.56	0.92	21.71
12/06	30.06	59 48	0.52	0.92	20.68
12/05	28.03	245 179	0.14	0.92	20.39
Annual Growth	**0.5%**	**— —**	**74.6%**	**0.0%**	**(0.6%)**

Medco Health Solutions

Administering some 700 million prescriptions each year, Medco Health Solutions is the country's top pharmacy benefits management company and, through its Accredo Health unit, its top specialty pharmacy as well. The company assists health plans in managing drug costs by designing drug formularies, negotiating discounts with pharmaceutical companies, and processing claims. Members may fill their prescriptions through a network of about 60,000 pharmacies, a mail-order program, or the company's call-center and Internet pharmacies. Medco Health Solutions manages drug benefits for clients that include unions, corporations, HMOs, insurance companies, and federal employees.

Customer cost containment is the cornerstone of the company's business strategy. Medco Health Solutions is able to control costs through the use of technology to process prescription claims, automation to fill and distribute prescriptions, and volume purchasing of pharmaceuticals. It also encourages the use of its mail order pharmacies and of generic equivalents in place of more expensive brand name drugs.

Within its mail order pharmacy segment, Medco has instituted what it calls Medco Therapeutic Resource Centers, which are specialized groups of pharmacists who are focused on certain chronic or complex diseases. One of its largest Therapeutic Resource Centers provides diabetes supplies under the Liberty Medical brand (which it gained through the 2007 purchase of PolyMedica). The company further enhanced the Liberty division when it bought the diabetes distribution assets of Owens & Minor subsidiary Access Diabetic Supply in 2009.

Another key component of the company's strategy is the growth of Accredo Health, which dispenses sensitive biotechnology drugs, usually injectable or infusion drugs, to patients with serious diseases such as cancer and hemophilia. Accredo delivers medications and related supplies either to patient homes or clinical sites from three main distribution centers in Tennessee and Pennsylvania.

Medco has been working to expand its complementary service offerings to help pharmacists, patients, and payers select the most cost-efficient and accurate medical regimen. In 2010 the company acquired personalized medicine company DNA Direct, a provider of advisory services for gene-based and biological medicines.

Medco went international in 2008 when it purchased a majority stake in Dutch firm Europa Apotheek Venlo, which provides mail-order pharmacy and other health care services in the Netherlands and Germany. Earlier the same year, the company partnered up with Apoteket, the Swedish government agency that oversees retail pharmacy operations in that country, to develop an automated prescription-review system. In 2009 Medco formed a partnership with United Drug to provide specialty pharmacy services in patients' homes in the UK.

To build up its information services arm, the company has announced plans to pay $730 million to acquire United BioSource, which conducts research on pharmaceuticals and medical devices that have already been approved, to analyze their use and effectiveness rates.

HISTORY

Medco Health Solutions (aka Medco Containment Services) was started in 1983 by former Wall Street investment banker Martin Wygod. Wygod believed that a mail-order pharmacy could improve efficiency, increase sales volume, and reduce prescription costs. Medco Containment Services became a publicly traded company in 1984. The firm acquired retail pharmacy management company PAID Prescriptions in 1985. As a result, the company became the first pharmacy in the nation to provide its customers with both retail and mail-order pharmacy services.

Wygod's vision proved to be right on target as the company exceeded $1 billion in sales in 1990 and had more than 25 million members by 1991. In 1993 the company was acquired by Merck & Co. and changed its name to Medco Health.

For Medco Health, 1996 proved to be a breakthrough year. The firm received a contract to provide pharmacy benefit management services to a purchasing group consisting of *FORTUNE* 500 companies. As a result, Medco Health managed more than 200 million prescriptions.

In the late 1990s the company used the Internet to improve its efficiency and cut costs. The firm opened its Internet pharmacy and formed partnerships with Healtheon (now part of WebMD Health), CVS, and Reader's Digest.

In 2000 the company acquired ProVantage Health Services, a health care information and benefits management company. The acquisition increased the company's customer base by 5 million members. The next year Medco Health became the first Internet pharmacy to exceed $1 billion in prescription sales.

Accounting issues with parent Merck delayed the planned 2002 spin-off of Medco. The next year, however, the deal was completed; Merck retained no ownership stake in Medco.

In 2005 Medco became the country's leading specialty pharmacy by acquiring Accredo Health for some $2.3 billion. The two companies had formed an alliance in 2004 to deliver biopharmaceuticals to Medco's clients.

The company's $1.5 billion acquisition in 2007 of PolyMedica, a mail-order distributor of blood-glucose monitors to diabetes patients, strengthened its Therapeutic Resource Center model, giving it resources dedicated to diabetes patients. Under a previous agreement, Medco had been supplying diabetes drugs to PolyMedica's patients.

Medco also grew its Accredo unit in 2007 with the acquisition of Critical Care Systems, a national provider of infusion services either in the home or at outpatient infusion sites.

EXECUTIVES

Chairman and CEO: David B. Snow Jr., age 55, $13,372,037 total compensation
President and COO: Kenneth O. Klepper, age 56, $5,037,128 total compensation
SVP Finance and CFO: Richard J. Rubino, age 52, $3,126,228 total compensation
SVP, Controller, and Chief Accounting Officer: Gabriel R. Cappucci, age 47
SVP Channel and Generic Strategy; President, Liberty Medical: Laizer D. Kornwasser, age 38
SVP and Chief Marketing Officer: Jack A. Smith, age 62
SVP Pharmaceutical Strategies and Solutions, General Counsel, and Secretary: Thomas M. Moriarty, age 46
SVP Human Resources: Karin V. Princivalle, age 52
Group President, Health Plans: Brian T. Griffin, age 50, $3,445,210 total compensation
Group President, Employer Accounts: Timothy C. Wentworth, age 49, $3,330,386 total compensation
Group President, Key Accounts: Glenn C. Taylor, age 58
Group President, Retiree Solutions: Mary T. Daschner, age 51
President, New Markets: John P. Driscoll, age 50, $3,224,636 total compensation
President, Accredo Health Group: Steven R. (Steve) Fitzpatrick, age 50
Chief Medical Officer; President, Medco Research Institute: Robert S. Epstein, age 54
Auditors: PricewaterhouseCoopers LLP

LOCATIONS

HQ: Medco Health Solutions, Inc.
   100 Parsons Pond Dr., Franklin Lakes, NJ 07417
Phone: 201-269-3400   **Fax:** 201-269-1109
Web: www.medcohealth.com

PRODUCTS/OPERATIONS

2009 Sales

	$ mil.	% of total
Products		
Retail	36,596.4	61
Mail order	22,365.0	38
Services		
Client & other	685.0	1
Manufacturer	157.8	—
Total	**59,804.2**	**100**

HISTORICAL FINANCIALS

Company Type: Public

Income Statement

FYE: Saturday nearest December 31

	REVENUE ($ mil.)	NET INCOME ($ mil.)	NET PROFIT MARGIN	EMPLOYEES
12/09	59,804	1,280	2.1%	22,850
12/08	51,258	1,103	2.2%	21,800
12/07	44,506	912	2.0%	20,800
12/06	42,544	630	1.5%	15,700
12/05	37,871	602	1.6%	15,300
Annual Growth	**12.1%**	**20.8%**	**—**	**10.5%**

2009 Year-End Financials

Debt ratio: 62.6%
Return on equity: 20.7%
Cash ($ mil.): 2,528
Current ratio: 1.29
Long-term debt ($ mil.): 4,000
No. of shares (mil.): 434
Dividends
   Yield: —
   Payout: —
Market value ($ mil.): 27,715

Stock History

Exchange:

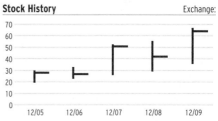

	STOCK PRICE ($) FY Close	P/E High/Low	PER SHARE ($) Earnings	Dividends	Book Value
12/09	63.91	25 14	2.61	—	14.73
12/08	41.91	26 14	2.13	—	13.74
12/07	50.70	32 16	1.63	—	15.85
12/06	26.72	31 23	1.04	—	17.30
12/05	27.90	28 20	1.02	—	17.81
Annual Growth	**23.0%**	**— —**	**26.5%**	**—**	**(4.6%)**

Medtronic, Inc.

Sometimes the best medicine is a short, sharp shock; that's why Medtronic's products reside in its customers' hearts and minds (among other places). A leading maker of implantable biomedical devices, the company makes defibrillators and pacemakers that shock the heart to help it beat normally. Subsidiary Medtronic Sofamor Danek makes spinal implant devices, while Medtronic CardioVascular produces catheters, stents, valves, balloons, and surgical ablation technologies used to treat vascular and heart disease. The company's neuromodulation division makes nerve and brain stimulation and drug delivery systems. Medtronic also makes devices for diabetes; ear, nose, and throat (ENT) conditions; and emergency medicine.

The Cardiac Rhythm Disease Management (CRDM) division makes pacemakers, defibrillators, heart monitors, and other products used to keep the heart beating properly. In 2008 the company expanded its CRDM division with the acquisition of Canada-based CryoCath Technologies, a maker of cryotherapy products to treat cardiac arrhythmias (irregular heartbeats), for about $374 million. Medtronic further expanded the division in 2009 by purchasing Ablation Frontiers, a maker of ablation therapies for cardiac rhythm disorders, for $225 million.

Medtronic's spinal and cardiovascular divisions have both been bolstered over the years through Medtronic's acquisition and development activities. The spinal division manufactures spinal devices and implants, as well as surgical instruments used in spine surgery; it also offers bone grafting tissue used in spinal, dental, and oral surgical procedures. This division expanded internationally when it formed a joint venture with orthopedics firm Shandong Weigao to market its products in China in 2009. In 2010 Medtronic made a move to expand its biologics operations when it agreed to purchase bone graft maker Osteotech.

The company has especially been building up the cardiovascular division, which focuses on minimally invasive technologies including drug-eluting stents (to prevent re-clogging of arteries), heart valves, and surgical ablation systems. The unit was augmented through the 2009 acquisitions of CoreValve and Ventor Technologies; both companies brought in technologies to facilitate aortic valve replacements using catheters instead of traditional surgical methods. Then in 2010 Medtronic acquired private interventional device maker Invatec for up to $500 million. The purchase added several drug-eluting balloon devices for coronary and lower-extremity vascular procedures to the cardiovascular division's offerings. Later that year Medtronic acquired ATS Medical, a maker of heart valves and cryoablation devices, for $370 million to further broaden its offering of cardiac surgery products.

The company's neuromodulation division makes electrical stimulation devices and drug delivery systems that help control conditions including chronic pain, tremors, and urinary incontinence. Additionally, Medtronic's diabetes segment manufactures and sells supplies including glucose monitors and insulin pumps.

Medtronic's ENT offerings are housed in its smaller surgical technologies segment and has steadily grown through acquisitions.

HISTORY

In 1949 electrical engineer Earl Bakken and his brother-in-law Palmer Hermundslie founded Medtronic in Minneapolis as a medical equipment repair outfit. After branching into custom-made products, Bakken made history in 1957 by crafting the world's first external, battery-powered cardiac pacemaker. In 1960 Medtronic began making and selling the first implantable pacemakers; the company quickly claimed about 80% of the market.

In the late 1960s and early 1970s Medtronic acquired other medical devices companies. Calamity struck in 1976 when the firm had to recall more than 35,000 Xytron pacemakers (some of which were already in patients) because body moisture was seeping into the battery chamber. Market share plunged to about 35%.

Medtronic recruited former Pillsbury COO Winston Wallin as chairman and CEO in 1985. The next year Medtronic released its Activitrax pacemaker, which snagged about 20% of the market. Under Wallin (who retired in 1996), the firm opened facilities in Europe and Asia and resumed acquisitions, adding companies in Italy, the Netherlands, and the US.

In the early 1990s Medtronic sought to expand its position in the vascular market. Its 1990 purchase of Bio-Medicus made the company the world's top maker of centrifugal blood pumps; it also entered the lucrative cardiac defibrillator market (1992) and increased other lines with the purchase of a maker of blood recycling devices and a company that produced disposable tubing and detection kits for breast and prostate cancer.

With an eye on the hot stent market, Medtronic in 1996 acquired InStent and AneuRx, makers of devices used to keep diseased arteries open. The company failed to become a leader in the market because its new units did not perform.

Using its expertise in implant devices, the company developed (and in 1997 received FDA approval for) devices aimed at the growing tremor control and incontinence markets.

In the late 1990s Medtronic undertook a flurry of acquisitions, both to solidify its leadership in the cardiovascular market and to broaden its operations. In 1999 Medtronic bought #1 spinal implant product maker Sofamor Danek to boost its neurosurgical business. The company took one more stab at the stent market, buying market-leader Arterial Vascular Engineering. Its share of the market fell after it was acquired, however, so Medtronic closed five facilities.

In 2001 the firm bought medical device makers MiniMed and Medical Research Group and combined them to form Medtronic MiniMed. In 2002 Medtronic bought VidaMed to grow its urology offerings.

In 2007 the company's CRDM division suspended sales of one of its defibrillator leads (the wires that connect the device to the heart), after determining that a flaw in the wire may have contributed to several deaths. The lead, called Sprint Fidelis, had been implanted in more than 200,000 patients. In 2008 Medtronic settled federal allegations that Kyphon had defrauded Medicare, agreeing to pay a $75 million fine.

Also in 2008 Medtronic bought Restore Medical, adding that company's soft palate implant system, which treats sleep breathing disorders such as snoring and obstructive sleep apnea, to its ENT lineup. Later that year it purchased a similar product line for the treatment of sleep-breathing disorders from InfluENT Medical.

EXECUTIVES

Chairman and CEO: William A. (Bill) Hawkins III, age 56, $7,512,626 total compensation
EVP; Group President, Cardiac and Vascular Group: Michael J. Coyle, age 48
EVP and Group President, Restorative Therapies Group: Christopher J. (Chris) O'Connell, age 43
EVP; Group President, International: Jean-Luc Butel, age 53, $3,611,055 total compensation
SVP and CFO: Gary L. Ellis, age 53, $3,323,976 total compensation
SVP Quality and Operations: H. James Dallas, age 51, $2,921,608 total compensation
SVP Medicine and Technology: Stephen N. (Steve) Oesterle, age 59
SVP; President, Cardiac Rhythm Disease Management: James Patrick (Pat) Mackin, age 43
SVP, General Counsel, and Corporate Secretary: D. Cameron Findlay, age 50
SVP and Chief Regulatory Officer: Susan Alpert, age 64
SVP and Chief Scientific, Clinical, and Regulatory Officer: Richard E. (Rick) Kuntz, age 53
SVP and Chief Talent Officer: Caroline Stockdale, age 46
SVP; President, Surgical Technologies: Bob Blankemeyer, age 63
SVP; President, Neuromodulation: Tom Tefft
SVP; President, Diabetes: Catherine M. (Katie) Szyman, age 43
Director Investor Relations: Jeff Warren
Senior Manager Corporate Public Relations: Chuck Grothaus
President, Physio-Control: Brian Webster
Auditors: PricewaterhouseCoopers LLP

LOCATIONS

HQ: Medtronic, Inc.
710 Medtronic Pkwy., Minneapolis, MN 55432
Phone: 763-514-4000   **Fax:** 763-514-4879
Web: www.medtronic.com

2010 Sales

	$ mil.	% of total
US	9,366	59
Europe	4,014	26
Asia/Pacific	1,903	12
Other regions	534	3
Total	**15,817**	**100**

PRODUCTS/OPERATIONS

2010 Sales

	$ mil.	% of total
Cardiac rhythm disease management (CRDM)	5,268	33
Spinal	3,500	22
CardioVascular	2,864	18
Neuromodulation	1,560	10
Diabetes	1,237	8
Surgical Technologies	963	6
Physio-Control	425	3
Total	**15,817**	**100**

Selected Products

CRDM
  Ablation systems
  Cardiac resynchronization therapy devices
  Electrophysiology catheters
  Implantable defibrillators
  Pacemakers, pacing systems, leads, and monitors
  Patient management tools
Spinal
  Balloon kyphoplasty instruments
  Bone graft substitutes
  Cervical and thoracolumbar fixation devices
  Minimal access retractor systems
  Neuro-monitoring systems

CardioVascular
  Cardiac surgery instruments and grafts
  Coronary stents
  Drug-eluting stents
  Embolic protection systems
  Endovascular stent grafts
  Heart stabilizers
  Heart valves
  Peripheral vascular stents
  Surgical tissue ablation systems
Neuromodulation
  Deep brain stimulation systems
  Implantable neurostimulation devices
  Implantable drug delivery systems
  Urology and gastroenterology stimulation therapies
Diabetes
  Blood glucose meters
  Glucose monitoring systems
  Insulin pumps
Surgical Technologies
  Computer-assisted surgery guidance systems
  Cranial fixation devices
  Ear ventilation tubes
  Hydrocephalus shunts
  Middle ear prostheses
  Nerve integrity monitors
  Palatal implants
  Sinus micro-endoscopy systems
Physio-Control
  Automated external defibrillators

COMPETITORS

Abbott Labs
American Medical Systems
Boston Scientific
Cardiac Science Corporation
Cook Incorporated
DexCom
Edwards Lifesciences
GE Healthcare
Gyrus ACMI
Integra LifeSciences
Johnson & Johnson
NuVasive
Philips Electronics
Roche Holding
Siemens Healthcare
Sorin
St. Jude Medical
Stryker
Synthes
Terumo Medical Corporation
Urologix
W.L. Gore
Zimmer Holdings
ZOLL

HISTORICAL FINANCIALS

Company Type: Public

Income Statement

FYE: Last Friday in April

	REVENUE ($ mil.)	NET INCOME ($ mil.)	NET PROFIT MARGIN	EMPLOYEES
4/10	15,817	3,099	19.6%	43,000
4/09	14,599	2,169	14.9%	41,000
4/08	13,515	2,231	16.5%	40,000
4/07	12,299	2,802	22.8%	38,000
4/06	11,292	2,547	22.6%	36,000
Annual Growth	8.8%	5.0%	—	4.5%

2010 Year-End Financials

Debt ratio: 47.5%
Return on equity: 22.6%
Cash ($ mil.): 1,400
Current ratio: 1.92
Long-term debt ($ mil.): 6,944

No. of shares (mil.): 1,083
Dividends
  Yield: 1.9%
  Payout: 29.4%
Market value ($ mil.): 47,315

HOOVER'S HANDBOOK OF AMERICAN BUSINESS 2011

Stock History

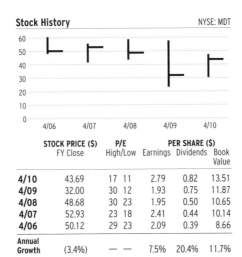

NYSE: MDT

	STOCK PRICE ($) FY Close	P/E High/Low		PER SHARE ($) Earnings	Dividends	Book Value
4/10	43.69	17	11	2.79	0.82	13.51
4/09	32.00	30	12	1.93	0.75	11.87
4/08	48.68	30	23	1.95	0.50	10.65
4/07	52.93	23	18	2.41	0.44	10.14
4/06	50.12	29	23	2.09	0.39	8.66
Annual Growth	(3.4%)	—	—	7.5%	20.4%	11.7%

Men's Wearhouse

With a business strategy tailored for growth, The Men's Wearhouse has made alterations even a haberdasher would be hard-pressed to follow. It's one of the largest discount retailers of men's business and formal attire with more than 1,250 stores throughout North America. Its primary operations are Men's Wearhouse, which has about 580 stores, Moores Clothing in Canada, and some 455 Men's Wearhouse and Tux stores (formerly MW Tux) that sell and rent tuxedos. Men's Wearhouse sells discounted tailored suits, as well as shoes, formal wear, and casual clothes. Its K&G unit caters to thriftier shoppers and sells women's careerwear in most of its 100-plus stores. Chairman and CEO George Zimmer founded the firm in 1973.

The deep recession in the US and resulting high levels of unemployment have decreased demand for professional attire and cut into sales. Amid the gloomy retail environment, the company is cutting back on store openings, and paying special attention to its value-priced K&G chain, by remodeling its stores.

The company also plans to increase its women's apparel offering at about 40% of its K&G outlets and launch a limited assortment of deeply discounted European luxury brand merchandise in some K&G stores. (Women's clothing currently accounts for about 5% of the company's apparel sales.)

Turning to Europe, in 2010 the company acquired two makers of corporate uniforms and work wear in the UK — Dimensions Clothing and Alexandra — and combined their operations into an as-yet unnamed entity. The purchase strengthens The Men's Wearhouse's corporate apparel presence in the UK. The two companies have strong sourcing operations in the Far East and offer popular brands.

The company has finished renaming — again — all of the After Hours Formalwear and Mr. Tux stores (acquired from Macy's, Inc. in 2007) as

Men's Wearhouse and Tux (formerly MW Tux shops). The acquisition landed Men's Wearhouse in first place in the tuxedo rental business in North America. The tux rental business attracted Men's Wearhouse because it attracts men younger than the retailer's typical customer. The newly renamed Men's Wearhouse and Tux stores carry an expanded selection of merchandise, including suit separates, denim, and sportswear targeted at younger men.

About 12% of The Men's Warehouse's sales come from Canada where it operates some 115 Moores Clothing for Men stores in 10 provinces. Like its US counterpart Men's Warehouse, Moores stores sells suits, sport coats, slacks, business casual attire, dress shirts, sportswear, shoes, and accessories. Moores stores also offer tuxedo rentals and "big and tall" merchandise.

Tailored clothing accounts for more than half of sales, although the firm is selling more casual apparel, shoes, and accessories. The Men's Wearhouse stresses attentive, low-pressure customer service to attract the man with little knowledge of buying suits.

In addition to its retail chains, The Men's Wearhouse also operates a corporate apparel and uniform program (Twin Hill) serving about 10 contract customers, as well as 30-plus MW Cleaners dry cleaning and laundry facilities in the Houston area.

HISTORY

George Zimmer, an apparel industry veteran at 23, founded The Men's Wearhouse in fast-growing Houston in 1973 with his father, Robert Zimmer, and college buddy Harry Levy. By the time George debuted on TV in 1986 with his now popular "I guarantee it" motto, the company had 25 stores. It went public in 1992 and continued to grow at a slower but more sustainable pace than its competitors, some of which went bankrupt as a result of overexpansion.

In 1997, through its newly formed Value Price Clothing division, The Men's Wearhouse bought C & R Clothiers, adding 17 stores and a new, lower-priced segment to its operations. The division added four Suit Warehouse stores in the Detroit area the next year.

An on-again-off-again deal to grow into Canada was back on (for good) in early 1999 when The Men's Wearhouse paid $127 million for the Montreal-based Moores Retail Group. The company later began offering tuxedo rentals at some of its Men's Wearhouse stores. Also that year The Men's Wearhouse bought K&G Men's Center, operator of 34 superstores in 16 states. In 2000 it combined its other discount operations with K&G, renaming most of the stores K&G Men's Center. After 2001's economic downturn hit the company hard, CEO Zimmer announced a return to focusing on the suits, rather than casualwear, and not carrying anything priced more than $500.

In 2002 the company acquired TwinHill, which became its global uniform and corporate apparel division. TwinHill supplies uniforms for clients in the transportation, hospitality, foodservice, banking, retail, security, and entertainment industries. That year The Men's Wearhouse purchased the Wilke-Rodriguez brand and became its sole distributor. Plans to launch a 100-store chain catering to Latino men under the Eddie Rodriguez name were abandoned in 2005.

On the lookout for complementary products and services, the company entered the dry-cleaning business in December 2003 when it bought Nesbit's Cleaners and Craig's Cleaners of Houston.

In April 2007 Men's Wearhouse acquired After Hours Formalwear from Federated Department Stores (now Macy's, Inc.) for about $100 million.

Citing the strengthening of the Canadian dollar, Men's Wearhouse closed its manufacturing facility in Montreal (Golden Brand Clothing), which supplied its Moores Clothing stores, in mid-2008. In early 2009 the firm changed the name of its MW Tux stores to Men's Wearhouse and Tux.

The Men's Wearhouse in mid-2009 bid for Filene's Basement at auction and had won until the judge reopened the auction to suitors Syms and Vornado Realty in a deal valued at $65 million.

EXECUTIVES

Chairman and CEO: George A. Zimmer, age 61, $1,498,911 total compensation
Vice Chairman: David H. Edwab, age 55, $973,699 total compensation
President and COO: Douglas S. (Doug) Ewert, age 46, $855,016 total compensation
EVP, CFO, Treasurer, and Principal Financial Officer: Neill P. Davis, age 53, $504,013 total compensation
EVP Distribution, Logistics, Tuxedo Operations, and Chief Compliance Officer: Gary G. Ckodre, age 60
EVP Marketing and Human Resources: Charles Bresler, age 62, $440,255 total compensation
EVP Employee Relations and Chief Legal Officer: Carole L. Souvenir, age 49
EVP Stores, Men's Wearhouse: Mark Neutze
EVP Stores, Men's Wearhouse: Dean A. Speranza
EVP Manufacturing: William C. (Will) Silveira, age 52
SVP Merchandising: James E. Zimmer, age 58, $370,615 total compensation
SVP Stores, K&G: William (Bill) Evans
SVP, Chief Accounting Officer, and Principal Accounting Officer: Diana M. Wilson, age 62
SVP Real Estate: Thomas L. Jennings
SVP and CIO: William Melvin
SVP and Chief Marketing Officer: Diane Ridgway-Cross
SVP E-Business and Digital Strategies: Susan G. Neal
Secretary: Michael W. Conlon
President, Moores Retail Store Operations: Dave Starrett
President, MW Cleaners: Michael Nesbit
President, K&G: Mary Beth Blake
President, TwinHill: Howard Wecksler
Auditors: Deloitte & Touche LLP

LOCATIONS

HQ: The Men's Wearhouse, Inc.
6380 Rogerdale Rd., Houston, TX 77072
Phone: 281-776-7200
Web: www.menswearhouse.com

2010 Stores

	Men's Wearhouse	Men's Wearhouse & Tux	K&G
US			
California	86	43	1
Texas	56	2	13
Florida	41	41	6
New York	31	14	4
Illinois	28	37	6
Pennsylvania	24	21	5
Michigan	20	26	7
Ohio	19	17	5
Virginia	18	22	3
Georgia	18	18	6
New Jersey	16	15	7
Massachusetts	15	24	5
Maryland	14	18	7
Colorado	14	3	3
Washington	14	2	3
Arizona	14	8	—
North Carolina	12	20	4
Tennessee	12	13	2
Missouri	11	9	2
Indiana	9	10	3
Connecticut	9	6	2
Minnesota	9	10	2
Wisconsin	9	11	1
Oregon	9	2	—
Louisiana	7	12	4
Utah	7	—	—
Nevada	6	4	—
Oklahoma	5	—	2
Alabama	5	9	1
Kansas	5	2	1
South Carolina	5	10	1
Iowa	4	2	—
New Mexico	4	—	—
Kentucky	3	6	1
Arkansas	3	—	—
Nebraska	3	—	—
New Hampshire	3	2	—
Other states	12	11	—
Total	**580**	**450**	**107**

2010 Moores Stores

	No.
Canada	
Ontario	50
Quebec	24
British Columbia	16
Alberta	12
Manitoba	5
New Brunswick	3
Nova Scotia	3
Saskatchewan	2
Newfoundland	1
Prince Edward Island	1
Total	**117**

PRODUCTS/OPERATIONS

2010 Sales

	$ mil.	% of total
MW	1,281.8	67
K&G	370.1	19
Moores	222.0	12
MW Cleaners	22.1	1
Twin Hill	13.5	1
Total	**1,909.5**	**100**

2010 Sales

	% of total
Apparel	76
Tuxedo rental	17
Alteration & other services	7
Total	**100**

Selected Merchandise

Corporate uniforms
Dress shirts
Formal wear
Outerwear
Shoes
Slacks
Sport coats
Sport shirts
Suits
Work wear

COMPETITORS

ARAMARK
Astor & Black
Brooks Brothers
Burlington Coat Factory
Casual Male Retail Group
Cintas
Dillard's
Eddie Bauer llc
Faithful Ltd.
G&K Services
Hudson's Bay
J. Crew
Jos. A. Bank
Kohl's
Macy's
Neiman Marcus
Nordstrom
Ross Stores
Saks
Sears
Sugdens & Sons
Syms

HISTORICAL FINANCIALS

Company Type: Public

Income Statement

FYE: Saturday nearest January 31

	REVENUE ($ mil.)	NET INCOME ($ mil.)	NET PROFIT MARGIN	EMPLOYEES
1/10	1,910	46	2.4%	15,900
1/09	1,972	59	3.0%	16,200
1/08	2,113	147	7.0%	18,400
1/07	1,882	149	7.9%	14,900
1/06	1,725	104	6.0%	13,800
Annual Growth	2.6%	(18.7%)	—	3.6%

2010 Year-End Financials

Debt ratio: 4.8%
Return on equity: 5.2%
Cash ($ mil.): 186
Current ratio: 3.16
Long-term debt ($ mil.): 43
No. of shares (mil.): 53
Dividends
Yield: 1.4%
Payout: 32.6%
Market value ($ mil.): 1,061

Stock History

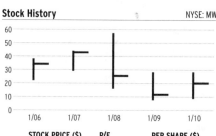

NYSE: MW

	STOCK PRICE ($) FY Close	P/E High/Low		PER SHARE ($) Earnings	Dividends	Book Value
1/10	20.15	32	11	0.86	0.28	17.14
1/09	11.65	24	7	1.13	0.28	16.00
1/08	25.49	21	6	2.73	0.23	15.50
1/07	42.94	16	11	2.71	0.20	14.32
1/06	34.17	20	12	1.88	—	11.92
Annual Growth	(12.4%)	—	—	(17.8%)	11.9%	9.5%

Merck & Co.

The new Merck (formerly Schering-Plough) makes medicines for a number of ailments, from stuffy noses and asthma to hypertension and arthritis. The compny's top prescription drugs include asthma medication Singulair, anti-inflammatory Remicade, hypertension fighters Cozaar and Hyzaar, and cholesterol combatants Vytorin, Zetia, and Zocor. It also makes animal health pharmaceuticals, as well as childhood and adult vaccines for such diseases as measles, mumps, hepatitis, and shingles. Its OTC drug and personal care offerings include Claritin allergy pills and Dr. Scholl's foot care products.

The predecessor Merck entity paid $41.1 billion to acquire Schering-Plough's operations in November 2009 through a reverse-merger transaction. The combined entity, which began operating under the Merck name immediately following the transaction, became the second-largest global pharmaceuticals manufacturer (behind Pfizer). Former Schering-Plough shareholders own nearly a third of the new Merck. Integration efforts to combine the two organizations will result in an estimated 15% reduction in its workforce by the end of 2012. The existing Merck CEO, Dick Clark, took the helm at the new Merck.

The merger created a stronger portfolio of marketed and development-stage pharmaceuticals in areas including cardiovascular, oncology, respiratory, neurology, inflammatory ailments, infectious disease, vaccines, and women's health.

Merck especially boosted its presence in the growing biotech drug business through the transaction by gaining access to Schering-Plough's biologics pipeline. The purchase also greatly expanded Merck's operations in the animal health and consumer health arenas, although Merck had to sell its stake in veterinary joint venture Merial to partner Sanofi-Aventis for about $4 billion to avoid anti-trust issues.

Best-selling drugs carried over from the old Merck include Singulair (topping $4 billion in annual sales), Cozaar/Hyzarr, diabetes drug Januvia, osteoporosis therapy Fosamax, and infant vaccines ProQuad and Varivax. The former Schering-Plough contributed Remicade, a treatment for rheumatoid arthritis and Crohn's disease earning over $2 billion in annual revenues, as well as allergy drugs Nasonex and Clarinex and cancer therapy Temodar.

As part of the merger integration efforts, the new Merck is focused on bringing its most promising late-stage development candidates to market. It is also increasingly seeking out collaboration, licensing, and outsourcing agreements in the R&D arena to cut costs. The research and development programs of the combined entities are focused on ailments in fields such as cancer, cardiology, women's health, immunology, infectious disease, metabolism, ophthalmology, respiratory ailments, and neurological conditions.

The success of Vytorin, a combination of two cholesterol drugs — Schering-Plough's Zetia and Merck's Zocor, was thwarted in 2008 when study results were released questioning the drug's effectiveness compared to Merck's older medication Zocor. The companies' troubles with Vytorin came to a head in 2009 when they agreed to pay about $42 million to settle class-action lawsuits filed by consumers and health plans over Vytorin's efficacy.

HISTORY

Merck was formed in 2009 when the former Merck acquired Schering-Plough in a reverse-merger transaction. Following the merger, Schering-Plough took on the Merck name.

Schering-Plough traced its roots back to 1851, when Berlin chemist Ernst Schering began to sell chemicals to apothecary shops.

The company went on to develop such new drugs as Chlor-Trimeton, one of the first antihistamines, and the cold medicine Coricidin. In the 1960s the company introduced Garamycin (antibiotic, 1964), Tinactin (antifungal, 1965), and Afrin (decongestant, 1967).

Schering's 1971 merger with Memphis-based Plough expanded the product line to include such cosmetics and consumer items as Coppertone and Di-Gel. Schering-Plough introduced many products after the merger, including Lotrimin AF (antifungal, 1975), antibiotic Netromycin (1980), and Drixoral (a cold remedy made nonprescription in 1982).

The company was one of the first drug giants to make significant investments in biotechnology: It bought DNAX Research Institute of Palo Alto, California, in 1982. Acquisitions in the late 1970s and 1980s included Scholl (foot care, 1979) and Cooper Companies (eye care, 1988).

In 1993 Schering-Plough began marketing its non-sedating antihistamine, Claritin, in the US. (Claritin became an OTC drug in 2002.) In 2000 Schering-Plough formed its first collaboration with Merck. In 2002 it paid a $500 million fine to the FDA over manufacturing concerns.

As Schering-Plough's revenues started to decline in 2003, the company brought in several executives from Pharmacia, including CEO Fred Hassan (who retired following the 2009 merger with Merck) to help streamline operations and expand its R&D programs and product offerings.

Merck was started in 1887 when German chemist Theodore Weicker came to the US to set up a branch of German firm E. Merck AG (which was founded in 1668 and later became Merck KGaA). At first the firm imported and sold drugs and chemicals from Germany, but in 1903 it began manufacturing its own products.

Merck opened its first research lab in 1933; Merck scientists there developed the first steroid, cortisone, in 1944. Five Merck scientists received Nobel Prizes in the 1940s and 1950s.

In the 1970s, an accelerated R&D organization created new products including Clinoril (antiarthritic), Flexeril (muscle relaxant), and Timoptic (for glaucoma). Merck introduced 10 major new drugs in the 1980s, including Mevacor (high cholesterol) and Vasotec (high blood pressure).

In 1997 Merck and Rhône-Poulenc (now part of Sanofi-Aventis) merged their animal health units to form Merial.

In 2004 Merck pulled its blockbuster pain medication Vioxx off the market after studies linked the drug to increased risks of strokes and heart attacks. (Merck settled thousands of class-action and personal injury lawsuits related to Vioxx in 2007 for $4.85 billion.) The Vioxx safety scandal, along with the pending loss of patent protection on some of its biggest sellers like Zocor (which began facing competition in 2006), sent the company into recovery mode. Merck announced restructuring plans to make the company's operations leaner and more cost-effective in 2005 under new CEO Richard (Dick) Clark, a long-time Merck executive. Between 2005 and 2008, the company eliminated more than 10,000 jobs and closed a handful of manufacturing plants.

EXECUTIVES

Chairman and CEO: Richard T. (Dick) Clark, age 63, $16,838,368 total compensation
President: Kenneth C. (Ken) Frazier, age 55, $5,298,169 total compensation
EVP and CFO: Peter N. Kellogg, age 54, $3,750,597 total compensation
EVP; President, Consumer Health Care: Bridgette P. Heller, age 48
EVP and General Counsel: Bruce N. Kuhlik, age 53, $2,656,937 total compensation
EVP; President, Animal Health: Raul E. Kohan, age 57
EVP; President, Merck Research Laboratories: Peter S. Kim, age 51, $4,147,401 total compensation
EVP and Chief Medical Officer: Michael Rosenblatt, age 62
EVP Global Services and CIO: J. Chris Scalet, age 51
EVP and Chief Compliance Officer: Richard S. Bowles III, age 58
EVP; President, Merck Manufacturing: Willie A. Deese, age 54
EVP The Merck Company Foundation: Ellen W. Lambert
EVP Human Resources: Miriam M. Graddick-Weir, age 55
SVP Global Medical Affairs: Hans M. Vemer
SVP External Manufacturing: Didier Colombeen
SVP Global Market Access: Jeffrey Berkowitz
SVP; President Global Supply Chain: Ian A.T. McInnes, age 56
SVP and Global Controller: John Canan, age 53
SVP and Chief Communications Officer: Adele D. Ambrose, age 53
VP Investor Relations: Alex Kelly
President, Merck Vaccines: Julie Louise Gerberding, age 54
President Director, P.T. Schering-Plough Indonesia: Thierry Powis
Auditors: PricewaterhouseCoopers LLP

LOCATIONS

HQ: Merck & Co., Inc.
 1 Merck Dr., Whitehouse Station, NJ 08889
Phone: 908-423-1000   **Fax:** 908-735-1253
Web: www.merck.com

2009 Sales

	$ mil.	% of total
US	14,401.2	52
Europe, Middle East & Africa	7,093.1	26
Japan	2,425.6	9
Other	3,508.4	13
Total	**27,428.3**	**100**

PRODUCTS/OPERATIONS

Selected Products

Pharmaceuticals
  Bone, Respiratory, Immunology, and Dermatology
    Arcoxia (arthritis and pain)
    Asmanex (from pre-merger Schering-Plough)
    Clarinex/Aerius (pre-merger Schering-Plough)
    Fosamax (osteoporosis)
    Nasonex (pre-merger Schering-Plough)
    Propecia (male-pattern hair loss)
    Remicade (pre-merger Schering-Plough)
    Singulair (asthma and allergic rhinitis)
  Mature Brands
    Claritin Rx (pre-merger Schering-Plough)
    Cozaar/Hyzaar (hypertension)
    Proscar (benign prostate enlargement)
    Proventil (pre-merger Schering-Plough)
    Vasotec/Vaseretic (hypertension/heart failure)
    Zocor (elevated cholesterol)
  Vaccines
    Gardasil (cervical cancer caused by HPV virus)
    M-M-R II (measles, mumps, and rubella)
    Pneumovax (pneumococcal disease)
    ProQuad (measles, mumps, rubella, varicella)
    RotaTeq (rotavirus gastroenteritis)
    Varivax (chicken pox)
    Zostavax (shingles)
  Infectious Disease
    Avelox (pre-merger Schering-Plough, with Bayer)
    Cancidas (antifungal)
    Crixivan (HIV)
    Invanz (antibacterial)
    Isentress (antifungal)
    Peg-Intron (pre-merger Schering-Plough)
    Primaxin (antibiotic)
    Rebetol (pre-merger Schering-Plough)
    Stocrin (HIV)
  Diabetes and Obesity
    Janumet (diabetes)
    Januvia (diabetes)
  Neurosciences and Ophthalmology
    Cosopt (glaucoma)
    Maxalt (migraine)
    Remeron (pre-merger Schering-Plough)
    Subutex/Suboxone (pre-merger Schering-Plough)
    Trusopt (glaucoma)
  Cardiovascular
    Integrilin (pre-merger Schering-Plough)
    Vytorin (Merck and pre-merger Schering-Plough)
    Zetia (Merck and pre-merger Schering-Plough)
  Oncology
    Caelyx (pre-merger Schering-Plough)
    Emend
    Intron A (pre-merger Schering-Plough)
    Temodar/Temodal (pre-merger Schering-Plough)
  Women's Health
    Follistim/Puregon (pre-merger Schering-Plough)
    NuvaRing (pre-merger Schering-Plough)

Animal Health (Intervet)
  Aquaflor (antibiotic for farm-raised fish)
  Banamine (nonsteroid anti-inflammatory)
  Coccivac (poultry vaccine)
  Exspot/Scalibor (canine topical insecticide)
  M+PAC (swine pneumonia vaccine)
  Nuflor (antimicrobial)
  Otomax (canine otitis)
  Paracox (poultry vaccine)

Consumer Health Care
  Afrin (nasal decongestant)
  Bain de Soleil (sun care)
  Claritin (allergy)
  Coppertone (sun care)
  Correctol (laxative)
  Drixoral (cold medicine)
  Dr. Scholl's (foot care products)
  Solarcaine (sun care)
  Tinactin (antifungal)

COMPETITORS

Abbott Labs
Alcon
Allergan
Amgen
AstraZeneca
Bausch & Lomb
Baxter International
Bayer AG
Biogen Idec
Boehringer Ingelheim
Bristol-Myers Squibb
Chattem
Eli Lilly
Forest Labs
Genzyme
Gilead Sciences
GlaxoSmithKline
Heska
Johnson & Johnson
Meda Pharmaceuticals
Merck KGaA
Mylan
Novartis
Perrigo
Pfizer
Roche Holding
Sandoz International GmbH
Sanofi-Aventis
Shire
Teva Pharmaceuticals
Three Rivers Pharmaceuticals
Valeant
Virbac Corporation
Warner Chilcott
Watson Pharmaceuticals

HISTORICAL FINANCIALS

Company Type: Public

Income Statement

FYE: December 31

	REVENUE ($ mil.)	NET INCOME ($ mil.)	NET PROFIT MARGIN	EMPLOYEES
12/09	27,428	12,901	47.0%	100,000
12/08	23,850	7,808	32.7%	51,000
12/07	24,198	3,275	13.5%	55,000
12/06	22,636	4,434	19.6%	33,500
12/05	22,012	4,631	21.0%	32,600
Annual Growth	5.7%	29.2%	—	32.3%

2009 Year-End Financials

Debt ratio: 27.2%
Return on equity: 33.2%
Cash ($ mil.): 9,311
Current ratio: 1.80
Long-term debt ($ mil.): 16,075

No. of shares (mil.): 3,074
Dividends
  Yield: 4.2%
  Payout: 26.9%
Market value ($ mil.): 112,309

Stock History

NYSE: MRK

	STOCK PRICE ($) FY Close	P/E High	P/E Low	PER SHARE ($) Earnings	PER SHARE ($) Dividends	PER SHARE ($) Book Value
12/09	36.54	7	4	5.65	1.52	19.21
12/08	30.40	57	21	1.07	1.52	6.10
12/07	58.11	41	28	1.49	1.52	5.92
12/06	43.60	23	16	2.03	1.52	5.71
12/05	31.81	17	12	2.10	1.52	5.83
Annual Growth	3.5%	—	—	28.1%	0.0%	34.7%

Meredith Corporation

Meredith may be the true domestic goddess of media. A home and family media firm, Meredith publishes magazines, special interest publications, and books. Its more than 25 subscription magazines include flagship title *Better Homes and Gardens*, as well as *Family Circle*, *Ladies' Home Journal*, *Parents*, *Fitness*, and *More*. The company is active in broadcasting with about a dozen network-affiliated TV stations across the US; it also has one AM radio station. Meredith additionally operates about 30 websites, offers integrated marketing services, and has a large consumer database. Family members of the late E. T. Meredith III — grandson of the firm's founder — control more than 50% of the company's voting power.

As a result of the economic recession that has ravaged the publishing industry, the company has been looking to cut costs and focus on other areas of the business. In 2008 Meredith sold WFLI, a CW affiliate serving Chattanooga, Tennessee. It next closed its *Country Home* magazine in 2009. And in 2010 it took further steps to diversity its business when it acquired the outstanding shares in mobile marketing firm The Hyperfactory. (Meredith took a minority stake in The Hyperfactory the previous year.)

The deal is one of Meredith's latest attempts at focusing on its digital offerings. In 2009 the company launched the Meredith Women's Network, a network of premium websites that includes The Better Homes and Gardens Network (made up of more than 20 sites, including *Better Homes and Gardens* and *Better Recipes*); The Parents Network (*Parents* and *Top Baby Name*); and The Real Girls Network (including Meredith's *Fitness*, *More*, and *Ladies' Home Journal*). Also in 2009 Meredith launched MixingBowl.com, a social network built around food, recipes, and entertaining. In 2009, the Company launched *Mixing Bowl* magazine as an extension of MixingBowl.com.

In addition, Meredith has been expanding its licensing operations to extend the reach of the Better Homes and Gardens brand and to focus on a revenue stream that isn't as dependent on advertising. The company has a licensing agreement with John Wiley & Sons to publish and distribute books based on Meredith's Better Homes and Gardens imprint.

In addition to its magazines, Meredith publishes some 135 special interest publications (*American Patchwork & Quilting*, *Decorating*), and has more than 200 books in print. The company maintains a focus on content related to the home, publishing books that cover topics such as cooking, gardening, remodeling, and decorating; its familiar red and white checkered *Better Homes and Gardens New Cook Book* has been on the cuisine scene since 1930.

Meredith has been active in broadcasting for more than 50 years, and its television stations reach about 10 million households. Among the 12 TV stations it owns are CBS affiliates WGCL (Atlanta), KPHO (Phoenix), and KCTV (Kansas City, Missouri). Meredith operates its websites through its Meredith Interactive Media unit. Through its Meredith Integrated Marketing, Meredith uses its database of information on some 85 million people to develop new integrated marketing products and create direct mail projects.

HISTORY

Around the turn of the century, Edwin Thomas (E. T.) Meredith's grandfather eschewed traditional gifts and gave his grandson a unique wedding present — a handful of $20 gold pieces, enough to buy the grandfather's controlling interest in the *Farmer's Tribune*, and a note instructing his grandson to "Sink or Swim" with the financially troubled publication. Meredith proceeded to revive the *Farmer's Tribune*, and after he sold it in 1902, he used the profits to found Meredith Corporation and launch *Successful Farming* magazine.

Following a stint as Secretary of Agriculture under President Woodrow Wilson, E. T. Meredith extended the company's publishing reach, introducing *Fruit, Garden and Home* in 1922. Two years later the publication became *Better Homes and Gardens*. E.T. Meredith died in 1928, but his company forged ahead, moving into book publishing in 1930 with the first issue of *Better Homes and Gardens Cook Book*, and branching into special interest publications in 1937.

After going public in 1946, Meredith wasted no time diversifying into the fledgling TV industry. It bought its first TV station (Syracuse, New York's WHEN-TV) in 1948, followed by KPHO (Phoenix) in 1952 and Kansas City's KCTV in 1953. Meredith launched a commercial printing business in 1957 and expanded its printing activities in 1969 by teaming with West Germany's Burda family to operate several US printing plants.

Accelerated expansion was the essence of Meredith's story in the 1980s. In addition to buying two more TV stations, the company acquired *Ladies' Home Journal* from Family Media in 1986 and introduced *Midwest Living* and *Traditional Home* in 1987 and 1989, respectively.

Meredith reacted to an advertising slump in the early 1990s by paring down its holdings. Among its divestitures were its printing business (1990), two television stations (1993), a book club (1995), and its cable TV interests (1996). In 1997 it launched its syndicated *Better Homes and Gardens* TV show, the same year William Kerr became CEO.

The company's 1999 purchase of Atlanta's TV station WGNX (changed to WGCL in a 2000 restructuring) brought the number of TV stations in its stable to one dozen. An advertising slump resulted in job reductions at the company. In mid-2001 the company hired a marketing company to better leverage its magazine brands.

Executive committee chairman E. T. Meredith III — grandson of the company's founder — died in early 2003.

In 2005 Meredith purchased the *Parents, Child, Fitness*, and *Family Circle* magazines from Bertelsmann's Gruner + Jahr for $350 million.

In 2006 president and COO Stephen Lacy succeeded Kerr as CEO. Later that year Meredith acquired the *ReadyMade* do-it-yourself lifestyle magazine. The following year the company closed the print edition of *Child*; the brand continues to exist online.

Boosting its presence in this area, in 2007 Meredith acquired four companies: online customer relationship marketing firm Genex, interactive word-of-mouth marketing company New Media Strategies, consumer health information search engine Healiea, and Directive Corporation, a provider of database strategy, analytics, and customer asset management services. In 2008 it purchased Big Communications, a health care marketing communications firm.

EXECUTIVES

Chairman, President, and CEO: Stephen M. (Steve) Lacy, age 55, $5,775,688 total compensation
Vice Chairman: D. Mell Meredith Frazier, age 53
Chief Development Officer, General Counsel, and Secretary: John S. Zieser, age 51, $1,768,214 total compensation
Chief Marketing Officer: Keith Sedlak
Chief Strategy Officer: Wendy P. Riches, age 66
VP and CFO: Joseph H. Ceryanec, age 48, $662,968 total compensation
VP and Publisher, *More*: Brenda Saget Darling
VP Advertising, Meredith Women's Network: Steve Hamkins
VP, Hispanic Ventures: Ruth Gaviria
VP and Publisher, *Parents* and *American Baby*: Diane Newman
VP Corporate Communications and Government Relations: Art Slusark, age 48
President, Local Media Group: Paul Karpowicz, age 56, $2,029,217 total compensation
Publisher, *Family Circle*: Diane Papazian
President, National Media Group: Tom Harty, age 47
Director Investor Relations: Mike Lovell
Corporate Controller: Steven M. Cappaert
Auditors: KPMG LLP

LOCATIONS

HQ: Meredith Corporation
1716 Locust St., Des Moines, IA 50309
Phone: 515-284-3000   **Fax:** 515-284-2700
Web: www.meredith.com

PRODUCTS/OPERATIONS

2009 Sales

	$ mil.	% of total
Publishing		
Advertising	530.2	38
Circulation	280.8	20
Other	323.3	23
Broadcasting	274.5	19
Total	**1,408.8**	**100**

Selected Magazines

American Baby (parenthood)
Better Homes and Gardens (home content)
Family Circle (women's content)
Fitness (women's content)
Ladies' Home Journal (women's content)
Midwest Living (regional travel and lifestyle)
More (aimed at women ages 40 and above)
Parents (parenthood)
ReadyMade (do-it-yourself lifestyle)
Siempre Mujer (Hispanic women's magazine)
Successful Farming (farm content)
Traditional Home (home decorating)
Wood (woodworking)

Selected Book Imprints

Better Homes and Gardens Books
The Home Depot Books

Selected TV Stations

KCTV (CBS; Kansas City, MO)
KPHO (CBS; Phoenix)
KPTV (FOX; Portland, OR)
KVVU (FOX, Las Vegas)
KSMO (MyNetworkTV, Kansas City, MO)
WFSB (CBS; Hartford/New Haven, CT)
WGCL (CBS; Atlanta)
WHNS (FOX; Greenville/Spartanburg/Asheville, NC)
WNEM (CBS; Flint/Saginaw/Bay City, MI)
WSMV (NBC; Nashville, TN)

Selected Websites

Meredith Women's Network
  Better Homes and Gardens
  Parents
  The Real Girls Network

COMPETITORS

ACME Communications
Advance Publications
American Media
Dwell, LLC
Dynamic Resource Group
E. W. Scripps
Essence Communications
F+W Media
Farm Journal
Freedom Communications
Gannett
Gruner + Jahr
Hearst Corporation
Krause Publications
Lagardère Active
Martha Stewart Living
Media General
News Corp.
Reader's Digest
Reed Elsevier Group
Rodale
Time Inc.
Tribune Company

HISTORICAL FINANCIALS

Company Type: Public

Income Statement

FYE: June 30

	REVENUE ($ mil.)	NET INCOME ($ mil.)	NET PROFIT MARGIN	EMPLOYEES
6/09	1,409	(107)	—	3,280
6/08	1,587	135	8.5%	3,570
6/07	1,616	162	10.0%	3,160
6/06	1,598	145	9.1%	3,160
6/05	1,221	128	10.5%	2,706
Annual Growth	**3.6%**	**—**	**—**	**4.9%**

2009 Year-End Financials

Debt ratio: 88.7%   No. of shares (mil.): 45
Return on equity: —   Dividends
Cash ($ mil.): 28   Yield: 3.4%
Current ratio: 0.97   Payout: —
Long-term debt ($ mil.): 540   Market value ($ mil.): 1,159

Stock History

NYSE: MDP

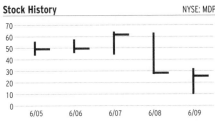

	STOCK PRICE ($) FY Close	P/E High/Low	PER SHARE ($) Earnings	Dividends	Book Value
6/09	25.55	— —	(2.38)	0.88	13.43
6/08	28.29	22 10	2.83	0.80	17.36
6/07	61.60	19 14	3.31	0.69	18.36
6/06	49.54	20 16	2.86	0.60	15.39
6/05	49.06	22 18	2.52	0.52	14.37
Annual Growth	**(15.0%)**	**— —**	**—**	**14.1%**	**(1.7%)**

MetLife, Inc.

Part of its name may stand for "metropolitan," but the company is found in villages, towns, and huge cities coast-to-coast and then some. MetLife is the US's largest life insurer; its flagship insurance subsidiary is Metropolitan Life Insurance Company. Its Insurance Products segment includes all of its group and individual life insurance and non-medical health insurance products (dental, disability, long-term care). Its Retirement Products segment includes its annuity products. MetLife's Auto & Home segment works through subsidiary Metropolitan Property and Casualty Insurance (MPC).

The company's Corporate Benefit Funding segment handles investment management for large employers that offer retirement benefits, including pension closeouts and specialized life insurance products used to fund such benefit plans. Its banking segment, MetLife Bank, offers residential mortgage loans and individual online banking services and has grown through acquisitions of smaller businesses.

Like all of its life insurance brethren, MetLife experienced some queasiness during the recession of 2008 and 2009. As its investments roller-coasted, some of its ratings also bobbed up and down and losses from its investments contributed to the company's first net income loss of the decade. However, the company's operations were never in serious trouble and it did not seek or receive any federal support. It even saw some of its business swell from increased mortgage refinancing and from an influx of nervous customers who switched from other insurers to MetLife.

MetLife has announced its planned acquisition of American Life Insurance Company (ALICO) from troubled American International Group (AIG). The US-based company provides life insurance in Asia and other developing markets — Japan is its largest market. MetLife has agreed to pay $6.8 billion in cash (which AIG will use to pay back some of the billions it owes the US government) and $8.7 billion in equity. That last half of the deal could potentially give AIG a 20% stake in MetLife.

While MetLife is primarily known as an insurance company, it also holds a solid real estate portfolio valued at more than $7 billion. However, the company has sold off some of its largest properties, including Chicago's Sears Tower (divested in 2004, the tower was renamed Willis Tower in 2009) and even its own landmark headquarters in New York (in 2005 for $1.5 billion). It also sold the Peter Cooper and Stuyvesant Town housing complexes that it helped build with government funding in 1947. Tishman Speyer Properties and BlackRock paid $5.4 billion for the property in late 2006; the sale boosted MetLife's 2006 net income to a record $6.29 billion. However, the buyers didn't fare as well and in 2010 they handed the keys to the iconic complexes over to their lenders.

HISTORY

New York merchant Simeon Draper tried to form National Union Life and Limb Insurance to cover Union soldiers in the Civil War, but investors were scared away by heavy casualties. After several reorganizations and name changes, the enterprise emerged in 1868 as Metropolitan Life Insurance (MetLife), a stock company.

Sustained at first by business from mutual assistance societies for German immigrants, MetLife went into industrial insurance with workers' burial policies. The firm was known for its aggressive sales methods. Agents combed working-class neighborhoods, collecting small premiums. If a worker missed one payment, the company could cancel the policy and keep all premiums paid, a practice outlawed in 1900.

MetLife became a mutual company (owned by its policyholders) in 1915 and began offering group insurance two years later.

After a period of conservative management under the Eckers family from 1929 to 1963, MetLife began to change, dropping industrial insurance in 1964. It started offering auto and homeowners insurance in 1974.

To diversify, the company bought State Street Research & Management (1983), Century 21 Real Estate (1985, sold 1995), London-based Albany Life Assurance (1985), and Allstate's group life and health business (1988). In 1987 it took over the annuities segment of the failed Baldwin United Co., and expanded into Spain and Taiwan in 1988. During the early 1990s, MetLife re-emphasized insurance, adding such new products as long-term-care insurance.

In 1993 MetLife was charged with improper sales practices in 13 states. Legal fees, fines, and refunds in these cases exceeded $100 million; bad publicity had a chilling effect on sales. MetLife in turn instituted new training and sales practices. (In 1998 it agreed to pay an additional $25 million civil penalty to settle the federal investigation.) MetLife's problems continued with a suit over its sales of insurance to Americans in Europe and an investigation in Florida related to churning (agents inducing customers to buy more expensive policies).

In 1998 it sold its UK insurance operations and its Canadian business, then cut 10% (about 1,900) of its administrative staff. In 1999 MetLife followed the industry trend of buying and selling single product lines rather than whole companies. Also in 1999, the company agreed to pay $1.7 billion to settle policyholder lawsuits related to churning allegations.

MetLife went public in 2000. It also bought fellow insurer GenAmerica, and purchased Grand Bank, a one-office nationally chartered bank in New Jersey, which was renamed MetLife Bank. Plans to use Grand Bank as a ticket into the financial services arena met with opposition from community and consumer groups concerned about how MetLife's ownership would comply with the Community Reinvestment Act. The Federal Reserve Board approved the acquisition in 2001.

Solidifying its position as a major group benefits provider, MetLife bought John Hancock's group life insurance operations in 2003.

MetLife in 2005 exited the asset management business when it sold State Street Research to BlackRock. That same year it acquired The Travelers Insurance Company and The Travelers Life and Annuity Company, from Citigroup in a cash and equity deal valued at $11.8 billion. The deal, which included Citigroup's international insurance businesses, made MetLife the largest individual life insurer in North America.

Until 2008 the company participated in reinsurance by holding 52% of Reinsurance Group of America. However, MetLife sold off its shares that year to focus on its core activities.

PRODUCTS/OPERATIONS

2009 Sales

	$ mil.	% of total
Life insurance products	23,483	57
Retirement products	3,543	9
Corporate benefit funding	5,669	14
Auto & Home	3,113	7
International	4,383	11
Banking, corporate, & other	867	2
Total	**41,058**	**100**

Selected Subsidiaries and Affiliates

GenAmerica Financial LLC (distribution)
Hyatt Legal Plans, Inc. (prepaid legal plans)
MetLife Bank, N.A. (consumer banking)
MetLife Insurance Company of Connecticut
MetLife Investors Group, Inc. (distribution)
Metropolitan Property and Casualty Insurance Company
New England Life Insurance Company
Texas Life Insurance Company
Tower Square Securities (affiliated broker)
Walnut Street Securities, Inc. (mutual funds, securities)

COMPETITORS

AEGON USA	John Hancock Financial
Aetna	Liberty Mutual
Aflac	Lincoln Financial Group
AIG	MassMutual
AIG American General	Mutual of Omaha
Allianz	Nationwide
Allstate	New York Life
Aon	Northwestern Mutual
AXA	Pacific Mutual
CIGNA	Principal Financial
COUNTRY Financial	Prudential
Genworth Financial	State Farm
Guardian Life	TIAA-CREF
The Hartford	USAA
ING	Zurich Financial Services

HISTORICAL FINANCIALS

Company Type: Public

Income Statement

FYE: December 31

	ASSETS ($ mil.)	NET INCOME ($ mil.)	INCOME AS % OF ASSETS	EMPLOYEES
12/09	539,314	(2,278)	—	54,000
12/08	501,678	3,209	0.6%	57,000
12/07	558,562	4,317	0.8%	49,000
12/06	527,715	6,293	1.2%	47,000
12/05	481,645	4,714	1.0%	65,500
Annual Growth	2.9%	—	—	(4.7%)

2009 Year-End Financials

Equity as % of assets: 6.1%
Return on assets: —
Return on equity: —
Long-term debt ($ mil.): 21,708
No. of shares (mil.): 820

Dividends
Yield: 2.1%
Payout: —
Market value ($ mil.): 28,992
Sales ($ mil.): 41,058

Stock History

NYSE: MET

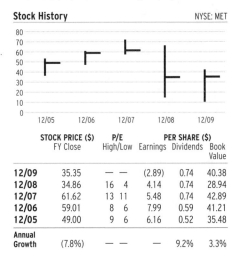

	STOCK PRICE ($) FY Close	P/E High/Low		PER SHARE ($) Earnings	Dividends	Book Value
12/09	35.35	—	—	(2.89)	0.74	40.38
12/08	34.86	16	4	4.14	0.74	28.94
12/07	61.62	13	11	5.48	0.74	42.89
12/06	59.01	8	6	7.99	0.59	41.21
12/05	49.00	9	6	6.16	0.52	35.48
Annual Growth	(7.8%)	—	—	—	9.2%	3.3%

MetroPCS Communications

MetroPCS Communications is marching to the beat of a different drummer. The regional wireless service provider offers use of its phone networks, which use CDMA (code division multiple access) technology, without chaining its customers to long-term contracts. Unlike other providers that charge by the minute, MetroPCS offers monthly unlimited usage flat-rate plans for local and domestic long distance services to its approximately 6.6 million customers. It operates in more than 10 states in such major metropolitan areas as Atlanta, Dallas/Fort Worth, Detroit, Las Vegas, Los Angeles, Miami, Sacramento, and San Francisco. Chairman and CEO Roger Linquist and CTO Malcolm Lorang founded MetroPCS in 1994.

MetroPCS has focused largely on serving densely populated markets, which creates efficiencies for the company in regard to network deployment and product distribution. In 2009 MetroPCS expanded its service area, which spans 11,000 cities and towns in the US, to include the New York and Boston metropolitan areas. The company's strategy has helped to make it one of the top five facilities-based wireless network operator by subscribers.

The company's revenue from wireless services and handset sales rose 28% in 2009 due to an increase in subscribers of more than 1 million. Profits also climbed nearly 20% that year as MetroPCS managed to bring down its operating expenses and its losses on investments.

MetroPCS plans to increase its subscriber numbers in part by continuing to simplify its billing as consumers look increasingly to mobile accounts to replace their landline telephones. The company introduced service plans in 2010 that include all taxes and fees in the advertised flat rates. Also that year, MetroPCS expanded its voice, text, and mobile Web services for new subscribers to include nationwide coverage.

HISTORY

CEO Roger Linquist and CTO Malcolm Lorang founded General Wireless in 1994 to bid on PCS licenses being auctioned by the US government. Linquist was formerly CEO of PacTel Personal Communications (later called AirTouch and now part of the Vodafone Group) and founded PageMart Wireless (now WebLink Wireless). In 1996 Japanese trading house Mitsui and audio-equipment maker Kenwood agreed to invest $10 million in General Wireless. The US electronics unit of Hyundai also made a substantial financial commitment, and Lucent Technologies said it would provide $300 million in vendor financing to build the networks.

Also in 1996 the firm successfully bid $1 billion for 14 PCS licenses. But before the licenses were awarded, the FCC held another auction during which similar licenses sold for far less. General Wireless scrapped its IPO in 1997 because of poor market conditions. A year later it filed for Chapter 11 bankruptcy protection and sought to reduce the price of its licenses. In 1999 a federal bankruptcy court ruled that the licenses were worth only $166 million and that the company could reorganize and keep the licenses. The FCC launched an appeal but the bankruptcy court's decision was upheld by a Texas district court. The FCC then lobbied the US Congress to reclaim the licenses, but the resulting bill was blocked.

After emerging from bankruptcy protection, the firm changed its name to MetroPCS Communications. The legal wrangling continued into 2000 when the FCC appealed the decision to the 5th US Circuit Court of Appeals in New Orleans, which ruled in favor of the company. The next year the Supreme Court denied a review of the case, upholding the lower court's decision. MetroPCS then began rolling out operations in its major markets.

In 2007 the company went public and bought $1.4 billion in spectrum licenses, covering regions such as Boston, New York, and Philadelphia, during the federal government's auction.

Also in 2007 the company's more than $5 billion bid to acquire Leap Wireless was rejected. MetroPCS had hoped to significantly expand its service area in order to better compete with nationwide carriers like Sprint Nextel and AT&T Mobility through a merger with Leap.

In late 2008 the company entered into a national roaming agreement with Leap Wireless (which MetroPCS unsuccessfully tried to acquire in 2007), as well as agreeing to settle outstanding litigation between the two companies. The pact also included a spectrum exchange agreement that saw Leap acquiring from MetroPCS spectrum rights in San Diego, Fresno, Seattle, and other Washington and Oregon markets, and MetroPCS acquiring from Leap additional spectrum in Dallas/Fort Worth and other markets in Louisiana and Florida.

EXECUTIVES

Chairman, President, and CEO: Roger D. Linquist, age 71, $8,990,792 total compensation
COO: Thomas C. Keys, age 51, $4,575,877 total compensation
EVP and CFO: J. Braxton Carter, age 51, $3,002,027 total compensation
EVP, General Counsel, and Secretary: Mark A. Stachiw, age 48, $2,076,000 total compensation
SVP and CTO: Malcolm M. Lorang, age 76, $1,350,610 total compensation
SVP Engineering and Network Operations: Ed Chao
SVP and CIO: John J. Olsen, age 53
SVP Corporate Development: Douglas S. (Doug) Glen, age 52
SVP, Chief Accounting Officer, and Controller: Christine B. Kornegay, age 46
SVP Corporate Marketing: Phillip R. (Phil) Terry
SVP Market Operations, West: Herbert (Chip) Graves IV, age 54
VP Corporate Engineering: Ron Unger
VP Network Operations: David Walker
VP Finance and Treasurer: Keith D. Terreri, age 45
VP Market Finance and Control: Charles Moore
VP Human Resources: Dennis T. (Tom) Currier, age 41
VP Customer Operations: Greg Pressly
Director Investor Relations: Jim Mathias
Auditors: Deloitte & Touche LLP

LOCATIONS

HQ: MetroPCS Communications, Inc.
2250 Lakeside Blvd., Richardson, TX 75082
Phone: 214-570-5800   **Fax:** 214-570-5859
Web: www.metropcs.com

2009 Sales

	$ mil.	% of total
Core markets	3,195.8	92
Northeast markets	284.7	8
Total	3,480.5	100

PRODUCTS/OPERATIONS

2009 Sales

	$ mil.	% of total
Service	3,130.4	90
Equipment	350.1	10
Total	3,480.5	100

COMPETITORS

AT&T
AT&T Mobility
Boost Mobile
Cellco
Clearwire
Comcast Cable
Cox Communications
Cricket Communications
Leap Wireless
Sprint Nextel
Time Warner Cable
T-Mobile USA
TracFone
Verizon
Virgin Mobile
Vonage
XO Holdings

HISTORICAL FINANCIALS

Company Type: Public

Income Statement

FYE: December 31

	REVENUE ($ mil.)	NET INCOME ($ mil.)	NET PROFIT MARGIN	EMPLOYEES
12/09	3,481	177	5.1%	3,600
12/08	2,752	149	5.4%	3,200
12/07	2,236	100	4.5%	2,498
12/06	1,547	54	3.5%	2,046
12/05	1,038	199	19.1%	—
Annual Growth	35.3%	(2.9%)	—	20.7%

2009 Year-End Financials

Debt ratio: 158.5%
Return on equity: 8.2%
Cash ($ mil.): 929
Current ratio: 1.87
Long-term debt ($ mil.): 3,626

No. of shares (mil.): 354
Dividends
  Yield: —
  Payout: —
Market value ($ mil.): 2,700

Stock History

NYSE: PCS

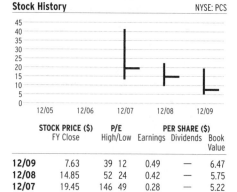

	STOCK PRICE ($) FY Close	P/E High/Low	PER SHARE ($) Earnings	Dividends	Book Value
12/09	7.63	39 12	0.49	—	6.47
12/08	14.85	52 24	0.42	—	5.75
12/07	19.45	146 49	0.28	—	5.22
Annual Growth	(37.4%)	— —	32.3%	—	11.3%

MGIC Investment

Since a pinkie-promise isn't good enough for most lenders, there's MGIC Investment's mortgage insurance to protect lenders from home buyers who don't hold up their end of the bargain. MGIC Investment owns Mortgage Guaranty Insurance Corporation, the largest US provider of private mortgage insurance. Such coverage allows otherwise qualified buyers who can't scrape up the standard 20% down payment to get mortgages. MGIC writes both primary insurance on individual loans, and pooled insurance on blocks of mortgages sold on the secondary market. The actual purchasers of its products are the mortgage lenders, including banks, mortgage brokers, and credit unions.

The subprime mortgage loan crisis that began in 2007 was brutal on MGIC and its competitors. MGIC responded by yanking hard on its own leash and tightening its underwriting standards to reduce its losses. The company stopped writing insurance on riskier loans, curbed its coverage in states hardest hit by the resulting housing slump, and raised its premium rates.

It also sold its 25% interest in debt collections firm Sherman Financial Group to Sherman for about $125 million in cash and an

$85 million promissory note. Around that same time Credit-Based Asset Servicing and Securitization LLC (C-BASS), of which MGIC owns less than a 50% interest, ceased operations. C-BASS purchased and securitized credit-sensitive and nonperforming single-family residential mortgages, investing in whole loans, subordinated securities, and properties that were on the verge of being foreclosed upon.

Now MGIC's businesses include a range of investment subsidiaries, reinsurance subsidiaries, and assurance corporations. MGIC also offers some online products: eMagic.com, a Web portal where mortgage providers can shop for a variety of loan origination tools, and Myers Internet, a Web hosting provider and lead generator.

Prior to the mortgage mess in the US, MGIC opened offices in Sydney, Australia, and Toronto, Canada, marking the company's entry into the global market. Less than two years later MGIC stopped issuing new policies and began searching for a buyer for its Australian operations and closed its Canadian office. Instead MGIC is focusing on its domestic operations.

Insurance holding company and mortgage guaranty competitor Old Republic International holds 10% of the company's stock.

HISTORY

Milwaukee lawyer Max Karl founded MGIC in 1957, reinventing private mortgage guaranty insurance, which had gone out of favor in the Depression. MGIC went public in 1961, suffered in the stagflated 1970s, and entered the 1980s ready to expand. But poorly underwritten loans in such trouble spots as Texas and Oklahoma slammed MGIC.

Piano builder Baldwin United made a fruitless foray into financial services in 1982, paying too much for MGIC and going bankrupt in 1983. Northwestern Mutual bankrolled a management LBO in 1985. Surviving the weak real estate market of the 1980s, MGIC went public again in 1991.

In 1995 MGIC debuted professional liability insurance products for lenders. Two years later it began selling homeowners extended warranties for appliances.

In the late 1990s changes in Fannie Mae and Freddie Mac mortgage insurance requirements hit MGIC hard. News reports that some insurers and lenders failed to inform homeowners when they could cancel their mortgage insurance also gave the industry a black eye.

In 1998 MGIC began insuring second mortgages and joined with Enhance Financial Services Group (now owned by Radian Group) to form C-BASS to buy and securitize nonperforming mortgages. Meanwhile, MGIC was busy buffing up its in-house appraisal, default, and prepayment prediction tools and bundling them with a variety of mortgage origination services that it began offering over its eMAGIC website in 1999. In 2000 the decision by Illinois to allow insurance of 100% home loans meant that MGIC could begin to insure such loans nationwide.

With low interest rates, high employment rates, and some key legislative pushes to encourage home ownership, lenders and homebuilders enjoyed a heyday from 2001 to late-2006. These were also good years for MGIC which wrote up a storm of mortgage insurance on all of those home purchases.

EXECUTIVES

Chairman and CEO, MGIC Investment and Mortgage Guaranty Insurance: Curt S. Culver, age 57, $3,118,969 total compensation

President and COO, MGIC Investment and Mortgage Guaranty Insurance: Patrick Sinks, age 53, $1,625,927 total compensation

EVP and CFO, MGIC Investment and Mortgage Guaranty Insurance: J. Michael Lauer, age 65, $1,149,177 total compensation

EVP Risk Management, Mortgage Guaranty Insurance: Lawrence J. Pierzchalski, age 57, $1,263,039 total compensation

EVP, General Counsel, and Secretary, MGIC Investment and Mortgage Guaranty Insurance: Jeffrey H. Lane, age 60, $1,204,316 total compensation

SVP Claims, Mortgage Guaranty Insurance: Carla A. Gallas

SVP Capital Markets, Mortgage Guaranty Insurance: Steven T. Snodgrass

SVP International Business Development, Mortgage Guaranty Insurance: Martin F. Wood

SVP Information Services and CIO, Mortgage Guaranty Insurance: Michael G. Meade, age 60

SVP, Chief Investment Officer, and Treasurer, MGIC Investment and Mortgage Guaranty Insurance: James A. Karpowicz, age 62

SVP Regulatory Relations, Assistant Secretary, and Associate General Counsel, MGIC Investment and Mortgage Guaranty Insurance: Joseph J. Ziino Jr.

SVP Investor Relations, Mortgage Guaranty Insurance: Michael J. (Mike) Zimmerman

VP Information Services and CTO, Mortgage Guaranty Insurance: James R. Stirling

VP Human Resources, Mortgage Guaranty Insurance: Kurt J. Thomas

VP and Controller: Timothy J. Mattke, age 34

Auditors: PricewaterhouseCoopers LLP

LOCATIONS

HQ: MGIC Investment Corporation
MGIC Plaza, 250 E. Kilbourn Ave.
Milwaukee, WI 53202
Phone: 414-347-6480   **Fax:** 888-601-4440
Web: www.mgic.com

PRODUCTS/OPERATIONS

2009 Sales

	$ mil.	% of total
Net premiums earned	1,302.3	76
Investment income	304.7	18
Realized investment gains	51.9	3
Other revenue	49.6	3
Total	**1,708.5**	**100**

COMPETITORS

Genworth Financial
PMI Group
Radian Group
Republic Mortgage Insurance
United Guaranty
VBA

HISTORICAL FINANCIALS

Company Type: Public

Income Statement

FYE: December 31

	REVENUE ($ mil.)	NET INCOME ($ mil.)	NET PROFIT MARGIN	EMPLOYEES
12/09	1,709	(1,322)	—	1,020
12/08	1,722	(519)	—	1,160
12/07	1,693	(1,670)	—	1,250
12/06	1,469	565	38.4%	1,200
12/05	1,527	627	41.1%	1,200
Annual Growth	2.9%	—	—	(4.0%)

Debt ratio: 51.4% No. of shares (mil.): 200
Return on equity: — Dividends
Cash ($ mil.): 1,186 Yield: 0.0%
Current ratio: — Payout: —
Long-term debt ($ mil.): 669 Market value ($ mil.): 1,159

Stock History NYSE: MTG

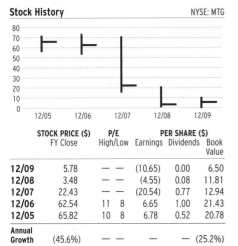

	STOCK PRICE ($) FY Close	P/E High/Low		PER SHARE ($) Earnings	Dividends	Book Value
12/09	5.78	—	—	(10.65)	0.00	6.50
12/08	3.48	—	—	(4.55)	0.08	11.81
12/07	22.43	—	—	(20.54)	0.77	12.94
12/06	62.54	11	8	6.65	1.00	21.43
12/05	65.82	10	8	6.78	0.52	20.78
Annual Growth	(45.6%)	—	—	—	—	(25.2%)

MGM Resorts

It's not your imagination — MGM Resorts International (formerly MGM MIRAGE) is one of the world's largest gaming firms. The company's more than 15 partially or wholly owned properties include Las Vegas' MGM Grand, Luxor, Bellagio, The Mirage, and the Monte Carlo. It also owns or has a stake in other casinos in Nevada, as well as in Illinois, Michigan, and Mississippi (Beau Rivage). It is selling its stake in the Borgata casino in Atlantic City, a joint venture with Boyd Gaming. Internationally, it operates in China and Dubai. The company changed its name from MGM MIRAGE in 2010 to better reflect its family of hotel brands and its expanding global presence. Founder Kirk Kerkorian owns about 40% of the firm.

Like all casino resorts, the company is struggling under large debt burdens amid falling gaming revenues. MGM Resorts' long-term debt is worth a staggering $13 billion, much of it incurred to finance its ambitious CityCenter project. The mega-resort, located on a 66-acre site between the company's Bellagio and Monte Carlo casinos in Las Vegas, was originally set to cost some $11 billion. However, as a result of the devastated tourism industry amid the economic recession, in 2009 the company scaled back the project, reducing its budget to $8.5 billion and delaying the opening of certain stages of development. MGM CityCenter eventually opened in late 2009 as a joint venture with Dubai World (a holding company for the Persian Gulf state).

A battle emerged between Kerkorian and activist investor Carl Icahn, who along with private-equity fund Oaktree Capital Management has been acquiring hundreds of millions of dollars in MGM Resorts debt in 2009. Icahn was reportedly pushing the company to file for bankruptcy, an action Kierkorian wanted to avoid. Later that year MGM Resorts sold some $2.5 billion in stock and notes in order to boost liquidity and improve its financials. Other efforts to lighten its debt include the 2009 sale of Treasure Island Hotel & Casino on the Las Vegas Strip to Ruffin Acquisition for $775 million.

Yet another step MGM Resorts expects to make to pay down debt is an initial public offering of the MGM Grand Macau. MGM Resorts owns 50% of the company that built the casino resort in China; the joint venture is with private Macao casino developer Pansy Ho. In 2009 New Jersey regulators issued a report declaring Ho an "unsuitable" business partner for MGM, because of allegations her father Stanley Ho has had ties to organized crime. The finding jeopardized MGM Resorts' license for its casino in Atlantic City, and in 2010 MGM Resorts announced that it is selling its 50% share in the New Jersey property in order to maintain its joint venture in Macau.

HISTORY

Billionaire Kirk Kerkorian purchased a stake in famed movie studio Metro-Goldwyn-Mayer (MGM; formed in 1924) for just over $80 million in 1970. Around the same time, he began acquiring property in Las Vegas and started construction on the city's largest hotel.

Financial difficulties led Kerkorian to sell his new hotel, as well as many of MGM's assets in the early 1970s. But he kept the MGM name and used it for MGM Grand hotels in Las Vegas and Reno, Nevada. In 1986 Kerkorian sold MGM Grand Hotels to Bally, but he retained the rights to the MGM Grand name and logo. That year Kerkorian founded MGM Grand, Inc., and took the company public in 1987. He set about snapping up Las Vegas property in the late 1980s and early 1990s.

In 1993 Kerkorian and company unveiled Las Vegas' MGM Grand, a $1.1 billion complex featuring a 33-acre theme park and, at the time, the largest casino on the planet (171,500 sq. ft.). The project was a success ($742 million in revenues its first year) and spawned expansion plans.

In 1996 MGM Grand began planning for an Atlantic City casino and signed on as developer and manager for gaming company Tsogo Sun, which was opening casinos in South Africa. The following year, through its joint venture with Primadonna Resorts, it opened the 2,035-room hotel and casino New York-New York. In 1998 MGM Grand narrowly won its bid to become one of three groups to build casinos in Detroit. (The MGM Grand Detroit opened the following year and pulled in $4.8 million in its first three days.)

In 1999 the company bought Primadonna Resorts, which gave MGM Grand complete ownership of New York-New York. The company appointed co-CEOs John Redmond and Daniel Wade to their posts in late 1999. (Both Redmond and Wade moved to other positions in the company when Terrence Lanni became CEO in 2001.)

In a landmark deal, MGM Grand bought rival Mirage Resorts for $6.4 billion (including $2 billion in debt) in 2000 and became one of the top gaming companies in the world.

The purchase of Mirage Resorts allowed MGM Grand to add a string of opulent casinos to its collection. Among the casinos the deal brought to the MGM Grand fold were Las Vegas strip properties Bellagio, a luxurious European-style casino, and The Mirage, a tropical-themed casino. The Mirage Resorts acquisition also put Las Vegas' Treasure Island, the Golden Nugget, and Monte Carlo (50%-owned with Mandalay Resort Group) under the MGM Grand umbrella. Mirage Resorts' Beau Rivage in Biloxi, Mississippi, and the Golden Nugget in Laughlin, Nevada, also became MGM Grand properties.

Steven Wynn, who had propelled Mirage Resorts from a single casino (the Golden Nugget) to its spot as one of the world's leading gaming companies, opted not to join the merged firm. Later in 2000 MGM Grand changed its name to MGM MIRAGE. MGM MIRAGE laid off more than 6,700 employees due to declining guest numbers in the wake of the September 11th terrorist attacks.

In 2004 the company sold its Golden Nugget properties in Las Vegas and Laughlin to a private investment firm. Also in 2004 MGM MIRAGE sold its MGM Grand Hotel and Casino in Darwin, Australia.

The following year MGM MIRAGE purchased rival Mandalay Resort Group for about $7.9 billion, briefly creating the world's largest gaming company. (It was surpassed later in 2005 when Harrah's bought Caesars.) In 2006 MGM Mirage and Boyd Gaming debuted a $200 million expansion of its Borgata casino.

In 2007 the company opened MGM Grand Macau, a hotel it jointly owns in China. The following year chairman and CEO Terrence Lanni resigned from his executive positions. James Murren, former COO, replaced him.

In 2009 the company opened CityCenter, an $8 billion-plus mixed-use development on the Las Vegas Strip that is a joint venture with Dubai World. Also that year MGM Mirage changed its name to MGM Resorts International.

EXECUTIVES

Chairman, President, and CEO: James J. (Jim) Murren, age 48, $13,752,443 total compensation
EVP, CFO, and Treasurer: Daniel J. D'Arrigo, age 41, $1,301,576 total compensation
EVP, Corporate Strategy, and Special Counsel: William M. (Bill) Scott IV, age 49, $1,884,853 total compensation
EVP and Chief Administrative Officer: Aldo Manzini, age 46, $1,443,651 total compensation
EVP and Chief Accounting Officer: Robert C. Selwood, age 54, $1,208,894 total compensation
EVP Special Counsel-Litigation and Chief Diversity Officer: Phyllis A. James, age 57
EVP, General Counsel, and Secretary: John M. McManus, age 42
Chief Design and Construction Officer and Director: Robert H. Baldwin, age 60, $5,132,846 total compensation
SVP and Treasurer: Cathryn Santoro, age 41
SVP and Corporate Controller: Rick Arpin, age 37
SVP Taxes: Shawn T. Sani, age 44
SVP Human Resources: Miriam Hammond
SVP Public Affairs: Alan Feldman, age 51
President and CEO, MGM Resorts Hospitality; President and COO, MGM Grand Las Vegas: Gamal Abdelaziz, age 53
President, MGM Resorts International Development: Kenneth (Ken) Rosevear
Chief Marketing Officer, MGM Resorts: William J. (Bill) Hornbuckle
Auditors: Deloitte & Touche LLP

LOCATIONS

HQ: MGM Resorts International
3600 Las Vegas Blvd. South, Las Vegas, NV 89109
Phone: 702-693-7111
Web: www.mgmresorts.com

PRODUCTS/OPERATIONS

2009 Sales

	$ mil.	% of total
Casino		
Slots	1,579	24
Table games	955	14
Other	84	1
Non-casino		
Rooms	1,370	21
Food & beverage	1,362	21
Entertainment, retail & other	1,294	19
Adjustments	(665)	—
Total	**5,979**	**100**

Selected Properties

Bellagio (Las Vegas)
Beau Rivage (Biloxi, MS)
Borgata (50%; Atlantic City, NJ)
Circus Circus (Las Vegas)
Circus Circus Reno (Nevada)
CityCenter (50%, Las Vegas)
Excalibur (Las Vegas)
Gold Strike (Tunica County, MS)
Gold Strike (Jean, NV)
Luxor (Las Vegas)
Mandalay Bay Resort & Casino (Las Vegas)
MGM Grand (Las Vegas)
MGM Grand Detroit
MGM Grand Macau (50%; Macau, China)
The Mirage (Las Vegas)
Monte Carlo (Las Vegas)
New York-New York (Las Vegas)
Railroad Pass (Henderson, NV)
Silver Legacy (50%; Reno, NV)

COMPETITORS

Boyd Gaming
Galaxy Entertainment
Harrah's Entertainment
Las Vegas Sands
Pinnacle Entertainment
Rio All-Suite Hotel & Casino
Riviera Holdings
Sahara Hotel and Casino
SJM
Star City
Station Casinos
Stratosphere
Tropicana Entertainment
Trump Resorts
Wynn Resorts

HISTORICAL FINANCIALS

Company Type: Public

Income Statement

FYE: December 31

	REVENUE ($ mil.)	NET INCOME ($ mil.)	NET PROFIT MARGIN	EMPLOYEES
12/09	5,979	(1,292)	—	62,000
12/08	7,209	(855)	—	61,000
12/07	7,692	1,584	20.6%	67,400
12/06	7,176	648	9.0%	70,000
12/05	6,482	443	6.8%	66,500
Annual Growth	**(2.0%)**	**—**	**—**	**(1.7%)**

2009 Year-End Financials

Debt ratio: 341.9%
Return on equity: —
Cash ($ mil.): 2,056
Current ratio: 1.28
Long-term debt ($ mil.): 13,233

No. of shares (mil.): 441
Dividends
  Yield: 0.0%
  Payout: —
Market value ($ mil.): 4,025

Stock History

NYSE: MGM

	STOCK PRICE ($) FY Close	P/E High/Low		PER SHARE ($) Earnings	Dividends	Book Value
12/09	9.12	—	—	(3.41)	0.00	8.77
12/08	13.76	—	—	(3.06)	0.00	9.01
12/07	84.02	19	11	5.31	0.00	13.73
12/06	57.35	27	15	2.22	0.00	8.72
12/05	36.67	31	22	1.50	0.00	7.33
Annual Growth	**(29.4%)**	**—**	**—**	**—**	**—**	**4.6%**

Micron Technology

Don't let Micron Technology's name mislead you: The circuits on its chips are well under one micron across, but the company is one of the largest memory chip makers in the world. It makes DRAM chips, flash memory chips, and memory modules. The company sells to customers in networking, consumer electronics, and telecommunications, but the bulk of its sales are in the computer market.

Through its Lexar Media subsidiary, Micron offers digital media products and flash memory storage devices, including memory cards and portable USB flash drives. The company sells products under its Lexar brand, as well as makes products sold under other brand names and resells third-party flash memory products. Micron has an agreement with Eastman Kodak to sell Kodak-branded digital media products.

Going head-to-head with Samsung Electronics and Hynix Semiconductor, the company acquired Numonyx in 2010. Numonyx (previously a joint venture between Intel and STMicroelectronics) specializes in making NOR flash memory chips used in mobile phones. The $1.2 billion stock-swap deal also promises to widen the door for Micron to the multichip package business.

Moving in another direction in 2009, Micron entered the microdisplay market through its acquisition of Displaytech, a designer of display panels and modules based on ferroelectric liquid crystal on silicon technology, which is manufactured with a CMOS process on a single chip.

The volatile semiconductor market hit another cyclical downturn in 2008 and a global economic downturn followed in 2009, making the year particularly painful for chip makers. Micron has reduced its workforce by about 20% and phased out production of 200mm wafers at its Boise plant. The company also cut executive salaries by 20% and suspended its performance-based bonus plan for officers.

Micron is engaged in joint technology development with Taiwan's Nanya Technology. The two memory device makers cooperate on DRAM development and design, focusing on sub-50nm process technologies. That is an advanced level of semiconductor manufacturing, as most microchips are made with features measuring 90nm or larger.

Micron produces photomasks through its MP Mask Technology joint venture with Photronics. Micron and Photronics each own about half of the venture, which sells the majority of its products to Micron.

In 2006 Micron joined with Intel to form a company devoted to NAND flash memory. Each contributed roughly $1.2 billion to create IM Flash Technologies, which manufactures memory at a plant in Utah exclusively for Micron and Intel. Apple prepaid $250 million to each company. Apple uses flash memory in some of its iPod digital music players. Micron owns a 51% interest in IM Flash.

The company sold its MicronPC business (now called MPC Computers), but continues to offer PC memory upgrades to consumers though its Crucial Technology subsidiary.

HISTORY

Micron Technology was founded in 1978 by twins Joe and Ward Parkinson and colleague Doug Pitman in the basement of a dentist's office. They started it as a semiconductor design firm but dreamed of manufacturing their own chips. In 1980 they persuaded several local businessmen, including J. R. Simplot and Allen Noble, to provide financial backing. They built their own production facility and in 1982 sold their first DRAM products.

Micron went public in 1984. The following year Japanese chip makers began dumping chips on the US market to capture market share, causing huge losses for US DRAM makers. Micron filed an antidumping petition with the International Trade Commission, and in 1986 the US and Japan agreed to a semiconductor trade pact to curb dumping.

By 1988 a shortage of memory chips had developed, and Micron cashed in. The company began to diversify into SRAM (static random-access memory) chips and add-in memory products for PCs. (The company wound down its SRAM product line in 2003 in the face of a dire industry slump.)

In the 1990s Micron expanded into PC manufacturing, in part to soften the impact of the volatile cycles of the memory chip industry. It bought PC manufacturer ZEOS in 1995, merging it with two other Micron units to form Micron Electronics, which it took public that year.

Also in 1995 Micron CEO and co-founder Joe Parkinson left the company after a clash with Simplot. Steve Appleton, who had started as a production operator in 1983, became the new CEO. In early 1996 an internal power struggle triggered by longtime director Noble resulted in Appleton's ouster. But within a few days, as several executives loyal to Appleton threatened to revolt, Simplot wooed the CEO back. Noble resigned.

In 2001 the company acquired full ownership of Japan-based DRAM maker KMT Semiconductor when it bought out joint venture partner Kobe Steel for about $350 million. (KMT was subsequently renamed Micron Japan, Ltd.)

Also that year the company acquired Photobit, a small developer of CMOS image sensors, an image-capturing chip that would become widely used in camera phones and digital still cameras, among other uses. The acquisition launched Micron into a new semiconductor business line that would help the company withstand the volatile cycles of the memory chip business.

At the end of 2001 Micron struck a surprise deal with Toshiba to acquire the Japanese giant's Dominion Semiconductor unit in Virginia. (The deal was closed in 2002; Micron paid about $300 million in cash and stock for Dominion.)

The company used a strong balance sheet to grow capacity during the steep industry swoon of the early 21st century, but also stumbled a bit with slow product introductions. Micron surprised the industry in 2002 by announcing an agreement to buy the DRAM operations of Toshiba. The Toshiba purchase, which cost Micron about $300 million in cash and stock, saddled Micron with too much production capacity in the midst of an especially soft DRAM market. Micron rose on improved industry conditions after the chip industry slump ended in 2003, and returned to black ink by 2004.

In 2004 Intel made a $450 million investment in Micron, giving the chip giant rights to a 5% ownership stake in the company.

In mid-2006 Micron acquired flash memory maker Lexar Media for about $850 million. The Lexar acquisition bolstered Micron's position in NAND flash memory.

EXECUTIVES

Chairman and CEO: Steven R. (Steve) Appleton, age 50, $2,499,958 total compensation
President and COO: D. Mark Durcan, age 48, $1,517,795 total compensation
VP Finance and CFO: Ronald C. (Ron) Foster, age 59, $980,010 total compensation
VP Worldwide Sales: Mark W. Adams, age 45, $1,292,511 total compensation
VP Memory: Brian M. Shirley, age 40, $1,014,898 total compensation
VP Worldwide Procurement and Chief Procurement Officer: Steven L (Steve) Thorsen
VP DRAM Development: John F. Schreck
VP DRAM Marketing: Robert A. Feurle
VP Human Resources: Patrick T. (Pat) Otte, age 47
VP Process Development: Scott J. DeBoer
VP Legal Affairs, General Counsel, and Corporate Secretary: Roderic W. Lewis, age 54
VP Memory System Development: Dean A. Klein
VP Investor Relations: Kipp A. Bedard, age 50
VP Information Systems: James E. (Ed) Mahoney
VP Worldwide Wafer Fabrication: Brian J. Shields, age 48
VP NAND Development: Frankie F. Roohparvar, age 45
VP OEM Sales: Michael W. Bokan
VP Backend Manufacturing; President, Italy, Japan, and Puerto Rico: Jay L. Hawkins, age 49
Director Global Government Affairs: Melika D. Carroll, age 36
Auditors: PricewaterhouseCoopers LLP

LOCATIONS

HQ: Micron Technology, Inc.
8000 S. Federal Way, Boise, ID 83716
Phone: 208-368-4000   **Fax:** 208-368-4617
Web: www.micron.com

2009 Sales

	$ mil.	% of total
Asia/Pacific		
China	1,242.0	26
Malaysia	542.0	11
Taiwan	447.0	9
Other countries	990.0	21
US	928.0	19
Europe	470.0	10
Other regions	184.0	4
Total	**4,803.0**	**100**

PRODUCTS/OPERATIONS

2009 Sales

	$ mil.	% of total
Memory	4,290.0	89
Imaging	513.0	11
Total	**4,803.0**	**100**

2009 Sales by Product

	% of total
DRAM memory	50
NAND flash memory	39
CMOS image sensors	11
Total	**100**

Semiconductor Products

Dynamic random-access memories (DRAMs)
  Direct Rambus DRAMs (RDRAMs)
  Synchronous DRAMs (SDRAMs)
  Double data rate synchronous DRAMs (DDR SDRAMs)
Flash memory devices
Memory modules
Photomasks

Selected Operations

Crucial Technology (memory module upgrade supplier)
IM Flash Technologies, LLC (joint venture with Intel; NAND flash memory devices)
Lexar Media, Inc. (memory cards, USB flash drives)
MP Mask Technology Center, LLC (joint venture with Photronics; photomask production)
TECH Semiconductor Singapore Pte. Ltd. (joint venture with Canon and Hewlett-Packard; wafer fabrication)

COMPETITORS

Atmel
Cypress Semiconductor
Elpida Memory
Hitachi Global Storage
Hynix
Integrated Device Technology
Kingston Technology
Mosel Vitelic
Nanya
PNY Technologies
Quantum Corporation
Rambus
Samsung Electronics
SanDisk
Seagate Technology
Sharp Corp.
SMART Modular Technologies
Spansion
Toshiba Semiconductor
Viking Modular Solutions
Western Digital

HISTORICAL FINANCIALS

Company Type: Public

Income Statement

FYE: Thursday nearest August 31

	REVENUE ($ mil.)	NET INCOME ($ mil.)	NET PROFIT MARGIN	EMPLOYEES
8/09	4,803	(1,835)	—	18,200
8/08	5,841	(1,619)	—	22,800
8/07	5,688	(320)	—	23,500
8/06	5,272	408	7.7%	23,500
8/05	4,880	188	3.9%	18,800
Annual Growth	**(0.4%)**	**—**	**—**	**(0.8%)**

2009 Year-End Financials

Debt ratio: 57.5%
Return on equity: —
Cash ($ mil.): 1,485
Current ratio: 1.77
Long-term debt ($ mil.): 2,674
No. of shares (mil.): 994
Dividends
  Yield: 0.0%
  Payout: —
Market value ($ mil.): 7,327

Stock History

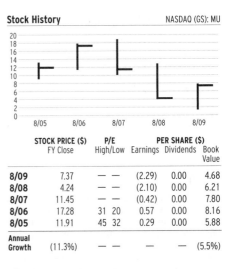

NASDAQ (GS): MU

	STOCK PRICE ($) FY Close	P/E High/Low		PER SHARE ($) Earnings	Dividends	Book Value
8/09	7.37	—	—	(2.29)	0.00	4.68
8/08	4.24	—	—	(2.10)	0.00	6.21
8/07	11.45	—	—	(0.42)	0.00	7.80
8/06	17.28	31	20	0.57	0.00	8.16
8/05	11.91	45	32	0.29	0.00	5.88
Annual Growth	**(11.3%)**	**—**	**—**	**—**	**—**	**(5.5%)**

Microsoft Corporation

Microsoft's ambitions are anything but small. The world's #1 software company provides a variety of products and services, including its ubiquitous Windows operating systems and Office software suite. Microsoft has expanded into markets such as video game consoles, customer relationship management applications, server and storage software, and digital music players. It has also used selective acquisitions to bulk up its presence in markets such as online advertising, mobile devices, and enterprise software.

Microsoft's bid to acquire Yahoo! would have marked the company's largest acquisition in its history, but Yahoo!'s board of directors refused multiple offers from Microsoft (including proposals to buy certain parts of Yahoo!), insisting that the offers undervalued the company.

Microsoft's primary interest in acquiring Yahoo! was to bulk up its search offerings, where the company has struggled to gain ground on Google. Amid persisting rumors that Yahoo! still might give in and sell its search business to the company, in 2009 Microsoft overhauled and rebranded its own search business as a new search engine called bing.com. Shortly after its launch, Yahoo! and Microsoft came to terms on an agreement that would see Microsoft take over the search engine responsibilities on Yahoo!

Competition between Microsoft and Google stands to heat up even further; in 2009 Google announced plans to launch an operating system targeted toward netbooks that will compete directly with Microsoft's OS software. Competition with an older foe, Apple, has also increased, with the companies now butting heads in digital media players and retail outlets, with Microsoft opening its first-ever retail store in late 2009.

In 2009 Microsoft rolled out Windows 7, the latest release of its ubiquitous operating system. Its predecessor was Windows Vista (released in 2007), which was plagued by criticism and negative reviews. Microsoft has high hopes for sales of Windows 7, as many enterprises and large organizations still using Windows XP avoided upgrading to Windows Vista but will likely need to migrate to Windows 7.

While desktop applications and platforms remain the cornerstone of its operations, Microsoft has expanded its product lines, which include video game consoles, its MSN division, digital media players, enterprise software, computer peripherals, and software development tools. By transforming itself from a traditional software provider to a broader technology services and media company, Microsoft hopes to position its operating systems, software, and services as a de facto standard for accessing, communicating, and doing business over the Internet.

HISTORY

Bill Gates founded Microsoft (originally named Micro-soft) in 1975 after dropping out of Harvard at age 19 and teaming with high school friend Paul Allen to sell a version of the programming language BASIC. While Gates was at Harvard, the pair wrote the language for Altair, the first commercial microcomputer. The company was born in an Albuquerque, New Mexico, hotel room and grew by modifying BASIC for other computers.

Gates moved Microsoft to his native Seattle in 1979 and began developing software that let others write programs. The modern PC era dawned in 1980 when IBM chose Microsoft to write the operating system for its new machines. Although hesitant at first, Gates bought QDOS, short for "quick and dirty operating system," for $50,000 from a Seattle programmer, renaming it the Microsoft Disk Operating System (MS-DOS).

Allen fell ill with Hodgkin's disease and left Microsoft in 1983. In the mid-1980s Microsoft introduced Windows, a graphics-based version of MS-DOS that borrowed from rival Apple's Macintosh system. The company went public in 1986, and Gates became the industry's first billionaire a year later. Microsoft introduced Windows NT in 1993 to compete with the UNIX operating system, popular on mainframes and large networks.

The early 1990s brought monopoly charges from inside and outside the industry. In 1995 antitrust concerns scotched a $1.5 billion acquisition of personal finance software maker Intuit.

When the Internet began transforming business practices, holdout Gates at last embraced the medium; the Microsoft Network (MSN) debuted in 1995. That year Microsoft introduced its Internet Explorer Web browser. It also launched Expedia, an online travel site.

The US Justice Department, backed by 18 states, filed antitrust charges in 1998 against the software giant, claiming that it stifled Internet browser competition and limited consumer choice. Gates turned over the president's job to longtime Microsoft executive Steve Ballmer.

In 1999 Microsoft agreed to invest $5 billion for a minority stake in AT&T as part of that company's move to acquire cable operator MediaOne. In addition, Microsoft bought Windows-based technical drawing software specialist Visio for $1.3 billion.

Gates named Ballmer CEO in 2000. Gates remained chairman and added the title of chief software architect. A federal judge's ruling later that year that Microsoft used its monopoly powers to violate antitrust laws left the prospect of two (smaller) Microsofts, a decision the company aggressively appealed. (The initial ruling to split Microsoft into two companies was later struck down, leading to a settlement between the company and the US Justice Department.)

Netscape Communications filed suit in 2002 against Microsoft, seeking unspecified damages and injunctions against the company's alleged antitrust actions. Microsoft settled the suit with Netscape in 2003, agreeing to pay AOL $750 million as part of a larger settlement that includes AOL licensing Microsoft's Internet Explorer browser and its digital media technology.

In 2003 the company declared its first ever dividend for common stock. Microsoft also eliminated stock options, instead moving to a system of distributing shares of its stock directly to employees.

In an attempt to keep pace with Google and other competitors in a consolidating online advertising and search market, the company acquired aQuantive for about $6 billion in 2007. Later in the year Microsoft reached an agreement to acquire a minority stake in social networking site Facebook for $240 million.

Microsoft put many of its legal woes from antitrust issues behind it from 2004-2008, reaching major settlement agreements with Sun Microsystems, Novell, IBM, and RealNetworks.

In 2007-2008 the company also partnered with mobile devices makers such as Hewlett-Packard and Motorola to develop handheld computers and mobile phones that utilize Microsoft Windows Mobile and Windows Media software.

EXECUTIVES

Chairman: William H. (Bill) Gates III, age 54
CEO and Director: Steven A. (Steve) Ballmer, age 54, $1,276,627 total compensation
COO: B. Kevin Turner, age 45, $7,936,018 total compensation
CFO: Peter Klein, age 47
Chief Software Architect: Raymond E. (Ray) Ozzie, age 53
Chief Strategy Officer: David Webster
Chief Research and Strategy Officer: Craig J. Mundie, age 60
Chief Creative Officer: Gayle Troberman
SVP; President, North America Sales and Marketing: Robert H. Youngjohns, age 58
SVP, Emerging Markets: Orlando Ayala, age 53
SVP Technical Strategy: Eric D. Rudder
SVP, General Counsel, and Secretary: Bradford L. (Brad) Smith, age 51
SVP, Windows Core Operating System Division: Jon S. DeVaan, age 48
SVP Mobile Communications Business: Andrew (Andy) Lees
SVP Human Resources: Lisa E. Brummel, age 50
SVP Research: Richard F. (Rick) Rashid, age 57
SVP Developer Division: Sivaramakichenane (Soma) Somasegar
VP and CIO: Tony Scott, age 58
VP Corporate Communications: Frank X. Shaw
Chairman, Microsoft Business Solutions Group: Douglas J. (Doug) Burgum, age 53
President, Entertainment and Devices Division: Robert J. (Robbie) Bach, age 47, $6,212,441 total compensation
President, Microsoft Business Division: Stephen A. Elop, age 46, $11,847,468 total compensation
President, Microsoft International: Jean-Philipe Courtois, age 50
Auditors: Deloitte & Touche LLP

LOCATIONS

HQ: Microsoft Corporation
1 Microsoft Way, Redmond, WA 98052
Phone: 425-882-8080 **Fax:** 425-936-7329
Web: www.microsoft.com

2010 Sales

	$ mil.	% of total
US	36,173	58
Other countries	26,311	42
Total	**62,484**	**100**

PRODUCTS/OPERATIONS

2010 Sales

	$ mil.	% of total
Microsoft Business	18,909	30
Windows & Windows Live	17,788	28
Server & tools	14,878	24
Entertainment & devices	8,114	13
Online services	2,198	4
Unallocated & other	597	1
Total	**62,484**	**100**

Selected Products

Desktop Applications
 Access (relational database management)
 Excel (integrated spreadsheet)
 FrontPage (website publishing)
 MS Office (business productivity software suite)
 Outlook (messaging and collaboration)
 PowerPoint (presentation graphics)
 Project (project scheduling and resource allocation)
 Word (word processing)
Enterprise Software
 BackOffice (server software suite)
 Content Management Server (content management)
 Exchange Server (messaging server)
 Proxy Server (Internet gateway)
 Site Server (website management)
 SQL Server (database and data analysis management)
 Systems Management Server (centralized management)
 Visio (visualization and diagramming suite)
Consumer Software, Services, and Devices
 Flight Simulator (flight simulation software)
 Xbox (video game console)
 Zune (digital media player)

COMPETITORS

Adobe Systems
Amazon.com
Apple Inc.
CA Technologies
EMC
Google
Hewlett-Packard
IBM
Logitech
Nintendo
Nokia
Novell
Oracle
Red Hat
salesforce.com
SAP
Sony
Symbian
Yahoo!

HISTORICAL FINANCIALS

Company Type: Public

Income Statement

FYE: June 30

	REVENUE ($ mil.)	NET INCOME ($ mil.)	NET PROFIT MARGIN	EMPLOYEES
6/10	62,484	18,760	30.0%	89,000
6/09	58,437	14,569	24.9%	93,000
6/08	60,420	17,681	29.3%	91,000
6/07	51,122	14,065	27.5%	79,000
6/06	44,282	12,599	28.5%	71,000
Annual Growth	**9.0%**	**10.5%**	**—**	**5.8%**

2010 Year-End Financials

Debt ratio: 10.7%
Return on equity: 43.8%
Cash ($ mil.): 5,505
Current ratio: 2.13
Long-term debt ($ mil.): 4,939
No. of shares (mil.): 8,654
Dividends
 Yield: 2.3%
 Payout: 24.8%
Market value ($ mil.): 199,119

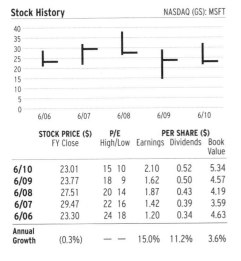

	STOCK PRICE ($)	P/E		PER SHARE ($)		
	FY Close	High/Low	Earnings	Dividends	Book Value
6/10	23.01	15 10	2.10	0.52	5.34
6/09	23.77	18 9	1.62	0.50	4.57
6/08	27.51	20 14	1.87	0.43	4.19
6/07	29.47	22 16	1.42	0.39	3.59
6/06	23.30	24 18	1.20	0.34	4.63
Annual Growth	(0.3%)	— —	15.0%	11.2%	3.6%

Mohawk Industries

Mohawk Industries doesn't mind being trampled under foot. The company is the second-largest maker of commercial and residential carpets, rugs, and other floor coverings in the US (after Shaw Industries) and one of the largest carpet makers in the world. It produces woven and tufted broadloom carpets and rugs under such names as Mohawk, Aladdin, Durkan, Karastan, and Bigelow. Mohawk's Dal-Tile International division is one of the US's largest makers of ceramic tile and stone flooring. Laminate, wood, and vinyl flooring, round out Mohawk's operations. The company sells its wares to about 40,000 customers, including carpet retailers, home centers, mass merchandisers, department stores, and dealers.

Once focused exclusively on carpets and rugs, Mohawk has evolved, adapting itself to changing customer tastes and budgets. It continues to confront the downturn in US home remodeling and new construction markets, as well as weak commercial real estate demand, at home and abroad. Although the company's makeover has resulted in a full-service operation, offering popular alternatives to carpet such as hardwood, laminate, and ceramic tile, 2009 sales slumped. The company has also struggled to reach outside of its premium-priced portfolio by rolling out a do-it-yourself flooring line that mimics the elegant look of materials like marble or limestone, without the coldness, chipping, or costly installation of real stone.

Hooking up with faster-growing, higher-margin businesses has diversified the company's goods. In 2007 Mohawk added the wood flooring assets of Columbia Forest Products for $147 million cash. The deal, which included three plants in the US and one in Malaysia, built upon an established relationship; Columbia manufactures the wood flooring that Mohawk distributes. Turning its attention to the East, Mohawk created a joint venture with China-based Sanfi Ceramics in 2010 to manufacture tile in that country, which some industry insiders believe will see tile sales grow 10% annually.

In addition to the economic environment coupled with building activity, Mohawk's business faces exposure to cyclical energy and raw material costs — the carpet maker uses oil-based textiles. In 2008 the cost of key raw materials jumped as much as 50%; passing the increase on to customers failed as many opted to trade down to lower-quality offerings. The flooring company was forced to shutter a plant in Dahlonega, Georgia, that made yarn for carpeting and employed 137 people. Its Dal-Tile segment cut close to 40% of its workforce at its Gettysburg, Pennsylvania, plant.

Chairman, president, and CEO Jeffrey Lorberbaum owns about a 17% stake in Mohawk. Formerly the company's president, he assumed the CEO helm in 2001.

HISTORY

Mohawk Carpet was an ailing unit of Mohasco until 1988, when division president David Kolb led an LBO to separate Mohawk from its parent and became CEO of the new company. Mohawk traces its origins to the Shuttleworth family who founded the company in Amsterdam, New York, in 1878, setting up their business with 14 second-hand looms imported from England. The company was incorporated as Shuttleworth Brothers in 1902. It introduced the popular Karnak carpet design in 1908.

The firm acquired carpet maker McLeary, Wallin and Crouse and began to consolidate the fragmented carpet industry in the Northeast. The company renamed itself Mohawk Carpet Mills and was the only maker of a complete line of domestic carpets, under the Wilton, Axminster, Velvet, and Chenille styles. Over the next three decades the company pioneered a number of carpet industry firsts: the first texture design (Shuttlepoint), the first sculptured weave (Raleigh), and the first knitted carpet (Woven Interlock).

Mohawk Carpet Mills, like the rest of the industry, moved into synthetics such as nylon and acrylics during the late 1940s and early 1950s. The company merged with Alexander Smith in 1956 to form Mohasco Industries, the largest carpet maker in the world at the time.

By 1980 the company was facing a fiercely competitive market. Mohasco had failed to keep up with changing fashions and was no longer the leading carpet maker. Allied Fibers veteran David Kolb was brought in to turn Mohasco's unprofitable Mohawk division around. He moved the company's headquarters to the carpet-making center of the US, Georgia. Kolb began modernizing equipment and refocused the company on its high-margin carpet products and emphasized direct sales to retailers.

Kolb took Mohawk public in 1992 and began acquiring other carpet makers, including Horizon Industries (carpet mills, 1992), American Rug Craftsmen (household rugs and mats, 1993), and Fieldcrest Cannon's Karastan and Bigelow divisions (carpets and rugs, 1993).

In 1994 Mohawk bought Aladdin Mills, then the fourth-largest carpet maker in the US. Jeffrey Lorberbaum, son of Aladdin founder Alan Lorberbaum, became Mohawk's president and COO.

The company's spending spree continued, acquiring Galaxy Carpet Mills in 1995. In 1996 Mohawk added capacity at all its plants: The

acquisition of Fiber One boosted Mohawk's annual polypropylene extrusion capacity by 40 million pounds, and in 1997 Mohawk added approximately 100 million pounds of annual polypropylene extrusion capacity by acquiring certain assets of Diamond Rug. In 1998 Mohawk purchased American Weavers and floorcoverings maker World Carpets.

In 1999 the company paid $232 million for Image Industries, a unit of Maxim Group that makes residential polyester carpet from recycled plastic bottles, and $98 million for commercial carpet supplier Durkan Patterned Carpets. Mohawk entered the market for hardwood floors by introducing a product line in 2000. Also that year the company purchased the Wovens Division of Crown Crafts (woven throws, bedspreads, and coverlets). Lorberbaum succeeded Kolb as CEO in 2001.

Early in 2002 Mohawk acquired ceramic tile maker Dal-Tile International for $1.5 billion. Dal-Tile added nearly $1 billion in sales (or nearly a quarter of Mohawk's total revenues) and gave the company an automatic stronghold in the hard flooring business. Mohawk followed that up by acquiring bankrupt Burlington Industries' carpet division, Lees Carpet, for about $350 million in 2003.

In 2005 Mohawk acquired Unilin Holding NV, a European manufacturer of laminate flooring for $2.6 billion.

EXECUTIVES

Chairman, President, and CEO: Jeffrey S. Lorberbaum, age 55, $1,499,887 total compensation
COO and Director: W. Christopher (Chris) Wellborn, age 55, $5,080,840 total compensation
VP Finance and CFO: Frank H. Boykin, age 54, $771,449 total compensation
VP, General Counsel, and Assistant Secretary: James T. Lucke, age 49
Corporate Controller and Chief Accounting Officer: James F. Brunk, age 45
Secretary: Barbara M. Goetz
President, Unilin: Bernard P. Thiers, age 54, $1,248,960 total compensation
President, Dal-Tile: Harold G. Turk, age 63
President, Mohawk Flooring: Frank T. Peters, age 61, $728,921 total compensation
Auditors: KPMG LLP

LOCATIONS

HQ: Mohawk Industries, Inc.
160 S. Industrial Blvd., Calhoun, GA 30701
Phone: 706-629-7721   **Fax:** 706-624-3825
Web: www.mohawkind.com

2009 Sales

	$ mil.	% of total
North America	4,516.8	85
Other regions	827.2	15
Total	**5,344.0**	**100**

PRODUCTS/OPERATIONS

2009 Sales

	$ mil.	% of total
Mohawk	2,856.7	53
Dal-Tile	1,426.8	26
Unilin	1,128.3	21
Adjustments	(67.8)	—
Total	**5,344.0**	**100**

Selected Operations

Mohawk
  Bath rugs
  Blankets
  Carpet
  Ceramic tile
  Decorative throws and pillows
  Doormats
  Hardwood flooring
  Laminate flooring
  Resilient flooring
  Rugs
  Woven and tufted rugs
  Woven bedspreads
Dal-Tile
  Ceramic tile
  Glazed floor tile
  Glazed wall tile
  Glazed and unglazed ceramic mosaic tile
  Porcelain tile
  Quarry tile
  Stone products
Unilin
  Insulated roofing
  Laminate flooring
  Wood paneling

Selected Brand Names

Mohawk
  Aladdin
  Bigelow Commercial
  Durkan
  Horizon
  Karastan
  Lees
  Merit
  Mohawk
  Mohawk Home
  Ralph Lauren
Dal-Tile
  American Olean
  Dal-Tile
Unilin
  Century Flooring
  Columbia Flooring
  Mohawk
  Quick-Step
  Universal Flooring

COMPETITORS

Armstrong World Industries
Beaulieu of America
Couristan
Dixie Group
Formica
Guilford Mills
Hollander Home Fashions
Interface, Inc.
Mannington Mills
Perstorp
Shaw Industries
Tarkett Inc.
Wilsonart International

HISTORICAL FINANCIALS

Company Type: Public

Income Statement

FYE: December 31

	REVENUE ($ mil.)	NET INCOME ($ mil.)	NET PROFIT MARGIN	EMPLOYEES
12/09	5,344	(6)	—	27,400
12/08	6,826	(1,458)	—	31,200
12/07	7,586	707	9.3%	36,200
12/06	7,906	456	5.8%	37,100
12/05	6,620	358	5.4%	37,700
Annual Growth	(5.2%)	—	—	(7.7%)

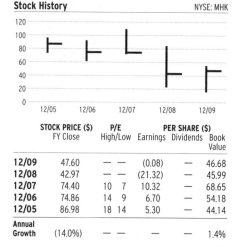

2009 Year-End Financials

Debt ratio: 56.3%
Return on equity: —
Cash ($ mil.): 531
Current ratio: 2.67
Long-term debt ($ mil.): 1,802
No. of shares (mil.): 69
Dividends
  Yield: —
  Payout: —
Market value ($ mil.): 3,264

Stock History

NYSE: MHK

	STOCK PRICE ($) FY Close	P/E High/Low		PER SHARE ($) Earnings	Dividends	Book Value
12/09	47.60	—	—	(0.08)	—	46.68
12/08	42.97	—	—	(21.32)	—	45.99
12/07	74.40	10	7	10.32	—	68.65
12/06	74.86	14	9	6.70	—	54.18
12/05	86.98	18	14	5.30	—	44.14
Annual Growth	(14.0%)	—	—	—	—	1.4%

Molex Incorporated

Molex makes mountains out of connections. The company is one of the world's largest makers of plugs and other electrical connectors. It makes more than 100,000 kinds of electronic, electrical, and fiber-optic connectors and switches. Its miniature plugs, jacks, and other complex connectors are used in a wide variety of products, including automobiles, computers, consumer electronics, home appliances, industrial machinery, and telecommunications equipment.

New product development is vital in a highly competitive industry like electronic components, where rapid advances in technology are required to keep pace with customer demand. Even in a challenging economic environment, Molex continues to introduce new products through internal development or acquisitions As part of its new product strategy, the company looks for adjacent markets that have growth potential, such as the medical imaging, solid state lighting, and solar energy industries.

Like many electronics manufacturers, Molex battled declining sales in 2009 due to weak demand in the mobile phone, consumer electronics, and data networking equipment markets. In fiscal 2010, however, sales across all the company's product lines improved. In consumer electronics, the recovery was led by demand for products such as flat-panel TVs, cameras, and appliances. In the automotive market segment, customers began to replenish their inventories as car sales rose worldwide. Molex has also benefited from the increase in automotive electronics, primarily those used in navigation systems, cameras, mobile communications, and entertainment systems.

Molex responded to the global economic downturn with corporate reorganizations and a variety of cost-cutting measures — including layoffs and plant closures — as well as moving manufacturing operations to lower cost regions outside the US, such as China, Eastern Europe, and Mexico. As the global recession deepened, Molex consolidated smaller plants, focusing instead on larger and more integrated facilities.

In spite of its cost-cutting measures, Molex has continued to invest in certain industries, such as the telecom and base station/wireless markets. The telecom market remains the largest market segment for Molex, representing a quarter of sales. During fiscal 2010, the company acquired China-based Zhenjiang Tean Telecom & Appliance Co., Ltd., enhancing its global position in the design and manufacture of an array of radio frequency (RF) and microwave products.

The Krehbiel family, including co-chairmen Fred and John Jr., grandsons of Molex's founder, owns a controlling interest in the company.

HISTORY

In 1938 Frederick Krehbiel, the son of Swiss Mennonites, on a lark began mixing waste substances coal tar and asbestos. The result was a thick, black plastic material that he called Molex, combining a reference to its "mol"-ded state with the modern-sounding "ex." That year he founded Molex Products Company in Brookfield, Illinois. Soon Molex was being used to make everything from flower pots and salt shakers to moisture-resistant bushings and radiator controls.

Frederick's son, John Sr. (known simply as Senior), joined the company in the 1940s and, recognizing the material's electrical insulating properties, expanded its uses to include coatings for US Army land mines (masking them from enemy detectors) and sheathing for electrical components. Senior also shifted the company's focus to connectors that linked electronic components. Because it was still unproven by the start of WWII, Molex was one of the few plastic substances not restricted to use by the war effort; manufacturers flocked to it as a substitute. (The original Molex product later became obsolete due to newer materials, such as nylon.)

By the 1950s and 1960s, Molex, under Senior's leadership, had targeted its connector sales toward manufacturers of televisions, ranges, washer-dryers, and other consumer electronics and appliances.

When Senior asked his son Frederick to use his foreign experience (he had attended school in England) to the company's advantage, Molex began an international expansion in the late 1960s. Frederick thought it wise to build plants overseas to lower costs and be closer to customers; in 1970 the company opened its first non-US factory, in Japan. Molex went public in 1972 and relocated its headquarters to Lisle, Illinois. Senior's older son, John Krehbiel Jr., was named president in 1975.

By the 1980s Molex was the world's tenth-largest maker of electronic connectors. Long cautious in dealings, the company in the late 1980s went on a spending spree. Molex bought stakes in a variety of small companies to position itself in such lucrative locations as China. In 1989 the company bought an 85% interest in Ulti Mate and gained a stronger connector presence in the military market. Fred Krehbiel was named CEO in 1988.

Chairman John Sr. died in 1993. Molex, which more than doubled its global manufacturing capacity in the 1990s, opened new factories in China and Puerto Rico in 1997. In 1999 Fred and John Jr. became co-chairmen and co-CEOs. Fred and John Jr. handed over the CEO reins to Joseph King in 2001 but remained co-chairmen.

Facing dismal conditions across its target markets in 2001-02, Molex instituted a variety of cost-cutting measures including reductions in executive pay, shortened work-weeks, and a small number of plant closures and layoffs. Molex closed facilities in Puerto Rico, Slovakia, the UK, and the US.

An accounting irregularity in inventory calculations — and the resulting request by company auditors for a management representation letter from a different CFO — led Molex to name an acting CFO in late 2004, make adjustments to 2004 financial results, and delay filing its quarterly SEC report. The auditors also asked that both the CEO and CFO no longer serve as officers of the company and requested additional disclosures; Molex initially refused, and auditor Deloitte & Touche resigned. Late in 2004, however, Molex announced King's resignation and Fred Krehbiel's assumption of the CEO post. (Fred served as CEO until mid-2005, when Martin Slark was named to the position.) Ernst & Young was appointed as auditor.

In 2006 Molex acquired Woodhead Industries (network and electrical infrastructure products) for $256 million. In 2008 it bought AFlextech, a Taiwan-based flexible circuit manufacturer.

EXECUTIVES

Co-Chairman: Frederick A. (Fred) Krehbiel, age 69
Co-Chairman: John H. Krehbiel Jr., age 72
Vice Chairman and CEO: Martin P. Slark, age 54, $4,007,820 total compensation
President and COO: Liam G. McCarthy, age 53, $2,261,175 total compensation
President, Senior Technology Officer, and Director: Frederick L. (Fred) Krehbiel, age 44
CIO: Gary Matula
EVP, CFO, and Treasurer: David D. Johnson, age 53, $1,917,242 total compensation
EVP; President, Global Micro Products Division: Katsumi Hirokawa, age 62, $1,808,207 total compensation
EVP; President, Global Commercial Products Division: James E. Fleischhacker, age 65
EVP; President, Global Sales and Marketing Division: Graham C. Brock, age 55, $1,793,019 total compensation
SVP; President, Global Integrated Products Division: J. Michael Nauman, age 47
SVP Corporate Human Resources: Ana G. Rodriguez
VP, Corporate Controller, and Chief Accounting Officer: K. Travis George, age 40
VP Investor Relations: Steve Martens
Secretary: Mark R. Pacioni
Director Employee Communications and Public Relations: Susan Armitage
Auditors: Ernst & Young LLP

LOCATIONS

HQ: Molex Incorporated
2222 Wellington Ct., Lisle, IL 60532
Phone: 630-969-4550   **Fax:** 630-968-8356
Web: www.molex.com

2010 Sales

	$ mil.	% of total
China	833.8	28
US	568.8	19
Japan	541.1	18
Other countries	1,063.5	35
Total	**3,007.2**	**100**

2010 Sales by Region

	% of total
Asia/Pacific	60
Americas	24
Europe	16
Total	**100**

PRODUCTS/OPERATIONS

2010 Sales

	$ mil.	% of total
Connector	2,177.0	72
Custom & electrical	828.9	28
Corporate & other	1.3	—
Total	**3,007.2**	**100**

2010 Sales by Market

	% of total
Telecommunications	25
Data	22
Consumer	20
Automotive	16
Industrial	14
Other	3
Total	**100**

COMPETITORS

3M	Kyocera
Alps Electric	Methode Electronics
Amphenol	Northrop Grumman
Cooper Industries	Oki Electric
Hirose Electric	Parlex
Hon Hai	Radiall
Hosiden	Thomas & Betts
Innovex	Tyco Electronics
ITT Corp.	Viasystems

HISTORICAL FINANCIALS

Company Type: Public

Income Statement

FYE: June 30

	REVENUE ($ mil.)	NET INCOME ($ mil.)	NET PROFIT MARGIN	EMPLOYEES
6/10	3,007	77	2.6%	35,519
6/09	2,582	(321)	—	25,240
6/08	3,328	215	6.5%	32,160
6/07	3,266	241	7.4%	33,200
6/06	2,861	237	8.3%	32,400
Annual Growth	**1.3%**	**(24.5%)**	**—**	**2.3%**

2010 Year-End Financials

Debt ratio: 9.2%
Return on equity: 3.8%
Cash ($ mil.): 376
Current ratio: 1.95
Long-term debt ($ mil.): 183
No. of shares (mil.): 174
Dividends
  Yield: 3.3%
  Payout: 138.6%
Market value ($ mil.): 3,178

Stock History

NASDAQ (GS): MOLX

	STOCK PRICE ($) FY Close	P/E High/Low		PER SHARE ($) Earnings	Dividends	Book Value
6/10	18.24	54	32	0.44	0.61	11.39
6/09	15.55	—	—	(1.84)	0.61	11.84
6/08	24.41	26	17	1.19	0.45	15.36
6/07	30.01	31	21	1.30	0.30	14.48
6/06	33.57	31	19	1.26	0.22	13.09
Annual Growth	**(14.1%)**	**—**	**—**	**(23.1%)**	**29.0%**	**(3.4%)**

Molson Coors Brewing

Molson Coors Brewing Company (MCBC) drinks with the big boys: The company is among the largest brewers by volume in the world, producing some 19 million hectoliters (502 million US gallons) of beer in 2009. With a portfolio of Molson-branded beers, led by the popular Molson Canadian, it dominates the Canadian beer market, accounting for 40% of the beer sold in that country. In the US, Molson Coors operates through joint venture MillerCoors (42%-owned with SABMiller), which markets Coors, Coors Light, and Molson products and is the second-largest US brewer by volume. MCBC operates in Canada; its international sales are handled by its Molson Coors International (MCI) segment.

Struggling to compete against the US beer juggernaut Anheuser-Busch, Molson Coors joined with UK-based SABMiller to form MillerCoors in 2008. The joint venture was formed in order to gain market share by combining both company's popular brands, while at the same time, boosting profits by centralizing their US marketing, sales, and distribution operations. MillerCoors, which also handles beer sales in Puerto Rico, boasts more than half a dozen breweries including Molson Coors' plant in Golden, Colorado, the world's largest single-site brewery. MillerCoors also brews, packages and ships beer for the Pabst Brewing Company under contract and also brews Miller and Foster's beers for the MCBC's MCI operations.

Also in 2008 Molson Coors and GRUPO MODELO established a joint venture, Modelo Molson Imports (MMI), to import, distribute, and market the Corona and Modelo beer brands in Canada. In addition, the company has agreement with Heineken N.V. to import, market, and sell Heineken products in Canada and with Miller Brewing Company (a US subsidiary of SABMiller) to brew, market, and sell several Miller brands, and distribute and sell imported Miller brands.

Outside North America, the company competes in the UK beer market with its flagship Coors brands, as well as Grolsch, which is produced and distributed through a joint venture with SABMiller's Royal Grolsch. Coors Brewers also markets beers and other beverages (mainly its Zima and Coors brands) in Asia. In China the company in 2010 agreed to pay $40 million to acquire a 51% stake in a new joint venture with the Hebei Si'hai Beer Company. The joint venture will have direct control over the Si'hai brewing operations, including its contract brewing business, and provide opportunities to expand the sales and distribution of a portfolio of emerging brands led by Coors Light and regional Si'hai beers in China.

In 2009 the company formed a joint venture with the Billimoria family (owners of Cobra Beer) whereby Molson Coors owns 50.1% of Cobra's UK operations. Cobra Beer is stocked in more than 6,000 restaurants and in all major supermarkets in the UK.

The Coors family owns about 12% of the company through the Adolph Coors Jr. Trust.

HISTORY

Adolph Coors landed in Baltimore in 1868, a 21-year-old stowaway fleeing Germany's military draft. He worked his way west to Denver, where he bought a bottling company in 1872 and became partners with Jacob Schueler, a local merchant, in 1873. The partners built a brewery in Golden, Colorado, a small town in the nearby Rocky Mountain foothills. Coors became sole owner of the Adolph Coors Company in 1880.

For most of its history, Coors confined its sales to western states. The cost of nationwide distribution was prohibitive because the company used a single brewery, natural brewing methods, and no preservatives; Coors beer was made, transported, and stored under refrigeration, with a shelf life of only one month.

The brewer survived Prohibition by making near beer and malted milk and by entering cement and porcelain chemical ware production. The Coors family built a vertically integrated company that did everything from growing brewing ingredients to pumping the oil that powered its breweries. By 1929, when Adolph died, son Adolph Jr. was running the company. After repeal of the 18th Amendment, beer sales grew steadily in the company's 11-state market.

By the 1960s Coors beer had achieved cult status. Another result of the company's national reputation was that the Coors family had become notoriously private. In 1960 Adolph III was kidnapped and murdered, sending the clan into an even deeper state of secrecy.

Adolph Jr. died in 1970; his son Bill was named chairman and started the country's first aluminum-recycling program. Coors beer was the top seller in 10 of its 11 state markets by 1975, when the company went public. However, sales began to decline as Miller Brewing and Anheuser-Busch introduced new light and super-premium beers. Coors responded by introducing its own light and super-premium brands and expanding its market area to 16 states.

In the late 1970s and 1980s, the company began rapid expansion while enduring boycotts and strikes due to alleged discriminatory labor practices. The brewer eventually developed progressive employment policies.

It spun off its packaging and ceramics firm ACX Technologies in 1992. Also that year it introduced Zima, a clear, malt-based brew. Leo Kiely became the first president of the company's brewing operations from outside the Coors family in 1993. The company also cut its workforce by nearly 700 positions; the severance program cost $70 million and resulted in its first loss in more than 10 years.

The company formed a partnership with Molson Breweries and Foster's in 1997 to manage the distribution of its brands in Canada. (Foster's later sold its stake to Molson.)

In 2000 Peter Coors (Adolph's great-grandson) was named president and CEO of Adolph Coors Company and chairman of Coors Brewing Company. In 2001 the brewer formed a joint venture with Molson to distribute Molson's beers in the US. In 2002 Belgium's Interbrew (now known as Anheuser-Busch InBev) sold the Carling division of its Bass Brewers holding to Coors for nearly $1.8 billion.

With the 2005 merger of Coors and Molson to form Molson Coors, the company added control of three more well-known brands: Coors Light, Carling, and Molson Canadian. Following the merger, 11 top executives left the company.

The company sold a 68% stake in its Brazilian brewing operation to FEMSA Cerveza in 2006.

EXECUTIVES

Chairman: Peter H. (Pete) Coors, age 63, $3,760,201 total compensation
Vice Chairman: Andrew T. Molson, age 42
President, CEO, and Director: Peter Swinburn, age 57, $9,422,784 total compensation
CFO: Stewart Glendinning, age 44, $3,153,563 total compensation
Chief Legal Officer and Corporate Secretary: Samuel D. (Sam) Walker, age 51
Chief Compliance Officer: Sherri Heckel Kuhlmann
Chief Legal Officer, Molson Coors Canada: Kelly Brown, age 39
Chief People Officer: Ralph P. Hargrow, age 58
Global Chief Supply Chain Officer: Gregory L. Wade, age 61
Controller and Chief Accounting Officer: William G. Waters, age 41
President and CEO, Molson Coors Canada: David (Dave) Perkins, age 56, $3,787,453 total compensation
President and CEO, Molson Canada: Kevin T. Boyce, age 52, $5,224,133 total compensation
President and CEO, Molson Coors Brewing Company (UK) Limited: Mark Hunter, age 47, $4,641,333 total compensation
President, Molson Coors International: Krishnan (Kandy) Anand, age 52
Investor Relations: Julie Frye
Auditors: PricewaterhouseCoopers LLP

LOCATIONS

HQ: Molson Coors Brewing Company
1225 17th St., Ste. 3200, Denver, CO 80202
Phone: 303-927-2337   **Fax:** 303-277-5415
Web: www.molsoncoors.com

2009 Sales

	$ mil.	% of total
Canada	1,687.0	56
UK	1,180.3	39
US & territories	46.3	2
Other countries	118.8	3
Total	**3,032.4**	**100**

PRODUCTS/OPERATIONS

Selected Brands
Canada
  Company owned
    Carling
    Coors Light
    Creemore Springs
    Molson Canadian
    Molson Dry
    Molson Export
    Rickard's Red Ale
  Licensed
    Amstel Brouwerij BV
      Amstel Light
      Heineken
      Murphy's
    Asahi Breweries, Ltd.
      Asahi
      Asahi Select
    Carlton & United Beverages Limited
      Foster's
      Foster's Special Bitter
    Cerveceria Modelo S.A. de C.V.
      Corona
    Miller Brewing Company
      Milwaukee's Best
      Miller Genuine Draft
      Milwaukee's Best Dry

UK
  Company owned
    C2
    Caffrey's
    Carling
    Coors Fine Light Beer
    Reef
    Screams
    Stones
    Worthington
  Licensed
    Boon Rawd Trading International
      Singha Beer
    SAB Miller
      Grolsch
US
  Company owned
    Blue Moon Belgian White Ale
    Coors
    Coors Light
    Coors Non-Alcoholic
    Keystone
    Keystone Ice
  Licensed
    George Killian's Irish Red
    Zima XXX

COMPETITORS

Anchor Brewers	Kingway Brewery
Anheuser-Busch InBev	Lion Nathan
Boston Beer	Michigan Brewing
Brick Brewing	Pabst
Carlsberg	Sleeman Breweries
Diageo	Sprecher
Foster's Group	Tsingtao
Gambrinus	Yanjing
Heineken	

HISTORICAL FINANCIALS

Company Type: Public

Income Statement

FYE: Last Sunday in December

	REVENUE ($ mil.)	NET INCOME ($ mil.)	NET PROFIT MARGIN	EMPLOYEES
12/09	3,032	723	23.8%	14,540
12/08	4,774	400	8.4%	14,180
12/07	6,191	497	8.0%	9,700
12/06	5,845	361	6.2%	9,550
12/05	5,507	139	2.5%	10,200
Annual Growth	**(13.9%)**	**51.1%**	**—**	**9.3%**

2009 Year-End Financials

Debt ratio: 20.0%
Return on equity: 11.1%
Cash ($ mil.): 734
Current ratio: 1.12
Long-term debt ($ mil.): 1,413
No. of shares (mil.): 186
Dividends
  Yield: 2.0%
  Payout: 23.8%
Market value ($ mil.): 8,396

Stock History

NYSE: TAP

	STOCK PRICE ($) FY Close	P/E High/Low		PER SHARE ($) Earnings	Dividends	Book Value
12/09	45.16	13	8	3.87	0.92	38.08
12/08	48.92	28	17	2.09	0.76	32.16
12/07	51.62	21	14	2.74	0.64	38.45
12/06	38.22	18	15	2.09	0.64	31.29
12/05	33.49	47	34	0.85	0.64	28.64
Annual Growth	**7.8%**	**—**	**—**	**46.1%**	**9.5%**	**7.4%**

Monsanto Company

An ear of corn the size of a Trident missile? Not quite, but Monsanto *is* all about bioengineered crops. The company helps farmers grow more crops by applying biotechnology and genomics to seeds and herbicides. It produces genetically altered seeds that tolerate Roundup (its flagship product and the world's #1 herbicide) and resist bugs. Monsanto estimates that more than 70% of the world's herbicide-resistant crops bear its stamp. The company also produces Asgrow, DEKALB, Deltapine, and Seminis seeds. During the past decade, Monsanto remade itself into a seed and biotech company, as opposed to one focused on agrochemicals.

The 2007 acquisition of Delta and Pine Land only furthered the seed build-up; the company is the #1 cotton seed producer in the US. The Delta deal, which was for $1.5 billion, required Monsanto to sell its Stoneville cottonseed business to Bayer CropScience for about $300 million. Also in 2007 the company formed a $1.5 billion joint R&D initiative with BASF to develop genetically modified crops with an emphasis on meeting the demand for biofuels.

The company acquired Netherlands-based De Ruiter Seeds Group in 2008 for some $850 million. De Ruiter sells to the greenhouse market, offering seeds for vegetable crops such as tomatoes, cucumbers, and melons.

Later in the year, it acquired Central America's largest corn seed company, Marmot, which operates Semillas Cristiani Burkard (SCB) in Guatemala City, Guatemala.

In 2009 the company partnered with Dole, the world's largest fresh produce company, to develop vegetables that are more appealing to consumers. Using plant breeding techniques, the companies hope to improve the nutrition, flavor, color, texture, taste, and aroma of broccoli, cauliflower, lettuce, and spinach.

Turning to wheat, in 2009 Monsanto acquired WestBred from Barkley Seed. The acquisition of the grain-seed developer will help Monsanto develop new seed technologies to improve crop yields for the amber, waving grain. Also that year, it sold its sunflower seed business to Syngenta Seeds. Late in 2009 the company agreed to purchase Pfizer's Chesterfield Village Research Center in Missouri for $435 million.

Investment firm FMR owns about 10% of the company; Marsico Capital Management owns 5%.

HISTORY

Realizing he had only a German source for saccharin and foreseeing growing US demand for the product, in 1901 drug firm buyer John Queeny spent $5,000 to found Monsanto Chemical Works (using his wife's maiden name) to make saccharin in St. Louis. Monsanto soon added caffeine, vanillin, antiseptic phenol, and aspirin; it went public in 1927.

Queeny's son Edgar became president in 1928. He branched out into rubber additives and plastics through acquisitions. In 1943 Monsanto began making styrene monomer used to produce the US Army's first synthetic rubber tires.

Monsanto and American Viscose joined forces to form synthetic-fiber firm Chemstrand in 1949 (Monsanto bought it in 1961). Chemstrand also developed Acrilan fibers (1952) and the synthetic surface AstroTurf (first used commercially in Houston's Astrodome, 1966). In 1954 Monsanto

and Bayer formed a joint venture to develop urethane foams (sold to Bayer, 1967). Monsanto debuted the herbicides Lasso (1969) and Roundup (1973) and stopped making saccharin in 1972.

Monsanto bought drugmaker G. D. Searle (founded 1868) in 1985, inheriting lawsuits relating to its Copper-7 contraceptive IUD. It also got the rights to artificial sweetener aspartame (NutraSweet). In 1993 Monsanto bought Chevron's Ortho lawn and garden business for $416 million. It launched its first biotech product (to increase milk yields) the next year.

Searle's Robert Shapiro became CEO in 1995 and set out to create genetically altered foods. That year Monsanto bought Merck's specialty chemicals unit, Syntex (birth-control pills), and 50% of biotech firm Calgene (it bought the rest in 1997).

In 1996 Monsanto bought a stake in DEKALB Genetics (it bought the rest in 1998). It bought Holden's Foundation Seeds (corn seed) in 1997 and spun off chemicals unit Solutia. After calling off a $35 million merger with drugmaker American Home Products in 1998, Monsanto laid off workers and sold Ortho to The Scotts Company (now Scotts Miracle-Gro).

In 1999 Monsanto launched Celebrex, an arthritis drug that set new prescription records. Meanwhile, concerns about genetically modified foods prompted bans in the UK and Brazil (and later in other countries). Negative public reaction led Monsanto to stop developing seeds with a terminator gene that rendered them sterile.

Late in 1999 activists stepped up protests over bioengineered crops, and lawyers filed a class-action suit alleging inadequate testing and unfair price influence.

Monsanto merged with Pharmacia & Upjohn in 2000, and the new entity, Pharmacia Corporation (with Monsanto now a wholly owned subsidiary), set about restructuring, selling Monsanto's NutraSweet, Equal, and Canderel sweeteners, as well as its biogums (food texturing and processing) business. The "new" Monsanto was now focused solely on using advanced technology to grow better crops — the pharmaceutical and other operations of the old Monsanto have been assumed by Pharmacia. Consumer apprehension over so-called "Frankenfoods" and the like prompted Pharmacia to spin off about 15% of Monsanto to the public in 2000; the company spun off the remainder as a dividend to shareholders in 2002.

After two disappointing years of results, in December 2002 CEO Hendrik Verfaillie resigned and chairman Frank AtLee assumed the position. In late May 2003 COO Hugh Grant was named president and CEO. The company elected Grant chairman at its annual meeting in October of that year.

In a more significant move Monsanto announced in the spring of 2005 that it had acquired fruit and vegetable seed maker Seminis for about $1.4 billion in cash and assumed debt. Seminis is among the world's largest fruit and vegetable seed producers, with about 3,500 varieties of seed sold in more than 150 countries. It continues as a wholly owned subsidiary of Monsanto with its own management remaining in place. The deal furthered the company's recent emphasis on growing its seeds business and changing its focus from agricultural chemicals.

Later in 2005 the company purchased the cotton business of Emergent Genetics for $300 million, giving Monsanto a foothold in the cotton seed business.

EXECUTIVES

Chairman, President, and CEO: Hugh Grant, age 51, $9,133,836 total compensation
EVP and CFO: Carl M. Casale, age 48, $3,532,681 total compensation
EVP and CTO: Robert T. (Robb) Fraley, age 56, $5,194,476 total compensation
EVP Seeds and Traits: Brett D. Begemann, age 48, $3,149,087 total compensation
EVP Manufacturing: Mark J. Leidy, age 53, $3,906,784 total compensation
EVP Sustainability and Corporate Affairs: Gerald A. (Jerry) Steiner, age 49
EVP Human Resources: Steven C. Mizell, age 49
SVP, Chief of Staff, and Community Relations: Janet M. Holloway, age 55
SVP, Secretary, and General Counsel: David F. (Dave) Snively, age 55
VP Vegetable Business: Consuelo E. Madere, age 48
VP Investor Relations: Scarlett Lee Foster, age 52
VP and Treasurer: Thomas D. (Tom) Hartley, age 50
VP Crop Protection: Kerry J. Preete, age 49
VP and Controller: Nicole M. Ringenberg, age 48
President, American Seeds: Michael Stern
President and Managing Director, Monsanto Brazil: Andre Dias
Auditors: Deloitte & Touche LLP

LOCATIONS

HQ: Monsanto Company
800 N. Lindbergh Blvd., St. Louis, MO 63167
Phone: 314-694-1000   **Fax:** 314-694-8394
Web: www.monsanto.com

2009 Sales

	$ mil.	% of total
US	6,434	55
Europe & Africa	1,763	15
Brazil	1,419	12
Argentina	597	5
Asia/Pacific	568	5
Canada	457	4
Mexico	332	3
Other	154	1
Total	**11,724**	**100**

PRODUCTS/OPERATIONS

2009 Sales

	$ mil.	% of total
Seeds & genomics		
Corn seed & traits	4,113	35
Soybean seed & traits	1,448	12
Vegetable seeds	808	7
Cotton seeds & traits	466	4
Other crop seeds & traits	462	4
Agricultural productivity		
Roundup & other glyphosate-based herbicides	3,527	30
All other agricultural products	900	8
Total	**11,724**	**100**

COMPETITORS

ADM
BASF SE
Bayer CropScience
Dow AgroSciences
DuPont Agriculture & Nutrition
Exelixis Plant Sciences
FMC
GROWMARK
NC Hybrids
Nippon Soda
Origin Agritech
Pfister Hybrid Corn
Pioneer Hi-Bred
Sakata Seed
Scotts Miracle-Gro
Syngenta
Syngenta Seeds

HISTORICAL FINANCIALS

Company Type: Public

Income Statement

FYE: August 31

	REVENUE ($ mil.)	NET INCOME ($ mil.)	NET PROFIT MARGIN	EMPLOYEES
8/09	11,724	2,109	18.0%	27,000
8/08	11,365	2,024	17.8%	26,400
8/07	8,563	993	11.6%	23,600
8/06	7,344	695	9.5%	17,500
8/05	6,294	255	4.1%	16,500
Annual Growth	16.8%	69.6%	—	13.1%

2009 Year-End Financials

Debt ratio: 17.1%
Return on equity: 21.7%
Cash ($ mil.): 1,956
Current ratio: 2.10
Long-term debt ($ mil.): 1,724

No. of shares (mil.): 540
Dividends
  Yield: 1.2%
  Payout: 26.6%
Market value ($ mil.): 45,333

Stock History

NYSE: MON

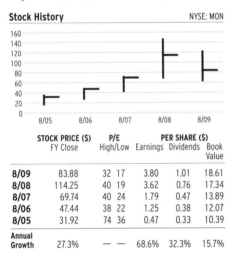

	STOCK PRICE ($) FY Close	P/E High/Low		PER SHARE ($) Earnings	Dividends	Book Value
8/09	83.88	32	17	3.80	1.01	18.61
8/08	114.25	40	19	3.62	0.76	17.34
8/07	69.74	40	24	1.79	0.47	13.89
8/06	47.44	38	22	1.25	0.38	12.07
8/05	31.92	74	36	0.47	0.33	10.39
Annual Growth	27.3%	—	—	68.6%	32.3%	15.7%

Moog Inc.

Moog (rhymes with "rogue") rules with its precision-control components and systems used in aerospace products, industrial machinery, and medical equipment. Servoactuators, Moog's core product, receive electrical signals from computers and then perform specific actions. Using its servoactuators, Moog builds flight and control systems for commercial and military aircraft, hydraulic and electrical controls for plastic-injection and blow-molding machines, and control systems for satellites and spacecraft. The company also makes medical devices including infusion therapy pumps, slip rings for CT scanners, and motors used in devices for sleep apnea.

Responding to the global recession, the company has restructured to get costs in line with lower sales and operating margins. Moog has reduced R&D spending, increased its contract loss reserves, and implemented workforce reductions primarily affecting staff in the US, Europe, and the Philippines. Business related to US military contracts (including sales to contractors such as Boeing and Lockheed Martin) accounts for more than a third of Moog's sales.

With defense spending on the rise, Moog saw an increase in sales related to its military aircraft components. In particular, sales in its Aircraft Controls

segment were boosted by the company's participation in the F-35 Joint Strike Fighter project (officially named the Lightning II) and the V-22 Osprey program. Aiming to build upon the uptick, Moog acquired the Wolverhampton, UK-based flight control actuation business of GE Aviation Systems, a unit of General Electric Co., in 2009 for $90 million. Moog also bought UK-based Fernau Avionics that year, adding a broad range of ground-based air navigation aids used to provide bearing and range information and extending its reach to customers in Europe and Asia.

While military-related sales were strong, they were not enough to offset declines in commercial aircraft sales brought on by the worldwide economic downturn. Moog saw sales drop in all of its major markets except power generation and wind energy, as businesses cut back on spending for capital equipment. Its acquisition of Germany-based LTi REEnery, which specializes in the design and manufacture of drive systems for electric rotor blades used in wind turbines, gave the company a boost in the alternative energy market and partially offset the negative impact on results of its plastics making, metal forming, and steel mill machinery businesses. In addition, Moog bought Invensys, a maker of pitch control and rotor blade monitoring systems for wind turbines.

The company expanded its products for the security and surveillance markets in early 2009 with the purchase of Videolarm Inc. (cameras, networking products, and protective housings for surveillance systems) for $45 million in cash.

Moog also expanded its Medical Devices segment through two acquisitions in 2009, adding syringe-style pumps, contract disposables manufacturing, and microbiology, toxicology, and sterilization services.

Employees hold about one-third of Moog through an employee compensation trust and the company's retirement plan. The founding Moog family controls a 5% voting stake in the company.

HISTORY

Engineer Bill Moog (second cousin of the creator of the Moog synthesizer) invented an electrohydraulic servovalve while working for Cornell Aeronautical Laboratories. He left in 1951 to start his own company, selling his products to missile builders and aircraft flight-control makers. In 1959 the business moved into the industrial machinery market. International expansion began in Germany in 1965. Sales slowed by the late 1980s as the end of the Cold War brought military cutbacks. Differences with the board caused Bill Moog to step down in 1988, trading in his company shares for its industrial controls unit — Moog Controls. (Moog headed the unit until his retirement in 1994; he died three years later.)

Flat sales continued, and in 1992 Moog closed three plants after the US government canceled or cut back on fighter and missile projects. Sales rebounded in 1995 due to a strong European market and the 1994 purchase of the hydraulic and mechanical actuation product lines of AlliedSignal (now Honeywell International).

Preparing for growth, Moog bought back its former Moog Controls unit and Parker Hannifin's satellite propellant valve product line in 1996. Moog also entered a joint venture to make industrial components with European integrated hydraulic manifold systems maker Hydrolux.

In 1998 Moog bought Schaeffer Magnetics (electromechanical actuation), Raytheon's Montek unit (flight controls), a 75% interest in Hydrolux, and a 66% interest in Microset (electronic controls, Italy).

Moog continued to grow through acquisitions in 2000 by purchasing Schenck Pegasus (industrial servovalves) from Carl B. Schenck AG and Vickers Electric (electric motors and controllers) from Eaton. Despite the acquisition activity, Moog's sales in 2000 had only a 2% gain in growth after years of double digit gains — primarily because of declines in the F-15 jet fighter and B-2 bomber production programs and declines in aircraft sales at Boeing.

Moog began supplying parts for the new F-35 Joint Strike Fighter in 2002. Late in 2003 the company bought Northrop Grumman's PolyScience division, a maker of data communications and motion control devices.

Moog expanded via acquisitions in 2005. In July of that year the company acquired Kaydon's Power and Data Transmission Products segment, a maker of electrical and fiber-optic products for a variety of applications. In August 2005 Moog bought Amsterdam-based FCS Control Systems, a designer and manufacturer of high-fidelity electromechanical and electrohydraulic flight and vehicle simulation equipment, as well as structural test systems for aerospace and automotive applications.

In 2006 the company paid $75 million for the assets of Curlin Medical, a maker of infusion pumps, and two affiliated companies.

Early in 2007 Moog purchased ZEVEX International, a maker of medical devices. ZEVEX became a subsidiary of Moog under its medical devices division. Later that year the company picked up cooling and air-moving systems maker Thermal Control Products.

EXECUTIVES

Chairman, President, and CEO: Robert T. (Bob) Brady, age 69, $1,742,883 total compensation
Vice Chairman and VP Strategy and Technology: Richard A. Aubrecht, age 65
CFO: John R. Scannell, age 46, $955,961 total compensation
EVP, Chief Administrative Officer, and Director: Joe C. Green, age 68, $1,449,364 total compensation
VP; President, Medical Devices Group: Martin J. Berardi, age 52, $1,269,263 total compensation
VP; President, Space and Defense Group: Jay K. Hennig, age 49
VP; President, International Group: Stephen A. Huckvale, age 60
VP; President, Components Group: Lawrence J. (Larry) Ball, age 55
VP Aircraft Group: Warren C. Johnson, age 50, $1,419,650 total compensation
VP Finance: Donald R. Fishback, age 53
VP Human Resources: John Grabon
VP; General Manager, Europe: Harald E. Seiffer, age 50
VP and Deputy General Manager, Aircraft Controls Group: Sasidhar Eranki, age 55
Controller and Principal Accounting Officer: Jennifer Walter, age 38
Secretary: John B. Drenning, age 72
Auditors: Ernst & Young LLP

LOCATIONS

HQ: Moog Inc.
Jamison Road, East Aurora, NY 14052
Phone: 716-652-2000   **Fax:** 716-687-5969
Web: www.moog.com

2009 Sales

	$ mil.	% of total
US	1,118.2	61
Germany	98.7	5
Japan	93.0	5
UK	62.7	3
Other countries	476.3	26
Total	**1,848.9**	**100**

PRODUCTS/OPERATIONS

2009 Sales

	$ mil.	% of total
Aircraft controls	663.5	36
Industrial systems	454.6	24
Components	345.5	19
Space & defense controls	274.5	15
Medical devices	110.8	6
Total	**1,848.9**	**100**

Selected Products

Aircraft controls
  Active vibration control systems
  Engine control servovalves and servoactuators
  Flight control servovalves
  Primary and secondary flight control actuation
  Stabilizer trim controls and elevator feel systems
  Wingfold and weapons bay actuation systems
Industrial systems
  Actuation packages
  Brushless servomotors and programmable servodrives
  Customized, integrated manifold valves
  Electronic controls for specialized automated
    machinery
  Electronically actuated motion simulators and
    platforms
  Linear and rotary electromechanical servoactuator
    packages
  Servovalves and proportional valves
Components
  Fiber-optic rotary joints
  Motors
  Slip rings
Space and defense controls
  Electric propulsion propellant management systems
    for satellites
  Fin controls for missiles
  Satellite propulsion control products
    Integrated manifolds
    Isolation valves
    Regulators
    Thruster valves
  Solar array drives and antenna pointing mechanisms
  Thrust vectoring controls
Medical devices
  Disposable ambulatory pumps
  Electronic ambulatory pumps
  Enteral feeding pumps
  Surgical handpieces
  Ultrasonic and optical sensors

COMPETITORS

Abbott Labs
Aeroflex
Aerojet
Alcon
Alliant Techsystems
Allied Motion Technologies
AMETEK
Astronautics
Axsys
B. Braun Melsungen
Baxter International
Bosch Rexroth
Cardinal Health
CareFusion
Covidien
Curtiss-Wright
Danaher
Eaton
Fresenius
GE
Goodrich Corp.
Hamilton Sundstrand
Honeywell International
Hospira
I-Flow
Indramat
Parker Hannifin
Pelco
Raytheon
S.A.B.C.A.
Siemens AG
Sierra Nevada Corp
Smiths Medical
Teijin
Textron
UQM Technologies
Whittaker Controls
Yaskawa Electric

HISTORICAL FINANCIALS

Company Type: Public

Income Statement

FYE: Last Saturday in September

	REVENUE ($ mil.)	NET INCOME ($ mil.)	NET PROFIT MARGIN	EMPLOYEES
9/09	1,849	85	4.6%	10,005
9/08	1,903	119	6.3%	8,844
9/07	1,558	101	6.5%	8,364
9/06	1,307	81	6.2%	7,273
9/05	1,051	65	6.2%	6,662
Annual Growth	15.2%	7.0%	—	10.7%

2009 Year-End Financials

Debt ratio: 76.5%
Return on equity: 8.3%
Cash ($ mil.): 81
Current ratio: 2.71
Long-term debt ($ mil.): 815
No. of shares (mil.): 45
Dividends
  Yield: 0.0%
  Payout: —
Market value ($ mil.): 1,338

Stock History

NYSE: MOG.A.A

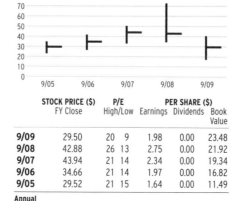

	STOCK PRICE ($) FY Close	P/E High/Low	PER SHARE ($) Earnings	PER SHARE ($) Dividends	Book Value
9/09	29.50	20 9	1.98	0.00	23.48
9/08	42.88	26 13	2.75	0.00	21.92
9/07	43.94	21 14	2.34	0.00	19.34
9/06	34.66	21 14	1.97	0.00	16.82
9/05	29.52	21 15	1.64	0.00	11.49
Annual Growth	(0.0%)	— —	4.8%	—	19.6%

Morgan Stanley

One of the world's top investment banks, Morgan Stanley serves up a smorgasbord of financial services. The company operates in three primary business segments: institutional securities (capital raising, corporate lending, financial advisory services for corporate and institutional investors); global wealth management group (brokerage and investment advisory services, financial planning for individual investors and businesses); and asset management (asset management services and products including alternative investments, equity, fixed income; merchant banking; investment activities).

Over the last couple of years, Morgan Stanley has been repositioning its asset management business. In 2009 the company merged its wealth management operations with those of Citigroup to form a new firm called Morgan Stanley Smith Barney. Morgan Stanley owns 51% of the combined company.

At the height of the financial crisis in 2008, the Federal Reserve mandated that Morgan Stanley and Goldman Sachs (the other remaining independent bulge-bracket US investment bank) convert to a bank holding company structure. The structure subjects them to tighter scrutiny but enables them to acquire a commercial bank to shore up their balance sheets if need be.

Morgan Stanley has taken advantage of its new bank holding status and is forming a private banking business to serve its wealthy Morgan Stanley Smith Barney customers.

In order to shore up the big banks during the financial crisis, the US government invested $250 billion in healthy banks to help them jumpstart their operations; Morgan Stanley received about $10 billion of that. The company announced in late 2008 that it would cut its staff by 10% in an effort to reduce costs. Morgan Stanley repaid the $10 billion in 2009.

It sold its retail asset management business, including Van Kampen, to Invesco for some $1.5 billion in 2010 in order to focus on its wealthiest clients and institutional investors.

Morgan Stanley also shook up its top leadership. John Mack stepped down as CEO in early 2010; he remains chairman. James Gorman, the firm's co-president, succeeded Mack.

Japanese bank Mitsubshi UFJ paid some $9 billion for a 21% stake in Morgan Stanley in 2008, making it the company's largest shareholder. Morgan Stanley and Mitsubsishi UFJ also combined their brokerage operations in Japan.

HISTORY

In 1934 the Glass-Steagall Act required the J. P. Morgan bank (now part of JPMorgan Chase & Co.) to sell its securities-related activities. The next year Henry Morgan, Harold Stanley, and others established Morgan Stanley as an investment bank. Capitalizing on old ties to major corporations, the firm handled $1 billion in issues its first year. By 1941, when it joined the NYSE, it had managed 25% of all bond issues underwritten since Glass-Steagall took effect.

In the 1950s Morgan Stanley was known for handling large issues alone. Clients included General Motors, U.S. Steel, General Electric, and DuPont.

The firm avoided the merger wave of the 1960s, but in the early 1970s it formed Wall

Street's first mergers and acquisitions (M&A) department. In 1974 Morgan Stanley handled its first hostile takeover, International Nickel's (now Inco) buy of ESB, the world's #1 battery maker.

Morgan Stanley went public in 1986. By 1994 it was talking to possible merger mates, including Dean Witter, and finally merged with Dean Witter, Discover in 1997, creating Morgan Stanley Dean Witter & Co.

The San Francisco brokerage founded by Dean Witter in 1924 had remained regional for 40 years, serving wealthy customers. In 1977 the firm merged with Reynolds Securities. The new company, Dean Witter Reynolds, became the #2 US brokerage after Merrill Lynch and one of the top 10 US underwriters.

Dean Witter needed capital in the early 1980s and sold itself to Sears, which hoped to turn it into a financial Allstate. Sears put in a retail-oriented management team and tried to shoehorn Dean Witter into in-store brokerages. Sears' indifference to the investment side hobbled operations. The Discover card, introduced by Sears and Dean Witter in 1986, was a hit, but by the late 1980s it was obvious Sears would never be a financial giant. The retailer spun off Allstate Insurance and the newly renamed Dean Witter, Discover in 1993.

In 2002 Morgan Stanley dropped "Dean Witter" from its name. When regulatory scrutiny fell on the mutual fund industry, Morgan Stanley was charged with failing to adequately disclose the incentives its brokers and managers received for selling certain funds. In 2003 the firm agreed to pay a $50 million fine and adopt a "plain English" approach to informing investors about its product fees and broker compensation.

In mid-2004 the firm agreed to pay $54 million to settle a sex discrimination lawsuit filed on behalf of more than 300 female employees who claimed they were denied promotions and salary raises.

Unhappy with the firm's performance, eight former Morgan Stanley executives (dubbed the Group of Eight) publicly called for the ouster of chairman and CEO Philip Purcell in 2005; Purcell was replaced by John Mack. That same year a jury ordered Morgan Stanley to pay more than $1.5 billion to Ronald Perelman, now the chairman of cosmetics giant Revlon. (Morgan Stanley in 2003 rejected an offer from Perelman to settle the dispute for $20 million.) Perelman contended that Morgan Stanley withheld knowledge of massive accounting fraud at appliance maker Sunbeam when he sold his camping gear firm, Coleman, to that company for some $1.5 billion in cash and stock in 1998; a Florida appeals court overturned the verdict in 2007.

In 2006 the firm agreed to pay a $15 million fine to settle charges that it was uncooperative and did not produce documents during investigations performed by the Securities and Exchange Commission (SEC). In addition, the company settled charges (while not pleading guilty) that it falsely claimed to arbitration claimants and regulators that it lost e-mails on September 11, 2001; it agreed to pay $12.5 million in 2007.

In 2007 Morgan Stanley spun off its Discover credit card operations, the last remnant of the company's merger with the venerable Dean Witter at the end of the previous century.

After the company wrote down more than $9 billion in mortgage-related investments in 2007, it was compelled to sell part of itself to an investment arm of the Chinese government, China Investment Corp., for some $5 billion. The equity units included in the deal could be converted to a nearly 10% stake in Morgan Stanley.

EXECUTIVES

Chairman: John J. Mack, age 65, $1,235,097 total compensation
Vice Chairman: Gary G. Lynch, age 59, $4,017,611 total compensation
President, CEO, and Director: James P. Gorman, age 51
COO: Thomas R. (Tom) Nides, age 48, $3,143,382 total compensation
EVP and CFO: Ruth Porat, age 52
CIO: Ivan Freeman
Finance Director: Paul C. Wirth
Chief Legal Officer: Francis P. Barron, age 59
Chief Risk Officer: Kenneth M. deRegt, age 54
Managing Director: John W. Pratt
Chairman, Morgan Stanley International: Walid Chammah, age 55, $1,204,598 total compensation
President and COO, Morgan Stanley Smith Barney: Charles Johnston
President and CIO, Morgan Stanley Real Estate Investing: Jay Mantz
Co-President, Institutional Securities: Colm Kelleher, age 52, $7,442,682 total compensation
Co-President, Institutional Securities: Paul J. Taubman, age 48
Global Head Private Wealth Management: Michael (Mike) Armstrong
Management Committee; General Counsel Americas; Global Head Litigation and General Counsel, Morgan Stanley Smith Barney: Eric F. Grossman, age 43
Auditors: Deloitte & Touche LLP

LOCATIONS

HQ: Morgan Stanley
1585 Broadway, New York, NY 10036
Phone: 212-761-4000   **Fax:** 212-761-0086
Web: www.morganstanley.com

PRODUCTS/OPERATIONS

2009 Sales

	$ mil.	% of total
Interest & dividends	7,702	26
Principal transactions	6,393	21
Asset management, distribution & administration fees	5,884	19
Investment banking	5,019	17
Commissions	4,234	14
Other	838	3
Total	**30,070**	**100**

COMPETITORS

Brown Brothers Harriman
Charles Schwab
CIBC
Citigroup
Citigroup Global Markets
Deutsche Bank
FMR
Franklin Resources
Goldman Sachs
JPMorgan Chase
Lehman Brothers
Marsh & McLennan
Merrill Lynch
MF Global
Nomura Securities
Oppenheimer Holdings
Raymond James Financial
State Street
T. Rowe Price
TD Bank
UBS
Wells Fargo Securities

HISTORICAL FINANCIALS

Company Type: Public

Income Statement

FYE: December 31

	REVENUE ($ mil.)	NET INCOME ($ mil.)	NET PROFIT MARGIN	EMPLOYEES
12/09*	30,070	1,406	4.7%	61,388
11/08	62,262	1,707	2.7%	46,964
11/07	85,328	3,209	3.8%	48,256
11/06	76,551	7,472	9.8%	55,310
11/05	51,770	4,890	9.4%	53,218
Annual Growth	**(12.7%)**	**(26.8%)**	**—**	**3.6%**

*Fiscal year change

2009 Year-End Financials

Debt ratio: 521.4%   No. of shares (mil.): 1,397
Return on equity: 4.1%   Dividends
Cash ($ mil.): 55,703   Yield: 1.4%
Current ratio: —   Payout: —
Long-term debt ($ mil.): 193,374   Market value ($ mil.): 41,350

Stock History

NYSE: MS

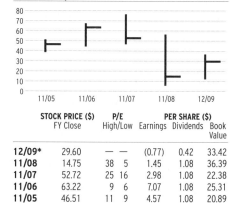

	STOCK PRICE ($) FY Close	P/E High/Low		Earnings	PER SHARE ($) Dividends	Book Value
12/09*	29.60	—	—	(0.77)	0.42	33.42
11/08	14.75	38	5	1.45	1.08	36.39
11/07	52.72	25	16	2.98	1.08	22.38
11/06	63.22	9	6	7.07	1.08	25.31
11/05	46.51	11	9	4.57	1.08	20.89
Annual Growth	**(10.7%)**	**—**	**—**	**—**	**(21.0%)**	**12.5%**

*Fiscal year change

Motorola, Inc.

Once a perennial favorite in the cell phone game, Motorola has lost some steam in that area as mobile phone users enjoy a wider selection of phones offered by industry leaders Nokia and Samsung, as well as Apple, Research in Motion, and LG. The company's home and network products include set-top boxes, digital video recorders, video broadcasting equipment, and IP telephony gear. Its products for business and government clients consist of broadband wireless systems used to build private voice and data networks and public safety communications systems. Motorola said in 2010 that it will spin off its handset and set-top box units into a new company called Motorola Mobility.

The company, which developed and sold the first mobile phone, has struggled to regain its momentum in the wireless handset market.

Motorola's cell phone business has lost about $5 billion in the past three years and contributed to annual losses for the company during the same period; the company hopes that the spinoff will give its remaining business a better chance for success. The restructuring, slated for completion in early 2011, would reduce the company's size by about two-thirds, and see it take on the name Motorola Solutions. Its products will include public safety radios, telecom network gear, and handheld scanners.

As part of this reorganization, the company agreed in 2010 to sell much of its wireless network infrastructure business to Nokia Siemens Networks for $1.2 billion in cash. The deal will include Motorola's product lines based on GSM, CDMA, and WiMAX wireless standards.

Motorola and its competitors were hit hard by the slumping global economy of 2008-2009, as growth slowed in emerging markets and phone replacement sales in mature markets dipped as consumers sharply curtailed their spending. The company responded by embarking on a series of cost-cutting restructuring moves during those two years that included limits on executive compensation, a freeze on pension plans, and a series of job cuts that eliminated about 8,000 positions

Motorola, originator of the clamshell handset, had its biggest hit with the RAZR phone model (introduced in 2003), which sold more units than any other wireless handset in history until it was surpassed by the iPhone in 2008. This milestone underscored the lack of smartphones in Motorola's product line up, a fact that contributed to the company's faltering position in the market.

The company has had to play catch-up in this area, but it has gained some ground since the introduction of a line of phones based on the Google Android operating system.

The company in 2010 acquired Israel-based video content management systems maker BitBand in a move to strengthen its IPTV product line and customer base, particularly in Europe where it wants to raise the profile of its video-on-demand products.

HISTORY

Born entrepreneur Paul Galvin started his first business as a popcorn vendor when he was 13. In 1928, at age 33, he founded Galvin Manufacturing in Chicago to make battery eliminators, so early radios could run on household current instead of batteries. The following year Galvin began making car radio receivers and trying to develop a mobile radio for the police. In 1940 the company developed the first handheld two-way radio for the US Army.

In 1947 Galvin renamed the company Motorola, after its car radios. In the late 1950s Motorola started making integrated circuits and microprocessors, stepping outside its auto industry mainstay. When Galvin died in 1959, his son Robert became CEO. The firm's purchase that year of a hospital communications systems maker led it to produce some of the first pagers.

Motorola began to change focus in the 1970s. The company invested in the data communications hardware market by acquiring Codex (1977) and Universal Data Systems (1978). In 1977 Motorola began developing its first cellular phone system. By 1985 sales of its cellular systems had taken off. In 1987 Motorola made its last car radio.

In 1990 Motorola organized the 66-satellite Iridium communication system (which went online in 1998). In 1996 China adopted Motorola's technology as its national paging standard.

The founder's grandson, Christopher Galvin, took over as CEO in 1997 on the heels of a major drop in profits — the result of increasing competition in the cellular phone market and a downturn in semiconductor sales. He began a restructuring that included the sale of noncore assets and the layoffs of 15,000 employees.

In 2000 Motorola acquired General Instrument in a deal valued at $17 billion. Also that year Motorola agreed to outsource about 15% of its manufacturing to Flextronics. As part of the $30 billion deal, Motorola took a small stake in Flextronics. In early 2001 Motorola cut more than 30,000 jobs amid slow sales of semiconductors and mobile phones. Motorola also cut back on its manufacturing outsourcing and sold its stake in Flextronics back to that company.

Faced with continuing weak sales, the company continued to make layoffs through 2002. Motorola ceased production of pagers in 2002 to focus on the development of new wireless handsets, but continued to license its pager technology to other manufacturers.

After disagreeing with the board of directors about Motorola's future in late 2003, Chris Galvin retired as chairman and CEO, and Ed Zander, the former head of Sun Microsystems, took over in 2004, becoming the first person from outside the Galvin family to lead the company.

In 2004 Motorola spun off its semiconductor operations as Freescale Semiconductor, a publicly traded company. Motorola's other restructuring efforts included selling some IT services units, shifting some production to contractors, and using extensive layoffs to reduce costs.

In 2007 activist investor Carl Icahn bought up Motorola shares, about 6% in total, in a successful attempt to obtain seats on the company's board of directors.

Early in 2008 Zander was replaced by COO and communications industry veteran Greg Brown; Zander stayed on as chairman. Former AT&T CEO David Dorman was named chairman upon Zander's retirement in mid-2008, and Sanjay Jha joined Brown as co-CEO that same year. The company also bought Symbol Technologies, a manufacturer of bar-code scanners and other devices, for about $3.9 billion. The Symbol purchase formed the core of Motorola's enterprise wireless products business.

In 2009 Motorola bought the iDEN (integrated digital enhanced network) business of RadioFrame Networks.

EXECUTIVES

Chairman: David W. Dorman, age 56
Co-CEO and Director; CEO, Mobile Devices and Home Business: Sanjay K. Jha, age 46, $3,774,885 total compensation
Co-CEO and Director; CEO, Enterprise Mobility Solutions and Networks: Gregory Q. (Greg) Brown, age 49, $8,462,544 total compensation
EVP; President, Enterprise Mobility Solutions: Eugene A. (Gene) Delaney, age 53, $6,602,006 total compensation
EVP, General Counsel, and Secretary: A. Peter Lawson, age 63, $3,294,503 total compensation
SVP Finance and CFO: Edward J. (Ed) Fitzpatrick, age 43, $3,677,391 total compensation
Corporate VP and Chief Accounting Officer: John K. Wozniak, age 38

SVP and General Manager, Networks: Bruce Brda
SVP Home & Networks Mobility: Fred Wright
SVP and General Manager: John Cipolla
SVP Human Resources: Michele A. Carlin, age 48
SVP Mobile Devices: Alain Mutricy
SVP and CIO: Leslie Jones
SVP Global Go-to-Market, Mobile Devices Business: Mark Shockley
SVP and General Manager, Motorola Mobile Devices and Home: Joe Cozzolino
SVP Public Affairs and Communications: Karen P. Tandy, age 56
VP Investor Relations: Dean Lindroth
President, Mobility: Daniel M. (Dan) Moloney, age 50, $3,556,737 total compensation
Auditors: KPMG LLP

LOCATIONS

HQ: Motorola, Inc.
   1303 E. Algonquin Rd., Schaumburg, IL 60196
Phone: 847-576-5000
Web: www.motorola.com

2009 Sales

	% of total
US	54
Asia	
China	6
Other countries	11
Latin America	11
Europe	9
Other regions	9
Total	**100**

PRODUCTS/OPERATIONS

2009 Sales

	% of total
Home & networks mobility	36
Mobile devices	32
Enterprise mobility	32
Total	**100**

Business Segments

Mobile Devices (wireless handsets and accessories)
Home and Networks Mobility (video and Internet products, systems for consumers and carriers)
Enterprise Mobility (radio, voice, data communications products for businesses and government customers)

COMPETITORS

Alcatel-Lucent	Intermec
Apple Inc.	Kenwood
ARRIS	LG Group
Cisco Systems	NEC
Delphi Automotive	Nokia
DENSO	Nokia Siemens Networks
EADS	Robert Bosch
EF Johnson Technologies	Samsung Group
Ericsson	Sony Ericsson Mobile
Harmonic	Technicolor
Harris Corp.	Visteon
Honeywell International	ZTE
Huawei Technologies	

HISTORICAL FINANCIALS

Company Type: Public

Income Statement				FYE: December 31
	REVENUE ($ mil.)	NET INCOME ($ mil.)	NET PROFIT MARGIN	EMPLOYEES
12/09	22,044	(28)	—	53,000
12/08	30,146	(4,244)	—	64,000
12/07	36,622	(49)	—	66,000
12/06	42,879	3,661	8.5%	66,000
12/05	36,843	4,578	12.4%	69,000
Annual Growth	**(12.1%)**	**—**	**—**	**(6.4%)**

Stock History NYSE: MOT

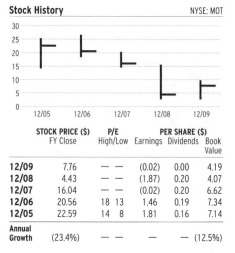

	STOCK PRICE ($) FY Close	P/E High/Low		PER SHARE ($) Earnings	Dividends	Book Value
12/09	7.76	—	—	(0.02)	0.00	4.19
12/08	4.43	—	—	(1.87)	0.20	4.07
12/07	16.04	—	—	(0.02)	0.20	6.62
12/06	20.56	18	13	1.46	0.19	7.34
12/05	22.59	14	8	1.81	0.16	7.14
Annual Growth	(23.4%)	—	—	—	—	(12.5%)

Mutual of Omaha Insurance Company

In the wild kingdom that is today's insurance industry, Mutual of Omaha Insurance Company wants to distinguish itself from the pack. The company provides individual, group, and employee benefits products through a range of affiliated companies. It offers Medicare supplement, disability, and long-term care coverage as well as life insurance and annuities through its United of Omaha Life Insurance unit. Mutual of Omaha, which is owned by its policyholders, offers its products through both its agency sales force and independent agents, as well as direct marketing.

The company's Mutual of Omaha Investor Services offers brokerage services, pension plans, and mutual funds, while the Mutual of Omaha Bank operates regionally.

Mutual of Omaha has remixed its health care insurance products. In 2007 it sold its employer-based group health business to Coventry Health Care, but it kept its employer-based life, disability, dental, and supplemental health coverage. It then launched its Medicare Supplement insurance products. It also agreed in 2010 to sell its employer stop-loss line of business to HM Life Insurance. The sale is another step in the company's decision to move away from health insurance sales.

Taking advantage of changes in regulatory restrictions, Mutual of Omaha is expanding into banking through acquisitions. Its key markets are rapidly growing cities where it already has high numbers of insurance customers. Operating as Mutual of Omaha Bank, it provides commercial and personal banking through locations in 10 states. The company intends to eventually offer Internet banking nationwide.

Like all insurance companies, Mutual of Omaha saw investment losses in 2008, but it was not badly shaken as it had not invested in the riskier products that undermined other companies.

The company's sponsorship of the long-running *Mutual of Omaha's Wild Kingdom* introduced it to a generation of Americans. Recognizing that the connection remained strong, the company has revived the television series which now runs on Discovery Communications' Animal Planet cable channel.

HISTORY

Charter Mutual Benefit Health & Accident Association got its start in Omaha, Nebraska, in 1909. A year later half of its founders quit, leaving a group headed by pharmaceuticals businessman H. S. Weller in charge. He tapped C. C. Criss as principal operating officer and general manager. Criss brought in his wife, Mabel, and brother Neil to help run the business.

Formed to offer accident and disability protection at a time when there were many fraudulent benefit societies, Charter Mutual Benefit Health faced consumer resistance that slowed growth in its first 10 years. By 1920 it was licensed in only nine states. Experience helped it refine its products and improve its policies' comprehensibility. By 1924 the firm had more than doubled its penetration, gaining licensing in 24 states.

The US was nearing the depths of the Depression when Weller died in 1932. Criss succeeded him as president. The stock crash had brought a steep decline in the value of the firm's asset base, and premium income dropped (accompanied by an increase in claims). Even so, Mutual Benefit Health expanded its agency force, the scope of its benefits, and its operations. It went into Canada in 1935 and began a campaign to obtain licensing throughout the US.

By 1939 the company was licensed in all 48 states. During WWII it wrote coverage for civilians killed or injured in acts of war in the US (including Hawaii) and Canada. With paranoia running high and consumer goods in short supply, the insurance industry boomed during the war (and payouts on stateside act-of-war claims were low to nonexistent). Criss retired in 1949.

Gearing up its postwar sales efforts, in 1950 the company changed its name to Mutual of Omaha and adopted its distinctive chieftain logo. During the 1950s it added specialty accident and group medical coverage. In 1963 it made an advertising coup when it launched *Mutual of Omaha's Wild Kingdom*. Hosted by zoo director Marlin Perkins and, later, naturalist sidekick Jim Fowler, the show was one of the most popular nature programs of all time. Later that decade the company added investment management to its services.

Changes in the health care industry during the 1990s led Mutual of Omaha to de-emphasize its traditional indemnity products in favor of building managed care alternatives. In 1993 it joined with Alegent Health System to form managed care company Preferred HealthAlliance. Mutual of Omaha also stopped writing new major medical coverage in such states as California, Florida, New Jersey, and New York, where state laws made providing health care onerous. This led the company to cut its workforce by about 10% in 1996.

In 1999 it bought out Alegent's interest in their joint venture and entered the credit card business (offering First USA Visa cards). The firm also lifted its $25,000 limit for coverage of AIDS-related illnesses (its standard limit is $1 million); the company had been sued over the policy.

In the new millennium, the company enhanced its products targeted towards seniors as well as introducing more flexible personal health care plans.

Focusing on its core individual and employer-based lines, in 2003 the company sold the renewal rights to all of its Omaha Property and Casualty Co. (OPAC) policies to Fidelity National Financial. After the actual operations had been transferred, in 2005 the UK's Beazley Group bought up the OPAC operating license. In 2006 the company sold its innowave water purification subsidiary to Waterlogic International.

EXECUTIVES

Chairman and CEO; Chairman and CEO, United of Omaha Life Insurance: Daniel P. (Dan) Neary, age 58
EVP, CFO, and Treasurer: David A. Diamond, age 54
EVP and General Counsel: Richard C. Anderl
EVP Information Services: James T. Blackledge
EVP Customer Service: Madeline R. Rucker
EVP Corporate Services: Stacy A. Scholtz
EVP Group Benefit Services: Daniel P. Martin
EVP Individual Financial Services; President, United World Life Insurance: Michael C. (Mike) Weekly
EVP and Chief Investment Officer: Richard A. (Rick) Witt
SVP and Corporate Chief Actuary: Paul Ochsner
SVP Individual Underwriting: Bill Vigliotte
SVP Private Investment Sourcing and Trading: Curt Caldwell
President, Mutual of Omaha Foundation: Christine Johnson
President and CEO, Omaha Financial Holdings; Chairman and CEO, Mutual of Omaha Bank: Jeffrey R. (Jeff) Schmid
Auditors: Deloitte & Touche LLP

LOCATIONS

HQ: Mutual of Omaha Insurance Company
Mutual of Omaha Plaza, Omaha, NE 68175
Phone: 402-342-7600 **Fax:** 402-351-2775
Web: www.mutualofomaha.com

PRODUCTS/OPERATIONS

2008 Revenues

	$ mil.	% of total
Health & accident	1,908.3	45
Life & annuity	1,322.6	31
Net investment income	909.7	22
Net realized investment losses	(133.7)	—
Other	65.9	2
Total	**4,072.8**	**100**

Selected Subsidiaries and Affiliates

Companion Life Insurance Company (insurance in New York)
Mutual of Omaha Investor Services, Inc. (mutual funds)
Omaha Financial Holdings (banking)
United of Omaha Life Insurance Company
United World Life Insurance Company

COMPETITORS

Aetna
Allstate
Assurant
CIGNA
Guardian Life
John Hancock Financial Services
MassMutual
MetLife

New York Life
Northwestern Mutual
Physicians Mutual Insurance
Prudential
State Farm
Unum Group
USAA

HISTORICAL FINANCIALS

Company Type: Mutual company

Income Statement
FYE: December 31

	ASSETS ($ mil.)	NET INCOME ($ mil.)	INCOME AS % OF ASSETS	EMPLOYEES
12/08	21,246	47	0.2%	—
12/07	19,447	217	1.1%	—
12/06	19,008	166	0.9%	4,619
12/05	18,374	121	0.7%	5,053
12/04	18,540	125	0.7%	—
Annual Growth	3.5%	(21.7%)	—	(8.6%)

2008 Year-End Financials

Equity as % of assets: —
Return on assets: 0.2%
Return on equity: —

Long-term debt ($ mil.): 570
Sales ($ mil.): 4,073

Net Income History

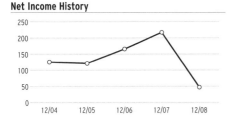

	12/04	12/05	12/06	12/07	12/08

Mylan Inc.

Mylan knows you may not recognize the names of their drugs, but it hopes you'll appreciate their prices. Through Mylan Pharmaceuticals, Generics (UK), and other subsidiaries, the company is one of the top global manufacturers of prescription generic drugs. Mylan's pharmaceutical cabinet holds antibiotics, antidepressants, anti-inflammatories, and laxatives in a range of delivery forms. Its specialty division makes branded nebulized and injectable drugs.

In addition to finished drugs, Mylan is a top producer of active pharmaceutical ingredients (APIs) for generic drugs through its Matrix subsidiary. The company's customers in 140 countries include wholesalers, distributors, retailers, and government agencies.

Mylan's specialty pharmaceutical division includes Dey whose top selling product is the EpiPen Auto-Injector, used to treat severe allergic reactions. The epinephrine auto-injector is a matter of life and death for some, and commands more than 95% of the US market share. Other products marketed by Dey include the anti-depressant EMSAM transdermal patch that was developed by sibling subsidiary Somerset Pharmaceuticals and manufactured by another sibling, Mylan Technologies.

A key piece of Mylan's strategy is to be the first to file with the FDA to manufacture generic versions of popular drugs as they become fair game. Being first in line gives a generics manufacturer a three-month window of exclusivity, while its competitors have to wait before they can produce an equivalent product.

Mylan formed a partnership with Indian biotech firm Biocon in 2009 to expand into the growing field of generic biotech drugs. While biologic drugs are trickier to copy and finicky to produce, they do promise considerable profits. The two companies will co-develop and market biologic therapies in numerous countries.

Back as recently as 2006, Mylan Laboratories was a mid-sized generics manufacturer making modest acquisitions. However, the company more than doubled its size in less than three years. To get there, it made a pair of ambitious acquisitions.

It got a running start in 2006 when it first bought 20% of Matrix Laboratories. Then, with an eye on global expansion Mylan secured control of 51% of the company in 2007. With 10 manufacturing facilities, Matrix was one of the largest companies in India and the world's largest supplier of the generic anti-retroviral pharmaceutical ingredients used to treat HIV/AIDS. Additionally, by having its own API producer in-house, Mylan sought to gain an edge over competitors, who must obtain their ingredients from outside manufacturers. Over the following two years Mylan slowly increased its holdings to 97% of Matrix.

Mylan then spent nearly $7 billion in 2007 to acquire Generics (UK) Ltd. from Merck. Mylan won out in a bidding war that included rivals Actavis Group and Teva, with the prize being a business almost twice Mylan's size. Following the acquisition, the company changed its name from Mylan Laboratories to just plain Mylan.

After a pause in acquisitions, in 2010 Mylan paid private-equity firm RoundTable Healthcare Partners $550 million in cash to acquire Bioniche Pharma Holdings. Adding Bioniche increased Mylan's presence in the North American injectables market. Following the acquisition, Mylan combined Bioniche with its existing unit dose business, UDL Laboratories, to form Mylan Institutional. The business now serves US institutional customers including group purchasing organizations, hospitals, and long-term care facilities.

Robert Coury was tapped to be the company's CEO in 2002 and in 2009 was chosen to also serve as its chairman.

HISTORY

Milan Puskar and a colleague founded Milan as a drug distributor in 1961 and shifted to vitamin manufacturing in 1965. It added generic penicillin in 1966 and tetracycline three years later. The next year Parke-Davis (now part of Pfizer) became the first major drug company to purchase Milan's products. Puskar left in 1972 after a management dispute, and the company changed its name to Mylan. The company went public in 1973. Chairman Roy McKnight brought Puskar back as president in 1976 when the two bought control of Mylan. In 1984 the company launched its first proprietary drug. Mylan became the #1 independent drugmaker in the US in 1985, specializing in generics.

In 1988 Mylan formed research joint venture Somerset Pharmaceuticals with Circa Pharmaceuticals (later bought by Watson Pharmaceuticals). The venture helped produce the successful anti-Parkinson's disease drug Eldepryl. The firm absorbed dermatological products maker Dow Hickam Pharmaceuticals in 1991 and drug-delivery specialist Bertek in 1993.

Puskar became chairman and CEO after McKnight died in 1993. Mylan launched cimetidine, a generic ulcer drug, in 1994, and by the following year it held 39% of the market for all new cimetidine prescriptions. Mylan got FDA approval for Etodolac, a generic version of arthritis drug Lodine, in 1997. The next year it bought Penederm Inc., maker of topical antifungal treatment Mentax.

In 2000 Mylan paid $135 million to settle price-fixing and antitrust charges relating to popular antianxiety drugs lorazepam and chlorazepate (generic versions of Ativan and Tranxene). On a happier note that year, the FDA approved the sale of Mylan's generic version of GlaxoSmithKline's Wellbutrin antidepressant. The following year, the company's generic version of Merck's cholesterol drug Mevacor was approved by the FDA, and in 2002 its version of Eli Lilly's Prozac won FDA approval.

The company's proposed acquisition of troubled King Pharmaceuticals rankled investor Carl Icahn, a minority stakeholder in Mylan. In late November 2004, Icahn made a buyout offer of Mylan to end its bid to buy King. That bid became moot after asset manager Perry Corp., led by Richard Perry, increased its stake in Mylan just enough to edge out Icahn as largest shareholder. However, Icahn filed suit against the company and Perry Corp., making charges of hedging to allow Mylan to complete its acquisition of King. The scuffle between shareholders was for naught.

At the end of February 2005, Mylan and King terminated their deal, and Perry announced plans to unload his entire near-10% stake in the company. Ichan dropped his lawsuit against Perry, and then re-set his sights on a hostile buyout of Mylan. In retaliation, the company bought back 25% of its stock and closed its Mylan Bertek division — the branded drug unit that would have benefited most from the King Pharmaceuticals acquisition. In the end, Mylan incurred $22.9 million in expenses related to the fizzled plan during its 2005 fiscal year.

EXECUTIVES

Chairman and CEO: Robert J. Coury, age 49, $16,481,387 total compensation
Vice Chairman: Rodney L. (Rod) Piatt, age 57
President: Heather Bresch, age 40, $4,850,166 total compensation
EVP and COO: Rajiv Malik, age 49, $3,449,797 total compensation
EVP and CFO: John D. Sheehan, age 49
EVP and Global General Counsel: Joe Haggerty
SVP; President, North America: Harry A. (Hal) Korman, age 52, $1,701,918 total compensation
SVP, Chief Accounting Officer, and Corporate Controller: Daniel C. Rizzo Jr., age 47, $1,206,668 total compensation
SVP and Global CIO: Greg Sheldon
SVP and Global Head Human Biologics: Patrick Vink
SVP and Chief Compliance Officer: Brian Roman
SVP and Global Head Human Resources: David A. Lillback
SVP and Treasurer: Brian Byala
VP Investor Relations: Kris King
VP Global Public Affairs: Michael Laffin
President, Europe, Middle East, and Africa: Didier Barret, age 45, $2,153,833 total compensation
President, Dey Pharma: Carolyn Myers, age 52
CEO and Managing Director, Matrix Laboratories: S. Srinivasan
Senior Director Government Relations: David Rice
Auditors: Deloitte & Touche LLP

LOCATIONS

HQ: Mylan Inc.
1500 Corporate Dr., Canonsburg, PA 15317
Phone: 724-514-1800   **Fax:** 724-514-1870
Web: www.mylan.com

2009 Sales

	% of total
Americas	
US	47
Other	3
Europe	37
Asia	13
Total	**100**

PRODUCTS/OPERATIONS

2009 Sales

	$ mil.	% of total
Generic drugs	4,677.8	92
Specialty drugs	414.9	8
Total	**5,092.7**	**100**

Selected Generic Products

Albuterol (Proventil, Ventolin)
Alprazolam (Xanax)
Cimetidine (Tagamet)
Diazepam (Valium)
Diltiazem Hydrochloride (Cardizem)
Estradiol (Estrace)
Fentanyl (Duragesic)
Fluoxetine (Prozac)
Haloperidol (Haldol)
Lorazepam (Ativan)
Lovastatin (Mevacor)
Metformin hydrochloride (Glucophage)
Naproxen (Naprosyn)
Nifedipine (Procardia)
Omeprazole (Prilosec)
Propanolol hydrochloride (Inderal)
Selegiline hydrochloride (Eldepryl)
Sertraline hydrochloride (Zoloft)
Tizanidine hydrochloride (Zanaflex)

COMPETITORS

Abbott Labs	Novartis
Bayer AG	Par Pharmaceutical
Bayer Schering Pharma	Companies
Bristol-Myers Squibb	Perrigo
Daiichi Sankyo	Pfizer
Dr. Reddy's	Roche Holding
Eisai	Roxane Laboratories
Eli Lilly	Sandoz International
GlaxoSmithKline	GmbH
Johnson & Johnson	Teva Pharmaceuticals
King Pharmaceuticals	Watson Pharmaceuticals
Merck	

HISTORICAL FINANCIALS

Company Type: Public

Income Statement

FYE: December 31

	REVENUE ($ mil.)	NET INCOME ($ mil.)	NET PROFIT MARGIN	EMPLOYEES
12/09	5,093	233	4.6%	15,500
12/08*	5,138	(181)	—	15,000
3/07	1,612	217	13.5%	6,400
3/06	1,257	185	14.7%	2,900
3/05	1,253	204	16.2%	3,000
Annual Growth	**42.0%**	**3.4%**	**—**	**50.8%**

*Fiscal year change

2009 Year-End Financials

Debt ratio: 159.3%
Return on equity: —
Cash ($ mil.): 381
Current ratio: 1.91
Long-term debt ($ mil.): 4,985

No. of shares (mil.): 309
Dividends
Yield: 0.0%
Payout: —
Market value ($ mil.): 5,702

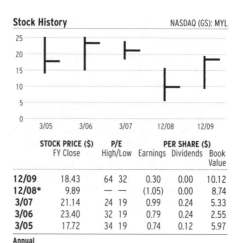

Stock History

NASDAQ (GS): MYL

	STOCK PRICE ($) FY Close	P/E High/Low		PER SHARE ($) Earnings	Dividends	Book Value
12/09	18.43	64	32	0.30	0.00	10.12
12/08*	9.89	—	—	(1.05)	0.00	8.74
3/07	21.14	24	19	0.99	0.24	5.33
3/06	23.40	32	19	0.79	0.24	2.55
3/05	17.72	34	19	0.74	0.12	5.97
Annual Growth	**1.0%**	**—**	**—**	**(20.2%)**	**—**	**14.1%**

*Fiscal year change

NACCO Industries

An unlikely combination of coal mines, toasters, and forklifts propels NACCO Industries. The holding company's independent operating subsidiaries do business in a diverse set of industries. NACCO Materials Handling Group manufactures and leases Hyster and Yale lift trucks and parts. Its Hamilton Beach (formerly Hamilton Beach/Proctor-Silex) subsidiary makes small kitchen appliances and commercial foodservice products; the Kitchen Collection operates retail kitchenware and gourmet food stores. North American Coal mines lignite coal in the US and sells it to utilities. NACCO Industries got its start back in 1913 as The Cleveland & Western Coal Company and has diversified its business through acquisitions.

Although it got its start in mining, the coal segment of NACCO — which also includes dragline operations at limestone quarries and oil and gas mineral royalty income — is now the company's smallest. The majority of NACCO's sales come from lift trucks, which are manufactured at plants located in the Americas, Europe, and Asia/Pacific. Its Materials Handling segment also includes the manufacture of aftermarket parts, repair services, and rental revenues. Most lift trucks and parts are sold through dealers or through a National Accounts sales program that targets large customers that operate across dealer territories. NACCO also has a small number of company-owned retail dealerships and rental companies acquired to boost its presence in specific geographic markets.

The flagship of NACCO's housewares segment, Hamilton Beach (HB) is a leading maker of small electric appliances such as blenders, coffeemakers, indoor grills, mixers, toasters, and slow cookers. It also sells Proctor Silex (appliances) and TrueAir (air purifiers) brand products. HB makes private-label products as well, selling GE-brand appliances to Wal-Mart, Michael Graves-brand products to Target, and Food Network-brand products to Kohls. Housewares also includes The Kitchen Collection and Le Gourmet Chef stores, located in factory outlet and traditional malls across the US.

With such diversified interests, the company regularly reorganizes and consolidates manufacturing operations, such as it has done in the US, Mexico, and Europe. Facing tough industry conditions across all of its segments in 2008 and 2009, NACCO moved to aggressively control costs through measures that included workforce reductions and suspended employee-benefits programs. The company, however, increased the capital provided to its subsidiaries and lowered the management fees it charges in order to provide adequate liquidity for their operations.

NACCO's chairman, president, and CEO, Alfred Rankin Jr., controls about 11% of the company.

HISTORY

King Coal ruled the early part of the 20th century, and Frank Taplin was ready to be a loyal subject. In 1913 the 38-year-old Cleveland native, formerly an office boy for John D. Rockefeller and later a VP at Standard Oil Company, formed distributor Cleveland & Western Coal. Four years later, spurred by WWI, the company bought three mines and began producing coal. It incorporated in 1925 as North American Coal Corporation (NACCO).

Taplin continued building his company until his death in 1938. Henry Schmidt took over as chairman in 1942, just as the company's sluggish sales began to rise, buoyed by demand for coal during WWII.

When home-heating coal sales declined, NACCO targeted electric utilities, signing its first long-term utility sales contract in 1951 with Ohio Edison. By 1952 NACCO had four underground coal-mining subsidiaries. During this time, strip mining became more common because of its efficiency and low cost. NACCO went public in 1956, and a year later bought its first lignite field for strip mining.

Profits stayed healthy in the 1980s despite frequent strikes and strict mine-safety laws. Pollution issues dimmed coal's prospects, and concerns about a potential buyout led Frank Taplin's heirs (sons Frank and Thomas, daughter Clara, son-in-law Alfred Rankin Sr., and grandson Alfred Rankin Jr.) to okay anti-takeover measures in the mid-1980s. NACCO became a holding company in 1986 and was renamed NACCO Industries. It sold some of its mines and began to diversify and to target simply made products that held top market positions.

During a two-year period beginning in 1988, NACCO bought electrical appliance specialist WearEver-ProctorSilex (it sold off the WearEver pots and pans operation in 1989), appliance factory outlet store chain The Kitchen Collection, and US maker of forklift trucks, Hyster Company. The Hyster buy doubled NACCO's sales and bolstered the company's 1985 purchase of forklift maker Yale Materials Handling. This purchase made NACCO a power in the growing forklift industry. Yale University graduate Alfred Jr., who had been the COO of Eaton, was named president in 1989 (and CEO in 1991).

In 1990 Proctor-Silex bought a majority stake in blender and mixer maker Hamilton Beach (it bought the remainder in 1996). The kitchen appliance foes merged to become a US market leader. By 1990 coal made up less than 15% of NACCO's sales. In 1997 NACCO reduced its US activities when it began production at a Hamilton Beach/Proctor-Silex plant in Mexico.

In 2000 NACCO's National American Coal unit purchased from Phillips Coal the remaining assets of the Mississippi Lignite Mining Company and the Red River Mining Company that it did not already own.

As a part of the company's restructuring plan, NACCO laid off about 150 employees from its Danville, Illinois, auto parts plant in 2001. In 2002 NACCO decided to phase out its Lenoir, North Carolina, lift truck component facility (by 2004) and restructure its Irvine, Scotland, lift truck assembly and component unit (by 2006). The company's Hamilton Beach/Procter-Silex unit also closed its Sotec plant in Juarez, Mexico, and its El Paso warehouse in 2004.

In 2006 NACCO's The Kitchen Collection subsidiary acquired Le Gourmet Chef, Inc., a kitchen goods retailer. Le Gourmet Chef operates nearly 80 retail stores across the US.

EXECUTIVES

Chairman, President, and CEO: Alfred M. Rankin Jr., age 68, $3,488,334 total compensation
VP and Controller; VP and CFO; NACCO Materials Holding Group: Kenneth C. Schilling, age 50, $447,017 total compensation
VP Corporate Development and Treasurer: J. C. Butler Jr., age 49
VP, General Counsel, and Secretary, NACCO Industries and NACCO Materials Handling Group: Charles A. Bittenbender, age 60
VP Consulting Services; SVP Marketing and Consulting, NMHG: Lauren E. Miller, age 55
President, The Kitchen Collection: Robert A. LeBrun, age 53
President and CEO, Hamilton Beach Brands and CEO, The Kitchen Collection: Gregory H. Trepp, age 48
President and CEO, NMHG: Michael P. Brogan, age 59, $725,287 total compensation
President and CEO, North American Coal: Robert L. (Bob) Benson, age 62, $1,629,033 total compensation
Auditors: Ernst & Young LLP

LOCATIONS

HQ: NACCO Industries, Inc.
5875 Landerbrook Dr., Ste. 300
Cleveland, OH 44124
Phone: 440-449-9600   **Fax:** 440-449-9607
Web: www.nacco.com

2009 Sales

	$ mil.	% of total
US	1,415.5	61
Europe, Africa & Middle East	410.6	18
Other regions	484.5	21
Total	**2,310.6**	**100**

PRODUCTS/OPERATIONS

2009 Sales

	$ mil.	% of total
Materials handling		
Wholesale	1,377.4	60
Retail	97.8	4
Housewares		
Hamilton Beach	492.0	21
Kitchen Collection	213.9	9
North American Coal	129.5	6
Total	**2,310.6**	**100**

Selected Subsidiaries

Materials Handling
Hyster-Yale Materials Handling, Inc.
NACCO Materials Handling, BV (The Netherlands)
NACCO Materials Handling Group, Inc.
NACCO Materials Handling Group, Ltd. (UK)
NACCO Materials Handling Group, Pty., Ltd. (Australia)
NACCO Materials Handling, Spa (Italy)
NHMG Mexico SA de CV
NHMG Oregon, Inc.

Housewares
Hamilton Beach Brands de Mexico, SA de CV
Hamilton Beach Brands, Inc.
Le Gourmet Chef
The Kitchen Collection, Inc.
Coal Mining
The Coteau Properties Company
The Falkirk Mining Company
Mississippi Lignite Mining Company
The North American Coal Corporation
The North American Coal Royalty Company
The Sabine Mining Company
San Miguel Lignite Mine

COMPETITORS

Arch Coal
Cascade Corp.
Caterpillar
CLARK Material Handling
CNH Global
Crown Equipment
Deere
Doosan Infracore
Gehl
Jungheinrich
Komatsu
Nissan Forklift
Peabody Energy
Russell Hobbs
Toyota Material Handling
Whirlpool

HISTORICAL FINANCIALS

Company Type: Public

Income Statement

FYE: December 31

	REVENUE ($ mil.)	NET INCOME ($ mil.)	NET PROFIT MARGIN	EMPLOYEES
12/09	2,311	8	0.4%	4,300
12/08	3,680	(438)	—	5,500
12/07	3,603	89	2.5%	10,200
12/06	3,349	93	2.8%	10,700
12/05	3,157	58	1.8%	10,700
Annual Growth	**(7.5%)**	**(38.3%)**	**—**	**(20.4%)**

2009 Year-End Financials

Debt ratio: 95.2%
Return on equity: 2.2%
Cash ($ mil.): 256
Current ratio: 2.02
Long-term debt ($ mil.): 378
No. of shares (mil.): 8
Dividends
  Yield: 4.2%
  Payout: 55.2%
Market value ($ mil.): 415

Stock History

NYSE: NC

	STOCK PRICE ($) FY Close	P/E High/Low		PER SHARE ($) Earnings	Dividends	Book Value
12/09	49.80	20	4	3.75	2.07	47.60
12/08	37.41	—	—	(52.84)	2.05	42.81
12/07	99.69	16	8	10.80	1.98	107.07
12/06	136.60	13	9	12.89	1.90	95.19
12/05	117.15	16	12	7.60	1.85	84.41
Annual Growth	**(19.3%)**	**—**	**—**	**(16.2%)**	**2.8%**	**(13.3%)**

Nalco Holding

Dirty water? Wastewater? Process-stream water? Nalco treats them all. The company is the world's largest maker of chemicals used in water treatment for industrial processes (ahead of #2 GE Water and Process Technologies). Nalco's Energy Services segment is also #1 worldwide, ahead of Baker Petrolite; it provides fuel additives, oilfield chemicals, and flow assurance services to energy companies. The company's chemicals help clarify water, conserve energy, prevent pollution, separate liquids from solids, and prevent corrosion in cooling systems and boilers. Its Energy Services segment has a third of the market, the Water Services segment a 20% market share, and Nalco's Paper Services unit ranks in the top three.

Customers include municipalities, hospitals, and makers of electronics, chemicals, paper, petroleum, and steel. Nalco also provides water management services and, through its Industrial Solutions unit, maintenance of water treatment operations.

It sells its wares in more than 150 countries worldwide; business outside of North America accounts for more than half of Nalco's sales. The company has targeted emerging geographical markets for growth, looking toward the BRIC countries — Brazil, Russia, India, and China — like every other respectable global giant, but also to areas like West Africa, the Middle East, and the region surrounding the Caspian Sea.

Nalco expanded its water pre-treatment services and related specialty equipment capabilities when it acquired Res-Kem Corporation and General Water Services of Philadelphia in 2010. The move improves Nalco's ability to provide customers in the northeastern US with industrial water equipment, supplies, and accessories.

Its Nalco Mobotec unit provides services to fight air pollution. Nalco Mobotec announced in 2009 a joint venture with Sonic Technology Solutions that will develop processes to use fly ash from coal-fired power stations as an ingredient in the manufacture of a cement substitute or concrete additives.

HISTORY

Nalco Chemicals got its start because, as its chief chemist would say, "You can put water in your stomach that you dare not put in a boiler." In the early 1920s Herbert Kern founded Chicago Chemical Company, and Wilson Evans started Aluminate Sales Corporation. Both companies sold liquid sodium aluminate, which is used to soften water — Chicago Chemical for water used in industrial boilers, and Aluminate Sales for steam locomotives. In 1928 Chicago Chemical, Aluminate Sales, and Alcoa's sodium aluminate unit merged to form National Aluminate Corporation.

In 1930 the company acquired Paige-Jones Chemical Company of New York, and with it the capability to supply its water-treatment products in the form of "ball briquettes." During the 1930s it began making gel-type water-softening agents at the urging of one of its chemists, Emmett Culligan. (Culligan left to start his own water-treatment firm in 1935.)

During WWII, Chicago Chemical was revived for a three-year stint making catalytic products for aviation fuel. At war's end, it again became a division of National Aluminate, bringing expertise in petroleum cracking and ion exchange materials. In 1947 National Aluminate went public. The postwar era brought a major challenge as railroads converted from steam to diesel locomotives; the changeover cost the company half its business in just a few years. In response, the company developed diesel catalysts and additives, cooling system treatments, and weed-control chemicals for the railroads. In the 1950s National Aluminate expanded into Europe and Latin America and added new customers such as papermakers and nuclear power plant operators. The company changed its name to Nalco Chemical Company in 1959.

In 1962 Nalco and UK-based Imperial Chemical Industries (ICI) formed Catoleum Pty. Ltd. in Australia. Later in the decade the company established Nalfloc in the UK and Katalco in the US (sold to joint venture partner ICI in 1986).

Nalco set up regional water-analysis laboratories throughout the US during the 1970s and continued overseas expansion. The company established itself as a star during a decade of dismal US stock performance. Nalco continued to acquire in the 1980s and moved into new markets such as chemicals for the electronics and auto industries. By 1989 Nalco's sales topped $1 billion.

To combat the recession of the early 1990s, Nalco sold some operations, increased its sales force, and continued to innovate, creating a process to detoxify crude oil sludge. Nalco's 1996 acquisitions included Molson Companies' water-treatment operations and UK-based chemicals firm Albright & Wilson. It soaked up the Netherlands-based International Water Consultants Beheer BV and the assets of Nutmeg Technologies in 1997. Nalco added more water-treatment companies in 1998, including Trident Chemicals, Dutch company USF Houseman Waterbehandling, and three Malaysian firms.

Nalco bought more water-treatment companies in Brazil, Finland, Italy, Sweden, the UK, and the US in 1999. That year French utility Suez bought Nalco for $4.1 billion in cash. In 2000 Suez tapped Nalco to integrate and control the operations of Calgon, Aquazur, and other group water-treatment companies.

Early in 2001 Suez added the Ondeo name to all of its water operations to build brand identity; Nalco Chemical became Ondeo Nalco. (Ondeo was derived from the word "water" in several languages.) The company also purchased GEO Specialty Chemicals' paper chemical business later in 2001.

Suez sold Nalco to a group of private equity firms — the Blackstone Group, Apollo Management, and Goldman Sachs Capital Partners — in 2003 for more than $4 billion. The acquiring group dropped the Ondeo from the company's name and hired former Hercules CEO William Joyce to take over as chairman and CEO. Until a secondary offering of shares in mid-2005 the consortium's ownership stake still had been well above the 50% mark. Joyce retired in 2008 and was replaced by J. Erik Fyrwald, who had been president of DuPont Agriculture & Nutrition.

EXECUTIVES

Chairman and CEO: J. Erik Fyrwald, age 50, $4,008,217 total compensation
SEVP; President, Water and Process Services: David E. Flitman, age 45, $789,060 total compensation
EVP; President, EAME (Europe, Africa, and Middle East): David Johnson, age 50, $1,245,420 total compensation
EVP; President, Energy Services Division: Stephen M. (Steve) Taylor, age 47, $905,039 total compensation
EVP; President, Asia Pacific: Eric G. Melin, age 49
EVP, CFO, and Treasurer: Bradley J. (Brad) Bell, age 57, $866,131 total compensation
Chief Marketing Officer: Mary Kay Kaufmann, age 50
CIO: Stewart H. McCutcheon
CTO: Manian Ramesh, age 52
Group VP Water Marketing and Development: Richard A. (Rich) Bendure, age 41
VP, General Counsel, and Corporate Secretary: Stephen N. (Steve) Landsman, age 50
VP Human Resources: Laurie M. Marsh
VP Energy Services Supply Chain: Mark R. Stoll, age 53
Division VP Communications and Investor Relations: Mike Bushman
Auditors: Ernst & Young LLP

LOCATIONS

HQ: Nalco Holding Company
1601 W. Diehl Rd., Naperville, IL 60563
Phone: 630-305-1000   **Fax:** 630-305-2900
Web: www.nalco.com

2009 Sales

	$ mil.	% of total
The Americas		
US	1,675.4	45
Other countries	521.4	14
Europe/Middle East/Africa	961.8	25
Asia/Pacific	588.2	16
Total	**3,746.8**	**100**

PRODUCTS/OPERATIONS

2009 Sales

	$ mil.	% of total
Water Services	1,662.4	44
Energy Services	1,418.4	38
Paper Services	666.0	18
Total	**3,746.8**	**100**

Selected Products

Lubricants and functional fluids
Process chemicals
Water-treatment chemicals

Selected Markets

Automobile industry
Chemical industry
Commercial buildings (hospitals, hotels)
Electronic industry
Food-processing industry
Paper industry
Petroleum industry
Steel industry
Water-treatment plants

COMPETITORS

Arch Chemicals
Ashland Hercules Water Technologies
Baker Petrolite
BASF Corporation
Champion Technologies
Cytec
Eka Chemicals
GE Water and Process Technologies
LANXESS
Rockwood Holdings

HISTORICAL FINANCIALS

Company Type: Public

Income Statement

FYE: December 31

	REVENUE ($ mil.)	NET INCOME ($ mil.)	NET PROFIT MARGIN	EMPLOYEES
12/09	3,747	61	1.6%	11,590
12/08	4,212	(343)	—	11,770
12/07	3,913	129	3.3%	11,560
12/06	3,603	99	2.7%	11,100
12/05	3,312	48	1.4%	10,900
Annual Growth	**3.1%**	**6.1%**	**—**	**1.5%**

2009 Year-End Financials

Debt ratio: 575.6%
Return on equity: 14.0%
Cash ($ mil.): 128
Current ratio: 1.34
Long-term debt ($ mil.): 2,714

No. of shares (mil.): 138
Dividends
  Yield: 0.5%
  Payout: 31.8%
Market value ($ mil.): 3,528

Stock History

NYSE: NLC

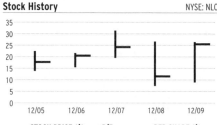

	STOCK PRICE ($) FY Close	P/E High/Low		PER SHARE ($) Earnings	Dividends	Book Value
12/09	25.51	59	21	0.44	0.14	3.41
12/08	11.54	—	—	(2.44)	0.14	2.84
12/07	24.18	35	23	0.88	0.14	8.08
12/06	20.46	32	24	0.67	—	6.44
12/05	17.71	67	43	0.33	—	5.10
Annual Growth	**9.6%**	**—**	**—**	**7.5%**	**0.0%**	**(9.6%)**

NASDAQ OMX Group

NASDAQ OMX isn't a place; it's a state of mind. OK, that's not exactly true, but NASDAQ OMX *is* the leader in floorless exchanges and has challenged NYSE Euronext as the world's largest stock exchange. The group was formed in 2008 when the NASDAQ Stock Market merged with OMX, the owner of Northern Europe's largest securities marketplace. Combined, the group trades in more than 3,600 companies, including Exchange-Traded Funds (ETFs), equities, options, futures, derivatives, commodities, and structured products. The group's market services segment, which includes quotations, order execution, and reporting services, accounts for about 90% of sales.

Its issuer services segment includes shareholder services, newswire services, and such financial products and derivatives as ETFs and the Nasdaq-100 Index. The market technology segment, the smallest division, offers systems integration, advisory, and other support services for exchanges.

Traditionally a heavy trader in smaller companies and tech stocks, the NASDAQ exchange lists its securities within a tiered structure. Elite stocks are traded on the NASDAQ Global Select Market, which represents about half of all listed firms; the other tiers are the NASDAQ Global Market and the NASDAQ Capital Market.

NASDAQ bolstered its status in the US by going head-to-head with the venerable New York Stock Exchange; the younger exchange successfully lured a number of companies to dual-list with both competitors (or, in some cases, to move totally to NASDAQ). It launched a trading platform to handle dual-listed companies, as well as all NYSE-listed stocks and ETFs. The exchange also aggressively courted IPOs and foreign company listings, with international firms accounting for some 10% of its total companies.

Close on the heels of NASDAQ's successful domestic strategy, however, was an international push that had more than its share of ups and downs. After a failed attempt to acquire the London Stock Exchange (LSE) in 2006, NASDAQ became the European exchange's largest shareholder, acquiring more than 25% of the LSE in several separate transactions. When NASDAQ's 2007 hostile takeover bid for the LSE also failed, the disappointment was particularly bitter in the face of domestic and transoceanic hookups being carried out by NASDAQ's rivals (including the vaunted deal that created NYSE Euronext). In a peculiar turn of events, NASDAQ in 2007 sold its interests in LSE.

NASDAQ finally caught a break later that year, inking an agreement to acquire OMX. As part of the deal, Borse Dubai, which acquired NASDAQ's stake in LSE, also acquired some 20% of NASDAQ OMX Group. Borse Dubai has since upped its ownership stake to approximately 30% of the group.

In terms of service offerings, the exchange has used acquisitions — BRUT, Instinet, Shareholder.com, and PrimeNewswire (now GlobeNewswire) — to strengthen its positions or add capabilities in such areas as electronic trading platforms, shareholder services, and newswire services. NASDAQ OMX used technology obtained in the Instinet acquisition to launch an options exchange. In 2007 NASDAQ purchased Directors Desk, which helps companies conduct daily communications.

The following year, the company acquired the Philadelphia Stock Exchange (now NASDAQ OMX PHLX), which carries about 15% of the US options market, in a $652 million deal. NASDAQ OMX Group then acquired the Boston Stock Exchange in a deal providing additional trading licenses and clearing licenses. It used the platform to launch a second cash equities market in the US, the NASDAQ OMX BX. Also in 2008 the company launched NASDAQ OMX Commodities, which offers energy and carbon derivatives products.

EXECUTIVES

Chairman: H. Furlong Baldwin, age 78
CEO and Director: Robert (Bob) Greifeld, age 52, $13,841,825 total compensation
EVP Corporate Strategy and CFO: Adena T. Friedman, age 40, $5,234,614 total compensation
EVP Global Corporate Client Group: Bruce E. Aust, age 46, $2,610,007 total compensation
EVP, General Counsel, and Chief Regulatory Officer: Edward S. Knight, age 59, $3,247,493 total compensation
EVP and Chief Marketing Officer, Global Index Products and Global Marketing Group: John L. Jacobs, age 51
EVP and CIO: Anna M. Ewing, age 49, $5,092,075 total compensation
EVP Transaction Services US and UK: Eric W. Noll, age 48
EVP Transaction Services Nordic: Hans-Ole Jochumsen, age 52

SVP Global IT Services: Carl-Magnus Hallberg, age 44
SVP, Controller, and Principal Accounting Officer: Ronald Hassen, age 58
SVP Global Corporate Communications: Frank De Maria
SVP Market Technology: Lars Ottersgård
Chairman, International Derivatives Clearing Group (IDCG): Vincent Viola
CEO, International Derivatives Clearing Group (IDCG): Garry N. O'Connor, age 39
Auditors: Ernst & Young LLP

LOCATIONS

HQ: The NASDAQ OMX Group, Inc.
1 Liberty Plaza, 165 Broadway, 50th Fl.
New York, NY 10006
Phone: 212-401-8700   **Fax:** 212-401-1024
Web: www.nasdaqomx.com

2009 Sales

	$ mil.	% of total
US	2,742	80
Other countries	667	20
Total	**3,409**	**100**

PRODUCTS/OPERATIONS

2009 Sales

	$ mil.	% of total
Market Services	2,929	86
Issuer Services	324	10
Market Technology	145	4
Other	11	—
Total	**3,409**	**100**

Selected Subsidiaries

Agora-X, LLC
AS Eesti Väärtpaberikeskus (Estonia)
AS Latvijas Centralais depozitaris (Latvia)
Carpenter Moore (San Francisco) LLC
Clearing Control CC AB (Sweden)
GlobeNewswire, Inc.
Independent Research Network, LLC
International Derivatives Clearing Group, LLC
Nasdaq Execution Services, LLC
NASDAQ OMX Copenhagen A/S
NASDAQ OMX Futures Exchange, Inc.
NASDAQ OMX Nordic Ltd. (Finland)
NASDAQ Options Services, LLC
Norway Acquisition LLC
OM London Exchange Ltd.
OMX AB (Sweden)
OMX Ltd. (China)
OMX Pte Ltd. (Singapore)
OMX Technology (Ireland) Ltd.
OMX Technology (UK) Ltd.
Power Clearing Systems AS (Norway)
The Trade Reporting Facility, LLC
Verdbrefaskraning Islands hf. (dba Icelandic Securities Depository, Iceland)

COMPETITORS

ASX
Bombay Stock Exchange
Citigroup
CME
Deutsche Börse
Investment Technology
Knight Capital
London Stock Exchange
NYSE Amex
NYSE Euronext
TRADEBOOK
TSX Group

HISTORICAL FINANCIALS

Company Type: Public

Income Statement

FYE: December 31

	REVENUE ($ mil.)	NET INCOME ($ mil.)	NET PROFIT MARGIN	EMPLOYEES
12/09	3,409	266	7.8%	2,216
12/08	3,649	320	8.8%	2,507
12/07	2,437	518	21.3%	891
12/06	1,658	128	7.7%	898
12/05	880	62	7.0%	917
Annual Growth	**40.3%**	**44.1%**	**—**	**24.7%**

2009 Year-End Financials

Debt ratio: 37.9%
Return on equity: 5.8%
Cash ($ mil.): 594
Current ratio: 1.20
Long-term debt ($ mil.): 1,867

No. of shares (mil.): 208
Dividends
  Yield: —
  Payout: —
Market value ($ mil.): 4,127

Stock History

NASDAQ (GS): NDAQ

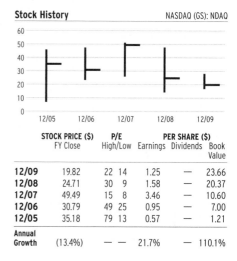

	STOCK PRICE ($) FY Close	P/E High/Low		PER SHARE ($) Earnings	Dividends	Book Value
12/09	19.82	22	14	1.25	—	23.66
12/08	24.71	30	9	1.58	—	20.37
12/07	49.49	15	8	3.46	—	10.60
12/06	30.79	49	25	0.95	—	7.00
12/05	35.18	79	13	0.57	—	1.21
Annual Growth	**(13.4%)**	**—**	**—**	**21.7%**	**—**	**110.1%**

Nash-Finch Company

Nash-Finch knows what's in store for food retailers. One of the largest US wholesale grocery distributors, the company supplies food and general merchandise to about 1,700 retail grocery stores in more than 25 states. It operates 15 distribution centers located in the Midwest, the Great Lakes region, and the Southeast. The company is also one of the leading suppliers to the US armed forces, distributing goods to approximately 250 military commissaries and exchanges in both the US and abroad. In addition to its food distribution businesses, Nash-Finch operates some 50 of its own supermarkets under such banners as Econofoods and Sun Mart.

The biggest plate on Nash-Finch's table is food distribution. It provides its customers with nationally branded and private-label grocery products and perishable food products, mainly meat and fresh produce. It has its own private labels — value-priced Our Family and Value Choice and a premium brand, Nash Brothers Trading Company. Nash-Finch has been focused on improving efficiencies within its warehouse and distribution system in order to cut costs and boost the bottom line. To this end, the firm in May 2010 completed an expansion of its Lima, Ohio, distribution center. The move enables Nash-Finch to triple the volume of frozen foods shipped from the facility.

The company has also been working to expand its military supply operations, acquiring three distribution centers from GSC Enterprises during 2009.

Retail food is a highly competitive business. Supercenters and other alternative formats compete for price-conscious consumers have affected the company's performance in the sector. Due to these conditions, Nash-Finch closed or sold three retail stores in 2007, four retail stores in 2008, and four retail stores in 2009. In order to improve the performance of its remaining retail food operations, the company is reformatting some of its retail stores into alternative formats. For example, that year it invested in a start-up retail grocery operation called AVANZA, designed to appeal to Hispanic consumers.

It's more than just steak and salad at Nash-Finch. The company offers a wide array of services, including promotional, advertising, and merchandising programs; consumer and market research; installation of computerized ordering, receiving, and scanning systems; and assistance with the procurement of retail equipment. It also provides remodeling and store-development services; contacts for accounting, budgeting, and payroll operations; and NashNet, an Internet service that offers supply-chain efficiencies.

Mutual fund company T. Rowe Price owns 10% of Nash-Finch.

HISTORY

Vermont farmers Warren and Mary Nash operated a small country store in the mid-1800s. In 1884 their son Fred followed the homesteading rush to the Dakota Territory, where the next year he opened a small confectionery and tobacco shop in railroad boomtown Devils Lake. His brothers Edgar and Willis soon joined him, and by 1887 there was a Nash Brothers store in Devils Lake and another in Grand Forks.

Two years later North Dakota entered the Union, and the Nash brothers bought an unclaimed boxcar of peaches and turned it into a quick profit. That year the company hired 14-year-old Harry Finch to sort lemons for $4 a week, a job he took to support his ailing father. Also in 1889 Edgar moved to California, where he established ties between the Nashes' wholesale business and California produce growers. He died in 1896; Finch became a manager that year.

Acquisitions expanded the company in the late 1890s and early 1900s. It partnered with local produce brokerage C. H. Robinson in 1905; Nash Brothers controlled it by 1913.

Over the next several decades, Nash Brothers expanded its growing, packaging, and shipping operations, forming companies in California and Texas. In 1916 it started the Nash Coffee Company and fruit and vegetable packager Nash DeCamp. Three years later the company moved its headquarters to Minneapolis. Nash Brothers' 60-plus companies incorporated as Nash-Finch in 1921. When Fred died in 1926, Finch became president. During the 1930s the company introduced its own brand, Our Family.

Nash-Finch returned to retailing in the 1950s with 17 supermarkets in Nebraska. Finch, by then a partner, retired in 1953 after 64 years

with the company. During the 1960s the FTC limited C. H. Robinson's role with Nash-Finch, and the grocer sold its remaining stake in the broker in 1976. The company reached $1 billion in sales in 1981 and was the US's 10th-largest grocery wholesaler by the mid-1980s.

It made acquisitions throughout the 1990s, including a division of military distributor B. Green & Co. (Maryland, 1992); Easter Enterprises, a 16-store Iowa chain (1993); and 23 Food Folks stores (1994). In 1994 chairman Harold Finch, grandson of Harry, died in an auto accident. President Alfred Flaten became chairman and CEO and separated the wholesale and retail divisions.

The company sold two convenience store subsidiaries (Thomas & Howard and T&H Service Merchandisers) in 1995. In 1996 Nash-Finch bought Military Distributors of Virginia, a distributor of groceries to military bases in the eastern US and Europe, and grocery wholesalers T. J. Morris and Super Food Services.

A year later it bought most of the assets of Nebraska-based grocery distributor United-A.G. Cooperative. Former Pathmark executive Ron Marshall succeeded Flaten as CEO in 1998.

In ensuing years it replaced most of its management team, consolidated distribution centers, and sold produce and dairy subsidiaries to focus more on retailing.

It purchased retailer Erickson's Diversified (18 stores in Minnesota and Wisconsin) and in 2000 bought Hinky Dinky Supermarkets (12 locations in Nebraska). In 2001 Nash-Finch announced that it would sell its North and South Carolina supermarkets as it continued focusing on the market in the Midwest. To that end, it acquired U Save Foods (14 supermarkets in Nebraska, Kansas, and Colorado) in mid-2001.

In 2003 the company purchased five Sunshine Food stores in South Dakota and converted some of those to the Econofoods banner. It also started two specialty retail food operations: Buy·n·Save (aimed at low-income customers) and AVANZA (aimed at the Hispanic market).

In the midst of an investigation into internal trading practices in 2006, Marshall stepped down as CEO. Alec Covington, formerly North American chief for Dutch food distributor Koninklijke Wessanen, was named as his replacement.

EXECUTIVES

Chairman: William R. Voss, age 56
President, CEO, and Director: Alec C. Covington, age 53, $5,001,958 total compensation
EVP, CFO, and Treasurer: Robert B. (Bob) Dimond, age 48, $1,405,170 total compensation
EVP Supply Chain Management: Jeffrey E. (Jeff) Poore, age 51, $1,021,878 total compensation
EVP and CIO: Calvin S. (Cal) Sihilling, age 60, $1,189,392 total compensation
EVP Food Distribution; President and COO, Wholesale: Christopher A. Brown, age 47, $1,547,848 total compensation
EVP, General Counsel, and Secretary: Kathleen M. (Kathy) Mahoney, age 55
SVP Merchandising: Howard Befort
SVP Military: Edward L. Brunot, age 46
VP Sales and Business Development: Gary Bickmore
VP Distribution: Dan M. Davidson
Auditors: Ernst & Young LLP

LOCATIONS

HQ: Nash-Finch Company
    7600 France Ave. South, Minneapolis, MN 55440
Phone: 952-832-0534   **Fax:** 952-844-1237
Web: www.nashfinch.com

PRODUCTS/OPERATIONS

2009 Sales

	$ mil.	% of total
Food distribution	2,655.0	51
Military	1,985.3	38
Retail	572.3	11
Total	**5,212.6**	**100**

2009 Retail Banners

	No.
Sun Mart	21
Econofoods	16
AVANZA	5
Family Thrift Center	5
Family Fresh Market	2
Pick n' Save	2
Prairie Market	1
Wholesale Food Outlet	1
Other stores	1
Total	**54**

COMPETITORS

ALDI	McLane
Alex Lee	Piggly Wiggly Midwest
Associated Wholesale	Purity Wholesale Grocers
Grocers	Roundy's Supermarkets
C&S Wholesale	ShopKo Stores
Coastal Pacific Food	Spartan Stores
Core-Mark	SUPERVALU
Costco Wholesale	UniPro Foodservice
Hy-Vee	United Natural
Kroger	Wal-Mart

HISTORICAL FINANCIALS

Company Type: Public

Income Statement			FYE: Saturday nearest December 31	
	REVENUE ($ mil.)	NET INCOME ($ mil.)	NET PROFIT MARGIN	EMPLOYEES
12/09	5,213	3	0.1%	7,563
12/08	4,704	36	0.8%	7,410
12/07	4,533	39	0.9%	7,475
12/06	4,632	(23)	—	8,227
12/05	4,556	41	0.9%	9,487
Annual Growth	**3.4%**	**(49.0%)**	**—**	**(5.5%)**

2009 Year-End Financials

Debt ratio: 79.6%	No. of shares (mil.): 12
Return on equity: 0.8%	Dividends
Cash ($ mil.): 1	Yield: 1.9%
Current ratio: 1.81	Payout: 342.9%
Long-term debt ($ mil.): 279	Market value ($ mil.): 457

Stock History

NASDAQ (GS): NAFC

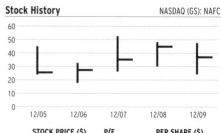

	STOCK PRICE ($)	P/E		PER SHARE ($)		
	FY Close	High/Low		Earnings	Dividends	Book Value
12/09	37.09	223	119	0.21	0.72	28.47
12/08	44.89	17	11	2.75	0.72	27.29
12/07	35.28	18	9	2.84	0.72	25.63
12/06	27.30	—	—	(1.72)	0.72	23.91
12/05	25.48	14	8	3.13	0.68	26.20
Annual Growth	**9.8%**	**—**	**—**	**(49.1%)**	**1.4%**	**2.1%**

National Fuel Gas

National Fuel Gas doesn't cover the nation, but it does touch all the bases in its industry: The company explores for, produces, stores, transmits, and distributes natural gas. The diversified energy concern's public utility, National Fuel Gas Distribution (more than half of the company's annual sales) distributes gas to about 727,000 customers in New York and Pennsylvania. National Fuel Gas has gas exploration, production, storage, and transportation units; it also engages in energy marketing, timber processing, independent power, and methane gas production. In 2009 oil and gas subsidiary Seneca Resources reported proved reserves of 248.9 billion cu. ft. of natural gas and 46.6 million barrels of oil.

The unit explores for, develops, and purchases natural gas and oil reserves in the Gulf Coast, Appalachia, the Southwest, and California.

Subsidiary National Fuel Gas Supply owns about 30 underground gas storage facilities and a 3,000-mile pipeline that runs from southwestern Pennsylvania to the New York-Canada border.

Growing its assets to meet demand, in 2008 the company extended the Empire State Pipeline by building a 78-mile stretch from near Rochester to Corning. That year the company proposed building a new gas pipeline, the Appalachian Lateral, that will provide transportation and storage services to major Northeast market interconnects (primarily in Pennsylvania). It was still actively pursuing the project in 2010.

Energy deregulation has changed the rules in recent years, and the firm's utility customers can now choose their own supplier. In response, National Fuel Gas has set up a gas marketing unit (National Fuel Resources) to compete for customers in the northeastern US.

HISTORY

The roots of National Fuel Gas go back to the 1820s in northwestern New York. The early days of natural gas exploitation were marked by varied uses of the fuel and creative transport methods. In 1821 Iroquois Gas (later a National Fuel Gas unit) laid lead pipe from a source beneath Canadaway Creek in New York to light street lamps in the village of Fredonia. Fifty years later an investor group tried (and failed) to pipe gas from Bloomfield, New York, to Rochester, some 25 miles away, using hollow logs connected by iron bands.

A more successful attempt was made in 1886 with an 87-mile iron pipeline that carried gas from McKean County, Pennsylvania, to Buffalo, New York. The Buffalo pipeline was bought by United Natural Gas, a predecessor of National Fuel Gas, and portions of it remained in use well into the 20th century.

Incorporated in 1902, National Fuel Gas bought smaller gas firms in the Buffalo area in the early 1900s and stretched its pipeline network into Pennsylvania. In 1916 Iroquois Gas established the US's first underground gas storage unit.

As gas reserves in the Appalachian region became depleted in the 1930s, the company joined other utilities to develop reserves in the Southwest and connect them through pipelines. Growth exploded in the 1940s, sparked by WWII increases in coal and oil prices, and in the 1950s, when home heating shifted to gas.

The industry was in a feast-or-famine period from the 1960s to the 1980s. The gas market matured in the 1960s, but the 1970s energy crisis increased demand, forcing National Fuel Gas to restrict new customer hookups. The next decade an aggressive industrywide development program glutted the market and prices plummeted. In response, National Fuel Gas diversified, moving away from retail and into storage and transport. In 1986 it bought Utility Constructors to build pipelines.

National Fuel Gas began looking beyond its utility business in 1991, when it set up gas marketing subsidiary National Fuel Resources. The next year the company cut staff and formed a joint venture with Citizens Gas Supply of Boston to purchase, transport, and sell gas to other utilities.

As part of the energy industry's globalization trend, National Fuel Gas established operations in China and the Czech Republic in 1996. The next year oil and gas exploration unit Seneca Resources bought interests in wells in California and Wyoming.

Also in 1997, as the oil and gas industry boomed, National Fuel Gas' exploration and pipeline operations were hampered by a scarcity of drilling rigs because of high demand. The petroleum industry slump in 1998 eliminated the rig shortage, and Seneca increased development drilling. The firm more than doubled its proved reserves in 1998 by acquiring energy exploration and production firms HarCor Energy, Bakersfield Energy, and M.H. Whittier.

The next year National Fuel Gas expanded its Czech Republic holdings and added timber and mineral rights in New York and Pennsylvania to its portfolio. Its National Fuel Resources moved into the electricity marketing business; it also bought a cogeneration plant in New York.

In 2000 the company increased its reserves 30% by acquiring Canada's Tri Link Resources. The next year it formed a joint venture with Canadian company Talisman Energy to explore in the Appalachian Basin. Subsidiary Seneca Resources also acquired another Canadian company, Player Petroleum.

In 2007, in order to focus on its US oil and gas operations, Seneca Resources sold its Canadian business unit.

EXECUTIVES

Chairman and CEO: David F. Smith, age 56, $4,556,049 total compensation
President and COO: Ronald J. (Ron) Tanski, age 58, $3,359,172 total compensation
Treasurer and Principal Financial Officer: Maj. David P. Bauer
Secretary and General Counsel: Paula M. Ciprich, age 49
SVP; President and CEO, Seneca Resources: Matthew D. Cabell, age 51, $2,430,681 total compensation
SVP National Fuel Gas Distribution: James D. Ramsdell, age 54, $1,253,640 total compensation
SVP Seneca Resources: John P. McGinnis, age 46
SVP Distribution: Carl M. Carlotti, age 55
SVP and Secretary, Seneca Resources: Barry L. McMahan
VP Business Development: Donna L. DeCarolis, age 50
President, National Fuel Gas Distribution: Anna Marie Cellino, age 56, $1,736,075 total compensation
President, National Fuel Gas Supply: John R. Pustulka, age 57, $888,355 total compensation
President, Highland Forest Resources: Duane A. Wassum

Principal Accounting Officer and Controller; Controller, National Fuel Gas Distribution and National Fuel Gas Supply: Karen M. Camiolo, age 50
Director Investor Relations: James C. Welch
Auditors: PricewaterhouseCoopers LLP

LOCATIONS

HQ: National Fuel Gas Company
6363 Main St., Williamsville, NY 14221
Phone: 716-857-7000 **Fax:** 716-857-7195
Web: www.natfuel.com

PRODUCTS/OPERATIONS

2009 Sales

	$ mil.	% of total
Utility	1,097.6	53
Energy marketing	397.8	19
Exploration & production	382.7	19
Pipeline & storage	137.5	7
Other & corporate	42.2	2
Total	**2,057.8**	**100**

Selected Subsidiaries

Empire State Pipeline (natural gas transportation)
Highland Forest Resources, Inc. (timber processing)
Horizon Energy Development, Inc. (foreign and domestic energy investment, wholesale electricity generation)
Horizon Power, Inc. (wholesale electricity generation)
National Fuel Gas Distribution Corporation (natural gas utility)
National Fuel Gas Supply Corporation (natural gas transportation and storage)
National Fuel Resources, Inc. (energy marketer and broker for utilities and retail customers)
Seneca Resources Corporation (natural gas and oil exploration and production)

COMPETITORS

Allegheny Energy
Anadarko Petroleum
Belden & Blake
Cabot Oil & Gas
Castle Oil
Con Edison
Duke Energy
Dynegy
El Paso Corporation
Enbridge
Energy Future
Exelon
Iberdrola USA
Niagara Mohawk
ONEOK
Petroleum Development
PPL Corporation
Rochester Gas and Electric
Southern Union
Southwestern Energy
TransCanada
UGI

HISTORICAL FINANCIALS

Company Type: Public

Income Statement				FYE: September 30
	REVENUE ($ mil.)	NET INCOME ($ mil.)	NET PROFIT MARGIN	EMPLOYEES
9/09	2,058	101	4.9%	1,949
9/08	2,400	269	11.2%	1,943
9/07	2,040	338	16.5%	1,952
9/06	2,312	138	6.0%	1,993
9/05	1,924	190	9.9%	2,044
Annual Growth	**1.7%**	**(14.6%)**	**—**	**(1.2%)**

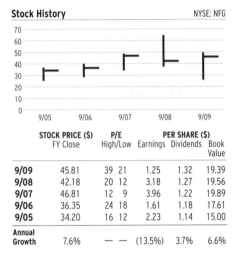
National Semiconductor

National Semiconductor has an international reputation for semiconductors. The pioneering chip maker offers a variety of integrated circuits (ICs), especially analog and mixed-signal (blending analog and digital functions) chips. Its varied offerings reflect its focus on analog chips, which transform physical information — light, sound, pressure, even radio waves — into data that a computer can use. National's chips are used in a host of wireless communications, networking, medical, solar, automotive, and industrial applications.

The global semiconductor industry began to recover from a prolonged downturn in 2010, and National's results reflected the overall conditions in the industry with a steady rise in revenues. The company's sales grew due to increased sales of power management products, as well as improved demand for analog products for the wireless handset and industrial market sectors.

In 2009, with the industry in a prolonged downturn and the global economy in a slump, the company consolidated facilities and idled more than a quarter of its worldwide workforce. National closed its assembly and test facility in Suzhou, China, in 2009. Its wafer fabrication facility in Arlington, Texas, was closed in 2010.

The company, however, remains active in acquisitions — and divestitures — as it shapes its product portfolio. Power management is the predominant theme for National, which continues to invest in products that boost energy efficiency, particularly for mobile electronics, communications infrastructure, renewable energy, medical, sensors, and detection equipment.

In 2010 the company bought GTronix to boost its expertise in programmable and adaptive analog sensor processors. GTronix's technology is designed to improve the efficiency of audio user-interface and voice processing applications in mobile phones and other electronics.

The company introduced its in-panel Solar-Magic power optimizer in 2010, a product that can be embedded in the junction box of both new and existing systems, allowing photovoltaic solar arrays to lose less energy due to shading and array mismatch problems.

In 2009 the company bought Act Solar expanding National's portfolio of power optimization technologies, diagnostics, and panel monitoring capabilities for solar arrays.

Brian L. Halla stepped down as CEO in 2009 as part of a planned succession, but retained his position as chairman. He was replaced by COO Donald Macleod. The following year Halla retired, and Macleod took over as chairman.

HISTORY

National Semiconductor was founded as a transistor maker in 1959 by eight engineers from Sperry Rand Corporation. The company was established in Danbury, Connecticut. In 1966, as the company was struggling with only $7 million in annual sales, Peter Sprague (heir to the Sprague Electric fortune) took over as chairman. The next year he hired manufacturing expert Charles Sporck away from Fairchild Semiconductor to be National's CEO.

Sporck transferred company headquarters to Silicon Valley (the Danbury facility closed in 1989), halved the company's transistor workforce, and plowed the savings into developing linear and digital logic chips. During the 1970s National's mass manufacturing of low-cost chips made the company the leading US semiconductor maker for a time; its no-frills management approach led to its employees being dubbed "the animals of Silicon Valley."

The company bought National Advanced Systems (NAS), a distributor and servicer of Hitachi mainframes, in 1979 and Data Terminal Systems, which made point-of-sale terminals, in 1983; the two were combined to form Datachecker. When Japanese manufacturers dumped memory chips on the market in 1984 and 1985, National pulled out of the memory business.

Sporck moved to transform his low-cost commodity chip maker into a higher-margin supplier of niche products. National bought troubled Fairchild in 1987 for its logic chip designs and the custom linear circuits it made for the US military.

With mounting mainframe competition from IBM and Amdahl, in 1989 National sold Datachecker. National left the high-speed, high-density static random-access memory (SRAM) business, and in early 1991 Sporck retired. Former Rockwell International (now Rockwell Automation) executive Gilbert Amelio became CEO and undertook another restructuring.

By 1993 National had shifted production to Arlington, Texas. When Amelio joined Apple Computer in 1996, National chose Intel veteran and LSI Logic EVP Brian Halla as its new leader. Halla consolidated National's operations and resurrected the Fairchild name for its commodity chip business. Soon after Halla's arrival, about 600 jobs were cut, two COOs left, and 14 of 56 VPs resigned or were fired.

In 1997 National sold Fairchild. It bought Cyrix (microprocessors for inexpensive computers) in 1997 and ComCore Semiconductor (communications ICs) in 1998. That year National cut another 10% of its workforce in the face of an industry slump.

Things looked up in late 1998 when heavy hitters IBM, Compaq, and Packard Bell signed on to use Cyrix chips. However, Intel's low-end Celeron chip hammered Cyrix's sales, and National exited the PC chip market. National sold its flat-panel display operations to Three-Five Systems, and Cyrix to Taiwan's VIA Technologies.

Also in 1999 National unveiled its Geode system-on-a-chip, targeting the handheld computer market. In 2000 the Geode processor debuted in a TV set-top box made by Philips Electronics for America Online's AOLTV service.

In 2001 the company cut 1,100 jobs — about 10% of its workforce — in response to another, particularly brutal, dropoff in the global chip market. In 2003 the company shuttered a unit that made baseband chips for wireless communications applications and sold the Geode processor line to AMD.

In 2004 National opened its semiconductor assembly and test plant in the Suzhou Industrial Park, located outside of Shanghai and employing about 400 people. In 2005 National Semi said it would sell its assembly and testing facility in Singapore. Four months later it said it would close the facility and transfer its equipment to plants in China and Malaysia.

In 2007 National acquired Xignal Technologies, a German developer of high-speed analog-to-digital converters.

EXECUTIVES

Chairman: Brian L. Halla, age 63, $1,956,259 total compensation
President, CEO, and Director: Donald (Don) Macleod, age 61, $1,513,618 total compensation
National Fellow and CTO, Analog: Dennis Monticelli
National Fellow and CTO, Labs: Ahmad Bahai
SVP Finance and CFO: Lewis Chew, age 47, $1,454,521 total compensation
SVP Worldwide Marketing and Sales: Suneil V. Parulekar, age 62
SVP Power Management Products Group: Detlev J. Kunz, age 59, $996,387 total compensation
SVP Worldwide Manufacturing: Chue Siak (C.S.) Liu, age 57, $1,396,645 total compensation
SVP Key Marketing Segments and Business Development: Michael S. (Mike) Polacek, age 45
SVP Worldwide Technology Development: Mohan Yegnashankaran, age 53
SVP, General Counsel, and Secretary: Todd M. DuChene, age 46
SVP Worldwide Human Resources: Edward J. (Eddie) Sweeney, age 53
VP Web Business: Phil Gibson
VP Operations, South Portland, Maine Facility: Paul Edmonds
VP Worldwide Distribution and Customer Support: Jennifer J. Bleakney
VP Information Services and CIO: Julie Wong
Consulting Staff Scientist: Bob Pease
Senior Manager Worldwide Public Relations and Corporate Communications: LuAnn Jenkins
Manager Investor Relations: Mark Veeh
Auditors: KPMG LLP

LOCATIONS

HQ: National Semiconductor Corporation
 2900 Semiconductor Dr., Santa Clara, CA 95052
Phone: 408-721-5000
Web: www.national.com

2010 Sales

	$ mil.	% of total
China	450.5	32
US	334.9	24
Germany	317.3	22
Singapore	192.7	13
Japan	124.0	9
Total	**1,419.4**	**100**

PRODUCTS/OPERATIONS

2010 Sales

	$ mil.	% of total
Analog	1,329.1	94
Other	90.3	6
Total	**1,419.4**	**100**

Selected Products

Aerospace and military integrated circuits (ICs)
Amplifiers and regulators
Audio circuits
Automotive ICs
Data acquisition circuits
Display circuits for monitors
Ethernet and Fast Ethernet digital signal processing
 devices
Interface circuits
Microcontrollers (automotive, communications, and
 industrial applications)
Power management circuits
Temperature sensors
Wireless circuits (radio and other functions)

COMPETITORS

Analog Devices
Atmel
Broadcom
Cypress Semiconductor
Fairchild Semiconductor
Freescale Semiconductor
IBM Microelectronics
Infineon Technologies
Intel
International Rectifier
Intersil
Linear Technology
Marvell Technology
Maxim Integrated Products
Micrel
Microchip Technology
Microsemi
NXP Semiconductors
ON Semiconductor
Qualcomm CDMA
Samsung Electronics
Sanken Electric
Sharp Corp.
STMicroelectronics
Texas Instruments
Toshiba Semiconductor

HISTORICAL FINANCIALS

Company Type: Public

Income Statement

FYE: Last Sunday in May

	REVENUE ($ mil.)	NET INCOME ($ mil.)	NET PROFIT MARGIN	EMPLOYEES
5/10	1,419	209	14.7%	5,800
5/09	1,460	73	5.0%	5,800
5/08	1,886	332	17.6%	7,300
5/07	1,930	375	19.4%	7,600
5/06	2,158	449	20.8%	8,500
Annual Growth	**(9.9%)**	**(17.4%)**	**—**	**(9.1%)**

2010 Year-End Financials

Debt ratio: 235.0%
Return on equity: 69.4%
Cash ($ mil.): 1,027
Current ratio: 2.68
Long-term debt ($ mil.): 1,001
No. of shares (mil.): 239
Dividends
 Yield: 2.3%
 Payout: 36.8%
Market value ($ mil.): 3,363

Stock History

NYSE: NSM

	STOCK PRICE ($) FY Close	P/E High/Low		PER SHARE ($) Earnings	Dividends	Book Value
5/10	14.05	19	13	0.87	0.32	1.78
5/09	13.88	80	29	0.31	0.28	0.74
5/08	21.05	24	13	1.26	0.20	0.82
5/07	26.92	25	18	1.12	0.14	7.31
5/06	25.68	25	15	1.26	0.10	8.05
Annual Growth	**(14.0%)**	**—**	**—**	**(8.8%)**	**33.7%**	**(31.4%)**

Navistar International

Navistar's gonna roll its truckin' convoy 'cross the USA and beyond. The company manufactures its products under brand names such as International (commercial trucks and military/defense vehicles), MaxxForce (diesel engines), IC (school and commercial buses), and Workhorse (chassis for motor homes). It also designs and manufactures diesel engines for the pickup truck, van, and SUV markets. Navistar's parts group supplies engine parts, and its financial sector offers sales and lease financing for its dealers and customers. Navistar derives most of its sales in North America — 25% of which come from the US government.

Navistar makes no bones about 2009 having been a rough-and-tumble year, especially for truck division sales. The company contained its costs in employee benefits, reduced its design expenses, and cut staff, while still pursuing acquisitions, alliances, and joint ventures to expand its share in international markets.

Caterpillar and Navistar engaged in a 50-50 alliance, beginning in 2010, to build Cat-branded construction trucks for the US market, as well as commercial trucks and engines for overseas markets.

Navistar agreed to purchase a stake in Amminex, a Danish technology company in 2009. It plans to use Amminex's proprietary technology, which uses a metal ammine-based NOx system to reduce exhaust gas. Earlier in the year Navistar bought privately held Continental Mfg. Company Inc., one of the largest cement mixer manufacturers in North America.

Also in 2009 Navistar bought the recreational vehicle manufacturing assets of Monaco RV, which had filed for Chapter 11 bankruptcy protection earlier in the year. Navistar plans to use two of Monaco RV's plants in Indiana to develop and build 400 all-electric delivery trucks in 2010, using in part a $39 million US Department of Energy grant.

The company is continuing to explore South, Central, and North America, with a primary focus on Brazil for manufacturing expansion opportunities. In 2008 Navistar partnered to manufacture public and commercial buses with Brazilian bus body maker San Marino Ônibus e Implementos Ltda., which sells internationally under the Neobus brand.

The company's Navistar Defense subsidiary in 2009 secured more than $1.6 billion in contracts with the US armed forces for military vehicles used to protect troops from roadside bombs in Iraq. It received orders for nearly 3,000 MaxxPro MRAP (mine-resistant ambush-protected) vehicles, more than any other supplier.

The company is also stepping up in hybrid technology by partnering with the EPA, UPS, and Eaton to develop a diesel "series" hydraulic urban delivery vehicle. The vehicle uses hydraulic pumps and hydraulic storage tanks to capture and store energy. Navistar is making school buses and midsized commercial vehicles with hybrid-electric powertrains, as well.

Three trusts for employees and retirees of International Truck and Engine together own about 10% of Navistar International.

HISTORY

Virginia-born inventor Cyrus McCormick perfected the reaper in 1831 and moved west to open a factory in Chicago in 1846. Before his death in 1884, McCormick had implemented such innovations as installment plans, written guarantees, and factory-trained repairmen. In 1902, with help from banker J. P. Morgan, the company merged with Deering Harvester (agricultural machinery) and several smaller companies to form International Harvester (IH); it soon controlled 85% of US harvester production.

IH set up its first overseas plant in 1905 in Sweden. It entered the tractor industry in 1906, and in 1907 it began making the forerunner of the truck — the Auto Buggy. By 1910 IH was making 1,300 trucks and 1,400 tractors annually and had exceeded $100 million in sales.

Cyrus Jr. borrowed $5 million from John D. Rockefeller in 1913 and took control of IH. In 1924 IH introduced the Farmall, the first all-purpose tractor. IH began making heavy trucks in 1928, and by 1937 it was the top US producer of medium and heavy trucks.

Overextended and underfinanced after WWII, IH's market share declined. It produced more trucks than agricultural equipment for the first time in 1955. By 1958 Deere had taken over the lead in farm equipment. IH lost its medium-duty industry sales lead to Ford in the 1960s, and its construction equipment business faltered as well.

A six-month strike by the UAW in 1980, coupled with a recession, sent IH to the edge of bankruptcy. Over the next two years IH lost $2.3 billion. In 1982 IH sold its construction equipment unit, and in 1985 it sold its agricultural equipment business and the International Harvester name. Employee numbers had dropped 85% by 1986, and plants decreased from 48 worldwide to six in North America.

The company was renamed Navistar International in 1986. It redesigned 85% of its truck line by 1987. In 1989 Navistar introduced a nine-speed heavy-truck transmission — its first all-new design in more than 25 years. In 1991 Navistar raised its stake in truck maker Dina Camiones (Mexico) to 17% and inked OEM deals for its engines with Perkins Group (UK) and its North American distributor, Detroit Diesel.

A boom in demand for heavy trucks in 1992 and 1993 resulted in Navistar's retail deliveries rising nearly 33%. Navistar unveiled an engine for vans and trucks in 1994 that was the cleanest burning of its kind, increasing the company's share of the diesel engine market. Company veteran John Horne became CEO in 1995.

In 1999 Navistar bought half of Maxion Motores, Brazil's largest maker of diesel engines. The joint venture was renamed Maxion International Motores. Maxion provided diesel engines to Ford and GM factories in South America.

In 2001 Navistar and Ford announced the formation of a 50-50 joint venture to produce commercial trucks in Mexico. The venture, named Blue Diamond Truck, began operation in 2002. In late 2003 the company created an operating unit for the sole purpose of conducting business with the US military.

An agreement to supply the US Postal Service with 1,700 medium-duty trucks was signed in early 2004. The following year, through subsidiary International Truck and Engine, Navistar bought Workhorse Custom Chassis for an undisclosed sum from Grand Vehicle Works Holdings Corporation, a Carlyle Group company.

The company was challenged to keep the delivery pace up in 2007 during a seven-week UAW strike against International Truck and Engine.

EXECUTIVES

Chairman, President, and CEO: Daniel C. (Dan) Ustian, age 60, $8,181,126 total compensation
EVP and CFO: Andrew J. (A.J.) Cederoth, age 45, $1,252,360 total compensation
SVP, General Counsel, and Chief Ethics Officer: Steven K. (Steve) Covey, age 59, $2,632,607 total compensation
SVP Human Resources and Administration: Gregory W. (Greg) Elliott, age 49
SVP and General Manager, Parts Division: Phyllis E. Cochran, age 57
SVP Sales Operations, North America: James L. Hebe, age 61
SVP; President and CEO, Navistar Financial: David Johanneson
Corporate Secretary: Curt A. Kramer, age 42
Chief Designer: Dave Allendorph
VP and Corporate Controller: John P. Waldron, age 45
VP and Treasurer: James M. (Jim) Moran, age 44
VP and CIO: Donald C. (Don) Sharp, age 42
VP Investor Relations: Heather Kos, age 39
VP and General Manager Heavy Vehicle Center: Thomas Baughman
VP and General Manager Light Duty Vehicles and Joint Ventures; CEO, Workhorse Custom Chassis: David Tarrant
President, North American Truck Operations: John J. (Jack) Allen
President, International Truck Group: Deepak T. (Dee) Kapur, age 56, $2,778,907 total compensation
President, Navistar Defense: Archie Massicotte
Auditors: KPMG LLP

LOCATIONS

HQ: Navistar International Corporation
4201 Winfield Rd., Warrenville, IL 60555
Phone: 630-753-5000   **Fax:** 630-753-2303
Web: www.navistar.com

2009 Sales

	$ mil.	% of total
North America		
US	9,262	80
Canada	748	6
Mexico	467	4
Brazil	638	6
Other countries	454	4
Total	**11,569**	**100**

PRODUCTS/OPERATIONS

2009 Sales

	$ mil.	% of total
Trucks	7,294	63
Engines	2,031	18
Parts	1,975	17
Financial services	269	2
Total	**11,569**	**100**

Selected Brands, Products, and Services

Engines
  MaxxForce
  MWM International
Services
  Navistar Electronics
  Navistar Financial
  Navistar Parts
Vehicles
  IC Bus
  International Trucks
  Mahindra Navistar
  Monaco RV
  Navistar Defense
  Workhorse

COMPETITORS

All American Group
BAE SYSTEMS
Blue Bird
Caterpillar
Cummins
Daimler
Detroit Diesel
Eaton
Force Protection
Ford Motor
Freightliner Custom Chassis
General Dynamics
General Dynamics Land Systems
General Motors
Hino Motors
Isuzu
Leyland Trucks
Mercedes-Benz U.S. International
Mitsubishi Motors North America
Oshkosh Truck
PACCAR
Scania
Spartan Motors
UD Trucks
Volvo
Volvo Trucks
Winnebago

HISTORICAL FINANCIALS

Company Type: Public

Income Statement

FYE: October 31

	REVENUE ($ mil.)	NET INCOME ($ mil.)	NET PROFIT MARGIN	EMPLOYEES
10/09	11,569	320	2.8%	17,900
10/08	14,724	134	0.9%	17,800
10/07	12,295	(120)	—	17,200
10/06	14,200	301	2.1%	18,200
10/05	12,124	139	1.1%	18,600
Annual Growth	**(1.2%)**	**23.2%**	**—**	**(1.0%)**

2009 Year-End Financials

Debt ratio: —
Return on equity: —
Cash ($ mil.): 1,212
Current ratio: 1.37
Long-term debt ($ mil.): 4,270

No. of shares (mil.): 72
Dividends
  Yield: 0.0%
  Payout: —
Market value ($ mil.): 2,373

Stock History

NYSE: NAV

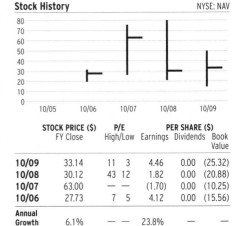

	STOCK PRICE ($) FY Close	P/E High/Low		PER SHARE ($) Earnings	Dividends	Book Value
10/09	33.14	11	3	4.46	0.00	(25.32)
10/08	30.12	43	12	1.82	0.00	(20.88)
10/07	63.00	—	—	(1.70)	0.00	(10.25)
10/06	27.73	7	5	4.12	0.00	(15.56)
Annual Growth	**6.1%**	**—**	**—**	**23.8%**	**—**	**—**

NBC Television

This company is hoping TV viewers will share in a little water cooler talk at *The Office* about *The Biggest Loser*. The flagship unit of media conglomerate NBC Universal (NBCU), NBC Television Network operates #4 broadcast network NBC, which reaches millions of viewers through more than 200 affiliate stations including 10 that are company-owned or -operated. Its schedule is anchored by such shows as *The Office*, *30 Rock*, and reality hits *The Biggest Loser* and *Celebrity Apprentice*. The Peacock network operates as part of NBC Television Group alongside TV production unit Universal Media Studios and Spanish-language broadcaster Telemundo. Cable TV giant Comcast is acquiring control of NBCU from General Electric.

The network has been mired in last place among the four major broadcasters for several years due to some unsuccessful programming choices and the fact that positions in the ratings race have become mostly entrenched.

NBC's woes have only added to the bleak overall picture for NBCU, which has also been dogged by poor performance within its Universal Studios feature film business. With its media division under-performing, GE decided to sell 51% control of NBCU to Comcast in 2009. The #1 cable TV systems operator agreed to pay $6.5 billion in cash and is contributing its portfolio of cable TV networks (E! Entertainment, The Golf Channel, VERSUS) to the new joint venture. NBCU is also buying back a 20% stake held by French telecommunications company Vivendi for $5.8 billion, leaving GE with the remaining 49% of the media conglomerate.

The 2009-10 television season was especially bleak for NBC with its very public failure to switch hosts on *The Tonight Show*. The network installed former late-night host Conan O'Brien as the new host that year while moving Jay Leno to his own hour-long variety show scheduled in the final hour of primetime each evening. Ratings failed to materialize, however, and the network was forced to cancel *The Jay Leno Show* to avoid a revolt by affiliates. But NBC created a public relations nightmare when it suggested pre-empting *The Tonight Show* in favor of a new late-night program hosted by Leno. O'Brien eventually exited the network after helming *The Tonight Show* for just seven months.

The episode provided for a rough beginning to Jeff Gaspin's tenure as chairman of NBC Universal Television Entertainment, a position he took up in 2009 as part of a reorganization that combined NBCU's broadcast and cable operations under one umbrella organization. The move was prompted by the resignation of NBC Entertainment chief Ben Silverman who departed the network after two mostly unsuccessful years. Gaspin previously built NBC Universal Cable into a successful portfolio of networks.

NBC is making big investments in online programming to promote and supplement its traditional broadcasting operations. The network distributes shows through its website, where it has also launched some online-only programs that offer a tie-in to its primetime schedule. In addition, parent NBCU is a joint venture partner in video streaming site Hulu along with News Corporation and Walt Disney.

HISTORY

In 1919 General Electric and Westinghouse formed Radio Corporation of America (RCA). Five years later RCA pioneered television with the transmission of the first radio-photo. Led by inventor-cum-entrepreneur David Sarnoff, RCA set up the National Broadcasting Company (NBC) in 1926 to develop quality radio programs.

The demand for radio network programming grew rapidly. The company split its programming into two networks to give listeners a choice of formats. In 1941 the Federal Communications Commission (FCC) ruled that companies could own only one network. NBC subsequently sold one of its networks, which formed the nucleus of rival American Broadcasting Company (ABC).

Sarnoff also pursued the development of TV. In 1939 NBC began the first regular TV service with coverage of President Roosevelt inaugurating the New York World's Fair. In 1941 NBC obtained a commercial TV license from the FCC, and its WBNT-TV (New York) became the world's first commercial TV station. NBC launched current affairs program *Meet the Press* in 1947. The company won FCC approval for its color TV system in 1953 and presented the first nationwide color broadcast that year.

During the 1970s NBC's ratings slumped, as did its radio business. Led by NBC Entertainment's young president Brandon Tartikoff, the network staged a comeback in the 1980s with an unparalleled string of hits, including *Miami Vice*, *The Cosby Show*, and *Cheers*.

In the midst of the network's resurrection, GE bought RCA for $6.4 billion in 1986. That year Robert Wright was named president and CEO of the NBC network. Despite a number of attempts to revive radio's popularity, the company decided to exit the business. It sold seven of its eight stations in 1988.

In 1990 Tartikoff aide Warren Littlefield took over as head of entertainment. In 1993 the network fell to third in the ratings, had to apologize

to General Motors for a fraudulent news demonstration, and lost late-night's David Letterman to rival CBS. But NBC bounced back with a slew of new programs (led by *ER*) in 1994 and 1995 to win back the top ratings spot. Littlefield left in 1998 and was replaced by Scott Sassa. NBC also ended its 33-year affiliation with the National Football League.

In 2002 NBC purchased Telemundo Communications, owner of the second-largest Spanish-language television network in the US, for about $2.6 billion.

In 2004 GE and Paris-based Vivendi Universal (now Vivendi) came together to merge their film and TV business, forming NBC Universal. The media conglomerate, 80%-owned by GE, encompassed broadcast and cable television networks, along with film and TV production studios. Wright was named chairman and CEO of NBCU.

Entertainment head Jeff Zucker was named CEO of NBC Universal Television in 2004, taking on responsibility for the NBC network, as well as NBCU's many cable outlets.

In 2007 Wright announced his departure from NBCU after 20 years of leading first the NBC network and later the entertainment conglomerate. Zucker was appointed his successor. Later that year, entertainment chief Kevin Reilly was ousted from his position due to NBC's sagging ratings; TV producer Ben Silverman was tabbed to lead the entertainment division. After two largely unsuccessful years, however, Silverman left NBC and was replaced by NBC Universal Cable chief Jeff Gaspin.

EXECUTIVES

Chairman, NBC Universal Television Entertainment: Jeff Gaspin
EVP Entertainment Strategy and Programs: Ted Frank
EVP Late Night and Primetime Series, NBC Entertainment: Rick Ludwin
EVP Current Series, NBC Entertainment: Erin Gough
EVP NBC Sports: Jonathan D. (Jon) Miller
EVP Advertising and Promotion, The NBC Agency: Frank Radice
EVP Alternative Programming: Paul Telegdy
EVP NBC Universal Television Group Publicity: Rebecca Marks
EVP Program Planning and Scheduling, NBC Universal: Mitch Metcalf
EVP Studios and Broadcast Operations: Derek Bond
EVP Casting, NBC Universal Television: Marc Hirschfeld
Chairman, NBC Universal Sports and Olympics: Dick Ebersol
Chairman, NBC Entertainment and Universal Media Studios: Marc Graboff
President, NBC Sports: Kenneth Schanzer
President, Primetime Entertainment: Angela Bromstad
President, Telemundo: Donald (Don) Browne
President, MSNBC: Phil Griffin
President, NBC News: Steve Capus
President NBC Program Planning, Scheduling and Strategy, NBC Universal: Vince Manze
Chief Marketing Officer; President, NBC Agency: John Miller
Auditors: KPMG LLP

LOCATIONS

HQ: The NBC Television Network
30 Rockefeller Plaza, New York, NY 10112
Phone: 212-664-4444   **Fax:** 212-664-4085
Web: www.nbc.com

PRODUCTS/OPERATIONS

Selected Shows
NBC News
Dateline NBC
Meet the Press
Today
NBC Entertainment
30 Rock
The Biggest Loser
Chase (Fall 2010)
Chuck
Community
The Event (Fall 2010)
Friday Night Lights
Law & Order: Criminal Intent
Law & Order: Los Angeles (Fall 2010)
Law & Order: Special Victims Unit
The Office
Outlaw (Fall 2010)
Outsourced (Fall 2010)
Parks and Recreation
Saturday Night Live
The Tonight Show with Jay Leno
Undercovers (Fall 2010)
NBC Sports
Football Night in America
Sunday Night Football

COMPETITORS

ABC, Inc.
CBS
The CW
Discovery Communications
FOX Broadcasting
MTV Networks
MyNetworkTV
Turner Broadcasting
Univision

NBTY, Inc.

NBTY draws upon nature's bounty to cash in on the market for preventive and alternative health care. As the largest vertically integrated source of nutritional supplements in the US, the company manufactures, wholesales, and retails more than 25,000 products including vitamins, minerals, herbs, and sports drinks. Brands include Ester-C, Nature's Bounty, Solgar, and Sundown. NBTY has manufacturing facilities in Canada, the UK, and the US and is able to produce and package capsules, tablets, powders, and liquids. The company sells its goods through pharmacies, wholesalers, supermarkets, and health food stores around the world. NBTY has agreed to be acquired by investment firm The Carlyle Group.

The Carlyle Group has offered to pay $3.8 billion to acquire NBTY. The company has agreed to the deal with an eye on future global growth.

In North America it operates more than 430 Vitamin World stores in US malls, and some 80 Le Naturiste stores in Canada. In the UK the company operates more than 900 Holland & Barrett, GNC, and Julian Graves stores. In the Netherlands the company operates more than 70 De Tuinen retail stores.

In addition to its retail stores, NBTY operates Puritan's Pride, which sells nutritional products through mail-order catalogs and over the Internet. Based upon the success of the Puritan's Pride site, the company is establishing additional websites to support its brick-and-mortar retail brands.

Unlike many of its competitors that rely upon third-party manufacturers, the company actually manufactures 90% of the nutritional supplements that it sells and also serves as a third-party manufacturer of private-label products for retailers. While the company keeps an eye out for new products, in recent years it hasn't spent much on research and development, preferring instead to simply acquire or copy products with proven sales.

NBTY has grown big and strong as the entire natural products industry has boomed, but a steady diet of acquisitions has supplemented its growth. In recent years the highly acquisitive company has bought Canadian vitamin manufacturer and distributor SISU (2005), premium-brand supplement maker Solgar Vitamin and Herb (2005), and Zila Nutraceuticals (2006, formerly a division of Zila). Zila Nutraceuticals was then renamed The Ester-C Company to reflect the business' primary product. In 2008 the company bought the assets of Leiner Health Products, a bankrupt maker of nutritional supplements and over-the-counter drugs, for $371 million.

To secure its spot as the UK's largest supplement retailer, NBTY paid $25 million to acquire natural foods retail chain Julian Graves in 2008. The purchase bumped the company's spread from 640 stores to more than 900 stores. However, it also caught the attention of the UK's Office of Fair Trading which launched an investigation to determine if the purchase would unfairly reduce competition. In mid-2009 the acquisition was cleared by the Office of Fair Trading. NBTY operates Julian Graves business separately from its existing UK business.

Chairman and CEO Scott Rudolph owns 8% of the company his father founded.

HISTORY

Arthur Rudolph founded NBTY in his garage in the early 1960s. Then called Nature's Bounty, the company went public in 1971 to market nutritional supplements. Rudolph was chairman and CEO until his 1993 resignation, when son Scott succeeded him.

Without so much as a glass of water, Nature's Bounty swallowed the mail-order business of General Nutrition Companies in 1989, and vitamin distributor Prime Natural Health Laboratories in 1993.

In 1995 the company agreed to settle Federal Trade Commission charges that it made deceptive claims about the effectiveness of 26 nutrient supplements. That year Nature's Bounty changed its name to that of its stock symbol, NBTY (the symbol changed to NTY in 2003 when the company moved to the NYSE).

In 1997 NBTY bought leading UK health foods chain Holland & Barrett, which operated more than 400 stores. The acquisition more than doubled NBTY's store count. After the buy, NBTY started stocking Holland & Barrett's shelves with its products. In 1998 the company bought a group of privately held vitamin companies and made a major push to open more Vitamin World stores in the US. In 1999 NBTY acquired Nutrition Warehouse, further bolstering its retail, e-commerce, and mail-order operations. Also

that year it bought network marketer Dynamic Essentials to broaden its distribution channels.

Acquisitions continued into the 21st century: SDV Vitamins, a division of Rexall Sundown, joined the family in 2000, and in 2001 NBTY bought the Knox NutraJoint and Knox for Nails nutritional supplement business from Kraft Foods for about $4 million, along with NatureSmart from Whole Foods Market. The company's Holland & Barrett subsidiary bought a chain of 12 vitamin retail stores (Nature's Way) in Ireland. To expand its wholesale business, NBTY in 2002 purchased a line of nutritional supplements sold under the Synergy Plus trademark, a well-known brand among health food aficionados.

A big move came in 2003. NBTY bought Rexall Sundown from Royal Numico N.V. that year. Also that year, the company disbanded its Dynamic Essentials subsidiary after receiving a letter of inquiry by the FTC regarding a weight-loss product marketed by Dynamic Essentials. In addition, the company ceased production of all weight-loss products that contained ephedra, prior to the FDA's eventual ban on the herb.

EXECUTIVES

Chairman and CEO: Scott Rudolph, age 52
President and CFO: Harvey Kamil, age 65
SVP and Assistant to CEO: Glenn Schneider, age 40
SVP Marketing and Advertising: James P. Flaherty, age 52
SVP Operations and Corporate Secretary: Hans Lindgren, age 49
Auditors: PricewaterhouseCoopers LLP

LOCATIONS

HQ: NBTY, Inc.
2100 Smithtown Ave., Ronkonkoma, NY 11779
Phone: 631-567-9500
Web: www.nbty.com

PRODUCTS/OPERATIONS

2009 Sales

	$ mil.	% of total
Wholesale	1,557.1	60
Retail		
Europe & UK	601.5	23
North America	201.9	8
Direct response	221.4	9
Total	**2,581.9**	**100**

Selected Retail Operations
DeTuinen (the Netherlands)
GNC (UK)
Holland & Barrett (Europe, South Africa)
Le Naturiste (Canada)
Nature's Way (Ireland)
Vitamin World (US)

Selected Brands
American Health
Body Fortress
Ester-C
Flex-A-Min
Knox
MET-Rx
Natural Wealth
Nature's Bounty
Osteo-Bi-Flex
Physiologics
Pure Protein
Puritan's Pride
Rexall
SISU
Solgar
Sundown
WORLDWIDE Sport Nutrition

COMPETITORS

Alere
Bactolac Pharmaceutical
GeoPharma
GNC
Herbalife Ltd.
Integrated BioPharma
NAI
Natrol
Nature's Sunshine

Nutraceutical International
Perrigo
Pharmavite LLC
Schiff Nutrition
Sunrider
Vitacost
Vitamin Shoppe
Whole Foods

HISTORICAL FINANCIALS
Company Type: Public

Income Statement
FYE: September 30

	REVENUE ($ mil.)	NET INCOME ($ mil.)	NET PROFIT MARGIN	EMPLOYEES
9/09	2,582	146	5.6%	13,950
9/08	2,180	153	7.0%	13,760
9/07	2,015	208	10.3%	10,800
9/06	1,880	112	5.9%	10,900
9/05	1,737	78	4.5%	11,200
Annual Growth	**10.4%**	**16.9%**	**—**	**5.6%**

2009 Year-End Financials
Debt ratio: 38.8%
Return on equity: 13.7%
Cash ($ mil.): 106
Current ratio: 3.08
Long-term debt ($ mil.): 438
No. of shares (mil.): 63
Dividends
  Yield: —
  Payout: —
Market value ($ mil.): 2,510

Stock History
NYSE: NTY

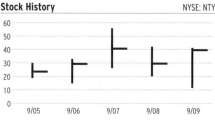

	STOCK PRICE ($) FY Close	P/E High	P/E Low	Earnings	Dividends	Book Value
9/09	39.58	18	5	2.30	—	17.79
9/08	29.52	18	9	2.33	—	15.74
9/07	40.60	18	9	3.00	—	16.65
9/06	29.27	20	10	1.62	—	13.24
9/05	23.50	26	17	1.13	—	11.29
Annual Growth	**13.9%**	**—**	**—**	**19.4%**	**—**	**12.0%**

NCI Building Systems

NCI's buildings are quite a "steel." NCI Building Systems, also known as NCI Group, engineers, designs, manufactures, and distributes metal buildings and components (doors, roofs, walls, and trim) for non-residential construction markets in North America. It sells its products to contractors, developers, and builders. The group also provides steel coil coating, which is used by manufacturers of HVAC systems, lighting fixtures, and other products. NCI has about 30 manufacturing facilities in the US and Mexico; it operates distribution and sales offices in the US and Canada. In 2009 investment firm Clayton, Dubilier & Rice acquired a controlling stake of 68% of NCI Group.

NCI was not immune to negative impacts of the tightened credit markets and industrywide construction declines in 2008 and 2009, which slowed down business significantly. Additionally, volatile price fluctuations in the steel market caused some customers to delay projects. To offset losses, the company closed several plants and cut 40% of its workforce. It also shuttered its residential overhead doors division, a noncore business.

To expand on its metal buildings and components operations — the heaviest hit as business declined — the group is expanding into new markets. It is converting at least one plant to an insulated panel systems manufacturing facility.

HISTORY

NCI Building Systems' founder Johnie Schulte Jr. began his career in the mid-1950s when he landed a job punching and shearing metal building pieces in Houston. In 1984 he founded NCI. The enterprise made only metal building components until 1987, when it began making metal buildings. That year NCI had sales of about $2 million. The company went public in 1992, and a year later its sales had reached more than $130 million. While competitors were shuttering plants in the soft market of the early 1990s, NCI was buying companies — including its 1992 purchase of A&S Building Systems, a metal building maker based in Caryville, Tennessee. NCI later expanded its product line to include self-storage buildings. It entered the market for roll-up steel overhead doors in 1995 when it bought Doors & Building Components (also a maker of interior steel parts) and started its own line of steel-frame homes.

NCI continued to make acquisitions in 1996, picking up a metal stud plant in Texas from Alabama Metal Industries, the equipment of Carlisle Engineered Metals, and Mesco Metal Buildings. The next year it bought the rest of Carlisle, including a manufacturing plant in Alabama, and began a 51%-owned joint venture in Mexico to manufacture framing systems. NCI bought the US metal building components business of UK-based BTR in 1998 for $593 million, doubling its size and adding painting and coating capabilities. The company spent 1999 integrating the large business.

NCI bought out Consolidated System's share in their DOUBLECOTE metal coil-coating joint venture for $26 million in 2000. Later that year NCI bought Midland Metals, a maker of metal building components. The move strengthened NCI's presence in the Midwest.

In 2001 NCI sold its 50% interest in Midwest Metal Coatings to its joint venture partner. The company closed five manufacturing facilities during the first quarter of fiscal 2002. NCI launched into direct selling to the public by opening a series of NCI Metal Depot retail factory stores that offer commercial and residential metal components (metal roof and wall panels, light structural and tubing shapes, and accessories) and a variety of small metal building packages (carports, storage sheds, and other metal buildings).

The company opened two retail stores in Texas in fiscal 2003. Also that year, NCI entered the residential garage door market by acquiring Texas-based Able Manufacturing and Wholesale Garage Door Company for about $3.3 million. NCI shortened the company's name to Able Door Manufacturing. Able operates distribution centers in the Dallas, Texas, area; Atlanta, Georgia; Oklahoma City, Oklahoma; and Ontario, California.

Founder, president, and CEO Johnie Schulte Jr. retired as an executive in November 2003 and retired as a director the next year; he was succeeded by A. R. Ginn. The following year NCI filed a suit against Schulte, alleging he had violated non-competitive agreements. Schulte filed a countersuit; an undisclosed settlement was reached in 2005.

To expand its retail and builder distribution channels for its small engineered buildings, NCI bought North Little Rock, Arkansas-based Heritage Building Systems and Steelbuilding.com for approximately $30 million in 2004. NCI also acquired the 49% minority stake held by its partners in its manufacturing plant in Monterrey, Mexico.

The next year NCI bought the intellectual property rights of metal building and components maker STEELOX Systems of Ohio, gaining the patents and trademarks, copyrights, common law rights, names, logos, websites, and customer lists of the established (by more than 70 years) company.

In 2006 NCI paid $370 million in cash for metal buildings maker Robertson-Ceco Corporation and its Robertson Building Systems, Ceco Building Systems, Star Building Systems, and Steelspec divisions. Late that year Ginn stepped down as CEO, with president and COO Norm Chambers becoming president and CEO. The next year Chambers assumed the chairmanship. NCI also bought Garco Building Systems in 2007.

EXECUTIVES

Chairman, President, and CEO:
Norman C. (Norm) Chambers, age 60, $2,266,175 total compensation
EVP and COO: Mark W. Dobbins, age 51, $770,461 total compensation
EVP, CFO, and Treasurer: Mark E. Johnson, age 43, $776,265 total compensation
EVP and CIO: Eric J. Brown, age 52
EVP, General Counsel, and Secretary: Todd R. Moore, age 50
VP Corporate Development: Mark T. Golladay, age 47
VP Finance and Corporate Controller: Richard W. Allen, age 34
President, Metal Components Division:
Charles W. Dickinson, age 58, $758,374 total compensation
President, NCI Buildings: Bradley D. (Brad) Robeson, age 47, $648,629 total compensation
President, Metal Coil Coatings: John L. Kuzdal, age 44
Auditors: Ernst & Young LLP

LOCATIONS

HQ: NCI Building Systems, Inc.
10943 N. Sam Houston Pkwy. West
Houston, TX 77064
Phone: 281-897-7788   **Fax:** 281-477-9674
Web: www.ncilp.com

PRODUCTS/OPERATIONS

2009 Sales

	$ mil.	% of total
Engineered building systems	541.6	46
Metal components	458.7	39
Metal coil coating	169.9	15
Adjustments	(202.3)	—
Total	**967.9**	**100**

Selected Subsidiaries

Building Systems de Mexico, S.A. de C.V.
NCI Group, Inc.
Robertson Building Systems Limited (Canada)
Robertson-Ceco II Corporation
Steelbuilding.com, Inc.

Selected Products and Services

Metal building components and complete buildings (carports, utility buildings, etc.)
Metal cladding and accessories
Mini-storage buildings
Modular offices
Roll-up doors, partitions, and panels

Selected Brands

A&S Building Systems
ABC (American Building Components)
Able Door Manufacturing
Ceco Building Systems
DBCI
Heritage Building Systems
MBCI
Mesco Building Solutions
Metal Coaters
Metal Depots
Metal Prep
Metallic Building Company
Mid-West Steelbuilding Company
Robertson Building Systems

COMPETITORS

American Buildings
Berger Building Products
Berlin Steel
Butler Manufacturing
Design Components
G-I Holdings
Gibraltar Industries
Horton Homes
Johns Manville
Nucor
Overhead Door
Varco Pruden Buildings
Williams Scotsman

HISTORICAL FINANCIALS

Company Type: Public

Income Statement

FYE: Saturday nearest October 31

	REVENUE ($ mil.)	NET INCOME ($ mil.)	NET PROFIT MARGIN	EMPLOYEES
10/09	968	(747)	—	3,673
10/08	1,764	79	4.5%	5,394
10/07	1,624	64	3.9%	5,721
10/06	1,571	74	4.7%	6,010
10/05	1,130	56	5.0%	3,800
Annual Growth	**(3.8%)**	**—**	**—**	**(0.8%)**

2009 Year-End Financials

Debt ratio: 274.0%
Return on equity: —
Cash ($ mil.): 90
Current ratio: 1.79
Long-term debt ($ mil.): 136
No. of shares (mil.): 20
Dividends
  Yield: —
  Payout: —
Market value ($ mil.): 192

Stock History

NYSE: NCS

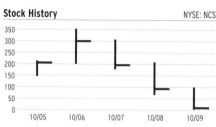

	STOCK PRICE ($) FY Close	P/E High/Low		PER SHARE ($) Earnings	Dividends	Book Value
10/09	9.80	—	—	(170.30)	—	2.54
10/08	93.05	10	4	20.25	—	31.88
10/07	195.90	20	12	15.30	—	27.58
10/06	299.25	20	12	17.25	—	25.47
10/05	205.30	16	11	13.40	—	22.69
Annual Growth	**(53.3%)**			**—**	**—**	**(42.2%)**

NCR Corporation

Want to find NCR? Follow the money. A leading maker of automated teller machines (ATMs), the company also makes point-of-sale (POS) terminals and bar code scanners. Other retail and financial systems offerings include self-service kiosks for such applications as gift registries; paper, ink, and other consumable media; DVDs; and check image processing systems. NCR's services unit provides maintenance and support, as well as professional services, such as systems integration and managed services.

The company reorganized its operational structure in 2008, shifting from product-based business units to geographic divisions. The restructuring allowed NCR to reduce redundancies and process inefficiencies. Continuing to struggle with profitability in 2009, due to the global economic downturn, the company is cutting up to 10% of its workforce, possibly eliminating more than 2,200 jobs.

While many companies continue the trend of outsourcing manufacturing to third-party contractors, NCR is going in the opposite direction, opening two new plants for making ATMs in Brazil and the US during 2009, taking some work away from Flextronics International, the giant contract electronics manufacturer.

NCR has come a long way since it was known as National Cash Register, and the company continues to broaden its product line and move into new markets. It has targeted such industries as entertainment, gaming, health care, and travel for expansion of its self-service systems. Examples of such systems include self-checkout kiosks in hotels and casinos, as well as ordering and payment systems for restaurants.

In 2009 the company acquired TNR Holdings, an operator of DVD rental kiosks. NCR made the purchase to expand its SelfServ Entertainment line, and it plans to install the units in supermarkets and convenience stores nationwide. The kiosks will operate under the Blockbuster Express brand. NCR's alliance with Blockbuster began in 2008 with a pilot kiosk program.

The company further expanded the Blockbuster partnership in 2009 with its acquisition of DVDPlay, which operates about 1,300 DVD rental kiosks in North America. Those kiosks will be rebranded as Blockbuster Express outlets, bringing NCR's total to around 3,800.

HISTORY

John Patterson bought control of a Dayton, Ohio, cash register factory in 1882 and founded National Cash Register (NCR). Colonel Edward Deeds (who later became chairman) joined NCR in 1889, and hired inventor Charles Kettering in 1904 to develop an electric cash register. (The duo also developed an electric car ignition system and left NCR to start Dayton Engineering Laboratories Co., or Delco.)

By the 1920s NCR controlled 90% of the cash register market. That decade NCR introduced accounting machines, which became almost as important to the company as cash registers. NCR's stock dropped from $154 to $6.87 in the crash of 1929, but by 1936 the company had fully recovered.

Responding to the commercialization of computers following WWII, NCR bought computer developer Computer Research in 1952. During the 1960s the company introduced mainframe computers, opened data processing centers, established microelectronics research facilities, and introduced disk-based computers. However, NCR failed to automate its primary products — cash registers and accounting machines. In 1969 the company had record profits of $50 million; by 1971 they had plunged to $2 million.

William Anderson, who became president in 1972, is credited with saving NCR. He slashed its Dayton workforce by 75% and focused the company on computing, with an emphasis on retail scanners and ATMs.

In the early 1980s NCR moved from proprietary to UNIX operating systems and introduced networking equipment. In 1990 it began developing parallel processing technologies with database management specialist Teradata. That year the company won a contract to supply workstations to JCPenney stores.

Hoping to become one of the world's top PC makers, in 1991 AT&T bought NCR in a $7.4 billion hostile takeover. AT&T also acquired Teradata and merged the two companies as Global Information Systems (GIS). Lars Nyberg, a Swede who had led a divisional turnaround at electronics giant Philips, took over GIS in 1995 and began a reorganization that would eventually cut 11,000 jobs. When he joined GIS, it was losing $2 million a day.

In 1996 AT&T spun off the company (renamed NCR); it had suffered losses totaling nearly $4 billion during its years with AT&T. Nyberg jettisoned NCR's financially draining PC operations but beefed up the company's ATM and retail automation business by acquiring Compris Technologies (grocery automation and management products) and Dataworks (check processing software).

But losses prompted NCR to restructure in 1997, and the company slimmed down its 130-country network of independent operating units into a handful of global business units. The next year it announced a partnership with Microsoft to further integrate NCR's Teradata systems with Microsoft's server technology, making it easier for companies to create data warehouses.

The following year, with a narrowed focus on ATM, banking, retail, and data warehousing systems, the company acquired IBM's financial self-service operations and financial industry automation software company Gaspar.

In 2000 NCR bought Ceres Integrated Solutions, a provider of customer relationship management software, and it acquired information technology and outsourcing service provider 4Front Technologies for $250 million. In 2003 Nyberg handed the CEO reins to NCR president and former Teradata head Mark Hurd. Nyberg retained his chairmanship.

In 2004 NCR acquired Kinetics, a provider of self-service check-in systems for airlines and hotels; Kinetics' products also included systems for restaurant preordering and event ticketing.

Early in 2005 Hurd resigned to become CEO of Hewlett-Packard; NCR director Jim Ringler was appointed chairman and interim CEO. Soon after, former Symbol Technologies CEO Bill Nuti was named CEO of NCR.

NCR acquired the ATM business of Tidel Technologies in 2006. NCR also acquired the assets of IDVelocity, a developer of RFID infrastructure and process management software in 2006.

The company purchased Touch Automation, a developer of kiosks used to distribute DVDs, in 2007. NCR also spun off its Teradata unit that year.

EXECUTIVES

Chairman, CEO, and Director: William R. (Bill) Nuti, age 46, $6,955,919 total compensation
EVP Industry Solutions Group: John G. Bruno, age 44, $2,907,035 total compensation
SVP, CFO, and Chief Accounting Officer: Robert (Bob) Fishman, age 46, $469,317 total compensation
SVP and General Manager, NCR Consumables: Daniel (Dan) Bogan, age 54
SVP Human Resources: Andrea Ledford, age 44
SVP, NCR Services: Christopher J. Askew, age 48
SVP Global Sales: Peter Leav, age 39, $3,054,717 total compensation
SVP Global Operations: Peter A. Dorsman, age 54, $1,489,186 total compensation
VP Corporate Development and Chief Marketing Officer: Richard (Rich) Bravman, age 50
VP Sales: Tushar Kothari
VP North American Channels: Juliann Larimer
VP European Channels: Dawn Calderbank
VP and General Manager, NCR Entertainment: Justin Hotard
General Counsel and Secretary: Jennifer M. Daniels, age 46
Director Corporate Communications: Peter Tulupman
Auditors: PricewaterhouseCoopers LLP

LOCATIONS

HQ: NCR Corporation
2651 Satellite Blvd., Duluth, GA 30096
Phone: 937-445-1936 **Fax:** 937-445-5541
Web: www.ncr.com

2009 Sales

	$ mil.	% of total
Americas		
US	1,609	35
Other countries	413	9
Europe, Middle East & Africa	1,649	36
Asia/Pacific		
Japan	328	7
Other countries	613	13
Total	**4,612**	**100**

PRODUCTS/OPERATIONS

2009 Sales

	$ mil.	% of total
Products	2,234	48
Support services	1,800	39
Professional & installation services	578	13
Total	**4,612**	**100**

Selected Products and Services

Customer Service
  Maintenance
  Professional and installation-related
Financial Self Service
  Automated teller machines (ATMs)
  Support services
Retail Store Automation
  Consulting, implementation, and maintenance services
  Electronic shelf labels
  Point-of-sale workstations and scanners
  Software
  Web-enabled kiosks
NCR Consumables
  Ink
  Paper
  Printer cartridges
Payment and Imaging
  Consulting, outsourcing, and support services
  Transactions processing systems

HISTORICAL FINANCIALS

Company Type: Public

Income Statement

FYE: December 31

	REVENUE ($ mil.)	NET INCOME ($ mil.)	NET PROFIT MARGIN	EMPLOYEES
12/09	4,612	(30)	—	21,500
12/08	5,315	228	4.3%	22,400
12/07	4,970	274	5.5%	23,200
12/06	6,142	382	6.2%	28,900
12/05	6,028	529	8.8%	28,200
Annual Growth	(6.5%)	—	—	(6.6%)

2009 Year-End Financials

Debt ratio: 2.0%
Return on equity: —
Cash ($ mil.): 451
Current ratio: 1.66
Long-term debt ($ mil.): 11

No. of shares (mil.): 161
Dividends
  Yield: —
  Payout: —
Market value ($ mil.): 1,786

Stock History

NYSE: NCR

	STOCK PRICE ($) FY Close	P/E High/Low		PER SHARE ($) Earnings	Dividends	Book Value
12/09	11.13	—	—	(0.21)	—	3.51
12/08	14.14	21	9	1.36	—	2.74
12/07	25.10	20	14	1.50	—	10.95
12/06	20.37	10	7	2.09	—	11.72
12/05	16.17	7	5	2.80	—	12.68
Annual Growth	(8.9%)	—	—	—	—	(27.4%)

New York Life Insurance Company

New York Life Insurance has been in the Big Apple since it was just a tiny seed. Although the top mutual life insurer in the US has branched out somewhat, it has retained its core business: life insurance and annuities. Its products include long-term care insurance and special group policies sold through AARP and other affinity groups and professional associations. New York Life Investments offers products and services ranging from mutual funds for individuals to investment management services for institutional investors. The company, through New York Life International, is also reaching out geographically, targeting areas such as Mexico and India where the life insurance markets are not yet mature.

The insurer is using its considerable capital reserves to further expand its international operations — Asia and Latin America are major expansion targets, and sales growth in both regions has been rapid. It is also expanding its investment management operations through its New York Life Investment Management (mutual funds, group and individual retirement plans, college savings products).

New York Life distributes its products primarily through its network of some 12,000 career agents in the US and internationally. A network of brokers represents the company's corporate and bank-owned products and products aimed at high net-worth customers.

In the late 1990's the company, like many of its rivals, considered demutualizing and turning itself into a public company. However, New York Life encountered resistance from legislators and eventually dropped plans for such a change. Demutualizing would have allowed it to make riskier investments, but also would have made it vulnerable to being gobbled up in a merger. As a result of remaining a staid old mutual, the company had a comfy cushion of capital reserves to see it through the economic crises of 2008 and 2009. Unlike its public competitors, New York Life retained its pristine ratings, and even saw earnings increase.

HISTORY

In 1841 actuary Pliny Freeman and 56 New York businessmen founded Nautilus Insurance Co., the third US policyholder-owned company. It began operating in 1845 and became New York Life in 1849.

By 1846 the company had the first life insurance agent west of the Mississippi River. Although the Civil War disrupted southern business, New York Life honored all its obligations and renewed lapsed policies when the war ended. By 1887 the company had developed its branch office system. By the turn of the century, the company had established an agent compensation plan that featured a lifetime income after 20 years of service (discontinued 1991). New York Life moved into Europe in the late 1800s but withdrew after WWI.

In the early 1950s the company simplified insurance forms, slashed premiums, and updated mortality tables from the 1860s. In 1956 it became the first life insurer to use data-processing equipment on a large scale.

New York Life helped develop variable life insurance, which featured variable benefits and level premiums in the 1960s; it added variable annuities in 1968. Steady growth continued into the late 1970s, when high interest rates led to heavy policyholder borrowing. The outflow of money convinced New York Life to make its products more competitive as investments.

The company formed New York Life and Health Insurance Co. in 1982. It acquired MacKay-Shields Financial, which oversees its MainStay mutual funds, in 1984. The company's first pure investment product, a real estate limited partnership, debuted that year. (When limited partnerships proved riskier than most insurance customers bargained for, investors sued New York Life; in 1996 the company negotiated a plan to liquidate the partnerships and reimburse investors.)

Expansion continued in 1987 when New York Life bought a controlling interest in a third-party insurance plan administrator and group insurance programs. The company also acquired Sanus Corp. Health Systems.

New York Life formed an insurance joint venture in Indonesia in 1992; it also entered South Korea and Taiwan. The next year it bought Aetna UK's life insurance operations.

In 1994 New York Life grew its health care holdings, adding utilization review and physician practice management units. Allegations of churning (agents inducing customers to buy more expensive policies) led New York Life to overhaul its sales practices in 1994; it settled the resulting lawsuit for $300 million in 1995. Soon came claims that agents hadn't properly informed customers that some policies were vulnerable to interest-rate changes and that customers might be entitled to share in the settlement. Some agents lashed out, saying New York Life fired them so it wouldn't have to pay them retirement benefits.

As health care margins decreased and the insurance industry consolidated, New York Life in 1998 sold its health insurance operations and said it would demutualize — a plan challenged by the state legislature.

In 2000 the company bought two Mexican insurance firms, including the nation's #2 life insurer, Seguros Monterrey. It received Office of Thrift Supervision permission to open a bank, New York Life Trust Company. Also that year the company created a subsidiary to house its asset management businesses and entered the Indian market through its joint venture with Max India.

In 2002 New York Life entered into a joint life insurance venture with China's Haier Group.

EXECUTIVES

Chairman, President, and CEO:
Theodore A. (Ted) Mathas, age 43
Vice Chairman and Chief Investment Officer;
Chairman, New York Life Investment Management:
Gary E. Wendlandt, age 59
EVP; Chairman and CEO, New York Life International:
Richard L. (Dick) Mucci, age 59
EVP; President and CEO, New York Life Investment Management: John Y. Kim, age 49
EVP and Chief Administrative Officer: Frank M. Boccio
EVP; CEO, Greater China: Gary R. Bennett
EVP and COO, New York Life International:
Russell G. Bundschuh
EVP and CFO: Michael E. Sproule
EVP, Chief Legal Officer, and General Counsel:
Sheila K. Davidson
EVP and CEO, Asia Sub-Region, New York Life
International: Arthur Belfer
EVP Retirement Income Security:
Christopher O. (Chris) Blunt

LOCATIONS

HQ: New York Life Insurance Company
  51 Madison Ave., New York, NY 10010
Phone: 212-576-7000
Web: www.newyorklife.com

PRODUCTS/OPERATIONS

2009 Revenue

	$ mil.	% of total
Premiums	11,496	52
Investment income	8,853	40
Fees	1,026	4
Investment gains	387	2
Other	484	2
Total	**22,246**	**100**

COMPETITORS

AIG American General	MassMutual
Allstate	MetLife
American National	Mutual of Omaha
Insurance	Northwestern Mutual
AXA	Principal Financial
CIGNA	Prudential
CNA Financial	T. Rowe Price
Guardian Life	TIAA-CREF
The Hartford	UBS Financial Services
John Hancock Financial	

HISTORICAL FINANCIALS
Company Type: Mutual company

Income Statement
FYE: December 31

	ASSETS ($ mil.)	NET INCOME ($ mil.)	INCOME AS % OF ASSETS	EMPLOYEES
12/09	208,153	1,290	0.6%	17,000
12/08	188,908	(1,197)	—	15,000
12/07	198,383	1,497	0.8%	14,847
12/06	182,343	2,298	1.3%	13,580
12/05	168,865	855	0.5%	13,180
Annual Growth	5.4%	10.8%	—	6.6%

2009 Year-End Financials

Equity as % of assets: —
Return on assets: 0.6%
Return on equity: —
Long-term debt ($ mil.): —
Sales ($ mil.): 22,246

Net Income History

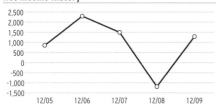

New York Times

"All the News That's Fit to Print and Post On-line" would be a more accurate motto for this media titan. The New York Times Company (The Times Co.) publishes *The New York Times*, one of the world's most respected newspapers boasting a circulation of about 950,000. It also owns *The Boston Globe* and the *Worcester Telegram & Gazette* (Massachusetts). Subsidiary International Herald Tribune, meanwhile, publishes its eponymous newspaper for English readers in 180 countries. The Times Co. distributes news online through NYTimes.com and other sites, and it owns online content portal About Group. Chairman Arthur Sulzberger and his family control the company through a trust.

The Times Co. is something of an anomaly in an industry led by diversified media conglomerates (Tribune Co.) and vast newspaper empires stretching coast to coast (Gannett). Without television stations or other media businesses to fall back on, the company's success hinges on its big city papers attracting readers and advertisers. Its flagship paper, known to many as The Grey Lady, fights for readership in a charged New York City media market against tabloids such as the *New York Post* (owned by News Corporation) and *The Daily News*. The Manhattan news business got a little tougher in 2010 when *The Wall Street Journal*, another News Corporation paper, launched a New York metro news section.

Having a venerable and highly respected masthead has not saved The Times Co. from the declines affecting the newspaper business, however. Both readership and ad sales have been declining for years as people turn to other sources for their news. The downturn in the economy has only served to exacerbate those problems. In response, The Times Co. raised cover prices and subscription rates for *The New York Times* in an effort to make up for declines in print advertising.

Cost-cutting efforts by the company have included both wage reductions and layoffs. In 2009 *The Boston Globe* was forced to cut about 10% of its workforce. The Times Co. also shuttered a distribution subsidiary that delivered more than 220 publications throughout the greater New York area. Meanwhile, the company is working to boost online readership by incorporating video and interactive features into its flagship nytimes.com website.

Losses from its publishing operations and the need to pay down debt have forced The Times Co. to take drastic action. During 2009 The Times Co. raised $250 million from Carlos Slim Helú through Inmobiliaria Carso (his family-controlled trust) and Grupo Financiero Inbursa. The deal made the Mexican billionaire the second-largest shareholder after Sulzberger. (However, the Ochs-Sulzberger family has an almost unbreakable lock on control through its special class of shares.) Carlos Slim and his family control Mexico's #1 telecommunications provider Teléfonos de México (Telmex) and retail holding company Grupo Carso.

Looking to shed other assets, the company sold part of its stake in New England Sports Ventures, a joint venture that owns the Boston Red Sox baseball team and 80% of cable channel New England Sports Network, to Henry McCance in 2010. The deal left The Times Co. with more than 15% interest in the sports business, which it continues to shop to prospective buyers.

HISTORY

In 1851 George Jones and Henry Raymond, former *New York Tribune* staffers, started *The New York Times*. The politically minded paper lost ground to the yellow journalism of Hearst and Pulitzer and was bought in 1896 by Tennessee newspaperman Adolph Ochs, who continued to encourage hard news and business coverage. Ochs coined the newspaper's now-famous slogan, "All the News That's Fit to Print."

Ochs' son-in-law Arthur Hays Sulzberger, who ran the paper from 1935 to 1961, diversified the company with the 1944 purchase of two New York City radio stations. In 1963 Ochs' grandson Arthur Ochs "Punch" Sulzberger took control of the company.

In the 1960s declining ad revenues and a newspaper strike sent the company into the red. To regain strength, Punch built the largest news-gathering staff of any newspaper. The *Times'* coverage of the Vietnam War helped change public sentiment, and the newspaper won a Pulitzer Prize in 1972 for publishing the Pentagon Papers. In the meantime Punch had taken the company public (1967), although the family retained solid control. In the late 1960s and 1970s the company began co-publishing the *International Herald Tribune* (1967, with The Washington Post) and bought magazines, publishing houses, TV stations, smaller newspapers, and cable TV systems.

In the 1980s the *Times* added feature sections to compete with suburban papers. The company bought *Golf World* in 1988, and the next year sold its cable systems.

Arthur Ochs Sulzberger Jr. succeeded his father as *Times* publisher in 1992. The next year The New York Times bought Affiliated Publications, owner of *The Boston Globe,* for $1.1 billion. In 1997 chairman and CEO Punch Sulzberger retired from executive duties but remained on the board as chairman emeritus. He was replaced by his son as chairman, and non-family member Russell Lewis as CEO.

Journalistic integrity took a nosedive at *The Boston Globe* in mid-1998: Within a span of two months the newspaper demanded the resignations of reporter Patricia Smith after she admitted to making up people and quotes for several stories, and columnist Mike Barnicle after he included jokes from a book by George Carlin in his column without attribution.

In 2001 the company was part of a group of investors calling themselves New England Sports Ventures, which bought the Boston Red Sox, Fenway Park, and cable network New England Sports Network.

Punch Sulzberger retired from the company's board in 2001, but he retained the titles of chairman emeritus of The Times Company and of co-chairman of the *International Herald Tribune*. His daughter, Cathy J. Sulzberger, replaced him on the board.

At the close of the company's 2004 fiscal year, Lewis announced his retirement as president, CEO, and director; former COO Janet Robinson was named his successor.

In 2005 the company acquired online information portal About.com from PRIMEDIA, and it bought a 49% stake in free daily paper *Metro Boston* (owned by Metro International). About 200 employees were laid off to help contain costs in the face of declining newspaper ad revenue. A further 250 jobs were cut the next year.

The New York Times Company further trimmed its noncore assets the following year, selling nine TV stations to Oak Hill Capital Partners for $575 million.

EXECUTIVES

Chairman; Publisher, The New York Times:
Arthur O. Sulzberger Jr., age 58,
$5,986,738 total compensation
Vice Chairman; President and COO, Regional Media Group: Michael Golden, age 59,
$2,400,841 total compensation
President, CEO, and Director: Janet L. Robinson,
age 59, $6,262,755 total compensation
SVP and CFO: James M. Follo, age 50,
$1,297,269 total compensation
SVP and CIO: Joseph N. Seibert, age 50
SVP, General Counsel, and Secretary:
Kenneth A. (Ken) Richieri, age 58
SVP Finance and Controller: R. Anthony (Tony) Benten,
age 46
SVP Human Resources: Todd C. McCarty, age 44
SVP Corporate Communications: Robert H. Christie
SVP Corporate Development: James C. Lessersohn
SVP Digital Operations: Martin A. Nisenholtz, age 54
**SVP Marketing and Circulation, The New York Times
Media Group:** Yasmin Namini, age 50
**SVP and Chief Advertising Officer, The New York
Times Media Group; General Manager, NYTimes.com:**
Denise F. Warren, age 45
President and CEO, About Group: Cella M. Irvine
President and General Manager, The New York Times:
Scott H. Heekin-Canedy, age 58,
$2,130,990 total compensation
Executive Editor, The New York Times: Bill Keller
Public Editor: Arthur S. (Art) Brisbane, age 59
Auditors: Ernst & Young LLP

LOCATIONS

HQ: The New York Times Company
620 8th Ave., New York, NY 10018
Phone: 212-556-1234
Web: www.nytco.com

PRODUCTS/OPERATIONS

2009 Sales

	$ mil.	% of total
Advertising	1,336.3	55
Circulation	936.5	38
Other	167.6	7
Total	**2,440.4**	**100**

2009 Sales

	$ mil.	% of total
New York Times Media Group	1,581.9	65
New England Media Group	440.6	18
Regional Media Group	296.9	12
About Group	121.0	5
Total	**2,440.4**	**100**

Selected Operations

The New York Times Media Group
  Baseline StudioSystems (database research service)
  International Herald Tribune (Paris)
  The New York Times
  NYTimes.com
  Other
    Digital Archive Distribution (database licensing)
    The New York Times Index
    The New York Times News Services (news
     syndication)
New England Media Group
  Newspapers
    The Boston Globe
    Worcester Telegram & Gazette (Massachusetts)
  Online content
    Boston.com
    Telegram.com

Regional Media Group
  The Courier (Houma, LA)
  Daily Comet (Thibodaux, LA)
  The Dispatch (Lexington, NC)
  The Gadsden Times (Alabama)
  The Gainesville Sun (Florida)
  Herald-Journal (Spartanburg, SC)
  The Ledger (Lakeland, FL)
  Petaluma Argus-Courier (weekly, California)
  The Press Democrat (Santa Rosa, CA)
  Sarasota Herald-Tribune (Florida)
  Star-Banner (Ocala, FL)
  Times-News (Hendersonville, NC)
  The Tuscaloosa News (Alabama)
  Wilmington Star-News (North Carolina)
About Group (online content, About.com)
Other operations and investments
  Donohue Malbaie (49%, newsprint manufacturing,
   Canada)
  Madison Paper Industries (40%, Maine)
  Metro Boston (49%, fee daily newspaper)
  New England Sports Ventures (17%)
    Boston Red Sox (Major League Baseball franchise)
    Fenway Park (sports stadium)
    New England Sports Network (80%, regional cable
     broadcasting)
    Roush Fenway Racing (50%, NASCAR racing team)
  quadrantONE (25%, online advertising)

COMPETITORS

Advance Publications
Agence France-Presse
AOL
BBC
CNN
Daily News
Financial Times
Gannett
Hearst Newspapers
Herald Media
MSN
News Corp.
Newsday
Tribune Company
Washington Post
Wikimedia Foundation
Yahoo!

HISTORICAL FINANCIALS

Company Type: Public

Income Statement

FYE: Last Sunday in December

	REVENUE ($ mil.)	NET INCOME ($ mil.)	NET PROFIT MARGIN	EMPLOYEES
12/09	2,440	20	0.8%	7,665
12/08	2,949	(58)	—	9,346
12/07	3,195	209	6.5%	10,231
12/06	3,290	(543)	—	11,585
12/05	3,373	266	7.9%	11,965
Annual Growth	**(7.8%)**	**(47.7%)**	**—**	**(10.5%)**

2009 Year-End Financials

Debt ratio: 127.3%
Return on equity: 3.6%
Cash ($ mil.): 37
Current ratio: 1.00
Long-term debt ($ mil.): 769

No. of shares (mil.): 146
Dividends
  Yield: 0.0%
  Payout: —
Market value ($ mil.): 1,803

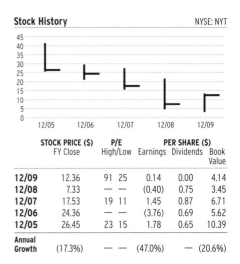

Stock History NYSE: NYT

	STOCK PRICE ($) FY Close	P/E High/Low		Earnings	PER SHARE ($) Dividends	Book Value
12/09	12.36	91	25	0.14	0.00	4.14
12/08	7.33	—	—	(0.40)	0.75	3.45
12/07	17.53	19	11	1.45	0.87	6.71
12/06	24.36	—	—	(3.76)	0.69	5.62
12/05	26.45	23	15	1.78	0.65	10.39
Annual Growth	**(17.3%)**	**—**	**—**	**(47.0%)**	**—**	**(20.6%)**

Newell Rubbermaid

Newell Rubbermaid wants to get its products into your drawers, your kitchen cabinets, and your workbench. The go-to firm for men, women, and children makes housewares (Rubbermaid plastic products, Calphalon cookware), hardware (Amerock cabinet hardware, IRWIN and Lenox hand tools), home furnishings (Levolor blinds), juvenile products (Graco), hair products (Goody), and office products (DYMO, Sanford, Sharpie). Newell Rubbermaid sells its products primarily to mass retailers (Target) and home and office supply stores (Staples). Mark Ketchum, from Procter & Gamble, heads the firm as CEO; Former Gillette executive Michael Cowhig is chairman.

The company aims to strengthen and transform the consumer products maker's portfolio. Citing rising resin costs, Newell Rubbermaid has targeted resin-intensive products for downsizing or elimination. It is also cutting some 5,000 employees from its workforce of 31,000 and shuttering a third of its 80 factories. To consolidate offices, the company in 2008 moved its headquarters to a 350,000-sq.-ft., 14-story building in Atlanta. Newell Rubbermaid also sold portions of its Home Decor Europe business to window-coverings giant Hunter Douglas. The sale included businesses in Portugal and the Nordic, Central, and Eastern European regions. (Previously, the company sold its Home Decor operations in the UK.)

In recent years Newell Rubbermaid has been whittling down its businesses and concentrating on core competencies. The company sold its preschool toys business, Little Tikes, to MGA Entertainment (maker of the Bratz line of dolls) in late 2006. It also sold off three of its businesses (Anchor Hocking Glass, Burnes Picture Frame, and Mirro Cookware) to Global Home Products, LLC, for an estimated $320 million, as well as its Curver division (European indoor organization and home storage business) to Jardin International Holding.

Known as Newell before its purchase of plastics giant Rubbermaid in 1999, the company has become a diversified manufacturer during the past 30 years, mostly by acquiring companies that produce brand-name, low-tech staples, such as American Saw & Manufacturing (manufacturer of power tools under the Lenox brand).

HISTORY

Businessmen in Ogdensburg, New York, advanced curtain rod maker W.F. Linton Co. $1,000 to relocate from Rhode Island in the early 1900s. Local wholesaler Edgar Newell signed off on the loan; when the company went bankrupt in 1903, he was forced to take over. The company, renamed Newell Manufacturing, set up plants in Canada and Freeport, Illinois, to ease shipping costs and speed delivery.

Production expanded into towel racks, ice picks, and other items; Woolworth's decision to carry Newell's products turned the company into a national supplier. Edgar Newell died in 1920. The company made its first acquisition in 1938, window treatment specialist Drapery Hardware.

The Newell companies were consolidated in the mid-1960s into a single corporation. Daniel Ferguson was named president in 1965 and served alongside his CEO father Leonard, one of Newell's original employees. During his tenure, Daniel hitched the company's future to the growing dominance of large discount stores. Newell went from a $14 million family business to a global, multiline conglomerate by acquiring products that it distributed to these big buyers. The company went public in 1972 and bought paint applicator maker EZ Paintr the next year. By 1978 sales reached $100 million.

Newell moved into housewares with the acquisitions of Mirro (cookware, 1983) and the much larger Anchor Hocking (glassware, 1987). It then bought office supply companies W.T. Rogers and Keene Manufacturing in 1991 and Sanford (writing instruments) in 1992. That year Daniel bowed out of active management.

The company began a global push with its purchase of Corning's European Consumer Products business (1994), and it kept busy at home by buying Insilco's Rolodex unit and Rubbermaid's office products business (both 1997). William Sovey succeeded Daniel as chairman in 1997, and John McDonough became CEO. Its 1998 acquisitions included Calphalon (upscale cookware), Panex (Brazil, bakeware), and Rotring Group (Germany, writing instruments).

Originally a balloon maker in the 1920s, by the mid-1930s Ohio's Wooster Rubber had acquired the Rubbermaid product line of rubber housewares. It went public in 1955 and two years later changed its name to Rubbermaid. During the 1980s the company enjoyed a decade of phenomenal growth. However — despite product innovations — increased material costs, a competitive retail climate, and weak customer service began dulling Rubbermaid's luster. Profits plunged even as it reached record sales.

Newell's $6 billion purchase of Rubbermaid in 1999 sealed its biggest deal yet and resulted in a name change: Newell Rubbermaid. Also that year Newell Rubbermaid bought the consumer products division of McKechnie (window furnishings and cabinet hardware) and three French firms: Ateliers 28 (drapery hardware), Reynolds (pens and pencils), and Ceanothe Holdings (picture frames).

In late 2000 CEO McDonough resigned and Sovey replaced him. In 2001 Newell Rubbermaid acquired Gillette's stationery business, including the Parker, Paper Mate, Liquid Paper, and Waterman brands. The same month Joseph Galli succeeded Sovey as CEO; Sovey reassumed his position as chairman (and left in mid-2004).

In 2003 Newell Rubbermaid acquired American Saw & Manufacturing for $450 million in cash, and then sold its Cosmolab business to CSI East, an affiliate of Cosmetic Specialties. The same year Newell Rubbermaid moved its corporate headquarters from Illinois to Alpharetta, Georgia (relocated again in 2004 to Atlanta).

In April 2004 Newell sold its Anchor Hocking Glass, Burnes Picture Frame, and Mirro Cookware divisions to Global Home Products, LLC.

To add depth to its office products portfolio the company acquired the DYMO brand from Esselte in late 2005 for $730 million.

CEO Joseph Galli resigned in 2005. A board member with three decades of experience at Procter & Gamble, Mark Ketchum stepped in as interim CEO. He was made permanent in 2006.

In a move that expanded the company's juvenile products business and positioned it to expand in Asia, Newell Rubbermaid acquired Japan's Aprica Kassai, a maker of strollers, car seats, and other children's gear, in April 2008.

Also in 2008 it acquired Technical Concepts, an Illinois-based firm that makes restroom hygiene systems for the away-from-home (AFH) market.

EXECUTIVES

Chairman: Michael T. Cowhig, age 63
President, CEO, and Director: Mark D. Ketchum, age 60, $8,416,539 total compensation
EVP and CFO: Juan R. Figuereo, age 54, $679,833 total compensation
EVP Human Resources and Corporate Communications and Chief Human Resources Officer: James M. (Jim) Sweet, age 57
SVP and Chief Marketing Officer: Theodore W. (Ted) Woehrle, age 48
SVP, General Counsel, and Secretary: John Stipancich, age 41
SVP Program Management Office and CIO: Gordon Steele, age 58
VP, Corporate Controller, and Chief Accounting Officer: John B. Ellis
VP E-Business and Interactive Marketing: Bert DuMars
VP Global Licensing: Nathaniel S. (Nat) Milburn, age 37
VP Investor Relations: Nancy O'Donnell
VP Corporate Communications: David Doolittle
President, Home and Family: Jay D. Gould, age 50, $1,725,621 total compensation
President, Office Products: Penny McIntyre, age 48, $1,725,621 total compensation
President, Corporate Development: Hartley D. (Buddy) Blaha, age 44, $1,271,678 total compensation
President, Rubbermaid Commercial Products: Larry McIsaac
President, Office Products North America: Ben Gadbois
President, Newell Rubbermaid International: J. Eduardo Senf, age 50
Group President, Tools, Hardware, and Commercial Products: William A. (Bill) Burke III, age 49
Auditors: Ernst & Young LLP

LOCATIONS

HQ: Newell Rubbermaid Inc.
   3 Glenlake Pkwy., Atlanta, GA 30328
Phone: 770-418-7000   **Fax:** 770-407-3970
Web: www.newellrubbermaid.com

2009 Sales

	$ mil.	% of total
US	3,881.4	70
Europe, Middle East & Africa	795.1	14
Canada	326.5	6
Asia/Pacific	311.7	5
Latin America	262.9	5
Total	**5,577.6**	**100**

PRODUCTS/OPERATIONS

2009 Sales

	$ mil.	% of total
Home & family	2,377.2	43
Office products	1,674.7	30
Tools, hardware & commercial products	1,525.7	27
Total	**5,577.6**	**100**

Selected Brands and Trade Names

Cleaning, organization, and decor
   Brute
   Kirsch
   Levolor
   Roughneck
   Rubbermaid
   TakeAlongs
   TC

Office products
   Accent
   Berol
   DYMO
   Eberhard Farber
   Expo
   Liquid Paper
   Paper Mate
   Parker
   rotring
   Sharpie
   Uni-Ball (under license)
   Vis-à-vis
   Waterman

Tools and hardware
   Amerock
   BernzOmatic
   Bulldog
   Irwin
   Lenox
   Quick-Grip
   Marathon
   Shur-Line
   Strait-Line
   Unibit
   Vise-Grip

Home and family
   Ace
   Aprica
   Calphalon
   Calphalon One
   Cooking with Calphalon
   Goody
   Graco
   Katana
   Kitchen Essentials
   Solano
   Teutonia

COMPETITORS

ACCO Brands	Knape & Vogt
Acme United	Lancaster Colony
Alticor	Libbey
Avery Dennison	Lifetime Brands
BIC	Myers Industries
Bridgestone	Owens-Illinois
Coleman	Springs Global
Cooper Industries	Step 2
Crayola	Sterilite
Decorator Industries	Tupperware Brands
Dixon Ticonderoga	Uniek
Faber-Castell	Wilton Brands
Fortune Brands	WKI Holding
Home Products International	ZAG Industries
Katy Industries	

HISTORICAL FINANCIALS

Company Type: Public

Income Statement

	REVENUE ($ mil.)	NET INCOME ($ mil.)	NET PROFIT MARGIN	EMPLOYEES
12/09	5,578	286	5.1%	19,500
12/08	6,471	(52)	—	20,400
12/07	6,407	467	7.3%	22,000
12/06	6,201	385	6.2%	23,500
12/05	6,343	251	4.0%	27,900
Annual Growth	(3.2%)	3.2%	—	(8.6%)

2009 Year-End Financials

Debt ratio: 113.3%
Return on equity: 16.8%
Cash ($ mil.): 278
Current ratio: 1.24
Long-term debt ($ mil.): 2,015
No. of shares (mil.): 278
Dividends
Yield: 1.7%
Payout: 25.8%
Market value ($ mil.): 4,177

Stock History

NYSE: NWL

	STOCK PRICE ($) FY Close	P/E High/Low	PER SHARE ($) Earnings	Dividends	Book Value
12/09	15.01	17 5	0.97	0.25	6.39
12/08	9.78	— —	(0.19)	0.84	5.80
12/07	25.88	19 14	1.68	0.84	8.08
12/06	28.95	21 17	1.40	0.84	6.79
12/05	23.78	28 23	0.91	0.84	5.90
Annual Growth	(10.9%)	— —	1.6%	(26.1%)	2.0%

Newmont Mining

Newmont Mining certainly goes for the gold. The company is among the world's top gold producers (with Barrick and Goldcorp), following acquisitions in Canada, Bolivia, and Australia. Newmont produces some 6.5 million ounces of gold annually; it has proved and probable reserves of more than 85 million ounces of gold. Other metals that the company mines include copper, silver, and zinc; it produces some 500 million pounds of copper each year. Operations in North America and South America account for about half of Newmont's production. It also has mining facilities in Australia, Indonesia, New Zealand, and Ghana.

The company's North American operations include mines in Nevada's Carlin Trend, one of the largest gold-mining areas in North America. The company also has stakes in gold mines in Peru, Mexico, and Indonesia (Batu Hijau, a 45%-owned mine that produces both copper and gold). In 2008 it bought Canadian gold producer Miramar Mining for about $1.5 billion. The move came a few years after an initial acquisition of a 10% stake in Miramar, whose primary mining focus is the Nunavut Territory in far northern Canada. It also bought, in 2009, Anglogold Ashanti out of its one-third stake in

the Australian Boddington mine for about $1 billion. The deal gave Newmont 100% of the Boddington project, Australia's largest gold mining property.

To weather price fluctuations, Newmont has tried to keep production costs low. The company has put off discretionary spending and remains largely unhedged, which enables it to profit from gold price increases but offers little protection from falling gold prices.

Once the clear #1 gold producing company in the world, Newmont now ranks #3 behind Barrick and Goldcorp. In 2007 Newmont spun off its royalty assets as Franco-Nevada Corporation. Those assets, acquired in 2002, have been operating since then as Newmont Mining Corporation of Canada. The spinoff was designed to allow the company to get the most value out of those investments, as well as to concentrate on its in-progress mining operations.

Newmont's operations in Ghana consist of one operating mine and a development project; it sees the country as the site of its next big operating district.

HISTORY

Colonel William Boyce Thompson, a flamboyant trader, founded the Newmont Co. in 1916 to trade his various oil and mining stocks. The Newmont name was a combination of New York and Montana, where Thompson grew up. The company was renamed Newmont Corporation in 1921 and Newmont Mining Corporation in 1925, when it went public. Thompson died five years later. During its first 10 years, Newmont focused on investing and trading stocks in promising mineral properties, including US copper and gold mines.

Newmont's gold mines bolstered the company throughout the Depression. During the 1940s its focus shifted to copper and Africa. It bought Idarado Mining in 1943 and Newmont Oil in 1944 (sold 1988). The company grew during the 1950s by acquiring stakes in North American companies involved in offshore oil drilling, nickel mining, and uranium oxide production. It also bought stakes in copper mines in South Africa and South America.

Newmont started producing gold from the Carlin Trend in Nevada in the mid-1960s. It bought a one-third stake in Foote Mineral (iron alloys and lithium) in 1967; by 1974 it controlled 83% of the company (sold 1987). In 1969 Newmont merged with Magma Copper, one of the US's largest copper companies. A Newmont-led consortium bought Peabody Coal, the US's largest coal producer, from Kennecott Copper in 1977 (sold 1990).

After its 1980 discovery of one of the century's most important gold stakes, Gold Quarry in the Carlin Trend, Newmont spent a decade fending off takeover attempts. The company began selling off noncore operations to focus on gold. Magma Copper was spun off to stockholders in 1988.

A proposed merger with American Barrick Resources, a major stockholder, collapsed in 1991. Former Freeport-McMoRan VP Ronald Cambre became CEO in 1993, and that year the company began mining in Peru. A 1994 action by the French government, one of Newmont's partners in Peru's Yanacocha Mine, kicked off a protracted battle over the property's ownership. The claim was upheld in 1998, raising Newmont's stake to more than 50%. Reflecting its increasing interest in Indonesia, in 1996 Newmont and Japan's

Sumitomo formed a joint venture to exploit gold reserves on Sumbawa Island. In 1997 the company increased its gold reserves and territory by acquiring Santa Fe Pacific Gold for about $2.1 billion.

For years Newmont and Barrick Gold Corporation operated interlocked mining claims in Nevada's Carlin Trend, which prevented optimal exploitation by either company. In 1999 both companies agreed to a mutually advantageous land swap in the region.

In 2000 an Indonesian court ordered the closure of the Minahasa mine over a local tax dispute; the company's joint venture agreed to pay a $500,000 penalty to settle the matter. Newmont was fined $500,000 after a mercury spill at its Yanacocha mine. That year Newmont settled the lingering ownership dispute over the Yanacocha.

Company president Wayne Murdy became CEO early in 2001 (he replaced Cambre as chairman in 2002). Newmont acquired Battle Mountain Gold in 2001 for nearly $600 million. Late that year Newmont moved to acquire Australia's top gold producer, Normandy Mining (setting off a bidding war with AngloGold), as well as Canadian gold miner France-Nevada Mining Corp. AngloGold bowed out of the "battle for Normandy" in early 2002, but later completed a three-way deal, in which it acquired Normandy and Franco-Nevada.

In 2003 Newmont reduced its stake in Kinross Gold from 14% to 5%, and it mulled selling off the Ghanaian interests it had gained in the Normandy merger. However, in 2004 Newmont literally discovered a gold mine in Ghana — a major district with some 16 million equity ounces of gold.

Murdy retired in 2007; taking the helm was former CEO Richard O'Brien. The next year the company acquired Miramar Mining, which controls the Hope Bay Project — a nearly 400-sq.-mi. project that includes one of the largest undeveloped gold projects in North America.

EXECUTIVES

Chairman: Vincent A. Calarco, age 67
President, CEO, and Director: Richard T. O'Brien, age 55, $7,067,920 total compensation
EVP and CFO: Russell D. Ball, age 41, $2,956,469 total compensation
EVP Discovery and Development: Guy Lansdown, age 49, $3,041,091 total compensation
EVP Strategic Development: Randy Engel, age 43, $2,564,364 total compensation
EVP Operations: Brian A. Hill, age 50, $2,347,862 total compensation
EVP Legal and External Affairs: Alan R. Blank, age 53
EVP Human Resources and Communications: Bill MacGowan
SVP South American Operations: Carlos Santa Cruz, age 54
SVP Asia Pacific Operation: Timothy Netscher
SVP African Operations: Jeffrey R. Huspeni, age 54
SVP North America Operations: Thomas R. Kerr
VP Investor Relations: John Seaberg
VP and CIO, Information Technology: Gerald Gluscic
VP Corporate Development: David R. Faley
VP and General Counsel: Stephen P. Gottesfeld
VP and Chief Accounting Officer: Roger Johnson, age 52
VP Environmental Affairs and Chief Sustainability Officer: David A. Baker
VP and Treasurer: Thomas P. Mahoney, age 54
VP and Secretary: Jeffrey K. Reeser
Auditors: PricewaterhouseCoopers LLP

LOCATIONS

HQ: Newmont Mining Corporation
6363 S. Fiddler's Green Cir., Ste. 800
Greenwood Village, CO 80111
Phone: 303-863-7414 **Fax:** 303-837-5837
Web: www.newmont.com

2009 Production

	% of total
Peru	26
US	25
Indonesia	24
Australia/New Zealand	16
Ghana	7
Mexico	2
Total	**100**

PRODUCTS/OPERATIONS

2009 Sales

	$ mil.	% of total
Gold	6,386	83
Copper	1,319	17
Total	**7,705**	**100**

Selected Products

Copper
Gold
Silver
Zinc

Selected Operations

North America
  Carlin, Nevada
  Midas, Nevada.
  Phoenix, Nevada
  Twin Creeks, Nevada
  Turquoise Ridge, Nevada
  La Herradura, Mexico

South America
  Conga, Peru
  Yanacocha, Peru
  Kori Kollo, Bolivia

Asia/Pacific
  Batu Hijau, Indonesia
  Boddington, Western Australia
  Jundee, Western Australia
  Kalgoorlie, Western Australia
  Waihi, New Zealand
  Tanami, Northern Territory

Africa
  Ahafo, Ghana
  Akyem, Ghana

COMPETITORS

AngloGold Ashanti
Barrick Gold
Freeport-McMoRan
Gold Fields
Goldcorp
Harmony Gold
Hecla Mining
Inmet Mining
Kinross Gold
Rio Tinto Limited

HISTORICAL FINANCIALS

Company Type: Public

Income Statement

FYE: December 31

	REVENUE ($ mil.)	NET INCOME ($ mil.)	NET PROFIT MARGIN	EMPLOYEES
12/09	7,705	2,093	27.2%	30,400
12/08	6,199	853	13.8%	15,450
12/07	5,526	(1,886)	—	15,000
12/06	4,987	791	15.9%	15,000
12/05	4,406	322	7.3%	15,000
Annual Growth	**15.0%**	**59.7%**	**—**	**19.3%**

2009 Year-End Financials

Debt ratio: 43.5%
Return on equity: 23.5%
Cash ($ mil.): 3,215
Current ratio: 2.51
Long-term debt ($ mil.): 4,652
No. of shares (mil.): 492
Dividends
  Yield: 0.8%
  Payout: 15.0%
Market value ($ mil.): 23,295

Stock History

NYSE: NEM

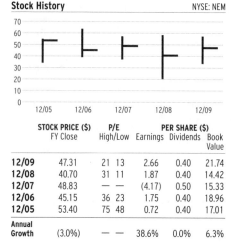

	STOCK PRICE ($) FY Close	P/E High/Low		PER SHARE ($) Earnings	Dividends	Book Value
12/09	47.31	21	13	2.66	0.40	21.74
12/08	40.70	31	11	1.87	0.40	14.42
12/07	48.83			(4.17)	0.50	15.33
12/06	45.15	36	23	1.75	0.40	18.96
12/05	53.40	75	48	0.72	0.40	17.01
Annual Growth	**(3.0%)**	**—**	**—**	**38.6%**	**0.0%**	**6.3%**

News Corporation

This News is heard, seen, and read all around the world. The world's #2 media conglomerate (behind Walt Disney), News Corporation has operations spanning film, television, and publishing. It produces and distributes movies through Fox Filmed Entertainment, while its FOX Broadcasting network boasts more than 200 affiliate stations in the US. The company also owns and operates more than 25 TV stations, as well as a portfolio of cable networks. Its publishing businesses include newspaper publishers Dow Jones (*The Wall Street Journal*) and News International (*The Times*, London), and book publisher HarperCollins. In addition, News Corporation has stakes in British Sky Broadcasting (BSkyB) and Sky Deutschland.

The company's individual media subsidiaries all rank highly in their respective sectors, but like its rival conglomerates News Corporation creates additional streams of revenue for itself by distributing its content through multiple channels. For example, a movie from one of its film studios can be released to theaters, aired on its broadcast and cable channels, sold to consumers on DVD, and later fill some afternoon or late night airtime on one of its local TV stations. Media mogul and CEO Rupert Murdoch and his family control about 40% of the company.

The company's newspapers including *The Times* and the *New York Post* have been struggling for several years as readership and advertising have declined, but the company expanded its holdings in 2007 when it acquired Dow Jones for $5.6 billion. In response to the losses, News Corporation is focused on cost-cutting measures throughout its newspaper operations, including some layoffs and wage freezes.

The one bright spot among its mastheads has been *The Wall Street Journal*, which continues to show strong circulation figures in defiance of industry trends. The company has been working to reposition the leading business paper as a rival to *The New York Times* in national news reporting. The *Journal* surpassed *USA TODAY* (owned by rival Gannett) as the #1 US daily in terms of circulation during 2009.

The *Journal's* value as a newspaper property is enhanced by the fact that its website is one of the few news sites to succeed as a subscription business. Looking to replicate that success, News Corporation put its flagship UK titles, *The Times* and *The Sunday Times*, behind a pay wall in 2010. Murdoch has also challenged the notion that content aggregation companies and search engines including Google should be allowed to freely index and link to newspaper content.

News Corporation's film and television units, which account for more than 50% of sales, have also been hampered by the recession, but the film *Avatar* released in late 2009 bested the economic woes to become the highest grossing motion picture of all time. Increased box office revenue has been somewhat offset, however, by declining DVD sales.

Despite good ratings, FOX and the company's local TV stations have been hurt by declining ad revenue. News Corporation's cable networks, particularly its popular Fox News channel, have performed well despite the downturn in advertising thanks to increasing carriage fees paid by cable system operators such as Comcast and Time Warner Cable.

HISTORY

In 1952 Rupert Murdoch inherited two Adelaide, Australia, newspapers from his father. After launching the *Australian,* the country's first national daily, in 1964 Murdoch moved into the UK market. He bought tabloid *News of the World,* a London Sunday paper, in 1968, and London's *Sun* the next year. In 1973 Murdoch hit the US, buying the *San Antonio Express-News* and founding the *Star* tabloid. He followed this up in 1976 by buying the *New York Post.* Murdoch formed News Corporation in Australia in 1979.

Moving upmarket in 1981, Murdoch bought the London *Times* and 40% of Collins Publishers, a London book publisher. After buying the *Chicago Sun-Times* in 1983 (sold 1986), Murdoch bought 13 US travel, hotel, and aviation trade magazines from Ziff-Davis, as well as film studio Twentieth Century Fox in 1985. In 1986 Murdoch bought six Metromedia stations and launched FOX Broadcasting, the first new US TV network since 1948.

Print was not forgotten, however, and in the late 1980s News Corp. picked up US book publisher Harper & Row as well as Triangle Publications (*TV Guide* and other magazines). It also bought textbook publisher Scott, Foresman and the rest of Collins Publishers. (Harper & Row was later merged with Collins to form HarperCollins.)

In 1996 Murdoch launched the FOX News Channel, an all-news cable channel. In 1998 the company bought the Los Angeles Dodgers and stakes in the new Los Angeles-area Staples Center sports arena. (It sold its stake in the Staples Center in 2004.) Also that year News Corp. spun off part of Fox Entertainment in one of America's largest IPOs, raising $2.7 billion.

That year News Corp. sold *TV Guide* to Tele-Communications Inc.'s United Video Satellite Group (now Gemstar-TV Guide International) for $800 million in cash and a 21% stake. The company also bought the 50% of FOX/Liberty Networks (now FOX Sports Net) it didn't own and transferred ownership to Fox Entertainment. The deal gave John Malone's Liberty Media holding company an 8% stake (later 19%) in News Corp.

In 2001, along with partner Haim Saban, News Corp. sold the Fox Family Channel to Disney for about $5.2 billion. That year the FCC approved the company's $4.8 billion purchase of TV station group Chris-Craft. The deal gave News Corp. an additional 10 TV stations.

News Corp. in 2003 finally realized its dream of owning a chunk of DIRECTV when it bought 34% of Hughes Electronics, the satellite television company's parent, from General Motors. The following year, in an effort to make its stock more attractive to US investors, News Corp. shifted its incorporation from Australia to the US. It also purchased the rest of Fox Entertainment that it didn't already own for $6.2 billion.

The company made another splash in the television industry when it launched MyNetworkTV in 2006. The startup network was established in response to rivals WB and UPN merging to form The CW Television Network. The following year News Corp. acquired newspaper giant Dow Jones and its flagship paper *The Wall Street Journal* for $5.6 billion.

In 2008 the company exchanged its 40% stake in DIRECTV along with some regional sports networks and $625 million in cash for Liberty Media's 19% stake in News Corp.

EXECUTIVES

Chairman and CEO: K. Rupert Murdoch, age 78, $19,887,610 total compensation
Deputy Chairman, President, and COO: Chase Carey, age 56
SEVP, CFO, and Director: David F. DeVoe, age 63, $7,824,564 total compensation
SEVP and Group General Counsel: Lawrence A. Jacobs, age 55
EVP and Chief Human Resources Officer: Beryl Cook, age 48
EVP and Deputy CFO: John P. Nallen
EVP Government Affairs: Michael Regan
EVP Business Affairs and General Counsel, Digital Media Group: Dan Fawcett
EVP Corporate Communications, FOX TV Stations, FOX Business Network, and FOX News Channel: Brian Lewis
SVP Investor Relations: Reed Nolte
SVP, Deputy General Counsel, and Chief Compliance and Ethics Officer: Genie Gavenchak
SVP Corporate Affairs and Communications: Teri Everett
Chairman and CEO, FOX News Channel and FOX Business Network; Chairman, Fox Television Stations and Twentieth Television: Roger Ailes, age 70, $23,683,140 total compensation
Chairman and CEO, Europe and Asia and Director; Chairman, British Sky Broadcasting Group: James R. Murdoch, age 37, $9,216,184 total compensation

Chairman, Fox Entertainment: Peter Rice
Co-Chairman, Fox Filmed Entertainment: James N. (Jim) Gianopulos
Co-Chairman, Fox Filmed Entertainment: Thomas E. (Tom) Rothman
Chairman and CEO, Fox Networks: Anthony J. (Tony) Vinciquerra, age 55
Chief Digital Officer; Chairman and CEO, Digital Media: Jonathan F. (Jon) Miller, age 53
CEO, Fox Television Stations Group: Jack Abernethy
CEO, Dow Jones; Publisher, The Wall Street Journal: Leslie F. (Les) Hinton
Senior Advisor to the Chairman and Director: Arthur M. Siskind, age 71
Auditors: Ernst & Young LLP

LOCATIONS

HQ: News Corporation
1211 Avenue of the Americas, New York, NY 10036
Phone: 212-852-7000   **Fax:** 212-852-7145
Web: www.newscorp.com

2010 Sales

	$ mil.	% of total
US & Canada	17,812	54
Europe	9,628	30
Australasia & other regions	5,338	16
Total	**32,778**	**100**

PRODUCTS/OPERATIONS

2010 Sales

	$ mil.	% of total
Filmed entertainment	7,631	23
Cable network programming	7,038	21
Newspapers & inserts	6,087	18
Television	4,228	13
Direct broadcast satellite	3,802	12
Integrated marketing services	1,192	4
Book publishing	1,269	4
Other	1,531	5
Total	**32,778**	**100**

Selected Operations

Filmed entertainment
　Feature film production and distribution
　　Fox Filmed Entertainment
　　　Fox Searchlight Pictures
　　　Twentieth Century Fox
　　　Twentieth Century Fox Animation
　Television production and distribution
　　Fox Television Studios
　　Twentieth Century Fox Television
　　Twentieth Television
Newspapers
　Dow Jones
　　Barron's (magazine)
　　Dow Jones Newswires
　　The Wall Street Journal
　　The Wall Street Journal Digital Network
　New York Post
　News International Limited (UK)
　　News of the World
　　The Sun
　　The Sunday Times
　　The Times
　News Limited (Australia)
Cable network programming
　Fox Business Network
　Fox Movie Channel
　Fox News Channel
　Fox Pan American Sports (33%)
　Fox Sports Net
　FX
　National Geographic Channel (67%, cable channel)

Television
　FOX Broadcasting
　Fox Television Stations
　　KCOP (MyNetworkTV, Los Angeles)
　　KDFI (MyNetworkTV, Dallas)
　　KDFW (FOX, Dallas)
　　KMSP (FOX, Minneapolis)
　　KRIV (FOX, Houston)
　　KSAZ (FOX, Phoenix)
　　KTBC (FOX; Austin, TX)
　　KTTV (FOX, Los Angeles)
　　KTXH (MyNetworkTV, Houston)
　　KUTP (MyNetworkTV, Phoenix)
　　WAGA (FOX, Atlanta)
　　WDCA (MyNetworkTV; Washington, DC)
　　WFLD (FOX, Chicago)
　　WFTC (MyNetworkTV, Minneapolis)
　　WFXT (FOX, Boston)
　　WHBQ (FOX, Memphis)
　　WJBK (FOX, Detroit)
　　WNYW (FOX, New York City)
　　WOFL (FOX; Orlando, FL)
　　WOGX (FOX; Gainesville, FL)
　　WPWR (MyNetworkTV, Chicago)
　　WTTG (FOX; Washington, DC)
　　WTVT (FOX, Tampa)
　　WTXF (FOX, Philadelphia)
　　WUTB (MyNetworkTV, Baltimore)
　　WWOR (MyNetworkTV, New York City)
　MyNetworkTV
　Star Group (international televison broadcasting, Asia)
Direct broadcast satellite
　British Sky Broadcasting (39%, UK)
　Sky Deutschland (45%, Germany)
　SKY Italia
Magazines and inserts
　Magazine publishing
　News America Marketing Group (insert publications and in-store marketing)
Book publishing
　HarperCollins Publishers

COMPETITORS

Advance Publications
Bertelsmann
Bloomberg L.P.
CBS Corp
Disney
Gannett
Hearst Corporation
MGM
NBC Universal
New York Times
Pearson plc
Reed Elsevier Group
Sony Pictures Entertainment
Thomson Reuters
Time Warner
Tribune Company
Viacom
Washington Post

HISTORICAL FINANCIALS

Company Type: Public

Income Statement

FYE: Sunday nearest June 30

	REVENUE ($ mil.)	NET INCOME ($ mil.)	NET PROFIT MARGIN	EMPLOYEES
6/10	32,778	2,539	7.7%	51,000
6/09	30,423	(3,378)	—	55,000
6/08	32,996	5,387	16.3%	64,000
6/07	28,655	3,426	12.0%	53,000
6/06	25,327	3,327	13.1%	47,300
Annual Growth	6.7%	(6.5%)	—	1.9%

2010 Year-End Financials

Debt ratio: 52.5%
Return on equity: 10.5%
Cash ($ mil.): 8,709
Current ratio: 2.03
Long-term debt ($ mil.): 13,191

No. of shares (mil.): 2,621
Dividends
　Yield: 1.0%
　Payout: 14.4%
Market value ($ mil.): 36,303

NASDAQ (GS): NWS

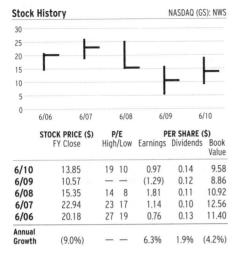

	STOCK PRICE ($) FY Close	P/E High/Low		PER SHARE ($)	
			Earnings	Dividends	Book Value
6/10	13.85	19 10	0.97	0.14	9.58
6/09	10.57	— —	(1.29)	0.12	8.86
6/08	15.35	14 8	1.81	0.11	10.92
6/07	22.94	23 17	1.14	0.10	12.56
6/06	20.18	27 19	0.76	0.13	11.40
Annual Growth	(9.0%)	— —	6.3%	1.9%	(4.2%)

NextEra Energy

For a Florida company without any oranges, NextEra Energy (formerly FPL Group) produces a lot of juice. Its operations across the US include an independent power production business, but most of its revenues are produced by its utility subsidiary, Florida Power & Light (FPL). The unit distributes electricity to 4.5 million customers, and has about 26,700 MW of generating capacity from its nuclear and fossil-fueled power plants. Subsidiary FPL Group Capital owns nonutility businesses, including NextEra Energy Resources, an independent power producer and energy marketer. Subsidiary FPL FiberNet leases wholesale fiber-optic capacity to telephone, cable, and Internet providers; it operates a 2,950-mile network.

In 2010 the company (the largest producer of power from wind and solar plants in North America) changed its corporate name to NextEra Energy in order to better reflect its strategic focus on green energy and to differentiate it from subsidiary Florida Power & Light. Its NYSE stock symbol changed to NEE.

NextEra Energy's 10-year strategic plan for meeting Florida's energy needs (released in 2008) combines additions in generating capacity while using renewable energy sources and energy efficiency programs to avoid the need to build four previously proposed midsized power plants.

NextEra Energy Resources (formerly FPL Energy) gets about 45% of its 18,000 MW generating capacity from wind, solar, hydroelectric, and waste-to-energy facilities; the rest comes from traditional nuclear and thermal plants. The unit operates 100-plus facilities in more than two dozen states and Canada, and it is expanding its generation portfolio. In 2009 the company acquired three wind power developments in South Dakota, Texas, and Wisconsin from Babcock & Brown for about $350 million.

In 2009 its Lone Star Transmission subsidiary was allocated $565 million of a $4.9 billion transmission grid improvement program to deliver wind power to West Texas and the Texas Panhandle. Lone Star will build and operate 250 miles of the 2,300-mile project, which is expected to begin operating in 2014.

HISTORY

During Florida's land boom of the early 1920s, new homes and businesses were going up fast. But electric utilities were sparse, and no transmission lines linked systems.

In 1925 American Power & Light Company (AP&L), which operated utilities throughout the Americas, set up Florida Power & Light (FPL) to consolidate the state's electric assets. AP&L built transmission lines linking 58 communities from Miami to Stuart on the Atlantic Coast and from Arcadia to Punta Gorda on the Gulf.

FPL accumulated many holdings, including a limestone quarry, streetcars, phone companies, and water utilities, and purchases in 1926 and 1927 nearly doubled its electric properties. In 1927 the company used an electric pump to demonstrate how swamplands could be drained and cultivated.

During the 1940s and 1950s, FPL sold its nonelectric properties. The Public Utility Holding Company Act of 1935 forced AP&L to spin off FPL in 1950. The company was listed on the NYSE that year.

FPL grew with Florida's booming population. In 1972 its first nuclear plant (Turkey Point, south of Miami) went on line. In the 1980s it began to diversify with the purchase of real estate firm W. Flagler Investment in 1981, and FPL Group was created in 1984 as a holding company. It subsequently acquired Telesat Cablevision (1985), Colonial Penn Group (1985, insurance), and Turner Foods (1988, citrus groves). FPL Group formed ESI Energy in 1985 to develop nonutility energy projects.

Diversification efforts didn't pan out, and in 1990 the firm wrote off about $750 million. That year, sticking to electricity, the utility snagged its first out-of-state power plant, in Georgia, acquiring a 76% stake (over five years). FPL Group sold its ailing Colonial Penn unit in 1991; two years later it sold its real estate holdings and some of its cable TV businesses.

The utility gave environmentalists cause to complain in 1995. First, the St. Lucie nuclear plant was fined by the Nuclear Regulatory Commission for a series of problems. FPL also wanted to burn orimulsion, a cheap, tar-like fuel. (Barred by the governor, the utility gave up the plan in 1998.)

In 1997 FPL Group created FPL Energy, an independent power producer (IPP), out of its ESI Energy and international operations; FPL Energy teamed up with Belgium-based Tractebel the next year to buy two gas-fired plants in Boston and Newark, New Jersey.

FPL Energy built wind-power facilities in Iowa in 1998 and in Wisconsin and Texas in 1999; it also bought 35 generating plants in Maine in 1999. That year FPL Group sold its Turner Foods citrus unit and the rest of its cable TV holdings. By 2000 FPL Energy owned interests in plants in 12 states.

Out of its fiber-optic operations, FPL Group in 2000 created subsidiary FPL FiberNet to market wholesale capacity. That year talks of Spanish utility giant Iberdrola purchasing FPL Group ended when Iberdrola's shareholders objected; in 2001 plans to merge with New Orleans-based Entergy fell through after a series of disagreements. The deal would have created one of the US's largest power companies.

In 2002 FPL Group purchased an 88% interest in the Seabrook Nuclear Generating Station in New Hampshire for $837 million from a consortium of US utilities, including Northeast Utilities and BayCorp Holdings. In 2005 FPL Group acquired Gexa Corp., a Houston-based electric utility.

Late in 2005 FPL agreed to buy rival power concern Constellation Energy Group Inc. in an $11 billion stock deal. However, the companies called the deal off in 2006, citing uncertainty about regulatory approvals.

FPL Energy had agreed to purchase British Energy's 50% stake in nuclear power generation firm AmerGen Energy in 2003; however, Exelon, which owns the other half of AmerGen, exercised its right of first refusal and purchased the remainder of AmerGen.

The company purchased the Point Beach Nuclear Plant in Two Rivers from Wisconsin Energy for $924 million in 2007.

EXECUTIVES

Chairman and CEO; Chairman, Florida Power & Light: Lewis (Lew) Hay III, age 54, $11,540,544 total compensation
Vice Chairman and Chief of Staff: Moray P. Dewhurst, age 54, $4,796,517 total compensation
President and COO: James L. (Jim) Robo, age 47, $4,954,019 total compensation
EVP Finance and CFO; EVP Finance and CFO, Florida Power & Light: Armando Pimentel Jr., age 47, $2,616,597 total compensation
EVP and President, Nuclear Division and Chief Nuclear Officer: Mano K. Nazar
EVP Federal Regulatory Affairs: Joseph T. Kelliher
EVP Power Generation Division: Antonio Rodriguez, age 67
EVP Engineering, Construction and Corporate Services: Robert L. (Bob) McGrath, age 56
EVP and General Counsel: Charles E. Sieving, age 37
EVP and Chief Strategy, Policy, and Business Process
EVP Human Resources: James W. Poppell Sr., age 59
VP and Corporate Secretary: Alissa E. Ballot
VP, Controller and Chief Accounting Officer: Chris N. Froggatt, age 52
VP Marketing and Communications: Timothy (Tim) Fitzpatrick
Director Investor Relations: Rebecca Kujawa
President and CEO, Florida Power & Light: Armando J. Olivera, age 60, $4,644,945 total compensation
President and CEO, NextEra Energy Resources: F. Mitchell (Mitch) Davidson, age 47
President, FPL FiberNet, LLC: Carmen Perez
President, Gexa Energy, NextEra Energy Resources: Mark Ianni
President, Commodities Marketing and Retail Markets, NextEra Energy Resources: Mark Maisto
Auditors: Deloitte & Touche LLP

LOCATIONS

HQ: NextEra Energy, Inc.
700 Universe Blvd., Juno Beach, FL 33408
Phone: 561-694-4000 **Fax:** 561-694-4620
Web: www.fplgroup.com

PRODUCTS/OPERATIONS

2009 Sales

	$ mil.	% of total
Florida Power & Light	11,491	73
NextEra Energy Resources	3,997	26
Corporate & other	155	1
Total	**15,643**	**100**

COMPETITORS

AES
Bangor Hydro-Electric
Calpine
Chesapeake Utilities
CMS Energy
Delmarva Power
Duke Energy
Edison International
Entergy
Exelon
Florida Public Utilities
JEA
MidAmerican Energy
Mirant
Oglethorpe Power
Progress Energy
Public Service Enterprise Group
SCANA
Seminole Electric
Sempra Energy
Southern Company
TECO Energy

HISTORICAL FINANCIALS

Company Type: Public

Income Statement

FYE: December 31

	REVENUE ($ mil.)	NET INCOME ($ mil.)	NET PROFIT MARGIN	EMPLOYEES
12/09	15,643	1,615	10.3%	10,500
12/08	16,410	1,639	10.0%	10,700
12/07	15,263	1,312	8.6%	10,500
12/06	15,710	1,281	8.2%	10,400
12/05	11,846	885	7.5%	10,200
Annual Growth	7.2%	16.2%	—	0.7%

2009 Year-End Financials

Debt ratio: 125.7%
Return on equity: 13.1%
Cash ($ mil.): 238
Current ratio: 0.67
Long-term debt ($ mil.): 16,300

No. of shares (mil.): 415
Dividends
  Yield: 3.6%
  Payout: 47.6%
Market value ($ mil.): 21,903

Stock History

NYSE: NEE

	STOCK PRICE ($) FY Close	P/E High/Low		PER SHARE ($) Earnings	Dividends	Book Value
12/09	52.82	15	10	3.97	1.89	31.27
12/08	50.33	18	8	4.07	1.78	28.17
12/07	67.78	22	16	3.27	1.64	25.89
12/06	54.42	17	12	3.23	1.50	23.95
12/05	41.56	21	16	2.29	1.42	20.50
Annual Growth	6.2%	—	—	14.7%	7.4%	11.1%

Nicor Inc.

Nicor heats the hearths of the Heartland and carries cargo in the Caribbean. The holding company's principal subsidiary, gas utility Northern Illinois Gas (doing business as Nicor Gas), has 34,000 miles of mains and service pipes that distribute natural gas to about 2.2 million residential, commercial, and industrial customers in Illinois, excluding the city of Chicago; it obtains its supply through long-term contracts and on the spot market. Nicor Gas also operates the Chicago Hub, which provides natural gas storage and transmission-related services to marketers and other gas distribution companies. Nicor also ships container cargo between Florida and the Caribbean through its Tropical Shipping subsidiary.

Its Tropical Shipping unit owns or charters about 15 ships that primarily transport freight between Florida and about 30 Caribbean locations; it also has routes to other locations in the Americas, Europe, and Asia. In 2009 Nicor added to this business by buying Deluxe Freight, a Miami-based logistic services company catering to Caribbean customers.

Thanks to an increase in its gas distribution margins, in 2009 the company was able to post a jump in operating income, despite seeing a significant slump in revenues due to the effect of the global recession in lowering commodity prices.

In response to electric utility deregulation in Illinois and nearby states and to hedge its bets by diversifying beyond its natural gas utility base, Nicor has been pursuing other nonutility businesses. Subsidiary Nicor Enerchange markets and trades wholesale gas; other Nicor subsidiaries offer energy-related retail services and pipeline operations.

In 2009 the company sold its 50% stake in construction services firm EN Engineering, L.L.C. for $16 million in order to focus on its other nonregulated businesses.

HISTORY

Nicor's history dates back to the 1850s, when one of its predecessors lit the Lincoln-Douglas debates by transporting gas through hollowed-out logs. By the early 1900s, it was transporting gas over longer distances in northern Illinois. Over the next half-century, the region's gas and electric companies were united in the Public Service Co. of Northern Illinois.

Utility Commonwealth Edison bought the company in 1953 and the next year created subsidiary Northern Illinois Gas to operate the gas business. In 1955 Northern Illinois Gas was spun off, and it immediately purchased Union Gas & Electric. A few years later, it built the world's largest underground storage system.

The utility enlarged its service area in the 1960s and began drilling its own gas with mediocre results. When the energy crisis of the early 1970s began affecting the firm's gas deliveries, it increased gas production and built a synthetic gas plant. A 1974 general rate increase (the company's first in two decades), coupled with cost-cutting measures, helped relieve financial pressures.

To diversify beyond the utility business, Northern Illinois Gas formed holding company Nicor in 1976. Over the next few years Nicor bought coal reserves, oil leases, a drilling company, an inland barge business, and an offshore drilling

services company. Nicor also acquired Caribbean shipper Tropical Shipping in 1982. When the energy bust of the 1980s hit, Nicor's diversification program lost its momentum; the company unloaded most of its purchases but kept Tropical Shipping.

The company took another, more cautious, stab at diversifying in 1992, when it began Nicor Energy Services to maintain and repair heating and air-conditioning equipment. In 1993 Northern Illinois Gas and gas wholesaler NGC (later named Dynegy) formed the Chicago Hub to provide various services to sellers and buyers of natural gas.

Nicor formed Nicor Technologies in 1994 to offer energy-related consulting services. Lower prices in the increasingly competitive natural gas market caused sales to fall. Nicor and NGC joined Pacific Enterprises (now Sempra Energy) and National Fuel Gas in 1995 to form Enerchange, to manage the Chicago Hub and others in California and the Northeast.

Northern Illinois Gas was granted a 2.8% rate increase in 1996, its first in 14 years. That year Tropical Shipping expanded into the Cayman Islands, Jamaica, and Puerto Rico by purchasing Thompson Shipping. In 1997 Nicor and NGC formed Nicor Energy, which offered energy services to industrial and commercial customers in the US Midwest. Nicor also joined TransCanada PipeLines to build a pipeline between Illinois and Manitoba, Canada; however, the project was later scrapped. That year Northern Illinois Gas began doing business as Nicor Gas.

Nicor and Dynegy teamed up in 1998 to build natural gas-fired electric power plants in six midwestern states; however, Nicor bailed out on its first joint project in 1999. Utility deregulation arrived in Illinois in 1999, and by early 2000 Nicor had more than 100,000 users in its customer choice program. Also that year Nicor announced plans with Texas-based pipeline company Kinder Morgan to build a 74-mile pipeline in Illinois, and construction activities commenced in 2001. (The pipeline was completed in 2002.)

Also in 2001 Nicor formed a pipeline engineering joint venture with A. Epstein & Sons, and Tropical Shipping acquired the container operations of Canadian firm Kent Line International.

Retail gas competition was implemented for all customers in Illinois in 2002. Nicor and former partner Dynegy liquidated the assets of their Nicor Energy joint venture, which marketed gas and electricity to retail customers in the Midwest, due to heavy losses at the unit. (Several former Nicor Energy officers were indicted on charges of inflating the unit's 2001 earnings.)

Thomas Fisher stepped down as CEO in early 2005 and was replaced by Russ Strobel.

EXECUTIVES

Chairman, President, and CEO, Nicor and Nicor Gas: Russ M. Strobel, age 57, $3,255,589 total compensation

EVP and CFO, Nicor and Nicor Gas: Richard L. (Rick) Hawley, age 60, $1,311,765 total compensation

EVP Diversified Ventures: Daniel R. Dodge, age 56, $843,740 total compensation

EVP Operations, Nicor Gas: Rocco J. D'Alessandro, age 51, $1,138,845 total compensation

SVP Human Resources and Corporate Communications, Nicor and Nicor Gas: Claudia J. Colalillo, age 60, $793,238 total compensation

SVP, General Counsel, and Secretary, Nicor and Nicor Gas: Paul C. Gracey Jr., age 50, $793,222 total compensation

SVP Finance and Strategic Planning, Nicor and Nicor Gas: Gerald P. O'Connor, age 58
VP Human Resources: Becky Bacidore
VP and Treasurer, Nicor and Nicor Gas: Douglas M. Ruschau, age 51
VP and Controller, Nico and Nico Gas: Karen K. Pepping, age 45
VP Information Technology, Nicor and Nicor Gas: Barbara A. Zeller, age 55
Chairman and President, Tropical Shipping and Construction: Rick Murrell, age 61, $893,666 total compensation
VP Governmental Relations, Nicor and Nicor Gas: D. Scott Lewis
Director Investor Relations: Kary D. Brunner
Director Corporate Communications: Annette Martinez
Auditors: Deloitte & Touche LLP

LOCATIONS

HQ: Nicor Inc.
1844 Ferry Rd., Naperville, IL 60563
Phone: 630-305-9500   **Fax:** 630-983-9328
Web: www.nicor.com

PRODUCTS/OPERATIONS

2009 Sales

	$ mil.	% of total
Gas distribution	2,140.8	78
Shipping	352.6	13
Other energy ventures	239.0	9
Adjustments	(80.3)	—
Total	**2,652.1**	**100**

Selected Operations

Birdall, Inc.
Tropical Shipping (freight transportation between Florida and the Caribbean)
Horizon Pipeline Co. LLC (50%, pipeline company, joint venture with Kinder Morgan)
Nicor Enerchange (energy trading)
Nicor Energy Services Company (Nicor Services, maintenance and repair for gas piping and HVAC equipment)
Nicor Solutions (energy-related financial and billing services)
Northern Illinois Gas Company (operates as Nicor Gas, gas utility)

COMPETITORS

AES
Alliant Energy
Ameren
AmerenCILCO
AmerenIP
Commonwealth Edison
Crowley Maritime
DTE
Duke Energy
Evergreen Marine
Exelon
Integrys Energy Group
MidAmerican Energy
NiSource
NRG Energy
Seaboard

HISTORICAL FINANCIALS

Company Type: Public

Income Statement

FYE: December 31

	REVENUE ($ mil.)	NET INCOME ($ mil.)	NET PROFIT MARGIN	EMPLOYEES
12/09	2,652	136	5.1%	3,900
12/08	3,777	120	3.2%	3,900
12/07	3,176	135	4.3%	3,900
12/06	2,960	128	4.3%	3,900
12/05	3,358	136	4.1%	3,700
Annual Growth	**(5.7%)**	**(0.1%)**	**—**	**1.3%**

2009 Year-End Financials

Debt ratio: 48.0%
Return on equity: 13.5%
Cash ($ mil.): 56
Current ratio: 0.86
Long-term debt ($ mil.): 498
No. of shares (mil.): 46
Dividends
  Yield: 4.4%
  Payout: 62.4%
Market value ($ mil.): 1,916

Stock History

NYSE: GAS

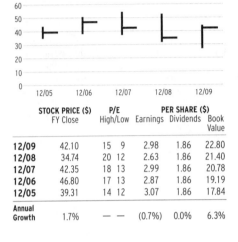

	STOCK PRICE ($) FY Close	P/E High/Low		PER SHARE ($) Earnings	Dividends	Book Value
12/09	42.10	15	9	2.98	1.86	22.80
12/08	34.74	20	12	2.63	1.86	21.40
12/07	42.35	18	13	2.99	1.86	20.78
12/06	46.80	17	13	2.87	1.86	19.19
12/05	39.31	14	12	3.07	1.86	17.84
Annual Growth	**1.7%**	**—**	**—**	**(0.7%)**	**0.0%**	**6.3%**

NIKE, Inc.

Nike, the Greek goddess of victory, helped others succeed in times of war. NIKE, the world's #1 maker of athletic footwear and apparel, does more dominating than assisting, to capture a hefty share of the US athletic shoe market. It designs and sells footwear for a wide variety of sports. It operates NIKETOWN shoe and sportswear stores, NIKE factory outlets, NIKE Women shops, and sells its products online. Overall, it sells its items in some 690 NIKE-owned retail stores worldwide and through some 23,000 retail accounts in the US and through independent distributors and licensees in other countries.

The balance of NIKE's sales came from its "Other Businesses," which include Cole Haan, Converse (known for its classic and retro-style shoes, including the Chuck Taylor brand), Hurley (sports apparel for skateboarding, snowboarding, and surfing), NIKE Golf, and Umbro (soccer apparel and equipment).

Given NIKE's ranking as a top athletic products firm, it's noteworthy that the behemoth logged only a modest decline in revenues among some of the more bleak results of some of its rivals and manufacturers in general. NIKE is working hard to climb out of the economic downturn and return to its status as a far-reaching retailer and manufacturer.

Before consumers began to tighten their belts in 2008, NIKE acquired UK-based global soccer brand Umbro for about $576 million. The deal has provided NIKE with a firm foundation in soccer in the US and England and has positioned the company for growth in emerging soccer markets, such as China, Russia, and Brazil, while its US business slowed. For a couple of decades, NIKE has built a $1.5 billion soccer business from its beginnings of about $40 million. Umbro, which sells directly and through licensees,

brought high-profile sports marketing agreements with soccer players, teams, and leagues and its own global reach.

To help fund its soccer purchase, NIKE shed its hockey business. More than a dozen years after acquiring Bauer NIKE Hockey, NIKE sold the hockey unit in 2008 to a group of investors, including Kohlberg & Company and W. Graeme Roustan, for $200 million. It divested its hockey unit after a strategic review of subsidiaries that didn't reach the $2 billion mark in sales, a long-term growth strategy for the company.

While North America accounts for about a third of NIKE's total revenue, domestic sales growth has slowed in recent years. To make sure it doesn't slip from its #1 spot atop the athletic shoe and apparel market, NIKE in 2009 adopted a new business model centered around half a dozen geographies: North America, Western Europe, Central/Eastern Europe, Greater China, Japan, and Emerging Markets. The company also slashed its global workforce by about 5% in a bid to streamline its operations.

NIKE is led by Mark Parker, a longtime brand executive with the company, who was named president and CEO in 2006. Parker succeeded short-lived CEO Bill Perez, who replaced NIKE co-founder Philip Knight in 2005. Chairman Knight controls the company.

HISTORY

Phil Knight, a good miler, and Bill Bowerman, a track coach who tinkered with shoe designs, met at the University of Oregon in 1957. The two men formed Blue Ribbon Sports in 1962 in an effort to make quality American running shoes. The next year they began selling Tiger shoes, manufactured by Japanese shoe manufacturer Onitsuka Tiger. They sold the running shoes out of cars at track meets.

The company became NIKE in 1972, named for the Greek goddess of victory. The NIKE "Swoosh" logo was designed by a graduate student named Carolyn Davidson, who was paid $35. The same year NIKE broke with Onitsuka in a dispute over distribution rights.

At the 1972 Olympic Trials in Oregon, Knight and Bowerman persuaded some of the marathoners to wear NIKE shoes. When some of these runners placed, the two advertised that NIKEs were worn by "four of the top seven finishers."

Bowerman tested a new sole in 1974 by stuffing a piece of rubber into a waffle iron. The result was the waffle sole, which NIKE added to its running shoes. NIKE grew as running's popularity surged in the 1970s. (NIKE even offered a red-and-silver shoe for disco dancing.) By 1979 it had 50% of the US running shoe market. NIKE went public the next year.

NIKE expanded with shoes for other sports, introducing the Air Jordan basketball shoe in 1985 (named for basketball star Michael Jordan) and the Cross Trainer two years later. NIKE's famous "Just Do It" slogan was introduced in 1988, the same year it bought dress-shoe maker Cole Haan.

In 1992 NIKE opened its first NIKETOWN store. It acquired Canstar Sports, which included hockey equipment maker Bauer, in 1995 (now Bauer NIKE Hockey). NIKE signed 20-year-old golf phenom Tiger Woods to a $40 million endorsement contract that year. Also in 1995 NIKE acquired a license to place its logo on NFL uniforms. (Reebok took over this license in 2002.)

NIKE launched a Jordan-branded athletic footwear and apparel division in 1997. Prompted by falling sales in Asia, NIKE cut 1,200 jobs in 1998 (about 5% of its workforce) to cut costs. With demand for athletic shoes weakening, in 1999 NIKE reported its first drop in sales since 1994. Also in 1999 the company began opening JORDAN store-within-a-store boutiques. Bowerman died in 1999; NIKE released a line of running shoes in his honor.

In 2000 the company launched a line of athletic electronics, including MP3 players, heart monitors, and two-way radios. A full year before Tiger Woods' contract expired, NIKE in 2000 signed the golfer to a five-year contract. The company said the new contract represented a "substantial raise" from his previous $40 million deal.

NIKE opened its first NIKEgoddess store in Newport Beach, California, in October 2001. The company acquired Hurley International, a distributor of action sports apparel, in April 2002.

In September 2003 NIKE acquired competitor Converse and left it as a separate operating unit to keep the Converse name intact. In October Bauer NIKE Hockey announced the closing of its hockey stick factory in Ontario and a staff reduction at its Quebec facilities.

In early 2008 NIKE bought international football star Umbro.

NIKE, which pays Tiger Woods millions of dollars in endorsements each year and has been one of his major sponsors since signing him in the 1990s, stood by the famed golfer in late 2009, when it was alleged that the athlete had been party to marital infidelity.

EXECUTIVES

Chairman: Philip H. Knight, age 72
President, CEO, and Director: Mark G. Parker, age 54, $13,118,834 total compensation
President, Global Operations: Gary M. DeStefano, age 53, $5,248,748 total compensation
VP and CFO: Donald W. Blair, age 52, $4,837,075 total compensation
VP Merchandising and Product: Eric D. Sprunk, age 46, $5,070,294 total compensation
VP Global Brand and Category Management: Trevor Edwards, age 47, $2,815,548 total compensation
VP Global Sports Marketing: John F. Slusher, age 40
VP Global Sales: Roland P. Wolfram, age 50
VP Global Human Resources: David J. Ayre
VP Global Merchandising: Dennis van Oossanen
VP and General Counsel: Hilary K. Krane, age 46
VP Global Operations and Technology: Hans van Alebeek, age 44
VP Global Planning and Development: Andy Campion
VP Global Sourcing and Manufacturing: Nicholas (Nick) Athanasakos, age 47
VP Creative Design: Tinker Hatfield, age 58
VP Corporate Communications: Nigel Powell
VP Investor Relations: Pamela Catlett, age 44
President, NIKE Affiliates: P. Eunan McLaughlin, age 52
President, NIKE Brand: Charles D. (Charlie) Denson, age 54, $9,433,486 total compensation
President and CEO, NIKE Foundation: Maria S. Eitel, age 48
President and CEO, Umbro: James (Jim) Allaker
President, Direct to Consumer: Jeanne P. Jackson, age 58
President, New Business Development: Thomas E. Clarke, age 58
Corporate Secretary: John F. Coburn III
Auditors: PricewaterhouseCoopers LLP

LOCATIONS

HQ: NIKE, Inc.
1 Bowerman Dr., Beaverton, OR 97005
Phone: 503-671-6453   **Fax:** 503-671-6300
Web: www.nikebiz.com

2010 Sales

	$ mil.	% of total
North America	6,696.0	35
Western Europe	3,892.0	20
Emerging Markets	2,041.6	11
Greater China	1,741.8	9
Central & Eastern Europe	1,149.9	6
Japan	882.0	5
Global Brand Divisions	105.3	1
Total NIKE brand	16,508.6	
Other businesses	2,529.5	13
Corporate	(24.1)	—
Total	**19,014.0**	**100**

PRODUCTS/OPERATIONS

2010 Sales

	$ mil.	% of total
Footwear	10,333.1	54
Apparel	5,036.6	26
Equipment	1,033.6	5
Other	2,610.7	15
Total	**19,014.0**	**100**

Selected Products

Athletic Shoes
  Aquatic
  Auto racing
  Baseball
  Basketball
  Bicycling
  Cheerleading
  Cross-training
  Fitness
  Football
  Golf
  Running
  Soccer
  Tennis
  Volleyball
  Wrestling
Athletic Wear and Equipment
  Accessories
  Athletic bags
  Bats
  Caps
  Fitness wear
  Gloves
  Headwear
  Jackets
  Pants
  Running clothes
  Shirts
  Shorts
  Skirts
  Snowboards and snowboard apparel
  Socks
  Sport balls
  Timepieces
  Uniforms
  Unitards

Selected Subsidiaries

Cole Haan (footwear and accessories)
Converse Inc. (footwear)
Hurley International LLC (action sports apparel)

COMPETITORS

Acushnet
adidas
Amer Sports
ASICS
Brown Shoe
Callaway Golf
Columbia Sportswear
Deckers Outdoor
Fila Korea
Fruit of the Loom
FUBU
Hanesbrands
Juicy Couture
K-Swiss
Levi Strauss
Mizuno
New Balance
Oakley
Phoenix Footwear
Polo Ralph Lauren
PUMA AG
Quiksilver
R. Griggs
Rawlings Sporting Goods
Rollerblade
Russell Brands
Saucony
Skechers U.S.A.
Stride Rite
Timberland
Timex
Tommy Hilfiger
Under Armour
VF
Victoria's Secret Stores
Wolverine World Wide

HISTORICAL FINANCIALS

Company Type: Public

Income Statement   FYE: May 31

	REVENUE ($ mil.)	NET INCOME ($ mil.)	NET PROFIT MARGIN	EMPLOYEES
5/10	19,014	1,907	10.0%	34,400
5/09	19,176	1,487	7.8%	34,300
5/08	18,627	1,883	10.1%	32,500
5/07	16,326	1,492	9.1%	30,200
5/06	14,955	1,392	9.3%	28,000
Annual Growth	**6.2%**	**8.2%**	**—**	**5.3%**

2010 Year-End Financials

Debt ratio: 4.6%
Return on equity: 20.7%
Cash ($ mil.): 3,079
Current ratio: 3.26
Long-term debt ($ mil.): 446
No. of shares (mil.): 483
Dividends
  Yield: 1.5%
  Payout: 27.5%
Market value ($ mil.): 34,961

Stock History   NYSE: NKE

	STOCK PRICE ($) FY Close	P/E High/Low		Earnings	Dividends	Book Value
5/10	72.38	20	13	3.86	1.06	20.19
5/09	57.05	23	13	3.03	0.98	18.00
5/08	68.37	19	14	3.74	0.88	16.20
5/07	56.75	19	13	2.93	1.05	14.54
5/06	40.15	17	14	2.64	0.56	13.01
Annual Growth	**15.9%**	**—**	**—**	**10.0%**	**17.3%**	**11.6%**

NiSource Inc.

NiSource is the main energy source for resourceful Americans living in the Midwest, the South, and New England. The company's utility subsidiaries distribute natural gas to about 3.3 million customers in seven states over 58,000 miles of pipeline. NiSource also generates, transmits, and distributes power to some 457,000 customers in 20 counties in its home state through its largest subsidiary, Northern Indiana Public Service Company (NIPSCO). NiSource owns one of the largest natural gas transmission and underground storage systems in the US (capable of storing 639 billion cu. ft. of natural gas), including a 15,000-mile interstate pipeline system.

NiSource's other utilities distribute natural gas in Kentucky, Maryland, Massachusetts, Ohio, Pennsylvania, and Virginia. Several of NiSource's utilities participate in customer choice programs in states with deregulated energy markets.

The company faced difficult economic conditions in 2009, including increased pension expenses, reduced electric demand in Indiana markets stemming from the economic recession, and increased interest expense. Despite a dramatic downturn in revenues, NiSource posted solid earnings thanks to aggressive cost-cutting measures, and careful debt management.

The company believes that its long-term success lies in developing a portfolio that balances creating more efficiencies in its regulated utility operations with expanding its gas transmission and storage businesses.

NiSource has sold noncore assets to pay down debt and focus on its core operations. In 2008 NiSource sold Northern Utilities and Granite State Gas Transmission to Unitil for about $202 million. It also sold its Whiting Clean Energy facility to BP Alternative Energy North America for $217 million. NiSource is also scaling back its unregulated natural gas marketing activities.

HISTORY

NiSource's earliest ancestor was the South Bend (Indiana) Gas Light Company, founded in 1868 by the Studebaker brothers (of later auto fame) to supply gas. In 1886 a natural-gas discovery near Kokomo, Indiana, led to a boom in northern Indiana's use of the fuel. By 1900 steel plants and other industries had set up shop along Lake Michigan in northwestern Indiana and in Illinois.

Another NiSource ancestor was formed in 1901 as Hammond Illuminating, but it changed its name to South Shore Gas and Electric. In 1909 Northern Indiana Gas and Electric was founded by merging South Shore with other regional utilities. The next year Northern Indiana acquired South Bend.

A third NiSource predecessor, Calumet Electric (founded in 1912), had acquired several utilities by the early 1920s when utility magnate Samuel Insull bought it to add to his huge Midland Utilities holding company. In 1923 Insull bought Northern Indiana Gas and Electric, which merged three years later with Calumet to form Northern Indiana Public Service Company (NIPSCO). NIPSCO acquired its current service territory in 1930 when it swapped some areas with another Midland subsidiary.

The Public Utility Holding Company Act of 1935, beginning the regulation of regional monopolies, forced Midland to divest NIPSCO in 1947. In the 1950s and 1960s NIPSCO built two power plants and tripled its natural gas supply through a contract with a Houston gas company.

Responding to rising demand, NIPSCO in 1970 applied to build a nuclear unit at its Bailly plant, estimated to cost $180 million. In 1981 the nuke was abandoned after its cost rose to $2.1 billion. Reorganizing in 1987, NIPSCO became part of holding company NIPSCO Industries.

The Energy Policy Act of 1992 ushered in wholesale-power competition. That year NIPSCO acquired Kokomo Gas and Fuel, and in 1993 it picked up Northern Indiana Fuel and Light and Crossroads Pipeline.

To prepare for oncoming retail competition, NIPSCO in 1993 divided the electric and gas utilities into competing units and increased NIPSCO's marketing force. In 1997 NIPSCO branched out, buying water utility holding company IWC Resources, and the next year it began a customer choice program for its natural gas customers (all gas was delivered through its distribution lines, however).

The company changed its name to NiSource in 1999 but did not alter its acquisition strategy. NiSource entered the US Northeast's gas market, where deregulation plans were under way, by purchasing New England utility Bay State Gas. A unit of Bay State Gas, EnergyUSA, bought natural gas marketer TPC, and NiSource began integrating its nonregulated operations into EnergyUSA.

After launching a hostile takeover, which it later withdrew, NiSource purchased natural gas giant Columbia Energy Group for $6 billion in 2000. NiSource then sold its salt cavern gas storage and pipeline construction subsidiaries, as well as certain Columbia electric generation and LNG facilities. In 2001 NiSource sold its Columbia Propane unit to AmeriGas Partners; it also agreed to sell water company IWC Resources (and its utility subsidiary Indianapolis Water) to the City of Indianapolis (the sale was completed in 2002).

In 2002 NiSource teamed up with the merchant services unit of Aquila (formerly UtiliCorp) to form an energy marketing and trading joint venture; however, NiSource later backed out of the partnership due to instability in the energy trading industry. It also shut down its coal-fired Mitchell Generating Station, and sold its SM&P Utility Resources subsidiary to The Laclede Group.

The following year NiSource sold its Columbia Transmission Communications (Transcom) subsidiary to Neon Communications (which itself was acquired by Globix in 2005).

EXECUTIVES

Chairman: Ian M. Rolland, age 76
President, CEO, and Director:
Robert C. (Bob) Skaggs Jr., age 55,
$4,138,377 total compensation
EVP and CFO: Stephen P. (Steve) Smith, age 48,
$1,693,214 total compensation
EVP; Group CEO, Gas Distribution Segment; Head, Indiana Gas and Electric Utilities: Jimmy D. Staton, age 49, $1,448,808 total compensation
EVP; Group CEO, NiSource Gas Transmission and Storage: Christopher A. (Chris) Helms, age 55, $1,664,539 total compensation
EVP and Chief Legal Officer: Carrie J. Hightman, age 52
SVP Distribution Operations: W. Harris Marple
SVP and CIO: Violet G. Sistovaris
SVP Human Resources: Robert D. (Rob) Campbell, age 50
SVP Corporate Affairs: Glen L. Kettering, age 55

VP, Controller, and Chief Accounting Officer:
Jon D. Veurink, age 45
VP, Chief Risk Officer, and Treasurer:
David J. (Dave) Vajda
VP Ethics and Compliance and Corporate Secretary:
Gary W. Pottorff
President, Columbia Gas of Maryland and Columbia Gas of Pennsylvania: M. Carol Fox
President, Columbia Gas of Ohio:
John W. (Jack) Partridge Jr.
President, Columbia Gas of Virginia: Carl Levander
President, Bay State Gas: Stephen H. (Steve) Bryant
President, Columbia Gas of Kentucky:
Herbert A. Miller Jr.
Auditors: Deloitte & Touche LLP

LOCATIONS

HQ: NiSource Inc.
801 E. 86th Ave., Merrillville, IN 46410
Phone: 219-647-5990   **Fax:** 219-647-5589
Web: www.nisource.com

NiSource distributes energy in Indiana, Kentucky, Maine, Maryland, Massachusetts, New Hampshire, Ohio, Pennsylvania, and Virginia.

PRODUCTS/OPERATIONS

2009 Sales

	$ mil.	% of total
Gas distribution	3,296.2	50
Electric	1,239.5	19
Gas transmission & storage	1,213.2	18
Other	900.5	13
Total	**6,649.4**	**100**

Selected Subsidiaries

Utility Operations
Bay State Gas Company (natural gas utility)
Colombia Gas of Kentucky, Inc. (natural gas utility)
Columbia Gas of Maryland, Inc. (natural gas utility)
Columbia Gas of Ohio, Inc. (natural gas utility)
Columbia Gas of Pennsylvania, Inc. (natural gas utility)
Columbia Gas of Virginia, Inc. (natural gas utility)
Kokomo Gas and Fuel Company (natural gas utility)
Northern Indiana Fuel and Light Company, Inc. (NIFL, natural gas utility)
Northern Indiana Public Service Company (NIPSCO, electric and natural gas utility, electric generation)
Gas Transmission and Storage Operations
Columbia Gas Transmission Corporation
Columbia Gulf Transmission Company
Crossroads Pipeline Company
Other Operations
EnergyUSA-TPC (energy marketing and asset management)
NiSource Energy Technologies (distributed power generation technologies)

COMPETITORS

AEP
Allegheny Energy
Atmos Energy
Baltimore Gas and Electric
Constellation Energy Group
Dominion Resources
Duke Energy
El Paso Corporation
E.ON U.S.
EQT Corporation
IPALCO Enterprises
National Grid USA
New Jersey Resources
Nicor
Northeast Utilities
NSTAR
RGC Resources
Southern Union
Unitil
Vectren

HISTORICAL FINANCIALS

Company Type: Public

Income Statement

FYE: December 31

	REVENUE ($ mil.)	NET INCOME ($ mil.)	NET PROFIT MARGIN	EMPLOYEES
12/09	6,649	218	3.3%	7,616
12/08	8,874	79	0.9%	7,981
12/07	7,940	321	4.0%	7,607
12/06	7,490	282	3.8%	7,439
12/05	7,899	307	3.9%	7,822
Annual Growth	(4.2%)	(8.2%)	—	(0.7%)

2009 Year-End Financials

Debt ratio: 122.9%
Return on equity: 4.5%
Cash ($ mil.): 16
Current ratio: 0.71
Long-term debt ($ mil.): 5,965

No. of shares (mil.): 278
Dividends
Yield: 6.0%
Payout: 116.5%
Market value ($ mil.): 4,275

Stock History

NYSE: NI

	STOCK PRICE ($) FY Close	P/E High/Low		PER SHARE ($) Earnings	Dividends	Book Value
12/09	15.38	20	10	0.79	0.92	17.46
12/08	10.97	68	36	0.29	0.92	17.01
12/07	18.89	22	15	1.17	0.92	18.26
12/06	24.10	24	19	1.03	0.92	18.04
12/05	20.86	23	18	1.12	0.92	18.04
Annual Growth	(7.3%)	—	—	(8.4%)	0.0%	(0.8%)

Noble Corporation

Noble Corporation may be heir to a fortune as demand increases for deepwater oil and gas contract drilling services. The company, with operations in waters off the coasts of five continents, has a fleet of 69 offshore drilling units: two submersibles, seven dynamically positioned drillships, two conventional drillships, 15 semisubmersibles, and 43 jack-up rigs. Many of its rigs are capable of operating in depths greater than 5,000 feet. About 87% of the company's drilling fleet is deployed in international markets, primarily in the Middle East, India, Mexico, the North Sea, Brazil, and West Africa. Noble (which is domiciled in Switzerland) also provides labor contract drilling, well site, and project management services.

The group, which derives most of its revenues from offshore contracts, has positioned itself to ride a global trend toward deepwater exploration. Through acquisitions and equipment upgrading, Noble has been extending its geographical reach and increasing its ability to drill in deeper offshore locations.

In 2010 Noble acquired drilling company FDR Holdings for $2.16 billion. Noble added six floating drilling units and adds about $2 billion to its contract backlog. The deal also includes a dynamically positioned floating production, storage, offloading vessel.

Expanding its fleet organically, Noble completed the construction of a jackup rig and a semisubmersible rig in 2009 and began construction of an ultra-deepwater drillship (due to commence operating in 2011). Two other ultra-deepwater semisubmersibles came online in 2010.

To secure long-term contracts, Noble has formed alliances with major state-owned drilling companies. It has a long-term drilling contract with PEMEX (which the company was renegotiating in 2010). PEMEX accounted for 23% of the company's total revenues in 2009. In 2008 Noble signed a memorandum of understanding for drilling contracts worth $4 billion with PETROBRAS. Future deals with the Brazil-based oil giant are likely as that company expands its deepwater drilling activities.

In 2009 the company sought a more financially advantageous position by relocating its place of incorporation from the Cayman Islands to the even more corporate-tax-friendly Switzerland.

HISTORY

Lloyd Noble and Art Olsen founded Noble-Olsen Oil in 1921 with one rig in Oklahoma. In 1929 Noble-Olsen ventured outside the US to perform contract drilling services in Canada. The next year Olsen left the firm, and the new Noble Oil formed subsidiary Noble Drilling to operate its contract drilling business. The firm began drilling along the Gulf Coast in 1933.

Oil was discovered in the UK in 1939, and Lloyd was called to Washington, DC, to discuss the best way to develop the fields. During WWII Noble crews completed more than 100 wells for the British as part of the war effort. The company also drilled wells in Canada's Northwest Territories near the Arctic Circle in the 1940s. Lloyd Noble died in 1950.

The company built its first jack-up rig in 1955 and began air drilling in 1958. In the mid-1960s new discoveries in North Dakota kept the firm busy, and it was also able to take advantage of increased drilling activity in the US caused by the Arab oil embargo of the early 1970s. Noble Drilling's parent, which had become Noble Affiliates, went public in 1972.

In the midst of the 1980s oil bust, Noble Affiliates spun off Noble Drilling, which went public in 1985. The contract driller began acquiring rigs that were being divested at a discount because of the suffering oil industry. Noble bought six offshore rigs and 20 land rigs in 1988. Three years later it bought 12 more offshore rigs. In 1994 the firm acquired Triton Engineering Services, and the next year Noble bought two more jack-up rigs and began operating in the Middle East.

The company added deepwater and harsh-environment capabilities to its fleet with the 1996 acquisition of Neddrill's oil and gas drilling division. Noble also announced that it had successfully completed studies on the conversion of submersibles into semisubmersibles with deepwater drilling capabilities.

As part of its focus on deepwater drilling, Noble sold 12 shallow-water rigs in 1997. That year and in 1998, the firm won contracts for its converted rigs from Shell Oil, PETROBRAS, and Amerada Hess (later renamed Hess), among others. One of the converted rigs, Noble Paul Wolff, set a new world record for water depth drilling at more than 8,000 feet off the coast of Brazil.

In 2000 Noble formed a joint venture with Lime Rock Partners to acquire a North Sea jack-up rig for $32.7 million. The company upgraded its technology options in 2001 with the acquisition of Houston-based Maurer Engineering, which it planned to integrate with its drilling technology subsidiary, Noble Engineering and Development.

The company boosted its fleet with the acquisition of two drilling rigs from Ocean Rig ASA, and two from Transocean's Sedco Forex in 2002. The company also purchased two additional jack-up rigs, the Trident III and Dhabi II, from a subsidiary of Schlumberger for about $95 million. It also expanded its technology assets by acquiring WELLDONE Engineering. Later that year Noble Drilling changed its name to Noble Corporation.

In 2005 Noble Corporation increased its stake in offshore drilling contractor Smedvig asa (Norway) to more than 39% by purchasing Smedvig family shares for about NOK 4.6 billion ($687.7 million), but sold its interests in 2006.

EXECUTIVES

Chairman, President, and CEO: David W. Williams, age 52
EVP and Secretary: Julie J. Robertson, age 53
SVP, CFO, Treasurer, and Controller:
  Thomas L. Mitchell, age 49
SVP Operations: Donald E. (Don) Jacobsen
SVP and General Counsel: William E. Turcotte, age 46
SVP Marketing and Contracts: Roger B. Hunt, age 59
VP Investor Relations and Planning: Lee M. Ahlstrom
Director Investor Relations: Brook Wootton
Director Corporate Communications: John S. Breed
Auditors: PricewaterhouseCoopers LLP

LOCATIONS

HQ: Noble Corporation
13135 S. Dairy Ashford, Ste. 800
Sugar Land, TX 77478
Phone: 281-276-6100   Fax: 281-491-2092
Web: www.noblecorp.com

2009 Sales

	$ mil.	% of total
Mexico	839.3	23
US	811.5	22
Brazil	372.8	10
Qatar	348.0	10
The Netherlands	333.4	9
UK	237.4	7
Nigeria	154.0	4
Libya	132.6	4
Other countries	411.8	11
Total	3,640.8	100

PRODUCTS/OPERATIONS

2009 Sales

	$ mil.	% of total
Contract drilling services	3,509.8	96
Reimbursables	99.2	3
Labor contract drilling services	30.3	1
Engineering, consulting & other	1.5	—
Total	3,640.8	100

HISTORICAL FINANCIALS

Company Type: Public

Income Statement

FYE: December 31

	REVENUE ($ mil.)	NET INCOME ($ mil.)	NET PROFIT MARGIN	EMPLOYEES
12/09	3,641	1,679	46.1%	5,700
12/08	3,447	1,561	45.3%	6,000
12/07	2,995	1,206	40.3%	6,600
12/06	2,100	732	34.8%	6,000
12/05	1,382	297	21.5%	5,600
Annual Growth	27.4%	54.2%	—	0.4%

2009 Year-End Financials

Debt ratio: 11.1%
Return on equity: 27.8%
Cash ($ mil.): 735
Current ratio: 3.42
Long-term debt ($ mil.): 751

No. of shares (mil.): 256
Dividends
  Yield: 0.3%
  Payout: 2.0%
Market value ($ mil.): 10,414

Stock History

NYSE: NE

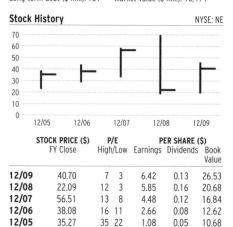

	STOCK PRICE ($) FY Close	P/E High	P/E Low	PER SHARE ($) Earnings	PER SHARE ($) Dividends	PER SHARE ($) Book Value
12/09	40.70	7	3	6.42	0.13	26.53
12/08	22.09	12	3	5.85	0.16	20.68
12/07	56.51	13	8	4.48	0.12	16.84
12/06	38.08	16	11	2.66	0.08	12.62
12/05	35.27	35	22	1.08	0.05	10.68
Annual Growth	3.6%	—	—	56.1%	27.0%	25.6%

Nordstrom, Inc.

Service with a smile is a part of Nordstrom's corporate culture. One of the nation's largest upscale apparel and shoe retailers, Nordstrom sells clothes, shoes, and accessories through about 110 Nordstrom stores and about 70 off-price outlet stores (Nordstrom Rack) in some 30 states. It also operates a pair of Jeffrey luxury boutiques, a "Last Chance" clearance store, and sells goods online and through catalogs. The retailer has sold its Façonnable boutiques. With its easy-return policy and touches such as thank-you notes from employees, Nordstrom has earned a reputation for top-notch customer service. Members of the Nordstrom family, who own more than 15% of the company's stock, closely supervise the chain.

Nordstrom, along with other upscale department store chains, has felt the effects of reduced consumer spending due to the deep recession in the US. While full-line Nordstrom stores saw same-store sales fall by more than 7% in 2009 vs. 2008, the off-price Rack stores posted their eighth consecutive year of positive sales growth. In response to reduced consumer spending, Nordstrom cut expenses by reducing the number of stores it remodels and delaying or canceling plans for several new Nordstrom department stores. (It also substantially increased its inventory turnover rate by carefully managing its stock.) The cautious approach to new store openings was a retreat from Nordstrom's previously stated five-year growth plan, which called for opening about 30 new or relocated Nordstrom department stores and remodeling some 30 others annually.

The family-run company has consolidated its catalog and Internet businesses into one unit called Nordstrom Direct. The firm also owns its own bank, Nordstrom fsb, through which it offers a private-label credit card, as well as two co-branded Nordstrom VISA cards.

HISTORY

In 1901 John Nordstrom, a lumberjack and successful gold miner, used his Alaska Gold Rush money to open Wallin & Nordstrom shoe store in Seattle with shoemaker Carl Wallin. Nordstrom retired in 1928 and sold his half of the business, which included a second store, to his sons Everett and Elmer. Wallin sold his share to the brothers after retiring the following year. A third Nordstrom son, Lloyd, joined in 1933. The shoe chain thrived and incorporated as Nordstrom's in 1946.

By 1963 Nordstrom's was the largest independent shoe chain in the country. The company diversified by acquiring Best Apparel's stores in Seattle and Portland, Oregon. Three years later Nordstrom's bought Portland's Nicholas Ungar, a fashion retailer, and merged it with one of its shoe stores in Portland under the name Nordstrom Best.

Renaming itself Nordstrom Best in 1966, the company went public in 1971 and changed its name again in 1973 to Nordstrom. The retailer grew steadily throughout the 1970s, opening new stores, boosting sales in existing stores, and diversifying. In 1976 Nordstrom started Place Two, featuring apparel and shoes in smaller stores than its traditional department layouts. It moved into Southern California (Orange County) two years later. Buoyed by almost

$300 million in new sales, Nordstrom executives planned an aggressive expansion.

Nordstrom opened its first store on the East Coast in 1988 in Virginia. The chain continued to expand, opening stores in Northern California and in the affluent Washington, DC, suburbs.

The 1989 San Francisco earthquake, along with a national downturn, hurt retail sales significantly. Nordstrom's much-touted focus on customer service had a downside: The company was investigated in 1990 for not paying employees for customer services they performed, including delivery of merchandise on their own time. (Three years later Nordstrom set aside $15 million to pay back wages to employees who had performed off-the-clock services.)

The company continued to expand in the East and Midwest, opening its first store in the New York City area in 1991. In 1993 the retailer opened a men's boutique in New York (Façonnable). Looking for new ways to attract customers, Nordstrom introduced a mail-order catalog the next year.

Following the family's business tradition, six members of Nordstrom's fourth generation began running the company in 1995. Third-generation members James Nordstrom, John Nordstrom, Bruce Nordstrom, and Jack McMillan retired as co-chairmen and were replaced by non-family members Ray Johnson and John Whitacre. (Johnson retired in 1996.)

In 1999 Nordstrom created Nordstrom.com, a partnership with Benchmark Capital and Madrona Investment Group, to consolidate its catalog and Internet operations.

In early 2000, amid slumping sales, the company dissolved the co-presidency. Less than a year later, however, the Nordstroms were back in charge. Chairman and CEO Whitacre resigned and Blake Nordstrom took over running the company as president. His father, Bruce, came out of retirement to take the chairman's role. Later the company bought the French design company Façonnable, which supplies the products for its Façonnable boutiques.

In 2002 the company bought out Benchmark's and Madrona's minority stake in Nordstrom.com.

In August 2005 Nordstrom bought a majority interest in luxury specialty stores Jeffrey New York and Jeffrey Atlanta. Terms of the agreement were not disclosed. The Jeffrey stores had about $35 million in sales in 2004. Also in 2005 the company opened stores in Atlanta; Dallas; Irvine, California; and San Antonio.

In late 2007 Nordstrom sold its four US Façonnable boutiques and 37 European locations to Lebanon-based M1 Group for about $210 million. Overall in 2007, Nordstrom opened three full-line department stores and a single Rack store.

In early 2008 Nordstrom opened its first full-line department store in Hawaii. In October, amid economic gloom, the retailer opened a store in Pittsburgh. Overall, the retailer opened eight new Nordstrom stores and half a dozen Rack outlets in 2008. In 2009 it added three full-line Nordstrom locations and 13 Rack outlets.

EXECUTIVES

EVP and Director; President, Merchandising:
Peter E. (Pete) Nordstrom, age 48,
$4,608,400 total compensation
EVP; President, Nordstrom Direct:
James F. (Jamie) Nordstrom Jr., age 37
EVP and Chief Administrative Officer:
Daniel F. (Dan) Little, age 48,
$1,980,640 total compensation
EVP; President, Nordstrom Rack: Geevy S. K. Thomas,
age 45
EVP; President, Nordstrom Product Group:
Mark J. Tritton
**EVP; Chairman and CEO, Nordstrom fsb; President,
Nordstrom Credit:** Kevin T. Knight, age 54
EVP Marketing: Anne Martin-Vachon
EVP Designer Merchandising: Jeffrey Kalinsky
EVP, General Counsel, and Corporate Secretary:
Robert B. Sari, age 54
EVP Human Resources and Diversity Affairs:
Delena M. Sunday, age 49
EVP Strategy and Development: Ken Worzel
VP and CIO: R. Michael Richardson, age 53
VP Investor Relations and Treasurer:
Robert E. (Rob) Campbell, age 54
VP Corporate Communications: Brooke White
Auditors: Deloitte & Touche LLP

LOCATIONS

HQ: Nordstrom, Inc.
1617 6th Ave., Seattle, WA 98101
Phone: 206-628-2111   **Fax:** 206-628-1795
Web: www.nordstrom.com

PRODUCTS/OPERATIONS

2010 Stores

	No.
Full-line	112
Rack & other	75
Total	**187**

2010 Sales

	% of total
Women's apparel	34
Shoes	22
Men's apparel	15
Women's accessories	12
Cosmetics	11
Children's apparel	3
Other	3
Total	**100**

Selected Retail Operations

Jeffrey (boutiques)
Last Chance (clearance stores)
Nordstrom (specialty stores selling apparel, shoes, and
accessories for women, men, and children)
Nordstrom Direct (catalogs and online ordering)
Nordstrom Rack (outlets selling merchandise from
Nordstrom specialty stores and manufacturers)

COMPETITORS

AnnTaylor	J. C. Penney
Astor & Black	J. Crew
Barneys	Jones Apparel
Benetton	Lands' End
Bloomingdale's	Loehmann's
Brooks Brothers	Macy's
Brown Shoe	Men's Wearhouse
Caché	Neiman Marcus
Dillard's	Saks Fifth Avenue
Donna Karan	Talbots
Eddie Bauer llc	Tiffany & Co.
The Gap	Von Maur

HISTORICAL FINANCIALS

Company Type: Public

Income Statement

FYE: January 31

	REVENUE ($ mil.)	NET INCOME ($ mil.)	NET PROFIT MARGIN	EMPLOYEES
1/10	8,627	441	5.1%	48,000
1/09	8,573	401	4.7%	52,000
1/08	8,828	715	8.1%	55,000
1/07	8,561	678	7.9%	57,400
1/06	7,723	551	7.1%	51,400
Annual Growth	**2.8%**	**(5.4%)**	**—**	**(1.7%)**

2010 Year-End Financials

Debt ratio: 143.6%
Return on equity: 31.7%
Cash ($ mil.): 795
Current ratio: 2.01
Long-term debt ($ mil.): 2,257
No. of shares (mil.): 219
Dividends
Yield: 1.9%
Payout: 31.8%
Market value ($ mil.): 7,567

Stock History

NYSE: JWN

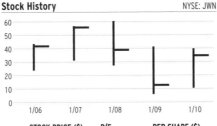

	STOCK PRICE ($) FY Close	P/E High/Low		PER SHARE ($) Earnings	Dividends	Book Value
1/10	34.54	19	6	2.01	0.64	7.18
1/09	12.69	22	4	1.83	0.64	5.52
1/08	38.85	21	10	2.88	0.54	5.09
1/07	55.71	22	12	2.55	0.42	9.90
1/06	41.72	22	12	1.98	0.32	9.55
Annual Growth	**(4.6%)**	**—**	**—**	**0.4%**	**18.9%**	**(6.9%)**

Norfolk Southern

Transportation titan Norfolk Southern is one
big train that could. Its main subsidiary, Norfolk
Southern Railway, transports freight over a network consisting of more than 21,000 route miles
in 22 states in the eastern, southeastern, and
midwestern US and in Ontario, Canada. The rail
system is made up of more than 16,000 route
miles owned by Norfolk Southern and about
5,000 route miles of trackage rights, which allow
the company to use tracks owned by other railroads. Norfolk Southern also offers intermodal
services (freight transportation by a combination of train and truck) through its Triple Crown
Services unit.

Amtrak passenger trains and other commuter
trains operate under contract on some Norfolk
Southern lines. The company's other operations
include commercial real estate development, the
sale and leasing of rail property and equipment,
and the leasing and management of coal, oil and
gas, and other minerals.

The economic downturn that began in 2008
and continued through 2009 caused traffic volumes to fall across all market groups. Norfolk
Southern also had lower average revenue per
unit because of decreased fuel surcharges. With
lower fuel prices and less product to ship, some

customers returned to truck transportation because of the flexibility.

To ensure the safety and efficiency of its rail
network, Norfolk Southern repairs infrastructure, increases track capacity, upgrades computer technology and crossing signals, and adds
intermodal terminals and equipment, bulk
transfer facilities, and mechanical repair shops.
Targets of the company's investment for 2010
include $110 million for the Heartland Corri-
dor, between Chicago and Norfolk, Virginia, and
the Chicago Regional Environmental and Transportation Efficiency (CREATE) project, a public-
private partnership working to add freight and
passenger capacity in the Chicago area — a
major hub for the railway industry.

In 2009 Norfolk Southern announced a proposed arrangement with the Canadian National
Railway (CN) to cooperate on the MidAmerica
Corridor, a partnership created for the railroads
to share track from Chicago to a new coal gateway in Corinth, Mississippi.

Other ongoing rail improvement projects include the Meridian Speedway LLC, a joint venture with Kansas City Southern, to improve
service and increase capacity on a rail line that
connects southeastern and southwestern markets. The company is also investing with Pan Am
Railways to improve the 436 miles of track in the
northeastern US known as the Patriot Corridor.

By far its biggest project is the Crescent Corridor, a proposed $2 billion improvement and
expansion of rail line from New Jersey to
Louisiana. Norfolk Southern is heralding the
railroad as a solution to environmental and infrastructure concerns, saying it would take up to
1 million trucks off the interstate highway system every year.

HISTORY

Norfolk Southern Corporation resulted from
the 1982 merger of two US rail giants — Norfolk & Western Railway Company (N&W) and
Southern Railway Company — which had
emerged from more than 200 and 150 previous
mergers, respectively.

N&W dates to 1838, when one track connected
Petersburg, Virginia, to City Point (now
Hopewell). This eight-miler became part of the
Atlantic, Mississippi & Ohio (AM&O), which was
created by consolidating three Virginia railways
in 1870.

In 1881 Philadelphia banker E.W. Clark bought
the AM&O, and renamed it the Norfolk & Western. N&W rolled into Ohio by purchasing two
other railroads (1892, 1901).

The company took over the Virginian Railway,
a coal carrier with track paralleling much of its
own, in 1959. In 1964 N&W became a key railroad in the Midwest by acquiring the New York,
Chicago & St. Louis Railroad and the Pennsylvania Railroad's line between Columbus and
Sandusky, Ohio. It also leased the Wabash Railroad, with lines from Detroit and Chicago to
Kansas City and St. Louis.

Southern Railway can be traced back to the
South Carolina Canal & Rail Road, a nine-mile
line chartered in 1827 and built by Horatio Allen
to win trade for Charleston's port. It began operating the US's first regularly scheduled passenger train in 1830 and became the world's
longest railway when it opened a 136-mile line
to Hamburg, South Carolina (1833).

Soon other railroads sprang up in the South,
including the Richmond & Danville (Virginia,

1847) and the East Tennessee, Virginia & Georgia (1869), which were combined to form the Southern Railway System in 1894. Southern eventually controlled more than 100 railroads, forging a system from Washington, DC, to St. Louis and New Orleans.

The 1982 merger of Southern and N&W created an extensive rail system throughout the East, South, and Midwest. Norfolk Southern (a holding company created for the two railroads) also bought North American Van Lines in 1985. Triple Crown Services, the company's intermodal subsidiary, was started in 1986. The company also made a failed attempt to take over Piedmont Aviation the next year.

Norfolk Southern revived North American Van Lines by selling its refrigerator truck operation, Tran-star (1993), and suspending its commercial trucking line. But it later sold the rest of the motor carrier (1998) to focus on rail operations.

When CSX announced its plans to buy Conrail in 1997, Norfolk Southern's counteroffer led to a split of the former Northeastern monopoly, between Norfolk Southern (58%) and CSX (42%). Problems with integrating Conrail's assets hurt Norfolk Southern's results. But by 2000 it had regained some of the traffic it had lost to service problems, and its intermodal shipping business also gained speed. In 2004 Norfolk Southern and CSX reorganized Conrail to give each parent company direct ownership of the portion of Conrail's assets that it operates. Conrail still operates switching facilities and terminals used by both Norfolk Southern and CSX.

Norfolk Southern got hit in the wallet in 2001: The company agreed to pay $28 million to settle a racial discrimination lawsuit brought by black employees in 1993. Norfolk Southern began rounds of layoffs and closed redundant depots and facilities in 2001.

In 2005 nine people died in South Carolina when chlorine gas leaked from a ruptured car on a Norfolk Southern freight train. The car was ruptured when the train crashed into a company-owned locomotive and two train cars that were parked on a siding.

EXECUTIVES

Chairman, President, and CEO, Norfolk Southern Corporation and Norfolk Southern Railway:
Charles W. (Wick) Moorman IV, age 58,
$12,756,176 total compensation
EVP and COO: Mark D. Manion, age 57,
$3,903,120 total compensation
EVP Finance and CFO: James A. (Jim) Squires, age 48,
$3,086,573 total compensation
EVP Planning and CIO: Deborah H. (Debbie) Butler, age 56, $3,557,542 total compensation
EVP and Chief Marketing Officer:
Donald W. (Don) Seale, age 57,
$3,800,662 total compensation
EVP Administration: John P. Rathbone, age 57,
$3,717,828 total compensation
EVP Law and Corporate Relations:
James A. (Jim) Hixon, age 56,
$3,511,591 total compensation
SVP Energy and Properties: Daniel D. (Danny) Smith, age 57
VP Engineering: Timothy J. Drake
VP Human Resources: Cindy C. Earhart
VP and Treasurer: Marta R. Stewart, age 52
VP Real Estate and Corporate Sustainability Officer:
F. Blair Wimbush
VP Industrial Products: David T. Lawson
VP Safety and Environmental: David F. Julian
Assistant VP Corporate Communications: Frank Brown
President, Triple Crown Services:
James A. (Jim) Newton
Director Investor Relations: Leanne D. Marilley
Auditors: KPMG LLP

LOCATIONS

HQ: Norfolk Southern Corporation
3 Commercial Place, Norfolk, VA 23510
Phone: 757-629-2600   **Fax:** 757-664-5069
Web: www.nscorp.com

PRODUCTS/OPERATIONS

2009 Sales

	$ mil.	% of total
Coal	2,264	29
Intermodal	1,530	19
General merchandise		
Agriculture, consumer & government	1,181	15
Chemicals	1,056	13
Metals & construction	745	9
Paper, clay & forest	666	8
Automotive	527	7
Total	**7,969**	**100**

COMPETITORS

American Commercial Lines	Ingram Industries
APL Logistics	J.B. Hunt
Burlington Northern Santa Fe	Kansas City Southern
Canadian National Railway	Kirby Corporation
Canadian Pacific Railway	Landstar System
CSX	Pacer International
Hub Group	Schneider National
	Union Pacific
	Werner Enterprises

HISTORICAL FINANCIALS
Company Type: Public

Income Statement
FYE: December 31

	REVENUE ($ mil.)	NET INCOME ($ mil.)	NET PROFIT MARGIN	EMPLOYEES
12/09	7,969	1,034	13.0%	28,593
12/08	10,661	1,716	16.1%	30,709
12/07	9,432	1,464	15.5%	30,806
12/06	9,407	1,481	15.7%	30,541
12/05	8,527	1,281	15.0%	30,294
Annual Growth	**(1.7%)**	**(5.2%)**	**—**	**(1.4%)**

2009 Year-End Financials
Debt ratio: 64.5%
Return on equity: 10.4%
Cash ($ mil.): 996
Current ratio: 1.26
Long-term debt ($ mil.): 6,679
No. of shares (mil.): 369
Dividends
  Yield: 2.6%
  Payout: 49.3%
Market value ($ mil.): 19,323

Stock History
NYSE: NSC

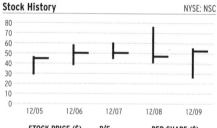

	STOCK PRICE ($) FY Close	P/E High/Low		PER SHARE ($) Earnings	Dividends	Book Value
12/09	52.42	20	10	2.76	1.36	28.09
12/08	47.05	17	9	4.52	1.22	26.06
12/07	50.44	16	12	3.68	0.96	26.39
12/06	50.29	16	11	3.57	0.68	26.08
12/05	44.83	15	10	3.11	0.48	25.20
Annual Growth	**4.0%**	**—**	**—**	**(2.9%)**	**29.7%**	**2.7%**

Northeast Utilities

Northeast Utilities (NU) uses a little Yankee ingenuity (and a number of power generation plants) to keep its customers powered up. The largest utility in New England, NU supplies power to more than 2 million customers in Connecticut, New Hampshire, and Massachusetts through subsidiaries Connecticut Light and Power, Public Service Company of New Hampshire, and Western Massachusetts Electric. The company's power grid encompasses more than 3,100 circuit miles of overhead transmission lines and more than 32,800 pole miles of distribution lines. NU's Yankee Gas utility provides natural gas to 205,000 customers in Connecticut.

NU's competitive businesses (under the NU Enterprises umbrella) consist of a few wholesale energy marketing contracts, Northeast Generation Services (which is being wound down), and an electrical contracting business.

The company's strategy is focused on increasing the scope and efficiency of its regulated operations by upgrading its infrastructure and by using new technologies (such as automated meters and other smart grid technologies) that enable customers to better manage their energy usage.

To give better access and service to its customers, in 2009 NU relocated its headquarters from Berlin, Connecticut, to a larger building in downtown Hartford.

Once a more diverse collection of businesses, in the mid-2000s NU decided to focus its future growth on its regulated power and gas distribution and transmission operations. As a result, it subsequently divested most of its non-regulated units (commercial plumbing, electrical, mechanical, telecommunications, contracting operations, wholesale energy marketing and energy services).

HISTORY

In 1966 three old, intertwined New England utilities merged. One was The Hartford Electric Light Company (HELCO), founded in 1883 by Austin Dunham in Hartford, Connecticut. In 1915 the company signed the first power exchange agreement in the US with Connecticut Power (CP), which HELCO acquired in 1920.

The second, founded in 1886, was Western Massachusetts Electric (WMECO), which merged with Western Counties in the 1930s to become WMECO. The third was Connecticut Light and Power (CL&P). Founded as Rocky River Power in 1905, it took the CL&P name in 1917. In 1929 it built the US's first large-scale pumped-storage hydroelectric plant.

In the 1950s HELCO formed Yankee Atomic Electric with CL&P, WMECO, and others to build an experimental nuclear reactor. In 1965 members of the group began jointly building the Connecticut Yankee nuke (on line in 1968). After years of cooperation, CL&P, HELCO, and WMECO merged in 1966, and Northeast Utilities (NU) was born. It was the first multistate utility holding company created since the Public Utility Holding Company Act of 1935 had broken up the old utility giants. Holyoke Water Power joined NU the following year.

The 1970s energy crisis spurred NU to continue building nukes, including Maine Yankee, Vermont Yankee, and two Millstone units. But by the 1980s, construction delays had raised the cost of the final unit, Millstone 3.

Regulators forced CL&P to spin off its gas utility, Yankee Energy System, in 1989. The next year NU acquired bankrupt utility Public Service Company of New Hampshire (PSNH) and its new Seabrook nuke. (PSNH emerged from bankruptcy in 1991.)

The 1995 shutdown of Millstone 1 began NU's nuclear troubles. In 1996 regulators closed all of its nukes except Seabrook because of safety concerns, and NU mothballed Connecticut Yankee. The next year Michael Morris replaced CEO Bernard Fox, who left after federal regulators ordered NU to comply with regulations and fix management problems — NU managers had routinely retaliated against whistleblowers — the first time a utility had been given such an order. New managers came in, including a former whistleblower, but NU couldn't avoid a record-setting $2.1 million fine. NU received permission to restart the Millstone units in 1998-99. But it had to absorb the $1 billion in power replacement associated with the shutdown.

Meanwhile, as deregulation loomed, NU created a retail marketer (now Select Energy) and a telecommunications arm (Mode 1 Communications) in 1996. Two years later retail competition began in Massachusetts and deregulation legislation was passed in Connecticut (deregulation went into effect there in 2000).

In 1999 NU sold its Massachusetts plants to New York's Consolidated Edison and auctioned off its non-nuclear plants in Connecticut to its subsidiary, Northeast Generation, and Northern States Power (now Xcel Energy). NU agreed to plead guilty to 25 federal felony counts and pay $10 million in penalties for polluting water near Millstone and lying to regulators.

That year Consolidated Edison agreed to buy NU for $3.3 billion in cash and stock and $3.9 billion in assumed debt. The deal broke down in 2001, however; Con Edison charged NU with misrepresenting information about power-supply contracts, and NU charged Con Edison with improperly attempting to renegotiate the terms of the acquisition.

Bringing an old family member home, NU bought Yankee Energy System for $679 million in 2000. Later that year Dominion Resources, which had helped NU restart Millstone 2 and Millstone 3 (Millstone 1 had been taken out of service), agreed to buy the Millstone complex for $1.3 billion. The sale closed in 2001.

Also in 2001 NU subsidiary Select Energy bought Niagara Mohawk's energy marketing unit; NU sold the distribution business of its Holyoke Water Power utility to the City of Holyoke for $18 million; and retail electric competition began in New Hampshire. NU agreed to sell CL&P's 10% stake in the Vermont Yankee nuclear facility to Entergy in 2001; the deal was completed the following year.

In 2002 NU sold its 40% interest in the Seabrook Nuclear Generating facility to FPL Group. In 2006 NU sold nonregulated subsidiary Select Energy, which marketed and traded energy to wholesale and retail customers, to Hess Corporation. That year the company also sold its competitive generation assets in Connecticut and Massachusetts to Energy Capital Partners for $1.34 billion.

In 2007 Connecticut Light and Power Company completed the installation of electric service to Yankee Gas Services Company's new liquefied natural gas facility in Waterbury.

EXECUTIVES

Chairman, President, and CEO:
Charles W. (Chuck) Shivery, age 64, $7,773,638 total compensation
EVP and COO; CEO, CL&P, PSNH, WMECO and Yankee Gas: Leon J. (Lee) Olivier, age 61, $2,086,533 total compensation
EVP and CFO: David R. McHale, age 49, $2,893,177 total compensation
SVP and General Counsel: Gregory B. Butler, age 52, $1,958,496 total compensation
VP Human Resources, Northeast Utilities Service Company: Jean M. LaVecchia, age 58, $867,091 total compensation
VP Customer Operations, WMECO: Robert S. Coates Jr.
VP Accounting and Controller: Jay S. Buth, age 40
VP and Treasurer: Randall A. (Randy) Shoop
President and COO, Western Massachusetts Electric Co.: Peter J. Clarke, age 48
President and COO, Connecticut Power and Light Co.: Jeffrey D. (Jeff) Butler, age 53
President and COO, Yankee Gas: Rodney O. (Rod) Powell, age 57
Secretary and Deputy General Counsel: Samuel K. Lee
Auditors: Deloitte & Touche LLP

LOCATIONS

HQ: Northeast Utilities
107 Selden St., Berlin, CT 06037
Phone: 800-286-5000 **Fax:** 860-665-5418
Web: www.nu.com

Northeast Utilities operates primarily in Connecticut, western Massachusetts, and New Hampshire.

PRODUCTS/OPERATIONS

2009 Sales

	$ mil.	% of total
Utilities		
Distribution		
Electric	4,359	80
Gas	449	8
Transmission	578	11
Competitive businesses	81	1
Adjustments	(28)	—
Total	**5,439**	**100**

Selected Subsidiaries

The Northeast Utilities System (regulated utilities)
  Connecticut Light and Power Company (CL&P, electric utility)
  Public Service Company of New Hampshire (PSNH, electric utility)
  Western Massachusetts Electric Company (WMECO, electric utility)
  Yankee Energy System, Inc. (natural gas utility, Connecticut)
    Yankee Gas Services Company (retail natural gas service)
Other Operations
  Northeast Utilities Service Company (administrative services for NU subsidiaries)
  NU Enterprises, Inc. (nonutility operations)

COMPETITORS

AEP
Bangor Hydro-Electric
Central Vermont Public Service
Con Edison
Green Mountain Power
Iberdrola USA
Massachusetts Municipal Wholesale Electric
National Grid USA
NiSource
NSTAR
PG&E Corporation
Public Service Enterprise Group
Southern Company
UIL Holdings
Unitil
USPowerGen

HISTORICAL FINANCIALS

Company Type: Public

Income Statement

FYE: December 31

	REVENUE ($ mil.)	NET INCOME ($ mil.)	NET PROFIT MARGIN	EMPLOYEES
12/09	5,439	336	6.2%	6,078
12/08	5,800	261	4.5%	6,189
12/07	5,822	247	4.2%	5,869
12/06	6,884	476	6.9%	5,869
12/05	7,397	(247)	—	6,879
Annual Growth	(7.4%)	—	—	(3.0%)

2009 Year-End Financials

Debt ratio: 125.6%
Return on equity: 10.2%
Cash ($ mil.): 27
Current ratio: 1.29
Long-term debt ($ mil.): 4,493
No. of shares (mil.): 176
Dividends
  Yield: 3.7%
  Payout: 49.7%
Market value ($ mil.): 4,543

Stock History

NYSE: NU

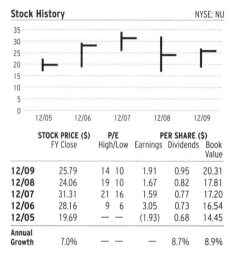

	STOCK PRICE ($) FY Close	P/E High/Low	PER SHARE ($) Earnings	Dividends	Book Value
12/09	25.79	14 10	1.91	0.95	20.31
12/08	24.06	19 10	1.67	0.82	17.81
12/07	31.31	21 16	1.59	0.77	17.20
12/06	28.16	9 6	3.05	0.73	16.54
12/05	19.69	— —	(1.93)	0.68	14.45
Annual Growth	7.0%	— —	—	8.7%	8.9%

Northern Trust

Since its founding in 1889, Northern Trust Corporation has been working hard to keep clients' trusts. Flagship subsidiary The Northern Trust Company and other units bearing the Northern Trust name provide banking and trust services to the affluent and to financial institutions and corporations from 85 offices in nearly 20 states and about a dozen countries. Operating in two segments, Corporate and Institutional Services and Personal Financial Services, the corporation is a leading personal trust manager in the US, in addition to specializing in master trust services and catering to corporate pension plans and institutional clients.

Northern Trust's Corporate and Institutional Services division administers assets for fund managers, foundations and endowments, and insurance companies. The Personal Financial Services segment offers trust and wealth management, banking, mortgages, and other services for small and midsized companies, executives, retirees, and the well-to-do. Subsidiary Northern Trust Global Investments oversees portfolio management, investment research, and other investment products, including the firm's proprietary mutual funds.

Abroad, Northern Trust has branches in Australia, Canada, Ireland, Luxembourg, the Netherlands, and the UK. The company is targeting Asia for growth, where it has offices in China, Hong Kong, India, Japan, and Singapore. All told, Northern Trust has approximately $3.5 trillion of assets under custody and more than $600 billion under management.

Northern Trust received nearly $1.6 billion from the US government's Troubled Asset Relief Program (TARP), but later returned the money after the public funds brought increased scrutiny, particularly over client perks and the company's sponsorship of a golf tournament.

Board member Harold Smith of the founding Smith family owns around 5% of Northern Trust.

HISTORY

When banker Byron Smith took time off to handle family concerns in 1885, friends turned to him for advice on trust and estate matters. It occurred to him that there was a market for such services within a banking framework.

Smith tested new Illinois banking and trust laws by arranging for state banking authorities to reject his charter application for Northern Trust. As Smith had hoped, the charter was upheld by the Illinois Supreme Court.

Northern Trust opened in 1889 in one of Chicago's new skyscrapers, the Rookery. With $1 million in capital — about 40% of it from Smith and the rest from the likes of Marshall Field (retailing), Martin Ryerson (steel), and Philip Armour (meatpacking) — the bank attracted $138,000 in deposits its first day.

By 1896 the bank was firmly established; Smith began taking a salary and the company issued its first dividend. Ten years later the firm built its solid granite edifice, the "Gray Lady of LaSalle Street," where it still resides.

The bank began buying commercial paper in 1912, joined the Federal Reserve System in 1917, and became a custodian for expropriated German assets during WWI. Byron Smith died in 1914 and was succeeded by his son, Solomon.

Northern Trust rejected the get-rich-quick ethos of the 1920s. It was so strong during the Depression that after the 1933 bank holiday people actually clamored to make deposits, and the bank administered the Depression-era scholarship fund that helped Ronald Reagan attend college. By 1941 almost half of Northern Trust's commercial deposits originated outside the Chicago area. The bank kept growing during and after WWII.

Solomon Smith retired in 1963; his son Edward took over and launched the company's expansion overseas (Northern Trust International was formed in 1968) and out of state (Florida in 1971, Arizona in 1974). The firm's business was helped by the 1974 passage by Congress of ERISA, which required company retirement plans to be overseen by an outside custodian. Edward retired in 1979.

Northern Trust expanded locally when Illinois legalized intrastate branch banking in 1981. In 1987 the company lost money, due in part to defaults on loans made to developing countries. It moved into California in 1988 and Texas in 1989.

Northern Trust navigated the early 1990s recession, expanded geographically in the mid-1990s, and added services through acquisitions. In 1995 the company became the first foreign trust company to operate throughout Canada. That year it bought investment management service RCB International (now Northern Trust

Global Advisors). It expanded in the Sun Belt with such acquisitions as Dallas' Metroplex Bancshares and was made first custodian for the Teacher Retirement System of Texas (1997).

In 1998 the company expanded into Michigan and broke into the Cleveland and Seattle markets in 1999. Northern Trust entered cyberspace as well, launching a website for its mutual funds. In 2000 the company opened locations in Nevada and Missouri and bought Florida-based investment adviser Carl Domino Associates (renamed Northern Trust Value Investors). Also that year the bank bought Ireland's Ulster Bank Investment Services.

In 2004 Northern Trust bought the fund management, custody, and trust operations of Baring Asset Management from Amsterdam-based ING Groep.

EXECUTIVES

Chairman, President, and CEO, Northern Trust Corporation and Northern Trust Company: Frederick H. (Rick) Waddell, age 56, $11,891,070 total compensation
EVP and CFO: William L. Morrison, age 59, $4,202,177 total compensation
EVP and Head of EMEA; President, Northern Trust Global Investments: Stephen N. Potter, age 53, $4,066,686 total compensation
EVP and President, Operations and Technology: Jana R. Schreuder, age 51, $4,262,286 total compensation
EVP and Controller: Aileen B. Blake, age 42
EVP Corporate Social Responsibility: Connie L. Lindsey
EVP and CTO, Northern Trust Company: Nirup N. Krishnamurthy
EVP and Chief Investment Officer: Robert P. (Bob) Browne, age 44
EVP and General Counsel: Kelly R. Welsh, age 57
EVP Human Resources and Administration: Timothy P. Moen, age 57
EVP; President, Wealth Management Group, The Northern Trust Company: Douglas P. (Doug) Regan
EVP, Northern Trust Global Marketing and Community Affairs: K. Kelly Mannard
EVP and General Auditor: Dan E. Phelps
EVP and Head of Corporate Risk Management: Joyce St. Clair, age 51
EVP and Treasurer: William R. Dodds Jr., age 57
SVP and Director Corporate Communications: Doug Holt
SVP and Director Investor Relations: Beverly J. (Bev) Fleming
President, Northern Trust Personal Financial Services: Sherry S. Barrat, age 60, $4,226,235 total compensation
President, Corporate and Institutional Services: Steven L. (Steve) Fradkin, age 48, $4,120,255 total compensation
Corporate Secretary and Assistant General Counsel: Rose A. Ellis
Auditors: KPMG LLP

LOCATIONS

HQ: Northern Trust Corporation
50 S. La Salle St., Chicago, IL 60603
Phone: 312-630-6000   **Fax:** 312-630-1512
Web: www.northerntrust.com

PRODUCTS/OPERATIONS

2009 Sales

	$ mil.	% of total
Noninterest income		
Trust, investment & other servicing fees	2,083.8	50
Foreign exchange trading	445.7	11
Treasury management fees	81.8	2
Security commissions & trading income	62.4	1
Other	113.4	3
Interest income	1,406.0	33
Total	**4,193.1**	**100**

COMPETITORS

HISTORICAL FINANCIALS

Company Type: Public

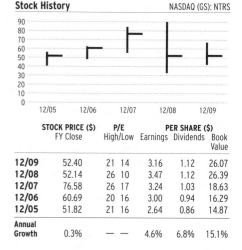

Income Statement				FYE: December 31
	ASSETS ($ mil.)	NET INCOME ($ mil.)	INCOME AS % OF ASSETS	EMPLOYEES
12/09	82,142	864	1.1%	12,400
12/08	82,054	795	1.0%	12,200
12/07	67,611	727	1.1%	10,918
12/06	60,712	665	1.1%	9,726
12/05	53,414	584	1.1%	9,008
Annual Growth	**11.4%**	**10.3%**	**—**	**8.3%**

2009 Year-End Financials

Equity as % of assets: 7.7%
Return on assets: 1.1%
Return on equity: 15.4%
Long-term debt ($ mil.): 4,666
No. of shares (mil.): 242

Dividends
Yield: 2.1%
Payout: 35.4%
Market value ($ mil.): 12,686
Sales ($ mil.): 4,193

Stock History

NASDAQ (GS): NTRS

	STOCK PRICE ($) FY Close	P/E High/Low	PER SHARE ($) Earnings	Dividends	Book Value
12/09	52.40	21 14	3.16	1.12	26.07
12/08	52.14	26 10	3.47	1.12	26.39
12/07	76.58	26 17	3.24	1.03	18.63
12/06	60.69	20 16	3.00	0.94	16.29
12/05	51.82	21 16	2.64	0.86	14.87
Annual Growth	**0.3%**	**— —**	**4.6%**	**6.8%**	**15.1%**

Northrop Grumman

Avast there! The acquisitions of Litton Industries, Newport News, and TRW made Northrop Grumman the world's #1 shipbuilder and a leading military contractor (behind Lockheed Martin and Boeing). It operates through five segments: Aerospace Systems (aircraft, spacecraft, laser systems, electronic subsystems), Electronic Systems (radar, sensors, chemical detection, countermeasure systems), Information Systems (C4ISR, or command, control, communications, computers, intelligence, surveillance, and reconnaissance), Shipbuilding (ships, nuclear submarines, aircraft carriers), and Technical Services (systems support, training and simulation). The US government is behind more than 90% of Northrop Grumman's sales.

With its eye on the changing priorities of the US Department of Defense, Northrop Grumman is streamlining its organizational structure in an effort to better align with the operations of its customers. In so doing, the company aims to enhance its competitiveness with respect to the Pentagon's short- and long-term strategic plans, contract bids, and contract scheduling.

While the company is the sole provider of nuclear-powered aircraft carriers, and one of two companies that build nuclear-powered submarines for the US Navy, competition for information systems contracts has become intense. Customers are shifting to commercial and multinational firms, rather than traditional defense contractors, to take on systems integration and support contracts.

In the meantime, the wars in Afghanistan and Iraq, and resulting military spending, have buoyed results for Northrop Grumman and other military contractors. The company expects that the increased military emphasis on information gathering, surveillance, battle management, and precision munitions will lead to heavy government spending on advanced electronics systems and software in the coming years.

On the other hand, the company's surface ships and submarines are prime targets for the federal budget's axe as the military looks to cut costs by switching to smaller, more nimble arsenals. In mid-2010 Northrop Grumman announced its plans to shutter one of its seven shipbuilding yards and decision to consider selling or spinning off the entire naval business.

No stranger to divestments, Northrop sold its TASC division (engineering and consulting services to the US military and state governments) in late 2009 to private equity investors General Atlantic LLC and KKR for about $1.65 billion.

HISTORY

Jack Northrop co-founded Lockheed Aircraft in 1927 and designed its record-setting Vega monoplane. He founded two more companies — Avion Corporation (formed in 1928 and bought by United Aircraft and Transportation) and Northrop Corporation (formed in 1932 with Douglas Aircraft, which absorbed it in 1938) — before founding Northrop Aircraft in California in 1939.

During WWII Northrop produced the P-61 fighter and the famous Flying Wing bomber, which failed to win a production contract. In the 1950s Northrop depended heavily on F-89 fighter and Snark missile sales. When Thomas Jones succeeded Jack Northrop as president (1959), he moved the company away from risky prime contracts in favor of numerous subcontracts and bought Page Communications Engineers (telecommunications, 1959) and Hallicrafters (electronics, 1966) to reduce its dependence on government contracts.

In the early 1970s Northrop was hit with a bribery scandal and the disclosure of illegal payments to Richard Nixon's 1972 campaign fund; Jones was eventually fined for an illegal contribution. As a result, a shareholder lawsuit forced Jones to resign as president (he was allowed to remain as chairman). In 1981 the company won the B-2 bomber contract. Jones retired as chairman in late 1990, and under the leadership of Kent Kresa (who became CEO in early 1990 and chairman when Jones retired), Northrop pleaded guilty to 34 counts related to fudging test results on some government projects; it was fined

$17 million. In a related shareholders' suit, Northrop paid $18 million in damages in 1991.

Northrop and private investment firm The Carlyle Group bought LTV's Vought Aircraft in 1992. In 1994 it paid $2.1 billion for Grumman Corporation, a premier electronic systems firm, and changed its name to Northrop Grumman.

In 1929 Roy Grumman, Jake Swirbul, and Bill Schwendler founded Grumman; within three months it had a contract to design a US Navy fighter. Grumman completed its first commercial aircraft (the Grumman Goose) in 1937 and went public in 1938. It soared during WWII on the wings of its Wildcat and Hellcat fighter planes.

Grumman built its first corporate jet (the Gulfstream) in 1958, and in 1963 began work on the Lunar Module for the Apollo space program. It was near bankruptcy during the 1970s due to costs related to its F-14 Tomcat fighter project. The company rebuilt its military business in the 1980s, achieving its greatest success in electronic systems.

In 1998 Northrop Grumman began a restructuring that cut 10,500 defense and aircraft jobs. In 2000 the company sold its underperforming commercial aerostructures business to The Carlyle Group in a $1.2 billion transaction in order to focus on its growing defense electronics and information technology segments.

In 2001 the company completed the deal to acquire Litton Industries for $3.8 billion, plus $1.3 billion in debt. While its wallet was open, the company agreed to match the $2.6 billion that General Dynamics had agreed to pay for submarine and aircraft carrier builder Newport News — a move that the US Defense Department endorsed. In December Honeywell agreed to pay Northrop Grumman $440 million to settle an antitrust and patent infringement lawsuit that Litton had filed against Honeywell in 1990.

In 2002 Northrop Grumman then made a hostile $6 billion bid for conglomerate TRW. After a bidding war, TRW accepted a sweetened $7.8 billion offer. Northrop sold 80.4% of TRW Automotive to Blackstone Group in February 2003. In April of the same year, Kresa stepped down as president and CEO, and Ronald Sugar took over those roles; Sugar added the chairmanship to his title when Kresa retired in October.

In 2006 Northrop Grumman agreed to buy Essex Corporation — a provider of signal, image, and information processing for defense and intelligence customers in the US.

Ronald Sugar stepped down as chairman and CEO at the end of 2009. He remained on the board as chairman emeritus. Wesley Bush, formerly president and COO, took over as CEO in January 2010, as part of a planned succession.

EXECUTIVES

Chairman: Lewis W. (Lew) Coleman, age 68
President, CEO, and Director: Wesley G. (Wes) Bush, age 48, $10,382,080 total compensation
VP and CFO: James F. (Jim) Palmer, age 60, $5,688,861 total compensation
VP and CIO: Bernard P. (Bernie) McVey Jr.
VP; President, Technical Services:
  Thomas E. (Tom) Vice
VP; President, Enterprise Shared Services:
  Gloria A. Flach
VP and Acting Chief Human Resources Officer:
  Debora Catsavas
VP Government Relations: Sid Ashworth, age 59
VP Enterprise Communications:
  Daniel J. (Dan) McClain
VP Investor Relations: Paul O. Gregory
VP, Controller, and Chief Accounting Officer:
  Kenneth N. (Ken) Heintz, age 63

Corporate VP; President, Aerospace Systems:
  Gary W. Ervin, age 52, $4,070,789 total compensation
Corporate VP; President, Northrop Grumman Electronic Systems: James F. Pitts, age 58, $3,765,112 total compensation
Corporate VP and General Counsel: Sheila C. Cheston
Corporate VP and CTO: Alexis C. Livanos, age 61
Corporate VP and Treasurer: Mark A. Rabinowitz, age 48
Corporate VP; President, Northrop Grumman Shipbuilding: C. Michael (Mike) Petters, age 50
Corporate VP; President, Technical Services Sector:
  James L. Cameron, age 52
Corporate VP; President, Information Systems:
  Linda A. Mills, age 60
Corporate VP, Secretary, and Deputy General Counsel:
  Joseph F. Coyne Jr., age 54
Corporate VP Communications: Darryl M. Fraser, age 51
Auditors: Deloitte & Touche LLP

LOCATIONS

HQ: Northrop Grumman Corporation
  1840 Century Park East, Los Angeles, CA 90067
Phone: 310-553-6262   **Fax:** 310-556-4561
Web: www.northropgrumman.com

PRODUCTS/OPERATIONS

2009 Sales

	$ mil.	% of total
Aerospace systems	10,419	29
Information systems	8,611	24
Electronic systems	7,671	22
Shipbuilding	6,213	17
Technical services	2,776	8
Adjustments	(1,935)	—
Total	**33,755**	**100**

2009 Sales by Customer

	$ mil.	% of total
US government	31,000	92
Other customers	2,755	8
Total	**33,755**	**100**

COMPETITORS

Aerojet
BAE SYSTEMS
Boeing
EADS
Elbit Systems
Finmeccanica
GE
GenCorp
General Dynamics
Hamilton Sundstrand
Hanjin Heavy Industries & Construction
Herley Industries
Honeywell Aerospace
ITT Defense
Lockheed Martin
Meggitt
Raytheon
Rockwell Collins
ThalesRaytheonSystems
Todd Shipyards

HISTORICAL FINANCIALS

Company Type: Public

Income Statement				FYE: December 31
	REVENUE ($ mil.)	NET INCOME ($ mil.)	NET PROFIT MARGIN	EMPLOYEES
12/09	33,755	1,686	5.0%	120,700
12/08	33,887	(1,262)	—	123,600
12/07	32,018	1,790	5.6%	122,600
12/06	30,148	1,542	5.1%	122,200
12/05	30,721	1,383	4.5%	123,600
Annual Growth	**2.4%**	**5.1%**	**—**	**(0.6%)**

Stock History   NYSE: NOC

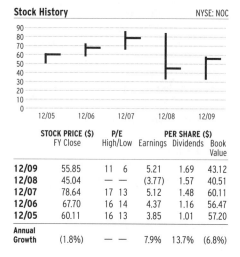

	STOCK PRICE ($) FY Close	P/E High/Low		PER SHARE ($) Earnings	Dividends	Book Value
12/09	55.85	11	6	5.21	1.69	43.12
12/08	45.04	—	—	(3.77)	1.57	40.51
12/07	78.64	17	13	5.12	1.48	60.11
12/06	67.70	16	14	4.37	1.16	56.47
12/05	60.11	16	13	3.85	1.01	57.20
Annual Growth	(1.8%)	—	—	7.9%	13.7%	(6.8%)

Novell, Inc.

Novell is a firm believer in the power of networking. The company's products include network server operating systems that connect desktop computers to corporate networks, integrating directories, storage systems, printers, servers, and databases. Novell also provides a version of the Linux operating system, and applications including network management software, collaborative tools, and directory services products. In addition, it offers a variety of services such as IT consulting, implementation, support, and training. Novell's strategic partners include CA, Dell, Intel, Microsoft, and SAP.

In 2010 hedge fund Elliott Associates (which owns a 7% stake in Novell) made an unsolicited bid to buy the remainder of the company for about $1.8 billion. Novell's board rejected the bid as financially inadequate, saying it undervalued the company's franchise and growth prospects. At the same time, the board stated it is reviewing alternatives to enhance shareholder value, including a possible sale of the company.

Much of Novell's product strategy has been driven by a push to expand past its roots as a provider of network operating systems. It has identified Linux, identity management software, and systems and resource management applications as its growth products. Novell has pursued strategic acquisitions to expand those lines.

It first built its Linux-based offerings with the acquisitions of Ximian, SuSE Linux, and Immunix. Novell's identity and access management division got a boost from the purchase of enterprise security software developer e-Security. Novell also acquired endpoint security management specialist Senforce Technologies, which bolstered its systems and resource management offerings. Novell further expanded its systems and resource management portfolio with three purchases in 2008-2009: data center software developer

PlateSpin, business service management software provider Managed Objects, and identity management provider Fortefi.

In addition to its Linux efforts, Novell has also announced plans to target what it calls the Intelligent Workload Management (IWM) market. IWM applications enable IT departments to manage and optimize hardware and software assets in virtualized cloud computing environments. This emerging market encompasses both its newer Linux products and its legacy networking tools, with Novell trying to position itself as a provider of tools to manage a wide range of computing environments, both physical and virtual.

HISTORY

Novell was woven from the remnants of Novell Data Systems, a maker of disk operating systems founded in 1980. (The name was chosen for its suggestion of newness.) High-tech investment firm Safeguard Scientifics bought a controlling stake in the venture in 1981. In 1983 Safeguard incorporated the company and shortened its name to Novell. It also recruited CEO Raymond Noorda, an experienced engineer and marketer who invested $125,000 of his own money.

Under Noorda, Novell focused on developing PC networking systems that designated one machine (the file server) to manage the network and control access to shared devices, such as disk drives and printers. In 1983 Novell introduced NetWare, the first networking software based on file server technology.

Safeguard sold half of its 51% stake to the public two years later and gradually sold off the rest. Novell began acquiring other companies to expand its product line, including Santa Clara Systems (microcomputer workstations, 1987) and Excelan (networking software and equipment, 1989). In 1988 Novell halted production of most hardware.

By the early 1990s Novell dominated the networking market with a nearly 70% share. Wanting to undermine Microsoft's dominant position, Noorda bought the rights to AT&T's UNIX operating system (1992), top word-processing software maker WordPerfect (1994), and Borland's spreadsheet business, Quattro Pro (1994). Novell in 1994 also transferred its database products (NetWare SQL, Xtrieve) to Btrieve Technologies (now Pervasive Software). The acquisitions failed to dent Microsoft's market share.

Noorda retired in 1994 and was succeeded by Hewlett-Packard executive Robert Frankenberg, who began to streamline the company and divest itself of units such as WordPerfect.

Frankenberg was ousted in 1996 after Novell posted flat sales for several consecutive quarters. Temporary CEO John Young began to focus the company's development efforts on the burgeoning Internet market, a push that was intensified when Young was replaced in 1997 by former Sun Microsystems engineer Eric Schmidt.

In 1997 Novell laid off 1,000 workers (18% of its workforce, including nearly half of its 66 VPs) and became the subject of IBM takeover rumors. The next year it shifted its focus to directory services and introduced a version of NetWare designed exclusively for Internet and intranet applications.

Novell bought Netoria, a privately held maker of software for computer network administrators, in 1999. Compaq and Dell began shipping servers with Novell's Internet caching software, which linked PCs to host Internet sites for delivery of content to corporate intranets.

In 2001 Novell (along with minority partners Nortel Networks and Accenture) announced the creation of Volera, a caching and content networking company. It also bought Cambridge Technology Partners in a deal valued at about $266 million; Cambridge CEO Jack Messman assumed the role of chief executive at Novell.

The company acquired SilverStream Software in 2002 for about $210 million. It also purchased Accenture and Nortel's stakes in Volera as part of a plan to integrate it into Novell's product lines.

In 2004 Novell agreed to accept a $536 million cash settlement from Microsoft in regards to possible antitrust action relating to Netware products. The following year the company announced a restructuring plan that included a 10% workforce reduction.

Messman was replaced as CEO by company president Ronald Hovsepian in 2006. That same year Novell sold off its management consulting firm Celerant Consulting for $77 million; the buyout group included Celerant management and Caledonia Investments.

The company forged an unlikely partnership with rival Microsoft in 2006. The terms of the deal included a reseller agreement that has Microsoft distributing subscriptions to Novell's SUSE Linux software, the conducting of joint research and development operations, the payment of royalties by Novell to Microsoft, and an agreement by Microsoft not to file patent infringement charges.

EXECUTIVES

Chairman: Richard L. (Rick) Crandall, age 66
President, CEO, and Director:
Ronald W. (Ron) Hovsepian, age 49,
$4,989,882 total compensation
SVP and CFO: Dana C. Russell, age 48,
$1,516,640 total compensation
SVP, Chief Marketing Officer, and Channel Chief:
John K. Dragoon, age 49,
$1,248,647 total compensation
SVP and General Manager, Collaboration Solutions and Global Services: Colleen A. O'Keefe, age 53,
$1,303,870 total compensation
SVP and General Manager, Security, Management, and Operating Platforms: James P. (Jim) Ebzery, age 50
SVP; General Manager, Open Platform Solutions:
Markus Rex
SVP and General Manager, Global Alliances:
Joe H. Wagner
SVP Human Resources: Russell C. Poole, age 55
SVP, General Counsel, and Secretary: Scott N. Semel, age 52
VP and CIO: José Almandoz
VP Finance: Bill Smith
President and General Manager, Europe, Middle East, and Africa: Javier Colado
President and General Manager, Novell Americas:
Timothy M. (Tim) Wolfe
President and General Manager, Novell Asia/Pacific:
Maarten Koster
Director Global Public Relations: Ian Bruce
Auditors: PricewaterhouseCoopers LLP

LOCATIONS

HQ: Novell, Inc.
  404 Wyman St., Ste. 500, Waltham, MA 02451
Phone: 781-464-8000   **Fax:** 781-464-8100
Web: www.novell.com

2009 Sales

	$ mil.	% of total
Americas		
US	424.6	49
Other countries	55.0	6
Europe, Middle East & Africa	300.9	35
Asia/Pacific	81.7	10
Total	**862.2**	**100**

PRODUCTS/OPERATIONS

2009 Sales

	$ mil.	% of total
Maintenance & subscriptions	640.8	74
Software licenses	116.9	13
Services	104.5	13
Total	**862.2**	**100**

Selected Software and Services

Data center management
Identity and access management
Security management

COMPETITORS

Avocent
BMC Software
CA Technologies
Cisco Systems
Hewlett-Packard
IBM
McAfee
Microsoft
Oracle
Red Hat
Symantec
VMware

HISTORICAL FINANCIALS

Company Type: Public

Income Statement

FYE: Last Saturday in October

	REVENUE ($ mil.)	NET INCOME ($ mil.)	NET PROFIT MARGIN	EMPLOYEES
10/09	862	(213)	—	3,600
10/08	957	(9)	—	4,000
10/07	933	(45)	—	4,100
10/06	967	20	2.0%	4,549
10/05	1,198	377	31.5%	5,066
Annual Growth	(7.9%)	—	—	(8.2%)

2009 Year-End Financials

Debt ratio: —
Return on equity: —
Cash ($ mil.): 592
Current ratio: 1.75
Long-term debt ($ mil.): —

No. of shares (mil.): 350
Dividends
  Yield: —
  Payout: —
Market value ($ mil.): 1,431

Stock History

NASDAQ (GS): NOVL

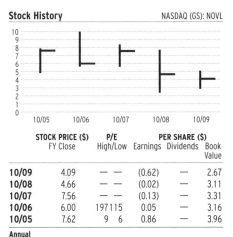

	STOCK PRICE ($) FY Close	P/E High/Low		PER SHARE ($) Earnings	Dividends	Book Value
10/09	4.09	—	—	(0.62)	—	2.67
10/08	4.66	—	—	(0.02)	—	3.11
10/07	7.56	—	—	(0.13)	—	3.31
10/06	6.00	197	115	0.05	—	3.16
10/05	7.62	9	6	0.86	—	3.96
Annual Growth	(14.4%)	—	—	—	—	(9.4%)

NSTAR

A giant star in the Massachusetts utility firmament, NSTAR is looking to outshine its rivals through the efficiency of its regulated electric and natural gas sales, distribution, and transmission operations. The utility holding company transmits and distributes electricity to almost 1.2 million homes and businesses through NSTAR Electric and serves some 300,000 natural gas customers in Massachusetts through NSTAR Gas. The company also markets wholesale electricity, and operates liquefied natural gas (LNG) processing and storage facilities. Its NSTAR Communications unit owns about 240 miles of fiber optic network.

NSTAR's power utilities — Boston Edison, Cambridge Electric Light, and Commonwealth Electric — which merged as NSTAR Electric in 2007, serve customers in more than 80 Massachusetts communities, including Boston. Subsidiary NSTAR Gas is present in more than 50 communities in central and eastern Massachusetts.

As part of its strategy of selling nonregulated businesses, in 2010 the company sold its district energy operations in the Boston Longwood Medical Area for $320 million to a joint venture led by a Veolia Environnment unit. The move allowed NSTAR to raise cash and focus on its core electric and gas delivery businesses and on growing its electric transmission operations.

Its other non-utitlity businesses are the LNG storage division and a telecom services unit. The latter owns and operates a wholesale transport network for other telecom service providers in the Boston area. Once a prominent part of its business model, unregulated businesses now provide NSTAR with only about 1% of its total sales.

NSTAR was formed by the 1999 merger of BEC Energy and Commonwealth Energy System.

HISTORY

NSTAR got its start in 1886 as the Edison Electric Illuminating Company of Boston. The company pushed the use of electricity (promoting and selling appliances in its early days) and helped to develop the first electric vehicles. In the 1920s the company launched radio stations WTAT and WEEI. It changed its name to Boston Edison in 1937.

In the 1970s Boston Edison's fortunes soured as it endured a three-month strike in 1971. In 1972 its nuclear-generated power plant, Pilgrim Station, went online, just in time for the OPEC oil embargo. The company spent about $300 million in the 1980s to fix problems at Pilgrim, which had been heavily fined by the Nuclear Regulatory Commission.

Utility deregulation began gaining momentum in the Northeast in the 1990s, and Boston Edison responded by selling its fossil-fueled power plants, reducing rates, and creating a holding company (BEC Energy) for new, unregulated businesses. In 1996 BEC Energy and the Williams Companies formed a power-marketing joint venture (Williams later took over). It also formed a joint venture with telecommunications company RCN to provide bundled telephone, cable, and Internet access over BEC Energy's fiber-optic networks in Boston.

BEC Energy sold its fossil fuel-generated plants to Sithe Energies in 1997. Still shedding assets in 1999, the company sold its Pilgrim nuke to Entergy. BEC Energy then merged with Commonwealth Energy System to form NSTAR. In 2000 the new holding company organized its three electric utilities under the NSTAR Electric brand, and renamed its gas unit NSTAR Gas.

In 2002 NSTAR sold its 3% interest in the Vermont Yankee nuclear plant to Entergy. That year the company sold its 4% interest in the Seabrook nuclear plant to FPL Group and exchanged its 23% interest in joint venture RCN-BecoCom for an 11% stake in the venture's parent, RCN Corporation. Due to low market value, NSTAR wrote off its investment in RCN in 2005.

NSTAR and Evergreen Solar, a maker of solar power products, formed an alliance in 2007 designed to increase the role of solar power in eastern Massachusetts.

EXECUTIVES

Chairman, President, and CEO: Thomas J. (Tom) May, age 62, $7,395,965 total compensation
SVP and CFO: James J. (Jim) Judge, age 53, $2,459,247 total compensation
SVP Customer and Corporate Relations: Joseph R. (Joe) Nolan Jr., age 46, $1,085,546 total compensation
SVP Strategy, Law, and Policy, Secretary, and General Counsel: Douglas S. (Doug) Horan, age 60, $2,425,644 total compensation
SVP Operations: Werner J. Schweiger, age 50, $1,875,464 total compensation
SVP Human Resources: Christine M. (Chris) Carmody, age 46
VP Engineering: Lawrence J. (Larry) Gelbien
VP Financial Strategic Planning and Policy: Geoffrey O. (Geoff) Lubbock
VP Electric Field Operations: Craig Hallstrom
VP Information Technology: Katherine (Kathy) Kountze-Tatum
VP Customer Care: Penelope M. (Penni) Conner
VP, Chief Accounting Officer, and Controller: Robert J. (Bob) Weafer Jr., age 62
VP and Treasurer: Philip J. (Phil) Lembo
VP Energy Supply and Supply Chain Management: Ellen K. Angley
VP Electric System Operations and Transmission Development: Paul D. Vaitkus
Director Investor Relations and Financial Reporting: John M. Moreira
Auditors: PricewaterhouseCoopers LLP

LOCATIONS

HQ: NSTAR
800 Boylston St., Boston, MA 02199
Phone: 617-424-2000   **Fax:** 781-441-8886
Web: www.nstaronline.com

PRODUCTS/OPERATIONS

2009 Sales

	$ mil.	% of total
Electric utility	2,551.6	84
Gas utility	482.1	16
Unregulated operations	16.3	—
Total	**3,050.0**	**100**

Selected Subsidiaries

Hopkinton LNG Corp. (liquefied natural gas services)
NSTAR Communications, Inc. (wholesale broadband network)
NSTAR Electric Company (electric utility)
NSTAR Gas Company (natural gas utility)

COMPETITORS

Bay State Gas
Con Edison
Green Mountain Power
Iberdrola USA
National Grid USA

NiSource
Northeast Utilities
PG&E Corporation
Unitil
USPowerGen

HISTORICAL FINANCIALS

Company Type: Public

Income Statement

FYE: December 31

	REVENUE ($ mil.)	NET INCOME ($ mil.)	NET PROFIT MARGIN	EMPLOYEES
12/09	3,050	255	8.4%	3,000
12/08	3,345	238	7.1%	3,250
12/07	3,262	222	6.8%	3,150
12/06	3,578	207	5.8%	3,100
12/05	3,243	196	6.0%	3,050
Annual Growth	(1.5%)	6.8%	—	(0.4%)

2009 Year-End Financials

Debt ratio: 116.5%
Return on equity: 13.9%
Cash ($ mil.): 143
Current ratio: 0.69
Long-term debt ($ mil.): 2,181

No. of shares (mil.): 104
Dividends
  Yield: 4.1%
  Payout: 64.1%
Market value ($ mil.): 3,812

Stock History

NYSE: NST

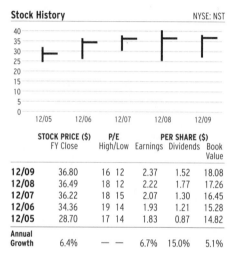

	STOCK PRICE ($) FY Close	P/E High/Low	PER SHARE ($) Earnings	PER SHARE ($) Dividends	PER SHARE ($) Book Value
12/09	36.80	16 12	2.37	1.52	18.08
12/08	36.49	18 12	2.22	1.77	17.26
12/07	36.22	18 15	2.07	1.30	16.45
12/06	34.36	19 14	1.93	1.21	15.28
12/05	28.70	17 14	1.83	0.87	14.82
Annual Growth	6.4%	— —	6.7%	15.0%	5.1%

Nu Skin Enterprises

Multilevel marketer Nu Skin Enterprises keeps itself busy exfoliating and polishing. It offers more than 100 namesake personal care products, including cleansers, toners, and moisturizers, through a global network of more than 760,000 independent distributors, sales reps, and preferred customers. It also sells cosmetics, fragrances, hair care items, and mouthwash. Nu Skin has its foot in the door in 50 global markets, including cherished China. Its Pharmanex unit sells LifePak nutritional supplements. Its Big Planet unit offers personal and small-business technology and communications products, as well as Internet and long-distance services. Nu Skin was founded in 1984 by chairman Blake Roney.

While the company is based in the US, nearly 85% of Nu Skin's 2009 revenue was generated internationally (including about 35% from Japan). The personal care products firm banks on breakaway items in its stable of brands for its bread and butter. One such line is Galvanic Spa, which consists of a handheld spa appliance that emits galvanic currents as well as anti-aging gels and skin care treatments. Introduced in 2005, Galvanic Spa generated about 20% of Nu Skin's total revenue in 2009. The line has helped the com-

pany retain its sales increases during the economic downturn and is part of Nu Skin's strategy to boost use of "unique tools." In 2009 Nu Skin added to its portfolio by launching a product that targets the signs and sources of aging under the ageLOC brand name. It's rolling out nutritional products under the ageLOC name by the end of 2010. Nu Skin's staff of 75 in-house scientists has helped to keep the company on the forefront of skin care research. The firm spends about $10 million in R&D each year.

The company believes its unique products help it to stand out. Nu Skin has its distributors use a laser-based scanner — called the Pharmanex BioPhotonic Laser Scanner — to measure the level of antioxidants in customers' skin after supplemental use. Another sales tool for distributors is the ProDerm Skin Analyzer, which gives customers a personalized report on four different skin features.

The company celebrated its 25th anniversary in 2009. It achieved the milestone, navigating through the downturn in the economy, by making some adjustments in recent years to stay afloat. Ensuring it's one step ahead of rivals Amway and Avon, Nu Skin shed jobs at its US corporate office in 2008 and shuttered about 70 of its 115 retail stores in China, shifting focus to open a handful of stores in Beijing, Guangzhou, and Shanghai soon thereafter. The company also closed its Brazil operations in 2007, after nearly 10 years of unprofitability in that market.

Nu Skin Enterprises has shed its motley organizational hide in favor of a smoother business veneer. The company once operated through a number of nationally separated licensees, but it now sells its personal care, nutritional, and technological products through its three divisions.

Chairman Roney and his wife Nancy own about 13% of the company's shares.

HISTORY

Brigham Young University graduate Blake Roney and his sister, Nedra, came up with the idea for Nu Skin in 1984 while pondering the amount of fillers in personal care products. They compiled a list of beneficial ingredients, came up with $5,000 (from friend and present SVP Sandra Tillotson), and found a manufacturer to make their product — and Nu Skin International was born. Roney was dead-set against incurring debt, so he decided to use multilevel marketing to push the products. Such marketing systems are often accused of being illegal pyramid schemes, and Nu Skin has drawn the attention of many attorneys general across the US.

Nevertheless the company expanded rapidly and soon entered other countries, including Canada (1990), Taiwan (1992), and Australia and Japan (1993). Nu Skin introduced Interior Design Nutritionals in 1992 and a line of plaque-fighting oral care products in 1993. Expansion continued as the company entered several European countries during 1996.

Roney formed Nu Skin Asia Pacific as a public company in 1995 and 1996 while maintaining Nu Skin International as a privately held affiliate. In 1996 the company introduced its Epoch line of products, containing ingredients used by indigenous cultures around the world. The following year supermodel Christie Brinkley signed on as Nu Skin spokeswoman, and in 1998 Nu Skin Asia Pacific acquired its parent — excluding its North American operations — for about $250 million, plus up to $100 million more in

performance-based payments. Nu Skin Asia Pacific was renamed Nu Skin Enterprises.

Nu Skin Enterprises bought the assets of Nu Skin USA in March 1999 in a continuing effort to simplify the Nu Skin organization and gain worldwide ownership and marketing rights. In August 1999 it bought technology and communications products maker Big Planet and later organized its personal care, nutritional, and technological products into three separate divisions.

Nu Skin expanded Pharmanex into the emergency food supply market through its 2002 acquisition of First Harvest International and began selling Vitameals, a dehydrated food product. It also established a humanitarian initiative (Nourish the Children) through which Vitameals can be distributed to malnourished children worldwide.

Nu Skin opened more than 100 retail outlets in China in January 2003.

The company increased revenue in 2005 with year-over-year growth in certain markets, including Korea, Taiwan, Europe, and the US, as well as with its expansion into Indonesia.

EXECUTIVES

Chairman: Blake M. Roney, age 52, $1,739,391 total compensation
Vice Chairman: Steven J. Lund, age 56
President, CEO, and Director: M. Truman Hunt, age 51, $3,049,698 total compensation
CFO: Ritch N. Wood, age 44, $1,085,858 total compensation
EVP Product Development and Chief Scientific Officer: Joseph Y. (Joe) Chang, age 57, $2,961,342 total compensation
General Counsel and Secretary: D. Matthew Dorny, age 45
CIO: Mark L. Adams, age 58
SVP and Director: Sandra N. (Sandie) Tillotson, age 53
VP Global Opportunity Marketing: Elizabeth Thibaudeau
VP Global Logistics and Fulfillment: Bradley R. (Brad) Morris
VP Corporate Administrative Services: Charles H. (Charlie) Allen
VP Global Product Marketing: Kevin Fuller
VP Global Government and Industry Affairs: Richard M. (Rich) Hartvigsen
VP and General Counsel: Tyler Whitehead
VP Human Resources: David Daines
VP Global Supply Chain: Jeff Henderson
President, Global Sales and Operations: Daniel R. (Dan) Chard, age 45, $1,085,633 total compensation
President, Greater China Region: Andrew Fan, age 46
President, Southeast Asia Region: Melisa T. Quijano
President, North Asia; President and General Manager, Korea: Luke B. Yoo
Senior Director Corporate Communications: Kara Schneck
Director Investor Relations: Scott Pond
Auditors: PricewaterhouseCoopers LLP

LOCATIONS

HQ: Nu Skin Enterprises, Inc.
75 W. Center St., Provo, UT 84601
Phone: 801-345-1000   **Fax:** 800-487-8000
Web: www.nuskinenterprises.com

2009 Sales

	$ mil.	% of total
North Asia	606.1	45
Americas	260.9	20
Greater China	210.4	16
Europe	133.6	10
South Asia/Pacific	120.1	9
Total	**1,331.1**	**100**

PRODUCTS/OPERATIONS

2009 Sales

	$ mil.	% of total
Nu Skin	752.7	57
Pharmanex	565.6	42
Other	12.8	1
Total	**1,331.1**	**100**

Selected Products

Nu Skin
  Body care products
  Cosmetics
  Facial care products
  Fragrances
  Hair care products
  Oral care products
Pharmanex
  Botanicals
  Emergency nutritional supply
  General nutrition
  Herbal products
  Multivitamin/mineral supplement
  Sports nutrition
  Water filtration systems
  Weight management
Big Planet
  Educational and training products
  E-commerce products
  Internet access products
  Long-distance and voice-messaging services
  Pagers
  Prepaid calling cards

COMPETITORS

Alticor
Amazon.com
AMS Health Sciences
Avon
Bath & Body Works
BeautiControl
Beiersdorf
Body Shop
Buy.com
CCA Industries
Clarins
Comcast
Del Laboratories
EarthLink
Estée Lauder
Forever Living
ForeverGreen Worldwide
GNC
Kodak Imaging Network
L'Oréal
Mannatech
Mary Kay
Melaleuca
Merle Norman
Microsoft
Murad, Inc.
Nature's Sunshine
Procter & Gamble
Revlon
Schiff Nutrition International
Shaklee
Shiseido
Sprint Nextel
The Stephan Co.
Sunrider
Time Warner Cable
Tom's of Maine
Unilever

HISTORICAL FINANCIALS

Company Type: Public

Income Statement

FYE: December 31

	REVENUE ($ mil.)	NET INCOME ($ mil.)	NET PROFIT MARGIN	EMPLOYEES
12/09	1,331	90	6.7%	8,900
12/08	1,248	65	5.2%	9,185
12/07	1,158	44	3.8%	8,700
12/06	1,115	33	2.9%	11,360
12/05	1,181	74	6.3%	9,000
Annual Growth	**3.0%**	**5.0%**	**—**	**(0.3%)**

2009 Year-End Financials

Debt ratio: 32.2%
Return on equity: 26.0%
Cash ($ mil.): 158
Current ratio: 1.82
Long-term debt ($ mil.): 121
No. of shares (mil.): 63
Dividends
  Yield: 1.7%
  Payout: 32.9%
Market value ($ mil.): 1,694

Stock History

NYSE: NUS

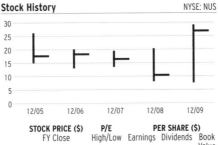

	STOCK PRICE ($) FY Close	P/E High/Low		PER SHARE ($) Earnings	Dividends	Book Value
12/09	26.87	21	6	1.40	0.46	5.96
12/08	10.43	20	8	1.02	0.44	5.02
12/07	16.43	29	21	0.67	0.42	4.36
12/06	18.23	42	29	0.47	0.40	5.06
12/05	17.58	25	15	1.04	0.36	5.63
Annual Growth	**11.2%**	**—**	**—**	**7.7%**	**6.3%**	**1.5%**

Nucor Corporation

Nucor continues to electrify the steel industry with a simple concept: The minimill is mighty. At its various minimills, Nucor produces about 15 million tons of steel annually, including hot- and cold-rolled steel, steel joists, and metal buildings. A major recycler of scrap metal, Nucor produces steel by melting scrap in electric arc furnaces. Most of its products are sold to steel service centers, manufacturers, and fabricators. Divisions such as Vulcraft — one of the US's largest producers of steel joists, girders, and decking — use the balance of the steel. The company has added greatly to its operations through acquisitions since 2006, including spending $1 billion to buy The David J. Joseph Company.

Nucor has dominated the minimill industry for more than two decades, but competitors in the sector are increasing. The company continues to expand its steel mills, add new facilities, and pursue a program of rapid external growth.

The company has always operated primarily in the US, but in 2008 it moved into the international market with the formation of a European joint venture with Duferco. The JV produces steel beams and merchant bar products from manufacturing locations in Italy and serves the European and North African markets. Nucor put

about $650 million into the new venture, called Nucor S.r.l. Duferdofin.

In 2010 it announced the formation of another joint venture, this one based in the US. Nucor and Mitsui & Co. formed NuMit LLC as a steel processing venture that will look to buy steel businesses in the United States and internationally. Nucor paid $225 million for its half of the venture. Its first move was to take in Mitsui subsidiary Steel Technologies.

Even though Nucor continues to face stiff domestic and foreign competition as well as pronounced economic difficulties, it has not laid off any employees in more than 30 years. The company's SOP is to modulate its output — and its employees' pay — according to demand; thus, in a downturn the company produces less steel and its employees make less than they do during stronger economic times.

HISTORY

Nucor started as the second carmaking venture of Ransom Olds, who built his first gasoline-powered car in 1897. Two years later, Samuel Smith, a Detroit copper and lumber magnate, put up $199,600 to finance Olds Motor Works. A fire destroyed the company's Detroit plant in 1901, so Olds moved production to Lansing, Michigan, where he built America's first mass-produced car — the Oldsmobile. In 1904 Olds left Olds Motor Works, which was bought by General Motors (GM) in 1908, and formed Reo Car Company (renamed Reo Motor Car in 1906). In addition to cars, it eventually made trucks and buses.

By the end of the Depression, Ford, GM, and Chrysler commanded over 85% of the US passenger car market. Reo stopped making cars in 1936 and sold its truck manufacturing operations in 1957. Meanwhile, it had formed Reo Holding, which in 1955 merged with Nuclear Consultants to form Nuclear Corporation of America. The new company offered services such as radiation studies and made nuclear instruments and electronics.

In 1962 Nuclear bought steel joist maker Vulcraft and gained the services of Kenneth Iverson. The diverse company was unprofitable, losing $2 million on $22 million in sales in 1965. That year Iverson took over as CEO, moved headquarters to Charlotte, North Carolina, and shut down or sold about half of the company's businesses. By focusing on its profitable steel joist operations, the firm ended 1966 in the black. Because the company depended on imports for 80% of its steel needs, Iverson decided to move into steel production. Nuclear Corporation built its first minimill in 1969.

The company was renamed Nucor in 1972. It started making steel deck (1977) and cold-finished steel bars (1979). Production tripled and sales more than doubled between 1974 and 1979.

Nucor began to diversify, adding grinding balls (used in the mining industry to process ores, 1981); steel bolts, steel bearings, and machined steel parts (1986); and metal buildings and components (1987). Nucor and Japanese steelmaker Yamato Kogyo formed Nucor-Yamato and built a mill in 1988 to produce wide-flange beams (for heavy construction). The following year Nucor opened a state-of-the-art mill in Crawfordsville, Indiana, and another mill near Hickman, Arkansas, in 1992.

Iverson turned over his CEO duties to company veteran John Correnti in 1996. The next year Nucor began building a steel beam mill in

South Carolina and added a galvanizing facility to its Hickman mill.

In 1998 Nucor announced plans to build its first steel plate mill, which became operational in 2000. The company slashed prices twice in 1998 to compete against low-cost imports from Russia, Japan, and Brazil. Differences with the board prompted Correnti to resign in 1999; chairman David Aycock assumed his duties. In September 2000 Aycock resigned from the company and Daniel DiMicco, formerly an EVP, was named CEO.

In 2002 Nucor teamed up with Companhia Vale do Rio Doce (Vale), a Brazilian producer and exporter of iron-ore pellets, to develop low-cost iron-based products. In late 2002 Nucor bought financially troubled Birmingham Steel for $615 million in cash and debt.

Its Vulcraft unit saw an increase in non-residential building construction in 2004, which boosted sales of joist girders, steel deck, and steel joists. Nucor bought Corus Tuscaloosa (now called Nucor Tuscaloosa) in mid-2004, a producer of coiled plate with an annual capacity of around 700,000 tons.

The company named CEO DiMicco chairman in 2006.

In the latter half of the last decade, it started a program of rapid external growth. It acquired the former Connecticut Steel, Verco Manufacturing, and Canadian steel products maker Harris Steel, which like Connecticut Steel had been a customer and partner of Nucor for years. Harris itself made an acquisition in 2008, when it bought rebar fabricator and distributor Ambassador Steel. Nucor also expanded its downstream operations with the 2007 acquisition of building systems maker MAGNATRAX for $280 million. Its largest acquisition was that of the David J. Joseph Company, a scrap metal broker that had supplied Nucor's minimills for 40 years.

EXECUTIVES

Chairman, President, and CEO:
Daniel R. (Dan) DiMicco, age 59,
$2,884,064 total compensation
COO Steelmaking Operations: John J. Ferriola, age 57,
$1,308,649 total compensation
EVP, CFO, and Treasurer: James D. (Jim) Frias, age 53
EVP Fabricated Construction Products:
Hamilton Lott Jr., age 60,
$1,152,048 total compensation
EVP Bar Products: D. Michael (Mike) Parrish, age 57,
$1,152,048 total compensation
EVP; President and CEO, DJJ: Keith B. Grass, age 53,
$2,264,776 total compensation
EVP Beam and Plate Products: R. Joseph Stratman,
age 53
EVP Flat Rolled Products: Ladd R. Hall, age 53
VP; President, Nucor Building Systems:
Jeffrey B. (Jeff) Carmean
VP; President, Nucor Buildings Group: Harry R. Lowe
VP; President, Vulcraft and Verco Group:
James R. Darsey
VP; President, Nucor Europe: K. Rex Query
VP; President, American Buildings Company:
Raymond S. Napolitan Jr.
President and CEO, Harris Steel Group: John Harris
General Manager and Secretary: A. Rae Eagle
Auditors: PricewaterhouseCoopers LLP

LOCATIONS

HQ: Nucor Corporation
1915 Rexford Rd., Charlotte, NC 28211
Phone: 704-366-7000   **Fax:** 704-362-4208
Web: www.nucor.com

PRODUCTS/OPERATIONS

2009 Sales

	$ mil.	% of total
Steel mills	7,159.5	64
Steel products	2,691.3	24
Raw materials	1,077.0	10
Other	262.5	2
Total	**11,190.3**	**100**

Selected Products

Alloy steel
  Cold-drawn steel bars
  Finished hex caps
  Hex-head cap screws
  Locknuts
  Structural bolts and nuts
Carbon steel
  Angles
  Beams
  Channels
  Cold-drawn steel bars
  Finished hex nuts
  Flats
  Floor plate
  Galvanized sheet
  Grinding balls
  Hexagons
  Hot-rolled sheet
  Reinforcing bars
  Structural bolts and nuts
  Wide-range beams
Engineered products
  Composite floor joists
  Floor deck
  Joists
  Joist girders
  Pre-engineered metal buildings
  Roof deck
  Special-profile steel trusses
Stainless steel
  Cold-rolled steel
  Hot-rolled steel
  Pickled sheet

COMPETITORS

AK Steel Holding Corporation
ArcelorMittal USA
BlueScope Steel
Commercial Metals
Corus Group
Gerdau Ameristeel
Renco
Schnitzer Steel
Steel Dynamics
United States Steel

HISTORICAL FINANCIALS

Company Type: Public

Income Statement

FYE: December 31

	REVENUE ($ mil.)	NET INCOME ($ mil.)	NET PROFIT MARGIN	EMPLOYEES
12/09	11,190	(294)	—	20,400
12/08	23,663	1,831	7.7%	21,700
12/07	16,593	1,472	8.9%	18,000
12/06	14,751	1,758	11.9%	11,900
12/05	12,701	1,310	10.3%	11,300
Annual Growth	**(3.1%)**	**—**	**—**	**15.9%**

2009 Year-End Financials

Debt ratio: 41.7%
Return on equity: —
Cash ($ mil.): 2,017
Current ratio: 4.22
Long-term debt ($ mil.): 3,080

No. of shares (mil.): 316
Dividends
  Yield: 3.0%
  Payout: —
Market value ($ mil.): 14,721

Stock History   NYSE: NUE

	STOCK PRICE ($) FY Close	P/E High/Low		PER SHARE ($) Earnings	Dividends	Book Value
12/09	46.65	—	—	(0.94)	1.41	23.42
12/08	46.20	14	4	5.98	1.51	25.13
12/07	59.22	14	8	4.94	1.13	16.20
12/06	54.66	12	6	5.68	0.40	15.29
12/05	33.36	8	6	4.13	0.43	13.56
Annual Growth	**8.7%**	**—**	**—**	**—**	**34.6%**	**14.6%**

NVIDIA Corporation

NVIDIA keeps staging new graphics chip invasions. The fabless semiconductor company designs high-definition 2-D and 3-D graphics processors for gaming and industrial design applications. Its graphics chips, especially the flagship GeForce line, are used by leading PC makers, such as Apple, Dell, and Hewlett-Packard, as well as in add-in boards and motherboards produced by ASUSTeK Computer, PNY Technologies, and other firms. NVIDIA also provides complementary graphics driver software, as well as graphics chipsets — clusters of components with integrated graphics functions that aid the operation of PC microprocessors.

Targeting the applications processor, desktop and notebook PC, high-performance computing, and professional workstation markets with its graphics processors and ultra-low-power mobile system-on-a-chip products, NVIDIA plans to continue dominance of its market niche through building on its expertise in digital media, sustaining product and technology leadership in 3-D graphics and high-def video, and increasing market share. The company is wading into the high-performance computing market with its Tesla line of graphics processors and the CUDA parallel computing architecture. NVIDIA wants to see developers build "personal supercomputers" and high-performance computing clusters with CUDA, which allows NVIDIA graphics processors to solve complex computational problems in a fraction of the time required on an average central processing unit.

AMD's acquisition of NVIDIA's archrival, ATI Technologies, complicated a number of relationships in the semiconductor industry. AMD and NVIDIA previously collaborated on making sure AMD's microprocessors and NVIDIA's graphics processors worked smoothly together. The purchase put AMD and NVIDIA in the awkward position of being both collaborators and competitors, as AMD is developing a new set of "Fusion" processors that meld the capabilities of the AMD and ATI product lines.

AMD and Intel are NVIDIA's biggest competitors. Intel is preparing a multiple-core architecture, code-named Arrandale, that may compete with various NVIDIA products. Intel's Atom processor for low-end PCs also presents a challenge to the company.

Intel filed suit against NVIDIA in 2009, claiming a licensing agreement the two companies signed in 2004 does not extend to certain media and communications processor (MCP) chipset products sold by NVIDIA. While not seeking any damages, Intel wants to bar NVIDIA from selling MCP chipsets for use with specific Intel processors. NVIDIA responded with legal counterclaims against Intel, and a trial is scheduled for 2010.

In 2008 NVIDIA acquired AGEIA Technologies, a developer of physics processing software for gaming. The company sees a complementary fit between its GeForce graphics processing units and PhysX for not only gaming, but also for applications in computer vision, physics research, and video/image processing.

NVIDIA's chips supply the graphics muscle for Microsoft's Xbox video game console, and the company has partnered with Sony to develop graphics processors for the PlayStation console. NVIDIA also supplies media processors used in phones from Motorola and Sony Ericsson.

HISTORY

Taiwan-born and Stanford-trained engineer Jen-Hsun Huang was already a veteran of Advanced Micro Devices and LSI Logic (now just LSI) when he decided to start his own company at age 30. He co-founded NVIDIA in 1992 with fellow engineers and industry veterans Chris Malachowsky (SVP) and Curtis Priem (former CTO). It was incorporated in 1993.

After its first try at a graphics chip failed miserably in 1995, NVIDIA hit the big time in 1997 when it introduced a graphics processor that set a new industry standard for speed. Good product timing and flawless execution kept the company growing in the years to come: After turning its first profit in 1998, NVIDIA crossed the $100 million, $300 million, and $700 million sales thresholds in successive years.

The company made its IPO in 1999. The following year Microsoft chose NVIDIA to supply the graphics chips for its Xbox video game console. Also in 2000 the company overtook archrival ATI Technologies in market share for desktop PC graphics chips.

In 2000 the company announced that it would acquire the assets of erstwhile rival 3dfx in a deal initially valued at $110 million. The transaction was completed in 2001 for $70 million in cash and a potential earnout payment of 1 million shares of NVIDIA common stock. In 2002 the company came under review by the SEC for potential accounting irregularities; when the company restated earnings a few months later, though, its financial results for the three-year period in question improved slightly.

Later that year NVIDIA bought privately held 3-D software company Exluna, which was founded by veterans of Pixar. The following year NVIDIA acquired MediaQ, whose handheld graphics and media products were rebranded as GoForce, for about $70 million. In 2004 NVIDIA acquired assets of privately held iReady Corp., primarily consisting of the intellectual property and patents related to its TCP/IP and iSCSI Ethernet technologies.

The company acquired Taiwanese circuit designer ULi Electronics for about $52 million in 2006. The company also acquired Hybrid Graphics, a developer of embedded graphics software for handheld devices, that year.

Adding to industry anxiety was an investigation into the graphics processor market by the Antitrust Division of the US Department of Justice. AMD and NVIDIA received subpoenas in 2006 from the Justice Department for materials related to competitive practices in the business for graphics processing units and cards. The Justice Department also had a longstanding antitrust case in the DRAM device market, which resulted in several industry executives going to prison and vendors paying hundreds of millions of dollars in fines for fixing prices on memory parts, and separate investigations into the static random-access memory (SRAM) and NAND flash memory device markets. The Department of Justice concluded the antitrust investigation into graphics processing units and cards in 2008 without taking any action against AMD or NVIDIA.

In 2007 the company purchased PortalPlayer, a supplier of chips that go into Apple's iPods, SanDisk's Sansa MP3 music players, and other portable electronics, for approximately $357 million in cash. The transaction was a financial bargain for NVIDIA, as PortalPlayer had about $196 million in cash among its assets, making up more than half of the purchase price.

EXECUTIVES

President, CEO, and Director: Jen-Hsun Huang, age 47, $3,482,145 total compensation
EVP and CFO: David L. White, age 54, $2,871,495 total compensation
EVP, General Counsel, and Secretary: David M. Shannon, age 54, $1,941,306 total compensation
EVP Operations: Debora C. Shoquist, age 55, $1,698,758 total compensation
EVP Worldwide Sales: Ajay K (Jay) Puri, age 55, $1,531,916 total compensation
CIO: Ranga Jayaraman
Chief Scientist: Bill Dally
SVP Human Resources: Scott P. Sullivan
SVP Mobile Business Unit: Philip J. (Phil) Carmack
SVP Engineering and Operations and NVIDIA Fellow: Chris A. Malachowsky, age 51
SVP Consumer Electronics Engineering: Frank Fox
SVP Content and Technology: Tony Tamasi
SVP Software Engineering: Dwight Diercks
SVP Investor Relations and Communications: Michael W. (Mike) Hara
SVP Systems and Application Engineering: Tommy Lee
VP Corporate Marketing: Rob Csongor
VP Corporate Communications: Robert (Bob) Sherbin, age 52
Auditors: PricewaterhouseCoopers LLP

LOCATIONS

HQ: NVIDIA Corporation
2701 San Tomas Expwy., Santa Clara, CA 95050
Phone: 408-486-2000   **Fax:** 408-486-2200
Web: www.nvidia.com

2010 Sales

	$ mil.	% of total
Asia/Pacific		
China	1,304.2	39
Taiwan	883.1	27
Other countries	406.3	12
Americas		
US	248.8	8
Other countries	280.3	8
Europe	203.7	6
Total	**3,326.4**	**100**

PRODUCTS/OPERATIONS

2010 Sales

	$ mil.	% of total
GPU Business	1,764.7	53
Media & Communications Processor	871.6	26
Professional Solutions Business	510.2	15
Consumer Products Business	163.9	5
Other	16.0	1
Total	**3,326.4**	**100**

Selected Products

Graphics processing unit (GPU) chips for PCs and workstations (GeForce, NVIDIA Quadro)
Media and communications processors (MCP) for PCs, workstations, and servers (nForce)
Consumer electronics processors for video game consoles and other devices
Handheld GPUs for handheld computers and mobile phones (GoForce)

COMPETITORS

AMD	MediaTek
ARM Holdings	QUALCOMM
Broadcom	Renesas Electronics
Creative Technology	Samsung Electronics
Epson	Sigma Designs
Freescale Semiconductor	Silicon Integrated Systems
Fujitsu Semiconductor	STMicroelectronics
Imagination Technologies	Texas Instruments
Intel	Toshiba America
Marvell Technology	VIA Technologies
Matrox Electronic Systems	

HISTORICAL FINANCIALS

Company Type: Public

Income Statement			FYE: Last Saturday in January	
	REVENUE ($ mil.)	NET INCOME ($ mil.)	NET PROFIT MARGIN	EMPLOYEES
1/10	3,326	(68)	—	3,940
1/09	3,425	(30)	—	5,420
1/08	4,098	798	19.5%	4,985
1/07	3,069	448	14.6%	4,083
1/06	2,376	303	12.7%	2,737
Annual Growth	8.8%	—	—	9.5%

2010 Year-End Financials

Debt ratio: 0.9%	No. of shares (mil.): 572
Return on equity: —	Dividends
Cash ($ mil.): 447	Yield: —
Current ratio: 3.16	Payout: —
Long-term debt ($ mil.): 24	Market value ($ mil.): 8,806

Stock History

NASDAQ (GS): NVDA

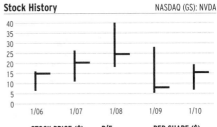

	STOCK PRICE ($)	P/E	PER SHARE ($)		
	FY Close	High/Low	Earnings	Dividends	Book Value
1/10	15.39	— —	(0.12)	—	4.66
1/09	7.95	— —	(0.05)	—	4.18
1/08	24.59	30 14	1.31	—	4.58
1/07	20.43	34 15	0.77	—	3.51
1/06	14.99	28 13	0.55	—	2.55
Annual Growth	0.7%	— —	—	—	16.3%

NVR, Inc.

From finished lot to signed mortgage, NVR offers homebuyers everything — including the kitchen sink. The company builds single-family detached homes, townhomes, and condominiums, mainly for first-time and move-up buyers, primarily in the eastern US. NVR markets its homes as Ryan Homes, Fox Ridge Homes, Rymarc Homes, and NVHomes. Its largest markets, the Washington, DC, and Baltimore areas, account for nearly half of sales. NVR sells about 15,000 homes annually. Sizes range from 1,000 sq. ft. to 7,300 sq. ft., and prices range from $56,000 to $2 million, averaging about $296,000. Subsidiary NVR Mortgage Finance offers mortgage and title services.

NVR had arranged to buy the assets of bankrupt Orleans Homebuilders, but the acquisition target later rejected the $170 million bid in favor of a restructuring plan. NVR is pursuing the matter in court.

Like other homebuilders, Orleans fell victim to the slumping housing market. NVR's sales have also dipped slightly, but the company is faring better than some of its competitors, in part because of its conservative land acquisition strategy. To control capital risk, it does not develop land, but instead buys option contracts on finished building lots from developers; it purchases finished lots through joint developments, as well. NVR also has remained profitable by lowering its prices and focusing on areas where it has a high market share.

NVR's Ryan Homes, Fox Ridge Homes, and Rymarc Homes divisions primarily market to first-time buyers. Ryan Homes operates in some two-dozen metropolitan areas along the eastern seaboard and in Indiana, Kentucky, Ohio, Pennsylvania, and West Virginia. Fox Ridge Homes is dedicated to the Nashville market, and Rymarc Homes operates solely in Columbia, South Carolina. NVHomes caters to upscale buyers and builds primarily in the Baltimore, Philadelphia, and Washington, DC, metro areas, as well as on Maryland's eastern shore.

HISTORY

NVR got its start when Dwight Schar founded NVHomes, Inc., in 1980. Schar had worked for Ryan Homes (founded 1948) since 1969. NVHomes, like Ryan Homes, specialized in single-family homes around Washington, DC. The strong economy of the 1980s and the deregulation of lending institutions — coupled with favorable partnership and real estate tax laws passed by the Reagan administration — resulted in rapid growth. The company was clearing income of more than $1 million a year by 1983 and soon branched into building townhomes and condominiums.

In 1986, when the company was reorganized as a limited partnership (NVH L.P.), income was up to $14 million. The new entity soon acquired a controlling interest in Ryan Homes; it completed its acquisition of that company in 1987. NVH reorganized as a holding company (NVRyan L.P.), and 1988 profits reached $33.5 million. Over the years the company formed or acquired almost 100 subsidiaries that were involved in all aspects of homebuilding — from land acquisition and construction to home finance and investment advice. It had also branched out into California, Florida, Indiana, Kentucky, North Carolina, Ohio, Pennsylvania, and Virginia.

Following an economic recession in 1989, demand for new housing dropped off in the US. The company shortened its name to NVR L.P., and its inventory of unsold land and houses started to grow. The situation was exacerbated by changes in the tax code that made real estate less attractive as an investment; sales from development and construction projects dropped from more than $1 billion in 1988 to about $600 million in 1991. NVR posted a $260 million loss in 1990 as sales and the value of its inventory nose-dived.

NVR reorganized in 1990 and 1991. Focused on eight mid-Atlantic states, it put homebuilding under one management structure, consolidated its finance activities, exited its land-development businesses, and offered its mortgage services to customers who weren't NVR homebuyers. It also organized its business into two product lines: upscale (NVHomes) and moderately priced (Ryan Homes) homes. Despite the reorganization and introduction of innovative marketing, NVR and several of its subsidiaries filed for Chapter 11 bankruptcy relief in 1992. That year the CFO of NVR's thrift (NVR Savings Bank) went on the lam to Malta after embezzling more than $750,000.

The company emerged from bankruptcy as NVR, Inc., in 1993 with less debt, new owners, and a new line of credit; it also had its IPO that year. The next year NVR sold NVR Savings Bank, which had four branches in northern Virginia. The robust mid-1990s economy aided NVR; as home sales rose, the company entered new markets, including the Cleveland and Nashville areas, in 1995. To reduce its vulnerability to downturns in the mid-Atlantic area, it continued its expansion outside that region, buying Fox Ridge Homes (the #2 builder in Nashville) in 1997.

In 1999 it merged its homebuilding subsidiary, NVR Homes, and mortgage banking holding company, NVR Financial Services, into NVR. It also acquired Rockville, Maryland-based First Republic Mortgage that year, but closed the subsidiary's retail operations in 2000 and realigned its mortgage banking business to serve NVR customers exclusively.

From 1994 through 2003 the company benefited from increased housing activity, recording steady increases in unit sales, backlog, and profits for nine years.

EXECUTIVES

Chairman: Dwight C. Schar, age 68
President and CEO: Paul C. Saville, age 54, $1,207,350 total compensation
SVP, CFO, and Treasurer: Dennis M. Seremet, age 54, $719,850 total compensation
VP and Controller: Robert W. Henley, age 43, $336,000 total compensation
VP Business Planning: Dan Malzahn
Secretary and General Counsel: James M. Sack
President, NVR Mortgage Banking System: Robert A. (Bob) Goethe, age 55
Auditors: KPMG LLP

LOCATIONS

HQ: NVR, Inc.
Tower 1, 11700 Plaza America Dr., Ste. 500
Reston, VA 20190
Phone: 703-956-4000 **Fax:** 703-956-4750
Web: www.nvrinc.com

PRODUCTS/OPERATIONS

2009 Sales

	$ mil.	% of total
Homebuilding		
Mid-Atlantic	1,661.3	60
Mid-East	505.4	18
Southeast	262.1	10
Northeast	254.7	9
Mortgage banking & other	72.7	3
Total	**2,756.2**	**100**

COMPETITORS

Beazer Homes
Brookfield Homes
Champion Enterprises
David Weekley Homes
D.R. Horton
Hovnanian Enterprises
John Wieland Homes
KB Home
Lennar
M.D.C.
M/I Homes
Orleans Homebuilders
PulteGroup
The Ryland Group
Toll Brothers

HISTORICAL FINANCIALS

Company Type: Public

Income Statement

FYE: December 31

	REVENUE ($ mil.)	NET INCOME ($ mil.)	NET PROFIT MARGIN	EMPLOYEES
12/09	2,756	192	7.0%	2,688
12/08	3,714	101	2.7%	2,845
12/07	5,129	334	6.5%	4,119
12/06	6,134	587	9.6%	4,548
12/05	5,275	698	13.2%	5,401
Annual Growth	**(15.0%)**	**(27.6%)**	**—**	**(16.0%)**

2009 Year-End Financials

Debt ratio: 7.7%
Return on equity: 12.3%
Cash ($ mil.): 1,250
Current ratio: 3.85
Long-term debt ($ mil.): 136
No. of shares (mil.): 6
Dividends
  Yield: —
  Payout: —
Market value ($ mil.): 4,383

Stock History

NYSE: NVR

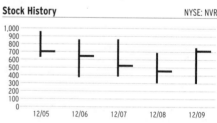

	STOCK PRICE ($) FY Close	P/E High/Low		PER SHARE ($) Earnings	Dividends	Book Value
12/09	710.71	24	10	31.26	—	284.94
12/08	456.25	40	19	17.04	—	222.76
12/07	524.00	16	7	54.14	—	183.13
12/06	645.00	10	4	88.05	—	186.81
12/05	702.00	11	7	89.61	—	109.80
Annual Growth	**0.3%**	**—**	**—**	**(23.1%)**	**—**	**26.9%**

NYSE Euronext

NYSE Euronext is one of the world's largest exchange groups, boasting trades totaling more than a third of the global cash equities volume. It operates such esteemed exchanges as the New York Stock Exchange (NYSE), one of the oldest and largest markets in the world; Euronext, the first cross-border exchange with markets in Amsterdam, Brussels, Lisbon, and Paris; NYSE Liffe, a leading international derivatives market with daily trading values exceeding $1.7 trillion; and NYSE Amex, formerly the American Stock Exchange. In 2007 NYSE acquired Euronext and its derivatives and futures markets (including Liffe) for some $10 billion to create the first transatlantic exchange. The following year it bought rival AMEX.

The NYSE lists some 2,000 companies, including most of the largest US corporations; it also recruits foreign firms seeking the greater liquidity available in US markets. Euronext lists some 1,500 companies and is a leading market for European IPOs. The NYSE Amex, the group's market for emerging US companies, has some 400 listings. NYSE Arca is a fully electronic exchange with more than 1,000 exchange-traded fund, exchange-traded vehicle, and exchange-traded note listings and certificates.

The company has been actively retooling itself to remain relevant in a world of electronic exchanges, cross-border trading, and alternative investment classes. In addition to buying up major exchanges around the world, NYSE Euronext has acquired businesses to help broaden its offerings. In 2009 it bought trading systems designer NYFIX for $144 million, strengthening its technological capabilities to provide faster trades in addition to cost savings.

In a move that will help raise capital, NYSE Euronext is selling a significant part of its NYSE AMEX options trading business to several investment banks in order to boost use and lift its market share. The company will continue to manage the unit's operations, as well as retaining the largest stake in the business.

HISTORY

To prevent a monopoly on stock sales by securities auctioneers, 24 New York stockbrokers and businessmen agreed in 1792 to avoid "public auctions," to charge a commission on sales of stock, and to "give preference to each other" in their transactions. The Buttonwood Agreement, named after a tree on Wall Street under which they met, established the first organized stock market in New York. The Bank of New York was the first corporate stock traded under the Buttonwood tree.

Excluded traders continued dealing on the streets of New York until 1921 and later formed the American Stock Exchange.

In 1817 the brokers created the New York Stock & Exchange Board, a stock market with set meeting times. The NYS&EB began to require companies to qualify for trading (listing) by furnishing financial statements in 1853. Ten years later the board became the New York Stock Exchange.

Stock tickers began recording trades in 1867, and two years later the NYSE consolidated with competitors the Open Board of Brokers and the Government Bond Department. Despite repeated panics and recessions in the late 1800s, the stock market remained unregulated until well into the 20th century.

In the 1920s the NYSE installed a centralized stock quote service. Postwar euphoria brought a stock mania that fizzled in the crash of October 1929. The subsequent Depression brought investigation and federal regulation to the securities industry.

The NYSE registered as an exchange in 1934. In 1938 it reorganized, with a board of directors representing member firms, nonmember brokers, and the public; it also hired its first full-time president, member William McChesney Martin. As a self-regulating body, the NYSE policed the activities of its members.

The NYSE began electronic trading in the 1960s; in 1968 it broke 1929's one-day record for trading volume (16 million shares). It became a not-for-profit corporation in 1971.

Despite upgrades, technology was at least partly to blame for the crash of 1987: A cascade of large sales triggered by computer programs fueled the market's fall. NYSE's income suffered, leading to a $3 million loss in 1990.

In 1995 Richard Grasso became the first NYSE staff employee named chairman. The NYSE followed the other US stock markets in 1997 by switching trade increments from one-eighth point to one-sixteenth point (known as a "teenie" by arbitrageurs).

In 1999 the exchange named Karen Nelson Hackett as its first woman governor.

In the wake of the terrorism attacks that shook Wall Street and the nation, the NYSE and Nasdaq in 2001 began discussing a disaster plan that would see the two cooperating should a future incident cripple either market. Also that year the NYSE moved entirely to decimal pricing in accordance with SEC mandates.

Grasso, who earned a reputation as something of a hero in the months following the 2001 terrorist attacks on New York City, resigned under fire two years later when his $187 million pay package was revealed. During the furor over Grasso's pay, the SEC launched an investigation, and many officials — including the heads of top pension funds — called for his resignation.

Former Citigroup chairman John Reed was named interim chairman and CEO following Grasso's departure; former Goldman Sachs president John Thain was subsequently tapped for the CEO role in 2004.

The company acquired ECN Archipelago in 2006 and finally went public.

Member-owned and not-for-profit for more than 200 years, the NYSE became a publicly traded company as part of the $10 billion transaction. NYSE stockholders got about 70% of the firm, while Archipelago shareholders got the rest. However, some traders became wary that the combination might lead to the extinction of the open-outcry floor auctions (where stock prices are set largely by a throng of traders on the exchange floor) that characterize the NYSE.

Less than three months after that transaction closed, the NYSE announced the deal for Euronext, which had also been courted by Deutsche Börse. Euronext rejected a larger $11 billion bid from the German exchange, claiming it carried too much debt.

Continuing its international aspirations, NYSE Euronext in 2007 purchased a 5% stake in India's largest stock exchange, Mumbai-based National Stock Exchange. Additionally, NYSE Euronext bought 20% of the Qatar Exchange (formerly Doha Securities Market) for $200 million.

HISTORICAL FINANCIALS

Company Type: Public

Income Statement

FYE: December 31

	REVENUE ($ mil.)	NET INCOME ($ mil.)	NET PROFIT MARGIN	EMPLOYEES
12/09	4,687	212	4.5%	3,367
12/08	4,703	(738)	—	3,757
12/07	4,158	643	15.5%	3,083
12/06	2,376	205	8.6%	2,578
12/05	493	16	3.3%	1,975
Annual Growth	75.6%	89.9%	—	14.3%

2009 Year-End Financials

Debt ratio: 31.5%
Return on equity: 3.2%
Cash ($ mil.): 423
Current ratio: 0.71
Long-term debt ($ mil.): 2,166

No. of shares (mil.): 261
Dividends
Yield: 4.7%
Payout: 142.9%
Market value ($ mil.): 6,603

Stock History

NYSE: NYX

	STOCK PRICE ($) FY Close	P/E High/Low	PER SHARE ($) Earnings	Dividends	Book Value
12/09	25.30	38 17	0.84	1.20	26.33
12/08	27.38	— —	(2.78)	1.15	25.12
12/07	87.77	41 24	2.70	0.75	35.95
12/06	97.20	82 36	1.36	—	6.39
12/05	50.00	183 41	0.34	—	1.62
Annual Growth	(15.7%)	— —	25.4%	26.5%	100.9%

Occidental Petroleum

Harnessing its heritage of Western technical know-how, Occidental Petroleum engages in oil and gas exploration and production and makes basic chemicals, plastics, and petrochemicals. In 2009 the oil giant reported proved reserves of 3.2 billion barrels of oil equivalent in the US, the Middle East, North Africa, and Latin America. Subsidiary Occidental Chemical (OxyChem) produces acids, chlorine, and specialty products; it also owns Oxy Vinyls, the #1 producer of polyvinyl chloride (PVC) resin in North America. Occidental Petroleum's midstream and marketing operations gather, treat, process, transport, store, trade, and market crude oil, natural gas, NGLs, condensate, and CO2, and generate and market power.

The global recession and the resulting low demand and low prices for oil and gas and chemical commodities saw a sharp decline in the company's sales figures across the board in 2009.

Undeterred, Occidental is focusing on large, mature oil and gas assets with long-term growth potential. Occidental has reworked its business and created two divisions, Eastern and Western hemispheres. It is investing heavily in the Middle East and North Africa. It has begun to import Libyan oil (after a 20-year absence from the US

market). In addition to its existing assets in Qatar and Yemen, the company is developing new fields in Oman and Abu Dhabi. In 2008 the company agreed to spend $5 billion in capital investment to increase gross production in Libya to more than 300,000 barrels per day from the current level of 100,000 barrels per day.

In North America, to finance its 2008 purchase of the US government's 78% interest in California's historic and underused Elk Hills oil field, the company has divested its natural gas pipeline and marketing operation, MidCon, and sold off noncore oil and gas properties in the US, Venezuela, and the Netherlands. All told, Occidental has shed assets producing some 46,000 barrels of oil per day and let go about a quarter of its workforce. Also in North America in 2008 the company bought a 15% stake in the Joslyn Oil Sands project for nearly $500 million. That project is based in Alberta, Canada, and is operated by Total. It also acquired $1.2 billion of assets in the Permian and Piceance basins in the US from Plains Exploration & Production.

Beefing up its investment vehicles, in 2009 the company purchased Citigroup's commodities trading unit (Philbro LLC).

HISTORY

Founded in 1920, Occidental Petroleum struggled until 1956, when billionaire industrialist Dr. Armand Hammer sank $100,000 into the company, then worth $34,000. It drilled two wells, and both came in. Hammer eventually gained control of the company.

Occidental's discovery of California's second-largest gas field (1959) was followed by a concession from Libya's King Idris (1966) and the discovery of a billion-barrel Libyan oil field. In 1968 Occidental bought Signal Oil's European refining and marketing business as an outlet for the Libyan oil. It also diversified, buying Island Creek Coal and Hooker Chemical.

In 1969 Occidental sold 51% of its Libyan production to the Libyan government under duress (after Idris was ousted). It soon began oil exploration in Latin America (1971) and in the North Sea (1972-73), where it discovered the lucrative Piper field. Other projects included a 20-year fertilizer-for-ammonia deal with the USSR (1974) and a coal joint venture with China (1985).

During the 1980s Occidental sold some foreign assets and bought US natural gas pipeline firm MidCon (1986). It also bought Iowa Beef Processors (IBP) for stock worth $750 million (1981) and then spun off 49% of it in 1987 for $960 million.

In 1983 Hammer hired Ray Irani to revive Occidental's ailing chemicals business (losses that year: $38 million). Irani integrated operations to ensure higher margins during industry downturns and purchased Diamond Shamrock Chemicals (1986), Shell's vinyl chloride monomer unit (1987), a DuPont chloralkali facility (1987), and Cain Chemical (1988). OxyChem's profits reached almost $1.1 billion by 1989.

Hammer died in 1990, and Irani became CEO. In 1991, to reduce debt, Occidental exited the Chinese coal business and sold the North Sea oil properties. Occidental also spun off IBP, the largest US red-meat producer, to its shareholders.

Occidental paid Irani $95 million in 1997 to buy out his employment contract; instead, his compensation (a minimum of $1.2 million a year) was tied to the company's fortunes. That year Occidental's $3.65 billion bid won the US government's auction of its 78% stake in California's

Elk Hills petroleum reserve, one of the largest in the continental US.

To help pay for Elk Hills, the company sold MidCon to K N Energy for $3.1 billion in 1998. Occidental traded its petrochemical operations to Equistar Chemicals, a partnership between Lyondell (now LyondellBasell) and Millennium Chemicals, for $425 million and a 29.5% stake.

In a venture with The Geon Company, Occidental in 1999 formed Oxy Vinyls, the #1 producer of polyvinyl chloride (PVC) resin in North America. That year also brought a windfall: Chevron agreed to pay Occidental $775 million to settle a lawsuit stemming from the 1982 withdrawal by Gulf (later acquired by Chevron) of an offer to buy Cities Service (later acquired by Occidental).

In 2000 Occidental sold its 29% stake in Canadian Occidental back to the company for $828 million to help fund the purchase of oil and gas producer Altura Energy, a partnership of BP and Shell Oil, for $3.6 billion. Later that year the company sold some Gulf of Mexico properties to Apache for $385 million.

Occidental acquired a new exploration block in Yemen in 2001.

The next year it sold its 30% of Equistar Chemicals to Lyondell in exchange for a 21% stake in Lyondell. In 2005 it acquired a stake in a gas and oil production site located in Texas' Permian Basin from ExxonMobil for a reported $972 million. Occidental closed the acquisition of Vintage Petroleum for a reported $3.8 billion in early 2006.

The government of Ecuador seized Occidental Petroleum's Ecuadorian assets in 2006 as part of a nationalization drive. That year Plains Exploration and Production sold non-core oil and gas properties to Occidental for $865 million.

Also in 2006 Occidental reduced its stake in Lyondell from 12% to 8%. The following year Occidental sold its remaining Lyondell shares on the open market.

EXECUTIVES

Chairman and CEO: Ray R. Irani, age 75, $31,401,356 total compensation
President, COO, and Director: Stephen I. (Steve) Chazen, age 63, $13,485,465 total compensation
EVP and CFO: James M. Lienert, age 58
EVP, General Counsel, and Secretary: Donald P. de Brier, age 69, $3,552,683 total compensation
EVP, Oil and Gas: John M. Winterman
EVP Human Resources: Martin A. Cozyn, age 49
VP; President, Oxy Oil and Gas, USA: William E. Albrecht, age 58, $2,842,381 total compensation
VP; President, International Production, Oil and Gas: Edward A. (Sandy) Lowe, age 58
VP; EVP Worldwide Exploration, Oil and Gas: Anita M. Powers
VP Communications and Public Affairs: Richard S. Kline
VP Government Relations: Ian M. Davis
VP Investor Relations: Christopher G. (Chris) Stavros
VP Internal Audit: Gary L. Daugherty
VP Health, Environment, and Safety: Charles F. Weiss
VP and CIO: Donald L. Moore Jr.
VP and Treasurer: Robert J. Williams Jr., age 50
VP, Controller, and Principal Accounting Officer: Roy Pineci, age 47
VP Tax: Michael S. Stutts
President, Occidental Chemical: B. Chuck Anderson, age 50
Auditors: KPMG LLP

LOCATIONS

HQ: Occidental Petroleum Corporation
10889 Wilshire Blvd., Los Angeles, CA 90024
Phone: 310-208-8800   **Fax:** 310-443-6690
Web: www.oxy.com

2009 Sales

	% of total
US	61
Qatar	14
Oman	6
Colombia	6
Yemen	4
Argentina	4
Libya	2
Other countries	3
Total	**100**

PRODUCTS/OPERATIONS

2009 Sales

	$ mil.	% of total
Oil & gas	11,598	73
Chemicals	3,225	20
Midstream, marketing & other	1,016	7
Adjustments	(308)	—
Total	**15,531**	**100**

Selected Subsidiaries

Occidental Chemical Corp. (OxyChem; chemicals,
  polymers, and plastics)
Occidental Energy Marketing, Inc. (energy marketing)
Occidental Exploration and Production Company
  (exploration and production)
OxyVinyls, LP (76%, polyvinyl chloride)

COMPETITORS

Apache
Ashland Inc.
BP
ConocoPhillips
Devon Energy
Dow Chemical
DuPont
Eastman Chemical
Exxon Mobil
Hess Corporation
Huntsman International
Imperial Oil
J.M. Huber
Koch Industries, Inc.
Marathon Oil
Olin
PEMEX
Royal Dutch Shell
Sunoco
TOTAL

HISTORICAL FINANCIALS

Company Type: Public

Income Statement

FYE: December 31

	REVENUE ($ mil.)	NET INCOME ($ mil.)	NET PROFIT MARGIN	EMPLOYEES
12/09	15,531	2,966	19.1%	10,100
12/08	24,480	6,857	28.0%	10,400
12/07	20,013	5,400	27.0%	9,700
12/06	18,160	4,182	23.0%	8,886
12/05	16,259	5,278	32.5%	8,017
Annual Growth	**(1.1%)**	**(13.4%)**	**—**	**5.9%**

2009 Year-End Financials

Debt ratio: 8.8%
Return on equity: 10.5%
Cash ($ mil.): 1,230
Current ratio: 1.33
Long-term debt ($ mil.): 2,557

No. of shares (mil.): 812
Dividends
  Yield: 1.6%
  Payout: 36.6%
Market value ($ mil.): 66,070

Stock History

NYSE: OXY

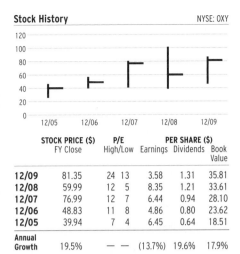

	STOCK PRICE ($) FY Close	P/E High/Low		PER SHARE ($) Earnings	Dividends	Book Value
12/09	81.35	24	13	3.58	1.31	35.81
12/08	59.99	12	5	8.35	1.21	33.61
12/07	76.99	12	7	6.44	0.94	28.10
12/06	48.83	11	8	4.86	0.80	23.62
12/05	39.94	7	4	6.45	0.64	18.51
Annual Growth	**19.5%**	**—**	**—**	**(13.7%)**	**19.6%**	**17.9%**

Office Depot

Paper clips add up to big money for Office Depot. The world's #2 office supply chain (behind Staples), Office Depot sells office supplies through about 1,130 company-owned and licensed locations throughout North America and at another 135 locations overseas. The big-box retail stores sell to both consumers and small and medium-sized businesses. In addition to typical office supplies, its stores offer computer hardware and software, office furniture, art and school supplies, and printing and copying services. It also sells goods through catalogs and call centers, the Internet, and a contract sales force. Amid the weak economy, Office Depot is closing stores and exiting markets.

While the company's sales had already begun to slow even before the financial crisis hit, 2009 and 2008 were discouraging years for the office products retailer. In response to the decreased demand for its products and services, Office Depot in 2009 closed 126 stores in North America and 27 in Japan, exiting that market. It also shuttered five distribution centers. To raise cash in lean times, Office Depot in mid-2009 sold about $350 million in preferred stock to BC Partners, a private-equity firm based in the Channel Islands. As a result, BC Partners owns about 21% of Office Depot's shares through CIE Management and LMBO Europe. AXA Financial, through various entities, owns about 15% of the company's shares.

To spur sales by making shopping easier for its customers, Office Depot has adopted a new store format, called Millennium2 (M2), used in all new store openings and remodels. The M2 minimizes construction costs and strategically locates products to encourage sales consultation. Office Depot plans to add about 20 new stores in 2010.

The decline in the company's international business reversed its previously growing contribution to Office Depot's coffers. To extend its reach into India, Office Depot in April 2008 partnered with Reliance Retail, a unit of India's Reliance Industries, in a joint venture to sell office products and services to business customers in India. The US office products giant sells to customers in about 50 countries, including France,

Hungary, Israel, South Korea, and now Sweden. Through its joint venture (formed in 1994) in Mexico, Office Depot de Mexico operates about 195 stores there, and in Colombia, Costa Rica, El Salvador, Guatemala, Honduras, and Panama.

Adding to its woes, Office Depot is likely to see increased competition in Europe and at home as a result of the 2008 acquisition of Corporate Express NV by Office Depot's larger rival Staples. Corporate Express is a major office products wholesaler, with more than half of its sales in the US through Corporate Express US.

To capture a larger share of the small business audience, Office Depot partnered with Google in 2008 to roll out an online Business Resource Center, which includes Google AdWords, Google Apps, and Google Local Business Center. The latter offers free online business listings that appear on Google search and Google Maps.

HISTORY

Pat Scher, Stephen Dougherty, and Jack Kopkin opened the first Office Depot, one of the first office supply superstores, in Lauderdale Lakes, Florida, in 1986. Scher was selected as chairman. By the end of the year the fledgling company had opened two more stores (both in Florida).

Office Depot opened seven more stores in 1987. When Scher died of leukemia that year, the company recruited David Fuente, former president of Sherwin-Williams' Paint Store Division, as chairman and CEO. Office Depot continued its breakneck expansion under Fuente. In 1988 — the year the company went public — it opened 16 stores and broke into new markets in four states.

The chain stepped up its pace, and by 1990 it had expanded into several other areas, including the South and Midwest. Office Depot also added computers and peripherals and opened its first delivery center.

In 1991 the company became North America's #1 office products retailer and expanded its presence in the West through the acquisition of Office Club, another warehouse-type office supply chain with 59 stores (most in California). Fuente remained chairman and CEO, while former Office Club CEO Mark Begelman became president and COO. (Begelman, who left in 1995 and eventually formed the MARS music chain, had founded the first Office Club in 1987 in Concord, California; he took it public in 1989.)

The company entered the international market with its 1992 purchase of Canada's H. Q. Office International and through licensing agreements in 1993 (in Colombia and Israel). Office Depot created its business services division by acquiring various contract stationers, including Eastman Office Products (the West Coast's #1 contract office supplier), in the mid-1990s, and added locations in Mexico and Poland; it established a joint venture in France with retailer Carrefour in 1996.

Also in 1996 Office Depot announced a $3.4 billion agreement to be acquired by Staples, which would have created a company with more than 1,100 stores. However, the government blocked the purchase on antitrust grounds in 1997 and the agreement dissolved.

In 1998 Office Depot acquired Viking Office Products in a $2.7 billion deal. With more than 60% of its sales coming from outside the US, Viking augmented Office Depot's already strong delivery network and international expansion. Office Depot acquired the remaining 50% of its French operations from Carrefour in 1998, and the remaining 50% of its Japanese operations from Deo Deo in 1999.

In July 2000 Bruce Nelson, CEO of Viking, replaced Fuente as CEO of Office Depot. Citing weak computer sales and high warehouse prices, the company closed about 70 stores and cut its workforce. In 2002 Nelson was named chairman as well as CEO after Fuente stepped down.

Office Depot sold its Australian operations to Officeworks, a unit of Coles Myer, in January 2003. Also that year the company acquired the retail operations of French office supplier Guilbert from Pinault-Printemps-Redoute, a move that doubled the company's business in Europe.

Nelson left the company and Neil Austrian served as interim head. Office Depot named AutoZone leader Steve Odland as CEO and chairman in 2005. During 2005 the company shuttered its Viking Office Products brand in the US, consolidating its catalog sales under the Office Depot banner.

In mid-2008 the company acquired 13 stores in Sweden through the acquisition of AGE Kontor & Data AB, a contract and retail office supply company operating there.

In 2009 the company closed about 125 stores in North America and exited the Japanese market.

EXECUTIVES

Chairman and CEO: Steve Odland, age 51, $3,394,551 total compensation
EVP and CFO: Michael D. (Mike) Newman, age 53, $1,427,775 total compensation
EVP Merchandising: Steve Mahurin
EVP, General Counsel, and Corporate Secretary: Elisa D. Garcia, age 52
EVP E-Commerce and Direct Marketing: Monica Luechtefeld, age 61
EVP Human Resources: Daisy L. Vanderlinde, age 58
SVP Marketing: Jeff Herbert
SVP and Chief Compliance Officer: Robert Brewer
SVP and Controller: Mark E. Hutchens, age 44
VP Furniture Merchandising: Richard Diamond
President, North American Business Solutions Division: Steven M. (Steve) Schmidt, age 55, $1,736,894 total compensation
President, International: Charles E. Brown, age 56, $1,545,863 total compensation
President, North American Retail: Kevin A. Peters, age 52
Senior Director Merchandising: Wade Eveleth
Senior Director Loyalty and Direct Marketing: Larry Wadford
Director Environmental Strategy: Yalmaz Siddiqui
Auditors: Deloitte & Touche LLP

LOCATIONS

HQ: Office Depot, Inc.
6600 N. Military Trail, Boca Raton, FL 33496
Phone: 561-438-4800   **Fax:** 561-438-4001
Web: www.officedepot.com

2009 International Retail Stores

	No.
France	49
Israel	46
Hungary	17
Sweden	13
South Korea	12
Total	**137**

PRODUCTS/OPERATIONS

2009 Sales

	% of total
Office supplies	66
Technology	22
Furniture & other	12
Total	**100**

2009 Sales

	$ mil.	% of total
North American Retail	5,113.6	42
North American Business Solutions	3,483.7	29
International	3,547.2	29
Total	**12,144.5**	**100**

Selected Products

Office supplies
  Basic supplies and labels
  Binders and accessories
  Breakroom and janitorial supplies
  Business cases
  Calendars and planners
  Desk accessories
  Executive gifts
  Filing and storage
  Paper and envelopes
  Pens, pencils, and markers
  School supplies
Technology products
  Audio-visual equipment and supplies
  Cameras
  Computers and related accessories (including monitors and printers)
  Copiers
  Data storage supplies
  Fax machines
  Networking supplies
  PDAs
  Software
Office furniture
  Armoires
  Bookcases
  Carts and stands
  Chair mats and floor mats
  Chairs
  Desks
  Filing cabinets
  Lamps and light bulbs
  Office furnishings
  Panel systems
  Tables
  Workstations

COMPETITORS

Best Buy
BJ's Wholesale Club
CDW
Costco Wholesale
FedEx Office
Fry's Electronics
IKON
Insight Enterprises
Lyreco
Mail Boxes Etc.
OfficeMax
RadioShack
School Specialty
Staples
Systemax
Unisource
United Stationers
Wal-Mart

HISTORICAL FINANCIALS

Company Type: Public

Income Statement

FYE: Saturday nearest December 31

	REVENUE ($ mil.)	NET INCOME ($ mil.)	NET PROFIT MARGIN	EMPLOYEES
12/09	12,145	(597)	—	41,000
12/08	14,496	(1,479)	—	43,000
12/07	15,528	396	2.5%	49,000
12/06	15,011	516	3.4%	52,000
12/05	14,279	274	1.9%	47,000
Annual Growth	**(4.0%)**	**—**	**—**	**(3.4%)**

2009 Year-End Financials

Debt ratio: 84.3%
Return on equity: —
Cash ($ mil.): 660
Current ratio: 1.32
Long-term debt ($ mil.): 663
No. of shares (mil.): 276
Dividends
  Yield: —
  Payout: —
Market value ($ mil.): 1,780

Stock History

NYSE: ODP

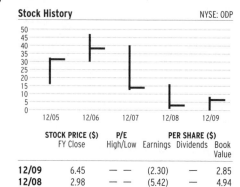

	STOCK PRICE ($) FY Close	P/E High/Low		PER SHARE ($) Earnings	Dividends	Book Value
12/09	6.45	—	—	(2.30)	—	2.85
12/08	2.98	—	—	(5.42)	—	4.94
12/07	13.91	28	9	1.43	—	11.17
12/06	38.17	26	17	1.79	—	9.46
12/05	31.40	37	19	0.87	—	9.93
Annual Growth	**(32.7%)**	**—**	**—**	**—**	**—**	**(26.8%)**

OfficeMax

This company is taking the office supply business to the max. OfficeMax is the #3 office products retailer in North America (far behind Staples and Office Depot), with more than 1,000 superstores in the US, Mexico, Puerto Rico, and the US Virgin Islands. The stores offer about 10,000 name-brand and OfficeMax-branded products, including paper, pens, forms, and organizers, as well as office furniture and a wide range of technology products. OfficeMax also provides printing and document services through its ImPress store-within-a-store. In addition to its retail outlets, the firm's contract division sells directly to business and government customers.

With consumers and businesses suffering from the recession in the US, OfficeMax's retail and contract divisions are taking the hit. (The demise of Lehman Brothers also led to a big write off by the office products retailer in 2008.) Indeed, same-store sales at its retail stores have shown negative comparisons since 2007. To control costs amid the decline, the firm eliminated about 245 corporate staff and field management positions in North America. Plans to grow its retail network and remodel existing stores have been put on hold until the economic outlook brightens.

OfficeMax operates about 930 retail locations throughout the US and more than 75 stores in Mexico (through its Grupo OfficeMax majority-owned joint venture there). To boost its international business, OfficeMax recently formed an alliance with the French stationery and office-supply giant Lyreco to supply customers in Europe and Asia through Lyreco and allowing Lyreco to supply customers in the US and Mexico through OfficeMax. OfficeMax has also launched a small-format store called Ink-Paper-Scissors that abandons the warehouse-style format and instead highlights small- and home-office solutions in a warmer atmosphere. The company opened three Ink-Paper-Scissors stores in 2008.

To make a challenging business climate even tougher, OfficeMax is likely to face increased competition in Europe and the US as a result of rival Staples' acquisition of Corporate Express NV in 2008.

Chairman and CEO Sam Duncan is slated to retire in 2011. The company has begun searching for his successor.

FMR LLC owns about 15% of OfficeMax's shares. Evercore Trust Co. owns about 11%.

HISTORY

Boise Cascade got its start in 1957 with the merger of two small lumber companies — Boise Payette Lumber Company (based in Boise, Idaho) and Cascade Lumber Company (Yakima, Washington). The business diversified in the 1960s under the leadership of Robert Hansberger, moving into office-products distribution in 1964. A number of acquisitions followed, including Ebasco Industries (1969), a consulting, engineering, and construction firm. By 1970 Boise Cascade had made more than 30 buys to diversify into building materials, paper products, real estate, recreational vehicles (RVs), and publishing.

In the early 1970s the company suffered a timber shortage as its access to public timberlands dwindled. Its plans to develop recreational communities in California, Hawaii, and Washington met opposition from residents, causing Boise Cascade to scrap all but six of the 29 projects.

In 1972 high costs related to the remaining projects left the company in debt. John Fery replaced Hansberger as president that year and sold companies not directly related to the company's core forest-product operations.

In the late 1980s and early 1990s, Boise sold more nonstrategic operations, including its Specialty Paperboard Division in 1989. It sold more than half of its corrugated-container plants in 1992 to focus on manufacturing forest products and distributing building materials and office supplies.

Boise Cascade also sold its wholesale office-product business in 1992 to focus on direct sales to big buyers such as IBM and Boeing. The company sold off its Canadian subsidiary, Rainy River Forest Products, during 1994 and 1995. Resurgent paper prices resulted in a profit in 1995, Boise Cascade's first since 1990.

Also in 1995, in a move into the international paper market, Boise Cascade signed a joint venture agreement with Shenzhen Leasing to form Zhuhai Hiwin Boise Cascade, a Chinese manufacturer of carbonless paper. That year it sold a minority stake in Boise Cascade Office Products (BCOP) to the public.

The company sold its coated-papers business to paper and packaging heavyweight Mead in 1996 for $639 million. The following year Boise began harvesting its first quick-growth cottonwood trees (specially grown to cut the cost of harvesting from traditional slow-growth hardwood plantations).

The low price of paper in 1998 prompted the company to close four sawmills and a research and development center. Restructuring costs associated with the closures and a fire at the company's Medford, Oregon, plywood plant led to a net income loss for the year.

In 1999 Boise bought Wallace Computer Services, a contract stationer business, and broadened its building-supply distribution network nationwide by acquiring Furman Lumber, a

building-supplies distributor. In 2000 Boise Cascade completed the purchase of the 19% of Boise Office Solutions that it didn't already own. The company also sold its European office products operations for $335 million.

Because of the decline in federal timber sales, in 2001 the company closed its plywood mill and lumber operations in Emmett, Idaho, and a sawmill in Cascade, Idaho. In 2002 lagging profits prompted Boise to implement cost-cutting procedures. In 2003 the company pinned its hopes for growth on the office product segment with the acquisition of OfficeMax for nearly $1.2 billion in cash and stock. The deal put Boise Cascade's office products business on par with industry leaders Staples and Office Depot.

The company sold its paper, forest products, and timberland assets to investment firm Madison Dearborn Partners for $3.7 billion in October 2004. That same year the company changed its name to OfficeMax and tagged Christopher Milliken, a former Boise Cascade executive, as CEO, but he resigned after only four months on the job. Former ShopKo Stores CEO Sam Duncan was tapped as his replacement.

In 2006 the company moved its headquarters from Itasca, Illinois, to nearby Naperville. Looking to improve its balance sheet, OfficeMax announced a major restructuring effort in 2006 that saw the company close about 110 underperforming locations in the US.

EXECUTIVES

Chairman and CEO: Sam K. Duncan, age 58, $5,211,186 total compensation
EVP, CFO, and Chief Administrative Officer: Bruce H. Besanko, age 52, $1,863,403 total compensation
EVP and Chief Merchandising Officer: Ryan T. Vero, age 40, $1,305,886 total compensation
EVP and General Counsel: Matthew R. (Matt) Broad, age 50
EVP Supply Chain: Reuben E. Slone
EVP North American Sales: Jim Durkin
EVP and CIO: Randy G. Burdick
SVP Finance and Chief Accounting Officer: Deborah A. (Deb) O'Connor, age 47, $605,165 total compensation
SVP and Secretary: Susan Wagner-Fleming
SVP Marketing and Advertising: Bob Thacker
SVP; Managing Director, Australasian Operations: David Armstrong
SVP Human Resources: Carter Knox
SVP E-Commerce and Direct Marketing: Julie Krueger
VP Global Loss Prevention and Chief Security Officer: John Voytilla
VP Investor Relations and Treasurer: Tony Giuliano, age 51
Chief Diversity Officer: Carolynn Brooks
Senior Director External Relations: William (Bill) Bonner
Auditors: KPMG LLP

LOCATIONS

HQ: OfficeMax Incorporated
263 Shuman Blvd., Naperville, IL 60563
Phone: 630-438-7800
Web: www.officemax.com

2009 Sales

	$ mil.	% of total
US	5,952.8	83
Other countries	1,259.3	17
Total	**7,212.1**	**100**

PRODUCTS/OPERATIONS

2009 Sales

	$ mil.	% of total
OfficeMax, Contract	3,656.7	51
OfficeMax, Retail	3,555.4	49
Total	**7,212.1**	**100**

2009 Contract Sales

	% of total
Office supplies & paper	59
Technology products	32
Office furniture	9
Total	**100**

2009 Retail Sales

	% of total
Technology products	53
Office supplies & paper	39
Office furniture	8
Total	**100**

COMPETITORS

Best Buy	Office Depot
BJ's Wholesale Club	RadioShack
CDW	Sam's Club
Container Store	Staples
Costco Wholesale	Systemax
FedEx Office	Unisource
IKON	United Stationers
Insight Enterprises	Wal-Mart
Mail Boxes Etc.	

HISTORICAL FINANCIALS

Company Type: Public

Income Statement

FYE: Last Saturday in December

	REVENUE ($ mil.)	NET INCOME ($ mil.)	NET PROFIT MARGIN	EMPLOYEES
12/09	7,212	1	0.0%	31,000
12/08	8,267	(1,658)	—	33,000
12/07	9,082	207	2.3%	36,000
12/06	8,966	92	1.0%	36,000
12/05	9,158	(74)	—	35,000
Annual Growth	**(5.8%)**	**—**	**—**	**(3.0%)**

2009 Year-End Financials

Debt ratio: 58.8%
Return on equity: 0.2%
Cash ($ mil.): 487
Current ratio: 1.85
Long-term debt ($ mil.): 275
No. of shares (mil.): 85
Dividends
  Yield: 0.0%
  Payout: —
Market value ($ mil.): 1,079

Stock History

NYSE: OMX

	STOCK PRICE ($) FY Close	P/E High/Low		PER SHARE ($) Earnings	Dividends	Book Value
12/09	12.69	—	—	(0.03)	0.00	5.92
12/08	7.64	—	—	(21.90)	0.45	3.41
12/07	20.66	21	8	2.66	0.60	26.80
12/06	49.65	44	21	1.19	0.60	23.36
12/05	25.36	—	—	(0.99)	0.60	20.42
Annual Growth	**(15.9%)**	**—**	**—**	**—**	**—**	**(26.6%)**

Olin Corporation

The making of bleach and bullets is all in a day's work for Olin. Olin Chlor Alkali Products manufactures chemicals used to make bleach, water purification and swimming pool chemicals, pulp and paper processing agents, and PVC plastics. Olin Chlor Alkali is one of the top chlor-alkali producers in North America along with Dow and OxyChem. Olin also makes Winchester-branded ammunition. US customers account for the great majority of Olin's sales, and company's manufacturing facilities are located primarily in the US, though it also has plants in Australia and Canada.

The company experienced the value of having a diverse product line in 2009. While a slumping economy depressed demand for Olin Chlor Alkali's chlorine and caustic soda products, sales of Winchester's ammunition jumped 16% for that year, with demand beginning to rise following the November 2008 US presidential election.

In 2007 Olin grew its core chemicals business, acquiring chlor-alkali producer Pioneer Companies for about $415 million. To help pay for the deal, in late 2007 Olin sold its former Metals unit to investment group KPS Capital Partners for almost $400 million. The Metals unit — which had accounted for about two-thirds of sales — made copper and copper alloy sheets, clad metal, foil, and stainless-steel strips.

HISTORY

Vermont-born engineer Franklin Olin founded Equitable Powder in East Alton, Illinois, in 1892 to make blasting powder for use in the midwestern coal fields. By 1898 the company, called Western Cartridge, was also making ammunition for small arms.

When WWI increased demand for military cartridges, Western Cartridge built a brass mill. After the war it began making custom brass and other copper alloys for industrial customers. The company bought Winchester Repeating Arms, maker of the famous Winchester Model 1876 repeating rifles, in 1931. During WWII Western Cartridge developed the US carbine and M-1 rifles.

The various businesses of Western Cartridge merged as Olin Industries in 1944. Franklin then retired, handing the company to sons John and Spencer.

Enriched by the war effort, Olin Industries grew. In 1949 it began making cellophane, and in 1951 it acquired Frost Lumber Industries and Ecusta Paper, a maker of cigarette papers. Olin Industries merged with Mathieson Chemical in 1954 to form Olin Mathieson Chemical, the fifth-largest US chemical company.

The Mathieson Alkali Works was founded in Saltville, Virginia, in 1892 to produce alkalis using a process acquired from English chemical firm Neil Mathieson. By 1909 the company began producing liquid chlorine, and in 1923 it built one of the earliest plants for producing synthetic ammonia. During WWII Mathieson manufactured chlorine for water purification and alkali chemicals for sanitation. In 1952 Mathieson acquired drugmaker Squibb.

Olin Mathieson continued to diversify in the mid-1950s, buying Blockson Chemical (industrial phosphates) and Brown Paper Mill (kraft paper bags and corrugated cardboard containers). Frost Lumber and Brown Paper Mill formed the Forest Products Division, later dubbed Olinkraft. In 1956 Olin Mathieson entered the aluminum business via a joint venture — just in time for a drop in aluminum demand.

In the 1960s the company began making urethane chemicals. It also created Olin-American, a subsidiary that built houses, and spun off Squibb. In 1969 it shortened its name to Olin Corporation and moved to Stamford, Connecticut.

The 1970s saw Olin reining in its diverse businesses. It spun off Olinkraft and sold its aluminum operations. During the 1980s Olin sold its sporting-arms business (but kept Winchester ammunition), as well as its paper, housing, and cellophane units. John Olin died in 1982. The company acquired Rockcor, which included Rocket Research, Pacific Electro Dynamics, and Physics International, in 1985.

Olin moved its headquarters to Norwalk, Connecticut, in 1995, the same year Spencer Olin died. In 1996, as the earnings potential of its ordnance and aerospace operations lagged, Olin spun them off as Primex Technologies. It also sold its isocyanate (used in plastics and adhesives) and other cyclical businesses. Olin bought the remaining 50% of its Niachlor chlor alkali joint venture from DuPont in 1997 after considering putting Niachlor up for sale.

Aspiring to become a leading basic-materials company, Olin spun off its specialty chemical business in early 1999 under the name Arch Chemicals. Citing regulatory issues, Olin cancelled plans in 2000 to form a chlor alkali chemicals joint venture with Occidental subsidiary OxyChem. Olin acquired Monarch Brass & Copper Corp. for about $49 million in 2001. The next year it bought brass rod maker Chase Industries. Olin closed its copper and copper alloy sheet plant in Indianapolis in 2003.

EXECUTIVES

Chairman, President, and CEO: Joseph D. Rupp, age 59, $5,721,354 total compensation
VP and CFO: John E. Fischer, age 54, $1,880,079 total compensation
VP; President, Winchester: Richard M. (Dick) Hammett, age 63, $1,022,838 total compensation
VP; President, Chlor Alkali Products Division: John L. McIntosh, age 55, $1,395,013 total compensation
VP, General Counsel, and Secretary: George H. Pain, age 59, $1,696,639 total compensation
VP and Controller: Todd A. Slater, age 46
VP Strategic Planning: G. Bruce Greer Jr., age 49
VP and Treasurer: Stephen C. Curley, age 58
VP Human Resources: Dolores J. Ennico, age 57
Assistant Treasurer and Director, Investor Relations: Larry P. Kromidas
Director, Government and Public Affairs: Elaine Patterson
Auditors: KPMG LLP

LOCATIONS

HQ: Olin Corporation
190 Carondelet Plaza, Ste. 1530, Clayton, MO 63105
Phone: 314-480-1400   **Fax:** 314-862-7406
Web: www.olin.com

2009 Sales

	$ mil.	% of total
US	1,375.9	90
Other countries	155.6	10
Total	**1,531.5**	**100**

PRODUCTS/OPERATIONS

2009 Sales

	$ mil.	% of total
Chlor Alkali Products	963.8	63
Winchester	567.7	37
Total	**1,531.5**	**100**

Selected Products

Chlor Alkali Products
Caustic soda
Chlorine
Hydrochloric acid
Sodium hydrochlorite (Industrial and institutional cleaning products)
Sodium hydrosulfite (bleaching)

Winchester
Ammunition (shot-shell, small-caliber, and rimfire)
Government-owned arsenal operation (maintenance for the US Army)
Industrial cartridges (eight-gauge loads and powder-actuated tool loads for the construction industry)

COMPETITORS

Alliant Techsystems	Honeywell Specialty
Arch Chemicals	Materials
Blount International	Mitsubishi Chemical
Dow Chemical	Occidental Chemical
FMC	PPG Industries
Formosa Plastics USA	Remington Arms
Georgia Gulf	Sterling Chemicals
Herstal	Sumitomo Chemical

HISTORICAL FINANCIALS

Company Type: Public

Income Statement

FYE: December 31

	REVENUE ($ mil.)	NET INCOME ($ mil.)	NET PROFIT MARGIN	EMPLOYEES
12/09	1,532	136	8.9%	3,700
12/08	1,765	158	8.9%	3,600
12/07	1,277	(9)	—	3,600
12/06	3,152	150	4.7%	6,000
12/05	2,358	140	5.9%	5,900
Annual Growth	(10.2%)	(0.7%)	—	(11.0%)

2009 Year-End Financials

Debt ratio: 48.4%
Return on equity: 17.8%
Cash ($ mil.): 459
Current ratio: 2.77
Long-term debt ($ mil.): 398

No. of shares (mil.): 79
Dividends
Yield: 4.6%
Payout: 46.2%
Market value ($ mil.): 1,388

Stock History

NYSE: OLN

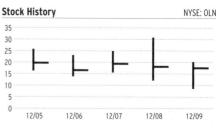

	STOCK PRICE ($) FY Close	P/E High/Low		PER SHARE ($) Earnings	Dividends	Book Value
12/09	17.52	11	5	1.73	0.80	10.38
12/08	18.08	15	6	2.07	0.80	8.90
12/07	19.33	—	—	(0.12)	0.80	8.38
12/06	16.52	11	7	2.06	0.80	6.86
12/05	19.68	14	9	1.86	0.80	5.39
Annual Growth	(2.9%)	—	—	(1.8%)	0.0%	17.8%

Omnicare, Inc.

Omnicare strives to be omnipresent in US nursing homes. The firm is the country's largest institutional pharmacy services provider, dispensing drugs to nursing homes, assisted-living centers, and other long-term care facilities in the US and parts of Canada. It also provides clinical and financial software and consulting services to long-term care facilities, as well as infusion and respiratory therapy products and services for nursing home residents and hospice patients. The company has some 250 pharmacy and distribution locations across the US, and it serves health care facility customers with a combined capacity of some 1.4 million patient beds.

The highly acquisitive Omnicare expands its operations by purchasing small, independent institutional pharmacies and integrating them into its organization; it made more than 20 such acquisitions in 2008 and 2009.

Omnicare has struggled against lower reimbursements on drugs from health insurers. It has responded to these challenges with a number of customer retention efforts and restructuring initiatives aimed at improving quality and efficiency. The company has been reorganizing its operations into a "hub-and-spoke" model, moving more administrative activities, as well as some routine prescription refilling, to larger regional hubs where scale, centralization, and automation can produce greater efficiency. The company has also been working to divest some small businesses, such as its home health operations, that don't fit in with its core operations.

Omnicare's Pharmacy Services division, which includes its institutional pharmacy operations, brings in more than 95% of the company's revenue. Serving nursing homes and their residents, the institutional pharmacy unit fills and dispenses prescriptions to customers, monitors medication safety and process efficiencies, and provides purchasing, billing, and inventory services. In addition, the Pharmacy Services division offers consulting, compliance, and data management services and operates divisions providing specialty pharmacy (infusion and other complex medications), pharmacy benefits management (PBM), and disease management services.

A second division, CRO Services (operating as Omnicare Clinical Research) provides contract clinical research and development to pharmaceutical, biotech, and medical device companies.

In late 2009 the company agreed to pay $98 million to settle allegations from the US Department of Justice that it had accepted kickback payments from drug manufacturers and nursing homes. Omnicare settled the charges without admitting any wrongdoing.

Omnicare sued UnitedHealth Group over reimbursement reductions in its Medicare Part D prescription drug coverage in 2006, but a summary judgment by an Illinois federal court dismissed the lawsuit in 2009. Omnicare has appealed the ruling.

In 2010 CEO Joel Gemunder retired. James Shelton, a board member and former CEO of Triad Hospitals, was named to replace him on an interim basis.

HISTORY

In 1981 W. R. Grace subsidiaries Daylin and Chemed merged some health care units to form Omnicare, which was then spun off. Omnicare began a restructuring process in 1985 that reshaped the firm around pharmacy services for long-term care facilities. It acquired 17 long-term care pharmacies in 1993 alone.

As the baby boomers age, the company will continue to have a growing market for the long run. Using economies of scale to keep costs down, Omnicare began pursuing an aggressive acquisition strategy.

In 1994 the company teamed with Health Care and Retirement Corp., one of the US's largest nursing home operators. It acquired 17 pharmacy units in 1996, including those of Revco and several other retailers. In 1997 Omnicare expanded its operations by targeting assisted living providers and small rural hospitals. It continued acquiring pharmacy service providers (20 in 1997 — including its largest deal up to that time, American Medserve — and CompScript in 1998), and it leveraged its treatment outcomes database with the addition of contract research organizations (Coromed, 1997; IBAH, 1998).

Also in 1998 Omnicare settled a lawsuit that alleged a company pharmacy had repackaged and resold unused medications originally sold to nursing homes (and paid for by Medicaid). That year the company acquired Extendicare's pharmacy operations. In 1999 Omnicare expanded its services for the drug development industry with the purchase of a German clinical research organization; the company also acquired the pharmaceutical division of nursing home operator Life Care Services of America.

Omnicare consolidated its three clinical research organizations into Omnicare Clinical Research in 2000 and it acquired NCS HealthCare and Sun Healthcare's SunScript Pharmacy business in 2003; the move was designed to strengthen its position as the largest supplier of pharmacy services to long-term care facilities in the US.

After a year-long pursuit, the company acquired NeighborCare in a hostile takeover in 2005. The deal, valued at nearly $2 billion, brought with it 300,000 patient beds and took Omnicare's annual revenue to more than $6 billion. Following the acquisition, Omnicare consolidated about 30 pharmacy locations. It also lost some nursing home customers who complained about bad service.

The same it year it won NeighborCare, Omnicare also bought RxCrossroads, a mail-order specialty pharmaceutical company that specializes in providing pricey drugs used to treat chronic conditions, and excelleRx, a distributor of pharmaceuticals and related products to hospice agencies in 47 states.

EXECUTIVES

Chairman: John T. Crotty, age 72
Interim President and CEO: James Shelton
EVP and CFO: John L. Workman, age 58, $4,819,311 total compensation
EVP, Advanced Care Scripts: Edward H. Hensley
SVP Pharmacy Operations: Jeffrey M. Stamps, age 50, $1,533,217 total compensation
SVP and CIO: Stephen S. Brown
SVP and Secretary: Cheryl D. Hodges, age 57, $4,875,198 total compensation
SVP Sales and Customer Development: Beth A. Kinerk, age 41, $1,940,370 total compensation
SVP Professional Pharmacies, Omnicare Senior Helath Outcomes: Stanton G. Ades
SVP Professional Services; President, Omnicare Senior Health Outcomes: W. Gary Erwin, age 57
SVP Strategic Planning and Development: Leo P. (Tracy) Finn III, age 51
Chief Compliance Officer: James S. Mathis
VP Internal Audit: John D. Stone
VP Purchasing: Daniel J. Maloney
VP and General Counsel: Mark G. Kobasuk, age 52
VP Government Affairs: Timothy L. Vordenbaumen Sr.
VP and Controller; Group Executive, Corporate Financial Services Group: Bradley S. Abbott
VP Management Information Systems: D. Michael Laney
VP; Group Executive, Operations Finance Group: Robert E. Dries
President and CEO, Advanced Care Scripts: Jeffrey P. Spafford
President and CEO, Omnicare Clinical Research: James M. Pusey, age 50
President and CEO, excelleRx: Gary W. Kadlec
Auditors: PricewaterhouseCoopers LLP

LOCATIONS

HQ: Omnicare, Inc.
1600 RiverCenter II, 100 E. RiverCenter Blvd.
Covington, KY 41011
Phone: 859-392-3300   **Fax:** 859-392-3333
Web: www.omnicare.com

2009 Sales

	$ mil.	% of total
US	6,111.7	99
Other countries	54.5	1
Total	**6,166.2**	**100**

PRODUCTS/OPERATIONS

2009 Sales

	$ mil.	% of total
Pharmacy services	6,009.5	97
CRO services	156.7	3
Total	**6,166.2**	**100**

2009 Sources of Revenue

	% of total
Federal Medicare programs (Part B & Part D)	44
Private pay, third-party & facilities (includes Medicare Part A)	42
State Medicaid programs	9
Other sources	5
Total	**100**

COMPETITORS

Accredo Health
AmerisourceBergen
Broadlane
Cardinal Health
Covance
Covenant Care
Express Scripts
Five Star Quality Care
The Harvard Drug Group
Kendle
Life Sciences Research
McKesson
Novation
Option Care
PAREXEL
Pharmaceutical Product Development
PharMerica
Quintiles Transnational
ResMed
Standard Management

HISTORICAL FINANCIALS

Company Type: Public

Income Statement

FYE: December 31

	REVENUE ($ mil.)	NET INCOME ($ mil.)	NET PROFIT MARGIN	EMPLOYEES
12/09	6,166	212	3.4%	15,200
12/08	6,311	156	2.5%	17,200
12/07	6,220	114	1.8%	17,800
12/06	6,493	184	2.8%	17,100
12/05	5,293	227	4.3%	17,900
Annual Growth	3.9%	(1.7%)	—	(4.0%)

2009 Year-End Financials

Debt ratio: 51.1%
Return on equity: 5.8%
Cash ($ mil.): 276
Current ratio: 3.58
Long-term debt ($ mil.): 1,980

No. of shares (mil.): 118
Dividends
Yield: 0.4%
Payout: 5.0%
Market value ($ mil.): 2,857

Stock History

NYSE: OCR

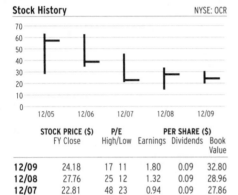

	STOCK PRICE ($) FY Close	P/E High/Low	PER SHARE ($) Earnings	Dividends	Book Value
12/09	24.18	17 11	1.80	0.09	32.80
12/08	27.76	25 12	1.32	0.09	28.96
12/07	22.81	48 23	0.94	0.09	27.86
12/06	38.63	41 24	1.50	0.09	26.77
12/05	57.22	30 14	2.10	0.09	24.90
Annual Growth	(19.4%)	— —	(3.8%)	0.0%	7.1%

Omnicom Group

While it might not be omnipotent, Omnicom Group can create advertising that is omnipresent. The company ranks as the world's #1 corporate media services conglomerate, with advertising, marketing, and public relations operations serving some 5,000 clients in more than 100 countries. It serves global advertising clients through its agency networks BBDO Worldwide, DDB Worldwide, and TBWA Worldwide, while such firms as GSD&M's Idea City, Merkley + Partners, and Zimmerman Advertising provide services for regional and national clients. More than 160 other firms in its Diversified Agency Services division, including Fleishman-Hillard, Integer, and Rapp, provide public relations and other marketing services.

Despite an economic downturn and a more cost-cautious approach on the part of advertisers, Omnicom has continued to grow both domestically and internationally. The company's fortunes have been buoyed in part by its agency networks and their consistently strong creative work (traditional media advertising accounts for more than 40% of revenue), but the bulk of its growth has come from such areas as customer relationship management (CRM) and specialty communications. Omnicom sees continued growth being tied to its ability to provide an ever expanding menu of services to its largest clients.

Following a long period of consolidation and acquisitions, Omnicom is slowly and quietly beginning to reorganize itself into a new kind of holding company. Longtime CEO John Wren sees the company's agency networks becoming more full-service communications firms; and he is looking to integrate (or in some cases reintegrate) Omnicom's specialized services units into its global agencies. Throughout 2009 Omnicom made four acquisitions, a far lower number than the 12 acquisitions the company made the year before.

Omnicom has also been focused on expanding its media planning and buying operations. OMD Worldwide is a leading media specialist firm (behind Publicis' Starcom MediaVest), but Omnicom still trails WPP Group, Publicis, and Interpublic in total media services billings. To help close the gap, OMD launched Full Circle Entertainment, a branded entertainment production unit that works with clients like DIRECTV and Pier 1. In addition, Omnicom's Prometheus Media Services unit is its third media specialist, alongside OMD Worldwide and PHD Media Limited.

HISTORY

Omnicom Group was created in 1986 to combine three leading ad agencies into a single group capable of competing in the worldwide market. BBDO Worldwide, founded in New York in 1928 as Batten, Barton, Durstine & Osborn, had a huge PepsiCo account and developed the Pepsi Generation campaign. Doyle Dane Bernbach Group (DDB), which had created the *fahrvergnügen* ads for Volkswagen, had strong ties in Europe. And Needham Harper Worldwide, which had served up the "You Deserve a Break Today" commercials for McDonald's, had connections in Asia. BBDO remained separate, but DDB and Needham Harper were merged to form DDB Needham Worldwide. The business services units (public relations firms and direct marketers) of each of these companies were tucked under the Diversified Agency Services (DAS) umbrella.

Bruce Crawford, a previous chairman of BBDO who had just finished a stint running New York's Metropolitan Opera, became chairman and CEO in 1989. He transformed DAS from a chaotic group of shops into an integrated marketing giant and ran Omnicom as a holding company of independent operating units working together through cross-referrals. By keeping costs low, especially interest expenses, Omnicom survived the 1990-91 recession with little pain. The company acquired Goodby, Berlin & Silverstein (now Goodby, Silverstein & Partners) in 1992. The next year TBWA Advertising (founded in Paris in 1970 by American Bill Tragos) was added to Omnicom's roster.

The merger spree continued in 1994 when Omnicom purchased WWAV Group, the largest direct-marketing agency in the UK. In 1995 Omnicom fused TBWA with Chiat/Day (founded in 1968 by Jay Chiat and Guy Day) to form TBWA International Network. Omnicom also acquired Michigan-based Ross Roy Communications (later Interone Marketing Group). In 1997 DDB Needham won back its McDonald's account after a 15-year hiatus. That year Crawford stepped down as CEO (though he remained chairman) and John Wren took control of Omnicom.

In 1998 the company acquired PR firm Fleishman-Hillard, adding to the PR clout it established with the acquisition of Ketchum Communications (now Ketchum) in 1996. Omnicom also acquired GGT Group of London for $235 million. (GGT's New York office, Wells BDDP, had lost a large Procter & Gamble account that year.) It merged GGT's BDDP Worldwide with TBWA to form TBWA Worldwide. BBDO landed a $200 million account with PepsiCo's Frito-Lay that year.

Omnicom's position in Europe was boosted in 1999 when it bought the Abbot Mead Vickers (now Abbot Mead Vickers BBDO) shares it didn't already own. That year TBWA founder William Tragos retired from the company (replaced by Lee Clow) and DDB Needham changed its moniker to DDB Worldwide Communications Group. Omnicom also bought market research firm M/A/R/C for about $95 million, and invested $20 million in pharmaceutical clinical trials company SCIREX. In 2000 BBDO scored a major coup over rival FCB Worldwide (now part of Interpublic) by landing the $1.8 billion DaimlerChrysler account. The next year it formed Seneca Investments to hold its stakes in several i-services shops, including Agency.com and Organic. (Omnicom acquired the interactive agencies outright in 2003.)

EXECUTIVES

Chairman: Bruce Crawford, age 81
Vice Chairman: Peter W. Mead, age 70
Vice Chairman; CEO, Omnicom Asia-Pacific, India, Middle East, and Africa (APIMA): Tim Love, age 60
President, CEO, and Director: John D. Wren, age 57, $2,953,384 total compensation
Chief Digital Officer: Jon Raj
Chief Creative Officer, TPN: Sharon Love
EVP and CFO: Randall J. Weisenburger, age 51, $2,771,754 total compensation
EVP: Asit Mehra
EVP: Bruce Redditt
EVP: Janet Riccio
SVP Finance and Controller: Philip J. Angelastro, age 45
SVP, General Counsel, and Secretary: Michael J. O'Brien, age 48
SVP: Tiffany R. Warren
SVP and Corporate Director of Public Affairs: Pat Sloan
Chairman and CEO, Diversified Agency Services: Thomas L. Harrison, age 62, $2,289,293 total compensation
President and CEO, BBDO Worldwide: Andrew Robertson, age 49, $1,855,490 total compensation
President and CEO, DDB Worldwide: Charles E. (Chuck) Brymer, age 50, $1,871,579 total compensation
Auditors: KPMG LLP

LOCATIONS

HQ: Omnicom Group Inc.
437 Madison Ave., New York, NY 10022
Phone: 212-415-3600   **Fax:** 212-415-3530
Web: www.omnicomgroup.com

2009 Sales

	$ mil.	% of total
US	6,178.4	53
Europe		
UK	1,045.3	9
Other countries	2,551.3	22
Other regions	1,945.7	16
Total	**11,720.7**	**100**

PRODUCTS/OPERATIONS

2009 Sales

	$ mil.	% of total
Traditional media advertising	5,195.0	44
Customer relationship management	4,383.1	38
Public relations	1,075.3	9
Specialty communications	1,067.3	9
Total	**11,720.7**	**100**

Selected Operations

Global advertising networks
  BBDO Worldwide
  DDB Worldwide
  TBWA Worldwide

National advertising agencies
  Goodby, Silverstein & Partners (San Francisco)
  GSD&M's Idea City (Austin, TX)
  Martin|Williams (Minneapolis)
  Merkley + Partners (New York City)
  Zimmerman Partners Advertising (Fort Lauderdale, FL)

Marketing and consulting agencies

Direct response
  Interbrand (brand identity)
  M/A/R/C Research (market research)
  Rapp (direct marketing)
  Targetbase (direct marketing)

Promotional marketing
  CPM (field marketing)
  The Integer Group (retail marketing)
  Kaleidoscope (sports and event marketing)
  Millsport (sports and event marketing)

Public relations
  Brodeur Partners
  Clark & Weinstock
  Cone
  Fleishman-Hillard
  Gavin Anderson & Company
  GPC International
  Ketchum
  Porter Novelli International
  Smythe Dorward Lambert

Specialty communications
  Adelphi Group (health care)
  Corbett Accel Healthcare (health care)
  Dieste (multicultural marketing)
  Doremus (business-to-business advertising)
  SafirRosetti (security and intelligence)

Media services
  Icon International
  Novus Print Media
  OMD Worldwide
  PHD Network

COMPETITORS

Aegis Group
Dentsu
Hakuhodo
Havas
Interpublic Group
Publicis Groupe
WPP

HISTORICAL FINANCIALS

Company Type: Public

Income Statement

FYE: December 31

	REVENUE ($ mil.)	NET INCOME ($ mil.)	NET PROFIT MARGIN	EMPLOYEES
12/09	11,721	793	6.8%	63,000
12/08	13,360	1,000	7.5%	68,000
12/07	12,694	976	7.7%	70,000
12/06	11,377	864	7.6%	66,000
12/05	10,481	791	7.5%	62,000
Annual Growth	**2.8%**	**0.1%**	**—**	**0.4%**

2009 Year-End Financials

Debt ratio: 52.9%
Return on equity: 20.6%
Cash ($ mil.): 1,587
Current ratio: 0.87
Long-term debt ($ mil.): 2,221
No. of shares (mil.): 301
Dividends
  Yield: 1.5%
  Payout: 23.7%
Market value ($ mil.): 11,798

Stock History

NYSE: OMC

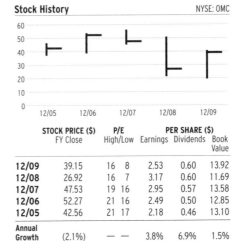

	STOCK PRICE ($) FY Close	P/E High/Low		PER SHARE ($) Earnings	Dividends	Book Value
12/09	39.15	16	8	2.53	0.60	13.92
12/08	26.92	16	7	3.17	0.60	11.69
12/07	47.53	19	16	2.95	0.57	13.58
12/06	52.27	21	16	2.49	0.50	12.85
12/05	42.56	21	17	2.18	0.46	13.10
Annual Growth	**(2.1%)**	**—**	**—**	**3.8%**	**6.9%**	**1.5%**

ONEOK, Inc.

One okey-dokey company, ONEOK (pronounced "one oak") is branching out across the energy industry. The company's regulated utilities — Oklahoma Natural Gas, Kansas Gas Service, and Texas Gas Service — distribute natural gas to more than 2 million customers. Through its 43%-owned ONEOK Partners (of which it is the general partner) it operates 15,000 miles of gas-gathering pipeline and 7,100 miles of transportation pipeline, as well as gas processing plants and storage facilities. The unit also owns one of the US's top natural gas liquids (NGL) systems. ONEOK's energy services unit focuses on marketing natural gas and related services across the US. ONEOK also has a parking garage and leases office space in Tulsa.

The company reported lower revenues in 2009 primarily due to the effect of the global recession suppressing commodity prices.

ONEOK's strategy is to deliver consistent growth and sustainable earnings via its ONEOK Partners, Distribution, and Energy Services segments through both internal growth and strategic acquisitions.

To generate cash and increase shareholder return, in 2006 ONEOK sold its gathering and processing, natural gas liquids, pipelines, and storage businesses to Northern Border Partners (renamed ONEOK Partners) for $3 billion and became that company's general partner.

The company's primary growth vehicle, ONEOK Partners, has targeted potential expansion projects (including NGLs pipelines) that will require $300 million to $500 million of capital investment between 2010 and 2015. Between 2006 and 2009 ONEOK invested some $2 billion to support ONEOK Partners' rapid development.

HISTORY

In 1906 Oklahoma Natural Gas (ONG) was founded to pipe natural gas from northeastern Oklahoma to Oklahoma City. A 100-mile pipeline was completed the next year. In 1921 ONG created two oil companies to pump out the oil it found as a result of its natural gas exploration.

In the 1920s ONG changed hands many times, ending up with utility financier G. L. Ohrstrom and Company, which milked it dry by brokering acquisitions (purchasing gas properties and then selling them to ONG) and collecting fees. Stock sales drove revenues, inflating the stock's price, and the inflated price triggered more stock sales. The bubble burst on October 29, 1929. A series of leadership changes ensued, and in 1932 the company was dissolved and reincorporated. Under president Joseph Bowes, ONG recovered, wooing back dissatisfied customers and upgrading its pipelines.

In the late 1930s the company pioneered a type of underground storage that injected gas into depleted gas reservoirs in the summer and withdrew it during winter's peak use times.

The 1950s and 1960s saw the company expand. In 1962 it created its first subsidiary, Oklahoma Natural Gas Gathering Company, selling gas out of state and therefore subject to federal regulation.

In the lean 1970s ONG was not affected by federal laws that kept wellhead prices low for gas transported across state lines because its main operations were confined to Oklahoma. Congress deregulated wellhead prices in 1978, spurring exploration but causing great price fluctuations in the 1980s. In 1980 ONG changed its name to ONEOK.

In the 1980s ONEOK signed take-or-pay contracts, which forced it to pay for gas offered by its suppliers even if it had no customers. When recession in the 1980s caused demand to drop, ONEOK had to pay for high-priced natural gas it couldn't sell. In 1988 the company was ordered to pay some $50 million to supplier Forest Oil of Denver. A year later ONEOK was sued for allegedly failing to tell stockholders about the take-or-pay agreements (settled in 1993 for $5.5 million). It later sold more than half of its oil and gas reserves to Mustang Energy for $52 million to finance the Forest Oil court award. The company was still settling lawsuits over the agreements into the 1990s; it settled the last of the claims by 1998.

ONEOK began buying gas transmission and production facilities in Oklahoma and creating drilling alliances in the 1990s. In 1997 ONEOK bought the natural gas assets of Westar Energy, formerly Western Resources, for $660 million and ONEOK stock worth $800 million. The acquisition doubled the number of ONEOK's customers and increased its gas marketing, gathering, and transmission operations.

In 1998 the company sold oil and gas reserves, processing plants, and gathering systems in Kansas, Louisiana, and Oklahoma to Duke Energy. With gas utility deregulation looming, ONEOK purchased producing oil and gas properties, primarily in Oklahoma and Texas.

President and COO David Kyle took over as chairman and CEO in 2000 after Larry Brummett died of cancer. In 2001 the company established a new unit, ONEOK Power, with the startup of a new power plant northwest of Oklahoma City.

Westar Energy reduced its stake to approximately 15% by selling shares back to ONEOK and to the public in mid-2003; it sold its remaining shares to Cantor Fitzgerald later that year.

ONEOK has been juggling assets to focus on profitable businesses. The firm, which gets a large slice of its revenues from its gas distribution, gathering, and processing operations, sold about 70% of its oil and gas production assets in Kansas, Oklahoma, and Texas to Chesapeake Energy for $300 million in 2003. Later that year, shifting its production focus to the Texas market (and focusing on development rather than exploration), it acquired oil and gas reserves and related gathering systems in East Texas from Wagner & Brown for about $240 million.

The company also acquired Southern Union's Texas natural gas distribution business (540,000 customers), as well as Southern Union's stake in a Mexican gas utility and its propane distribution, gas marketing, and gas transmission operations in the southwestern US, for $420 million.

ONEOK acquired Northern Plains Natural Gas, a general partner of pipeline operator Northern Border Partners (later renamed ONEOK Partners), from CCE Holdings (a joint venture of Southern Union and GE Commercial Finance) for $175 million in 2004.

In 2005 the company bought Koch Industries' natural gas liquids assets for $1.35 billion. That year ONEOK sold properties to TXOK Acquisition Inc. for $645 million, and some Texas natural gas assets to Eagle Rock Energy for $528 million to help pay down debt.

EXECUTIVES

Chairman: David L. Kyle, age 57
President, CEO, and Director; Chairman, President, and CEO, ONEOK Partners: John W. Gibson, age 58, $6,571,790 total compensation
COO: Robert F. (Rob) Martinovich, age 52
EVP and Director; COO, ONEOK Partners: Terry K. Spencer, age 51
SVP, CFO, and Treasurer; EVP, CFO, Treasurer and Director, ONEOK Partners: Curtis L. Dinan, age 42, $1,280,587 total compensation
SVP, General Counsel, and Assistant Secretary; EVP, General Counsel and Secretary, ONEOK Partners: John R. Barker, age 62, $1,476,272 total compensation
SVP Compliance: D. Lamar Miller, age 50
SVP Corporate Planning and Development: Caron A. Lawhorn, age 49
SVP Administrative Services: David E. Roth, age 55
SVP Origination, Retail and Business Development, ONEOK Energy Services: Charles (Chuck) Kelley
SVP and Chief Accounting Officer, ONEOK and ONEOK Partners: Derek S. Reiners, age 39
VP and Controller, Oklahoma Natural Gas, Kansas Gas Service and Texas Gas Service: Beverly C. Monnet, age 50
VP and CIO: Kevin L. Burdick, age 45
President Energy Services: Patrick J. (Pat) McDonie, age 49
President, Natural Gas Pipelines, Natural Gas, ONEOK Partners: W. Kent Shortridge, age 43
President, Kansas Gas Service: Bradley O. (Brad) Dixon, age 57
President, Texas Gas Service: Gregory A. (Greg) Phillips, age 47
President, Oklahoma Natural Gas: Roger N. Mitchell, age 58
President, Viking Trans, Guardian MW, Northern Plains Natural Gas: Paul F. Miller, age 41
President ONEOK Distribution Companies: Pierce H. Norton II, age 50
Auditors: PricewaterhouseCoopers LLP

LOCATIONS

HQ: ONEOK, Inc.
100 W. 5th St., Tulsa, OK 74103
Phone: 918-588-7000   **Fax:** 918-588-7960
Web: www.oneok.com

PRODUCTS/OPERATIONS

2009 Sales

	$ mil.	% of total
ONEOK Partners	5,998.7	54
Energy Services	3,266.5	29
Distribution	1,843.4	17
Adjustments	3.0	—
Total	**11,111.6**	**100**

Selected Subsidiaries, Affiliates, and Divisions

Energy Services
  ONEOK Energy Services Company (formerly ONEOK Energy Marketing and Trading Company; natural gas, oil, and electricity sales)
Natural Gas Liquids
  ONEOK NGL Pipeline, L.P.
Distribution
  Kansas Gas Service Company
  Oklahoma Natural Gas Company
  Texas Gas Service Company (formerly Southern Union Gas Company)
Gathering and Processing
  ONEOK Partners, L.P. (48%)
  ONEOK Field Services Company
  ONEOK NGL Marketing L.P.
Pipelines and Storage
  MidContinent Market Center, Inc.
  Northern Plains Natural Gas Company, LLC
  ONEOK Gas Gathering, L.L.C. (nonprocessable gas gathering services)
  ONEOK Gas Storage, L.L.C.
  ONEOK Gas Transportation, L.L.C.
  ONEOK Texas Gas Storage L.P.
  ONEOK WesTex Transmission, L.P.
Other
  ONEOK Leasing Company (leases space in corporate headquarters building)
  ONEOK Parking Company (owns and operates parking lot adjacent to headquarters)

COMPETITORS

Adams Resources	EQT Corporation
AEP	Exxon Mobil
Atmos Energy	FirstEnergy
BP	Hess Corporation
CenterPoint Energy	National Fuel Gas
CMS Energy	OGE Energy
Duncan Energy	Southern Union
Dynegy	Southwest Gas
Energen	Williams Companies
Energy Future	

HISTORICAL FINANCIALS

Company Type: Public

Income Statement

FYE: December 31

	REVENUE ($ mil.)	NET INCOME ($ mil.)	NET PROFIT MARGIN	EMPLOYEES
12/09	11,112	306	2.7%	4,758
12/08	16,157	312	1.9%	4,742
12/07	13,477	305	2.3%	4,555
12/06	11,896	306	2.6%	4,536
12/05	12,676	547	4.3%	4,558
Annual Growth	**(3.2%)**	**(13.5%)**	**—**	**1.1%**

2009 Year-End Financials

Debt ratio: 196.4%
Return on equity: 14.2%
Cash ($ mil.): 29
Current ratio: 0.78
Long-term debt ($ mil.): 4,334

No. of shares (mil.): 106
Dividends
  Yield: 3.7%
  Payout: 57.1%
Market value ($ mil.): 4,738

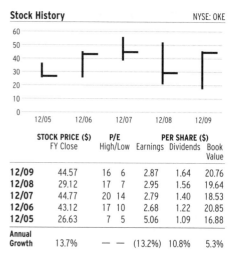
Oracle Corporation

According to this Oracle, consolidation in the business software industry is the wisest move. The enterprise software giant provides a range of tools for managing business data, supporting business operations, and facilitating collaboration and application development. Oracle also offers business applications for data warehousing, customer relationship management, and supply chain management. In recent years the company has aggressively used acquisitions to expand, including the purchases of PeopleSoft, Siebel Systems, and BEA Systems. In early 2010 the company completed its most ambitious acquisition to date, the purchase of Sun for about $7.4 billion.

The Sun acquisition was not only one of the larger deals Oracle has undertaken, but also marks its first significant foray into the world of hardware and chips. Oracle hopes to extend its software expertise to Sun's servers, Solaris operating system, and SPARC chips, enabling Oracle to offer customers an integrated offering of both hardware and software (much like Oracle rivals IBM and Hewlett Packard do).

In August 2010 the company acquired Phase Forward for about $685 million. The deal expands Oracle's presence in the health care and life sciences market, as Phase Forward's clinical drug trial management software has been used by clients such as AstraZeneca, Eli Lilly, and Boston Scientific.

In recent years the company has faced a similar pleasurable dilemma encountered by its rival Microsoft: what to do with a mountain of cash. Oracle's dominant position in the lucrative world of databases produces a steady stream of cash flow and profits, but it also has generated pressure from shareholders to put the company's cash hoard to use. In response the company has embarked on an extended spending spree with one primary goal: to expand its business applications product line, customer base, and market share through acquisitions, both large and small. The company has spent more than $20 billion on acquisitions since 2004.

International sales and operations are a major area of focus for Oracle. Unlike some software firms that have come to rely on services related to their software as their primary source of revenue, software licenses accounted for more than 80% of Oracle's sales in fiscal 2009. Its strong licensing sales and distributed geographic presence have allowed Oracle to successfully weather the economic downturn of 2008-2009.

Founder and CEO Larry Ellison holds a 23% stake in the company, a holding that (along with other assets) routinely places the flashy and outspoken billionaire among the world's richest people. Ellison was vocal in his support of Mark Hurd when Hurd was forced out of his role as CEO of Hewlett-Packard, leading in part to Hurd being named co-president of Oracle in September 2010.

HISTORY

Larry Ellison, Robert Miner, Bruce Scott, and Edward Oates founded System Development Laboratories in 1977 to create a database management system according to theoretical specifications published by IBM. Ellison had studied physics at the University of Chicago but dropped out in the 1960s to seek his fortune in Silicon Valley. He was part of the team that developed the first IBM-compatible mainframe. Miner, an experienced programmer, was the main developer of Oracle's database manager, which was able to run on many computer brands and was introduced in 1979. The company also changed its name that year to Relational Software.

In 1983 the company changed its name again, this time to Oracle, in order to more closely align itself with its primary product. Oracle went public in 1986 and within two years had a 36% share of Uncle Sam's PC database market. It also added financial management, graphics, and human resource management software.

Oracle's rapid growth came at a great cost. It gained notoriety as a leader in vaporware — that is, announced products that actually had not yet been developed. When the company's software was released, it was sometimes bug-ridden and lacking promised features. Duplicate billings and the booking of unconsummated sales inflated revenues.

Oracle recorded a loss for fiscal 1991, accompanied by a downward restatement of earnings for past years. Its stock nosedived. The company laid off 400 employees and revised its growth estimates. Ellison stabilized the company with $80 million in financing from Nippon Steel.

Thanks to Oracle7 (launched 1992), the company within two years became the #1 database management software maker. Sales for fiscal 1994 hit $2 billion. Ellison by that time had developed a reputation as an extravagant adventurer (his hobbies included yacht racing and piloting disarmed fighter planes).

Oracle formed affiliate Network Computer Inc. in 1997 to market Internet appliances (with no disk drive and local memory) that Ellison envisioned would strip Microsoft of its operating system ubiquity. Oracle and Netscape (now owned by Time Warner) merged joint venture Navio Communications one year later into Network Computer (renamed Liberate Technologies, redesigned around interactive software, and spun off in 1999).

In 1999 the company bought three niche front-office software specialists and took its Oracle Japan subsidiary public. The next year it partnered with rival Commerce One to provide software and support for a giant online venture

merging the Web-based procurement exchanges of General Motors, Ford Motor, and Daimler.

Oracle continued to expand its portfolio of business applications in 2001, introducing warehouse, supply chain, and customer relationship management software, as well as software suites targeted at small businesses.

The company launched a hostile takeover bid for PeopleSoft in 2003, just days after the rival software maker had disclosed plans to acquire J.D. Edwards. PeopleSoft's board unanimously rejected the initial all-cash offer of $5.1 billion, deeming the unsolicited bid inadequate and citing antitrust concerns. After bitter negotiations that included a number of rejected bids, Oracle finally reached an agreement to acquire PeopleSoft for $10.3 billion in December 2004; the deal closed the following month.

Soon after the PeopleSoft deal closed, Oracle again pursued a takeover. After a brief bidding war with SAP, Oracle purchased retail software developer Retek for about $670 million in 2005.

EXECUTIVES

Chairman: Jeffrey O. (Jeff) Henley, age 64
CEO and Director: Lawrence J. (Larry) Ellison, age 65, $56,810,852 total compensation
Co-President and Director: Mark Hurd, age 53
Co-President and Director: Safra A. Catz, age 48, $24,298,692 total compensation
EVP and CFO: Jeffrey E. Epstein, age 53, $2,185,152 total compensation
EVP Oracle Customer Services: Juergen Rottler, age 41, $8,475,698 total compensation
EVP Microelectronics: Michael E. (Mike) Splain, age 53
EVP North America Sales and Consulting: Keith G. Block, age 48, $8,273,205 total compensation
EVP Oracle Latin America Sales and Consulting: Luiz Meisler
EVP Oracle Product Development: Thomas Kurian
EVP Oracle Europe, Middle East, and Africa Sales and Consulting: Loïc le Guisquet
EVP Oracle Product Development: Charles A. (Chuck) Rozwat
EVP Systems: John F. Fowler, age 48
Chief Corporate Architect: Edward Screven
Chief Marketing Officer: Judith Sim
Chief Customer Officer: Jeb Dasteel
Chief Security Officer: Mary Ann Davidson
SVP and CIO: Mark E. Sunday, age 55
SVP Human Resources: Joyce Westerdahl
SVP, Office of the CEO: Ken Glueck
SVP, General Counsel, and Secretary; President and CEO, Sun Microsystems: Dorian E. Daley, age 51
Auditors: Ernst & Young LLP

LOCATIONS

HQ: Oracle Corporation
500 Oracle Pkwy., Redwood City, CA 94065
Phone: 650-506-7000   **Fax:** 650-506-7200
Web: www.oracle.com

2010 Sales

	$ mil.	% of total
Americas	13,819	52
EMEA	8,938	33
Asia/Pacific	4,063	15
Total	26,820	100

PRODUCTS/OPERATIONS

2010 Sales

	$ mil.	% of total
Software	20,625	77
Services	3,905	15
Hardware Systems	2,290	8
Total	26,820	100

Selected Software Lines

Business applications
    Corporate performance management
    Customer relationship management
    Financial management
    Human capital management
    Procurement
    Project management
    Supply chain management
Databases
Enterprise application integration
Middleware

COMPETITORS

Accenture
ADP
Autonomy
BMC Software
CA Technologies
CDC Software
Ceridian
Cisco Systems
Courion
EMC
Fujitsu Technology Solutions
Hewlett-Packard
Hitachi
HP Enterprise Services
IBM
Infor Global
Informatica
JasperSoft
JDA Software
Lawson Software
Manhattan Associates
Microsoft
MicroStrategy
NCR
Netezza
Novell
Open Text
Pegasystems
Progress Software
Quest Software
Red Hat
Sage Group
salesforce.com
SAP
SAS Institute
Siemens IT Solutions and Services
SOA Software
Software AG
SuccessFactors
Taleo
Teradata
TIBCO Software

HISTORICAL FINANCIALS

Company Type: Public

Income Statement

FYE: May 31

	REVENUE ($ mil.)	NET INCOME ($ mil.)	NET PROFIT MARGIN	EMPLOYEES
5/10	26,820	6,135	22.9%	105,000
5/09	23,252	5,593	24.1%	86,000
5/08	22,430	5,521	24.6%	84,233
5/07	17,996	4,274	23.7%	74,674
5/06	14,380	3,381	23.5%	56,133
Annual Growth	16.9%	16.1%	—	16.9%

2010 Year-End Financials

Debt ratio: 37.4%	No. of shares (mil.): 5,026
Return on equity: 22.0%	Dividends
Cash ($ mil.): 9,914	Yield: 0.9%
Current ratio: 1.84	Payout: 16.5%
Long-term debt ($ mil.): 11,510	Market value ($ mil.): 113,442

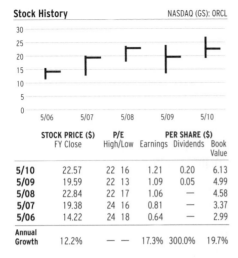

	STOCK PRICE ($) FY Close	P/E High/Low		PER SHARE ($)	
			Earnings	Dividends	Book Value
5/10	22.57	22 16	1.21	0.20	6.13
5/09	19.59	22 13	1.09	0.05	4.99
5/08	22.84	22 17	1.06	—	4.58
5/07	19.38	24 16	0.81	—	3.37
5/06	14.22	24 18	0.64	—	2.99
Annual Growth	12.2%	— —	17.3%	300.0%	19.7%

Oshkosh Corporation

Whether you need to plow through Sahara sands or Buffalo snow, Oshkosh has your ride. The company makes and sells heavy-duty vehicles and vehicle bodies for commercial, access, fire and emergency, and military applications. Oshkosh's commercial and emergency vehicles include concrete carriers and refuse trucks (McNeilus brand), snow blowers, aircraft rescue and firefighting vehicles (Pierce), and towing equipment (Jerr-Dan). Vehicles are sold worldwide through dealers to airport, institutional, construction, and municipal markets. The company also makes heavy-payload trucks, and other vehicles for the US Department of Defense. Oshkosh nets more than 50% of its sales from the US government.

For more than nine decades Oshkosh has channeled its efforts into strengthening marketplace reach and portfolio breadth. It attributes its growth and cost reductions, in part, to having completed 15 acquisitions since 1996. The company benefits particularly from an 80-year long relationship with the US Department of Defense. Oshkosh continues to win an array of defense contracts; these reinforce the company's hold in manufacturing a range of severe-duty, heavy- and medium-payload tactical trucks. Rolling forward, the company sets its sights on diversifying the applications and vehicle body styles of its tactical lineup.

Beyond the defense market, the company touts its lineup as meeting a broad customer-base, thereby serving to shore up against a downturn in any one market. Oshkosh's vehicle development and distribution might is, moreover, reinforced by access equipment maker JLG. JLG's some 3,500 dealers and independent rentals, for example, have helped to drive product launches.

Tie ups with big brands, including Caterpillar prove powerful, too. In 2009 Oshkosh inked a 20-year lease to build CAT-branded telehandlers, routed to market through Caterpillar's global dealer network. Oshkosh is also partnering with Daimler Trucks North America; Daimler supplies the 2010 EPA emission standards compliant engines for Oshkosh's Pierce Manufacturing.

The deal strengthens Pierce's position as North America's largest manufacturer of fire and rescue equipment.

The Oshkosh fire and emergency segment relies as well upon relationships cultivated with an array of major players, from municipal entities to airports, institutions, and industrial companies. Oshkosh manufacturing facilities and service locations crisscross North America, enabling quick turnaround for these demanding markets.

Among Oshkosh's disappointments is its European refuse collection vehicle operation, Geesink. After three years of restructuring, this business continued to perform poorly. In 2009 Oshkosh shed Geesink to Platinum Equity, retaining only Geesink's plant in Romania. Oshkosh's European fire apparatus and equipment company, BAI, also failed to meet expectations. Oshkosh sold off its 75% stake to BAI management.

In a move to simplify its name and reflect the company's more diverse operations, Oshkosh changed its name from Oshkosh Truck Corporation to Oshkosh Corporation in 2008.

HISTORY

Bernhard Mosling and William Besserdich founded Oshkosh Truck in 1917, attracting investors with *Old Betsy*, a four-wheel-drive, 3,000-pound truck. Over the next few decades, the company developed a range of heavy-duty vehicles. Sales took off when the US Army gave truck contracts to Oshkosh during WWII. Commercial sales increased after the war, the result of demand from mining and plantation companies. Oshkosh Truck went public in 1985.

Defense cutbacks prompted the company to diversify. It acquired Deere & Company's motorhome chassis business in 1989 and Miller Trailers the next year.

In 1995 Oshkosh formed a strategic alliance with Daimler-Benz's (now Daimler AG) Freightliner Corporation (now Daimler Trucks North America), although the transfer of Oshkosh's chassis business caused the company's sales to drop by more than $100 million in fiscal 1995. The following year Oshkosh bought fire truck maker Pierce Manufacturing for $158 million. Robert Bohn became CEO in 1997, succeeding Eugene Goodson, who quit in a disagreement with the board. Oshkosh also bought Quebec-based Nova Quintech's firefighting ladder technology that year.

The company acquired McNeilus Companies, a leading maker of concrete mixers and bodies for refuse trucks, for $250 million in 1998. It also won the initial contract for the US Marine Corps' Medium Tactical Truck Replacement program, potentially worth up to $1.2 billion. In 1999 Oshkosh bought Kewaunee Engineering, which made parts for aerial devices, for $6.3 million. The next year Oshkosh picked up Viking Truck and Equipment (concrete mixer sales and service). Later in 2000 Oshkosh diversified into ambulances with the purchase of Medtec Ambulance Corporation.

Oshkosh expanded its European presence in 2001 when it bought the Geesink Norba Group (refuse collection truck bodies, mobile and stationary compactors, and transfer stations) from Powell Duffryn Ltd. In 2004 Oshkosh acquired Jerr-Dan, a towing equipment manufacturer, from Littlejohn & Co. Later that year the company acquired 75% of two Italy-based firefighting equipment manufacturers, BAI Brescia Antcendi International and BAI Tecnica.

Oshkosh acquired access equipment manufacturer JLG Industries in 2006. The acquisition of JLG marked Oshkosh's expansion into the aerial platform market, and JLG instantly became Oshkosh's largest product segment. The move also gave Oshkosh purchasing leverage, and gave it exposure to complementary markets.

Not surprisingly, the company's defense products also enjoyed brisk sales of parts and services for the thousands of Oshkosh trucks currently in service in Iraq. Oshkosh also won market share for its line of emergency vehicles, including response vehicles used in homeland security applications.

Also in 2006 Oshkosh acquired AK Specialty Vehicles from HealthTronics. The purchase brought a lineup of mobile medical, broadcast, and homeland-security command and control vehicles — new specialty vehicle markets for Oshkosh. Later that year Oshkosh bought Iowa Mold Tooling, a maker of tire service, general mechanics, and lubrication trucks.

EXECUTIVES

Chairman and CEO: Robert G. (Bob) Bohn, age 56, $5,740,014 total compensation
President, COO, and Director: Charles L. (Charlie) Szews, age 52, $2,232,491 total compensation
EVP and CFO: David M. Sagehorn, age 47, $925,641 total compensation
EVP Government Operations and Industry Relations: Joseph H. (Jay) Kimmitt, age 59, $1,128,276 total compensation
EVP; President, Fire and Emergency; President, Pierce Manufacturing: Wilson R. Jones, age 48
EVP; President, Defense: R. Andrew (Andy) Hove, age 47, $1,034,791 total compensation
EVP and President, Fire & Emergency Segment; President, Pierce Manufacturing: Jim Johnson
EVP; President, Commercial: Frank Nerenhausen
EVP Technology: Donald H. Verhoff, age 63
EVP Global Manufacturing Services: Thomas D. Fenner, age 53
EVP, General Counsel, and Secretary: Bryan J. Blankfield, age 48
EVP and Chief Administration Officer: Matthew J. Zolnowski, age 56
EVP and Chief Administration Officer-Elect: Michael K. Rohrkaste, age 51
SVP and Chief Procurement Officer: Gregory L. (Greg) Fredericksen
SVP Global Operating Systems and Lean Deployment: Josef Matosevic
SVP Finance and Controller: Thomas J. Polnaszek
VP Oshkosh Corporation Foundation and Assistant Secretary: Connie S. Stellmacher
VP Investor Relations: Patrick N. Davidson
VP Marketing Communications: Ann T. Stawski
President, Asian Operations: Desmond Soh
Auditors: Deloitte & Touche LLP

LOCATIONS

HQ: Oshkosh Corporation
2307 Oregon St., Oshkosh, WI 54902
Phone: 920-235-9151   **Fax:** 920-233-9268
Web: www.oshkoshcorporation.com

2009 Sales

	$ mil.	% of total
North America		
US	4,487.1	85
Other countries	89.7	2
Europe, Africa & Middle East	510.7	9
Other regions	207.7	4
Total	**5,295.2**	**100**

PRODUCTS/OPERATIONS

2009 Sales

	$ mil.	% of total
Defense	2,594.8	47
Fire & emergency	1,169.0	21
Access equipment	1,139.4	21
Commercial	590.0	11
Adjustments	(198.0)	—
Total	**5,295.2**	**100**

Selected Products

Defense
  Heavy equipment transporter (HET)
  Heavy expanded mobility tactical trucks (HEMTT)
  Load handling systems (LHS)
  Logistic vehicle system (LVS)
  Medium tactical vehicle replacements (MTVR)
  Palletized load system (PLS)

Fire and emergency
  Aircraft rescue vehicles
  Airport snow removal vehicles
  Custom ambulances
  Firefighting vehicles
  Rescue and homeland security vehicles
  Snow blowing and plow trucks
  Towing and recovery equipment

Access equipment
  Aerial work platforms
  Excavators
  Telehandlers
  Trailers

Commercial
  Portable concrete batch plants
  Rear- and front-discharge concrete mixers
  Refuse truck bodies

COMPETITORS

AM General
American LaFrance
BAE Systems Land & Armaments
Collins Industries
Daimler
Daimler Trucks North America
Dover Corp.
E-ONE
Federal Signal
Force Protection
General Dynamics Land Systems
Haulotte
Heil Environmental Industries
Hyundai Motor
Iveco S.p.A.
J C Bamford Excavators
L-3 Communications
Leyland Trucks
Mack Trucks
MAN
MANITOU BF
Miller Industries
Navistar
Navistar International
PACCAR
Skyjack
Spartan Motors
Terex
Trinity Industries
UD Trucks
Volvo

HISTORICAL FINANCIALS

Company Type: Public

Income Statement

FYE: September 30

	REVENUE ($ mil.)	NET INCOME ($ mil.)	NET PROFIT MARGIN	EMPLOYEES
9/09	5,295	(1,100)	—	12,300
9/08	7,138	79	1.1%	14,000
9/07	6,307	268	4.3%	14,200
9/06	3,427	206	6.0%	9,387
9/05	2,960	160	5.4%	7,960
Annual Growth	**15.7%**	**—**	**—**	**11.5%**

2009 Year-End Financials

Debt ratio: 393.5%
Return on equity: —
Cash ($ mil.): 530
Current ratio: 1.29
Long-term debt ($ mil.): 2,023
No. of shares (mil.): 91
Dividends
  Yield: 0.6%
  Payout: —
Market value ($ mil.): 2,800

Stock History

NYSE: OSK

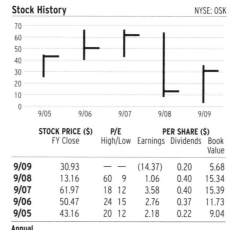

	STOCK PRICE ($) FY Close	P/E High/Low		PER SHARE ($) Earnings	Dividends	Book Value
9/09	30.93	—	—	(14.37)	0.20	5.68
9/08	13.16	60	9	1.06	0.40	15.34
9/07	61.97	18	12	3.58	0.40	15.39
9/06	50.47	24	15	2.76	0.37	11.73
9/05	43.16	20	12	2.18	0.22	9.04
Annual Growth	**(8.0%)**	**—**	**—**	**—**	**(2.4%)**	**(11.0%)**

Owens & Minor

Owens & Minor (O&M) makes sure hospitals are prepared for major surgeries. A leading distributor of medical and surgical supplies, the company carries some 200,000 products from about 1,400 manufacturers. Products distributed by O&M include surgical dressings, endoscopic and intravenous products, needles, syringes, sterile procedure trays, gowns, gloves, and sutures. The firm also offers software, consulting, and other services to help customers manage their supplies. O&M's customers are primarily hospitals and health systems and the purchasing organizations that serve them. It delivers products to roughly 4,600 health care providers from some 50 distribution centers across the US.

The company's major suppliers include Covidien and Johnson & Johnson, whose products account for about 15% and 10% of O&M's revenues, respectively. The distributor sells some 2,400 value products under its own MediChoice label.

Most of O&M's sales come from acute-care hospitals, which are often represented by group purchasing organizations (GPOs) or integrated health care networks (IHNs). GPO Novation accounts for around 35% of the company's earnings, and GPOs Premier and Broadlane account for about 20% and 10%, respectively. The company also has an ongoing exclusive supplier agreement with the US Department of Defense.

As the health care industry has consolidated, so have the industries that serve it, and the company has tried to remain competitive by providing supply chain management tools and services in addition to supplies to help its customers control costs. Its OMSolutions business unit provides outsourcing and resource management services, including one-on-one consultations and physical inventory reviews. O&M's technology offerings include WISDOM, which allows customers to track inventory, usage, and other information to keep costs down, and PANDAC, which helps operating rooms track and control their inventory.

O&M doesn't shy away from acquisitions as another way to help boost sales. To help bolster its core distribution business, in 2008 O&M acquired private Midwest distributor The Burrows Company for $30 million plus debt assumptions.

In 2009, in a move designed to focus on its core acute-care distribution operations, the company sold its direct-to-consumer (DTC) diabetes supply business, Access Diabetic Supply, to Liberty Medical (a division of Medco Health Solutions) for $63 million. O&M has exited its other DTC operations as well.

HISTORY

George Gilmer Minor Jr.'s great-grandfather was an apothecary and surgeon in colonial Williamsburg, Virginia. His grandfather was Thomas Jefferson's personal physician. Minor himself worked as a wholesale drug salesman in Richmond after the Civil War. In 1882 he and rival wholesaler Otho Owens partnered to form the Owens & Minor Drug Company. The company was both a retail and wholesale business, with a storefront that filled prescriptions and sold sundries, paints, oils, and window glass. When Owens died in 1906, Minor became the company's president.

During the 1920s, the Owens family sold their stake in the firm. George Gilmer Minor III served briefly as the company's president in the early 1940s; his son, George Gilmer Minor IV (called Mr. Minor Jr. to differentiate him from his father), became president in 1947.

In 1954 Owens & Minor installed its first computerized order fulfillment system. The following year the firm became Owens, Minor & Bodeker when it bought the Bodeker Drug Company, which was both older and larger than Owens & Minor.

After 84 years in the drug wholesale business, the company entered the medical and surgical distribution business after buying A&J Hospital Supply in 1966 and Powers & Anderson in 1968. In 1971 Owens, Minor & Bodeker went public. By the end of the decade, the company had operations in 10 states.

The fourth Minor to run the firm, G. Gilmer Minor III (Mr. Minor Jr.'s son), was named president in 1981 (he became CEO in 1984). Under his direction Owens, Minor & Bodeker would complete the transition from a drug wholesaler to a medical supplies distributor. In 1981 it purchased the Will Ross subsidiary of G.D. Searle (then the country's #2 medical and surgical supplies distributor).

The company reverted to its original name on its 100th anniversary in 1982. By 1984 medical supplies supplanted wholesale drugs as its primary source of income. In 1988 Owens & Minor listed on the NYSE.

The company passed the $1 billion revenue mark in 1990 and later sold its wholesale drug business. It extended its reach with the purchase of Lyons Physician Supply in 1993 and Stuart Medical (the #3 national distributor) in 1994.

The company consolidated its warehouse operations and upgraded its computer system in 1995. To make up for losses attributed to restructuring costs and discounting prices for large accounts, Owens & Minor eliminated or reassigned jobs at several distribution centers.

In 1998 it lost its biggest customer when embattled Columbia/HCA (now HCA) canceled its contract. Owens & Minor replaced this business by contracting with such providers as Sutter Health.

In 1999 the company formed an alliance with drug distributor AmeriSource Health (now AmerisourceBergen) to streamline transactions with Sutter Health. In 2002 Owens & Minor launched an initiative to offer automated supply chain management services to its clients.

Chairman and CEO G. Gilmer Minor III stepped down from the CEO post after 21 years in July 2005 but remained the company's chairman; Craig R. Smith, the company's former COO, was named CEO.

Also in 2005, the company expanded into the diabetic direct-to-consumer supply business by acquiring Access Diabetic Supply. (That division was later divested, however.)

The company in 2006 acquired the acute care medical and surgical supply business of McKesson Medical-Surgical, a subsidiary of McKesson Corporation, for $165 million.

EXECUTIVES

Chairman: G. Gilmer Minor III, age 69
President, CEO, and Director: Craig R. Smith, age 58, $4,043,065 total compensation
EVP and COO: Charles C. Colpo, age 52, $1,436,259 total compensation
EVP Distribution: E. V. Clarke, age 49, $1,358,189 total compensation
SVP and CFO: James L. (Jim) Bierman, age 58, $2,105,643 total compensation
SVP, General Counsel, and Corporate Secretary: Grace R. den Hartog, age 58, $1,017,680 total compensation
SVP Strategic Planning and Business Development: Mark A. Van Sumeren, age 52, $1,450,477 total compensation
SVP and CIO: Richard W. Mears, age 49
SVP Sales and Operations: W. Marshall Simpson, age 41
SVP Human Resources: Erika T. Davis, age 46
Corporate VP, Controller, and Chief Accounting Officer: D. Andrew (Drew) Edwards, age 51
Operating VP, Corporate Development: Robert K. Snead
VP Quality and Communications: Hugh F. Gouldthorpe Jr., age 71
Director Investor and Media Relations: Truitt (Trudi) Allcott
Director Finance: Chuck Graves
Auditors: KPMG LLP

LOCATIONS

HQ: Owens & Minor, Inc.
9120 Lockwood Blvd., Mechanicsville, VA 23116
Phone: 804-723-7000   **Fax:** 804-723-7100
Web: www.owens-minor.com

PRODUCTS/OPERATIONS

Selected Subsidiaries

Medical Supply Group, Inc.
O&M Funding Corp.
OMI International, Ltd. (British Virgin Islands)
OM Solutions International, Inc.
Owens & Minor Canada, Inc.
Owens & Minor Distribution, Inc.
Owens & Minor Healthcare Supply, Inc.
Owens & Minor Medical, Inc.

COMPETITORS

AmerisourceBergen
Buffalo Supply
Cardinal Health
Henry Schein
Invacare Supply Group
Kerma Medical Products
McKesson
Medisavers
Medline Industries
Metro Medical Supply
Patterson Companies
PSS World Medical
Surgical Express
Tri-anim

HISTORICAL FINANCIALS

Company Type: Public

Income Statement

	REVENUE ($ mil.)	NET INCOME ($ mil.)	NET PROFIT MARGIN	EMPLOYEES
12/09	8,038	105	1.3%	4,800
12/08	7,243	93	1.3%	5,300
12/07	6,801	73	1.1%	4,800
12/06	5,534	49	0.9%	4,600
12/05	4,822	64	1.3%	3,700
Annual Growth	13.6%	12.9%	—	6.7%

FYE: December 31

2009 Year-End Financials

Debt ratio: 27.1%
Return on equity: 14.4%
Cash ($ mil.): 96
Current ratio: 1.92
Long-term debt ($ mil.): 208
No. of shares (mil.): 63
Dividends
  Yield: 2.1%
  Payout: 36.5%
Market value ($ mil.): 1,806

Stock History

NYSE: OMI

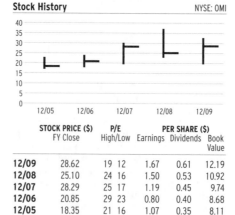

	STOCK PRICE ($) FY Close	P/E High/Low		PER SHARE ($) Earnings	Dividends	Book Value
12/09	28.62	19	12	1.67	0.61	12.19
12/08	25.10	24	16	1.50	0.53	10.92
12/07	28.29	25	17	1.19	0.45	9.74
12/06	20.85	29	23	0.80	0.40	8.68
12/05	18.35	21	16	1.07	0.35	8.11
Annual Growth	11.8%	—	—	11.8%	14.9%	10.7%

Owens Corning

Owens Corning operates in the PINK. Famous for its Pink Panther mascot and its trademarked PINK glass fiber insulation, the company is a top global maker of building and composite material systems. Its building materials segment, which accounts for about two-thirds of sales, makes insulation, roofing and asphalt, and other building materials for the residential and commercial markets. Its composite products segment makes glass fiber reinforcement materials for the transportation, industrial, infrastructure, marine, wind energy, and consumer markets.

As a result of the global financial crisis in 2008 and 2009, building materials suppliers in general experienced a significant downturn in sales. Owens Corning took cost-cutting actions to weather the storm including reducing production and cutting its workforce by about 10%.

The company's composites business supplies the industrial, energy, and residential markets. Its OCV Reinforcements and OCV Technical Fabrics units provide lightweight alternatives for steel, wool, and aluminum. Owens Corning strengthened its composite operations in late 2007 when it acquired the reinforcements and composite fabrics business of materials giant Saint-Gobain in late 2007. After that transaction, the company restructured, including selling its Norandex siding business and a handful of manufacturing and distribution facilities.

Asbestos-related lawsuits sunk Owens Corning deep into debt and the company operated under Chapter 11 bankruptcy from 2000 until late 2006. As part of the reorganization the company's paid some $5 billion in asbestos claims, along with an additional $2.4 billion earmarked for debt holders.

The Owens Corning/Fibreboard Asbestos Personal Injury Trust, an entity formed to pay all valid asbestos personal injury claims, owns 11% of the company.

HISTORY

In the 1930s Corning Glass Works and Owens-Illinois Glass independently found that glass fiber has special resilience and strength. Realizing the potential market, they formed joint venture Owens-Corning Fiberglas in 1938. The companies expanded rapidly in the 1940s and 1950s, establishing several US plants and one in Canada. Their products included fine fibers, thermal wool, textiles, and continuous filaments.

A US antitrust decree in 1949 denied the two founding firms any control over Owens-Corning. Each retained one-third ownership when the company went public in 1952. During the 1950s Owens-Corning developed new uses for fiberglass in automobile bodies, shingles, and insulation. In the 1960s the company expanded overseas. Fiberglass uses multiplied as applications developed in aerospace, tires, and underground tanks.

By 1980 the company had invested more than $700 million in acquisitions and made the Pink Panther its mascot. Owens-Corning introduced a rolled insulation in 1982.

The company successfully fended off a takeover attempt by Wickes Companies in 1986, but the effort left Owens-Corning with $2.6 billion in debt. It sold 10 businesses, halved its research budget, and laid off or lost to divestitures 46% of its workforce.

The company bought Fiberglas Canada, that country's largest fiberglass-insulation maker, in 1989. To expand globally, Owens-Corning formed alliances in 1990 with BASF, Lucky-Goldstar, and Siam Cement.

Owens-Corning spent $65 million in 1991 on restructuring and took an $800 million charge to cover its liability to asbestos-exposure lawsuits (the company stopped making asbestos in 1972). That same year it exchanged its commercial roofing business for the residential roofing business of Schuller International.

In 1994 Owens-Corning acquired UC Industries, a maker of foam board insulation, and bought Pilkington's insulation and industrial supply business. It also formed joint venture Alpha/Owens-Corning, the largest producer of polyester resin in North America.

The company bought Western Fiberglass Group in 1995. That year Owens-Corning Fiberglas changed its name to Owens Corning and recouped part of its asbestos-related charge when it received a $330 million arbitration settlement from one of its insurers. Owens Corning formed a joint venture in India in 1995. Asbestos-litigation charges led to another loss in 1996.

In 1998 falling insulation prices led the company to announce layoffs and a restructuring plan that included plant closures. To pay off debt, the company sold its half of Alpha/Owens-Corning to Alpha Corporation, marking its exit from polyester-resin manufacturing.

Seeking to end a liability issue that had dogged the company for a quarter of a century, Owens Corning agreed in 1998 to pay out $1.2 billion to settle 176,000 asbestos-related lawsuits. However, the deal dissolved in 1999 when the US Supreme Court disallowed the settlement. Owens Corning then set up a $2.6 billion reserve fund to settle the claims. Also that year the company formed a joint venture (Decillion) with Geon to make fiberglass and PVC composites. Still dogged by lawsuits that could eventually cost the company billions, the company filed for bankruptcy protection late in 2000.

In 2001 Owens Corning sold its engineered pipe systems business to joint venture partner Saudi Arabian Amiantit Company. Seeking a foothold in the growing acoustic ceiling market, it bought Wall Technology later that year.

Owens Corning increased its loose fill and thermacube insulation products line and capacity in 2002 in response to growing demand. It also acquired Woodbridge, Virginia-based Certified Basements, a basement finishing systems franchise.

Following a period of falling stock prices for the company, the New York Stock Exchange suspended its trading in December 2002. In early 2003 the company filed a bankruptcy reorganization plan to settle asbestos litigation. Under the plan, Owens Corning provided partial payments to its creditors (mainly through distributing common stock and notes of the new reorganized company) and its existing common stock was canceled. The company emerged from bankruptcy in 2006.

In 2007 it acquired Saint-Gobain's reinforcements and composite fabrics business, strengthening its position in the composites industry.

While the company focused growth on its composites business, it began trimming off other operations. Saint-Gobain acquired Owens Corning's vinyl siding business, Norandex, in 2007. Also that year, it sold its continuous filament mat business to AGY and its Fabwel composite panels business to Crane.

EXECUTIVES

Chairman, President, and CEO: Michael H. (Mike) Thaman, age 46, $7,263,190 total compensation
SVP and CFO: Duncan J. Palmer, age 45, $1,941,147 total compensation
SVP and Chief Supply Chain and Information Technology Officer: David L. Johns, age 51, $1,660,470 total compensation
SVP, General Counsel, and Secretary: Stephen K. (Steve) Krull, age 45, $1,624,880 total compensation
SVP Human Resources: Daniel T. (Dan) Smith
VP; President, Owens Corning Construction Services: William E. LeBaron, age 53
VP; President, Roofing and Asphalt Business: Sheree L. Bargabos, age 54, $1,782,950 total compensation
VP Sales, North American Building Materials Distribution: Curt A. Barker, age 53
VP and Chief Accounting Officer: Mark W. Mayer, age 52
VP Sales, North American Building Materials Distribution: Curt A. Barker, age 53
VP and Chief Innovation Officer: John Hillenbrand
VP Investor Relations and Corporate Communications: Scott A. Deitz, age 54
VP and Managing Director, Asia/Pacific Building Materials: Daniel Zhang, age 47
Group President, Composite Solutions Business: Charles E. (Chuck) Dana, age 54, $2,096,060 total compensation
Group President, Building Materials: Karel K. Czanderna, age 53
President, Insulating Systems Business: Roy D. Dean, age 50
Director, Building Science: Achilles Karagiozis
Auditors: PricewaterhouseCoopers LLP

LOCATIONS

HQ: Owens Corning
1 Owens Corning Pkwy., Toledo, OH 43659
Phone: 419-248-8000
Web: www.owenscorning.com

2009 Sales

	$ mil.	% of total
US	3,261	68
Asia/Pacific	604	12
Europe	523	11
Other	415	9
Total	**4,803**	**100**

PRODUCTS/OPERATIONS

2009 Sales by Segment

	$ mil.	% of total
Building Materials		
Roofing	1,898	38
Insulation	1,285	26
Other	141	3
Adjustments	(10)	—
Composites	1,633	33
Adjustments	(144)	—
Total	**4,803**	**100**

COMPETITORS

Associated Materials
CertainTeed
Champion Window
Deceuninck
GAF Materials
Johns Manville
PPG Industries
Saint-Gobain
SIG plc
TAMKO

HISTORICAL FINANCIALS

Company Type: Public

Income Statement

FYE: December 31

	REVENUE ($ mil.)	NET INCOME ($ mil.)	NET PROFIT MARGIN	EMPLOYEES
12/09	4,803	67	1.4%	16,000
12/08	5,847	(839)	—	18,000
12/07	4,978	96	1.9%	20,000
12/06	909	(65)	—	19,000
12/05	6,323	(4,099)	—	20,000
Annual Growth	**(6.6%)**	**—**	**—**	**(5.4%)**

2009 Year-End Financials

Debt ratio: 77.2%
Return on equity: —
Cash ($ mil.): 564
Long-term debt ($ mil.): 2,177
No. of shares (mil.): 128
Dividends
　Yield: —
　Payout: —
Current ratio: 1.97
Market value ($ mil.): 3,290

Stock History

NYSE: OC

	STOCK PRICE ($) FY Close	P/E High/Low		PER SHARE ($) Earnings	Dividends	Book Value
12/09	25.64	54	10	0.50	—	21.98
12/08	17.30	—	—	(6.56)	—	21.30
12/07	20.22	49	26	0.75	—	31.08
12/06	29.90	0	0	113.25	—	28.73
Annual Growth	**(5.0%)**			**—**	**—**	**—**

Owens-Illinois

Owens-Illinois (O-I) is involved in more toasts than Dick Clark and all Irish writers combined. The world's largest maker of glass containers, it touts a leading market presence in the regions in which it operates — North and South America, Europe, and the Asia/Pacific. O-I's glass containers include bottles in a wide range of shapes, sizes, and colors, used to hold beer, wine, liquor, as well as soft drinks, juice, and other beverages. It also makes glass containers for foods, such as soups, salad dressings, and dairy products, and for pharmaceuticals. Major customers include Anheuser-Busch, H.J. Heinz, and SABMiller.

Despite its depth of operations and industry dominance, the economic recession's impact on customer spending as well as unfavorable currency exchange rates chipped O-I's sales.

O-I is placing a priority on winning over customers that have shied away from glass packaging as well as encouraging existing ones to use more. To this end, its marketing efforts piggyback on the wave of sustainable packaging practices. Along with a variety of features and functions, the company highlights the benefits of glass recyclability. Moreover, O-I rolled out a wine bottle in 2009 that weighs roughly 28%

less than standard ones, boasting reduced manufacturing and transportation emissions, and delivery costs. The company is shrinking its own environmental footprint, as well. In 2007 O-I initiated a 10-year plan to cut its energy use by 50% and its carbon dioxide-equivalent emissions by 65%, in tandem with boosting its use of postconsumer recycled glass to 60%.

The company's plans for improved performance include acquisitions, new partnerships, and new plant construction that expand its presence in the Asia/Pacific region and Latin America. Since 1990 O-I has acquired more than 20 glass container businesses. Moving forward, O-I announced in mid-2010 that it is partnering with Thailand-based Berli Jucker Public Co. to purchase four beverage and food container manufacturing plants located in China and Southeast Asia. Of the total purchase price (around $222 million), O-I will pay $132 million.

O-I's expansion into developing, operationally less costly economies is accompanied by its consolidation of its more expensive manufacturing facilities, due to their older and less efficient equipment, located in regions where demand is maturing. In 2010 the company closed plants in Pennsylvania, Michigan, and California, cumulatively eliminating 760 jobs. The company shuttered a plant in Finland in 2009, cutting 100 jobs. Meanwhile in South America, the company has expanded its plant in Lurin, Peru, adding a second furnace that doubles the plant's capacity. O-I also is transferring its engineering resources from the US to a newly built facility neighboring its Peruvian plant and one in Argentina.

HISTORY

The Owens Bottle Machine Corp. was incorporated in Toledo, Ohio, in 1907 as the successor to a four-year-old New Jersey company of the same name. It initially grew by acquiring small glass companies. In 1929 Owens bought the Illinois Glass Co. (medical and pharmaceutical glass) and became Owens-Illinois Glass.

The company bought Libbey Glass (tableware) in 1935. Three years later Owens-Illinois and Corning Glass, which were both studying uses for glass fiber, began Owens-Corning Fiberglass, a joint venture with a virtual industry monopoly.

After WWII Owens-Illinois (O-I) started to diversify beyond glass. The company went public in 1952. In 1956 it bought National Container (cardboard boxes). It also created a semi-rigid plastic container that was adopted by bleach and detergent companies.

The introduction of the non-returnable bottle in the 1960s gave new life to the glass industry. During the late 1960s the company bought Lily Tulip Cups (sold in 1981). In the 1970s the company started producing specialty optical and TV glass.

With the glass industry foundering at the beginning of the 1980s, O-I invested over $600 million in its glass operations. In 1986 O-I refused an initial purchase offer by Kohlberg Kravis Roberts & Co. (KKR), but KKR raised the offer and O-I was sold and went private. Total debt after the LBO was $4.4 billion.

In the years following the LBO, the company sold its forest products, mortgage banking, and health care businesses. O-I went public again in 1991 and expanded its plastics business with the purchase of Specialty Packaging Products in 1992, which added trigger sprayers and finger pumps to its line. The next year the company expanded its South American operations. O-I spun off Libbey Glass as a separate public firm and sold 51% of its interest in Kimble Glass (specialty packaging and laboratory ware; the rest was sold in 1997). The company acquired a majority stake in Ballarpur Industries, one of India's largest makers of glass containers.

In 1997 O-I acquired assets of a bankrupt competitor, Anchor Glass, which gave it more than a 40% share of the US glass container market. In 1999 the company sold its UK-based glass container maker, Rockware Group, to Ireland-based container maker Ardagh, and its Chicago Heights pharmaceutical glass business to Germany-based glassmaker Gerresheimer Glas.

In 2000, following a short-lived victory for the company in asbestos-related litigation, a US district judge in Texas overturned a $1.6 billion default judgment to be awarded the company by former asbestos maker T&N Ltd. Charges related to asbestos litigation and restructuring fees cost the company dearly in 2000 as it posted a $270 million loss for the year.

In 2001 O-I sold its Harbor Capital Advisors business to the Netherlands-based Robeco Groep for an estimated $490 million.

In 2003 Joseph Lemieux stepped down as CEO of the company. Steven McCracken was named president and CEO. McCracken replaced Lemieux as chairman in 2004.

O-I completed its acquisition of BSN Glasspack, Europe's #2 glass container maker, for about $1.3 billion the same year. The deal made O-I Europe's largest container company. Late in 2004 O-I sold its American and European blow-molded plastics operations to Graham Packaging Company.

Late in 2006 Steven McCracken resigned as chairman and CEO. Company board member Albert Stroucken, who held similar leadership roles at H.B. Fuller, succeeded McCracken.

In 2007 the company sold its plastics packaging business (O-I Plastics), which manufactured prescription bottles, tamper-proof closures, and injection-molded containers, to Rexam for $1.8 billion.

EXECUTIVES

Chairman, President, and CEO:
Albert P. L. (Al) Stroucken, age 62,
$8,762,311 total compensation
SVP and CFO: Edward C. (Ed) White, age 62,
$2,680,345 total compensation
SVP and Chief Human Resources Officer:
Stephen P. (Steve) Malia
SVP Strategic Planning and General Counsel:
James W. Baehren, age 59,
$1,762,366 total compensation
SVP and Chief Process Improvement Officer:
Ed Snyder
VP Sustainability: Jay Scripter
VP and Chief Strategy Officer: Gregory T. (Greg) Sipla, age 43
VP and CIO: Ron White
VP Global Product Innovation: Michael Lonsway
VP and General Counsel: Philip McWeeny
VP Global Quality: Shaun McMackin
VP Glass Container Research and Development:
Robert E. Lachmiller
VP and Chief Procurement Officer: Radhika Batra
VP Sales and Marketing, O-I North America:
Abbott Wolfe
VP and Treasurer: Catherine E. Neel, age 48
VP Investor Relations: John Haudrich
VP and Chief Communications Officer: Barbara Owens

President, O-I North America: Miguel Escobar
President, O-I Europe: Jose A. Lorente,
$2,097,633 total compensation
President, Global Glass Operations:
L. Richard (Rich) Crawford, age 49,
$2,095,790 total compensation
President, O-I Asia Pacific: Greg W. J. Ridder,
$1,165,691 total compensation
President, O-I Latin America: Andres Lopez
Auditors: Ernst & Young LLP

LOCATIONS

HQ: Owens-Illinois, Inc.
1 Michael Owens Way, Perrysburg, OH 43551
Phone: 567-336-5000   **Fax:** 419-247-7107
Web: www.o-i.com

2009 Sales

	$ mil.	% of total
Europe	2,917.6	41
North America	2,074.3	29
South America	1,104.1	16
Asia/Pacific	925.0	13
Other regions	45.5	1
Total	**7,066.5**	**100**

COMPETITORS

Alcoa
Amcor
Anchor Glass
AptarGroup
Ball Corp.
Bemis
Berry Plastics
BWAY
Consolidated Container
Constar International
Crown Holdings
Graham Packaging
Jarden
Newell Rubbermaid
Plastipak Holdings
Rexam
Saint-Gobain
Saint-Gobain Containers
Sealed Air Corp.
Silgan
Sonoco Products
Tetra Pak
Tupperware Brands
Vitro

HISTORICAL FINANCIALS

Company Type: Public

Income Statement

	REVENUE ($ mil.)	NET INCOME ($ mil.)	NET PROFIT MARGIN	EMPLOYEES
			FYE: December 31	
12/09	7,067	198	2.8%	22,000
12/08	7,885	258	3.3%	23,000
12/07	7,679	1,341	17.5%	24,000
12/06	7,524	(28)	—	28,000
12/05	7,190	(559)	—	28,200
Annual Growth	(0.4%)	—	—	(6.0%)

2009 Year-End Financials

Debt ratio: 211.8%
Return on equity: 15.3%
Cash ($ mil.): 812
Current ratio: 1.37
Long-term debt ($ mil.): 3,258

No. of shares (mil.): 164
Dividends
  Yield: —
  Payout: —
Market value ($ mil.): 5,376

Stock History

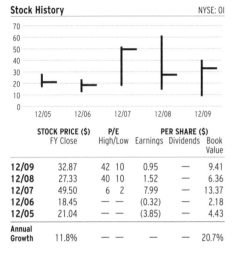

NYSE: OI

	STOCK PRICE ($) FY Close	P/E High/Low		PER SHARE ($) Earnings	Dividends	Book Value
12/09	32.87	42	10	0.95	—	9.41
12/08	27.33	40	10	1.52	—	6.36
12/07	49.50	6	2	7.99	—	13.37
12/06	18.45	—	—	(0.32)	—	2.18
12/05	21.04	—	—	(3.85)	—	4.43
Annual Growth	**11.8%**	—	—	—	—	**20.7%**

PACCAR Inc

Old PACCARs never die, they just get a new Peterbilt. PACCAR is one of the world's largest designers and manufacturers of big rig trucks. Its lineup of light-, medium-, and heavy-duty trucks includes the Kenworth, Peterbilt, and DAF nameplates. The company also manufactures and distributes aftermarket truck parts for these brands. PACCAR's other products include Braden, Carco, and Gearmatic industrial winches. With the exception of a few company-owned branches, PACCAR's trucks and parts are sold through independent dealers. The company's PACCAR Financial Services and PacLease subsidiaries offer financing and truck leasing, respectively.

The company delivers products and services to customers in more than 100 countries through a dealer network of about 1,800 locations. PACCAR competes in the European light/medium market with DAF cab-over-engine trucks assembled in the UK by Leyland. PACCAR's trucks are used worldwide for hauling freight, petroleum, wood products, and construction and other materials. The truck segment manufactures from three plants in the US (the Peterbilt plant in Nashville was shuttered in 2009), three in Europe, and one each in Australia, Canada, and Mexico. PACCAR continues to examine business opportunities in Asia, with a primary focus on China and India.

Commercial trucks and related replacement parts comprise the largest segment of the company's business. With the onslaught of the 2008 economic recession and a drop in commercial truck sales, the company responded by reducing its headcount by 14%. Regardless of the downturn, PACCAR continues to increase its capital investments and related research and development spending in order to design and launch a new range of vehicles, increase global production capacity, and develop a new line of engines. The latter it achieved in 2010 with the introduction of its diesel MX Engine, which will be installed in Kenworth and Peterbilt trucks in the summer. The engine was designed to meet the emissions regulations set forth by the Environmental Protection Agency (EPA) in 2010.

The company views the implementation of updated North American engine emission standards as positive; some operators may be encouraged to advance their truck purchases. To meet demand, PACCAR completed its engine assembly plant in Mississippi and is installing machinery and assembly lines; additionally, it expanded its manufacturing capacity in Australia. In 2008 the company unveiled an enhanced engine research and development facility at PACCAR's Technical Center and opened a new parts distribution center in Budapest.

The Pigott family, descendants of PACCAR's founder, owns about 7% of the company.

HISTORY

William Pigott founded the Seattle Car Manufacturing Company in 1905 to produce railroad cars for timber transport. Finding immediate success, Pigott began to make other kinds of railcars in 1906. When the Seattle plant burned the next year, the company moved near Renton, Washington. In 1911 Pigott renamed the company Seattle Car & Foundry.

In 1917 Seattle Car merged with the Twohy Brothers of Portland. The new company, Pacific Car & Foundry, was sold to American Car & Foundry in 1924. Pacific Car then diversified into bus manufacturing, structural steel fabrications, and metal technology.

Pacific Car was in decline by 1934 when William's son Paul bought it; since then the company has remained under family management. Paul Pigott added Hofius Steel and Equipment and Tricoach, a bus manufacturer, in 1936. The company entered the truck-making business with the 1945 purchase of Seattle-based Kenworth.

In the 1950s Pacific Car became the industry leader in mechanical refrigerator car production. It began producing off-road, heavy trucks and acquired Peterbilt Trucks of Oakland (1958). To augment its winch business, Pacific Car bought Canada's Gearmatic in 1963.

The company moved its headquarters to Bellevue, Washington, in 1969 and changed its name to PACCAR in 1971. Acquisitions in the 1970s included Wagner Mining Equipment (1973); International Car, the largest US caboose producer (1975); and Braden Winch (1977). In 1980 PACCAR acquired UK-based Foden Trucks.

Demand for smaller trucks caused heavy-truck sales to drop 35% between 1979 and 1986, leading PACCAR to close two factories, its first closures in 41 years. In 1987 PACCAR bought Trico Industries (oil-drilling equipment). Also that year PACCAR entered the auto parts sales market, buying Al's Auto Supply; in 1988, it bought Grand Auto.

Truck demand hit a nine-year low in 1990. PACCAR responded by cutting its workforce by 11% that year and withdrawing from the auto parts wholesale market in 1991. The following year PACCAR acquired an interest in Wood Group ESP, a maker and servicer of oil-field equipment. In 1993 PACCAR bought Caterpillar's line of winches.

In 1995 PACCAR opened a truck assembly plant in South Africa and bought the rest of VILPAC, its truck-making joint venture in Mexico. When workers in Quebec went on strike, the company closed the plant after eight months and shifted production to Mexico.

PACCAR expanded in Europe in 1996 by acquiring medium- and heavy-duty truck maker DAF Trucks (the Netherlands). Charles Pigott retired in 1996, and his son Mark became chairman and CEO. In 1997 PACCAR sold Trico Industries to EVI. The next year PACCAR bought light- and medium-duty truck maker Leyland Trucks (UK). After an $80 million renovation, the company began producing medium-duty trucks in 1999 at its Quebec plant, which was idled after the strike. That year the company sold its Al's Auto Supply and Grand Auto parts retail operations to CSK Auto for $143 million.

Slow sales of large trucks prompted the company to lay off about one-third of its hourly — and almost one-fifth of its salaried — Peterbilt workers in 2000. In 2001 PACCAR entered a long-term contract with Cummins for the supply of heavy-duty engines. Later that year, in order to bring production in line with worldwide demand, PACCAR closed two truck manufacturing facilities — the Seattle Kenworth plant and a Foden plant in the UK.

In an effort to dedicate production efforts of its DAF branded trucks, PACCAR retired the Foden Trucks line in 2006.

EXECUTIVES

Chairman and CEO: Mark C. Pigott, age 56, $4,198,201 total compensation
Vice Chairman: Thomas E. (Tom) Plimpton, age 60, $2,716,027 total compensation
President: James G. (Jim) Cardillo, age 61, $2,249,315 total compensation
EVP: Daniel D. (Dan) Sobic, age 56, $1,114,667 total compensation
SVP: Robert J. (Bob) Christensen, age 53
SVP: Ronald E. (Ron) Armstrong, age 54, $999,388 total compensation
VP and CIO: T. Kyle Quinn, age 48
VP and Controller: Michael T. Barkley, age 54
VP and General Counsel: David C. Anderson, age 56
VP Human Resources: Jack LeVier
VP; President, DAF Trucks N.V.: Aad L. Goudriaan, age 50
Secretary: Janice M. D'Amato
Treasurer: Robin E. Easton
Auditors: Ernst & Young LLP

LOCATIONS

HQ: PACCAR Inc
777 106th Ave. NE, Bellevue, WA 98004
Phone: 425-468-7400   **Fax:** 425-468-8216
Web: www.paccar.com

2009 Sales

	$ mil.	% of total
US	3,594.4	44
Europe	2,828.3	35
Other regions	1,663.8	21
Total	**8,086.5**	**100**

PRODUCTS/OPERATIONS

2009 Sales

	$ mil.	% of total
Trucks & other	7,076.7	87
Financial services	1,009.8	13
Total	**8,086.5**	**100**

2009 Sales by Product

	$ mil.	% of total
Trucks	5,103.3	63
Aftermarket parts	1,890.7	23
Other	1,092.5	14
Total	**8,086.5**	**100**

Selected Divisions and Subsidiaries

DAF Trucks N.V. (The Netherlands)
Dynacraft (battery cables, hose assemblies, and air conditioning hardlines)
Kenworth
Kenworth Mexicana S.A. de C.V.
Leyland Trucks Limited (UK)
PACCAR Australia Pty. Ltd.
PACCAR Engines
PACCAR Financial Corp.
PACCAR Mexico, S.A. de C.V.
PACCAR of Canada Ltd.
  Canadian Kenworth Co.
  Peterbilt of Canada
PACCAR Parts
PACCAR Winch

COMPETITORS

Daimler
Fiat
Ford Motor
General Motors
Hino Motors
Isuzu
Iveco S.p.A.
Mack Trucks
Morris Material Handling
Navistar International
Oshkosh Truck
Scania
UD Trucks
Volvo
Volvo Trucks

HISTORICAL FINANCIALS

Company Type: Public

Income Statement

FYE: December 31

	REVENUE ($ mil.)	NET INCOME ($ mil.)	NET PROFIT MARGIN	EMPLOYEES
12/09	8,087	112	1.6%	15,200
12/08	14,973	1,018	6.8%	18,700
12/07	15,222	1,227	8.1%	21,800
12/06	16,454	1,496	9.1%	21,000
12/05	14,057	1,133	8.1%	21,900
Annual Growth	(12.9%)	(43.9%)	—	(8.7%)

2009 Year-End Financials

Debt ratio: 64.6%
Return on equity: 2.3%
Cash ($ mil.): 1,837
Current ratio: 2.33
Long-term debt ($ mil.): 3,062
No. of shares (mil.): 365
Dividends
  Yield: 1.5%
  Payout: 174.2%
Market value ($ mil.): 13,235

Stock History

NASDAQ (GS): PCAR

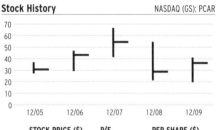

	STOCK PRICE ($) FY Close	P/E High/Low		PER SHARE ($) Earnings	Dividends	Book Value
12/09	36.27	130	66	0.31	0.54	13.99
12/08	28.60	19	8	2.78	0.72	13.28
12/07	54.48	20	13	3.29	0.65	13.74
12/06	43.27	12	8	3.97	0.51	12.21
12/05	30.77	12	10	2.92	0.39	10.69
Annual Growth	4.2%	—	—	(42.9%)	8.5%	6.9%

Pall Corporation

Pall takes liquids and gases to the cleaners. The company makes filtration and separation systems designed to remove solid, liquid, and gaseous contaminants from a variety of materials. Pall's industrial business segment makes filtration products for general industrial applications, including water purification, as well as for use in the aerospace and microelectronics industries. The company's industrial business units include Pall Aeropower. Products of Pall's life sciences segment are used to help develop and manufacture drugs and for medical functions such as removing white blood cells from blood. Most of Pall's sales are made outside the US.

The company also makes filter media from chemical film, metals, paper, and plastics, and makes metal and plastic housings for its filters. In 2010 Pall's strategic plan called for it to focus on geographic expansion and on beefing up its high-growth markets (such as biotechnology) by making complementary acquisitions and by developing more specially engineered filtration systems, which offer long-term revenue potential.

In 2008 Pall acquired GeneSystems, a France-based biotechnology company that has developed an easy-to-use and cost-effective molecular diagnostics platform. In 2010 it bought MicroReactor Technologies, a US-based biotechnology firm specializing in miniature bioreactor equipment and disposables.

HISTORY

Canadian-born chemist David Pall worked on the Manhattan Project, helping develop systems to refine uranium for the first atomic bomb. In 1946 he founded Micro Metallic to develop filters for commercial applications. Pall added Abraham Krasnoff, a CPA, in 1950. The company went public in 1957 and was renamed Pall Corporation. During the 1960s it specialized in aircraft hydraulics and fuel systems for the defense industry. In 1969 Krasnoff became CEO.

In the late 1970s and during the 1980s, the company moved into the growing semiconductor and biotechnology industries. This process accelerated after the defense industry was hit by budget cuts late in the 1980s.

Pall researchers announced in 1995 the development of a filter that reduces the levels of HIV in blood serum to below detectable levels. In 1997 the company bought Gelman Sciences, maker of polymeric membranes and specialized medical disposable filters.

In 1998 Pall acquired Germany-based Rochem, an osmosis filtration system manufacturer, and entered a technology partnership with VI Technologies (Vitex) for exclusive marketing rights to Vitex's viral and bacterial inactivation chemistry. The following year Pall signed a $6 million water-purification deal with the Pittsburgh Water and Sewer Authority. Also in 1999 Pall announced a restructuring plan calling for job cuts and other spending reductions. The company sold its Well Technology division (filtration equipment and drilling services to oil and gas companies) to Oiltools International in 1999.

The German Red Cross Transfusion Center awarded Pall a $6 million contract for blood filtration equipment in 2000 after the German government mandated that all transfused blood must be filtered. Highlights in 2001 included alliances with biopharmaceutical companies

QIAGEN N.V. and Stedim SA. In early 2002 Pall completed the acquisition of the Filtration and Separations Group from US Filter (now Siemens Water Technologies) for about $360 million. In 2003 Pall purchased Whatman HemaSure, the blood filtration business of Whatman plc.

Pall expanded in 2004 by buying BioSepra, a provider of chromatography technologies (used for protein purification and optimization), from Ciphergen Biosystems for about $32 million.

EXECUTIVES

Chairman, President, and CEO: Eric Krasnoff, age 58, $5,842,621 total compensation
COO: Roberto Perez, age 60, $1,845,411 total compensation
CFO and Treasurer: Lisa McDermott, age 44, $1,872,352 total compensation
CTO: Michael Egholm
SVP Pall Water Processing: Tony Wachinski
SVP, General Counsel, and Secretary: Sandra Marino, age 39, $1,334,512 total compensation
VP; President, Life Sciences: Yves Baratelli
VP Investor Relations and Communications: Patricia Iannucci
VP, Corporate Controller, and Chief Accounting Officer: Francis (Frank) Moschella
Applications Manager, Water Systems, Middle-East North Africa: Jan Bultiauw
Global Marketing Manager, Wine and Spirits: Nicole Madrid
Auditors: KPMG LLP

LOCATIONS

HQ: Pall Corporation
  25 Harbor Park Dr., Port Washington, NY 11050
Phone: 516-484-5400   **Fax:** 516-801-9754
Web: www.pall.com

2009 Sales

	$ mil.	% of total
Europe	960.3	41
Western Hemisphere	769.7	33
Asia	599.2	26
Total	**2,329.2**	**100**

PRODUCTS/OPERATIONS

2009 Sales

	$ mil.	% of total
Industrial		
Energy, Water & Process Technologies	887.7	38
Aerospace & Transportation	290.0	12
Microelectronics	211.0	9
Life Sciences		
BioPharmaceuticals	550.6	24
Medical	389.9	17
Total	**2,329.2**	**100**

COMPETITORS

3M Purification
CLARCOR
Donaldson Company
Entegris
ESCO Technologies
GE Healthcare
Merck Millipore
Parker Hannifin
Sartorius
Siemens Water Technologies

HISTORICAL FINANCIALS
Company Type: Public

Income Statement
FYE: July 31

	REVENUE ($ mil.)	NET INCOME ($ mil.)	NET PROFIT MARGIN	EMPLOYEES
7/09	2,329	196	8.4%	10,200
7/08	2,572	217	8.4%	10,600
7/07	2,250	128	5.7%	10,700
7/06	2,017	146	7.2%	10,828
7/05	1,902	141	7.4%	10,400
Annual Growth	5.2%	8.6%	—	(0.5%)

2009 Year-End Financials
Debt ratio: 51.8%
Return on equity: 17.4%
Cash ($ mil.): 414
Current ratio: 2.19
Long-term debt ($ mil.): 578
No. of shares (mil.): 117
Dividends
Yield: 1.9%
Payout: 34.1%
Market value ($ mil.): 3,509

Stock History
NYSE: PLL

	STOCK PRICE ($) FY Close	P/E High/Low		PER SHARE ($) Earnings	Dividends	Book Value
7/09	30.08	26	11	1.64	0.56	9.55
7/08	40.42	25	19	1.76	0.62	9.77
7/07	41.52	48	25	1.02	0.35	9.09
7/06	26.08	28	22	1.16	0.43	10.10
7/05	30.97	28	20	1.12	0.39	9.77
Annual Growth	(0.7%)	—	—	10.0%	9.5%	(0.6%)

Panera Bread

Panera Bread is ready for an epochal change in American eating habits. The company is a leader in the quick-casual restaurant business with about 1,400 bakery-cafes in 40 states and Canada. Its locations, which operate under the banners Panera Bread, Saint Louis Bread Co., and Paradise Bakery & Café, offer made-to-order sandwiches using a variety of artisan breads, including Asiago cheese bread, focaccia, and its classic sourdough bread. The chain's menu also features soups, salads, and gourmet coffees. In addition, Panera sells its bread, bagels, and pastries to go. More than 580 of its locations are company-operated, while the rest are run by franchisees.

Like many other dining operators, Panera (which is Latin for "time for bread") relies on a mix of corporate-run locations and franchising to expand and operate its restaurant chain. The company-owned stores account for the lion's share of Panera's sales (about 85%) and give the company a significant footprint from which to control the consistency of food and service quality. Panera's franchising efforts, meanwhile, allow the company to expand into new markets

without the expense of construction and operation. Local franchisees pay the company royalties and other fees in order to use the Panera brand and other intellectual property. The company also supplies its franchise locations with fresh dough and other ingredients through a network of more than 20 production and distribution facilities.

Panera was a pioneer in the quick-casual dining segment, which offers quick counter service but boasts higher-quality ingredients. The chain built significant brand loyalty by targeting suburban markets with its menu of European-inspired sandwich creations. It competes with other national fast-casual chains such as California Pizza Kitchen, Chipotle Mexican Grill, and Einstein Bros. Bagels (operated by Einstein Noah Restaurant Group), as well as #1 coffee house chain Starbucks.

Once focused on rapid expansion, Panera has slowed the growth of its chain to focus on cost containment and boosting traffic at its existing locations due in part to the economic slowdown that took its toll on the restaurant business during 2009. The company has used special menu offers to help draw new customers while price increases have helped boost revenue.

The company did expand its brand portfolio during 2009, acquiring the remaining 49% of Paradise Bakery it didn't already own for about $22 million. The company had purchased its original stake in the business in 2007. Paradise Bakery boasts about 70 bakery cafés mostly in the Southwest. Panera also added about 50 new locations during 2009 compared to about 100 bakery openings the previous year.

Bill Moreton took over as CEO of Panera in 2010, replacing Ron Shaich who remained chairman. A veteran of the company, Moreton was promoted from co-COO. Shaich co-founded the business under the name Au Bon Pain, a brand now owned by Boston-based ABP Corporation. He controls more than 10% of Panera's voting stock.

HISTORY

Panera Bread traces its roots to a restaurant opened in Boston by French commercial oven manufacturer Pavailler. Au Bon Pain, opened in 1976, was intended as a showcase for Pavailler's ovens. The scent of hot croissants (and money) caught the attention of Louis Kane, who bought the business in 1978 and began expanding in Boston. Ron Shaich (pronounced "shake") joined Kane in 1981, and together they formed Au Bon Pain Co., Inc. The chain grew rapidly until the early 1990s, saturating the high-traffic areas in eastern US cities. After its IPO in 1991, Au Bon Pain began making acquisitions, including Saint Louis Bread in 1993.

Saint Louis Bread was founded in 1987 when Ken Rosenthal, spurred into the restaurant business by his brother, opened his first cafe in Kirkwood, Missouri. Based on sourdough bakeries in San Francisco, the concept eventually spread to five stores by 1990 and nearly 20 units two years later. In 1993 the company made *Inc.* magazine's list of the 500 fastest-growing companies. At the end of that year, Au Bon Pain paid $24 million for the company, franchising its new units outside of the St. Louis area as Panera Bread. Rosenthal stayed on with Au Bon Pain as chairman of its new chain before leaving to become a major franchisee.

By 1995 the company was facing new competition from coffee and bagel shops. Flat sales and

sharp price increases for butter hurt the chain's bottom line. By 1997 the company had added bagels to its menu and was considering extensive renovations. It ultimately decided the chain had peaked in the US, and it limited expansion to countries with dense urban areas and emerging middle classes, such as Brazil and Indonesia.

During 1998 Au Bon Pain's Panera Bread unit perked up with new stores and growing sales. But that success was offset by the company's namesake chain, where sales continued to struggle. The company eventually sold the Au Bon Pain chain in 1999 to investment firm Bruckmann, Rosser, Sherrill, and Co. for $73 million. (Bruckmann, Rosser later sold the chain to UK-based Compass Group, which ran the eateries through its subsidiary ABP Corporation until it sold a majority stake to a management group.) Shaich remained with the company, which was renamed Panera Bread, as chairman and CEO. Panera Bread later moved its headquarters back to the St. Louis area.

In 2001 president and COO Rich Postle resigned to run a joint venture with Panera Bread to build and manage 40 bakery-cafes in the northern Virginia and central Pennsylvania regions.

The company introduced its new upscale takeout program, Via Panera, in 2004. With Via Panera, the company simplified the to-go ordering process while upgrading its customization, particularly for larger orders. Panera Bread also released its first cookbook that year, *The Panera Bread Cookbook: Breadmaking Essentials and Recipes from America's Favorite Bakery-Cafe*.

In 2007 the company acquired a 51% stake in Paradise Bakery & Café, the operator of a small bakery-cafe chain in the Southwest, for about $20 million. (Panera acquired the remaining stake for about $22 million two years later.)

EXECUTIVES

Chairman: Ronald M. (Ron) Shaich, age 56, $1,919,351 total compensation
President, CEO, and Director: William W. (Bill) Moreton, age 50
EVP and Co-COO: John M. Maguire, age 44, $874,681 total compensation
EVP and Co-COO: Cedric J. (Rick) Vanzura, age 46
EVP and Chief Concept Officer: Scott G. Davis, age 46
SVP and CFO: Jeffrey W. (Jeff) Kip, age 42, $677,556 total compensation
SVP, Chief Franchise Officer, and Assistant Secretary: Michael J. (Mike) Kupstas, age 53, $729,154 total compensation
SVP and Chief Supply Chain Officer: Mark A. Borland, age 57
SVP and Chief Development Officer: Michael J. Nolan, age 50
SVP and Chief People Officer: Rebecca A. Fine, age 47
SVP and Chief Company and Joint Venture Operations Officer: William H. (Hank) Simpson, age 47
SVP and Chief Marketing Officer: Michael Simon
SVP and CIO: Thomas C. (Tom) Kish, age 44
SVP, Chief Legal Officer, General Counsel, and Secretary: Scott G. Blair, age 52
VP and Controller: Amy L. Kuzdowicz, age 40
Chief Accounting Officer and Assistant Controller: Mark D. Wooldridge, age 35
Director Product Development: John Taylor
Auditors: PricewaterhouseCoopers LLP

LOCATIONS

HQ: Panera Bread Company
6710 Clayton Rd., Richmond Heights, MO 63117
Phone: 314-633-7100   **Fax:** 314-633-7200
Web: www.panerabread.com

2009 Locations

	No.
US	
Florida	116
Illinois	103
Ohio	98
California	91
New York	70
Pennsylvania	69
Missouri	66
Virginia	63
Michigan	62
New Jersey	48
Texas	47
Massachusetts	44
Maryland	42
North Carolina	42
Indiana	38
Arizona	35
Colorado	35
Georgia	32
Tennessee	28
Minnesota	26
Wisconsin	24
Connecticut	21
Kansas	18
Iowa	17
Kentucky	17
Oklahoma	17
Alabama	14
South Carolina	14
Nebraska	13
Washington	12
New Hampshire	9
Oregon	9
West Virginia	27
Canada	3
Total	**1,380**

PRODUCTS/OPERATIONS

2009 Sales

	$ mil.	% of total
Restaurants	1,153.2	85
Foodservice distribution	121.9	9
Franchising	78.4	6
Total	**1,353.5**	**100**

2009 Locations

	No.
Franchised	795
Company-owned	585
Total	**1,380**

COMPETITORS

ABP Corporation	Einstein Noah
Boston Market	Fresh Enterprises
Bruegger's	Potbelly Sandwich Works
California Pizza Kitchen	Qdoba Restaurants
Caribou Coffee	Quiznos
CBC Restaurant	Starbucks
Chipotle	Subway

HISTORICAL FINANCIALS

Company Type: Public

Income Statement				FYE: Last Tuesday in December
	REVENUE ($ mil.)	NET INCOME ($ mil.)	NET PROFIT MARGIN	EMPLOYEES
12/09	1,354	86	6.4%	12,100
12/08	1,299	67	5.2%	23,300
12/07	1,067	58	5.4%	23,400
12/06	829	59	7.1%	17,400
12/05	640	52	8.2%	13,900
Annual Growth	**20.6%**	**13.3%**	**—**	**(3.4%)**

2009 Year-End Financials

Debt ratio: 4.3%
Return on equity: 15.8%
Cash ($ mil.): 246
Current ratio: 2.26
Long-term debt ($ mil.): 26

No. of shares (mil.): 31
Dividends
  Yield: —
  Payout: —
Market value ($ mil.): 2,083

Stock History

NASDAQ (GS): PNRA

	STOCK PRICE ($) FY Close	P/E High/Low		PER SHARE ($) Earnings	Dividends	Book Value
12/09	66.94	25	15	2.78	—	19.19
12/08	52.24	29	14	2.22	—	15.91
12/07	35.82	35	19	1.79	—	14.34
12/06	55.91	41	25	1.84	—	12.78
12/05	65.68	44	24	1.65	—	10.19
Annual Growth	**0.5%**	**—**	**—**	**13.9%**	**—**	**17.2%**

The Pantry

If you've ever passed through the Carolinas on business, or made the drive to Disney World, chances are The Pantry has provided fuel for your car and body. The company is the leading convenience store operator in the southeastern US with more than 1,660 shops in about a dozen states. (Florida accounts for more than a quarter of the company's sales.) Most of the company's stores do business under the Kangaroo Express banner. Other store names include Golden Gallon, Lil' Champ, The Pantry (naturally), and Petro Express. The stores sell beverages, candy, gasoline, magazines, and tobacco products, among other items. Fuel accounts for about three-quarters of the company's sales.

About a third of the company's outlets, which are conventional in size (about 2,800 sq. ft.), are located near such tourist destinations as Myrtle Beach and Hilton Head, South Carolina, and Orlando, Florida, and another 25% along major interstates and highways.

Over the past few years the convenience store operator has been busy converting stores to the Kangaroo Express name in an effort to establish a consistent identity in the Southeast, much like its rivals 7-Eleven and Couche-Tard (Circle K) have developed consistent national brands. Currently, more than 1,550 of its locations are branded Kangaroo or Kangaroo Express.

The fast-growing firm has used a roll-up strategy of acquiring other businesses within its industry in order to grow in the Southeast. After a brief hiatus in 2008 due to tough retail environment and record gas prices, in mid-2009 The Pantry acquired 38 convenience stores from Herndon Oil. The purchase included about 30 shops in Mobile, Alabama, as well as locations in Florida, Louisiana, and Mississippi. Previously, the company purchased about 150 stores, including 66 Petro Express convenience stores in North and South Carolina, in 2007.

The Pantry is working to increase merchandise sales, especially foodservice and private label products, which carry substantially higher margins than gasoline sales. To this end, the company in 2010 began test marketing freshly made to-go food items (such as sandwiches and salads) and coffee at about 45 of its Raleigh, North Carolina, stores; it plans to extend the offerings to some 60 stores in Charlotte by December.

About 230 stores have fast-food outlets, including Subway, Church's, and Hardee's.

HISTORY

North Carolina businessmen Sam Wornom and Truby Proctor (president of Lee Moore Oil Co.) founded The Pantry in 1967 in Sanford, North Carolina. The chain added new stores by borrowing against its existing stores, paying the debt with new sales.

The Pantry had grown to about 480 outlets in 1987 when investment firm Montrose Capital bought Wornom's stake. Founded by former Duke University business professor Clay Hamner, Montrose's shareholders included J. B. Fuqua (after whom the Duke business school is named), the late Dave Thomas (the Wendy's fast-food chain founder), and Wayne Rogers (Trapper John in the TV series M*A*S*H). Montrose gained control of The Pantry when it acquired half of Proctor's shares in 1990. Proctor remained as CEO.

With poor sales, the company restructured during the early 1990s, closing unprofitable stores and cutting costs. After struggling in 1991 and 1992, The Pantry made a slim profit in 1993. However, burdened by debt, the company was without the cash to make further substantive acquisitions, and it resumed its annual losses the following year.

In 1995 Proctor sold his remaining shares to Freeman Spogli & Co., a California-based investment firm specializing in management-led buyouts, and Chase Manhattan Capital. The next year Freeman Spogli and Chase Manhattan acquired the rest of the company from Montrose. Freeman Spogli owned 76% of The Pantry and Chase Manhattan owned 23% until more shares were issued to management and directors. Peter Sodini, a former CEO with supermarket chain Purity Supreme (acquired by Stop & Shop), became CEO that year.

After a string of small acquisitions in early 1997, The Pantry more than doubled in size by paying about $135 million to Docks U.S.A. for the Lil' Champ Food Stores convenience store chain. Lil' Champ — named after founder Julian Jackson, a bantamweight boxing champion in the 1930s — had 489 outlets, including 150 outlets in Jacksonville, Florida.

The Pantry continued to bulk up in 1998, acquiring nearly 155 stores through seven separate purchases of small chains. The biggest purchases among them included Quick Stop, a 75-store chain in the Carolinas, and 41 Zip Mart stores in North Carolina and eastern Virginia. The company exited the Georgia market that year.

In early 1999 The Pantry acquired 121 Handy Way stores in central Florida, many of which operated fast-food outlets such as Hardee's and Subway. The Pantry went public that year to raise money to pay nearly $450 million in debt stemming from its acquisitions. Shortly thereafter, the company bought 53 Depot Food Store outlets in Georgia and South Carolina from R & H Maxxon.

In late 1999 The Pantry added the 49-store Kangaroo chain in Georgia, and in early 2000 it purchased the On-The-Way Foods Stores chain of 12 stores in Virginia and North Carolina. Other purchases in 2000 furthering the company's southeastern US expansion included 33 MiniMart and Big K chain stores, and 26 Fast Lane convenience stores in Louisiana and Mississippi from R.R. Morrison and Son.

In 2003 The Pantry reached agreements with BP Products and Citgo Petroleum to brand and supply most of its gasoline for the next five years. In October the company completed the acquisition of the 138-store Golden Gallon chain from Ahold USA. The Pantry acquired D & D Oil Co. (operator of 53 convenience stores under the Cowboys banner in Alabama, Georgia, and Mississippi) in 2005.

In 2006 the company acquired the 38-store Shop-A-Snak Food Mart convenience store chain in Alabama, doubling its store count in the state. It closed on 66 Petro Express convenience stores in North and South Carolina and its affiliated wholesale fuels business Carolina Petroleum Distributors in 2007.

In June 2009 the company acquired 38 convenience stores from Herndon Oil Co. Also that summer, the company moved its corporate headquarters from Sanford to Cary, North Carolina. In September CEO Peter Sondini retired after 10 years at the helm. He was succeeded by Terrance Marks, previously an executive with Coca-Cola Enterprises.

EXECUTIVES

Chairman: Edwin J. (Ed) Holman, age 63
President, CEO, and Director:
 Terrance M. (Terry) Marks, age 49
EVP, CFO, and Secretary: Frank G. Paci, age 52, $1,324,394 total compensation
SVP Field Operations: R. Brad Williams, age 39, $761,484 total compensation
SVP Fuels and Contruction: Keith S. Bell, age 46, $837,590 total compensation
CIO: Paul M. Lemerise, age 64
VP Food Service: Brandon Frampton
VP Marketing: Michael Knight, age 53
Corporate Controller: Berry Epley
Director, Total Rewards: Diana King
Auditors: Deloitte & Touche LLP

LOCATIONS

HQ: The Pantry, Inc.
 305 Gregson Dr., Cary, NC 27511
Phone: 919-774-6700   **Fax:** 919-774-3329
Web: www.thepantry.com

2009 Stores

	No.
Florida	440
North Carolina	384
South Carolina	284
Georgia	132
Alabama	114
Tennessee	104
Mississippi	100
Virginia	50
Kentucky	29
Louisiana	27
Indiana	9
Total	**1,673**

PRODUCTS/OPERATIONS

2009 Sales

	$ mil.	% of total
Gasoline	4,731.2	74
Merchandise	1,658.9	26
Total	**6,390.1**	**100**

2009 Merchandise Sales

	% of total
Tobacco products	34
Packaged beverages	16
Beer & wine	16
General merchandise, health & beauty care	6
Fast food service	5
Self-service fast foods & beverages	5
Salty snacks	4
Candy	4
Services	3
Dairy products	2
Bread & cakes	2
Grocery & other merchandise	2
Newspapers & magazines	1
Total	**100**

Selected Banners and Trademarks

Aunt M's
Bean Street Coffee Company
Big Chill
Celeste
Cowboys
Golden Gallon
Kangaroo
Kangaroo Express
Market Express
Mini Mart
The Chill Zone
The Pantry
Petro Express
Quickstop
Sprint
Worth

COMPETITORS

7-Eleven
BI-LO
Couche-Tard
Crown Central
Cumberland Farms
Delhaize America
Exxon Mobil
Gate Petroleum
Publix
Racetrac Petroleum
Spinx
Winn-Dixie
Worsley

HISTORICAL FINANCIALS

Company Type: Public

Income Statement

	REVENUE ($ mil.)	NET INCOME ($ mil.)	NET PROFIT MARGIN	EMPLOYEES
9/09	6,390	59	0.9%	13,694
9/08	8,996	32	0.4%	14,221
9/07	6,911	27	0.4%	13,232
9/06	5,962	89	1.5%	12,005
9/05	4,429	58	1.3%	10,803
Annual Growth	**9.6%**	**0.6%**	**—**	**6.1%**

FYE: Last Thursday in September

2009 Year-End Financials

Debt ratio: 273.2%
Return on equity: 14.0%
Cash ($ mil.): 170
Current ratio: 1.60
Long-term debt ($ mil.): 1,246

No. of shares (mil.): 23
Dividends
 Yield: —
 Payout: —
Market value ($ mil.): 356

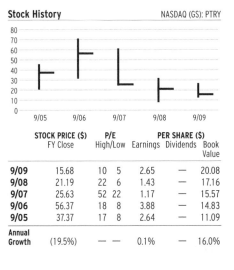

	STOCK PRICE ($) FY Close	P/E High/Low		PER SHARE ($) Earnings	Dividends	Book Value
9/09	15.68	10	5	2.65	—	20.08
9/08	21.19	22	6	1.43	—	17.16
9/07	25.63	52	22	1.17	—	15.57
9/06	56.37	18	8	3.88	—	14.83
9/05	37.37	17	8	2.64	—	11.09
Annual Growth	**(19.5%)**	**—**	**—**	**0.1%**	**—**	**16.0%**

Parker Hannifin

Motion-control equipment made by Parker Hannifin helped sink a replica of the *Titanic* in the Academy Award-winning film. Parker Hannifin's motion-control products use hydraulic (liquid) or pneumatic (gas or air) systems to move and position materials or to control equipment. Its Industrial segment manufactures fluid connectors, purification systems, hydraulic and automation systems, electromechanical devices, seals and filters, and process instrumentation. The other two business segments include Climate & Industrial Controls (refrigeration and air conditioning components) and Aerospace (hydraulics, and fuel and engine systems).

Of the three business segments, Industrial is the largest; it is made up of the Automation, Filtration, Fluid Connectors, Hydraulics, Instrumentation, and Seal groups. Customers for industrial products are generally in the manufacturing, transportation, and food processing industries. The Aerospace segment designs and manufactures aircraft wheels and brakes for military and general aviation markets. In addition to refrigeration, Climate & Industrial Controls produces systems and components for use in fluid control applications, such as fuel dispensing, beverage dispensing, and mobile emissions.

The negative worldwide economic conditions and the credit market crunch have impacted the company, along with its distributors, customers, and suppliers. In response, Parker Hannifin reduced its workforce, froze salaries, and implemented shorter work weeks.

Still, the company seeks international expansion. In October 2008 the company acquired the Legris SA division from Groupe Legris Industries. Legris SA complements Parker Hannifin with its strong brand recognition in pneumatic, hydraulic, and chemical processing applications, as well as its fluid command and control systems technology. Legris SA has a well-established distribution network and presence in the European market.

Continuing with international acquisitions, Parker Hannifin purchased Origa Group (actuators, cylinders, and valves), which has operations in Germany and Austria. The company acquired the 51% in Parker Seal de México it did not already own. The acquisition was meant to strengthen Parker Hannifin's foothold in Mexico. The company also bought Malaysian firm EmiTherm, which makes shielding materials used by electronics manufacturers.

The 2008 acquisition of Vansco Electronics gave the company additional global distribution capacity and expanded the company's electronic controls and sensors product lines. Parker Hannifin also bought Titan Industries, which makes rubber products and custom-made and composite hoses.

The company inked a major deal with French aircraft maker Airbus. The deal, which is worth more than $2 billion, calls for Parker Hannifin to provide the fuel system equipment and hydraulic systems for Airbus' A350 aircraft.

HISTORY

Entrepreneurial engineer Arthur Parker founded the Parker Appliance Company in 1918 to make pneumatic brake boosters. Its products were designed to help trucks and buses stop more easily. Unfortunately, Parker's own truck slid off an icy road and over a cliff in 1919, destroying the company's inventory and ending that line of business.

Undeterred, Parker started a hydraulics and pneumatic components business in 1924 to serve automotive and industrial clients. In 1927 the fuel-linkage system the company developed for the *Spirit of St. Louis* helped Lindbergh cross the Atlantic. The company prospered during the Depression; sales reached $2 million in 1934. Two of Parker's long-term clients were Douglas Aircraft and Lockheed.

The company went public in 1938. It employed 5,000 defense workers during WWII. After Parker died in 1945, his wife Helen hired new management to focus on the automation market. The firm bought cylinder maker Hannifin in 1957 and became Parker Hannifin.

In 1960 Parker Hannifin formed an international unit in Amsterdam, and it set up a German subsidiary in 1962. Overseas acquisitions and increased demand from the space program and the aviation market spurred growth in the 1960s. Patrick Parker, the founder's son, became president in 1968 and chairman in 1977. Parker Hannifin expanded its aerospace business in 1978 with the purchase of Bertea (electrohydraulic flight controls). Patrick Parker continued as CEO until 1983 and as chairman until 1999.

During the 1980s Parker Hannifin bought several smaller companies in niche markets, including Schrader Bellows (pneumatics, 1985), Compumotor (electromechanical applications, 1986), and Stratoflex and Gull Corp. (hoses and fittings and aerospace electronics, respectively, 1988).

The company again pushed into Europe during the 1990s, buying Sweden-based Trelleborg (hydraulic hoses) in 1992 and Atlas Automation (pneumatic components for automation equipment) in 1993.

Parker Hannifin expanded into the medical, petrochemical, and semiconductor markets in 1988 by purchasing Veriflo (high-purity valves and regulators) and into mobile equipment makers with Fluid Power Systems (hydraulic valves and electrohydraulic systems).

Overseas expansion included the 1998 purchase of Sempress Pneumatics (pneumatic cylinders, the Netherlands).

In 2000 Parker Hannifin acquired motion-control maker Commercial Intertech in a deal worth around $473 million. It also bought Whatman's industrial business (purification products and gas generators) and Wynn's International (industrial sealing products, in a $498 million deal).

President and COO Donald Washkewicz succeeded Duane Collins as CEO in 2001. (Collins remained chairman until his retirement in 2004, when Washkewicz replaced him in that role, too.) Parker Hannifin acquired Eaton's air conditioning unit, Aeroquip, the same year.

Parker Hannifin completed the acquisition of Denison International early in 2004 for about $2.4 billion.

Early in 2005 Parker Hannifin sold Wynn Oil (chemical car care products) to Illinois Tool Works for an undisclosed sum. Wanting to secure its foothold in the water filtration market, Parker Hannifin acquired UK-based domnick hunter group after winning a bidding war with Eaton Corporation. domnick hunter drew such avid interest in part because it had developed products designed to protect against nuclear, biological, and chemical weapons.

EXECUTIVES

Chairman, President, and CEO:
Donald E. (Don) Washkewicz, age 59,
$8,110,109 total compensation
EVP Finance and Administration and CFO:
Timothy K. Pistell, age 62,
$4,064,945 total compensation
EVP Sales, Marketing, and Operations Support:
Marwan M. Kashkoush, age 55,
$2,416,442 total compensation
EVP and Operating Officer: Lee C. Banks, age 46,
$2,153,585 total compensation
EVP and Operating Officer; President, Aerospace Group: Robert P. (Bob) Barker, age 59
EVP and Operating Officer: Thomas L. (Tom) Williams, age 51
SVP Finance: Dana A. Dennis, age 61
VP: Heinz Droxner, age 64,
$2,440,238 total compensation
VP, General Counsel, and Secretary:
Thomas A. Piraino Jr., age 60
VP and CIO: William G. Eline, age 53
VP Human Resources: Daniel S. (Dan) Serbin, age 55
VP; President, Fluid Connectors Group:
Robert W. (Bob) Bond, age 51
VP; President, Latin America Group:
A. Ricardo Machado, age 61
VP; President, Seal Group: Kurt Keller, age 52
VP; President, Filtration Group: Peter Popoff, age 57
VP; President, Climate and Industrial Controls Group:
Thomas F. Healy, age 49
VP; President, Automation Group: Roger S. Sherrard
VP; President, Instrumentation Group: John R. Greco
VP; President, Hydraulics Group: Jeffrey A. Cullman
VP; President, Asia/Pacific Group: Michael Y. Chung
VP; President, Europe, Middle East, and Africa Group:
Charly Saulnier
VP Corporate Communications: Christopher M. Farage
Auditors: Deloitte & Touche LLP

LOCATIONS

HQ: Parker Hannifin Corporation
6035 Parkland Blvd., Cleveland, OH 44124
Phone: 216-896-3000 **Fax:** 216-896-4000
Web: www.parker.com

2009 Sales

	$ mil.	% of total
North America	6,090.2	59
Other regions	4,218.8	41
Total	**10,309.0**	**100**

PRODUCTS/OPERATIONS

2009 Sales

	$ mil.	% of total
Industrial		
International	3,895.9	38
North America	3,734.6	36
Aerospace	1,883.3	18
Climate & industrial controls	795.2	8
Total	**10,309.0**	**100**

Operating Groups and Selected Products

Aerospace
   Aircraft wheels and brakes
   Flight control components
   Fuel systems
   Pneumatic pumps and valves
Climate and Industrial Controls
   Expansion valves
   Filter-dryers
   Hose assemblies
   Pressure regulators
   Solenoid valves
Industrial
   Automation
      Air preparation units
      Electric actuators
      Human/machine interface hardware and software
      Indexers
      Multi-axis positioning tables
      Pneumatic valves
      Stepper and servo drives
      Structural extrusions
      Vacuum products
   Filtration
      Cabin air filters
      Compressed-air and gas-purification filters
      Fuel conditioning filters
      Fuel filters/water separators
      Gas generators
      Hydraulic, lubrication, and coolant filters
      Lube oil and fuel filters
      Nitrogen and hydrogen generators
      Process, chemical, and microfiltration filters
      Water desalinization and purification
   Fluid Connectors
      Couplers
      Diagnostic equipment
      Hoses and hose fittings
      Tube fittings
      Valves
   Hydraulics
      Accumulators
      Cylinders
      Electrohydraulic systems
      Hydrostatic steering units
      Metering pumps
      Motors and pumps
      Power units
      Rotary actuators
      Sensors
      Valves
   Instrumentation
      Ball, plug, and needle valves
      Cylinder connections
      Fluoropolymer fittings
      Miniature solenoid valves
      Multi-solenoid manifolds
      Packless ultra-high-purity valves
      Quick connects
      Regulators
      Spray guns
      Transducers
      Tubing
      Ultra-high-purity tube fittings
   Seals
      Gaskets and packings
      Metal and plastic composite seals
      Medical devices, seals, and instruments
      O-rings
      O-seals
      Thermal management products

HISTORICAL FINANCIALS

Company Type: Public

Income Statement

FYE: June 30

	REVENUE ($ mil.)	NET INCOME ($ mil.)	NET PROFIT MARGIN	EMPLOYEES
6/09	10,309	509	4.9%	51,639
6/08	12,146	950	7.8%	61,722
6/07	10,718	830	7.7%	57,338
6/06	9,386	673	7.2%	57,073
6/05	8,215	605	7.4%	50,638
Annual Growth	5.8%	(4.2%)	—	0.5%

2009 Year-End Financials

Debt ratio: 43.0%
Return on equity: 10.7%
Cash ($ mil.): 188
Current ratio: 1.56
Long-term debt ($ mil.): 1,840

No. of shares (mil.): 161
Dividends
 Yield: 2.3%
 Payout: 31.9%
Market value ($ mil.): 6,918

Stock History

NYSE: PH

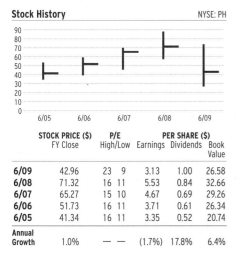

	STOCK PRICE ($) FY Close	P/E High/Low		PER SHARE ($) Earnings	Dividends	Book Value
6/09	42.96	23	9	3.13	1.00	26.58
6/08	71.32	16	11	5.53	0.84	32.66
6/07	65.27	15	10	4.67	0.69	29.26
6/06	51.73	16	11	3.71	0.61	26.34
6/05	41.34	16	11	3.35	0.52	20.74
Annual Growth	1.0%	—	—	(1.7%)	17.8%	6.4%

Patterson Companies

Patterson Companies helps doctors look at gift horses and mouths. The company is a leading North American wholesaler of dental products, including X-ray film and machines, hand instruments, sterilization products, dental chairs and lights, and diagnostic equipment. Additionally, it sells office supplies, computer equipment, software, and other products and services for dental offices and laboratories. In the US, Patterson also distributes animal health supplies (including equine products) through its Webster Veterinary division. A third unit, Patterson Medical, distributes physical therapy and other rehabilitation medical equipment worldwide.

Patterson has been in the dental supply business since 1877. The company offers its customers some 90,000 different items, including about 4,000 private-label products marketed under the Patterson name, through direct sales and marketing representatives.

Patterson Dental has expanded its network through selective acquisitions, including the purchase of Canadian dental distributor Denesca and US dental distributor Leventhal & Sons in 2008. To bump up into the specialty dental segment, in early 2009 the company acquired 3-D imaging provider Dolphin Imaging Systems and sister software company Dolphin Practice Management, which together serve orthodontic, oral surgery, and other specialty offices.

Though its dental segment is still its largest business, Patterson has diversified its offerings in the 21st century to also include animal health and rehabilitation equipment. In each of its segments, Patterson uses its size and breadth to present itself as a full-service partner to its customers, providing services such as technology consulting and equipment repair, in addition to a full complement of consumables, equipment, and software.

Patterson's animal health division, Webster Veterinary, is a leading US distributor of health products for household pets and horses, with a particularly strong presence in the eastern part of the country. It sells more than 11,000 products — including vaccines and drugs, consumables, and diagnostic supplies — made by more than 550 suppliers. Webster also offers a growing line of value-priced, private-label items.

In 2008 Webster Veterinary acquired Columbus Serum Company, a regional distributor of pet veterinary equipment and drugs. It also bought software developer Odyssey Veterinary Software, which makes programs designed to communicate diagnoses and treatment plans to pet owners.

Patterson Medical sells equipment and supplies used by physical and occupational therapists, such as home health aids (bathing and dressing devices), orthopedic soft goods, walkers and canes, exam and therapy tables, and exercise equipment.

The company grew in the UK rehabilitation market by acquiring distribution firm Mobilis Healthcare Group in 2009. Patterson Medical also expanded by acquiring Empi Therapy Solutions — a rehabilitation equipment and supply catalog business — from Empi's parent company, DJO Incorporated.

The company's employee stock option plan, managed by Delaware Charter Guarantee & Trust, controls 17% of the company's stock.

HISTORY

In 1877 brothers Myron and John Patterson bought a Milwaukee drugstore and later added dental supplies to the inventory. Myron bought the dental side of the business from his brother in 1891, moved to St. Paul, Minnesota, and started a dental supply store. His business later became a subsidiary of diversified manufacturer Esmark, which sold Patterson to food giant Beatrice in 1982. Recognizing that food and dental supplies were an odd mix, Patterson executives initiated a leveraged buyout in 1985.

In an industry as fragmented as some dental patients' smiles, the firm used acquisitions to secure a leading position as a full-service provider. In 1987 Patterson bought D.L. Saslow, then the #3 distributor. Between 1989 and 1993 it bought smaller distributors in eight states and Washington, DC. In 1993, a year after it went public, Patterson bought the Canadian arm of bankrupt rival Healthco International.

During the mid- and late 1990s, Patterson continued to buy small local dental-supply distributors, branching out across the US and Canada. In 1996 and 1997 Patterson expanded into front-office products with the purchase of Colwell Systems and EagleSoft. It took a few more bites out of the market with purchases of two more local distributors in 1998. In 2000 it bought Micheli Dental Supply, a dental products distributor in California, and eCheck-Up.com, an online provider of payroll, human resources, payables processing, and other services.

In 2001 Patterson expanded beyond dental products distribution when it purchased J. A. Webster, a distributor of veterinary supplies. Patterson broadened its operations further in 2003, acquiring AbilityOne Products, a provider of medical rehabilitation supplies. It also acquired Smith & Nephew's rehab division, and with it the Rolyan and Homecraft brand names. The following year the company changed its name from Patterson Dental to Patterson Companies to reflect this expansion.

Patterson has continued to grow through acquisitions in its various units. Patterson Dental expanded with the 2005 purchase of Michigan-based distributor Accu-Bite. And Patterson Medical acquired Medco Supply Company, a distributor of sports medicine products, in 2004. Additionally, Patterson's veterinary unit added pet supply company ProVet from Lextron in 2004, equine distributor Milburn Distributions in 2005, and veterinary practice management software maker Intra in 2006. It also introduced its own private-label veterinary products line in 2005.

EXECUTIVES

Chairman: Peter L. Frechette, age 72, $210,663 total compensation
President, CEO, and Director: Scott P. Anderson, age 43, $466,203 total compensation
EVP, CFO and Treasurer: R. Stephen Armstrong, age 59, $561,675 total compensation
VP Human Resources: Jerome E. Thygesen, age 52
Secretary and General Counsel: Matthew L. Levitt
President, Webster Veterinary Supply: George L. Henriques, age 49, $506,628 total compensation
President, Patterson Dental: Paul A. Guggenheim, age 50
President, Patterson Medical Products: David P. (Dave) Sproat, age 43, $497,444 total compensation
VP Management Information Systems: Lynn E. Askew, age 47
Auditors: Ernst & Young LLP

LOCATIONS

HQ: Patterson Companies, Inc.
  1031 Mendota Heights Rd., St. Paul, MN 55120
Phone: 651-686-1600   **Fax:** 651-686-9331
Web: www.pattersoncompanies.com

2010 Sales

	$ mil.	% of total
US	2,903.4	90
Other countries	334.0	10
Total	**3,237.4**	**100**

PRODUCTS/OPERATIONS

2010 Sales

	$ mil.	% of total
Dental supply	2,167.5	67
Veterinary supply	643.6	20
Rehabilitative supply	426.3	13
Total	**3,237.4**	**100**

2010 Sales

	$ mil.	% of total
Consumable & printed products	2,124.6	66
Equipment & software	839.4	26
Other	273.4	8
Total	**3,237.4**	**100**

Selected Subsidiaries

Accu-Bite, Inc.
Ausmedic Australia Pty Limited
Country Footwear Ltd. (UK)
Direct Dental Supply Co.
Dolphin Imaging Systems, LLC
Dolphin Practice Management, LLC
Halo Healthcare Ltd (UK)
Homecraft Rolyan Limited (UK)
Kinetec S.A. (France)
Midland Manufacturing Company Inc.
Mobilis Healthcare Group Ltd. (UK)
Patterson Dental Canada, Inc.
Patterson Dental Supply, Inc.
Patterson Logistics Services, Inc.
Patterson Medical Limited (UK)
Patterson Medical Supply, Inc.
Patterson Office Supplies, Inc.
Patterson Technology Center, Inc.
Physio Med Services Limited (UK)
Sammons Preston Canada, Inc.
Strategic Dental Marketing, Inc.
Tumble Forms, Inc.
Webster Veterinary Supply, Inc.
Williamston Industrial Center, LLC

COMPETITORS

A.C. Graham
Animal Health International
Benco Dental
Buffalo Supply
Burkhart Dental
Cardinal Health
Cardinal Health Medical
Central Garden & Pet
Darby Dental
DENTSPLY
The Harvard Drug Group
Henry Schein
IVESCO
McKesson
McKesson Medical-Surgical
Medline Industries
MWI Veterinary Supply
Owens & Minor
Professional Veterinary Product
PSS World Medical
TW Medical
Universal Medical Systems

HISTORICAL FINANCIALS

Company Type: Public

Income Statement

FYE: Last Saturday in April

	REVENUE ($ mil.)	NET INCOME ($ mil.)	NET PROFIT MARGIN	EMPLOYEES
4/10	3,237	212	6.6%	6,890
4/09	3,094	200	6.5%	7,010
4/08	2,999	225	7.5%	6,850
4/07	2,798	208	7.4%	6,580
4/06	2,615	198	7.6%	6,440
Annual Growth	**5.5%**	**1.7%**	**—**	**1.7%**

2010 Year-End Financials

Debt ratio: 36.4%
Return on equity: 16.2%
Cash ($ mil.): 341
Current ratio: 3.25
Long-term debt ($ mil.): 525
No. of shares (mil.): 124
Dividends
  Yield: 0.3%
  Payout: 5.6%
Market value ($ mil.): 3,959

Stock History

NASDAQ (GS): PDCO

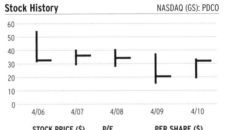

	STOCK PRICE ($) FY Close	P/E High/Low		PER SHARE ($) Earnings	Dividends	Book Value
4/10	31.96	18	11	1.78	0.10	11.64
4/09	20.46	22	9	1.69	—	9.58
4/08	34.20	24	17	1.69	—	8.11
4/07	36.06	26	20	1.51	—	11.13
4/06	32.58	38	22	1.43	—	10.03
Annual Growth	**(0.5%)**	**—**	**—**	**5.6%**	**—**	**3.8%**

Paychex, Inc.

If Johnny Paycheck had founded Paychex, his song might have been, "Take This Job and . . . Let Us Do Your Payroll." The company processes payrolls of about 535,000 clients, making it the second-largest payroll accounting firm in the US after Automatic Data Processing. Paychex also provides automatic tax payment, direct deposit, and wage garnishment processing. Paychex Business Solutions (a professional employer organization) offers such services as 401(k) record-keeping, risk management, benefits administration, and group insurance management. Established in 1971, Paychex focuses on small and midsized businesses (ones with fewer than 100 employees) and owns more than 100 offices worldwide.

The global economic recession has hurt Paychex, causing revenues and its number of clients to tumble. To counter these effects, Paychex plans to beef up its sales force for its payroll services, as well as for health and benefits services. Paychex also wants to sell existing clients more services and products, such as outsourced wage and tax compliance. Paychex has also expanded its German operations to include offices in Berlin, Hamburg, Munich, and Dusseldorf. The

Germany offices alone bring in about 1,700 clients for Paychex.

In mid-2010, president and CEO Jonathan Judge resigned. He joined Paychex in late 2004 and was only the second person to serve as president and CEO. An executive committee led by founder and chairman Thomas Golisano would run the company in the interim. Golisano (owner of the Buffalo Sabres NHL team) owns about 10% of Paychex.

HISTORY

Before founding Paychex in 1971, Thomas Golisano worked in a payroll accounting company that solicited the business of large firms. After discovering that 98% of all US businesses had 200 or fewer employees, he started his own company to cater to small business needs. Several friends started branches in other cities, and by 1979 the enterprise had grown to 17 locations, some company-owned, some joint ventures, and some franchised. Golisano began consolidating Paychex, buying out his partners and friends. In 1983 the company went public. (In 1994, 1998, and 2002 Golisano made unsuccessful bids for the New York governorship.)

The company has bolstered its market share through acquisitions, including Pay-Fone Systems (payroll processing, 1995), Olsen Computer Systems (software development, 1995) and National Business Solutions (benefit services, 1996). The company sought to entice more clients in the 1990s through such new services as a wage debit card that lets users draw upon salaries deposited in a special account.

Paychex also launched 401(k) plan administration for small businesses and new-hire compliance reporting. In 1999 Paychex unveiled Internet Report Service, its first online product. The following year it launched a series of products and services geared toward accountants, including access to Internet-based payroll reports. In 2002 the company bought Advantage Payroll Services for $240 million. Paychex purchased payroll and human resource services provider InterPay in 2003. In 2004 the company expanded operations outside the US by opening an office in Germany.

EXECUTIVES

Chairman: B. Thomas Golisano, age 68
SVP, CFO, and Secretary: John M. Morphy, age 62, $1,181,486 total compensation
SVP Operations: Martin Mucci, age 50, $922,214 total compensation
SVP Sales and Marketing: Delbert (Del) Humenik, age 48
VP Organizational Development: William G. Kuchta, age 63, $564,951 total compensation
VP Major Market Services: Michael A. McCarthy, $573,434 total compensation
VP Information Technology Operations and Support: Daniel A. Canzano
VP Insurance Operations: Kevin N. Hill
VP and Controller: Jennifer R. Vossler, age 47
VP and Chief Legal Officer: Stephanie L. Schaeffer
VP Human Resource Services: Martin Stowe
VP Product Management and Development: Michael E. (Mike) Gioja
Director Training: Kimberly Kelly
Investor Relations: Terri Allen
Director Corporate Communications: Laura S. Lynch
Corporate Communications Manager: Becky Cania
Director Marketing: Neil Rhorer
Auditors: Ernst & Young LLP

LOCATIONS

HQ: Paychex, Inc.
   911 Panorama Trail South, Rochester, NY 14625
Phone: 585-385-6666   **Fax:** 585-383-3428
Web: www.paychex.com

PRODUCTS/OPERATIONS

2010 Sales

	$ mil.	% of total
Payroll	1,404.9	70
Human resource & benefits	540.9	27
Other	55.0	3
Total	**2,000.8**	**100**

Selected Services and Products

Payroll
   Direct deposit (deposit of salary directly into
      employee's bank account)
   New hire reporting
   Paychex Access Card (direct deposit and debit card
      service)
   Payroll (processing of employee paychecks and
      earnings statements, payroll records, and tax
      returns)
   Taxpay (automatic filing of local, state, and federal
      payroll tax returns)
   Wage garnishment processing
Human resources/Professional employer organization
   401(k) plan record-keeping
   Employee benefits and related administration
   Employer regulatory compliance management
   Human resources administration
   Risk management
   Workers' compensation insurance

COMPETITORS

Administaff
ADP
Barrett Business Services
CBIZ
Ceridian
CompuPay
Hewitt Associates
SurePayroll
TeamStaff
TriNet Group

HISTORICAL FINANCIALS

Company Type: Public

Income Statement

FYE: May 31

	REVENUE ($ mil.)	NET INCOME ($ mil.)	NET PROFIT MARGIN	EMPLOYEES
5/10	2,001	477	23.8%	12,200
5/09	2,083	534	25.6%	12,500
5/08	2,066	576	27.9%	12,200
5/07	1,887	515	27.3%	11,700
5/06	1,675	465	27.8%	10,900
Annual Growth	**4.5%**	**0.6%**	**—**	**2.9%**

2010 Year-End Financials

Debt ratio: —
Return on equity: 34.8%
Cash ($ mil.): 284
Current ratio: 1.11
Long-term debt ($ mil.): —

No. of shares (mil.): 361
Dividends
   Yield: 4.3%
   Payout: 93.9%
Market value ($ mil.): 10,316

Stock History

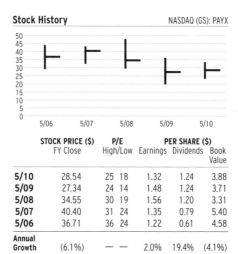

NASDAQ (GS): PAYX

	STOCK PRICE ($) FY Close	P/E High/Low		PER SHARE ($) Earnings	Dividends	Book Value
5/10	28.54	25	18	1.32	1.24	3.88
5/09	27.34	24	14	1.48	1.24	3.71
5/08	34.55	30	19	1.56	1.20	3.31
5/07	40.40	31	24	1.35	0.79	5.40
5/06	36.71	36	24	1.22	0.61	4.58
Annual Growth	**(6.1%)**	**—**	**—**	**2.0%**	**19.4%**	**(4.1%)**

PC Connection

You may not see a store on every street corner, but PC Connection is just a click away. A leading direct marketer of computer products in the US, the company sells hardware, software, networking devices, and peripherals. It offers more than 180,000 items from Apple, Hewlett-Packard, Lenovo, and Microsoft, among others. Through its catalogs, websites, and direct sales force, PC Connection targets small and midsized businesses, large corporations, government agencies, and educational institutions, as well as individual consumers. PC Connection was founded in 1982 by Patricia Gallup (chairman and CEO) and David Hall (director).

The global recession and slump in spending on information technology products has led to declining sales in recent years. Since reaching a high point of $1.8 billion in 2007, PC Connection saw its revenues slide to about $1.6 billion in 2009, a more than 10% drop. Also that year, the company posted a loss of $1 million (down from $23 million in profits in 2007). The dip in demand from small and midsized businesses and large corporate clients has been lessened slightly by increased spending from PC Connection's public sector customers (government agencies and educational institutions). In 2009 the company saw a nearly 10% increase in public sector sales, which account for 25% of net revenue. While demand from the public sector has grown in recent years, small and midsized businesses remain PC Connection's largest customer segment, generating about half of net revenue; large corporate accounts bring in the remaining roughly 25%.

Though its sales have taken a hit, PC Connection has focused on maintaining strong customer relations and providing good service. About 90% of sales are made to repeat customers each year. Most of its revenue (roughly 70%) is generated through telemarketing and field sales, while the balance comes from its owned websites.

Gallup, a nature lover whose father was a union organizer, built a company respected for its treatment of employees and the environment.

PC Connection's mascot is a raccoon, and a converted strip shopping center serves as its headquarters. Gallup and Hall each control about a third of the company's shares.

HISTORY

Patricia Gallup, an anthropologist, and David Hall, an audio engineer, met while hiking on the Appalachian Trail. She later went to work at his family-owned audio business in rural New Hampshire. When the duo decided to buy a PC for the audio store, long drives to city computer outlets, plus surly salespeople, inspired them to go into direct marketing.

Gallup and Hall pooled $8,000 in savings and started PC Connection in 1982, specializing at first in software and computer accessories with an emphasis on customer service. He served as the technical expert, she as the manager. Their ad in *Byte* magazine drew an immediate response, and the company saw first-year sales of $233,000. In 1984 they created *MacConnection* to sell Apple-related software.

PC Connection played on its pastoral surroundings, adopting as its mascot a raccoon and informing customers in one ad that from PC Connection it was "only a five-day drive to Silicon Valley." In 1987 *Inc.* magazine named the company the second-fastest-growing private company in the US.

Gallup built the company with an emphasis on frugality and hard work (she celebrated her honeymoon at a company dinner) and ample respect for its staff. During the 1980s real estate boom, PC Connection built a handful of single-family homes and sold them at cost to employees.

In 1988 the company started making instructional videotapes for its customers, showing, for example, how to install an internal disk drive. The tapes boosted sales, so the company created PCTV in 1989, building a studio and a satellite link to produce videos for other companies (spun off in 1994).

In 1992 PC Connection signed its first deal — with Compaq — to sell computer systems, and several other deals followed. Three years later the company began focusing on business customers, particularly small and midsized companies.

The company continued to shine in customer service, receiving its seventh consecutive Best Company award from readers of *PC World* in 1997. PC Connection went public without any venture capital funds in 1998 and inked a deal to sell Compaq products to the lucrative small and midsized business market. In 1999 the company unveiled its own line of computers and monitors (EPIQ), increasing its cost-effectiveness. Also that year the company bought ComTeq Federal, a computer supplier to federal government agencies (it was renamed GovConnection in early 2002).

PC Connection in 2001 cut about 125 nonsales jobs (almost 8% of its workforce). That year it agreed to acquire consumer technology products e-tailer Cyberian Outpost, but the deal later fell through. In 2001 the former president of Ziff-Davis, Kenneth Koppel, was named as CEO; Gallup remained chairman.

The economic downturn in the US and a slowing in the demand for IT products hurt PC Connection's sales and bottom line in 2001. In April 2002 the company acquired MoreDirect, a leading e-procurement supplier of IT products. In September Koppel became president, and Gallup reassumed the CEO title.

681

Koppel resigned for personal reasons in 2003, and Gallup took on the presidential role. That same year the company lost a $56 million government contract due to incorrect procedures discovered during a routine audit by the Government Services Administration (GSA). As a result, a new president (Don Weatherson) was appointed to head up GovConnection. The following year the unit was again granted permission to sell to government agencies through the General Services Administration.

In 2005 the company bought Amherst Technologies, a multiplatform implementation and support services company focusing on midsized to large corporations.

EXECUTIVES

Chairman and CEO: Patricia Gallup, age 56, $657,296 total compensation
Vice Chairman: David Hall, age 60
President and COO: Timothy J. (Tim) McGrath, age 51, $969,325 total compensation
EVP, CFO, and Treasurer: Jack L. Ferguson, age 71, $875,307 total compensation
SVP Human Resources: Bradley G. (Brad) Mousseau, age 58, $284,348 total compensation
SVP and CIO: John A. Polizzi
SVP Finance and Corporate Controller: Stephen Baldridge
Public Relations Director: Karin Bakis
Auditors: Deloitte & Touche LLP

LOCATIONS

HQ: PC Connection, Inc.
Rt. 101A, 730 Milford Rd., Merrimack, NH 03054
Phone: 603-683-2000   **Fax:** 603-423-5748
Web: www.pcconnection.com

PRODUCTS/OPERATIONS

2009 Sales

	$ mil.	% of total
Small & midsized businesses	752.5	52
Large account	427.9	27
Public sector	389.3	21
Total	**1,569.7**	**100**

2009 Sales

	$ mil.	% of total
Notebooks & PDAs	234.3	15
Software	219.6	14
Video, imaging & sound	212.9	13
Desktops & servers	212.1	13
Net/Com products	167.3	11
Printers & printer supplies	133.9	9
Storage devices	128.9	8
Memory & system enhancements	60.3	4
Accessories & other	200.4	13
Total	**1,569.7**	**100**

Selected Products

Computers (desktops, notebooks, PDAs, servers)
Monitors (projectors, plasma displays)
Printers and scanners (laser, ink-jet, dot-matrix)
Electronics (digital cameras, home audio and video)
Networking (adapters, hubs, modems, routers)
Storage (CD drives, DVD drives, media)
Upgrades (audio and video hardware)
Accessories (batteries, cables, furniture)

COMPETITORS

Apple Inc.	IBM
Austin Ribbon & Computer	Insight Enterprises
Best Buy	Lenovo
CDW	Newegg
CompuCom	PC Mall
Dell	Systemax
Gateway, Inc.	Zones
Hewlett-Packard	

HISTORICAL FINANCIALS

Company Type: Public

Income Statement

FYE: December 31

	REVENUE ($ mil.)	NET INCOME ($ mil.)	NET PROFIT MARGIN	EMPLOYEES
12/09	1,570	(1)	—	1,448
12/08	1,754	10	0.6%	1,625
12/07	1,785	23	1.3%	1,616
12/06	1,636	14	0.8%	1,635
12/05	1,444	4	0.3%	1,571
Annual Growth	**2.1%**	**—**	**—**	**(2.0%)**

2009 Year-End Financials

Debt ratio: 1.2%
Return on equity: —
Cash ($ mil.): 46
Current ratio: 2.18
Long-term debt ($ mil.): 3
No. of shares (mil.): 27
Dividends
  Yield: —
  Payout: —
Market value ($ mil.): 183

Stock History

NASDAQ (GM): PCCC

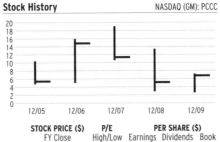

	STOCK PRICE ($) FY Close	P/E High/Low		PER SHARE ($) Earnings	Dividends	Book Value
12/09	6.75	—	—	(0.05)	—	8.69
12/08	5.12	34	8	0.39	—	8.69
12/07	11.35	22	13	0.85	—	8.28
12/06	14.83	29	10	0.54	—	7.27
12/05	5.38	56	27	0.18	—	6.33
Annual Growth	**5.8%**	**—**	**—**	**—**	**—**	**8.2%**

The Pep Boys

Still an automotive paradise for do-it-yourselfers, The Pep Boys — Manny, Moe & Jack now hears increasing cries of "Do it for me!" The company operates about 585 stores in 35 states and Puerto Rico, selling brand-name and private-label automotive parts and offering on-site service facilities. Pep Boys stores stock about 25,000 car parts and accessories, including tires, and combined operate over 6,000 service bays for parts installation, repair, and vehicle inspection. The company serves four segments of the automotive aftermarket: do-it-yourself, do-it-for-me (service), buy-for-resale (sales to professional garages), and tire sales. Pep Boys sales have lost their pep, and the firm is cutting expenses.

While total sales have declined for the past four years at Pep Boys, auto repair and maintenance service has increased as a proportion of the company's total revenue. That's because cars have become more complex, thereby limiting the growth of the do-it-yourself segment, the company's primary customers. As a result, Pep Boys has turned more toward do-it-for-me (DIFM) customers as well as commercial services, including sales to professional installers through its parts delivery service, Pep Express

Parts, which operates in about 450 stores. In addition to its Pep Boys Supercenters and Service & Tire Centers, the company operates about 10 smaller Pep Boys Express locations, which do not offer service or sell tires. To grow its service operation, in 2009 the company launched a pilot program in about 20 stores offering mobile electronics and installation services. The program, which sells and installs radios, speakers, amplifiers, remote starters, and alarm systems, was expanded to 150 stores in 2010.

Still, merchandise (including tires) accounts for about 80% of Pep Boys' sales. In an effort to revive sales growth at the chain, Pep Boys has put more emphasis on customer service and has spent heavily to improve its stores and add new locations.

Leading the turnaround effort at Pep Boys is CEO Mike Odell, who was promoted to the top job at the company in 2008. His appointment marked the end of a tumultuous time for the firm, which due to poor performance came under pressure from dissatisfied investors and led to changes in board and top leadership.

HISTORY

Philadelphians Emanuel (Manny) Rosenfeld, Maurice (Moe) Strauss, Graham (Jack) Jackson, and Moe Radavitz founded Pep Auto Supplies in 1921, named in part from a product, Pep Valve Grinding Compound. (Radavitz pulled out after a few years.) Two years later the men renamed the store The Pep Boys — Manny, Moe & Jack. A friend created the corporate caricature of the three, though the version that became famous is actually of Manny, Moe, and Izzy (Moe's brother); it was drawn after Jack left.

By 1928 there were 12 Pep Boys stores in the Philadelphia area. In 1932 the car-friendly West Coast beckoned, and the boys dispatched Murray Rosenfeld to launch Pep Boys West. Intense competition in California spurred Pep Boys West to increase parts selection, while the Philadelphia stores focused more on service. The company went public in 1946 with Manny as president and Moe as chairman, but its growth was hindered by overly conservative management; Pep Boys would not lease stores and avoided debt like a crowded freeway. Moe became president after Manny's death in 1959, and as the fiscal caution continued, the company grew by only two stores between 1964 and 1984.

Moe held both posts until 1973, when his son Ben became president. In 1977 Moe stepped down as chairman but remained on the board until his death in 1982. That year Ben became chairman and CEO, and Moe's son-in-law Morton Krause became president. In 1984 Krause retired, and two years later Ben tapped Mitchell Leibovitz as president — the first from outside the founding families. As head of eastern operations, Leibovitz had closed 32 small stores between 1979 and 1984. Between 1984 and 1986 he opened 60 bond-financed stores.

In 1986 Pep Boys was the #2 parts retailer in the US, behind Western Auto, and Leibovitz set up a plan to modernize and overhaul the entire business. Between 1986 and 1991 Pep Boys spent $477 million improving distribution, merchandising, and marketing: The number of stores doubled to 337, and the number of items offered went from about 9,000 to 24,000. The company adopted an everyday-low-price strategy, and many locations were expanded into 23,000-sq.-ft. superstores with more service bays and related services.

Leibovitz was named CEO in 1990. Pep Boys topped $1 billion in annual sales the following year. The recession of the early 1990s hurt profits; however, cash flow picked up, and the company was able to retire some debt and to open 30 stores in 1992. In 1993 Leibovitz put mechanics on commission, with safeguards to prevent overcharging.

Store count doubled during the next five years. In 1994 Leibovitz became chairman. Also that year the company began opening Parts USA stores (renamed Pep Boys Express in 1997), which had no service bays or tires. The conversion, along with tightening margins, adversely impacted profits in fiscal 1998, and Pep Boys decided in 1998 to sell 100 of its Pep Boys Express stores to AutoZone.

In 2000 Pep Boys closed 38 unprofitable stores and two distribution centers, citing stagnant sales. It also cut about 5% of its workforce (1,500 jobs). Pep Boys settled a lawsuit in 2002 alleging that it received discriminatory prices from auto parts manufacturers.

Leibovitz retired in 2003. Lawrence Stevenson, formerly the CEO of Chapters, a Canadian book retailer, became CEO. In 2004 Stevenson also assumed the company chairmanship.

Under pressure from dissatisfied investors, in February 2006 Stevenson relinquished the chairman's title, which was bestowed on director William Leonard. In mid-July Leonard was named interim CEO when Stevenson resigned from that position as well. (Leonard left the company in 2008 and James Mitarotonda took over as chairman.) In 2007 former Sonic Automotive president Jeffrey Rachor took over as CEO.

Rachor left the company in 2008. In September Mike Odell, who had served as interim CEO since April, was named to the post permanently.

In May 2010 Pep Boys signed a settlement agreement with the Environmental Protection Agency (EPA), after previously agreeing to pay a $5 million fine related to the sale of certain small-engine merchandise. Pep Boys also implemented a formal compliance program to ensure that all small-engine merchandise complies with the Clean Air Act.

EXECUTIVES

Chairman: Max L. Lukens, age 62
CEO and Director: Michael R. (Mike) Odell, age 46, $3,007,923 total compensation
EVP Stores: William E. (Bill) Shull III, age 51, $726,507 total compensation
EVP Merchandising and Marketing: Scott A. Webb, age 46, $831,576 total compensation
EVP and CFO: Raymond L. (Ray) Arthur, age 51, $1,493,742 total compensation
SVP, General Counsel, and Secretary: Brian D. Zuckerman, age 40
SVP Human Resources: Troy E. Fee, age 41, $454,737 total compensation
SVP Business Development: Joseph A. (Joe) Cirelli, age 51, $679,234 total compensation
VP Marketing: Ronald J. Stoupa
Manager Communications: Alexandra Spooner
Auditors: Deloitte & Touche LLP

LOCATIONS

HQ: The Pep Boys — Manny, Moe & Jack
3111 W. Allegheny Ave., Philadelphia, PA 19132
Phone: 215-430-9000   **Fax:** 215-227-7513
Web: www.pepboys.com

2010 Stores

	No.
California	124
Florida	53
Texas	47
Pennsylvania	45
New Jersey	31
New York	29
Illinois	25
Arizona	22
Georgia	22
Maryland	18
Virginia	16
Nevada	12
Ohio	10
Louisiana	8
New Mexico	8
North Carolina	8
Indiana	7
Colorado	7
Connecticut	7
Delaware	7
Tennessee	7
Massachusetts	6
South Carolina	6
Utah	6
Other states	29
Puerto Rico	27
Total	**587**

PRODUCTS/OPERATIONS

2010 Sales

	$ mil.	% of total
Parts & accessories	1,219.4	64
Service	377.3	20
Tires	314.2	16
Total	**1,910.9**	**100**

Selected Products

Additives
Air-conditioning parts
Air filters
Alarms
Antifreeze
Batteries
Belts
Brake parts
Engines and engine parts
Floor mats
Gauges
Hand tools
Hoses
Ignition parts
Mobile electronics
Motor oil
Mufflers
Oil filters
Paints
Polishes
Seat covers
Sound systems
Suspension parts
Truck and van accessories

Selected Private-Label Brands

CORNELL
FUTURA
Pep Boys
PROCOOL
PROLINE
PROSTART
PROSTOP
PROSTEER
VARSITY

COMPETITORS

Advance Auto Parts
AutoZone
Bridgestone Retail Operations
CARQUEST
Commercial Tire
Cottman Transmission Systems
Discount Tire
General Parts
Goodyear Tire & Rubber
Jeg's
Jiffy Lube
Les Schwab Tire Centers
Meineke
Midas
Monro Muffler Brake
O'Reilly Automotive
Precision Auto
Sears
Snap-on
TBC
VIP
Wal-Mart

HISTORICAL FINANCIALS

Company Type: Public

Income Statement

FYE: Saturday nearest January 31

	REVENUE ($ mil.)	NET INCOME ($ mil.)	NET PROFIT MARGIN	EMPLOYEES
1/10	1,911	23	1.2%	17,718
1/09	1,928	(30)	—	18,458
1/08	2,138	(41)	—	18,564
1/07	2,272	(3)	—	18,794
1/06	2,235	(36)	—	19,980
Annual Growth	**(3.8%)**	**—**	**—**	**(3.0%)**

2010 Year-End Financials

Debt ratio: 69.1%
Return on equity: 5.3%
Cash ($ mil.): 39
Current ratio: 1.40
Long-term debt ($ mil.): 306
No. of shares (mil.): 52
Dividends
  Yield: 1.4%
  Payout: 27.3%
Market value ($ mil.): 438

Stock History

NYSE: PBY

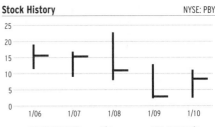

	STOCK PRICE ($) FY Close	P/E High/Low		PER SHARE ($) Earnings	Dividends	Book Value
1/10	8.35	25	6	0.44	0.12	8.45
1/09	2.89	—	—	(0.58)	0.27	8.06
1/08	10.97	—	—	(0.86)	0.27	8.97
1/07	15.31	—	—	(0.05)	0.27	10.82
1/06	15.60	—	—	(0.69)	0.27	11.33
Annual Growth	**(14.5%)**	**—**	**—**	**—**	**(18.4%)**	**(7.1%)**

PepsiCo, Inc.

The PepsiCo challenge (to keep up with archrival The Coca-Cola Company) never ends for the world's #2 carbonated soft-drink maker. Its soft drinks include Pepsi, Mountain Dew, and Mug. Cola is not the company's only beverage: Pepsi sells Tropicana orange juice brands, Gatorade sports drink, SoBe tea, and Aquafina water. The company also owns Frito-Lay, the world's #1 snack maker with offerings such as Lay's, Ruffles, Doritos, and Fritos. Its Quaker Foods unit offers breakfast cereals (Life, Quaker Oats), rice (Rice-A-Roni), and side dishes (Near East). Pepsi's products are available in some 200 countries. In 2010 the company acquired its two largest bottlers, Pepsi Bottling Group and PepsiAmericas.

PepsiCo announced plans to consolidate its bottling and distribution operations in 2009, offering to acquire 100% of both The Pepsi Bottling Group (PBG) and PepsiAmericas (PAS). PepsiCo already owned 33% of PBG and 43% of PepsiAmericas. However, PBG initially rejected the offer as being "grossly inadequate," in particular, with regard to price. PepsiAmericas rejected the offer on the same grounds. Not content with a "no," PepsiCo submitted an offer again some months later, this time upping its cash and stock proposal to a deal valued at $7.8 billion. This time the offer was accepted by both companies.

The takeover of PBG and PAS gave PepsiCo control over the majority of its North American bottling and distribution volume. It allowed the company to cut significant costs and also allow it to make any desired changes to the supply-chain more rapidly. In addition, the takeover created one of the largest food and beverages businesses in the world.

With the purchase of its two largest soda bottlers completed, the company is taking a healthful approach to boosting its food business. It has smaller acquisitions and alliances in mind to complement its portfolio of nutrition-oriented brands, such as Tropicana and Quaker Oats. The shift comes amid flattening soda sales in the US and greater demand for wholesome food options.

PepsiCo has also been looking overseas for areas of growth. In 2009 its joint venture with Saudi dairy company Almarai, called International Dairy and Juice Limited (IDJ), purchased a 75% stake in top Jordanian dairy and juice company, Teeba Investment for Developed Food Processing Company (or Teeba). Pepsi owns 52% of IDJ, and Almarai owns 48%.

Other international deals included PepsiCo and the former PBG's acquisition of the #1 Russian juice maker, JSC Lebedyansky, for about $1.4 billion in 2008. PepsiCo controlled a 75% stake, while PBG owned the rest. PepsiCo and PBG also acquired another Russian beverage manufacturer, Sobol-Aqua, that same year.

HISTORY

Pharmacist Caleb Bradham invented Pepsi in 1898 in New Bern, North Carolina. He named his new drink Pepsi-Cola (claiming it cured dyspepsia, or indigestion) and registered the trademark in 1903. Following The Coca-Cola Company's example, Bradham developed a bottling franchise system. By WWI, 300 bottlers had signed up. After the war, Bradham stockpiled sugar to safeguard against rising costs, but in 1920 sugar prices plunged, forcing him into bankruptcy in 1923.

Pepsi existed on the brink of ruin under various owners until Loft Candy bought it in 1931. Its fortunes improved in 1933 when, in the midst of the Depression, it doubled the size of its bottles to 12 ounces without raising the five-cent price. In 1939 Pepsi introduced the world's first radio jingle. Two years later Loft Candy merged with its Pepsi subsidiary and became The Pepsi-Cola Company.

Donald Kendall, who became Pepsi-Cola's president in 1963, turned the firm's attention to young people ("The Pepsi Generation"). It acquired Mountain Dew in 1964 and became PepsiCo in 1965, when it acquired Frito-Lay.

In 1972 PepsiCo agreed to distribute Stolichnaya vodka in the US in exchange for being the only Western firm allowed to bottle soft drinks in the USSR. With the purchases of Pizza Hut (1977), Taco Bell (1978), and Kentucky Fried Chicken (1986), it became a major force in the fast-food industry.

When Coca-Cola changed its formula in 1985, Pepsi had a short-lived victory in the cola wars (until the splashy return of Coca-Cola classic). The rivalry was extended to ready-to-drink tea in 1991 when, in response to Coca-Cola's Nestea venture with Nestlé, PepsiCo teamed up with Lipton. Between 1991 and 1996 PepsiCo aggressively expanded its overseas bottling operations. Roger Enrico became CEO in 1996. A year later PepsiCo spun off its $10 billion fast-food unit as TRICON Global Restaurants (now known as YUM! Brands, Inc.), putting itself in a better position to sell its soft drinks at other restaurants.

In 1998 the company bought Seagram's market-leading Tropicana juices (rival of Coca-Cola's Minute Maid) for $3.3 billion. The firm sold a 65% stake in its new Pepsi Bottling Group to the public in 1999.

Its more than $13 billion purchase of The Quaker Oats Company in 2001 added the dominant Gatorade sports drink brand to its lineup. Later that year the company named president and COO Steve Reinemund as chairman and CEO; Enrico stayed as vice chairman (where he remained through 2002).

PepsiCo also found opportunities for growth overseas in 2003. However, claims surfaced that year that both Coke and Pepsi products bottled in India contained traces of DDT, malathion, and other pesticides that exceeded government limits. Coke and Pepsi denied the reports in a rare joint press conference. Government labs cleared the colas, saying the drinks were safe, but not before both soft-drink companies saw sales dip by as much as 50% in a two-week period.

PepsiCo bought General Mills' stake of their joint venture, Snack Ventures Europe (SVE), in 2005 for $750 million. The deal gave Pepsi control of Europe's largest snack food company.

Later that year the company revealed it was subject to an SEC investigation involving transactions it had with Kmart. Allegedly, lower-level employees within its cola and snack divisions signed documents that Kmart used to improperly record nearly $6 million in revenue. PepsiCo cooperated with the investigation, which led to the resignations of a PepsiCo national account manager and a sales director.

CEO Steve Reinemund stepped down as CEO in 2006 in order to spend more time with his family. His replacement, Indra Nooyi, had served as the company's president and CFO.

EXECUTIVES

Chairman and CEO: Indra K. Nooyi, age 54, $15,768,350 total compensation
EVP Sales and Marketing: A. Salman Amin
EVP PepsiCo Global Operations: Richard A. Goodman, age 62, $3,655,457 total compensation
EVP and Chief Commercial Officer, Pepsi Beverages: Thomas R. (Tom) Greco
CFO: Hugh F. Johnston, age 48
Chief Marketing Officer and President, Joint Ventures, PepsiCo Beverages America: Jill Beraud
SVP PepsiCo Human Resources and Chief Personnel Officer: Cynthia M. Trudell, age 56
SVP Government Affairs, General Counsel, and Secretary: Larry D. Thompson, age 64
SVP and CIO: Robert Dixon
SVP and Chief Procurement Officer: Mitch Adamek
SVP Chief Global Diversity and Inclusion Officer: Ronald C. (Ron) Parker
SVP and Controller: Peter A. Bridgman, age 57
SVP Corporate Strategy and Development: Vivek Sankaran
SVP Investor Relations: Lynn A. Tyson
SVP and Chief Scientific Officer: Mehmood Khan
SVP and Chief Communications Officer: Julie A. Hamp
President and CEO, Frito-Lay North America: Albert P. (Al) Carey, age 58, $6,626,964 total compensation
CEO, PepsiCo Americas Foods: John C. Compton, age 48, $4,921,468 total compensation
President, Tropicana: Neil Campbell
President, Quaker Foods & Snacks: Jaya Kumar
CEO, PepsiCo Americas Beverages: Massimo F. d'Amore, age 53
CEO, PepsiCo Bottling North America: Eric J. Foss, age 51
Auditors: KPMG LLP

LOCATIONS

HQ: PepsiCo, Inc.
700 Anderson Hill Rd., Purchase, NY 10577
Phone: 914-253-2000   **Fax:** 914-253-2070
Web: www.pepsico.com

2009 Sales

	$ mil.	% of total
US	22,446	52
Mexico	3,210	7
Canada	1,996	5
UK	1,826	4
Other	13,754	32
Total	**43,232**	**100**

PRODUCTS/OPERATIONS

Selected North American Brands

Frito-Lay
  Baken-ets fried pork skins
  Cheetos cheese flavored snacks
  Chester's popcorn
  Cracker Jack candy coated popcorn
  Doritos tortilla chips
  Fritos corn chips
  Funyuns onion flavored rings
  Grandma's cookies
  Hickory Sticks
  Hostess Potato Chips
  Lay's potato chips
  Maui Style potato chips
  Munchos potato crisps
  Oberto meat snacks
  Rold Gold pretzels and snack mix
  Ruffles potato chips
  Rustler's meat snacks
  Sabritones puffed wheat snacks
  Santitas tortilla chips
  Smartfood popcorn
  Sunchips multigrain snacks
  Tostitos tortilla chips

Pepsi Cola
  AMP energy drink
  Aquafina
  Dole juices and juice drinks (licensed)
  Ethos Water (licensed)
  Frappuccino ready-to-drink coffee (partnership)
  Gatorade
  Jazz Diet Pepsi
  Lipton Brisk (partnership)
  Mountain Dew
  Mug Root Beer
  No Fear Motherload
  Ocean Spray juices and juice drinks (licensed)
  Pepsi
  Propel Fitness Water
  Sierra Mist
  Slice
  SoBe juice drinks, dairy, and teas
  Starbucks (partnership)
  Tropicana lemonade and punches
Quaker
  Aunt Jemima mixes and syrups
  Cap'n Crunch cereal
  Crisp'ums baked crisps
  Harvest Crunch cereal
  King Vitaman cereal
  Life cereal
  Near East side dishes
  Pasta Roni side dishes
  Puffed Wheat
  Quisp cereal
  Rice-A-Roni side dishes
  Spudz snacks

COMPETITORS

American Beverage	Impulse Energy USA
Anadolu Efes	Inventure foods
Asahi Breweries	Jones Soda
Avani International Group	Kellogg
Beer Nuts	Kellogg U.S. Snacks
Big Red	Kettle Foods
Britvic	Kraft Foods
Campbell Soup	Lance Snacks
Carolina Beverage	Merisant
Celestial Seasonings	Monarch Beverage
Chiquita Brands	Monarch Beverage (GA)
Clearly Canadian	Mountain Valley
Coca-Cola	National Beverage
Coca-Cola FEMSA	National Grape Cooperative
ConAgra	Nestlé
Cott	Nestlé Waters
Cranberries Limited	New Leaf
Cumberland Packing	Odwalla
Danone Water	Polar Beverages
Dr Pepper Snapple Group	Princes Limited
DS Waters	Procter & Gamble
Energy Brands	Ralcorp
Evans Food Products	Red Bull
Faygo	Reed's
Florida's Natural	Snapple
Fraser & Neave	Snyder's of Hanover
General Mills	Sunny Delight
Golden Enterprises	Sweet Leaf Tea
Grupo Bimbo	Tree Top
Hansen Natural	Weaver Popcorn Company
Hawaiian Springs	Wet Planet Beverages
Hornell Brewing	XELR8

HISTORICAL FINANCIALS

Company Type: Public

Income Statement

FYE: Last Saturday in December

	REVENUE ($ mil.)	NET INCOME ($ mil.)	NET PROFIT MARGIN	EMPLOYEES
12/09	43,232	5,946	13.8%	203,000
12/08	43,251	5,142	11.9%	198,000
12/07	39,474	5,658	14.3%	185,000
12/06	35,137	5,642	16.1%	168,000
12/05	32,562	4,078	12.5%	157,000
Annual Growth	7.3%	9.9%	—	6.6%

HOOVER'S HANDBOOK OF AMERICAN BUSINESS 2011

2009 Year-End Financials

Debt ratio: 44.1%
Return on equity: 41.1%
Cash ($ mil.): 3,943
Current ratio: 1.44
Long-term debt ($ mil.): 7,400

No. of shares (mil.): 1,591
Dividends
  Yield: 2.9%
  Payout: 46.9%
Market value ($ mil.): 96,729

Stock History

NYSE: PEP

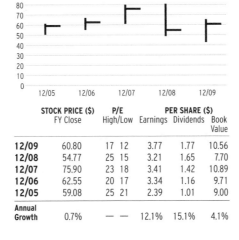

	STOCK PRICE ($) FY Close	P/E High/Low		PER SHARE ($) Earnings	Dividends	Book Value
12/09	60.80	17	12	3.77	1.77	10.56
12/08	54.77	25	15	3.21	1.65	7.70
12/07	75.90	23	18	3.41	1.42	10.89
12/06	62.55	20	17	3.34	1.16	9.71
12/05	59.08	25	21	2.39	1.01	9.00
Annual Growth	0.7%	—	—	12.1%	15.1%	4.1%

PerkinElmer, Inc.

If you know the difference between covalent and ionic bonds, you can probably appreciate the products from PerkinElmer. It makes a wide range of instruments used for chemical and thermal analysis, including calorimeters, chromatographs, and spectrometers.

In 2010 PerkinElmer purchased the 50% stake in a joint venture in inductively coupled plasma mass spectrometry (ICP-MS) held by MDS Inc.'s Analytical Technologies business, which was acquired by Danaher. The ICP-MS technology opens the door to detection of individual chemical elements, simultaneously in a sample. Its applications are broad, ranging from environmental to nutraceutical, biomonitoring, semiconductor, and geochemical research.

In the meantime, PerkinElmer picked up Analytica of Branford, Inc. The deal increases PerkinElmer's human health and environmental health portfolio with know-how in mass spectrometry and ion source technology. In 2009 PerkinElmer also bought Shanghai Sym-Bio LifeSciences, a maker of diagnostic products based in China. The acquisition adds to PerkinElmer's Human Health segment with fluorometry instruments and diagnostic reagents, as well as a manufacturing facility for both instruments and drug production in China.

Another acquisition bolstered its lighting equipment business: PerkinElmer acquired Opto Technology Inc. in 2009. Opto Technology makes lighting components and subsystems based on light-emitting diodes (LEDs).

PerkinElmer Optoelectronics makes fiber-optic test systems and lithography systems used in medical, industrial, and telecommunications applications. PerkinElmer Life and Analytical Sciences makes products used for drug discovery and genetic disease screening, including labeling reagents and cell imaging systems.

Looking to improve its international reach, particularly in the Asia/Pacific region, PerkinElmer in 2008 opened an R&D center in Singapore. The Center of Excellence manufactures a variety of instruments and specifically supports the corporate EcoAnalytix program. EcoAnalytix is aimed at providing products for applications in food quality, water purity, and renewable energy, such as the development of biofuels. Later in the year, PerkinElmer opened an EcoAnalytix application and technical center in Mumbai, India.

In 2008 PerkinElmer bought the newborn metabolic screening laboratory of Pediatrix Medical. Later the same year, the company expanded its hydrocarbon processing abilities with the acquisition of long-time partner Arnel, Inc.

HISTORY

PerkinElmer traces its roots back to the invention of the strobe light in 1931. MIT professor Harold Edgerton, who invented the strobe light while doing research on electric motors, formed a consulting business with former student Kenneth Germeshausen that used strobe lights and high-speed photography to solve manufacturing problems. As business picked up, they brought in another former student, Herbert Grier, and in 1947 formed Edgerton, Germeshausen and Grier. Their first contract job was to photograph nuclear weapons tests for the US government. The company went public in 1959 and changed its name to EG&G in 1966.

Over the next 30 years, EG&G bought scores of companies involved in electronic instruments and components, biomedical services, energy and nuclear weapons R&D, seal and gasket manufacturing, automotive testing, and the aerospace industry. Key acquisitions included Reynolds Electrical & Engineering (1967), which provided support services for the Department of Defense (including the nuclear weapons testing program); Sealol (1968), a maker of seals for industrial applications; and Automotive Research Associates (1973).

Company veteran John Kucharski became CEO in 1987 and chairman in 1988. The company took over operation of Department of Energy (DOE) facilities in Miamisburg, Ohio (1988) and Rocky Flats, Colorado (1990). The company bought the optoelectronics businesses of General Electric Canada in 1990, and the next year it purchased Heimann, a German maker of optoelectronic devices, from Siemens. EG&G acquired Finland's Wallac Group (analytical and diagnostic systems) from Procordia AB in 1993. The following year it bought IC Sensors (sold in 1999).

The close of the Cold War put an end to DOE-sponsored nuclear weapons programs, while activists' questions about worker safety and environmental protection measures led to lawsuits against the company. In 1994 EG&G announced that it would discontinue its nuclear business (which had accounted for about half of sales) as its contracts ran out.

In 1998 the company sold its mechanical components businesses (Sealol, Rotron) and created a separate life sciences unit. Kucharski retired that year and president Gregory Summe, a former AlliedSignal (now Honeywell International) and General Electric executive, was named CEO.

In 1999 the company bought Lumen Technologies, a maker of specialty light sources, and paid $425 million for the analytical instruments division of PE Corporation (formerly Perkin-Elmer, then Applied Biosystems, and later Life Technologies). EG&G later changed its name to

PerkinElmer. That same year the company sold its technical services business to The Carlyle Group in a $250 million deal.

In 2001 the company acquired Packard BioScience, a maker of drug discovery products, for $650 million. Later that year PerkinElmer sold two units, Voltarc Technologies (specialty lighting products) and Instruments for Research and Applied Science (scientific instrumentation).

In 2005 PerkinElmer divested the operations that comprised its fluid sciences business segment to focus on products related to health sciences and photonics. It sold the Automotive Research Laboratory segment of its fluid sciences division to Intertek Caleb Brett, a division of Intertek Group. The company also sold its aerospace business to Eaton for approximately $333 million.

In 2006 PerkinElmer acquired the assets of Spectral Genomics, a supplier of molecular karyotyping technology. The company acquired ViaCell (now ViaCord) for about $300 million in 2007, in order to expand its offerings in neonatal and prenatal markets.

President/COO Robert Friel was promoted to CEO in 2008, succeeding Gregory Summe, who remained executive chairman until the 2009 annual meeting. Friel joined the company in 1999 as CFO.

EXECUTIVES

Chairman, President, and CEO: Robert F. (Rob) Friel, age 54, $4,853,169 total compensation
SVP, CFO, and Chief Accounting Officer: Frank A. (Andy) Wilson, age 51, $979,333 total compensation
SVP; President, Environmental Health: John A. Roush, age 44, $1,572,571 total compensation
SVP and Chief Scientific Officer; President, Greater China: Daniel R. (Dan) Marshak, age 52, $1,182,875 total compensation
SVP, General Counsel, and Secretary: Joel S Goldberg, age 41
SVP Human Resources: John R. Letcher, age 48
SVP and Chief Marketing Officer: Lapo Paladini
CIO: Eric Lindgren
VP; CFO, Human Health: Michael L. Battles, age 41, $789,287 total compensation
VP Chromatography and Mass Spectrometry, Analytical Sciences and Laboratory Services: Eric Ziegler
VP Business Development, Bio-discovery: Alan Fletcher
VP Corporate Communications: Stephanie R. Wasco
VP Spectroscopy, Analytical Sciences and Laboratory Services: Martin Long
VP Automation and Detection Solutions, Bio-discovery: Nance Hall
VP Business Development: Aaron Geist
President, Genetic Screening: Ann-Christine Sundell
President, Analytical Sciences and Laboratory Services: Maurice H. (Dusty) Tenney
President, Emerging Technologies: Richard F. (Dick) Begley, age 61
President, PerkinElmer India: Fedja Bobanovic
President, Illumination and Detection Solutions: David Nislick
President, Bio-discovery: Richard Eglen
Auditors: Deloitte & Touche LLP

LOCATIONS

HQ: PerkinElmer, Inc.
940 Winter St., Waltham, MA 02451
Phone: 781-663-6900   **Fax:** 203-944-4904
Web: www.perkinelmer.com

2009 Sales

	$ mil.	% of total
US	732.9	40
Europe		
Germany	130.0	7
UK	119.0	7
France	79.5	4
Italy	76.5	4
China	117.8	7
Japan	83.3	5
Other countries	473.2	26
Total	**1,812.2**	**100**

PRODUCTS/OPERATIONS

2009 Sales

	$ mil.	% of total
Environmental Health	1,075.7	59
Human Health	736.5	41
Total	**1,812.2**	**100**

Selected Products

Analytical Instruments
  Chromatography
    Gas chromatographs
    Hybrid gas chromatography/mass spectrometers
    Liquid chromatographs
    Consumables and accessories
  Informatics
    Chromatography Data Systems software (TotalChrom)
    Laboratory information management systems (LABWORKS)
    Web-based instrument and data management systems (Sombrilla)
  Inorganic analysis
    Atomic absorption spectrometers
    Inductively coupled plasma (ICP) mass spectrometers
    ICP optical emission spectrometers
    Sample preparation equipment
  Molecular spectroscopy
    Fourier transform-infrared (FT-IR) spectroscopes
    Luminescence spectrometers
    Polarimeters
    Ultraviolet-visible spectroscopes
  Thermal and elemental analysis
    Elemental
      Carbon, hydrogen, nitrogen, sulfur, and oxygen (CHNS/O) analyzers
      Nitrogen analyzers
    Thermal
      Differential scanning calorimeters
      Dynamic mechanical analyzers
      Thermogravimetric analyzers
      Thermomechanical analyzers
Life Sciences
  Automated liquid handling high-throughput screening (HTS) systems
  Chemical reagents for heterogenous and homogenous assays
  Live cell imaging systems for proteomics research
  Multilabel counters and plate readers
  Parallel plate processing systems
Optoelectronics
  Health sciences
    Endoscopic surgical lamps
    Gas sensors for patient monitoring equipment
    Single photon counting modules (SPCMs)
    Thermopiles
  Industrial
    Charge-coupled display cameras
    Mercury ultraviolet lamps
    Ultraviolet laser-based direct imaging systems for newspaper printing

COMPETITORS

Agilent Technologies
Beckman Coulter
Bio-Rad Labs
Bruker
Danaher
Dionex
Harvard Bioscience
Honeywell International
IDEXX Labs
Kaydon
MDS
Mettler-Toledo
MTS Systems
Nanosphere
OSI Systems
Roper Industries
Shimadzu Scientific Instruments
Siemens AG
Thermo Fisher Scientific
Tyco
Varian Medical Systems
Waters Corp.

HISTORICAL FINANCIALS

Company Type: Public

Income Statement

FYE: Sunday nearest December 31

	REVENUE ($ mil.)	NET INCOME ($ mil.)	NET PROFIT MARGIN	EMPLOYEES
12/09	1,812	86	4.7%	8,200
12/08	1,938	126	6.5%	7,900
12/07	1,787	132	7.4%	8,700
12/06	1,546	120	7.7%	8,500
12/05	1,474	268	18.2%	8,000
Annual Growth	**5.3%**	**(24.8%)**	**—**	**0.6%**

2009 Year-End Financials

Debt ratio: 34.3%
Return on equity: 5.4%
Cash ($ mil.): 180
Current ratio: 1.78
Long-term debt ($ mil.): 558
No. of shares (mil.): 118
Dividends
  Yield: 1.4%
  Payout: 38.4%
Market value ($ mil.): 2,428

Stock History

NYSE: PKI

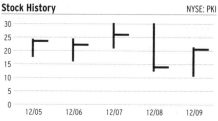

	STOCK PRICE ($) FY Close	P/E High/Low		PER SHARE ($) Earnings	Dividends	Book Value
12/09	20.59	29	15	0.73	0.28	13.82
12/08	13.91	28	12	1.07	0.28	13.30
12/07	26.02	28	20	1.09	0.28	13.36
12/06	22.23	25	17	0.95	0.28	13.38
12/05	23.56	12	9	2.04	0.28	14.00
Annual Growth	**(3.3%)**	**—**	**—**	**(22.7%)**	**0.0%**	**(0.3%)**

Perrigo Company

Perrigo makes its name by making sure you never see it. One of the US's largest manufacturers of generic and private-label over-the-counter pharmaceuticals and supplements, Perrigo makes products that use similar packaging and discount pricing to compete with leading national brands. The company makes more than 1,300 products, including pain relievers, cough and cold remedies, dietary supplements, and smoking cessation products — some of which are sold under its own Good Sense brand. It also makes more than 250 generic prescription products for other companies. Its Active Pharmaceutical Ingredients (API) division manufactures the raw materials used by generic and branded pharmaceutical companies worldwide. Wal-Mart accounts for more than 20% of sales.

Perrigo's international consumer health care product subsidiaries Quimica y Farmacia (Mexico) and Wrafton (UK) offer over-the-counter and store-brand pharmaceutical products. Perrigo manufactures generic prescription drugs at facilities in the US and Israel, and subsidiary Chemagis makes APIs in Israel, Germany, and China. In 2010 it divested its consumer products operations (but not its manufacturing operations) in Israel. The business primarily sold consumer products to the Israeli market, including cosmetics, toiletries, and detergents.

In a departure from all things pharmaceutical, in 2010 Perrigo purchased PBM Holdings, a US-based private manufacturer and marketer of store-brand infant formulas and baby foods. The $808 million acquisition took advantage of Perrigo's existing private-label relationships with retailers, and gave it a deeper presence in the OTC consumer products market.

To expand internationally, the firm has made purchases abroad including the acquisition of UK company Galpharm Healthcare, a manufacturer of store brand products, in 2008. It then bought Mexican drugmaker Laboratorios Diba to expand its manufacturing capacity. In 2010 the company agreed to acquire Australian OTC products maker Orion Laboratorie.

Perrigo's ongoing efforts to introduce a generic version of Mucinex (guaifenesin) have been stymied by Mucinex maker Adams Respiratory, which has filed a blizzard of patent infringement lawsuits seeking to protect its lucrative market niche. The company won the rights to begin selling a version of Johnson & Johnson's Monistat vaginal infection product after a similar series of lawsuits. It plans to begin marketing the products in 2010.

Perrigo in 2010 acquired from Teva Pharmaceuticals the exclusive US store brand rights to sell and distribute generic versions of blockbuster allergy drug Allegra. Though Allegra is currently a prescription drug (for which Teva has held the rights until this sale), Sanofi-Aventis has applied to the FDA to switch the drug to an over-the-counter product.

Along with snapping up other companies' products, Perrigo has its own in-house research and development team that whips up generic formulations of name brand products, and also responds to changes in existing national brand products by reformulating its own products.

Vice Chairman Moshe Arkin owns about 10% of Perrigo, and director Michael Jandernoa holds just over a 3% stake.

HISTORY

Brothers Luther and Charles Perrigo moved from New York to Michigan in 1887 and opened a general store. Soon they began packaging home remedies. Charles left the company, but Luther continued, incorporating in 1892. Their family ran the business for most of the next century.

After WWII Perrigo began making drugs and personal products. In 1979 Michael Jandernoa became VP of finance for the firm, which by the next year led the store-brand products industry. In 1984 it bought Bell Pharmacal Labs.

Perrigo went public in 1986 as part of manufacturing conglomerate the Grow Group, then was bought by management in 1988 and taken public again in 1991. Perrigo built its own packaging and labeling plant in 1992.

After several years of growth, Perrigo slipped in 1995 and 1996, in part because of restructuring, ongoing lawsuits, and costs associated with its 1994 purchase of product lines and facilities from rival Vi-Jon Laboratories. But sales picked up with the launches of off-patent versions of popular brand-name drugs (such as Aleve and Rogaine).

In 1997 Perrigo bought 88% of Mexican drugmaker Quimica y Farmacia and took a stake in the largest drug distributor in Russia and Ukraine. The latter's failure (spurred by Russia's economic crisis) and slumping OTC drug sales walloped the company in 1998. Perrigo responded by restructuring and closing facilities to cut costs. It sold its personal care products line in 1999. The next year the company hired CEO David Gibbons, a 3M and Rubbermaid veteran known as a turnaround specialist.

Perrigo acquired Israeli pharmaceutical company Agis in 2005. The move expanded its reach into Israel and gave Perrigo a large foothold in the active pharmaceutical ingredients (APIs) market.

Perrigo took a big hit in late 2006, when more than 10 million packages of the company's acetaminophen were recalled from drug retailers across the US because the pills were found to contain metal fragments. Some of the packaged containers of 500-milligram tablets were distributed more than three years prior; more than 120 retail chains were affected.

That same year, prompted by concerns of misuse, Congress mandated a limit on the production and distribution of products containing the decongestant pseudoephedrine. Perrigo's sales of pseudoephedrine dropped more than two-thirds in a two-year period, and the company scrambled (along with the entire industry) to reformulate its products with an alternative decongestant.

The company named Joseph Papa CEO in 2006; Gibbons remained as chairman until late 2007, when Papa became chairman, as well.

Perrigo purchased Qualis, manufacturer primarily of head lice treatment products, in 2007. It followed that buy-up by acquiring nine generic dermatological products and four pipeline products from Stiefel Laboratories subsidiary Glades Pharmaceuticals. It then added several smoking cessation products, including a nicotine gum meant to compete as a store brand with GlaxoSmithKline's Nicorette.

EXECUTIVES

Chairman, President, and CEO: Joseph C. Papa, age 54, $3,674,023 total compensation
EVP and CFO: Judy L. Brown, age 41, $1,168,219 total compensation
EVP; President, Perrigo Israel: Refael Lebel, age 51, $1,244,086 total compensation
EVP, General Counsel and Secretary: Todd W. Kingma, age 50, $1,222,256 total compensation
EVP Global Operations and Supply Chain: John T. Hendrickson, age 46, $1,096,589 total compensation
EVP U.S. Generics: Sharon Kochan, age 42
SVP and CIO: Thomas M. (Tom) Farrington, age 53
SVP Commercial Business Development: Jeffrey R. Needham, age 54
SVP and Chief Scientific Officer: Jatin Shah
SVP Consumer Healthcare Sales: James C. Tomshack, age 59
SVP Global Quality and Compliance: Louis W. Yu, age 60
SVP Global Human Resources: Michael R. Stewart, age 57
VP Investor Relations and Communication: Arthur J. Shannon
Auditors: BDO Seidman, LLP

LOCATIONS

HQ: Perrigo Company
515 Eastern Ave., Allegan, MI 49010
Phone: 269-673-8451   **Fax:** 269-673-9128
Web: www.perrigo.com

2010 Sales

	$ mil.	% of total
US	1,800.0	79
Israel, UK, Mexico, Australia	468.9	21
Total	**2,268.9**	**100**

PRODUCTS/OPERATIONS

2010 Sales

	$ mil.	% of total
Consumer health care	1,833.0	81
Prescription pharmaceuticals	237.6	10
Active pharmaceutical ingredients	139.3	6
Other	59.0	3
Total	**2,268.9**	**100**

Selected Products

Analgesics
Antacids
Cough/cold remedies
Diagnostic test kits
Feminine hygiene products
First aid
Laxatives
Nutritional drinks
Nutritional supplements
Sleep aids
Smoking cessation
Vitamins

Subsidiaries

Arginet Investments and Property (2003) Ltd. (Israel)
Barum Limited (UK)
Careline (Pharmagis) Ltd. (Israel)
ChemAgis B.V. (Netherlands)
Clay Park Industries Inc.
Dovechem Ltd. (Israel)
Elite Soap Manufacturers (1986) (Israel)
Enprofen Ltd. (UK)
Galpharm Healthcare Ltd. (UK)
Healthy Ideas Ltd. (UK)
Indo-China Trading Ltd. (UK)
Kiteacre Ltd. (UK)
L. Perrigo Company
Neca Chemicals (1952) Ltd. (Israel)
Neca Cosmetics Products (1990) Ltd. (Israel)
Pan-European Pharmaceuticals Ltd. (UK)
Pharma Clal Ltd. (Israel)
Quimica y Farmacia S.A. de C.V. (Mexico)
Vesteck Ltd. (Israel)
Wrafton Laboratories Limited (UK)

COMPETITORS

Actavis
Apotex
Bayer AG
Bristol-Myers Squibb
Caraco Pharmaceutical
Chattem
Dr. Reddy's
GlaxoSmithKline
Hi-Tech Pharmacal
Mylan
NBTY
Novartis
Nycomed US
Paddock Laboratories
Par Pharmaceutical Companies
Pfizer
PureTek
Roxane Laboratories
Sandoz International GmbH
Stiefel Laboratories
Taro
Teva Pharmaceuticals
Watson Pharmaceuticals

HISTORICAL FINANCIALS

Company Type: Public

Income Statement

FYE: June 30

	REVENUE ($ mil.)	NET INCOME ($ mil.)	NET PROFIT MARGIN	EMPLOYEES
6/10	2,269	223	9.8%	7,700
6/09	2,007	144	7.2%	7,250
6/08	1,822	136	7.5%	6,200
6/07	1,447	74	5.1%	6,200
6/06	1,367	71	5.2%	5,969
Annual Growth	13.5%	32.9%	—	6.6%

2010 Year-End Financials

Debt ratio: 86.0%
Return on equity: 22.2%
Cash ($ mil.): 98
Current ratio: 1.52
Long-term debt ($ mil.): 935

No. of shares (mil.): 92
Dividends
  Yield: 0.4%
  Payout: 10.0%
Market value ($ mil.): 5,416

Stock History

NASDAQ (GS): PRGO

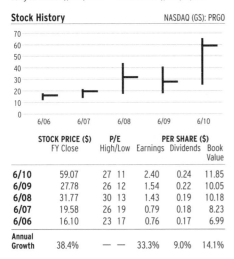

	STOCK PRICE ($) FY Close	P/E High/Low		PER SHARE ($) Earnings	Dividends	Book Value
6/10	59.07	27	11	2.40	0.24	11.85
6/09	27.78	26	12	1.54	0.22	10.05
6/08	31.77	30	13	1.43	0.19	10.18
6/07	19.58	26	19	0.79	0.18	8.23
6/06	16.10	23	17	0.76	0.17	6.99
Annual Growth	38.4%	—	—	33.3%	9.0%	14.1%

Peter Kiewit Sons'

Peter Kiewit Sons' is a heavyweight in the heavy construction industry. The general contractor and its subsidiaries have a breadth of expertise, building everything from roads and dams to high-rise office towers and power plants throughout the US and Canada. Its transportation projects, which include bridges, rail lines, airport runways, and mass transit systems, account for a majority of its sales. Kiewit also serves the oil and gas, electrical, power, and waterworks industries. Public contracts, most of which are awarded by government agencies, are handled by its Kiewit Federal Group. The company, which was founded in 1884, is owned by current and former employees and Kiewit family members.

As a leader in transportation construction, Kiewit is responsible for several notable highway and bridge projects, from replacing a segment of the San Francisco-Oakland Bay Bridge Skyway to upgrading the Sea-to-Sky Highway between Vancouver and Whistler, British Columbia. Water supply and dam projects include the Olivenhain and East dams in California, underground storage tanks for the Hollywood Hills Quality Improvement Project, and an intake valve at Lake Mead in Nevada.

Kiewit also has steadily built its expertise working on environmentally sensitive projects in the power sector. Through its Kiewit Power Engineers Co., the company has been contracted by Plutonic Energy Corporation and GE Energy Financial Services to work on one of British Columbia's largest renewable energy projects — building six hydroelectric projects with intakes, penstocks, and a transmission line that will reduce dependence on non-renewable imported energy. The firm is working with the local Native American community, First Nations, creating jobs to help complete the project. Kiewit also has experience working on wind energy farms in Canada.

The company's mining operations (Kiewit Mining Group) include ownership of coal mines in Texas, Montana, and Wyoming and management of two additional mines, all of which are surface mines.

Subsidiary Kiewit Offshore Services fabricates complex offshore oil production platforms at a facility in Texas. The company counts many of the world's largest oil companies as its clients. Another subsidiary, Kiewit Energy Group, focuses on the petroleum refining business.

In 2008 the group acquired TIC Holdings, a heavy industrial construction and engineering firm based in Colorado. TIC operates more than 40 area and district offices throughout North America. It provides construction services in the power, mining, oil/gas/chemicals, renewable energy, water, marine, food and beverage, and pulp and paper industries.

HISTORY

Born to Dutch immigrants, Peter Kiewit and brother Andrew founded Kiewit Brothers, a brickyard, in 1884 in Omaha, Nebraska. By 1912 two of Peter's sons worked at the yard, which was named Peter Kiewit & Sons. When Peter Kiewit died in 1914, his son Ralph took over, and the firm took the name Peter Kiewit Sons'. Another son, Peter, joined Ralph at the helm in 1924 after dropping out of Dartmouth, and later took over.

During the Depression, Kiewit managed huge federal public works projects, and in the 1940s it focused on war-related emergency construction projects.

One of the company's most difficult projects was top-secret Thule Air Force Base in Greenland, above the Arctic Circle. For more than two years 5,000 men worked around the clock, beginning in 1951; the site was in development for 15 years. In 1952 the company won a contract to build a $1.2 billion gas diffusion plant in Portsmouth, Ohio. It also became a contractor for the US interstate highway system (begun in 1956).

Peter Kiewit died in 1979, after stipulating that the largely employee-owned company should remain under employee control and that no one employee could own more than 10%. His 40% stake, when returned to the company, transformed many employees into millionaires. Walter Scott Jr., whose father had been the first graduate engineer to work for Kiewit, took charge. Scott made his mark by parlaying money from construction into successful investments.

When the construction industry slumped, Kiewit began looking for other investment opportunities, and in 1984 it acquired packaging company Continental Can Co. (selling off noncore insurance, energy, and timber assets). Continental was saddled with a 1983 class action lawsuit alleging that it had plotted to close plants and lay off workers before they were qualified for pensions. In 1991 Kiewit agreed to pay $415 million to settle the lawsuit. In the face of a consolidating packaging industry, the company sold Continental in the early 1990s.

In 1986 Kiewit loaned money to a business group to build a fiber-optic loop in Chicago; by 1987 it had launched MFS Communications to build local fiber loops in downtown districts. In 1992 Kiewit split its business into two pieces: the construction group, which was strictly employee-owned; and a diversified group, to which it added a controlling stake in phone and cable TV company C-TEC in 1993. That year Kiewit took MFS public; by 1995 it had sold all its shares, and the next year MFS was bought by telecom giant WorldCom.

In 1996 Kiewit assisted CalEnergy (now MidAmerican Energy) in a hostile $1.3 billion takeover of the UK's Northern Electric. Kiewit got stock in CalEnergy and a 30% stake in the UK electric company, all of which is sold to CalEnergy in 1998.

That year Kiewit spun off its telecom and computer services holdings into Level 3 Communications. Scott, who had been hospitalized the year before for a blood clot in his lung, stepped down as CEO, and Ken Stinson, CEO of Kiewit Construction Group, took over Peter Kiewit Sons'.

Kiewit spun off its asphalt, concrete, and aggregates operations in 2000 as Kiewit Materials. Also that year it created Kiewit Offshore Services to focus on construction for the offshore drilling industry. Kiewit made history in 2002 for the fastest completion of a project of its type when it completed the rebuilding of Webbers Falls I-40 Bridge in Oklahoma at the end of July. (The bridge had collapsed in May after being hit by a pair of barges, resulting in 14 fatalities.)

In 2004 Kiewit greatly increased its coal sales and reserves with the acquisition of the Buckskin Mine in Wyoming from Arch Coal.

Also that year 22-year veteran Bruce Grewcock took the reins as the company's fourth CEO since its founding. Stinson stayed on as the company's chairman.

EXECUTIVES

Chairman Emeritus: J. Walter (Walter) Scott Jr., age 78
Chairman: Kenneth E. (Ken) Stinson, age 67
President and CEO: Bruce E. Grewcock, age 55
EVP; EVP, Kiewit Corporation and Kiewit Pacific Co.:
Richard W. Colf, age 65
**EVP and Division Manager and Director; EVP, Kiewit
Corporation, Kiewit Construction, Kiewit Pacific Co.,
and Kiewit Western Co.:** R. Michael Phelps, age 55
EVP: Douglas E. Patterson, age 57
**EVP and Division Manager; EVP, Kiewit Corporation
and Kiewit Construction; President, Gilbert Industrial
Corp.:** Scott L. Cassels, age 50
**SVP and Hawaii Area Manager, Kiewit Building Group;
VP Kiewit Pacific:** Lance K. Wilhelm
SVP, General Counsel, and Secretary: Tobin A. Schropp,
age 46
SVP and CFO: Michael J. Piechoski, age 54
VP and Treasurer: Ben E. Muraskin, age 44
VP Human Resources and Administration:
Michael Gary
**Division Manager, VP, and Director; SVP, Kiewit
Corporation; President, Kiewit Mining Group:**
Christopher J. Murphy, age 54
**Division Manager and Director; SVP, Kiewit
Corporation and Kiewit Construction; President,
Kiewit Energy Group:** Thomas S. Shelby, age 50
**Leader, Structural Design Team, Keiwit Engineering
Co.:** Dave Sinsheimer
**Leader, Structural Design Team, Keiwit Engineering
Co.:** Dave Anderson
**Controller and Assistant Secretary; VP and Controller,
Kiewit Corporation:** Michael J. Whetstine, age 42
President, Kiewit Engineering Co. (KECo):
Gary Pietrok
CEO, Kiewet Federal Group: Kirk R. Samuelson, age 51
Auditors: KPMG LLP

LOCATIONS

HQ: Peter Kiewit Sons', Inc.
Kiewit Plaza, 3555 Farnam St., Omaha, NE 68131
Phone: 402-342-2052　　**Fax:** 402-271-2939
Web: www.kiewit.com

PRODUCTS/OPERATIONS

Selected Subsidiaries and Affiliates
Aero Automatic Sprinkler
Buckskin Mining Company
Black Butte Company
Continental Fire Sprinkler Company
Decker Coal Company
Ganotec Corporation
General Construction Company
Kiewit Building Group
Kiewit Constructors Inc.
Kiewit Energy, Inc.
Kiewit Engineering Co.
Kiewit Federal Group
Kiewit Mining Group
Kiewit New Mexico Co.
Kiewit Offshore Services Ltd.
Kiewit Pacific Co.
Kiewit Power
Kiewit Southern Co.
Kiewit Texas Construction L.P.
Kiewit Western Co.
Mass. Electric Construction Co.
TIC Holdings, Inc.
Walnut Creek Mining Company

COMPETITORS

ABB	Jacobs Engineering
Ames Construction	KBR
Balfour Beatty	Lane Construction
Bechtel	Parsons Corporation
Black & Veatch	Raytheon
Bovis Lend Lease	Rio Tinto plc
CH2M HILL	Skanska USA Civil
Fluor	Turner Corporation
Foster Wheeler	Tutor Perini
Granite Construction	Walsh Group
Halliburton	Whiting-Turner
Hubbard Group	Williams Companies

HISTORICAL FINANCIALS
Company Type: Private

Income Statement				FYE: Last Saturday in December
	REVENUE ($ mil.)	NET INCOME ($ mil.)	NET PROFIT MARGIN	EMPLOYEES
12/08	8,000	—	—	15,000
12/07	6,200	—	—	15,000
12/06	5,049	—	—	14,700
12/05	4,145	—	—	14,500
12/04	3,352	—	—	14,000
Annual Growth	24.3%	—	—	1.7%

Revenue History

PetSmart, Inc.

PetSmart is the top dog and the cat's meow in its industry. The #1 US specialty retailer of pet food and supplies boasts about 1,150 stores in the US and Canada. Both pets and their masters may lay paws, claws, or hands on its 10,000 products, which range from scratching posts to iguana harnesses, and are sold under national brands and PetSmart's own private labels. The retailer offers products through its PetSmart website. PetSmart stores also provide in-store boarding facilities (PetsHotels), grooming services, and obedience training. Veterinary services are available in more than 750 shops through pet hospital operator Medical Management International (known as Banfield).

While most of PetSmart's sales come from pet food and supplies, the service side (grooming, pet training, boarding, and day camp) of its business has been growing. The company operates more than 160 in-store PetsHotels boarding facilities and Doggie Day Camps. The company plans to eventually add more than 400 PetsHotels.

As the pet products firm chases after more profitable services business, it has looked to shed operations that don't satisfy its strategy. To this end, PetSmart in 2007 sold its State Line Tack subsidiary — exiting the equine niche altogether — to Web-based retailer PetsUnited.

Meanwhile, the company's concentrating on its brick-and-mortar retail business. PetSmart thinks there is room for at least 1,400 of its PetSmart stores throughout North America. However, the weak economy continues to stall its expansion goals. PetSmart plans to maintain its slower growth as it seeks out additional investments under the new leadership of Robert Moran. Moran, formerly president and COO of the company, was promoted to CEO in mid-2009. He retained the title of president.

The pet supplier generates 2% of its sales through peddling pets, such as fresh-water tropical fish, birds, reptiles, and small animals. The company, on occasion, has shunned from selling certain types of pets to its customers. PetSmart temporarily suspended sales of birds in its stores nationwide in 2008 after discovering that birds with the bacterial infection psittacosis could spread the disease to humans. PetSmart does not sell dogs or cats. To encourage adoption of dogs and cats, PetSmart sponsors in-store adoption programs with local humane organizations.

As of 2010, PetSmart owns about 21% of Banfield's parent company, MMI Holdings, Inc.

HISTORY

In the mid-1980s the owner of a California pet supply wholesaler had an idea: If the company opened its own retail stores, it could make a bundle supplying itself. Not wanting to compete with its own retail customers in California, the company hired Jim and Janice Dougherty to run the first store in Las Vegas, called Pet Food Supermarket. In response to customer requests, the store began offering a broader range of products and soon business was booming. The store moved to a larger location, and four more stores were eventually opened in Phoenix.

While managing the Pet Food Supermarkets, the Doughertys met Ford Smith, a retailer who had developed a plan for giant pet-supply stores while in business school. Together they agreed to give the Toys "R" Us superstore format a try for pet supplies. They opened two PetFood Warehouse stores in Arizona in 1987. The next year there were seven stores in Arizona, Colorado, and Texas.

In 1989 PetFood Warehouse officially became PETsMART, Jim left the company due to health reasons (Janice followed shortly thereafter), and supermarket executive Sam Parker came on as CEO. His management team recrafted the PETsMART business strategy and gave the store a new look: brightly lit, low shelves with various pet supplies in the front of the store, and high warehouse-style shelves with bulk pet food in the back.

The 1990s saw PETsMART adding services such as in-store grooming, obedience training, veterinary exams, and adoption programs; it also began selling birds and fish. In 1991 the company added 15 new stores. The following year 32 stores were opened.

PETsMART went public in 1993. The company added more than 40 stores that year. In 1994 PETsMART bought the Weisheimer Companies, which operated about 30 pet superstores in the Midwest under the name Petzazz.

A year later the company went on an acquisition spree, buying two pet superstore operators (56-store, Georgia-based Petstuff and 10-store, New Jersey-based Pet Food Giant) and two specialty-catalog retailers of pet and animal supplies. Some 80 stores were added in 1995, and Mark Hansen replaced Parker as CEO; Parker remained chairman.

Hansen took PETsMART overseas in 1996 through the acquisition of Pet City Holdings, which operated more than 50 stores in the UK. The company also entered Canada that year. But the aggressive expansion campaign diverted the company's attention from daily operations and inventory management, eroding PETsMART's earnings in fiscal year 1998. In response, the company instituted a back-to-basics strategy of improved customer service and lower prices. Phil Francis, formerly with Shaw's Supermarkets, became CEO in 1998.

In 1999 PETsMART launched PETsMART.com in conjunction with PetJungle.com, an online pet retailer backed by Internet incubator idealab!. The move intensified a catfight with several lavishly funded online pet supply stores, including now-defunct Pets.com, which was backed by dominant e-tailer Amazon.com.

The company sold its 92 UK stores to Pets At Home for more than $40 million in late 1999. PETsMART acquired full ownership of PETsMART.com in 2002. Carrefour sold its 9.9% stake in PETsMART for $194.3 million through a public offering that year.

In 2003 PETsMART finished remodeling its stores; the company replaced the traditional warehouse feel with a specialty-store shopping atmosphere. The company added 100 new stores in 2005. In line with those changes, in 2006 PETsMART changed how its name is styled to PetSmart, with the emphasis on "smart" rather than "mart."

In 2007 PetSmart boosted its Canadian presence with the acquisition of 19 stores from the Super Pet chain. It exited the equine products business in May 2007 when it sold State Line Tack to PetsUnited.

In June 2009, PetSmart promoted president and COO Robert Moran to CEO of the company. He retained his title as president. Phil Francis, who led the company for more than a decade, was named executive chairman of PetSmart.

EXECUTIVES

Chairman: Philip L. (Phil) Francis, age 63, $5,547,530 total compensation
President, CEO, and Director: Robert F. (Bob) Moran, age 59, $5,298,326 total compensation
SVP and CFO: Lawrence P. (Chip) Molloy, age 48, $2,187,462 total compensation
SVP Store Services and Store Operations and Human Resources: David K. Lenhardt, age 40, $2,569,074 total compensation
SVP Supply Chain and Merchandising: Joseph D. (Joe) O'Leary, age 51, $2,342,089 total compensation
SVP and Chief Marketing Officer: John Alpaugh
SVP: Kenneth T. (Ken) Hall, age 41
SVP Human Resources: Neil H. Stacey, age 56
SVP, General Counsel, and Secretary: Emily D. Dickinson, age 50
SVP and CIO: Donald E. (Don) Beaver, age 51
SVP Supply Chain: Bruce K. Thorn, age 42
SVP Real Estate and Development: Jaye D. Perricone, age 51
VP Investor Relations: David (Dave) Cone
Director Corporate Planning and Reporting: Christina Vance
Auditors: Deloitte & Touche LLP

LOCATIONS

HQ: PetSmart, Inc.
  19601 N. 27th Ave., Phoenix, AZ 85027
Phone: 623-580-6100
Web: www.petsmart.com

2010 Stores

	No.
US	1,086
Canada	63
Total	**1,149**

PRODUCTS/OPERATIONS

2010 Sales

	$ mil.	% of total
Merchandise	4,761.0	89
Pet services	575.4	11
Total	**5,336.4**	**100**

Selected Merchandise

Animal carriers
Aquariums
Bedding
Bird cages
Books
Cat furniture
Collars
Dog houses
Freshwater tropical fish
Greeting cards
Health aids
Leashes
Litter
Magazines
Medications
Pet food
Reptiles
Shampoos
Toys
Treats

Selected Services

Boarding
Doggie day camp
Grooming
Obedience training
Veterinary services

Private Labels

Pet Food
  Authority (cat and dog food, treats)
  Grreat Choice (dog treats)
  SophistaCat (cat food)
Pet Supplies
  Top Fin
  Top Paw
  Top Wing

COMPETITORS

Ahold USA	PETCO
Albertsons	Petland
Costco Wholesale	PetMed
Drs. Foster & Smith	Sears Holdings
Fat Cat	Target
J&J Commerce	United Pharmacal
Pet Supermarket	VCA Antech
Pet Valu	Wal-Mart
PetCareRx	Weis Markets

HISTORICAL FINANCIALS

Company Type: Public

Income Statement

FYE: Sunday nearest January 31

	REVENUE ($ mil.)	NET INCOME ($ mil.)	NET PROFIT MARGIN	EMPLOYEES
1/10	5,336	198	3.7%	45,000
1/09	5,065	193	3.8%	46,000
1/08	4,673	259	5.5%	43,000
1/07	4,234	185	4.4%	38,400
1/06	3,761	183	4.9%	34,600
Annual Growth	**9.1%**	**2.1%**	**—**	**6.8%**

2010 Year-End Financials

Debt ratio: 45.5%
Return on equity: 17.1%
Cash ($ mil.): 308
Current ratio: 1.89
Long-term debt ($ mil.): 534
No. of shares (mil.): 118
Dividends
  Yield: 1.3%
  Payout: 20.8%
Market value ($ mil.): 3,047

Stock History

NASDAQ (GS): PETM

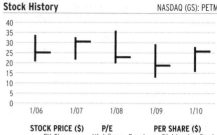

	STOCK PRICE ($) FY Close	P/E High/Low		PER SHARE ($) Earnings	Dividends	Book Value
1/10	25.75	17	10	1.59	0.33	9.91
1/09	18.77	19	9	1.52	0.12	9.67
1/08	22.87	18	10	1.95	0.12	8.34
1/07	30.54	24	17	1.33	0.12	8.46
1/06	25.06	27	17	1.25	0.12	7.95
Annual Growth	**0.7%**	**—**	**—**	**6.2%**	**28.8%**	**5.7%**

Pfizer Inc.

Pfizer pfabricates pfarmaceuticals pfor quite a pfew inpfirmities. The company is the world's largest research-based pharmaceuticals firm. Its best-known products include cholesterol-lowering Lipitor, pain management drugs Celebrex and Lyrica, pneumonia vaccine Prevnar, high-blood-pressure therapy Norvasc, and erectile dysfunction treatment Viagra. Pfizer also keeps Fluffy and Fido in mind with its animal health products, including Revolution (antiparasitic). Pfizer acquired pharma rival Wyeth in a $68 billion deal in 2009.

The combination of the two drug giants — the largest pharmaceuticals merger in nearly a decade — was designed to help both companies deal with upcoming patent losses on top-selling drugs. The acquisition of Wyeth broadened Pfizer's traditional and biological product offerings in areas including vaccines, antibiotics, women's health, inflammatory and cardiovascular conditions, and gastroenterology. Wyeth's top sellers include Prevnar, antidepressant Effexor, and arthritis treatment Enbrel. The combined company also has an expanded development pipeline for targets including Alzheimer's disease, cancer, pain, and psychosis.

The company launched a 10% workforce reduction to prepare for the transaction, and it estimates that the integration efforts will eventually result in an overall 15% reduction of the combined workforce.

The acquisition of Wyeth brought Pfizer back into the consumer health arena, adding products such as analgesic Advil and cough medicine Robitussin. (Pfizer sold its consumer unit — which made such sniffle-and-sneeze treatments as Benadryl and Sudafed — to Johnson & Johnson in 2006.)

Pfizer's largest patent threat has been over cash cow Lipitor, the world's top-selling drug that brings Pfizer over $12 billion in annual sales. After a years-long court battle over a proposed generic equivalent release by Ranbaxy, Pfizer reached a settlement agreement with the generics maker in 2008 allowing Ranbaxy to sell a generic Lipitor version in the US after November 30, 2011.

The drug giant claims that it will be able to launch new blockbusters from its robust pipeline to make up for the off-patent losses. Pfizer spends about $8 billion annually on R&D in order to bolster its pipeline, which includes about 130 projects in clinical stages of development, including drugs for diabetes, breast cancer, epilepsy, pain, and anxiety disorders.

Vaccines have taken on a new luster for many large drugmakers looking for the next big therapeutic treatment. Wyeth brings a strong foothold in the vaccines market; Pfizer also purchased Coley Pharmaceutical in early 2008 to gain access to Coley's vaccine technologies.

Pfizer took a financial hit, however, in 2009 when it agreed to pay $2.3 billion to settle allegations that it improperly marketed several drugs, including discontinued painkiller Bextra. In a recent crackdown effort against pharmaceutical marketing fraud (promoting drugs for unapproved uses), the federal government has reached several settlement agreements with large pharmaceutical companies (including smaller deals with Pfizer); however, Pfizer's 2009 settlement was the largest to date.

HISTORY

Charles Pfizer and his cousin, confectioner Charles Erhart, began making chemicals in Brooklyn in 1849. Products included camphor, citric acid, and santonin (an early antiparasitic). The company, incorporated in 1900 as Chas. Pfizer & Co., was propelled into the modern drug business when it was asked to mass-produce penicillin for the war effort in 1941.

Pfizer discovered Terramycin and introduced it in 1950. Three years later it bought drugmaker Roerig, its first major acquisition. In the 1950s the company opened branches in Belgium, Canada, Cuba, Mexico, and the UK and began manufacturing in Asia, Europe, and South America. By the mid-1960s Pfizer had worldwide sales of more than $200 million.

Beginning in the late 1950s, Pfizer made Salk and Sabin polio vaccines and added new drugs, such as Diabinese (antidiabetic, 1958) and Vibramycin (antibiotic, 1967). It moved into consumer products in the early 1960s, buying BenGay, Desitin, and cosmetics maker Coty (sold 1992). It bought hospital products company Howmedica in 1972 (sold 1998) and heart-valve maker Shiley in 1979.

When growth slowed in the 1970s, new chairman Edmund Pratt increased R&D expenditures, resulting in Minipress (antihypertensive, 1975), Feldene (arthritis pain reliever, 1980), and Glucotrol (antidiabetic, 1984). Licensing agreements with foreign companies let Pfizer sell antihypertensive Procardia XL and antibiotic Cefobid. In the 1980s Pfizer expanded its hospital products division, buying 18 product lines and companies.

Lawsuits over the failure of about 500 heart valves and the alleged falsification of records led Pfizer to divest most of Shiley's operations in 1992. Drugs released that year included antidepressant Zoloft, antibiotic Zithromax, and cardiovascular agent Norvasc.

In 1997 Pfizer began promoting Lipitor, the cholesterol-lowering drug discovered by Warner-Lambert; it grabbed nearly 13% of the market in its first four months. Pfizer made headlines (and lots of happy men) when the company won FDA approval for Viagra in 1998. The little blue pill became a pop icon, and made the company a household name.

When Warner-Lambert said in 1999 that it would merge with American Home Products (now Wyeth), Pfizer sued to prevent the union and eventually succeeded with its own hostile bid. The merger with Warner-Lambert was completed, and CEO William Steere retired.

In 2003 Pfizer purchased rival Pharmacia for $54 billion, making it the world's largest research-based pharmaceutical company. Following its two giant acquisitions, the company trimmed some 20,000 people.

While acquiring new holdings on the pharmaceutical front, the company trimmed its non-pharmaceutical businesses between 2003 and 2005, including operations it acquired with Pharmacia and its European generics portfolio.

Pfizer sold its consumer unit to Johnson & Johnson in 2006, including such brands as Benadryl, Listerine, Nicorette, Rolaids, and Sudafed, for $16.6 billion.

Pfizer's board dismissed Hank McKinnell as its CEO in 2006, replacing him with general counsel Jeffrey Kindler. Kindler began restructuring the company. By the end of 2007, about 12% of Pfizer's workforce had been cut.

Bestsellers Norvasc and antidepressant Zoloft lost patent protection in 2007. New products launched in 2007 included AIDS drug Selzentry and smoking-cessation aid Chantix.

EXECUTIVES

Chairman Emeritus: William C. Steere Jr., age 73
Chairman Emeritus: M. Anthony Burns, age 67
Chairman and CEO: Jeffrey B. (Jeff) Kindler, age 54, $14,898,038 total compensation
SVP Business Operations and CFO: Frank A. D'Amelio, age 52, $7,858,969 total compensation
SVP and Chief Medical Officer: Freda C. Lewis-Hall, age 54, $5,087,263 total compensation
SVP; Group President, Pfizer BioPharmaceutical Businesses: Ian C. Read, age 56, $9,447,036 total compensation
SVP and Chief Compliance Officer: Douglas (Doug) Lankler
SVP and General Counsel: Amy W. Schulman, age 49
SVP Worldwide Policy: Greg Simon
SVP Worldwide Clinical Development: Briggs W. Morrison
SVP; President, Pfizer Worldwide Research and Development: Mikael Dolsten, age 51
SVP; President, Pfizer Global Manufacturing: Natale S. (Nat) Ricciardi, age 61
SVP; Group President, Diversified Businesses: Cavan M. Redmond, age 49
SVP Investor Relations: Charles E. (Chuck) Triano
SVP Worldwide Business Development, Strategy, and Innovation: Kristin C. Peck
SVP Worldwide Human Resources: Mary S. McLeod, age 53
SVP and Chief Communications Officer: Sally Susman, age 48
SVP, Chief Accounting Officer, and Controller: Loretta V. Cangialosi
VP and Chief Talent Officer: Tanya Clemons
President, US Primary Care: Adele Gulfo
President, Pfizer Vaccines: Mark Swindell
Auditors: KPMG LLP

LOCATIONS

HQ: Pfizer Inc.
235 E. 42nd St., New York, NY 10017
Phone: 212-733-2323
Web: www.pfizer.com

2009 Sales

	$ mil.	% of total
US	21,749	44
Europe	14,561	29
Japan & Asia	7,988	16
Canada, Latin America, Africa & Middle East	5,711	11
Total	**50,009**	**100**

PRODUCTS/OPERATIONS

Selected Products

Pharmaceuticals
Aricept (Alzheimer's disease)
Aromasin (breast cancer)
BeneFIX (hemophilia, from Wyeth acquisition)
Caduet (high cholesterol and blood pressure dual therapy)
Camptosar (colorectal cancer)
Cardura (hypertension and enlarged prostate disease)
Celebrex (arthritis pain)
Chantix/Champix (smoking cessation)
Detrol (overactive bladder)
Diflucan (antifungal)
Effexor (antidepressant and anxiety disorder treatment, from Wyeth acquisition)
Enbrel (arthritis treatment, from Wyeth acquisition)
Genotropin (growth hormone deficiency)
Geodon (schizophrenia and bipolar disorder, Zeldox outside of the US)
Lipitor (cholesterol)
Lybrel (oral contraceptive, from Wyeth acquisition)
Lyrica (nerve pain)
Neurontin (epilepsy)
Norvasc (hypertension)
Premarin (hormone replacement therapy, from Wyeth acquisition)
Prempro (hormone replacement therapy, from Wyeth acquisition)
Prevnar (pneumococcus vaccine, from Wyeth acquisition)
Pristiq (antidepressant, from Wyeth acquisition)
Protonix (protein pump inhibitor, from Wyeth acquisition)
Rapamune (organ rejection preventative, from Wyeth acquisition)
Rebif (multiple sclerosis)
ReFacto AF/Xyntha (hemophilia, from Wyeth acquisition)
Relpax (migraines)
Revatio (hypertension)
Selzentry (HIV)
Spiriva (chronic obstructive pulmonary disease)
Sutent (carcinoma and tumors)
Tygacil (anti-infective, from Wyeth acquisition)
Vfend (fungal infections)
Viagra (impotence)
Xalatan/Xalacom (glaucoma)
Xanax (anti-anxiety treatment)
Zithromax/Zmax (antibiotic)
Zoloft (depression)
Zosyn/Tazocin (anti-infective, from Wyeth acquisition)
Zyvox (antibiotic)

Animal Health
Convenia (canine and feline antibiotics)
Draxxin (cattle and swine antibiotic)
Excede (cattle and swine antibiotic)
Improvac (swine vaccine for boar taint)
Palladia (dog cancer treatment)
Revolution/Stronghold (antiparasitic for dogs and cats)
Rimadyl (canine osteoarthritis treatment)
Suvaxyn PCV2 (swine vaccine, from Wyeth acquisition)
Zulvac (cattle vaccine, from Wyeth acquisition)

Consumer Health (from Wyeth acquisition)
Advil (analgesic)
Anbesol (oral pain relief)
Caltrate (nutritional supplement)
Centrum (vitamins)
ChapStick (lip care)
Dimetapp (cough/cold remedy)
FiberCon (laxative)
Preparation H (hemorrhoid treatment)
Robitussin (cough/cold remedy)
ThermaCare (aches and pains)

Nutrition (from Wyeth acquisition)
  Progress Gold (nutritional formula)
  Promil Gold (nutritional formula)
  S-26 Gold (nutritional formula)

COMPETITORS

Abbott Labs
Amgen
Apotex
Astellas
AstraZeneca
Baxter International
Bayer AG
Biogen Idec
Boehringer Ingelheim
Bristol-Myers Squibb
Carma Laboratories
Chattem
Crucell
Eli Lilly
Forest Labs
Genzyme
GlaxoSmithKline
Johnson & Johnson
Merck
Merck KGaA
Mylan
Novartis
Novo Nordisk
Perrigo
Prestige Brands
Procter & Gamble
Ranbaxy Laboratories
Roche Holding
Sanofi-Aventis
Sun Pharmaceutical
Teva Pharmaceuticals
Watson Pharmaceuticals

HISTORICAL FINANCIALS

Company Type: Public

Income Statement

FYE: December 31

	REVENUE ($ mil.)	NET INCOME ($ mil.)	NET PROFIT MARGIN	EMPLOYEES
12/09	50,009	8,644	17.3%	116,500
12/08	48,296	8,104	16.8%	81,800
12/07	48,418	8,144	16.8%	86,600
12/06	48,371	19,337	40.0%	98,000
12/05	51,298	8,110	15.8%	106,000
Annual Growth	(0.6%)	1.6%	—	2.4%

2009 Year-End Financials

Debt ratio: 58.0%
Return on equity: 11.7%
Cash ($ mil.): 1,978
Current ratio: 1.66
Long-term debt ($ mil.): 52,193

No. of shares (mil.): 8,066
Dividends
  Yield: 4.4%
  Payout: 65.0%
Market value ($ mil.): 146,723

Stock History

NYSE: PFE

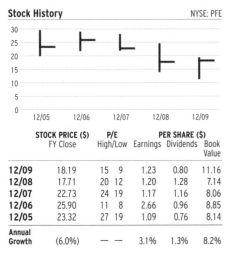

	STOCK PRICE ($) FY Close	P/E High/Low		PER SHARE ($) Earnings	Dividends	Book Value
12/09	18.19	15	9	1.23	0.80	11.16
12/08	17.71	20	12	1.20	1.28	7.14
12/07	22.73	24	19	1.17	1.16	8.06
12/06	25.90	11	8	2.66	0.96	8.85
12/05	23.32	27	19	1.09	0.76	8.14
Annual Growth	(6.0%)	—	—	3.1%	1.3%	8.2%

PG&E Corporation

Utility holding company PG&E Corporation is well on the way to fully recharging its batteries after losing power and declaring bankruptcy following California's energy crisis and the ensuing collapse of the wholesale energy trading industry. Its venerable Pacific Gas and Electric utility serves approximately 5.1 million electric customers and 4.3 million natural gas customers in California. The utility (which was founded in 1905) is also engaged in electricity generation; procurement and transmission; and natural gas procurement, transportation, and storage.

To help comply with the State of California's long-term carbon emission requirements, PG&E is pushing energy efficiency (both at its plants and its customers' facilities), but it is also breaking new ground. In 2008 it announced a 15-year purchase agreement with Canada's Finavera Renewables to use wave power captured off the Northern California coastline. PG&E is the first US utility company that has committed to purchasing wave-generated power. The company is also working with Topaz Solar Farms, a subsidiary of OptiSolar, for 550 MW of thin-film PV solar power and has signed a deal with High Plains Ranch II, a subsidiary of SunPower Corporation for 250 MW of high-efficiency PV solar energy. PG&E is also looking to develop wind farms with IBERDROLA RENEWABLES.

PG&E emerged from Chapter 11 in 2004 after reaching agreement with the California Public Utilities Commission (CPUC) in a dispute over the two entities' opposing reorganization plans. PG&E's original plan would have split the utility into several companies. The agreed-upon plan, which won bankruptcy court approval, left the utility intact under the CPUC's jurisdiction.

HISTORY

Peter Donahue founded the first gas company in the western US, San Francisco Gas, in 1852, which merged with Edison Light & Power to become San Francisco Gas & Electric (SFG&E) in 1896. Meanwhile, also in San Francisco, money broker George Roe and other investors founded California Electric Light (1879). The first electric utility in the US, it predated Edison's New York Pearl Street Station by three years. California Electric and SFG&E consolidated in 1905 to form Pacific Gas and Electric (PG&E).

In 1928 PG&E discovered natural gas in California, and in 1930 it began converting more than 2.5 million appliances to burn this fuel. The company started exploring for out-of-state gas supplies in the 1950s, first in Texas and New Mexico and then in western Canada.

The utility opened the world's first private atomic power plant (Vallecitos) in 1957, and in 1960 it developed the first geothermal plant (The Geysers) in North America. Its Humboldt Bay facility (completed 1963) was one of the first nukes to produce electricity at a cost comparable to that of conventional plants. Stanley Skinner began his 33-year career at PG&E in 1964 (he became CEO in 1995).

By the late 1970s PG&E had acquired some 500 electric, gas, and water utilities, but it left the water business in the 1980s. That year Unit

1 of the Diablo Canyon nuclear facility went on line, despite protests over its earthquake-fault location. Unit 2 was operating by 1986. PG&E fell on hard times in the mid-1980s as industrial customers began to generate their own electricity or buy gas directly from suppliers. In response, PG&E cut 2,500 jobs in 1987 and formed an independent power producer, which became U.S. Generating, with construction giant Bechtel. In 1995, as deregulation accelerated in California, the company formed an energy services division to serve large customers.

In 1996 PG&E was hit by an outage originating in the Pacific Northwest that affected nine western states and raised doubts over the power grid's stability. That year PG&E's gas unit bought a pipeline in Australia.

PG&E Corporation was formed as a holding company in 1997, and utility Pacific Gas and Electric became a subsidiary. The company also bought Bechtel's 50% stake in U.S. Generating. That year Skinner retired and president Robert Glynn became CEO. PG&E also settled a lawsuit filed in 1993 that claimed it had polluted groundwater by discharging toxic wastewater. (The case was the subject of a movie, *Erin Brockovich,* released in 2000.)

As its home state deregulated in 1998, PG&E was required to sell off most of its California power plants. The company auctioned off some of its hydro plants, and Duke Energy picked up three of the utility's fossil-fuel plants in California and its Australian pipeline. (The divestiture requirement was reversed by regulatory agencies in 2000.) PG&E also bought 18 power plants (4,800 MW) from New England Electric System.

In 1999 the company sold its Texas gas operations to El Paso Corporation, agreed to sell most of its retail marketing arm (PG&E Services) to Enron, and moved the headquarters of its nonregulated operations (PG&E National Energy Group) to Bethesda, Maryland. PG&E suffered a loss that fiscal year.

A price squeeze brought on in part by deregulation battered Pacific Gas and Electric in 2000. Prices on the wholesale power market soared, but a California rate freeze prevented the utility from passing along increasing costs to customers. In 2001 it suspended payments to creditors and suppliers to conserve cash, but gained some prospect of relief when California's governor signed legislation to allow a state agency to buy power from wholesalers under long-term contracts. Also that year PG&E sold its nonregulated energy services unit and its natural gas liquids businesses.

Later in 2001 the California Public Utilities Commission (CPUC) approved a significant increase in retail electricity rates, and the Federal Energy Regulatory Commission (FERC) approved a plan to limit wholesale energy prices during periods of severe shortage in 11 western states. The moves didn't come quickly enough for Pacific Gas and Electric, which filed for bankruptcy protection. The unit completed its reorganization in 2004.

Poor conditions in the wholesale power market drove PG&E National Energy Group into bankruptcy in 2003; the unit changed its name to National Energy & Gas Transmission shortly after to signify separation from PG&E following its emergence from bankruptcy.

EXECUTIVES

Chairman, President, and CEO: Peter A. Darbee, age 57, $10,559,428 total compensation
SVP, CFO, and Treasurer; SVP Financial Services, Pacific Gas and Electric Company: Kent M. Harvey, age 51, $1,929,571 total compensation
SVP Corporate Strategy and Development: Rand L. Rosenberg, age 56, $2,214,754 total compensation
SVP and General Counsel: Hyun Park, age 48, $2,703,384 total compensation
SVP and Senior Advisor to the Chairman and CEO: Nancy E. McFadden, age 51
SVP Energy Procurement: Fong Wan, age 48
SVP Corporate Affairs, PG&E Corporation and Pacific Gas and Electric Company: Greg S. Pruett, age 52
SVP Human Resources, PG&E Corporation and Pacific Gas and Electric Company: John R. Simon, age 45
VP and Chief Risk and Audit Officer, PG&E Corporation and Pacific Gas and Electric Company: Anil K. Suri
VP Internal Audit and Compliance, PG&E Corporation and Pacific Gas and Electric Company: Stephen J. Cairns
VP Corporate Governance and Corporate Secretary, PG&E Corporation and Pacific Gas and Electric Company: Linda Y. H. Cheng, age 50
VP Investor Relations: Gabriel B. (Gabe) Togneri, age 54
Director; President, Pacific Gas and Electric Company: Christopher P. (Chris) Johns, age 49, $3,497,730 total compensation
SVP and COO, Pacific Gas and Electric Company: John S. (Jack) Keenan, age 61, $3,387,000 total compensation
SVP and CIO, Pacific Gas and Electric Company: Patricia M. (Pat) Lawicki, age 49
Auditors: Deloitte & Touche LLP

LOCATIONS

HQ: PG&E Corporation
1 Market Spear Tower, Ste. 2400
San Francisco, CA 94105
Phone: 415-267-7000 **Fax:** 415-267-7268
Web: www.pgecorp.com

PRODUCTS/OPERATIONS

2009 Sales

	$ mil.	% of total
Electric	10,257	73
Natural gas	3,142	27
Total	**13,399**	**100**

COMPETITORS

AEP
AES
Avista
Calpine
Constellation Energy Group
Duke Energy
Edison International
Entergy
Exelon
FirstEnergy
Mirant
Modesto Irrigation District
North Baja Pipeline
Northern California Power Agency
NV Energy
PacifiCorp
RRI Energy
Sacramento Municipal Utility
Sempra Energy
Southern Company
SUEZ-TRACTEBEL
Turlock Irrigation District
Western Area Power Administration

HISTORICAL FINANCIALS

Company Type: Public

Income Statement

FYE: December 31

	REVENUE ($ mil.)	NET INCOME ($ mil.)	NET PROFIT MARGIN	EMPLOYEES
12/09	13,399	1,234	9.2%	19,425
12/08	14,628	1,338	9.1%	14,649
12/07	13,237	1,006	7.6%	20,050
12/06	12,539	991	7.9%	20,400
12/05	11,703	917	7.8%	19,800
Annual Growth	**3.4%**	**7.7%**	**—**	**(0.5%)**

2009 Year-End Financials

Debt ratio: 108.5%
Return on equity: 12.5%
Cash ($ mil.): 527
Current ratio: 0.83
Long-term debt ($ mil.): 11,208
No. of shares (mil.): 372
Dividends
Yield: 3.8%
Payout: 52.5%
Market value ($ mil.): 16,625

Stock History

NYSE: PCG

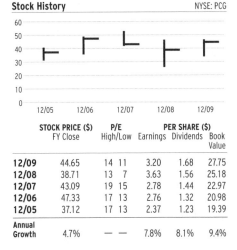

	STOCK PRICE ($) FY Close	P/E High/Low		Earnings	Dividends	Book Value
12/09	44.65	14	11	3.20	1.68	27.75
12/08	38.71	13	7	3.63	1.56	25.18
12/07	43.09	19	15	2.78	1.44	22.97
12/06	47.33	17	13	2.76	1.32	20.98
12/05	37.12	17	13	2.37	1.23	19.39
Annual Growth	**4.7%**	**—**	**—**	**7.8%**	**8.1%**	**9.4%**

Phillips-Van Heusen

Phillips-Van Heusen (PVH) has the buttoned-down look all sewn up. A top apparel firm worldwide and key US dress-shirt maker, PVH sells clothes, accessories, and shoes for men, women, and children under its own brands, such as Calvin Klein, Van Heusen, Tommy Hilfiger, IZOD, and ARROW. It sells other brands under license, including Geoffrey Beene, CHAPS, DKNY, and Nautica, and offers private-label goods. PVH distributes to department stores; it generates nearly a third of its revenue from wholesale clients Macy's, Kohl's, JCPenney, and Wal-Mart. The apparel manufacturer peddles its products through some 650 outlet stores located mostly in US malls. PVH acquired Tommy Hilfiger Group (THG) in May 2010.

The company, which already had been selling the Tommy Hilfiger brand under license, wrote a check to London-based private equity firm Apax Partners for about $3 billion to fold the brand into its bulging portfolio. Both companies, which boast well-known iconic brands, create an international apparel powerhouse with an expected annual revenue of about $4.6 billion.

While PVH expands its business, it's keeping an eye on expenses. Looking to keep ahead of the US economic downturn and lower its operating

costs, PVH has shuttered some 175 stores and shed about 400 employees.

PVH's long-standing strategy is to grow its Calvin Klein brands globally. The firm has three brand tiers that cater to different markets, positioning, and channels. Its Calvin Klein business comprises brand names Calvin Klein Collection, ck Calvin Klein, and Calvin Klein (white label) to capture several marketing opportunities. To give it greater control, PVH in 2008 acquired CMI, the licensee of the high-end collection of apparel and accessories for men and women. It's using its bridge brand, ck Calvin Klein, to help PVH extend its reach into Europe and Asia, which supports the brand's upper-moderate price range. The company's also opening stores in China, Southeast Asia, Japan, Europe, and the Middle East under the ck Calvin Klein banner. PVH believes its white-label Calvin Klein brand offers it the most growth opportunities in North America by showcasing its men's sportswear business, licensing men's and women's apparel and accessories, adding new fragrances and underwear brands, and pursuing licensing deals for new products.

To extend its reach into niche markets, PVH bought privately held necktie maker Superba for more than $110 million in 2007 to market Calvin Klein and IZOD neckwear. The company offers men's and women's sunglasses through a licensing agreement with Marchon Eyewear. Other licensing deals include watches, footwear, and handbags.

While PVH is entering new markets, the company has been fine-tuning its licensing and international strategies. In 2008 PVH partnered with Timberland in a licensing agreement to make men's apparel (in 2008) and women's apparel (in 2009).

PVH has made several moves in recent years in an effort to gain global control of the Van Heusen brand. PVH acquired the Van Heusen label for Europe and Asia from UK-based Coats Viyella. PVH licensed the brand back to the previous owner, giving the company distribution rights in the UK and Ireland.

HISTORY

In 1881 Moses Phillips came to America from Poland. While living in a one-room apartment in Pottsville, Pennsylvania, he sold flannel shirts (which his wife sewed) to coal miners from a pushcart. He soon brought the rest of his family to the US and upgraded the pushcart to a horse and buggy. Business continued to grow, and the Phillips-Jones Corporation was formed in 1907.

The company moved to New York in 1914, and control passed from father to son for four generations. Isaac followed Moses, then Seymour took over in 1941 until he handed the reins to Lawrence, who joined the company in 1948 and became president and CEO in 1969. Ads in the 1950s featured such actors as Anthony Quinn, Burt Lancaster, and Ronald Reagan in Van Heusen shirts. In 1957 the company received its present name. Phillips-Van Heusen (PVH) grew via acquisitions throughout the 1970s and began selling its merchandise at its own outlet stores in 1979, but it didn't want its products sold at the off-price outlets that became popular in the early 1980s. The company stopped doing business with stores and distributors that allowed PVH merchandise to reach cut-price vendors.

In 1987 PVH acquired G. H. Bass & Co., maker of Bass and Weejun shoes, for $79 million. It also bought back over 5 million shares of stock in order to fend off an acquisition bid by the

Hunt family of Texas. Lawrence stepped down in 1993, ending the unbroken chain of Phillipses at the helm. Bruce Klatsky, a human rights supporter who had started work at the company 22 years earlier as a merchandising trainee, took over as CEO. In 1995 the Phillips family sold its stake in the business. PVH acquired the Gant and IZOD brands (and about 90 outlet stores) from Crystal Brands.

During 1995 and 1996 PVH closed 218 of its poorest performing stores. Klatsky also closed three US shirt factories in 1995 as the company moved more of its production overseas.

PVH decided to close 150 more outlet stores (affecting 700 jobs), reposition Gant as a premium brand, and exit the private-label sweater manufacturing business in 1997. Klatsky ended an organized labor controversy at PVH's Guatemala operation in 1997 by meeting with union officials and ratifying a union contract.

After a repositioning attempt failed to move Bass upscale, the company in 1998 cited the expense of doing business in the US when it closed its Bass shoe manufacturing plant in Wilton, Maine (where Bass had been founded in 1876). PVH then shifted the manufacturing to plants in Puerto Rico and the Dominican Republic.

In 2000 the company purchased Cluett Designer Group (a licensee for Kenneth Cole dress shirts) from Cluett American; it also licensed the Arrow shirts and sportswear brand from Cluett American. That November the company announced it would lay off 1,200 employees due to a sluggish retail environment.

PVH bought most of fashion design giant Calvin Klein in 2003, renewing its commitment to apparel and divesting of its footwear endeavors. Bruce Klatsky stepped down as CEO of the company (but remained chairman) in mid-2005. COO Mark Weber was tapped as his replacement. He lasted about eight months in that position. Emanuel Chirico was named to the top spot in 2006, when Weber left the company.

In April 2008 PVH acquired the rights to produce neckwear under the Kenneth Cole, New York, and Liz Claiborne brands, among others, from privately held Mulberry Thai Silks.

EXECUTIVES

Chairman and CEO: Emanuel (Manny) Chirico, age 53, $12,557,366 total compensation
President and COO: Allen E. Sirkin, age 68, $5,043,663 total compensation
EVP and CFO: Michael A. (Mike) Shaffer, age 47, $1,917,096 total compensation
EVP Logistics and Technology: Jon D. Peters
EVP Logistics Services: Kevin Urban
EVP Marketing: Michael Kelly
SVP and Controller: Bruce Goldstein
SVP, Investor Relations, and Treasurer: Pamela N. (Pam) Hootkin, age 62
SVP, General Counsel, and Secretary: Mark D. Fischer
SVP Human Resources: David F. Kozel
Vice Chairman, Wholesale: Francis Kenneth (Ken) Duane, age 53, $3,196,319 total compensation
President and CEO, Calvin Klein: Paul Thomas (Tom) Murry III, age 59, $2,995,465 total compensation
President, IZOD and Timberland Sportswear: Cheryl Dapolito
President, Van Heusen and Arrow Sportswear: Geoffrey Barrett
President, IZOD Retail: Donna Patrick
President, Van Heusen Retail: Margaret P. Lachance
President, Bass Retail: Scott H. Orenstein

President and COO, Calvin Klein Retail: Steven B. Shiffman
President, Licensing and Public Relations: Kenneth L. (Ken) Wyse
Auditors: Ernst & Young LLP

LOCATIONS

HQ: Phillips-Van Heusen Corporation
200 Madison Ave., New York, NY 10016
Phone: 212-381-3500 **Fax:** 212-381-3950
Web: www.pvh.com

2010 Sales

	$ mil.	% of total
Domestic	2,129.3	89
Foreign	269.4	11
Total	**2,398.7**	**100**

PRODUCTS/OPERATIONS

2010 Sales

	$ mil.	% of total
Net sales	2,070.8	86
Royalty revenue	245.9	10
Advertising & other revenue	82.0	4
Total	**2,398.7**	**100**

Selected Brands

Arrow (owned)
Bass/GH Bass (owned)
BCBG Max Azria (licensed)
Calvin Klein (owned)
DKNY (licensed)
Geoffrey Beene (licensed)
IZOD (owned)
Reaction by Kenneth Cole (licensed)
Tommy Hilfiger (owned)
Van Heusen (owned)

COMPETITORS

Allen-Edmonds	Kellwood
Armani	Kenneth Cole
Berkshire Hathaway	Levi Strauss
Brown Shoe	Luxottica
Capital Mercury Apparel	Oxford Industries
Donna Karan	Perry Ellis International
Eddie Bauer llc	Polo Ralph Lauren
The Gap	Prada
Genesco	Reebok
Gucci	Stride Rite
Haggar	Timberland
Hugo Boss	VF
J. Crew	Warnaco Group
Jones Apparel	

HISTORICAL FINANCIALS

Company Type: Public

Income Statement			FYE: Sunday nearest February 1	
	REVENUE ($ mil.)	NET INCOME ($ mil.)	NET PROFIT MARGIN	EMPLOYEES
1/10	2,399	162	6.7%	10,800
1/09	2,492	92	3.7%	11,100
1/08	2,425	183	7.6%	11,600
1/07	2,091	155	7.4%	10,900
1/06	1,909	112	5.9%	9,700
Annual Growth	**5.9%**	**9.7%**	**—**	**2.7%**

2010 Year-End Financials

Debt ratio: 34.2%
Return on equity: 14.9%
Cash ($ mil.): 481
Current ratio: 2.74
Long-term debt ($ mil.): 400
No. of shares (mil.): 66
Dividends
  Yield: 0.4%
  Payout: 4.9%
Market value ($ mil.): 2,605

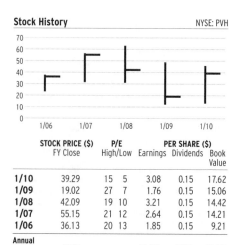

Stock History　　　　　　　　NYSE: PVH

	STOCK PRICE ($) FY Close	P/E High/Low		PER SHARE ($)		
				Earnings	Dividends	Book Value
1/10	39.29	15	5	3.08	0.15	17.62
1/09	19.02	27	7	1.76	0.15	15.06
1/08	42.09	19	10	3.21	0.15	14.42
1/07	55.15	21	12	2.64	0.15	14.21
1/06	36.13	20	13	1.85	0.15	9.21
Annual Growth	**2.1%**	**—**	**—**	**13.6%**	**0.0%**	**17.6%**

Pier 1 Imports

When shoppers fish for home decor, Pier 1 wants to be sure they catch something. The company sells about 4,000 items (imported from more than 50 countries) through some 1,050 Pier 1 Imports stores in the US and Canada. Stores offer a wide selection of indoor and outdoor furniture, lamps, vases, baskets, ceramics, dinnerware, candles, and other decorative accessories. In addition, the company supplies merchandise to about 30 stores in Mexico owned by Grupo Sanborns. In a bid to boost profits, the retailer has been closing underperforming stores, slashing spending, and refining its product assortment.

The moves, part of a turnaround plan rolled out in 2007, are paying off. In fiscal 2010 Pier 1's profits soared above $85 million, signaling its first profitable year since 2005. Aiming for greater efficiency through leaner operations, the plan has guided other significant decisions the retailer has made along the way, including the shutdown of its e-commerce site, the closing of its Pier 1 Kids chain, and the sale of its proprietary credit card business to JPMorgan Chase.

Even before the severe downturn in the US economy, Pier 1 has struggled with sagging demand for its home furnishings and decor. The retailer hit a high point in fiscal 2005, recording some $1.8 billion in sales, but those figures fell steadily in the years since. The company has been stung by competitors, including discounters Target and Wal-Mart Stores, moving in on its market for trendy, inexpensive merchandise. To kick up sales and set itself apart from the mass merchandisers, Pier 1 has cleaned its house of exotic furniture and funky tchotchkes and replaced them with a less cluttered look that features more contemporary pieces.

Right-sizing its retail and distribution network has also been part of Pier 1's restructuring. In fiscal 2010 the company closed nearly 40 stores and halted operations at a distribution center it owns in St. Charles, Illinois. Also that year Pier 1 cut about 10% of the full-time equivalent positions in its distribution center, home office, and field administration divisions. In 2009 it shuttered about 25 retail locations. As part of further cost-cutting efforts, Pier 1 continues to negotiate rent reductions with landlords and to consider early terminations at underperforming locations where reductions cannot be granted.

HISTORY

Attracted by a Fisherman's Wharf import outlet called Cost Plus, marketing guru Charles Tandy (founder of RadioShack) made a loan to its owner and obtained the right to open other Cost Plus stores. Opening his first Cost Plus store in 1962 in San Francisco, Tandy leveraged the strength of the US dollar against weaker foreign currencies. He bought inexpensive wicker furniture, brass candlesticks, and other items from countries such as India, Mexico, and Thailand and gave them healthy markups, yet still managed to price them attractively for US customers.

The store was a hit with the peace and free-love generation of the 1960s, which dug its beads, incense, and wicker furniture. In 1965, with 16 locations, the company changed its name to Pier 1 Imports. Pressed by the demands of RadioShack, Tandy sold Pier 1 the next year. In 1969, with 42 stores, including its first store in Canada, the company went public on AMEX.

By 1971 Pier 1 had 123 stores and was celebrating 100% sales gains for four consecutive years. It expanded its international presence, adding locations in Australia and Europe, and moved to the NYSE the next year. The chain experimented with alternative retail formats, including art supply, rug outlet, and fabric stores, but had abandoned them, as well as its foreign stores, by the mid-1970s. Pier 1 boasted nearly 270 locations by 1975.

Baby boomers, key to the chain's success, grew up and acquired different tastes, however. The dollar had also weakened, thereby increasing costs. Performance faltered, and in 1980 the company brought in Robert Camp, who had successfully operated his own Pier 1 stores in Canada, to give it a makeover. Camp closed poorly performing stores, opened larger stores in more profitable areas, and began changing the merchandise mix from novelties to higher-quality goods.

In 1983 investment group Intermark bought more than a third of the company. The next year Pier 1 acquired 36 Nurseryland Garden Centers from Intermark (boosting Intermark's stake in Pier 1 to about 50%) and merged the stores with its Wolfe's Nursery to form Sunbelt Nursery Group, which was spun off in 1985. That year Pier 1 named Clark Johnson its CEO. At the time, it operated nearly 265 locations, showing little growth in store count in a decade.

Johnson initiated an ambitious plan to double the number of Pier 1 stores, which reached 500 in early 1989. With Intermark struggling, Pier 1 bought back Sunbelt (including a 50% stake in Sunbelt from Intermark) in 1990. The following year Intermark sold its stake in Pier 1 to pay back debt (the ailing investment group declared bankruptcy in 1992). That year Pier 1 took Sunbelt public, keeping a 57% stake (Sunbelt has

since been dissolved). In 1993 the company launched The Pier, a chain of stores in the UK, and opened boutiques in Sears stores in Mexico.

Having spruced up stores, the chain continued to adjust the merchandise mix, dumping apparel in 1997 in favor of higher-margin goods. That year Pier 1 purchased a national bank charter from Texaco (now Chevron Corp.) to standardize the interest rates and fees on its private-label credit card. Marvin Girouard replaced Johnson as CEO in 1998 and as chairman in 1999.

In 2001 the company acquired the 21-store Cargo Furniture chain (later renamed Pier 1 Kids) from home furnishings manufacturer Tandycrafts. In the summer of 2004 Berkshire Hathaway, billionaire Warren Buffett's investment vehicle, bought 8 million shares of Pier 1.

In 2006 the company sold its UK subsidiary, The Pier (Retail) Ltd., to Palli Limited. The business operated 40-plus stores in the UK and Ireland. Later in the year, the firm sold its proprietary credit card business to JPMorgan Chase for $155 million.

In February 2007 Marvin Girouard retired as chairman and CEO of the company after 32 years with the firm. The retailer recruited Alex Smith, formerly with off-price retailer TJX Cos., to succeed him as chief executive. Soon after Smith arrived, Pier 1 announced that it would cut about 175 jobs in an attempt to make the company leaner and return it to profitability.

Also in 2007 Pier 1 closed 83 stores, including the remaining 36 Pier 1 Kids stores and 22 clearance outlets, as well as its direct-to-consumer business.

EXECUTIVES

Chairman: Michael R. Ferrari, age 70
President, CEO, and Director:
Alexander W. (Alex) Smith, age 57,
$8,001,925 total compensation
EVP Finance and CFO: Charles H. (Cary) Turner,
age 53, $1,395,883 total compensation
EVP Stores: Sharon M. Leite, age 47,
$825,993 total compensation
EVP Human Resources: Gregory S. (Greg) Humenesky,
age 58, $853,328 total compensation
EVP Merchandising: Catherine A. (Cathy) David, age 46
SVP Planning and Allocations: Michael R. Benkel,
age 41, $806,545 total compensation
SVP Marketing and Visual Merchandising:
Donald L. Kinnison, age 52
SVP, General Counsel, and Secretary: Michael A. Carter,
age 51
SVP Information Systems and CIO: Andy Laudato
Principal Accounting Officer: Laura A. Schack, age 44
Public Relations Manager: Kelly Keenum
Senior Manager International Marketing: Kalen Ruiz
Auditors: Ernst & Young LLP

LOCATIONS

HQ: Pier 1 Imports, Inc.
100 Pier 1 Place, Fort Worth, TX 76102
Phone: 817-252-8000   **Fax:** 817-252-8174
Web: www.pier1.com

2010 Stores

	No.
US	
California	110
Texas	79
Florida	74
New York	45
Illinois	39
Pennsylvania	38
North Carolina	34
Virginia	34
New Jersey	33
Michigan	31
Ohio	30
Washington	28
Georgia	27
Arizona	24
Massachusetts	24
Maryland	22
Connecticut	20
Wisconsin	19
Minnesota	18
Missouri	18
Tennessee	18
Indiana	17
South Carolina	17
Colorado	15
Louisiana	15
Alabama	14
Oregon	14
Kentucky	11
Other states	105
Canada	81
Total	**1,054**

PRODUCTS/OPERATIONS

2010 Sales

	% of total
Decorative accessories	60
Furniture	40
Total	**100**

2010 Sales

	$ mil.	% of total
Stores	1,279.7	99
Other	11.1	1
Total	**1,290.8**	**100**

Selected Merchandise

Baskets
Bed and bath accessories
Candles
Ceramics
Dinnerware
Dried and silk flowers
Fragrance products
Furniture
Lamps
Seasonal products
Vases
Wall decor

COMPETITORS

Bed Bath & Beyond	Kirkland's
Container Store	Longaberger
Cost Plus	Michaels Stores
Costco Wholesale	Restoration Hardware
Decorize	Room & Board
Eddie Bauer llc	Rooms To Go
Euromarket Designs	Target
Eurway	Tuesday Morning
Garden Ridge	Corporation
Hobby Lobby	Wal-Mart
IKEA	Williams-Sonoma

HISTORICAL FINANCIALS

Company Type: Public

Income Statement FYE: Saturday nearest last day in February

	REVENUE ($ mil.)	NET INCOME ($ mil.)	NET PROFIT MARGIN	EMPLOYEES
2/10	1,291	87	6.7%	16,200
2/09	1,321	(129)	—	16,700
2/08	1,512	(96)	—	16,400
2/07	1,623	(228)	—	15,400
2/06	1,777	(40)	—	19,100
Annual Growth	(7.7%)	—	—	(4.0%)

2010 Year-End Financials

Debt ratio: 6.3%
Return on equity: 38.8%
Cash ($ mil.): 188
Current ratio: 2.34
Long-term debt ($ mil.): 19

No. of shares (mil.): 117
Dividends
 Yield: 0.0%
 Payout: —
Market value ($ mil.): 716

Stock History

NYSE: PIR

	STOCK PRICE ($) FY Close	P/E High/Low		PER SHARE ($) Earnings	Dividends	Book Value
2/10	6.11	7	0	0.86	0.00	2.59
2/09	0.21	—	—	(1.45)	0.00	1.23
2/08	5.24	—	—	(1.09)	0.00	2.29
2/07	6.79	—	—	(2.60)	0.20	3.08
2/06	10.53	—	—	(0.46)	0.40	5.04
Annual Growth	(12.7%)	—	—	—	—	(15.3%)

Pinnacle West Capital

Pinnacle West Capital is at the peak of the energy pyramid in Arizona. It is the holding company for the state's largest electric utility, Arizona Public Service (APS), which transmits and distributes electricity to 1.1 million residential, commercial, and industrial customers throughout most of the state. The utility also has more than 6,280 MW of generating capacity. Through APS and other subsidiaries, Pinnacle West markets wholesale and retail power in Arizona and the western US. The company also develops and manages real estate and invests in energy ventures.

Its SunCor Development subsidiary builds residential communities and commercial building projects (including resort facilities and nine master-planned communities around Phoenix and the western US). However, the collapse of the housing market and the global recession prompted Pinnacle West to sell almost all of SunCor's assets in 2009 to pay down debt.

Pinnacle West also participates in deregulated retail markets in the western US through subsidiary APS Energy Services, which provides energy commodities and related products and services to commercial and industrial customers, and which through venture capital firm El Dorado Investment has stakes in a number of companies providing energy-related services. The company in 2009 reported that these units would have no material impact on the company for the next three years.

In terms of its core business, Pinnacle West sees APS adding another 600,000 customers by 2025, and the company is gearing up to meet the increased demand by adding new capacity and by encouraging more efficient use of power by end users. APS is committed to get 10% of its power from renewable sources by 2015.

HISTORY

In 1906 three Phoenix businessmen organized Pacific Gas & Electric (no connection with the California utility), which served the city's power needs until 1920, when Central Arizona Light & Power (Calapco) was formed to assume operations. In 1924 Calapco became a subsidiary of American Power & Light. After WWII the Public Utility Holding Company Act of 1935, which strictly curtailed the sprawling utility industry, finally forced American Power & Light to sell Calapco to the public in 1945.

In 1949 Calapco expanded northward by purchasing Northern Arizona Light & Power. It merged in 1951 with Arizona Edison, formed in the 1920s, to create Arizona Public Service (APS). Unprecedented population growth befell Arizona in the 1950s, and APS built three gas-fired plants between 1955 and 1960 to keep up with demand.

CEO Keith Turley reorganized APS in 1985 as a subsidiary of AZP Group, a holding company. Turley implemented a diversification plan and in 1986 bought a Phoenix-based savings and loan (MeraBank), a real estate firm (SunCor), and Mobil Oil's Wyoming uranium mines (sold 1990). In 1987 AZP became Pinnacle West Capital.

In the late 1980s an economic downturn hit Arizona, and bad real estate deals rocked the company. These included several investments by SunCor just after APS bought it, and the purchase by MeraBank of three Texas savings and loans in a 1988 diversification attempt. But in 1989 Pinnacle West had to cover about $510 million of MeraBank's bad loan losses. As Turley stepped down and power broker Richard Snell assumed the CEO post, MeraBank was taken over in 1990 by federal regulators, who released Pinnacle West from further obligation after a $450 million infusion.

The company had rejected several takeover bids from utility PacifiCorp, but in the early 1990s the two companies finally reached an agreement that included much-needed seasonal power sharing.

SunCor finally posted a profit in 1994 and bought the Sedona Golf Resort the following year. To prepare for utility deregulation, APS overhauled both management and operations by separating its generation and distribution divisions.

APS launched the first commercial solar power plant in the Phoenix area in 1998. After APS and publicly owned utility Salt River Project (which was protected from competitors) both agreed to open their territories to competition, Arizona legislators passed the Electric Power Competition Act.

Snell stepped down as CEO in 1999 (replaced by president Bill Post) but remained as chairman to see the company through the regulatory changes. The legislation originally required the transfer of APS's regulated power plants to independent production subsidiary Pinnacle West Energy, which operated 2,200 MW of nonregulated generating capacity. However, the Arizona Corporation Commission later revoked the rule due to a lack of competition in the state. As a result, Pinnacle West instead transferred its wholesale energy marketing and trading operations to APS, and dissolved Pinnacle West Energy in 2006.

In 2009 Pinnacle West Capital president Donald Brand succeeded long-serving top executive William Post as chairman, president, and CEO.

EXECUTIVES

Chairman, President, and CEO; CEO, Arizona Public Service: Donald E. (Don) Brandt, age 55, $2,210,449 total compensation
EVP Customer Service and Regulation, APS: Steven M. (Steve) Wheeler, age 61, $2,489,231 total compensation
EVP, General Counsel, and Secretary, Pinnacle West Capital and Arizona Public Service: David P. Falck, age 56
EVP and Chief Nuclear Officer, APS: Randall K. (Randy) Edington, age 56
SVP and CFO, Pinnacle West Capital and Arizona Public Service: James R. (Jim) Hatfield, age 52, $694,324 total compensation
Chief Compliance Officer; VP Rates and Regulation, Arizona Public Service: Jeff Guldner
VP, Controller, and Chief Accounting Officer, Pinnacle West Capital and Arizona Public Service: Denise R. Danner, age 54
VP Federal Affairs: Robert S. (Robbie) Aiken, age 52
VP and Treasurer, Pinnacle West and Arizona Public Service: Lee R. Nickloy, age 43
VP Government Affairs: Martin L. Shultz, age 62
Director Investor Relations: Rebecca L. Hickman
Manager Corporate Communications: Alan Bunnell
Auditors: Deloitte & Touche LLP

LOCATIONS

HQ: Pinnacle West Capital Corporation
 400 N. 5th St., Phoenix, AZ 85004
Phone: 602-250-1000   **Fax:** 602-250-2430
Web: www.pinnaclewest.com

PRODUCTS/OPERATIONS

2009 Sales

	$ mil.	% of total
Regulated electric	3,149.2	96
Real estate	103.1	3
Other	44.8	1
Total	**3,297.1**	**100**

Major Subsidiaries

APS Energy Services Company, Inc. (unregulated retail energy sales and information and management services)
Arizona Public Service Company (APS, electric utility)
El Dorado Investment Company (energy-related investments)
SunCor Development Company (real estate company that develops land, primarily in the Phoenix area, and operates family entertainment locations, golf courses, and resorts)

COMPETITORS

A.G. Spanos
Calpine
Capital Pacific
CenterPoint Energy
Duke Energy
NV Energy
PacifiCorp

Panda Energy
PG&E Corporation
PNM Resources
Sempra Energy
Southwest Gas
SRP
UniSource Energy

HISTORICAL FINANCIALS

Company Type: Public

Income Statement
FYE: December 31

	REVENUE ($ mil.)	NET INCOME ($ mil.)	NET PROFIT MARGIN	EMPLOYEES
12/09	3,297	54	1.6%	7,200
12/08	3,367	242	7.2%	7,500
12/07	3,524	307	8.7%	7,600
12/06	3,402	327	9.6%	7,400
12/05	2,988	176	5.9%	7,300
Annual Growth	2.5%	(25.7%)	—	(0.3%)

2009 Year-End Financials

Debt ratio: 101.6%
Return on equity: 1.6%
Cash ($ mil.): 145
Current ratio: 0.86
Long-term debt ($ mil.): 3,371

No. of shares (mil.): 109
Dividends
Yield: 5.7%
Payout: 313.4%
Market value ($ mil.): 3,974

Stock History
NYSE: PNW

	STOCK PRICE ($) FY Close	P/E High/Low		PER SHARE ($) Earnings	Dividends	Book Value
12/09	36.58	57	33	0.67	2.10	30.52
12/08	32.13	18	11	2.40	2.10	31.72
12/07	42.41	17	12	3.05	2.10	32.51
12/06	50.69	16	12	3.27	2.03	31.72
12/05	41.35	26	22	1.82	1.92	31.53
Annual Growth	(3.0%)	—	—	(22.1%)	2.3%	(0.8%)

Pioneer Natural Resources

Oil and gas explorer Pioneer Natural Resources' frontier is not in the Western prairies, but below them, and below the Rocky Mountains, the Midcontinent, West Texas, South Texas, and elsewhere. The large independent exploration and production company holds proved reserves of 959.6 million barrels of oil equivalent. The vast majority of the exploration and production company's reserves are found within the US (including in Alaska), but Pioneer also explores for and produces oil and gas in South Africa and Tunisia, and has additional assets in Equatorial Guinea and Nigeria.

The bulk of the company's revenues come from its US operations where the oil firm focuses on exploiting low-risk, long-lived basins. It complements these with riskier international exploration in a handful of countries.

Realigning its exploration portfolio, the company sold all of its operations in Argentina in 2006 to Apache for $675 million. That year Pioneer sold the bulk of its Gulf of Mexico oil and gas assets to Marubeni Offshore Production for $1.3 billion. In 2007 the company sold its Canadian subsidiary to Abu Dhabi National Energy Company PJSC for $540 million.

In 2009 it sold its assets in the Spraberry field to subsidiary Pioneer Southwest Energy Partners for $171.2 million. The next year it entered a joint venture to sell a 45% stake in its southern Texas gas field, Eagle Ford Shale, to the USA subsidiary of India's Reliance Industries for $1.15 billion.

HISTORY

The 1997 merger of MESA and Parker & Parsley moved quickly to pull itself out of the dry hole created by its own debt and the industry's late-1990s dropoff. Parker & Parsley began in 1962 as a partnership between geologist Howard Parker and engineer Joe Parsley. In 1977 it began drilling wells in West Texas. Southmark, a Dallas real estate firm, bought the company in 1984; in 1989 management purchased it from Southmark. The company went public in 1991.

T. Boone Pickens founded Petroleum Exploration in 1956. In 1964 Petroleum Exploration and Pickens' Canadian holding, Altair Oil and Gas, merged as MESA and went public. With gas prices declining in the 1990s, MESA began selling assets. Pickens resigned as CEO in 1996.

Richard Rainwater took control of MESA and then merged the firm into Parker & Parsley, which became Pioneer Natural Resources. The company moved into Argentina when it paid $1.2 billion for Calgary-based Chauvco Resources in 1997.

To streamline operations and reduce debt, Pioneer cut its workforce, and in 1999 it sold 400 US properties to Prize Energy.

Pioneer sold oil and gas properties in Texas and Canada in 1999 and moved to consolidate its Permian Basin operations by offering to buy out limited partners. It also drilled its first deepwater well in the Gulf of Mexico and acquired additional properties in Argentina.

In 2000 the company disposed of noncore natural gas assets in Louisiana, New Mexico, and Oklahoma. At the same time, it boosted its deepwater holdings in the Gulf of Mexico. The next year the company announced successful test drilling in its prospects in Argentina and South Africa.

Pioneer also announced an oil discovery in 2001 on its Ozona Deep prospect in the Gulf of Mexico, indicating another deepwater production asset for the company. In 2003 Pioneer teamed up with Woodside Energy to conduct a joint exploration program in the shallow-water Texas Shelf region of the Gulf of Mexico.

In 2005 Pioneer sold the Martin Creek, Conroy Black, and Lookout Butte oil and gas properties in Canada to Ketch Resources for $199 million. That year it acquired oil and gas assets in the Permian Basin and South Texas for a total of $177 million.

EXECUTIVES

Chairman and CEO: Scott D. Sheffield, age 57, $4,969,705 total compensation
President and COO: Timothy L. (Tim) Dove, age 53, $2,277,338 total compensation
EVP and CFO: Richard P. (Rich) Dealy, age 44, $1,488,250 total compensation
EVP Business Development and Technology: Chris J. Cheatwood, age 49, $1,293,885 total compensation
EVP and General Counsel: Mark S. Berg, age 51, $1,301,716 total compensation
EVP Domestic Operations: Jay P. Still
EVP International Operations: David McManus, age 56
EVP Permian Operations: Danny L. Kellum, age 55

EVP South Texas Operations: William F. (Bill) Hannes, age 50
VP and CIO: Thomas C. Halbouty
VP Administration and Risk Management: Larry N. Paulsen
VP, Corporate Secretary, and Chief Compliance Officer: Mark H. Kleinman, age 43
VP Operations Services: Denny B. Bullard
VP Government Affairs: Roger W. Wallace
VP and Chief Accounting Officer: Frank W. Hall, age 59
VP Land: Robert C. Hagens
VP Investor Relations: Frank E. Hopkins
Senior Director Corporate Communications and Public Affairs: Susan A. Spratlen
Auditors: Ernst & Young LLP

LOCATIONS

HQ: Pioneer Natural Resources Company
5205 N. O'Connor Blvd., Ste. 200, Irving, TX 75039
Phone: 972-444-9001 **Fax:** 972-969-3576
Web: www.pioneernrc.com

2009 Sales

	$ mil.	% of total
US	1,402.5	82
Tunisia	150.3	9
South Africa	57.2	3
Corporate	101.5	6
Total	**1,711.5**	**100**

COMPETITORS

Anadarko Petroleum	Marathon Oil
Apache	Newfield Exploration
BP	Noble Energy
Chesapeake Energy	Royal Dutch Shell
Exxon Mobil	TOTAL
Hess Corporation	YPF

HISTORICAL FINANCIALS

Company Type: Public

Income Statement
FYE: December 31

	REVENUE ($ mil.)	NET INCOME ($ mil.)	NET PROFIT MARGIN	EMPLOYEES
12/09	1,712	(42)	—	1,888
12/08	2,338	220	9.4%	1,824
12/07	1,741	373	21.4%	1,702
12/06	1,633	740	45.3%	1,624
12/05	2,373	535	22.5%	1,694
Annual Growth	(7.8%)	—	—	2.7%

2009 Year-End Financials

Debt ratio: 78.1%
Return on equity: —
Cash ($ mil.): 27
Current ratio: 1.08
Long-term debt ($ mil.): 2,761

No. of shares (mil.): 116
Dividends
Yield: 0.2%
Payout: —
Market value ($ mil.): 5,587

Stock History
NYSE: PXD

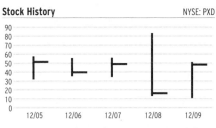

	STOCK PRICE ($) FY Close	P/E High/Low		PER SHARE ($) Earnings	Dividends	Book Value
12/09	48.17	—	—	(0.46)	0.08	30.49
12/08	16.18	44	8	1.85	0.30	30.88
12/07	48.84	18	12	3.06	0.27	26.23
12/06	39.69	9	6	5.81	0.25	25.73
12/05	51.27	15	9	3.80	0.22	19.11
Annual Growth	(1.5%)	—	—	—	(22.3%)	12.4%

Pitney Bowes

Pitney Bowes has a measured approach to the mail management industry. The world's largest producer of postage meters, the company also makes other mailing equipment and provides shipping and weighing systems. Pitney Bowes offers online postage services, financing for office equipment purchases, and facilities management services. It also develops software to create mailers and manage shipping, transportation, and logistics for government agencies and corporations. The company provides document management outsourcing services through its Pitney Bowes Management Services subsidiary.

Pitney Bowes is reducing costs by $150 million to $200 million over two years, partly through a workforce reduction of up to 10%. The restructuring also will include streamlining corporate processes through implementation of enterprise-wide systems and common platforms, and an increase in shared services across business units, including more outsourcing.

The majority of the company's revenues are subject to regulation by the US Postal Service and foreign postal authorities. Its revenues and profitability could be affected by changes in postal regulations, at home or abroad. E-mail, electronic document transmission, and electronic messaging services continue to erode the volume of physical mail (or "snail mail") worldwide. Mail services are sometimes the means of delivering terrorist attacks, and such events could further erode consumer confidence in postal systems. A significant interruption in mail services as a result of such attacks could have an adverse effect on the company's business.

Pitney Bowes relies on third-party providers for components, services, some product manufacturing, and supplies — in certain cases, depending on single sources or limited sources. Interruptions in delivery of those goods and services could disrupt the company's manufacturing and operations, including product shortages.

The company's growth strategy has included acquisitions that augment its software and mail services segments. It acquired location information and software provider MapInfo for $408 million in 2007.

In mid-2010 Pitney Bowes further expanded into software, adding Portrait Software plc, a UK provider of CRM software, for about £44.4 million (around $65 million). Portrait specializes in software that lets companies design more effective customer service and marketing campaigns using customer behavior data. The software complements Pitney Bowes' existing customer relationship systems and will be integrated into other suites of software tools the company offers.

HISTORY

In 1912 Walter Bowes, an address machine salesman, gained control of Universal Stamping Machine, which made stamp canceling machines. In 1920 Bowes joined with Arthur Pitney, who had developed a postage metering machine. After creating a market by forcing through Congress legislation that outlawed the sale of meters, the Pitney-Bowes Postage Meter Company began leasing new machines in 1921. During the 1920s Pitney-Bowes built a large service fleet with leasing and repair expertise; added mail handling machines, including stampers and counters, to its product line; and expanded into Canada, the UK, and Germany.

Pitney left in 1924 to start a competing company. Other competitors, including IBM and NCR, entered the market, but they were never able to catch up with Pitney-Bowes. The company was so successful that almost no competitors remained. The Justice Department investigated the business practices of the company, which agreed to license its patents to potential competitors, free of charge.

Facing the prospect of increased competition, Pitney-Bowes began to diversify its operations. In 1967 the company took on Xerox with a line of copiers. In the late 1960s it moved into pricing and inventory control equipment and credit and ID card products. It also established a joint venture with Alpex for point-of-sale terminals that proved a flop. In 1973 the company wrote off its investment, resulting in its first-ever loss.

But Pitney Bowes (the hyphen was dropped in 1970) continued to add operations. In 1979 it bought Dictaphone Corp. (voice processing). In 1981 the company consolidated Dictaphone subsidiary Grayarc with *The Drawing Board* (an office-supply catalog it acquired in 1980) to form Wheeler Group, a direct-mail marketer of office supplies.

With its long history of meter leasing, the company moved into the commercial arena, eventually leasing such big-ticket items as airplanes and barges under the aegis of Pitney Bowes Financial Services. The company also continued to widen its product line with its 1981 introduction of Postage By Phone and a line of fax machines.

In the late 1980s the company began whittling its holdings, selling its Dictaphone-related operations in pieces between 1988 and 1995. Meanwhile, as its US markets matured, Pitney Bowes added a variety of mailing services and electronic products, and bolstered its overseas operations in 1994 with pacts to help China and Mexico update their postal systems. Vice chairman Michael Critelli was named CEO in 1996.

In 1998 the company introduced a system that generates, addresses, and stuffs mass-mailing materials. The next year it filed a patent-infringement lawsuit against e-postage rivals Stamps.com and E-Stamp. Also in 1999 the Justice Department launched another antitrust investigation into the company's activities in the postage meter and online postage markets. In 2000 Pitney Bowes sold its mortgage servicing business, Atlantic Mortgage & Investment Corporation, to a subsidiary of Netherlands-based ABN AMRO for about $490 million.

The next year Pitney Bowes acquired Danka Business Systems' outsourcing unit, Danka Services International, for $290 million. The company also received a $400 million settlement from a 1995 patent infringement suit against Hewlett-Packard (related to laser-jet printer technology). Pitney Bowes spun off its copier and fax business, Pitney Bowes Office Systems, in 2001. In 2004 Pitney Bowes bought Group 1 Software for approximately $321 million.

Pitney Bowes sold its Océ Imagistics lease portfolio to Rabobank Group subsidiary De Lage Landen for about $288 million in 2006. It also sold its Capital Services business to an affiliate of Cerberus Capital Management for about $750 million.

Pitney Bowes president Murray Martin was named CEO in 2007; Critelli assumed the role of executive chairman. Martin added the title of chairman in 2009.

EXECUTIVES

Chairman, President, and CEO: Murray D. Martin, age 62, $6,189,196 total compensation
EVP and CFO: Michael (Mike) Monahan, age 49, $1,922,953 total compensation
EVP and President, Mailing Solutions Management: Leslie R. Abi-Karam, age 51, $1,939,576 total compensation
EVP and President, Mailstream International: Patrick J. Keddy, age 55, $1,390,687 total compensation
EVP and President, Pitney Bowes Management Services and Goverment & Postal Affairs: Vicki A. O'Meara, age 52, $1,197,244 total compensation
EVP and President, Global Financial Services: Elise R. (Lisa) DeBois, age 54
EVP and Chief Strategy and Innovation Officer: Joseph H. (Joe) Timko, age 49
EVP, Chief Human Resources Officer, and Interim Chief Legal and Compliance Officer: Johnna G. Torsone, age 59
EVP and CIO: Gregory E. Buoncontri, age 62
VP; President, Pitney Bowes Business Management: John O'Hara
VP and Chief Marketing and Communications Officer: Juanita T. James, age 57
VP Finance and Chief Accounting Officer: Steven J. Green
VP, Corporate Secretary, and Chief Governance Officer: Amy C. Corn
VP Investor Relations: Charles F. McBride
VP Corporate Communications: Sheryl Y. Battles
President, Pitney Bowes Marketing Solutions: Art Fiordaliso
President, Pitney Bowes Mail Services: John Ward
President, Pitney Bowes Government Solutions: Jon Love
Auditors: PricewaterhouseCoopers LLP

LOCATIONS

HQ: Pitney Bowes Inc.
1 Elmcroft Rd., Stamford, CT 06926
Phone: 203-356-5000   **Fax:** 203-351-7336
Web: www.pb.com

2009 Sales

	$ mil.	% of total
US	3,979.5	71
Other countries	1,589.7	29
Total	**5,569.2**	**100**

PRODUCTS/OPERATIONS

2009 Sales

	$ mil.	% of total
Business services	1,804.9	32
Equipment sales	1,006.6	18
Support services	714.4	13
Financing	694.5	12
Rentals	647.4	12
Software	365.2	7
Supplies	336.2	6
Total	**5,569.2**	**100**

2009 Sales

	$ mil.	% of total
Mailstream Solutions		
US mailing	2,016.3	36
International mailing	920.4	17
Production mail	525.8	9
Software	345.7	6
Mailstream Services		
Management	1,060.9	19
Mail	559.2	10
Marketing	140.9	3
Total	**5,569.2**	**100**

HISTORICAL FINANCIALS

Company Type: Public

Income Statement				FYE: December 31
	REVENUE ($ mil.)	NET INCOME ($ mil.)	NET PROFIT MARGIN	EMPLOYEES
12/09	5,569	445	8.0%	33,004
12/08	6,262	420	6.7%	35,140
12/07	6,130	367	6.0%	36,165
12/06	5,730	105	1.8%	34,454
12/05	5,492	527	9.6%	34,165
Annual Growth	0.3%	(4.1%)	—	(0.9%)

2009 Year-End Financials

Debt ratio: 10,000.0%
Return on equity: —
Cash ($ mil.): 413
Current ratio: 1.16
Long-term debt ($ mil.): 4,214
No. of shares (mil.): 207
Dividends
  Yield: 6.3%
  Payout: 70.6%
Market value ($ mil.): 4,704

Stock History

NYSE: PBI

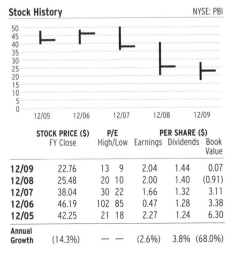

	STOCK PRICE ($) FY Close	P/E High/Low		PER SHARE ($) Earnings	Dividends	Book Value
12/09	22.76	13	9	2.04	1.44	0.07
12/08	25.48	20	10	2.00	1.40	(0.91)
12/07	38.04	30	22	1.66	1.32	3.11
12/06	46.19	102	85	0.47	1.28	3.38
12/05	42.25	21	18	2.27	1.24	6.30
Annual Growth	(14.3%)	—	—	(2.6%)	3.8%	(68.0%)

Plains All American Pipeline

The term "All American" includes Canada for Plains All American Pipeline, which has expanded its pipeline operations north of the border. The limited partnership is engaged in the transportation, storage, terminalling and marketing of crude oil, refined products, and LPG, and owns extensive gathering, terminal, and storage facilities in California, Louisiana, Oklahoma, Texas, and in Alberta and Saskatchewan. Plains All American Pipeline owns about 16,000 miles of gathering and mainline crude oil pipelines throughout the US and Canada, operates a large fleet of trucks and barges, and owns storage capacity of 28 million barrels. Paul Allen's Vulcan Energy holds just over 50% of its general partner.

Plains All American Pipeline handles more than 3 million barrels of crude oil, refined products, and LPG per day through its extensive network based in key North American producing basins and transportation gateways. It has steadily built its network through acquisitions, and has also expanded into refining and marketing.

Further expanding its asset base in 2009, the company acquired joint venture partner Vulcan Capital's 50% stake in PAA Natural Gas Storage, which owns 40 billion cu. ft. of natural gas storage capacity in Michigan and Louisiana, for $62 million. It also acquired an additional 21% in the Capline Pipeline System (in which it held 22%) on the Gulf Coast for $215 million. A year earlier, the company boosted its Canadian midstream assets with the acquisition of Rainbow Pipeline (crude oil gathering and pipelines) for $687 million.

Despite decreased revenues in 2009, primarily due to the global recession negatively impacting demand in its supply and logistics segment, the company posted improved profits, mainly as the result of acquisitions, favorable supply financing, and increased operational efficiencies.

In 2008 Occidental Petroleum acquired 10% of the company's general partner, boosting the amount of new capital available for Plains All American Pipeline to pay down debt and make further acquisitions.

HISTORY

Goodyear Tire & Rubber subsidiary Celeron began designing the All American Pipeline in 1983 to bring heavy crude from California to the less-regulated refineries of Texas. It was completed in 1987 at a cost of $1.6 billion, but by 1991 only a trickle of oil was dribbling through. The pipeline did not post a profit until 1994.

Prospects began to look up in the mid-1990s when Chevron, Texaco, and Exxon signed contracts to use the pipeline, beginning in 1996. Plains Resources bought the pipeline in 1998 for $400 million; the company created Plains All American Pipeline to acquire and operate the pipeline, then sold off a 43% stake in an IPO that raised $260 million. The next year Plains All American bought Scurlock Permian (2,300 miles of pipeline) from Marathon Ashland Petroleum for $141 million and the West Texas Gathering System from Chevron (450 miles) for $36 million.

Shareholders sued Plains All American in 1999 after it reported that an employee's unauthorized crude-oil trading would cost the company about $160 million. (In 2000 the company agreed to pay $29.5 million, plus interest, to settle the cases.)

Plains All American announced plans to mothball all but the California section of the All American Pipeline in 1999. The next year El Paso Energy bought the 1,088-mile section of the pipeline that was to be deactivated, plus the right to run fiber-optic cable over the entire pipeline, for $129 million.

Targeting Canada as part of its expansion strategy, in 2001 Plains All American bought about 450 miles of oil pipeline and other midstream assets from Murphy Oil and acquired crude oil and LPG marketing firm CANPET Energy. Also that year Plains Resources reduced its stake in Plains All American from 44% to 29%.

In 2002 the company acquired the Wapella Pipeline System, located in southeastern Saskatchewan and southwestern Manitoba. It also bought Shell Pipeline's West Texas crude oil pipeline assets for $315 million. Plains All American Pipeline continued its acquisition streak in 2003 with the acquisitions of the South Saskatchewan pipeline system in Canada and the ArkLaTex pipeline system originating in Sabine, Texas.

In 2004 Plains All American continued its expansion with the acquisition of interests in the Capline and Capwood pipeline systems from Shell Pipeline Company for about $158 million. It also acquired the crude oil and pipeline operations of Link Energy for about $330 million and the Cal Ven pipeline system from Unocal Canada for about $19 million. Later that year, the company continued its system expansion by acquiring the Schaefferstown propane storage facility from Koch Hydrocarbon for about $32 million.

In 2006 the company acquired Andrews Petroleum and Lone Star Trucking for $205 million. It also acquired stakes in a number of Gulf Coast crude oil pipeline systems from BP Oil Pipeline Company for $133.5 million. That year, in a major deal, the company acquired Pacific Energy Partners for $2.4 billion, moving the company beyond crude oil and into the refined products and barging businesses.

In 2007 Plains All American Pipeline acquired LPG storage facilities in Arizona and South Carolina.

EXECUTIVES

Chairman and CEO: Greg L. Armstrong, age 51, $3,390,800 total compensation
President and COO: Harry N. Pefanis, age 52, $3,215,800 total compensation
EVP: Phillip D. (Phil) Kramer, age 53
SVP and CFO: Al Swanson, age 46, $1,642,246 total compensation
SVP Commercial Activities: John P. vonBerg, age 55, $3,485,800 total compensation
SVP Operations and Business Development: Mark J. Gorman, age 55
SVP Technology, Process, and Risk Management: Alfred A. (Al) Lindseth, age 40
VP Refinery Supply: James B. (Jim) Fryfogle, age 58
VP, Secretary, and General Counsel: Tim Moore, age 52
VP Engineering: Daniel J. Nerbonne, age 52
VP Human Resources: Roger D. Everett, age 64
VP and Treasurer: Charles Kingswell-Smith, age 58
VP Acquisitions: James G. (Jim) Hester, age 50
VP Accounting and Chief Accounting Officer: Chris Herbold, age 38
VP, General Counsel Commercial and Litigation, and Assistant Secretary: Lawrence J. (Larry) Dreyfuss, age 55

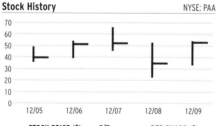

VP Environmental, Health, and Safety:
Troy E. Valenzuela, age 48
President, PMC (Nova Scotia): W. David (Dave) Duckett,
age 54, $3,712,941 total compensation
President, Natural Gas Storage, LLC:
Constantine S. (Dean) Liollio, age 51
Director, Investor Relations: Roy I. Lamoreaux
Auditors: PricewaterhouseCoopers LLP

LOCATIONS

HQ: Plains All American Pipeline, L.P.
333 Clay St., Ste. 1600, Houston, TX 77002
Phone: 713-646-4100   **Fax:** 713-646-4572
Web: www.plainsallamerican.com

2009 Sales

	$ mil.	% of total
US	15,439	83
Canada	3,081	17
Total	**18,520**	**100**

PRODUCTS/OPERATIONS

2009 Sales

	$ mil.	% of total
Supply & logistics	17,757	96
Transportation	536	3
Facilities	227	1
Total	**18,520**	**100**

COMPETITORS

Buckeye Partners	Kinder Morgan
Enbridge	Sunoco Logistics
Enterprise Products	TransMontaigne

HISTORICAL FINANCIALS

Company Type: Public

Income Statement   FYE: December 31

	REVENUE ($ mil.)	NET INCOME ($ mil.)	NET PROFIT MARGIN	EMPLOYEES
12/09	18,520	579	3.1%	3,400
12/08	30,061	437	1.5%	3,302
12/07	20,394	365	1.8%	3,100
12/06	22,444	279	1.2%	2,900
12/05	31,177	218	0.7%	2,000
Annual Growth	**(12.2%)**	**27.7%**	**—**	**14.2%**

2009 Year-End Financials

Debt ratio: —	No. of shares (mil.): 136
Return on equity: —	Dividends
Cash ($ mil.): 25	Yield: 6.9%
Current ratio: 0.97	Payout: 109.0%
Long-term debt ($ mil.): 4,142	Market value ($ mil.): 7,210

Stock History   NYSE: PAA

	STOCK PRICE ($) FY Close	P/E High/Low	PER SHARE ($) Earnings	Dividends	Book Value
12/09	52.85	16 10	3.32	3.62	—
12/08	34.69	19 9	2.67	3.49	26.04
12/07	52.00	26 18	2.52	3.28	25.10
12/06	51.20	18 14	2.88	2.87	21.82
12/05	39.57	18 13	2.72	2.58	9.75
Annual Growth	**7.5%**	**— —**	**5.1%**	**8.8%**	**38.7%**

Plexus Corp.

Plexus isn't perplexed by even complex contract electronics manufacturing. The company develops and manufactures electronic products for companies in the telecommunications, medical, industrial, and defense markets. Plexus provides product design, engineering, and assembly of printed circuit boards (PCBs), test equipment, and other electronic components. The company also offers prototyping, materials procurement, warehousing and distribution, and other support services. Its customers include networking equipment maker Juniper Networks and General Electric. While Plexus manufactures in China, Malaysia, Mexico, Romania, and the UK, the company gets more than half of its sales from operations in the US.

In the economic turmoil of 2009, Plexus sales and profits plunged due to lower demand from customers across the board. With a limited number of customers — the company's top 10 customers historically account for around 60% of sales — even the loss of one customer can be brutal. Though Plexus lost a significant defense customer during 2009, the company added The Coca-Cola Company as an industrial customer. Plexus will manufacture the Coca-Cola Freestyle fountain dispenser. The company's strategy is to focus on mid-to-low volume, high mix turnkey manufacturing services in its primary markets, along with offering value-added services such as logistics management and repair services.

In response to the global economic downturn, Plexus restructured its North American operations, including workforce reductions in the US and Mexico. Plexus also completed closing its Ayer, Massachusetts plant, transferring production to other facilities. The company expanded plants in China and Romania, however, as it looks to move production to regions with lower labor and materials costs in the future.

In 2008 Plexus completed the implementation of an enterprise resource planning (ERP) system covering all manufacturing sites around the world. The ERP installation augments other management information systems the company uses and includes software from Oracle and other vendors.

HISTORY

In the 1970s Peter Strandwitz needed a contract electronics manufacturer when his small electronics business suffered from a lack of engineering expertise. He founded Plexus in 1979 and marketed its services to electronics companies that could not efficiently operate their own manufacturing facilities. The company went public in 1986. Three years later it discontinued its faltering International Communications subsidiary, which made pay phones, to concentrate on its core business.

Plexus grew throughout the early 1990s, and in 1994 doubled its manufacturing capabilities with a new facility in Neenah, Wisconsin. In 1996 Plexus and Oneida Nation Electronics, a company owned by the Native American Oneida tribe, built an electronics fabrication plant in Green Bay, Wisconsin. The next year, Plexus acquired NEI Electronics and computer parts maker Tertronics.

In 1998 Plexus began building components for General Motors' test electric vehicles. The following year the company boosted its reach into the Pacific Northwest when it bought SeaMED, a Seattle-area designer and manufacturer of electronic equipment for the medical industry.

In 2000 the company continued its acquisition binge, purchasing manufacturing facilities in Mexico and the UK, as well as US-based electronic manufacturing services providers Agility and e2E.

In 2001 COO John Nussbaum succeeded Strandwitz as CEO (Strandwitz remained chairman until the next year). Also in 2001 Plexus agreed to acquire most of the assets of contract manufacturer MCMS; the deal, which closed early in 2002, expanded Plexus' reach into Asia thanks to MCMS's plants in Malaysia and China.

In 2002 COO Dean Foate succeeded Nussbaum as CEO (Nussbaum remained chairman).

Plexus lined up AuthenTec, the developer of biometric chips, as a customer in 2003, providing design, engineering, and integration services to the supplier of fingerprint sensors.

The company went through a corporate restructuring in 2004, closing a plant in the Seattle area. Plexus also mothballed facilities in New Hampshire and Oregon.

In 2006 Plexus expanded its manufacturing capacity in China and Malaysia.

Plexus decided in 2008 to close its facility in Ayer, Massachusetts, primarily transferring production to Neenah, Wisconsin. The company expanded plants in Buffalo Grove, Illinois, and Fremont, California, during the year, and leased about 106,000 sq. ft. at an industrial park in Hangzhou, China.

EXECUTIVES

Chairman: John L. Nussbaum, age 66
President, CEO, and Director: Dean A. Foate, age 50,
$2,744,922 total compensation
SVP Global Market Development:
Michael T. (Mike) Verstegen, age 50,
$613,159 total compensation
SVP Global Manufacturing Operations:
Michael D. (Mike) Buseman, age 47,
$638,608 total compensation
SVP Global Engineering Services:
Steven J. (Steve) Frisch, age 42
SVP Global Customer Services: Todd P. Kelsey, age 43
VP and CFO: Ginger M. Jones, age 44,
$689,768 total compensation
**VP, Secretary, General Counsel, and Corporate
Compliance Officer:** Angelo M. Ninivaggi Jr., age 41
VP Global Human Resources: Joseph E. (Joe) Mauthe,
age 46
CIO: Steve Gearhart
Corporate Treasurer and Chief Treasury Officer:
George W. F. Setton, age 63
Sales and New Business Development, Asia: Mandy Lin
Corporate Investor Relations: Dianne Boydstun
Regional President, Plexus Asia/Pacific:
Yong Jin (Y. J.) Lim, age 48,
$639,780 total compensation
Auditors: PricewaterhouseCoopers LLP

LOCATIONS

HQ: Plexus Corp.
55 Jewelers Park Dr., Neenah, WI 54957
Phone: 920-722-3451   **Fax:** 920-751-5395
Web: www.plexus.com

2009 Sales

	$ mil.	% of total
US	1,007.1	58
Malaysia	512.6	30
Mexico	77.2	5
China	75.5	4
UK	55.6	3
Adjustments	(111.4)	—
Total	**1616.6**	**100**

PRODUCTS/OPERATIONS

2009 Sales

	% of total
Wireline & networking	44
Medical	22
Industrial & commercial	13
Wireless infrastructure	11
Defense, security & aerospace	10
Total	**100**

Selected Services

Assembly
Design (printed circuit boards, product housings)
Distribution
Materials procurement
New product introduction
Product development and testing
Product manufacture and assembly
Prototyping
Support
Warehousing

COMPETITORS

Avnet	Nam Tai
Benchmark Electronics	Quanta Computer
Celestica	Sanmina-SCI
Cofidur	Saturn Electronics
CTS Corp.	Silicon Forest Electronics
Flextronics	SMTC Corp.
Hon Hai	Sparton
Jabil	Suntron
Key Tronic	SYNNEX
Kimball International	TTM Technologies
LaBarge	Viasystems

HISTORICAL FINANCIALS

Company Type: Public

Income Statement

FYE: September 30

	REVENUE ($ mil.)	NET INCOME ($ mil.)	NET PROFIT MARGIN	EMPLOYEES
9/09	1,617	46	2.9%	7,100
9/08	1,842	84	4.6%	7,900
9/07	1,546	66	4.2%	7,500
9/06	1,461	101	6.9%	7,800
9/05	1,229	(12)	—	6,800
Annual Growth	7.1%	—	—	1.1%

2009 Year-End Financials

Debt ratio: 25.4%	No. of shares (mil.): 40
Return on equity: 9.2%	Dividends
Cash ($ mil.): 258	Yield: —
Current ratio: 2.35	Payout: —
Long-term debt ($ mil.): 134	Market value ($ mil.): 1,063

Stock History

NASDAQ (GS): PLXS

	STOCK PRICE ($) FY Close	P/E High/Low		PER SHARE ($) Earnings	Dividends	Book Value
9/09	26.34	23	9	1.17	—	13.07
9/08	20.70	17	9	1.92	—	11.74
9/07	27.40	20	11	1.41	—	14.20
9/06	19.20	22	7	2.15	—	11.93
9/05	17.09	—	—	(0.29)	—	8.42
Annual Growth	11.4%	—	—	—	—	11.6%

PNC Financial Services

PNC Financial Services has returned to its traditional banking roots. One of the 10 largest banks in the US, its flagship PNC Bank subsidiary operates about 2,500 branches in some 15 states in the mid-Atlantic region and the Midwest. In addition to retail and corporate banking, the company offers insurance, investments, personal and institutional asset management, and capital markets products and services. It owns boutique investment bank Harris Williams and about a quarter of money management giant BlackRock. In 2010 PNC sold its Global Investment Servicing unit to Bank of New York Mellon for some $2.3 billion in cash.

The divestment was necessary for PNC as it looked to repay money it received from the government. PNC acquired troubled rival National City for some $6.1 billion of cash and stock after months of speculation that the two companies would join. Following the completion of the deal in late 2008, the US Treasury bolstered the combined firm by investing some $7.6 billion through the acquisition of preferred shares in the company as part of the government's Troubled Asset Relief Program (TARP). (PNC repaid the money in 2010.) The purchase doubled PNC's branch network and extended it westward to Chicago and Milwaukee.

The company divested about 60 National City bank branches in western Pennsylvania in a 2009 sale to First Niagara Financial in order to settle antitrust concerns stemming from the larger deal. PNC also sold the Ohio, Kentucky, and Missouri offices of National City Insurance, a retail employee benefits insurance brokerage business, to USI Holdings.

PNC had been growing by acquisitions even prior to buying National City. In 2007 the company acquired Yardville National Bancorp and its 35 branches in central New Jersey and eastern Pennsylvania, and Mercantile Bankshares, which added some 240 branches in the mid-Atlantic region. Also that year PNC expanded its commercial mortgage operations with the acquisition of multifamily housing lender ARC Commercial Mortgage (now PNC ARCS).

The following year PNC finalized its acquisition of multibank holding company Sterling Financial, which provided banking, leasing, trust, investment, and brokerage services to individuals and businesses through nearly 70 branches in Delaware, Maryland, and Pennsylvania.

As the dust settles from its flurry of acquisitions and divestitures, PNC has recommitted itself to its core retail, corporate, and mortgage banking activities. PNC is also focusing on new technologies as an increasing number of customers migrate to electronic banking and payment channels.

HISTORY

First National Bank of Pittsburgh opened in 1863. In 1913 the bank consolidated with Second National Bank of Pittsburgh, and in 1921 it bought Peoples National.

The company changed its name to Pittsburgh National after a long expansion following the Depression and WWII. It entered the credit card business in 1965 and joined the BankAmericard program (Visa's forerunner) four years later. In the inflationary 1970s Pittsburgh National diversified, moving into commercial paper financing (1972),

lease financing (1979), and credit life, health, and accident reinsurance (1979).

In 1983 Pittsburgh National merged with Provident National of Philadelphia (founded by Quakers in 1865) to form PNC Corp. The union combined Pittsburgh National's corporate lending strength with Provident's money management and trust operations. PNC expanded through the 1980s by buying more Pennsylvania banks and then moved into Kentucky in 1987. That year PNC, with $37 billion in assets, passed Mellon Bank as Pennsylvania's largest bank.

This growth was accompanied by investment in risky commercial mortgages, so when the real estate market unraveled in 1989-90, PNC was stuck with millions of dollars in problem loans. It soon began selling its bad loans and property and tightening underwriting standards.

PNC reorganized in 1991, operating its several state-chartered banks as if they were a single entity. Acquisitions continued, including BlackRock Financial Management, Sears Mortgage, 84 banking branches orphaned by the Chase Manhattan/Chemical Bank merger, and New Jersey-based Midlantic Corp (founded in 1804 as Newark Banking and Insurance).

PNC's acquisitions focused more sharply on mortgages in 1997 and 1998; it bought Midland Loan Services, as well as the mortgage origination offices of what became FleetBoston. The former purchase moved the company strongly into servicing and securitization to become a major buyer in the secondary commercial-mortgage market.

In addition to consolidating its asset management operations under the BlackRock subsidiary in 1998 (spun off the next year), PNC bought BTM Capital, an asset-based lender headquartered in Boston. After rules separating banking from securities activities were relaxed in 1998, the firm bought Louisville, Kentucky-based securities brokerage Hilliard Lyons. Also that year the company paid $30 million to attach its name to the Pittsburgh Pirates' baseball stadium for 20 years. Christened PNC Park, it opened in 2001.

In 1999 PNC agreed to pay $375,000 to 31 women employees in response to a Labor Department charge that PNC had a "glass ceiling."

PNC exited the vehicle leasing and residential mortgage businesses in 2001. The following year the company sold BillingZone, a joint venture with Perot Systems that provided electronic bill payment and presentment services; it was purchased by eONE Global, a unit of First Data.

Belying speculation that it was a takeover target itself, PNC bought United National Bancorp in 2004.

PNC had originally agreed to buy Riggs National in 2004, but lowered its bid after Riggs pleaded guilty to Bank Secrecy Act violations in early 2005. (Riggs also paid millions in fines and technology upgrades to comply with the anti-terrorism measure.) Riggs sued PNC for damages for backing out on the deal, but dropped the charges after agreeing on a renegotiated sale price.

In 2005 the company bought boutique investment bank Harris Williams, which specializes in mergers and acquisitions advisory services. Harris Williams kept its name and became a subsidiary of PNC after the deal was completed.

PNC sold part of its 70% share in BlackRock to Merrill Lynch in 2006, netting some $1.6 billion from the transaction. PNC sold brokerage firm Hilliard Lyons to Houchens Industries in 2008.

EXECUTIVES

Chairman and CEO: James E. (Jim) Rohr, age 61, $18,027,856 total compensation
Senior Vice Chairman; Head, Corporate and Institutional Banking: William S. (Bill) Demchak, age 47, $12,534,835 total compensation
Vice Chairman; Chairman, PNC Global Investment Servicing: Timothy G. (Tim) Shack, age 58, $4,577,332 total compensation
Vice Chairman and Chief Risk Officer: Thomas K. (Tom) Whitford, age 53
President: Joseph C. (Joe) Guyaux, age 59, $6,989,668 total compensation
EVP and CFO: Richard J. Johnson, age 53, $3,918,126 total compensation
EVP and Chief Credit Officer: Michael J. Hannon, age 53
EVP and Chief Human Resources Officer: Joan L. Gulley, age 62
EVP and Director Investor Relations: William H. Callihan
EVP and General Counsel: Helen P. Pudlin, age 60
EVP Asset Management Group: Robert Q. Reilly, age 45
CIO: Anuj Dhanda
Director Corporate Communications: Brian Goerke
Corporate Secretary: George P. Long III
Auditors: PricewaterhouseCoopers LLP

LOCATIONS

HQ: The PNC Financial Services Group, Inc.
1 PNC Plaza, 249 5th Ave., Pittsburgh, PA 15222
Phone: 412-762-2000   **Fax:** 412-762-7829
Web: www.pnc.com

PRODUCTS/OPERATIONS

2009 Sales

	$ mil.	% of total
Interest		
Loans	8,919	46
Investment securities	2,688	14
Other	479	2
Noninterest		
Consumer Services	1,290	7
Net gain on Black Rock/Barclays		
Global Investors transaction	1,076	6
Corporate services	1,021	5
Residential mortgage	990	5
Service charges on deposits	950	5
Asset management	858	5
Net gain on sales of securities	550	3
Other	410	2
Total	**19,231**	**100**

Selected Subsidiaries

PNC Bancorp, Inc.
    PNC Bank, National Association
        PNC Bank Capital Securities, LLC
        PNC Capital Leasing, LLC
        PNC Preferred Funding LLC
        PNC REIT Corp.
PNC Holding, LLC
    PNC Funding Corp
    PNC Investment Corp.
    PNC Venture, LLC

COMPETITORS

Bank of America
Capital One
Citigroup
Citizens Financial Group
Fifth Third
Harris Bankcorp
Huntington Bancshares
JPMorgan Chase
KeyCorp
M&T Bank
Sovereign Bank
TD Bank USA
U.S. Bancorp
Wells Fargo

HISTORICAL FINANCIALS

Company Type: Public

Income Statement
FYE: December 31

	ASSETS ($ mil.)	NET INCOME ($ mil.)	INCOME AS % OF ASSETS	EMPLOYEES
12/09	269,863	2,403	0.9%	55,820
12/08	291,081	882	0.3%	59,595
12/07	138,920	1,467	1.1%	28,320
12/06	101,820	2,595	2.5%	23,783
12/05	91,954	1,325	1.4%	25,348
Annual Growth	**30.9%**	**16.0%**	**—**	**21.8%**

2009 Year-End Financials

Equity as % of assets: 11.1%
Return on assets: 0.9%
Return on equity: 8.7%
Long-term debt ($ mil.): 20,668
No. of shares (mil.): 525
Dividends
Yield: 1.8%
Payout: 22.0%
Market value ($ mil.): 27,736
Sales ($ mil.): 19,231

Stock History
NYSE: PNC

	STOCK PRICE ($) FY Close	P/E High	P/E Low	Earnings	Dividends	Book Value
12/09	52.79	13	4	4.36	0.96	56.99
12/08	49.00	36	16	2.46	2.61	48.39
12/07	65.65	18	15	4.35	2.44	28.27
12/06	74.04	9	7	8.73	2.15	20.53
12/05	61.83	14	11	4.55	2.00	16.30
Annual Growth	**(3.9%)**	**—**	**—**	**(1.1%)**	**(16.8%)**	**36.7%**

Polaris Industries

Rough roads are no enemy of commerce for Polaris Industries. The company is one of the world's top makers of off-road vehicles, comprising all-terrain vehicles (ATVs) and side-by-side recreational and utility RANGER-branded vehicles. The company is also known for snowmobiles, on-road vehicles such as Victory branded motorcycles, and low-emission vehicles (LEV). Polaris' offerings include replacement parts, accessories (covers, tow hitches, cargo racks), and riding gear (boots and helmets). The company partners with Fuji Heavy Industries on building Polaris engines as well as products for OEMs in non-competitive industries. Polaris' youth ATVs and snowmobile engines are made for OEMs in Taiwan and Germany, too.

To shore up weak demand driven by the global recession and its slow recovery, Polaris is focusing on whittling costs, as well as developing its product portfolio and market presence, through both internal investments and acquisitions.

Polaris began the new decade by acquiring Swissauto Powersports, maker of the Weber engine, which is used in several Polaris snowmobile models. The deal follows Polaris' sale of its dismal investment in KTM Power Sports AG, an Austrian motorcycle maker that has supplied four-stroke engines for Polaris ATVs.

In the meantime, Polaris has shifted its resources. The company is expanding its marketing efforts in Europe, the Middle East, and Africa, as well as new opportunities in China. At home, declining sales — attributed to the continuing recession — forced the company to reduce its workforce by about 14%. Making do with less, Polaris formed an On-Road Vehicle Division, which is intended to drive cohesive and strategic growth for the Victory Motorcycles brand, and other on-road brands.

The company introduced its first series of luxury touring motorcycles in 2009. An electric-powered low-emission vehicle, the Polaris Breeze, was also rolled out to master planned communities in the US's Sun Belt region. Off-road vehicles, however, continue to account for about two-thirds of Polaris' sales. Since 2007 the company has courted the defense market with a line of military ATVs and side-by-side vehicles, designed for light-duty tactical applications.

HISTORY

Originally called Hetteen Hoist & Derrick, Polaris Industries was founded in Roseau, Minnesota, in 1945 by Edgar Hetteen and David Johnson. The friends did welding and repair work and made custom machinery for local farmers.

In the early 1950s Johnson invented a gas-powered sled to ride to his winter hunting ground. The contraption attracted the attention of a neighbor, who bought the machine. In 1954 the company began making snowmobiles under the Polaris brand. It built five machines in the winter of 1954-55 and was up to 300 per year within three years. Hetteen's younger brother Allen also joined the firm during the 1950s.

Snowmobiles made inroads as utility vehicles, but didn't catch on as recreational vehicles. To spur interest, in 1960 Edgar Hetteen led a snowmobile team on a thousand-mile trip across Alaska. When the company's backers complained about the expense of the trip, Hetteen left Polaris. He later founded Arctic Enterprises, which produced the Arctic Cat snowmobile and was, for a time, the top US snowmobile maker.

With Edgar's departure, Allen Hetteen became president of Polaris. The firm's fortunes rose as the snowmobile gained popularity, and in 1968 diversified manufacturer Textron (Bell helicopters, Schaefer pens, Talon zippers) acquired Polaris.

The snowmobile industry peaked in 1971, with sales topping 495,000 units; the industry declined through the rest of the 1970s. Polaris continued to introduce new models and to sponsor snowmobile racing teams. In 1981 Textron refocused on its defense segments and planned to shut Polaris down. Company president Hall Wendel, an outdoorsman who would later climb Mt. Everest, led a management buyout.

In 1982 Polaris tried to buy Arctic Cat; Arctic Enterprises temporarily closed soon after, leaving Polaris as the US's sole snowmobile maker for a time.

Under Wendel, Polaris began looking for another product to fill production during snowmobiling's off-season. In 1985 it entered the ATV market, going up against several established Japanese manufacturers, including Honda and Suzuki. The company positioned its ATVs not as recreational vehicles, but as utility vehicles, and soon Polaris slipped into the #2 spot behind Honda. It became the world's #1 snowmobile maker in 1991. The next year Polaris began marketing personal watercraft, which made up about 10% of sales in 1993 (dropped to 4% in 1998). The company went public in 1994.

Polaris and Fuji Heavy Industries formed a joint venture — Robin Manufacturing, USA — in 1995 to build engines for its products and noncompeting companies. In 1997 Polaris announced its plans for the Victory motorcycle. In 1998 the company was slapped with a nearly $45 million judgment in a trade-secret lawsuit brought by the inventor of an engine fuel-injection system. Partner Fuji Heavy Industries was ordered to pay $11.6 million.

Polaris became the first American manufacturer in 50 years to enter the motorcycle market when it unveiled the Victory, a cruiser-style cycle, in 1998. *Cycle World* magazine named Victory the cruiser of the year. Thomas Tiller, a 15-year veteran of General Electric, succeeded Wendel as CEO that year.

The following year Victory sales tripled and a second model was introduced. In 2000 company founders and septuagenarians Hetteen and Johnson, along with Tiller, trekked across Alaska in snowmobiles, hoping the publicity would increase snowmobile sales (similar to the trip Hetteen made to boost sales 40 years earlier).

The following year Polaris introduced its first true sport ATV, the Predator. The first Arlen Ness limited-edition cruiser motorcycle (named after motorcycle designers Arlen and Corey Ness) rolled off the assembly line in 2003.

Citing increasing costs and competitive pressures, Polaris decided to liquidate its unprofitable watercraft unit in 2004. In 2005 Polaris purchased a 25% stake in Austrian motorcycle maker KTM Power Sports AG. The move was to give Polaris a better foothold in Europe through KTM's extensive dealer network. Polaris sold most of that stake two years later in an effort to pay down debt.

Tiller stepped down as CEO in 2008 and resigned from the board in 2009. He was succeeded as CEO by Scott Wine, a former executive of Danaher and United Technologies.

EXECUTIVES

Chairman: Gregory R. Palen, age 54
CEO and Director: Scott W. Wine, age 42,
$1,948,514 total compensation
President and COO: Bennett J. Morgan, age 46,
$1,446,954 total compensation
VP Finance, CFO, and Secretary: Michael W. Malone,
age 51, $1,159,892 total compensation
VP and CIO: William C. Fisher, age 55
VP and CTO: David C. Longren, age 51
VP Sales and Marketing: Michael P. Jonikas, age 49,
$943,979 total compensation
VP Operations: Wes Barker,
$1,007,752 total compensation
VP Human Resources: John B. Corness, age 55,
$890,246 total compensation
VP, General Counsel, and Corporate Secretary:
Stacy Bogart
VP Off-Road Vehicle Division:
Matthew J. (Matt) Homan, age 38
VP Snowmobile and PG&A Divisions:
Scott A. Swenson, age 46
VP Motorcycles: Mark E. Blackwell, age 56
VP Corporate Development: Todd Balan
VP Supply Chain and Integration: Suresh Krishna
VP Global New Market Development:
Michael D. Dougherty, age 42
Director Investor Relations: Richard Edwards
Auditors: Ernst & Young LLP

LOCATIONS

HQ: Polaris Industries Inc.
2100 Hwy. 55, Medina, MN 55340
Phone: 763-542-0500   **Fax:** 763-542-0599
Web: www.polarisindustries.com

2009 Sales

	$ mil.	% of total
US	1,074.2	69
Canada	239.3	15
Other countries	252.4	16
Total	**1,565.9**	**100**

PRODUCTS/OPERATIONS

2009 Sales

	$ mil.	% of total
Off-road vehicles	1,021.1	65
Parts, garments & accessories	312.7	20
Snowmobiles	179.3	12
Motorcycles	52.8	3
Total	**1,565.9**	**100**

Selected Products

All-terrain vehicles (four-wheel, six-wheel utility, and side-by-side)
On-road vehicles (motorcycles, low-emission vehicles)
Parts, garments, and accessories
  Boots
  Bumpers
  Cabs
  Handlebars
  Helmets
  Jackets
  Motorcycle backrests and seats
  Mowers
  Oil and lubricants
  Tires
  Winches
  Windshields
Snowmobiles

COMPETITORS

Arctic Cat
BMW
Deere
E-Z-GO
Harley-Davidson
Honda
Kawasaki Heavy Industries
Kubota
Suzuki Motor
Yamaha Motor

HISTORICAL FINANCIALS

Company Type: Public

Income Statement

FYE: December 31

	REVENUE ($ mil.)	NET INCOME ($ mil.)	NET PROFIT MARGIN	EMPLOYEES
12/09	1,566	101	6.4%	3,000
12/08	1,948	117	6.0%	3,300
12/07	1,780	112	6.3%	3,200
12/06	1,657	107	6.4%	3,400
12/05	1,870	143	7.7%	3,600
Annual Growth	**(4.3%)**	**(8.4%)**	**—**	**(4.5%)**

2009 Year-End Financials

Debt ratio: 97.8%	No. of shares (mil.): 33
Return on equity: 59.1%	Dividends
Cash ($ mil.): 140	Yield: 3.6%
Current ratio: 1.43	Payout: 51.1%
Long-term debt ($ mil.): 200	Market value ($ mil.): 1,445

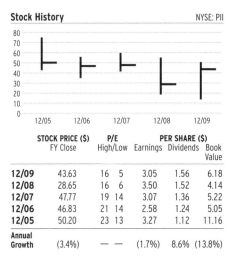

Stock History

NYSE: PII

	STOCK PRICE ($) FY Close	P/E High/Low		PER SHARE ($) Earnings	Dividends	Book Value
12/09	43.63	16	5	3.05	1.56	6.18
12/08	28.65	16	6	3.50	1.52	4.14
12/07	47.77	19	14	3.07	1.36	5.22
12/06	46.83	21	14	2.58	1.24	5.05
12/05	50.20	23	13	3.27	1.12	11.16
Annual Growth	**(3.4%)**	—	—	**(1.7%)**	**8.6%**	**(13.8%)**

Polo Ralph Lauren

Polo Ralph Lauren is galloping at a faster clip than when founder Ralph Lauren first entered the arena more than 40 years ago. With golden mallet brands such as Polo by Ralph Lauren, RRL, Rugby, and Club Monaco, the company designs and markets apparel and accessories, home furnishings, and fragrances. Its collections are available at some 9,000 locations worldwide, including many upscale and mid-tier department stores. It also operates about 350 Ralph Lauren, Club Monaco, and Rugby retail stores worldwide. American style icon and CEO Lauren controls the company.

In recent years Polo Ralph Lauren has been expanding its business through acquisitions, extending the reach of its retail operations, and growing organically. To give the apparel maker more control of its operations in Asia, Polo Ralph Lauren has been buying out its licensees there. In July 2010 it agreed to buy its South Korean wholesale and retail distribution operation from licensee Doosan Corp. Previously, it bought out licensing partner Dickson Concepts in late 2009. Dickson was a licensee for the Polo brand in China, Hong Kong, Indonesia, Malaysia, the Philippines, Singapore, Taiwan, and Thailand.

Polo Ralph Lauren purchased the remaining 50% stake in Polo.com from both Ralph Lauren Media, a unit of NBC Universal, and ValueVisions Media for about $175 million in 2007. The move gave Polo full control over its plans to develop its online presence domestically and abroad, where the company has seen an uptick in traffic.

To further extend its reach into accessories, Polo Ralph Lauren has partnered with its licensees, including Richemont SA (to form Ralph Lauren Watch and Jewelry Co.) and the Italian eyewear giant Luxottica Group, which designs, manufactures, and distributes Polo Ralph Lauren-branded prescription frames and sunglasses. Luxottica's US arm also makes Club Monaco-branded prescription frames and sunglasses sold in the US and Canada.

Other major licensing partners include WestPoint Home, Peerless, Inc., and J.C. Penney, which launched the American Living lifestyle brand (designed by Polo Ralph Lauren's new Global Brand Concepts group) in 2008.

Polo Ralph Lauren's push to extend its classic American style to the global market got a big boost with the selection of the company to outfit the US Olympic team at the 2008 summer games in Beijing. Under the terms of the agreement, Polo clothed some 1,500 American athletes during the opening and closing ceremonies, and during downtime in the Olympic Village. The firm has its eye on extending the deal to the Winter Olympics in 2010, the 2012 Summer Olympics in London, and beyond.

Ralph Lauren controls the company through his ownership of more than 85% of the voting shares of the company. In mid-2010 Lauren disclosed plans to sell more than a quarter of his holdings as "part of his individual asset diversification plan." He will maintain a stake sizeable enough to remain in control of the company.

HISTORY

Ralph Lauren, suave Manhattanite, was actually born Ralph Lifschitz in the Bronx, New York. It is said that his father, Frank, an immigrant Russian housepainter and muralist, informally changed the family's name to Lauren and inspired his son to recreate himself in the image of a mythic upper class.

After high school Ralph, who formally changed his name to Lauren, became a salesman at Brooks Brothers and then a sales representative for Rivetz, a Boston tie maker. In 1967 he landed a job as a tie designer for Beau Brummel of New York. The company gave him his own style division, which he named Polo because of the sport's refined image. The next year Lauren started Polo Fashions to make tailored menswear. Partner Peter Strom teamed up with Lauren in the early 1970s. Although its designs received critical acclaim, Polo Fashions had a bumpy start as Lauren adjusted to the business aspect of his fashion label.

Lauren's profile rose in the 1970s when he won three Coty Awards for design and produced costumes for the movie *The Great Gatsby*. In 1971 Lauren adopted his polo-player-on-a-horse logo and introduced a line for women. That year the first licensed Polo store opened (on Rodeo Drive in Beverly Hills), along with his first in-store boutique (at Bloomingdale's in New York City). He added shoes to the lineup in 1972, licensed his womenswear line the next year, and launched a licensed fragrance line in 1978.

By 1980 Polo Fashions had become Polo Ralph Lauren. Encouraged by the success of the licensed products, Lauren led the designer charge into home furnishings, introducing his Home Collection in 1983. He opened his flagship store in New York City three years later.

Lauren sold 28% of Polo to a Goldman Sachs investment fund for $135 million in 1994. The company expanded upmarket with its Purple Label and downmarket with Polo Jeans denims and a line of paints in 1996.

Following the stampede of fashion-house IPOs, Polo went public in 1997. The next year, moving

to reduce expenses, the company restructured its divisions. The reorganization included closing nine stores and cutting about 4% of its workforce, resulting in a $65 million charge.

In May 1999 Polo paid $85 million for hip Canadian retailer Club Monaco to compete in the burgeoning youth market. It also opened RL, a fine-dining restaurant adjacent to its retail outlet in Chicago's famed shopping district.

In early 2000 Polo purchased its European licensee, Poloco, for $230 million, giving the company greater control of its brand. Then, in a 50-50 joint venture with NBC and its affiliates, Polo formed Ralph Lauren Media Company to sell its products via the Internet as well as broadcast, cable, and print media. Also that year the company closed 11 underperforming Club Monaco locations and announced plans to shut down all of its jeans stores. To extend its European reach even further, Polo bought its Italian licensee, PRL Fashions of Europe, in 2001.

Polo Ralph Lauren entered a licensing agreement with Luxottica in 2006 that's valued at more than $1.75 billion over a 10-year period.

Initiatives for 2007 included the launch of a new group named Global Brand Concepts formed to develop lifestyle brands for specialty and department stores, including J.C. Penney's new American Living Collection, which launched in early 2008. The group designs and markets new products, including accessories, home decor, and women's, men's, and children's apparel.

EXECUTIVES

Chairman and CEO: Ralph Lauren, age 70, $20,303,522 total compensation
EVP and Director: Jackwyn L. (Jacki) Nemerov, age 58, $1,866,547 total compensation
SVP Finance and CFO: Tracey T. Travis, age 47, $1,866,547 total compensation
SVP Human Resources: Mitchell A. Kosh, age 60, $1,514,283 total compensation
Auditors: Deloitte & Touche LLP

LOCATIONS

HQ: Polo Ralph Lauren Corporation
650 Madison Ave., New York, NY 10022
Phone: 212-318-7000   **Fax:** 212-888-5780
Web: www.ralphlauren.com

2010 Sales

	$ mil.	% of total
US & Canada	3,462.3	70
Europe	1,052.6	21
Asia	459.7	9
Other regions	4.3	—
Total	**4,978.9**	**100**

PRODUCTS/OPERATIONS

2010 Sales

	$ mil.	% of total
Wholesale	2,532.4	51
Retail	2,263.1	45
Licensing	183.4	4
Total	**4,978.9**	**100**

Selected Brand Names and Licenses

Wholesale
  Lauren by Ralph Lauren
  Pink Pony
  Polo by Ralph Lauren
  Ralph by Ralph Lauren
  Ralph Lauren Black Label
  Ralph Lauren Blue Label
  Ralph Lauren/Purple Label
  Ralph Lauren Polo Sport
Retail
  Club Monaco
  Ralph Lauren
  Rugby
  Polo Ralph Lauren
  Polo Sport
Licensing Partners
  Fitz and Floyd, Inc.
  Hanesbrands
  Kohl's Department Stores, Inc.
  L'Oréal S.A.
  Luxottica Group
  Peerless, Inc.
  Schnadig International Corp.
  Town & Country Linen Corp.
  The Warnaco Group
  WestPoint Home, Inc.

COMPETITORS

Abercrombie & Fitch	Hugo Boss
American Eagle Outfitters	J. Crew
AnnTaylor	Jones Apparel
Armani	Jos. A. Bank
Benetton	Kenneth Cole
Brand Matter	Lands' End
Burberry	Laura Ashley
Calvin Klein	Levi Strauss
Christian Dior	Liz Claiborne
Coach, Inc.	L.L. Bean
Donna Karan	Luxottica
Ermenegildo Zegna	LVMH
Escada	Martha Stewart Living
Estée Lauder	Nautica Apparel
The Gap	Perry Ellis International
Gianni Versace	Phillips-Van Heusen
Gucci	PPR SA
Guess?	Richemont
H&M	St. John Knits
Haggar	Tiffany & Co.
Hermès	Tommy Bahama
HMX	Warnaco Group

HISTORICAL FINANCIALS

Company Type: Public

Income Statement		FYE: Saturday nearest March 31		
	REVENUE ($ mil.)	NET INCOME ($ mil.)	NET PROFIT MARGIN	EMPLOYEES
3/10	4,979	480	9.6%	19,000
3/09	5,019	406	8.1%	17,000
3/08	4,880	420	8.6%	15,000
3/07	4,295	401	9.3%	14,000
3/06	3,746	308	8.2%	12,800
Annual Growth	**7.4%**	**11.7%**	**—**	**10.4%**

2010 Year-End Financials

Debt ratio: 9.1%   No. of shares (mil.): 98
Return on equity: 16.4%   Dividends
Cash ($ mil.): 563   Yield: 0.4%
Current ratio: 3.05   Payout: 6.3%
Long-term debt ($ mil.): 282   Market value ($ mil.): 8,350

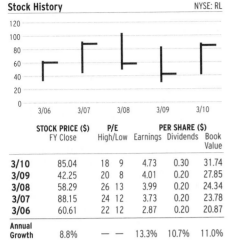

PPG Industries

You won't catch PPG Industries painting itself into a corner. Coatings — such as paints (Pittsburgh Paints, Lucite, and Monarch), stains (Olympic), and sealants — account for most of its sales; the remainder comes from glass, chemicals, and specialty materials. PPG's glass offerings include flat glass for buildings, fabricated glass, and continuous-strand fiberglass used in aircraft and buildings. Its chemicals segment makes chlor-alkali chemicals, and the specialty materials unit provides silica products. The company also makes optical products like Transitions brand lenses. PPG operates more than 120 manufacturing facilities worldwide and owns 450 retail centers in the US and Australia.

One of PPG's major markets is automakers and their suppliers, who buy the company's adhesives, sealants, and coatings. It also supplies automotive refinishes through distributors. The company tried to sell its auto glass business to Platinum Equity for $500 million in 2007, but the private equity firm pulled out of the agreement at the end of that year. The next year, PPG finally managed to sell the auto glass business to a private equity group. This time it was Kohlberg & Company, which set the unit up as a standalone company called Pittsburgh Glass Works. PPG received $330 million plus a 40% interest in the company.

Relatively stable before 2005, the company stepped out a little that year and acquired Singapore-based Crown Coating Industries, which made radiation-cured coatings for wood flooring. That started a prolonged streak of acquisitions throughout Europe, Asia, and Australia over the next few years. The biggest of these deals was the 2008 acquisition of SigmaKalon for $3 billion. SigmaKalon itself was among the top 10 paint manufacturers in the world and did business almost entirely outside the US.

Since the divestiture of the auto glass business, PPG's M&A activities have slowed considerably. Primarily, the company seems to have concentrated on integrating SigmaKalon —

both operationally and financially — and weathering the global economic crisis of 2008-2009. It did the latter by closing a small number of manufacturing facilities and decreasing production at many of the others.

HISTORY

After the failure of his first two plate-glass manufacturing plants, John Ford persuaded former railroad superintendent John Pitcairn to invest $200,000 in a third factory in 1883 in Creighton, Pennsylvania. The enterprise, Pittsburgh Plate Glass (PPG), became the first commercially successful US plate-glass factory.

Ford left in 1896 after Pitcairn established a company distribution system, replacing glass jobbers. Ford went on to found a predecessor of competitor Libbey-Owens-Ford (now owned by glassmaker Pilkington).

Pitcairn built a soda ash plant in 1899, bought a Milwaukee paint company the following year, and began producing window glass in 1908. Pitcairn died in 1916, leaving his stock to his sons.

Strong automobile and construction markets in the early 20th century increased demand for the company's products. In 1924 PPG revolutionized glass production with the introduction of a straight-line conveyor manufacturing method. In the 1930s and 1940s, PPG successfully promoted structural glass for use in the commercial construction industry.

PPG was listed on the NYSE in 1945. In 1952 it started making fiberglass, and in 1968 the company adopted its present name.

Vincent Sarni (CEO, 1984-93) recognized that 85% of the company's sales were to the maturing construction and automobile industries. Sarni decided to move the company into growing industries, such as electronics.

In 1986 PPG spent $154 million on acquisitions, including the medical electronics units of Litton Industries and Honeywell. It acquired the medical technology business of Allegheny International in 1987 and bought Casco Nobel, a coatings distributor, and the Olympic and Lucite paint lines from Clorox in 1989.

The company, which owned one-third of Dutch fiberglass producer Silenka BV, acquired the rest in 1991. In 1992 PPG acquired a silica plant in the Netherlands, its first in Europe. Two years later it acquired the European automotive coatings business of Netherlands-based Akzo Nobel.

In the 1990s PPG backed away from Sarni's earlier strategies for greater diversification and unloaded a number of high-tech businesses. The firm refocused on its core coatings, glass, and chemicals operations. PPG acquired Matthews Paints, a leading maker of paints for outdoor signs, and the refinish coating business of Lilly Industries in 1995.

The company bolstered its chemical operations in 1997 with the addition of France's Sipsy Chime Fine. That same year President and COO Raymond LeBoeuf took over as CEO. In 1998 PPG sold its European flat and automotive glass business to Belgium-based Glaverbel. Acquisitions that year included Australia-based Orica's technical coatings unit and the US paint operations (Porter Paints) of Akzo Nobel.

In 1999 PPG expanded its European coatings business with the purchase of Belgium-based Sigma Coatings' commercial transport coatings unit and Akzo Nobel's aircraft coatings and sealants company, PRC-DeSoto International. That year PPG also bought Imperial Chemical Industries' Germany-based coatings business for large commercial vehicles and its US-based auto

refinish and industrial coatings businesses. PPG's acquisition spree continued in 2000 with architectural coating maker Monarch Paint.

Early in the new decade, PPG suffered from flat or declining earnings from existing operations. Amid falling sales and lower prices for chemicals and glass, PPG began to cut jobs and closed some facilities. Still the company recorded its first loss in more than 10 years in 2002 and its second straight year of declining sales.

Like many manufacturers in its industry, PPG has been exposed to potentially costly asbestos litigation, mainly because of its 50% stake in the bankrupt Pittsburgh Corning, a joint venture with Corning that made insulation with asbestos. In 2002 PPG and its insurers agreed to pay roughly $2.7 billion to settle its asbestos claims.

LeBoeuf retired in 2005. He was replaced by president and COO Charles Bunch, who had joined the company in 1979 and worked up through the ranks of, first, the finance department, and then the coatings operations.

EXECUTIVES

Chairman and CEO: Charles E. (Chuck) Bunch, age 60, $8,422,427 total compensation
EVP Information Technology: Pierre-Marie de Leener, age 53, $2,119,513 total compensation
EVP: J. Rich Alexander, age 54, $2,204,292 total compensation
SVP Finance and CFO: Robert J. (Bob) Dellinger, age 50, $2,017,407 total compensation
SVP Optical and Specialty Materials: Richard C. (Rick) Elias, age 56
SVP Commodity Chemicals: Michael H. McGarry, age 51
SVP Packaging Coatings: Viktor R. Sekmakas
SVP Glass and Fiber Glass: Victoria M. (Vicki) Holt, age 52
SVP: Cynthia A. Niekamp, age 50
CTO and VP Coatings Research and Development: Charles F. Kahle II
VP Government and Community Affairs: Lynne D. Schmidt
VP Human Resources: Charles W. (Bud) Wise
VP and Controller: David B. Navikas
VP Tax Administration: Donna Lee Walker
VP Strategic Planning and Treasurer: Aziz S. Giga
VP Information Technology: Werner Baer
VP Global Refinish and Corporate Supply Chain: Reginald (Reg) Norton
Director Investor Relations: Vince Morales
Supervisor Public Relations: K.C. McCrory
Auditors: Deloitte & Touche LLP

LOCATIONS

HQ: PPG Industries, Inc.
1 PPG Place, Pittsburgh, PA 15272
Phone: 412-434-3131   **Fax:** 412-434-2011
Web: www.ppg.com

2009 Sales

	$ mil.	% of total
The Americas		
US	5,113	42
Other countries	867	7
Europe/Middle East/Africa	4,458	36
Asia	1,801	15
Total	12,239	100

PRODUCTS/OPERATIONS

2009 Sales

	$ mil.	% of total
Performance Coatings	4,095	34
Industrial Coatings	3,068	25
Architectural Coatings EMEA	1,952	16
Commodity Chemicals	1,273	10
Optical & Specialty Materials	1,002	8
Glass	849	7
Total	12,239	100

Selected Products

Performance Coatings
Aerospace coatings
Architectural coatings (Lucite paints, Olympic stains)
Refinish

Industrial Coatings
Automotive coatings, chemicals, adhesives, and sealants
Industrial coatings
Packaging coatings (food and beverage containers)

Commodity Chemicals
Calcium hypochlorite
Caustic soda
Chlorine
Chlorine derivatives
Phosgene derivatives

Optical and Specialty Materials
Optical products (Transitions variable-tint lenses)
Silica products

Glass
Aircraft transparencies
Coated glass
Continuous-strand fiberglass
Flat glass

COMPETITORS

3M	Guardian Industries
Akzo Nobel	Kelly-Moore
Asahi Glass	Nippon Paint
BASF Coatings AG	Nippon Sheet Glass
BEHR	Pilkington Group
Benjamin Moore	Quanex Building Products
Dow Chemical	RPM International
DuPont Performance	Saint-Gobain
Coatings	Sherwin-Williams
Ferro	

HISTORICAL FINANCIALS

Company Type: Public

Income Statement

FYE: December 31

	REVENUE ($ mil.)	NET INCOME ($ mil.)	NET PROFIT MARGIN	EMPLOYEES
12/09	12,239	426	3.5%	39,900
12/08	15,849	538	3.4%	44,900
12/07	11,206	834	7.4%	34,900
12/06	11,037	711	6.4%	32,200
12/05	10,201	596	5.8%	30,800
Annual Growth	4.7%	(8.1%)	—	6.7%

2009 Year-End Financials

Debt ratio: 81.9%
Return on equity: 12.0%
Cash ($ mil.): 1,057
Current ratio: 1.67
Long-term debt ($ mil.): 3,074

No. of shares (mil.): 165
Dividends
Yield: 3.6%
Payout: 104.9%
Market value ($ mil.): 9,668

Stock History

NYSE: PPG

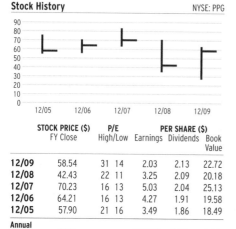

	STOCK PRICE ($) FY Close	P/E High/Low		PER SHARE ($) Earnings	Dividends	Book Value
12/09	58.54	31	14	2.03	2.13	22.72
12/08	42.43	22	11	3.25	2.09	20.18
12/07	70.23	16	13	5.03	2.04	25.13
12/06	64.21	16	13	4.27	1.91	19.58
12/05	57.90	21	16	3.49	1.86	18.49
Annual Growth	0.3%	—	—	(12.7%)	3.4%	5.3%

PPL Corporation

PPL packs a powerful punch in Pennsylvania and the UK, where it distributes electricity to about 4 million customers through regulated subsidiaries PPL Electric Utilities (1.4 million customers) and Western Power Distribution Holdings (2.6 million electricity customers). The company has 11,720 MW of generating capacity in the US and sells energy in key US markets through its PPL EnergyPlus subsidiary. Once a global power player with interests in distribution companies in a number of countries, the company has opted for the UK as its sole non-US focus. Western Power Distribution operates two of the 15 distribution networks providing electricity service in the UK — WPD (South West) and WPD (South Wales).

Anticipating a rebounding economy, in 2010 PPL agreed to buy E.ON U.S., the owner of Kentucky's two major utilities, Louisville Gas & Electric and Kentucky Utilities, for $7.2 billion. The utilities serve 1.2 million customers, primarily in Kentucky. The deal will make PLL stronger (with 20,000 MW of generating capacity) and more geographically diverse.

The global recession suppressed demand, weakening the company's revenues in 2009. During an earlier economic slump PPL shed noncore businesses and focused on its power operations, and aggressively reduced its operation and maintenance spending. In 2007 the company sold its Latin American companies, as well as its domestic telecommunications and synthetic fuels businesses. In 2008 PPL sold its US propane and gas distribution unit.

HISTORY

PPL's wires reach back to Lehigh Coal & Navigation, which was formed in 1822 to mine Pennsylvania coal and build a canal to deliver it to Philadelphia. Heavy industry and steel mills flourished in the Lehigh Valley, and Thomas Edison formed small electric companies to serve the area in the early 1880s. Rivals soon followed, and by 1900 there were 64 companies in what would become PPL's territory.

Lehigh formed Lehigh Navigation Electric in 1912 to provide power to its coal mines, only to lose control of the company in 1917 to conglomerate Electric Bond & Share. S. Z. Mitchell, Electric Bond & Share's president, merged the renamed Lehigh Valley Light & Power with six other utilities to form Pennsylvania Power & Light (PP&L) in Allentown in 1920. The next year PP&L became a subsidiary of National Power & Light.

PP&L bought more than 60 neighboring utilities in a decade, and by 1930 industrial customers accounted for 70% of power sales. The company also built a 220,000-volt transmission interconnection line with neighbors Philadelphia Electric (now PECO Energy, a unit of Exelon) and Public Service Electric and Gas of New Jersey (now part of Public Service Enterprise Group). During the Depression the company offset falling industrial sales with residential sales.

The Public Utility Holding Company Act of 1935 forced large utility holding companies to streamline their businesses, and by 1948 National Power & Light had unloaded PP&L.

To keep up with postwar demand, PP&L built several coal-fired power plants. By 1964 industry still accounted for about a third of sales, but suburbs assumed greater importance. PP&L began operating coal mines in the early 1970s and started building the Susquehanna nuclear plant.

Although its proprietary coal supply helped PP&L weather skyrocketing fuel costs in the 1970s, huge construction delays endemic to nukes hit the utility for $4 billion by the time Susquehanna was completed in 1982. Flat sales in the late 1980s led to 2,000 job cuts and to a reorganization by CEO William Hecht.

In 1992 the federal Energy Policy Act signaled the end of the monopoly era by promoting wholesale competition. PP&L formed Power Markets Development (now PPL Global) in 1994 to make energy investments worldwide. The next year it created holding company PP&L Resources to house both regulated and nonregulated businesses.

The Customer Choice Act was passed in Pennsylvania in 1996, ushering in competition, and the utility formed its non-regulated retail power sales arm, PP&L EnergyPlus. PP&L also bought 25% of Chile's Empresas Emel in 1997 (upped to 67%, 1999). Fellow US utility Southern Company, which bought UK utility SWEB in 1995, had turned over a 51% stake in SWEB to PP&L Resources by 1998.

PP&L Resources began buying mechanical contracting firms in 1998 to complement its electric business, and it purchased natural gas and propane distributor Penn Fuel Gas.

In 1999 the company bought generating facilities with a total capacity of 1,315 MW from Montana Power. Also that year PP&L Resources and Southern sold SWEB's supply business and the SWEB brand name to London Electricity, a unit of Electricité de France. PP&L Resources and Southern retained their stakes in SWEB's distribution network, which was renamed Western Power Distribution (later changed to WPD Holdings UK after it acquired British utility Hyder in 2000).

PP&L Resources changed its name to PPL Corporation in 2000 and reorganized into four major operating subsidiaries: PPL Utilities, PPL EnergyPlus, PPL Generation, and PPL Global. PPL's restructuring separated its regulated distribution operations from its non-regulated generation, supply, and services operations.

In 2002 PPL's Brazilian utility, Companhia Energética do Maranhão (Cemar), filed for bankruptcy protection and fell under the control of the Brazilian government. (PPL divested its interest in Cemar in 2004.) Also in 2002 PPL purchased the remaining 49% stake in WPD Holdings UK (now Western Power Distribution Holdings) from Mirant for $235 million.

EXECUTIVES

Chairman, President, and CEO: James H. Miller, age 61, $6,676,874 total compensation
EVP and CFO: Paul A. Farr, age 42, $1,601,615 total compensation
EVP and COO; President, Generation: William H. (Bill) Spence, age 53, $2,420,708 total compensation
SVP, General Counsel, and Secretary: Robert J. Grey, age 59, $1,693,210 total compensation
VP Risk Management and Chief Risk Officer: J. Matt Simmons Jr., age 44
VP and Controller: Vincent (Vince) Sorgi, age 38
VP and CIO: James E. (Jim) Schinski, age 50
VP Customer Service, PPL Gas Utilities: Robert M. Geneczko
VP External Affairs: Joanne H. Raphael
VP Finance and Treasurer: James E. Abel, age 58

President, PPL Electric Utilities:
David G. (Dave) DeCampli, age 52
President, PPL EnergyPlus: Robert D. (Rob) Gabbard
President, PPL Global and President, PPL Energy
 Services Group: Rick L. Klingensmith, age 49
President, PPL Nuclear Development:
Victor N. Lopiano, age 59
General Manager Corporate Communications:
Daniel J. (Dan) McCarthy
Director Investor Relations: Timothy J. (Tim) Paukovits
Auditors: Ernst & Young LLP

LOCATIONS

HQ: PPL Corporation
2 N. 9th St., Allentown, PA 18101
Phone: 610-774-5151   **Fax:** 610-774-4198
Web: www.pplweb.com

2009 Sales

	$ mil.	% of total
US	6,840	91
UK	716	9
Total	**7,556**	**100**

PRODUCTS/OPERATIONS

2009 Sales

	$ mil.	% of total
Supply	3,618	48
Pennsylvania delivery	3,222	43
International delivery	716	9
Total	**7,556**	**100**

Selected Subsidiaries

PPL Development Corporation (acquisition and
 divestiture activities)
PPL Electric Utilities Corporation (electricity
 distribution)
PPL Energy Supply (nonregulated operations)
 PPL EnergyPlus, LLC (wholesale and retail energy
  marketing)
 PPL Generation, LLC (electricity generation)
  PPL Montana, LLC (electricity generation)
 PPL Global, LLC (international utility operations)
  Western Power Distribution Holdings Limited
   (formerly WPD Holdings UK, electricity
   distribution)
PPL Services Corporation (shared services for PPL Corp.
 and other subsidiaries)

COMPETITORS

ABB
AEP
Allegheny Energy
Canadian Utilities
Centrica
Con Edison
Constellation Energy Group
Covanta
Delmarva Power
Dominion Resources
Duke Energy
Duquesne Light Holdings
EnergySolve
Environmental Power
Exelon
FirstEnergy
Green Mountain Energy
HC Energía
Iberdrola USA
Maine & Maritimes
Midwest Generation
Ontario Power Generation
Orange & Rockland Utilities
Pepco Holdings
Public Service Enterprise Group
Scottish and Southern Energy
South Jersey Industries
Southern Company
TransAlta
UIL Holdings

HISTORICAL FINANCIALS

Company Type: Public

Income Statement

FYE: December 31

	REVENUE ($ mil.)	NET INCOME ($ mil.)	NET PROFIT MARGIN	EMPLOYEES
12/09	7,556	426	5.6%	10,489
12/08	8,044	948	11.8%	10,554
12/07	6,498	1,306	20.1%	11,149
12/06	6,899	865	12.5%	12,620
12/05	6,219	686	11.0%	12,276
Annual Growth	**5.0%**	**(11.2%)**	**—**	**(3.9%)**

2009 Year-End Financials

Debt ratio: 130.0%
Return on equity: 8.1%
Cash ($ mil.): 801
Current ratio: 1.14
Long-term debt ($ mil.): 7,143
No. of shares (mil.): 379
Dividends
 Yield: 4.3%
 Payout: 127.8%
Market value ($ mil.): 12,232

Stock History

NYSE: PPL

	STOCK PRICE ($) FY Close	P/E High/Low	Earnings	PER SHARE ($) Dividends	Book Value
12/09	32.31	32 22	1.08	1.38	14.52
12/08	30.69	22 11	2.47	1.34	13.41
12/07	52.09	16 10	3.35	1.22	14.68
12/06	35.84	17 12	2.24	1.10	13.53
12/05	29.40	19 14	1.77	0.96	11.80
Annual Growth	**2.4%**	**— —**	**(11.6%)**	**9.5%**	**5.3%**

Praxair, Inc.

At Praxair, doing business is always a gas. The company produces and sells atmospheric gases (oxygen, nitrogen, argon, and others), as well as process and specialty gases (CO2, helium, and hydrogen) for the chemicals, food and beverage, semiconductor, and health care industries worldwide. Depending on a client company's gas needs, Praxair can build an on-site gas plant or provide gases by the cylinder. The company's Praxair Surface Technologies subsidiary supplies high-temperature and corrosion-resistant metallic, ceramic, and powder coatings mainly to the aircraft, plastics, and primary metals industries. Praxair's Healthcare Services unit supplies hospitals and the medical homecare industry.

The company has grown through an aggressive acquisition program, completing more than two dozen, mostly small, deals since 2007. For example, the 2008 acquisition of Kirk Welding Supply was one of several purchases that advanced the company in the Midwest, while its 2007 acquisition of Wilson Welding in Michigan helped its Great Lakes operations. Another 2007 acquisition expanded Praxair's Canadian operations when the company bought Blue Rhino's tank-exchange business, with the goal of rebranding using Praxair's own PropanQuikSwap

name. (Blue Rhino is a part of Ferrellgas Partners.) The 2009 acquisition of SermaTech brought Praxair Surface technologies new business with the oil and gas, aerospace, and power generation industries.

The 2007 acquisition of 50% of Yara International's industrial gas business led to the creation of a joint venture that gave Praxair entry to the Scandinavian market, and its acquisition of Linde's industrial gas business in Mexico broadened its geographic reach in that country. Other international acquisitions were made in South America and Europe.

The company's international growth is being fueled organically through new plant construction and expansion of existing facilities, especially throughout the Asia/Pacific region.

HISTORY

The origins of Praxair date to the work of Karl von Linde, a professor of mechanical engineering at the College of Technology in Munich, Germany, in the late 1800s. In 1895 he created the cryogenic air liquefier. Von Linde built his first oxygen-production plant in 1902 and a nitrogen plant in 1904, and in the first decade of the 20th century he built a number of air-separation plants throughout Europe.

By 1907 von Linde had moved to the US and founded Linde Air Products in Cleveland, to extract oxygen from air. Linde Air Products joined rival Union Carbide in 1911 in experimenting with the production of acetylene; it became a unit of Union Carbide in 1917. America's war effort and economic expansion in the 1920s spurred the development of new uses for industrial gases. Union Carbide's Linde unit also contributed to the development of the atomic bomb in the 1940s, when its scientists perfected a process for refining uranium.

As Union Carbide expanded worldwide over the next two decades, Linde became America's #1 producer of industrial gases. In the 1960s Linde expanded into oxygen-fired furnaces for steel production and the use of nitrogen in refrigerators. By the early 1980s Linde accounted for 11% of Union Carbide's annual sales.

The disastrous 1984 chemical accident at Union Carbide's plant in Bhopal, India, coupled with heavy debt and falling sales, forced Union Carbide to reorganize. In 1992 Linde was spun off as Praxair. William Lichtenberger, former president of Union Carbide, headed the new company and pushed global expansion. Two years later Praxair set up China's first helium transfill plants for medical magnetic resonance imaging. In 1995 the company began operations in India and Peru.

In 1996 Praxair Surface Technologies bought Miller Thermal (thermal spray coatings) and Maxima Air Separation Center (industrial and specialty gases, Israel). Also that year the company picked up $60 million when it sold the Linde name and trademark to Linde, a German engineering and industrial gas company. Praxair purchased and then spun off Chicago Bridge & Iron. The company kept only its Liquid Carbonic division, the world's leading supplier of carbon dioxide for processing. The move opened up a new market in carbonated beverages for Praxair.

In 1997 and 1998 Praxair constructed plants and, to control its own delivery systems, acquired 20 packaged-gases distributors in the US and one in Germany. The company also formed a joint venture in China to produce high-purity nitrogen and other specialty gases for electronics and then teamed up with rival L'Air Liquide in a production joint venture.

Praxair supplied an argon-based protection system for the Shroud of Turin's public display in Italy in 1998. It also installed the industry's first small on-site hydrogen-generating system at an Indiana powdered-metals plant. In 1999 the company formed a global alliance with German pharmaceutical and chemicals company Merck KGaA to provide gases and chemicals to the semiconductor industry. The same year Praxair acquired Materials Research Corporation, a maker of thin-film deposition materials for semiconductors, and the TAFA Group, which makes thermal-spray equipment and related products.

In 2001 Praxair underwent a restructuring that included layoffs in its surface technologies unit (hurt by the decline in jet orders) and Brazilian operations. The next year the company started work on a new plant to serve Singapore's high-tech industry.

In 2004 Praxair Healthcare Services bought Home Care Supply for $245 million. With Home Care Supply joining the company's existing operations, the combined Healthcare Services unit grew its sales to $750 million worldwide, slightly more than 10% of Praxair's total annual sales. The home care market became more important for Praxair as the company saw high growth potential in it (and high margins) and wanted to be able to compete with rivals L'Air Liquide and Air Products and Chemicals.

The company bought some of L'Air Liquide's German assets for about $650 million later that year. Due to antitrust requirements, the French company needed to dispose of the businesses after buying much of Messer Group earlier in the year. The acquisition put Praxair's European sales over $1 billion annually.

In 2006 Praxair sold the aviation repair business of the Surface Technologies unit to Gridiron Capital and Skyview Capital. Also that year, Praxair acquired Medical Gas of Illinois and Withrow Oxygen Service of California.

EXECUTIVES

Chairman, President, and CEO:
Stephen F. (Steve) Angel, age 54,
$10,184,304 total compensation
EVP and CFO: James S. (Jim) Sawyer, age 53,
$2,817,706 total compensation
EVP: Ricardo S. Malfitano, age 51,
$3,289,320 total compensation
SVP, General Counsel, and Secretary:
James T. (Jim) Breedlove, age 62,
$2,087,668 total compensation
SVP; President, North American Industrial Gases, Praxair Canada, and Praxair Mexico:
James J. (Jim) Fuchs, age 57,
$2,107,747 total compensation
SVP and CTO: Raymond P. (Ray) Roberge
SVP Global Sales: Anne K. Roby
SVP: Scott E. Telesz
VP and Treasurer: Michael J. (Mike) Allan
VP Human Resources: Sally A. Savoia
VP Strategic Planning and Marketing: Sunil Mattoo
VP; President, Praxair Europe: Eduardo F. Menezes, age 46
VP; President, Praxair Distribution: George P. Ristevski, age 50
VP Communications and Public Relations; President, The Praxair Foundation: Nigel D. Muir

President, Praxair Surface Technologies:
Mark F. Gruninger, age 45
President, Praxair China: David H. Chow
President, Praxair Healthcare Services:
Scott W. Kaltrider
President, Global Hydrogen: Daniel H. (Dan) Yankowski
President, Praxair Electronics: Mark J. Murphy
President, Praxair Asia: Joseph S. (Joe) Cappello
President and General Director, Praxair Mexico:
Murilo Melo
Director Investor Relations: Elizabeth T. (Liz) Hirsch
Auditors: PricewaterhouseCoopers LLP

LOCATIONS

HQ: Praxair, Inc.
39 Old Ridgebury Rd., Danbury, CT 06810
Phone: 203-837-2000   **Fax:** 800-772-9985
Web: www.praxair.com

2009 Sales

	$ mil.	% of total
North America	4,626	52
South America	1,645	18
Europe	1,283	14
Asia	885	10
Surface Technologies	517	6
Total	**8,956**	**100**

PRODUCTS/OPERATIONS

2009 Sales by Distribution Method

	% of total
Packaged gases (cylinders)	31
Merchant (delivered liquids)	29
On-site (includes non-cryogenics)	24
Other	16
Total	**100**

2009 Sales by End Market

	% of total
Manufacturing	23
Metals	15
Energy	12
Health Care	11
Chemicals	10
Electronics	8
Food & beverage	7
Aerospace	3
Other	11
Total	**100**

Selected Products and Services

Atmospheric Gases
　Argon
　Nitrogen
　Oxygen
　Rare gases
Process Gases
　Acetylene
　Carbon dioxide
　Carbon monoxide
　Electronic gases
　Helium
　Hydrogen
　Specialty gases
Surface Technologies
　Ceramic coatings and powders
　Electric arc, plasma, and high-velocity oxygen fuel spray equipment
　Industrial gas-production equipment
　Metallic coatings and powders

Selected Subsidiaries

Home Care Supply, Inc.
Praxair Asia, Inc. (China)
Praxair Canada Inc.
Praxair Europe Finance-Consultadoria e Projectos Lda. (Portugal)
Praxair Healthcare Services, Inc.
Praxair Mexico Holdings S. de R.L. de C.V.
Praxair Puerto Rico, LLC
Praxair Surface Technologies, Inc.
White Martins Gases Industriais Ltda. (Brazil)

COMPETITORS

Air Products
Airgas
Balchem
Chromalloy Gas Turbine Corporation
GKN Aerospace Chem-tronics
L'Air Liquide
The Linde Group
Teleflex

HISTORICAL FINANCIALS

Company Type: Public

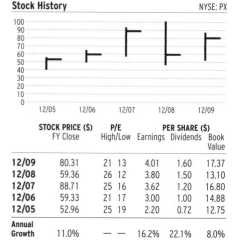

Income Statement				FYE: December 31
	REVENUE ($ mil.)	NET INCOME ($ mil.)	NET PROFIT MARGIN	EMPLOYEES
12/09	8,956	1,254	14.0%	26,164
12/08	10,796	1,211	11.2%	26,936
12/07	9,402	1,177	12.5%	27,992
12/06	8,324	988	11.9%	27,042
12/05	7,656	732	9.6%	27,306
Annual Growth	4.0%	14.4%	—	(1.1%)

2009 Year-End Financials

Debt ratio: 89.5%
Return on equity: 26.9%
Cash ($ mil.): 45
Current ratio: 1.23
Long-term debt ($ mil.): 4,757

No. of shares (mil.): 306
Dividends
　Yield: 2.0%
　Payout: 39.9%
Market value ($ mil.): 24,580

Stock History

NYSE: PX

	STOCK PRICE ($) FY Close	P/E High/Low		PER SHARE ($) Earnings	Dividends	Book Value
12/09	80.31	21	13	4.01	1.60	17.37
12/08	59.36	26	12	3.80	1.50	13.10
12/07	88.71	25	16	3.62	1.20	16.80
12/06	59.33	21	17	3.00	1.00	14.88
12/05	52.96	25	19	2.20	0.72	12.75
Annual Growth	11.0%	—	—	16.2%	22.1%	8.0%

Precision Castparts

You won't find Precision Castparts Corp. (PCC) offering Tom Cruise any movie roles. The company is a leading maker of investment castings used in jet aircraft, satellite launches, armaments, and medical applications (prostheses). Its Investment Cast Products segment makes jet engine parts, fluid management valves, and deep-hole boring tools. Forged Products and Fastener Products round out the company's three segments and cover the power generation and paper and pulp industries, as well as general industry. The cyclical aerospace market still accounts for more than half of PCC's sales. PCC's aerospace customers include jet engine makers General Electric and Pratt & Whitney.

Since the dark days immediately after the terrorist attacks of 9/11, the commercial aerospace industry has paradoxically enjoyed a cyclical upswing. PCC's aerospace fortunes have improved with contracts related to the Airbus A380 and the Boeing 787 Dreamliner. The company, however, has felt the effects of a slower-than-expected recovery due to the global economic crisis, the 2008 Boeing strike, and the lower-than-average metal selling prices.

As one way to offset the cyclical nature of the aerospace industry, the company has entered other markets. It has adapted its existing knowhow to industrial uses and/or acquired market leaders in niche metals and precision metalworking sectors. Overall, the company's mantra is growth by acquisition, with each of its segments augmenting their portfolios and capabilities with products and technologies from complementary companies. Even with a decrease in revenues brought on by the global economic recession, the company has not stopped expanding.

Some recent acquisitions include a 49% stake in China-based Yangzhou Chengde Steel Tube in 2010 — a maker of boiler pipes used for coal-fired power plants and in other energy applications. In 2009 the company spent $847 to acquire Carlton Forge Works, which makes aircraft engines for Boeing and Airbus. PCC also picked up Airdrome Holdings (fluid fittings), Fatigue Technology (cold expansion technology), and Hackney Ladish (forged pipe fittings) in 2009.

The Investment Cast Products division works with specialty materials and alloys, such as nickel- and cobalt-base alloys and stainless steel, to create large structural castings including aircraft engines, gas turbines, airfoils, and airframes. Other products from this segment include medical prostheses, artificial hips and knees, and components for pumps and compressors, as well as large titanium components for armament systems.

The Fasteners segment produces specialty fasteners, and assemblies primarily for use in aerospace applications. Its products are also used in automotive, farm and construction equipment, transportation, and power generation markets.

The Forged Products division works with special metals such as titanium and steel alloys to manufacture components for commercial and military aircraft (landing gear, wing structures, and airframes) and general industrial markets, as well as piping for the energy market.

HISTORY

The history of Precision Castparts Corp. (PCC) is not as precise as its castings. The Oregon Saw Company was founded in 1949 and sold in 1953; its buyer wanted neither the future PCC nor a power tools unit, so the two became Omark Industries. In 1956 a buyer purchased the power tool business but wasn't interested in castings; that operation was spun off as Precision Castparts Corp.

In the early 1950s a group of Oregon Saw's casting employees developed a process for producing parts as large as 60 inches by use of investment casting, making products that rivaled the strength of forged and machined parts at a fraction of the cost. After a two-year search, they landed their first aerospace customer — Air Research Corp. — with many to follow. The higher operating temperatures generated by aircraft engines led the company to buy a vacuum furnace in 1959 to fabricate parts that could tolerate greater heat; two more vacuum furnaces were added and sales vaulted toward $10 million by

1967. PCC went public in 1968 and continued to grow. In 1976 the company acquired Centaur Cast Alloys (small investment castings, UK) to make parts for the European aerospace industry. By that time General Electric (GE) and Pratt & Whitney accounted for most of PCC's business. Edward Cooley, who had masterminded the company's growth since incorporation, forged ahead with plans to double production capacity.

In 1980 the airline industry crashed, but PCC's sales held at about $90 million. Structural airplane products soon picked up, and in 1984 the company bought two titanium foundries in France. To diversify, it added TRW's cast airfoils (used in aircraft engines and industrial gas turbines) division in 1986. That acquisition, renamed PCC Airfoils, increased PCC's annual sales by about 80%.

The company broadened its offerings again in 1991 when it acquired Advanced Forming Technology, which made small, complex, metal-injection molded parts used in everything from adding machines to military ordnance. The early 1990s recession hit the airline industry and sales dropped. Cooley retired as chairman in 1994 and GE veteran William McCormick replaced him. The next year PCC acquired Quamco, Inc. (industrial tools and machines). In 1996 PCC flowed into the fluid management market with the acquisition of NEWFLO for about $300 million.

In 1997 PCC spent $437 million to acquire seven more companies that helped boost sales 75% from 1996 levels. The next year it purchased four metalworking companies that served industries other than aerospace. Having reduced dependence on sales to the aerospace industry to just over 50%, PCC began consolidating operations and closing plants to reduce costs.

The company continued to diversify through acquisitions in 1999, but it also expanded its aerospace operations with the purchase of Wyman-Gordon, a leading maker of advanced metal forgings for the aerospace market.

In 2003 Precision Castparts' PCC Structurals unit reached a $400 million agreement with Rolls-Royce to supply large titanium and steel castings. PCC acquired Air Industries Corporation in early 2005. In 2006 PCC bought Special Metals Corporation (SMC), a maker of nickel alloys and super alloys.

Early in 2007 PCC completed the purchase of GSC, a leading maker of aluminum and steel structural investment casting for the aerospace, energy, and medical markets. It also acquired Cherry Aerospace, which expanded its fastener products portfolio.

EXECUTIVES

Chairman and CEO: Mark Donegan, age 53, $10,873,091 total compensation
EVP; President, PCC Airfoils and Wyman-Gordon: Kenneth D. (Ken) Buck, age 50, $4,817,729 total compensation
EVP and President, Fastener Products: Kevin M. Stein, age 44, $3,123,481 total compensation
EVP; President, Investment Cast Parts: Steven G. (Steve) Hackett, age 53, $3,075,686 total compensation
SVP, CFO, and Assistant Secretary: Shawn R. Hagel, age 44, $3,489,219 total compensation
SVP; President, Special Metals: Joseph I. Snowden, age 53
SVP; President, Structurals Casting Operations: Ross M. Lienhart, age 57
SVP Corporate Training and Organizational Development: John W. Ericksen, age 48
SVP, General Counsel, and Secretary: Roger A. Cooke, age 62, $1,913,996 total compensation

VP, Treasurer, and Assistant Secretary: Steven C. Blackmore, age 48
VP and CIO: Byron J. Gaddis, age 53
VP Strategic Planning and Corporate Development: Kirk G. Pulley, age 41
VP Internal Audit: Mark E. Ellis, age 50
VP Corporate Taxes and Assistant Secretary: Roger P. Becker, age 56
VP, Corporate Controller, and Assistant Secretary: Russell S. Pattee, age 46
Director Communications: Dwight E. Weber
President, PCC Airfoils: Jhn P. O'Neill
Auditors: Deloitte & Touche LLP

LOCATIONS

HQ: Precision Castparts Corp.
4650 SW Macadam Ave., Ste. 400
Portland, OR 97239
Phone: 503-417-4800   **Fax:** 503-417-4817
Web: www.precast.com

2010 Sales

	$ mil.	% of total
US	4,497.5	82
UK	673.4	12
Other countries	315.7	6
Total	**5,486.6**	**100**

PRODUCTS/OPERATIONS

2010 Sales

	$ mil.	% of total
Forged products	2,283.0	42
Investment cast products	1,851.3	34
Fastener products	1,352.3	24
Total	**5,486.6**	**100**

2010 Sales by Industry

	$ mil.	% of total
Aerospace	2,991.4	54
Power Generation	1,454.6	27
General Industrial	1,040.6	19
Total	**5,486.6**	**100**

Selected Products and Services

Fasteners
  Advanced forming technology
  E/One (for the disposal of residential sanitary waste)
  J&L fiber services (for pulp and paper industry)
  PCC Precision Tool Group
  SPS aerospace fasteners (for commercial/military aircraft)
  SPS engineered fasteners (high strength for automotive and construction applications)
Forged products
  Special Metals Corporation
  Wyman-Gordon Forgings
Investment Cast Products
  PCC Airfoils (high-temperature blades and vanes)
  PCC Structurals (structural investment castings)
  Specialty materials and alloys (alloys, waxes, and metal processing for investment casting)

COMPETITORS

Alcoa	Haynes International
Allegheny Technologies	Hitachi Metals
BAE Systems Steel Products	Kennametal
Carpenter Technology	LISI
Chicago Rivet	Mettis Aerospace
Crane Co.	Pacific Aerospace
Curtiss-Wright	Sumitomo Metal Industries
ESCO	Swagelok
Farwest Steel Corporation	Teleflex
Federal Screw Works	ThyssenKrupp
Georg Fischer	United Technologies
Goodrich Corp.	Universal Stainless
Hawk Corp.	V & M Tubes (USA)
	Volvo Aero

HISTORICAL FINANCIALS

Company Type: Public

Income Statement

FYE: Sunday nearest March 31

	REVENUE ($ mil.)	NET INCOME ($ mil.)	NET PROFIT MARGIN	EMPLOYEES
3/10	5,487	925	16.9%	18,100
3/09	6,828	1,045	15.3%	20,300
3/08	6,852	987	14.4%	21,600
3/07	5,361	633	11.8%	19,800
3/06	3,546	351	9.9%	16,000
Annual Growth	11.5%	27.5%	—	3.1%

2010 Year-End Financials

Debt ratio: 4.0%
Return on equity: 17.2%
Cash ($ mil.): 112
Current ratio: 2.82
Long-term debt ($ mil.): 235

No. of shares (mil.): 142
Dividends
  Yield: 0.1%
  Payout: 1.8%
Market value ($ mil.): 18,018

Stock History

NYSE: PCP

	STOCK PRICE ($) FY Close	P/E High/Low		PER SHARE ($) Earnings	Dividends	Book Value
3/10	126.71	20	4	6.49	0.12	41.41
3/09	59.90	18	6	7.43	0.12	34.18
3/08	102.08	23	13	7.04	0.12	28.45
3/07	104.05	23	11	4.59	0.12	19.95
3/06	59.40	24	14	2.58	0.10	15.05
Annual Growth	20.9%	—	—	25.9%	4.7%	28.8%

priceline.com

priceline.com would like to name itself the king of online travel. At priceline.com's website, buyers can "name their own price" for airline tickets, hotel rooms, rental cars, cruises, and vacation packages for destinations in more than 90 countries. Customers can also choose set-price options. With its patented business model, priceline.com generates most of its revenue from travel-related services. In the case of airline tickets and hotel reservations, priceline.com generates sales on the margin, keeping the difference between the price paid by the individual and what priceline.com paid for the ticket or hotel room (the firm also charges airline ticket buyers a handling fee).

Like many firms focused on the travel business, priceline.com saw fewer customers hit the road and take to the skies during the downturn in the economy. But based on the company's business model, its profit margins rise when travel partners discount their prices. Because the industry anticipates an uptick in consumer travel by the end of 2010, priceline.com, in turn, expects its business to become slightly more difficult. If 2010 repeats 2009, however, priceline.com anticipates that travel suppliers will stimulate demand for leisure travel by discounting fares and rates during the latter half of the year. Therefore, the online travel firm is banking on more of the same in 2010. Continued discounting by suppliers would benefit the online travel retailer, as price drops spur demand.

While priceline.com generates most of its revenue in the US, the threat of slimmer profit margins as travel picks up has the company looking to international markets for growth. To this end, it operates Booking.com worldwide and Agoda in Asia. Most of this business comes from commissions earned from hotel reservations. priceline.com's international business represented 61% of its gross bookings in 2009 and some 75% of the firm's consolidated operating income. The online travel retailer attributes its international success to the hotel market, which isn't as consolidated as it is in the US, and to the firm's strategy of targeting smaller, independent hotels and chains with set prices.

In the cut-throat travel industry, priceline.com keeps an eye on its rivals and its marketing strategy as more consumers book their own travel online. When priceline.com in 2007 eliminated processing fees for certain airline tickets and reduced processing fees for some merchant hotel room services, competitors Expedia, Travelocity, and Orbitz followed suit with similar deals in 2008 and 2009.

Not everyone who hooks up with priceline.com gets his or her ticket to ride, however. The firm limits how it accepts offers. priceline.com considers an individual's named price for a plane ticket "reasonable" if it's no more than 30% lower than the lowest fare for the route.

HISTORY

priceline.com founder Jay Walker launched a string of ventures before making the leap into e-commerce. In 1994 he founded Walker Digital, an entrepreneurial think tank formed to develop business models that could germinate into new companies.

In 1996 Walker Digital found the impetus that would drive priceline.com: Each day major airlines have more than 500,000 empty seats. Walker's team reasoned that if the airlines were offered even a discounted price for these empty seats, they'd jump at the chance to cut their losses. Based on that premise, Walker Digital developed a "name your price" system and founded priceline.com in 1997.

The company launched its airfare service in 1998 and obtained financing from General Atlantic Partners and Paul Allen's Vulcan Ventures (now called Vulcan Northwest). That year it expanded into hotel reservations and added a car-buying service. Richard Braddock became chairman and CEO in 1998.

priceline.com added home financing services to its offerings in 1999. The company went public with a chart-busting IPO later that year. priceline.com also launched a rental car service. Branching into the retail arena, it licensed its technology to WebHouse Club for use in selling grocery products. The company sued Microsoft in 1999, claiming that company's Expedia unit's name-your-own-price hotel reservation service violated priceline.com's patent.

In 2000 the company licensed its business model to several international ventures including General Atlantic Partners' Priceline.com Europe (headed by former Burger King CEO Dennis Malamatinas), SOFTBANK's Priceline.com Japan (a deal that was later cancelled), MyPrice in Australia and New Zealand (also cancelled), and Asian conglomerate Hutchinson Whampoa. In collaboration with Alliance Capital (now AllianceBernstein), priceline.com created subsidiary pricelinemortgage to act as mortgage broker.

Daniel Schulman became CEO later that year. Jay Walker resigned as vice chairman at the end of 2000, after taking on the role of CEO at Walker Digital. After deciding it would probably never be profitable, WebHouse Club shut down, ending priceline.com's foray into grocery sales. Known for its splashy ads, priceline.com dumped pop icon William Shatner as its TV spokesperson in favor of *Sex and the City* star Sarah Jessica Parker. (Shatner returned in 2002.) Later that year the company fired Schulman and reappointed Braddock as CEO.

In 2002 the company joined with National Leisure Group to offer cruises from its website. Later that year priceline.com purchased the assets of discount travel site Lowestfare.com. It also announced plans to sell cars under a marketing agreement with Autobytel. In late 2002 Braddock passed his CEO responsibilities to president Jeffery H. Boyd. (Braddock remained as chairman.)

In 2002 the company purchased the assets of discount travel site Lowestfare.com. In August 2003 a handful of new international destinations (Australia, Japan, Indonesia, Malaysia, South Korea, Taiwan) were added to priceline.com's hotel reservation service. In April 2004 chairman Richard Braddock (former president of Citicorp and one of the last remaining high-profile board members, resigned from the company. Director Ralph Bahna was then named chairman. The following month priceline.com acquired most of Travelweb.com. In September 2004 it bought Active Hotels of Britain for about $161 million in cash. In December 2004 priceline.com acquired the remaining stake in Travelweb for about $4 million.

EXECUTIVES

Chairman: Ralph M. Bahna, age 67
Vice Chairman; Head Worldwide Strategy and Planning: Robert J. (Bob) Mylod Jr., age 43, $2,917,061 total compensation
President, CEO, and Director: Jeffery H. (Jeff) Boyd, age 53, $4,279,963 total compensation
EVP, General Counsel, and Corporate Secretary: Peter J. Millones Jr., age 40, $1,904,450 total compensation
EVP Corporate Development: Glenn D. Fogel
SVP, CFO, and Chief Accounting Officer: Daniel J. Finnegan, age 48, $1,647,640 total compensation
SVP Hotels: Tim Gordon
SVP Air: Mark Koehler
SVP Customer Service and Operations: Lisa Gillingham
SVP Finance and Investor Relations: Matthew N. Tynan, age 33
SVP Rental Cars: Patricia (Patti) D'Angelo
SVP Vacation Packages: Thomas L. (Tom) Trotta, age 47
CIO North America: Michael Diliberto
Chief Marketing Officer: Brett Keller, age 42
Chief Distribution Officer: Paul J. Hennessy
CEO Booking.com B.V.: Kees Koolen, age 44, $3,198,354 total compensation
President, North American Travel: Christopher L. (Chris) Soder, age 50, $1,713,640 total compensation
Auditors: Deloitte & Touche LLP

LOCATIONS

HQ: priceline.com Incorporated
  800 Connecticut Ave., Norwalk, CT 06854
Phone: 203-299-8000   **Fax:** 203-299-8948
Web: www.priceline.com

2009 Sales

	$ mil.	% of total
US	1,486.2	64
The Netherlands	558.4	24
UK & other	293.6	12
Total	**2,338.2**	**100**

PRODUCTS/OPERATIONS

2009 Sales

	$ mil.	% of total
Merchant	1,447.6	62
Agency	868.4	37
Other	22.2	1
Total	**2,338.2**	**100**

Selected Products

Airline tickets
Cruises
Hotel rooms
Rental cars
Vacation packages

Selected Participating Airlines

America West Airlines
American Airlines
Continental Airlines
Delta
United Airlines
US Airways

Selected Participating Hotels

Hilton
Hyatt
Marriott
Starwood Hotels & Resorts

Selected Participating Rental Car Services

Avis
Budget
Hertz
National

COMPETITORS

Amadeus IT	Internet Brands
American Express	Intuit
Autobytel	Kayak.com
AutoNation	lastminute.com
AutoTrader	Microsoft
BCD Travel	Orbitz Worldwide
Carlson Wagonlit	Prestige Travel
Expedia	Sabre Holdings
GetThere	Travelocity
Google	Travelzoo
Hotels.com	TripAdvisor
Hotwire, Inc.	

HISTORICAL FINANCIALS

Company Type: Public

Income Statement

FYE: December 31

	REVENUE ($ mil.)	NET INCOME ($ mil.)	NET PROFIT MARGIN	EMPLOYEES
12/09	2,338	490	20.9%	2,010
12/08	1,885	194	10.3%	1,780
12/07	1,409	157	11.1%	1,324
12/06	1,123	75	6.6%	696
12/05	963	193	20.0%	532
Annual Growth	**24.8%**	**26.2%**	**—**	**39.4%**

2009 Year-End Financials

Debt ratio: 2.7%
Return on equity: 47.7%
Cash ($ mil.): 202
Current ratio: 2.50
Long-term debt ($ mil.): 36

No. of shares (mil.): 48
Dividends
  Yield: —
  Payout: —
Market value ($ mil.): 10,568

Stock History

NASDAQ (GS): PCLN

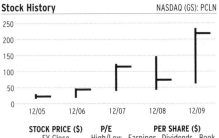

	STOCK PRICE ($) FY Close	P/E High	P/E Low	Earnings	Dividends	Book Value
12/09	218.41	23	7	9.88	—	27.31
12/08	73.65	36	11	3.98	—	15.09
12/07	114.86	35	12	3.42	—	11.97
12/06	43.61	26	13	1.68	—	7.20
12/05	22.32	6	4	4.21	—	7.63
Annual Growth	**76.9%**	**—**	**—**	**23.8%**	**—**	**37.6%**

PriceSmart, Inc.

PriceSmart is wise in the ways of members-only club retailing. The retailer runs about 25 membership stores under the PriceSmart names in about a dozen countries and one US territory in Central America and the Caribbean. It sells low-cost food, pharmacy, and basic consumer items. In each store, nearly half of the merchandise comes from the US, and the other half is sourced locally. In-store services include auto/tire centers, banking, and photo developing. PriceSmart stores are typically smaller than wholesale clubs in the US, averaging about 40,000-50,000 sq. ft., and the membership fees vary by market from around $25 up to $35. PriceSmart was founded in 1976 by father-and-son team Sol and Robert Price.

PriceSmart has been steadily acquiring property on which to build new stores for several years now. In 2008 it acquired land in Panama and Costa Rica and in April 2009 opened its newest warehouse store in Costa Rica — its fifth in the country. An existing store in Panama will be relocated to the newly acquired site there in 2010. Also, new PriceSmart stores are slated to open in Trinidad and the Dominican Republic in 2010. The company is considering entering Colombia as a potential location for multiple warehouse clubs. It is also expanding its reach by offering online shopping to customers in Costa Rica, El Salvador, Guatemala, and Panama.

Chairman and CEO Robert Price individually and through The Price Group, which he manages, owns about 40% of PriceSmart's shares. Sol Price died in December 2009 at the age of 93. The late Mr. Price was credited with pioneering the retail models — Fed-Mart in 1954 and Price Club in 1976 — that were the inspiration for companies such as Wal-Mart, Sam's Club, and Costco Wholesale. Indeed, Wal-Mart founder Sam Walton admitted he "borrowed" many of his innovations.

HISTORY

Sol Price created the members-only warehouse retail concept in the mid-1950s when he started Fedmart. In 1976 he and son Robert began Price Club. Facing pressure in the warehouse club niche, Price Club and competitor Costco merged in 1993, forming Price/Costco. But their managements disagreed over direction and policy, and the next year Price/Costco spun off Price Enterprises, Inc. (PEI). PEI assets included commercial real estate and international development projects. Eventually, Price/Costco resumed its maiden name, Costco.

In mid-1997 PEI split into two companies, Price Enterprises (a real estate investment trust, now Price Legacy) and PriceSmart. PriceSmart was built from subsidiaries Price Quest, Price Global Trading, and Price Ventures. During a busy 1998 the company closed stores in Indonesia and Guam and opened locations in China and Panama. In addition, it formed a joint venture (60% owned by PriceSmart) with Panamanian firm PSC to open nine new warehouse clubs in Central America and the Caribbean. That year the company's joint venture with PSC opened warehouses in Costa Rica, the Dominican Republic, El Salvador, Guatemala, and Honduras.

PriceSmart entered an agreement in fiscal 1999 with investors from Trinidad and Tobago to open two warehouses in Trinidad. (One opened a year later.) The company sold its domestic auto referral program in 1999 and its travel program in 2000. Also in 2000, the company announced a joint-venture with Philippine investors to open five to 10 stores in the Philippines. In 2001 the company received more than $30 million in loans to build 13 stores in Central America and the Caribbean. PriceSmart opened six stores in 2001, including two in the Philippines.

In 2002 PriceSmart opened four new warehouse stores in Trinidad, Guam, and two outlets in the Philippines.

In April 2003 president and CEO Gilbert A. Partida resigned from the company and its board of directors. Chairman Robert E. Price took on the additional role of interim president and CEO during the search for Partida's replacement. In 2003 the company opened three warehouse stores (one each in Jamaica, Nicaragua, and the Philippines) and closed four clubs.

In October 2004 Jose Luis Laparte became president of the company, while chairman Robert E. Price remained interim CEO of PriceSmart. The company opened one new store in the Philippines and closed its warehouse club in Guam in 2004.

PriceSmart closed its Mexican operations and terminated its licensing agreement in China in 2005. In 2006 the retailer sold its interest in its PSMT Philippines subsidiary, the operator of four warehouse clubs there.

In February 2008 PriceSmart agreed to pay $17.9 million to settle a lawsuit with PSC SA, Tecnicard Inc., and Banco de la Produccion. Under the terms of the settlement, PriceSmart will acquire PSC's 49% interest in PSMT Nicaragua (BVI) Inc. and become sole owner of the PriceSmart Nicaragua business. PriceSmart will also get land next to warehouse clubs in Nicaragua and Zapote and San Jose, Costa Rica. PSC will sell its PriceSmart shares.

Sol Price died in 2009 at the age of 93.

EXECUTIVES

President, CEO, and Director: Jose Luis Laparte,
age 43, $1,944,274 total compensation
EVP and COO: William J. (Bill) Naylon, age 47,
$469,415 total compensation
EVP and CFO: John M. Heffner,
$447,447 total compensation
EVP, Secretary, and General Counsel: Robert M. Gans,
age 60, $462,179 total compensation
EVP Construction Management: Brud E. Drachman,
age 54
EVP Merchandising: Thomas D. Martin, age 53
EVP Information Technology and Logistics:
A. Edward Oats, age 48
EVP Central America and Trinidad Operations:
John D. Hildebrandt, age 51
SVP and Corporate Controller: Michael McCleary
SVP Real Estate: Rodrigo Calvo
SVP Merchandising: Jose López
SVP Treasury: Atul Patel
SVP Latin America and Caribbean Legal Affairs:
Ernesto Grijalva
Auditors: Ernst & Young LLP

LOCATIONS

HQ: PriceSmart, Inc.
9740 Scranton Rd., San Diego, CA 92121
Phone: 858-404-8800   **Fax:** 858-404-8848
Web: www.pricesmart.com

2009 Stores

	No.
Costa Rica	5
Panama	4
Guatemala	3
Trinidad	3
Dominican Republic	2
El Salvador	2
Honduras	2
Aruba	1
Barbados	1
Jamaica	1
Nicaragua	1
U.S. Virgin Islands	1
Total	**26**

2009 Sales

	% of total
Central America	59
Caribbean	41
Total	**100**

PRODUCTS/OPERATIONS

2009 Sales

	% of total
Food (dry & fresh)	46
Sundries	32
Hardlines	13
Softlines	8
Other	1
Total	**100**

COMPETITORS

Amazon.com
Carrefour
IGA
Wal-Mart

HISTORICAL FINANCIALS

Company Type: Public

Income Statement

FYE: August 31

	REVENUE ($ mil.)	NET INCOME ($ mil.)	NET PROFIT MARGIN	EMPLOYEES
8/09	1,252	43	3.4%	4,385
8/08	1,120	38	3.4%	4,200
8/07	889	13	1.5%	3,434
8/06	735	12	1.6%	2,937
8/05	619	(42)	—	2,961
Annual Growth	**19.3%**	**—**	**—**	**10.3%**

2009 Year-End Financials

Debt ratio: 13.5%
Return on equity: 14.8%
Cash ($ mil.): 44
Current ratio: 1.30
Long-term debt ($ mil.): 41

No. of shares (mil.): 30
Dividends
  Yield: 3.7%
  Payout: 45.5%
Market value ($ mil.): 530

Stock History

NASDAQ (GM): PSMT

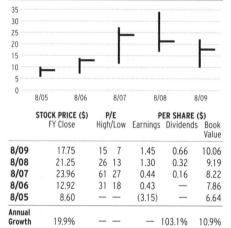

	STOCK PRICE ($) FY Close	P/E High/Low		PER SHARE ($) Earnings	Dividends	Book Value
8/09	17.75	15	7	1.45	0.66	10.06
8/08	21.25	26	13	1.30	0.32	9.19
8/07	23.96	61	27	0.44	0.16	8.22
8/06	12.92	31	18	0.43	—	7.86
8/05	8.60	—	—	(3.15)	—	6.64
Annual Growth	**19.9%**	**—**	**—**	**—**	**103.1%**	**10.9%**

Pricewaterhouse Coopers International

Not merely the firm with the longest one-word name, PricewaterhouseCoopers (PwC) is also one of the world's largest accounting networks. PwC was formed when Price Waterhouse merged with Coopers & Lybrand in 1998, bypassing then-leader Andersen. With some 770 offices in more than 150 countries, the accountancy provides clients with services in three business lines: assurance (including financial and regulatory reporting), tax, and advisory. The firm provides services in some capacity for most of the world's largest companies as well as smaller businesses.

PwC's member firms are locally owned and operated. The largest geographic segment is western Europe, followed by the North America/Caribbean region. PricewaterhouseCoopers International oversees the strategic growth and development activities for the network and provides support services to the member firms.

In 2009 PwC acquired several units of management consultant firm BearingPoint, which months earlier had entered bankruptcy and begun selling itself off. It bought BearingPoint's

Japanese operations, adding some 1,500 professionals and setting PwC up as an advisory services leader there. The firm also acquired most of BearingPoint's North American commercial services business and offices in China and India.

The accounting business received a boost from the implementation of such regulatory and financial reporting rules as the International Financial Reporting Standards (IFRS) and the Sarbanes-Oxley Act. More recently, the industry faced criticism for the practice of mark-to-market accounting, which many say contributed to the global economic crisis in 2008. PwC stands behind the practice as the best accounting method of complex financial instruments.

In 2009 Samuel DiPiazza retired as CEO. Dennis Nally, a senior partner of the US firm, was elected to serve as PwC's global chairman.

HISTORY

In 1850 Samuel Price founded an accounting firm in London and in 1865 took on partner Edwin Waterhouse. The firm and the industry grew rapidly, thanks to the growth of stock exchanges that required uniform financial statements from listees. By the late 1800s Price Waterhouse (PW) had become the world's best-known accounting firm.

US offices were opened in the 1890s, and in 1902 United States Steel chose the firm as its auditor. PW benefited from tough audit requirements instituted after the 1929 stock market crash. In 1935 the firm was given the prestigious job of handling Academy Awards balloting. It started a management consulting service in 1946. But PW's dominance slipped in the 1960s, as it gained a reputation as the most traditional and formal of the major firms.

Coopers & Lybrand, the product of a 1957 transatlantic merger, wrote the book on auditing. Lybrand, Ross Bros. & Montgomery was formed in 1898 by William Lybrand, Edward Ross, Adam Ross, and Robert Montgomery. In 1912 Montgomery wrote *Montgomery's Auditing,* which became the bible of accounting.

Cooper Brothers was founded in 1854 in London by William Cooper, eldest son of a Quaker banker. In 1957 Lybrand joined up to form Coopers & Lybrand. During the 1960s the firm expanded into employee benefits and internal control consulting, building its technology capabilities in the 1970s as it studied ways to automate the audit process.

Coopers & Lybrand lost market share as mergers reduced the Big Eight accounting firms to the Big Six. After the savings and loan debacle of the 1980s, investors and the government wanted accounting firms held liable not only for the form of audited financial statements but for their veracity. In 1992 the firm paid $95 million to settle claims of defrauded investors in MiniScribe, a failed disk-drive maker. Other hefty payments followed, including a $108 million settlement relating to the late Robert Maxwell's defunct media empire.

In 1998 Price Waterhouse and Coopers & Lybrand combined PW's strength in the media, entertainment, and utility industries, and Coopers & Lybrand's focus on telecommunications and mining. But the merger brought some expensive legal baggage involving Coopers & Lybrand's performance of audits related to a bid-rigging scheme involving former Arizona governor Fife Symington.

The year 2000 began on a sour note: An SEC conflict-of-interest probe turned up more than

8,000 alleged violations, most involving PwC partners owning stock in their firm's audit clients. As the SEC grew ever more shrill in its denunciation of the potential conflicts of interest arising from auditing companies that the firm hoped to recruit or retain as consulting clients, PwC saw the writing on the wall and in 2000 began making plans to split the two operations. As part of this move, the company downsized and reorganized many of its operations.

In 2001 PwC paid $55 million to shareholders of MicroStrategy, who charged that the audit firm defrauded them by approving the client firm's inflated earnings and revenues figures.

The separation of PwC's auditing and consulting functions finally became a reality in 2002, when IBM bought the consulting business. (The acquisition took the place of a planned spinoff.)

Like the other members of the Big Four, PwC picked up business and talent as scandal-felled Andersen was winding down its operations in 2002. The former Andersen organization in China and Hong Kong joined PwC, accounting for about 70% of the approximately 3,500 Andersen alumni that came aboard.

In 2003 former client AMERCO (parent of U-Haul) sued PwC for $2.5 billion, claiming negligence and fraud in relation to a series of events that led to AMERCO restating its results. The suit was settled for more than $50 million the following year.

PwC endured a two-month suspension in Japan in 2006 after three partners of its firm there were implicated in a fraud investigation involving a PwC client, Kanebo. To distance itself from the scandal, PwC's existing Japanese firm was renamed and a second firm was launched.

In 2007 US arm PricewaterhouseCoopers agreed to pay $225 million to settle a class-action lawsuit related to the Tyco International financial scandal. The suit asserted that the auditors should have uncovered a $5.8 billion overstatement of earnings during the four years ending in 2002. The fraud sent Tyco's top executives to prison.

EXECUTIVES

Chairman: Dennis M. Nally, age 57
Chairman and Senior Partner US:
  Robert E. (Bob) Moritz
Chairman, Regional Asia Board: Silas S.S. Yang
Global Leader Operations: Paul Boorman
Global Assurance Leader: Donald A. McGovern Jr.
Global and US Human Capital Leader: Dennis J. Finn
Global Strategy and Transformation Leader:
  Christopher (Chris) Kelkar
Global Board Member, Tokyo: Matthew Wyborn
Global Leader for Risk and Quality: Pierre Coll
Global Leader Advisory Services: Juan Pujadas
Chairman India: Gautam Banerjee
Global Leader Tax; Managing Partner,
  PricewaterhouseCoopers, UK: Richard Collier-Keywood
Global Leader Clients and Markets: Donald V. Almeida
Global Leader Public Policy and Regulation:
  Peter L. Wyman
Global General Counsel: Javier H. Rubinstein
Chairman and Senior Partner, United Kingdom:
  Ian Powell
Director Global Public Relations: Mike Davies

LOCATIONS

HQ: PricewaterhouseCoopers International Limited
  300 Madison Ave., New York, NY 10017
Phone: 646-471-4000   **Fax:** 813-286-6000
Web: www.pwcglobal.com

PRODUCTS/OPERATIONS

2009 Sales

	% of total
Assurance	50
Tax	27
Advisory	23
Total	**100**

2009 Sales by Industry

	% of total
Industrial products	22
Banking & capital markets	13
Asset management	12
Retail & consumer	10
Energy, utilities & mining	9
Technology	6
Insurance	5
Entertainment & media	4
Government	4
Professional services	4
Pharmaceuticals	3
Automotive	3
Information & communications	3
Health care	2
Total	**100**

Selected Products and Services

Audit and assurance
  Actuarial services
  Assistance on capital market transactions
  Corporate reporting improvement
  Financial accounting
  Financial statement audit
  IFRS reporting
  Independent controls and systems process assurance
  Internal audit
  Regulatory compliance and reporting
  Sarbanes-Oxley compliance
  Sustainability reporting
Crisis management
  Business recovery services
  Dispute analysis and investigations
Human resources
  Change and program effectiveness
  HR management
  International assignments
  Reward
Performance improvement
  Financial effectiveness
  Governance, risk, and compliance
  IT effectiveness
Tax
  Compliance
  EU direct tax
  International assignments
  International tax structuring
  Mergers and acquisitions
  Transfer pricing
Transactions
  Accounting valuations
  Advice on fundraising
  Bid support and bid defense services
  Commercial and market due diligence
  Economics
  Financial due diligence
  Independent expert opinions
  Mergers and acquisitions advisory
  Modeling and business planning
  Post deal services
  Private equity advisory
  Privatization advice
  Project finance
  Public company advisory
  Structuring services
  Tax valuations
  Valuation consulting

COMPETITORS

Bain & Company	Grant Thornton
Baker Tilly International	H&R Block
BDO International	Hewitt Associates
Booz Allen	KPMG
Boston Consulting	Marsh & McLennan
Deloitte	McKinsey & Company
Ernst & Young Global	

HISTORICAL FINANCIALS
Company Type: Partnership

Income Statement

FYE: June 30

	REVENUE ($ mil.)	NET INCOME ($ mil.)	NET PROFIT MARGIN	EMPLOYEES
6/09	26,171	—	—	163,545
6/08	28,185	—	—	155,693
6/07	25,150	—	—	146,767
6/06	21,986	—	—	142,162
6/05	18,998	—	—	130,203
Annual Growth	**8.3%**	—	—	**5.9%**

Revenue History

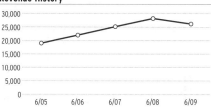

Principal Financial

Ah, the circle of life. For a child in elementary school, avoiding the principal is paramount. However, folks looking toward retirement may actually seek out The Principal. Principal Financial Group (or The Principal) offers pension products and services (the company is a top administrator of employer-sponsored retirement plans), mutual funds, annuities, asset management, trust services, and investment advice. Its insurance segment provides group and individual life, health, disability, dental, and vision coverage. To compete with banks encroaching on the company's territory and to maximize customer asset retention, subsidiary Principal Bank offers online banking.

The Principal has about 19 million customers and more than $275 billion of assets under management. Its products are offered through a network of about 7,600 independent brokers and agents, as well as through its own sales force at more than 40 offices nationwide.

With operations in about a dozen countries, The Principal aims to become a global player in retirement services, targeting countries in Asia and Latin America that rely on private-sector defined-contribution pension plans to accommodate their growing number of retirees. It also does business in Australia and Europe.

In the US, the company courts firms with fewer than 500 employees for its insurance and pension products and large institutional clients for its asset management operations, which include Principal Global Investors. The company serves approximately 33,000 pension plans.

HISTORY

Principal Financial was founded as the Bankers Life Association in 1879 by Edward Temple, a Civil War veteran and banker. Life insurance became popular after the war, but some dishonest insurers canceled customers' policies before they had to pay out benefits. Bankers Life, an assessable association (members shared the cost of death benefits as the claims arose), was intended to provide low-cost protection to bankers and their families. The company soon began offering life insurance to nonbankers, but it refused to insure women because of the high mortality rate among mothers during childbirth.

Bankers Life relied on volunteer workers until 1893. By 1900 it was operating in 21 states. Temple died in 1909, and two years later the company converted to a legal reserve mutual life insurance company with a new name: the Bankers Life Company. The conversion scared many customers away, however. About 50,000 policies were lost over the next three years. In 1915 Bankers Life began insuring women.

WWI slowed growth, and the 1918-1919 influenza epidemic, which killed many policyholders, hit the company hard. The Depression also stunted growth. In 1941 the firm started offering group life insurance, and during WWII it became a major force in that area.

Bankers Life grew through the 1950s and 1960s, adding individual accident and health insurance (1952) and other products. In 1968 it began offering variable annuities for profit-sharing plans and mutual funds, forming what are now Princor Financial Services and Principal Management. In 1977 Bankers Life introduced an adjustable life insurance product that allowed policyholders to change both premium costs and coverage.

In 1986 the company made a few name changes, becoming The Principal Financial Group and renaming its largest unit Principal Mutual Life Insurance (now Principal Life Insurance). That year Principal Financial acquired Eppler, Guerin & Turner, the largest independent stock brokerage firm in the Southwest.

In 1993 Principal Financial was issued Mexico's first new insurance license in 50 years; subsequent expansion included Argentina, China, and Spain.

In 1996 Principal Financial expanded its health care operations, purchasing third-party administrator The Admar Group. The next year the company bought the 76,000-member FHP of Illinois health plan. Despite this fast buildup, Principal Financial decided to exit the direct provision of health care; in 1997 it sold these operations to what is now Coventry Health Care for a 40% stake in the firm, which it also later sold.

Continuing to refocus, the company in 1998 sold its Principal Financial Securities brokerage and bought ReliaStar Mortgage to build a mortgage banking franchise. The company also launched online banking services. Also that year Principal Financial converted to a mutual holding structure. It formed joint ventures in such countries as Chile, Mexico, and India as part of its move into asset management overseas.

The company went public in 2001, when it started trading on the New York Stock Exchange.

As with its health care operations, Principal Financial made a hasty exit from the mortgage business after building that part of its business through acquisitions. Amid rising interest rates and an industrywide decrease in loan volume, the company sold its retail mortgage branches to American Home Mortgage in 2003, then sold its remaining mortgage banking business to Citigroup the following year. Also in 2004 the company bolstered its core operations by purchasing health care claims processor J.F. Molloy & Associates and the US trust operations of Dutch banking giant ABN AMRO.

At the end of 2006 The Principal finalized its purchase of WM Advisors, the former mutual fund operations of Washington Mutual.

EXECUTIVES

Chairman, President, and CEO, Principal Financial Group and Principal Life: Larry D. Zimpleman, age 58, $4,909,023 total compensation
EVP and General Counsel, Principal Financial and Principal Life: Karen E. Shaff, age 55
SVP and CFO: Terry J. Lillis, age 57, $1,067,500 total compensation
SVP and Chief Marketing Officer, Principal Financial and Principal Life: Mary A. O'Keefe, age 53
SVP Human Resources and Corporate Services: Ralph C. Eucher
SVP and Controller: Gregory B. (Greg) Elming
SVP and CIO, Principal Financial and Principal Life: Gary P. Scholten, age 52
SVP and Corporate Secretary: Joyce Nixson Hoffman
SVP and Chief Investment Officer, Principal Financial and Principal Life: Julia M. Lawler, age 50
SVP and Chief Risk Officer, Principal Financial and Principal Life: Ellen Z. Lamale, age 56
SVP; President, Principal Financial Group Latin America: Luis Valdés
SVP; President, Asia Principal International, Inc: Rex Auyeung
SVP Retirement and Investor Services; President, Principal Funds: Nora M. Everett
SVP Investor Relations: Thomas J. (Tom) Graf
President, Retirement, Insurance, and Financial Services: Daniel J. (Dan) Houston, age 48, $2,295,139 total compensation
President, International Asset Management and Accumulation; President and CEO, Principal International: Norman R. Sorensen, age 64, $1,187,476 total compensation
President, Global Asset Management, Principal Financial and Principal Life: James P. (Jim) McCaughan, age 56, $3,608,035 total compensation
Auditors: Ernst & Young LLP

LOCATIONS

HQ: Principal Financial Group, Inc.
711 High St., Des Moines, IA 50392
Phone: 515-247-5111 **Fax:** 515-246-5475
Web: www.principal.com

PRODUCTS/OPERATIONS

2009 Sales

	$ mil.	% of total
Premiums & other considerations	3,750.6	40
Net investment income	3,400.8	37
Fees & other revenues	2,096.0	23
Net capital losses	(398.3)	—
Total	**8,849.1**	**100**

COMPETITORS

Aetna	Manulife Financial
AIG	MassMutual
Allianz	MetLife
AXA	Morgan Stanley
BlackRock	Investment Management
Blue Cross	Nationwide Financial
CIGNA	PIMCO
FMR	T. Rowe Price
ING	UnitedHealth Group
John Hancock Financial	Unum Group
JPMorgan Chase	The Vanguard Group
Lincoln Financial Group	

HISTORICAL FINANCIALS

Company Type: Public

Income Statement
FYE: December 31

	ASSETS ($ mil.)	NET INCOME ($ mil.)	INCOME AS % OF ASSETS	EMPLOYEES
12/09	137,759	646	0.5%	14,487
12/08	128,182	458	0.4%	16,234
12/07	154,520	860	0.6%	16,585
12/06	143,658	1,064	0.7%	15,289
12/05	127,035	919	0.7%	14,507
Annual Growth	2.0%	(8.4%)	—	(0.0%)

2009 Year-End Financials

Equity as % of assets: 5.7%	Dividends
Return on assets: 0.5%	Yield: 2.1%
Return on equity: 12.5%	Payout: 25.4%
Long-term debt ($ mil.): 1,585	Market value ($ mil.): 7,686
No. of shares (mil.): 320	Sales ($ mil.): 8,849

Stock History
NYSE: PFG

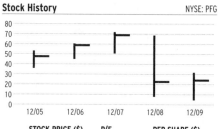

	STOCK PRICE ($) FY Close	P/E High/Low		PER SHARE ($) Earnings	Dividends	Book Value
12/09	24.04	16	3	1.97	0.50	24.69
12/08	22.57	41	5	1.63	0.45	7.73
12/07	68.84	23	17	3.09	0.90	23.21
12/06	58.70	16	12	3.74	0.80	24.59
12/05	47.43	17	12	3.11	0.65	24.42
Annual Growth	(15.6%)	—	—	(10.8%)	(6.3%)	0.3%

Procter & Gamble

The Procter & Gamble Company (P&G) boasts boatloads of brands. The world's #1 maker of household products courts market share and billion-dollar names. It's divided into three global units: health and well being, beauty, and household care. The company also makes pet food and water filters and produces a soap opera. Some two-dozen of P&G's brands are billion-dollar sellers, including Fusion, Always/Whisper, Braun, Bounty, Charmin, Crest, Downy/Lenor, Gillette, Iams, Olay, Pampers, Pantene, Pringles, Tide, and Wella, among others. P&G shed its coffee brands in late 2008. Being the acquisitive type, with Clairol and Wella as notable conquests, P&G's biggest buy in company history was Gillette in 2005.

Few people worldwide go a day without using at least one product made by P&G. Its hundreds of brands are available in more than 180 countries. With P&G's product depth and breadth has come a consistent tweaking of its products portfolio in its effort to regularly pump out profits. In recent years, the company has been turning to its highest revenue generators for the most growth potential.

As the recession was gaining momentum in 2008, P&G initiated several changes. In a push to increase productivity, P&G shed about 15% of its management staff. (Most of the job cuts came through attrition.) P&G also kicked its coffee (brand) habit in 2008, when the company sold its Folgers business to The J. M. Smucker Company in an all-stock transaction valued at more than $3 billion. The deal involved P&G's entire coffee business, including Folgers and Millstone, as well as its licensing agreement with Dunkin' Donuts to distribute that company's coffee.

A successor for the company's longtime top executive, Alan G. Lafley, took over in 2010. Robert McDonald became the next in line to Lafley when he was named president and chief executive in 2009. When Lafley retired in 2010, McDonald took on the additional role of chairman.

In recent years, P&G has been focused on expanding its beauty business to improve its worldwide market share. To fortify itself as a leader in the shaving industry, the firm purchased The Art of Shaving, a high-end brand of men's shaving and skin care products, in 2009.

The consumer products giant in July 2010 bought Sara Lee's European air-freshener business, Ambi Pur, for €320 million ($470 million).

Also in mid-2010 P&G acquired Natura Pet Products, a California-based maker of holistic and natural pet foods. Natura's brand portfolio includes Evo, Healthwise, Innova, and Karma.

In 2009 P&G 2009 sold its prescription drug unit to drug maker Warner Chilcott for about $3 billion. Also that year CBS announced that it was canceling P&G's last on-air soap opera, *As The World Turns* (*ATWT*) after 54 years on television. Previously, through its partnership with CBS, P&G produced *Guiding Light* (which began as a radio program in 1937).

HISTORY

Candle maker William Procter and soap maker James Gamble merged their small Cincinnati businesses in 1837, creating The Procter & Gamble Company (P&G), which incorporated in 1905. By 1859 P&G had become one of the largest companies in Cincinnati, with sales of $1 million. It introduced Ivory, a floating soap, in 1879, and Crisco shortening in 1911.

The Ivory campaign was one of the first to advertise directly to the consumer. Other advertising innovations included sponsorship of daytime radio dramas in 1932. P&G's first TV commercial, for Ivory, aired in 1939.

Family members headed the company until 1930, when William Deupree became president. In the 29 years that he served as president and then chairman, P&G became the largest US seller of packaged goods.

After years of researching cleansers for use in hard water, in 1947 P&G introduced Tide detergent. It began a string of acquisitions when it picked up Spic and Span (1945; sold 2001), Duncan Hines (1956; sold 1998), Charmin Paper Mills (1957), and Folgers Coffee (1963). P&G launched Crest toothpaste in 1955 and Head & Shoulders shampoo and Pampers disposable diapers in 1961.

Rely tampons were pulled from shelves in 1980 when investigators linked them to toxic shock syndrome. In 1985 P&G moved into health care when it purchased Richardson-Vicks (NyQuil, Vicks) and G.D. Searle's nonprescription drug division (Metamucil). The acquisitions of Noxell (1989; CoverGirl, Noxzema) and Max Factor (1991) made it a top cosmetics company in the US.

P&G began a major restructuring in 1993, cutting 13,000 jobs and closing 30 plants. The firm in 1996 sued rival Amway over rumors connecting P&G and its moon-and-stars logo to Satanism. (The suit was dismissed in 1999.) Also in 1996 the FDA approved the use of olestra, a controversial fat substitute developed by P&G.

In 1997 it acquired Tambrands (Tampax tampons), making P&G #1 in feminine sanitary protection. Chairman John Pepper handed over his chairman and CEO title in 1999 to president Durk Jager, who promised five new products a year and a shakeup of the corporate culture.

In 1999 the company announced further reorganization plans, including 15,000 job cuts worldwide by 2005. That same year P&G bought The Iams Company (maker of Eukanuba- and Iams-brand dog and cat foods).

With earnings flat, Jager resigned in 2000. P&G insider Alan G. Lafley immediately assumed the president and CEO duties, and Pepper returned to succeed Jager as chairman.

In 2001 P&G announced job cuts for 9,600 employees to further reduce costs. It also sold its Comet cleaner business. That year P&G completed its purchase of the Clairol hair care unit from Bristol-Myers Squibb for nearly $5 billion.

In 2003 P&G entered the premium pet food market with its purchase of The Iams Company for $2.3 billion. And to secure its foothold in China, it bought the remaining 20% stake in its joint venture with Hutchison Whampoa China Ltd. in 2004 for $1.8 billion.

Further expanding its luxury hair-care portfolio, in 2008 P&G purchased Frédéric Fekkai & Co. from Chrysallis. The acquisition gave P&G a foothold in department store hair care. Fekkai caters to prestige stores such as Neiman Marcus, Nordstrom, and Sephora. Later that year, P&G purchased NIOXIN Research Laboratories to add volume to its haircare business.

In 2010 P&G sold Iams Pet Imaging (IPI) to AnimalScan, LLC. IPI fell under the company's P&G Pet Care North America division.

EXECUTIVES

Chairman, President, and CEO:
Robert A. (Bob) McDonald, age 57, $6,828,396 total compensation
Vice Chairman Global Operations: Werner Geissler, age 57, $6,805,170 total compensation
Vice Chairman Global Household Care:
E. Dimitri Panayotopoulos, age 58, $6,047,291 total compensation
Vice Chairman Global Beauty and Grooming:
Edward D. (Ed) Shirley, age 53
Vice Chairman Global Health and Well-Being:
Robert A. (Rob) Steele, age 55
CFO: Jon R. Moeller, age 46, $2,287,990 total compensation
CTO: Bruce Brown, age 52
Chief Legal Officer and Secretary:
Deborah Platt Majoras, age 46
Global Consumer and Market Knowledge Officer:
Joan Lewis
Global Customer Business Development Officer:
Robert L. Fregolle Jr., age 53
Global Business Services: Lucy Hodgson
Global Brand Building Officer: Marc S. Pritchard, age 50
Global Business Services: Laura Lewis
Global Product Supply Officer: R. Keith Harrison Jr., age 62
Global Human Resources Officer: Moheet Nagrath, age 51
Global Design Officer: Philip J Duncan, age 45

SVP Global Diversity and Global Business Services:
Linda Clement-Holmes
VP Corporate: Nancy Swanson
VP Business Development: Jeff Weedman
Corporate External Relations and Financial Communications: Jennifer Chelune
Director Investor Relations: John T. Chevalier
Auditors: Deloitte & Touche LLP

LOCATIONS

HQ: The Procter & Gamble Company
1 Procter & Gamble Plaza, Cincinnati, OH 45202
Phone: 513-983-1100   **Fax:** 513-983-9369
Web: www.pg.com

2010 Sales

	% of total
North America	42
Western Europe	21
Asia	15
Central & Eastern Europe, Middle East & Africa	13
Latin America	9
Total	**100**

2010 Sales

	% of total
Developed markets	66
Developing markets	34
Total	**100**

PRODUCTS/OPERATIONS

2010 Sales

	% of total
Household care	48
Beauty & grooming	34
Health & well-being	18
Total	**100**

Selected Brand Names by Global Business Unit

Beauty Care
  Braun
  Clairol
  CoverGirl
  Frédéric Fekkai & Co.
  Fusion
  Gillette
  Head & Shoulders
  Herbal Essence
  I-Iman
  Ivory
  Mach3
  Max Factor
  Nice 'n Easy
  Olay
  Old Spice
  Pantene
  Safeguard
  Secret
  Ultresse
  Wella
  Zest

Health & Well Being
  Actonel
  Always
  Crest
  Iams
  Oral-B
  Prilosec
  Pringles

Household Care
  Ambi Pur
  Ariel
  Bounty
  Charmin
  Dawn
  Downy
  Duracell
  Gain
  Pampers
  P&G Pro Line (commercial cleaning)
  Swiffer
  Tide

COMPETITORS

Alberto-Culver	Kraft Foods
Alticor	L'Oréal
American Safety Razor	Mary Kay
Amway	Meda Pharmaceuticals
Avon	Nestlé
Bath & Body Works	PepsiCo
Baxter of California	Pfizer
BIC	Philips Electronics
Body Shop	Revlon
Bristol-Myers Squibb	Russell Hobbs
Church & Dwight	Sanofi-Aventis
Clorox	SANYO
Colgate-Palmolive	Sara Lee
Discus Dental	S.C. Johnson
Dr. Bronner's	Scott's Liquid Gold
Energizer Holdings	SEB
Estée Lauder	Shiseido
Frito-Lay	Spectrum Brands
Hain Celestial	Tom's of Maine
Heinz	Turtle Wax
Henkel	Unilever
Johnson & Johnson	VIVUS
Kimberly-Clark	

HISTORICAL FINANCIALS

Company Type: Public

Income Statement

FYE: June 30

	REVENUE ($ mil.)	NET INCOME ($ mil.)	NET PROFIT MARGIN	EMPLOYEES
6/10	78,938	12,736	16.1%	127,000
6/09	79,029	13,436	17.0%	135,000
6/08	83,503	12,075	14.5%	138,000
6/07	76,476	10,340	13.5%	138,000
6/06	68,222	8,684	12.7%	138,000
Annual Growth	3.7%	10.0%	—	(2.1%)

2010 Year-End Financials

Debt ratio: 35.7%
Return on equity: 20.9%
Cash ($ mil.): 2,879
Current ratio: 0.77
Long-term debt ($ mil.): 21,360

No. of shares (mil.): 2,838
Dividends
  Yield: 3.0%
  Payout: 43.8%
Market value ($ mil.): 170,252

Stock History

NYSE: PG

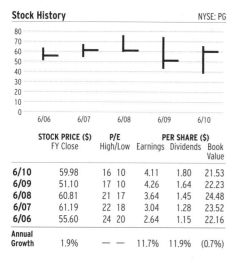

	STOCK PRICE ($) FY Close	P/E High/Low		PER SHARE ($) Earnings	Dividends	Book Value
6/10	59.98	16	10	4.11	1.80	21.53
6/09	51.10	17	10	4.26	1.64	22.23
6/08	60.81	21	17	3.64	1.45	24.48
6/07	61.19	22	18	3.04	1.28	23.52
6/06	55.60	24	20	2.64	1.15	22.16
Annual Growth	1.9%	—	—	11.7%	11.9%	(0.7%)

Progress Energy

Without progress, millions of people would be without energy. Progress Energy provides electricity to 3.1 million customers. It serves customers in North and South Carolina, through utility Carolina Power & Light (dba Progress Energy Carolinas), and in Florida, through Florida Power (or Progress Energy Florida). The company generates most of its energy from nuclear and fossil-fueled plants and has a total capacity of more than 22,000 MW. Progress Energy is pursuing a strategy of improving its operational efficiency while seeking to expand its alternative energy power sources in order to reduce its greenhouse gas emissions.

In 2010 its Progress Energy Carolinas unit brought online the largest solar array in the region, Evergreen Solar Farm. Other green energy initiatives by Progress Energy companies include swine waste-to-energy projects, and customer conservation programs such as appliance recycling and air duct upgrading.

In a move to refocus on its core retail and wholesale power businesses, in 2007 the company shut down its Competitive Commercial Operations unit and exited its synthetic fuels business, and in 2008 it sold its remaining coal mine and coal terminal services. It sold its nonregulated power plants, hedges, and contracts for $480 million and its Powell Mountain Coal Company, Dulcimer Land Company, and Kanawha River Terminals to an investor group for $94 million.

HISTORY

Central Carolina Power was incorporated in 1908. Later that year, under the aegis of the Electric Bond and Share Co. (EBS, a subsidiary of General Electric), Central Carolina Power crossed lines with Raleigh Electric and Consumers Light & Power to form Carolina Power & Light (CP&L).

EBS president S. Z. Mitchell was a leader in the young industry, espousing economies of scale through mergers and promoting lower rates to encourage sales. CP&L had three hydroelectric plants by 1911, and by 1912 it had acquired three neighboring utilities, including Asheville Power & Light. The company began selling power wholesale to municipal utilities, in addition to its retail sales.

Demand soared after WWI as textile mills switched from steam engines to electricity and residential customers became enamored of modern appliances sold by CP&L. The company merged with four other utilities and reincorporated in 1926. The next year it became part of National Power & Light, a huge utility holding company created by EBS.

CP&L struggled during the Depression as demand slackened. To add legislative insult to financial injury, Congress passed the Public Utility Holding Company Act of 1935 (repealed in 2005) to break up vast utility trusts. The act inaugurated 60 years of regional monopolies regulated by state and federal authorities. In 1948 CP&L was divested from EBS and went public.

The postwar boom increased the demand for power, and to keep up CP&L built several large coal-fired plants. By the early 1960s the company had begun building its first nuclear facility, the Robinson plant, which was completed in

1971. CP&L also continued to build huge, coal-fired plants.

The company completed its second nuke (Brunswick) in 1977. But two years later the accident at Pennsylvania's Three Mile Island cast a pall on the industry. After numerous delays CP&L decided to complete just one more nuke (Harris). The plant went on line in 1987, and CP&L requested a 13% rate increase to help cover its $3.8 billion cost. In contrast to its brothers, Harris ran quite well. But problems continued to plague CP&L's nuclear program into the early 1990s.

The Federal Energy Policy Act of 1992 dramatically changed the utility industry by allowing wholesale power competition. The following year CP&L hired new nuke management to turn around its troubled Brunswick plant.

In 1996 the utility lost $100 million to damages from Hurricane Fran. The next year the company unveiled Strategic Resource Solutions, a nonregulated energy services company created out of the former Knowledge Builders. In 1998 CP&L began marketing wholesale power.

To expand into natural gas distribution, CP&L bought North Carolina Natural Gas (NCNG) in 1999 for about $354 million in stock. The company also agreed to buy utility holding company Florida Progress for $5.4 billion in cash and stock and $2.7 billion in assumed debt. In preparation for its Florida Progress purchase, CP&L adopted a holding company structure in 2000 and was renamed CP&L Energy Inc. The Florida Progress deal was completed later that year, and CP&L Energy became Progress Energy. In 2000 it also formed a new unregulated energy marketing subsidiary, Progress Energy Ventures.

As a condition of the merger, Progress Energy agreed to divest some noncore assets; in 2001 it sold its MEMCO Barge Line unit to American Electric Power for $270 million. In 2002 Progress Energy Ventures purchased two Georgia power plants (one operational and one under construction) for $345 million from LG&E Energy.

Progress Energy exited the natural gas distribution business in 2003 with the sale of its North Carolina Natural Gas utility to Piedmont Natural Gas for about $425 million. The company has also sold its transportation assets, and a portion of its oil and gas production operations. Also that year Progress Energy merged its telecom unit with broadband provider Epik Communications; Progress Energy owned 55% of the combined company, but subsequently exited the field.

In 2004 Progress Energy sold its Progress Rail Services to One Equity Partners for $405 million. (One Equity turned around 18 months later and sold the railroad maintenance and repair service company to Caterpillar for a cool $1 billion.)

Progress Energy sold its Winchester Energy natural gas exploration and production business in 2006 to EXCO Resources for $1.2 billion.

EXECUTIVES

Chairman, President, and CEO, Progress Energy and Florida Progress: William D. (Bill) Johnson, age 56, $6,454,010 total compensation
EVP and Secretary: John R. McArthur, age 54, $1,797,802 total compensation
EVP Energy Supply: Jeffrey J. (Jeff) Lyash, age 48, $1,950,396 total compensation
SVP and CFO, Progress Energy, PEC and PEF: Mark F. Mulhern, age 50, $1,767,180 total compensation
SVP Compliance and General Counsel, Progress Energy: Frank A. Schiller, age 49
SVP Corporate Development and Improvement: Paula J. Sims, age 48, $1,873,640 total compensation

SVP and Chief Nuclear Officer, PEC and PEF:
James (Jim) Scarola, age 54
Chief Accounting Officer and Controller; VP and Controller Accounting, Progress Energy Service Company; Chief Accounting Officer, Progress Energy Carolinas and Progress Energy Florida:
Jeffrey M. (Jeff) Stone, age 48
VP, Chief Risk Officer, and Treasurer, Progress Energy Carolinas, Progress Energy Florida, Treasury & Enterprise Risk Management, Progress Energy Service Company: Thomas R. (Tom) Sullivan
VP Investor Relations, Progress Energy Service Company: Robert F. (Bob) Drennan Jr.
VP Information Technology and Telecommunications and CIO, Progress Energy Service Company:
Dede F. Ramoneda
VP Human Resources, Progress Energy Service Company, Progress Energy Carolinas, and Progress Energy Florida: Anne M. Huffman
VP Corporate Communications, Progress Energy Service Company: Cari P. Boyce
President and CEO, Progress Energy Carolinas:
Lloyd M. Yates, age 49, $1,829,776 total compensation
President and CEO, Progress Energy Florida:
Vincent M. (Vinny) Dolan, age 55
Auditors: Deloitte & Touche LLP

LOCATIONS

HQ: Progress Energy, Inc.
410 S. Wilmington St., Raleigh, NC 27601
Phone: 919-546-6111   **Fax:** 919-546-2920
Web: www.progress-energy.com

PRODUCTS/OPERATIONS

2009 Sales

	% of total
Residential	39
Commercial	27
Wholesale	16
Industrial	16
Other	2
Total	**100**

2009 Sales

	$ mil.	% of total
PEF	5,249	53
PEC	4,627	47
Corporate & other	9	—
Total	**9,885**	**100**

Selected Subsidiaries

Carolina Power & Light Company (operates as Progress Energy Carolinas, electric utility; PEC)
Florida Power Corporation (operates as Progress Energy Florida, electric utility; PEF)

COMPETITORS

ACES Power Marketing
AEP
ALLETE
CenterPoint Energy
Dominion Resources
Duke Energy
Entergy
JEA
Mississippi Power
NextEra Energy
North Carolina Electric Membership
Oglethorpe Power
Piedmont Natural Gas
Santee Cooper
SCANA
Seminole Electric
Southern Company
TECO Energy
TVA

HISTORICAL FINANCIALS

Company Type: Public

Income Statement

FYE: December 31

	REVENUE ($ mil.)	NET INCOME ($ mil.)	NET PROFIT MARGIN	EMPLOYEES
12/09	9,885	761	7.7%	11,000
12/08	9,167	830	9.1%	11,000
12/07	9,153	504	5.5%	11,000
12/06	9,570	571	6.0%	11,000
12/05	10,108	696	6.9%	11,600
Annual Growth	**(0.6%)**	**2.3%**	**—**	**(1.3%)**

2009 Year-End Financials

Debt ratio: 129.9%
Return on equity: 8.4%
Cash ($ mil.): 725
Current ratio: 1.33
Long-term debt ($ mil.): 12,272
No. of shares (mil.): 287
Dividends
Yield: 7.6%
Payout: 114.4%
Market value ($ mil.): 11,777

Stock History

NYSE: PGN

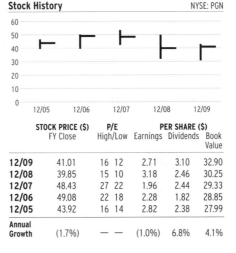

	STOCK PRICE ($) FY Close	P/E High/Low	PER SHARE ($) Earnings	PER SHARE ($) Dividends	PER SHARE ($) Book Value
12/09	41.01	16 12	2.71	3.10	32.90
12/08	39.85	15 10	3.18	2.46	30.25
12/07	48.43	27 22	1.96	2.44	29.33
12/06	49.08	22 18	2.28	1.82	28.85
12/05	43.92	16 14	2.82	2.38	27.99
Annual Growth	**(1.7%)**	**— —**	**(1.0%)**	**6.8%**	**4.1%**

Progressive Corporation

It's risky business, and Progressive loves it. Long a leader in nonstandard, high-risk personal auto insurance, The Progressive Corporation has motored beyond its traditional business into standard-risk and preferred auto insurance, as well as other personal-use vehicle coverage (motorcycles, recreational vehicles, and snowmobiles). Progressive also offers commercial policies for heavy trucks, vans, and lighter trucks. It writes a bit of professional liability insurance for directors' and officers' insurance of community banks. The company markets directly to consumers online and by phone, and through 30,000 independent agents who account for roughly 60% of the company's business.

Focusing on its core auto business, Progressive stopped writing homeowners insurance years ago, but continues to offer coverage to its auto insurance customers, underwritten by third party Homesite Insurance. Progressive also offers personal umbrella insurance that provides coverage for the extras in life, such as personal injury and legal defense.

Unlike some insurers who, in fat markets, earn more from their investments than their premiums, more than 90% of Progressive's revenues have historically come from policy premiums. This quirk allowed the company to maintain a bit more serenity than its competitors during most market fluctuations. However, it loaded up on subprime investments in 2007, which proved a regrettable strategy. Subsequently, in 2008 Progressive experienced its first loss in 26 years.

Despite that loss, the company's actual insurance operations have remained profitable and grown as it has entered into new geographic markets and expanded distribution of its personal auto products online. Already among the leading US auto insurers based on premiums (just behind State Farm and Allstate), Progressive is aiming to be on top.

By 2009 the company had bounced back sufficiently to afford a bold move: launching personal auto insurance online in Australia. International expansion has not been a key strategy for Progressive, but apparently the time was right for such growth.

Colorful chairman Peter Lewis (who supports legalizing marijuana and holds that contemporary art in the company's hallways stimulates innovation) is the son of one of the insurer's founders. He built Progressive up from a regional operation to a national player and controls more than 5% of the company.

HISTORY

Attorneys Jack Green and Joseph Lewis founded Progressive Mutual Insurance in Cleveland in 1937. Initially offering standard auto insurance, the company attracted customers through such innovations as installment plans for premiums (a payment method popularized during the Depression) and drive-in claims services (the company was headquartered in a garage). Progressive's early years were uncertain — at one point the founders were even advised to go out of business — but the advent of WWII bolstered business: Car and insurance purchases were up, but accidents were down as gas rationing limited driving.

Then came the suburbs and cars of the 1950s. While most competitors sought low-risk drivers, Progressive exploited the high-risk niche through careful underwriting and statistical analysis. Subsidiary Progressive Casualty was founded in 1956 (the year after Joseph Lewis died) to insure the best of the worst. Lewis' son Peter joined the company in 1955 and helped engineer its early-1960s expansion outside Ohio. After Green retired in 1965, Peter gained control of the company through a leveraged buyout and renamed it The Progressive Corporation. Six years later, Lewis took it public and formed subsidiary Progressive American in Florida.

In the mid-1970s the industry went into a funk as it was hit by a wave of consolidations and rising interest rates. Lewis set a goal for the company to always earn an underwriting profit instead of depending on investments to make a profit. Progressive achieved stellar results during the 1970s, especially after states began requiring drivers to be insured and other insurers began weeding out higher risks.

Competition in nonstandard insurance grew in the 1980s, as major insurers such as Allstate and State Farm joined the fray with their larger sales forces and deeper pockets. In 1988 California's Proposition 103 retroactively reduced rates;

Progressive fought California's demand for refunds but set aside reserves to pay them.

That year Lewis hired Cleveland financier Alfred Lerner to guide company investments. Lerner invested $75 million in Progressive via a convertible debenture; five years later he converted it to stock, half of which he sold for $122 million. Soon after, he was asked to resign. In 1993 Progressive settled with California for $51 million and applied to earnings the remaining $100 million in refund reserves. (Company soul-searching related to Proposition 103 led to the launch of Progressive's now-famous "Immediate Response" vehicles, which provide 24-hour claims service at accident sites.)

In 1995 Progressive's practice of using consumer credit information to make underwriting decisions drew the attention of Arkansas and Vermont insurance regulators, who said the company might be discriminating against people who didn't have the credit cards Progressive used to evaluate creditworthiness. In 1996 insurance regulators in Alaska, Maryland, and Texas also began probing Progressive's credit information practices.

In 1997 Progressive bought nonstandard auto insurer Midland Financial Group. As competition grew in 1999, the company cut rates and said it would write no new policies in Canada. In 2000 — with underwriting margins dropping industry-wide — the company continued advertising aggressively. Progressive stopped writing new homeowners insurance in 2002, instead concentrating on its core operations. In 2006 the company began offering personal umbrella coverage.

EXECUTIVES

Chairman: Peter B. Lewis, age 76
President, CEO, and Director: Glenn M. Renwick, age 54, $9,128,036 total compensation
VP and CFO: Brian C. Domeck, age 51, $1,555,132 total compensation
VP, Chief Legal Officer, and Secretary: Charles E. Jarrett, age 53, $1,257,148 total compensation
VP and Chief Accounting Officer: Jeffrey W. Basch, age 52
VP and Treasurer: Thomas A. King, age 50
CIO: Raymond M. Voelker, age 46, $1,170,457 total compensation
Chief Investment Officer: William M. Cody, age 48, $1,559,574 total compensation
Chief Human Resource Officer: Valerie Krasowski, age 44
General Manager, Centralized Claims Operations: Richard H. Watts, age 55
General Manager, Personal Lines: David J. Skove
Director Accounting and Assistant Secretary: Mariann Wojtkun Marshall, age 48
Director Communications: Mari Pumarejo
Senior Manager Investor Relations: Patrick Brennan
Group President, Personal Lines: John P. Sauerland, age 45, $1,535,832 total compensation
Claims Group President: Susan P. Griffith, age 45, $1,535,832 total compensation
President, Commercial Lines Group: John A. Barbagello, age 50
Auditors: PricewaterhouseCoopers LLP

LOCATIONS

HQ: The Progressive Corporation
6300 Wilson Mills Rd., Mayfield Village, OH 44143
Phone: 440-461-5000   **Fax:** 800-456-6590
Web: www.progressive.com

PRODUCTS/OPERATIONS

2009 Revenues

	$ mil.	% of total
Premiums		
Personal lines	12,365.9	85
Commercial auto	1,623.3	11
Other	23.6	—
Service businesses	16.7	—
Investment income & gains on securities	534.1	4
Total	**14,563.6**	**100**

COMPETITORS

21st Century Insurance
Allstate
American Family Insurance
Cincinnati Financial
Farmers Group
GEICO
Liberty Mutual
Nationwide
Ohio Casualty
Old Republic
State Auto Financial
State Farm
Travelers Companies
USAA
White Mountains Insurance Group

HISTORICAL FINANCIALS

Company Type: Public

Income Statement

FYE: December 31

	ASSETS ($ mil.)	NET INCOME ($ mil.)	INCOME AS % OF ASSETS	EMPLOYEES
12/09	20,049	1,058	5.3%	24,661
12/08	18,251	(70)	—	25,929
12/07	18,843	1,183	6.3%	26,851
12/06	19,482	1,648	8.5%	27,778
12/05	18,899	1,394	7.4%	28,336
Annual Growth	1.5%	(6.7%)	—	(3.4%)

2009 Year-End Financials

Equity as % of assets: 28.7%
Return on assets: 5.5%
Return on equity: 21.2%
Long-term debt ($ mil.): 2,177
No. of shares (mil.): 670
Dividends
  Yield: 0.0%
  Payout: —
Market value ($ mil.): 12,061
Sales ($ mil.): 14,564

Stock History

NYSE: PGR

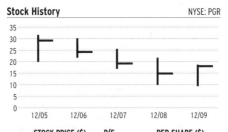

	STOCK PRICE ($) FY Close	P/E High/Low		PER SHARE ($) Earnings	Dividends	Book Value
12/09	17.99	12	6	1.57	0.00	8.57
12/08	14.81	—	—	(0.10)	0.14	6.29
12/07	19.16	15	10	1.65	0.00	7.36
12/06	24.22	14	11	2.10	0.03	10.21
12/05	29.19	18	12	1.75	0.03	9.11
Annual Growth	(11.4%)	—	—	(2.7%)	—	(1.5%)

Protective Life

Protective Life wants to cushion its customers from the nasty blows of life and death. The company focuses on life insurance products sold through its Life Marketing business segment (via independent agents, worksite plans, and financial institutions). Its Acquisitions segment brings in blocks of life insurance policies sold elsewhere. The company's Asset Protection segment sells extended service contracts and credit life insurance through auto and marine dealers nationwide, while its Annuities segment provides fixed and variable annuities sold through brokers and independent agents. The company operates through subsidiaries Protective Life Insurance and West Coast Life Insurance.

Protective Life's combined life insurance operations (Life Marketing and Acquisitions) account for nearly 70% of the company's revenue. Protective Life has aggressively capitalized on the industry trend of consolidation, carefully selecting small and midsized firms that complement its existing operations. It has acquired more than 40 insurance companies or blocks of policies in the past three decades, allowing the company to gain premiums without expensive commissions.

Protective briefly considered acquiring The Bank of Bonifay, a small Florida bank, in early 2009. The purchase would have helped it obtain status as a bank holding company, potentially allowing it to tap into the US Treasury's Troubled Asset Relief Program (TARP). However, after observing the glacial speed with which the Treasury was considering such applications, Protective scrapped the plan and stuck with insurance.

Nonetheless, by 2009 the company had stopped marketing its Stable Value Products, including funding agreements for financial instruments, such as municipal bonds and money market funds, and guaranteed investment contracts (GICs) for 401(k) plans. While it has stopped selling such products, Protective does maintain those products which it sold earlier.

Prior to the implosions in the lending and credit markets, the company invested a significant portion of its assets into mortgage-backed securities, preferring to invest in pools of prime residential mortgages and non-speculative commercial properties such as strip-center retailers.

HISTORY

In 1907 — when former Alabama governor William Jelks founded Protective Life in Birmingham — the South had not yet risen again, and most insurance business was controlled by northern companies. Protective Life survived the financial panic that year and grew steadily, paying its first dividends in 1916. It was sorely tested in 1918, as were most insurance companies, when the influenza pandemic took thousands of lives, particularly in large cities.

In 1927 Protective Life merged with another Birmingham-based insurance company, Alabama National Insurance, founded in 1908 as Great Southern Life Insurance. Alabama National's Samuel Clabaugh, a former banker, was appointed president, and under his guidance the company passed through the Depression intact, having cautiously conserved its capital. Another Alabama National alumnus, William Rushton, whose family name would become synonymous with Protective Life in Birmingham, took over as CEO in 1937. Colonel Rushton, as he became known after his stint in WWII, continued to lead the company for the next 20 years, investing in southern economic development.

In 1963 Protective Life formulated a new strategy, concentrating on the upper-income market, advanced underwriting, business insurance, and estate planning. The company planned to expand geographically, with hopes of going nationwide. Protective Life was operating in 14 states by 1969, the year that Rushton's son, William Rushton III, assumed command from the colonel.

Under the younger Rushton, Protective expanded its operations to all 50 states. The firm purchased 39 companies and numerous blocks of policies between 1970 and 1997.

In 1992 Rushton was named chairman and Drayton Nabers was appointed CEO. In 1994 Protective teamed with Indonesia's Lippo Group (which has interests in securities, banking, and insurance) to form Hong Kong-based Lippo Protective Life Insurance, now CRC Protective Life Insurance. The joint venture introduced US-style universal life insurance to Hong Kong. Denomination of policies in US dollars attracted clients wary of unstable Asian currencies.

In the early 1990s Protective pioneered the concept of selling indemnity dental insurance on a voluntary payroll-deduction basis. In 1995 the company purchased National Health Care Systems of Florida, operating under the trade name DentiCare, and entered the managed dental care business.

In 1997 Protective acquired West Coast Life Insurance and Western Diversified Group. It also continued to build its dental care operations through the 1997 acquisitions of three more small, managed dental care companies and its 1998 purchase of United Dental Care, making it the third-largest managed dental care company in the US. In 1999 Nabers took on the additional role of chairman, taking over after William Rushton resigned. That year the company began distributing term life insurance over the Internet through agreements with HomeCom Communications and Matrix Direct Insurance Services. (Matrix was sold to American International Group in 2007.)

In 2000 Protective bought specialty insurer Lyndon Insurance Group from Frontier Insurance Group. Then Protective's subsidiary Protective Life Insurance acquired 70,000 life insurance policies from Standard Insurance. Nabers stepped down as CEO at the end of 2001.

The company sold its dental benefits division to Fortis Inc. in 2002. The following year Nabers resigned as chairman to become Alabama's finance director and Protective CEO John Johns was named chairman.

EXECUTIVES

Chairman, President, and CEO: John D. Johns, age 57, $2,561,186 total compensation
Vice Chairman and CFO: Richard J. (Rich) Bielen, age 49
EVP and COO: Carolyn M. Johnson, age 49, $747,946 total compensation
EVP, General Counsel, and Secretary: Deborah J. Long, age 56, $681,480 total compensation
EVP and Chief Risk Officer: Edward M. Berko
EVP and Chief Investment Officer: Carl S. Thigpen, age 53, $900,340 total compensation

SVP and Chief Human Resources Officer: D. Scott Adams, age 45
SVP Asset Protection: Brent E. Griggs, age 54
SVP Acquisitions: Carolyn King, age 60
SVP Stable Value Products: Judy Wilson, age 51
SVP, Controller, and Chief Accounting Officer: Steven G. Walker, age 50
Auditors: PricewaterhouseCoopers LLP

LOCATIONS

HQ: Protective Life Corporation
2801 Hwy. 280 South, Birmingham, AL 35223
Phone: 205-268-1000   **Fax:** 205-268-3196
Web: www.protective.com

PRODUCTS/OPERATIONS

2009 Revenues

	$ mil.	% of total
Life Marketing	1,096.4	36
Acquisitions	777.2	25
Annuities	508.8	17
Asset Protections	277.0	9
Stable Value Products	220.9	7
Corporate & other	187.7	6
Total	**3,068.0**	**100**

Selected Subsidiaries

Lyndon Insurance Group (in Massachusetts)
Protective Life and Annuity Insurance Company
Protective Life Insurance Company
West Coast Life Insurance Company

COMPETITORS

AEGON USA
AIG
APCO
C.A.R.S. Protection Plus
CNO Financial
Hartford Life
ING Americas
Interstate National Dealer Services
MassMutual
MetLife
Nationwide
New York Life
Northwestern Mutual
Pacific Mutual
Principal Financial
Prudential
UNIFI Companies
Warrantech

HISTORICAL FINANCIALS

Company Type: Public

Income Statement

FYE: December 31

	ASSETS ($ mil.)	NET INCOME ($ mil.)	INCOME AS % OF ASSETS	EMPLOYEES
12/09	42,312	272	0.6%	2,317
12/08	39,572	(42)	—	2,372
12/07	41,786	290	0.7%	2,406
12/06	39,795	282	0.7%	2,743
12/05	28,967	247	0.9%	2,192
Annual Growth	**9.9%**	**2.4%**	**—**	**1.4%**

2009 Year-End Financials

Equity as % of assets: 5.9%
Return on assets: 0.7%
Return on equity: 17.0%
Long-term debt ($ mil.): 2,170
No. of shares (mil.): 86
Dividends
  Yield: 2.9%
  Payout: 14.4%
Market value ($ mil.): 1,418
Sales ($ mil.): 3,068

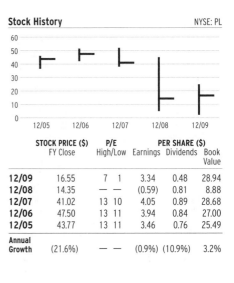

Stock History   NYSE: PL

	STOCK PRICE ($) FY Close	P/E High/Low		PER SHARE ($) Earnings	Dividends	Book Value
12/09	16.55	7	1	3.34	0.48	28.94
12/08	14.35	—	—	(0.59)	0.81	8.88
12/07	41.02	13	10	4.05	0.89	28.68
12/06	47.50	13	11	3.94	0.84	27.00
12/05	43.77	13	11	3.46	0.76	25.49
Annual Growth	**(21.6%)**	**—**	**—**	**(0.9%)**	**(10.9%)**	**3.2%**

Prudential Financial

Prudential Financial wants to make sure its position near the top of the life insurance summit is set in stone. Prudential, known for its Rock of Gibraltar logo, is one of the top US life insurers and also one of the largest insurance companies worldwide. The firm is perhaps best known for its individual life insurance, though it also sells group life, long-term care, and disability insurance, as well as annuities. Prudential also offers investment products and services, including asset management services, mutual funds, and retirement planning. Other lines include a national real estate brokerage franchise and relocation services.

Prudential's International Insurance and Investments business offers individual life insurance policies to affluent and middle income customers in Asian, European, and Latin American countries. Its also provides asset management and investment advice in non-US markets. The international division has shed some asset and investment management operations in non-core markets, but it is seeking to expand its insurance and retirement operations in emerging markets such as China and India.

Up until late 2009, Prudential's 38% ownership of Wells Fargo Advisors (formerly Wachovia Securities) allowed its customers access to securities brokerage and financial advice; however, the company sold its holdings in Wells Fargo Advisors to Wells Fargo for some $4.5 billion.

The company acquired specialty commercial insurer MullinTBG in 2008 to pad its retirement business. And Gibraltar Life expanded in its home market of Japan through the acquisition of bankrupt insurer Yamato Life (now Prudential Financial of Japan Life) in 2009. Prudential invested in an insurance venture in India that commenced operations in 2008.

Like many in the insurance industry, the company took a hit financially in 2008 due to its investments in asset- and mortgage-backed securities. As the global credit markets deteriorated, Prudential suffered losses and had to take action to shore up its finances.

HISTORY

In 1873 John Dryden founded the Widows and Orphans Friendly Society in New Jersey to sell workers industrial insurance (low-face-value weekly premium life insurance). In 1875 it became The Prudential Friendly Society, taking the name from England's Prudential Assurance Co. The next year Dryden visited the English company and copied some of its methods, such as recruiting agents from its targeted neighborhoods.

Prudential added ordinary whole life insurance in 1886. By 1900 the firm was selling more than 2,000 such policies annually and had 3,000 agents in eight states. In 1896 the J. Walter Thompson advertising agency (now the WPP Group) designed Prudential's Rock of Gibraltar logo.

The firm issued its first group life policy in 1916 (Prudential became a major group life insurer in the 1940s). In 1928 it introduced an Accidental Death Benefit, which cost it an extra $3 million in benefits the next year alone (death claims rose drastically early in the Depression).

In 1943 Prudential mutualized. The company began decentralizing operations in the 1940s. Later it introduced a Property Investment Separate Account (PRISA), which gave pension plans a real estate investment option. By 1974 the firm was the US's group pension leader.

The insurer bought securities brokerage The Bache Group to form Pru Bache (now Prudential Securities) in 1981. Bache's forte was retail investments, an area expected to blend well with Prudential's insurance business. Under George Ball, Pru Bache tried to become a major investment banker — but failed. In 1991 Ball resigned, leaving losses of almost $260 million and numerous lawsuits involving real estate limited partnerships.

Despite the 1992 settlement of the real estate partnership suits, Prudential remained under scrutiny by several states because of "churning," a process in which agents generated commissions by inducing policyholders to trade up to more expensive policies. In 1995 new management, led by former Chase Manhattanite Arthur Ryan, brought sales under control, sold such units as reinsurance and mortgage servicing, and put its $6 billion real estate portfolio on the block. (In 1997 it sold its property management unit and Canadian commercial real estate unit; in 1998 it sold its landmark Prudential Center complex in Boston.)

In 1996 regulators from 30 states found that Prudential knew about the churning earlier than it had admitted, had not stopped the perpetrators, and had even promoted them. A 1997 settlement called for the company to pay restitution, but the more than $2 billion estimated cost was thought to be less than the losses customers had suffered.

As the financial services industry continued to restructure, Prudential in 1998 announced plans to demutualize. To focus on life insurance, the company sold its health care unit to Aetna in 1999. The same year, Prudential paid $62 million to resolve more churning claims, revamped itself into international, institutional, and retail divisions, and trimmed jobs.

Ending its attempts to originate business, the company cut 75% of its investment banking staff in 2000.

Demutualized Prudential Financial's 2001 IPO — one of the largest ever in the insurance industry — raised more than $3 billion. Prudential Financial became the holding company name for all operations, making Prudential Insurance (the company's former name) a subsidiary and pure life insurer.

Following the IPO, Prudential got busy at rearranging its portfolio. It sold off its property/casualty insurance businesses to Liberty Mutual in 2003. Prudential also sold its brokerage division to banking powerhouse Wachovia in 2003.

Variable annuities and retirement held a special allure for the company. It bought Swedish insurer Skandia's US annuities operations in 2003 and during 2004 it bought CIGNA's retirement business. The company added to its substantial Japanese operations (which include subsidiary Gibraltar Life) by acquiring Aoba Life Insurance Company in 2004. Its acquired South Korean asset management firm Hyundai Investment and Securities in 2004.

In late 2006 the company agreed to pay $19 million ($16.5 million in restitution and $2.5 million as penalty) after the New York Attorney General determined that certain payments to insurance brokers amounted to collusion.

Prudential acquired Allstate's variable annuity business in 2006. In 2007 it purchased some retirement assets from Union Bank of California.

EXECUTIVES

Chairman, President, and CEO: John R. Strangfeld Jr., age 56, $18,425,632 total compensation
Vice Chairman: Mark B. Grier, age 57, $14,284,044 total compensation
EVP and CFO: Richard J. Carbone, age 62, $4,778,094 total compensation
EVP and COO, International Businesses: Edward P. (Ed) Baird, age 61, $5,312,076 total compensation
EVP and COO, US Businesses: Bernard B. Winograd, age 59, $8,093,785 total compensation
EVP and Head of Life Insurance, Japan: Kazuo Maeda
EVP Operations and Systems: Robert C. Golden, age 63
CIO: Barbara G. Koster
Chief Investment Officer: Michael Lillard
Chief Security Officer: Lori Hennon-Bell
Chief Medical Officer: K. Andrew Crighton
Chief Domestic Investment Officer: Scott G. Sleyster
Chief Communications Officer: Robert (Bob) DeFillippo
Treasurer: Robert F. Falzon
SVP and General Counsel: Susan L. Blount, age 52
SVP Operations and Systems: Joyce Leibowitz
SVP Corporate Human Resources: Sharon C. Taylor, age 55
SVP and Head Defined Contribution Business, JennisonDryden: Michael Rosenberg
VP Community Resources; President, The Prudential Foundation: Gabriella Morris
President, Prudential Mortgage Capital Company: David A. (Dave) Twardock, age 52
President and CEO, Prudential Investment Management: Charles F. (Charlie) Lowrey
President, Prudential Annuities: Stephen (Steve) Pelletier
Chairman and CEO, Prudential International Investments: Christopher (Chris) Cooper
Auditors: PricewaterhouseCoopers LLP

LOCATIONS

HQ: Prudential Financial, Inc.
751 Broad St., Newark, NJ 07102
Phone: 973-802-6000
Web: www.prudential.com

PRODUCTS/OPERATIONS

2009 Sales

	$ mil.	% of total
Financial Services		
International Insurance & Investments		
Insurance	10,466	31
Investments	422	1
US Retirement Solutions & Investment Management		
Retirement	4,676	14
Individual annuities	2,871	9
Asset management	1,257	4
US Individual Life & Group Insurance		
Group	5,285	15
Individual life	2,768	9
Real Estate & Relocation Services	162	1
Corporate operations	(167)	—
Closed Block Business	5,245	16
Adjustments	(297)	—
Total	**32,688**	**100**

COMPETITORS

AEGON
Aetna
Aflac
AIG
Allianz
American Financial Group
Aviva
AXA
Berkshire Hathaway
Charles Schwab
Citigroup
COUNTRY Financial
Dai-ichi Mutual Life
FMR
Great-West Lifeco
The Hartford
HomeServices
ING
John Hancock Financial Services
Legal & General Group
MassMutual
Merrill Lynch
MetLife
Nationwide Life Insurance
Nippon Life Insurance
Northwestern Mutual
Principal Financial
Prudential plc
The Vanguard Group
Zurich Financial Services

HISTORICAL FINANCIALS

Company Type: Public

Income Statement

	ASSETS ($ mil.)	NET INCOME ($ mil.)	INCOME AS % OF ASSETS	EMPLOYEES
12/09	480,203	3,090	0.6%	41,943
12/08	445,011	(1,073)	—	41,844
12/07	485,814	3,704	0.8%	40,703
12/06	454,266	3,428	0.8%	39,814
12/05	417,776	3,540	0.8%	38,853
Annual Growth	3.5%	(3.3%)	—	1.9%

FYE: December 31

2009 Year-End Financials

Equity as % of assets: 5.2%
Return on assets: 0.7%
Return on equity: 16.0%
Long-term debt ($ mil.): 21,037
No. of shares (mil.): 466
Dividends
Yield: 1.4%
Payout: 9.2%
Market value ($ mil.): 23,188
Sales ($ mil.): 32,688

Stock History

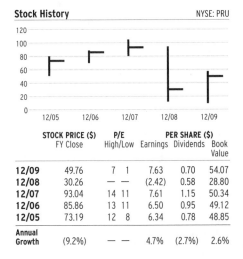

	STOCK PRICE ($) FY Close	P/E High/Low		PER SHARE ($) Earnings	Dividends	Book Value
12/09	49.76	7	1	7.63	0.70	54.07
12/08	30.26	—	—	(2.42)	0.58	28.80
12/07	93.04	14	11	7.61	1.15	50.34
12/06	85.86	13	11	6.50	0.95	49.12
12/05	73.19	12	8	6.34	0.78	48.85
Annual Growth	(9.2%)	—	—	4.7%	(2.7%)	2.6%

PSS World Medical

From basic supplies to sophisticated equipment, PSS World Medical keeps doctors and nursing homes fully stocked. The company distributes medical supplies, equipment, and pharmaceuticals to doctors' offices, long-term care facilities, and home health care providers nationwide through a network of about 40 distribution centers. The company operates in two business segments. Its Physician Sales & Service unit distributes products to primary care doctors, while its Elder Care segment (represented by subsidiary Gulf South Medical Supply) sells medical supplies to nursing homes and home health care providers. PSS reaches its customers through its team of more than 850 sales representatives.

PSS World Medical has supplier agreements with about 90 manufacturers in multiple countries (primarily in Asia and Europe) to distribute both branded and private-label products. The company's Physician segment offers more than 55,000 different products (70% of which are medical supplies, 20% equipment, and 10% pharmaceuticals). Gulf South Medical Supply sells more than 20,000 items. Expanding its private label Select Medical Products brand is part of the company's growth strategy, and key to this plan is securing contracts with less-expensive non-US manufacturers, particularly those based in Asia.

The company has also placed an emphasis on its technology infrastructure and services. It distributes information technology solutions through its Physician segment, and offers Medicare Part B billing services through its Elder Care unit's ProClaim subsidiary.

Acquisitions have historically been part of PSS World Medical's growth strategy, but the company became more selective after a spree in the late 1990s that eventually hurt earnings. Today, acquisitions are not a big part of PSS World Medical's growth strategy. The company has only made two in the past few years since it bought the Washington-based Cascade Medical Supply, a distributor of nursing home supplies (2008), and Activus Healthcare Solutions, a California-based medical supply distributor (2007).

Perhaps it was that conservative spending strategy that helped the company see a profit in 2010, even as the economy was crashing around it. Also helping profits that year were soaring sales of influenza test kits, surgical masks, medical gloves, and hand sanitizers to medical providers who were preparing for the threat of the H1N1/swine flu pandemic.

In early 2010, CEO David Smith left the company unexpectedly after he and the company "terminated his employment by mutual agreement." Gary Corless, formerly executive vice president and COO, was named to replace Smith.

HISTORY

Like an inner tube hooked to an air compressor, PSS expanded from a shoestring-budget medical supply company into a major player in just five years. Former chairman Patrick Kelly and two others founded Physician Sales & Service (PSS) in 1983 to supply physicians; the company made deliveries by U-Haul in the early days. By 1988 the company was the largest supplier of its type in Florida, with $13 million in revenues. The company expanded into other states by acquisition. PSS went public in May 1994.

Improved medical technology and cost-saving efforts by insurance companies led PSS to ink an exclusive agreement with US pharmaceutical and diagnostics powerhouse Abbott Laboratories in 1995. PSS began to sell Abbott's diagnostic equipment to offices of up to 25 doctors; Abbott bought 4% of PSS. That year Taylor Medical, the #4 medical supplies distributor in the US, merged with PSS, forming the first national physician supply company.

In 1996 PSS formed its WorldMed subsidiary to assimilate acquisitions. PSS also expanded its radiology and imaging equipment operations by purchasing distributor Diagnostic Imaging; in 1997 and 1998 acquisitions moved the imaging unit into Arizona, California, Florida, Minnesota, New Mexico, New York, and Wisconsin.

PSS changed its name to PSS World Medical in 1998 and bought nursing home supplier Gulf South Medical Supply. However, unforeseen expenses related to the purchase and reorganization (as well as SEC-mandated accounting adjustments) led to a drop in the company's overall earnings; this prompted shareholder lawsuits in 1999. To reverse the tide, PSS streamlined its distribution centers and back-office functions. Nonetheless, the company continued to acquire, buying Salt Lake City-based Physician Supply Co. in 1999.

The following year Fisher Scientific International made plans to buy PSS, but the acquisition fell through. About a month later, PSS founder Patrick Kelly resigned as chairman and CEO, along with COO Frederick "Gene" Dell.

Disappointments in sales prompted the company to sell its European operations in 2001. Also that year PSS was charged with securities fraud in a class-action suit on behalf of shareholders. The company sold its Diagnostic Imaging business in 2002. In 2003 PSS acquired ProClaim, a provider of billing services to the long-term care industry, and Highpoint Healthcare, a marketing and distribution organization for assisted living, long-term health, and home care businesses.

EXECUTIVES

Chairman: Delores M. Kesler, age 69
President, CEO, and Director: Gary A. Corless, age 45, $2,861,639 total compensation
EVP and Chief Marketing Officer: John F. Sasen Sr., age 67, $1,869,768 total compensation
EVP and CFO: David M. Bronson, age 57, $2,306,420 total compensation
Chief Service Officer: Bradley J. Hilton, age 39, $1,587,935 total compensation
Chief Sourcing Officer: Kevin P. English, age 41, $1,582,478 total compensation
VP and CIO: Carl A. Duhnoski, age 40
VP and Treasurer: David D. Klarner, age 40
VP Internal Audit: John G. Kammlade
VP and Corporate Controller: Andrew E. Behrends
VP Operational Compliance: Andrew S. Woods
VP, General Counsel, and Corporate Secretary: Joshua H. DeRienzis, age 41
VP Investor Relations: Robert C. Weiner, age 47
President, Extended Care Business, Gulf South Medical Supply: Mark E. Steele, age 38
President, Physician Business, Physician Sales and Service: Edward D. (Eddie) Dienes, age 50
Senior Associate Public Relations: Brian C. Kosoy
Auditors: KPMG LLP

LOCATIONS

HQ: PSS World Medical, Inc.
4345 Southpoint Blvd., Jacksonville, FL 32216
Phone: 904-332-3000 **Fax:** 904-332-3213
Web: www.pssworldmedical.com

PRODUCTS/OPERATIONS

2010 Sales

	$ mil.	% of total
Physician business	1,437.8	70
Elder care business	614.9	30
Corporate shared services	2.5	—
Total	**2,055.2**	**100**

COMPETITORS

AmerisourceBergen
Cardinal Health Medical
Kimberly-Clark Health
McKesson
McKesson Medical-Surgical
Medline Industries
Metro Medical Supply
Moore Medical
Owens & Minor
SourceOne
Surgical Express
Tri-anim
Universal Hospital

HISTORICAL FINANCIALS

Company Type: Public

Income Statement				FYE: Friday nearest March 31
	REVENUE ($ mil.)	NET INCOME ($ mil.)	NET PROFIT MARGIN	EMPLOYEES
3/10	2,055	69	3.4%	3,650
3/09	1,953	58	3.0%	3,680
3/08	1,856	57	3.1%	3,593
3/07	1,742	51	2.9%	3,349
3/06	1,619	44	2.7%	3,269
Annual Growth	**6.1%**	**11.9%**	**—**	**2.8%**

2010 Year-End Financials

Debt ratio: 46.1%
Return on equity: 18.4%
Cash ($ mil.): 53
Current ratio: 2.91
Long-term debt ($ mil.): 188
No. of shares (mil.): 56
Dividends
Yield: —
Payout: —
Market value ($ mil.): 1,327

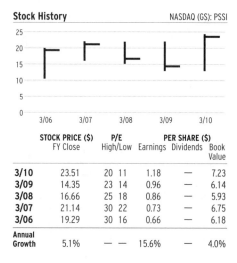

	STOCK PRICE ($) FY Close	P/E High/Low		PER SHARE ($) Earnings	Dividends	Book Value
3/10	23.51	20	11	1.18	—	7.23
3/09	14.35	23	14	0.96	—	6.14
3/08	16.66	25	18	0.86	—	5.93
3/07	21.14	30	22	0.73	—	6.75
3/06	19.29	30	16	0.66	—	6.18
Annual Growth	5.1%	—	—	15.6%	—	4.0%

Public Service Enterprise Group

In the Garden State, Public Service Enterprise Group's (PSEG) diversified business model has it smelling like a rose. Regulated subsidiary Public Service Electric and Gas (PSE&G) transmits and distributes electricity to 2.1 million customers and natural gas to 1.7 million customers in New Jersey. Nonregulated subsidiary PSEG Power operates PSEG's generating plants. PSEG Power's 13,300-MW generating capacity comes mostly from nuclear and fossil-fueled plants in the US Northeast. Other operations (under PSEG Energy Holdings) include energy infrastructure investments and wholesale energy marketing.

PSEG Global (a unit of PSEG Energy Holdings) owns stakes in 16 power plants (1,245 MW of capacity) primarily in Texas and California, but also in Venezuela.

In order to focus on its core North American power businesses, PSEG has sold most of its overseas independent power plant interests, and it has scaled down plans to expand its energy generation and marketing businesses. In 2006 PSEG Global sold its 32% stake in RGE, a Brazilian electric distribution company with approximately 1.1 million customers, to Companhia Paulista de Força e Luz. In 2008 it sold the SAESA Group of Companies (a power distribution group) in southern Chile to a consortium formed by Morgan Stanley Infrastructure and the Ontario Teachers' Pension Plan for $887 million. By the end of 2009 PSEG Global's international generation portfolio consisted of three plants in Venezuela with a collective capacity of 160 MW.

In 2009 PSEG announced plans to invest in solar energy and wind power initiatives to help meet its commitment to reduce greenhouse gas emissions. The company's revenues took a hit that year when the global recession and an unusually cool summer in its service region conspired to suppress power demand.

HISTORY

Tragedy struck Newark, New Jersey, in 1903 when a trolley slid down an icy hill and collided with a train, killing more than 30 people. While investigating the accident, state attorney general Thomas McCarter discovered the mismanagement of the trolley company and many of New Jersey's other transportation, gas, and electric companies. Planning to buy and consolidate these companies, McCarter resigned and established the Public Service Corporation in 1903 with several colleagues.

The company formed divisions for gas utilities, electric utilities, and transportation companies. The trolley company generated almost half of Public Service's sales during its first year.

In 1924 the gas and electric companies consolidated as Public Service Electric and Gas (PSE&G). A new company was formed that year to operate buses, and in 1928 it merged with the trolley company to form Public Service Coordinated Transport (later Transport of New Jersey). PSE&G signed interconnection agreements with two Pennsylvania electric companies in 1928 to form the first integrated power pool — later known as the Pennsylvania-New Jersey-Maryland Interconnection. The Public Utility Holding Company Act of 1935 ushered in the era of regulated regional monopolies, ensuring PSE&G a captive market.

During the 1960s PSE&G joined Philadelphia Electric to build its first nuclear plant, at Peach Bottom, Pennsylvania. The company completed a second nuke in 1977, at Salem, New Jersey. Its third one went on line at Hope Creek, New Jersey. However, plant mismanagement earned PSE&G a slew of fines in the 1980s and 1990s.

The company sold its transportation system to the State of New Jersey in 1980. Five years later PSE&G formed holding company Public Service Enterprise Group (PSEG) to move into nonutility enterprises and created Community Energy Alternatives (CEA, now PSEG Global) to invest in independent power projects. In 1989 Enterprise Diversified Holdings (now PSEG Energy Holdings) was formed to handle activities ranging from real estate to oil and gas production.

CEA and three partners acquired a Buenos Aires power plant in 1993. Taking advantage of overseas privatization in the late 1990s, it expanded into Asia and, with AES, purchased two Argentine electric companies.

PSE&G's nuclear problems resurfaced when the Salem plant was shut down in 1995 to rectify equipment breakdowns. In 1997 PSEG paid Salem partners Delmarva Power & Light and PECO Energy $82 million to settle their lawsuits charging mismanagement of Salem; both units were back on line by 1998.

Continuing to diversify in the late 1990s, PSEG formed PSEG Energy Technologies in 1997 to market power and acquired five mechanical services companies in 1998 and 1999.

In 1999 PSEG Global teamed up with Panda Energy International to build three merchant plants in Texas (to be completed by 2001). It also planned plants in India and Venezuela and joined Sempra Energy to buy 90% of Chilquinta Energía, an energy distributor in Chile and Peru. In 2000 it bought 90% of a distributor serving Argentina and Brazil.

New Jersey's electricity markets were deregulated in 1999; a year later the company transferred PSE&G's generation assets to nonregulated unit PSEG Power. PSEG Power also took charge of PSEG Global's plants under development in Illinois, Indiana, and Ohio; announced plans for

new plants in New Jersey; and acquired an Albany, New York, plant from Niagara Mohawk.

In 2001 PSEG Global completed a power plant in Texas. It also bought 94% of generator and distributor Saesa from Chile's largest conglomerate, Copec, for $460 million; it later acquired the rest. It also purchased a Peruvian generation firm, ElectroAndes, for $227 million.

In 2002 PSEG Power acquired two Connecticut plants from Wisconsin Energy for approximately $270 million.

PSEG had agreed to be acquired by Exelon, but both New Jersey and Pennsylvania opposed the merger, and the deal fell through in 2006.

EXECUTIVES

Chairman, President, and CEO: Ralph Izzo, age 52, $8,715,970 total compensation
EVP and CFO: Caroline Dorsa, age 51, $4,610,450 total compensation
EVP Strategy and Development: Randall E. (Randy) Mehrberg, age 54, $2,520,192 total compensation
EVP Law: J. A. (Lon) Bouknight Jr.
SVP Public Affairs and Sustainability, PSEG Services Corporation: Anne E. Hoskins
SVP Human Resources and Chief Human Resources Officer, PSEG Services: Margaret M. Pego
VP Risk Management and Chief Risk Officer: Laura L. Brooks
VP Communications and Advertising, PSEG Services: J. Brian Smith
VP IT and CIO, PSEG Services: Manoj S. Chouthai
VP Investor Relations: Kathleen A. Lally
President and COO, PSE&G: Ralph A. LaRossa, age 46, $3,267,943 total compensation
President and COO, PSEG Power: William (Bill) Levis, age 53, $2,495,109 total compensation
President, PSEG Energy Resources and Trade: Clarence J. (Joe) Hopf Jr., age 53
President and Chief Nuclear Officer, PSEG Power: Thomas P. Joyce, age 57
President, PSEG Resources: Eileen A. Moran, age 54
President, PSEG Fossil: Richard P. Lopriore, age 60
Director; President and COO, PSEG Services: Elbert C. Simpson, age 61
Auditors: Deloitte & Touche LLP

LOCATIONS

HQ: Public Service Enterprise Group Incorporated
80 Park Plaza, Newark, NJ 07101
Phone: 973-430-7000   **Fax:** 973-824-7056
Web: www.pseg.com

PRODUCTS/OPERATIONS

2009 Sales

	$ mil.	% of total
PSE&G	8,243	53
Power	7,143	46
Energy Holdings	221	1
Adjustments	(3,201)	—
Total	**12,406**	**100**

Selected Subsidiaries

PSEG Energy Holdings Inc. (nonutility companies)
    PSEG Global Inc. (international development of independent power plants and distribution operations)
    PSEG Resources Inc. (energy infrastructure investments)
PSEG Power LLC
    PSEG Fossil LLC (operator of PSEG's fossil fuel plants)
    PSEG Nuclear LLC (operator of PSEG's nuclear plants)
    PSEG Energy Resources and Trade LLC (energy marketing)
PSEG Services Corporation (management and administrative services for PSEG)
Public Service Electric and Gas Company (PSE&G, distribution of electricity and gas)

HISTORICAL FINANCIALS

Company Type: Public

Income Statement

FYE: December 31

	REVENUE ($ mil.)	NET INCOME ($ mil.)	NET PROFIT MARGIN	EMPLOYEES
12/09	12,406	1,592	12.8%	10,352
12/08	13,322	1,192	8.9%	6,069
12/07	12,853	1,335	10.4%	2,538
12/06	12,164	739	6.1%	6,154
12/05	12,430	678	5.5%	6,335
Annual Growth	(0.0%)	23.8%	—	13.1%

2009 Year-End Financials

Debt ratio: 87.0%
Return on equity: 19.2%
Cash ($ mil.): 350
Current ratio: 1.13
Long-term debt ($ mil.): 7,645

No. of shares (mil.): 506
Dividends
  Yield: 4.0%
  Payout: 42.4%
Market value ($ mil.): 16,823

Stock History

NYSE: PEG

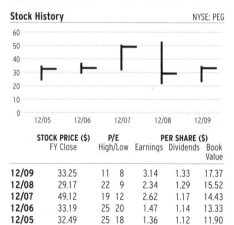

	STOCK PRICE ($) FY Close	P/E High	P/E Low	PER SHARE ($) Earnings	PER SHARE ($) Dividends	PER SHARE ($) Book Value
12/09	33.25	11	8	3.14	1.33	17.37
12/08	29.17	22	9	2.34	1.29	15.52
12/07	49.12	19	12	2.62	1.17	14.43
12/06	33.19	25	20	1.47	1.14	13.33
12/05	32.49	25	18	1.36	1.12	11.90
Annual Growth	0.6%	—	—	23.3%	4.4%	9.9%

Publix Super Markets

Publix Super Markets tops the list of privately owned supermarket operators in the US. By emphasizing service and a family-friendly image over price, Publix has grown faster and been more profitable than Winn-Dixie Stores and other rivals. More than two-thirds of its 1,000-plus stores are in Florida, but it also operates in Alabama, Georgia, South Carolina, and Tennessee. Publix makes some of its own bakery, deli, and dairy goods, and many stores house pharmacies and banks. It also operates liquor stores, convenience stores, and Crispers restaurants in Florida. Founder George Jenkins began offering stock to Publix employees in 1930. Employees own about 30% of Publix, which is still run by the Jenkins family.

The fast-growing grocery chain opened its 1,000th supermarket in early 2009 and went on to add about a dozen more supermarkets — including about a dozen locations acquired from Albertsons — before the year was out. It also added liquor stores, but trimmed the number of Crispers restaurants in operation. While the purchase of Albertsons' Florida stores eliminated one rival, Publix is facing increased competition from a resurgent Winn-Dixie, following its stint in bankruptcy; Sweetbay; and supercenter operator Wal-Mart. (Low-cost ALDI is also expanding in Florida.)

To stay on top of the competitive Florida grocery market, Publix keeps up with national trends in grocery retailing. In 2009 the company teamed up with NCR to install DVD rental kiosks in its supermarkets, saving customers a trip to the video store and giving Netflix a bit of competition. In 2007 it began offering free antibiotics at its 680-plus in-store pharmacies. The grocery chain also fills other generic prescriptions for $4 (upon customer request), thereby matching Wal-Mart's low-cost generic drug program. To better serve its Latino customers, Publix has launched its own line of pre-packaged Hispanic foods, including frozen plantains and ready-to-eat black beans.

In 2007 the company launched a new store format called GreenWise Market (the name Publix has already given to its store-within-a-store natural/organic sections and private-label line of specialty foods) to court more health-conscious consumers and compete with national organic chains, such as Whole Foods.

In addition to grocery stores, Publix also operates liquor stores next to about 100 of its supermarkets in Florida. Other ventures include its majority-owned restaurant chain Crispers in Florida. Currently, the soup-salad-and-sandwich chain operates about three dozen locations.

HISTORY

George Jenkins, age 22, resigned as manager of the Piggly Wiggly grocery in Winter Haven, Florida, in 1930. With money he had saved to buy a car, he opened his own grocery store, Publix, next door to his old employer. The small store (named after a chain of movie theaters) prospered despite the Depression, and in 1935 Jenkins opened another Publix in the same town.

Five years later, after the supermarket format had become popular, Jenkins closed his two smaller locations and opened a new, more modern Publix Market. With pastel colors and electric-eye doors, it was also the first US store to feature air conditioning.

Publix Super Markets bought the All-American chain of Lakeland, Florida (19 stores), in 1944 and moved its corporate headquarters to that city. The company began offering S&H Green Stamps in 1953, and in 1956 it replaced its original supermarket with a mall featuring an enlarged Publix and a Green Stamp redemption center. Publix expanded into South Florida in the late 1950s.

As Florida's population grew, Publix continued to expand, opening its 100th store in 1964. Publix was the first grocery chain in the state to use bar-code scanners — all its stores had the technology by 1981. The company beat Florida banks in providing ATMs and during the 1980s opened debit card stations.

Publix continued to grow in the 1980s, safe from takeover attempts because of its employee ownership. In 1988 it installed the first automated checkout systems in South Florida, giving patrons an always-open checkout lane.

In 1989 the chain stopped offering Green Stamps, and most of the $19 million decrease in Publix advertising expenditures was attributed to the end of the 36-year promotion. That year, after almost six decades, "Mr. George," as founder Jenkins was known, stepped down as chairman in favor of his son Howard. (George died in 1996.)

In 1991 Publix opened its first store outside Florida, in Georgia, as part of its plan to become a major player in the Southeast. Publix entered South Carolina in 1993 with one supermarket; it also tripled its presence in Georgia to 15 stores.

The United Food and Commercial Workers Union began a campaign in 1994 against alleged gender and racial discrimination in Publix's hiring, promotion, and compensation policies.

Publix opened its first store in Alabama in 1996. That year a federal judge allowed about 150,000 women to join a class-action suit filed in 1995 by 12 women who had sued Publix, charging that the company consistently channeled female employees into low-paying jobs with little chance for good promotions. The case, which at the time was said to be the biggest sex discrimination lawsuit ever, was set to go to trial, but in 1997 the company paid $82.5 million to settle and another $3.5 million to settle a complaint of discrimination against black applicants and employees.

Publix promised to change its promotion policies, but two more lawsuits alleging discrimination against women and blacks were filed in 1997 and 1998. The suit filed on behalf of the women was denied class-action status in 2000. Later that year the company settled the racial discrimination lawsuit for $10.5 million. Howard Jenkins stepped down as CEO in mid-2001; his cousin Charlie Jenkins took the helm.

In 2002 Publix entered the Nashville, Tennessee, market with the purchase of seven Albertsons supermarkets, a convenience store, and a fuel center. In mid-2003 Publix pulled the plug on its online store PublixDirect, which offered delivery service in parts of Florida, citing disappointing sales.

In 2007 the chain began offering seven popular antibiotics free at some 685 Publix Pharmacies. CEO Charlie Jenkins Jr. retired at the end of March 2008. Jenkins was succeeded by his cousin and Publix president Ed Crenshaw. In September Publix completed the acquisition of 49 Albertsons stores in Florida.

EXECUTIVES

Chairman: Charles H. (Charlie) Jenkins Jr., age 66, $540,093 total compensation
Vice Chairman: Hoyt R. (Barney) Barnett, age 66
CEO and Director: William E. (Ed) Crenshaw, age 59, $916,705 total compensation
President: R. Todd Jones Sr., age 47, $737,749 total compensation
CFO and Treasurer: David P. Phillips, age 50, $724,693 total compensation
SVP and CIO: Laurie Z. Douglas, age 46, $616,920 total compensation
SVP, General Counsel, and Secretary:
John A. Attaway Jr., age 51, $500,005 total compensation
SVP: John T. Hrabusa, age 54
VP Retail Operations: Charles B. Roskovich Jr.
VP Manufacturing: Michael R. (Mike) Smith, age 50
VP and Assistant Secretary: Linda S. Kane, age 44
VP and Controller: Sandra J. (Sandy) Estep, age 50
VP Facilities: David S. (Dave) Duncan, age 56
VP and Controller: G. Gino DiGrazia, age 47
VP Risk Management: Marc H. Salm, age 49
Assistant Secretary and Executive Director Publix Super Markets Charities: Sharon A. Miller, age 66
Director Media and Community Relations: Maria Brous
Director Marketing and Advertising: Kevin Lang
Chairman and CEO, Crispers Restaurants: Ron Fuller
Auditors: KPMG LLP

LOCATIONS

HQ: Publix Super Markets, Inc.
3300 Publix Corporate Pkwy., Lakeland, FL 33811
Phone: 863-688-1188   **Fax:** 863-284-5532
Web: www.publix.com

2009 Supermarkets

	No.
Florida	729
Georgia	177
South Carolina	42
Alabama	39
Tennessee	27
Total	**1,014**

PRODUCTS/OPERATIONS

2009 Stores

	No.
Supermarkets	1,014
Liquor stores	103
Crispers restaurants	37
Pix convenience stores	11
Total	**1,165**

COMPETITORS

ALDI
BI-LO
Costco Wholesale
CVS Caremark
IGA
Ingles Markets
Kerr Drug
Kmart
Kroger
Nash-Finch
The Pantry
Rite Aid
Ruddick
Sedano's
Sweetbay
Walgreen
Wal-Mart
Whole Foods
Winn-Dixie

HISTORICAL FINANCIALS

Company Type: Private

Income Statement

FYE: Last Saturday in December

	REVENUE ($ mil.)	NET INCOME ($ mil.)	NET PROFIT MARGIN	EMPLOYEES
12/09	24,515	1,161	4.7%	142,000
12/08	24,110	1,090	4.5%	144,000
12/07	23,194	1,184	5.1%	144,000
12/06	21,820	1,097	5.0%	140,000
12/05	20,745	989	4.8%	134,000
Annual Growth	**4.3%**	**4.1%**	**—**	**1.5%**

2009 Year-End Financials

Debt ratio: 0.0%
Return on equity: —
Cash ($ mil.): —
Current ratio: —
Long-term debt ($ mil.): 0

Net Income History

PulteGroup

PulteGroup pulls its weight in providing homes for American families. The company became the top homebuilder in the US when it merged with rival Centex in 2009. The company, which targets a cross-section of homebuyers around the country, buys land to build single-family houses, duplexes, townhouses, and condominiums. The Centex brand is focused on entry-level buyers, while the Pulte Homes name is used for customers looking to trade up. PulteGroup also builds Del Webb retiree communities, mostly in Sun Belt locales, for the growing number of buyers in the 55-plus age range. The company sells its homes in nearly 70 markets across 30 states.

The stock-for-stock deal (valued at $3.1 billion) with Centex helped PulteGroup strengthen its focus on first-time homebuyers — a market that has some of the most promise for growth. The combination also gave PulteGroup access to the Centex Homes label and the Fox & Jacobs brand in Texas. The merger occurred during one of the worst economic downturns in history, when home construction was at extremely low levels. PulteGroup is hoping that the combination of its expertise in retirement housing and Centex's focus on new homebuyers will help it weather the bad housing market and return the company to profitability.

Upon the merger, CEO Richard Dugas became chairman and chief executive of the combined company. As part of the transition, PulteGroup has streamlined operations by cutting jobs and discontinuing or moving Centex operations to other PulteGroup offices. The company also changed its name to PulteGroup in 2010.

The downturn in the US housing market — due to a toxic cocktail of higher home prices, increased foreclosures, high unemployment, and constraints on mortgage lending — led to weakened demand for new homes and higher cancellation rates. For PulteGroup, this trend has meant decreased profitability and a decline in homebuilding activity. PulteGroup has responded to the downturn and has adjusted its operations by cutting jobs and shuttering plants to meet lower demand levels. To add to its woes, the company also was named in lawsuits by subcontractors alleging breach of overtime payment and by homebuyers alleging shoddy construction of homes.

PulteGroup has maintained a diverse land portfolio. It controls more than 150,000 lots. It has pursued a fast-growth strategy, acquiring land and smaller competitors such as Pratt Building System and DiVosta Homes. Its DiVosta Homes brand continues to offer houses for sale in Florida. However, in light of the recession, PulteGroup scaled back its land acquisitions and development practices (though the Centex acquisition added tracts in Texas and the Carolinas). Some planned developments have been delayed and construction has slowed.

Founder William Pulte owns about 11% of the company. He retired from the company and the board of directors in 2010.

HISTORY

William Pulte built his first home in Detroit in 1950 and incorporated his business in 1956 as William J. Pulte, Inc. In 1961 the company built its first subdivision, in Detroit. During that decade Pulte moved into Washington, DC (1964), Chicago (1966), and Atlanta (1968). In 1969 Pulte merged with Colorado's American Builders to form the Pulte Home Corporation, a publicly traded company.

Originally a builder of high-priced, single-family homes, Pulte began expanding into affordable and midrange housing markets. To lower costs, it pioneered modular designs and prebuilt components. Pulte architects designed the Quadrominium, a large structure with four separate two-bedroom units, each with its own entrance and garage (priced at a mere $20,000 per unit in the 1970s).

Pulte formed Intercontinental Mortgage (later renamed ICM Mortgage) and began making home loans in 1972. The company ran into trouble in 1988 when it was accused of forcing Pulte homebuyers in Baltimore to use ICM financing instead of cheaper loans from the county. Pulte settled by repaying the difference in loan costs.

By the mid-1980s Pulte was one of the US's largest on-site homebuilders. PHM Corporation was created in 1987 as a holding company for the Pulte group of companies. That year PHM entered the thrift business by assisting the Federal Savings and Loan Insurance Corp.'s S&L bailout. It acquired five Texas S&Ls (with assets of $1.3 billion) for $45 million and eventually combined them to form First Heights (finally discontinuing the business in 1994).

Renamed Pulte Corporation in 1993, the company soon faced rising interest rates, which dampened the US housing market and affected the Mexican peso. Nonetheless, it began a second joint venture in that country in 1995 and helped form mortgage bank Su Casita with nine Mexican homebuilders to finance home construction on its border.

In 1996 its Mexican joint venture Condake-Pulte began building thousands of affordable homes for General Motors and Sony employees in *maquiladora* residential areas near the US-Mexico border. Pulte in 1998 acquired DiVosta, one of Florida's largest homebuilders, and Radnor Homes, based in Tennessee.

Pulte's 1988 foray into S&Ls came back to haunt it in 1998: the Federal Deposit Insurance Corp. won a lawsuit that accused the builder of abusing tax benefits associated with the S&Ls. (Pulte settled in 2001, paying $41.5 million.)

The company changed its name to Pulte Homes in 2001. That year Mark O'Brien became the company's CEO. He directed Pulte through the major acquisition of retirement community developer Del Webb for about $800 million in stock and $950 million in assumed debt. The combined company became the largest US homebuilder.

Pulte expanded its operations in the fast-growing San Diego area in 2003 by purchasing assets of ColRich Communities. It boosted its presence in the Albuquerque, Phoenix, and Tucson markets by acquiring Sivage-Thomas Homes (Albuquerque), with about 7,000 lots in the region. O'Brien left the company in 2003. EVP and COO Richard Dugas stepped up to become the company's president and CEO at that time.

In September 2003 the US Court of Federal Claims awarded Pulte and related parties $48.7 million as a result of a breach of contract by the US government related to Pulte's acquisition of five savings and loans in 1988.

At the close of 2004, Pulte sold some operations in Argentina to real estate developer Grupo Farallon. The next year it sold its Mexican and remaining Argentine homebuilding enterprises to focus exclusively on US operations.

EXECUTIVES

Chairman, President, and CEO: Richard J. Dugas Jr., age 44, $5,855,510 total compensation
Vice Chairman: Timothy R. (Tim) Eller, age 61
EVP and CFO: Roger A. Cregg, age 53, $3,693,984 total compensation
EVP Human Resources: James R. (Jim) Ellinghausen, age 51, $2,549,448 total compensation
SVP, General Counsel, and Secretary: Steven M. Cook, age 51, $1,474,427 total compensation
SVP Project Management Office: Peter J. Keane, age 44, $2,753,597 total compensation
SVP and Chief Marketing Officer: Deborah Wahl Meyer, age 47
VP and Controller: Michael J. Schweninger, age 41
VP and Treasurer: Bruce E. Robinson, age 48
VP and CIO: Jerry R. Batt, age 58
VP Finance and Homebuilding Operations: James L. Ossowski
VP Strategic Marketing: Steven A. Burch
VP Homebuilder Operations: Anthony C. Koblinski
VP Merchandising: Janice M. Jones
VP Investor Relations and Corporate Communications: James P. (Jim) Zeumer
President and CEO, Pulte Mortgage: Debra W. (Deb) Still
Auditors: Ernst & Young LLP

LOCATIONS

HQ: PulteGroup, Inc.
100 Bloomfield Hills Pkwy., Ste. 300
Bloomfield Hills, MI 48304
Phone: 248-647-2750   **Fax:** 248-433-4598
Web: www.pultegroupinc.com

2009 Sales

	$ mil.	% of total
Gulf Coast	921.0	23
Northeast	640.6	16
Southwest	640.6	16
West	598.1	15
Southeast	561.2	14
Midwest	445.1	11
Financial services	117.8	3
Land sales	97.2	2
Other homebuilding	62.8	—
Total	**4,084.4**	**100**

US Homebuilding Regions

Gulf Coast (Florida, Texas)
Midwest (Colorado, Illinois, Indiana, Michigan, Minnesota, Missouri, Ohio)
Northeast (Connecticut, Delaware, Maryland, Massachusetts, New Jersey, New York, Pennsylvania, Rhode Island, Virginia)
Southeast (Georgia, North Carolina, South Carolina, Tennessee)
Southwest (Arizona, Nevada, New Mexico)
West (California, Oregon, Washington)

PRODUCTS/OPERATIONS

2009 Sales

	$ mil.	% of total
Homebuilding	3,966.6	97
Financial Services	117.8	3
Total	**4,084.4**	**100**

Selected Brands

Centex
Del Webb
DiVosta Homes
Fox & Jacobs
Pulte Homes

COMPETITORS

Ball Homes
Beazer Homes
Capital Pacific
D.R. Horton
Hovnanian Enterprises
J.F. Shea
KB Home
Lennar
M.D.C.
Meritage Homes
M/I Homes
NVR
Pardee Homes
The Ryland Group
Standard Pacific
Toll Brothers
Woodbridge Holdings

HISTORICAL FINANCIALS

Company Type: Public

Income Statement

FYE: December 31

	REVENUE ($ mil.)	NET INCOME ($ mil.)	NET PROFIT MARGIN	EMPLOYEES
12/09	4,084	(1,183)	—	5,700
12/08	6,290	(1,473)	—	5,300
12/07	9,263	(2,256)	—	8,500
12/06	14,274	688	4.8%	12,400
12/05	14,695	1,492	10.2%	13,400
Annual Growth	(27.4%)	—	—	(19.2%)

2009 Year-End Financials

Debt ratio: 134.0%
Return on equity: —
Cash ($ mil.): 1,858
Current ratio: 3.09
Long-term debt ($ mil.): 4,282
No. of shares (mil.): 383
Dividends
   Yield: 0.0%
   Payout: —
Market value ($ mil.): 3,827

Stock History

NYSE: PHM

	STOCK PRICE ($) FY Close	P/E High/Low		Earnings	PER SHARE ($) Dividends	Book Value
12/09	10.00	—	—	(3.94)	0.00	8.35
12/08	10.93	—	—	(5.81)	0.16	7.41
12/07	10.54	—	—	(8.94)	0.16	11.29
12/06	33.12	17	10	2.66	0.16	17.19
12/05	39.36	8	5	5.68	0.13	15.57
Annual Growth	(29.0%)	—	—	—	—	(14.4%)

Quad/Graphics, Inc.

Your mailbox may be filled with Quad/Graphics' handiwork. A leading US printing company, Quad/Graphics produces catalogs, magazines, books, direct mail, and other commercial material. Its full range of services includes design, photography, desktop production, printing, binding, wrapping, distribution, and related software. The company owns more than 80 printing facilities throughout North America, Europe, and Latin America and has produced catalogs for Bloomingdale's and L.L. Bean, books for National Geographic, and magazines such as *People* and *Newsweek*. In mid-2010 Quad/Graphics expanded significantly by acquiring rival World Color Press.

In a move that combined two of the largest players in the highly fragmented commercial printing industry, Quad/Graphics acquired its Canadian rival World Color Press (WCP) in the summer of 2010 in a deal initially valued at $1.2 billion. After the deal's completion, Quad/Graphics became a publicly traded company, with WCP shareholders receiving about 40% of the newly issued shares of Quad/Graphics and Quad/Graphics shareholders owning the rest. The purchase added about 70 printing plants to Quad/Graphics' network and expanded its reach into Canada and certain Latin American markets. It also brought *Rolling Stone, Sports Illustrated,* and *Forbes* on board its client roster. CEO Joel Quadracci leads the combined company.

Before that monster deal, Quad/Graphics' growth strategy was focused on consistent contract wins and renewals. In March 2010 the printing company extended its multiyear contract with J. Crew. Quad/Graphics prints 40 million catalogs each year for the apparel retailer. During that same time period, Quad/Graphics inked a five-year deal with Hearst Magazines. As per the agreement, Quad/Graphics is printing five of the publisher's magazines: *Good Housekeeping*; *O, The Oprah Magazine*; *Harper's Bazaar*; *House Beautiful*; and *Veranda*.

As demand has fallen for printing services, Quad/Graphics in 2009 laid off about 550 plant workers nationwide. The company linked the reduction to dwindling sales of catalogs and other media. After the dust settled on its 2010 purchase of World Color Press, Quad/Graphics announced it was closing five plants, resulting in the elimination of 2,200 jobs.

It has extended its reach into Europe to strengthen its presence, acquiring Ireland-based Vigitek in 2008. Vigitek, whose scanners and inspection systems detect printing defects, was renamed Quad/Tech following the purchase. In 2007 the company bought Poland-based Winkowski, a leading commercial printer. In addition to its European business lines, Quad/Graphics maintains partnerships with printers in Argentina and Brazil.

HISTORY

Ink runs in the Quadracci family. Harry R. Quadracci founded Standard Printing in Racine, Wisconsin, in 1930, when he was 16. Four years later Quadracci sold out to William A. Krueger. Though he worked to build Krueger into a major regional printer, Quadracci had little equity in the company.

In the 1960s Harry R. Quadracci's son Harry V. Quadracci joined Krueger as a company lawyer. Within a few years he had worked his way up to plant manager. Krueger was a union shop, and in those days unions dictated the work rules and often salary levels. In 1970 there was a three-and-a-half-month strike. At odds with new management and reportedly dissatisfied with the way Krueger caved in to union demands and the adversarial relationship between company and union, the younger Quadracci left.

After 18 months of unemployment, in 1971 Quadracci formed a limited partnership with 12 others to get a loan to buy a press, which was installed in a building in Pewaukee, Wisconsin. The next year his father joined the company as chairman. Within two years the partners had recouped their initial investment, but the business' future remained in question until about 1976. One of its most innovative moves was to make its delivery fleet drivers into entrepreneurs by requiring them to find cargo to haul on their return trips.

Working on a shoestring, Quadracci hired inexperienced workers and trained them, moving them up as the company grew. The need to improvise fostered a flexibility that Quadracci institutionalized by keeping management layers flat and remaining accessible to his employees. Beginning in 1974, Quadracci rewarded his workers with equity in the company.

In the 1980s Quad/Graphics' commitment to technology enabled it to offer better service than many of its competitors. It was also immune to the merger-and-acquisition fever of the time. Free of acquisition debt, the company had excellent credit and was able to finance equipment upgrades with bank loans. Quad/Graphics expanded by opening a plant in Saratoga Springs, New York (1985), and buying a plant in Thomaston, Georgia (1989).

But there were missteps, such as its 1985 attempt to break into the newspaper coupon insert business dominated by Treasure Chest Advertising. Quad/Graphics sold that operation three years later. The company could not avoid the national economic downturn that began about that time, which forced it to lay off employees in the late 1980s and early 1990s and prompted it to reduce weekend overtime pay (from double time to time-and-a-half). The firm was also hit when a major customer consolidated its printing outside the Midwest. In response, Quad/Graphics increased its capacity in other regions of the US during the 1990s.

Benefiting from the UPS strike and changes in the postal regulations, in 1997 Quad/Graphics expanded its shipping services with Parcel Direct, targeting parcels for large shippers such as catalog merchants, in cooperation with the US Postal Service.

The company was shocked in 2002 when Harry V. Quadracci drowned at age 66. His brother, Tom, was then appointed president. In 2004 Tom Quadracci assumed the role of chairman and CEO, while Harry's son, Joel, took over as president. Quad/Graphics sold its package delivery business, Parcel Direct, to FedEx in 2004.

Tom Quadracci stepped down as CEO in late 2006, and Joel Quadracci succeeded him. Tom Quadracci remained executive chairman through the end of 2006 before retiring.

In mid-2010 Quad/Graphics acquired one of its biggest rivals, World Color Press, for about $1.2 billion. It also became a publicly traded company at that time, listing on the New York Stock Exchange.

EXECUTIVES

President, CEO, and Director: J. Joel Quadracci
SVP and CFO: John C. Fowler
SVP Sales and Administration: David A. Blais
SVP Manufacturing; President, QuadWinkowski: Thomas J. (Tom) Frankowski
VP Information Systems and Infrastructure; President, QuadDirect: Steve Jaeger
VP Customer Service: Ron Nash
VP Finishing Operations: Bill Graushar
VP Employee Services: Emmy M. LaBode
VP and Treasurer: Kelly Vanderboom
VP Press Operations: Tim Sands
VP and General Counsel: Andy Schiesl
VP Distribution: David (Dave) Riebe

LOCATIONS

HQ: Quad/Graphics, Inc.
N63 W23075 State Hwy. 74, Sussex, WI 53089
Phone: 414-566-6000   **Fax:** 414-566-4650
Web: www.qg.com

PRODUCTS/OPERATIONS

Selected Services

Binding and finishing
Color correction
Defect detection
Design
Desktop production
Direct mailing
Imaging and photography
Ink jetting
Integrated circulation
Mailing and distribution
Mailing list management
Printing
Scanning

COMPETITORS

Angstrom Graphics
Arandell
Brown Printing
Cenveo
Consolidated Graphics
Dai Nippon Printing
Merrill
R.R. Donnelley
Toppan Printing

HISTORICAL FINANCIALS

Company Type: Public

Income Statement

FYE: December 31

	REVENUE ($ mil.)	NET INCOME ($ mil.)	NET PROFIT MARGIN	EMPLOYEES
12/08	2,000	—	—	11,000
12/07	2,050	—	—	12,000
12/06	2,030	—	—	12,000
12/05	1,950	—	—	12,000
Annual Growth	0.8%	—	—	(2.9%)

Revenue History

NYSE: QUAD

QUALCOMM

Cell phone makers, wireless carriers, and governments worldwide call on QUALCOMM to engineer a quality conversation. The company pioneered the commercialization of the code-division multiple access (CDMA) technology used in digital wireless communications equipment and satellite ground stations mainly in North America. It licenses CDMA semiconductor technology and system software to equipment and cell phone makers. QUALCOMM's OmniTRACS satellite vehicle tracking system is used by the trucking industry to manage vehicle fleets. QUALCOMM Ventures invests in wireless communications and Internet startups.

In addition to equipment and software, the company has a plethora of intellectual property (patents, copyrights, trademarks, and trade secrets) for its technologies. It holds about 3,600 US patents and around 18,500 patents issued by other countries.

A short list of QUALCOMM's other technologies include Orthogonal Frequency Division Multiplexing Access (OFDMA), which allows multiple access on the same channel — WiMAX uses OFDMA. Its next-generation WCDMA (Wideband Code Division Multiple Access) chips, designed to ease the transmission of multimedia content, are used by Kyocera (which took over SANYO's mobile phone business) and Samsung. The company is also using its BREW (Binary Runtime Environment for Wireless) custom mobile-phone software to face off against Nokia.

Business lines, in addition to Licensing, include Integrated Circuits (CDMA-based); Asset Tracking and Services (equipment and software for fleet management); FLO (Forward Link Only) TV (mobile TV); and Display (technology for consumer mobile products). Its Wireless Device Software and Related Services supplies its products to the wireless industry. Its Mobile Banking business provides software for mobile banking services on cell phones and other wireless devices.

The International Trade Commission (ITC) ruled in 2007 that new mobile phones being imported into the US with certain QUALCOMM chipsets were barred from sale because they infringed on a Broadcom patent. In 2009 Broadcom and QUALCOMM reached a settlement, dismissing all patent claims against each other and granting each certain rights under their patent portfolios. The company agreed to pay Broadcom $891 million in cash over four years.

Nokia not only filed a patent infringement claim against the company, but it joined with other vendors to nudge the European Commission, the European Union's antitrust regulator, to upgraded its investigation into QUALCOMM's royalty practices. The two companies reached a legal settlement on patents in 2008. The settlement called for Nokia to assign certain patents related to QUALCOMM, and for the handset giant to pay a lump sum and royalties to QUALCOMM. Nokia later reported the lump-sum payment totaled about $2.5 billion. In November 2009 the European Commission closed the formal antitrust case against the company.

Although the US was long QUALCOMM's main market in CDMAs, the company has sown the seeds of expansion in Asia — particularly China and South Korea — and South America by partnering with such wireless service providers as China Unicom and Brazil-based Vésper.

HISTORY

Professors Irwin Mark Jacobs and Andrew Viterbi founded digital signal processing equipment company Linkabit in 1968. M/A-COM acquired the company in 1980. Led by Jacobs, Viterbi and five other executives left M/A-COM Linkabit in 1985 to start engineer-focused QUALCOMM (for "quality communications") to provide contract R&D services. The company's first home was located above a strip mall pizza parlor in San Diego. CEO Jacobs dreamed of modifying code-division multiple access (CDMA) — a secure wireless transmission system developed during WWII — for commercial use.

In 1988 QUALCOMM introduced OmniTRACS, a satellite-based system that tracks the location of long-haul truckers. By 1989, when QUALCOMM unveiled its version of CDMA, the company was working on military contracts worth $15 million.

In 1990 the company interrupted the Cellular Telecommunications Industry Association's (CTIA) plans to adopt a rival technology called time-division multiple access when communications service providers NYNEX (now part of Verizon) and Ameritech (later part of SBC Communications and now part of AT&T) adopted QUALCOMM's maverick technology. QUALCOMM initiated a public relations blitz and by 1991 Motorola, AT&T, Clarion, and Nokia had signed product development and testing agreements.

The company went public in 1991 and introduced the Eudora e-mail software program (named for "Why I Live at the P.O." author Eudora Welty), which it licensed from the University of Illinois. That year QUALCOMM and Loral Corporation unveiled plans for Globalstar, a satellite telecommunications system similar to the Iridium system. The CTIA adopted CDMA as a North American standard for wireless communications in 1993.

In 1996 most of the major US cellular carriers upgraded to CDMA. In 1997 Russia charged a QUALCOMM technician with espionage but allowed him to return to the US. The company spun off its wireless phone service operations in 1998 as Leap Wireless International.

In 1999 QUALCOMM and rival Ericsson settled a bitter dispute over the use of CDMA as an industry standard when they signed a cross-licensing deal. QUALCOMM sold its cell phone operations to Kyocera in 2000. The company also signed a potentially huge deal with China Unicom. In 2001 the Chinese government, after years of balking at CDMA in favor of 3G, granted QUALCOMM and China Unicom permission to install a CDMA-based network.

EVP Paul Jacobs, son of co-founder Irwin Mark Jacobs, took over as CEO in mid-2005; his father remained chairman of the company. In 2006 it acquired Flarion Technologies, a developer of a proprietary version of OFDM (orthogonal frequency-division multiplexing) technology called FLASH-OFDM. An alternative to WiMAX, FLASH-OFDM is a cellular broadband technology used to connect mobile devices to networks.

The Eudora e-mail program became an open-source product in May 2007, with QUALCOMM ceasing commercial sales of the product. At the end of 2007 QUALCOMM acquired Firethorn Holdings for about $210 million in cash. Firethorn, previously a unit of ITC Holding, is a developer of software for mobile banking services on cell phones and other wireless devices.

EXECUTIVES

Chairman and CEO: Paul E. Jacobs, age 47, $18,896,412 total compensation
President: Steven R. (Steve) Altman, age 48, $12,266,734 total compensation
EVP and CFO: William E. Keitel, age 57, $8,066,760 total compensation
EVP and Chief Marketing Officer: Jeffrey A. (Jeff) Jacobs, age 44
EVP and CTO: Roberto Padovani, age 55
EVP; President, CDMA Technologies: Steven M. (Steve) Mollenkopf, age 40, $4,761,497 total compensation
EVP; President, Qualcomm Technology Licensing: Derek K. Aberle, age 39
EVP Asia/Pacific and Middle East and Africa: Jing Wang, age 47
EVP; EVP, Americas and India: Margaret L. (Peggy) Johnson, age 48
EVP Human Resources: Daniel L. Sullivan, age 58
EVP; General Manager, Qualcomm CDMA Technologies (QCT): James Lederer, age 49
EVP, General Counsel, and Corporate Secretary: Donald J. Rosenberg, age 58
EVP; President, Europe: Andrew M. Gilbert, age 46
SVP Government Affairs: William (Bill) Bold
SVP Global Marketing and Investor Relations: William F. (Bill) Davidson Jr.
SVP and CIO: Norm Fjeldheim
SVP; President, Firethorn: Rocco J. Fabiano, age 52
SVP; President, QUALCOMM Government Technologies: Kimberly M. Koro
SVP; President, Greater China: Xiang Wang
Corporate Communications: Bertha Agia
VP Investor Relations: Warren Kneeshaw
President and CEO, Qualcomm Enterprise Services: Rich Sulpizio
Auditors: PricewaterhouseCoopers LLP

LOCATIONS

HQ: QUALCOMM Incorporated
5775 Morehouse Dr., San Diego, CA 92121
Phone: 858-587-1121   **Fax:** 858-658-2100
Web: www.qualcomm.com

2009 Sales

	$ mil.	% of total
Asia/Pacific		
South Korea	3,655	35
China	2,378	23
Japan	1,098	11
US	632	6
Other countries	2,653	25
Total	**10,416**	**100**

PRODUCTS/OPERATIONS

2009 Sales

	$ mil.	% of total
Equipment & services	6,466	62
Licensing & royalty fees	3,950	38
Total	**10,416**	**100**

2009 Sales

	$ mil.	% of total
QUALCOMM CDMA Technologies (QCT)	6,135	59
QUALCOMM Technology Licensing (QTL)	3,605	35
QUALCOMM Wireless & Internet (QWI)	641	6
QUALCOMM Strategic Initiatives (QSI)	29	—
Other	6	—
Total	**10,416**	**100**

Selected Operations and Products

Code-Division Multiple Access (CDMA) Technologies Group
  Integrated circuits
    Baseband
    Intermediate-frequency
    Power management
    Radio-frequency
  Systems software
Engineering Services Group
Enterprise Services
Firethorn Holdings
Flarion Technologies
FLO TV Incorporated
Government Technologies
Innovation Center
Internet Services
MediaFLO Technologies
MEMS Technologies
Qualcomm Ventures
Strategic Initiatives
Technology Licensing Group
  CDMA technologies and patents (cdmaOne, CDMA2000, WCDMA, TD-SCDMA)
  Royalties from products incorporating CDMA technology
Wireless and Internet Group
  Digital Media
    Digital motion picture delivery systems (under development)
    Government systems (development and analysis services; wireless base stations and phones)
  Internet Services
    Applications development software for wireless devices (BREW)
  Wireless Systems
    Low-Earth-orbit satellite-based telecommunications system (Globalstar)
    Satellite and terrestrial two-way data messaging and position reporting systems and services (OmniTRACS, OmniExpress, TruckMAIL)

COMPETITORS

Apple Inc.	MediaTek
Atheros	Motorola
Broadcom	NAVTEQ
Freescale Semiconductor	Nokia
Fujitsu	Nortel Networks
IBM Microelectronics	NXP Semiconductors
Icera	Panasonic Corp
Infineon Technologies	Samsung Electronics
Intel	ST-Ericsson
InterDigital	STMicroelectronics
Marvell Technology	Texas Instruments
Maxim Integrated Products	Trimble Navigation

Income Statement

FYE: Last Sunday in September

	REVENUE ($ mil.)	NET INCOME ($ mil.)	NET PROFIT MARGIN	EMPLOYEES
9/09	10,416	1,592	15.3%	16,100
9/08	11,142	3,160	28.4%	15,400
9/07	8,871	3,303	37.2%	12,800
9/06	7,526	2,470	32.8%	11,200
9/05	5,673	2,143	37.8%	9,300
Annual Growth	16.4%	(7.2%)	—	14.7%

2009 Year-End Financials

Debt ratio: —
Return on equity: 8.3%
Cash ($ mil.): 2,717
Current ratio: 4.47
Long-term debt ($ mil.): —
No. of shares (mil.): 1,605
Dividends
  Yield: 1.5%
  Payout: 69.5%
Market value ($ mil.): 72,202

Stock History

NASDAQ (GS): QCOM

	STOCK PRICE ($) FY Close	P/E High/Low		PER SHARE ($) Earnings	Dividends	Book Value
9/09	44.98	51	30	0.95	0.66	12.66
9/08	42.97	30	16	1.90	0.60	11.18
9/07	42.26	24	17	1.95	0.52	9.86
9/06	36.35	37	23	1.44	0.42	8.35
9/05	44.75	36	25	1.26	0.32	6.93
Annual Growth	0.1%	—	—	(6.8%)	19.8%	16.3%

Quest Diagnostics

Quest Diagnostics is testing its ability to be the world's leading clinical lab. The company performs diagnostics on about 150 million specimens each year, including routine clinical tests such as cholesterol checks, Pap smears, HIV screenings, and drug tests. Quest Diagnostics also performs esoteric testing (such as genetic screening) and anatomic pathology testing (such as tissue biopsies for cancer study). The company directly serves doctors and patients, as well as corporations, government agencies, and other clinical labs. It has more than 2,000 patient service centers where samples are collected, along with 30 primary labs and 150 rapid response labs throughout the US, as well as internationally.

While more than 90% of Quest's revenue comes from routine clinical and esoteric testing services, mostly in the US market, the company offers a number of other products, including online data management system Care360 physician portal, which lets doctors order diagnostic tests, review results, prescribe medication, and manage patient files. Quest also offers software that helps patients schedule tests and assess their results.

A small portion of sales comes from providing testing services to international drug companies for their clinical trials; GlaxoSmithKline, which owns nearly 20% of Quest, accounts for about 35% of such revenue. Additionally, Quest provides global testing and risk assessment services for the life insurance industry.

Quest strives to make itself ubiquitous, with a comprehensive menu of tests (more than 3,000) and a network of labs and collection sites that blanket the country. It keeps looking to grow its service offering, however, by acquiring firms with complementary testing capabilities and through developing its own novel tests. Quest is especially focused on growing its product line in the esoteric and genetic testing markets, which are experiencing increasing product demand in areas such as cancer diagnostics and personalized medicine (using genetic tests to determine proper medication regimens).

The company has made a number of acquisitions that have increased its presence in specific testing categories. Quest has especially been working to enhance its line of cancer biopsy tests and point-of-care diagnostics by purchasing other diagnostics companies. Point-of-care tests are increasing in popularity because they can be performed at the bedside or in the doctor's office and produce results more quickly.

While more than 95% of sales come from the US market, Quest aims for its international operations to eventually account for more than 10% of revenues. Key growth markets outside the US include Mexico, Ireland, Puerto Rico, and the UK. One international target for Quest is the developing world, where the diagnostic testing market is more fragmented. It began providing testing services in India in 2008, including esoteric testing for hospitals, tests for the life insurance industry, and diagnostics for global clinical trials.

HISTORY

Quest Diagnostics began as one man's quest to make clinical tests more affordable. Pathologist Paul Brown started Metropolitan Pathological Laboratory (MetPath) in his Manhattan apartment in 1967. To help his business take off, in 1969 he bought two $55,000 blood analyzers that could automatically perform a dozen common tests; the machines allowed him to charge patients $5.50 while hospitals and other labs were charging upwards of $40. Investments in emerging lab technology helped MetPath continue to beat competitors' prices and grow its business. It made its first profit in 1971 and eventually attracted the attention of Corning Glass Works, which bought 10% of the company in 1973.

MetPath's growth was due in part to investments in technology. The company built a state-of-the-art central lab in New Jersey in 1978 that could process some 30,000 specimens daily; it also went on an acquisition spree to expand across the US. These investments left the firm swamped with debt, and Corning bought the company in 1982.

An autonomous unit of Corning, MetPath continued to grow as Medicare reimbursement for lab tests went up and more doctors ordered more tests to catch and prevent disease before it happened. To cut costs in the mid-1980s, the company reorganized its facilities to create a regional lab network. A reorganization in 1990 at its parent placed MetPath in the Corning Lab Services subsidiary.

Corning Lab Services strengthened its operations in the early 1990s by buying labs from regional operators. In 1994 MetPath became Corning Clinical Laboratories. Around the same time, the company found itself besieged with demands from HMOs and other managed care providers to lower its costs. Also during this time, the company settled a handful of federal suits accusing it of fraudulent Medicare billing. In the face of increasing pressure, parent Corning spun off its lab testing business to the public as Quest Diagnostics in 1996.

On its own, Quest aimed to grow through acquisitions. In 1999 it bought rival SmithKline Beecham Clinical Laboratories and has continued its growth strategy in the 21st century. It bought American Medical Laboratories to expand its esoteric testing operations in 2002. The company was finally able to close its acquisition of Unilab in early 2003 after the deal ran into delays with the FTC. Quest sold some labs and service contracts in northern California to LabCorp to appease FTC regulators.

Quest Diagnostics acquired LabOne, a provider of risk assessment services for life insurance companies, in 2005. The following year it purchased point-of-care test makers Enterix (colorectal cancer screens) and Focus Diagnostics (infectious disease and esoteric testing). In 2007 the company purchased another point-of-care testing provider, Sweden-based HemoCue, for $344 million.

In 2007 the company acquired laboratory services firm AmeriPath in a deal worth about $2 billion. The purchase strengthened Quest's operations in a number of areas, including anatomic pathology (especially cancer testing) and molecular diagnostics.

EXECUTIVES

Chairman, President, and CEO: Surya N. Mohapatra, age 60, $12,474,784 total compensation
SVP and CFO: Robert A. Hagemann, age 53, $4,253,909 total compensation
SVP and General Counsel: Michael E. Prevoznik, age 48, $2,384,204 total compensation
SVP Pathology and Hospital Services: Joan E. Miller, age 55, $2,633,267 total compensation
SVP and Chief Medical Officer: Jon R. Cohen, age 55, $2,710,775 total compensation
VP Operations: Wayne R. Simmons, age 54, $2,135,960 total compensation
VP Information Technology: Rich Bevan
VP and Chief Laboratory Officer: Stephen Suffin
VP Compliance: Timothy (Tim) Sharpe
VP Health and Wellness Services: Steve Burton
VP Hospital Services: Catherine T. Doherty
VP and General Manager, Focus Diagnostics: John G. R. Hurrell, age 60
VP Human Resources: David W. Norgard
VP Physician Sales and Marketing: John Nosenzo
VP Clinical Trials and International Operations: Mary Hall Gregg
VP Office of the Chairman: Dermot Shorten
VP Communications and Investor Relations: Laure E. Park
Secretary: William J. O'Shaughnessy Jr.
Auditors: PricewaterhouseCoopers LLP

LOCATIONS

HQ: Quest Diagnostics Incorporated
3 Giralda Farms, Madison, NJ 07940
Phone: 973-520-2700
Web: www.questdiagnostics.com

2009 Sales

	% of total
US	97
Other countries	3
Total	**100**

PRODUCTS/OPERATIONS

2009 Sales

	$ mil.	% of total
Clinical laboratory testing	6,824.1	92
Other	631.1	8
Total	**7,455.2**	**100**

Selected Products and Services

Clincial laboratory testing
  Anatomic pathology testing (cancer biopsies, tissue
    and cell testing)
  Esoteric testing
    Endocrinology
    Genetics
    Hematology
    Immunology
    Microbiology
    Oncology
    Serology
    Toxicology
  Routine testing (body fluid testing)
    Alcohol and other substance-abuse tests
    Allergy tests
    Blood cholesterol
    Complete blood cell counts
    Pap smears
    Pregnancy testing
    Urinalyses
Other products and services
  Clinical trials testing
  Medical data management systems
  Life insurance risk assessment services

COMPETITORS

Associated Regional and University Pathologists
Bio-Reference Labs
Celera
Covance
Genomic Health
Genzyme
Kroll Background America
LabCorp
Medtox Scientific
Mid America Clinical Laboratories
Oncolab
Orchid Cellmark
PAREXEL
Pathology Associates Medical Laboratories
Pharmaceutical Product Development
Psychemedics
Quintiles Transnational
Sonic Healthcare
Spectrum Laboratory Network

HISTORICAL FINANCIALS

Company Type: Public

Income Statement

FYE: December 31

	REVENUE ($ mil.)	NET INCOME ($ mil.)	NET PROFIT MARGIN	EMPLOYEES
12/09	7,455	766	10.3%	43,000
12/08	7,249	582	8.0%	42,800
12/07	6,705	340	5.1%	43,500
12/06	6,269	586	9.4%	41,000
12/05	5,504	546	9.9%	41,500
Annual Growth	**7.9%**	**8.8%**	**—**	**0.9%**

2009 Year-End Financials

Debt ratio: 73.6%
Return on equity: 20.2%
Cash ($ mil.): 534
Current ratio: 1.59
Long-term debt ($ mil.): 2,937

No. of shares (mil.): 177
Dividends
  Yield: 0.7%
  Payout: 10.3%
Market value ($ mil.): 10,700

Stock History

NYSE: DGX

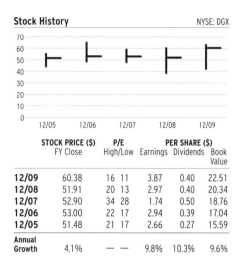

	STOCK PRICE ($) FY Close	P/E High/Low		PER SHARE ($) Earnings	Dividends	Book Value
12/09	60.38	16	11	3.87	0.40	22.51
12/08	51.91	20	13	2.97	0.40	20.34
12/07	52.90	34	28	1.74	0.50	18.76
12/06	53.00	22	17	2.94	0.39	17.04
12/05	51.48	21	17	2.66	0.27	15.59
Annual Growth	**4.1%**	**—**	**—**	**9.8%**	**10.3%**	**9.6%**

Quiksilver, Inc.

Quiksilver rides the wave of youth appeal. It caters to the young and athletic with surfwear, snowboardwear, sportswear, and swimwear sold under such names as Quiksilver, Roxy, Raisins, Hawk, Radio Fiji, and Gnu. Quiksilver owns the DC Shoes brand of footwear and apparel for young men and juniors. It sells its products worldwide in specialty and department stores. The retailer boasts about 470 of its own stores under the Boardriders Clubs (board sports), Roxy (junior apparel), and Quiksilver Youth banners. Quiksilver has expanded its products to include eyewear, watches, and personal care items, while shedding its Rossignol wintersports equipment business.

The company has cut 200 jobs and taken other steps to reduce expenses in its Americas division in response to the dismal retail climate in the US. It relies on California, Florida, and Hawaii — some of its biggest markets — for its sales, but these states have been hit with a noteworthy housing collapse.

Until November 2008, Quiksilver also sold snow skis, boots, and bindings through its Rossignol business under the Rossignol, Dynastar, Lange, and Look brands. Since acquiring Rossignol in 2005, however, the company grew to dislike its exposure to the hardgoods manufacturing side of business and longed to return to its roots as an apparel and footwear maker. The company eventually sold the underperforming business to Chartreuse & Mont Blanc, a company headed by Rossignol's former CEO Bruno Cercley. Quiksilver had sold its golf equipment unit (Roger Cleveland Golf Company), which was part of the Rossignol buy, to SRI Sports Limited in late 2007 for more than $132 million.

In recent years, Quiksilver has been busy extending its reach into many new, potentially lucrative markets. The company in 2005 acquired Australia's top boardriding retailer, Surfection, to pave the way for its expansion into the Asia/Pacific region. To enter the Mexican market, Quiksilver formed a joint venture in late 2006 with PBM International (of which Quiksilver owns a majority stake) to peddle the Quiksilver and Roxy brands in Mexico. Quiksilver entered the Russian wholesale and retail markets in mid-2006

through its joint venture with Sprandi International, a top sports and outdoor products manufacturer in Russia and Eastern Europe that specializes in footwear, apparel, and accessories.

Like many surf/skate/snowboarding companies, Quiksilver promotes its brands not so much through advertising as through sponsorship of events featuring its products, e.g., major surf and skateboard competitions. It forms associations with well-known athletes in the field, such as skateboarder Tony Hawk, to promote its products. Another division, Quiksilver Entertainment, produces programming that covers these events, while also promoting the boardriding (and hence Quiksilver) lifestyle.

Quiksilver also has ventured into personal care products for its namesake and Roxy lines. Through a worldwide licensing agreement, Inter Parfums develops and distributes Roxy fragrance, sun care, skin care, and related items.

In February 2008 Robert McKnight took over as president of the company when Bernard Mariette, with the firm for some 15 years, resigned. McKnight became chairman, CEO, and president.

HISTORY

Australian surfers Alan Green and John Law started Quiksilver in 1969 to make "boardshorts" for surfers. In 1976 surfers Jeff Hakman and Bob McKnight bought the US rights to the Quiksilver name — Hakman displayed his enthusiasm for the line by eating a doily at a dinner with Green — and established Quiksilver, USA. The firm went public in 1986.

The recession of the early 1990s and the dominance of grunge as the fashion du jour hurt Quiksilver and prompted it to restructure. It acquired French affiliate Na Pali in 1991 and began building its European operations. To gain surer footing in the fickle teen fashion market, Quiksilver broadened its product offerings. It added the Roxy women's swimwear line in 1991, expanding it to clothing in 1993. It also launched the Boardriders Club concept — stores featuring Quiksilver merchandise but owned by independent retailers. In 1994 the company acquired swimwear maker The Raisin Company. In 1997 Quiksilver began advertising nationally and entered the snowboard market, buying Mervin Manufacturing, maker of Lib Technologies, Gnu, and Bent Metal snowboard products.

With its women's lines making waves and a strong current from European sales, Quiksilver began opening its own Boardriders Club stores in 1998. In 1999 it launched the Quik Jeans and Roxy Jeans denim lines, and the next year it added the Alex Goes line for women 25 to 40. In 2000 the company acquired Fidra men's golf apparel; Freestyle, the European licensee of rival youth wear label Gotcha; and pro-skateboarder Tony Hawk's apparel and accessories business. In a tail-that-wags-the-dog move, it bought its progenitor, Quiksilver International, the same year; in doing so, Quiksilver gained sole possession of the Quiksilver name worldwide.

In June 2002 Quiksilver launched Quiksilver Entertainment, a production company that creates actionsport-based programming for the entertainment industry. Later that year Quiksilver acquired Ug Manufacturing in Australia and Quiksilver Japan, in an effort to gain control over nearly all its global business. At about the same time, the company purchased and integrated Beach Street, the owner and operator of 26 Quiksilver outlet stores.

The company formed a 50-50 joint venture in 2003 with Glorious Sun Enterprises to expand into China.

Quiksilver's entertainment unit in 2004 launched an actionsport film distribution company, Union, which is a supplier to more than 1,000 retail locations in Australia, China, Europe, Japan, and the US. In 2004 Quiksilver completed its purchase of DC Shoes and bought the footwear firm's Canadian distributor, Centre Skateboard Distribution, Ltd., in 2005. The footwear company's popularity in the skate and surf community serves to embed Quiksilver further in that market, while ensuring its ability to compete with Nike and adidas in the footwear arena.

In 2005 Quiksilver flipped its board in a new direction, however, and broadened its reach into the mainstream. The company announced it has signed an exclusive licensing deal with Kohl's and Tony Hawk to give traction to its apparel, outerwear, and accessories.

Quiksilver exited the sports equipment manufacturing business in November 2008 when it sold its Rossignol unit.

EXECUTIVES

Chairman, President, and CEO:
Robert B. (Bob) McKnight Jr., age 56, $1,795,162 total compensation
EVP and CFO: Joseph (Joe) Scirocco, age 53, $1,186,600 total compensation
EVP Global Marketing, Roxy: Randy Hild
EVP Quiksilver Sales: Tom Holbrook
EVP Human Resources: Carol Sherman
Chief Administrative Officer, General Counsel, Secretary, and Director: Charles S. Exon, age 60, $910,300 total compensation
SVP Sales, Quiksilver Brands and Quiksilver Americas: John Mills
VP Investor Relations: Bruce Thomas
President, Quiksilver Europe: Pierre Agnes, age 45, $1,519,400 total compensation
President, Quiksilver Brands, Americas: Stephen R. (Steve) Tully
President, Quiksilver Americas: Craig Stevenson, age 49, $1,044,102 total compensation
President, DC Shoes, Americas: Anton Nistl
Auditors: Deloitte & Touche LLP

LOCATIONS

HQ: Quiksilver, Inc.
15202 Graham St., Huntington Beach, CA 92649
Phone: 714-889-2200 **Fax:** 714-889-2315
Web: www.quiksilver.com

2009 Sales

	% of total
Americas	47
Europe	40
Asia/Pacific	13
Total	**100**

PRODUCTS/OPERATIONS

Selected Brands

DC Shoes (men's and women's extreme sportswear and footwear)
Hawk Clothing (men's and boys' skateboard apparel and accessories)
Leilani (women's swimwear)
Quiksilver (sportswear, beachwear, activewear, and outerwear)
Quiksilver Boys (boys' sportswear)
Quiksilver Roxy (junior sportswear, footwear, accessories, and swimwear)
Quiksilver Silver Edition (men's sportswear, beachwear, activewear, and outerwear)
Quiksilver Toddler (children's sportswear)
Radio Fiji (junior swimwear)
Raisins (junior swimwear)

COMPETITORS

Abercrombie & Fitch
adidas
Amer Sports
Amerex
Bauer Hockey
Billabong
Body Glove
Burton
Calvin Klein
Columbia Sportswear
Fat Face
FUBU
Head N.V.
Levi Strauss
Life is good
Nautica Apparel
NIKE
Oakley
Orange 21
Pacific Sunwear
Sole Technology
Stüssy
Tecnica
Tommy Hilfiger
VF
Volcom
Warnaco Swimwear

HISTORICAL FINANCIALS

Company Type: Public

Income Statement

FYE: October 31

	REVENUE ($ mil.)	NET INCOME ($ mil.)	NET PROFIT MARGIN	EMPLOYEES
10/09	1,978	(192)	—	7,650
10/08	2,265	(226)	—	8,400
10/07	2,426	(121)	—	9,600
10/06	2,362	93	3.9%	9,200
10/05	1,781	107	6.0%	7,875
Annual Growth	**2.7%**	**—**	**—**	**(0.7%)**

2009 Year-End Financials

Debt ratio: 199.6%
Return on equity: —
Cash ($ mil.): 100
Current ratio: 2.30
Long-term debt ($ mil.): 911
No. of shares (mil.): 133
Dividends
  Yield: —
  Payout: —
Market value ($ mil.): 264

Stock History

NYSE: ZQK

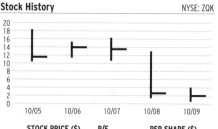

	STOCK PRICE ($) FY Close	P/E High/Low		PER SHARE ($) Earnings	Dividends	Book Value
10/09	1.99	—	—	(1.51)	—	3.44
10/08	2.59	—	—	(1.75)	—	4.52
10/07	13.50	—	—	(0.98)	—	6.69
10/06	13.95	21	16	0.73	—	6.65
10/05	11.53	21	12	0.86	—	5.53
Annual Growth	**(35.5%)**	**—**	**—**	**—**	**—**	**(11.2%)**

RadioShack

These stores are tuned to your electronics needs and desires. RadioShack is a leading consumer electronics retail chain with some 4,475 stores in the US, Puerto Rico, and the Virgin Islands. Its shops and website offer a variety of products, including wireless and residential telephones, computers, DVD players, electronic toys, and, of course, radios. The stores also sell third-party services such as wireless calling plans and direct satellite service. In addition, RadioShack sells a wide range of electronics parts and components. The chain also runs about 1,300 dealer outlets and some 560 wireless phone kiosks located primarily inside SAM'S CLUB and Target stores (kiosks are not RadioShack-branded).

Increased sales in its wireless business helped RadioShack post a modest gain in revenues. The addition of T-Mobile as its third wireless carrier, and the consolidation of its business in Mexico, helped fuel the increase.

Wireless has given the chain, long-known as a seller of gadgets and batteries, a profitable new line of business, and it is working hard to establish itself as a leader in mobility products and services. (Sales of wireless products account for more than a third of the company's revenue, exceeding any other product segment.) Radio-Shack stores offer postpaid rate plans from three national carriers — Sprint Nextel, T-Mobile, and AT&T — as well as those of several prepaid carriers. The stores also offer smartphones, including Apple's iPhone.

The long-struggling firm — which lost ground to rivals Best Buy, Wal-Mart, and others over the past decade — may finally be turning its business around. Under the leadership of CEO Julian Day, a turnaround specialist with experience at Safeway and Kmart, who was recruited by the company in mid-2006, RadioShack has undertaken a major rebranding effort to update its old-fashioned image. It has dropped the antiquated term "radio" from its name and adopted the nickname "THE SHACK." It also hoped to get some mileage from its sponsorship of seven-time Tour de France winner Lance Armstrong's cycling team in 2010.

Unlike its big-box competitors, RadioShack has built its chain with smaller but more numerous locations. (Its stores are about 2,500 sq. ft. on average.) FMR owns more than 12% of RadioShack's shares.

HISTORY

During the 1950s Charles Tandy expanded his family's small Fort Worth, Texas, leather business (founded 1919) into a nationwide chain of leather craft and hobby stores. By 1960 Tandy stock was being traded on the NYSE. In the early 1960s Tandy began to expand into other retail areas, buying Leonard's, a Fort Worth department store.

In 1963 Tandy purchased RadioShack, a nearly bankrupt electronics parts supplier with a mail-order business and nine retail stores in the Boston area. Tandy collected part of the $800,000 owed the company and started expanding. Between 1961 and 1969 Tandy's sales grew from $16 million to $180 million; the bulk of the growth was due to the expansion of RadioShack. Between 1968 and 1973 Tandy ballooned from 172 to 2,294 stores; RadioShack provided over 50% of sales and 80% of earnings in 1973.

Tandy sold its department store operations to Dillard's in 1974. The next year Tandy spun off its leather products business to its shareholders as Tandy Brands and its hobby and handicraft business as Tandycrafts, focusing Tandy on the consumer electronics business. During 1976 the boom in CB radio sales pushed income up 125% as Tandy opened 1,200 stores. The following year it introduced the first mass-marketed PC.

In 1984 the company introduced the Tandy 1000, the first IBM-compatible PC priced under $1,000. Then came acquisitions — electronics equipment chain stores Scott/McDuff and VideoConcepts (1985), laptop specialist GRiD Systems (1988), and microcomputer makers Victor Microcomputer and Micronic (1989, later merged as Victor Technologies).

In 1987 Tandy spun off its foreign retail operations as InterTAN. Realizing that RadioShack had nearly exhausted its expansion possibilities, the company focused on alternate retail formats such as GRiD Systems Centers and in 1991 opened Computer City and the Edge in Electronics. Also that year it introduced name-brand products into RadioShack stores.

Tandy sold Memtek Products (magnetic tape), LIKA (printed circuit boards), and its computer manufacturing and marketing operations in 1993 and spun off O'Sullivan Industries (ready-to-assemble furniture) to the public in 1994. As part of the restructuring, Tandy began to scale back VideoConcepts and McDuff Electronics.

A year later the company announced that it would close all of its VideoConcepts mall stores and half of its McDuff electronics stores. Also in 1995 it sold its credit card business.

In 1996 and 1997 Tandy closed down its 19-store Incredible Universe "gigastores" chain, shuttered the 53-store McDuff chain, and closed about 20 of its Computer City stores and sold others in Europe.

Longtime CEO John Roach stepped down in 1998, and president Leonard Roberts replaced him. Tandy then sold the Computer City chain to CompUSA for $211 million.

The company changed its name to RadioShack in 2000. In 2001 RadioShack announced plans to sell products in about 5,000 Blockbuster video stores; the plan included kiosks and store-within-a-store shops. In December the company sold its headquarters building (the Charles D. Tandy Center), exited the commercial installation business, and closed 35 stores.

After a six-month trial, RadioShack halted plans to install boutiques in Blockbuster video stores in January 2002. RadioShack completed construction of a new headquarters in downtown Fort Worth in 2004.

Roberts retired as CEO in 2005 and turned the reins of the company over to David Edmondson, who had joined RadioShack from direct marketer ADVO in 1994. However, Edmondson was forced to resign the following year after it was revealed he may have misrepresented his academic record on his resume. The company in July 2006 named former Sears executive Julian Day as Edmonson's replacement. Later that month CFO David Barnes announced he would leave the electronics retailer to take a job with The Western Union Company.

In 2006 the company closed 500 of its traditional retail outlets and cut some 1,500 jobs.

In December 2008 the company acquired 100% ownership of its joint venture in Mexico with Grupo Gigante, S.A.B.

EXECUTIVES

Chairman and CEO: Julian C. Day, age 57, $8,066,133 total compensation
EVP and CFO: James F. (Jim) Gooch, age 42, $3,189,501 total compensation
EVP Store Operations: Bryan Bevin, age 47, $2,524,116 total compensation
EVP and Chief Marketing Officer: Lee Applbaum, age 39, $1,937,916 total compensation
EVP and Chief Merchandising Officer: Scott E. Young, age 48
SVP Supply Chain: John G. Ripperton, $1,034,202 total compensation
SVP Human Resources: Mary Ann Doran, age 54
VP Investor Relations: Molly Salky
VP and Corporate Controller: Martin O. Moad, age 53
Auditors: PricewaterhouseCoopers LLP

LOCATIONS

HQ: RadioShack Corporation
300 RadioShack Cir., Fort Worth, TX 76102
Phone: 817-415-3011 **Fax:** 817-415-2647
Web: www.radioshack.com

PRODUCTS/OPERATIONS

2009 Locations

	No.
Company-operated	
US Stores	4,476
Kiosks	562
Mexico stores	204
Dealer & other	1,321
Total	**6,563**

2009 Sales

	$ mil.	% of total
Company-operated		
US Stores	3,650.9	85
Kiosks	250.0	6
Other sales	375.1	9
Total	**4,276.0**	**100**

2009 Sales

	$ mil.	% of total
Wireless	1,633.3	38
Accessory	1,058.6	25
Modern home	561.0	13
Personal electronics	454.9	11
Power	227.6	5
Technical	181.1	4
Service	115.3	3
Service centers & other	44.2	1
Total	**4,276.0**	**100**

COMPETITORS

Amazon.com
Apple Inc.
Best Buy
Brookstone
Costco Wholesale
Dell
Fry's Electronics
GameStop
Gateway, Inc.
Home Depot
Office Depot
PC Mall
Sears
Staples
Systemax
Target
TSIC
Verizon
Wal-Mart

HISTORICAL FINANCIALS

Company Type: Public

Income Statement

FYE: December 31

	REVENUE ($ mil.)	NET INCOME ($ mil.)	NET PROFIT MARGIN	EMPLOYEES
12/09	4,276	205	4.8%	36,700
12/08	4,225	192	4.6%	36,800
12/07	4,252	237	5.6%	35,800
12/06	4,778	73	1.5%	40,000
12/05	5,082	270	5.3%	47,000
Annual Growth	**(4.2%)**	**(6.6%)**	**—**	**(6.0%)**

2009 Year-End Financials

Debt ratio: 59.9%
Return on equity: 22.0%
Cash ($ mil.): 908
Long-term debt ($ mil.): 628
No. of shares (mil.): 125
Dividends
  Yield: 1.3%
  Payout: 15.3%
Current ratio: 3.08
Market value ($ mil.): 2,445

Stock History

NYSE: RSH

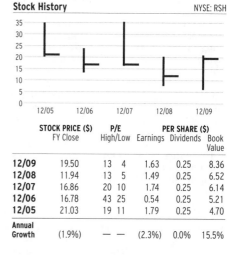

	STOCK PRICE ($) FY Close	P/E High/Low		PER SHARE ($)		
				Earnings	Dividends	Book Value
12/09	19.50	13	4	1.63	0.25	8.36
12/08	11.94	13	5	1.49	0.25	6.52
12/07	16.86	20	10	1.74	0.25	6.14
12/06	16.78	43	25	0.54	0.25	5.21
12/05	21.03	19	11	1.79	0.25	4.70
Annual Growth	**(1.9%)**	**—**	**—**	**(2.3%)**	**0.0%**	**15.5%**

Ralcorp Holdings

Ralcorp Holdings reminds us that you can't judge food by its cover. The company is a top US maker of private-label or "store-brand" ready-to-eat and hot breakfast cereals. Ralcorp has also stocked its pantry with a variety of private-label cookies, crackers, peanut butter, ketchup, snack nuts, candy, and breakfast cereal. In addition, the company makes branded products: Ralston Hot Cereal, Post dry cereals, Ry Krisp crackers, and Rippin' Good cookies. Its Carriage House unit produces private-label dressings, syrups, jellies, and sauces, and its Lofthouse and Parco businesses offer frozen cookies to in-store bakeries. In 2010 Ralcorp acquired American Italian Pasta Company (AIPC), adding pasta to its menu.

The company's strategy is to round out its larder through acquisitions. (It has acquired more than 20 companies during the past 10 years.) And it kept to that strategy with its $1.2 billion purchase of one of the US's leading dry pasta manufacturers. By adding AIPC's branded and private-label products to its offerings, Ralcorp enhanced its ability to provide a boader array of foods. It adds strategically located production facilities, solid brands, and a top-tier customer base. A tender offer for about 85% of AIPC's shares was completed in July, at which time AIPC became a wholly owned subsidiary of Ralcorp, although it will operate as an independent division of the company. Previously, Ralcorp completed the acquisition in 2010 of Sepp's Gourmet Foods, a maker of frozen breakfast foods for the retail food and foodservice sectors. Sepp's, which is based in Canada, has operations in Delta, British Columbia, and in Richmond Hill, Ontario.

The acquisition of Post cereals from Kraft Foods in 2008 was a real shot in the arm for Ralcorp. The Post brand is the #3 US breakfast cereal (behind Kellogg and General Mills). (It brought in more than $1 billion in 2006 for Kraft.) Post makes such well-known brands as Honey Bunches of Oats (the third-best-selling breakfast cereal in the US), Pebbles, Shredded Wheat, Grape-Nuts, and Honeycomb. The all-stock transaction was worth some $2.6 billion.

The company's operating divisions include cereals (Post Foods, Ralston Foods, and Bloomfield Bakers); frozen bakery products (Krusteaz, Lofthouse, Parco, and Panne Provincio); snacks (Bremner, Medallion, Harvest Manor Farms, and Nutcracker); and sauces and spreads (Carriage House). Contributing to Ralcorp's success is its wide customer base, which ranges from retail grocery stores, mass merchandisers, warehouse club stores, supercenters, drugstores, restaurant chains, and foodservice distributors in the US and Canada.

Wal-Mart accounts for about 19% of the company's sales.

The mutual fund investment firm FMR owns about 6% of Ralcorp; Wellington Management Company also owns about 6%.

HISTORY

Ralston Purina spun off Ralcorp Holdings, then a maker of name-brand and private-label foods, in 1994 under co-CEOs Richard Pearce and Joe Micheletto. Ralston was concerned that its huge pet food and Eveready battery interests had overshadowed its smaller consumer foods and ski resort businesses.

A cereal price war in 1996 ate at Ralcorp's price advantage and devoured margins. To focus on its core private-label business, in 1997 the firm sold its branded snack and cereal businesses (which included Cookie Crisp and Chex) to General Mills for about $570 million, and its ski resort holdings to Vail Resorts for $310 million (it received a 22% stake in Vail; shares were gradually reduced until by 2009, Ralcorp owned less than 5%). Pearce resigned while the sales were in progress; Micheletto stayed on as CEO.

The company expanded its cookie and cracker division by adding the Wortz Company (the #2 US private-label cracker and cookie maker) for about $46 million in 1997 and Sugar Kake Cookie the following year. In 1998 Ralcorp entered a new private-label category, snack nuts, by purchasing nut makers Flavor House and Nutcracker Brands. Faced with price competition and decreasing demand, it sold its Beech-Nut baby food business that year for $68 million to the Milnot company.

To broaden its private-label portfolio further, in early 1999 Ralcorp bought Martin Gillet (mayonnaise and salad dressings) and Southern Roasted Nuts of Georgia. In late 1999 the company bought Ripon Foods (cookies, sugar wafers, breakfast bars). And, seeing breakfast cereal sales shrinking, Ralcorp purchased Ripon Foods in 1999 — in part, for its ability to make private-label breakfast bars.

In 2000 Ralcorp purchased private-label chocolate candy maker James P. Linette and the Cascade Cookie Company. That same year it bought Red Wing (syrups, peanut butter, jelly, barbecue sauce) from Tomkins for about $132 million. Also in 2000 Ralcorp said it would merge with animal feed company Agribrands International, but the agreement fell through. Additionally that year the company said it would buy Genesee Corporation's Ontario Foods business (powdered drinks, soups, prepared meals) for $50 million, but called off that deal too.

During 2002 Ralcorp purchased cookie-maker Lofthouse Foods. Early in 2003 it sold off its industrial tomato paste facility. Later that same year, Ralcorp purchased frozen breakfast foods company Bakery Chef for $287.5 million. In 2004 the company acquired Concept 2 Bakers (C2B), a frozen, par-baked artisan bread maker, from McGlynn Bakeries. The next year it purchased private-label corn-snack (tortillas) manufacturer Medallion Foods and Canadian private-label griddle-product maker Western Waffles.

It purchased Parco Foods, a Chicago-based cookie maker for in-store bakeries, and Cottage Bakeries, a frozen bread dough maker, in 2006. Its 2007 purchase of Bakery Chef (frozen foodservice pancakes and waffles) allowed Ralcorp to reach people eating breakfast at restaurants. It bought Bloomfield Bakers for about $140 million that year as well. The deal included Bloomfield affiliate Lovin Oven. Bloomfield makes nutritional and cereal bars.

In 2009 Ralcorp purchased Harvest Manor Farms, a Cedar Rapids, Iowa-based maker of private-label and Hoody's-branded nuts. Harvest Manor products strengthened Ralcorp's snack food portfolio.

In July 2010 Ralcorp acquired American Italian Pasta Company, a leading US manufacturer of dry pasta.

EXECUTIVES

Chairman: William P. (Bill) Stiritz, age 75
Co-CEO, President, and Director: Kevin J. Hunt, age 58, $1,486,410 total compensation
Co-CEO, President, and Director; CEO and Interim President, Post Foods: David P. Skarie, age 63, $1,969,031 total compensation
Corporate VP and Chief Accounting Officer: Thomas G. Granneman, age 60, $556,312 total compensation
Corporate VP; President, Cereal Products: Ronald D. (Ron) Wilkinson, age 59, $655,065 total compensation
Corporate VP; President, Carriage House, Bremner Food Group, and Nutcracker Brands: Richard R. Koulouris, age 53, $705,665 total compensation
Corporate VP, Treasurer, Corporate Development Officer: Scott D. Monette, age 48
VP; President, Ralcorp Frozen Bakery Products: Charles G. (Chuck) Huber Jr., age 45
VP, General Counsel, and Secretary: Gregory A. (Greg) Billhartz
VP and Director Human Resources: Jack Owczarczak
President and CEO, American Italian Pasta: John P. (Jack) Kelly, age 58
EVP and COO, American Italian Pasta: Walter N. (Walt) George, age 54
Director Business Development: Matt Pudlowski
Auditors: PricewaterhouseCoopers LLP

LOCATIONS

HQ: Ralcorp Holdings, Inc.
800 Market St., St. Louis, MO 63101
Phone: 314-877-7000   **Fax:** 314-877-7900
Web: www.ralcorp.com

PRODUCTS/OPERATIONS

2009 Sales

	$ mil.	% of total
Cereals	1,873.9	48
Snacks	793.7	20
Frozen bakery products	694.8	18
Sauces & spreads	529.5	14
Total	**3,891.9**	**100**

Selected Branded Products

3 Minute Brand (instant breakfast cereal)
Bremner (snacks)
Cascade (cookies)
Champagne (crackers)
Flavor House (snack nuts)
Golden Grain (pasta)
Heartland (pasta)
Hoody's (snack nuts)
JERO (bottled non-alcoholic cocktail mixes)
Lofthouse (cookies)
Krusteaz (frozen breakfast foods)
Major Peters' (bottled non-alcoholic cocktail mixes)
Medallion (corn and tortilla chips)
Mrs. Grass (pasta)
Nutcracker (snack nuts)
Panne Provincio (in-store bakery bread)
Parco (cookies)
Post (ready-to-eat breakfast cereal)
  Grape-Nuts
  Honey Bunches of Oats
  Honeycomb
  Pebbles
  Post Selects
  Raisin Bran
  Shredded Wheat
  Spoon Size Shredded Wheat
  Trail Mix Crunch
Ralson (hot breakfast cereal)
Rippin' Good (cookies)
Ry Krisp (crackers)

COMPETITORS

ak-mak Bakeries	Malt-O-Meal
Annie's, Inc.	Marzetti
Barilla	McKee Foods
Campbell Soup	National Grape Cooperative
Cento	New World Pasta
Colavita	NORPAC
Dakota Growers	Otis Spunkmeyer
Eden Foods	Pepperidge Farm
Fehr Foods	PepsiCo
Frito-Lay	Renée's Gourmet Foods
General Mills	Rossi Pasta
Gilster-Mary Lee	Sara Lee
Heinz	Silver Lake Cookie
Interbake Foods	Smucker
John Sanfilippo & Son	Unilever PLC
Kellogg	Voortman Cookies
Kraft Foods	Welch's
Lance Snacks	

HISTORICAL FINANCIALS

Company Type: Public

Income Statement

FYE: September 30

	REVENUE ($ mil.)	NET INCOME ($ mil.)	NET PROFIT MARGIN	EMPLOYEES
9/09	3,892	290	7.5%	9,350
9/08	2,824	168	5.9%	9,000
9/07	2,233	32	1.4%	7,800
9/06	1,850	68	3.7%	6,500
9/05	1,675	71	4.3%	6,370
Annual Growth	**23.5%**	**42.0%**	**—**	**10.1%**

2009 Year-End Financials

Debt ratio: 59.6%
Return on equity: 11.4%
Cash ($ mil.): 283
Current ratio: 1.99
Long-term debt ($ mil.): 1,611

No. of shares (mil.): 55
Dividends
  Yield: —
  Payout: —
Market value ($ mil.): 3,210

NYSE: RAH

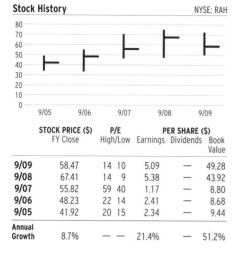

	STOCK PRICE ($) FY Close	P/E High/Low		PER SHARE ($) Earnings	Dividends	Book Value
9/09	58.47	14	10	5.09	—	49.28
9/08	67.41	14	9	5.38	—	43.92
9/07	55.82	59	40	1.17	—	8.80
9/06	48.23	22	14	2.41	—	8.68
9/05	41.92	20	15	2.34	—	9.44
Annual Growth	8.7%	—	—	21.4%	—	51.2%

Raymond James Financial

You could call it Ray. You could call it Ray Jay. But Raymond James Financial will do just fine. The company offers investment and financial planning services primarily through subsidiary Raymond James & Associates (RJA), which provides securities brokerage, investment banking, and financial advisory services throughout the US; and Raymond James Financial Services, which offers financial planning and brokerage services through independent contractors, as well as through alliances with community banks. Other divisions provide asset management, trust, and retail banking services. Raymond James Financial has approximately 2,300 offices worldwide.

The company's business is divided into seven primary segments. The Private Client Group is the largest, accounting for more than half of the company's sales; it provides retail brokerage and financial planning services to nearly 2 million customers in the US, Canada, and the UK. The Asset Management segment includes Eagle Asset Management, Eagle Fund Management (formerly Heritage Asset Management), and Eagle Boston Investment Management. Building its capital markets business, which performs investment banking and equity research services, Raymond James Financial acquired Boston-based boutique investment bank Lane, Berry & Co. International in 2009.

Raymond James Bank (RJBank), securities lending, proprietary investments, and the Emerging Markets segment, which is involved in joint ventures in Latin America, round out Raymond James Financial's operations.

In response to turmoil in the financial markets, the firm plans to switch to a financial services holding company structure. Raymond James has said it had been mulling the move for a while, and that economic conditions hastened its decision. The move should help the company continue to build its burgeoning portfolio of usually more-profitable commercial loans.

In 2006 Raymond James extended its deal to attach its name to the home stadium of the NFL's Tampa Bay Buccaneers through 2015.

Chairman Thomas James owns about 18% of Raymond James Financial. James stepped down as CEO in 2010; he was succeeded by Paul Reilly, a former CEO of executive recruitment company Korn/Ferry and Big Four accounting firm KPMG International.

HISTORY

Robert James, often called the "founder of financial planning," first started a construction business in Ohio after his WWII service in the US Navy, and then began a Florida home-building company. He got into the financial services business in 1954 with Florida Mutual Fund, a company he and Gerard Jobin formed that eventually became American National Growth Fund. But when most companies were selling just stocks or mutual funds, James saw a need for a more comprehensive approach to investing. He decided to focus on helping individual clients, learning about their financial needs and goals and then working with them on everything from investments to taxes. To that end, he began offering seminars for retirees.

In 1960 those seminars had turned into a new company, James and Associates, which two years later became Robert A. James Investments. In 1964 James acquired Raymond and Associates, a firm started by Edward Raymond in 1962; the newly merged firm was renamed Raymond James & Associates (RJA).

James' son Thomas joined the firm in 1966, the year the company's revenues first surpassed $1 million. Over the next several years, the company expanded its investment offerings and set up new divisions. It added Investment Management & Research as an affiliate broker/dealer in 1967 and Planning Corporation of America as a general insurance agency in 1968.

Raymond James Financial (RJF) incorporated as a holding company in 1969, and Thomas James became CEO the next year. RJA formed Eagle Asset Management in 1975, RJ Oil & Gas (subsidiary for oil and gas limited partnerships) in 1977, securities and real estate subsidiaries in 1980 (Robert Thomas Securities and RJ Properties, respectively), and an equipment leasing subsidiary (RJ Leasing) in 1982.

RJF went public in 1983, the year Robert James died. Two years later the company organized its Heritage Family of Funds. RJA became an international company in the late 1980s, opening an office in Paris in 1987 and in Geneva the next year. It also began offering a cash management program in 1988 and began its Stock Loan Department. Trust and banking subsidiaries were begun in 1992 and 1994, respectively, followed by the creation of Equity Capital Markets Group in 1996.

In 2000 RJF crossed the billion-dollar-mark, hitting $1.7 billion in sales. That year it acquired Canadian investment firm Goepel McDermid Inc., (renamed Raymond James Ltd.) to offer individual and institutional investment services to the Canadian market, and it launched Raymond James Killik (a UK joint venture that became Raymond James Investment Services in 2002). In 2006 RJF reduced front-end commissions with variations of variable annuity products; the next year it kicked off its Wealth Solutions department, a unit designed to help high-net-worth clients and their advisors.

EXECUTIVES

Chairman: Thomas A. (Tom) James, age 67, $2,750,931 total compensation
Vice Chairman: Francis S. (Bo) Godbold, age 66
President, CEO, and Director: Paul C. Reilly, age 54
COO and Director: Chester B. (Chet) Helck, age 57, $1,692,135 total compensation
EVP Finance and CFO: Jeffrey P. (Jeff) Julien, age 53, $1,063,094 total compensation
EVP Asset Management; CEO, Eagle Asset Management: Richard K. Riess, age 60, $1,739,581 total compensation
EVP Equity Capital Markets: Jeffrey E. Trocin, age 50
SVP and Chief Risk Officer: George Catanese, age 50
SVP, General Counsel, and Director Compliance, and Secretary: Paul L. Matecki, age 53
SVP, Controller, and Chief Accounting Officer: Jennifer C. Ackart, age 45
SVP and CIO: J. Timothy (Tim) Eitel, age 60
SVP Human Resources: Pam Ward
Chief Administrative Officer: Angela M. Biever, age 56
Chairman and CEO, Raymond James Financial Services: Richard G. (Dick) Averitt III, age 64
President, Raymond James & Associates: Dennis W. Zank, age 55
EVP Operations and Administration, Raymond James & Associates: Thomas R. (Thom) Tremaine, age 53
SVP and Manager Fixed Income Department, Raymond James and Associates: Van C. Sayler, age 54, $3,211,780 total compensation
President and CEO, Raymond James Bank: Steven M. Raney, age 44
President and CEO, Raymond James Ltd.: Paul D. Allison, age 53
Senior Managing Director and Head, Investment Banking, Raymond James Ltd.: Jason Holtby
Managing Director, Investment Banking and Head of Mergers and Acquisitions: Jeremy Rakusin
Manager Public Relations: Anthea Penrose
Auditors: KPMG LLP

LOCATIONS

HQ: Raymond James Financial, Inc.
880 Carillon Pkwy., St. Petersburg, FL 33716
Phone: 727-567-1000   **Fax:** 727-567-8915
Web: www.rjf.com

2009 Sales

	$ mil.	% of total
US	2,359.6	91
Canada	186.9	7
Europe	41.4	2
Other	14.6	—
Total	**2,602.5**	**100**

PRODUCTS/OPERATIONS

2009 Sales

	$ mil.	% of total
Securities commissions & fees	1,634.3	63
Interest	443.6	17
Investment advisory fees	147.8	6
Financial service fees	126.5	5
Investment banking	95.1	3
Net trading profits	48.0	2
Other	107.2	4
Total	**2,602.5**	**100**

2009 Sales By Segment

	$ mil.	% of total
Private Client Group	1,557.5	58
Capital Markets	533.2	20
RJBank	343.4	13
Asset Management	177.4	7
Other	45.0	2
Intersegment eliminations	(54.0)	—
Total	**2,602.5**	**100**

Selected Subsidiaries

Eagle Asset Management, Inc.
Lane, Berry & Co. International
Raymond James & Associates
Raymond James Bank, FSB (dba RJBank)
Raymond James Capital Partners, L.P.
Raymond James Financial Services
Raymond James Investment Services Limited (UK, 75%)
Raymond James Ltd. (Canada)
Raymond James Trust, N.A.

COMPETITORS

Charles Schwab
Citigroup
Deutsche Bank Alex. Brown
E*TRADE Financial
Edward Jones
FMR
Legg Mason
LPL Investment Holdings
Merrill Lynch
Morgan Keegan
Morgan Stanley
Piper Jaffray
Principal Financial
TD Ameritrade
UBS Financial Services
Wells Fargo Advisors

HISTORICAL FINANCIALS

Company Type: Public

Income Statement

FYE: September 30

	REVENUE ($ mil.)	NET INCOME ($ mil.)	NET PROFIT MARGIN	EMPLOYEES
9/09	2,603	153	5.9%	7,100
9/08	3,205	235	7.3%	6,900
9/07	3,110	250	8.1%	5,788
9/06	2,633	214	8.1%	6,616
9/05	2,157	151	7.0%	6,790
Annual Growth	4.8%	0.3%	—	1.1%

2009 Year-End Financials

Debt ratio: 70.3%
Return on equity: 7.8%
Cash ($ mil.): 2,306
Current ratio: —
Long-term debt ($ mil.): 1,428

No. of shares (mil.): 124
Dividends
Yield: 1.9%
Payout: 34.1%
Market value ($ mil.): 2,888

Stock History

NYSE: RJF

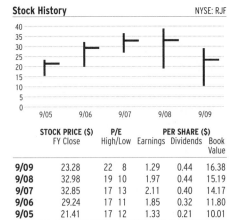

	STOCK PRICE ($) FY Close	P/E High/Low		PER SHARE ($) Earnings	Dividends	Book Value
9/09	23.28	22	8	1.29	0.44	16.38
9/08	32.98	19	10	1.97	0.44	15.19
9/07	32.85	17	13	2.11	0.40	14.17
9/06	29.24	17	11	1.85	0.32	11.80
9/05	21.41	17	12	1.33	0.21	10.01
Annual Growth	2.1%	—	—	(0.8%)	20.3%	13.1%

Raytheon Company

Raytheon ("light of the gods") took a shine to its place in the upper pantheon of US military contractors; the company regularly places among the Pentagon's top 10 prime contractors. Its air/land/sea defense offerings include reconnaissance, targeting, and navigation systems, as well as missile systems (Patriot, Sidewinder, and Tomahawk), unmanned ground and aerial systems, sensing, and radars. Additionally, Raytheon makes systems for communications (satellite) and intelligence, radios, cybersecurity, and air traffic control. It also offers commercial electronics products and services, as well as food safety processing technologies.

While the US government accounts for around 88% of sales, the company has contracts with South Korea to provide air and missile defense systems, with Japan for training, Saudi Arabia for surveillance systems, and Australia for joint standoff weapons. Other main global clients include the United Arab Emirates, Taiwan, Germany, and Finland. The company is gaining a greater presence in the Indian market, having provided air traffic systems to the country, as well as infrared imaging sights and electronics for T-72 tanks to the Indian army.

Raytheon's diverse product lineup is in a better position to weather government budget cuts than some of its competitors that may handle a limited number of defense products and services. Its offerings run the gamut from kill vehicles (ballistic missile interceptors) to pasteurization technology and GPS satellites.

The world's #1 missile maker, Raytheon is a key player in US efforts to construct a comprehensive missile defense system. Such systems need intercept vehicles, sensors, command and control systems, and systems integration expertise, and it is a leader in all those markets.

Raytheon's Intelligence and Information Systems (IIS) segment's products include space-based radars, satellite systems, and communications systems. As for homeland security, the systems Raytheon makes for traditional defense applications are readily transferable to homeland security applications.

Raytheon develops avionics systems, electronic warfare technologies, and fire control radars within its Space and Airborne Systems segment. The company designs and manufactures sensor payload for national programs used in defense and commercial space applications.

Multiple acquisitions reflect Raytheon's focus on building up its security and intelligence services portfolio. The company moved to acquire BBN Technologies in 2009, adding an array of advanced networking, and technologies for speech and language and information, as well as sensor systems, and cyber security. In 2008 it bought Telemus Solutions, a provider of information security and intelligence services and support for military customers.

HISTORY

In 1922 Laurence Marshall and several others founded American Appliance Company to produce home refrigerators. When their invention failed, Marshall began making Raytheon (meaning "light of/from the gods") radio tubes. Raytheon was adopted as the company's name in 1925. It bought the radio division of Chicago's Q. R. S. Company in 1928 and formed Raytheon Production Company with National Carbon Company (makers of the Eveready battery) to market Eveready Raytheon tubes in 1929.

Growing rapidly in WWII, Raytheon became the first producer of magnetrons (tubes used in radar and later in microwave ovens). Wartime sales peaked at $173 million but dwindled by 1947. Amid rumors of bankruptcy, Charles Adams became Raytheon's president. He sold Raytheon's unprofitable radio and TV business in 1956.

In 1964 Adams (then chairman) named missile engineer Thomas Phillips president. Phillips oversaw several purchases designed to balance Raytheon's commercial and military earnings, beginning with Amana Refrigeration (1965), D.C. Heath (textbooks, 1966), Caloric (stoves, 1967), and three petrochemical firms (1966-69).

Raytheon began making computer terminals in 1971 (exited 1984). In 1980 it bought Grumman's Beech Aircraft division. Despite efforts to diversify, Raytheon still relied on missiles, radar, and communications systems for most of its sales in 1987. In 1991 it won an $800 million US Army contract to upgrade Patriot missiles used in the Persian Gulf War. After 43 years with Raytheon, Phillips retired that year, and president Dennis Picard became chairman.

Raytheon expanded as it bought the business jet division of British Aerospace (1993), E-Systems (advanced electronics and surveillance equipment, 1995), and most of Chrysler's aerospace and defense holdings (1996).

By 1997 Raytheon doubled in size and became the #1 US missile maker, after buying Texas Instruments' missile and defense electronics holdings for about $3 billion and Hughes Electronics' (now The DIRECTV Group) defense business for $9.5 billion. Weak sales in Asia hurt Raytheon in 1998, and it announced cuts of some 14,000 defense jobs (16% of the unit's workforce) and the closure of 28 plants over two years. Former AlliedSignal VC Daniel Burnham became CEO in 1998, succeeding Picard. Raytheon also began a legal battle with Hughes, claiming it had been overcharged $1 billion in 1997 for Hughes' defense unit (the suit was settled for about $650 million in 2001).

In 1999 Raytheon cut more jobs, made plans to close or combine 10 facilities, and took a $668 million charge to correct financial problems in its defense electronics business.

Raytheon sold its flight simulation and training business to L-3 Communications for $160 million in 2000 and its engineering and construction unit to Washington Group International (formerly Morrison Knudsen) for about $500 million. Raytheon also sold its optical systems business to BFGoodrich (now Goodrich) and agreed to a joint venture with France-based Thales (formerly Thomson-CSF) to form a joint air defense venture, ThalesRaytheonSystems.

In 2002 Raytheon sold its aircraft integration unit to L-3 Communications for over $1 billion in cash and made a bid for TRW's satellite and missile defense operations. It continued to sell noncore units, including its commercial infrared unit (to L-3 Communications) in 2004.

In 2005 Raytheon agreed to team up with EADS North America to bid on the Army's $1 billion Future Cargo Aircraft program.

In 2007 Raytheon sold Raytheon Aircraft to a new company, Hawker Beechcraft, formed by Goldman Sachs and Onex Corporation, for $3.3 billion. In late 2007 Raytheon sold Flight Options, which provided fractional jet ownership services, to H.I.G. Capital.

EXECUTIVES

Chairman and CEO: William H. Swanson, age 61, $18,636,872 total compensation
EVP Business Development; CEO, Raytheon International: Thomas M. Culligan
SVP and CFO: David C. Wajsgras, age 50, $4,204,945 total compensation
SVP, General Counsel, and Secretary: Jay B. Stephens, age 63, $4,519,451 total compensation
SVP Human Resources: Keith J. Peden, age 59
VP; President, Network Centric Systems: Colin J. R. Schottlaender, age 54, $3,616,240 total compensation
VP; President, Missile Systems: Taylor W. Lawrence, age 46, $3,221,794 total compensation
VP; President, Technical Services: John D. Harris II, age 48
VP; President, Space and Airborne Systems (SAS): Richard R. (Rick) Yuse, age 58
VP; President, Intelligence and Information Systems: Lynn A. Dugle, age 50
VP and Chief Accounting Officer: Michael J. Wood, age 41
VP Engineering, Technology, and Mission Assurance: Mark E. Russell, age 48
VP Investor Relations: Marc Kaplan
VP Corporate Public Affairs: Kristin Hilf
VP Corporate Affairs and Communications: Pamela A. (Pam) Wickham
VP and CIO: Rebecca B. Rhoads
VP and CTO: William F. Kiczuk
VP Global Marketing Communications: Lucy A. Flynn, age 56
Director Investor Relations: Jim Singer
President, Integrated Defense Systems: Thomas A. (Tom) Kennedy, age 55
President, Asia, Raytheon International: Walter F. Doran
Auditors: PricewaterhouseCoopers LLP

LOCATIONS

HQ: Raytheon Company
870 Winter St., Waltham, MA 02451
Phone: 781-522-3000   **Fax:** 781-522-3001
Web: www.raytheon.com

2009 Sales

	$ mil.	% of total
US	19,618	79
Asia/Pacific	2,470	10
Europe & other regions	1,577	6
Middle East & North Africa	1,216	5
Total	**24,881**	**100**

PRODUCTS/OPERATIONS

2009 Sales

	$ mil.	% of total
Missile Systems	5,561	21
Integrated Defense Systems	5,525	20
Network Centric Systems	4,822	18
Space & Airborne Systems	4,582	17
Intelligence & Information Systems	3,204	12
Technical Services	3,161	12
Adjustments	(1,974)	—
Total	**24,881**	**100**

Selected Products

Integrated Defense Systems
  Aegis Weapon Systems radar equipment
  AN/AQS Minehunting Sonar System
  Joint Land Attack Cruise Missile Defense Elevated
    Netted Sensor (JLENS)
  Landing Platform Dock Amphibious Ship LPD-17
  Patriot Air and Missile Defense System
  Sea-Based X-Band Radar (SBX)
  Ship Self-Defense System (SSDS)
  Surface-Launched AMRAAM (SLAMRAAM)
  Terminal High Altitude Area Defense (THAAD) Radar
Intelligence and Information Systems
  Army Research Lab
  Communications systems
  Department of Education programs

Distributed Common Ground System
Emergency Patient Tracking System
Global Broadcast Service
Global Hawk Ground Segment
Information solutions programs
Managed data storage solutions
Mobile Very Small Aperture Satellite Terminal
National Polar-Orbiting Operational Environmental
  Satellite System Program
RedWolf telecommunications surveillance
Signal and imagery intelligence programs
Supercomputing
U-2 (field support)
UAV systems and ground stations
Missile Systems
  Advanced Medium-Range Air-to-Air missile (AMRAAM)
  AIM-9X Sidewinder
  Evolved SeaSparrow (ESSM)
  Excalibur long-range artillery system
  Exoatmospheric Kill Vehicle
  Extended Range Guided Munition (ERGM)
  High-Speed Anti-Radiation Missile Targeting System
  Paveway laser-guided bombs
  Maverick AGM-65 missiles
  Tomahawk and Tactical Tomahawk cruise missiles
  TOW, Javelin, Phalanx, Standard, and SeaRAM missiles
Network Centric Systems
  Airspace management and homeland security
  Command and control systems
  Combat systems
  Integrated communications systems
  Precision technologies and components
Space and Airborne Systems
  Active electronically scanned array radars
  Airborne radars and processors
  Electronic warfare systems
  Electro-optic/infrared sensors
  Intelligence, surveillance, and reconnaissance systems
  Space and missile defense technology
Technical Services
  Base operations
  Logistics support
  Maintenance support
  Professional services
  Treaty compliance monitoring
  Weapons security and destruction

COMPETITORS

BAE Systems Inc.	L-3 Avionics
Boeing	Lockheed Martin
Crane Aerospace	MBDA
Emerson Electric	Meggitt USA
Fluor	Northrop Grumman
GE	Olin
Harris Corp.	Rockwell Collins
Herley Industries	Saab AB
Honeywell Aerospace	Sierra Nevada Corp
Interstate Electronics	Sperry Marine
ITT Defense	

HISTORICAL FINANCIALS

Company Type: Public

Income Statement

FYE: December 31

	REVENUE ($ mil.)	NET INCOME ($ mil.)	NET PROFIT MARGIN	EMPLOYEES
12/09	24,881	1,976	7.9%	75,000
12/08	23,174	1,672	7.2%	73,000
12/07	21,301	2,578	12.1%	72,100
12/06	20,291	1,283	6.3%	80,000
12/05	21,894	871	4.0%	80,000
Annual Growth	3.2%	22.7%	—	(1.6%)

2009 Year-End Financials

Debt ratio: 23.7%
Return on equity: 20.9%
Cash ($ mil.): 2,642
Current ratio: 1.42
Long-term debt ($ mil.): 2,329

No. of shares (mil.): 374
Dividends
  Yield: 2.4%
  Payout: 25.4%
Market value ($ mil.): 19,274

HOOVER'S HANDBOOK OF AMERICAN BUSINESS 2011

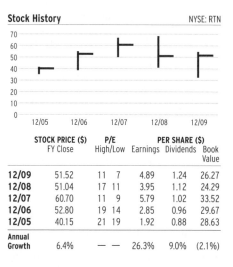

Stock History   NYSE: RTN

	STOCK PRICE ($) FY Close	P/E High/Low		PER SHARE ($) Earnings	Dividends	Book Value
12/09	51.52	11	7	4.89	1.24	26.27
12/08	51.04	17	11	3.95	1.12	24.29
12/07	60.70	11	9	5.79	1.02	33.52
12/06	52.80	19	14	2.85	0.96	29.67
12/05	40.15	21	19	1.92	0.88	28.63
Annual Growth	6.4%	—	—	26.3%	9.0%	(2.1%)

Regions Financial

Regions Financial ain't just whistling Dixie anymore. The holding company for Regions Bank, which sprouted in the South, has grown by acquiring other financial services firms over the years. Regions has some 1,900 branches in 16 states, roughly stretching from the Southeast and Texas northward through the Mississippi River Valley in the US heartland. It also owns investment bank and brokerage Morgan Keegan, which has more than 300 offices on its parent's turf, plus New York and Massachusetts. In addition to traditional banking, Regions offers a variety of other services, including mortgage banking (Regions Mortgage), and life, health, and property/casualty insurance (Regions Insurance).

Another unit, Regions Interstate Billing Service, factors accounts receivable and performs billing and collection services, primarily for the automotive service industry. Regions Financial has stated that it is seeking growth in non-banking operations such as check card and merchant services, treasury management, and capital markets.

Since its inception in 1971, the company has looked for acquisitions in order to grow geographically and diversify its product and services mix. It fortified its foothold in the South and expanded into the Midwest with its blockbuster merger with Union Planters in 2004. Regions Financial later acquired fellow Birmingham-based bank AmSouth for nearly $10 billion in stock. The AmSouth deal created one of the 10 largest banks in the US and helped the company keep pace with other megabanks in its markets, such as Bank of America and SunTrust. The deals also helped entrench Regions in states such as Alabama, Arkansas, Mississippi, and Tennessee, where it is a market leader.

However, economic conditions have forced Regions Financial to shed some of its weight. After the mortgage sector got battered by the housing bust and rising interest rates, the company in 2007 sold its subprime mortgage origination unit EquiFirst to Barclays Bank (the flagship subsidiary of UK-based Barclays). Regions Financial has also been disposing of problem assets and has reduced its portfolio of loans secured by investment real estate and construction.

The market turmoil also has provided opportunities. In 2008 Regions Financial assumed control of the branches and deposits of failed Atlanta-area financial institution Integrity Bank in an FDIC-assisted transaction; it did the same with another failed Georgia bank, FirstBank Financial Services, in 2009.

HISTORY

Regions Financial was created out of three venerable Alabama banks. The oldest, First National Bank of Huntsville, was founded in 1855. When, 10 years later, the bank was besieged by Union troops, a loyal cashier hid securities in the chimney and refused to tell the soldiers where they were. A few years later it was robbed by Jesse James (for years the bank kept in its vaults a gun purported to belong to a James gang member). First National Bank of Montgomery was founded in 1871, and Exchange Security Bank in 1928.

Banking veteran Frank Plummer consolidated the three banks to form Alabama's first multibank holding company, First Alabama Bancshares, in 1971. The combined firm then became the bank that ate Alabama. But even as it gobbled up other banks, its diet remained bland: Its lending programs were modest and focused on a narrow range of business.

The bank's growth in the 1980s was solid, if unexciting, as it picked up community banks in Alabama (Anniston National Bank and South Baldwin Bank, among others) and Georgia (Georgia Co., a mortgage subsidiary of Columbus Bank and Trust). Before he died in 1987, Plummer brought in Willard Hurley as chairman. Hurley put the brakes on acquisitions when they overloaded the bank's data-processing systems. He also put the company up for sale, igniting its stock price for a while, but there were no serious suitors.

When Hurley passed the baton to Stanley Mackin in 1990 the bank was still rumored to be for sale. But Mackin had other ideas. He put the bank back on its acquisition track and raised the bar on profitability expectations for each department. In 1993 Mackin orchestrated First Alabama's purchase of Secor, a failed New Orleans thrift, outbidding rival AmSouth Bancorporation. The Secor purchase raised eyebrows, but First Alabama sold some branches and folded other operations into its organization.

In 1994 First Alabama changed its name to Regions Financial in order to reflect its out-of-state operations. The next year Regions rolled into Georgia in a big way, leaping from a few banks to holdings with approximately $4 billion in assets. Rumors of a merger with either Wachovia or SunTrust Banks popped up in 1996, but the bank continued on its independent course. The next year the company's tank-like progress was halted when it was outbid for Mississippi's Deposit Guaranty Corp. by First American.

By way of consolation, Regions in 1998 bought First Commercial Corp. of Little Rock, paying a premium price for its 26 banks, mortgage company, and investment company. Regions also acquired 13 other companies that year and began a major overhaul of its systems concurrently with the assimilation of these operations. This effort included the consolidation of the back-office aspects of its retail and indirect lending operations.

Mackin retired in 1998, and banking veteran Carl Jones Jr. became CEO. Under his direction the bank continued its geographic infill strategy with acquisitions of banks and branches in Arkansas, Florida, Louisiana, Tennessee, and Texas in 1999 and 2000. The company also sold its credit card portfolio to MBNA (since acquired by Bank of America) and in 2001 acquired Memphis-based investment bank Morgan Keegan.

Jones helped mastermind the $6 billion acquisition of Union Planters in 2004; he stepped down as CEO after the merger, but remained Regions' chairman until 2006. Jackson Moore, chairman and CEO of Union Planters, took over the reins of Regions as president and CEO. The company's acquisition of AmSouth for $10 billion in 2006 saw yet another change in leadership, with Moore becoming executive chairman and AmSouth's top executive, C. Dowd Ritter, becoming chairman, president, and CEO.

In 2009 Ritter stepped down as CEO. He was succeeded by former company president Grayson Hall, who initially joined Regions Financial's management trainee program in 1980. Ritter will continue to provide consulting services to the company until 2015.

EXECUTIVES

Chairman: Earnest W. (Earnie) Deavenport Jr., age 72
President, CEO, and Director: O. B. Grayson Hall Jr., age 53, $4,227,745 total compensation
SEVP and CFO: David J. Turner Jr., age 46
SEVP; President, Business Services Banking Group: G. Timothy (Tim) Laney, age 49, $2,175,026 total compensation
SEVP; Chief Risk Officer and Head, Risk Management Group: William C. (Bill) Wells II, age 50, $1,652,011 total compensation
SEVP, Corporate Secretary, and General Counsel: John D. Buchanan
SEVP Consumer Services Group: John B. Owen, age 49
Chief Administrative Officer: David B. Edmonds, age 56, $2,785,601 total compensation
Chief Marketing Officer: Scott Peters
Controller and Chief Accounting Officer: Brad Kimbrough, age 45
EVP Capital Markets: Chris Grubbs
EVP Commercial and Industrial Banking: Sam Tortorici
EVP Corporate Security: William Burch
EVP eBusiness: Pat Scott
EVP Bank Operations: Cindy Rogers
EVP Private Banking: James B. (Jim) Nonnengard
EVP Community Banking: Mike Hart
EVP Regions Mortgage: E. Todd Chamberlain
EVP HR Systems and Administration: Christine Germanson
EVP Compliance: Jim Pihera
Investor Relations: M. List Underwood Jr.
Corporate Communications: Evelyn Mitchell
CEO Morgan Keegan: John C. Carson Jr., age 53
Auditors: Ernst & Young LLP

LOCATIONS

HQ: Regions Financial Corporation
1900 5th Ave. North, Birmingham, AL 35203
Phone: 205-944-1300 **Fax:** 901-580-3915
Web: www.regions.com

2009 Branches

	No.	% of total
Florida	420	22
Tennessee	296	16
Alabama	248	13
Georgia	159	8
Mississippi	155	8
Louisiana	129	7
Arkansas	112	6
Texas	84	4
Illinois	71	4
Missouri	69	4
Indiana	66	4
South Carolina	37	2
Kentucky	19	1
Iowa	18	1
North Carolina	9	—
Virginia	3	—
Total	**1,895**	**100**

PRODUCTS/OPERATIONS

2009 Sales

	$ mil.	% of total
Interest		
Loans, including fees	4,199	46
Securities	985	11
Other	148	1
Noninterest		
Service charges on deposit accounts	1,156	13
Brokerage, investment banking & capital markets	989	11
Mortgage income	259	3
Trust department income	191	2
Other	1,160	13
Total	**9,087**	**100**

COMPETITORS

Arvest Bank
Bank of America
BB&T
Capital One
Citigroup
Compass Bancshares
First Citizens BancShares
First Horizon
JPMorgan Chase
RBC Bank
SunTrust
Synovus Financial
Trustmark
Wells Fargo
Woodforest Financial

HISTORICAL FINANCIALS

Company Type: Public

Income Statement

FYE: December 31

	ASSETS ($ mil.)	NET INCOME ($ mil.)	INCOME AS % OF ASSETS	EMPLOYEES
12/09	142,318	(1,031)	—	30,000
12/08	146,248	(5,596)	—	30,784
12/07	141,042	1,251	0.9%	33,161
12/06	143,369	1,353	0.9%	35,900
12/05	84,786	1,001	1.2%	25,000
Annual Growth	**13.8%**	**—**	**—**	**4.7%**

2009 Year-End Financials

Equity as % of assets: 10.0%   Dividends
Return on assets: —   Yield: 2.5%
Return on equity: —   Payout: —
Long-term debt ($ mil.): 18,464   Market value ($ mil.): 6,308
No. of shares (mil.): 1,192   Sales ($ mil.): 9,087

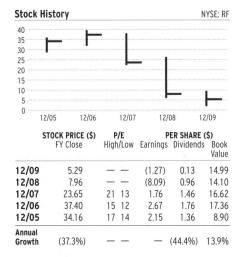

Stock History   NYSE: RF

	STOCK PRICE ($)	P/E		PER SHARE ($)		
	FY Close	High/Low	Earnings	Dividends	Book Value
12/09	5.29	— —	(1.27)	0.13	14.99
12/08	7.96	— —	(8.09)	0.96	14.10
12/07	23.65	21 13	1.76	1.46	16.62
12/06	37.40	15 12	2.67	1.76	17.36
12/05	34.16	17 14	2.15	1.36	8.90
Annual Growth	(37.3%)	— —	—	(44.4%)	13.9%

Regis Corporation

Regis is hair, there, and everywhere. It is the world's largest operator of hair salons, with about 12,900 company-owned or franchised salons (primarily in the US) and about 95 Hair Club for Men and Women hair restoration centers. Formats range from mall-based to Wal-Mart-based (2,400 SmartStyle and Cost Cutters). The salons sell hair care products branded under the Regis, MasterCuts, and Cost Cutters names. Regis also runs a variety of store formats in strip malls, including more than 5,400 franchised and company-owned shops. The sale of hair care products accounts for more than 20% of sales. Headquartered in Minneapolis, Minnesota, the company has more than 440 locations in the UK and Germany.

The company's North American salons account for more than 85% of its revenues. Most of those sales are to women, but the company is testing a new concept, Raze, aimed at men looking for a more sophisticated experience than typical sport-related men's hair cutters and barbershops. Regis's varied salon concepts also target different price points, with walk-in Supercuts and Cost Cutters locations offering low-priced haircuts, Regis and Sassoon brand salons charging a bit more, and appointment-needed Jean Louis David salons at the high end of the price spectrum.

Despite its size, Regis still commands only a small percentage of the highly fractured US market. It has been sweeping up market share through the construction of new salons and acquisitions both internationally and at home. Since 1995, Regis has acquired more than 8,000 salons. However, competition within the personal hair care industry is prompting Regis to evaluate its 10,000-plus company-owned salons; it closed more than 300 salons in fiscal 2009 to help enhance profitability. It laid off 150 people from corporate HQ about the same time. Also, Regis sold its Trade Secret beauty products retail division to Premier Salon in early 2009 in a bid to focus the company on its salon operations as opposed to hair care product sales.

The salon closures came on the heels of the company's efforts to boost its stake in the European hair care market. It completed a merger of its continental European franchise salon operations with the Franck Provost Salon Group in early 2008. As part of the deal, Regis owns a 30% minority interest in the newly formed Provalliance Group, now the largest hair salon company in Europe. Regis retained sole ownership of its salons in the UK and Germany. In Japan, Regis owns an equity interest in My Style salons. Regis also owns a 49% stake in Intelligent Nutrients, a business that provides a wide variety of certified organic products for health and beauty.

To keep its shops stocked with trained professionals, the company owns a majority stake in Empire Education Group, which runs nearly 100 cosmetology training centers.

HISTORY

Russian-born immigrant Paul Kunin started with one local barbershop in Minneapolis in 1922. Within the next three decades he owned 60 salons, which were mainly leased departments in stores. Paul sold the business in 1954 to his son Myron and daughter Diana. Myron bought Diana's share some years later.

Once at the helm, Myron shifted stores into the enclosed malls that sprouted during the 1960s. Eschewing franchising, Regis benefited from the complete control of its stores, maintaining an upscale image that fared well against small-time salons. By 1975 the company had 161 salons and it grew during the late 1970s and early 1980s. Regis went public in 1983.

The next year it attempted to diversify from its largely female clientele with the purchase of Your Father's Mustache, a chain of 60 barbershops. However, the unsuccessful attempt caused earnings to suffer for two years while Regis converted the shops into other formats.

Wanting to reward its managers with company ownership, Regis went private again in 1988, taking on a heavy load of debt. This hindered Myron's efforts to expand in the department store niche. In response, in 1990 he joined MEI Diversified, a cash-rich investment company, to form MEI-Regis Salon (of which MEI owned 80%) in order to buy Essanelle (department store salons).

However, the deal quickly gave all parties a bad hair day: Lawsuits, claims of mismanagement and misrepresentation, and poor earnings conspired to destroy the partnership. MEI-Regis went public again in 1991, but the offering did not make enough to pay bank debt, and it posted a loss. MEI and Regis sued each other in 1992, and Regis called for unpaid expenses related to management while MEI accused Regis of fraud and racketeering.

While all this was going on, Regis continued to expand. Acquisitions such as Trade Secret (1993) moved Regis into higher-margin beauty products. MEI went into Chapter 11 in 1993 and the dispute between the companies was finally settled in bankruptcy court, costing Regis $15 million.

Over the next two years, Regis expanded both in the US and abroad. Overseas, the company bought some 170 UK salons in 1995 and 1996. It moved away from its mall stronghold with the purchase of competitor Supercuts in 1996, adding more than 1,100 stores, mainly in strip malls. Then #2, Supercuts was struggling; ousted CEO David Lipson sued and won a $6.7 million settlement from Regis in 1997. Also in 1996 Regis

bought 154 salons operating inside Wal-Mart stores from National Hair Centers. That year COO Paul Finkelstein was promoted to CEO.

The firm took another giant step forward in 1999 when it bought The Barbers, Hairstyling for Men & Women, an operator of about 980 salons, including the Cost Cutters and We Care Hair chains. The deal made Regis the only provider of salon services in Wal-Mart stores.

Regis continued making acquisitions, including Haircrafters, about 550 salons mostly in Canada, and 523 franchised salons in France.

International expansion continued in 2002 with its acquisition of Jean Louis David, Europe's #1 salon chain (nearly 1,200 salons). In May 2004 Myron Kunin stepped down as chairman, passing his title to longtime CEO Finkelstein. Kunin assumed the role of vice chairman.

In December 2004 Regis added significantly to its hair restoration operations when it inked a deal to make Hair Club for Men and Women a wholly owned subsidiary.

In 2007 Regis combined its beauty school business with that of a rival school operator, Empire Education Group. It took a 49% stake in the expanded Empire Education Group, which following the transaction owns nearly 90 schools.

EXECUTIVES

Chairman, President, and CEO: Paul D. Finkelstein, age 67, $7,628,470 total compensation
SEVP, Chief Administrative Officer, and CFO: Randy L. Pearce, age 54, $1,828,403 total compensation
EVP Design and Construction: Bruce D. Johnson, age 55, $1,022,263 total compensation
EVP Fashion, Education, and Marketing: Gordon B. Nelson, age 58, $1,308,905 total compensation
EVP; President, Franchise Division: Mark Kartarik, age 53, $1,129,164 total compensation
EVP Merchandising: Norma Knudsen, age 51
SVP and President, SmartStyle Family Hair Salons: C. John Briggs, age 65
SVP and International Managing Director, UK: Jackie Lang
SVP Law, General Counsel, and Secretary: Eric A. Bakken, age 42
President and CEO, Hair Club for Men and Women: Darryll Porter, age 46
President, International Division: Andrew Cohen, age 46
COO, Promenade Salon Concepts: Amy Edwards, age 40
COO, SmartStyle Family Hair Care: John Exline, age 46
COO, Supercuts: Diane Calta, age 40
COO, MasterCuts: David Bortnem, age 42
Public Relations: Leann Dake
Auditors: PricewaterhouseCoopers LLP

LOCATIONS

HQ: Regis Corporation
7201 Metro Blvd., Minneapolis, MN 55439
Phone: 952-947-7777   **Fax:** 952-947-7600
Web: www.regiscorp.com

2009 Salons

	No.
North America	
Company-owned	7,537
Franchised	2,045
International (company-owned)	444
Total	**10,026**

2009 Sales

	$ mil.	% of total
North America (includes Hair Club)	2,258.2	93
International	171.6	7
Total	**2,429.8**	**100**

PRODUCTS/OPERATIONS

2009 Sales

	$ mil.	% of total
Salons		
North America	2,117.7	87
International	171.6	7
Hair restoration centers	140.5	6
Total	**2,429.8**	**100**

2009 Company-Owned Salons

	No.
Promenade	3,351
SmartStyle/Cost Cutters	2,422
Supercuts	2,136
Regis	1,071
International	444
Mastercuts	602
Total	**10,026**

2009 Sales

	% of total
Service	75
Product	23
Royalties & fees	2
Total	**100**

Selected Stores

BoRics (regional strip-center salons)
Cost Cutters (national strip-center salons and Wal-Mart store salons)
Famous Hair (national strip-center salons)
First Choice Haircutters (national strip-center salons)
Hair Masters (regional strip-center salons)
Jean Louis David (international salons)
Magicuts (national strip-center salons)
MasterCuts Family Haircutters (regional-mall salons)
Mia & Maxx Hair Studios (regional-mall salons)
Raze (salons for men)
Regis Hairstylists (international salons)
Regis Salons (regional-mall salons)
Saint Algue (international salons)
Sassoon (international salons)
SmartStyle (Wal-Mart store salons)
Supercuts (national strip-center salons in the US and international salons)
We Care Hair (national strip-center salons)

COMPETITORS

Alberto-Culver
Bath & Body Works
Body Shop
Cool Cuts
L'Oréal
Mascolo
Premier Salons
Procter & Gamble
Ratner Companies
Shiseido
Sport Clips
Ulta
Wella AG

HISTORICAL FINANCIALS

Company Type: Public

Income Statement

FYE: June 30

	REVENUE ($ mil.)	NET INCOME ($ mil.)	NET PROFIT MARGIN	EMPLOYEES
6/09	2,430	(125)	—	59,000
6/08	2,739	85	3.1%	65,000
6/07	2,627	83	3.2%	62,000
6/06	2,431	110	4.5%	59,000
6/05	2,194	65	2.9%	55,000
Annual Growth	**2.6%**	**—**	**—**	**1.8%**

2009 Year-End Financials

Debt ratio: 72.1%
Return on equity: —
Cash ($ mil.): 43
Current ratio: 1.29
Long-term debt ($ mil.): 579
No. of shares (mil.): 57
Dividends
  Yield: 0.9%
  Payout: —
Market value ($ mil.): 1,000

Stock History

NYSE: RGS

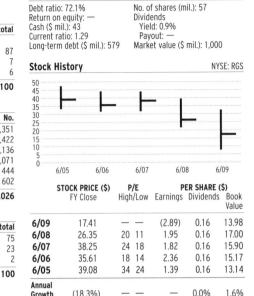

	STOCK PRICE ($) FY Close	P/E High/Low		PER SHARE ($) Earnings	Dividends	Book Value
6/09	17.41	—	—	(2.89)	0.16	13.98
6/08	26.35	20	11	1.95	0.16	17.00
6/07	38.25	24	18	1.82	0.16	15.90
6/06	35.61	18	14	2.36	0.16	15.17
6/05	39.08	34	24	1.39	0.16	13.14
Annual Growth	**(18.3%)**	**—**	**—**	**—**	**0.0%**	**1.6%**

Rent-A-Center

Rent-A-Center (RAC) wants its customers to rent while it buys. The firm became the #1 rent-to-own chain nationwide through a slew of acquisitions. It owns and operates about 3,000 stores (down from 3,400 in 2007) throughout North America and Puerto Rico under the Rent-A-Center, Get It Now, and Home Choice names, and franchises some 210 through subsidiary ColorTyme. The stores rent name-brand home electronics, furniture, accessories, appliances, and computers. While customers have the option to eventually own their rented items, only about 25% ever do. RAC also offers financial services, including loans, check cashing and money transfer services, and tax preparation, to its customers in some 350 stores.

The store closings (about 400 over the past three years) represent a retreat for RAC, which climbed to the top of the US rent-to-own industry through the acquisition of more than 3,300 stores between 1993 and 2006. (Its purchase of rival Rent-Way in 2006 eliminated one of the firm's primary competitors.) Since then RAC has been in what it calls a "store consolidation" phase during which it has closed or merged hundreds of redundant stores in overcrowded markets. While RAC plans to continue opening and acquiring locations in new and existing markets, it doesn't anticipate a return to its prior bout of acquisitiveness. International growth is also on the table.

Given the high number of store closures, it's no surprise that RAC's net sales declined more than 4% in 2009 vs. 2008, and was essentially flat in the year earlier period. However, same-store sales at existing units also fell as its customers spent less. (About three-quarters of RAC's customers have household incomes between $15,000 and $50,000 per year, a group hit hard by the deep recession in the US.) On the bright side, the company's operating profit rose significantly (by about 4% between 2007 and 2009) as it stems the losses from unprofitable stores.

To grow sales and attract new customers, the rent-to-own chain has been expanding its offerings of upscale brands (Sony Electronics, Ashley Furniture) and rolling out a line of financial services products (introduced in 2005) to more of its stores. The products include loans, bill paying, debit cards, check cashing, and money transfer services under the RAC Financial Services and Cash AdvantEdge banners. The company expects to offer financial services in about 400 of its stores by the end of 2010.

RAC also operates about 40 stores under the Get It Now and Home Choice banners in Illinois, Minnesota, and Wisconsin that sell merchandise on an installment plan.

HISTORY

Ernest Talley is a pioneer in the rent-to-own industry, having founded one of the first rent-to-own chains in 1963. He sold that business in 1974 and went into commercial real estate in Dallas. In 1987, after the Texas real estate crash, Talley and his son Michael started Talley Leasing, which rented appliances to apartment complex owners.

Talley bought Vista Rent To Own, a chain of 22 stores in New Jersey and Puerto Rico, in 1989. He upgraded merchandise, increased selection, updated information and data systems, and improved store management. In 1993 the company acquired DEF, an 84-store chain, and repeated the upgrading process. That year the company changed its name to Renters Choice. It went public in 1995 and used the proceeds to make more acquisitions.

The purchases of Crown Leasing and Pro Rental (parent of Magic Rent-to-Own) moved Renters Choice into the southern US and increased its store count from just more than 100 to 322. In 1996 the company acquired Texas-based competitor ColorTyme, adding another 320 stores (most of them franchises). Renters Choice acquired Trans Texas Capital, another rental purchase enterprise, the following year.

In 1998 the company bought Central Rents, owner of about 180 stores, for $103 million and paid $900 million (most of it borrowed) for rival Thorn Americas, which operated some 1,400 stores under the Rent-A-Center, Remco, and U-Can-Rent brands. Renters Choice then changed its name to Rent-A-Center. Also that year it settled a class-action lawsuit with 20,000 customers for $12 million; the suit alleged that the company had misled consumers about actual finance costs.

Rent-A-Center lost an appeal of another lawsuit in 1999 and was ordered to pay $30 million to 30,000 consumers for charging interest rates as high as 750%.

After making no acquisitions in 1999, Rent-A-Center announced in 2000 that it would be adding 100-plus stores annually. The company also began offering Internet service (originally for $5.95 per week through BellSouth and then, in 2001, offering free service through NetZero).

In October 2001 Ernest Talley retired and Mark Speese was named chairman and CEO. In February 2003 Rent-A-Center bought 295 stores (located in 38 states) from rival Rent-Way for just more than $100 million. In 2004 the company acquired Rent Rite (90 stores in 11 states) and Rainbow Rentals (124 stores in 15 states). Also that year Rent-A-Center broke into the Canadian market with the purchase of five stores in Alberta for $2.4 million.

In April 2005 the company settled a lawsuit related to its business practices in California — *Benjamin Griego, et al. v. Rent-A-Center, Inc.* — by agreeing to pay the plaintiff's attorneys' fees as well as about $37.5 million cash to eligible customers who entered into rental-purchase agreements with the company between early 1999 and late 2004.

In December 2005 the company sold the rental contracts and merchandise of 19 stores to Aaron's for about $4.4 million.

In November 2006 Rent-A-Center acquired Rent-Way for about $600 million. Rent-Way became a wholly owned indirect subsidiary.

In December 2007 Rent-A-Center closed or merged about 275 stores. Another dozen or so locations met with a similar fate in early 2008. The closings were designed to relieve oversaturation in some of the company's markets.

EXECUTIVES

Chairman and CEO: Mark E. Speese, age 52, $1,982,944 total compensation
President, COO, and Director: Mitchell E. Fadel, age 52, $1,365,224 total compensation
EVP Finance, CFO, and Treasurer: Robert D. Davis, age 38, $854,177 total compensation
EVP Operations: Christopher A. Korst, age 50, $748,950 total compensation
EVP Operations: Theodore V. DeMarino, age 48, $692,311 total compensation
EVP, General Counsel, and Secretary: Ronald D. DeMoss, age 59
EVP Operational Services: David E. West, age 59
SVP Strategic Planning and Development: Joel M. Mussat
SVP Human Resources: Robert D. Brockman, age 55
SVP Information Technology and CIO: Tony F. Fuller
SVP Marketing and Advertising and Chief Marketing Officer: Ann L. Davids
SVP Public Affairs: Dwight D. Dumler
VP Information Technology and CTO: Robert W. (Bob) Rapp Jr., age 56
VP Spend Management and Chief Procurement Officer: Michael S. Wilding
VP Inventory Management: John Butler
VP Marketing: Tim Pitt
VP Field Human Resources: Rebecca O. Crawford
VP Merchandise: Dan Glasky
VP Sales: Joe T. Arnette
VP Investor Relations: David E. (Dave) Carpenter
President and CEO, ColorTyme: Robert F. (Bob) Bloom, age 56
Auditors: Grant Thornton LLP

LOCATIONS

HQ: Rent-A-Center, Inc.
5501 Headquarters Dr., Plano, TX 75024
Phone: 972-801-1100   **Fax:** 866-260-1424
Web: www.rentacenter.com

2009 Stores

	Co.-Owned	Franchised	Fin. Services
Texas	289	37	112
New York	176	3	—
Ohio	175	4	54
Florida	172	19	—
Pennsylvania	151	3	—
California	140	5	—
North Carolina	129	12	—
Illinois	110	8	—
Michigan	104	7	—
Indiana	97	2	—
Tennessee	90	4	37
Georgia	83	7	—
Massachusetts	69	1	—
Virginia	68	12	—
Kentucky	65	4	20
Missouri	65	—	16
South Carolina	64	4	—
Maryland	63	11	—
Alabama	59	3	—
Arizona	57	—	6
Louisiana	45	6	—
Oklahoma	45	6	—
Puerto Rico	45	—	—
New Jersey	44	—	—
Washington	44	5	26
Colorado	43	—	12
Connecticut	40	1	—
Arkansas	39	1	—
Mississippi	35	1	—
West Virginia	35	—	—
Kansas	34	8	13
Maine	28	9	—
Oregon	27	4	—
Iowa	27	—	13
New Mexico	27	9	10
Nevada	23	—	3
Wisconsin	23	—	—
New Hampshire	20	1	—
Delaware	20	—	—
Canada	18	—	—
Rhode Island	16	2	—
Utah	16	—	6
Nebraska	14	—	—
Other states	72	11	19
Total	**3,007**	**210**	**353**

PRODUCTS/OPERATIONS

2009 Sales

	$ mil.	% of total
Store		
Rentals & fees	2,346.8	85
Merchandise sales	261.6	10
Installment sales	53.0	2
Other	57.6	2
Franchise		
Merchandise sales	28.0	1
Royalty income & fees	4.9	—
Total	**2,751.9**	**100**

2009 Sales

	% of total
Consumer electronics	36
Furniture & accessories	31
Appliances	17
Computers	16
Total	**100**

Store Names
ColorTyme
Get It Now
Home Choice
Rent-A-Center

Selected Merchandise
Appliances
Computers
Furniture
Home accessories
Home electronics

COMPETITORS

Aaron's, Inc.	Dollar Financial
Advance America	EZCORP
Best Buy	Family Dollar Stores
Bestway	First Cash Financial
Brook Furniture Rental	Sears
Cash America	Wal-Mart

HISTORICAL FINANCIALS

Company Type: Public

Income Statement

FYE: December 31

	REVENUE ($ mil.)	NET INCOME ($ mil.)	NET PROFIT MARGIN	EMPLOYEES
12/09	2,752	168	6.1%	17,400
12/08	2,884	140	4.8%	17,900
12/07	2,906	76	2.6%	18,600
12/06	2,434	103	4.2%	19,740
12/05	2,339	136	5.8%	15,480
Annual Growth	4.1%	5.5%	—	3.0%

2009 Year-End Financials

Debt ratio: 57.0%
Return on equity: 14.4%
Cash ($ mil.): 102
Current ratio: 2.00
Long-term debt ($ mil.): 711
No. of shares (mil.): 66
Dividends
  Yield: —
  Payout: —
Market value ($ mil.): 1,169

Stock History

NASDAQ (GS): RCII

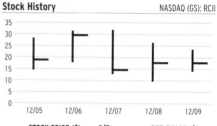

	STOCK PRICE ($) FY Close	P/E High/Low		PER SHARE ($) Earnings	Dividends	Book Value
12/09	17.72	9	6	2.52	—	18.91
12/08	17.65	13	5	2.08	—	16.36
12/07	14.52	29	12	1.10	—	14.35
12/06	29.51	21	12	1.46	—	14.29
12/05	18.86	15	8	1.83	—	12.48
Annual Growth	(1.5%)	—	—	8.3%	—	10.9%

Republic Services

Homeowners and businesses in 40 states pledge allegiance to Republic Services and the trash collection for which it stands. In late 2008 the once #3 industry player acquired #2 company Allied Waste for $6 billion to place it closer to industry leader Waste Management in terms of revenues and geographic coverage. Republic provides waste disposal services for commercial, industrial, municipal, and residential customers through its network of 400 collection companies. Republic owns or operates more than 210 solid waste landfills, 240 transfer stations, and about 80 recycling centers. The company serves millions of customers through its waste collection contracts with more than 3,000 municipalities.

To better address the local variables of the waste collection business, Republic organizes its operations into four regions: eastern, central, southern, and western. Each region is further divided into several operating areas, each of which provides collection, transfer, disposal, and recycling services. Regional and area managers are given considerable authority under the company's decentralized management structure.

Republic had grown by buying smaller waste management operations in its existing service areas and in new regions. Likely candidates included assets of municipalities that were privatizing their waste management services. After swallowing the large national business of Allied Waste, the company is looking to grow organically by integrating and streamlining its operations to increase efficiency. However, it will continue to make "tuck-in" acquisitions of landfills and transfers stations and other complementary assets, and will divest some properties if they prove inefficient.

In 2008, prior to its megadeal with Allied Waste, Republic rebuffed a takeover bid by industry leader Waste Management. Following the acquisition, Republic divested assets in seven markets (six municipal solid waste landfills, six collection businesses, and three transfer stations) in order to meet US antitrust regulations.

In 2007 the company sold Living Earth Technology Company (a noncore, stand-alone business in Texas) for about $37 million.

Republic's largest shareholder is Microsoft chairman Bill Gates, who owns about 14% of Republic through Cascade Investment LLC.

HISTORY

Republic Services began in 1980 as Republic Resources, an oil exploration and production company. In 1989, after a stockholder group tried to force Republic into liquidation, Browning-Ferris (BFI) founder Thomas Fatjo stepped in, gained control of Republic Resources, and refocused it on a field he knew well — solid waste. Renamed Republic Waste, the company began making acquisitions.

In 1990 Michael DeGroote, founder of BFI competitor Laidlaw, bought into Republic Waste. In 1995 Wayne Huizenga — who co-founded Waste Management in 1971 and was beginning to develop a national auto sales organization in the mid-1990s after his tenure as chairman and CEO of Blockbuster Entertainment — approached DeGroote about a deal. They rejected an immediate merger of the waste and auto businesses because the latter was not well-enough developed and would drag down Republic's numbers. Instead, they agreed to merge Republic and the Hudson Companies (a trash business owned by Huizenga's brother-in-law, Harris Hudson), to sell Huizenga a large interest in Republic through a private offering, and to give him control of the board (in 1995). The company became Republic Industries.

Huizenga's investment brought a flood of new investors. With new resources, Republic Industries became a driving force in the garbage industry's consolidation binge, and the company bought more than 100 smaller waste haulers between 1995 and 1998. Republic Industries spun off about 30% of its waste business as Republic Services in 1998; the IPO raised $1.3 billion. Republic's acquisition trend continued, as it agreed to buy 16 landfills, 136 commercial collection routes, and 11 transfer stations from Waste Management for $500 million. Later that year Waste Management veteran James O'Connor succeeded Huizenga as CEO, although Huizenga continued as chairman.

Investors filed class-action lawsuits against Republic in 1999, claiming the Waste Management purchases held far more integration problems than the company admitted. In 2000 the company swapped nine of its solid waste operations for eight Allied Waste businesses, which Allied needed to divest in order to gain federal approval for its merger with BFI.

While many firms in the industry were selling off assets in 2001, Republic was expanding its operations in the northern California market by acquiring Richmond Sanitary Services. Huizenga retired as chairman at the end of 2002 and was once again succeeded by O'Connor. Huizenga stayed on the board as a director until May 2004.

EXECUTIVES

Chairman and CEO: James E. (Jim) O'Connor, age 60, $5,676,620 total compensation
President, COO, and Director: Donald W. (Don) Slager, age 48, $3,760,792 total compensation
EVP and CFO: Tod C. Holmes, age 61, $2,097,605 total compensation
EVP Communications: William C. (Will) Flower
EVP, General Counsel, and Corporate Secretary: Michael P. Rissman, age 49, $812,417 total compensation
EVP Business Development: Brian A. Bales
EVP Marketing and Sales: Gary L. Sova
EVP Human Resources: Jeffrey A. Hughes
SVP Environmental Development and Compliance: James G. VanWeelden
SVP and Treasurer: Edward A. Lang III
SVP Operations and Controller: Jerome S. Clark
SVP and CIO: William G. Halnon
SVP and Chief Accounting Officer: Charles F. Serianni
VP Labor Relations: Dean Burrell
VP Procurement: Tom Piersa
VP Tax: Lawrence Focazio
Auditors: Ernst & Young LLP

LOCATIONS

HQ: Republic Services, Inc.
18500 N. Allied Way, Phoenix, AZ 82054
Phone: 480-627-2700
Web: www.republicservices.com

2009 Sales

	$ mil.	% of total
Western	2,170.0	26
Eastern	2,115.0	26
Southern	2,046.2	25
Midwest	1,777.0	22
Corporate	90.9	1
Total	**8,199.1**	**100**

PRODUCTS/OPERATIONS

2009 Sales

	$ mil.	% of total
Collection		
Commercial	2,553.4	31
Residential	2,187.0	27
Industrial	1,541.4	19
Other	26.9	—
Transfer & disposal	1,549.4	19
Other	341.0	4
Total	**8,199.1**	**100**

COMPETITORS

Casella Waste Systems
IESI-BFC
Recology
Rumpke
Veolia ES Solid Waste
Waste Connections
Waste Industries USA
Waste Management

HISTORICAL FINANCIALS

Company Type: Public

Income Statement

FYE: December 31

	REVENUE ($ mil.)	NET INCOME ($ mil.)	NET PROFIT MARGIN	EMPLOYEES
12/09	8,199	495	6.0%	31,000
12/08	3,685	74	2.0%	35,000
12/07	3,176	290	9.1%	13,000
12/06	3,071	280	9.1%	13,000
12/05	2,864	254	8.9%	13,000
Annual Growth	30.1%	18.2%	—	24.3%

2009 Year-End Financials

Debt ratio: 84.9%
Return on equity: 6.7%
Cash ($ mil.): 48
Current ratio: 0.50
Long-term debt ($ mil.): 6,420
No. of shares (mil.): 383
Dividends
Yield: 2.7%
Payout: 58.5%
Market value ($ mil.): 10,843

Stock History

NYSE: RSG

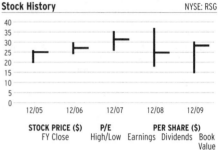

	STOCK PRICE ($) FY Close	P/E High/Low		PER SHARE ($) Earnings	Dividends	Book Value
12/09	28.31	23	12	1.30	0.76	19.75
12/08	24.79	99	49	0.37	0.72	19.01
12/07	31.35	23	17	1.51	0.55	3.40
12/06	27.11	21	18	1.38	0.40	3.71
12/05	25.03	22	17	1.17	0.35	4.19
Annual Growth	3.1%	—	—	2.7%	21.4%	47.3%

Res-Care, Inc.

Through its residential, training, and support services, ResCare offers RESpect and CARE to people with physical and mental disabilities. ResCare has residential and nonresidential facilities in more than 35 states and Canada. The company operates through four primary segments: ResCare HomeCare Services, ResCare Residential Services, ResCare Workforce Services, and ResCare Youth Services. Combined, the segments provide in-home personal care and training in social, vocational, and functional skills, as well as counseling and therapy programs. In addition to these services, Res-Care runs correctional and care programs for at-risk youth and assistance for adults.

Investment firm Onex owns a 25% stake in the company; in 2010 Onex made an offer to purchase the remaining shares in ResCare.

ResCare's HomeCare and Residential segments (formerly called Community Services Group) is one of the largest players in the US special-needs industry (and the company's biggest business segment). It operates thousands of group homes for people with intellectual and developmental disabilities, and also provides home care and pharmacy services to the elderly and developmentally disabled. ResCare depends on federal, state, and local government agencies to reimburse it for services delivered to the disabled through Medicaid programs.

ResCare's Workforce Services (formerly called the Training Services Group) provides training and job placement services in the US, Germany, the Netherlands, and the UK. In the US it operates some 100 career centers in two dozen states to offer vocational assessment, career counseling, and job search assistance, and makes up about 13% of the company's sales. Its international employment training services remain a tiny slice of company revenues, but it is seeking to expand that area.

The company serves disadvantaged youths at training centers under the federal Job Corps program through its Youth Services segment. It also helps teens and adults transitioning from juvenile facilities or welfare into the workforce

ResCare is focused on broadening its range and reach through acquisitions of local and regional care providers and job training operations. In 2009 Res-Care made more than 15 acquisitions, primarily in the Community Services segment. Previously, ResCare acquired Kelly Home Care Services, a subsidiary of Kelly Services that provides home care to the elderly and disabled in 18 states.

In 2010 the company reorganized and renamed its operations into its current four operating segments to focus on its long-term goal of adding services through organic growth and through acquisitions. It also hopes the change will diversify its revenue stream.

ResCare provides pharmacy services through its Pharmacy Alternatives (PAL) partnership with Pharmapro and Community Alternatives Pharmacy. PAL began operations in 2006 and is one of a handful of pharmacies in the nation that specialize in serving people with intellectual and developmental disabilities. In addition to providing traditional pharmacy services, PAL provides clinical support including seminars, conferences, webinars, e-mail education, and individualized educational support.

HISTORY

In 1974 James Fornear founded ResCare to run the Whitney Young Job Corps Center in Shelbyville, Kentucky. He expanded the operations to Mississippi in 1977 and 1978. Also in 1978 ResCare diversified, establishing a Kentucky center to service mentally disabled clients. The company co-founded in-home nursing service provider Home Care Affiliates in 1985. ResCare went public three years later and had facilities for the mentally disabled in six states by 1989.

In the early 1990s ResCare rode the shift from large health care institutions to in-home care, entering Colorado (1992) and California (1994). ResCare bought Beverly Enterprises' Mental Retardation/Developmental Disabilities operations in 1995, extending into Illinois and Kansas. It also moved into New Jersey, Ohio, and Oklahoma that year and sold its 68% interest in Home Care Affiliates.

In 1996 ResCare contracted to run up to 10 intermediate-care group homes for disabled individuals in Orange County, California. ResCare in 1998 made its largest buy ever with the purchase of Normal Life, a group home provider; it also bought Florida's Gator Human Services (youth services). The buying spree ran into 1999, with Georgia's American Patient Care and the planned acquisition of California-based Social Vocational Services.

The company focused on organic growth and improving its financial management, compliance, and quality systems between 2000 and 2004. A unit of Onex bought a 30% equity interest in the company in 2004. The investment was expected to fuel further expansion of ResCare's services; the company bought around 130 homes that year.

EXECUTIVES

Chairman: Ronald G. Geary, age 62
President, CEO, and Director: Ralph G. Gronefeld Jr., age 51, $440,000 total compensation
COO: Patrick G. (Pat) Kelley, age 45, $375,000 total compensation
CFO: David W. Miles, age 44, $300,000 total compensation
CTO: George Watts
Chief Development Officer: Richard L. Tinsley, age 38, $230,000 total compensation
Chief Compliance Officer and General Counsel: David S. Waskey, age 58, $225,000 total compensation
Chief Business Services Officer: Michael J. Reibel
Chief Communication Officer: Nel Taylor
Chief People Officer: Nina P. Seigle
Auditors: KPMG LLP

LOCATIONS

HQ: Res-Care, Inc.
9901 Linn Station Rd., Louisville, KY 40223
Phone: 502-394-2100   **Fax:** 502-394-2206
Web: www.rescare.com

PRODUCTS/OPERATIONS

2009 Revenues

	$ mil.	% of total
Community Services	1,152.7	73
Employment Training Services	232.7	15
Job Corps Training Services	145.8	9
Other	47.7	3
Total	**1,579.1**	**100**

Selected Subsidiaries

Arbor E&T, LLC
The Academy for Individual Excellence, Inc.
Alternative Youth Services, Inc.
Capital TX Investments, Inc.
CATX Properties, Inc.
CNC/Access, Inc.
Community Advantage, Inc.
Community Alternatives Illinois, Inc.
Community Alternatives Indiana, Inc.
Community Alternatives Kentucky, Inc.
Community Alternatives Missouri, Inc.
Community Alternatives Nebraska, Inc.
Community Alternatives New Mexico, Inc.
Community Alternatives Texas Partner, Inc.
Community Alternatives Virginia, Inc.
Creative Networks, L.L.C.
Normal Life, Inc.
PeopleServe, Inc.
RSCR West Virginia, Inc.
Southern Home Care Services, Inc.
Tangram Rehabilitation Network, Inc.
Texas Home Management, Inc.
THM Homes, Inc.
Youthtrack, Inc.

COMPETITORS

Care UK	Life Care Centers
Comprehensive Care	Magellan Health
Elwyn	Mosaic (Nebraska)
FHC Health Systems	PHC
GEO Group	Providence Service
Horizon Health	Sun Healthcare

HISTORICAL FINANCIALS

Company Type: Public

Income Statement

FYE: December 31

	REVENUE ($ mil.)	NET INCOME ($ mil.)	NET PROFIT MARGIN	EMPLOYEES
12/09	1,579	(10)	—	45,700
12/08	1,544	37	2.4%	46,400
12/07	1,433	44	3.1%	42,000
12/06	1,302	37	2.8%	37,000
12/05	1,089	21	1.9%	35,000
Annual Growth	**9.7%**	**—**	**—**	**6.9%**

2009 Year-End Financials

Debt ratio: 50.7%
Return on equity: —
Cash ($ mil.): 21
Current ratio: 1.79
Long-term debt ($ mil.): 196
No. of shares (mil.): 29
Dividends
Yield: —
Payout: —
Market value ($ mil.): 329

Stock History

NASDAQ (GS): RSCR

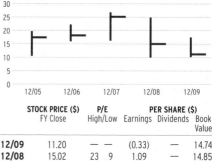

	STOCK PRICE ($) FY Close	P/E High/Low		PER SHARE ($) Earnings	Dividends	Book Value
12/09	11.20	—	—	(0.33)	—	14.74
12/08	15.02	23	9	1.09	—	14.85
12/07	25.16	20	13	1.31	—	13.83
12/06	18.15	20	15	1.11	—	11.95
12/05	17.37	29	16	0.66	—	10.27
Annual Growth	**(10.4%)**	**—**	**—**	**—**	**—**	**9.5%**

Revlon, Inc.

Revlon has the look of a leader in the US mass-market cosmetics business, alongside L'Oréal's Maybelline and Procter & Gamble's Cover Girl. In addition to its Almay and Revlon brand makeup and beauty tools, the company makes Revlon ColorSilk hair color, Mitchum antiperspirants and deodorants, Charlie and Jean Naté fragrances, and Ultima II and Gatineau skincare products. Its beauty aids are distributed in more than 100 countries, though the US is its largest market, generating about 60% of revenue. Wal-Mart accounts for some 20% of sales.

What started as a company that marketed nail polish has become nails on a chalkboard to some investors. Revlon's sales have progressed downward in recent years, driven by weak demand for its core Revlon and Almay cosmetics in the US and Europe (especially the UK), which have struggled through economic downturns. The results are disappointing to Revlon, which has focused its strategy on building the mainstay brands, and run counter to the belief that cosmetics are recession-proof products. (Proposed by Estée Lauder chairman Leonard Lauder, the Lipstick Effect theory dictates that during tough economic times women will opt for inexpensive "luxuries," like lipstick or mascara, to lift their spirits.) All the same, Revlon has seen an uptick in demand from Latin America, Africa, and the Asia/Pacific region, where the company has worked to build its brand.

To oversee and steer its strategy, the company established an "office of the vice chairman" executive structure in mid-2009. The structure comprises three executives. CEO David Kennedy was promoted to vice chairman and tapped as EVP at MacAndrews & Forbes, Revlon's largest shareholder. Alan Ennis took the CEO title, and Chris Elshaw, the US region's EVP and general manager, was elected EVP and COO.

The revised executive arrangement complements a global restructuring also implemented that year. About 400 jobs were cut, including 75 unfilled positions. Revlon's latest undertaking follows other moves in years past to improve its stubbornly poor financial performance. In 2008 the company sold its noncore brands in Brazil, including its men's skin care brand Bozzano, for nearly $110 million to Hypermarcas. Revlon consolidated facilities in 2007 to cut costs, after announcing it would cut about 10% of its workforce and cancel its newly developed Vital Radiance line of cosmetics.

New York socialite Ron Perelman owns about 60% of Revlon — and controls about 80% of its voting power — through holding companies, including MacAndrews & Forbes. FMR owns about 15% of Revlon.

HISTORY

Legend has it that, jobless in New York City in the depths of the Depression, Charles Revson became a cosmetics salesman by the toss of a coin — tails, he'd apply for a job selling household appliances; heads, he'd answer an ad for a cosmetics salesman. It was heads, and in 1931 Revson began selling Elka nail polish to beauty salons. He painted his own nails with different colors so he wouldn't need a color chart.

Revson and his brother Joseph decided to start their own nail polish company. They scraped together $300, hooked up with nail polish supplier Charles Lachman, and in 1932 began Revlon (the "L" in the name came from Lachman). The nail polish, emulating Elka's, was opaque rather than transparent, available in many colors, and an immediate hit with beauty salons. Revlon grew rapidly, and by 1937 Revson was selling his nail polish in upscale department stores.

Seeing nail polish as a fashion accessory, Revson introduced new colors twice a year, giving them — and the matching lipsticks introduced in 1940 — names like Kissing Pink and Fifth Avenue Red. More opportunist than innovator, he let his competitors do the research and make the mistakes, and then he would make a better version of the product, outpackaging and outadvertising his rivals.

Revlon introduced Fire & Ice in 1952, one of its most successful launches ever. Its sole sponsorship of The $64,000 Question quiz show in 1955 boosted sales of some products by 500%. Later that year Revlon went public. To diversify and expand its markets, it began making acquisitions (although many were soon dumped) and selling its products overseas.

The company bought deodorant maker Mitchum in 1970, and three years later it introduced Charlie, its wildly popular fragrance. In 1974 a dying Revson handpicked his successor, Michel Bergerac, president of European operations for IT&T. Revson died the next year. Bergerac began a new push for diversification and

lower costs. Acquisitions included ophthalmic and pharmaceuticals companies. However, while Revlon's health care operations were rising, its cosmetics star was losing market share and profits were falling.

Social-climbing conglomateur Ron Perelman bought Revlon in an LBO in 1985 with funds raised by friend Michael Milken. Hoping to restore the firm as a beauty business, Perelman began selling off the profitable health care businesses and buying beauty companies.

In 1994 Revlon introduced ColorStay lipstick, which quickly became the top-selling brand. Revlon went public in 1996. George Fellows was promoted to CEO the next year. The company merged its Prestige Fragrance & Cosmetics chain into Perelman's Cosmetic Center chain in 1997; Revlon sold its 85% stake in the combination at a loss in 1998.

Still deep in debt and suffering from domestic competition, too much inventory, and troubles in Russia and Brazil, Revlon closed three plants and cut 3,000 jobs in 1998. Fellows resigned in 1999 and was replaced by Jeff Nugent, the former president of Neutrogena (and brother of rocker Ted Nugent). Sales fell as retailers cut inventory.

Revlon sold its professional products business in 2000 to an investment group led by the unit's chairman, Carlos Colomer (now chairman of Colomer USA). Also in 2000 Revlon sold its Plusbelle line (Argentina) to consumer products company Dial. In 2001 it sold its Colorama brand of cosmetics and hair care products to rival L'Oréal.

In February 2002 CEO Nugent abruptly resigned after it was reported that chairman Ron Perelman planned to replace him with Jack Stahl, former president and COO at The Coca-Cola Company; Stahl took office that month. The same year Perelman offered a cash infusion of $150 million to the struggling company. Revlon's board accepted the proposal in 2003.

Stahl left the troubled company in September 2006 to pursue other interests and was succeeded as president and CEO of Revlon by David Kennedy, the firm's CFO.

EXECUTIVES

Chairman: Ronald O. (Ron) Perelman, age 67
Vice Chairman: David L. Kennedy, age 63, $1,005,093 total compensation
President, CEO, and Director: Alan T. Ennis, age 39, $1,311,797 total compensation
EVP and COO: Chris Elshaw, age 49, $1,180,106 total compensation
EVP and CFO: Steven Berns, age 45, $598,270 total compensation
EVP Human Resources, Chief Legal Officer, and General Counsel: Robert K. Kretzman III, age 58, $1,738,086 total compensation
EVP and Chief Science Officer: Alan J. Meyers, age 52
EVP North American Sales: Karl Obrecht
CIO: David Giambruno
SVP, Corporate Controller, and Chief Accounting Officer: Gina Mastantuono
SVP Taxes: Mark M. Sexton
SVP and Managing Director, Europe: Simon Worraker
SVP and Managing Director, Asia/Pacific: Graeme Howard
SVP and Managing Director, Latin America: Manuel Blanco
SVP New Product Support and Engineering: John Butcher
SVP, Deputy General Counsel, and Secretary: Michael T. Sheehan
SVP Worldwide Manufacturing: Arthur Franson
SVP Investor Relations and Treasurer: Elise A. Garofalo
Auditors: KPMG LLP

LOCATIONS

HQ: Revlon, Inc.
237 Park Ave., New York, NY 10017
Phone: 212-527-4000   **Fax:** 212-527-4995
Web: www.revloninc.com

2009 Sales

	$ mil.	% of total
US	747.9	58
Asia/Pacific	266.7	21
Europe	172.4	13
Latin America	108.9	8
Total	**1,295.9**	**100**

PRODUCTS/OPERATIONS

2009 Sales

	$ mil.	% of total
Color cosmetics	785.5	61
Beauty care & fragrance	510.4	39
Total	**1,295.9**	**100**

Selected Products and Brands

Cosmetics
  Almay Bright Eyes
  Almay Intense i-Color
  Almay Smart Shade
  Almay TLC Truly Lasting Color
  Revlon Age Defying
  Revlon Beyond Natural
  Revlon ColorStay
  Revlon Fabulash
  Revlon PhotoReady
  Revlon Super Lustrous
Beauty tools
  Revlon
Deodorants and antiperspirants
  Mitchum
Fragrance
  Charlie
  Jean Naté
Hair
  Revlon ColorSilk
Skin Care
  Gatineau
  Ultima II

COMPETITORS

Alberto-Culver
Alticor
Avlon
Avon
Bath & Body Works
Beiersdorf
Body Shop
Bristol-Myers Squibb
Clarins
Colgate-Palmolive
Colomer USA
Combe
Coty Inc.
Estée Lauder
Joh. A. Benckiser
John Paul Mitchell
Johnson & Johnson
L'Oréal
LVMH
Mary Kay
Nu Skin
Orly International
Procter & Gamble
Puig Beauty & Fashion
Shiseido
SoftSheen/Carson
Unilever NV

HISTORICAL FINANCIALS

Company Type: Public

Income Statement

FYE: December 31

	REVENUE ($ mil.)	NET INCOME ($ mil.)	NET PROFIT MARGIN	EMPLOYEES
12/09	1,296	49	3.8%	4,800
12/08	1,347	58	4.3%	5,600
12/07	1,400	(16)	—	5,600
12/06	1,331	(251)	—	6,000
12/05	1,332	(84)	—	6,800
Annual Growth	(0.7%)	—	—	(8.3%)

2009 Year-End Financials

Debt ratio: —
Return on equity: —
Cash ($ mil.): 55
Current ratio: 1.30
Long-term debt ($ mil.): 1,186

No. of shares (mil.): 51
Dividends
  Yield: —
  Payout: —
Market value ($ mil.): 874

Stock History

NYSE: REV

	STOCK PRICE ($) FY Close	P/E High/Low	PER SHARE ($) Earnings	Dividends	Book Value
12/09	17.01	21 2	0.94	—	(20.12)
12/08	6.67	13 5	1.13	—	(21.66)
12/07	11.80	— —	(0.30)	—	(21.06)
12/06	12.80	— —	(6.20)	—	(23.94)
12/05	31.00	— —	(2.30)	—	(21.34)
Annual Growth	(13.9%)	— —	—	—	—

Reynolds American

We're #2! That slogan is an apt description of Reynolds American Inc. (RAI), the holding company for the US's second-largest cigarette maker (RJR Tobacco) and smokeless tobacco manufacturer (American Snuff Company). RJR Tobacco boasts five of the 10 best-selling cigarette brands in the US: Camel, Doral, Kool, Pall Mall, and Winston. RJR Tobacco also makes and markets smoke-free Camel brand tobacco products. American Snuff makes moist snuff under the value-priced Grizzly and premium-priced Kodiak brands. Other RAI subsidiaries include cigarette maker Santa Fe Natural Tobacco Co. and nicotine gum maker Niconovum. RAI was formed by the merger of R.J. Reynolds Tobacco Holdings and Brown & Williamson.

RAI is reorganizing with the aim of maximizing the efficiency of its cigarette manufacturing operations, while expanding its smokeless tobacco production capacity. It is closing cigarette factories in North Carolina and Puerto Rico and transferring production to the company's largest factory in Tobaccoville, North Carolina. Meanwhile, American Snuff is expanding its tobacco processing and manufacturing capacity in Memphis and Clarksville, Tennessee. A new plant in

Memphis in currently under construction and is slated to begin operating in early 2012.

Unlike the market for cigarettes in the US, which is mature and declining, the market for moist snuff and other smokeless tobacco products is growing. American Snuff (formerly Conwood Co.), makes the top-selling Grizzly and Kodiak brands of moist snuff. It also distributes a variety of tobacco products manufactured by Lane, Limited, including cigars and roll-your-own tobacco.

RAI's archrival Altria (the parent company of Philip Morris USA) acquired American Snuff's largest competitor UST in January 2009, bumping RAI from the #1 spot to the #2 spot in the smokeless tobacco market. After Altria combined Copenhagen and Skoal snuff with its Marlboro cigarettes business, RAI announced restructuring changes and the elimination of some 570 jobs at its headquarters and its R.J. Reynolds' tobacco subsidiary in Winston-Salem. The changes at RAI and R.J. Reynolds are designed to streamline noncore business processes and programs to free up additional resources for growth initiatives.

The Altria/UST merger and the passage six months later of landmark legislation giving the U.S. Food and Drug Administration unprecedented authority to regulate tobacco products is reshaping the tobacco industry and RAI's future. Balking at "unprecedented restrictions" on First Amendment rights, RAI and rival Lorillard filed a lawsuit against the FDA in August 2009. RAI's position in that it isn't against the decision to give FDA authority to regulate tobacco, but it is protesting several provisions in the legislation.

The company is looking to further diversify its products portfolio by helping smokers to quit. To that end, in late 2009 RAI acquired Niconovum, AB, a Swedish maker of smoking cessation products, for about $44 million. Niconovum's nicotine replacement therapy (NRT) items include nicotine gum, mouth spray, and pouches made under the Zonnic brand name, and are sold in Sweden and Denmark. The newly-acquired firm will operate as a separate company.

Brown & Williamson's former parent British American Tobacco owns about 42% of RAI. Invesco Ltd. owns about 12%.

HISTORY

R. J. Reynolds formed the R.J. Reynolds Tobacco Company in 1875 in Winston, North Carolina, to produce chewing tobacco. In the late 1890s, Reynolds lost two-thirds of the company to the American Tobacco Trust, but he regained control in 1911 after the trust was dismantled by the government. Two years later the company introduced Camel.

After Reynolds died in 1918, leadership passed to Bowman Gray, whose family ran the company for the next 50 years. Camel held the #1 or #2 cigarette position throughout the 1930s and 1940s, and Reynolds became the largest domestic cigarette company. In response to growing health concerns in the 1950s, the company introduced its filtered Winston (1954) and Salem (1956) brands.

In response to growing antismoking sentiment, Reynolds Tobacco began diversifying into foods and other nontobacco businesses beginning in the 1960s. Acquisitions included Chun King, Patio Foods, American Independent Oil, Del Monte, Inglenook wines, Smirnoff vodka, Kentucky Fried Chicken, Sunkist beverages, and Canada Dry, all of which it had sold by 1991. In September 1985, Reynolds acquired Nabisco

Brands (Newtons, Oreo, Planters nuts) for $4.9 billion. In 1986, the parent company was renamed RJR Nabisco Inc.

In November 1988, RJR Nabisco agreed to be acquired by Kohlberg Kravis Roberts (KKR). The deal, valued in excess of $25 billion, closed in April 1989. After being privately held for a period, KKR took RJR Nabisco Holdings public in 1991. In early 1995, KKR divested its remaining holdings in RJR Nabisco. Also that year Andrew Schindler was promoted to CEO of the firm.

The tobacco business ended the much-criticized Joe Camel campaign in the US in 1997 and cut its tobacco workforce by 10%. The big US tobacco companies reached a $206 billion settlement in 1998 covering 46 states (four states had already settled for $40 billion).

Prior to 1999, RJR was a subsidiary of RJR Nabisco Holdings Corp. (RJRN). In 1999, following the sale of the company's international tobacco business to Japan Tobacco for $8 billion, the remaining tobacco and food businesses were separated and RJRN was renamed Nabisco Group Holdings Corp. (NGH). In June the former parent company, RJRN, was renamed RJ Reynolds Tobacco Holdings, Inc., and became an independent, publicly traded company again, with RJ Reynolds Tobacco Company as its wholly owned subsidiary.

A Florida jury rendered a $35 billion punitive damages verdict against RJRT in 2000. It filed an appeal, as it and four other Big Tobacco firms claimed the verdict — totaling $145 billion — would put them out of business (which violates Florida tort law). A state appeals court later threw out the verdict, saying the thousands of Florida smokers named in the case could not lump their complaints into one lawsuit.

In 2000 RJRT acquired its former parent company, Nabisco Group Holdings Corp., for $9.8 billion. In 2002 RJRT acquired the Santa Fe Natural Tobacco Company, maker of the Natural American Spirit additive-free cigarette brand, for $340 million in cash.

In June 2003 NASCAR and RJRT parted ways, signaling the end to NASCAR's Winston Cup series. The race circuit is now called the Sprint Cup. In September 2003 the company launched a two-year plan to cut costs by $1 billion, which included cutting jobs by 40%. By the end of 2003, RJRT had cut 1,400 jobs. Shortly thereafter, the company announced merger plans with Brown & Williamson.

Before combining with RJRT to create Reynolds American in July 2004, Brown & Williamson had been ordered to cut back on promoting its Kool brand, which was associated with hip-hop music. The issue carried over to Reynolds American, which agreed in October 2004 to settle several related lawsuits in New York, Illinois, and Maryland by paying $1.5 million toward antismoking campaigns and severely restricting Kool promotions that critics said targeted black youths.

In 2009 RAI acquired Niconovum AB, a Swedish maker of smoking cessation products.

EXECUTIVES

Chairman, President, and CEO; President, RAI Services: Susan M. Ivey, age 51, $16,442,578 total compensation
EVP and CFO: Thomas R. (Tom) Adams, age 59, $3,662,461 total compensation
EVP Operations and Chief Scientific Officer: Jeffery S. (Jeff) Gentry, age 52, $2,626,498 total compensation

EVP and Chief Human Resources Officer, Reynolds America and Reynolds American Services:
Lisa J. Caldwell, age 49
EVP Consumer Marketing, R.J. Reynolds Tobacco Company: Brice O'Brien, age 41
EVP Corporate Affairs, General Counsel, and Assistant Secretary, Reynolds American and Reynolds American Services: E. Julia (Judy) Lambeth, age 58, $3,615,643 total compensation
EVP, Trade Marketing, R.J. Reynolds Tobacco Company: Robert D. Stowe, age 52
SVP and Chief Accounting Officer, Reynolds American and Reynolds American Services:
Frederick W. Smothers, age 46
SVP Strategy and Planning, R.J. Reynolds Tobacco Company: Walton T. Carpenter, age 56
SVP Research and Development, R.J. Reynolds Tobacco Company: Daniel J. Herko, age 49
SVP, General Counsel, and Secretary, R.J. Reynolds Tobacco Company and RAI Services Company:
Martin L. (Mark) Holton III
SVP, Deputy General Counsel, and Secretary, Reynolds American and Reynolds American Services: McDara P. Folan III, age 51
SVP Strategy and Business Development:
E. Kenan (Ken) Whitehurst, age 53
President and CEO, Santa Fe Natural Tobacco:
Nicholas A. (Nick) Bumbacco, age 45
President and CEO, American Snuff Company:
Bryan K. Stockdale, age 51
President and CEO, R.J. Reynolds Tobacco Company: Daniel M. (Dan) Delen, age 44, $5,911,129 total compensation
President, Niconovum USA: Tommy J. Payne, age 52, $1,570,631 total compensation
Auditors: KPMG LLP

LOCATIONS

HQ: Reynolds American Inc.
401 N. Main St., Winston-Salem, NC 27101
Phone: 336-741-2000　　**Fax:** 336-741-4238
Web: www.reynoldsamerican.com

PRODUCTS/OPERATIONS

2009 Sales

	$ mil.	% of total
RJR Tobacco	7,334	87
American Snuff	673	8
Other	412	5
Total	**8,419**	**100**

Selected Brands

Cigarettes
　Camel
　Capri
　Doral
　Kool
　Misty
　Pall Mall
　Salem
　Winston
Smokeless tobacco
　Grizzly
　Kodiak

COMPETITORS

British American Tobacco
Commonwealth Brands
GSK Italy
JT International
Lorillard
Nat Sherman
Philip Morris USA
Smokin Joes
Star Scientific
Swisher International
UST llc
Vector Group
Wellstone Filter Sciences

HISTORICAL FINANCIALS

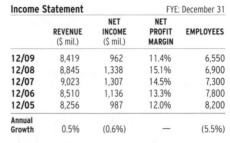

Company Type: Public

Income Statement

FYE: December 31

	REVENUE ($ mil.)	NET INCOME ($ mil.)	NET PROFIT MARGIN	EMPLOYEES
12/09	8,419	962	11.4%	6,550
12/08	8,845	1,338	15.1%	6,900
12/07	9,023	1,307	14.5%	7,300
12/06	8,510	1,136	13.3%	7,800
12/05	8,256	987	12.0%	8,200
Annual Growth	0.5%	(0.6%)	—	(5.5%)

2009 Year-End Financials

Debt ratio: 63.7%　　　　No. of shares (mil.): 292
Return on equity: 15.1%　Dividends
Cash ($ mil.): 2,723　　　Yield: 6.5%
Current ratio: 1.27　　　　Payout: 104.5%
Long-term debt ($ mil.): 4,136　Market value ($ mil.): 15,442

Stock History

NYSE: RAI

	STOCK PRICE ($) FY Close	P/E High/Low		PER SHARE ($) Earnings	Dividends	Book Value
12/09	52.97	16	10	3.30	3.45	22.29
12/08	40.31	16	8	4.57	3.40	21.39
12/07	65.96	16	13	4.43	3.20	25.61
12/06	65.47	16	12	4.10	2.75	24.16
12/05	47.67	15	11	3.53	2.10	22.48
Annual Growth	2.7%	—	—	(1.7%)	13.2%	(0.2%)

Rite Aid

Rite Aid is clinging to its position as a distant third (behind CVS and Walgreen) in the US retail drugstore business. The ailing company runs more than 4,780 drugstores in about 30 states and the District of Columbia. Rite Aid stores fill prescriptions (about two-thirds of sales) and sell health and beauty aids, convenience foods, greeting cards, and other items, including some 3,300 Rite Aid brand private-label products. About 60% of all Rite Aid stores are free-standing and about 50% have drive-through pharmacies. Rite Aid acquired more than 1,850 Brooks and Eckerd drugstores from Canada's Jean Coutu Group for about $4 billion

Rite Aid's heavy debt load, negative cash flow, the recession, and tight credit markets have put the company in a vulnerable position and even led to speculation about its survival. In an effort to right its ship, Rite Aid is making changes within its executive suite. In June 2010 president and COO John Standley became president and CEO. The succession plan has Mary Sammons stepping down as CEO and retaining her title as chairman until June 2012.

The new CEO will face the tough job of turning the business around and proving that the Brooks and Eckerd purchase was not a colossal mistake. (Rite Aid has lost money every quarter since acquiring Brooks Eckerd in 2007.) While Rite Aid has completed integrating the acquired stores (and thus put those expenses behind it), there is still work to be done to make some of them profitable. To reduce its debt, the drugstore chain has closed about 280 underperforming and overlapping stores since early 2008, reduced inventory and costs, and cut its budget for capital expenditures.

Partnering with General Nutrition Companies, Inc. (GNC), about 40% of Rite Aid stores have GNC concessions inside, and the two firms jointly market a line of vitamins and supplements (PharmAssure). It plans to open an additional 625 GNC LiveWell stores-within-a-store inside Rite Aid locations by the end of 2014, including more than 100 in 2010. Rite Aid also sells online through drugstore.com.

Jean Coutu, which received a 32% stake in Rite Aid in the Brooks/Eckerd deal, holds about 28% of the total Rite Aid voting power.

HISTORY

Wholesale grocer Alex Grass founded Rack Rite Distributors in Harrisburg, Pennsylvania, in 1958 to provide health and beauty aids and other sundries to grocery stores. He offered the same products at his first discount drugstore, Thrif D Discount Center, opened in 1962 in Scranton, Pennsylvania. Four years later the company began placing pharmacies in its 36 stores. Rite Aid went public and adopted its current name in 1968, and the next year it made the first of many diverse acquisitions: Daw Drug, Blue Ridge Nursing Homes, and plasma suppliers Immuno Serums and Sero Genics.

Purchases in the 1970s included Sera-Tec Biologicals of New Jersey (blood plasma) and nearly 300 stores. By 1981 Rite Aid was the #3 drugstore chain, and sales exceeded $1 billion. In 1984 it bought the American Discount Auto Parts chain and Encore Books discount chain and spun off its wholesale grocery operation in 1984 as Super Rite, retaining a 47% stake (sold 1989).

Acquisitions added almost 900 stores during the 1980s. Expansion costs eroded Rite Aid's profit margins, and the company focused on integrating its buys in 1990.

Martin Grass took Rite Aid's reins from his dad in 1995. That year the company agreed to buy Revco, the #2 drugstore operator, but the deal was derailed by FTC and Department of Justice objections. Rite Aid bounced back and acquired Thrifty PayLess (with more than 1,000 stores) for about $2.3 billion in 1996. The deal gave the company more than 3,600 stores and a presence in the western US. In 1998 it bought PCS Health Systems (the #1 US pharmacy benefits manager) from drug maker Eli Lilly.

In 1999, after a *Wall Street Journal* investigation, Rite Aid revealed that Martin Grass, Alex Grass, and other family members held stakes in several suppliers and real estate interests doing business with the company. That year Rite Aid partnered with General Nutrition Companies, Inc. (GNC) and took a 25% stake in the Internet retailer drugstore.com. Later in 1999 Rite Aid began slashing its $5.1 billion debt by cutting corporate staff and selling off some stores in California and the Pacific Northwest. CEO Martin Grass resigned, and a team of former Fred Meyer officers — led by Robert Miller — took over.

In July 2000 the company announced it would restate profits that, over the past two years, had been inflated in excess of $1 billion. Later that year Rite Aid sold PCS Health Systems to pharmacy benefits manager Advance Paradigm for more than $1 billion (about $500 million less than what Rite Aid originally paid for it).

To raise cash Rite Aid sold large blocks of its drugstore.com stock, trimming its original 25% stake to less than 10% by April 2002. Former chairman and CEO Martin Grass, former general counsel and vice chairman Franklin Brown, and former CFO Frank Bergonzi, among others, were indicted on June 21, 2002, for allegedly falsifying Rite Aid's books.

In April 2003 former chairman and CEO Martin Grass agreed to pay nearly $1.5 million to settle a lawsuit in which shareholders alleged that Rite Aid's books were falsified, inflating the stock's value. In June Grass and former CFO Bergonzi both pleaded guilty to conspiracy to defraud shareholders. Eric Sorkin, Rite Aid's former VP of Pharmacy Services, pleaded guilty to conspiring to obstruct justice. The following month Rite Aid began mailing checks totaling nearly $140 million to thousands of its current and former shareholders damaged by the accounting scandal at the company. In October, former chief counsel Brown was convicted of conspiracy and lying to the Securities and Exchange Commission, among other charges.

In May 2004 Grass, whose father founded Rite Aid, struck a plea deal with prosecutors under which he was sentenced to eight years in prison. Also in May, several other former company executives, including ex-CFO Bergonzi and vice president Sorkin, were sentenced in the accounting scandal. In June, Rite Aid agreed to pay the US government $5.6 million (plus another $1.4 million to more than 20 states) to settle a federal lawsuit alleging the drugstore chain submitted false prescription claims to government insurance programs. In October, former vice chairman Brown was sentenced to 10 years in prison, the longest sentence of six Rite Aid officials charged in the accounting scandal.

Rite Aid founder Alex Grass died in August 2009 at the age of 82.

EXECUTIVES

Co-Chairman: Mary F. Sammons, age 63, $3,203,815 total compensation
Co-Chairman: Michel Coutu, age 56
President, CEO, and Director: John T. Standley, age 47, $4,537,844 total compensation
COO: Kenneth A. (Ken) Martindale, age 50, $1,326,331 total compensation
SEVP, CFO, and Chief Administrative Officer: Frank G. Vitrano, age 54, $1,601,852 total compensation
EVP Store Operations: Brian R. Fiala, age 49, $1,277,001 total compensation
EVP, General Counsel, and Secretary: Marc A. Strassler, age 62
EVP Pharmacy: Robert I. Thompson, age 56

SVP and Chief Compliance Officer: Anthony J. (Tony) Bellezza, age 42
SVP and Chief Accounting Officer: Douglas E. (Doug) Donley, age 47
SVP Human Resources: Steve Parsons, age 45
SVP Corporate Communications: Karen Rugen
SVP and CIO: Don P. Davis
SVP Pharmacy Business Development: Christopher S. (Chris) Hall, age 45
SVP Category Management: Tony Montini, age 57
SVP Managed Care and Government Affairs: William (Bill) Wolfe, age 46
SVP Pharmacy Operations: Dan Miller, age 53
SVP Supply Chain: Wilson A. Lester Jr., age 50
SVP Marketing: John Learish, age 44
Group VP Strategy and Investor Relations and Treasurer: Matt Schroeder, age 40
Director Public Relations: Cheryl Slavinsky, age 55
Auditors: Deloitte & Touche LLP

LOCATIONS

HQ: Rite Aid Corporation
30 Hunter Ln., Camp Hill, PA 17011
Phone: 717-761-2633   **Fax:** 717-975-5871
Web: www.riteaid.com

2010 Stores

	No.
New York	656
California	600
Pennsylvania	570
Michigan	286
New Jersey	270
North Carolina	242
Ohio	229
Georgia	195
Virginia	195
Massachusetts	159
Maryland	145
Washington	139
Kentucky	117
West Virginia	104
South Carolina	98
Alabama	95
Tennessee	88
Maine	81
Connecticut	78
Oregon	71
New Hampshire	68
Louisiana	66
Rhode Island	47
Delaware	43
Vermont	38
Mississippi	27
Utah	22
Colorado	20
Idaho	13
Indiana	10
District of Columbia	7
Nevada	1
Total	**4,780**

PRODUCTS/OPERATIONS

2010 Sales

	% of total
Prescription drugs	68
General merchandise & other	18
Over-the-counter medications & personal care	9
Health & beauty aids	5
Total	**100**

2010 Sales

	$ mil.	% of total
Pharmacy	17,356.0	67
Front-end	8,213.3	33
Other	99.8	—
Total	**25,669.1**	**100**

Selected Merchandise and Services

Beverages
Convenience foods
Cosmetics
Designer fragrances
Greeting cards
Health and personal care products
Household items
Over-the-counter drugs
Photo processing
Prescription drugs
Private-label products
Seasonal merchandise
Vitamins and minerals

COMPETITORS

A&P
Ahold USA
Costco Wholesale
CVS Caremark
Discount Drug
Dollar General
Family Dollar Stores
Kmart
Kroger
Marc Glassman
Medicine Shoppe
Publix
Safeway
Target
Walgreen
Wal-Mart

HISTORICAL FINANCIALS

Company Type: Public

Income Statement FYE: Saturday nearest last day of February

	REVENUE ($ mil.)	NET INCOME ($ mil.)	NET PROFIT MARGIN	EMPLOYEES
2/10	25,669	(507)	—	97,500
2/09	26,289	(2,915)	—	103,000
2/08	24,327	(1,079)	—	112,800
2/07	17,508	27	0.2%	69,700
2/06	17,271	1,273	7.4%	70,200
Annual Growth	**10.4%**	**—**	**—**	**8.6%**

2010 Year-End Financials

Debt ratio: —
Return on equity: —
Cash ($ mil.): 104
Current ratio: 2.07
Long-term debt ($ mil.): 6,319

No. of shares (mil.): 887
Dividends
  Yield: 0.0%
  Payout: —
Market value ($ mil.): 1,348

Stock History

NYSE: RAD

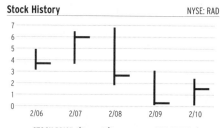

	STOCK PRICE ($) FY Close	P/E High	P/E Low	PER SHARE ($) Earnings	PER SHARE ($) Dividends	PER SHARE ($) Book Value
2/10	1.52	—	—	(0.59)	0.00	(1.89)
2/09	0.28	—	—	(3.49)	0.00	(1.35)
2/08	2.67	—	—	(1.54)	0.00	1.93
2/07	5.97	—	—	(0.01)	0.00	1.88
2/06	3.69	3	2	1.89	0.00	1.81
Annual Growth	**(19.9%)**	**—**	**—**	**—**	**—**	**—**

Robert Half

Robert Half International carries the full load of personnel services. The company places temporary and permanent staff through seven divisions: Accountemps, Robert Half Finance and Accounting, Robert Half Legal, OfficeTeam (general administrative), Robert Half Technology (information technology), Robert Half Management Resources (senior level professionals), and The Creative Group (advertising, marketing, and Web design). The firm has also established internal audit and risk consulting subsidiary Protiviti. Robert Half operates from more than 370 offices in some 40 states and 20 countries.

The firm placed about 157,000 employees in temporary assignments in 2009, recruiting them through direct marketing and print, radio, and Internet advertising. (This number was down from 220,000 employees placed in 2008.) Robert Half also has joint marketing agreements with many tech-related companies to coordinate joint mailings, cooperative advertising, and other promotions.

CEO Harold "Max" Messmer moonlights as an author and has published several popular employment books, including *Human Resources Kit For Dummies*. The company also publishes job reports and surveys on the latest employment trends and annual salary guides to track pay trends.

HISTORY

Robert Half founded Robert Half Inc. in 1948 as an employment agency for accountants. He developed Accountemps on the side to supply firms with accountants and other finance professionals on a temporary basis. His concept was a hit, and Half became known as a pioneer in the specialized employment services industry. He started franchising his business nationwide. The temp industry grew slowly in the 1960s and 1970s, until the 1980s brought a rapid expansion. By 1985 there were 150 independent Accountemps and Robert Half franchises.

Harold "Max" Messmer joined the company in 1985 for what would prove to be a tumultuous first couple of years. In 1986 Boothe Financial Corporation bought all of Robert Half's outstanding stock, and Messmer launched a program to buy all the Robert Half franchises. A year later Boothe sold Robert Half, which then went public as Robert Half International, placing Messmer at the helm as CEO and president.

Robert Half's focus on the accounting and financial services niche helped the company avoid the industry's price war of the early 1990s. The company's permanent placement operations accounted for nearly 20% of Robert Half's business in 1990. As corporate downsizing lessened the demand for permanent employees, the company's business slumped. The slow economy brought on some changes (reduced overhead and advertising cuts) and facilitated buybacks of Robert Half and Accountemps franchises.

In 1991 Robert Half started its OfficeTeam division to place temporary administrative office personnel. The division got off to a fast start in its initial year, earning some $2 million. Its success continued the following year, with sales rising to about $12 million. The permanent placement business, however, wasn't faring as well, and the company attempted to streamline

those operations by combining its Robert Half and Accountemps facilities.

Robert Half bought The Affiliates, a firm specializing in temporary legal support staff, in 1992. The company then expanded in the eastern US and Europe (through new offices in France, Belgium, and the UK) the next year. In 1994 Robert Half founded RHI Consulting, which provided information technology workers. By then the company had bought all but four of the original 150 Robert Half and Accountemps franchises. Messmer, meanwhile, had *Job Hunting For Dummies* published in 1995 (other books followed).

Robert Half announced a new division in 1997: RHI Management Resources, an operation that targets start-up companies in need of executive-level financial personnel. In 1999 the company added The Creative Group division, which provides advertising, marketing, and Web design staff, to its collection of services. Robert Half made its first foray into Eastern Europe in 2000 when it bought a Czech recruitment agency. The following year it began offering free online courses to finance and accounting professionals through an affiliation with SmartForce, which has been acquired by SkillSoft.

In 2002 Robert Half created Protiviti, an internal audit and risk consulting subsidiary, by hiring more than 750 former employees of Arthur Andersen's internal audit and risk consulting practice. The company bought the two remaining independent Robert Half franchises in 2003.

EXECUTIVES

Chairman and CEO: Harold M. (Max) Messmer Jr., age 64, $7,061,886 total compensation
Vice Chairman, President, and CFO: M. Keith Waddell, age 52, $4,031,505 total compensation
CIO: Sean Perry
EVP, Chief Administration Officer, and Treasurer: Michael C. Buckley, age 43, $2,175,925 total compensation
EVP, Secretary, and General Counsel: Steven Karel, age 60, $1,019,214 total compensation
EVP Corporate Development: Robert W. Glass, age 51, $1,143,360 total compensation
SVP and Associate General Counsel: Evelyn Crane-Oliver
SVP Operational Finance and Accounting: Paula Streit
SVP Marketing: Elena West
SVP Corporate Communications: Reesa M. Staten
SVP and Corporate Controller: Lex Doherty
President and COO, Staffing Services: Paul F. Gentzkow, age 54, $3,059,274 total compensation
President, Western U.S. and Canadian Operations: Rita Steel
President and CEO, Protiviti: Joseph A. Tarantino
Auditors: PricewaterhouseCoopers LLP

LOCATIONS

HQ: Robert Half International Inc.
2884 Sand Hill Rd., Menlo Park, CA 94025
Phone: 650-234-6000   **Fax:** 650-234-6999
Web: www.rhii.com

2009 Sales

	$ mil.	% of total
Domestic	2,161.8	71
Foreign	874.7	29
Total	**3,036.5**	**100**

PRODUCTS/OPERATIONS

2009 Sales

	$ mil.	% of total
Temporary & consultant staffing	2,471.1	81
Risk consulting & internal audit services	383.6	13
Permanent placement staffing	181.8	6
Total	**3,036.5**	**100**

Selected Operating Units

Accountemps (temporary accounting and finance personnel)
The Creative Group (advertising, marketing, and Web design)
OfficeTeam (temporary administrative and office personnel)
Protiviti (internal audit and risk consulting)
Robert Half Finance and Accounting (temporary accounting and finance personnel)
Robert Half Legal (temporary and full-time legal support personnel)
Robert Half Management Resources (senior-level accounting and finance personnel)
Robert Half Technology (temporary and contract IT personnel)

COMPETITORS

Adecco	Kforce
Deloitte Consulting	KPMG
Ernst & Young Global	Manpower
General Employment	PricewaterhouseCoopers
Enterprises	Randstad Holding
Headway Corporate	SFN Group
Resources	Solomon Page
Kelly Services	Winston Resources

HISTORICAL FINANCIALS

Company Type: Public

Income Statement

FYE: December 31

	REVENUE ($ mil.)	NET INCOME ($ mil.)	NET PROFIT MARGIN	EMPLOYEES
12/09	3,037	35	1.2%	166,900
12/08	4,601	250	5.4%	13,300
12/07	4,646	296	6.4%	272,300
12/06	4,014	283	7.1%	255,400
12/05	3,338	238	7.1%	230,000
Annual Growth	(2.3%)	(38.0%)	—	(7.7%)

2009 Year-End Financials

Debt ratio: 0.2%	No. of shares (mil.): 148
Return on equity: 3.7%	Dividends
Cash ($ mil.): 366	Yield: 1.8%
Current ratio: 2.51	Payout: 200.0%
Long-term debt ($ mil.): 2	Market value ($ mil.): 3,945

Stock History

NYSE: RHI

	STOCK PRICE ($) FY Close	P/E High/Low	PER SHARE ($) Earnings	Dividends	Book Value
12/09	26.73	117 59	0.24	0.48	6.10
12/08	20.82	18 9	1.63	0.44	6.67
12/07	27.04	23 13	1.81	0.40	6.67
12/06	37.12	27 18	1.65	0.32	7.06
12/05	37.89	29 18	1.36	0.28	6.58
Annual Growth	(8.4%)	— —	(35.2%)	14.4%	(1.9%)

Rock-Tenn Company

A rock-solid reputation? You betcha. One of North America's folding carton giants, Rock-Tenn produces packaging for food, paper goods, hardware, apparel, and many other consumer goods. Its lineup includes recycled and bleached paperboard, containerboard, consumer and corrugated packaging, and point-of-purchase displays. Specialty paperboard is also converted into book cover and laminated paperboard goods and sold to other manufacturers for end applications such as furniture, storage, and automotive components. Rock-Tenn's 100 facilities dot North America, Chile, and Argentina, serving Procter & Gamble, its largest single customer, and thousands of other companies, predominantly in the US.

The company is pursuing a combination of cost-cutting efforts and strategic acquisitions to build upon its mix of packaging products. Despite the economic downturn during 2008 and 2009, Rock-Tenn's business model, along with lower prices in 2009 for recycled fiber, natural gas, chemicals, and transportation, has moved operations in a positive direction. (Raw material costs that climbed in 2008 were passed on in price increases to Rock-Tenn customers.)

Rock-Tenn is benefiting particularly from its 2008 acquisition of Southern Container Corp., a New York-based private containerboard and corrugated packaging manufacturer. Southern Container operates one mill, eight corrugated box plants, two sheet plants, and four graphics facilities. Its capacity boosts Rock-Tenn's annual bleached and recycled paperboard production to some 2.4 million tons. Moreover, Southern Container's low operating cost assets are helping to increase the corrugated packaging segment's profit margins. Rock-Tenn's performance has also enjoyed a federal tax credit, available to paper producers who burn a byproduct of the papermaking process to generate electricity.

In 2007, the consumer packaging segment grew, too. Rock-Tenn picked up its remaining 40% interest in Fold-Pak (formerly GSD Packaging), giving Rock-Tenn a 100% stake in the food container maker, a relatively recession-proof business.

HISTORY

Former preacher Arthur Morris founded Rock-Tenn in 1936 as Southern Box Co., a folding carton maker. Acquisitions fueled the company's growth in the following years. During WWII it became Rock City Box Co. Morris' son-in-law, Worley Brown, was appointed CEO in 1967.

The company adopted its current name in 1973, after merging with Tennessee Paper Mills. Rock-Tenn bought Mead's recycled products unit in 1988 and began book cover production. Brad Currey, a banker who was recruited by Brown in 1976, became CEO in 1989.

Rock-Tenn bought a folding carton plant in Canada in 1993, and in 1994 the company went public. It acquired Olympic Packaging (folding cartons) and Alliance Display & Packaging (corrugated displays) in 1995. The company boosted its position as a leading maker of folding cartons in 1997 with its $414 million purchase of Waldorf Corporation, its largest acquisition to date. That year Rock-Tenn also bought two paperboard companies and formed RTS Packaging, its 65%-owned joint venture with Sonoco Products.

To cut costs and compensate for stagnant demand, Rock-Tenn closed several US plants in 1999. The following year CEO Brad Currey retired and was replaced by Jim Rubright, formerly an EVP at energy firm Sonat (El Paso Energy). Also in 2000 Rock-Tenn entered the gypsum paperboard liner business through a joint venture with Lafarge. In 2001 the company announced additional plant closings as demand for its products bottomed out.

In 2002 in a rebounding market Rock-Tenn bought point-of-purchase display and fixture maker Athena Industries, increasing annual sales by an estimated $12 million.

Pactiv purchased Rock-Tenn's packaging business in 2003 for about $60 million. The next year Rock-Tenn acquired a corrugated sheet facility located in Athens, Alabama, from Menasha Packaging Company. That move was part of an effort to expand its geographic reach. In 2005 the company acquired pulp and packaging assets from Gulf States Paper (now The Westervelt Company).

EXECUTIVES

Chairman and CEO: James A. (Jim) Rubright, age 62, $11,009,647 total compensation
EVP, CFO, and Chief Administrative Officer: Steven C. Voorhees, age 55, $2,049,234 total compensation
EVP Containerboard and Corrugated Packaging: Jim Porter Jr., age 58, $2,718,994 total compensation
EVP: Michael E. (Mike) Kiepura, age 53, $2,311,355 total compensation
EVP and General Manager, Recycled Fiber Division: Erik Deadwyler
EVP Specialty Paperboard Products Division: President and CEO, RTS: Richard E. (Dick) Steed
EVP and General Manager Alliance: Craig A. Gunckel
Chief Accounting Officer: A. Stephen Meadows, age 59
SVP, General Counsel, and Secretary: Robert B. McIntosh, age 52, $1,360,122 total compensation
VP Risk Management and Supply Chain: Gregory L. (Greg) King
VP Employee Services: Jennifer Graham-Johnson
VP Six Sigma: George W. Turner
VP and CIO: Paul W. Stecher
VP and Treasurer: John Stakel
President and CEO, RTS Packaging, LLC: Alan P. Bosma
Auditors: Ernst & Young LLP

LOCATIONS

HQ: Rock-Tenn Company
504 Thrasher St., Norcross, GA 30071
Phone: 770-448-2193   **Fax:** 678-291-7666
Web: www.rocktenn.com

PRODUCTS/OPERATIONS

2009 Sales

	$ mil.	% of total
Consumer packaging	1,478.0	53
Corrugated packaging	715.6	26
Merchandising displays	320.2	11
Specialty paperboard products	298.5	10
Total	**2,812.3**	**100**

Selected Products

Packaging products
  Folding cartons (for food items, hardware products, paper goods, and other items)
  Protective packaging (solid fiber partitions)
Paperboard
  100% recycled coated and uncoated grades
  Laminated paperboard (for book covers, book binders, and furniture products)
Specialty corrugated packaging and displays
  Corrugated packaging and sheet
  Point-of-purchase displays

COMPETITORS

Caraustar	Kapstone Paper and
Clearwater Paper	Packaging
Georgia-Pacific	Shorewood Packaging
Graphic Packaging Holding	Smurfit-Stone Container
Green Bay Packaging	Sonoco Products
International Paper	Temple-Inland

HISTORICAL FINANCIALS
Company Type: Public

Income Statement
FYE: September 30

	REVENUE ($ mil.)	NET INCOME ($ mil.)	NET PROFIT MARGIN	EMPLOYEES
9/09	2,812	222	7.9%	10,300
9/08	2,839	82	2.9%	10,700
9/07	2,316	82	3.5%	9,300
9/06	2,138	29	1.3%	9,500
9/05	1,734	18	1.0%	9,600
Annual Growth	**12.9%**	**88.5%**	**—**	**1.8%**

2009 Year-End Financials
Debt ratio: 166.0%
Return on equity: 31.4%
Cash ($ mil.): 12
Current ratio: 1.47
Long-term debt ($ mil.): 1,289
No. of shares (mil.): 39
Dividends
  Yield: 0.8%
  Payout: 7.0%
Market value ($ mil.): 1,835

Stock History
NYSE: RKT

	STOCK PRICE ($) FY Close	P/E High/Low		PER SHARE ($) Earnings	Dividends	Book Value
9/09	47.11	9	4	5.75	0.40	19.94
9/08	39.98	22	10	2.14	0.40	16.44
9/07	28.90	21	9	2.07	0.39	15.12
9/06	19.80	27	16	0.77	0.36	13.06
9/05	15.10	34	20	0.49	0.36	11.71
Annual Growth	**32.9%**	**—**	**—**	**85.1%**	**2.7%**	**14.2%**

Rockwell Automation

Rockwell Automation is rocking along as one of the world's largest industrial automation companies, serving the automotive, food and beverage (including dairies), personal care, life sciences, oil and gas, mining, and paper and pulp markets. The company's Control Products & Solutions unit makes industrial automation products, such as motor starters and contactors, relays, timers, signaling devices, and variable-speed drives. To complement its automation product offerings, Rockwell's Architecture & Software unit offers factory management software and motion control, sensor, and machine safety components.

Acquisitions are a key link to the company's growth. It bought a majority of Canadian engineering firm Rutter Hinz Inc.'s North American assets for an undisclosed price in 2009. Rutter

Hinz is a subsidiary of Rutter Inc. The deal will add engineering expertise in industrial automation, process control, and power distribution, specifically for the oil and gas industry, as well as boost the company's growth in the oil and gas industry in Canada. Earlier that year Rockwell Automation acquired certain assets and liabilities of Xi'an Hengsheng Science & Technology to advance its global footprint and to better serve its customers in China.

Additionally, it purchased CEDES Safety & Automation (machine safety products), as well as software makers Incuity Software (factory control systems) and Pavilion Technologies (process control systems) in 2008. All three deals helped strengthen its product portfolio in automation and enterprise intelligence software.

The company's Architecture & Software unit markets products under such brand names as Rockwell Software and FactoryTalk. The Control Products unit markets the ICS Triplex brand. Both units manufacture components with the Allen Bradley and A-B brand names.

HISTORY

Rockwell Automation is the legacy of two early-20th-century entrepreneurs: Willard Rockwell and Clement Melville Keys. Rockwell gained control of Wisconsin Parts Company, an Oshkosh, Wisconsin, maker of automotive axles, in 1919. He went on to buy a number of industrial manufacturers, merging them in 1953 to create Rockwell Spring & Axle. Renamed Rockwell-Standard in 1958, it led the world in the production of mechanical automotive parts by 1967.

In 1928 Keys founded North American Aviation (NAA) as a holding company for his aviation interests. General Motors bought NAA in 1934 and named James Kindelberger as its president. The company moved in 1935 from Maryland to Inglewood, California, where it built military training planes.

NAA made more than 15,000 AT-6 trainers during WWII, and it produced the B-25 bomber and the P-51 fighter planes. By the end of the war, NAA had built nearly 43,000 aircraft, more than any other US manufacturer. NAA's sales plunged at the end of WWII. In 1948 GM took its subsidiary public; Kindelberger revitalized the company with new factories in California and Ohio. Major products included the F-86 (1948) and its successor, the F-100 (1953). NAA also produced the X-15 rocket plane (1959).

In the 1960s NAA built rocket engines and spacecraft for the Apollo program. NAA merged with Rockwell-Standard, creating North American Rockwell in 1967. The company adopted the Rockwell International name in 1973.

Rockwell won the contract for the B-1 bomber in 1970 and the space shuttle orbiter in 1972. The following year it bought Collins Radio, the backbone of its avionics segment. Rockwell briefly ventured into consumer goods, buying Admiral (appliances) in 1974 and selling it in 1979.

The company bought Allen-Bradley (industrial electronics) in 1985. Facing declining military-related revenues as B-1 production ended, Don Beall, who became CEO in 1988, spent billions on modernizing plants and research and development for Rockwell's electronics and graphics units. In 1989 Rockwell sold its Measurement & Flow Control Division and bought the Baker Perkins printing machinery business in the UK.

Rockwell sold its fiber-optic transmission equipment unit to Alcatel (now Alcatel-Lucent) in 1991. It acquired industrial automation supplier Sprecher + Schuh in 1993 and Reliance Electric (which was merged with Allen-Bradley) in 1995. The next year Rockwell sold its aerospace and defense divisions to Boeing for $3.2 billion and its Graphic Systems business to investment firm Stonington Partners. It also acquired integrated circuit maker Brooktree Corp. in 1996.

A 1997 federal court order forced Rockwell to pay Celeritas Technologies nearly $58 million for breaching patent protections and misappropriating trade secrets related to computer and cell phone communication technology. That year Rockwell acquired Hughes Electronics' airline passenger communications and entertainment systems unit (now The DIRECTV Group), and it spun off its automotive unit as Meritor Automotive (now ArvinMeritor). President Don Davis also became CEO in 1997.

Rockwell spun off its sluggish semiconductor business to shareholders (as Conexant Systems) in 1998 in a move to cut losses and focus on its faster-growing industrial automation operations.

In 1999 Rockwell moved its headquarters from California to Milwaukee, the base of its automation division. That year the company's Rockwell Collins unit bought out Kaiser Aerospace and Electronics' interest in their avionics joint venture, Flight Dynamics. In 2001 it spun off its Rockwell Collins avionics and communications unit to its shareholders. Concurrently, Rockwell International changed its name to Rockwell Automation to reflect its new focus.

Davis stepped down as CEO in 2004 and was replaced by Keith Nosbusch, head of Rockwell's Control Systems unit. He also took on the chairman's role the following year.

In 2007 the company sold most of the operations of its former power systems unit, which offered motors and motor repair services, as well as bearings, bushings, clutches, and brakes. Rockwell sold its Dodge mechanical power transmission division, as well as the industrial motors unit of its Reliance Electric subsidiary to Baldor Electric for $1.8 billion. (Rockwell retained the rest of Reliance, which makes electrical drives.)

Internationally, Rockwell Automation bought UK firm Industrial Control Services (ICS Triplex) in 2007 to help expand its Control Products & Solutions unit.

EXECUTIVES

Chairman, President, and CEO: Keith D. Nosbusch, age 59, $7,246,189 total compensation
SVP and CFO: Theodore D. Crandall, age 54, $2,111,527 total compensation
SVP: Steven A. Eisenbrown, age 56, $2,235,763 total compensation
SVP: Robert A. Ruff, age 61, $1,904,668 total compensation
SVP: John P. McDermott, age 51, $1,741,519 total compensation
SVP, General Counsel, and Secretary: Douglas M. Hagerman, age 48, $1,500,890 total compensation
SVP Human Resources: Susan J. Schmitt, age 46
SVP Operations and Engineering Services: Martin Thomas, age 51
SVP and CTO: Sujeet Chand, age 51
SVP Strategic Development and Communications: John D. Cohn, age 55

VP and Chief Intellectual Property Counsel: John M. Miller, age 42
VP and General Tax Counsel: Kent G. Coppins, age 56
VP and Treasurer: Steven W. Etzel, age 49
VP and Controller: David M. Dorgan, age 45
VP and General Auditor: A. Lawrence Stuever, age 57
VP Investor Relations and Corporate Development: Rondi Rohr-Dralle, age 53
President Asia/Pacific: Keiran Coulton
Director External Communications: John Bernaden
Auditors: Deloitte & Touche LLP

LOCATIONS

HQ: Rockwell Automation, Inc.
1201 S. 2nd St., Milwaukee, WI 53204
Phone: 414-382-2000   **Fax:** 414-382-4444
Web: www.rockwellautomation.com

2009 Sales

	$ mil.	% of total
Americas		
US	2,209.2	51
Latin America	324.8	8
Canada	257.1	6
Europe, Middle East & Africa	962.1	22
Asia/Pacific	579.3	13
Total	**4,332.5**	**100**

PRODUCTS/OPERATIONS

2009 Sales

	$ mil.	% of total
Control Products & Solutions	2,609.0	60
Architecture & Software	1,723.5	40
Total	**4,332.5**	**100**

Selected Products and Services

Condition sensors and switches
Drive systems
Motion control systems
Motor control centers
Motor starters and contactors
Programmable controls
Push buttons
Relays, timers, and temperature controllers
Signaling devices
Software (Rockwell Software)
Termination and protection devices
Transformers
Variable-speed drives

COMPETITORS

ABB	Metso
Baldor Electric	Mitsubishi Corp.
Danaher	OMRON
Dematic GmbH	Schneider Electric
Eaton	Select Business Solutions
Emerson Electric	Siemens AG
Hitachi	Toshiba
Honeywell ACS	Weiss Instrument
Invensys	Wonderware

HISTORICAL FINANCIALS

Company Type: Public

Income Statement				FYE: September 30
	REVENUE ($ mil.)	NET INCOME ($ mil.)	NET PROFIT MARGIN	EMPLOYEES
9/09	4,333	221	5.1%	19,000
9/08	5,698	578	10.1%	21,000
9/07	5,004	1,488	29.7%	20,000
9/06	5,561	625	11.2%	23,000
9/05	5,003	540	10.8%	21,000
Annual Growth	(3.5%)	(20.0%)	—	(2.5%)

2009 Year-End Financials

Debt ratio: 68.7%
No. of shares (mil.): 143
Return on equity: 14.7%
Dividends
Cash ($ mil.): 644
Yield: 2.7%
Current ratio: 2.25
Payout: 74.8%
Long-term debt ($ mil.): 905
Market value ($ mil.): 6,075

Stock History
NYSE: ROK

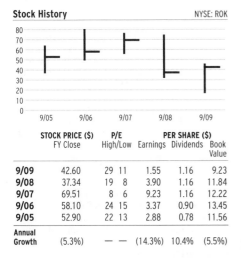

	STOCK PRICE ($) FY Close	P/E High/Low		PER SHARE ($) Earnings	Dividends	Book Value
9/09	42.60	29	11	1.55	1.16	9.23
9/08	37.34	19	8	3.90	1.16	11.84
9/07	69.51	8	6	9.23	1.16	12.22
9/06	58.10	24	15	3.37	0.90	13.45
9/05	52.90	22	13	2.88	0.78	11.56
Annual Growth	(5.3%)	—	—	(14.3%)	10.4%	(5.5%)

Roper Industries

Control, pump, scan, authorize, and analyze: Roper Industries is an amalgamation of activities. The company designs, manufactures, and distributes a slew of industrial high-tech tools, scientific imaging equipment and software, energy systems and controls, and radio frequency (RF) devices. Its lines are used in niche markets engaged in RF, as well as water, energy, research and medical, education, and security applications. Roper divides its operations into four business segments: Energy Systems and Controls, Scientific and Industrial Imaging, Industrial Technology Products, and RF Technology.

Roper's recent direction has focused on complementing or extending its product portfolio coupled with increasing its market exposure, both in the US and abroad. Although the economic downturn eroded sales, Roper has kept its eye out for acquisitions that position the company for a recovery. In mid-2010 the company agreed to acquire iTradeNetwork, a provider of Software-as-a-Service (SaaS)-based trading network and information services used by the food industry, from private equity Accel-KKR, for $525 million.

Also meeting Roper's acquisition criteria for recovery, Alabama-based United Toll Services (UTS) beckoned. UTS makes toll and traffic systems and software vital to transportation infrastructure projects, which are anticipated to receive an uptick in funding. Swelling its Scientific and Industrial Imaging lineup, Roper acquired Washington-based Verathon, a medical device provider. Verathon brings a number of proprietary products, notably a noninvasive BladderScan and GlideScope video laryngoscope, promising an increased market as the global population ages. The investment for both transactions totaled over $350 million.

In 2008 Roper purchased The CBORD Group for $375 million. CBORD makes electronic ID and debit cards for colleges and universities, hospitals, supermarkets, and other businesses and institutions. The acquisition diversifies the company's RF Technology interests beyond transportation and water utilities to health care and education end-markets.

HISTORY

George Roper founded the company in 1919 in Rockford, Illinois, to make gas stoves and gear pumps. In the late 1950s the stove works were spun off to Sears as the Roper Corporation, and the pump-making operations were moved to Georgia. Roper was a public company until a 1981 LBO. UK-born Derrick Key, who joined Roper in 1982, became CEO in 1991. The company went public again the next year as Roper Industries.

During the 1990s Roper grew by acquisitions both at home and abroad. However, it gained entry into Eastern Europe in 1993 by winning a seven-year contract worth $350 million with Russian gas czar OAO Gazprom to install advanced control systems across Russia's vast pipeline system.

The company added digital-imaging and analytical systems for electron microscopes in 1996 by purchasing Gatan International, a California company with branches in Germany and the UK. Roper's 1997 purchases included Industrial Data Systems (leak-testing equipment, Utah); Petrotech (systems integration for fluid-control products; Louisiana, with an Indonesian unit); and Princeton Instruments (spectral and imaging cameras; New Jersey, with locations in France and the UK).

Roper expanded its digital-imaging line in 1998 by acquiring Photometrics, Ltd. (digital cameras and detectors) and PMC/Beta Limited (vibration sensing and control equipment). Roper's bid to buy Leach Holding fell through, impeding its effort to boost its industrial components offerings. In 1999 it bought Varlen's petroleum analysis instrumentation unit and Eastman Kodak's motion analysis operations (digital video equipment).

Roper's focus on providing high-margin products to niche markets spurred growth through acquisitions that included Eastman Kodak's high-speed and high-resolution digital video equipment unit, as well as makers of testing equipment for the petroleum industry. And, in its largest acquisition to date, the company bought Struers Holdings' two operating units, which provided preparation equipment used in quality inspection (Struers A/S), and material shaping equipment used to make semiconductors and optoelectronics (Logitech).

Roper didn't rest after acquiring Hansen Technologies and adding Streurs' operating units in 2001; in 2002 it spent about $83 million on Zetec (industrial testing equipment), Duncan Technologies (industrial digital cameras), AiCambridge/"Qualitek" (leak detection equipment), Quantitative Imaging (industrial and scientific digital cameras), and Definitive Imaging (image analysis software). At the same time, however, Roper exited some of its Petrotech businesses and was hit by the downturn in the semiconductor industry, the oil and gas exploration markets, and the generally weak economy.

At the end of 2003 Roper acquired Neptune Technology Group Holdings (meter-reading technology) for $475 million. Expanding beyond its core controls, pumps, and analytical tools businesses, Roper acquired radio-frequency identification technology and related services provider TransCore Holdings for $597 million in 2004.

In 2005 the company purchased Louisville, Colorado-based security applications technologies provider Inovonics Wireless Corporation for $45 million. Roper strengthened its presence in the medical imaging market in 2005 by acquiring Kalona, Iowa-based CIVCO Medical Instruments Co., Inc., a supplier of specialized medical products, from KRG Capital Partners, LLC. It also bought Orange City, Iowa-based MEDTEC, Inc., a maker of technology used in diagnosing and treating cancer, for about $150 million, to fold into its CIVCO operations.

In late 2006 the company acquired Dynisco LLC for $243 million from the Audax Group, a private equity investment firm. Also known as Dynisco Instruments, the business made pressure and temperature measurement and control instruments, primarily for the plastics industry, with applications in life sciences. In recent years Dynisco acquired Alpha Technologies and Viatran Corp., suppliers of analytical instruments and sensors for various applications.

In 2008 Roper acquired Horizon Software, a provider of transaction software for the corporate dining, health care, K-12 education, military, and senior living markets

EXECUTIVES

Chairman, President, and CEO: Brian D. Jellison, age 64, $3,154,943 total compensation
VP and CFO: John Humphrey, age 44, $2,991,933 total compensation
VP Industrial Technology: Nigel W. (Will) Crocker, age 55, $1,377,056 total compensation
VP, General Counsel, and Secretary: David B. Liner, age 54, $1,177,448 total compensation
VP Scientific and Industrial Imaging: Benjamin W. (Ben) Wood, age 49, $1,394,336 total compensation
VP Energy Systems and Controls: Timothy J. Winfrey, age 49, $1,541,368 total compensation
VP and Controller: Paul J. Soni
Auditors: PricewaterhouseCoopers LLP

LOCATIONS

HQ: Roper Industries, Inc.
6901 Professional Pkwy. East, Ste. 200, Sarasota, FL 34240
Phone: 941-556-2601   **Fax:** 941-556-2670
Web: www.roperind.com

2009 Sales

	$ mil.	% of total
US	1,526.4	74
Other countries	523.2	26
Total	**2,049.6**	**100**

PRODUCTS/OPERATIONS

2009 Sales

	$ mil.	% of total
RF Technology	717.7	35
Industrial Technology	536.2	26
Energy Systems & Controls	440.9	22
Scientific & Industrial Imaging	354.8	17
Total	**2,049.6**	**100**

Selected Products

Energy Systems and Controls
Control systems
Fluid properties testing equipment
Industrial valves and controls
Nondestructive inspection and measurement
    instrumentation
Sensors and controls

Industrial Technology
Flow measurement equipment
Industrial leak testing equipment
Industrial pumps
Materials analysis equipment and consumables
Water meter and AMR products and systems

RF Technology
Card systems/integrated security solutions
Freight matching
Toll and traffic systems

Scientific and Industrial Imaging
Digital imaging products and software
Handheld and vehicle mount computers and software
Medical products and software

COMPETITORS

ABB
Agilent Technologies
Ampco-Pittsburgh
Cameron International
CEM
CIRCOR International
Coherent, Inc.
Colfax
Curtiss-Wright
DXP Enterprises
Emerson Electric
Entegris
Flowserve
Gorman-Rupp
Halliburton
Hamilton Sundstrand
Haskel
Honeywell International
IBM Software
IDEX
IMI plc
Itron
ITT Corp.
Microsoft
Newport Corp.
Oracle
Parker Hannifin
PerkinElmer
Precision Castparts
Robbins & Myers
Rotork
Schneider Electric
SpiraxSarco
SPX
Sumitomo Electric
Thermo Fisher Scientific
Transcat
Tuthill
Tyco
Varian

HISTORICAL FINANCIALS

Company Type: Public

Income Statement

FYE: December 31

	REVENUE ($ mil.)	NET INCOME ($ mil.)	NET PROFIT MARGIN	EMPLOYEES
12/09	2,050	240	11.7%	7,650
12/08	2,306	287	12.4%	7,900
12/07	2,102	250	11.9%	7,100
12/06	1,701	193	11.4%	6,900
12/05	1,454	153	10.5%	6,000
Annual Growth	9.0%	11.8%	—	6.3%

2009 Year-End Financials

Debt ratio: 43.0%
Return on equity: 10.8%
Cash ($ mil.): 168
Current ratio: 1.82
Long-term debt ($ mil.): 1,041

No. of shares (mil.): 94
Dividends
  Yield: 0.7%
  Payout: 13.2%
Market value ($ mil.): 4,921

Stock History

NYSE: ROP

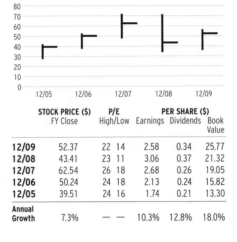

	STOCK PRICE ($) FY Close	P/E High/Low		PER SHARE ($) Earnings	Dividends	Book Value
12/09	52.37	22	14	2.58	0.34	25.77
12/08	43.41	23	11	3.06	0.37	21.32
12/07	62.54	26	18	2.68	0.26	19.05
12/06	50.24	24	18	2.13	0.24	15.82
12/05	39.51	24	16	1.74	0.21	13.30
Annual Growth	7.3%	—	—	10.3%	12.8%	18.0%

Ross Stores

Ross wants to let you dress (and lots more) for less. The #2 off-price apparel retailer (behind TJX Cos.) operates about 1,000 Ross Dress for Less and dd's DISCOUNTS stores that sell mostly closeout merchandise, including men's, women's, and children's clothing, at prices well below those of department and specialty stores. While apparel accounts for more than 50% of sales, Ross also sells small furnishings, toys and games, luggage, and jewelry in select stores. Featuring the Ross "Dress for Less" trademark, the chain targets 18- to 54-year-old white-collar shoppers from primarily middle-income households. Ross stores are located in strip malls in 27 states, mostly in the western US, and Guam.

Ross Stores' off-price business model has served the company well as the US economy entered a deep recession and consumers searched for bargains. The company believes that its dd's DISCOUNTS chain (launched in 2004) serves one of the fastest-growing demographic markets in the US. The ultra-low-price spinoff, which offers brand-name apparel at a 20%-70% discount, has grown to number more than 50 locations in Arizona, California, Florida, and Texas. The 25,000-sq.-ft. stores are located in strip shopping centers in urban and suburban neighborhoods.

About a quarter of Ross Stores are in California, where discount department store operator Kohl's is expanding rapidly after acquiring about 30 stores that once belonged to defunct discount retailer Mervyn's. On the East Coast, Ross recently opened a new 1.3-million-sq.-ft. distribution center in South Carolina to support its growth in the Southeastern US.

To boost its relationships with suppliers, Ross does not require them to provide markdown/promotional allowances or return privileges. This, combined with opportunistic purchases (closeouts such as manufacturer overruns and canceled orders), allows the company to obtain large discounts on merchandise. As a result, Ross Stores' customers typically pay 20% to 60% less than department and specialty store prices. Ross holds down costs by offering minimal service and few frills inside its stores.

HISTORY

In 1957 the Ross family founded Ross Stores and opened its first junior department store; by 1982 there were six of the stores in the San Francisco area. That year two retailing veterans, Stuart Moldaw (founder of Country Casuals and The Athletic Shoe Factory) and Donald Rowlett (creator of Woolworth's off-price subsidiary, J. Brannam), led the acquisition of the company. Moldaw (chairman) and Rowlett (president) wanted to create an off-price chain in California, where — despite the success such endeavors were having in the rest of the country — such stores were largely absent. The duo intended to establish a foothold by saturating California markets before competitors muddied the waters.

They restocked the stores with brand-name men's, women's, and children's apparel, shoes, accessories, and domestics merchandise at reduced prices. Before the end of 1982, they opened two more Ross "Dress for Less" stores; the next year 18 more were added, including the chain's first non-California store, in Reno, Nevada (much of the chain's expansion came through the acquisition of existing strip mall stores). Another 40 stores were added in 1984.

The company went public in 1985 to help fund its expansion and extended its reach to include Colorado, Florida, Georgia, New Mexico, and Oregon; that year it opened 41 stores. In 1986, 39 new stores were opened, including locations in Maryland, North Carolina, and Virginia, though the company was forced to close 25 unprofitable stores, primarily in recession-hammered Texas and Oklahoma. Ross lost more than $41 million for the year, and the honeymoon was over.

Rowlett resigned in 1987, and company veteran Norman Ferber was soon named CEO. Ross opened only 11 stores that year, all of which were located in markets the company had already broached. It also decided to focus its expansion efforts in three markets: the West Coast; the Washington, DC, area; and Florida. On the merchandise side, housewares were dropped and cosmetics, fragrances, and high-end clothing were added. Ross returned to the black in 1987, posting an $11 million profit. The company continued refining its merchandising strategy, and by 1989 it had more than 150 stores, making it one of the largest off-price retailers.

Ross opened 72 stores between 1990 and 1992, bringing its total to more than 220 stores as sales passed the $1 billion mark. Ferber became chairman in 1993 and continued to focus the company on existing markets. The chain grew to more than 290 stores by the end of 1995. VP Michael Balmuth was named CEO the next year.

The company's buying department had more than tripled in size by 1998, allowing it to have buyers in the right place at the right time to take advantage of buying opportunities. The nonapparel business tripled during the same time, both keys to the retailer's success. That year Ross added fine jewelry, maternity wear, sporting goods, small furnishings, and educational toys to its list of product offerings. With its stock price sagging in late 1998, Ross began a $120 million stock repurchase program in 1999. After repurchasing 5.4 million shares of its stock, the company pledged to continue the program through 2001. Ross opened 30 stores in 1999; its 34 openings in 2000 included its first non-US store in Guam.

In 2001 the company entered new markets in Georgia, Montana, North Carolina, South Carolina, and Wyoming, and opened new stores in existing markets, for a total of 45 new stores.

Ross opened 60 new stores in 2002 and closed five others, followed in 2003 by 61 new stores, some of which were in new markets such as Louisiana and Tennessee.

In August 2004 Ross opened its first three dd's DISCOUNTS stores in Vallejo, San Leandro, and Fresno, California. The retailer moved its headquarters from Newark, California, to Pleasanton in mid-2004 and then sold the Newark property for about $17 million.

The company opened 10 dd's DISCOUNTS stores and about 75 Ross stores in 2005. Ross also purchased a 685,000-sq.-ft. warehouse in Moreno Valley, California, that year.

The retailer's deal with supermarket operator Albertsons, inked in late 2006, fueled its 2007 expansion plans and secured 46 Albertsons stores located in Arizona, California, Colorado, Florida, Oklahoma, and Texas. dd's DISCOUNTS expanded beyond California in 2007, with its first stores in Arizona, Florida, and Texas.

EXECUTIVES

Chairman: Norman A. Ferber, age 61
Vice Chairman and CEO: Michael A. Balmuth, age 59,
  $10,599,729 total compensation
President and COO: Michael B. O'Sullivan, age 46,
  $6,688,922 total compensation
President and Chief Merchandising Officer, Ross Dress for Less: Barbara Rentler, age 52,
  $7,513,392 total compensation
President and Chief Development Officer:
  James S. Fassio, age 55
Group EVP Merchandising, Ross Home, Men's, and Children's: Lisa Panattoni, age 47,
  $5,772,529 total compensation
EVP Stores and Loss Prevention: Gary L. Cribb, age 45
EVP Supply Chain and Allocation and CIO:
  Michael K. (Mike) Kobayashi
EVP Merchandising: Jennifer Vecchio, age 44
EVP Merchandising: Bernie Brautigan
EVP Merchandising: Dan Cline
EVP Strategy, Marketing, and Human Resources:
  Ken Caruana
EVP Merchandising, dd's DISCOUNTS:
  Douglas (Doug) Baker
SVP and CFO: John G. Call, age 51,
  $1,366,849 total compensation
SVP Property Development: Gregg McGillis
SVP Stores: Mary Walter
SVP Human Resources: D. Jane Marvin
SVP Merchandise Control: Art Roth
SVP, General Counsel, and Corporate Secretary:
  Mark LeHocky
SVP Supply Chain: Michael L. Wilson
Senior Director Investor Relations: Bobbi Chaville
Auditors: Deloitte & Touche LLP

LOCATIONS

HQ: Ross Stores, Inc.
  4440 Rosewood Dr., Pleasanton, CA 94588
Phone: 925-965-4400
Web: www.rossstores.com

2010 Stores

	No.
US	
California	259
Texas	153
Florida	125
Arizona	52
Georgia	44
North Carolina	32
Pennsylvania	32
Virginia	32
Washington	30
Colorado	28
Oregon	25
Tennessee	25
South Carolina	20
Nevada	20
Maryland	18
Oklahoma	18
Alabama	17
Hawaii	12
Utah	12
Louisiana	11
New Jersey	10
Idaho	9
Montana	6
New Mexico	6
Mississippi	5
Wyoming	2
Delaware	1
Guam	1
Total	**1,005**

PRODUCTS/OPERATIONS

2010 Stores

	No.
Ross Dress for Less	953
dd's DISCOUNTS	52
Total	**1,005**

2010 Sales

	% of total
Women's apparel	30
Home accents, bed & bath	24
Men's apparel	13
Fine jewelry, accessories, lingerie & fragrances	13
Shoes	11
Children's apparel	9
Total	**100**

Selected Merchandise

Bed and bath
Children's apparel
Cookware
Educational toys
Fine jewelry
Fragrances
Gourmet foods
Home accents
Ladies' apparel
  Accessories
  Dresses
  Junior
  Lingerie
  Maternity
  Misses sportswear
  Petites
  Women's World
Luggage
Men's apparel
  Traditional men's
  Young men's
Shoes
Small electronics
Small furnishings
Sporting goods and exercise equipment

COMPETITORS

Big Lots	J. C. Penney
Burlington Coat Factory	Kmart
Cato	Kohl's
Charming Shoppes	Men's Wearhouse
Dress Barn	Sears
Family Dollar Stores	Target
Filene's Basement	TJX Companies
Fred's	Wal-Mart

HISTORICAL FINANCIALS

Company Type: Public

Income Statement				FYE: Saturday nearest January 31
	REVENUE ($ mil.)	NET INCOME ($ mil.)	NET PROFIT MARGIN	EMPLOYEES
1/10	7,184	443	6.2%	45,600
1/09	6,486	305	4.7%	40,000
1/08	5,975	261	4.4%	39,100
1/07	5,570	242	4.3%	35,800
1/06	4,944	200	4.0%	33,200
Annual Growth	9.8%	22.0%	—	8.3%

2010 Year-End Financials

Debt ratio: 13.0%
Return on equity: 41.1%
Cash ($ mil.): 768
Current ratio: 1.47
Long-term debt ($ mil.): 150

No. of shares (mil.): 122
Dividends
  Yield: 1.0%
  Payout: 12.4%
Market value ($ mil.): 5,608

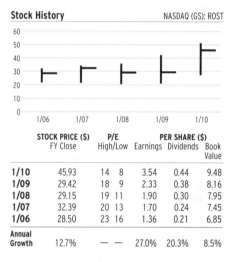

Stock History				NASDAQ (GS): ROST

	STOCK PRICE ($) FY Close	P/E High/Low		PER SHARE ($) Earnings	Dividends	Book Value
1/10	45.93	14	8	3.54	0.44	9.48
1/09	29.42	18	9	2.33	0.38	8.16
1/08	29.15	19	11	1.90	0.30	7.95
1/07	32.39	20	13	1.70	0.24	7.45
1/06	28.50	23	16	1.36	0.21	6.85
Annual Growth	12.7%	—	—	27.0%	20.3%	8.5%

Rowan Companies

Where does a gorilla drill for oil? Anywhere it wants if it is one of Rowan Companies' *Gorilla*-class heavy-duty offshore drilling rigs. Rowan performs contract drilling of oil and gas wells. Its fleet consists of more than 20 jack-up rigs and 30 land drilling rigs. The company performs contract drilling primarily in the Middle East, Texas, the Gulf of Mexico, and in the North Sea. Rowan plans to maintain its competitive edge by beefing up its current fleet of equipment. Subsidiary LeTourneau Technologies operates a mini-steel mill and manufactures heavy equipment including front-end loaders, log stackers, and gantry cranes. LeTourneau's marine group builds offshore jack-up drilling rigs, pumps, and motors.

Rowan Companies' combination of contract drilling and an in-house manufacturing company that supplies rigs gives the company a distinct edge over its drilling rivals, most of which have to rely solely on third-party manufacturers to supply its rigs. The manufacturing unit also provides it with a more diverse base of customers and a second major revenue stream.

In a move to further expand its fleet, in 2010 the company agreed to acquire Norway-based Skie Drilling, which has three high-specification jack-up rigs on order (being built by Keppel FELS in Singapore) and which are expected to commence operating in 2010 and 2011.

Diversifying its fleet, the company added *Tarzan*-class jack-up rigs designed for deep drilling in shallow water on the outer continental shelf of the Gulf of Mexico. Its fourth *Tarzan*-class rig was completed in 2008. That year the company secured a term drilling contract for work offshore in Saudi Arabia. In 2009 Saudi Aramco accounted for 15% of total revenues.

The global recession and the resulting lower oil prices and the slump in oil and gas exploration and other industrial activities pulled down the company's overall revenues in 2009.

HISTORY

Rowan Drilling Company was founded in 1923 as a contract drilling business. In 1947 it incorporated as Rowan Companies. Twenty years later Rowan acquired Era Aviation, a small, Alaska-based helicopter company. Rowan began to concentrate on jack-up rigs in 1970. Two years later Bob Palmer, who had started with the company in 1953 as a roughneck, became president.

The boom times for the oil industry went bust in the mid-1980s, and so did Rowan's net income. In 1991 Era acquired 49% of KLM Helikopters, a subsidiary of KLM Airlines. The company bought Marathon LeTourneau from General Cable Corp. in 1994 and rechristened it LeTourneau. In 1996 Rowan sold its Argentine drilling subsidiary. Two years later Era dumped its 49% stake in KLM ERA Helicopters to facilitate KLM's exit from the helicopter business.

With oil prices rebounding from a slump, the company had most of its 15 Gulf of Mexico rigs hired out by the end of 1999, up from only one-third in action earlier in the year. In 2000 the company relocated its rigs remaining in the North Sea to the Gulf of Mexico and added a new rig, the *Gorilla VI* super-jack-up, to its drilling fleet. The company reached 97% utilization of its total offshore fleet in 2001.

In 2002 Rowan expanded its manufacturing capacity with the acquisition of assets from Oilfield-Electric-Marine and Industrial Logic Systems. That year it also won a $175 million settlement from BP as part of resolving a 3-year dispute over a Rowan *Gorilla*-class drilling rig contract.

Refocusing on its core businesses, in 2005 Rowan sold its Era Aviation aircraft services subsidiary to Seacor Holdings for $118 million.

EXECUTIVES

Chairman: Henry E. (Jack) Lentz Jr., age 65
President, CEO, and Board Member:
  W. Matthew (Matt) Ralls, age 61,
  $4,913,559 total compensation
EVP Drilling Operations: David P. Russell, age 49,
  $2,200,320 total compensation
EVP Legal: John L. Buvens, age 55,
  $1,487,624 total compensation
EVP Business Development: Mark A. Keller, age 58,
  $1,724,845 total compensation

SVP, CFO, and Treasurer: William H. Wells, age 48,
  $1,420,546 total compensation
VP Human Resources: Terry D. Woodall, age 62
VP Engineering: Michael J. (Mike) Dowdy, age 51
VP Strategic Planning: Kevin Bartol, age 51
VP Health, Safety, and Environmental Affairs:
  Barbara Carroll, age 56
Corporate Secretary and Special Assistant to the CEO:
  Melanie M. Trent, age 46
Director Investor Relations: Suzanne M. McLeod
Controller: Gregory M. (Greg) Hatfield, age 41
President and CEO, LeTourneau Technologies:
  Thomas P. Burke, age 44
Auditors: Deloitte & Touche LLP

LOCATIONS

HQ: Rowan Companies, Inc.
  2800 Post Oak Blvd., Ste. 5450, Houston, TX 77056
Phone: 713-621-7800   **Fax:** 713-960-7660
Web: www.rowancompanies.com

2009 Sales

	$ mil.	% of total
US	952.0	54
Middle East	379.1	21
Europe	172.6	10
West Africa	116.0	7
Australia	58.6	3
Other regions	91.9	5
Total	**1,770.2**	**100**

PRODUCTS/OPERATIONS

2009 Sales

	$ mil.	% of total
Drilling services	1,214.9	69
Manufacturing sales & services	555.3	31
Total	**1,770.2**	**100**

Major Subsidiary

LeTourneau Technologies, Inc.

COMPETITORS

Acergy
Diamond Offshore
Ensco
Helmerich & Payne
Nabors Industries
Noble
Nucor
Oshkosh Truck
Precision Drilling
Pride International
Terex
Transocean

HISTORICAL FINANCIALS

Company Type: Public

Income Statement

FYE: December 31

	REVENUE ($ mil.)	NET INCOME ($ mil.)	NET PROFIT MARGIN	EMPLOYEES
12/09	1,770	368	20.8%	4,846
12/08	2,213	428	19.3%	6,023
12/07	2,095	484	23.1%	5,704
12/06	1,511	318	21.1%	5,160
12/05	1,069	230	21.5%	4,577
Annual Growth	**13.4%**	**12.5%**	**—**	**1.4%**

2009 Year-End Financials

Debt ratio: 25.3%
Return on equity: 12.7%
Cash ($ mil.): 640
Current ratio: 2.73
Long-term debt ($ mil.): 787
No. of shares (mil.): 115
Dividends
  Yield: 0.0%
  Payout: —
Market value ($ mil.): 2,595

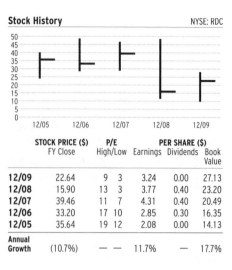

Stock History   NYSE: RDC

	STOCK PRICE ($) FY Close	P/E High/Low		Earnings	PER SHARE ($) Dividends	Book Value
12/09	22.64	9	3	3.24	0.00	27.13
12/08	15.90	13	3	3.77	0.40	23.20
12/07	39.46	11	7	4.31	0.40	20.49
12/06	33.20	17	10	2.85	0.30	16.35
12/05	35.64	19	12	2.08	0.00	14.13
Annual Growth	**(10.7%)**	**—**	**—**	**11.7%**	**—**	**17.7%**

Royal Caribbean Cruises

Royal Caribbean Cruises takes to the waves and drops anchor to see the sights. The world's second-largest cruise line (behind the combined Carnival Corporation and Carnival plc behemoth), the company operates nearly 40 ships with more than 84,000 berths overall. Its three main cruise brands — Royal Caribbean International, Celebrity Cruises, and Pullmantur Cruises — carry about 4 million passengers a year to about 400 ports, including ones in Alaska, Asia, Australia, Canada, the Caribbean, Europe, and Latin America. Its other brands include Azamara Club Cruises and CDF Croisières de France. In addition, Royal Caribbean operates land-based tours and expeditions through Royal Celebrity Tours.

Battered by the multiyear economic downturn and high fuel prices in 2008, Royal Caribbean has been working to stem its losses by diversifying its customer base in international markets. The company continues to extend its reach abroad as it awaits a rebound within its US market. It has expanded in the Asian, European, Latin American, and Caribbean markets with additional cruises from the UK, Spain, and Italy as well as new itineraries from Australia, New Zealand, the South Pacific, Panama, Singapore, and Shanghai. Royal Caribbean entered a joint venture with TUI AG in 2008, forming TUI Cruises, to serve the growing and relatively untapped German cruise market. Operations began in 2009 with the 1,900-berth ship *Mein Schiff* (My Ship).

Looking to the future, the firm's Royal Caribbean International has been going full steam ahead by adding two massive ships to its line: *Oasis of the Seas* and *Allure of the Seas*. Touted as the world's largest cruise ships, the gigantic vessels weigh 220,000 gross tons, boast 5,400 berths, span 16 decks, and include themed "neighborhood" areas and amphitheaters. *Oasis of the Seas* started service to the eastern Caribbean in late 2009.

In 2008 Royal Caribbean sold its stake in Island Cruises, a joint venture with UK-based tour operator TUI Travel, to First Choice Holidays Ltd., a subsidiary of TUI. Island Cruises operates two vessels, one of which belongs to Royal Caribbean. That vessel, *Island Star*, was redeployed to Pullmantur, renamed *Pacific Dream*, and serves the Latin American market.

Co-founder Arne Wilhelmsen owns about 20% of Royal Caribbean and the Pritzker family owns about 16%.

HISTORY

When Arne Wilhelmsen (director) and Edwin Stephan (former vice chairman) helped found Royal Caribbean Cruise Lines in 1969, they created an entire industry. Royal Caribbean's first vessel, *Song of Norway* (1970), touted endless sun decks and glass-walled dining rooms, initiating the concept of year-round cruising. Stephan, inspired by Seattle's Space Needle and its revolving restaurant, designed a cocktail lounge cantilevered from the ship's smokestack. The panoramic observation point became the signature of Royal Caribbean vessels. The company operated three ships during the 1970s; by 1972 it was the largest Caribbean cruise line.

Through the 1970s and early 1980s, it launched larger and more modern cruise ships and introduced air/sea inclusive vacations, fitness programs, and other industry firsts. Royal Caribbean moved out of the Caribbean for the first time in 1985 with Bermuda cruises from New York. The company bought Admiral Cruises in 1988 (sold in 1992, though it retained rights to the name) and Richard Fain, Admiral's chairman, became chairman and CEO of Royal Caribbean. With the goal of turning the company from a regional party fleet into an international vacation powerhouse, he expanded the company's fleet by four vessels in four years, including the world's first megaship, *Sovereign of the Seas,* with 2,250 berths.

In 1990 Royal Caribbean broadened its destination list to include Mexico, Alaska, and Europe. To enhance its relationship with the travel agents who booked its cruises, Royal Caribbean developed the industry's first computerized booking system. However, a fire that year severely damaged one of its under-construction vessels. Unstable earnings and ship construction and refurbishing costs left Royal Caribbean with almost $1 billion in long-term debt by 1992; the company went public in 1993 to ease its burden.

Royal Caribbean's next class of vessels, introduced in 1995, included high-tech movie theaters, shopping malls, and other accoutrements. In 1996 the company changed its name from Royal Caribbean Cruise Lines to Royal Caribbean Cruises Ltd., in order to reflect its growing breadth.

In 1997 the company acquired Celebrity Cruise Lines and its four working ships at a cost of $1.3 billion. (Rival Carnival had earlier bid $525 million for Celebrity.) In 1998 Royal Caribbean pleaded guilty to obstruction of justice in federal court for covering up its illegal dumping of oil off the coasts of Florida and Puerto Rico between 1990 and 1994. The company agreed to pay a $9 million fine and was put on probation for five years.

Royal Caribbean was again indicted in 1999 on oil-dumping charges and eventually pleaded guilty to 21 felony counts. It was slapped with a record $18 million fine. The following year it agreed to pay the State of Alaska another $3.3 million to settle similar charges. In 2001 it

began offering land-based tours in Alaska through Royal Celebrity Tours.

In an effort to trim costs and better compete with airlines, Royal Caribbean announced that year that it would halve the commissions paid to travel agents for the air-travel part of cruise bookings. In 2002 the company launched Island Cruises, a joint venture with First Choice Holidays. (First Choice Holidays became TUI Travel after it was acquired by TUI in 2007.)

Royal Caribbean hoped to reduce administrative costs and increase buying power by merging with P&O Princess Cruises, but P&O dropped the deal in favor of an acquisition by Carnival in 2003.

Celebrity Xpeditions (Celebrity Cruises' limited-capacity cruise line) debuted in 2004, offering service to the Galapagos Islands.

One of the largest cruise ships in the world, *Freedom of the Seas*, set sail from England in mid-2006. The Royal Caribbean ship holds more than 3,600 guests. Also that year Royal Caribbean expanded its tour operations in Spain with the $900 million purchase of the Pullmantur line.

EXECUTIVES

Chairman and CEO: Richard D. Fain, age 62, $5,418,660 total compensation
EVP and CFO: Brian J. Rice, age 51, $2,050,235 total compensation
EVP International: Michael Bayley, age 52
EVP Maritime: Harri U. Kulovaara, age 57, $1,673,814 total compensation
SVP, General Counsel, and Secretary: Bradley Stein
SVP Revenue Management: Douglas R. Santoni
SVP Land Operations; President, Royal Celebrity Tours: Craig S. Milan
VP and CIO: Bill Martin
VP Investor Relations: Ian M. Bailey Jr.
VP Global Corporate Communications: Michele Nadeem
VP Strategy and Corporate Planning: Jason Liberty
VP and Corporate Controller: Henry J. Pujol, age 42
VP Government Relations: Michael Ronan
VP and Global Chief Human Resources Officer: Maria Del Busto
VP Commercial Development: John Tercek
President and CEO, Royal Caribbean International: Adam M. Goldstein, age 50, $2,702,898 total compensation
President and CEO, Celebrity Cruises: Daniel J. (Dan) Hanrahan, age 52, $2,426,840 total compensation
President and CEO, Azamara Cruises: Lawrence (Larry) Pimentel
President and CEO, Pullmantur: Gonzalo Chico Barbier, age 49
Investor Relations Contact: Carlos Moya
Auditors: PricewaterhouseCoopers LLP

LOCATIONS

HQ: Royal Caribbean Cruises Ltd.
1050 Caribbean Way, Miami, FL 33132
Phone: 305-539-6000   **Fax:** 305-539-0562
Web: www.royalcaribbean.com

2009 Passenger Ticket Revenue

	% of total
US	54
Other countries	46
Total	**100**

PRODUCTS/OPERATIONS

2009 Sales

	$ mil.	% of total
Passenger tickets	4,205.7	71
Onboard & other	1,684.1	29
Total	**5,889.8**	**100**

Selected Cruise Ships

Azamara Cruises
Journey (2004, Europe and South America, 700 berths)
Quest (2006; Asia, Caribbean, Europe, and Panama Canal; 700 berths)
CDF Croisières de France
Bleu de France (2005, Caribbean and Mediterranean, 750 berths)
Celebrity Cruises
Century (1995, Caribbean and Europe, 1,800 berths)
Constellation (2002; Caribbean, Europe, and Canada/New England; 2,050 berths)
Eclipse (2010; Caribbean and Europe, 2,850 berths)
Equinox (2009; Caribbean and Europe, 2,850 berths)
Galaxy (1996, Southern Caribbean and Europe, 1,850 berths)
Infinity (2001; Hawaii, Alaska, Panama Canal, and South America; 2,050 berths)
Mercury (1997; Alaska, Pacific Coastal, California, and Mexican Riviera; 1,850 berths)
Millennium (2000, Eastern Caribbean and Europe, 2,050 berths)
Solstice (2008, Eastern Caribbean, 2,850 berths)
Summit (2001; Caribbean, Alaska, Panama Canal, and Pacific Coastal; 2,050 berths)
Xpedition (2004, Galapagos Islands, 100 berths)
Pullmantur Cruises
Empress (1990, Caribbean and Bermuda, 1,600 berths)
Ocean Dream (2008, Western Mediterranean, 1,000 berths)
Oceanic (2001, Western Mediterranean, 1,150 berths)
Sovereign (1988, Bahamas, 2,300 berths)
Zenith (1992; Caribbean, Bahamas, and Bermuda; 1,400 berths)
Royal Caribbean
Adventure of the Seas (2001, Caribbean, 3,100 berths)
Allure of the Seas (2010; Caribbean, 5,400 berths)
Brilliance of the Seas (2002; Caribbean, Europe, and Panama Canal; 2,100 berths)
Enchantment of the Seas (1997, Caribbean, 2,250 berths)
Explorer of the Seas (2000, Caribbean, 3,100 berths)
Freedom of the Seas (2006, Caribbean, 3,600 berths)
Grandeur of the Seas (1996; Caribbean, Bahamas, and Canada/New England; 1,950 berths)
Independence of the Seas (2008, Caribbean and Europe, 3,600 berths)
Jewel of the Seas (2004; Caribbean, Canada/New England, and Europe; 2,100 berths)
Legend of the Seas (1995; Hawaii, Mexican Riviera, and Panama Canal; 1,800 berths)
Liberty of the Seas (2007, Caribbean, 3,600 berths)
Majesty of the Seas (1992, Bahamas, 2,350 berths)
Mariner of the Seas (2003, Caribbean, 3,100 berths)
Monarch of the Seas (1991; Baja, Mexico; 2,350 berths)
Navigator of the Seas (2002, Caribbean, 3,100 berths)
Oasis of the Seas (2009; Caribbean, 5,400 berths)
Radiance of the Seas (2001; Caribbean, Pacific Northwest, Alaska, Hawaii, and Panama Canal; 2,100 berths)
Rhapsody of the Seas (1997, Caribbean, 2,000 berths)
Serenade of the Seas (2003; Alaska, Caribbean, Panama Canal, and Hawaii; 2,100 berths)
Splendour of the Seas (1996; Caribbean, Panama Canal, and Europe; 1,800 berths)
Vision of the Seas (1998; Hawaii, Alaska, Mexican Riviera, and Pacific Northwest; 2,000 berths)
Voyager of the Seas (1999, Caribbean and Canada, 3,100 berths)

COMPETITORS

Carnival Corporation
Carnival plc
Club Med
Disney Parks & Resorts
Genting Hong Kong
Holland America
NCL
Princess Cruise Lines
Siem Industries
Vard

HISTORICAL FINANCIALS

Company Type: Public

Income Statement

FYE: December 31

	REVENUE ($ mil.)	NET INCOME ($ mil.)	NET PROFIT MARGIN	EMPLOYEES
12/09	5,890	162	2.8%	60,300
12/08	6,533	574	8.8%	49,650
12/07	6,149	603	9.8%	5,068
12/06	5,230	634	12.1%	42,958
12/05	4,903	664	13.5%	39,400
Annual Growth	4.7%	(29.7%)	—	11.2%

2009 Year-End Financials

Debt ratio: 102.2%
Return on equity: 2.3%
Cash ($ mil.): 285
Current ratio: 0.37
Long-term debt ($ mil.): 7,664

No. of shares (mil.): 215
Dividends
  Yield: 0.0%
  Payout: —
Market value ($ mil.): 5,438

Stock History

NYSE: RCL

	STOCK PRICE ($) FY Close	P/E High/Low	PER SHARE ($) Earnings	Dividends	Book Value
12/09	25.28	37 7	0.75	0.00	34.86
12/08	13.75	16 2	2.68	0.45	31.62
12/07	42.44	16 12	2.82	0.60	31.41
12/06	41.38	16 11	2.94	0.60	28.32
12/05	45.06	17 12	3.26	0.56	25.82
Annual Growth	(13.5%)	— —	(30.7%)	—	7.8%

RPM International

If you've ever done any sort of home improvement, there's a good chance you've used RPM International's products. Maker of home repair favorites like Rust-Oleum, Zinsser, and DAP, RPM is divided into two units: industrial and consumer products. Industrial offerings, which account for about two-thirds of sales, include products for waterproofing, corrosion resistance, floor maintenance, and wall finishing. RPM's do-it-yourself items include caulks and sealants, rust-preventatives and general-purpose paints, repair products, and hobby paints. The company operates 90 manufacturing facilities worldwide and does more than a third of its business outside the US.

RPM's industrial products include roofing systems (Tremco, Republic, Vulkem, and Dymeric), corrosion control coatings (Carboline, Nullifire, and Plasite), flooring systems (Stonhard and Fibergrate), concrete and masonry additives (Euco), fluorescent pigments (Day-Glo), exterior insulation finishing systems (Dryvit), commercial carpet cleaning products (Chemspec), wood treatments (Kop-Coat), and marine coatings (Pettit, Woolsey, and Z-Spar). The industrial segment accounts for a vast majority of RPM's international sales.

For the do-it-yourselfer, RPM offers rust-preventatives and paints (Rust-Oleum), caulks and sealants (DAP), primer-sealers and wall-covering preparation and removal products (Zinsser), interior stains and finishes (Varathane), patch and repair products (Plastic Wood), deck coatings (Wolman), wall coverings and fabrics (Thibaut), and hobby products (Testors).

In 2010 two RPM subsidiaries, Bonded International and its holding company Specialty Products Holding Corp., filed for Chapter 11 reorganization in a move to resolve asbestos claims against Bondex. The process will allow the companies to establish a trust fund and a court order directing all present and future claims to the fund for compensation.

Also that year RPM's Performance Coatings Group acquired Hummervoll Industribelegg AS, a supplier and installer of industrial flooring systems based in Bergen, Norway. The deal will broaden RPM's presence in the Scandinavian market.

The company tendency is to grow its operations through acquisitions, keeping the acquired name brands intact. In 2008 the company acquired UK-based Flowcrete Group, which makes flooring products for industrial and commercial applications. The next year saw the acquisition of a just-less-than-half stake in Chinese licensee Carboline Dalian Paint Production Co. by subsidiary Carboline Company. RPM also made smaller deals for a Swiss sealants maker and a US weatherproofing agents manufacturer.

As can be expected, consumer home centers account for much of the company's business; retailers such as Home Depot, Lowe's, Wal-Mart, and Ace Hardware represent about 65% of the Consumer segment's sales.

HISTORY

Frank Sullivan founded Republic Powdered Metals in 1947 to make an industrial aluminum paint. The company went public in 1963, and three years later it bought Reardon Co. (household coatings), the first of more than 50 acquisitions. After his father's death in 1971, Thomas Sullivan took over and reorganized RPM as a holding company.

By 1979 RPM, though successful, was taken to task by its board for lack of formal planning. In 1985 it bought Sun Oil's Carboline coating and tank-lining subsidiary. This purchase forced RPM to lay off employees for the first time.

RPM bought Rust-Oleum in 1994. In its largest acquisition at that time, the company bought roofing-product expert Tremco in 1996 for $236 million. The purchase amassed debt, and to compensate, RPM sold its Craft House hobby activity subsidiary and Swiggle Insulating Glass in 1997.

The company resumed acquisitions and overseas expansion in 1998 by purchasing Flecto (wood finish), the UK's Nullifire (fireproof coatings), and Germany's Alteco Technik (floors); it also established joint ventures in Russia and China. In 1999 RPM paid $290 million for UK-based Wassall's DAP adhesives division. Softer sales in the Americas and Asia, plus increased distribution expenses that fiscal year, prompted the company to begin restructuring its operations.

RPM sold its Alox metalworking additive business to Lubrizol in 2000. The next year the company finished its restructuring — which had resulted in 17 plant closures and a 10% workforce reduction — and set its sights on reducing debt.

Thomas C. Sullivan's son — and the grandson of the company's founder — Frank Sullivan took the chief executive reins in 2002; Thomas Sullivan remained with the company as chairman.

The company went through a spate of acquisitions in the middle of the decade. Its flooring services division acquired National Building Facilities Services and Harsco's fiberglass-reinforced plastics business, and its corrosion control division acquired AD Fire Protection Systems. Tremco acquired German sealant manufacturer Illbruck Sealant Systems. In early 2007 Rust-Oleum acquired the UK's Tor Coatings in an effort to grow the unit's European coatings operations. Later that year the company sold its auto restoration products subsidiary, Bondo, to 3M.

EXECUTIVES

Chairman and CEO: Frank C. Sullivan, age 49, $2,672,473 total compensation
President, COO, and Assistant Secretary: Ronald A. Rice, age 47, $1,285,622 total compensation
SVP and CFO: Robert L. (Bob) Matejka, age 67
SVP Manufacturing and Operations and CIO: Paul G. P. Hoogenboom, age 50, $727,055 total compensation
VP, General Counsel, and Secretary: Edward W. Moore
VP Corporate Planning: Russell L. Gordon
VP Corporate Benefits and Risk Management: Janeen B. Kastner
VP and Controller: Barry M. Slifstein
VP Public Affairs: Randell McShepard
VP Corporate Development: Thomas C. Sullivan Jr.
VP, Treasurer, and Assistant Secretary: Keith R. Smiley, age 46
VP Corporate Development: John F. Kramer
VP Information Technology: Lonny R. DiRusso
VP Global Taxes: Matthew T. (Matt) Ratajczak, age 42
Manager Investor Relations: Kathie M. Rogers
Auditors: Ernst & Young LLP

LOCATIONS

HQ: RPM International Inc.
2628 Pearl Rd., Medina, OH 44258
Phone: 330-273-5090   **Fax:** 330-225-8743
Web: www.rpminc.com

2010 Sales

	$ mil.	% of total
US	2,148.9	63
Europe	728.1	21
Canada	308.4	9
Other regions	227.3	7
Total	**3,412.7**	**100**

PRODUCTS/OPERATIONS

2010 Sales

	$ mil.	% of total
Industrial	2,328.2	68
Consumer	1,084.5	32
Total	**3,412.7**	**100**

Selected Products

Industrial
  Carboline (industrial coatings)
  Chemspec (commercial carpet cleaning chemicals)
  Day-Glo (fluorescent colorants and pigments)
  Dryvit (exterior finishing systems)
  Dymeric (sealants)
  Fibergrate (reinforced plastic grating)
  Kop-Coat (wood and lumber treatments)
  Nullifire (fireproofing coatings)
  Republic (roofing products)
  Stonhard (flooring products)
  TCI (powder coatings)
  Tremco (industrial and commercial sealants)
  Vulkem (sealants)
  Woolsey/Z-Spar (marine coatings)

Consumer
American Accents (decorative finishes)
Chemical Coatings (industrial coatings)
DAP (sealants, caulks, and patch and repair products)
OKON (sealants and stains)
Painter's Touch (general purpose coatings)
Rust-Oleum (rust preventative coatings)
Testors (hobby and leisure products)
Tremclad (coatings)
Varathane (wood finishes)
Watco (wood finishes)
Zinsser (primer-sealers and wallcovering removers)

COMPETITORS

3M
Akzo Nobel
Ameron
Benjamin Moore
DuPont Performance Coatings
Ferro
H.B. Fuller
Henkel
Masterchem Industries
PPG Industries
Sherwin-Williams
Tennant
Valspar
Zep Inc.

HISTORICAL FINANCIALS

Company Type: Public

Income Statement

FYE: May 31

	REVENUE ($ mil.)	NET INCOME ($ mil.)	NET PROFIT MARGIN	EMPLOYEES
5/10	3,413	180	5.3%	8,873
5/09	3,368	120	3.6%	9,674
5/08	3,644	48	1.3%	10,360
5/07	3,339	208	6.2%	9,424
5/06	3,008	(76)	—	9,213
Annual Growth	3.2%	—	—	(0.9%)

2010 Year-End Financials

Debt ratio: 85.6%
Return on equity: 16.2%
Cash ($ mil.): 215
Current ratio: 2.29
Long-term debt ($ mil.): 924
No. of shares (mil.): 130
Dividends
Yield: 4.1%
Payout: 58.3%
Market value ($ mil.): 2,576

Stock History

NYSE: RPM

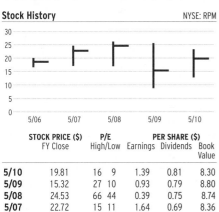

	STOCK PRICE ($) FY Close	P/E High/Low		PER SHARE ($) Earnings	Dividends	Book Value
5/10	19.81	16	9	1.39	0.81	8.30
5/09	15.32	27	10	0.93	0.79	8.80
5/08	24.53	66	44	0.39	0.75	8.74
5/07	22.72	15	11	1.64	0.69	8.36
5/06	18.63	—	—	(0.65)	0.63	7.12
Annual Growth	1.5%	—	—	—	6.5%	3.9%

R.R. Donnelley

If you can read it, R.R. Donnelley & Sons can print it. A leading full-service printing company, R.R. Donnelley produces magazines, catalogs, and books, as well as advertising material, business forms, financial reports, and telephone directories. The company offers graphics and prepress services in conjunction with printing. In addition, it provides logistics, distribution, and business process outsourcing services related to getting printed material to its audience. Along with publishers, R.R. Donnelley's customers include companies in the advertising, financial services, health care, retail, and technology industries.

The global economic slowdown and technological changes (such as the migration of print from paper to the digital realm) have impacted R.R. Donnelley and other printing companies as they scramble to adjust to a fast-changing and challenging business environment. In 2009 the company experienced significant declines in volume across nearly all of R.R. Donnelley's products and services. The company has been streamlining operations and selling noncore holdings to focus on commercial printing and business process outsourcing. Cost control initiatives have included some facility consolidations and reducing expenses, such as the continued suspension of the matching contribution under its employee 401(k) savings plan.

Despite the gloomy economic backdrop, the company has been and plans to continue bolstering its operations at home and abroad through acquisitions in order to implement its long-term growth strategy. In 2010 R.R. Donnelley agreed to purchase Bowne & Co., a New York-based financial documents printer, for about $480 million. The deal follows R.R. Donnelley's 2009 acquisition of Prospectus Central, which provides electronic delivery of investment prospectuses. Also that year the company purchased the assets of Santiago, Chile-based PROSA, a Web-based printing company. In 2008 it bought newspaper inserts printer Pro Line Printing in Irving, Texas, for about $120 million.

HISTORY

In 1864 Canadian Richard Robert Donnelley joined Chicago publishers Edward Goodman and Leroy Church to form what eventually would become Lakeside Publishing and Printing. The company's building and presses were destroyed in the 1871 Chicago fire but soon were rebuilt.

By 1890 Richard Donnelley's son Thomas was leading the company, which was incorporated as R.R. Donnelley & Sons. The company spun off its phone directory publishing subsidiary, the Chicago Directory Company, in 1916. (Renamed the Reuben H. Donnelley Corporation after another of Richard Donnelley's sons, the business was acquired by Dun & Bradstreet — now D&B — in 1961, which spun it off as R.H. Donnelley, now Dex One, in 1998.)

R.R. Donnelley began printing *Time* in 1928 and *LIFE* in 1936. The company endured limits on commercial printing and paper shortages during WWII. It went public in 1956. Thomas Donnelley's son Gaylord steered the company from 1964 until 1975, when Charles Lake, the first CEO who was not a member of the Donnelley family, replaced him.

During the 1980s R.R. Donnelley developed the Selectronic process, which allowed magazine publishers to tailor content and ads to different geographic audiences. The company acquired Metromail, the largest US mailing list business, in 1987. John Walter became CEO in 1988. R.R. Donnelley's South Side Chicago plant, its oldest, was shuttered in 1993 when Sears stopped publishing its catalogs.

R.R. Donnelley merged its software operations with Corporate Software to form Stream International (technical support, software licensing, and fulfillment) in 1995. That year Donnelley expanded internationally into Chile, China, India, and Poland.

In 1996 Donnelley took both its Donnelley Enterprise Solutions subsidiary (IT services) and its Metromail subsidiary public, retaining about 43% and 38% of each company, respectively. Controversy erupted that year when it was revealed that Metromail had sold personal information in its customer database and, through contracting, had given prison inmates access to its database. In the wake of these revelations, Walter resigned in 1996. Former Emerson Electric executive William Davis was appointed CEO in 1997. Davis restructured the company, reorganized Stream's operations, and integrated digital printing into R.R. Donnelley's other operations. He also pushed the company to jettison underperforming units. In 1998 the company sold its interests in Metromail and Donnelley Enterprise Solutions.

Sharpening its focus in commercial printing, R.R. Donnelley continued divesting in 1999, selling most of its stake in Stream International and its stakes in software distributor Corporate Software & Technology and manufacturing and fulfillment firm Modus Media International.

In early 2000 the company doubled the size of its logistics unit when it bought business-to-home parcel mailer CTC Distribution Direct. It also expanded its digital services through the purchase of premedia services firm Iridio. In 2001 the company announced closures of a handful of plants as part of a streamlining effort. It also cut about 1,700 jobs.

In 2004 R.R. Donnelley bought business forms and label printer Moore Wallace for about $2.8 billion. Moore Wallace CEO Mark Angelson took over leadership of the combined company. In its continuing efforts to divest itself of noncore assets, R.R. Donnelley sold off its package logistics business, including CTC Distribution Direct, in 2004; it retained its print logistics and distribution businesses.

In 2005 R.R. Donnelley sold Peak Technologies, a former Moore Wallace company that integrated and resold automated data capture and identification systems, to Platinum Equity. It also bought The Astron Group, a UK-based provider of outsourced document and information management services, for $990 million.

Angelson retired in early 2007 and CFO Thomas Quinlan replaced him as president and CEO in April 2007. The firm acquired the business forms company Cardinal Brands for $130 million in late 2007, as well as rival Banta for $1.3 billion in early 2007, gaining printing operations in the US, Europe, and Asia, as well as a supply chain management business that serves technology companies. Also in 2007 R.R. Donnelley acquired textbook printer Von Hoffman for $413 million.

EXECUTIVES

Chairman: Stephen M. Wolf, age 68
President, CEO, and Director:
Thomas J. (Tom) Quinlan III, age 47,
$7,889,992 total compensation
COO: John R. Paloian, age 51,
$3,405,569 total compensation
EVP and CFO: Miles W. McHugh, age 45,
$1,632,609 total compensation
EVP; Group President: Daniel L. (Dan) Knotts, age 45,
$2,444,742 total compensation
EVP, General Counsel, Corporate Secretary, and Chief Compliance Officer: Suzanne S. (Sue) Bettman, age 45,
$1,512,240 total compensation
SVP, Controller, and Chief Accounting Officer:
Andrew B. Coxhead, age 41
Auditors: Deloitte & Touche LLP

LOCATIONS

HQ: R.R. Donnelley & Sons Company
111 S. Wacker Dr., Chicago, IL 60606
Phone: 312-326-8000   **Fax:** 312-326-7156
Web: www.rrdonnelley.com

2009 Sales

	$ mil.	% of total
US	7,647.1	77
Europe	1,063.9	11
Asia	470.5	5
Other regions	675.9	7
Total	**9,857.4**	**100**

PRODUCTS/OPERATIONS

2009 Sales

	$ mil.	% of total
US print & related services	7,437.0	75
International	2,420.4	25
Total	**9,857.4**	**100**

Selected Operations

US print and related services
Book (consumer, religious, educational and specialty, and telecommunications)
Direct mail (content creation, database management, printing, personalization, finishing, and distribution in North America)
Directories (yellow and white pages)
Logistics (consolidation and delivery of printed products; expedited distribution of time-sensitive and secure material; print-on-demand, warehousing, and fulfillment services)
Magazine, catalog, and retail inserts
Short-run commercial print (annual reports, marketing brochures, catalog and marketing inserts, pharmaceutical inserts and other marketing, retail point-of-sale and promotional materials and technical publications)
International
Business process outsourcing
Global Turnkey Solutions (product configuration, customized kitting, and order fulfillment)

COMPETITORS

Accenture	M & F Worldwide
Arandell	Merrill
Bowne	Penn Lithographics
Capgemini	Quad/Graphics
Cenveo	St Ives
Consolidated Graphics	St. Joseph
Courier Corporation	Communications
Dai Nippon Printing	Taylor Corporation
Deluxe Corporation	Toppan Printing
EBSCO	Transcontinental Inc.
Harte-Hanks	Valassis
IBM Global Services	Vertis Inc
Infosys	

HISTORICAL FINANCIALS

Company Type: Public

Income Statement

FYE: December 31

	REVENUE ($ mil.)	NET INCOME ($ mil.)	NET PROFIT MARGIN	EMPLOYEES
12/09	9,857	(21)	—	56,800
12/08	11,582	(190)	—	62,000
12/07	11,587	(49)	—	65,000
12/06	9,317	401	4.3%	53,000
12/05	8,430	137	1.6%	50,000
Annual Growth	**4.0%**	**—**	**—**	**3.2%**

2009 Year-End Financials

Debt ratio: 139.8%
Return on equity: —
Cash ($ mil.): 499
Current ratio: 1.45
Long-term debt ($ mil.): 2,983
No. of shares (mil.): 206
Dividends
Yield: 4.7%
Payout: —
Market value ($ mil.): 4,594

Stock History

NASDAQ (GS): RRD

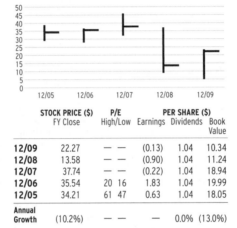

	STOCK PRICE ($) FY Close	P/E High/Low		PER SHARE ($) Earnings	Dividends	Book Value
12/09	22.27	—	—	(0.13)	1.04	10.34
12/08	13.58	—	—	(0.90)	1.04	11.24
12/07	37.74	—	—	(0.22)	1.04	18.94
12/06	35.54	20	16	1.83	1.04	19.99
12/05	34.21	61	47	0.63	1.04	18.05
Annual Growth	**(10.2%)**	**—**	**—**	**—**	**0.0%**	**(13.0%)**

Ryder System

When it comes to commercial vehicles and distribution, Ryder System wants to be the designated driver. Its Fleet Management Solutions (FMS) segment acquires, manages, maintains, and disposes of fleet vehicles for commercial customers. Similarly, the Supply Chain Solutions (SCS) segment provides logistics and supply chain services from industrial start (raw material supply) to finish (product distribution). Ryder also offers Dedicated Contract Carriage (DCC) services by supplying trucks, drivers, and management and administrative services to customers on a contract basis. Ryder's worldwide fleet of more than 150,000 vehicles ranges from tractor-trailers to light-duty trucks.

Ryder's FMS business provides full service leasing, contract maintenance, and commercial rental to customers from small businesses to large national enterprises. FMS maintains over 700 locations in the US, Puerto Rico, and Canada, along with more than 200 on-site maintenance facilities. Its also operates over 90 repair and warehousing facilities in Germany, Mexico, China, and Singapore.

Ryder continues to grow through a steady stream of FMS acquisitions. The Northeast US represents a particularly strong region for

growth; Ryder in 2008 acquired such companies as Lily Transportation and Pennsylvania-based Gordon Truck Leasing; both are regional full-service truck leasing firms. Also in 2008 Ryder acquired Gator Leasing and its fleet of approximately 2,300 vehicles, which will extend network service in Florida. The acquisition of Connecticut-based Edart Leasing in 2009 gives Ryder further coverage throughout Connecticut, Massachusetts, and New Jersey.

The SCS segment provides professional services, distribution operations, and transportation solutions to customers who operate in electronics, high-tech, telecommunications, industrial, consumer goods, paper and paper products, office equipment, food and beverage, and general retail industries.

Ryder added Transpacific Container Terminal Ltd. and CRSA Logistics Ltd. in late 2008, which included CRSA Logistics' operations in Hong Kong and Shanghai, China. These acquisitions are intended to help strengthen Ryder's role in moving commerce to and from North America and Asia. To further strengthen its role in import/export services, Ryder entered into a joint venture with Cargo Services Far East Limited, a logistics solutions provider based in Asia.

Ryder spent 2009 reducing costs by discontinuing certain of its SCS operations in South America and Europe to focus on serving the US, Canada, Mexico, UK, and Asia markets. Additionally, it eliminated almost 6,000 jobs from its worldwide workforce, representing a reduction of approximately 20%.

The DDC unit offers equipment, maintenance, and administrative services to customers in industries with time-sensitive deliveries or special handling requirements, such as newspapers.

In 2008 the company launched its RydeGreen Hybrid medium-duty straight truck line, which offers reduced fuel consumption and emissions. In addition to the lease offering, a limited supply of RydeGreen trucks will be available in 2009 to commercial customers in the US.

HISTORY

Ryder Truck Rental, founded in Miami by Jim Ryder in 1933, was the first truck leasing company in the US. It rented trucks in four southern states until 1952, when it bought Great Southern Trucking (renamed Ryder Truck Lines), doubling its size. In 1955, the year it went public as Ryder System, Ryder bought Carolina Fleets (a South Carolina trucking company) and Yellow Rental (a northeastern leasing service). More purchases over the next decade extended its truck rental business across the US and into Canada. Ryder Truck Lines was sold to International Utilities in 1965.

After establishing One-Way truck rental services for self-movers in 1968, the company entered several new markets, including new automobile transport (1968), truck driver and heavy-equipment operator training (1969), temporary services (1969), insurance (1970), truck stops (1971), and oil refining (1974).

Leslie Barnes, the former president of Allegheny Airlines (later part of US Airways), replaced Jim Ryder as CEO in 1975 and sold the oil refinery and other company assets by the end of the year.

Anthony Burns, Ryder's president, became CEO in 1983. Burns sold Ryder's truck stops (1984) and, through 65 acquisitions, moved the firm into aviation sales and service (1982), freight hauling (1983), aircraft leasing (1984), aircraft engine overhauling (1985), and school busing (1985). By 1987 Ryder was the US leader in truck leasing and automobile hauling, the world's #1 non-airline provider of aviation maintenance and parts, and second only to Canada's Laidlaw in school bus fleet management.

Ryder sold its freight hauling business and most of its insurance interests in 1989. Responding to the weak economy and financial turmoil in the airline industry, the company began withdrawing from its aircraft operations in 1991 with the discontinuation of its leasing business. Unfortunately, the company's name was linked to two tragedies in the 1990s: Ryder trucks were used in the 1993 World Trade Center bombing in New York and the 1995 bombing of the Oklahoma City federal building.

To expand its logistics capabilities, Ryder acquired LogiCorp in 1994 and bought two UK logistics businesses from FedEx. But the consumer truck rental unit, once a bright spot on the balance sheet, was dragging down earnings. Ryder sold its bright yellow trucks in 1996 to investor group Questor Partners.

In 1997 Ryder sold its faltering automotive carrier business to industry leader Allied Holdings. The next year Ryder bought Companhia Transportadora e Comercial Translor, a leading logistics company in Brazil.

Burlington Northern Santa Fe SVP Gregory Swienton became Ryder's president and COO in 1999; Burns remained chairman and CEO. That year, as part of the long restructuring initiative, Ryder sold its school-bus unit to UK-based FirstGroup for $940 million.

Burns retired as CEO in 2000, remaining chairman, and Swienton took over. In 2003 Ryder added to its fleet support services operations when it acquired Vertex Services, a Houston-based fuel storage tank management company.

In 2004 Ryder acquired General Car and Truck Leasing System based in Davenport, Iowa. The company purchased Canadian transportation and supply chain management provider Pollock NationaLease in 2007.

EXECUTIVES

Chairman and CEO: Gregory T. (Greg) Swienton, age 59, $4,115,885 total compensation
President, Global Fleet Management Solutions: Anthony G. (Tony) Tegnelia, age 64, $1,276,765 total compensation
President, Global Supply Chain Solutions: John H. Williford, age 53, $1,014,035 total compensation
EVP and CFO: Robert E. Sanchez, age 44, $1,653,229 total compensation
EVP and Chief Human Resources Officer: Gregory F. (Greg) Greene, age 50
EVP, Chief Legal Officer, and Secretary: Robert D. (Bob) Fatovic, age 44, $873,104 total compensation
SVP Sales and Marketing, North America, Fleet Management Solutions: John J. Gleason, age 53
SVP and CIO: Kevin Bott
SVP and Controller: Art A. Garcia, age 48
SVP Global Finance: John J. Diez
SVP Sales and Marketing, Supply Chain Solutions: Steve Dean
SVP and General Manager, U.S. Supply Chain Solutions: Tom Jones
SVP Finance and Treasurer: W. Daniel Susik
SVP Operations, Fleet Management Solutions, North America: Michael J. Brannigan
VP Investor Relations and Public Affairs: Robert (Bob) Brunn
VP Corporate Communications: David Bruce
Auditors: PricewaterhouseCoopers LLP

LOCATIONS

HQ: Ryder System, Inc.
11690 NW 105th St., Miami, FL 33178
Phone: 305-500-3726   **Fax:** 305-500-3203
Web: www.ryder.com

2009 Sales

	$ mil.	% of total
US	4,127.0	84
Canada	424.1	9
Europe	223.9	5
Latin America	97.6	2
Asia	14.6	—
Total	**4,887.2**	**100**

PRODUCTS/OPERATIONS

2009 Sales

	$ mil.	% of total
Fleet Management Solutions	3,567.8	67
Supply Chain Solutions	1,139.9	23
Dedicated Contract Carriage	471.0	10
Adjustments	(291.5)	—
Total	**4,887.2**	**100**

COMPETITORS

Arkansas Best	Penske Truck Leasing
Barloworld Handling	Schenker, Inc.
C.H. Robinson Worldwide	Schneider National
Con-way Inc.	Trailer Fleet Services
FedEx	UniGroup
J.B. Hunt	UPS
Landstar System	YRC Worldwide

HISTORICAL FINANCIALS

Company Type: Public

Income Statement

FYE: December 31

	REVENUE ($ mil.)	NET INCOME ($ mil.)	NET PROFIT MARGIN	EMPLOYEES
12/09	4,887	62	1.3%	22,900
12/08	6,204	200	3.2%	28,000
12/07	6,566	254	3.9%	28,800
12/06	6,307	249	3.9%	28,600
12/05	5,741	229	4.0%	27,800
Annual Growth	(3.9%)	(27.9%)	—	(4.7%)

2009 Year-End Financials

Debt ratio: 158.7%	No. of shares (mil.): 52
Return on equity: 4.5%	Dividends
Cash ($ mil.): 99	Yield: 2.3%
Current ratio: 1.04	Payout: 86.5%
Long-term debt ($ mil.): 2,265	Market value ($ mil.): 2,158

Stock History

NYSE: R

	STOCK PRICE ($) FY Close	P/E High/Low		PER SHARE ($) Earnings	Dividends	Book Value
12/09	41.17	42	17	1.11	0.96	27.22
12/08	38.78	22	8	3.52	0.92	25.66
12/07	47.01	14	9	4.24	0.84	36.01
12/06	51.06	15	10	4.04	0.72	32.83
12/05	41.02	14	9	3.52	0.64	29.14
Annual Growth	0.1%	—	—	(25.1%)	10.7%	(1.7%)

The Ryland Group

Building the American dream is home sweet home for The Ryland Group. The homebuilder, founded by James Ryan and Bob Gaw in 1967, constructs single-family detached homes, as well as attached condominiums for entry-level, first- and second-time move-up, and retired buyers. Ryland has constructed more than 285,000 homes in hundreds of communities around the US. The average price for a Ryland Home is around $240,000. The company offers services that span the homeownership process. Homebuyers can select custom home finishes at a My Style Design Center. The group also provides mortgage financing, including title, settlement, escrow, and insurance services, through Ryland Mortgage.

The Ryland Group's financial services unit focuses on retail mortgage loan originations, including conventional, Federal Housing Administration (FHA), and Veterans Administration (VA) mortgages. More than 99% of the loans originated by the subsidiary are for homes built by the company.

Its homebuilding segment oversees the building of homes in some 30 cities across the country. Ryland focuses on diversification, with no more than 10% of its capital resources allocated to any given market, since it believes that strategy minimizes vulnerability to economic and market fluctuations.

Following several years of solid earnings growth, Ryland began to feel the effects of declining demand for new homes in 2006. Since then Ryland's revenues steadily fell. An increase in foreclosures created an oversaturated housing market. That, coupled with a tight credit market, lagging consumer confidence, and high unemployment rates, forced housing demand and prices down.

In response to the downturn, Ryland made several changes to its operations. Compared to peak levels, the company cut its workforce by nearly 70%. In 2008 the company also decreased the number of communities that it was active in (leaving markets such as Northern California and Cincinnati), and it slashed its inventory of lots by about 40%. Ryland also created a new portfolio of smaller homes that cater to demand, while at the same time reduce construction costs. By 2010 Ryland began seeing the housing market start to rebound slightly, and the company grew its lot count for the first time since 2006. Home sales figures also began to improve.

Along with the challenges presented by the recession, there also came opportunity. In early 2009 Ryland formed a joint venture with Oaktree Capital to buy distressed residential real estate projects in an effort to take advantage of deals in the troubled market. The joint venture plans to buy residential and commercial properties, improve them, and then sell them.

Chad Dreier retired as the company's CEO in 2009. Ryland's president, Larry Nicholson, took over the executive position. William Jews replaced Dreier as chairman in 2010.

HISTORY

The Ryland Group was founded in 1967 by entrepreneur James Ryan in the new planned community of Columbia, Maryland. Ryan got the idea for the company name after seeing "Maryland" on a sign with the first two letters covered up, so in

1970 the James P. Ryan Co. changed its name to The Ryland Group. Ryan took Ryland public in 1971, and the company expanded to a new planned community near Atlanta that year. In 1974 the company opened its first panel-building plant (Ryland Building Systems). By 1977 Ryland had moved into the Midwest and Philadelphia, completing 10,000 homes by year's end.

Ryland purchased Crest Communities (Cincinnati) in 1978. Crest's financial subsidiary became the basis for Ryland's mortgage operations (later known as Ryland Mortgage). Ryan retired in 1980, and Charles Peck became CEO. In 1981 the company entered the loan servicing business with the purchase of Guardian Mortgage. The following year Ryland formed Ryland Acceptance as an administrator and distributor of mortgage-backed securities. By 1985 the company had completed 50,000 homes.

It formed Cornerstone Title in 1989 to conduct real estate closing services in Maryland. The following year Ryland teamed up with American Loyalty Insurance to offer homeowners' insurance. In the 1990s the firm entered the fast-growing California and Florida housing markets. It also dabbled in overseas markets, building homes in Israel in 1991 and Russia in 1992.

A recession and overexpansion led to the company's loss in 1993. Chad Dreier, a former Kaufman and Broad EVP, was appointed as Ryland CEO in late 1993 and took the company in a new direction. He recognized that while Ryland's center-hall colonial-style house formed the foundation for the company's success, that fixed image of a "Ryland Home" was also an impediment to its future growth. Under Dreier's leadership, the company began enlisting the services of top architectural firms such as Bloodgood, Sharp, Buster, and Kaufman Meeks to introduce new house designs and to offer Ryland's customers a greater degree of customization in house design. The company also placed a stronger emphasis on market research after securing plots of land to better determine the best house designs for any given area.

In 1995, as part of its plan to focus on its core homebuilding and retail mortgage finance operations, the company sold its institutional mortgage-securities administration business (which included master servicing, investor information services, securities administration, tax calculation, and reporting). A year later it sold its wholesale mortgage operations.

The company purchased The Regency Organization, a private Florida homebuilder, in 1998 to expand into the growing retirement market and acquired Thomas Builders to expand operations in the Baltimore area. In 2000 Ryland relocated its corporate headquarters to California.

Also in 2000 Ryland joined other major US homebuilders in an Internet-based marketing cooperative. The builder continued to surf the Net the next year as it invested $1 million in online sales company iBidCo, after using iBidCo's system to sell 14 California homes for a total of nearly $11 million.

Ryland opened 152 new communities in fiscal 2003. At the close of 2003, Ryland began operating in California's Inland Empire (Riverside and San Bernardino counties), and in 2004 the company opened communities in Las Vegas. In 2006 Ryland split its Northern California division and created two new divisions in Sacramento and the Central Valley.

EXECUTIVES

Chairman: William L. (Bill) Jews, age 58
President, CEO, and Director: Larry T. Nicholson, age 52, $7,312,976 total compensation
EVP and CFO: Gordon A. Milne, age 58, $2,204,502 total compensation
SVP; President, North/West Region, Ryland Homes: Peter G. (Pete) Skelly, age 46, $1,483,950 total compensation
SVP; President, Ryland Mortgage Company: Daniel G. (Dan) Schreiner, age 52, $1,931,192 total compensation
SVP; President, South Region, Ryland Homes: Keith E. Bass, age 45, $1,471,838 total compensation
SVP, Secretary, and General Counsel: Timothy J. (Tim) Geckle, age 57, $1,230,284 total compensation
SVP Marketing and Communications: Eric E. Elder, age 52
SVP, Controller, and Chief Accounting Officer: David L. Fristoe, age 53
SVP Human Resources: Robert J. (Bob) Cunnion III, age 54
VP Investor Relations: Drew P. Mackintosh
VP and CIO: Craig McSpadden
VP Sales Training: Charles W. (Charlie) Jenkins
VP Tax: René L. Mentch
VP Internal Audit: Thomas M. (Tom) Pearson
VP Purchasing: Steven M. (Steve) Dwyer
President, Ryland Mortgage: David A. Brown
Auditors: Ernst & Young LLP

LOCATIONS

HQ: The Ryland Group, Inc.
24025 Park Sorrento, Ste. 400, Calabasas, CA 91302
Phone: 818-223-7500   **Fax:** 818-223-7667
Web: www.ryland.com

2009 Sales

	$ mil.	% of total
Homebuilding		
North	437.9	34
Southeast	315.1	25
Texas	332.1	26
West	156.6	12
Financial services	41.9	3
Total	**1,283.6**	**100**

Major Markets Served by Region

North
  Baltimore
  Chicago
  Delaware
  Indianapolis
  Minneapolis
  Northern Virginia
  Washington, DC

Southeast
  Atlanta
  Charleston, SC
  Charlotte, NC
  Jacksonville
  Orlando, FL
  Tampa

Texas
  Austin
  Dallas
  Houston
  San Antonio

West
  Central Valley of California
  Coachella Valley of California
  Denver
  Inland Empire of California
  Las Vegas
  Phoenix

PRODUCTS/OPERATIONS

2009 Sales

	$ mil.	% of total
Homebuilding	1,241.7	97
Financial services	41.9	3
Total	**1,283.6**	**100**

Selected Subsidiaries

Columbia National Risk Retention Group, Inc.
Cornerstone Title Company (operates as Ryland Title Company)
LPS Holdings Corporation
Ryland Homes Insurance Company
Ryland Homes of California, Inc.
Ryland Homes of Texas, Inc.
Ryland Mortgage Company
Ryland Organization Company

COMPETITORS

Beazer Homes
Champion Enterprises
D.R. Horton
Hovnanian Enterprises
J.F. Shea
KB Home
Lennar
M.D.C.
M/I Homes
NVR
PulteGroup
Standard Pacific
Toll Brothers

HISTORICAL FINANCIALS

Company Type: Public

Income Statement

FYE: December 31

	REVENUE ($ mil.)	NET INCOME ($ mil.)	NET PROFIT MARGIN	EMPLOYEES
12/09	1,284	(163)	—	1,019
12/08	1,976	(397)	—	1,303
12/07	3,033	(334)	—	2,026
12/06	4,757	360	7.6%	2,810
12/05	4,818	447	9.3%	3,217
Annual Growth	**(28.2%)**	**—**	**—**	**(25.0%)**

2009 Year-End Financials

Debt ratio: 147.1%
Return on equity: —
Cash ($ mil.): 285
Current ratio: 6.37
Long-term debt ($ mil.): 856
No. of shares (mil.): 44
Dividends
  Yield: 0.6%
  Payout: —
Market value ($ mil.): 868

Stock History

NYSE: RYL

	STOCK PRICE ($) FY Close	P/E High/Low		PER SHARE ($) Earnings	Dividends	Book Value
12/09	19.70	—	—	(3.74)	0.12	13.21
12/08	17.67	—	—	(9.33)	0.48	16.47
12/07	27.55	—	—	(7.92)	0.48	25.53
12/06	54.62	11	4	7.83	0.48	34.30
12/05	72.13	9	6	9.03	0.24	31.24
Annual Growth	**(27.7%)**	**—**	**—**	**—**	**(15.9%)**	**(19.4%)**

Safeway Inc.

For many Americans, "going to Safeway" is synonymous with "going to the grocery store." Safeway is one of North America's largest food retailers, with some 1,725 stores located mostly in the western, midwestern, and mid-Atlantic regions of the US, as well as western Canada. It also operates regional supermarket companies, including The Vons Companies (primarily in Southern California), Dominick's Finer Foods (Chicago), Carr-Gottstein Foods (Alaska's largest retailer), Genuardi's Family Markets (eastern US), and Randall's Food Markets (Texas). Safeway owns grocery e-retailer GroceryWorks.com. Outside the US, Safeway owns 49% of Casa Ley, which operates about 155 food and variety stores in western Mexico.

Safeway's sales decreased as cautious shoppers cut back on spending, traded down to less expensive products, and shopped at stores operated by wholesale clubs and discounters. Profitability also suffered as the company cut prices and increased its advertising to hang on to customers. Safeway is heavily promoting its less expensive private-label brands and has adopted an everyday pricing policy for some items to match its competitors.

Another expense for Safeway — and a key element of its long-term marketing plan — is the conversion of its store base to the *Lifestyle* format, which features expanded perishables departments, warm lighting, custom flooring, superior customer service, and other amenities. The company is betting that when the economy improves shoppers will prefer its spruced-up *Lifestyle* stores to those of discounters.

The company is taking two of its successful inhouse brands — Eating Right and O Organics — beyond the shelves of its own stores to market them to foodservice operators and internationally. The "O Organics" line of food and beverages was launched, in part, to win back sales from natural and organic chains, including Whole Foods Market and Trader Joe's. The company's Bright Green brand of 20-plus home care products (launched in 2008) is designed to appeal to environmentally conscious consumers.

With pharmacies inside more than three-quarters of its stores, Safeway is a leader in pharmacy sales among US grocery retailers. In mid-2008 the retailer launched a $4 generic prescription-drug program at in-store pharmacies on the East Coast.

Following labor trouble and failure to find a buyer for struggling Dominick's, Safeway took the chain off the market. Randall's, which competes in Texas against powerhouse H-E-B, has also struggled. As a result, Safeway closed 26 stores — including 16 Randall's locations — in the Lone Star State.

HISTORY

Founded in 1914 by Sam Seelig, Safeway had grown to about 300 stores in California and Hawaii by 1926. That year investment banker Charles Merrill, one of the founders of Merrill Lynch, bought Safeway. Merrill convinced M. B. Skaggs — of the famous grocery retailing Skaggs family — to become president, and his brother L. S. Skaggs (founder of what became American Stores) became VP. M. B. merged his 430 or so Skaggs stores with Safeway and took the Safeway name.

Safeway bought Arizona Grocery, Eastern Stores, and Piggly Wiggly Pacific in 1928 and Piggly Wiggly Western States, a grocer operating in California, Texas, and Nevada, in 1929. Two years later the chain had its greatest number of stores (3,527); this number was reduced as smaller stores were converted into larger supermarkets. In addition, the company expanded internationally into western Canada, the UK, and Australia. Peter Magowan, grandson of Merrill, became chairman and CEO in 1980. (His father, Robert Magowan, ran the chain for about 15 years.) The company acquired 49% of Mexican retailer Casa Ley in 1981. Safeway sold its Australian and German operations four years later.

In 1986 Safeway received an unsolicited buy-out bid from the Dart Group. In response, Peter and takeover specialist Kohlberg Kravis Roberts (KKR) took Safeway private in a leveraged deal. Saddled with debt, in 1987 and 1988 the company sold more than 1,350 stores. Included in that number were 162 Southern California stores (sold to The Vons Companies in exchange for stock) and about 120 stores in the UK to food and beverage company Argyll Group (now Safeway plc). A slimmer Safeway re-emerged as a public company in 1990.

Steven Burd became president in 1992 and CEO the next year. He has played hardball with the unions representing about 90% of Safeway's employees. In 1995, with 87 stores in Alberta, Canada, he replaced 4,000 full-time union employees with part-time workers, a move that saved the company $40 million. Burd also reduced corporate and store staff, consolidated distribution centers, and restructured the debt left over from the 1986 LBO.

Safeway acquired the rest of Vons it didn't already own in 1997. Burd took over the title of chairman from the retiring Peter the next year. Late in 1998 Safeway acquired the Dominick's Supermarkets chain, and the grocer acquired the Texas-based 115-store Randall's Food Markets (largely owned by KKR) in 1999.

In 2000 Safeway bought a majority stake in GroceryWorks.com. Also that year KKR reduced its stake in Safeway to less than 5%.

A four-and-a-half month strike by grocery workers in Safeway's second-largest market, Southern California, affecting nearly 300 Safeway-owned Vons and Pavilions stores, ended in March 2004. The dispute pitted workers' demands for generous health care benefits against Safeway's drive to cut costs and remain profitable in the face of mounting competition, particularly from non-unionized Wal-Mart. The strike took its toll on Safeway's bottom line, but it achieved a key goal: the establishment of a two-tier pay and benefits scheme under which new hires will receive substantially less in wages and benefits than veteran employees.

Several public pension funds, including the nation's two largest (California Public Employees' Retirement System and the New York State fund), agitated for the ouster of Burd, citing the purchase of Dominick's and steep losses from the Southern California grocery strike among Burd's missteps. Soon after, Burd survived a shareholder vote attempting to uncouple his dual roles of chairman and CEO.

In 2004 the grocery chain settled a lawsuit filed by the California attorney general alleging that Safeway sold tobacco products to minors at its Pack N' Save, Pavilions, Safeway, and Vons stores. In 2005 it launched the "O Organics" line of more than 150 organic products, including bread, cereal, coffee, frozen foods, and milk.

EXECUTIVES

Chairman, President, and CEO: Steven A. (Steve) Burd, age 60, $10,901,895 total compensation
EVP and CFO: Robert L. Edwards, age 54, $3,023,111 total compensation
EVP and Chief Strategist and Administrative Officer: Larree M. Renda, age 51, $3,227,110 total compensation
EVP and Chief Marketing Officer: Diane M. Dietz, age 43, $3,890,834 total compensation
EVP Retail Operations: Bruce L. Everette, age 58, $3,192,110 total compensation
SVP Finance and Control and Chief Accounting Officer: David F. Bond, age 56
SVP, Secretary, General Counsel, and Chief Governance Officer: Robert A. Gordon, age 58, $1,514,211 total compensation
SVP Internal Audit: John A. Lewis
SVP Planning and Business Development: David R. Stern, age 55
SVP Consumer Brands: Joseph (Joe) Ennen
SVP and CIO: David T. Ching, age 57
SVP Finance and Investor Relations: Melissa C. Plaisance, age 50
SVP Marketing Planning: Carl Graziani
SVP Human Resources: Russell M. Jackson, age 52
SVP Government Relations, Public Affairs, Corporate Social Responsibility, and Philanthropy: Jonathan Mayes, age 52
SVP Strategic Initiatives, Health Initiatives, and Reengineering: Kenneth M. Shachmut, age 61
SVP Real Estate and Engineering: Donald P. Wright, age 57
SVP Supply Operations: Jerry Tidwell, age 58
Chairman, Casa Ley, S.A. De C.V. (Mexico): Juan Manuel Ley Lopez
Auditors: Deloitte & Touche LLP

LOCATIONS

HQ: Safeway Inc.
5918 Stoneridge Mall Rd., Pleasanton, CA 94588
Phone: 925-467-3000   **Fax:** 925-467-3321
Web: www.safeway.com

2009 Sales

	$ mil.	% of total
US	34,980.3	86
Canada	5,870.4	14
Total	**40,850.7**	**100**

2009 Manufacturing and Processing Plants

	US	Canada
Milk	6	3
Bakery	6	2
Soft drink bottling	4	—
Ice cream	2	2
Fruit & vegetable processing	1	3
Cake commissary	1	—
Cheese & meat packaging	—	2
Total	**20**	**12**

2009 Stores

	No.
Southern California (Vons)	293
Northern California	272
Seattle (includes Alaska)	206
Eastern (Genuardi's)	177
Denver	142
Phoenix	117
Portland	117
Texas (Randall's & Tom Thumb)	112
Alberta	95
Chicago (Dominick's)	80
Vancouver	74
Winnipeg	54
Total	**1,739**

2009 Sales

	$ mil.	% of total
Non-perishables	18,998.1	47
Perishables	15,328.6	37
Pharmacy	3,835.3	9
Fuel	2,688.7	7
Total	**40,850.7**	**100**

COMPETITORS

Acme Markets	Raley's
Ahold USA	Rite Aid
Albertsons	Sam's Club
Bashas'	Save Mart
BJ's Wholesale Club	Smart & Final
Comerci	Sobeys
Costco Wholesale	Soriana
CVS Caremark	Stater Bros.
Fiesta Mart	SUPERVALU
Giant Food	Target
GNC	Tesco
H-E-B	Trader Joe's
IGA	Unified Grocers
Katz Group	Walgreen
Kroger	Wal-Mart
Loblaw	Wal-Mart de México
Meijer	Wegmans
Overwaitea	Whole Foods
PETCO	WinCo Foods

HISTORICAL FINANCIALS

Company Type: Public

Income Statement			FYE: Saturday nearest December 31
	REVENUE ($ mil.)	NET INCOME ($ mil.)	NET PROFIT MARGIN	EMPLOYEES
12/09	40,851	(1,098)	—	186,000
12/08	44,104	965	2.2%	197,000
12/07	42,286	888	2.1%	201,000
12/06	40,185	871	2.2%	207,000
12/05	38,416	561	1.5%	201,000
Annual Growth	1.5%	—	—	(1.9%)

2009 Year-End Financials

Debt ratio: 88.2%
Return on equity: —
Cash ($ mil.): 472
Current ratio: 0.90
Long-term debt ($ mil.): 4,361

No. of shares (mil.): 382
Dividends
  Yield: 1.8%
  Payout: —
Market value ($ mil.): 8,124

Stock History

NYSE: SWY

	STOCK PRICE ($)	P/E		PER SHARE ($)		
	FY Close	High	Low	Earnings	Dividends	Book Value
12/09	21.29	—	—	(2.66)	0.38	12.96
12/08	23.77	16	8	2.21	0.32	17.78
12/07	34.21	19	15	1.99	0.26	17.56
12/06	34.56	18	11	1.94	0.22	14.85
12/05	23.66	21	14	1.25	0.15	12.89
Annual Growth	(2.6%)	—	—	—	26.2%	0.1%

SAIC, Inc.

SAIC pledges its allegiance to the US government. A leading government services contractor, the company provides a wide range of information technology services, including systems engineering and project management, to federal and state agencies, including all branches of the US military. It specializes in such areas as consulting and technical support related to defense systems, custom software development, network security management, intelligence gathering, and logistics. While SAIC does provide its services to some commercial customers, the government sector accounts for more than 90% of its revenues.

Examples of the company's contracts include support of command, control, and communications programs for Department of Defense customers, and integration of vehicle and cargo inspections systems used for border security. SAIC added the Department of Energy to its customer roster in 2010 when it was awarded a contract to provide technical and managerial support services for the agency's statistical analysis and modelling efforts.

Though sales have largely increased organically, SAIC also attributes growth to acquired businesses. The company has a long history of expansion through acquisition; it has bought more than 20 companies in the past five years. It purchased technical and business consulting firm R.W. Beck Group and cyber security product testing services provider Atlan in 2009. Atlan validates hardware and software components using US government security standards.

SAIC continued to make acquisitions to support and expand its security products and services business the following year. It bought X-ray security scanning systems maker Spectrum San Diego; data security specialist CloudShield; and data analysis and surveillance systems maker Science, Engineering and Technology Associates Corporation in early 2010. In August 2010 the company boosted its homeland security business when it acquired Reveal Imaging Technologies, which provides the Transportation Security Administration with explosives detection equipment for baggage scanning in airports.

Ken Dahlberg stepped down as SAIC's CEO in 2009, remaining chairman of the board until mid-2010. Walter Ravenstein, the former president and CEO of BAE Systems, succeeded him as CEO.

HISTORY

Physicist Robert Beyster, who worked at Los Alamos National Laboratory in the 1950s, was hired by General Atomics in 1957 to establish and manage its traveling wave linear accelerator. When the company was sold to Gulf Oil in 1968, research priorities changed and Beyster left. He founded Science Applications Inc. (SAI) the following year and built his business from consulting contracts with Los Alamos and Brookhaven National Laboratory. During the first year Beyster instituted an employee-ownership plan that rewarded workers who brought on board new business with stock in SAI. Beyster's idea was to share the success of SAI and to raise capital.

In 1970 the company established an office in Washington, DC, to court government contracts. Despite a recession, SAI continued to grow during the 1970s, and by 1979 sales topped

$100 million. The following year SAI restructured, becoming a subsidiary of Science Applications International Corporation (SAIC), a new holding company.

During the 1980s defense buildup, an emphasis on high-tech weaponry, and SAIC's high-level Pentagon connections (directors have included former defense secretaries William Perry and Melvin Laird and former CIA director John Deutch) brought in contracts for submarine warfare systems and technical development for the Strategic Defense Initiative ("Star Wars"). As defense spending slowed with the end of the Cold War, though, SAIC began casting a wider net. By 1991 computer systems integration and consulting accounted for 25% of sales, which surpassed the $1 billion mark.

SAIC made several purchases during the mid-1990s, including transportation communications firm Syntonic and Internet domain name registrar Network Solutions, Inc. (NSI). It also began merger talks with The Aerospace Corporation, a government-funded research center, in 1996 until the Air Force scotched the deal a few months later. In 1997 SAIC acquired Bellcore (the research lab of the regional Bells, later renamed Telcordia Technologies), and reduced its stake in NSI through a public offering. SAIC formed several alliances in 1998, including a joint venture with Rolls-Royce to service the aerospace, energy, and defense industries.

The next year SAIC expanded its IT expertise with the acquisition of Boeing's Information Services unit. It also acquired the call center software operations of Elite Information Group. SAIC in 2000 realized a significant gain on its $5 million purchase of NSI when e-commerce software maker VeriSign bought the minority-owned (23%) subsidiary for about $20 billion in stock. SAIC signed a variety of large contracts the next year, including an outsourcing agreement with BP to manage that company's North American application and hosting services, as well as a $3 billion deal to provide support (in conjunction with Bechtel Group) for the US Department of Energy's civilian radioactive waste management program.

The omnipresent and self-described workaholic Beyster retired as CEO in 2003, turning the position over to Kenneth Dahlberg, a former executive of General Dynamics. (Dahlberg became chairman of SAIC the following year.) In 2005 the company sold its Telcordia subsidiary to investment firms Warburg Pincus and Providence Equity Partners for $1.3 billion.

SAIC's IPO in late 2006 ended the company's reign as the largest employee-owned research and engineering firm.

SAIC acquired Applied Marine Technology — a company with expertise in special operations, special mission units, and other areas of special warfare operations, as well as in homeland security and terrorism — in 2006. Other 2006 acquisitions included AETC, a San Diego-based provider of remote sensing systems for the Department of Defense, and Applied Ordnance Technology, a provider of technical products and services catering to weapons systems.

In 2007 SAIC acquired Benham Investment Holdings, a provider of consulting, engineering, architecture, design/build, and other related services, as well as Scicom Technologies. The company bought IT services provider SM Consulting in 2008. It also purchased Icon Systems, a developer of laser-based systems for military training and testing.

EXECUTIVES

Chairman: A. Thomas Young, age 72
CEO and Director: Walter P. (Walt) Havenstein, age 61, $8,053,810 total compensation
EVP and CFO: Mark W. Sopp, age 44, $2,254,035 total compensation
EVP Business Development: James E. (Jim) Cuff
EVP Communications and Government Affairs: Deborah L. (Debbie) James
EVP Operations and Performance Excellence: Tony Moraco
EVP and General Counsel: Vincent A. Maffeo, age 59
EVP Human Resources: Brian F. Keenan, age 53
SVP and CTO: Amy E. Alving, age 47
SVP and Corporate Controller: John R. Hartley, age 49
SVP and Treasurer: Steven P. Fisher, age 49
SVP Investor Relations: Paul E. Levi
President, Intelligence, Surveillance and Reconnaissance Group: K. Stuart (Stu) Shea, age 53, $1,899,302 total compensation
President, Information Technology and Network Solutions Group: Charles F. Koontz, age 48
President, Defense Solutions Group: Deborah H. (Deb) Alderson, age 53, $1,949,510 total compensation
President, Infrastructure, Energy, Health, and Product Solutions Group: Joseph W. (Joe) Craver III, age 51, $1,899,302 total compensation
Secretary: Douglas E. Scott, age 53
Auditors: Deloitte & Touche LLP

LOCATIONS

HQ: SAIC, Inc.
1710 SAIC Dr., McLean, VA 22102
Phone: 703-676-4300
Web: www.saic.com

PRODUCTS/OPERATIONS

2010 Sales by Market

	$ mil.	% of total
Government	10,390.0	96
Commercial	462.0	4
Adjustments	(6)	—
Total	**10,846**	**100**

COMPETITORS

Accenture
Affiliated Computer Services
American Science and Engineering
BAE Systems Technology Solutions
Battelle Memorial
Booz Allen
CACI International
CH2M HILL
Computer Sciences Corp.
General Dynamics
Honeywell Technology Solutions
HP Enterprise Services
IBM Global Services
KEYW
L-3 Communications Titan
Lockheed Martin Information Systems
ManTech
Northrop Grumman Info Systems
OSI Systems
Raytheon Technical Services
Serco
SRA International
Unisys

HISTORICAL FINANCIALS

Company Type: Public

Income Statement

FYE: January 31

	REVENUE ($ mil.)	NET INCOME ($ mil.)	NET PROFIT MARGIN	EMPLOYEES
1/10	10,846	497	4.6%	46,200
1/09	10,070	452	4.5%	45,400
1/08	8,935	415	4.6%	43,800
1/07	8,294	391	4.7%	44,100
1/06	7,792	927	11.9%	43,100
Annual Growth	**8.6%**	**(14.4%)**	**—**	**1.8%**

2010 Year-End Financials

Debt ratio: 48.1%
Return on equity: —
Cash ($ mil.): 861
Current ratio: 1.87
Long-term debt ($ mil.): 1,103
No. of shares (mil.): 380
Dividends
 Yield: —
 Payout: —
Market value ($ mil.): 6,965

Stock History

NYSE: SAI

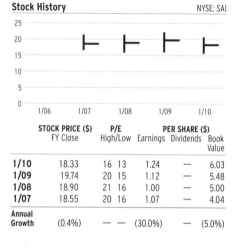

	STOCK PRICE ($) FY Close	P/E High/Low		PER SHARE ($) Earnings	Dividends	Book Value
1/10	18.33	16	13	1.24	—	6.03
1/09	19.74	20	15	1.12	—	5.48
1/08	18.90	21	16	1.00	—	5.00
1/07	18.55	20	16	1.07	—	4.04
Annual Growth	**(0.4%)**	**—**	**—**	**(30.0%)**	**—**	**(5.0%)**

St. Jude Medical

If your heart has trouble catching the beat, St. Jude Medical's got rhythm to spare. The company's main products are pacemakers and implantable cardioverter defibrillators (ICDs), both of which use electrical impulses to shock irregularly beating hearts back into rhythm. St. Jude, which was founded in 1976, also makes mechanical and tissue heart valves; items used in interventional cardiology procedures, such as catheters and guidewires; and ablation systems used to treat atrial fibrillation. Its neuromodulation business makes implantable devices (similar to pacemakers) that treat chronic pain using electrical stimulation.

St. Jude started out in life making mechanical heart valves, but most of its revenue these days comes from its Cardiac Rhythm Management (CRM) division, which makes pacemakers and ICDs. ICDs correct for tachycardia, or overly fast heartbeats, and the company has been aggressively introducing new ICD products and taking market share from its larger competitors in the field, Medtronic and Boston Scientific. A recall in 2010 of some of Boston Scientific's defibrillators helped shuttle St. Jude into a top industry position, and the company is counting on the continued introduction of new products (it

invests just over 10% of its annual income in research and development of new products) and a vigorous marketing campaign to keep it there.

Pacemakers, in contrast to ICDs, are used to treat patients whose hearts beat too slowly. In 2009 St. Jude received FDA and European approval for one of the industry's first pacemakers with wireless telemetry — which in this case allows the patient to be monitored from a distance from the time of implantation to follow-up.

The company has a number of CRM products entering clinical trials in 2010 including an MRI-compatible pacemaker and a quadripolar pacing system, which allows physicians to better manage pacing complications without having to intervene surgically.

The Cardiovascular division makes mechanical and tissue heart valves, annuloplasty rings that repair damaged valves, and products used in interventional cardiology procedures. The unit acquired Radi Medical Systems in 2008 to gain that company's closure products used to help arrest arterial bleeding. The company expanded its cardiovascular division even more with its 2010 acquisition of medical imaging developer LightLab Imaging.

Of other divisions, the company's Atrial Fibrillation unit makes diagnostic products and ablation systems, as well as cardiac mapping technology, used to treat irregular rhythms in the heart's upper chambers. The ablation systems use catheters and radiofrequency energy to zap away heart tissue that is causing arrhythmias. In a move to expand its Atrial Fibrillation business, St. Jude acquired EP Medsystems for about $92 million and MediGuide for $283 million in 2008. EP Medsystems makes the EP WorkMate, an electrophysiology recording system, as well as cardiac stimulators, and an intracardiac ultrasound system called ViewMate.

St. Jude's neuromodulation business got a boost when the company acquired Northstar Neuroscience in 2009.

HISTORY

Manuel Villafana, who started Cardiac Pacemakers in 1972, founded St. Jude Medical four years later to develop the bileaflet heart valve. In 1977 patient Helen Heikkinen received the first St. Jude heart valve. The firm also went public that year.

Villafana left in 1981 and established competitor Helix Biocore. St. Jude expanded into tissue valves with its purchase of BioImplant in 1986.

In the mid-1980s St. Jude gained market share when devices from Pfizer and Baxter International had problems. Concerns that the company hadn't diversified led to a joint venture in 1992 with Hancock Jaffe Laboratories to develop a bioprosthetic (constructed of animal tissue) heart valve. In 1994 it bought Siemens' pacemaker unit, doubling revenues and tripling its sales force.

The firm continued diversifying, buying Daig (cardiac catheters) in 1996 and Ventritex (cardiac defibrillators) in 1997. In 1997 the FDA approved St. Jude's Toronto SPV tissue valve, marking its entry into that market. In 1999 St. Jude landed on CalPERS' list of worst-performing companies as it lagged behind rivals Guidant and Medtronic. A management shake-up followed, and the firm strengthened its product lines, buying Tyco International's Angio-Seal subsidiary (cardiac sealant) and Vascular Science (artery connectors). The next year the FDA stepped up its regulatory oversight after the company and its competitors recalled or issued warnings regarding defective or potentially defective devices.

In 2002 St. Jude bought Getz Bros., its largest distributor in Japan. The firm scooped up two other firms, Irvine Biomedical and Epicor Medical, in 2004.

The company acquired both Endocardial Solutions, which makes diagnostic and therapeutic catheters marketed under the EnSite System brand, and Velocimed, a privately owned maker of interventional cardiology devices, in early 2005. Velocimed's products included the Venture catheter and the Premere system, used to seal a tiny hole between the left and right upper chambers of the heart that fails to close in some babies.

Also in 2005 St. Jude spent more than $1.3 billion to acquire Advanced Neuromodulation Systems, establishing its presence in the neurostimulation market.

EXECUTIVES

Chairman, President, and CEO: Daniel J. Starks, age 55, $7,938,920 total compensation
EVP and CFO: John C. Heinmiller, age 55, $4,097,313 total compensation
SVP Clinical Affairs, Cardiac Rhythm Management Division and Chief Medical Officer: Mark D. Carlson
VP and Corporate Controller: Donald J. Zurbay, age 42
VP Global Quality: Behzad (Ben) Khosravi, age 53
VP Corporate Relations: Angela D. Craig, age 38
VP, General Counsel, and Corporate Secretary: Pamela S. Krop, age 51
VP Information Technology and CIO: Thomas R. Northenscold, age 52
Group President: Michael T. Rousseau, age 54, $3,552,048 total compensation
President, Cardiac Rhythm Management Division: Eric S. Fain, age 49, $2,761,971 total compensation
President, Cardiovascular Division: Frank J. Callaghan, age 56
President, Atrial Fibrillation: Jane J. Song, age 47
President, Neuromodulation Division: Christopher G. (Chris) Chavez, age 54
President, International: Denis M. Gestin, age 46, $2,403,425 total compensation
Manager Investor Relations: J. C. Weigelt
Auditors: Ernst & Young LLP

LOCATIONS

HQ: St. Jude Medical, Inc.
1 St. Jude Medical Dr., St. Paul, MN 55117
Phone: 651-756-2000   **Fax:** 651-756-3301
Web: www.sjm.com

2009 Sales

	$ mil.	% of total
US	2,468.2	53
Europe	1,197.9	26
Japan	480.9	10
Asia/Pacific	254.4	5
Other regions	279.9	6
Total	**4,681.3**	**100**

PRODUCTS/OPERATIONS

2009 Sales

	$ mil.	% of total
Cardiac rhythm management	2,769.0	59
Cardiovascular	953.6	21
Atrial fibrillation	627.9	13
Neuromodulation	330.8	7
Total	**4,681.3**	**100**

COMPETITORS

Abbott Labs	Edwards Lifesciences
ATS Medical	Empi
Bard	Johnson & Johnson
Biosense Webster	Medtronic
Boston Scientific	Sorin
Cyberonics	

HISTORICAL FINANCIALS
Company Type: Public

Income Statement

FYE: Saturday nearest December 31

	REVENUE ($ mil.)	NET INCOME ($ mil.)	NET PROFIT MARGIN	EMPLOYEES
12/09	4,681	777	16.6%	14,000
12/08	4,363	384	8.8%	14,000
12/07	3,779	559	14.8%	12,000
12/06	3,302	548	16.6%	11,000
12/05	2,915	394	13.5%	10,000
Annual Growth	**12.6%**	**18.5%**	**—**	**8.8%**

2009 Year-End Financials

Debt ratio: 47.8%	No. of shares (mil.): 327
Return on equity: 23.7%	Dividends
Cash ($ mil.): 393	Yield: 0.0%
Current ratio: 2.40	Payout: —
Long-term debt ($ mil.): 1,588	Market value ($ mil.): 12,042

Stock History

NYSE: STJ

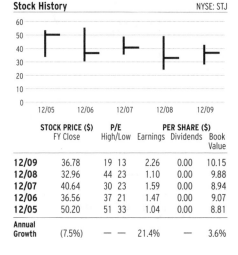

	STOCK PRICE ($) FY Close	P/E High/Low	PER SHARE ($) Earnings	Dividends	Book Value
12/09	36.78	19 13	2.26	0.00	10.15
12/08	32.96	44 23	1.10	0.00	9.88
12/07	40.64	30 23	1.59	0.00	8.94
12/06	36.56	37 21	1.47	0.00	9.07
12/05	50.20	51 33	1.04	0.00	8.81
Annual Growth	**(7.5%)**	**— —**	**21.4%**	**—**	**3.6%**

Sanderson Farms

Sanderson Farms has steadily scratched its way up the pecking order of poultry processors. The company sells fresh, chill-pack, and frozen chicken in whole, cut-up, and boneless forms under the Sanderson Farms label. Its customers include food retailers, distributors, and restaurants and other foodservice operators located mainly in the southeastern, southwestern, northeastern, and western US. In addition to buying chicks from about 180 breeders, the company maintains its own breeder flocks and contracts with about 750 independent chicken farmers, who raise the chicks for Sanderson. Its prepared-foods division sells value-added processed and prepared food items, including frozen entrées.

Vertically integrated, Sanderson Farms operates seven hatcheries, six feed mills, and eight processing facilities — four in Mississippi and one each in Louisiana, Georgia, and Texas. In 2009 the company processed some 397 million chickens and produced more than 2.4 billion pounds of chicken products.

While many chicken processors serve the small bird markets (i.e., primarily fast-food purveyors), Sanderson follows a strategy of concentrating its production in the retail and big bird deboning markets, which service the retail grocery and foodservice sectors. Therefore, the average weight of Sanderson's birds is more than that of other companies' and its total production in pounds is greater as well.

While most of its sales are generated in the US, Sanderson's major foreign markets include Asia, the Caribbean, Eastern Europe, Mexico, and Russia. In 2009 the company ran afoul of the Russian authorities, which reported finding antibiotic and anti-parasitic drug residue in the products originating from three separate plants belonging to three US chicken companies, Sanderson being one of the three. In March of that year, Russia banned the companies' products. (The other companies included in the ban are Tyson and Peco Foods.)

The company spread its wings in 2009 with the opening of new poultry operations in North Carolina. Located in the town of Kingston, the plant processes 1.25 million birds per week for the retail chill pack market.

Investment firm Royce & Associates owns about 12% of the company; an employee trust owns about 8%.

HISTORY

Sanderson Farms began in 1947 when Dewey Sanderson started a Mississippi farm supply business to sell seed, feed, fertilizer, and other supplies. His sons Dewey Jr. and Joe Frank Sanderson joined the company in 1951, when it became Sanderson Brothers. It began breeding poultry and was incorporated four years later as Sanderson Brothers Farms. The company became vertically integrated with its 1961 purchase of broiler processor Miss Goldy.

Throughout the 1960s and 1970s, the company expanded, constructing new plants in Mississippi and acquiring facilities in Louisiana. Sanderson Farms expanded into the processed and prepared foods business with the 1986 acquisition of National Prepared Foods. It went public the following year.

From 1987 to 1992 the company expanded existing facilities, constructed new sites, and added shifts at processing facilities. Joe Jr. was named president and CEO in 1989. In 1993 Sanderson Farms built its second complete poultry-processing complex.

Sanderson Farms completed a $68 million poultry complex in 1997 in Texas' Brazos and Robertson counties (eking out only a small profit as a result of the expense). Co-founder Joe died in 1998, and his son took the additional role of chairman. Dewey Jr. died in 1999.

The Russian embargo on US poultry hit Sanderson Farms' export business hard during 2002.

EXECUTIVES

Chairman and CEO: Joseph F. (Joe) Sanderson Jr., age 62, $3,317,921 total compensation
President, COO, and Director: Lampkin Butts, age 58, $1,752,652 total compensation
CFO, Treasurer, and Director: D. Michael (Mike) Cockrell, age 52, $1,110,666 total compensation

Secretary and Chief Accounting Officer:
 James A. (Jimmy) Grimes, age 61,
 $538,682 total compensation
Chief Financial Analyst: Robert (Bob) Rosa
Director Technical Services: John Rice
Director Organization Development and Corporate
 Communication: Robin Robinson
Director Production: Randy Pettus
Director Development and Engineering:
 Robert (Bob) Billingsley
Director Processing: Doug Lee
Director Administration: Brian Romano
Director Sales: Neil Morgan
Auditors: Ernst & Young LLP

LOCATIONS

HQ: Sanderson Farms, Inc.
 127 Flynt Rd., Laurel, MS 39440
Phone: 601-649-4030   **Fax:** 601-426-1461
Web: www.sandersonfarms.com

2009 Processing Plants

	Pounds per Week (at full capacity)
Georgia	
Mountrie — Chill Pack Retail	1,250,000
Hammond — Big Bird Deboning	625,000
Mississippi	
Collins — Big Bird Deboning	1,250,000
Hazelhurst — Big Bird Deboning	625,000
Laurel — Big Bird Deboning	625,000
McComb — Chill Pack Retail	1,250,000
Texas	
Bryan — Chill Pack Retail	1,250,000
Waco — Big Bird Deboning	1,250,000
Total	**8,125,000**

PRODUCTS/OPERATIONS

2009 Sales

	% of total
Value-added chicken	
Fresh bulk pack	50
Chill pack	31
Frozen	10
Prepared chicken	8
Non-value-added chicken	
Ice pack	1
Total	**100**

COMPETITORS

Allen Family Foods
Cagle's
Coleman Natural Foods
Cooper Farms
Fieldale Farms
Lincoln Poultry
New Market Poultry
On-Cor Frozen Foods
Perdue Incorporated
Pilgrim's Pride
Raeford Farms
Tecumseh Poultry
Townsends
Tyson Foods
Wayne Farms LLC

HISTORICAL FINANCIALS

Company Type: Public

Income Statement				FYE: October 31
	REVENUE ($ mil.)	NET INCOME ($ mil.)	NET PROFIT MARGIN	EMPLOYEES
10/09	1,790	82	4.6%	9,965
10/08	1,724	(43)	—	10,739
10/07	1,475	79	5.3%	9,705
10/06	1,048	(12)	—	8,711
10/05	1,006	71	7.0%	8,645
Annual Growth	**15.5%**	**3.9%**	**—**	**3.6%**

2009 Year-End Financials
Debt ratio: 24.5%
Return on equity: 21.0%
Cash ($ mil.): 8
Current ratio: 3.10
Long-term debt ($ mil.): 106
No. of shares (mil.): 23
Dividends
 Yield: 1.6%
 Payout: 14.3%
Market value ($ mil.): 831

Stock History   NASDAQ (GS): SAFM

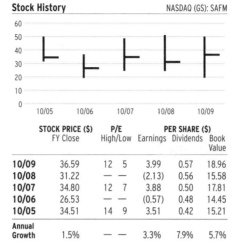

	STOCK PRICE ($) FY Close	P/E High/Low		PER SHARE ($) Earnings	Dividends	Book Value
10/09	36.59	12	5	3.99	0.57	18.96
10/08	31.22	—	—	(2.13)	0.56	15.58
10/07	34.80	12	7	3.88	0.50	17.81
10/06	26.53	—	—	(0.57)	0.48	14.45
10/05	34.51	14	9	3.51	0.42	15.21
Annual Growth	**1.5%**	**—**	**—**	**3.3%**	**7.9%**	**5.7%**

SanDisk Corporation

If forgetting things drives you crazy, SanDisk's products might help preserve your sanity. The company is a top producer of data storage products based on flash memory, which retains data even when power is interrupted. Its products include removable and embedded memory cards used in digital cameras, medical devices, networking equipment, notebook computers, and other electronics. The company sells to such manufacturers as Canon, Eastman Kodak, and Siemens, as well as through retailers, including Best Buy and Office Depot. About half of its sales are from the Asia/Pacific region. SanDisk, which holds more than 1,400 US patents and 700 foreign patents, licenses its technology to customers such as Intel, Sharp, and Sony.

The company is branching out into other product areas that use flash memory, such as its G3 solid-state drives (a smaller alternative to hard-disk drives) and slotRadio cards, which contain 1,000 preloaded songs that can be played on mobile phones or its Sansa fuze music player. SanDisk once heavily relied on retailers and distributors, but its sales are now evenly divided between OEM and retail channels.

In 2008 Samsung Electronics made a hostile takeover bid for SanDisk. The unsolicited acquisition offer, valued at $5.85 billion in cash, came amid turbulent business conditions in the memory device industry, with oversupply in the DRAM and NAND flash memory markets continually driving down prices and causing red ink for several memory chip makers. Samsung and SanDisk discussed a possible combination earlier in 2008, but after nearly four months of negotiations, Samsung grew impatient with the progress of such talks.

Samsung withdrew the offer in late 2008, citing "growing uncertainties" in SanDisk's business and the worldwide financial crisis. Samsung is one of SanDisk's biggest customers.

The company has become a leading competitor in the market for music/video players with its Sansa brand. To strengthen the Sansa product line, in 2008 it bought MusicGremlin, a developer of digital content distribution technologies.

The company further delved into the digital music market in 2008 with the unveiling of its slotMusic microSD cards. Best Buy and Wal-Mart sell the fingernail-sized memory cards, which can plug into mobile phones and MP3 players, loaded with full albums. SanDisk signed licensing deals with the four biggest recording companies — EMI Music, Sony Music, Universal Music, and Warner Music.

SanDisk has signed joint product development deals with Hynix Semiconductor and Microsoft, among other companies. Microsoft and SanDisk collaborated on developing USB flash drives and flash memory cards incorporating SanDisk's U3 Smart Technology drive platform (which is supported by independent software developers) and TrustedFlash security technology.

SanDisk outsources its chip manufacturing to silicon foundries (contract semiconductor manufacturers). The company also has joint ventures with Toshiba to produce NAND flash memory in Japan. The joint ventures produce finished wafers that they sell to SanDisk and Toshiba.

HISTORY

SanDisk was founded as SunDisk in 1988 by Eli Harari (now CEO), an expert on nonvolatile memory technology. SunDisk's first product, based on a four-megabit flash chip, was developed with AT&T Bell Labs and released in 1991. In 1992 the company formed a development partnership with disk drive maker Seagate Technology; as part of the pact, Seagate acquired 25% of SunDisk.

Because SunDisk was being confused with Sun Microsystems, in 1995 the company changed its name to SanDisk. It went public that year and introduced the industry's smallest Type II (a PC card slot size designation) flash storage card — the CompactFlash. Sales increased by nearly 80% in 1995, SanDisk's first profitable year. The next year SanDisk and Matsushita (now Panasonic) developed double-density flash, a breakthrough technology that doubled the capacity of flash storage products.

In 1997 SanDisk started production of its double-density flash series, investing $40 million in a semiconductor plant in Taiwan with United Microelectronics. In 1999 SanDisk said it would move about 75% of its production to China, partly through a partnership with Celestica.

Seagate divested the last of its ownership stake in SanDisk in 2000. Also that year SanDisk and Toshiba formed a joint venture, FlashVision, to produce advanced flash memory at a Toshiba semiconductor plant in Virginia. FlashVision commenced production the following year. (The joint venture's operations were moved to one of Toshiba's Japanese plants after Toshiba announced the sale of the Virginia factory — which primarily made DRAM chips — to Micron Technology in 2001.) SanDisk and Toshiba consolidated manufacturing at Toshiba's Yokkaichi memory fab in 2002.

In 2004 SanDisk opened a retail distribution center in China and formed a new joint venture with Toshiba, Flash Partners, for the purpose of adding manufacturing capacity. The following year Toshiba began operation of a new fab in Yokkaichi for making NAND flash memory devices. The semiconductors were produced on silicon wafers measuring 300mm (12 inches) across.

In 2006 SanDisk acquired Matrix Semiconductor, a developer of 3-D, one-time programmable (OTP) chip technology, for about $300 million in stock and cash. The companies began working together on integrating the Matrix technology into SanDisk's product line.

SanDisk purchased rival msystems in 2006 for about $1.5 billion in stock. After passing on an opportunity to acquire competitor Lexar Media (which went to chip maker Micron Technology earlier that year), SanDisk pursued msystems instead, widening its portfolio of flash memory-based data storage products.

Responding to the dramatic collapse of prices in the NAND flash memory market, SanDisk set a number of cost-cutting measures in 2007. These included the layoff of up to 10% of the worldwide staff (approximately 250 employees), salary cuts for senior executives, salary freezes for all other employees, and a hiring freeze for most areas.

EXECUTIVES

Director: Michael E. Marks, age 59
Chairman and CEO: Eli Harari, age 64, $4,079,099 total compensation
Vice Chairman: Irwin Federman, age 74
President, COO, and Director: Sanjay Mehrotra, age 51, $2,141,984 total compensation
EVP Administration and CFO: Judy Bruner, age 51, $1,649,384 total compensation
EVP OEM Business and Corporate Engineering: Yoram Cedar, age 57, $1,396,470 total compensation
Chief Intellectual Property Counsel: E. Earle Thompson, age 53
SVP Strategy and Business Development: Sumit Sadana, age 41
SVP Memory Technology and Product Development: Khandker Nazrul Quader
SVP Human Resources: Tom Baker
SVP, General Counsel, and Corporate Secretary: James (Jim) Brelsford
SVP Technology and Fab Operations: Atsuyoshi Koike, age 57
Director Public Relations: Mike Wong
Director Investor Relations: Jay Iyer
Auditors: Ernst & Young LLP

LOCATIONS

HQ: SanDisk Corporation
601 McCarthy Blvd., Milpitas, CA 95035
Phone: 408-801-1000 **Fax:** 408-801-8657
Web: www.sandisk.com

2009 Sales

	$ mil.	% of total
Asia/Pacific		
South Korea	428.4	12
Taiwan	397.3	11
Other countries	1,010.1	28
US	940.6	27
Europe, Middle East & Africa	707.8	20
Other regions	82.6	2
Total	**3,566.8**	**100**

PRODUCTS/OPERATIONS

2009 Sales

	$ mil.	% of total
Products	3,154.3	88
Licenses & royalties	412.5	12
Total	**3,566.8**	**100**

2009 Product Sales by Channel

	$ mil.	% of total
OEM	1,586.8	50
Retail	1,567.5	50
Total	**3,154.3**	**100**

Selected Products

Embedded data storage devices (FlashDrive)
MP3 music players (Sansa)
Portable storage devices (Cruzer)
Removable storage cards (used in cellular phones, digital cameras, digital music players, digital voice recorders, and personal digital assistants)
  CompactFlash
  Memory Stick
  MultiMedia
  Secure Digital
  SmartMedia

COMPETITORS

Apple Inc.
Archos
Atmel
Buffalo Technology
Creative Technology
Eastman Kodak
FUJIFILM
Gemalto
Hynix
IM Flash Technologies
Imation
Iomega
Iriver
Kingston Technology
Lexar
Macronix International
Microsoft
Netlist
Panasonic Corp
Philips Electronics
PNY Technologies
Samsung Electronics
Seagate Technology
Silicon Motion
Silicon Storage
SMART Modular Technologies
SMDK
Sony
STEC
STMicroelectronics
Toshiba Semiconductor
Verbatim Corp.
Viking Modular Solutions
Western Digital

HISTORICAL FINANCIALS

Company Type: Public

Income Statement

FYE: Sunday closest to December 31

	REVENUE ($ mil.)	NET INCOME ($ mil.)	NET PROFIT MARGIN	EMPLOYEES
12/09	3,567	415	11.6%	3,267
12/08	3,351	(2,057)	—	3,565
12/07	3,896	218	5.6%	3,172
12/06	3,258	199	6.1%	2,586
12/05	2,306	386	16.8%	1,083
Annual Growth	**11.5%**	**1.8%**	**—**	**31.8%**

2009 Year-End Financials

Debt ratio: 23.9%
Return on equity: 11.7%
Cash ($ mil.): 1,100
Current ratio: 3.35
Long-term debt ($ mil.): 935
No. of shares (mil.): 230
Dividends
  Yield: —
  Payout: —
Market value ($ mil.): 6,667

Stock History

NASDAQ (GS): SNDK

	STOCK PRICE ($) FY Close	P/E High/Low		PER SHARE ($) Earnings	Dividends	Book Value
12/09	28.99	17	4	1.79	—	17.00
12/08	9.60	—	—	(9.13)	—	13.80
12/07	33.17	64	35	0.93	—	21.57
12/06	43.03	83	39	0.96	—	20.73
12/05	62.82	33	10	2.00	—	10.97
Annual Growth	**(17.6%)**	**—**	**—**	**(2.7%)**	**—**	**11.6%**

Sanmina-SCI

Sanmina-SCI's services help keep electronics makers sane. The company is a top contract manufacturer of sophisticated electronic components, including printed circuit boards and backplane assemblies (circuit boards with slots and sockets for plugging in other boards and cables). Other products include cable and wiring harness assemblies, custom enclosures, optical components, and memory modules. In addition, the company provides services such as design and engineering, materials management, order fulfillment, and in-circuit testing. Sanmina-SCI has manufacturing facilities in 18 countries on five continents.

In order to reduce costs and exert greater control over production, the company locates components plants in lower cost regions and final system assembly plants near customers and their end markets. It provides vertically integrated manufacturing services — producing components that can be used in subassemblies that it builds — for products that include wireless and networking communications gear, MRI and CT scanners, servers, storage devices, and semiconductor manufacturing equipment.

Responding to turmoil in the global economy, in 2009 Sanmina-SCI implemented a restructuring plan that included closing or consolidating six facilities and terminating about 4,000 employees, about a 10% workforce reduction. Operating in a highly cyclical industry, however, means the company is constantly restructuring in order to provide more cost-efficient products to its customers. The company also purchases manufacturing operations being divested by OEMs, often as part of an agreement to supply the products back to the customer. These deals provide expanded capacity and technologies, and access to new customers and geographic markets, with less investment than organic growth.

In early 2009 Sanmina-SCI scored JDS Uniphase's Shenzhen, China, optical facility. Subsequently, Sanmina-SCI inked an agreement with OneChip Photonics to manufacture Photonic Integrated Circuit (PIC)-based Fiber-to-the-Premises (FTTP) transceivers.

In 2008 Sanmina-SCI sold its PC manufacturing business, saying the barely profitable business was no longer integral to the company's long-term strategy. The company transferred its PC plant in Monterrey, Mexico, to Lenovo Group and sold certain assets to the giant Chinese PC maker. Other assets of the PC business in Hungary, Mexico, and the US were sold to Foxteq Holdings, a unit of Foxconn Technology Group, which is part of Hon Hai Precision Industry, the world's largest contract electronics manufacturer. The PC business previously represented nearly a third of Sanmina-SCI's revenues.

The company's $6 billion acquisition of rival SCI Systems in 2001 vaulted Sanmina-SCI into the top ranks of contract manufacturers such as Flextronics and Celestica. The deal also capped a buying spree that expanded the company into Europe and Asia.

HISTORY

Bosnian immigrants Jure Sola (chairman and CEO) and Milan Mandaric founded Sanmina in 1980 to provide just-in-time manufacturing of printed circuit boards (PCBs). The name Sanmina comes from the names of Mandaric's children.

During the late 1980s and early 1990s Sanmina shifted production to higher-margin components, such as backplane assemblies and subassemblies. Mandaric, an entrepreneur with other interests, left in 1989. The company went public in 1993.

Like other contract manufacturers, Sanmina began bolstering its operations through acquisitions. The company bought manufacturing plants from Comptronix (1994), Assembly Solutions (1995), Golden Eagle Systems (1996), and Lucent Technologies (1996). In 1997 the company bought contract electronics maker Elexsys International, which was headed by Milan Mandaric. Sanmina also opened a plant in Ireland.

Sanmina's 1998 acquisitions included Massachusetts-based Altron, its #1 competitor in backplane manufacturing. In 1999 the company acquired assets from Nortel Networks and Devtek Electronics Enclosure, a designer of enclosure systems for the telecommunications and networking industries.

In 2000 Sanmina acquired PCB maker Hadco in a $1.3 billion deal, expanding its global presence. That year the company also purchased Swedish contract manufacturer Essex AB, entered into a joint venture with Siemens to manufacture complex PCBs, and acquired some plants from Nortel and Lucent.

In mid-2001 Sanmina agreed to buy rival SCI Systems, one of the world's largest contract manufacturers, for about $4.5 billion. (Sanmina also assumed $1.5 billion of SCI's debt.) Later that year it also acquired a facility in Texas from (and signed a multiyear supplier agreement with) French telecom titan Alcatel (now Alcatel-Lucent). When its acquisition of SCI Systems closed late in the year, Sanmina changed its name to Sanmina-SCI. (Sola and SCI Systems chairman and CEO Eugene Sapp became co-chairmen; Sola remained CEO of the combined company.)

Sanmina-SCI forged several deals in early 2002. The company announced a three-year, $5 billion agreement with IBM to produce desktop PCs. As part of the deal, Sanmina-SCI acquired two US plants from IBM. In addition, Sanmina-SCI and HP penned a deal whereby the company produces some HP products and acquired HP's manufacturing operations in France for $65.8 million. Also that year Sanmina-SCI ac-

quired plants in France, Germany, and Spain from Alcatel for $129.9 million as part of a multiyear supply agreement. All three deals were completed by mid-year.

After a year as co-chairman, Eugene Sapp stepped down from that post in late 2002, while remaining a director of the company.

Like dozens of other tech companies, Sanmina-SCI found problems in 2006 with its past practices in granting stock options to executives and other employees. An internal investigation by a special board committee, going back to the beginning of 1997, found that most grants in the prior decade were not correctly dated or accounted for, requiring the company to restate financial results and record non-cash compensation charges.

Among other changes recommended by the special committee, the board adopted a policy of establishing fixed dates for granting equity-based awards, reducing or eliminating the possibility of backdating or springloading options.

Sanmina-SCI shuttered Newisys in 2007, laying off 87 employees.

EXECUTIVES

Chairman and CEO: Jure Sola, age 58, $1,784,043 total compensation
President and COO: Hari Pillai, age 50, $1,365,004 total compensation
EVP and CFO: Robert K. (Bob) Eulau, age 48, $16,923 total compensation
EVP Worldwide Sales and Marketing: Dennis Young, age 58, $697,072 total compensation
EVP, General Counsel, and Secretary: Michael R. (Mike) Tyler, age 54, $620,307 total compensation
EVP Global Human Resources: David L. Pulatie, age 68
VP Enterprise Services: Manesh Patel
Marketing and Strategic Business Development, Europe: Ulrike Winter
Director Worldwide Marketing and Public Relations: Michael Kovacs
Investor Relations: Paige Bombino
Auditors: KPMG LLP

LOCATIONS

HQ: Sanmina-SCI Corporation
2700 N. 1st St., San Jose, CA 95134
Phone: 408-964-3500   **Fax:** 408-964-3636
Web: www.sanmina-sci.com

2009 Sales

	$ mil.	% of total
US	1,198.1	23
China	1,137.0	22
Mexico	1,104.4	21
Singapore	521.3	10
Other countries	1,216.7	24
Total	**5,177.5**	**100**

PRODUCTS/OPERATIONS

Selected Services

Backplane assembly
Cable assembly
Circuit assembly
Circuit fabrication
Configuration
Distribution
Enclosures
Engineering
In-circuit testing
Materials management
Order fulfillment
Printed circuit board design
System assembly and testing

COMPETITORS

Benchmark Electronics
BenQ
Cal-Comp Electronics
Celestica
CTS Corp.
Elcoteq
Flextronics
Hon Hai
IBM Canada
Inventec
Jabil
Jurong Technologies
Nam Tai
Plexus
SMTC Corp.
Suntron
SYNNEX
TTM Technologies
Universal Scientific
Venture Corp.
Viasystems
Wistron

HISTORICAL FINANCIALS

Company Type: Public

Income Statement

FYE: September 30

	REVENUE ($ mil.)	NET INCOME ($ mil.)	NET PROFIT MARGIN	EMPLOYEES
9/09	5,178	(136)	—	38,602
9/08	7,202	(486)	—	45,610
9/07	10,384	(1,135)	—	52,607
9/06	10,955	(144)	—	54,397
9/05	11,735	(1,006)	—	48,621
Annual Growth	**(18.5%)**	**—**	**—**	**(5.6%)**

2009 Year-End Financials

Debt ratio: 232.4%
Return on equity: —
Cash ($ mil.): 899
Current ratio: 2.07
Long-term debt ($ mil.): 1,262

No. of shares (mil.): 80
Dividends
  Yield: —
  Payout: —
Market value ($ mil.): 684

Stock History

NASDAQ (GS): SANM

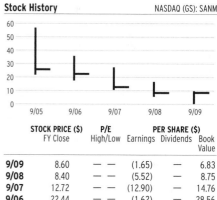

	STOCK PRICE ($) FY Close	P/E High/Low	PER SHARE ($) Earnings	Dividends	Book Value
9/09	8.60	— —	(1.65)	—	6.83
9/08	8.40	— —	(5.52)	—	8.75
9/07	12.72	— —	(12.90)	—	14.76
9/06	22.44	— —	(1.62)	—	28.56
9/05	25.74	— —	(11.58)	—	29.92
Annual Growth	**(24.0%)**	**— —**	**—**	**—**	**(30.9%)**

Sara Lee

Sara Lee chose cheesecake over clothing. Jettisoning the apparel business, Sara Lee now peddles mostly food and drink, along with some household goods, though it's selling off that business too. Its North American Retail unit is a major packaged meat maker (Ball Park, Jimmy Dean) and a leading manufacturer of frozen bakery products, including Ms. Lee's famous raid-the-fridge-at-midnight frozen cheesecakes. The fresh bakery segment supplies North America with prepackaged bread and other baked goods. Sara Lee International oversees coffee, tea, and bakery items in Europe, Australia, and Brazil. The North American Foodservice unit supplies coffee, meat, and baked goods to foodservice operators across the continent.

In 2010 CEO Brenda Barnes stepped down permanently after suffering a stroke. The company began the search for her replacement. In the meantime, Marcel Smits will serve as interim CEO. Barnes has been credited with transforming Sara Lee by exiting low-margin businesses. During her tenure, she focused on businesses like food and coffee, while divesting lines such as the Hanes underwear business.

To streamline Sara Lee's operations into cohesive units, Barnes first oversaw the spinoff of its $4.5 billion Americas/Asia Branded Apparel group (consisting of Hanes, Champion, Playtex, and other brands) to form an independent, public company called Hanesbrands Inc., which began trading in 2006.

The company also sold its $1.2 billion European apparel business to Florida's Sun Capital Partners. The deal included the Dim, Playtex, Wonderbra, Abanderado, and Unno brands.

In 2007 the company laid off some 1,700 workers at its Mississippi pork plant. It also cut about 500 other jobs throughout the rest of the company. And it sliced about a dozen top management jobs in 2007 as well, including the chief of its international business operations.

Sara Lee sold its foodservice sauce and salad dressing business to Richelieu Foods in 2008; it also disposed of its Mexican meat operations that year. It bought Brazilian coffee producer Cafe Moka later in the year in order to strengthen its position in the Brazilian coffee market.

Sara Lee accepted a cash bid of €1.28 billion ($1.88 billion) from Unilever for the purchase of its global body-care business in 2009. Tupperware Brands bought Sara Lee's international direct-selling operation for $557 million in 2010.

BlackRock owns about 6% of Sara Lee; Brandes Investment Partners, Capital Group International, and ValueAct Capital each own approximately 5%.

HISTORY

Businessman Nathan Cummings bought the C. D. Kenny Co., a Baltimore coffee, tea, and sugar wholesaler, in 1939. Cummings soon purchased several grocery firms and later changed the company's name to Consolidated Grocers (1945). The operation went public in 1946 and was renamed Consolidated Foods Corp. (CFC) in 1954.

Two years later CFC bought the Kitchens of Sara Lee, a Chicago bakery founded by Charles Lubin in 1951. Introduced in 1949 and named after Lubin's daughter, Sara Lee cheesecake had become the bakery's most popular product.

In 1968 CFC sold its Eagle Complex, which included Piggly Wiggly Midwest supermarkets and Eagle Food Centers, and it bought Bryan Foods. The firm continued to buy and sell businesses in the US, including beverage, appliance, and chemical companies. Some major US purchases were Hanes Corp. (1979), Jimmy Dean Meat Co. (1984), Coach Leatherware International (1985), and Champion Products (athletic knitwear, 1989). Cummings served as president until 1970.

CFC began building its international markets with its first European acquisition in 1962. Following that purchase, it expanded its global presence with the purchases of Douwe Egberts (coffee, tea, and tobacco; the Netherlands; 1978), Nicholas Kiwi (shoe care and pharmaceuticals, Australia, 1984), and Dim (hosiery and underwear, France, 1989).

Using one of its most respected brand names to enhance the public's awareness of the company, CFC changed its name to Sara Lee in 1985. It continued making acquisitions in the 1990s, including Playtex Apparel.

In 1997 Sara Lee began a restructuring that included selling noncore businesses and increasing its use of outsourcing, closed more than 90 manufacturing and distribution facilities, and laid off 9,400 employees.

Sara Lee sold its loose tobacco business (Amphora, Drum, Van Nelle) in 1998 to the UK's Imperial Tobacco for $1.1 billion; bought undergarments maker Strouse, Adler; and purchased Quaker Oats' coffee marketer, Continental Coffee Products. Also that year Sara Lee recalled hot dogs and packaged meats produced by its Bil Mar Foods unit after the items were linked to nearly two dozen fatal food-poisoning cases. (The company settled class-action suits over the incident in 2000.)

While closing more than 100 facilities, during 1999 Sara Lee continued acquiring, including coffee company Chock full o'Nuts, and the Hills Bros., MJB, and Chase & Sanborn coffee operations from Nestlé. It also bought Royal Ahold's Dutch meat processing units, Meester and Nistria; J.E. Morgan Knitting Mills (maker of Duofold thermal underwear); and the UK's leading intimate apparel and underwear producer, Courtaulds Textiles.

During 2000 Sara Lee spun off its Coach (leather goods) business and sold off its foodservice operation, PYA/Monarch, to a Royal Ahold subsidiary as the first move to refocus on its core brands. In 2000 president Steven McMillan added the CEO title to his duties; he was named chairman that October.

In 2001 Sara Lee continued to dispose of noncore operations. However, in that August it acquired The Earthgrains Company, the second-largest fresh-bread company in the US; the combined bakery operations of the companies were renamed the Sara Lee Bakery Group.

Due to falling sales caused by more casual dressing habits, the company sold off its Italian hosiery business in 2003.

In 2005 McMillan retired and handed over the titles of president, CEO, and chairman to Brenda Barnes, who instituted a total reorganization of the company.

In mid-2010 Sara Lee sold its European air-freshener business, including Ambi Pur, to Procter & Gamble for €320 million ($470 million). Additionally, in 2010 the company completed the sale of its 51% stake in the Godrej joint venture in India to its partner there for $230 million.

EXECUTIVES

Chairman: James S. Crown, age 56
Interim CEO: Marcel H. M. Smits, age 48
Interim CFO: Mark A. Garvey, age 45, $1,715,727 total compensation
EVP; CEO, International Beverage and Bakery: Frank van Oers, age 50, $2,059,945 total compensation
EVP; CEO, North American Retail and Foodservice: Christopher J. (CJ) Fraleigh, age 46, $2,846,492 total compensation
EVP; CEO, International Household and Body Care: Vincent H. A. M. Janssen, age 56
EVP, General Counsel, and Corporate Secretary: Brett J. Hart, age 41
EVP Human Resources: Stephen J. Cerrone, age 46
CIO: Anne Teague, age 50
SVP Strategic Planning and Corporate Development: B. Thomas Hansson, age 49
SVP Global Communications: Jon Harris
VP International Communications, Sara Lee International: Joost den Haan
VP Investor Relations: Aaron Hoffman
VP Breakfast and Snacking, Sara Lee North American Retail: Andy Callahan
President, Household and Beverage: Martin Lind
Auditors: PricewaterhouseCoopers LLP

LOCATIONS

HQ: Sara Lee Corporation
3500 Lacey Rd., Downers Grove, IL 60515
Phone: 630-598-8100 **Fax:** 630-598-8482
Web: www.saralee.com

2009 Sales

	$ mil.	% of total
North America	7,059	55
Other regions	5,856	45
Adjustments	(34)	—
Total	**12,881**	**100**

PRODUCTS/OPERATIONS

2009 Sales

	$ mil.	% of total
International beverage	3,041	24
North American retail	2,767	21
North American fresh bakery	2,200	17
North American foodservice	2,092	16
International household & body care	2,025	16
International bakery	790	6
Adjustments	(34)	—
Total	**12,881**	**100**

Selected Brands and Products

Foodservice
 Bakery
  Bagels
  Bread
  Buns
  Frozen pies, cakes, and cheesecakes
  Muffins
  Refrigerated dough
  Rolls
  Specialty breads
 Beverages
  Roast, ground and liquid coffee, cappuccinos, lattes, and teas
 Condiments
  Sauces and dressings
 Meats
  Bacon
  Breakfast sausages and sandwiches
  Cooked and dry hams
  Corn dogs
  Deli and luncheon meats
  Hot dogs
  Meat snacks
  Smoked and dinner sausages

Household and Body Care
Bloom
Catch
Duschdas
GoodKnight
Kiwi
Monsavon
Radox
Ridsect
Sanex
Vapona
Zendium

International Bakery
Bimbo
BonGateaux
CroustiPate
Ortiz
Sara Lee

North American Retail Bakery
Colonial
Earth Grains
Healthy Choice
Heiner's
Holsum
IronKids
Mother's
Rainbo
Roman Meal
Sara Lee
Sunbeam
Sun-Maid

North American Retail Meats
Ball Park
Bryan
Hillshire Farm
Jimmy Dean
Kahn's
Sara Lee
State Fair

COMPETITORS

Canada Bread Company	King's Hawaiian
Cheesecake Factory	Kraft Foods
Church & Dwight	Maple Leaf Foods
Clorox	Millstone
Colgate-Palmolive	Nestlé
ConAgra	Pepperidge Farm
Farmland Foods	Plumrose USA
Flowers Foods	Procter & Gamble
George Weston Bakeries	Reckitt Benckiser
Heinemann's Bakeries	S.C. Johnson
Hormel	Smucker
Hostess Brands	Starbucks
Johnsonville Sausage	SYSCO
Jones Dairy Farm	Tyson Foods
Karl Ehmer	Usinger's

HISTORICAL FINANCIALS
Company Type: Public

Income Statement
FYE: Saturday nearest June 30

	REVENUE ($ mil.)	NET INCOME ($ mil.)	NET PROFIT MARGIN	EMPLOYEES
6/09	12,881	364	2.8%	41,000
6/08	13,212	(79)	—	44,000
6/07	12,278	504	4.1%	52,400
6/06	15,944	555	3.5%	109,000
6/05	19,254	719	3.7%	137,000
Annual Growth	(9.6%)	(15.6%)	—	(26.0%)

2009 Year-End Financials
Debt ratio: 134.8%
Return on equity: 15.0%
Cash ($ mil.): 959
Current ratio: 1.35
Long-term debt ($ mil.): 2,745
No. of shares (mil.): 661
Dividends
  Yield: 4.5%
  Payout: 84.6%
Market value ($ mil.): 6,454

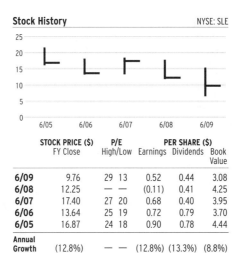

	STOCK PRICE ($) FY Close	P/E High/Low		PER SHARE ($) Earnings	Dividends	Book Value
6/09	9.76	29	13	0.52	0.44	3.08
6/08	12.25	—	—	(0.11)	0.41	4.25
6/07	17.40	27	20	0.68	0.40	3.95
6/06	13.64	25	19	0.72	0.79	3.70
6/05	16.87	24	18	0.90	0.78	4.44
Annual Growth	(12.8%)	—	—	(12.8%)	(13.3%)	(8.8%)

S.C. Johnson

S.C. Johnson & Son helped to replace the fly-swatter with the spray can. It's one of the world's largest makers of consumer chemical products, boasting big names such as Glade, Mr. Muscle, Raid, Pledge, Brise, Drano, Fantastik, Kabbikiller, OFF!, Scrubbing Bubbles, Shout, Vanish, Windex, Saran, and Ziploc. S.C. Johnson, founded in 1886, peddles its products in more than 110 countries. The founder's great-grandson and once one of the richest men in the US, Samuel Johnson, died in 2004. His immediate family owns about 60% of S.C. Johnson; descendants of the founder's daughter own about 40%. Chairman Dr. Fisk Johnson assumed the title of CEO when president, CEO, and director Bill Perez left for NIKE in late 2004.

Many of S.C. Johnson's products have been and remain top sellers in their markets. However, after seeing its Edge and Skintimate shave preparation brands lose market share to rival Procter & Gamble's Gillette, the company in June 2009 sold the two brands to Energizer, which already competes with P&G in the razors business with its Schick-Wilkinson Sword unit.

A top supplier of air fresheners globally, S.C. Johnson was jockeying to purchase the European air freshener business of Sara Lee Corporation in late 2009. The deal would have extended S.C. Johnson's reach overseas and solidified its scents niche. However, behemoth P&G elbowed the Glade-products maker and offered Sara Lee some $470 million for the business in December 2009.

S.C. Johnson met Sara Lee at the table again in mid-2010, when the consumer chemical company agreed to expand its insecticides portfolio with the cheesecake maker's Ridsect and Bloom branded items. S.C. Johnson plans to pick up the brands for $188 million.

While its competitors dip their toes in the commercial side of the cleaning and air freshener products business, S.C. Johnson has fined-tuned its focus on the consumer side. The company's commercial products division was spun off as a private company owned by the Johnson family.

The company boasts operations in more than 70 countries, including Canada, Australia, Costa Rica, Mexico, and Puerto Rico. For three years since 2006, *Working Mother* magazine has recognized S.C. Johnson as one of the 100 best companies for working mothers.

HISTORY

Samuel C. Johnson, a carpenter whose customers were as interested in his floor wax as in his parquet floors, founded S.C. Johnson in Racine, Wisconsin, in 1886. Forsaking carpentry, Johnson began to manufacture floor care products. The company, named S.C. Johnson & Son in 1906, began establishing subsidiaries worldwide in 1914. By the time Johnson's son and successor, Herbert Johnson, died in 1928, annual sales were $5 million. Herbert Jr. and his sister, Henrietta Lewis, received 60% and 40% of the firm, respectively. The original section of S.C. Johnson's headquarters, designed by Frank Lloyd Wright and called "the greatest piece of 20th-century architecture" in the US, was finished in 1939.

In 1954, with $45 million in annual sales, Herbert Jr.'s son Samuel Curtis Johnson joined the company as new products director. Two years later it introduced Raid, the first water-based insecticide, and soon thereafter, OFF! insect repellent. Each became a market leader. The company unsuccessfully attempted to diversify into paint, chemicals, and lawn care during the 1950s and 1960s. The home care products segment prospered, however, with the introduction of Pledge aerosol furniture polish and Glade aerosol air freshener.

After Herbert Jr. suffered a stroke in 1965, Samuel became president. In 1975 the firm banned the use of the chlorofluorocarbons (CFCs) in its products, three years before the US government banned CFCs. Samuel started a recreational products division that was bought by the Johnson family in 1986. That company went public in 1987 as Johnson Worldwide Associates, with the family retaining control.

The company launched Edge shaving gel and Agree hair products in the 1970s but had few products as successful in the 1980s. It moved into real estate with Johnson Wax Development (JWD) in the 1970s, but sold JWD's assets in the late 1980s.

S. Curtis Johnson, Samuel's son, joined the company in 1983. In 1986 S.C. Johnson bought Bugs Burger Bug Killers, moving into commercial pest control; in 1990 it entered into an agreement with Mycogen to develop biological pesticides for household use.

In 1993 it bought Drackett, bringing Drano and Windex to its product roster along with increased competition from heavyweights such as Procter & Gamble and Clorox. That year S.C. Johnson sold the Agree and Halsa lines to DEP. In 1996 it launched a line of water-soluble pouches for cleaning products that allow work to be done without touching hazardous chemicals. President William Perez became CEO the next year (and left in late 2004 to become president, CEO, and director of Nike, Inc.).

S.C. Johnson bought Dow Chemical's DowBrands unit, maker of bathroom cleaner (Dow), plastic bags (Ziploc), and plastic wrap (Saran Wrap), for $1.2 billion in 1998. It then sold off other Dow brands (cleaners Spray 'N Wash, Glass Plus, Yes, and Vivid) to the UK's Reckitt & Colman to settle antitrust issues.

A year later S.C. Johnson sold its skin care line, including Aveeno, to health care products maker Johnson & Johnson, and spun off its commercial products unit as a private firm owned by the Johnson family.

In 2000 S.C. Johnson pulled its AllerCare carpet powder and allergen spray from store shelves after some consumers had negative reactions to the fragrance additive in the products. That year H. Fisk Johnson succeeded his father (who became chairman emeritus) as chairman.

In 2001 the company was fined $950,000 for selling banned Raid Max Roach Bait traps in New York after agreeing to pull them from store shelves. Also that year S.C. Johnson's Japanese subsidiary agreed to buy that country's leading drain cleaner brand, Pipe Unish, from Unicharm.

In October 2002 the company acquired the household insecticides unit of German drug giant Bayer Group for $734 million. The following year S.C. Johnson invested in Karamchand Appliances Private Limited, which owns India's second-leading insect control brand *AllOut*.

Chairman emeritus Samuel C. Johnson died in 2004 at the age of 76.

In June 2009 S. C. Johnson sold its Edge and Skintimate pre-shave brands to Energizer Holdings for $275 million.

EXECUTIVES

Chairman and CEO: H. Fisk Johnson
Vice Chairman: Michael W. Wright, age 71
EVP Worldwide Corporate and Environmental Affairs: Jane M. Hutterly
EVP Worldwide Human Resources: Gayle P. Kosterman
SVP Global Product Supply: Tim Bailey
VP and General Manager, Mexico and Central America: Eduardo Ortiz-Tirado
VP Global Public Affairs and Communications: Kelly M. Semrau
Director Global Procurement: Ted Abrahamson
President, Developed Markets: Patrick J. O'Brien
President, Developing Markets: Steven P. Stanbrook, age 52

LOCATIONS

HQ: S.C. Johnson & Son, Inc.
1525 Howe St., Racine, WI 53403
Phone: 262-260-2000   **Fax:** 262-260-6004
Web: www.scjohnson.com

PRODUCTS/OPERATIONS

Selected Products and Brands

Air Care
   Air freshener (Glade, Glade Duet)
Home Cleaning
   Bathroom/drain (Drano, Scrubbing Bubbles, Vanish)
   Cleaners (Fantastik, Windex, Windex Multi-Surface Cleaner with Vinegar)
   Floor care (Pledge, Johnson)
   Furniture care (Pledge, Pledge Wipes, Pledge Grab-it Dry Dusting Mitts)
   Laundry/carpet care (Shout)
Home Storage
   Plastic bags (Ziploc)
   Plastic wrap (Handi-Wrap, Saran Wrap)
Insect Control
   Insecticides (Raid, Raid Max)
   Repellents (Deep Woods OFF!, OFF!, OFF! Mosquito Lamp)

COMPETITORS

3M	Henkel Corp.
Alticor	IWP International
Blyth	Procter & Gamble
Church & Dwight	Reckitt Benckiser
Clorox	Shaklee
Colgate-Palmolive	Unilever
Dow Chemical	Yankee Candle
DuPont	

HISTORICAL FINANCIALS

Company Type: Private

Income Statement				FYE: Friday nearest June 30
	ESTIMATED REVENUE ($ mil.)	NET INCOME ($ mil.)	NET PROFIT MARGIN	EMPLOYEES
6/09	8,880	—	—	12,000
6/08	8,000	—	—	12,000
6/07	8,750	—	—	12,000
6/06	7,000	—	—	12,000
6/05	6,500	—	—	12,000
Annual Growth	8.1%	—	—	0.0%

Revenue History

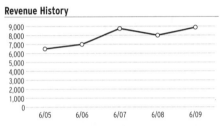

SCANA Corporation

SCANA is cooking with (natural) gas and electricity all over South and North Carolina, and Georgia. The holding company serves 659,000 electricity customers and more than 1 million gas customers in the neighboring states through utilities South Carolina Electric & Gas (SCE&G), Public Service Company of North Carolina, and SCANA Energy (in Georgia). SCANA has an electric generating capacity of about 4,900 MW, derived from fossil-fueled power plants and hydroelectric and nuclear generation facilities. Unregulated operations include retail and wholesale energy marketing and trading, gas transportation, power plant management, fiber-optic telecommunications services, and appliance and HVAC maintenance.

SCANA (which derives its name from the letters in "South CAroliNA") has a strong market position in three states. It also has the advantage of a deregulated segment to offset the limited growth curve of its regulated utilities. The company operates in Georgia's deregulated gas market, where it has emerged as a distribution leader with 455,000 customers (a 30% market share).

On the regulated side of the ledger, in 2009 SCANA won a competitive bid to continue serving as Georgia's sole regulated provider of natural gas, a role the company has had since the Georgia Public Service Commission launched the regulated provider program in 2002.

The global recession with the resulting low commodity prices and demand pulled down SCANA's revenues and income in 2009. In 2010 the company was looking to a rebounding economy and increased rate adjustments to boost its bottom line.

HISTORY

SCANA's earliest ancestors include Charleston Gas Light Company (1846) and Columbia Gas Light Company (1852), formed to light those cities' streets. After barely surviving the Civil War, the companies rebuilt, only to face the greater challenge posed by Thomas Edison's lightbulb in 1879.

Electric utilities such as Charleston Electric Light Company (1886) began to emerge, and they also introduced electric trolleys, which were commonly operated by electric utilities to boost power consumption. After a series of mergers among utilities in South Carolina, the Columbia Electric Street Railway, Light and Power Company (1892) and Charleston Consolidated Railway, Gas and Electric Company (1897) were formed to handle energy and transit needs in their respective cities.

The 1920s brought another wave of utility mergers and consolidation in South Carolina. Columbia Electric Street Railway became part of the Broad River Power Company in 1925, and Charleston Consolidated Railway became a part of South Carolina Power Company the next year. In 1937 Broad River was renamed South Carolina Electric & Gas (SCE&G).

SCE&G went public in 1948. After a two-year fight with the South Carolina Public Service Authority, SCE&G finally gained approval to purchase South Carolina Power Company in 1950. During the 1950s it built several power plants and natural gas distribution lines and joined other utilities to build the Southeast's first nuclear plant prototype in 1959.

A dozen years later SCE&G and the South Carolina Public Service Authority began building a nuke near the pilot plant. Because of delays related to the Three Mile Island accident and stricter regulations, the plant cost $1.3 billion by the time it was completed in 1984.

SCE&G and Carolina Energies merged in 1982 under the SCE&G name. SCANA Corporation was formed two years later to allow the company to separate its utility business from nonregulated activities. The company formed an energy marketing subsidiary in 1988.

In 1989 Hurricane Hugo wiped out power to 300,000 customers. SCE&G's efforts to quickly restore power in its storm-ravaged territory won it industry praise.

Moving into telecommunications, SCANA in 1994 joined ITC Holding (now ITC^DeltaCom) to build a fiber-optic network in the Southeast. In 1996 SCANA invested in Powertel, which launched PCS wireless phone service in the Southeast later that year.

Meanwhile, in 1995 SCANA and Westvaco formed a joint venture, Cogen South, to build a cogeneration plant to provide power to a Westvaco paper mill in Charleston. SCANA sold its oil and gas subsidiary, Petroleum Resources, to Kelley Oil in 1997.

As deregulation overtures became stronger in 1998, SCANA expanded its natural gas business by entering Georgia's deregulated market, where it quickly became a leader. In 1999 it began planning to extend its gas pipeline into North Carolina, sold its propane assets to Suburban Propane to reduce debt, and agreed to buy natural gas distributor Public Service Company of

North Carolina in a $900 million deal, which closed in 2000.

Also in 2000 SCANA sold its home security business and swapped its 27% stake in Powertel for stock in Deutsche Telekom, which took control of the PCS provider. The following year SCANA agreed to sell its 800 MHz emergency radio network to Motorola; the deal was completed in 2002. Also that year SCANA sold its Deutsche Telecom interest.

SCANA purchased 50,000 retail customer accounts in Georgia from Energy America, a unit of UK utility Centrica, in 2004.

SCANA in 2006 merged its two gas transportation units (SCG Pipeline and South Carolina Pipeline) as Carolina Gas Transmission.

EXECUTIVES

Chairman, President, and CEO:
William B. (Bill) Timmerman, age 63,
$5,033,358 total compensation
SVP and CFO: James E. (Jimmy) Addison, age 49,
$1,324,335 total compensation
SVP Governmental Affairs and Economic Development:
Charles B. McFadden, age 65
SVP; President and COO, Carolina Gas Transmission:
Paul V. Fant Sr., age 56
SVP, General Counsel, and Assistant Secretary:
Ronald T. (Ron) Lindsay, age 59
SVP Fuel Procurement and Asset Management:
Sarena D. Burch, age 52
VP Communications and Planning: Cathy Love
CIO: Randal M. (Randy) Senn
SVP and Chief Nuclear Officer, South Carolina Electric & Gas: Jeffrey B. (Jeff) Archie, age 52
President and COO, South Carolina Electric & Gas:
Kevin B. Marsh, age 54, $2,108,101 total compensation
President and COO, SCANA Energy Marketing, SCANA Energy, SCANA Communications, and ServiceCare; Senior Executive Oversight, PSNC Energy and South Carolina Electric & Gas Powering Marketing:
George J. Bullwinkel Jr., age 61,
$1,567,752 total compensation
President and COO, PSNC Energy:
D. Russell (Rusty) Harris
EVP Generation South Carolina Electric & Gas:
Stephen A. Byrne, age 50,
$1,434,329 total compensation
Corporate Secretary, Associate General Counsel, and Director Corporate Governance: Gina S. Champion
Risk Management Officer and Treasurer:
Mark R. Cannon
Controller: James E. Swan IV
Manager Public Affairs: Eric Boomhower
Manager Investor Relations: Bryan D. Hatchell
Auditors: Deloitte & Touche LLP

LOCATIONS

HQ: SCANA Corporation
100 SCANA Pkwy., Cayce, SC 29033
Phone: 803-217-9000   **Fax:** 803-217-8119
Web: www.scana.com

PRODUCTS/OPERATIONS

2009 Sales

	$ mil.	% of total
Electric operations	2,141	50
Gas (nonregulated)	1,138	27
Gas (regulated)	958	23
Total	**4,237**	**100**

Selected Operations

Carolina Gas Transmission Corp. (gas transportation and natural gas purchase, transmission, and sale; LNG liquefaction, storage, and regasification plants)
Public Service Company of North Carolina, Incorporated (dba PSNC Energy, natural gas distribution)
SCANA Communications, Inc. (fiber-optic telecommunications, tower construction, and investments)

SCANA Energy Marketing, Inc. (electricity and natural gas marketing)
SCANA Energy (retail natural gas marketing)
SCANA Services, Inc. (support services)
ServiceCare, Inc. (maintenance for home appliances)
South Carolina Electric & Gas Company (SCE&G, electric and gas utility)
South Carolina Fuel Company, Inc. (financing for SCE&G's nuclear fuel, fossil fuel, and sulfur dioxide emission allowances)
South Carolina Generating Company, Inc. (GENCO, owns and operates Williams power plant and sells electricity to SCE&G)

COMPETITORS

AEP
AGL Resources
CenterPoint Energy
Dominion Resources
Duke Energy
Dynegy
El Paso Corporation
Entergy
Green Mountain Energy
Laclede Group
NextEra Energy
North Carolina Electric Membership
Piedmont Natural Gas
Progress Energy
PS Energy
Santee Cooper
Sempra Energy
Southern Company
TVA

HISTORICAL FINANCIALS

Company Type: Public

Income Statement

FYE: December 31

	REVENUE ($ mil.)	NET INCOME ($ mil.)	NET PROFIT MARGIN	EMPLOYEES
12/09	4,237	355	8.4%	5,828
12/08	5,319	346	6.5%	5,786
12/07	4,621	320	6.9%	5,703
12/06	4,563	304	6.7%	5,683
12/05	4,777	320	6.7%	5,628
Annual Growth	**(3.0%)**	**2.6%**	**—**	**0.9%**

2009 Year-End Financials

Debt ratio: 131.5%
Return on equity: 11.0%
Cash ($ mil.): 162
Current ratio: 1.21
Long-term debt ($ mil.): 4,483
No. of shares (mil.): 127
Dividends
  Yield: 5.0%
  Payout: 66.0%
Market value ($ mil.): 4,771

Stock History

NYSE: SCG

	STOCK PRICE ($) FY Close	P/E High/Low		PER SHARE ($) Earnings	Dividends	Book Value
12/09	37.68	14	9	2.85	1.88	26.92
12/08	35.60	15	9	2.95	1.84	24.94
12/07	42.15	17	13	2.74	1.76	24.27
12/06	40.62	16	14	2.68	1.68	22.54
12/05	39.38	16	13	2.81	1.56	22.04
Annual Growth	**(1.1%)**	**—**	**—**	**0.4%**	**4.8%**	**5.1%**

ScanSource, Inc.

There are more than a few fine lines between ScanSource and its competitors. The company is a leading distributor of automatic identification and data capture (AIDC) products, such as bar code scanners, label printers, and portable data collection terminals. It also provides point-of-sale (POS) products, including PC-based alternatives to cash registers. In addition, ScanSource distributes voice and data communications products and electronic security equipment. The company sells products from vendors such as Avaya, IBM, NCR, and Zebra Technologies to resellers and systems integrators. ScanSource generates about a fifth of its revenues outside North America.

ScanSource has used acquisitions to build its international business, which primarily serves Europe and Latin America. It acquired UK-based MTV Telecom, a distributor of voice and data products, in 2008. The following year ScanSource bought Cologne, Germany-based communications products distributor Algol Europe. The company said the acquisition will boost its profile among European resellers.

The company sells through four sales units in North America: Catalyst Telecom, ScanSource Communications, ScanSource POS & Barcoding, and ScanSource Security Distribution.

In fiscal 2009 Catalyst Telecom was stung by negative market reaction to a program rollout by Avaya; resellers delayed purchases or placed orders with other vendors as a result. While Avaya made changes in its programs, products, and services later in the year, ScanSource was hurt by the uncertain economic climate and a resulting lack of big orders.

HISTORY

In 1992 — as bar codes were evolving from checkout counter aids into tools used for managing distribution and inventory — Steven Owings and Mike Baur started ScanSource as a joint venture with a PC products distributor. The next year the company bought point-of-sale (POS) distributor Alpha Data Systems. ScanSource went public in 1994 and acquired the hardware distribution business of Micro-Biz. ScanSource was named the first US distributor for IBM's POS division.

The company unveiled its own warehousing and management information services operation in 1995 (previously handled by computer distributor MicroAge). That year it became one of two distributors of Seiko Epson's Intelligent Terminals and added Zebra Technologies (bar code equipment), among others, to its supplier roster. In 1996 ScanSource bought out its joint venture partner. The following year it entered into an agreement with Lucent to distribute telephony products.

ScanSource bought distributor POS ProVisions in 1998 and broadened its distribution of computer telephony integration (CTI) products with the purchase of CTI Authority. The next year the company opened a distribution center in Tennessee, tripling capacity. In 2000 ScanSource named president Michael Baur to the additional post of CEO, replacing Owings, who remained chairman. The company also that year reorganized its logistics and fulfillment services and Web-based development organizations into subsidiary ChannelMax.

In 2001 ScanSource acquired the Pinacor CTI sales unit from ailing MicroAge for about $21 million. Also that year the company acquired Miami-based distributor Netpoint International, and began exporting into the Latin American market.

In 2002 the company further expanded its operations by opening its ScanSource Europe division with a headquarters office and distribution center in Belgium. Later that year the company acquired UK-based ABC Technology Distribution. Founder Owings resigned as chairman in 2005.

EXECUTIVES

Chairman: Steven R. Fischer, age 64
President, CEO, and Director: Michael L. (Mike) Baur, age 52, $3,623,024 total compensation
EVP Operations and Corporate Development: Andrea D. Meade, age 39, $630,064 total compensation
VP and CFO: Richard P. (Rich) Cleys, age 58, $568,738 total compensation
VP, General Counsel, and Secretary: John J. Ellsworth, $319,259 total compensation
VP Sales: Brian Cuppett
VP and Treasurer: Linda B. Davis
VP Information Systems: P. Christopher Elrod
VP and CTO: Gregory B. (Greg) Dixon
VP Human Resources: Marsha M. Madore
VP and Controller: Gerald Lyons
VP Marketing: Robert S. (Bobby) McLain Jr., age 49
VP Reseller Financial Services: Timothy M. (Tim) Ramsey
President, ScanSource Communications: Glen D. (Buck) Baker
President, Catalyst Telecom: John K. Black
President, Worldwide Operations: R. Scott Benbenek, age 54, $1,013,101 total compensation
President, ScanSource POS and Barcoding: Jeffrey E. (Jeff) Yelton, age 48
President, ScanSource Latin America: Elias Botbol
President, Europe: Xavier Cartiaux
Director, Reverse Logistics and System Integration: James Sommese, age 39
Auditors: Ernst & Young LLP

LOCATIONS

HQ: ScanSource, Inc.
6 Logue Ct., Greenville, SC 29615
Phone: 864-288-2432   **Fax:** 864-288-1165
Web: www.scansource.com

2009 Sales

	$ mil.	% of total
North America	1,500.2	81
Other regions	347.8	19
Total	**1,848.0**	**100**

PRODUCTS/OPERATIONS

2009 Sales

	$ mil.	% of total
AIDC, POS & security	1,162.0	63
Communications products	686.0	37
Total	**1,848.0**	**100**

Selected Products

Automatic identification and data capture (AIDC)
Bar code printers and labeling devices
Contact wands
Light pens
Handheld and fixed-mount laser scanners
Keyboard wedges
Magnetic stripe readers
Portable data collection devices

Point-of-sale (POS)
Cash drawers
Computer-based terminals
Keyboards
Monitors
Peripheral equipment
Pole displays
Receipt printers
Retail application-based processing units
Converged communications
Business telephone systems (PBXs, key systems, handsets, cabling)
Components used in voice, fax, data, voice recognition, other applications
Electronic security equipment

COMPETITORS

Anixter International
Avnet
Barcoding, Inc.
Honeywell International
Ingram Micro
McRae Industries
Nimans
Northern Video
PEAK Technologies
SYNNEX
Tech Data
Westcon

HISTORICAL FINANCIALS

Company Type: Public

Income Statement

FYE: June 30

	REVENUE ($ mil.)	NET INCOME ($ mil.)	NET PROFIT MARGIN	EMPLOYEES
6/09	1,848	48	2.6%	1,017
6/08	2,176	56	2.6%	1,059
6/07	1,987	43	2.1%	992
6/06	1,666	40	2.4%	916
6/05	1,469	36	2.4%	887
Annual Growth	**5.9%**	**7.5%**	**—**	**3.5%**

2009 Year-End Financials

Debt ratio: 6.8%
Return on equity: 11.3%
Cash ($ mil.): 128
Current ratio: 2.52
Long-term debt ($ mil.): 30

No. of shares (mil.): 27
Dividends
  Yield: —
  Payout: —
Market value ($ mil.): 658

Stock History

NASDAQ (GS): SCSC

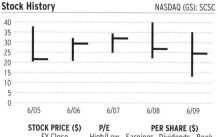

	STOCK PRICE ($) FY Close	P/E High/Low		PER SHARE ($) Earnings	Dividends	Book Value
6/09	24.52	19	8	1.79	—	16.59
6/08	26.76	19	11	2.10	—	14.74
6/07	31.99	21	15	1.63	—	12.10
6/06	29.32	21	14	1.53	—	10.23
6/05	21.47	27	15	1.38	—	8.41
Annual Growth	**3.4%**	**—**	**—**	**6.7%**	**—**	**18.5%**

Schlumberger Limited

No sleeper, Schlumberger is one of the world's largest oil field services companies, along with Halliburton. The company — whose name is more or less pronounced SHLUM-ber-ZHAY — provides a full range of oil and gas services, including seismic surveys, drilling, wireline logging, well construction and completion, and project management. Schlumberger's Oilfield Services unit provides reservoir evaluation, reservoir development, and reservoir management services, and is working to develop new technologies for reservoir optimization. Through its WesternGeco business, the company provides seismic services to customers worldwide. In 2010 Schlumberger agreed to buy oil and gas services giant Smith International.

The $11 billion deal will add Smith International's drilling services and equipment to Schlumberger's portfolio of services, allowing the company to better serve oil and gas majors as they search for hydrocarbons in ever more difficult environments.

Waiting for the giant Smith purchase to go through did not slow down Schlumberger's acquisitive ways. To expand its portfolio of services, in 2010 the company spent $1 billion to acquire drilling mud expert Nexus Geosciences, which delivers integrated seismic software and services for data imaging, modeling, and analysis. It also bought GeothermEx, a California-based geothermal consulting firm.

In 2009 Schlumberger acquired Techsia SA, a supplier of petrophysical software based in France. Techsia was converted into the Schlumberger Petrophysics Software Center for Excellence and will work toward developing high-tech answers for the oil and gas exploration and production industry. Further extending its data management portfolio, in 2010 it acquired integrated seismic software and services firm Nexus Geosciences. That same year, Schlumberger acquired IGEOSS, a developer of structural geology software.

HISTORY

In a Paris basement in 1912, physicist Conrad Schlumberger experimented with wire and a sand-filled bathtub, eventually hoping to use electric current to find ore deposits. With his father's money, Conrad and his brother Marcel began "electrical prospecting" in 1919. Société de Prospection Électrique (SPE) began using the methods for oil exploration in 1923. In 1927 Conrad asked son-in-law Henri Doll to design a tool to chart where oil lay in a well, and wireline logging was born.

To survive the Depression, SPE teamed with rival SGRM in 1931. SPE handled logging, and the two firms formed Compagnie Générale de Géophysique (CGG) for subsurface operations. After entering the US in 1932, the Schlumbergers formed a company in Houston in 1934 and moved headquarters there in 1940.

Also in the 1930s SPE and CGG moved into the Soviet Union, which was desperate for industry. While developing the nation's oil fields, SPE began its policy of adapting to other cultures. Stalin banished the firms in 1936. Conrad died that year, and Marcel followed in 1953.

Led by chairman Doll and Marcel's son Pierre (CEO), the company went public as Schlumberger Limited in 1956. It also bought 50% of

Forex, a drilling rig firm, in 1959. The next year Schlumberger sold its stake in CGG and formed an oil services venture with Dow Chemical.

Schlumberger nearly doubled in size with the 1962 acquisition of electronics maker Daystrom. In 1964 the firm combined its 50% stakes in Forex and Languedocienne to create drilling company Neptune. After Jean Riboud became CEO in 1966, the company moved to New York. Doll retired the next year; by then some 40% of the firm's sales stemmed from his inventions. Schlumberger bought a utility meter manufacturer in 1970.

Continuing to build its drilling operations, it bought the rest of Forex in 1972 and SEDCO in 1984 (to form Sedco Forex Drilling in 1985). Also in 1984 Schlumberger combined its 1977 purchase, The Analysts (computerized mud logging), with Dowell's drilling unit to form directional driller Anadrill. (Schlumberger took over Anadrill in 1993.) When oil prices crashed, Schlumberger merged its wireline logging businesses with Flopetrol (acquired 1971) in 1986. It also began seismic analysis, buying GECO (50% in 1984, the rest in 1988) and PRAKLA-SEISMOS (1991, folded into GECO).

Meanwhile, the firm introduced smart cards in 1982. Schlumberger bought GeoQuest (well data management software) in 1992 and formed the Omnes communications venture with Cable & Wireless in 1995. (Schlumberger took over Omnes in 1999.)

In 1998 Schlumberger bought Camco International (drilling services and equipment). Facing the 1999 oil slump, the firm cut staff and combined four engineering and consulting units into Holditch-Reservoir Technologies. It also created a drilling fluids joint venture with Smith International's M-I. Schlumberger finished the year by spinning off Sedco Forex, which then merged with Transocean.

Schlumberger boosted its utility meter business in 2000 by buying CellNet, a UK telemetry services firm, and it acquired control of information technology company Convergent Group.

In 2001 SchlumbergerSema was formed when Schlumberger bought Sema, a software and support provider for electronic payment systems, for about $5 billion. It also acquired UK-based Phoenix Petroleum Services, a leading player in optimizing production in artificially lifted wells.

Schlumberger began expanding its IT assets and reorganizing its SchlumbergerSema operations in 2002 in an effort to expand its IT offerings to its Oilfield Service customers.

In 2003 Andrew Gould was promoted to the position of chairman and CEO following the resignation of Euan Baird. The company began its exit from the chip-testing business by selling off its Schlumberger Verification Systems business unit to Soluris.

In 2004 Schlumberger sold its electricity meter business to Itron. In an effort to expand its Information Solutions units, the company acquired Austria-based Decision Team, a provider of oil and gas software and consulting

services. It expanded its oil and gas services division by acquiring a 26% stake (increased to 100% in 2006) in PetroAlliance Services, Russia's largest oilfield services company.

The company bought Baker Hughes' 30% stake in WesternGeco in 2006 for $2.4 billion, giving it full control of the company. The next year Schlumberger acquired seismic surveying firm Eastern Echo Holdings for $679 million.

EXECUTIVES

Chairman and CEO: Andrew Gould, age 63, $14,063,353 total compensation
COO: Paal Kibsgaard, age 42, $4,328,780 total compensation
Senior Executive Advisor to Chairman and CEO: Chakib Sbiti, age 55, $7,346,309 total compensation
EVP and CFO: Simon Ayat, age 55, $3,393,619 total compensation
Chief Accounting Officer: Howard Guild, age 38
VP and CTO; President, Reservoir Characterization Group: Ashok Belani, age 51
VP Operations, Oilfield Services: Satish Pai, age 48, $3,731,100 total compensation
VP Investor Relations: Malcolm Theobald, age 48
VP Communications: Rodney (Rod) Nelson, age 51
VP Personnel: Stephanie Cox, age 41
Secretary and General Counsel: Alexander (Alex) Juden, age 49
President, Wireline: Catherine MacGregor, age 37
President, North America: Steve Fulgham
President, Schlumberger Information Solutions: Tony Bowman
President, Completions, Oilfield Services: Eric Larson
President, Well Services, Oilfield Services — Technologies: Patrick Schorn
President, Testing Services: Jesus Grande
President, North America Offshore: Robert Drummond
President, Data and Consulting Services: Sophie Zurquiyah-Rousset, age 43
President, Integrated Project Management: Miguel Galuccio
Auditors: PricewaterhouseCoopers LLP

LOCATIONS

HQ: Schlumberger Limited
5599 San Felipe, 17th Fl., Houston, TX 77056
Phone: 713-513-2000
Web: www.slb.com

2009 Sales

	$ mil.	% of total
Europe/CIS/Africa	7,150	32
Latin America	5,234	23
Middle East & Asia	4,225	19
North America	3,707	16
Other regions	202	1
WesternGeco	2,122	9
Corporate services	62	—
Total	**22,702**	**100**

PRODUCTS/OPERATIONS

2009 Sales

	$ mil.	% of total
Oilfield services	20,518	91
WesternGeco	2,122	9
Corporate services	62	—
Total	**22,702**	**100**

Selected Subsidiaries and Affiliates

Schlumberger Antilles N.V. (Netherlands Antilles)
  Schlumberger Offshore Services N.V. (Limited) (Netherlands Antilles)
Schlumberger B.V. (The Netherlands)
  Schlumberger Canada Limited
  Schlumberger SA (France)
    Services Petroliers Schlumberger (France)
  WesternGeco B.V. (The Netherlands)
    WesternGeco A.S. (Norway)

Schlumberger Oilfield Holdings Limited (British Virgin Islands)
  Dowell Schlumberger Corporation (British Virgin Islands)
  Schlumberger Holdings Limited (British Virgin Islands)
    Schlumberger Middle East S.A. (Panama)
    Schlumberger Overseas, S.A (Panama)
    Schlumberger Seaco, Inc. (Panama)
    Schlumberger Surenco, S.A. (Panama)
  WesternGeco Seismic Holdings Limited (British Virgin Islands)
Schlumberger Technology Corporation
  WesternGeco L.L.C.

COMPETITORS

Baker Hughes
Core Laboratories
Fortum
Halliburton
National Oilwell Varco
Petroleum Geo-Services
Stolt-Nielsen
Technip
Weatherford International

HISTORICAL FINANCIALS

Company Type: Public

Income Statement
FYE: December 31

	REVENUE ($ mil.)	NET INCOME ($ mil.)	NET PROFIT MARGIN	EMPLOYEES
12/09	22,702	3,142	13.8%	77,000
12/08	27,565	5,435	19.7%	87,000
12/07	23,277	5,177	22.2%	80,000
12/06	19,231	3,710	19.3%	70,000
12/05	14,309	2,207	15.4%	60,000
Annual Growth	**12.2%**	**9.2%**	**—**	**6.4%**

2009 Year-End Financials

Debt ratio: 22.8%
Return on equity: 17.5%
Cash ($ mil.): 243
Current ratio: 1.88
Long-term debt ($ mil.): 4,355
No. of shares (mil.): 1,193
Dividends
  Yield: 1.3%
  Payout: 32.4%
Market value ($ mil.): 77,668

Stock History
NYSE: SLB

	STOCK PRICE ($) FY Close	P/E High/Low		PER SHARE ($) Earnings	Dividends	Book Value
12/09	65.09	27	14	2.59	0.84	16.02
12/08	42.33	25	8	4.45	0.84	14.13
12/07	98.37	27	13	4.20	0.70	12.47
12/06	63.16	25	16	3.01	0.50	8.73
12/05	48.58	28	17	1.82	0.42	6.36
Annual Growth	**7.6%**	**—**	**—**	**9.2%**	**18.9%**	**26.0%**

Schnitzer Steel Industries

Your old car could end up in a Malaysian office building if Schnitzer Steel Industries gets its steel jaws on it. The company processes scrap steel and iron, which it obtains from sources such as auto salvage yards, industrial manufacturers, and metals brokers. The company sells more of that scrap to steelmakers in Asia than anywhere else; much of the rest goes to Schnitzer Steel's own steelmaking business, including Cascade Steel Rolling Mills, which produces merchant bar, steel reinforcing bar, and other products at its minimill in Oregon. Schnitzer Steel's Pick-N-Pull Auto Dismantlers unit operates auto salvage yards. The family of founder Sam Schnitzer controls the company through a voting trust.

Considering itself primarily a ferrous metals recycling business, Schnitzer Steel plans to continue to expand this business segment through acquisitions in North America. It has regularly made acquisitions throughout the US, primarily focusing on buying small, regional operations. In addition to growing through acquisitions, Schnitzer Steel hopes to improve the efficiency of its recycling operations by investing in new processing technology.

Schnitzer enhanced its recycling operations in 2010, acquiring Golden Recycling & Salvage of Billings, Montana. The deal will give Schnitzer a presence in the Montana market and expand the number of products and services it offers. The facility will be operated as Schnitzer Steel Billings.

In 2009 the company divested its full-service auto parts operations, selling the business to LKQ Corporation in exchange for that company's self-service auto parts business. Schnitzer then rebranded the former LKQ businesses with the Pick-N-Pull name.

Toward the end of 2008 president and CEO John Carter was named chairman of Schnitzer, and executive Tamara Lundgren moved up the ladder and took over as president and CEO. Lundgren joined Schnitzer in 2005 after a career spent primarily in investment banking.

HISTORY

Sam Schnitzer, a draftee into the Russian army, found his way to Austria, then to the US in 1904. The next year he moved to Portland, where he and partner Henry Wolf formed Alaska Junk in 1908. The enterprise grew, buying sawmills, logging camps, and shipyards. Sam's son, Morris, formed Schnitzer Steel Products on his own in 1936. After WWII the patriarch turned Alaska Junk over to sons Gilbert, Leonard, Manuel, and Morris.

The brothers changed the company's name to Alaska Steel and acquired Woodbury, a local steel distributor, in 1956. The Schnitzers formed Lasco Shipping in 1963. Morris' Schnitzer Steel Products returned to family control, and in 1978 Alaska Steel and Woodbury combined to make Metra Steel. The company boosted its vertical integration by acquiring the Cascade Steel minimill in 1984.

Leonard Schnitzer's son-in-law Robert Philip became president in 1991. Two years later the family's steel businesses went public as Schnitzer Steel Industries. In 1994 the company launched a $42 million expansion program. It bought Manufacturing Management (then Washington's #1 scrap processor, 1995) and Proler International (scrap-related environmental services, 1996), adding 17 scrap-collecting and -processing facilities, primarily on the East Coast.

Schnitzer Steel Industries began producing wire rod and coiled rebar at its Oregon facility in 1997. The next year Schnitzer Steel Industries and joint venture partner Hugo Neu added facilities in Maine, Massachusetts, and New Hampshire. Also in 1998 a marked drop in scrap export prices due to an economic downturn in Asia hurt the company's earnings. Its Asian exports declined some 20% in 1999.

To maximize its potential and reduce costs, Schnitzer Steel Industries installed an automobile shredder capable of processing 2,000 tons per day at its Tacoma, Washington, facility in 2000. In 2001 the company experienced improvements in its metal recycling business, the result of a temporary backlog that helped boost sales. However, the slowdown in the economy hurt sales at its steel manufacturing segment.

In 2002 the company's Portland, Oregon, metals recycling facility went through a $4.4 million renovation to increase efficiency in loading recycled metal cargoes. The next year, Schnitzer Steel Industries purchased Pick-N-Pull, a major operator of auto salvage yards, for about $71 million.

Schnitzer Steel Industries unwound its joint ventures with Hugo Neu in 2005. That same year the company named John Carter as its new president and CEO.

EXECUTIVES

Chairman: John D. Carter, age 64, $6,638,057 total compensation
President, CEO, and Director: Tamara L. Lundgren, age 52, $3,725,171 total compensation
EVP Business Development: Gary A. Schnitzer, age 67
SVP and Chief Administrative Officer: George P. Nutwell, age 62
SVP; President, Auto Parts Business: Thomas D. (Tom) Klauer Jr., age 56
SVP, General Counsel, and Secretary: Richard C. (Rich) Josephson, age 61, $1,046,734 total compensation
SVP; President, Metals Recycling Business: Donald W. (Don) Hamaker, age 57, $1,619,850 total compensation
SVP and CFO: Richard D. Peach, age 46, $834,341 total compensation
SVP; President, Steel Manufacturing Business: Jeffrey (Jeff) Dyck, age 46
VP and Corporate Controller: Jeff P. Poeschl, age 45
VP Environmental and Public Affairs: Thomas (Tom) Zelenka, age 60
Health and Safety: Dru Silva
Compliance: Callie Pappas
Investor Relations: Rob Stone
Auditors: PricewaterhouseCoopers LLP

LOCATIONS

HQ: Schnitzer Steel Industries, Inc.
3200 NW Yeon Ave., Portland, OR 97210
Phone: 503-224-9900
Web: www.schnitzersteel.com

2009 Sales

	$ mil.	% of total
Asia	993.4	49
North America	818.2	40
Europe	176.8	9
Africa	48.7	2
Adjustments	(136.9)	—
Total	**1,900.2**	**100**

PRODUCTS/OPERATIONS

2009 Sales

	$ mil.	% of total
Metals Recycling	1,507.6	74
Auto Parts	266.2	13
Steel Manufacturing	263.3	13
Adjustments	(136.9)	—
Total	**1,900.2**	**100**

COMPETITORS

AK Steel Holding Corporation
Aleris International
Commercial Metals
LKQ
Nippon Steel
Nucor
SHV Holdings
Sims Metal Management
Steel Dynamics
United States Steel

HISTORICAL FINANCIALS

Company Type: Public

Income Statement

FYE: August 31

	REVENUE ($ mil.)	NET INCOME ($ mil.)	NET PROFIT MARGIN	EMPLOYEES
8/09	1,900	(32)	—	3,323
8/08	3,642	249	6.8%	3,669
8/07	2,572	131	5.1%	3,499
8/06	1,855	143	7.7%	3,252
8/05	853	147	17.2%	1,799
Annual Growth	**22.2%**	**—**	**—**	**16.6%**

2009 Year-End Financials

Debt ratio: 12.0%
Return on equity: —
Cash ($ mil.): 41
Current ratio: 2.93
Long-term debt ($ mil.): 110
No. of shares (mil.): 28
Dividends
  Yield: 0.1%
  Payout: —
Market value ($ mil.): 1,502

Stock History

NASDAQ (GS): SCHN

	STOCK PRICE ($) FY Close	P/E High/Low		PER SHARE ($) Earnings	Dividends	Book Value
8/09	54.01	—	—	(1.14)	0.07	33.07
8/08	68.41	14	5	8.61	0.07	35.18
8/07	58.43	15	7	4.32	0.07	27.52
8/06	31.75	9	6	4.65	0.07	26.40
8/05	28.60	9	4	4.72	0.07	20.84
Annual Growth	**17.2%**	**—**	**—**	**—**	**0.0%**	**12.2%**

Scholastic Corporation

Once upon a time, a company grew up to become one of the world's leading children's book publishers. Scholastic Corporation sells more than 320 million books (including the *Harry Potter* series) annually to children in the US. It also sells products in more than 140 other countries. It operates through four divisions: Children's Book Publishing and Distribution; Educational Publishing; Media, Licensing and Advertising; and International. It publishes reference material (*Encyclopedia Americana*) through Scholastic Classroom and Library Group. Known for its school book fairs, Scholastic also publishes magazines, textbooks, and software for students and teachers, and produces children's TV programming and films.

The recession has caused a decrease in spending among families and school districts. As a result, Scholastic has cut costs by reducing salaries, offering a voluntary retirement program, freezing hiring, and reducing costs for paper, printing, and postage. The company is also increasing the price of children's books in select categories, and hopes to see sales boosted by federal stimulus money allotted to school districts in 2009 and 2010.

Scholastic created some sales magic when it agreed to be the US distributor of the J.K. Rowling *Harry Potter* series, which has broken sales records and become the best-selling children's series of all time. Scholastic also paid close to $10 million for the rights to the popular spooky kids' series *Goosebumps* by R.L. Stine. Other big-name brands include *Clifford the Big Red Dog, I Spy*, and *The Baby-Sitters Club*.

The company had been busy growing the business through deals and acquisitions. It struck a deal to license some of its publications to DreamWorks, which will produce animated movies based on Scholastic properties. On the horizon is the big screen version of Scholastic's *The 39 Clues*. In addition, Scholastic partnered up with NBC and Telemundo (along with other content and broadcasting companies) to produce and distribute television for children through a venture called Qubo. Spots reinforcing the importance of books and reading play throughout the Qubo programming block, which airs on NBC, i network, and Telemundo in English and Spanish. The company also partnered with LEGO Group to publish books and other products using LEGO brands, such as *Lego Reader: Space Adventures: Mars Alien Attack!*.

The company generates more than 20% of sales outside of the US. Scholastic has long-established operations in Australia, Canada, New Zealand, and the UK, with newer holdings in China, India, and Ireland.

Chairman and CEO Richard Robinson (a descendant of founder Maurice Robinson) owns about 20% of the company.

HISTORY

Fresh from a stint on his college newspaper, Maurice Robinson returned to his hometown of Wilkinson, Pennsylvania, in 1920 and launched *The Western Pennsylvania Scholastic,* a newspaper geared toward high school students. By 1922 its circulation had grown to 4,000 — prompting Robinson to incorporate his business as Scholastic Publishing Company and launch *Scholastic,* a national version of the newspaper.

The Depression found the unprofitable Scholastic struggling to improve its financial picture. In 1932 the company changed its name to Scholastic Corporation. A cost-cutting program helped it achieve a profit for the first time four years later. Profitability, however, would be fleeting: Accusations that Scholastic's publications promoted Communism prompted some schools to ban them.

During WWII paper rationing compelled Scholastic to print slimmer publications and turn away subscribers. Following the war the company introduced a string of publications and initiated a sales push that permitted it to pay its first dividend in 1951. In the 1950s, while weathering another spate of accusations that the company had Communist leanings, Scholastic continued to expand its list of publications. The company also created two book clubs that decade, launching what would become one of its most successful endeavors.

During the 1960s Scholastic broadened its interests to include instructional materials and hardcover books. The company went public in 1969 and continued its expansion during the 1970s with ventures into record production and filmstrips. In 1974 Maurice's son Richard was appointed president.

Scholastic began producing educational software and TV programming during the 1980s. In 1987 Richard took the company private again in order to help it regain financial stability. His timing was fortuitous — the children's book market was on an upswing, and by the time he took Scholastic public again in 1992, the company's book sales had doubled.

The 1992 launch of its *Goosebumps* books initially met with great success. But by 1996, when kids had grown weary of *Goosebumps,* book returns caused profits to take a nosedive. Robinson responded by instituting cost-cutting and layoffs, and Scholastic divested itself of products not associated with its core business. The company continued to expand its TV and film interests during the 1990s, producing TV shows such as *Scholastic's The Magic School Bus* and feature films such as *The Indian in the Cupboard* for worldwide audiences.

Scholastic created a new publishing unit to issue professional and parenting magazines in 1998. Also that year it published the first *Harry Potter* book by then-unknown British author J.K. Rowling. In addition, the company inked a deal with Warner Brothers Worldwide Publishing to create children's books based on Warner Brothers' movie and TV properties. The next year it relaunched its six-year-old subscription-based Internet site as a free site.

In 2000 Scholastic purchased children's book and reference publisher Grolier from Lagardére for $400 million. (It later changed Grolier's name to Scholastic Library Publishing.) In 2001 the company bought the assets of book fair company Troll Book Fairs Inc. It also bought educational software maker Tom Snyder Productions and animated TV producer Soup2Nuts.

In 2002 the company acquired Klutz, a maker of children's products and books, from Corus Entertainment and bought a 15% interest in The Book People, a UK book distributor. Citing poor industry conditions, Scholastic cut about 400 employees in 2003.

In 2007 the last book in the *Harry Potter* series, *Harry Potter and the Deathly Hallows*, set sales records after 8.3 million copies vanished from shelves in 24 hours.

EXECUTIVES

Chairman, President, and CEO:
Richard (Dick) Robinson, age 73,
$3,595,707 total compensation
EVP, CFO, and Chief Administrative Officer:
Maureen E. O'Connell, age 48,
$1,796,215 total compensation
EVP, General Counsel, Secretary, and Director:
Andrew S. (Andy) Hedden, age 69
EVP; President, Scholastic Education:
Margery W. Mayer, age 58,
$1,086,710 total compensation
EVP; President, International: Shane Armstrong
EVP; President, Book Clubs: Judith A. (Judy) Newman,
age 52, $1,209,045 total compensation
EVP; President, Scholastic Media: Deborah A. Forte,
age 56
**EVP; President, Consumer and Professional
Publishing:** Hugh Roome, age 58
SVP and Chief Accounting Officer: Robert J. Jackson,
age 55
SVP Human Resources and Employee Services:
Cynthia H. (Cindy) Augustine, age 52,
$607,248 total compensation
SVP Education and Corporate Relations:
Ernest B. (Ernie) Fleishman, age 73
**SVP Marketing and Consumer Products, Scholastic
Media:** Leslye Schaefer
SVP; President, Klutz: Matt Brown
SVP, E-Commerce: Thomas P. (Tom) Burke
VP Corporate Communications and Media Relations:
Kyle Good
President, Book Fairs: Alan Boyko
President, Trade Publishing Division: Ellie Berger
President, Scholastic Classroom and Library Group:
Greg Worrell
Auditors: Ernst & Young LLP

LOCATIONS

HQ: Scholastic Corporation
557 Broadway, New York, NY 10012
Phone: 212-343-6100   **Fax:** 212-343-6934
Web: www2.scholastic.com

PRODUCTS/OPERATIONS

2010 Sales

	$ mil.	% of total
Children's book publishing & distributing	910.6	48
Educational publishing	476.5	25
International	412.0	22
Media, licensing & advertising	113.8	6
Total	**1,912.9**	**100**

Selected Products and Services

Audiovisual children's books
  Make Way for Ducklings
  Where the Wild Things Are
Book Fairs
  Scholastic Book Fairs
Educational software and programs
  I Spy
  Literacy Place
  Read 180
  Solares
  Success with Writing
  WiggleWorks
Feature films
  The Baby-Sitters Club
  Clifford's Really Big Movie
  Indian in the Cupboard
Products
  Klutz (book and toy packages)
School-based book clubs
  Arrow
  Firefly
  Honeybee
  Lucky
  SeeSaw
  TAB

Television properties
Animorphs
Clifford the Big Red Dog
Dear America
Goosebumps
I Spy
Maya & Miguel
Scholastic's The Magic School Bus

Selected Book Titles

Animorphs
The Baby-Sitters Club
Captain Underpants
Clifford the Big Red Dog
Dear America
Goosebumps
Harry Potter
The Magic School Bus
Miss Spider
The Scholastic Encyclopedia of Presidents
The Scholastic Encyclopedia of Women

Scholastic Library Publishing

Kids Clubs
  Barbie book club
  Beginning Reader's Program (featuring Dr. Seuss
    books)
  Disney book club
Publishing
  Cumbre (Spanish-language encyclopedia)
  Encyclopedia Americana
  New Book of Knowledge

COMPETITORS

Addison-Wesley
American Girl
The Aristotle Corporation
Cengage Learning
Channel One Network
Cookie Jar Group
Disney Publishing
Educational Development
HarperCollins
Highlights for Children
HIT Entertainment
John Wiley
LeapFrog
Little, Brown Book Group
McGraw-Hill
Pearson plc
Random House
RD School & Educational Services
Simon & Schuster

HISTORICAL FINANCIALS

Company Type: Public

Income Statement

FYE: May 31

	REVENUE ($ mil.)	NET INCOME ($ mil.)	NET PROFIT MARGIN	EMPLOYEES
5/10	1,913	56	2.9%	8,900
5/09	1,849	(14)	—	9,100
5/08	2,206	(17)	—	10,200
5/07	2,179	61	2.8%	10,200
5/06	2,284	69	3.0%	10,400
Annual Growth	(4.3%)	(4.9%)	—	(3.8%)

2010 Year-End Financials

Debt ratio: 31.0%
Return on equity: 6.9%
Cash ($ mil.): 244
Current ratio: 2.27
Long-term debt ($ mil.): 258
No. of shares (mil.): 36
Dividends
Yield: 1.1%
Payout: 19.7%
Market value ($ mil.): 945

Stock History

NASDAQ (GS): SCHL

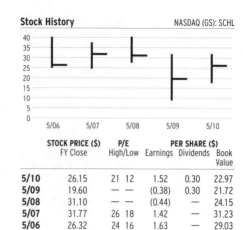

	STOCK PRICE ($) FY Close	P/E High/Low		PER SHARE ($) Earnings	Dividends	Book Value
5/10	26.15	21	12	1.52	0.30	22.97
5/09	19.60	—	—	(0.38)	0.30	21.72
5/08	31.10	—	—	(0.44)	—	24.15
5/07	31.77	26	18	1.42	—	31.23
5/06	26.32	24	16	1.63	—	29.03
Annual Growth	(0.2%)	—	—	(1.7%)	0.0%	(5.7%)

Scotts Miracle-Gro

The grass sure seems greener over at Scotts Miracle-Gro (SMG), the world's largest maker and marketer of horticultural and turf products. Its garden and indoor plant care items include grass seeds, fertilizers, herbicides, potting soils, and related tools. Brand names include Ortho, Miracle-Gro, Hyponex, and Turf Builder. SMG markets Monsanto's Roundup herbicide products for the consumer market and has a lawn and shrub care service. Siblings James Hagedorn (chairman and CEO) and Katherine Littlefield (a director) own a third of SMG. Hagedorn and Littlefield are the children of Horace Hagedorn, the creator of Miracle-Gro plant food.

Scotts also sells directly to professionals (i.e., nurseries, greenhouses, and specialty crop growers). To broaden its portfolio, Scotts has a business development group that focuses on three main areas: improving sales and profits in businesses such as hardware and independent garden centers; expanding the company's presence into grocery and drug stores; and expanding into ancillary products such as tools, pottery, and watering equipment. It also had owned upscale garden retailer Smith & Hawken, which had retail stores throughout the country in addition to doing business through catalog and online sales. In 2009 Scotts Miracle-Gro shuttered the Smith & Hawken business, another casualty of the troubled economy. (It did sell the Smith & Hawken brand to Target, however, at the end of 2009.)

While the company has international operations, the North American market accounts for more than 80% of sales. As well, while the company does target professional landscapers, its consumer business accounts for three-quarters of its sales. Within that market, Scotts' largest customers are The Home Depot (about a third of sales), Wal-Mart (almost 20%), and Lowe's (almost 20%). Because of this reliance on such a small number of businesses, the company focuses mightily on its relationships with the retailers.

The Scotts LawnService unit has grown — through both acquisitions and internal growth — from $42 million in sales in 2001 to well more than $200 million in 2009. It is the #2 lawn care services company in the US, after TruGreen.

SMG has been able to profit from competitor Spectrum Brands' decision to stop providing private-label lawn fertilizer and growing products to retailers. The company stepped into that market and was able to provide its retail customers with its own products.

HISTORY

Founded by Orlando Scott in Marysville, Ohio, in 1868 as O.M. Scott & Sons, the firm originally cleaned crop seed. It later began selling grass seed, and in 1928 debuted the US's first lawn fertilizer, Turf Builder. The family-owned business became a subsidiary of conglomerate ITT in 1971; it broke away in a 1986 management-led LBO. It went public as The Scotts Company in 1992.

Acquisitions include Hyponex (1988), lawn and garden equipment maker Republic Tool and Manufacturing (1992), and specialty fertilizer maker Grace-Sierra Horticultural Products (1993). In 1995 Scotts merged with Stern's Miracle-Gro, a company that Horace Hagedorn had started in 1951; the deal married the #1 lawn care company with the #1 garden plant food firm. The company simplified its product line by cutting more than 300 products in 1996.

Scotts launched an acquisition program in 1997 to increase sales in Europe. That year Scotts acquired the UK's Levington Horticulture (fertilizers and pesticides) and 80% of Sanford Scientific (genetically engineered grasses and plants). The next year Scotts landed a deal to market Monsanto's Roundup herbicide products internationally and bought two European lawn and garden product firms — ASEF and Rhone-Poulenc Jardin (#1 in Europe). International sales jumped almost 75% for the year. In 1999 Scotts bought Monsanto's lawn and garden businesses (including its Ortho line) for $300 million.

In 2000 Scotts bought the distribution rights for peat products manufactured by Bord na Mona, one of Europe's largest peat producers. It also sold its US and Canadian professional turf operations to The Andersons, Inc. The same year Scotts acquired Henkel's European fertilizer and plant care brand, Substral. Due to sluggish growth, Scotts reorganized its European operations in 2002, pledging an investment of about $50 million by 2005. The company took a $9 million charge as a result in 2003.

President and COO James Hagedorn was named CEO in 2001; James, Horace's son, retained the title of president. He assumed the additional role of chairman in 2003. The following year Scott's ventured into the gardening retail market with the acquisition of Smith & Hawken. In the fall of 2004 Scotts paid $72 million for the high-end gardening retail chain.

Horace Hagedorn died in early 2005. The Scotts Company changed its name to The Scotts Miracle-Gro Company that same year.

EXECUTIVES

Chairman and CEO: James (Jim) Hagedorn, age 54,
$7,548,657 total compensation
President, COO, and Director: Mark R. Baker, age 53,
$4,789,350 total compensation
EVP and CFO: David C. (Dave) Evans, age 47,
$1,746,697 total compensation
EVP Global Consumer: Barry W. Sanders, age 45,
$2,032,491 total compensation
EVP International: Claude L. Lopez, age 49,
$996,241 total compensation
EVP: Michael P. (Mike) Kelty, age 60

EVP, General Counsel, Chief Ethics and Compliance Officer, and Secretary: Vincent C. Brockman, age 47
EVP Global Human Resources: Denise S. Stump, age 56
SVP Regulatory and Government Affairs and Chief Environmental Officer: Richard (Rich) Shank
SVP and Chief Sustainability Officer: Janet E. (Jan) Valentic
SVP Global Purchasing: Pete Supron
SVP Global Research and Development: Jeff Garascia
SVP Global Professional: Fred Bosch
SVP Global Pro Seed, Asia/Pacific, and Emerging Markets: Korbin Riley
SVP Marketing: Dan Paradiso
SVP North America Finance: Randy Coleman
SVP North America Sales: Brian Kura
SVP Global Supply Chain: Dave Swihart
Auditors: Deloitte & Touche LLP

LOCATIONS

HQ: The Scotts Miracle-Gro Company
14111 Scottslawn Rd., Marysville, OH 43041
Phone: 937-644-0011   **Fax:** 937-644-7614
Web: www.scotts.com

2009 Sales

	$ mil.	% of total
North America	2,626.2	84
Other regions	515.3	16
Total	**3,141.5**	**100**

PRODUCTS/OPERATIONS

2009 Sales

	$ mil.	% of total
Global Consumer	2,457.6	78
Global Professional	293.1	9
Scotts Lawn Service	231.1	7
Corporate & other	160.8	6
Adjustments	(1.1)	—
Total	**3,141.5**	**100**

Selected Products

Garden and indoor plant care items
Garden tools
Grass seed
Herbicides
Insecticides
Lawn fertilizers
Lawn spreaders and other application devices
Pesticides
Plant foods
Potting soils
Wild bird seed

Selected Brands

ASEF (Benelux countries)
Bug-B-Gon
Celaflor (Germany and Austria)
Earthgro (growing media such as potting mix)
Evergreen (lawn fertilizer, UK)
Fertiligene (France)
Hyponex (growing media such as potting mix)
KB (France and Benelux countries)
Levington (growing media, UK)
Miracle-Gro (plant food)
Morning Song (bird seed)
Nature Scapes (growing media such as potting mix)
Nexa-Lotte (Germany and Austria)
Ortho (weed, insect, and disease control)
Osmocote
Pathclear (herbicide, UK)
Peters Professional
Roundup (licensed by Monsanto, herbicide)
Scotts
Shamrock (Europe)
Substral (Europe)
Turf Builder (lawn fertilizer and weed control)
Weed-B-Gon
Weedol (herbicide, UK)

COMPETITORS

Acuity Brands	Home Depot
Applied Energetics	K+S
BASF SE	LESCO
Bayer CropScience	Spectrum Brands
Central Garden & Pet	Trans-Resources
Dow AgroSciences	TruGreen Landcare

HISTORICAL FINANCIALS

Company Type: Public

Income Statement

FYE: September 30

	REVENUE ($ mil.)	NET INCOME ($ mil.)	NET PROFIT MARGIN	EMPLOYEES
9/09	3,142	153	4.9%	6,851
9/08	2,982	(11)	—	6,378
9/07	2,872	113	3.9%	6,120
9/06	2,697	133	4.9%	5,720
9/05	2,369	101	4.2%	5,291
Annual Growth	**7.3%**	**11.1%**	**—**	**6.7%**

2009 Year-End Financials

Debt ratio: 111.2%
Return on equity: 30.0%
Cash ($ mil.): 72
Current ratio: 1.44
Long-term debt ($ mil.): 650
No. of shares (mil.): 67
Dividends
  Yield: 1.2%
  Payout: 21.6%
Market value ($ mil.): 2,872

Stock History

NYSE: SMG

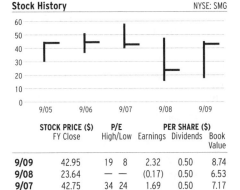

	STOCK PRICE ($) FY Close	P/E High/Low		PER SHARE ($) Earnings	Dividends	Book Value
9/09	42.95	19	8	2.32	0.50	8.74
9/08	23.64	—	—	(0.17)	0.50	6.53
9/07	42.75	34	24	1.69	0.50	7.17
9/06	44.49	26	19	1.91	0.50	16.18
9/05	43.97	30	21	1.47	0.13	15.35
Annual Growth	**(0.6%)**	**—**	**—**	**12.1%**	**40.0%**	**(13.1%)**

Seaboard Corporation

With pork from Oklahoma, flour from Haiti, and sugar from Argentina, Seaboard has a lot on its plate. The diversified agribusiness and transportation firm has operations in some 40 countries in the Americas, the Caribbean, and Africa. Seaboard sells pork in the US and foreign markets. Overseas it trades grain (wheat, soya), operates power plants and feed and flour mills, and grows and refines sugar cane. Seaboard operates a shipping service for containerized cargo between the US, the Caribbean, and South America; it owns shipping terminals in Miami and Houston and a fleet of 40 vessels (12 owned, others chartered) that ship worldwide to some 40 ports. Seaboard is run by descendants of founder Otto Bresky who own 72% of the company.

It was rough sailing for Seaboard in 2009 as the worldwide recession and the havoc created by the H1N1 virus (aka the swine flu) in the pork industry caused sales to plummet. The company, which operates a flour mill near Port-au-Prince, lost 15 employees in the massive earthquake in January 2010. Seaboard expects to resume milling operations in Haiti in early 2011.

In the US, Seaboard is a leading producer and processor of pork (with about a 9% market share of all pork processed in the US) with operations in Oklahoma, Kansas, Texas, and Colorado. Despite what some consider to be an industry oversupply of pork, Seaboard has significantly expanded its pork business with an emphasis on private-label preseasoned pork products. It markets some of its pork products under the Prairie Fresh (in the US), Seaboard Farms (international), and Daily's brands.

As its name suggests, Seaboard is engaged in ocean transportation, which is sensitive to the global economy. Demand for its transportation services has dipped as global trade contracted. year-over-year unit volume fell for the first time in more than a decade.

Overseas, the company operates mainly commodity merchandising, grain processing, sugar production, and electric power generation. In addition to shipping and the trading of sugar, pork and commodities, Seaboard grows and processes citrus and sugar and has distillery operations in Argentina; it manufactures ethanol and has trucking transportation operations in the US. It also owns jalapeño farms in Texas and Honduras.

HISTORY

Otto Bresky founded his company as a flour broker in 1916. He acquired his first flour mill in Atchison, Kansas, in 1918 and the following year purchased the Imperial Brewery Co. in Kansas City and converted it to a flour mill. Over the next four decades, Bresky ground out a series of acquisitions of milling companies. In 1928 he purchased Rodney Milling Co. and retained the name as the identity for the family business. The company then purchased Ismert-Hincke Milling Co. (1938) and the Consolidated Flour Mills Co. (1950). In 1959 Rodney Milling merged with publicly traded Hathaway Industries and changed its name to Seaboard Allied Milling Corp.

In the 1960s Seaboard Allied became one of the first millers to shift flour milling from the source of the raw materials (the wheat fields of the Great Plains) to the population centers in the Southeast and on the East Coast. In 1962 Seaboard Allied built a flour mill in Chattanooga, Tennessee. It then purchased George Urban Milling Company in Buffalo, New York (1965), and built a flour mill in Jacksonville, Florida (1966). But Bresky's expansionist strategy did not stop at the Atlantic Seaboard. The company acquired a flour mill in Guayaquil, Ecuador, in 1966 (a joint venture with Continental Grain Co.), then constructed flour mills in Freetown, Sierra Leone (1968), and Georgetown, Guyana (1969).

Bresky retired in 1973 and was succeeded by his son Harry. A chip off the old block, Harry acquired a flour mill in Cleveland, Tennessee, and built flour mills in Buchanan, Liberia, and in Sapele, Nigeria, that year. In 1978 Seaboard Allied acquired Mochasa, Ecuador's leading producer of animal feed, and launched Top Feeds, a mixed-feed plant in Sapele.

Facing stiff competition in the mill business from agribusiness giants, in 1982 Seaboard Allied sold all its US flour mills to Cargill. The company changed its name to Seaboard that year and began expanding outside the US. In 1983 the company formed Seaboard Marine, a shipping business in Florida, to serve its increasingly far-flung enterprises.

In addition to geographic diversification, the company expanded into new agribusiness areas. Seaboard acquired Central Soya's poultry unit in 1984, and it bought the Elberton Poultry Company the next year. Seaboard commenced shrimp farming operations in Ecuador in 1986 and in Honduras in 1987. Two years later Transcontinental Capital Corporation (Bermuda), a subsidiary, began supplying power from a floating power barge to the Dominican Republic.

Seaboard entered the hog business in 1990 by acquiring a pork-processing plant in Albert Lea, Minnesota. It opened a hog-processing facility in Guymon, Oklahoma, in 1996 and closed the Minnesota plant. That year the company bought a stake in Ingenio y Refinerio San Martin del Tabacal, an Argentina-based sugar cane and citrus company. It then acquired flour-mill, pasta-plant, and cookie operations in Mozambique.

During 1998 Seaboard bought a controlling interest in the Argentine sugar business, purchased a Bulgarian winery, and acquired a flour and feed milling business in Zambia.

In 2000 Seaboard sold its poultry division to ConAgra for $375 million. Also that year the company acquired a 35% stake in Unga Group, (feed milling, Kenya) and the JacintoPort marine terminal in Houston.

During 2001 the company traded its non-controlling interest in a joint-venture salmon processor (ContiSea LLC) to Norway's Fjord Seafood ASA for stock, and swapped its majority ownership of one Bulgarian winery for minority ownership in a larger one.

Seaboard purchased more of Fjord Seafood in 2002; with 20% of the company, it became the largest shareholder. However, by the end of 2003 Seaboard sold off its entire investment in Fjord Seafood for $37 million. In 2004 the company acquired a controlling stake in a Mozambique grain milling business.

Seaboard acquired Daily's Foods for $45 million in 2005; the bacon processor and foodservice supplier has been added to the company's Seaboard Foods (formerly Seaboard Farms) unit.

After serving as CEO for more than 30 years, in 2006 Harry Bresky stepped down as CEO and turned over the company's reins to his son, Steven. Harry Bresky died in 2007.

EXECUTIVES

President, CEO, and Director: Steven J. Bresky, age 56,
 $2,784,860 total compensation
SVP and CFO: Robert L. Steer, age 50,
 $2,728,278 total compensation
VP Governmental Affairs: Ralph L. Moss, age 64
VP Taxation and Business Development:
 David S. Oswalt, age 42
VP Engineering: James L. (Jim) Gutsch, age 56
VP, Corporate Controller, and Chief Accounting Officer:
 John A. Virgo, age 49
VP, General Counsel, and Secretary: David M. Becker,
 age 48
VP Audit Services: Ty Tywater
VP Finance and Treasurer: Barry E. Gum, age 43

President, Seaboard Overseas Trading Group:
 David M. Dannov, age 48,
 $1,733,021 total compensation
President, Seaboard Foods:
 Rodney K. (Rod) Brenneman, age 45,
 $1,955,682 total compensation
President, Seaboard Marine:
 Edward A. (Eddie) Gonzalez, age 44,
 $1,503,373 total compensation
Auditors: KPMG LLP

LOCATIONS

HQ: Seaboard Corporation
 9000 W. 67th St., Shawnee Mission, KS 66202
Phone: 913-676-8800 **Fax:** 913-676-8872
Web: www.seaboardcorp.com

2009 Sales

	$ mil.	% of total
Caribbean, Central & South America	1,406.8	39
Africa	969.3	27
North America		
US	855.4	24
Canada & Mexico	165.7	4
Pacific Basin & Far East	146.6	4
Europe	42.5	1
Eastern Mediterranean	15.0	1
Total	**3,601.3**	**100**

PRODUCTS/OPERATIONS

2009 Sales

	$ mil.	% of total
Commodity trading & milling	1,531.6	43
Pork	1,065.3	30
Marine	737.6	20
Sugar	143.0	4
Power	107.1	3
Other	16.7	—
Total	**3,601.3**	**100**

Selected Operations

Cargo shipping
Citrus production and processing
Commodity merchandising (wheat, corn, and soybean meal)
Domestic trucking transportation
Electric power generation
Flour, maize, and feed milling
Jalapeño-pepper processing
Pork production and processing
Sugar production and refining

Selected Subsidiaries

Cape Fear Railways, Inc.
Cayman Freight Shipping Services, Ltd.
Chestnut Hill Farms Honduras, S. de R.L. de C.V.
Eureka Chickens Limited (Zambia)
Fairfield Rice Incorporated (Guyana)
Gloridge Bakery (PTY) Limited (South Africa)
Green Island Maritime, Inc.
High Plains Bioenergy, LLC
Hybrid Poultry (Mauritius) Limited
JacintoPort International LLC
Lesotho Flour Mills Limited (Lesotho)
Life Flour Mill Ltd. (Nigeria)
Mount Dora Farms de Honduras, S.R.L.
Mount Dora Farms Inc.
National Milling Company of Guyana, Inc.
National Milling Corporation Limited (Zambia)
Sea Cargo, S.A. (Panama)
SSI Ocean Services, Inc.
Top Feeds Limited (Nigeria)
Unga Farmcare (East Africa) Limited (Kenya)

COMPETITORS

ADM	Johnsonville Sausage
American Crystal Sugar	Kraft Foods
APL	Louis Dreyfus Group
Bay State Milling	M. A. Patout
Bunge Limited	Makino
Cargill	Neptune Orient
Carr's Milling	Nicor
CGC	Nitto Flour
Chelsea Milling	Nutreco
Chiquita Brands	NYK Line
CHS	Organic Milling
Colonial Group	Overseas Shipholding
Crowley Maritime	Südzucker
CSX	Sara Lee
Della Natura Commodities	Sempra Energy Trading
Dole Food	Smithfield Foods
Evergreen Marine	Southern States
Evergreen Mills	Star of the West
Farmers Rice Milling	Sunkist
Fresh Del Monte Produce	Tate & Lyle
Genco Shipping and	Tyson Foods
Trading	U.S. Sugar
Horizon Milling	Viterra Inc.
Hormel	Western Sugar Cooperative
Imperial Sugar	

HISTORICAL FINANCIALS

Company Type: Public

Income Statement
FYE: December 31

	REVENUE ($ mil.)	NET INCOME ($ mil.)	NET PROFIT MARGIN	EMPLOYEES
12/09	3,601	93	2.6%	10,734
12/08	4,268	147	3.4%	10,734
12/07	3,213	181	5.6%	10,663
12/06	2,707	259	9.6%	10,363
12/05	2,689	267	9.9%	10,357
Annual Growth	**7.6%**	**(23.3%)**	**—**	**0.9%**

2009 Year-End Financials

Debt ratio: 5.0%
Return on equity: 6.2%
Cash ($ mil.): 62
Current ratio: 2.75
Long-term debt ($ mil.): 77
No. of shares (mil.): 1
Dividends
 Yield: 0.2%
 Payout: 4.0%
Market value ($ mil.): 1,658

Stock History
NYSE Amex: SEB

	STOCK PRICE ($) FY Close	P/E High/Low	PER SHARE ($) Earnings	Dividends	Book Value
12/09	1,349.00	21 11	74.74	3.00	1,254.66
12/08	1,194.00	16 6	118.19	3.00	1,187.67
12/07	1,470.00	19 9	144.15	3.00	1,102.11
12/06	1,765.00	9 6	205.09	3.00	979.29
12/05	1,511.00	9 4	211.94	3.00	795.82
Annual Growth	**(2.8%)**	**— —**	**(22.9%)**	**0.0%**	**12.1%**

SEACOR Holdings

SEACOR Holdings' core business is anchored in the sea. Operating through various subsidiaries, the diversified company operates one of the world's largest fleets of marine support vessels serving the global offshore oil and gas industry. Its vessels deliver cargo and crew to offshore platforms and handle anchors for drilling rigs. Other marine operations include US coastal tanker transportation of fuel and chemicals and inland river barge transportation of chemicals and bulk agricultural products. Under the Era name, SEACOR provides aviation services that include helicopter and air medical transportation. Its environmental services unit specializes in emergency fire, hazardous material, and oil spill response.

That unit, which additionally offers waste and wastewater remediation and pipeline repair services, is an emergency responder to some of the worst crises, including the Haiti earthquake in early 2010. Working with Haitian conglomerate WIN Group, which owns a key Port-au-Prince marine shipping terminal, SEACOR helped make repairs that are allowing the terminal to resume bulk fuel and cargo shipping and receiving. This effort was necessary to replenish dwindling supplies of fuel oil for power plants, gas and diesel fuel for cars, and propane gas and edible oils for cooking.

SEACOR's sixth main business segment, but second largest in terms of revenue overall, focuses on commodity trading and logistics. Subsidiaries that comprise this group buy, store, sell, and transport energy-related and agricultural commodities, such as ethanol, rice, and sugar. They are exported to destination ports mainly in Africa and Latin America.

Globally, SEACOR Holdings maintains joint ventures and offices in Africa, Asia, Europe, Latin America, the Middle East, and North America. Within its largest segment, the company focuses on deploying its offshore marine support vessels in oil-rich regions amidst its customers' exploration and production operations. In the US, the Gulf of Mexico is a major market, where more than a third of its vessels are operating.

HISTORY

With only two vessels, SEACOR was founded in 1989 to service offshore oil rigs in the Gulf of Mexico. It quickly expanded its fleet by buying 36 vessels from midwestern utility holding company Nicor, which had diversified into oil services in the late 1970s.

When the *Exxon Valdez* oil spill prompted a 1990 federal law requiring energy companies to have cleanup plans, SEACOR was among the first to enter the safety business. In 1991 the company joined a joint venture that operated safety standby vessels in the North Sea. By the time SEACOR went public in 1992, it had formed a similar joint venture in the US.

SEACOR expanded its Gulf operations throughout the 1990s. In 1994 it formed a joint venture with Transportación Maritima Mexicana to operate off the coast of Mexico. The company also gained some 165 ships by acquiring John E. Graham & Sons (1995) and McCall Enterprises (1996).

Also in 1996 SEACOR bought 45 offshore support vessels from the Netherlands' SMIT Internationale. As a result of the deal, the company changed its name to SEACOR SMIT Inc. in 1997. That year the firm created another joint venture to operate offshore Argentina, and SEACOR grabbed a 55% stake in Chiles Offshore, which began building two jack-up offshore drilling rigs.

SEACOR paid $37 million in 1998 for SMIT Internationale's 5% stake in the company. It also sold 34 vessels for $144 million (11 of these were chartered back to SEACOR) and accepted delivery of 10 new vessels. Also that year SEACOR invested in Globe Wireless, a marine telecommunications company concentrating on e-mail and data transfer. In 1999 SEACOR bought Kvaerner's Marinet Systems, which provides communications services to the shipping industry, with the intent of integrating its operations into Globe Wireless.

Chiles Offshore went public in 2000; SEACOR retained a 27% stake. In 2001 SEACOR acquired UK shipping firm Stirling Shipping. The next year SEACOR sold its stake in Chiles Offshore to Ensco and acquired the remaining 80% of Tex-Air Helicopters, expanding its air support operations.

SEACOR SMIT changed its name in 2004 to SEACOR Holdings. That year SEACOR acquired Era Aviation, including its fleet of 128 helicopters, 16 aircraft, and 14 operating bases, from Rowan Companies for about $118 million.

In 2005 the company acquired former rival Seabulk International for $1 billion, including assumed debt. It sold its Globe Wireless unit two years later, exiting the maritime telecommunications business.

EXECUTIVES

Chairman, President, and CEO: Charles L. Fabrikant, age 65, $7,096,537 total compensation
SVP and CFO: Richard Ryan, age 55, $982,359 total compensation
SVP; Chairman, President, and CEO, Environmental Services: Randall Blank, age 59, $2,108,758 total compensation
SVP International: John Gellert, age 39, $2,860,226 total compensation
SVP Corporate Development and Treasurer: Dick Fagerstal, age 49, $998,164 total compensation
SVP Strategy and Corporate Development: James A. F. Cowderoy, age 50
SVP, General Counsel, and Corporate Secretary: Paul L. Robinson, age 42
VP and Chief Accounting Officer: Matthew Cenac, age 44
Corporate Communications and Investor Relations: Molly Hottinger
Auditors: Ernst & Young LLP

LOCATIONS

HQ: SEACOR Holdings Inc.
2200 Eller Dr., Fort Lauderdale, FL 33316
Phone: 954-523-2200   **Fax:** 954-524-9185
Web: www.seacorholdings.com

2009 Sales

	$ mil.	% of total
North America	1,190.2	68
Africa	191.4	10
Latin America	115.7	7
Middle East	82.0	5
UK	73.8	5
Asia	35.7	3
Other regions	22.5	2
Total	**1,711.3**	**100**

PRODUCTS/OPERATIONS

2009 Sales

	$ mil.	% of total
Offshore marine services	562.3	32
Commodity trading	472.6	27
Aviation services	235.7	14
Inland river services	155.1	9
Environmental services	145.8	9
Marine transportation services	92.8	5
Other	64.3	4
Adjustments	(17.3)	—
Total	**1,711.3**	**100**

Selected Services

Cargo delivery
Commodity trading of agricultural and energy products
Crew transportation
Environmental services
Helicopter and air medical services
Inland river barge transportation
Line handling (assisting tankers while loading)
Logistics services
Offshore construction support
Offshore maintenance work support
Oil spill response services
Salvage
Seismic data gathering support
Towing and anchor handling for drill rigs
Well stimulation support

COMPETITORS

Bristow Group Inc
BUE Marine
CHC Helicopter
Crowley Maritime
Global Industries
GulfMark Offshore
Hornbeck Offshore
Kirby Corporation
Louis Dreyfus Commodities
Martin Resource Management
PHI, Inc.
Siem Offshore
Stolt-Nielsen
Tidewater Inc.
Trico Marine

HISTORICAL FINANCIALS

Company Type: Public

Income Statement

FYE: December 31

	REVENUE ($ mil.)	NET INCOME ($ mil.)	NET PROFIT MARGIN	EMPLOYEES
12/09	1,711	144	8.4%	4,956
12/08	1,656	224	13.5%	5,316
12/07	1,359	242	17.8%	5,268
12/06	1,323	234	17.7%	4,994
12/05	972	171	17.6%	5,035
Annual Growth	15.2%	(4.2%)	—	(0.4%)

2009 Year-End Financials

Debt ratio: 38.6%
Return on equity: 8.1%
Cash ($ mil.): 466
Current ratio: 3.31
Long-term debt ($ mil.): 755

No. of shares (mil.): 21
Dividends
  Yield: —
  Payout: —
Market value ($ mil.): 1,618

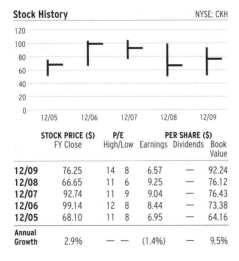

	STOCK PRICE ($) FY Close	P/E High/Low		PER SHARE ($) Earnings	Dividends	Book Value
12/09	76.25	14	8	6.57	—	92.24
12/08	66.65	11	6	9.25	—	76.12
12/07	92.74	11	9	9.04	—	76.43
12/06	99.14	12	8	8.44	—	73.38
12/05	68.10	11	8	6.95	—	64.16
Annual Growth	2.9%	—	—	(1.4%)	—	9.5%

Seagate Technology

Seagate Technology knows that if you want to survive in the storage market, you'd better have drive. The company is a leading independent maker of rigid disk drives (or hard drives) used to store data in computers. Its drives are used in systems ranging from personal computers and consumer electronics to high-end servers and mainframes. Seagate sells directly to computer manufacturers and through distributors. About two-thirds of Seagate's sales are to computer hardware manufacturers, which include Hewlett-Packard (16% of sales), Dell (11%), EMC, IBM, and Sun Microsystems; distributors and retailers account for the rest. Seagate gets around three-quarters of its sales outside the US.

The global recession and accompanying credit crisis have had several effects on Seagate's operations. Key suppliers have become insolvent, resulting in product delays, and some customers are unable to finance purchases of Seagate products.

In an industry that sees constantly falling PC prices, Seagate managed to stay at the front of the disk drive market by significantly undercutting competitors' prices, instituting global layoffs, and consolidating facilities.

Investment firms Silver Lake Partners and Texas Pacific Group took Seagate private in 2000. Prior to being taken private — a transaction that allowed Seagate to realize the value of its large holding in VERITAS Software while avoiding certain tax liabilities — the company had operations that included a business intelligence software developer (Crystal Decisions), a subsidiary that develops storage networking products (Biotech), and a unit devoted to tape storage products. The reorganized Seagate generates virtually all of its sales from its core hard-drive business. It went public again in 2002.

HISTORY

Seagate Technology was founded in 1979 by Alan Shugart, an 18-year veteran of IBM who made floppy disks standard on microcomputers; manufacturing expert and longtime technology industry veteran Tom Mitchell; design engineer

Douglas Mahon; and Finis Conner. Seagate pioneered the miniaturizing of larger mainframe hard disk drives for PCs.

Seagate's first product, a 5.25-inch. hard disk, sold briskly. With IBM as a customer, the company had grabbed half of the market for small disk drives by 1982; sales reached $344 million by 1984. But Seagate's heavy dependence on IBM showed its double edge as dwindling PC demand prompted IBM to cut orders. Sales in 1985 dropped to $215 million and profits to $1 million (from $42 million). Seagate transferred its manufacturing to Singapore and cut its California workforce in half. That year Conner, after a quarrel with Shugart, left Seagate to start his own disk drive company, Conner Peripherals. (Mitchell later joined him.)

Using acquisitions to grow, the company purchased Grenex (thin-film magnetic media, 1984), Aeon (aluminum substrates, 1987), and Integrated Power Systems (custom semiconductors, 1987). Seagate also lured back IBM, which had turned to an alternate supplier in the interim.

With sales more than doubling in 1986 and again in 1987, Seagate continued to invest in 5.25-inch. production, ignoring signs of a coming 3.5-inch. drive standard. The strong market in 1988 for the smaller drives prompted Seagate's quick shift to 3.5-inch. production. Seagate's purchase of Imprimis in 1989 made it the world's premier independent drive maker and a leader in high-capacity drives.

In 1993 the company acquired a stake in flash memory storage specialist SunDisk (now SanDisk). That year, when Sun Microsystems accounted for 11% of sales, Seagate was the only profitable independent disk drive company. In 1994 it began pursuing its software initiative, acquiring companies including Palindrome and Crystal Computer Services.

Shugart, an iconoclast who once ran his dog for Congress, had a small comeuppance in 1996 when Seagate paid just over $1 billion for Conner Peripherals, which banked on 3.5-inch. disk drives from the start and went public in 1988. By the time of the acquisition, Conner was a leading maker of disk and tape drives, storage systems, and software.

Seagate merged Conner's software subsidiary with its own holdings to form Seagate Storage Management Group, and continued to expand by buying management software companies. In 1997 the company bought disk drive developer Quinta. Seagate took a charge that year following a ruling that it had sold faulty drives to Amstrad PLC.

An industry slump, production problems, and lowered PC demand prompted Seagate to cut 20% of its workforce, streamline development, fire Shugart, and replace him with president and COO — and former investment banker — Stephen Luczo. The downturn took its toll when the company suffered a $530 million loss for fiscal 1998. The next year Seagate gained a stake of about 33% in VERITAS Software when it sold its network and storage management software operations to that company for $3.1 billion. Seagate also laid off another 10% of its workforce of nearly 80,000.

In 2000 the company acquired XIOtech, a maker of virtual storage and storage area network systems, for about $360 million. Later that year Seagate entered into an intricate deal with VERITAS, whereby the software maker bought back the stake owned by Seagate. As part of the deal, Seagate was taken private in a buyout led by Silver Lake Partners and Texas Pacific Group.

Also in 2000 COO William Watkins, who joined Seagate when it bought Conner Peripherals, replaced Luczo as president; Luczo remained CEO. The company went public again in 2002 in an IPO that raised $870 million. In 2004 Luczo passed the CEO reins to Watkins, but retained his chairmanship. At the beginning of 2009, however, Watkins stepped down as CEO and Luczo reprised his role as head of the company.

In a major step to expand its operations, the company agreed in 2005 to acquire rival storage device maker Maxtor for about $1.9 billion in stock; the deal closed in mid-2006. Seagate retained the Maxtor brand. Early in 2007 Seagate completed its purchase of online backup services provider EVault for approximately $186 million. Seagate acquired MetaLINCS late in 2007; MetaLINCS helped companies responding to litigation or regulatory issues search large volumes of data for relevant information. The following year Seagate combined the operations of MetaLINCS and EVault with its Seagate Recovery Services business to form a unit called i365.

Co-founder Alan Shugart died in 2006.

EXECUTIVES

Chairman, President, and CEO:
Stephen J. (Steve) Luczo, age 52,
$1,178,553 total compensation
EVP and CFO: Patrick J. O'Malley, age 48,
$1,130,070 total compensation
EVP Product and Process Development and CTO:
Robert (Bob) Whitmore, age 47,
$2,265,132 total compensation
EVP Sales, Marketing, and Product Line Management:
William D. (Dave) Mosley,
$1,990,503 total compensation
EVP Sales: D. Kurt Richarz, age 49,
$1,209,571 total compensation
Business Development Officer, Strategic Planning and Corporate Development: Charles C. Pope, age 55,
$2,469,841 total compensation
SVP, General Counsel, and Corporate Secretary:
Kenneth M. (Ken) Massaroni, age 49
SVP Operations and Materials: Douglas DeHaan, age 51
SVP Human Resources: Karen Hanlon
SVP Branded Solutions and i365:
Terence R. (Terry) Cunningham, age 50
SVP Worldwide Sales and Marketing, i365:
Larry Sheffield
VP Finance, Treasurer, and Principal Accounting Officer: David Z. Anderson, age 45
VP Investor Relations: Rod Cooper
Auditors: Ernst & Young LLP

LOCATIONS

HQ: Seagate Technology LLC
Arthur Cox Building, Earlsfort Terrace
Dublin, Ireland
Phone: 353-1-618-0517
US HQ: 920 Disc Dr., Scotts Valley, CA 95066
US Phone: 831-438-6550   **US Fax:** 831-429-6356
Web: www.seagate.com

2009 Sales

	$ mil.	% of total
Singapore	4,186	43
Netherlands	2,849	29
US	2,695	27
Other countries	75	1
Total	**9,805**	**100**

PRODUCTS/OPERATIONS

2009 Sales

	% of total
OEM	64
Distributors	27
Retailers	9
Total	**100**

Selected Products

Personal computing disk drives
   Desktop (Barracuda, DiamondMax)
   Notebook (Momentus)
Enterprise computing disk drives (Barracuda, Cheetah, Savvio)
Online backup, data protection, and recovery services (EVault)

COMPETITORS

Fujitsu
Hitachi Global Storage
Imation
Intel
Iomega
LaCie
Micron Technology
Samsung Electronics
SanDisk
STEC
Toshiba
Western Digital

HISTORICAL FINANCIALS

Company Type: Public

Income Statement

	REVENUE ($ mil.)	NET INCOME ($ mil.)	NET PROFIT MARGIN	EMPLOYEES
			FYE: Friday nearest June 30	
6/09	9,805	(3,086)	—	47,000
6/08	12,708	1,262	9.9%	54,000
6/07	11,360	913	8.0%	54,000
6/06	9,206	840	9.1%	60,000
6/05	7,553	707	9.4%	44,000
Annual Growth	6.7%	—	—	1.7%

2009 Year-End Financials

Debt ratio: 128.3%
Return on equity: —
Cash ($ mil.): 1,427
Current ratio: 1.34
Long-term debt ($ mil.): 1,956

No. of shares (mil.): 487
Dividends
   Yield: 2.6%
   Payout: —
Market value ($ mil.): 5,099

Stock History

NASDAQ (GS): STX

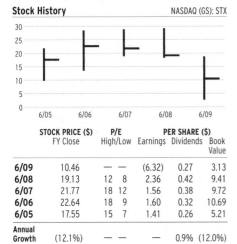

	STOCK PRICE ($) FY Close	P/E High/Low		PER SHARE ($) Earnings	Dividends	Book Value
6/09	10.46	—	—	(6.32)	0.27	3.13
6/08	19.13	12	8	2.36	0.42	9.41
6/07	21.77	18	12	1.56	0.38	9.72
6/06	22.64	18	9	1.60	0.32	10.69
6/05	17.55	15	7	1.41	0.26	5.21
Annual Growth	(12.1%)	—	—	—	0.9%	(12.0%)

Sealed Air Corp.

Pop-Pop-Pop is the same sound to Sealed Air as *cha-ching* is to other companies. From the company that introduced Bubble Wrap, Sealed Air makes it, along with Instapak foam, Jiffy mailers, and Fill-Air inflatable packaging systems, through its Protective Packing segment. Its largest segment, Food Packaging, makes Cryovac bags, trays, and absorbent pads for use by food processors and supermarkets to protect meat and poultry. Other products include shrink packaging for consumer goods, such as toys and CDs; medical packaging for pacemakers and IV fluid; and specialty packaging for the construction and transportation industries. The company operates through its two subsidiaries: Sealed Air and Cryovac.

Sealed Air is relying on diversification for its growth. With its broad reach and varied product lines, the company reduces its exposure to an economic downturn in the event that sales in a particular region or particular industry drop. Geographically, the company's two primary subsidiaries run more than 100 manufacturing facilities worldwide.

While Sealed Air's business is best known for its food and protective packaging, it is broadening its interest in new market segments that utilize specialty and performance-based materials for use in antistatic, acoustic, moisture/gas barrier, formable, printable, and adhesive applications. The foams, films, and composites are marketed under name brands including Cellu-Cushion, Stratocell, and Ethafoam HRC.

These new materials are being used in medical and pharmaceutical applications. The health care industry in the US is experiencing a growth spurt, due in part to Baby Boomers reaching that age when more medical attention is required, and also because the US Food and Drug Administration has suggested using disposable wares in hospitals and nursing homes for better hygiene.

Building on the company's diverse offerings, it bought selected assets in 2007 of The Dow Chemical Company's Ethafoam HRC (High Recycled Content) polyethylene foam product line, which contains at least 65% recycled content. The company opened a new manufacturing facility in Louisville, Kentucky, in November 2009 where it will manufacture Ethafoam and its Cell-Aire polyethylene foam packaging products.

In order to continue to develop and introduce new products, Sealed Air decided to outsource some of its technically less complex product lines, such as foam and plastic trays, to third-party manufacturers. In 2009 Sealed Air launched several new products, including the Deli-Snap! tray and Oven Ease (cook-in bag).

Davis Selected Advisers holds a 36% stake in the company.

HISTORY

In the late 1950s, after US engineer Al Fielding and Swiss inventor Marc Chavannes found no takers for their plastic air-bubble-embossed wallpaper, they looked for another use for the material. They came up with Bubble Wrap, the first product of Sealed Air, which they founded in 1960 and took public soon after. AirCap, as the material was first known, didn't just protect products from damage; it also reduced storage and shipping costs.

Sealed Air expanded in the early 1970s into bubble-lined mailers and adhesive products with subsidiary PolyMask. With the $5 million company in the doldrums, Dublin-born packaging veteran Dermot Dunphy was brought in as CEO in 1971. New products followed Dunphy's entrance, including the Bubble Wrap-based Solar Pool Blanket. Sealed Air's sales moved beyond the US in the 1970s into Canada, Japan, and Western Europe. The company bought Instapak in 1977.

The purchase in 1983 of the Dri-Loc product line moved Sealed Air into food packaging. It began selling static-control packaging in 1984, and in 1987 it bought padded-mailer maker Jiffy Packaging. Fielding and Chavannes both retired in 1987. Sealed Air pleaded guilty in 1989 to making illegal chemical shipments to Libya (made by a division the company has since sold).

By 1989 Sealed Air had plenty of cash on hand, but with no appealing acquisitions to spend it on, the company was a potential takeover target. It had also grown complacent. To provide greater incentive to the company's rank and file while warding off any buyout overtures, Dunphy and CFO Bill Hickey took Sealed Air through a risky recapitalization. This plunged the company into debt but more than doubled its employees' ownership stake. The newly inspired company became more efficient, the cost of Sealed Air's raw materials dropped, and the company brought its debt back down over the next several years.

The acquisition of Korrvu in 1991 gave Sealed Air a gateway to innovative packaging for electronics manufacturers. The company made a host of mostly small purchases in Asia, Australia, Europe, and North America between 1993 and 1996. When Sealed Air bought New Zealand-based Trigon Industries in 1995, its food-packaging business nearly doubled in size, along with sales outside the US.

In 1998 Sealed Air combined with W. R. Grace's packaging business (including the Cryovac, Formpac, and Omicron lines). Grace structured a deal with Sealed Air that gave Grace's shareholders about two-thirds of the resulting packaging-only company. Sealed Air tripled its sales and number of employees with the purchase.

The company restructured its operations in 1999 to integrate its newly acquired businesses. It closed facilities with overlapping operations and eliminated 750 jobs (5% of its workforce). Dunphy retired in 2000 and president William Hickey became CEO.

In 2001, more than three years after the company combined its operations with W. R. Grace's packaging business, Sealed Air continued to defend itself against asbestos lawsuits related to Grace's past operations. (In 2005 the company's definitive settlement agreement was accepted by the bankruptcy court.)

Another lawsuit was prompted by a 2003 fire in a New Jersey nightclub that killed 100 people. The fire occurred during a concert by the rock band Great White. Their pyrotechnics set fire to soundproofing material on the walls inside the club. The material was allegedly supplied by Sealed Air, which did not admit to any wrongdoing. However, the company agreed to pay $25 million to the victims' families in 2008.

Sealed Air cut nearly 400 employees and consolidated some of its operations in 2004.

Early in 2006 Sealed Air acquired Nelipak Holdings, a Netherlands-based rigid packaging company. The company sold its security bag business (Trigon) to Ampac in 2007.

EXECUTIVES

President, CEO, and Director: William V. Hickey, age 65, $2,490,424 total compensation
SVP and CFO: David H. Kelsey, age 58, $1,037,125 total compensation
VP: Jean-Marie Demeautis, age 59, $778,448 total compensation
VP Technology and Innovation: Ann C. Savoca, age 51
VP, General Counsel, and Secretary: H. Katherine White, age 64
VP: J. Ryan Flanagan, age 46
VP: Ruth Roper, age 55
VP: Christopher C. Woodbridge, age 58
VP: Karl R. Deily, age 52
VP: Cheryl Fells Davis, age 57
VP: James Donald Tate, age 58
VP: Hugh L. Sargant, age 61
VP: James P. Mix, age 58
VP: Mary A. Coventry, age 56
VP: Manuel Mondragón, age 60
VP: Jonathan B. Baker, age 56
Director Investor Relations: Amanda Butler
Treasurer: Tod S. Christie, age 51
Controller: Jeffrey S. Warren, age 56
Auditors: KPMG LLP

LOCATIONS

HQ: Sealed Air Corporation
200 Riverfront Blvd., Elmwood Park, NJ 07407
Phone: 201-791-7600   **Fax:** 201-703-4205
Web: www.sealedair.com

2009 Sales

	$ mil.	% of total
International	2,273.7	54
US	1,969.1	46
Total	**4,242.8**	**100**

PRODUCTS/OPERATIONS

2009 Sales

	$ mil.	% of total
Food packaging	1,839.8	43
Protective packaging	1,192.9	28
Food solutions	891.7	21
Other	318.4	8
Total	**4,242.8**	**100**

Selected Brands

Bubble Wrap
CRYOVAC
Ethafoam
Fill-Air
Instapak
Jiffy Mailer
Korrvu
Shanklin

Selected Products

Food Packaging
 Absorbent pads and case liners
 Bulk packaging
 Foam trays
 Laminates
 Lidstock
 Pouches
 Rollstock
 Vacuum bags
Medical Packaging
 Cleanroom blisters
 Films
 Lidding material
 Medical device packaging
 Sealing machines

Protective Packaging
 Air cushioning (Bubble Wrap)
 Cushioned mailing bags (Jiffy Mailer)
 Foam packaging (Instapak)
 Inflatable packaging and cushioning (Fill-Air and FillTeck)
 Paper cushioning (PackTiger)
 Paper packaging (Kushion Kraft and Custom Wrap)
 Polyethylene fabrication foam (Cellu-Cushion, CelluPlank, Stratocell)
 Polyethylene foam (Cell-Aire)
 Suspension and retention packaging (Korrvu)
Shrink Packaging
 Equipment
 Films
Specialty Materials
 Foams
 Solar pool heating

COMPETITORS

3M
AEP Industries
Bemis
Curwood
Huhtamäki
Intertape Polymer
Packaging Dynamics
Pactiv
Pliant Corporation
Polyair Inter Pack
Printpack
Reynolds Food Packaging
Sonoco Products
Tekni-Plex
Winpak

HISTORICAL FINANCIALS

Company Type: Public

Income Statement

FYE: December 31

	REVENUE ($ mil.)	NET INCOME ($ mil.)	NET PROFIT MARGIN	EMPLOYEES
12/09	4,243	244	5.8%	16,200
12/08	4,844	180	3.7%	17,000
12/07	4,651	353	7.6%	17,700
12/06	4,328	274	6.3%	17,400
12/05	4,085	256	6.3%	17,000
Annual Growth	**1.0%**	**(1.1%)**	**—**	**(1.2%)**

2009 Year-End Financials

Debt ratio: 73.9%
Return on equity: 11.8%
Cash ($ mil.): 695
Current ratio: 1.45
Long-term debt ($ mil.): 1,626
No. of shares (mil.): 159
Dividends
 Yield: 2.2%
 Payout: 35.6%
Market value ($ mil.): 3,486

Stock History

NYSE: SEE

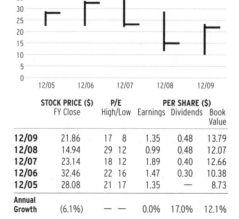

	STOCK PRICE ($) FY Close	P/E High/Low		PER SHARE ($) Earnings	Dividends	Book Value
12/09	21.86	17	8	1.35	0.48	13.79
12/08	14.94	29	12	0.99	0.48	12.07
12/07	23.14	18	12	1.89	0.40	12.66
12/06	32.46	22	16	1.47	0.30	10.38
12/05	28.08	21	17	1.35	—	8.73
Annual Growth	**(6.1%)**	**—**	**—**	**0.0%**	**17.0%**	**12.1%**

Sealy Corporation

Sealy is a slumbering giant. It's the world's largest maker of bedding products and a leading US manufacturer, with about a 20% wholesale market share. Sealy makes mattresses and box springs under the Sealy, Bassett, and Stearns & Foster names and sells them through about 7,000 stores. Its customers include sleep shops, furniture and department stores, warehouse clubs, and mass merchandisers, as well as the hospitality industry. Sealy also licenses its name to makers of other bedding products and home furnishings. Sealy, formerly owned by Bain Capital, was bought by Kohlberg Kravis Roberts (KKR) in 2004. KKR owns some 49% of Sealy.

The recession has put an indentation in Sealy's overall mattress sales. The firm was hit hardest in the specialty bedding category, which comprises latex foam and memory foam bedding, and the above-$1,000 price point. To boost its higher-priced lines, Sealy is working to capture these customers by launching new products at luxury price points. The company's sweet spot, where it generates some 63% of its domestic sales, comes from sales of mattresses priced at $750 and up.

The bedding company also is looking over its shoulder. Top rivals Simmons and Serta came together in January 2010 under the same owner. While Simmons and Serta operate separately and under different management teams, both mattress firms stand to benefit from the deep pockets of their shared investor owner as they work to expand in the US.

While the majority of Sealy's sales come from the US, the company also boasts licensees and sales operations worldwide. Sealy is making acquisitions and building plants to expand its business in Latin America.

The mattress maker has been working to expand its US operations. In 2007 Sealy created a North American division as it realigned its business to ensure continued sales gains. Amid the worsening US economy, Sealy reorganized its US operations in 2008 by reducing the number of regional divisions and by eliminating an unspecified number of jobs.

In early 2008 David McIlquham, a 20-year Sealy veteran, resigned as chairman and CEO. He was replaced on an interim basis by Larry Rogers, another Sealy long-timer who had been president of the company's North American operations. Rogers became the company's permanent president and CEO in July 2008.

HISTORY

Daniel Haynes, a cotton gin builder, first made a new, more resilient type of cotton-filled mattress in 1881 in Sealy, Texas. In 1889 he patented a machine to mass-produce his increasingly popular product. Haynes sold manufacturing rights to firms in other cities, and in 1906 he sold his patents to a Texas firm that renamed itself Sealy.

Sealy expanded by advertising in national magazines and finding licensees to open mattress factories. By 1920 the company had 28 licensed plants. When doctors in the 1940s advised that people with back problems sleep on firm mattresses, Sealy designed the Orthopedic Firm-O-Rest; it was renamed the Posturepedic in 1950 after the FTC banned the use of the medical term "orthopedic" in brand names.

In the 1950s Sealy sprung out geographically (it added Canadian licensees in 1954) and financially (sales quintupled to $48 million during the decade). During the 1960s it became the first mattress firm to advertise on prime-time TV.

The princess had her uncomfortable pea; Sealy had The Ohio Mattress Company, one of its independent licensees. In the 1950s Ohio Mattress began entering other licensees' territories (despite exclusive territory agreements) and lowering its prices to force its new rivals to sell out. In 1963 Ernest Wuliger succeeded his father as president of Ohio Mattress and began an aggressive expansion campaign. He acquired a Sealy licensee in Texas and Oklahoma in 1967, but Sealy bought some of the licensees that Wuliger wanted. The Supreme Court found Sealy guilty that year of antitrust violations regarding price-fixing and exclusive territories. Still, by the end of the 1960s, Sealy had sales of $113 million and additional international licensees.

Wuliger took Ohio Mattress public in 1970. The next year Wuliger began a series of antitrust lawsuits against Sealy that lasted fifteen years. Ohio Mattress acquired bedding maker Stearns & Foster (1983) and Woodstuff Manufacturing (1985). In 1986 the legal bedding battle ended, and Ohio Mattress was awarded $77 million. In 1987 Ohio Mattress opted to buy Sealy and all but one of Sealy's nine US licensees. It acquired the holdout licensee's Sealy license later in 1987 and became the leading mattress manufacturer.

Investment firm Gibbons Goodwin van Amerongen led a $965-million, junk-bond-financed LBO of Ohio Mattress in 1989; it renamed the company Sealy in 1990. Amid a downturn in the junk-bond market, from 1991 to 1993 Sealy changed owners twice, ending up with investment fund Zell/Chilmark. It also found itself in bed with a variety of new CEOs. Right after the LBO, Wuliger resigned due to conflicts with the new owners. COO Malcolm Candlish was promoted to CEO. In 1992 Candlish resigned and was replaced by Lyman Beggs, who lasted until 1995, when he was replaced by Ronald Jones, former head of Masco Home Furnishings.

In 1997 investment firm Bain Capital bought a majority stake in Sealy. Sealy also sold its Samuel Lawrence bedroom furniture unit (formerly Woodstuff Manufacturing) that year. The company relocated from Ohio to North Carolina in 1998. Sealy lost $34 million that fiscal year, in part due to early debt repayment related to the Bain Capital buyout.

In 2000 Sealy acquired the Bassett bedding license and Carrington-Chase brand from Premier Bedding; the deal included the corresponding factory. Sealy also bought control of Argentina-based bedding maker Rosen and built a factory in Brazil. In 2001 Sealy announced it would close its Tennessee bedding plant because it wasn't profitable. Marking its entrance into Europe, Sealy acquired Paris-based Sapsa Bedding the same year. In April 2002 David McIlquham replaced Jones as CEO; Jones remained as chairman until 2004.

In April 2004 Sealy was bought by Kohlberg Kravis Roberts (KKR) for about $1.5 billion. It went public in 2006.

In 2008 McIlquham resigned his posts and was replaced by company executive Larry Rogers as president and CEO.

Heating up competition in the mattress industry, Sealy's top rivals Serta and Simmons came under the same ownership umbrella in 2010.

EXECUTIVES

Chairman: Paul J. Norris, age 62
President and CEO: Lawrence J. (Larry) Rogers, age 61, $5,945,305 total compensation
EVP and CFO: Jeffrey C. (Jeff) Ackerman, age 46, $2,272,003 total compensation
EVP Operations, North America: G. Michael Hofmann, age 51, $1,441,254 total compensation
EVP Sales: Louis R. Bachicha, age 54
SVP and Chief Marketing Officer: Jodi Allen
SVP Human Resources: Carmen J. Dabiero
SVP, General Counsel, and Secretary: Michael Q. Murray
Auditors: Deloitte & Touche LLP

LOCATIONS

HQ: Sealy Corporation
1 Office Pkwy. at Sealy Dr., Trinity, NC 27370
Phone: 336-861-3500   **Fax:** 336-861-3501
Web: www.sealy.com

2009 Sales

	% of total
Americas	
US	73
Canada	12
Europe	9
Other regions	6
Total	**100**

PRODUCTS/OPERATIONS

Brand Names

Bassett
Carrington Chase
MirrorForm
PurEmbrace
Reflexions
Sealy
Sealy Posturepedic
SpringFree
Stearns & Foster
TrueForm

COMPETITORS

Mattress Giant
Mattress Holding
Select Comfort
Serta
Simmons
Spring Air
Tempur-Pedic
W. S. Badcock

HISTORICAL FINANCIALS

Company Type: Public

Income Statement

FYE: Sunday nearest November 30

	REVENUE ($ mil.)	NET INCOME ($ mil.)	NET PROFIT MARGIN	EMPLOYEES
11/09	1,290	14	1.0%	4,848
11/08	1,498	(3)	—	4,817
11/07	1,702	79	4.7%	6,099
11/06	1,583	74	4.7%	6,233
11/05	1,470	69	4.7%	6,208
Annual Growth	**(3.2%)**	**(33.4%)**	**—**	**(6.0%)**

2009 Year-End Financials

Debt ratio: —
Return on equity: —
Cash ($ mil.): 131
Current ratio: 1.69
Long-term debt ($ mil.): 834

No. of shares (mil.): 98
Dividends
  Yield: 0.0%
  Payout: —
Market value ($ mil.): 261

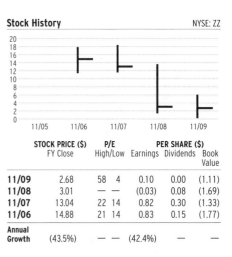

Stock History

NYSE: ZZ

	STOCK PRICE ($) FY Close	P/E High/Low		PER SHARE ($) Earnings	Dividends	Book Value
11/09	2.68	58	4	0.10	0.00	(1.11)
11/08	3.01	—	—	(0.03)	0.08	(1.69)
11/07	13.04	22	14	0.82	0.30	(1.33)
11/06	14.88	21	14	0.83	0.15	(1.77)
Annual Growth	**(43.5%)**	**—**	**—**	**(42.4%)**	**—**	**—**

Sears, Roebuck

Sears, Roebuck and Co. hasn't outgrown the mall scene, but it's spending more time in other places. Beyond its 850 US mall-based stores, Sears has more than 1,300 other locations nationwide. The company operates more than 900 independently owned Sears Hometown Stores (formerly known as dealer stores) in small towns and about 105 Sears hardware stores and some 85 Orchard Supply Hardware shops. Sears' stores sell apparel, tools, and appliances, and provide home services (remodeling, appliance repairs) under the Sears Parts & Repair Services and A&E Factory brands. It also sells appliances and tools online. Sears was acquired by Kmart Holding Corp. in 2005. The deal formed Sears Holdings, which owns both chains.

So far it's hard to see how the megamerger orchestrated by the chairman of Sears Holdings — Edward Lampert (whose hedge fund ESL Investments controls Sears Holdings) — has improved the performance of either Sears or Kmart. Overall sales at Sears' US stores have fallen, as have same-store sales (generally considered the best indicator of a retailer's health). Following the sales declines, Sears Holdings closed more than 40 underperforming stores.

While its bricks-and-mortar stores struggle, the retailer has been hard at work improving its e-commerce platform Sears.com. The updated website features appliances and offers merchandise available in both Sears and Kmart stores and is designed to drive Web customers to its stores and store customers to the website.

The combination of Sears and Kmart was a response to the pounding both companies endured at the hands of Wal-Mart and other discount and mass merchandisers. Sears' status as the nation's largest seller of home appliances has been under siege from big-box chains, including Best Buy, Home Depot, and Lowe's, for years. Its latest effort to defend its appliance business is an aggressive move into the market for high-end kitchens. To that end, it signed a deal in 2009 to become the only national retail chain to carry Whirlpool's Jenn-Air appliance brand.

The company's freestanding off-the-mall format — 60 Sears Essentials/Grand stores — is designed to compete directly with supercenters by selling consumables, health and beauty aids, housewares, and toys, among other offerings, all under one very large roof. About half the locations have in-store pharmacies. The superstores average about 116,000 sq. ft. and are present in some 25 states.

To breathe new life into what some see as a stale image, Sears is ramping up efforts to tap into the youth market. With a focus on hip and urban youth consumers, the company began stocking teen footwear line Skechers and is adding a line of street clothes and accessories designed by hip-hop artist LL Cool J. Sears also hopes to make an impression on younger customers by bringing toys back to its lineup.

HISTORY

Richard Sears, a Minnesota railway agent, bought a load of watches in 1886 that were being returned to the maker. He started the R. W. Sears Watch Company six months later, moved to Chicago, and in 1887 hired watchmaker Alvah Roebuck. Sears sold the watch business in 1889 and two years later formed the mail-order business that in 1893 became Sears, Roebuck and Co. It issued its first general catalog in 1896, targeting mainly farmers.

Roebuck left the company in 1895, and Sears found two new partners: Aaron Nussbaum (who left in 1901) and Julius Rosenwald. In 1906 the company went public to finance expansion. Differences soon arose between Sears and Rosenwald; Sears departed in 1908, and Rosenwald became president.

In 1925 the firm brought out a line of tires under the name Allstate. That year it opened its first retail store, and by 1931 the company's catalog sales trailed its retail sales. The rapid growth of Sears' retail operations was instrumental in the development of its prominent lines of store-brand merchandise. Sears began offering Allstate auto insurance in 1931.

Sales shot up after WWII, passing the $1 billion mark in 1945 and doubling just a year later. Sears targeted the fast-growing Sun Belt and nascent suburbs for expansion. By the early 1950s, sales of durable goods had fallen off, and the company began stocking more clothing.

After struggling through the late 1970s, Sears diversified. It acquired Coldwell Banker (real estate sales) and Dean Witter Reynolds (stock brokerage) in 1981 and launched the Discover credit card in 1985.

In reaction to falling market share in the 1980s, Sears lurched from one retail strategy to another and diversified into auto supplies and repairs. In 1993 the company sold its remaining stake in Coldwell Banker and spun off Dean Witter and Discover.

In 2005 the firm spun off insurer Allstate. Sears' top merchandiser, Arthur Martinez, became CEO that year. He gave Sears a makeover, catering especially to its mainly female clientele.

In 1996 and 1997 Sears abandoned a pair of ventures with IBM, including Prodigy (an online service that the two companies sold at a huge loss).

Again revamping its retail strategy, in 1998 the company sold its Western Auto wholesale business (which also operated about 600 Parts America stores) to Advance Holding. In 1998 a stream of high-ranking officers left the company. The executive departures continued in 1999 as Sears reorganized its automotive and direct-marketing units and eventually cut some 1,400 jobs at headquarters.

In 2000 Martinez stepped down as CEO; president of services Alan Lacy assumed the role in October 2000. In 2002 the company laid off about 22% of its workforce. In June of the same year Sears bought catalog retailer Lands' End for almost $2 billion.

In September 2003 Sears sold its giant credit-card business to Citigroup for about $6 billion. To better focus on core operations, Sears sold its National Tire & Battery (NTB) chain to TBC Corporation for $225 million in December 2003.

In 2005 Kmart Holding Corp acquired Sears, Roebuck. The deal formed a new company, Sears Holdings, which is now the parent company of both chains.

In January 2008 Aylwin Lewis, who served as president and CEO of the company since September 2005, stepped down. Lewis was replaced on an interim basis by EVP W. Bruce Johnson.

In July 2009 the landmark Sears Tower was renamed Willis Tower, after its parent the global insurer Willis Group Holdings. According to Willis, the name change reflects Chicago's rise as a global financial capital (and perhaps also Sears' decline in the American retail landscape).

EXECUTIVES

Interim President, Interim CEO, and Director: W. Bruce Johnson, age 58
EVP Operating and Support Businesses: Scott J. Freidheim, age 44
EVP Apparel and Home; President, Kmart: John D. Goodman, age 44
EVP; President, Retail Services: James H. (Jim) Haworth, age 47
SVP and CFO: Michael D. (Mike) Collins, age 46
SVP; President, Tools, Lawn, and Garden: John W. Froman, age 55
SVP, Controller, and Chief Accounting Officer: William K. Phelan, age 47
SVP; President, Appliances: Douglas T. (Doug) Moore, age 53
SVP, General Counsel, and Corporate Secretary: Dane A. Drobny
VP and Chief Marketing Officer, Appliances: Kevin Brown
VP Tools, Hardware, and Paint: Dave Figler
VP and General Merchandise Manager: Steven Light
VP and General Manager, Kenmore: Betsy Owens
President, Home Electronics: Karen A. Austin, age 48
Auditors: Deloitte & Touche LLP

LOCATIONS

HQ: Sears, Roebuck and Co.
3333 Beverly Rd., Hoffman Estates, IL 60179
Phone: 847-286-2500   **Fax:** 800-326-0485
Web: www.sears.com

PRODUCTS/OPERATIONS

2010 Stores

	No.
Specialty	1,284
Full-line mall	848
Sears Essentials/Grand	60
Total	**2,192**

Selected Brands

Hard Goods
  Craftsman
  DieHard
  Kenmore
  WeatherBeater
Soft Goods
  Apostrophe
  Canyon River Blues
  Covington
  Lands' End

Selected Specialty Stores

Lands' End (casual apparel and accessories)
Orchard Supply Hardware (neighborhood hardware stores)
Sears Auto Centers
Sears Home Appliance Showrooms (appliance only)
Sears Hometown Stores (independently owned)
Sears Hardware
The Great Indoors (home decorating and remodeling superstores)

COMPETITORS

Ace Hardware	Kohl's
Army and Air Force	L.L. Bean
Exchange	Lowe's
AutoZone	Macy's
Bed Bath & Beyond	Men's Wearhouse
Belk	Pep Boys
Best Buy	RadioShack
Big 5	Ross Stores
Big Lots	ShopKo Stores
Brown Shoe	Snap-on
Burlington Coat Factory	Target
Collective Brands	TJX Companies
Family Dollar Stores	Toys "R" Us
Foot Locker	True Value
Home Depot	Wal-Mart
J. C. Penney	

Sempra Energy

Sempra Energy isn't joining the Marines, but it is faithful to making money in utility markets in the US and around the world. In the US Sempra distributes natural gas to some 5.8 million customers and electricity to 1.4 million customers through its Southern California Gas (SoCalGas) and San Diego Gas & Electric (SDG&E) utilities. Unregulated subsidiaries include Sempra Pipelines & Storage, Sempra Generation, and Sempra LNG, which have global energy projects and serve power and gas customers (mainly in Latin America). Sempra Energy companies serve more than 29 million customers worldwide.

The company develops and acquires merchant power plants (Sempra Generation, formerly Sempra Energy Resources), liquefied natural gas (LNG) regasification facilities (Sempra LNG), and affordable housing properties.

In addition to investing in its utilities and its commodities marketing business in North America, the company's future strategy calls for developing its natural gas and renewable energy infrastructure. In a move to expand its midstream and distribution assets in the Southeastern US, in 2008 the company acquired EnergySouth for $510 million. Further building its midstream portfolio, in 2010 the company acquired El Paso's Mexico-based pipeline and compression assets for $300 million.

Sempra had formed a partnership with The Royal Bank of Scotland to operate RBS Sempra Commodities, including Sempra Energy Trading, which trades and markets wholesale energy commodities in Asia, Europe, and North America. However, to refocus its operations primarily around its more financially reliable North American businesses, and to pay down debt, in 2010 the company sold the European and Asian segments of this partnership to JP Morgan Chase for about $1.6 billion.

HISTORY

Sempra Energy is the latest incarnation of some of California's leading lights. Formed by the $6.2 billion merger between Enova and Pacific Enterprises, the company traces its roots back to the 1880s.

Enova began as San Diego Gas, which lit its first gaslights in 1881 and added electricity in 1887 (when it became San Diego Gas & Electric Light). Massive utility holding company Standard Gas & Electric bought the company in 1905 and renamed it San Diego Consolidated Gas & Electric. Over the next few decades, San Diego Consolidated expanded through acquisitions and even stayed profitable during the Depression. But the 1935 Public Utilities Holding Company Act forced Standard to divest many of its widespread utilities, and in 1940 San Diego Consolidated went public as San Diego Gas & Electric (SDG&E).

SDG&E grew quickly until the 1970s, when new environmental laws slowed plans to build more power plants, and rates soared because the company had to purchase power. The company finally added more generating capacity in the 1980s, and the state of California allowed SDG&E to diversify into real estate, software, and oil and gas distribution. In 1995 it created Enova to serve as its holding company.

Meanwhile, up the coast in San Francisco, Pacific Enterprises began as gas lamp rental firm Pacific Lighting in 1886; it quickly moved into gas distribution to defend its market against electricity. The firm bought three Los Angeles gas and electric utilities in 1889 and continued to grow through acquisitions; it consolidated all of its utilities in the 1920s. Pacific Lighting sold its electric properties to the city of Los Angeles in 1937 in exchange for a long-term gas franchise.

The company entered oil and gas exploration in 1960. A decade later it merged its gas utility operations into Southern California Gas (SoCalGas). Pacific Lighting continued to diversify in the 1980s, buying two oil and gas companies and three drugstore chains. Renamed Pacific Enterprises in 1988, the company launched an unsuccessful diversification effort that cost it $88 million in 1991. Over the next two years it sold off noncore businesses to focus on SoCalGas, and in the mid-1990s it began moving into South and Central America. This included a joint venture with Enova and Mexico's Proxima SA to build and operate Mexico's first private utility.

Pacific Enterprises and Enova agreed in 1997 to a $6.2 billion merger; Sempra Energy was born in 1998. That year California began deregulating its retail power market. In response, Sempra sold SDG&E's non-nuclear power plants (1,900 MW) in 1999. It used the proceeds to eliminate its competitive transition charge and, in turn, lowered its electric rates.

But under deregulation, rates tripled by mid-2000; that summer the California Public Utilities Commission (CPUC) implemented a rate freeze for electric customers. Wholesale power prices soared, and rolling blackouts occurred in 2000 and 2001 as a result of the state's inadequate energy supply. In 2001 the CPUC began allowing utilities to increase their rates, and SDG&E agreed to sell its transmission assets to the state for about $1 billion.

Sempra sold its 72.5% share in power marketing firm Energy America to British energy company Centrica in 2001. In 2002 the company purchased bankrupt utility Enron's London-based metals trading unit for about $145 million; later that year it purchased Enron's metals concentrates and metals warehousing businesses.

The company restructured its competitive energy business units in 2005, renaming several divisions and dividing the former Sempra Energy Solutions operations (retail energy marketing and services for commercial and industrial customers) under the Commodities and Generation divisions. That year Sempra sold one of its gas storage units to Vulcan Capital, an investment company headed up by Microsoft co-founder Paul Allen, for a reported $250 million.

In 2006 the company settled class-action litigation that claimed that two of its subsidiaries, Southern California Gas and San Diego Gas & Electric, helped to create the 2000-2001 energy crises in California by restricting the supply of natural gas to the state.

In 2007 Sempra was awarded a $172 million settlement arising from a 2002 dispute over the company's minority stakes in two Argentine natural gas holding companies.

EXECUTIVES

Chairman and CEO: Donald E. Felsinger, age 62, $20,894,518 total compensation
President, COO, and Director: Neal E. Schmale, age 63, $6,266,066 total compensation
EVP and CFO: Mark A. Snell, age 53, $4,547,825 total compensation
EVP: Debra L. (Debbie) Reed, age 53
EVP and General Counsel: M. Javade Chaudhri, age 57, $2,956,332 total compensation
SVP, Controller, and Chief Accounting Officer: Joseph A. (Joe) Householder, age 54, $2,853,707 total compensation
SVP Human Resources: G. Joyce Rowland, age 55
VP Tax and Chief Tax Counsel: Paul Yong
VP Audit Services: Lisa Urick
VP Corporate Planning: Monica Haas
VP Risk Analysis and Management: Amy H. Chiu
VP Corporate Relations and Corporate Secretary: Randall L. Clark
VP Mergers and Acquisitions: Richard A. Vaccari
VP Investor Relations: Steven D. Davis, age 54
President and CEO, Sempra Generation: Jeffery W. (Jeff) Martin, age 47
President and CEO, Sempra Pipelines & Storage: George S. Liparidis
President and CEO, Southern California Gas: Michael W. Allman, age 49
CEO, San Diego Gas & Electric: Jessie J. Knight Jr., age 59
President and COO, San Diego Gas & Electric: Michael R. (Mike) Niggli, age 60
President and CEO, Sempra LNG: Darcel L. Hulse, age 57
Auditors: Deloitte & Touche LLP

LOCATIONS

HQ: Sempra Energy
101 Ash St., San Diego, CA 92101
Phone: 619-696-2000   **Fax:** 619-696-2374
Web: www.sempra.com

2009 Sales

	$ mil.	% of total
US	7,476	92
Latin America	630	8
Total	**8,106**	**100**

PRODUCTS/OPERATIONS

2009 Sales

	$ mil.	% of total
Sempra Utilities		
Natural gas	3,801	47
Electric	2,419	30
Sempra Global & parent	1,886	23
Total	**8,106**	**100**

Selected Subsidiaries

Sempra Energy Utilities
San Diego Gas & Electric (SDG&E, regulated gas and electric utility)
Southern California Gas Company (SoCalGas, regulated gas utility)
Sempra Global (formerly Sempra Energy Global Enterprises)
RBS Sempra Commodities (50%; wholesale and retail energy trading and marketing, metals trading; Sempra Energy Trading)
Sempra Generation (formerly Sempra Energy Resources, independent power production)
Sempra LNG (formerly Sempra Energy LNG, acquisition and development of liquefied natural gas facilities)
Sempra Pipelines & Storage (formerly Sempra Energy International, power generation and distribution and gas distribution, transportation, and compression)
Other operations
Sempra Energy Financial (affordable housing properties and alternative fuel projects)

COMPETITORS

AEP
AES
AT&T
Avista
Calpine
CenterPoint Energy
CMS Energy
Constellation Energy Group
Dominion Resources
Duke Energy
Edison International
El Paso Corporation
Endesa S.A.
Entergy
IBERDROLA
Los Angeles Water and Power
Mirant
NV Energy
PacifiCorp
PG&E Corporation
PSEG Global
Public Service Enterprise Group
RRI Energy
Sacramento Municipal Utility
Southwest Gas
Tenaska
Williams Companies

HISTORICAL FINANCIALS

Company Type: Public

Income Statement				FYE: December 31
	REVENUE ($ mil.)	NET INCOME ($ mil.)	NET PROFIT MARGIN	EMPLOYEES
12/09	8,106	1,122	13.8%	13,839
12/08	10,758	1,113	10.3%	13,673
12/07	11,438	1,099	9.6%	14,314
12/06	11,761	1,406	12.0%	14,061
12/05	11,737	920	7.8%	13,420
Annual Growth	**(8.8%)**	**5.1%**	**—**	**0.8%**

Debt ratio: 82.8% | No. of shares (mil.): 248
Return on equity: 13.2% | Dividends
Cash ($ mil.): 110 | Yield: 2.8%
Current ratio: 0.59 | Payout: 34.5%
Long-term debt ($ mil.): 7,460 | Market value ($ mil.): 13,875

Stock History NYSE: SRE

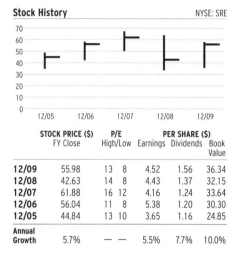

	STOCK PRICE ($) FY Close	P/E High/Low		PER SHARE ($) Earnings	Dividends	Book Value
12/09	55.98	13	8	4.52	1.56	36.34
12/08	42.63	14	8	4.43	1.37	32.15
12/07	61.88	16	12	4.16	1.24	33.64
12/06	56.04	11	8	5.38	1.20	30.30
12/05	44.84	13	10	3.65	1.16	24.85
Annual Growth	**5.7%**	—	—	**5.5%**	**7.7%**	**10.0%**

Seneca Foods

Seneca Foods has a can-do attitude. The company primarily cans and freezes vegetables, but it also makes apple chips, maraschino cherries, and candied fruits used in baked goods. A top US producer of canned vegetables, its brands include Aunt Nellie's, Blue Boy, Diamond, Libby's, Seneca, and Stokely. About 19% of the company's sales come from processing Green Giant vegetables for General Mills. Seneca sells private-label and name-brand veggies and fruit to food retailers, mass merchandisers, and club and dollar stores, as well as foodservice providers and other food manufacturers. It also exports to customers in 75 countries. The company operates 20 processing plants located near growing areas throughout the US.

Although Seneca produces a supermarket-full of its own well-known national brands, at 9% of 2010 sales, these are dwarfed by the company's private-label sales, which accounted for 51% of its sales for 2010. Sales to foodservice customers rang up at 21%; the remaining 19% was generated by sales to General Mills. Overall, the company's total sales remained essentially flat for fiscal 2009 and 2010. Its 2010 net sales decreased only $0.6 million when compared to 2009. Seneca attributed the decrease to reduced sales to the U.S. Department of Agriculture (USDA), to which Seneca sells its foods for school lunch and other governmental programs.

During Seneca's 61 years of operations, it has made more than 50 strategic acquisitions. Recent acquisitions include the 2010 addition to its private-label operations of Unilink, a maker of packaged frozen fruits and vegetables for the private-label and foodservice markets. The deal also included Unilink's cold-storage facilities, Lebanon Valley Cold Storage. Both operations are located in Pennsylvania.

Chairman Arthur Wolcott and president and CEO Kraig Kayser and their families control a majority stake of the company.

HISTORY

Arthur Wolcott and his father purchased the Dundee Grape Juice Co. in 1949. The company went public in the 1950s but has long been notorious for behaving more like a tight-lipped private firm. It merged in 1971 with a textile and paint business run by one of its investors, Julius Kayser. Two years later the company, then Seneca Grape Juice Corp., bought food company S.S. Pierce, including its mushroom canning business; it took that name in 1977. The company acquired Nestlé's Libby vegetable business in 1982 and was renamed Seneca Foods in 1986.

Kraig Kayser, Julius' son, joined the company in 1991 and was named CEO in 1993. That year Seneca Foods divested itself of all nonfood operations except for its tiny charter airline. In 1995 it purchased six vegetable processing plants from Grand Metropolitan's Pillsbury unit and entered into a 20-year agreement to supply its Green Giant line of canned and frozen vegetables.

In 1997 the company acquired Grand Met's Aunt Nellie's Farm Kitchen unit and the private-label canned vegetable business of Curtice-Burns. After three years of losses, Seneca Foods sold most of its juice operations (TreeSweet and Awake brands and the Seneca brand license) to Northland Cranberries for about $30 million in 1998.

The firm sold its nonbranded specialty fruit concentrate business and Seneca applesauce license to Tree Top Inc. in 1999 for about $29 million. Seneca Foods also bought a private-label canned vegetable business in the Midwest from Pro-Fac Cooperative that year for about $48 million.

The new private-label business, combined with better prices and Y2K-induced hoarding, helped boost Seneca's sales in 2000. That year the company obtained the rights to sell the Libby brand of products internationally.

Sales in 2001 were weaker, despite its introduction of raspberry-flavored pickled beets. The company moved its headquarters to Marion, New York, that year.

In 2003 Seneca purchased Chiquita Processed Foods (CPF), the vegetable canning subsidiary of Chiquita Brands International, for $110 million in cash, stock, and debt assumption. The sale involved 12 US processing plants in the upper Midwest and West. Later that year Seneca sold off four of the former Chiquita canning plants to Lakeside Foods.

Seneca Foods' 20-year alliance agreement with General Mills (begun in 1995) prompted it to shift its focus to vegetable production. (The company divested its juice, applesauce, and flavorings businesses.) However, it still continues to expand its fruit product lines. In 2006 Seneca acquired Signature Fruit, a producer of shelf-stable fruit products for $20 million in cash and $25 million in stock.

EXECUTIVES

Chairman: Arthur S. (Art) Wolcott, age 84, $711,640 total compensation
President, CEO, and Director: Kraig H. Kayser, age 49, $716,096 total compensation
EVP and COO: Paul L. Palmby, age 48, $491,940 total compensation
SVP, CFO, and Treasurer: Roland E. Breunig, age 58, $305,419 total compensation
SVP Sales: Dean E. Erstad, age 47, $309,936 total compensation

CIO: Carl A. Cichetti, age 52
Chief Administrative Officer: Cynthia L. Fohrd, age 47
General Counsel: John D. Exner, age 48
VP Food Service: Stephen J. Ott
VP Customer Service: Richard L. Waldorf
VP Branded Sales: James E. Blair
VP Procurement: Vincent J. Lammers
VP Accounting: Craig W. Knapp
VP, Secretary, and Controller: Jeffrey L. Van Riper, age 53
VP Marketing: Bruce S. Wolcott
VP International: Barbara J. deJong
VP Human Resources: Jim Uttech
VP Technical Services and Development: Matt J. Henschler
VP Transportation: Gene W. Schaetten
President, Seneca Flight Operations: Richard Leppert
Auditors: BDO Seidman, LLP

LOCATIONS

HQ: Seneca Foods Corporation
3736 S. Main St., Marion, NY 14505
Phone: 315-926-8100 **Fax:** 315-926-8300
Web: www.senecafoods.com

2010 Sales

	$ mil.	% of total
US	1,178.5	92
Other	101.6	8
Total	**1,280.1**	**100**

PRODUCTS/OPERATIONS

2010 Sales

	$ mil.	% of total
Canned vegetables	750.8	59
Green Giant vegetables	239.6	19
Fruit	200.4	15
Frozen vegetables	48.3	4
Snack	21.3	2
Other	19.7	1
Total	**1,280.1**	**100**

Selected Brands and Products

Aunt Nellie's Farm Kitchen (glass-packed vegetables, relishes, and bean salads)
Blue Boy (canned vegetables)
Diamond A (canned vegetables)
Festal (canned vegetables)
Green Giant (licensed from General Mills, canned and frozen vegetables)
Le Suer (licensed from General Mills, canned vegetables)
Libby's (canned fruits and canned and frozen vegetables)
Read (canned potato and bean salads)
Seneca (apple and sweet potato snack chips)
Stokely's (canned vegetables)

COMPETITORS

Allens
Birds Eye
Del Monte Foods
Dole Food
Faribault Foods
Frito-Lay
Goya
Hain Celestial
Hanover Foods
Heinz
Lakeside Foods
NORPAC
Pictsweet

HISTORICAL FINANCIALS

Company Type: Public

Income Statement

FYE: March 31

	REVENUE ($ mil.)	NET INCOME ($ mil.)	NET PROFIT MARGIN	EMPLOYEES
3/10	1,280	48	3.8%	3,300
3/09	1,281	19	1.5%	3,200
3/08	1,081	8	0.7%	3,201
3/07	1,025	32	3.1%	3,358
3/06	884	22	2.5%	2,906
Annual Growth	**9.7%**	**21.8%**	**—**	**3.2%**

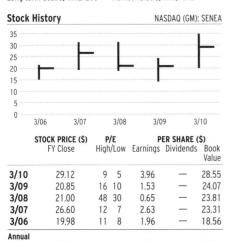

Stock History   NASDAQ (GM): SENEA

	STOCK PRICE ($) FY Close	P/E High/Low		PER SHARE ($) Earnings	Dividends	Book Value
3/10	29.12	9	5	3.96	—	28.55
3/09	20.85	16	10	1.53	—	24.07
3/08	21.00	48	30	0.65	—	23.81
3/07	26.60	12	7	2.63	—	23.31
3/06	19.98	11	8	1.96	—	18.56
Annual Growth	9.9%	—	—	19.2%	—	11.4%

Service Corporation

Service Corporation International (SCI) is to death what H&R Block is to taxes. SCI, the largest funeral and cemetery services company in North America, operates more than 1,260 funeral homes and about 370 cemeteries in more than 43 US states, eight Canadian provinces, the District of Columbia, Puerto Rico, and Germany. The company's primary services include embalming, burial, and cremation. As part of its business, SCI also sells traditional funeral necessities, including prearranged funeral services, caskets, burial vaults, cremation receptacles, flowers, and burial garments.

In 2010 SCI acquired Keystone North America. As North America's fifth-largest provider of death care products and services, Keystone operates about 200 funeral homes and 15 cemeteries in some 30 US states, as well as in Ontario, Canada.

Acquisitions have fueled SCI's growth and enabled the company to operate clusters of funeral homes in the same geographic regions, which allows them to share personnel, vehicles, and preparation services, thereby lowering their operating costs. SCI maintains the local identity of each home, allowing it to handle services for different religious and ethnic groups.

In 2008 the firm made an $881 million bid to acquire rival Stewart Enterprises. Stewart rejected SCI's initial offer as inadequate. Not one to give up easily, SCI sweetened the offer but eventually gave up and withdrew its bid.

During the past few years, SCI has been reducing its international holdings to focus on its core business: North American funeral service locations and cemeteries. To that end, it has sold its minority interest in its UK operation and its funeral homes in Argentina, Chile, Singapore, and Uruguay. SCI also is looking to sell about a dozen funeral homes in Germany, which represents its only remaining international holding.

As the popularity of lower-cost cremation has increased to about 41% of SCI's business (up from about a third 10 years ago), the company has focused on adding products and services, including online memorials and themed ceremonies, in an attempt to boost revenue. Other parties cutting into SCI's profits include competition from casket wholesalers and online retailers.

Call it unburied treasure: SCI has more than $6 billion worth of backlogged unfulfilled funeral contracts.

HISTORY

When Robert Waltrip was just 20, in the early 1950s, he inherited Houston's Heights Funeral Home, which his father and aunt had founded in 1926. Waltrip acquired several other funeral homes, modeling his operations on other popular service chains, such as Holiday Inn and McDonald's. In 1962 he incorporated Service Corporation International (SCI) and began expanding across the country.

SCI went public in 1969, and by 1975 it was the largest provider of funeral services in the US. However, that year the FTC accused the company of overcharging customers for flowers, cremation, and other services. SCI was ordered to refund overcharges it had made to cremation customers (it had charged them for caskets), and the FTC issued industry guidelines to prevent deceptive practices.

Two years later SCI began offering advance sales of funeral services so that clients could avoid the effects of inflation by reserving future services and caskets at current prices. While it was barred from using the prepaid funds until funerals were performed, some states allowed the use of investment profits from those funds.

The company moved into flower shops in 1982, and two years later SCI bought Amedco, a top casket maker and a major supplier of embalming fluid, burial clothing, and mortuary furniture. (Amedco was later sold.)

SCI spun off 71 rural funeral homes as Equity Corporation International (ECI) in 1991 (it sold its remaining 40% stake in 1996). The company continued its rapid pace of acquisitions, buying 342 homes and 57 cemeteries from 1991 to 1993. It made its first acquisition outside North America in 1993 with the purchase of Pine Grove Funeral Group, the largest funeral and cremations provider in Australia. SCI entered the European market by acquiring Great Southern Group and Plantsbrook of the UK in 1994, as well as the funeral operations of Lyonnaise des Eaux of France a year later.

In 1997 and 1998 it swallowed up 602 funeral homes, 98 cemeteries, and 37 crematoria. SCI bought American Annuity Group's prearranged funeral services unit in 1998. In 1999 it bought back all of Equity Corporation International (about 440 US funeral homes and cemeteries).

With SCI's earnings slumping — which the company attributed in part to declining mortality rates — president and COO William Heiligbrodt resigned in 1999. Also in 1999 SCI deep-sixed about 2,000 jobs and consolidated its funeral home and cemetery groups in the US down to 87 (from 200).

To help pay down its debt, SCI sold its French insurance subsidiary and its Northern Ireland funeral operations in 2000 and sold more than 500 funeral locations and cemeteries the next year.

A class-action lawsuit filed in December 2001 claimed the company broke open burial vaults and dumped the contents, crushed vaults to make room for others, and mixed body parts from different individuals; the company denied the charges. In May 2003 SCI agreed to pay penalties of approximately $10 million stemming from the lawsuit and faced felony charges filed against the company and two of its Florida cemetery executives. SCI agreed in December 2003 to pay $100 million to settle the class-action lawsuit and individual lawsuits pending regarding its Florida cemetery operations.

In early 2004 SCI sold its French funeral operation, OGF Group, to Vestar Capital Partners in a management buyout transaction. Vestar and SCI reinvested in the operation and took about a 25% ownership.

In November 2006 SCI acquired its chief rival, Alderwoods Group, for about $856 million and assumed some $374 million in debt. To gain regulatory approval for the transaction, SCI agreed to sell some 40 funeral homes and 15 cemeteries in areas where the combined company's market share would have been too large.

SCI's aggressive acquisition program led to daunting debt, causing the firm to sell off certain assets in 2007. It sold its Mayflower National Life Insurance Company, acquired alongside Alderwoods, to Assurant for more than $67 million. SCI also sold its stake in disaster-recovery company Kenyon International Emergency Services that year. It ended 2007 by selling 46 cemeteries and 30 funeral homes to competitor StoneMor Partners for $71 million.

EXECUTIVES

Chairman: Robert L. (Bob) Waltrip, age 79, $3,988,818 total compensation
President, CEO, and Board Member: Thomas L. Ryan, age 44, $4,227,500 total compensation
EVP and COO: Michael R. (Mike) Webb, age 51, $2,567,094 total compensation
SVP, CFO, and Treasurer: Eric D. Tanzberger, age 41, $1,215,787 total compensation
SVP and Chief Marketing Officer: Philip C. (Phil) Jacobs, age 55
SVP Operations: Sumner J. Waring III, age 41, $1,226,367 total compensation
SVP Middle Market Operations: Stephen M. Mack, age 58
SVP Sales: J. Daniel Garrison, age 58
SVP Operation Services: Elisabeth G. Nash, age 48
SVP, General Counsel, and Secretary: Gregory T. Sangalis, age 54
VP Information Technology: John Del Mixon II
VP and Controller: Tammy R. Moore, age 43
VP Business Development: John Faulk
VP Main Street Market Operations: Steve Tidwell
VP Human Resources: Jane D. Jones, age 54
VP Litigation and Risk Management: Albert R. Lohse, age 49
Managing Director Corporate Communications: Lisa Marshall
Director Investor Relations: Debbie Young
Auditors: PricewaterhouseCoopers LLP

LOCATIONS

HQ: Service Corporation International
  1929 Allen Pkwy., Houston, TX 77019
Phone: 713-522-5141   **Fax:** 713-525-5586
Web: www.sci-corp.com

2009 Sales

	$ mil.	% of total
US	1,869.0	91
Canada	177.7	9
Germany	6.8	—
Total	**2,053.5**	**100**

PRODUCTS/OPERATIONS

2009 Sales

	$ mil.	% of total
Funeral	1,391.8	67
Cemetery	661.7	33
Total	**2,053.5**	**100**

Selected Products

Burial garments
Burial vaults
Caskets
Coffins
Cremation receptacles
Flowers
Lawn crypts
Mausoleum spaces
Stone and bronze memorials

Selected Services

Bereavement travel
Cremation
Development loans
Floral arrangements
Grief counseling
Grounds management and maintenance
Interment
Perpetual care
Prearranged funeral services
Transportation

COMPETITORS

Alcor
Arbor Memorial Services
Aurora Casket
Batesville Casket
Carriage Services, Inc.
Eternal Reefs
Matthews International
Rock of Ages
Security National Financial
Stewart Enterprises
StoneMor
Wilbert
York Group

HISTORICAL FINANCIALS

Company Type: Public

Income Statement

FYE: December 31

	REVENUE ($ mil.)	NET INCOME ($ mil.)	NET PROFIT MARGIN	EMPLOYEES
12/09	2,054	123	6.0%	20,176
12/08	2,156	97	4.5%	20,771
12/07	2,285	248	10.8%	20,591
12/06	1,747	57	3.2%	22,623
12/05	1,716	61	3.5%	16,722
Annual Growth	**4.6%**	**19.3%**	**—**	**4.8%**

2009 Year-End Financials

Debt ratio: 124.1%
Return on equity: 8.9%
Cash ($ mil.): 180
Current ratio: 1.03
Long-term debt ($ mil.): 1,841

No. of shares (mil.): 247
Dividends
  Yield: 2.0%
  Payout: 32.7%
Market value ($ mil.): 2,021

Stock History

NYSE: SCI

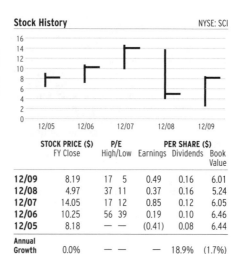

	STOCK PRICE ($) FY Close	P/E High/Low		PER SHARE ($) Earnings	Dividends	Book Value
12/09	8.19	17	5	0.49	0.16	6.01
12/08	4.97	37	11	0.37	0.16	5.24
12/07	14.05	17	12	0.85	0.12	6.05
12/06	10.25	56	39	0.19	0.10	6.46
12/05	8.18	—	—	(0.41)	0.08	6.44
Annual Growth	**0.0%**	**—**	**—**	**—**	**18.9%**	**(1.7%)**

SFN Group

This group seeks to circumvent your personnel problems. SFN Group (formerly Spherion) provides traditional temporary staffing along with services such as professional and executive recruitment and employee consulting and assessment. Through several subsidiaries and specialized staffing units, SFN Group offers staffing and technology services in such areas as project management, quality assurance, and data center and network operations. It operates through a network of some 600 locations in the US and Canada, serving more than 8,000 clients ranging from small businesses to *FORTUNE* 500 companies. Known as Spherion for about 10 years, the company changed its name to SFN Group in early 2010.

The company changed its name from Spherion to SFN Group in February 2010 in order to better reflect one single unified company which operates a family of specialized businesses, including Technisource, Tatum, Mergis, Todays Office Professionals, SourceRight Solutions, and Spherion Staffing Services. The company acquired Tatum a few months earlier, and the deal gave it greater expertise for providing CFO staffing services. Purchasing Tatum also expanded its Professional Services segment, which places professionals with skill sets in IT, finance, legal, engineering, human resources, administrative, and sales and marketing. (IT professionals accounted for 66% of this segment in 2009.) Its Staffing Services segment, represented primarily by Spherion Staffing Services and accounting for 60% of the company's total revenue in 2009, places workers with administrative, clerical, and light industrial skill sets.

In addition to acquisitions, the company has been growing by expanding its product portfolio. Through its Mergis Group division, the company formed a Troubled Assets Relief Program and government bailout team in early 2009 to supply recruiting and staffing for the federal government's efforts to stimulate the weak US economy. The team provides services including executive recruitment, project management, staffing in accounting and finance, information

technology, and other professional-office management roles.

Over the years, SFN Group has discontinued its staffing operations in Australia, the Netherlands, and the UK in order to focus on its business in North America. The company also cut some operations in the US, including its call center outsourcing division and court reporting business. In mid-2007 it sold its HR consulting business to IMPACT Group, a career-transition services firm. As demand for its services declined as a result of the recession, SFN Group has focused on adjusting its cost structure; it reduced its expenses by $122.9 million in 2009 when compared to the same period the year before.

HISTORY

LeRoy Dettman founded City Car Unloaders in 1946 to provide railroad car workers in Chicago. As it grew, the company added industrial and clerical workers; it moved into health care staffing in 1966. H&R Block acquired the company (then named Personnel Pool) in 1978, bought personnel placement firm Interim Systems in 1991, and combined the two under the Interim name. Also that year Raymond Marcy became CEO of the company. In 1994 Interim went public.

Interim used the proceeds of its IPO to fund more acquisitions, particularly in the higher-margin professional staffing fields such as medicine and law. In 1995 it began targeting information technology by acquiring Computer Power Group and a year later, computer staffing company Brandon Systems. Also in 1996 the company acquired Netherlands-based staffing companies Allround and Interplan.

In a move to expand internationally, Interim acquired London-based Michael Page Group for about $574 million in 1997. Also that year Interim bought AimExecutive Holdings, adding outplacement services to its business. In 1998 the company acquired London-based staffing company Crone Corkill Group. The following year it bought rival Norrell in a $550 million deal, adding nearly 400 offices to its operations.

To broaden its e-business services, Interim bought Applied Internet Consultancy in 2000 and soon changed its name to Spherion. It also expanded its online recruiting services with its launch of CareerZone.com, a website for job seekers, and its acquisition of an 80% stake in JobOptions.com.

In 2001 Spherion spun off Michael Page as a public company. Later that year the company announced a broad reorganization plan, including office closures, job cuts, and the divestiture of noncore or underperforming units. In 2002 Spherion sold consulting businesses in the UK and the Netherlands. In 2003 the company reorganized its operations into two divisions, Staffing Services and Professional Services. Spherion sold its noncore businesses in Australia, the Netherlands, and the UK in 2004.

In 2007 the company made some big moves to expand; it bought administrative, legal, and financial staffing firm Todays Staffing, Resulté Universal, and Technisource, which added to its IT consulting operations. Years later it obtained Tatum, an executive search firm targeting CFOs.

In early 2010 the company changed its name again, to SFN Group.

EXECUTIVES

Chairman: James J. Forese, age 74
President, CEO, and Director: Roy G. Krause, age 63,
$1,495,927 total compensation
EVP and COO: William J. (Bill) Grubbs, age 52,
$939,469 total compensation
EVP and CFO: Mark W. Smith, age 47,
$865,222 total compensation
SVP and Chief Human Resources Officer:
John D. Heins, age 50, $536,970 total compensation
VP and CIO: Richard Harris, age 50
VP Legal and Corporate Secretary: Thad Florence
VP Finance: Teri Miller
Director Public Relations and Corporate Marketing:
Lisa McCarthy
Investor Contact: Randy Atkinson
President, SourceRight Solutions: Rebecca Callahan
President, Spherion Staffing Services: Loretta A. Penn,
age 60, $298,735 total compensation
Auditors: Deloitte & Touche LLP

LOCATIONS

HQ: SFN Group, Inc.
2050 Spectrum Blvd., Fort Lauderdale, FL 33309
Phone: 954-308-7600   **Fax:** 954-308-7666
Web: www.sfngroup.com

PRODUCTS/OPERATIONS

2009 Sales

	$ mil.	% of total
Staffing Services	1,029.2	60
Professional Services	681.7	40
Total	**1,710.9**	**100**

Selected Staffing Areas

Staffing services
  Administrative
  Clerical
  Light industrial
Professional services
  Administrative
  Engineering
  Finance and accounting
  Human resources
  Information technology
  Legal
  Sales and marketing

COMPETITORS

Accenture
Adecco
ADP
Allegis Group
Butler America
COMFORCE
Diversified Search
Egon Zehnder
Express Employment
Heidrick & Struggles
HP Enterprise Services
Hudson Highland Group
IBM Global Services
Keane
Kelly Services
Kforce
Korn/Ferry
Manpower
Randstad Holding
Robert Half
Spencer Stuart
TAC Worldwide
Volt Information
WJM Associates

HISTORICAL FINANCIALS

Company Type: Public

Income Statement

FYE: Last Friday in December

	REVENUE ($ mil.)	NET INCOME ($ mil.)	NET PROFIT MARGIN	EMPLOYEES
12/09	1,711	(6)	—	161,000
12/08	2,189	(119)	—	215,000
12/07	2,017	25	1.3%	258,000
12/06	1,933	55	2.8%	273,000
12/05	1,972	12	0.6%	302,000
Annual Growth	**(3.5%)**	**—**	**—**	**(14.6%)**

2009 Year-End Financials

Debt ratio: 0.4%
Return on equity: —
Cash ($ mil.): 8
Current ratio: 1.81
Long-term debt ($ mil.): 1

No. of shares (mil.): 53
Dividends
  Yield: —
  Payout: —
Market value ($ mil.): 296

Stock History

NYSE: SFN

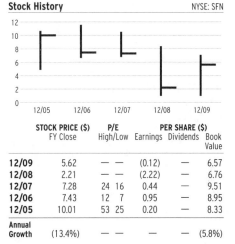

	STOCK PRICE ($) FY Close	P/E High/Low		PER SHARE ($) Earnings	Dividends	Book Value
12/09	5.62	—	—	(0.12)	—	6.57
12/08	2.21	—	—	(2.22)	—	6.76
12/07	7.28	24	16	0.44	—	9.51
12/06	7.43	12	7	0.95	—	8.95
12/05	10.01	53	25	0.20	—	8.33
Annual Growth	**(13.4%)**	**—**	**—**	**—**	**—**	**(5.8%)**

The Shaw Group

The Shaw Group is one of the largest engineering and construction contractors for the power generation market as well as a top environmental services firm. Shaw designs, engineers, builds, and maintains fossil fuel and nuclear power plants; provides consulting services to the chemical industry; performs environmental rehabilitation services; manages US government facilities; and manufactures pipe fittings. The group's largest segments are its power unit and remediation/infrastructure arm Shaw Environmental & Infrastructure. Clients include multinational oil companies, industrial corporations and manufacturers, utilities, and government agencies.

Shaw claims to have worked on 95% of the nuclear power facilities in the US. With rising oil prices and a growing focus on alternative energy sources, interest in nuclear energy has seen a serious boost. Shaw has scaled up its operations to meet demand by Duke Energy and other companies that may be restarting their nuclear construction programs. The company also owns a 20% stake in nuclear reactor designer Westinghouse Electric.

On the other hand, the company has scaled back in the noncore areas of transmission and distribution in order to focus on engineering and construction. In 2008 it sold powerline services business Energy Delivery Services to Pike Electric for some $24 million.

The group serves clients across the Americas, Middle East, Europe, and Pacific Rim through more than 150 offices.

HISTORY

James Bernhard formed National Fabricators in 1986. After visiting the Benjamin F. Shaw Company's plant in South Carolina to bid on its inventory, he established The Shaw Group in 1987 and bought the 100-year-old maker of power-station piping systems. From 1988 to 1990 Shaw expanded its business by leasing three plants in Louisiana and Texas. The company bought a plant in 1992.

Shaw formed a joint venture with Venezuela-based Formiconi in 1993 to open a plant there. The company began making pipes for chemicals and oil refining with its purchase of Sunland Fabricators. Shaw also went public that year.

In 1994 Shaw acquired Fronek Company (pipe engineering and design services), bought out its Venezuelan partner, and watched its domestic fiscal earnings bend south when its South Carolina plant had to repair a botched fabrication job.

Shaw expanded plant capacity and added more induction bending machines to its inventory in 1996 and 1997. It purchased NAPTech (industrial piping systems) in 1997. Company spending continued with the 1998 acquisitions of Lancas (construction, Venezuela), Cojafex BV (induction bending equipment, the Netherlands), and Bagwell Brothers (offshore platforms, heliports, and vessels for the petroleum industry). The Cojafex buy proved to be one of the company's best acquisitions, because its pipe-bending machines eliminated much of the cost of welding. Also in 1998 Shaw sold its NAPTech Pressure Systems (pressure vessels) subsidiary and others that provided welding supplies, boiler steam leak-detection devices, and corrosion-resistant pipe systems.

In 1999 Shaw won a five-year contract to supply 90% of the piping for GE's gas turbines for power plants. In 2000 Shaw signed a letter of intent with a US power developer to build a $380 million power plant in central Texas. It also created EntergyShaw, a joint venture with Entergy Corporation, to build cookie-cutter power plants in North America and Europe in hopes of driving down costs and speeding construction time. That year the company purchased Stone & Webster, Inc., for about $38 million and around 2.5 million shares of stock.

In 2002 Shaw acquired the assets of The IT Group (which was in bankruptcy) for about $105 million in cash and up to $95 million in assumed debt and made the environmental services firm a subsidiary, Shaw Environmental & Infrastructure (Shaw E&I). It also entered into an agreement to buy industrial construction group Turner Industries, but quickly terminated discussions with its hometown rival.

Shaw divested its hanger engineering and pipe support businesses in 2004 and its Roche consulting operations the following year. In 2006 it acquired a 20% stake in nuclear reactor designer Westinghouse Electric. It also established investment and transaction arm Shaw Capital to handle the group's growth and assets.

EXECUTIVES

Chairman, President, and CEO: James M. Bernhard Jr.,
age 55
EVP and CFO: Brian K. Ferraioli, age 54
EVP, General Counsel, and Corporate Secretary:
John Donofrio, age 48
EVP and COO: Gary P. Graphia, age 47
EVP: Robert L. (Bob) Belk, age 60
**SVP Environmental & Infrastructure Group, Northeast
Central Region and National Director Transportation:**
Vahid Ownjazayeri
SVP Procurement, Power Group: Eli Smith
SVP and Chief Accounting Officer: Michael J. Kershaw,
age 60
VP Investor Relations: Chris D. Sammons
President, Construction: R. Monty Glover, age 56
**President, Environmental and Infrastructure (E & I)
Group:** George P. Bevan, age 62
**President, Nuclear Division, Fossil and Nuclear
Segment:** David P. (Dave) Barry, age 58
President, Energy and Chemicals:
Louis J. (Lou) Pucher, age 66
President, Power Group: Frederick W. (Fred) Buckman,
age 63
President, Maintenance: D. Ron McCall, age 61
President, Fossil and Renewables: Ron Barnes
President, Fabrication and Manufacturing:
David L. Chapman Sr., age 64
Managing Director, Shaw Group UK Holdings:
Ronald W. (Ron) Oakley, age 59
Director, Corporate Communications: Gentry Brann
Auditors: KPMG LLP

LOCATIONS

HQ: The Shaw Group Inc.
4171 Essen Ln., Baton Rouge, LA 70809
Phone: 225-932-2500   **Fax:** 225-987-3328
Web: www.shawgrp.com

2009 Sales

	$ mil.	% of total
US	5,669.7	78
Asia/Pacific Rim	978.4	13
Middle East	386.3	5
Europe	127.9	2
South America & Mexico	51.8	1
Canada	37.7	1
Other regions	27.9	—
Total	**7,279.7**	**100**

PRODUCTS/OPERATIONS

2009 Sales by Segment

	$ mil.	% of total
Fossil, Renewables & Nuclear	2,581.2	35
Environmental & Infrastructure	1,835.5	25
Energy & Chemicals	1,371.5	19
Maintenance	864.1	12
Fabrication & Manufacturing	623.4	9
Corporate	4.0	—
Total	**7,279.7**	**100**

2009 Sales by Industry

	$ mil.	% of total
Power Generation	3,168.5	44
Chemicals	2,120.0	29
Environmental & Infrastructure	1,835.5	25
Other	155.7	2
Total	**7,279.7**	**100**

Selected Services

Biomass conversion
Computer modeling
Decommissioning
Decontamination
Engineering
Feasibility studies
New plant design/build
Operator training
Permitting support
Pipe fabrication
Plant maintenance
Plant rehabilitation, upgrading, and expansion
Procurement
Scaffolding
Site appraisal

COMPETITORS

Austin Industries	Parsons Corporation
Bechtel	Senior plc
Black & Veatch	Siemens Water
CH2M HILL	Technologies
Fluor	Tetra Tech
Foster Wheeler	Turner Industries
Jacobs Engineering	URS
KBR	Willbros
McJunkin Red Man	

HISTORICAL FINANCIALS

Company Type: Public

Income Statement

FYE: August 31

	REVENUE ($ mil.)	NET INCOME ($ mil.)	NET PROFIT MARGIN	EMPLOYEES
8/09	7,280	15	0.2%	28,000
8/08	6,998	141	2.0%	26,000
8/07	5,724	(19)	—	27,000
8/06	4,776	51	1.1%	22,000
8/05	3,266	16	0.5%	1,900
Annual Growth	**22.2%**	**(2.2%)**	**—**	**95.9%**

2009 Year-End Financials

Debt ratio: 0.5%
Return on equity: 1.0%
Cash ($ mil.): 1,029
Current ratio: 1.15
Long-term debt ($ mil.): 8
No. of shares (mil.): 84
Dividends
  Yield: —
  Payout: —
Market value ($ mil.): 2,477

Stock History

NYSE: SHAW

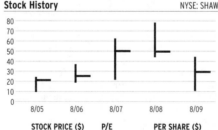

	STOCK PRICE ($) FY Close	P/E High/Low		PER SHARE ($) Earnings	Dividends	Book Value
8/09	29.33	241	64	0.18	—	16.85
8/08	49.54	46	27	1.67	—	17.64
8/07	50.05	—	—	(0.24)	—	14.64
8/06	25.16	57	31	0.63	—	14.72
8/05	21.10	101	45	0.23	—	13.55
Annual Growth	**8.6%**	**—**	**—**	**(5.9%)**	**—**	**5.6%**

Sherwin-Williams

No matter how you coat it, Sherwin-Williams is the largest paint manufacturer in the US and #2 worldwide, after Akzo Nobel. Sherwin-Williams' products include a variety of paints, finishes, coatings, applicators, and varnishes sold under the names Dutch Boy, Krylon, Martin-Senour, Red Devil, Sherwin-Williams, Thompson's WaterSeal, and Minwax. The company operates more than 3,350 paint stores throughout North America. It sells automotive finishing and refinishing products through wholesale branches throughout the Americas, as well as in Asia and Europe. Other distribution outlets (and competitors) include mass merchandisers, home centers, and independent retailers.

Sherwin-Williams continually adds to its retail operations, which account for 60% of sales. The company typically opens between 50 and 100 new stores every year, primarily in the US but also in Canada and Puerto Rico. In 2009, though it opened 53 stores, it shut down 45, citing the global economic downturn.

In addition to that type of internal, organic growth, Sherwin-Williams has also been active in the M&A market. The company moved into India in 2007 with the acquisition of Nitco Paints and expanded its reach at home as well with the acquisition of regional paint makers M.A. Bruder and Columbia Paint & Coatings. Since then, it has acquired a powder coatings company in the US, the liquid coatings subsidiaries of Singapore-based Inchem Holdings, and protective coatings companies in Poland and Portugal.

Expanding its Global Chemical Coatings Division even further, in 2010 Sherwin-Williams bought Arch Chemicals' Sayerlack, a leading Italian wood care coating company, and agreed to acquire Becker Acroma Industrial Wood Coatings, a Swedish manufacturer of industrial wood coatings.

Also in 2010, the company acquired all the shares of AlSher Titania (a joint venture with Altair Nanotechnologies) it did not already own, giving it a 100% stake in the technology company. AlSher Titania is developing the Altairnano Hydrochloride Process, a promising titanium dioxide technology that Sherwin-Williams plans to develop towards commercialization.

HISTORY

In 1870 Henry Sherwin bought out paint materials distributor Truman Dunham and joined Edward Williams and A. T. Osborn to form Sherwin, Williams & Company in Cleveland. The business began making paints in 1871 and became the industry leader after improving the paint-grinding mill in the mid-1870s, patenting a reclosable can in 1877, and improving liquid paint in 1880.

In 1874 Sherwin-Williams introduced a special paint for carriages, beginning the concept of specific-purpose paint. (By 1900 the company had paints for floors, roofs, barns, metal bridges, railroad cars, and automobiles.) Sherwin-Williams incorporated in 1884 and opened a dealership in Massachusetts in 1891 that was the forerunner of its company-run retail stores. The company obtained its "Cover the Earth" trademark in 1895.

Before the Depression, Sherwin-Williams bought a number of smaller paint makers: Detroit White Lead (1910), Martin-Senour (1917), Acme Quality Paints (1920), and The Lowe

Brothers (1929). Responding to wartime restrictions, the company developed a fast-drying and water-reducible paint, called Kem-Tone, and the forerunner of the paint roller, the Roller-Koater.

Sales doubled during the 1960s as the company made acquisitions, including Sprayon (aerosol paint, 1966), but rising expenses kept earnings flat. In 1972 the company expanded its stores to include carpeting, draperies, and other decorating items. But long-term debt ballooned from $80 million in 1974 to $196 million by 1977, when the company lost $8.2 million and suspended dividends for the first time since 1885.

John Breen became CEO in 1979, reinstated the dividend, purged over half of the top management positions, and closed inefficient plants. He also focused stores on paint and wallpaper merchandise and purchased Dutch Boy (1980).

In 1990 Sherwin-Williams began selling Dutch Boy in Sears stores and Kem-Tone in Wal-Marts. Acquisitions that year included Borden's Krylon and Illinois Bronze aerosol operations and DeSoto's architectural coatings segment, which made private-label paints for Sears and Home Depot. In 1991 Sherwin-Williams bought two coatings business units from Cook Paint and Varnish and the Cuprinol brand of coatings.

Sherwin-Williams purchased paint manufacturer Pratt & Lambert in 1996. That year it introduced several new products, including Low Temp 35, a paint for low temperatures; Healthspec, a low-odor paint; and Ralph Lauren designer paints. Prep-Rite do-it-yourself interior primers debuted in 1997. Also that year Sherwin-Williams bought Thompson Minwax (Thompson's Water Seal, Minwax Wood Products) from Forstmann Little, and Chile-based Marson Chilena, a spray paint maker.

The company streamlined some of its business segments and trimmed jobs in 1998. Christopher Connor, president of the Paint Stores group, replaced Breen as CEO in 1999 and chairman in 2000. Also in 2000, Sherwin-Williams moved into the European automotive coatings market by acquiring Italy-based ScottWarren.

In late 2001 the company acquired Wisconsin-based Mautz Paint Company.

After a rough but still profitable 2001, the company grew revenues and profits for its consumer units (consumer paints and paint stores) in 2002, thanks largely to a healthy do-it-yourself market. Sales for its automotive finishes and international units, however, were down because of a slow collision-repair market and currency-exchange effects.

EXECUTIVES

Chairman and CEO: Christopher M. (Chris) Connor, age 54, $7,495,810 total compensation
President and COO: John G. Morikis, age 47, $3,393,867 total compensation
SVP Finance and CFO: Sean P. Hennessy, age 53, $2,741,449 total compensation
SVP Strategic Excellence Initiatives: Thomas W. Seitz, age 62, $2,291,049 total compensation
SVP, General Counsel, and Secretary: Louis E. Stellato, age 60
SVP Corporate Communications and Public Affairs: Robert J. Wells, age 53
SVP Corporate Planning and Development: Timothy A. Knight, age 46
SVP Human Resources: Thomas E. Hopkins, age 53
VP and Treasurer: Cynthia D. Brogan, age 59
VP Administration: Richard M. Weaver, age 56
President, Paint Stores Group: Steven J. Oberfeld, age 58, $2,291,049 total compensation
President, Global Finishes Group: George E. Heath, age 45

President and General Manager, Diversified Brands Division, Consumer Group: Harvey P. Sass, age 53
President and General Manager, Protective and Marine Coatings Division, Global Finishes Group: Peter J. Ippolito, age 46
President and General Manager, Chemical Coatings Division, Global Finishes Group: Drew A. McCandless
President and General Manager, Paint and Coatings Division, Consumer Group: Joel Baxter, age 50
President and General Manager, Automotive Division, Global Finishes Group: Thomas C. Hablitzel, age 48
Director, Corporate Communications and Investor Relations: Mike Conway
Auditors: Ernst & Young LLP

LOCATIONS

HQ: The Sherwin-Williams Company
101 W. Prospect Ave., Cleveland, OH 44115
Phone: 216-566-2000   **Fax:** 216-566-2947
Web: www.sherwin-williams.com

2009 Sales

	$ mil.	% of total
US	6,068	86
Other countries	1,026	14
Total	**7,094**	**100**

PRODUCTS/OPERATIONS

2009 Sales

	$ mil.	% of total
Paint Stores Group	4,209	60
Global Group	1,653	23
Consumer Group	1,225	17
Administrative	7	—
Total	**7,094**	**100**

Operations

Paint Stores
  Products
    Architectural coatings
    Industrial maintenance
    Marine products
  Brands
    ArmorSeal
    Brod-Dugan
    Con-Lux
    FlexBon Paints
    Hi-Temp
    Kem
    Mautz
    Mercury
    Old Quaker
    Powdura
    Pro-Line
    SeaGuard
    Sherwin-Williams
Consumer
  Products
    Architectural paints
    Industrial maintenance
    Paints
    Private-label coatings
    Stains
    Wood finishings
    Varnishes
  Brands
    Cuprinol
    Dupli-color
    Dura Clad
    Dutch Boy
    EverLast
    Formby's
    H&C
    Krylon
    Martin Senour
    Maxwood Latex Stains
    Minwax
    Plastic Kote
    Pratt & Lambert
    Red Devil
    Rubberset
    Signature Select
    Thompson's
    White Lightning

Automotive Finishes
  Products
    Finishing, refinishing, and touch-up products for motor vehicles
  Brands
    Baco
    Excelo
    Lazzuril
    Martin Senour
    ScottWarren
    Sherwin-Williams
    Western
International Coatings
  Products
    Architectural paints
    Industrial maintenance products
    Stains
    Varnishes
    Wood finishing products
  Brands
    Andina
    Colorgin
    Dutch Boy
    Globo
    Kem-Tone
    Krylon
    Marson
    Martin Senour
    Minwax
    Pratt & Lambert
    Pulverlack
    Ronseal
    Sherwin-Williams
    Sumare

COMPETITORS

Akzo Nobel
BASF SE
BEHR
Benjamin Moore
California Products
Comex Group
Coronado Paint
Diamond Vogel Paint
Dunn-Edwards
DuPont
Ferro
H.B. Fuller
Home Depot
Kelly-Moore
Lowe's
PPG Industries
RPM International
True Value
Valspar
Wal-Mart

HISTORICAL FINANCIALS

Company Type: Public

Income Statement

FYE: December 31

	REVENUE ($ mil.)	NET INCOME ($ mil.)	NET PROFIT MARGIN	EMPLOYEES
12/09	7,094	436	6.1%	29,220
12/08	7,980	477	6.0%	30,677
12/07	8,005	616	7.7%	31,572
12/06	7,810	576	7.4%	30,767
12/05	7,191	463	6.4%	29,434
Annual Growth	**(0.3%)**	**(1.5%)**	**—**	**(0.2%)**

2009 Year-End Financials

Debt ratio: 61.4%   No. of shares (mil.): 109
Return on equity: 32.7%   Dividends
Cash ($ mil.): 69   Yield: 2.3%
Current ratio: 1.27   Payout: 37.6%
Long-term debt ($ mil.): 783   Market value ($ mil.): 6,707

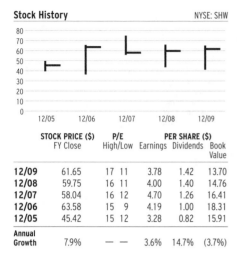
Sigma-Aldrich Corporation

Check the shelves of any research (or mad) scientist and you'll likely find Sigma-Aldrich's chemical products. The company is a leading supplier of chemicals to research laboratories. It has more than 90,000 customers, including labs involved in government and commercial research, for its more than 130,000 chemical and 40,000 equipment products. The products are divided into three categories: research chemicals (further divided into essentials and specialties), fine chemicals (for commercial applications), and biotech products (for immunochemical and molecular biology applications). The company operates in 35 countries, sells its wares worldwide, and manufactures about a third of its chemical products itself.

Sigma-Aldrich gets about three-quarters of its sales from its research chemicals business, which includes biochemicals, organic chemicals, and reagents. The unit's sales are divided among government institutions, nonprofits, universities, and pharmaceutical, diagnostic, and biotech companies and chemical companies and hospitals. Small orders from labs account for more than 70% of the company's total sales.

Sigma-Aldrich's organizational structure is split into three units: specialties (traditional line of lab products), essentials (large pharmaceutical, academic, and commercial research customers), and biotech (for genomic, proteomic, and other life science research uses).

In 2010 Sigma-Aldrich subsidiary SAGE Labs acquired Ace Animals, a rodent husbandry firm. The deal will enhance SAGE Labs' rat and mouse breeding capabilities, which feature specific gene deletions, insertions, repressions, and modifications created using proprietary technology.

HISTORY

The sugar shortage caused by WWII led biochemist Dan Broida to begin a storefront saccharin-manufacturing business, Sigma Chemical Company, in St. Louis in 1945. The firm later branched into biochemicals and diagnostic products. Six years after Broida started turning out saccharin, Aldrich Chemical Company, founded by future collaborator and Harvard-educated chemist Dr. Alfred Bader, started making organic chemicals in a Milwaukee garage. At first, Bader specialized in chemicals not offered by Eastman Kodak, then a leading chemical producer. Soon, however, he went head-to-head with larger chemical companies, offering a full range of research and pharmaceutical organic chemicals.

Sigma-Aldrich was formed by the merger of the two companies in 1975. Broida became the new enterprise's chairman and Bader its president. Though dwarfed by some of its competitors, through astute management the company claimed about 35% of the market for specialty chemicals used in research by 1979. Much of Sigma-Aldrich's success can be traced to its catalogs. Bader had begun compiling simple chemical listings in the early 1950s. In 1979 the company distributed 300,000 copies of the free catalog, which doubled as a laboratory reference tool listing 40,000 chemicals and their physical properties. By that time the company had subsidiaries in Canada, Germany, Israel, and the UK, and sold to customers — mostly academicians and researchers — in 125 countries. In 1980 metal forming firm B-Line Systems became a subsidiary of Sigma-Aldrich.

The company paralleled the fast growth of the biomedical research market in the 1980s, keeping up with new developments and supplying researchers with specialty chemicals and resisting opportunities in the bulk-chemicals market. After Broida died in 1981, his relatives sold much of their stock in Sigma-Aldrich, making it more widely held. Then-CEO Tom Cori took charge and the company continued to grow, with sales of $215 million and a catalog circulation of about 1.5 million by 1986. In 1989 Sigma-Aldrich acquired Fluka Chemical AG (Switzerland), a maker of biochemicals and organic chemicals for use in research and development, from Ciba-Geigy, Hoffmann-La Roche, and others. By 1993 Sigma-Aldrich had more than eight times the catalog sales of any of its competitors. That year it acquired Supelco, a supplier of chromatography products used in chemical research and production, from Rohm and Haas.

In 1996 Sigma-Aldrich was fined $480,000 for exporting 48 shipments of biotoxins without a license in 1992 and 1993 (the company said it had misinterpreted regulations passed in the wake of the Gulf War that were designed to stop the spread of biological weapons). Sigma-Aldrich stepped into the bulk market in 1997 with the construction of a large-scale manufacturing plant in the UK.

Sigma-Aldrich in 1999 bought the remaining 25% interest in Germany-based RdH Laborchemikalien Gmbh (laboratory chemicals) from partner Riedelde-Haen and also acquired Genosys Biotechnologies, a private Texas-based supplier of synthetic DNA products, for $39.5 million. That year COO David Harvey replaced CEO Cori.

To boost concentration on chemicals, in 2000 Sigma-Aldrich sold its B-Line subsidiary (metal conduits and cable trays) to Cooper Industries for about $425 million and reorganized its chemicals business into four units: laboratory products, life-science products, fine chemicals, and diagnostics. The sale of B-Line resulted in a one-time gain of about $170 million (which was over 50% of 2000 net income); most of that cash was used to buy company stock.

Early in 2001 the company bought isotope maker Isotec Inc. from Nippon Sanso for $35.6 million. In 2002 the company reorganized into its present three divisions.

In early 2002 Sigma-Aldrich began divesting its poorly performing diagnostics business in an effort to focus on research chemicals, fine chemicals, and biotech.

The company acquired the JRH Biosciences division of Australian biotech firm CSL Limited for $370 million in 2005. It also bought Degussa's genomics research division, Proligo. The following year it pushed heavily into the Chinese market with the acquisition of Beijing Superior Chemicals and Instruments, which had been Sigma-Aldrich's primary distributor in China, and the creation of Sigma-Aldrich (Shanghai) Trading Co. to head up its operations in the country.

In 2005 Harvey retired as CEO and was replaced by Jai Nagarkatti, who also took on the role of chairman in 2009.

EXECUTIVES

Chairman, President, and CEO: Jai P. Nagarkatti, age 64, $3,196,782 total compensation
SVP, CFO, and Chief Administrative Officer: Rakesh Sachdev, age 53, $1,917,290 total compensation
SVP Strategy and Corporate Development: Karen J. Miller, age 52
SVP, General Counsel, and Secretary: George L. Miller, age 55
VP and CIO: Magnus Borg, age 50
VP and Corporate Controller: Michael F. (Mike) Kanan, age 47
VP Supply Chain: Joseph Porwoll
VP Human Resources: Douglas W. (Doug) Rau, age 53
VP and Treasurer: Kirk A. Richter, age 63
VP Research and Development, Research Biotech: Patrick M. (Pat) Sullivan
VP Marketing, Research Biotech: Helge Bastian
VP Environmental Health and Safety: Steven G. (Steve) Walton, age 42
VP Sales, U.S. and Canada: Gerrit van den Dool, age 56
Investor Relations: Carrie Fields
President, SAFC: Gilles A. Cottier, age 51, $971,899 total compensation
President, SAFC Hitech: Philip Rose
President, Research Biotech: David A. (Dave) Smoller, age 46
Managing Director, U.S. and Canada; President, Research Specialties and Research Essentials: Franklin D. (Frank) Wicks Jr., age 56, $1,274,819 total compensation
Senior Marketing Communications Coordinator: Sean Battles
Auditors: KPMG LLP

LOCATIONS

HQ: Sigma-Aldrich Corporation
3050 Spruce St., St. Louis, MO 63103
Phone: 314-771-5765 **Fax:** 314-771-5757
Web: www.sigmaaldrich.com

2009 Sales

	$ mil.	% of total
US	784.8	36
Germany	236.3	11
UK	148.2	7
Other countries	978.3	46
Total	**2,147.6**	**100**

PRODUCTS/OPERATIONS

2009 Sales

	$ mil.	% of total
Research chemicals		
Specialties	793.4	37
Essentials	417.5	19
Biotech	332.3	16
Fine chemicals	604.4	28
Total	**2,147.6**	**100**

COMPETITORS

Aceto
Ashland Distribution
Atrium Innovations
Bayer AG
Becton, Dickinson
Brenntag
Cambrex
Cambridge Isotope Laboratories
Chemtura
Clariant
DSM
Life Technologies Corporation
Mediatech
Promega
QIAGEN
TECHNE
VWR International

HISTORICAL FINANCIALS

Company Type: Public

Income Statement

FYE: December 31

	REVENUE ($ mil.)	NET INCOME ($ mil.)	NET PROFIT MARGIN	EMPLOYEES
12/09	2,148	347	16.1%	7,740
12/08	2,201	342	15.5%	7,900
12/07	2,039	311	15.3%	7,862
12/06	1,798	277	15.4%	7,299
12/05	1,667	258	15.5%	6,849
Annual Growth	**6.5%**	**7.6%**	**—**	**3.1%**

2009 Year-End Financials

Debt ratio: 5.9%	No. of shares (mil.): 121
Return on equity: 22.6%	Dividends
Cash ($ mil.): 373	Yield: 1.1%
Current ratio: 1.86	Payout: 20.7%
Long-term debt ($ mil.): 100	Market value ($ mil.): 6,133

Stock History

NASDAQ (GS): SIAL

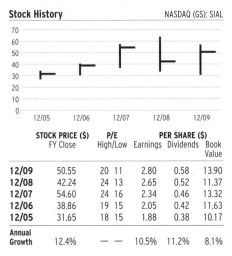

	STOCK PRICE ($) FY Close	P/E High/Low		PER SHARE ($) Earnings	Dividends	Book Value
12/09	50.55	20	11	2.80	0.58	13.90
12/08	42.24	24	13	2.65	0.52	11.37
12/07	54.60	24	16	2.34	0.46	13.32
12/06	38.86	19	15	2.05	0.42	11.63
12/05	31.65	18	15	1.88	0.38	10.17
Annual Growth	**12.4%**	**—**	**—**	**10.5%**	**11.2%**	**8.1%**

Simon Property Group

Simon says: "Shop!" And millions do. Simon Property Group is the largest shopping mall owner in the US, with a portfolio of more than 320 commercial properties totaling some 250 million sq. ft. of leasable space. The self-managed real estate investment trust (REIT) owns, develops, and manages shopping malls, outlet malls (under the Premium Outlet and Prime Outlet brands), boutique malls, and shopping centers. Its portfolio is concentrated in the Southeast, Midwest, and Northeast. The REIT also has stakes in some 50 properties in Europe, as well as outlet centers in Japan, South Korea, and Mexico. In 2010 Simon lost its bid to acquire struggling General Growth Properties, the nation's second-largest mall owner.

The owner of some 200 malls, General Growth found itself mired in debt after years of buying and developing new properties. It filed for bankruptcy in 2009 and weighed its options before selecting a bid from a group of investors led by Brookfield Asset Management. If Simon had won the bid for General Growth, the combined company would have far eclipsed its competitors with about a third of the US retail market.

The REIT further expanded its outlet mall holdings in 2009 by agreeing to acquire Prime Outlets in a $2.3 billion transaction. Prime Outlets' portfolio includes 22 outlet centers located in major metropolitan markets and tourist destinations. Simon has also pursued more international expansion in Europe and Asia, primarily in joint venture investments. With property interests already established in Japan and South Korea, the REIT pursued investments in China but decided to cut its losses there and sold those assets in late 2009.

The founding Simon family, owners of the Indiana Pacers NBA franchise, holds a 12% ownership in the company.

HISTORY

Simon Property Group helped change the face of the US retail landscape from mom-and-pop stores to shopping malls. The original Simon Property Group (formed in 1993) was the offshoot of brothers Melvin and Herbert Simon's Melvin Simon & Associates (MSA, founded in 1959). MSA's first project was Southgate Plaza, a strip center in Bloomington, Indiana, consisting of a half-dozen small tenants anchored by a food store.

To get started, the Simons sometimes borrowed cash from friends, but during the 1960s and 1970s developers could usually borrow 100% of a shopping center's construction costs after securing an anchor tenant. Leases then provided money to repay debt and make a down payment on the next project. The Simons consistently retained equity, developing a huge asset base that they used as collateral for larger projects.

The new strip malls lacked the prestige of big-city stores such as Macy's; they also lacked the personal touch of the neighborhood shops they put out of business. But they boasted retail's two most important virtues — price and convenience — and in time they developed into the modern mall. MSA built its first indoor mall in the mid-1960s in snowy Fort Collins, Colorado. By the late 1960s, MSA and other developers were consumed with mall projects.

Unlike many developers, the Simons were genial, honest negotiators, appealing to merchants and bankers put off by city slickers or hucksters. Yet Mel and Herb were often compared to the Marx brothers for bickering between themselves. During one negotiation, Mel allegedly took off his shoe and threw it at Herb.

In the mid-1970s Mel packed up and headed west to become a Hollywood producer. After a string of such Oscar noncontenders as *Porky's* and *Love at First Bite,* Mel returned to the family company in the 1980s, and in 1983 the brothers bought pro basketball's Indiana Pacers. Melvin Simon died in 2009.

As the 1989 real estate slump hit, the Simons were busy building the largest mall in the country, just outside Minneapolis. Completed in 1992, the Mall of America included a roller coaster, a two-story miniature golf course, and a walk-through aquarium. In 1993 Simon Property Group went public in one of the largest IPOs of its time.

In 1996 the company became the Simon DeBartolo Group after merging with DeBartolo Realty, founded to hold the retail and residential properties of another sporting family, the DeBartolos (San Francisco 49ers).

After its record-setting purchase of private paired-share REIT Corporate Property Investors in 1998, the company reverted to the Simon Property Group name (Edward DeBartolo's name had been soiled in a Louisiana casino scandal) and added more than 20 midwestern properties to its fold, giving the company a firm lock on the top mall REIT spot.

In 1999 Simon bought stakes in 14 malls in the northeastern US and became 50%-owner of the Mall of America after buying a 27% stake in the development held by financing partner TIAA-CREF. The following year it formed a joint venture with Kimco Realty to buy 250 stores from the bankrupt Montgomery Ward chain.

In 2002 the company bought part of the mall portfolio of Rodamco North America. That year, Simon also pulled out of a much-ballyhooed project — building a family entertainment complex at Penn's Landing in Philadelphia's Center City — after a deadline to lease 50% of the center was not met. Later that year, the company merged with SPG Realty Consultants, ending the companies' paired share corporate structure.

In 2003 the company bought out the 42% stake in The Forum Shops held by joint venture partner Sheldon Gordon. That same year Simon dropped a bid with Westfield America (now Westfield Group) to acquire rival Taubman Centers after a legal battle was ended by the passage of an antitakeover bill in Michigan.

In 2004 the company was forced to sell a controlling interest in the Mall of America to Canadian real estate firm Triple Five, an original partner in the development, after a court ruled that Simon improperly acquired control of the mall from TIAA-CREF in 1999. (The case is still pending appeals.) Later that year Simon acquired outlet mall developer Chelsea Property Group for about $3.5 billion.

Also in 2004 the REIT acquired Chelsea Property Group, allowing it to open its first Premium Outlet center in Mexico. Three years later it acquired The Mills Corporation, giving it 37 additional properties across the country.

EXECUTIVES

Chairman Emeritus: Herbert (Herb) Simon, age 75
Chairman and CEO: David Simon, age 48,
  $4,633,583 total compensation
President, COO, and Director:
  Richard S. (Rick) Sokolov, age 60,
  $2,600,599 total compensation
SEVP Leasing: Gary L. Lewis, age 51,
  $1,739,409 total compensation
Secretary and General Counsel: James M. Barkley,
  age 58, $1,707,155 total compensation
EVP and CFO: Stephen E. Sterrett, age 54,
  $1,580,729 total compensation
EVP and Chief Administrative Officer; President,
  Simon Management Group: John Rulli, age 53,
  $1,288,511 total compensation
EVP Leasing, The Mills: Gary Duncan
EVP and Treasurer: Andrew A. (Andy) Juster, age 57
EVP Development Operations: Michael E. McCarty
EVP Leasing, Premium Outlet Centers:
  Richard N. Lewis
EVP Real Estate, Premium Outlet Centers:
  Mark J. Silvestri
EVP, Simon Management Group: Timothy G. Earnest
EVP Property Management, The Mills:
  Paul C. Fickinger
SVP and Chief Accounting Officer: Steve Broadwater
Chief Marketing Officer; President, Simon Brand
  Ventures: Mikael Thygesen
President, Community/Lifestyle Centers:
  Myles H. Minton
President, The Mills: Gregg M. Goodman, age 46
President, Premium Outlet Centers: John R. Klein
President, International Division; Chairman, Simon
  Global Limited: Hans C. Mautner, age 69
Auditors: Ernst & Young LLP

LOCATIONS

HQ: Simon Property Group, Inc.
  225 W. Washington St., Indianapolis, IN 46204
Phone: 317-636-1600   **Fax:** 317-263-2318
Web: www.simon.com

PRODUCTS/OPERATIONS

2009 Sales

	$ mil.	% of total
Minimum rent	2,316.8	62
Tenant reimbursements	1,062.2	28
Overage rent	84.9	2
Management fees & other	124.1	3
Other	187.2	5
Total	**3,775.2**	**100**

COMPETITORS

Belz	Kimco Realty
Cadillac Fairview	Lincoln Property
CBL & Associates	Macerich
General Growth Properties	Taubman Centers
Glimcher Realty	Vornado Realty
Horizon Group Properties	Weingarten Realty

HISTORICAL FINANCIALS

Company Type: Public

Income Statement

FYE: December 31

	REVENUE ($ mil.)	NET INCOME ($ mil.)	NET PROFIT MARGIN	EMPLOYEES
12/09	3,775	387	10.3%	5,200
12/08	3,783	464	12.3%	5,300
12/07	3,651	519	14.2%	5,100
12/06	3,332	564	16.9%	4,300
12/05	3,167	613	19.3%	4,700
Annual Growth	**4.5%**	**(10.8%)**	**—**	**2.6%**

2009 Year-End Financials

Debt ratio: 422.2%	No. of shares (mil.): 289
Return on equity: 11.0%	Dividends
Cash ($ mil.): 3,958	Yield: 1.2%
Current ratio: 12.34	Payout: 87.6%
Long-term debt ($ mil.): 18,630	Market value ($ mil.): 23,068

Stock History

NYSE: SPG

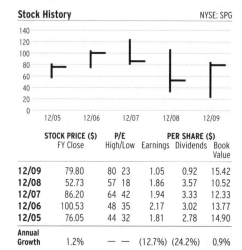

	STOCK PRICE ($) FY Close	P/E High/Low		PER SHARE ($) Earnings	Dividends	Book Value
12/09	79.80	80	23	1.05	0.92	15.42
12/08	52.73	57	18	1.86	3.57	10.52
12/07	86.20	64	42	1.94	3.33	12.33
12/06	100.53	48	35	2.17	3.02	13.77
12/05	76.05	44	32	1.81	2.78	14.90
Annual Growth	**1.2%**	**—**	**—**	**(12.7%)**	**(24.2%)**	**0.9%**

Skadden, Arps, Slate, Meagher & Flom

Have you heard about the law firm that sued the business-information publisher for a profile that opened with a wickedly clever lawyer joke? Neither have we, and we would like to keep it that way. Skadden, Arps, Slate, Meagher & Flom, a leading US law firm and one of the largest in the world, has some 2,000 attorneys in some 25 offices around the globe, from Boston to Beijing and from London to Los Angeles. The firm is best known for its work in mergers and acquisitions, corporate restructuring, and corporate finance, but it represents businesses in a wide variety of practice areas, including intellectual property and litigation. Skadden was founded in 1948.

Skadden has worked for a number of *FORTUNE* 500 companies. High-profile clients have included JPMorgan Chase and State Farm, as well as Arcelor, Merrill Lynch, and Toshiba.

Over the years Skadden has grown organically rather than by merging with other firms. The New York office is the firm's largest, but offices outside the US have been growing faster. As part of its plan to expand outside the US, Skadden opened offices in Shanghai and São Paulo in 2008 — giving the firm greater access to growing markets less affected by the economic downturn.

HISTORY

Marshall Skadden, Leslie Arps, and John Slate hung out their shingle in New York City on April Fool's Day, 1948. Skadden and Arps came from a Wall Street law firm, and Slate had been counsel to Pan American World Airways. Without the reputation and connections of the established New York law firms, the firm found work one case at a time from referrals, handling mainly commercial, corporate, and litigations work. Marshall Skadden died in 1958.

Denied the luxury of steady clients, the firm was forced to be innovative and, at times, unorthodox. Joe Flom, who had joined as the firm's first associate, specialized in corporate law and proxy fights. During the 1960s, when tender offers and hostile takeovers increased, many of the more venerable firms referred clients engaged in the undignified corporate raids to Flom to preserve their gentlemanly reputations. With "white shoe" lawyers on Wall Street hesitant to tread into the uncivilized region of corporate takeovers, Skadden, Arps went for it, and the firm virtually pioneered the business of mergers and acquisitions (M&A) under Flom.

When Congress passed the Williams Act in 1968, which "legitimized" tender offers by providing regulation, other law firms started to get in on the act. Skadden, Arps was way ahead of the game, however, and as corporations and lawyers realized that aggressive legal tactics helped win corporate takeover battles, it also became apparent that Joe Flom was the expert. As takeover fights became more frequent in the early 1970s, the firm earned more than just respect. Earnings came not just from some of the highest hourly rates in the industry, but from hefty retainers (now a common practice at many firms) on the theory that association with Flom would scare raiders off. The only other name that could strike such fear in people's hearts was Marty Lipton of rival takeover specialists Wachtell, Lipton, Rosen & Katz. From the late 1970s through the 1980s, Skadden, Arps was involved in almost every important M&A case in the US.

The firm used its success in mergers and acquisitions to build its practice in other areas. In the early 1980s it branched into bankruptcy, product liability, and real estate law. By then it had opened offices in Boston; Chicago; Los Angeles; Washington, DC; and Wilmington, Delaware. Les Arps died in 1987.

With the boom in mergers and acquisitions activity and bankruptcies in the late 1980s, the firm grew to almost 2,000 lawyers by 1989. Then came the recession, and M&A work virtually dried up. Skadden, Arps responded by shedding more than 500 lawyers between 1989 and 1990. It also scrambled to diversify and expand internationally. As takeover activity rebounded in the mid-1990s, the diversification strategy actually began to work against Skadden, Arps because profits didn't skyrocket like those of M&A specialist firms.

The firm opened an office in Singapore in 1995 to coordinate its Asian business, signaling that city's growing importance as a financial center. Two years later two-thirds of the firm's Beijing team defected to a rival firm. Headquarters shrugged it off and flew in replacements. Representing President Bill Clinton, Skadden, Arps won one of its highest-profile cases in 1998 when the sexual harassment suit brought by Paula Jones was thrown out.

With its M&A practice in full swing again, Skadden, Arps was involved in 70 announced M&A deals in 1999, including the $75 billion merger of oil companies Exxon and Mobil. It also became the first US law firm to reach $1 billion in revenue in 2000. The company announced an alliance with Italian law firm Studio Chiomenti the following year and took part in three of the top 10 M&A deals of 2002. Skadden, Arps helped struggling discount retailer Kmart emerge from its titanic bankruptcy the next year.

EXECUTIVES

Executive Partner: Eric J. Friedman, age 45
CFO: Noah J. Puntus
CTO: Harris Z. Tilevitz
Chief Administrative Officer: Laurel E. Henschel
Corporate Partner: Joseph H. Flom
Managing Attorney: Robert Abrams
Manager Employee Benefits: Lisa Gross
Manager Business Systems and Information Projects:
  Nitin Trivedi
Director Human Resources: Vaughn Burke
Director Marketing and Business Development:
  Sally J. Feldman
Of Counsel: Wayne W. Whalen

LOCATIONS

HQ: Skadden, Arps, Slate, Meagher & Flom LLP
  4 Times Sq., New York, NY 10036
Phone: 212-735-3000   **Fax:** 212-735-2000
Web: www.skadden.com

PRODUCTS/OPERATIONS

Selected Practice Areas

Alternative dispute resolution
Antitrust
Appellate litigation and legal issues
Banking and institutional investing
Biological and chemical technology diligence and
  transactions
CFIUS
Class action litigation
Climate change
Communications
Consumer financial services enforcement and litigation
Corporate
Corporate compliance programs
Corporate finance
Corporate governance
Corporate restructuring
Crisis management
Derivative financial products, commodities, and futures
Energy and infrastructure projects
Energy regulation and litigation
Environmental
Environmental litigation
European Union/international competition
Executive compensation and benefits
Exempt and nonprofit organizations
False Claims Act defense
Financial institutions
Financial institutions regulation and enforcement
Foreign Corrupt Practices Act defense
Franchise law
Gaming
Government contract disputes
Government enforcement and white collar crime
Health care
Health care and life sciences
Information technology and e-commerce
Insurance
Intellectual property and technology
International law and policy
International litigation and arbitration
International tax
International trade
Investment management
Labor and employment law
Lease financing
Litigation
Mass torts and insurance litigation
Media and entertainment
Mergers and acquisitions
Outsourcing
Patent and technology litigation and counseling
Pharmaceutical, biotechnology, and medical device
  licensing
Political law
Private equity
Private equity funds
Pro bono
Public policy
Real estate
Real estate investment trusts

Russia and CIS
Securities enforcement and compliance
Securities litigation
Sports
Structured finance
Tax
Tax controversy and litigation
Trademark, copyright, and advertising litigation and
  counseling
Trusts and estates
UCC and secured transactions
Utilities mergers and acquisitions

COMPETITORS

Baker & McKenzie	McDermott Will & Emery
Clifford Chance	O'Melveny & Myers
Davis Polk	Shearman & Sterling
Gibson, Dunn & Crutcher	Sidley Austin
Hogan Lovells	Sullivan & Cromwell
Jones Day	Wachtell, Lipton
Kirkland & Ellis	Weil, Gotshal & Manges
Latham & Watkins	White & Case
Mayer Brown	WilmerHale

HISTORICAL FINANCIALS

Company Type: Partnership

Income Statement

FYE: December 31

	REVENUE ($ mil.)	NET INCOME ($ mil.)	NET PROFIT MARGIN	EMPLOYEES
12/09	2,100	—	—	4,000
12/08	2,200	—	—	4,500
12/07	2,170	—	—	4,721
12/06	1,850	—	—	4,520
12/05	1,610	—	—	4,400
Annual Growth	11.0%	—	—	0.8%

Revenue History

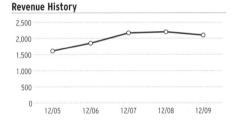

SkyWest, Inc.

SkyWest flies in every direction. The company's main subsidiaries, regional carriers SkyWest Airlines and Atlantic Southeast Airlines (ASA), serve about 220 destinations in the US, Canada, Mexico and the Caribbean, mainly for Delta Air Lines and UAL's United Airlines. SkyWest Airlines flies as Delta Connection from Atlanta and Salt Lake City and as United Express from hubs in Chicago, Denver, Los Angeles, and San Francisco. ASA flies for Delta, mainly from Atlanta and Cincinnati. Combined, the carriers operate a fleet of about 450 aircraft, consisting of more than 400 Canadair regional jets (CRJs, made by Bombardier) and about 50 turboprops.

Amid growing demand by airline giants to cut costs by outsourcing regional flights, SkyWest is moving to further diversify its operations and bolster its marketplace presence. Owning both SkyWest Airlines and ASA makes SkyWest a strong competitor for more business from Delta

and United or for contracts from other carriers. Industry turbulence, however, is growing as Continental and United plan to combine and, if successful, create the world's largest airline. Through ASA, SkyWest inked a $133 million deal in mid-2010 to buy rival regional carrier ExpressJet. SkyWest had made an offer in 2008; ExpressJet rejected it as too low, but left the door open for negotiations. The expanded regional family has its sights set on continuing to serve Continental and United hubs.

In the meantime, SkyWest entered into a marketing alliance in late 2009 with AirTran. SkyWest Airlines operates five aircraft for AirTran Airways between Milwaukee and six destinations, primarily located in the Midwestern US. The AirTran partnership lets SkyWest continue to provide regional service from Milwaukee, a hub that the carrier served through a former Midwest contract.

In mid-2009 SkyWest announced it was pulling the plug on its contract to provide regional service for Midwest Airlines. SkyWest became a Midwest Connect carrier in 2007, but the relationship began to falter in 2008, after Midwest (along with the rest of the airline industry) ran into trouble with high fuel prices followed by the economic downturn. The companies agreed to reduce the number of aircraft from 21 to 12, and SkyWest deferred weekly payments for a handful of months, but the change wasn't enough to convince SkyWest to continue. The carrier cancelled a $9.3 million unsecured note from Midwest in exchange for a $4 million payment. SkyWest removed the last of its aircraft from Midwest's routes in early 2010.

Along with regional passenger transportation, which accounts for nearly all of its sales, SkyWest provides ground handling services — loading and unloading of aircraft — for other airlines at several of the airports where it operates.

HISTORY

In 1972 Ralph Atkin founded SkyWest with one airplane that served three points in Utah. The company doubled in size in 1984 when it bought California-based Sun Aire Lines; two years later it went public. Growth also was fueled by the trend toward code-sharing agreements between major airlines and regional airlines serving rural markets. SkyWest jumped on board with Delta in 1987 to become one of four Delta Connection carriers.

Atkin stepped down as chairman in 1991 and was replaced by his nephew, CEO Jerry Atkin. By 1993 SkyWest had assembled a fleet of about 50 turboprop aircraft; that year it placed an order for 10 Canadair Regional Jets (CRJs) from Bombardier. The jets would prove to be popular among travelers.

SkyWest became a United affiliate in 1997 with 120 daily United Express departures from Los Angeles. The next year SkyWest expanded its United Express service into additional markets in California, Oregon, and Washington. Meanwhile, the company sold most of its air tours business, Scenic Airlines, to Eagle Canyon Airlines in 1998; it sold the rest in 1999.

With business booming, SkyWest placed orders for 55 more CRJs in 1999. Amid unusually cordial labor relations for an airline, SkyWest fliers voted down a chance to join the pilots' union. Also in 1999 SkyWest and Delta terminated their Los Angeles code-sharing agreement because of SkyWest's close ties to United in the city. The following year SkyWest agreed to sell the outstanding shares of subsidiary National Parks Transportation, a provider of rental car services at six airports served by the airline.

SkyWest began providing regional service for Continental Airlines in 2003, but the companies ended the deal in 2005.

In a major expansion, SkyWest in 2005 bought fellow regional carrier Atlantic Southeast Airlines (ASA) from Delta for about $425 million and some $1.25 billion in debt. The purchase was completed just before Delta filed for Chapter 11 bankruptcy protection. The acquisition diversified SkyWest's operations geographically and added Delta business to a revenue mix that had leaned heavily toward United. In conjunction with the acquisition, SkyWest negotiated new, 15-year Delta Connection contracts for both SkyWest Airlines and ASA.

SkyWest attempted to further diversify its operations when it made an unsolicited bid to buy rival regional carrier ExpressJet in 2008. ExpressJet rejected the offer of about $182 million as too low, but left the door open for negotiations; SkyWest withdrew its bid, however, after ExpressJet signed a new agreement to provide feeder service for Continental.

EXECUTIVES

Chairman, President, and CEO; Chairman and CEO, SkyWest Airlines: Jerry C. Atkin, age 61, $1,268,826 total compensation
EVP, CFO, and Treasurer, SkyWest and SkyWest Airlines: Bradford R. Rich, age 48, $890,770 total compensation
VP and Controller: Eric Woodward
VP Planning, SkyWest, SkyWest Airlines, and Atlantic Southeast Airlines: Eric D. Christensen
VP Information Technology, SkyWest, SkyWest Airlines, and Atlantic Southeast Airlines: James B. Jensen
Director Application Development: Justin Esplin
Director Risk Management and Compensation: Brad Wood
Director Communications and Development: Amber Hunter
President and COO, Atlantic Southeast Airlines: Bradford R. (Brad) Holt, $613,411 total compensation
President and COO, SkyWest Airlines: Russell A. (Chip) Childs, age 42, $718,930 total compensation
General Counsel, SkyWest Airlines: Todd Emerson
Director Operations Control Center, Skywest Airlines: Bill Mostowy
Director Stations, SkyWest Airlines: Steve Black
Director Internal Culture, SkyWest Airlines: Greg Burton
Director Training, SkyWest Airlines: Robin L. Wall
Director Flight Operations, SkyWest Airlines: Christopher C. Brown
Director Midwest Connect, SkyWest Airlines: Randy Mulvey
Director Multimedia and Business Development, SkyWest Airlines: Spencer N. Hyde
Director Aircraft Spares, SkyWest Airlines: Joe Sigg
Director, Operations Safety and Compliance, SkyWest Airlines: David W. Faddis
Auditors: Ernst & Young LLP

LOCATIONS

HQ: SkyWest, Inc.
444 S. River Rd., St. George, UT 84790
Phone: 435-634-3000   **Fax:** 435-634-3105
Web: www.skywest.com

PRODUCTS/OPERATIONS

2009 Sales

	$ mil.	% of total
Passenger	2,582.2	99
Ground handling & other	31.4	1
Total	**2,613.6**	**100**

COMPETITORS

Air Wisconsin Airlines
American Eagle
Comair
ExpressJet
Horizon Air
Mesa Air
Pinnacle Airlines
Republic Airways
Trans States

HISTORICAL FINANCIALS

Company Type: Public

Income Statement			FYE: December 31	
	REVENUE ($ mil.)	NET INCOME ($ mil.)	NET PROFIT MARGIN	EMPLOYEES
12/09	2,614	84	3.2%	8,654
12/08	3,496	113	3.2%	13,335
12/07	3,374	159	4.7%	10,249
12/06	3,115	146	4.7%	8,792
12/05	1,964	112	5.7%	13,647
Annual Growth	**7.4%**	**(7.1%)**	**—**	**(10.8%)**

2009 Year-End Financials

Debt ratio: 134.3%
Return on equity: 6.4%
Cash ($ mil.): 76
Current ratio: 2.79
Long-term debt ($ mil.): 1,816
No. of shares (mil.): 56
Dividends
Yield: 0.9%
Payout: 10.9%
Market value ($ mil.): 950

Stock History

NASDAQ (GS): SKYW

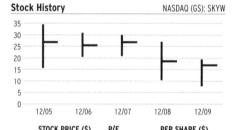

	STOCK PRICE ($) FY Close	P/E High/Low		PER SHARE ($) Earnings	Dividends	Book Value
12/09	16.92	13	6	1.47	0.16	24.09
12/08	18.60	14	6	1.93	0.13	22.72
12/07	26.85	12	9	2.49	0.12	22.19
12/06	25.51	13	9	2.30	0.12	20.99
12/05	26.86	18	8	1.90	0.12	16.27
Annual Growth	**(10.9%)**	**—**	**—**	**(6.2%)**	**7.5%**	**10.3%**

SLM Corporation

Those who graduated *magna cum payments* may not be familiar with SLM, but they probably know its more common moniker, Sallie Mae. The company, which manages some 10 million student loans, is one of the US's largest sources of funding and servicing for education loans. Formerly primarily a wholesale acquirer, SLM now originates more than half its loans. The company also originates private student loans, which are not guaranteed by the government. In addition, SLM earns fees for its servicing and collections services as well as processing and administrative offerings through various subsidiaries. The company is one of four private entities providing servicing for the Department of Education.

Founded in 1974 as a government-sponsored enterprise, SLM borrowed money at near-government rates to purchase government-guaranteed loans. In the 1990s, though, Congress took away SLM's funding edge, making privatization attractive. SLM completed the separation in 2004, but more changes followed.

In 2007 the College Cost Reduction and Access Act (CCRAA) was signed into law. Intended to reform student lending and cut costs for borrowers, the act slashed subsidies for lenders participating in the Federal Family Education Loan Program (FFELP). The reform cut into the company's interest-earning operations. As a result, SLM increased its focus on higher-yielding private education loans, which carry a lower risk.

Further student lending reforms were to follow. In 2010 the FFELP program was eliminated in efforts to save the government an estimated $4 billion annually. SLM will no longer originate loans under the program but still manages a $150 billion portfolio of existing FFELP loans. To cut costs, SLM shut down subsidiary Nellie Mae, cut its workforce, and moved remaining employees to its Upromise subsidiary. It plans further job cuts as it restructures its operations.

HISTORY

The Student Loan Marketing Association was chartered in 1972 as a response to problems in the Guaranteed Student Loan Program of 1965. For years the GSL program had tinkered with rates to induce banks to make loans, but servicing the small loans was expensive and troublesome. Sallie Mae began operations in 1973, buying loans from their originators; its size provided economies of scale in loan servicing.

Originally, only institutions making educational or student loans were allowed to own stock in Sallie Mae. This was later changed so that anyone could buy nonvoting stock. In 1993 voting stock was listed on the NYSE.

Sallie Mae was always a political football, altered again and again to reflect the education policies of the party in power. When it was founded during the Nixon administration, its loans were restricted by a needs test, which was repealed during the Carter years. The Reagan administration reimposed the needs test and at the same time sped up the schedule under which the company was to become self-supporting, which it did by late 1981.

Forced to rely on its own resources, Sallie Mae turned to creative financing. One of its traditional advantages was that its loan interest rates were linked to Treasury bills, traditionally about 3% above the T-bill rate. The company became a master at riding the spread between its cost of funds and the interest rates it charged. (Since 2000, rates have been linked to the average three-month commercial paper rate.)

Between 1983 and 1992 Sallie Mae's assets swelled by more than 400% and its income rose by almost 500%. As the firm grew, management became more visible, with high pay and extravagant perks. Although salaries were not inconsistent with those of executives at comparable private corporations, the remuneration level and perks irked Congress. But Sallie Mae kept growing — in 1992 it expanded its facilities and added 900 new staff members.

The 1993 Omnibus Budget Reconciliation Act, with its transfer of the student loan program directly to the government and its surcharge on Sallie Mae, began to adversely affect earnings in 1994. While awaiting permission to alter its charter, the company stepped up its marketing efforts, especially to school loan officers who advised students on loan options.

In 1995 then-COO Albert Lord led a group of stockholders in a push to cut operating expenses and repackage student loans as securities, à la Freddie Mac and Fannie Mae. Lord and some of his supporters won seats on the board (as well as the enmity of Lawrence Hough, who resigned as CEO in the midst of the melee). That year Sallie Mae bought HICA Holding, one of two private insurers of education loans. In 1996 Congress passed legislation forcing Sallie Mae's privatization. Despite SLM's rising stock, shareholders were unhappy with chairman William Arceneaux's status quo business plan. Lord gained control in 1997.

In 1998 the organization became SLM Holding. Assets and earnings were muted that year when unfavorable market conditions prevented Sallie Mae from securitizing its loans.

The firm the next year expanded its lending operations by buying Nellie Mae. Also in 1999 Sallie Mae teamed with Answer Financial to sell insurance. In 2000 the company also cut some 1,700 jobs, approximately 25% of its workforce.

The following year Sallie Mae teamed with Intuit, allowing the financial software company access to Sallie Mae's 7 million customers.

In 2002 it bought Pioneer Credit Recovery and General Revenue Corporation, two of the nation's largest student loan collection agencies. It also reverted to the SLM moniker.

The privatization plan put into place in the mid-1990s (orchestrated in large part by then-CEO Lord) came to fruition nearly four years ahead of schedule when SLM transitioned to a private organization in December 2004.

In 2007 SLM that year became ensnared in a student-lending industry probe led by New York attorney general Andrew Cuomo. The company agreed to a $2 million settlement and to abide by a code of conduct regarding its dealings with college employees.

One of the most dramatic results of the troubles was the collapse of a planned acquisition by a consortium of investment firms. The planned $8.8 billion deal included buyers J.C. Flowers (which would own about half of SLM), Bank of America, and JPMorgan Chase. In the midst of the industry probe, J.C. Flowers sought a change in SLM's leadership in an effort to secure regulatory approval for the acquisition; Thomas J. (Tim) Fitzpatrick was ousted as CEO. Ultimately, the buyers canceled the deal, citing the reduced potential value of SLM. It later cut more than 10% of its workforce.

EXECUTIVES

Chairman: Anthony P. (Tony) Terracciano, age 71
Vice Chairman and CFO: John F. (Jack) Remondi, age 47, $7,974,419 total compensation
Vice Chairman and CEO: Albert L. Lord, age 64, $5,433,192 total compensation
SEVP and Chief Lending Officer: John (Jack) Hewes, age 61, $3,150,484 total compensation
EVP and Treasurer: Jonathan (Jon) Clark, age 51, $1,088,478 total compensation
EVP and Chief Marketing Officer: Joseph (Joe) DePaulo, $1,079,084 total compensation
EVP and General Counsel: Mark L. Heleen
SVP Corporate Finance: Kenneth (Ken) Fischbach
Auditors: PricewaterhouseCoopers LLP

LOCATIONS

HQ: SLM Corporation
12061 Bluemont Way, Reston, VA 20190
Phone: 703-810-3000   **Fax:** 703-984-5042
Web: www.salliemae.com

PRODUCTS/OPERATIONS

2009 Sales

	$ mil.	% of total
Interest		
FFELP consolidation loans	1,882.2	28
Private education loans	1,582.5	24
FFELP Stafford & other student loans	1,211.6	18
Other loans	56.0	1
Cash & investments	26.1	—
Contingency fees	295.9	4
Servicing & securitization	295.3	4
Net gains on sales of loans & securities	283.8	4
Guarantor servicing fees	135.6	2
Collections	51.1	1
Other	929.1	14
Adjustments	(604.5)	—
Total	**6,144.7**	**100**

Selected Subsidiaries

AFS US, Inc.
AFS Holdings, LLC
Arrow Financial International, LLC
Cavalier Funding, LLC
Crimson Funding, LLC
Nellie Mae Corporation
Sallie Mae UK Holding Corporation
SLM Grammercy Corporation
Student Loan Finance Association, Inc.
VL Funding LLC

COMPETITORS

Bank of America
Brazos Higher Education Service Corp.
Educational Funding of The South
First Marblehead
FirstCity Financial
Great Lakes Higher Education
KeyCorp
Mohela
Nelnet
Pennsylvania Higher Education Assistance Agency
Student Loan Corp.
SunTrust
Texas Guaranteed

HISTORICAL FINANCIALS

Company Type: Public

Income Statement

FYE: December 31

	ASSETS ($ mil.)	NET INCOME ($ mil.)	INCOME AS % OF ASSETS	EMPLOYEES
12/09	169,985	325	0.2%	8,000
12/08	168,768	(213)	—	8,000
12/07	155,565	(896)	—	11,000
12/06	116,136	1,157	1.0%	11,000
12/05	99,339	1,382	1.4%	11,000
Annual Growth	**14.4%**	**(30.4%)**	**—**	**(7.7%)**

2009 Year-End Financials

Equity as % of assets: 2.3%
Return on assets: 0.2%
Return on equity: 9.0%
Long-term debt ($ mil.): 130,546
No. of shares (mil.): 486
Dividends
Yield: 0.0%
Payout: —
Market value ($ mil.): 5,474
Sales ($ mil.): 6,145

Stock History

NYSE: SLM

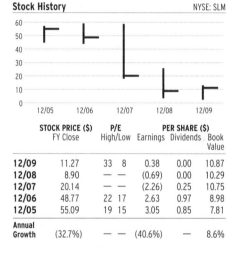

	STOCK PRICE ($) FY Close	P/E High/Low		PER SHARE ($) Earnings	Dividends	Book Value
12/09	11.27	33	8	0.38	0.00	10.87
12/08	8.90	—	—	(0.69)	0.00	10.29
12/07	20.14	—	—	(2.26)	0.25	10.75
12/06	48.77	22	17	2.63	0.97	8.98
12/05	55.09	19	15	3.05	0.85	7.81
Annual Growth	**(32.7%)**	**—**	**—**	**(40.6%)**	**—**	**8.6%**

Smithfield Foods

When Smithfield Foods waddles up to the trough, the other porkers stand back. Fat from acquisitions, the company is the world's largest hog producer and pork processor. Its products include fresh pork and processed, value-added pork products sold under the Armour, Cook's, John Morrell, Lykes, Patrick Cudahy, Roegelein, and Cumberland Gap names. Smithfield distributes its meats in the US and internationally, mainly in Mexico, Western Europe, the UK, Poland, Romania, and China. In addition to pork, the company produces turkey and turkey products through its Armour-Eckrich operations and its 49% stake in the largest US turkey producer Butterball.

Looking to get back in the black following the economic downturn, Smithfield has been eyeing its Butterball joint venture with Maxwell Farms, which holds a 51% stake. Smithfield hopes to either gain full ownership of the flagship turkey brand or cash out of its minority stake. As part of the deal, Smithfield would either buy out its joint venture partner with an offer of $200 million or Maxwell Farms would acquire Smithfield's share.

Besides turkey, beef was an important part of Smithfield's diet. Once one of the largest beef processors in the US, in 2008 it sold its beef operations, Smithfield Beef Group (now JBS Packerland), and its feedlot joint venture, Five Rivers Ranch Cattle Feeding, to Brazilian meat giant JBS. To sell the feedlot joint venture, Smithfield bought out the 50% interest that was owned by ContiGroup for some 2 million shares of its stock. (Smithfield still has some minimal live cattle operations, which it is in the process of selling off.)

To stay competitive, the company has streamlined its operations. It merged its Groupe Smithfield Holdings with Spanish meat processor Campofrio Alimentacion in 2008. The all-stock transaction created a leading European meat processor. Smithfield owns 37% of the combined companies, which operate under the Campofrio Food Group name. And the following year it sold Maverick Food Co. (a Chinese meat joint venture with Belgium's Artal Group) to China's largest grain trader, COFCO.

The company also closed half a dozen plants and moved their operations to other facilities. Some 1,800 jobs were eliminated.

Its biggest deal in recent years was the acquisition of Premium Standard Farms for $810 million in 2007. As the US's #1 pork processor and marketer, Smithfield's takeover of Premium Standard (the nation's #2 pork producer) created a pig-production powerhouse. Premium Standard brought brands such as All Natural, Fresh & Tender, Lundy's, Natural Excellence, and Premium Farms to the Smithfield roster. (In 2010 Smithfield paid a $900,000 fine levied by the US Department of Justice for violating antitrust procedures because it took took control of a large segment of Premium Standard before the legal waiting period expired.)

HISTORY

Joseph Luter's father and grandfather set up Smithfield Foods in 1936 and built it into a regional pork producer. Luter began to manage the business in 1962 after his father died. In 1969 he sold the company to conglomerate Liberty Equities for $20 million and was retained as its manager, but he was soon dismissed.

Smithfield Foods floundered in his absence and grew weak from overexpansion and non-pork diversifications. Luter bought the business back in 1975, paying a fraction of what he had sold it for. At that time the company was a wholesaler of pork and fish products and was operating 27 seafood restaurants. Luter trimmed the fat to pay down debt, leaving only the pork operations. He then began to expand in the pork business through acquisitions, including Gwaltney Packing in 1982, thereby doubling its size. Other purchases included pork processors Patrick Cudahy (1985) and Esskay (1986).

The company formed a joint venture with pork producer Carroll's Foods in 1987 to help lessen its dependence on Midwestern hog farmers. To move toward higher-quality pork, the joint venture acquired North American rights from National Pig Development (a UK-based, family-owned firm) for a long and lean English breed — the NPD hog, which became the basis for the company's flagship brand, Smithfield Lean Generation Pork.

The company co-founded Circle Four Farms, a giant hog farm in Utah, in 1994 with partners Murphy's Family Farms, Carroll's, and Prestage

Farms. (Two years later it bought out the other partners.) Smithfield Foods also bought regional processors Valleydale Foods (1993) and John Morrell (1995) and struggling Lykes Meat Group (1996), thereby transforming it into a national concern. In 1997 the company was ticketed with $12.6 million in fines by the EPA for water violations. The fine was later lowered by $6 million by an appellate court.

Beginning in 1998, Smithfield Foods went shopping abroad, starting with Canadian meat processor Canada's Schneider Corporation and Société Bretonne de Salaisons, France's largest private-label maker of hams and bacon.

In 2000 the company acquired Murphy Family Farms for about $460 million, doubling its pig production. Now with a taste for beef, in 2001 Smithfield acquired midsized beef processors Moyer Packing Company (MOPAC) and Packerland Holdings. Smithfield began a joint venture in late 2001 with Artal Holland to distribute processed meat products in China.

Despite cries of antitrust, in late 2003 Smithfield spent $367 million to purchase the Farmland Foods pork production and processing businesses from ailing cooperative Farmland Industries. The purchase gave Smithfield control of 27% of the US pork industry.

In 2005 Smithfield acquired MF Cattle Feeding, which has operations in Colorado and Idaho. Later that year MF and ContiGroup subsidiary ContiBeef formed a 50-50 joint venture cattle-feeding business named Five Rivers Ranch Cattle Feeding.

Extending its reach into Europe, in 2005 Smithfield purchased French meat processor Jean Caby. In 2006 the company purchased Cook's Ham from ConAgra and the bulk of ConAgra's refrigerated meats business. The deal included the Eckrich, Armour, Longmont, LunchMakers, and Margherita brands. The Butterball brand was sold to Carolina Turkeys (now Butterball, LLC), of which Smithfield owns 49%.

After 31 years as Smithfield's CEO and chairman, Joseph Luter stepped down as CEO in 2006. However, he remained as non-executive chairman of the company. President and COO C. Larry Pope, a 25-year veteran of Smithfield, succeeded Luter as CEO.

EXECUTIVES

Chairman: Joseph W. Luter III, age 71
President, CEO, and Director: C. Larry Pope, age 55, $2,320,616 total compensation
EVP and CFO: Robert W. (Bo) Manly IV, age 57, $1,670,940 total compensation
EVP: Richard J. M. Poulson, age 71, $1,080,648 total compensation
EVP: Joseph W. (Joe) Luter IV, age 45, $940,845 total compensation
SVP Corporate Affairs and Chief Sustainability Officer: Dennis H. Treacy, age 55
CIO: Mansour T. Zadeh, age 55
Senior Corporate VP Operations and Engineering: Henry L. Morris, age 67
VP Finance: Carey J. Dubois, age 50, $560,639 total compensation
VP Sales and Marketing: James D. Schloss, age 64
VP and Chief Accounting Officer: Kenneth M. Sullivan, age 46
VP and Senior Counsel: Michael D. Flemming, age 61
VP, Chief Legal Officer, and Secretary: Michael H. Cole, age 50
VP and Corporate Controller: Jeffrey A. Deel, age 52
VP Investor Relations and Corporate Communications: Jerry Hostetter, age 65

President, John Morrell: Joseph B. Sebring, age 62, $1,626,186 total compensation
President, Farmland Foods: James C. (Jim) Sbarro, age 49, $1,465,281 total compensation
President, Smithfield Packing Company: Timothy O. (Tim) Schellpeper, age 45, $1,454,902 total compensation
President, Murphy-Brown: Jerry H. Godwin, age 63, $1,139,218 total compensation
President and COO, Pork Group: George H. Richter, age 65, $3,478,475 total compensation
Manager Investor Relations: Keira Ullrich
Corporate Treasurer: Houghton Lewis
Auditors: Ernst & Young LLP

LOCATIONS

HQ: Smithfield Foods, Inc.
200 Commerce St., Smithfield, VA 23430
Phone: 757-365-3000   **Fax:** 757-365-3017
Web: www.smithfieldfoods.com

2010 Sales

	$ mil.	% of total
US	9,960.9	89
International	1,241.7	11
Total	**11,202.6**	**100**

PRODUCTS/OPERATIONS

2010 Pork Sales

	% of total
Packaged	55
Fresh, by-products & rendering	45
Total	**100**

Selected Brands

Aoste	Krakus
Armour	Kretschmar Deli
Basse's Choice	Krey
Big 8's	La Abuelita
Bistro	LunchMakers
Butterball	Lundy's
Campofrío	Lykes
Carando	Marcassou
Carolina Turkey	Margherita
Casa Taraneasca	Maverick
Cochonou	Mayrose
Comtim	Mazury
Cook's	Milano's Italian Grille
Cumberland Gap	Morliny
Curly's Foods	Mosey's Corned Beef
Del Mare	Nobre
Dinner Bell	Norson
Eckrich	Olde Kentucky
El Miño	Party Dipper
Ember Farms	Patrick Cudahy
Esskay	Paula Deen Collection
E-Z-Cut Hams	Pavone
Farmland	Peyton's
Farmstead	Premium Standard Farms
Flavoré	Pure Farms
Genuine Smithfield Ham	Quick-N-Easy
Great	Rath Black Hawk
Gwaltney	Ready Crisp
Healthy Ones	Realean
Higüeral	Riojano
Hunter	Rip-n-Dip
Jean Caby	Rodeo
John Morrell	Simply Natural
John Morrell Off the Bone	Sizzle & Serve
Justin Bridou	

HISTORICAL FINANCIALS

Company Type: Public

Income Statement

FYE: Sunday nearest April 30

	REVENUE ($ mil.)	NET INCOME ($ mil.)	NET PROFIT MARGIN	EMPLOYEES
4/10	11,203	(101)	—	48,000
4/09	12,488	(190)	—	52,400
4/08	11,351	129	1.1%	58,100
4/07	11,911	167	1.4%	53,100
4/06	11,404	173	1.5%	52,500
Annual Growth	(0.4%)	—	—	(2.2%)

2010 Year-End Financials

Debt ratio: 105.9%
Return on equity: —
Cash ($ mil.): 451
Current ratio: 2.79
Long-term debt ($ mil.): 2,918

No. of shares (mil.): 166
Dividends
  Yield: 0.0%
  Payout: —
Market value ($ mil.): 3,111

Stock History

NYSE: SFD

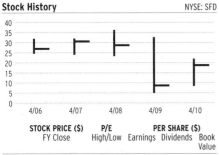

	STOCK PRICE ($) FY Close	P/E High/Low		PER SHARE ($) Earnings	Dividends	Book Value
4/10	18.74	—	—	(0.65)	0.00	16.60
4/09	8.64	—	—	(1.35)	0.00	15.43
4/08	28.68	37	25	0.96	0.00	18.36
4/07	30.57	21	16	1.49	0.00	13.50
4/06	26.90	20	16	1.54	0.00	12.22
Annual Growth	(8.6%)	—	—	—	—	8.0%

Smurfit-Stone Container

Smurfit-Stone Container doesn't think outside the box — it thinks *about* the box. Its operating company, Smurfit-Stone Container Enterprises, makes corrugated containers, containerboard, kraft paper for bags, market pulp, and solid bleached sulfate (SBS) for folding cartons. It also provides graphic design services. Vertically integrated, the company is one of the world's largest recyclers of paper fiber, a key raw material in manufacturing the company's products. Smurfit-Stone buys its wood fiber on the open market, as well as indirectly owns timberland in Canada and operates nurseries and harvesting facilities in the US and Canada. The company filed for Chapter 11 bankruptcy relief in 2009, emerging in 2010.

Under the plan of reorganization, Smurfit-Stone merges with its operating subsidiary, Smurfit-Stone Container Enterprises, forming one new company (Reorganized Smurfit-Stone). In Canada a newly formed subsidiary of Reorganized Smurfit-Stone acquired all Canadian assets. Management changes are in the works, as well; Chairman and CEO Patrick Moore intends to retire within a year of the company's bankruptcy exit, June 2011.

Smurfit-Stone has cited the worsening economy, slumping sales, and too much debt, more so than operational issues, for its inability to restructure its debt through means other than bankruptcy. The company relies heavily on Main Street spending, as its cardboard boxes are used by manufacturers of consumer and industrial products to package items ranging from computers and high-definition TV sets to pizza and office furniture. Millions of tons of market pulp and containerboard are sold to third parties, too.

The company squeezed operating costs by closing 11 converting facilities and halting production at two mills, and cutting its workforce by more than 10%.

Smurfit-Stone Container operates some 150 container plants, paper mills, and recycling centers in the US, Canada, Mexico, Puerto Rico, and China, and a lamination plant in Canada. In addition to selling a range of paper-based packaging products, it handles some 7 million tons of recycled fiber. Its sustainable practices include distribution of more than 24 million pine seedlings annually from its nurseries for cultivating private and public properties.

HISTORY

Joseph Stone left Russia in 1888 and headed for America. In 1926 he and his sons launched J.H. Stone & Sons as a jobber for shipping supplies. It soon began making corrugated boxes. The company incorporated as Stone Container Corporation in 1945; it went public in 1947. Roger Stone, Joseph's grandson, became president in 1975. Under Roger the company bought competitors during industry slumps in the 1980s.

In 1989 the firm bought leading newsprint manufacturer Consolidated-Bathhurst of Canada. Soon after that, prices slumped and interest expenses soared, and Stone began to pile on debt. It began divesting assets in 1993 and spun off Stone-Consolidated, its Canadian subsidiary. Stone Container merged its retail paper-bag operations with

rival Gaylord Container in 1996 as oversupply and falling pulp and paper prices drove revenues down. The next year it merged its 46%-owned Stone-Consolidated with Canada's Abitibi-Price to create Abitibi-Consolidated (the world's #1 newsprint company), in which it owned a 25% stake.

John Jefferson Smurfit, a young Englishman, moved to Belfast, Northern Ireland, in 1934 and became an advisor to a box-making business. By 1938 he controlled the box business.

Jefferson Smurfit & Sons (later Jefferson Smurfit Group, now Smurfit Kappa Group) grew through acquisitions in the 1960s, and it went public in 1964. The enterprise diversified and nearly doubled in size by buying the Hely Group (radio and TV distribution, packaging, and educational and office supplies) in 1970.

Keen to make inroads in the US market, the group acquired 40% of paper and plastic maker Time Industries in 1974, adding the rest in 1977. Smurfit's son Michael continued to acquire during the 1980s.

Jefferson Smurfit Corporation (JSC) was formed to consolidate the Irish company's US holdings; it went public in 1983. JSC diversified into newsprint with the 80% purchase of Publishers Paper in 1986. It teamed up with Morgan Stanley to purchase Container Corporation of America for $1.2 billion. JSC bought out Morgan Stanley's 50% of Container Corporation in 1989 and reorganized as a privately held corporation. After struggling with high-cost debt and weak paper markets in the early 1990s, JSC went public again in 1994.

JSC purchased Ohio recycler Grossman Industries and Michigan Can and Tube in 1995. The combination of higher selling prices and a cost-reduction program that year led JSC to its first profitable year in half a decade.

Late in 1998 JSC merged with Stone Container in a $1.3 billion deal to form Smurfit-Stone Container, a containerboard company. The new company moved to cut costs by consolidating operations in 1999. It shut down eight containerboard and corrugated-container facilities and cut about 5% of its workforce. Also in 1999 the company sold its southeastern timberland holdings (969,000 acres) to Rayonier for $710 million and sold its newsprint mill in Newberg, Oregon, to a partnership of three newspaper publishers for $220 million.

Smurfit-Stone acquired specialty containerboard manufacturer St. Laurent Paperboard in 2000 in a deal worth around $1.4 billion. In September Jefferson Smurfit Group distributed its remaining shares in Smurfit-Stone, some 29%, to its shareholders.

Smurfit-Stone in 2005 closed down a US paper mill and two Canadian containerboard mills and cut more than 550 jobs. Later that year the company shut down four more facilities and reduced its workforce by nearly 800.

In 2006 Smurfit-Stone sold its consumer packaging operations — including more than 40 production facilities — to Texas Pacific Group for more than $1 billion. It also shut down approximately 20 corrugating and converting facilities and reduced its workforce by about 2,000 that year. The company sold its Brewton, Alabama, linerboard and bleached board mill to Georgia-Pacific for $355 million in 2007.

In 2008 the company acquired a 90% interest in Calpine Corrugated, a manufacturer of corrugated containers, in exchange for guaranteeing Calpine's $45 million in third-party debt.

EXECUTIVES

Chairman: Ralph F. Hake, age 61
CEO and Director: Patrick J. Moore, age 55, $5,614,026 total compensation
President, COO, and Director: Steven J. (Steve) Klinger, age 51, $2,661,137 total compensation
SVP, Secretary, and General Counsel: Craig A. Hunt, age 49, $1,117,691 total compensation
SVP and General Manager, Corrugated Container Division: Steven C. Strickland, age 58, $1,027,456 total compensation
SVP and General Manager, Board Sales Division: Matthew J. Blanchard, age 50
SVP and General Manager, Recycling Division: Michael R. Oswald, age 53
SVP and General Manager, Containerboard Mill Division: Michael P. (Mike) Exner, age 56
SVP Supply Chain and Board Sales: John L. Knudsen
SVP Corporate Communications and Public Affairs: Susan M. (Sue) Neumann, age 56
SVP and Corporate Controller: Paul K. Kaufmann, age 47
SVP Strategic Initiatives and CIO: Mark R. O'Bryan, age 47
SVP Human Resources: Ronald D. Hackney, age 63
SVP Business Planning and Analysis: Matthew T. Denton, age 47
VP Innovation and Chief Marketing Officer: Douglas M. Keim
VP Research and Development: James D. (Jim) Cutter
VP Environmental Affairs: Nina E. Butler
VP Investor Relations and Treasurer: Timothy T. Griffith
Director Corporate Communications and Public Affairs: Lisa Esneault
Auditors: Ernst & Young LLP

LOCATIONS

HQ: Smurfit-Stone Container Corporation
222 N. LaSalle St., Chicago, IL 60601
Phone: 312-346-6600   **Fax:** 312-580-2272
Web: www.smurfit.com

2009 Sales

	$ mil.	% of total
US	4,823	87
Canada	562	10
Other countries	189	3
Total	**5,574**	**100**

PRODUCTS/OPERATIONS

2009 Sales

	% of total
Food/Beverage	53
Light Manufacturing/Distribution	17
Household	15
Durables	11
Other non-durables	4
Total	**100**

Selected Products and Services

Automated Packaging Systems
Containerboard
  Kraft Linerboard
  Corrugating Medium
  White Top Linerboard
  Premium White Top Linerboard
  Coated White Top Liner
Corrugated Containers
  Bulk Bins
  Pallets
Food Service
  Cup Stock
  Plate Stock
  Bacon Board
Global Packaging Solutions
Image Pac
Kraft Paper
Pulp
  Market Pulp
  Specialty Pulp
Solid Bleached Sulfate (SBS)
Recycling and Waste Solutions

COMPETITORS

Amcor	Oji Paper
Boise Cascade	Packaging Corp.
Georgia-Pacific	of America
Greif	Potlatch
International Paper	Pratt Industries USA
Longview Fibre	Smurfit Kappa
Louisiana-Pacific	Sonoco Products
MeadWestvaco	Temple-Inland
M-real	Weyerhaeuser

HISTORICAL FINANCIALS

Company Type: Public

Income Statement

FYE: December 31

	REVENUE ($ mil.)	NET INCOME ($ mil.)	NET PROFIT MARGIN	EMPLOYEES
12/09	5,574	8	0.1%	19,000
12/08	7,042	(2,818)	—	21,300
12/07	7,420	(103)	—	22,700
12/06	7,157	(59)	—	25,200
12/05	8,396	(327)	—	33,500
Annual Growth	**(9.7%)**	**—**	**—**	**(13.2%)**

2009 Year-End Financials

Debt ratio: —
Return on equity: —
Cash ($ mil.): 704
Current ratio: 0.92
Long-term debt ($ mil.): 4,389
No. of shares (mil.): 257
Dividends
Yield: —
Payout: —
Market value ($ mil.): 71

Stock History

NYSE: SSCC

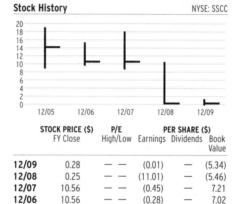

	STOCK PRICE ($) FY Close	P/E High/Low	Earnings	PER SHARE ($) Dividends	Book Value
12/09	0.28	— —	(0.01)	—	(5.34)
12/08	0.25	— —	(11.01)	—	(5.46)
12/07	10.56	— —	(0.45)	—	7.21
12/06	10.56	— —	(0.28)	—	7.02
12/05	14.17	— —	(1.33)	—	7.32
Annual Growth	**(62.5%)**	**— —**	**—**	**—**	**—**

Snap-on Incorporated

Snap-on understands the mechanics of the automotive repair business. It's a leading maker and distributor of high-quality hand tools, as well as auto diagnostic equipment and "undercar" shop implements, such as hydraulic lifts and tire changers. Snap-on serves mechanics, car manufacturers, and government and industrial organizations. Other products — with brand names Snap-on, Blackhawk, Mitchell, ShopKey, and Sun — include collision repair equipment, management software, roll cabinets, tool chests, wheel balancers, and wrenches. Snap-on operates finance subsidiaries in international markets where it has franchises.

Overall, Snap-on's business has been hit by the economic slowdown and a tightened credit market. Since 2009 the tools firm has jockeyed for immediate growth opportunities to right its ship. To this end, Snap-on in 2009 boosted its manufacturing capacity in China and Eastern Europe.

Snap-on is working to balance its desire to invest in growth opportunities with its need to reduce costs as it moves to climb out of the global recession. Its last investment was in China. To boost its CIG business segment and expand its manufacturing to low-cost regions, Snap-on acquired a 60% stake in Zhejiang Wanda Tools Co. for more than $15 million. In one of its larger acquisitions in recent years, Snap-on bought the automotive parts and services information systems business of Voyager Learning Center (then ProQuest) for about $527 million.

Snap-on originated the mobile-van tool distribution channel in the automotive repair market. Snap-on's US van salespeople are primarily franchisees who buy tools at a discount, then sell them to mechanics at a price they determine. The company publishes *Fuel*, a lifestyle magazine that's free and hand-delivered by dealers to technicians.

Snap-on's finance operations serves two primary customers: the buyers of its tools and services and its franchisees. The toolmaker offers loans and vehicle leases to franchisees, as well as financing to customers who wish to purchase tools, equipment, or diagnostic products.

Snap-on has made changes to its executive suite. Chairman, president, and CEO Jack Michaels in December 2007 handed his titles of president and CEO to Nicholas Pinchuk. Michaels gave his chairman title to Pinchuk in April 2009. Pinchuk was initially hired in 2002 to head the company's Worldwide Commercial and Industrial Group. Pinchuk came to Snap-on from Carrier Corporation, a unit of United Technologies Corporation, and Ford Motor Company.

Harris Associates and Janus Capital management each own a 7% stake (more or less) in Snap-on.

HISTORY

Joe Johnson's boss at American Grinder Manufacturing rejected his idea for interchangeable wrench handles and sockets in 1919, and Snap-on Tools was born. With practically no capital, Joe and co-worker William Seidemann made a set of five handles and 10 sockets, and two Wisconsin salesmen sold over 500 orders. Snap-on Wrench Company was incorporated in 1920. Stanton Palmer and Newton Tarble, both salesmen, developed a distribution business based on demonstrations at customer sites and formed Motor Tool Specialty Company in 1920. The next year they bought out Johnson's original supporters, and Palmer became president, holding the office until his death in 1931.

By 1925 Snap-on had salesmen working out of 17 branches; by 1929 it had about 300 salesmen and 26 branches. Overextended when the Depression hit, Snap-on was rescued by Forged Steel Products. Later, during WWII, tool shortages forced salesmen to carry excess stock in their vehicles. By 1945 walk-in vans loaded with tools were commonplace. Salesmen retailing to mechanics became independent dealers with their own regions.

In the 1960s Snap-on started buying branch outlets, giving it complete control over distribution and marketing. Research and development during the 1960s produced pneumatic, hydraulic, and electric tools, as well as the patented

Flank Drive wrench with superior gripping. The company went public in 1978.

During the 1980s Snap-on became the sole supplier of tools to NASA for the space shuttles. In 1985 it had 4,000 dealers, and by 1990 over 5,000.

Robert Cornog became CEO in 1991, the same year Snap-on began signing new dealers as franchisees and offering existing dealers the option to convert. The changeover was prompted by several lawsuits from dealers claiming the company misrepresented their earnings potential. Snap-on purchased all of its minority-owned affiliate, Balco (engine diagnostic and wheel service equipment), in 1991 and acquired Sun Electric (automotive diagnostic, test, and service equipment) in 1992. The following year it acquired J. H. Williams Industrial Products (hand tools).

The company changed its name to Snap-on Incorporated in 1994. It also launched its first national advertising campaign. The next year Snap-on increased its stake in Edge Diagnostic Systems (automobile diagnostic software) to 90%. The company also acquired Consolidated Devices (torque application and measuring equipment) in 1995 and Spain-based Herramientas Eurotools SA (hand tools), doubling its European sales.

In 1996 Snap-on purchased the automotive service equipment division of FMC Corp. The next year it moved head-on into the collision repair industry by purchasing Breco Collision Repair System.

Snap-on in 1998 bought Hein-Werner (collision repair equipment) and formed Snap-on Credit LLC, a joint venture with Newport Credit Group, to offer customer financing services. After difficulty integrating new acquisitions and the company-wide computer system, Snap-on announced in 1998 that it would "simplify" its operations by cutting 8% of its workers and 10% of its product line.

In 1999 Snap-on bought Sandvik Saws and Tools, a division of Sweden's Sandvik AB, for $400 million; the deal helped Snap-on expand in Asia and South America. In mid-2001 executive Dale Elliott was promoted to president and CEO; Cornog remained as chairman until 2002, when Elliott took that position. In late 2001 Snap-on lost a $44 million arbitrator's decision to industrial products and services company SPX Corp. in a case involving alleged patent infringement.

In November 2004 Elliott resigned and director Jack Michaels was named as his replacement. Michaels became chairman in late 2007, when Nicholas Pinchuk was named CEO.

EXECUTIVES

Chairman, President, and CEO:
Nicholas T. (Nick) Pinchuk, age 63,
$4,310,254 total compensation
SVP; President, Commercial Group: Thomas L. Kassouf, age 57, $995,968 total compensation
SVP, Snap-on Incorporated and President, Snap-on Tools Group: Thomas J. Ward, age 57, $2,006,101 total compensation
SVP and CFO: Aldo Pagliari, age 55
SVP Finance and Accounting, Snap-on Tools Company: Blaine A. Metzger, age 51
VP and CIO: Jeanne M. Moreno, age 49, $874,383 total compensation
VP and Chief Marketing Officer:
Andrew R. (Andy) Ginger
VP, General Counsel, and Secretary: Irwin Shur
VP Diagnostics and Information: Bradley R. Lewis, age 46
VP Human Resources: Iain Boyd, age 47
VP Investor Relations: Leslie H. Kratcoski

President, Tool Storage: Christopher H. Potter
President, Snap-on Credit: Joseph R. (Joe) Burger
President, Snap-on Business and Equipment Solutions: Tim Chambers
President, Hand Tools, Snap-on Tools Company: Mike G. Gentile
President, Snap-on Diagnostics: David R. Ellingen, age 49
President, Merchandise Products: Richard V. Caskey, age 56
President, Snap-on Industrial Worldwide: Donald E. Broman, age 60
President, Sales and Franchising: Barrie Young
Manager Corporate Communications: Richard Secor
Auditors: Deloitte & Touche LLP

LOCATIONS

HQ: Snap-on Incorporated
2801 80th St., Kenosha, WI 53143
Phone: 262-656-5200 **Fax:** 262-656-5577
Web: www.snapon.com

2009 Sales

		% of total
US	1,440.1	59
UK	193.2	8
All other	787.5	33
Total	**2,420.8**	**100**

PRODUCTS/OPERATIONS

2009 Sales

	$ mil.	% of total
Commercial & Industrial Group	1,083.8	45
Snap-on Tools Group	998.5	41
Diagnostics & Information Group	530.6	22
Financial services	58.3	2
Adjustments	(250.4)	(10)
Total	**2,420.8**	**100**

2009 Product Sales

	% of total
Tools	56
Diagnostic & repair information	23
Equipment	21
Total	**100**

Selected Products and Services

Diagnostic and shop equipment
  Air-conditioning service equipment
  Brake testers
  Collision repair equipment
  Engine and emissions analyzers
  Lifts and hoists
  Wheel-balancing and alignment equipment
Hand tools
  Cutting tools
  Pliers
  Ratchets
  Screwdrivers
  Sockets
  Wrenches
Information services
  Management software
  Vehicle service information
Power tools
  Battery-powered tools
  Electric tools
  Pneumatic tools
Tool storage products
  Roll cabinets
  Tool chests

COMPETITORS

Ace Hardware
Atlas Copco
Atlas Copco USA Holdings
AutoZone
Cooper Industries
Cornwell Parker
Danaher
Dover Corp.
Emerson Electric
Fluke Corporation
Home Depot
Hunter Engineering
Illinois Tool Works
Industrial Distribution Group
Ingersoll-Rand
IRWIN Industrial Tool
Klein Tools
L. S. Starrett
Lowe's
Makita
MSC Industrial Direct
Myers Industries
Newell Rubbermaid
Pep Boys
Robert Bosch Tool
Rotary Lift
Sears
SPX
Stanley Black and Decker
Techtronic
W.W. Grainger

HISTORICAL FINANCIALS

Company Type: Public

Income Statement

FYE: Saturday nearest December 31

	REVENUE ($ mil.)	NET INCOME ($ mil.)	NET PROFIT MARGIN	EMPLOYEES
12/09	2,421	144	5.9%	11,000
12/08	2,853	237	8.3%	11,500
12/07	2,841	181	6.4%	11,600
12/06	2,522	100	4.0%	12,400
12/05	2,362	93	3.9%	11,400
Annual Growth	**0.6%**	**11.5%**	**—**	**(0.9%)**

2009 Year-End Financials

Debt ratio: 69.9%
Return on equity: 11.6%
Cash ($ mil.): 699
Current ratio: 2.27
Long-term debt ($ mil.): 902
No. of shares (mil.): 58
Dividends
  Yield: 2.8%
  Payout: 51.7%
Market value ($ mil.): 2,455

Stock History

NYSE: SNA

	STOCK PRICE ($) FY Close	P/E High/Low		PER SHARE ($) Earnings	Dividends	Book Value
12/09	42.26	19	9	2.32	1.20	22.21
12/08	39.38	15	7	4.07	1.20	20.42
12/07	48.24	19	14	3.09	1.11	22.03
12/06	47.64	29	22	1.69	1.08	18.53
12/05	37.56	24	19	1.59	1.00	16.56
Annual Growth	**3.0%**	**—**	**—**	**9.9%**	**4.7%**	**7.6%**

Solutia Inc.

Solutia looks to provide solutions across a range of markets, by manufacturing plastics, films, and chemicals for the construction, automotive, and rubber manufacturing industries. The company operates through three segments. Its Technical Specialties unit manufactures specialty chemicals for rubber and transmission fluids customers through its Flexsys, Terminol, and Skydrol businesses. Solutia's Saflex unit produces polyvinyl butyral (PVB) sheet, which is used as an interlayer in the manufacture of glass. CPFilms makes various plastic films for use in glass, tapes, and packaging products. A global company, Solutia has operations in 50 locations across five continents.

In 2010 Solutia began to grow its specialty chemicals business with the acquisition of German company Etimax Solar for $325 million. That company manufactures ethylene vinyl acetate (EVA) encapsulants for the photovoltaic market. Solutia combined the new unit with its own polyvinyl butyral encapsulants, which are also used by the solar photovoltaic market.

Solutia had entered Chapter 11 bankruptcy protection in late 2003, after years of litigation and a load of debt remaining from its spinoff from the former Monsanto. It emerged from bankruptcy finally in early 2008. Not long after that, the company announced a new strategic direction, which included the divestment of its nylon business. Solutia had decided it preferred the relatively high margins of its performance materials and specialty chemicals business and so chose to sell the larger nylon segment. That business made fibers for carpets, space shuttle tires, upholstery, and dental floss, accounting for more than half of Solutia's annual sales. In 2009 the company sold the business to private equity group SK Capital Partners for about $50 million. Solutia also received a small stake in the company SK Capital set up to operate the business. The company used the $50 million to pay down debt.

HISTORY

Before going solo, Solutia was the chemical side of the former Monsanto (which had merged with Pharmacia & Upjohn and changed its name to Pharmacia; the new entity spun off its seeds and crop protection business as the new Monsanto before Pharmacia itself was acquired by Pfizer in 2003). John Queeny, dubbing the company with his wife's maiden name, started Monsanto in St. Louis after seeing an opening in the artificial-sweetener market. Saccharin was its first product (1902), followed by caffeine (1904), vanillin (1904), and aspirin (1917).

The company acquired R. A. Graesser Chemical Works, the UK's leading producer of phenol (an ingredient in nylon), in 1919. It went public in 1927. A year later Queeny's son, Edgar, became president and expanded the company through aggressive licensing and acquisitions.

In 1938 the company entered the plastics and resins market. It bought Fiberloid (producer of celluloid, the first man-made plastic) and 50% of Shawinigan Resins (it bought the rest in 1963). In 1943 Monsanto produced styrene monomer, a key material for synthetic rubber needed by the US in WWII.

Seven years later Monsanto and American Viscose formed Chemstrand to make Acrilan acrylic

fiber and nylon. An agricultural division was created in 1960.

Monsanto created AstroTurf (based on Monsanto's carpet-fiber technology) in 1966 to surface Houston's Astrodome field. In 1976 it produced the first plastic pop bottles, which were promptly taken off the market for possible cancer risks. A reformulated bottle gained approval in 1983, but the market had already been lost to other bottle makers.

The company restructured in the 1980s and early 1990s. It sold its largest chemical business and purchased G.D. Searle (producer of Nutrasweet, 1985). Monsanto cut its workforce and divided its business into three life-sciences units and one chemical group. Monsanto used the chemical unit's strong cash flow to fund high-risk ventures in life sciences. Recognizing that investments in the chemical side of the company would take funds away from the agricultural aspect, Monsanto spun off the chemicals division in 1997. As part of the breakup, Solutia took $1 billion of Monsanto's corporate debt and $1 billion in retirement medical benefit payments.

Solutia's then-CEO, Robert Potter, eliminated some excess administrative levels, cut 800 jobs, and linked executive pay to financial performance. He also started overhauling Solutia's entire supply chain and business processes.

In 1998 Solutia teamed with Bayer, Novus, and a Japanese company to double the size of its acrylonitrile (used in nylon carpet fibers, acrylic fibers, and other products) plant in Alvin, Texas. It also introduced an ingredient that prevents animal feed from becoming rancid.

In 1999 the company bought the window films business of chemical firm Akzo Nobel for $200 million and purchased Germany-based Vianova Resins for $640 million from Morgan Grenfell Private Equity Ltd. Potter retired that year, and John Hunter, a Monsanto veteran since 1969, was named CEO.

By mid-1999, using the strong cash flow from its established businesses and cost reductions, Solutia managed to retire nearly half the debt it inherited at the time of the spinoff. Meanwhile, the company continued to make acquisitions.

Solutia bought Switzerland-based pharmaceutical R&D companies CarboGen Laboratories and AMCIS in 2000. It also combined its phosphorus operations with FMC to form joint venture Astaris. On the divestiture side, Solutia sold its polymer modifiers business to Ferro Corporation and its light denier industrial nylon fibers business to South African Nylon Spinners (SANS).

In 2002 Solutia sold its 50% stake in an elastomer joint venture with ExxonMobil Chemical for about $100 million. In early 2003 the company sold several specialty products businesses to UCB.

Solutia filed for Chapter 11 at the end of 2003 as a result of legacy costs associated with its spinoff from Monsanto, including Monsanto retiree health care obligations. In the middle of 2005 the company reached an agreement-in-principal with unsecured creditors and the new Monsanto to resolve historical liabilities. (The present-day Monsanto agreed to take over certain liabilities from Pharmacia when it was spun off in 2000.) One step toward solvency was the company's sale of ICL Performance Products (formerly Astaris), its joint venture with FMC Corporation, to Israel Chemicals Limited for $255 million.

It finally emerged from Chapter 11 in 2008.

EXECUTIVES

Chairman, President, and CEO: Jeffry N. (Jeff) Quinn, age 52, $5,711,007 total compensation
EVP and COO: James R. Voss, age 43, $2,178,712 total compensation
EVP, CFO, and Treasurer: James M. Sullivan, age 50, $1,695,996 total compensation
SVP Legal and Governmental Affairs and General Counsel: Paul J. Berra III, age 42, $1,051,623 total compensation
SVP Business Operations: Robert T. DeBolt, age 50, $1,204,846 total compensation
VP and Corporate Controller: Timothy J. Spihlman, age 39
VP Corporate Strategy and Development: Nadim Z. Qureshi
President and General Manager, CPFilms: Ray J. Kollar
President and General Manager, Saflex: Timothy J. (Tim) Wessel
President and General Manager, Technical Specialties: D. Michael (Mike) Donnelly
Director Investor Relations: Susannah Livingston
Auditors: Deloitte & Touche LLP

LOCATIONS

HQ: Solutia Inc.
575 Maryville Centre Dr., St. Louis, MO 63141
Phone: 314-674-1000   **Fax:** 314-674-1585
Web: www.solutia.com

2009 Sales

	% of total
Europe	35
Asia/Pacific	27
US	25
Other regions	13
Total	**100**

PRODUCTS/OPERATIONS

2009 Sales

	% of total
Technical Specialties	46
Saflex	42
CPFilms	11
Other	1
Total	**100**

COMPETITORS

3M
Bekaert Corp.
Chemtura
DuPont
ExxonMobil Chemical
Mitsubishi Chemical
Nitto Denko
Sekisui Chemical

HISTORICAL FINANCIALS

Company Type: Public

Income Statement				FYE: December 31
	REVENUE ($ mil.)	NET INCOME ($ mil.)	NET PROFIT MARGIN	EMPLOYEES
12/09	1,667	(109)	—	3,400
12/08	2,110	786	37.3%	3,700
12/07	3,535	(208)	—	6,000
12/06	2,905	11	0.4%	5,100
12/05	2,825	11	0.4%	5,400
Annual Growth	**(12.4%)**	**—**	**—**	**(10.9%)**

2009 Year-End Financials

Debt ratio: 213.2%	No. of shares (mil.): 122
Return on equity: —	Dividends
Cash ($ mil.): 243	Yield: —
Current ratio: 1.98	Payout: —
Long-term debt ($ mil.): 1,264	Market value ($ mil.): 1,549

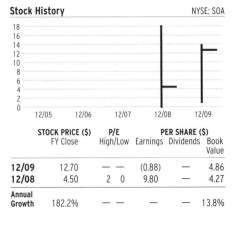

	STOCK PRICE ($) FY Close	P/E High/Low		PER SHARE ($) Earnings	Dividends	Book Value
12/09	12.70	—	—	(0.88)	—	4.86
12/08	4.50	2	0	9.80	—	4.27
Annual Growth	182.2%	—	—	—	—	13.8%

Sonoco Products

Sonoco Products is a package deal. The company is one of the world's largest makers of industrial and consumer packaging used by the food, consumer products, construction, and automotive industries. Sonoco's largest segment, consumer packaging, specializes in round and shaped composite cans for snack foods, powdered beverages, and pet food. It also makes flexible and rigid packaging using both paper and plastic for food, personal care items, and chemicals. Sonoco produces paperboard tubes and cores, too, for industrial protective packaging. The company's slate of end-to-end packaging services includes brand artwork management, supply chain management, and point-of-purchase display design and assembly.

Faced with declining profits, the company is tackling an aggressive strategy that aims to shift 60% of its business to less cyclical, consumer-related demand and away from lower-growth industrial markets by 2012. The recession's corrosive effect on commerce weakened Sonoco's industrial tubes and core/paper segment. Its sales slumped by 20%, forcing the shutter of one US paper mill, five tube and core plants in the US, Europe, and Canada, and one wooden reel plant. It has also reduced its workforce by 15% since 2008.

The company aims to position its consumer segment as a low-cost leader in the packaging industry. Underpinning the effort, the company is developing new products and services that extend its portfolio; in 2009 Sonoco introduced a branded Flavor Lock Lid and composite paperboard can for coffee (made by Kraft Foods).

Sonoco's geographic footprint is another driver for Sonoco's growth. Although the US accounts for a majority of its sales, the company has operations planted in key developing regions where business activity is rapidly expanding, thereby positioning Sonoco for new opportunities. Sonoco is relying on its reach into South America, Eastern Europe, and Asia, to help its industrial segment rebound.

Sonoco's paper-based protective packaging business (part of the company's "other" operating segment) is testing the international waters, as well. The line, which is used in wrapping household appliances, heating and air-conditioning units, and garden equipment, has been well re-

ceived in several developing markets. Protective product advances include an all-paper protective packaging for Haier washing machines. The innovation delivers a low-waste, lighter-weight shipping alternative. The "other" operations include making reels for wire and cable manufacturers. In 2009 Sonoco expanded this segment by acquiring EconoReel Corporation.

HISTORY

Sonoco Products originated during the South's industrial renewal after the Civil War. Major James Coker and son James Jr. (who had been badly wounded at the Battle of Chickamauga) founded the Carolina Fiber company in Hartsville, South Carolina, to make pulp and paper from pine trees. The business was based on a thesis James Jr. wrote in 1884 at Stevens Institute of Technology in Hoboken, New Jersey. The essay explained how to make paper pulp using the sulfite process.

After failing to sell the pulp commercially, the Cokers decided to use it to make paper cones for the textile industry, which was seeing rapid growth in the southern US. In 1899 Major Coker and investor W. F. Smith formed the Southern Novelty Company. Major Coker's son Charles became president in 1918. As sales neared $1 million in 1923, the company changed its name to Sonoco.

In the 1920s Sonoco formed a joint venture in the UK to make Sonoco-style textile carriers. The venture became the Textile Paper Tube Company, which later set up plants in Germany, India, Ireland, the Netherlands, and South Africa.

When Charles died in 1931, his 27-year-old son James became president. James eventually set up eight plants in the US and established a Canadian subsidiary. With the introduction of man-made fibers, the textile industry expanded dramatically, and Sonoco kept pace with the technological changes. By the late 1940s it had eight paper machines in operation at its Hartsville mill.

In the 1950s Sonoco formed a Mexican subsidiary; began tube operations in California, Indiana, and Texas; and diversified into corrugated materials. The company forged a business relationship in 1964 with Showa Products Company of Japan.

Charles Coker, great-grandson of the founder, became president in 1970. The company entered the wastepaper-packing business in 1972 and the folding-carton and fiber-partitions businesses in 1973. It expanded rapidly, and by 1986 Sonoco had 150 plants. The next year it acquired the consumer packaging division of Boise Cascade, which was then the country's #1 producer of composite cans. By 1989 Sonoco was the world's top maker of uncoated, recycled cylinder paperboard.

Charles became CEO in 1990. The company set up a Singapore office and a tube and core plant in Malaysia in 1992 and acquired specialty packager Engraph the following year. In 1995 Sonoco formed a joint venture to produce paperboard in China and bought a paper mill and a tube-making plant in France. The company acquired paper-mill assets in Brazil in 1996 and entered a joint venture in Indonesia to make composite cans.

The next year saw further expansion as Sonoco entered a joint venture in Chile and a second joint venture in Brazil. In 1997 packaging maker Greif Bros. bought most of Sonoco's industrial

container division, and in 1998 Sonoco sold its North American pressure-sensitive-labels business to CCL Industries. President Peter Browning also replaced Charles as CEO (Charles remained chairman). Also in 1998 the company cut about 13% of its workforce and closed five plants to trim costs and consolidate operations.

In 1999 Sonoco doubled its flexible packaging business with the purchase of Graphic Packaging International's flexible packaging unit. CEO Peter Browning retired in 2000 and was replaced by company veteran Harris DeLoach. Sonoco announced several plant closures in 2001.

In 2003 Sonoco purchased Australian Tube Company (ATC), a maker of paper-based tubes and cores. In 2004 the company acquired CorrFlex Graphics, which offers point-of-purchase displays and related products, for about $250 million.

Sonoco bought The Cin-Made Packaging Group, which makes rigid composite containers in 2006. In 2007 it acquired private Canadian rigid plastic container maker Matrix Packaging for $210 million. It also acquired six manufacturing facilities from Caraustar Industries.

EXECUTIVES

Chairman, President, and CEO: Harris E. DeLoach Jr., age 65, $8,717,164 total compensation
EVP Consumer: M. Jack Sanders, age 56, $3,251,633 total compensation
SVP and CFO: Charles J. Hupfer, age 63, $2,637,915 total compensation
SVP Primary Materials Group: Jim C. Bowen, age 59, $1,177,264 total compensation
SVP Human Resources: Cynthia A. (Cindy) Hartley, age 61
VP Global Flexibles and Packaging Services: Robert C. (Rob) Tiede, age 51, $1,213,652 total compensation
VP Global Industrial Converting: John M. Colyer Jr., age 49
VP Global Rigid Paper and Closures: Rodger D. Fuller, age 48
VP Global Manufacturing, Industrial: Marty F. Pignone, age 53
VP Global Corporate Accounts: Vicki B. Arthur, age 52
VP Global Plastics: Robert L. Puechl
VP and CIO: Bernard W. (Bernie) Campbell
VP Corporate Planning: Kevin P. Mahoney, age 54
VP Investor Relations and Corporate Affairs: Roger P. Schrum, age 54
VP, Corporate Controller, and Chief Accounting Officer: Barry L. Saunders, age 50
VP North American Industrial Carriers: James A. Harrell III, age 48
Staff VP, Treasurer, and Corporate Secretary: Ritchie L. Bond, age 53
Auditors: PricewaterhouseCoopers LLP

LOCATIONS

HQ: Sonoco Products Company
1 N. 2nd St., Hartsville, SC 29550
Phone: 843-383-7000   Fax: 843-383-7008
Web: www.sonoco.com

2009 Sales

	$ mil.	% of total
US	2,315.1	64
Europe	616.7	17
Canada	315.9	9
All other	349.6	10
Total	**3,597.3**	**100**

PRODUCTS/OPERATIONS

2009 Sales

	$ mil.	% of total
Consumer packaging	1,550.6	43
Tubes & cores/paper	1,339.1	37
Packaging services	426.5	12
All other	281.1	8
Total	**3,597.3**	**100**

Selected Products and Services

Consumer packaging
  Printed flexible packaging
    Flexographic and combination printed film
      (laminations and rotogravure cylinder engraving)
    Thin-gauge packaging
  Rigid packaging — paper
    Paperboard cans
    Paperboard pails
    Fiber cartridges
  Rigid packaging — blow molded plastics
    Monolayer and multilayer bottles, jars, tubs, and
      squeeze tubes
  Rigid packaging — thermoformed plastic
    Laminated tubs, cups, and consumer and
      institutional trays
  Ends and closures
    Aluminum, steel and peelable membrane closures
      for composite, metal, and plastic containers
  Printed flexible packaging

Other
  Molded and extruded plastics
  Paperboard specialties (coasters, glass covers)
  Protective packaging
  Wire and cable reels

Packaging services
  Point-of-purchase displays
  Supply chain management

Tubes and cores/paper
  Boxboard
  Chipboard
  Concrete forms
  Linerboard
  Lightweight corestock
  Molded plugs
  Pallet components
  Paperboard tubes and cores
  Recycled paperboard
  Roll packaging
  Rotary die boards
  Tubeboard

COMPETITORS

Amcor	MeadWestvaco
AptarGroup	The Newark Group
Avery Dennison	Owens-Illinois
Ball Corp.	Pactiv
Bemis	Rock-Tenn
Caraustar	Sealed Air Corp.
Crown Holdings	Silgan
Graphic Packaging	Smurfit-Stone Container
Greif	Temple-Inland
International Paper	

HISTORICAL FINANCIALS

Company Type: Public

Income Statement

FYE: December 31

	REVENUE ($ mil.)	NET INCOME ($ mil.)	NET PROFIT MARGIN	EMPLOYEES
12/09	3,597	152	4.2%	16,500
12/08	4,122	165	4.0%	17,500
12/07	4,040	214	5.3%	18,600
12/06	3,657	195	5.3%	17,700
12/05	3,529	162	4.6%	17,600
Annual Growth	**0.5%**	**(1.6%)**	**—**	**(1.6%)**

2009 Year-End Financials

Debt ratio: 33.9%
Return on equity: 12.0%
Cash ($ mil.): 185
Current ratio: 1.24
Long-term debt ($ mil.): 463

No. of shares (mil.): 101
Dividends
  Yield: 3.7%
  Payout: 72.0%
Market value ($ mil.): 2,944

Stock History

NYSE: SON

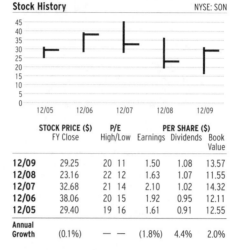

	STOCK PRICE ($) FY Close	P/E High/Low		PER SHARE ($) Earnings	Dividends	Book Value
12/09	29.25	20	11	1.50	1.08	13.57
12/08	23.16	22	12	1.63	1.07	11.55
12/07	32.68	21	14	2.10	1.02	14.32
12/06	38.06	20	15	1.92	0.95	12.11
12/05	29.40	19	16	1.61	0.91	12.55
Annual Growth	**(0.1%)**	**—**	**—**	**(1.8%)**	**4.4%**	**2.0%**

Sotheby's

Sotheby's believes that every man's trash (or treasure) is another man's treasure — especially when that trash just so happens to be a pricey antique, a rare collectible, or anyone's idea of art. The company (along with rival Christie's International) dominates the world's auction house market. Sotheby's orchestrates hundreds of sales each year at its auction centers around the world dealing mainly in fine art, antiques, and collectibles. The company collects commissions and fees from both the buyer and the seller on each sale. Sotheby's also provides loans (secured against works of art) to clients as part of its finance services and acts as an art dealer through its Noortman Master Paintings business.

The past decade has been a bit of a wild ride for Sotheby's, which while recovering from the dot-com bust of the early 2000s was hit by an alleged commission fixing scandal involving its former CEO and chairman. Having put its tarnished past behind it and riding high on the booming market for Impressionist and Contemporary art, Sotheby's then fell victim to the global economic downturn.

With the international art market in decline, Sotheby's has scrambled to respond to the marked decline in its fortunes (and those of its wealthy clients). In response, the art and antiques auctioneer has reduced operating expenses through salary cuts and layoffs. The firm has also been looking to emerging markets, such as Turkey and Qatar, for growth.

Live auctions account for the bulk of Sotheby's revenues. The company has overseen the sales of such items as Picasso's *Femme Assise dans un Jardin,* Degas' *Petite Danseuse de Quatorze Ans,* and the last baseball glove used by Lou Gehrig. Sotheby's has leveraged its expertise and profile in art circles to offer such

services as secured financing and insurance, as well as serving as a broker for private sales. Additionally, the company offers restoration and appraisal services and operates two art institutes in New York City and London. In 2006 Sotheby's expanded when it acquired Noortman Master Paintings (NMP), an art dealer specializing in Dutch, Flemish, and French paintings.

HISTORY

Sotheby's Holdings traces its roots to Samuel Baker, a London bookseller, who held his first auction in 1744 to dispose of an English nobleman's library. After Baker died in 1778, his nephew John Sotheby took over, placing his name over the door of the business. During the 19th century Sotheby's expanded into antiquities, paintings, jewelry, and furniture. Business boomed as newly wealthy Americans swarmed across the Atlantic seeking the status symbols of the Old World.

By the end of WWI, Sotheby's had become fully entrenched in the art market, and in 1917 the company moved to New Bond Street (where its London office still stands). Following WWII, Sotheby's expanded into the US, opening its first office in New York City in 1955. It later acquired Parke-Bernet, a leading US art auction house, in 1964. The company prospered and expanded during the 1970s as rising interest rates and inflation fueled an art market boom, and in 1977 Sotheby's went public.

A collapse of the art market left Sotheby's a target for corporate raiders in the early 1980s. The company's board asked US shopping center magnate Alfred Taubman to lead a buyout group in 1983. After weathering the storm, the company was well-positioned when the art market rebounded, a turnaround driven in part by the desire of newly wealthy Japanese to confirm their status — just as Americans had done a century before. In 1988 the company went public again, with Taubman as chairman.

After the boom peaked in 1990 (Christie's International sold van Gogh's *Portrait of Dr. Gachet* that year for a record $82.5 million), Sotheby's earnings plummeted, and its share price tanked. In 1994 Diana Brooks became president and CEO. The company posted solid results in 1995, but the company slipped to the #2 auctioneer in the world for the first time in more than 20 years.

In 1997 Sotheby's acquired Chicago-based Leslie Hindman Auctioneers and Chicago wine auctioneers Davis & Co. in 1998. The next year Sotheby's created a co-branded auction website with Amazon.com. The site never turned a profit and was scaled back in 2000 and the partnership terminated in 2001. In 2002 Sotheby's partnered with eBay to sell high-end merchandise online within the eBay website.

In 2000 the US Justice Department reopened a 1997 investigation of an alleged price fixing scheme involving Sotheby's and Christie's. After the allegations became public, Taubman and Brooks resigned, replaced by Michael Sovern (chairman) and William Ruprecht (CEO). The probe sparked additional lawsuits and investigations. Both companies agreed to pay $256 million each to settle the civil claims. Brooks pleaded guilty to violating antitrust laws but testified against Taubman in exchange for leniency. Taubman pleaded innocent and was convicted and sentenced to one year in prison after a vicious trial.

In 2001 Sotheby's laid off about 8% of its staff and raised fees in 2002 in its efforts to offset losses. The bleeding continued into 2002 as the company sold its Upper East Side headquarters in New York for $175 million and laid off 7% of its staff. In 2004 Sotheby's sold its International Realty operations to Cendant for about $100 million. (Cendant spun off its real estate businesses as Realogy in 2006.)

Sotheby's dropped "Holdings" from its official name in mid-2006.

The auction house's legal woes continued in August 2007 when a Canadian antitrust entity obtained a restrictive order against Sotheby's, claiming that the company had agreed with competitors to fix the prices it charged to customers (between the years of 1993 to 2000).

EXECUTIVES

Chairman: Michael I. Sovern, age 78
Deputy Chairman: The Duke of Devonshire, age 65
President, CEO, and Director:
William F. (Bill) Ruprecht, age 54,
$2,354,242 total compensation
EVP and COO: Bruno Vinciguerra, age 47,
$1,508,649 total compensation
EVP and CFO: William S. Sheridan, age 56,
$1,107,886 total compensation
EVP and Director; Chairman, Sotheby's International:
Robin G. Woodhead, age 58,
$1,897,412 total compensation
EVP and Worldwide Director Press and Corporate Affairs: Diana Phillips, age 63
EVP, Secretary, and Worldwide General Counsel:
Gilbert L. Klemann II, age 59
EVP and Worldwide Head Human Resources:
Susan Alexander, age 56
SVP and Chief Technology and Strategy Officer; COO, North America: David Ulmer, age 53
SVP, Controller, and Chief Accounting Officer:
Kevin M. Delaney
SVP and Worldwide Director Compliance:
Jane A. Levine
SVP and Worldwide Director Taxes:
Vincent L. Montagnino
SVP and Treasurer: Michael L. Gillis
CEO, Sotheby's Asia: Kevin S. H. Ching, age 53,
$1,062,672 total compensation
Chairman, Sotheby's Financial Services; President, Sotheby's Venture: Mitchell Zuckerman, age 63,
$793,799 total compensation
Managing Director Sotheby's Europe:
Patrick van Maris van Dijk, age 48
Managing Director Sotheby's Americas:
Maarten ten Holder, age 39
Investor Relations: Jennifer Park
Auditors: Deloitte & Touche LLP

LOCATIONS

HQ: Sotheby's
1334 York Ave., New York, NY 10021
Phone: 212-606-7000   **Fax:** 212-606-7107
Web: www.sothebys.com

2009 Sales

	$ mil.	% of total
US	203.1	42
UK	145.3	30
China	50.1	10
France	29.2	6
Other countries	60.8	12
Adjustments	(3.6)	—
Total	**484.9**	**100**

PRODUCTS/OPERATIONS

2009 Sales

	$ mil.	% of total
Auction	448.8	92
Dealer segment	22.3	4
Finance segment	9.1	2
License fees	3.2	1
Other	1.5	1
Total	**484.9**	**100**

Selected Operations

Acquavella Modern Art (50%, art sale brokerage)
Noortman Master Paintings B.V. (art dealer, The Netherlands)
Sotheby's (live auctions)
Sotheby's Financial Services (art financing)
Sotheby's Insurance Brokerage Services

COMPETITORS

Bonhams
Christie's
eBay
Finarte-Semenzato
GoIndustry-DoveBid
Phillips, de Pury & Company
SinoCoking
Spectrum Group
Tiffany & Co.

HISTORICAL FINANCIALS

Company Type: Public

Income Statement

FYE: December 31

	REVENUE ($ mil.)	NET INCOME ($ mil.)	NET PROFIT MARGIN	EMPLOYEES
12/09	485	(7)	—	1,323
12/08	692	28	4.1%	1,638
12/07	918	213	23.2%	1,555
12/06	665	107	16.1%	1,497
12/05	514	63	12.2%	1,443
Annual Growth	**(1.4%)**	**—**	**—**	**(2.1%)**

2009 Year-End Financials

Debt ratio: 88.9%
Return on equity: —
Cash ($ mil.): 322
Current ratio: 2.19
Long-term debt ($ mil.): 513
No. of shares (mil.): 67
Dividends
　Yield: 1.3%
　Payout: —
Market value ($ mil.): 1,506

Stock History

NYSE: BID

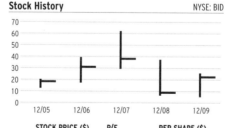

	STOCK PRICE ($) FY Close	P/E High/Low		PER SHARE ($) Earnings	Dividends	Book Value
12/09	22.48	—	—	(0.10)	0.30	8.61
12/08	8.89	85	17	0.43	0.60	8.26
12/07	38.10	19	9	3.25	0.50	9.01
12/06	31.02	22	11	1.72	0.20	4.50
12/05	18.36	19	13	1.00	0.00	1.88
Annual Growth	**5.2%**	**—**	**—**	**—**	**—**	**46.2%**

Southern Company

Southern Company isn't just whistling Dixie. The holding company is one of the largest electricity distributors in the US. It operates regulated utilities Alabama Power, Georgia Power, Gulf Power, and Mississippi Power, which combined have a generating capacity of more than 42,900 MW and serve more than 4.4 million electricity customers in the southeastern US. The good ol' power company also has energy marketing operations, and it provides energy consulting and management services for businesses and institutions. Through its Southern LINC Wireless unit, it provides wireless communications services in its US utility territory; its Southern Telecom unit offers wholesale fiber-optic services.

Southern Company also participates in the nonregulated energy sector: it markets excess energy from its retail plants and is building competitive plants across the southeastern US through subsidiary Southern Power.

The global recession and the reduced use of power, especially by industry, hurt the company's sales revenues in 2009.

In keeping with the federal regulatory framework, which demands that utilities cut back on carbon emissions, in 2009 Southern Company's Mississippi Power filed plans to build a 582-MW integrated gasification combined cycle power plant near Orlando, Florida. This is one of the first advanced gasification generating facilities with carbon capture capabilities in the US.

In 2010 Southern Company teamed up with Ted Turner's Turner Renewable Energy to bring online one of the largest solar photovoltaic power plants in the US. The 30 MW plant, built by First Solar, will supply electricity to 9,000 homes in New Mexico.

Southern has announced that CEO Ronnie Bates will retire in December 2010. Company veteran and COO Oscar Harper, who was promoted to President in mid-2010, has been named to succeed him.

HISTORY

Steamboat captain W. P. Lay founded the Alabama Power Company in 1906 to develop electric power on the Coosa River. James Mitchell took over in 1912, moved headquarters from Montgomery to Birmingham, and bought a number of Alabama's utilities, consolidating them with Alabama Power under his Canadian holding company, Alabama Traction Light & Power (ATL&P).

In 1920 ATL&P became Southeastern Power & Light, forming Mississippi Power (1924) and Georgia Power (1927) to take over electric utilities in those states, and Gulf Power to do the same in northern Florida (1925).

Southeastern merged with Penn-Ohio Edison to form Commonwealth & Southern in 1929. But by 1942 Commonwealth & Southern was dissolved under the Public Utilities Holding Company Act of 1935 since it owned 11 unrelated, unconnected utilities. Alabama Power, Georgia Power, Gulf Power, and Mississippi Power were placed under a new holding company, Southern Company, which began full operations in 1949.

In 1975, amid an anti-utility political environment created by energy shortages, Georgia Power was near bankruptcy; Alabama Power stopped work on new construction and laid off

4,000 employees in 1978. That year, when Alabama governor and utility critic George Wallace left office, state regulators granted Southern long-sought rate relief.

The SEC allowed Southern to diversify into unregulated operations — a first in the US — with the 1981 formation of Southern Energy, which began investing in independent power projects and companies. In 1988 Southern bought Savannah Electric and Power.

Meanwhile, the industry was undergoing major changes, and utilities were venturing outside their territories. Southern sold a Georgia power plant to two Florida utilities in 1990. Two years later it bought 50% of Bahamian utility Freeport Power, and by 1994 Southern had a 49% stake in three power plants in Trinidad and Tobago. At home the company formed Southern LINC in 1995 to offer wireless telecom services in the southeastern US via specialized mobile radio (SMR) technology.

Also that year the company joined other US electric companies in raiding Britain's deregulated electricity larder. It bought UK utility South Western Electricity (SWEB) in 1995, though it later turned over a 51% stake to partner PP&L Resources. In 1996 it acquired 80% of Hong Kong's Consolidated Electric Power Asia, buying the rest the next year.

The first US company to enter Germany's electric utility market, Southern bought a 25% stake in Berlin's electric utility, Bewag, in 1997. That year and the next Southern expanded into the northeastern US and California, buying power plants from Commonwealth Energy, Eastern Utilities, ConEd, PG&E, and Orange and Rockland Utilities.

Focusing on power transmission in the UK, Southern and PP&L Resources (which became PPL in 2000) sold SWEB's power supply business and the SWEB brand name to London Electricity, an Electricité de France unit, in 1999. The former SWEB's distribution network was renamed Western Power Distribution.

In 2000 Southern sold a 20% stake in Southern Energy, which included the company's merchant energy operations (excluding those in the southeastern US) and its overseas investments, to the public. Southern Energy changed its name to Mirant in 2001, and that year Southern spun off its remaining stake in the unit to its shareholders. To improve operating efficiencies, in 2006 the company merged its Savannah Electric unit into another subsidiary, Georgia Power.

EXECUTIVES

Chairman, President, and CEO: David M. Ratcliffe, age 61, $10,804,474 total compensation
President: Thomas A. (Tom) Fanning, age 53, $3,200,638 total compensation
EVP and COO: Anthony J. Topazi, age 60
EVP and CFO: Art P. Beattie, age 56
EVP, General Counsel, and Corporate Secretary: G. Edison Holland Jr., age 57
EVP; President and CEO, Alabama Power: Charles D. McCrary, age 58, $3,713,816 total compensation
EVP and Chief Transmission Officer: William O. (Billy) Ball
EVP; COO, Georgia Power: W. Paul Bowers, age 53, $3,048,931 total compensation
EVP; President, External Affairs: Christopher C. (Chris) Womack, age 51

EVP; President and CEO, SCS: C. Alan Martin, age 61
EVP; President and CEO, Georgia Power: Michael D. (Mike) Garrett, age 60, $3,785,012 total compensation
EVP: Steven R. (Steve) Spencer, age 54
EVP Engineering and Construction Services, Generation: Penny M. Manuel, age 45
SVP Southern Company Services; SVP and Senior Production Officer, Alabama Power: Theodore J. (Ted) McCullough, age 46
SVP and General Counsel: John Pemberton
SVP Human Resources: Marsha S. Johnson
President and CEO, Mississippi Power: Edward Day VI, age 50
President and CEO, Southern Nuclear: James H. (Jim) Miller III, age 60
President and CEO, SouthernLINC Wireless and Southern Telecom: Robert G. Dawson, age 64
CEO, Southern Power: Ronnie L. Bates, age 50
President and CEO, Gulf Power: Susan N. Story, age 50
Investor Relations Contact: Glen A. Kundert
Auditors: Deloitte & Touche LLP

LOCATIONS

HQ: Southern Company
30 Ivan Allen Jr. Blvd. NW, Atlanta, GA 30308
Phone: 404-506-5000   **Fax:** 404-506-0455
Web: www.southernco.com

PRODUCTS/OPERATIONS

2009 Sales

	$ mil.	% of total
Electric		
Retail	13,307	85
Wholesale	1,802	11
Other revenues	634	4
Total	**15,743**	**100**

Selected Subsidiaries and Affiliates

Alabama Power Company (electric utility)
Georgia Power Company (electric utility)
Gulf Power Company (electric utility)
Mississippi Power Company (electric utility)
Southern Company Energy Solutions LLC (energy services)
Southern Company Services, Inc. (administrative services, limited energy trading)
SouthernLINC Wireless (wireless services)
Southern Nuclear Operating Company, Inc. (operates and maintains Alabama Power's and Georgia Power's nuclear plants)
Southern Power Company (independent power production)
Southern Telecom (fiber-optic telecommunications)

COMPETITORS

AEP
AGL Resources
CenterPoint Energy
Cleco
Constellation Energy Group
Duke Energy
Energen
Entergy
FirstEnergy
Florida Public Utilities
JEA
MEAG Power
NextEra Energy
Oglethorpe Power
PacifiCorp
Progress Energy
SCANA
TECO Energy
TVA
Xcel Energy

HISTORICAL FINANCIALS

Company Type: Public

Income Statement

FYE: December 31

	REVENUE ($ mil.)	NET INCOME ($ mil.)	NET PROFIT MARGIN	EMPLOYEES
12/09	15,743	1,708	10.8%	26,112
12/08	17,127	1,742	10.2%	27,276
12/07	15,353	1,734	11.3%	26,742
12/06	14,356	1,573	11.0%	26,091
12/05	13,554	1,591	11.7%	25,554
Annual Growth	**3.8%**	**1.8%**	**—**	**0.5%**

2009 Year-End Financials

Debt ratio: 116.3%
Return on equity: 11.8%
Cash ($ mil.): 690
Current ratio: 1.05
Long-term debt ($ mil.): 18,131

No. of shares (mil.): 831
Dividends
  Yield: 5.2%
  Payout: 84.0%
Market value ($ mil.): 27,679

Stock History

NYSE: SO

	STOCK PRICE ($) FY Close	P/E High/Low		PER SHARE ($) Earnings	Dividends	Book Value
12/09	33.32	18	13	2.06	1.73	18.76
12/08	37.00	18	13	2.25	1.66	15.98
12/07	38.75	17	15	2.28	1.60	14.91
12/06	36.86	18	15	2.10	1.53	13.69
12/05	34.53	17	15	2.13	1.48	12.87
Annual Growth	**(0.9%)**	**—**	**—**	**(0.8%)**	**4.0%**	**9.9%**

Southern Union

One of the largest diversified natural gas operations in the US, Southern Union is looking to form a more perfect union of natural gas transportation, storage, gathering, processing, and distribution assets. The company's major utility, Missouri Gas Energy, distributes natural gas to customers in four states. Southern Union has interests in gas storage facilities and more than 20,000 miles of pipeline throughout the US (primarily through Panhandle Energy and its 50% ownership of Florida Gas). Subsidiary Southern Union Gas Services is a transmission and gathering unit that operates in Texas and New Mexico.

It was able to ward off a proxy fight by institutional investor Sandell Asset Management, which owns about 9% of Southern Union, in 2009 by giving Sandell the right to nominate two candidates to stand for election to Southern Union's Board in 2009 and 2010.

HISTORY

Southern Union's earliest predecessor was the Wink Gas Co., formed in 1929 in Wink, Texas, during the West Texas oil boom. Although its first customer had to lay his own pipeline, the company grew, and in 1932 it became the Southern Union Company. In 1949 Southern Union won the Austin, Texas, gas franchise by merging with Texas Public Service Co.

The energy crisis of the 1970s led Southern Union to diversify into unrelated areas (such as real estate) that turned sour by the 1980s. Shortly after the natural gas industry was deregulated in the 1980s, the company formed Mercado Gas Services in 1986 to market gas to commercial and industrial customers.

Four years later, New York entrepreneur George Lindemann acquired Southern Union and installed Peter Kelley as president. Kelley wasted no time in shifting the corporate culture from a lethargic, top-heavy bureaucracy to an efficient sales organization.

Southern Union bought several Texas natural gas companies in 1993 and nearly doubled its customer base in 1994 with the purchase of Gas Service of Kansas City (now Missouri Gas Energy, or MGE). Moving into Florida in 1997, Southern Union acquired gas distributor Atlantic Utilities.

Continuing to look for acquisitions, Southern Union in 1999 submitted a bid to buy Las Vegas-based Southwest Gas, which instead accepted a lower offer from ONEOK. Southern Union sued Southwest Gas to block the ONEOK deal, and ONEOK terminated the agreement in 2000. Southern Union also filed fraud claims against ONEOK and Southwest Gas. (Southwest Gas paid Southern Union $17.5 million in 2002 to settle the suits.)

Southern Union decided to move north in 1999, when it bought natural gas distributor Pennsylvania Enterprises (150,000 customers). The next year Southern Union gained nearly 300,000 customers in New England by buying two Rhode Island gas utilities, Valley Resources and Providence Energy, and Massachusetts-based Fall River Gas. In 2001 the three utilities began operating as New England Gas.

Kelley resigned for health reasons in 2001, and Thomas Karam moved from the company's Pennsylvania operations to replace him. In a cost-cutting effort, Southern Union that year offered early retirement programs to 400 employees and laid off 48 workers in a reorganization of corporate management functions.

The company also began selling noncore assets, including the gas marketing business of PG Energy Services, its Keystone Pipeline Services unit, two small propane/heating oil distribution units, and a plumbing and heating services unit (Morris Merchants).

The company sold its Texas gas distribution utility (Southern Union Gas), as well as SUPro Energy (propane distribution in Texas and New Mexico), Mercado Gas Services (natural gas marketing), its Mexican gas utility interest, and some gas pipeline interests, to ONEOK for about $420 million. Southern Union has also sold its Florida gas distribution businesses, its propane distribution operations in Florida and Pennsylvania, and its outsourced energy management unit, ProvEnergy. New England Gas was sold to National Grid USA for a reported $575 million (and $77 million of assumed debt).

Proceeds from the asset sales were applied to the 2003 purchase from CMS Energy of the Panhandle Energy companies, which together operated a 10,000-mile gas pipeline system. The $1.8 billion deal included the assumption of nearly $1.2 billion in debt.

In 2004 Southern Union subsidiary CCE Holdings purchased Enron's CrossCountry Energy

unit for $2.45 billion (including debt assumption). CrossCountry Energy owned the Transwestern Pipeline (sold in 2006) and holds a 50% stake in Citrus Corp. (the owner of Florida Gas Transmission). Following this transaction, CCE Holdings sold CrossCountry subsidiary Northern Plains Natural Gas, a general partner of Northern Border Partners (now ONEOK Partners), to ONEOK for $175 million.

In 2006 Southern Union sold its PG Energy operating division and its interests in PG Energy Services to UGI Corporation for a reported $580 million. It also went in the other direction that year with the acquisition of natural gas gathering and processing firm Sid Richardson Energy Services for $1.6 billion.

EXECUTIVES

Chairman Emeritus: Franklin W. (Frank) Denius, age 85
Chairman and CEO: George L. Lindemann, age 74
Vice Chairman, President, and COO:
Eric D. Herschmann, age 46
SVP and CFO: Richard N. (Rick) Marshall, age 51
SVP Pipeline Operations; President and COO, Panhandle Energy and CrossCountry Energy:
Robert O. (Rob) Bond, age 51
SVP Associate General Counsel: Monica M. Gaudiosi, age 47
VP, Controller, and Chief Accounting Officer:
George E. Aldrich, age 60
VP Investor Relations: John F. (Jack) Walsh
VP, Assistant General Counsel, and Secretary:
Robert M. Kerrigan III
President, Gathering and Processing Business:
Roger A. Farrell, age 51
Director External Affairs: John P. Barnett
Auditors: PricewaterhouseCoopers LLP

LOCATIONS

HQ: Southern Union Company
5444 Westheimer Rd., Houston, TX 77056
Phone: 713-989-2000   **Fax:** 713-989-1121
Web: www.southernunionco.com

PRODUCTS/OPERATIONS

2009 Sales

	$ mil.	% of total
Gas transportation & storage	749.2	35
Gas gathering & processing	732.2	34
Gas distribution	692.9	31
Other	4.7	—
Total	**2,179.0**	**100**

Selected Subsidiaries

CCE Holdings, LLC (natural gas transportation)
   Citrus Corp. (50%)
      Florida Gas Transmission Company (50%)
Missouri Gas Energy (natural gas utility)
New England Gas Company (natural gas utility)
Panhandle Energy (natural gas transportation)
   Panhandle Eastern Pipe Line Company
   Sea Robin Pipeline Company
   Pan Gas Storage (dba Southwest Gas Storage)
   Trunkline Gas Company
   Trunkline LNG Company
PEI Power Corporation (independent power production)

COMPETITORS

Ameren	Great Plains Energy
Atmos Energy	Laclede Group
Dominion Resources	National Fuel Gas
Dominion Transmission	NiSource
Duke Energy	ONEOK
El Paso Corporation	Peoples Natural Gas
Empire District Electric	Transcontinental Gas
Exelon	Pipe Line

HISTORICAL FINANCIALS

Company Type: Public

Income Statement

FYE: December 31

	REVENUE ($ mil.)	NET INCOME ($ mil.)	NET PROFIT MARGIN	EMPLOYEES
12/09	2,179	180	8.2%	2,446
12/08	3,070	295	9.6%	2,413
12/07	2,617	229	8.7%	2,337
12/06	2,340	64	2.7%	2,312
12/05	2,019	21	1.0%	2,888
Annual Growth	**1.9%**	**71.6%**	**—**	**(4.1%)**

2009 Year-End Financials

Debt ratio: 145.3%
Return on equity: 7.8%
Cash ($ mil.): 11
Current ratio: 0.82
Long-term debt ($ mil.): 3,421
No. of shares (mil.): 124
Dividends
   Yield: 2.6%
   Payout: 43.8%
Market value ($ mil.): 2,826

Stock History

NYSE: SUG

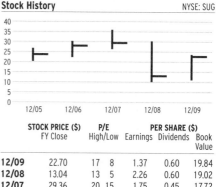

	STOCK PRICE ($) FY Close	P/E High/Low		PER SHARE ($) Earnings	Dividends	Book Value
12/09	22.70	17	8	1.37	0.60	19.84
12/08	13.04	13	5	2.26	0.60	19.02
12/07	29.36	20	15	1.75	0.45	17.72
12/06	27.95	74	57	0.40	0.40	16.47
12/05	23.63	876	692	0.03	—	14.89
Annual Growth	**(1.0%)**	**—**	**—**	**160.0%**	**14.5%**	**7.4%**

Southwest Airlines

Southwest Airlines will fly any plane, as long as it's a Boeing 737, and let passengers sit anywhere they like, as long as they get there first. Sticking with what has worked, Southwest has expanded its low-cost, no-frills, no-reserved-seats approach to air travel throughout the US to serve almost 70 cities in some 35 states. Now among the leading US airlines, Southwest nevertheless stands as an inspiration for scrappy low-fare upstarts the world over.

Southwest is looking to expand its discount flight capabilities, announcing a definitive agreement in late 2010 to acquire Florida-based Air-Tran Airways for about $1.4 billion. By adding AirTran, Southwest would have access to more airports in the Southeastern US, as well as to destinations in the Caribbean and Mexico.

In 2009 Southwest made a move to expand westward when it placed a $170 million bid to buy troubled airline Frontier, but the bid was rejected. The bankruptcy court (Frontier has been under bankruptcy protection since April 2008) ruled in favor of a proposal by Republic Airways.

Southwest and its industry peers have struggled through disastrous market conditions brought on by volatile fuel prices, a severe drop-off in consumer demand, and an economic recession. Southwest responded by slashing capacity, retiring older aircraft, postponing delivery of new planes, offering early retirement to some 1,400 employees, and implementing a hiring freeze.

Simplicity has been a key to Southwest's success. Most of the carrier's flights are less than two hours, and it usually lands at small airports to avoid congestion at competitors' larger hubs. Southwest's fleet of more than 500 aircraft consists only of one type — the Boeing 737 — to minimize training and maintenance costs.

In the wake of the recession, airlines have been searching for new revenue streams. Protective of its low-cost image, Southwest staunchly has resisted fees and remains one of the few airlines that does not charge for checking a second piece of luggage. However, in May 2009 Southwest saw the value in fees and rolled out measures, such as charging for a third bag and for bringing small pets on board, that are expected to eventually add tens of millions of dollars to its annual revenues.

In late 2008 Southwest inked an agreement for an alliance with Canada-based WestJet to begin a joint code-sharing program and with Mexican carrier Volaris. Both deals are set to begin in 2011. WestJet offers scheduled service to more than 50 cities in North America and the Caribbean, and Volaris flies to some 25 cities throughout Mexico. Southwest has said it would consider service to the Caribbean.

HISTORY

Texas businessman Rollin King and lawyer Herb Kelleher founded Air Southwest in 1967 as an intrastate airline linking Dallas, Houston, and San Antonio. The now-defunct Braniff and Texas International sued, questioning whether the region needed another airline, but the Texas Supreme Court ruled in Southwest's favor. In 1971 the company, renamed Southwest Airlines, made its first scheduled flight.

Operating from Love Field in Dallas, Southwest adopted "love" as the theme of its early ad campaigns, serving love potions (drinks) and love bites (peanuts). When other airlines moved to the new Dallas/Fort Worth Airport (DFW) in 1974, Kelleher insisted on staying at Love Field, gaining a virtual monopoly there.

When Kelleher decided to fly outside Texas, Congress passed the Wright Amendment in 1979. Designed to protect DFW, the law restricted the states served directly from Love Field. (Arkansas, Louisiana, New Mexico, and Oklahoma were on the original list; a 1997 amendment added Alabama, Kansas, and Mississippi. In 2000 a federal court removed the restrictions for planes with 56 or fewer seats. Later, Missouri was added to the list of states eligible for direct service from Love Field.)

When Lamar Muse, Southwest's president, resigned in 1978 because of differences with King, Kelleher assumed control. (Muse later took over his son Michael's nearly bankrupt airline, Muse Air, which was sold in 1985 to Southwest. The airline was liquidated in 1987.)

An industry maverick, Kelleher introduced advance-purchase Fun Fares in 1986 and a frequent-flier program in 1987 based on the number of flights taken instead of mileage. He gained attention in 1992 for starring in Southwest's TV commercials and for arm wrestling Stevens Aviation chairman Kurt Herwald for the rights to the "Just Plane Smart" slogan. When

Southwest became the official airline of Sea World in Texas, Kelleher had a 737 painted as a killer whale.

Southwest took on the East Coast with service to Baltimore in 1993 and bought Salt Lake City-based Morris Air in 1994. That year it launched a ticketless system and adopted its own passenger reservation system to cut costs. Agreements with Icelandair in 1996 and 1997 allowed Southwest passengers to connect from four US cities to Europe through Icelandair's Baltimore hub.

In 2001 Southwest experienced a rare labor dispute when stalled contract negotiations led to picketing by the airline's ground crew union.

Kelleher stepped down as president and CEO in 2001. General counsel Jim Parker took over as CEO, and EVP Colleen Barrett — who first worked for Kelleher as his secretary and is given much of the credit for maintaining Southwest's corporate spirit — was named COO.

Parker would reign over the airline during one of the most tumultuous times in its history. Despite an industrywide downturn resulting from the lagging US economy and exacerbated by the September 11 terrorist attacks, Southwest managed to post a profit for 2001 as well as 2002, but it did not come easily.

Increased Internet sales led the airline to close its call centers in Dallas, Little Rock, and Salt Lake City in 2003. Nearly 2,000 workers were given the choice of relocating to another call center or accepting a severance package.

Union negotiations with flight attendants began in 2002 and lasted for two years, during which time Parker was publicly chastised for being uncooperative. A resolution was not reached until Kelleher and Barrett were asked to step in by Parker, who resigned in 2004, after negotiations ended. He was replaced by former CFO Gary Kelly.

After intense lobbying from both Southwest and American Airlines, Congress revisited the Wright Amendment in 2006. A compromise measure signed into law that year allowed Southwest to offer direct, one-stop service from Love Field to states not covered by the original Wright law or its revisions.

Marking a milestone for Southwest, Kelleher and Barrett stepped down from the board in 2008, and Kelly replaced Kelleher as chairman.

After a year of tense meetings with FAA officials, Southwest agreed in early 2009 to pay a $7.5 million fine over missed required structural inspections in 2008 on 46 planes.

EXECUTIVES

Chairman, President, and CEO: Gary C. Kelly, age 54, $1,559,431 total compensation
EVP and COO: Michael G. (Mike) Van de Ven, age 48, $1,037,602 total compensation
EVP Corporate Services and Corporate Secretary: Ron Ricks, age 60, $1,044,835 total compensation
EVP Strategy and Planning: Robert E. (Bob) Jordan, age 49, $976,720 total compensation
SVP Finance and CFO: Laura H. Wright, age 49, $819,844 total compensation
SVP Administration and Chief People Officer: A. Jeff Lamb III
SVP Operations: Greg Wells
SVP Marketing and Revenue Management: Davis S. (Dave) Ridley, age 56
SVP Customer Services: Daryl Krause
SVP Corporate Communications: Ginger C. Hardage
VP Technology and CIO: Jan Marshall
VP and General Counsel: Madeleine Johnson
VP Labor Relations: Michael (Mike) Ryan

VP Communications and Strategic Outreach: Linda B. Rutherford
VP and Controller: Leah Koontz
VP Inflight Services: Mike Hafner
VP Flight Operations: Chuck Magill
VP Marketing, Sales, and Distribution: Kevin M. Krone
VP Customer Support and Services: Ellen Torbert
VP Safety and Security: Scott Halfmann
Auditors: Ernst & Young LLP

LOCATIONS

HQ: Southwest Airlines Co.
  2702 Love Field Dr., Dallas, TX 75235
Phone: 214-792-4000 **Fax:** 214-792-5015
Web: www.southwest.com

PRODUCTS/OPERATIONS

2009 Sales

	$ mil.	% of total
Passenger	9,892	96
Freight	118	1
Other	340	3
Total	**10,350**	**100**

COMPETITORS

AirTran Holdings
Alaska Air
AMR Corp.
Continental Airlines
Delta Air Lines
Frontier Airlines
JetBlue
UAL
US Airways

HISTORICAL FINANCIALS

Company Type: Public

Income Statement

FYE: December 31

	REVENUE ($ mil.)	NET INCOME ($ mil.)	NET PROFIT MARGIN	EMPLOYEES
12/09	10,350	99	1.0%	34,726
12/08	11,023	178	1.6%	35,499
12/07	9,861	645	6.5%	34,378
12/06	9,086	499	5.5%	32,664
12/05	7,584	548	7.2%	31,729
Annual Growth	8.1%	(34.8%)	—	2.3%

2009 Year-End Financials

Debt ratio: 60.8%
Return on equity: 1.9%
Cash ($ mil.): 1,114
Current ratio: 1.25
Long-term debt ($ mil.): 3,325
No. of shares (mil.): 744
Dividends
  Yield: 0.2%
  Payout: 15.4%
Market value ($ mil.): 8,509

Stock History

NYSE: LUV

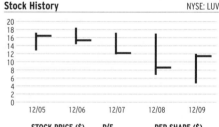

	STOCK PRICE ($) FY Close	P/E High/Low		PER SHARE ($) Earnings	Dividends	Book Value
12/09	11.43	91	38	0.13	0.02	7.34
12/08	8.62	70	29	0.24	0.02	6.65
12/07	12.20	20	14	0.84	0.02	9.32
12/06	15.32	30	24	0.61	0.02	8.66
12/05	16.43	25	19	0.67	0.02	8.97
Annual Growth	(8.7%)	—	—	(33.6%)	0.0%	(4.9%)

Spartan Stores

Spartan Stores operates primarily in Michigan and Indiana. Its holdings include 96 retail supermarkets, all of which are located in Michigan. They operate under the banners Glen's Markets, Family Fare Supermarkets, D&W Fresh Markets, Felpausch Food Centers, and VG's Food and Pharmacy. In addition to selling national brands, the stores offer private-label goods under the Spartan, Top Care, Valu Time, and Full Circle brand names. Spartan is also a leading grocery wholesaler, distributing 43,000 food and general merchandise items to about 375 independent grocery stores in Michigan and Indiana.

The company has been focused on boosting its retail grocery business through a series of acquisitions. It purchased more than 15 properties from V.G.'s Food Center in 2008 after acquiring G&R Felpausch and its chain of 20 Felpausch Food Centers the previous year. At the same time, Spartan Stores divested some noncore properties, including its chain of drug stores (operating under the name The Pharm), which were sold to Rite Aid. Retail supermarkets now account for more than 50% of Spartan's sales.

Sixty-six Spartan's food stores offer pharmacy services and 24 have fuel centers. The fuel centers — named D&W Quick Stop, Family Fare Quick Stop, Glen's Quick Stop, Felpausch Quick Stop and V.G.'s Quick Stop — offer refueling facilities and adjacent convenience stores. Spartan has seen increases in its supermarket sales as a result of fuel-center operation and related cross-merchandising activities. The company plans to open additional fuel centers at its supermarket locations during the next few years.

Meanwhile, the company has been investing in efforts to lower costs within its wholesale distribution business, including implementing new software systems and other improvements at its distribution facilities. Other initiatives have included wage controls and hiring freezes. It also improved its supply chain operations, installing a new on-board transportation management system in its trucks and a new inventory optimization system at its warehouse.

Dennis Eidson was promoted to CEO in 2008 replacing Craig Sturken, who stepped down. Sturken, who had also joined the company from A&P, remained with Spartan Stores as chairman. Investment firm Blackrock owns 8% of the company.

HISTORY

Making dinner in the early 1900s often required several shopping stops: the grocer for canned goods, a butcher for meat, and yet another place for produce. Eventually the big grocery chains began offering one-stop shopping, not to mention better prices due to greater buying power. Worrying about how to compete, in 1917 approximately 100 small grocers met in Grand Rapids, Michigan, to discuss organizing a cooperative; almost half of those formed the Grand Rapids Wholesale Grocery Co. The stores remained independent, operating under different names but achieving economies of scale and volume buying through the co-op. They also began developing a variety of services for member stores. Sales topped $1 million in 1934.

Over the years the company expanded beyond its Grand Rapids origins. In 1950 it formed subsidiary United Wholesale, which served independent grocers on a cash-and-carry basis. It acquired the Grand Rapids Coffee Company in 1953. The next year the co-op launched its first private-label item, Spartan Coffee, with a green Spartan logo reminiscent of the Michigan State University mascot. The company changed its name to Spartan Stores in 1957.

Spartan Stores entered retailing in the early 1970s when it bought 19 Harding's stores. It became a for-profit company in 1973, but continued to provide rebates to customers based on their purchases. Spartan Stores began offering insurance to its customers in 1979.

Concerned about the direction of the company, customers named Patrick Quinn, formerly a VP at a small chain of grocery stores, as president and CEO in 1985. To focus on the wholesale business, and to avoid any appearance of conflict of interest in both supplying member stores and operating competing stores, Spartan Stores sold its 23 retail stores between 1987 and 1994, giving customer stores the first option on them. It entered the convenience store wholesale business with its 1987 acquisition of L&L/Jiroch. Two years later the co-op acquired Associated Grocers of Michigan (later known as Capistar, closed in 1996).

Sales topped $2 billion in 1991. Spartan Stores expanded its convenience store operations in 1993 by buying wholesaler J.F. Walker. Despite record sales in 1996, a $46 million restructuring charge that included extensive technological improvements led to a $21.7 million loss, the largest in the company's history. The following year Jim Meyer, who had joined Spartan Stores in 1973, replaced the retiring Quinn as president and CEO. Also in 1997 the company stopped giving its customers rebates, finally doing away with the last remnants of its co-op years.

To keep Michigan customers out of the clutches of its wholesaling rivals, Spartan Stores re-entered retailing in 1999 by acquiring eight Ashcraft's Markets. It bought 13 Family Fare stores and 23 Glen's grocery stores that year. In early 2000 the company sold off its insurance business. Later that year Spartan Stores acquired food and drug chain Seaway Food Town (Michigan and Ohio) for about $180 million and began publicly trading.

In 2001 the company purchased longtime customer Prevo's Family Markets, a supermarket chain with 10 stores in western Michigan. In an effort to reduce debt and improve profitability in mid-2002 the company announced plans to close its Food Town stores, which suffered from competitors such as Meier, Kroger, and Farmer Jack's. (By mid-2003, Spartan had sold the last of its 26 Food Town stores. Spartan Stores' retail operations had accounted for about 40% of the company's sales.)

In 2003 Spartan Stores sold seven shopping centers in Michigan for $46 million as part of its strategy to sell noncore properties and focus on its retail and distributions businesses. That year James Meyer retired as president and CEO of Spartan Stores and was succeeded by Craig Sturken, a former executive of the Great Atlantic & Pacific Tea Company.

Spartan Stores sold the assets of United Wholesale Grocery Co., a privately held firm in Michigan in 2004, marking its exit from the convenience store distribution business.

In 2005 the company acquired D&W Food Centers and purchased about 20 stores from G&R Felpausch in 2007. Spartan Stores' retail expansion continued in 2008 when it acquired more than 15 stores from V.G.'s Food Center.

EXECUTIVES

Chairman: Craig C. Sturken, age 66, $2,885,199 total compensation
President, COO, and Director: Dennis Eidson, age 56, $1,512,627 total compensation
EVP and CFO: David M. (Dave) Staples, age 47, $914,414 total compensation
EVP Retail Operations: Theodore C. (Ted) Adornato, age 56, $672,511 total compensation
EVP, General Counsel, and Corporate Secretary: Alex J. DeYonker, age 60, $688,145 total compensation
EVP Wholesale Operations: Derek Jones, age 41
EVP Merchandising: Alan Hartline
VP Center Store Merchandising: Larry Pierce
VP Operations and Finance: Francis Wong
VP Corporate Affairs: Jeanne Norcross
VP Fresh Merchandising: Scott R. Ruth
VP Information Technology: David deS. (Dave) Couch, age 59
VP Marketing: Ken Thewes
VP Center Store Merchandising: Brian Haaraoja
VP Finance: Thomas A. (Tom) Van Hall, age 54
Auditors: Deloitte & Touche LLP

LOCATIONS

HQ: Spartan Stores, Inc.
850 76th St. SW, Grand Rapids, MI 49518
Phone: 616-878-2000   **Fax:** 616-878-8561
Web: www.spartanstores.com

2010 Retail Stores

	No. of stores
Glen's Markets	34
Family Fare Supermarkets	27
VG's Food & Pharmacy	16
D&W's Fresh Markets	11
Felpausch Food Centers	8
Total	**96**

PRODUCTS/OPERATIONS

2010 Sales

	$ mil.	% of total
Retail	1,461	57
Distribution	1,091	43
Total	**2,552**	**100**

Selected Retail Brands

Full Circle
Spartan
Spartan Fresh Selections
Top Care
Valu Time

Selected Retail Stores

D&W Fresh Markets
Family Fare Supermarkets
Felpausch Food Centers
Glen's Markets
VG's Food and Pharmacy

COMPETITORS

Associated Wholesale Grocers
C&S Wholesale
Costco Wholesale
IGA
Kroger
McLane
Meijer
Miner's
Nash-Finch
S. Abraham & Sons
SUPERVALU
Wal-Mart

HISTORICAL FINANCIALS

Company Type: Public

Income Statement

FYE: Last Saturday in March

	REVENUE ($ mil.)	NET INCOME ($ mil.)	NET PROFIT MARGIN	EMPLOYEES
3/10	2,552	26	1.0%	8,800
3/09	2,577	39	1.5%	9,700
3/08	2,477	34	1.4%	8,100
3/07	2,370	25	1.1%	7,300
3/06	2,040	18	0.9%	7,500
Annual Growth	5.8%	8.9%	—	4.1%

2010 Year-End Financials

Debt ratio: 76.0%
Return on equity: 10.1%
Cash ($ mil.): 9
Current ratio: 1.09
Long-term debt ($ mil.): 208

No. of shares (mil.): 23
Dividends
  Yield: 1.4%
  Payout: 17.5%
Market value ($ mil.): 326

Stock History

NASDAQ (GS): SPTN

	STOCK PRICE ($) FY Close	P/E High/Low		PER SHARE ($) Earnings	Dividends	Book Value
3/10	14.42	15	10	1.14	0.20	12.11
3/09	15.41	16	7	1.78	0.20	10.36
3/08	20.85	22	11	1.58	0.20	9.13
3/07	26.80	23	10	1.18	0.20	7.63
3/06	12.75	18	10	0.86	0.05	6.43
Annual Growth	3.1%	—	—	7.3%	41.4%	17.2%

Spectrum Brands

Spectrum Brands runs the spectrum of brands — more than 15 of them. They include batteries (Rayovac and VARTA), pet foods and supplies (Tetra, Marineland, Dingo), personal care (Remington), and garden care (Spectracide, Cutter, Hot Shot). The company operates from four divisions, which include Global Batteries & Personal Care, United Pet Group, Home Appliance, and the Home & Garden Business. Spectrum Brands markets its products in about 120 countries and is a leader in the sale of rechargeable batteries and hearing aid batteries to manufacturers. It gets more than half of its sales in the US; 20% comes from Wal-Mart. The company completed a bankruptcy reorganization in 2009.

After guiding Spectrum through its financial restructuring and leading the company back to profitability over three years, CEO Kent Hussey retired, although he remained chairman. Co-COO David Lumley was promoted to CEO to succeed Hussey; he was previously responsible for Spectrum's Global Batteries & Personal Care and Home & Garden businesses.

The company implemented a financial restructuring, which canceled out old equity and approximately $840 million in debt. New stock was issued, and the company agreed to pay all

outstanding invoices from suppliers in full. Several financial institutions led by GE Capital provided exit financing to make available working capital for the company. Spectrum adopted initiatives to lower manufacturing and operating costs by reducing employee numbers, and it exited some of its pet product facilities in 2009. It shuttered its Chinese operations of battery manufacturer Ningbo Baowang Battery in 2008.

After Spectrum posted a net loss of nearly $500 million for the fourth quarter and a net loss of about $932 million for 2008 (mostly on writing off impaired goodwill and intangibles, such as trade names), the company decided to shut down the growing products portion of its Home & Garden division. The business included fertilizers, enriched soils, mulch, and grass seed.

Best known for its general-purpose alkaline batteries, Spectrum Brands also makes hearing aid batteries (Beltone, Miracle Ear, and Starkey brands), as well as zinc carbon, nickel metal hydride, lithium, silver oxide, and coin cell (used in cameras and computer clocks) batteries. The company serves European markets through its VARTA battery brand.

HISTORY

Spectrum Brands traces its roots to 1906, when a trio of Wisconsin entrepreneurs created the French Battery Company. Radio and government orders during WWI galvanized the firm. Its products included Ray-O-Vac radio batteries, and the company adopted that name in the 1930s. In 1937 Ray-O-Vac patented the first wearable vacuum tube hearing aid. Two years later it introduced the sealed dry cell battery, a vital part in mine detectors and bazookas during WWII. The advent of the transistor radio during the 1950s sparked more growth. Ray-O-Vac merged with the much larger Electric Storage Battery Co. in 1957.

The company lost its market lead during the 1960s and 1970s, when it failed to push alkaline batteries. In 1982 husband-and-wife marketers Thomas and Judith Pyle bought the company, changed its name to Rayovac, and introduced new products such as a zinc hearing-aid battery. During the early 1990s it introduced the Workhorse fluorescent lantern. In 1995 basketball superstar Michael Jordan became the company's pitchman.

Investment firm Thomas H. Lee Partners acquired 80% of Rayovac in 1996. David Jones, who had headed Lee's Thermoscan unit, was chosen to head the company, and he began consolidating its operations. Rayovac went public in 1997. The next year the firm entered the Chinese market.

In 1999 the company bought back the battery business of ROV — which Rayovac had spun off in 1982 — for $155 million. Jordan announced his retirement from endorsements in 2000 but said he would honor existing contracts.

In 2001, as part of a plan to cut costs, Rayovac closed its Honduras facility, as well as a US flashlight and lantern assembly plant, and began buying those items from outside suppliers. Also that year 8% of its global workforce lost their jobs.

In 2002 Jones reported that virtually all of the company's earnings in the first quarter of fiscal 2002 were wiped out by Kmart's Chapter 11 bankruptcy filing. Kmart represented more than 6% of Rayovac's 2001 revenues.

Rayovac closed its plant in the Dominican Republic in 2002. The company acquired VARTA's portable battery business later that year. Restruc-

turing in the wake of the acquisition, Rayovac closed its plant in Mexico the same month. In 2003 Rayovac acquired electric shaver maker Remington Products for about $322 million.

In 2004 the company acquired 85% of Ningbo Baowang Battery, which made alkaline and heavy-duty batteries and distributed them in China. Later the same year it acquired Microlite S.A., which owned the Rayovac brand name in Brazil, for about $28 million. The transaction gave Rayovac worldwide rights to the Rayovac brand name. Also in 2004 the company moved its corporate headquarters from Madison, Wisconsin, to Atlanta.

In a deal intended to further diversify its product offerings, in 2005 the company bought United Industries Corp., a privately held maker of lawn and garden products, for around $500 million in cash and stock. Including debt assumption, the deal had a value of about $1.2 billion. It changed its name in 2005 to Spectrum Brands, using a trade name that had been employed by United Industries.

Spectrum Brands then acquired Germany's Tetra Holding AG for approximately $485 million. Tetra was a supplier of foods, equipment, and care products for fish and reptiles, along with accessories for home aquariums and ponds.

After Spectrum posted a big loss in fiscal 2006, David Jones stepped down as CEO in 2007, while remaining nonexecutive chairman of the board for a short period. Vice chairman Kent Hussey, who formerly served as the company's president/COO, was tapped as CEO.

In 2006 the company put up for sale its Home & Garden business, which represented about one-quarter of sales. Spectrum sold the Canadian division of its Home & Garden business, which operated as Nu-Gro, to a new company formed by RoyCap Merchant Banking Group and Clarke Inc.

In 2009, unable to contain its growing losses and ballooning debt, Spectrum filed for Chapter 11 bankruptcy protection and emerged later that same year.

EXECUTIVES

Interim Chairman: David M. Maura
CEO and Director; President, Global Batteries, Personal Care, and Home and Garden:
David R. (Dave) Lumley, age 55,
$4,062,951 total compensation
EVP, CFO, and Chief Accounting Officer:
Anthony L. (Tony) Genito, age 53,
$2,579,237 total compensation
SVP, Secretary, and General Counsel: John T. Wilson
VP Business Technology: Allen Benson
Divisional VP Investor Relations: Carey Phelps
President, Global Pet Supplies: John A. Heil, age 58,
$3,034,949 total compensation
Director; President, Small Appliances:
Terry L. Polistina, age 46
Auditors: KPMG LLP

LOCATIONS

HQ: Spectrum Brands, Inc.
  601 Rayovac Dr., Madison, WI 53711
Phone: 608-275-3340
Web: www.spectrumbrands.com

2009 Sales

	$ mil.	% of total
US	1,280.3	57
Other countries	950.2	43
Total	**2,230.5**	**100**

2009 Sales

	$ mil.	% of total
Batteries & personal care	1,335.0	60
Pet supplies	573.9	26
Home & garden	321.6	14
Total	**2,230.5**	**100**

2009 Sales by Product Line

	% of total
Consumer batteries	37
Pet supplies	26
Home & garden	14
Electric shaving & grooming	10
Electric personal care products	9
Portable lighting	4
Total	**100**

Selected Products by Product Line

Consumer batteries (alkaline, zinc carbon, rechargeable, hearing aid, and specialty)
Electric personal care and styling devices
Electric shaving and grooming
Home and garden (insecticides, insect repellants, herbicides)
Pet supplies (aquatic, dog and cat treats, small animal food, training aids, health and grooming, bedding)
Portable lighting

COMPETITORS

American Vanguard
Bayer AG
BYD
Central Garden & Pet
Coleman
Conair
Energizer Holdings
EnerSys
GP Batteries
Hartz Mountain
Helen of Troy
Henkel
Hong Kong Highpower Technology
Mag Instrument
Mars Petcare
Panasonic Corp
Philips Electronics
Procter & Gamble
S.C. Johnson
Scotts Miracle-Gro
Ultralife
Wahl Clipper

HISTORICAL FINANCIALS

Company Type: Public

Income Statement

FYE: September 30

	REVENUE ($ mil.)	NET INCOME ($ mil.)	NET PROFIT MARGIN	EMPLOYEES
9/09	2,231	943	42.3%	5,700
9/08	2,688	(932)	—	7,000
9/07	1,995	(597)	—	7,100
9/06	2,552	(434)	—	8,400
9/05	2,359	47	2.0%	9,800
Annual Growth	**(1.4%)**	**111.9%**	**—**	**(12.7%)**

2009 Year-End Financials

Debt ratio: 231.5%
Return on equity: —
Cash ($ mil.): 98
Current ratio: 1.65
Long-term debt ($ mil.): 1,530

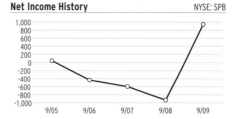

Net Income History   NYSE: SPB

Sprint Nextel

Running to keep up in the US telecom race, Sprint Nextel is the #3 wireless carrier behind Verizon Wireless and AT&T Mobility in terms of subscribers. Sprint Nextel serves nearly 40 million customers with mobile voice, data, and Web services over its nationwide network. While the namesake brand is reserved for postpaid accounts, the company also offers prepaid mobile access through its Boost Mobile subsidiary. Sprint Nextel also provides cellular access to other carriers and resellers on a wholesale basis. The company's smaller legacy wireline business provides long-distance voice, Internet, and data network services primarily to corporate customers and other carriers.

Sprint Nextel is partnering with other telecommunications companies and shedding physical assets in order to cut operational costs and increase liquidity while also making acquisitions to extend the reach of its brand. The company in 2009 announced an agreement with Sweden-based wireless networking equipment and services stalwart Ericsson in which the daily operation, resource provisioning, and maintenance of Sprint Nextel's core wireless and wireline networks will be outsourced to Ericsson.

The previous year, the company formed a joint venture with Kirkland, Washington-based wireless ISP Clearwire that combined the infrastructure of Sprint Nextel's next-generation, wireless broadband network (based on the emerging WiMAX transmission protocol) with Clearwire's network. In return for contributing its WiMAX network (constructed at a cost of more than $3 billion), Sprint Nextel received a 51% stake in the venture, which operates under the Clearwire name. Other investors include Google, Comcast, Time Warner Cable, and Bright House Networks.

The increased data capacity of the emerging WiMAX protocol is seen as something of a gamble for Sprint Nextel due to its largely unproven efficacy for large-scale deployment. Sprint Nextel is betting on strong demand for next-generation (fourth generation or 4G) wireless Internet services to justify the expense. It is intended not only to deliver video and other advanced services to cell phones, but to enable wireless broadband service for residential and business users as an alternative to cable or DSL.

The company paid about $483 million in stock for Virgin Mobile USA in late 2009; Sprint Nextel also paid off Virgin Mobile USA's debt (estimated to be greater than $200 million) as part of the deal. The acquisition was intended to give a bump to Sprint Nextel's prepaid business.

The company hopes to entice new customers by offering converged communications and broadcast entertainment services. As part of a joint venture with cable titans including Advance/Newhouse Communications, Comcast, Cox Communications, and Time Warner, Sprint Nextel is testing a program to provide cable television, home phone, and wireless phone services in a single package.

HISTORY

In 1899 Jacob Brown and son Cleyson began operating the Brown Telephone Company, one of the first non-Bell phone companies in the western US, in Abilene, Kansas. Cleyson later formed Union Electric (phone equipment, 1905) and Home Telephone and Telegraph (long-distance, 1910). In 1911 he consolidated his company with other Kansas independents as United Telephone, then obtained capital from rival Missouri and Kansas Telephone (later Southwestern Bell), which bought 60% of United's stock.

Cleyson sold his electric utility to finance expansions in telephone services, and in 1925 he incorporated United Telephone and Electric. Reorganized as United Utilities after the Depression, United continued to buy local exchanges. A post-WWII order backlog halted United's acquisition activity until 1952, but the company soon began further expansion, becoming the second largest non-Bell phone company in the US before 1960.

During the 1960s United focused on satellites, nuclear power plants, and cable TV, and it bought North Electric (1965), the US's oldest independent phone equipment maker. The company was renamed United Telecommunications in 1972. Meanwhile, Southern Pacific had developed the telegraph system along its railroad tracks into a microwave long-distance network called Southern Pacific Communications (1970) and known as SPRINT (for Southern Pacific Railroad Internal Telecommunications). In 1983 GTE acquired the network and renamed it GTE Sprint Communications. The next year United acquired U.S. Telephone, the Dallas-based reseller of long-distance services and the eighth-largest US long-distance company.

A year after the 1984 AT&T Corp. breakup, United bought 50% of GTE Sprint (United bought another 30% in 1989 and the balance in 1992). United and GTE teamed up to combine their long-distance systems — GTE Sprint and US Telecom — to form US Sprint. The new unit began offering long-distance in 1986 and completed a nationwide fiber-optic network the next year (The US was later dropped from the partnership's name, leaving Sprint). It was renamed Sprint Corporation in 1992.

In 1998 Sprint Spectrum, a wireless partnership with several cable firms, was combined with PhillieCo (another cable partnership) and SprintCom (its PCS subsidiary) to form Sprint PCS Group.

Selling a 10% stake in PCS Group to the public, Sprint split its stock into the FON Group (non-wireless operations) and the PCS Group. In 2003 Sprint named BellSouth vice chairman Gary Forsee as its CEO.

Sprint has not been immune to the economic despair that has plagued the telecom industry. Its reorganization plans, designed to cut expenses, included deep job cuts — it eliminated more than 20,000 jobs in two years. Sprint FON in early 2003 completed the sale of its directory-publishing unit to R. H. Donnelley for $2.1 billion in a move to pay down its $21 billion debt.

Sprint Nextel in 2005 began leasing its cell phone tower business to Global Signal in a deal valued at $1.2 billion.

Chairman William Kennard resigned in early 2007. Forsee added chairman to his title, but resigned from the company later that year. Board member James Hance Jr. was named non-executive chairman, and Terabeam CEO Daniel Hesse was hired as the new chief executive.

As it struggled under its own weight to keep pace with rivals, the company used layoffs during 2007 and 2008 to cut costs. Additionally, it closed about 10% of its 1,400 retail shops and 20% of its 20,000 distribution points to bring down expenses. Sprint Nextel spun off its local consumer wireline voice operations to focus on its wireless broadband services in 2008.

EXECUTIVES

Chairman: James H. (Jim) Hance Jr., age 65
President, CEO, and Director: Daniel R. (Dan) Hesse, age 56, $12,334,096 total compensation
CFO: Robert H. (Bob) Brust, age 66, $3,006,936 total compensation
Chief Service Officer: Robert L. (Bob) Johnson, age 51, $3,608,038 total compensation
SVP Corporate Marketing: William Morgan
SVP Corporate Communications: William (Bill) White
SVP and Controller: Charles L. (Charlie) Hall
SVP Human Resources: Sandra J. (Sandy) Price
VP Emerging Solutions: Wayne Ward
VP Product Development: Fared Adib
General Counsel and Corporate Secretary: Charles Wunsch, age 53
President, Prepaid: Daniel H. (Dan) Schulman, age 51, $3,792,926 total compensation
President, Network Operations and Wholesale: Steven L. (Steve) Elfman, age 54, $4,671,328 total compensation
President, Strategy and Corporate Initiatives: Keith O. Cowan, age 54, $5,195,632 total compensation
President, Integrated Solutions Group: Danny L. Bowman, age 44
President, 4G: Matthew Carter, age 49
President, CDMA Business Unit: Robert H. (Bob) Johnson, age 56
President, Business Markets Group: Paget A. Alves, age 55
Director, Financial and Corporate Communications: Leigh Horner
Investor Relations Contact: Yijing Brentano
Auditors: KPMG LLP

LOCATIONS

HQ: Sprint Nextel Corporation
6200 Sprint Pkwy., Overland Park, KS 66251
Phone: 913-624-6000
Web: www.sprint.com

PRODUCTS/OPERATIONS

2009 Sales

	$ mil.	% of total
Wireless	27,786	86
Wireline	4,474	14
Total	**32,260**	**100**

COMPETITORS

AT&T Mobility
Cellco
CenturyTel
Cincinnati Bell
Level 3 Communications
MetroPCS
Qwest Communications
T-Mobile USA
U.S. Cellular
Verizon

HISTORICAL FINANCIALS

Company Type: Public

Income Statement

FYE: December 31

	REVENUE ($ mil.)	NET INCOME ($ mil.)	NET PROFIT MARGIN	EMPLOYEES
12/09	32,260	(2,436)	—	40,000
12/08	35,635	(2,796)	—	56,000
12/07	40,146	(29,580)	—	60,000
12/06	41,028	1,329	3.2%	103,483
12/05	34,680	1,801	5.2%	79,900
Annual Growth	**(1.8%)**	**—**	**—**	**(15.9%)**

2009 Year-End Financials

Debt ratio: 112.1%
Return on equity: —
Cash ($ mil.): 3,819
Current ratio: 1.27
Long-term debt ($ mil.): 20,293

No. of shares (mil.): 2,950
Dividends
Yield: 0.0%
Payout: —
Market value ($ mil.): 10,795

Stock History

NYSE: S

	STOCK PRICE ($) FY Close	P/E High/Low		PER SHARE ($) Earnings	Dividends	Book Value
12/09	3.66	—	—	(0.84)	0.00	6.13
12/08	1.83	—	—	(0.98)	0.00	6.65
12/07	13.13	—	—	(10.31)	0.10	7.46
12/06	18.89	55	35	0.45	0.10	18.01
12/05	21.19	28	22	0.87	0.30	17.61
Annual Growth	**(35.5%)**	**—**	**—**	**—**	**—**	**(23.2%)**

SPX Corporation

SPX Corporation likes to control the flow. The company's business segments include Flow Technology (pumps, valves, and other fluid handling devices), Test and Measurement (diagnostic tools, fare-collection, and cable/pipe locators), Thermal Equipment and Services (cooling, heating, and ventilation), and Industrial Products and Services (compactors, power systems, broadcast antenna systems, and aerospace components). These segments serve developing and emerging end markets, such as global infrastructure, food and beverage, and process control equipment industries.

The company is reinventing itself into a global industrial equipment manufacturer through acquisitions and divestments, spurred by the global economic challenges of 2009, which affected many of its customers. As part of its operating initiatives, SPX typically looks to buy what it terms "bolt-on" businesses that easily mesh with existing activities, many of which are located in countries with developing economies.

In early 2010 the company acquired Denmark-based Gerstenberg Schröder, a manufacturer of machinery for food processing lines, such as mixers and emulsification equipment. The acquisition expands the company's footprint into

new international markets, as well as builds up its process equipment portfolio and process line installation capabilities. In mid-2010 Flow expanded its geographic reach with its purchase of the majority of Anhydro, a Danish company that makes dewatering plants and equipment (used in dairy, food, and pharmaceutical applications).

The company's Thermal Equipment and Services segment acquired Yuba Heat Transfer from holding company Connell Limited Partnership for about $125 million in late 2009. Yuba manufactures and services feedwater heaters and condensers used by power generation companies, including nuclear, solar, geothermal, gas, and coal facilities.

SPX has additionally entered into a joint venture with Thermax Limited, which broadens its Thermal Equipment and Services segment predominantly in Indian markets, but also in Southeast Asia. SPX will hold a 49% stake in the deal to Thermax's 51%. Another important joint venture is EGS Electrical Group, of which SPX owns 44.5%. Along with partner Emerson Electric, EGS Electrical makes electrical fittings and industrial lighting products primarily in the US, Canada, and France.

In 2010 SPX sold its Premier Mill brand of grinding and dispersing equipment to NETZSCH Fine Particle Technology. In 2009 SPX sold its interest in Filtran (automatic transmission filters and other products for the auto market) to investment group Madison Capital Partners. The deal marked SPX's exit from the automotive industry.

HISTORY

Paul Beardsley and Charles Johnson founded SPX in 1911 as The Piston Ring Company. The company, which had its start making piston rings for major automakers, expanded through a series of acquisitions. In 1931 it changed its name to Sealed Power to reflect the increasing diversity of its products. Expansion continued after WWII, and the company went public in 1955. By 1959 Sealed Power made half of its sales from replacement parts.

Following further diversification and international growth in the 1960s and 1970s, the company moved its stock listing to the New York Stock Exchange in 1972 and changed its name to SPX Corporation in 1988.

SPX ran into trouble in the early 1990s when a US recession resulted in losses. The company restructured, however, and by the time the auto industry rebounded in 1994, it was focused on specialty service tools and components.

Flat sales and losses in 1995-96 prompted the ouster of Dale Johnson (CEO from 1991 to 1995). He was replaced by GE veteran John Blystone, who set about streamlining the business, selling inefficient units and beefing up profitable lines. In 1997 SPX sold the Sealed Power division (its original business) for $223 million.

In 1998 SPX paid $2.3 billion for General Signal, a company nearly twice its size that provided SPX the opportunity to lower its exposure to the auto parts industry and to expand its offerings. SPX later announced it would cut 1,000 jobs and close about two dozen factories and warehouses it had picked up in the deal.

In 2001 SPX acquired United Dominion Industries Limited (flow technology, machinery, specialty engineered products, and test instrumentation) in a deal valued at $1.83 billion. In August of that year, SPX announced plans to close 49 facilities and cut 2,000 jobs (about 7% of its workforce) by 2003.

Following the security trend, SPX acquired the US-based IDenticard Systems in early 2003. SPX sold Inrange Technologies to Computer Network Technology (CNT) that year.

In 2004 SPX acquired Bill-Jay Machine Tool (rotor head components for helicopters) to augment its Fenn Technologies aerospace components business. It also acquired the assets of Actron Manufacturing, a maker of automotive test equipment and instruments under the Actron, KAL-EQUIP, and Faze brand names, among others. Late 2004 chairman and CEO Blystone abruptly resigned. The company separated the board and officer positions, naming director Charles Johnson as chairman, and VP Christopher Kearney as president and CEO.

In 2006 the company acquired AB Custos, a Swedish manufacturer of pumps for industrial and marine markets, and aerator filters and regulators for the HVAC heating and plumbing market. It paid about $184 million.

Johnson retired from the board at the annual meeting in 2007. The board designated Kearney to succeed him as chairman, reuniting the top board and management posts. The board named J. Kermit Campbell, an SPX director since 1993, as lead director for a two-year term. Campbell was CEO of Herman Miller.

In late 2007 SPX acquired the APV division of Invensys for nearly $516 million (about £250 million) in cash. APV made pumps, valves, heat exchangers, and homogenizers for the beverage, dairy, food, and pharmaceutical industries. APV became part of SPX's Flow Technology segment.

In 2007 the company sold its Contech automotive components business to Marathon Automotive Group for about $146 million in cash. SPX saw the business as no longer strategic to its long-term interests. Marathon Automotive Group was an entity formed by a private equity firm, Marathon Asset Management.

Also in 2007 SPX put its Air Filtration business unit on the auction block. It sold the business to The Riverside Company in 2008.

EXECUTIVES

Chairman, President, and CEO:
Christopher J. (Chris) Kearney, age 55, $13,267,330 total compensation
EVP, CFO, and Treasurer: Patrick J. O'Leary, age 52, $7,677,116 total compensation
EVP Global Business Systems and Services; President, Asia/Pacific: Robert B. Foreman, age 53, $5,523,431 total compensation
Chief Marketing Officer: Erin Hall
SVP, Secretary, and General Counsel: Kevin L. Lilly, age 57, $1,974,759 total compensation
VP Business Development: J. Michael Whitted, age 38
VP and CFO, Flow Technology: Jeremy W. Smeltser, age 35
VP, Corporate Controller, and Chief Accounting Officer: Michael A. Reilly
Segment President, Thermal Equipment and Services: Drew T. Ladau, age 50
Segment President, Test and Measurement: David A. (Dave) Kowalski, age 52
Segment President, Flow Technology: Don L. Canterna, age 59, $2,021,343 total compensation
Segment President, Industrial Products and Services: Lee Powell, age 52
Director Investor Relations: Ryan Taylor
Auditors: Deloitte & Touche LLP

LOCATIONS

HQ: SPX Corporation
13515 Ballantyne Corporate Place
Charlotte, NC 28277
Phone: 704-752-4400   **Fax:** 704-752-4505
Web: www.spx.com

2009 Sales

	$ mil.	% of total
US	2,469.6	51
Germany	717.2	15
China	288.2	6
UK	253.0	5
Other countries	1,122.8	23
Total	**4,850.8**	**100**

PRODUCTS/OPERATIONS

2009 Sales

	$ mil.	% of total
Flow technology	1,634.1	34
Thermal equipment & services	1,600.7	33
Test & measurement	810.4	17
Industrial products & services	805.6	16
Total	**4,850.8**	**100**

Selected Products

Analyzers
Bacon press
Closures and pipeline pigging
Dispersion equipment
Dehydration equipment
Fittings
Filtration equipment
Heat exchangers
HVAC
Mixers
Pumps
Strainers
Valves

COMPETITORS

ABB	GEA Group
ALSTOM	Glen Dimplex
AMETEK	Harris Corp.
Baltimore Aircoil	Harsco
BBT Thermotechnik	Honeywell International
Broan-NuTone	Ingersoll-Rand
Converteam	Interpump
Cubic Transportation	ITT Corp.
Danaher	Johnson Controls
Dresser, Inc.	Parker Hannifin
Eaton	Robbins & Myers
Endress + Hauser	Robert Bosch
Evapco	Roper Industries
Fisher Controls	Siemens AG
Franklin Electric	Snap-on
GE	Trippe Manufacturing

HISTORICAL FINANCIALS

Company Type: Public

Income Statement

FYE: December 31

	REVENUE ($ mil.)	NET INCOME ($ mil.)	NET PROFIT MARGIN	EMPLOYEES
12/09	4,851	14	0.3%	15,000
12/08	5,856	248	4.2%	17,800
12/07	4,822	294	6.1%	17,800
12/06	4,313	171	4.0%	14,300
12/05	4,292	1,090	25.4%	18,300
Annual Growth	**3.1%**	**(66.1%)**	**—**	**(4.8%)**

2009 Year-End Financials

Debt ratio: 59.7%
Return on equity: 0.7%
Cash ($ mil.): 523
Current ratio: 1.41
Long-term debt ($ mil.): 1,129

No. of shares (mil.): 50
Dividends
  Yield: 1.8%
  Payout: 156.3%
Market value ($ mil.): 2,729

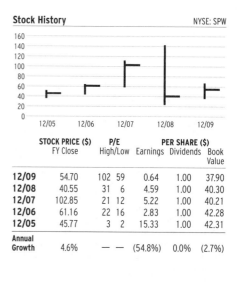

Stock History   NYSE: SPW

	STOCK PRICE ($) FY Close	P/E High/Low		Earnings	PER SHARE ($) Dividends	Book Value
12/09	54.70	102	59	0.64	1.00	37.90
12/08	40.55	31	6	4.59	1.00	40.30
12/07	102.85	21	12	5.22	1.00	40.21
12/06	61.16	22	16	2.83	1.00	42.28
12/05	45.77	3	2	15.33	1.00	42.31
Annual Growth	**4.6%**	**—**	**—**	**(54.8%)**	**0.0%**	**(2.7%)**

Stage Stores

If the world is a stage, Stage Stores wants to dress the actors. The company operates about 775 department stores, mainly in rural towns in some 40 US states. About a third of its stores are in Texas. Through its Peebles, Bealls, Stage, Palais Royal, and recently acquired Goody's chains, the company offers small-town America moderately priced apparel and accessories, cosmetics, and footwear. Nationally recognized brands such as Tommy Hilfiger, Carter's, Levi Strauss, Chaps, and Polo account for about 85% of sales and are sold alongside Stage Stores' private-label merchandise. Stage Stores acquired the Goody's Family Clothing name at a bankruptcy auction in 2009.

Goody's is the most recent addition to Stage Stores' growing family of department store chains. It acquired the B.C. Moore & Sons chain of more than 75 stores in four states and converted most to the Peebles name in 2006; in 2003 it bought the 136-store Peebles chain. (With more than 330 stores, Peebles is Stage Stores' largest department store chain.) In 1988 Bealls Brothers merged with Palais Royal to form predecessor firm Specialty Retailers Inc. In 1996 the retailer went public under the name Stage Stores.

After shrinking from 688 stores in 1999 to about 550 by 2006, Stage Stores has resumed opening new stores in new markets and acquiring others. In fiscal 2010 it opened about 20 new stores, despite sliding sales as a result of the deep recession in the US.

About 65% of the company's stores are found in small towns and communities with populations below 50,000 people. Another 17% of the retailer's department stores are in metropolitan areas, including Houston and San Antonio, Texas. The remainder are in midsized markets.

In November 2008 chairman Jim Scarborough retired as CEO and was succeeded by Andrew Hall, president and former COO of the company. Scarborough retained the chairman's title.

The retailer's target customers are women who are 25 and older with annual household incomes of more than $45,000.

HISTORY

Palais Royal and Bealls were successful clothing chains in their own right before they were bought by a group led by Boston investment company Bain Capital in 1988. Palais Royal was founded in Houston in 1921 by Isadore Erlich and had grown into a chain of 28 stores.

In contrast to Palais Royal's big-city style, Bealls (owned by 3 Bealls Brothers 3) focused on the fashion needs of small-town residents. The retailer was founded in Henderson, Texas, in 1923 by Bealls brothers Robbie and Archie (Willie joined soon thereafter) and had 152 stores in Alabama, New Mexico, Oklahoma, and Texas when it was acquired by Bain Capital.

Bain Capital combined the two chains under newly formed holding company Specialty Retailers Inc. (SRI). Palais Royal CEO Bernie Fuchs became the head of SRI, which closed several Bealls stores and converted others to the Palais Royal format.

SRI bought 76-store retailer Fashion Bar, whose stores included a juniors' chain called Stage, in 1992. Fashion Bar had been founded in 1933 in Denver by German immigrant siblings Jack and Hannah Levy under the name Hosiery Bar. SRI scrapped a planned IPO in 1992 after receiving a tepid response. Carl Tooker, a veteran of department store operators May Department Stores and Federated Department Stores, took over as president of the company in 1993 and as CEO in 1994.

Recognizing that the Fashion Bar purchase had been a mistake, SRI closed most of that chain's poorly faring stores in 1994 and renamed some Stage. (The last closed in 1997.) When SRI began to further develop its small-market approach by acquiring Beall-Ladymon (45 stores in Louisiana, Arkansas, and Mississippi), it renamed the stores Stage. (SRI wanted to differentiate Beall-Ladymon from the unrelated Bealls chain and avoid the "hard to pronounce" Palais Royal moniker.)

The company changed its name to Stage Stores and went public in 1996. Also that year it bought F. W. Uhlman, a 34-store retailer (founded in 1867) with locations in Indiana, Michigan, and Ohio. It increased its store count dramatically in 1997 and built up its small-town base by buying 246 C. R. Anthony stores in the southwestern and Rocky Mountain regions. The stores in the chain, which was founded by Charles Ross Anthony in 1922 in Oklahoma, were converted to the Stage or Bealls names.

Stage Stores continued its small-town march in 1998 when it acquired the leases and other assets of 15 stores in Montana, Nevada, Oregon, and Washington — mostly under the Hub Clothing name — from Tri-North Department Stores. It also opened new stores. Beset by a sales slump blamed on scorching heat in the Southwest, the company saw its stock value drop in 1998. Late in the year Stage Stores' chief merchandising officer resigned, and the company announced that it would take a break from acquisitions while it focused on improving sales.

In 1999 Stage Stores closed more than 25 poorly performing locations. Tooker resigned in early 2000; board member Jack Wiesner was appointed interim chairman, president, and CEO. Stage Stores then filed for Chapter 11 bankruptcy in June, citing low sales and vendor payment troubles. (The retailer closed some 300 stores since entering bankruptcy.) James Scarborough took over as president and CEO that year. Stage Stores exited bankruptcy protection

in August 2001 and was listed on the NASDAQ stock exchange in January 2002.

In 2002 the retailer opened 14 new stores in Texas (10), Arkansas (2), and Louisiana (2). In November 2003 Stage Stores greatly enhanced the company's total store count with its acquisition of Peebles Inc., a privately held retailer similarly catering to small-town America.

In February 2006 Stage Stores acquired the 78-store B.C. Moore & Sons chain for about $37 million. Of those, 69 were converted to Peebles locations, while the rest were closed. The privately owned company operated stores in small markets throughout Alabama, Georgia, and North and South Carolina. Overall, in 2006 the retailer opened more than 100 shops.

In 2007 the company opened its first locations in Utah and Wisconsin. In 2008 Jim Scarborough retired as CEO of the company and was succeeded by Andrew Hall. Scarborough retained the chairman's title. New markets for the company in 2008 included Idaho, Minnesota, and Nevada.

EXECUTIVES

Chairman: James R. (Jim) Scarborough, age 59, $1,782,553 total compensation
President, CEO, and Director: Andrew T. (Andy) Hall, age 49, $1,692,285 total compensation
COO and CFO: Edward J. (Ed) Record, age 41, $1,054,538 total compensation
EVP and CIO: Steven Hunter, age 39
EVP Store Operations: Ernest R. Cruse, age 59, $510,213 total compensation
EVP Advertising and Sales Promotion: Joanne Swartz, age 50
EVP Human Resources: Ron D. Lucas, age 62
EVP and CIO: Jeffrey J. (Jeff) Kish, age 45
Chief Merchandising Officer: Richard A. Maloney, age 60
SVP Finance and Controller: Richard E. Stasyszen, age 49
SVP Cosmetics: Christine Johnston
SVP Store Operations, South Hill: Russell A. Lundy II, age 47
SVP Real Estate: Mel B. Ward, age 56
SVP Logistics and Distribution: Gough H. Grubbs, age 61
VP Investor Relations: Bob Aronson
Auditors: Deloitte & Touche LLP

LOCATIONS

HQ: Stage Stores, Inc.
10201 Main St., Houston, TX 77025
Phone: 713-667-5601   **Fax:** 713-663-9780
Web: www.stagestores.com

2010 Stores

	No.
South Central	345
Southeast	148
Mid-Atlantic	139
Midwest	62
Southwest	37
Northeast	24
Northwest	3
Total	**758**

PRODUCTS/OPERATIONS

2010 Stores

	No.
Peebles	334
Bealls	210
Stage	144
Palais Royal	55
Goody's	15
Total	**758**

2010 Sales

	% of total
Men/Young Men's	18
Misses sportswear	17
Children's	12
Footwear	12
Accessories	8
Junior sportswear	8
Cosmetics	7
Special sizes	6
Dresses	5
Intimates	4
Home & gifts	2
Outerwear, swimwear & other	1
Total	**100**

COMPETITORS

The Buckle
Casual Male Retail Group
Dillard's
Dress Barn
Family Dollar Stores
J. C. Penney
Kohl's
Macy's
Men's Wearhouse
Ross Stores
Saks
Sears
Stein Mart
Target
TJX Companies
Wal-Mart

HISTORICAL FINANCIALS

Company Type: Public

Income Statement

FYE: Saturday nearest January 31

	REVENUE ($ mil.)	NET INCOME ($ mil.)	NET PROFIT MARGIN	EMPLOYEES
1/10	1,432	29	2.0%	13,100
1/09	1,516	(66)	—	14,058
1/08	1,546	53	3.4%	14,458
1/07	1,550	55	3.6%	14,608
1/06	1,344	56	4.2%	13,304
Annual Growth	**1.6%**	**(15.4%)**	**—**	**(0.4%)**

2010 Year-End Financials

Debt ratio: 8.1%
Return on equity: 6.2%
Cash ($ mil.): 94
Current ratio: 2.33
Long-term debt ($ mil.): 38
No. of shares (mil.): 38
Dividends
　Yield: 1.5%
　Payout: 26.7%
Market value ($ mil.): 494

Stock History

NYSE: SSI

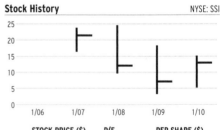

	STOCK PRICE ($) FY Close	P/E High/Low		PER SHARE ($) Earnings	Dividends	Book Value
1/10	12.92	20	7	0.75	0.20	12.45
1/09	7.15	—	—	(1.71)	0.20	11.77
1/08	12.03	20	8	1.24	0.20	13.63
1/07	21.39	19	13	1.25	0.12	14.95
Annual Growth	**(15.5%)**	**—**	**—**	**(12.3%)**	**60.7%**	**(1.3%)**

Stanley Black & Decker

Stanley Black & Decker, the result of the 2010 merger of Stanley Works and rival Black & Decker, has the tools that neighbors envy. As a top US toolmaker, it markets hand tools, mechanics' tools, power tools, pneumatic tools, and hydraulic tools. Since the merger, the company's tool shed is bulging with additional items, such as garden tools, plumbing products (Price Pfister), and cleaning items (Dustbuster), as well as security hardware (Kwikset) and door products. Besides the Stanley and Black & Decker names, it boasts such brands as Bostitch, Mac Tools, and DEWALT. Stanley Black & Decker peddles its products through home centers and mass-merchant distributors, as well as through third-party distributors.

Stanley Works and Black & Decker merged their operations in an all-stock deal worth about $4.5 billion. The new firm is led by former Stanley Works CEO John Lundgren as its president and CEO alongside Nolan Archibald, most recently Black & Decker CEO, as executive chairman. As part of the deal, it's speculated that Archibald could leave the company after three years with an estimated $89 million pay package. Former Stanley investors own a narrow majority stake in the new business, with about a 51% holding; Black & Decker's shareholders own the remainder. With complementary product portfolios, the companies expect to save about $350 million annually as the combined Stanley Black & Decker.

Prior to the merger, Stanley Works had been facing sharp sales declines because of the severe financial crisis in the US and abroad. As a result, the company shed about 10% of its global workforce in late 2008 and shuttered a few manufacturing plants.

Black & Decker saw sales slide as the US housing market stalled and retailers such as Home Depot and Lowe's (two of its top customers) slashed their inventory levels in response to lighter foot traffic. Thanks to its business overseas, Black & Decker was able to offset losses in the US with a rise in revenue in Europe.

Both companies have been working to extend their reach abroad. Black & Decker marketed its products in more than 100 countries. Stanley Works operated manufacturing and distribution facilities in the US and about 14 other countries.

HISTORY

In 1843 Frederick Stanley opened a bolt shop in a converted early-19th-century armory in New Britain, Connecticut. In 1852 he teamed with his brother and five friends to form The Stanley Works to cast, form, and manufacture various types of metal.

The business prospered during the 1860s when the Civil War and westward migration created a need for hardware and tools. When Stanley turned his attention to political and civic affairs, company management fell to William Hart. He engaged in a "knuckles-bared" fight with four bigger competitors (Stanley was the sole survivor) and led the firm into steel strapping production, which would become a major element in the company's operations. Hart was named president in 1884.

During WWI the company produced belt buckles and rifle and gas mask parts. Along with making numerous domestic acquisitions, it established operations in Canada (1914) and Germany (1926). In 1920 the company merged with Stanley Rule and Level (a local tool company formed in 1857 by a cousin of Frederick Stanley), and in 1925 it opened a new hydroelectric plant near Windsor, Connecticut, to provide power for all its operations.

Stanley struggled through the Depression, but following WWII, the toolmaker embarked on four decades of expansion. Staying within its traditional product line, Stanley acquired a myriad of companies, including Berry Industries (garage doors, 1965), Ackley Manufacturing and Sales (hydraulic tools, 1972), Mac Tools (1980), and National Hand Tool (1986). The company grew globally in the late 1980s by establishing high-tech plants in Europe and the Far East.

After twice fending off takeover attempts by rival Newell (now Newell Rubbermaid) in the early 1990s, Stanley returned to acquisitions. In 1992 it acquired LaBounty Manufacturing (large hydraulic tools), American Brush (paintbrushes and decorator tools), and Goldblatt Tool (masonry and dry-wall tools). The following year the company sold its Taylor Rental subsidiary, the largest system of general rental centers in the US, to SERVISTAR.

When weak sales hit Stanley's primary markets in mid-1995, the company responded with a massive restructuring program, including $150 million in expense cuts.

As part of the restructuring, Stanley sold the Creative Rivets division of Stanley-Bostitch to rival rivet maker Marson in 1996. In 1997 Stanley sold its garage-related products unit to radar-detector manufacturer Whistler. Stanley alas announced that it would cut 4,500 jobs — almost a quarter of its workforce.

While continuing to close plants in 1999, Stanley settled charges with the FTC for selling Made-in-USA tools that had foreign components.

The company closed about 90 facilities, with about 4,000 job cuts, in 2002. In 2003 it cut another 1,000 jobs and discontinued MacDirect, the Mac Tools retail channel.

In 2004 John Lundgren, a former executive with Georgia-Pacific, became chairman and CEO. Also in 2004 Stanley sold its residential entry-door business to Masonite International, and its Home Decor division to Wellspring Capital Management.

In January 2006 the company acquired France's Facom, a leading European maker of hand and mechanics tools, for about $486 million. That July, Stanley purchased a 67% stake in Besco Pneumatic Corp., a Taiwan-based maker of pneumatic tools, for $42 million in cash. Stanley has the option to acquire an additional 15% stake in the company over the next five years. Stanley sold its CST/berger business, consisting of leveling and measuring devices, to Robert Bosch Tool Corporation for $205 million in July 2008.

Partnering with fellow toolmaker, Stanley Works merged its operations with Black & Decker in early 2010 and renamed the new entity Stanley Black & Decker. The blended businesses are led by Stanley's Lundgren and Black & Decker's Nolan Archibald as executive chairman.

EXECUTIVES

Chairman: Nolan D. Archibald, age 66
President, CEO, and Director: John F. Lundgren, age 58, $9,602,517 total compensation
EVP and COO: James M. (Jim) Loree, age 51, $4,809,429 total compensation
SVP and CFO: Donald (Don) Allan Jr., age 46, $1,786,789 total compensation
SVP; Group Executive, Construction and DIY: Jeffery D. (Jeff) Ansell, age 42, $1,933,306 total compensation
SVP and CIO/SFS: Hubert W. (Bert) Davis Jr., age 61, $1,846,825 total compensation
SVP Human Resources: Mark J. Mathieu, age 57, $1,995,008 total compensation
SVP; Group Executive, Convergent Security Solutions; Integration Co-Leader: D. Brett Bontrager, age 47
SVP; Group Executive, Mechanical Access Systems: Justin C. Boswell, age 42
SVP, General Counsel, and Secretary: Bruce H. Beatt, age 58
VP and Treasurer: Craig A Douglas, age 55
VP Human Resources: Joe Voelker
President, Consumer Power Tools and Products: Jeff Cooper
President, Engineered Fastening Solutions: Michael A. (Mike) Tyll, age 53
President, Professional Power Tools and Products: William S. (Bill) Taylor, age 54
President, Accessory Products, Construction and DIY: Beau Parker
President, Infrastructure Solutions: Tim Jones
President, Hand Tools and Pneumatic Products: Kyle Dancho
President, Hardware and Home Improvement, Mechanical Security Segment: Greg Gluchowski
President, Industrial and Auto Repair: Massimo Grassi
Director Investor Relations: Kathryn H. (Kate) White
Director Global Communications: Tim Perra
Auditors: Ernst & Young LLP

LOCATIONS

HQ: Stanley Black & Decker, Inc.
1000 Stanley Dr., New Britain, CT 06053
Phone: 860-225-5111   **Fax:** 860-827-3895
Web: www.stanleyblackanddecker.com

2009 Sales

	$ mil.	% of total
US	2,168.0	58
Other Americas	352.8	9
France	498.5	13
Other Europe	505.3	14
Asia	212.5	6
Total	**3,737.1**	**100**

PRODUCTS/OPERATIONS

2009 Sales

	$ mil.	% of total
Security	1,560.2	42
Construction & D-I-Y	1,295.3	35
Industrial	881.6	23
Total	**3,737.1**	**100**

Selected Brand Names

Atro	Mac Tools
Black & Decker	Powerlock
Blackhawk	Price Pfister
Bostitch	Proto
DEWALT	Scumbuster
Dustbuster	SnakeLight
Facom	Stanley
FatMax	Vidmar
Jensen	Virax
Kwikset	ZAG
LaBounty	

HISTORICAL FINANCIALS

Company Type: Public

Income Statement

FYE: Saturday nearest December 31

	REVENUE ($ mil.)	NET INCOME ($ mil.)	NET PROFIT MARGIN	EMPLOYEES
12/09	3,737	226	6.1%	16,700
12/08	4,426	313	7.1%	18,225
12/07	4,484	337	7.5%	18,400
12/06	4,019	290	7.2%	17,600
12/05	3,285	270	8.2%	15,800
Annual Growth	3.3%	(4.3%)	—	1.4%

2009 Year-End Financials

Debt ratio: 54.6%
Return on equity: 12.3%
Cash ($ mil.): 401
Current ratio: 1.18
Long-term debt ($ mil.): 1,085

No. of shares (mil.): 166
Dividends
  Yield: 2.5%
  Payout: 46.6%
Market value ($ mil.): 8,534

Stock History

NYSE: SWK

	STOCK PRICE ($) FY Close	P/E High/Low		PER SHARE ($) Earnings	Dividends	Book Value
12/09	51.51	19	8	2.79	1.30	11.99
12/08	34.10	13	6	3.92	1.26	10.19
12/07	48.48	16	12	4.00	1.22	10.43
12/06	50.29	16	12	3.46	1.18	9.37
12/05	48.04	16	13	3.16	1.14	8.72
Annual Growth	1.8%	—	—	(3.1%)	3.3%	8.3%

Staples, Inc.

Staples is clipping along as the #1 office supply superstore operator in the US. It sells office products, furniture, computers, and other supplies through its chain of 2,240-plus Staples and Staples Express stores in the Americas, Europe, Asia, and Australia. (More than 1,870 of its superstores are located in North America.) In addition to its retail outlets, Staples sells office products via the Internet and through its catalog and direct sales operations, including subsidiary Quill Corporation. Staples also provides document management and copying services through its retail chain, as well as promotional products. It targets customers worldwide through its Corporate Express business.

In a move that enlarged its footprint in Europe significantly, Staples acquired Netherlands-based business supply wholesaler Corporate Express NV in 2008 in a deal valued at about $2.7 billion. Corporate Express is a major office products wholesaler, with more than half of its sales in the US through Corporate Express US. The Dutch office supplies distributor finally accepted Staples sweetened buyout offer after Staples raised its bid three times.

International expansion is a priority for the office products retailer as sales in North America slow as a result of the deep recession. To that end, Staples is focused on further expanding its operations in Europe, where it already has about 325 retail locations. Other new markets for the company include Argentina and China, and the office products retailer is looking to other emerging markets, such as India and Brazil. In early 2007 the chain formed a 50-50 joint venture with India's largest retailer, Pantaloon, to bring office supply warehouse stores to India. In China, where the company has 20-plus stores, Staples has partnered with United Parcel Service to launch co-branded stores there. Australia is also on Staples' short list for international expansion. The firm looks to take full control of Corporate Express Australia by mid-2010, after bidding A$390 million for the roughly 40% it didn't already own. Adding Finland to its locations map, in 2010 Staples acquired Oy Lindell Ab.

Staples' North American retail operation had been expanding at a rapid pace but now is slowing. Some of the newer stores are smaller in size than Staples' traditional warehouse locations and designed to target urban and other niche markets. The company is also expanding the number of proprietary products — under the Staples, Quill, and other in-house brands — sold in its stores.

The office supplies retailer has also expanded its five-year-old electronics waste recycling program to cover used computers and monitors. All Staples stores in the US stores now accept used computer hardware for a $10 fee. (There's no charge for recycling smaller devices, such as cell phones and digital cameras.)

A large part of the company's growth, though, has come from its North American delivery business, which brings office products and services directly to businesses and consumers. The acquisition of Corporate Express helped to expand this business by adding new products and services. As a result, the North American delivery business now rings up a greater share of sales than Staples' retail operation in the US and Canada. Staples expects Corporate Express to be a key driver of growth in this area.

HISTORY

A veteran of the supermarket industry (and the man who developed the idea for generic food), Thomas Stemberg was fired from his executive position with Connecticut supermarket Edwards-Finast in 1985. Stemberg began searching for a niche retail market — he found one in office supplies, which he estimated at $100 billion.

While large companies could buy in bulk from dealers, smaller businesses were served by mom-and-pop office supply stores that charged much higher prices. Applying the supermarket model to office supply, Stemberg founded Staples in late 1985 with Leo Kahn, a former competitor in the supermarket business. With money from Kahn and venture capital firms, Staples opened its first store in a Boston suburb the next year.

In 1987 the retailer moved into the New York City area and continued to expand throughout the Northeast. By early 1989 — the year it went public — it had 23 stores.

Aggressive expansion began the following year when Staples opened three stores in Southern California and introduced two new concepts: Staples Direct (delivery operations for midsized businesses) and Staples Express (downtown stores offering smaller merchandise selections). International growth included buying a stake in Canada's Business Depot (1991) and 48% of MAXI-Papier, a European office supply store chain (1992). It also paired up with Kingfisher to establish stores in the UK (Kingfisher sold its interest to Staples in 1996).

Additional acquisitions gave Staples more than 200 stores by the end of 1993. The next year Staples entered Arizona, Virginia, and Kentucky (by acquiring selected Office America stores); acquired the rest of Canada's Business Depot; and began expanding into the contract stationer business. It started Staples Business Advantage, a regional stationer, in 1995. The company agreed to buy Office Depot, its biggest rival, in 1996, but the FTC rejected the $4.3 billion deal on antitrust grounds.

In 1998 Staples acquired privately held Quill to expand its direct-sales business. In 2001 the company continued its international expansion, introducing its Quill catalog business in the UK and buying three European office supply companies (which added about 40 stores, extending the company's presence in Germany and moving it into the Netherlands and Portugal).

During 2002 Staples acquired Medical Arts Press (specialized medical software and forms to medical providers) and the mail-order business of Guilbert, a subsidiary of French retailer PPR (formerly Pinault-Printempts-Redoute); the $815 million Guilbert deal provided entrée for Staples in France, Italy, Spain, and Belgium. Company veteran Ron Sargent took over as CEO that same year.

CEO Sargent took on the added title of chairman when Stemberg resigned in 2005.

A 2006 joint venture with UB Office Systems brought the company into the Taiwan market.

In 2007 Staples entered China and India through partnerships in both countries. In late 2007 the company reached a settlement in a California class-action lawsuit brought by store managers seeking overtime pay dating back to 1995. Staples has agreed to pay $38 million, subject to court approval. Again, in early 2009, the firm was ordered to pay almost $2.5 million to 343 plaintiffs in a case brought under the Fair Labor Standards Act. A federal court jury ruled that Staples violated the law by classifying employees as exempt and failing to pay them overtime.

EXECUTIVES

Chairman and CEO: Ronald L. (Ron) Sargent, age 54, $8,377,420 total compensation
Vice Chairman and CFO: John J. Mahoney, age 58, $4,363,376 total compensation
President and COO; President, Staples Foundation for Learning: Michael A. (Mike) Miles Jr., age 48, $2,967,014 total compensation
EVP International Development: John K. Barton
EVP and CIO: Brian T. Light, age 46
EVP Human Resources: Shira D. Goodman, age 49
SVP Business Delivery: Steven (Steve) Bussberg
SVP and Corporate Controller: Christine T. Komola, age 42
SVP, General Counsel, and Secretary: Kristin A. Campbell, age 48
SVP Global Brand Marketing: Steven Fund
SVP, Southern Europe: Pete Howard
SVP Finance, Staples North American Delivery: Elaine Bruzios
SVP Finance, US Retail Business: Nick Hotchkin
VP and Treasurer: Lisa Scopa
President, US Stores: Demos Parneros, age 47, $1,830,384 total compensation
President, Staples North American Delivery: Joseph G. (Joe) Doody, age 57, $3,403,470 total compensation
President, China: Anders Kristiansen
President, Staples Business Depot: Steven E. Matyas
Auditors: Ernst & Young LLP

LOCATIONS

HQ: Staples, Inc.
500 Staples Dr., Framingham, MA 01702
Phone: 508-253-5000   **Fax:** 508-253-8989
Web: www.staples.com

2010 Sales

	$ mil.	% of total
US	16,343.4	67
Canada	2,661.2	11
Other countries	5,270.9	22
Total	**24,275.5**	**100**

2010 Locations

	No.
US	
California	216
New York	140
Florida	97
Pennsylvania	94
New Jersey	90
Massachusetts	77
Ohio	61
Texas	55
Illinois	53
North Carolina	51
Maryland	45
Arizona	44
Michigan	43
Virginia	42
Georgia	39
Connecticut	38
Indiana	32
Washington	30
New Hampshire	22
Colorado	21
Tennessee	21
Oregon	20
South Carolina	20
Kentucky	17
Oklahoma	17
Iowa	15
Maine	13
Utah	13
Other states	138
Canada	316
UK	137
Germany	58
The Netherlands	47
Portugal	35
Sweden	22
China	22
Other countries	51
Total	**2,242**

PRODUCTS/OPERATIONS

2010 Sales

	% of total
Office supplies & services	48
Business machines & related products	32
Computers & related products	15
Office furniture	5
Total	**100**

2010 Sales

	$ mil.	% of total
North American delivery	9,640.4	40
North American retail	9,364.2	38
International	5,270.9	22
Total	**24,275.5**	**100**

Selected Operations

Corporate Express (US, Europe, office products wholesale)
Office Centre (stores, The Netherlands)
Quill Corporation (US, catalog)
Staples (stores, North America and Europe)
Staples Business Advantage (contract stationers for midsized to large businesses)
Staples Business Delivery
Staples Express (smaller-store format)
Staples National Advantage (contract stationers for large multiregional businesses)
Staples The Office Superstore (stores, Canada)
Staples.com (Internet shopping site)

COMPETITORS

Amazon.com
Best Buy
BJ's Wholesale Club
CDW
Costco Wholesale
Dell
FedEx Office
Fry's Electronics
Hewlett-Packard
IKON
Insight Enterprises
Lyreco
Mail Boxes Etc.
Office Depot
OfficeMax
RadioShack
S.P. Richards
Systemax
Tesco
Unisource
United Stationers
Wal-Mart

HISTORICAL FINANCIALS

Company Type: Public

Income Statement

FYE: Saturday nearest January 31

	REVENUE ($ mil.)	NET INCOME ($ mil.)	NET PROFIT MARGIN	EMPLOYEES
1/10	24,276	739	3.0%	91,095
1/09	23,084	805	3.5%	91,125
1/08	19,373	996	5.1%	75,588
1/07	18,161	974	5.4%	73,646
1/06	16,079	834	5.2%	68,533
Annual Growth	**10.8%**	**(3.0%)**	**—**	**7.4%**

2010 Year-End Financials

Debt ratio: 36.9%
Return on equity: 12.0%
Cash ($ mil.): 1,416
Current ratio: 1.63
Long-term debt ($ mil.): 2,500

No. of shares (mil.): 730
Dividends
    Yield: 1.4%
    Payout: 32.4%
Market value ($ mil.): 17,124

Stock History

NASDAQ (GS): SPLS

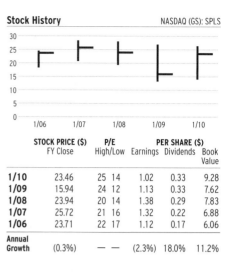

	STOCK PRICE ($) FY Close	P/E High/Low		PER SHARE ($) Earnings	Dividends	Book Value
1/10	23.46	25	14	1.02	0.33	9.28
1/09	15.94	24	12	1.13	0.33	7.62
1/08	23.94	20	14	1.38	0.29	7.83
1/07	25.72	21	16	1.32	0.22	6.88
1/06	23.71	22	17	1.12	0.17	6.06
Annual Growth	**(0.3%)**	**—**	**—**	**(2.3%)**	**18.0%**	**11.2%**

Starbucks Corporation

Wake up and smell the coffee — Starbucks is everywhere. The world's #1 specialty coffee retailer, Starbucks has more than 16,600 coffee shops in about 40 countries. The outlets offer coffee drinks and food items, as well as roasted beans, coffee accessories, and teas. Starbucks operates more than 8,800 of its shops, which are located in about 10 countries (mostly in the US), while licensees and franchisees operate more than 7,800 units worldwide (primarily in shopping centers and airports). It also owns the Seattle's Best Coffee and Torrefazione Italia coffee brands. In addition, Starbucks markets its coffee through grocery stores and licenses its brand for other food and beverage products.

What was once a simple chain of coffeehouses has become a force of nature in the retail business. Starbucks has used its chain to branch out into other retail segments, including CDs, books, and similar lifestyle products. It also licenses the Starbucks brand for such products as ice cream (made by Nestlé's Dreyer's Grand Ice Cream subsidiary), coffee flavored liqueur (Beam Global Spirits), and bottled Frappuccino (PepsiCo).

Being a global phenomenon did not immunize the company from the economic slowdown during 2008, however. Starbucks shuttered about 800 company-run locations in the US as part of an effort to cut costs and eliminate underperforming stores. The restructuring move was prompted by chairman Howard Schultz who returned as CEO in 2008 (replacing Jim Donald). It has also cut back on plans for new domestic locations while putting an emphasis on the growth of international markets with a particular focus on the growing consumer market in Brazil, China, India and Vietnam.

In addition to weak consumer spending, Starbucks has faced growing competition in the coffee sector. Both Dunkin' Donuts (owned by Dunkin' Brands) and fast food giant McDonald's are marketing their coffee selections as cost-effective morning java alternatives, cutting in on the company's gourmet coffee market. In response, Starbucks is looking to steal some market share in the quick-service segment by promoting its Seattle's Best Coffee brand to restaurant chains and other counter-service outlets. It has deals with sub sandwich chain Subway and #2 hamburger franchise Burger King.

Starbucks is also looking to new products to boost sales. The company rolled out an expanded menu of breakfast items and other hot foods, as well as a new menu of cold drink options. In the retail sector, the company launched an instant coffee product called Via during 2009.

HISTORY

Starbucks was founded in 1971 in Seattle by coffee aficionados Gordon Bowker, Jerry Baldwin, and Ziv Siegl, who named the company for the coffee-loving first mate in *Moby Dick* and created its famous two-tailed siren logo. They aimed to sell the finest-quality whole bean and ground coffees. By 1982 Starbucks had five retail stores and was selling coffee to restaurants and espresso stands in Seattle. That year Howard Schultz joined Starbucks to manage retail sales and marketing. In 1983 Schultz traveled to Italy and was struck by the popularity of coffee bars. He convinced Starbucks' owners to open a downtown Seattle coffee bar in 1984. It was a success; Schultz left the company the following year to open his own coffee bar, Il Giornale, which served Starbucks coffee.

Frustrated by its inability to control quality, Starbucks sold off its wholesale business in 1987. Later that year Il Giornale acquired its retail operations for $4 million. (Starbucks' founders held on to their other coffee business, Peet's Coffee & Tea.) Il Giornale changed its name to Starbucks Corporation, prepared to expand nationally, and opened locations in Chicago and Vancouver. In 1988 the company published its first mail-order catalog.

Starbucks lost money in the late 1980s as it focused on expansion (it tripled its number of stores to 55 between 1987 and 1989). Schultz brought in experienced managers to run Starbucks' stores. In 1991 it became the nation's first privately owned company to offer stock options to all employees.

In 1992 Starbucks went public and set up shops in Nordstrom's department stores. The following year it began operating cafes in Barnes & Noble bookstores. The company had nearly 275 locations by the end of 1993. Starbucks inked a deal in 1994 to provide coffee to ITT/Sheraton hotels (later acquired by Starwood Hotels & Resorts). The next year it capitalized on its popular in-house music selections by selling compact discs. Also in 1995 Starbucks joined with PepsiCo to develop a bottled coffee drink and agreed to produce a line of premium coffee ice cream with Dreyer's.

Starbucks expanded into Japan and Singapore in 1996. Also that year the company created Caffe Starbucks, an online store located on AOL's marketplace. In 1998 Starbucks expanded into the UK when it acquired that country's Seattle Coffee Company chain (founded in 1995) for about $86 million and converted its stores into Starbucks locations. It also announced plans to sell coffee in supermarkets nationwide through an agreement with Kraft Foods. In 1999 Starbucks bought Tazo, an Oregon-based tea company, as well as music retailer Hear Music, and opened its first store in China.

In 2000 Schultz ceded the CEO post to president Orin Smith, remaining chairman but focusing primarily on the company's global strategy. Starbucks jumpstarted its worldwide expansion the next year, opening about 1,100 stores worldwide, including locations in a handful of new European countries such as Austria and Switzerland. It also spun off its Japanese operations as a public company.

In 2003 Starbucks acquired Seattle Coffee Company from AFC Enterprises. The deal gave Starbucks an additional 150 coffee shops (as if it needed them), but more importantly it gave the coffee giant the Seattle's Best Coffee brand and wholesale coffee business. It also got something new out of the deal: franchised locations.

Starbucks was one of the first national retailers to jump on the Wi-Fi bandwagon, teaming with Hewlett-Packard and Deutsche Telekom's T-Mobile unit to offer high-speed wireless Internet access at 1,200 of its locations in the US, London, and Berlin.

In 2005 in conjunction with Jim Beam Brands (now Beam Global Spirits & Wine) it introduced Starbucks Coffee Liqueur and Starbucks Cream Liqueur. Smith retired as president and CEO in 2005; he was replaced by Starbucks' North American president Jim Donald.

While Starbucks continued to dominate the coffee business, traffic at its stores began to decline in 2007. The company brought Schultz back as CEO in 2008, replacing Donald.

EXECUTIVES

Chairman, President, and CEO: Howard D. Schultz, age 56, $12,109,792 total compensation
EVP, CFO, and Chief Administrative Officer: Troy Alstead, age 46, $1,299,761 total compensation
EVP Global Supply Chain Operations: Peter D. Gibbons, age 48
EVP Partner Resources: Kalen Holmes
EVP, General Counsel, and Secretary: Paula E. Boggs, age 50
Chief Marketing Officer: Annie Young-Scrivner, age 40
SVP and CIO; General Manager, Digital Ventures: Stephen Gillett
SVP; President, Asia/Pacific: Maria (Mercy) Corrales
SVP; President, Starbucks Coffee EMEA: Buck Hendrix
SVP; President, Starbucks Coffee Americas: Colin Moore
SVP Marketing: Terry Davenport, age 53
SVP Public Affairs: Vivek Varma
SVP Operations: Clarice Turner
SVP Store Design: Tim Pfeiffer
President, Starbucks Coffee U.S.: Clifford Burrows, age 50, $2,286,855 total compensation
President, Global Development: Arthur Rubinfeld, age 55, $1,768,605 total compensation
President, Global Consumer Products and Foodservice: Jeff Hansberry
President, Seattle's Best Coffee; Interim President, Global Consumer Products and Foodservice: Michelle Gass, age 42
President, Starbucks Coffee International: John Culver, age 49
Auditors: Deloitte & Touche LLP

LOCATIONS

HQ: Starbucks Corporation
2401 Utah Ave. South, Seattle, WA 98134
Phone: 206-447-1575   **Fax:** 206-447-0828
Web: www.starbucks.com

2009 Locations

	No.
US	11,128
International	5,507
Total	**16,635**

PRODUCTS/OPERATIONS

2009 Sales

	$ mil.	% of total
Company-operated retail	8,180.1	84
Licensing	1,222.3	12
Foodservice & other	372.2	4
Total	**9,774.6**	**100**

2009 Locations

	No.
Company-owned	8,832
Licensed	7,803
Total	**16,635**

COMPETITORS

Caffè Nero
Caribou Coffee
Cinnabon
The Coffee Bean
Community Coffee
Dunkin
Einstein Noah Restaurant Group
Farmer Bros.
Green Mountain Coffee
Greggs
illy
Lavazza
McDonald's
Nestlé
Panera Bread
Tim Hortons
Van Houtte
Whitbread

HISTORICAL FINANCIALS

Company Type: Public

Income Statement	FYE: Sunday nearest September 30			
	REVENUE ($ mil.)	NET INCOME ($ mil.)	NET PROFIT MARGIN	EMPLOYEES
9/09	9,775	391	4.0%	142,000
9/08	10,383	316	3.0%	176,000
9/07	9,412	673	7.1%	172,000
9/06	7,787	582	7.5%	145,800
9/05	6,369	495	7.8%	115,000
Annual Growth	**11.3%**	**(5.7%)**	**—**	**5.4%**

2009 Year-End Financials

Debt ratio: 18.0%	No. of shares (mil.): 740
Return on equity: 14.1%	Dividends
Cash ($ mil.): 600	Yield: —
Current ratio: 1.29	Payout: —
Long-term debt ($ mil.): 549	Market value ($ mil.): 15,283

Stock History

NASDAQ (GS): SBUX

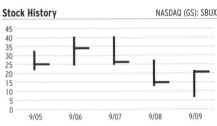

	STOCK PRICE ($) FY Close	P/E High/Low		PER SHARE ($) Earnings	Dividends	Book Value
9/09	20.65	40	14	0.52	—	4.12
9/08	14.87	62	31	0.43	—	3.37
9/07	26.20	46	29	0.87	—	3.09
9/06	34.05	56	35	0.71	—	3.01
9/05	25.05	53	37	0.61	—	2.82
Annual Growth	**(4.7%)**	**—**	**—**	**(3.9%)**	**—**	**9.9%**

Starwood Hotels & Resorts

Starwood Hotels & Resorts Worldwide knows how to shine a light on hospitality. One of the world's largest hotel and leisure companies, it has about 980 properties in some 100 countries. Starwood's hotel empire consists of luxury and upscale brands such as Four Points, Sheraton, and Westin. Starwood operates 80 high-end resorts and hotels through its St. Regis and Luxury Collection, while its chain of about 30 W Hotels offers ultra-modern style for sophisticated business travelers. Other brands include Le Méridien, Aloft, and Element. Its Starwood Vacation Ownership subsidiary operates nearly 15 time-share resorts.

Notable Starwood hotels include the St. Regis in New York and the Hotel Gritti Palace in Venice. Starwood expanded its portfolio in 2008 with the introduction of new brands Aloft (select-service hotels) and Element (extended stay hotels).

Some 440 of Starwood's hotels are owned and operated by franchisees; the company owns or leases about 70 locations, and manages another 440 hotels on behalf of third parties. The company continues to reduce its investment in owned real estate and increase its focus on the management and franchise business.

In early 2010 Starwood sold its Bliss spa and product company to Steiner Leisure Limited for $100 million. Despite the sale, Bliss and Remede spas and amenities remain in W Hotels and St. Regis Hotels. Starwood made the sale in order to focus on its core hospitality business.

Steven Heyer, who took over as CEO from founder Barry Sternlicht in 2004, resigned his post in 2007. Chairman Bruce Duncan served as interim chief until Frits van Paasschen, formerly an executive at Molson Coors Brewing Company, was brought in as his replacement.

HISTORY

Barry Sternlicht earned his MBA from Harvard in 1986 and joined the fast track at JMB Realty, bringing the company a UK real estate deal involving Randsworth Trust in 1989. He left two years later to start Starwood Capital Group, with backers including the wealthy Burden and Ziff families. (JMB and its pension fund partners, meanwhile, lost their shirts when Randsworth went belly-up during the recession of the early 1990s.) In 1995 Starwood Capital joined Goldman Sachs and Nomura Securities to buy Westin Hotel (renamed Westin Hotels & Resorts) from Japanese construction firm Aoki. Founded in Washington State in 1930, Westin was acquired by UAL in 1970, then Aoki bought it in 1988 during a boom in Japanese investments in US real estate.

Also in 1995 Sternlicht bought Hotel Investors Trust (a hotel REIT) and Hotel Investors Corp. (hotel management), two struggling firms whose chief attraction was their rare paired-share status, allowing management company profits to flow through the REIT to investors exempt from corporate income tax. (The structure was banned in 1984, but four such entities were grandfathered in under the law.) The companies were renamed Starwood Lodging Trust and Starwood Lodging Corp. (together, Starwood Lodging).

Through more acquisitions, Starwood had amassed a collection of about 110 hotels by 1997.

Starwood's industry standing took a quantum leap in early 1998 when it acquired the 50% of the Westin hotel chain that Starwood Capital didn't already own and bought lodging giant ITT, the former telephone industry conglomerate and owner of the Sheraton hotel chain. ITT — with more than 400 hotels and gaming properties (Desert Inn, Caesars) — fought off a hostile takeover bid from Hilton Hotels (now Hilton Worldwide) and accepted Starwood Lodging's $14.6 billion offer. (Starwood Capital made $22 million in advising fees on the deal.) Later that year the firm changed its name to Starwood Hotels & Resorts, bought four former Ritz-Carlton hotels, and sold eight all-suite hotels to FelCor Suite Hotels (now FelCor Lodging Trust). Sternlicht then chose Walt Disney executive and Harvard classmate Richard Nanula to take the reins of Starwood's operating company. In late 1998 it launched W Hotels.

Before Congress closed the paired-share loophole for new acquisitions, Starwood Hotels went on a shopping spree, becoming a standard corporation in 1999. Nanula resigned that year, apparently after repeated clashes with Sternlicht. The company bought time-share resort company Vistana — renamed Starwood Vacation Ownership (SVO) — and purchased the portion of European hotel operator Ciga (part of which Sheraton had acquired in 1994) that it didn't already own.

Gaming profits had begun to fall off in 1999, however, as the Asian economic crisis stymied the flow of gambling-hungry tourists. The following year Starwood sold its Caesars unit to Park Place Entertainment (later Caesars Entertainment, now owned by Harrah's) for $3 billion and its Desert Inn hotel and casino to Mirage Resorts founder Steve Wynn for about $270 million. That year SVO began building new resorts in Arizona, Colorado, and Hawaii. Starwood saw its business begin to suffer following the September 11, 2001, terrorist attacks, which kept many potential travelers at home. Starwood cut about 12,000 jobs, roughly 25% of its workforce.

To pay down its debt, Starwood raised about $1.5 billion in capital by selling bonds (2002), and sold its Italian Ciga assets — including luxury hotels, a golf club, and other real estate interests — to Colony Capital (2003).

In 2004 Steven Heyer, former president and COO of Coca-Cola, was named CEO as Sternlicht began setting the stage for his retirement from the company. He stayed on for nearly another year as executive chairman, however, before leaving the company altogether.

The company's expansion efforts in 2005 included the acquisition of the Le Meridien brand for $225 million. In 2006 Starwood sold some 30 properties to Host Hotels & Resorts for about $4 billion. New hotels added in 2006 included The Westin Chicago North Shore (Wheeling, Illinois), The U.S. Grant (San Diego, California), and The Westin St. Maarten, Dawn Beach Resort & Spa (St. Maarten, Netherland Antilles).

Heyer resigned from the company in 2007; chairman Bruce Duncan was tapped to serve as interim CEO. Later that year Frits van Paasschen was named CEO. Starwood sold its Bliss spas in 2010.

EXECUTIVES

Chairman: Bruce W. Duncan, age 58
Vice Chairman and CFO: Vasant M. Prabhu, age 50, $3,902,606 total compensation
President, CEO, and Director: Frits D. van Paasschen, age 49, $8,240,034 total compensation
EVP and Chief Brand Officer: Phil P. McAveety, age 43, $1,690,598 total compensation
EVP and Chief Human Resources Officer: Jeffrey M. (Jeff) Cava, age 58
CIO: Todd Thompson
Chief Administrative Officer, Secretary, and General Counsel: Kenneth S. (Ken) Siegel, age 54, $3,126,843 total compensation
SVP Brand Management; SVP Global Brand Management, Sheraton Hotels & Resorts: Hoyt H. Harper II
SVP Global Brand Design: Mike Tiedy, age 49
SVP and Corporate Controller: Alan M. Schnaid
SVP Global Sales: Christie Hicks
SVP Owner Relations and Franchise: Lynne Dougherty
VP Investor Relations: Jason Koval
President, Hotel Group: Matthew E. (Matt) Avril, age 49, $2,859,688 total compensation
President, Global Development: Simon M. Turner, age 48, $3,661,254 total compensation
CEO, Starwood Vacation Ownership: Sergio D. Rivera, age 47
President, North America Division: Denise M. Coll
President, Latin America: Osvaldo V. Librizzi
President, Europe, Africa, and Middle East Division: Roeland Vos
Chairman and President, Asia/Pacific: Miguel Ko
Senior Director Consumer Affairs: Helen Horsham-Bertels
Auditors: Ernst & Young LLP

LOCATIONS

HQ: Starwood Hotels & Resorts Worldwide, Inc.
1111 Westchester Ave., White Plains, NY 10604
Phone: 914-640-8100   **Fax:** 914-640-8310
Web: www.starwoodhotels.com

2009 Sales

	$ mil.	% of total
US	3,401	72
Italy	175	4
Other countries	1,136	24
Total	**4,712**	**100**

PRODUCTS/OPERATIONS

2009 Sales

	$ mil.	% of total
Owned, leased & consolidated joint venture hotels	1,584	34
Management fees, franchise fees & other income	658	14
Vacation ownership & residential	523	11
Other revenues from managed & franchise properties	1,947	41
Total	**4,712**	**100**

2009 Sales

	$ mil.	% of total
Hotel	4,038	86
Vacation ownership & residential	674	14
Total	**4,712**	**100**

Selected Brands

Aloft
Element
Four Points by Sheraton
Luxury Collection
Le Méridien
Sheraton
Westin

COMPETITORS

Accor	InterContinental Hotels
Bluegreen	Loews Hotels
Carlson Hotels	LXR Luxury Resorts
Diamond Resorts	Marriott
Fairmont Raffles	Millennium & Copthorne
Four Seasons Hotels	Omni Hotels
Hilton Worldwide	Silverleaf Resorts
Hyatt	Wyndham Worldwide

HISTORICAL FINANCIALS
Company Type: Public

Income Statement
FYE: December 31

	REVENUE ($ mil.)	NET INCOME ($ mil.)	NET PROFIT MARGIN	EMPLOYEES
12/09	4,712	71	1.5%	145,000
12/08	5,907	329	5.6%	145,000
12/07	6,153	542	8.8%	155,000
12/06	5,979	1,113	18.6%	145,000
12/05	5,977	422	7.1%	145,000
Annual Growth	(5.8%)	(36.0%)	—	0.0%

2009 Year-End Financials

Debt ratio: 162.0%
Return on equity: 4.1%
Cash ($ mil.): 87
Current ratio: 0.74
Long-term debt ($ mil.): 2,955

No. of shares (mil.): 190
Dividends
Yield: 0.5%
Payout: 48.8%
Market value ($ mil.): 6,953

Stock History
NYSE: HOT

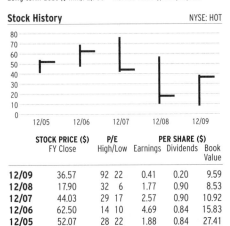

	STOCK PRICE ($) FY Close	P/E High/Low	PER SHARE ($) Earnings	Dividends	Book Value
12/09	36.57	92 22	0.41	0.20	9.59
12/08	17.90	32 6	1.77	0.90	8.53
12/07	44.03	29 17	2.57	0.90	10.92
12/06	62.50	14 10	4.69	0.84	15.83
12/05	52.07	28 22	1.88	0.84	27.41
Annual Growth	(8.5%)	— —	(31.7%)	(30.1%)	(23.1%)

State Farm Mutual

Like an enormous corporation, State Farm is everywhere. The leading US personal lines property/casualty company (by premiums), State Farm Mutual Automobile Insurance Company is the #1 provider of auto insurance. It also is the leading home insurer and offers nonmedical health and life insurance through its subsidiary companies. Its products are marketed via some 17,000 agents in the US and Canada.

Competition has increased with the fall of barriers between the banking, securities, and insurance industries. State Farm's efforts to diversify include a federal savings bank charter (State Farm Bank) that offers consumer and business loans through its agents and by phone, mail, and the Internet.

The company also established itself as a financial services provider in 1999, and its mutual funds have since built up $3.7 billion in assets. However, insurance is still its main source of income. And, while State Farm already insures 15% of the automobiles on US roads, it is scrambling to hang on to that much while attempting to grab an even larger portion of the pie. Competition and market weakness has spurred the company to refocus its efforts on the segment that makes up over 50% of its policies and accounts.

State Farm's size and stability has made it easier for the insurer to stretch out to new, hard-to-reach customers such as immigrant ethnic groups and younger people. It has also made ethnic diversity in its workforce a priority and has actively recruited bilingual agents and employees.

With increasingly severe weather in recent years, the company has been busily readjusting its homeowners' strategy. State Farm still insures more than 20% of the single-family homes in the US, but the insurer stopped writing new homeowners policies in some 15 states in an effort to improve profitability.

Hurricanes Katrina, Wilma, and Rita brought State Farm customer claims totaling $6.3 billion in property and casualty losses. Midwestern storms along with Hurricanes Gustav and Ike accounted for another $6.3 billion losses in 2008. For residents along the Gulf Coast, at first it seemed like State Farm would stay put. However, as the claims rolled in the company quickly began revising its underwriting guidelines to limit its risk. New homeowner policies in places such as New Orleans now have steeper deductibles and less coverage, and the company has completely stopped offering new homeowners and commercial property policies in the state of Mississippi. State Farm is still a major insurer along the Alabama coast, and its 2009 threats to pull out of Florida subsided following a noisy tussle with state insurance regulators.

Since its founding, the group's companies have been run by only two families, the Mecherles (1922-54) and the Rusts (1954-present).

HISTORY

Retired farmer George Mecherle formed State Farm Mutual Automobile Insurance in Bloomington, Illinois, in 1922. State Farm served only members of farm bureaus and farm mutual insurance companies, charging a one-time membership fee and a premium to protect an automobile against loss or damage.

Unlike most competitors, State Farm offered six-month premium payments. The insurer billed and collected renewal premiums from its home office, relieving the agent of the task. In addition, State Farm determined auto rates by a simple seven-class system, while competitors varied rates for each model.

State Farm in 1926 started City and Village Mutual Automobile Insurance to insure nonfarmers' autos; it became part of the company in 1927. Between 1927 and 1931 it introduced borrowed-car protection, wind coverage, and insurance for vehicles used to transport schoolchildren.

State Farm expanded to California in 1928 and formed State Farm Life Insurance the next year. In 1935 it established State Farm Fire Insurance. George Mecherle became chairman in 1937, and his son Ramond became president. In 1939 George challenged agents to write "A Million or More (auto policies) by '44." State Farm saw a 110% increase in policies.

During the 1940s State Farm focused on urban areas after most of the farm bureaus formed their own insurance companies. In the late 1940s and 1950s it moved to a full-time agency force. Homeowners coverage was added to the insurer's offerings under the leadership of Adlai Rust, who led State Farm from 1954 until 1958, when Edward Rust took over. He died in 1985 and his son, Edward Jr., currently holds the top spot.

Between 1974 and 1987 the insurer was hit by several gender-discrimination suits (a 1992 settlement awarded $157 million to 814 women). State Farm has since tried to hire more women and minorities.

Serial disasters in the early 1990s, including Hurricane Andrew and the Los Angeles riots, proved costly. The 1994 Northridge earthquake alone generated more than $2.5 billion in claims and contributed to a 72% decline in earnings.

State Farm — the top US home insurer since the mid-1960s — canceled 62,500 residential policies in South Florida in 1996 to cut potential hurricane loss an estimated 11%. In response, Florida's insurance regulators rescinded a previously approved rate hike. That year the company agreed to open more urban neighborhood offices to settle a discrimination suit brought by the Department of Housing and Urban Development, which accused State Farm of discriminating against potential customers in minority-populated areas.

Legal trouble continued. In 1997 State Farm settled with a California couple who alleged the company forged policyholders' signatures on forms declining coverage and concealed evidence to avoid paying earthquake damage claims. That year a policyholder sued to keep State Farm from "wasting company assets" on President Clinton's legal defense against Paula Jones' sexual harassment charges (Clinton held a State Farm personal liability policy).

Relations with its sales force were already rocky, but in 1998 State Farm proposed to reduce up-front commissions and cut base pay in favor of incentives for customer retention and cross-selling. Reduced auto premiums and increased catastrophe claims from across the US eroded State Farm's bottom line that year. A federal thrift charter obtained in 1998 let the company launch banking operations the next year.

In 2000 the company was hit with a class-action lawsuit about its denial of personal-injury claims; previous suits had been individual cases. In 2002 State Farm Indemnity, the company's auto-only New Jersey subsidiary, withdrew from the Garden State's auto insurance market but began phasing back into the market in 2005.

Like all reinsurers, State Farm's reinsurance business was tested by the 2005 hurricane season. It underwrote losses of $2.8 billion.

EXECUTIVES

Chairman and CEO: Edward B. (Ed) Rust Jr., age 59
Vice Chairman and Chief Agency and Marketing Officer: Michael C. Davidson
Vice Chairman, CFO, and Treasurer: Michael L. Tipsord, age 50
Vice Chairman and Chief Administrative Officer: James E. (Jim) Rutrough
EVP: Willie G. Brown
EVP: Barbara Cowden
EVP: Deborah Traskell
EVP: Brian V. Boyden
EVP, General Counsel, and Secretary: Kim M. Brunner
EVP: William K. (Bill) King

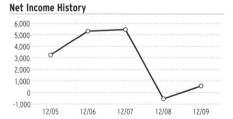
State Street Corporation

Ol' Blue Eyes sang about the State Street (that great street) in Chicago, but investors may find Boston's State Street more melodious. Its flagship State Street Bank provides custody, shareholder services, brokerage, securities finance, research, and other management services for institutional clients around the world. Customers include mutual funds, pension plans, and investment managers. At the top of the custody-services heap, State Street has more than $18.7 trillion in assets under custody. It also has some $1.9 trillion in assets under administration. Other subsidiaries include asset manager State Street Global Advisors and State Street Alternative Investment Solutions.

Boston Financial Data Services, a joint venture with DST Systems, provides shareholder services to mutual funds and other clients. In 2007 State Street added bulk by acquiring another Boston-based fund accounting and servicing provider Investors Financial Services. The following year State Street and Citigroup sold their CitiStreet retirement and pension plan management joint venture to ING Groep for some $900 million.

In the distressed economic climate beginning in mid-2007, the company's servicing and management revenues declined due to lower equity market valuations and lending volumes and an increase in bankruptcies. The declines were somewhat offset in 2008 by gains from the CitiStreet sale. In a sign of the much-anticipated economic turnaround, State Street's assets under custody have also been climbing (by nearly $3 trillion in 2009).

The US Treasury invested some $2 billion in the company in 2008 as part of a broader bailout plan to restore confidence and increase liquidity. State Street was among eight other top banks that received a combined $250 billion; the company repaid the full amount within months.

At the vanguard of financial services technology, State Street banks on its computerized analytical and organizational tools to woo and retain clients. Among its offerings are foreign exchange trading platform FX Connect and Global Link, which provides market research and portfolio analysis.

State Street has also been investing in international growth. It expanded its global fund administration and alternative asset servicing capabilities in 2010 when it acquired Channel Islands-based Mourant International Finance Administration. The company also bought the securities services business of Italian bank Intesa Sanpaolo, further increasing its presence in markets outside the US.

Ron Logue retired as State Street's CEO in 2010 but remains chairman. He was succeeded by Jay Hooley, formerly the company's president and COO.

HISTORY

The US's chaotic postrevolutionary era gave birth to the first ancestor of State Street Corporation. Union Bank was founded in 1792 by Boston businessmen, breaking the eight-year monopoly held on Boston banking by Massachusetts Bank (a forerunner of FleetBoston, which was acquired by Bank of America in 2004). Governor John Hancock's distinctive signature graced Union's charter; the bank set up shop at 40 State Street near the port and enjoyed the glory days of New England's shipping trade.

In the mid-19th century, Boston's financial eminence faded as New York flexed its economic muscle. In 1865 the bank was nationally chartered and changed its name to National Union Bank of Boston. It got a new neighbor in 1891: Directors of Third National Bank set up State Street Deposit & Trust to engage in the newfangled business of trusts.

In 1925 National Union Bank merged with State Street and inherited its custodial business. The bank grew through the 1950s; acquisitions included the Second National Bank and the Rockland-Atlas National Bank.

In 1970 State Street converted to a holding company — the State Street Boston Financial Corp. (State Street Boston Corp. as of 1977). The company also went international that decade, opening an office in Munich, Germany.

Soaring inflation and the recession of the 1970s forced the company to radically rethink its mission. The 1974 passage of the Employee Retirement Income Security Act changed the laws governing the management of pension funds and created an opportunity. State Street was one of the first banks to move aggressively into high-tech information processing, and affiliate Boston Financial Data Services began servicing pension assets in 1974.

Encouraged by that success, in 1975 new CEO William Edgerly (who served until 1992) steered State Street away from branch banking and into investments, trusts, and securities processing. An early achievement was designing PepsiCo's retirement plan. Fee-based sales approached 50% of revenues; the company could now quit focusing on lending. In the 1980s and 1990s the company built its administration and investment management businesses overseas and moved into software.

Evolving in the late 1990s, State Street left noncore businesses but expanded globally. In 1997 it formed European Direct Capital Management to invest in eastern and central Europe. State Street Global Advisors opened a London office in 1998 to serve wealthy individuals outside the US.

The company sold its commercial banking business to Royal Bank of Scotland in 1999, signaling an exit from that business and narrowing State Street's scope to the asset and investment management businesses. The company also bought Wachovia's custody and institutional trust business and teamed with Citigroup to sell 401(k) retirement products.

In 2000 State Street created FX Connect, an electronic foreign exchange trading system. Also that year David Spina took over as CEO from the retiring Marshall Carter.

The firm bought Bel Air Investment Advisors and its broker/dealer affiliate Bel Air Securities in 2001 to cater to the ultrawealthy. In 2003 State Street sold its corporate trust business to U.S. Bancorp and its private asset management business to Charles Schwab's U.S. Trust. Spina retired in 2004; his protégé, Ron Logue, stepped in as chairman and CEO.

The company was reappointed as the financial advisor for the $2.4 billion Suffolk County (New York) Council Pension Fund in 2007. Also that year, State Street boosted its foreign exchange offerings with the acquisition of Currenex.

EXECUTIVES

Chairman: Ronald E. (Ron) Logue, age 64,
$7,994,758 total compensation
President, CEO, and Director: Joseph L. (Jay) Hooley,
age 53, $13,903,548 total compensation
**EVP and Vice Chairman; Head, North American
Investor Services and Global Investment Manager
Outsourcing Services:** Joseph C. Antonellis, age 55,
$11,401,905 total compensation
EVP and CFO: Edward J. Resch, age 57,
$9,046,940 total compensation
**EVP; Head, Global Operations, Technology and Product
Development:** James S. Phalen, age 59,
$7,603,956 total compensation
EVP and Head Global Marketing: Hannah Grove
EVP and CIO: Christopher (Chris) Perretta
EVP and Chief Compliance Officer: Tracy Atkinson
EVP and Chief Administrative Officer: David C. O'Leary,
age 63
EVP and General Counsel: David C. Phelan, age 52
EVP, Chief Legal Officer, and Secretary:
Jeffrey N. (Jeff) Carp, age 53,
$8,558,286 total compensation
EVP Investment Services: Gunjan Kedia
EVP and General Auditor: Jayne Donahue
EVP and Head, Global Human Resources:
Alison A. Quirk
**EVP; Head, Investment Manager Services for North
America:** Anne P. Tangen
EVP; Head, Institutional Investor Services:
Michael L. Williams
**EVP and CTO; Chairman and General Manager, State
Street Zhejiang Technology Company (SSTZ):**
Albert J. (Jerry) Cristoforo
EVP and Head Regulatory and Industry Affairs:
Stefan M. Gavell
**EVP, Corporate Controller, and Chief Accounting
Officer:** James J. Malerba, age 55
SVP Investor Relations: S. Kelley MacDonald
President and CEO, State Street Global Advisors:
Scott F. Powers, age 50
Auditors: Ernst & Young LLP

LOCATIONS

HQ: State Street Corporation
1 Lincoln St., Boston, MA 02111
Phone: 617-786-3000   **Fax:** 617-664-4299
Web: www.statestreet.com

PRODUCTS/OPERATIONS

2009 Sales

	$ mil.	% of total
Fees		
Servicing	3,276	35
Trading	1,094	12
Management	824	9
Securities finance	570	6
Processing & other	171	2
Interest	3,286	35
Net gains related to investment securities	141	1
Total	**9,362**	**100**

COMPETITORS

Bank of New York Mellon
Citigroup
Credit Suisse (USA)
Deutsche Bank
First Data
Fiserv
JPMorgan Chase
Morgan Stanley
Northern Trust
Principal Financial
SEI Investments
UBS Financial Services

HISTORICAL FINANCIALS

Company Type: Public

Income Statement

FYE: December 31

	ASSETS ($ mil.)	NET INCOME ($ mil.)	INCOME AS % OF ASSETS	EMPLOYEES
12/09	157,946	(1,881)	—	27,000
12/08	173,631	1,811	1.0%	28,475
12/07	142,543	1,261	0.9%	27,110
12/06	107,353	1,106	1.0%	21,700
12/05	97,968	722	0.7%	20,965
Annual Growth	**12.7%**	**—**	**—**	**6.5%**

2009 Year-End Financials

Equity as % of assets: 9.2%
Return on assets: —
Return on equity: —
Long-term debt ($ mil.): 8,838
No. of shares (mil.): 502
Dividends
  Yield: 0.1%
  Payout: —
Market value ($ mil.): 21,851
Sales ($ mil.): 9,362

Stock History

NYSE: STT

	STOCK PRICE ($) FY Close	P/E High/Low		PER SHARE ($) Earnings	Dividends	Book Value
12/09	43.54	—	—	(4.31)	0.04	28.87
12/08	39.33	20	7	4.30	0.95	25.45
12/07	81.20	24	17	3.45	0.88	22.51
12/06	67.44	21	17	3.29	0.80	14.45
12/05	55.44	24	16	2.50	0.72	12.69
Annual Growth	**(5.9%)**	**—**	**—**	**—**	**(51.5%)**	**22.8%**

Steelcase Inc.

For those really tough office meetings, there's Steelcase, a top office furniture maker worldwide. The company manufactures a wide variety of products, from file cabinets that come with a lifetime warranty to premium Coalesse-branded contemporary furnishings. Steelcase also sells staples, such as tables, desks, and lighting. Its brands include Brayton, Designtex, Details, Metro, PolyVision, Steelcase, Turnstone, and Vecta, among others. Steelcase offers a variety of services, including workspace planning, interior construction, and project management. In addition the company focuses on high-end furniture and specialty markets through various subsidiaries and affiliates.

The company extended its reach into premium furniture in 2009 with its launch of the Coalesse brand in its effort to target the more recession-proof luxury clientele. The collection is targeted to corporate, hospitality, and residential clients. It's a blend of Steelcase's Metro Furniture, Brayton International, and Vecta product lines. Coalesse sells through a dealer network in North America.

Despite the increases for its Coalesse collection, Steelcase cites the global economic downturn as one reason its revenue dipped by 28% in 2010 compared to 2009. An upheaval in the capital markets, too, kept companies' office furniture purchases on the backburner for most of the year. Indeed, as US joblessness mounted, the demand for office furniture fell. In response, the firm cut costs through layoffs, salary cuts, and the consolidation of facilities.

Steelcase has expanded its operations globally through acquisitions during the past few years to diversify its business and reduce its risk in any one region. The company acquired the office furniture business of China-based Ultra Group Holdings in 2007 to expand its business in Asia. The purchase added about 1,000 employees to Steelcase's operations in China and beefed up the company's international sales. About 70% of its international business was generated in Western Europe.

It's also reaching into new niches to diversify. Steelcase's purchase of whiteboard maker PolyVision expanded the company's business in the corporate learning and higher education markets. It also made inroads into the automotive sector with its agreement with Johnson Controls to improve vehicle seats with Steelcase technology. In 2006 the company acquired hospital furniture maker Softcare Innovations and its sister company DJRT Manufacturing. The companies were folded into Steelcase's health care furniture line, Nurture by Steelcase.

Steelcase in 2008 entered an agreement with IDEO, a Steelcase subsidiary that specializes in innovation and "human-centered" design. As part of the agreement, IDEO management is able to purchase a controlling equity interest in IDEO in two phases ending in 2013.

Descendants of Steelcase's founders control the company.

HISTORY

In the early 1900s, when wooden office furniture was the rule, sheet-metal designer Peter Wege began espousing the benefits of fireproof steel furniture. In 1912 Wege persuaded a group of investors, led by Grand Rapids, Michigan, banker Walter Idema, to create the Metal Office Furniture Company. Salesman David Dyer Hunting — a onetime vaudeville press agent who is considered the company's third founder — joined in 1914. Metal Office Furniture's first big hit was a metal wastepaper basket.

Businesses were slow to switch from wood to the more expensive metal furniture, but US government architects, concerned with fire safety, began specifying metal furniture in their designs. Metal Office Furniture won its first government contract in 1915.

Wege hired media consultant Jim Turner in 1921 to tout the benefits of metal furniture. Turner came up with a trademark to describe the indestructible nature of the company's products — Steelcase. The company patented the suspension cabinet in 1934 and teamed with Frank Lloyd Wright in 1937 to create office furniture for the Johnson Wax headquarters building. Metal Office Furniture provided the US Navy with shipboard furniture during WWII and sold Navy-inspired modular furniture after the war.

In 1954 the company changed its name to Steelcase. Five years later it introduced Convertibles and Convertiwalls, a system of frames, cabinets, and panels that could tailor a work area to an individual worker's needs. By 1968 Steelcase had become the world's #1 maker of metal office furniture.

To boost its presence overseas, the company signed deals with firms such as Strafor Facom (1974, France). Steelcase began a series of acquisitions in 1978, fueling growth that helped triple its sales during the 1980s.

In 1987 Steelcase positioned itself as a more design-oriented company by creating the Steelcase Design Partnership. The partnership, which was made up of seven companies, provided products for special market niches such as fabrics. The firm was hit hard by the recession of the early 1990s as many businesses postponed buying new furniture. Steelcase was forced to lay off hourly workers, but by 1992 it was able to recall them all.

In 1993 Steelcase launched Turnstone, serving small businesses and home office workers. Turnstone president James Hackett was named president and CEO of Steelcase the next year.

In 1996 Steelcase joined with computer mouse pioneer IDEO to co-design furniture for computers. Steelcase went public in 1998 at the urging of the Wege and Hunting families; Peter Wege, son of one of the company's founders, gave nearly $140 million (of the $214 million he gained from the IPO) to his charity, the Wege Foundation.

Acquisitions in the late 1990s included Germany's wood office furniture maker Werndl BuroMobel and the remaining 50% stake of its French joint venture, Steelcase Strafor, from Strafor Facom.

The company acquired Custom Cable Industries (data and voice cabling) and PolyVision (whiteboards) in 2002. In the face of declining office furniture sales, however, Steelcase was also laying off workers. More than 6,600 hourly, temporary, and salaried positions were eliminated between December 2000 and March 2002, or 27% of the workforce. The company temporarily closed its North American operations for one week in April 2003. The shutdown was the company's first in its 90-year history.

In September 2003 Steelcase sold Attwood Corporation, a marine parts manufacturing subsidiary, to leisure products industry leader Brunswick Corporation.

EXECUTIVES

Chairman Emeritus: Robert C. Pew II, age 84
Chairman: Robert C. (Rob) Pew III, age 59
President, CEO, and Director: James P. Hackett, age 55, $2,240,371 total compensation
SVP and Chief Administrative Officer: Nancy W. Hickey, age 58
SVP and Global Operations Officer: Mark A. Baker, age 49, $1,480,235 total compensation
VP and CFO: David C. (Dave) Sylvester, age 45, $1,355,416 total compensation
VP, Chief Legal Officer, and Secretary: Lizbeth S. O'Shaughnessy, age 48
VP Growth Initiatives: John S. Malnor, age 48
VP WorkSpace Futures and Corporate Strategy: Sara E. Armbruster, age 39
VP Global Design: James Ludwig
VP Global Corporate Community Relations: Brian Cloyd
Corporate Controller and Chief Accounting Officer: Mark T. Mossing, age 52
Design Director, Turnstone: Kirt Martin
Director Global Environmental Sustainability: Angela Nahikian
Director Corporate Strategy and Development: Raj Mehan
Director UK Sales: Nikos Liapis
Corporate Communications: Jeanine Holquist

President, Steelcase Group: James P. (Jim) Keane, age 50, $1,436,029 total compensation
President, Steelcase International: James G. (Jim) Mitchell, age 60, $1,498,913 total compensation
President, Coalesse: Frank H. Merlotti Jr., age 59, $918,979 total compensation
Auditors: BDO Seidman, LLP

LOCATIONS

HQ: Steelcase Inc.
901 44th St. SE, Grand Rapids, MI 49508
Phone: 616-247-2710   **Fax:** 616-475-2270
Web: www.steelcase.com

2010 Sales

	$ mil.	% of total
US	1,469.7	64
Other countries	822.0	36
Total	**2,291.7**	**100**

PRODUCTS/OPERATIONS

2010 Sales

	$ mil.	% of total
Systems & storage	944.1	41
Seating	595.9	26
Other	751.7	33
Total	**2,291.7**	**100**

Selected Products

Desks and suites (standard, executive)
Interior architecture (flooring, space dividers)
Lighting (task, ambient, accent)
Seating (general, executive, guest, lounge)
Storage (shelves, cabinets, files)
Systems (workstation, panel systems)
Tables (meeting, personal, cafe)
Technology (appliances)
Textiles (seating upholstery, panel fabric)
Worktools (organizers, boards and easels)

Selected Brand Names

Brayton International
Braytonspaces
Coalesse
Designtex
Details
Metro
PolyVision
Steelcase
Turnstone
Vecta

COMPETITORS

ABCO Office Furniture   Inscape corp
CFGroup   KI
Design Within Reach   Kimball International
Haworth, Inc.   Knoll, Inc.
Herman Miller   Shelby Williams
HNI   Teknion
The HON Company

HISTORICAL FINANCIALS

Company Type: Public

Income Statement

FYE: Last Friday in February

	REVENUE ($ mil.)	NET INCOME ($ mil.)	NET PROFIT MARGIN	EMPLOYEES
2/10	2,292	(14)	—	11,400
2/09	3,184	(12)	—	13,000
2/08	3,421	133	3.9%	13,500
2/07	3,097	107	3.5%	13,000
2/06	2,869	49	1.7%	13,000
Annual Growth	**(5.5%)**	**—**	**—**	**(3.2%)**

2010 Year-End Financials

Debt ratio: 42.1%   No. of shares (mil.): 133
Return on equity: —   Dividends
Cash ($ mil.): 111   Yield: 3.0%
Current ratio: 1.48   Payout: —
Long-term debt ($ mil.): 293   Market value ($ mil.): 874

Stock History

NYSE: SCS

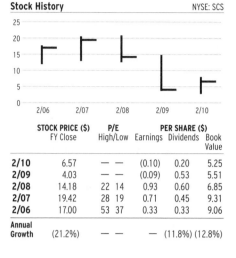

	STOCK PRICE ($) FY Close	P/E High/Low		PER SHARE ($) Earnings	Dividends	Book Value
2/10	6.57	—	—	(0.10)	0.20	5.25
2/09	4.03	—	—	(0.09)	0.53	5.51
2/08	14.18	22	14	0.93	0.60	6.85
2/07	19.42	28	19	0.71	0.45	9.31
2/06	17.00	53	37	0.33	0.33	9.06
Annual Growth	**(21.2%)**	**—**	**—**	**—**	**(11.8%)**	**(12.8%)**

Sun Healthcare

Sun Healthcare Group shines its rays on nursing homes across the US. The company provides long-term, subacute, and related health care services at about 200 inpatient facilities in 25 states (totaling some 23,000 beds) through its SunBridge Healthcare subsidiary. SunBridge's facilities are primarily skilled nursing centers for seniors; it also offers assisted and independent living arrangements and behavioral health services. The firm's SunDance Rehabilitation unit offers physical, occupational, and speech therapy, and its SolAmor division provides hospice services. Sun Healthcare also provides temporary medical staffing through its CareerStaff Unlimited unit.

The company gets roughly 90% of its revenues from its inpatient facility operations, and most of that comes from Medicaid and Medicare. Sun Healthcare is focused on growing its inpatient business (primarily within the Medicare and high-need market) in select geographic areas in order to reduce overhead and maximize synergies in its operating markets.

Sun Healthcare is also adding Rehab Recovery Suites (for Medicare and managed care patients) and Alzheimer's care wings to several of its skilled nursing homes.

The company also anticipates further growing its hospice and rehabilitation businesses through acquisitions and internal efforts, as it feels the two units complement its focus on providing integrated, full-time inpatient care. To that end, SolAmor Hospice acquired New Jersey-based Holisticare Hospice in 2008. In 2009 SolAmor expanded once again by acquiring Massachusetts-based Allegiance Hospice Group. Following that transaction SolAmor has a presence in eight states.

In 2008 and 2009 the company sold or closed seven skilled nursing centers, two hospitals, a regional provider of adolescent rehabilitation and special education services, and an assisted living facility. Sun Healthcare continues to evaluate its various operations to identify those that should be sold or closed because they are not performing up to par.

HISTORY

In 1987 Andrew Turner left long-term care chain Hillhaven Corp. to form a smaller, similar operation named Horizon Healthcare. Two years later he formed another health care business, Sunrise Healthcare, by buying and turning around seven unprofitable facilities in Washington and Connecticut. Sunrise Healthcare was based in Albuquerque, New Mexico.

Acquisitive Sunrise Healthcare bought some 20 facilities between 1990 and 1992 and added a therapy services division, SunDance Rehabilitation (1991). But the company went supernova in 1993, when Turner added SunScript Pharmacy and bundled Sunrise, SunDance, and SunScript into Sun Healthcare Group, taking the holding company public. Sun Healthcare used the proceeds to acquire 42 nursing homes, including Honorcare, which had 14 facilities in four states. That year the group added subacute care, a lucrative market with higher reimbursement rates, to its services.

The growth continued throughout the mid-1990s. Sun added 60 more facilities to its network in 1994, including 36 nursing homes from its merger with The Mediplex Group. By combining the two companies' subacute care facilities, Sun became one of the US's largest subacute care providers. Recognizing the potential in less-developed markets outside the US, the company ventured overseas. Sun acquired Exceler, which had 20 nursing homes in the UK.

As the long-term-care industry continued to consolidate, Sun realigned its operations in 1995, selling off the mental health and substance abuse facilities it had acquired with Mediplex. That year the group also acquired CareerStaff Unlimited, broadening SunDance's ability to provide a continuum of care to affiliated and nonaffiliated facilities. Sun continued to expand overseas, acquiring UK long-term-care providers Ashbourne and Hesslewood Nursing & Residential Care Home.

The company reorganized its management in 1996 to better control its diverse health care services. Sun strengthened its pharmacy unit by adding a medical/surgical supply business and buying 10% of OmniCell, which makes medical supply distribution software.

In the late 1990s Sun continued its bigger-is-better strategy, acquiring US nursing home operators Regency (1997) and Retirement Care Associates and Contour Medical (1998), Spain's Eurosar (1997), Australia's Alpha Healthcare Ltd. (38%, 1997) and Moran Health Care Group (1997). Shadows loomed in 1998, however, when the company was accused in a California lawsuit of giving substandard care; a comatose patient in a Massachusetts facility was raped and impregnated; and Sun Healthcare employees in New England went on strike.

But Sun faced its darkest hours in 1999, when major losses due to changes in Medicare reimbursement led to a reorganization and prompted it to file for Chapter 11 protection. Shareholders also filed suit over these losses. That year and into 2000 the company cut its workforce, sold nonperforming homes, and sold its operations in Spain to shore up its bottom line.

The selling spree continued in 2001 when the company shed its remaining overseas operations and its medical supplies unit. In early 2002, Sun Healthcare emerged from Chapter 11 bankruptcy after securing a $150 million senior credit line with lenders, led by Heller Healthcare Finance, a GE Capital company.

Sun Healthcare divested more than 130 underperforming facilities in 2003 and 2004. The company also sold its SunScript Pharmacy unit and its software development operations.

In 2005, as finances improved, the company beefed up its health care staffing business. Its CareerStaff Unlimited subsidiary acquired SingleSource Staffing and Goddard Healthcare Consulting, both based in Texas. Later CareerStaff Unlimited bought ProCare One Nurses, which provides staffing services for nursing professionals.

Sun Healthcare also acquired Peak Medical Corporation in 2005. The company acquired hospice operator SolAmor Hospice in 2006. Sun Healthcare also sold its home health division that year, as well as its remaining laboratory and radiology businesses.

Sun Healthcare acquired Harborside Healthcare in early 2007 from majority shareholder Investcorp and other investors. Harborside added some 75 skilled nursing and assisted living facilities (9,000 beds) in nine eastern US states to SunBridge Healthcare's operations.

EXECUTIVES

Chairman and CEO: Richard K. Matros, age 55, $2,839,709 total compensation
EVP and CFO: L. Bryan Shaul, age 65, $1,094,353 total compensation
EVP and General Counsel: Michael Newman, age 61, $789,328 total compensation
SVP Human Resources: Cindy Chrispell, age 49
SVP Corporate Communications: Terri Kern
VP and CIO: Slayton E. Austria
VP and Treasurer: Brandi Riddle
VP and Corporate Controller: Jeffrey M. Kreger
President, SunDance Rehabilitation:
Susan E. (Sue) Gwyn, age 58, $774,844 total compensation
President and COO, SunBridge HealthCare and SHG Services: William A. (Bill) Mathies, age 50, $1,627,269 total compensation
President, CareerStaff Unlimited: Richard L. Peranton, age 61, $687,289 total compensation
President, SolAmor Hospice: Glen R. Cavallo
Chief Risk Officer and Chief Compliance Officer:
Chauncey J. Hunker, age 59
Secretary: Michael Berg
Manager Public Relations: Bernadette G. Bell
Auditors: Ernst & Young LLP

LOCATIONS

HQ: Sun Healthcare Group, Inc.
18831 Von Karman, Ste. 400, Irvine, CA 92612
Phone: 949-255-7100   **Fax:** 949-255-7054
Web: www.sunh.com

2009 Inpatient Facilities

	No.
Kentucky	20
Massachusetts	18
Ohio	17
California	15
New Hampshire	15
New Mexico	12
Connecticut	10
Idaho	10
Colorado	9
Florida	9
Georgia	9
Oklahoma	9
North Carolina	8
Tennessee	8
Alabama	7
West Virginia	7
Washington	6
Montana	5
Maryland	3
Indiana	2
Rhode Island	2
Arizona	1
New Jersey	1
Utah	1
Wyoming	1
Total	**205**

PRODUCTS/OPERATIONS

2009 Sales

	$ mil.	% of total
Inpatient	1,675.7	86
Rehabilitation therapy	179.5	9
Medical staffing	102.5	5
Adjustments	(75.9)	—
Total	**1,881.8**	**100**

2009 Sales

	$ mil.	% of total
Medicaid	753.4	40
Medicare	555.6	30
Private pay & other	471.2	25
Managed care & commercial insurance	101.6	5
Total	**1,881.8**	**100**

COMPETITORS

Advocat	Kelly Services
AMN Healthcare	Kindred Healthcare
Assisted Living Concepts	Life Care Centers
ATC Healthcare	Magellan Health
Brookdale Senior Living	Manor Care
Consulate Health Care	Medical Staffing Network
Covenant Care	Odyssey HealthCare
Cross Country Healthcare	Psychiatric Solutions
Emeritus Corporation	RehabCare
Ensign Group	SavaSeniorCare
Extendicare REIT	Skilled Healthcare Group
Five Star Quality Care	Sunrise Senior Living
Gentiva	Tenet Healthcare
Golden Horizons	Ventas
HealthSouth	VITAS Healthcare
InteliStaf Healthcare	

HISTORICAL FINANCIALS

Company Type: Public

Income Statement

	REVENUE ($ mil.)	NET INCOME ($ mil.)	NET PROFIT MARGIN	EMPLOYEES
12/09	1,882	39	2.1%	30,029
12/08	1,824	109	6.0%	29,845
12/07	1,587	58	3.6%	36,850
12/06	1,046	27	2.6%	19,350
12/05	882	3	0.3%	22,000
Annual Growth	**20.9%**	**92.8%**	**—**	**8.1%**

FYE: December 31

Debt ratio: 148.5%
Return on equity: 9.1%
Cash ($ mil.): 104
Current ratio: 1.67
Long-term debt ($ mil.): 667

No. of shares (mil.): 44
Dividends
  Yield: —
  Payout: —
Market value ($ mil.): 403

Stock History   NASDAQ (GS): SUNH

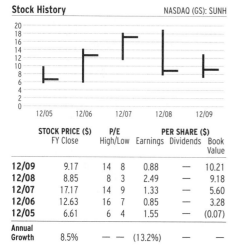

	STOCK PRICE ($) FY Close	P/E High/Low		PER SHARE ($) Earnings	Dividends	Book Value
12/09	9.17	14	8	0.88	—	10.21
12/08	8.85	8	3	2.49	—	9.18
12/07	17.17	14	9	1.33	—	5.60
12/06	12.63	16	7	0.85	—	3.28
12/05	6.61	6	4	1.55	—	(0.07)
Annual Growth	8.5%	—	—	(13.2%)	—	—

Sunoco, Inc.

A leading independent oil refiner and marketer, Sunoco has screened its operations, shed nonperforming ones, and buffed the others in hopes that the sun will shine on future profits. The company operates three refineries, which have a combined processing capacity of 675,000 barrels of crude oil a day, and it has more than 6,000 miles of oil and refined products pipelines and more than 40 product terminals. More than half of its crude oil is sourced from West Africa. It markets its Sunoco gasoline through more than 4,700 retail outlets (including Ultra Service Centers and APlus convenience stores) in 23 states. Sunoco also produces lubricants, mines coal for coke processing, and operates a chemicals business. The company's Sunoco Chemicals unit produces phenol and plasticizers.

To raise cash to pay down debt, in 2010 Sunoco Chemicals sold its polypropylene business to Brazilian-based Braskem S.A. in a $350 million stock transaction. That year Sunoco also announced plans to spin off its coal unit, Sunoco Coke, in order to raise cash and to focus on its core oil and petroleum products transportation operations.

Some of Sunoco's pipeline, terminal, and storage assets are held through publicly traded Sunoco Logistics Partners, which is 32% controlled by Sunoco unit Sunoco Partners.

In the last five years Sunoco has implemented its Retail Portfolio Management (RPM) program, which was created to decrease investment in outlets leased or owned by the company while retaining fuel sales to those locations through long-term contracts. In 2009, as part of rationalizing and streamlining its refining business in the light of a weakened global economy and the oversupply of petroleum products, the company sold its 85,000-barrels-per-day Tulsa, Oklahoma, refinery to regional player Holly Corporation, and shut down its Westville, New Jersey, refinery.

Sunoco also sold its retail heating oil and propane business to Superior Plus for $86 million. These moves, along with slumping demand and lower oil prices, saw the company's revenues drop sharply in 2009.

Looking to lock in an affordable ethanol supply, that year it acquired the largest ethanol plant in the Northeast, which is targeted to provide a quarter of the company's ethanol production.

Veteran oil industry executive Lynn Laverty Elsenhans was elected CEO in 2008.

HISTORY

Joseph Newton Pew began his energy career in 1876 when he helped form a Pennsylvania gas pipeline partnership that became Pittsburgh's first natural gas system. When oil discoveries in northwestern Ohio sparked an 1886 boom, Pew began buying oil leases and pipelines and organized the assets into The Sun Oil Company of Ohio in 1890. Four years later the company bought Diamond Oil and its refinery in Toledo, Ohio. The firm traces its trademark diamond pierced by an arrow to the short-lived Diamond subsidiary.

After the 1901 Spindletop gusher, Pew dispatched nephew Edgar Pew to Texas, where he bought the oil-rich properties of a bankrupt firm. Back East, the elder Pew bought Delaware River acreage in Pennsylvania for a shipping terminal and refinery to process Texas crude into Red Stock. The lubricating oil carved Sun Oil a place in the Standard Oil-dominated petroleum industry.

Joseph Pew died in 1912 and was succeeded by sons Howard and Joseph Newton Jr. The company moved into shipbuilding (1916) and gasoline stations (1920). Sun Oil's gasoline was dyed blue (legend says it matched a Chinese tile chip Joseph Jr. and his wife had received on their honeymoon) and sold as Blue Sunoco. The firm went public as Sun Oil in 1925.

When Howard retired in 1947, Joseph Jr. became chairman, and Robert Dunlop became the first non-Pew president of Sun Oil. The company had its first major foreign oil strike in Venezuela in 1957.

In 1967 Dunlop's chance meeting with a Sunray DX Oil executive led to Sun Oil's acquisition of that company the next year. The Sunray DX addition diluted the Pew family's stake in the company. Sun Oil's Venezuelan holdings were nationalized in 1975. The next year the company dropped "Oil" from its name.

In the early 1980s the company sold its shipbuilding arm (1982) and began building its oil holdings, gaining interests in the North Sea and offshore China. In the US Sun purchased Seagram's Texas Pacific Oil for $2.3 billion (1980) and acquired Exeter Oil, Victory Oil, and the interests of Petro-Lewis (1984).

Sun began to shed exploration and production assets in 1988 to focus on refining and marketing. That year it spun off its domestic oil and gas properties into what became Oryx Energy (acquired by Kerr-McGee in 1999). Sun also acquired Atlantic Petroleum and gained more than 1,000 service stations in the process.

In 1993 Sun sold Cordero Mining to Kennecott and cut its stake in Canadian petroleum company Suncor from 68% to 55%. The next year Sun bought a refinery in Philadelphia from Chevron and a stake in a pipeline connecting that refinery to New York Harbor.

In 1995 Sun sold its 55% interest in Suncor, and the following year sold its international oil and gas production business. It also bought the Kendall/Amalie motor oils and lubricants unit of Witco Corporation. In 1998 the company changed its name to Sunoco. Sunoco acquired a Philadelphia phenol plant from AlliedSignal that year.

The company experienced a strike (settled after five months) at its Yabucoa, Puerto Rico, lubricants refinery in 1999. (In 2001 it decided to close the plant.) CEO Robert Campbell retired in 2000 and was replaced by COO John Drosdick.

In 2001 Sunoco bought Mitsubishi subsidiary Aristech Chemical, which operated five chemical plants in the US. It also beefed up its retail operations that year, acquiring more than 230 outlets in 12 eastern states from Coastal Corp.

That year the company formed Sunoco Logistics Partners to acquire, own, and operate a major portion of its midstream and downstream assets.

The company acquired 193 gas stations in the southeastern US in 2003 from Marathon Ashland Petroleum's (now Marathon Petroleum) Speedway SuperAmerica unit. That year Sunoco also bought the Eagle Point refinery (adjacent to its own Philadelphia refining complex) from El Paso Corp. for $111 million and related assets for $135 million.

In 2004 the company acquired 340 gas stations in Delaware; Maryland; Washington, DC; and Virginia from ConocoPhillips.

EXECUTIVES

Chairman, President, and CEO; Chairman, Sunoco Partners: Lynn L. Elsenhans, age 53, $1,875,911 total compensation
SVP and CFO: Brian P. MacDonald, age 44, $4,631,890 total compensation
SVP Refining: Anne-Marie Ainsworth, age 53, $2,423,699 total compensation
SVP; President, SunCoke Energy: Michael J. (Mike) Thomson, age 51, $1,981,898 total compensation
SVP Engineering and Technology: Vincent J. (Vince) Kelley, age 50, $1,662,890 total compensation
SVP Marketing: Robert W. Owens, age 56, $1,869,529 total compensation
SVP and General Counsel: Stacy L. Fox, age 56
SVP Strategy and Portfolio: Bruce D. Rubin, age 54
SVP and Chief Human Resources Officer: Dennis Zeleny, age 54, $1,506,700 total compensation
VP and Treasurer: Charmian Uy
Chief Governance Officer, Assistant General Counsel, and Corporate Secretary: Ann C. Mulé
General Auditor: Marie A. Natoli
Management Attorney: Wanda E. Flowers
Comptroller: Joseph P. Krott, age 46
Auditors: Ernst & Young LLP

LOCATIONS

HQ: Sunoco, Inc.
  1735 Market St., Ste. LL, Philadelphia, PA 19103
Phone: 215-977-3000   **Fax:** 215-977-3409
Web: www.sunocoinc.com

PRODUCTS/OPERATIONS

2009 Sales

	$ mil.	% of total
Refining & supply	12,305	39
Retail marketing	11,458	36
Logistics	4,696	15
Chemicals	1,616	5
Coke	1,616	5
Other income	(379)	—
Total	**31,312**	**100**

COMPETITORS

BP	Koch Industries, Inc.
CITGO Refining	Marathon Oil
ConocoPhillips	Motiva Enterprises
Eni	Shell Oil Products
Exxon Mobil	United Refining
Hess Corporation	U.S. Oil
HOVENSA	Valero Energy
Imperial Oil	

HISTORICAL FINANCIALS

Company Type: Public

Income Statement

FYE: December 31

	REVENUE ($ mil.)	NET INCOME ($ mil.)	NET PROFIT MARGIN	EMPLOYEES
12/09	31,312	(200)	—	11,200
12/08	54,146	776	1.4%	13,700
12/07	44,728	891	2.0%	14,200
12/06	38,715	979	2.5%	14,000
12/05	33,764	974	2.9%	13,800
Annual Growth	(1.9%)	—	—	(5.1%)

2009 Year-End Financials

Debt ratio: 80.6%	No. of shares (mil.): 121
Return on equity: —	Dividends
Cash ($ mil.): 377	Yield: 4.6%
Current ratio: 0.85	Payout: —
Long-term debt ($ mil.): 2,061	Market value ($ mil.): 3,147

Stock History

NYSE: SUN

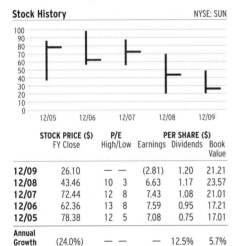

	STOCK PRICE ($) FY Close	P/E High/Low		PER SHARE ($) Earnings	Dividends	Book Value
12/09	26.10	—	—	(2.81)	1.20	21.21
12/08	43.46	10	3	6.63	1.17	23.57
12/07	72.44	12	8	7.43	1.08	21.01
12/06	62.36	13	8	7.59	0.95	17.21
12/05	78.38	12	5	7.08	0.75	17.01
Annual Growth	(24.0%)	—	—	—	12.5%	5.7%

SunTrust Banks

Coca-Cola, fast cars, and SunTrust Banks — this Sun Belt financial holding company is southern to its core. Its SunTrust Bank subsidiary operates about 1,700 bank branches in about a dozen southeastern states, including the Carolinas, Florida, Georgia, Maryland, Tennessee, Virginia, and the District of Columbia. SunTrust Bank offers standard retail and commercial banking services as well as trust services, asset management, insurance, lease financing, and securities brokerage. The company participated in the underwriting of fellow Atlanta icon Coca-Cola's IPO and was one of its largest shareholders for many years.

SunTrust was impacted by the economic crisis of 2008 and 2009, as credit markets froze and unemployment levels increased. The bank suffered losses related to bad loans, both on the consumer and commercial levels, and a softening of demand for loans. Like many of its peers, SunTrust took part in the Federal Reserve's bailout in 2008, selling the government about $4.9 billion in preferred shares.

To raise money and streamline operations, SunTrust has been spinning off noncore operations. It is selling the assets of nine funds managed by subsidiary RidgeWorth Capital Management (totaling some $17 billion in managed assets) to Federated Investors.

SunTrust bought GB&T Bancshares in 2008, adding about 20 branches in north and central Georgia. The following year it acquired three small wealth and investment management businesses. To augment capital, the company sold its interests in Lighthouse Investment Partners, an investment brokerage; First Mercantile Trust Company, a retirement-plan services firm; and TransPlatinum, a fuel-card services firm.

Legend has it that the only written copy of the Coke formula lies in a SunTrust vault. The company began slowly selling off its shares in 2007. It contributed some 3.6 billion of Coca-Cola's common shares to its SunTrust Foundation and sold another 8.1 million shares. SunTrust now holds an agreement to sell all or part of the shares to another financial institution. In the meantime, though, the shares are a solid source of dividends for the company.

SunTrust helped fund the construction of the home of the Daytona 500, Daytona International Speedway in Florida.

HISTORY

SunTrust was born from the union of old-money Georgia and new-money Florida. Founded in 1891, the Trust Company of Georgia (originally Commercial Traveler's Savings Bank) served Atlanta's oldest and richest institutions. It helped underwrite Coca-Cola's IPO in 1919; the bank's ownership stake in Coke stemmed from its early involvement with the beverage maker.

Beginning in 1933, Trust acquired controlling interests in five other Georgia banks. As regulation of multibank ownership relaxed in the 1970s, Trust acquired the remaining interests in its original banks and bought 25 more. At the height of the Sun Belt boom in 1984, Trust was the most profitable bank in the nation. The next year it united with Sun Banks.

Sun Banks was formed in 1934 as the First National Bank at Orlando. It grew into a holding company in 1967, and in the early 1970s helped assemble the land for Walt Disney World. The Sun name was adopted in 1973.

Under president and CEO Joel Wells, Sun Banks began an acquisition-fueled expansion within Florida. Between 1976 and 1984, Sun Banks' approximate asset growth was an astronomical 500%, and branch count grew fivefold (51 to 274).

After a lingering courtship, Sun and Trust formed a super holding company over the two organizations. When the marriage was consummated in 1985, Sun brought a dowry of $9.4 billion in assets, and Trust contributed $6.2 billion. Trust's chairman, Bob Strickland, became chairman and CEO for the new Atlanta-based SunTrust, and Wells became president.

In 1986 SunTrust bought Nashville, Tennessee-based Third National Bank, the #2 banking company in the Volunteer State. But problems with Tennessee real estate loans plagued SunTrust. In 1990 it increased the amount of loans it wrote off; the bank's ratings suffered because of nonperforming loans on properties in overbuilt Florida. While nonperforming assets decreased in Tennessee in 1991, they climbed in Florida and Georgia.

Strickland stepped down as chairman and CEO in 1990. Wells died in 1991, and James Williams, a conservative banker who instilled strict fiscal management in the Trust banks, became chairman and CEO. Under his direction the company reduced its nonperforming assets and began diversifying its business lines.

In 1993 the bank adopted accounting rules that caused it to revalue its Coca-Cola stock from its historic value of $110,000 to almost $1.1 billion. SunTrust continued developing its non-banking financial services: It expanded its investment services outside its traditional southern US market and bought Equitable Securities (now SunTrust Equitable Securities) in 1998. That year president Phillip Humann succeeded Williams as chairman and CEO. SunTrust also nearly doubled its branch count when it bought Crestar Financial, a banking powerhouse in the mid-Atlantic and Southeast.

In 1999 the company created a new trust business to serve high-net-worth clients, and it consolidated its 27 banking charters in six states into one based in Georgia the following year. In 2001 SunTrust bought the institutional business of investment bank Robinson-Humphrey, a unit of Citigroup's Salomon Smith Barney.

SunTrust bought National Commerce Financial in 2004 for some $7 billion. The deal helped the bank expand in existing territories, as well as provide entry into the growing North Carolina market, where SunTrust had been conspicuously absent. The company divested its 49% stake in First Market Bank (Ukrop's Super Markets owns the rest), which it acquired in the National Commerce deal. SunTrust unloaded the unit in part because it has branches in Kroger, Publix, Safeway, and Wal-Mart stores.

The company placed on administrative leave or dismissed several financial officers after it had to restate its earnings for the first two quarters of 2004 due to miscalculations of its loan loss reserves. (The SEC concluded an investigation into the matter in 2006 without recommending penalties.) Former president and COO Jim Wells became CEO in 2007; Humann remained as chairman but stepped down the following year.

SunTrust bought GB&T Bancshares in 2008, adding about 20 branches in Georgia.

EXECUTIVES

Chairman and CEO: James M. (Jim) Wells III, age 63, $7,672,822 total compensation
President: William H. (Bill) Rogers Jr., age 52, $4,283,062 total compensation
Corporate EVP and CFO: Mark A. Chancy, age 45, $3,354,446 total compensation
Corporate EVP and Chief Administrative Officer: David F. Dierker, age 52, $2,080,565 total compensation
Corporate EVP and CIO: Timothy E. Sullivan, age 59, $1,698,634 total compensation
Corporate EVP and Chief Risk Officer: Thomas E. (Tom) Freeman, age 58, $2,178,382 total compensation
Corporate EVP, Commercial Line of Business: Gay O. Abbott
Corporate EVP, General Counsel, and Corporate Secretary: Raymond D. Fortin, age 57
Corporate EVP, Corporate Sales Administration: Dennis M. Patterson
Corporate EVP and Director Human Resources: Frances L. (Mimi) Breeden, age 59
Corporate EVP: E. Jenner Wood III, age 58

Corporate EVP: Charles T. (C. T.) Hill, age 59
Chief Marketing Officer: Rilla Delorier, age 43
EVP and Head Private Wealth Management:
 Willem Hattink
EVP and Head Business Banking: Bill Holt
SVP, Controller, and Chief Accounting Officer:
 Thomas E. Panther, age 38
President and CEO, SunTrust Mortgage:
 Sterling Edmunds Jr.
Chairman, President, and CEO, SunTrust Robinson
 Humphrey: Hugh S. (Beau) Cummins III
Chairman, SunTrust Investment Services:
 John T. Rhett III
Director Investor Relations: Steven P. Shriner
Auditors: Ernst & Young LLP

LOCATIONS

HQ: SunTrust Banks Inc.
 303 Peachtree St. NE, Atlanta, GA 30308
Phone: 404-588-7711   Fax: 404-332-3875
Web: www.suntrust.com

PRODUCTS/OPERATIONS

2009 Sales

	$ mil.	% of total
Interest		
Loans, including fees	5,530.2	53
Securities available for sale,		
including dividends	829.7	8
Loans held for sale	232.8	2
Trading accounts	114.7	1
Other	2.4	—
Noninterest		
Service charges on deposit accounts	848.4	8
Trust & investment management	486.5	5
Mortgage production-related income	376.1	4
Mortgage servicing-related income	329.9	3
Card fees	323.8	3
Investment banking	272.0	3
Retail investment services	217.8	2
Gain from ownership in Visa	112.1	1
Net securities gains	98.0	1
Other charges & fees	522.7	5
Other	163.6	1
Adjustments	(40.7)	—
Total	**10,420.0**	**100**

2009 Assets

	$ mil.	% of total
Cash & equivalents	6,997	4
Trading assets	4,980	3
Securities available for sale	28,477	16
Loans held for sale	4,670	3
Net loans	110,555	63
Other	18,486	11
Total	**174,165**	**100**

COMPETITORS

BancorpSouth	First Horizon
Bank of America	JPMorgan Chase
BankAtlantic	RBC Bank
BB&T	Regions Financial
Citigroup	Synovus Financial
Compass Bancshares	Wells Fargo
First Citizens BancShares	

HISTORICAL FINANCIALS

Company Type: Public

Income Statement

FYE: December 31

	ASSETS ($ mil.)	NET INCOME ($ mil.)	INCOME AS % OF ASSETS	EMPLOYEES
12/09	174,165	(1,564)	—	28,001
12/08	189,138	796	0.4%	29,333
12/07	179,574	1,634	0.9%	32,323
12/06	182,162	2,118	1.2%	33,599
12/05	179,713	1,987	1.1%	33,406
Annual Growth	**(0.8%)**	**—**	**—**	**(4.3%)**

2009 Year-End Financials

Equity as % of assets: 10.1%	Dividends
Return on assets: —	Yield: 1.1%
Return on equity: —	Payout: —
Long-term debt ($ mil.): 17,490	Market value ($ mil.): 10,143
No. of shares (mil.): 500	Sales ($ mil.): 10,420

Stock History

NYSE: STI

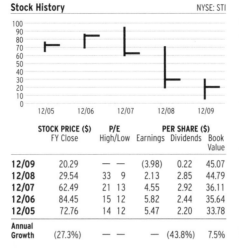

	STOCK PRICE ($) FY Close	P/E High/Low		PER SHARE ($) Earnings	Dividends	Book Value
12/09	20.29	—	—	(3.98)	0.22	45.07
12/08	29.54	33	9	2.13	2.85	44.79
12/07	62.49	21	13	4.55	2.92	36.11
12/06	84.45	15	12	5.82	2.44	35.64
12/05	72.76	14	12	5.47	2.20	33.78
Annual Growth	**(27.3%)**	**—**	**—**	**—**	**(43.8%)**	**7.5%**

SUPERVALU INC.

SUPERVALU is feeling pretty super following the acquisition of more than 1,100 supermarkets from fallen grocery giant Albertsons. Its purchase of the Albertsons' stores catapulted the chain to second place in the traditional grocery retail market (behind Kroger) with about 4,290 stores in some 40 US states. The deal added half a dozen new banners, including Albertsons, Acme Markets, and Shaw's, to SUPERVALU's store roster (which includes Shoppers Food & Pharmacy, Cub Foods, Shop 'n Save). SUPERVALU also bought Albertsons' in-store pharmacy operations. The company is also one of the nation's largest food wholesalers, supplying some 2,000 grocery stores nationwide with brandname and private-label goods.

SUPERVALU's blueprint for success in the retail grocery market — known for its razor-thin profit margins — is to leverage its increased size and supply chain operation to realize efficiencies and economies of scale. Leading the charge is SUPERVALU's new president and CEO Craig Herkert, who joined the company in 2009 from Wal-Mart, where he served as president and CEO of The Americas.

However, falling sales suggest that the company may be having trouble dealing with the twin challenges of digesting its big Albertsons purchase and responding to the weak US economy. Indeed, net sales fell more than 8% in 2009. The grocery chain sold or closed 112 locations last year (including 36 Albertsons stores in Utah), and in 2010 sold six of its Bigg's stores (acquired in 1994) in the Cincinnati area and closed the rest. Also, it sold all 18 of its Shaw's stores in Connecticut to rival Stop & Shop. The firm has announced it will reduce the size of its board of directors, while bringing in two new outside directors to provide a fresh perspective.

SUPERVALU has come under increasing pressure from supercenters and warehouse clubs, such as Wal-Mart and Costco, which have stolen sales from conventional grocery retailers. To better compete with big discounters, it's expanding its extreme-value Save-A-Lot format, which already holds the #1 spot (based on revenues) in the extreme-value grocery market. The 1,180 Save-A-Lot limited assortment stores (about 320 are company owned) sell mostly private-label goods. SUPERVALU has big plans for Save-A-Lot, including more than doubling the number of outlets in a nationwide expansion.

SUPERVALU's wholesale customers include conventional and upscale supermarkets, combination food and drugstores, supercenters, convenience stores, limited assortment stores, and e-tailers. SUPERVALU offers its retailers private labels in every price range and in virtually every store category, from the value-priced Shoppers Value brand to the premium Preferred Selection line. It added a private label organic food line, called Wild Harvest, in 2008. SUPERVALU also offers retailers support services, such as store design and construction.

The company's Total Logistics subsidiary offers retailers and manufacturers logistics services, including warehouse and transportation management, and supply chain integration and technology services through its Advantage Logistics operation. In March 2010, SUPERVALU sold off its Payson Store Fixtures division, which makes fixtures, millwork, and decor items, to DGS Retail, based in Boston.

HISTORY

SUPERVALU's predecessor was formed in Minneapolis in the 1870s — and again in 1926. In 1871 wholesalers Hugh Harrison, George Newell, and W. D. Washburn joined forces to create Newell and Harrison. Newell bought out his partners in 1874 and renamed the firm George R. Newell Co. Five years later Harrison formed his own operation, H. G. Harrison Co. In 1926 the companies merged, creating Winston & Newell Co., the largest grocery distributor to independent grocers in the Midwest.

The company was part of the Independent Grocers Alliance from 1928-1942 before adopting the name Super Valu Stores in 1954. It expanded by acquiring chains such as Piggly-Wiggly Midland (1958, Wisconsin) and a number of wholesale operations across the US.

Super Valu entered nonfood retailing in 1971 by acquiring ShopKo, a discount department store chain. Two years later it founded clothing chain County Seat (sold 1983). Super Valu added a new format to its food operations by purchasing Cub Stores (warehouse-style groceries) in 1980; it later combined its Cub Stores and ShopKo formats. More acquisitions followed, including Atlanta's Food Giant chain. Super Valu named Michael Wright CEO in 1981 and chairman in 1982.

Super Valu acquired Scott's, an Indiana food store chain, in 1991 and sold a 54% interest in ShopKo to the public. The company changed its name to SUPERVALU in 1992 and bought food wholesaler Wetterau, making it the #1 independent food distributor in the US and giving it the Save-A-Lot franchise (launched in 1978).

Experiencing sluggish distribution growth, SUPERVALU continued to expand its retail holdings. Acquisitions in 1994 included Sweet Life Foods (280 stores) and 30 Texas T Stores. In 1996 it acquired Fleming's Sav-U-Foods, converting the 21 stores to Save-A-Lots and establishing a presence in California. SUPERVALU sold its remaining 46% stake in ShopKo the next year.

SUPERVALU later announced plans to cut 7% of its workforce and close some of its distribution centers and stores, including its Laneco stores in Pennsylvania and New Jersey, and its central Indiana Cub stores. Wright retired as CEO in mid-2001 and remained as chairman; president and CFO Jeff Noddle became CEO.

Later in the month, Wright retired as chairman and was succeeded by Noddle. In June the company announced it would take a charge of up to $21 million because of accounting irregularities in its pharmacy division.

SUPERVALU expanded its agreement in 2003 with Target Corporation to supply all Super Target stores. In 2004 it sold off its minority interest in the regional grocery chain WinCo Foods.

In February 2005 SUPERVALU acquired Total Logistics, a provider of third-party logistics services and maker of refrigeration systems.

The company completed its acquisition of 1,124 stores from Albertsons in June 2006. Looking to take back sales lost to natural and organic grocery chains, SUPERVALU launched its own natural foods division, called Sunflower Market, in 2006; but in early 2008 the company announced it would close its five Sunflower Markets as they did not deliver expected results.

In 2007 SUPERVALU sold its 18 Scott's Food & Pharmacy stores in Indiana to rival Kroger.

In 2009 the company named Craig Herkert, a former Wal-Mart executive, as its new president and CEO, succeeding Jeff Noddle. As part of the executive shift, president and COO Mike Jackson retired in August 2009 after more than 30 years with the company. Throughout the course of the year, SUPERVALU closed or sold more than 100 stores nationwide, including about 40 Albertsons stores in Utah to grocery wholesaler Associated Food Stores. The closings were part of an effort by the company to scale back spending.

EXECUTIVES

Chairman: Wayne C. Sales, age 60
President, CEO, and Director: Craig R. Herkert, age 50, $10,790,012 total compensation
EVP; President and COO, Supply Chain Services: Janel S. Haugarth, age 54, $2,809,695 total compensation
EVP; President, Retail Operations: Peter J. (Peter) Van Helden, age 49
EVP: David L. (Dave) Boehnen, age 63, $1,557,753 total compensation
EVP and CIO: Wayne Shurts, age 50
EVP and Chief Marketing Officer: Julie Dexter Berg, age 53
EVP Merchandising: Steven J. (Steve) Jungmann, age 47
EVP Market and Real Estate Development: J. Andrew (Andy) Herring, age 51
EVP, Human Resources and Communications: David E. (Dave) Pylipow, age 52, $1,677,856 total compensation
SVP Finance and Interim CFO: Sherry M. Smith, age 48
SVP Specialty Retail: Brian Huff, age 51
Group VP and Controller: Adrian J. Downes, age 46
Group VP, Fresh Food Merchandising: Jim Smits
VP and Controller: Daniel J. Zvonek, age 45
VP Strategic Planning: Chuck Golias
VP Investor Relations: David M. Oliver
President, Shaw's Supermarkets: Mike Witynski, age 47
President, W. Newell: Greg McNiff, age 46
President, Cub Foods: Keith R. Wyche, age 49
President, Acme Markets: Dan Sanders
Auditors: KPMG LLP

LOCATIONS

HQ: SUPERVALU INC.
11840 Valley View Rd., Eden Prairie, MN 55344
Phone: 952-828-4000   **Fax:** 952-828-8998
Web: www.supervalu.com

2010 Stores

	No.
East	1,594
West	463
Midwest	277
Other regions	15
Total	**2,349**

PRODUCTS/OPERATIONS

2010 Sales

	% of total
Retail food	
Nonperishable grocery	43
Perishable grocery	21
Pharmacy	6
General merchandise &health & beauty care	5
Fuel	2
Other	1
Supply chain services	
Product sales	22
Total	**100**

2010 Sales

	$ mil.	% of total
Retail food	31,637	78
Supply chain service	8,960	22
Total	**40,597**	**100**

2010 Stores

	No.
Company-owned	1,494
Licensed	855
Total	**2,349**

Selected Retail Food Stores and Formats

Extreme Value Stores
    Save-A-Lot (licensed)

Price Superstore
    Cub Foods
    Shop 'n Save
    Shoppers Food & Pharmacy

Supermarkets
    Acme Markets
    Albertsons
    Bristol Farms
    Farm Fresh
    Hornbacher's
    Jewel-Osco
    Lucky
    Shaw's Supermarkets
    Star Markets

Selected Services

Accounting
Category management
Consumer and market research
Financial assistance
Insurance
Merchandising assistance
Personnel training
Private-label program
Retail operations counseling
Site selection and purchasing or leasing assistance
Store design and construction
Store equipment
Store management assistance
Store planning
Strategic and business planning

COMPETITORS

A&P	Krasdale Foods
Ahold USA	Kroger
ALDI	Marsh Supermarkets
Alex Lee	McLane
Arden Group	Meijer
Associated Wholesale Grocers	Nash-Finch
	Piggly Wiggly Midwest
Associated Wholesalers	Ralphs Grocery
Big Y Foods	Rite Aid
Bozzuto's	Roundy's Supermarkets
C&S Wholesale	Safeway
Costco Wholesale	Schnuck Markets
CVS Caremark	Sherwood Food
Delhaize America	Spartan Stores
Di Giorgio	Stop & Shop
Dierbergs Markets	Vons
Dollar General	Wakefern Food
Dollar Tree	Walgreen
Family Dollar Stores	Wal-Mart
Giant Eagle	Whole Foods
Hannaford Bros.	Winn-Dixie
Jetro Cash & Carry	

HISTORICAL FINANCIALS
Company Type: Public

Income Statement
FYE: Last Saturday in February

	REVENUE ($ mil.)	NET INCOME ($ mil.)	NET PROFIT MARGIN	EMPLOYEES
2/10	40,597	393	1.0%	160,000
2/09	44,564	(2,855)	—	178,000
2/08	44,048	593	1.3%	192,000
2/07	37,406	452	1.2%	191,400
2/06	19,864	206	1.0%	52,400
Annual Growth	**19.6%**	**17.5%**	**—**	**32.2%**

2010 Year-End Financials

Debt ratio: 243.2%	No. of shares (mil.): 212
Return on equity: 14.4%	Dividends
Cash ($ mil.): 211	Yield: 4.0%
Current ratio: 0.89	Payout: 33.0%
Long-term debt ($ mil.): 7,022	Market value ($ mil.): 3,240

Stock History
NYSE: SVU

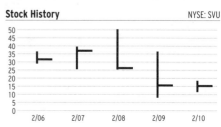

	STOCK PRICE ($) FY Close	P/E High/Low		PER SHARE ($) Earnings	Dividends	Book Value
2/10	15.27	10	7	1.85	0.61	13.61
2/09	15.61	—	—	(13.51)	0.69	12.17
2/08	26.25	18	9	2.76	0.68	28.06
2/07	36.96	17	11	2.32	0.66	25.01
2/06	31.60	25	20	1.46	0.64	12.35
Annual Growth	**(16.6%)**	**—**	**—**	**6.1%**	**(1.2%)**	**2.5%**

Symantec Corporation

Symantec never has a problem with insecurity. The company provides security, storage, and systems management software for consumers and businesses. Its applications handle such functions as virus protection, PC maintenance, data backup and recovery, intrusion detection, data loss prevention, spam control, content filtering, and remote server management. Symantec sells its products through a direct sales force, as well as through distributors, resellers, OEMs, and systems integrators. The company also provides consulting, managed services, and training. Customers in the Americas account for more than half of sales.

Symantec may be best known for its popular Norton family of consumer security software, but the company generates more of its revenues from enterprise infrastructure management, security and compliance applications, and services. Delving into the market for cloud computing, where users access applications over the Internet rather than installing software on their own computers, the company offers a variety of applications through Symantec Hosted Services. Also known as software-as-a-service (SaaS), the field is seen as a growth area by Symantec.

Symantec has pursued an aggressive acquisition strategy to grow its enterprise business. The company expanded its enterprise security and compliance line when it purchased longtime partner AppStream in 2008. AppStream developed application streaming technology that allows for remote program deployment and management. The purchase bolstered the company's SaaS offerings. The company also grew its professional services portfolio with the acquisition of MessageLabs for $695 million in cash in 2008. MessageLabs provided Symantec with a managed service for protecting e-mail and other electronic communications. Symantec also holds a 49% stake in a joint venture with Huawei Technologies that develops security and storage products for telecom service providers. In 2010 Symantec purchased Gideon Technologies, a provider of security software and services for public sector clients. Also that year it bought PGP Corporation for about $300 million and GuardianEdge Technologies for around $70 million, extending its data protection capabilities.

In a transaction that would substantially grow the company's online security portfolio, Symantec bought the Authentication Services business of VeriSign in 2010 for about $1.28 billion. The purchase strengthens Symantec's offerings in a number of areas, including identity security, mobile device security, and security for private and public computing clouds. The deal also includes a majority stake in VeriSign Japan.

Consumer products still account for about 30% of Symantec's revenues, and the company continues to develop technologies and make acquisitions that supplement that segment of its business. Symantec augmented its consumer product line with the purchases of PC Tools and SwapDrive in 2008. PC Tools provides privacy and security software for Windows-based PCs. SwapDrive developed file sharing and data backup services.

The company saw its top leadership change in 2009. Chairman John Thompson stepped down as CEO after a 10-year stint; Symantec COO Enrique Salem took over as chief executive.

HISTORY

Artificial intelligence expert Gary Hendrix founded Symantec in 1982. Gordon Eubanks, a former student of the late industry pioneer Gary Kildall and founder of C&E Software, was appointed CEO in 1983 and bought the company in 1984. Realizing that Symantec could not compete against Microsoft and Lotus, Eubanks began buying niche-market software firms. In 1990, a year after going public, Symantec merged with DOS utilities market leader Peter Norton Computing. It bought 13 companies between 1990 and 1994.

Symantec bought Delrina (maker of WinFax) in 1995. Symantec slowed its acquisition pace and concentrated on the growing Internet market. In 1996 it sold Delrina's electronic forms business to JetForm.

Symantec filed copyright-infringement charges against Network Associates (now McAfee) in 1997. The next year a suit was filed against Symantec on behalf of antivirus product users, alleging that it ignored its warranty by charging to fix a year-2000 software glitch.

The company went on another acquisition binge, buying the antivirus operations of both IBM and Intel in 1998 and acquiring rival Quarterdeck in 1999. When Eubanks left that year to head an enterprise software startup, IBM exec John Thompson stepped in and became the first African-American CEO of a major software firm.

In 2000 Symantec sold its Internet tools division to BEA Systems in a deal valued at about $75 million. It also acquired L-3 Communications' network security operations. Late that year it bought rival network security software maker AXENT Technologies in a $975 million deal.

The company divested its Web access management product line in 2001. Later that year the company acquired Foster-Melliar's enterprise security management division.

In 2002 the company continued its acquisitive ways, purchasing Recourse Technologies, Riptech, and SecurityFocus. The following year the company acquired Nexland, PowerQuest, and SafeWeb. The company purchased infrastructure management software provider ON Technology for about $100 million in 2004. Later that year Symantec also purchased antispam software provider Brightmail for $370 million.

Symantec announced plans to purchase VERITAS Software for about $11 billion in 2004. The deal was completed in the following year.

It purchased WholeSecurity, Inc. (a maker of security software used to thwart viruses, worms, and other malicious code) and Sygate Technologies (network access control solutions) in 2005. The following year it bought BindView Development Corporation (computer network management and security), IMlogic (enterprise instant messaging), and Relicore (data center change and configuration management). It also acquired UK-based Company-i, a data center services firm focused on the finance sector, as well as data protection software developer Revivio.

In 2007 Symantec acquired IT asset management software maker Altiris for approximately $830 million, and data loss prevention specialist Vontu for $350 million. The company also formed a joint venture with China-based Huawei Technologies in 2007. In 2008 Symantec sold its Application Performance Management (APM) division to Vector Capital.

Thompson stepped down as CEO in 2009; he remained chairman. COO Enrique Salem was promoted to chief executive.

EXECUTIVES

Chairman: John W. Thompson, age 60, $7,025,792 total compensation
President, CEO, and Director: Enrique T. Salem, age 44, $3,884,744 total compensation
EVP and CFO: James A. Beer, age 48, $3,436,994 total compensation
EVP and CTO: Mark F. Bregman, age 52
EVP Worldwide Sales: William T. (Bill) Robbins, age 41
EVP and Chief Human Resources Officer: Rebecca A. Ranninger, age 51
EVP, General Counsel, and Secretary: Scott C. Taylor, age 45
SVP and Chief Marketing Officer: Carine Clark
SVP Endpoint Security and Management: Brad Kingsbury, age 42
SVP Enterprise Services: Anil S. Chakravarthy
SVP, Americas Geography: Rich Spring
SVP Information Management Group: Deepak Mohan
SVP Enterprise Security Group: Francis deSouza
SVP Hosted Services: Rowan M. Trollope
Group President and CIO, Symantec Services Group: J. David Thompson, age 42, $2,697,234 total compensation
Group President, Consumer Business Unit: Janice D. Chaffin, age 55
President Symantec Software, Beijing and VP Greater China Region, Symantec: Andy Wu
Senior Director Product Management and Engineering: Aaron Aubrecht
Director Corporate Communications: Genevieve Haldeman
Investor Relations: Helyn Corcos
Auditors: KPMG LLP

LOCATIONS

HQ: Symantec Corporation
350 Ellis St., Mountain View, CA 94043
Phone: 650-527-8000
Web: www.symantec.com

2010 Sales

	$ mil.	% of total
Americas	3,241	54
Europe, Middle East & Africa	1,838	31
Asia/Pacific	906	15
Total	**5,985**	**100**

PRODUCTS/OPERATIONS

2010 Sales

	$ mil.	% of total
Content, subscriptions & maintenance	5,034	84
Licenses	951	16
Total	**5,985**	**100**

2010 Sales

	$ mil.	% of total
Storage & server management	2,287	38
Consumer products	1,871	31
Security & compliance	1,411	24
Services	416	7
Total	**5,985**	**100**

Selected Products

Storage and server management
  Data protection
  Endpoint security
  Storage and server management
Consumer products
  Backup
  Fraud detection service
  Identity protection authentication
  Internet security
  PC tune-up
Security and compliance
  Compliance and security management
  Messaging management
Services
  Consulting
  Maintenance and support
  Training

Avocent
CA Technologies
Check Point Software
Cisco Systems
CommVault
Courion
DataCore
EMC
F5 Networks
FalconStor
F-Secure
Google
Hewlett-Packard
IBM
Kaspersky Lab
McAfee
Microsoft
Novell
NTRU
Oracle
Quest Software
SecureWorks
Smith Micro
Sophos
Trend Micro
VeriSign
Zone Labs

HISTORICAL FINANCIALS

Company Type: Public

Income Statement

FYE: Friday closest to March 31

	REVENUE ($ mil.)	NET INCOME ($ mil.)	NET PROFIT MARGIN	EMPLOYEES
3/10	5,985	714	11.9%	17,400
3/09	6,150	(6,729)	—	17,400
3/08	5,874	464	7.9%	17,600
3/07	5,199	404	7.8%	17,100
3/06	4,143	157	3.8%	16,000
Annual Growth	9.6%	46.1%	—	2.1%

2010 Year-End Financials

Debt ratio: 41.1%
Return on equity: 16.8%
Cash ($ mil.): 3,029
Current ratio: 1.15
Long-term debt ($ mil.): 1,871

No. of shares (mil.): 789
Dividends
  Yield: —
  Payout: —
Market value ($ mil.): 13,362

Stock History

NASDAQ (GS): SYMC

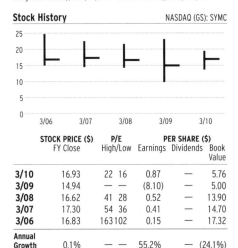

	STOCK PRICE ($) FY Close	P/E High/Low	PER SHARE ($) Earnings	Dividends	Book Value
3/10	16.93	22 16	0.87	—	5.76
3/09	14.94	— —	(8.10)	—	5.00
3/08	16.62	41 28	0.52	—	13.90
3/07	17.30	54 36	0.41	—	14.70
3/06	16.83	163 102	0.15	—	17.32
Annual Growth	0.1%	— —	55.2%	—	(24.1%)

Synopsys, Inc.

Let's cut to the chase — Synopsys is a leading provider of electronic design automation (EDA) software and services. Its products are used by designers of integrated circuits (ICs) to develop, simulate, and test the physical design of ICs before production, and then to test finished products. The company also provides semiconductor intellectual property (SIP) for the basic building blocks of circuit design. Customers come from a variety of markets, including the semiconductor, consumer electronics, and aerospace industries. Synopsys offers time-based software licenses, where customers make yearly payments for use and support, rather than pay traditional upfront fees followed by ongoing maintenance costs.

The company has used acquisitions to expand its product lines and SIP assets, including the purchases of Sigma-C Software, Virtio, and HPL Technologies, as well as buying Sandwork Design, ArchPro Design Automation, and the SIP assets of MOSAID Technologies.

In 2010 the company extended its virtual prototyping portfolio into automotive and consumer applications through the acquisition of VaST Systems Technology, a developer of models and tools for designing embedded electronics. Virtual prototypes enable pre-silicon software development and complement traditional hardware/software verification approaches. The designing of semiconductors and electronic subsystems for portable electronics and other products with small form factors is becoming key for many electronics manufacturers, which want to develop software while they're designing new products. Among VaST's competitors, Wind River Systems was acquired by Intel in 2009, while MontaVista Software was purchased by Cavium Networks that same year.

Also that year Synopsys acquired CoWare, a provider of software and services for electronic systems design. The purchase expands the company's portfolio of system-level design and verification packages for automotive, consumer, and wireless electronics. It expanded its portfolio of high-level synthesis tools through the purchase of Synfora. Looking to broaden its SIP portfolio, Synopsys agreed to acquire Virage Logic in 2010 for about $315 million in cash, adding embedded memories with test and repair, nonvolatile memories (NVMs), standard cell libraries, and programmable cores for control and multimedia subsystems.

HISTORY

Aart de Geus founded Optimal Solutions in 1986 with funding from General Electric, where he had been a manager in the company's Advanced Computer-Aided Engineering Group. The group built the prototype of a product that saved chip designers time by automating much of the design work.

In 1987 the company changed its name to Synopsys (an abbreviation of "synthesis and optimization systems") and moved to California. It went public in 1992, and two years later it introduced software that engineers used to design chips by function rather than structure.

As chips grew more complicated, Synopsys bolstered its product development efforts through acquisitions. In 1995 the company purchased hardware emulation developer Silicon Architects. Synopsys bought transistor-level tool specialist

EPIC Design Technology in 1997 to improve its submicron-level design capabilities. It acquired Viewlogic Systems to increase its design automation prowess. (Synopsys later sold Viewlogic's printed circuit board design software segment.)

Synopsys' acquisitions continued in 1998 with the purchase of Radiant Design Tools, a supplier of technology for designing simulation performance, and Everest Design Automation, which specialized in system-on-a-chip devices. In 1999 Synopsys bought Stanza Systems, which developed physical layout products; Smartech, a developer of wireless market design products; and several others. It also introduced several products, including one that combines design and physical layout of system-on-a-chip devices in one package.

In 2001 the company sold its Silicon Library Business. Synopsys' attempt to acquire IKOS Systems in 2002 was stymied by Mentor Graphics. However, Synopsys did acquire troubled software developer Avant! for nearly $730 million, and purchased inSilicon for $64 million.

In 2003 Synopsys acquired Numerical Technologies, whose software helps prepare chip designs for manufacturing, for about $250 million. Looking to beef up its design capabilities for analog and mixed-signal chips, Synopsys in 2004 acquired the assets of Analog Design Automation (ADA), a company founded in 1999. Also in 2004 Synopsys bought Accelerant Networks, Inc., of Beaverton, Oregon, a fabless semiconductor company. The purchase price was $22.5 million in cash. Later that year, Synopsys acquired Integrated Systems Engineering AG (ISE) of Zurich, Switzerland, for about $95 million in cash, plus another $20 million in future earnout payments. At the same time, Synopsys acquired the assets of Monterey Design Systems and hired most of the engineers working in Armenia for Monterey. Synopsys did not acquire Monterey's software products. Synopsys added even more Armenian engineers with its 2004 asset acquisition of LEDA Design, which had more than 80 people working in Yerevan, Armenia.

Synopsys agreed to acquire Monolithic System Technology (MoSys) for about $432 million in cash, but called off the deal in 2004. MoSys sued; the companies settled the case after the trial began a few months later. Synopsys also agreed in 2004 to acquire rival Nassda for around $192 million in cash. The acquisition was completed in 2005.

In 2008 the company purchased Synplicity, a provider of field programmable gate array (FPGA), IC design, and verification software. Later that year the company also bought the CHIPit business unit of ProDesign. The move boosted Synopsys' aim to provide end-to-end products for the design and verification markets, enhancing its system validation and embedded software development capabilities.

EXECUTIVES

Chairman and CEO: Aart J. de Geus, age 55, $4,536,831 total compensation
President, COO, and Director: Chi-Foon Chan, age 60, $2,872,419 total compensation
CFO: Brian M. Beattie, age 57, $2,253,267 total compensation
SVP Worldwide Sales: Joseph W. (Joe) Logan, age 50, $1,695,723 total compensation
SVP; General Manager, Implementation: Antun Domic, age 58, $1,605,737 total compensation
SVP; General Manager, Silicon Engineering Group: Howard Ko, age 54
SVP; General Manager, Analog/Mixed Signal Group: Sheng-Chun (Paul) Lo

SVP; General Manager, Verification Group:
Manoj Gandhi, age 49
SVP Marketing and Strategic Development:
John Chilton, age 52
SVP Global Technical Services: Deirdre Hanford, age 47
SVP Human Resources and Facilities:
Janet S. (Jan) Collinson, age 49
VP, General Counsel, and Secretary: Brian E. Cabrera, age 44, $1,037,896 total compensation
VP; President and Managing Director, Synopsys (India): Pradip K. Dutta
VP IT and CIO: Debra Martucci
VP Marketing, Solutions Group: John Koeter
VP Product Marketing, Design and Manufacturing Products: Bijan Kiani
VP, Corporate Controller, and Principal Accounting Officer: Esfandiar (Essie) Naddaf, age 56
VP Investor Relations: Lisa L. Ewbank
VP Global Real Estate and Facilities:
Barbara Donaldson
Manager Worldwide Public Relations: Sheryl M. Gulizia
Auditors: KPMG LLP

LOCATIONS

HQ: Synopsys, Inc.
700 E. Middlefield Rd., Mountain View, CA 94043
Phone: 650-584-5000   **Fax:** 650-584-4249
Web: www.synopsys.com

2009 Sales

	$ mil.	% of total
US	665	49
Japan	264	19
Europe	197	15
Other regions	234	17
Total	**1,360**	**100**

PRODUCTS/OPERATIONS

2009 Sales

	% of total
Core EDA	74
Manufacturing solutions	12
Intellectual property & system-level solutions	10
Professional services & other	4
Total	**100**

2009 Sales

	% of total
Time-based licenses	84
Upfront licenses	5
Maintenance	6
Professional services & other	5
Total	**100**

Selected Products

Astro (place and route)
Chip Architect (planning and analysis of various design phases)
coreBuilder (reusable design data)
CoCentric System Studio (system-level design and verification)
Design Compiler (logic synthesis)
Design Vision (design management and analysis)
DesignWare (implementation and verification design library)
Hercules (physical verification)
Module Compiler (synthesis of data paths)
NanoSim (memory and mixed-signal verification)
PathMill (static timing analysis)
Physical Compiler (physical synthesis)
PowerMill (circuit simulation and design)
Scirocco (VHDL-based simulation)
VCS (Verilog language-based simulation)

Selected Services

Design consulting services
Systems development

COMPETITORS

Agilent EEsof	MoSys
Altium	PDF Solutions
Ansoft	Rambus
Cadence Design	Sagantec
CEVA	Silvaco
Intrinsix	SynTest
Magma Design	Virage Logic
Mentor Graphics	

HISTORICAL FINANCIALS

Company Type: Public

Income Statement

FYE: Saturday nearest to October 31

	REVENUE ($ mil.)	NET INCOME ($ mil.)	NET PROFIT MARGIN	EMPLOYEES
10/09	1,360	168	12.3%	5,928
10/08	1,337	190	14.2%	952
10/07	1,213	131	10.8%	5,196
10/06	1,096	25	2.3%	5,130
10/05	992	(16)	—	4,756
Annual Growth	**8.2%**	**—**	**—**	**5.7%**

2009 Year-End Financials

Debt ratio: —
Return on equity: 9.9%
Cash ($ mil.): 702
Current ratio: 1.80
Long-term debt ($ mil.): —
No. of shares (mil.): 148
Dividends
    Yield: —
    Payout: —
Market value ($ mil.): 3,258

Stock History

NASDAQ (GS): SNPS

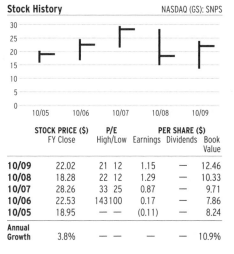

	STOCK PRICE ($) FY Close	P/E High/Low		PER SHARE ($) Earnings	Dividends	Book Value
10/09	22.02	21	12	1.15	—	12.46
10/08	18.28	22	12	1.29	—	10.33
10/07	28.26	33	25	0.87	—	9.71
10/06	22.53	143	100	0.17	—	7.86
10/05	18.95	—	—	(0.11)	—	8.24
Annual Growth	**3.8%**			**—**	**—**	**10.9%**

Synovus Financial

Synovus has a nose for community banking. The holding company owns about 30 banks offering deposit accounts and consumer and business loans in Alabama, Florida, Georgia, South Carolina, and Tennessee. Through more than 325 locations, the banks and other Synovus subsidiaries provide deposits, loans, credit cards, insurance, and asset management services. It has traditionally maintained separate charters and local boards of directors for its subsidiary banks. However, in 2010 Synovus consolidated all of its charters into one. The change was made in order to reduce complexity and improve efficiency.

The company has been making such changes in order to better position itself and emerge stronger from the economic downturn. Synovus

has been looking for ways to cut costs, raise capital, and improve efficiency as it has been plagued by the residential and commercial real estate bust that hit the southeastern US particularly hard.

Synovus has also consolidated by merging some of its banks in Georgia and Florida; two of its Florida banking subsidiaries (one *de novo* and the other formed in the merger of three subsidiaries' banking charters) have taken the Synovus Bank brand, a new strategy for the company.

Synovus also has been cutting costs and selling nonperforming assets. Between 2008 and 2009 it slashed about 10% of its workforce. Fred Green abruptly stepped down as president of Synovus in 2009. CEO Richard Anthony assumed his responsibilities until early 2010 when Kessel Stelling was named president and COO of the company.

The shift in leadership came amid allegations by shareholders that Synovus executives had misrepresented the company's credit exposure to Sea Island, an ailing Georgia luxury resort. At least three lawsuits were filed by shareholders against Synovus. In 2010 the company also announced that it was facing an informal inquiry by the Securities and Exchange Commission.

HISTORY

In 1885 W. C. Bradley founded his eponymous company (today a manufacturing and development concern). Three years later he invested in a new bank that would eventually bear the name of its Georgia hometown: Columbus Bank and Trust. (Bradley's investment in Atlanta-based Coca-Cola today accounts for the lion's share of his family's wealth.) When Bradley died, his son-in-law Abbott Turner joined the bank's board of directors, followed by Turner's son William.

In 1958 the bank hired James Blanchard as president. The next year Columbus Bank and Trust became one of the first banks to issue credit cards. The company's credit processing business grew, leading it to computerize the process in 1966 and train its own employees to operate the equipment. (It decided to go it alone after a failed joint-venture attempt with corporate cousin W.C. Bradley Co.)

In a little more than a decade, Blanchard led the bank to triple its assets. When he died in 1969, the search for a new leader took the bank's directors in a surprising direction: They offered the position to Blanchard's son Jimmy, a young attorney with no banking experience. The board pressed him to take the job, which he did in 1971 after a brief apprenticeship.

From the start, the younger Blanchard emphasized the company's financial services operations, such as credit card processing. Taking advantage of new laws opening up the banking and financial services industry in the early 1970s, the bank reorganized in 1972, incorporating CB&T Bancshares to serve as a holding company for Columbus Bank and Trust. In 1973 CB&T's financial services division finished a new software product called the Total System, which allowed electronic access to account information. CB&T used the groundbreaking software to start processing other banks' paperwork, including an ever-growing number of credit card accounts. In 1983 CB&T spun off financial services division Total System Services (TSYS), but retained a majority stake in the company.

Blanchard helped win passage of Georgia's multibank holding law, and further deregulation in the early 1980s allowed the company to operate across state lines. It bought four banks in

Florida and Georgia in 1983 and 1984, and snapped up six more (including an Alabama bank) in 1985. Meanwhile, TSYS benefited from the trend to outsource credit card processing.

In 1989 CB&T changed its name to Synovus, a combination of the words "synergy" and "novus," the latter word meaning (according to the company) "of superior quality and different from the others listed in the same category."

During the early 1990s Synovus swept up 20 banks in its market area after the bank bust. After 1993, acquisitions dropped off until 1998, when Synovus announced three acquisitions in two weeks. That year it also said it was planning to move further into Internet and investment banking, as well as auto and life insurance. In 1999 the company bought banks in Georgia and Florida; it also moved into debt collection with its purchase of Wallace & de Mayo, which was renamed Total System Services (TSYS). In 2007 Synovus spun off TSYS.

The company grew its retail investment operations with the acquisitions of Atlanta-area asset managers Creative Financial Group in 2001 and GLOBALT in 2002. Jimmy Blanchard, who had ultimately become Synovus Financial's chairman, retired as an executive in 2005, but remained on the board. President Richard Anthony was promoted to chairman and CEO that year. In 2010 Kessel Stelling was named president and COO of Synovus.

EXECUTIVES

Chairman and CEO: Richard E. Anthony, age 63, $1,196,487 total compensation
Vice Chairman, Chief People Officer, and Secretary: Elizabeth R. (Lee Lee) James, age 48, $561,739 total compensation
President, COO, and Director: Kessel D. Stelling Jr., age 53
EVP and CFO: Thomas J. Prescott, age 55, $538,069 total compensation
EVP and Chief Credit Officer: Mark G. Holladay, age 54, $395,419 total compensation
EVP, General Counsel, and Corporate Secretary: Samuel F. Hatcher, age 64, $335,875 total compensation
EVP; President, Financial Management Services: J. Barton Singleton, age 46
EVP and Chief Commercial Officer: R. Dallis (Roy) Copeland Jr., age 41
EVP Corporate Affairs: Calvin Smyre, age 62
EVP and Chief Retail Officer: Leila S. Carr, age 48
EVP and Chief Credit Officer: Kevin J. Howard, age 45
Chief Commercial Officer: Curtis J. Perry
Chief Accounting Officer: Liliana C. McDaniel, age 45
External Communications Manager: Greg Hudgison
President, GLOBALT Investments: William H. Roach
Director; Chairman and CEO, Total System Services: Philip W. (Phil) Tomlinson, age 63
Auditors: KPMG LLP

LOCATIONS

HQ: Synovus Financial Corp.
1111 Bay Ave., Ste. 500, Columbus, GA 31901
Phone: 706-649-2311 **Fax:** 706-641-6555
Web: www.synovus.com

PRODUCTS/OPERATIONS

2009 Sales

	$ mil.	% of total
Interest		
Loans, including fees	1,323.9	69
Investment securities available for sale	168.9	9
Other	16.3	1
Noninterest		
Service charges on deposit accounts	117.8	6
Gain on sale of Visa shares	51.9	3
Fiduciary & asset management fees	44.2	2
Mortgage banking income	38.5	2
Bankcard fees	36.1	2
Brokerage & investment banking	28.5	1
Other	93.8	5
Total	**1,919.9**	**100**

Select Subsidiaries and Affiliates

AFB&T
Bank of Coweta
The Bank of Nashville
Bank of North Georgia
The Bank of Tuscaloosa
CB&T Bank of East Alabama
CB&T Bank of Middle Georgia
Citizens First Bank
The Coastal Bank of Georgia
Cohutta Banking Company of Tennessee
Columbus Bank and Trust Company
Commercial Bank
Commercial Bank & Trust Company of Troup County
Community Bank & Trust of Southeast Alabama
Creative Financial Group, LTD
First Commercial Bank
First Commercial Bank of Huntsville
First Community Bank of Tifton
First State Bank and Trust Company of Valdosta
Georgia Bank & Trust
GLOBALT, Inc.
The National Bank of Jasper
SB&T Bank
Sea Island Bank
Sterling Bank
Synovus Bank
Synovus Securities, Inc.
The Tallahassee State Bank
Total Technology Ventures, LLC
Trust One Bank

COMPETITORS

Bank of America
BB&T
Citigroup
Compass Bancshares
Fidelity Southern
Georgia Bancshares
Regions Financial
SunTrust

HISTORICAL FINANCIALS

Company Type: Public

Income Statement

FYE: December 31

	ASSETS ($ mil.)	NET INCOME ($ mil.)	INCOME AS % OF ASSETS	EMPLOYEES
12/09	32,831	(1,429)	—	6,385
12/08	35,786	(582)	—	6,876
12/07	33,019	526	1.6%	6,807
12/06	31,855	617	1.9%	13,178
12/05	27,621	516	1.9%	6,603
Annual Growth	**4.4%**	**—**	**—**	**(0.8%)**

2009 Year-End Financials

Equity as % of assets: 5.9%
Return on assets: —
Return on equity: —
Long-term debt ($ mil.): 1,752
No. of shares (mil.): 785
Dividends
Yield: 2.0%
Payout: —
Market value ($ mil.): 1,609
Sales ($ mil.): 1,920

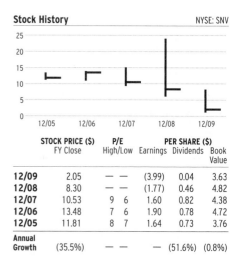

Stock History

NYSE: SNV

	STOCK PRICE ($) FY Close	P/E High/Low		Earnings	PER SHARE ($) Dividends	Book Value
12/09	2.05	—	—	(3.99)	0.04	3.63
12/08	8.30	—	—	(1.77)	0.46	4.82
12/07	10.53	9	6	1.60	0.82	4.38
12/06	13.48	7	6	1.90	0.78	4.72
12/05	11.81	8	7	1.64	0.73	3.76
Annual Growth	**(35.5%)**	**—**	**—**	**—**	**(51.6%)**	**(0.8%)**

SYSCO Corporation

This company has the menu that restaurants depend on. SYSCO is the #1 foodservice supplier in North America, serving about 400,000 customers through more than 180 distribution centers in the US and Canada. Its core broadline distribution business supplies food and non-food products to restaurants, schools, hotels, health care institutions, and other foodservice customers, while its SYGMA Network focuses on supplying chain restaurants. SYSCO distributes both nationally branded products and its own private-label goods. In addition, SYSCO supplies customers with specialty produce and meat products, and it distributes kitchen equipment and supplies for the hospitality industry.

The wholesale foodservices distribution business is highly fragmented with a patchwork of regional and local suppliers to compete against. On a national scale, meanwhile, SYSCO competes for customers with rivals U.S. Foodservice and Performance Food Group. The company claims to have more than 15% of the market. Customers in the restaurant industry account for more than 60% of sales, with fast food giant Wendy's/Arby's Group accounting for almost 5% of SYSCO's business.

With the downturn in the economy hurting many dining operators, SYSCO and other suppliers have been forced to cut costs to help offset sales declines. The company has consolidated some of its regional operations and reduced headcount as part of that effort.

Poor economic conditions have also slowed the company's expansion activities, which have traditionally focused on acquiring local distributors that specialize in items such as premium steaks and hotel supplies. Meanwhile, SYSCO made its first bold move toward expansion outside North America in 2009 when it acquired Pallas Foods, a leading broadline supplier serving the foodservice industry in Ireland.

Bill DeLaney was promoted to CEO in 2009, replacing Richard Schnieders who retired from the company after about seven years at the helm.

HISTORY

SYSCO was founded in 1969 when John Baugh, a Houston wholesale food distributor, formed a national distribution company with the owners of eight other US wholesalers. Joining Baugh's Zero Foods of Houston to form SYSCO were Frost-Pack Distributing (Grand Rapids, Michigan), Louisville Grocery (Louisville, Kentucky), Plantation Foods (Miami), Thomas Foods and its Justrite subsidiary (Cincinnati), Wicker (Dallas), Food Service Company (Houston), Global Frozen Foods (New York), and Texas Wholesale Grocery (Dallas). The company went public in 1970. SYSCO, which derives its name from Systems and Services Company, benefited from Baugh's recognition of the trend toward dining out. Until SYSCO was formed, small, independent operators almost exclusively provided food distribution to restaurants, hotels, and other non-grocers.

The company expanded through internal growth and the acquisition of strong local distributors, benefiting through buyout agreements requiring the seller to continue managing its own operation while earning a portion of the sale price with future profits.

In 1988, when SYSCO was already the largest North American foodservice distributor, it acquired CFS Continental, the third-largest North American food distributor. The CFS acquisition added a large truck fleet and increased the company's penetration along the West Coast of the US and into Canada. Also that year SYSCO purchased Olewine's, a Pennsylvania-based distributor. In 1990 the company bought Oklahoma City-based Scrivner, later renamed SYSCO Food Services of Oklahoma.

In 1992 SYSCO acquired Collins Foodservice (serving the Northwest) and Benjamin Polakoff & Son and Perloff Brothers (both serving the Northeast). In 1994 it bought Woodhaven Foods, a distributor owned by ARA (now ARAMARK), one of the nation's largest cafeteria and concession operators.

In 1997 the company formed an alliance with National Healthcare Logistics to improve distribution to hospitals and integrated health care systems. Baugh, at age 81, retired from his senior chairman post later that year.

The company completed a number of large acquisitions in 1999, including Atlanta-based Buckhead Beef Company, Newport Meat Company of Southern California, and Virginia-based Doughtie's Foods (renamed SYSCO Food Services of Hampton Roads).

SYSCO president Charles Cotros succeeded Bill Lindig as CEO in 2000. That year SYSCO bought Dallas-based produce distributor FreshPoint. It also purchased Canadian foodservice distributor North Douglas Distributors. In 2001 SYSCO acquired specialty meat supplier The Freedman Companies and Guest Supply, which distributes personal care amenities and housekeeping supplies to the lodging industry.

In 2002 SYSCO acquired SERCA Foodservice, which distributes to 80,000 customers in Canada, from Canada's Sobeys. It also completed the acquisition of privately held Abbott Foods, a broadline foodservice distributor located in Columbus, Ohio.

SYSCO's chairman and CEO Charles Cotros retired at the end of 2002, passing the torch to then president and COO Richard Schnieders. In 2003 SYSCO acquired Maine-based Reed Distributors

and the specialty meat-cutting division of the Colorado Boxed Beef Company and its Florida broadline foodservice operation, J&B Foodservice.

SYSCO unit SYSCO Food Services of Central Alabama announced in 2004 that it planned to expand its foodservice agreement with Cuba and had signed a letter of intent with the Cuban food import agency Alimport. The unit had generated $500,000 in sales in Cuba since the previous year. Within the same month, though, the SYSCO subsidiary retracted its offer, reporting that the agreement asked for SYSCO to assist "in normalizing trade relations" between the US and Cuba.

SYSCO acquired International Food Group, a foodservice distributor to chain restaurants in international markets, in mid-2004. The company added to its specialty meat offerings with the 2005 acquisitions of California-based Facciola Meat Company and Florida-based Royalty Foods. That year it also acquired specialty-food importer Walker Foods, and fresh fruit and vegetable distributor Piranha Produce.

In 2006 SYSCO acquired the foodservice assets of Bunn Capitol, a supplier to restaurants and other customers in Illinois. Founder Baugh died in 2007.

In July 2010, SYSCO acquired Nebraska-based Lincoln Poultry & Egg Co., a broadline foodservice provider with more than 800 customers primarily in the central US.

EXECUTIVES

Chairman: Manuel A. (Manny) Fernandez, age 63
President, CEO, and Director:
William J. (Bill) DeLaney III, age 53,
$1,724,983 total compensation
EVP and CFO: Robert C. (Chris) Kreidler
EVP Foodservice Operations: Michael W. Green, age 50,
$1,098,704 total compensation
EVP Global Sourcing and Supply Chain:
Larry G. Pulliam, age 53,
$1,765,452 total compensation
EVP Merchandising and Supply Chain: William B. Day, age 54
EVP Business Transformation: James D. Hope, age 49
SVP, Controller, and Chief Accounting Officer:
G. Mitchell Elmer, age 50
SVP Finance and Treasurer: Kirk G. Drummond, age 54
SVP Foodservice Operations, North Central and Northeast Regions: Charles W. Staes, age 54
SVP Canadian Foodservice Operations:
G. Kent Humphries
SVP Administration and General Counsel:
Michael C. Nichols, age 57
SVP and CIO: Twila M. Day, age 44
SVP Foodservice Operations, South and West Regions:
Scott A. Sonnemaker
SVP Merchandising: Alan E. Hasty, age 51
VP; Chairman, SYSCO Specialty Meat Companies:
Andrew L. (Andy) Malcolm
VP; Chairman and CEO, SYGMA Network:
Alan W. Kelso, age 59
VP; President and CEO, FreshPoint: Brian M. Sturgeon
VP Human Resources: Mark Wisnoski
VP Investor Relations: Neil A. Russell, age 39
VP Organizational Effectiveness and Corporate Communications: Mark A. Palmer, age 46
Auditors: Ernst & Young LLP

LOCATIONS

HQ: SYSCO Corporation
1390 Enclave Pkwy., Houston, TX 77077
Phone: 281-584-1390   **Fax:** 281-584-2721
Web: www.sysco.com

2009 Sales

	$ mil.	% of total
US	33,378.5	91
Canada	3,135.0	8
Other countries	339.8	1
Total	**36,853.3**	**100**

PRODUCTS/OPERATIONS

2009 Sales

	$ mil.	% of total
Broadline	29,234.2	78
SYGMA	4,839.0	13
Other	3,242.1	9
Adjustments	(462.0)	—
Total	**36,853.3**	**100**

2009 Sales

	$ mil.	% of total
Canned & dry products	7,091.4	19
Fresh & frozen meats	6,394.4	17
Frozen fruits, vegetables, bakery & other	5,122.4	14
Dairy products	3,750.7	10
Poultry	3,709.6	10
Fresh produce	3,017.0	8
Paper & disposables	2,911.0	8
Seafood	1,740.3	5
Beverage products	1,322.3	4
Janitorial products	940.1	3
Equipment & smallwares	661.3	2
Medical supplies	192.8	—
Total	**36,853.3**	**100**

2009 Sales

	% of total
Restaurants	62
Hospitals & nursing homes	11
Hotels & motels	6
Schools & colleges	5
Other	16
Total	**100**

COMPETITORS

Ben E. Keith
Clark National
Edward Don
Foodbuy
Golden State Foods
Gordon Food Service
MAINES
McLane Foodservice
Meadowbrook Meat Company
Performance Food
PrimeSource FoodService
Reinhart FoodService
Shamrock Foods
UniPro Foodservice
U.S. Foodservice

HISTORICAL FINANCIALS

Company Type: Public

Income Statement			FYE: Saturday nearest June 30	
	REVENUE ($ mil.)	NET INCOME ($ mil.)	NET PROFIT MARGIN	EMPLOYEES
6/09	36,853	1,056	2.9%	47,000
6/08	37,522	1,106	2.9%	50,000
6/07	35,042	1,001	2.9%	50,900
6/06	32,628	846	2.6%	49,600
6/05	30,282	962	3.2%	47,500
Annual Growth	**5.0%**	**2.4%**	**—**	**(0.3%)**

2009 Year-End Financials

Debt ratio: 71.5%
Return on equity: 30.8%
Cash ($ mil.): 1,087
Current ratio: 1.67
Long-term debt ($ mil.): 2,467

No. of shares (mil.): 592
Dividends
  Yield: 4.2%
  Payout: 53.1%
Market value ($ mil.): 13,299

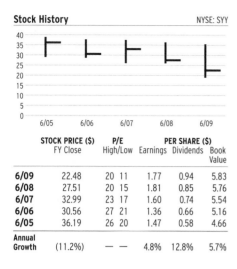

	STOCK PRICE ($)	P/E		PER SHARE ($)		
	FY Close	High/Low	Earnings	Dividends	Book Value
6/09	22.48	20　11	1.77	0.94	5.83
6/08	27.51	20　15	1.81	0.85	5.76
6/07	32.99	23　17	1.60	0.74	5.54
6/06	30.56	27　21	1.36	0.66	5.16
6/05	36.19	26　20	1.47	0.58	4.66
Annual Growth	(11.2%)	—　—	4.8%	12.8%	5.7%

T. Rowe Price Group

T. Rowe Price Group administers an eponymous family of mutual funds, offering a variety of investment styles, as well as asset management advisory services (including retirement plan advice for individuals) and discount brokerage. Other services include corporate retirement plan management and transfer agency and shareholder services. T. Rowe Price manages approximately 100 funds in all. Traditionally oriented toward growth investing, the funds offer products in many risk and taxation profiles, including small-, mid-, and large-cap stock funds; money market funds; and bond funds, both taxable and nontaxable.

Some three-fourths of the company's approximately $390 billion of assets under management are held in retirement plans and variable annuities. Most of the firm's clients — individual and institutional investors, retirement plans, third-party distributors — are in the US, but T. Rowe Price Group also has offices in Asia, Europe, and South America and serves clients in some 30 countries. It is pursuing growth in India and China by introducing new products and services there. The company also acquired more than a quarter of India-based UTI Asset Management in 2009.

HISTORY

Thomas Rowe Price Jr. left a brokerage job at Mackubin, Goodrich & Co. to found his own investment advisory firm in 1937. He pushed investing for the long haul, choosing stocks of promising young companies (the firm invested in IBM in 1950). Price's company was incorporated in 1947 and was employee-owned until it went public in 1986.

The firm moved into international investments in 1979. T. Rowe Price was primarily an institutional pension fund manager until the 1980s. Creativity lagged as fund managers made investments from a list selected by the research department, and the Growth Stock Fund underperformed the S&P 500. In 1987 the firm opened its funds to individual investors.

Thereafter it introduced a slew of new funds, slicing and dicing the market to appeal to the broadest possible industry and risk investment profiles, including offerings in emerging market stocks and health and science stocks. In 1996 longtime president and CEO George Collins retired, and was succeeded by then-CFO George Roche, who eventually became the company's chairman.

In the late 1990s, however, the company's value investing strategy brought lagging fund results, and a stagnant corporate stock price. Nevertheless, cash continued to pour into the company's funds until the collapse of Russian and Asian markets in 1998. US investors got the willies, slowing asset flows to T. Rowe Price and other mutual fund managers.

In response, Roche began moving the company into overseas asset management markets. In 1999 the firm joined with Sumitomo Bank (now part of Sumitomo Mitsui Financial Group) and Daiwa Securities to form asset manager Daiwa SB Investments in Japan. It also targeted Europe, where the growth of private retirement plans opened up new opportunities. Nevertheless, the company missed out on many of the explosive returns of the high-tech boom.

In 2000, however, the high-tech bubble burst, seeming to vindicate T. Rowe Price's conservative approach. That year the company bought out the remaining 50% of its Rowe Price-Fleming International asset management joint venture with Robert Fleming (which is now part of JPMorgan Chase). Also that year the company reorganized itself into holding company T. Rowe Price Group. The company's UK subsidiary received regulatory approval to expand to the European continent in 2001.

Long-time company executive James Kennedy succeeded the retiring George Roche as CEO in 2007, while chief investment officer Brian Rogers succeeded Roche as chairman.

EXECUTIVES

Chairman and Chief Investment Officer:
Brian C. Rogers, age 55, $4,724,744 total compensation
Vice Chairman and VP: Edward C. Bernard, age 55, $4,427,244 total compensation
President, CEO, and Board Member:
James A. C. Kennedy, age 57, $4,729,805 total compensation
VP, CFO, and Treasurer: Kenneth V. Moreland, age 54, $1,215,549 total compensation
VP and Director of Equities and Global Equity Research: William J. Stromberg, age 50, $4,435,406 total compensation
VP Marketing, Web Strategy, and Development, Third Party Distribution: Bill Weker
VP and Director Fixed Income: Mike Gitlin, age 40
VP, Australia and New Zealand: Murray Brewer
VP and Principal Accounting Officer: Jessica M. Hiebler, age 35
VP; Manager, Growth Stock Fund:
P. Robert (Rob) Bartolo
VP; President, T. Rowe Price International:
Christopher D. Alderson, age 48
President, T. Rowe Price Retirement Plan Services:
Cynthia L. Egan
Secretary: Barbara A. Van Horn
Auditors: KPMG LLP

LOCATIONS

HQ: T. Rowe Price Group, Inc.
100 E. Pratt St., Baltimore, MD 21202
Phone: 410-345-2000　　**Fax:** 410-345-2394
Web: www.troweprice.com

PRODUCTS/OPERATIONS

2009 Sales

	$ mil.	% of total
Investment advisory fees	1,546.1	83
Administrative fees	318.8	17
Savings bank subsidiary	7.0	—
Total	**1,871.9**	**100**

Selected Subsidiaries

T. Rowe Price Advisory Services, Inc.
T. Rowe Price Associates, Inc.
　T. Rowe Price (Canada), Inc. (US)
　T. Rowe Price Investment Services, Inc.
　T. Rowe Price Retirement Plan Services, Inc.
　T. Rowe Price Savings Bank
　T. Rowe Price Services, Inc.
　TRP Suburban Second, Inc.
T. Rowe Price Global Investment Services Ltd. (UK)

COMPETITORS

AllianceBernstein	Legg Mason
American Century	MFS
AXA Financial	Morgan Stanley
BlackRock	Northwestern Mutual
Capital Group	Old Mutual (US)
Charles Schwab	Prudential
FAF Advisors	Putnam
FMR	Raymond James Financial
Franklin Resources	UBS Financial Services
Invesco	USAA
Janus Capital	The Vanguard Group

HISTORICAL FINANCIALS

Company Type: Public

Income Statement

FYE: December 31

	ASSETS ($ mil.)	NET INCOME ($ mil.)	INCOME AS % OF ASSETS	EMPLOYEES
12/09	3,210	434	13.5%	4,802
12/08	2,819	491	17.4%	5,385
12/07	3,177	671	21.1%	5,081
12/06	2,765	530	19.2%	4,605
12/05	2,311	431	18.6%	4,372
Annual Growth	8.6%	0.2%	—	2.4%

2009 Year-End Financials

Equity as % of assets: 89.8%
Return on assets: 14.4%
Return on equity: 16.1%
Long-term debt ($ mil.): —
No. of shares (mil.): 256
Dividends
　Yield: 1.9%
　Payout: 60.6%
Market value ($ mil.): 13,651
Sales ($ mil.): 1,872

Stock History

NASDAQ (GS): TROW

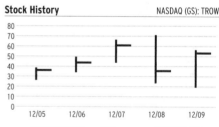

	STOCK PRICE ($)	P/E		PER SHARE ($)		
	FY Close	High/Low	Earnings	Dividends	Book Value
12/09	53.25	34　12	1.65	1.00	11.24
12/08	35.44	39　13	1.82	0.96	9.71
12/07	60.88	27　19	2.40	0.75	10.83
12/06	43.77	26　18	1.90	0.59	9.47
12/05	36.01	24　17	1.58	0.49	7.94
Annual Growth	10.3%	—　—	1.1%	19.5%	9.1%

Target Corporation

Purveyor of all that is cheap, yet chic, Target Corporation is the nation's #2 discount chain (behind Wal-Mart). The fashion-minded discounter operates about 1,745 Target and SuperTarget stores in 49 states, as well as an online business called Target.com. Target and its larger grocery-carrying incarnation, SuperTarget, have carved out a niche by offering more upscale, fashion-forward merchandise than rivals Wal-Mart and Kmart. Target also issues its proprietary Target credit card, good only at Target. After a reversal in fortune that coincided with the onset of the deep recession in the US, Target is growing its grocery business, remodeling stores, and — in a few years — looking to grow outside the US.

Historically a stellar performer in the retail arena, Target has missed the bull's eye of late, posting slower sales and earnings growth than investors have come to expect. Sales of consumables and household essentials have risen as cash-strapped consumers stick to the basics. To capitalize on the new frugality, Target has taken a page from archrival Wal-Mart's playbook and opened new formats that devote more space to food, especially its house brands Archer Farms and Market Pantry, and other household basics.

In early 2010 Target announced in a strategy update that it plans to spend $1 billion to renovate about 340 of its existing stores in 2010. The remodels will make more room for more groceries, as well as beauty, home, and electronic products. The discounter will also develop a smaller store format with an edited selection of merchandise tailored for urban areas. Farther down the road, Target announced plans to expand outside the US (most likely in Canada, Mexico, or Latin America) in three to five years.

The retailer extended its cheap-chic appeal to the kitchen in 2010 when it introduced an exclusive line of cookware from Food Network chef Giada De Laurentiis. Besides promoting her line, De Laurentiis will also formulate cooking tips that tie together with Target's private-label brands, such as Archer Farms. Also that year Target acquired the brand and related intellectual property assets of the defunct Smith & Hawken, which made upscale patio furniture and gardening products.

Target's online division, Target.com, is growing at a slightly faster rate than its in-store sales. To give it more control over this part of its business, Target announced in late 2009 that it plans to build its own retail website by the 2011 holiday season, essentially ending its relationship with e-commerce provider Amazon.com.

The retailer's business-to-business subsidiary — Target Commercial Interiors — operates about a half-dozen showrooms in Illinois, Minnesota, and Wisconsin that provide products and services for office environments. The interior design company, whose clients include some of America's largest companies, is attempting to expand its business by reaching out to small and midsized companies.

In May 2008 Bob Ulrich, who had been chairman and CEO since 1994, handed his CEO title to president Gregg Steinhafel. Steinhafel, who joined the retailer in 1979 and worked his way up the ranks, added the chairman's title in early 2009 following Ulrich's retirement from Target's board of directors.

HISTORY

The panic of 1873 left Joseph Hudson bankrupt. After he paid his debts at 60 cents on the dollar, he saved enough to open a men's clothing store in Detroit in 1881. Among his innovations were merchandise-return privileges and price marking in place of bargaining. By 1891 Hudson's was the largest retailer of men's clothing in the US. Hudson repaid his creditors from 1873 in full, with interest. When Hudson died in 1912, four nephews expanded the business.

Former banker George Dayton established a dry-goods store in 1902 in Minneapolis. Like Hudson, he offered return privileges and liberal credit. His store grew to a 12-story, full-line department store.

After WWII both companies saw that the future lay in the suburbs. In 1954 Hudson's built Northland in Detroit, then the largest US shopping center. Dayton's built the world's first fully enclosed shopping mall in Edina, a Minneapolis suburb, in 1956. In 1962 Dayton's opened its first discount store in Roseville (naming the store Target to distinguish the discounter from its higher-end department stores).

Dayton's went public in 1966, the same year it began the B. Dalton bookstore chain. Three years later it merged with the family-owned Hudson's, forming Dayton Hudson. Dayton Hudson purchased more malls and invested in such specialty areas as consumer electronics and hard goods. Target had 24 stores by 1970.

The Target chain became the company's top moneymaker in 1977. The next year Dayton Hudson bought California-based Mervyn's (later Mervyns). In the late 1970s and 1980s, it sold nine regional malls and several other businesses, including the 800-store B. Dalton chain to Barnes & Noble. The Target stores division purchased Indianapolis-based Ayr-Way (1980) and Southern California-based Fedmart stores (1983). In the late 1980s Dayton Hudson took Target to Los Angeles and the Northwest. Robert Ulrich, who began with the company as a merchandise trainee in 1967, became president and CEO of the Target stores division in 1987 and chairman and CEO of Dayton Hudson in 1994.

Dayton Hudson opened the first Target Greatland store in 1990. By this time it had 420 Target stores. Also that year Dayton Hudson bought the Marshall Field's chain of 24 department stores from B.A.T Industries. Marshall Field's began as a dry-goods business that Marshall Field bought in 1865 and subsequently built into Chicago's premier upscale retailer.

In 2000 Dayton Hudson renamed itself Target Corporation. The year 2004 was a time of divestments for Target. In January the discounter announced it was exiting the catalog business. In July Target sold its Marshall Field's business to The May Department Stores Co. for about $3.2 billion in cash. In September Target completed the sale of 257 Mervyns stores in 13 states to an investment group that includes Cerberus Capital Management, Lubert-Adler/Klaff and Partners, and Sun Capital Partners, as well as its Mervyns credit card receivables to GE Consumer Finance for a combined sum of approximately $1.65 billion in cash.

In the largest mass opening in Target's history, the retailer opened 60 new stores on October 9, 2005.

In May 2008 Ulrich, who had served as chairman and CEO since 1994, handed his CEO title to president Gregg Steinhafel. (Steinhafel joined the retailer in 1979 and worked his way up the executive ranks.) Also that year Target closed on the sale of a 47% stake in its credit-card receivables to JPMorgan Chase for $3.6 billion. The five-year deal allows Target to buy back the stake at the end of the term. In October the company opened a pair of stores in Alaska, thereby expanding its retail presence to 48 states.

Ulrich retired from the board in January 2009 and Steinhafel added the chairman's title to his job description.

EXECUTIVES

Chairman, President, and CEO: Gregg W. Steinhafel, age 55, $16,103,433 total compensation
EVP and CFO: Douglas A. Scovanner, age 54, $8,018,439 total compensation
EVP and Chief Marketing Officer: Michael R. Francis, age 47, $6,126,089 total compensation
EVP Stores: Troy H. Risch, age 42, $4,759,361 total compensation
EVP Merchandising: Kathryn A. (Kathee) Tesija, age 47, $5,461,449 total compensation
EVP Property Development: John D. Griffith, age 48
EVP Human Resources: Jodeen A. Kozlak, age 46
EVP Target Technology Services and CIO: Beth M Jacob, age 48
EVP, General Counsel, and Corporate Secretary: Timothy R. (Tim) Baer, age 49
SVP Treasury and Accounting: John Mulligan
SVP Store Design: Rich Varda
SVP Store Operations: Janna Adair-Potts
SVP Real Estate: Scott Nelson
SVP Marketing: Karen Gershman
SVP Communications and Publicity: Susan D. Kahn
President, Target.com: Stephen (Steve) Eastman
President, Target Financial Services: Terrence J. (Terry) Scully, age 52
President, Target Sourcing Services: Annette Miller
President, Community Relations and Target Foundation: Laysha Ward, age 42
President and Managing Director, Target India: Lalit Ahuja
Auditors: Ernst & Young LLP

LOCATIONS

HQ: Target Corporation
1000 Nicollet Mall, Minneapolis, MN 55403
Phone: 612-304-6073   **Fax:** 612-696-5400
Web: www.target.com

2010 Locations

	No.
California	244
Texas	148
Florida	126
Illinois	86
Minnesota	73
New York	64
Ohio	63
Michigan	60
Pennsylvania	59
Virginia	56
Georgia	55
Arizona	48
North Carolina	47
New Jersey	43
Colorado	42
Wisconsin	37
Maryland	36
Missouri	36
Washington	35
Indiana	33
Massachusetts	33
Tennessee	32
Iowa	22
Alabama	20
Connecticut	20
Kansas	19
Nevada	19
Oregon	19
South Carolina	18
Louisiana	15
Nebraska	14
Oklahoma	14
Kentucky	13
Utah	11
Other states	80
Total	**1,740**

PRODUCTS/OPERATIONS

2010 Sales

	% of total
Household essentials	23
Hardlines	22
Apparel & accessories	20
Home furnishings & décor	19
Food & pet supplies	16
Total	**100**

2010 Stores

	No.
Target	1,489
SuperTarget	251
Total	**1,740**

Selected Designer Private Labels

Amy Coe (children's bedding and accessories)
Liz Lange (maternity)
Michael Graves Design (housewares)
Mossimo (junior fashions)
Sonia Kashuk (cosmetics and fragrances)
Todd Oldham (bedding and furniture)

Selected Private Labels

Archer Farms (food)
Cherokee (apparel)
Choxie (candy)
Furio (housewares)
Honors (apparel)
In Due Time (maternity wear)
Market Pantry
Merona (apparel)
Nick & Nora (apparel)
Playwonder (toys)
Utility (apparel)
Xhilaration (apparel)

Other Operations

Rivertown Trading (catalogs and e-commerce)
  Britannia (British video and gifts)
  I Love A Deal (apparel, housewares, and jewelry)
  Seasons (traditional)
Target Capital Corp.
Target Commercial Interiors
Target Receivables Corp.

COMPETITORS

Bed Bath & Beyond
Best Buy
Burnes Home Accents
Container Store
Costco Wholesale
CVS Caremark
Dillard's
Dollar General
eBay
Euromarket Designs
Foot Locker
The Gap
Home Depot
J. C. Penney Company
Kmart
Kohl's
Kroger
Limited Brands
Macy's
PETCO
Ross Stores
Sears
SUPERVALU
TJX Companies
Toys "R" Us
Walgreen
Wal-Mart
Williams-Sonoma

HISTORICAL FINANCIALS

Company Type: Public

Income Statement

FYE: Saturday nearest January 31

	REVENUE ($ mil.)	NET INCOME ($ mil.)	NET PROFIT MARGIN	EMPLOYEES
1/10	65,357	2,488	3.8%	351,000
1/09	64,948	2,214	3.4%	351,000
1/08	63,367	2,849	4.5%	366,000
1/07	59,490	2,787	4.7%	352,000
1/06	52,620	2,408	4.6%	338,000
Annual Growth	**5.6%**	**0.8%**	**—**	**0.9%**

2010 Year-End Financials

Debt ratio: 98.5%
Return on equity: 17.1%
Cash ($ mil.): 583
Current ratio: 1.63
Long-term debt ($ mil.): 15,118

No. of shares (mil.): 736
Dividends
  Yield: 1.3%
  Payout: 20.0%
Market value ($ mil.): 37,759

Stock History

NYSE: TGT

	STOCK PRICE ($) FY Close	P/E High/Low		PER SHARE ($) Earnings	Dividends	Book Value
1/10	51.27	16	8	3.30	0.66	20.84
1/09	31.20	21	9	2.86	0.60	18.62
1/08	55.42	21	14	3.33	0.52	20.78
1/07	61.36	20	14	3.21	0.44	21.23
1/06	54.75	22	17	2.71	0.36	19.29
Annual Growth	**(1.6%)**	**—**	**—**	**5.0%**	**16.4%**	**2.0%**

TD Ameritrade

If your stock makes a big move while you're stuck in traffic, don't worry — TD AMERITRADE lets you buy and sell even when you're on the go. Through numerous subsidiaries, it provides electronic discount brokerage and related financial services for active traders, investment advisors, and long-term investors. Products include common and preferred stocks of US companies, fixed-income assets, ETFs, mutual funds, and option trades. TD AMERITRADE Clearing provides clearing and execution services. In addition to its online offerings, the group provides services through a retail network of more than 100 branches nationwide and via independent advisors.

Throughout its history, TD AMERITRADE has grown through acquiring other businesses and expanding its offerings. In 2009 it acquired online brokerage thinkorswim Group, a specialist in options trading and investor education, for some $600 million in cash and stock. The year before that, it acquired most of the business and assets of Fiserv ISS for $225 million, adding some $25 billion in client assets and $10 billion in third-party administered plans. Also in 2008, it bulked up its TD AMERITRADE Institutional business, which has more than $100 billion in assets under management.

TD AMERITRADE's expanded account base has helped it keep the pressure on competitors E*TRADE and Charles Schwab. The company remains focused on its core business of online trading, supplementing its growth with products such as mutual funds and money market accounts, as well as multimillion-dollar brand-building advertising campaigns.

Founder Joe Ricketts retired as chairman in 2008. Ricketts and his family sold some of their stakes to Canada-based TD Bank, which is now the largest shareholder with 45% ownership. Ricketts' son Tom used proceeds of the sale to help fund his acquisition of the Chicago Cubs from the Tribune Company. The Ricketts family still owns some 15% of TD AMERITRADE. Company CEO Joe Moglia took over as chairman when Ricketts retired; former COO Fred Tomczyk stepped into the CEO position.

Money market sweep arrangements with major owner TD Bank account for about a quarter of TD AMERITRADE's sales.

HISTORY

Ameritrade began in 1971 as investment bank TransTerra. Dean Witter veteran Joe Ricketts transformed the firm into a discount broker in 1975. TransTerra formed Televest/Bancvest (now AmeriVest) in 1982 and Ameritrade Clearing (now TD AMERITRADE Clearing) in 1983.

In 1988 the company became the first to offer Touch-Tone telephone trading, and added Internet trading in 1994. TransTerra formed Ceres Securities, a deep-discount brokerage service that added research to its services when it bought brokerage firms K. Aufhauser and All American in 1995. The company formed its eBroker all-Internet brokerage service in 1996, and became Ameritrade late that year.

In 1997 the company went public and combined its service-oriented subsidiaries. It also formed an alliance that directed users of America Online's investor site to Ameritrade's websites. The company grew rapidly in the late

1990s, but like most technology-based companies, suffered the impact of the subsequent tech wreck and the struggling economy.

Later, TD AMERITRADE led a wave of consolidation within the electronic brokerage industry. It purchased rivals National Discount Brokers and Datek in 2001 and 2002, but didn't stop there. In 2003 the company acquired the accounts of Mydiscountbroker.com from SWS Group, and the retail accounts of BrokerageAmerica, which together helped push the company's account base past the 3 million mark. It gained another 145,000 accounts from brokerage firms Bidwell & Company and JB Oxford Holdings in 2004 and 2005.

E*TRADE offered to buy Ameritrade for more than $6 billion in mid-2005, but the company refused, saying it wasn't up for sale. The following year, Ameritrade made its own purchase. It bought the US operations of TD Waterhouse and added the "TD" to its name (in addition to the all-caps style it now uses), as well as some 100 branch locations.

As part of the company's deal to acquire TD Waterhouse's US business, Canada-based TD Bank assumed a 40% stake in the firm.

EXECUTIVES

Chairman: Joseph H. (Joe) Moglia, age 60, $9,936,460 total compensation
Vice Chairman: W. Edmund (Ed) Clark, age 62
President, CEO, and Director:
Fredric J. (Fred) Tomczyk, age 54, $8,096,773 total compensation
EVP and COO: David M. (Dave) Kelley, age 49, $1,907,218 total compensation
EVP and CFO: William J. (Bill) Gerber, age 52, $1,189,094 total compensation
EVP Product, Marketing, and Client Experience:
Peter Sidebottom, age 47, $2,141,856 total compensation
EVP, General Counsel, and Secretary:
Ellen L.S. Koplow, age 50
EVP Retail Distribution: John B. Bunch, age 43
Chief Risk Officer: David Kimm
Chief Human Resources Officer: Karen Ganzlin
SVP and Chief Marketing Officer: Laurine M. Garrity, age 48
SVP Trading: Tom Sosnoff, age 53
SVP Trader Group: Steven (Steve) Quirk
President, TD AMERITRADE Institutional:
J. Thomas Bradley Jr., age 47
Managing Director, Finance and Treasurer:
Michael D. Chochon, age 41
Manager Corporate Communications: Kim Hillyer
Auditors: Ernst & Young LLP

LOCATIONS

HQ: TD AMERITRADE Holding Corporation
4211 S. 102nd St., Omaha, NE 68127
Phone: 402-331-7856
Web: www.amtd.com

PRODUCTS/OPERATIONS

2009 Sales

	$ mil.	% of total
Commissions & transaction fees	1,253.2	52
Insured deposit account fees	568.1	23
Interest	362.1	15
Investment product fees	184.3	8
Other	53.4	2
Total	**2,421.1**	**100**

Selected Subsidiaries

Ameritrade Advisory Services, LLC
Ameritrade International Company, Inc. (Cayman Islands)
Amerivest Investment Management, LLC
Datek Online Management Corp.
Financial Passport, Inc.
Investools Inc.
TD AMERITRADE Clearing, Inc.
TD AMERITRADE, Inc.
TD AMERITRADE IP Company, Inc.
TD AMERITRADE Online Holdings Corp.
TD AMERITRADE Services Company, Inc.
TD Waterhouse Canadian Call Center, Inc.
TD Waterhouse Capital Markets, Inc.
TenBagger, Inc.
thinkorswim Holdings Inc.
ThinkTech, Inc.
TOS Trading LLC
TradeBridge, Inc.

COMPETITORS

Bank of America
Charles Schwab
Citigroup Global Markets
E*TRADE Financial
Edward Jones
FMR
JPMorgan Chase
Morgan Stanley
Scottrade
ShareBuilder
The Vanguard Group

HISTORICAL FINANCIALS

Company Type: Public

Income Statement

FYE: Friday nearest September 30

	REVENUE ($ mil.)	NET INCOME ($ mil.)	NET PROFIT MARGIN	EMPLOYEES
9/09	2,421	644	26.6%	5,196
9/08	2,788	804	28.8%	4,660
9/07	2,638	646	24.5%	3,882
9/06	2,221	527	23.7%	3,947
9/05	1,145	340	29.7%	2,052
Annual Growth	**20.6%**	**17.3%**	**—**	**26.1%**

2009 Year-End Financials

Debt ratio: 40.6%
Return on equity: 19.9%
Cash ($ mil.): 6,605
Current ratio: —
Long-term debt ($ mil.): 1,443
No. of shares (mil.): 576
Dividends
  Yield: —
  Payout: —
Market value ($ mil.): 11,308

Stock History

NASDAQ (GS): AMTD

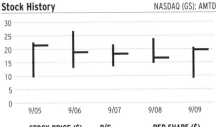

	STOCK PRICE ($) FY Close	P/E High/Low		PER SHARE ($) Earnings	Dividends	Book Value
9/09	19.63	18	8	1.10	—	6.16
9/08	16.67	18	11	1.33	—	5.08
9/07	18.22	20	13	1.06	—	3.74
9/06	18.85	28	14	0.95	—	3.00
9/05	21.47	27	12	0.82	—	2.64
Annual Growth	**(2.2%)**	**—**	**—**	**7.6%**	**—**	**23.7%**

Tech Data Corporation

Tech Data is 100% committed to IT products distribution. One of the world's largest distributors of computer products, Tech Data provides thousands of different items to more than 125,000 resellers in 100-plus countries. Its catalog of products includes computer components (disk drives, keyboards, and video cards), networking equipment (routers and bridges), peripherals (printers, modems, and monitors), systems (PCs and servers), and software. Tech Data also provides technical support, configuration, integration, financing, electronic data interchange (EDI), and other logistics and product fulfillment services. More than half of Tech Data's revenues are generated in Europe.

Tech Data distributes products from such vendors as Apple, Cisco Systems, Hewlett-Packard (which accounts for nearly 30% of sales), IBM, Microsoft, and Sony.

As the global recession continued to grind on, Tech Data saw its fiscal 2010 sales contract by about 8% from the prior year. The IT distributor was able to eke its usual paper-thin profit margin, however. While the lengthy economic downturn may be coming to an end, the general instability might continue to have an effect on Tech Data's financial results, operations, and prospects for new business. The company operates in a highly competitive market and must contend not only with other large distributors, but also with companies entering into the e-commerce supply chain services, logistics services, and product fulfillment services markets.

As manufacturers have promoted more direct relationships with their customers, the need for middlemen in the industry has dwindled and many tech product distributors went under. Tech Data was spared this fate due to its size and scope, but it continually looks to cut costs in order to survive in a business characterized by thin margins. It has also expanded its service offerings, which range from pre- and post-sale technical support to customized shipping documents and electronic commerce integration.

Tech Data announced it would buy Triade Holding, a Netherlands-based distributor of consumer electronics and IT products, in August 2010. The purchase will expand Tech Data's reach in Denmark and the Benelux region, as well as support its operations across Europe by adding new speciality products, vendors, and customers. As part of the transaction, Tech Data's joint venture with Brightstar, Brightstar Europe, will acquire Triade subsidiary Mobile Communication Company, a mobility products distributor in Benelux.

The company previously increased its presence in Northern Europe with the purchase of Swedish technology distributor Scribona Nordic for $78 million in 2008.

HISTORY

Tech Data grew out of an electronics distribution business founded by Edward Raymund, a University of Southern California graduate who started out as a representative for electronics manufacturers. By the early 1960s he had established an industrial electronics distribution business in Florida. In 1974 he incorporated that business as Tech Data.

In 1981 Raymund's 25-year-old son, Steven, who had earned master's degrees in economics and international politics from Georgetown University's School of Foreign Service, joined Tech Data on a temporary basis to work on the company's catalog. At that time Tech Data sold diskettes and other computer supplies to local companies and had about $2 million in sales.

Steven Raymund's favored status at the company angered a group of managers. Shortly after he arrived at Tech Data, they copied the company's client list and walked out. The defection nearly sank Tech Data, but Steven Raymund stayed on when his father handed him two-thirds of the company.

With the PC industry beginning to take off, Steven Raymund positioned Tech Data as a middleman between computer and peripheral manufacturers and resellers. Steven was named COO in 1984. He became CEO in 1986, the year the company went public.

In 1990 fast growth strained Tech Data's resources, and earnings slumped. The company cut inventory and management costs. The following year Steven Raymund became chairman when his father retired.

Tech Data began to distribute software in 1992, and a year later the company signed up Microsoft and inked a distribution deal for IBM computer systems. In 1994 Tech Data purchased U.S. Software Resource, a California-based distributor of more than 500 business and entertainment software titles, thereby increasing its software list and gaining high-profile publishers such as Borland International (now Borland Software) and Corel as suppliers. Also in 1994 Tech Data began a global expansion when it bought France's largest distributor of wholesale computer products, Softmart International.

Tech Data won US distribution rights for Apple subsidiary Claris (now named FileMaker) and its software line in 1995. The company one-upped its rivals that year when, through a deal with MCI (later part of WorldCom), it became the first distributor to resell telephone line service employing advanced data transmission technologies. Tech Data resellers packaged line services with their computer networks; the resellers and Tech Data earned monthly usage fees on the services.

Tech Data in 1998 bought VIAG AG's majority stake in European distributor Computer 2000 for about $390 million. (To avoid geographic overlap, the company sold its controlling stake in Germany-based Macrotron, acquired in 1997, to rival Ingram Micro.) Also in 1998 Tech Data began direct assembly and shipping at its distribution centers. In 1999 the company inked an estimated $2 billion outsourcing deal with GE Capital and expanded its Canadian presence with the purchase of Globelle Corporation.

In 2000 the company purchased the remainder of Computer 2000 and expanded its outsourcing offerings with a new business division. The next year Tech Data introduced an online software license purchasing and upgrade program; it also cut about 20% of its staff to keep costs down.

Tech Data broadened its menu of outsourcing services and added to its international operations with the acquisition of the UK's Azlan Group in 2003.

In 2006 the company named Robert Dutkowsky, a veteran of data center infrastructure specialist Egenera, as its CEO; Steven Raymund retained his chairmanship.

EXECUTIVES

Chairman: Steven A. (Steve) Raymund, age 54
CEO and Director: Robert M. (Bob) Dutkowsky, age 55, $4,568,139 total compensation
EVP and CIO: John Tonnison
EVP, CFO, and Director: Jeffery P. (Jeff) Howells, age 53, $2,268,661 total compensation
SVP and Controller: Joseph B. (Joe) Trepani, age 49, $941,199 total compensation
SVP US Sales: Pete Peterson
SVP US Marketing and Vendor Partner Relations: Joseph H. (Joe) Quaglia
SVP Real Estate and Corporate Services: Benjamin B. (Ben) Godwin, age 55
SVP and Treasurer: Charles V. Dannewitz, age 55
SVP, General Counsel, and Secretary: David R. (Dave) Vetter, age 50
SVP US Purchasing and Supply Chain Management: Brooke D. Powers
VP Client Systems Product Marketing: Greg Parsonson
VP Software Product Marketing: Stacy Nethercoat
VP Human Resources, The Americas: Caryl N. Lucarelli
VP Marketing Services: Katie Dumala
VP Networking: John O'Shea
President, Europe: Néstor Cano, age 46, $2,504,037 total compensation
President, Americas: Murray Wright
President, Canada: Rick Reid
Director Investor Relations and Shareholder Services: Arleen Quinones
Auditors: Ernst & Young LLP

LOCATIONS

HQ: Tech Data Corporation
   5350 Tech Data Dr., Clearwater, FL 33760
Phone: 727-539-7429   **Fax:** 727-538-7803
Web: www.techdata.com

2010 Sales

	$ mil.	% of total
Europe	12,529.8	57
Americas	9,570.1	43
Total	**22,099.9**	**100**

PRODUCTS/OPERATIONS

2010 Sales

	% of total
Peripherals	35
Systems	31
Networking	17
Software	17
Total	**100**

2010 Sales by Channel

	% of total
VARs	50
Direct marketers & retailers	30
Corporate resellers	20
Total	**100**

COMPETITORS

Agilysys	Ingram Micro
ARQUES Industries	Integralis
Arrow Electronics	MA Laboratories
ASI Computer	MicroAge
Technologies	New Age Electronics
Avnet	Optical Laser
Bell Microproducts	ScanSource
Black Box	SED International
Communications Supply	Softmart
CompuCom	Software House
D&H Distributing	International
Dell	SYNNEX
GTSI	Westcon
IBM	ZT Group
IKON	

HISTORICAL FINANCIALS

Company Type: Public

Income Statement

FYE: January 31

	REVENUE ($ mil.)	NET INCOME ($ mil.)	NET PROFIT MARGIN	EMPLOYEES
1/10	22,100	180	0.8%	7,600
1/09	24,081	124	0.5%	8,000
1/08	23,423	108	0.5%	8,300
1/07	21,440	(97)	—	8,000
1/06	20,483	27	0.1%	8,200
Annual Growth	**1.9%**	**61.3%**	**—**	**(1.9%)**

2010 Year-End Financials

Debt ratio: 16.2%	No. of shares (mil.): 51
Return on equity: 9.5%	Dividends
Cash ($ mil.): 1,117	Yield: —
Current ratio: 1.66	Payout: —
Long-term debt ($ mil.): 338	Market value ($ mil.): 2,067

Stock History

NASDAQ (GS): TECD

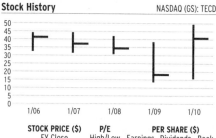

	STOCK PRICE ($) FY Close	P/E High/Low		PER SHARE ($) Earnings	Dividends	Book Value
1/10	40.75	14	5	3.54	—	41.18
1/09	18.11	16	6	2.40	—	33.90
1/08	34.38	21	16	1.96	—	37.87
1/07	37.14	—	—	(1.76)	—	33.57
1/06	41.23	97	73	0.45	—	34.71
Annual Growth	**(0.3%)**	**—**	**—**	**67.5%**	**—**	**4.4%**

Telephone & Data Systems

One of the top US phone companies without a regional Bell lineage, Telephone and Data Systems (TDS) has more than 7 million local phone and wireless customers in 36 states. The company's core business unit, United States Cellular, serves about 6 million customers in 26 states; key markets are located in the central and mid-Atlantic regions of the US. The company also offers fixed-line and Internet services in rural and suburban markets in several states through its TDS Telecommunications (TDS Telecom) and TDS Metrocom subsidiaries. TDS Telecom provides local service through more than 1 million access lines in 30 states.

In the future, the company hopes to grow its operations by strengthening its cellular business in its existing markets and by expanding into adjacent markets. It has also expressed intentions to begin offering new services such as Voice over Internet Protocol (VoIP) through its fixed-line business.

Through subsidiary TDS Telecom, the company expanded its service area in rural New Hampshire when it bought Farmington-based Union Telephone Company in late 2009. The deal brought the number of phone companies in the state owned by TDS up to five. The next year, the company bought Minneapolis-based data center and managed hosting services provider VISI Incorporated in a move to broaden its network and data service portolio for business customers and increase its presence in the state. The VISI business will be overseen by TDS Telecom.

Aside from its core telecom operations, TDS also has an 80% interest in commercial printing business Suttle-Straus, which provides corporate communications, direct mail, advertising materials, and distribution services to customers primarily in the midwestern US.

Founder and chairman emeritus LeRoy Carlson and his family occupy the top executive and directorial spots and control more than half of the company's voting power.

HISTORY

LeRoy Carlson learned the ins and outs of rural phone operators when he owned a small firm that supplied equipment and forms to independent phone companies. In the mid-1950s he began buying some of these small phone companies, which he consolidated with a phone book publisher and his equipment company to form Telephones Inc. Carlson sold the company to Contel in 1966.

Carlson continued to buy and sell rural carriers, allowing them to retain local management while he provided centralized purchasing and system upgrades. In 1969 he bought 10 rural providers in Wisconsin and consolidated all of his companies into Telephone and Data Systems (TDS).

Between 1970 and 1975 TDS acquired 32 rural phone companies. When smaller companies in its established regions became scarce, TDS bought rural phone providers from large independents. As TDS diversified, the wireline subsidiary became TDS Telecommunications.

The company began offering paging services in Wisconsin in 1972 and later created subsidiary American Paging (1981). In 1975 TDS moved into cable TV service, eventually creating TDS Cable Communications (1984), but it sold the holdings in 1986.

Getting a head start on the big Bells in the cellular race, TDS began seeking licenses in the early 1980s, eventually winning a 5% stake in the Los Angeles market. Although buffeted by larger independents, it placed a high priority on cellular operations and formed subsidiary United States Cellular Corporation (now doing business as U.S. Cellular) in 1983. Two years later the subsidiary launched services in Tennessee and Oklahoma.

Carlson named his son, LeRoy Jr., to replace him as CEO in 1986 but remained chairman. TDS reduced its ownership in U.S. Cellular to about 80% in 1988 when it took the subsidiary public. Coditel, a Belgian cable TV company, secured a minority stake in U.S. Cellular that year.

In 1993 TDS created subsidiary American Portable Telecom to bid for the new PCS wireless licenses. Three years later the subsidiary, renamed Aerial Communications, went public; TDS kept an 82% stake. Aerial began providing PCS service in 1997.

Expansion, financed mainly through stock, caused Michael Price's Franklin Mutual Advisers to complain that its shares were undervalued. To gain more leverage with management, in 1997 Franklin organized a proxy contest to gain a seat on the board, and veteran private investor Martin Solomon was elected.

That year, in response to investor demand for more liquidity, TDS planned to buy the shares in U.S. Cellular and Aerial that it didn't already own and to create three tracking stocks for its cellular, PCS, and wireline phone units. However, TDS withdrew the proposal in 1998 because of poor market conditions. That year it acquired the 18% of American Paging that it didn't own and joined the company with TSR Paging. The deal left TDS with a 30% stake in the new TSR Wireless (but the company ceased operations in 2000 and declared bankruptcy).

Sonera Group (formerly Telecom Finland) acquired a significant minority stake in Aerial when it invested $200 million in the company in 1998. That year TDS made plans to spin off Aerial in an effort to raise cash. However, TDS dropped the idea and sold its Aerial stake to VoiceStream Wireless for $1.8 billion in 2000. TDS took a 14% stake in VoiceStream, which it swapped to Deutsche Telekom for cash and stock in 2001.

To add to its holdings, in 2001 Telephone and Data Systems bought Wisconsin local telephone service provider Chorus Communications for $195 million and $30 million in assumed debt. The next year the company acquired two local phone service providers in New Hampshire.

EXECUTIVES

Chairman Emeritus: LeRoy T. Carlson Sr., age 93, $1,374,785 total compensation
Chairman: Walter C. D. Carlson, age 56
President, CEO, and Board Member: LeRoy T. (Ted) Carlson Jr., age 63, $6,316,091 total compensation
EVP, CFO, and Board Member: Kenneth R. (Ken) Meyers, age 56, $3,100,713 total compensation
SVP Acquisitions and Corporate Development: Scott H. Williamson, age 59, $2,355,070 total compensation
SVP and Corporate Controller: Douglas D. Shuma, age 48
SVP and CIO: Kurt B. Thaus, age 51
VP Internal Audit: Frieda E. Ireland, age 54
VP Technology Planning and Services: Joseph R. Hanley, age 43
VP Acquisitions and Corporate Development: Kenneth M. Kotylo, age 45
VP Corporate Relations: Jane W. McCahon
VP and Corporate Secretary: Kevin C. Gallagher
VP Corporate Development: Bryon A. Wertz, age 60
VP and Treasurer: Peter L. Sereda, age 48
VP Corporate Finance: James W. Twesme, age 54
VP Human Resources: C. Theodore Herbert, age 74
President and CEO, TDS Telecommunications Corporation: David A. (Dave) Wittwer, age 49, $1,863,852 total compensation
President and CEO, United States Cellular Corporation: Mary N. Dillon, age 48
Auditors: PricewaterhouseCoopers LLP

LOCATIONS

HQ: Telephone and Data Systems, Inc.
30 N. LaSalle St., Ste. 4000, Chicago, IL 60602
Phone: 312-630-1900 **Fax:** 312-630-1908
Web: www.teldta.com

PRODUCTS/OPERATIONS

Selected Subsidiaries and Affiliates

Suttle-Straus, Inc. (commercial printing)
TDS Telecommunications Corporation (wireline phone services)
TDS Metrocom, LLC (competitive local-exchange carrier)
United States Cellular Corporation (cellular phone service)

COMPETITORS

AT&T
CenturyTel
NTELOS
Sprint Nextel
T-Mobile USA
Verizon

HISTORICAL FINANCIALS

Company Type: Public

Income Statement				FYE: December 31
	REVENUE ($ mil.)	NET INCOME ($ mil.)	NET PROFIT MARGIN	EMPLOYEES
12/09	5,021	254	5.1%	12,400
12/08	5,092	94	1.8%	8,470
12/07	4,829	343	7.1%	11,800
12/06	4,365	162	3.7%	11,800
12/05	3,960	223	5.6%	11,500
Annual Growth	6.1%	3.3%	—	1.9%

2009 Year-End Financials

Debt ratio: 39.5%
Return on equity: 6.7%
Cash ($ mil.): 671
Current ratio: 2.11
Long-term debt ($ mil.): 1,493
No. of shares (mil.): 105
Dividends
 Yield: 1.3%
 Payout: 24.3%
Market value ($ mil.): 3,564

Stock History NYSE: TDS

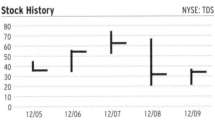

	STOCK PRICE ($) FY Close	P/E High/Low		PER SHARE ($) Earnings	Dividends	Book Value
12/09	33.92	20	12	1.77	0.43	35.95
12/08	31.75	83	27	0.80	0.41	35.86
12/07	62.60	23	16	3.22	0.39	37.37
12/06	54.33	40	26	1.37	0.37	33.98
12/05	36.03	23	19	1.91	0.35	31.89
Annual Growth	(1.5%)	—	—	(1.9%)	5.3%	3.0%

Tellabs, Inc.

Tellabs provides communications service providers with the nuts and bolts of networks. The company's equipment is used around the world to transmit data, video, and voice signals. Its broadband network access and transport systems enable carriers to build fiber-optic backbone networks, while its digital cross-connect systems help connect incoming and outgoing digital and fiber-optic lines. Tellabs also provides such services as product deployment, training, and technical support. The company's customers include incumbent local telephone carriers, including the regional phone service providers, cable companies, corporations, and government agencies.

The company turned a profit in 2009, despite a double digit drop in revenue, after reporting a fiscal loss in 2008. It cited reduced overall spending by customers resulting from the economic downturn as a contributing factor to its losses for 2008. Tellabs credits the dramatic reduction of its operating expenses among reasons for the improvement in 2009.

Tellabs is putting much of its R&D effort into products that address the growing market for wireless Internet services, driven by users of smartphones and mobile computers. The strategy has paid off as the company has seen sales of wireless data-centric products increase.

The company used the 2009 acquisition of WiChorus for about $165 million in cash to supplement its R&D efforts. WiChorus makes the SmartCore mobile packet core platform, which supports fourth-generation (4G) wireless data communications standards, like Long Term Evolution (LTE) and WiMAX, as well as the 3G standards currently in place. Tellabs said SmartCore offers faster speeds and more simultaneous connections for mobile Internet users.

Tellabs' largest customers — AT&T and Verizon — account for about half of its sales. The company makes around one-third of its sales to customers outside North America. Tellabs primarily sells directly to customers, particularly in the US, but it also works with distributors, resellers, and systems integrators.

HISTORY

Tellabs (shortened from Telecommunications Laboratories) was founded in 1975 by Michael Birck, Charles Cooney, and several others. Birck was an Indiana farm boy who later became a Bell Labs engineer before working at Continental Telephone and telecommunications equipment manufacturer Wescom. At nascent Tellabs, Birck developed an echo suppressor on the company's homemade plywood workbench. (Echo suppressors improve the quality of long-distance calls by eliminating voice echoes caused by slight transmission delays.) Before long the increased use of satellites for phone transmission had created a growth market for the product, and sales jumped from $300,000 in Tellabs' first year to almost $8 million in 1977. AT&T competitor Western Union became one of the company's first major customers.

Tellabs went public in 1980. When the creation of the regional Bell companies and several long-distance services providers in the mid-1980s led to a surge of competition, Tellabs

boosted R&D spending and refocused on high-end products. It entered the data communications market in 1983. However, cost overruns and delays in development of its TITAN long-distance routing system threatened to sink the company, and TITAN was jokingly compared with the *Titanic*.

In 1987 a $10 million contract from Sprint for digital echo cancelers helped revive Tellabs, which began marketing to overseas telecom service providers and making acquisitions, including Delta Communications (Ireland, 1987). Birck's faith in Tellabs bore fruit in 1991, when the company finally introduced its TITAN line.

Tellabs shifted its focus from the mature North American market to central and eastern Europe. In 1993 the company acquired Martis Oy, a Finnish maker of multiplexers. It debuted the CABLESPAN distribution system in 1994. Tellabs purchased wireless network system maker Steinbrecher Corp. and synchronous optical network (SONET) technology from Canadian firm TRANSYS Networks in 1996. The next year it bought multiplexing and optical networking technology from IBM and increased its push into Latin America.

In 1998 Tellabs bought Coherent Communications Systems (now Tellabs Virginia, voice enhancement products). It called off its deal (originally valued at about $7 billion) to acquire telecom equipment maker Ciena after a key Ciena contract fell through. Also in 1998, Bell Atlantic awarded Tellabs a five-year contract as its sole supplier of SONET-based digital cross-connect systems. Tellabs sales rose nearly 38% in 1998, partly on the strength of the once-disparaged TITAN line.

Tellabs in 1999 won supply agreements with telecom operators in Brazil and Mexico, and it opened a factory in Ireland. Also that year Tellabs acquired Internet backbone specialist NetCore. Continuing its push for globalization, it also bought the European high-speed telephone networking equipment operations of Alcatel USA (formerly DSC Communications). In 2000 the company acquired privately held telephony switch maker SALIX. Later that year Birck turned over the day-to-day operations of Tellabs to former Ameritech chief Richard Notebaert, who became president and CEO. Birck remained chairman.

In 2001 Tellabs closed facilities and laid off about 30% of its staff, amid slow sales. In 2002 Tellabs acquired privately held Ocular Networks. In 2004 the company acquired network access product maker Advanced Fibre Communications (AFC) in a cash and stock deal valued at $1.5 billion.

EXECUTIVES

Chairman: Michael J. Birck, age 72
President, CEO, and Director: Robert W. (Rob) Pullen, age 47, $2,600,264 total compensation
EVP and CFO: Timothy J. Wiggins, age 53, $1,404,014 total compensation
EVP and CTO: Vikram R. Saksena, age 53, $1,784,693 total compensation
EVP Global Operations: John M. Brots, age 49, $841,510 total compensation
EVP Global Product: Daniel P. (Dan) Kelly, age 48, $1,253,962 total compensation
EVP, General Counsel, Secretary, and Chief Administrative Officer: James M. (Jim) Sheehan, age 47, $1,059,156 total compensation
EVP and CIO: Jean K. Holley, age 51
EVP Global Sales and Services: Roger J. Heinz, age 47
EVP Global Marketing: Rizwan Khan, age 43
SVP Mobile Internet: Rehan Jalil

VP, China: Chenhong Huang
VP and General Manager, Transport Products: Mark Pashan
VP Government Systems: Joseph Shilgalis
VP and General Manager, Global Customer Service: Rich Tatara
VP Product Development, Finland: Mika Heikkinen
VP, North America Sales: Charles S. (Chuck) Bernstein
VP Finance and Chief Accounting Officer: Thomas P. Minichiello
Senior Manager Investor Relations: Tom Scottino
Auditors: Ernst & Young LLP

LOCATIONS

HQ: Tellabs, Inc.
1415 W. Diehl Rd., Naperville, IL 60563
Phone: 630-798-8800   **Fax:** 630-798-2000
Web: www.tellabs.com

2009 Sales

	$ mil.	% of total
North America	1,005.3	66
Other regions	520.4	34
Total	**1,525.7**	**100**

PRODUCTS/OPERATIONS

2009 Sales

	$ mil.	% of total
Broadband	785.8	52
Transport	509.6	33
Services	230.3	15
Total	**1,525.7**	**100**

Selected Operations

Products
  Access networking systems
  Broadband data systems
  Digital cross-connects
  Transport switching
  Voice-quality enhancement
Services
  Engineering
  Installation and integration
  Maintenance
  Material procurement
  Program management
  Technical assistance

COMPETITORS

ADTRAN	Huawei Technologies
ADVA	Juniper Networks
Alcatel-Lucent	Network Equipment
Ciena	Technologies
Cisco Systems	Nokia Siemens Networks
Ditech	Samsung
ECI Telecom	Telecommunications
Ericsson	America
Fujitsu Network	UTStarcom
Communications	ZTE

HISTORICAL FINANCIALS

Company Type: Public

Income Statement

FYE: Friday nearest Dec. 31

	REVENUE ($ mil.)	NET INCOME ($ mil.)	NET PROFIT MARGIN	EMPLOYEES
12/09	1,526	114	7.4%	3,295
12/08	1,729	(930)	—	3,228
12/07	1,913	65	3.4%	3,716
12/06	2,041	194	9.5%	3,713
12/05	1,883	176	9.3%	3,609
Annual Growth	**(5.1%)**	**(10.3%)**	**—**	**(2.2%)**

2009 Year-End Financials

Debt ratio: 0.4%
Return on equity: 6.0%
Cash ($ mil.): 154
Current ratio: 3.11
Long-term debt ($ mil.): 7

No. of shares (mil.): 381
Dividends
Yield: —
Payout: —
Market value ($ mil.): 2,166

Stock History

NASDAQ (GS): TLAB

	STOCK PRICE ($) FY Close	P/E High/Low		PER SHARE ($) Earnings	Dividends	Book Value
12/09	5.68	27	12	0.29	—	5.02
12/08	4.12	—	—	(2.32)	—	4.84
12/07	6.54	91	43	0.15	—	7.64
12/06	10.26	40	21	0.43	—	7.70
12/05	10.90	29	17	0.39	—	7.38
Annual Growth	(15.0%)	—	—	(7.1%)	—	(9.2%)

Temple-Inland

Whether you have something to box or something to build, Temple-Inland has it covered. One of North America's top producers of corrugated packaging, the company also makes building products for residential and commercial construction. It manufactures fiberboard, gypsum wallboard, lumber, and particleboard panels. Its corrugated packaging segment, which accounts for the majority of sales, makes containerboard boxes for agricultural and industrial use, linerboard, retail displays, and specialty wood and foam containers.

Supplying corrugated packaging to customers within its manufacturing footprint is Temple-Inland's bread and butter. Brown boxes, bulk containers, and related products are sold predominantly to US customers in the chemical, food, glass container, household appliance, paper, and plastics industries — sectors all hurt by the economic recession and credit crisis rampant in 2008 and 2009. Albeit a less significant market, core customers of its building products have fared poorly, too, including distributors and retailers, as well as OEMs operating in the construction repair and remodeling markets.

Temple-Inland has responded to the tough times by doing more with less. It cut operating costs, largely through box plant improvements that increased production and energy efficiency, and workforce reductions (more than 20% in two years). Temple-Inland's bottom line also received a $213 million boost from an alternative fuel mixture tax credit allowed by the Internal Revenue Service for mixing diesel with an alternative fuel to run its operations.

Temple-Inland has lessened its exposure to the volatile housing market, as well, by driving a portion of its building products through a 50-50 joint venture, Del-Tin Fiber, which produces Temple-Inland medium density fiberboard. Its

shift also aims to leverage a $62 million investment made in 2008 for Premier Boxboard LLC (PBL), a former 50-50 joint venture with Caraustar Industries. PBL manufactures containerboard (white top linerboard) and gypsum facing paper — lines that have continued to sell during the economic downturn.

In 2007 the company split three of its former operations into stand-alone public companies; the corrugated packaging and building products remained as Temple-Inland businesses, with Guaranty Financial Group and Forestar Real Estate Group leaving the group. Temple-Inland also netted more than $2 billion that year by selling off its timberland.

HISTORY

Temple-Inland dates back to 1893, when Thomas Temple, a native Virginian, purchased 7,000 acres of Texas timberland from J. C. Diboll. Temple founded Southern Pine Lumber and built his mill in the town of Diboll, Texas. In 1894 he opened his first sawmill. The company set up a second sawmill in 1903 and a hardwood mill in 1907. Temple formed the Temple Lumber Company three years later. When Temple died in 1934, his son, Arthur, inherited a company heavily in debt. In 1937 a fire destroyed the company's sawmill in Hemphill, Texas.

The Temple family's Southern Pine business fared better, producing basic hardwood and pine lumber items for the construction and furniture industries during the housing boom following WWII. By the early 1950s the company had begun converting chips, sawdust, and shavings into panel products. The company subsequently pioneered southern pine plywood production and branched into making particleboard, gypsum wallboard, and other building materials. Temple Lumber merged with Southern Pine Lumber in 1956 under the Southern Pine name. In 1962 Southern Pine moved into finance with the purchase of the controlling interest of Lumbermen's Investment.

The company changed its name to Temple Industries in 1964. It expanded in the early 1970s by opening a particleboard mill in Diboll in 1971 and acquiring AFCO, a manufacturer of do-it-yourself products, in 1972. The next year media titan Time Inc. acquired Temple Industries and merged it with Eastex Pulp and Paper, creating Temple-Eastex. Time bought Inland Container, a fully integrated packaging company, in 1978 for $272 million.

Inland traces its roots back to 1918, when Herman Krannert started Anderson Box Company in Indiana to make ventilated corrugated products for baby chicks. It had grown into a major manufacturer of packaging materials for the agricultural, horticultural, and poultry industries.

Time spun off the Temple and Inland operations as Temple-Inland in 1983. The company expanded its financial businesses in the late 1980s by acquiring a Kansas insurance company (1985) and three insolvent Texas S&Ls (1988).

Following the retirement of Arthur Temple Jr., Temple-Inland appointed Clifford Grum as chairman and CEO (the first non-family chairman) in 1991. Temple-Inland grew by adding plants and resources. In 1994 it bought Rand-Whitney Packaging. It expanded its Latin American production capacity in 1995 with the opening of a box plant in Chile and a corrugated container sheet facility in Mexico. In 1996 it bought a wallboard plant and gypsum quarry in

Texas with joint venture partner Caraustar Industries (building products).

Temple-Inland acquired California Financial Holding and Knutson Mortgage in 1997. In 1999 it paid $120 million for HF Bancorp (parent of California's 18-branch Hemet Federal Savings and Loan), which became part of Guaranty Federal Bank. The company also sold its bleached-paperboard mill in Evadale, Texas, to forestry product company Westvaco for $625 million.

CFO Kenneth Jastrow became CEO in 2000. In April 2002 the company acquired Gaylord Container, a maker of paper packaging products, in a deal that included about $65 million in Temple-Inland stock and the assumption of $847 million in Gaylord debt.

Between mid-2003 and the end of 2004 the company closed seven converting plants and axed more than 300 jobs, and in October 2004 Temple-Inland announced that it would eliminate 1,500 jobs. Late in 2005 it announced that it would cut a further 250 jobs by restructuring its Financial Services unit.

In 2007 Temple-Inland announced a restructuring initiative in which it would spin off its real estate and finance businesses into two new public entities while retaining its packaging and building products manufacturing operations.

The company initiative was launched shortly after breakup and spinoff rumors surfaced when famed corporate raider Carl Icahn announced plans to nominate four new directors. Icahn dropped the proxy battle effort after Temple-Inland announced its restructuring plans.

EXECUTIVES

Chairman and CEO: Doyle R. Simons, age 46, $5,616,171 total compensation
President, COO, and Director: J. Patrick Maley III, age 48, $4,942,445 total compensation
CFO and Treasurer: Randall D. Levy, age 58, $2,423,922 total compensation
CIO: Scott Smith, age 55
Chief Administrative Officer: J. Bradley Johnston, age 54
Chief Governance Officer: Grant F. Adamson, age 51
Chief Accounting Officer and Corporate Controller: Troy L. Hester, age 53
General Counsel: C. Morris Davis, age 67
SVP and Secretary: Leslie K. O'Neal, age 54
Group VP: Larry C. Norton, age 50, $2,028,807 total compensation
Group VP: Dennis J. Vesci, age 62, $2,804,523 total compensation
VP Investor Relations and Treasury: Chris Mathis, age 36
VP Internal Audit: Carolyn C. Ferguson
Auditors: Ernst & Young LLP

LOCATIONS

HQ: Temple-Inland Inc.
1300 S. Mopac Expwy., 3rd Fl., Austin, TX 78746
Phone: 512-434-5800   **Fax:** 512-434-3750
Web: www.templeinland.com

2009 Sales

	$ mil.	% of total
US	3,379	94
Mexico	198	6
Total	3,577	100

PRODUCTS/OPERATIONS

2009 Sales

	$ mil.	% of total
Corrugated packaging	3,001	84
Building products	576	16
Total	3,577	100

HISTORICAL FINANCIALS

Company Type: Public

Income Statement — FYE: Saturday nearest December 31

	REVENUE ($ mil.)	NET INCOME ($ mil.)	NET PROFIT MARGIN	EMPLOYEES
12/09	3,577	207	5.8%	11,000
12/08	3,884	(8)	—	11,000
12/07	3,926	1,305	33.2%	12,000
12/06	5,558	468	8.4%	15,500
12/05	4,888	176	3.6%	15,500
Annual Growth	(7.5%)	4.1%	—	(8.2%)

2009 Year-End Financials

Debt ratio: 89.4%
Return on equity: 28.0%
Cash ($ mil.): 36
Current ratio: 2.11
Long-term debt ($ mil.): 710

No. of shares (mil.): 108
Dividends
  Yield: 1.9%
  Payout: 21.2%
Market value ($ mil.): 2,271

Stock History

NYSE: TIN

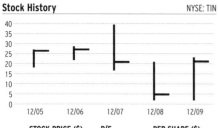

	STOCK PRICE ($) FY Close	P/E High/Low		PER SHARE ($) Earnings	Dividends	Book Value
12/09	21.11	12	1	1.89	0.40	7.38
12/08	4.80	—	—	(0.08)	0.40	6.38
12/07	20.85	3	1	12.08	1.12	7.25
12/06	27.06	7	5	4.22	1.00	20.35
12/05	26.36	17	12	1.54	0.90	19.33
Annual Growth	(5.4%)	—	—	5.3%	(18.4%)	(21.4%)

Tenet Healthcare

Tenet Healthcare is here to spread the doctrine of good health. The for-profit company owns or leases about 50 acute care hospitals with roughly 14,000 beds in a dozen US states. The majority of Tenet's hospitals (60%) are in California, Florida, and Texas. The hospitals range from small community facilities offering basic care to major teaching and research hospitals. In addition to its acute care holdings, Tenet also operates specialty hospitals, skilled nursing facilities, physician practices, outpatient centers, and other health care facilities that form regional networks around its main hospitals.

Although the company is slowly beginning to see some improvements, Tenet has been hit by declining patient volumes during the past few years, in part, due to increased competition between health care providers to recruit physicians and attract patients.

Tenet has stepped up doctor recruitment efforts and has implemented a number of quality initiatives to lure in doctors and patients. It has also negotiated managed care contracts with national HMO and PPO companies that account for about $5 billion (or more than half) of its annual revenue.

Despite its success with negotiating managed care contracts, Tenet, like most other hospital operators, has seen an increase in uninsured patients (which often results in more services being written off as unpaid or bad debt) as a direct result of the nation's high rate of unemployment over the past few years.

To finance its various capital improvement programs (and offset some of the financial losses related to the increase in uninsured patients) Tenet has shed low-performing hospitals. In recent years it has sold or closed five hospitals in California and one in Florida. In 2009 it also sold the USC University Hospital and Kenneth Norris Jr. Cancer Hospital to the University of Southern California for $275 million.

While Tenet is shedding holdings that aren't performing well, it is expanding where it sees room for growth. The company opened a 100-bed general hospital in El Paso, Texas, and is building another in Fort Mill, South Carolina.

Tenet has also been making money outside the hospital, by spinning off logistics firm Broadlane, selling its stake in Medicare Advantage provider People's Health Network, and forming Conifer Health Solutions, a patient billing and communications company, that serves Tenet and other hospitals.

HISTORY

Hospital attorney Richard Eamer, along with attorneys Leonard Cohen and John Bedrosian, founded National Medical Enterprises (NME) in 1969. After its IPO, NME bought 10 hospitals, nursing homes, an office building, and land in California. Within six years the company owned, operated, and managed 23 hospitals and a home health care business. It sold medical equipment and bottled oxygen, and provided vocational training for nurses.

In the 1970s NME expanded into hospital construction and bought five Florida hospitals. By 1981 NME was the #3 health care concern in the US, owning or managing 193 hospitals and nursing homes. In the 1980s NME diversified further, buying nursing homes and mental health

centers. By the end of the decade the company's Specialty Hospital Group brought in more than 50% of revenues. NME was the second-largest publicly owned health care company in the US (after HCA) by 1985.

In 1990 NME reversed course, spinning off most of its long-term-care businesses, but kept 19 UK nursing facilities operated by its Westminster Health Care subsidiary (sold 1996). In 1992 the company acquired an Australian hospital management firm.

That year several insurance companies sued NME, alleging fraudulent psychiatric claims; NME settled the suits in 1993. Federal agents later raided company headquarters, seizing papers related to the suspected fraud. That year investment banker Jeff Barbakow took over as CEO, forcing out Eamer and Cohen.

In 1993 and 1994 NME dumped most of its psychiatric and rehabilitation facilities, using the proceeds to help pay penalties stemming from the federal investigation into alleged insurance fraud, kickbacks, and patient abuse at its psychiatric facilities. NME paid another $16 million in related state fines. (Related civil lawsuits were settled in 1997.)

The company's name change to Tenet Healthcare coincided with new purchases throughout the South in 1995 and 1996.

In 1998 the company was dogged by another investigation, this time by the Health and Human Services Inspector General's office over allegations the company paid more than fair market value for a physician practice in return for kickbacks. Tenet in 2004 agreed to pay around $31 million to settle two lawsuits stemming from these allegations.

Like many companies in the industry, in 1999 Tenet began feeling the effects of the Balanced Budget Act of 1997, which mandated more scrutiny of Medicare expenditures to health care providers. In response, the company began divesting some of its hospitals; it also shed its practice management business.

Federal investigations into the company's billing practices, particularly those related to Medicare, began late in 2002. In 2003 the company settled claims brought by the Department of Justice that doctors performed unnecessary cardiac surgeries at its Redding Medical Center (now Shasta Regional Medical Center) in California; the settlement cost Tenet $54 million (plus millions more to settle patients' claims).

An even larger sell-off began in 2004 and included nearly 20 hospitals in California and others in Louisiana, Massachusetts, Missouri, and Texas. Additionally, Tenet sold about a dozen home health agencies and hospice providers to Amedisys. The company moved its headquarters from Santa Barbara, California, to Dallas in 2005.

Tenet saw some hard times in 2005 and spent years struggling to emerge from several subsequent years of investigations, lawsuits, and bad publicity. Its New Orleans and Mississippi facilities were hit hard by Hurricane Katrina in 2005, and its Memorial Medical Hospital in New Orleans became a symbol of the city's devastation after several dozen bodies were found there in the aftermath of the storm. The company has since sold both locations.

In 2006 it resolved multiple federal investigations regarding its billing practices by agreeing to a $900 million deal with the Justice Department. Its sale of hospitals post-Katrina was part of a larger plan announced in 2006 to sell off about a dozen facilities, ridding itself of some low-performing operations.

EXECUTIVES

Chairman: Edward A. (Ed) Kangas, age 65
President, CEO, and Director: Trevor Fetter, age 50, $10,700,750 total compensation
COO: Stephen L. Newman, age 59, $4,764,360 total compensation
CFO: Biggs C. Porter, age 56, $2,945,356 total compensation
EVP and CIO: Stephen F. Brown, age 55
SVP, General Counsel, and Secretary: Gary K. Ruff, age 50, $1,288,172 total compensation
SVP Human Resources: Cathy Fraser, age 45, $1,222,501 total compensation
SVP and Chief Medical Officer: Kelvin A. Baggett, age 38
SVP and Chief Compliance Officer: Audrey T. Andrews, age 42
SVP Investor Relations: Thomas R. (Tom) Rice
SVP and Chief Managed Care Officer: Clint Hailey, age 45
SVP and Controller: Daniel J. (Dan) Cancelmi, age 47
VP Outpatient Services: Kyle Burtnett
VP and Treasurer: Tyler Murphy, age 39
VP Government Relations: Daniel R. Waldmann, age 41
VP Corporate Communications: Jeff Eller
Auditors: Deloitte & Touche LLP

LOCATIONS

HQ: Tenet Healthcare Corporation
1445 Ross Ave., Ste. 1400, Dallas, TX 75202
Phone: 469-893-2200 **Fax:** 469-893-8600
Web: www.tenethealth.com

PRODUCTS/OPERATIONS

2009 Sales

	% of total
Managed care	56
Medicare	25
Indemnity, self-pay & other	11
Medicaid	8
Total	**100**

COMPETITORS

Ascension Health
Banner Health
Baylor Health
Carolinas HealthCare System
Catholic Health Initiatives
Catholic Healthcare West
CHRISTUS Health
Community Health Systems
HCA
Health Management Associates
HealthSouth
Kindred Healthcare
LifePoint Hospitals
Memorial Health Services
Sisters of Mercy Health System
SSM Health Care
Sun Healthcare
Sutter Health
Universal Health Services
WellStar Health System

HISTORICAL FINANCIALS

Company Type: Public

Income Statement

FYE: December 31

	REVENUE ($ mil.)	NET INCOME ($ mil.)	NET PROFIT MARGIN	EMPLOYEES
12/09	9,014	197	2.2%	57,613
12/08	8,663	25	0.3%	60,297
12/07	8,852	(89)	—	63,264
12/06	8,701	(805)	—	68,952
12/05	9,614	(708)	—	73,434
Annual Growth	**(1.6%)**	**—**	**—**	**(5.9%)**

2009 Year-End Financials

Debt ratio: 1,369.2%	No. of shares (mil.): 485
Return on equity: 94.9%	Dividends
Cash ($ mil.): 690	Yield: 0.0%
Current ratio: 1.39	Payout: —
Long-term debt ($ mil.): 4,272	Market value ($ mil.): 2,615

Stock History

NYSE: THC

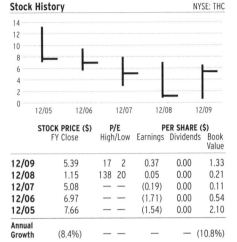

	STOCK PRICE ($) FY Close	P/E High/Low		PER SHARE ($) Earnings	Dividends	Book Value
12/09	5.39	17	2	0.37	0.00	1.33
12/08	1.15	138	20	0.05	0.00	0.21
12/07	5.08	—	—	(0.19)	0.00	0.11
12/06	6.97	—	—	(1.71)	0.00	0.54
12/05	7.66	—	—	(1.54)	0.00	2.10
Annual Growth	**(8.4%)**	**—**	**—**	**—**	**—**	**(10.8%)**

Tenneco Inc.

No Peter Fonda, Tenneco is still an easy rider, of sorts, in the automotive industry. The auto parts maker designs and distributes ride-control equipment (including shock absorbers, struts, and suspensions) under the Monroe brand and emissions-control systems (catalytic converters, exhaust pipes, and mufflers) under the Walker brand. It also makes Clevite elastomer products (bushings, mounts, and springs) for vibration control in cars and heavy trucks. Tenneco supplies both OEMs and aftermarket wholesalers and retailers.

The global economic recession coupled with tightening access to credit, begun in 2008, has continued to hammer the automotive industry and, consequently, Tenneco's performance. Tenneco has had to make a series of hard choices in its restructuring and ongoing program to reduce costs and streamline manufacturing operations. Late in 2008 the company called for furloughs and temporary pay cuts for salaried employees and eliminated temporary workers; it also closed three North American manufacturing plants and an Australian engineering facility. Simultaneously, the company has relocated several of its operations to countries such as Brazil, China, India, and Russia with lower manufacturing costs.

Along with capturing new business, Tenneco is banking on its extensive geographic footprint to smooth the way toward financial recovery. The company is among the major manufacturers of original equipment emission controls for China's rising automotive industry.

The company has also established itself as a European kingpin of supplying emission control systems. The company claims that its emission control products are used in six of the top 10 passenger cars produced for sale in Europe. Tenneco's rank in North America is as prominent;

eight of the top 10 light trucks built in North America incorporate its lines.

Tenneco is expanding its customer roster as well as zeroing in on a competitive cost base through a series of key alliances. In March 2010 Tenneco entered into a joint venture with Changchun FAW Sihuan Group (owned by FAW Group), a manufacturer of light and commercial vehicles in China. The JV — Tenneco's seventh in China and its third focused on emissions control — aims to capture a large share of the country's promising commercial vehicle demand.

Sales to the OEM market constitute nearly 80% of Tenneco's total revenues. Tenneco is working to expand its aftermarket business and develop a more balanced mix of products and markets. New lines of quick struts and brake pads have been introduced. It is also looking to ramp up sales to the heavy-duty truck, agricultural equipment, and specialty vehicle markets.

HISTORY

Tennessee Gas and Transmission began in 1943 as a division of the Chicago Corporation, headed by Gardiner Symonds and authorized to build a pipeline from West Virginia to the Gulf of Mexico. With the US facing WWII fuel shortages, the group finished the project in 11 months.

After WWII, Tennessee Gas went public with Symonds as president. It merged its oil and gas exploration interests into Tennessee Production Company (1954), which with Bay Petroleum (bought 1955) became Tenneco Oil in 1961. Symonds acquired complementary firms and entered the chemical industry by buying 50% of Petro-Tex Chemical in 1955.

Tenneco Oil moved its headquarters to Houston in 1963 to better ship natural gas from the Texas Gulf Coast. Symonds bought Packaging Corporation of America, a maker of shipping containers, pulp, and paperboard products, in 1965. A year later the company, which had become a conglomerate, adopted the Tenneco name. In 1967 it bought Kern County Land Company, which owned 2.5 million acres of California farmland and two Racine, Wisconsin, manufacturers: J. I. Case (tractors and construction equipment) and automotive firm Walker Manufacturing.

In 1968 Symonds bought Newport News Shipbuilding. The shipbuilder began making submarines and nuclear-powered aircraft carriers in the 1960s.

Symonds died in 1971. In 1977 Tenneco bought shock-absorber maker Monroe of Monroe, Michigan, and Philadelphia Life Insurance Company (sold to ICH Corporation in 1986). In 1985 it bought UK chemical company Albright & Wilson, and Case bought International Harvester's farm-equipment business. A farming recession prompted Tenneco to sell its agricultural operations in 1987. It sold its oil exploration and production business in 1988.

In the early 1990s Tenneco restructured. It sold its natural gas liquids business to Enron, its pulp chemicals business to Sterling Chemicals, and a US soda ash plant to Belgium's Solvay. It bought gas marketer EnTrade.

Under Dana Mead, a former International Paper executive appointed COO in 1992, Tenneco sold some businesses to focus on automotive parts and packaging. It divested Case through a 1994 IPO and sold the rest in 1996. In 1995 Tenneco bought Mobil's plastics division (Hefty, Baggies) for nearly $1.3 billion. In 1996 the firm spun off Newport News Shipbuilding and sold its natural gas unit to El Paso Energy for $3.7 billion.

Also in 1996 Tenneco moved to Greenwich, Connecticut; formed joint ventures in China and India; and opened a plant in Mexico. It formed a joint venture with Shanghai Automotive Industry Group to make exhaust systems in China.

In 1999 Tenneco sold 55% of its container board business to investment firm Madison Dearborn Partners for $2.2 billion, forming joint venture Packaging Corporation of America. Tenneco split into two companies in 1999, both based in Lake Forest, Illinois. Tenneco's packaging unit was spun off as Pactiv Corporation, and Tenneco was renamed Tenneco Automotive. Former president of automotive operations, Mark Frissora, became CEO that year.

In 2000, amid poor results, Tenneco Automotive announced that it would cut 700 jobs (about 16% of its workforce). In 2001 the company announced that more than 400 more jobs would be eliminated. To further cut costs and pay down debt incurred by the spinoff of Pactiv, in 2002 Tenneco Automotive announced 900 more job cuts as well as the closure of eight plants in North America and Europe.

In keeping with its strategy to transfer some manufacturing operations to low-labor-cost regions, Tenneco Automotive opened a new plant in Togliatti, Russia, in 2003. In 2004 the company said it would spend several million dollars to build an engineering center to provide support for the company's joint ventures in China.

In 2008 Tenneco acquired Gruppo Marzocchi, an Italy-based supplier of suspension products for two-wheeled vehicles.

EXECUTIVES

Chairman and CEO: Gregg M. Sherrill, age 57, $2,021,349 total compensation
COO and Director: Hari N. Nair, age 50, $721,535 total compensation
EVP and CFO: Kenneth R. Trammell, age 49, $872,680 total compensation
EVP North America: Neal A. Yanos, age 48, $859,564 total compensation
SVP and CTO: Timothy E. (Tim) Jackson, age 52, $967,964 total compensation
SVP Global Administration: Richard P. Schneider, age 62
SVP, General Counsel, and Secretary: James Harrington
SVP and General Manager, North American Original Equipment Emission Control Group: Brett J. Bauer, age 54
SVP Global Supply Chain Management and Manufacturing: Michael J. (Mike) Charlton, age 51
SVP, Europe, South America, and India: Josep Fornos, age 57
VP and Managing Director China: Patrick Guo
VP and Controller: Paul D. Novas, age 51
VP and CIO: H. William Haser, age 53
VP Global Human Resources: Barbara A. Kluth
VP Global Communications: James K. Spangler
VP Tax and Treasurer: John E. Kunz
VP North America Aftermarket: Joseph Pomaranski
VP Strategic Planning and Business Development: Maritza Gibbons
Executive Director, Global Communications: Jane Ostrander
Auditors: PricewaterhouseCoopers LLP

LOCATIONS

HQ: Tenneco Inc.
500 North Field Dr., Lake Forest, IL 60045
Phone: 847-482-5000   **Fax:** 847-482-5940
Web: www.tenneco.com

2009 Sales

	$ mil.	% of total
North America	2,092	45
Europe, South America, India	2,047	44
Asia/Pacific	510	11
Total	**4,649**	**100**

PRODUCTS/OPERATIONS

2009 Sales

	$ mil.	% of total
Emission-control systems & products		
OEM	2,604	56
Aftermarket	315	7
Ride-control systems & products		
OEM	1,009	22
Aftermarket	721	15
Total	**4,649**	**100**

Selected Brands and Products

Elastomers (Clevite)
  Engine and body mounts
  Exhaust isolators
  Leaf and coil springs
  LiteningRod
  Spring seats
  Suspension, control arm, link and stabilizer bar bushings
Emission-control systems (DNX, DynoMax, Fonos, Gillet, Thrush, and Walker)
  Catalytic converters
  Catalytic burner with secondary hydrocarbon dosing
  Cross-channel filters
  DeNOx converter aftertreatment systems
  Diesel particulate filters
  Downpipes and tailpipes
  Fabricated manifolds
  High-frequency turbo decoupler
  Manifold converters
  Mufflers
  Resonators
  Selective catalytic reduction
  Tubing
  Woven metal filter
Ride-control systems (DNX, Fric-Rot, Kinetic, Monroe, and Rancho)
  Cab shock absorbers
  Coil and leaf springs
  Computerized electronic suspension (CES)
  Corner and full axle modules
  Heavy duty truck and train shocks
  Kinetic passive stability systems
  Seat shock absorbers
  Shock absorbers and struts
  Suspensions
  Top moounts

COMPETITORS

Arvin Sango	Faurecia Exhaust Systems
ArvinMeritor	Kolbenschmidt Pierburg
Benteler Automotive	Letts Industries
Cooper-Standard	Metaldyne
Automotive	Wescast Industries
Edelbrock	ZF Group NAO
Faurecia	

HISTORICAL FINANCIALS

Company Type: Public

Income Statement

	REVENUE ($ mil.)	NET INCOME ($ mil.)	NET PROFIT MARGIN	EMPLOYEES
12/09	4,649	(54)	—	21,000
12/08	5,916	(415)	—	21,000
12/07	6,184	(5)	—	21,000
12/06	4,685	51	1.1%	19,000
12/05	4,441	58	1.3%	19,000
Annual Growth	**1.2%**	**—**	**—**	**2.5%**

FYE: December 31

2009 Year-End Financials

Debt ratio: —
Return on equity: —
Cash ($ mil.): 167
Current ratio: 1.16
Long-term debt ($ mil.): 1,145

No. of shares (mil.): 60
Dividends
  Yield: 0.0%
  Payout: —
Market value ($ mil.): 1,060

Stock History

NYSE: TEN

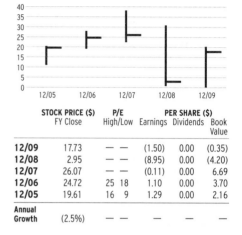

	STOCK PRICE ($) FY Close	P/E High/Low		PER SHARE ($) Earnings	Dividends	Book Value
12/09	17.73	—	—	(1.50)	0.00	(0.35)
12/08	2.95	—	—	(8.95)	0.00	(4.20)
12/07	26.07	—	—	(0.11)	0.00	6.69
12/06	24.72	25	18	1.10	0.00	3.70
12/05	19.61	16	9	1.29	0.00	2.16
Annual Growth	**(2.5%)**	**—**	**—**	**—**	**—**	**—**

Tennessee Valley Authority

The Tennessee Valley Authority (TVA) may not be an expert on Tennessee attractions like Dollywood and the Grand Ole Opry, but it is an authority on power generation. Government-owned, TVA is the largest public power producer in the US, generating more than 35,000 MW of capacity. Its facilities include 11 fossil fuel-powered plants, 29 hydroelectric dams, three nuclear plants, and six combustion turbine plants. The federal corporation transmits electricity to about 160 local distribution utilities, which serve some 9 million consumers, as well as industrial facilities and government agencies, in most of Tennessee and neighboring parts of Alabama, Georgia, Kentucky, Mississippi, North Carolina, and Virginia.

Since 1999, when government appropriations for the authority ceased, the company has funded its activities almost entirely from the sale of electricity. In addition, the TVA manages the Tennessee River system for flood control and navigation.

The TVA benefits from its exempt federal and state income tax status, nonetheless, its financial footing teeters under a $20 billion-plus debt load. Moreover, the TVA has some of the oldest generating equipment of any utility in its region. As of 2009, the average age of TVA's coal fired generation assets was 47 years. Though the agency has plans to increase maintenance expenditures in 2010, it is projecting increased downtime for several of its power plants due to their age.

Most of TVA's power comes from traditional generation sources, but the company is also exploring alternative energy technologies. In 2009, more than half of its generating capacity came from coal-fired generators, with roughly a third coming from nuclear plants. In addition, it has developed nearly 20 solar, wind, and methane gas facilities. TVA is working toward obtaining 50% of its power supply from low or zero carbon-emitting or renewable sources by 2020.

TVA has an agreement to produce tritium, a radioactive gas that boosts the power of nuclear weapons, for the US Department of Energy at its Watts Bar nuclear plant. The company plans to add three more nuclear plants by 2020 and is working with the DOE to reprocess waste from its existing plants.

Various environmental issues challenge the TVA. In 2008 a holding pond at TVA's coal-burning Kingston Fossil Plant failed and dumped some 5.4 million cu. yd. of fly ash over 400 acres in eastern Tennessee's Roane County. The slide knocked down utility poles and trees, and damaged at least a dozen homes (some beyond repair). Although no one was hurt, some residents were cut off by the spill, prompting officials to build a new road. The flooding was the pond's third reported incident in six years. The cleanup will likely cost more than $1 billion and be completed by 2013. Some 14 lawsuits are pending against the TVA as a result of the incident.

HISTORY

In 1924 the Army Corps of Engineers finished building the Wilson Dam on the Tennessee River in Alabama to provide power for two WWI-era nitrate plants. With the war over, the question of what to do with the plants became a political football.

An act of Congress created the Tennessee Valley Authority (TVA) in 1933 to manage the plants and Tennessee Valley waterways. New Dealers saw TVA as a way to revitalize the local economy through improved navigation and power generation. Power companies claimed the agency was unconstitutional, but by 1939, when a federal court ruled against them, TVA had five operating hydroelectric plants and five under construction.

During the 1940s TVA supplied power for the war effort, including the Manhattan Project in Tennessee. During the postwar boom between 1945 and 1950, power usage in the Tennessee Valley nearly doubled. Despite adding dams, TVA couldn't keep up with demand, so in 1949 it began building a coal-fired unit. Because coal-fired plants weren't part of TVA's original mission, in 1955 a Congressional panel recommended the authority be dissolved.

Though TVA survived, its funding was cut. In 1959 it was allowed to sell bonds, but it no longer received direct government appropriations for power operations. In addition, it had to pay back the government for past appropriations.

TVA began to build the first unit of an ambitious 17-plant nuclear power program in Alabama in 1967. However, skyrocketing costs forced it to raise rates and cut maintenance on its coal-fired plants, which led to breakdowns. In 1985 five reactors had to be shut down because of safety concerns.

In 1988 former auto industry executive Marvin Runyon was appointed chairman of the agency. "Carvin' Marvin" cut management, sold three airplanes, and got rid of peripheral businesses, saving $400 million a year. In 1992 Runyon left to go to the postal service and was replaced by Craven Crowell, who began preparing TVA for competition in the retail power market.

TVA ended its nuclear construction program in 1996 after bringing two nuclear units on line within three months, a first for a US utility. The

next year it raised rates for the first time in 10 years, planning to reduce its debt. In response to a lawsuit filed by neighboring utilities, it agreed to stop "laundering" power by using third parties to sell outside the agency's legally authorized area.

In 1999 the authority finished installing almost $2 billion in scrubbers and other equipment at its coal-fired plants so that it could buy Kentucky coal along with cleaner Wyoming coal. That year, however, the EPA charged TVA with violating the Clean Air Act by making major overhauls on some of its older coal-fired plants without getting permits or installing updated pollution-control equipment. It ordered TVA to bring most of its coal-fired plants into compliance with more current pollution standards. The next year TVA contested the order in court, stating compliance would jack up electricity rates.

TVA was fined by the US Nuclear Regulatory Commission in 2000 for laying off a nuclear plant whistleblower. The next year saw the beginning of a revolving door to the chairman's office — Crowell resigned in 2001, and Glenn McCullough Jr. was named chairman; he served in that role until May 2005. McCullough was replaced by Bill Baxter (who served until March 2006) and then by William Sansom (who served until February 2009). Mike Duncan served until May 2010, when Dennis Bottorff became chairman.

EXECUTIVES

Chairman: Dennis C. Bottorff, age 65
CEO: Tom D. Kilgore, age 61,
$1,163,620 total compensation
COO: William R. (Bill) McCollum Jr., age 58,
$1,795,469 total compensation
Group President: Kimberly (Kim) Scheibe-Greene,
age 43, $1,227,943 total compensation
Chief Nuclear Officer and EVP, Nuclear Power Group:
Preston D. Swafford, age 49,
$1,506,865 total compensation
EVP Administrative Services and Chief Administrative
Officer: John E. Long Jr., age 57
EVP PowerSystem Operations:
Robin E. (Rob) Manning, age 53
EVP, TVA Nuclear and Chief Nuclear Officer:
William R. (Bill) Campbell Jr., age 58
EVP Strategy and Business Planning: Van M. Wardlaw,
age 49
EVP Customer Resources: Kenneth R. Breeden, age 61
SVP, Interim CFO, and Treasurer: John M. Hoskins,
age 54
SVP Nuclear Generation Development and
Construction: Ashok S. Bhatnagar, age 53,
$1,244,939 total compensation
SVP Government Relations: Emily J. Reynolds, age 53
SVP, Fossil Operations: John J. McCormick Jr., age 48
SVP, Fossil Generation: Robert Fisher
SVP Corporate Governance and Compliance:
John M. Thomas III, age 46
SVP Office of Environment and Research: Anda A. Ray,
age 53
SVP Communications: David R. Mould, age 52
SVP Corporate Responsibility and Diversity,
Ombudsman, Chief Ethics and Compliance Officer,
and External Ombudsman: Peyton T. Hairston Jr.,
age 54
VP and CIO: Daniel Traynor
Auditors: Ernst & Young LLP

LOCATIONS

HQ: Tennessee Valley Authority
400 W. Summit Hill Dr., Knoxville, TN 37902
Phone: 865-632-2101 **Fax:** 888-633-0372
Web: www.tva.gov

2009 Sales

	$ mil.	% of total
Electricity sales		
Tennessee	6,970	62
Alabama	1,526	14
Kentucky	1,252	11
Mississippi	1,017	9
Georgia	264	2
North Carolina	58	1
Virginia	51	—
Other revenues	117	1
Total	**11,255**	**100**

PRODUCTS/OPERATIONS

2009 Sales

	$ mil.	% of total
Electricity sales		
Municipalities & cooperatives	9,644	86
Industries directly served	1,367	12
Federal agencies & other	131	1
Other revenues	113	1
Total	**11,255**	**100**

HISTORICAL FINANCIALS

Company Type: Government-owned

Income Statement				FYE: September 30
	REVENUE ($ mil.)	NET INCOME ($ mil.)	NET PROFIT MARGIN	EMPLOYEES
9/09	11,255	726	6.5%	12,219
9/08	10,382	817	7.9%	11,584
9/07	9,244	383	4.1%	12,013
9/06	9,175	329	3.6%	12,600
9/05	7,794	85	1.1%	12,703
Annual Growth	**9.6%**	**71.0%**	**—**	**(1.0%)**

Net Income History

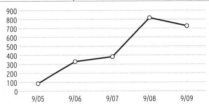

Terex Corporation

Terex lifts and digs for pay dirt; the company manufactures a slew of cranes, construction equipment, aerial platforms, and materials processing equipment. Its construction business makes compaction equipment, such as compact track loaders and excavators, as well as off-highway trucks, and road building equipment. Another arm makes various aerial lifts, from articulating to telescopic booms used in industrial and construction overhead jobs. The lines are sold worldwide to construction, as well as forestry, recycling, shipping, and utility industries, under brands Genie, Powerscreen, and Bid-Well. In 2010 the company sold its mining business to Bucyrus International.

The company has been been hammered by a deteriorating worldwide economy and tightening credit markets. Terex aims to shift its role as an equipment manufacturer to one that focuses on specialty machinery and industrial equipment. It is eyeing product lines other than construction equipment due to a lack of acquisition targets in the market; its target list includes related machinery and industrial products, particularly in Europe.

The company is actively pursuing attempts to increase its operations in China. To that end, Terex entered into an agreement in 2010 to acquire a 65% stake in Jinan-based boom crawler crane maker Shandong Topower Heavy Machinery Company. It has also announced plans to form a joint venture with Fujian South Highway Machinery Company to make mobile materials processing equipment. Other recent forays into China include its Terex Port Equipment facility in Xiamen and the Aerial Work Platforms factory in Changzhou.

In order to regain its financial footing, Terex is using $1.3 billion from the sale of its mining division to Bucyrus to retire some of its debt as well as reposition itself for other investments. Terex also divested its construction trailer business (formerly part of its aerial work platforms segment), a power buggy lineup, and, subsequently in 2010, its generator set assets to Cummins Power Generation.

As part of its long-term effort to reposition its business, Terex is offloading its parts of its heavy construction equipment business, Terex Atlas. Terex succeeded in selling the Atlas line and its Germany-based knuckle-boom crane manufacturing facility to Atlas Maschinen GmbH.

Terex's acquisition of rubber track loader manufacturer ASV Inc. for about $488 million in 2008 was poorly timed; both divisions were dented by the economic downturn. Terex was forced to reduce its workforce and slow production at some of its plants and shutter others. Spying longer term opportunities in manufacturing and servicing port equipment, Terex acquired the niche crane businesses of Fantuzzi Industries, and Noell Crane in 2009.

Litigation has also had a negative effect on Terex's performance. It has been under investigation by the SEC for circumstances surrounding restatement of Terex financial statements for 2000-2004, and for transactions between the company and United Rentals in 2000-2001. Terex reached a final settlement during 2009 with the SEC to pay a civil penalty of $8 million. No action was recommended against any current or former employee of the company, including chairman and CEO Ronald DeFeo.

HISTORY

Real estate entrepreneur Randolph Lenz moved into heavy equipment manufacturing with the purchase of bankrupt snowplow maker FWD Corporation in 1981. That was followed the same year with the acquisition of Northwest Engineering, a maker of construction equipment started in the 1920s.

In 1986 the company acquired Terex USA, the North American distributor of parts for off-highway Terex trucks, from General Motors, and later Terex Equipment, the UK-based truck maker. The company changed its corporate name to Terex Corporation in 1987. That year Terex entered the mobile-crane market with the purchase of Koehring Cranes. Terex acquired

mining-truck maker Unit Rig in 1988 and trailer maker Fruehauf in 1989. It moved into aerial work platforms in 1991 with the acquisition of Mark Industries and picked up the forklift business of Clark Equipment the following year. (Clark invented the forklift truck in 1928.)

Overexpansion and heavy debt led to losses as the US slipped into recession in the early 1990s, and Terex teetered on the brink of bankruptcy. The losses prompted the 1993 installation of new management led by former Case executive Ron DeFeo, who refocused Terex on its core earthmoving and lifting businesses. In 1995 the company sold its stake in Fruehauf. It sold Clark Material Handling in 1996.

Terex added to its lifting-product business with the acquisition of PPM Cranes in 1995 and Simon Access and Baraga Products in 1997. It strengthened its earthmoving product line with the 1998 purchases of O&K Mining, a maker of hydraulic mining excavators, and Gru Comedil, a maker of tower cranes. That year Lenz stepped down as chairman and DeFeo replaced him.

The company settled long-lived SEC and IRS investigations in 1999, which had negatively affected the company's stock price. (The IRS had audited the company; the SEC was probing its accounting methods.)

Terex began piling on new earthmoving businesses in 1999, including Amida Industries, a maker of front-end dumpers and mobile floodlight towers. Also in 1999 Terex bought UK-based Powerscreen International, a maker of screening and crushing equipment for quarries, and Cedarapids, Raytheon's road construction-equipment business.

Early in 2001 Terex acquired Fermec Holdings Limited, a UK-based maker of loader backhoes, from CNH Global. Later the same year, it added CMI Corporation, a maker of large-scale construction equipment, and cut operating costs (about 30% of its workforce). The company also entered the power generation business, selling diesel generators under the name Terex Power. In addition, Terex expanded its reach into Europe by acquiring Atlas Weyhausen (cranes and excavators, Germany) in 2001.

In 2002 Terex initiated investments in Tatra a.s. (heavy-duty trucks with commercial and military applications, Czech Republic), increasing its share to 71% in 2003.

The company continued to buy in 2003, adding utility equipment distributors Commercial Body and Combatel.

In late 2006 Terex sold its interest in Czech truck maker Tatra a.s. to Blue River s.r.o., a Czech-based private investment concern.

EXECUTIVES

Chairman and CEO: Ronald M. (Ron) DeFeo, age 57, $4,699,980 total compensation
President and COO: Thomas J. (Tom) Riordan, age 53, $1,974,495 total compensation
CIO: Greg Fell
SVP and CFO: Phillip C. Widman, age 54, $1,483,892 total compensation
SVP Human Resources: Kevin A. Barr, age 50
SVP Finance and Business Development:
Brian J. Henry, age 51
SVP, Secretary, and General Counsel: Eric I. Cohen, age 51
SVP Product Development and Marketing, Terex Business System: Jacob Thomas

VP and Chief Ethics and Compliance Officer:
Stacey Babson-Smith
VP Investor Relations: Tom Gelston
VP, Controller, and Chief Accounting Officer:
Mark I. Clair, age 49
President, Terex Cranes: Richard (Rick) Nichols, age 48, $1,076,167 total compensation
President, Terex Aerial Work Platforms:
Timothy A. Ford, age 48, $2,226,986 total compensation
President, Developing Markets and Strategic Accounts:
Stoyan (Steve) Filipov, age 41, $1,353,760 total compensation
President, Terex Financial Services: Kevin Bradley
President, Terex Construction: George Ellis, age 49
President, Terex Materials Processing: Kieran Hegarty
Director Corporate Communications:
Michael G. (Mike) Bazinet
Auditors: PricewaterhouseCoopers LLP

LOCATIONS

HQ: Terex Corporation
200 Nyala Farm Rd., Westport, CT 06880
Phone: 203-222-7170   **Fax:** 203-222-7976
Web: www.terex.com

2009 Sales

	$ mil.	% of total
US	1,012.2	25
Europe		
Germany	420.0	11
UK	288.9	7
Other countries	973.4	24
Other regions	1,348.6	33
Total	**4,043.1**	**100**

PRODUCTS/OPERATIONS

2009 Sales

	$ mil.	% of total
Cranes	1,964.2	48
Construction	951.9	23
Aerial work platforms	838.1	20
Materials processing	353.6	9
Adjustments	(64.7)	—
Total	**4,043.1**	**100**

Selected Products

Attachments and tools
Aerial devices
Aerial work platforms
Asphalt production and paving
Backhoe loaders
Bridge inspection platforms
Cable placers
Compaction
Concrete preparation and finishing
Concrete production and paving
Cranes
Crushing and screening
Digging derricks
Drilling
Dumpers
Excavators
Graders
Highwall mining
Lighting
Material handlers
Scrapers
Telehandlers
Track loaders
Tracked Utility vehicles
Trucks (off highway)
Wheel loaders

COMPETITORS

Altec Industries
Astec Industries
Atlas Copco
Blount International
Caterpillar
Charles Machine Works
CNH Global
Deere
Doosan Heavy Industries
Dynapac
Fontaine Trailer
Furukawa
Gehl
Haulotte
Hitachi Construction Machinery
Hyundai Heavy Industries
Instant UpRight
J C Bamford Excavators
JLG Industries
Kobelco Construction Machinery America
Komatsu
Legris Industries Group
Liebherr International
MANITOU BF
Manitowoc
Marmon Group
Metso
Multiquip
Oshkosh Truck
Sandvik
Skyjack
Sumitomo
Textron
Trail King Industries
Volvo
Wacker Neuson

HISTORICAL FINANCIALS

Company Type: Public

Income Statement

FYE: December 31

	REVENUE ($ mil.)	NET INCOME ($ mil.)	NET PROFIT MARGIN	EMPLOYEES
12/09	4,043	(397)	—	15,900
12/08	9,890	72	0.7%	20,000
12/07	9,138	614	6.7%	21,000
12/06	7,648	401	5.2%	18,000
12/05	6,380	189	3.0%	17,600
Annual Growth	(10.8%)	—	—	(2.5%)

2009 Year-End Financials

Debt ratio: 114.7%
Return on equity: —
Cash ($ mil.): 930
Current ratio: 2.52
Long-term debt ($ mil.): 1,893

No. of shares (mil.): 109
Dividends
  Yield: 0.0%
  Payout: —
Market value ($ mil.): 2,153

Stock History

NYSE: TEX

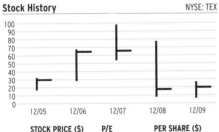

	STOCK PRICE ($) FY Close	P/E High/Low		PER SHARE ($) Earnings	Dividends	Book Value
12/09	19.81	—	—	(3.88)	0.00	15.18
12/08	17.32	106	12	0.72	0.00	15.84
12/07	65.57	17	9	5.85	0.00	21.56
12/06	64.58	17	8	3.88	0.00	16.11
12/05	29.70	17	10	1.85	0.00	10.68
Annual Growth	(9.6%)	—	—	—	—	9.2%

Tesoro Corporation

Once a player in the exploration and production field, Tesoro Corporation (formerly Tesoro Petroleum) has been enjoying a more refined existence in recent years. The independent oil refiner and marketer operates seven US refineries — in Alaska, California (two), Hawaii, North Dakota, Utah, and Washington — with a combined capacity of 665,000 barrels per day. It produces gasoline, jet fuel, diesel fuel, fuel oil, liquid asphalt, and other fuel products. Tesoro markets fuel to more than 880 branded retail gas stations (including 380 company-owned stations under the Tesoro, Shell, Mirastar, and USA Gasoline brands), in Alaska, Hawaii, and 15 western states.

The global economic slowdown and an excess refining capacity caused a major slump in the industry's (and the company's) revenues and profits in 2009.

In 2010 the company appointed industry veteran Greg Goff as president and CEO to replace the retiring Bruce Smith.

As part of a strategy to step up its marketing efforts on the US West Coast, Tesoro has an agreement with Wal-Mart to build and operate up to 200 Mirastar-branded gas stations at Wal-Mart locations in 13 states.

In a significant supply agreement, the company has a throughput deal that allows it to transport crude oil in a pipeline owned by Petroterminal de Panamá (PTP). In 2009 PTP reversed the flow of its 81-mile trans-Panamanian pipeline to allow Tesoro to more economically transport crude oils produced in Africa, the Atlantic coast of South America and the North Sea to Tesoro's five refineries on the Pacific Rim.

Tesoro acquired a Los Angeles refinery and some 276 gas stations from Shell Oil Products US for about $1.6 billion in 2007. It then acquired more than 130 USA Petroleum gas stations, primarily in California; these acquisitions nearly doubled Tesoro's retail presence.

HISTORY

Founded by Robert West in 1964 as a spinoff of petroleum producer Texstar, Tesoro Petroleum was hamstrung by debt from the get-go. In 1968 West merged Tesoro with Intex Oil and Sioux Oil to invigorate its financial standing.

Reborn, the company constructed an Alaska refinery and began a 10-year stretch of petroleum-related acquisitions, usually at bargain prices, including almost half of the oil operations of British Petroleum (BP) in Trinidad, which became Trinidad-Tesoro Petroleum. By 1973 earnings had quintupled.

In 1975 Tesoro paid $83 million for about a third of Commonwealth Oil Refining Company (Corco), a troubled Puerto Rican oil refiner one-and-a-half times its size. Debt soon was troubling Tesoro again, and the company divested many of its holdings, including refineries in Montana and Wyoming. Corco declared bankruptcy in 1978. That year Tesoro was hit with tax penalties and revealed it had bribed officials in foreign countries.

The company fought takeover attempts and bankruptcy in the 1980s and sold its half of Trinidad-Tesoro in 1985. In the 1990s it expanded its natural gas operations and returned to profitability.

In 1998 Tesoro bought a refinery and 32 retail outlets in Hawaii from an affiliate of BHP, and a refinery in Washington from an affiliate of Shell. To concentrate on its downstream businesses, the company in 1999 sold its exploration and production operations in the US (to EEX for $215 million) and in Bolivia (to BG for about $100 million).

Tesoro West Coast Co., a Tesoro subsidiary, entered into a lease agreement with Wal-Mart in 2000 to build and operate retail fueling facilities at Wal-Mart locations in 11 western states (subsequently expanded to 13 states). That year the company reviewed the possibility of closing part or all of its Alaska properties, including its underperforming refinery. But boosted by higher crude prices and its new deal with Wal-Mart, Tesoro decided to leave its Alaska operations untouched.

In 2001 Tesoro bought refineries in North Dakota and Utah, plus 45 gas stations and contracts to supply 300 others, from BP for about $675 million. Tesoro bought the Golden Eagle (San Francisco-area) refinery and 70 retail service stations in Northern California from Valero Energy for $945 million in 2002. At the end of the year Tesoro sold 47 of those gas stations to help pay down debt. It also sold its Northern Great Plains Products System to Kaneb Pipe Line Partners L.P. for $100 million.

The 2003 sale of its marine services unit for $32 million was also part of the company's plan to focus on its refining and marketing operations and pay down debt. Tesoro achieved its goal of shedding some $500 million of debt by the end of 2003 through asset sales and cost reductions.

EXECUTIVES

Chairman: Steven H. Grapstein, age 52
President, CEO, and Director: Greg J. Goff, age 53
EVP and COO: Everett D. Lewis, age 62, $3,219,074 total compensation
EVP, General Counsel, and Secretary: Charles S. (Chuck) Parrish, age 52, $1,682,729 total compensation
SVP, CFO, and Treasurer: G. Scott Spendlove, age 46
SVP Marketing: Claude P. Moreau, age 55
SVP Administration: Susan A. Lerette, age 51
SVP System Optimization: Claude A. (Chuck) Flagg, age 56
SVP Logistics and Marine: Joseph M. (Joe) Monroe, age 55
SVP Supply and Trading: Joe G. McCoy, age 61
SVP External Affairs and Chief Economist: Lynn D. Westfall, age 57
VP and Controller: Arlen O. Glenewinkel Jr., age 53
VP Heavy Oils and Specialty Products: William Weimer
VP International Crude: Lewis Schwartz
VP Heavy Fuels Marketing: Phil Wing
VP Arbitrage Trading: Doug Koskie
VP Marine: Charles Parks
VP Product Supply and Trading: Ed Peters
VP Trading and Risk Management: Mark Smith
Director North American Crude Supply and Trading: Damon Van Zandt
Managing Director Finance and Investor Relations: Scott Phipps
Auditors: Deloitte & Touche LLP

LOCATIONS

HQ: Tesoro Corporation
19100 Ridgewood Pkwy, San Antonio, TX 78259
Phone: 210-626-6000   **Fax:** 210-579-4574
Web: www.tsocorp.com

PRODUCTS/OPERATIONS

2009 Sales

	$ mil.	% of total
Refining		
Refined products	15,674	80
Crude oil resales & other	691	4
Retail		
Fuel	3,000	15
Merchandise & other	235	1
Adjustments	(2,728)	—
Total	**16,872**	**100**

Major Subsidiaries

Tesoro Alaska Company
Tesoro Hawaii Corporation
Tesoro Refining and Marketing Company

COMPETITORS

Arctic Slope Regional Corporation
BP
Branch & Associates
Chevron
ConocoPhillips
Exxon Mobil
Shell Oil Products
Valero Energy

HISTORICAL FINANCIALS

Company Type: Public

Income Statement

FYE: December 31

	REVENUE ($ mil.)	NET INCOME ($ mil.)	NET PROFIT MARGIN	EMPLOYEES
12/09	16,872	(140)	—	5,500
12/08	28,309	278	1.0%	5,620
12/07	21,915	566	2.6%	5,500
12/06	18,104	801	4.4%	3,950
12/05	16,581	507	3.1%	3,928
Annual Growth	**0.4%**	**—**	**—**	**8.8%**

2009 Year-End Financials

Debt ratio: 59.5%
Return on equity: —
Cash ($ mil.): 413
Current ratio: 1.18
Long-term debt ($ mil.): 1,837

No. of shares (mil.): 143
Dividends
  Yield: 2.6%
  Payout: —
Market value ($ mil.): 1,934

Stock History

NYSE: TSO

	STOCK PRICE ($) FY Close	P/E High/Low		PER SHARE ($) Earnings	Dividends	Book Value
12/09	13.55	—	—	(1.01)	0.35	21.63
12/08	13.17	22	3	2.00	0.40	22.55
12/07	47.70	16	8	4.06	0.35	21.39
12/06	32.88	7	5	5.73	0.20	17.53
12/05	30.77	10	4	3.60	0.10	13.22
Annual Growth	**(18.5%)**	**—**	**—**	**—**	**36.8%**	**13.1%**

Tetra Tech

Tetra Tech puts technical know-how to work. The environmental management, consulting, and technical services group focuses on resource management and infrastructure development. Services include environmental engineering, restoration, groundwater cleanup, watershed management, and operations and maintenance support. Tetra Tech provides architectural, engineering, and construction services for public and private facilities and designs and builds water supply systems and other infrastructure systems. US federal contracts account for almost half of its annual revenues. In addition, Tetra Tech brings in another 15% from state and local government clients.

Commercial customers include companies in the chemical, energy, mining, and pharmaceutical industries.

Revenues from government contracts have helped position the company among the top environmental firms worldwide. Tetra Tech's strategy has been to establish its consulting practice in a new business area and then offer additional technical services.

Tetra Tech expanded its international energy and infrastructure consulting services by agreeing to purchase the U.S.-based international development consulting business practice from London-based PA Consulting Group. The deal will double Tetra Tech's energy management consulting business. It also acquired Alberta-based EBA Engineering Consultants, expanding its Canadian holdings. EBA provides natural science, engineering, and arctic engineering services to the mining, energy, and infrastructure sectors.

It builds out its skill set and product offerings through acquisitions — such as the 2008 purchase of Vermont-based international engineering consulting firm ARD and of Tennessee-based nuclear services provider Haselwood Enterprises the next year. In 2009 it also acquired construction management firm Tesoro Corporation, environmental consulting firm Mussetter Engineering of Fort Collins, Canadian power engineering specialists ACI Engineering, and the Californian consulting and engineering firm Bryan A. Stirrat.

HISTORY

Tetra Tech was founded in 1966 by Nicholas Boratynski as a coastal and marine engineering firm. One of its first jobs was measuring water waves to determine the damage an offshore nuclear bomb could do to the coastline. The company developed expertise in water management in the 1970s. Honeywell bought the company in 1982, and Tetra Tech management in turn bought out Honeywell in 1988. Tetra Tech went public in 1991.

Since 1993 Tetra Tech has grown largely through acquisitions. In 1997 the company expanded into infrastructure and telecommunications. Tetra Tech acquired two site development firms — CommSite Development Corp. and Whalen & Company — to capitalize on the growing telecom market. It also enlarged its environmental business with the purchase of Halliburton's Brown & Root and Halliburton NUS environmental service units.

Continuing to build up its telecom business in 1998, it bought Sentrex Cen-Comm Communications Systems, an engineering firm serving the cable TV, telephone, and data networking industries.

A year later the company won a $105 million contract from the US Department of Energy to help monitor the nation's nuclear weapons stockpile. In 2000 Tetra Tech won a $375 million contract from WideOpenWest, a leading broadband wired access provider in the Denver area. It also snapped up nine companies that fiscal year.

In 2001 Tetra Tech expanded its energy services to include power plant relicensing projects in the US. The company also expanded its consulting services to the energy and mining industries through acquisitions. In 2002 the company acquired The Thomas Group, a leading designer of educational and health care facilities. It also picked up Florida-based consulting engineering firm Ardaman & Associates, adding to its water resources management operations.

The next year the group expanded even more by acquiring nearly all the assets of environmental services management firm Foster Wheeler Environmental Corp., a unit of Foster Wheeler. Tetra Tech renamed the group, which provides hazardous and nuclear waste management primarily to the federal government, Tetra Tech FW. In 2003 it strengthened its position in the federal market even more by acquiring California-based engineering firm Engineering Management Concepts (EMC), which provides weapons test range services and systems logistics support to the Department of Defense.

The group was buying again in 2004 with its purchase of Advanced Management Technology Inc., which enhanced its position in the security and defense market. In 2005, however, Tetra Tech exited the wireless communications arena and began consolidating its infrastructure operations.

EXECUTIVES

Chairman, CEO, and President: Dan L. Batrack, age 51, $2,490,723 total compensation
EVP, CFO, and Treasurer: David W. King, age 53, $1,172,209 total compensation
SVP; President, Engineering and Architecture Services: Douglas G. (Doug) Smith, age 60, $834,606 total compensation
SVP; President, Remediation and Construction Group: Donald I. Rogers Jr., age 65, $818,712 total compensation
SVP; President, Environmental Consulting Services: James R. Pagenkopf, age 58
SVP; President, Technical Support Services: Ronald J. Chu, age 52
SVP; President, Systems Support and Security Group: Patrick D. Haun, age 49
SVP and Chief Engineer: William R. Brownlie, age 56
SVP and Corporate Controller: Steven M. Burdick, age 45
SVP Corporate Administration: Richard A. Lemmon, age 50
VP, General Counsel, and Secretary: Janis B. Salin, age 56, $731,310 total compensation
VP Investor Relations: Jorge Casado
VP Corporate Development: Michael A. (Mike) Bieber, age 41
VP and CIO: Craig L. Christensen, age 56
VP Strategic Initiatives: Leslie L. Shoemaker, age 52
VP Project Risk Management: Sam W. Box, age 64
Director Corporate Communications: Talia Starkey
Auditors: PricewaterhouseCoopers LLP

LOCATIONS

HQ: Tetra Tech, Inc.
  3475 E. Foothill Blvd., Pasadena, CA 91107
Phone: 626-351-4664   **Fax:** 626-351-5291
Web: www.tetratech.com

PRODUCTS/OPERATIONS

2009 Sales

	% of total
Environmental consulting services	32
Remediation & construction management	28
Technical support services	23
Engineering & architecture services	17
Total	**100**

2009 Sales

	% of total
Federal government	45
Commercial	32
State & local government	15
International	8
Total	**100**

Selected Subsidiaries

Advanced Management Technology, Inc.
Ardaman & Associates, Inc.
Cosentini Associates, Inc.
Engineering Management Concepts, Inc. (EMC)
Evergreen Utility Contractors, Inc.
FHC, Inc.
Hartman & Associates, Inc.
MFG, Inc.
Rizzo Associates, Inc.
Sciences International, Inc.
SCM Consultants, Inc.
Tetra Tech EM Inc.
Tetra Tech NUS, Inc
The Thomas Group of Commpanies, Inc.
Vector Colorado, LLC.
Western Utility Cable, Inc.
Western Utility Contractors, Inc.
Whalen & Company, Inc.
Whalen/Sentrex LLC

COMPETITORS

AECOM
AMEC
ARCADIS
Baran Telecom
Black & Veatch
Brown and Caldwell
Camp Dresser McKee
CH2M HILL
EA Engineering
Ecology and Environment
ERM
Foster Wheeler
Geocon Group
Jacobs Engineering
Kratos Defense & Security Solutions
MasTec
MWH Global
Quanta Services
RECON Environmental
SCS Tracer Environmental
Shaw Group
Stantec
TRC Companies
URS
Weston Solutions

HISTORICAL FINANCIALS

Company Type: Public

Income Statement

FYE: Sunday nearest September 30

	REVENUE ($ mil.)	NET INCOME ($ mil.)	NET PROFIT MARGIN	EMPLOYEES
9/09	2,288	87	3.8%	10,000
9/08	2,145	61	2.8%	9,200
9/07	1,554	46	3.0%	7,800
9/06	1,415	37	2.6%	7,300
9/05	1,286	(100)	—	7,200
Annual Growth	**15.5%**	**—**	**—**	**8.6%**

2009 Year-End Financials

Debt ratio: 1.0%
Return on equity: 15.0%
Cash ($ mil.): 89
Current ratio: 1.52
Long-term debt ($ mil.): 7
No. of shares (mil.): 62
Dividends
  Yield: —
  Payout: —
Market value ($ mil.): 1,638

Stock History

NASDAQ (GS): TTEK

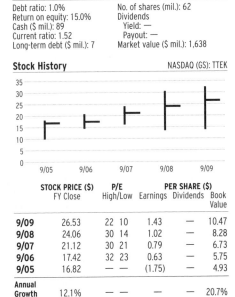

	STOCK PRICE ($) FY Close	P/E High/Low		PER SHARE ($) Earnings	Dividends	Book Value
9/09	26.53	22	10	1.43	—	10.47
9/08	24.06	30	14	1.02	—	8.28
9/07	21.12	30	21	0.79	—	6.73
9/06	17.42	32	23	0.63	—	5.75
9/05	16.82	—	—	(1.75)	—	4.93
Annual Growth	**12.1%**	**—**	**—**	**—**	**—**	**20.7%**

Texas Instruments

Say hello to the big Texan. One of the world's oldest and largest semiconductor makers, Texas Instruments (TI) is the market leader in digital signal processors (DSPs). Many of the wireless phones sold worldwide contain TI's DSPs, which are also found in other products, such as DVD players, automotive systems, and computer modems. Additional TI semiconductor offerings include logic chips, microprocessors, microcontrollers, and display components. The company also makes calculators. Nokia accounts for about 20% of sales.

TI jockeys back and forth with European chip giant STMicroelectronics to be the world's top maker of analog chips; both companies far outpace other analog rivals.

The semiconductor industry is historically notorious for its cyclicality, and the global recession dampened demand for consumer electronics. During 2009 TI cut its workforce by about 3,000 positions, a 10% reduction in force. As the electronics industry started to recover from the prolonged downturn in 2010, TI began to boost its capacity for the analog chips used in electronic gadgets. In mid-2010 the company announced it would buy two wafer fabs in Japan from the Japanese unit of Spansion.

In 2010 TI agreed to sell its cable modem product line to Intel. The unit supplies customers such as Motorola, ARRIS, and Cisco's Scientific Atlanta brand with chips for cable modems.

While TI signaled that it will be spending less money on R&D for semiconductor process development in the future, the giant chip maker is flexing its financial muscle in other ways. In 2009 it scored the microcontroller (MCU) portfolio of Luminary Micro, a power player in supplying ARM Cortex-M3-based 32-bit MCUs. The company previously committed to spending $1 billion over 10 years to expand its chip assembly and test operations in the Philippines. TI built a new facility in the Clark Freeport Zone, the site of a former US Air Force base.

During the late 1990s and the early 21st century, TI sold off noncore businesses and made a series of acquisitions to focus on its analog and DSP lines. TI touts its combination of expertise in analog and DSP technologies as a key advantage in allowing it to deliver more highly integrated components for customers in areas such as wireless and broadband communications.

TI began shipping its Digital Light Processing (DLP) device in 1996. The part is a microelectromechanical system (MEMS) device, also known as a digital micromirror device. It contains more than 2 million microscopic mirrors on the surface of the device, mirrors that can individually move to create a sharper image. For years, the DLP seemed to be a product in search of an application, but it eventually found its way into HDTV sets, digital projectors, and digital cinema equipment. TI has shipped more than 20 million DLP subsystems to manufacturers. TI is finding more applications for the DLP device in such areas as 3-D metrology, confocal microscopy, and holographic data storage.

HISTORY

Clarence "Doc" Karcher and Eugene McDermott founded Geophysical Service, Inc. (GSI) in Newark, New Jersey, in 1930 to develop reflective seismology, a new technology for oil and gas exploration. In 1934 GSI moved to Dallas. The company produced military electronics during WWII, including submarine detectors for the US Navy. GSI changed its name to Texas Instruments (TI) in 1951.

TI began making transistors in 1952 after buying a license from Western Electric. The company went public on the New York Stock Exchange in 1953. In 1954 it introduced the Regency Radio, the first pocket-sized transistor radio. (That year TI also produced the first commercial silicon transistor.) Impressed by the radio, IBM president Thomas Watson made TI a major supplier to IBM in 1957. That year the company opened a plant in the UK — its first foreign operation.

TI engineer Jack Kilby invented the integrated circuit (IC) in 1958. (Working independently, Intel co-founder Robert Noyce developed an IC at the same time, while working at Fairchild Semiconductor; the two men are credited as co-inventors. In 2000 Kilby was awarded the Nobel Prize in Physics for his work; Noyce could not be awarded the prize, since he had died 10 years earlier.)

Other breakthroughs for the company included terrain-following airborne radar (1958), handheld calculators (1967), and single-chip microcomputers (1971). During the 1970s TI introduced innovative calculators, digital watches, home computers, and educational toys such as the popular Speak & Spell — the first TI product to use digital signal processors (DSPs), which decades later would become a major driver of TI's growth.

Low-cost foreign competition led TI to abandon its digital watch and PC businesses. Price competition in the chip market contributed to the company's first loss in 1983. In 1988 the company sold most of its remaining oil and gas operations to Halliburton.

As the chip market toughened, TI leveraged its DRAM device know-how through strategic alliances, including a 1993 agreement with Hitachi (the venture ended in 1998). TI sold its line of educational toys to Tiger Electronics in 1995.

When company head Jerry Junkins, who built TI into a semiconductor force, died unexpectedly in 1996, he was replaced by company veteran Thomas Engibous as president and CEO. (Engibous became chairman in 1998.)

Engibous refocused TI, which in 1996 sold its custom manufacturing business to Solectron and acquired Silicon Systems (chips for mass storage devices). In 1997 TI sold its notebook computer business to Acer, its defense electronics operation to Raytheon, and its enterprise applications software unit to Sterling Software (now part of CA).

A global chip slump and the loss of the memory chip business lowered TI's results in 1998 and led to the layoff of 3,500 employees.

In 2001 TI began to lay off about 2,500 workers in reaction to a softening market for its chips. In 2004 COO Richard Templeton succeeded Engibous as president and CEO; Engibous remained chairman.

In 2006 TI sold its Sensors and Controls business to Bain Capital for $3 billion in cash. The business was rechristened Sensata Technologies. In selling the sensors and controls business, TI held on to its radio-frequency identification (RFID) tags business, making chips used in contactless payment systems, health care, manufacturing, retail supply chain management, and other applications.

In 2008 Engibous retired as chairman and was succeeded by Templeton.

EXECUTIVES

Chairman, President, and CEO:
Richard K. (Rich) Templeton, age 51,
$9,865,657 total compensation
SVP and CFO: Kevin P. March, age 52,
$3,397,575 total compensation
SVP and General Manager, Wireless Business Unit:
R. Gregory (Greg) Delagi,
$3,566,673 total compensation
SVP Analog Business Unit: Gregg A. Lowe, age 47,
$4,654,884 total compensation
SVP Technology and Manufacturing Group:
Kevin J. Ritchie, age 53, $4,111,175 total compensation
SVP and Manager, Application Specific Products:
Michael J. (Mike) Hames, age 51,
$2,991,260 total compensation
SVP and General Manager, DLP (R) Products:
Kent Novak
SVP, Secretary, and General Counsel:
Joseph F. (Joe) Hubach, age 52
SVP and Worldwide Manager, Power Management:
Stephen (Steve) Anderson
SVP and Manager Worldwide Sales and Marketing:
John Szczsponik
SVP and Manager High-Volume Analog and Logic:
David K. (Dave) Heacock, age 49
SVP; President, Education Technology: Melendy Lovett, age 52
SVP and Manager Worldwide Human Resources:
Darla Whitaker, age 44
SVP and Worldwide Manager, High-Performance Analog Business Unit: Arthur L. (Art) George, age 48
SVP and Manager Communications and Investor Relations; VP, Texas Instruments Foundation:
Teresa L. (Terri) West, age 49
Auditors: Ernst & Young LLP

LOCATIONS

HQ: Texas Instruments Incorporated
12500 TI Blvd., Dallas, TX 75266
Phone: 972-995-3773   **Fax:** 972-927-6377
Web: www.ti.com

2009 Sales

	$ mil.	% of total
Asia/Pacific		
Japan	976	9
Other countries	6,575	63
Europe	1,408	14
US	1,140	11
Other regions	328	3
Total	**10,427**	**100**

PRODUCTS/OPERATIONS

2009 Sales

	$ mil.	% of total
Analog	4,270	41
Wireless	2,558	25
Embedded Processing	1,471	14
Other	2,128	20
Total	**10,427**	**100**

Selected Products

Semiconductors
 Analog and mixed-signal
  Amplifiers and comparators
  Clocks and timers
  Data converters
  Power management chips
  Radio-frequency (RF) chips
 Application-specific integrated circuits (ASICs)
 Digital light processors (DLPs, micro-mirror-based devices for video displays)
 Digital signal processors (DSPs)
 Microcontrollers
 Reduced instruction set computer (RISC) microprocessors
 Standard logic
Educational Technology
 Calculators (including graphing, handheld, and printing models)

COMPETITORS

Analog Devices
Atmel
Avago Technologies
Broadcom
Canon
CASIO COMPUTER
Conexant Systems
CSR plc
Cypress Semiconductor
Fairchild Semiconductor
Freescale Semiconductor
Fujitsu Semiconductor
Hewlett-Packard
Hitachi
IBM Microelectronics
Infineon Technologies
Intel
International Rectifier
Linear Technology
LSI Corp.
Marvell Technology
Maxim Integrated Products
MediaTek
Microchip Technology
National Semiconductor
NVIDIA
NXP Semiconductors
Oki Semiconductor
ON Semiconductor
QUALCOMM
SANYO Semiconductor
ST-Ericsson
STMicroelectronics
Toshiba Semiconductor
Vishay Intertechnology
Xilinx

HISTORICAL FINANCIALS

Company Type: Public

Income Statement

FYE: December 31

	REVENUE ($ mil.)	NET INCOME ($ mil.)	NET PROFIT MARGIN	EMPLOYEES
12/09	10,427	1,470	14.1%	26,584
12/08	12,501	1,920	15.4%	29,537
12/07	13,835	2,657	19.2%	30,175
12/06	14,255	4,341	30.5%	30,986
12/05	13,392	2,324	17.4%	32,507
Annual Growth	**(6.1%)**	**(10.8%)**	**—**	**(4.9%)**

2009 Year-End Financials

Debt ratio: —
Return on equity: 15.4%
Cash ($ mil.): 1,182
Current ratio: 3.85
Long-term debt ($ mil.): —
No. of shares (mil.): 1,195
Dividends
 Yield: 1.7%
 Payout: 39.1%
Market value ($ mil.): 31,147

Stock History

NYSE: TXN

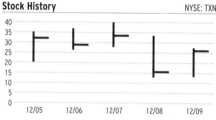

	STOCK PRICE ($) FY Close	P/E High/Low		PER SHARE ($) Earnings	Dividends	Book Value
12/09	26.06	23	12	1.15	0.45	8.13
12/08	15.52	23	9	1.45	0.41	7.80
12/07	33.40	22	15	1.84	0.30	8.35
12/06	28.80	13	10	2.78	0.13	9.50
12/05	32.07	25	15	1.39	0.10	9.99
Annual Growth	**(5.1%)**	**—**	**—**	**(4.6%)**	**45.6%**	**(5.0%)**

Textron Inc.

Executives should like Textron: The company's E-Z-GO golf carts enrich their golfing jaunts, its Cessna airplanes and Bell helicopters whisk them around, its auto parts keep their cars running, and its finance subsidiary provides loans. Besides golf carts and car parts, Textron's Industrial segment makes power tools, electrical and fiber optic assemblies, and turf maintenance equipment. Its Textron Systems segment sells smart weapons, surveillance systems, and unmanned aerial vehicles to the Defense Department. The US government accounts for about one-third of Textron's sales

While Textron enjoyed healthy sales growth and good profit margins for several years, the global recession has brought lower demand for its products, particularly in its Cessna and Industrial segments. In response, it slashed 10,400 employees in 2009 and closed 23 facilities. Other restructuring measures included employee furloughs and temporary plant shutdowns.

Cessna was hurt by numerous order cancellations for business jets during 2009, including a $1.3 billion cancellation from a single customer.

The decision to cancel development of the Citation Columbus aircraft (part of Textron's restructuring program) had a $2.1 billion negative impact on Cessna's results.

Not all businesses were negatively affected by the global economy. Its defense business remains strong. Bell is a leading helicopter supplier to the US and international militaries. Working with Boeing, Bell is the only supplier of military tiltrotor aircraft. Its major programs are the V-22 tiltrotor and the H-1 helicopter. It also supplies commercial helicopters and support for offshore petroleum, utility, fire, rescue, and emergency medical applications. Its support operations provide logistics support and maintenance, repair, and overhaul (MRO) services, along with customization, modification, and product engineering services. In its defense-oriented Textron Systems segment, demand for unmanned aerial vehicles, sensor fused weapons, and armored security vehicles has also been strong.

CEO Lewis Campbell retired in 2009, but remained chairman until September 2010. President and COO Scott Donnelly was named president and CEO (the COO position was eliminated); he added the chairman's title in 2010. Donnelly previously served as CEO of GE Aviation, one of the world's largest manufacturers of engines for commercial and military aircraft.

In 2009 Textron sold its HR Textron unit to Woodward Governor for $365 million. HR Textron makes actuators and other products for aircraft, armored vehicles, guided weapons, and turbine engines.

The company's Greenlee unit was also busy with acquisitions in 2008 with the additions of the UK-based Utilux (cable connectors and assemblies) and Telefonix, a cable testing equipment maker headquartered in California. The same year Textron sold its Fluid & Power business unit to the UK-based Clyde Blowers Ltd.

In 2007 Textron paid $1.1 billion for United Industrial Corporation, a maker of avionics testing equipment, combat systems training simulators, and perhaps most importantly — unmanned aerial vehicles (UAVs). The US military is expected to spend plenty on UAVs in the future as they have proven themselves on the battlefields of Iraq and Afghanistan.

HISTORY

Pioneer conglomerate builder Royal Little founded Special Yarns Corporation, a Boston textile business, in 1923 and merged it with the Franklin Rayon Dyeing Company in 1928. The result, Franklin Rayon Corporation, moved its headquarters to Providence, Rhode Island, in 1930 and changed its name to Atlantic Rayon in 1938.

The company expanded during WWII to make parachutes, and in 1944 adopted the name Textron to reflect the use of synthetics in its textiles. Between 1953 and 1960 Textron bought more than 40 businesses, including Bell Helicopter, before banker Rupe Thompson took over in 1960.

Thompson sold weak businesses, such as Amerotron, Textron's last textile business (1963), but also bought 20 companies between 1960 and 1965. By 1968, when former Wall Street attorney William Miller replaced Thompson as CEO, Textron made products ranging from chain saws to watchbands. Miller sold several companies and bought Jacobsen Manufacturers (lawn care equipment, 1978) before leaving Textron in 1978

to head the Federal Reserve and become treasury secretary under President Jimmy Carter.

B. F. Dolan, who became president in 1980, sold Textron's least profitable businesses. The company bought Avco Corporation (aerospace and financial services, 1985) and UK-based Avdel (metal fastening systems, 1989).

In 1992 Textron bought Cessna Aircraft. The company sold its Lycoming Turbine Engine division in 1994 and acquired Orag Inter AG of Switzerland, Europe's #1 distributor of golf and turf care equipment. In 1995-96 Textron bought Household Finance of Australia and three fastening systems companies. Also in 1996 Textron acquired Kautex Werke Reinold Hagen AG (plastic fuel tanks) and sold most of its aircraft wing division to The Carlyle Group.

In 1997 Provident (now part of Unum Group) bought Textron's 83% stake in Paul Revere Corp. (insurance). The following year Textron bought UK-based Ransomes plc (turf care machinery and Cushman brand transports) and David Brown Group plc (industrial gears and hydraulic systems). Lewis Campbell, Textron's president and COO, became CEO in 1998 and added chairman to his duties in 1999.

In 1999 the company bought 18 companies for about $2.5 billion; the largest of these purchases included Flexalloy (vendor-managed inventory services), Omniquip International (telescopic material handling equipment), InteSys Technologies (plastic and metal assemblies), and the industry and aircraft finance divisions of Green Tree Financial Servicing.

Textron announced plans to close or consolidate operations at about 20 manufacturing sites and cut more than 3,600 jobs in 2001. Later that year it closed more plants and cut more jobs, running the total announced layoffs for the year to around 7,500. The company also sold its TAC-Trim automotive trim unit to Collins & Aikman in a deal worth about $1.34 billion.

Restructuring continued in 2003 and 2004 and the cost savings goal grew to a reduction of 10,000 jobs and 99 facilities.

Textron sold Fastening Systems for $630 million to Platinum Equity in 2006. Near the end of 2006 Textron bought Overwatch Systems, a maker of communications products and intelligence analysis tools for the US Department of Defense, the US Department of Homeland Security, and certain friendly foreign militaries.

EXECUTIVES

Chairman, President, CEO, and Director:
Scott C. Donnelly, age 48,
$5,115,739 total compensation
EVP and CFO: Frank T. Connor, age 50,
$3,186,121 total compensation
EVP, General Counsel, Corporate Secretary, and Chief Compliance Officer: Terrence (Terry) O'Donnell, age 66, $1,631,095 total compensation
EVP Administration and Chief Human Resources Officer: John D. Butler, age 62,
$2,358,138 total compensation
SVP and Corporate Controller: Richard L. (Dick) Yates, age 59, $2,276,935 total compensation
SVP Washington Operations: Robert O. Rowland
SVP International: Tony Vernaci
VP and CIO: Gary Cantrell
VP Investor Relations: Douglas R. Wilburne
VP Human Resources and Benefits: Cathy A. Streker
VP Communications: Adele Suddes
VP Operations: Frank Brittain
VP and Treasurer: Mary F. Lovejoy

Chairman, President, and CEO, Cessna Aircraft Company: Jack J. Pelton
President and CEO, Textron Financial Corporation: Warren R. Lyons
President and CEO, Textron Systems: Frederick M. (Fred) Strader
President, Jacobsen: Daniel F. (Dan) Wilkinson
President, E-Z-GO: Kevin P. Holleran
President, Industrial Segment and Greenlee: J. Scott Hall
President and CEO, Bell Helicopter: John L. Garrison Jr.
Director Investor Relations: William Pitts
Auditors: Ernst & Young LLP

LOCATIONS

HQ: Textron Inc.
40 Westminster St., Providence, RI 02903
Phone: 401-421-2800   **Fax:** 401-457-2220
Web: www.textron.com

2009 Sales

	$ mil.	% of total
Americas		
US	6,563	63
Canada	344	3
Latin America & Mexico	815	8
Europe	1,625	15
Middle East & Africa	600	6
Asia & Australia	553	5
Total	**10,500**	**100**

PRODUCTS/OPERATIONS

2009 Sales

	$ mil.	% of total
Cessna	3,320	32
Bell	2,842	27
Industrial		
Fuel systems & functional components	1,287	12
Golf & turf care products	491	5
Powered tools, testing & measurement equipment & other	300	3
Textron Systems	1,899	18
Finance	361	3
Total	**10,500**	**100**

Selected Products

Cessna
  Business jets
  Overnight express package carrier aircraft
  Single engine piston aircraft
  Single engine turboprops
Bell
  Commercial helicopters
  Military helicopters
  Tiltrotor aircraft and spare parts
Industrial
  Kautex
    Blow-molded fuel tank systems
    Catalytic reduction systems
    Engine camshafts
    Plastic bottles and containers
    Windshield and headlamp washer systems
  E-Z-GO
    Golf carts
    Multipurpose utility vehicles
    Off-road utility vehicles
  Jacobsen
    Professional turf maintenance equipment
    Turf-care vehicles
  Greenlee
    Electrical connectors
    Electrical test and measurement instruments
    Fiber optic assemblies
    Hand and hydraulic power tools
    Powered equipment

Textron Systems
  Airborne and ground-based sensors and surveillance
    systems
  Aircraft engines
  Armament systems
  Armored combat vehicles
  Automated aircraft test and maintenance equipment
  Countersniper detection devices
  Intelligence and situational awareness software
  Light armored combat vehicles
  Marine craft
  Multi-source intelligence framework systems
  Smart weapons
  Training and simulation systems
  Turrets
  Unattended ground sensors
  Unmanned aircraft systems
Finance (captive commercial finance for new aircraft,
  helicopter, golf, and turf-care equipment)

COMPETITORS

AgustaWestland	Kaman
Boeing	Lockheed Martin
Bombardier	Magna International
Claverham	Moog
Deere	Northrop Grumman
EADS	Northstar Aerospace
Eaton	Piper Aircraft
Embraer	Raytheon
GE	Rolls-Royce
General Dynamics	Spirit AeroSystems
Honda	Sun Hydraulics
Honeywell International	Terex
Illinois Tool Works	Toro Company
Ingersoll-Rand	TRW Automotive
Johnson Controls	United Technologies

HISTORICAL FINANCIALS

Company Type: Public

Income Statement

FYE: Saturday nearest December 31

	REVENUE ($ mil.)	NET INCOME ($ mil.)	NET PROFIT MARGIN	EMPLOYEES
12/09	10,500	(31)	—	32,000
12/08	14,246	486	3.4%	43,000
12/07	13,225	917	6.9%	44,000
12/06	11,490	601	5.2%	40,000
12/05	10,043	203	2.0%	37,000
Annual Growth	1.1%	—	—	(3.6%)

2009 Year-End Financials

Debt ratio: 322.6%	No. of shares (mil.): 274
Return on equity: —	Dividends
Cash ($ mil.): 1,748	Yield: 0.4%
Current ratio: 2.07	Payout: —
Long-term debt ($ mil.): 9,117	Market value ($ mil.): 5,158

Stock History

NYSE: TXT

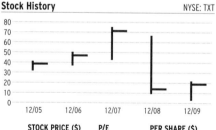

	STOCK PRICE ($) FY Close	P/E High/Low		PER SHARE ($) Earnings	Dividends	Book Value
12/09	18.81	—	—	(0.12)	0.08	10.31
12/08	13.87	34	5	1.95	0.92	8.63
12/07	71.30	21	12	3.60	0.85	12.79
12/06	46.88	21	16	2.31	0.78	9.66
12/05	38.49	54	44	0.75	0.70	11.95
Annual Growth	(16.4%)	—	—	—	(41.9%)	(3.6%)

Thermo Fisher Scientific

Whether for research, analysis, discovery, or diagnostics, Thermo Fisher Scientific gets the laboratory ready to assist mankind. The company makes and distributes analytical instruments, equipment, and laboratory supplies — from chromatographs to Erlenmeyer flasks. Thermo Fisher serves more than 350,000 customers worldwide in biotech and pharmaceutical companies, clinical diagnostic labs and hospitals, government agencies, research organizations, and universities, as well as environmental quality and industrial process control applications. The company was formed in an $11 billion merger of Thermo Electron with Fisher Scientific International in 2006.

As separate entities, Thermo and Fisher were among the biggest companies in the scientific and technical instruments field. The merger worked because Thermo Electron was, for the most part, a manufacturer of scientific instruments, while Fisher Scientific was largely a distributor of laboratory equipment and supplies. Together as Thermo Fisher Scientific, the company pushes a one-stop catalog of products and services that captures a large roster of drug companies and laboratories.

Through its continuing acquisitions and organic growth, Thermo Fisher barely slowed down during the global recession. The company is looking more nervously at health care reform in the US, which could have an adverse effect on Thermo Fisher. The reforms may lead American health care firms to purchase fewer products and obtain fewer services from the company, or to reduce what they pay for those products and services. Congress may enact a new tax on the sale of medical devices, which Thermo Fisher expects would have an adverse impact on its results.

The company's product portfolio for measuring critical gases was boosted in 2010 as Thermo Fisher acquired chemical sensor maker NovaWave Technologies. NovaWave's products are used in environmental monitoring, and industrial and safety systems. The transaction follows Thermo Fisher's purchase of Ahura Scientific, a Massachusetts-based analytical instruments manufacturer. Also that year the company bought Fermentas International for $260 million in cash. Fermentas makes enzymes, reagents, and kits for molecular and cellular biology research.

Expanding its presence internationally, Thermo Fisher purchased Finland-based Finnzymes. The 2010 acquisition gives Thermo Fisher a broader lineup of tools for molecular biology analysis. The move follows Thermo Fisher's 2009 purchase of B.R.A.H.M.S. AG (Germany, diagnostic tests and instruments).

CEO and president Marijn Dekkers resigned from the company that year in order to serve as CEO of Bayer AG. EVP/COO Marc Casper was tapped to take the helm.

HISTORY

In 1902, 20-year-old Chester Fisher bought the stockroom of Pittsburgh Testing Laboratories (established 1884) and formed Scientific Materials Co. The company's earliest products, supplied from Europe, included simple tools such as mi-

croscopes, balances, and calorimeters. It published its first catalog in 1904.

When the outbreak of WWI disrupted supplies from Europe, Scientific Materials established its own R&D and manufacturing facilities. It acquired Montreal-based Scientific Supplies in 1925 and the following year changed its name to Fisher Scientific Company. By 1935 Fisher had doubled its size, adding glass-blowing operations and an instrument shop.

During the German occupation of Greece in WWII, George Hatsopoulos, part of a well-to-do family packed with politicians and engineering professors, made radios for the Greek resistance. After the war he came to the US and became a professor of mechanical engineering at MIT. With a $50,000 loan, Hatsopoulos founded Thermo Electron in 1956 to identify emerging technology needs and create solutions for them.

That year he built a machine that would turn heat directly into electrons. This thermionic converter, though itself never commercialized, formed the basis of many of the company's successful products, including a battery-operated heart pump and a process for incinerating toxic material in polluted soils.

Thermo Electron went public in 1967 and in the early 1970s introduced efficient industrial furnaces for the paper and metals markets.

Chester Fisher died in 1965 — the same year Fisher Scientific went public — leaving Fisher to sons Aiken, Benjamin, and James.

Aiken retired as chairman in 1975 and was replaced by Benjamin. That year former Pfeiffer Glass president Edward Perkins was appointed president and CEO — the first non-family member to hold this position.

Besides developing its own business lines, Thermo Electron expanded through several acquisitions in the 1990s. The company bought the analytical instrument and process-control businesses of Baker Hughes (1994), the scientific-instruments division of Fisons (now part of Sanofi-Aventis, 1995), and respiratory-care equipment maker Sensormedics (1996).

In 1992 Fisher bought Hamilton Scientific, the top US maker of laboratory workstations, as well as a majority interest in Kuhn + Bayer, a German supplier of scientific equipment.

Former American Stock Exchange CEO Richard Syron replaced Hatsopoulos as CEO of Thermo Electron in 1999. The next year Syron announced a reorganization in which the Thermo Electron family would be reduced to three companies: Thermo Electron would concentrate on measurement and detection instruments, while Thermo Fibertek (renamed Kadant in 2001) and a medical products company (later dubbed Viasys Healthcare) would be spun off to shareholders.

Late in 2002 Syron was named executive chairman, and replaced as CEO by president and COO Marijn Dekkers. The next year Syron resigned as chairman and was replaced by board member Jim Manzi.

In 2003 Fisher acquired Sweden-based Perbio Science (consumable tools for protein-related research) for about $700 million. In 2004, Fisher acquired Apogent Technologies, a maker of laboratory and life sciences equipment for health care and scientific research applications, for nearly $4 billion.

In 2005 Thermo Electron acquired SPX's Kendro Laboratory Products business for approximately $834 million.

In late 2006 Thermo Electron merged with Fisher Scientific International in a stock-swap transaction valued at nearly $11 billion.

EXECUTIVES

Chairman: Jim P. Manzi, age 58
President, CEO, and Director: Marc N. Casper, age 42, $34,283,776 total compensation
SVP and CFO: Peter M. Wilver, age 50, $2,996,295 total compensation
SVP; President, Laboratory Products: Alan J. Malus, age 50, $3,284,615 total compensation
SVP; President, Customer Channels: Edward A. Pesicka, age 42, $3,082,124 total compensation
SVP and President, Analytical and Scientific Instruments: Gregory J. (Greg) Herrema, age 44, $3,057,665 total compensation
SVP; President, Specialty Diagnostics: Kenneth Berger
SVP, General Counsel, and Secretary: Seth H. Hoogasian, age 55, $2,071,310 total compensation
SVP Human Resources: Elizabeth S. Bolgiano
SVP Global Business Services: Alexander G. Stachtiaris, age 46
VP and Chief Accounting Officer: Peter E. Hornstra, age 50
VP Tax and Treasurer: Anthony H. Smith
VP and CIO: Ina B. Kamenz
VP Investor Relations: Kenneth J. Apicerno
VP Global Research and Development: Ian D. Jardine
VP Financial Operations: Stephen Williamson
VP Corporate Communications: Karen A. Kirkwood
Auditors: PricewaterhouseCoopers LLP

LOCATIONS

HQ: Thermo Fisher Scientific Inc.
81 Wyman St., Waltham, MA 02454
Phone: 781-622-1000 **Fax:** 781-622-1207
Web: www.thermofisher.com

2009 Sales

	$ mil.	% of total
US	6,848.6	58
Germany	1,166.2	10
UK	891.1	7
Other countries	2,942.5	25
Adjustments	(1,738.7)	—
Total	**10,109.7**	**100**

PRODUCTS/OPERATIONS

2009 Sales

	$ mil.	% of total
Laboratory Products & Services	6,426.6	61
Analytical Technologies	4,153.9	39
Adjustments	(470.8)	—
Total	**10,109.7**	**100**

2009 Sales

	$ mil.	% of total
Products	8,523.7	84
Services	1,586.0	16
Total	**10,109.7**	**100**

Selected Products

Analytical Instrumentation
  Analysis instruments
    Electron backscattered diffraction systems
    Gas chromatography equipment
    High-performance liquid chromatography/ion chromatography (HPLC/IC) systems
    Ion energy analyzers
    Mass spectrometers (hybrid, ion trap, quadrupole)
    Microscopes
Laboratory Equipment
  Clinical diagnostics
  Lab furnishings
  Laboratory consumables
  Laboratory information management systems
  Laboratory instrument services
  Liquid handling equipment
  Meters, monitors, and electrochemical equipment
  Sample preparation equipment
  Vacuum equipment

Process Equipment
  Analysis instruments
    Chromatographs
    Elemental analyzers
    Fourier transform infrared analyzers
    Gas measurement
    Guided microwave spectrometry
    Mass spectrometers
    Moisture analyzers
    Near infrared analyzers
    Particle analyzers
    Surface analyzers
    X-ray spectrometers
  Coding and marking systems
  Foreign object detection equipment
  Nuclear radiation
    Neutron flux monitoring systems
    Neutron sources
    Reactor protection systems
  Nuclear reactor instrumentation systems
  Physical measurement and control systems
  Polymer testing equipment
  Process monitoring and control equipment
Security and Detection Devices
  Chemical and biological detection
    Aerosol monitors
    Ambient air analyzers
    Particle sizing impactors
    Unknown material identification instruments
  Explosives trace detection systems
  Radiological and nuclear detection
    Contamination survey meters
    Isotope identifiers
    Mobile gamma radiation monitors
    Neutron generators
    Nuclear incident emergency response kit
    Personal dosimeters
    Radioactivity monitors
    Rapid response vans
    SecurScan

COMPETITORS

Abbott Labs	Life Technologies
Agilent Technologies	MDS
Beckman Coulter	Mettler-Toledo
Becton, Dickinson	Newport Corp.
Bio-Rad Labs	PerkinElmer
Bruker	QIAGEN
Corning	Roche Diagnostics
Danaher	Roper Industries
Emerson Electric	Shimadzu
Harvard Bioscience	Sigma-Aldrich
Hitachi	Tektronix
Honeywell International	VWR International
IDEXX Labs	Waters Corp.
Johnson & Johnson	Yokogawa Electric

HISTORICAL FINANCIALS

Company Type: Public

Income Statement

FYE: December 31

	REVENUE ($ mil.)	NET INCOME ($ mil.)	NET PROFIT MARGIN	EMPLOYEES
12/09	10,110	850	8.4%	35,400
12/08	10,498	994	9.5%	34,500
12/07	9,746	761	7.8%	33,000
12/06	3,792	169	4.5%	30,500
12/05	2,633	223	8.5%	11,500
Annual Growth	**40.0%**	**39.7%**	**—**	**32.5%**

2009 Year-End Financials

Debt ratio: 13.4%
Return on equity: 5.6%
Cash ($ mil.): 1,564
Current ratio: 2.76
Long-term debt ($ mil.): 2,066

No. of shares (mil.): 407
Dividends
  Yield: —
  Payout: —
Market value ($ mil.): 19,430

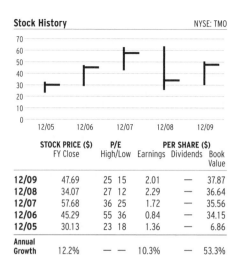

Stock History

NYSE: TMO

	STOCK PRICE ($) FY Close	P/E High/Low		Earnings	PER SHARE ($) Dividends	Book Value
12/09	47.69	25	15	2.01	—	37.87
12/08	34.07	27	12	2.29	—	36.64
12/07	57.68	36	25	1.72	—	35.56
12/06	45.29	55	36	0.84	—	34.15
12/05	30.13	23	18	1.36	—	6.86
Annual Growth	**12.2%**	**—**	**—**	**10.3%**	**—**	**53.3%**

Thomas & Betts

Thomas & Betts (T&B) is betting on its good connections. T&B provides electrical connectors, HVAC equipment, and transmission towers to the commercial construction, communications, industrial, and utility markets. It has three business segments: electrical (electrical connectors, enclosures, raceways, installation tools); HVAC (heaters, gas-fired duct furnaces, and evaporative cooling products); and steel structures (poles and transmission towers for power and telecommunications companies). T&B's many brands include Color-Keyed, Elastimold, Kindorf, Red Dot, Reznor, Sta-Kon, Snap-N-Seal, and Steel City. Sales outside the US account for about one-third of its revenues.

T&B started 2010 with the acquisition of power protection equipment provider JT Packard & Associates (based in Wisconsin). The deal expands T&B's service capacity in preventative maintenance and emergency service for a variety of power sources in both commercial and industrial markets. T&B also took over PMA AG, a privately held European maker of cable protection systems used in a variety of industrial applications. The acquisition gives T&B greater access to markets in Asia, Europe, and the Middle East, as well as boosting its portfolio of industrial cable products.

T&B's challenges include its dependence on the US market, where the economy was struggling through an extended recession. Volatile costs for commodity raw materials (aluminum, copper, rubber compounds, steel, and zinc among them) and for energy are another challenge. The credit crisis is forcing the company to keep a close eye on the creditworthiness of leading customers, although T&B doesn't have any customers with a large amount of trade receivables owed.

T&B streamlined its operations, consolidating production and distribution facilities and divesting stakes in joint ventures in Belgium and Japan. The company also made sizable strategic acquisitions to supplement its product portfolio.

HISTORY

In 1898 in New York City, Princeton engineering graduates Hobart D. Betts and Robert McKean Thomas founded a distribution company for the infant electrical industry; they quickly moved into designing conduits and fittings. In 1905 the company incorporated as Thomas and Betts Company, and in 1912 it began manufacturing with the purchase of Standard Electric Fittings. In 1917 the two merged to form The Thomas & Betts Company, consolidating operations in Elizabeth, New Jersey.

Thomas & Betts was one of the first manufacturers of electrical products to embrace electrical distributors as marketing and sales partners, not competitors. In the early 1930s the company adopted its first marketing slogan: "Wherever Electricity Goes, So Do We."

The company made products that were used to wire the Hoover Dam and the New York City subway system, and by the US military during WWII. During this period Thomas & Betts grew internally and through acquisitions. In 1959 the company went public. It changed its name to Thomas & Betts Corporation (T&B) in 1968.

In 1992 T&B acquired American Electric, an electrical products manufacturer, and relocated its corporate offices to American Electric's headquarters in Memphis. The company acquired Augat, a maker of electronic connectors, in 1996; consolidation expenses brought a severe drop in profits for the year.

President Clyde Moore was named CEO in 1997. T&B made another 15 acquisitions in 1997 and 1998, continuing to expand upon its product offerings for fiber-optic and telecommunications companies. Among the acquisitions were Pride Product Services, a maker of fiber-optic sleeves; and Kaufel Group, a Canadian manufacturer of industrial and emergency lighting products. The latter more than doubled the extent of T&B's lighting product line. Also in 1998 T&B entered a new market with its $74 million acquisition of Telecommunications Devices, a maker of batteries for cell phones and laptops.

The company's 1999 acquisitions included Ocal, which makes plastic-coated conduits and components, and L.E. Mason, a manufacturer of electrical boxes and related products. But its bid to acquire cable maker AFC Cable was topped by rival Tyco International. That year losses caused T&B to exit the active-components portion of its cable TV business; the company sold its Megaflex, Photon, and broadband radio-frequency amplifier product lines.

In 2000 T&B sold its electronics manufacturing operations to Tyco for $750 million, and Moore was elected chairman. He later resigned his post, and director T. Kevin Dunnigan (who had previously served as both chairman and CEO of T&B), assumed Moore's position.

In early 2001 T&B announced that the SEC was investigating its accounting practices; the company also announced it was restating earnings for 2000.

Five class-action lawsuits over the accounting issues were filed in 2000, and they were consolidated into one action late in the year. A US District Court ordered formal mediation in the litigation in mid-2002, which resulted in a settlement agreement later that year. Without T&B admitting any liability or wrongdoing, the parties agreed to dismiss the lawsuit and the company paid $46.5 million to the plaintiffs.

Dominic Pileggi, president of T&B's main electrical business, was promoted to president and COO of the company at the beginning of 2003.

Later in 2003 the company reached a settlement with the SEC, basically agreeing to more closely follow accounting and financial reporting regulations, while the commission brought no charges against the company.

Pileggi succeeded Dunnigan as CEO in early 2004. Dunnigan became non-executive chairman of the board.

In 2005 T&B acquired the assets of Southern Monopole and Utilities, a subsidiary of Qualico Steel Company. Pileggi succeeded Dunnigan as chairman at the end of 2005, as Dunnigan retired as chairman and a member of the board.

In 2007 the company acquired competitor Lamson & Sessions for around $450 million in cash. In the biggest acquisition in its history, T&B saw a strategic fit with the Lamson & Sessions product portfolio of non-metallic electrical boxes, fittings, flexible conduit, and industrial PVC pipe.

Following the L&S acquisition, T&B decided to divest its portfolio of PVC and high-density polyethylene (HDPE) conduits, ducts, and pressure pipes used in the construction, industrial, municipal, utility, and telecommunications markets. Also in 2007 T&B acquired the power quality business of Danaher for $280 million in cash.

EXECUTIVES

Chairman and CEO: Dominic J. Pileggi, age 57, $9,106,706 total compensation
SVP and CFO: William E. Weaver Jr., age 46, $1,412,033 total compensation
SVP Global Operations: Imad Hajj, age 49, $2,355,785 total compensation
SVP and Group President, Electrical: Charles L. (Chuck) Treadway, age 44, $2,783,469 total compensation
SVP Human Resources and Administration: Peggy P. Gann
VP Business Development and Strategic Planning: Stanley P. (Stan) Locke, age 50, $769,054 total compensation
VP, General Counsel, and Secretary: James N. (Jim) Raines, age 66, $1,588,162 total compensation
VP Tax: Michael W. Arney
VP and Controller: David L. Alyea
VP Treasury: Joseph F. (Joe) Warren Jr.
VP Information Technologies: Joseph (Joe) DiCianni
VP Investor and Corporate Relations: Patricia A. (Tricia) Bergeron
President, U.S. Electrical: E. F. (Ned) Camuti
President, Steel Structures: James R. (Jim) Wiederholt
President, Europe, Middle East, Africa, and Asia: Fabrice Van Belle
President, Canada: Nathalie Pilon
Auditors: KPMG LLP

LOCATIONS

HQ: Thomas & Betts Corporation
8155 T&B Blvd., Memphis, TN 38125
Phone: 901-252-8000   **Fax:** 901-252-1354
Web: www.tnb.com

2009 Sales

	$ mil.	% of total
US	1,244.3	66
Canada	331.8	17
Europe	209.2	11
Other regions	113.4	6
Total	**1,898.7**	**100**

PRODUCTS/OPERATIONS

2009 Sales

	$ mil.	% of total
Electrical	1,554.3	82
Steel structures	234.5	12
HVAC	109.9	6
Total	**1,898.7**	**100**

Selected Segments and Brands

Electrical
  Boxes and covers (Bowers, Commander, Steel City)
  Cable ties (Catamount, Ty-Fast, Ty-Rap)
  Cable tray systems (Canstrut, Cen-Tray, Electrotray, Pilgrim, T&B)
  Communications connectors, grounding products, meter sockets (Anchor, Blackburn)
  Conduit and cable fittings (Carlon, Iberville, Ocal, Red Dot, T&B)
  Connectors (Blackburn, Color-Keyed)
  Electrical maintenance products (Valon)
  Electricians' supplies (T&B)
  Fittings and grounding systems (T&B)
  Industrial connectors (Russellstoll)
  Lighting (Carlon, Red Dot, Lumacell)
  Metal framing (Kindorf, Superstrut)
  Outlet boxes (Bowers, Union)
  Terminals and connectors (STA-KON)
  Timers and relays (Agastat)
  Wire management systems (Carlon, T&B)
  Wiring ducts (Taylor)
Steel Structures
  Power connectors and accessories (Elastimold)
  Steel poles (Meyer)
  Transmission towers (Lehigh)
HVAC
  Evaporative cooling and energy recovery equipment (International Energy Saver)
  Heaters (EK Campbell, Reznor)
  Heating, mechanical, and refrigeration supplies (T&B)

COMPETITORS

3M
Amphenol
Beghelli
Cembre
Channell Commercial
Cooper Industries
Corning
Eaton
Encore Wire
Fujikura Ltd.
GE Appliances & Lighting
Gewiss
Hubbell
ITT Corp.
Legrand
Methode Electronics
Molex
Panasonic Corp
Sabre Industries
Siemens AG
Smiths Group
Spirent
Sumitomo Electric
Tyco
Valmont Industries

HISTORICAL FINANCIALS

Company Type: Public

Income Statement

FYE: December 31

	REVENUE ($ mil.)	NET INCOME ($ mil.)	NET PROFIT MARGIN	EMPLOYEES
12/09	1,899	108	5.7%	8,500
12/08	2,474	265	10.7%	10,000
12/07	2,137	183	8.6%	11,000
12/06	1,869	175	9.4%	9,000
12/05	1,695	113	6.7%	9,000
Annual Growth	**2.9%**	**(1.2%)**	**—**	**(1.4%)**

2009 Year-End Financials

Debt ratio: 47.6%
Return on equity: 8.7%
Cash ($ mil.): 479
Current ratio: 3.46
Long-term debt ($ mil.): 638

No. of shares (mil.): 52
Dividends
Yield: 0.0%
Payout: —
Market value ($ mil.): 1,871

Stock History   NYSE: TNB

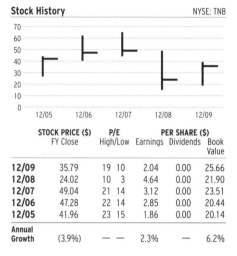

	STOCK PRICE ($) FY Close	P/E High/Low		PER SHARE ($) Earnings	Dividends	Book Value
12/09	35.79	19	10	2.04	0.00	25.66
12/08	24.02	10	3	4.64	0.00	21.90
12/07	49.04	21	14	3.12	0.00	23.51
12/06	47.28	22	14	2.85	0.00	20.44
12/05	41.96	23	15	1.86	0.00	20.14
Annual Growth	(3.9%)	—	—	2.3%	—	6.2%

Thomson Reuters

Financial information is king and Thomson Reuters Corporation holds the crown. The financial data powerhouse was created as the result of the $16 billion cash and stock purchase of news service Reuters by niche information provider The Thomson Corporation. The combined entity is the leader in financial data, with approximately 34% of the market share. (Information service Bloomberg is a close second with 33% of the market.) Thomson Reuters provides electronic information and services to businesses and professionals worldwide, serving the legal, financial services, tax and accounting, health care and science, and media markets. Data is offered online and through CD-ROM; most revenues come from subscription sales.

The acquisition of Reuters (which occurred in 2008) significantly expanded the geographic reach of the business, with the former Thomson having earned most of its revenue from the US, while the majority of Reuters' revenue came from Europe. Tom Glocer, former CEO of Reuters, was named head of Thomson Reuters and has been overseeing the integration. His first order in the consolidation was to cut some 1,500 jobs.

Thomson Reuters is organized into two units, the Markets division and the Professional division. The company's Markets division consists of Sales & Trading, Investment & Advisory, Enterprise, and Media businesses, and includes established brands and products such as Reuters, Omgeo, Lipper, Tradeweb, First Call, Datastream, and Thomson ONE. The company's Professional division includes non-financial business segments devoted to Legal, Tax & Accounting, and Healthcare & Science. Professional operations include Thomson Reuters, Legal; Elite (business management software); Thomson Scientific

(technical information and applications); Thomson Tax & Accounting (tax and accounting information, software, and services); and Baker Robbins & Company (technology consulting).

As part of an effort to expand its content offerings, the company acquired some 30 companies in 2009. Within the Markets division, it bolstered its editorial operations with the purchase of Breakingviews, a financial commentary website managed by Reuters. Following the completion of the acquisition, Thomson Reuters overhauled Reuters.com. The redesign features more analysis and opinion, as well as fewer but more prominent ads. Further additions to the Markets division in 2009 included Vhayu Technologies, a provider of analytics and storage technology. The company also acquired Hugin Group, a provider of regulatory and news distribution services, from NYSE Euronext. It purchased Hugin to expand its investor relations and corporate communications offerings.

Thomson Reuters is also acquiring many businesses within its Professional division. In 2010 it expanded the Legal division with the acquisition of Round Table Group, a provider of expert witness consulting services to litigators, and Complinet, a provider of compliance information solutions. In early 2010 Thomson Reuters acquired Discovery Logic, a provider of customizable analytics solutions for scientific research, in order to bolster its Healthcare & Science offerings.

Previous changes to the Professional division include the global expansion of its Legal and Tax & Accounting businesses to accommodate the growth of international products and customers. The company in 2009 combined all of that division's offerings related to patents, trademarks, and standards to form an intellectual property (IP) business. The IP business is part of the Legal segment, which includes such brands as Westlaw and FindLaw. (The Legal segment was the former Thomson Corporation's largest unit, and had accounted for 45% of that company's business.)

In its first major strategic move after its formation, Thomson Reuters sold its Dialog subsidiary to information provider ProQuest Information and Learning in 2008. Dialog offered a broad source of aggregated information; the divestiture reflects Thomson Reuters' goal of building deeper content within specialized markets.

After the combination of Thomson and Reuters, the Thomson family, through its Woodbridge investment firm, took a 53% economic and voting interest in Thomson Reuters. Former Reuters shareholders have a 24% stake in the company, while former Thomson shareholders own 23%. The company was previously owned through a complex dual listing and had traded on the London Stock Exchange and Nasdaq. In 2009 it unified its ownership structure in order to simplify trading. As a result, the company ceased to be listed on the London Stock Exchange and Nasdaq.

HISTORY

The Thomson Corporation was established when Roy Thomson started a radio station in Ontario in 1930. He next began purchasing town newspapers, venturing outside Ontario in 1949 and into the US in 1952.

The Thomson newspaper empire grew rapidly, and the company next entered into a North Sea oil drilling venture. Oil accounted for the bulk of Thomson's profits by 1976, when Thomson died, and the company used its oil earnings to expand and diversify its publishing interests.

Purchases included American Banker and Bond Buyer (financial publications, 1983), Gale Research (library reference materials, 1985), and several online information providers. Thomson then completed the sale of its oil and gas holdings. In 1991 it bought Maxwell's Macmillan Professional and Business Reference Publishing. It bought law and textbook publisher West Publishing in 1996. Continuing its selective divestment of newspapers, the company sold 43 daily papers in the US and Canada in 1996. In 2000 Thomson announced it would sell its newspapers to focus on the Internet.

Other Thomson purchases included a pair of tax and law publishing units from UK's Pearson; Knight-Ridder's Technimetrics financial information unit; Sylvan Learning Systems' Prometric division, which provided computer-based testing services; and Wave Technologies International, a provider of multimedia instructional products. Thomson also bought the online data services division of Dialog, and it acquired rival financial data provider Primark for $1 billion. In 2001 the company bought the higher education and corporate training businesses of Harcourt General (which later became Harcourt Education) from Reed Elsevier Group plc (formerly Reed Elsevier plc), and acquired business content provider NewsEdge.

Thomson started trading on the New York Stock Exchange in mid-2002. Later that year it beefed up its Internet education group with the purchase of certain e-learning assets from McGraw Hill. In 2003 the company purchased Elite Information Group, a maker of law firm practice software, for more than $100 million. (The software firm later dropped the "Information Group" portion of its name to become simply Elite.)

In 2006 Thomson purchased Solucient LLC, a provider of data and advanced analytics to hospitals and health systems; Quantitative Analytics, Inc., a provider of financial database integration and analysis solutions; and LiveNote Technologies, a provider of transcript and evidence management software to litigators and court reporters. Kenneth Thomson died at the age of 82 that year.

The following year Thomson exited the educational information market when it sold Thomson Learning to investment groups Apax Partners and OMERS Capital for $7.7 billion. Thomson cited a lack of growth potential as its primary rationale for selling Thomson Learning (now called Cengage Learning). It used the proceeds of the sale to help acquire Reuters in 2008 in a $16.2 billion deal that created the largest player in the field of financial data.

Later in 2008 Thomson Reuters sold Dialog to ProQuest Information and Learning. At the end of the year it acquired financial software firm Paisley. In 2009 it unified its dual-listed ownership structure in order to simplify trading.

EXECUTIVES

Chairman: David K. R. Thomson, age 52
Deputy Chairman: W. Geoffrey (Geoff) Beattie, age 50
Deputy Chairman: Niall FitzGerald, age 64
CEO and Director: Thomas H. (Tom) Glocer, age 50
EVP and CFO: Robert D. (Bob) Daleo, age 60
EVP and CTO: James Powell
EVP and Chief Human Resources Officer:
 Stephen G. Dando, age 48
EVP and Global Chief Marketing Officer:
 Gustav Carlson
EVP and Chief Strategy Officer: David Craig
EVP and General Counsel: Deirdre Stanley, age 45

EVP: Jonathan S. Newpol
Chief Medical Officer: Raymond J. (Ray) Fabius, age 56
SVP Investor Relations: Frank J. Golden
SVP and CIO: Kelli Crane
CEO, Scientific: Vin Caraher
CEO, Reuters Foundation: Monique Villa
CEO, Professional Division: James C. (Jim) Smith
CEO, Tax and Accounting: Roy M. Martin Jr.
CEO, Markets Division: Devin N. Wenig, age 43
CEO, Healthcare and Science: Mike Boswood
CEO, Legal: Peter Warwick
President, Investment and Advisory: Eric Frank
President, Enterprise: Jon Robson
President Business of Law, Legal: Chris Kibarian
President, Reuters Media: Chris Ahearn
President, Sales and Trading: Mark Redwood

LOCATIONS

HQ: Thomson Reuters Corporation
3 Times Square, New York, NY 10036
Phone: 646-223-4000
Web: www.thomsonreuters.com

2009 Sales

	$ mil.	% of total
Americas (North America, Latin America, South America)	7,699	59
Europe, Middle East & Africa	3,948	30
Asia/Pacific	1,350	11
Total	**12,997**	**100**

PRODUCTS/OPERATIONS

2009 Sales

	$ mil.	% of total
Markets	7,535	58
Professional		
Legal	3586	28
Tax & Accounting	1006	8
Healthcare & Science	878	6
Adjustments	(8)	—
Total	**12,997**	**100**

Selected Offerings

Markets
Reuters (business newswire service)
Thomson Financial (content, analytical applications, and transaction platforms to financial professionals)
Thomson ONE (flagship financial product)
Professional
Legal
West (legal, regulatory, and compliance information)
FindLaw (legal directory)
Elite (law firm management software)
Healthcare and Science
Baker Robbins & Company (technology consulting)
PDR (Physicians Desk Reference)
Solucient (databases and analytics)
Thomson Scientific (technical information and applications)
Tax & Accounting
Thomson Tax & Accounting (tax and accounting information, software, and services)

COMPETITORS

Agence France-Presse
Associated Press
Bloomberg L.P.
D&B
Dow Jones
FactSet
Forbes
IHS
MarketWatch
Pearson plc
Reed Elsevier Group
Track Data
United Business Media
UPI
Wolters Kluwer

HISTORICAL FINANCIALS

Company Type: Public

Income Statement

FYE: December 31

	REVENUE ($ mil.)	NET INCOME ($ mil.)	NET PROFIT MARGIN	EMPLOYEES
12/09	12,997	867	6.7%	55,000
12/08	11,707	1,321	11.3%	—
Annual Growth	**11.0%**	**(34.4%)**	**—**	**—**

Net Income History

NYSE: TRI

Thor Industries

The Norse gods might have laughed at the idea of bedrooms on wheels, but that doesn't stop Thor Industries, a recreation vehicle builder. Through its subsidiaries, the company makes and sells a range of RVs, from motor homes to travel trailers, as well as related parts. Brands include Airstream and Dutchmen. Thor is also a major US producer of small and midsize buses. Bus and RV manufacturing plants generally produce vehicles to dealer order; Thor's independent dealers dot the US and Canada catering to private purchasers and municipalities. The company drives a joint venture with Cruise America, renting vacation RVs. Thor rolled out in 1980 when Wade Thompson and Peter Orthwein purchased Airstream's business.

In 2010 Thor acquired SJC Industries, a privately held manufacturer of ambulances. A natural fit with Thor's bus and RV manufacturing operations, SJC gives the company access to the emergency vehicle market, which is less subject to economic ups and downs than the RV market.

RVs continue to be Thor's thoroughbred in terms of revenue. Competitively, the company touts a 31% share of the travel trailer and fifth wheels market, and an 18% share of the motor home. Although Thor's bus sales come in a distant second on its bottom line, the company captures about 40% of small and midsize bus demand in the US and Canada.

Thor's business is based upon a decentralized operation of RV and bus making subsidiaries. Each subsidiary, encompassing a network of small plants, is managed by objectives tied to employee incentives, including manufacturing processes, products, and customer service.

The company faces exposure to downturns in consumer buying and limited avenues for credit, as well as volatile fuel prices. During 2008 and 2009 vehicle sales plunged, although bus demand has fared better. Bus customers, largely government agencies, are subject to public budgetary constraints. Its commercial customers, including rental car companies and hotels, are influenced by the health of the travel industry.

In light of deteriorating RV and bus sales, the company dialed back operations and cut head-count in 2009 — at its Keystone subsidiary, for example, by as much as 30%. Thor's rapid response, coupled with its decentralized operating structure, has helped it dodge the financial pitfalls that forced rivals Fleetwood and Monaco into bankruptcy. In fact, despite the tough economic and RV industry environment, the company made a profit in 2009, and has done so since its founding.

Thor also dealt with GE Consumer Finance's decision in late 2008 to end their relationship. Thor bounced back by reviving Thor Credit retail financing. Through Thor dealers, the unit aims to build sales by assisting customers in financing their purchases of new and used RVs. In 2009, FreedomRoads, LLC, a dealer with 47 locations in 26 US states, capped 15% of Thor's consolidated RV net sales.

Prior to his death in late 2009, Thompson stepped down as chairman and CEO, passing the torch to Orthwein. Thompson owned more than 25% of the company.

HISTORY

Mergers and acquisitions specialist Wade Thompson and investment banker Peter Orthwein saw the potential of the RV market after buying Hi-Lo Trailer in 1977. Thor Industries was formed when they bought the troubled Airstream Trailers unit (founded in 1931) from Beatrice Foods in 1980. Named after the mythical Norse god of thunder and containing the first two letters of the founders' last names, Thor Industries formed Citair in 1982 to buy the RV division of Commodore Corp. (founded 1948). The company went public in 1984, and it entered the bus business with the acquisitions of ElDorado Bus company in 1988 and National Coach in 1991. Thor expanded its RV line with the purchases of Dutchmen Manufacturing in 1991 and Four Winds International in 1992.

The company continued acquisitions in 1995, buying Skamper Corp. (folding trailers) and Komfort Trailers. In 1996 its bus operations received significant orders from National Car Rental and the suburban Chicago transit company, PACE.

Bus sales did well in 1997, but RV sales were flat. That year Thor sold its Henschen Axle manufacturing operation. In response to weak sales, the company opened new channels, such as its RV rental joint venture. In 1998 it bought Champion Motor Coach (small and midsize buses) from manufactured-home company Champion Enterprises for about $10 million. It also sold its unprofitable motor homes unit, Thor West, to the division's managers.

In 1999 Thor won a $45 million contract to build 1,135 buses for the state of California. The following year the company made a bid to buy rival RV company Coachmen Industries; that bid was later rejected and withdrawn.

Thor regained its thunder in 2001 with the $145 million purchase of Keystone RV Company. The deal made the company the US's leading manufacturer of travel trailers and third wheels (with 25% of the market), as well as the largest builder of small and midsize buses (with 37% of the market).

In 2003 Thor paid nearly $30 million for Damon Corporation, a maker of class-A motor homes and park models. Thor paid $27 million for fifth wheel and travel trailer manufacturer CrossRoads RV in 2004.

EXECUTIVES

Chairman, President, and CEO: Peter B. Orthwein, age 64, $235,991 total compensation
COO and Senior Group President, Bus Group: Richard E. (Dickey) Riegel III, age 43, $977,503 total compensation
EVP, Chief Administrative Officer, and Secretary: Walter L. Bennett, age 64, $479,988 total compensation
SVP, CFO, and Treasurer: Christian G. (Chris) Farman, age 50, $965,351 total compensation
Senior Group President, Recreational Vehicle Group: Ronald J. (Ron) Fenech, age 52
Group President, Thor Bus: Andrew Imanse
Chairman, Airstream: Lawrence J. Huttle
President, Crossroads: Mark R. Lucas
President, Champion Bus: John A. Resnik
President, Goshen Coach: Troy Snyder
President, Dutchmen: Donald J. Clark
President, Komfort: John P. Attila
President, Airstream: Robert H. Wheeler III
President, Thor Motor Homes: William C. (Bill) Fenech
President, Breckenridge: Tim J. Howard
President, ElDorado National, California: Anthony W. Wayne
President, ElDorado National, Kansas: Sheldon E. Walle
President, General Coach, Ontario: Roger W. Faulkner
Auditors: Deloitte & Touche LLP

LOCATIONS

HQ: Thor Industries, Inc.
419 W. Pike St., Jackson Center, OH 45334
Phone: 937-596-6849   **Fax:** 937-596-6539
Web: www.thorindustries.com

PRODUCTS/OPERATIONS

2009 Sales

	$ mil.	% of total
Recreation vehicles		
Towables	953.3	63
Motorized	161.7	10
Buses	406.9	27
Total	**1,521.9**	**100**

Selected Products

Ambulances
 Marque
 McCoy-Miller
 Premiere
Buses
 Champion (small and midsize buses)
 ElDorado National (small and midsize buses for shuttles, tour and charter operations, community transit systems)
 General Coach (small and midsize buses)
 Goshen Coach (small and midsize buses)
Recreational vehicles
 Motorized
  Damon (gasoline and diesel class-A motor homes)
  Four Winds (motor homes)
 Towables
  Airstream (premium and medium-high-priced travel trailers and motor homes)
  Breckenridge (factory-built cottage homes)
  Citair, dba General Coach (park trailers and models, cabins, mobile homes, theatrical trailers)
  CrossRoads (travel trailers, fifth wheels, ultra lite trailers, and destination trailers/park models)
  Dutchmen (travel trailers and fifth wheels)
  Keystone (travel trailers and fifth wheels)
  Komfort (travel trailers and fifth wheels for sale in the western US and Canada)

COMPETITORS

All American Group
Blue Bird
Champion Enterprises
Collins Industries
Daimler Buses
Featherlite
Forest River
FTCA
Hino Motors
Jayco, Inc.
Monaco RV
Motor Coach Industries
Prevost Car
Rexhall Industries
Skyline
Volvo
Winnebago

HISTORICAL FINANCIALS

Company Type: Public

Income Statement

FYE: July 31

	REVENUE ($ mil.)	NET INCOME ($ mil.)	NET PROFIT MARGIN	EMPLOYEES
7/09	1,522	17	1.1%	5,378
7/08	2,641	93	3.5%	7,064
7/07	2,856	135	4.7%	8,689
7/06	3,066	173	5.6%	9,363
7/05	2,558	122	4.8%	8,473
Annual Growth	**(12.2%)**	**(38.8%)**	**—**	**(10.7%)**

2009 Year-End Financials

Debt ratio: —
Return on equity: 2.4%
Cash ($ mil.): 222
Current ratio: 3.27
Long-term debt ($ mil.): —
No. of shares (mil.): 51
Dividends
 Yield: 1.2%
 Payout: 90.3%
Market value ($ mil.): 1,230

Stock History

NYSE: THO

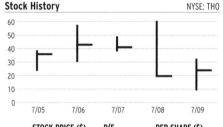

	STOCK PRICE ($) FY Close	P/E High/Low		PER SHARE ($) Earnings	Dividends	Book Value
7/09	23.91	103	31	0.31	0.28	13.70
7/08	19.62	36	12	1.66	0.28	13.60
7/07	41.02	20	16	2.41	0.28	14.89
7/06	42.84	19	10	3.03	0.24	13.86
7/05	35.80	18	11	2.13	0.12	11.61
Annual Growth	**(9.6%)**	**—**	**—**	**(38.2%)**	**23.6%**	**4.2%**

TIAA-CREF

It's punishment enough to write the name once on a blackboard. Teachers Insurance and Annuity Association — College Retirement Equities Fund (TIAA-CREF) is one of the largest, if not longest-named, private retirement systems in the US, providing for more than 3.5 million members of the academic, cultural, medical, and research communities and for investors outside academia's ivied confines. It also serves institutional investors. TIAA-CREF's core offerings include financial advice, investment information, retirement plans and accounts, annuities, life insurance, brokerage, and trust services (through TIAA-CREF Trust). The system, a not-for-profit organization, also manages a line of mutual funds.

TIAA-CREF is one of the nation's heftiest institutional investors, with some $400 billion in assets under management, and it has not been afraid to throw its weight around corporate boardrooms. The organization is known for active and choosy investing and is a vocal critic of extravagant executive compensation packages. It invests with an eye toward social responsibility, as well, taking into account companies' policies and practices toward such issues as human rights, labor, and global warming.

TIAA-CREF also owns one of the nation's largest portfolios of real estate investments. The company agreed to sell a $503 million portfolio of commercial mortgages to real estate investment trust Starwood Property Trust for $510 plus accrued interest in early 2010.

That same year, TIAA-CREF and joint venture partner Developers Diversified Realty sold a portfolio of 16 shopping centers to Inland Real Estate Acquisitions for $424 million. The centers, with some 3.5 million sq. ft. of retail space, are located in Florida, Georgia, and North and South Carolina.

HISTORY

With $15 million, the Carnegie Foundation for the Advancement of Teaching in 1905 founded the Teachers Insurance and Annuity Association (TIAA) in New York City to provide retirement benefits and other forms of financial security to educators. When Carnegie's original endowment was found to be insufficient, another $1 million reorganized the fund into a defined-contribution plan in 1918. TIAA was the first portable pension plan, letting participants change employers without losing benefits and offering a fixed annuity. The fund required infusions of Carnegie cash until 1947.

In 1952 TIAA CEO William Greenough pioneered the variable annuity, based on common stock investments, and created the College Retirement Equities Fund (CREF) to offer it. Designed to supplement TIAA's fixed annuity, CREF invested participants' premiums in stocks. CREF and TIAA were subject to New York insurance (but not SEC) regulation.

During the 1950s, TIAA led the fight for Social Security benefits for university employees and began offering group total disability coverage (1957) and group life insurance (1958).

In 1971 TIAA-CREF began helping colleges boost investment returns from endowments, then moved into endowment management. It helped found a research center to provide objective investment information in 1972.

For 70 years retirement was the only way members could exit TIAA-CREF. Their only investment choices were stocks through CREF or a one-way transfer into TIAA's annuity accounts based on long-term bond, real estate, and mortgage investments. In the 1980s CREF indexed its funds to the S&P average.

By 1987's stock crash, TIAA-CREF had a million members, many of whom wanted more protection from stock market fluctuations. After the crash, Clifton Wharton (the first African-American to head a major US financial organization) became CEO; the next year CREF added a money market fund, for which the SEC required complete transferability, even outside TIAA-CREF. Now open to competition, TIAA-CREF became more flexible, adding investment options and long-term-care plans.

John Biggs became CEO in 1993. After the 1994 bond crash, TIAA-CREF began educating members on the ABCs of retirement investing, hoping to persuade them not to switch to flashy short-term investments and not to panic during such cyclical events as the crash.

In 1996 it went international, buying interests in UK commercial and mixed-use property. TIAA-CREF filed for SEC approval of more mutual funds in 1997. Although federal tax legislation took away TIAA-CREF's tax-exempt status in 1997, the change was made without decreasing annuity incomes for the year.

The status change let TIAA-CREF offer no-load mutual funds to the public in 1998. A trust company and financial planning services were added; all new products were sold at cost, with TIAA-CREF waiving fees. TIAA-CREF in 1998 became the first pension fund to force out an entire board of directors (that of sputtering cafeteria firm Furr's/Bishop's). Also that year TIAA-CREF's crusade to curb "dead hand" poison pills (an antitakeover defense measure) found favor with the shareholders of Bergen Brunswig (now AmerisourceBergen), Lubrizol, and Mylan Laboratories.

Biggs retired in 2002. He was succeeded by Herbert Allison, who was replaced in 2008 by Roger Ferguson.

EXECUTIVES

Chairman, TIAA Board of Trustees:
Ronald L. Thompson, age 60
Chairman, CREF Board of Trustees: Nancy L. Jacob, age 65
Director Corporate Media Relations: Chad Peterson
President, CEO, TIAA Trustee and Overseer, and CREF Overseer: Roger W. Ferguson Jr., age 58
COO: Edward (Ed) Van Dolsen, age 52
Senior Managing Director and Chief Investment Officer: Edward J. Grzybowski
EVP and Chief Legal Officer: Brandon Becker
EVP and Chief Integration Officer:
Georganne C. Proctor, age 53
EVP Shared Services: Marvin W. (Marv) Adams, age 53
EVP and CFO: Virginia M. (Gina) Wilson, age 55
EVP Asset Management; CEO, Teachers Advisors and TIAA-CREF Investment Management: Scott C. Evans
EVP and Chief Marketing and Communications Officer: Connie K. Weaver
EVP Risk Management: Stephen B. (Steve) Gruppo
EVP Technology and Operations: Cara L. Schnaper
EVP Human Resources and Corporate Services:
Dermot J. O'Brien
Senior Managing Director and Chief Strategy Officer: Keith Stock, age 57
Managing Director and Head TIAA-CREF Institute:
Stephanie Bell-Rose
Director Corporate Media Relations: Chad Peterson

LOCATIONS

HQ: Teachers Insurance and Annuity Association — College Retirement Equities Fund
730 3rd Ave., New York, NY 10017
Phone: 212-490-9000   **Fax:** 212-916-4840
Web: www.tiaa-cref.org

PRODUCTS/OPERATIONS

Selected Mutual Funds
Bond
Bond Index
Bond Plus
Equity Index
Growth & Income
High-Yield
Inflation-Linked Bond
International Equity
Large-Cap Growth
Large-Cap Value
Lifecycle Retirement Income Fund
Managed Allocation
Mid-Cap Growth
Mid-Cap Value
Money Market
Real Estate Securities
Short-Term Bond
Small-Cap Equity
Social Choice Equity
Tax-Exempt Bond

COMPETITORS

Aetna
Ameriprise
AXA Financial
CalPERS
Charles Schwab
CIGNA
Citigroup
FMR
John Hancock Financial Services
JPMorgan Chase
MassMutual
MetLife
New York Life
Northwestern Mutual
Principal Financial
Prudential
T. Rowe Price
USAA
VALIC
The Vanguard Group

HISTORICAL FINANCIALS

Company Type: Private

Income Statement				FYE: December 31
	REVENUE ($ mil.)	NET INCOME ($ mil.)	NET PROFIT MARGIN	EMPLOYEES
12/08	12,740	(3,060)	—	7,500
12/07	13,187	1,465	11.1%	7,500
12/06	12,378	3,453	27.9%	5,500
12/05	11,703	1,878	16.0%	5,500
12/04	10,864	540	5.0%	6,000
Annual Growth	4.1%	—	—	5.7%

Net Income History

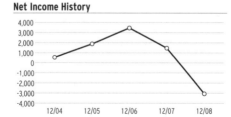

Tiffany & Co.

Breakfast at Tiffany & Co. has turned into a bountiful buffet, complete with the finest crystal and flatware, as well as more ubiquitous fare. Its specialty is fine jewelry, but the company also puts its name on timepieces, silverware, china, stationery, and other luxury items. Many products are packaged in the company's trademarked Tiffany Blue Box. Tiffany has broadened its merchandise mix to include key chains and other items that sell for much less than the typical Tiffany price tag. The firm sells its goods exclusively through more than 220 Tiffany & Co. stores and boutiques worldwide, its website, business-to-business accounts, and catalogs.

Tiffany has been expanding its retail presence, as well, while diversifying its customer reach through other retail venues. About 90 stores are located in the US and the company plans to add a handful of new shops on its home turf by the end of 2010. Its famed flagship location on Manhattan's Fifth Avenue accounted for 9% of 2009 sales. Tiffany also markets through its iconic annual Blue Book catalog, through its Selections and Collections catalogs, and through its website.

Despite a tough selling environment in 2009, Tiffany saw steady sales and even a rebound, of sorts, during the last quarter of the year. Overall, while the jewelry retailer lost its firm footing in the Americas, Tiffany was able to eke out near-pre-recession revenue figures thanks to a boost in sales in other regions, such as Asia/Pacific and Europe.

While jewelry is its primary business, Tiffany wants to strengthen its products portfolio and reach into other niches of the market. Aiming to broaden its accessories collections, Tiffany acquired luxury handbag and footwear brand Lambertson Truex from Samsonite in 2009. The high-end design firm had filed for Chapter 11 bankruptcy protection earlier in the year. Lambertson Truex's classic designs are expected to be a perfect complement to the Tiffany brand. In a bid to re-enter the watch business, Tiffany in 2007 formed an alliance with The Swatch Group to create a new company to make and distribute Tiffany-branded timepieces.

Tiffany in late 2006 inked a 10-year exclusive deal with eyewear behemoth Luxottica to make and market Tiffany-branded ophthalmic and sun eyewear. The products began distribution worldwide in 2008 in Tiffany's stores and in retail locations in North America, Japan, Hong Kong, South Korea, the Middle East, and Mexico.

Pointing to the mounting recession in the US, the company shuttered its nearly 20-store Iridesse chain in 2009. Iridesse stores focused exclusively on high-end pearl jewelry.

Tiffany sold its store in Tokyo's tony Ginza district to Goldman Sachs for about $318 million. The jeweler purchased the nine-story building for $140 million in 2003. Tiffany now leases the property (through 2032) from Goldman.

Peter May and his Trian Fund Management own about a 17% stake in Tiffany.

HISTORY

Charles Lewis Tiffany and John Young founded Tiffany & Young in New York City in 1837. The store sold stationery and costume jewelry and offered a unique, no-haggling approach (prices were clearly marked). In 1845 the company began selling real jewelry and also published its first mail-order catalog. During the late 1840s it added silverware, timepieces, perfumes, and other luxury offerings.

In 1851 Tiffany & Young bought the operations of silversmith John Moore, adding the design and manufacture of silver to its business (its standard for sterling silver was later adopted as the US standard). Tiffany bought out his partners (including a third partner, J. L. Ellis) two years later, renaming the company Tiffany & Co.

Although it served European royalty, Tiffany found its primary clientele in the growing number of wealthy Americans. In 1878 it acquired the Tiffany Diamond, one of the largest yellow diamonds in the world, weighing 128.5 carats (on display in its flagship New York City store). By 1887 the company had more than $40 million in precious stones in its vaults.

Tiffany died in 1902, and his son Louis Comfort Tiffany joined the firm that year as artistic director. Louis designed jewelry and stained glass patterned after nature and art, and remains one of the most celebrated glass designers (Tiffany lamps are very popular with collectors). Tiffany's sales hit nearly $18 million in 1919, then stalled during the 1920s. Because of the Depression, sales dropped to less than $3 million in 1932, forcing the company to lay off employees and dip into its cash reserves to pay dividends. Louis died in 1933.

The company moved in 1940 to its present Fifth Avenue location, which was showcased in Truman Capote's 1958 novella *Breakfast at Tiffany's* (the story became an Audrey Hepburn movie in 1961). To keep Bulova Watch Co., which owned a 30% stake, from controlling Tiffany, in 1955 the Tiffany heirs sold their share of the company to Hoving Corp., which owned retailer Bonwit Teller. Walter Hoving, Tiffany's new chairman and CEO, and other investors bought the chain from Hoving's parent, Genesco, and Bulova in 1961. The company opened its first store outside of New York City, in San Francisco, two years later, and it added locations in Beverly Hills, California, and Houston in 1964.

Sales grew through the 1970s. Tiffany was sold to cosmetics seller Avon Products in 1979, and Hoving retired as chairman and CEO the next year. Avon increased the stores' selection of less expensive items, a decision some felt hurt Tiffany. In 1984 Avon sold Tiffany to a group of investors led by Tiffany's then chairman William Chaney and backed by Bahrain-based Investcorp. Chaney set about improving Tiffany's tarnished image with affluent shoppers. In 1986 the company expanded into Europe, opening a store in London. To retire debt, it went public the next year with about 30 retail locations worldwide.

Japanese retailer Mitsukoshi, a seller of Tiffany's items in department stores and Tiffany & Co. boutiques in Japan, increased its stake in the company to 10% in 1989. The company expanded dramatically in the US during the 1990s, opening stores in more than 20 cities.

President and COO Michael Kowalski became CEO in 1999 and Mitsukoshi sold its stake in the company. Tiffany then paid $72 million for a 15% stake in diamond supplier Aber Resources. In an attempt to gain greater control of its brand, Tiffany discontinued sales to retailers in the US and Europe in 2000. In May 2001 Tiffany purchased 45% of duty-free store operator Little Switzerland and raised its stake to about 98% in 2002. In 2003 Chaney retired and Kowalski added the title of chairman.

In 2007 Tiffany sold its Little Switzerland unit.

EXECUTIVES

Chairman and CEO: Michael J. Kowalski, age 57, $7,873,135 total compensation
President: James E. Quinn, age 58, $3,947,622 total compensation
EVP and CFO: James N. Fernandez, age 54, $4,335,823 total compensation
EVP: Beth O. Canavan, age 55, $3,199,566 total compensation
EVP: Jon M. King, age 53, $3,095,537 total compensation
SVP and Chief Marketing Officer: Caroline D. Naggiar, age 52
SVP Operations: John S. Petterson, age 51
SVP Global Human Resources: Victoria Berger-Gross, age 54
SVP Merchandising: Pamela H. Cloud, age 40
SVP Finance: Patrick F. McGuiness, age 44
SVP, General Counsel, and Secretary: Patrick B. Dorsey, age 59
Group VP, Europe: Melvyn Kirtley
Group VP, Asia-Pacific: Darren Chen
VP and Treasurer: Michael Connolly
VP Investor Relations: Mark L. Aaron
VP, Japan: Stephan Lafay
VP and Controller: Henry Iglesias
Auditors: PricewaterhouseCoopers LLP

LOCATIONS

HQ: Tiffany & Co.
727 5th Ave., New York, NY 10022
Phone: 212-755-8000
Web: www.tiffany.com

2010 Sales

	$ mil.	% of total
Americas	1,410.8	52
Asia/Pacific	957.2	35
Europe	311.8	12
Other regions	29.9	1
Total	**2,709.7**	**100**

2010 Sales

	$ mil.	% of total
US	1,338.2	49
Japan	513.0	19
Other countries	858.5	32
Total	**2,709.7**	**100**

PRODUCTS/OPERATIONS

2010 Sales

	$ mil.	% of total
Non-gemstone sterling silver jewelry	824.6	31
Gemstone jewelry & band rings	715.3	26
Diamond rings & wedding bands	575.3	21
Non-gemstone gold or platinum jewelry	329.5	12
Other	265.0	10
Total	**2,709.7**	**100**

Selected Merchandise and Brands

China and other tableware
Crystal
Fashion and personal accessories
Fine jewelry
Fragrances (Tiffany, Pure Tiffany, Tiffany for Men)
Glassware
Stationery
Sterling silver (desk accessories, flatware, holloware, key holders, picture frames, trophies)
Watches and clocks
Writing instruments

COMPETITORS

ARC International
Armani
Asprey
Aurum Holdings
Blue Nile, Inc.
Bulgari
Cartier
Chanel
Christie's
Citizen
Coach, Inc.
Cole Haan
Elizabeth Arden Inc
Gucci
H. Stern
Hermès
Inter Parfums
LVMH
Movado Group
Neiman Marcus
Nordstrom
Parlux Fragrances
Richard-Ginori 1735
Richemont
Rolex
Royal Doulton
Saks Fifth Avenue
Shiseido
Signet
Société du Louvre
Union Diamond
Van Cleef & Arpels
WWRD Holdings
Yves Saint-Laurent Groupe
Zale

HISTORICAL FINANCIALS

Company Type: Public

Income Statement

FYE: January 31

	REVENUE ($ mil.)	NET INCOME ($ mil.)	NET PROFIT MARGIN	EMPLOYEES
1/10	2,710	265	9.8%	8,400
1/09	2,860	220	7.7%	9,000
1/08	2,939	304	10.3%	8,800
1/07	2,648	254	9.6%	8,800
1/06	2,395	255	10.6%	8,120
Annual Growth	**3.1%**	**1.0%**	**—**	**0.9%**

2010 Year-End Financials

Debt ratio: 27.6%
Return on equity: 15.3%
Cash ($ mil.): 786
Current ratio: 4.07
Long-term debt ($ mil.): 520
No. of shares (mil.): 127
Dividends
  Yield: 1.7%
  Payout: 32.2%
Market value ($ mil.): 5,164

Stock History

NYSE: TIF

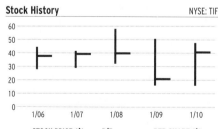

	STOCK PRICE ($) FY Close	P/E High/Low		PER SHARE ($) Earnings	Dividends	Book Value
1/10	40.61	22	8	2.11	0.68	14.81
1/09	20.75	29	10	1.74	0.66	12.49
1/08	39.79	26	15	2.20	0.52	12.88
1/07	39.26	23	16	1.80	0.38	14.19
1/06	37.70	25	16	1.75	0.30	14.40
Annual Growth	**1.9%**	**—**	**—**	**4.8%**	**22.7%**	**0.7%**

The Timberland Company

Even non-hikers can get a kick out of Timberlands. The Timberland Company is best known for making men's, women's, and kids' footwear. Its footwear includes yellow hiking boots, boat shoes, dress and outdoor casual footwear, and sandals. Timberland also makes apparel (outerwear, shirts, pants, socks) and accessories, such as sunglasses, watches, and belts. Its brands include SmartWool, howies, IPATH, and Timberland. The firm sells its products through about 220 company-owned stores and through department and athletic shops in Asia, Canada, Europe, Latin America, the Middle East, and the US. The founding Swartz family, including CEO Jeffrey Swartz, controls about 73% of its voting power.

Footwear, Timberland's top product segment, accounted for some 72% of its 2009 sales. The company's acquisitions of IPATH (2007) and howies (2006), along with a 2008 boost in sales of casual and outdoor performance footwear, have collectively helped to raise the segment's revenue and offset a decline in sales of boots and kids' footwear during the economic downturn.

About 48% of the company's sales come from North America; however, Timberland is pushing into global markets, such as Europe and Asia, to diversify its revenue streams. Growth in its European distribution operation and gains in Scandinavia were key to balancing stalled sales across Europe. In Asia, Timberland saw its distribution business gain a foothold, showing some traction in China. The company continued to expand its brand into China and India during 2009 and opened its first company-owned retail store in China in 2010.

Licensing deals and a debt-free balance sheet have helped to keep Timberland's head above water during the global economic downturn. Indeed, sales in both North America and abroad are down by double digits. Licensing revenue, which represents 2% of its business, has risen in recent years due, in part, to the company's licensed Timberland PRO apparel and licensed kids' apparel. Getting into the bling of things, Timberland's agreement with Endura brought a collection of performance and casual watches. The company holds a licensing agreement with top clothing manufacturer Phillips-Van Heusen (inked in 2007) to add Timberland-branded apparel.

Not only was Timberland's purchase of SmartWool a strategic acquisition for a footwear manufacturer, but the sock maker allowed Timberland to expand into international outlets. Timberland bought the Colorado-based maker of wool socks, apparel, and accessories from RAF Industries and the Stripes Group for about $82 million. SmartWool items are sold in outdoor specialty stores in the US and through independent distributors in Canada, Europe, and Asia.

Timberland has been paring down its retail locations, opting for a smaller, more footwear-focused concept. The company in 2008 shuttered about 40 of its larger specialty stores in the US, Europe, and Asia and closed several underperforming US factory outlet stores soon thereafter.

HISTORY

After buying a 50% interest in the Abington Shoe Company in 1952, Nathan Swartz purchased the rest three years later and brought his 19-year-old son Sidney on board. Abington Shoe made handmade private-label footwear during the 1950s and 1960s.

In 1968 Nathan retired, leaving sons Sidney and Herman in charge. The brothers persuaded Goodyear to make a synthetic rubber sole, which the Swartzes then bonded to blond leather, creating the first waterproof Timberland boot in 1973. Because of the boot's popularity, the company changed its name to The Timberland Company five years later.

The boots were a cult hit on US college campuses, but they really kicked up a following when they reached Italy in 1980. Spurred by the success overseas, US retailers gave the boots an increased focus, and by the late 1980s Timberland was riding the crest of the outdoors craze. The company opened its first store in 1986 and went public a year later.

Timberland's success brought competition from NIKE and Reebok. As the "brown shoes" market became saturated, the company closed its US plants and started outsourcing production in 1994. Timberland streamlined its product lines and announced plans to revamp retail stores in 1997. The next year it introduced the "beige shoe," a boot and sneaker hybrid under the Gorge MPO brand. Also in 1998 Jeffrey Swartz stepped into his father's Timberlands as CEO.

In 1999 Timberland unveiled the Mountain Athletics product line aimed at the 18- to 25-year-old outdoor athlete market and Timberland Pro — footwear for the tradesperson (construction workers, factory foremen). Timberland reacquired the Asian distribution of its products from Inchcape in February 2000. In 2001 the company launched its "Around the World" ad campaign, the company's most ambitious ever.

In 2003 Timberland penned a licensing agreement with Italy's Marcolin, S.p.A, to make and distribute Timberland-brand eyewear.

EXECUTIVES

Chairman: Sidney W. Swartz, age 74
President, CEO, and Director: Jeffrey B. Swartz, age 50, $3,990,705 total compensation
Chief Brand Officer and Co-President, Timberland Brand: Michael J. (Mike) Harrison, age 49, $1,309,317 total compensation
SVP, Chief Administrative Officer, and Director: Carden N. Welsh, age 56, $1,300,192 total compensation
VP and CFO: Carrie W. Teffner, age 43, $632,236 total compensation
VP, General Counsel, and Secretary: Danette Wineberg, age 63
VP, Corporate Controller, and Chief Accounting Officer: John J. Fitzgerald Jr., age 47
Co-President, Timberland brand: Eugene R. (Gene) McCarthy, age 53, $924,771 total compensation
Manager Investor Relations and Strategic Planning: Kaitlyn Bruder
Auditors: Deloitte & Touche LLP

LOCATIONS

HQ: The Timberland Company
200 Domain Dr., Stratham, NH 03885
Phone: 603-772-9500 **Fax:** 603-773-1640
Web: www.timberland.com

2009 Sales

	% of total
North America	48
Europe	41
Asia	11
Total	**100**

PRODUCTS/OPERATIONS

2009 Sales

		% of total
Footwear	931.2	72
Apparel & accessories	328.6	26
Royalties & other	26.1	2
Total	**1,285.9**	**100**

COMPETITORS

Billabong
Birkenstock Distribution USA
Columbia Sportswear
Deckers Outdoor
Eddie Bauer llc
Fossil, Inc.
L.L. Bean
NIKE
Norm Thompson
North Face
Patagonia, Inc.
Phillips-Van Heusen
Polo Ralph Lauren
R. Griggs
Reebok
Rocky Brands
Skechers U.S.A.
Wolverine World Wide

HISTORICAL FINANCIALS

Company Type: Public

Income Statement

FYE: December 31

	REVENUE ($ mil.)	NET INCOME ($ mil.)	NET PROFIT MARGIN	EMPLOYEES
12/09	1,286	57	4.4%	5,700
12/08	1,365	43	3.1%	6,000
12/07	1,437	40	2.8%	6,300
12/06	1,568	106	6.8%	6,300
12/05	1,566	165	10.5%	5,300
Annual Growth	**(4.8%)**	**(23.4%)**	**—**	**1.8%**

2009 Year-End Financials

Debt ratio: —	No. of shares (mil.): 54
Return on equity: 9.7%	Dividends
Cash ($ mil.): 290	Yield: —
Current ratio: 2.94	Payout: —
Long-term debt ($ mil.): —	Market value ($ mil.): 961

Stock History

NYSE: TBL

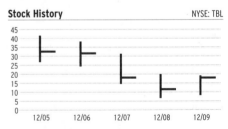

	STOCK PRICE ($) FY Close	P/E High/Low		PER SHARE ($) Earnings	Dividends	Book Value
12/09	17.93	18	9	1.01	—	11.11
12/08	11.55	27	10	0.73	—	10.76
12/07	18.08	47	23	0.65	—	10.77
12/06	31.58	23	15	1.67	—	10.46
12/05	32.55	17	11	2.43	—	9.85
Annual Growth	**(13.8%)**	**—**	**—**	**(19.7%)**	**—**	**3.0%**

Time Warner

Even among media titans, this company is a giant. Time Warner is the world's third-largest media conglomerate behind Walt Disney and News Corporation, with operations spanning television, film, and publishing. Through subsidiary Turner Broadcasting, the company runs a portfolio of popular cable TV networks including CNN, TBS, and TNT. Time Warner also operates pay-TV channels HBO and Cinemax. The company's Warner Bros. Entertainment, meanwhile, includes films studios (Warner Bros. Pictures, New Line Cinema), TV production units (Warner Bros. Television Group), and comic book publisher DC Entertainment. In the magazine world, venerable Time Inc. is the top publisher of consumer titles including *FORTUNE, People,* and *Time.*

Cable television continues to be a leading source of revenue for Time Warner. Its TBS and TNT channels rank among the most watched ad-supported channels. While advertising has been weak due to the recession, the cable networks have been able to make up the difference in higher carriage fees charged to cable system operators. Its flagship HBO pay-TV service has managed to hold the interest of cable subscribers despite the loss of hit series *The Sopranos*, thanks to such shows as *Entourage.*

Time Warner's filmed entertainment division, meanwhile, has been delivering at the box office with such hits as *The Hangover, Harry Potter and the Half-Blood Prince*, and *Sherlock Holmes.* The global economic slowdown, however, forced Warner Bros. to focus on cost reduction measures early in 2009 when it cut about 10% of its workforce, outsourcing many positions to consulting firm Capgemini.

Time Warner's magazine publishing unit, however, has not fared well in an environment of declining readership and print advertising. Time Inc. is focused primarily on reducing operating costs for its magazines, an effort that has included the elimination of some jobs. It is also looking for new ways to distribute content, particularly through digital media.

Once ranked as the world's largest media company, Time Warner disposed of some significant businesses during 2009 in order to focus on its core entertainment and publishing operations. The biggest shake-up came at the end of the year when the company shed its AOL Internet portal subsidiary, closing the long and torturous chapter of Time Warner's history that began when it merged with AOL (then called America Online) in 2001. The enlarged business, briefly known as AOL-Time Warner, was never able to achieve significant synergies between the online media and traditional film and TV content arms despite several restructuring attempts, leaving Time Warner burdened with debt and suffering losses.

Time Warner finally spun off the Internet business to shareholders as a separate, publicly traded company. The stock swap and separation valued AOL at less than $3 billion, far less than the $124 billion valuation of the original AOL-Time Warner merger.

Time Warner also got out of the cable-TV system business in 2009 when the company spun off its 84% stake in Time Warner Cable.

This latest transformation for Time Warner is being led by Jeffrey Bewkes, who replaced Richard Parsons as CEO in 2008 after overseeing the company's entertainment divisions.

HISTORY

Though formed in 2001, AOL Time Warner was the product of decades of media history. An elder statesman compared to relative newcomer America Online, Time Warner's roots extend back to 1922 — the year that Henry Luce and Briton Hadden founded Time Inc. to publish *Time* magazine, and brothers Harry, Abe, Jack, and Sam Warner established the origins of Warner Bros., which later became Warner Communications.

America Online's ancestry stretches back to the early 1980s when Stephen Case joined the management of a company called Control Video. Later renamed Quantum Computer Services, the company created the online service that would become America Online in 1985. Quantum Computer Services changed its name to America Online in 1991. It went public the next year.

As America Online was germinating, Time Inc. and Warner Communications were eyeing each other. The two companies merged in 1990 to form Time Warner. Gerald Levin was appointed CEO in 1992. To shave off debt, Time Warner grouped several of its properties into Time Warner Entertainment in 1992, in which U S West (which later became MediaOne Group) bought a 25% interest.

Time Warner's 1996 acquisition of Ted Turner's Turner Broadcasting System further elevated Time Warner's profile on the media stage. After AT&T's announcement that it would acquire MediaOne, MediaOne gave up its 50% management control of Time Warner Entertainment but retained its 25% ownership interest. AT&T's acquisition of MediaOne was completed in 2000, thus giving AT&T 25% of Time Warner Entertainment. (AT&T later boosted its stake to 27%.)

America Online announced that it would acquire Time Warner in early 2000. After a lengthy review by regulatory bodies, America Online acquired Time Warner for $106 billion and formed AOL Time Warner in 2001. Case became chairman, and Levin was appointed CEO. The newly formed company soon began streamlining, cutting more than 2,400 jobs in the process. (It cut another 1,700 jobs at America Online later that year.)

Levin retired from the company in 2002 and was replaced by co-COO Richard Parsons. The following year AOL Time Warner finally succeeded in buying Comcast's stake in Time Warner Entertainment (Comcast gained its share of TWE when it bought the cable assets of AT&T in 2002). The following year Case and Turner both resigned their executive positions with the company. And in a move to distance itself from the struggling online unit, the company dropped AOL from its moniker and returned to being known as Time Warner Inc.

Time Warner started off 2004 by ridding itself of Warner Music Group, which it sold for $2.6 billion to a group led by former Seagram executive Edgar Bronfman Jr. and investment firm Thomas H. Lee Partners.

In 2006 Time Warner sold its book publishing unit, Time Warner Book Group, to French media firm Lagardère. Time Warner Cable joined with Comcast to acquire Adelphia Communications for $17.6 billion in cash and stock;

as part of the deal, Adelphia shareholders sold part of their newly acquired stake in TWC through an IPO in 2007.

Parsons retired as CEO at the beginning of 2008 and was replaced by Jeffery Bewkes.

Time Warner spun off its remaining stake in Time Warner Cable in 2009.

EXECUTIVES

Chairman and CEO: Jeffrey L. (Jeff) Bewkes, age 57, $19,562,284 total compensation
EVP and CFO: John K. Martin Jr., age 42, $6,276,230 total compensation
EVP and General Counsel: Paul T. Cappuccio, age 48, $5,040,144 total compensation
EVP, Warner Bros. Theatre Ventures: Gregg Maday
EVP: Olaf Olafsson, age 47, $2,885,394 total compensation
EVP Global Public Policy: Carol A. Melton, age 55
EVP Administration: Patricia (Pat) Fili-Krushel, age 56, $4,271,488 total compensation
EVP Business Affairs and President, Film Programming, Home Box Office: Bruce Grivetti
SVP Global Public Policy: Steve Vest, age 44
SVP; President and Chief Creative Officer, Global Media Group: Mark D'Arcy
VP Corporate Communications: Keith Cocozza
VP Investor Relations: Douglas (Doug) Shapiro
President, Warner Bros. Pictures Group: Jeff Robinov
President, Warner Bros. Television Group: Bruce Rosenblum, age 51
President and CEO, Retail Sales and Marketing: Richard A. (Rich) Jacobsen
President, Time Media Group: Wayne Powers
Chairman and CEO, Time: Jack Griffin
Chairman and CEO, Home Box Office: Bill Nelson, age 61
Chairman and CEO, Turner Broadcasting System: Philip I. (Phil) Kent, age 55
President, DC Entertainment: Diane Nelson
President, CNN Worldwide: Jim Walton, age 51
Editor-in-Chief, Time: John Huey
Auditors: Ernst & Young LLP

LOCATIONS

HQ: Time Warner Inc.
1 Time Warner Center, New York, NY 10019
Phone: 212-484-8000
Web: www.timewarner.com

2009 Sales

	$ mil.	% of total
US	18,085	70
UK	1,495	6
Canada	646	3
Germany	643	2
France	580	2
Japan	471	2
Other countries	3,865	15
Total	**25,785**	**100**

PRODUCTS/OPERATIONS

2009 Sales

	$ mil.	% of total
Content	11,020	43
Subscriptions	8,859	34
Advertising	5,161	20
Other	745	3
Total	**25,785**	**100**

2009 Sales

	$ mil.	% of total
Networks	11,703	44
Filmed entertainment	11,066	42
Publishing	3,736	14
Adjustments	(720)	—
Total	**25,785**	**100**

Selected Operations

Networks
Cinemax (pay-television service)
Home Box Office (HBO, pay-television service)
Turner Broadcasting System
Boomerang (classic cartoons)
Cartoon Network
Cable News Network (CNN)
TBS
truTV
Turner Classic Movies (TCM)
Turner Network Television (TNT)
Filmed entertainment
Warner Bros. Entertainment
The CW Network (50%, broadcast television network)
DC Entertainment
New Line Cinema
Warner Bros.
Castle Rock Entertainment
Warner Bros. Pictures
Warner Bros. Consumer Products (product licensing)
Warner Bros. Home Entertainment
Warner Bros. Digital Distribution
Warner Bros. Interactive Entertainment
Warner Home Video
Warner Bros. Television Group
Telepictures Productions
Warner Bros. Animation
Warner Bros. Television
Warner Horizon Television
Publishing
Time Inc.
Entertainment Weekly
FORTUNE
InStyle
People
Real Simple
Southern Living
Sports Illustrated
Time

COMPETITORS

CBS Corp
Discovery Communications
Disney
Hearst Corporation
Lagardère Active
Meredith Corporation
NBC Universal
News Corp.
Sony Pictures Entertainment
Viacom

HISTORICAL FINANCIALS

Company Type: Public

Income Statement

FYE: December 31

	REVENUE ($ mil.)	NET INCOME ($ mil.)	NET PROFIT MARGIN	EMPLOYEES
12/09	25,785	2,517	9.8%	31,000
12/08	46,984	(13,402)	—	87,000
12/07	46,482	4,387	9.4%	86,400
12/06	44,224	6,527	14.8%	92,700
12/05	43,652	2,905	6.7%	87,850
Annual Growth	(12.3%)	(3.5%)	—	(22.9%)

2009 Year-End Financials

Debt ratio: 46.0%
Return on equity: 6.7%
Cash ($ mil.): 4,800
Current ratio: 1.48
Long-term debt ($ mil.): 15,357

No. of shares (mil.): 1,124
Dividends
Yield: 2.6%
Payout: 36.2%
Market value ($ mil.): 32,760

Stock History

NYSE: TWX

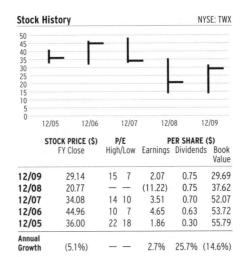

	STOCK PRICE ($) FY Close	P/E High/Low		PER SHARE ($) Earnings	Dividends	Book Value
12/09	29.14	15	7	2.07	0.75	29.69
12/08	20.77	—	—	(11.22)	0.75	37.62
12/07	34.08	14	10	3.51	0.70	52.07
12/06	44.96	10	7	4.65	0.63	53.72
12/05	36.00	22	18	1.86	0.30	55.79
Annual Growth	(5.1%)	—	—	2.7%	25.7%	(14.6%)

The Timken Company

The Timken Company tries to keep its bearings straight. The company makes bearings that find their way into products from consumer appliances to railroad cars. It also makes power transmission components, from automotive gear shafts and connecting rods to aircraft engine components. In addition, Timken makes more than 450 grades of alloy and carbon steels, producing bars, billets, tubing, and custom components for automotive and industrial applications. It also offers power transmission components, lubricants, seals, and motion control systems. Five generations of the Timken family have served the company since its founding by one-time carriage maker Henry Timken in 1899.

The company's Bearings & Power Transmission group is divided into three market-based divisions: Mobile Industries targets manufacturers of cars, light and heavy-duty trucks, rail cars and locomotives, as well as construction, agricultural, and mining vehicles; Process Industries serves the energy, power transmission, and heavy machinery and equipment industries; Aerospace & Defense sells to customers in the civilian and military aviation markets.

In its Aerospace & Defense division, Timken has added rotor head assemblies, turbine engine components, gears, and other flight components to its bearing and helicopter transmission systems product lines. It has also added aftermarket services such as repair and overhaul of engines, transmissions, and fuel controls; bearing repair; and component rebuilding.

The company's sales were rocked by the global economy and capital market crises in 2009. As the worldwide recession took hold, it trimmed its headcount by more than 10% and cut production by shortening work weeks and operating hours. While sales fell across all of its other operations, Timken's Aerospace & Defense segment held its own, and the company plans to continue to invest in the business through acquisitions and product development.

Meanwhile, Timken is fortifying its presence in China. Acquisitions and joint ventures there, coupled with Timken's businesses in India, are part of a plan to grow its Asian business. In 2009

Timken inked a five-year production arrangement with Japan's Daido Steel Co. Ltd. The arrangement gives Timken more routes to market its precision steel lineup to Asian industrial customers. Timken also moved ahead with plans to build a new plant in Chennai, India.

The Timken family, through individual holdings and its foundation, controls 11% of the company. The company's pension plan owns another 7%.

HISTORY

Veteran St. Louis carriage maker Henry Timken patented a design in 1898 for tapered roller bearings (enclosed bearings between a pair of concentric rings). The following year Timken and his sons, William and Henry (H. H.) Timken, founded the Timken Roller Bearing Axle Company to make bearings for carriage axles.

In 1902 the company moved to Canton, Ohio, to be near the growing steelworks of Pittsburgh and the new auto industries of Buffalo, New York; Cleveland; and Detroit. With the debut of the Ford Motor Model T in 1908, the Timkens' business soared. In 1909 Henry Timken died. That year a separate company, the Timken-Detroit Axle Company, was formed in Detroit to serve the auto industry. The original company changed its name to the Timken Roller Bearing Company and continued to produce bearings. Also in 1909 Vickers began making bearings and axles under license from Timken (Timken acquired that operation in 1959).

Suffering steel shortages during WWI, in 1916 the company began making its own steel. By the 1920s the rail industry had adopted Timken bearings to increase the speed of trains. Timken stock was sold to the public for the first time in 1922.

WWII created increased demand for Timken's products, and the company opened several new plants. The AP bearing — a revolutionary prelubricated, self-contained railroad bearing unveiled by Timken in 1954 — boosted the company's railroad segment, and a new plant, the Columbus Railroad Bearing Plant, opened in 1958.

H. H. Timken's son, W. Robert Timken, became president in 1960 and chairman in 1968. The company continued to grow during the 1960s by opening plants in Brazil and France. It adopted its current name in 1970. W. R. Timken Jr., grandson of the founder, became chairman in 1975. That year the company bought specialty alloy maker Latrobe Steel.

In 1982, with increasing competition from Europe and Japan, the company suffered its first loss since the Depression. Five years later it established Indian joint venture Tata Timken to make bearings for agricultural equipment, heavy machinery, and railcars.

Timken bought precision-bearing maker MPB Corporation in 1990. The company opened its first European steel operations in 1993 and the following year introduced its environmentally progressive Dynametal steel products. It bought the Rail Bearing Service Corporation in 1995.

Timken formed joint venture Yantai Timken in 1996 to make bearings in China. In 1997 Timken purchased Gnutti Carlo SpA (bearings, Italy) and the aerospace bearing operations of UK-based Torrington.

In 1999 Timken cut production capacity to 80% and continued to consolidate operations and restructure into global business units. The company closed plants in Australia, restructured operations in South Africa (cutting about 1,700 jobs), and transferred its European distribution to an outside company in France.

In 2001 the company announced that it would lay off more than 7% of its workforce. Timken's 2003 acquistion of Ingersoll-Rand unit, The Torrington Co., for $840 million, made Timken the third-largest bearing company in the world.

Blaming the woes of the North American automotive industry, Timken laid off approximately 700 employees, or about 5% of its Automotive Group, in the fall of 2006. Soon after, the company said it would close the group's factory in São Paulo, Brazil, by the end of 2007, eliminating manufacturing redundancies. The company then closed down its unprofitable plant in Desford, UK, which made seamless steel tubes. Four hundred employees lost their jobs as a result.

Timken supplemented its aerospace business in 2007 by acquiring the assets of The Purdy Corp, a maker of transmissions, gears, rotorhead systems, and other components for helicopters and fixed-wing aircraft.

In 2007 Timken formed a joint venture with Xiangtan Electric Manufacturing Co., Ltd., to manufacture ultra-large-bore bearings for the main rotor shafts of multi-megawatt wind turbines for the Chinese wind energy market.

EXECUTIVES

Chairman: Ward J. (Tim) Timken Jr., age 42, $2,599,795 total compensation
President, CEO, and Director: James W. Griffith, age 56, $3,960,155 total compensation
EVP; President, Bearings and Power Transmission Group: Michael C. Arnold, age 53, $1,825,986 total compensation
EVP Finance and Administration: Glenn A. Eisenberg, age 48, $1,644,154 total compensation
SVP Human Resources and Organizational Advancement: Donald L. Walker
SVP, Asia-Pacific, Bearings and Power Transmission Group: Roger W. Lindsay
SVP Tax and Treasury: Philip D. (Phil) Fracassa, age 40
SVP and Controller: J. Ted Mihaila, age 55
SVP and General Counsel: William R. Burkhart, age 44
SVP Technology: Douglas H. Smith
SVP Strategy and CIO: Daniel E. Muller
VP Communications and Public Relations: Kari Groh
VP Corporate Development: Michael T. Schilling
VP Ethics and Compliance and Corporate Secretary: Scott A. Scherff, age 52
President, Steel Group: Salvatore J. Miraglia Jr., age 59, $1,624,957 total compensation
President, Process Industries, Bearings and Power Transmission Group: Christopher A. Coughlin
President, Mobile Industries, Bearings and Power Transmission Group: Richard G. Kyle
President, Aerospace and Defense, Bearings and Power Transmission Group: J. Ron (Ron) Menning
Director Capital Markets and Investor Relations: Steve D. Tschiegg
Auditors: Ernst & Young LLP

LOCATIONS

HQ: The Timken Company
1835 Dueber Ave. SW, Canton, OH 44706
Phone: 330-438-3000   **Fax:** 330-458-6006
Web: www.timken.com

2009 Sales

	$ mil.	% of total
US	1,943.2	62
Europe	536.2	17
Other regions	662.2	21
Total	**3,141.6**	**100**

PRODUCTS/OPERATIONS

2009 Sales

	$ mil.	% of total
Bearings & Power Transmission group		
Mobile Industries	1,245.0	40
Process Industries	806.0	26
Aerospace & Defense	417.7	13
Steel group	672.9	21
Total	**3,141.6**	**100**

Selected Products

Bearings & Power Transmission
  Aerospace bearing repair and component reconditioning
  Aftermarket distribution
  Bearing maintenance tools
  Condition monitoring equipment
  Cylindrical bearings
  Gears
  Helicopter transmission systems
  Lubricants
  Power transmission components
  Repair and overhaul of engine, fuel controls, and transmissions
  Rotor head assemblies
  Seals
  Spherical bearings
  Straight ball bearings
  Super-precision ball and roller bearings
  Turbine engine components
  Tapered bearings
Steel
  Custom precision steel components
  Mechanical seamless steel tubing
  Specialty steels and alloys
  Tool steel

COMPETITORS

Allegheny Technologies
Amatsuji Steel Ball
ArcelorMittal
BÖHLER-UDDEHOLM
Corus Group
General Bearing
JTEKT
Kaydon
Linamar Corp.
Macsteel Service Centres
MINEBEA
Nippon Bearing
NSK
NTN
Nucor
PAV Republic
Plymouth Tube
Quanex Building Products
RBC Bearings
RBS Global
Schaeffler
SKF
Steel Dynamics
Tenaris
United States Steel
Universal Stainless
V & M Tubes (USA)

HISTORICAL FINANCIALS

Company Type: Public

Income Statement

FYE: December 31

	REVENUE ($ mil.)	NET INCOME ($ mil.)	NET PROFIT MARGIN	EMPLOYEES
12/09	3,142	(134)	—	16,667
12/08	5,664	268	4.7%	25,662
12/07	5,236	220	4.2%	25,175
12/06	4,973	223	4.5%	25,418
12/05	5,168	260	5.0%	27,000
Annual Growth	**(11.7%)**	**—**	**—**	**(11.4%)**

2009 Year-End Financials

Debt ratio: 29.7%	No. of shares (mil.): 97
Return on equity: —	Dividends
Cash ($ mil.): 756	Yield: 1.9%
Current ratio: 3.74	Payout: —
Long-term debt ($ mil.): 469	Market value ($ mil.): 2,294

Stock History

NYSE: TKR

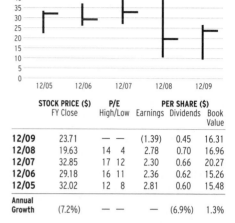

	STOCK PRICE ($) FY Close	P/E High/Low		Earnings	PER SHARE ($) Dividends	Book Value
12/09	23.71	—	—	(1.39)	0.45	16.31
12/08	19.63	14	4	2.78	0.70	16.96
12/07	32.85	17	12	2.30	0.66	20.27
12/06	29.18	16	11	2.36	0.62	15.26
12/05	32.02	12	8	2.81	0.60	15.48
Annual Growth	**(7.2%)**	**—**	**—**	**—**	**(6.9%)**	**1.3%**

TJX Companies

Rifling through the racks is an art at TJX stores. The TJX Companies operates eight retail chains, including the two largest off-price clothing retailers in the US, T.J. Maxx and Marshalls. T.J. Maxx sells brand-name family apparel, accessories, women's shoes, domestics, giftware, and jewelry at discount prices at some 890 stores nationwide. Marshalls offers a full line of shoes and a broader selection of menswear through 800-plus stores. Its HomeGoods chain of about 325 stores nationwide focuses on home furnishings, while 150 A.J. Wright clothing stores aim for lower-income shoppers. T.K. Maxx is the company's European retail arm with about 265 stores in the UK, Ireland, Germany, and now Poland.

TJX Companies' focus on value across its eight chains appears to be the right retail formula for recessionary times. The retailer targets middle-to-upper income, fashion-conscious females between the ages of 25 and 54 who tend to shop at high-end department and specialty stores, but have traded down as budgets tighten.

Despite continued economic pressures in Europe and North America, all of the company's retail chains added stores. Buoyed by its recent strong results, TJX Companies plans to add locations across all eight chains. It is also experimenting with new formats. Recent additions include three free-standing ShoeMegaShops by Marshalls stores in the US, which sell family footwear, as well as several StyleSense stores in Canada that sell shoes and accessories. The company opened four T.K. Maxx shops in Poland in 2009 and exported its Canadian HomeSense chain to the UK in 2008.

T.J. Maxx and Marshalls (together known as Marmaxx) operate more than 1,700 stores between them and contribute about two-thirds of TJX's total sales. They share similar retail concepts, and sell merchandise generally priced 20% to 60% below similar items at department stores.

However, Marshalls offers a bigger men's department than T.J. Maxx, a larger shoe department, and costume jewelry. Marshalls has stores in more than 40 states and about a dozen locations in Puerto Rico. Both chains target deal-seeking consumers who usually shop at full-priced chains.

Its HomeGoods stores are both stand-alone outlets and located within superstores such as T.J. Maxx 'N More and Marshalls Mega-Stores. In Canada TJX operates HomeSense, with about 80 stores, and a chain of family clothing stores called Winners Apparel (210 stores).

HISTORY

Cousins Stanley and Sumner Feldberg opened the first Zayre (Yiddish for "very good") store in Hyannis, Massachusetts, in 1956. During the next 15 years the number of stores grew to nearly 200.

Zayre purchased the Hit or Miss chain, which sold upscale women's clothing at discounted prices, in 1969. When the recession of the early 1970s hit, superb results at Hit or Miss prompted Zayre to look for further opportunities in the off-price apparel marketplace. Zayre hired Ben Cammarata to create a new store concept, and in March 1977 he opened the first T.J. Maxx, in Auburn, Massachusetts, to market discounted upscale family clothing. Six years later Zayre formed the catalog retailer Chadwick's of Boston to sell Hit or Miss apparel by mail.

The company came to rely increasingly on its specialty operations to provide consistent sales and income as its flagship general merchandise stores often struggled. By 1983 the specialty chains were producing almost half of Zayre's sales.

In the second half of the 1980s, Zayre's upscale (yet still off-priced) retailers' sales rose, while its general merchandise stores (targeting lower-income customers) dropped. To keep its specialty stores unhindered by its flagging Zayre stores, it established The TJX Companies as a public company in 1987. Zayre sold about 17% of its new subsidiary to the public, with Cammarata as CEO. Zayre sold its 400 general merchandise stores in 1988 to Ames for about $430 million in cash, $140 million in Ames stock, and a receivable note. The next year the company merged with its subsidiary, The TJX Companies, taking that name.

TJX acquired Winners Apparel, a Toronto-based five-store apparel chain, in 1990. That year, in the same month that Ames declared bankruptcy, TJX established a $185 million reserve against losses it might suffer through its ownership of Ames' stock. Ames emerged from bankruptcy two years later, and TJX was left with 4% of Ames' voting shares and over 100 empty Ames stores. TJX sold or leased most of them.

Also in 1992 TJX opened HomeGoods gift and houseware outlets in three of its remaining Ames stores and closed about 70 Hit or Miss stores. Encouraged by the success of its off-price operations in Canada, in 1994 TJX opened five T.K. Maxx stores (similar to T.J. Maxx and Winners Apparel) in the UK.

A year later TJX paid $550 million for Melville's ailing chain of 450 Marshalls clothing stores. In addition, the company sold its Hit or Miss apparel chain. To help pay for Marshalls, TJX sold the Chadwick's of Boston catalog in 1996 to retailer Brylane. It debuted the A.J. Wright discount chain in New England in 1998.

In 1999 TJX elected Cammarata to the additional post of chairman and elevated Ted English

to president and COO. In 2000 Cammarata relinquished his CEO post to English but remained chairman. Citing the successes of its new stores, the company announced in early 2001 it expected to increase its total number of stores 12% annually for the next several years. Seven TJX employees perished on September 11, 2001, when their flight, bound for Los Angeles, crashed into the World Trade Center during the worst terrorist attack in US history.

In 2002 the company opened HomeSense, a new Canadian home furnishings chain fashioned after its US counterpart HomeGoods.

In September 2005 English resigned abruptly after five years as the company's CEO. TJX named company president Carol Meyrowitz to the post. In March 2006 TJX cut about 250 jobs in its corporate and divisional offices and reduced the salaries of a dozen senior executives, including its chairman and acting CEO and its president, by 10%.

In 2007 TJX reached a settlement with Visa and Fifth Third Bancorp stemming from a breach of its computer systems in which customer data was stolen. Under the terms of the agreement, TJX will fund up to $40.9 million for recovery payments for US Visa issuers. Also in 2007 the retailer's European arm, T.K. Maxx, entered the German market with five stores there.

In 2008 TJX sold money-losing Bob's Stores, which has about 35 locations in the Northeast, to the private equity firms Versa Capital Management and Crystal Capital.

EXECUTIVES

Chairman: Bernard (Ben) Cammarata, age 70
President, CEO, and Director: Carol M. Meyrowitz, age 56, $17,362,112 total compensation
SEVP, CFO, and Chief Administrative Officer: Jeffrey G. (Jeff) Naylor, age 51, $3,876,268 total compensation
SEVP and Group President: Ernie Herrman, age 49, $3,184,744 total compensation
SEVP and Group President: Jerome Rossi, age 66, $3,601,649 total compensation
SEVP; Group President, Europe: Paul Sweetenham, age 45, $2,855,915 total compensation
SEVP and COO, The Marmaxx Group: Richard Sherr, age 52
EVP and Chief Logistics Officer: Peter Lindenmeyer
EVP and Chief Human Resources Officer: Gregorio R. (Greg) Flores III
EVP, General Counsel, and Secretary: Ann McCauley, age 59
EVP, Real Estate and New Business Development: Michael Skirvin
EVP Finance: Scott Goldenberg
EVP and CIO: Kathy S. Lane
SVP Brand Development: Barry Zelman
SVP Real Estate and Property Development: Christina Lofgren
SVP Global Procurement: Marc Boesch
SVP Global Communications: Sherry Lang
President, The Marmaxx Group: Michael MacMillan
President, A.J. Wright: Celia Clancy, age 53
President, Winners/HomeSense: Robert Cataldo, age 51
President, HomeGoods: Nan Stutz, age 52
Managing Director U.K. and Ireland: Susanne Given
Auditors: PricewaterhouseCoopers LLP

LOCATIONS

HQ: The TJX Companies, Inc.
770 Cochituate Rd., Framingham, MA 01701
Phone: 508-390-1000 **Fax:** 508-390-2828
Web: www.tjx.com

2010 Stores

	No.
US	2,176
Canada	290
Europe	277
Total	**2,743**

2010 Sales

	$ mil.	% of total
US		
Marmaxx	13,270.9	65
HomeGoods	1,794.4	9
A.J. Wright	779.8	4
UK		
T.K. Maxx/HomeSense	2,275.4	11
Canada		
Winners/HomeSense/StyleSense	2,167.9	11
Total	**20,288.4**	**100**

PRODUCTS/OPERATIONS

2010 Stores

	No.
T.J. Maxx	890
Marshalls	813
HomeGoods	323
T.K. Maxx	263
Winners & StyleSense	211
A.J. Wright	150
HomeSense (Canada & UK)	93
Total	**2,743**

2010 Sales

	% of total
Clothing & footwear	61
Home fashions	26
Jewelry & accessories	13
Total	**100**

Selected Stores

A.J. Wright (discount chain aimed at moderate-income shoppers)
HomeGoods (off-price home fashion chain)
HomeSense (off-price home fashion chain, Canada and UK)
Marshalls (off-price retailer of apparel, shoes, home fashions)
Marshalls Mega-Stores (combination Marshalls and HomeGoods stores)
StyleSense (family footwear and accessories, Canada)
T.J. Maxx (off-price retailer of apparel, shoes, home fashions)
T.J. Maxx 'N More (combination T.J. Maxx and HomeGoods stores)
T.K. Maxx (off-price retailer of apparel, shoes, home fashions, Europe)
Winners Apparel (off-price family apparel chain, Canada)

COMPETITORS

ASDA	J. C. Penney
Bed Bath & Beyond	Kmart
Belk	Kohl's
Big Lots	Loehmann's
Brown Shoe	Macy's
Burlington Coat Factory	Men's Wearhouse
Cato	Primark
Charming Shoppes	Ross Stores
The Children's Place	Sears
Claire's Stores	ShopKo Stores
Collective Brands	Stage Stores
Dillard's	Stein Mart
Dollar General	Target
Eddie Bauer llc	Tesco
Foot Locker	Wal-Mart
The Gap	Zellers
Inditex	

HISTORICAL FINANCIALS

Company Type: Public

Income Statement

	REVENUE ($ mil.)	NET INCOME ($ mil.)	NET PROFIT MARGIN	EMPLOYEES
1/10	20,288	1,214	6.0%	154,000
1/09	19,000	881	4.6%	133,000
1/08	18,647	772	4.1%	129,000
1/07	17,405	738	4.2%	125,000
1/06	16,058	690	4.3%	119,000
Annual Growth	6.0%	15.1%	—	6.7%

FYE: Last Saturday in January

2010 Year-End Financials

Debt ratio: 27.3%
Return on equity: 48.3%
Cash ($ mil.): 1,615
Current ratio: 1.66
Long-term debt ($ mil.): 790

No. of shares (mil.): 408
Dividends
  Yield: 1.2%
  Payout: 16.5%
Market value ($ mil.): 15,507

Stock History

NYSE: TJX

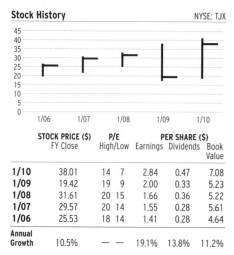

	STOCK PRICE ($) FY Close	P/E High/Low		PER SHARE ($) Earnings	Dividends	Book Value
1/10	38.01	14	7	2.84	0.47	7.08
1/09	19.42	19	9	2.00	0.33	5.23
1/08	31.61	20	15	1.66	0.36	5.22
1/07	29.57	20	14	1.55	0.28	5.61
1/06	25.53	18	14	1.41	0.28	4.64
Annual Growth	10.5%	—	—	19.1%	13.8%	11.2%

Toll Brothers

Ask not for whom the Tolls build, because if you have to ask you probably can't afford it. Toll Brothers builds luxury homes in the US, targeting move-up, second-home, and retired buyers. Its single-family detached houses and apartments range in price from about $230,000 to some $2 million. The company also develops communities for active adults and operates country club communities. Subsidiaries offer related services and products including insurance coverage, title and mortgage services, and landscaping. Like its peers, Toll Brothers closed on fewer homes with the housing downturn and financial crisis: It went from delivering nearly 8,600 homes in fiscal 2006 to fewer than 3,000 in fiscal 2009.

Toll Brothers finished up 2007 with a backlog of around 3,950 homes for sale but managed to reduce that figure by about half in 2008. Those years were somber ones for the housing industry as a whole, as builders overbuilt and were left holding large inventories. Compounding the issue, the subprime mortgage meltdown left many borrowers in default and homes in foreclosure. Hoping to profit from the economic crisis the company joined with Oaktree Capital Management in 2010 to acquire at a discount some $1.7 billion worth of troubled loans from the FDIC. The assets were formerly held by AmTrust Bank, which failed and was seized by regulators in late 2009.

Toll Brothers has also unloaded some noncore operations. It sold its subsidiary Advanced Broadband, which provided fiber-optic networks in its communities, to Comcast in 2007. It also divested its security monitoring operations.

Co-founder Robert Toll stepped down as CEO after more than 40 years in 2010. He was succeeded by Douglas Yearley, a member of the firm's management team since the 1990s. Robert Toll remains chairman.

HISTORY

Homebuilder Albert Toll's two sons, Robert and Bruce Toll, founded their own business in 1967. The duo began by building starter homes in the Philadelphia suburbs of Elkins Park and Yardley. As Philadelphia's population began to sprawl beyond these older suburban areas, the company grew, and in 1982 it moved beyond Pennsylvania to build houses in New Jersey. The young firm also began to distinguish itself by catering to upmarket customers.

Toll Brothers, Inc., went public in 1986 and later expanded around New York City, north to the Boston area, and south to the suburbs of Washington, DC. The firm survived the late 1980s real estate recession in the Northeast because, unlike many builders, it did not overextend itself.

Until the 1990s Toll Brothers operated primarily in the northeastern US, but it expanded as the housing market began an upward cycle. It entered California and North Carolina in 1994, and Arizona, Florida, and Texas in 1995. Toll Brothers began work in Nashville, Tennessee, and Las Vegas in 1997. The next year the company entered the active adult market, building its first two age-qualified communities in New Jersey. Also in 1998 the company joined other investors, including the Pennsylvania State Employees Retirement System, and formed the Toll Brothers Realty Trust to acquire and develop commercial property.

In 1999 Toll Brothers acquired Silverman Companies, a leading homebuilder and developer of luxury apartments with more than 80 years of experience in Detroit. The company also began building homes in the Chicago, San Diego, and San Francisco markets that year, and it teamed with Marriott International to begin developing an assisted-living community in Reston, Virginia.

It also set up its cable and broadband subsidiary, Advanced Broadband, that year, to provide its communities with Internet connectivity. Toll Brothers sold those operations to Comcast in 2007.

The company began operating in Rhode Island and New Hampshire in 2000, and the next year entered Colorado. In 2002 the company entered South Carolina in the Hilton Head area to develop Hampton Hall, a luxury country club community with a master-planned golf course.

In 2003 Toll Brothers acquired Jacksonville, Florida-based homebuilder Richard R. Dostie, Inc., for an undisclosed cash amount. The company also expanded its luxury urban in-fill market operations by acquiring The Manhattan Building Company, a developer of luxury mid- and high-rise condos on northern New Jersey's waterfront. The next year Toll Brothers and Pinnacle Ltd. jointly began development of an 832-home luxury condominium community (Maxwell Place on the Hudson) on the waterfront of Hoboken, New Jersey, overlooking Manhattan.

For its 12th consecutive year, Toll Brothers produced record fiscal-year-end results for earnings, revenues, contracts, and backlog in 2004. The company's net income grew 57% over the previous year's earnings, and it operated in more communities and offered more product lines than it had in previous years. Another record was set in 2005; revenue from home sales increased 50% and net income increased 97%. That year Toll Brothers began operations in West Virginia but stopped selling homes in Ohio.

Toll correctly predicted an industry slowdown in 2006, and for both 2006 and 2007 the number of homes it built dropped from 8,600 to around 6,700. As numbers continued to sink, it sold land holdings, reduced its backlog, and divested its cable, Internet, and home security businesses.

EXECUTIVES

Chairman: Robert I. Toll, age 69, $4,155,495 total compensation
Vice Chairman: Bruce E. Toll, age 66
CEO and Director: Douglas C. (Doug) Yearley Jr., age 49
President, COO, and Director: Zvi Barzilay, age 63, $4,739,990 total compensation
EVP, CFO, Treasurer, and Director: Joel H. Rassman, age 64, $3,820,890 total compensation
EVP Land Development and Country Club Operations: Joseph J. Palka
SVP and Chief Accounting Officer: Joseph R. Sicree
SVP Tax: Joseph DeSanto
SVP Finance and Investor Relations: Frederick N. Cooper
SVP and General Counsel: John K. McDonald
SVP and CIO: George W. Nelson
SVP and Controller: Kevin J. McMaster
SVP Toll Brothers Realty Trust: James M. Steuterman
SVP Acquisitions: Werner Thiessen
SVP, Secretary, and Chief Planning Officer: Michael I. Snyder
SVP Human Resources: Jonathan C. Downs
President, Westminster Security Company: Felicia Ratka
President, TBI Mortgage Company: Donald L. Salmon
President, Westminster Title Company: William T. Unkel
President, Toll Architecture: Jed Gibson
Auditors: Ernst & Young LLP

LOCATIONS

HQ: Toll Brothers, Inc.
  250 Gibraltar Rd., Horsham, PA 19044
Phone: 215-938-8000   **Fax:** 215-938-8010
Web: www.tollbrothers.com

2009 Sales

	$ mil.	% of total
North	585.3	33
Mid-Atlantic	492.7	28
West	389.1	22
South	288.2	17
Total	**1,755.3**	**100**

2009 Homes Closed

	No. units	% of total
North	983	33
Mid-Atlantic	862	30
West	576	19
South	544	18
Total	**2,965**	**100**

Selected Operations

Architectural design services
Golf course development and operation
Engineering services
House component assembly
Land development
Landscape services
Lumber distribution
Mortgage lending
Title insurance

COMPETITORS

David Weekley Homes
D.R. Horton
Hovnanian Enterprises
John Wieland Homes
KB Home
Lennar
Orleans Homebuilders
PulteGroup
The Ryland Group
Shapell Industries
Standard Pacific
William Lyon Homes

HISTORICAL FINANCIALS

Company Type: Public

Income Statement

	REVENUE ($ mil.)	NET INCOME ($ mil.)	NET PROFIT MARGIN	EMPLOYEES
			FYE: October 31	
10/09	1,755	(756)	—	2,066
10/08	3,158	(298)	—	3,160
10/07	4,647	36	0.8%	4,329
10/06	6,124	687	11.2%	5,542
10/05	5,793	806	13.9%	5,581
Annual Growth	(25.8%)	—	—	(22.0%)

2009 Year-End Financials

Debt ratio: 85.0%
Return on equity: —
Cash ($ mil.): 1,808
Current ratio: 5.35
Long-term debt ($ mil.): 2,135

No. of shares (mil.): 165
Dividends
Yield: —
Payout: —
Market value ($ mil.): 2,865

Stock History

NYSE: TOL

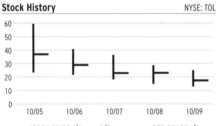

	STOCK PRICE ($) FY Close	P/E High/Low		PER SHARE ($) Earnings	Dividends	Book Value
10/09	17.32	—	—	(4.68)	—	15.19
10/08	23.12	—	—	(1.88)	—	19.57
10/07	22.91	162	86	0.22	—	21.32
10/06	28.91	10	5	4.17	—	20.65
10/05	36.91	12	5	4.78	—	16.70
Annual Growth	(17.2%)	—	—	—	—	(2.3%)

Torchmark Corporation

Torchmark aims to be a beacon in the world of insurance. It is the holding company for a family of firms; its member companies specialize in lower-end individual life insurance, supplemental health insurance, and annuities. Torchmark subsidiaries, which include flagship Liberty National Life, offer annuities, whole and term life insurance, health insurance, accidental death insurance, Medicare supplements, and long-term care health policies for the elderly. Its American Income Life sells life insurance policies to labor union and credit union members in the US, Canada, and New Zealand. Torchmark sells its products through direct marketing, as well as a network of exclusive and independent agents.

Targeting middle-income citizens, Liberty National Life operates primarily in the southeastern US. A smaller subsidiary, Globe Life and Accident, offers sells life insurance and supplemental health products direct to consumers through print, online, and television ads.

Beginning in 2007 Torchmark moved the incorporation of its subsidiaries to Nebraska to take advantage of lower tax rates. However, all of its actual operations are based in Alabama, Oklahoma, and Texas.

HISTORY

It began as a scam, plain and simple. In 1900 the Heralds of Liberty was founded as a fraternal organization — but its real reason for existence was to funnel money to its founders, according to Frank Samford, Torchmark's CEO from 1967 until 1985; Samford was also the great-grandson of the governor who signed the group's charter, and the son of the state insurance commissioner who oversaw the Heralds of Liberty's rehabilitation into a real insurance company.

The Heralds offered a joint life distribution plan, under which policyholders were divided by age; when a person died, his or her beneficiary was paid along with the holder of the lowest-numbered insurance certificate in the class (if they were paid at all; the Heralds were not scrupulous about that). Postal authorities called this plan a lottery and it was illegal in many states. But the Heralds' fraternal order status allowed it to circumvent Alabama insurance laws until 1921, when its infractions could no longer be ignored.

The organization operated under state supervision until 1929, when it was recapitalized as stock company Liberty National. By 1934, despite the Depression, the company was financially sound.

In 1944 Liberty National merged with funeral insurance company Brown-Service, whose large sales force began selling Liberty National's policies. The added sales helped the company grow and make acquisitions from the 1950s through the 1970s. Even after it discontinued funeral insurance, the company still paid out benefits. (As late as 1985, half of all Alabamans who died had the policies.)

Liberty National reorganized itself as a holding company in 1980 to accommodate the purchase of Globe Life And Accident. In 1981 it acquired Continental Investment Corp., which owned United Investors Life Insurance, Waddell & Reed (financial services), and United American Insurance. In 1982 the holding company became

Torchmark. Throughout its growth spurt it refrained from offering high-yield financial products and thus escaped the worst effects of the economic disruptions of the late 1980s. Its 1990 acquisition of Family Service Life Insurance put it back in the funeral insurance business (it exited again in 1995 and sold the unit in 1998).

Sales in the 1990s were affected by a decline in cash-value life insurance and Medicare supplements. Slack sales forced the company to stop having agents collect premiums personally, and by 1996 all accounts were handled by mail.

In 1998 the company sought to sell its 28% stake in property insurer Vesta Insurance Group after that company became the target of numerous lawsuits. Torchmark was only able to reduce its stake to 24% on the open market, but in 2000 Vesta bought out Torchmark's holdings.

Torchmark was haunted in 2000 by its own version of the undead — burial policies. An investigation by Alabama regulators was sparked by a Florida court order forcing the company to stop collecting premiums on old burial policies for which African-Americans had been charged higher premiums. In 2001 and 2002 Torchmark was hit by another dozen lawsuits, including allegations of overcharging.

EXECUTIVES

Chairman and CEO: Mark S. McAndrew, age 56, $2,836,298 total compensation
EVP and CFO: Gary L. Coleman, age 57, $1,741,005 total compensation
EVP and Chief Administrative Officer; CEO, United American: Vern D. Herbel, age 52, $1,387,150 total compensation
EVP and Chief Actuary: Rosemary J. Montgomery, age 60, $1,838,894 total compensation
EVP and General Counsel: Larry M. Hutchison, age 56, $1,638,985 total compensation
EVP and Chief Marketing Officer: Glenn D. Williams, age 50
VP and Director Human Resources: Arvelia Bowie
VP and Chief Investment Officer: W. Michael Pressley, age 58
VP, Associate Counsel, and Secretary: Carol A. McCoy
VP and Chief Accounting Officer: Danny H. Almond, age 58
VP Investor Relations: Mike Majors
VP and Actuary: Ben W. Lutek
VP and Director Tax: Frank M. Svoboda
CEO, Liberty National Life; President and CEO, United Investors Life: Anthony L. McWhorter, age 60
President and CEO, Globe Life: Charles F. Hudson, age 53
President and CEO, American Income Life: Roger C. Smith, age 57
President and Chief Marketing Officer, Liberty National Life and United American: Andrew W. King, age 52
Controller: Spencer H. Stone
Auditors: Deloitte & Touche LLP

LOCATIONS

HQ: Torchmark Corporation
3700 S. Stonebridge Dr., McKinney, TX 75070
Phone: 972-569-4000
Web: www.torchmarkcorp.com

PRODUCTS/OPERATIONS

2009 Revenue

	$ mil.	% of total
Premiums		
Life	1,659.8	49
Health	1,017.7	30
Other	9.7	1
Net investment income	674.9	20
Losses & other	(139.7)	—
Total	**3,222.4**	**100**

HISTORICAL FINANCIALS

Company Type: Public

Income Statement				FYE: December 31
	ASSETS ($ mil.)	NET INCOME ($ mil.)	INCOME AS % OF ASSETS	EMPLOYEES
12/09	16,024	405	2.5%	3,505
12/08	13,529	452	3.3%	3,605
12/07	15,241	528	3.5%	3,596
12/06	14,980	519	3.5%	3,758
12/05	14,769	495	3.4%	4,530
Annual Growth	2.1%	(4.9%)	—	(6.2%)

2009 Year-End Financials

Equity as % of assets: 21.2%
Return on assets: 2.7%
Return on equity: 14.4%
Long-term debt ($ mil.): 920
No. of shares (mil.): 83

Dividends
Yield: 1.3%
Payout: 11.7%
Market value ($ mil.): 3,627
Sales ($ mil.): 3,222

Stock History

NYSE: TMK

	STOCK PRICE ($) FY Close	P/E High/Low		PER SHARE ($) Earnings	Dividends	Book Value
12/09	43.95	10	3	4.88	0.57	41.19
12/08	44.70	13	5	5.11	0.56	26.94
12/07	60.53	13	11	5.50	0.52	40.29
12/06	63.76	13	11	5.13	0.50	41.92
12/05	55.60	12	11	4.68	0.44	41.60
Annual Growth	(5.7%)	—	—	1.1%	6.7%	(0.2%)

The Toro Company

Need to repair the 13th green after wild, rampaging bulls run through? Give The Toro Company a call. Toro makes lawn mowers and other products for professional and residential use. Toro's professional products include irrigation equipment, mowers for commercial use, riding and walk-behind power mowers for golf course fairways and greens, trimmers, and utility vehicles. Some professional brands are Toro, Rain Master, Exmark, Irritrol, and Dingo. Its residential products, sold to distributors, home centers, and mass retailers, include walk-behind and riding lawn mowers, lawn tractors, electrical trimmers, and snow blowers. Brand names in this sector include Toro, Rain Master, Irritrol, Lawn Genie, and Lawn-Boy.

Toro has been focused on expanding its business in recent years in its effort to stay on top of the latest technologies and to maintain its position alongside its competition. (In 2008 competitor Deere & Company passed Toro in the micro-irrigation products market when it completed its acquisitions of T-Systems International and Israel-based Plasto Irrigation that year.)

To get a foothold in the sports field and golf course markets, Toro has made several acquisitions. In late 2009 Toro acquired certain assets from TY-Crop Manufacturing Ltd., which makes equipment to maintain golf courses and sports fields. In 2008 Toro acquired Southern Green, a top maker of deep-tine aeration equipment under the Soil Reliever name. And to help its customers monitor their turf, the company expanded its soil technology. In 2008 it purchased the Turf Guard wireless monitoring technology from JLH Labs. The system measures soil moisture, salinity, and temperature, and stores and communicates the data. In 2007 Toro purchased Rain Master Irrigation Systems. A leader for some 25 years, Rain Master also boosts Toro's distribution network, with its established presence in the western US.

It's working to steer itself more toward the rental niche of the industry. Toro in 2010 purchased certain assets of USPraxis, maker of outdoor power equipment. The deal added stump grinders, wood chippers, and log splitters to the Toro products portfolio and strengthened its presence in the rental and landscape markets.

Michael Hoffman — promoted from group VP to president and COO in late 2004 — succeeded Ken Melrose as CEO in 2005. Hoffman added the chairman title when Melrose retired that March.

HISTORY

Toro — Spanish for "bull" — was founded in 1914 as The Toro Motor Company to make engines for The Bull Tractor Company. In 1921 Toro provided a tractor fitted with 30-inch lawn mower blades to replace a horse-drawn grass-cutting machine at a Minneapolis country club, and the modern power mower industry was born. By 1925 Toro turf maintenance machines were used on many of the US's major golf courses and parks, and by 1928 its products were used in Europe.

The company went public in 1935. Toro introduced its first walk-behind power mower for consumers four years later. In 1948 the company entered the rotary mower market when it bought Whirlwind. Toro started making snow removal equipment in 1951. With its 1962 purchase of

Moist O' Matic, the company's offerings included automatic irrigation for golf courses.

It was renamed The Toro Company in 1971. Consumer sales of snow removal equipment began to pile up, but those sales melted away when little snow fell during the winters of 1980 and 1981, and Toro suffered immense losses.

Kendrick Melrose, a 13-year Toro veteran, became CEO in 1983. He cut staff, closed plants, and revamped the company's inventory system. During the 1980s Toro diversified, acquiring two lighting manufacturers, including Lunalite (1984). The company also established an outdoor electrical appliance division.

In 1986 Toro purchased lawn tractor manufacturer Wheel Horse, and it entered the mid-priced market with the acquisition of rival Lawn-Boy three years later. Toro kept the Lawn-Boy brand, trying to capitalize on its name recognition in mass-merchandise retail channels.

Sales fell during the recession of the early 1990s, causing another round of plant closures and layoffs. The company introduced its "environmentally friendly" bagless Toro Recycler mower (1990), entered the fertilizer market with its Toro BioPro line (1992), and formed a Recycling Equipment division (1994). Toro found success with such new products as cordless electric mowers in 1995.

Trying to insulate itself against weather-related downturns, the company bought a unit (now called Irritrol) from irrigation products maker James Hardie Industries (1996); professional landscaping equipment maker Exmark (1997); and Motorola's OSMAC irrigation unit (1997). Toro's other acquisitions included the US rights of Dingo Digging Systems and micro-irrigation products maker Drip In (1998).

Despite the company's growing sales of commercial products, earnings plunged in 1998 in part because of declining consumer products sales (particularly snow blowers, thanks to uncooperative weather patterns), troubled sales in Asia, and restructuring costs.

Breaking with its policy to sell mainly through independent dealers, Toro opted to distribute its Toro-brand lawn mowers to selected home centers, adding nearly 1,500 distribution outlets in 1998. To mow down costs, in 1998 and 1999 it sold its Recycling Equipment business and fertilizer products business. Also in 1999 the company bought Multi-Core Aerators, a European distributor of large turf aeration equipment, and stopped making outdoor lighting products.

In 2000 the company acquired Sitework Systems (US sales representative of the Dingo compact utility loader) and completed the purchase of two distributors of turf maintenance and creation products.

Toro formed a financing unit with GE Capital in 2002 to help cities and golf courses buy irrigation systems and grounds maintenance equipment. Additionally that year Toro expanded facilities in Nebraska and Juarez, Mexico, where it also opened a plant for the production of walk-behind lawn mowers. During the same year Toro closed facilities in Evansville, Indiana, and Riverside, California.

Toro acquired R & D Engineering, which markets wireless rain and freeze switches for residential irrigation systems, in 2003.

EXECUTIVES

Chairman, President, and CEO: Michael J. Hoffman, age 54, $2,077,470 total compensation
VP Finance and CFO: Stephen P. Wolfe, age 61, $723,306 total compensation
VP Residential and Landscape Contractor Businesses: William E. (Bill) Brown Jr., age 48, $533,851 total compensation
VP Human Resources and Business Development: Peter M. (Pete) Ramstad, age 52, $584,325 total compensation
VP, Secretary, and General Counsel: Timothy P. (Tim) Dordell, age 47, $557,351 total compensation
VP Operations: Judy Altmaier, age 48
VP and Corporate Controller: Blake M. Grams, age 42
VP Commercial Business: Michael J. Happe, age 38
VP International Business: Darren Redetzke, age 45
VP Irrigation Business: Philip A. Burkart, age 47
VP Contractor Business and CIO: Michael D. Drazan, age 52
VP and Treasurer: Thomas J. Larson, age 52
Director Investor Relations: John Wright
Manager Public Relations: Branden Happel
Auditors: KPMG LLP

LOCATIONS

HQ: The Toro Company
8111 Lyndale Ave. South, Bloomington, MN 55420
Phone: 952-888-8801   **Fax:** 952-887-8258
Web: www.thetorocompany.com

2009 Sales

	$ mil.	% of total
US	1,036.2	68
Other countries	487.2	32
Total	**1,523.4**	**100**

PRODUCTS/OPERATIONS

2009 Sales

	$ mil.	% of total
Professional	965.9	63
Residential	532.7	35
Other	24.8	2
Total	**1,523.4**	**100**

2009 Sales

	$ mil.	% of total
Equipment	1,227.0	81
Irrigation	296.4	19
Total	**1,523.4**	**100**

Selected Products

Professional
  Agricultural irrigation
    Aqua-TraXX irrigation tape
    Blue Stripe polyethylene tubing
    Drip In drip line
  Golf course
    Bunker maintenance equipment
    Turf aerators
    Walking and riding mowers
  Landscape contractor
    Backhoes
    Compact utility loaders
    Heavy-duty walk-behind mowers
    Trenchers
    Zero-turning-radius riding mowers
  Sports fields and grounds
    Blowers
    Multipurpose vehicles
    Sweepers
    Vacuums

Residential
  Home solutions
    Electric blower-vacuums
    Grass trimmers
  Riding products
    Garden tractor models
    Lawn tractor models
    Zero-turning-radius mowers
  Snow removal
    Single-stage snow throwers
    Two-stage snow throwers
  Walk power mowers
    Bagging mowers
    Mulching mowers
    Side discharging mowers

COMPETITORS

Alamo Group
Deere
Emak Group
Honda
Kubota
LESCO
MTD Products
Tecumseh Products
Textron

HISTORICAL FINANCIALS

Company Type: Public

Income Statement

FYE: October 31

	REVENUE ($ mil.)	NET INCOME ($ mil.)	NET PROFIT MARGIN	EMPLOYEES
10/09	1,523	63	4.1%	4,414
10/08	1,878	120	6.4%	5,133
10/07	1,877	142	7.6%	5,320
10/06	1,836	129	7.0%	5,343
10/05	1,799	114	6.3%	5,185
Annual Growth	**(4.1%)**	**(13.9%)**	**—**	**(3.9%)**

2009 Year-End Financials

Debt ratio: 71.4%
Return on equity: 18.5%
Cash ($ mil.): 188
Current ratio: 1.84
Long-term debt ($ mil.): 225
No. of shares (mil.): 32
Dividends
  Yield: 1.6%
  Payout: 34.7%
Market value ($ mil.): 1,203

Stock History

NYSE: TTC

	STOCK PRICE ($) FY Close	P/E High/Low		PER SHARE ($) Earnings	PER SHARE ($) Dividends	PER SHARE ($) Book Value
10/09	37.02	24	12	1.73	0.60	9.70
10/08	33.64	19	9	3.10	0.60	11.22
10/07	55.66	19	13	3.40	0.48	11.40
10/06	43.16	18	13	2.91	0.36	12.07
10/05	36.53	20	14	2.45	0.24	12.00
Annual Growth	**0.3%**	**—**	**—**	**(8.3%)**	**25.7%**	**(5.2%)**

Total System Services

Total System Services (TSYS) helps consumers go paperless. The company is one of the largest electronic payment processors in the world. Through its TSYS Acquiring Solutions unit, it serves financial institutions and other companies that issue bank, private-label, prepaid, health care, or other types of cards. Products and services include credit authorization, payment processing, e-commerce services, card issuance, and such customer-relations services as call-center operations and fraud monitoring. TSYS (pronounced tee-sis) also has units that market processing equipment and software, perform commercial printing services, and sell Internet payment processing software.

While TSYS relished opportunities for growth in the payments industry presented by new technologies (such as mobile phones and the Internet), the company also had to contend with the fallout from the global economic crisis. High unemployment rates drove down consumer spending, tight credit markets meant fewer credit cards in circulation, and several financial institutions and retailers that TSYS counted as customers failed or underwent massive restructuring. All of those factors led to a drop in profits for the company.

TYSYS lost a major customer in 2010 as Bank of America began to provide its own merchant services. Bank of America accounted for about 5% of the company's revenues. However, not all of Bank of America's business will be going away. TYSYS still provides the company with services such as commercial and small-business card processing, and card production.

In order to offset some of the negative impact, TSYS is busy readapting to the marketplace by diversifying its revenue streams and geographic reach. The company has operations in 85 countries and is looking to further expand overseas.

Several past acquisitions and partnerships have helped the company grow abroad. Its 2006 acquisition of what is now TSYS Card Tech gave TSYS a foothold in dozens of new countries in the Asia/Pacific region, Europe, the Middle East, and Africa. One year before, an alliance also put TSYS on the ground in China, where it has a 45% stake in China UnionPay Data Services. Through the partnership, the company provides credit card processing for several large Chinese financial institutions, making it the leading outsourced payment solutions provider in that country. TSYS also has expanded operations to Brazil and made progress in the Asia/Pacific region. In 2009 the company opened an office in New Delhi, India, which is at the center of one of the fastest growing card markets in the world.

In addition to growing its international operations, TSYS is expanding its merchant services capabilities. An example includes the acquisition of technology firm Infonox in 2009. The acquisition provided the company with new payment technology and acceptance capabilities such as a new service that allows clients to accept payments through their smart phones.

TSYS has been cautious about its growth and has reduced some operations in order to focus on its payments business and reduce costs. One such cut came in 2009 when it sold its TSYS Total Debt Management subsidiary. The unit handled collection and bankruptcy processing.

HISTORY

Created in 1959 to handle the bank card operations of Columbus Bank and Trust, Total System Services was spun off in 1982 and went public the following year. Its growth was spurred by increased credit card use, a growing tendency by banks to outsource data processing, and the company's ability to snag such big customers as NationsBank (later part of Bank of America) and AT&T Universal Card Services.

As the US credit card processing market matured, TSYS began looking to expand overseas — and taking other companies' business. Despite Mexico's economic downturn, in 1993 TSYS formed a joint venture with Mexican card processor PROSA; in 1995 it snagged part of BankAmerica's business. The following year TSYS upgraded its data-processing system to let its banking and retail customers tailor cards to their clients.

Alliances helped position TSYS as a one-stop support shop for banks. These included a joint venture with Visa International in 1996 that created Vital Processing Services, a merchant transaction processing and data services firm.

In 1998 TSYS agreed to process 60 million Sears credit card accounts. It was TSYS's biggest deal ever and one passed over by rival First Data. The pact helped compensate for the 1999 loss of major client Universal Card Services, which AT&T sold to Citicorp. Also in 1999 TSYS added call-center and other customer services to its offerings when it acquired Partnership Card services from Synovus Financial.

TSYS entered Europe and Japan in a big way in 2000. It inked a deal to process cards for The Royal Bank of Scotland Group (the UK's #2 card issuer). It also bought a majority stake in Japanese credit card issuer GP Network (leading Japanese card issuers also had a stake in the card processor).

In 2005 TSYS bought from Visa U.S.A. the 50% it didn't own in merchant transaction clearing and settlement firm TSYS Acquiring Solutions (formerly Vital Processing Services).

TSYS became an independent company in 2008 after it was spun off by Synovus.

In 2010 the company acquired a 51% stake in the merchant-acquiring business of First National Bank of Omaha. The new partnership, which does business as First National Merchant Solutions, allowed TSYS better access to consumers and merchants and additional channels of revenue.

EXECUTIVES

Chairman and CEO: Philip W. (Phil) Tomlinson, age 63, $4,038,473 total compensation
President, COO, and Director: M. Troy Woods, age 58, $3,089,161 total compensation
SEVP and CFO: James B. (Jim) Lipham, age 61, $1,199,395 total compensation
SEVP, General Counsel, and Secretary: G. Sanders Griffith III, age 56
SEVP and Chief Client Officer: William A. (Bill) Pruett, age 56, $1,326,903 total compensation
SEVP and CIO: Kenneth L. (Ken) Tye, age 57, $1,319,919 total compensation
EVP and Chief Human Resource Officer: Ryland L. Harrelson
EVP, Chief Accounting Officer, and Controller: Dorenda K. Weaver
EVP Customer Care: Colleen W. Kynard
EVP and CTO: Stephen W. (Steve) Humber
EVP Mergers, Acquisitions, and Strategy: Paul M. Todd
EVP Sales, Strategy, and Emerging Markets: Gaylon M. Jowers Jr.

EVP Product and Client Development: Connie C. Dudley
Group Executive and Chief Sales and Marketing Officer: Bruce L. Bacon
Group Executive; President, TSYS Loyalty and Prepaid: Rodney Q. (Rod) Boyer
Group Executive, TSYS International: Robert E. (Bob) Evans
Group Executive; CIO, TSYS Acquiring Solutions: Ashim K. Banerjee
Group Executive, TSYS Commercial Services: Keith D. Pierce
Group Executive, Output Services: Richard L. (Rick) St. John
Group Executive, Relationship Management: W. Allen Pettis
Investor Relations: Shawn Roberts
Media Relations and Corporate Communications: Cyle Mims
Auditors: KPMG LLP

LOCATIONS

HQ: Total System Services, Inc.
1 TSYS Way, Columbus, GA 31902
Phone: 706-649-2310   **Fax:** 706-649-4266
Web: www.tsys.com

2009 Sales

	$ mil.	% of total
US	1,194.4	71
Europe	269.4	16
Canada	139.7	8
Japan	48.9	3
Mexico	8.2	—
Other regions	27.5	2
Total	**1,688.1**	**100**

PRODUCTS/OPERATIONS

2009 Sales

	$ mil.	% of total
Electronic payment processing services	946.3	56
Merchant services	277.4	16
Reimbursable items	270.2	16
Other services	194.2	12
Total	**1,688.1**	**100**

Selected Subsidiaries

China UnionPay Data Services Company Limited (45%)
Columbus Depot Equipment Company
Enhancement Services Corporation
GP Network Corporation
Merlin Solutions LLC
ProCard, Inc.
TSYS Acquiring Solutions, LLC
TSYS Loyalty, Inc.

COMPETITORS

Banc of America Merchant Services
Chase Paymentech Solutions
ECHO, Inc.
Elavon
Equifax
First Data
Fiserv
MasterCard

HISTORICAL FINANCIALS

Company Type: Public

Income Statement

FYE: December 31

	REVENUE ($ mil.)	NET INCOME ($ mil.)	NET PROFIT MARGIN	EMPLOYEES
12/09	1,688	219	13.0%	7,620
12/08	1,939	250	12.9%	8,110
12/07	1,806	237	13.1%	6,921
12/06	1,787	249	13.9%	6,644
12/05	1,603	195	12.1%	6,603
Annual Growth	**1.3%**	**3.0%**	**—**	**3.6%**

2009 Year-End Financials

Debt ratio: 17.4%
Return on equity: 20.2%
Cash ($ mil.): 450
Current ratio: 3.67
Long-term debt ($ mil.): 205
No. of shares (mil.): 197
Dividends
  Yield: 1.6%
  Payout: 25.7%
Market value ($ mil.): 3,409

Stock History

NYSE: TSS

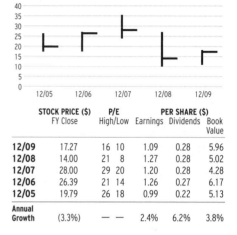

	STOCK PRICE ($) FY Close	P/E High/Low		PER SHARE ($) Earnings	Dividends	Book Value
12/09	17.27	16	10	1.09	0.28	5.96
12/08	14.00	21	8	1.27	0.28	5.02
12/07	28.00	29	20	1.20	0.28	4.28
12/06	26.39	21	14	1.26	0.27	6.17
12/05	19.79	26	18	0.99	0.22	5.13
Annual Growth	**(3.3%)**	**—**	**—**	**2.4%**	**6.2%**	**3.8%**

Travelers Companies

Running a business is a risk The Travelers Companies will insure. While it does offer personal auto and homeowners insurance, the company's largest segment is commercial property/casualty insurance to businesses big and small. It is one of the largest business insurers in the US, providing commercial auto, property, workers' compensation, marine, and general and financial liability coverage to companies in North America and the UK. The company also offers surety and fidelity bonds as well as professional and management liability coverage for commercial operations. The Travelers distributes its products through independent agencies and brokers.

In addition to serving general commercial accounts, The Travelers maintains a group of industry-specific underwriting units serving the agribusiness, construction, oil and gas, and technology industries, as well as the public sector.

While the vast majority (over 90%) of the company's business is in the US, it does have a presence in the UK, where it operates through two arms: Travelers Insurance Company and Travelers Syndicate 5000, whose operations are connected with Lloyd's of London. The two businesses offer commercial property/casualty and risk management services.

The Travelers has been pruning itself of any noncore operations, including most of its international businesses. It has sold its non-standard personal property/casualty and medical malpractice lines. The company uses outside reinsurers to control its exposure to catastrophic losses, but The Travelers itself exited the reinsurance business.

The Travelers got back to insurance basics long before getting back to basics was cool (or in some cases desperately necessary). The company sold off its nearly 80% stake in asset management business Nuveen Investments in a series of transactions during 2005.

HISTORY

St. Paul, Minnesota, was a boomtown in 1852 thanks to traffic on the Mississippi. Settlers knew fire insurance was a must in their wooden town, but there were no local insurers. Buying policies from eastern companies and getting claims processed was difficult — especially in the winter, when river traffic stopped.

In 1853 a group of local investors led by George and John Farrington and Alexander Wilkin formed St. Paul Mutual Insurance, a mixed stock and mutual company (mutual members shared in the firm's profits and losses, while stockholders could benefit by selling if the company's value rose). St. Paul Mutual sold its first policy the following year.

The company changed its name in 1865 to St. Paul Fire and Marine Insurance, stopped offering mutual policies, and expanded throughout the Midwest. Claims from the Chicago Fire in 1871 nearly sank the company, which assessed its shareholders $15 for each share of stock, but prompt and full payment of claims resulted in more business. By the turn of the century, St. Paul Fire and Marine was operating nationwide.

Although the company was hard hit by shipping losses in WWI, it continued expanding, joining other US insurers in the American Foreign Insurance Association to market insurance in Europe.

In 1926 St. Paul Fire and Marine organized its first subsidiary, St. Paul Mercury Indemnity, to write liability insurance policies. Other additions included coverage for automobiles, aircraft, burglary and robbery, and, in 1940, turkey farming.

During WWII, St. Paul Fire and Marine joined the War Damage Corp., a government-financed consortium that paid claims for war damage. The St. Paul Companies was formed in 1968 as the umbrella organization for the various subsidiaries, and the firm grew through purchases.

Lines of business blossomed during the 1970s, including life and title insurance, leasing, a mail-order consumer finance company, oil and gas, and real estate. Many of these were sold during the 1980s, but one, The John Nuveen Co. (1974), became the nucleus of St. Paul's financial services operations.

St. Paul posted a loss in 1992 after paying out huge claims related to Hurricane Andrew. In 1995 the company expanded its malpractice line when it bought NML Insurance. The Minet unit (a brokerage business) started Global Media Services that year to focus on insurance for the telecommunications industry. The division also bought London-based Special Risk Service, a top insurance broker, and Boston-based William Gallagher Associates, a high-tech and biotechnology insurer.

In 1997 St. Paul sold its unprofitable Minet division. That year and the next the company was struck by catastrophic losses, more than $150 million total.

St. Paul acquired USF&G in 1998. The purchase triggered a round of job cuts as the company assimilated its new operations; the deal also slammed the insurer's earnings. To focus on its more profitable commercial business, the firm sold its personal insurance business (1999) and jettisoned its nonstandard auto insurance business (2000). In 2000 it bought MMI Companies to build its health care risk operations and decided later that year to close Unionamerica Holdings, an unprofitable subsidiary of MMI. In 2001 St. Paul sold F&G Life, a subsidiary of USF&G, to UK-based insurer Old Mutual.

The World Trade Center attacks (in which the company paid out almost $1 billion in claims) and other disasters combined to make reinsurance a costlier game of dice. The company spun off its reinsurance business, St. Paul Re, into Bermuda-based Platinum Underwriters in 2002.

In a $16 billion blockbuster deal, The St. Paul Companies acquired Travelers Property Casualty in 2004. (Travelers had been a subsidiary of Citigroup until its IPO in early 2002.) Reflecting the acquisition, the company then changed its name to The St. Paul Travelers Companies. Then, in early 2007 the company changed its name to The Travelers Companies, Inc. and reclaimed the trademarked red umbrella logo used in previous Travelers incarnations.

EXECUTIVES

Chairman and CEO: Jay S. Fishman, age 57, $20,628,968 total compensation
Vice Chairman: Charles J. (Chuck) Clarke, age 74
Vice Chairman, Chief Legal Officer, and EVP Financial, Professional, and International Insurance:
Alan D. Schnitzer, age 44, $5,122,574 total compensation
Vice Chairman and CFO: Jay S. Benet, age 57, $6,030,166 total compensation
Vice Chairman and Chief Investment Officer:
William H. Heyman, age 61, $6,290,249 total compensation
Vice Chairman: Irwin R. Ettinger, age 71
President and COO: Brian W. MacLean, age 56, $7,310,228 total compensation
EVP and Chief Administrative Officer: Andy F. Bessette, age 56
EVP Business Insurance:
William E. (Bill) Cunningham Jr., age 44
EVP Human Resources: John P. Clifford Jr.
EVP Enterprise Risk Management and Business Conduct Officer: Bill Hannon
EVP and General Counsel: Kenneth F. (Ken) Spence III, age 54
EVP Public Policy: Joan Kois Woodward
EVP; CEO, Claim Services and Personal Insurance: Doreen Spadorcia, age 52
EVP and Chief Marketing Officer: Anne MacDonald, age 53
EVP Strategic Development and Treasurer: Maria Olivo, age 45
SVP Investor Relations: Gabriella Nawi
SVP and Corporate Secretary: Matthew S. Furman
CEO, Travelers Insurance: Martin P. Hudson
Auditors: KPMG LLP

LOCATIONS

HQ: The Travelers Companies, Inc.
485 Lexington Ave., New York, NY 10017
Phone: 917-778-6000
Web: www.travelers.com

PRODUCTS/OPERATIONS

2009 Revenues

	$ mil.	% of total
Premiums		
Business insurance	10,968	44
Personal insurance	7,117	29
Financial, professional & international insurance	3,333	14
Net investment income	2,776	11
Fee income	306	1
Net realized investment losses	17	—
Other	163	1
Total	**24,680**	**100**

Selected Subsidiaries

St. Paul Fire and Marine Insurance Company
Travelers Property Casualty Corp.
The Standard Fire Insurance Company
Travelers Casualty and Surety Company
Travelers Casualty and Surety Company of America
The Travelers Indemnity Company
First Floridian Auto and Home Insurance Company
First Trenton Indemnity Company (Travelers of New Jersey)
The Premier Insurance Co. of Massachusetts
Travelers Insurance Company Ltd. (UK)

COMPETITORS

ACE Limited
AIG
Allianz
Allstate
American Financial Group
AXA
Chubb Corp
CNA Financial
The Hartford
Lexington Insurance
Markel
Nationwide
W. R. Berkley
Zurich Financial Services

HISTORICAL FINANCIALS

Company Type: Public

Income Statement

FYE: December 31

	ASSETS ($ mil.)	NET INCOME ($ mil.)	INCOME AS % OF ASSETS	EMPLOYEES
12/09	109,560	3,622	3.3%	32,000
12/08	109,751	2,924	2.7%	33,000
12/07	115,224	4,601	4.0%	33,300
12/06	113,761	4,208	3.7%	32,800
12/05	113,187	1,622	1.4%	31,900
Annual Growth	**(0.8%)**	**22.2%**	**—**	**0.1%**

2009 Year-End Financials

Equity as % of assets: 25.0%
Return on assets: 3.3%
Return on equity: 13.8%
Long-term debt ($ mil.): 6,527
No. of shares (mil.): 470
Dividends
Yield: 2.5%
Payout: 19.4%
Market value ($ mil.): 23,434
Sales ($ mil.): 24,680

Stock History

NYSE: TRV

	STOCK PRICE ($) FY Close	P/E High/Low		PER SHARE ($) Earnings	Dividends	Book Value
12/09	49.86	9	5	6.33	1.23	58.33
12/08	45.20	12	6	4.82	1.19	53.87
12/07	53.80	8	7	6.86	1.13	56.63
12/06	53.69	9	7	5.91	1.01	53.48
12/05	44.67	20	14	2.33	0.91	47.45
Annual Growth	**2.8%**	**—**	**—**	**28.4%**	**7.8%**	**5.3%**

Trinity Industries

If Trinity Industries had a theme song, it would be sung by Boxcar Willie. The company manufactures auto carriers, box cars, gondola cars, hopper cars, intermodal cars, and tank cars — in short, railcars for hauling everything from coal to corn syrup. Trinity also leases and manages railcar fleets. Its Inland Barge unit builds barges used to transport coal, grain, and other commodities. In addition to transportation, other Trinity businesses provide products and services to the industrial, energy (structural towers for wind turbines, metal containers for liquefied petroleum gas and fertilizer), and construction (concrete, aggregates, highway guardrails) sectors.

The rail supply industry as a whole suffered economic derailment throughout 2008 and 2009. Along with volatile market steel prices came the compounding factor of a global economic crisis and subsequent decreases in demand. The company responded by idling significant production facilities — closing railcar manufacturing plants in Georgia, Missouri, Oklahoma, Texas, and Mexico, as well as a barge-making facility in Louisiana. Trinity reduced its workforce in the railcar and energy groups, which included a 15% cut at the wind turbine plant in Oklahoma in early 2009.

While the 2010 economic forecast for the railcar industry remains dim, the company has been able to limit a full impact by its contract purchases of steel, as well as its diversified product lineup. However, its construction division (Trinity's third largest) took a crushing blow when the housing market bottomed out.

Trinity Rail Group still holds an approximate 42% market share of the North American railcar industry by shipment. The division manufactures freight railcars that transport liquids, gases, and dry cargo. Trinity's Railcar and Leasing Management Services Group operates primarily through Trinity Industries Leasing Company (TILC). It provides leasing options to companies involved in petroleum, chemical, agricultural, and energy industries, among others. Trinity's fleet numbers over 50,000 railcars.

The Construction Products Group produces concrete, aggregates, and asphalt; it manufactures highway products, which include beams and girders used in highway bridge construction. Other highway products include guardrails, cable barrier systems, and crash cushions. Trinity owns mining operations in Texas, Arkansas, and Louisiana, which produce sand, gravel, and limestone base. Armor Materials provides asphalt and base products for construction.

Inland Barge Group, with its four barge production facilities, manufactures dry cargo barges (flat-deck and hopper), which transport products such as grain, coal, and aggregates. Tank barges carry petroleum, fertilizer, chemicals, and other liquid cargoes. This business makes fiberglass barge covers and deck hardware (brand name Nabrico), including hatches, castings, and winches for other watercraft and dock facilities.

Energy Equipment Group makes tank containers and tank heads for pressure vessels, propane tanks, and structural wind towers. Trinity Industries de Mexico, under the brand name TATSA, manufactures containers for liquefied petroleum gas. It also manufactures containers for fertilizers, comestibles, and ammonia.

HISTORY

Trinity Industries resulted from the 1958 merger of Trinity Steel, a maker of metal products for the petroleum industry, and Dallas Tank Co. The enterprise was headed by Ray Wallace, a Trinity Steel veteran since the 1940s.

The company, which took the name Trinity Industries in 1966, acquired related tank, welding, and steel companies in the 1960s and quickly became the leading manufacturer of metal storage containers for liquefied petroleum gas. During this period it also applied its expertise to containers for another rapidly growing industry — fertilizer — and made custom products for the oil and chemical industries. Other products included hopper bodies and tanks for use on railcars.

During the 1970s Trinity diversified into building seagoing vessels by purchasing Equitable Equipment and its Louisiana shipyards in 1972. The next year the company bought Mosher Steel (steel beams and framing products). By the mid-1970s it was producing highway guardrails and other road construction products. Trinity expanded its railcar parts manufacturing in 1977 to building complete cars and created a railcar-leasing subsidiary.

The company was a leading producer of railcars by the early 1980s, but a change in federal tax laws and a glut of railcars caused demand to plummet; in 1985 Trinity suffered its first loss in 27 years. Still, Trinity managed to snap up failing competitors, including Pullman Standard, once the US's top freight car maker. The company also bought Greenville Steel Car (1986), Ortner Freight (1987), and Standard Forgings (locomotive axles, 1987). Trinity tripled its manufacturing capacity, so that it controlled more than half of the US freight car production capacity in the early 1990s.

The company also expanded its marine division with such acquisitions as Halter Marine (1983) and Bethlehem Steel's manufacturing plant and marine facilities in Beaumont, Texas (1989).

Trinity expanded its construction products line in 1992 with the purchase of Syro Steel (fabricated steel products) and added the Texas and Louisiana operations of Lafarge (concrete) in 1994. The company expanded into Mexico in 1995 by acquiring Grupo TATSA (fabricated steel products).

To fund expansion in other segments, Trinity spun off its Halter Marine Group in 1996. In 1997 Trinity acquired two manufacturing facilities from pipe fitting, flange, and valve industry specialist Ladish.

Ray Wallace retired as chairman and CEO in 1999 and was replaced by his son, Timothy Wallace. That year Trinity bought McConway and Torley (railcar couplers) and Excell Materials (ready-mix concrete). It also set up a railcar joint venture in Brazil. In the summer of 2001 Trinity agreed to acquire privately held railcar maker Thrall Car Manufacturing.

In 2006 the company focused on its core businesses and sold its Trinity Fittings Group to the division's management and investment firm Levine Leichtman Capital Partners.

Trinity strengthened its construction products business in 2007 with the acquisition of a number of holdings operating under the name Armor Materials. The operations included asphalt, ready mix concrete, and aggregates businesses.

Trinity bolstered its construction products business again in 2010 with the acquisition of Quixote, a maker of highway crash cushions, anti-icing systems for bridges, and other transportation safety related products.

EXECUTIVES

Chairman, President, and CEO: Timothy R. Wallace, age 56, $4,241,760 total compensation
SVP; Group President, Construction Products, Inland Barge, and Rail Components:
William A. (Bill) McWhirter II, age 46, $1,420,204 total compensation
SVP and Group President, TrinityRail:
D. Stephen (Steve) Menzies, age 54, $1,595,601 total compensation
VP Finance, Treasurer, and CFO: James E. Perry, age 38
VP and Chief Audit Executive: Donald G. Collum, age 61
VP and Chief Legal Officer: S. Theis Rice, age 59, $963,093 total compensation
VP: Antonio Carrillo
VP Information Technology: Madhuri A. Andrews, age 43
VP Business Development: John M. Lee, age 49
VP Organizational Development: Virginia C. Gray, age 50
VP Human Resources and Shared Services:
Andrea F. Cowan, age 47
Associate General Counsel and Secretary:
Jared S. Richardson
Corporate Controller: Mary E. Henderson, age 51
President, Parts and Components: Patrick S. Wallace
Auditors: Ernst & Young LLP

LOCATIONS

HQ: Trinity Industries, Inc.
2525 Stemmons Fwy., Dallas, TX 75207
Phone: 214-631-4420   **Fax:** 214-589-8810
Web: www.trin.net

PRODUCTS/OPERATIONS

2009 Sales

	$ mil.	% of total
Rail	895.3	29
Construction	538.5	18
Inland Barge	527.3	17
Railcar Leasing & Management Services	524.5	17
Energy Equipment	510.0	17
Other	48.4	2
Adjustments	(468.8)	—
Total	**2,575.2**	**100**

Selected Products and Services

Rail
  Box cars
  Freight cars
  Gondola cars
  Hopper cars
  Intermodal cars
  Tank cars
Construction products
  Aggregates
  Anti-icing systems for bridges
  Beams
  Flexible post delineators
  Girders
  Highway crash cushions
  Highway guardrails
  Highway safety devices
  Ready-mix concrete
  Truck-mounted attenuators
Inland barge
  Deck barges
  Fiberglass barge covers
  Hopper barges
  Tank barges
Energy equipment
  Container heads
  Fertilizer containers
  Liquefied petroleum gas containers
  Wind towers
Railcar leasing and management services
  Railcar leasing, repair, and management

HISTORICAL FINANCIALS

Company Type: Public

Income Statement				FYE: December 31
	REVENUE ($ mil.)	NET INCOME ($ mil.)	NET PROFIT MARGIN	EMPLOYEES
12/09	2,575	(138)	—	7,200
12/08	3,883	286	7.4%	13,070
12/07	3,833	293	7.6%	14,400
12/06	3,219	230	7.1%	13,800
12/05	2,902	86	3.0%	15,224
Annual Growth	(2.9%)	—	—	(17.1%)

2009 Year-End Financials

Debt ratio: —
Return on equity: —
Cash ($ mil.): 612
Current ratio: 0.47
Long-term debt ($ mil.): —

No. of shares (mil.): 80
Dividends
  Yield: 1.8%
  Payout: —
Market value ($ mil.): 1,391

Stock History

NYSE: TRN

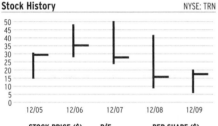

	STOCK PRICE ($) FY Close	P/E High	P/E Low	PER SHARE ($) Earnings	PER SHARE ($) Dividends	PER SHARE ($) Book Value
12/09	17.44	—	—	(1.81)	0.32	22.65
12/08	15.76	11	3	3.59	0.30	22.96
12/07	27.76	14	7	3.65	0.25	21.65
12/06	35.20	16	10	2.90	0.21	17.60
12/05	29.38	27	14	1.13	0.17	13.97
Annual Growth	(12.2%)	—	—	—	17.1%	12.8%

True Value

To survive against home improvement giants such as The Home Depot and Lowe's, True Value (formerly TruServ) is relying on the true value of service. Formed by the 1997 merger of Cotter & Company (which supplied the True Value chain) and ServiStar Coast to Coast, the retailer-owned hardware cooperative serves more than 5,000 retail outlets in some 55 countries. Stores offer home improvement and garden supplies, as well as appliances, housewares, sporting goods, and toys. In addition to the flagship True Value banner, members operate under the names of Taylor Rental, Grand Rental Station, Home & Garden Showplace, and Induserve Supply, among others.

The merger of Cotter & Company and ServiStar Coast to Coast gave members — many of them mom-and-pop outlets — more buying clout to compete against the do-it-yourself mega-retailers, plus retail advice and advertising support. Connecting with customers is central to True Value's business, especially as it fights for foot traffic following the collapse of the housing market and subsequent economic downturn.

Essential to the company's growth strategy has been the rollout of its Destination True Value (DTV) retail format, which aims to simplify shopping in its hardware stores, particularly for its female clientele (who hold sway when it comes to tackling home improvement projects). The format features a "racetrack" layout for easy navigation as well as color-coded signs, brighter lighting, and an expanded array of decorative hardware and paint. Also, the format is relatively flexible and allows owners to customize their store layouts for their particular local markets.

In addition to the DTV plan, the company is working to woo younger do-it-yourselfers into its stores through the reach of digital marketing. Stores produce area-specific online circulars, and True Value's website offers a project library, product guides, and bargains of the month.

While the organization is focused on expanding its retail presence, the weak housing market in the US has kept growth in check. Over the years, its smaller in-town locations have taken a beating at the hands of the big-box hardware chains. True Value's store count has declined from nearly 7,200 outlets in 2001. Yet, high gas prices and shoppers' increasing ambivalence toward the big-box shopping experience may bode well for the co-op's future.

HISTORY

Noting that hardware retailers had begun to form wholesale cooperatives to lower costs, John Cotter, a traveling hardware salesman, and associate Ed Lanctot started pitching the wholesale co-op idea in 1947 to small-town and suburban hardware retailers, and by early 1948 they had enrolled 25 merchants for $1,500 each. Cotter became chairman of the new firm, Cotter & Company.

The co-op created the Value & Service (V&S) store trademark in 1951 to emphasize the advantages of an independent hardware store. Acquisitions included the 1963 purchase of Chicago-based wholesaler Hibbard, Spencer, Bartlett, giving Cotter 400 new members and the well-known True Value trademark, which soon replaced V&S signs. Four years later Cotter broadened its focus by buying the General Paint & Chemical Company (Tru-Test paint).

The V&S name was revived in 1972 for a five-and-dime store co-op, V&S Variety Stores.

In 1989 Cotter died and Lanctot retired. (Lanctot died in October 2003.) By 1989 there were almost 7,000 True Value Stores. Cotter moved into Canada in 1992 by acquiring hardware distributor and store operator Macleod-Stedman (275 outlets).

Juggling variety-store and hardware merchandise and delivering very small amounts of merchandise to a lukewarm co-op membership did not allow for economies of scale, so in 1995 the company quit its manufacturing operations and its US variety stores (though it still serves variety stores in Canada, operating as C&S Choices), tightened membership requirements, and introduced new services.

Two years later Cotter formed TruServ by merging with hardware wholesaler ServiStar Coast to Coast. ServiStar had its origins in the nation's first hardware co-op, American Hardware Supply, which was founded in Pittsburgh in 1910 by M. R. Porter, John Howe, and E. S. Corlett. By 1988, the year it changed its name to ServiStar, the co-op topped $1 billion in sales.

ServiStar expanded in the upper Midwest and on the West Coast in 1990 when it acquired the assets of the Coast to Coast chain (founded in 1928 as a franchise hardware store in Minneapolis); ServiStar brought Coast to Coast out of bankruptcy two years later, making it a co-op. Merging its 1992 acquisition of Taylor Rental Center with its Grand Rental Station stores in 1993 made ServiStar the #1 general rental chain. In 1996 it consolidated Coast to Coast's operations into its own and changed its name to ServiStar Coast to Coast.

President Don Hoye became CEO of the company in 1999. That year TruServ slashed 1,000 jobs and declared it would convert all its hardware store chains to the True Value banner. But TruServ lost $131 million in 1999 over bookkeeping gaffes, and co-op members received no dividends. Of 2,800 ServiStar dealers, only 1,900 raised the True Value flag. Others either declined to switch or were never offered the change because other True Value stores already shared their market area. In addition, stores began deserting the co-op because of inventory and other problems.

As competition continued to increase in 2001, the company was facing falling sales, lawsuits from shareholders, and accusations by retailers of unfair practices intended to pressure them into adopting the cooperative's flagship True Value banner. TruServ also had to confront a $200 million loan default. It made cuts in its corporate staff and divested its Canadian interests. In July 2001 Hoye resigned. The company's CFO and COO, Pamela Forbes Lieberman, was named new CEO that November.

TruServ, under SEC investigation for alleged inventory, accounting, and other internal-control problems, failed in 2002 to meet a government requirement to swear by their past financial results. TruServ settled the SEC's allegations in 2003, without admitting or denying them, and agreed to follow measures intended to ensure compliance with securities laws.

Lieberman resigned in 2004. Director Thomas Hanemann was named interim CEO. TruServ changed its name to True Value in January 2005. In June 2005 Hanemann turned over the reins to Sears veteran Lyle G. Heidemann.

The year 2008 marked the first time in over a decade that revenue from new stores exceeded lost revenue from terminated stores.

EXECUTIVES

Chairman; CEO, Krueger's True Value, Neenah, Wis.:
Brian A. Webb
President, CEO, and Director: Lyle G. Heidemann,
age 65
SVP and CFO: David A. (Dave) Shadduck
SVP Retail Operations: Steve Poplawski
SVP Logistics and Supply Chain Management:
Stephen Poplawski
SVP and Chief Merchandising Officer: Michael Clark
SVP Human Resources, General Counsel, and
Secretary: Cathy C. Anderson
VP Marketing: Carol Wentworth, age 50
VP and Corporate Treasurer: Barbara L. Wagner
VP Specialty Businesses: Fred L. Kirst, age 56
VP Retail Growth: Mark Flowers
VP Retail Finance: Jon Johnson
VP Logistics: Donald J. (Don) Deegan
Director; CEO, Campbell's True Value, Madison, Maine:
Brent A. Burger
Director; CEO, True Value Hardware House, Annapolis,
MD: Kenneth A. Niefeld, age 66
Director; CEO, Welch's True Value Hardware, South
Royalton, VT: Charles M. Welch, age 58
Director; CEO, Shively True Value Hardware, Saratoga,
WY: Michael S. Glode, age 59
Auditors: PricewaterhouseCoopers LLP

LOCATIONS

HQ: True Value Company
8600 W. Bryn Mawr Ave., Chicago, IL 60631
Phone: 773-695-5000
Web: www.truevaluecompany.com

PRODUCTS/OPERATIONS

Selected Operations

Grand Rental Station (general rental)
Home & Garden Showplace (nursery and giftware)
Induserve Supply (commercial and industrial)
Party Central (parties and corporate events)
Taylor Rental (general rental)
True Value (hardware)

COMPETITORS

84 Lumber	Northern Tool
Ace Hardware	Orgill
Akzo Nobel	Reno-Depot
Benjamin Moore	Sears
Do it Best	Sherwin-Williams
Fastenal	Stock Building Supply
Home Depot	Sutherland Lumber
Kmart	United Rentals
Lowe's	Valspar
McCoy Corp.	Wal-Mart
Menard	

HISTORICAL FINANCIALS

Company Type: Cooperative

Income Statement				FYE: December 31
	REVENUE ($ mil.)	NET INCOME ($ mil.)	NET PROFIT MARGIN	EMPLOYEES
12/09	1,823	65	3.6%	3,000
12/08	2,013	64	3.2%	3,000
12/07	2,041	64	3.1%	3,000
12/06	2,050	73	3.6%	3,000
12/05	2,043	48	2.3%	2,800
Annual Growth	(2.8%)	8.3%	—	1.7%

2009 Year-End Financials

Debt ratio: 57.9%
Return on equity: —
Cash ($ mil.): —
Current ratio: —
Long-term debt ($ mil.): 91

Net Income History

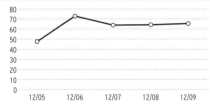

Tupperware Brands

Tupperware Brands Corporation (TBC) knows that there's more than one way to party. The company makes and sells household products and beauty items. Tupperware parties became synonymous with American suburban life in the 1950s, when independent salespeople organized gatherings to peddle their plasticware. TBC deploys a sales force of about 2.4 million people in about 100 countries. The company also sells its products online. Brands include Armand Dupree, Avroy Shlain, BeautiControl, Fuller, NaturCare, Nutrimetics, Nuvo, Swissgarde, and, of course, Tupperware. Its BeautiControl unit sells beauty and skin care products and fragrances in North America, Latin America, and the Asia/Pacific region.

TBC's direct sales force logged 16.5 million Tupperware parties worldwide in 2009. Though many consider the Tupperware brand to be something of an American institution, some 68% of the company's 2009 sales (up from 65% in 2008 and 2007's 62%) were generated outside the US. TBC has pushed into new and developing markets (such as China, Eastern Europe, India, Japan, and Indonesia), offering region-specific products such as Kimono Keepers. The direct seller often targets areas where jobs are scarce and family ties are strong — the better for developing its sales network.

Its international growth and beauty segment have been gaining momentum, as well. The company's beauty segment accounted for about 33% of sales in 2009. TBC built its global beauty presence through one strategic acquisition. In 2005 it doubled its sales force of independent consultants who sell beauty and personal care products in the Asia/Pacific region and Latin America with the acquisition of Sara Lee Corporation's international direct-selling unit. As part of the agreement, TBC paid $557 million and acquired the direct selling unit's staff of 884,000 consultants, as well. The company then changed its name from Tupperware Corporation to Tupperware Brands Corporation to reflect the firm's growing portfolio of brands. While the Tupperware brand accounted for 83% of 2005 sales, in 2009 it brought in about 67%, while its beauty segment blossomed.

FMR owns about an 11% stake in Tupperware. BlackRock, a group of investors, has an 8% share.

HISTORY

Earl Tupper was a self-styled inventor with only a high school education when he went to work for DuPont in the 1930s. He left DuPont in 1938 to start his own company, taking with him an unwanted, smelly chunk of polyethylene, a by-product of the oil refining process. Tupper eventually developed his own refining process, and in 1942 he created a clear, lightweight, unbreakable, odorless, nontoxic plastic, which he called Poly-T.

Tupper continued to do contract work for DuPont during the war, making parts for gas masks and Navy signal lamps. He continued to work with Poly-T and founded Tupperware in 1946. The next year, inspired by a paint can lid, Tupper developed the Tupperware Seal, which creates an airtight, partial vacuum. The Tupperware food storage container was born and began to move onto retail shelves.

At the same time, a secretary in Detroit named Brownie Wise was selling Stanley Home Products' appliances through parties at her home to raise money for her son's medical bills. (The party system was actually developed in the 1920s to introduce communities to aluminum cookware.) Wise added a Tupperware set to her product mix, and sales took off. By the early 1950s Tupperware parties began to spread.

Wise, hired as VP and general manager, became Tupperware's inspirational leader. In 1951 all Tupperware products were removed from retail shelves, and subsidiary Tupperware Home Parties was officially founded. By 1954 sales multiplied 25 times and the company had about 9,000 independent sellers.

By 1958 Tupperware expanded into Canada. That year Wise left and Tupper sold the company to Rexall Drug. In 1969 Rexall became Dart Industries; by this time Tupperware had entered Western Europe, Latin America, and parts of Asia. In 1976 international sales pushed revenue past $500 million.

In 1980 Dart merged with Kraft to become Dart and Kraft, Inc. By 1984 sales began to slip due to the number of women entering the workforce. Tupperware introduced a catalog and revised the party plan to include gatherings in the workplace. Dart and Kraft split in 1986, and Dart became Premark International. Tupperware's national ad campaign the next year inadvertently increased the sales of retail competitors such as Rubbermaid. By 1990 sales were slowing across the US, Latin America, and Japan.

Tupperware restructured in 1992 and former Avon executive Rick Goings became president. Wall Street's belief that Tupperware was languishing as a subsidiary led to its spinoff from Premark as a public company in 1996. Tupperware established operations in China that year and began holding parties in Russia in 1997. The Asian economic crisis and domestic organizational problems led to slumping sales in 1997 and 1998.

The company experimented with new sales channels in 1998 and 1999, including infomercials, mall kiosks, a website, and catalogs. Tupperware made the best of Asia's troubled economy in 1998 by recruiting laid-off workers and launching "I Save With Tupperware" campaigns to help consumers stretch food budgets. German direct seller Vorwerk bought an 11% stake in Tupperware in 2000 (and sold it in early 2005). In October 2000 Tupperware purchased cosmetics company BeautiControl.

Tupperware's first foray into store retailing was short-lived. The company began selling some products in SuperTarget stores in October 2001, but the negative impact felt by Tupperware's direct sales channel quickly prompted the company to pull the items from Target stores' shelves in June 2003.

In December 2005 the company acquired Sara Lee Corporation's direct selling businesses — International Beauty — and at the same time changed its name from Tupperware Corp. to Tupperware Brands Corporation. The acquisition boosted the direct seller's sales force at the time to about 1.9 million independent consultants.

EXECUTIVES

Chairman and CEO: E.V. (Rick) Goings, age 64, $14,053,109 total compensation
President and COO: Simon C. Hemus, age 60, $5,268,475 total compensation
EVP, Chief Legal Officer, and Secretary: Thomas M. Roehlk, age 59
EVP and CFO: Michael S. (Mike) Poteshman, age 45, $1,392,663 total compensation
SVP Global Product Marketing: Rashit Ismail, age 47
SVP Worldwide Market Development: Christian E. Skröder, age 61, $2,671,083 total compensation
SVP Tax and Governmental Affairs: Josef Hajek, age 51
VP and CTO: Robert F. Wagner, age 49
VP and Controller: Nicholas Poucher, age 47
VP and Treasurer: Edward R. Davis III, age 47
EVP and President, Fuller Argentina: Lillian D. Garcia, age 53
VP Investor Relations: Nicole Decker
SVP Worldwide Human Resources: Anna Braungardt
EVP Supply Chain Worldwide: José R. Timmerman
Group President, Europe, Africa, and the Middle East: R. Glenn Drake, age 56, $2,769,091 total compensation
VP Internal Audit and Enterprise Risk Management: Carl Benkovich, age 53
Auditors: PricewaterhouseCoopers LLP

LOCATIONS

HQ: Tupperware Brands Corporation
14901 S. Orange Blossom Trail, Orlando, FL 32837
Phone: 407-826-5050   **Fax:** 407-826-8268
Web: www.tupperwarebrands.com

2009 Sales

	$ mil.	% of total
Europe	749.6	35
North America	683.9	32
Asia/Pacific	385.0	18
Beauty other	309.0	15
Total	**2,127.5**	**100**

PRODUCTS/OPERATIONS

2009 Sales

	$ mil.	% of total
Tupperware	1,426.9	67
Beauty	700.6	33
Total	**2,127.5**	**100**

Selected Product Lines
Children's educational toys
Cooking products
Cosmetics and skin care
Food storage containers
Serving and preparation products

Selected Trademarks
BeautiControl
Expressions
FridgeSmart
Modular Mates
One Touch
OvenWorks
Rock 'N Serve
Tupperware

COMPETITORS

Alticor
Avon
Body Shop
Clorox
Container Store
CPAC
Discovery Toys
Hasbro
Home Products International
Kmart
Learning Curve
Lifetime Brands
Mary Kay
Mattel
Newell Rubbermaid
Owens-Illinois
Pampered Chef
Princess House
Sterilite
Target
Tastefully Simple
Wal-Mart
Williams-Sonoma
Wilton Brands
WKI Holding
ZAG Industries

HISTORICAL FINANCIALS

Company Type: Public

Income Statement

FYE: Last Saturday in December

	REVENUE ($ mil.)	NET INCOME ($ mil.)	NET PROFIT MARGIN	EMPLOYEES
12/09	2,128	175	8.2%	12,900
12/08	2,162	161	7.5%	14,740
12/07	1,981	117	5.9%	12,800
12/06	1,744	94	5.4%	12,300
12/05	1,279	86	6.7%	11,700
Annual Growth	**13.6%**	**19.4%**	**—**	**2.5%**

2009 Year-End Financials

Debt ratio: 66.8%
Return on equity: 31.5%
Cash ($ mil.): 112
Current ratio: 1.51
Long-term debt ($ mil.): 426
No. of shares (mil.): 63
Dividends
  Yield: 2.0%
  Payout: 33.1%
Market value ($ mil.): 2,938

Stock History

NYSE: TUP

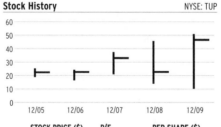

	STOCK PRICE ($) FY Close	P/E High/Low		PER SHARE ($) Earnings	Dividends	Book Value
12/09	46.57	18	4	2.75	0.91	10.11
12/08	22.70	18	6	2.56	0.88	7.51
12/07	33.03	20	12	1.87	0.88	8.28
12/06	22.61	15	11	1.54	0.88	6.35
12/05	22.40	18	14	1.41	0.88	5.32
Annual Growth	**20.1%**	**—**	**—**	**18.2%**	**0.8%**	**17.4%**

Tyco International

Water and fire: Tyco International ties together two of the four elements of nature. The company comprises five divisions devoted to security, fire protection, safety, valves, and tubing. Security system equipment, installation, and monitoring fall under Tyco's largest business, ADT Worldwide. Tyco offers fire detection and suppression systems through Fire Protection Services (through subsidiary SimplexGrinnell); Tyco Flow Control makes valves and related devices for water, wastewater, and the oil and gas markets. Other Tyco units include Electrical and Metal Products (steel tubing, pipes, and cables for commercial construction) and Tyco Safety Products (protective gear).

Despite a difficult global economy, the company is continuing to expand its presence through select acquisitions that complement its core security, fire, and flow control platforms. In 2010 Tyco acquired Brinks Home Security, dba Broadview. The deal, which is worth approximately $2 billion in cash and stock, joins together two of North America's top residential and commercial security companies under the ADT nameplate, opening the door for Tyco to dominate the market.

In addition to Broadview, other notable acquisitions include Vue Technology, a provider of radio frequency identification ("RFID") technology. ADT Worldwide also acquired FirstService Security (to strengthen its systems integration capabilities), and two franchises of its Sensormatic (anti-theft systems) product: Winner Security Services and Sensormatic Security Corp.

But along with acquisitions come divestitures. Tyco is looking to transition its business from that of industrial to a service-oriented company. In 2010 Tyco sold its Flow Control segment to private equity firm Triton for $245 million. Earlier exits included a subsidiary that makes and sells fire protection products in Japan, a European manufacturer of building products for the construction industry, and substantially all of its Infrastructure Services business.

In the meantime, Tyco has disassociated itself from the free-spending ways of former CEO Dennis Kozlowski, who is serving jail time for taking millions of dollars from the company. In mid-2007 Tyco split into three publicly held companies: Tyco International, Covidien (formerly Tyco Healthcare Group), and Tyco Electronics. Tyco is legally domiciled in Switzerland but run primarily from Princeton, New Jersey.

HISTORY

Arthur Rosenberg founded Tyco, Inc., in 1960 to conduct experimental research for the government and commercial sectors. It successfully developed the Dynalux battery charger, the first blue-light laser, and the first laser with a nonstop beam. Under a new name, Tyco Laboratories (changed in 1965), the firm boosted sales through acquisitions in the mid-1960s to reach $41 million by 1969, up from $1 million in 1963. Rosenberg left Tyco Labs in 1970.

In 1974 Tyco Labs acquired venerable Simplex Wire & Cable, whose predecessor had developed water-resistant Anhydrex cables in the 1920s, made submarine cables during WWII, and began installing undersea cables in 1966. Tyco Labs almost tripled its sales in 1975 by acquiring ITT's Grinnell.

Tyco Labs bought polyethylene producer Armin in 1979 and packaging maker Ludlow two years later. It acquired Grinnell Flow Control, a valve distributor, from ITT in 1986 and Allied Pipe & Tube the next year. In 1988 Tyco Labs acquired Mueller, a water and gas pipe maker founded in 1885 by industry pioneer Hieronymous Mueller.

In 1993 Tyco replaced "Laboratories" with "International" in its name to reflect its multinational operations. The next year it bought Kendall International, which moved Tyco into the disposable health care products market.

Security giant ADT bought Tyco for $6.6 billion in a 1997 deal that left Tyco in control of the combined company. In 1999 it bought AMP, the world's largest supplier of electrical and electronic connectors, for $12.2 billion, and Raychem, a top electronic component maker.

Digesting its acquisitions, Tyco laid off more than 9,000 workers in 1998 and 1999. Also in 1999 Tyco's method of accounting for its acquisitions prompted an SEC inquiry, but no action was taken against the company.

In 2000 the company expanded its health care business with several purchases, including the $4.2 billion acquisition of Mallinckrodt, a leading maker of respiratory care equipment. At the end of 2000 Tyco bought Lucent's Power Systems division for $2.5 billion. In 2001 Tyco completed the $1.15 billion purchase of security products manufacturer Simplex Time Recorder and bought SecurityLink (security monitoring) from Cambridge Protection Industries for about $1 billion. Tyco also acquired Sensormatic, a manufacturer of electronic article surveillance systems, for about $2.3 billion.

Tyco moved into the financial services industry in 2001 by buying commercial lender CIT Group for $9.2 billion in stock and cash.

CEO Dennis Kozlowski resigned in 2002 after a newspaper reported that New York prosecutors suspected him of using family trusts to avoid paying state sales taxes. His predecessor, John Fort, stepped in as interim CEO. Later that year Kozlowski and two other former Tyco executives, including former CFO Mark Swartz, were indicted on charges that they took millions of dollars in unauthorized compensation.

In 2005 Kozlowski and Swartz were both convicted of grand larceny and conspiracy, falsifying business records, and violating business law. They each were sentenced to serve from 100 months to 25 years in state prison and were ordered to repay $134 million to Tyco. Kozlowski was also fined $70 million, and Swartz was fined $35 million.

Tyco spun off CIT Group in 2002. Also that year the company announced that former Motorola COO Edward Breen would take the helm at Tyco as the new chairman and CEO. In 2003 Tyco announced plans to reorganize its operations and cut costs by closing about 300 plants and by disposing of about 50 business units.

In 2006 the company settled with the SEC, agreeing to pay a fine of $50 million over accounting practices under the former management regime.

In 2008 the company agreed to pay $250 million to settle a lawsuit from bondholders who claimed Tyco failed to get their approval when it spun off its electronics and health-care businesses. The bondholders alleged the breakup plan was merely a scheme to shield assets, and had filed a lawsuit aimed at stopping the plan after it was announced in 2006, claiming Tyco required their approval.

EXECUTIVES

Chairman and CEO: Edward D. (Ed) Breen Jr., age 54, $19,439,652 total compensation
EVP and CFO: Christopher J. Coughlin, age 58, $6,304,457 total compensation
SVP and Chief Tax Officer: John E. Evard Jr., age 63, $3,608,512 total compensation
EVP and General Counsel: Judith A. Reinsdorf, age 46
SVP and Treasurer; CFO, ADT Worldwide: Arun Nayar
SVP Strategy and Investor Relations: Edward C. (Ed) Arditte, age 54
SVP, Controller, and Chief Accounting Officer: Carol A. (John) Davidson, age 54
SVP Operational Excellence and Chief Procurement Officer: Shelley Stewart Jr., age 56
SVP Human Resources and International Communications: Laurie A. Siegel, age 53
VP Corporate Communications: Paul Fitzhenry
VP Supply Chain Management: Jaime Bohnke
VP and Corporate Secretary: John S. Jenkins Jr.
President, Tyco Safety, Electrical, and Metal Products: George R. Oliver, age 49, $3,897,986 total compensation
President, ADT Worldwide: Naren K. Gursahaney, age 48, $3,872,211 total compensation
President, SimplexGrinnell: James (Jim) Spicer
President, Tyco Flow Control: Patrick Decker, age 45
Auditors: Deloitte & Touche LLP

LOCATIONS

HQ: Tyco International Ltd.
9 Roszel Rd., Princeton, NJ 08540
Phone: 609-720-4200　　**Fax:** 609-720-4208
Web: www.tyco.com

2009 Sales

	$ mil.	% of total
Americas		
US	8,304	48
Other countries	1,520	9
Europe, Middle East & Africa	4,706	27
Asia/Pacific	2,707	16
Total	**17,237**	**100**

PRODUCTS/OPERATIONS

2009 Sales

	$ mil.	% of total
ADT Worldwide	7,015	41
Flow Control	3,850	22
Fire Protection Services	3,428	20
Safety Products	1,552	9
Electrical & Metal Products	1,392	8
Total	**17,237**	**100**

Selected Products and Operations

ADT Worldwide (security system equipment, installation, monitoring)
　Sensormatic

Electrical and Metal Products
　AFC Cable
　Allied Tube & Conduit

Fire Protection Services
　SimplexGrinnell
　Wormald

Flow Control
　Keystone
　Vanessa

Safety Products
　Ansul
　Scott

COMPETITORS

Anvil International
Belden
Cooper Industries
Crane Co.
Dresser, Inc.
Flowserve
G4S
GE
Honeywell International
Hubbell
Illinois Tool Works
Ingersoll-Rand
ITT Corp.
Johnson Controls
Parker Hannifin
Raytheon
Rentokil Initial
Roper Industries
Securitas
Siemens AG
Stryker
Sumitomo Electric
Thomas & Betts
United Technologies

HISTORICAL FINANCIALS

Company Type: Public

Income Statement

	REVENUE ($ mil.)	NET INCOME ($ mil.)	NET PROFIT MARGIN	EMPLOYEES
			FYE: September 30	
9/09	17,237	(1,798)	—	106,000
9/08	20,199	1,553	7.7%	113,000
9/07	18,781	(1,742)	—	118,000
9/06	40,960	3,727	9.1%	238,200
9/05	39,727	3,011	7.6%	247,900
Annual Growth	**(18.8%)**	**—**	**—**	**(19.1%)**

2009 Year-End Financials

Debt ratio: 31.1%　　　No. of shares (mil.): 498
Return on equity: —　　Dividends
Cash ($ mil.): 2,354　　　Yield: 1.8%
Current ratio: 1.69　　　Payout: —
Long-term debt ($ mil.): 4,029　Market value ($ mil.): 17,160

Stock History

NYSE: TYC

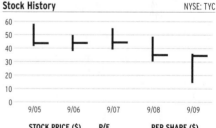

	STOCK PRICE ($) FY Close	P/E High/Low	Earnings	PER SHARE ($) Dividends	Book Value
9/09	34.48	— —	(3.80)	0.62	26.00
9/08	35.02	15 10	3.19	0.65	31.13
9/07	44.34	— —	(3.52)	1.35	31.39
9/06	43.90	7 5	7.20	1.60	71.17
9/05	43.68	10 7	5.72	1.60	65.20
Annual Growth	**(5.7%)**	**— —**	**—**	**(21.1%)**	**(20.5%)**

Tyson Foods

Think of Tyson Foods as a 600-pound chicken with a bullish attitude. One of the largest US chicken producers, Tyson's Fresh Meats division makes it a giant in the beef and pork sectors as well. In addition to fresh meats, Tyson offers value-added processed and pre-cooked meats, and refrigerated and frozen prepared foods. Its chicken operations are vertically integrated — the company hatches the eggs, supplies contract growers with the chicks and feed, and brings them back for processing when ready. Tyson processes 41 million chickens, 393,000 head of pork, and 139,000 head of beef every week.

Beef is Tyson's biggest revenue maker. Although the company was knocked off its top perch as the US's biggest poultry producer with the 2007 merger of GoldKist and Pilgrim's Pride, Tyson still remains a poultry powerhouse.

The company's fresh meat operations process beef, and pork. In addition, it offers processed pork products such as sausage, ham, and bacon. The company's prepared foods unit produces pizza toppings and frozen entrées. It also has a significant foodservice operation. Other Tyson activities include rendering meat by-products and tortilla and pizza-crust manufacturing.

Saying that it no longer fit the company's long-term international strategy, in 2009 Tyson sold its Canadian beef operations (Lakeside Farm Industries) to XL Foods. Due to what the company called challenging conditions in the pork market, the company downsized its pork operations with the sale of five of its hog farms that same year.

President and CEO Dick Bond resigned from the company in 2009. Tyson veteran, Donnie Smith, who has been with the company since 1980, replaced him. Just one day after announcing Bond's departure, the company was fined $500,000 by a US District Court for safety violations that resulted in a Tyson worker's death at its animal-feed plant in Texarkana, Texas. The worker was killed as a result of exposure to hydrogen sulfide gas. Prosecutors, who charged the company with "willful violation of an OSHA standard resulting in the death of an employee," said an identical exposure injured a Tyson worker at the same facility in 2002.

Things weren't going well on the foreign front for Tyson either. In March 2009 the largest export market for US chicken, Russia reported finding antibiotic and anti-parasitic drug residue in the products from plants belonging to three US chicken companies, Tyson among them. Russia immediately banned the companies' chicken products. (The other companies involved in the ban were Peco and Sanderson Farms.)

Biofuels are among the company's more recent interests. In 2010 Tyson began supplying the animal fats and greases from its meat production operations to Dynamic Fuels, its joint venture with Syntroleum that aims to produce renewable fuels from the by-products.

Former chairman Don Tyson is the controlling owner of the company.

HISTORY

During the Great Depression, Arkansas poultry farmer John Tyson supported his family by selling vegetables and poultry. In 1935, after developing a method for transporting live poultry (he installed a food-and-water trough and nailed small feed cups on a trailer), he bought 500 chickens in Arkansas and sold them in Chicago.

For the next decade Tyson bought, sold, and transported chickens. By 1947, the year he incorporated the company as Tyson Feed & Hatchery, he was raising the chickens himself. He emphasized chicken production, opening his first processing plant in 1958, where he implemented an ice-packing system that allowed the company to send its products greater distances.

John's son Don took over as manager in 1960, and in 1963 it went public as Tyson Foods. Tyson Country Fresh Chicken (packaged chicken that would become the company's mainstay) was introduced in 1967.

Rapid expansion included a new egg processing building (1970), a new plant and computerized feed mill (1971), and the acquisitions of Prospect Farms (1969, precooked chicken) and the Ocoma Foods Division (1972, poultry), as well as hog operations.

Health-conscious consumers increasingly turned from red meats to poultry during the 1980s. Tyson became the industry leader with several key acquisitions of poultry operations, including the Tastybird division of Valmac (1985), Lane Processing (1986), and Heritage Valley (1986). Its 1989 purchase of Holly Farms added beef and pork processing.

Don Tyson relinquished the CEO position to Leland Tollett in 1991. In 1992 the firm plunged into seafood with the purchase of Arctic Alaska Fisheries and Louis Kemp Seafood.

In 1997 the company pleaded guilty to charges that it illegally gave former Agriculture Secretary Mike Espy thousands of dollars' worth of gifts; the settlement included $6 million in fines and fees. In 1998 John H. Tyson, grandson of the founder, was elected chairman. He became CEO in 2000.

As the winner in a bidding war with Smithfield Foods, in 2001 Tyson agreed to buy IBP, Inc., the #1 beef processor and #2 pork processor in the US, for nearly $3.2 billion.

In late 2001 Tyson Foods and six managers were indicted for conspiring to smuggle illegal immigrants from Mexico and Central America to work for lower than legal wages in 15 of its US poultry processing plants. Two managers made plea bargains and testified for the government; another manager committed suicide. Tyson and the remaining three managers were acquitted of the conspiracy charges in 2003.

Following the discovery of bird flu on a Texas chicken farm in February 2004 and the resultant banning of the importation of US chicken products by other countries, Tyson consolidated and automated its poultry operations, resulting in hundreds of layoffs at the company.

In 2004 the SEC recommended civil action against the company for its failure to disclose $1.7 million in corporate perks given to Don Tyson without authorization from Tyson's compensation committee. With neither the company nor Tyson admitting any guilt, the case was settled in 2005 with Tyson paying the SEC $700,000 in fines and the company, $1.5 million.

In 2006 Don's son, John Tyson, stepped down as CEO; COO Richard L. Bond replaced him. Tyson remained as chairman. Soon thereafter, Bond announced $200 million in cost reductions. The plan included the elimination of 850 primarily managerial positions. Later that year, the company announced it would cut another 770 jobs as it closed and consolidated several meat slaughtering and processing plants in the northwestern US.

EXECUTIVES

Chairman: John H. Tyson, age 56
President and CEO: Donnie Smith, age 50, $862,939 total compensation
COO: James V. (Jim) Lochner, age 57, $1,967,054 total compensation
EVP and CFO: Dennis Leatherby, age 50, $927,066 total compensation
EVP and General Counsel: David L. Van Bebber, age 54
EVP Corporate Affairs: Archie Schaffer III
Chief Marketing Officer: Sue Quillin
SVP and Chief Environmental, Health, and Safety Officer: Kevin J. Igli
SVP, Controller, and Chief Accounting Officer: Craig J. Hart, age 54
SVP Food Quality Assurance: Rick Roop
SVP Corporate Research and Development: Craig Bacon
SVP and CIO: Gary Cooper
SVP Poultry and Prepared Foods: Donnie D. King, age 48
SVP Beef Production Operations: Dan Brooks
SVP and Chief Human Resources Officer: Kenneth J. Kimbro, age 56
SVP Fresh Meats: Noel White, age 51
SVP International Operations: Mike Baker
VP, Associate General Counsel, and Secretary: R. Read Hudson
VP Investor Relations and Assistant Secretary: Ruth Ann Wisener
Director Community Relations: Ed Nicholson
Auditors: Ernst & Young LLP

LOCATIONS

HQ: Tyson Foods, Inc.
2200 Don Tyson Pkwy., Springdale, AR 72762
Phone: 479-290-4000   **Fax:** 479-290-4061
Web: www.tysonfoodsinc.com

2009 International Sales

	% of total
Mexico	21
China	13
Japan	10
South Korea	6
Canada	5
Russia	5
Other	40
Total	**100**

PRODUCTS/OPERATIONS

2009 Sales

	$ mil.	% of total
Beef	10,782	40
Chicken	9,660	37
Pork	3,426	13
Prepared foods	2,836	10
Total	**26,704**	**100**

2009 Production Plants

	No.
Chicken	63
Prepared foods	23
Beef	12
Pork	9
Total	**107**

Selected Products and Brands

Meats, fresh
Certified Angus Beef
Chairman's Reserve (beef)
Golden Trophy Steaks (beef)
Open Prairie Angus Beef
Star Ranch Angus Beef
Supreme Tender (pork)
Tyson (beef, chicken, Cornish game hens, pork)
Tyson Holly Farms (chicken)

Meats, processed
  Bonici (foodservice; chicken wings, pizza toppings)
  Chicken Twists (foodservice)
  Premium Chunk (canned chicken)
  Right Size (foodservice; beef patties, chicken patties)
  Tyson (bacon, beef, chicken, pork)
  Wright (bacon)
Prepared foods
  Any'Tizers (chicken snacks)
  Doskocil (value-added meats for pizza industry)
  Heat 'N Eat Entrees (beef, chicken, pork)
  Lady Aster (entrees)
  Mexican Original (flour and corn tortilla products)
  Skillet Creations (beef and chicken meal kits)

COMPETITORS

Buckhead Beef
Cargill
Casa de Oro Foods
CGC
Clougherty Packing
Coleman Natural Foods
ConAgra
Cooper Farms
Del Monte Foods
Eberly Poultry
Empire Kosher Poultry
Foster Farms
Freedman Meats
Gruma
Gusto Packing
H. J. Heinz Limited
Hormel
JBS
Koch Foods
Kraft Foods
Kraft North America
Laura's Lean Beef Co.
Mars, Incorporated
National Beef Packing
New Market Poultry
Perdue Incorporated
Petaluma Poultry
Pilgrim's Pride
Plainville Farms
Raeford Farms
Sanderson Farms
Sara Lee North American Retail
Shelton's
Smithfield Foods
Tecumseh Poultry
U.S. Premium Beef

HISTORICAL FINANCIALS

Company Type: Public

Income Statement				FYE: Saturday nearest September 30
	REVENUE ($ mil.)	NET INCOME ($ mil.)	NET PROFIT MARGIN	EMPLOYEES
9/09	26,704	(537)	—	117,000
9/08	26,862	86	0.3%	107,000
9/07	26,900	268	1.0%	104,000
9/06	25,559	(191)	—	107,000
9/05	26,014	353	1.4%	114,000
Annual Growth	0.7%	—	—	0.7%

2009 Year-End Financials

Debt ratio: 76.6%
Return on equity: —
Cash ($ mil.): 1,004
Current ratio: 2.20
Long-term debt ($ mil.): 3,333

No. of shares (mil.): 377
Dividends
  Yield: 1.3%
  Payout: —
Market value ($ mil.): 4,767

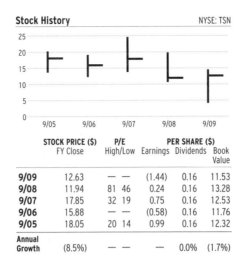

Stock History   NYSE: TSN

	STOCK PRICE ($) FY Close	P/E High/Low		PER SHARE ($) Earnings	Dividends	Book Value
9/09	12.63	—	—	(1.44)	0.16	11.53
9/08	11.94	81	46	0.24	0.16	13.28
9/07	17.85	32	19	0.75	0.16	12.53
9/06	15.88	—	—	(0.58)	0.16	11.76
9/05	18.05	20	14	0.99	0.16	12.32
Annual Growth	(8.5%)	—	—	—	0.0%	(1.7%)

UAL Corporation

UAL unites cities around the globe through subsidiary United Airlines, one of the world's leading passenger and cargo carriers. United Airlines also provides regional feeder service in the US via United Express. United serves more than 230 destinations in about 30 countries from hubs in Chicago, Denver, L.A., San Francisco, and Washington, DC. The airline leads the Star Alliance, a marketing and code-sharing group that includes Continental and Lufthansa. In May 2010 UAL announced plans to merge United with Continental in a $3 billion stock swap.

The deal would create the world's largest airline, one that would be about 8% larger than Delta Air Lines in terms of traffic and command a 21% share of the US market. The new airline would retain the United name and be based in Chicago, but use Houston-based Continental's logo and aircraft branding. UAL shareholders will hold 55% of the new company, which will be led by Continental CEO Jeff Smisek. The at-market stock swap is intended to avoid additional debt for the carriers, which have only recently reported stronger financial results.

The two airlines see opportunities to boost revenue and cut costs through the merger, which will expand access to new markets for both companies. United has a strong presence across the Asia/Pacific region, while Continental is big in Europe and Latin America. United flies to 100 cities not served Continental, while Continental would add 136 cities not served by United. The company had been in discussions with US Airways about a possible merger, when USAir ended the talks in April 2010. Rumors of a deal with Continental had been flying since those talks broke off.

Hammered by losses related to high fuel costs and lower passenger demand, UAL announced plans in 2009 to cut as many as 2,000 jobs by year's end — bringing the total of job cuts since 2008 to about 9,000. Also that year about 2,100 flight attendants agreed to take voluntary furloughs from 10 to 30 months that will help the airline avoid some layoffs.

In 2009, UAL reduced United's domestic mainline capacity by about 10% and its international capacity by 9%; the company's workforce was reduced to match lower capacity. United also shut down its one-class, low-fare carrier, Ted, and reconfigured the unit's 55-plus aircraft to include first-class sections for mainline use.

HISTORY

In 1929 aircraft designer Bill Boeing and engine designer Fred Rentschler of Pratt & Whitney joined forces to form United Aircraft and Transport. Renamed United Air Lines in 1931, the New York-based company offered one of the first coast-to-coast airline services. In 1934 United's manufacturing and transportation divisions split. Former banker Bill Patterson became president of the latter, United Air Lines, and moved it to the Chicago area.

Led by Patterson until 1963, United was slow to move and began offering jet service in 1959, after rival American. But in 1961 United bought Capital Airlines and became the US's #1 airline.

In 1969 UAL Corp. was formed as a holding company. In 1979, a year after airline deregulation, hotelier Richard Ferris became CEO. Dreaming of a travel conglomerate, he bought Hertz (1985) and Hilton International (1987). Angered by the diversification, the pilots struck in 1985 and then tried to buy the airline in 1987. That year, after dropping $7.3 million to change United's name to Allegis, Ferris left when leading shareholder Coniston Partners threatened to oust the board and liquidate the firm. Assuming its old name and a new CEO, Stephen Wolf (former chief of cargo carrier Flying Tigers), UAL shed its hotels and car rental business and 50% of its computer reservation partnership, Covia.

A 1989 takeover bid by Los Angeles billionaire Marvin Davis and Coniston triggered an unsuccessful buyout effort by United pilots, management, and British Airways. Gerald Greenwald, a turnaround expert from Chrysler, headed the attempt. Coniston later sold most of its stake in exchange for two seats on the board.

United began expanding globally and added routes in the Asia/Pacific region (bought from Pan Am in 1986 and 1991). It also laid off thousands of employees and cut executive pay. Finally, the 1993 sale of United's kitchen operations (slashing 5,800 union jobs) brought the unions to the table with an employee stock ownership plan (ESOP). The ESOP, which ceded 55% of UAL to employees in exchange for $4.8 billion in wage concessions, was approved in 1994. The deal effectively ended Wolf's reign at UAL, since he had fallen out of favor with employees; Greenwald became CEO. United also launched its low-fare carrier that year.

In 1997 United formed the Star Alliance with Lufthansa, Scandinavian Airlines System, Air Canada, and Thai Airways. President James Goodwin, a 32-year United veteran, took over as CEO after Greenwald's 1999 retirement.

Also that year United Airlines lost two planes in the September 11 terrorist attacks on New York and Washington, DC. As demand for air travel slumped after the attacks, UAL eliminated flights and laid off more than 20% of its workforce. A month after the attacks, chairman and CEO James Goodwin resigned under pressure from employee unions; UAL director and former Weyerhaeuser chief John Creighton replaced him on an interim basis. The cutbacks, however, were not enough to prevent the airline from posting a $2.1 billion loss for 2001.

The following year UAL avoided a potentially disastrous strike by its mechanics when they approved a new contract giving them their first raise since 1994. The airline managed to convince its pilots and salaried managers to take a pay cut in 2002 to alleviate some of its debt. Also that year UAL applied for a $1.8 billion loan under the federal loan guarantee program created to help airlines in the aftermath of the September 11 attacks. Creighton retired and was replaced by Glenn Tilton, an oil industry executive. UAL's financial troubles continued to mount, however, and it filed for Chapter 11 bankruptcy protection in December 2002.

To assist with its emergence from bankruptcy, UAL petitioned for an additional loan from the US government in 2004, but it was denied. Instead, the government extended the repayment deadline. In the course of its reorganization, UAL launched low-fare carrier Ted, renegotiated labor agreements, and won court permission to terminate its four employee pension plans. Employees also lost their controlling stake in the company. The federal Pension Benefit Guaranty Corporation wound up with responsibility for the pension plans and a stake in UAL.

UAL emerged from bankruptcy protection in February 2006.

EXECUTIVES

Chairman, President, and CEO: Glenn F. Tilton, age 61, $6,471,062 total compensation
EVP and Chief Administrative Officer: Peter D. (Pete) McDonald, age 58, $4,193,340 total compensation
EVP and CFO: Kathryn A. Mikells, age 44, $1,017,746 total compensation
EVP and President, Mileage Plus: Graham W. Atkinson, age 58
EVP; President, United Airlines: John P. Tague, age 47, $3,165,827 total compensation
SVP and CIO, United Airlines: R. Keith Halbert
SVP Strategic Sourcing and Chief Procurement Officer, United Airlines: Grace M. Puma
SVP Corporate Planning and Strategy, United Airlines: Gregory T. (Greg) Taylor
SVP Corporate Strategy and Business Development, United Airlines: Rohit Philip
SVP Worldwide Sales and Marketing, United Airlines: Jeffrey T. (Jeff) Foland
SVP Corporate and Government Affairs, United Airlines: Rosemary Moore, age 59
SVP Human Resources, United Airlines: Marc L. Ugol, age 51
SVP, Office of the Chairman, United Airlines: Sara A. Fields, age 66
SVP and Chief Marketing Officer, United Airlines: Thomas F. (Tom) O'Toole, age 52
SVP Labor Relations, United Airlines: P. Douglas (Doug) McKeen
SVP, General Counsel, and Corporate Secretary, UAL and United Airlines: Thomas J. (Tom) Sabatino Jr., age 50
SVP Corporate Communications and Chief Communications Officer, United Airlines: Antonio B. (Tony) Cervone
Managing Director Investor Relations: Tyler Reddien
Auditors: Deloitte & Touche LLP

LOCATIONS

HQ: UAL Corporation
77 W. Wacker Dr., Chicago, IL 60601
Phone: 312-997-8000
Web: www.united.com

2009 Sales

	$ mil.	% of total
Domestic (US & Canada)	10,775	66
Pacific	2,628	16
Atlantic	2,538	16
Latin America	394	2
Total	**16,335**	**100**

PRODUCTS/OPERATIONS

2009 Sales

	$ mil.	% of total
Passenger		
United Airlines	11,910	73
United Express (regional affiliates)	3,064	19
Cargo	536	3
Other	825	5
Total	**16,335**	**100**

COMPETITORS

Air France-KLM
Alaska Air
Alitalia
AMR Corp.
British Airways
Delta Air Lines
FedEx
Frontier Airlines
Japan Airlines
JetBlue
Qantas
Southwest Airlines
UPS
US Airways
Virgin Atlantic Airways

HISTORICAL FINANCIALS

Company Type: Public

Income Statement

FYE: December 31

	REVENUE ($ mil.)	NET INCOME ($ mil.)	NET PROFIT MARGIN	EMPLOYEES
12/09	16,335	(651)	—	47,000
12/08	20,194	(5,348)	—	50,000
12/07	20,143	403	2.0%	55,000
12/06	19,340	22,876	118.3%	55,000
12/05	17,379	(21,176)	—	57,000
Annual Growth	**(1.5%)**	**—**		**(4.7%)**

2009 Year-End Financials

Debt ratio: —
Return on equity: —
Cash ($ mil.): 3,042
Current ratio: 0.79
Long-term debt ($ mil.): 7,572

No. of shares (mil.): 168
Dividends
 Yield: 0.0%
 Payout: —
Market value ($ mil.): 2,174

Stock History

NASDAQ (GS): UAUA

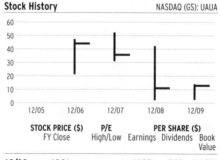

	STOCK PRICE ($) FY Close	P/E High/Low		PER SHARE ($) Earnings	Dividends	Book Value
12/09	12.91	—	—	(4.32)	0.00	(16.70)
12/08	11.02	—	—	(42.21)	0.00	(14.64)
12/07	35.66	18	11	2.79	0.00	14.36
12/06	44.00	0	0	131.94	0.00	12.76
Annual Growth	**(33.6%)**			**—**	**—**	**—**

UGI Corporation

Energy services, marketing, and distribution company UGI distributes propane across the US and abroad. Its 44%-owned propane distributor, AmeriGas Partners, is the largest source of the holding company's sales and is one of the top two US propane marketers (along with Ferrellgas). Its UGI Utilities subsidiary distributes electricity to 62,000 customers and gas to about 563,000 customers in Pennsylvania. Other UGI operations include energy marketing in the mid-Atlantic region, propane distribution in Asia and Europe, electricity generation, and energy services.

Subsidiary AmeriGas sells propane to 1.3 million retail and wholesale customers a year from about 1,200 locations in 50 states. AmeriGas also offers propane-related products and services and provides propane storage services. UGI subsidiary UGI Enterprises, which operates as the company's Energy Services division, markets natural gas and electricity and offers HVAC (heating, ventilation, and air-conditioning) and energy management services to more than 150,000 customers in the mid-Atlantic region of the US. Another subsidiary, UGI Development, is involved in power generation ventures in Pennsylvania.

UGI is focused on expanding its core natural gas, electric, and propane operations. It is also seeking complementary opportunities to continue its growth in the US and abroad. To expand its base of gas customers in Pennsylvania, in 2008 UGI Utilities acquired PPL Gas Utilities for $32 million. It soon changed that company's name to UGI Central Penn Gas. In 2010 it took advantage of BP's need to raise cash due to its oil spill problems and agreed to acquire the liquefied petroleum gas distribution business of BP in Denmark. The deal, when closed, will expand UGI's footprint in the European LPG market.

Internationally UGI has interests in propane distributors in Austria, China, the Czech Republic, Denmark, France, Hungary, Poland, Romania, Slovakia, and Switzerland, primarily through its Antargaz and Flaga subsidiaries. In 2009 Antargaz sold 290 million gallons of propane; Flaga, almost 70 million gallons.

HISTORY

United Gas Improvement was set up in 1882 by Philadelphia industrialist Thomas Dolan and other investors to acquire a gasworks and a new coal-gas manufacturing process. The firm also bought electric utilities and street railways across the US and moved into construction. The 1935 Public Utility Holding Company Act led to United Gas Improvement's restructuring when the SEC ordered the divestiture of many of its operations in 1941. The company converted to natural gas in the 1950s and entered the liquefied petroleum gas (LPG) business in 1959. It became UGI Corporation in 1968.

UGI shifted its emphasis to propane in the late 1980s, buying Petrolane in 1995 and combining it with AmeriGas Propane to create AmeriGas Partners, which then went public. Overseas, UGI launched a joint venture in 1996 to build an LPG import project in Romania. The next year it signed a deal to distribute propane in China.

In 1999 UGI moved into consumer products by opening its first Hearth USA retail store in Rockville, Maryland, which offered hearth items, spas, grills, and patio accessories. It ventured into a growing European market by purchasing

FLAGA GmbH, a leading gas distributor in Austria and the Czech Republic.

That year a 1997 Pennsylvania law kicked in, restructuring the state's electricity industry and enabling customers to choose their electricity provider. In response, UGI separated its distribution and power generation operations, and in 2000 contributed the bulk of its generation assets to a partnership with Allegheny Energy that sells power to UGI Utilities and other distributors.

In 2001 UGI Enterprises purchased a 20% interest in French propane distributor Antargaz. Also that year UGI closed its Hearth USA retail stores. Through its UGI Energy Services subsidiary, UGI completed the acquisition of TXU Energy, in 2003.

In 2004 UGI acquired the remaining 80% interest in Antargaz, expanding its operations in France. Later that year the company continued its European expansion through the acquisition of BP's retail propane distribution business in the Czech Republic.

In 2006 the company acquired the natural gas utility assets of PG Energy for about $580 million. During the next year its Gas Utility unit purchased approximately 79 billion cu. ft. of natural gas for sale to retail core market and off-system sales customers.

EXECUTIVES

Chairman and CEO: Lon R. Greenberg, age 58, $9,948,066 total compensation
VP Finance and CFO: Peter Kelly, age 51, $2,135,954 total compensation
VP Accounting and Financial Control and Chief Risk Officer: Davinder Athwal, age 42
VP and Treasurer: Robert W. (Bob) Krick
VP, General Counsel, and Assistant Secretary: Robert H. Knauss, age 55, $2,200,217 total compensation
VP New Business Development; President, UGI Enterprises: Bradley C. Hall, age 56
VP, UGI HVAC Enterprises: Robert L. Pistor
Chairman and CEO, Antargaz: François Varagne, age 54
President, COO, and Director; Vice Chairman, President, and CEO, UGI Utilities: John L. Walsh, age 53, $3,762,308 total compensation
President and CEO, AmeriGas Propane: Eugene V. N. Bissell, age 55, $2,234,201 total compensation
Associate General Counsel and Corporate Secretary: Margaret M. Calabrese
Director, Corporate Accounting and Reporting: Richard R. Eynon
Investor Relations: Brenda Blake
Auditors: PricewaterhouseCoopers LLP

LOCATIONS

HQ: UGI Corporation
460 N. Gulph Rd., King of Prussia, PA 19406
Phone: 610-337-1000 **Fax:** 610-992-3254
Web: www.ugicorp.com

2009 Sales

	% of total
US	84
Other countries	16
Total	**100**

PRODUCTS/OPERATIONS

2009 Sales

	$ mil.	% of total
AmeriGas propane	2,260.1	38
Energy services	1,241.0	21
Gas utility	1,224.7	21
International propane	955.3	16
Electric utility	138.5	2
Corporate & other	90.7	2
Adjustments	(172.5)	—
Total	**5,737.8**	**100**

Selected Subsidiaries and Affiliates

AmeriGas, Inc.
AmeriGas Propane, Inc.
    AmeriGas Partners, L.P. (44%)
    AmeriGas Propane L.P.
    AmeriGas Technology Group, Inc.
    Petrolane Incorporated
Four Flags Drilling Company, Inc.
Ashtola Production Company
UGI Ethanol Development Corporation
Newbury Holding Company
UGI Enterprises, Inc. (energy marketing and services)
CFN Enterprises, Inc.
Eastfield International Holdings, Inc.
    FLAGA GmbH (propane distribution; Austria, the Czech Republic, and Slovakia)
Eurogas Holdings, Inc.
McHugh Service Company
UGI Energy Services, Inc.
    GASMARK (gas marketing)
    POWERMARK (electricity marketing)
UGI International Enterprises, Inc.
    UGI Europe, Inc.
        Antargaz (propane distribution, France)
        FLAGA GmbH (propane distribution, Austria)
UGI Properties, Inc.
UGI Utilities, Inc. (natural gas and electric utility)
United Valley Insurance Company

COMPETITORS

Chesapeake Utilities
Dominion Resources
Duquesne Light Holdings
Energy Transfer
Exelon
Ferrellgas Partners
National Fuel Gas
NorthWestern
PPL Corporation
Suburban Propane

HISTORICAL FINANCIALS

Company Type: Public

Income Statement

FYE: September 30

	REVENUE ($ mil.)	NET INCOME ($ mil.)	NET PROFIT MARGIN	EMPLOYEES
9/09	5,738	259	4.5%	9,700
9/08	6,648	216	3.2%	5,900
9/07	5,477	204	3.7%	6,200
9/06	5,221	176	3.4%	5,900
9/05	4,889	188	3.8%	6,000
Annual Growth	**4.1%**	**8.4%**	**—**	**12.8%**

2009 Year-End Financials

Debt ratio: 128.1%
Return on equity: 17.2%
Cash ($ mil.): 280
Current ratio: 1.08
Long-term debt ($ mil.): 2,039
No. of shares (mil.): 110
Dividends
    Yield: 3.1%
    Payout: 33.5%
Market value ($ mil.): 2,755

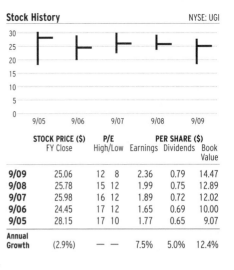

Stock History   NYSE: UGI

	STOCK PRICE ($) FY Close	P/E High/Low		PER SHARE ($) Earnings	Dividends	Book Value
9/09	25.06	12	8	2.36	0.79	14.47
9/08	25.78	15	12	1.99	0.75	12.89
9/07	25.98	16	12	1.89	0.72	12.02
9/06	24.45	17	12	1.65	0.69	10.00
9/05	28.15	17	10	1.77	0.65	9.07
Annual Growth	**(2.9%)**	**—**	**—**	**7.5%**	**5.0%**	**12.4%**

Union Pacific

Venerable Union Pacific (UP) keeps on chugging down the track, just as it has since the 19th century. The company's Union Pacific Railroad is one of the nation's leading rail freight carriers (along with rival Burlington Northern Santa Fe). Union Pacific Railroad transports coal, chemicals, industrial products, and other bulk freight over a system of more than 32,000 route miles in 23 states in the western two-thirds of the US. The company owns more than 26,000 route miles of its rail network; leases and trackage rights, which allow UP to use other railroads' tracks, account for the rest. UP's biggest customers are container shipping company APL Limited, followed by automaker General Motors.

To offset a 16% drop in freight volumes across all commodity groups fueled by the US economic downturn, UP raised its rates by about 6 percent in 2009. The company also parked approximately 26% of its locomotives, 18% of its freight car stock, and furloughed about 3,000 employees. Government regulations requiring installation of positive train control (PTC) by 2015 is also hitting the company's bottom line. PTC, a collision prevention tool, overrides the train's controls, stopping it before an accident. UP is dedicating some $200 million to develop PTC in 2010.

In the meantime, UP is keeping up with the future of transportation demand by investing in upgrades to its infrastructure and its equipment fleet. A significant growth driver for UP, its intermodal business transports containerized freight that will travel by at least one additional mode of transportation, such as a truck or a ship. In 2009 the company broke ground on a new intermodal terminal in Joliet, Illinois. The facility is positioned to ramp up railroad capacity for domestic and international containers, as well as enhance traffic efficiencies at the largest rail center in the US, Chicago.

UP also expects growth along its Sunset Corridor, a 760-mile route between Los Angeles and El Paso, Texas. In 2008 the company added 45 miles of double track to the corridor, which carries about 20% of UP's traffic. In addition, the company is jockeying to serve US power plants' growing demand for coal; its lines serve major coal production areas, particularly the Southern Powder River Basin of Wyoming. Rising demand for ethanol also has been a boon for UP in its shipping of agricultural products.

HISTORY

In 1862 the US Congress chartered the Union Pacific Railroad (UP) to build part of the first transcontinental railway. The driving of the Golden Spike at Promontory, Utah, in 1869 marked the linking of the East and West coasts, as UP's rails met those of Central Pacific Railroad (predecessor of Southern Pacific, or SP), which had been built east from Sacramento, California.

In 1872 the *New York Sun* revealed the Credit Mobilier scandal: UP officials had pocketed excess profits during the railroad's construction. Debt and lingering effects of the scandal forced UP into bankruptcy in 1893.

A syndicate headed by E. H. Harriman purchased UP in 1897. After reacquiring the Oregon branches it lost in the bankruptcy, UP gained control of SP (1901) and Chicago & Alton (1904). The Supreme Court ordered UP to sell its SP holdings in 1913 on antitrust grounds. In the 1930s UP diversified into trucking, and in the 1970s and 1980s it moved into oil and gas production.

UP bought trucking firm Overnite Transportation in 1986. During the 1980s UP also built up its rail operations, acquiring the Missouri Pacific and Western Pacific railroads in 1982 and the Missouri-Kansas-Texas Railroad in 1988. It joined Chicago and North Western (CNW) Railway managers in an investment group led by Blackstone Capital Partners that bought CNW in 1989.

CNW traced its roots to the Galena & Chicago Union Railroad, which was founded by Chicago's first mayor, W. B. Ogden, in 1836, and merged with CNW in 1864. By 1925 the North Western (as it was then known) had tracks throughout the Midwest. In 1995 UP completed its purchase of CNW and made a bid for SP.

SP was founded in 1865, but its history dates to 1861, when four Sacramento merchants founded Central Pacific. By building new track and buying other railroads (including SP, in 1868), Central Pacific had expanded throughout California, Texas, and Oregon by 1887. The two railroads merged in 1885 under the SP name. In 1983 SP was sold to a holding company controlled by Philip Anschutz, which in 1995 agreed to sell the company to UP.

UP completed its SP acquisition in 1996, but assimilation of the purchase led to widespread rail traffic jams. UP also sold its remaining interest in Union Pacific Resources, an oil company it had spun off the year before. In 1997 UP moved from Bethlehem, Pennsylvania, to Dallas and joined a consortium led by mining company Grupo Mexico that won a bid to run two major Mexican rail lines. In the US, however, UP's fatal collisions led to a federal review, which found a breakdown in rail safety, such as overworked employees and widespread train defects. Meanwhile, regulators, seeking to resolve UP's massive freight backlog, ordered the railroad to open its Houston lines to competitors.

UP decentralized its management into three regions (north, south, and west) in 1998 to improve traffic flow. It also hired more workers, added new trains, and realigned routes, while selling Skyway Freight Systems, its logistics services unit. In 1999 UP moved its headquarters from Dallas to Omaha, Nebraska, where Union Pacific Railroad offices already were located.

UP sold its trucking unit, Overnite Corporation (a holding company for Overnite Transportation and Motor Cargo Industries), in an IPO in 2003. (Overnite Corporation was acquired by United Parcel Service in 2005 and renamed UPS Freight the next year.) UP sold its Timera subsidiary (workforce management software) in 2004.

Traffic congestion in the UP system, brought on by a shortage of train crews, caused some freight from UPS and other customers to be rerouted onto trucks in 2004. The crew shortage was attributed in part to a greater-than-expected number of retirements in 2003. UP accelerated its hiring and training efforts, but the company still had to restrict freight volume in an effort to minimize bottlenecks.

In 2006 Union Pacific Railroad reorganized its operating structure, going from four regions to three: northern, southern, and western. Service units of the company's central region were reassigned to the northern and southern regions.

EXECUTIVES

Chairman, President, and CEO, Union Pacific Corporation and Union Pacific Railroad: James R. (Jim) Young, age 57, $15,284,347 total compensation
Vice Chairman Operations: Dennis J. Duffy, age 59, $5,767,825 total compensation
EVP Finance and CFO, Union Pacific Corporation and Union Pacific Railroad: Robert M. Knight Jr., age 52, $4,327,273 total compensation
SVP Law and General Counsel, Union Pacific Corporation and Union Pacific Railroad: J. Michael (Mike) Hemmer, age 60, $3,480,277 total compensation
SVP Strategic Planning and Administration, Union Pacific Corporation and Union Pacific Railroad: Charles R. Eisele
SVP and CIO, Union Pacific Corporation and Union Pacific Railroad: Lynden L. Tennison
SVP Human Resources and Secretary, Union Pacific Corporation and Union Pacific Railroad: Barbara R. Schaefer, age 56
SVP Corporate Relations, Union Pacific Corporation and Union Pacific Railroad: Robert W. Turner
Chief Mechanical Officer: Barry J. Kanuch
VP Operations: Lance M. Fritz, age 47
VP and Controller; Chief Accounting Officer and Controller, Union Pacific Railroad: Jeffrey P. Totusek, age 51
VP Harriman Dispatching Center and Network Operations: Stephen R. Barkley
VP Intermodal Operations: Barry Michaels
Assistant VP Corporate Communications: Donna Kush
Assistant VP Investor Relations: Jennifer Hamann
Auditors: Deloitte & Touche LLP

LOCATIONS

HQ: Union Pacific Corporation
 1400 Douglas St., Omaha, NE 68179
Phone: 402-544-5000   **Fax:** 402-501-2133
Web: www.up.com

PRODUCTS/OPERATIONS

2009 Sales

	$ mil.	% of total
Commodity		
Energy	3,118	22
Agricultural	2,666	19
Intermodal	2,486	18
Industrial products	2,147	15
Chemicals	2,102	15
Automotive	854	6
Other	770	5
Total	**14,143**	**100**

COMPETITORS

American Commercial Lines
Burlington Northern Santa Fe
Canadian National Railway
Canadian Pacific Railway
CSX
Hub Group
Ingram Industries
J.B. Hunt
Kansas City Southern
Kirby Corporation
Landstar System
Norfolk Southern
Pacer International
Schneider National
Werner Enterprises

HISTORICAL FINANCIALS

Company Type: Public

Income Statement
FYE: December 31

	REVENUE ($ mil.)	NET INCOME ($ mil.)	NET PROFIT MARGIN	EMPLOYEES
12/09	14,143	1,898	13.4%	43,531
12/08	17,970	2,338	13.0%	48,242
12/07	16,283	1,855	11.4%	50,089
12/06	15,578	1,606	10.3%	50,739
12/05	13,578	1,026	7.6%	49,747
Annual Growth	**1.0%**	**16.6%**	**—**	**(3.3%)**

2009 Year-End Financials

Debt ratio: 56.9%
Return on equity: 11.7%
Cash ($ mil.): 1,850
Current ratio: 1.37
Long-term debt ($ mil.): 9,636

No. of shares (mil.): 498
Dividends
 Yield: 1.7%
 Payout: 28.8%
Market value ($ mil.): 31,794

Stock History
NYSE: UNP

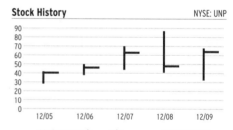

	STOCK PRICE ($) FY Close	P/E High/Low		PER SHARE ($) Earnings	Dividends	Book Value
12/09	63.90	18	9	3.75	1.08	34.05
12/08	47.80	19	9	4.54	0.98	31.05
12/07	62.81	20	13	3.45	0.75	31.32
12/06	46.01	16	13	2.95	0.60	30.77
12/05	40.26	21	15	1.92	0.60	27.55
Annual Growth	**12.2%**	**—**	**—**	**18.2%**	**15.8%**	**5.4%**

Unisys Corporation

Information systems of the world, unite! Unisys is among the top global players in the IT consulting business. Its operations are split into two main segments: Services and Technology. The company's Services unit handles outsourcing, systems integration and consulting, infrastructure services, and core maintenance. Its Technology division develops enterprise-class servers and related operating systems and middleware. Unisys is among the largest government IT contractors, serving local, state, and federal agencies, as well as foreign governments. Other key sectors include communications, financial services, and transportation.

Unisys has seen its revenues slip in recent years as the weakened economy has slowed spending on technology services and computer servers, particularly in the financial services market. After taking over as CEO in 2008, Edward Coleman spearheaded a turnaround program designed to cut costs and improve the company's bottom line. In addition to the continuation of a multiyear reduction in staff, cost-cutting measures included facility consolidation, reduction of benefits, and salary freezes.

Unisys' growth strategy has focused on investments in the areas of IT and physical security, data center transformation and outsourcing services, end-user outsourcing, and application modernization and outsourcing services. It is working to secure more long-term outsourcing contracts for applications, data center, and network management as a way to offset cyclical downturns in the technology services sector.

International business is a key contributor to overall sales, with more than half of Unisys' revenues coming from outside the US.

The company has used divestitures to unload noncore business lines. In 2010 Unisys sold its health information management business to Molina Healthcare for about $135 million. Also that year, Unisys sold its Michigan-based check and cash automation business to Marlin Equity Partners.

The company continues to capitalize on its legacy as a provider of mainframe computers and high-end network servers through its Technology division. The unit designs and markets servers and related software primarily for use in commercial data centers. Unisys has sales partnerships with a wide range of IT companies including such key vendors as Cisco Systems, Dell, EMC, Oracle, and SAP.

HISTORY

Unisys was formed in 1986 when struggling mainframe computer giant Burroughs swallowed fellow mainframe maker Sperry Corporation. Burroughs traced its roots back to American Arithmometer (St. Louis, 1886), later Burroughs Adding Machine (Detroit, 1905), and then Burroughs Corporation (1953). It entered data processing by purchasing Electrodata (1956) and many other firms, including Memorex (1982).

Sperry was the product of the 1955 merger of Sperry Gyroscope (founded in 1910 by Elmer

Sperry) and Remington Rand, an old-line typewriter manufacturer and maker of the first commercially viable computer, the UNIVAC. Sperry later bought RCA's faltering computer unit in 1971.

In 1986 Burroughs president Michael Blumenthal sought to achieve efficiency in parts and development by merging Burroughs' small-database managers with Sperry's defense-related number crunchers. The new company was called Unisys, a contraction of "United Information Systems."

As president of Unisys, Blumenthal quickly disposed of $1.8 billion in assets (Sperry Aerospace and Marine divisions and Memorex), closed plants, and cut jobs. He continued to support Sperry's flagship line of mainframes and nurtured Burroughs' prized "A" series of computers. The initial results were positive, with 1986's $43 million loss followed by 1987's $578 million profit.

Amid an industry trend toward stronger, smaller systems, Unisys in 1988 equipped its U line of servers with the open UNIX operating system and moved to smaller networked systems by acquiring Timeplex (voice/data networks) and Convergent (UNIX workstations). That year the US Department of Justice launched an investigation of illegal defense procurement practices committed by Sperry prior to its merger with Burroughs (Unisys settled the charges in 1991).

Plummeting mainframe demand in 1989 and 1990 led to heavy losses. Blumenthal left the company in 1990, and continuing losses prompted layoffs the following year (Unisys eventually laid off nearly two-thirds of its workforce). The company pared its product line and closed seven of its 15 plants.

In 1995 Unisys sold its defense unit to Loral for $862 million. Restructuring charges contributed to losses for the year. In 1996 shareholders rejected a proposal to split Unisys into three separate companies (computer manufacturing, consulting, and services).

Former Andersen Worldwide CEO Larry Weinbach (who left the accounting giant long before it was brought down by scandal) took over as chairman, president, and CEO that year. He immediately began boosting employee morale — easing the company's travel policy, among other changes — and remaking Unisys in the image of his old consulting firm. Charges of more than $1 billion (largely to write off the value of the 1986 Sperry purchase, a move cheered by many analysts) led to a loss for 1997. Unisys hired about 7,000 workers in 1999 to install and maintain corporate computer networks.

In 2000 Unisys signed co-branding deals with Compaq and other manufacturers to market its high-end servers. The economy in general and technology spending in particular began to deteriorate in 2000, leading to smaller profits and eventually a loss in 2001. Unisys responded by placing more emphasis on long-term outsourcing contracts as a hedge against further economic decline. The company also took steps to reduce costs, including cutting staff.

Following the terrorist attacks of September 11, 2001, Unisys expanded its public sector business units as government agencies began focusing on homeland security issues.

In 2004 the company joined the widespread outsourcing trend, announcing its decision to relocate its technology development operations to India. Weinbach stepped down as CEO in 2005, tapping Joe McGrath as his replacement.

Unisys sold its 28% stake in Japanese affiliate Nihon Unisys early in 2006. A year later it sold its media business to UK media software firm Atex Group.

McGrath was replaced as CEO by Edward Coleman, former CEO of Gateway, in 2008. Coleman was also named chairman of the board.

EXECUTIVES

Chairman and CEO: J. Edward (Ed) Coleman, age 58, $3,697,575 total compensation
SVP and CFO: Janet Brutschea Haugen, age 51, $1,661,653 total compensation
SVP; President, Federal Systems: Edward (Ted) Davies, age 50, $1,181,389 total compensation
SVP; President, Technology, Consulting, and Integration Solutions and Worldwide Strategic Services: Dominick Cavuoto, age 56, $1,248,049 total compensation
SVP, General Counsel, and Secretary: Nancy Straus Sundheim, age 58, $754,680 total compensation
SVP Worldwide Human Resources: Patricia A. (Pat) Bradford, age 59
SVP Corporate Development: M. Lazane Smith, age 55
SVP and CIO: Suresh V. Mathews, age 56
VP and General Manager, IT Outsourcing Global Operations: William L. (Bill) Bancroft
VP and Managing Director Global Services, India; Country Manager, India: Kumar Prabhas
VP Marketing Programs Unisys Systems and Technology: Janis Cooper
VP and Controller: Scott W. Hurley, age 51
VP and Unisys Partner, Passenger Services: Mike McNamara
VP and Treasurer: Scott A. Battersby, age 51
VP Investor Relations: Niels Christensen
President, Global Transportation: Olivier Houri
President, Global Outsourcing and Infrastructure Services: Ron Frankenfield
Auditors: KPMG LLP

LOCATIONS

HQ: Unisys Corporation
Unisys Way, Blue Bell, PA 19424
Phone: 215-986-4011   **Fax:** 215-986-2312
Web: www.unisys.com

2009 Sales

	$ mil.	% of total
US	2,117.1	46
UK	569.5	12
Other countries	1,911.1	42
Total	**4,597.7**	**100**

PRODUCTS/OPERATIONS

2009 Sales

	$ mil.	% of total
Services		
Outsourcing	1,804.2	39
Systems integration & consulting	1,360.0	30
Infrastructure	563.9	12
Core maintenance	308.8	7
Technology		
Enterprise-class servers	464.6	10
Specialized technologies	96.2	2
Total	**4,597.7**	**100**

Selected Products and Services

Services
- Application modernization and outsourcing
- Business process outsourcing
- Communication and collaboration
- End-user outsourcing
- Enterprise and asset modernization
- Enterprise content management
- Global commerce
- Infrastructure
- Security
- Supply chain management
- Systems integration

Technology
- Enterprise servers
- Mainframes
- Open Source
- Software
- Storage

COMPETITORS

Accenture
Affiliated Computer Services
Atos Origin
Bull
Capgemini
Capita
Computer Sciences Corp.
Dell
Deloitte Consulting
Fujitsu
Hewlett-Packard
Hitachi
IBM
L-3 Communications Titan
Logica
NEC
SAIC

HISTORICAL FINANCIALS

Company Type: Public

Income Statement

FYE: December 31

	REVENUE ($ mil.)	NET INCOME ($ mil.)	NET PROFIT MARGIN	EMPLOYEES
12/09	4,598	189	4.1%	25,600
12/08	5,233	(130)	—	29,000
12/07	5,653	(79)	—	30,000
12/06	5,757	(279)	—	31,500
12/05	5,759	(1,732)	—	36,100
Annual Growth	(5.5%)	—	—	(8.2%)

2009 Year-End Financials

Debt ratio: —
Return on equity: —
Cash ($ mil.): 648
Current ratio: 1.22
Long-term debt ($ mil.): 846

No. of shares (mil.): 43
Dividends
Yield: 0.0%
Payout: —
Market value ($ mil.): 1,643

Stock History

NYSE: UIS

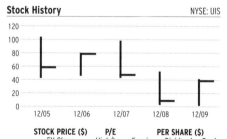

	STOCK PRICE ($) FY Close	P/E High	P/E Low	Earnings	Dividends	Book Value
12/09	38.56	8	1	4.75	0.00	(29.76)
12/08	8.50	—	—	(3.60)	0.00	(34.13)
12/07	47.30	—	—	(2.30)	0.00	8.60
12/06	78.40	—	—	(8.10)	0.00	(1.51)
12/05	58.30	—	—	(50.90)	0.00	(0.76)
Annual Growth	(9.8%)			—	—	—

United Natural Foods

This distribution network comes together to serve healthy food fans. United Natural Foods is a leading wholesale distributor of natural and organic foods and other products in the US. It has about 20 distribution centers supplying more than 60,000 items to 17,000 customers, including independently owned retail stores, supermarket chains, and buying clubs. The company offers natural groceries, personal care products, supplements, and frozen foods. In addition to wholesale distribution, United Natural Foods operates more than a dozen natural-products retail stores under the name NRG (mostly locations in Florida) and it produces roasted nuts, dried fruits, and other snack items through subsidiary Woodstock Farms.

Like other wholesale distributors, United Natural Foods is constantly focused on operating costs and improving efficiency because success depends on its ability to deliver goods to its customer stores at a low price. It invests heavily in automation and information systems to help track expenses and to keep the goods flowing. At the same time, United Natural Foods is trying to stay a step ahead of the competition, expanding its distribution network through new facilities as well as through targeted acquisitions.

To this end, United Natural Foods in June 2010 acquired the food distribution assets of Ontario-based rival SunOpta, the largest supplier of organic, kosher, and specialty foods in Canada. United Natural Foods has been working to build its operations in the country, which it sees as a dynamic market.

United Natural Foods' broadline distribution business is augmented by specialty products units such as subsidiary Albert's Organics, which supplies more than 5,000 customers with fruits, vegetables, and other perishable items. United Natural Foods also supplies ethnic food items and related products through its UNFI Specialty Distribution unit.

The bulk of the company's business comes from independently owned retail stores (more than 40% of sales) and from supermarket chains that specialize in natural food products. Its single largest customer is Whole Foods Market, which accounts for about a third of sales. The company also supplies natural products to traditional supermarkets including Kroger, Publix and Wegman's.

The company buys products from more than 5,000 suppliers, mostly in the United States; Hain Celestial Group accounts for more than 5% of its purchases. United Natural Foods has also been focused on building its own food brands through subsidiary Blue Marble Brands. The unit offers a portfolio of goods to retailers and third party distributors that includes Moosewood, Rising Moon Organics, and Tumaro's Gourmet Tortillas.

In the natural and organic foods segment, United Natural Foods competes most directly with Kehe Food, which acquired another rival, Tree of Life, from Dutch food giant Wessanen in 2010. The company also competes with traditional grocery wholesalers such as C & S Wholesale and Nash-Finch that distribute a growing number of organic food items.

Company veteran Michael Funk stepped down as CEO in 2008 (remaining with the company as chairman) and was replaced by former Performance Food Group chief Steven Spinner.

HISTORY

Rhode Island retailer Norman Cloutier founded Cornucopia Natural Foods in 1978 and soon focused on distribution. During the 1980s Cornucopia grew by acquiring other natural foods distributors. It bought suppliers Natural Food Systems (seafood) and BGS Distributing (vitamins) in 1987 and 1990, respectively. Cornucopia expanded into the Southeast in 1991, when it opened a distribution center in Georgia.

Reviving its interest in retailing, Cornucopia formed Natural Retail Group in 1993 to buy and run natural foods stores. During the next two years it acquired several retailers. The company expanded its distribution operations in the West in 1995, adding Denver-based Rainbow Distributors. In 1996 Cornucopia merged with the leading natural foods distributor in the western US, Sacramento-based Mountain People's, which Michael Funk had founded 20 years earlier. The combined company became United Natural Foods, with Cloutier as chairman and CEO and Funk as president and vice chairman; it went public later that year.

United Natural Foods became the largest natural foods distributor when it bought New Hampshire-based Stow Mills in 1997. The next year it added Hershey Imports, an importer and processor of nuts, seeds, and snacks, and Albert's, a distributor of organic produce. With the purchase of Mother Earth Markets in 1998, the company's retailing operations had grown to 16 stores, but by mid-1999 it had sold four stores. That year United Natural Foods' East Coast consolidation problems became so profound that top customer Whole Foods announced it was finding backup distribution sources.

Funk replaced Cloutier as CEO, and the company handed the chairman's post to board member Thomas Simone in 1999. In 2000, after the resignation of Cloutier from the board of directors, United Natural Foods adopted a poison-pill plan to block potential takeovers. The company leased a distribution center in the Los Angeles area in 2001 to increase market share in the Southwest. It also acquired Florida's Palm Harbor Natural Products.

In mid-2002 United Natural Foods lost one of its two largest customers — Wild Oats Markets — when that company defected to rival specialty foods distributor Tree of Life. However, United Natural Foods soon won that business back. In October the company completed the acquisition of privately held Blooming Prairie Cooperative for approximately $31 million. In late 2002 the company merged with Northeast Cooperatives, a natural foods distributor in the Midwest and Northeast.

That year, United Natural Foods discontinued the management, sales, and support operations at its Hershey Imports subsidiary, but continued to manufacture and distribute products from the Edison, New Jersey, plant.

In 2004 the company renewed its distribution agreement with Wild Oats with a five-year pact. United Natural Foods later announced a new three-year distribution agreement with Whole Foods, which it renewed in 2006. Whole Foods later acquired Wild Oats in 2007. That same year United Natural Foods acquired ethnic and specialty food distributor Millbrook Distribution Services for about $85 million.

EXECUTIVES

Chairman: Michael S. Funk, age 55,
$887,572 total compensation
Vice Chairman: Gordon D. Barker, age 63
President, CEO, and Director:
Steven L. (Steve) Spinner, age 50
SVP, CFO, and Treasurer: Mark E. Shamber, age 41,
$736,997 total compensation
SVP and CIO: John Stern, age 43,
$507,570 total compensation
SVP National Distribution: Sean Griffin
SVP, General Counsel, and Chief Compliance Officer:
Joseph J. (Joe) Traficanti, age 58
VP and Chief Human Resources Officer:
Carl F. Koch III, age 42
VP Sales: Kate Tierney
VP Sustainable Development: Thomas A. Dziki, age 48
President, Eastern Region: David A. Matthews
President, Western Region: Kurt Luttecke, age 42
President, Specialty Foods; President, Millbrook
Distribution Services: Casey Van Rysdam
Corporate Controller: Lisa N'Chonon
Auditors: KPMG LLP

LOCATIONS

HQ: United Natural Foods, Inc.
313 Iron Horse Way, Providence, RI 02908
Phone: 401-528-8634
Web: www.unfi.com

PRODUCTS/OPERATIONS

2009 Sales

	$ mil.	% of total
Wholesale	3,393.0	96
Other	142.8	4
Adjustments	(80.9)	—
Total	**3,454.9**	**100**

2009 Sales

	% of total
Independently owned retailers	42
Natural foods supermarkets	33
Conventional supermarkets	20
Other	5
Total	**100**

Selected Operations

Albert's Organics (fresh produce distribution)
Blue Marble Brands (marketing and branding services)
Natural Retail Group (NRG, natural products retail
stores)
Select Nutrition (health and beauty products
distribution)
UNFI Specialty Distribution Services (wholesale ethnic
and natural foods distribution)
Woodstock Farms (dried fruit and nuts packaging and
distribution)

COMPETITORS

Associated Wholesale Grocers
Associated Wholesalers
C&S Wholesale
DPI Specialty Foods
KeHE Distributors
Nash-Finch
SUPERVALU
Wal-Mart

HISTORICAL FINANCIALS

Company Type: Public

Income Statement

FYE: July 31

	REVENUE ($ mil.)	NET INCOME ($ mil.)	NET PROFIT MARGIN	EMPLOYEES
7/09	3,455	59	1.7%	6,000
7/08	3,366	49	1.4%	6,300
7/07	2,754	50	1.8%	4,800
7/06	2,434	43	1.8%	4,500
7/05	2,060	42	2.0%	4,030
Annual Growth	**13.8%**	**9.2%**	**—**	**10.5%**

2009 Year-End Financials

Debt ratio: 9.9%
Return on equity: 11.6%
Cash ($ mil.): 10
Current ratio: 1.40
Long-term debt ($ mil.): 54
No. of shares (mil.): 43
Dividends
  Yield: —
  Payout: —
Market value ($ mil.): 1,171

Stock History

NASDAQ (GS): UNFI

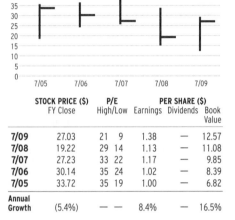

	STOCK PRICE ($) FY Close	P/E High/Low		Earnings	Dividends	Book Value
7/09	27.03	21	9	1.38	—	12.57
7/08	19.22	29	14	1.13	—	11.08
7/07	27.23	33	22	1.17	—	9.85
7/06	30.14	35	24	1.02	—	8.39
7/05	33.72	35	19	1.00	—	6.82
Annual Growth	**(5.4%)**	**—**	**—**	**8.4%**	**—**	**16.5%**

United Parcel Service

The ubiquitous Brown is more than chocolate-colored trucks or a plain-vanilla ground delivery business. United Parcel Service (UPS) is the world's largest package delivery company, transporting some 15 million packages and documents per business day throughout the US and to more than 200 countries and territories. Its delivery operations use a fleet of about 100,000 motor vehicles and about 500 aircraft. In addition to package delivery, the company offers services such as logistics and freight forwarding through UPS Supply Chain Solutions, and less-than-truckload (LTL) freight transportation through UPS Ground Freight. (LTL carriers combine freight from multiple shippers into a single truckload.)

Domestic package delivery remains UPS's largest business segment, but growth in the segment has slowed along with the US economy. Archrival FedEx, through its FedEx Ground unit, has expanded its US ground delivery business.

Package delivery revenue, however, is increasing overseas, where UPS continues to expand through infrastructure investments and selected acquisitions. Although Europe remains the company's largest market outside the US, its sights are set on the Asia/Pacific region. UPS is

adding facilities to offer direct air service in China. In 2010 the company opened an intra-Asia hub in southern China; the Shenzhen facility operates as the company's primary transit center in Asia and replaces an intra-Asia hub at Clark Air Force Base in the Philippines.

The company formed a joint venture in Vietnam with P&T Express, a subsidiary of VN Post. UPS Vietnam takes root in Hanoi, a fertile site for growing UPS's transportation and logistics businesses. The deal follows the company's move to add flights between the US and Japan, and open a new air hub in Shanghai, linking Chinese domestic and international routes.

In 2009 UPS expanded its reach into Eastern Europe and Central Asia. That year it acquired the small package operations of its shipping contractors in Turkey and Slovenia. UPS set up a joint venture based in Dubai, United Arab Emirates, that coordinates services across the Middle East, Turkey, and parts of Central Asia.

Freight forwarding and logistics customers are a potential source of small-package revenue; UPS also hopes to sell supply chain management services to more of its package delivery and freight transportation customers. Along with logistics and trucking, the company's supply chain and freight segment includes mail expediting (UPS Mail Innovations) and financial services (UPS Capital) businesses, as well as postal and business services store franchiser Mail Boxes Etc.

HISTORY

Seattle teens Jim Casey and Claude Ryan started American Messenger Company, a delivery and errand service, in 1907. They were soon making small-parcel deliveries for local department stores, and in 1913 changed the company's name to Merchants Parcel Delivery. Casey, who led the company for 50 years, established a policy of manager ownership, best service, and lowest rates. In 1916 new employee Charlie Soderstrom chose the brown paint still used on the company's vehicles.

Service expanded outside Seattle in 1919 when Merchants Parcel bought Oakland, California-based Motor Parcel Delivery, later changing its name to United Parcel Service (UPS). By 1930 the company served residents in New York City (its headquarters from 1930 to 1975) and New Jersey, as well as all major cities along the Pacific Coast.

Offering small-package delivery within a 125-mile radius of certain cities, starting with Los Angeles in 1927, UPS grew in relative obscurity as it expanded westward from the East Coast and eastward from the West Coast. The company gained notice in 1952 when the U.S. Postal Service named UPS as a competitor. Noted for its employee-oriented culture, the company through the 1960s required all executives to start as drivers.

In 1975, after becoming the first package delivery company to serve every address in the 48 contiguous US states, UPS crossed the border to Canada, and Germany followed the next year. (UPS had been offering two-day air parcel delivery service to major cities on both coasts via cargo holds on regularly scheduled airline flights since 1953.) By 1977 UPS Blue Label Air (now UPS Next Day Air) guaranteed 48-hour delivery anywhere on the mainland.

Overnight service began in 1981 and was nationwide by 1985 (also serving six European countries). It started air express delivery from its hub in Louisville, Kentucky, in 1982. After purchasing its own jet cargo fleet and getting authorization from the FAA to operate its own aircraft, in 1988 UPS Airlines officially became an airline (and the fastest-growing one in FAA history). By 1990 UPS Airlines was delivering to more than 175 countries in North and South America, Africa, Europe, and Asia.

Moving to its headquarters in Atlanta in 1991, the company began to work on its customer service. As part of a technology revamp, UPS created the electronic clipboard still used by drivers to track packages and digitize signatures. In 1994 UPS went online, allowing customers to track packages in transit.

In 1994 Teamsters staged a one-day strike to protest UPS's new per-package weight limit (raised from 70 to 150 pounds). The next year the firm allowed rank-and-file employees to buy UPS stock. In 1997 UPS was hit by a 15-day Teamsters strike that cost the company hundreds of millions of dollars. UPS settled the strike by combining part-time jobs into 10,000 new full-time positions; in 1998 the company headed off another labor threat by giving its pilots a five-year contract with pay raises.

Chinese government-owned logistics giant Sinotrans proved more friendly than the IRS, teaming up with UPS in 1999 to expand UPS-branded service across China. To fund global expansion, UPS sold about 10% of its stock in 1999 in a public offering valued at more than $5 billion — then the largest IPO in US history.

In 2001 UPS bought Mail Boxes Etc., a franchiser of stores that offer mail, packing, and shipping services.

UPS in 2004 expanded its freight forwarding business by buying Menlo Worldwide Forwarding from Con-Way. The next year UPS bought trucking company Overnite for about $1.2 billion. The acquisition brought UPS into the less-than-truckload (LTL) freight transportation business and — not coincidentally — countered a move by FedEx, which formed nationwide LTL carrier FedEx Freight in 2001.

CFO Scott Davis took over as chairman and CEO in 2008, succeeding Mike Eskew.

EXECUTIVES

Chairman and CEO; Chairman and CEO, UPS Supply Chain Solutions: D. Scott Davis, age 58, $6,242,055 total compensation
SVP and COO: David P. Abney, age 54, $2,479,315 total compensation
SVP, CFO, and Treasurer: Kurt P. Kuehn, age 55, $1,855,566 total compensation
SVP US Operations: Myron A. Gray, age 52, $2,136,831 total compensation
SVP Global Transportation Services and Labor Relations: John J. McDevitt, age 51, $1,789,491 total compensation
SVP Engineering, Strategy, Supply Chain Distribution, and Sustainability: Robert E. (Bob) Stoffel, age 54, $1,658,726 total compensation
SVP Worldwide Sales and Marketing: Alan Gershenhorn, age 51
SVP Communications and Brand Management: Christine M. Owens, age 54
SVP Strategy, UPS Freight: Kevin Hartman
SVP Legal, Compliance, and Public Affairs, General Counsel, and Corporate Secretary: Teri P. McClure, age 46
SVP; President, UPS International: Daniel J. (Dan) Brutto, age 53
SVP Human Resources: Allen E. Hill, age 54
SVP and CIO: David A. (Dave) Barnes, age 54

VP Investor Relations: Andy Dolny, age 52
VP Finance: Rich Peretz, age 48
VP Human Resources: Amy Whitley
Director Customer Communications: Maureen Healy
Auditors: Deloitte & Touche LLP

LOCATIONS

HQ: United Parcel Service, Inc.
  55 Glenlake Pkwy. NE, Atlanta, GA 30328
Phone: 404-828-6000
Web: www.ups.com

2009 Sales

	$ mil.	% of total
US	34,375	76
Other countries	10,922	24
Total	**45,297**	**100**

PRODUCTS/OPERATIONS

2009 Sales

	$ mil.	% of total
US domestic package		
Ground	19,843	44
Next day air	5,456	12
Deferred	2,859	6
International package		
Export	7,176	16
Domestic	2,111	5
Cargo	412	1
Supply chain & freight		
Forwarding & logistics	5,080	11
Freight	1,943	4
Other	417	1
Total	**45,297**	**100**

COMPETITORS

AMR Corp.
Canada Post
Con-way Inc.
Deutsche Post
FedEx
Japan Post
La Poste
Lufthansa
Nippon Express
Panalpina
Royal Mail
Ryder System
TNT
UAL
US Postal Service
YRC Worldwide

HISTORICAL FINANCIALS

Company Type: Public

Income Statement

FYE: December 31

	REVENUE ($ mil.)	NET INCOME ($ mil.)	NET PROFIT MARGIN	EMPLOYEES
12/09	45,297	2,152	4.8%	408,000
12/08	51,486	3,003	5.8%	426,000
12/07	49,692	382	0.8%	425,300
12/06	47,547	4,202	8.8%	428,000
12/05	42,581	3,870	9.1%	407,000
Annual Growth	**1.6%**	**(13.6%)**	**—**	**0.1%**

2009 Year-End Financials

Debt ratio: 113.6%
Return on equity: 29.9%
Cash ($ mil.): 1,542
Current ratio: 1.49
Long-term debt ($ mil.): 8,668
No. of shares (mil.): 991
Dividends
  Yield: 3.1%
  Payout: 84.1%
Market value ($ mil.): 56,836

Stock History NYSE: UPS

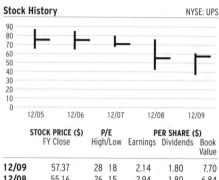

	STOCK PRICE ($) FY Close	P/E High/Low	PER SHARE ($) Earnings	Dividends	Book Value
12/09	57.37	28 18	2.14	1.80	7.70
12/08	55.16	26 15	2.94	1.80	6.84
12/07	70.72	219191	0.36	1.68	12.30
12/06	74.98	22 17	3.86	1.52	15.63
12/05	75.15	25 19	3.47	1.32	17.04
Annual Growth	**(6.5%)**	**— —**	**(11.4%)**	**8.1%**	**(18.0%)**

United Rentals

No cash to buy a bulldozer? No worries — just lease one from United Rentals. The company is the #1 commercial and construction equipment renter in the world, serving more than a million customers. Leveraging an integrated network of more than 550 locations in Canada, Mexico, and the US, United Rentals offers thousands of equipment items — from heavy construction and industrial equipment to hand tools, special-event items such as light towers, and trench-safety equipment. It also sells new and used equipment, rental-related and contractor supplies, and parts.

After a potential buyout by Cerberus Capital Management fell through, the company has refocused its core rental business, optimizing its fleet, and trimming operating costs and boosting cash flow from operations. The effort maximizes resource usage by shifting fleet assets from low return locations to high return locations. Operations that fail to yield desired returns are closed, or downsized. United Rentals has also reduced the scope of equipment sales tied to its contractor supplies business. In 2009 the company cut its rental locations by nearly 9% and headcount by almost 20%.

United Rentals champions the equipment-rental industry in North America by uniting with its mom-and-pop rivals; the company has purchased more than 200 other leasing firms since its founding. In 2008 the company acquired U-Rent-It. Because of its size, United Rentals rallies more resources over smaller businesses.

United Rental's joint ventures also give it a competitive edge. In mid-2010 it agreed to form a partnership with Fluor Corporation's AMECO unit (construction equipment and tools) in order to expand its presence in the energy market and to offer more comprehensive products to oil and gas customers along the Gulf Coast.

Operating efficiencies are also ramped up through consolidation of functions, including payroll and accounting. In order to manage the age, composition and size of its fleet, the company routinely sells used rental equipment and invests in new equipment. Also on the company's sale rack are equipment and supplies that no longer generate high demand. The company acts as a dealer of new equipment for many leading equipment makers like DeWalt, Honda USA, and Genie Industries. At most branches United Rentals sells various supplies and merchandise and offers repair and maintenance services.

Although United Rentals' customers range from *FORTUNE* 500 companies to small businesses and homeowners, it targets larger customers, which tend to rent for longer terms and are timely in payment. Based on this platform, it exited its traffic control business in 2007 for $85 million to HTS Acquisition, an entity formed by Wynnchurch Capital Partners and Oak Hill Special Opportunities Fund.

Investment firm BlackRock holds a 10% stake in the rental business.

HISTORY

Bradley Jacobs had made a fortune in the garbage business, having used United Waste Systems as a roll-up company to buy small trash-hauling firms in that fragmented industry. Flush with cash after he sold United Waste Systems in 1997 to USA Waste Services (now Waste Management), Jacobs launched the same roll-up strategy to consolidate the equipment-rental industry. He and his management team bought six leasing companies and started United Rentals. The company, which went public in 1997, had acquired 38 rental companies in 20 states by mid-1998.

United Rentals landed its biggest rival — U.S. Rentals — that year. U.S. Rentals had been founded in 1957, and by the 1960s it had become part of Leasing Enterprises, which was buying rental yards in western states. Richard Colburn bought a majority stake in 1975 and became the company's chairman. Leasing Enterprises and U.S. Rentals merged as U.S. Rentals; by 1984 Colburn owned the entire company. Between 1992 and 1995, U.S. Rentals bought 13 yards and opened 12 more. In 1997 U.S. Rentals went public and added 43 locations, expanding into the midwestern and southeastern US.

United Rentals bought U.S. Rentals for $1.1 billion in stock and assumed debt in 1998, forming the largest equipment-rental company in North America. Colburn quit, and Jacobs became chairman and CEO. In 1999 United Rentals continued its consolidation strategy, buying more than 60 competitors and moving into traffic-safety equipment rental. The next year it offered to buy a majority stake in lessor Neff Corp. for $37 million in stock and $277 million in debt, but the deal fell through in 2001. However, by 2001 the company had acquired more than 200 companies in four years.

In 2002 the company continued its growth-by-acquisition strategy, acquiring S&R Equipment, an equipment-rental unit of construction giant Fluor. It also acquired the trench shoring business (with 34 branches in 12 states) of rival NES Rentals for about $110 million. In 2003 chairman and CEO Bradley Jacobs stepped down from the position of CEO for the company. COO Wayland Hicks was his replacement.

The company was forced to delay its financial statements for 2004 due to an SEC investigation into accounting discrepancies. The problem reached a head in the summer of 2005 when the board of directors fired president and CFO John Milne, one of United Rentals' founding officers, after Milne declined to answer specific questions about the investigation.

Hicks retired as CEO in June 2007, and COO Michael Kneeland was named as his interim replacement. In August, Jacobs stepped down as chairman. In 2008 Kneeland was designated by the board as the company's president and CEO, and additionally was appointed to the board. Also that year United Rentals reached a deal with the SEC, agreeing to pay a civil penalty of $14 million, without admitting or denying any wrongdoing.

EXECUTIVES

Chairman: Jenne K. Britell, age 67
President, CEO, and Director: Michael J. Kneeland, age 56, $1,108,731 total compensation
EVP and CFO: William B. Plummer, age 51, $747,580 total compensation
SVP, General Counsel, and Corporate Secretary: Jonathan M. Gottsegen, age 43, $658,799 total compensation
SVP Trench Safety, Power, and HVAC: Paul I. McDonnell
SVP Operations: Matthew J. (Matt) Flannery, age 45
VP and CIO: Kenneth E. (Ken) DeWitt, age 60, $472,239 total compensation
VP, Controller, and Principal Accounting Officer: John J. Fahey, age 43, $699,522 total compensation
VP Sales: Joseph A. (Joe) Dixon, age 52, $478,072 total compensation
VP Corporate Systems: Daniel T. Higgins
VP and CTO: Patrick A. Stephens
VP Human Resources: Craig A. Pintoff
VP Service and Maintenance: Bruce W. Lafky
VP Risk Management: Raymond J. Alletto
VP Strategy and Planning: Kenneth B. Mettel
VP Supply Chain: Dale A. Asplund
VP and Treasurer: Irene Moshouris
VP Business Development: Ned Graham
VP Corporate Communications and Investor Relations: Fred B. Bratman
Auditors: Ernst & Young LLP

LOCATIONS

HQ: United Rentals, Inc.
5 Greenwich Office Park, Greenwich, CT 06831
Phone: 203-622-3131   **Fax:** 203-622-6080
Web: www.ur.com

2009 Sales

	$ mil.	% of total
US	2,046	87
Other countries (primarily Canada)	312	13
Total	**2,358**	**100**

PRODUCTS/OPERATIONS

2009 Sales

	$ mil.	% of total
General rentals	2,202	93
Trench safety, pump & power	156	7
Total	**2,358**	**100**

2009 Sales

	$ mil.	% of total
Equipment rental	1,830	77
Rental equipment sales	229	10
Contractor supply sales	121	5
New equipment sales	86	4
Service & other	92	4
Total	**2,358**	**100**

Selected Products

Aerial lifts
Backhoes
Barricades
Compressors
Cones
Contractor supplies
Ditching equipment
Earth-moving equipment
Forklifts
Generators
Hand tools
Heaters
Light towers
Material-handling equipment
Message boards
Pavement-marking systems
Portable power units
Power washers
Pumps
Skid-steer loaders
Trench shields
Warning lights
Water pumps

COMPETITORS

AMECO
Atlas Lift Truck Rentals
Case Power & Equipment
Hertz
Neff
NES Rentals
RDO Equipment
RSC Equipment Rental
Sunbelt Rentals
Ziegler inc

HISTORICAL FINANCIALS

Company Type: Public

Income Statement				FYE: December 31
	REVENUE ($ mil.)	NET INCOME ($ mil.)	NET PROFIT MARGIN	EMPLOYEES
12/09	2,358	(62)	—	8,000
12/08	3,267	(704)	—	9,900
12/07	3,731	362	9.7%	10,900
12/06	3,640	224	6.2%	12,000
12/05	3,563	187	5.2%	13,400
Annual Growth	**(9.8%)**	**—**	**—**	**(12.1%)**

2009 Year-End Financials

Debt ratio: —
Return on equity: —
Cash ($ mil.): 169
Current ratio: 1.53
Long-term debt ($ mil.): 2,950

No. of shares (mil.): 61
Dividends
   Yield: —
   Payout: —
Market value ($ mil.): 594

Stock History

NYSE: URI

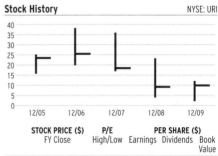

	STOCK PRICE ($) FY Close	P/E High/Low		PER SHARE ($) Earnings	Dividends	Book Value
12/09	9.81	—	—	(1.02)	—	(0.31)
12/08	9.12	—	—	(12.62)	—	(0.48)
12/07	18.36	11	5	3.25	—	33.34
12/06	25.43	18	10	2.06	—	25.41
12/05	23.39	14	9	1.80	—	20.30
Annual Growth	**(19.5%)**	**—**	**—**	**—**	**—**	**—**

United States Cellular

United States Cellular takes calls from sea to shining sea. Doing business as U.S. Cellular, the company provides wireless phone service to about 6 million customers in more than two dozen states in the US, largely in the Midwest and the South, where it has nearly 4 million customers. Its products and services — marketed directly, through the Internet, and from about 400 retail stores — include mobile messaging, prepaid calling, international long distance, mobile Internet, and directory assistance. U.S. Cellular service is also sold through contracts with resellers. The company offers phones from HTC, LG Electronics, Research In Motion, and Samsung Electronics, among other vendors.

U.S. Cellular is taking steps to improve its operational systems and reduce future costs by upgrading its billing, customer support, and service provisioning systems. The company is also expanding and upgrading its wireless network to reach more callers and better handle the increased data demands driven by rising customer adoption of smartphones. It hopes that more robust customer management systems and better network performance will enable it to retain and add subscribers amid brisk competition from other national and regional wireless carriers.

While U.S. Cellular's subscribers and revenues decreased somewhat in 2009, its income was up for the year over 2008. Results were lower in 2008 due largely to impairment losses incurred from older wireless spectrum licenses.

Jack Rooney retired in 2010; he had joined U.S. Cellular as president and CEO in 2000. The company hired the executive recruiting firm of Spencer Stuart to help find a successor for Rooney. Mary Dillon, EVP and global chief marketing officer for McDonald's Corporation, was named to succeed Rooney as president and CEO.

Telephone and Data Systems owns 82% of U.S. Cellular.

HISTORY

LeRoy Carlson, a Chicago-based investor, formed Telephone and Data Systems (TDS) in 1969 by consolidating the rural phone companies he owned. In the early 1980s TDS began acquiring cellular licenses, including the rights to operate 5% of the Los Angeles market. Getting a jumpstart on the Bells, TDS created United States Cellular as a subsidiary in 1983.

United States Cellular commenced operations in Knoxville, Tennessee, and Tulsa, Oklahoma, in 1985. Three years later TDS took the company public and reduced its stake to 82%. Belgian cable television operator Coditel was an initial investor.

Hefty startup and acquisition costs kept the company from making a profit until 1993. After moving into the black, it began selling its phones (purchased from suppliers) at kiosks in Wal-Mart stores in 1995. Meanwhile, it continued to add networks: In 1995 and 1996 United States Cellular added markets in Arizona, Florida, Iowa, Texas, and Virginia.

In 1997 United States Cellular traded its controlling interests in 10 markets, primarily in Indiana and Kentucky, for BellSouth's controlling interests in 12 markets in Illinois and Wisconsin (including Milwaukee). That year the firm

also began converting its network to digital technologies (both TDMA, time division multiple access, and the newer CDMA, code division multiple access).

In 1998 United States Cellular acquired majority interests in six more markets. That year the firm also sold several minority interests in markets in which it did not operate to Vodafone. The following year the company introduced a new logo and began doing business as U.S. Cellular. Also in 1999 it began providing CDPD (cellular digital packet data) service, which allows for data transmission over cellular networks, to police departments and government agencies in Illinois.

The company agreed in 2001 to acquire PCS licenses in Illinois, Iowa, and Nebraska from McLeodUSA for $74 million to bolster its Midwest operations. It purchased PrimeCo Wireless Communications in a 2002 deal valued at $610 million, gaining entrance into the Chicagoland market, as well as Bloomington-Normal, Champaign-Urbana, Decatur, and Springfield, Illinois, with expanded service to Peoria and Rockford, Illinois. Additionally, U.S. Cellular provided service to South Bend and Fort Wayne, Indiana, and Benton Harbor, Michigan.

In a 2003 swap agreement with AT&T Wireless, the company acquired wireless licenses and properties in 13 states in the Midwest and northeastern US in exchange for assets in northern Florida and southern Georgia.

U.S. Cellular in 2008 exchanged surplus wireless spectrum licenses covering parts of Illinois for licenses held by Sprint Nextel for areas of Oklahoma, West Virginia, Maryland, and Iowa.

EXECUTIVES

Chairman: LeRoy T. (Ted) Carlson Jr., age 63
President, CEO, and Director: Mary N. Dillon, age 48
EVP Finance, CFO, and Treasurer: Steven T. Campbell, age 59, $1,310,033 total compensation
EVP and Chief Human Resources Officer:
Jeffrey J. (Jeff) Childs, age 53,
$1,186,746 total compensation
EVP Engineering and CTO: Michael S. (Mike) Irizarry, age 48, $1,698,566 total compensation
EVP Operations: Alan D. Ferber, age 42
VP Organizational Learning and Chief Teaching Officer: Thomas J. Griffin, age 52
VP Public Affairs and Communications:
Karen C. Ehlers
VP Financial and Real Estate Services:
Thomas (Tom) Weber
VP Customer Service: R. Lynn Costlow
VP Information Technology Delivery: John M. Cregier
VP Legal and Regulatory Affairs: John C. Gockley, age 54
VP National Network Operations: Kevin R. Lowell
VP Financial Planning and Analysis: Jeffrey S. Hoersch, age 43
VP Corporate Relations, Telephone and Data Systems: Jane W. McCahon
VP Marketing and Sales Operations: Edward C. Perez
Chief Accounting Officer and Director; EVP and CFO, Telephone & Data Systems: Kenneth R. (Ken) Meyers, age 56
Auditors: PricewaterhouseCoopers LLP

LOCATIONS

HQ: United States Cellular Corporation
8410 W. Bryn Mawr, Ste. 700, Chicago, IL 60631
Phone: 773-399-8900   **Fax:** 773-399-8936
Web: www.uscellular.com

COMPETITORS

AT&T Mobility	MetroPCS
Boost Mobile	Sprint Nextel
Cellco	T-Mobile USA
CenturyTel	Virgin Mobile USA
Leap Wireless	

HISTORICAL FINANCIALS

Company Type: Public

Income Statement

FYE: December 31

	REVENUE ($ mil.)	NET INCOME ($ mil.)	NET PROFIT MARGIN	EMPLOYEES
12/09	4,215	216	5.1%	9,200
12/08	4,243	33	0.8%	8,470
12/07	3,946	315	8.0%	8,400
12/06	3,473	180	5.2%	8,100
12/05	3,036	135	4.4%	7,700
Annual Growth	8.5%	12.5%	—	4.6%

2009 Year-End Financials

Debt ratio: 25.5%
Return on equity: 6.5%
Cash ($ mil.): 294
Current ratio: 1.56
Long-term debt ($ mil.): 868

No. of shares (mil.): 86
Dividends
  Yield: —
  Payout: —
Market value ($ mil.): 3,654

Stock History

NYSE: USM

	STOCK PRICE ($) FY Close	P/E High/Low	PER SHARE ($) Earnings	Dividends	Book Value
12/09	42.41	19 12	2.48	—	39.51
12/08	43.24	224 72	0.38	—	37.22
12/07	84.10	29 19	3.56	—	37.09
12/06	69.59	35 24	2.04	—	34.74
12/05	49.40	37 27	1.54	—	31.93
Annual Growth	(3.7%)	— —	12.7%	—	5.5%

United States Steel

Steel crazy after all these years, Pittsburgh-based United States Steel is the nation's #2 integrated steelmaker (behind ArcelorMittal). The company operates mills throughout the Midwest in the US; in Ontario, Canada; and in Serbia and Slovakia. U.S. Steel makes sheet and semifinished steel, tubular and plate steel, and tin products; its annual production capacity is more than 30 million tons of raw steel (though its actual production rate is less than that). The company's customers are primarily in the automotive, construction, chemical, and steel service center industries. In addition, U.S. Steel offers services such as mineral resource management and engineering and consulting.

After making a number of acquisitions in the middle of the last decade, the company had built up its capacity significantly. But, as the global economic nightmare hit several of its target markets especially hard — the automotive and construction industries, for example — U.S. Steel severely curtailed production.

The company's European operations consist of two companies, U.S. Steel Serbia (which produces limestone, sheets, strip mill plate, and tin) and U.S. Steel Kosice in Slovakia (which manufactures sheet, strip mill plate, tin mill, tubular, and specialty steel products).

Other units and subsidiaries include U.S. Steel Canada, which maintains the company's two facilities in Ontario, and U.S. Steel's tubular steel operations, which serve the energy industry primarily, providing both seamless and electric resistance welded (ERW) products (commonly called oil country tubular goods, or OCTG). U.S. Steel also owns both iron ore mining and coke production operations that provide the raw materials used in the manufacture of steel. The company, too, participates in joint ventures with a number of its industry competitors. They include the world's #1 steelmaker ArcelorMittal, Japanese producer Kobe Steel, Korean giant POSCO, Russian metals company Severstal, and US steel service center Worthington Industries.

U.S. Steel Canada sold its Bar Mill and Bloom and Billet Mill at its Ontario operations to Max Aicher (North America) in 2010. The deal will allow U.S. Steel Canada to focus on core operations at its Hamilton Works facility.

HISTORY

United States Steel Corporation was conceived through a 1901 merger of 10 steel companies that combined their furnaces, ore deposits, railroad companies, and shipping lines. The deal involved industrial pioneers Andrew Carnegie, Charles Schwab, Elbert Gary, and J. P. Morgan.

Morgan had helped organize the Federal Steel Company in 1898, and he then wanted to create a centralized trust to dominate the soaring steel market. Carnegie owned the largest US steel company at the time, Carnegie Steel, but wanted to retire.

In 1900 Schwab, Carnegie Steel's president, outlined the idea of the steel trust based on a merger of the Carnegie and Federal steel companies. Morgan asked Schwab to persuade Carnegie to sell his steel mills and name his price. Morgan didn't haggle when Carnegie responded that he would sell for almost half a billion dollars. The Carnegie-Morgan combination created the world's first billion-dollar company. It produced 67% of the country's steel in its first year (its steel complex and the Indiana town where it was located were named after Gary, who was CEO until 1927).

The company boomed during WWI and WWII. But its market share fell to about 30% by the 1950s, although it set new profit records in 1955. During the 1970s prospects for long-term growth in steel became dismal in light of rising costs, foreign competition, and competitive pricing.

In 1982 U.S. Steel doubled its size when it bought Marathon Oil, a major integrated energy company with huge oil and gas reserves in the US and abroad. It continued to cut back its steelmaking capacity, laying off 100,000 employees, closing steel mills, and selling off assets.

The company bought Texas Oil & Gas in 1986 and renamed itself USX Corporation to reflect the decreasing role of steel in its business. Also that year corporate raider Carl Icahn, USX's largest single shareholder, unsuccessfully tried to get the company to sell its steel operations. In 1988 USX bought 49% of Transtar, a group of rail and water transport providers. (It purchased the remaining stake in 2001, making Transtar a wholly owned subsidiary.)

Stockholders in 1991 approved splitting the company into two separate units under the USX umbrella: U.S. Steel and Marathon. During the 1990s U.S. Steel continued to close steelmaking facilities. In 1992 USX joined five other leading US steel producers in a suit against subsidized foreign steelmakers.

The company agreed to pay $106 million in fines and improvements in 1996 to settle charges of air pollution violations involving its Indiana plant. U.S. Steel began upgrading several of its facilities in 1997 and 1998 and entered into a number of domestic and foreign joint ventures, including one in Slovakia and another in Mexico. Seeing prices drop in 1998 and 1999, the company cut production and joined other US steelmakers in charging rivals in Brazil, Japan, and Russia with unlawfully dumping low-priced steel in the US.

In early 2001 USX spun off its steel operations as United States Steel Corporation; the remaining energy businesses begain operating as Marathon Oil Corporation. The breakup left the company with over $1.3 billion in debt.

U.S. Steel, along with other US steelmakers, received concessions (40% import tariffs and assistance with its huge retiree health-care costs) from the Bush administration. In early 2002 the administration imposed tariffs between 8 to 30 percent providing temporary relief to U.S. Steel and the US steel industry. The Bush administration rejected any retiree bailout plan and in December 2003 ended the tariffs 16 months ahead of schedule.

In 2003 U.S. Steel made the monumental move to purchase National Steel for roughly $1.1 billion in cash. With the combined manufacturing capabilities of National Steel and U.S. Steel, the company's raw steel production came in at around 20 million tons of steel annually, both domestically and internationally, which made it the nation's largest steel producer until the formation of Mittal Steel USA in 2005. The year 2003 also saw the expansion of U.S. Steel's European businesses with the acquisition of Serbian steelmaker Sartid.

U.S. Steel again jumped into the industrywide consolidation game in 2007, when it spent a combined $3.3 billion to buy tubular goods maker Lone Star Technologies and the former Stelco in separate deals.

EXECUTIVES

Chairman and CEO: John P. Surma Jr., age 55, $3,561,001 total compensation
EVP and COO: John H. Goodish, age 61, $7,703,149 total compensation
EVP and CFO: Gretchen R. Haggerty, age 54, $3,075,901 total compensation
SVP Strategic Planning, Business Services, and Administration: David H. (Dave) Lohr, age 56, $2,633,343 total compensation
SVP Corporate Affairs and General Counsel: James D. Garraux, age 57, $2,615,395 total compensation
SVP North American Flat-Roll Operations: Michael S. Williams, age 49
SVP, European Operations; President, U. S. Steel Kosice: George F. Babcoke, age 54

VP Human Resources: Susan M. (Sue) Suver, age 50
VP Tubular Operations; President, U.S. Steel Tubular Products: Douglas R. Matthews, age 44
VP Sales: Joseph R. (Joe) Scherrbaum Jr., age 53
VP Procurement, Raw Material, and Real Estate: Michael J. Hatcher, age 52
VP and Controller: Gregory A. Zovko, age 49
VP Supply Chain and Customer Service: Anton Lukac, age 48
VP Engineering and Technology: Anthony R. Bridge, age 56
Auditors: PricewaterhouseCoopers LLP

LOCATIONS

HQ: United States Steel Corporation
600 Grant St., Pittsburgh, PA 15219
Phone: 412-433-1121   **Fax:** 412-433-5733
Web: www.ussteel.com

2009 Sales

	$ mil.	% of total
North America	8,104	73
Europe	2,944	27
Adjustments	(2)	—
Total	**11,048**	**100**

2009 Raw Steel Production

	Net tons (thou.)	% of total
North America		
Gary, Indiana	5,379	33
Mon Valley, Pennsylvania	2,460	15
Fairfield, Alabama	1,586	9
Granite City, Illinois	906	5
Hamilton, Ontario	564	3
Great Lakes, Michigan	473	3
Lake Erie, Ontario	356	2
Europe		
U.S. Steel Kosice	3,897	23
U.S. Steel Serbia	1,180	7
Total	**16,801**	**100**

PRODUCTS/OPERATIONS

2009 Sales

	$ mil.	% of total
Flat-rolled	6,814	62
US Steel Europe	2,944	27
Tubular Products	1,216	11
Other	74	—
Total	**11,048**	**100**

Selected Subsidiaries

Acero Prime S. R. L de CV (44%, steel processing and warehousing)
Delray Connecting Railroad Company (transportation)
Double Eagle Steel Coating Company (50%, steel processing, with Severstal)
PRO-TEC Coating Co. (50%, steel processing, with Kobe Steel, Ltd.)
Transtar, Inc. (transportation)
U. S. Steel Kosice sro (steelmaking, Slovakia)
USS-POSCO Industries (50%, steel processing, with Pohang Iron & Steel Co., Ltd.)
Worthington Specialty Processing (50%, steel processing, with Worthington Industries Inc.)

COMPETITORS

AK Steel Holding Corporation	Nucor
Allegheny Technologies	POSCO
ArcelorMittal	Salzgitter
BÖHLER-UDDEHOLM	Severstal North America
BlueScope Steel	Simec
Carpenter Technology	SSAB North America
Gerdau Ameristeel	SSAB Svenskt
JFE Holdings	Steel Dynamics
Kobe Steel	Ternium
Nippon Steel	ThyssenKrupp Steel

HISTORICAL FINANCIALS

Company Type: Public

Income Statement

FYE: December 31

	REVENUE ($ mil.)	NET INCOME ($ mil.)	NET PROFIT MARGIN	EMPLOYEES
12/09	11,048	(1,401)	—	43,000
12/08	23,754	2,112	8.9%	49,000
12/07	16,873	879	5.2%	28,000
12/06	15,715	1,374	8.7%	44,000
12/05	14,039	910	6.5%	46,000
Annual Growth	(5.8%)	—	—	(1.7%)

2009 Year-End Financials

Debt ratio: 71.5%
Return on equity: —
Cash ($ mil.): 1,218
Current ratio: 2.03
Long-term debt ($ mil.): 3,345

No. of shares (mil.): 144
Dividends
Yield: 0.8%
Payout: —
Market value ($ mil.): 7,913

Stock History

NYSE: X

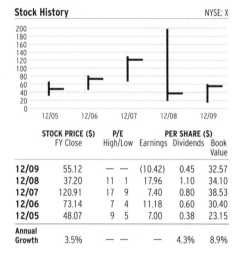

	STOCK PRICE ($) FY Close	P/E High/Low		PER SHARE ($) Earnings	Dividends	Book Value
12/09	55.12	—	—	(10.42)	0.45	32.57
12/08	37.20	11	1	17.96	1.10	34.10
12/07	120.91	17	9	7.40	0.80	38.53
12/06	73.14	7	4	11.18	0.60	30.40
12/05	48.07	9	5	7.00	0.38	23.15
Annual Growth	3.5%	—	—	—	4.3%	8.9%

United Stationers

Don't think that United Stationers is just another paper pusher. The company is the leading wholesale distributor of office supplies and equipment in North America, offering more than 100,000 products to more than 25,000 customers. Through subsidiaries United Stationers Supply (USS), Lagasse, and ORS Nasco, United Stationers supplies such items as business machines, computer products and peripherals, janitorial supplies, and office products and furniture. It also offers office furniture for such markets as education and health care. United Stationers sells primarily to resellers through catalogs and over the Internet, as well as through its direct sales force.

Sales of technology products, including printers and print cartridges, data storage devices, and other computer peripherals, account for more than one-third of the company's sales, making United Stationers one of the top computer products distributors in the country. Traditional office supplies make up about 27% of the company's business. Office supply retailer Staples accounted for some 11% of 2009 sales.

As part of its key merchandising strategy, United Stationers keeps its costs low through high-volume purchasing. It orders products from more than 1,000 manufacturers. Some 20% of the company's purchases were made from Hewlett-Packard in 2009.

To strengthen its foothold in product distribution, United Stationers has acquired the assets of its rivals. Most recently, the company's USS subsidiary acquired Denver-based MBS Dev, a software solutions provider to business products resellers for $15 million in early 2010. The purchase is expected to bolster the company's online merchandising and marketing capabilities. In 2008 United Stationers purchased Emco Distribution, a New Jersey-based business product distributor, for $15 million. It acquired ORS Nasco, a wholesale distributor of industrial supplies, for about $180 million in 2007.

Neuberger Berman is owner of about 10% of the company.

HISTORY

Morris Wolf and Harry Hecktman, former office supply salesmen, and Israel Kriloff, a grocer, purchased Utility Supply Company (founded in 1906) and began selling office supplies in downtown Chicago in 1921. Weathering the Depression, Utility Supply's business grew steadily during the 1930s. In 1935 the company published its first catalog, and it opened its first retail store in downtown Chicago two years later. The partners bought out Kriloff in 1939.

WWII created a scarcity of raw materials, and Utility Supply had difficulty in obtaining merchandise. The company tried selling non-office products, unsuccessfully. Fortunately, the war's end brought an end to the inventory drought. During the postwar era, Utility Supply began mailing a series of catalogs to retailers nationwide. By 1948 mail-order business accounted for 40% of sales. A wholesale division to sell products to independent resellers was created in the 1950s.

In 1960 the company adopted the name United Stationers Supply, and the retail stores became the Utility Stationery Stores. Business increased as independent retailers began to appreciate the advantages of ordering through a wholesaler instead of a manufacturer — purchasing goods on an as-needed basis. Howard Wolf, the founder's son, became CEO in 1967 and began emphasizing computers and automation to track inventory and costs.

By 1970 wholesale trade accounted for about two-thirds of sales. United Stationers introduced a series of abridged catalogs targeting specific groups and marketing segments, such as furniture and electronics. The following year United Stationers developed regional redistribution centers that offered overnight delivery. The company sold its retail outlets in 1978.

Three years later United Stationers went public. During the 1980s the advent of warehouse clubs and office supply superstores threatened independent retailers. The company developed marketing concepts to help its independent resellers, even as it aggressively targeted mail-order houses and superstores. The downsizing trend in the late 1980s caused the corporate market to shrink, and United Stationers lowered prices; it instituted a decentralization plan in 1990.

The next year the company expanded into Canada, opening its first non-US subsidiary, and it acquired archrival Stationers Distributing and its distribution centers across the US in 1992. In 1994 it established its United Facility Supply unit to distribute maintenance supplies.

Investment firm Wingate Partners, which controlled rival Associated Stationers, bought United Stationers in 1995 and combined the operations of the two companies under the United Stationers name. United Stationers acquired janitorial supplies wholesaler Lagasse Bros. in 1996. In 1998 the company acquired the US and Mexican operations of Abitibi-Consolidated, including Azerty. (It acquired Azerty Canada in 2000.)

United Stationers launched a venture with E-Commerce Industries in 1999 to help customers sell products over the Internet. The next year the company started The Order People, a third-party call center fulfillment business aimed at online retailers; however, the dot-com bust and higher losses than planned led United Stationers to curtail operations in 2001. Also that year it bought Peerless Paper Mills (merging the wholesale distributor of janitorial and paper products into Lagasse).

The company sold its Canadian operations in 2006, following an accounting scandal. United Stationers discovered that its Canadian operation was incorrectly accounting for supplier allowances and other receivables.

EXECUTIVES

Chairman: Frederick B. (Fred) Hegi Jr., age 66
CEO and Director: Richard W. Gochnauer, age 60, $2,351,597 total compensation
President and COO: P. Cody Phipps, age 48, $1,016,244 total compensation
SVP and CFO: Victoria J. Reich, age 52, $1,122,057 total compensation
SVP Sales and Marketing: Patrick T. (Pat) Collins, age 49, $656,279 total compensation
SVP and CIO: S. David Bent, age 49
SVP Human Resources: Barbara Kennedy, age 43
SVP Inventory Management: Ronald C. Berg, age 50
SVP Merchandising: James K. Fahey, age 59
SVP, General Counsel, and Secretary: Eric A. Blanchard, age 53
SVP Trade Development: Joseph R. Templet, age 62
SVP National Accounts and Channel Management: Jeffrey G. Howard, age 54
SVP Operations: Timothy P. Connolly, age 46
VP, Controller, and Chief Accounting Officer: Kenneth M. Nickel, age 42
Group President, LagasseSweet and ORS Nasco: Stephen A. (Steve) Schultz, age 43, $806,731 total compensation
President, United Stationers Supply: Todd Shelton
Investor Relations Specialist: Mary Disclafani
Auditors: Cowan, Gunteski & Co., P.A.

LOCATIONS

HQ: United Stationers Inc.
1 Parkway N. Blvd., Ste. 100, Deerfield, IL 60015
Phone: 847-627-7000   **Fax:** 847-627-7001
Web: www.unitedstationers.com/home

2009 Sales

	% of total
Domestic	98
International	2
Total	**100**

PRODUCTS/OPERATIONS

2009 Sales

	$ mil.	% of total
Technology products	1,636	35
Traditional office products	1,282	27
Janitorial & breakroom supplies	1,117	24
Office furniture	354	7
Industrial supplies	231	5
Freight revenue	81	2
Other	9	—
Total	**4,710**	**100**

Selected Products

Technology products
  Computer monitors
  Copiers and fax machines
  Data storage
  Digital cameras
  Printers and printer cartridges
Traditional office products
  Calendars
  Organizers
  Paper products
  Writing instruments
Office furniture
  Computer furniture
  Leather chairs
  Vertical and lateral file cabinets
  Wooden and steel desks
Janitorial and sanitation products
  Food service disposables
  Janitorial and sanitation supplies
  Paper and packaging supplies
  Safety and security items
Industrial supplies
  Hand and power tools
  Safety and security supplies
  Janitorial equipment and supplies
  Maintenance, repair and operations items
  Oil field and welding supplies

COMPETITORS

Corporate Express NV	Newell Rubbermaid
D&H Distributing	SED International
Gould Paper	S.P. Richards
Ingram Micro	Supplies Network

HISTORICAL FINANCIALS

Company Type: Public

Income Statement

FYE: December 31

	REVENUE ($ mil.)	NET INCOME ($ mil.)	NET PROFIT MARGIN	EMPLOYEES
12/09	4,710	101	2.1%	5,700
12/08	4,987	98	2.0%	5,800
12/07	4,646	107	2.3%	6,100
12/06	4,547	132	2.9%	5,700
12/05	4,409	98	2.2%	6,000
Annual Growth	1.7%	0.9%	—	(1.3%)

2009 Year-End Financials

Debt ratio: 62.5%	No. of shares (mil.): 23
Return on equity: 15.9%	Dividends
Cash ($ mil.): 19	Yield: 0.0%
Current ratio: 2.28	Payout: —
Long-term debt ($ mil.): 442	Market value ($ mil.): 1,329

Stock History

NASDAQ (GS): USTR

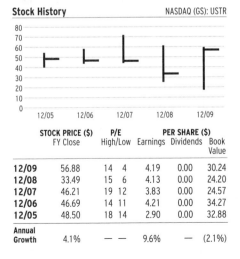

	STOCK PRICE ($) FY Close	P/E High/Low		PER SHARE ($) Earnings	Dividends	Book Value
12/09	56.88	14	4	4.19	0.00	30.24
12/08	33.49	15	6	4.13	0.00	24.20
12/07	46.21	19	12	3.83	0.00	24.57
12/06	46.69	14	11	4.21	0.00	34.27
12/05	48.50	18	14	2.90	0.00	32.88
Annual Growth	4.1%	—	—	9.6%	—	(2.1%)

United Technologies

United Technologies (UTC) lifts you up and cools you down. Through flagships Carrier, Otis, Pratt & Whitney, and Sikorsky, UTC makes and supplies a global slate of technologies and services to the building systems and aerospace markets. Carrier is the world's largest maker of HVAC units. Otis is the world's largest elevator and escalator manufacturer. Pratt & Whitney is a leading global supplier of commercial and military engines, while Sikorsky makes helicopters. Hamilton Sundstrand is a leading producer of engine controls, auxiliary power units, propellers, and flight systems for military, commercial, and space industries.

Worsening business conditions for the commercial aerospace and construction markets forced UTC to initiate a $830 million restructuring program, adopting a "less is more" strategy. All of the company's subsidiaries were streamlined to cut costs; manufacturing, service and sales facilities were consolidated, and in some cases moved to regions with lower labor costs; and its workforce was cut by 14,600 employees.

UTC's commercial and industrial businesses take the brunt of swings in construction activity, interest rates, and access to credit, as well as raw materials and energy costs — all of which were negatively impacted by the global recession. The recession had a diverse impact on the company's individual sectors. While its commercial and industrial division saw sales drop, demand remained strong for its military aerospace sector — particularly Sikorsky, which makes Black Hawk and Medevac helicopters. The US government accounts for about 18% of sales, primarily from its Pratt & Whitney, Hamilton Sundstrand, and Sikorsky units.

As economic recovery is felt, the company is venturing out in 2010 to take advantage of acquisition opportunities. UTC bought GE Security, the electronic security and fire safety division of GE, for about $1.82 billion. The deal adds commercial and residential products and a strong North American presence . UTC also bought GST Holdings Limited (GST), a China-based fire alarm provider, furthering its global reach in the fire safety industry.

In addition to expansion in China, UTC also sees Argentina, Brazil, India, Russia, and South Africa as areas of interest. Sikorsky Aircraft is scoring work in the Middle East. In mid-2009 the helicopter-maker agreed to joint control of a new venture with United Arab Emirates investment fund Mubadala Development.

HISTORY

In 1925 Frederick Rentschler and George Mead founded Pratt & Whitney Aircraft (P&W) to develop aircraft engines. P&W merged with Seattle-based Boeing Airplane Company and Chance Vought Corporation in 1929 to form United Aircraft & Transport. United Aircraft soon bought aviation companies Hamilton Aero, Standard Steel Propeller, and Sikorsky.

In 1934, after congressional investigations led to new antitrust laws, United Aircraft split into three independent entities: United Airlines, Boeing Airplane Company, and United Aircraft. United Aircraft retained P&W and several other manufacturing interests.

During WWII United Aircraft produced half of all the engines used in US warplanes. Sikorsky

developed helicopters, and Vought made the Corsair and Cutlass planes. After a postwar decline in sales, the company retooled for jet engine production. United Aircraft spun off Chance Vought in 1954 and bought Norden-Ketay (aeronautical electronics) in 1958.

A design flaw in engines produced for Boeing 747s sent P&W on an expensive trip back to the drawing board in the late 1960s. A concerned board of directors appointed Harry Gray, a 17-year veteran of Litton Industries, as president in 1971. Gray transformed the company into a conglomerate; it adopted its present name in 1975.

To decrease UTC's dependence on government contracts, Gray diversified the company by acquiring Otis Elevator (1975) and Carrier (1979). Acquisitions expanded sales to $15.7 billion by 1986. Under pressure from his board, Gray tapped Bob Daniell to head the company in 1986. Gray retired a year later.

Daniell, a 25-year Sikorsky veteran, stressed profitability over growth and sold businesses, cut jobs, and changed management. UTC enjoyed record earnings in 1990. However, the next year reduced orders from the military and the auto and building industries resulted in UTC's first operating loss in 20 years.

UTC paid a $6 million fine in 1992 for hiring advisers to illegally inform it about competing bids for a Pentagon contract. The company sold its Norden radar unit and its stake in the Westland Helicopter Company in 1994. George David, UTC president and COO, became CEO that year (eventually replacing Daniell as chairman in 1997).

P&W introduced the most-powerful jet engine in history in 1995, and Sikorsky flew the prototype of the world's first radar-evading helicopter.

In 1996 Ford recalled 8.7 million vehicles — the most in its history — due to faulty auto ignition switches made by UT Automotive.

UTC bought Sundstrand (aerospace components) for $4.3 billion in 1999. Sundstrand's operations were rolled into UTC's Hamilton Standard unit to form Hamilton Sundstrand Corporation. The company sold its auto parts unit (headliners, door and instrument panels) to Lear for $2.3 billion. It paid more than $700 million for air-conditioning and heat-pump maker International Comfort Products. The purchases were accompanied by consolidation, primarily in the Otis and Carrier businesses. About 15,000 jobs were cut; the company's overall employee count dropped 17%.

UTC cut an additional 4,600 jobs in 2001. Restructuring continued in 2002 as UTC continued reducing costs and cut about 7,000 more jobs.

In 2003 UTC spent about $1.3 billion on acquisitions, including its purchase of security service provider Chubb plc. In 2004 UTC acquired British fire-fighting equipment maker Kidde PLC for $3 billion. In 2005 Pratt & Whitney bought up Boeing's Rocketdyne unit for around $700 million. Rocketdyne designed and manufactured rocket propulsion systems and made the rocket boosters for the Space Shuttle.

In mid-2006 UTC agreed to pay $283 million to the US Department of Defense to settle a contract accounting dispute with the government over Pratt & Whitney's cost accounting for engine parts on commercial engine collaboration programs from 1984 through 2004.

In 2007 UTC acquired the Initial Electronic Security Group of Rentokil Initial for £595 million ($1.2 billion). Louis Chênevert, who was named president and COO in 2006, was promoted to CEO in 2008, retaining the president's title. George David remained as chairman.

EXECUTIVES

Chairman, President, and CEO: Louis R. Chênevert, age 52, $20,501,712 total compensation
EVP; President, Commercial Companies: Ari Bousbib, age 48, $8,838,094 total compensation
SVP and CFO: Gregory J. Hayes, age 49, $5,956,747 total compensation
SVP Human Resources and Organization: J. Thomas Bowler Jr., age 57
SVP and General Counsel: Charles D. Gill Jr., age 45
SVP Science and Technology: J. Michael McQuade, age 53
SVP Government Affairs: Gregg Ward
VP, Secretary, and Associate General Counsel: Kathleen M. Hopko
VP Operations: Eileen P. Drake
VP and CIO: Nancy M. Davis
VP and Controller: Margaret M. (Peggy) Smyth, age 46
VP Transportation Business, UTC Power: Ken Stewart
VP and Treasurer: Thomas I. Rogan, age 57
President, Carrier: Geraud Darnis, age 50, $6,879,975 total compensation
President, Fire and Security: William M. (Bill) Brown, age 47, $4,889,311 total compensation
President, Sikorsky: Jeffrey P. (Jeff) Pino, age 55
President, Otis: Didier Michaud-Daniel, age 52
President, Pratt & Whitney: David P. Hess, age 54
President, Sikorsky Aerospace Services: David Adler
President, Sikorsky Global Helicopters and Chief Marketing Officer: Carey E. Bond
Auditors: PricewaterhouseCoopers LLP

LOCATIONS

HQ: United Technologies Corporation
1 Financial Plaza, Hartford, CT 06103
Phone: 860-728-7000   **Fax:** 860-565-5400
Web: www.utc.com

2009 Sales

	$ mil.	% of total
US	28,337	54
Europe	12,269	23
Asia/Pacific	7,138	13
Other regions	5,040	10
Adjustments	136	—
Total	**52,920**	**100**

PRODUCTS/OPERATIONS

2009 Sales

	$ mil.	% of total
Pratt & Whitney	12,577	24
Otis	11,779	22
Carrier	11,413	21
Sikorsky	6,318	12
Hamilton Sundstrand	5,599	11
UTC Fire & Security	5,531	10
Adjustments	(297)	—
Total	**52,920**	**100**

2009 Sales

	$ mil.	% of total
Products	37,332	71
Services	15,093	28
Financing & other	495	1
Total	**52,920**	**100**

Selected Operations, Products, and Services

Pratt & Whitney
  Commercial and military aircraft engines, parts, and services
  Geothermal power systems
  Industrial gas turbines
  Space propulsion systems
Otis
  Elevators
  Escalators
  Installation, maintenance, and repair services
  Moving sidewalks

Carrier
  Commercial and residential heating, ventilation, and air-conditioning (HVAC) equipment
  Commercial and transport refrigeration equipment
  HVAC replacement parts and services
  Micro-turbine-based HVAC and power systems
Sikorsky (commercial and military helicopters and maintenance)
Hamilton Sundstrand
  Aerospace equipment (engine and flight controls, environmental controls, space life support, propulsion systems)
  Industrial equipment (air compressors, fluid-handling equipment, metering devices)
  Space and defense fuel cell power plants
UTC Fire & Security
  Electronic security
  Fire detection
  Rapid response systems
  Security personnel services
  Security system monitoring services
UTC Power Systems (fuel cells for stationary and transportation applications)

COMPETITORS

AAR Corp.
AgustaWestland
BAE SYSTEMS
Boeing
DynCorp International
Eaton
Emerson Electric
GE
GenCorp
General Dynamics
Goodrich Corp.
Hitachi
Honeywell International
IDEX
Kaman
L-3 Communications
Lennox
Lockheed Martin
Middleby
Mitsubishi Electric
Northrop Grumman
Parker Hannifin
Precision Castparts
Raytheon
Rolls-Royce
SAFRAN
SANYO
Siemens AG
SPX
Textron
ThyssenKrupp
Tomkins
Trane Inc.
Tyco

HISTORICAL FINANCIALS

Company Type: Public

Income Statement

FYE: December 31

	REVENUE ($ mil.)	NET INCOME ($ mil.)	NET PROFIT MARGIN	EMPLOYEES
12/09	52,920	3,829	7.2%	206,700
12/08	58,681	4,689	8.0%	223,100
12/07	54,759	4,224	7.7%	225,600
12/06	47,829	3,732	7.8%	214,500
12/05	42,725	3,164	7.4%	222,200
Annual Growth	**5.5%**	**4.9%**	**—**	**(1.8%)**

2009 Year-End Financials

Debt ratio: 41.1%
Return on equity: 21.3%
Cash ($ mil.): 4,449
Current ratio: 1.29
Long-term debt ($ mil.): 8,257

No. of shares (mil.): 929
Dividends
  Yield: 2.2%
  Payout: 37.4%
Market value ($ mil.): 64,487

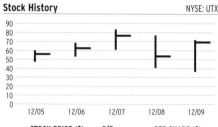

Stock History   NYSE: UTX

	STOCK PRICE ($) FY Close	P/E High/Low		PER SHARE ($) Earnings	Dividends	Book Value
12/09	69.41	17	9	4.12	1.54	21.60
12/08	53.60	15	9	4.90	1.35	17.13
12/07	76.54	19	14	4.27	1.17	22.99
12/06	62.52	18	15	3.71	1.01	18.62
12/05	55.91	19	16	3.03	0.88	18.29
Annual Growth	**5.6%**	**—**	**—**	**8.0%**	**15.0%**	**4.2%**

UnitedHealth Group

UnitedHealth Group wants to keep you connected with your health. A leading US health insurer, it offers a variety of plans and services to tens of millions of customers in the US. Its health care services segment manages HMO, PPO, and POS (point-of-service) plans, as well as various Medicare and Medicaid options, through UnitedHealthcare, AmeriChoice (for public-sector programs), and Ovations (for members of AARP). Large employer groups are served by UnitedHealthcare National Accounts. Its OptumHealth division offers vision and dental care and other products and services. Ingenix provides health care information, while the Prescription Solutions unit provides pharmacy benefit management services.

UnitedHealth is prospering in a market increasingly unfriendly to managed care in part by expanding into new regions through the purchase of smaller rivals and corporate health plans. UnitedHealth Group's sales are primarily composed of premiums derived from risk-based health insurance arrangements in which the premium is fixed, usually for a period of a year.

As a provider of workplace benefits, United-Health was particularly vulnerable to massive layoffs that occurred during the economic meltdown that occurred over the past couple of years. The company expects the decline to continue until the nation's unemployment rate begins to reverse course.

The highly acquisitive company bought up the northeastern US operations of rival Health Net to solidify its position in the region in 2009. The deal, which included health plans in Connecticut, New Jersey, and New York, was valued at close to $630 million.

UnitedHealth completed several large acquisitions in 2008, spending $730 million to purchase Fiserv's health-related businesses, including Fiserv Health (benefits administration for 2 million members), Avidyn Health (care facilitation), Fiserv Health Specialty Solutions (administration), and Innoviant Pharmacy Benefits Management. UnitedHealth also paid $980 million to acquire Unison Health Plans and used it to expand its AmeriChoice unit.

The company completed its controversial purchase of Nevada insurance provider Sierra Health Services for approximately $2.6 billion in 2008, gaining some 600,000 health plan members in the state and boosting UnitedHealth's position in the growing Southwest market. The acquisition took nearly a year to receive approval due to political opposition in Nevada and extended antitrust reviews.

At the start of 2009 UnitedHealth found its Ingenix subsidiary at the root of several class-action lawsuits filed by state attorneys general in Connecticut, New York, and Texas. The suits allege that information Ingenix provided to health insurers resulted in underpayments of out-of-network physicians, and placed undue financial burdens on customers. UnitedHealth reached a settlement in New York by agreeing to pay $50 million and stop using the Ingenix product.

HISTORY

Dr. Paul Ellwood became known as the Father of the HMO for his role as an early champion of the health care concept. As a neurology student in the 1950s, Ellwood recognized that applying business principles to medicine could minimize costs and make health care more affordable. Although the HMO was considered a radical approach to health care reform, Ellwood got Congress and the Nixon administration to approve his HMO model in 1970; the next year he hired Richard Burke to put the model into action. Burke established United HealthCare (UHC) in 1974 to manage the not-for-profit Physicians Health Plan of Minnesota (PHP). UHC incorporated in 1977.

The company bought HMOs and began managing others, operating 11 HMOs in 10 states by 1984, the year it went public. Its expansion continued with the purchases of HMOs Share Development (1985) and Peak Health Care (1986). Unfortunately, acquisitions and startups began to eat away at UHC's financial health. Meanwhile, Burke, CEO of both UHC and PHP, was accused by PHP doctors of having a conflict of interest after a change in the HMO's Medicare policy threatened to cut off patients from some member hospitals. Burke resigned in 1987 and was replaced by Kennett Simmons.

UHC lost nearly $16 million in 1987, largely from a restructuring that axed the company's Phoenix HMO, as well as startups in six other markets. In the late 1980s UHC adopted a new strategy of acquiring specialty companies that provided fee income. It also continued building its HMO network through acquisitions, hoping to gain critical mass in such varied markets as the Midwest and New England.

Physician William (Bill) McGuire was named UHC's chairman and CEO in 1991. The company's expansion accelerated in the 1990s with a string of purchases in the Midwest, but there were also divestitures. In 1994 UHC sold subsidiary Diversified Pharmaceutical Services, providing cash for still more purchases, including GenCare (St. Louis), Group Sales and Service of Puerto Rico, and MetraHealth.

The company in 1999 (now called United-Health Group) added UK-based contract research organization ClinPharm International to Ingenix. It also announced it would let doctors — not administrators — choose what treatment patients would get, partially because it was

spending more on care scrutiny than the practice saved. Nevertheless, many doctors claimed the process was still restrictive.

In 2000 the American Medical Association sued the company, claiming it used faulty data to reduce payments to member doctors.

To expand its Medicaid services business, the firm bought AmeriChoice in 2002. Golden Rule was acquired in late 2003 so UnitedHealth could enter the individual health insurance market by providing medical savings accounts. To increase its market share in the northeastern US, the company bought Oxford Health Plans that year.

The company acquired PacifiCare Health Systems in 2005. The $8.8 billion acquisition brought UnitedHealth 3 million more customers, including a strong foothold in the California Medicare market.

Bill McGuire became the focus of inquiry in 2006 over a scandal involving the back-dating of stock options awarded to him and other company executives. Following a board inquiry, McGuire was replaced by Stephen Hemsley, formerly the company's COO. The back-dating brouhaha continued to be a distraction for UnitedHealth, and in 2008 it opted to settle several related shareholder lawsuits by agreeing to pay more than $900 million.

EXECUTIVES

Chairman: Richard T. Burke Sr., age 66
President, CEO, and Director:
Stephen J. (Steve) Hemsley, age 57,
$8,901,916 total compensation
EVP and CFO: George L. (Mike) Mikan III, age 38,
$5,756,390 total compensation
EVP; President, Public and Senior Markets Group:
Anthony Welters, age 55,
$6,039,861 total compensation
EVP; CEO, Public and Senior Markets Group:
Larry C. Renfro, age 56, $6,770,671 total compensation
EVP; President, Enterprise Services Group:
William A. Munsell, age 57,
$5,716,168 total compensation
EVP; President, UnitedHealth Group Operations:
David S. Wichmann, age 47,
$4,638,870 total compensation
EVP; President, Global Health: Simon Stevens
EVP; President, UnitedHealthcare: Gail K. Boudreaux, age 49
EVP and Chief Medical Affairs: Reed V. Tuckson
EVP and Acting Executive Director, United Health Foundation: Jeannine M. Rivet
EVP Human Capital: Lori K. Sweere, age 51
EVP, General Counsel, and Assistant Secretary:
Mitchell E. (Mitch) Zamoff, age 42
Chief Ethics Officer: Jack Radke
SVP and Chief Accounting Officer: Eric S. Rangen, age 53
SVP and Chief Communications Officer: Don Nathan
Executive Assistant, Investor Relations: Frances Jacobs
Auditors: Deloitte & Touche LLP

LOCATIONS

HQ: UnitedHealth Group Incorporated
UnitedHealth Group Center, 9900 Bren Rd. East
Minnetonka, MN 55343
Phone: 952-936-1300   **Fax:** 952-936-1819
Web: www.unitedhealthgroup.com

Selected Operations

AmeriChoice (public-sector programs)
Ingenix (information technology, consulting services)
OptumHealth (specialty benefits)
Ovations (benefits for people age 50 and older)
Prescription Solutions (pharmacy benefit management)
UnitedHealthcare (health plans; individuals, businesses, employers)

PRODUCTS/OPERATIONS

2009 Sales

	$ mil.	% of total
Health benefits	81,341	79
Prescription solutions	14,452	14
OptumHealth	5,528	5
Ingenix	1,823	2
Adjustments	(16,006)	—
Total	**87,138**	**100**

COMPETITORS

Aetna
Blue Cross
CIGNA
Coventry Health Care
CVS Caremark
Delta Dental Plans
Express Scripts
Health Insurance of New York
Health Net
Humana
Kaiser Foundation Health Plan
Medco Health
WellPoint

HISTORICAL FINANCIALS

Company Type: Public

Income Statement

FYE: December 31

	REVENUE ($ mil.)	NET INCOME ($ mil.)	NET PROFIT MARGIN	EMPLOYEES
12/09	87,138	3,822	4.4%	80,000
12/08	81,186	2,977	3.7%	75,000
12/07	75,431	4,654	6.2%	67,000
12/06	71,542	4,159	5.8%	58,000
12/05	45,365	3,300	7.3%	55,000
Annual Growth	**17.7%**	**3.7%**	**—**	**9.8%**

2009 Year-End Financials

Debt ratio: 48.0%
Return on equity: 17.2%
Cash ($ mil.): 9,800
Current ratio: 0.82
Long-term debt ($ mil.): 11,334

No. of shares (mil.): 1,124
Dividends
  Yield: 0.1%
  Payout: 0.9%
Market value ($ mil.): 34,268

Stock History

NYSE: UNH

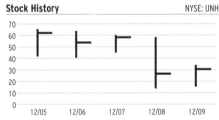

	STOCK PRICE ($) FY Close	P/E High	P/E Low	PER SHARE ($) Earnings	PER SHARE ($) Dividends	PER SHARE ($) Book Value
12/09	30.48	10	5	3.24	0.03	21.00
12/08	26.60	24	6	2.40	0.03	18.48
12/07	58.20	17	13	3.42	0.03	17.85
12/06	53.73	21	14	2.97	0.03	18.51
12/05	62.14	26	17	2.48	0.01	15.77
Annual Growth	**(16.3%)**	**—**	**—**	**6.9%**	**31.6%**	**7.4%**

Universal Corporation

Smoking may be hazardous to your health, but providing the tobacco for the smokes has proven safe and profitable so far for Universal Corporation. The company selects, buys, processes, and ships leaf tobacco in the US and some 35 other nations, including Brazil, Canada, and Zimbabwe. The leaf is sold to cigarette makers. Universal also procures and processes dark tobacco used in cigars and smokeless products. A pure play in tobacco, the firm has sold its lumber and building products as well as its agricultural products businesses, which provided the food industry with such products as tea, dried fruit, and seeds. The firm's Universal Leaf subsidiaries are active in Africa, Europe, South America, and the US.

Acting as an intermediary between tobacco growers and cigarette and smokeless tobacco companies, Universal primarily deals in flue-cured (processed by artificial heat), burley (air-cured), and oriental (small-leafed) tobaccos, all of which are the major ingredients in American blend cigarettes. Philip Morris International and Japan Tobacco are among its biggest customers. However, Japan Tobacco's pending purchase of the UK's Triback Leaf and a pair of Brazilian firms will likely reduce the volume of tobacco it purchases from Universal. Also, the effects of the trend toward consolidation among tobacco product manufacturers, which involves some of Universal's customers, remains unclear. While consolidation increases the tobacco broker's reliance on a few key customers, it's unclear whether those customers will buy more or less tobacco from Universal.

In recent years Universal's sales have suffered as the number of US smokers has decreased and some US cigarette makers increasingly have bought tobacco abroad or directly from US farmers. In response, the company has ceased operations at its dark tobacco processing facility in Kenbridge, Virginia, and consolidated all of its domestic dark tobacco processing at its plant in Lancaster, Pennsylvania. Previously, Universal closed its Danville, Virginia, plant and consolidated its US burley leaf processing to its North Carolina facility in late 2005.

In 2006 and 2007 Universal Corporation shed businesses unrelated to its tobacco operations and refocused its attention to the tobacco market. (The company's non-tobacco activities had brought in almost half of its revenues.)

HISTORY

Jaquelin Taylor founded Universal Leaf Tobacco Company in 1918 by combining six tobacco dealers, including his own J.P. Taylor Company of Virginia, and the company went public a few years later. The company launched subsidiaries in China in 1924 and in Canada the following year.

Philip Morris became a customer during the 1930s, and the cigarette maker's association with Universal became instrumental in its growth. By 1940 the company was the leading purchaser of leaf tobacco in the US. That year the US government filed antitrust charges against Universal and seven other tobacco companies. American, Liggett & Myers, and Reynolds stood trial for the whole group, and four years later each of the eight companies was fined $15,000.

Universal expanded into South America and Asia during the next several decades, and by the

end of the 1960s it was operating in 15 countries outside the US. The company diversified under Gordon Crenshaw, who became president in 1965 and CEO soon thereafter. Universal made several small acquisitions between 1966 and 1980, including fertilizer producer Royster in 1980 (sold in 1984). Its first significant venture outside agriculture came in 1984 when it bought both Lawyers Title and Continental Land Title for a total of $115 million. Two years later Universal bought Netherlands-based Deli-Maatschappij, which traded in tobacco and commodities such as tea, rubber, sunflower seeds, and timber.

In 1987 the company changed its name to Universal Corporation to reflect its diversifying interests. Henry Harrell replaced Crenshaw as CEO in 1988 (and as chairman in 1991). Also in 1988 Universal bought tobacco processors Thope and Ricks, and two years later it purchased Gebreder Kulenkampffag (tobacco, Germany), giving Universal a greater presence in the developing market in Eastern Europe.

The company acquired Kliemann (tobacco, Brazil) in 1991, ensuring access to Brazilian flue-cured tobacco. Also that year a depressed real estate market led the company to spin off its title insurance operation, Lawyers Title, to shareholders. Universal bought the Casalee Group, a UK tobacco processor with key operations in Brazil and Africa and trading operations in Europe and the Far East, for about $100 million in 1993. A global surplus in the tobacco markets hurt profits the following year.

In 1996 Universal formed a joint venture with COSUN, a Dutch sugar cooperative, creating the #1 spice enterprise in the Benelux market. As part of its plan to grow in emerging markets, the next year Universal acquired leaf-processing plants in Tanzania and Poland. Despite strong sales and profits, Universal's stock had flagged, and in 1998 the company bought back $100 million of its shares to improve their value.

Sales fell in 1999 amid a worldwide glut of leaf tobacco. In 2000 Universal said it would close several US plants, eliminating about 175 full-time and 1,400 seasonal jobs. In 2001 the transition from the traditional auction market to direct contracting with farmers caused increases in the cost of doing business for Universal.

In January 2003 Harrell retired as chairman and CEO. He was succeeded by Allen King who had been with the company since 1969.

Universal sold its Dutch non-tobacco businesses, which included its lumber and building products distribution segment and most of its agri-products operations in September 2006. In December of that year George Freeman, III was named president and CEO of the company, while King remained chairman.

The remainder of Universal's ag-operations and assets were sold in 2007 and early 2008. The divestitures, which were effected to increase shareholder value and return to core competencies, involved selling a UK trading company, as well as trading companies in Virginia, Washington, and California. In its role as an agricultural products merchant, the company had provided the food industry with a number of products, including tea, dried fruit, and sunflower seeds. It also provided the tire manufacturing industry with rubber. Universal distributed building materials and lumber to wholesale/do-it-yourself chains and to the construction and prefabrication industries in the Netherlands and Belgium through regional outlets.

EXECUTIVES

Chairman, President, and CEO: George C. Freeman III, age 46, $2,313,894 total compensation
EVP and COO: W. Keith Brewer, age 51, $2,031,199 total compensation
SVP, CFO, and Chief Administrative Officer: David C. Moore, age 54, $1,724,330 total compensation
VP, General Counsel, Secretary. and Chief Compliance Officer: Preston D. (P. D.) Wigner, age 41, $739,120 total compensation
VP and Treasurer: Karen M. L. Whelan, age 63, $883,155 total compensation
VP: William J. Coronado
Controller: Robert M. Peebles, age 52
Auditors: Ernst & Young LLP

LOCATIONS

HQ: Universal Corporation
9201 Forest Hill Ave., Richmond, VA 23235
Phone: 804-359-9311   **Fax:** 804-254-3584
Web: www.universalcorp.com

2010 Sales

	$ mil.	% of total
Belgium	469.1	19
US	305.4	12
Other countries	1,717.2	69
Total	**2,491.7**	**100**

PRODUCTS/OPERATIONS

2010 Sales

	$ mil.	% of total
Flue-cured & burley tobacco	2,253.0	90
Other tobacco	238.7	10
Total	**2,491.7**	**100**

Selected Subsidiaries

Beleggings-en Beheermaatschappij "DE Amstel" B.V (The Netherlands)
Continental Tobacco, S.A (Switzerland)
Deltafina, S.p.A (Italy)
Ermor Tabarama-Tabacos do Brasil Ltda (Brazil)
Gebrueder Kulenkampff AG (Germany)
Indoco International B.V (The Netherlands)
Industria AG (Switzerland)
Itofina, S.A (Switzerland)
L'Agricola, S.r.L. (Italy)
Mozambique Leaf Tobacco Import & Export Limitada
Simcoe Leaf Tobacco Company, Limited (Canada)
Tabacos del Pacífico Norte, S.A. De C.V. (Mexico)
Tanzania Leaf Tobacco Co., Ltd
Tobacco Trading International, Inc. (British Virgin Islands)
Toutiana, S.A (Switzerland)
Uganda Leaf Tobacco Co. Limited
Ultoco, S.A (Switzerland)
Universal Leaf International S.A. (Switzerland)
Universal Leaf Tabacos Ltda. (Brazil)
Zambia Leaf Tobacco Co., Ltd.

HISTORICAL FINANCIALS

Company Type: Public

Income Statement

	REVENUE ($ mil.)	NET INCOME ($ mil.)	NET PROFIT MARGIN	EMPLOYEES
3/10	2,492	170	6.8%	28,000
3/09	2,555	132	5.2%	24,000
3/08	2,146	119	5.6%	25,000
3/07	2,007	44	2.2%	25,000
3/06	3,511	8	0.2%	30,000
Annual Growth	**(8.2%)**	**115.5%**	**—**	**(1.7%)**

FYE: March 31

2010 Year-End Financials

Debt ratio: 45.6%
Return on equity: 19.7%
Cash ($ mil.): 246
Current ratio: 2.75
Long-term debt ($ mil.): 415

No. of shares (mil.): 24
Dividends
  Yield: 3.5%
  Payout: 32.6%
Market value ($ mil.): 1,273

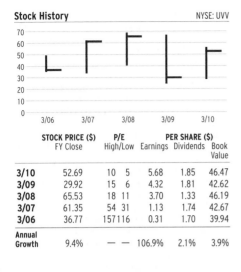

	STOCK PRICE ($) FY Close	P/E High/Low		PER SHARE ($) Earnings	Dividends	Book Value
3/10	52.69	10	5	5.68	1.85	46.47
3/09	29.92	15	6	4.32	1.81	42.62
3/08	65.53	18	11	3.70	1.33	46.19
3/07	61.35	54	31	1.13	1.74	42.67
3/06	36.77	157	116	0.31	1.70	39.94
Annual Growth	9.4%	—	—	106.9%	2.1%	3.9%

Unum Group

Unum Group is undoubtedly a top disability insurer in the US and the UK. The company offers short-term and long-term disability insurance, as well as life and accidental death and dismemberment, to individuals and groups in a workplace benefits setting. Specialty coverage offerings include long-term care, cancer, and travel insurance. US subsidiaries include Unum Life Insurance Company of America, Provident Life and Accident, First Unum Life, Colonial Life & Accident Insurance, and The Paul Revere Life Insurance Company. Unum Group, which operates as Unum Limited in the UK, sells its products through field agents and independent brokers.

Unum Group seeks to achieve a competitive edge by providing group, individual, and voluntary workplace products that can be combined with other coverage to better integrate benefits for customers. The company strives to maintain close relationships with its sales force and independent agents and brokers, as it relies on these representatives to market its products to employers.

Unum Group has also stayed ahead of the game in the disability market by sticking to conservative investment and growth strategies. It has also focused its operations on long-term growth opportunities in the employee benefits market. Over the years, the company has shifted away from selling individual disability policies through non-workplace settings, and in 2009 it also stopped offering new individual long-term care policies.

As part of a rebranding effort following years of corporate restructuring to focus on core operations, the company changed its name from UnumProvident to Unum Group in 2007.

HISTORY

Coal was discovered in eastern Tennessee in the 1870s; in 1887 several Chattanooga professional men formed the Provident Life & Accident Insurance Co. to provide medical insurance to miners. But it was a case of the inexperienced serving the uninsurable, and by 1892 the company was on the brink of ruin. The founders sold half the company for $1,000 to Thomas Maclellan and John McMaster, two Scotsmen who had failed at banking in Canada.

While Maclellan handled the business end, McMaster scoured the coalfields for customers. He even went into the mines, pitching to individual miners and bringing along someone to dig coal for them so they wouldn't lose money by stopping work to listen.

In 1895 the partners bought the rest of the company. Provident grew, thanks to the cooperation of mining companies, which deducted premiums from miners' pay. Provident added sickness and industrial insurance (low-benefit life policies). In 1900, after a period of strained relations, Maclellan bought out McMaster.

After 1905 northern insurers began moving into the industrializing South. To meet the competition, Provident reorganized and added capital, and its stepped-up sales efforts brought in such lucrative business as railroad accounts. Provident added life insurance in 1917. The first policy was bought by Robert Maclellan, who became president when his father died in 1916.

In 1931 Provident acquired the Southern Surety Co. During and after WWII, group sales exploded as employee benefit packages proliferated. Provident, which by then operated nationally, entered Canada in 1948. Four years later R. L. Maclellan succeeded his father as president (R. L. stepped down in 1971). Provident's growth in the 1970s stemmed from its life units, but it also developed a large health insurance operation.

The health care operations were hammered by rising medical costs in the 1980s, so the company moved into managed care. But the combination of increased health care costs and a real estate crash gave the company a one-two punch in the late 1980s and early 1990s. An accounting change in 1993 further hit profits. In 1994 new president Harold Chandler initiated a reevaluation of Provident's operations and future, which resulted in Provident's exit from the health care business beginning in 1995.

In 1997 Provident began a major move into disability insurance. It bought 83% of rival disability insurer The Paul Revere Corporation from Textron. About 10,000 Paul Revere insurance brokers later filed suit alleging they were denied millions of dollars in commissions. In exchange for its $300 million aid in the purchase, Switzerland's Zurich Insurance (now Zurich Financial Services) received about 15% of Provident. The company also acquired GENEX Services (vocational rehabilitation and related services) and sold its dental insurance business to Ameritas Life Insurance. In 1998 Provident sold its annuity business to American General (now a subsidiary of AIG).

In 1998, with both Provident and Unum Corporation looking for ways to enhance business, the companies commenced merger negotiations and completed the transaction the next year. But the merger was more expensive than anticipated, and problems in integrating the companies' sales forces slowed policy sales.

Company operations began melding more smoothly and UnumProvident began addressing the problems with its sales force, as well as adding customer service staff in 2000. It pulled money out of reserves by reinsuring several blocks of acquisition-related businesses and sold an inactive shell subsidiary licensed to sell annuities in most states to Allstate. In 2001 the company sold its Provident National Assurance subsidiary to Allstate. UnumProvident faced accusations that the company denied valid disability claims in 2002. These accusations resulted in legal actions in a number of states.

UnumProvident acquired Sun Life Financial's UK life insurance group in 2003 in a move designed to expand the company's operations in the UK. UnumProvident sold its Unum Japan Accident Insurance subsidiary to Hitachi Capital Corporation (Hitachi) in 2004.

In 2007 the company divested its GENEX Services unit, a provider of disability management and workers' compensation services. GENEX's specialty services no longer fit into Unum's strategy to focus on its primary disability insurance operations.

EXECUTIVES

Chairman: Jon S. Fossel, age 68
President, CEO, and Director; President and CEO, First Unum Life: Thomas R. (Tom) Watjen, age 55, $13,943,923 total compensation
EVP and COO: Robert O. (Bob) Best, age 60, $2,251,634 total compensation
EVP and CFO: Richard P. (Rick) McKenney, age 41, $4,335,229 total compensation
EVP; President and CEO, Unum US: Kevin P. McCarthy, age 54, $3,832,361 total compensation
EVP; President and CEO, Colonial Life & Accident Insurance Company: Randall C. (Randy) Horn, age 57, $1,658,066 total compensation
EVP and General Counsel: Liston (Bo) Bishop III
Interim Chief Investment Officer: David G. Fussell
SVP Investor Relations: Thomas A. H. (Tom) White
SVP and Controller: Vicki Corbett
SVP and Deputy Chief Investment Officer: Martha Leiper
SVP and Chief Government Affairs Officer: Scott Maker
SVP and Treasurer: Kevin McMahon
SVP Integrated Underwriting, Unum US: Tim Arnold
SVP National Client Group, Unum US: Don Boutin
SVP and Chief Marketing Officer: Joseph R. (Joe) Foley
SVP Human Resources: Eileen C. Farrar
SVP and Chief Risk Officer: Mike Temple
VP Corporate Communications: Jim Sabourin
Auditors: Ernst & Young LLP

LOCATIONS

HQ: Unum Group
1 Fountain Sq., Chattanooga, TN 37402
Phone: 423-294-1011
Web: www.unum.com

PRODUCTS/OPERATIONS

2009 Sales

	$ mil.	% of total
Unum US	6,192.3	62
Closed block individual disability	1,739.9	17
Colonial Life	1,129.9	11
Unum UK	813.0	8
Corporate & other	215.9	2
Total	**10,091.0**	**100**

Selected Subsidiaries

Colonial Life & Accident Insurance Company
Duncanson & Holt, Inc.
  Duncanson & Holt Services, Inc.
  Duncanson & Holt Syndicate Management Ltd. (UK)
    Trafalgar Underwriting Agencies Ltd. (UK)
  Duncanson & Holt Underwriters, Ltd. (UK)
First Unum Life Insurance Company
Provident Investment Management, LLC
Provident Life and Accident Insurance Company
Provident Life and Casualty Insurance Company
The Paul Revere Life Insurance Company
  The Paul Revere Variable Annuity Insurance Company
Unum Life Insurance Company of America

Unum European Holding Company Limited (UK)
  Claims Services International Limited (UK)
  Group Risk Insurance Services Limited (UK)
  Unum Limited (UK)
UnumProvident International Ltd. (Bermuda)

COMPETITORS

AEGON
Aflac
AIG American General
Allianz
Aon
AXA Financial
CIGNA
CNA Financial
CNO Financial
GatesMcDonald
Guardian Life
Hartford Life
John Hancock Financial Services
Liberty Mutual
Lincoln Financial Group
MassMutual
MetLife
Mutual of Omaha
Nationwide
New York Life
Northwestern Mutual
Old Republic
Principal Financial
Prudential

HISTORICAL FINANCIALS

Company Type: Public

Income Statement			FYE: December 31
	ASSETS ($ mil.)	NET INCOME ($ mil.)	INCOME AS % OF ASSETS	EMPLOYEES
12/09	54,477	853	1.6%	9,700
12/08	49,417	553	1.1%	9,800
12/07	52,433	679	1.3%	9,700
12/06	52,823	411	0.8%	11,100
12/05	51,867	514	1.0%	11,300
Annual Growth	1.2%	13.5%	—	(3.7%)

2009 Year-End Financials

Equity as % of assets: 15.6%
Return on assets: 1.6%
Return on equity: 11.4%
Long-term debt ($ mil.): 2,550
No. of shares (mil.): 333
Dividends
  Yield: 1.6%
  Payout: 12.1%
Market value ($ mil.): 6,497
Sales ($ mil.): 10,091

Stock History

NYSE: UNM

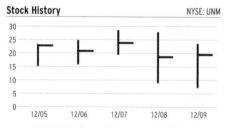

	STOCK PRICE ($) FY Close	P/E High/Low		PER SHARE ($) Earnings	Dividends	Book Value
12/09	19.52	9	3	2.57	0.31	25.54
12/08	18.60	17	6	1.62	0.30	19.22
12/07	23.79	15	10	1.91	0.30	24.16
12/06	20.78	20	13	1.23	0.30	23.19
12/05	22.75	14	9	1.64	0.30	22.13
Annual Growth	(3.8%)	—	—	11.9%	0.8%	3.7%

Urban Outfitters

If you're a metropolitan hipster, Urban Outfitters has your outfit. The firm's 150-plus namesake stores — mainly in the US, but also in Canada and Europe — sell casual clothes, accessories, gifts, housewares, and shoes. The retailer also courts older women (30- to 45-year-olds) at about 135 Anthropologie shops. Urban Outfitters and Anthropologie also distribute catalogs and operate e-commerce sites. Its wholesale division makes, sells, and distributes clothing under the Free People label at 35 of its own stores and about 1,400 better department and specialty stores worldwide.

The fast-growing retailer has been increasing the number of Free People stores — opening half a dozen in 2009 with more planned in 2010 — while cutting back on wholesale customers, which include the upscale department stores Bloomingdales, Nordstrom, and Belk. Free People targets a narrow market — women ages 25 to 30 — with apparel, accessories, and gifts.

Indeed, overall company sales increased more than 6% in 2009, buoyed by a healthy rise on the retail side that compensated for about a 5% drop in its wholesale segment sales. Capitalizing on the strength of its retail business, Urban Outfitters plans to open another 45 stores in 2010. On the international front, Anthropologie's eclectic mix of apparel and housewares made its European debut with a store opening in London in fall 2009.

About 10% of the company's sales originate overseas, where it operates about two dozen Urban Outfitters stores in the UK and half a dozen other countries. Also, the firm has been busy adding wholesale customers and growing its e-commerce sales overseas. Together the company's three retail brands mail about 36 million catalogs each year. While Urban Outfitters has trimmed the number of catalogs it puts in the mail as it directs its efforts more toward online marketing, the count will creep up in 2010.

Ever on the lookout for new brand opportunities, Urban Outfitters recently launched two more in the form of Terrain, a mix of home and garden products targeting the well-heeled set, and Leifsdottir, a wholesale apparel brand for its Anthropologie chain, which debuted in Nordstrom, Bergdorf Goodman, and other high-end department stores in 2009. Terrain, which grew out of Urban Outfitters' 2008 acquisition of J. Franklin Styer Nurseries, operates a single store in Glen Mills, Pennsylvania.

Chairman and president Richard Hayne founded the company as The Free People's Store in 1970. He owns about 19% of the company.

HISTORY

Richard Hayne and his first wife opened the Free People Store in 1970 near the University of Pennsylvania campus in Philadelphia. Aimed at the student age group, Free People sold used clothes, jeans, ethnic apparel, and housewares, such as Indian bedspreads. Six years later Hayne and his second wife changed the name to Urban Outfitters. A second store was opened in 1980 in Harvard Square in Cambridge, Massachusetts, and seven more opened near other college campuses during the 1980s. The company's wholesale business was established in 1984.

Urban Outfitters opened its first Anthropologie store in Wayne, Pennsylvania, in 1992. The company went public the next year and opened two more Anthropologie stores in 1995. In 1997 it opened five more Anthropologie stores and its first two Urban Outfitters stores in Canada. That year Hayne closed the original Urban Outfitters store and opened another in a more bustling area six blocks away. The company originally had placed a cap of 35 Urban Outfitters stores in the US, but it has decided to enter smaller markets with smaller stores.

In 1998 the retailer debuted an Anthropologie catalog and website and opened its first Urban Outfitters store in the UK. Urban Outfitters in 1999 bought a minority stake in MXG Media (formerly HMB Publishing), but that venture was bankrupt by the end of 2000.

Urban Outfitters opened more than 40 stores from 2000 to 2002, with plans to continue openings at the same pace in the years to come, adding Free People retail stores into the mix. In 2003 it tacked on about 20 Anthropologie stores and 20 Urban Outfitters stores. In March 2003 the company launched its Urban Outfitters catalog. Also that year the company was caught up in an odd but short-lived trend of exploiting the politically incorrect: By October of that year the company had discontinued sales of Ghettopoly, a Monopoly-like board game that, critics charged, made light of poverty and other social problems.

Urban Outfitters moved to a new headquarters, at the Navy Yard in Philadelphia, in August 2006.

In May 2007 the firm promoted EVP and director Glen Senk to the newly created post of CEO. Richard Hayne retained the titles of chairman and president.

In 2008 Urban Outfitters acquired Franklin Styer Nurseries in Pennsylvania, laying the foundation for the company's fourth retail concept Terrain: upscale garden centers.

In 2009 the company launched Leifsdottir, a sophisticated wholesale brand of women's apparel.

EXECUTIVES

Chairman and President: Richard A. Hayne, age 62, $625,006 total compensation
CEO and Director: Glen T. Senk, age 53, $29,944,180 total compensation
CFO: Eric Artz, age 42
General Counsel and Secretary: Glen A. Bodzy, age 57, $498,905 total compensation
Chief Administrative Officer: Freeman M. Zausner, age 62
CIO and Chief Logistics Officer: Calvin Hollinger
Chief Talent Officer: Bill Cody
President, Free People: Margaret (Meg) Hayne, age 52, $462,011 total compensation
Co-President, Anthropologie: Wendy B. McDevitt, age 45
Co-President, Anthropologie: Wendy Wurtzburger, age 52
Global President, Urban Outfitters Brand: Steve Murray, age 50
Managing Director, Free People Division: Krissy Meehan
Managing Director, Anthropologie Europe: James Bidwell
COO, European Operating Divisions: Andrew McLean
Controller and Principal Accounting Officer: Frank J. Conforti, age 34
Director Investor Relations: Oona McCullough
Auditors: Deloitte & Touche LLP

LOCATIONS

HQ: Urban Outfitters, Inc.
  5000 S. Broad St., Philadelphia, PA 19112
Phone: 215-454-5500   **Fax:** 215-454-5163
Web: www.urbanoutfittersinc.com

2010 Sales

	$ mil.	% of total
US	1,752.8	90
International	185.0	10
Total	**1,937.8**	**100**

2010 Stores

	Urban Outfitters	Anthropologie	Free People
US	132	133	34
England	9	1	—
Canada	7	3	—
Ireland	2	—	—
Denmark	1	—	—
Belgium	1	—	—
Germany	1	—	—
Scotland	1	—	—
Sweden	1	—	—
Total	**155**	**137**	**34**

PRODUCTS/OPERATIONS

2010 Sales

	$ mil.	% of total
Retail	1,833.7	94
Wholesale	109.3	6
Adjustments	(5.2)	—
Total	**1,937.8**	**100**

2010 Sales

	% of total
Urban Outfitters	39
Anthropologie	36
Direct-to-consumer	17
Free People (including wholesale) & other	8
Total	**100**

Selected Operations

Anthropologie, catalog, stores, and website (decorative accessories, gifts, home furnishings, women's casual apparel, and accessories)

Terrain, stores (outdoor living and gardening)

Urban Outfitters, catalog, stores and website (accessories, housewares, fashion apparel, footwear, and gifts)

Wholesale (distribution of apparel, apartment wares, gifts, accessories, and shoes under the Free People brand name)

COMPETITORS

Abercrombie & Fitch
Aéropostale
Alloy, Inc.
American Eagle Outfitters
Banana Republic
bebe stores
Benetton
Casual Male Retail Group
Cost Plus
dELiA*s
Dillard's
Eddie Bauer llc
Euromarket Designs
French Connection
The Gap
Guess?
H&M
Hot Topic
J. Jill Group
Jones Apparel
Lands' End
Levi Strauss
Liz Claiborne
L.L. Bean
Macy's
Nautica Apparel
Old Navy
Pacific Sunwear
Polo Ralph Lauren
Target
Williams-Sonoma
Zara

HISTORICAL FINANCIALS

Company Type: Public

Income Statement

FYE: January 31

	REVENUE ($ mil.)	NET INCOME ($ mil.)	NET PROFIT MARGIN	EMPLOYEES
1/10	1,938	220	11.3%	14,000
1/09	1,835	199	10.9%	12,500
1/08	1,508	160	10.6%	10,000
1/07	1,225	116	9.5%	8,400
1/06	1,092	131	12.0%	7,500
Annual Growth	**15.4%**	**13.9%**	**—**	**16.9%**

2010 Year-End Financials

Debt ratio: —
Return on equity: 18.7%
Cash ($ mil.): 159
Current ratio: 4.28
Long-term debt ($ mil.): —
No. of shares (mil.): 169
Dividends
   Yield: —
   Payout: —
Market value ($ mil.): 5,340

Stock History

NASDAQ (GS): URBN

	STOCK PRICE ($) FY Close	P/E High/Low		PER SHARE ($) Earnings	Dividends	Book Value
1/10	31.57	28	11	1.28	—	7.67
1/09	15.58	33	11	1.17	—	6.23
1/08	29.00	32	20	0.94	—	5.05
1/07	24.40	42	20	0.69	—	3.99
1/06	27.31	44	26	0.77	—	3.32
Annual Growth	**3.7%**	**—**	**—**	**13.5%**	**—**	**23.3%**

URS Corporation

URS Corporation provides engineering, construction, and technical services for public and private customers around the world. Through its infrastructure and environmental business, URS builds, manages, operates, and maintains projects for government agencies and private corporations. Its federal services division (formerly operating as EG&G) provides management, decommissioning, and technical support services to US agencies including the Department of Defense and the Department of Homeland Security. Finally, its energy and construction segment (formerly the Washington Division) provides design, management, construction, maintenance, and closure services for domestic and international clients.

A key federal defense contractor, URS provides operations, management, and maintenance services to all branches of the military and such entities as NASA. The US Army is its largest customer, accounting for more than 15% of all sales. For the military, URS refurbishes military vehicles, modernizes weapons systems, manages military facilities, provides logistic support, trains pilots, and is trained to decommission nuclear, chemical, and biological weapons.

For the industrial and commercial sectors, URS offers a range of services including construction, modification, and decommissioning for facilities including oil and gas refineries, biotechnology and other research laboratories, and manufacturing facilities. URS is also a leading nuclear plant remediation and decommissioning services provider.

The company has expanded through significant acquisitions including the Washington Division and EG&G (both rebranded under the URS name in 2010). URS also agreed to acquire UK-based Scott Wilson Group in 2010. However, CH2M Hill also entered a competing bid for the company. But URS upped its offer to $333 million and CH2M Hill withdrew. The deal will bolster URS's presence in the UK infrastructure market and give it entry into other geographic markets overseas.

Other recent acquisitions include the 2008 purchases of Tryck Nyman Hayes, which helped URS build its presence in Alaska infrastructure, and LopezGarcia, a Texas-based group focused on infrastructure engineering. In 2009 URS acquired oil and gas pipeline services provider ForeRunner Corporation.

URS operates in more than 30 countries. Much of its business is derived from US government agency operations overseas.

HISTORY

Founded as an engineering research partnership in 1951 and incorporated as Broadview Research Corp. in 1957, the company won its first big contract (which lasted until 1971) with the US Army to automate logistical and personnel systems. In 1962 it changed its name to United Research Services, shortening it to URS two years later. Through the 1960s the firm tried to reduce its reliance on the Army contract by diversifying into leasing and training (even owning Evelyn Wood Reading Dynamics at one point). URS went public in 1976.

Diversification was not the answer, however, and in 1984 URS returned to its engineering and architecture roots. Laden with debt from the earlier acquisitions and overextended overseas, it was ill-equipped to deal with lower construction spending in the late 1980s on public infrastructure and the environment. The firm was near bankruptcy in 1989 when CEO Martin Koffel took the helm. URS sold noncore assets and cut foreign operations, settled shareholder lawsuits, and pared down debt. By 1991 it was profitable again.

Focused on its core business, in 1995 URS bought E.C. Driver & Associates, specialists in highway and bridge design. The following year URS acquired Greiner Engineering, forming URS Greiner, which doubled its US offices and gave it a presence in Asia. On a roll, in 1997 URS doubled its private-sector business by acquiring geotechnical and environmental engineering specialists Woodward-Clyde.

Continuing to grow through acquisitions, the company bought Thorburn Colquhoun, the UK civil and structural engineering consulting firm, in 1999. Also that year URS won a major prize when it purchased Los Angeles-based engineering and construction services firm Dames & Moore in a $600 million deal. The acquisition more than doubled URS's size again and strengthened the company's presence in Asia, Australia, and Europe.

URS projects in 2000 included a contract to provide environmental services to U.S. Air Force installations worldwide and a contract to design a water treatment plant in Lancaster, Ohio. Among the projects URS began working on in 2001 was the design of downtown Atlanta's 17th Street Bridge. The firm also won contracts to provide environmental consulting to the US Postal Service and the US Coast Guard. After helping both public and private companies with their heightened security concerns following the September 11 attacks, URS decided in 2002 to form a security services group to help protect buildings, airports, and infrastructure against natural disasters and terrorist attacks.

To gain even more earnings from federal defense contracts (particularly for national and homeland defense projects), URS in 2002 acquired outsourced operations and maintenance provider EG&G from Carlyle Group, a DC-based investing firm with several ties to the defense industry. In 2007 URS acquired Washington Group International (renamed The Washington Division) for $2.6 billion in 2007. That deal made URS a powerhouse in the nuclear industry sector just in time for the growing resurgence in nuclear power. In 2010 the company integrated EG&G and the Washington Division under the URS brand.

EXECUTIVES

Chairman, President, and CEO: Martin M. Koffel, age 71, $6,576,899 total compensation
EVP Public Sector Business Development: Martin S. Tanzer
EVP Public Sector Business Development: Dhamo S. Dhamotharan
VP and CFO: H. Thomas (Tom) Hicks, age 59, $2,568,315 total compensation
VP; President, Federal Services: Randall A. (Randy) Wotring, age 53, $2,237,349 total compensation
VP; President, Infrastructure and Environment: Gary V. Jandegian, age 57, $2,121,522 total compensation
VP; President, Energy and Construction: Thomas H. (Tom) Zarges, age 61, $5,223,840 total compensation
VP; Chairman, URS Division: Irwin L. Rosenstein, age 67
VP and Treasurer: Judy L. Rodgers
VP Corporate Information Technology: Thomas J. Lynch
VP Strategy; SVP, Construction Services: Thomas W. (Tom) Bishop, age 63
VP, General Counsel, and Secretary: Joseph Masters, age 53
VP, Controller, and Chief Accounting Officer: Reed N. Brimhall, age 56
VP Communications: Susan B. Kilgannon, age 51
VP Investor Relations: Sreeram (Sam) Ramraj
Auditors: PricewaterhouseCoopers LLP

LOCATIONS

HQ: URS Corporation
600 Montgomery St., 26th Fl.
San Francisco, CA 94111
Phone: 415-774-2700   **Fax:** 415-398-1905
Web: www.urscorp.com

2009 Sales

	$ mil.	% of total
US	8,451.2	91
International	811.3	9
Adustments	(13.4)	—
Total	**9,249.1**	**100**

PRODUCTS/OPERATIONS

2009 Sales by Segment

	$ mil.	% of total
Energy & Construction	3,583.9	38
Infrastructure & Environment	3,170.4	34
Federal Services	2,561.3	28
Adjustments	(66.5)	—
Total	**9,249.1**	**100**

2009 Sales by Sector

	$ mil.	% of total
Federal	4,140.8	45
Industrial & commercial	2,052.9	22
Infrastructure	1,663.2	18
Power	1,392.2	15
Total	**9,249.1**	**100**

Selected Services

Design
Architectural and interior design
Civil, structural, mechanical, electrical, sanitary, environmental, water resource, geotechnical/underground, dam, mining, and seismic engineering
Engineering and design studies for the upgrade and maintenance of military hardware
Operations and maintenance
Management of base logistics
Operation and maintenance of chemical agent disposal systems
Oversight of construction, testing, and operation of base systems and processes
Support of high-security systems
Planning
Archaeological and cultural resources studies
Coordination of community involvement programs
Development and analysis of alternative concepts
Environmental impact studies
Environmental site analyses
Facilities planning
Master planning
Permitting
Programming
Technical and economic feasibility studies
Traffic and revenue studies
Program and construction management
Cash flow analyses
Constructability reviews
Construction and bid management
Construction and life-cycle cost estimating
Construction or demolition of buildings

COMPETITORS

AECOM	Foster Wheeler
Babcock & Wilcox	Jacobs Engineering
Baran Group	KBR
Bechtel	Lockheed Martin
Black & Veatch	Morganti
Camp Dresser McKee	Parsons Brinckerhoff
CH2M HILL	Skidmore Owings
DynCorp International	Tetra Tech
Fluor	

HISTORICAL FINANCIALS

Company Type: Public

Income Statement

FYE: Friday closest to Dec. 31

	REVENUE ($ mil.)	NET INCOME ($ mil.)	NET PROFIT MARGIN	EMPLOYEES
12/09	9,249	269	2.9%	45,000
12/08	10,086	220	2.2%	50,000
12/07	5,383	132	2.5%	56,000
12/06	4,240	113	2.7%	29,300
12/05	3,918	83	2.1%	29,200
Annual Growth	**24.0%**	**34.4%**	**—**	**11.4%**

2009 Year-End Financials

Debt ratio: 17.7%	No. of shares (mil.): 83
Return on equity: 7.1%	Dividends
Cash ($ mil.): 721	Yield: —
Current ratio: 1.88	Payout: —
Long-term debt ($ mil.): 690	Market value ($ mil.): 3,687

Stock History

NYSE: URS

	STOCK PRICE ($) FY Close	P/E High/Low		PER SHARE ($) Earnings	Dividends	Book Value
12/09	44.52	16	8	3.29	—	47.16
12/08	40.77	20	7	2.66	—	43.77
12/07	54.33	27	17	2.35	—	42.00
12/06	42.85	23	17	2.19	—	18.19
12/05	37.61	25	16	1.72	—	16.24
Annual Growth	**4.3%**	**—**	**—**	**17.6%**	**—**	**30.6%**

US Airways

US Airways Group takes wing with its US Airways unit, one of the nation's leading passenger carriers. Along with its regional affiliates, US Airways serves about 200 cities, mainly in the US and Canada, but also in Latin America, the Caribbean, the Middle East, and Europe. It uses about 350 jets on mainline routes; regional service is provided by subsidiaries Piedmont Airlines, PSA, and several independent carriers with about 300 aircraft. US Airways extends its network via the Star Alliance, a marketing and codesharing partnership led by UAL subsidiary United Airlines and Lufthansa.

US Airways Group entered into talks with UAL (parent of United Airlines) in 2010 about a possible merger. The combined company would have been the second largest in the US, trailing only Delta. By the end of April, US Airways put an end to the merger talks. UAL and Continental agreed to merge the following month.

The economic recession, which caused major turbulence for the airline industry, got its start when high fuel prices changed the trajectory for all air carriers. Even though fuel prices dropped it was not enough to mitigate for decreased passenger demand. In 2008 the carrier joined peers in cutting domestic capacity by selling aircraft, reducing its workforce, and imposing new fees (including charges for checked bags, premium seats, and pillow-and-blanket sets).

Those fees helped US Airways stem losses. Other fees implemented include charging for inflight beverages that were once complimentary and increases to the cost of call center/airport ticketing fees. (Sensitive to passenger complaints, US Airways returned to offering free soft drinks in March 2009.)

The carrier said it would shut down its crew base at Boston Logan airport in 2010; crew bases in New York and Las Vegas fall under the knife, too, as US Airways seeks to reduce costs. Cost-cutting measures include job reductions (including 200 pilot positions) in 2010.

Even though its realignment caused the suspension of five European destinations, US Airways hopes to grow by adding international flights. The carrier added its first flight to South America in 2009 with service from Philadelphia to Rio de Janeiro, Brazil. US Airways also added service to Oslo, Norway; Tel Aviv, Israel; and Montego Bay, Jamaica.

HISTORY

Richard du Pont (of the DuPont chemical dynasty) founded All American Aviation as an airmail service in 1939 to serve Pennsylvania and the Ohio Valley. Pilots used a system of hooks and ropes to pick up and drop off mail "on the fly." Ten years later the company expanded its service, began carrying passengers, and changed its name to All American Airways.

The carrier became Allegheny Airlines in 1953. It bought smaller airlines in 1968 and 1972, expanding into the Midwest and up the East Coast. In 1978 the US airline industry was deregulated; Allegheny became USAir in 1979 and began flying across the South and to California.

In 1987 USAir bought two major regional carriers — Pacific Southwest Airlines and Piedmont Airlines. The USAir/Piedmont merger was at the time the largest in US airline history. It also gave USAir its hub in Charlotte, North Carolina; its first international route (Charlotte-London); and an East Coast commuter airline.

High fuel prices and fare wars in the early 1990s put USAir in the red for six years (and forced it to lay off 9,000 workers by 1996). Seth Schofield became CEO in 1991, and USAir acquired TWA's London routes in 1992. Taking a 40% stake in Trump Shuttle, USAir began a joint marketing effort under the name USAir Shuttle. (It bought the shuttle outright in 1997.) The next year USAir and British Airways (BA) began code-sharing, and BA took a stake in USAir, which gave up its London routes.

The year 1994 was not one of USAir's best: It took a beating as it lowered fares to compete with Continental Airlines, which by then challenged USAir in almost half its routes. The airline tried in vain to wring wage concessions from its unions. Then disaster struck: A jet carrying 132 passengers crashed at Pittsburgh — USAir's second fatal crash that year.

Though USAir returned to profitability in 1996, Schofield resigned. The new CEO Stephen Wolf, a UAL veteran, demanded labor concessions. USAir, which became US Airways in 1997, finally won a new contract with its pilots.

The company's relationship with BA soured after US Airways sued BA to gain access to London's Heathrow. The two canceled code-sharing in 1997, and by 1998 BA had sold its US Airways stock. The next year Wolf disciple Rakesh Gangwal became CEO; Wolf remained chairman. US Airways suffered a pilot shortage after more than 300 pilots took early retirement and others were called up by the US military to support the Kosovo conflict.

To remain aloft after the terrorist attacks in New York and Washington, DC, in 2001 the carrier announced that it would cut back on its flights and lay off about 20% of its workforce. Later that year Gangwal resigned, and Wolf stepped back in as CEO until March 2002, when Avis Rent A Car CEO David Siegel, a Continental Airlines veteran, replaced him.

The group filed for bankruptcy protection in 2002; in conjunction with its filing, the company received a bid from Texas Pacific Group, and it won a $900 million loan guarantee from the federal government. The Texas Pacific deal was replaced by The Retirement Systems of Alabama, which invested $240 million in exchange for a 36% ownership (and a 72% voting) stake in the company. It emerged from bankruptcy in 2003.

US Airways strengthened its European presence in 2003 when it began a code-sharing agreement with top German airline Lufthansa, which eventually led to its inclusion in the Star Alliance. Its new structure, however, didn't prove viable, and the carrier found itself overwhelmed by heavy costs, primarily record-high fuel prices. It was forced once again to seek the protection of bankruptcy courts in 2004. US Airways merged with America West and emerged from Chapter 11 the following year.

To accelerate its growth, US Airways offered to buy rival Delta in 2006. Delta failed to bite, however, spoiling US Airways' dreams of creating the world's largest airline.

In January 2009 US Airways Flight 1549 had just taken off from New York on its way to Charlotte, North Carolina, when it struck a flock of Canada geese, causing failure in both the plane's engines. Captain Chesley "Sully" Sullenberger made international news by skillfully "ditching" the plane in the Hudson River, saving the lives of all 155 people aboard.

EXECUTIVES

Chairman and CEO: W. Douglas (Doug) Parker, age 48, $5,426,702 total compensation
Vice Chairman: Bruce R. Lakefield, age 66
President: J. Scott Kirby, age 42, $3,638,463 total compensation
EVP and COO: Robert D. Isom Jr., age 46, $2,006,186 total compensation
EVP and CFO: Derek J. Kerr, age 45, $1,608,063 total compensation
EVP Corporate: Stephen L. (Steve) Johnson, age 53, $1,417,263 total compensation
EVP People and Communications: Elise R. Eberwein, age 44, $1,213,718 total compensation
SVP Public Affairs: C. A. Howlett, age 66
SVP and CIO: Brad Jensen
SVP Marketing and Planning: Andrew P. Nocella
SVP Airport Customer Service, International and Cargo: Suzanne Boda
SVP Flight Operations and Inflight:
Edward W. (Ed) Bular
SVP Technical Operations: David Seymour
VP IT Infrastructure: Alan Ferayorni
VP Flight Operations: Capt. Lyle Hogg
VP; President, US Airways Express: Dion Flannery
VP Human Resources: Daniel (Dan) Pon, age 57
VP Corporate Communications: James (Jim) Olson, age 41
President and CEO, Piedmont:
Stephen R. (Steve) Farrow
President and CEO, PSA: Keith D. Houk
Director Investor Relations: Daniel E. Cravens
Secretary: Caroline B. Ray
Auditors: KPMG LLP

LOCATIONS

HQ: US Airways Group, Inc.
111 W. Rio Salado Pkwy., Tempe, AZ 85281
Phone: 480-693-0800
Web: www.usairways.com

2009 Sales

	$ mil.	% of total
US	8,285	79
Other countries	2,173	21
Total	**10,458**	**100**

PRODUCTS/OPERATIONS

2009 Sales

	$ mil.	% of total
Mainline passenger	6,752	64
Express passenger	2,503	24
Cargo	100	1
Other	1,103	11
Total	**10,458**	**100**

Selected Subsidiaries

Airways Assurance Limited (AAL)
Material Services Company, Inc. (MSC)
Piedmont Airlines, Inc.
PSA Airlines, Inc.
US Airways, Inc.

COMPETITORS

Air France-KLM
AirTran Holdings
Alaska Air
Allegiant Travel
AMR Corp.
British Airways
Delta Air Lines
Frontier Airlines
JetBlue
Southwest Airlines
Virgin Atlantic Airways

HISTORICAL FINANCIALS

Company Type: Public

Income Statement

	REVENUE ($ mil.)	NET INCOME ($ mil.)	NET PROFIT MARGIN	EMPLOYEES
12/09	10,458	(205)	—	31,300
12/08	12,118	(2,210)	—	37,500
12/07	11,700	427	3.6%	39,600
12/06	11,557	303	2.6%	37,000
12/05	5,077	(335)	—	36,600
Annual Growth	19.8%	—	—	(3.8%)

FYE: December 31

2009 Year-End Financials

Debt ratio: —
Return on equity: —
Cash ($ mil.): 1,299
Current ratio: 0.84
Long-term debt ($ mil.): 4,024
No. of shares (mil.): 161
Dividends
Yield: —
Payout: —
Market value ($ mil.): 781

Stock History

NYSE: LCC

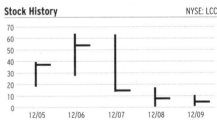

	STOCK PRICE ($) FY Close	P/E High/Low		Earnings	PER SHARE ($) Dividends	Book Value
12/09	4.84	—	—	(1.54)	—	(2.20)
12/08	7.73	—	—	(22.06)	—	(3.13)
12/07	14.71	14	3	4.52	—	8.92
12/06	53.85	19	8	3.33	—	6.01
12/05	37.14	—	—	(17.06)	—	2.60
Annual Growth	(39.9%)	—	—	—	—	—

U.S. Bancorp

Not quite a bank for the entire US, U.S. Bancorp has more than 3,000 locations and 5,000 branded ATMs in two dozen midwestern and western states. The bank holding company, one of the 10 largest in the country, owns U.S. Bank and other subsidiaries that provide consumer and commercial banking, as well as credit card and ATM processing, mortgage banking, mutual funds, wealth management, equipment leasing, trust services, corporate payments, and insurance. California is its largest market.

In 2009 the company acquired the nine banking subsidiaries of the failed FBOP Corporation; the FDIC-assisted transaction added some 150 locations in Arizona, California, and Illinois to U.S. Bank's network. U.S. Bancorp also acquired the banking operations of the failed California-based banks Downey Savings & Loan and PFF Bank & Trust in FDIC-assisted transactions in late 2008. In 2010 it bought approximately $850 million in deposits and some branches in Nevada from BB&T, which had acquired the operations from the failed Colonial BancGroup.

The company has made purchases of stable institutions, as well, to deepen its presence in the West. Prior to the Downey and PFF acquisitions, the bank bought Los Angeles-based Mellon 1st Business Bank from The Bank of New York Mellon; Montana-based bank United Financial; and Colorado's Vail Banks, owners of WestStar Bank. U.S. Bancorp is also selling its FAF Advisors asset management subsidiary to investment services firm Nuveen Investments in exchange for a 10% stake in Nuveen.

U.S. Bancorp has also been expanding its fee-based business services such as treasury management, corporate trust, institutional custody, merchant processing, and freight payment services. Its largest fee-gathering subsidiaries include FAF Advisors and Elavon (formerly NOVA Information Systems), a leading processor of merchant credit card transactions in the US, Canada, and Europe. U.S. Bancorp is also one of the largest providers of corporate credit cards and payment services to the US government.

In 2009 U.S. Bank agreed to buy the corporate trust bond administration business of AmeriServ Financial and the bond trustee business of First Citizens Bancshares. It arranged to buy the corporate trust administration business of F.N.B. Corporation the following year.

Warren Buffett's Berkshire Hathaway owns about 4% of U.S. Bancorp.

HISTORY

When Farmers and Millers Bank was founded in 1853, it operated out of a strongbox in a rented storefront. After surviving a panic in the 1850s, the bank became part of the national banking system in 1863 as First National Bank of Milwaukee. The bank grew and in 1894 it merged with Merchants Exchange Bank (founded 1870).

In 1919 the bank merged again, with Wisconsin National Bank (founded 1892), to form First Wisconsin National Bank of Milwaukee, a leading financial institution in the area from the 1920s on.

First Wisconsin grew through purchases over the next decade, though the number of banks fell

after the 1929 stock market crash; by the end of WWII it had 11 banks. State and federal legislation, particularly the 1956 Bank Holding Company Act (which proscribed acquisitions and branching), constrained postwar growth. In the 1970s Wisconsin eased restrictions on intrastate branching and the bank began to grow again.

Growth accelerated in the late 1980s after Wisconsin and surrounding states legalized interstate banking in adjoining states in 1987. That year First Wisconsin bought seven Minnesota banks and then moved into Illinois. The company focused on strong, well-run institutions. Also that year, it sold its headquarters and used the proceeds to fund more buys. In 1988, in its first foray outside the Midwest, the company bought Metro Bancorp in Phoenix, targeting midwestern retirees moving to Arizona.

In 1989 First Wisconsin changed its name to Firstar. The early 1990s saw the company move into Iowa (Banks of Iowa, 1990), buy in-state rivals (Federated Bank Geneva Capital Corporation, 1992), and then roll into Illinois (DSB Corporation, 1993). The next year it bought First Southeast Banking Corp. (Wisconsin) and merged it, along with Firstar Bank Racine and Firstar Bank Milwaukee, into one bank. In 1994 the company was hit with a $13 million charge to cover losses from a check-kiting fraud.

Firstar continued its buying spree in 1995 and 1996, buying banks in Chicago and Minneapolis. The acquisitions left the company bloated. In 1996 Firstar began a restructuring designed to cut costs and increase margins. The restructuring project ended in 1997, but by then its performance lagged behind other midwestern banks considerably. Under pressure from major stockholders to seek a partner, Firstar began looking for a buyer.

It found Star Banc. Established in 1863 as The First National Bank of Cincinnati under a bank charter signed by Abraham Lincoln, Star Banc over the years added branches and bought other banks. The company renamed all of its subsidiary banks Star Bank in 1988 and took the name Star Banc in 1989.

In 1998 Star Banc chairman Jerry Grundhofer approached Firstar about a combination. Negotiations proceeded quickly, and a new Firstar was born. The next year Firstar bought Mercantile Bancorporation. The purchase enabled the bank to expand its international banking services into such markets as Kansas, Nebraska, and Missouri. In 2000 the company made arrangements to buy U.S. Bancorp, a Minneapolis-based bank with roots dating back to 1929. Under the terms of the acquisition, Firstar would shed its own name in favor of the more appropriate U.S. Bancorp moniker.

When the merger was completed in 2001, Firstar's Jerry Grundhofer became CEO of U.S. Bancorp, taking a seat next to his brother John, the company's chairman. Later that year the company bolstered its credit and debit card processing operations with the purchase of NOVA Corporation (now NOVA Information Systems). At the end of 2002 John Grundhofer retired from his chairman's post.

In late 2003 U.S. Bancorp unloaded its investment bank subsidiary Piper Jaffray in a spinoff to U.S. Bancorp shareholders.

Near the end of 2006 vice chairman Richard Davis succeeded CEO Jerry Grundhofer, who had been leading the company for more than a dozen

years. Davis succeeded Grundhofer as chairman the following year.

In 2008 U.S. Bancorp received $6.6 billion from the US government under the Treasury Department's program to invest some $250 billion in banks to help encourage more lending.

EXECUTIVES

Chairman, President, and CEO: Richard K. Davis, age 52, $4,973,769 total compensation
Vice Chairman: Joseph C Hoesley, age 55
Vice Chairman and CFO: Andrew Cecere, age 49, $2,559,818 total compensation
EVP and Chief Credit Officer: P. W. (Bill) Parker, age 53
EVP, General Counsel, and Secretary: Lee R. Mitau, age 61, $3,537,687 total compensation
EVP and Chief Risk Officer: Richard J. Hidy, age 47
EVP Corporate Investor and Public Relations: Judy Murphy
EVP Enterprise Revenue Office: Howell D. (Mac) McCollough III, age 50
EVP Human Resources: Jennie P. Carlson, age 49
SVP Media Relations: Steve Dale
Vice Chairman and Head Consumer Banking: Richard C. (Rick) Hartnack, age 64, $2,637,798 total compensation
Vice Chairman Payment Services: Pamela A. (Pam) Joseph, age 51
Vice Chairman, Wealth Management and Securities Services Division: Terrance R. (Terry) Dolan, age 47
Vice Chairman, Technology Services and Operations: Jeffry (Jeff) von Gillern, age 44
Vice Chairman and Head Commercial Banking: Joseph M. Otting, age 52
President and CEO, Elavon: Mike Passilla
Auditors: Ernst & Young LLP

LOCATIONS

HQ: U.S. Bancorp
800 Nicollet Mall, Minneapolis, MN 55402
Phone: 651-466-3000   **Fax:** 612-303-0782
Web: www.usbancorp.com

PRODUCTS/OPERATIONS

2009 Sales

	$ mil.	% of total
Interest		
Loans	9,841	51
Investment securities	1,606	8
Other	91	1
Noninterest		
Trust & investment management fees	1,168	6
Merchant processing services	1,148	6
Credit & debit card revenue	1,055	5
Mortgage banking	1,035	5
Deposit service charges	970	5
Corporate payment products	669	3
Commercial products	615	3
Treasury management fees	552	3
ATM processing services	410	2
Other	330	2
Total	**19,490**	**100**

2009 Assets

	$ mil.	% of total
Cash & due from banks	6,206	2
Mortgage-backed securities	32,152	12
State & municipal bonds	6,693	2
Other securities	5,923	2
Loans		
Loans held for sale	4,772	2
Commercial	48,792	17
Commercial real estate	34,093	12
Residential mortgages	26,056	9
Retail	63,955	22
Covered assets	22,512	8
Allowance for loan losses	(5,079)	—
Other	35,101	12
Total	**281,176**	**100**

COMPETITORS

BancWest	Huntington Bancshares
Bank of America	JPMorgan Chase
Capital One	KeyCorp
Citigroup	Marshall & Ilsley
Fifth Third	TCF Financial
First National of Nebraska	UnionBanCal
Great Western	Wells Fargo
Bancorporation	Zions Bancorporation

HISTORICAL FINANCIALS

Company Type: Public

Income Statement

FYE: December 31

	ASSETS ($ mil.)	NET INCOME ($ mil.)	INCOME AS % OF ASSETS	EMPLOYEES
12/09	281,176	2,205	0.8%	58,229
12/08	265,912	2,946	1.1%	57,000
12/07	237,615	4,324	1.8%	54,000
12/06	219,232	4,751	2.2%	50,000
12/05	209,465	4,489	2.1%	49,684
Annual Growth	7.6%	(16.3%)	—	4.0%

2009 Year-End Financials

Equity as % of assets: 8.7%	Dividends
Return on assets: 0.8%	Yield: 0.9%
Return on equity: 10.3%	Payout: 20.6%
Long-term debt ($ mil.): 32,580	Market value ($ mil.): 43,155
No. of shares (mil.): 1,917	Sales ($ mil.): 19,490

Stock History

NYSE: USB

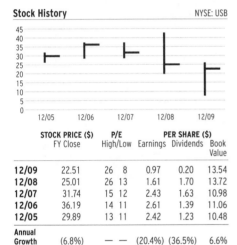

	12/05	12/06	12/07	12/08	12/09

	STOCK PRICE ($) FY Close	P/E High/Low	PER SHARE ($) Earnings	Dividends	Book Value
12/09	22.51	26 8	0.97	0.20	13.54
12/08	25.01	26 13	1.61	1.70	13.72
12/07	31.74	15 12	2.43	1.63	10.98
12/06	36.19	14 11	2.61	1.39	11.06
12/05	29.89	13 11	2.42	1.23	10.48
Annual Growth	(6.8%)	— —	(20.4%)	(36.5%)	6.6%

US Postal Service

The United States Postal Service (USPS) handles cards, letters, and packages sent from sea to shining sea. The USPS delivers 203 billion pieces of mail a year (at an average of 667 million per day) to some 149 million addresses in the US and its territories. The independent government agency relies on postage and fees to fund operations. Though it has a monopoly on delivering the mail, the USPS faces competition for services such as package delivery. The US president appoints nine of the 11 members of the board that oversee the USPS. The presidential appointees select the postmaster general, and together they name the deputy postmaster general; the two also serve on the board.

A challenge for the agency is the growing use of the Internet, which has led to lower volume of some types of mail. To keep pace, the USPS has worked to gain delivery business generated by online shopping. It also is investing in the development of the Intelligent Mail Barcode, a mini-GPS system for tracking mail. In 2009 the USPS introduced its new mobile phone application allowing phone users to locate post offices, track and confirm packages, and look up zip codes.

At the same time the agency is looking to technical advancements, it is also attentively working to cut costs. In 2008 USPS reduced its workforce by more than 20,000 positions through attrition and by cutting hours of operation at some of its 32,000-plus post offices and other retail and delivery facilities. Transportation is also a major expense for the agency, and high fuel prices have pumped up costs for operating the agency's 221,000 vehicles.

With an eye on its bottom line, the USPS has accelerated the pace of its rate increases. Between January 2006 and May 2009 the price of a first-class stamp went from 37 cents to 44 cents. To cater to customers who get stuck with some of the out-of-date stamps, USPS introduced a new concept in April 2007 — the Forever Stamp. The Liberty Bell-imaged stamp is sold at the same price as a first-class stamp but it can then be used, as the name says, forever, even as the price of first-class postage goes up.

The USPS was given some flexibility in setting rates, as well as some new restrictions, by the Postal Accountability and Enhancement Act of 2006, considered the farthest-reaching postal reform legislation since the agency became independent in 1970. The goal of the law was to enable the USPS to adopt some private-sector management practices in order to ensure the agency's long-term financial health and to preserve universal mail service. Among the short-term effects of the legislation was a requirement that the agency pay into a new fund for retiree health benefits. The $5.6 billion payment caused the USPS to record a loss in 2007, the agency's first since 2002.

Affected by the skyrocketing fuel prices and diminished demand for its postal and shipping services, the USPS recorded another loss in 2008.

The USPS's 72nd Postmaster General of the US is John E. Potter, who took the position in 2001.

HISTORY

The second-oldest agency of the US government (after Indian Affairs), the Post Office was created by the Continental Congress in 1775 with Benjamin Franklin as postmaster general. The postal system came to play a vital role in the development of transportation in the US.

At that time, postal workers were riders on muddy paths delivering letters without stamps or envelopes. Letters were delivered only between post offices. Congress approved the first official postal policy in 1792: Rates ranged from six cents for less than 30 miles to 25 cents for more than 450. Letter carriers began delivering mail in cities in 1794.

First based in Philadelphia, in 1800 the Post Office moved to Washington, DC. In 1829 Andrew Jackson elevated the position of postmaster general to cabinet rank — it became a means of rewarding political cronies. Mail contracts subsidized the early development of US railroads. The first adhesive postage stamp appeared in the US in 1847.

Uniform postal rates (not varying with distance) were instituted in 1863, the year free city delivery began. The start of free rural delivery in 1896 spurred road construction in isolated US areas. Parcel post was launched in 1913, and new mail-order houses such as Montgomery Ward and Sears, Roebuck flourished.

The famous pledge beginning "Neither snow nor rain . . ." — not an official motto — was first inscribed at the main New York City post office in 1914. Scheduled airmail service between Washington, DC, and New York City began in 1918, stimulating the development of commercial air service. The ZIP code was introduced in 1963.

As mail volume grew, postal workers became increasingly militant under work stress. (Franklin's pigeonhole sorting method had barely changed.) A work stoppage in the New York City post office in 1970 spread within nine days to 670 post offices, and the US Army was deployed to handle the mail. Later that year the Postal Reorganization Act was passed. The new law established a board of governors to handle postal affairs and choose the postmaster general, who became CEO of an independent agency, the US Postal Service (USPS). The next year USPS negotiated the first US government collective-bargaining labor contract. Express mail service began in 1977, and USPS stepped up automation efforts.

In 1995 USPS launched Global Package Link, a program to expedite major customers' shipments to Canada, Japan, and the UK. The next year it overhauled rates, cutting prices for larger mailers who prepared their mail for automation and raising prices for small mailers who didn't.

Postmaster General Marvin Runyon — whose six-year tenure took the agency from the red into the black — retired in 1998 and was succeeded by USPS veteran William Henderson. In a nod to the Internet, USPS in 1999 contracted with outside vendors to enable customers to buy and print stamps online.

In 2001 USPS formed a strategic alliance with rival FedEx through which FedEx agreed to provide air transportation for USPS mail, in return for the placement of FedEx drop boxes in post offices. Henderson stepped down at the end of May 2001, and EVP Jack Potter was named to replace him. That year several postal workers in a Washington, DC, branch office were exposed to anthrax-tainted letters.

Potter launched a series of cost-cutting programs, which together with rate increases enabled the USPS to post a profit in 2003 — the agency's first year in the black since 1999.

EXECUTIVES

Chairman: Louis J. Giuliano
Vice Chairman: Thurgood Marshall Jr., age 53
Chief Postal Inspector: William P. (Bill) Gilligan
Postmaster General, CEO, and Governor:
John E. (Jack) Potter
Deputy Postmaster, COO, and Governor:
Patrick R. Donahoe
EVP and CFO: Joseph (Joe) Corbett, age 50
EVP and CIO: Ross Philo
EVP and Chief Human Resources Officer:
Anthony J. (Tony) Vegliante
SVP and General Counsel: Mary Anne Gibbons
SVP Intelligent Mail and Address Quality:
Thomas G. (Tom) Day
SVP Strategy and Transition: Linda A. Kingsley
SVP Customer Relations: Stephen M. (Steve) Kearney
SVP Operations: Steven J. Forte
VP and Controller: Vincent H. (Vince) DeVito
VP Engineering: David E. Williams
VP Employee Development and Diversity:
Susan M. LaChance

VP Government Relations and Public Policy:
Marie Therese Dominguez
VP Corporate Communications: Mitzi R. Betman
President, Mailing and Shipping Services: Paul Vogel
Acting President, Mailing and Shipping Services:
Susan M. Plonkey
Secretary: Julie S. Moore
Auditors: Ernst & Young LLP

LOCATIONS

HQ: United States Postal Service
475 L'Enfant Plaza SW, Washington, DC 20260
Phone: 202-268-2500 **Fax:** 202-268-4860
Web: www.usps.com

PRODUCTS/OPERATIONS

2009 Sales

	$ mil.	% of total
Mail		
First-class mail	35,873	53
Standard mail	17,364	26
Periodicals	2,038	3
Shipping services	8,132	12
Package services	1,683	2
Other mailing services	3,000	4
Total	**68,090**	**100**

HISTORICAL FINANCIALS

Company Type: Government agency

Income Statement				FYE: September 30
	REVENUE ($ mil.)	NET INCOME ($ mil.)	NET PROFIT MARGIN	EMPLOYEES
9/09	68,090	(3,740)	—	623,128
9/08	74,932	(2,806)	—	663,238
9/07	74,973	(5,142)	—	684,762
9/06	72,650	900	1.2%	696,138
9/05	69,907	1,445	2.1%	704,716
Annual Growth	(0.7%)	—	—	(3.0%)

Net Income History

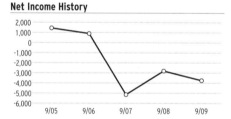

USEC Inc.

USEC beats radioactive swords into enriched uranium plowshares. The company processes used uranium — about half of which comes from old Russian atomic warheads — into enriched uranium, which it then supplies for commercial nuclear power plants. USEC is the radioactive recycler of choice for the "Megatons-to-Megawatts" program, a US-Russian agreement to convert uranium from warheads into nuclear fuel. USEC also processes uranium for the US Department of Energy. The company's NAC subsidiary provides consulting services to nuclear power plant operators and transportation of nuclear materials. The company works with Babcok & Wilcox to manufacture centrifuge components for the American Centrifuge Project.

The Project provides highly efficient uranium enrichment gas centrifuge technology to develop low enriched uranium for the nuclear industry.

Contracts from the US government, Exelon, and Entergy each account for more than 10% of the company's sales. Fully three-quarters of USEC's business comes from the US; Japan is its other main source of business.

In an unusual move, China acquired an indirect stake in USEC in 2010. Hong Kong-based Noble Group bought 5% of the American-owned uranium processor. The Chinese government's sovereign wealth fund is one of Noble's minority owners. While the Chinese investment was passive (it only owns a 15% stake in Noble), the move still raised eyebrows at the US State Department.

HISTORY

The US government's uranium enrichment program was born during WWII to produce material for the atomic bomb. Originally part of the Atomic Energy Commission, the program eventually came under the aegis of the Department of Energy (DOE). The Energy Policy Act of 1992 created the United States Enrichment Corporation (USEC) to encourage privatization. The act gave USEC four mandates: a consistent domestic supply of enriched uranium, competitive prices, support of US national security goals, and a transition into a fully privatized commercial business. USEC officially took over uranium enrichment operations in 1993.

In 1993 two of the USEC's mandates ran head-on into each other. As cash-poor, missile-laden Russia struggled to revive its economy, President Clinton and Russian President Boris Yeltsin made a deal for the US to pay Russia for nuclear fuel derived from its atomic warheads. The 1994 contract locked USEC into a 20-year, $12 billion contract with the Russian Ministry for Atomic Energy to buy 500 metric tons of enriched uranium from nuclear warheads. Although this was good for national security, it was bad business because US material was cheaper. USEC balked, but the "Megatons-to-Megawatts" agreement went through, and by 1995 USEC had received six metric tons of the warhead uranium.

USEC's 1995 privatization plan faced a major production concern. Built in the 1950s, USEC's gaseous diffusion plants required vast amounts of electricity, while European competitors were using a much less expensive centrifuge process. To improve competitiveness, the US government transferred its Atomic Vapor Laser Isotope Separation (AVLIS) process to USEC, giving the firm a technology the government had spent $1.5 billion and 30 years in developing. (The company shelved the AVLIS project in 1999 because building such a plant would cost $2.5 billion.)

The USEC Privatization Act was ratified in 1996; its transition was approved a year later, and the company was put up for sale. The US government received only two bids for USEC; both were unacceptable, so the government sold stock to the public in 1998, and the sale raised $1.4 billion for the US Treasury.

The next year USEC took over management of its facilities from Lockheed Martin, marking the first time the program would not be run by contractors. The troubled company (facing high prices for raw material, low prices for finished products, and an in-depth government investigation into the company's long-term operations) eliminated 500 jobs and announced it would consider other job cuts.

In 2000 USEC signed a fuel supply contract with the Tennessee Valley Authority and invested heavily into laser-enrichment technology developed by Australian firm Silex Systems. Also that year a DOE report outlined many historically unsafe practices at the company's Paducah, Kentucky, plant, including experiments that intentionally exposed workers to radioactivity.

The next year USEC negotiated the rate at which it purchases commercial uranium from its Russian partner, Tenex; however, the Bush administration delayed approval of the deal. Also, the US Department of Commerce decided to work toward imposing duties on imported uranium from European companies (it ruled that the companies were selling uranium at unfairly low prices). Also in 2001 USEC repurchased 20% of its common stock.

In early 2004 USEC announced that it selected Piketon, Ohio, as the site for its American Centrifuge plant. In late 2004 CEO William Timbers left the company, and chairman James Mellor took over as interim CEO.

General Dynamics veteran John Welch was named president and CEO of USEC in 2005.

EXECUTIVES

Chairman: James R. (Jim) Mellor, age 79
President and CEO: John K. Welch, age 59, $4,273,161 total compensation
SVP and CFO: John C. Barpoulis, age 45, $1,042,893 total compensation
SVP Human Resources and Administration: W. Lance Wright, age 62, $1,137,837 total compensation
SVP, Uranium Enrichment: Robert Van Namen, age 48, $1,060,333 total compensation
SVP, American Centrifuge and Russian HEU: Philip G. Sewell, age 63, $1,656,076 total compensation
SVP, General Counsel, and Secretary: Peter B. Saba, age 48
SVP External Relations: Christine M. Ciccone
VP Marketing and Sales: John M. A. Donelson, age 45
VP Finance and Treasurer: Stephen S. Greene, age 52
VP Government Relations: E. John Neumann, age 62
VP American Centrifuge: Paul Sullivan, age 49
VP Corporate Communications: Paul E. Jacobson, age 51
Controller and Chief Accounting Officer: J. Tracy Mey, age 49
Director Sales: Marisa Vilardo
Director Investor Relations: Steven Wingfield
Director Corporate Communications: Elizabeth Stuckle
Auditors: PricewaterhouseCoopers LLP

LOCATIONS

HQ: USEC Inc.
2 Democracy Center, 6903 Rockledge Dr.
Bethesda, MD 20817
Phone: 301-564-3200 **Fax:** 301-564-3201
Web: www.usec.com

2009 Sales

	$ mil.	% of total
US	1,402.2	69
Japan	305.0	15
Other countries	329.6	16
Total	**2,036.8**	**100**

PRODUCTS/OPERATIONS

2009 Sales

	$ mil.	% of total
Separative work units	1,647.0	81
US government contracts	209.1	10
Uranium	180.7	9
Total	**2,036.8**	**100**

COMPETITORS

AREVA
Belgonucleaire
BNFL
Cameco
Japan Nuclear Fuel

HISTORICAL FINANCIALS

Company Type: Public

Income Statement

FYE: December 31

	REVENUE ($ mil.)	NET INCOME ($ mil.)	NET PROFIT MARGIN	EMPLOYEES
12/09	2,037	59	2.9%	2,908
12/08	1,615	49	3.0%	2,978
12/07	1,928	97	5.0%	2,866
12/06	1,849	106	5.7%	2,677
12/05	1,559	22	1.4%	2,762
Annual Growth	6.9%	27.3%	—	1.3%

2009 Year-End Financials

Debt ratio: 45.1%
Return on equity: 4.8%
Cash ($ mil.): 131
Current ratio: 1.82
Long-term debt ($ mil.): 575
No. of shares (mil.): 114
Dividends
Yield: 0.0%
Payout: —
Market value ($ mil.): 440

Stock History

NYSE: USU

	STOCK PRICE ($) FY Close	P/E High	P/E Low	PER SHARE ($) Earnings	PER SHARE ($) Dividends	PER SHARE ($) Book Value
12/09	3.85	20	9	0.37	0.00	11.17
12/08	4.49	27	7	0.35	0.00	10.18
12/07	9.00	27	8	0.94	0.00	11.47
12/06	12.72	13	8	1.22	0.00	8.63
12/05	11.95	72	35	0.26	0.55	7.95
Annual Growth	(24.7%)	—	—	9.2%	—	8.9%

USG Corporation

Where there's a wall, there's likely SHEET-ROCK. USG, the maker of the world's top brand of wallboard, is one of the largest building products manufacturers and distributors in the US. The company operates in three divisions. Its North American gypsum unit, which accounts for about half of sales, manufactures wallboard, gypsum fiberboard, and other products for finishing interior walls, ceilings, and floors. The worldwide ceilings division makes ceiling systems and acoustic tile, used mainly in commercial buildings. USG's building products distribution arm distributes building products through L&W Supply. USG operates more than 140 plants, quarries, and other facilities in North America, Europe, and Asia.

The past several years have been challenging for USG. It was first struck by asbestos-related claims, then bankruptcy followed by major shifts in the business brought on by the economic recession. USG emerged from Chapter 11 bankruptcy protection in 2006 after establishing a $4 billion trust to pay asbestos claims. The company was one of several companies, including Owens Corning and W. R. Grace, that sought shelter from asbestos-related litigation in Chapter 11 to keep lawsuits from draining value from the company.

In a case of bad timing, the company emerged from bankruptcy a year before the construction industry suffered a severe downturn in 2007. USG's sales dropped and its shipments of wallboard and other products fell.

To deal with the US downturn brought on by overbuilding and the subprime mortgage crisis, the company has been scaling back operations and programs. It also reduced its workforce by a third in 2008. A year later USG closed two plants in California and idled another in New Jersey. The company also has shut down nearly 100 distribution centers since 2007.

New home construction (a major source of demand for USG) was at historically low levels in 2009, but managed to stabilize by the end of the year. Instead of relying on new home construction, the company looked to the repair and remodel market to spur sales.

USG isn't all about downsizing, however. Its L&W Supply unit continues to consider opportunities to grow its specialty dealer business. In 2007 L&W purchased the inventory of California Wholesale Material Supply (CALPLY), which sells building products in seven western states and Mexico.

Warren Buffett's Berkshire Hathaway owns about 35% of USG, and German firm Gebr. Knauf Verwaltungsgesellschaft and Fairfax Financial Holdings each own some 15%. USG was lifted in 2009 when Berkshire Hathaway, along with Fairfax purchased 26 million new convertible debt shares, injecting $400 million of much needed cash into the company.

HISTORY

In 1901 a group of 35 companies joined to form U.S.G., the largest gypsum producing and processing business in the industry. Sewell Avery became CEO in 1905 (he led U.S.G. until 1951).

U.S.G. began producing lime in 1915. It became United States Gypsum (U.S. Gypsum) in 1920 and began making paint in 1924. By 1931 it was producing insulating board and metal lath fields. It also added two lime businesses and two gypsum concerns.

Also in 1931 Avery became chairman of Montgomery Ward, managing both companies simultaneously. U.S. Gypsum entered asphalt roofing, mineral wool, hardboard, and asbestos-cement siding during the thirties. It made profits and paid dividends throughout the Depression.

Beginning in the late 1960s, U.S. Gypsum diversified into building materials and remodeling, buying such companies as Wallace Manufacturing (prefinished wood panels, 1970) and Kinkead Industries (steel doors and frames, 1972). U.S. Gypsum formed L&W Supply in 1971.

The company bought Masonite in 1984 and changed its name to USG the next year. It acquired Donn (remodeling materials) in 1986 and DAP (caulk and sealants) in 1987.

USG led a $776 million buyback of 20% of its stock to ward off a takeover that year. In 1988 Desert Partners of Midland, Texas, tried another takeover; the attempt was foiled nine months later when shareholders approved a management plan (including taking on $2.5 billion of new debt) to keep control of the company. By the end of 1989, USG had sold several assets and had shrunk by about 25%. Proceeds from the sale of Masonite (to International Paper Company), Kinkead, and Marlite netted $560 million, which was used to pay debt. USG defaulted on $40 million of scheduled payments to bondholders and banks in 1991, however, and sold its profitable DAP unit to the UK's Wassall for just $90 million.

The firm was among 20 manufacturers that agreed to a $1.3 billion class-action asbestos settlement in 1993. (The US Supreme Court voided the pact in 1997.) Also that year USG filed one of the largest prepackaged Chapter 11 bankruptcy cases on record. As a result of restructuring, USG cut its debt by $1.4 billion and its annual interest payments by $200 million. In 1994 USG sold 7.9 million new shares, raising $224 million to further reduce debt. Charges related to the sale or closure of certain operations contributed to another loss in 1995.

In 1997 USG announced a joint venture with Zhongbei Building Material Products Company; USG acquired 60% of the Chinese ceiling-grid manufacturer. In late 1999 the company acquired Sybex and The Synkoloid Company of Canada, both leading North American manufacturers of paper-faced metal corner bead (used to protect and strengthen the exposed edges of drywall).

In 2000 investor Warren Buffett revealed that he had built a 15% stake in USG. USG announced in 2001 that it would take an $850 million charge (for the fourth quarter of 2000) to cover against asbestos litigation. In June 2001 USG and 10 of its subsidiaries filed for bankruptcy protection.

The company closed a gypsum fiber panel plant in Nova Scotia, Canada, and a ceiling tile plant in Aubange, Belgium, in 2002.

USG sold its UK-based access floor systems business in 2003. The next year subsidiary USG Interiors sold its relocatable walls business and ULTRAWALL System product line to California-based Ultrawall, LLC; USG Interiors also agreed to supply the gypsum baseboard for use in the systems.

In 2005 USG took a $3.1 billion charge and outlined a plan to emerge from bankruptcy by settling outstanding claims; in 2006 it funded a trust with $900 million in cash and a $3.05 billion contingent note. That year it emerged from bankruptcy.

EXECUTIVES

Chairman and CEO: William C. Foote, age 59, $7,135,480 total compensation
President, COO and Director: James S. Metcalf, age 51, $2,829,181 total compensation
EVP and General Counsel: Stanley L. Ferguson, age 57, $1,672,253 total compensation
EVP and CFO: Richard H. (Rick) Fleming, age 62, $1,724,057 total compensation
SVP; President and CEO, L&W Supply: Brendan J. Deely, age 44
SVP Human Resources: Brian J. Cook, age 52, $1,253,637 total compensation
SVP Finance: D. Rick Lowes, age 55
SVP; President, International: Christopher R. Griffin, age 48
SVP Communications: Marcia S. (Marci) Kaminsky, age 51

VP; President, USG Building Systems: Fareed A, Khan, age 44, $968,793 total compensation
VP and CIO: Jennifer F. Scanlon, age 43
VP and CTO; Lead, Research and Development Center: Dominic A. Dannessa, age 53
VP, Corporate Secretary, and Associate General Counsel: Ellis A. Regenbogen, age 63
VP Employee Benefits, Safety and Corporate Services: Jeffrey P. Rodewald
VP and Controller: William J. Kelley Jr., age 45
VP and Treasurer: Karen L. Leets, age 53
Auditors: Deloitte & Touche LLP

LOCATIONS

HQ: USG Corporation
550 W. Adams St., Chicago, IL 60661
Phone: 312-436-4000   **Fax:** 312-436-4093
Web: www.usg.com

2009 Sales

	$ mil.	% of total
US	2,725	80
Canada	339	10
Other foreign	335	10
Adjustments	(164)	—
Total	**3,235**	**100**

PRODUCTS/OPERATIONS

2009 Sales

	$ mil.	% of total
North American Gypsum	1,770	48
Building Products Distribution	1,289	35
Worldwide Ceilings	663	17
Adjustments	(487)	—
Total	**3,235**	**100**

Selected Products

North American Gypsum
DIAMOND (plaster products)
DUROCK (cement board)
FIBEROCK (fiber panels)
LEVELROCK (poured gypsum underlayments)
IMPERIAL (plaster products)
RED TOP (plaster products)
SHEETROCK (gypsum wallboard)

Worldwide Ceilings Products & Brands
ACOUSTONE (ceiling tile)
AURATONE (ceiling tile)
CENTRICITEE (ceiling grid)
COMPASSO (ceiling grid)
CURVATURA (ceiling grid)
DONN (ceiling grid)
DX (ceiling grid)
FINELINE (ceiling grid)

Selected Subsidiaries

CGC Inc. (Canada)
L&W Supply Corporation
United States Gypsum Company
USG Interiors, Inc.
USG Mexico SA de CV (Mexico)

COMPETITORS

Allied Building Products	Industrial Acoustics
American Gypsum	James Hardie Industries
Armstrong World	Knauf Gips KG
Industries	Lafarge
BPB	Lafarge North America
CertainTeed	Louisiana-Pacific
CSR Limited	New NGC
Eagle Materials	Pacific Coast Building
Georgia-Pacific	Products
Gypsum Products	Temple-Inland
HeidelbergCement	Worthington Industries

HISTORICAL FINANCIALS
Company Type: Public

Income Statement
FYE: December 31

	REVENUE ($ mil.)	NET INCOME ($ mil.)	NET PROFIT MARGIN	EMPLOYEES
12/09	3,235	(787)	—	10,100
12/08	4,608	(463)	—	12,800
12/07	5,202	76	1.5%	14,800
12/06	5,810	288	5.0%	14,700
12/05	5,139	(1,425)	—	14,100
Annual Growth	**(10.9%)**	**—**	**—**	**(8.0%)**

2009 Year-End Financials

Debt ratio: 210.2%
Return on equity: —
Cash ($ mil.): 690
Current ratio: 2.91
Long-term debt ($ mil.): 1,955

No. of shares (mil.): 100
Dividends
Yield: 0.0%
Payout: —
Market value ($ mil.): 1,398

Stock History
NYSE: USG

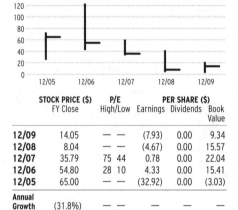

	STOCK PRICE ($) FY Close	P/E High/Low		Earnings	PER SHARE ($) Dividends	Book Value
12/09	14.05	—	—	(7.93)	0.00	9.34
12/08	8.04	—	—	(4.67)	0.00	15.57
12/07	35.79	75	44	0.78	0.00	22.04
12/06	54.80	28	10	4.33	0.00	15.41
12/05	65.00	—	—	(32.92)	0.00	(3.03)
Annual Growth	**(31.8%)**	**—**	**—**	**—**	**—**	**—**

Valassis Communications

Valassis Communications offers door-to-door marketing without taking a toll on its shoes. A giant in the marketing services industry, Valassis is a leading producer of newspaper inserts, selling space for advertising and coupons in its four-color booklets. Each week its consumer brand RedPlum delivers coupons and deals to more than 100 million households through the mailbox, in the newspaper, on the doorstep, or on the Internet. Outside the US, Valassis' products and services reach about 5 million Canadian households. In order to provide its services, the company works in collaboration with more than 15,000 advertisers worldwide. It has about 25 operations facilities in the US and eight internationally.

Valassis made industry news in 2007 when it acquired direct mail marketing leader ADVO for $1.2 billion. After the monster deal, Valassis inherited the ability to reach nine out of 10 US households through its shared mail distribution services. The ADVO acquisition was an effort by Valassis to look for growth beyond the US

newspaper insert business, which the company dominates. (News Corporation's News America is the industry's other major player.) In early 2008 the company changed the name of ADVO to Valassis Direct Mail and integrated its product portfolio into its own. At the same time, Valassis launched its RedPlum offering, which it intends to grow by launching its products across multiple platforms.

As News America controls over half of the $1 billion market, Valassis represents most of the rest. In fact, throughout 2006 and 2007, Valassis sued News America, claiming it was acting as a monopoly. News America filed motions to dismiss the complaints, and after years of back and forth, a trial was finally set to settle the matter beginning in early 2010. However, before the case went to trial, both parties agreed to settle all lawsuits, and News America's parent company News Corp. capitulated to paying Valassis a $500 million settlement. As part of the deal, News America also entered a 10-year shared mail distribution agreement with Valassis Direct Mail.

HISTORY

George F. Valassis started commercial printing firm GFV Communications in 1969. Knowing that publishers had the technology to insert TV listings, Valassis joined with ad man Ted Isaacs in 1972 to pioneer free-standing newspaper inserts as a way to get full-color ads circulated at a lower cost. The idea was slow to catch on and Isaacs bailed out in the mid-1970s. By 1979, however, sales had reached $35 million.

That year Valassis turned the business over to son-in-law Larry Johnson, who recruited school chum David Brandon to help run the company. The industry exploded during the 1980s, leading to brutal price wars, but GFV remained the market leader. In 1986 Valassis sold the company for $400 million to Consolidated Press Holdings (CPH). Brandon was appointed president in 1989. Changing its name to Valassis Communications, the company went public in 1992 with CPH holding a 49% stake.

In 1993 Sullivan Marketing, backed by Morgan Stanley, tried muscling into the market, forcing prices down. Valassis cut prices to protect its market share, and Sullivan exited the business the next year. The company made several expansion efforts, including establishing Valassis of Canada through its 1995 acquisition of Canadian sale promoter McIntyre & Dodd. But in 1997 it ended its Mexican joint venture (begun in 1994) and French operations (acquired in 1994).

In 1997 Consolidated Press Holdings sold its stake in the company to the public, and Brandon added chairman to his title. Valassis put $13 million into capital improvements to gear up for future growth. The next year Alan Schultz replaced Brandon as chairman, president, and CEO.

Valassis acquired 50% of startup Save.com in 1999 to offer coupons over the Internet. It also bought a majority stake in Independent Delivery Services, which provides e-commerce software to grocery stores, and a 30% stake in Relationship Marketing Group. In 2000 Valassis expanded its online holdings with a minority investment in Coupons.com. Save.com shut down in 2001 amid the dot-com shake-out.

Keeping the acquisitions going, in 2002 the company bought the remaining stakes of Valassis Retail Marketing Systems. In 2003 Valassis acquired PreVision Marketing, LLC. The following year Catalina Marketing sold its direct mail division to Valassis, strengthening the company's own 1-to-1 loyalty-building direct mail business.

Valassis made huge waves in the marketing services industry in March 2007 when it acquired direct mail marketing leader ADVO for about $1.2 billion.

EXECUTIVES

Chairman, President, and CEO: Alan F. Schultz, age 51, $3,948,846 total compensation
EVP, CFO, Treasurer, and Director: Robert L. Recchia, age 53, $1,413,782 total compensation
EVP Manufacturing and Client Services: William F. (Bill) Hogg Jr., age 63, $1,127,610 total compensation
EVP Sales and Marketing: Richard P. Herpich, age 57, $961,814 total compensation
Chief Marketing Officer: Suzanne C. (Suzie) Brown, age 50
Chief Sales Officer: Robert A. Mason, age 52
SVP Administration, General Counsel, and Secretary: Todd L. Wisely, age 40
VP New Account Development: Gabrielle Austin
President and CEO, NCH Marketing Services: Brian J. Husselbee, age 58, $600,988 total compensation
President, Digital Media: John Lieblang, age 52
Director Investor Relations and Corporate Communications: Mary Broaddus
Auditors: Deloitte & Touche LLP

LOCATIONS

HQ: Valassis Communications, Inc.
19975 Victor Pkwy., Livonia, MI 48152
Phone: 734-591-3000   **Fax:** 734-591-4994
Web: www.valassis.com

2009 Sales

	$ mil.	% of total
US	2,193.0	98
Other countries	51.2	2
Total	**2,244.2**	**100**

PRODUCTS/OPERATIONS

2009 Sales

	$ mil.	% of total
Shared mail (ADVO)	1,279.1	57
Neighborhood targeted products	444.7	20
Free-standing inserts	361.4	16
International, digital media & services	159.0	7
Total	**2,244.2**	**100**

Selected Subsidiaries

Marketing Systems, LLC
NCH Marketing Services, Inc.
Promotion Watch
Valassis Canada
Valassis Direct Mail, Inc.
Valassis Relationship

Selected Products and Services

Household targeted
 Direct mail advertising and sampling
 Internet-delivered promotions
 Software and analytics
International and services
 Coupon clearing, promotion, and marketing
 Promotion security and consulting services
Market delivered products
 Cooperative free-standing inserts
 Run of Press
Neighborhood targeted products
 Door Hangers
 Preprinted inserts
 Newspaper delivered product sampling
 Newspaper Polybag advertising

COMPETITORS

Acxiom
Catalina Marketing
Grey Group
Harte-Hanks
HighQ BPO
MailSouth
News America Marketing
News Corp.
Norwood Promotional Products
Outlook Group
Penn Lithographics
Quebecor
R.R. Donnelley
SPAR Group
Sunflower Group
Valpak Direct Marketing Systems
Vertis Inc
yesmail

HISTORICAL FINANCIALS

Company Type: Public

Income Statement

FYE: December 31

	REVENUE ($ mil.)	NET INCOME ($ mil.)	NET PROFIT MARGIN	EMPLOYEES
12/09	2,244	67	3.0%	7,440
12/08	2,382	(208)	—	7,200
12/07	2,242	58	2.6%	7,500
12/06	1,044	51	4.9%	3,600
12/05	1,131	95	8.4%	3,600
Annual Growth	**18.7%**	**(8.5%)**	**—**	**19.9%**

2009 Year-End Financials

Debt ratio: 1,026.8%
Return on equity: 129.4%
Cash ($ mil.): 130
Current ratio: 1.27
Long-term debt ($ mil.): 1,005
No. of shares (mil.): 50
Dividends
 Yield: 0.0%
 Payout: —
Market value ($ mil.): 910

Stock History

NYSE: VCI

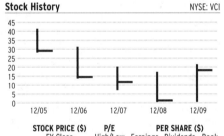

	STOCK PRICE ($) FY Close	P/E High	P/E Low	PER SHARE ($) Earnings	PER SHARE ($) Dividends	PER SHARE ($) Book Value
12/09	18.26	15	1	1.36	0.00	1.96
12/08	1.32	—	—	(4.32)	0.00	0.11
12/07	11.69	16	6	1.21	0.00	4.41
12/06	14.50	29	13	1.07	0.00	3.36
12/05	29.07	21	15	1.90	0.00	2.08
Annual Growth	**(11.0%)**	**—**	**—**	**(8.0%)**	**—**	**(1.4%)**

Valero Energy

Valero Energy is on a mission. Named after the Alamo (the Mission San Antonio de Valero), Valero is the largest independent oil refiner in the US. Valero refines low-cost residual oil and heavy crude into cleaner-burning, higher-margin products, including low-sulfur diesels. It operates 16 refineries (with a total production capacity of about 3 million barrels per day) located in California, Louisiana, New Jersey, Oklahoma, Tennessee, Texas, and in Aruba and Canada. It also has a network of some 5,800 retail gas stations and wholesale outlets bearing the Corner Store, Diamond Shamrock, Shamrock, Ultramar, Valero, Stop N Go, and Beacon names in 44 US states and in Canada.

Because of the global economic slowdown limiting fuel demand, Valero is pursuing a long-term strategy of selling about a third of its high-cost North American refineries, and exploring projects in faster-growing markets in Europe, the Middle East, and Asia. To cut costs, in 2008 the company sold its Krotz Springs, Louisiana, refinery to Alon USA Energy for $333 million, and in 2009 it closed its Delaware City refinery (and sold it in 2010).

Hedging its bets, Valero has moved into the alternative fuel business. Given that ethanol is a requirement in many of the gasoline fuel mixes it sells, the company decided that it could cut costs by owning ethanol plants, rather than buying ethanol wholesale. It made its first foray into ethanol production in 2009, buying seven ethanol production facilities from VeraSun Energy, which was operating under Chapter 11 bankruptcy protection. Valero paid about $475 million for the facilities. Acquiring other ethanol companies, by early 2010 the company owned a total of 10 ethanol plants, with a collective capacity of 1.1 billion gallons a year.

In 2009 Valero had an opportunity for international refinery expansion and a foothold in Europe, when it agreed to acquire Dow Chemical's 45% interest in Dutch refinery Total Raffinaderij Nederland N.V. However, the deal fell through, and the stake was sold to LUKOIL.

Valero became a retail giant overnight with its Ultramar Diamond Shamrock purchase in 2001. The 2005 acquisition of Premcor made Valero, the largest independent refiner on the Gulf Coast, a major national player.

HISTORY

Valero Energy was created as a result of the sins of its father, Houston-based Coastal States Gas Corporation. Led by flamboyant entrepreneur Oscar Wyatt, energy giant Coastal had established Lo-Vaca Gathering Company as a gas marketing subsidiary. Bound by long-term contracts to several Texas cities, Coastal was not able to meet its contractual obligations when gas prices rose in the early 1970s, and major litigation against the company resulted. The Texas Railroad Commission (the energy-regulating authority) ordered Coastal to refund customers $1.6 billion.

To meet the requirements, 55% of Lo-Vaca was spun off to disgruntled former customers as Valero Energy at the end of 1979. The new company was born fully grown — as the largest intrastate pipeline in Texas — with accountant-cum-CEO Bill Greehey, the court-appointed chief of Lo-Vaca, at its head. Greehey relocated the company to San Antonio, where it took its Valero name (from the Alamo, or Mission San Antonio de Valero) and put some distance between itself and its discredited former parent. Under Greehey's direction, Valero developed a squeaky-clean image by giving to charities, stressing a dress code, and keeping facilities clean.

Greehey diversified the company into refining unleaded gasoline. Valero bought residual fuel oil from Saudi Arabian refiners and in 1981 built a refinery in Corpus Christi, Texas, which went on line two years later. But in 1984 a glut of unleaded gasoline on the US market from European refiners undercut Valero's profits. To stay afloat, Valero sold pipeline assets, including 50% of its West Texas Pipeline in 1985 and 51% of its major pipeline operations in 1987. Refining margins finally began to improve in 1988. With one of the most modern refineries in the US, Valero did not have to spend a bundle to upgrade its refining processes to meet the tougher EPA requirements of the 1990s.

In 1992 Valero expanded its refinery's production capacity and acquired two gas processing plants and several hundred miles of gas pipelines from struggling oil firm Oryx Energy (acquired by Kerr-McGee in 1999). That year Valero became the first non-Mexican business engaged in Mexican gasoline production when it signed a deal with state oil company Petróleos Mexicanos S.A. to build a gasoline additive plant there.

To expand its natural gas business substantially, in 1994 Valero bought back the 51% of Valero Natural Gas Partners it didn't own. Valero also teamed up with regional oil company Swift Energy in a transportation, marketing, and processing agreement. As part of that arrangement, Valero agreed to build a pipeline linking Swift's Texas gas field with a Valero plant.

In 1997 the company sold Valero Natural Gas to California electric utility PG&E, gaining $1.5 billion for expansion. It then purchased Salomon's oil refining unit, Basis Petroleum (two refineries in Texas and one in Louisiana), and the next year picked up Mobil's refinery in Paulsboro, New Jersey.

With low crude oil prices hurting its bottom line in 1999, Valero explored partnerships with other refiners as a way to cut operating costs. In 2000 the company bought Exxon Mobil's 130,000-barrel-per-day Benicia, California, refinery, along with 340 retail outlets, for about $1 billion.

In 2001 Valero gained two small refineries when it bought Huntway Refining, a leading supplier of asphalt in California. Dwarfing that deal, Valero also bought Ultramar Diamond Shamrock for $4 billion in cash and stock (it assumed about $2.1 billion of debt in the deal). As part of the deal, and to comply with the demands of regulators, in 2002 Valero sold the Golden Eagle (San Francisco-area) refinery and 70 retail service stations in Northern California to Tesoro for $945 million.

In 2003 the company acquired Orion Refining's Louisiana refinery for about $530 million, and in 2004 it acquired an Aruba refinery from asset-shedding El Paso Corp. for $640 million. Suncor Energy bought a Colorado-based refinery from Valero for a reported $30 million in 2005.

Greehey turned over the leadership reins to another company veteran, Bill Klesse, in early 2006. The next year the company sold its Lima, Ohio, refinery to Husky Energy.

EXECUTIVES

Chairman, President, and CEO: William R. (Bill) Klesse, age 63, $11,698,231 total compensation
EVP and COO: Richard J. (Rich) Marcogliese, age 57, $5,940,686 total compensation
EVP and CFO: Michael S. (Mike) Ciskowski, age 52, $5,010,106 total compensation
EVP and General Counsel: Kimberly S. (Kim) Bowers, age 45, $2,115,756 total compensation
EVP Marketing and Supply: Joseph W. (Joe) Gorder, age 52, $1,999,153 total compensation
EVP Corporate Development and Strategic Planning: S. Eugene (Gene) Edwards, age 53
SVP and Controller: Clayton E. (Clay) Killinger
SVP Supply and Wholesale Marketing: Dave Parker
SVP and CIO: Hal Zesch
SVP Retail Marketing: Gary L. Arthur Jr.
SVP Corporate Law and Secretary: Jay D. Browning
SVP Human Resources: R. Michael (Mike) Crownover
VP and Treasurer: Donna M. Titzman
VP and General Manager, Valero Port Arthur Refinery: Greg Gentry
VP Investor Relations and Corporate Communications: Eric Fisher
Auditors: KPMG LLP

LOCATIONS

HQ: Valero Energy Corporation
1 Valero Way, San Antonio, TX 78249
Phone: 210-345-2000   **Fax:** 210-345-2646
Web: www.valero.com

2009 Sales

	$ mil.	% of total
US	58,792	86
Canada	6,048	9
Other countries	3,304	5
Total	**68,144**	**100**

PRODUCTS/OPERATIONS

2009 Sales

	$ mil.	% of total
Refining	59,061	87
Retail	7,885	11
Ethanol	1,198	2
Total	**68,144**	**100**

2009 Sales

	$ mil.	% of total
Refining		
Gasolines & blendstocks	29,830	44
Distillates	21,911	32
Petrochemicals	2,275	4
Lubes & asphalts	1,576	2
Other	3,469	5
Retail		
Fuel sales (gasoline & diesel)	6,148	9
Merchandise sales & other	1,505	2
Home heating oil	232	—
Ethanol		
Ethanol	1,032	2
Distllers grains	166	—
Total	**68,144**	**100**

Selected Products

Asphalt
Bunker oils
CARB Phase II gasoline
Clean-burning oxygenates
Conventional gasoline
Crude mineral spirits
Customized clean-burning gasoline blends for export markets
Gasoline blendstocks
Home heating oil
Jet fuel
Kerosene
Low-sulfur diesel
Lube oils
Petrochemical feedstocks
Petroleum coke
Premium reformulated and conventional gasolines
Reformulated gasoline
Sulfur

COMPETITORS

ADM
Aventine
BP
Chevron
CITGO
ConocoPhillips
Exxon Mobil
Frontier Oil
Hess Corporation
Holly Corporation
Marathon Petroleum
Motiva Enterprises
National Cooperative Refinery Association
Shell Oil Products
Sinclair Oil
Sunoco
Tesoro
TOTAL
TPC Group

HISTORICAL FINANCIALS

Company Type: Public

Income Statement

FYE: December 31

	REVENUE ($ mil.)	NET INCOME ($ mil.)	NET PROFIT MARGIN	EMPLOYEES
12/09	68,144	(1,982)	—	20,920
12/08	119,114	(1,131)	—	21,765
12/07	95,327	5,234	5.5%	21,651
12/06	91,832	5,462	5.9%	21,836
12/05	82,161	3,589	4.4%	22,068
Annual Growth	**(4.6%)**	**—**	**—**	**(1.3%)**

2009 Year-End Financials

Debt ratio: 48.6%
Return on equity: —
Cash ($ mil.): 825
Current ratio: 1.40
Long-term debt ($ mil.): 7,163

No. of shares (mil.): 565
Dividends
  Yield: 3.6%
  Payout: —
Market value ($ mil.): 9,472

Stock History

NYSE: VLO

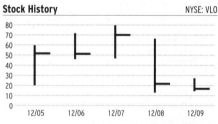

	STOCK PRICE ($) FY Close	P/E High/Low		PER SHARE ($) Earnings	Dividends	Book Value
12/09	16.75	—	—	(3.67)	0.60	26.04
12/08	21.64	—	—	(2.16)	0.57	27.62
12/07	70.03	9	5	8.88	0.48	32.73
12/06	51.16	8	5	8.64	0.30	32.90
12/05	51.60	10	3	6.10	0.19	26.61
Annual Growth	**(24.5%)**	**—**	**—**	**—**	**33.3%**	**(0.5%)**

The Valspar Corporation

Valspar wants you to put on a coat. The firm, founded in 1806, makes a variety of coatings and paints for manufacturing, automotive, and food-packaging companies, as well as for consumers. The company's industrial coatings — used by OEMs including building product, appliance, and furniture makers — include coatings for metal, wood, plastic, and glass. Packaging products include coatings and inks for rigid containers, such as food and beverage cans. Its consumer paints include interior and exterior paints, primers, stains, and varnishes sold through mass merchandisers like Wal-Mart and Lowe's. Valspar also makes auto paints, colorants, and gelcoats. It is active in Asia, the Americas, and Europe.

Valspar has boosted its core business through acquisitions of coatings companies around the world; in the past decade it made more than 20 acquisitions around the world, including joint venture interests. That strategy has made Valspar one of the top global industrial coatings makers. Among the most notable of these acquisitions was of an 80% stake in Chinese coatings manufacturer Huarun Paints, a maker of wood and furniture coatings. (In 2007 Valspar's sales in China reached 10% of total sales for the first time.) It also acquired businesses in Brazil, Mexico, and the US.

Lowe's accounts for more than 10% of the company's sales, and the hardware and home repair giant has named Valspar paint supplier of the year eight times. In 2007 Valspar began to use its own brand at Lowe's (replacing three fairly generic-sounding store brands) in an effort to boost consumer recognition. Valspar has made a point to tailor its products to the needs of retail customers, to the point of placing in-store employees to answer paint questions.

HISTORY

Samuel Tuck began the company as Paint and Color in Boston in 1806. It was known as Valentine & Co. by 1866. Then-owner Lawson Valentine hired chemist Charles Homer (brother of artist Winslow Homer), who perfected finishing varnishes. In 1903 Valentine's grandson, L. Valentine Pulsifer, invented the first clear varnish — dubbed Valspar — which became the company's name in 1932. Valspar grew by mergers including Rockcote Paint (1960) and Minnesota Paints (1970). CEO Angus Wurtele became chairman in 1973. Valspar's sales tripled by the time it acquired Mobil Oil's packaging coatings business in 1984.

Valspar formed a joint venture with China Merchants in 1994 (packaging coatings) and then bought US-based Sunbelt Coatings (auto refinishing, 1995), Gordon Bartels (packaging coatings, 1996), and Sureguard (industrial coatings, 1997). Valspar swapped its maintenance coatings business in 1997 with Ameron International's product finishes unit and formed a joint venture in Brazil with Renner Herrmann SA.

President and CEO Richard Rompala replaced Wurtele as chairman in 1998. Acquisitions that year included Plasti-Kote (consumer aerosol and specialty paints), Australia-based Anzol (packaging and industrial coatings), and Dyflex Polymers (specialty water-based polymers).

The company began divesting noncore businesses, selling its functional powder coatings unit in 1998 and its marine and packaging coatings product lines in 1999. Also in 1999 it bought the packaging coatings business of Dexter Corporation (now a part of Life Technologies) and its subsidiary in France and the Netherlands-based resins maker Dyflex. The next year Valspar bought rival coatings maker Lilly Industries in a $975 million deal, which made Valspar a top global maker of coatings for wood, mirrors, and coils (used in doors and appliances).

From 1996 to 2001 in a four-phase deal, the company acquired packaging coatings firm Coates Coatings, which operated in North America, Europe, Australia, Africa, and Asia. This acquisition boosted Valspar into the top of the market for metal packaging coatings.

In 2004 the company acquired Dutch automotive coatings maker De Beer Lakfabrieken, as well as the Forest Products division of wood coatings firm Associated Chemists.

William Mansfield became CEO in February 2005, but Rompala stayed on as chairman until his retirement in mid-2005. Thomas McBurney assumed the chairmanship for two years before Mansfield was named chairman in 2007.

EXECUTIVES

Chairman and CEO: William L. (Bill) Mansfield, age 61
President, COO, and Director: Gary E. Hendrickson, age 53, $2,631,150 total compensation
EVP: Steven L. Erdahl, age 57, $2,322,899 total compensation
EVP, General Counsel, and Secretary: Rolf Engh, age 56, $1,926,731 total compensation
SVP and CFO: Lori A. Walker, age 52, $1,669,349 total compensation
SVP Human Resources: Anthony L. Blaine, age 42
SVP Global Architectural: Howard C. Heckes, age 44
Group VP Global Packaging; President Europe, Middle East and Africa: Bern Ouimette
Group VP General Industrial and Composites: Brian Falline
Group VP Architectural: Kenneth H. Arthur
VP and Controller: Tracy C. Jokinen
VP Sales and Marketing Architectural Group: Steve Person
VP Packaging North America: Andrew Hecker
VP Corporate Purchasing: Thomas V. Kelliher
VP Research and Development: Larry B. Brandenburger
VP Coil Coatings: Jeff Alexander
VP Coil and Extrusion Coatings: Alfred N. (Al) Dunlop
VP Marketing: Scot Karstens
VP and Treasurer: Tyler N. Treat
Color Stylist: Sue Kim
Auditors: Ernst & Young LLP

LOCATIONS

HQ: The Valspar Corporation
901 3rd Ave. South, Minneapolis, MN 55402
Phone: 612-851-7000　　**Fax:** 612-851-3535
Web: www.valspar.com

2009 Sales

	$ mil.	% of total
US	1,790.1	62
China	328.6	12
Other countries	760.3	26
Total	**2,879.0**	**100**

PRODUCTS/OPERATIONS

2009 Sales

	$ mil.	% of total
Coatings	1,582.8	53
Paints	1,072.3	36
Other	316.3	11
Adjustments	(92.4)	—
Total	**2,879.0**	**100**

Selected Products

Industrial
　Fillers
　Mirror coatings
　Primers
　Stains
　Topcoats
Architectural, automotive, and specialty
　Aerosols
　Enamels
　Faux finishes
　Interior and exterior paints
　Primers
　Sealers
　Stains
　Varnishes
Packaging
　Coatings
　Inks
Other
　Colorants
　Composites
　Powder coatings for metal surfaces
　Specialty polymers

Selected Brands

Cabot
De Beer
Goof Off
House of Kolor
McCloskey
Mr. Spray
Plasti-Kote
Tempo
Valspar

COMPETITORS

Akzo Nobel
BASF Coatings AG
BEHR
Benjamin Moore
Detrex
Dunn-Edwards
DuPont
Ferro
H.B. Fuller
Kelly-Moore
NL Industries
PPG Industries
RPM International
Sherwin-Williams
Spraylat

HISTORICAL FINANCIALS

Company Type: Public

Income Statement

FYE: Last Friday in October

	REVENUE ($ mil.)	NET INCOME ($ mil.)	NET PROFIT MARGIN	EMPLOYEES
10/09	2,879	160	5.6%	8,800
10/08	3,482	151	4.3%	9,400
10/07	3,249	172	5.3%	10,000
10/06	2,978	175	5.9%	9,556
10/05	2,714	148	5.4%	7,540
Annual Growth	**1.5%**	**2.1%**	**—**	**3.9%**

2009 Year-End Financials

Debt ratio: 58.0%
Return on equity: 10.8%
Cash ($ mil.): 188
Current ratio: 1.49
Long-term debt ($ mil.): 873

No. of shares (mil.): 99
Dividends
  Yield: 2.4%
  Payout: 40.3%
Market value ($ mil.): 2,520

Stock History

NYSE: VAL

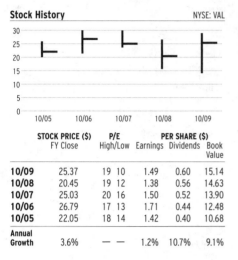

	STOCK PRICE ($) FY Close	P/E High/Low		PER SHARE ($) Earnings	Dividends	Book Value
10/09	25.37	19	10	1.49	0.60	15.14
10/08	20.45	19	12	1.38	0.56	14.63
10/07	25.03	20	16	1.50	0.52	13.90
10/06	26.79	17	13	1.71	0.44	12.48
10/05	22.05	18	14	1.42	0.40	10.68
Annual Growth	3.6%	—	—	1.2%	10.7%	9.1%

The Vanguard Group

If you buy low and sell high, invest for the long term, resist the urge to panic, and generally disapprove of those whippersnappers at Fidelity, then you may end up in the Vanguard of the financial market. The Vanguard Group offers individual and institutional investors a line of popular mutual funds and brokerage services. Claiming more than $1.2 trillion of assets under management, the firm is battling FMR (dba Fidelity) for the title of largest retail mutual fund manager on the planet. Vanguard's fund options include more than 200 stock, bond, mixed, and international offerings, as well as variable annuity portfolios; its Vanguard 500 Index Fund is one of the largest in the US.

The company is known as much for its puritanical thriftiness and conservative investing as for its line of index funds, which track the performance of such groups of stock as the S&P 500. Retired company founder John Bogle is sometimes derisively called "St. Jack" for his zealous criticism of industry practices, but the company's reputation for being squeaky clean appears to have kept it unscathed by the mutual fund industry scandals of recent years.

Unlike other fund managers, Vanguard is set up like a mutual insurance company. The funds (and by extension, their more than 9 million investors) own the company, so fees are low to nonexistent; funds are operated on a tight budget so as not to eat into results. The company spends next to nothing on advertising, relying instead on strong returns and word-of-mouth. And despite its no-broker, no-load background, Vanguard has developed cheap ways to dole out advice, especially through the use of toll-free numbers and the Internet and by quietly touting its online brokerage service.

In 2008 Vanguard joined the government's money-market guarantee program, which was designed to keep nervous investors from emptying their funds by safeguarding deposits. The program ended the following year, signalling growing confidence in the economy as well as the relative security of money-market funds.

Also in 2008 John Brennan retired as CEO but remained chairman of Vanguard. William McNabb, formerly the managing director of Vanguard's institutional investor group, succeeded Brennan as CEO.

HISTORY

A distant cousin of Daniel Boone, Walter Morgan knew a few things about pioneering. He was the first to offer a fund with a balance of stocks and bonds, serendipitously introduced early in 1929, months before the stock market collapsed. Morgan's balanced Wellington fund (named after Napoleon's vanquisher) emerged effectively unscathed.

John Bogle's senior thesis on mutual funds impressed fellow Princeton alum Morgan, who hired Bogle in 1951. Morgan retired in 1967 and picked Bogle to replace him. That year Bogle engineered a merger with old-school investment firm Thorndike, Doran, Paine and Lewis. After culture clashes and four years of shrinking assets, the Thorndike-dominated board fired Bogle, who appealed to the mutual funds and their separate board of directors. The fund directors decided to split up the funds and the advisory business.

Bogle named the fund company The Vanguard Group, after the flagship of Lord Nelson, another Napoleon foe. Vanguard worked like a cooperative; mutual fund shareholders owned the company, so all services were provided at cost. Wellington Management Company remained Vanguard's distributor until 1977, when Bogle convinced Vanguard's board to drop the affiliation. Without Wellington as the intermediary, Vanguard sold its funds directly to consumers as no-load funds (without service charges). In 1976 the company launched the Vanguard Index 500, the first index fund. These measures attracted new investors in droves.

Vanguard rode the 1980s boom. Its Windsor fund grew so large the company closed it, launching Windsor II in 1985. Vanguard weathered the 1987 crash and began the 1990s as the US's #4 mutual fund company. The actively managed funds of FMR (better known as Fidelity), most notably its Magellan fund, led the market then. The retirement of legendary Magellan manager Peter Lynch and the fund's consequential underperformance spurred a rush to index funds. Vanguard moved up to #2.

Vanguard played against type in 1995 when it introduced the Vanguard Horizon Capital Growth stock fund, an aggressively managed fund designed to vie directly with Fidelity's funds.

In 1997 Vanguard added brokerage services and began selling its own and other companies' funds on the Internet to allow clients to consolidate their financial activities. In 1998 Bogle passed the chairmanship to CEO John Brennan, a soft-spoken technology wonk. Morgan died that year at age 100.

Investors' feathers were ruffled when 70-year-old Bogle announced that corporate age limits would force him to leave the board of directors at the end of 1999. (Bogle retains an office at Vanguard headquarters and remains popular on the speaker circuit.)

Despite Vanguard's stated commitment to the little guy, by late 2002 the company was forced to mitigate realities of the economy and started courting investors with bigger bankrolls; it also raised fees for some customers with smaller accounts.

In another concession to changing times, the company began managing exchange-traded funds (ETFs) in 2001. Within a decade, Vanguard became the third-largest ETF sponsor in the US, thanks largely to its low fees.

EXECUTIVES

Chairman, President, and CEO:
 F. William (Bill) McNabb III, age 52
Managing Director and CIO: Paul Heller
Managing Director and Chief Investment Officer:
 George U. (Gus) Sauter
Managing Director, Human Resources:
 Kathleen C. Gubanich
Managing Director, Strategy and Finance Group:
 Glenn Reed
Managing Director, Institutional Investor Group:
 R. Gregory Barton
Managing Director, International Operations:
 James M. Norris
Managing Director, Planning and Development Group:
 Michael S. Miller
Managing Director, Retail Investor Group:
 Mortimer J. (Tim) Buckley
General Counsel: Heidi Stam
Principal, Retail Services: Alba Martinez

LOCATIONS

HQ: The Vanguard Group, Inc.
  100 Vanguard Blvd., Malvern, PA 19355
Phone: 610-648-6000   Fax: 610-669-6605
Web: www.vanguard.com

PRODUCTS/OPERATIONS

Selected Funds

500 Index Fund
Asset Allocation Fund
Balanced Index Fund
California Intermediate-Term Tax-Exempt Fund
California Long-Term Tax-Exempt Fund
California Tax-Exempt Money Market Fund
Capital Value Fund
Diversified Equity Fund
Dividend Appreciation Index Fund
Emerging Markets Stock Index Fund
Energy Fund
Equity Income Fund
European Stock Index Fund
Explorer Fund
Florida Long-Term Tax-Exempt Fund
FTSE Social Index Fund
Global Equity Fund
Growth and Income Fund
Growth Equity Fund
Growth Index Fund
Health Care Fund
High-Yield Corporate Fund
High-Yield Tax-Exempt Fund
Inflation-Protected Securities Fund
Intermediate-Term Bond Index Fund
Intermediate-Term Tax-Exempt Fund
International Explorer Fund
International Growth Fund
International Value Fund
Large-Cap Index Fund
LifeStrategy Growth Fund
LifeStrategy Income Fund
Limited-Term Tax-Exempt Fund
Long-Term Bond Index Fund
Long-Term Investment-Grade Fund
Long-Term Treasury Fund
Massachusetts Tax-Exempt Fund
Mid-Cap Growth Fund
Mid-Cap Value Index Fund
Morgan Growth Fund
New Jersey Long-Term Tax-Exempt Fund
New Jersey Tax-Exempt Money Market Fund

New York Long-Term Tax-Exempt Fund
New York Tax-Exempt Money Market Fund
Ohio Long-Term Tax-Exempt Fund
Ohio Tax-Exempt Money Market Fund
Pacific Stock Index Fund
Pennsylvania Long-Term Tax-Exempt Fund
Pennsylvania Tax-Exempt Money Market Fund
Precious Metals and Mining Fund
PRIMECAP Fund
REIT Index Fund
Short-Term Bond Index Fund
Short-Term Investment-Grade Fund
Small-Cap Growth Index Fund
Small-Cap Index Fund
STAR Fund
Strategic Equity Fund
Target Retirement 2010 Fund
Target Retirement 2015 Fund
Target Retirement 2020 Fund
Target Retirement 2025 Fund
Target Retirement 2030 Fund
Target Retirement 2035 Fund
Target Retirement 2040 Fund
Target Retirement 2045 Fund
Target Retirement 2050 Fund
Tax-Managed Growth and Income Fund
Tax-Managed International Fund
Total Bond Market Index Fund
Total International Stock Index Fund
Total Stock Market Index Fund
Treasury Money Market Fund
U.S. Growth Fund
U.S. Value Fund
Value Index Fund

COMPETITORS

AIG
AllianceBernstein
American Century
AXA Financial
BlackRock
Charles Schwab
FMR
Franklin Resources
Invesco
Invesco Aim
Janus Capital
Legg Mason
MFS
Principal Financial
Putnam
T. Rowe Price
TIAA-CREF
USAA

VeriSign, Inc.

VeriSign gives directions to land on the Internet. The company is a big part of what makes the Internet work. It operates two of the world's 13 root nameservers, which assign Internet protocol addresses to devices communicating across the Internet. VeriSign is also the only issuer of the .com and .net domain names that are sold to users by companies such as domain registrars Go Daddy and Register.com. As part of a plan to focus on its Internet naming business, VeriSign sold its security division, which provided digital certificate and secure socket layer (SSL) services for online communications and transactions, to Symantec in 2010.

VeriSign maintains its exclusive grip on website naming rights under agreements with ICANN and the US Department of Commerce.

Originally granted that right in 2001, the company's contract was renewed in 2006, extending its rights to maintain the .com (and .net) registries until 2012. In 2008 VeriSign negotiated with ICANN for a fee increase for .com and .net domain registration, resulting in increases from $6.42 to $6.86 and $3.85 to $4.23, respectively. These fees are paid by the domain name registrars. (VeriSign is not itself a registrar — it exited that business with the sale of Network Solutions in 2003.)

In 2007 VeriSign announced a major restructuring that included plans to divest all of its business lines in the Communications Services Group, encompassing connectivity and interoperability services, billing, and mobile commerce. The company sold the unit to Transaction Network Services for $230 million in 2009.

Continuing to hone its focus on Internet naming and authentication services, the company divested other noncore assets in 2009, including its Managed Security Services business, sold to security services company SecureWorks, and its Real-Time Publisher Services (RTP) business, which provided content aggregation and business intelligence services. Later in the year it sold its Messaging Business to network engineering services firm Syniverse Holdings for $175 million in cash. It also sold its global security consulting business to AT&T.

Completing its divestitures, in 2010 VeriSign sold its Identity and Authentication Services business to Symantec for about $1.28 billion in cash. The business had accounted for nearly 40% of VeriSign's revenues. More than 90,000 domains in 145 countries used its digital certificates and 96 of the world's 100 largest banks used its SSL protection.

HISTORY

VeriSign was founded by Stratton Sclavos and Jim Bidzos in 1995. Sclavos, a veteran of MIPS Computer Systems and two failed Silicon Valley startups, ran the company as RSA's digital certification division until it was spun off in 1995. Its early backers included Ameritech, Mitsubishi, and Visa. Apple and Netscape were among its first customers.

In 1996 VeriSign formed a Japanese subsidiary. The next year the company debuted its Financial Server ID, a digital certificate for use with the Open Financial Exchange, a home banking standard backed by Microsoft. VeriSign went public in early 1998 and added Sumitomo Bank and UPS as customers. Also in 1998 the company bought Secure It (Internet security consulting services).

In early 2000 the company stepped up expansion efforts, buying South Africa-based Thawte Consulting (digital certification products) and Signio (Internet payment services). Later that year VeriSign acquired Internet domain registrar Network Solutions for about $20 billion.

Looking to expand its communications service offerings, in 2001 the company acquired network service provider Illuminet Holdings for $1.3 billion. Also in 2001 VeriSign reached an agreement with ICANN to become the exclusive operator of the top level .com domain registry until 2007.

The company continued its acquisitive ways in 2002 and 2003, purchasing H.O. Systems ($350 million) and UNC-Embratel ($16 million). In late 2003 the company sold the portion of Network Solutions that sells domain names and provides Web-hosting services to Pivotal Private Equity for about $100 million.

In 2004 the company acquired managed security services provider Guardent for about $140 million, and later that year purchased Germany-based wireless content service provider Jamba! for about $273 million.

The company moved beyond its legacy encryption and digital certificate products with a string of purchases in 2005. Verisign bought LightSurf, a provider of multimedia messaging and interoperability solutions for the wireless market, for $270 million. Later that year Verisign purchased Authorize.Net Holdings' PrePay INS business (wireless phone rate plan and calling plan tracking products) for about $17 million. Quick on the heels of the PrePay INS deal came VeriSign's purchase of iDEFENSE for $40 million in cash. Other 2005 purchases included Moreover Technologies (news aggregation), Weblogs.com (blog tracking), and Retail Solutions (point-of-sale tracking). The company sold its payment gateway business to Pay Pal, a subsidiary of eBay, for $370 million in 2005.

VeriSign's acquisition tear continued in 2006. It purchased Web-based billing and client management software company CallVision, as well as m-Qube, a developer of software for delivering content and connectivity services to wireless subscribers. It also acquired Internet transaction security specialist GeoTrust.

Also in 2006 VeriSign renewed its contract with ICANN, extending its rights to the .com registry until 2012. It also bought Kontiki, a developer of technology for speeding up large downloads on the Internet.

In 2006 News Corporation acquired a majority stake in VeriSign's Jamba unit, which provides ring tones and other mobile phone content, for $188 million. (Jamba, also known as Jamster, operated as a joint venture between the two companies until 2008, when VeriSign sold its remaining stake to News Corp for $200 million.)

In 2007 Sclavos resigned and director William Roper was named president and CEO.

After only about a year on the job, CEO William Roper resigned in 2008. He was replaced by company founder Jim Bidzos on an interim basis. Early the following year, VeriSign named Mark McLaughlin as president and COO. McLaughlin had been heavily involved in the company's strategy to focus on its core Internet infrastructure business; while he ran the Naming Services business, he led contract negotiations that successfully extended VeriSign's hold on the .com and .net registries.

In August of 2009 McLaughlin was named president and CEO; Bidzos remained chairman.

EXECUTIVES

Chairman: D. James (Jim) Bidzos, age 55, $2,755,739 total compensation
President, CEO, and Director: Mark D. McLaughlin, age 44, $3,872,360 total compensation
EVP and CFO: Brian G. Robins, age 40, $1,717,025 total compensation
EVP Strategy and Technical Operations: Russell S. (Rusty) Lewis, age 55, $1,008,716 total compensation
SVP, General Counsel, and Secretary: Richard H. (Rick) Goshorn, age 53, $1,130,893 total compensation
SVP Corporate Development and Strategy: Kevin A. Werner, age 49, $1,081,302 total compensation
SVP Marketing: Greg Jorgensen

SVP Product Management: Raynor Dahlquist
SVP Network Availability: Ben Petro
SVP Business Authentication: Fran Rosch
SVP and CTO: Kenneth J. (Ken) Silva
SVP User Authentication: Atri Chatterjee
SVP Human Resources: Christine C. Brennan, age 57
VP Product Development: Nico Popp
VP Corporate Marketing: John Talbot
VP Media Relations: Brad Williams
VP Compensation and Benefits Design:
 Kathryn K. Cross
Director Investor Relations: Nancy Fazioli
Auditors: KPMG LLP

LOCATIONS

HQ: VeriSign, Inc.
 487 E. Middlefield Rd., Mountain View, CA 94043
Phone: 650-961-7500 **Fax:** 650-961-7300
Web: www.verisign.com

2009 Sales

	$ mil.	% of total
US	592.8	58
Asia/Pacific	193.6	19
Europe, Middle East & Africa	168.5	16
Other regions	75.7	7
Total	**1,030.6**	**100**

PRODUCTS/OPERATIONS

2009 Sales

	$ mil.	% of total
Naming Services	615.9	60
Authentication Services	410.1	40
Other	4.6	—
Total	**1,030.6**	**100**

COMPETITORS

Go Daddy
Microsoft
Network Solutions
Register.com
Tucows
Verio
WorldSite.ws

HISTORICAL FINANCIALS

Company Type: Public

Income Statement

FYE: December 31

	REVENUE ($ mil.)	NET INCOME ($ mil.)	NET PROFIT MARGIN	EMPLOYEES
12/09	1,031	249	24.2%	2,328
12/08	962	(375)	—	3,297
12/07	1,496	(140)	—	4,251
12/06	1,575	379	24.1%	5,331
12/05	1,610	407	25.3%	4,076
Annual Growth	**(10.5%)**	**(11.5%)**	**—**	**(13.1%)**

2009 Year-End Financials

Debt ratio: 104.5%
Return on equity: 83.0%
Cash ($ mil.): 1,477
Current ratio: 1.93
Long-term debt ($ mil.): 574

No. of shares (mil.): 174
Dividends
 Yield: —
 Payout: —
Market value ($ mil.): 4,221

Stock History

NASDAQ (GS): VRSN

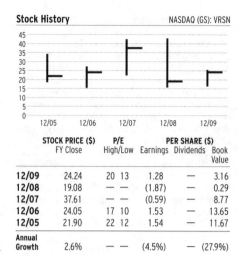

	STOCK PRICE ($) FY Close	P/E High/Low		PER SHARE ($) Earnings	Dividends	Book Value
12/09	24.24	20	13	1.28	—	3.16
12/08	19.08	—	—	(1.87)	—	0.29
12/07	37.61	—	—	(0.59)	—	8.77
12/06	24.05	17	10	1.53	—	13.65
12/05	21.90	22	12	1.54	—	11.67
Annual Growth	**2.6%**	**—**	**—**	**(4.5%)**	**—**	**(27.9%)**

Verizon Communications

The number two US telecom services provider (after AT&T) has taken the top spot in wireless services (ahead of AT&T Mobility). Verizon Wireless (known legally as Cellco Partnership), the company's joint venture with Vodafone, serves about 90 million customers. Meanwhile, with about 30 million access lines in service, Verizon's wireline business provides local telephone, long-distance, broadband Internet access, and digital TV services to residential, corporate, and wholesale customers. Verizon Business provides a wide range of telecom, managed network, and information technology services to business and government clients in the US and abroad.

Verizon has steadily used the acquisition of regional mobile phone companies to transform itself from a wireline telephone company into a leading US wireless carrier. It has responded to the migration of callers to cell phone and Internet telephony accounts, such as those offered by cable companies, by downsizing its landline business to cut costs. This included layoffs of thousands of workers from that segment during 2009, which will save the company money in the long run, but ate away at its annual profits.

To build up its wireless business, Verizon bought smaller rival Rural Cellular Corporation in 2009 for about $2.6 billion; the purchase increased Verizon's wireless subscriber base by more than 600,000. The company made another, much larger investment later that year with the acquisition of Alltel for $28.1 billion. The deal added about 13 million subscribers and created the largest cellular provider in the US in terms of sales and subscribers. It also boosted the company's retail presence with the addition of 750 Alltel-branded distribution points.

To earn regulatory approval Verizon sold some assets, including 1.6 million lines in 18 states, to AT&T for $2.3 billion. The largest transaction, however, was with Frontier Communications, which paid $8.6 billion in cash and stock in mid-2010 for wireline assets spun off by Verizon that

included about 4 million landline phone and broadband subscriber lines in 14 states. The deal gave Verizon ownership of more than two-thirds of Frontier's stock.

Despite its success in grabbing more wireless market share in the US, Verizon has not entirely given up hope on its wireline business. With an eye toward the continued convergence of wireline communications and digital broadcasting services, Verizon is building out its fiber-to-the-premises (FTTP) network, at a cost of $18 billion, to increase broadband capacity. Verizon is exploiting the boost in bandwidth with its digital television and video-on-demand service. Known as FiOS TV, the service is used by about 11 million customers in 14 states and includes digital music programming and high-definition TV, as well as broadband Internet options.

HISTORY

Verizon Communications (the name is a combination of *veritas*, the Latin word for truth, and horizon) was born in 2000 when Bell Atlantic bought GTE, but the company's roots are as old as the telephone. What is now Verizon began as one of the 1870s-era phone companies that evolved into AT&T Corp. and its Bell System of regional telephone operations.

AT&T lived happily as a regulated monopoly until a US government antitrust suit led to its breakup in 1984. Seven regional Bell operating companies (RBOCs, or Baby Bells) emerged in 1984, including Bell Atlantic. The new company, based in Philadelphia, received local phone service rights in six states and Washington, DC; cellular company Bell Atlantic Mobile Systems; and one-seventh of Bellcore, the R&D subsidiary (now Telcordia).

Bell Atlantic pursued unregulated businesses such as wireless, Internet, directory publishing, and catalog sales of computer parts and office supplies. It invested heavily in data-transport markets to supplement existing voice services, offering the first CO-LAN (central-office local area network) system in 1985. A year later it introduced a switched public data network and began testing integrating services digital network (ISDN) technology that combined voice and data transmissions over the same lines.

Bell Atlantic partnered with U S WEST to offer cellular services in the former Czechoslovakia in 1991, and in 1993 it bought a stake in Mexico's Grupo Iusacell (sold in 2003). Its 1992 acquisition of Metro Mobile gave it extensive East Coast cellular phone coverage.

In 1994 Bell Atlantic formed the PrimeCo partnership with NYNEX, AirTouch, and U S WEST. Enjoying freedom from wires, Bell Atlantic and NYNEX combined their cellular and paging operations in 1995. In 1996 Bell Atlantic and the six other RBOCs sold Bellcore to Science Applications International.

Bell Atlantic doubled in size with the $25.6 billion purchase of New York City-based NYNEX in 1997, moving from the Cradle of Liberty to the Big Apple. The deal created the second-largest US telecom services firm (after AT&T Corp.) but brought with it NYNEX's reputation for poor service.

In 1999 Bell Atlantic agreed to buy GTE, the giant non-Bell local phone company, in a $53 billion deal. To gain regulatory clearance to be acquired by Bell Atlantic, GTE sold off 90% of its Genuity Internet backbone operation (formerly GTE Internetworking). Later in 1999 the FCC granted Bell Atlantic permission to sell long-distance phone service in New York, making the company the first of the Baby Bells to be allowed to offer long-distance in its home territory.

Bell Atlantic and Vodafone AirTouch combined their US wireless operations, including PrimeCo, to form Verizon Wireless in 2000. Regulators later that year approved Bell Atlantic's acquisition of GTE, and Verizon Communications was formed. Tapped to run the new company were chairman and co-CEO Charles Lee, formerly of GTE, and president and co-CEO Ivan Seidenberg, formerly of Bell Atlantic (Lee later gave up the co-CEO position and announced he would step down as chairman in 2003).

In 2002 Verizon completed the sale of 675,000 access lines in Alabama and Missouri to CenturyTel, and it sold 600,000 access lines in Kentucky to ALLTEL, in deals valued at just over $4 billion. The company sold its wireline business in Hawaii to The Carlyle Group in 2005 for $1.65 billion.

Verizon paid nearly $8.5 billion for MCI in 2006. The deal enabled Verizon to expand its broadband data services, but led to about 7,000 job cuts at the combined company. Also that year, Verizon sold its Caribbean region and Latin American operations to companies controlled by Mexican entrepreneur Carlos Slim Helú in deals valued at a combined $3.7 billion.

EXECUTIVES

Chairman and CEO: Ivan G. Seidenberg, age 63, $17,534,332 total compensation
EVP; President and CEO, Verizon Wireless: Lowell C. McAdam, age 55, $10,272,787 total compensation
EVP and CFO: John F. Killian, age 55, $9,793,921 total compensation
EVP Strategy, Development, and Planning: John W. Diercksen, age 60, $4,946,155 total compensation
EVP and Chief Marketing Officer, Verizon Wireless: John G. Stratton, age 48
EVP and CTO: Richard J. (Dick) Lynch, age 61
EVP and CIO: Shaygan Kheradpir, age 49
EVP Human Resources: Marc C. Reed, age 51
EVP and General Counsel: Randal S. (Randy) Milch, age 51
EVP Public Affairs, Policy, and Communications: Thomas J. (Tom) Tauke, age 59
SVP, Deputy General Counsel, and Corporate Secretary: Marianne Drost
SVP Federal Regulatory Affairs: Kathleen Grillo
SVP Internal Auditing: Kathleen H. Leidheiser
SVP and Treasurer: Holly Hess Groos
SVP and Controller: Robert J. (Bob) Barish, age 48
SVP Investor Relations: Ronald H. (Ron) Lataille
President, Verizon Services Operations: Virginia P. Ruesterholz, age 48
President, Verizon Foundation: Patrick R. Gaston, age 52
President, Telecom and Business: Francis J. (Fran) Shammo, age 49
Executive Director Investor Relations: Kevin R. Tarrant
Auditors: Ernst & Young LLP

LOCATIONS

HQ: Verizon Communications Inc.
140 West St., New York, NY 10007
Phone: 212-395-1000
Web: www.verizon.com

PRODUCTS/OPERATIONS

2009 Sales

	$ mil.	% of total
Domestic wireless		
Service	53,426	50
Equipment & other	8,604	8
Wireline		
Mass markets	19,744	18
Global enterprise	14,988	14
Global wholesale	8,387	8
Other	1,626	2
Adjustments	1,033	—
Total	**107,808**	**100**

Selected Services

Business
  Conferencing
  Customer premises equipment design and maintenance
  Data center outsourcing
  Hosted messaging
  Information technology (IT)
  Systems integration
  Voice and data networking
Telecom
  Billing and collections
  Directory assistance
  Internet access services
  Local exchange access
  Long-distance
  Public telephones
Wireless
  Equipment sales
  Paging
  Wireless voice and data services

COMPETITORS

360networks
AT&T
Charter Communications
Comcast
Cox Communications
Global Crossing
Leap Wireless
Level 3 Communications
MetroPCS
Qwest Communications
Sprint Nextel
Time Warner Cable
T-Mobile USA
tw telecom
U.S. Cellular
XO Holdings
Yellow Book USA

HISTORICAL FINANCIALS

Company Type: Public

Income Statement

FYE: December 31

	REVENUE ($ mil.)	NET INCOME ($ mil.)	NET PROFIT MARGIN	EMPLOYEES
12/09	107,808	3,651	3.4%	222,900
12/08	97,354	6,428	6.6%	223,900
12/07	93,469	5,652	6.0%	235,000
12/06	88,144	6,239	7.1%	242,000
12/05	75,112	7,397	9.8%	250,000
Annual Growth	**9.5%**	**(16.2%)**	**—**	**(2.8%)**

2009 Year-End Financials

Debt ratio: 132.3%
Return on equity: 8.8%
Cash ($ mil.): 2,009
Current ratio: 0.78
Long-term debt ($ mil.): 55,051

No. of shares (mil.): 2,827
Dividends
  Yield: 6.0%
  Payout: 145.0%
Market value ($ mil.): 87,557

Stock History

NYSE: VZ

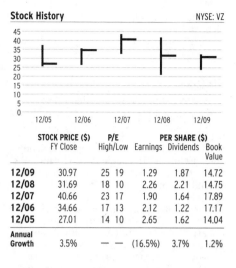

	STOCK PRICE ($) FY Close	P/E High/Low		PER SHARE ($) Earnings	Dividends	Book Value
12/09	30.97	25	19	1.29	1.87	14.72
12/08	31.69	18	10	2.26	2.21	14.75
12/07	40.66	23	17	1.90	1.64	17.89
12/06	34.66	17	13	2.12	1.22	17.17
12/05	27.01	14	10	2.65	1.62	14.04
Annual Growth	**3.5%**	**—**	**—**	**(16.5%)**	**3.7%**	**1.2%**

V.F. Corporation

V.F. Corporation is the name behind the names. The #1 jeans maker worldwide boasts a bevy of denim brands, such as Lee, Riders, Rustler, Wrangler, and 7 For All Mankind. Its other holdings include JanSport and Eastpak (backpacks), The North Face and Eagle Creek (outdoor gear and apparel), Red Kap and Bulwark (work clothes), Nautica (sportswear), Lucy Activewear (athletic apparel), John Varvatos (upscale menswear), and Vans (footwear). V.F.'s Majestic label features licensed MLB, NFL, and NBA apparel. The firm also runs e-commerce sites for its brands and operates more than 750 stores worldwide.

The company is the top jeans maker in the US, controlling about a quarter of the market. It is also a leading producer of sportswear, industrial workwear, licensed clothing, and outdoor and action sports products. In recent years V.F. has made inroads into offering more premium-priced apparel. Going forward, the firm is concentrating on building activity-based brands with a global reach.

While many of its rivals pulled back in the face of the economic downturn, V.F. charged ahead with its growth strategy, which included expansion of its brand portfolio and retail footprint. The firm added to its division of upper-tier contemporary brands by acquiring Mo Industries Holdings, the maker of premium sportswear brands Splendid and Ella Moss. It first purchased a 33% stake in 2008 and then snapped up the remaining 67% interest the following year; the investment totaled about $240 million. Also in 2008 VF bought out its former partner in a joint venture that marketed Lee products in Spain and Portugal.

Despite the expansion efforts and improved demand from its own retail operations, V.F.'s revenue has fallen recently. The company said sluggish consumer spending was to blame, a result of continued uncertainty in financial markets worldwide. To make up for the decline, it cut operational costs and reduced inventories by more than 15%.

V.F. saw its leadership change in 2008. In January Mackey McDonald stepped down as CEO, but he remains the company's chairman. He was replaced by Eric Wiseman, who'd served as president and COO.

Trusts established by founder John Barbey control about 20% of V.F.'s shares.

HISTORY

In 1899 six partners, including banker John Barbey, started the Reading Glove and Mitten Manufacturing Company. Barbey bought out his five partners in 1911 and changed the name of the Reading, Pennsylvania, company to Schuylkill Silk Mills in 1913. Barbey expanded the mills' production to include underwear and changed the mills' name to Vanity Fair Silk Mills (after a contest with a $25 prize in 1919).

Barbey (who banned the word "underwear") and his son J. E. led their lingerie company to national prominence. The mills made only silk garments until the 1920s, when synthetics were developed. In response to the US embargo on silk in 1941, Vanity Fair changed to rayon, finally converting to the new wonder fabric, nylon tricot, in 1948. Vanity Fair was then manufacturing all stages of its nylon products, from filament to finished garment. It won awards for its innovative advertising with photographs of live models in Vanity Fair lingerie.

J. E. Barbey owned all of Vanity Fair's stock until 1951, when he sold one-third of his holdings to the public. In 1966 the stock, previously traded over the counter, was listed on the NYSE.

The company used acquisitions to expand its lingerie business and to begin producing sportswear and blue jeans. It bought Berkshire International (hosiery, 1969) and H.D. Lee (jeans, 1969). To better reflect its diverse offerings, the company changed its name to VF Corporation that year.

VF doubled in size in 1986 by purchasing Blue Bell, a North Carolina maker of branded apparel by Wrangler, Rustler, Jantzen, Jansport, and Red Kap. VF then added the Vassarette brand name from Munsingwear (1990) and Healthtex (infants' and children's apparel, 1991). In 1992 VF acquired European lingerie brands Lou, Bolero, Intimate Cherry, and Variance.

The company bought sports apparel makers Nutmeg Industries and H.H. Cutler in 1994. The next year it cut costs by laying off 7,800 workers, closing 14 plants, and moving production operations to Mexico and the Caribbean. Also in 1995 VF began licensing swimwear and sportswear from NIKE.

Mackey McDonald became CEO in 1996. In 1998 VF moved from Pennsylvania to North Carolina, closer to the company's production facilities. The firm also acquired Bestform Intimates (Lily of France) in 1998.

VF acquired Bulwark Protective Apparel (flame-resistant apparel, 1996), Penn State textiles (kitchen and hospitality apparel, 1998), Horace Small (public safety and postal apparel, 1999), and American Household's Eastpak (backpacks, 2000). Later VF purchased the Chic and H.I.S. jeans names from Chic by H.I.S., Gitano jeanswear brand from bankrupt Fruit of the Loom, and troubled outdoor apparel retailer The North Face.

In 2000 VF combined its workwear and knitwear units and took action to exit certain underperforming businesses, including Fibrotek and its private-label knitwear group. VF cut its global workforce by 18% in November 2001, and in March 2002 the company completed its sale of swimwear unit Jantzen to Perry Ellis International. Adding to its rash of large-scale acquisitions, in 2003 VF entered into an

agreement to acquire sportswear maker Nautica Enterprises; the deal was intended to enable Nautica to focus on strengthening its menswear line. VF also acquired David Chu and Company, Inc.'s rights to 50% of royalty from licensing the Nautica trademark, and placed Chu at the helm of Nautica. With the sizable acquisition came the restructuring of the company to include a Sportswear Coalition that includes the Nautica, Earl Jean, John Varvatos, and E. Magrath brands.

The company sold its Earl Jean brand to Jordache Enterprises and an investor group in 2006. Continuing its divestment of noncore brands, in April 2007 VF sold its intimates apparel business to Fruit of the Loom for about $350 million. The deal involved US brands (Vanity Fair, Lily of France, Vassarette, Bestform, Curvation) as well as those in Europe (Lou, Gemma, Belcor). In August VF completed two acquisitions: Lucy Activewear (for $110 million), which operates some 50 stores in about a dozen states and lucy.com; and premium denim firm 7 For All Mankind LLC (for $775 million).

EXECUTIVES

Chairman, President, and CEO: Eric C. Wiseman, age 54, $7,243,127 total compensation
SVP and CFO: Robert K. (Bob) Shearer, age 58, $2,841,737 total compensation
VP and President, VF International: Karl Heinz Salzburger, age 52, $3,118,248 total compensation
VP; President, Supply Chain: Boyd Rogers, age 60, $1,425,856 total compensation
VP VF Direct/Customer Teams: Michael T. (Mike) Gannaway, age 58, $1,375,424 total compensation
VP Administration and General Counsel: Candace S. Cummings, age 63, $2,251,110 total compensation
VP and CIO: Martin Schneider
VP Strategy: Stephen F. Dull
VP Mergers and Acquisitions: Franklin L. (Frank) Terkelson
VP, Controller, and Chief Accounting Officer: Bradley W. (Brad) Batten, age 54
VP Human Resources: Susan L. Williams
VP and Treasurer: Frank C. Pickard III, age 65
President, VF Outdoor Americas: Steve Rendle, age 50
President, Action Sports Americas: Stephen M. (Steve) Murray, age 49
President, Contemporary Brands: Susan Kellogg
President, Mo Industries: Jonathan Saven
Founder and CEO, Mo Industries: Moise (Mo) Emquies
President, Outdoor and Action Sports, EMEA: Patrik Frisk
President, VF Retail Licensed Brands: David Conn, age 41
President, Sportswear and Contemporary Brands, EMEA: Martino Scabbia Guerrini, age 46
Director Corporate Communications: Paul Mason
Auditors: PricewaterhouseCoopers LLP

LOCATIONS

HQ: V.F. Corporation
105 Corporate Center Blvd., Greensboro, NC 27408
Phone: 336-424-6000 **Fax:** 336-424-7631
Web: www.vfc.com

2009 Sales

	$ mil.	% of total
US	5,078	70
Foreign, primarily Europe	2,142	30
Total	**7,220**	**100**

PRODUCTS/OPERATIONS

2009 Sales

	$ mil.	% of total
Outdoor & Action Sports	2,752	38
Jeanswear	2,522	35
Imagewear	865	12
Sportswear	498	7
Contemporary Brands	472	6
Other	111	2
Total	**7,220**	**100**

2009 Sales

	$ mil.	% of total
Net sales	7,143	99
Royalty income	77	1
Total	**7,220**	**100**

Selected Brands

Outdoor and action sports
  Eagle Creek
  Eastpak
  JanSport
  Kipling
  Napapijri
  The North Face
  Reef
  Vans

Jeanswear
  Lee
  Riders
  Rustler
  Timber Creek by Wrangler
  Wrangler
  Wrangler Hero

Imagewear
  Bulwark
  Harley-Davidson (licensed)
  Majestic
  MLB (licensed)
  NFL (licensed)
  Red Kap

Sportswear
  Kipling
  Nautica

Contemporary brands
  7 For All Mankind
  Ella Moss
  John Varvatos
  Lucy
  Splendid

Selected Licenses

Harley-Davidson Motor Company
Major League Baseball
NASCAR
National Basketball Association
National Football League
National Hockey League

COMPETITORS

Abercrombie & Fitch	Liz Claiborne
American Eagle Outfitters	L.L. Bean
Calvin Klein	OshKosh B'Gosh
Columbia Sportswear	Patagonia, Inc.
Diesel SpA	Reebok
The Gap	REI
Guess?	Rocky Brands
Gymboree	Russell Brands
H&M	Sears Holdings
Inditex	Target
J. C. Penney	Timberland
Joe's Jeans	Tommy Hilfiger
Johnson Outdoors	True Religion Apparel
Kellwood	Wal-Mart
Koos Manufacturing	Williamson-Dickie
Levi Strauss	Manufacturing
Limited Brands	

HISTORICAL FINANCIALS

Company Type: Public

Income Statement

FYE: Saturday nearest December 31

	REVENUE ($ mil.)	NET INCOME ($ mil.)	NET PROFIT MARGIN	EMPLOYEES
12/09	7,220	459	6.4%	45,700
12/08	7,643	603	7.9%	46,600
12/07	7,219	592	8.2%	54,200
12/06	6,216	534	8.6%	45,000
12/05	6,429	519	8.1%	52,300
Annual Growth	2.9%	(3.0%)	—	(3.3%)

2009 Year-End Financials

Debt ratio: 24.6%
Return on equity: 12.4%
Cash ($ mil.): 732
Current ratio: 2.41
Long-term debt ($ mil.): 938

No. of shares (mil.): 110
Dividends
  Yield: 3.2%
  Payout: 57.4%
Market value ($ mil.): 8,064

Stock History

NYSE: VFC

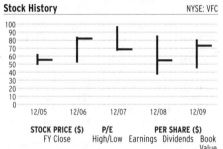

	STOCK PRICE ($) FY Close	P/E High/Low	PER SHARE ($) Earnings	PER SHARE ($) Dividends	PER SHARE ($) Book Value
12/09	73.24	19 11	4.13	2.37	34.65
12/08	54.77	16 7	5.42	2.33	32.30
12/07	68.66	18 13	5.22	2.23	32.49
12/06	82.08	18 11	4.72	1.94	29.65
12/05	55.34	14 11	4.44	1.10	25.50
Annual Growth	7.3%	— —	(1.8%)	21.2%	8.0%

Viad Corp

Viad (pronounced VEE-ahd) makes sure convention-goers get to their events. Viad offers convention and event services, exhibit design and construction, and travel and recreation services. Its event services operations are organized under its Global Experience Specialists (GES) brand, which provides convention services to trade associations and exhibitors. It also offers custom exhibit designers for corporations, museums, trade shows, and retail stores. Viad's Travel & Recreation Group operates through its Brewster unit (Canadian accommodations and tour provider) and Glacier Park division (mountain lodge operator). The firm has operations across Canada, Germany, the UK, the United Arab Emirates, and the US.

Before the recession took hold, Viad logged noteworthy revenue gains in 2008. Its income per share (before other items) grew by more than 20% and was in line with its guidance. However, revenue in 2009 tanked by 28% and the company suffered a net loss of $104.7 million. The company attributes the losses to overall declines in spending in the event marketing and tourism industries. Throughout 2009 it worked to reduce costs by restructuring and by centralizing its legal and human resources functions. In 2010

Viad consolidated its Exhibitgroup/Giltspur and Becker Group operations under the Global Experience Specialists name. In addition to reorganizing its exhibit operations, Viad formed the Travel & Recreation Group in 2009, which brought together its Brewster and Glacier Park units under one umbrella.

Viad acquired Baltimore-based experiential marketer Becker Group in 2008 to extend its reach beyond the tradeshow environment. It specialized in creating holiday-themed events and exhibits in such venues as retail centers, movie studios, museums, leading consumer brands, and casinos. The firm operated about 30 client care centers in the US, UK, Germany, and Canada, and works with partner agencies in other international markets. The deal was worth about $25 million.

GES typically brings in about three-quarters of the company's sales each year. Its offerings include event planning, exhibit and furniture rentals, and exhibit installation and dismantling. GES has added to Viad's international presence by extending the reach of its business to the United Arab Emirates and Germany. With its growing global footprint, Viad has likewise seen increasing revenue from its international operations. The company conducts its foreign affairs largely from offices in Canada and the UK. These locations account for about 25% of revenue. Additionally, its Canada operations generate a majority of its Travel & Recreation Group's revenue.

HISTORY

Although this company has only carried the Viad name since 1996, it has a decades-long lineage illustrative of corporate penchants for acquisitions and spinoffs. In the 1960s Greyhound Corporation (later renamed Greyhound Lines and subsequently acquired by Laidlaw) began diversifying beyond transportation as airline and auto travel became less expensive and more popular. Greyhound bought a string of companies that eventually would come under the Viad umbrella. Among its purchases were Restaura (contract foodservice, 1964), Brewster Transport Company (Canadian travel services, 1965), Travelers Express (financial services, 1965), Aircraft Service International (aircraft fueling, 1968), Exhibitgroup (exhibit products and services, 1968), and GES Exposition Services (convention services, 1969).

When Greyhound acquired Armour and Company in 1970, it branched into meat processing and added the US's most popular soap, Dial, to its holdings. Greyhound subsequently sold all but the meat processing and consumer businesses acquired in the deal. Diversification in the 1980s brought into the fold Glacier Park (lodging in Glacier National Park, 1981), Jetsave (travel agency, 1986), and Dobbs International (airline catering, 1987). Greyhound also launched Premier Cruise Lines in 1983.

Greyhound sold its bus line in 1987 and changed its name to Dial Corporation in 1991. Five years later Dial split into two publicly traded companies: a new Dial, which retained all of Dial's consumer products, and Viad (from the Latin "via," signifying movement), the renamed original company, which retained Dial's service companies (Restaura, Dobbs International, Brewster Transport Company, Travelers Express, Greyhound Leisure Services, Aircraft Service International, Exhibitgroup/Giltspur, GES Exposition Services). Viad also kept a $10 million investment in baseball's Arizona Diamondbacks.

In 1997-1998 Viad began narrowing its focus, shedding UK-based travel agencies Jetsave and Crystal Holidays, as well as Premier Cruise Lines, and Greyhound Leisure Services and Aircraft Services International. It strengthened its existing focus by buying trade show contractor ESR Exposition Services, German exhibit company Voblo, and wire-transfer giant MoneyGram.

Viad continued divesting noncore holdings in 1999 by selling most of Restaura to ARAMARK. It also exited the airline catering business by selling Dobbs to SAirGroup. In 2000 a Missouri jury awarded a former Burlington Northern railroad worker about $500,000 in damages related to asbestos exposure that occurred while working for Baldwin-Lima Hamilton, a predecessor of Viad that manufactured locomotives. Also that year the company sold its ProDine unit, which had provided concessions at Phoenix's America West Arena and Bank One Ballpark, to the Compass Group. In 2001 Viad's MoneyGram entered an agreement with Bancomer SA to provide electronic money transfer services to about 1,500 locations in Mexico, and its Brewster Tours began offering air travel from 36 US cities.

However, Moneygram and Travelers Express were spun off in 2004, forming MoneyGram International. In January 2008 Viad acquired Becker Group for $24.3 million. The Baltimore-based Becker Group is a provider of large-scale, holiday-themed events and experiences for retail real estate developers in North America.

Later in 2008 CEO and president Paul Dykstra took on the additional role of chairman with the retirement of chairman Robert Bohannon.

EXECUTIVES

Chairman, President, and CEO; President, GES Exposition Services and Interim President, Marketing and Events: Paul B. Dykstra, age 48, $2,672,017 total compensation
CFO: Ellen M. Ingersoll, age 45, $1,239,216 total compensation
VP, Controller, and Chief Accounting Officer: G. Michael Latta, age 47
VP, General Counsel, and Secretary: Scott E. Sayre, age 63, $840,171 total compensation
VP Corporate Development and Strategic Planning: Thomas M. Kuczynski, age 45
VP Human Resources and Administration: Suzanne J. (Sue) Pearl, age 47
Chairman, Brewster: David G. Morrison, age 61
President, Becker Group Creative Studio: Eddie Newquist
President and CEO, The Becker Group: Glenn W. Tilley, age 48
President, Travel and Recreation Group: Michael Hannan, age 44
President and General Manager, Glacier Park: Cindy J. Ognjanov, age 60
IT Director: Mike Ouwerkerk
Treasurer: Elyse A. Newman
Director Investor Relations: Carrie Long
Auditors: Deloitte & Touche LLP

LOCATIONS

HQ: Viad Corp
  1850 N. Central Ave., Ste. 800, Phoenix, AZ 85004
Phone: 602-207-4000   **Fax:** 602-207-5900
Web: www.viad.com

2009 Sales

	$ mil.	% of total
US	589.3	73
Canada	106.1	13
UK	90.4	11
Other International	20.0	3
Total	**805.8**	**100**

PRODUCTS/OPERATIONS

2009 Sales

	$ mil.	% of total
Convention & event services	583.0	73
Exhibits & environments	147.5	18
Travel & recreation services	75.3	9
Total	**805.8**	**100**

Selected Operations

Brewster Transport (Canadian tour operator)
Exhibitgroup/Giltspur (exhibit design and production)
GES Exposition Services (convention, exhibition, and event services)
Glacier Park (mountain lodge services)
The Becker Group (experiential marketing services)

COMPETITORS

AIRworks
Czarnowski
dmg world media
Freeman Decorating Services
George P. Johnson
PSAV Presentation Services
Sparks Marketing Group
TBA Global

HISTORICAL FINANCIALS

Company Type: Public

Income Statement			FYE: December 31	
	REVENUE ($ mil.)	NET INCOME ($ mil.)	NET PROFIT MARGIN	EMPLOYEES
12/09	806	(104)	—	3,210
12/08	1,121	43	3.9%	3,950
12/07	1,004	45	4.4%	4,110
12/06	856	64	7.4%	3,620
12/05	826	38	4.6%	3,390
Annual Growth	(0.6%)	—	—	(1.4%)

2009 Year-End Financials

Debt ratio: 2.2%
Return on equity: —
Cash ($ mil.): 116
Current ratio: 2.00
Long-term debt ($ mil.): 8

No. of shares (mil.): 21
Dividends
  Yield: 0.8%
  Payout: —
Market value ($ mil.): 424

Stock History

NYSE: VVI

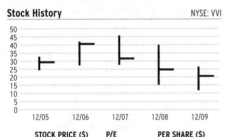

	STOCK PRICE ($) FY Close	P/E High/Low		PER SHARE ($) Earnings	Dividends	Book Value
12/09	20.63	—	—	(5.25)	0.16	18.37
12/08	24.74	19	7	2.12	0.16	22.42
12/07	31.58	21	13	2.14	0.16	22.87
12/06	40.60	14	10	2.91	0.16	20.93
12/05	29.33	19	15	1.70	0.16	19.32
Annual Growth	(8.4%)	—	—	—	0.0%	(1.2%)

Visa Inc

Paper or plastic? Visa hopes you choose the latter. Visa operates the world's largest consumer payment system (ahead of MasterCard and American Express) with some 1.7 billion credit and other payment cards in circulation. It licenses the Visa name to member institutions, which issue and market their own Visa products and participate in the VisaNet payment system (authorization, processing, and settlement services). Visa also provides its customers with debit cards, Internet payment systems, value-storing smart cards, and traveler's checks. Visa Inc. was formed in the 2007 merger of entities including Visa International, Visa Canada, and Visa U.S.A.; it went public in 2008, raising $17 billion.

Previously a cooperative run by its member banks, Visa's new corporate structure allows the company to implement a nimble and consistent global strategy that previously wasn't possible. Visa Inc. is now the parent of Visa Canada, Visa U.S.A., and a new version of Visa International (composed of Visa Central and Eastern Europe, Middle East and Africa, and Visa Latin America and the Caribbean).

Visa's filing to go public followed a similar move by MasterCard, whose public offering in 2006 was that year's most lucrative. Visa dedicated some of the funds raised towards exploring new payment-related technologies and expanding its credit card business into more regions. It has established joint ventures with payment processors and banks to improve its global payment platform. Other funds were set aside to cover costs resulting from legal settlements with American Express and Discover Financial totaling more than $4 billion.

The stake Visa Europe once held in Inovant, the company responsible for the VisaNet payment system, was acquired by Visa Inc. as a part of the restructuring. Visa Europe, which is owned and managed by its European member banks and utilizes a different authorization process, was not included in the reorganization. Visa Europe remains a minority stakeholder in Visa Inc.

On the technology front, the company is continuing to expand its contactless Visa Smart card program that does not require the card to be swiped when used. The company also is increasing its e-commerce business. In 2010 it acquired CyberSource, an online payments service, for $2 billion. The deal increased the amount of payments Visa can process online and help it expand into emerging markets where people often use cash rather than cards.

HISTORY

Although the first charge card was issued by Western Union in 1914, it wasn't until 1958 that Bank of America (BofA) issued its BankAmericard, which combined the convenience of a charge account with credit privileges. When BofA extended its customer base outside California, the interchange system controlling payments began to falter because of design problems and fraud.

In 1968 Dee Hock, manager of the BankAmericard operations of the National Bank of Commerce in Seattle, convinced member banks that a more reliable system was needed. Two years later National BankAmericard Inc. (NBI) was created as an independent corporation (owned by 243 banks) to buy the BankAmericard system from BofA.

With its initial ad slogan, "Think of it as Money," the Hock-led NBI developed BankAmericard into a widely used form of payment in the US. A multinational corporation, IBANCO, was formed in 1974 to carry the operations into other countries. People outside the US resisted BankAmericard's nominal association with BofA, and in 1977 Hock changed the card's name to Visa. NBI became Visa USA, and IBANCO became Visa International.

By 1980 Visa had debuted debit cards, begun issuing traveler's checks, and created an electromagnetic point-of-sale authorization system. Visa developed a global network of ATMs in 1983; it was expanded in 1987 by the purchase of a 33% stake in the Plus System of ATMs, then the US's second-largest system. Hock retired in 1984 with the company well on its way to realizing his vision of a universal payment system.

The company built the Visa brand image with aggressive advertising, such as sponsorship of the 1988 and 1992 Olympics, and by co-branding (issuing cards through other organizations with strong brand names, such as Blockbuster and Ford).

In 1994 Visa teamed up with Microsoft and others to develop home banking services and software. Visa Cash was introduced during the 1996 Olympics. Visa pushed its debit cards in 1996 and 1997 with humorous ads featuring presidential also-ran Bob Dole and showbiz success story Daffy Duck.

Visa expanded its smart card infrastructure in 1997. It published, with MasterCard, encryption and security software for online transactions. The gloves came off the next year as the companies vied to convince the world to rally around their respective e-purse technology standards.

During the 1990s, Visa fought American Express' attempts to introduce a bank credit card of its own by forbidding Visa members in the US from issuing the product; the Justice Department responded with an antitrust suit against Visa and MasterCard. The case went to trial in 2000 with the government claiming that Visa and MasterCard stifle competition and enjoy an exclusive cross-ownership structure.

The company continued its technology push in 2000 with a deal with Financial Services Technology Consortium to test biometrics — the use of fingerprints, irises, and voice recognition to identify cardholders. The company also launched a prepaid card, Visa Buxx, targeted at teenagers.

Also in 2000 the European Union launched an investigation into the firm's transaction fees, alleging that the fees could restrict competition. The following year Visa International agreed to drop its fee to 0.7% of the transaction value over five years.

Led by retail giant Wal-Mart, some 4 million merchants claimed Visa and MasterCard violated antitrust laws and attempted to monopolize a legally defined market for debit cards. The plaintiffs sought up to $200 billion in damages in their class-action suit. Just as the 1996 lawsuit was to go to trial in early 2003, Visa settled, agreeing to pay $2 billion (twice that of co-defendant MasterCard) over the next decade. Both agreed to pay $25 million immediately, as well as reduce the fee merchants pay for signature-based debit cards.

Visa settled a similar case with Discover Financial in 2008. Visa's net share of the deal totaled some $1.8 billion; MasterCard, which was also named, agreed to pay $862.5 million.

EXECUTIVES

Chairman and CEO: Joseph W. (Joe) Saunders, age 64, $13,736,895 total compensation
President: John M. Partridge, age 60, $7,952,979 total compensation
CFO: Byron H. Pollitt Jr., age 58, $4,630,035 total compensation
General Counsel and Secretary: Joshua R. (Josh) Floum, age 51, $3,325,354 total compensation
Chief Marketing Officer: Antonio Lucio, age 50
CIO: Michael L. Dreyer
Chief Enterprise Risk Officer: Ellen Richey, age 60
Global Head of Strategy and Corporate Development: Oliver Jenkyn
Global Head Customer Service and Implementation: Una Somerville
Global Head Operations: Keith Hunter
Global Head Corporate Relations: Douglas (Doug) Michelman
Global Head Human Resources: Richard A. (Rick) Leweke
Group President, The Americas: William M. (Bill) Sheedy, age 42
Group Executive, International: Elizabeth L. Buse, age 48
Head of Mobile: Bill Gajda
Head Global Investor Relations: Jack Carsky
Auditors: KPMG LLP

LOCATIONS

HQ: Visa Inc.
900 Metro Center Blvd., Foster City, CA 94404
Phone: 650-432-3200   **Fax:** 650-432-7436
Web: corporate.visa.com

PRODUCTS/OPERATIONS

2009 Sales

	$ mil.	% of total
Service fees	3,174	39
Data processing fees	2,430	30
International transaction fees	1,916	23
Other	625	8
Adjustments	(1,234)	—
Total	**6,911**	**100**

Selected Products and Services

Commercial
  Visa Business Credit Card (small business)
  Visa Business Debit Card (small business)
  Visa Business Electron (international)
  Visa Business Line of Credit
  Visa Commercial One Card
  Visa Corporate Card (travel and entertainment)
  Visa Gift Card
  Visa Incentive Card
  Visa Purchasing Card
  Visa Signature Business Card

Consumer Credit
  Visa Classic
  Visa Gold
  Visa Infinite
  Visa Platinum

Consumer Deposit
  Interlink Debit (POS debit network)
  Prepaid
  Visa Debit
    Visa Classic
    Visa Gold
    Visa Infinite
    Visa Platinum
  Visa Electron Debit

COMPETITORS

American Express
Citigroup
Discover
JCB International
MasterCard
Rewards Network

HISTORICAL FINANCIALS

Company Type: Public

Income Statement

FYE: September 30

	REVENUE ($ mil.)	NET INCOME ($ mil.)	NET PROFIT MARGIN	EMPLOYEES
9/09	6,911	2,353	34.0%	5,700
9/08	6,263	804	12.8%	5,765
9/07	3,590	(1,076)	—	5,479
9/06	2,948	455	15.4%	—
9/05	2,665	360	13.5%	—
Annual Growth	**26.9%**	**59.9%**	**—**	**2.0%**

2009 Year-End Financials

Debt ratio: 0.2%
Return on equity: —
Cash ($ mil.): 4,617
Current ratio: 2.08
Long-term debt ($ mil.): 44
No. of shares (mil.): 840
Dividends
  Yield: 0.6%
  Payout: 13.5%
Market value ($ mil.): 58,058

Stock History

NYSE: V

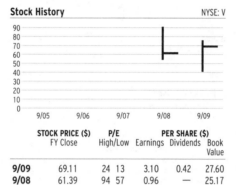

	STOCK PRICE ($) FY Close	P/E High/Low		PER SHARE ($) Earnings	Dividends	Book Value
9/09	69.11	24	13	3.10	0.42	27.60
9/08	61.39	94	57	0.96	—	25.17
Annual Growth	**12.6%**	**—**	**—**	**222.9%**	**—**	**9.7%**

Vishay Intertechnology

Vishay Intertechnology is aggressive when it comes to passives. The company is one of the top makers of passive electronic components, such as capacitors and resistors, in the world. It is also a top player in the market for discrete semiconductor components, including diodes and transistors, and it makes power integrated circuits and optoelectronic components. Vishay's components are used in everything from cars to spacecraft to wireless phones. The company's customers include tech giants such as Cisco, IBM, Nokia, and Sony. Vishay gets most of its sales outside the US.

The passive component business, like the semiconductor industry in general, is highly cyclical in market conditions. Chip makers around the world saw a dramatic downturn in orders beginning in late 2008, as sales of consumer electronics plummeted. Vishay continued restructuring during 2009 in response to poor market conditions, which caused sales to drop by more than one-quarter during the year. The company reduced its workforce by 10% as it went into the red for the second consecutive year, albeit with a narrower loss than 2008's.

In order to concentrate on its discrete electronic components (semiconductors and passive components) business, in mid-2010 Vishay spun off its noncore measurements and foil resistor divisions into a publicly traded company, Vishay

Precision Group (VPG). The spinoff was structured as a stock dividend to shareholders, who will receive one share in VPG for every 14 shares they own in Vishay Intertechnology.

Passive components are widely used in automobiles, computers, and consumer electronics to regulate the flow of electrical current and to store energy in such products. Vishay touts its line of passive components as the broadest in the industry, though its line of active semiconductor components accounts for slightly more than half of sales. While it continues to develop new products within its existing operations, the company also expands by acquiring well-positioned rivals with established brand names, such as Sprague in the US, Sfernice in France, and BCcomponents in the Netherlands.

In 2008 Vishay offered to buy all of competitor International Rectifier (IR) for about $1.6 billion in cash. The move came soon after competitor TDK bought EPCOS, a combination that created one of the biggest suppliers of passive electronic components in the world. IR's board rejected the buyout, and after raising its offer and being rejected again, Vishay ended its bid.

Founder and CTO Felix Zandman controls nearly half of Vishay's voting power.

HISTORY

Felix Zandman, Poland native and Holocaust survivor, earned his doctorate in physics at the Sorbonne. As a student, Zandman developed PhotoStress, a plastic coating that revolutionized stress testing of railcars and airplane wings. In the mid-1950s Zandman worked for the Budd Co., a Philadelphia-based steelmaker. During that period he developed a breakthrough resistor whose performance wasn't affected by temperature.

In 1962 Zandman borrowed $200,000 from cousin Alfred Slaner, the creator of nylon support hose, to start Vishay, which was named for the family's ancestral village in Lithuania. Zandman and associate James Starr made significant developments in resistors. Vishay opened its first plant in Israel in 1969 and went public in 1974. By the early 1980s it was a world leader in ultra-precise resistors and resistive sensors.

In 1985 the company and British financiers Mezzanine Capital formed a joint venture to buy Dale Electronics, a US maker of resistors whose parent company, Lionel, had filed for bankruptcy. Dale was nearly three times Vishay's size. Vishay soon added Draloric Electronic (1987, Germany) and Sfernice (1988, France). The company bought Mezzanine's half of Dale in 1988.

In 1992 Vishay purchased parts of the STI Group, formerly Sprague Technologies. Sprague, a specialist in compact, highly stable tantalum capacitors, was the US's top capacitor maker for several decades. The next year Vishay completed its purchase of Roederstein, a German capacitor and resistor maker. When sales of small specialty tantalum capacitors heated up in 1993, the company acquired the tantalum capacitor segment of Philips Electronics North America. It added Vitramon, the multilayer ceramic chip capacitor business of rival Thomas & Betts, in 1994. Vishay bought a 65% stake in Taiwan-based diode maker Lite-On Power Semiconductor in 1997.

Vishay bought TEMIC Telefunken, the semiconductor unit of German conglomerate Daimler-Benz (later DaimlerChrysler and now Daimler), for about $550 million in 1998. The purchase included 80% of TEMIC subsidiary Siliconix, a leading maker of discrete semiconductors. Vishay then sold most of TEMIC's integrated circuit operations to Atmel.

In 2000 the company sold its stake in Lite-On, saying it would focus on its Siliconix and Telefunken operations. It also acquired Electro-Films, a maker of thin-film components.

The next year began smoothly for Vishay — it acquired Infineon Technologies' infrared components business for about $120 million — but then the company hit an unexpected bump in the road. Vishay made a bid to acquire General Semiconductor (electrical protection products that control power surges) for about $463 million, but was twice rejected — a decision that drew Zandman's public ire. Vishay upped the ante when Siliconix (a top rival of General) subsequently sued General for patent infringement. Vishay finally acquired General for about $540 million in stock and the assumption of $229 million in debt.

In 2002 Vishay plunged into the transducer market, acquiring Sensortronics, Tedea-Huntleigh, and two businesses from Thermo Electron (now Thermo Fisher Scientific) to form its Vishay Transducers Group.

Zandman announced that he would step down as CEO in 2005. Vishay COO Gerald Paul succeeded Zandman as CEO. (Zandman stayed on as vice chairman and chief administrative officer.) In 2005 Vishay acquired the assets of CyOptics Israel and bought Alpha Electronics, a Japanese manufacturer of foil resistors.

Also in 2005 Vishay acquired SI Technologies for about $18 million in cash, plus the assumption of $12 million in debt. That same year the company acquired the 20% of Siliconix it didn't previously own, swapping Vishay common shares for those of Siliconix. Vishay's tender offer yielded enough shares to give the company ownership of more than 95% of Siliconix.

In 2007 competitor International Rectifier sold its Power Control Systems (PCS) business to Vishay for about $290 million in cash.

EXECUTIVES

Chairman, CTO, and Chief Business Development Officer: Felix Zandman, age 81, $11,884,966 total compensation
President, CEO, and Director: Gerald Paul, age 61, $1,303,516 total compensation
Vice Chairman and Chief Administration Officer; President, Vishay Israel: Marc Zandman, age 48, $703,638 total compensation
EVP and CFO: Lior E. Yahalomi, age 51, $362,650 total compensation
EVP Finance and Chief Accounting Officer: Lori Lipcaman, age 52
SVP, Corporate General Counsel, and Corporate Secretary: Marc L. Frohman
SVP and Corporate Controller: David L. Tomlinson
SVP, Corporate Communications, and Treasurer: Peter G. Henrici
Manager Global Communications: Andrew Post
Public Relations Associate and Director: Ruta Zandman, age 72
Corporate Investor Relations: Brenda R. Tate
Auditors: Ernst & Young LLP

LOCATIONS

HQ: Vishay Intertechnology, Inc.
63 Lancaster Ave., Malvern, PA 19355
Phone: 610-644-1300 **Fax:** 610-889-9429
Web: www.vishay.com

2009 Sales

	$ mil.	% of total
Europe		
Germany	544.4	27
Other countries	195.2	10
Asia/Pacific	777.7	38
US	312.2	15
Israel	212.5	10
Total	**2,042.0**	**100**

PRODUCTS/OPERATIONS

2009 Sales

	$ mil.	% of total
Passive components	1,037.1	51
Semiconductors	1,004.9	49
Total	**2,042.0**	**100**

2009 Sales by Market

	% of total
Industrial	38
Computer	17
Automotive	15
Consumer products	10
Telecommunications	13
Military & aerospace	5
Medical	2
Total	**100**

Selected Products

Semiconductors (active components)
  Diodes
    Rectifiers
    Small-signal diodes
    Transient voltage suppressors
    Zener diodes
  Integrated circuits (ICs)
    Analog switches
    Infrared data communication (IrDC) transceivers
    Multiplexers
    Power ICs
  Optoelectronic components
    Displays
    Infrared emitters
    Light-emitting diodes (LEDs)
    Optocouplers
    Optosensors
    Photo detectors
  Transistors
    Bipolar power transistors
    Junction field-effect transistors (JFETs)
    Power MOSFETs (metal oxide semiconductor FETs)
    Radio-frequency transistors
    Small-signal FETs
Passive components
  Capacitors
    Aluminum
    Ceramic
    Film
    Tantalum
  Magnetics
    Custom magnetics
    Inductors
    Transformers
  Resistors
    Bulk metal foil resistors
    Fuse resistors
    Metal-film resistors and networks
    Panel controls
    Panel potentiometers
    Thermistors
    Thick-film resistors and networks
    Thin-film resistors and networks
    Trimming potentiometers
    Varistors

COMPETITORS

Allegro MicroSystems
Avago Technologies
AVX
Diodes
Fairchild Semiconductor
Freescale Semiconductor
Infineon Technologies
International Rectifier
KEMET
Maxim Integrated Products
Murata Manufacturing
NXP Semiconductors
ON Semiconductor
ROHM
Samsung Electronics
Sanken Electric
Sharp Corp.
Shindengen Electric Manufacturing
STMicroelectronics
SunPower
TDK
Texas Instruments
Toshiba Semiconductor
Tyco Electronics

HISTORICAL FINANCIALS

Company Type: Public

Income Statement

FYE: December 31

	REVENUE ($ mil.)	NET INCOME ($ mil.)	NET PROFIT MARGIN	EMPLOYEES
12/09	2,042	(57)	—	22,300
12/08	2,822	(1,731)	—	24,800
12/07	2,833	131	4.6%	27,900
12/06	2,582	140	5.4%	27,000
12/05	2,297	62	2.7%	26,100
Annual Growth	**(2.9%)**	**—**	**—**	**(3.9%)**

2009 Year-End Financials

Debt ratio: 21.1%
Return on equity: —
Cash ($ mil.): 579
Current ratio: 3.45
Long-term debt ($ mil.): 320
No. of shares (mil.): 187
Dividends
  Yield: 0.0%
  Payout: —
Market value ($ mil.): 1,402

Stock History

NYSE: VSH

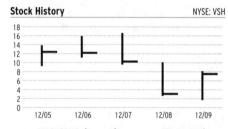

	STOCK PRICE ($) FY Close	P/E High/Low		PER SHARE ($) Earnings	Dividends	Book Value
12/09	7.51	—	—	(0.31)	0.00	8.12
12/08	3.08	—	—	(9.29)	0.00	8.28
12/07	10.26	24	14	0.69	0.00	17.99
12/06	12.18	22	16	0.73	0.00	16.51
12/05	12.38	40	28	0.34	0.00	15.30
Annual Growth	**(11.7%)**	**—**	**—**	**—**	**—**	**(14.6%)**

Volt Information Sciences

A jolt from Volt can discharge your personnel needs. Volt Information Sciences generates most of its sales by offering temporary and permanent employees to 10,000 clients through more than 300 branch and on-site offices in Asia, Europe, and North and South America. Volt's staffing segment also includes businesses that provide project management and information technology services (VMC Consulting) and outsourced procurement services (ProcureStaff Technologies). In addition, the company provides telecommunications network engineering and construction services, as well as information systems, including directory assistance systems. The founding Shaw family owns a controlling stake in Volt.

Volt aims to grow by continuing to focus on large corporate customers that need staffing help at multiple locations. Because the company competes for that business with lower-cost providers based outside the US, Volt is moving to expand internationally. In 2008 several divisions of Microsoft accounted for 10% of Volt's total sales.

To reduce debt and to free capital for investment in core operations, Volt in September 2008 sold its telephone directory systems and services business and its US-based telephone directory publishing operations to Yellow Pages for about $180 million. Volt retained a directory publishing business based in Uruguay. It acquired Advice Consulting, a firm also based in Uruguay that year.

In 2009 the company strengthened its product portfolio with the launch of Volt Consulting — Managed Service Programs. The new unit provides human capital supply chain management expertise and caters to each client's specific sourcing and vendor management needs. Similar services provided by VMC Consulting and ProcureStaff were consolidated into the new unit.

HISTORY

Brothers William and Jerome Shaw started their business in 1950 to provide freelance technical publication assistance; they chose the name Volt because it sounded technical. The company established a temporary technical staffing division in 1956 and went public in 1962.

Volt had expanded into clerical and administrative staffing, as well as telephone directory printing, by the late 1960s; it established a telecommunications services division in 1976. The company acquired Delta Resources (computerized directory assistance systems) in 1980 and began printing telephone directories in Uruguay and Australia several years later (the Australian operation was sold in 1997).

Volt's personnel segment grew in the 1990s as companies relied more on outside agencies to help staff their businesses, and increased telephone industry competition drove expansion in the telecommunications market. Electronic publishing was more problematic, however, and in 1996 the company merged its subsidiaries in that segment with Information International to form Autologic Information International (Volt took a 59% stake). In 1997 it expanded its breadth with the purchase of 11 US community telephone directories in North Carolina and West Virginia.

In 1999 Volt acquired UK-based Gatton Group. Also that year it bought the wired services business (installation of cable, wire, and small telecommunications systems) and professional staffing divisions of a Lucent Technologies unit. In 2000 the company created subsidiary ProcureStaff to provide supplemental staffing procurement services. In 2001 Agfa Corporation bought the company's 59%-owned subsidiary, Autologic Information International, for about $24 million. Volt combined its telecommunications services units to form Volt Telecommunications Group in 2002. In 2003 the company's VMC Consulting subsidiary merged with IT consulting division Volt Integrated Solutions Group.

Volt acquired Volt Delta, the directory and operator services unit of Nortel, in 2004 to boost its computer systems segment. In 2007 the company merged one of its Volt Delta subsidiaries with LSSi Corp. The combined company was renamed LSSi Data.

William Shaw died in 2006.

EXECUTIVES

President, CEO, COO, and Director: Steven A. (Steve) Shaw, age 50, $581,970 total compensation
EVP and Secretary: Jerome Shaw, age 83, $564,504 total compensation
SVP and CFO: Jack Egan, age 60, $346,093 total compensation
SVP and General Counsel: Howard B. Weinreich, age 67, $361,139 total compensation
SVP and Treasurer: Ludwig M. Guarino, age 58
SVP and General Manager, VoltDelta Enterprise Services and Solutions: Terry Saeger
SVP and Managing Director, Volt Europe: Stephanie Elliott
SVP LSSiDATA: Brad Schorer
VP Human Resources: Louise Ross, age 61
VP Accounting Operations: Daniel G. Hallihan, age 61
President, Volt Workforce Solutions: Thomas (Tom) Daley, age 55, $494,520 total compensation
President, Maintech: Frank D'Alessio
President, ProcureStaff Technologies: Allen Rittscher
President, Volt Telecom Group: R.J. (Chip) Anderson
President, VoltDelta: Joe DiAngelo
President, Volt Consulting and Managed Service Programs: Larry Kaylor
Auditors: Ernst & Young LLP

LOCATIONS

HQ: Volt Information Sciences, Inc.
1600 Stewart Ave., 4th Fl., Westbury, NY 11590
Phone: 212-704-2400   **Fax:** 212-704-2413
Web: www.volt.com

2008 Sales

	$ mil.	% of total
US	2,236.2	92
Europe	191.1	8
Total	**2,427.3**	**100**

PRODUCTS/OPERATIONS

2008 Sales

	$ mil.	% of total
Staffing	2,043.8	84
Computer systems	212.7	9
Telecommunications	171.7	7
Printing & other	16.9	—
Adjustments	(17.8)	—
Total	**2,427.3**	**100**

Selected Products and Services

Computer systems
  Directory assistance
  Information technology
Staffing
  Information technology services
  Professional placement
  Staffing procurement
  Temporary and contract staffing
Telecommunications
  Construction
  Design
  Engineering
  Installation
  Maintenance

COMPETITORS

Adecco
Aquent
Barrett Business Services
Butler America
Edgewater Technology
Express Employment
Joulé
Kelly Services
Manpower
SFN Group
TAC Worldwide
TeamStaff

HISTORICAL FINANCIALS

Company Type: Public

Income Statement
FYE: Sunday nearest October 31

	REVENUE ($ mil.)	NET INCOME ($ mil.)	NET PROFIT MARGIN	EMPLOYEES
10/08	2,427.3	64.2	2.6%	42,000
10/07	2,353.1	39.3	1.7%	43,000
10/06	2,338.5	30.6	1.3%	46,000
10/05	2,177.6	17.0	0.8%	48,000
10/04	1,924.8	33.7	1.8%	45,000
Annual Growth	**6.0%**	**17.5%**	**—**	**(1.7%)**

2008 Year-End Financials

Debt ratio: 3.1%
Return on equity: 17.3%
Cash ($ mil.): 121
Current ratio: 1.48
Long-term debt ($ mil.): 12
No. of shares (mil.): 21
Dividends
  Yield: 0.0%
  Payout: —
Market value ($ mil.): 159

Stock History
NYSE: VOL

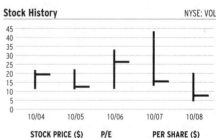

	STOCK PRICE ($) FY Close	P/E High/Low		PER SHARE ($) Earnings	Dividends	Book Value
10/08	7.65	7	2	2.92	0.00	18.86
10/07	15.55	25	8	1.71	0.00	16.91
10/06	26.33	25	9	1.31	0.00	15.60
10/05	12.53	29	16	0.74	0.00	14.15
10/04	19.37	15	8	1.47	0.00	13.27
Annual Growth	**(20.7%)**	**—**	**—**	**18.7%**	**—**	**9.2%**

Vulcan Materials

The road to just about everywhere is paved with Vulcan Materials' aggregates. The company is the largest producer of construction aggregates — crushed stone, gravel, and sand — in the US. Vulcan produces and distributes aggregates, asphalt mixes, ready-mixed concrete, and cement at more than 330 production plants in the US (primarily the Southeast and Mid-Atlantic), Canada, the Bahamas, and Mexico. Vulcan serves more than 20 states from coast to coast. A majority of its aggregates are used to build and maintain highways, bridges, railways, airports, and other public works systems; they're also used in residential, commercial, and industrial construction. Aggregates account for nearly 70% of Vulcan's sales.

Vulcan has not been immune to the economic downturn. The housing crash in states such as Florida and California, coupled with decreased commercial construction, led to dwindling demand and impacted sales volumes and earnings. As a result Vulcan has been focused on controlling costs and it has trimmed some operations and reduced its workforce by about 10%.

However, increased spending by the federal government on infrastructure and highway projects has helped Vulcan's aggregates sales. Stimulus spending for highway construction is expected to create an uptick in demand. Vulcan Materials also expects that the multi-year nature of highway and infrastructure projects will continue to offset the downturn in the residential construction industry and drive recovery.

To stay ahead of rival Martin Marietta Materials, the acquisitive Vulcan plans to keep buying quarries. The company has made a string of acquisitions over the years in order to grow. Its biggest deal came in 2007 when it acquired Florida Rock Industries for some $4.6 billion. In addition to increasing Vulcan's presence in Florida, the acquisition boosted its aggregates reserves by about 20%. The company expanded its Newberry, Florida-based cement plant, which produces portland and masonry cement. The expansion doubled the plant's production capacity.

Like many big corporations, the company has jumped on the corporate sustainability bandwagon, monitoring the amount of pollutants it generates. It has been commended in the state of California for tracking its greenhouse gas emissions and for building aggregates plants (such as its Corona, California, facility) that attempt to reduce and prevent those emissions by using a downhill conveyor that generates electricity as it carries rock to the processing plant below.

State Farm Mutual Automobile Insurance owns about 10% of Vulcan Materials.

HISTORY

In 1916 the Ireland family purchased a 75% interest in Birmingham Slag, a small Alabama company established in 1909 to process slag from a Birmingham steel plant. For several decades the company prospered by selling its processed slag to the construction industry.

Third-generation Charles Ireland became president in 1951 and transformed Birmingham Slag from a regional operation into a national one. In 1956 the company bought Vulcan Detinning, renamed itself Vulcan Materials, and went public. By 1959 Vulcan was the largest producer of aggregates in the US, with sales over $100 million.

Vulcan owned 90 quarries by 1981 and claimed sales of some $780 million. It added about 50 operations and plants in the 1980s and in 1987 entered into a joint venture, the Crescent Market Project, with Mexico's Grupo ICA, largely to supply aggregates from a Yucatan quarry to US Gulf Coast markets.

In 1990 Vulcan bought Reed Crushed Stone and Reed Terminal, which included the largest US crushed-rock quarry (in Paducah, Kentucky). The Yucatan plant was fully operational in 1991 and was supported by two company-owned ships that moved materials to the US Gulf Coast. Also that year Vulcan entered a venture with Tetra Technologies to produce calcium chloride from hydrochloric acids; this new use for the acid eased Vulcan's status as a major polluter.

Vulcan built a sodium chlorite plant in Wichita in 1993 and plants in Port Edwards, Wisconsin, to produce potassium carbonate and sodium hydrosulfite. In 1994 the company bought Peroxidation Systems of Tucson (water-purification technology, chemicals, and related equipment). That year Vulcan also acquired Callaway Chemical, boosting its specialty chemical line.

The company bought three food-processing chemical companies and Rio Linda Chemical (chlorine dioxide) in 1995. Acquisitions continued in 1996 as Vulcan purchased three chemical companies and several quarries. Also that year Vulcan sold its chlorine cylinder repackaging business and consolidated its paper and water-treatment businesses. In 1997 the company sold its coal-handling business, added several quarries, and bought the textile chemical business of Laun-Dry Supply.

Vulcan bought six aggregate operations in Georgia, Illinois, and Tennessee in 1998 and started three new aggregate operations in Alabama, Georgia, and Indiana. It also formed a joint venture with Mitsui to build a chlor-alkali plant. In 1999 Vulcan paid about $890 million for rival aggregate producer CalMat. The company also bought 20 quarries throughout the US. Vulcan merged its specialty chemicals businesses into one unit — Vulcan Performance Chemicals — in 2000. The company also acquired Texas-based Garves W. Yates & Sons, adding six quarries. Also in 2000 Vulcan acquired the North American aggregates production and transportation assets that Anglo American's Titan Cement Company obtained from its purchase of Tarmac plc. In 2001 the company bought two aggregates facilities in Tennessee, two recycling facilities in Illinois, and its Mexico-based Crescent Markets joint venture.

In 2003 Vulcan divested its Performance Chemicals business unit, concluding with the sale of its industrial water treatment and pulp and paper operations. It did retain the sodium

chlorite business and moved it under its Chloralkali operations. Vulcan expanded in central Tennessee with the purchase of Columbia Rock Products in 2004. In October 2004 the company agreed to sell the remainder of its chemical operations to Basic Chemical Company for an undisclosed sum; the deal was completed in 2005.

Vulcan spent $94 million on acquisitions in 2005, including 11 aggregate operations and five asphalt plants in Arizona, Georgia, Indiana, and Tennessee.

EXECUTIVES

Chairman and CEO: Donald M. (Don) James, age 61, $11,089,819 total compensation
SVP and CFO: Daniel F. Sansone, age 57, $2,199,150 total compensation
SVP and General Counsel: Robert A. Wason IV, age 58, $1,516,219 total compensation
SVP Construction Materials, East: Danny R. Shepherd, age 58, $1,860,073 total compensation
SVP Construction Materials, West:
Ronald G. (Ron) McAbee, age 63, $1,882,424 total compensation
SVP Human Resources: J. Wayne Houston, age 57
VP Business Development: James P. Daniel, age 54
VP, Controller, and CIO: Ejaz A. Khan, age 52
VP Marketing Support Services: Sidney F. Mays, age 65
VP Safety, Health and Environment, and Engineering Services: Randal C. Hall, age 54
VP Tax and Assistant Treasurer: James W. O'Brien, age 52
President, Southwest Division: J. Thomas (Tom) Hill, age 51
President, Midwest Division: Robert R. Vogel, age 51
President, Midsouth Division: Stanley G. (Stan) Bass, age 49
President, Western Division: Alan D. Wessel, age 50
President, Southeast Division: Michael R. Mills, age 48
Secretary: Jerry F. Perkins Jr.
Investor Relations: Mark Warren
Manager Public Affairs: John English
Treasurer: J. Philip Alford, age 59
Auditors: Deloitte & Touche LLP

LOCATIONS

HQ: Vulcan Materials Company
1200 Urban Center Dr., Birmingham, AL 35242
Phone: 205-298-3000   **Fax:** 205-298-2960
Web: www.vulcanmaterials.com

PRODUCTS/OPERATIONS

2009 Sales

	$ mil.	% of total
Aggregates	1,838.6	64
Asphalt mix & concrete	833.1	28
Cement	72.5	3
Delivery revenues	146.8	5
Eliminations	(200.5)	—
Total	**2,690.5**	**100**

Selected Products

Construction materials
Agricultural limestone
Asphalt coating (Guardtop)
Asphalt paving materials
Chemical stone (high-calcium and -magnesium stone)
Concrete
Construction aggregates
Crushed stone
Gravel
Sand
Recrushed concrete
Railroad ballast
Ready-mix concrete (portland cement)
Recycled materials

COMPETITORS

Aggregate Industries
Ash Grove Cement
Buzzi Unicem USA
Cementos Portland Valderrivas
CEMEX
Continental Materials
CRH
Cytec
Doan Construction
Eagle Materials
Edw. C. Levy
Giant Cement
Hanson Limited
HeidelbergCement
Holcim Apasco
Holcim (Australia)
Holcim Canada
Holcim (US)
Knife River
Lafarge North America
Lehigh Hanson
Martin Marietta Aggregates
Martin Marietta Materials
MDU Resources
New Enterprise Stone & Lime
Ready Mix USA
RMX Holdings
Rogers Group
Superior Ready Mix
Transit Mix Concrete
Trinity Industries
TXI
U.S. Lime & Minerals

HISTORICAL FINANCIALS

Company Type: Public

Income Statement

FYE: December 31

	REVENUE ($ mil.)	NET INCOME ($ mil.)	NET PROFIT MARGIN	EMPLOYEES
12/09	2,691	30	1.1%	8,227
12/08	3,651	(4)	—	9,320
12/07	3,328	451	13.5%	10,522
12/06	3,343	468	14.0%	7,983
12/05	2,895	389	13.4%	8,051
Annual Growth	(1.8%)	(47.2%)	—	0.5%

2009 Year-End Financials

Debt ratio: 52.2%
Return on equity: 0.8%
Cash ($ mil.): 22
Current ratio: 0.87
Long-term debt ($ mil.): 2,116

No. of shares (mil.): 128
Dividends
  Yield: 2.8%
  Payout: 592.0%
Market value ($ mil.): 6,756

Stock History

NYSE: VMC

	STOCK PRICE ($) FY Close	P/E High/Low		PER SHARE ($) Earnings	Dividends	Book Value
12/09	52.67	284	137	0.25	1.48	31.59
12/08	69.58	—	—	(0.04)	1.96	27.46
12/07	79.09	28	17	4.54	1.84	29.31
12/06	89.87	20	14	4.69	1.48	15.60
12/05	67.75	20	14	3.73	1.16	16.58
Annual Growth	(6.1%)	—	—	(49.1%)	6.3%	17.5%

Wakefern Food

Some might say you aren't shopping right if you don't get your groceries from stores supplied by this company. Wakefern Food is the largest member-owned wholesale distribution cooperative in the US, supplying groceries and other merchandise to a chain of more than 200 ShopRite supermarkets in five eastern states, including parts of New Jersey, New York, and Pennsylvania. The company supplies both national brands and private-label products (ShopRite, Chef's Express, Readington Farms) to its member stores; Wakefern also offers advertising, merchandising, and other business support services. The co-op, which boasts more than 40 members, was founded by seven grocers in 1946.

Like other wholesale distributors, Wakefern Food's success depends on its ability to distribute goods at the lowest possible cost to its customers, meaning the company focuses on keeping expenses low and improving efficiencies throughout its supply operation. But as a member-owned cooperative, the company differs from other wholesalers such as Nash-Finch in that its primary focus is on its member stores. Wakefern Food also has the added responsibility of promoting its ShopRight retail chain and helping its member retailers expand the chain's footprint.

The ShopRite chain boasts a loyal following in its core markets, but the supermarkets have been feeling the pinch from rivals in the price-competitive grocery business. The company is especially feeling pressure from non-supermarket chains such as Wal-Mart, CVS/Caremark, and Wawa. To help boost customer loyalty, Wakefern has turned to new technology in the form of mobile applications (developed in partnership with technology firm MyWebGrocer) for the Apple iPhone that allow users to get alerts about weekly store specials in their area. The company also rolled out an online pharmacy where customers can place orders through the Internet.

HISTORY

Wakefern Food was founded in 1946 by seven New York- and New Jersey-based grocers: Louis Weiss, Sam and Al Aidekman, Abe Kesselman, Dave Fern, Sam Garb, and Albert Goldberg. The company name was created by taking letters from the names of five of the founders (Weiss, the two Aidekmans, Kesselman, and Fern). Like many cooperatives, the association sought to lower costs by increasing its buying power as a group.

They each put in $1,000 and began operating a 5,000-sq.-ft. warehouse, often putting in double time to keep both their stores and the warehouse running. The shopkeepers' collective buying power proved valuable, enabling the grocers to stock many items at the same prices as their larger competitors.

In 1951 Wakefern members began pooling their resources to buy advertising space. A common store name — ShopRite — was chosen, and each week co-op members met to decide which items would be sale priced. Within a year, membership had grown to over 50. Expansion became a priority, and in the mid-1950s co-op members united in small groups to take over failed supermarkets. One such group, called the Supermarkets Operating Co. (SOC), was formed in 1956. Within 10 years it had acquired a number of failed stores, remodeled them, and given them the ShopRite name.

During the late 1950s sales at ShopRite stores slumped after Wakefern decided to buck the supermarket trend of offering trading stamps (which could then be exchanged for gifts), figuring that offering the stamps would ultimately lead to higher food prices. The move initially drove away customers, but Wakefern cut grocery prices across the board and sales returned. The company did embrace another supermarket trend: stocking stores with nonfood items.

The co-op was severely shaken in 1966 when SOC merged with General Supermarkets, a similar small group within Wakefern, becoming Supermarkets General Corp. (SGC). SGC was a powerful entity, with 71 supermarkets, 10 drugstores, six gas stations, a wholesale bakery, and a discount department store. Many Wakefern members opposed the merger and attempted to block the action with a court order. By 1968 SGC had beefed up its operations to include department store chains as well as its grocery stores. In a move that threatened to break Wakefern, SGC broke away from the co-op, and its stores were renamed Pathmark.

Wakefern not only weathered the storm, it grew under the direction of chairman and CEO Thomas Infusino, elected shortly after the split. The co-op focused on asserting its position as a seller of low-priced products. Wakefern developed private-label brands, including the ShopRite brand. In the 1980s members began operating larger stores and adding more nonfood items to the ShopRite product mix. With its number of superstores on the rise and facing increased competition from club stores in 1992, Wakefern opened a centralized, nonfood distribution center in New Jersey.

In 1995, 30-year Wakefern veteran Dean Janeway was elected president of the co-op. The company debuted its ShopRite MasterCard, co-branded with New Jersey's Valley National Bank, in 1996. The following year the co-op purchased two of its customers' stores in Pennsylvania, then threatened to close them when contract talks with the local union deteriorated. In 1998 Wakefern settled the dispute, then sold the stores.

The company partnered with Internet bidding site priceline.com in 1999, offering customers an opportunity to bid on groceries and then pick them up at ShopRite stores. Big V, Wakefern's biggest customer, filed for Chapter 11 bankruptcy protection in 2000 and said it was ending its distribution agreement with the co-op. In July 2002, however, Wakefern's ShopRite Supermarkets subsidiary acquired all of Big V's assets for approximately $185 million in cash and assumed liabilities.

Infusino retired in May 2005 after 35 years with Wakefern Food. He was succeeded by former vice chairman Joseph Colalillo. The cooperative added to its footprint in 2007 when it acquired about 10 underperforming retail locations from Stop & Shop. The stores, located mostly in South Jersey, were rebranded under the ShopRite banner.

EXECUTIVES

Chairman and CEO: Joseph S. (Joe) Colalillo, age 49
President and COO: Dean Janeway
CFO: Douglas (Doug) Wille
EVP: Joseph Sheridan
SVP and CIO: Natan Tabak
VP Logistics: Peter (Pete) Rolandelli
VP Information Services Division: Alan Aront
VP Human Resources: Ann Marie Burke
VP Corporate and Consumer Affairs: Karen Meleta
VP Quality Assurance: Mike Ambrosio

VP Strategic Development and Member Relations:
William (Bill) Crombie
Director Wholesale Division: Dave Baer
Director Consumer Affairs: Cheryl Macik
Director Advertising: Karen McAuvic
Director Private Label Branding: Loren Weinstein
Corporate Communications and Media Relations
 Specialist: Jeannette Castaneda

LOCATIONS

HQ: Wakefern Food Corp.
 5000 Riverside Dr., Keasbey, NJ 08832
Phone: 908-527-3300   **Fax:** 908-527-3397
Web: www.wakefern.com

COMPETITORS

A&P	Krasdale Foods
Acme Markets	Nash-Finch
Associated Wholesalers	Stop & Shop
C&S Wholesale	SUPERVALU
CVS Caremark	Wal-Mart
IGA	Wawa, Inc.

HISTORICAL FINANCIALS

Company Type: Cooperative

Income Statement				FYE: September 30
	REVENUE ($ mil.)	NET INCOME ($ mil.)	NET PROFIT MARGIN	EMPLOYEES
9/09	11,700	—	—	50,000
9/08	10,600	—	—	50,000
9/07	9,900	—	—	50,000
9/06	7,500	—	—	50,000
9/05	7,239	—	—	50,000
Annual Growth	12.8%	—	—	0.0%

Revenue History

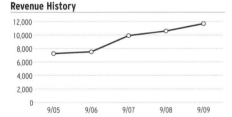

Walgreen Co.

Walgreen offers an old-fashioned tonic for fiscal fitness: quality over quantity and homespun growth rather than growth through acquisitions. It works. It operates nearly 7,500 drugstores in all 50 US states, the District of Columbia, Guam, and Puerto Rico, as well as two mail-order facilities. Prescription drugs account for about two-thirds of sales; the rest comes from general merchandise, over-the-counter medications, cosmetics, and groceries. Walgreen usually builds rather than buys stores, so it can pick prime locations. In 2010 Walgreen paid about $1 billion to acquire New York-based drugstore chain Duane Reade.

The Duane Reade purchase made Walgreen the instant market leader in New York City, adding its 250-plus stores in the metro area to Walgreen's 70 locations. The move is a strategic one for Walgreen, which is looking to grow by expanding in urban areas. In recent years, the regional chain has worked to develop a new "urban box" store format to maximize sales per square foot in densely-populated Manhattan. Walgreen plans to retain the Duane Reade name.

The acquisition was an exception to Walgreen's historical preference to grow organically. The sick US economy slowed sales and earnings growth, along with prescription drug sales, and caused Walgreen to curtail its break-neck pace of growth. Indeed, the chain has slowed store openings to focus on strengthening existing stores and has undertaken an aggressive store remodeling plan intended to help make stores more customer friendly. The company has also begun selling beer and wine as it procures liquor licenses. (Rivals CVS and Rite-Aid also stock alcohol in their stores.)

Walgreen's strategic shift follows a defeat by archrival CVS in a takeover battle for Longs Drug Stores in late 2008. Walgreen proved more successful in its acquisition of the specialty pharmacy business of McKesson Corporation, completed in December 2008.

Walgreen also aims to play an increasingly important role in the solution to America's health care crisis through about 375 convenient care in-store clinics operated by Take Care Health Systems. In a bid to diminish its reliance on retail stores for growth and expand its in-store network of health clinics, Walgreen formed a new Health and Wellness division to operate clinics and pharmacies at large-company worksites. To that end, it has acquired two operators of worksite health centers, I-trax, Inc and Whole Health Management. Previously, Walgreen acquired in-store health clinic operator Take Care Health Systems, which managed about 145 clinics in about a dozen states.

HISTORY

In 1901 Chicago pharmacist Charles Walgreen borrowed $2,000 from his father for a down payment on his first drugstore. He sold a half interest in his first store in 1909 and bought a second, where he installed a large soda fountain and began serving lunch. In 1916 seven stores consolidated under the corporate name Walgreen Co. By 1920 there were 20 stores in Chicago, with sales of $1.55 million.

Walgreen popularized the milk shake in the early 1920s, and he promoted his chain with the first company-owned-and-operated airplane. The firm was first listed on the NYSE in 1927; two years later its 397 stores in 87 cities had sales of $47 million.

The company did comparatively well during the Great Depression. Although average sales per store dropped between 1931 and 1935, per-store earnings went up, thanks to a chainwide emphasis on efficiency. By 1940 Walgreen had 489 stores, but the chain shrank during WWII when unprofitable stores were closed.

The 1950s saw a major change in the way drugstores did business. Walgreen was an early leader in self-service merchandising, opening its first self-serve store in 1952; it had 22 by the end of 1953. Between 1950 and 1960, as small, older stores were replaced with larger, more efficient, self-service units, the total number of stores in the chain increased only about 10%, but sales grew by more than 90%.

By 1960 Walgreen had 451 stores, half of which were self-service. The company bought three Globe discount department stores in Houston in 1962 and expanded the chain to 13 stores by 1966, but Globe struggled in the early 1970s and was sold in 1975. During the 1960s Walgreen began phasing out its soda fountains, which had become unprofitable.

The 1970s and 1980s brought rapid growth and modernization to the chain. It opened its 1,000th store in 1984.

Walgreen began its Healthcare Plus subsidiary in 1992 to provide prescriptions by mail. Along with other independent drugstores, it helped set up Pharmacy Direct Network in 1994 to manage prescription drug programs for group health plans. In 1995 Walgreen launched a prescription benefits management company, WHP Health Initiatives, to target small to midsized employers and HMOs.

President (and pharmacist) L. Daniel Jorndt was promoted to CEO in early 1998 after the founder's grandson, Charles Walgreen III, stepped down; Jorndt became chairman in 1999.

Jorndt retired in January 2003. CEO David Bernauer added chairman to his job description. In 2006 Walgreens Home Care acquired Oklahoma City-based Canadian Valley Medical Solutions, a provider of home care services to patients in central and western Oklahoma.

In 2007 Bernauer was succeeded by Jeffrey Reins. Also, Charles R. Walgreen, Jr. — son of the company founder, president of the company from 1939 to 1963, and chairman from 1963 until 1976 — died at the age of 100. Also that year the company agreed to pay $20 million to settle a class-action lawsuit filed by the US Equal Employment Opportunity Commission alleging that Walgreen discriminated against thousands of its black employees. Also in 2007 Walgreen purchased Illinois-based Option Care, a specialty pharmacy and home infusion provider with more than 100 stores in 34 states, for about $850 million.

In 2009 Gregory Wasson, formerly the president and COO of Walgreen, ascended to the office of CEO. Wasson succeeded chairman Alan McNally, who had served as interim CEO since Reins' departure in 2008. In July the company opened its first drugstore in Alaska, making its coverage of all 50 US states complete.

At the company's 2010 annual meeting in January, Charles R. "Cork" Walgreen, chairman emeritus and grandson of the company's founder, retired after serving on the board of directors for 46 years.

EXECUTIVES

Chairman: Alan G. McNally, age 64,
 $1,478,126 total compensation
President, CEO, and Director:
 Gregory D. (Greg) Wasson, age 51,
 $4,026,590 total compensation
EVP and CFO: Wade D. Miquelon, age 45
EVP Pharmacy Services: Kermit R. Crawford, age 50
EVP Operations and Community Management:
 Mark A. Wagner, age 48, $2,267,414 total compensation
EVP and General Counsel: Dana I. Green, age 60
SVP Health Care Innovation:
 Donald C. (Don) Huonker Jr., age 48
SVP Store Operations: Debra M. (Debbie) Ferguson, age 52
SVP and CIO: Timothy J. (Tim) Theriault, age 49
SVP Supply Chain and Logistics:
 J. Randolph (Randy) Lewis, age 60
SVP E-Commerce: Sona Chawla, age 42
SVP Eastern Store Operations:
 William M. (Bill) Handal, age 60

SVP Human Resources: Kenneth R. (Ken) Weigand, age 52
SVP and Chief Human Resources:
Kathleen Wilson-Thompson, age 52
SVP and President, Walgreens Health and Wellness:
Hal F. Rosenbluth, age 58
VP, Chief Accounting Officer, and Controller:
Mia M. Scholz, age 43
VP and Chief Sales Officer: Jeffrey J. Zavada
VP and Chief Marketing Officer: Kimberly L. Feil, age 50
VP Corporate Affairs and Communications:
Charles V. (Chuck) Greener, age 55
Chief Medical Officer: Cheryl Pegus, age 46
Auditors: Deloitte & Touche LLP

LOCATIONS

HQ: Walgreen Co.
200 Wilmot Rd., Deerfield, IL 60015
Phone: 847-914-2500   **Fax:** 847-914-2804
Web: www.walgreens.com

2009 Locations

	No.
Florida	824
Texas	679
Illinois	571
California	570
Ohio	266
Arizona	250
Tennessee	250
New York	245
Wisconsin	230
Michigan	225
Indiana	212
Missouri	192
Georgia	190
New Jersey	175
North Carolina	169
Colorado	165
Massachusetts	165
Minnesota	138
Louisiana	134
Pennsylvania	123
Washington	122
Connecticut	117
Oklahoma	109
Virginia	109
South Carolina	102
Alabama	99
Kentucky	95
Nevada	84
Iowa	72
Mississippi	70
Oregon	69
Delaware	64
Kansas	63
New Mexico	59
Nebraska	59
Maryland	56
Arkansas	55
Utah	39
Idaho	37
Other states	144
Puerto Rico	98
Guam	1
Total	**7,496**

PRODUCTS/OPERATIONS

2009 Sales

	% of total
Prescription drugs	65
General merchandise	25
Nonprescription drugs	10
Total	**100**

2009 Locations

	No.
Drugstores	6,997
Worksite facilities	377
Home care facilities	105
Specialty pharmacies	15
Mail service facilities	2
Total	**7,496**

COMPETITORS

7-Eleven
99 Cents Only
A&P
Concentra
Costco Wholesale
CVS Caremark
Dollar General
drugstore.com
Express Scripts
Family Dollar Stores
Food Lion
GNC
Health Fitness
Healthways, Inc.
H-E-B
Kerr Drug
Kmart
Kroger
Medicine Shoppe
Meijer
Publix
Randall's
Rite Aid
Ritz Camera
Safeway
SHPS
Smith's Food & Drug
SUPERVALU
Target
Wal-Mart
Winn-Dixie

HISTORICAL FINANCIALS

Company Type: Public

Income Statement

FYE: August 31

	REVENUE ($ mil.)	NET INCOME ($ mil.)	NET PROFIT MARGIN	EMPLOYEES
8/09	63,335	2,006	3.2%	238,000
8/08	59,034	2,157	3.7%	237,000
8/07	53,762	2,041	3.8%	226,000
8/06	47,409	1,751	3.7%	195,000
8/05	42,202	1,560	3.7%	179,000
Annual Growth	**10.7%**	**6.5%**	**—**	**7.4%**

2009 Year-End Financials

Debt ratio: 16.2%
Return on equity: 14.7%
Cash ($ mil.): 2,087
Current ratio: 1.78
Long-term debt ($ mil.): 2,336

No. of shares (mil.): 973
Dividends
   Yield: 1.4%
   Payout: 23.3%
Market value ($ mil.): 32,971

Stock History

NYSE: WAG

	STOCK PRICE ($) FY Close	P/E High/Low		PER SHARE ($) Earnings	Dividends	Book Value
8/09	33.88	18	11	2.02	0.47	14.77
8/08	36.43	22	14	2.17	0.40	13.22
8/07	45.07	25	20	2.03	0.33	11.41
8/06	49.46	29	23	1.72	0.27	10.39
8/05	46.33	32	23	1.52	0.22	9.13
Annual Growth	**(7.5%)**	**—**	**—**	**7.4%**	**20.9%**	**12.8%**

Wal-Mart Stores

Wal-Mart Stores is an irresistible (or at least unavoidable) retail force that has yet to meet any immovable objects. Bigger than Europe's Carrefour, Tesco, and Metro AG combined, it's the world's #1 retailer with 2.1 million employees in more than 8,400 stores, including about 800 discount stores, 3,100 combination discount and grocery stores (Wal-Mart Supercenters in the US and ASDA in the UK), and 595 Sam's Club warehouses. Wal-Mart's international division is growing at a fast pace; it's the #1 retailer in Canada and Mexico and it has operations in Asia (where it owns a 95% stake in Japanese retailer SEIYU), Europe, and South America. Founder Sam Walton's heirs own about 45% of Wal-Mart.

The recession and dismal retail climate in the US has been a boon for Wal-Mart, which is outperforming rival discounters (including Target), and most other retailers to boot. Already the nation's #1 seller of groceries prior to the onset of the recession, Wal-Mart has seen its share of the grocery market grow as newly budget-conscious shoppers flocked to its supercenters.

Wal-Mart Stores are famous for their low prices and breadth of merchandise, including more than 30 private-label and licensed brands. In 2009 the retailer revamped its private-label brand Great Value, which boasts more than 5,250 items across about 100 categories.

The retailer's online incarnation, Walmart.com (launched in 2000), offers more than 1,000,000 products, as well as music and video downloads and digital photo services. The e-tailer is expanding by offering merchandise from other retailers at its new virtual mall called Walmart Marketplace. It offers apparel, baby, home, and sporting goods items from other sellers in return for a share of the revenue.

While Wal-Mart has enjoyed a bit of a respite of late from negative publicity over labor relations, the certification by a federal appeals court of the largest gender discrimination class action lawsuit in US history threatens to bring back bad times. In 2010 a federal court ruled that more than 1 million female Wal-Mart employees could proceed with the lawsuit (filed back in 2001) that seeks billions of dollars in damages and accuses Wal-Mart of paying women less than men and promoting fewer females to management positions. Wal-Mart plans to appeal to the US Supreme Court.

Perhaps in a bid to go out on top, CEO Lee Scott retired in early 2009. Mike Duke, who ran Wal-Mart's international operation, succeeded Scott as president and CEO of the company.

As growth of its US division has slowed, Wal-Mart's sales are growing abroad. Through joint ventures in China the company operates about 280 stores. To support its growth there, Wal-Mart is building its Asian headquarters in the coastal city of Shenzhen, the site of its first supercenter and Sam's Club in China. And in a move that demonstrates how important the vast Chinese market is to the world's largest retailer, staunchly anti-union Wal-Mart has announced that it will work with officials there to establish labor unions in all Wal-Mart stores in China.

Following the death of Helen Robson Walton in 2007, the Walton family announced that much of the Wal-Mart stock held by Mrs. Walton will be donated to charity over several years. Once her shares are distributed, the Walton family's stake will slip from about 45% to about 33%.

HISTORY

Sam Walton began his retail career as a J. C. Penney management trainee and later leased a Ben Franklin-franchised dime store in Newport, Arkansas, in 1945. In 1950 he relocated to Bentonville, Arkansas, and opened a Walton 5 & 10. By 1962 Walton owned 15 Ben Franklin stores under the Walton 5 & 10 name.

After Ben Franklin management rejected his suggestion to open discount stores in small towns, Walton, with his brother James "Bud" Walton, opened the first Wal-Mart Discount City in Rogers, Arkansas, in 1962. Wal-Mart Stores went public in 1970 with 18 stores and sales of $44 million. Avoiding regional retailers, Walton opened stores in small and midsized towns in the 1970s. The company sold its Ben Franklin stores in 1976. By 1980 Wal-Mart's 276 stores had sales of $1.2 billion.

In 1983 Wal-Mart opened SAM'S Wholesale Club, a concept based on the successful cash-and-carry, membership-only warehouse format pioneered by the Price Company of California (now Costco Wholesale Corp.). It started Hypermart*USA in 1987 as a joint venture with Dallas-based supermarket chain Cullum Companies. The discount store/supermarket hybrid was later retooled as Wal-Mart Supercenters. Sam stepped down as CEO in 1988 and president David Glass was appointed CEO. Wal-Mart bought out Cullum the next year.

Wal-Mart acquired wholesale distributor McLane Company in 1990. In 1992, the year Sam died, the company expanded into Mexico through a joint venture to open SAM'S CLUBS with Mexico's largest retailer Cifra (renamed Wal-Mart de México in 2000). Wal-Mart acquired 122 former Woolco stores in Canada in 1994. Co-founder Bud died a year later.

More international expansion included entering China in 1996; the acquisition of German hypermarket chain Wertkauf in 1997; the purchase of Brazilian retailer Lojas Americanas' 40% interest in a joint venture (1998); and the addition of four stores and other sites in South Korea. In 1999 Wal-Mart bought 74 German-based Interspar hypermarkets and acquired ASDA Group, the UK's third-largest supermarket chain.

COO Lee Scott succeeded Glass as CEO in 2000. In June 2001 a group of six current and former female Wal-Mart employees filed a sex-discrimination lawsuit (seeking to represent up to 500,000 current and former Wal-Mart workers) against the company.

In 2002 the company was crowned America's largest corporation by *FORTUNE* magazine. In 2003 Wal-Mart sold its McLane grocery distribution business to Berkshire Hathaway.

In 2005 the retailer settled a high-profile lawsuit by agreeing to pay $11 million to the US government to close an investigation into the use of illegal immigrants by Wal-Mart contractors to clean its stores.

Wal-Mart's former vice chairman Thomas Coughlin, who was accused of misusing more than $500,000 in company funds, pleaded guilty to fraud and tax charges in 2006. He was sentenced to 27 months of house arrest and ordered to pay $400,000 in restitution to his former employer. Wal-Mart itself was ordered by a Pennsylvania jury to pay more than $78 million in damages in a class-action suit brought by employees alleging they were forced to work during breaks and off the clock.

In 2009 Wal-Mart acquired a majority stake in Chile's largest food retailer, Distribución y Servicio. In May of that year it opened its first location in India.

EXECUTIVES

Chairman: S. Robson (Rob) Walton, age 65
Vice Chairman; President and CEO Global.com and Global Sourcing: Eduardo Castro-Wright, age 55, $13,942,274 total compensation
President, CEO, and Director: Michael T. (Mike) Duke, age 60, $19,234,268 total compensation
EVP and CFO: Thomas M. (Tom) Schoewe, age 57, $7,216,307 total compensation
EVP; President and CEO, SAM'S CLUB: Brian C. Cornell, age 51, $14,322,200 total compensation
EVP; President and CEO, Wal-Mart International Division: C. Douglas (Doug) McMillon, age 43, $11,229,880 total compensation
EVP; President and CEO, Latin America; Chairman, Mexico: Eduardo Solorzano Morales, age 52
EVP and Chief Marketing Officer, Walmart U.S.: Stephen F. Quinn
EVP and Co-Chief Merchandising Officer: Jack L. Sinclair, age 49
EVP and Co-Chief Merchandising Officer: John T. Westling
EVP and Chief Merchandising Officer, Sam's Club: Linda P. Hefner, age 50
EVP, General Counsel, and Corporate Secretary: Jeffrey J. (Jeff) Gearhart, age 45
EVP Legal, Compliance, and Ethics and Corporate Secretary: Thomas D. (Tom) Hyde, age 61
EVP Corporate Affairs and Government Relations: Leslie A. Dach, age 55
EVP Finance and Treasurer: Charles M. Holley Jr.
EVP and CIO: Rollin Lee Ford, age 47
President and CEO, US: William S. (Bill) Simon, age 50
Director Investor Relations: Mike Beckstead
Auditors: Ernst & Young LLP

LOCATIONS

HQ: Wal-Mart Stores, Inc.
  702 SW 8th St., Bentonville, AR 72716
Phone: 479-273-4000 **Fax:** 479-277-1830
Web: www.walmartstores.com

2010 Stores

	No.
US	4,304
International	
Argentina	43
Brazil	434
Canada	317
Chile	252
Costa Rica	170
El Salvador	77
Guatemala	164
Honduras	53
India	1
Japan	371
Mexico	1,469
Nicaragua	55
Puerto Rico	56
United Kingdom	371
China	279
Total	**8,416**

PRODUCTS/OPERATIONS

2010 Sales

	$ bil.	% of total
Wal-Mart US	258.2	64
International	100.1	25
SAM'S CLUB	46.7	11
Membership & other	3.2	—
Total	**408.0**	**100**

2010 US Sales

	% of total
Grocery	51
Entertainment	13
Hardlines	11
Apparel	10
Health & wellness	10
Home	5
Total	**100**

2010 Stores

	No.
US	
Supercenters	2,747
Discount stores	803
SAM'S CLUB	596
Neighborhood Markets	158
International stores	3,833
Chinese joint venture stores	279
Total	**8,416**

Retail Divisions

ASDA (large, combination general merchandise and food stores)
Neighborhood Markets (traditional supermarkets)
SAM'S CLUB (members-only warehouse clubs)
Supercenters (large, combination general merchandise and food stores)
Wal-Mart International Division (foreign operations)
Wal-Mart Stores (general merchandise)

COMPETITORS

Ace Hardware	Kmart
AEON	Kohl's
Albertsons	Kroger
ALDI	Lianhua Supermarket
Apple Inc.	Loblaw
Army and Air Force Exchange	Lowe's
Aurora Wholesalers	Maruetsu
AutoZone	Meijer
Bed Bath & Beyond	METRO AG
Best Buy	Office Depot
Big Lots	Pep Boys
BJ's Wholesale Club	PETCO
Bridgestone Retail	Publix
Carrefour	RadioShack
Costco Wholesale	Rite Aid
CVS Caremark	Royal Ahold
Delhaize	Safeway
Dollar General	Sears
Eby-Brown	Staples
Family Dollar Stores	SUPERVALU
The Gap	Target
Home Depot	Tesco
Hudson's Bay	TJX Companies
J. C. Penney	Toys "R" Us
Katz Group	True Value
	Walgreen

HISTORICAL FINANCIALS

Company Type: Public

Income Statement

FYE: January 31

	REVENUE ($ mil.)	NET INCOME ($ mil.)	NET PROFIT MARGIN	EMPLOYEES
1/10	408,214	14,848	3.6%	2,100,000
1/09	405,607	13,400	3.3%	2,100,000
1/08	378,799	12,731	3.4%	2,100,000
1/07	348,650	11,284	3.2%	1,900,000
1/06	315,654	11,231	3.6%	1,800,000
Annual Growth	**6.6%**	**7.2%**	**—**	**3.9%**

2010 Year-End Financials

Debt ratio: 51.5%
Return on equity: 21.8%
Cash ($ mil.): 7,907
Current ratio: 0.87
Long-term debt ($ mil.): 36,401
No. of shares (mil.): 3,710
Dividends
  Yield: 2.0%
  Payout: 29.5%
Market value ($ mil.): 198,207

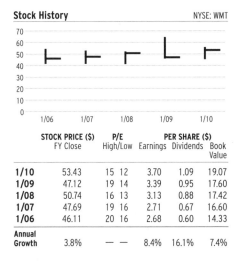

	STOCK PRICE ($) FY Close	P/E High/Low		PER SHARE ($) Earnings	Dividends	Book Value
1/10	53.43	15	12	3.70	1.09	19.07
1/09	47.12	19	14	3.39	0.95	17.60
1/08	50.74	16	13	3.13	0.88	17.42
1/07	47.69	19	16	2.71	0.67	16.60
1/06	46.11	20	16	2.68	0.60	14.33
Annual Growth	3.8%	—	—	8.4%	16.1%	7.4%

The Walt Disney Company

The monarch of this magic kingdom is no man but a mouse — Mickey Mouse. The Walt Disney Company is the world's largest media conglomerate with assets encompassing movies, television, publishing, and theme parks. Its TV holdings include the ABC television network and 10 broadcast stations, as well as a portfolio of cable networks including ABC Family, Disney Channel, and ESPN (80%-owned). Walt Disney Studios produces films through imprints Walt Disney Pictures, Touchstone, and Pixar, while Marvel Entertainment is a top comic book publisher and film producer. In addition, Walt Disney Parks and Resorts operates the company's popular theme parks including Walt Disney World and Disneyland.

While each of Disney's divisions — film, television, and theme parks — are among the leaders in their respective industries, the company, like other media conglomerates, generates additional revenue by distributing its content through multiple channels. A substantial part of its business also comes from ancillary products, mostly aimed at children, created from its trove of characters and other intellectual property.

Disney has traditionally relied on its existing creative units to continually produce new original properties in order to fuel that consumer products engine, but in 2009 the media giant acquired comic book company Marvel for $4.3 billion. The deal gave Disney such characters as Iron Man, Spider-Man, and the X-Men, all of which have been turned into successful Hollywood blockbusters.

As it looks to a future with superhero powers, Disney is dealing with weaknesses brought on by the economic downturn. The company's filmed entertainment division has been stung by weak DVD sales and disappointments at the box office, while its popular theme parks have been struggling with lower attendance and visitor spending. Disney's flagship ABC network, stuck in third place in the ratings behind CBS and FOX for several years, has also suffered declines in commercial advertising revenue.

Disney continues to invest in improvements to its theme parks, including a $1 billion effort through 2012 to renovate and upgrade its California Adventure park (adjacent to Disneyland). Looking to expand its presence in the Asia, the company plans to build a $3.6 billion theme park in Shanghai, and it is investing an additional $800 million to expand its Hong Kong park.

Disney-ABC Television, which oversees all of the company's broadcast, production, and distribution units, announced significant job cuts in 2009. Like other media companies, Disney is focused on the promise that new technologies hold for digital entertainment. It acquired a 30% stake in Hulu in 2009, joining fellow media giants News Corporation and NBCU as a partner in the online video venture. Earlier that same year, Disney formed a partnership with video sharing Web site YouTube (owned by Google) to distribute clips from shows on ABC and ESPN. Disney also distributes films and TV shows through Apple's iTunes store. (Apple CEO Steve Jobs is Disney's largest individual stockholder with a 7% holding he acquired when the company purchased Pixar.)

HISTORY

After getting started as an illustrator in Kansas City, Walt Disney and his brother Roy started Disney Brothers Studio in Hollywood, California, in 1923. Walt directed the first Mickey Mouse cartoon, *Plane Crazy*, in 1928 (the third, *Steamboat Willie*, was the first cartoon with a soundtrack). The studio produced its first animated feature film, *Snow White and the Seven Dwarfs*, in 1937. Walt Disney Productions went public in 1940 and later produced classics such as *Fantasia* and *Pinocchio*. The Disneyland theme park opened in 1955.

Roy Disney became chairman after Walt died of lung cancer in 1966. Disney World opened in Florida in 1971, the year Roy died. His son, Roy E., became the company's principal individual shareholder. Walt's son-in-law, Ron Miller, became president in 1980. Two years later Epcot Center opened in Florida. In 1984 the Bass family of Texas, in alliance with Roy E., bought a controlling interest in the company. New CEO Michael Eisner (from Paramount) and president Frank Wells (from Warner Bros.) ushered in an era of innovation, prosperity, and high executive salaries. The company later launched The Disney Channel and opened new theme parks, including Tokyo Disneyland (1984) and Disney-MGM Studios (1989; later renamed Hollywood Studios). In 1986 the company changed its name to The Walt Disney Company. Disneyland Paris (originally Euro Disney) opened in 1992.

Following Wells' death in a helicopter crash in 1994, boardroom infighting led to the acrimonious departure of studio head Jeffrey Katzenberg. (He was awarded $250 million in compensation in 1999.) The next year Eisner appointed Hollywood agent Michael Ovitz as president. (Ovitz left after 16 months with a severance package of more than $100 million.) Disney bought Capital Cities/ABC (now ABC, Inc.) for $19 billion in 1996, and two years later it bought Web services firm Starwave from Microsoft co-founder Paul Allen.

In 2001 Disney bought Fox Family Channel, which it renamed ABC Family, from News Corp.

and Haim Saban for $2.9 billion in cash and assumption of $2.3 billion in debt. At Disney's annual shareholder meeting in 2004, about 45% of stock owners voted not to re-elect the embattled Eisner to the board. In response, Disney directors stripped Eisner of the chairman title and named director and former US senator George Mitchell to that position.

Disney boosted its children's entertainment properties in 2004 by purchasing the Muppet and *Bear in the Big Blue House* characters, along with their film and television libraries, from The Jim Henson Company.

In 2005 Eisner passed the CEO torch after more than 20 years to former COO Robert Iger. That same year Disney Parks opened Hong Kong Disneyland. In mid-2006 Walt Disney completed a crucial acquisition — the $7.4 billion purchase of Pixar Animation. Disney almost lost Pixar as a production partner in the animation house's blockbuster films, but Iger successfully dodged the bullet.

In 2007 Disney spun off ABC's radio broadcasting operations to Citadel Broadcasting for $2.7 billion. Disney re-acquired its chain of retail stores in 2008, purchasing the Disney Store business from Hoop Holdings, a subsidiary of The Children's Place. The following year, the company purchased a 30% stake in video streaming website Hulu.

Roy E. died in late 2009 at age 79.

EXECUTIVES

Chairman: John E. Pepper Jr., age 72
President, CEO, and Director: Robert A. (Bob) Iger, age 58, $29,028,362 total compensation
SEVP and CFO: James A. (Jay) Rasulo
SEVP, General Counsel, and Secretary: Alan N. Braverman, age 61, $6,649,581 total compensation
EVP Corporate Finance, Real Estate, and Treasurer: Christine M. McCarthy, age 54, $2,196,411 total compensation
EVP Corporate Strategy, Business Development, and Technology: Kevin A. Mayer, age 47, $3,036,577 total compensation
EVP Disney Media Sales and Marketing: Rita Ferro
EVP and Chief Human Resources Officer: Jayne Parker
EVP Corporate Communications: Zenia Mucha
Chairman, Walt Disney Parks and Resorts: Thomas O. (Tom) Staggs, age 48, $9,276,302 total compensation
Chairman, The Walt Disney Studios: Rich Ross, age 48
Co-Chairman, Disney Media Networks; President, Disney-ABC Television: Anne M. Sweeney
Co-Chairman Disney Media Networks; President, ESPN and ABC Sports: George W. Bodenheimer, age 51
Chairman, Walt Disney International: Andy Bird, age 46
Chairman, Disney Consumer Products: Andrew P. (Andy) Mooney
President, Motion Picture Production, Walt Disney Studios: Sean Bailey, age 40
President, ABC-Owned Television Stations: Rebecca Campbell
President, Walt Disney and Pixar Animation Studios: Edwin E. (Ed) Catmull, age 65
President, Disney Interactive Media Group: Stephen H. (Steve) Wadsworth
Auditors: PricewaterhouseCoopers LLP

LOCATIONS

HQ: The Walt Disney Company
500 S. Buena Vista St., Burbank, CA 91521
Phone: 818-560-1000　　**Fax:** 818-560-1930
Web: disney.go.com

2009 Sales

	$ mil.	% of total
US & Canada	27,508	76
Europe	6,012	17
Asia/Pacific	1,860	5
Latin America & other regions	769	2
Total	**36,149**	**100**

PRODUCTS/OPERATIONS

2009 Sales

	$ mil.	% of total
Media networks	16,209	45
Parks & resorts	10,667	29
Studio entertainment	6,136	17
Consumer products	2,425	7
Interactive media	712	2
Total	**36,149**	**100**

Selected Operations

Consumer products
  Disney Publishing Worldwide
  Disney Stores (retail outlets)
Interactive media
  Disney Interactive Studios (video games)
  Disney Online
    Club Penguin (social networking for children)
    Disney.com
    DisneyFamily.com

Media networks
  A&E Television Networks (42%)
    A&E
    Bio (The Biography Channel)
    The History Channel
    History International
    Lifetime
    Lifetime Movie Network
    Lifetime Real Women
    The Military History Channel
  ABC Family Channel
  ABC Television Network
  Disney Channel
  ESPN (80%)
    ESPN2
    ESPN Classic
    ESPNEWS
  JETIX Europe
  SOAPnet
  Television broadcast stations
    KABC (Los Angeles)
    KFSN (Fresno, CA)
    KGO (San Francisco)
    KTRK (Houston)
    WABC (New York City)
    WJRT (Flint, MI)
    WLS (Chicago)
    WPVI (Philadelphia)
    WTVD (Raleigh-Durham, NC)
    WTVG (Toledo, OH)
  Toon Disney
Studio entertainment
  Dimension
  Disney Music Group (music production, distribution)
  Disney Theatrical Group (live entertainment events)
  Marvel Entertainment
  Pixar
  Touchstone Pictures
  Walt Disney Pictures

Theme parks and resorts
  Adventures by Disney (vacation packages)
  Disney Cruise Line
  Euro Disney (40%)
  Disneyland Resort (Anaheim, CA)
  Hong Kong Disneyland (47%)
  Tokyo Disney Resort (owned and operated by Oriental
    Land Co.; Disney earns royalties)
  Walt Disney Imagineering (planning and development)
  Walt Disney World Resort (Orlando, FL)
    Disney Vacation Club
    Disney's Animal Kingdom
    Disney's Hollywood Studios
    Disney's Wide World of Sports
    Downtown Disney
    Epcot
    Magic Kingdom

COMPETITORS

AOL
CBS Corp
Discovery Communications
DreamWorks Animation
Liberty Media
Lucasfilm
MGM
NBC Universal
News Corp.
SeaWorld Parks
Six Flags
Sony Pictures Entertainment
Time Warner
Viacom
Yahoo!

HISTORICAL FINANCIALS

Company Type: Public

Income Statement

FYE: September 30

	REVENUE ($ mil.)	NET INCOME ($ mil.)	NET PROFIT MARGIN	EMPLOYEES
9/09	36,149	3,307	9.1%	144,000
9/08	37,843	4,427	11.7%	150,000
9/07	35,510	4,687	13.2%	137,000
9/06	34,285	3,374	9.8%	133,000
9/05	31,944	2,569	8.0%	133,000
Annual Growth	**3.1%**	**6.5%**	**—**	**2.0%**

2009 Year-End Financials

Debt ratio: 34.1%
Return on equity: 10.0%
Cash ($ mil.): 3,417
Current ratio: 1.33
Long-term debt ($ mil.): 11,495

No. of shares (mil.): 1,913
Dividends
  Yield: 1.3%
  Payout: 19.9%
Market value ($ mil.): 52,520

Stock History

NYSE: DIS

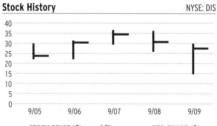

	STOCK PRICE ($) FY Close	P/E High/Low		PER SHARE ($) Earnings	Dividends	Book Value
9/09	27.46	17	9	1.76	0.35	17.64
9/08	30.69	16	12	2.28	0.35	16.90
9/07	34.39	16	13	2.25	0.31	16.08
9/06	30.33	19	14	1.64	0.27	16.64
9/05	23.67	24	18	1.22	0.24	13.70
Annual Growth	**3.8%**	**—**	**—**	**9.6%**	**9.9%**	**6.5%**

Warnaco Group

Underwear has long been The Warnaco Group's foundation. One of the leading marketers of bras, the firm designs and distributes intimates, swimwear, and sportswear under its own and licensed brands, including Calvin Klein, Speedo, Olga, and Warner's. Warnaco also makes menswear under the Chaps by Ralph Lauren brand. In addition, The Warnaco Group operates about 1,100 Calvin Klein retail stores worldwide, and it markets Calvin Klein and Speedo brand merchandise online.

Faced with increased competition from retailers and tough economic conditions in certain markets, the company has seen demand for its offerings rise and fall in recent years. To help stabilize its business going forward, Warnaco has been shedding its manufacturing operations and other less-profitable divisions. In 2009 the company discontinued its Calvin Klein Golf and Calvin Klein Collection businesses. A year earlier Warnaco sold its Lejaby business to Palmers Textil, effectively unloading the remainder of its own manufacturing operations. Also in 2008 the firm exited the designer swimwear category (except for the Calvin Klein brand); it formerly marketed swimwear under license by Nautica, Michael Kors, and OP. (The move did not affect Warnaco's Speedo brand.)

Another part of Warnaco's strategic alignment calls for the company to build its retail presence in the high-growth markets of South America and China. To this end, Warnaco in 2009 acquired a dozen retail stores in Brazil, Chile, and Peru for a total of $12 million. In 2008 it purchased a business that operates about a dozen retail stores in China, just in time for the Beijing Olympic Games, where the company's Speedo brand got plenty of exposure. Warnaco has increased its international business substantially over the years, from about 40% of revenue in fiscal 2006 to roughly 55% in fiscal 2009.

Another growth area for the company is direct sales, which typically accounts for about 20% of net revenue. Calvin Klein brand merchandise remains the company's cash cow, however, generating upwards of 70% of net revenue.

HISTORY

The Warnaco Group was founded in 1874 by brothers DeVer and Lucien Warner. As doctors, they were concerned about the unhealthy effects of boned and tight-fitting women's corsets. After much research, DeVer came up with a new corset made only from cloth. Within a few weeks of selling their first goods from a one-room tailor shop in McGrawville, New York, the brothers had a flourishing business, which they called Warner Brother's or Warner's.

In a business largely dependent on the changing trends of fashion, Warner's tried to adapt to the corsetless era of the 1920s with wraparound undergarments and by making greater use of rubber and elastic, but sales soured. After WWII, however, Warner's surged ahead.

Warner's apparel division acquired shirtmaker Hathaway in 1960. The firm was renamed Warnaco in 1968. Despite expansion and diversification in the 1970s, it lost ground to cheaper imports. Warnaco succumbed to a $550 million hostile takeover in 1986 led by a group of investors, including Linda Wachner, who had worked for Warnaco in the mid-1970s.

As chairman and CEO, Wachner transformed Warnaco from a maker of a mishmash of apparel products to a highly focused branded-apparel producer. Wachner and a group of investors bought Warnaco's Speedo swimwear division in 1990 (taking it public as Authentic Fitness in 1992, only to purchase it again in 1999). In 1991 the firm held its own IPO. It bought Calvin Klein's underwear business in 1994.

In 1996 Warnaco acquired GJM Group (private-label sleepwear and lingerie), Bodyslimmers (shapeware), and French lingerie maker Lejaby Euralis. It also sold its prestigious but underperforming Hathaway men's dress shirt operations. Sales topped $1 billion in 1996, but costs associated with the Hathaway sale and restructuring led to an $8 million loss.

Warnaco bought Designer Holdings, a maker of Calvin Klein jeans and sportswear, in 1997. By 1999 Warnaco owned distribution rights for Calvin Klein jeans in Canada, giving the company control over Calvin Klein jeans production and distribution throughout the Americas.

In 1998 Warnaco took a $69 million charge to discontinue Valentino and other brands and close a dozen outlet stores and a warehouse. The following year it bought 70% of UK perfume retailer Penhaligon and in 1999 added ABS by Allen Schwartz, a lower-priced designer womenswear maker.

A lawsuit came between Wachner and her Calvins in 2000 when Calvin Klein sued both Warnaco and Wachner for trademark violation and breach of trust. Wachner returned fire, suing Klein and his company for trademark violations, defamation, and trade libel. The firms settled in the hours before their trial was set to begin in 2001.

After dismal 2000 year-end results, Warnaco announced in April 2001 its plans to end its licensed Fruit of the Loom bra operations. In 2001 Warnaco filed for Chapter 11 bankruptcy protection. The board of directors ousted Wachner and replaced her with Antonio ("Tony") Alvarez as CEO and Stuart Buchalter as chairman. Alvarez began a restructuring program, which led to the sale of noncore assets such as GJM's sleepwear division and the closure of Calvin Klein outlet stores in 2002.

Wachner sued Warnaco to get $25 million she says the company owed her. An agreement was reached in November 2002 in which Wachner received $3.5 million in stock in the reorganized company and $200,000 in cash. She remained on the board of directors until the company emerged from bankruptcy in early 2003.

The year 2002 also brought the first round of paring down retail outlets: the company closed 47 Speedo retail outlets, 64 domestic outlet stores, and almost half of its 26 Calvin Klein underwear stores. The next round came in late 2003, with closure of all remaining Speedo stores and sale of its White Stag line to Wal-Mart.

In April 2003 Alvarez left and Joe Gromek (former CEO of Brooks Brothers) took over as president and CEO.

The company acquired the license, wholesale, and retail units for Calvin Klein jeans and accessories in Europe and Asia in January 2006 for about €240 million ($292 million).

In 2007 Warnaco sold its OP women's and junior's swimwear brand (bought in 2004) to Iconix Brand Group for $54 million. (Previously, Warnaco had hoped to morph Op into a $1 billion brand.)

In early 2008 Warnaco acquired about a dozen retail stores in China for about $2.5 million.

EXECUTIVES

Chairman: Charles R. Perrin, age 64
President, CEO, and Director: Joseph R. (Joe) Gromek, age 63, $6,431,639 total compensation
EVP and CFO: Lawrence R. Rutkowski, age 52, $1,992,937 total compensation
EVP International Strategy and Business Development: Stanley P. Silverstein, age 57, $2,027,287 total compensation
SVP Human Resources: Elizabeth Wood, age 48
SVP, General Counsel, and Secretary: Jay L. Dubiner, age 46
SVP Retail: Robert F. (Bob) Dakin, age 51
VP Investor Relations: Deborah Abraham
Group President, Intimate Apparel and Swimwear: Helen McCluskey, age 54, $2,670,298 total compensation
President, Sportswear Group: Frank Tworecke, age 63, $2,806,243 total compensation
President, Chaps: Michael Prendergast
President, Swimwear Division: James B. (Jim) Gerson
President, Calvin Klein Underwear: Kay LeGrange
President, Global Sourcing, Distribution, and Logistics: Dwight F. Meyer, age 57
President, Calvin Klein Jeans: David Cunningham
Chief Creative Officer, Calvin Klein Underwear: Robert A. Mazzoli
Auditors: Deloitte & Touche LLP

LOCATIONS

HQ: The Warnaco Group, Inc.
501 7th Ave., New York, NY 10018
Phone: 212-287-8000   **Fax:** 212-287-8297
Web: www.warnaco.com

2009 Sales

	$ mil.	% of total
US	916.7	45
Europe	551.6	27
Asia	322.9	16
Mexico, Central & South America	119.1	6
Canada	109.3	6
Total	**2,019.6**	**100**

PRODUCTS/OPERATIONS

2009 Sales

	$ mil.	% of total
Sportswear group	1,091.2	54
Intimate apparel	677.3	34
Swimwear group	251.1	12
Total	**2,019.6**	**100**

Selected Brands

Intimate apparel
 Body Nancy Ganz/Bodyslimmers
 Calvin Klein
 Olga
 Warner's

Sportswear and accessories
 CK/Calvin Klein (licensed)
 Chaps by Ralph Lauren (licensed)
 Lifeguard (licensed)
 Speedo/Fastskin (licensed)

COMPETITORS

adidas	Liz Claiborne
Benetton	Maidenform
Delta Galil Industries Ltd.	NIKE
Donna Karan	Perry Ellis International
Frederick's of Hollywood	Polo Ralph Lauren
Fruit of the Loom	Russell Brands
Guess?	Tommy Hilfiger
Hanesbrands	Top Form
Jockey International	Triumph Apparel
Kellwood	Under Armour
Levi Strauss	VF
Limited Brands	

HISTORICAL FINANCIALS

Company Type: Public

Income Statement		FYE: Saturday nearest December 31		
	REVENUE ($ mil.)	NET INCOME ($ mil.)	NET PROFIT MARGIN	EMPLOYEES
12/09	2,020	99	4.9%	5,400
12/08	2,065	47	2.3%	5,200
12/07	1,860	79	4.3%	4,656
12/06	1,828	51	2.8%	10,287
12/05	1,504	52	3.5%	10,156
Annual Growth	**7.6%**	**17.3%**	**—**	**(14.6%)**

2009 Year-End Financials

Debt ratio: 12.3%
Return on equity: 11.6%
Cash ($ mil.): 321
Current ratio: 2.27
Long-term debt ($ mil.): 113
No. of shares (mil.): 45
Dividends
 Yield: 0.0%
 Payout: —
Market value ($ mil.): 1,879

Stock History

NYSE: WRC

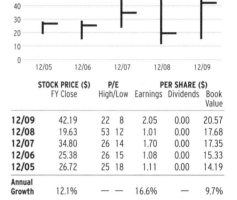

	STOCK PRICE ($) FY Close	P/E High/Low		PER SHARE ($) Earnings	Dividends	Book Value
12/09	42.19	22	8	2.05	0.00	20.57
12/08	19.63	53	12	1.01	0.00	17.68
12/07	34.80	26	14	1.70	0.00	17.35
12/06	25.38	26	15	1.08	0.00	15.33
12/05	26.72	25	18	1.11	0.00	14.19
Annual Growth	**12.1%**	**—**	**—**	**16.6%**	**—**	**9.7%**

Warner Music Group

These records were made to be listened to, not broken. Warner Music Group (WMG) is one of the largest recording companies in the world and ranks #3 in terms of US market share (behind Universal Music Group and Sony Music Entertainment). It operates through two businesses: Recorded Music and Music Publishing. Its Recorded Music catalog includes best-selling albums *The Eagles: Their Greatest Hits 1971-1975* and *Led Zeppelin IV*. Its Music Publishing business holds more than one million copyrights from more than 65,000 songwriters. The company's traditional A&R (artist and repertoire) work of finding and developing artists has helped WMG score hits from musicians such as Green Day and Faith Hill.

WMG's Recorded Music business produces, markets, and distributes recordings primarily through units Atlantic Records Group and Warner Bros. Records, and its Music Publishing business operates through Warner/Chappell Music. The company also has a stake in music firms and record labels such as Sub Pop, Roadrunner Records, and Rykodisc, and distributes its music through subsidiaries such as Rhino Entertainment (compilations and reissues) and Alternative Distribution Alliance. Its Independent

Label Group (ILG) is composed of WMG's Asylum Records (urban), East West Records (rock), and Cordless Recordings (digital-only).

Like all companies in the music business, WMG has struggled in the face of plummeting CD sales and slow growth in paid digital downloading. The company has responded with cost cutting and embracing new technologies. In 2009 the company began outsourcing certain IT, finance, and accounting functions. On the new technologies front, sales of digital music products, such as ringtones, videos, and downloaded songs and albums, now account for about 20% of the company's business (up from 17% and 13% the previous two years). And while sales of physical albums and CDs continue to wither, WMG has committed to increasing its marketing and development efforts to expand into new digital media formats.

WMG sells music online without copy protection (in the popular MP3 format) on Amazon.com's digital music store and through other online retail outlets. WMG has also embraced new video sharing mediums through its revenue-sharing deal with YouTube; the video site distributes and licenses copyrighted songs, videos, and other materials from WMG. In addition, to compete with Apple's iTunes service, WMG is part of the MySpace Music joint venture with News Corp. and the other major labels. It offers a range of new music-listening and merchandising features.

Thomas H. Lee Partners, a private equity firm based in Boston, owns more than 35% of WMG. The current iteration of the business was formed in 2004 when Thomas H. Lee, along with former Vivendi executive Edgar Bronfman, Jr., led the buyout of Warner from Time Warner for $2.6 billion, topping a bid from UK rival EMI Group in the twelfth hour. The deal marked a return to the entertainment business for Bronfman, WMG's chairman and CEO. (In the 1990s he led Seagram (the distilled liquor business controlled by his family) to buy Universal Studios and later PolyGram.) WMG went public in 2005.

HISTORY

Warner Bros. co-founder Jack Warner expanded his film company's operations into music when he created Warner Bros. Records in 1958. Initially focused on sound tracks and comedy albums, the company soon expanded its scope by issuing recordings by the Everly Brothers and Peter, Paul & Mary. Warner bought Reprise Records in 1963, the label started by Frank Sinatra in 1961. Warner sold his entertainment empire in 1966 to Seven Arts Productions, which became Warner-Seven Arts. That year the company bought Atlantic Records, a label co-founded in 1947 by famed music producer Ahmet Ertegun. (Ertegun died in 2006.) Steven Ross' Kinney National Services purchased Warner-Seven Arts in 1969 and changed its name to Warner Communications.

Former Reprise Records chief Mo Ostin became CEO of Warner Bros. Records in the early 1970s and is credited with propelling the company into the forefront of the music industry. Reorganized as Warner Music, the company battled rival CBS Records (now part of Sony BMG Music Entertainment) for dominance in the music business by adding to its collection of labels, acquiring Elektra Records in 1970 and Asylum Records in 1974. The company later created a distribution

arm, WEA (Warner-Electra-Atlantic), expanded internationally, and established a record pressing plant. Warner Music prospered in the 1980s, scoring hits with artists like R.E.M. and Madonna.

Parent Warner Communications was acquired by publisher Time Inc. in 1990, and Warner Music became part of media giant Time Warner. However, the company was losing market share and executive infighting was reaching a fevered pitch. Several top executives jumped ship. HBO chief Michael Fuchs took over in 1995 and cleaned house, but he himself was ousted later that year. Warner film studio chiefs Bob Daly and Terry Semel were later appointed co-CEOs.

While Daly and Semel helped restore order to the music group, they failed to revive sales. They announced their resignation in 1999, and Warner Music International executive Roger Ames was appointed chairman and CEO. To regain market share, Time Warner agreed to combine Warner Music with the UK's struggling EMI Group. Under the proposed deal, each would have held 50% of the resulting company. However, European regulators began to balk at the combination in light of America Online's offer to buy Time Warner. To save the larger deal, the combination with EMI was called off.

Following the merger of AOL and Time Warner in 2001, Ames began tightening the belt, cutting some 600 staff members and centralizing label operations.

In 2003 Warner sold the DVD and CD manufacturing businesses of WEA to Cinram for $1 billion. The following year Warner was taken private when a group of investors led by Edgar Bronfman, Jr., with backing from Thomas H. Lee Partners, Bain Capital, and Providence Equity Partners purchased the music company from Time Warner for $2.6 billion. The company went public in 2005.

Also that year the company signed a distribution deal with Sean "Diddy" Combs, taking a 50% stake in his Bad Boy Records.

In 2006 Warner purchased Ryko Corporation and its Rykodisc label, one of the top independent record companies in the US.

WMG acquired a nearly 75% stake in Roadrunner Music Group BV, which runs heavy metal label Roadrunner Records, in 2007.

EXECUTIVES

Chairman and CEO: Edgar M. Bronfman Jr., age 54, $7,010,044 total compensation
Vice Chairman; Chairman and CEO, Recorded Music — Americas and the U.K.: Lyor Cohen, age 50, $7,300,182 total compensation
Vice Chairman, Strategy and Operations: Michael D. Fleisher, age 45, $2,461,482 total compensation
EVP and CFO: Steven Macri, age 40, $1,387,098 total compensation
EVP and General Counsel: Paul M. Robinson, age 52
EVP, Digital Strategy and Business Development: Michael Nash, age 53
EVP, Human Resources and Chief Compliance Officer: Mark Ansorge, age 46
EVP and Chief Communications Officer: Will Tanous, age 41
SVP and CIO: Maggie Miller
Chairman and CEO, Warner/Chappell Music: David H. (Dave) Johnson, age 64, $1,574,970 total compensation
CEO, Warner Music Europe; Vice-Chairman, Warner Music International: John Reid
CEO, Warner Music UK and Chairman, Warner Bros Records UK: Christian Tattersfield

President, Alternative Distribution Alliance: Mitchell Wolk
President, Warner Music Nashville: John Esposito
President and CEO, WEA: Mike Jbara, age 43
President, Warner Music Asia/Pacific: Lachie Rutherford
Auditors: Ernst & Young LLP

LOCATIONS

HQ: Warner Music Group Corp.
75 Rockefeller Plaza, New York, NY 10019
Phone: 212-275-2000 **Fax:** 212-757-3985
Web: www.wmg.com

2009 Sales

	$ mil.	% of total
International	1,786	56
US	1,416	44
Adjustments	(26)	—
Total	**3,176**	**100**

PRODUCTS/OPERATIONS

2009 Sales

	$ mil.	% of total
Recorded Music		
Digital	656	20
Licensing	223	7
Physical sales & other	1,745	55
Music Publishing		
Performance	226	7
Mechanical	192	6
Synchronization	97	3
Digital & other	63	2
Adjustments	(26)	—
Total	**3,176**	**100**

Selected Operations

Recorded music
  Distribution
    Alternative Distribution Alliance
    Rhino Entertainment
  Recording labels
    Atlantic Records
    Elektra Records
    Lava Records
    Maverick Recording Company
    Nonesuch Records
    Roadrunner Records (75%)
    Reprise
    Rykodisc
    Sire
    Warner Bros. Nashville
    Warner Bros. Records
    Word Records
Music publishing
  Warner/Chappell Music

HISTORICAL FINANCIALS

Company Type: Public

Income Statement

FYE: September 30

	REVENUE ($ mil.)	NET INCOME ($ mil.)	NET PROFIT MARGIN	EMPLOYEES
9/09	3,176	(100)	—	3,400
9/08	3,491	(56)	—	3,800
9/07	3,385	(21)	—	3,800
9/06	3,516	60	1.7%	4,000
9/05	3,502	(169)	—	4,000
Annual Growth	**(2.4%)**	**—**	**—**	**(4.0%)**

2009 Year-End Financials

Debt ratio: — No. of shares (mil.): 155
Return on equity: — Dividends
Cash ($ mil.): 384 Yield: 0.0%
Current ratio: 0.65 Payout: —
Long-term debt ($ mil.): 1,939 Market value ($ mil.): 856

Stock History   NYSE: WMG

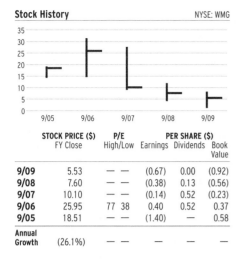

	STOCK PRICE ($) FY Close	P/E High/Low		PER SHARE ($)	
			Earnings	Dividends	Book Value
9/09	5.53	— —	(0.67)	0.00	(0.92)
9/08	7.60	— —	(0.38)	0.13	(0.56)
9/07	10.10	— —	(0.14)	0.52	(0.23)
9/06	25.95	77 38	0.40	0.52	0.37
9/05	18.51	— —	(1.40)	—	0.58
Annual Growth	(26.1%)	— —	—	—	—

Washington Post

It might be said this company can teach you something about newspapers. Best known as the publisher of *The Washington Post* newspaper, The Washington Post Company actually gets the lion's share of its revenue from Kaplan, a well-known source of test preparation materials. Washington Post's flagship newspaper, meanwhile, boasts a circulation of about 570,000 in the Washington, DC, area. Other media operations include famous weekly magazine Newsweek (which the company agreed to sell in mid-2010), a portfolio of six TV stations, and online publishing operations such as Slate. Washington Post also owns cable TV systems operator Cable One. The company is controlled by chairman Donald Graham and his family.

Like other newspaper and magazine publishers, Washington Post struggles to manage the long, slow decline of print publications. Its saving grace, though, is its Kaplan education and Cable One units, which help keep the rest of the business afloat. Kaplan is best known for its test preparation materials, but it also runs a popular online university that boasts about 65,000 students. Cable One, meanwhile, is focused on rolling out additional voice and data services to its subscribers. Together, the two operations account for about 75% of the company's sales.

The company's advertising supported media present a wholly different picture. Although its *Newsweek* magazine is the #2 weekly news magazine (after Time Inc's *Time*), it has suffered declines in readership and advertising, forcing the company to make hard choices regarding layoffs and other cost-cutting efforts. However, in mid-2010 Washington Post agreed to sell the weekly news magazine to Sidney Harmon, the founder of audio equipment maker Harman International Industries. *Newsweek* boasts 1.5 million subscribers in the US and Canada. Washington Post's television stations also suffered from the downturn in advertising during 2009.

The Washington Post, meanwhile, took aggressive steps to manage steep declines in advertising and circulation revenue through staff reductions and by closing its news bureaus outside Washington, DC, and shuttering a printing plant in Maryland. Also focused on boosting readership online, the *Post* integrated its print and digital media operations in 2010.

Chairman Donald Graham is the son of the late Katharine Graham, who had taken over the business after her husband died in the early 1960s and became a legend in the publishing business. She led the *Post* in its decisions to publish the Pentagon papers and pursue the Watergate story. Investment icon Warren Buffett owns almost 20% of the company through Berkshire Hathaway.

HISTORY

The Washington Post was first published in 1877, focusing on society columns, color comics, and sensational headlines. Hard news coverage took a back page to crime and scandal — by 1916 the *Post* was filled with yellow journalism. Any credibility the paper had was ruined by owner Ned McLean's lying to a Senate committee in 1924 about his involvement in the Teapot Dome oil scandal.

Eugene Meyer bought the bankrupt *Post* for $825,000 in 1933 and built a first-class news staff. By 1946, when Meyer's son-in-law Philip Graham took over as publisher, the *Post* was in the black again. In 1948 Meyer transferred his stock to his daughter Katharine and to Philip, her husband. Graham bought radio and TV stations and established overseas bureaus. In 1961 he bought *Newsweek* magazine and started a news service with the *Los Angeles Times*. In 1963 Graham lost a struggle with manic depression and killed himself.

An editor since 1939, Katharine became publisher after her husband's death. The Washington Post Company began publishing the *International Herald Tribune* with The New York Times Company in 1967. In 1971 the company went public, though the Graham family retained control. The next year reporters Bob Woodward and Carl Bernstein broke the Watergate story, which led to President Richard Nixon's resignation and a Pulitzer Prize for the *Post*. In the 1970s and 1980s, under the tutelage of investor (and former *Post* paper boy) Warren Buffett, Katharine Graham bought TV and radio stations, cable TV firms, newspapers, newsprint mills, and Stanley H. Kaplan Educational Centers.

The guard changed at The Washington Post Company in 1991 when the Grahams' son Donald became CEO. In 1992 it invested in ACTV (interactive television) and bought 84% of Gaithersburg Gazette, Inc. (community newspapers, upped to 100% in 1993) and a sports cable TV system. Donald Graham became chairman when his mother stepped down in 1993.

In the search for a place in new media, The Washington Post Company made some mammoth errors. In 1995 the firm wrote off the $28 million it had invested in Mammoth Micro Products, a CD-ROM maker it had purchased in 1994. Also that year, blaming costs and delays, the company sold its 80% stake (acquired 1990) in American Personal Communications (wireless telephone systems).

In 1996 *Newsweek* columnist Joe Klein resigned after it was revealed that he was the anonymous author of *Primary Colors,* a thinly veiled satire of the 1992 Clinton campaign. Two years later the company completed the sale of its 28% interest in Cowles Media, publisher of the Minneapolis *Star Tribune,* and sought to bolster its coverage of information technology by buying two magazines and two Washington, DC-based conferences from Reed Elsevier.

The company sold key assets of its Legi-Slate service to Congressional Quarterly in 1999. Later that year it formed a partnership with TV network NBC in which the two firms agreed to share news content, technology, and promotional resources. The company branched out into travel information with its purchase of *Arthur Frommer's Budget Travel* near the end of 1999. In 2000 its Kaplan subsidiary created Kaplan Ventures to invest in education and career services companies and subsequently acquired postsecondary school operator Quest Education.

The company's 2001 contract dispute with *Post* employees made headlines when reporters refused to allow their bylines to be used above their stories for several editions. Katharine Graham died later that year at age 84. In 2002 the company sold its stake in the *International Herald Tribune*.

Looking to expand its online publishing operations, Washington Post acquired Slate Magazine from Microsoft in 2005. It shed its Post Newsweek Tech unit (trade publications and trade shows) in 2006. It also sold its 49% stake in online recruitment firm BrassRing to Kenexa.

EXECUTIVES

Chairman and CEO: Donald E. (Don) Graham, age 65, $472,997 total compensation
Vice Chairman; Chairman *Washington Post* Newspaper: Boisfeuillet (Bo) Jones, age 63, $1,466,836 total compensation
SVP Finance and CFO: Hal S. Jones, age 57, $1,631,211 total compensation
SVP Planning and Development: Gerald M. Rosberg, age 63, $1,582,673 total compensation
SVP Human Resources: Ann L. McDaniel, $2,261,210 total compensation
SVP; Publisher, Express and WhoRunsGov.com: Christopher Ma
SVP, General Counsel, and Secretary: Veronica Dillon, age 60
SVP and Chief Digital Officer: Vijay Ravindran
VP Finance and Chief Accounting Officer: Wallace R. Cooney, age 47
VP Communications and External Relations: Rima Calderon
VP Technology and Chief Technology Officer: Yuvinder (Yuvi) Kochar
Chairman, Newsweek: Richard M. Smith, age 63
CEO, Newsweek: Thomas (Tom) Ascheim, age 47
President and CEO, Cable One: Thomas O. (Tom) Might
Chairman and CEO, Kaplan: Andrew S. (Andy) Rosen
President and General Manager, The Washington Post: Stephen P. (Steve) Hills
Chairman and Editor-in-Chief, The Slate Group: Jacob Weisberg, age 46
Publisher and CEO, Washington Post Media and The Washington Post: Katharine Weymouth, age 43
Managing Editor, The Washington Post: Raju Narisetti, age 43
Editor, Newsweek: Jon Meacham, age 40
VP At Large, The Washington Post: Benjamin C. Bradlee
Auditors: PricewaterhouseCoopers LLP

LOCATIONS

HQ: The Washington Post Company
1150 15th St. NW, Washington, DC 20071
Phone: 202-334-6000   **Fax:** 202-334-4536
Web: www.washpostco.com

PRODUCTS/OPERATIONS

2009 Sales

	$ mil.	% of total
Education	2,636.6	58
Circulation & subscribers	932.4	20
Advertising	858.1	19
Other	142.6	3
Total	**4,569.7**	**100**

2009 Sales

	$ mil.	% of total
Education	2,636.6	58
Cable television	750.4	16
Newspaper publishing	679.3	15
Television broadcasting	272.7	6
Magazine publishing	184.2	4
Other	53.9	1
Adjustments	(7.4)	—
Total	**4,569.7**	**100**

Selected operations

Education
  Kaplan Higher Education
  Kaplan International
  Kaplan Test Preparation
Cable television systems
  Cable ONE
Newspaper publishing
  The Herald (Everett, WA)
  Express Publications
    Express (free weekly)
  Greater Washington Publishing (free advertisers)
  Post-Newsweek Media (community newspapers)
    Fairfax County Times
    The Gazette Newspapers
    Southern Maryland Newspapers
  The Slate Group (online publishing)
    The Big Money
    Foreign Policy
    Slate
  El Tiempo Latino (Spanish-language newspaper;
    Washington, DC)
  The Washington Post
Television broadcasting
  KPRC (NBC, Houston)
  KSAT (ABC, San Antonio)
  WDIV (NBC, Detroit)
  WJXT (Ind.; Jacksonville, FL)
  WKMG (CBS; Orlando, FL)
  WPLG (ABC, Miami)
Magazine publishing
  Newsweek
Other
  Avenue100 Media Solutions (digital marketing
    services)
  Bowater Mersey Paper Company (newsprint
    manufacturing, Canada)

COMPETITORS

A. H. Belo
Advance Publications
Apollo Group
DeVry
DIRECTV
DISH Network
Educate
Gannett
ITT Educational
Laureate Education
McClatchy Company
McGraw-Hill
New York Times
News Corp.
News World Communications
Pearson plc
Princeton Review
Seattle Times
Strayer Education
Time Inc.
Tribune Company
U.S. News & World Report

HISTORICAL FINANCIALS

Company Type: Public

Income Statement

FYE: Sunday nearest December 31

	REVENUE ($ mil.)	NET INCOME ($ mil.)	NET PROFIT MARGIN	EMPLOYEES
12/09	4,570	93	2.0%	21,500
12/08	4,462	66	1.5%	20,000
12/07	4,180	289	6.9%	19,000
12/06	3,905	330	8.4%	17,100
12/05	3,554	314	8.8%	16,400
Annual Growth	**6.5%**	**(26.3%)**	**—**	**7.0%**

2009 Year-End Financials

Debt ratio: 13.5%
Return on equity: 3.2%
Cash ($ mil.): 478
Current ratio: 1.40
Long-term debt ($ mil.): 396
No. of shares (mil.): 9
Dividends
  Yield: 2.0%
  Payout: 87.9%
Market value ($ mil.): 4,044

Stock History

NYSE: WPO

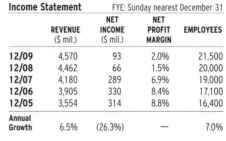

	STOCK PRICE ($) FY Close	P/E High/Low		PER SHARE ($) Earnings	Dividends	Book Value
12/09	439.60	51	31	9.78	8.60	319.53
12/08	390.25	120	47	6.87	8.60	310.61
12/07	791.43	29	24	30.19	8.20	376.22
12/06	745.60	24	20	33.68	7.80	343.44
12/05	765.00	30	22	32.59	7.40	286.79
Annual Growth	**(12.9%)**	**—**	**—**	**(26.0%)**	**3.8%**	**2.7%**

Waste Management

Holding company Waste Management tops the heap in the US solid waste industry. Through subsidiaries, the company serves about 20 million residential, industrial, municipal, and commercial customers in the US and Canada. Its four geographic groups and two functional groups (Recycling and Wheelabrator) provide waste collection, transfer, recycling and resource recovery, and disposal services. Its sites include 265 landfills, 345 transfer stations, 120 beneficial-use landfill gas projects, 90 material recovery facilities, and 15 waste-to-energy plants. Collection and landfill services account for three-quarters of sales.

Waste Management manages its core North American Solid Waste operations through four more-or-less equally sized geographic groups (Eastern, Midwest, Southern, and Western) and runs waste-to-energy facilities through Wheelabrator Technologies. It carries out recycling operations through Recycle America Alliance, L.L.C. To reduce the costly layers of management, the group has restructured most of its operations into market areas, which oversee each district's sales, marketing, and delivery services. Other company operations include the rental and servicing of portable restroom facilities to

municipalities and commercial customers (Port-O-Let) and providing street and parking lot sweeping services and in-plant services. Wheelabrator also operates six independent power producers (IPPs) that convert waste and conventional fuels into electricity and produce steam.

Waste Management also operates one of the largest trucking fleets in the industry for its collection services. At its hazardous waste sites, the group accepts hazardous waste primarily in a stable, solid form. Some of its secure sites accept hazardous waste that has been treated before disposal. The group operates one facility that isolates treated hazardous waste in liquid form and injects it into deep wells.

As part of its expansion of health care disposal services, in 2009 the company acquired PharmEcology Associates, a national pharmaceutical waste management consulting services firm, and Mountain High Medical Disposal Services. In 2010 it also acquired some medical waste assets from MedServe, following that company's acquisition by Stericycle. It also acquired a medical waste processing facility and other assets from Milum Textile Services in Phoenix.

HISTORY

In 1956 Dean Buntrock joined his in-laws' business, Ace Scavenger Service, an Illinois company that Buntrock expanded into Wisconsin.

Waste Management, Inc., was formed in 1971 when Buntrock joined forces with his cousin, Wayne Huizenga, who had purchased two waste routes in Florida in 1962. In the 1970s Waste Management bought companies in Michigan, New York, Ohio, Pennsylvania, and Canada. By 1975 it had an international subsidiary.

The company divided into specialty areas by forming Chemical Waste Management (1975) and offering site-cleanup services (ENRAC, 1980) and low-level nuclear-waste disposal (Chem-Nuclear Systems, 1982).

USA Waste was founded in 1987 to run disposal and collection operations in Oklahoma. It went public in 1988, and in 1990 Don Moorehead, a founder and former CEO of Mid-American Waste Systems, bought a controlling interest (most of which he later sold). Moorehead moved the business to Dallas and began buying companies in the fragmented industry. John Drury, a former president of Browning-Ferris, joined USA Waste in 1994 as CEO.

As USA Waste gathered steam, Waste Management got off track. It diversified, and Buntrock renamed the company WMX Technologies in 1993 to de-emphasize its waste operations. In 1997, however, the company reverted to the Waste Management name and, pressured by disappointed investor George Soros, CEO Phillip Rooney resigned. After more management changes, turnaround specialist Steve Miller became CEO, the fourth one in eight months, and Buntrock retired.

USA Waste picked up market share with large acquisitions, including Envirofill (1994), Chambers Development Corporation (1995), and Western Waste Industries and Sanifill (1996). In 1996 the company moved to Houston. During the next two years it bought United Waste Systems, Mid-American Waste, the Canadian operations of Allied Waste and Waste Management, and TransAmerican Waste Industries.

1998 saw the $20-billion merger between USA Waste and Waste Management. The new company, bearing the Waste Management name and led by Drury and other former USA Waste executives, controlled nearly a quarter of North America's waste business. The company finished the year by agreeing to pay shareholders $220 million in a suit over overstated earnings.

The new Waste Management bought Eastern Environmental Services for $1.3 billion in 1999. (A legal battle over negotiations between Eastern and Waste Management executives was settled out of court in 2000.) Drury took leave in 1999 because of an illness that would claim his life, and director Ralph Whitworth, known as a shareholder activist, stepped in as acting chairman.

The company faced shareholder lawsuits after it was reported that executives had sold shares before a second-quarter earnings shortfall was announced. Waste Management said it would investigate the sales; later, so did the SEC. (By 2001 the company had settled with both the SEC and shareholders.) In the fallout, president and COO Rodney Proto, who had sold shares before the earnings announcement, was fired. Later that year the company tapped Maury Myers, CEO of trucking company Yellow Corp., to take over as chairman and CEO.

In 2000, to concentrate on its core business in North America, Waste Management sold operations in Europe, Asia, and South America in a series of transactions that raised about $2.5 billion.

In 2002 Waste Management announced plans to restructure by reorganizing its operating areas and cutting its workforce of 57,000 by about 3.5%. Also that year the SEC sued six former Waste Management executives, charging that they had enriched themselves through accounting fraud between 1992 and 1997.

The company formed a new recycling unit, Recycle America Alliance, in 2003, after acquiring Milwaukee-based The Peltz Group, the largest privately held recycler in the US. The company also acquired 75 complementary collection businesses for about $337 million. That year two former executives of Waste Management, Proto and CFO Earl DeFrates, agreed to a settlement with the SEC on allegations that they had profited from insider trading in 1999.

EXECUTIVES

Chairman: John C. (Jack) Pope, age 61
President, CEO, and Director: David P. Steiner, age 49, $5,624,746 total compensation
SVP and CFO: Robert G. (Bob) Simpson, age 57, $1,978,916 total compensation
SVP Western Group: Duane C. Woods, age 58, $1,611,375 total compensation
SVP Southern Group: James E. (Jim) Trevathan Jr., age 57, $1,638,561 total compensation
SVP Eastern Group: Brett Frazier
SVP Midwestern Group: Jeff M. Harris, age 55
SVP Sales and Marketing: David A. (Dave) Aardsma, age 53
SVP and CIO: Puneet Bhasin
SVP, General Counsel, and Chief Compliance Officer: Richard L. (Rick) Wittenbraker, age 61
SVP People: Michael J. (Jay) Romans, age 59
SVP Government Affairs and Corporate Communications: Barry H. Caldwell, age 49
SVP Organic Growth: Carl V. Rush Jr.
VP and Chief Accounting Officer: Greg A. Robertson, age 56
VP Finance and Treasurer: Cherie C. Rice, age 45
VP Corporate Communications: Lynn C. Brown
President, Waste Management Recycle America: Patrick J. (Pat) DeRueda, age 48
President, Wheelabrator Technologies: Mark A. Weidman, age 53
Director Investor Relations: Jim Alderson
Corporate Secretary: Linda J. Smith
Auditors: Ernst & Young LLP

LOCATIONS

HQ: Waste Management, Inc.
1001 Fannin St., Ste. 4000, Houston, TX 77002
Phone: 713-512-6200   **Fax:** 713-512-6299
Web: www.wm.com

2009 Sales

	$ mil.	% of total
United States & Puerto Rico	11,137	94
Canada	654	6
Total	**11,791**	**100**

PRODUCTS/OPERATIONS

2009 Sales

	$ mil.	% of total
Southern	2,897	24
Western	2,713	23
Midwest	2,429	21
Eastern	2,427	21
Wheelabrator	718	6
Other	607	5
Total	**11,791**	**100**

2009 Sales

	$ mil.	% of total
Collection	7,980	58
Landfill	2,547	19
Transfer	1,383	10
Wheelabrator	841	6
Recycling	741	5
Other	245	2
Adjustments	(1,946)	—
Total	**11,791**	**100**

Selected Services

Collection
Disposal
Hazardous waste management
Landfill management
Portable sanitation services
Recycling
Transfer stations
Treatment

COMPETITORS

Casella Waste Systems
IESI-BFC
Republic Services
Rumpke
Safety-Kleen
Veolia ES Solid Waste
Waste Connections
WCA Waste

HISTORICAL FINANCIALS

Company Type: Public

Income Statement

FYE: December 31

	REVENUE ($ mil.)	NET INCOME ($ mil.)	NET PROFIT MARGIN	EMPLOYEES
12/09	11,791	994	8.4%	43,400
12/08	13,388	1,087	8.1%	45,900
12/07	13,310	1,163	8.7%	47,400
12/06	13,363	1,149	8.6%	48,000
12/05	13,074	1,182	9.0%	50,000
Annual Growth	**(2.5%)**	**(4.2%)**	**—**	**(3.5%)**

2009 Year-End Financials

Debt ratio: 129.3%
Return on equity: 16.3%
Cash ($ mil.): 1,140
Current ratio: 1.04
Long-term debt ($ mil.): 8,124
No. of shares (mil.): 483
Dividends
 Yield: 3.4%
 Payout: 57.7%
Market value ($ mil.): 16,331

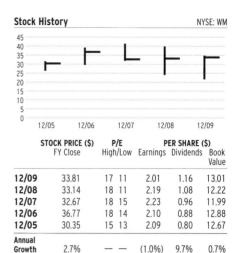

	STOCK PRICE ($) FY Close	P/E High/Low		PER SHARE ($) Earnings	Dividends	Book Value
12/09	33.81	17	11	2.01	1.16	13.01
12/08	33.14	18	11	2.19	1.08	12.22
12/07	32.67	18	15	2.23	0.96	11.99
12/06	36.77	18	14	2.10	0.88	12.88
12/05	30.35	15	13	2.09	0.80	12.67
Annual Growth	**2.7%**	**—**	**—**	**(1.0%)**	**9.7%**	**0.7%**

Watsco, Inc.

Keeping the Sun Belt cool makes Watsco a hot company. It is one of the largest independent distributors of residential heating, air conditioning, and refrigeration equipment in the US, with more than 500 distribution locations in more than 35 states. Through its group of subsidiaries Watsco also provides installation and repair equipment for its products. Its primary customers are contractors and dealers who install and replace HVAC equipment in homes. While it does not maintain any international facilities, Watsco does export products to Latin America and the Caribbean, which account for less than 5% of sales.

Sales of HVAC equipment account for about half of Watsco's revenues. Its key product suppliers include Rheem, Carrier, Nordyne, Goodman, Trane, and Lennox.

Watsco also sells products to the industrial and commercial refrigeration market. It distributes condensing units, compressors, evaporators, valves, coolers, and ice machines manufactured by Emerson Electric's Copeland Compressor, E. I. du Pont de Nemours and Company, Mueller Industries, and The Manitowoc Company.

Since air conditioning units have a working lifespan from eight to 20 years, the replacement market is the most lucrative part of Watsco's business, with higher growth margins. The replacement market makes up about 85% of Watsco's sales. Sales in that segment are expected to increase as older models wear out and are replaced by more energy-efficient ones. Demand for Watsco's products fell during the economic recession, which impacted sales. However, the industry and the company also got a boost in the replacement market as homeowners were given federal tax credits and other local utility rebates to replace their old units with high-efficiency air conditioners or furnaces.

Watsco is continuously examining opportunities for expansion, but also makes cuts where needed. In 2009 Watsco formed a joint venture with Carrier to distribute Carrier, Bryant, Payne, and Totaline residential and light commercial products in the US Sun Belt region and territories in the Caribbean and Latin America. The deal added 95 locations in those areas. The firm said the venture would boost revenue and profitability by improving parts distribution and cutting costs. The following year Watsco built up its presence on the US East Coast when it acquired Tennessee-based HVAC distributor The Bill Voorhees Company, which sells equipment manufactured by Goodman.

Chairman, president, and CEO Albert Nahmad controls more than 50% of Watsco.

HISTORY

Watsco was founded in 1945 as a maker of climate-control components. The company grew slowly until the mid-1980s, when a building boom and aggressive marketing increased sales. Albert Nahmad, the company's president since 1973, began looking for acquisitions, and in 1988 Watsco acquired Dunhill. When Dunhill didn't provide the profits Watsco wanted, Nahmad moved into residential air-conditioning (AC) distribution. Watsco bought 80% of Florida's Gemaire (1989) and 50% of Heating and Cooling Supply, the #1 residential central AC distributor in Southern California and Arizona (1990).

The company moved into the Texas market with the acquisition of distributor Comfort Supply in 1993. It then acquired H.B. Adams, a Florida distributor of air conditioners, in 1995. Purchases the following year added another 25 distribution branches. Watsco picked up four locations from heating and AC manufacturer Inter-City Products in 1997 and acquired Coastline Distribution (21 branches), as well as two midwestern distribution operations (Central Plains Distributing and Comfort Products Distributing) from Carrier. Watsco's acquisition streak heated up in 1998 when it bought Oklahoma-based Superior Supply Company, Tennessee-based KingAire, and Kaufman Supply, an AC distributor for the manufactured-housing market.

Acquisitions continued into 1999 as Watsco purchased Homans Associates and Heat Inc., both of which served New England, and Atlantic Air, which served several western states. Watsco signed an agreement in 2000 with Ariba (Web-based procurement software) to enable customers to order products online. The next year, the company closed seven facilities.

After Pameco filed for bankruptcy in 2003, Watsco purchased the company's HVAC and related parts and supplies operations, which sold from more than 40 locations in Arkansas, Louisiana, Mississippi, and Texas.

Acquisitions continued in 2005, when Watsco bought family-owned East Coast Metal Distributors, a distributor of air-conditioning and heating products operating from 27 locations that served more than 3,500 contractors throughout the Carolinas, Georgia, Virginia, and Tennessee.

In an effort to build a national network and streamline its core operations, Watsco acquired rival ACR Group, another HVAC distributor, which gave it an additional 54 locations and more than 12,000 customers across the country. In 2007 the company also disposed of Dunhill Staffing Systems, a temporary and permanent staffing business.

EXECUTIVES

Chairman, President, and CEO: Albert H. Nahmad, age 69, $4,861,842 total compensation
CFO, Treasurer, and Assistant Secretary: Ana M. Menendez, age 45, $186,446 total compensation
SVP and Secretary: Barry S. Logan, age 47, $339,463 total compensation
VP and Head Business Development: Paul W. Johnston, age 57, $233,058 total compensation
President, Gemaire Distributor: Stephen R. Combs, age 66, $908,995 total compensation
President, East Coast Metal Distributors: Al Lendino
President, Baker Distributing: Carole J. Poindexter, age 54
Auditors: KPMG LLP

LOCATIONS

HQ: Watsco, Inc.
2665 S. Bayshore Dr., Ste. 901
Coconut Grove, FL 33133
Phone: 305-714-4100   **Fax:** 305-858-4492
Web: www.watsco.com

2009 Sales Locations

	No.
Florida	101
Texas	94
Georgia	39
North Carolina	39
California	38
South Carolina	28
Tennessee	25
Louisiana	19
Virginia	18
Mississippi	13
Alabama	8
Arizona	8
Missouri	8
Maryland	7
Puerto Rico	7
Arkansas	6
Kansas	6
Massachusetts	5
Oklahoma	5
Utah	5
Colorado	3
Iowa	2
Kentucky	2
Maine	2
Nebraska	2
Nevada	2
New York	2
South Dakota	2
Other states	9
Total	**505**

PRODUCTS/OPERATIONS

Selected Subsidiaries

ACR Group, Inc.
Air Systems Distributors LLC
Atlantic Service & Supply LLC
Baker Distributing Company LLC
Coastline Distribution
Comfort Products Distributing LLC
East Coast Metal Distributors LLC
Gemaire Distributors LLC
Heating & Cooling Supply LLC
Homans Associates LLC/Heat Incorporated LLC
NSI Supply
Prime Supply
SPS Supply
Three States Supply Company LLC
Tradewinds Distributing Company LLC

COMPETITORS

Gensco	Mestek
Gustave A. Larson	Russell Sigler
HD Supply	US Airconditioning
Johnson Controls	WinWholesale
Johnstone Supply	

HISTORICAL FINANCIALS

Company Type: Public

Income Statement

FYE: December 31

	REVENUE ($ mil.)	NET INCOME ($ mil.)	NET PROFIT MARGIN	EMPLOYEES
12/09	2,002	52	2.6%	4,050
12/08	1,700	60	3.6%	3,100
12/07	1,758	66	3.7%	3,300
12/06	1,801	82	4.6%	3,300
12/05	1,683	70	4.2%	3,200
Annual Growth	4.4%	(7.3%)	—	6.1%

2009 Year-End Financials

Debt ratio: 1.8%
Return on equity: 7.9%
Cash ($ mil.): 58
Current ratio: 3.37
Long-term debt ($ mil.): 13
No. of shares (mil.): 32
Dividends
Yield: 3.9%
Payout: 135.0%
Market value ($ mil.): 1,587

Stock History

NYSE: WSO

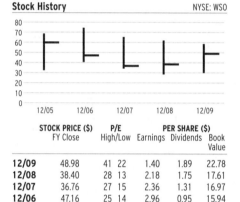

	STOCK PRICE ($) FY Close	P/E High/Low	PER SHARE ($) Earnings	Dividends	Book Value
12/09	48.98	41 22	1.40	1.89	22.78
12/08	38.40	28 13	2.18	1.75	17.61
12/07	36.76	27 15	2.36	1.31	16.97
12/06	47.16	25 14	2.96	0.95	15.94
12/05	59.81	27 13	2.52	0.62	13.91
Annual Growth	(4.9%)	— —	(13.7%)	32.1%	13.1%

Watson Pharmaceuticals

Watson Pharmaceuticals tries to have the best of both worlds, with operations in the US generics market and the higher-profit-margin branded drug business. The company's broad generics portfolio of about 140 products includes treatments for hypertension and pain, as well as smoking cessation products, antidepressants, and oral contraceptives. Its line of about 30 branded drugs focuses on urology and nephrology; it markets its branded products, including treatments for iron deficiency anemia and overactive bladder, to specialist physicians in the US.

Watson Pharmaceuticals' bread and butter is its generics line. An important part of that business is its oral contraceptive line. It has a leading position in the US in generic oral contraceptives with roughly two dozen different oral contraceptive products and about a 35% market share.

The generics business overall has struggled with the loss of a key product and the general decline of generics revenue over time. The big loss came a few years ago when a distribution agreement with Purdue Pharma for oxycodone HCl (generic OxyContin) ended. Name-brand drug companies sometimes authorize an "official" generic form when a drug goes off-patent. Watson had distributed the authorized generic of OxyContin since the drug lost patent protection in 2005, and the drug was a big contributor to the company's revenue.

Watson's strategy for combating declining sales is to develop and acquire new products to beef up its pipeline. In 2009 alone, the company launched about a dozen new products including Metoprolol ER to treat angina, emergency contraceptive NextChoice, and Galantamine for the treatment of Alzheimer's disease.

The previous year Watson introduced a generic version of Biovail's antidepressant Wellbutrin XL, Johnson & Johnson's Duragesic pain patch and its Alzheimer drug Razadyne, and GSK's Nicorette smoking cessation gum. Additionally, the company co-promotes AndroGel, a male hormone replacement therapy, with Unimed and distributes an authorized generic of Merck's Fosamax.

To pick up a few more products, expand its development pipeline, and broaden its geographic presence, Watson spent about $1.75 billion to acquire privately held Arrow Group in 2009. Arrow develops and manufactures generic pharmaceuticals in Canada, Malta, and Brazil and distributes its products in more than 20 countries.

Major products in the company's branded drug segment include prostate therapies Trelstar and Rapaflo. Watson is building its branded product line through partnerships and joint ventures, as well as through acquisitions of later-stage drug candidates. Because it relies on partnerships to augment its product line, the company's bottom line is also vulnerable to the expiration of those deals. For example, Watson lost a key product in 2009 when its license agreement with Sanofi-Aventis for anemia drug Ferrlecit ended.

To stave off losses related to losing licenses, Watson has been trimming costs by consolidating some operations and moving some manufacturing operations overseas.

HISTORY

As a youth, Watson Pharmaceuticals founder Allen Chao worked at his parents' Taiwan drug factory. After taking a PhD in pharmacology in the US and working at G.D. Searle for 10 years, Chao co-founded Watson in 1984 with $4 million raised from family and friends. Watson (an anglicized version of "Hwa's son" — based on his mother's name) introduced its first generic drug, a furosemide tablet (a diuretic), in 1985. The company went public in 1993.

At first Watson focused on products that posed manufacturing challenges or had limited markets. In the mid-1990s it diversified into drug development in cooperation with other firms, such as Rhône-Poulenc (now part of Sanofi-Aventis). It bought competitors (Circa Pharmaceuticals, 1995) and invested in drug research companies. In 1996 the company launched its first proprietary drug, Microzide, an antihypertensive. Watson acquired Royce Laboratories (generic drugs) and Oclassen Pharmaceuticals (dermatology products) and boosted its sales force substantially in 1997. It also acquired rights to several products, including Dilacor XR.

In 1998 Watson bought drug-delivery systems maker TheraTech (taking immediate steps to regain control of its transdermal hormone-replacement system) and Rugby Group, the US generic drug unit of Hoechst (now part of Sanofi-Aventis). The 1999 launch of the company's Nicotine Polacrilax (an off-patent version of the nicotine gum made by SmithKline Beecham, now GlaxoSmithKline) was hampered by SmithKline's claim that accompanying instructional materials breached its copyrights (the courts ruled in favor of Watson in 2000). To boost its research activities, in 2000 the firm bought Makoff R&D Laboratories and Schein Pharmaceutical. Three years later it bought Amarin Corp.'s Swedish R&D subsidiary.

Watson had marketed a Parkinson's disease treatment through a 50-50 joint venture with Mylan Laboratories, but in 2008 Mylan bought out Watson's share of the venture, known as Somerset Pharmaceuticals. Somerset had also developed depression treatment EmSam, which is marketed by Bristol-Myers Squibb.

To fatten up its product pipeline, in 2008 Watson picked up a portfolio of products from Teva. Teva needed to offload them as part of its acquisition of Barr Pharmaceuticals. Watson paid $36 million for the portfolio which included 15 approved products and two products in development.

EXECUTIVES

Chairman: Andrew L. Turner, age 63
President, CEO, and Director: Paul M. Bisaro, age 49, $4,277,180 total compensation
EVP Global Brands: G. Frederick (Fred) Wilkinson, age 53, $1,398,684 total compensation
EVP Global Generics and Global Operations: Thomas R. (Tom) Russillo, age 66, $1,796,123 total compensation
EVP and President, Brand Division: Edward F. Heimers Jr., age 63, $919,034 total compensation
EVP Global Generics: Sigurdur O. Olafsson
EVP Global Operations: Robert A. (Bob) Stewart, age 42
EVP and COO, Anda: Albert Paonessa III, age 50
SVP and CFO: R. Todd Joyce, age 52, $1,099,116 total compensation
SVP, General Counsel, and Secretary: David A. Buchen, age 45, $1,227,164 total compensation
SVP Generics Research and Development: Francois A. Menard, age 50
SVP Human Resources: Clare M. Carmichael, age 50
SVP and CIO: Thomas R. Giordano, age 59
SVP Research and Development: Charles D. Ebert, age 56
SVP Sales and Marketing, U.S. Generics Division: Andrew Boyer
SVP Quality Assurance: Gordon Munro, age 63
VP Sales: Allan Slavsky
VP Investor Relations and Corporate Communications: Patricia L. (Patty) Eisenhaur, age 47
Auditors: PricewaterhouseCoopers LLP

LOCATIONS

HQ: Watson Pharmaceuticals, Inc.
311 Bonnie Cir., Corona, CA 92880
Phone: 951-493-5300   **Fax:** 973-355-8301
Web: www.watsonpharm.com

PRODUCTS/OPERATIONS

2009 Sales

	$ mil.	% of total
Generic drugs	1,668.2	60
Distribution	663.8	24
Branded drugs	461.0	16
Total	**2,793.0**	**100**

Selected Products

Branded
Androderm (male hormone replacement)
Condylox (antiviral)
Ferrlecit (anemia in dialysis patients)
Fioricet (analgesic)
Gelnique (overactive bladder)
INFeD (anemia)
Oxytrol (overactive bladder)
Rapaflo (prostate cancer)
Trelstar DEPOT (prostate cancer)
Trelstar LA (prostate cancer)
Generic
Alendronate Sodium (Fosamax, osteoporosis)
Bupropion hydrochloride SR (Zyban, smoking cessation)
Bupropion hydrochloride SR (Wellbutrin SR, antidepressant)
Bupropion hydrochloride XL (Wellbutrin XL, antidepressant)
Cartia XT (Cardizem CD, anti-hypertensive)
Glipizide ER (Glucotrol XL, anti-diabetic)
Hydrocodone bitartrate/acetaminophen (Lorcet, Vicodin, Lortab, Norco; analgesic)
Levora (Nordette, oral contraceptive)
Low-Ogestrel (Lo-Ovral, oral contraceptive)
Lutera (Alesse, oral contraceptive)
Microgestin/Microgestin Fe (Loestrin/Loestrin Fe, oral contraceptive)
Necon (Ortho-Novum, Modicon; oral contraceptive)
Nicotine polacrilex gum (Nicorette, smoking cessation)
Nicotine transdermal system (Habitrol, smoking cessation)
Oxycodone/acetaminophen (Percocet, analgesic)
TriNessa (Ortho Tri-Cyclen, oral contraceptive)
Trivora (Triphasil, oral contraceptive)

COMPETITORS

Abbott Labs
Allergan Limited
AmerisourceBergen
Amgen
Auxilium Pharmaceuticals
Bayer Schering Pharma
Biovail
Boehringer Ingelheim Corporation
Bristol-Myers Squibb
Cardinal Health
Covidien
Dr. Reddy's
Endo Pharmaceuticals
Forest Labs
GlaxoSmithKline
Johnson & Johnson
King Pharmaceuticals
Kinray
McKesson
Merck
Mylan
Novartis
Par Pharmaceutical Companies
Pfizer
Purdue Pharma
Sanofi-Aventis
Shire
Teva Pharmaceuticals

HISTORICAL FINANCIALS

Company Type: Public

Income Statement				FYE: December 31
	REVENUE ($ mil.)	NET INCOME ($ mil.)	NET PROFIT MARGIN	EMPLOYEES
12/09	2,793	222	7.9%	5,830
12/08	2,536	238	9.4%	5,070
12/07	2,497	141	5.6%	5,640
12/06	1,979	(445)	—	5,830
12/05	1,646	138	8.4%	3,844
Annual Growth	14.1%	12.6%	—	11.0%

2009 Year-End Financials

Debt ratio: 38.0%
Return on equity: 8.7%
Cash ($ mil.): 201
Current ratio: 1.68
Long-term debt ($ mil.): 1,150

No. of shares (mil.): 125
Dividends
Yield: —
Payout: —
Market value ($ mil.): 4,946

Stock History

NYSE: WPI

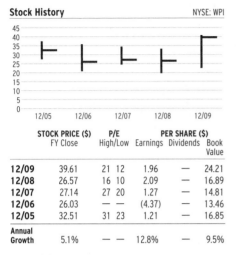

	STOCK PRICE ($) FY Close	P/E High/Low		PER SHARE ($) Earnings	Dividends	Book Value
12/09	39.61	21	12	1.96	—	24.21
12/08	26.57	16	10	2.09	—	16.89
12/07	27.14	27	20	1.27	—	14.81
12/06	26.03	—	—	(4.37)	—	13.46
12/05	32.51	31	23	1.21	—	16.85
Annual Growth	**5.1%**	**—**	**—**	**12.8%**	**—**	**9.5%**

Weatherford International

Weatherford International can weather the natural and economic storms that affect the oil and gas market. The company, which is domiciled in Switzerland but operationally based in Houston, supplies a wide range of equipment and services used in the oil and gas drilling industry, and operates in 100 countries. Weatherford provides well installation and completion systems, equipment rental, and fishing services (removing debris from wells). It provides pipeline services and oil recovery and hydraulic lift and electric submersible pumps to the oil and gas industry. The company also offers contract land drilling services.

Weatherford has 800 service bases and 16 training and development offices worldwide.

Operating in a volatile market, Weatherford has strengthened its broad base of product offerings through acquisitions and geographic expansion, including the purchase of Williams Tool (control flow products), Scotland-based Petroline Wellsystems (provider of completion products), Canadian firm Alpine Oil Services (under-balanced drilling equipment), US-based CAC (control systems), UK company Orwell (oil field services), and Louisiana-based Eclipse Packer (coiled tubing and gravel packing systems). The company has also created WellServ, a full services well intervention unit.

In 2007 Weatherford began to sell its oil and gas development and production business (completed in 2008) to raise cash to invest in its core oil field services businesses. To that end, the company in 2008 acquired International Logging, Inc., a provider of surface logging, formation evaluation, and drilling related services. It also bought the oilfield services unit of TNK-BP for about $500 million in stock in 2009.

Seeking the most favorable financial business location for its registered office, in 2009 Weatherford shifted its domicile from Bermuda to Switzerland.

HISTORY

Energy Ventures was founded in 1972 as an offshore oil and gas explorer and producer. In 1981 it became a 50-50 partner with Northwest Energy in an oil field located in Hockley County, Texas. By 1982 Northwest had increased its ownership in Energy Ventures to about 25%.

Majority stockholder Appalachian attempted a takeover in 1984, but later agreed to drop the takeover in exchange for the liquidation of Energy Ventures. A slump in oil and gas prices in 1985 derailed the plan.

By the late 1980s Energy Ventures was vertically integrating by buying oil field product makers such as Grant Oil Country Tubular (1990) and Prideco (1995). Grant and Prideco were combined in 1995, solidifying the company's position as a leading supplier of drill pipe and tubulars. In 1997 the company built a manufacturing facility in Canada and changed its name to EVI.

EVI doubled its size in 1998 by merging with oil field services firm Weatherford Enterra, which had been formed by the 1995 combination of Houston-based firms Weatherford International and Enterra. The newly combined company adopted the Weatherford International name shortly thereafter.

In 1999 Weatherford acquired Christiana Companies, whose 33% interest in Total Logistic Control introduced Weatherford to the warehousing and trucking business. Also, Weatherford bought Scotland-based Petroline Wellsystems, which makes oil and gas well completion products.

The following year the company spun off its drill pipe and casings maker, Grant Prideco. Also in 2000 the company continued its geographic expansion with the purchase of Gas Services International (compression systems serving Asia and the Middle East), Oakwell Compressor Packages of the Netherlands, and Alpine Oil Services of Canada.

In 2001, after buying out GE Capital's 36% interest in its natural gas compression joint venture, Weatherford exchanged the subsidiary for a 48% stake in Universal Compression Holdings. That year the company's acquisitions included US-based CAC, a maker of control systems for the oil and gas industry, and Scottish oil field services company Orwell, which widened its presence in the North Sea, Asia/Pacific, and Middle East regions.

To reduce its US tax obligations, Weatherford reincorporated in Bermuda in 2002. Later that year it formed a pipeline and specialty service group within its Drilling and Intervention Services division to offer pipe cleaning, testing, and inspection services.

In 2003 Weatherford completed the formation of WellServ, a full services well intervention group, through its Drilling & Intervention Services division. Also that year the company completed its acquisition of Eclipse Packer, a Louisiana-based provider of coiled tubing and gravel packer systems.

In 2005 Weatherford acquired two divisions of Canada's Precision Drilling for $2.3 billion.

Weatherford reorganized its operations in an effort to provide seamless services to its customers. The company sold its compression fabrication business to Universal Compression Holdings (now called Exterran) in 2004.

EXECUTIVES

Chairman, President, and CEO:
Bernard J. Duroc-Danner, age 55,
$17,535,040 total compensation
SVP and CFO: Andrew P. Becnel, age 42,
$3,909,979 total compensation
SVP Well Construction and Operations Support and Chief Safety Officer: Keith R. Morley, age 59,
$4,560,866 total compensation
SVP, General Counsel, and Secretary: Burt M. Martin, age 46, $3,999,578 total compensation
SVP Reservoir and Production and CTO:
Stuart E. Ferguson, age 43,
$2,781,266 total compensation
SVP Global Human Resources: Neal Gillenwater
VP Accounting and Chief Accounting Officer:
M. Jessica Abarca, age 38
VP Production Operations Systems: John Jameson
VP Tax: James M. Hudgins
VP Marketing: Christine McGee
VP Drilling Methods: Paul Timmins
VP Core Evaluation Services: Chris Bechtel
VP Well Construction Services: Carel Hoyer
VP Finance: Danielle Nicholas
VP Global Market and Sales Support: Pat Bond
VP Investor Relations: Karen David-Green
Auditors: Ernst & Young LLP

LOCATIONS

HQ: Weatherford International Ltd.
515 Post Oak Blvd., Ste. 600, Houston, TX 77027
Phone: 713-693-4000   **Fax:** 713-693-4323
Web: www.weatherford.com

2009 Sales

	% of total
North & South America	
US	40
Canada	16
Latin America	9
Eastern Hemisphere	35
Total	**100**

PRODUCTS/OPERATIONS

2009 Sales

	% of total
Production Systems	57
Drilling Services	43
Total	**100**

COMPETITORS

Baker Hughes
CE Franklin
Dover Corp.
Halliburton
National Oilwell Varco
Precision Drilling
Robbins & Myers
Schlumberger
Smith International
Tesco Corporation
Wilson

HISTORICAL FINANCIALS

Company Type: Public

Income Statement				FYE: December 31
	REVENUE ($ mil.)	NET INCOME ($ mil.)	NET PROFIT MARGIN	EMPLOYEES
12/09	8,827	280	3.2%	52,000
12/08	9,601	1,354	14.1%	50,000
12/07	7,832	1,071	13.7%	38,000
12/06	6,579	896	13.6%	33,000
12/05	4,333	467	10.8%	25,100
Annual Growth	**19.5%**	**(12.0%)**	**—**	**20.0%**

2009 Year-End Financials

Debt ratio: 60.2%	No. of shares (mil.): 741
Return on equity: 3.1%	Dividends
Cash ($ mil.): 253	Yield: —
Current ratio: 2.20	Payout: —
Long-term debt ($ mil.): 5,847	Market value ($ mil.): 13,265

Stock History NYSE: WFT

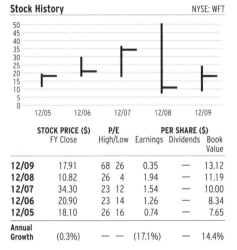

	STOCK PRICE ($) FY Close	P/E High/Low		PER SHARE ($) Earnings	Dividends	Book Value
12/09	17.91	68	26	0.35	—	13.12
12/08	10.82	26	4	1.94	—	11.19
12/07	34.30	23	12	1.54	—	10.00
12/06	20.90	23	14	1.26	—	8.34
12/05	18.10	26	16	0.74	—	7.65
Annual Growth	(0.3%)	—	—	(17.1%)	—	14.4%

WellPoint, Inc.

Like B. B. King but without the guitar, health benefits provider WellPoint is the king of the Blues. Through its subsidiaries, the firm provides health coverage, primarily under the Blue Cross and Blue Shield (BCBS) name, to about 34 million members. The largest health insurer in the US, it is a Blue Cross or BCBS licensee in more than a dozen states and provides plans under the Unicare name in other parts of the country. WellPoint offers a broad range of managed care plans (including PPO, HMO, indemnity, and hybrid plans) to employers, individuals, and Medicare and Medicaid recipients. It also provides administrative services to self-insured groups, as well as specialty insurance products.

The company's specialty products include dental, vision, long-term care, and group life insurance. Through several of its subsidiaries, WellPoint performs claims processing and other administrative tasks for government-run Medicare plans. It also provides fraud prevention services to the federal health care system and to private payors through two of its subsidiaries, TrustSolutions and Etico.

WellPoint's Unicare subsidiary gives the company the ability to sell group and individual health coverage in geographic areas where it is not a Blue Cross licensee. Unicare stopped providing health coverage in Illinois and Texas (previously two of its biggest markets) in 2009, citing competitive pressure. In 2010 WellPoint began providing Blue Cross-branded products in those states through an agreement with Health Care Services Corporation.

Blue-branded health coverage remains the company's core business. Many of the company's Blue subsidiaries (including plans in Kentucky,

Missouri, Wisconsin, and elsewhere) operate under the name Anthem Blue Cross Blue Shield. Other Blue subsidiaries include Empire Blue Cross Blue Shield (in New York) and Blue Cross Blue Shield of Georgia.

WellPoint provided pharmacy benefit management (PBM) services through its NextRx unit until 2009 when it was sold to Express Scripts for nearly $4.7 billion. Express Scripts will provide PBM services to WellPoint for 10 years through the deal, which it hopes will improve the cost-effectiveness of PBM services for its customers.

Also in 2009 the company acquired DeCare, a dental benefits administrator operating in the US and Ireland. The acquisition expanded WellPoint's dental operations significantly, adding some 4 million new members. The same year it set up an office in Beijing to explore opportunities in the Chinese market.

Following audits conducted by the company and the Centers for Medicare and Medicaid Services (CMS), in 2009 WellPoint was temporarily suspended by the CMS from adding new Medicare patients to its programs until certain compliance problems were remedied. The programs resumed enrollment later that year.

HISTORY

Anthem's earliest predecessor, prepaid hospital plan Blue Cross of Indiana, was founded in 1944. Unlike other Blues, Blue Cross of Indiana never received tax advantages or mandated discounts, so it competed as a private insurer. Within two years it had 100,000 members; by 1970 there were nearly 2 million.

Blue Shield of Indiana, another Anthem precursor, also grew rapidly after its 1946 formation as a mutual insurance company to cover doctors' services. The two organizations shared expenses and jointly managed the state's Medicare and Medicaid programs.

The 1970s and early 1980s were difficult as Indiana's economy stagnated and health insurance competition increased. In 1982 the joint operation restructured, adding new management and service policies to improve its performance.

Following the 1982 merger of the national Blue Cross and Blue Shield organizations, the Indiana Blues merged in 1985 as Associated Insurance Companies. The next year the company moved outside Indiana, began diversifying to help insulate itself from such industry changes as the shift to managed care, and renamed itself Associated Group to reflect a broader focus.

By 1990 Associated Group had more than 25 operating units with nationwide offerings, including health insurance, HMO services, life insurance, insurance brokerage, financial services, and software and services for the insurance industry. The group grew throughout the mid-1990s, buying health insurer Southeastern Mutual Insurance (including Kentucky Blue Cross and Blue Shield) in 1992, diversified insurer Federal Kemper in 1993, and Seattle-based property/casualty brokerage Pettit-Morry in 1994. In 1995 the company merged with Ohio Blues licensee Community Mutual and took the Anthem name.

Anthem divested its individual life insurance and annuity business and its Anthem Financial subsidiaries in 1996. In 1997 Anthem acquired Blue Cross and Blue Shield of Connecticut. That year Anthem was involved in court battles regarding the Blue mergers in Kentucky, as well as in Connecticut, where litigants feared a rise in their premiums.

Anthem shed the rest of its noncore operations in 1998, selling subsidiary Anthem Health and Life Insurance Company to Canadian insurer Great-West Life Assurance. Its proposed purchase of Blue Cross and Blue Shield of Maine (which it acquired in 2000) and merger with the Blues in Rhode Island were met with outcries similar to those that dogged earlier pairings.

Larry Glasscock was appointed president and CEO of the company in 1999. Under Glasscock's leadership, Anthem aggressively expanded through mergers and acquisitions. It bought Blues plans in Colorado, Nevada, and New Hampshire in 1999, and finalized the acquisition of Maine's Blue plan in 2000. In 2001 it became a publicly traded company and sold its military insurance business to Humana.

And in 2004 Anthem made its biggest leap yet, deciding to merge with WellPoint Health Networks in a deal that would make it the nation's largest health insurer. After the merger — which added Blue plans in California, Georgia, Missouri, and Wisconsin — Anthem changed its name to WellPoint.

The company continued its growth-by-acquisition strategy with the 2005 purchases of WellChoice (parent of New York insurer Empire Blue Cross Blue Shield) and Lumenos (a provider of consumer-directed health plans).

In 2007 Glasscock resigned as CEO and was succeeded by Angela Braly. Braly became chairman as well in 2010.

EXECUTIVES

Chairman, President, and CEO: Angela F. Braly, age 48, $13,108,198 total compensation
EVP and CFO: Wayne S. DeVeydt, age 40, $7,246,339 total compensation
EVP and Chief Actuary: Cynthia S. Miller, age 53
EVP; President and CEO, Comprehensive Health Solutions Business Unit: Dijuana K. Lewis, age 51, $4,459,971 total compensation
EVP; President and CEO, Commercial Business Unit: Ken R. Goulet, age 50, $4,426,907 total compensation
EVP; President and CEO, Consumer Business Unit: Brian A. Sassi, age 49, $4,091,630 total compensation
EVP and Chief Strategy and External Affairs Officer: Bradley M. (Brad) Fluegel, age 48, $2,264,581 total compensation
EVP Clinical Health Policy and Chief Medical Officer: Samuel R. (Sam) Nussbaum, age 61
EVP, General Counsel, and Corporate Secretary: John Cannon III, age 56
EVP and CIO: Lori A. Beer, age 42
EVP and Chief Human Resources Officer: Randal L. (Randy) Brown, age 51
SVP, Chief Accounting Officer, Chief Risk Officer, and Controller: Martin L. (Marty) Miller, age 47
SVP Senior Business and Consumer Business Marketing: Krista A. Bowers
VP Information Technology Security and Chief Information Security Officer: Roy R. Mellinger
VP Diversity and Inclusion and Chief Diversity Officer: Linda Jimenez
VP Investor Relations: Michael Kleinman
Auditors: Ernst & Young LLP

LOCATIONS

HQ: WellPoint, Inc.
120 Monument Cir., Indianapolis, IN 46204
Phone: 317-532-6000 **Fax:** 317-488-6028
Web: www.wellpoint.com

PRODUCTS/OPERATIONS

2009 Sales

	$ mil.	% of total
Commercial	37,363.4	57
Consumer	16,141.8	25
Other	7,323.4	11
Gain on sale of business	3,792.3	6
Net investment income	801.0	1
Gains on investments	56.4	—
Adjustments	(450.2)	—
Total	**65,028.1**	**100**

COMPETITORS

Aetna
Catalyst Health Solutions
CIGNA
ConnectiCare
Coventry Health Care
Delta Dental Plans
Harvard Pilgrim
HCSC
Health Net
Humana
Kaiser Foundation Health Plan
Kaiser Foundation Health Plan of Colorado
Kaiser Foundation Health Plan of the Northwest
Kaiser Permanente
Medco Health
Medical Mutual
MetLife
Molina Healthcare
Southern California Permanente Medical Group
UnitedHealth Group

HISTORICAL FINANCIALS

Company Type: Public

Income Statement

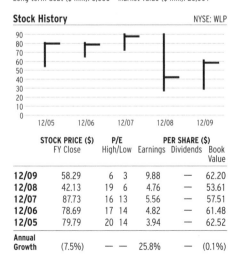

	REVENUE ($ mil.)	NET INCOME ($ mil.)	NET PROFIT MARGIN	EMPLOYEES
12/09	65,028	4,746	7.3%	40,500
12/08	61,251	2,491	4.1%	42,900
12/07	61,134	3,345	5.5%	41,700
12/06	56,953	3,095	5.4%	42,000
12/05	45,136	2,464	5.5%	42,000
Annual Growth	**9.6%**	**17.8%**	**—**	**(0.9%)**

FYE: December 31

2009 Year-End Financials

Debt ratio: 33.5%
Return on equity: 20.5%
Cash ($ mil.): 4,816
Current ratio: —
Long-term debt ($ mil.): 8,338

No. of shares (mil.): 400
Dividends
  Yield: —
  Payout: —
Market value ($ mil.): 23,301

Stock History

NYSE: WLP

	STOCK PRICE ($) FY Close	P/E High	P/E Low	PER SHARE ($) Earnings	Dividends	Book Value
12/09	58.29	6	3	9.88	—	62.20
12/08	42.13	19	6	4.76	—	53.61
12/07	87.73	16	13	5.56	—	57.51
12/06	78.69	17	14	4.82	—	61.48
12/05	79.79	20	14	3.94	—	62.52
Annual Growth	**(7.5%)**	**—**	**—**	**25.8%**	**—**	**(0.1%)**

Wells Fargo

This stagecoach likely makes a stop near you. One of the largest banks in the US, Wells Fargo has about 6,600 bank branches in some 40 states and more than 4,000 mortgage and consumer finance offices nationwide. Activities include retail, commercial, and corporate banking; investment management; insurance; equipment leasing; and venture capital investment. A top residential mortgage lender in the US, Wells Fargo is also one of the largest mortgage servicers. The company owns Wells Fargo Insurance Services, one of the world's largest insurance brokerage firms. It is also a leader in mutual funds and online brokerage services. Wells Fargo acquired Wachovia at the end of 2008, which doubled the company in size.

Wachovia was facing collapse as troubled mortgages threated to bring the bank billions of dollars of losses. Wells Fargo had long been looking to make a big acquisition *à la* its rivals JPMorgan Chase and Bank of America, and thus far the banks make a good fit. Both are big mortgage lenders, and the deal expanded Wells Fargo's West and Southwest banking presence to 15 additional states in the Mid-Atlantic and Southeast, where Wachovia Bank maintains its corporate identity as Wells Fargo painstakingly integrates its operations. Wells Fargo announced it would merge the business of consumer finance company Wells Fargo Financial into its banking operations and close more than 630 Wells Fargo Financial locations.

In 2009 Wells Fargo agreed to buy back about $1.4 billion in adjustable-rate bonds that had been frozen since the credit crisis struck in early 2008. Before the crisis, small investors bought billions of dollars of so-called auction-rate securities that Wells Fargo and others had marketed as being as safe as savings accounts and money market funds. The company agreed to buy the affected securities back at par value.

Also in 2009 long-time executive and chairman Dick Kovacevich retired from the company after 23 years at Wells Fargo. CEO John Stumpf took on the additional role of chairman.

Warren Buffett's Berkshire Hathaway owns about 7% of Wells Fargo. In 2008 the US government bought some $25 billion worth of Wells Fargo preferred shares as part of a $250 billion stimulus plan to help grease the wheels of US credit markets. Wells Fargo repaid the government, including interest, in late 2009.

HISTORY

Wells Fargo predecessor Norwest's history begins with the Depression, which came early to the Great Plains. Farmers overexpanded in WWI and went bust as demand fell, soon followed by the banks that held their mortgages. To protect themselves from eastern financial interests, several Midwest banks in 1929 joined Northwestern National Bank of Minneapolis to form a holding company-type banking cooperative, Northwest Bancorp (known as Banco). Each bank assigned its ownership to the company in return for an interest in the new public company. Banco, in turn, provided services to its members, though it could not unify them operationally because of interstate banking bans.

Banco added 90 banks in its first year and by 1932 had 139 affiliates. The Depression thinned membership: By 1940 only 83 remained. Postwar

prosperity didn't help, and by 1952 the number had dwindled to 70 as members consolidated, were sold, or quit.

It experienced functional problems in the 1960s because each member had its own system. In the 1970s Banco developed centralized data processing, but struggled against national competition.

In the 1980s Banco member Northwestern National of Minneapolis began buying financial services firms and formed several new business units. Banco, which had become a conventional bank holding company, reorganized along regional lines, and in 1983 it and its affiliates became Norwest.

Forecasts of food shortages had many farmers expanding production through debt financing in the 1970s, and many went bankrupt when the shortages failed to appear. Norwest needed most of the 1980s to reduce its bad loan portfolio. In response the bank diversified into mortgage banking and consumer finance and entered such markets as Nevada and Texas.

In 1997 Norwest bought banks in Nebraska, Minnesota, and Texas. The next year Norwest Financial entered South America, buying a Buenos Aires-based lender. The bank agreed to merge with Wells Fargo in 1998.

Wells Fargo (descended from the famous Old West stagecoach line) was primed for a merger after watching other pairings (NationsBank with BankAmerica to form Bank of America; BANC ONE with First Chicago). Norwest came a-courting with an attractive proposal: complementary regional coverage and expected cost savings of $650 million. Norwest was the surviving entity (touted as a merger of equals), but the new company adopted the Wells Fargo name.

Since the 1998 merger, Wells Fargo has not put on the brakes — it has made some 50 purchases, including Seattle brokerage Ragen MacKenzie; Dallas-area financial planner H.D. Vest; other companies' mortgage portfolios; and a host of community banks.

In 1999 the bank agreed to sell almost all mortgages it originates to Freddie Mac in exchange for a streamlined approval process. Wells Fargo bought banks in Alaska, California, Michigan, Nebraska, and Utah in 2000, as well as student loan writer Servus Financial; securities brokerage firm Ragen McKenzie, and leasing firm Charter Financial.

The company in 2002 moved its retail banking headquarters from San Francisco to Los Angeles, targeting that market's growing Hispanic and Asian communities and hoping to take advantage of the dearth of superregional banks based there.

Wells Fargo bought most of the funds and assets under management of troubled mutual fund manager Strong Financial in 2005. A week prior to the announcement of the deal, Strong Financial and its founder (Richard Strong, who has been banned from the industry) paid $175 million in fines to settle securities fraud charges. Because of the troubles, Wells Fargo was able to buy the company at a substantial discount and in the process became one of the largest mutual fund managers in the banking industry.

Wells Fargo continued to augment its presence in fast-growing states like Arizona, California, Colorado, and Texas. It bought the banking operations (five banks in Wyoming and Idaho) of United Bancorporation of Wyoming in 2008, and also bought Century Bancshares, expanding Wells Fargo's presence in the Dallas-Fort Worth metroplex and into Arkansas.

EXECUTIVES

Chairman, President, and CEO: John G. Stumpf, age 56,
$21,340,548 total compensation
SEVP and CFO: Howard I. Atkins, age 59,
$11,623,311 total compensation
SEVP Wealth, Brokerage, and Retirement Services:
David M. Carroll, age 53,
$14,302,770 total compensation
SEVP Wholesale Banking: David A. Hoyt, age 54,
$13,477,231 total compensation
SEVP Home and Consumer Finance: Mark C. Oman,
age 55, $12,721,630 total compensation
SEVP and Chief Loan Examiner: Eric D. Shand
SEVP and Chief Auditor: Kevin McCabe
SEVP Community Banking: Carrie L. Tolstedt, age 50
SEVP Investment Portfolio: Ellen Haude
SEVP and Treasurer: Paul R. Ackerman, age 48
SEVP Corporate Development: Bruce E. Helsel
SEVP Customer Connection: Diana L. Starcher
SEVP and Corporate Secretary: Laurel A. Holschuh
SEVP Social Responsibility: Jon R. Campbell
**EVP Legal Affairs and Government Relations and
General Counsel:** James M. (Jim) Strother, age 58
EVP and Chief Credit Officer:
Michael J. (Mike) Loughlin, age 54
EVP Technology and Operations and CIO:
Avid Modjtabai, age 48
EVP and Controller: Richard D. (Rich) Levy, age 52
EVP Card Services and Consumer Lending:
Kevin A. Rhein, age 56
EVP Corporate Communications: Oscar Suris
**Co-Head, Investment Banking and Capital Markets
Group:** Jonathan Weiss
**Co-Head, Investment Banking and Capital Markets
Group:** Robert A. (Rob) Engel
Auditors: KPMG LLP

LOCATIONS

HQ: Wells Fargo & Company
420 Montgomery St., San Francisco, CA 94163
Phone: 866-878-5865   **Fax:** 626-312-3015
Web: www.wellsfargo.com

PRODUCTS/OPERATIONS

2009 Sales

	$ mil.	% of total
Interest		
Loans	41,589	42
Securities available for sale	11,319	11
Loans & mortgages held for sale	2,113	2
Other	1,253	1
Noninterest		
Mortgage banking	12,028	12
Trust & investment fees	9,735	10
Service charges on deposit accounts	5,741	6
Card fees	3,683	4
Net gains on debt securities for sale	2,674	3
Insurance	2,126	2
Other fees	3,804	4
Other	2,698	3
Adjustments	(127)	—
Total	**98,636**	**100**

COMPETITORS

Bank of America
Bank of New York Mellon
BB&T
Capital One
Citigroup
JPMorgan Chase
PNC Financial
State Street
SunTrust
UnionBanCal
U.S. Bancorp

HISTORICAL FINANCIALS

Company Type: Public

Income Statement   FYE: December 31

	ASSETS ($ mil.)	NET INCOME ($ mil.)	INCOME AS % OF ASSETS	EMPLOYEES
12/09	1,243,646	12,275	1.0%	281,000
12/08	1,309,639	2,655	0.2%	281,000
12/07	575,442	8,057	1.4%	159,800
12/06	481,996	8,482	1.8%	158,000
12/05	481,741	7,671	1.6%	153,500
Annual Growth	26.8%	12.5%	—	16.3%

2009 Year-End Financials

Equity as % of assets: 8.3%
Return on assets: 1.0%
Return on equity: 14.4%
Long-term debt ($ mil.): 203,861
No. of shares (mil.): 5,210
Dividends
Yield: 1.8%
Payout: 28.0%
Market value ($ mil.): 140,622
Sales ($ mil.): 98,636

Stock History   NYSE: WFC

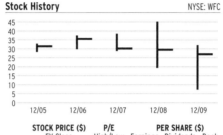

	STOCK PRICE ($) FY Close	P/E High/Low	Earnings	PER SHARE ($) Dividends	Book Value
12/09	26.99	18 4	1.75	0.49	21.46
12/08	29.48	64 28	0.70	1.30	19.02
12/07	30.19	16 12	2.38	1.18	9.14
12/06	35.56	15 12	2.49	1.08	8.81
12/05	31.42	14 13	2.25	1.00	7.80
Annual Growth	(3.7%)	— —	(6.1%)	(16.3%)	28.8%

Wendy's/Arby's Group

You might say this restaurant company has doubled down on the beef. Wendy's/Arby's Group is one of the largest fast-food companies in the world with more than 10,200 locations encompassing its two brands, Wendy's and Arby's. The #3 hamburger chain behind McDonald's and Burger King, Wendy's oversees more than 6,500 restaurants in the US and about 20 other countries. Arby's, with more than 3,700 eateries specializing in roast beef sandwiches, trails only Subway and Quiznos as one of the largest sandwich outlets. About three-fourths of Wendy's/Arby's restaurants are franchised. Chairman Nelson Peltz and vice chairman Peter May together own more than 20% of the company through investment firm Trian Partners.

Whether it's burgers or roast beef sandwiches, Wendy's/Arby's focuses on providing quality menus for value-minded consumers looking for a quick meal. The company does take two different tacks with marketing its chains, however. Wendy's promotes its use of fresh beef patties and made-to-order sandwiches as being superior to other burger joints, while Arby's touts its menu as an alternative to traditional burgers and fries. In both cases, the company faces stiff competition from larger chains including McDonald's,

Burger King, Subway, and the YUM! Brands empire of chicken (KFC), tacos (Taco Bell), and pizza (Pizza Hut).

The economic downturn hampered the company's growth plans during 2009 as consumer spending in general decreased due to the recession and high unemployment. In response, Wendy's/Arby's is focused on improving the profitability of its company-owned restaurants mostly through efforts to keep food costs low.

Even without the larger economic hurdles, Wendy's/Arby's faces the challenge of turning around its chains, each with its own particular problems. Wendy's has floundered somewhat in recent years searching for an identity in the shadow of its two larger rivals. The chain has tried several different marketing campaigns to boost its image but those efforts have mostly failed, much to the dismay of local franchisees.

Arby's, meanwhile, faces the bigger challenge of redefining an aging brand that has gotten lost in the fast-food shuffle. In 2010 the company announced a remodeling effort aimed at updating the roast beef restaurants. It is also expanding the chain's menu of value items to help drive additional traffic to the eateries.

Wendy's/Arby's was formerly known as Triarc Companies, a diversified holding company. Reorganizing to become a pure-play restaurant business, Triarc sold its 64% stake in investment manager Deerfield & Company. The following year the company purchased Wendy's International for $2.3 billion in stock and changed its name to Wendy's/Arby's.

A well-known activist investor, Peltz had owned about 10% of Wendy's through his Trian Fund Management. He began making buyout overtures after pressuring the company in 2006 to shed two of its non-hamburger businesses: donut chain Tim Hortons and Baja Fresh quick-service Mexican operator Fresh Enterprises.

HISTORY

Brothers Forrest and Leroy Raffel opened the first Arby's restaurant in Youngstown, Ohio, in 1964. (The name was derived from the phonetic spelling of the initials R.B., for Raffel Brothers.) Seeking money for expansion, the Raffels merged their company with soft-drink maker Royal Crown Cola Company in 1976.

Royal Crown had started as a ginger ale brewer by pharmacist Claude Hatcher, who founded the Union Bottling Works in 1905. Early successes included Chero-Cola and a variety of Nehi soda flavors (the company became Nehi Corporation in 1928), but when the firm returned to the Royal Crown name for a new cola in 1933, it had a hit. It became Royal Crown Cola Company in 1959 and Royal Crown Companies in 1978.

Victor Posner acquired Royal Crown in 1984 through an affiliate of his publicly traded holding company DWG and began bleeding his new cash cow. Top management quit in disgust, and the Arby's chain began to suffer from neglect and mismanagement. In the late 1980s Posner was investigated and sued by shareholders for draining company coffers to line Posner family pockets. (Posner settled out of court in 1990, and in 1993 was banned by a federal judge from running any public company.)

Junk bond magnates (and former protégés of convicted felon Michael Milken) Nelson Peltz and Peter May stepped forward and bought about 29% of DWG in 1993, changing its name to Triarc Companies (Posner retained a nonvoting stake, which Triarc gradually repurchased from 1999 through 2001). In addition to RC and Arby's, the company owned Graniteville (textiles, sold in 1996), C.H. Patrick (textile chemicals and dyes, sold in 1997), and National Propane (propane retailer, sold in 1999 to Columbia Propane). Triarc hired a new management team, renovated many Arby's locations, and built new restaurants.

To jump-start the RC brand, the company worked to placate long-disgruntled bottlers and bought complementary beverage lines. Triarc purchased the Mistic fruit and tea beverage business in 1995. Triarc also sold off its 355 company-owned Arby's restaurants to its largest franchisee, RTM Restaurant Group.

In 1997 the company picked up fruit juice maker Snapple (now Snapple Beverage Corporation) from Quaker Oats for $300 million. Quaker Oats had purchased Snapple for $1.7 billion in 1994 from Thomas H. Lee Company (which paid $130 million for it in 1992), but a series of missteps began a spectacular tumble in value. Also in 1997 Triarc acquired Cable Car Beverage (later Stewart's Beverages), maker of Stewart's soft drinks, a small national brand.

Saying they wanted to buoy Triarc's stagnant stock price, in 1998 Peltz and May offered to take Triarc private; they withdrew the offer in early 1999, saying it wasn't in the best interest of shareholders. (Both have since settled a lawsuit with disgruntled shareholders.) Later in 1999 the company signed an agreement with United States Beef Corporation, a franchisee of Arby's restaurants, to develop more than 100 Arby's during the next 12 years. Also in 1999 Triarc bought Millrose Distributors, then the largest independent bottler of Snapple, and launched RC Edge, containing ginseng and caffeine, its first new RC product in four years.

In 2000 Triarc sold Snapple to Cadbury Schweppes for about $1.45 billion. In 2002 Arby's franchisee I.C.H. Corporation filed for Chapter 11 bankruptcy, prompting Triarc initially to scale down expansion plans for the chain. Late that year, however, Triarc bought Sybra and its 300 restaurants. In 2005 it acquired Arby's franchisee RTM Restaurant Group and its 775 locations.

EXECUTIVES

Chairman: Nelson Peltz, age 67
Vice Chairman: Peter W. May, age 67
President, CEO, and Director; Interim President, Arby's Restaurant Group: Roland C. Smith, age 55, $3,436,781 total compensation
SVP and CFO: Stephen E. Hare, age 56, $1,324,945 total compensation
SVP and Chief Administrative Officer: Sharron L. Barton, age 58, $1,264,614 total compensation
SVP, General Counsel, and Secretary: Nils H. Okeson, age 44, $1,087,967 total compensation
SVP Strategic Development: Darrell G. van Ligten, age 45
SVP and Chief Accounting Officer: Steven B. Graham, age 56
SVP and Chief Communications Officer: John D. Barker, age 47
President, Wendy's International: J. David Karam, age 52, $2,148,116 total compensation
President, Arby's Restaurant Group: Hala G. Moddelmog, age 54
Auditors: Deloitte & Touche LLP

LOCATIONS

HQ: Wendy's/Arby's Group, Inc.
1155 Perimeter Center West, Atlanta, GA 30338
Phone: 678-514-4100   **Fax:** 212-451-3134
Web: www.wendysarbys.com

2009 Sales

	$ mil.	% of total
US	3,330.8	93
Canada	236.1	7
Other countries	13.9	—
Total	**3,580.8**	**100**

2009 Locations

	No.
US	
Ohio	713
Florida	664
Texas	576
Michigan	460
Georgia	442
Pennsylvania	409
California	402
North Carolina	394
Indiana	359
Illinois	333
Virginia	324
New York	309
Tennessee	293
Kentucky	276
South Carolina	205
Alabama	199
Colorado	190
Arizona	183
Missouri	167
New Jersey	166
Maryland	162
Louisiana	158
Utah	158
Minnesota	155
Wisconsin	153
Washington	137
Oklahoma	133
Kansas	126
Mississippi	120
West Virginia	109
Arkansas	108
Iowa	99
Massachusetts	98
Oregon	89
Nebraska	84
Nevada	77
New Mexico	68
Connecticut	64
Idaho	52
Montana	35
Delaware	34
Other states	180
International	786
Total	**10,259**

PRODUCTS/OPERATIONS

2009 Sales

	$ mil.	% of total
Restaurants	3,198.3	89
Franchising	382.5	11
Total	**3,580.8**	**100**

2009 Sales

	$ mil.	% of total
Wendy's	2,437.1	68
Arby's	1,143.7	32
Total	**3,580.8**	**100**

2009 Locations

	No.
Franchised	7,699
Company-owned	2,560
Total	**10,259**

2009 Locations

	No.
Wendy's	6,541
Arby's	3,718
Total	**10,259**

COMPETITORS

AFC Enterprises
Burger King
Chick-fil-A
Chipotle
Church's Chicken
CKE Restaurants
Dairy Queen
Jack in the Box
McDonald's
Panda Restaurant Group
Panera Bread
Quiznos
Sonic Corp.
Subway
YUM!

HISTORICAL FINANCIALS

Company Type: Public

Income Statement

FYE: December 31

	REVENUE ($ mil.)	NET INCOME ($ mil.)	NET PROFIT MARGIN	EMPLOYEES
12/09	3,581	5	0.1%	67,500
12/08	1,823	(480)	—	70,000
12/07	1,264	16	1.3%	26,605
12/06	1,243	(11)	—	24,372
12/05	727	(56)	—	25,203
Annual Growth	**49.0%**	**—**	**—**	**27.9%**

2009 Year-End Financials

Debt ratio: 64.2%
Return on equity: 0.2%
Cash ($ mil.): 593
Current ratio: 1.85
Long-term debt ($ mil.): 1,501
No. of shares (mil.): 418
Dividends
  Yield: 1.3%
  Payout: 600.0%
Market value ($ mil.): 1,962

Stock History

NYSE: WEN

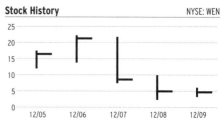

	STOCK PRICE ($) FY Close	P/E High/Low		PER SHARE ($) Earnings	Dividends	Book Value
12/09	4.69	580	355	0.01	0.06	5.59
12/08	4.94	—	—	(4.29)	0.25	5.70
12/07	8.56	134	48	0.16	0.32	1.07
12/06	21.31	—	—	(0.13)	0.32	1.13
12/05	16.41	—	—	(0.79)	0.29	0.95
Annual Growth	**(26.9%)**	**—**	**—**	**—**	**(32.6%)**	**55.9%**

Werner Enterprises

Transportation and logistics is Werner Enterprises' game; hauling truckload shipments — both interstate and intrastate — is its fame. Among the five largest truckload carriers in the US, Werner operates about 7,250 tractors and 23,880 trailers. Its trailer fleet consists of dry vans and, to a lesser extent, temperature-controlled vans and flatbeds. Werner's truckload transportation offerings include dedicated contract carriage, in which drivers and equipment are assigned to a customer. It also offers freight brokerage, intermodal freight transportation arrangement, and other value-added logistic services, as well as freight forwarding. Retailers, consumer and grocery products companies represent 75% of sales.

Whipsawed by high fuel prices and a low demand for freight transportation, Werner has trimmed its medium-to-long-haul fleet in an effort to control costs and maintain profitability. The company has reduced its fleet by two-thirds since 2007, and continued to cut costs, including non-driver headcount. Simultaneously, shorter-haul regional fleets have been expanded. Although revenues slumped by more than 20% and earning by more than 15% in 2009 from 2008, cash flow from operations, which tumbled by nearly 25%, still managed to exceed capital expenditures.

Moving forward Werner is planning to hold on to some 7,300 trucks to transport freight, mostly retail merchandise, various consumer goods and manufactured products, and groceries. It is maintaining its presence in the premium end of the transportation market, concentrating on shippers that require broad geographic coverage and customized services, and consequently are less rate-sensitive. In addition, the company is looking for the road to open up demand for dedicated fleet services and regional truckload transportation, along with freight brokerage opportunities. Werner also is counting on its freight forwarding business, which the company launched to help bring customers' cargo from China to the US.

Founder and chairman Clarence Werner and his family own about 40% of the company.

HISTORY

In 1956, 19-year-old Clarence Werner sold the family car to buy his first truck. Nine years later he was operating a modest, but profitable, 10-truck fleet. Werner focused on customer service in the medium- to long-haul segment of the industry and was well-positioned for the 1980 deregulation of the trucking industry. By 1986, when the company went public, its fleet had grown to about 630 tractors.

Werner sought to broaden its customer base and services in the early 1990s, and in 1992 it began offering three new services: dedicated fleet service, temperature-controlled freight service, and regional short-haul service. The next year the company added rail intermodal transportation to its portfolio of services, and in 1995 it created a Werner Logistics Services division. In 1997 Werner began providing dedicated trucking services to Dollar General's Oklahoma distribution center; a 1998 deal expanded the contract to include the retailer's Georgia and Kentucky hubs.

In a move reflecting a buoyant US economy, Werner added 900 trucks to its fleet in 1999.

However, high oil prices and a weak used truck market put the squeeze on Werner's financial performance in 2000.

In 2006 the company formed Werner Global Logistics U.S. to provide air and ocean freight forwarding services between China and the US.

Clarence Werner stepped down as CEO in 2007 but remained chairman. His son Greg Werner, already the company's president, took over as CEO.

EXECUTIVES

Chairman: Clarence L. (C. L.) Werner, age 72, $746,570 total compensation
Vice Chairman: Gary L. Werner, age 51, $1,140,113 total compensation
President, CEO, and Director:
Gregory L. (Greg) Werner, age 50, $1,614,744 total compensation
SEVP Value Added Services and International and COO: Derek J. Leathers, age 40, $1,191,042 total compensation
SEVP Specialized Services: H. Marty Nordlund, age 48
EVP, Treasurer, and CFO: John J. Steele, age 51, $526,524 total compensation
EVP and CIO: Robert E. (Bob) Synowicki Jr., age 51
EVP Sales and Marketing: Jim S. Schelble, age 48
EVP, Chief Accounting Officer, and Coporate Secretary: James L. Johnson
SVP Brokerage and Intermodal Operations, Value Added Services: Warren L. Schollaert Jr.
SVP Van Division: Steven L. Phillips
VP Analysis and Information Systems:
Anthony M. DeCanti
VP Government Relations: Richard S. Reiser, age 63
VP TCU and Dedicated Operations: Matthew E. Parry
VP Flatbed and Dedicated Operations: Todd A. Struble
VP Risk: Charles R. (Chuck) Stevens
VP Operations: Guy M. Welton
VP Safety and Compliance: Della M. Sanders
VP Driver School Relations: John W. Frey
Director Corporate Communications: Fred Thayer
Auditors: KPMG LLP

LOCATIONS

HQ: Werner Enterprises, Inc.
14507 Frontier Rd., Omaha, NE 68138
Phone: 402-895-6640 **Fax:** 402-894-3927
Web: www.werner.com

2009 Sales

	$ mil.	% of total
US	1,509.5	91
Mexico	84.4	5
Other countries	72.5	4
Total	**1,666.4**	**100**

PRODUCTS/OPERATIONS

2009 Sales

	$ mil.	% of total
Trucking revenues	1,256.3	75
Trucking fuel surcharge	176.7	11
Value-added services	222.2	13
Other	11.2	1
Total	**1,666.4**	**100**

COMPETITORS

C.H. Robinson Worldwide	Knight Transportation
Covenant Transportation	Landstar System
C.R. England	Prime, Inc.
Crete Carrier	Schneider National
Expeditors	Swift Transportation
Frozen Food Express	UPS Supply Chain
Heartland Express	Solutions
J.B. Hunt	U.S. Xpress

HISTORICAL FINANCIALS
Company Type: Public

Income Statement
FYE: December 31

	REVENUE ($ mil.)	NET INCOME ($ mil.)	NET PROFIT MARGIN	EMPLOYEES
12/09	1,666	57	3.4%	9,094
12/08	2,166	68	3.1%	13,526
12/07	2,071	75	3.6%	13,608
12/06	2,081	99	4.7%	15,146
12/05	1,972	99	5.0%	14,552
Annual Growth	**(4.1%)**	**(12.9%)**	**—**	**(11.1%)**

2009 Year-End Financials

Debt ratio: —
Return on equity: 7.4%
Cash ($ mil.): 18
Current ratio: 1.94
Long-term debt ($ mil.): —

No. of shares (mil.): 73
Dividends
  Yield: 1.3%
  Payout: 31.6%
Market value ($ mil.): 1,438

Stock History
NASDAQ (GS): WERN

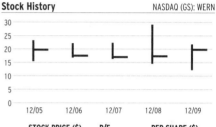

	STOCK PRICE ($) FY Close	P/E High/Low		PER SHARE ($) Earnings	Dividends	Book Value
12/09	19.80	27	16	0.79	0.25	9.70
12/08	17.34	31	16	0.94	0.15	11.47
12/07	17.03	22	16	1.02	0.19	11.47
12/06	17.48	17	14	1.25	0.17	11.98
12/05	19.70	19	13	1.22	0.16	11.88
Annual Growth	**0.1%**	**—**	**—**	**(10.3%)**	**11.8%**	**(4.9%)**

WESCO International

When contractors and manufacturers need parts, it's WESCO to the wescue. The company distributes electrical products (fuses, terminals, connectors, enclosures, fittings, circuit breakers, transformers, switchboards); industrial supplies (tools, abrasives, filters, safety equipment); lighting wares (lamps, fixtures, ballasts); wire and conduit materials; automation equipment (motors, drives, logic controllers); and data communication apparatus (patch panels, terminals, connectors). WESCO offers more than a million products from some 17,000 suppliers, with about 113,000 customers worldwide.

Through acquisitions and organic growth, WESCO plans to resume growing its business in 2010. The company plans to focus on its global account and integrated supply programs to increase its customer base and to extend its use of supply services to customers. It targets customers in the fields of construction contracting; education; engineering, procurement, and construction firms; government; health care; and utilities. Among product growth areas, WESCO looks toward data communications and security systems, and to clean tech lighting systems.

The recessionary year of 2009 was rough on WESCO, like it was on many companies. It saw sales decline and profits fall. The company reduced its workforce by about 15% as a result.

The electrical distribution industry serves electrical contractors, utilities, and commercial, institutional, and government customers, in addition to the industrial market. Electrical distribution provides products and services for MRO (maintenance, repair, operations) and OEM use. WESCO's largest supplier, Eaton Corporation, accounts for about 12% of the company's total purchases.

Sales to electrical contractors range from major industrial, commercial, and data communication projects, to small residential contractors. Utilities and specialty utility contractors include large and rural electric cooperatives and municipal power authorities, which maintain transmission, distribution lines, and power plants. Commercial, institutional, and governmental customers includes schools, hospitals, property management firms, retailers, and government agencies of all types. WESCO sells integrated lighting control and distribution equipment in a single package for multisite specialty retailers, restaurant chains, and department stores.

WESCO also offers a wide range of services and solutions to enhance its product sales. These services include national accounts programs, integrated supply programs, and construction project management capabilities.

In 2009 the company announced that CEO Roy Haley would assume the role as executive chairman for two years. COO John Engel succeeded Haley as CEO.

HISTORY

WESCO International got its start as a subsidiary of electrical power pioneer Westinghouse Electric Company. George Westinghouse founded the company bearing his name in Pittsburgh in 1886. The company installed the nation's first alternating current power system in Telluride, Colorado, in 1891. Two years later Westinghouse built the generating system that powered the Chicago World's Fair. The company also was chosen to provide generators for the hydroelectric power station at Niagara Falls.

George Westinghouse was ousted in 1910 after the company was unable to meet its debt obligations. He died four years later at the age of 67. During the next decade the company added the burgeoning radio and appliance markets to its portfolio of electrical distribution and production operations.

In 1922 the firm established Westinghouse Electric Supply Company (WESCO) to distribute power products and appliances. Westinghouse had its share of troubles over the years, many of which were caused by ill-advised diversification attempts. These included forays into uranium supply, financial services, and real estate.

By the 1990s Westinghouse was buried under nearly $10 billion in debt and too busy putting out fires to tend to day-to-day operations properly. Not surprisingly, WESCO was caught up in Westinghouse's problems: Sales declined four years in a row, and employee turnover was around 25% a year.

Westinghouse embarked on a divestiture program and sold WESCO to investment firm Clayton, Dubilier & Rice (CD&R) in 1994 for about $340 million. At the time, WESCO had about 250 branch locations. The new owners brought in Roy Haley, a veteran insurance and finance executive, to turn the ailing business around. Haley

tied pay and bonuses to performance and emphasized multisite customers, such as contractors and companies with multiple retail, industrial, or administrative locations. WESCO grew through acquisitions, and in 1995 sales reached $2 billion.

By 1996 the company had added 1,000 employees; it operated about 300 distribution branches throughout the world. Sales reached $2.6 billion in 1997 as WESCO continued acquiring complementary companies and formed an alliance with Australian mining and steel company BHP (now BHP Billiton). Managers led a $1.1 billion buyout of the company in 1998, increasing their stake in WESCO from 15% to 33%. The company opened sales offices in the UK, Singapore, and Mexico.

As it geared up for its IPO in 1999, WESCO bought distributors Industrial Electric Supply Company and Statewide Electrical Supply. The firm continued to shop during 2000, adding electrical distributors Orton Utility Supply (Tennessee), Control Corporation of America (Virginia), and KVA Supply Company (Colorado and California).

In 2001 WESCO acquired two distributors (Herning Underground Supply and Alliance Utility Products) that supplied contractors who install gas, lighting, and communication utility infrastructure in Arizona, California, Utah, and Washington.

The Cypress Group, the private equity firm that helped lead the $1.1 billion management buyout in 1998, sold most of its shares in WESCO in 2004 and 2005. Cypress owned nearly half of WESCO prior to those sales.

WESCO acquired fastener distributor Fastec Industrial and electronics distributor Carlton-Bates in 2005. The following year WESCO acquired Communications Supply Corporation (CSC), a distributor of low-voltage network infrastructure and industrial wire and cable products, for about $525 million in cash.

Roy Haley stepped aside as CEO in 2009, becoming WESCO's executive chairman. SVP/COO John Engel was promoted to president and CEO.

EXECUTIVES

Chairman: Roy W. Haley, age 63,
$4,880,133 total compensation
President, CEO, and Director: John J. Engel, age 48,
$3,190,637 total compensation
SVP, COO, and Director: Stephen A. Van Oss, age 55,
$2,398,276 total compensation
VP and CFO: Richard P. Heyse, age 47,
$522,561 total compensation
VP Operations: Andrew J. Bergdoll, age 47,
$589,967 total compensation
VP Operations: Ronald P. Van Jr., age 49,
$594,449 total compensation
VP Operations: David Bemoras, age 52
VP Operations: James R. Griffin, age 48
VP Operations: Robert B. Rosenbaum, age 52
VP Legal Affairs: Diane E. Lazzaris, age 43
VP Human Resources: Robert J. Powell, age 48
VP Investor Relations and Treasurer: Daniel A. Brailer, age 52
Corporate Controller: Timothy A. (Tim) Hibbard, age 53
Director Internal Audit: Allen A. Duganier, age 54
Auditors: PricewaterhouseCoopers LLP

LOCATIONS

HQ: WESCO International, Inc.
225 W. Station Square Dr., Ste. 700
Pittsburgh, PA 15219
Phone: 412-454-2200 **Fax:** 412-454-2505
Web: www.wesco.com

2009 Sales

	$ mil.	% of total
US	3,928.2	85
Canada	559.4	12
Other countries	136.4	3
Total	**4,624.0**	**100**

PRODUCTS/OPERATIONS

2009 Sales

	% of total
Industrial customers	40
Electrical contractors	36
Utilities & special utility contractors	17
Commercial, institutional & governmental customers	7
Total	**100**

Selected Products

Automation equipment
Ballasts
Boxes
Busways
Cable
Circuit breakers
Connectors
Data communications products
Drives
Electrical products
Fittings
Fixtures
Fuses
Industrial supplies
Light bulbs
Lighting
Lugs
Metallic and nonmetallic conduits
Motor control devices
MRO supplies
Operator interfaces
Panelboards
Patch panels
Premise wiring
Programmable logic controllers
Pushbuttons
Switchboards
Tape
Terminals
Tools
Transformers
Wire
Wire and conduit products

COMPETITORS

Anixter International	McNaughton-McKay
Bearing Distributors	Premier Farnell
Border States Electric	Rexel, Inc.
Consolidated Electrical	Richardson Electronics
Electrocomponents	Sonepar USA
Electro-Wire	SUMMIT Electric Supply
Graybar Electric	W.W. Grainger
HWC	

HISTORICAL FINANCIALS

Company Type: Public

Income Statement				FYE: December 31
	REVENUE ($ mil.)	NET INCOME ($ mil.)	NET PROFIT MARGIN	EMPLOYEES
12/09	4,624	105	2.3%	6,100
12/08	6,111	213	3.5%	7,200
12/07	6,004	241	4.0%	7,300
12/06	5,321	217	4.1%	7,100
12/05	4,421	104	2.3%	6,000
Annual Growth	1.1%	0.4%	—	0.4%

2009 Year-End Financials

Debt ratio: 60.0%
Return on equity: 12.2%
Cash ($ mil.): 112
Current ratio: 1.95
Long-term debt ($ mil.): 598
No. of shares (mil.): 42
Dividends
  Yield: —
  Payout: —
Market value ($ mil.): 1,147

Stock History   NYSE: WCC

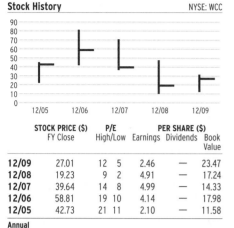

	STOCK PRICE ($) FY Close	P/E High/Low		PER SHARE ($) Earnings	Dividends	Book Value
12/09	27.01	12	5	2.46	—	23.47
12/08	19.23	9	2	4.91	—	17.24
12/07	39.64	14	8	4.99	—	14.33
12/06	58.81	19	10	4.14	—	17.98
12/05	42.73	21	11	2.10	—	11.58
Annual Growth	(10.8%)	—	—	4.0%	—	19.3%

Westar Energy

Westar Energy wished upon a star, and the answer was — "focus on power utility resources." Westar Energy has a generating capacity of more than 7,100 MW (mostly from fossil-fueled facilities) and serves about 685,000 electricity customers in Kansas through its utility subsidiaries. Westar Energy supplies power to 368,000 retail customers in central and northeast Kansas, and subsidiary Kansas Gas and Electric (KGE) supplies power to 317,000 retail customers in south-central and southeastern Kansas. The company operates 34,200 miles of transmission and distribution lines. It supplies wholesale electric power to more than 30 cities in Kansas and four electric cooperatives that serve rural areas.

Like other utilities, the company faces the challenge of needing to increase power capacity while decreasing carbon emissions in order to meet stricter environmental regulations. In 2009 some 50% of its Westar Energy's strategic plan to meet future demand includes investing in renewable power plants and in cleaner-burning traditional generation plants. It is also investing in transmission projects, upgrading environmental controls at existing plants, and providing customers with the tools (smart meters) and knowledge (conservation information) to help them to become more energy efficient.

In 2009 the company developed 300 MW of wind energy resources, and plans to bring an additional 500 MW of the wind generation online by the end of 2012. On the traditional side of its generation business, in 2009 Westar Energy completed the construction of Emporia Energy Center (a 660-MW-capacity natural gas-fired peaking power plant in Emporia, Kansas).

HISTORY

Although Western Resources was created in 1992, it has roots deep in the history of the US energy industry. Its acquisitive ancestors, Kansas Power & Light (KPL) and Kansas Gas and Electric (KGE), had been providing electricity and natural gas since the early years of the 20th century. KGE was founded in 1909 by holding company American Power & Light to provide energy to three Kansas towns. By 1925 KGE had sold its natural gas service to focus on providing electricity to 50 towns.

The 1930s and 1940s saw KGE grow through acquisitions and internal expansion. In 1948 American Power & Light offered a few shares of KGE stock and then sold the remaining shares in 1949. In 1954 KGE built its first gas-powered plant; a year later it was listed on the New York Stock Exchange. In 1970 KGE entered the nuclear age by planning a nuke for Coffey County, Kansas.

KPL was originally financed by holding company North American Light and Power, which incorporated the firm in 1924. KPL built a generating plant and transmission lines from Tecumseh to Topeka and Atchison, and a coal-powered facility at Neosho, Kansas. In 1927 KPL bought out the Kansas Public Service Company, then United Power and Light (UPL) in the 1930s, which gave KPL a service area covering most of central Kansas. KPL bought Kansas Electric Power in the 1940s, bringing eastern Kansas under its wing.

KPL was listed on the New York Stock Exchange in 1949, and its parent was dissolved. Within a decade, KPL had broadened its service from providing electricity for rural Kansas to also providing energy for industry. In 1968 KPL installed the nation's first power plant scrubber system. KPL grew quickly during the 1970s and 1980s, building technologically up-to-date power plants, including the Wolf Creek nuclear plant.

KPL and KGE's 1992 merger was debated by those who feared major rate hikes, but the SEC approved it and KGE became a subsidiary of KPL. The company changed its name to Western Resources, but each utility operated under its own name. After the merger, Western Resources sold most of its natural gas operations and focused on electricity generation. In 1996 the firm set out to acquire another utility, Kansas City Power & Light. Western Resources transferred its natural gas holdings to ONEOK in 1996 for 45% of the Oklahoma gas company's stock.

In 1997 Western Resources diversified in preparation for utility deregulation that could hurt its energy business. In 2000 it announced plans to spin off its nonregulated businesses to shareholders as a new company, Westar Industries, and its utility units to Public Service Company of New Mexico (now PNM Resources).

In 2001 PNM Resources filed suit to cancel its agreement to acquire KPL and KGE, and Western Resources filed a countersuit alleging a breach of the merger agreement. In 2002 PNM Resources terminated the agreement; however, both lawsuits were still pending. PNM Resources' termination of the agreement prompted Western Resources' decision to retain and focus on these assets. Later that year Western Resources changed its name to Westar Energy.

In 2003 the company filed a debt reduction plan with the Kansas Corporation Commission (KCC) to avoid a bankruptcy filing. The plan required the divestment of Westar Energy's nonutility assets and has replaced the company's earlier plans to spin off subsidiary Westar Industries, which held the company's ONEOK and Protection One stakes.

To begin reducing debt, the company in 2003 divested its 45% stake in ONEOK, selling shares back to ONEOK as well as to the public and to investment firm Cantor Fitzgerald.

Former CEO David Wittig had been indicted in 2002 on fraud charges in connection with a real estate deal and a loan he received from Capital City Bank (the charges were not related to Westar Energy); shortly after the indictment, Wittig resigned from the company. He was later convicted for these charges.

In 2003 Wittig and former EVP Douglas Lake were indicted on conspiracy, fraud, and other criminal charges for allegedly looting more than $37 million in corporate funds for personal uses, including house renovations and travel expenses, and for attempting to cover up the scheme. The indictment also accused the executives of criminal activities related to the structuring of the Westar Industries spinoff. During the executives' tenure, Westar's debt rose to $3 billion and the company was pushed to the brink of bankruptcy. The executives' 2004 fraud trial was declared a mistrial due to a hung jury. In 2005 prosecutors announced that they would retry the case. At the retrial, both men were found guilty.

In 2007 Westar Energy and energy co-op Kansas Electric Power Cooperative (KEPCo) announced that KEPCo will continue to purchase a major amount of its electricity requirements from Westar Energy for the next 38 years.

EXECUTIVES

Chairman: Charles Q. (Charlie) Chandler IV, age 56
President, CEO, and Director: William B. (Bill) Moore, age 57, $1,714,032 total compensation
EVP and COO: Douglas R. (Doug) Sterbenz, age 46, $1,134,311 total compensation
EVP and CFO: Mark A. Ruelle, age 48, $955,535 total compensation
EVP Public Affairs and Consumer Services: James J. (Jim) Ludwig, age 50, $474,067 total compensation
VP Operations Strategy and Support: Bruce A. Akin, age 45
VP Generation: Ken Johnson
VP Regulatory Affairs: Michael Lennen, age 64
VP Corporate Compliance and Internal Audit: Jeffrey L. Beasley, age 52
VP and Controller: Leroy P. (Lee) Wages, age 61
VP Distribution Power Delivery: Caroline A. Williams
VP Transmission Operations and Environmental Services: Kelly B. Harrison
VP Construction Services: Greg A. Greenwood
VP Customer Care: Peggy S. Loyd
VP, General Counsel, and Corporate Secretary: Larry D. Irick, age 53, $570,833 total compensation
Director Corporate Communications: Karla Olsen
Director Investor Relations: Bruce Burns
Treasurer: Anthony D. (Tony) Somma
Auditors: Deloitte & Touche LLP

LOCATIONS

HQ: Westar Energy, Inc.
  818 S. Kansas Ave., Topeka, KS 66612
Phone: 785-575-6300   **Fax:** 785-575-1796
Web: www.wr.com

PRODUCTS/OPERATIONS

2009 Sales

	$ mil.	% of total
Retail		
Residential	576.9	31
Commercial	529.9	29
Industrial	291.7	16
Wholesale marketing	305.3	16
Transmission	132.4	7
Energy marketing	15.4	1
Other	3.6	—
Adjustments	3.0	—
Total	**1,858.2**	**100**

Selected Operations

Kansas Gas and Electric Company (KGE, operates as Westar Energy, electric utility and marketer)

COMPETITORS

AES
Ameren
Atmos Energy
Dynegy
Edison International
Empire District Electric
Great Plains Energy
MidAmerican Energy
OGE Energy
Southern Company
Xcel Energy

HISTORICAL FINANCIALS

Company Type: Public

Income Statement

FYE: December 31

	REVENUE ($ mil.)	NET INCOME ($ mil.)	NET PROFIT MARGIN	EMPLOYEES
12/09	1,858	175	9.4%	2,397
12/08	1,839	178	9.7%	2,415
12/07	1,727	168	9.8%	2,323
12/06	1,606	165	10.3%	2,223
12/05	1,583	135	8.5%	2,191
Annual Growth	4.1%	6.7%	—	2.3%

2009 Year-End Financials

Debt ratio: 115.8%
Return on equity: 7.9%
Cash ($ mil.): 4
Current ratio: 0.92
Long-term debt ($ mil.): 2,600
No. of shares (mil.): 111
Dividends
　Yield: 5.5%
　Payout: 75.9%
Market value ($ mil.): 2,406

Stock History

NYSE: WR

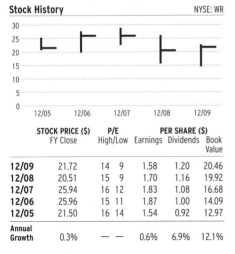

	STOCK PRICE ($) FY Close	P/E High/Low		PER SHARE ($) Earnings	Dividends	Book Value
12/09	21.72	14	9	1.58	1.20	20.46
12/08	20.51	15	9	1.70	1.16	19.92
12/07	25.94	16	12	1.83	1.08	16.68
12/06	25.96	15	11	1.87	1.00	14.09
12/05	21.50	16	14	1.54	0.92	12.97
Annual Growth	0.3%	—	—	0.6%	6.9%	12.1%

Western Digital

When it comes to data storage, Western Digital has drive. The company is one of the largest independent makers of hard-disk drives, which record, store, and recall volumes of data. Drives for PCs account for most of Western Digital's sales, although the company also makes devices for entry-level servers and home entertainment products, such as set-top boxes and video game consoles. The company sells to manufacturers and through retailers and distributors. About half of its sales are to OEMs. The company counts PC giant Dell among its customers. Western Digital gets around half of its sales in Asia.

Western Digital is one of a handful of manufacturers that dominate the hard-disk drive market — a sector characterized by harsh competition, short product life cycles, and aggressive price cuts.

The worldwide economic downturn and credit crisis are making it difficult for the company and its customers and suppliers to forecast market demand. There are signs that the recession is starting to lift, yet the economic recovery may take some time. The average selling prices of Western Digital products normally decline over time due to competition and product obsolescence, and it remains to be seen how global economic conditions will affect operations. The consumer market favors lower-priced computers during downturns, and Western Digital must remain competitive in supplying hard drives for low-cost PCs.

Western Digital acquired disk component maker Komag for $1 billion in 2007. The purchase allowed Western Digital to manufacture the media and substrates used in its drives. In 2009 the company sold its media substrate manufacturing facility in Sarawak, Malaysia, which it acquired from Komag, to competitor Hitachi Global Storage Technologies. Western Digital, which is looking to cut costs, will continue to manufacture the majority of its magnetic media requirements at other Malaysian facilities.

It moved into the solid-state drive market in 2009 when it purchased SiliconSystems. Used primarily in embedded systems, SiliconSystems' drives can be found in products ranging from network routers to automotive assembly line robotics. Western Digital plans to use the acquisition to develop solid-state products for the enterprise market.

In 2010 Western Digital bought the magnetic media operations of Hoya for about $233 million.

In recent years the company has seen significant growth in its non-desktop PC segment, which includes devices used in notebook computers and consumer electronics such as DVRs.

HISTORY

Western Digital was founded in 1970 as a manufacturer of specialized semiconductors and electronic calculators. The company filed for Chapter 11 bankruptcy in 1976. However, it reorganized and emerged successfully in 1978. Roger Johnson, after a succession of executive positions at Memorex, Measurex, and Burroughs, came to Western Digital as EVP and COO in 1982. Sales were merely $34 million, hurt by the acquisition of several ill-fitting computer and electronics businesses. By 1984 Johnson became president and CEO; he sold off several companies to concentrate on storage control devices.

A contract with IBM contributed to Western Digital's sales topping $460 million in 1987.

Anticipating a change in technology that would have disk drive makers building storage control into the drives themselves, Western Digital began to shift its efforts toward making disk drives in 1988. Ten-year company veteran Kathy Braun oversaw the purchase of Tandon's disk drive operations. Tandon was considered a second-rate manufacturer using aging technology, but its drives continued to sell well for a period following the acquisition. This created a false sense of security for Western Digital and delayed the development of more competitive drives. In 1990 the market for storage controller boards essentially disappeared. Losses prompted a restructuring that in turn violated Western Digital's credit agreements.

In 1991 the US economy slowed, and the disk drive industry began a price war. That year Western Digital, appearing close to bankruptcy, sold its profitable departmental network business to Standard Microsystems.

As the PC market improved in 1992, so did Western Digital's prospects. A big boost came when the cash-strapped company introduced a line of disk drives with a commonality of parts. In 1993 Western Digital's IPO and sale of its wafer factory to Motorola reduced its high debt. That year the Clinton administration appointed CEO Johnson head of the General Services Administration. IBM veteran Charles Haggerty, who joined Western Digital in 1992, assumed the company's top post.

In 1994 Western Digital enjoyed its first profit in four years. The company sold off its Microcomputer Products Group, which made proprietary semiconductors, in 1996 and introduced its first hard drives aimed at the corporate network computing market.

In 1997 a number of Asian manufacturers jumped into the market at the same time that computer makers were taking on sales approaches to eliminate the need for large inventories of hard drives and other stock. Those factors, combined with stalled PC demand and Western Digital's slow transition to newer recording head technologies, caused a loss for fiscal 1998. To respond, Western Digital cut more than 20% of its workforce and slashed production. Braun, by then second in command at the company and one of the industry's highest-paid women, retired in 1998.

In 1999 Western Digital took a financial hit following its recall of 400,000 defective disk drives; it announced it would lay off another 2,500 employees, primarily in Singapore. In 2000 Haggerty retired from the CEO post; COO Matthew Massengill was tapped to replace him.

In 2001 Western Digital sold Connex to former rival Quantum after that company exited the hard drive market. Massengill was named chairman later that year.

Massengill stepped down as CEO in 2005, while remaining executive chairman. Arif Shakeel, Western Digital's president and COO since 2002, succeeded Massengill as CEO.

Shakeel stepped down as CEO in 2007. John Coyne, a Western Digital employee since 1983, succeeded him in both posts. Also in 2007, Massengill stepped down as chairman, while remaining on the board, and was succeeded by Thomas Pardun, a veteran telecommunications executive who served as Western Digital's chairman for two years earlier in the decade.

EXECUTIVES

Chairman: Thomas E. Pardun, age 66
President, CEO, and Director: John F. Coyne, age 59, $11,590,374 total compensation
COO: Timothy M. (Tim) Leyden, age 58, $2,503,760 total compensation
EVP Operations: Martin W. (Marty) Finkbeiner
SVP and CFO: Wolfgang U. Nickl, age 41
SVP Administration, General Counsel, and Secretary: Raymond M. (Ray) Bukaty, age 53, $1,285,582 total compensation
SVP and General Manager Branded Products and Consumer Electronics Groups: Jim Welsh
VP and General Manager Enterprise Storage Solutions: Thomas (Tom) McDorman
VP Marketing, Branded Products Group: Dale Pistilli
VP, Controller, and Principal Accounting Officer: Joseph R. Carrillo
VP Investor Relations: Bob Blair, age 59
VP and General Manager PC Components Group: Richard E. Rutledge
Public Relations: Heather Skinner
Auditors: KPMG LLP

LOCATIONS

HQ: Western Digital Corporation
20511 Lake Forest Dr., Lake Forest, CA 92630
Phone: 949-672-7000   **Fax:** 949-672-5408
Web: www.wdc.com

2010 Sales

	% of total
Asia	53
Americas	24
Europe, Middle East & Africa	23
Total	**100**

PRODUCTS/OPERATIONS

2010 Sales by Channel

	% of total
Manufacturers	51
Distributors	31
Retailers	18
Total	**100**

2010 Sales by Product

	% of total
Non-desktop	64
Desktop	36
Total	**100**

Selected Products

Internal Hard Drives
  Audio/Video hard drives (Performer)
  Desktop PCs and entry-level servers (Caviar, Protégé)
  Servers and storage systems (Raptor)
External Hard Drives
  FireWire for PCs and Macs
Accessories
  Desktop (FireWire adapter)
  Mobile (FireWire CardBus PC card)

COMPETITORS

EMC
Fujitsu
Hitachi Global Storage
IM Flash Technologies
Iomega
LaCie
Samsung Electronics
Seagate Technology
SMART Modular Technologies
STEC
TEAC
Toshiba

HISTORICAL FINANCIALS

Company Type: Public

Income Statement

FYE: Saturday nearest June 30

	REVENUE ($ mil.)	NET INCOME ($ mil.)	NET PROFIT MARGIN	EMPLOYEES
6/10	9,850	1,382	14.0%	62,500
6/09	7,453	470	6.3%	45,991
6/08	8,074	867	10.7%	50,072
6/07	5,468	564	10.3%	29,572
6/06	4,341	395	9.1%	24,750
Annual Growth	**22.7%**	**36.8%**	**—**	**26.1%**

2010 Year-End Financials

Debt ratio: 6.2%
Return on equity: 35.0%
Cash ($ mil.): 2,734
Current ratio: 2.33
Long-term debt ($ mil.): 294
No. of shares (mil.): 229
Dividends
  Yield: —
  Payout: —
Market value ($ mil.): 6,916

Stock History

NYSE: WDC

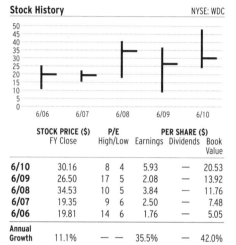

	STOCK PRICE ($) FY Close	P/E High/Low		PER SHARE ($) Earnings	Dividends	Book Value
6/10	30.16	8	4	5.93	—	20.53
6/09	26.50	17	5	2.08	—	13.92
6/08	34.53	10	5	3.84	—	11.76
6/07	19.35	9	6	2.50	—	7.48
6/06	19.81	14	6	1.76	—	5.05
Annual Growth	**11.1%**	**—**	**—**	**35.5%**	**—**	**42.0%**

Westinghouse Air Brake Technologies

More powerful than a speeding locomotive, Westinghouse Air Brake Technologies pulls out all the stops. The company, doing business as Wabtec, manufactures braking equipment and other parts for locomotives, freight cars, and passenger railcars. Products made by Wabtec's freight group include air brake systems, draft gears, hand brakes, slack adjusters, heat exchanges, railroad electronics, and monitoring and control equipment. Wabtec's transit business supplies replacement parts and repair services to operators of passenger transit systems. Major customers include ALSTOM, Electro-Motive Diesel, GE Infrastructure, and Trinity Industries. Wabtec garners about 70% of its sales in North America.

The global economic recession, which directly impacts the activity of the freight rail industry, has hammered the company's objectives for growth. In 2009 net sales decreased more than 10% from 2008. Wabtec's freight business took the brunt, slumping more than 20% as railroads tightened the purse on new equipment purchases. The erosion was offset, in part, by a 1.5%

increase in transit sales. Net income fell by more than 15% in 2009 from 2008.

Moving forward, Wabtec is keeping a close eye on the US federal government's $20 billion spending package dedicated to simulating freight and passenger transportation (passed in 2009). Its cost control measures include continuing to consolidate plant operations, cut headcount, and streamline manufacturing processes. Simultaneously, Wabtec is focused on extending its geographic presence along with speeding up development of new and aftermarket products and services though selective business acquisitions. Acquisitions are particularly scrutinized for their potential to increase Wabtec's customer base; currently, the company's five biggest customers collectively account for about 20% of sales.

To these ends, the company agreed to buy rail track and signal product supplier G&B Specialties for $35 million and electronic instrument maker Bach-Simpson for $45 million in late 2010. In 2009 the company's investment activities totaled more than $115 million, $92 million of which was used to acquire Unifin International, and its affiliate Cardinal Pumps and Exchangers. In 2008 investments topped $417 million. Wabtec acquired Poli SpA, an Italy-based rail-braking equipment company, for around $82 million. Taking a larger step, Standard Car Truck, an Illinois-based rail equipment supplier, was also purchased for about $302 million in cash.

HISTORY

The original Westinghouse Air Brake Company was one of 60 firms started by inventor extraordinaire George Westinghouse Jr., who first demonstrated his straight air brake in 1869. Before then, trains were stopped by workers in various cars turning brake wheels, a process that required stopping distances of up to a quarter-mile. American Standard (bathroom and kitchen fixtures, car braking systems — now named Trane Inc.) acquired the company during the 1960s.

WABCO was formed in 1990 when investors acquired the North American operations of American Standard's Railway Products Group (air brakes). Since its rebirth, WABCO expanded its worldwide presence with acquisitions such as Pulse (1995, event records and fuel-measuring devices), Australian firm Futuris Industrial Products (1996, rail brake shoes and disc brake pads), and Vapor (1996, railcar electronic door control systems). In 1997 WABCO added passenger transit air conditioning systems through its acquisitions of Stone Safety Service, Stone UK, and H.P. Srl, Italy's largest maker of door systems for passenger transit cars and buses.

In 1998 WABCO went on a buying spree, acquiring UK-based RFS, a rail engineering and services firm, the transit coupler product line of Hadady Corporation, the assets of Lokring (pipe fittings), Comet Industries' service centers (air brake repair), and the railroad electronics unit of Rockwell Collins. The final bill totaled some $113 million. That year WABCO also formed two joint ventures — WABCO/MPI de Mexico and Greysham Railway Friction Products (low-friction brake shoes, India).

WABCO laid off more than 185 workers in 1999 as it consolidated its acquisitions. It then announced it would merge with MotivePower Industries and take its name in a deal valued at

$634 million. An earnings shortfall at Motive-Power derailed that deal, and WABCO bought MotivePower for $475 million; the combined company changed its name to Westinghouse Air Brake Technologies and began doing business as Wabtec.

In keeping with its strategy to increase its international presence, the company signed a five-year supply contract with one of Australia's largest railroads, Freight Australia, in 2000.

William Kassling stepped down as CEO in 2001 but remained chairman, and Gregory Davies was promoted from president and COO to president and CEO. Davies stepped down for health reasons in 2004, however, and Kassling reassumed the reins as president and CEO. Davies died from a brain tumor that year.

In 2005 the company bought the assets of Italy-based railroad equipment maker Rütgers Rail.

In 2006 Kassling once again handed over the company's top executive role, this time to Albert Neupaver of AMETEK, an electronics manufacturer. Later that year the company's MotivePower subsidiary was awarded contracts worth $180 million to build locomotives for commuter rail lines in Utah and Southern California.

In 2006 Wabtec announced a restructuring plan that aimed to increase efficiency. The plan shuttered two Canadian production plants and moved their operations to lower-cost facilities. Some of the plants' production was outsourced. Later that year Wabtec paid $36 million to acquire forged brake rigging component manufacturer Schaefer Equipment.

As 2006 wound to a close, Wabtec acquired Germany's Becorit GmbH, a manufacturer of railway friction products (brake shoes, pads, and linings) for the European market. Wabtec paid the UK's BBA Aviation plc about $50 million for Becorit.

The following year Wabtec purchased California-based Rincon Corp., which made handicap ramps and lifts for North American and European markets, for nearly $74 million.

EXECUTIVES

Chairman: William E. Kassling, age 66
Vice Chairman: Emilio A. Fernandez, age 65
President, CEO, and Director: Albert J. Neupaver, age 59, $3,514,072 total compensation
SVP, CFO, and Secretary: Alvaro Garcia-Tunon, age 57, $1,326,702 total compensation
VP and Group Executive: Charles F. Kovac, age 53, $1,087,869 total compensation
VP and Group Executive: Richard A. Mathes, age 55, $842,704 total compensation
VP, Senior Counsel, and Assistant Secretary: David M. Seitz, age 45
VP Corporate Development: R. Mark Cox, age 42
VP and Treasurer: Keith P. Hildum, age 47
VP Transit Sales and Marketing: Michael J. Cassidy
VP Global Sourcing: John D. Whiteford
VP Sales, Freight: Mark J. Pace
VP Sales, Freight Group: Jeff W. Stearns
VP Wabtec Performance System: Jeffrey Langer
VP Human Resources: Scott E. Wahlstrom, age 46
VP International: Ronald L. Witt
VP Finance and Corporate Controller: Patrick D. Dugan, age 43
VP Investor Relations and Corporate Communications: Timothy R. Wesley, age 48
Auditors: Ernst & Young LLP

LOCATIONS

HQ: Westinghouse Air Brake Technologies Corporation
1001 Air Brake Ave., Wilmerding, PA 15148
Phone: 412-825-1000   **Fax:** 412-825-1019
Web: www.wabtec.com

2009 Sales

	$ mil.	% of total
North America		
US	838.3	60
Canada	134.8	10
Mexico	31.5	2
UK	139.8	10
Australia	59.0	4
Germany	33.5	2
Other countries	164.7	12
Total	**1,401.6**	**100**

PRODUCTS/OPERATIONS

2009 Sales

	$ mil.	% of total
Transit group	813.2	58
Freight group	588.4	42
Total	**1,401.6**	**100**

Selected Products

Transit group
  Air compressors
  Climate control and door equipment
  Collection equipment
  Couplers
  Disc brakes
  Electronic brake equipment
  Monitoring equipment
  Pneumatic controls
  Tread brakes
  Wheels
Freight group
  Electronics (on-board systems and braking)
  Freight Cars
    Air brake equipment
    Articulated couplers
    Brake valves
    Composite brake shoes
    Draft gears
    Hand brakes
    Slack adjusters
  Locomotives
    Air brake equipment
    Air dryers
    Alternators
    Brake cylinders
    Cooling equipment
    Diesel engines
    Gearing
    Generators
    Monitoring and control equipment
    Traction motors
    Turbochargers

COMPETITORS

A. Stucki Company
ALSTOM
Cardo
Construcciones y Auxiliar de Ferrocarriles
Electro-Motive
Faiveley
GE Infrastructure
Greenbrier Rail Services
L. B. Foster
New York Air Brake
SORL Auto Parts
Standard Steel
Trinity Industries
Vossloh
Woodward Governor

HISTORICAL FINANCIALS

Company Type: Public

Income Statement

FYE: December 31

	REVENUE ($ mil.)	NET INCOME ($ mil.)	NET PROFIT MARGIN	EMPLOYEES
12/09	1,402	115	8.2%	5,812
12/08	1,575	131	8.3%	7,295
12/07	1,360	110	8.1%	6,023
12/06	1,088	85	7.8%	5,317
12/05	1,034	56	5.4%	5,229
Annual Growth	**7.9%**	**19.8%**	**—**	**2.7%**

2009 Year-End Financials

Debt ratio: 46.2%
Return on equity: 16.2%
Cash ($ mil.): 189
Current ratio: 2.26
Long-term debt ($ mil.): 359
No. of shares (mil.): 48
Dividends
  Yield: 0.1%
  Payout: 1.7%
Market value ($ mil.): 1,957

Stock History

NYSE: WAB

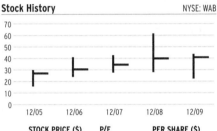

	STOCK PRICE ($) FY Close	P/E High/Low		PER SHARE ($) Earnings	Dividends	Book Value
12/09	40.84	18	10	2.39	0.04	16.21
12/08	39.75	23	11	2.67	0.04	13.47
12/07	34.44	19	13	2.23	0.04	12.88
12/06	30.38	23	14	1.73	0.04	9.80
12/05	26.90	25	14	1.17	0.04	7.91
Annual Growth	**11.0%**	**—**	**—**	**19.6%**	**0.0%**	**19.6%**

Weyerhaeuser Company

If a tree falls in a Weyerhaeuser forest, someone *is* there to hear it — and he has a chainsaw. Weyerhaeuser, one of the top US forest products companies, operates along several business lines, including wood products (lumber, plywood, and other building materials) and cellulose fibers or pulp products. Also, its timberlands division manages some 6 million acres of company-owned US timberland and more than 15 million acres of leased Canadian timberland. Its real estate unit develops housing and master-planned communities.

Weyerhaeuser has spent the last few years responding to the economic downturn. Most of its business is strongly dependent on the housing market and when it crashed, Weyerhaeuser was forced to drastically reduce costs, retool some of its operations, and sell other noncore assets.

In the housing business, the company and its Weyerhaeuser Real Estate division have been severely affected by the downturn in the home building market. It scaled back on its housing business, delayed land purchases, and limited housing starts in 2007 and 2008. In the company's timberland division it has shuttered plants and deferred harvest levels by more than 30%.

Since 2007 Weyerhaeuser has sold a slew of businesses including its fine paper operations and dozens of distribution centers in Canada and the US. It also sold its containerboard packaging and recycling operations to International Paper for $6 billion. The company pulled out of New Zealand and Australia, opting to focus much of its overseas timber operations in Uruguay. Weyerhaeuser used much of the proceeds from the sale of its businesses to pay down debt.

As part of its ongoing efforts to streamline operations, the company sold its Trus Joist commercial business, including four manufacturing plants, to Atlas Holdings. In 2009 Weyerhaeuser announced it was closing its trucking division, based in Millersburg, Oregon. Also that year Weyerhaeuser announced plans to sell non-strategic timberland in Oregon. In 2010 Weyerhaueser announced plans to sell its short line freight railroad holdings to Patriot Rail. The deal includes 160 miles of track in four states.

HISTORY

Frederick Weyerhaeuser, a 24-year-old German immigrant, bought his first lumberyard in 1858 in Illinois. He also participated in joint logging ventures in Illinois, Minnesota, and Wisconsin. In 1900 he and 15 partners bought 900,000 timbered acres from the Northern Pacific Railway. The venture was named Weyerhaeuser Timber Company.

During the Depression the business recouped losses in the deflated lumber market by selling wood pulp. Frederick's grandson, J. P. "Phil" Weyerhaeuser Jr., took over as CEO in 1933.

Diversification into the production of containerboard (1949), particleboard (1955), paper (1956), and other products led the company to drop "Timber" from its name in 1959. In 1963 Weyerhaeuser went public and opened its first overseas office in Tokyo.

In the 1970s George Weyerhaeuser (Phil's son) diversified further to insulate the company from the forest-product industry's cyclical nature and ended up with a mishmash of businesses and products, from private-label disposable diapers to pet supplies.

The eruption of Mount St. Helens in 1980 destroyed 68,000 acres of Weyerhaeuser timber. That disaster and the soft US lumber market depressed the company's earnings through 1982. Weyerhaeuser reduced its workforce by 25% during this period.

Under John Creighton (president since 1988 and CEO from 1991 until 1998), Weyerhaeuser refocused on forest products and organized along product lines rather than by geographic region. Less-successful ventures were put up for sale, including milk carton, hardwood, and gypsum board plants. The company took a $497 million pretax charge in 1989 related to the decision to close unprofitable operations.

In 1992 the company outbid Georgia-Pacific, paying $600 million for two pulp mills, three sawmills, and more than 200,000 acres of forest land to boost its market-pulp capacity by 40%. The following year the company sold its disposable-diaper business through a public offering in a new company, Paragon Trade Brands.

The federal government in 1995 allowed the company to harvest trees in an area inhabited by the endangered northern spotted owl. The move angered environmental groups. In 1998 Steve Rogel, a veteran from competitor Willamette, succeeded Creighton as CEO and became the first outsider to head Weyerhaeuser.

In 1999 Weyerhaeuser paid $2.45 billion for Canada's MacMillan Bloedel, and early in 2000 it acquired TJ International, 51% owner of leading engineered lumber products company Trus Joist MacMillan (Weyerhaeuser already owned the other 49%).

After a protracted courtship, in March 2002 Weyerhaeuser acquired Oregon-based Willamette Industries in a $6.1 billion cash deal. The company closed three North American plants (in Colorado, Louisiana, and Oregon) later that year. On the heels of the deals for MacMillan Bloedel, Trus Joist MacMillan, and Willamette, Weyerhaeuser moved to pay down debt. It sold more than 320,000 acres of the timberland (in the Carolinas and Tennessee) that it acquired with the Willamette purchase.

In 2003 Weyerhaeuser sold its Nipigon Multiply hardwood plywood underlayment operation in Ontario, Canada, to Columbia Forest Products. Late in the year the company closed its fine-paper operations in Longview, Washington (eliminating 119 jobs there). Altogether, Weyerhaeuser closed 12 facilities and sold about 444,000 acres of non-strategic timberlands in 2003.

In 2004 Weyerhaeuser sold roughly 270,000 acres of timberlands in central Georgia for about $400 million to investment and property firms in Georgia and South Carolina. Early in 2005 Weyerhaeuser agreed to sell five Canadian sawmills, two finishing plants, 635,000 acres of timber, and some government land-cutting rights to Brascan for $970 million. Weyerhaeuser also closed a Saskatchewan pulp and paper mill in 2006, cutting 690 jobs.

In 2007 Weyerhaeuser merged its fine paper business with Domtar. According to the terms of the $3.3 billion deal, Weyerhaeuser shareholders got a 55% stake in the renamed company, Domtar Corporation. Weyerhaeuser controls the board, and several Weyerhaeuser executives manage the company.

EXECUTIVES

Chairman: Charles R. (Chuck) Williamson, age 61
President, CEO, and Director: Daniel S. (Dan) Fulton, age 61, $4,870,566 total compensation
EVP and CFO: Patricia M. (Patty) Bedient, age 56, $1,444,921 total compensation
EVP Forest Products: Thomas F. (Tom) Gideon, age 58, $2,386,329 total compensation
SVP Timberlands: James M. (Mike) Branson, age 53, $1,416,553 total compensation
SVP Cellulose Fibers:
  Srinivasan (Shaker) Chandrasekaran, age 60, $1,282,127 total compensation
SVP Corporate Affairs: Ernesta Ballard, age 64
SVP Research and Development and CTO:
  Miles P. Drake, age 60
SVP and General Counsel: Sandy D. McDade, age 58
SVP Human Resources: John Hooper, age 55

VP Information Technology and CIO: Kevin Shearer, age 54
VP and Chief Accounting Officer: Jeanne M. Hillman, age 50
VP Investor Relations: Kathryn F. McAuley
VP and Treasurer: Jeffrey W. Nitta
VP, Secretary, and Assistant General Counsel:
  Claire S. Grace
President and CEO, Weyerhaeuser Real Estate Company (WRECO): Lawrence B. (Larry) Burrows, age 57, $1,390,621 total compensation
Manager Investor Relations: April Meier
Director Company Communications: Bruce Amundson
Auditors: KPMG LLP

LOCATIONS

HQ: Weyerhaeuser Company
33663 Weyerhaeuser Way South
Federal Way, WA 98003
Phone: 253-924-2345   **Fax:** 253-924-2685
Web: www.weyerhaeuser.com

2009 Sales

	$ mil.	% of total
US	3,961	71
Japan	485	9
Europe	277	5
China	209	4
Canada	209	4
Other countries	387	7
Total	**5,528**	**100**

PRODUCTS/OPERATIONS

2009 Sales

	$ mil.	% of total
Forest products	4,624	84
Real estate	904	16
Total	**5,528**	**100**

Selected Products and Services

Wood and Building Products
  Engineered lumber products
  Flooring
  Lumber (softwood and hardwood)
  Oriented Strand Board
  Plywood
  Structural panels
  Veneer

Cellulose Fiber and White Paper
  Paper and liquid packaging
  Paper
  Pulp
  Textiles

Real Estate and Related Assets
  Master-planned communities
  Multifamily homes
  Residential lots
  Single-family homes

Timberlands
  Chips
  Logs
  Mineral resources
  Seedlings
  Weyerhaeser Select Douglas Fir seed

Other
  Recycling
  Transportation

Selected Subsidiaries

Columbia & Cowlitz Railway Company
DeQueen & Eastern Railroad Company
Golden Triangle Railroad
MacMillan Bloedel Pembroke Limited Partnership
  (Canada)
Mississippi & Skuna Valley Railroad Company
North Pacific Paper Corporation (50%, joint venture
  with Nippon Paper)
Westwood Shipping Lines, Inc.
Weyerhaeuser Real Estate Company

HISTORICAL FINANCIALS

Company Type: Public

Income Statement

FYE: Last Sunday in December

	REVENUE ($ mil.)	NET INCOME ($ mil.)	NET PROFIT MARGIN	EMPLOYEES
12/09	5,528	(568)	—	14,900
12/08	8,018	(1,176)	—	19,850
12/07	16,308	790	4.8%	37,900
12/06	21,896	453	2.1%	46,700
12/05	22,629	733	3.2%	49,900
Annual Growth	(29.7%)	—	—	(26.1%)

2009 Year-End Financials

Debt ratio: 140.5%
Return on equity: —
Cash ($ mil.): 1,869
Current ratio: 3.88
Long-term debt ($ mil.): 5,683

No. of shares (mil.): 212
Dividends
　Yield: 1.4%
　Payout: —
Market value ($ mil.): 9,129

Stock History

NYSE: WY

	STOCK PRICE ($) FY Close	P/E High/Low	PER SHARE ($) Earnings	PER SHARE ($) Dividends	PER SHARE ($) Book Value
12/09	43.14	— —	(2.58)	0.60	19.11
12/08	30.61	— —	(5.57)	2.40	22.75
12/07	73.74	24 17	3.59	2.40	37.72
12/06	70.65	41 29	1.84	2.20	42.93
12/05	66.34	24 20	2.98	1.90	46.31
Annual Growth	(10.2%)	— —	—	(25.0%)	(19.9%)

Whirlpool Corporation

With brand names recognized by just about anyone who has ever separated dark colors from light, Whirlpool is one of the world's top home appliance makers. It manufactures washers, dryers, refrigerators, air conditioners, dishwashers, freezers, microwave ovens, ranges, trash compactors, air purifiers, and more. In addition to Whirlpool, the company sells its products under a bevy of brand names, including KitchenAid, Maytag, Jenn-Air, Roper, Amana, and Magic Chef.

To stay competitive, Whirlpool continues to pump out new products and improve existing ones by investing in research and development. Despite the effort, revenues have fallen. The company has pointed to turbulent economic conditions worldwide, especially in its largest markets (the US and Europe), regarding the declining demand.

Whirlpool has continued to grow in Latin America, where it is a key player, as well as in emerging Asian markets, primarily India, where the appliance industry has made steady gains over the years. Whirlpool's also expanding its portfolio of brand names in 2010 by purchasing the rights to the Privileg home appliances brand from Otto, a German mail order company.

Whirlpool, whose manufacturing footprint covers a dozen countries, has been streamlining its operations in response to reduced consumer spending on its big-ticket items. To this end, the company closed its refrigerator factory in Evansville, Indiana, in June 2010 and moved production to Mexico, where costs are lower; some 1,100 jobs were lost as a result of the move. It's also looking to stop production at a machining plant in Benton Harbor, Michigan, by early 2011, eliminating about 215 jobs there. The two shutdowns follow roughly 5,000 job cuts worldwide from 2008 to the end of 2009 as part of Whirlpool's restructuring efforts.

Although it markets its goods in nearly every country worldwide, Whirlpool benefits from a healthy relationship with American mainstay Sears. The retailer stocks the Whirlpool and KitchenAid brands and generates about 10% of Whirlpool's revenue.

HISTORY

Brothers Fred and Lou Upton and their uncle, Emory Upton, founded the Upton Machine Company, manufacturer of electric motor-driven washing machines, in 1911 in St. Joseph, Michigan. Sears, Roebuck and Co. began buying their products five years later, and by 1925 the company was supplying all of Sears' washers. The Uptons combined their company with the Nineteen Hundred Washer Company in 1929 to form the Nineteen Hundred Corporation, the world's largest washing machine company.

Sears and Nineteen Hundred prospered during the Great Depression, and during WWII Nineteen Hundred's factories produced war materials. In 1948 it began selling its first automatic washing machine (introduced a year earlier) under the Whirlpool brand. In 1950 the company changed its name to Whirlpool following the success of the product, and introduced its first automatic dryer.

During the 1950s and 1960s Whirlpool became a full-line appliance manufacturer while continuing as Sears' principal Kenmore appliance supplier. In 1955 the company bought

Seeger Refrigerator Company and the stove and air-conditioning interests of RCA. Three years later it made its first investment in Multibras Eletrodomésticos, an appliance maker in Brazil. (It has increased that investment over the years.) Other purchases included the gas refrigeration and ice-maker manufacturing facilities of Servel (1958); a majority interest in Heil-Quaker, makers of central heaters and space heaters (1964); Sears' major television set supplier, Warwick Electronics (1966); and 33% of Canadian appliance maker John Inglis Company (1969). It made a deal with Sony in 1973 for the distribution of Whirlpool-brand products in Japan. Whirlpool sold its TV manufacturing business to SANYO of Japan three years later.

Between 1981 and 1991, despite a static US market, Whirlpool's sales tripled to almost $6.6 billion. In 1986 the firm bought top-end appliance manufacturer KitchenAid (from Dart and Kraft). David Whitwam was appointed CEO in 1987. Whirlpool took over total ownership of Inglis in 1990.

The company formed Whirlpool Europe, a joint venture with Philips Electronics, in 1989; in 1991 it bought out Philips. In 1993 it took control of appliance marketer SAGAD of Argentina.

Whirlpool acquired control of Kelvinator of India in 1994 and formed a joint venture in China with Shenzhen Petrochemical Holdings in 1995 to produce air conditioners.

In 1997 Whirlpool initiated a restructuring (due to losses from its foreign operations) that included plant closures and substantial layoffs (as much as 10% of its workforce). The next year Whirlpool sold its appliance financing subsidiary to Transamerica. The company also began using a new, more efficient product development model in 1998, similar to one used in the auto industry. In 2000 Whirlpool launched the Cielo Bath line of jetted tubs.

Another global restructuring plan swept through the company in 2000, resulting in significant pretax charges ($373 million, incurred in 2001 and 2002) and the elimination of about 6,000 employees by October 2003.

In February 2002 Whirlpool bought the remaining 51% of Vitromatic it didn't already own. (Vitromatic — the second-largest appliance manufacturer in Mexico — is now called Whirlpool Mexico.) In March the company purchased 95% of Polar, Poland's second-largest appliance maker.

Whirlpool acquired Maytag in early 2006 for about $1.9 billion. Buying Maytag also spurred Whirlpool to streamline operations and purge staff. In 2006 it laid off some 4,500 employees, consolidated duplicate functions related to administration and manufacturing, and shuttered some offices, including a Maytag research and development center based in Newton, Illinois. Whirlpool shuttered Maytag's Iowa-based administrative offices and moved them to Michigan and other locations. The company cut 700 jobs at several Tennessee plants the following year.

In December 2007 Whirlpool acquired a minority stake in Elica Group in its effort to extend its reach into the global air ventilation market.

In 2008 the company formed a 50-50 joint venture with China's Hisense-Kelon Electrical Holdings to make and sell home appliances there.

In June 2010 Whirlpool closed its refrigerator factory in Evansville, Indiana; some 1,100 US jobs were lost as a result of the move.

EXECUTIVES

Chairman and CEO: Jeff M. Fettig, age 52,
$12,510,916 total compensation
EVP and CFO: Roy W. Templin, age 49,
$2,932,841 total compensation
EVP; President, Whirlpool North America:
Marc R. Bitzer, age 45, $2,826,785 total compensation
EVP; President, Latin America: Jose A. Drummond,
age 45
EVP; President, Europe: Bracken Darrell, age 47
EVP Global Product Organization:
David T. (Dave) Szczupak, age 54
SVP Global Human Resources: David A. (Dave) Binkley
SVP Corporate Affairs, General Counsel, and Secretary:
Daniel F. Hopp, age 62
VP Human Resources, North American Region:
Lynanne Kunkel
VP Government Relations: Tom Catania
VP Technology: Henry (Hank) Marcy
VP Innovation and Whirlpool University:
Nancy A. Tennet
VP North American Manufacturing Operations:
Al Holaday
Corporate Secretary and Group Counsel:
Robert J. LaForest
Investor Relations: Gregory A. (Greg) Fritz
Director; President, Whirlpool International:
Michael A. (Mike) Todman, age 53,
$4,044,413 total compensation
Auditors: Ernst & Young LLP

LOCATIONS

HQ: Whirlpool Corporation
2000 N. M-63, Benton Harbor, MI 49022
Phone: 269-923-5000 **Fax:** 269-923-3722
Web: www.whirlpoolcorp.com

2009 Sales

	$ mil.	% of total
North America	9,592	56
Latin America	3,705	21
Europe	3,338	19
Asia	654	4
Adjustments	(190)	—
Total	**17,099**	**100**

PRODUCTS/OPERATIONS

2009 Sales

	$ mil.	% of total
Home laundry appliances	5,345	31
Home refrigerators & freezers	5,200	30
Home cooking appliances	2,809	17
Other	3,745	22
Total	**17,099**	**100**

Selected Product Lines

Air conditioning equipment
Cooking appliances
Dishwashers
Freezers
Laundry appliances
Mixers
Refrigerators
Small household appliances

Selected Brands

Acros	Kenmore
Admiral	KIC
Amana (excluding	KitchenAid
commercial business)	Laden
Bauknecht	Magic Chef
Brastemp	Maytag
Consul	Polar
Eslabon de Lujo	Roper
Estate	Supermatic
Inglis	Whirlpool
Jenn-Air	

COMPETITORS

BSH Bosch und Siemens Hausgeräte
Candy Group
Daewoo Electronics
Electrolux
Electrolux Home Appliances China
Fisher & Paykel Appliances Holdings
GE Appliances & Lighting
Goodman Manufacturing
Gree Electrical Appliances
GuangDong Midea
Haier Group
Hitachi
Indesit
LG Electronics
Panasonic Corp
Samsung Electronics America
SANYO
Sears Holdings
Sharp Corp.
Sub-Zero
Viking Range

HISTORICAL FINANCIALS

Company Type: Public

Income Statement

FYE: December 31

	REVENUE ($ mil.)	NET INCOME ($ mil.)	NET PROFIT MARGIN	EMPLOYEES
12/09	17,099	354	2.1%	67,000
12/08	18,907	418	2.2%	70,000
12/07	19,408	640	3.3%	73,000
12/06	18,080	433	2.4%	73,000
12/05	14,317	422	2.9%	66,000
Annual Growth	**4.5%**	**(4.3%)**	**—**	**0.4%**

2009 Year-End Financials

Debt ratio: 68.3%   No. of shares (mil.): 76
Return on equity: 10.6%   Dividends
Cash ($ mil.): 1,380   Yield: 2.1%
Current ratio: 1.18   Payout: 39.6%
Long-term debt ($ mil.): 2,502   Market value ($ mil.): 6,131

Stock History

NYSE: WHR

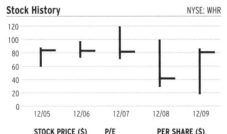

	STOCK PRICE ($) FY Close	P/E High/Low		PER SHARE ($) Earnings	Dividends	Book Value
12/09	80.66	20	4	4.34	1.72	48.20
12/08	41.35	18	5	5.50	1.72	39.55
12/07	81.63	15	9	8.01	1.72	51.45
12/06	83.02	17	13	5.67	1.72	43.19
12/05	83.76	14	10	6.19	1.72	22.96
Annual Growth	**(0.9%)**	**—**	**—**	**(8.5%)**	**0.0%**	**20.4%**

Whole Foods Market

With food and other items that are free of pesticides, preservatives, sweeteners, and cruelty, Whole Foods Market knows more about guiltless eating and shopping than most retailers. The world's #1 natural foods chain by far — now that it has digested its main rival Wild Oats Markets — the company operates about 295 stores in 38 US states, as well as in Canada and the UK. The stores emphasize perishable products, which account for about two-thirds of sales. Whole Foods Market offers more than 2,400 items in four lines of private-label products (such as the premium Whole Foods line). Founded in 1980, Whole Foods Market pioneered the supermarket concept in natural and organic foods retailing.

Rising food prices, increased competition from traditional supermarket operators, and the sharp downturn in the US economy put the brakes on Whole Foods Market's impressive track record of outperforming the rest of the grocery market. The company got a shot in the arm in late 2008 when the private equity firm Green Equity Investors invested $425 million in Whole Foods, thereby acquiring about a 17% stake in the chain. In response to the decrease in consumer confidence that sent many grocery shoppers to Wal-Mart and other discount grocery chains in search of bargains, Whole Foods has worked hard to emphasize its value proposition and shed its pricey image as "Whole Paycheck." Also, to lure shoppers and boost profit margins, Whole Foods has been aggressively expanding its range of private-label items, which includes the 365 Everyday Value and 365 Organic brands.

While growth has slowed from historic levels, natural and organic food is still one of the fastest-growing segments of the grocery business. However, with the incursion of traditional grocery chains such as Safeway and Kroger, and retail giant Wal-Mart (the nation's #1 seller of groceries) into the natural and organic food space, Whole Foods is facing a more mature and crowded retail market going forward.

In another move to put its recent troubles behind it, in late 2009 Whole Foods' enigmatic founder, vegan-capitalist John Mackey, voluntarily relinquished the chairman's title to lead director John Elstrott. (The move came about two years after the company's shareholders proposed splitting the offices of chairman and CEO.) In May 2010 the board promoted Walter Robb to co-CEO, a job he now shares with Mackey.

Recent troubles for Mackey included an investigation by the Securities and Exchange Commission over his use of a fake online identity, and a battle with the Federal Trade Commission over the Wild Oats takeover. The $565 million acquisition of Wild Oats in 2007 firmly anchored Whole Foods atop the natural and organic food chain and gave Whole Foods about 70 new stores in each of its operating regions, as well as stores in desirable new regions, such as the Pacific Northwest and Florida. However, the purchase sparked a protracted battle with the FTC, which attempted to block and later undo the merger on antitrust grounds. The dispute was eventually settled in 2009, with Whole Foods agreeing to close 32 Wild Oats stores.

After announcing plans to open hundreds more stores across Europe, international growth appears to have stalled, at least for now. Expanding across the Pacific, the organic grocer opened its first stores in Hawaii in 2010.

HISTORY

With a $10,000 loan from his father, John Mackey started Safer Way Natural Foods in Austin, Texas, in 1978. Despite struggling, Mackey dreamed of opening a larger, supermarket-sized natural foods store. Two years later Safer Way merged with Clarksville Natural Grocery, and Whole Foods Market was born. Led by Mackey, that year it opened an 11,000-sq.-ft. supermarket in a counterculture hotbed of Austin. The store was an instant success, and a second store was added 18 months later in suburban Austin.

The company slowly expanded in Texas, opening or buying stores in Houston in 1984 and Dallas in 1986. Whole Foods expanded into Louisiana in 1988 with the purchase of like-named Whole Food Co., a single New Orleans store owned by Peter Roy (who served as the company's president from 1993 to 1998). Sticking to university towns, Whole Foods added another store in California the next year and acquired Wellspring Grocery (two stores, North Carolina) in 1991. In 1992 it debuted its first private-label products under the Whole Foods name. Seeking capital to expand even more, the company raised $23 million by going public in early 1992 with 12 stores.

Every competitor in the fragmented health foods industry became a potential acquisition, and the chain began growing rapidly. In 1992 Whole Foods bought the six-store Bread & Circus chain in New England. The next year it added Mrs. Gooch's Natural Foods Markets (seven stores in the Los Angeles area). Its biggest acquisition came in 1996, when it bought Fresh Fields, the second-largest US natural foods chain (22 stores on the East Coast and in Chicago). In 1997 it introduced the less-expensive 365 brand private labels.

The company paid $146 million in 1997 for Amrion, a maker of nutraceuticals and other nutritional supplements. In 1998 Roy resigned as president and was replaced by Chris Hitt. Hitt resigned in mid-2001, and Mackey took over his duties. In 2002 Whole Foods crossed the border to Canada. Its first foreign store opened in downtown Toronto in May of that year.

In 2003 Mackey was named Entrepreneur of the Year by consulting firm Ernst & Young. In February 2004 Whole Foods opened a 59,000-sq.-ft. store in the new Time Warner Center in Manhattan. The new store, which includes a 248-seat cafe, sushi bar, wine shop, and gourmet bakery, is the largest supermarket in New York City. That month the company acquired the UK organic-food retailer Fresh & Wild.

In January 2005 Whole Foods launched the Animal Compassion Foundation, an independent, not-for-profit organization dedicated to the compassionate treatment of livestock.

In August 2007 Whole Foods acquired its main competitor, Boulder, Colorado-based Wild Oats Markets. In early October the company sold 35 Henry's Farmers Market and Sun Harvest stores to a subsidiary of Los Angeles-based Smart & Final. The stores, in California and Texas, were acquired along with Wild Oats.

Blaming the poor economy, the company announced the layoffs of some 50 employees at its Austin headquarters in August 2008.

For the first time in its 29-year history, Whole Foods reported negative same-store sales in the quarter ended December 2008 as traffic in its stores fell.

EXECUTIVES

Chairman: John B. Elstrott, age 61
Co-CEO: Walter E. Robb IV, age 57, $781,352 total compensation
Co-CEO and Director: John P. Mackey, age 56, $710,076 total compensation
President and COO: A. C. Gallo, age 56, $782,535 total compensation
EVP and CFO: Glenda J. Chamberlain, age 56, $655,261 total compensation
EVP Growth and Business Development: James P. (Jim) Sud, age 57, $802,864 total compensation
VP and CIO: Michael (Mike) Clifford
Senior Global VP Purchasing, Distribution, and Marketing: Michael Besancon, age 63
Global VP Construction and Store Development: Lee Matecko
Global VP Quality Standards and Public Affairs: Margaret Wittenberg
Global VP Investor Relations: Cynthia M. (Cindy) McCann
Global VP Distribution: Bart Beilman
Global VP Procurement and Perishables: Edmund LaMacchia
Global VP Procurement, Non Perishables: Jim Speirs
Global VP, Private Label: Bruce Silverman
Auditors: Ernst & Young LLP

LOCATIONS

HQ: Whole Foods Market, Inc.
550 Bowie St., Austin, TX 78703
Phone: 512-477-4455   **Fax:** 512-482-7000
Web: www.wholefoodsmarket.com

2009 Sales

	% of total
US	97
Canada & UK	3
Total	**100**

2009 Stores

	No.
US	
California	54
Massachusetts	20
Colorado	19
Florida	16
Illinois	16
Texas	14
New Jersey	10
New York	9
Virginia	9
Arizona	7
Georgia	7
Maryland	7
Pennsylvania	7
Ohio	6
Oregon	6
Connecticut	5
Michigan	5
Nevada	5
North Carolina	5
Washington	5
New Mexico	4
Utah	4
District of Columbia	3
Louisiana	3
Missouri	3
Rhode Island	3
Tennessee	3
Indiana	2
Kansas	2
Kentucky	2
Minnesota	2
South Carolina	2
Wisconsin	2
Other states	6
Canada	6
UK	5
Total	**284**

PRODUCTS/OPERATIONS

2009 Sales

	% of total
Grocery	34
Prepared foods	19
Other perishables	47
Total	**100**

COMPETITORS

Ahold USA	Loblaw
Albertsons	Marks & Spencer
AMCON Distributing	Minyard Group
Arden Group	NBTY
Bristol Farms	Publix
Costco Wholesale	Safeway
Delhaize America	Shaw's
Earth Fare	Sobeys
Fiesta Mart	SUPERVALU
Forever Living	Trader Joe's
GNC	United Supermarkets
H-E-B	Wal-Mart
Kroger	Winn-Dixie

HISTORICAL FINANCIALS

Company Type: Public

Income Statement

FYE: Last Sunday in September

	REVENUE ($ mil.)	NET INCOME ($ mil.)	NET PROFIT MARGIN	EMPLOYEES
9/09	8,032	147	1.8%	52,500
9/08	7,954	115	1.4%	52,900
9/07	6,592	183	2.8%	52,600
9/06	5,607	204	3.6%	39,500
9/05	4,701	136	2.9%	38,000
Annual Growth	**14.3%**	**1.9%**	**—**	**8.4%**

2009 Year-End Financials

Debt ratio: 45.4%
Return on equity: 9.4%
Cash ($ mil.): 430
Current ratio: 1.54
Long-term debt ($ mil.): 739
No. of shares (mil.): 171
Dividends
　Yield: 0.0%
　Payout: —
Market value ($ mil.): 5,227

Stock History

NASDAQ (GS): WFMI

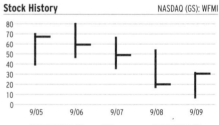

	STOCK PRICE ($) FY Close	P/E High/Low		PER SHARE ($) Earnings	Dividends	Book Value
9/09	30.49	37	8	0.85	0.00	9.49
9/08	20.03	65	21	0.82	0.78	8.78
9/07	48.96	51	28	1.29	0.69	8.51
9/06	59.43	57	33	1.41	0.57	8.19
9/05	67.22	71	40	0.99	0.34	7.97
Annual Growth	**(17.9%)**	**—**	**—**	**(3.7%)**	**—**	**4.5%**

Williams Companies

Williams Companies has several parts, but they all add up to the delivery of energy and profits. Williams is engaged in gas marketing, and exploration and production. Its midstream unit gathers, stores, and processes natural gas and natural gas liquids (NGLs) and operates refineries, ethanol plants, and terminals. Williams has proved reserves of 4.3 trillion cu. ft. of natural gas equivalent. The company's gas pipeline unit operates three pipeline companies (Transco, Northwest, and Gulfstream). Williams' US pipeline operations are concentrated in the Northwest, the Rockies, the Gulf Coast, and the East. In 2010 the company merged its Williams Pipeline Partners unit into Williams Partners.

The move allows The Williams Companies to pool its pipelines assets (including 14,600 miles of interstate natural gas pipeline and 8,500 miles of gas gathering lines), streamline its operations, and cut costs. The $12 billion restructuring establishes Williams Partners as a major integrated interstate pipeline and midstream player. The Williams Companies owns 84% of the new expanded entity, up from 24% of Williams Partners in early 2010.

The restructuring, coupled with the impact of the global recession putting downward pressure on commodity prices, meant The Williams Companies' 2009 sales and income were significantly lower than in 2008.

In 2008 the company acquired assets amounting to 175 billion cu. ft. of natural gas reserves in the Barnett Shale from Aspect Abundant Shale for about $147 million. The move increased Williams' holdings in the Barnett Shale by nearly two-thirds, bolstering its reserve base.

Williams planned to sell its power business (Williams Power) as part of a strategic plan to emphasize its core natural gas businesses, but dropped the idea in 2004, citing poor market conditions. However, in 2007 it finally did sell this unit to Bear Stearns' energy division for about $500 million. In 2007 Williams expanded its gas supply service to the US Northeast.

HISTORY

David Williams and his brother Miller were working for a construction contractor in 1908 when the contractor pulled out of a job paving sidewalks in Fort Smith, Arkansas. The brothers formed the Williams Brothers Corporation and completed the job themselves. As the oil industry grew in Oklahoma, the brothers cashed in on the boom by building pipelines. Williams Brothers relocated its head office to Tulsa in 1924.

The two brothers sold the company in 1949 to David Jr., nephews John and Charles, and six company managers. It went public in 1957. In 1966 Williams Brothers bought its first gas pipeline network (the longest in the US), the Great Lakes Pipe Line Company (renamed Williams Brothers Pipe Line Company).

In 1969 Williams Brothers began entering new markets. It bought a metals processor, a propane dealer, and fertilizer companies, including Agrico Chemical (1972), and changed its name to The Williams Companies to reflect its new diversity. In the wake of the Arab oil embargo, it formed Williams Exploration in 1974 to find natural gas. Two years later Williams became part-owner of the US's #1 coal producer, Peabody Coal.

During a 1980s energy sales slump, Williams began dumping its commodity businesses (including Agrico and Peabody in 1987). Instead, it went into telecommunications in 1985, forming Williams Telecommunications (WilTel) to install fiber optics inside abandoned pipelines. Its 1989 purchase of fiber-optic firm LIGHTNET brought its network miles to 11,000.

In 1995 the company acquired Transcontinental Gas Pipe Line Corp. (Transco), extending its reach into the East, and Pekin Energy, the country's #2 ethanol producer.

The Williams Companies sold WilTel's fiber-optic network in 1995 to telecom company LDDS (which became WorldCom) for $2.5 billion — but excluded from the sale a 9,700-mile single fiber-optic strand along the original network. In 1996 Williams acquired telecom services company Cycle-Sat, and the next year Williams Communications and Northern Telecom (later Nortel Networks) formed Williams Communications Solutions to distribute and integrate telecom networking equipment.

In 1998 Williams bought fellow Tulsa company MAPCO for more than $3 billion, giving it the US's largest US pipeline system moving propane and butane, a leading US propane retailer (ThermoGas), refineries, and gas stations.

To re-enter the telecom business, Williams established a new subsidiary, Williams Communications, in 1998. To raise money to build out its network, the company sold a minority stake in Williams Communications in a 1999 IPO. That year it also sold ThermoGas to Ferrellgas in a $444 million deal. The next year it joined Duke Energy in a $1.5 billion venture to build a gas pipeline across the Gulf of Mexico to link Alabama to Florida markets.

Williams spun off its stake in Williams Communications (later renamed WilTel Communications) to shareholders in 2001. Williams also shed energy assets that year: Its Williams Express sold its 186 MAPCO gas stations to The Israel Fuel Corporation for about $147 million. The company moved to expand its natural gas reserves significantly by buying producer Barrett Resources for about $2.5 billion in cash and stock and $300 million in assumed debt.

Also in 2001 Williams chairman and CEO Keith Bailey announced plans to retire the next year. The heir apparent, EVP Steven Malcolm, was given Bailey's title of president. The day after Malcolm's promotion, he announced that the company's energy marketing and trading operations would become a separate business unit. Malcolm was named CEO in January 2002.

As a way to pare down its debt load, that year Williams sold its Kern River interstate natural gas pipeline to Berkshire Hathaway's MidAmerican Energy Holdings unit for $450 million in cash and $510 million in assumed debt. It also sold its Williams Pipe Line unit (refined petroleum products) to Williams Energy Partners LP for $1 billion, and its stakes in two pipeline companies (Mid-America Pipeline and Seminole Pipeline) to Enterprise Products Partners, for about $1.2 billion.

Also in 2002, in addition to raising cash from asset sales, Williams secured commitments from mega-investor Warren Buffett and a number of banks to pony up $2 billion in new financing to help it restructure its operations.

In 2003 Williams sold its wholesale propane assets and marketing business to SemGroup. It also sold a gas processing plant in Oklahoma to Eagle Rock Energy.

EXECUTIVES

Chairman, President, and CEO:
 Steven J. (Steve) Malcolm, age 61,
 $9,479,835 total compensation
SVP and CFO: Donald R. (Don) Chappel, age 58,
 $3,650,843 total compensation
SVP Midstream Gas: Alan S. Armstrong, age 47,
 $2,877,407 total compensation
SVP, Gas Pipeline; Director, Williams Pipeline GP and General Partner Williams Pipeline Partners:
 Phillip D. (Phil) Wright, age 54,
 $3,011,514 total compensation
SVP Exploration and Production; Director, Apco Argentina: Ralph A. Hill, age 50,
 $3,117,283 total compensation
SVP Strategic Services and Administration and Chief Administrative Officer: Robyn L. Ewing, age 54
SVP and General Counsel: James J. (Jim) Bender, age 53
VP Commercial Operations, Transco: Frank J. Ferazzi
VP Onshore Gathering and Processing: Rory Miller
VP Piceance Basin: Alan Harrison
VP Commercial Management and Gas Operations:
 Neal Buck
Controller and Chief Accounting Officer:
 Ted T. Timmermans, age 52
Senior Counsel and Corporate Secretary:
 Brian K. Shore
Assistant General Counsel and Corporate Secretary:
 La Fleur C. Browne
Head Investor Relations: Travis Campbell
Manager Communications: Julie Gentz
Auditors: Ernst & Young LLP

LOCATIONS

HQ: The Williams Companies, Inc.
 1 Williams Center, Tulsa, OK 74172
Phone: 918-573-2000   **Fax:** 918-573-6714
Web: www.williams.com

2009 Sales

	$ mil.	% of total
US	8,065	98
Other countries	190	2
Total	**8,255**	**100**

PRODUCTS/OPERATIONS

2009 Sales

	$ mil.	% of total
Midstream gas & liquids	3,588	35
Gas marketing services	3,052	29
Exploration & production	2,219	21
Gas pipeline	1,591	15
Other	27	—
Adjustments	(2,222)	—
Total	**8,255**	**100**

COMPETITORS

Adams Resources
Avista
BP
CenterPoint Energy
Chevron
Constellation Energy Group
Dynegy
El Paso Corporation
Enbridge Energy
Energy Future
Enron
Entergy
Exxon Mobil
Kinder Morgan
Koch Industries, Inc.
Occidental Petroleum
OGE Energy
ONEOK
PG&E Corporation
ProLiance Energy
SandRidge Energy
Sempra Energy
Southern Company
U.S. Transmission

HISTORICAL FINANCIALS

Company Type: Public

Income Statement

	REVENUE ($ mil.)	NET INCOME ($ mil.)	NET PROFIT MARGIN	EMPLOYEES
12/09	8,255	361	4.4%	4,801
12/08	12,352	1,418	11.5%	4,704
12/07	10,558	990	9.4%	4,319
12/06	11,813	309	2.6%	4,313
12/05	12,584	315	2.5%	3,913
Annual Growth	(10.0%)	3.4%	—	5.2%

FYE: December 31

2009 Year-End Financials

Debt ratio: 97.8%
Return on equity: 4.3%
Cash ($ mil.): 1,867
Current ratio: 1.53
Long-term debt ($ mil.): 8,259

No. of shares (mil.): 585
Dividends
Yield: 2.1%
Payout: 89.8%
Market value ($ mil.): 12,325

Stock History

NYSE: WMB

	STOCK PRICE ($) FY Close	P/E High/Low		PER SHARE ($) Earnings	Dividends	Book Value
12/09	21.08	44	19	0.49	0.44	14.45
12/08	14.48	17	5	2.40	0.43	14.44
12/07	35.78	23	15	1.63	0.39	10.90
12/06	26.12	56	38	0.51	0.34	10.39
12/05	23.17	49	29	0.53	0.25	9.28
Annual Growth	(2.3%)	—	—	(1.9%)	15.2%	11.7%

Williams-Sonoma

Epicureans are at home at Williams-Sonoma, a leading retailer of high-end goods for well-appointed kitchens, bedrooms, and baths. Home products include bath and storage products, bedding, cookware, furniture, and tableware. The company's retail chains, Williams-Sonoma and Williams Sonoma Home (upscale cookware and furniture), West Elm (housewares), and Pottery Barn and Pottery Barn Kids (housewares, furniture), sell wares through about 615 stores in some 45 states, Washington, DC, Canada, and Puerto Rico. In addition, Williams-Sonoma distributes half a dozen catalogs. It also operates outlet stores, which sell goods from all five chains, six e-commerce sites, and an online bridal registry.

Weak demand for its wares, brought on by the housing crisis and deep recession in the US, led to a decline in Williams-Sonoma's sales. While the company's Pottery Barn and Pottery Barn Kids shops led the decline, all five retail brands suffered negative same-store sales comparisons. In response to weak sales, the retailer closed more than 15 stores in 2009 and announced plans to restructure its Williams-Sonoma Home (WSH) furniture business in 2010. The restructuring will include the closure of the 11 WSH retail stores, and the incorporation of some of the merchandise into the company's bridal registry.

WSH was one of the company's emerging retail concepts. The company hopes to have considerably more success with another emerging concept: West Elm. The three dozen West Elm locations carry more popularly priced merchandise than its sister chains. Also in response to consumer frugality, the company has tried to reposition Pottery Barn as a more affordable destination for housewares, a shift from its traditional upscale focus. To that end, in 2009 the shops stocked more lower-priced merchandise and increased promotional activity.

Looking for growth abroad, the company — through a franchise agreement with M.H. Alshaya — opened its first Pottery Barn and Pottery Barn Kids stores in Dubai, UAE, in 2010, with two more shops slated to open in Kuwait.

Howard Lester retired from his duties as chairman and CEO in May 2010 after 31 years with the company. (Lester purchased Williams-Sonoma from its founder Chuck Williams in 1978.) He continues as chairman emeritus through December 2012, serving in an advisory capacity and consulting with Laura Alber, who was named CEO. Alber joined Williams-Sonoma in 1995 and served as its president starting in 2006.

HISTORY

Food lover and hardware store owner Charles Williams founded a cookware store in 1956 in Sonoma, California, moving it to San Francisco in 1958.

Edward Marcus (of Neiman Marcus) acquired a third of the company in 1972, which then began adding new stores and started its first catalog, A Catalog for Cooks. Marcus died in 1976, and Williams, unable to manage the burgeoning enterprise, sold it to Howard Lester, owner of several computer service firms. Williams, a nonagenarian, remains a board member.

Lester acquired Gardeners Eden, a mail-order merchandiser of home gardening and related products, in 1982. The next year he bought the rights to a new catalog, Hold Everything (expanded into retailing later). Williams-Sonoma went public that year. In 1986 it acquired Pottery Barn from The Gap and soon added a catalog business. The company moved into bed and bath goods three years later when it introduced its Chambers catalog.

Williams-Sonoma bought California Closets, an operator of franchises that design and build custom closets, in 1990. (It sold the franchiser four years later to its management and an investor group.) Recession and heavy expansion spending hurt profits in the early 1990s, so the company slowed growth and focused on improving operations at the Williams-Sonoma and Pottery Barn stores.

In 1996 new management revamped Williams-Sonoma's inventory and distribution system, leading to a sharp earnings drop. The next year the company expanded the number of Pottery Barns, bringing that chain's sales to the level of its Williams-Sonoma stores. Expansion continued in 1998 with a focus on large-store formats Grande Cuisine and Design Studio.

The company sold its Gardeners Eden catalog business to retailer Brookstone in 1999.

Williams-Sonoma then launched a special Pottery Barn catalog featuring linens and furniture for children and began selling merchandise online via its wswedding.com bridal registry website and through Williams-Sonoma.com. In 2000 the first Pottery Barns Kids store was opened. The next year two Williams-Sonoma, two Pottery Barn, and one Pottery Barn Kids stores opened up shop in Toronto.

In 2001 Lester stepped down as CEO (he remained chairman) and was replaced by Dale Hilpert, a former Venator Group (now Foot Locker) executive. That year the company launched its Pottery Barn Kids website, Pottery Barn online gift and bridal registry, and Pottery Barn Kids online gift registry. In 2002 Williams-Sonoma discontinued TASTE, its quarterly magazine that focused on travel and fine dining.

Also in 2002 Williams-Sonoma launched its West Elm catalog, targeting young, design-conscious customers. In January 2003 Hilpert left the company, and Edward Mueller, former head of Ameritech, was named CEO. That April Williams-Sonoma released PBteen, a catalog featuring furniture, lighting, bedding, and accessories designed for the teenage market. Williams-Sonoma launched its West Elm e-commerce website the same year and opened its first retail location.

In 2004 the Chambers catalog was discontinued and replaced by Williams-Sonoma Home, offering classic home furnishings and decorative accessories. Following on the heels of the Williams-Sonoma Home catalog launched that fall, a corresponding website devoted to upscale furniture debuted in the spring of 2005. Also, the company opened its first Williams-Sonoma Home in West Hollywood, California.

Williams-Sonoma closed its chain of 11 Hold Everything stores in 2006. Chairman Howard Lester, who served as CEO of the company from 1979 to 2001, replaced retiring CEO Edward Mueller in mid-2006.

To control costs in lean times, Williams-Sonoma in 2009 cut about 18% of its workforce, reduced inventories, and closed a Pennsylvania call center and distribution facility in Tennessee. It also reduced its store count by 17 locations over the course of the year.

EXECUTIVES

Chairman: Adrian D. P. Bellamy, age 68
Chairman Emeritus: W. Howard Lester, age 74, $12,832,993 total compensation
President, CEO and Director: Laura J. Alber, age 41, $2,384,506 total compensation
EVP, COO, CFO, and Director: Sharon L. McCollam, age 47, $2,309,755 total compensation
EVP, Chief Marketing Officer, and Director: Patrick J. (Pat) Connolly, age 63, $1,084,897 total compensation
SVP, General Counsel, and Secretary: Seth R. Jaffe, age 53
Director Public Relations: Leigh Oshirak
Director Investor Relations: Stephen C. Nelson
President, Williams-Sonoma Brand: Richard Harvey, age 47, $1,156,949 total compensation
Auditors: Deloitte & Touche LLP

LOCATIONS

HQ: Williams-Sonoma, Inc.
3250 Van Ness Ave., San Francisco, CA 94109
Phone: 415-421-7900 **Fax:** 415-616-8359
Web: www.williams-sonomainc.com

PRODUCTS/OPERATIONS

2010 Stores

	No.
Williams-Sonoma	259
Pottery Barn	199
Pottery Barn Kids	87
West Elm	36
Williams-Sonoma Home	11
Outlet stores	18
Total	**610**

2010 Sales

	$ mil.	% of total
Retail	1,878.0	61
Direct-to-consumer	1,224.7	39
Total	**3,102.7**	**100**

Retail

PBteen (teen home furnishings)
Pottery Barn (home furnishings, flatware, and table accessories)
Pottery Barn Kids (children's home furnishings)
West Elm (home furnishings, decorative accessories, tabletop items, and textile collection)
Williams-Sonoma (cookware, cookbooks, cutlery, dinnerware, glassware, and table linens)

Selected Catalogs

PBteen (home furnishings for teenage market)
Pottery Barn (home furnishings and housewares)
Pottery Barn Bed + Bath (bed and bath products)
Pottery Barn Kids (children's linens and furniture)
West Elm (home furnishings and housewares)
Williams-Sonoma (kitchen products)
Williams-Sonoma Home (home furnishings)

COMPETITORS

Ashley Furniture	King Arthur Flour
Bed Bath & Beyond	Lands' End
Brookstone	Levenger
Container Store	Longaberger
Cornerstone Brands	Macy's
Cost Plus	Neiman Marcus
Dean & DeLuca	Pampered Chef
Decorize	Pier 1 Imports
Eddie Bauer llc	Restoration Hardware
Ethan Allen	Room & Board
Euromarket Designs	Target
Garden Ridge	Tuesday Morning
Hanover Direct	Z Gallerie
IKEA	

HISTORICAL FINANCIALS

Company Type: Public

Income Statement

FYE: Sunday nearest January 31

	REVENUE ($ mil.)	NET INCOME ($ mil.)	NET PROFIT MARGIN	EMPLOYEES
1/10	3,103	77	2.5%	26,000
1/09	3,362	30	0.9%	30,000
1/08	3,945	196	5.0%	39,000
1/07	3,728	209	5.6%	38,800
1/06	3,539	215	6.1%	37,200
Annual Growth	**(3.2%)**	**(22.5%)**	**—**	**(8.6%)**

2010 Year-End Financials

Debt ratio: 0.7%
Return on equity: 6.6%
Cash ($ mil.): 514
Current ratio: 2.09
Long-term debt ($ mil.): 9
No. of shares (mil.): 108
Dividends
  Yield: 2.5%
  Payout: 66.7%
Market value ($ mil.): 2,053

Stock History

NYSE: WSM

	STOCK PRICE ($) FY Close	P/E High/Low		PER SHARE ($) Earnings	Dividends	Book Value
1/10	18.98	32	10	0.72	0.48	11.20
1/09	7.92	106	16	0.28	0.48	10.61
1/08	26.88	21	11	1.76	0.46	10.78
1/07	35.00	25	16	1.79	0.40	10.65
1/06	39.78	25	18	1.81	—	10.40
Annual Growth	**(16.9%)**	**—**	**—**	**(20.6%)**	**6.3%**	**1.9%**

Windstream Corporation

Instead of relying on the prevailing breeze to deliver services to its customers, Windstream makes use of more tangible connections, such as fiber optics and copper wire. The company provides local and long-distance telephone service, as well as broadband data transmission and Internet access, to residential and business customers in 23 states. It also offers satellite television in all of its service areas through an agreement with DISH Network. Windstream makes sales directly in part from about 55 retail locations. The company's local and long-distance voice services together account for around half of sales.

Windstream is expanding its network and subscriber base through acquisitions. In early 2010 the company completed the purchase of privately held NuVox, for about $647 million. The deal boosted Windstream's business communications and broadband service segments and widened the company's footprint in the Southeast and Midwest regions. NuVox, based in South Carolina, served about 90,000 business customers in 16 states.

Windstream bought Iowa Telecom for about $1.2 billion in mid-2010. The purchase expanded Windstream's presence in the rural markets of Iowa and Minnesota, adding residential and business telephone, Internet, and digital TV customers. Later that year, the company agreed to acquire privately held local phone carrier and fiber transport services provider Q-Comm for about $782 million. The purchase will include Overland Park, Kansas-based Q-Comm's Kentucky Data Link and Norlight subsidiaries, and will approximately double Windstream's fiber network infrastructure. The company sees the deal as an opportunity to improve its capacity to provide signal transport services over landlines for wireless carriers.

In 2009 Windstream paid about $333 million in stock for Pennsylvania-based D&E Communications in 2009. The deal added about 160,000 rural access lines, including about 40,000 broadband subscriptions. Windstream also acquired North Carolina-based Lexcom that year for $141 million in cash.

While it bulked up in the area of core communications services during 2009, the company sold its Windstream Supply distribution business to Walker and Associates. Windstream Supply distributed telephony and communications equipment, largely to affiliated carriers and institutions. In late 2008 Windstream sold its small wireless business in North Carolina to AT&T Mobility.

HISTORY

Windstream was formed in 2006 through the combination of ALLTEL's wireline business with VALOR Communications Group after Little Rock-based ALLTEL turned its full attention to wireless communications services. Its decision to spin off its wireline operations came after several acquisitions of smaller wireless carriers, including Western Wireless and Midwest Wireless, both in 2005; and its purchase of First Cellular the following year. With its acquisition of VALOR and subsequent spin-off of its wireline operations as Windstream, ALLTEL became a purely wireless communications service provider.

In 2007 Windstream boosted its subscriber numbers by about 160,000 phone lines through its acquisition of North Carolina-based CT Communications for $584 million. Later that year, the company spun off its publishing business, Windstream Yellow Pages, to affiliates of Welsh, Carson, Anderson & Stowe for about $500 million. The following year the company sold its wireless business to AT&T Mobility for about $57 million.

EXECUTIVES

Chairman: Dennis E. Foster, age 69
President, CEO, and Director: Jeffery R. (Jeff) Gardner, age 50, $6,019,817 total compensation
COO: Brent K. Whittington, age 39, $1,838,083 total compensation
CFO: Anthony W. (Tony) Thomas, age 38, $742,944 total compensation
CIO: Cynthia B. (Cindy) Nash, age 45
EVP and Chief Marketing Officer: Richard J. (Ric) Crane, age 55, $950,054 total compensation
EVP, General Counsel, and Secretary: John P. Fletcher, age 44, $1,318,835 total compensation
EVP Network Operations: W. Grant Raney, age 49
SVP and Treasurer: Robert G. (Rob) Clancy Jr., age 45, $938,011 total compensation
SVP Consumer Sales: Gregg Richey
SVP Service Delivery and Operations: Jack Norris
SVP Customer Services: Joe Marano
SVP Governmental Affairs: Michael D. (Mike) Rhoda, age 49
SVP Human Resources: Susan Bradley, age 58
SVP Business Sales: A. John Leach Jr., age 46
Auditors: PricewaterhouseCoopers LLP

HQ: Windstream Corporation
4001 Rodney Parham Rd., Little Rock, AR 72212
Phone: 501-748-7000
Web: www.windstream.com

PRODUCTS/OPERATIONS

2009 Sales

	$ mil.	% of total
Voice service	1,116.2	37
Data & special access	825.9	27
Switched access & Universal Service Fund	534.1	18
Long distance	258.7	9
Miscellaneous	137.9	5
Product sales	123.8	4
Total	**2,996.6**	**100**

COMPETITORS

AT&T
Cox Communications
Hickory Tech
Momentum Telecom
Onvoy Voice Services
Sprint Nextel
Verizon

HISTORICAL FINANCIALS

Company Type: Public

Income Statement

FYE: December 31

	REVENUE ($ mil.)	NET INCOME ($ mil.)	NET PROFIT MARGIN	EMPLOYEES
12/09	2,997	335	11.2%	7,385
12/08	3,172	413	13.0%	7,349
12/07	3,261	917	28.1%	7,570
12/06	3,033	446	14.7%	8,017
12/05	506	36	7.0%	1,288
Annual Growth	**56.0%**	**75.1%**	**—**	**54.7%**

2009 Year-End Financials

Debt ratio: 2,405.6%
Return on equity: 130.4%
Cash ($ mil.): 1,063
Current ratio: 2.05
Long-term debt ($ mil.): 6,271

No. of shares (mil.): 483
Dividends
  Yield: 9.1%
  Payout: 131.6%
Market value ($ mil.): 5,310

Stock History

NASDAQ (GS): WIN

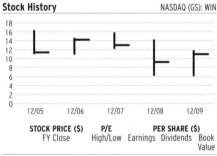

	STOCK PRICE ($) FY Close	P/E High/Low		PER SHARE ($) Earnings	Dividends	Book Value
12/09	10.99	15	8	0.76	1.00	0.54
12/08	9.20	15	7	0.93	1.00	0.52
12/07	13.02	8	6	1.94	1.00	1.45
12/06	14.22	12	9	1.25	1.24	0.97
12/05	11.40	31	22	0.52	1.26	1.18
Annual Growth	**(0.9%)**	**—**	**—**	**10.0%**	**(5.6%)**	**(17.8%)**

Winn-Dixie Stores

Winn-Dixie Stores has found — as Jefferson Davis did long ago — that winning Dixie ain't easy. The Deep South supermarket chain operates about 515 combination food and drug stores throughout Alabama, Florida, Georgia, Louisiana, and Mississippi under the Winn-Dixie, Winn-Dixie Marketplace, and SaveRite (warehouse stores) banners. More than 400 of Winn-Dixie's supermarkets have pharmacies, some 75 house liquor stores, and about a half-dozen sell gas. To fend off rivals (including Wal-Mart and Publix Super Markets) and stem the flow of red ink, Winn-Dixie has retrenched by exiting noncore markets and selling assets, including more than 500 supermarkets, during a bankruptcy restructuring.

The regional grocery chain is going after a different customer in its post-bankruptcy incarnation. Instead of the blue-collar workers it had traditionally targeted, Winn-Dixie is moving up market by emphasizing better customer service, freshness, quality, and cleanliness. It's also aggressively remodeling stores on a market-by-market basis with plans to renovate essentially all of them by mid-2013. By mid-2010, the chain had remodeled nearly half of its stores. On the merchandising front, it's emphasizing "fresh and local" goods and expanding selection.

It's a strategy that has worked well for archrival Publix, which is known for its high levels of service. Whether Winn-Dixie can pull it off remains to be seen. It's trying nevertheless. In 2010 the grocery chain opened a new upscale prototype store in Margate, Florida (its first new store in the state since 2004). The new supermarket has twice as many specialty items as any other Winn-Dixie, including a wider selection of gourmet, Latin, Kosher, Latin American, and Caribbean food.

In a bid to rebuild the Winn-Dixie brand, the supermarket operator has added more than 2,500 new private-label products to its store shelves. Meanwhile, Winn-Dixie continues to shutter underperforming locations, and in 2010 it eliminated 120 corporate and field-support staff positions in order to help cut costs.

HISTORY

In 1925 William Davis borrowed $10,000 to open the cash-and-carry Rockmoor Grocery in Lemon City, Florida, near Miami. After a slow start, he had expanded his chain of Table Supply Stores to 34 by the time of his death in 1934. His four sons — A. D., J. E., M. Austin, and Tine — took over. In 1939 they purchased control of Winn & Lovett Grocery, which operated 78 stores in Florida and Georgia. The company, incorporated in 1928, was a leader in the 1930s in building new supermarket-type stores. The combined company settled in Jacksonville in 1944 and formally took the name Winn & Lovett.

After WWII the company, still controlled by the Davis family, acquired grocery chains throughout the South, including Steiden (Kentucky), Margaret Ann (Florida), Wylie (Alabama), Penney (Mississippi), King (Georgia), and Eden and Ballentine (South Carolina). The company consolidated with Dixie Home Stores of the Carolinas in 1955 and changed its name to Winn-Dixie Stores, Inc.

The most profitable company in the industry during the 1950s and early 1960s, Winn-Dixie

continued to expand through acquisitions, adding Ketner and Milner (the Carolinas) and Hill (Louisiana and Alabama). Also in the 1960s Winn-Dixie entered the manufacturing, processing, and distribution arenas.

By 1966, under the leadership of chairman J. E. Davis, the company controlled so much of the grocery business in the South that, for antitrust reasons, the FTC imposed a 10-year moratorium on acquisitions. Winn-Dixie responded by growing internally and improving its existing stores. It also bought nine stores outside the US (in the Bahamas). When the expansion moratorium ended in 1976, the company bought Kimbell of Texas (sold 1979), adding stores and extensive support facilities in Texas, Oklahoma, and New Mexico.

William Davis' grandson Robert Davis took control as chairman of the company in 1983. After years of lackluster profits, Robert resigned in 1988 and was replaced by his cousin, Dano Davis. In the mid-1980s Winn-Dixie debuted a large combination store format called Marketplace, which offered services such as pharmacies and specialty shops. The company began replacing smaller stores with Marketplace stores; about 55 had been opened by the late 1980s.

In 1995 A. D., the only surviving son of the founder, died. In the first quarter of fiscal 1999 Winn-Dixie ended a 54-year streak of raising its dividends. The company settled a sex and race discrimination lawsuit filed by former and current employees for about $33 million in 1999. The company also hired Allen Rowland, the former president of Smith's Food & Drug, as president and CEO.

In 2000 Winn-Dixie started a restructuring plan — cutting 8% of its workforce, closing more than 100 supermarkets, and shuttering some manufacturing and warehouse facilities. By mid-2002 the company had exited the Texas (71 stores) and Oklahoma (five stores) markets entirely, laying off 5,300 workers.

In June 2003 Rowland retired from the company and was replaced by COO Frank Lazaran, previously president of Randall's Food Markets.

In August 2004 Winn-Dixie announced it had sold or closed 32 stores as part of its purge of underperforming assets, including nine stores in the Cincinnati area as well as stores in Kentucky, North and South Carolina, and Virginia.

Dano Davis retired as chairman in October 2004 after more than 35 years with the company. Davis was succeeded by Jay Skelton, president and CEO of DDI Inc., a diversified holding company owned by the Davis family. In December Lazaran was replaced (after only 18 months on the job) as CEO by Albertson's veteran Peter Lynch.

In February 2005 Winn-Dixie filed for Chapter 11 bankruptcy protection. Soon after, the supermarket chain sold 18 Georgia stores to Atlanta-based Wayfield Foods, All-American Quality Foods, and a partnership between holding company Alex Lee and Associated Wholesale Grocers, among other buyers. It also sold 81 supermarkets to various acquirers, including SUPERVALU. In August Winn-Dixie was hit by a storm of another sort: Hurricane Katrina, which caused property damage and inventory losses at about 110 of the 125 supermarkets operating in the New Orleans region.

In August 2006 Winn-Dixie completed the sale of a dozen stores operated by Winn-Dixie Bahamas to BSL Holdings Limited. Overall in 2006, the company closed or sold 374 stores. After 21 months in bankruptcy, Winn-Dixie emerged from Chapter 11 in late November 2006.

EXECUTIVES

Chairman, President, and CEO: Peter L. Lynch, age 57, $5,909,125 total compensation
SVP and CFO: Bennett L. Nussbaum, age 63, $2,115,333 total compensation
SVP Retail Operations: Frank O. Eckstein, age 63, $1,320,436 total compensation
SVP and Chief Merchandising and Marketing Officer: Daniel (Dan) Portnoy, age 53, $1,682,853 total compensation
SVP Human Resources and Legal, General Counsel, and Secretary: Laurence B. (Larry) Appel, age 49, $1,722,335 total compensation
Group VP Development: Philip E. (Phil) Pichulo, age 61
Group VP Information Technology: Charles M. (Charlie) Weston, age 62
Group VP Logistics and Distribution: Christopher L. (Chris) Scott, age 47
VP Non-Perishables: Matt Gutermuth
VP Marketing: Mary Kellmanson, age 42
VP Finance and Treasurer: Sheila C. Reinken, age 49
VP, Corporate Controller, and Chief Accounting Officer: D. Michael Byrum, age 57
Manager Communications: Joshua (Josh) Whitton
Director Investor Relations: Eric Harris
Auditors: KPMG LLP

LOCATIONS

HQ: Winn-Dixie Stores, Inc.
5050 Edgewood Ct., Jacksonville, FL 32254
Phone: 904-783-5000 **Fax:** 904-370-7224
Web: www.winn-dixie.com

2009 Stores

	No.
Florida	353
Alabama	71
Louisiana	52
Georgia	23
Mississippi	16
Total	**515**

PRODUCTS/OPERATIONS

2009 Stores

	No.
Winn Dixie/Marketplace	505
SaveRite	10
Total	**515**

Selected Items Produced or Processed

Carbonated beverages
Cheese
Coffee
Cookies
Crackers
Cultured products
Eggs
Frozen pizza
Ice cream
Jams and jellies
Margarine
Mayonnaise
Meats
Milk
Peanut butter
Salad dressing
Snacks
Spices
Tea

COMPETITORS

Albertsons	Kmart
ALDI	Kroger
BI-LO	The Pantry
CVS Caremark	Publix
Dollar General	Sweetbay
Farm Fresh	Target
Harris Teeter	Walgreen
IGA	Wal-Mart
Kerr Drug	

HISTORICAL FINANCIALS

Company Type: Public

Income Statement

FYE: Last Wednesday in June

	REVENUE ($ mil.)	NET INCOME ($ mil.)	NET PROFIT MARGIN	EMPLOYEES
6/09	7,367	40	0.5%	50,000
6/08	7,281	13	0.2%	50,000
6/07	4,525	29	0.6%	52,000
6/06	7,194	(365)	—	55,000
6/05	9,921	(833)	—	80,000
Annual Growth	(7.2%)	—	—	(11.1%)

2009 Year-End Financials

Debt ratio: 2.8%	No. of shares (mil.): 55
Return on equity: 4.7%	Dividends
Cash ($ mil.): 183	Yield: —
Current ratio: 1.45	Payout: —
Long-term debt ($ mil.): 24	Market value ($ mil.): 691

Stock History

NASDAQ (GS): WINN

	STOCK PRICE ($) FY Close	P/E High/Low	PER SHARE ($) Earnings	Dividends	Book Value
6/09	12.54	27 11	0.73	—	15.96
6/08	16.02	131 60	0.24	—	14.99
6/07	29.30	61 21	0.53	—	14.47
Annual Growth	(34.6%)	— —	17.4%	—	5.0%

World Fuel Services

You can't fuel all the people all the time, but World Fuel Services tries hard to do just that. The company provides fuel and services to commercial and corporate aircraft, petroleum distributors, and ships at more than 2,500 locations around the world, 24 hours a day. The company estimates it holds more than 10% of the global marine fuels market. Its aviation fueling business focuses on serving small to midsized air carriers, cargo and charter carriers, and private aircraft. World Fuel Services also markets fuel and related services to petroleum distributors operating in the land transportation market. All told, it has more than 40 offices in more than 20 countries, and does business in 200.

World Fuel Services maintains its competitive edge by offering a range of support services (such as fuel market analysis, flight planning, ground-handling services, and weather reports) to its aviation and marine customers.

As part of its marine fueling services business, World Fuel Services arranges fueling for ships on a brokered basis and extends credit to a global customer base, which includes container lines, cruise ships, dry bulk carriers, fishing fleets, refrigerated vessels, and tankers. The company also provides financial credit for aviation fuels.

World Fuel Services is increasing its geographic coverage and the depth of its portfolio through acquisitions. In 2008 World Fuel Services acquired Texor Petroleum. In 2009 it bought wholesale motor fuel distributor TGS Petroleum. The company combined TGS with Texor to expand World Fuel Services' presence as the largest independent wholesale motor fuel distributor in Illinois.

Expanding its UK market share, in 2009 the company acquired the Henty Oil Group of Companies, a leading independent provider of marine and land fuels in the UK. In 2010 it beefed up its position in the branded onshore wholesale market to 1 billion gallons a year by acquiring Lakeside Oil Company, based in Milwaukee.

Sales took a hit in 2009 because of the global recession, low commodity prices, and the slump in global transportation triggered by the weak economy. Though it is World Fuel Services' smallest segment in terms of revenues, its land-based fuel marketing business, with higher margins, has proven to be the company's most profitable since 2005.

HISTORY

Neighbors Ralph Weiser and Jerrold Blair founded International Oil Recovery, an oil recycling company, in Florida in 1984. The company moved into aviation fueling by acquiring Advance Petroleum in 1986. Two years later International Oil Recovery diversified further, entering the hazardous waste market by buying Resource Recovery of America, a soil remediation company. In 1989 the firm acquired JCo Energy Partners, an aviation fuel company, and subsequently renamed its aviation fueling division World Fuel Services. The company set up International Petroleum in 1993 to operate a Delaware used-oil and water-recycling plant.

The company changed its name to World Fuel Services Corporation in 1995 to reflect its expanded range of operations. Also that year it nearly doubled its revenue base with the purchase of Trans-Tec, the world's #1 independent marine fuel services company. World Fuel also exited the environmental services business in 1995 to focus on its fuel services and oil recycling businesses.

The following year the company formed World Fuel International, a subsidiary based in Costa Rica that serves World Fuel's aviation customers in South and Central America, Canada, and the Caribbean. In 1998 it acquired corporate jet fuel provider Baseops International, which has offices in the UK and Texas. In 1999 the company expanded its share of the marine fuel market with the acquisition of the Bunkerfuels group of companies, one of the world's top marine fuel brokerages.

To focus on its marine and aviation fueling businesses, World Fuel exited the oil recycling segment in 2000 when it sold its International Petroleum unit to waste services company EarthCare for about $33 million.

The company expanded into the United Arab Emirates with its 2001 acquisition of fuel services provider Marine Energy of Dubai. World Fuel acquired Rotterdam-based marine fuel reseller Oil Shipping Group in 2002.

In 2004 World Fuel Services acquired UK-based marine fuel reseller Tramp Holdings for $83 million.

The company diversified further in 2007, acquiring AVCARD, a leading provider of contract fuel sales and charge card services to the aviation industry, for $55 million.

EXECUTIVES

Chairman and CEO: Paul H. Stebbins, age 53,
$6,089,643 total compensation
Vice Chairman: Ken Bakshi, age 60
President, COO, and Director: Michael J. Kasbar,
age 53, $6,095,665 total compensation
EVP and CFO: Ira M. Birns, age 47,
$1,876,390 total compensation
EVP and Chief Risk and Administration Officer:
Francis X. (Frank) Shea, age 69,
$1,522,228 total compensation
SVP and Chief Accounting Officer: Paul M. Nobel,
age 42
General Counsel and Corporate Secretary:
R. Alexander Lake
President, World Fuel Services, Inc.:
Michael S. Clementi, age 48,
$1,966,262 total compensation
Auditors: PricewaterhouseCoopers LLP

LOCATIONS

HQ: World Fuel Services Corporation
9800 NW 41st St., Ste. 400, Miami, FL 33178
Phone: 305-428-8000 **Fax:** 305-392-5600
Web: www.wfscorp.com

2009 Sales

	$ mil.	% of total
US	5,041.8	45
Singapore	3,323.9	29
UK	1,619.9	14
Other countries	1,309.6	12
Total	**11,295.2**	**100**

PRODUCTS/OPERATIONS

2009 Sales

	$ mil.	% of total
Marine	6,040.6	53
Aviation	4,049.6	36
Land	1,205.0	11
Total	**11,295.2**	**100**

Selected Subsidiaries

Baseops Europe Ltd. (UK)
Baseops International, Inc.
Bunkerfuels Corp.
Bunkerfuels UK Ltd.
Casa Petro SA (Costa Rica)
Henty Oil Group of Companies (UK)
Marine Energy Arabia (United Arab Emirates)
PetroServicios de Costa Rica SA
Texor Petroleum
TGS Petroleum
Tramp Holdings Limited (UK)
Trans-Tec International SA (Costa Rica)
World Fuel International SA (Costa Rica)
World Fuel Services, Inc.
World Fuel Services, Ltd. (UK)
World Fuel Services (Singapore) Pte. Ltd.

COMPETITORS

BBA Aviation
BP Marine
Mercury Air Group
Sun Coast Resources

HISTORICAL FINANCIALS

Company Type: Public

Income Statement

FYE: December 31

	REVENUE ($ mil.)	NET INCOME ($ mil.)	NET PROFIT MARGIN	EMPLOYEES
12/09	11,295	117	1.0%	1,249
12/08	18,509	105	0.6%	1,164
12/07	13,730	65	0.5%	916
12/06	10,785	64	0.6%	743
12/05	8,734	40	0.5%	647
Annual Growth	**6.6%**	**31.1%**	**—**	**17.9%**

2009 Year-End Financials

Debt ratio: 1.4%
Return on equity: 17.5%
Cash ($ mil.): 299
Current ratio: 1.54
Long-term debt ($ mil.): 10
No. of shares (mil.): 60
Dividends
Yield: 0.6%
Payout: 7.7%
Market value ($ mil.): 1,594

Stock History

NYSE: INT

	STOCK PRICE ($) FY Close	P/E High/Low		PER SHARE ($) Earnings	Dividends	Book Value
12/09	26.79	15	6	1.96	0.15	12.32
12/08	18.50	11	4	1.81	0.08	10.21
12/07	14.52	22	13	1.12	0.08	8.13
12/06	22.23	24	14	1.11	0.08	7.16
12/05	16.86	24	14	0.79	0.08	5.94
Annual Growth	**12.3%**	**—**	**—**	**25.5%**	**17.0%**	**20.0%**

Worthington Industries

At least when it comes to steel, Worthington Industries may be considered a shape-shifter. One of the largest steel processors in the US, Worthington Industries shapes and processes flat-rolled steel for industrial customers, including automotive, appliance, and machinery companies. The company also forms flat-rolled steel to exact customer specifications, filling a niche not usually served by steelmakers and steel service centers with limited processing capabilities. Worthington's subsidiaries make products such as pressure cylinders, metal framing, and automotive panels. Through joint ventures, the company also makes steel products such as metal ceiling grid systems and laser-welded blanks.

Worthington's processed steel segment accounts for almost half of sales. The unit consists of Worthington Steel, which is an intermediate processor of flat-rolled steel. Worthington Steel is one of the largest flat-rolled steel processors in the US. Another unit, Gerstenslager, supplies automotive exterior body panels to North American automotive OEMs and other past model service businesses.

The company's metal framing unit, Dietrich Industries, designs and manufactures metal framing components and systems used in the

US commercial and residential construction markets. Worthington Pressure Cylinders, the company's pressure cylinder unit, makes pressure cylinders such as low-pressure liquefied petroleum gas, refrigerant gas cylinders, and high-pressure industrial gas cylinders. The cylinders are sold to automotive manufacturers, refrigerant gas producers and distributors, industrial forklift makers, and commercial and residential cookware producers.

Throughout much of the past decade, Worthington implemented an active acquisition and divestiture strategy, focusing on the processing of flat-rolled steel as the company's core business. It has invested more than $1 billion in several acquisitions and the modernization of its existing plants.

In 2010 the company purchased the assets of Hy-Mark Cylinders, a manufacturer of extruded aluminum cylinders for medical oxygen, scuba, beverage service, industrial, specialty, and professional racing applications. That same year Worthington acquired the metals processing unit of Gibraltar Industries. The acquired unit consists of a minority interest in a steel joint venture, a processing facility in Ohio, and the assets of another facility that will actually be shuttered.

Worthington added Piper Metal Forming to its Worthington Pressure Cylinders unit in 2009. Piper operates through subsidiaries and manufactures and distributes cylinders for the medical, defense, and automotive markets.

HISTORY

In 1955 John H. McConnell, son of a steelworker, borrowed money on his car and started the Worthington Steel Company in the garage of his Worthington, Ohio, home. McConnell had noticed that large steel mills would not fill small, specialized steel orders — a market he decided to serve. Worthington posted an $11,000 profit its first year.

Worthington moved into its processing facility in Columbus, Ohio, in 1959 and continued to grow during the next decade. It went public in 1968.

The company bought Lennox's pressure-cylinder business and renamed itself Worthington Industries in 1971. Worthington continued to expand its profitable pressure-cylinder business through acquisitions. Its 1980 purchase of Buckeye International provided the framework for what would become Worthington's two other business segments: custom products and castings. The company further expanded operations with purchases of machine maker Capital Die, Tool and Machine Co. and recycled metals processing company I. H. Schlezinger & Sons.

Worthington formed a joint venture with U.S. Steel in 1986 for a specialty steel-processing plant; two years later it teamed with Nissen Chemitec and Sumitomo to make molded plastic parts for automakers. To ensure a steady supply of steel, Worthington purchased an interest in Rouge Steel in 1989 (sold in 2000).

In 1992 Worthington formed WAVE, a joint venture with Armstrong World Industries, to produce and sell suspended ceiling-grid systems in Europe. That year John P. McConnell, founder John H.'s son, became vice chairman of the company. He succeeded his father as CEO a year later.

Forging into new markets, Worthington formed a joint venture in 1994 with Mexico's Hylsa SA to operate a steel-processing facility in Monterey, Mexico. (In 2006 it sold its stake in the JV.) The company also entered new markets for existing product lines: Its 1996 purchase of metal-framing maker Dietrich Industries moved Worthington into the residential and commercial building markets, while in 1997 the company expanded its line of automotive parts by acquiring aftermarket body panel maker Gerstenslager in a stock swap worth about $113 million. Worthington also began constructing a new plant in Alabama designed to process one million tons of steel annually.

In 1998 Worthington expanded its international operations again by acquiring Austrian cylinder maker Joseph Heiser. That year the company sold its automotive metals unit, Worthington Precision Metals, to the investor group Veritas Capital Fund, and its share of London Industries (plastic parts for transplant automakers) to Japan-based partner Nissen Chemitec. In 1999 Worthington sold its Buckeye Steel Castings subsidiary to a management group that includes investment firm Key Equity Capital.

To increase its global presence, in 1999 the company bought Portugal-based Metalurgica Progresso de Vale de Cambra and a 51% interest in the Czech Republic's Gastec, both makers of pressure cylinders. Despite steady sales in fiscal 1999, profits fell by half, in part from low prices for cold-rolled steel, start-up costs at the company's new Alabama facility, and the General Motors strike.

Worthington acquired three independent galvanized steel producers in Pennsylvania — MetalTech, NexTech, and GalvTech — during 2000. Along the same vein, in 2002 the company purchased construction steel maker, Unimast Incorporated (subsidiary of WHX Corporation).

In 2003 Worthington formed a joint venture with Ohio-based Viking Industries, an intermediate steel processor of hot-rolled steel coils.

Founder John H. McConnell died in 2008.

EXECUTIVES

Chairman and CEO: John P. McConnell, age 59
President and COO: George P. Stoe, age 64
SVP Marketing; President, Worthington Integrated Building Systems, LLC: Ralph V. Roberts, age 63
SVP Manufacturing: Virgil L. Winland, age 62
VP and CFO: B. Andrew Rose, age 39
VP Human Resources: Eric M. Smolenski, age 40
VP Communications: Catherine M. (Cathy) Lyttle
VP Administration, General Counsel, and Secretary: Dale T. Brinkman, age 57
VP Purchasing: Andrew J. Billman
VP Corporate Development and Treasurer: Matthew A Lockard, age 40
CIO: Robert (Rob) Richardson
President, The Worthington Steel Company: Mark A. Russell, age 47
President, Dietrich Industries: John E. Roberts, age 55
President, Worthington Cylinder: Harry A. Goussetis, age 56
Controller: Richard G. Welch, age 52
Auditors: KPMG LLP

LOCATIONS

HQ: Worthington Industries, Inc.
200 Old Wilson Bridge Rd., Columbus, OH 43085
Phone: 614-438-3210   **Fax:** 614-438-7948
Web: www.worthingtonindustries.com

2009 Sales

	$ mil.	% of total
North America		
US	2,395.4	91
Canada	66.5	3
Europe	169.4	6
Total	**2,631.3**	**100**

PRODUCTS/OPERATIONS

2009 Sales

	$ mil.	% of total
Steel Processing	1,183.0	45
Metal Framing	661.0	25
Pressure Cylinders	537.4	20
Other	249.9	10
Total	**2,631.3**	**100**

Selected Subsidiaries

Dietrich Industries, Inc. (metal framing)
GalvTech (galvanized steel)
MetalTech (galvanized steel)
NexTech (galvanized steel)
The Gerstenslager Company (aftermarket body panels)
Worthington Cylinder Corporation (pressure cylinders)
Worthington Steel Company (steel processing)

Joint Ventures and Other Holdings

Spartan Steel Coating, LLC (52%, joint venture with Rouge Steel Coating; sheet steel)
TWB Company, LLC (45%, joint venture with ThyssenKrupp; laser-welded blanks for cars)
Worthington Armstrong Venture (50%, joint venture with Armstrong World Industries; suspended ceiling grid systems)
Worthington Specialty Processing (51%, joint venture with United States Steel; wide-sheet steel for the auto industry)

COMPETITORS

AK Steel Holding Corporation
Gibraltar Industries
Harsco
INTERMET
Nippon Steel
Nucor
O'Neal Steel
Reliance Steel
Russel Metals
Ryerson
Shiloh Industries
Steel Technologies
ThyssenKrupp Steel
United States Steel

HISTORICAL FINANCIALS

Company Type: Public

Income Statement

FYE: May 31

	REVENUE ($ mil.)	NET INCOME ($ mil.)	NET PROFIT MARGIN	EMPLOYEES
5/09	2,631	(108)	—	6,400
5/08	3,067	107	3.5%	6,900
5/07	2,972	114	3.8%	6,900
5/06	2,897	146	5.0%	8,200
5/05	3,079	179	5.8%	6,450
Annual Growth	**(3.9%)**	—	—	**(0.2%)**

2009 Year-End Financials

Debt ratio: 14.2%
Return on equity: —
Cash ($ mil.): 56
Current ratio: 1.61
Long-term debt ($ mil.): 100
No. of shares (mil.): 79
Dividends
  Yield: 4.9%
  Payout: —
Market value ($ mil.): 1,109

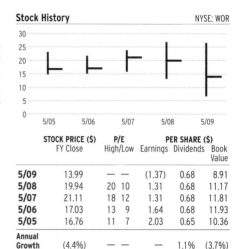

	Stock History				NYSE: WOR

	STOCK PRICE ($) FY Close	P/E High/Low		PER SHARE ($) Earnings	Dividends	Book Value
5/09	13.99	—	—	(1.37)	0.68	8.91
5/08	19.94	20	10	1.31	0.68	11.17
5/07	21.11	18	12	1.31	0.68	11.81
5/06	17.03	13	9	1.64	0.68	11.93
5/05	16.76	11	7	2.03	0.65	10.36
Annual Growth	**(4.4%)**	—	—	—	**1.1%**	**(3.7%)**

W. R. Grace

W. R. Grace & Co. operates through two major units. Grace's Davison unit — which accounts for about two-thirds of sales — makes silica-based products, chemical catalysts, packaging sealants, and refining catalysts that help produce refined products from crude oil. This unit has a refining joint venture with Chevron Products Company. Grace's second major business, Construction Products, manufactures concrete and cement additives, fireproofing chemicals, and specialty building materials, such as roofing underlayments and deck protectors. The company's customers include chemicals companies, oil refiners, and construction firms.

Grace has been wrestling with a reorgainzation and emergence-from-bankruptcy plan for most of a decade. It filed for bankruptcy protection in 2001 after an unexpected increase in asbestos litigation (injury claims nearly doubled in 2000, leading to a total of 130,000 unresolved claims); the company no longer makes such products. Approval of its exit plan was still pending in 2010.

The company has expanded manufacturing and sales operations in key regions (including China, India, the Middle East, Latin America, and Eastern Europe) to take advantage of growth in these markets. It is also pursuing global acquisitions to enhance existing product offerings and penetrate desirable segments. In the last half of this decade Grace has aquired businesses in Venezuela and Sweden in addition to several in North America.

A slumping global economy hurt demand for Grace's products in 2009, but despite a dip in sales, the company posted higher profits by raising the price of its products.

HISTORY

W. R. Grace & Co. grew from the businesses of Irishman William R. Grace, who fled the potato famine and moved to Peru in 1854 to charter ships trading guano fertilizer. In 1866 he moved his headquarters to New York and established shipping routes linking New York, South

America, and Europe. The company traded fertilizer, agricultural products, and US manufactured goods.

Grace, mayor of New York City in the 1880s, died in 1904. His son Joseph became president in 1907, and he expanded the firm's business in South America and started the Grace National Bank in 1916. The company entered aviation in 1928 in a joint venture with Pan American Airlines, forming Pan American-Grace Airways (Panagra) to serve Latin America.

In 1945 Joseph's son Peter took the helm at age 32. He took the company public in 1953. The next year Grace expanded into chemicals, buying Davison Chemical and Dewey & Almy Chemical (sealants, batteries, and packaging). Peter then sold Grace National Bank (1965), Panagra (1967), and the Grace Line (1969).

Purchases during the 1960s and 1970s included American Breeders Service (1967), Herman's (56%, sporting goods, 1970; sold 1986), Baker & Taylor (wholesale books, 1970), Sheplers (western wear, 1976; sold 1986), El Torito-La Fiesta Restaurants (1976; sold 1995), and home-improvement store Handy City (1976). Grace sold its agricultural and fertilizer businesses in 1988 and added three European water-treatment firms to its holdings in 1990. In 1992 it sold Baker & Taylor and bought DuPont Canada's North American food-service packaging operations.

Peter Grace left in 1993 after nearly 50 years as CEO. J. P. Bolduc succeeded him but was brought down by a sexual harassment scandal two years later. Grace acquired Riggers Medizintechnik of Germany (dialysis products) and Florida-based Home Intensive Care and sold its oil field services and liquid storage and terminal businesses.

Grace began divesting businesses in 1995, selling its Dearborn business to Betz Laboratories and the plant biotechnology portion of its Agracetus subsidiary to Monsanto. That year the company reclassified its health care business as discontinued; that move resulted in a dramatic drop in revenues. Albert Costello, a veteran executive from drug firm American Cyanamid, succeeded Bolduc.

In 1998 the company sold its biggest division, food packaging, to Sealed Air for about $4.9 billion in cash and stock (Grace shareholders wound up with more than 60% of Sealed Air). It also agreed to buy Imperial Chemical's Crosfield catalysts and silicas business but terminated the deal after US regulators raised antitrust issues. Grace relocated its headquarters to Columbia, Maryland, in 1999 and set up a $1 million financial education fund to settle an SEC lawsuit alleging the company socked away profits in the 1990s to mask poor earnings. The company upped its stake in Grace Chemicals K.K. (formerly Denka Grace), a Japanese joint venture to produce concrete admixture.

Also in 1999 Paul Norris, former president of AlliedSignal's specialty chemicals division, succeeded Costello as CEO. Early in 2001 Grace announced that it had filed for bankruptcy protection because of an unexpected 80% increase in asbestos-related litigation; previously, the company had managed to settle claims, which had come at a relatively manageable rate.

Grace continued to expand its presence in core markets in 2001; acquisitions included European companies Akzo-PQ Silicas (silica products) and Pieri S.A. (specialty construction chemicals). Also in 2001 Grace and Chevron Products (a unit of Chevron, formerly ChevronTexaco) formed catalyst developer Advanced Refining Technologies.

In 2002 Grace acquired catalyst manufacturing assets from Sweden's Borealis A/S. The next year Grace continued to expand internationally through the acquisition of German construction chemicals firm Tricosal Beton-Chemie.

In addition to acquisitions, Grace grew in 2002 and 2003 through improved sales for catalysts used in refining and increased volume at its Performance Chemicals unit, especially in the Asia/Pacific region.

In 2004 the company acquired Benelux firm Pieri N.V. It bought up sealants and adhesives maker Liquid Control later that year. It also acquired pharmaceutical chemical firm Alltech International as part of a strategy to build up its biotechnology and pharmaceutical customer base for silica-based products.

EXECUTIVES

Chairman, President, and CEO: Alfred E. (Fred) Festa, age 50, $5,620,988 total compensation
SVP and CFO: Hudson La Force III, age 45, $1,572,962 total compensation
SVP: W. Brian McGowan, age 60
VP; President, Grace Davison: Gregory E. (Greg) Poling, age 54, $2,724,851 total compensation
VP; President, Grace Construction Products: D. Andrew Bonham, age 49, $2,119,530 total compensation
VP, General Counsel, and Secretary: Mark A. Shelnitz, age 51, $1,622,135 total compensation
VP Public and Regulatory Affairs: William M. (Bill) Corcoran, age 60
VP Operations: J. P. (Butch) Forehand
VP and Chief Human Resources Officer: Pamela K. Wagoner, age 46
CIO: Gloria L. Keesee, age 55
Investor Relations: Susette Smith
Auditors: PricewaterhouseCoopers LLP

LOCATIONS

HQ: W. R. Grace & Co.
7500 Grace Dr., Columbia, MD 21044
Phone: 410-531-4000   **Fax:** 410-531-4367
Web: www.grace.com

2009 Sales

	$ mil.	% of total
Europe/Africa/Middle East	1,097.5	39
North America		
US	879.9	31
Canada & Puerto Rico	78.6	3
Asia/Pacific	514.9	18
Latin America	254.1	9
Total	**2,825.0**	**100**

PRODUCTS/OPERATIONS

2009 Sales

	$ mil.	% of total
Grace Davison	1,935.4	69
Grace Construction Products	889.6	31
Total	**2,825.0**	**100**

Selected Operations

Grace Davison
  Can and closure sealants
  Chemical catalysts
  Refining catalysts
  Silicas and absorbents
Grace Construction Products
  Air and vapor barriers
  Cement additives
  Coatings and sealants
  Concrete admixtures
  Fireproofing materials
  Masonry products
  Waterproofing materials

COMPETITORS

Albemarle	CRI/Criterion Catalyst
Ameron	DuPont
BASF Catalysts	Evonik Degussa
Cabot	H.B. Fuller
Clariant	UOP

HISTORICAL FINANCIALS

Company Type: Public

Income Statement

FYE: December 31

	REVENUE ($ mil.)	NET INCOME ($ mil.)	NET PROFIT MARGIN	EMPLOYEES
12/09	2,825	71	2.5%	5,940
12/08	3,317	122	3.7%	6,300
12/07	3,115	80	2.6%	6,500
12/06	2,827	18	0.6%	6,500
12/05	2,570	67	2.6%	6,400
Annual Growth	**2.4%**	**1.4%**	**—**	**(1.8%)**

2009 Year-End Financials

Debt ratio: —
Return on equity: —
Cash ($ mil.): 893
Current ratio: 3.29
Long-term debt ($ mil.): 11
No. of shares (mil.): 73
Dividends
  Yield: —
  Payout: —
Market value ($ mil.): 1,845

Stock History

NYSE: GRA

	STOCK PRICE ($) FY Close	P/E High/Low		PER SHARE ($) Earnings	Dividends	Book Value
12/09	25.35	27	4	0.98	—	(4.11)
12/08	5.97	18	2	1.68	—	(5.87)
12/07	26.18	29	14	1.12	—	(5.31)
12/06	19.80	76	29	0.27	—	(7.55)
12/05	9.40	14	7	1.00	—	(8.18)
Annual Growth	**28.1%**	**—**	**—**	**(0.5%)**	**—**	**—**

W.W. Grainger

Home, home on the Grainger is a well-stocked place. W.W. Grainger distributes more than 900,000 facilities maintenance and other products in categories such as electrical, fasteners, fleet maintenance, hand tools, hardware, janitorial, lighting, office supplies, power tools, plumbing, safety, security, and test instruments. Its two million customers include contractors, service and maintenance shops, manufacturers, resellers, hotels, and government, health care, and educational facilities. The company sells through a network of branches, distribution centers, catalogs, and websites in Canada, China, India, Japan, Mexico, Panama, Puerto Rico, and the US.

Grainger is growing its market share organically by adding new products, investing in sales and marketing programs, and by offering value-added inventory and logistics services. Since 2006 the company has added more than 230,000 new products as part of a multiyear product expansion in the US. In addition to services such as KeepStock (on-site stockroom management) and inventory scan (automated ordering through a self-managed inventory program), Grainger increasingly offers third-party services, including lighting retrofits, energy audits, and safety training, which Grainger hopes will encourage customers to consolidate their spending with the company.

Dealing with a tough economy in North America, the company saw its 2009 year-over-year sales fall by around 10% in its US and Canadian businesses. Sales to customers in the heavy manufacturing, reseller, and contractor sectors led the decline, while sales to government customers remained essentially flat. In its businesses outside North America, acquisitions in India and Japan and growth in China contributed to an increase in sales of more than 45% in 2009 compared to 2008. Grainger cuts costs primarily by closing local branches and adjusting its investment in distribution facilities.

Grainger's Industrial Supply unit distributes products for safety and security, lighting and electrical, power and hand tools, pumps and plumbing, and cleaning and maintenance industries in the US. Its Lab Safety Supply unit sells safety products businesses in the US and Canada, mostly through its branded catalogs. The unit, which had operated independently since it was acquired in 1992, was integrated into the Industrial Supply business in 2009.

Grainger entered the Latin America market in 2010 by acquiring an 80% stake in Torhefe, a maintenance parts distributor in Colombia. The joint venture increases its Latin American presence. Grainger's other international operations include operating units in China, India, Japan, Mexico, Panama, and Puerto Rico. In 2009 the company bought the rest of its joint venture in India, Asia Pacific Brands India, one of that country's largest industrial and electrical wholesale distributors. In Japan, Grainger has a 53% stake in MonotaRO, a catalog and Web-based direct marketer of facilities maintenance products aimed at small and midsized businesses.

Further expanding its offerings, Grainger bought vehicle maintenance product distributor Imperial Supplies, along with its 20,000 fleet maintenance products, from American Capital in October 2009.

Director James Slavik owns about 6% of the company.

HISTORY

In 1919 William W. Grainger, a motor designer and salesman, saw the opportunity to develop a wholesale electric-motor sales and distribution company. He set up an office in Chicago in 1927 and incorporated the business a year later. With sales generated primarily through postcard mailers and an eight-page catalog called *MotorBook*, Grainger started shipping motors to mail-order customers.

Utilities and factories began to shift from direct-current to alternating-current power systems in the late 1920s. Uniform DC-powered assembly lines gave way to individual workstations, each powered by a separate AC motor. This burgeoning market opened the way for distributors

such as W.W. Grainger to tap into segments that high-volume manufacturers found difficult to reach. In the early 1930s W.W. Grainger opened offices in Atlanta, Dallas, Philadelphia, and San Francisco; by 1936 it had 15 sales branches.

W.W. Grainger entered a boom period after WWII, and by 1949 it had branches in 30 states. The company continued to expand in the 1950s and 1960s, then went public in 1967.

William Grainger retired in 1968, and his son David succeeded him as CEO. The company expanded into electric motor manufacturing with the purchase of the Doerr Companies in 1969. Ten years later it opened its 150th branch.

Grainger's distribution became decentralized with the 1983 opening of its 1.4-million-sq.-ft. automated regional distribution center in Kansas City. The next year Grainger surpassed $1 billion in sales. The company sold its Doerr Electric subsidiary to Emerson Electric in 1986. It added 91 branches in 1987 and 1988.

After a 17-year hiatus, the company started making acquisitions again, buying Vonnegut Industrial Products in 1989; Bossert Industrial Supply and Allied Safety in 1990; Ball Industries, a distributor of sanitary and janitorial supplies, in 1991; and Lab Safety Supply in 1992. Grainger began integrating its sanitary supply business with its core activities in 1993.

For the first time in company history, no Grainger held the CEO position when president Richard Keyser was appointed in 1995, replacing David Grainger. That year the company moved its headquarters to Lake Forest, Illinois.

In 1995 Grainger put its catalog on the World Wide Web. The next year it announced new supply agreements with American Airlines, Emerson Electric Co., Lockheed Martin, and Procter & Gamble. Also in 1996 the company paid about $289 million for a unit of Canada's Acklands Ltd., distributor of automotive aftermarket products and industrial safety products.

Grainger launched several online stores through its home page in 1999 (TotalMRO.com launched in 2000) and began negotiations in 2001 to split its Internet segment off as a separate entity (dubbed Material Logic). However, citing a slow economy, it later abandoned those plans and closed all Internet sites except FindMRO.com. Grainger took a $38 million writedown related to its Internet investments.

In 2002 Grainger was recognized by *FORTUNE* magazine as one of "America's Most Admired Companies," ranked fourth among the US's largest diversified wholesalers. The company completed the acquisition of Gempler's direct marketing division (tools and safety equipment) in 2003.

EXECUTIVES

Chairman Emeritus: Richard L. (Dick) Keyser, age 67, $6,555,335 total compensation
Chairman, President, and CEO: James T. (Jim) Ryan, age 51, $5,005,497 total compensation
SVP and CFO: Ronald L. Jadin, age 49, $1,459,655 total compensation
SVP and General Counsel: John L. Howard, age 52, $1,284,176 total compensation
SVP; President, Grainger US: Michael A. Pulick, age 45, $1,422,072 total compensation
SVP Global Supply Chain: Donald G. Macpherson, age 42, $1,411,572 total compensation

SVP; President, Grainger International: Court D. Carruthers, age 37, $1,897,067 total compensation
SVP Human Resources: Lawrence J. Pilon, age 57
SVP Enterprise Processes and Systems: Timothy M. Ferrarell, age 49
SVP Communications and Investor Relations: Nancy A. Hobor, age 63
VP Specialty Brands; President, Lab Safety Supply, Inc.: Larry J. Loizzo, age 55, $1,461,129 total compensation
VP and Controller: Gregory S. Irving, age 51
VP Investor Relations: Ernest Duplessis
VP Grainger Industrial Supply Brand: Debra (Deb) Oler, age 53
President, Acklands-Grainger: Sean O'Brien
Auditors: Ernst & Young LLP

LOCATIONS

HQ: W.W. Grainger, Inc.
 100 Grainger Pkwy., Lake Forest, IL 60045
Phone: 847-535-1000   **Fax:** 847-535-0878
Web: www.grainger.com

2009 Sales

	$ mil.	% of total
US	5,362.7	86
Canada	654.0	11
Other countries	205.3	3
Total	**6,222.0**	**100**

PRODUCTS/OPERATIONS

2009 Sales

	$ mil.	% of total
US-based business	5,406.3	87
Canada-based business	651.0	10
Other businesses	164.7	3
Total	**6,222.0**	**100**

Selected Products

Adhesives
Air compressors
Air-filtration equipment
Electric motors
Electrical products
Fasteners
Fleet and vehicle maintenance products
Hand tools
Heating and ventilation equipment
Janitorial and plumbing supplies
Lab supplies
Library equipment
Lighting equipment
Material handling
Pneumatics and hydraulics
Power tools
Pumps
Safety products
Security products
Spray paints
Test instruments

COMPETITORS

Ace Hardware
Applied Industrial Technologies
Fastenal
Genuine Parts
Gexpro
Graybar Electric
Industrial Distribution Group
International Library Furniture
Kaman Industrial Technologies
Lowe's
McMaster-Carr
MSC Industrial Direct
WESCO International
Wilson

Income Statement

FYE: December 31

	REVENUE ($ mil.)	NET INCOME ($ mil.)	NET PROFIT MARGIN	EMPLOYEES
12/09	6,222	431	6.9%	18,000
12/08	6,850	475	6.9%	18,334
12/07	6,418	420	6.5%	18,036
12/06	5,884	383	6.5%	17,074
12/05	5,527	346	6.3%	16,732
Annual Growth	3.0%	5.6%	—	1.8%

2009 Year-End Financials

Debt ratio: 20.2%
Return on equity: 20.5%
Cash ($ mil.): 460
Current ratio: 2.74
Long-term debt ($ mil.): 438

No. of shares (mil.): 71
Dividends
  Yield: 1.8%
  Payout: 31.7%
Market value ($ mil.): 6,871

Stock History

NYSE: GWW

	STOCK PRICE ($) FY Close	P/E High/Low	PER SHARE ($) Earnings	Dividends	Book Value
12/09	96.83	18 11	5.62	1.78	30.49
12/08	78.84	16 10	6.04	1.55	28.66
12/07	87.52	20 14	4.94	1.34	29.57
12/06	69.94	19 14	4.24	1.11	30.69
12/05	71.10	19 14	3.78	0.92	32.26
Annual Growth	8.0%	— —	10.4%	17.9%	(1.4%)

Xcel Energy

Xcel Energy has accelerated its energy engine into utility markets across the US. The utility holding company distributes electricity to 3.4 million customers and natural gas to 1.9 million in eight states; Colorado and Minnesota account for the majority of its customers. Its regulated utilities — Northern States Power, Public Service Company of Colorado, and Southwestern Public Service — have more than 20,500 MW of primarily fossil-fueled generating capacity. Xcel also has 35,200 miles of natural gas transmission and distribution pipelines. Pushing green energy sources, in 2008 Xcel announced that it would develop solar-generated power plants in Colorado as part of its green energy initiative.

Xcel is an energy company in transition, with long-term plans to move from coalfired plants to natural gas, and on to alternative fuels such as wind, solar, and biomass to develop its power.

The largest US provider of wind energy, Xcel had almost 3,000 MW of wind energy in its portfolio by the end of 2008 and plans to have 7,400 MW by 2020. The company also plans to add 200 MW to 600 MW of solar energy sources.

Xcel plans to construct one of the largest biomass generating plants in the Midwest in Ashland, Wisconsin. The proposed plant will generate power from burning wood waste in all three operating units by 2012. Xcel currently has 67 MW of biomass generating power in Minnesota and Wisconsin.

The company spent more than $1 billion converting three coal-fired plants in Minnesota to natural gas units in 2008 and 2009. In the same time period, Xcel added gas-fired units to several of its other operations in Colorado and Minnesota. It is also working to develop so-called "smart grid" technology, which will provide customers with more reliability and control over their energy use. It completed the US's first fully integrated SmartGridCity in Boulder, Colorado.

In 2010 Xcel agreed to buy two gas-fired power plants from Calpine Corporation for $739 million. The two Denver area plants have a generating capacity of more than 900 MW and were already providing power to Public Service Company of Colorado under a contract agreement.

HISTORY

The Minnesota Electric Light & Electric Motive Power Company was founded in 1881 and changed its name to Minnesota Brush Electric the next year. In the 1890s it provided street lighting and power for trolleys and became Minneapolis General Electric.

In 1909 Henry Byllesby formed rival firm Washington County Light and Power Co. (soon renamed Consumers Power Company), then created holding company Northern States Power Company of Delaware (NSPD). In 1910 he founded Standard Gas and Electric, a holding company overseeing NSPD and many other US utilities.

NSPD bought Minneapolis General Electric in 1912, and Consumers Power was renamed the Northern States Power Company (NSP) in 1916. During the 1920s NSPD connected its subsidiaries via transmission lines. Byllesby died in 1924.

In 1931 NSP was placed under NSPD, but the Public Utility Holding Company Act of 1935 dissolved Standard and NSPD. NSP became independent in the 1940s and spent $335 million on new facilities after WWII.

During the 1960s NSP moved into Michigan, South Dakota, and Wisconsin, and brought its first nuclear power plant on line in 1964 (converted to natural gas in 1968). It began operating the Monticello and Prairie Island nukes in the early 1970s.

Company sales nearly doubled in the 1980s. In 1989 NSP created NRG Energy (incorporated 1992) to invest in independent power projects. The Federal Energy Policy Act allowed wholesale power competition in 1992, and NSP lost nine of its 19 municipal customers.

NSP acquired Viking Gas Transmission, which owned an interstate pipeline, in 1993. It also began developing affordable housing. NRG Energy began a shopping spree abroad in 1994, buying interests in plants in Germany and Australia. In 1996 it bought a 48% stake in Bolivia's COBEE (increased to 99% in 2001). Also that year it acquired PacifiCorp's Pacific Generating unit, which owned stakes in a dozen geographically scattered plants

In 1999 NRG Energy gained nearly 7,600 MW of capacity through power plant acquisitions in California, Connecticut, Massachusetts, and New York. The next year NRG Energy picked up another 1,700 MW in Louisiana, and it agreed to buy fossil-fueled plants (1,875 MW) from Delaware's Conectiv for $800 million (half of the deal was completed in 2001, the other half was canceled the following year). NSP spun off part of NRG in 2000 in an IPO.

Meanwhile, as the utility-merger trend gathered steam in 1999, NSP agreed to acquire Denver-based New Century Engines in a $4.9 billion deal. The acquisition was completed in 2000, and the expanded company changed its name to Xcel Energy.

The next year Xcel sold nearly all of its stake in UK-based Yorkshire Power Group, which had been held by New Century Energies, to Innogy (now RWE npower). It sold its remaining 5% stake in Yorkshire Power in 2002. NRG purchased several Latin American projects from Swedish utility Vattenfall in 2001. NRG also agreed to purchase four coal-fired plants (2,500 MW) in Ohio from FirstEnergy for $1.5 billion; however, the deal was later canceled.

In 2002 Xcel repurchased the 26% stake in NRG that it sold to the public in 2000-01.

Downturns in the wholesale energy industry (spurred by Enron's collapse and the ensuing financial scrutiny of other energy trading companies) led to serious financial difficulties for NRG in 2002. NRG entered into debt restructuring talks with its creditors, and in 2003 the unit filed for Chapter 11 bankruptcy. Its reorganization plan, which was completed that December, included a settlement agreement in which Xcel Energy agreed to pay $752 million to NRG and its creditors and then divest its interest in NRG.

In 2003 the company sold pipeline company Viking Gas Transmission to Northern Border Partners (now ONEOK Partners) and its Arizona utility, Black Mountain Gas (10,000 gas and propane customers), to Las Vegas-based utility Southwest Gas.

The company sold off the assets of subsidiary Xcel Energy International (primarily Latin American power investments) in 2004 and its Seren Innovations business (cable TV, phone, and high-speed Internet access networks in California and Minnesota) in 2006.

EXECUTIVES

Chairman and CEO: Richard C. (Dick) Kelly, age 63, $11,340,182 total compensation
President, COO, and Director: Benjamin G. S. (Ben) Fowke III, age 51, $3,384,850 total compensation
CFO: David M. Sparby, age 55, $2,046,940 total compensation
VP and Chief Energy Supply Officer: Kent T. Larson
VP and General Counsel: Michael C. Connelly, age 48, $1,872,946 total compensation
VP and Treasurer: George E. Tyson II, age 44
VP and Controller: Teresa S. Madden, age 53
VP and Chief Administrative Officer: Marvin E. McDaniel, age 49
VP Transmission: Teresa M. Mogensen
VP Regulatory and Resource Planning: Scott Wilensky
VP and Corporate Secretary: Cathy J. Hart, age 60
President and CEO, Northern States Power Company, Minnesota: Cynthia L. (Cyndi) Lesher, age 62
President, CEO, and Director, SPS: C. Riley Hill, age 50
President, CEO, and Director, Northern States Power Company, Wisconsin: Michael L. (Mike) Swenson, age 59
President, CEO, and Director NSP Minnesota: Judy M. Poferl, age 49
CEO, Public Service Company of Colorado: David L. Eves, age 51
Director Investor Relations: Jack E. Nielsen
Auditors: Deloitte & Touche LLP

LOCATIONS

HQ: Xcel Energy Inc.
414 Nicollet Mall, Minneapolis, MN 55401
Phone: 612-330-5500   **Fax:** 800-895-2895
Web: www.xcelenergy.com

PRODUCTS/OPERATIONS

2009 Sales

	$ mil.	% of total
Electric utility	7,704.7	80
Gas utility	1,865.7	19
Nonregulated & other	73.9	1
Total	**9,644.3**	**100**

Selected Subsidiaries and Affiliates

Regulated operations
  Northern States Power Company (Minnesota)
  Northern States Power Company (Wisconsin)
  Public Service Company of Colorado
  Southwestern Public Service Company
  WestGas InterState Inc. (interstate pipeline)

Nonregulated operations
  Eloigne Company (affordable housing projects)

COMPETITORS

AEP	DTE
ALLETE	Dynegy
Alliant Energy	Entergy
Atmos Energy	Integrys Energy Group
Basin Electric Power	Minnesota Power
CenterPoint Energy	OGE Energy
CMS Energy	Southern Company

HISTORICAL FINANCIALS

Company Type: Public

Income Statement

	REVENUE ($ mil.)	NET INCOME ($ mil.)	NET PROFIT MARGIN	EMPLOYEES	FYE: December 31
12/09	9,644	681	7.1%	11,351	
12/08	11,203	646	5.8%	11,223	
12/07	10,034	577	5.8%	10,917	
12/06	9,840	572	5.8%	9,735	
12/05	9,626	513	5.3%	9,781	
Annual Growth	**0.0%**	**7.3%**	**—**	**3.8%**	

2009 Year-End Financials

Debt ratio: 108.3%	No. of shares (mil.): 460
Return on equity: 9.6%	Dividends
Cash ($ mil.): 108	Yield: 4.6%
Current ratio: 0.92	Payout: 65.5%
Long-term debt ($ mil.): 7,889	Market value ($ mil.): 9,754

Stock History

NYSE: XEL

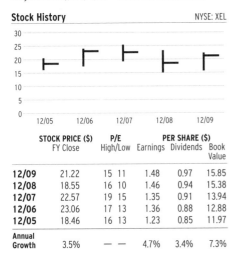

	STOCK PRICE ($) FY Close	P/E High/Low		PER SHARE ($) Earnings	Dividends	Book Value
12/09	21.22	15	11	1.48	0.97	15.85
12/08	18.55	16	10	1.46	0.94	15.38
12/07	22.57	19	15	1.35	0.91	13.94
12/06	23.06	17	13	1.36	0.88	12.88
12/05	18.46	16	13	1.23	0.85	11.97
Annual Growth	**3.5%**	**—**	**—**	**4.7%**	**3.4%**	**7.3%**

Xerox Corporation

You won't find many companies listed in the dictionary as a verb. Xerox, best known for its color and black-and-white copiers, also provides printers, scanners, multifunction devices, and a panoply of services. The company sells document management software and copier supplies and offers consulting and document management outsourcing services.

In 2010 Xerox acquired Affiliated Computer Services (ACS) for about $6.4 billion in cash and stock. Through the purchase, the company expanded its portfolio in document management services and delved deeper into business process outsourcing, IT services, and other business services. The acquisition tripled the amount of revenue Xerox derives from services.

The global recession helped knock down Xerox's sales. Through stringent cost control measures, which were a corporate watchword through the past decade, the company was able to remain profitable, although not with the margins seen earlier in the decade.

Once synonymous with copying, Xerox now generates most of its product sales from printers and multifunction devices. Though black-and-white systems traditionally accounted for the majority of Xerox's equipment sales, the company increased the number of color systems across its product lines, with a greater emphasis on higher-margin services and high-end printing systems. To that end, the company phased out its consumer product lines, including its personal ink jet printers.

Xerox generates more than three-quarters of its revenues from post-sale sources, which include maintenance and document management services, consumable supplies, and financing. Xerox also built a leading document management consulting business. It helps companies cut costs by monitoring and managing device usage and migrating businesses to multifunction machines (preferably replacing competitors' products with their own).

Addressing the Asia/Pacific region, Xerox holds a 25% stake in a joint venture with FUJIFILM called Fuji Xerox. The JV develops and manufactures document processing products in Australia, China, Japan, New Zealand, and other areas of the Pacific Rim.

Ursula Burns was promoted from president to CEO in 2009. Burns, who got her start at the company as a mechanical engineering summer intern, previously held roles in product development, manufacturing and supply chain operations, marketing, human resources, and strategy. Her predecessor, Anne Mulcahy, had served as CEO since 2001.

HISTORY

The Haloid Company was incorporated in 1906 to make and sell photographic paper. In 1935 it bought photocopier company Rectigraph, which led Haloid to buy a license for a new process called electrophotography (renamed xerography from the ancient Greek words for "dry" and "writing") from the Battelle Memorial Institute in 1947. Battelle backed inventor Chester Carlson, who had worked to perfect a process for transferring electrostatic images from a photoconductive surface to paper.

Haloid commercialized xerography with the Model A copier in 1949 and the Xerox Copyflo

in 1955, and by 1956 xerographic products represented 40% of sales. The company changed its name to Haloid Xerox in 1958 (Haloid was dropped from the name in 1961), and in 1959 it introduced the first simplified office copier. That machine took the world by storm, beating out such competing technologies as mimeograph (A.B.Dick), thermal paper (3M), and damp copy (Kodak). Sales soared to nearly $270 million in 1965.

Xerox branched out in the 1960s by buying three publishing companies and a computer unit; all were later sold or disbanded. In the 1970s Xerox bought printer, plotter, and disk drive businesses, as well as record carrier Western Union (1979; sold in 1982). In 1974 the FTC, believing Xerox was too market-dominant, forced the company to license its technology.

In the 1980s Xerox bought companies specializing in optical character recognition, scanning, faxing, and desktop publishing. It also diversified by buying insurance and investment banking firms, among others. In 1986 Paul Allaire, who had joined Xerox in 1966, was elected president. He was named CEO in 1990 and became chairman in 1991.

Eyeing future alliances, Xerox agreed to supply computer print engines to Compaq (1992) and Apple (1993). In 1995 it introduced networked color laser printers and software for printing Web documents.

Xerox bought Rank's 20% stake in Rank Xerox, the two companies' 41-year-old global marketing joint venture, in 1997. That year Xerox launched a $500 PC printer, copier, and scanner — its first product specifically for home use — and Allaire hired IBM CFO Richard Thoman as president and COO to spearhead a push into network and digital products.

In 1999 Xerox named Thoman CEO to replace Allaire, who remained chairman. Layoffs also continued, totaling 14,000 for 1998 and 1999.

Xerox bought Tektronix's ailing color printing and imaging division in 2000. With profits shrinking and market value flagging, Thoman resigned in May 2000 amid pressure from the board. Allaire assumed the CEO post once again. Also that year the company sold its operations in China and Hong Kong to Fuji Xerox.

Early in 2001 the company laid off 4,000 more employees. That year Xerox sold half of its 50% stake in Fuji Xerox to Fuji Photo Film, and it discontinued its product lines aimed at consumer and small office users, including its personal copiers and ink jet printers. Allaire stepped down as chief executive; COO Anne Mulcahy was named his successor. Looking to reduce its massive debt, Xerox transferred most of its US customer financing operations to GE Capital in a deal including $1 billion in cash financing from the lending giant (it later formed similar arrangements with GE Capital for many of its international operations).

In 2002 CEO Mulcahy replaced Allaire as chairman. Also that year Xerox agreed to pay a $10 million fine to settle a complaint brought by the SEC alleging financial reporting violations. After the settlement, Xerox — which had fired KPMG as its auditors the previous year and brought in PricewaterhouseCoopers — initiated an audit of its financial statements from 1997 through 2001; as a result of the audit, in June 2002 the company restated about $2 billion in revenues over the five-year period.

In 2007 Xerox acquired office equipment vendor Global Imaging Systems for approximately $1.5 billion.

EXECUTIVES

Chairman and CEO: Ursula M. Burns, age 51,
$11,172,774 total compensation
Vice Chairman and CFO:
Lawrence A. (Larry) Zimmerman, age 67,
$2,954,589 total compensation
EVP; President and CEO, Affiliated Computer Services:
Lynn R. Blodgett, age 55
EVP; President, Xerox North America:
James A. (Jim) Firestone, age 55,
$4,480,303 total compensation
EVP; President, Xerox Global Customer Operations and Xerox Europe: Armando Zagalo de Lima, age 51
SVP; President, North America: Russell M. Peacock, age 51
SVP Xerox Services: Bill Steenburgh
SVP; President, Xerox Global Services: Stephen Cronin, age 56
SVP, General Counsel, and Corporate Secretary:
Don H. Liu, age 48
SVP; President, Xerox Global Business and Services Group: Willem T. (Wim) Appelo, age 45
SVP Global Accounts Operations: Cameron Hyde
VP and Chief Accounting Officer: Gary R. Kabureck, age 56
VP and Chief Strategy Officer: Uta Werner, age 51
VP and CIO: John E. McDermott, age 56
VP and CTO; President, Xerox Innovation Group:
Sophie Vandebroek, age 47
VP Marketing and Communications and Chief Marketing Officer: Christa Carone, age 41
VP Human Resources: Tom Maddison, age 46
VP Global Public Relations: Carl Langsenkamp
VP Investor Relations: James H. Lesko, age 58
President and Director, Fuji Xerox Co., Ltd.:
Tadahito Yamamoto
Auditors: PricewaterhouseCoopers LLP

LOCATIONS

HQ: Xerox Corporation
45 Glover Ave., Norwalk, CT 06850
Phone: 203-968-3000
Web: www.xerox.com

2009 Sales

	$ mil.	% of total
US	8,156	54
Europe	4,971	33
Other regions	2,052	13
Total	**15,179**	**100**

PRODUCTS/OPERATIONS

2009 Sales

	$ mil.	% of total
Post-sale revenue	11,629	77
Equipment sales	3,550	23
Total	**15,179**	**100**

2009 Sales

	$ mil.	% of total
Office	8,576	56
Production	4,545	30
Other	2,058	14
Total	**15,179**	**100**

2009 Sales

	$ mil.	% of total
Service, outsourcing & rentals	7,820	51
Sales	6,646	44
Finance income	713	5
Total	**15,179**	**100**

Selected Products

Office (commercial, government, and education sectors)
Copiers
Displays
Multifunction devices (copy, fax, print, scan)
Printers
Projectors
Scanners
Production (graphics communications industry and large corporations)
Digital presses
High-volume printers
Software
Other
Paper
Services
Wide-format printers

COMPETITORS

Accenture	Infosys
Agfa	Konica Minolta
Brother Industries	Kyocera Mita
Canon	Lexmark
Capgemini	NEC
Computer Sciences Corp.	Océ
Dell	Oki Data
Eastman Kodak	Olivetti
Epson	Panasonic Corp
FUJIFILM	Pitney Bowes
Fujitsu	Ricoh Company
Heidelberger	Sharp Corp.
Druckmaschinen	Tata Consultancy
Hewlett-Packard	Toshiba
Hitachi	Unisys
IBM	Wipro

HISTORICAL FINANCIALS

Company Type: Public

Income Statement

FYE: December 31

	REVENUE ($ mil.)	NET INCOME ($ mil.)	NET PROFIT MARGIN	EMPLOYEES
12/09	15,179	485	3.2%	53,600
12/08	17,608	230	1.3%	57,100
12/07	16,406	1,135	6.9%	57,400
12/06	15,895	1,210	7.6%	53,700
12/05	15,701	986	6.3%	55,200
Annual Growth	**(0.8%)**	**(16.3%)**	**—**	**(0.7%)**

2009 Year-End Financials

Debt ratio: 117.4%
Return on equity: 7.3%
Cash ($ mil.): 3,799
Current ratio: 2.18
Long-term debt ($ mil.): 8,276
No. of shares (mil.): 1,383
Dividends
  Yield: 2.0%
  Payout: 30.9%
Market value ($ mil.): 11,701

Stock History

NYSE: XRX

	STOCK PRICE ($) FY Close	P/E High/Low		Earnings	PER SHARE ($) Dividends	Book Value
12/09	8.46	18	7	0.55	0.17	5.10
12/08	7.97	62	19	0.26	0.13	4.51
12/07	16.19	17	13	1.19	0.04	6.21
12/06	16.95	14	11	1.22	0.00	5.12
12/05	14.65	18	13	0.94	0.00	5.21
Annual Growth	**(12.8%)**	**—**	**—**	**(12.5%)**	**—**	**(0.6%)**

Xilinx, Inc.

Xilinx is programmed to give you control. The California company is a top supplier of field-programmable gate arrays (FPGAs) and complex programmable logic devices (CPLDs). Customers program these integrated circuits to perform specific functions, thereby achieving greater design flexibility and cutting time to market. Xilinx also offers a broad range of design software and intellectual property used to customize its chips. The company sells to manufacturers — including Cisco, IBM, Raytheon, Samsung, and Sony — in the aerospace, automotive, communications, computer, consumer electronics, medical, networking, and optical markets. Customers outside the US account for about two-thirds of the company's sales.

Mega-distributor Avnet handles about half of Xilinx's sales.

Consumers around the world were spending less on electronics during the recession, resulting in a prolonged downturn for the semiconductor industry, always a highly cyclical business. The global economic conditions hit Xilinx hard during the second half of fiscal 2009. The company is restructuring its operations in response to the downturn, reducing headcount and cutting other costs. While new products make up more of the chip maker's sales now than in the past, the company has limited market visibility on which new products will be in demand. Xilinx must continue to develop and introduce new products to remain competitive with its industry peers.

Through all the up-and-down cycles of the semiconductor industry, Xilinx is one of the most consistently profitable chip makers in the business. Its sales have remained essentially flat in the past four fiscal years, but that's a significant achievement in light of the general industry downturn during late 2008 and much of 2009.

Xilinx outsources manufacturing to Samsung Electronics, Seiko Epson, Toshiba Semiconductor, and United Microelectronics, among others. In 2010 it signed up Taiwan Semiconductor Manufacturing, the top silicon foundry (contract semiconductor manufacturer) in the world, to make its devices with 28-nanometer features, the leading edge in chip design. Like other fabless semiconductor companies, Xilinx plows money into R&D, since it is free of capital expenditures for wafer fabrication. The company spends about 20% of annual sales on R&D, which is typical for leading-edge semiconductor suppliers. It also formed scores of development alliances with other chip makers, chip equipment manufacturers, and suppliers of design software and services.

Xilinx has operations in Ireland, Singapore, and the US, and sales offices worldwide.

HISTORY

In 1984 Bernie Vonderschmitt, Ross Freeman, and Jim Barnett started Xilinx when ZiLOG, their employer, rejected the idea of investing in a programmable chip operation. Xilinx introduced the first field-programmable gate array (FPGA) the next year. Successive products featured more logic gates, providing greater computing power. A chip with up to 5,000 usable logic gates came out in 1987; three years later that number quadrupled. (Freeman died in 1989; Barnett left the company in 1990, the year Xilinx went public.)

Xilinx acquired FPGA software developer NeoCAD in 1995. That year Xilinx formed a joint venture with United Microelectronics to build a wafer operation, United Silicon, in Taiwan. Xilinx brought in Hewlett-Packard veteran Willem (Wim) Roelandts as CEO in 1996, replacing Vonderschmitt, who remained chairman until his retirement in 2003. (Roelandts then succeeded him in the chairman's role as well; Vonderschmitt died the next year.)

In 1999 Xilinx acquired the programmable chips business of Philips Semiconductors (now NXP). Also that year the company created the $75 million Technology Growth Fund, which was used to invest in chip design software companies, such as AccelChip and Synplicity (later acquired by Synopsys).

Buoyed by a strong market and record sales, Xilinx expanded its Colorado plant in 2000 and acquired several small chip-design and software companies, including RocketChips (high-speed networking and telecom transceivers).

In 2001 it began another plant expansion that doubled the size of its Irish facility. The next year Xilinx announced a multi-year deal with IBM Microelectronics under which IBM used some of its most advanced manufacturing techniques to produce high-end Xilinx FPGAs.

In 2004 Xilinx created the Ecosystem Growth Fund, a $100 million corporate venture capital fund targeted at investing in companies specializing in design software, digital signal processors, embedded processors, and high-speed connectivity. Xilinx was looking to grow beyond the $5 billion market for programmable logic into the much larger market for application-specific integrated circuits and application-specific standard parts, estimated at $36 billion.

Xilinx sharpened its product focus that year by creating two new divisions to deal with embedded processing devices and with digital signal processors (DSPs). The company expanded its offerings with its purchase of Triscend Corp., a maker of configurable microcontroller chips.

The company acquired AccelChip in 2006 for around $19 million in cash. Most of AccelChip's employees joined Xilinx's DSP division. Also that year Xilinx chartered another VC fund, the $75 million Asia Pacific Technology Fund. The company invested in ventures creating applications for programmable logic or developing technologies to increase the adoption of programmable logic in a variety of electronics markets. Xilinx put $500,000 to $5 million into startups based in China, India, Singapore, South Korea, and Taiwan, among other Asia/Pacific countries.

In 2007 Wim Roelandts set plans to retire as president and CEO, after guiding the company through a threefold increase in sales over 11 years as CEO. Moshe Gavrielov, an EVP/GM of Cadence Design Systems, was picked to succeed him as president and CEO in 2008. Roelandts remained chairman of Xilinx until 2009.

EXECUTIVES

Chairman: Philip T. (Flip) Gianos, age 60
President, CEO, and Director: Moshe N. Gavrielov, age 55, $3,232,717 total compensation
SVP Finance and CFO: Jon A. Olson, age 56, $1,304,738 total compensation
SVP Programmable Platforms Development: Victor Peng, age 49, $1,132,669 total compensation
SVP Worldwide Marketing: Vincent F. (Vin) Ratford, age 58, $1,023,990 total compensation

SVP Worldwide Sales: Frank A. Tornaghi, age 55, $1,031,865 total compensation
SVP and CTO: Ivo Bolsens
SVP Worldwide Quality and New Product Introductions: Vincent Tong
SVP Worldwide Operations: Raja Petrakian
VP and CIO; Managing Director, EMEA: Kevin Cooney
VP Corporate Strategic Planning: Krishna Rangasayee
VP Product Solutions and Management: Mustafa Veziroglu
VP, General Counsel, and Secretary: Scott Hover-Smoot, age 55
VP Worldwide Human Resources: Kathy Borneman, age 51
Investor Relations: Lori Owen
Corporate Communications, Corporate and Executive Programs: Lisa Washington
Auditors: Ernst & Young LLP

LOCATIONS

HQ: Xilinx, Inc.
2100 Logic Dr., San Jose, CA 95124
Phone: 408-559-7778   **Fax:** 408-559-7114
Web: www.xilinx.com

2010 Sales

	$ mil.	% of total
Asia/Pacific		
China	327.3	18
Japan	160.9	9
Other countries	321.8	17
North America		
US	578.3	31
Other countries	50.2	3
Europe	395.1	22
Total	**1,833.6**	**100**

PRODUCTS/OPERATIONS

2010 Sales

	$ mil.	% of total
Mainstream products	604.6	33
New products	580.0	32
Base products	559.1	30
Support products	89.9	5
Total	**1,833.6**	**100**

2010 Sales by Application

	% of total
Communications	47
Consumer & automotive	15
Data processing	7
Industrial & other	31
Total	**100**

Selected Products

Integrated circuits
  Complex programmable logic devices (CoolRunner)
  Field-programmable gate arrays (EasyPath, Spartan, Virtex)
Software design tools
  Alliance series (logic device design tool)
  Foundation series (low-cost design tool for logic devices)
  WebPACK (free, downloadable CPLD and FPGA design tools)

COMPETITORS

Actel	LOGIC Devices
Altera	LSI Corp.
Altium	ON Semiconductor
Atmel	PLX Technology
Cypress Semiconductor	PMC-Sierra
Fujitsu Semiconductor	QuickLogic
IBM Microelectronics	Texas Instruments
Lattice Semiconductor	

HISTORICAL FINANCIALS

Company Type: Public

Income Statement

FYE: March 31

	REVENUE ($ mil.)	NET INCOME ($ mil.)	NET PROFIT MARGIN	EMPLOYEES
3/10	1,834	358	19.5%	2,948
3/09	1,825	376	20.6%	3,145
3/08	1,841	374	20.3%	3,415
3/07	1,843	351	19.0%	3,353
3/06	1,726	354	20.5%	3,295
Annual Growth	**1.5%**	**0.2%**	**—**	**(2.7%)**

2010 Year-End Financials

Debt ratio: 19.4%
Return on equity: 18.5%
Cash ($ mil.): 1,031
Long-term debt ($ mil.): 411
No. of shares (mil.): 274
Dividends
  Yield: 2.4%
  Payout: 46.5%
Market value ($ mil.): 6,983

Stock History

NASDAQ (GS): XLNX

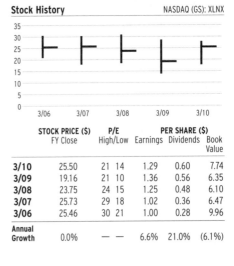

	STOCK PRICE ($) FY Close	P/E High/Low	PER SHARE ($) Earnings	Dividends	Book Value
3/10	25.50	21 14	1.29	0.60	7.74
3/09	19.16	21 10	1.36	0.56	6.35
3/08	23.75	24 15	1.25	0.48	6.10
3/07	25.73	29 18	1.02	0.36	6.47
3/06	25.46	30 21	1.00	0.28	9.96
Annual Growth	**0.0%**	**— —**	**6.6%**	**21.0%**	**(6.1%)**

Yahoo! Inc.

Yahoo! wants to spread some cheer to Internet users around the world. A leading online portal, Yahoo! draws people to its network of websites with a mix of news, entertainment, and shopping, as well as the revitalized Bing search engine (powered by Microsoft). The company also offers registered users personalized Web pages, e-mail, and message boards. Yahoo! publishes content in more than 25 languages. It generates most of its revenue through advertising and online marketing sales, but it also charges fees for premium services (such as personals and music) to about 8.5 million users.

A pioneer in Internet search and navigation, Yahoo!'s ever-growing collection of content and services has made it one of the best-known online brands and one of the most popular Internet destinations; however, it is facing intense competition. Google is capitalizing on its position as the most popular search engine to rapidly expand its range of content and services, while Microsoft's MSN portal has launched its own search engine technology and search-targeted ad capabilities.

Yahoo! dealt with its rivals in 2010 by uniting with Microsoft to face Google head on. Microsoft and Yahoo! formed a 10-year partnership in which Microsoft's new Bing search engine became the search provider on Yahoo!'s websites. As part of the deal, Yahoo! handles sales of search ads for both companies, and the two firms share search revenue. The deal was announced in 2009; the two companies formed the partnership after Yahoo! rejected Microsoft's unsolicited bid to buy Yahoo! in 2008.

Yahoo! revenues declined as a result of the troubled economy. In response, Yahoo! has rolled out major cost-cutting measures. It has been shedding noncore assets, such as the 2010 sale of Yahoo! Hot Jobs to Monster Worldwide for some $225 million. It also sold e-mail technology unit Zimbra to virtualization technology firm VMware. Yahoo! has been exiting international markets as well. In 2009 it sold its direct investment in Chinese search firm Alibaba.

After shedding these noncore assets, Yahoo! began buying up companies related to content and technology growth, and/or geographic areas that help strengthen or increase its market presence. Its first acquisition of this nature was announced in 2010, when it purchased social sports startup Citizen Sports, owner of a series of popular sports apps on Apple's iPhone and on social networking sites such as Facebook. Later in 2010 it beefed up the content it offers across its sites when it acquired Associated Content, an online publisher of articles, videos, audio, and images from about 380,000 contributors.

Yahoo!'s strategy is being spearheaded by outspoken CEO Carol Bartz, who was hired in 2009. The former executive at software firm Autodesk replaced co-founder Jerry Yang, who left after a short and tumultuous tenure as CEO.

HISTORY

David Filo and Jerry Yang began developing the Yahoo! search engine and directory while students at Stanford in 1994. By the end of that year, their website was attracting hundreds of thousands of visitors. The next year they incorporated the business and tapped former Motorola executive Timothy Koogle as president. Revenue also began flowing in 1995 when Yahoo! started selling ad space on its website. The company went public the next year and share prices soared. Yahoo! teamed with SOFTBANK and its affiliates to form Yahoo! Japan and Yahoo! Europe in 1996.

Branching into audio, the company launched its Yahoo! Radio broadcast Internet radio service in 1999. Yahoo's $3.7 billion acquisition of GeoCities and the more than $5 billion purchase of broadcast.com in 1999 stoked the Internet consolidation trend. Koogle was also named chairman in 1999.

The company also took a minority stake in Internet phone services firm Net2Phone and acquired e-mail communications firm eGroups for about $430 million in 2000.

In the wake of a November 2000 French court order requiring Yahoo! to bar French users from accessing Nazi-related items for sale on its auction sites, the company banned hate material from its auction websites in 2001. (It also stopped the sale of adult videos on its shopping sites that year.) To add a new source of revenue, Yahoo! announced it would begin charging fees to list items; 90% of its users later abandoned the site. With advertising revenue declining and profits in danger, Koogle said that year he would step down, and the company announced that it would lay off about 400 staff members (later adding another 300 to that figure).

Former Warner Bros. executive Terry Semel was tapped as Koogle's replacement in 2001. In other efforts to diversify its revenue streams, Yahoo! won an unsolicited takeover bid for HotJobs.com (which had already agreed to be acquired by TMP Worldwide) late in 2001.

Yahoo! paid $1 billion for a 40% stake in Alibaba.com, a Chinese e-commerce company, in 2005. Also that year it bought Flickr, a service for posting and sharing photos online, as well as del.icio.us, a service used to store and share Internet bookmarks. It also launched its own Web logging (blogging) service called Yahoo! 360 and picked up entertainment polling site Bix.com in 2006. The company continues to expand its music downloading service and is looking to create additional digital media services.

On the international front, in 2006 Yahoo! formed a strategic partnership with Seven Network Limited, an Australian media company, to form Yahoo! 7, the result of a combination of Yahoo! Australia, and Seven's online, TV, and magazine operations. Also that year Yahoo! combined its Spanish-language US website with Telemundo's site in order to target the growing Hispanic audience on the Web.

In 2007 Yahoo! introduced Yahoo Smart Ads, a product that includes tools to help marketers create custom online advertising aimed at specific groups of buyers. It also acquired online advertising exchange Right Media for $650 million.

In 2008 the company first cut 7% of its 14,300-employee work force, equaling some 1,000 jobs. A troubled economy called for even more belt-tightening, including a second round of layoffs (representing at least 10% of its work force) that occurred at the end of 2008.

Longtime advertising executive Roy Bostock was named chairman in early 2008. He had barely enough time to settle into his new office when Microsoft made another bid to buy the company; this time it offered nearly $45 billion. The offer increased the company's value more than 60%. Yahoo! rejected Microsoft, and the software giant eventually walked away from its pursuit of the company.

EXECUTIVES

Chairman: Roy J. Bostock, age 69
President, CEO, and Director; CEO, Yahoo! Search Marketing Group: Carol A. Bartz, age 61, $47,229,272 total compensation
Chief Yahoo and Director: Jerry Yang, age 40, $1 total compensation
Chief Yahoo: David Filo, age 43
EVP and CFO: Timothy R. (Tim) Morse, age 41, $6,170,193 total compensation
EVP Yahoo! Americas: Hilary A. Schneider, age 49, $5,261,775 total compensation
EVP, General Counsel, and Secretary: Michael J. (Mike) Callahan, age 41, $3,925,049 total compensation
EVP and Chief Marketing Officer: Elisa Steele
EVP and Chief Product Officer: Blake Irving, age 50
EVP and Chief Human Resources Officer: David Windley
EVP Product Architecture and Strategy: Ashvinkumar (Ash) Patel, age 44
EVP Service Engineering and Operations: David E. Dibble, age 48
EVP Customer Advocacy: Jeff Russakow

SVP Cloud Computing: Shelton Shugar
SVP, Chief Scientist, and Head, Yahoo! Labs: Prabhakar Raghavan, age 49
SVP and CTO: Raymie Stata
SVP Search Engineering: Tuoc V. Luong, age 46
SVP Global Integrated Marketing and Brand Management: Penny Baldwin
SVP Global Communications: Eric C. Brown
VP and Chief of Staff to CEO: Joel Jones
VP, Global Controller, and Chief Accounting Officer: Aman S. Kothari, age 37
Investor Relations: Cathy La Rocca
Auditors: PricewaterhouseCoopers LLP

LOCATIONS

HQ: Yahoo! Inc.
701 1st Ave., Sunnyvale, CA 94089
Phone: 408-349-3300 **Fax:** 408-349-3301
Web: www.yahoo.com

2009 Sales

	$ mil.	% of total
US	4,714	73
Other countries	1,746	27
Total	**6,460**	**100**

Selected International Subsidiaries

Yahoo! 7 (Australia & New Zealand)
Yahoo! Argentina
Yahoo! Asia
Yahoo! Brasil
Yahoo! Canada
Yahoo! China
Yahoo! Danmark (Denmark)
Yahoo! España (Spain)
Yahoo! Europe
  Yahoo! Deutschland (Germany)
  Yahoo! France
  Yahoo! UK
Yahoo! Hong Kong
Yahoo! India
Yahoo! Italia (Italy)
Yahoo! Japan (35%)
Yahoo! Korea
Yahoo! México
Yahoo! Norge (Norway)
Yahoo! Singapore
Yahoo! Sverige (Sweden)
Yahoo! Telemundo (United States Hispanic)

PRODUCTS/OPERATIONS

2009 Sales

	$ mil.	% of total
Marketing services		
Owned & operated sites	3,553	55
Affiliated sites	2,121	33
Fees	786	12
Total	**6,460**	**100**

Selected Offerings

Applications
  Communications
    Yahoo! Mail
    Yahoo! Messenger
  Communities
    Yahoo! Groups
    Flickr
Integrated Consumer Experiences
  My Yahoo!
  Yahoo! Home Page
  Yahoo! Local
  Yahoo! Toolbar
Media Products and Solutions
  Yahoo! Entertainment & Lifestyles
  Yahoo! Finance
  Yahoo! News
  Yahoo! Sports
Search
  Yahoo! Search

COMPETITORS

24/7 Real Media	Disney Online
About.com	eBay
Amazon.com	Facebook
AOL	Google
Apple Inc.	InfoSpace
Ask.com	LookSmart
CBS Interactive	MSN
CityGrid Media	MySpace
craigslist	RealNetworks
Daum Communications	Vertro

HISTORICAL FINANCIALS

Company Type: Public

Income Statement				FYE: December 31
	REVENUE ($ mil.)	NET INCOME ($ mil.)	NET PROFIT MARGIN	EMPLOYEES
12/09	6,460	598	9.3%	13,900
12/08	7,209	424	5.9%	13,600
12/07	6,969	660	9.5%	14,300
12/06	6,426	751	11.7%	11,400
12/05	5,258	1,896	36.1%	9,800
Annual Growth	5.3%	(25.1%)	—	9.1%

2009 Year-End Financials

Debt ratio: 0.7%
Return on equity: 5.0%
Cash ($ mil.): 1,275
Current ratio: 2.67
Long-term debt ($ mil.): 83

No. of shares (mil.): 1,348
Dividends
 Yield: —
 Payout: —
Market value ($ mil.): 22,624

Stock History

NASDAQ (GS): YHOO

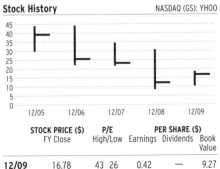

	STOCK PRICE ($) FY Close	P/E High/Low	PER SHARE ($) Earnings	Dividends	Book Value
12/09	16.78	43 26	0.42	—	9.27
12/08	12.20	104 31	0.29	—	8.34
12/07	23.26	73 47	0.47	—	7.07
12/06	25.54	84 44	0.52	—	6.79
12/05	39.18	34 24	1.28	—	6.35
Annual Growth	(19.1%)	— —	(24.3%)	—	9.9%

YRC Worldwide

As one of the largest providers of less-than-truckload (LTL) transportation in North America, holding company YRC Worldwide wants the "YRC" to stand for "Your Regional Carrier." (LTL carriers consolidate freight from multiple shippers into a single trailer.) About two-thirds of the company's revenue is generated from its national transportation segment, YRC, which operates some 12,900 tractors and 53,300 trailers from a network of about 340 service centers. YRC Worldwide also has a collection of regional LTL carriers. The company's YRC Logistics (formerly Meridian IQ) unit provides logistics services. Its newly formed YRC Truckload subsidiary oversees truckload carrier USF Glen Moore.

The company's YRC segment was formed in March 2009 with the integration of its two former LTL truck units: Roadway Express and Yellow Transportation. YRC Worldwide merged the two networks in an effort to reduce administrative costs and make its long-haul units more profitable and efficient. Newly created YRC is one of the major unionized long-haul LTL carriers in the US, along with smaller Arkansas Best. The segment also includes Canadian LTL shipper YRC Reimer (formerly Reimer Express Lines), which provides service in Canada and between Canada, Mexico, and the US. They face competition from increasingly strong regional LTL carriers, which generally are not unionized and thus are able to offer lower-cost services.

Bruised by slumping demand for freight shipping in the economic downturn, and with around $1 billion in secured outstanding debt, YRC Worldwide is working to improve its liquidity. In 2010 the company inked a deal to sell a portion of its YRC Logistics to Austin Ventures for about $36 million.

YRC Worldwide will keep YRC Logistics' China-based operations, which comprise a controlling stake in Shanghai Jiayu Logistics, a leading LTL carrier in China (acquired in 2008). Freight handled by Jiayu that is destined for US markets represents a solid source of revenue for YRC Worldwide's trucking businesses. Also staying with YRC Worldwide, its logistics business has a 50% stake in JHJ International Transportation, a China-based freight forwarder.

YRC Worldwide also implemented wage reductions and temporarily stopped pension contributions (the deferral will end at the close of 2010) to improve its cost structure. The company also is working to trim costs in its regional transportation business, and in 2009 it closed about 18 service centers.

HISTORY

In 1924 A. J. Harrell established a trucking company in conjunction with his Oklahoma City bus line and Yellow Cab franchise. Harrell's Yellow Transit trucking operation hauled less-than-truckload (LTL) shipments between Oklahoma City and Tulsa. By 1944 Yellow had more than 50 independent subsidiaries in Illinois, Indiana, Kansas, Kentucky, Missouri, and Texas. That year the company was sold to an investment firm and renamed Yellow Transit Freight Lines. But Yellow's policy of paying high dividends stunted its growth, and by 1951 it faced bankruptcy.

In 1952 George Powell Sr. took over and turned Yellow around. His son George Powell Jr. became CEO in 1957, and the company went public two years later. George Jr. focused the company on long-haul interstate shipments and started buying up other trucking companies.

In 1965 Yellow expanded to the West Coast and the Southeast by purchasing Watson-Wilson Transportation System. Changing its name to Yellow Freight System (1968), the company acquired part of Norwalk Truck Lines and its routes in the Northeast (1970), and Adley Express (1972), providing new East Coast routes. Yellow extended routes into the Pacific Northwest by buying Republic Freight Systems in 1975. Its 1978 purchase of Braswell Motor Freight Lines consolidated its routes in California, Texas, and the Southeast. Yellow's only deviation from route acquisitions was its $4 million investment in oil firm Overland Energy in 1976, which it dissolved in the early 1980s.

The company was unprepared, however, when Congress deregulated trucking routes and shipping rates in 1980. Yellow upgraded its aging depots and terminals, but profits still declined by 1983. In 1982 Yellow Freight formed a holding corporation (renamed Yellow Corporation in 1992). George Powell III took over from his father as CEO in 1990. Yellow purchased Preston Trucking, an overnight freight hauler, in 1992.

In 1994 Yellow Freight was hit by a 24-day Teamsters' strike that allowed nonunion carriers to gain a chunk of its market. The next year, struggling during industry price wars, it reported a $30 million loss. Yellow laid off about 250 employees, mostly from Yellow Freight. George III resigned in 1996, and Maurice "Mr. Fix-it" Myers became CEO. Myers began moving the firm from a one-size-fits-all LTL trucker to a more flexible, customer-responsive trucking and logistics firm.

In 1997 Yellow Freight was restructured into decentralized business units to improve customer service, and hundreds of workers were laid off. To expand international operations, Yellow created YCS International in 1998 (renamed Yellow Global in 2000). It also secured a five-year labor contract with its unions, ending the danger of a strike. Loss-making Preston was sold to three company executives, and Yellow acquired regional carriers Action Express (1998) and Jevic Transportation (1999).

Myers drove off into the sunset in 1999 to take over another troubled giant, Waste Management, and Yellow Freight president William Zollars became CEO of Yellow Corp. In 2000 Yellow and two venture capital firms set up online transportation marketplace transportation.com to provide freight-forwarding and brokerage services.

Yellow integrated Action Express and WestEx into Saia Motor Freight Line in 2001. The next year Yellow renamed its Yellow Freight subsidiary Yellow Transportation. In 2002 Yellow combined transportation.com with its other logistics services to form Meridian IQ.

Yellow spun off SCS Transportation (later Saia, Inc.) in 2002. The next year, Yellow and other leading LTL carriers negotiated a new contract with the Teamsters union.

Also in 2003, Yellow bought rival Roadway and became Yellow Roadway Corporation. The company expanded in 2005 with the acquisition of USF. Yellow Roadway changed its name to YRC Worldwide in January 2006.

EXECUTIVES

Chairman, President, and CEO:
 William D. (Bill) Zollars, age 62,
 $2,472,871 total compensation
COO; President, YRC Inc.: Michael J. (Mike) Smid,
 age 54, $1,020,890 total compensation
EVP and CFO: Sheila K. Taylor, age 36,
 $210,353 total compensation
EVP and Chief Sales Officer: John A. Garcia, age 56
EVP and Chief Marketing Officer:
 Gregory A. (Greg) Reid
EVP, General Counsel, and Secretary:
 Daniel J. (Dan) Churay, age 47,
 $514,575 total compensation
EVP Human Resources: James G. (Jim) Kissinger,
 age 53, $417,187 total compensation
SVP Finance and Chief Accounting Officer:
 Phillip J. (Phil) Gaines, $477,464 total compensation
VP Investor Relations and Treasurer: Paul F. Liljegren,
 age 55, $295,134 total compensation
Chief Strategy Officer: Richard M. Williamson, age 53
President, Holland: Jeffrey A. Rogers

President, Customer Care and Chief Customer Officer: Michael J. (Mike) Naatz
President, YRC Logistics: John E. Carr
Auditors: KPMG LLP

LOCATIONS

HQ: YRC Worldwide Inc.
 10990 Roe Ave., Overland Park, KS 66211
Phone: 913-696-6100   **Fax:** 913-696-6116
Web: www.yrcw.com

2009 Sales

	$ mil.	% of total
US	5,012.6	95
Other countries	270.2	5
Total	**5,282.8**	**100**

PRODUCTS/OPERATIONS

2009 Sales

	$ mil.	% of total
National Transportation	3,489.3	66
Regional Transportation	1,322.4	25
YRC Logistics	399.6	8
YRC Truckload	71.5	1
Total	**5,282.8**	**100**

COMPETITORS

Arkansas Best	Landstar System
Central Freight Lines	Menlo Worldwide
C.H. Robinson Worldwide	Old Dominion Freight
Con-way Inc.	Saia
Estes Express	Schneider National
FedEx Freight	UPS
J.B. Hunt	

HISTORICAL FINANCIALS

Company Type: Public

Income Statement

FYE: December 31

	REVENUE ($ mil.)	NET INCOME ($ mil.)	NET PROFIT MARGIN	EMPLOYEES
12/09	5,283	(622)	—	36,000
12/08	8,940	(974)	—	55,000
12/07	9,621	(638)	—	63,000
12/06	9,919	277	2.8%	66,000
12/05	8,742	288	3.3%	68,000
Annual Growth	(11.8%)	—	—	(14.7%)

2009 Year-End Financials

Debt ratio: 574.6%	No. of shares (mil.): 1,183
Return on equity: —	Dividends
Cash ($ mil.): 98	Yield: 0.0%
Current ratio: 0.85	Payout: —
Long-term debt ($ mil.): 936	Market value ($ mil.): 994

Stock History

NASDAQ (GS): YRCW

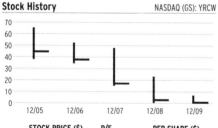

	STOCK PRICE ($) FY Close	P/E High/Low		PER SHARE ($) Earnings	Dividends	Book Value
12/09	0.84	—	—	(10.44)	0.00	0.14
12/08	2.87	—	—	(16.92)	0.00	0.40
12/07	17.09	—	—	(11.17)	0.00	1.36
12/06	37.73	11	7	4.74	0.00	1.85
12/05	44.61	13	8	5.07	0.00	1.64
Annual Growth	(63.0%)	—	—	—	—	(45.8%)

YUM! Brands

This company puts fast-food yummies in a whole lot of tummies. YUM! Brands is the largest fast-food operator in the world in terms of number of locations, with more than 37,000 outlets in about 110 countries. (It trails only hamburger giant McDonald's in sales.) The company's flagship chains include #1 chicken fryer KFC (with more than 16,200 units), top pizza joint Pizza Hut (more than 13,200), and quick-service Mexican leader Taco Bell (more than 5,800). YUM! also operates the Long John Silver's seafood chain, along with several hundred A&W root beer and burger stands. Franchisees, affiliates, and licensed operators run about 80% of the company's restaurants.

YUM! Brands has become a dominant player in the fast-food industry thanks in large part to its multi-concept strategy combined with strong marketing and franchising efforts. With its multiple chains, the company appeals to a wider variety of consumer tastes than single-concept operators such as McDonald's and Burger King. It can further refine its marketing to promote each chain to a different dining segment. Pizza Hut, for instance, appeals primarily to families and large groups, while Taco Bell targets the younger demographic and snacking segment.

With successful marketing campaigns and almost ubiquitous presence, YUM! Brands' flagship chains dominate their respective markets. Taco Bell holds more than 50% market share in the Mexican fast-food segment, while KFC commands more than 40% of the quick-service chicken business. Pizza Hut leads its fragmented segment with about 15% of the market, and Long John Silver's represents more than a third of the limited-service seafood segment.

YUM! Brands is focusing its expansion efforts on international locations, where it added almost 1,500 new units during 2009. It is specifically targeting the emerging market in China where it has more than 4,000 eateries, mostly company-owned KFC locations. To tailor the eateries to local tastes in China, the company has been experimenting with fish and beef menu items, as well as afternoon tea. Its Taco Bell chain is growing into a global brand as well, through franchising efforts in such markets as France, India, and Russia. During 2009 the company purchased a 20% stake in Little Sheep Group, which operates a chain of 375 eateries specializing in Mongolian-style soup and lamb dishes.

Domestically, YUM! Brands has been focused primarily on improving efficiencies and cutting costs. Part of that effort has involved selling some corporate locations to franchisees. More than 540 locations were refranchised during 2009. To drive additional traffic to its restaurants and boost sales, the company is continually rolling out new menu items. Its Pizza Hut chain is promoting a line of pasta dishes, while KFC has been marketing a menu of grilled chicken items in an attempt to appeal to health-conscious consumers.

HISTORY

Yum! Brands took its original name, TRICON, from the three brand icons — KFC, Pizza Hut, and Taco Bell — it inherited from former parent PepsiCo. The soft drink company entered the fast-food business with its acquisition of Pizza Hut in 1977. The pizza chain had begun in 1958 when brothers Dan and Frank Carney borrowed $600 from their mother and opened the first Pizza Hut in Wichita, Kansas, with partner John Bender. Their first franchise opened the next year in Topeka, Kansas. By 1971 the company had become the world's largest pizza chain, with more than 1,000 restaurants. Pizza Hut went public the following year. The chain had grown to 3,000 locations by the time it was acquired.

In 1978 PepsiCo acquired Taco Bell. After trying other fast-food formats, Glen Bell settled on the Mexican-style market. He bought and sold several chains before beginning Taco Bell in Downey, California, in 1962. The first franchise was sold two years later, and by 1967 — the year after it went public — Taco Bell had more than 335 restaurants, most of them franchised.

KFC was acquired in 1986. It had been founded by Harland Sanders — that's Colonel Sanders to you — who developed his secret, 11-herbs-and-spices recipe and method of pressure-frying chicken during the 1930s. The Colonel began franchising the secret in 1952 and founded Kentucky Fried Chicken in 1955. More than 600 outlets in the US and Canada were open by 1963. It went public in 1969 and was operating some 6,600 units in 55 countries when it was acquired by PepsiCo.

Through these acquisitions, PepsiCo hoped to diversify and build sales channels for its beverages, but the company had also incurred a huge debt load and fast-food competition had intensified. As same-store sales faltered, shareholders clamored for PepsiCo to spin off the restaurants. Restaurant officials grumbled that PepsiCo put more effort into marketing blitzes than into building restaurants (its 1991 renaming of Kentucky Fried Chicken as KFC didn't fool many health-conscious consumers).

In 1997 PepsiCo created a new restaurant subsidiary, which it spun off in the fall as TRICON Global Restaurants. To improve cash flow, it stepped up efforts to close or franchise underperforming Pizza Huts and KFCs. TRICON also began opening "three-in-one" restaurants featuring all its brands under one roof. In 1998 it launched a Taco Bell advertising campaign featuring a bilingual Chihuahua; the sassy pooch quickly became a cultural icon.

In 1999 TRICON spent some $2 billion on a massive *Star Wars: Episode I — The Phantom Menace* promotion that failed to increase traffic at its restaurants. Vice chairman David Novak took over as CEO in 2000.

In 2002 TRICON acquired Yorkshire Global Restaurants for $320 million, which brought Long John Silver's and A&W All-American Food Restaurants into the fold. Now a five-pack of well-known brands rather than a trio, TRICON changed its name to YUM! Brands.

Being market leaders did not save YUM!'s chains from the overall downturn in the economy, however, nor from the effects of changing eating habits as Americans sought healthier meal alternatives. KFC was hit particularly hard, prompting the company to appoint veteran Gregg Dedrick the chain's new president in 2003.

The company acquired the 50% stake it didn't already own in Pizza Hut (UK) from joint venture partner Whitbread in 2006.

The following year YUM! was stung by an *E. coli* outbreak at some of its Taco Bell outlets. The source of the outbreak was traced to a lettuce supplier; the company announced new steps to test its food supply. YUM! also sold its 31% stake in KFC Japan to Mitsubishi that same year.

EXECUTIVES

Chairman, President, and CEO: David C. Novak, age 57, $13,131,292 total compensation
Vice Chairman; Chairman and CEO, YUM! Brands China Division: Samuel J.S. (Sam) Su, age 58, $6,721,208 total compensation
CFO: Richard T. (Rick) Carucci, age 53, $4,458,698 total compensation
CIO: Delaney Bellinger
Chief People Officer: Anne P. Byerlein, age 51
SVP Public Affairs: Jonathan D. Blum, age 52
SVP, General Counsel, Secretary, and Chief Franchise Policy Officer: Christian L. (Chris) Campbell, age 59
SVP Finance and Corporate Controller: Ted F. Knopf, age 58
SVP Investor Relations and Treasurer: Timothy P. (Tim) Jerzyk
President, YUM! Restaurants International: Graham D. Allan, age 54, $4,407,577 total compensation
President and Chief Concept Officer, Taco Bell: Greg Creed, age 52, $3,360,111 total compensation
President, Global Branding; Chief Marketing Officer, YUM! Restaurants International: Micky Pant, age 55
President and Chief Concept Officer, Pizza Hut: Scott O. Bergren, age 63
President and Chief Concept Officer, KFC: Roger Eaton, age 49
President and COO, China Division: Mark Chu
General Manager, KFC France: Ivan Schofield
General Manager, United Kingdom; CEO, Pizza Hut UK: Jens Hofma
COO; President, LJS/A&W: Emil J. Brolick, age 62
COO, KFC: Laurance (Larry) Roberts
COO, Taco Bell: Rob Savage, age 49
COO, Pizza Hut: Patrick C. (Pat) Murtha
Director Public Affairs: Karen Sherman
Auditors: KPMG LLP

LOCATIONS

HQ: YUM! Brands, Inc.
1441 Gardiner Ln., Louisville, KY 40213
Phone: 502-874-8300   **Fax:** 502-874-8790
Web: www.yum.com

2009 Sales

	$ mil.	% of total
International		
China	3,682	34
Other countries	2,713	25
US	4,473	41
Adjustments	(32)	—
Total	**10,836**	**100**

2009 Locations

	No.
US	19,665
International	
China	4,055
Other countries	13,360
Total	**37,080**

PRODUCTS/OPERATIONS

2009 Sales

	$ mil.	% of total
Restaurants	9,413	87
Franchising	1,423	13
Total	**10,836**	**100**

2009 Locations

	No.
Franchised & licensed	
Franchised	26,745
Licensed	2,200
Affiliated	469
Company-owned	7,666
Total	**37,080**

COMPETITORS

AFC Enterprises	Domino's
Burger King	Jack in the Box
Chick-fil-A	Little Caesar's
Chipotle	McDonald's
Church's Chicken	Papa John's
CKE Restaurants	Quiznos
Dairy Queen	Subway
Del Taco	Wendy's/Arby's Group, Inc.

HISTORICAL FINANCIALS

Company Type: Public

Income Statement

FYE: Last Saturday in December

	REVENUE ($ mil.)	NET INCOME ($ mil.)	NET PROFIT MARGIN	EMPLOYEES
12/09	10,836	1,071	9.9%	350,000
12/08	11,279	964	8.5%	336,000
12/07	10,416	909	8.7%	301,000
12/06	9,561	824	8.6%	280,000
12/05	9,349	762	8.2%	272,000
Annual Growth	**3.8%**	**8.9%**	**—**	**6.5%**

2009 Year-End Financials

Debt ratio: 312.9%
Return on equity: 233.6%
Cash ($ mil.): 353
Current ratio: 0.73
Long-term debt ($ mil.): 3,207
No. of shares (mil.): 467
Dividends
Yield: 2.2%
Payout: 35.1%
Market value ($ mil.): 16,331

Stock History

NYSE: YUM

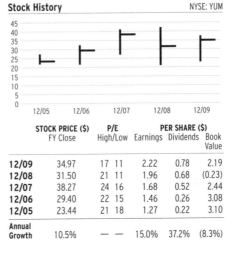

	STOCK PRICE ($) FY Close	P/E High/Low		Earnings	PER SHARE ($) Dividends	Book Value
12/09	34.97	17	11	2.22	0.78	2.19
12/08	31.50	21	11	1.96	0.68	(0.23)
12/07	38.27	24	16	1.68	0.52	2.44
12/06	29.40	22	15	1.46	0.26	3.08
12/05	23.44	21	18	1.27	0.22	3.10
Annual Growth	**10.5%**	**—**	**—**	**15.0%**	**37.2%**	**(8.3%)**

Zale Corporation

Zale is multifaceted. One of North America's largest specialty jewelry retailers, Zale sells diamond, colored stone, and gold jewelry (diamond fashion rings, semi-precious stones, earrings, gold chains); watches; and gift items at some 1,250 stores and 685 kiosks, mostly in malls, throughout the US, Canada, and Puerto Rico. The firm, which targets the value-oriented customer, has three large chains aimed at different jewelry markets: Gordon's Jewelers, flagship chain Zales Jewelers, and Piercing Pagoda. Zale also operates about 140 jewelry outlet stores, runs more than 200 stores in Canada under the Peoples Jewellers and Mappins Jewellers names, sells online, and offers jewelry insurance.

The downturn in the US economy, where Zale rings up about 85% of its sales, and consequent pinch on discretionary spending has hit jewelry retailers especially hard and has hindered Zale's turnaround efforts. CEO Neal Goldberg resigned, followed by two other executives (Zale's chief merchandising officer and head of stores). President Theo Killion was named interim CEO after the departure of Goldberg, the company's sixth chief executive in 10 years.

Several consecutive years of weak holiday sales have left Zale in a perilous financial position and led to changes in its management. In a bid to raise cash, in early 2010 Zale took the unusual step of asking its vendors to buy some of its inventory. The struggling company also canceled much of the advertising it had planned for Valentine's Day and Mother's Day, two of the biggest jewelry buying occasions after Christmas. In February, the company hired the investment bank Peter J. Solomon to help it find new investors. Private equity firm Golden Gate Capital (GGC) purchased about 20% of struggling Zale in May 2010 and lent the firm $150 million. In July GGC exercised warrants to increase its stake to more than 34%, making it the chain's largest shareholder (ahead of Breeden Capital Management, which owns about 28% of Zale).

Still, the company is betting it can hang on as regional jewelry chains are calling it quits. To ride out the downturn, Zale has taken cost-saving measures, including the closing of about 190 stores and the elimination of 245 jobs. Previously, Zale sold its upscale Bailey Banks & Biddle chain to Finlay Enterprises in 2007.

HISTORY

Russian immigrant Morris Zale opened his first jewelry store in Wichita Falls, Texas, in 1924. The store's most popular items were fountain pens. Zale advertised and offered credit ("a penny down, a dollar a week"); the two concepts were novel for the jewelry business of the day, and by 1937 the budding chain had seven stores.

The firm managed to survive the Depression — people were still getting married — and by 1941 it had 12 shops. It added upscale Houston jeweler Corrigan's three years later. Zale established buying offices in the diamond capitals of New York City and Antwerp, Belgium, which allowed it to buy wholesale. Sales were $10 million in 1946, the year the company moved its headquarters to Dallas.

Zale grew rapidly following WWII and had 50 stores by the mid-1950s. During that time the company became a fully integrated jeweler, buying raw goods and manufacturing its jewelry (including cutting and polishing its diamonds). Zale went public in 1957. It acquired Philadelphia-based Bailey Banks & Biddle in 1962 and became the world's largest retailer, with more than 400 stores, by the mid-1960s.

Spooked by the introduction of synthetic diamonds, the company began to diversify in 1965. It acquired a drugstore chain (Skillern); a line of airport tobacco/newsstand shops; and retailers of apparel, shoes (Butler), furniture, and sporting goods. By 1974 these operations represented half of Zale's sales.

Morris' son Donald became chairman in 1980. Zale began selling off its non-jewelry operations. Skillern went to Revco, Butler to Sears, and the sporting goods business to Oshman's.

The stumbling economy of the 1980s and the gold and diamond industries' uncharacteristic weakness rocked Zale. An $80 million restructuring charge contributed to its $60 million loss in 1986. That year Irving Gerstein, head of Canada's Peoples Jewellers and a 15% owner of Zale, joined with Austrian crystal firm Swarovski to buy Zale. Issuing junk bonds to finance the $650 million deal, each took an equal stake in the company.

Gerstein sold manufacturing operations, liquidated the company's diamond inventory, and cut its advertising budget. Zale looked healthy enough in 1989 to buy the 650-store Gordon's Jewelers chain. But a recession hurt sales in the early 1990s, and debt hindered the company's fiscal health.

Unable to make a junk bond payment in late 1991, Zale filed for bankruptcy protection early the next year. It emerged from bankruptcy in 1993 as a debt-free public company with 700 fewer stores. The following year Zale chose former Bon Marche CEO Robert DiNicola to lead its revival. DiNicola began adding new stores (especially the higher-end Bailey Banks & Biddle shops) and repositioned existing ones.

In 1999 the company bought Peoples Jewellers (177 stores in Canada). COO Beryl Raff succeeded DiNicola as CEO that year. In 2000 the company partnered with WeddingChannel.com to offer wedding planning services online. Zale also sold its private-label credit card business to Associates First Capital Corporation. It then bought about 95% of US kiosk jeweler Piercing Pagoda. In 2001 DiNicola once again became chairman and CEO after Raff resigned, but DiNicola stepped down as CEO in 2002 and Mary Forté replaced him.

The company closed about 30 Bailey Banks & Biddle stores after the 2005 holiday season, citing poor performance.

Forté resigned in 2006 after 11 years with the company and was replaced, on an interim basis, by director Betsy Burton. An investigation of the company's accounting practices launched in April by the Securities and Exchange Commission was dropped with no action taken in September. Soon after the probe was announced, CFO Mark Lenz was put on indefinite administrative leave and later terminated for failing to disclose vendor payments in a timely manner. In July Burton, a former chief executive of Supercuts and PIP Printing, was named president and CEO permanently.

In November 2007 Zale sold its 70-store Bailey Banks & Biddle Fine Jewelry division (12% of sales) to Finlay Enterprises for $200 million.

EXECUTIVES

President and Interim CEO: Theophlius (Theo) Killion, age 58, $1,032,754 total compensation
EVP and CFO: Matthew (Matt) Appel, age 54, $98,538 total compensation
EVP and Chief Merchant and Sourcing Officer: Gilbert P. (Gil) Hollander, age 56, $890,634 total compensation
EVP and Chief Marketing and E-Commerce Officer: Richard A. Lennox, age 45
SVP Supply Chain: Susann C. Mayo, age 57
SVP and Chief Stores Officer: Becky Mick
SVP, General Counsel, and Corporate Secretary: Hilary Molay, age 55
SVP and Treasurer: Stephen C. Massanelli, age 53
VP, Controller, and Chief Accounting Officer: James E. (Jim) Sullivan, age 45
VP Quality Assurance: Eric Christopher
Manager Investor Relations: Rhett Butler
Auditors: Ernst & Young

LOCATIONS

HQ: Zale Corporation
901 W. Walnut Hill Ln., Irving, TX 75038
Phone: 972-580-4000 **Fax:** 972-580-5523
Web: www.zalecorp.com

PRODUCTS/OPERATIONS

2009 Sales by Brand

	$ mil.	% of total
Zales & Gordon's (includes zales.com & gordonsjewelers.com)	1,110.4	62
Peoples Jewellers & Mappins Jewellers	256.7	14
Piercing Pagoda	232.8	13
Zales Outlet	168.5	10
Insurance	11.3	1
Total	**1,779.7**	**100**

2009 Stores and Kiosks

	No.
Zales & Gordon's	895
Piercing Pagoda	684
Peoples Jewellers & Mappins Jewellers	212
Zales Outlet	140
Total	**1,931**

2009 Sales

	$ mil.	% of total
Fine jewelry	1,535.6	86
Kiosk jewelry	232.8	13
Other	11.3	1
Total	**1,779.7**	**100**

Selected Operations and Merchandise

Gordon's Jewelers (mid-priced items, including regional and contemporary fashion-oriented jewelry)
Peoples Jewellers (Canada)
  Mappins Jewellers (Canada)
Piercing Pagoda (mall-based, lower-priced jewelry kiosks)
Zales Jewelers (lower-priced items, including engagement rings, wedding bands, bridal sets, anniversary bands, cocktail rings, earrings, chains, watches, and pearls)
Zales the Diamond Store Outlet (discounted new jewelry, pre-owned jewelry)
Zales.com (online sales)

COMPETITORS

Amazon.com	QVC
Birks and Mayors	Reeds Jewelers
Blue Nile, Inc.	Saks
Costco Wholesale	Sam's Club
DGSE Companies	Samuels Jewelers
Elegant Illusions	Sears
Fred Meyer Jewelers	Sterling Jewelers
Helzberg Diamonds	Tiffany & Co.
J. C. Penney	Ultra Stores
Macy's	Wal-Mart

HISTORICAL FINANCIALS

Company Type: Public

Income Statement

FYE: July 31

	REVENUE ($ mil.)	NET INCOME ($ mil.)	NET PROFIT MARGIN	EMPLOYEES
7/09	1,780	(190)	—	14,500
7/08	2,138	11	0.5%	15,500
7/07	2,437	59	2.4%	17,600
7/06	2,439	54	2.2%	16,900
7/05	2,383	107	4.5%	16,300
Annual Growth	**(7.0%)**	**—**	**—**	**(2.9%)**

2009 Year-End Financials

Debt ratio: 83.1%	No. of shares (mil.): 32
Return on equity: —	Dividends
Cash ($ mil.): 25	Yield: —
Current ratio: 2.29	Payout: —
Long-term debt ($ mil.): 311	Market value ($ mil.): 190

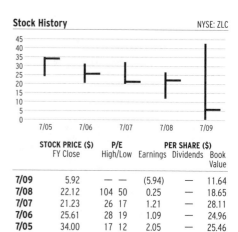

Stock History NYSE: ZLC

	STOCK PRICE ($) FY Close	P/E High/Low		PER SHARE ($) Earnings	Dividends	Book Value
7/09	5.92	—	—	(5.94)	—	11.64
7/08	22.12	104	50	0.25	—	18.65
7/07	21.23	26	17	1.21	—	28.11
7/06	25.61	28	19	1.09	—	24.96
7/05	34.00	17	12	2.05	—	25.46
Annual Growth	**(35.4%)**			**—**	**—**	**(17.8%)**

Zions Bancorporation

Multibank holding company Zions Bancorporation operates eight bank subsidiaries with approximately 500 branches in 10 western and southwestern states; the banks operate under their own brands and leadership rather than sharing one corporate identity. They focus on commercial and retail banking and mortgage lending; their products and services include deposit accounts, home mortgages and home equity lines of credit, residential and commercial development loans, credit cards, and trust and wealth management services. Zions is also a leading Small Business Administration (SBA) and agricultural lender.

The company lets its eight subsidiaries keep their own names and branding because it believes customers are more comfortable banking at a local level. Its subsidiary banks include Zions First National Bank, Nevada State Bank, National Bank of Arizona, and Vectra Bank Colorado. Additionally, it owns The Commerce Bank of Washington, California Bank & Trust, The Commerce Bank of Oregon, and Texas-based Amegy Corporation.

Zions, which built its empire on acquisitions, has managed to expand its reach during the economic downturn, partly by helping the FDIC clean up failed banks. The company acquired some $800 million in deposits in 2008 from failed Nevada-based Silver State Bank, whose 17 branches became either Nevada State Bank or National Bank of Arizona locations.

The following year Zions added another five branches to Nevada State Bank's network by picking up Great Basin Bank after the FDIC declared it insolvent. It later stepped in at the FDIC's request to help transition customers of the failed Community Bank of Nevada. Also in 2009 California Bank & Trust added some 20 branches from the acquisitions of Alliance Bank and Vineyard Bank, which had been seized by regulators, as well.

Though Zions is largely shielded from problem loans in its FDIC-assisted transactions, the company has been hit by nonperforming loans in its own portfolio, particularly in residential land acquisition, development, and construction lending in the Southwest. Its provision for loan losses for 2009 totaled more than $2 billion, more than triple the amount set aside the year before.

Zions also owns money manager Contango Capital Advisors and online brokerage Zions Direct. In addition, the company controls a handful of venture capital funds working with start-ups in the West and invests in financial services technologies, including check processing subsidiary NetDeposit.

HISTORY

Zions' history is entwined with that of the Mormon Church. Founded by the church in 1873 to take over the savings department of the Bank of Deseret when it obtained a national charter, the new bank was headed by Brigham Young and other church leaders. The church kept control of the bank until 1960, when it sold its interest to a group of investors led by Roy Simmons, who moved it into the holding company that became Zions Bancorporation. It went public in 1966.

The company fared well in Utah, and when regulations changed in the mid-1980s to allow expansion into contiguous states, it moved quickly into Arizona (1986). Zions was hit by the commercial real estate crash and a downturn in the copper industry. Nevertheless, it remained healthy enough to pick up some Arizona bargain banks as they folded. In the 1990s it moved into California, Colorado, Idaho, and New Mexico. Acquisitions in 1997 and 1998 included Colorado's Aspen Bancshares, Tri-State Bank, and Vectra Banking Corp.; California's GB Bancorporation; and Nevada's Sun State Bank. None of the new family members adopted the Zions name.

In 1998 the company bought Sumitomo Bank of California, the state's #6 bank, and merged it with Grossmont Bank to form California Bank & Trust. The firm increased its presence in 1999 in California and Nevada with the purchases of Regency Bancorp and Pioneer Bancorp, respectively.

In 2005 Zions bought Amegy Bancorporation, giving it a presence in Dallas and Houston, two of the more attractive banking markets in the US. Zions' wealth management unit Contango Capital Advisors acquired Phoenix-based BG Associates in 2006.

In 2007 Zions bought Arizona-based Stockmen's Bancorp (and its 43 Stockmen's Bank branches), merged it into National Bank of Arizona, then sold 11 Stockmen's branches located in California later that year. Also in 2007 it acquired Texas-based Intercontinental Bank Shares and its three Intercon Bank branches in San Antonio, which were rolled into Amegy Bank.

EXECUTIVES

Chairman, President, and CEO; Chairman, Zions First National Bank; Chairman, President, and CEO, Zions Management Services: Harris H. Simmons, age 55, $1,373,352 total compensation
Vice Chairman and CFO: Doyle L. Arnold, age 61, $919,451 total compensation
EVP Wealth Management; President and CEO, Contango Capitol Advisors: George M. Feiger, age 60, $945,306 total compensation
EVP; President and CEO, Zions First National Bank: A. Scott Anderson, age 63, $877,256 total compensation
EVP; Chairman, President, and CEO, California Bank & Trust: David E. Blackford, age 61, $779,693 total compensation
EVP and Chief Human Resources Officer: Connie Linardakis, age 45
EVP; President, Amegy Bank: Steve D. Stephens

EVP; President and CEO, NetDeposit: Danne L. Buchanan, age 52
EVP; President and CEO, National Bank of Arizona: Keith D. Maio, age 52
EVP, General Counsel, and Secretary: Thomas E. (Thom) Laursen, age 58
EVP Capital Markets and Investments; EVP, Zions First National Bank: W. David Hemingway, age 62
EVP; Chairman, President and CEO, Nevada State Bank: Dallas E. Haun, age 56
EVP; Chairman, President and CEO, Vectra Bank Colorado: Bruce K. Alexander, age 57
EVP; Chairman, President, and CEO, The Commerce Bank of Washington: Stanley D. Savage, age 64
EVP and CIO; Vice Chairman, Zions Management Services Company: John T. Itokazu, age 49
EVP; CEO, Amegy Bank: Scott J. McLean, age 53
SVP Investor Relations and External Communications: James R. Abbott, age 36
President, Zions Credit Corporation: Alan Ralphs
President and CEO, The Commerce Bank of Oregon: Larry B. Ogg
Chairman, Amegy Corporation and Amegy Bank of Texas: Walter E. Johnson, age 73
Chairman, National Bank of Arizona: John J. Gisi
Auditors: Ernst & Young LLP

LOCATIONS

HQ: Zions Bancorporation
1 S. Main St., Salt Lake City, UT 84133
Phone: 801-524-4787   **Fax:** 801-524-4805
Web: www.zionsbancorporation.com

2009 Branches

	No.
California	106
Utah	103
Texas	82
Arizona	76
Nevada	58
Colorado	37
Idaho	26
New Mexico	1
Oregon	1
Washington	1
Total	**491**

PRODUCTS/OPERATIONS

2009 Sales

	$ mil.	% of total
Interest		
Loans, including fees	2,319.3	61
Securities	157.4	4
Other	38.7	1
Noninterest		
Gain on subordinated debt modification	508.9	13
Service charges & fees on deposit accounts	212.6	6
Acquisition-related gains	169.2	4
Other service charges, commissions & fees	156.5	4
Fair value & non-hedge derivative income	113.8	3
Capital markets & foreign exchange	50.3	1
Trust & wealth management	29.9	1
Other	55.4	2
Valuation losses on securities purchased	(212.1)	—
Net impairment losses on investment securities	(280.5)	—
Total	**3,319.4**	**100**

2009 Assets

	$ mil.	% of total
Cash & due from banks	1,370.2	3
Money market investments	731.5	1
Investment securities	4,548.8	9
Net loans & leases	38,866.2	76
Other assets	5,606.3	11
Total	**51,123.0**	**100**

Selected Subsidiaries

Amegy Corporation
California Bank & Trust
Cash Access, Inc.
Great Western Financial Corporation
National Bank of Arizona
NetDeposit, Inc.
Nevada State Bank
The Commerce Bank of Oregon
The Commerce Bank of Washington
Vectra Bank Colorado
Zions First National Bank
Zions Insurance Agency, Inc.
Zions Management Services Company

COMPETITORS

Bank of America
Bank of the West
BOK Financial
Capital One
Citigroup
Cullen/Frost Bankers
First National of Nebraska
Great Western Bancorporation
JPMorgan Chase
Prosperity Bancshares
UnionBanCal
U.S. Bancorp
Washington Federal
Wells Fargo

HISTORICAL FINANCIALS

Company Type: Public

Income Statement

FYE: December 31

	ASSETS ($ mil.)	NET INCOME ($ mil.)	INCOME AS % OF ASSETS	EMPLOYEES
12/09	51,123	(1,216)	—	10,529
12/08	55,093	(266)	—	11,011
12/07	52,947	494	0.9%	10,933
12/06	46,970	583	1.2%	10,618
12/05	42,780	480	1.1%	10,102
Annual Growth	**4.6%**	—	—	**1.0%**

2009 Year-End Financials

Equity as % of assets: 11.1%
Return on assets: —
Return on equity: —
Long-term debt ($ mil.): 2,153
No. of shares (mil.): 160
Dividends
Yield: 0.8%
Payout: —
Market value ($ mil.): 2,056
Sales ($ mil.): 3,319

Stock History

NASDAQ (GS): ZION

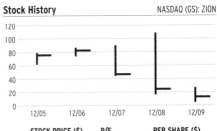

	STOCK PRICE ($) FY Close	P/E High/Low		PER SHARE ($) Earnings	Dividends	Book Value
12/09	12.83	—	—	(9.92)	0.10	35.52
12/08	24.51	—	—	(2.66)	1.61	40.57
12/07	46.69	20	10	4.42	1.68	33.03
12/06	82.44	16	14	5.36	1.47	31.12
12/05	75.56	15	12	5.16	1.44	26.44
Annual Growth	**(35.8%)**	—	—	—	**(48.7%)**	**7.7%**

Hoover's Handbook of

American Business

The Indexes

Index by Industry

Index by Headquarters

Index of Executives

A

Aardsma, David A. 925
Aaron, Mark L. 857
Abarca, M. Jessica 928
Abate, Peter 321
Abbott, Bradley S. 663
Abbott, Gay O. 824
Abbott, James R. 961
Abdelaziz, Gamal 603
Abel, James E. 706
Abendschein, Robert D. 89
Aberle, Derek K. 727
Abernathy, Kathleen Q. 384
Abernathy, Robert E. 513
Abernethy, Jack 380, 637
Abi-Karam, Leslie R. 698
Abney, David P. 882
Abraham, Deborah 921
Abraham, Thomas R. 314
Abraham, Todd 524
Abramowicz, Daniel A. 268
Abrams, Robert 793
Abramson, Josh D. 458
Abud, Joao Jr. 296
Achermann, Hubert 523
Ackart, Jennifer C. 733
Ackerman, Jeffrey C. 781
Ackerman, Patricia K. 94
Ackerman, Paul R. 931
Acton, Elizabeth S. 243
Adair-Potts, Janna 833
Adam, Donald F. 144
Adamek, Mitch 684
Adamonis, Richard C. 657
Adams, D. Scott 719
Adams, J. Dann 343
Adams, John 182
Adams, Katherine L. 448
Adams, Kent M. 194
Adams, Mark L. (Nu Skin) 652
Adams, Mark W. (Micron
  Technology) 605
Adams, Marvin W. 856
Adams, Mike 136
Adams, Peter T. 50
Adams, Robin J. 158
Adams, Ted 544
Adams, Thomas R. 743
Adamson, Grant F. 839
Adderley, Terence E. 509
Addicks, Mark W. 395
Addison, Brian M. 291
Addison, James E. 769
Aderhold, Ronald K. 229
Ades, Stanton G. 663
Adib, Fared 810
Adkerson, Richard C. 383
Adkins, Rodney C. 470
Adler, David 888
Adler, Robert L. 330
Adornato, Theodore C. 807
Adrean, Lee 343
Adriaenssens, Luc 245
Advani, Vijay C. 382

Aertker, Gayle 304
Afflerbach, Mary 54
Afzal, Zahid 456
Agar, Richard 414
Aghdaei, Amir 276
Aghili, Aziz 275
Agia, Bertha 727
Agnes, Pierre 730
Agnew, Dan 115
Agosta, Jeffrey A. 292
Aguirre, Fernando G. 213
Ahearn, Chris (Thomson Reuters) 854
Ahearn, Chris C. (Lowe's) 555
Ahearn, Joseph 559
Ahlstrom, Lee M. 643
Ahmad, Tanzim 313
Ahmed, Mumtaz 285
Ahuja, Lalit 833
Aiello, Liz 571
Aijala, Ainar D. Jr. 285
Aiken, Robert S. 696
Ainsworth, Anne-Marie 823
Ainsworth, William P. 194
Akers, Gregory 224
Akerson, Daniel F. 396
Akin, Bruce A. 935
Akins, Nicholas K. 75
Akkad, Susan 347
Alario, Richard J. 511
Alban, Carlos 33
Albano, Robert J. 491
Albaugh, James F. 154
Alber, Karen L. 442
Alber, Laura J. 944
Albers, Mark W. 357
Alberts, Shannon K. 59
Albrecht, William E. 658
Albright, Clarence H. Jr. 198
Alderson, Deborah H. 761
Alderson, Jim 925
Aldrich, George E. 805
Alexander, Bradley K. 369
Alexander, Bruce K. 961
Alexander, Forbes I. J. 484
Alexander, J. Rich 705
Alexander, Jeff 903
Alexander, Jim (Equity Residential) 344
Alexander, Jimmy (Ace Hardware) 39
Alexander, Mark 183
Alexander, Paul J. 513
Alexander, Penelope S. 382
Alexander, Robert M. 185
Alexander, Susan 803
Alexandrou, Anthony G. 475
Alfonso, Humberto P. 432
Alford, J. Philip 914
Alford, Sandra E. 123
Alger, Eugene K. 354
Alger, Montgomery 54
Allaker, James 641
Allan, Donald Jr. 813
Allan, Graham D. 959
Allan, Michael J. 708
Allan, Susan 484
Allcott, Truitt 670

Alleman, James 244
Allen, Barry K. 416
Allen, Bryan D. 415
Allen, Charles H. 652
Allen, David W. 283
Allen, Frances 290
Allen, Jay L. 207
Allen, Jodi 781
Allen, John J. 626
Allen, Keith 238
Allen, Mark W. 43
Allen, Paul J. 254
Allen, Peter A. 247
Allen, Richard W. 629
Allen, Samuel R. 281
Allen, Terri 680
Allendorph, Dave 626
Alletto, Raymond J. 883
Allin, Mark 495
Allison, Paul D. 733
Allison, Robert J. Jr. 89
Allman, Michael W. 783
Almeida, Donald V. 713
Almond, Danny H. 864
Aloia, Albert A. 250
Alonso, Carlos 131
Alonso, Mario E. 320
Alonso, Steve 364
Alpaugh, John 690
Alpert, Susan 594
Alpert-Romm, Adria 301
Alroy, Liore 461
Alseth, Becky 118
Alstead, Troy 816
Altabef, Peter A. 284
Alterio, Sharon M. 264
Altmaier, Judy 866
Altman, Steven R. 727
Altman, William M. 515
Altmeyer, John W. 188
Alton, Gregg H. 402
Altschul, Wayne 462
Altshuler, Barry 344
Alvarado, Joseph 244
Alvarez, Pablo A. 575
Alves, Paget A. 810
Alving, Amy E. 761
Alyea, David L. 852
Alziari, Lucien 121
Amalfi, Peter 149
Ambler, John O. 175
Ambrose, Adele D. 597
Ambrose, Brian 523
Ambrosio, Anthony G. 197
Ambrosio, Mike 915
Amello, Jason A. 400
Ames, Marshall H. 536
Ames, Richard D. 191
Amick, Rebecca K. 145
Amin, A. Salman 684
Amlung, Ray J. 271
Ammann, Daniel 396
Amoroso, Edward G. 111
Amoroso, Richard M. 71
Amos, Daniel P. 50

Amos, Paul S. II 50
Amundson, Bruce 939
Anand, Krishnan 610
Anderl, Richard C. 616
Andersen, Eric 96
Anderson, A. Scott 961
Anderson, B. Chuck (Occidental
  Petroleum) 658
Anderson, Bradley R. 284
Anderson, Cathy C. 871
Anderson, Chuck (HSN) 452
Anderson, Dave (Peter Kiewit
  Sons') 689
Anderson, David C. (PACCAR) 673
Anderson, David G. (HCA) 423
Anderson, David J. (Honeywell
  International) 448
Anderson, David Z. (Seagate
  Technology) 778
Anderson, Gary D. 561
Anderson, Gerard M. 315
Anderson, Jeremy 523
Anderson, R. John 540
Anderson, Richard H. 288
Anderson, R.J. 913
Anderson, Scott P. 679
Anderson, Stephen 848
Anderson, Timothy J. 444
Anderson, William T. 574
Andersson, Curt J. 406
Andrade, Juan C. 420
Andre, Erin M. 37
Andre, Kenneth B. III 409
Andreotti, Lamberto 167
Andres, Michael 587
Andrew, T. Peter 168
Andrews, A. Michael II 527
Andrews, Alan R. 507
Andrews, Audrey T. 841
Andrews, Madhuri A. 869
Anenen, Steven J. 113
Ang, Abel 440
Angel, Stephen F. 708
Angelakis, Michael J. 242
Angelastro, Philip J. 664
Angelini, Michael P. 415
Angelle, Evelyn M. 412
Angelo, Scott M. 296
Angerami, John 233
Angley, Ellen K. 651
Angus, Dan 157
Anik, Ruby 489
Ansell, Jeffery D. 813
Anstice, Martin B. 528
Anthony, Richard E. 830
Antonellis, Joseph C. 820
Anzaldua, Ricardo A. 420
Apicerno, Kenneth J. 851
Apodaca, Steven E. 209
Appel, Andrew M. 96
Appel, Laurence B. 947
Appel, Matthew 960
Appelo, Willem T. 954
Applbaum, Lee 731
Apple, Robert E. 575

Bogart, Stacy 703
Boggs, Paula E. 816
Bohlen, Lori 307
Bohn, Robert G. 668
Bohnert, Brad 452
Bohnke, Jaime 873
Bojalad, Ronald 277
Boje, James 472
Bokan, Michael W. 605
Bolch, James R. 353
Bold, William 727
Boles, Donna M. 138
Bolgiano, Elizabeth S. 851
Bollenbach, Stephen F. 506
Bolles, Albert D. 248
Bolsens, Ivo 955
Bolt, Jennifer J. 382
Bolzenius, Beda-Helmut 498
Bombara, Beth A. 420
Bombino, Paige 765
Bonach, Edward J. 234
Bonanni, Fabrizio 86
Bond, Carey E. 888
Bond, David F. 759
Bond, Derek 627
Bond, Michael 161
Bond, Pat 928
Bond, Ritchie L. 801
Bond, Robert W. 678
Bond, Timothy G. 117
Bondar, Lori J. 117
Bondur, Thomas J. 528
Bonham, D. Andrew 950
Boni, Eric N. 110
Boniface, Christopher 39
Bonner, William 661
Bonzani, Andrew 470
Boocock, Richard 54
Boomhower, Eric 769
Boor, Anthony W. 163
Boor, David A. 269
Boor, William C. 229
Boorman, Paul 713
Boorn, Andrew W. 276
Booth, Lewis W.K. 375
Booth, Stuart W. 199
Bordes, Michael P. 337
Borel, James C. 319
Boren, Jennifer A. 363
Boretz, J. Craig 255
Borg, Magnus 790
Borgen, Luis 278
Borland, Mark A. 675
Borneman, Kathy 955
Bornhorst, Donald T. 288
Borok, Gil 196
Boroughf, Barbara 532
Borras, Maria Claudia 123
Borsboom, Dick 120
Borzi, James 537
Bosch, Joe 300
Bosco, S. Y. 338
Bosler, Gregory J. 464
Bosma, Alan P. 747
Bossick, Jerry 578
Bossmann, Lori L. 39
Bostic, Mark R. 552
Bostick, Russell M. 234
Bostock, Roy J. 288, 956
Bostrom, Susan L. 224
Boswell, Gina R. 60
Boswell, Justin C. 813
Boswood, Mike 854
Botsford, Jon D. 385
Bott, Kevin 757
Bottini, Mark 130
Bottle, Lisa 404
Bottorff, Dennis C. 843
Boubel, Gary 435
Bouchard, Angelee F. 425
Boughner, Robert L. 161
Bouknight, J. A. Jr. 722
Boulier, Paul R. 27
Boultwood, Brenda 254
Bourdon, Lynn L. III 341

Bousbib, Ari 888
Bouta, Robert 118
Boutin, Don 891
Bowcock, Jennifer 99
Bowdish, Ellie J. 161
Bowen, Jim C. 801
Bowen, Lane M. 515
Bowers, Brian 505
Bowers, Kimberly S. 902
Bowers, Krista A. 929
Bowers, W. Paul 804
Bowers, William 361
Bowes, Tim 108
Bowie, Arvelia 864
Bowler, J. Thomas Jr. 888
Bowler, Mary E. 319
Bowles, Richard S. III 597
Bowling, David 269
Bowman, Danny L. 810
Bowman, Roberta B. 316
Bowman, Steven P. 83
Bowman, Tony 771
Box, Sam W. 846
Boyanowski, Kevin 358
Boyce, Cari P. 717
Boyce, Kevin T. 610
Boyd, Colin 498
Boyd, Iain 799
Boyd, Jeffery H. 710
Boyd, Larry C. 466
Boyd, Lois I. 434
Boyd, William S. 161
Boyd Johnson, Marianne 161
Boyden, Brian V. 818
Boydstun, Dianne 700
Boydstun, J. Herbert 185
Boyer, Andrew 927
Boyer, Herbert W. 64
Boyer, Rodney Q. 867
Boykin, Frank H. 607
Boyko, Alan 773
Boylson, Michael J. 488
Brace, Philip G. 556
Bracken, Richard M. 423
Brackenridge, Alec 344
Bradford, Darryl M. 352
Bradford, Douglas K. 126
Bradford, Patricia A. 879
Bradford, Steven M. 444
Bradlee, Benjamin C. 923
Bradley, Daniel R. 385
Bradley, Joseph W. 213
Bradley, Keith W. F. 466
Bradley, Kevin 844
Bradley, Susan 945
Bradley, Todd 437
Bradshaw, Chris 112
Bradway, Robert 86
Brady, Bryan 247
Brady, David J. 446
Brady, Robert T. 612
Brady, Sharon M. 463
Brailer, Daniel A. 934
Brake, William A. Jr. 229
Braly, Angela F. 929
Brand, Bill 452
Brand, Kevin F. 323
Brand, Mike 404
Brand, Robert R. 263
Brand, Stephen R. 249
Brandenburger, Larry B. 903
Brandewie, Brian 404
Brandman, Andrew T. 657
Brandon, David A. 307
Brandow, Paul 350
Brandt, Donald E. 696
Brandt, Eric K. 168
Brannigan, Michael J. 757
Branson, James M. 939
Bratman, Fred B. 883
Braungardt, Anna 872
Braunstein, Douglas L. 503
Brause, Kenneth A. 226
Brautigan, Bernie 751
Braverman, Alan N. 919

Bravman, Richard 630
Brda, Bruce 615
Brearton, David A. 524
Breaux, Randall P. 124
Breber, Pierre R. 212
Breed, John S. 643
Breeden, Frances L. 824
Breeden, Kenneth R. 843
Breeden, Richard C. 414
Breedlove, James T. 708
Breen, Edward D. Jr. 873
Bregman, Mark F. 827
Bregman, Mitchell S. 353
Breier, Benjamin A. 515
Breig, Geralyn R. 121
Breitbard, Mark 389
Brelsford, James 764
Brenn, James E. 162
Brennan, Aidan 523
Brennan, Christine C. 906
Brennan, Daniel J. 160
Brennan, David 600
Brennan, Donald A. 522
Brennan, Patrick 718
Brennan, Robert T. 479
Brennan, Seamus 91
Brennan, Troyen A. 272
Brenneman, Rodney K. 776
Brenner, James 385
Brentano, Yijing 810
Bresch, Heather 617
Bresky, Steven J. 776
Breslawski, James P. 430
Bresler, Charles 596
Bretches, David C. 90
Breunig, Roland E. 784
Brewer, John E. 575
Brewer, Murray 832
Brewer, Robert 660
Brewer, W. Keith 890
Brezovec, Daniel T. 101
Briamonte, Frank 588
Bridge, Anthony R. 885
Bridgeford, Gregory M. 555
Bridges, Shirley W. 288
Bridgman, Peter A. 684
Brienza, Dottie 441
Brigeman, Benjamin L. 207
Briggs, Timothy W. 116
Brimhall, Reed N. 894
Brin, Mitchell F. 64
Brin, Sergey 407
Brinkley, Charlie W. Jr. 364
Brinkley, Cynthia J. 111
Brinkley, Scott 365
Brinkman, Dale T. 949
Brinks, Greg A. 531
Brisbane, Arthur S. 633
Briskman, Louis J. 197
Britanik, Thomas P. 230
Britchfield, Michael 91
Britell, Jenne K. 883
Brittain, Frank 849
Brlas, Laurie 229
Broad, Matthew R. 661
Broadbent, Peregrine C. de M. 491
Broaddus, Mary 901
Broadwater, Steve 792
Brock, Graham C. 609
Brock, John F. 238
Brockman, Kevin 34
Brockman, Robert D. 739
Brockman, Vincent C. 775
Broderick, Dennis J. 560
Brodsky, Julian A. 242
Brogan, Cynthia D. 789
Brogan, Michael P. 619
Broger, Armin 540
Brolick, Emil J. 959
Bromstad, Angela 627
Bronczek, David J. 362
Brondeau, Pierre 372
Bronfin, Kenneth A. 428
Bronfman, Edgar M. Jr. 922
Bronson, David M. 721

Brooke, Charles 472
Brooklier, John L. 463
Brooks, Carolynn 661
Brooks, Dan 874
Brooks, Douglas H. 165
Brooks, Joyce L. 584
Brooks, Laura L. 722
Brooks, Redus Woodrow 444
Broome, J. Tol Jr. 132
Broome, Richard D. 434
Bross, Richard A. 450
Brossart, Darcie M. 489
Brothers, Ellen L. 578
Brotman, Jeffrey H. 261
Brots, John M. 838
Brotz, Melissa 33
Broughton, Philip J. 543
Brous, Maria 724
Brouwer, Wilfridus 94
Brova, Jacquelin J. 217
Brown, Bruce 715
Brown, Cathy (A. Schulman) 28
Brown, Charles E. 660
Brown, Christopher A. 622
Brown, David A. (The Ryland Group) 758
Brown, David C. (Exelon) 352
Brown, Eric C. (Yahoo!) 956
Brown, Eric F. (Electronic Arts) 332
Brown, Eric J. (NCI Building Systems) 629
Brown, Frank 646
Brown, G. Garvin IV 171
Brown, Gregory Q. 615
Brown, Hal D. 193
Brown, James S. 412
Brown, Jeffrey T. 414
Brown, Jody A. 180
Brown, Joseph W. 580
Brown, Judy L. 645
Brown, Kathleen J. (American Financial Group) 78
Brown, Kelly 610
Brown, Kevin 782
Brown, Lynn C. 925
Brown, Marc 283
Brown, Matt 773
Brown, Michael K. 555
Brown, Paul 441
Brown, Peter D. (Foot Locker) 374
Brown, Peter S. (Arrow Electronics) 107
Brown, Randal L. 929
Brown, Ricky K. 132
Brown, Robert 96
Brown, Ronald L. 409
Brown, Shona L. 407
Brown, Stephen F. (Tenet Healthcare) 841
Brown, Stephen S. (Omnicare) 663
Brown, Suzanne C. 901
Brown, Thomas K. 375
Brown, Tod D. 363
Brown, William (Iron Mountain Inc) 479
Brown, William E. (Central Garden & Pet) 199
Brown, William E. Jr. (Toro Company) 866
Brown, William M. (United Technologies) 888
Brown, Willie G. (State Farm) 818
Browne, Donald 627
Browne, La Fleur C. 943
Browne, Robert P. 648
Browning, Jay D. 902
Browning, Jeffery G. 316
Browning, Keith D. 190
Brownlee, Harvey Jr. 153
Brownlie, William R. 846
Bruce, David 757
Bruce, Ian 650
Bruder, Ann J. 244
Bruder, Kaitlyn 858
Bruder, Scott P. 138

Curlander, Paul J. 541
Curler, Jeffrey H. 142
Curley, Stephen C. 662
Curran, Christopher 218
Currault, Douglas N. II 383
Currier, Dennis T. 601
Curry, Kelly E. 424
Curry, P. R. 264
Curry, William L. 310
Curtis-McIntyre, Amy 389
Curwin, Ronald 140
Cusick, Mary L. 153
Cusolito, John 543
Cutbirth, Jason 43
Cutler, Alexander M. 326
Cutler, Stephen M. 503
Cutter, James D. 798
Cyprus, Nicholas S. 396
Cyr, Annette 163
Czanderna, Karel K. 671
Czudak, Bob 253

D

Dabiero, Carmen J. 781
Dabney, Donna C. 61
Dach, Leslie A. 918
Dacier, Paul T. 335
Daeninck, Yolande 591
Dahlquist, Raynor 906
Dail, Baljit 96
Dailey, Dell L. 553
Daines, David 652
Dake, Leann 737
Dakin, Robert F. 921
Dale, Steve 896
Daleo, Robert D. 853
Daley, Dorian E. 667
Daley, Thomas 913
Dalhoff, John J. 281
Dalhuisen, Jan 285
Dallas, H. James 594
Dally, Bill 655
Dalton, Hunter R. 62
Damaska, Phillip A. 353
Damilatis, Chris 106
Damiris, George J. 445
Dana, Charles E. 671
Dancho, Kyle 813
Dandini, Michael 420
Dando, Stephen G. 853
Dandy, William 157
Daniel, James P. 914
Daniel, Laree 50
Daniel, William K. II 276
Daniels, Brian 167
Daniels, Jennifer M. 630
Daniels, Laird K. 272
Daniels, Michael E. 470
Daniels, Robert P. 89
Danielson, Gilbert L. 31
Dannehl, William B. 416
Danner, Denise R. 696
Dannessa, Dominic A. 900
Dannewitz, Charles V. 836
Dannov, David M. 776
Danoff, William 373
Dansky, Ira M. 499
Danzig, Deborah 135
Dapolito, Cheryl 694
Darbee, Peter A. 693
Darcy, Joseph 420
Darnell, David C. 127
Darnis, Geraud 888
Darnold, Richard A. 161
Darrell, Bracken 941
Darrow, Kurt L. 531
Darsey, James R. 654
Daschner, Mary T. 593
Dasher, Wes 132
Dasteel, Jeb 667
Daugherty, Darren 554
Daugherty, Gary L. 658
Daurelle, Lawrence E. 286

Davenport, Terry 816
David, Catherine A. 695
David, Daryl D. 330
David, Leonard A. 430
David, Paul 580
David, Robert P. 182
David-Green, Karen 928
Davids, Ann L. 739
Davidson, Ann D. 481
Davidson, Bradford J. 507
Davidson, Carol A. 873
Davidson, Dan M. 622
Davidson, Mary Ann 667
Davidson, Michael C. 818
Davidson, Patrick N. 668
Davidson, Sheila K. 631
Davidson, Stephen 657
Davidson, William F. Jr. 727
Davies, Christa 96
Davies, Edward 879
Davies, Karen 66
Davies, Mike 713
Davis, C. Morris 839
Davis, D. Scott 882
Davis, Darryl W. 154
Davis, Don P. 745
Davis, Edward R. III 872
Davis, Elliot S. 62
Davis, Erika T. 670
Davis, George F. (Hershey) 432
Davis, George S. (Applied Materials) 102
Davis, Gregory S. 293
Davis, Hubert W. Jr. 813
Davis, Ian M. 658
Davis, Jack M. 315
Davis, Julie K. 266
Davis, Linda B. 770
Davis, Lynn D. 62
Davis, Marion T. 392
Davis, Mary 157
Davis, Michael L. 395
Davis, Nancy M. 888
Davis, Neill P. 596
Davis, Paula 61
Davis, Preston A. 34
Davis, Richard K. 896
Davis, Rob (Green Bay Packers) 408
Davis, Robert D. (Rent-A-Center) 739
Davis, Robert M. (Baxter International) 131
Davis, Robin A. 351
Davis, Scott G. 675
Davis, Steven A. (Bob Evans) 153
Davis, Steven D. (Sempra Energy) 783
Davis, Susan F. 498
Davis, Tony 200
Davis, Vandy T. 369
Davis, Wayne 182
Dawson, Charles T. 559
Dawson, Pat D. 310
Dawson, Peter 136
Day, Edward VI 804
Day, Julian C. 731
Day, Michael H. 42
Day, Thomas G. (US Postal Service) 897
Day, Thomas R. (Hormel) 450
Day, Twila M. 831
Day, William B. 831
De Alvarez, Alex C. 97
de Araujo, Beatriz P. 122
de Bok, Arthur 406
de Brier, Donald P. 658
de Cardenas, Alberto 575
de Chabert, Ralph 171
de Geus, Aart J. 828
de Halleux, Sebastien 332
de la Vega, Ralph 111
de Leener, Pierre-Marie 705
De Maria, Frank 621
De May, Stephen G. 316
de Maynadier, Patrick D. 440
de Notaristefani, Carlo 167
De Respino, Laurence J. 71

de Saint-Quentin, Thibaud 40
De Shon, Larry 118
de Varona, Ani 575
Deadwyler, Erik 747
Deal, Clifford M. III 235
Dealy, Richard P. 697
Dean, Roy D. 671
Dean, Steve 757
Deane, Frank M. 334
Dear, Joseph A. 182
Deas, Thomas C. Jr. 372
Deason, David S. 130
Deaton, Chad C. 123
Deavenport, Earnest W. Jr. 736
Deaver, W. Scott 118
Debertin, Jay D. 215
Deblaere, Johan G. 38
DeBoer, Scott J. 605
DeBois, Elise R. 698
DeBolt, Robert T. 800
Debrowski, Thomas A. 578
Debs, Michael E. 509
DeBuck, Donald G. 247
DeCampli, David G. 707
DeCanti, Anthony M. 933
DeCarli, Earl 440
DeCarlo, Don D. 292
DeCesare, Michael P. 581
Deckelman, William L. Jr. 247
Decker, Edward P. 447
Decker, Nicole 872
Decker, Patrick 873
DeClouet, Gladys H. 174
DeCourcy, Debra 364
Dedo, Jacqueline A. 274
Deegan, Donald J. 871
Deel, Jeffrey A. 796
Deely, Brendan J. 899
Deese, George E. 369
Deese, Willie A. 597
DeFeo, Ronald M. 844
DeFillippo, Robert 720
DeFontes, Kenneth W. Jr. 254
DeFord, John A. 264
DeFranco, James 302
DeGiorgio, Kenneth D. 365
Degnan, John J. 216
DeHaan, Douglas 778
Deignan, John M. 296
Deily, Karl R. 780
Deitz, Scott A. 671
DeIuliis, Nicholas J. 250
deJong, Barbara J. 784
Del Busto, Maria 753
Del Valle, Thomas R. 88
Delagi, R. Gregory 848
DeLand, Daniel F. 531
Delaney, Eugene A. 615
Delaney, James H. 318
Delaney, Kevin M. 803
DeLaney, William J. III 831
Delgado, Joaquin 26
Delker, Wayne L. 230
Dell, Michael S. 284
Dellaquila, Frank J. 338
Dellinger, Robert J. 705
Delly, Gayla J. 144
DeLoach, Harris E. Jr. 801
DeLorenzo, David A. 303
Delorier, Rilla 825
DelVacchio, Michael J. Jr. 516
DeMarie, Donald J. Jr. 574
DeMarino, Theodore V. 739
DeMattei, David M. 551
DeMatteo, Daniel A. 386
Demchak, William S. 702
Demeautis, Jean-Marie 780
DeMoss, Ronald D. 739
DeMuro, Gerard J. 392
den Haan, Joost 766
den Hartog, Grace R. 670
Denault, Leo P. 340
Deneffe, James H. 162
Denius, Franklin W. 805
Denman, John W. 492

Dennis, Dana A. 678
Dennis, Robert J. 398
Denniston, Brackett B. III 393
Denny, J. Henry 65
Denson, Charles D. 641
Dentinger, Mark P. 518
Denton, David M. 272
Denton, Matthew T. 798
Denton, Mike 154
Denton, Stephanie 548
Denzel, Nora M. 476
dePadua, Antonio Z. 415
DePaulo, Joseph 795
DeRango Wicks, Judy 368
Dere, Willard H. 86
deRegt, Kenneth M. 614
Derhaag, Gregory J. 142
DeRienzis, Joshua H. 721
Derksen, Henk 141
DeRoma, Nicholas J. 61
Derry, John E. 505
Dersidan, Christian 307
DeRueda, Patrick J. 925
DeSalvo, Joseph 479
DeSantis, Paul F. 27
DeSanto, Joseph 863
DeSimone, Lisa Marie 547
DeSimone, Samuel R. Jr. 323
Desoer, Barbara J. 127
DeSonier, David M. 535
deSouza, Francis 827
DesParte, Duane M. 352
Despeaux, Kimberly 340
Desrochers, Mark R. 415
DesRosier, Thomas J. 400
Dessau, Nigel 46
DeStefano, Gary M. 641
Determan, Bradley D. 444
Detrick, Edwin J. 218
Dettinger, Warren W. 296
DeTurk, Nanette P. 439
DeVaan, Jon S. 606
DeVeydt, Wayne S. 929
Devine, John M. 274
DeVito, Vincent H. 897
DeVoe, Darrell 93
DeVoe, David F. 380, 637
Devonshire, The Duke of 803
DeVries, James D. 67
Dew, Lyndol I. 295
DeWalt, David G. 581
Dewhurst, Moray P. 638
Dewhurst, Ronald R. 533
DeWitt, Bruce 66
DeWitt, Kenneth E. 883
Deyo, Russell C. 496
DeYonker, Alex J. 807
DeYoung, Caitlin 83
DeYoung, Mark W. 66
Dhamotharan, Dhamo S. 894
Dhanda, Anuj 702
Dhillon, Janet L. 488
Di Fronzo, Pascal W. 112
Diamond, David A. 616
Diamond, Richard 660
Diana, Shana 467
Dias, Andre 611
Diaz, Anthony (CIT Group) 226
Diaz, Anthony J. (Fortune Brands) 378
Diaz, Paul J. 515
DiBartolomeo, Joseph M. 318
Dibble, David E. 956
DiCandilo, Michael D. 85
DiCianni, Joseph 852
Dickerson, Lawrence R. 295
Dickerson, Michael P. 390
Dickey, Robert J. 398
Dickinson, Charles W. 629
Dickinson, Emily D. 690
Dickson, Richard 499
Dickson, Stephen 288
DiDonato, Thomas A. 74
Diehr, George 182
Dieker, John K. 409
Dienes, Edward D. 721

HOOVER'S HANDBOOK OF AMERICAN BUSINESS 2011

Von Thaer, Lewis A. 392
vonBerg, John P. 699
Voorhees, Steven C. 747
Vordenbaumen, Timothy L. Sr. 663
Vorpahl, Larry L. 450
Vorwaller, Gregory S. 196
Vos, Roeland 817
Voss, James R. 800
Voss, Thomas (Masco) 574
Voss, Thomas R. (Ameren) 72
Voss, William R. 622
Vossler, Jennifer R. 680
Votek, Glenn A. 226
Voytilla, John 661
Vucinic, Thomas J. 293

W

Wachinski, Tony 674
Waddell, Frederick H. 648
Waddell, John C. 107
Waddell, M. Keith 746
Wade, Gregory L. 610
Wadford, Larry 660
Wadhams, Timothy 574
Wadhwani, David 44
Wadle, Libby 482
Wadleigh, Doug 578
Wadsworth, Stephen H. 919
Waechter, Thomas H. 490
Wages, Leroy P. 935
Wagner, Amy E. 174
Wagner, Barbara L. 871
Wagner, Joe H. 650
Wagner, Loren 258
Wagner, Mark (Johnson Controls) 498
Wagner, Mark A. (Walgreen) 916
Wagner, Robert F. (Lowe's) 555
Wagner, Robert F. (Tupperware Brands) 872
Wagner-Fleming, Susan 661
Wagoner, Pamela K. 950
Wahl Meyer, Deborah 725
Wahlstrom, Scott E. 938
Wainscott, James L. 57
Wajda, Edward J. 162
Wajsgras, David C. 735
Wakenight, Matt 344
Walchirk, Mark 589
Waldmann, Daniel R. 841
Waldo, Dana E. 384
Waldo, Kurt R. 61
Waldorf, Richard L. 784
Waldron, John P. 626
Waleski, Anne G. 566
Walker, Andre K. 182
Walker, Brian C. 431
Walker, Danny Sr. 31
Walker, David (Bechtel) 136
Walker, David (MetroPCS) 601
Walker, Donald L. 861
Walker, Donna Lee 705
Walker, F. Borden 435
Walker, Joan H. 67
Walker, John E. 288
Walker, Kellye L. 82
Walker, Kent 407
Walker, Lori A. 903
Walker, Mark A. 205
Walker, P. Michael 319
Walker, R. A. 89
Walker, Samuel D. 610
Walker, Steven G. 719
Walker, Thomas K. 261
Wall, Barbara W. 388
Wall, Daniel R. 354
Wall, Della 526
Wall, John C. 271
Wall, Karen 350
Wall, Timothy O. 97
Wallace, Beverly B. 423
Wallace, Gary R. 37
Wallace, Henry D. G. 532
Wallace, Mark E. 275

Wallace, Michael J. 254
Wallace, Patrick S. 869
Wallace, Richard P. 518
Wallace, Roger W. 697
Wallace, Timothy R. 869
Wallach, Russell 550
Walling, Kevin R. 510
Wallis, John 457
Wallis, Michael G. 61
Walljasper, William J. 193
Walsh, Fionnuala 334
Walsh, John F. 805
Walsh, Kevin 376
Walsh, Michael 201
Walsh, Nicholas C. 80
Walter, Jennifer 612
Walter, Jim 578
Walter, Mary 751
Walter, William G. 372
Walters, Beth A. 484
Walters, Greg 122
Walther, Chris B. 40
Waltman, Randal G. 124
Walton, Jim 859
Walton, Jon D. 62
Walton, S. Robson 918
Walton, Steven G. 790
Waltrip, Robert L. 785
Waltzinger, G. William Jr. 140
Walz, Jim 462
Wambold, Stephen L. 363
Wan, Fong 693
Wandell, Keith E. 416
Wang, Geri 34
Wang, James L. K. 354
Wang, Jing 727
Wang, Mark 441
Wang, Xiang 727
Wanner, Kevin M. 140
Warady, Timothy S. 291
Warburg, Paul J. 199
Ward, Andrew 154
Ward, B. Holt 65
Ward, Earl L. 546
Ward, Gregg 888
Ward, Jay L. 308
Ward, John 698
Ward, Laysha 833
Ward, Mel B. 812
Ward, Michael J. 269
Ward, Pam 733
Ward, Patrick J. 271
Ward, Tana 74
Ward, Thomas 163
Ward, Wayne 810
Warden, Steven N. 226
Wardlaw, Van M. 843
Ware, Richard 569
Waring, Sumner J. III 785
Waring, Susan D. 819
Warnecke, David N. 104
Warner, Jane L. 463
Warner, Peter 551
Warner, Timothy 222
Warnock, John E. 44
Warren, Andrew C. 551
Warren, Jeff (Medtronic) 594
Warren, Jeffrey S. (Sealed Air Corp.) 780
Warren, Joseph F. Jr. 852
Warren, Mark 914
Warren, Tiffany R. 664
Warrior, Padmasree 224
Warsop, Thomas W. III 368
Warwick, Peter 854
Wasco, Stephanie R. 686
Washington, Lisa 955
Washington, Robin L. 402
Washkewicz, Donald E. 678
Waskey, David S. 741
Wason, Robert A. IV 914
Wasson, Gregory D. 916
Wasson, Wesley R. 228
Wassum, Duane A. 623
Waterman, Robert A. 423

Waters, John F. Jr. 539
Waters, Martin 544
Waters, Paula 340
Waters, Simon 421
Waters, Tina 242
Waters, William G. 610
Watjen, Thomas R. 891
Watkins, Carole S. 186
Watkins, Mark T. 592
Watson, Charles E. 485
Watson, John S. 212
Watson, Kevin 178
Watson, Noel G. 486
Watts, Eric 320
Watts, George 741
Watts, Richard H. 718
Watts, Russ 365
Watts, Wayne 111
Watzinger, Gerhard 581
Waxman-Lenz, Michael 79
Waz, Joseph W. Jr. 242
Weafer, Robert J. Jr. 651
Weaver, Connie K. 856
Weaver, Dorenda K. 867
Weaver, Jeffery J. 512
Weaver, Richard M. 789
Weaver, William E. Jr. 852
Webb, Darrell D. 494
Webb, David C. 343
Webb, Michael R. 785
Webb, Robert J. (Hilton Worldwide) 441
Webb, Robert W. K. (Hyatt) 457
Webb, Scott A. 683
Webb, Thomas J. 232
Webberman, Michael B. 165
Weber, Dwight E. 709
Weber, Jennifer L. 316
Weber, Jim H. 243
Weber, Lawrence J. 75
Weber, Robert C. 470
Weber, Thomas 884
Weber, Tracey 130
Webster, David (EMC) 335
Webster, David (Microsoft) 606
Webster, Michael S. 509
Weeden, Jeffrey B. 512
Weedman, Jeff 715
Weekly, Michael C. 616
Weeks, Christopher E. 580
Weeks, Wendell P. 259
Weicher, Richard E. 175
Weideman, William H. 310
Weidman, Mark A. 925
Weidner, Diane P. 78
Weigand, James R. 319
Weigand, Kenneth R. 917
Weigelt, J. C. 762
Weihl, Philip H. 510
Weil, Robert J. 583
Weil, William S. 535
Weiland, John H. 264
Weimer, William 845
Weinbach, Arthur F. 176
Weinberger, Mark A. 346
Weinberger, Peter 45
Weinberger, Rita 376
Weinblatt, Brett D. 118
Weiner, Robert C. 721
Weiner, Russell J. 307
Weinheimer, Don D. 511
Weinreich, Howard B. 913
Weinstein, Herschel S. 376
Weinstein, Loren 916
Weisenburger, Randall J. 664
Weiser, Ann E. 40
Weiskopf, Paul 44
Weismann, Gary W. 510
Weiss, Charles F. 658
Weiss, David I. 475
Weiss, Erwin 79
Weiss, Jeffrey M. 79
Weiss, Jonathan 931
Weiss, Morry 79
Weiss, Steven H. 180

Weiss, Zev 79
Weissberg, Jed 504
Weisz, Stephen P. 567
Weker, Bill 832
Welburn, Edward T. Jr. 396
Welch, Dennis E. 75
Welch, James C. (National Fuel Gas) 623
Welch, James S. Jr. (Brown-Forman) 171
Welch, John K. 898
Welch, Richard G. 949
Weldon, William C. 496
Wellborn, W. Christopher 607
Wells, Ben K. 174
Wells, Darren R. 406
Wells, Greg 806
Wells, James M. III 824
Wells, Robert J. 789
Wells, Ronald 28
Wells, William C. II (Regions Financial) 736
Wells, William H. (Rowan Companies) 752
Welsh, Carden N. 858
Welsh, Jim 937
Welsh, John E. III 390
Welsh, Kelly R. 648
Welsh, Sherry 108
Welters, Anthony 889
Welton, Guy M. 933
Wendland, Dennis 215
Wendlandt, Gary E. 631
Wenig, Devin N. 854
Wenker, Kristen S. 395
Wenokur, Bob 548
Wentworth, Carol 871
Wentworth, Timothy C. 593
Wermers, Markus 361
Werner, Clarence L. 933
Werner, Gary L. 933
Werner, Gregory L. 933
Werner, Kevin A. 905
Werner, Tony G. 242
Werner, Uta 954
Werning, David P. 281
Wertheim, Ram D. 580
Wertz, Bryon A. 837
Wesley, Timothy R. 938
Wessel, Alan D. 914
Wessel, Thomas 91
Wessel, Timothy J. 800
West, David (Arrow Electronics) 107
West, David E. (Rent-A-Center) 739
West, David J. (Hershey) 432
West, Elena 746
West, Gil 288
West, Mary Beth 524
West, Robert T. 210
West, Roderick K. 340
West, Teresa L. 848
Westbrock, Leon E. 215
Westerdahl, Joyce 667
Westerlund, David A. 126
Westerman, Bryan 575
Westfall, Kevin P. 115
Westfall, Lynn D. 845
Westin, David 34
Weston, Charles M. 947
Weston-Webb, Andy 569
Westphal, Steven D. 235
Wetekam, Donald J. 30
Wetzel, Joseph M. 323
Wexner, Leslie H. 544
Weyandt, Paul J. 505
Weyers, Larry L. 408
Weymouth, Katharine 923
Whalen, Wayne W. 793
Wheat, William W. 312
Wheatley, Arthur E. 166
Wheeler, Robert H. III 855
Wheeler, Steven M. 696
Wheeler, William J. 600
Whelan, Karen M. L. 890
Whelley, Eileen G. 420